Features

You may visit us on the Web at
http://www.census.gov/compendia/ccdb

ACKNOWLEDGMENTS

Aonghas M. St. Hilaire of the Statistical Compendia Branch was responsible for the technical supervision and coordination of this volume under the general direction of **Lars B. Johanson**. **Myra D. Smith** was responsible for text preparation and the processing of city and place tables. **Kathleen P. Denton** was responsible for text preparation and processing of state and county tables. **Kathleen A. Siemer** was responsible for computer operations and data processing. Assisting with data compilation and review was **Kristen M. Iversen**. Data entry and other support activities were provided by **Connie J. Nadzadi** and **Daphanie M. Smallwood**. **Connie J. Nadzadi** was responsible for the coding and preparation of all tables for printing and for the formatting of front matter and appendix content. Subject development and analytical review were provided by **Lars B. Johanson**, **Rosemary E. Clark**, **Richard P. Kersey**, and **Jean F. Mullin**.

Maps were designed and produced by **Connie Beard**, **Scott Wilcox**, and **Jessica Dobrowolski** of the Cartographic Products Management Branch within the Geography Division.

Jamie A. Peters, **Linda Chen**, and **Donald J. Meyd** of the Administrative and Customer Services Division, **Walter C. Odom**, Chief, provided publications and printing management, graphics design and composition, and editorial review for print and electronic media. General direction and production management were provided by **Wanda Cevis**, Chief, Publications Services Branch.

The cooperation of many contributors to this volume is gratefully acknowledged. The source notes below each table and in Appendix A credit the various government and private agencies that have furnished information for the *County and City Data Book*. In a few instances, contributors have requested that their data be designated as subject to copyright restrictions as indicated in the source notes. Permission to use copyright material should be obtained directly from the copyright owner.

County and City
Data Book: 2007

14th Edition

A Statistical Abstract Supplement

Issued November 2007

U.S. Department of Commerce
Carlos M. Gutierrez,
Secretary

Vacant,
Deputy Secretary

**Economics and Statistics
Administration
Cynthia A. Glassman**,
Under Secretary for Economic Affairs

U.S. CENSUS BUREAU
Charles Louis Kincannon,
Director

SUGGESTED CITATION

U.S. Census Bureau,
County and City Data Book: 2007
(14th edition).
Washington, DC, 2007.

ECONOMICS
AND STATISTICS
ADMINISTRATION

**Economics
and Statistics
Administration**

Cynthia A. Glassman,
Under Secretary
for Economic Affairs

U.S. CENSUS BUREAU

Charles Louis Kincannon,
Director

Preston Jay Waite,
Deputy Director and
Chief Operating Officer

Ted A. Johnson,
Associate Director for Administration
and Chief Financial Officer

Walter C. Odom,
Chief, Administrative
and Customer Services Division

For sale by National Technical Information Service (NTIS), Springfield, VA
Internet: www.ntis.gov   Phone (toll-free): 1-800-553-NTIS (6847)
Phone (local area): 703-605-6000   Fax: 703-605-6900

Reprinted without alteration on acid-free paper
February 2008

ISBN 978-0-934213-03-5
PB Number PB2008-105137

Preface

The *County and City Data Book* (CCDB), published intermittently since 1944, is a local area supplement to the *Statistical Abstract of the United States*. This 2007 edition is the fourteenth in the series. The first edition featured city data only; the second, in 1947, county data only. Beginning with the third edition in 1949, the book was redesigned to include both county and city data and renamed the *County and City Data Book*. Subsequent editions were published in 1952, 1956, 1962, 1972, 1977, 1983, 1988, 1994, and 2000.

The *County and City Data Book* is a convenient summary of statistics on the social and economic structure of the counties and cities of the United States. It is designed to serve as a statistical reference and guide to other data publications and sources. The latter function is served by the source citations appearing below each table and Appendix A, Source Notes and Explanations.

This volume includes a selection of data from many statistical publications and electronic sources, both government and private. Publications and Internet sites listed as sources usually contain additional detail and more comprehensive discussions of definitions and concepts than can be presented here. Data not available in publications issued by the contributing agency but obtained from unpublished records are identified in the source notes as "unpublished data." More information on the subjects covered in the tables so noted may generally be obtained from the source.

Although emphasis in this publication is primarily given to county and city data, Table A includes U.S. and state totals.

Statistics in this edition—Data are generally shown for the most recent year or period available by spring of 2007.

States—Data are presented for the United States, the 50 states, and the District of Columbia. 188 data items are presented for these areas in 15 tables, A-1 through A-15. The states and the District of Columbia are presented in alphabetic order under the U.S. total.

Counties—Data are presented for 3,141 counties and county equivalents defined as of February 22, 2005, as well as the United States, the 50 states, and District of Columbia. 188 data items are presented for these areas in 15 tables, B-1 through B-15. The counties and county

equivalents are presented in Federal Information Processing Standards (FIPS) code order, which lists counties alphabetically under their respective states; independent cities in Maryland, Missouri, Nevada, and Virginia are listed alphabetically at the end of the respective county listing.

Cities—Data are presented for states and the 1,265 incorporated places with 25,000 or more population as of April 1, 2000. Two census designated places (CDPs) are also included (Honolulu CDP in Hawaii and Arlington CDP in Virginia). 82 data items are presented for these areas in six tables, C-1 through C-6. The cities and CDPs are presented in FIPS code order, which lists these areas alphabetically under their respective states.

Places—Table D comprises six individual tables with 79 items of data. These tables present data for states and 242 incorporated places of 100,000 or more population as of April 1, 2000, in all states except Hawaii, which has no incorporated places recognized by the U.S. Census Bureau. Two CDPs are also included (Honolulu CDP in Hawaii and Arlington CDP in Virginia).

Statistical reliability and responsibility—The contents of this volume were taken from many sources. All data from either censuses and surveys or from administrative records are subject to error arising from a number of factors: sampling variability (for statistics based on samples), reporting errors in the data for individual units, incomplete coverage, nonresponse, imputations, and processing error. The Census Bureau cannot accept the responsibility for the accuracy or limitations of the data presented here, other than those for which it collects. The responsibility for selection of the material and for proper presentation, however, rests with the Census Bureau.

Maps—For a map of the United States with the 50 states and the District of Columbia, as well as census regions and divisions, see the inside of the front cover. Maps of all 50 states and the District of Columbia showing county and metropolitan area boundaries and names, as well as the locations of incorporated places of 25,000 or more population, can be found in Appendix D.

Appendixes—Appendix A presents a discussion of source notes and explanations for the data items in Tables A through D. Appendix B presents a discussion of the limitations of data and methodology. Appendix C presents a discussion of the geographic information relevant to this volume, as well as the current definitions for metropolitan areas. Appendix D is a set of state maps with county and metropolitan area boundaries and names, as well as locations of incorporated places of 25,000 or more population. Appendix E is a guide to subjects by geographic area.

For additional information on data presented—
Please consult the source publications available in local libraries, write to the agency indicated in the source notes, or visit the Internet site listed. Contact the Census Bureau only if it is cited as the source.

Statistics for the nation—Extensive data at the national level can be found in the *Statistical Abstract of the United States: 2007*, an annual national data book, released each fall. Several editions of this publication are available on the Internet at <http://www.census.gov/compendia/statab>.

USA Statistics in Brief, a pocket-size pamphlet highlighting many statistical series in the *Abstract*, is available separately; single copies of this pamphlet can be obtained free from U.S. Census Bureau, Customer Services Center, Washington, DC 20233 (telephone 301-763-4636).

Statistics for states and metropolitan areas—Data for states and metropolitan areas may be found in the *State and Metropolitan Area Data Book: 2006*; available in print or on the Internet at <http://www.census.gov/compendia/smadb/>.

Additional statistics for counties—While this book contains approximately 188 data items for all counties and county equivalents in the United States, an extensive county database featuring over 6,000 data items for these areas can be found in USA Counties on the Internet at <http://censtats.census.gov/usa/usa.shtml>.

Suggestions and comments—Users of the *County and City Data Book* and related publications (see inside back cover) are urged to make their data needs known for consideration in planning future editions. Suggestions and comments for improving coverage and presentation of data should be sent to the Director, U.S. Census Bureau, Washington, DC 20233.

CONTENTS

Cities

Places

APPENDIXES

Guide to Tabular Presentation

EXAMPLE OF TABLE STRUCTURE

Table B-9. Counties — **Personal Income and Earnings by Industries**

[Includes United States, states, and 3,141 counties/county equivalents defined as of February 22, 2005. For more information on these areas, see Appendix C, Geographic Information]

County	Personal income												
	Total, by place of residence					Per capita[1] (dol.)		Earnings, by place of work, 2005					
				Percent change					Percent by selected major industries				
	2005 (mil. dol.)	2004 (mil. dol.)	2000 (mil. dol.)	2004–2005	2000–2005	2005	2000	Total[2] (mil. dol.)	Construction	Retail trade	Professional and technical services	Health care and social assistance	Government
UNITED STATES	10,220,942	9,716,351	8,422,074	5.2	21.4	34,471	29,845	7,983,652	6.4	6.5	9.4	9.4	16.5
ALABAMA	134,736	126,655	105,807	6.4	27.3	29,623	23,764	98,672	6.4	7.3	7.6	9.4	20.2
Autauga	1,336	1,242	1,011	7.6	32.2	27,567	23,018	529	8.1	12.0	3.2	5.7	18.3
Baldwin	5,029	4,561	3,694	10.3	36.2	30,899	26,119	2,424	12.7	12.7	4.6	9.8	16.5
Barbour	660	626	547	5.4	20.7	23,343	18,820	469	2.5	6.2	(NA)	5.5	17.3
Bibb	466	437	353	6.6	31.9	21,732	17,724	184	18.6	7.1	3.6	(NA)	29.1
Blount	1,306	1,233	1,023	5.9	27.7	23,492	19,967	433	9.8	9.3	3.4	(NA)	19.9

NA Not available.

[1]Based on resident population estimated as of July 1, 2000, and 2005.   [2]Includes other industries not shown separately.

Survey, Census, or Data Collection Method: Based on the Regional Economic Information System; for more information, see <http://www.bea.gov/regional/methods.cfm/>.

Source: U.S. Bureau of Economic Analysis, Regional Economic Information Systems (REIS), download estimates and software, accessed June 5, 2007 (related Internet site <http://www.bea.gov/regional/docs/reis2005dvd.cfm>).

Headnotes immediately below table titles provide information on the geographic areas presented in the table.

Unit indicators show the specified quantities in which data items are presented. They are used for two primary reasons. Sometimes data are not available in absolute form.

Other times we round the numbers in order to save space to show more data, as in the case above.

If no unit indicator is shown, data presented are in absolute form (see Table B-5 for an example). When needed, unit indicators are found in the column or spanner headings for the data items as shown above.

Example of Unit Indicator Interpretation From Table

Geography or area	Year	Item	Unit indicator	Number shown	Multiply by
UNITED STATES	2005	Personal income	(mil. dol.)	10,220,942	$1,000,000

To Determine the Figure it Is Necessary to Multiply the Number Shown by the Unit Indicator:

Personal income, 2005 = 10,220,942 * 1,000,000 or 10,220,942,000,000
(over 10 trillion dollars)

In many tables, details will not add to the totals shown because of rounding.

EXPLANATION OF SYMBOLS AND TERMS

The following symbols are used in the tables throughout this book:

–	Represents zero.
B	Base figure too small to meet statistical standards for reliability of a derived figure.
D	Data withheld to avoid disclosure pertaining to a specific organization or individual.
NA	Data not enumerated, tabulated, or otherwise available separately.
S	Figure does not meet publication standards for reasons other than that covered by symbol B, above.
X	Not applicable.
Z	Entry would amount to less than half the unit of measurement shown.

The following terms are also used throughout this publication:

Averages. An average is a single number or value that is often used to represent the "typical value" of a group of numbers. It is regarded as a measure of "location" or "central tendency" of a group of numbers.

The *arithmetic* mean is the type of average used most frequently. It is derived by summing the individual item values of a particular group and dividing the total by the number of items. The arithmetic mean is often referred to simply as the "mean" or "average."

The *median* of a group of numbers is the middle number or value when each item in the group is arranged according to size (lowest to highest or visa versa); it generally has the same number of items above it as well as below it. If there is an even number of items in the group, the median is taken to be the average of the two middle numbers.

Rates. Rate is a quantity or amount of an item measured in relation to a specified number of units of another item. For example, unemployment rate is the number of unemployed persons per 100 persons in the civilian labor force. Examples of other rates found in this publication include birth rate, which is the number of births per 1,000 population; infant death rate, the number of infant deaths per 1,000 live births; and crime rate, which is the number of serious offenses per 100,00 population.

A *per capita* figure represents a specific type of rate computed for every person in a specified group (or population). It is derived by taking the total for a data item (such as income, taxes, or retail sales) and dividing it by the number of persons in the specified population.

Major Federal Data Contacts

To help *County and City Data Book* users find more data and information about statistical publications, we are issuing this list of contacts for federal agencies with major statistical programs. The intent is to give a single, first-contact point of entry for users of statistics. These agencies will provide general information on their statistical programs and publications, as well as specific information on how to order their publications. We are also including the Internet (World Wide Web) addresses for many of these agencies. These URLs were current in May 2007.

Executive Office of the President

Office of Management and Budget
Administrator
Office of Information and Regulatory Affairs
Office of Management and Budget
725 17th Street, NW
Washington, DC 20503
Information: 202-395-3080
Internet address: http://www.whitehouse.gov/omb

Department of Agriculture

Economic Research Service
U.S. Department of Agriculture
1800 M Street, NW
Room North 3050
Washington, DC 20036-5831
Information and Publications: 202-694-5050
Internet address: http://www.ers.usda.gov/

National Agricultural Statistics Service
U.S. Department of Agriculture
1400 Independence Avenue, SW
Room 5829
Washington, DC 20250
Information hotline: 1-800-727-9540
Internet address: http://www.nass.usda.gov/

Department of Commerce

U.S. Census Bureau
Customer Services Branch
U.S. Census Bureau
U.S. Department of Commerce
Washington, DC 20233
Information and Publications: 301-763-4636
Internet address: http://www.census.gov/

Bureau of Economic Analysis
U.S. Department of Commerce
Washington, DC 20230
Information and Publications: 202-606-9900
Internet address: http://www.bea.gov/

Department of Commerce—Con.

International Trade Administration
Trade Statistics Division
Office of Trade and Economic Analysis
Room 2814 B
Washington, DC 20230
Information and Publications: 202-482-2185
Internet address: http://www.ita.doc.gov/

Department of Defense

Department of Defense
Office of the Assistant Secretary of Defense (Public Affairs)
Room 3A750
Attention: Directorate for Public Communications
1400 Defense Pentagon
Washington, DC 20301-1400
Information: 703-697-5737
Internet address: http://www.defenselink.mil/

Department of Education

National Center for Education Statistics
U.S. Department of Education
400 Maryland Avenue, SW
Washington, DC 20202-5621
Education Information and Statistics:
 1-800-424-1616
Education Publications: 1-877-433-7827
Internet address: http://www.ed.gov/

Department of Energy

Energy Information Administration
National Energy Information Center
U.S. Department of Energy
1000 Independence Avenue, SW
1E238-EI-30
Washington, DC 20585
Information and Publications: 202-586-8800
Internet address: http://www.eia.doe.gov/

Department of Health and Human Services

Health Resources and Services Administration
HRSA Office of Communications
5600 Fishers Lane
Room 14-45
Rockville, MD 20857
Information Center: 301-443-3376
Internet address: http://www.hrsa.gov/

Substance Abuse Mental Health Services Administration
U.S. Department of Health and Human Services
5600 Fishers Lane
Room 12-105
Rockville, MD 20857
Information: 301-443-4795
Publications: 1-800-729-6686
Internet address: http://www.samhsa.gov/

Centers for Disease Control and Prevention
Office of Public Affairs
1600 Clifton Road, NE
Atlanta, GA 30333
Public Inquiries: 1-800-311-3435
Internet address: http://www.cdc.gov/

Centers for Medicare and Medicaid Services (CMS)
Office of Public Affairs
U.S. Department of Health and Human Services
Humphrey Building
200 Independence Avenue, SW
Room 303D
Washington, DC 20201
Media Relations: 202-690-6145
Internet address: http://www.cms.gov/

National Center for Health Statistics
U.S. Department of Health and Human Services
Centers for Disease Control and Prevention
National Center for Health Statistics
Data Dissemination Branch
6525 Belcrest Road
Room 1064
Hyattsville, MD 20782
Information: 301-458-INFO
Internet address: http://www.cdc.gov/nchs

Administration for Children and Families
370 L'Enfant Promenade, SW
Washington, DC 20201
Information and Publications: 202-401-2337
Internet address: http://www.acf.hhs.gov/

Department of Homeland Security

Bureau of Citizenship and Immigration Services
U.S. Department of Homeland Security
425 I Street, NW
Room 4034
Washington, DC 20536
Information and Publications: 202-305-1613
Internet address: http://www.uscis.gov/

Department of the Interior

Geological Survey
Earth Science Information Center
Geological Survey
U.S. Department of the Interior
507 National Center
Reston, VA 20192
Information and Publications: 1-888-275-8747
Internet address for minerals:
  http://minerals.usgs.gov/
Internet address for other materials:
  http://ask.usgs.gov/

National Park Service
WASO-TNT
P.O. Box 25287
Denver, CO 80225-0287
Information and Publications: 303-751-3727
Internet address: http://www2.nature.nps.gov/

Department of Justice

Bureau of Justice Statistics
Statistics Division
810 7th Street, NW
2nd Floor
Washington, DC 20531
Information and Publications: 202-307-0765
Internet address: http://www.ojp.usdoj.gov/bjs/

National Criminal Justice Reference Service
Box 6000
Rockville, MD 20849-6000
Information and Publications: 301-519-5500
Publications: 1-800-732-3277
Internet address: http://www.ncjrs.org/

Federal Bureau of Investigation
U.S. Department of Justice
J. Edgar Hoover FBI Building
935 Pennsylvania Avenue, NW
Washington, DC 20535-0001
National Press Office: 202-324-3000
Information and Publications: 202-324-3691
Research and Communications Unit: 202-324-5611
Internet address: http://www.fbi.gov/

Department of Labor
Bureau of Labor Statistics
Office of Publications and Special Studies Services
Division of Information
Bureau of Labor Statistics
2 Massachusetts Avenue, NE
Room 2850
Washington, DC 20212
Information and Publications: 202-691-5200
Internet address: http://www.bls.gov/

Department of Transportation
Bureau of Transportation Statistics
400 7th Street, SW
Room 3430
Washington, DC 20590
Products: 202-366-3282
Statistical Information: 1-800-853-1351
Internet address: http://www.bts.gov/

Federal Highway Administration
Office of Public Affairs
Federal Highway Administration
U.S. Department of Transportation
400 7th Street, SW
Washington, DC 20590
Information: 202-366-0660
Internet address: http://www.fhwa.dot.gov/

National Highway Traffic Safety Administration
Office of Public and Consumer Affairs
U.S. Department of Transportation
400 7th Street, SW
Washington, DC 20590
Information: 202-366-4000
Publications: 202-366-8892
Internet address: http://www.nhtsa.dot.gov/

Department of the Treasury
Internal Revenue Service
Statistics of Income Division
Internal Revenue Service
P.O. Box 2608
Washington, DC 20013-2608
Information and Publications: 202-874-0410
Internet address:
  http://www.irs.gov/taxstats/index.html

Department of Veterans Affairs
Office of Public Affairs
Department of Veterans Affairs
810 Vermont Avenue, NW
Washington, DC 20420
Information: 202-273-5400
Internet address: http://www.va.gov/

Independent Agencies
Environmental Protection Agency
Information Resource Center, Room M2904
Environmental Protection Agency
1200 Pennsylvania Ave., NW
Mail Code 3201
Washington, DC 20460
Information: 202-260-9152
Internet address: http://www.epa.gov/

National Science Foundation
Office of Legislation and Public Affairs
National Science Foundation
4201 Wilson Boulevard
Arlington, VA 22230
Information: 703-292-5111
Publications: 703-292-8129
Internet address: http://www.nsf.gov/

Social Security Administration
6400 Security Boulevard
Baltimore, MD 21235
Information and Publications: 1-800-772-1213
Internet address: http://www.ssa.gov/

Federal Communications Commission
445 12th Street, SW
Washington, DC 20554
Information and Publications: 1-888-225-5322
Internet address: http://www.fcc.gov/

National Credit Union Administration
1775 Duke Street
Alexandria, VA 22314-3428
Information and Publications: 703-518-6300
Internet address: http://www.ncua.gov/

Federal Deposit Insurance Corporation
550 17th Street, NW
Washington, DC 20429-9990
Information and Publications: 202-736-0000
Internet address: http://www.fdic.gov/

Other Related Internet Sites
http://www.fedstats.gov/
http://firstgov.gov/

States

Table A

Page

You may visit us on the Web at
http://www.census.gov/compendia/ccdb

States

Table A

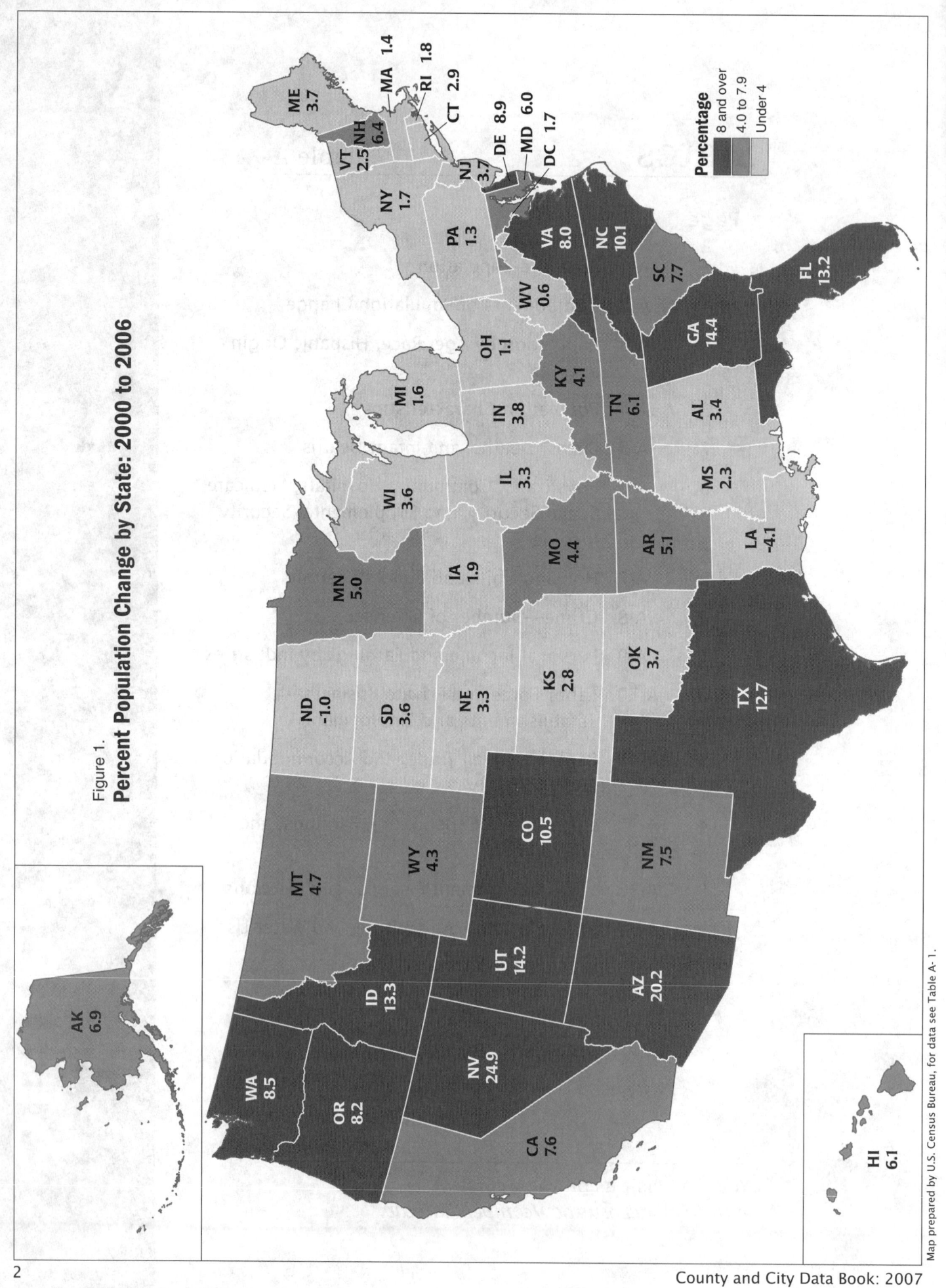

Figure 1.
Percent Population Change by State: 2000 to 2006

Percentage
- 8 and over
- 4.0 to 7.9
- Under 4

ME 3.7
NH 6.4
VT 2.5
MA 1.4
RI 1.8
CT 2.9
NY 1.7
NJ 3.7
PA 1.3
DE 8.9
MD 6.0
DC 1.7
WV 0.6
VA 8.0
NC 10.1
SC 7.7
FL 13.2
GA 14.4
OH 1.1
KY 4.1
TN 6.1
AL 3.4
MI 1.6
IN 3.8
IL 3.3
WI 3.6
MS 2.3
LA -4.1
MO 4.4
AR 5.1
IA 1.9
MN 5.0
ND -1.0
SD 3.6
NE 3.3
KS 2.8
OK 3.7
TX 12.7
CO 10.5
NM 7.5
WY 4.3
MT 4.7
UT 14.2
AZ 20.2
ID 13.3
NV 24.9
CA 7.6
WA 8.5
OR 8.2
AK 6.9
HI 6.1

Map prepared by U.S. Census Bureau, for data see Table A-1.

2

FIPS code[1]	State	Area, 2000 (square miles) Total	Area, 2000 (square miles) Rank[2]	Population 2006 (July 1)	Population 2005 (July 1)	Population 2000[3] (April 1 estimates base)	Population 1990[3] (April 1 estimates base)	Rank[2] 2006	Rank[2] 2000	Rank[2] 1990	Persons per square mile of land area 2006[4]	Persons per square mile of land area 2000	Persons per square mile of land area 1990
00	UNITED STATES . .	3,794,083	(X)	299,398,484	296,507,061	281,424,602	248,790,925	(X)	(X)	(X)	84.6	79.8	70.4
01	Alabama	52,419	30	4,599,030	4,548,327	4,447,351	4,040,389	23	23	22	90.6	87.7	79.6
02	Alaska.	663,267	1	670,053	663,253	626,931	550,043	47	48	49	1.2	1.1	1.0
04	Arizona	113,998	6	6,166,318	5,953,007	5,130,632	3,665,339	16	20	24	54.3	45.5	32.3
05	Arkansas	53,179	29	2,810,872	2,775,708	2,673,398	2,350,624	32	33	33	54.0	51.4	45.1
06	California.	163,696	3	36,457,549	36,154,147	33,871,653	29,811,427	1	1	1	233.8	218.1	191.1
08	Colorado	104,094	8	4,753,377	4,663,295	4,302,015	3,294,473	22	24	26	45.8	41.5	31.8
09	Connecticut	5,543	48	3,504,809	3,500,701	3,405,602	3,287,116	29	29	27	723.4	704.4	678.4
10	Delaware.	2,489	49	853,476	841,741	783,600	666,168	45	45	46	436.9	402.6	340.8
11	District of Columbia	68	(X)	581,530	582,049	572,059	606,900	(X)	(X)	(X)	9,471.2	9,300.4	9,882.8
12	Florida.	65,755	22	18,089,888	17,768,191	15,982,824	12,938,071	4	4	4	335.5	297.6	239.6
13	Georgia.	59,425	24	9,363,941	9,132,553	8,186,816	6,478,149	9	10	11	161.7	142.1	111.8
15	Hawaii.	10,931	43	1,285,498	1,273,278	1,211,537	1,108,229	42	42	41	200.2	188.7	172.5
16	Idaho	83,570	14	1,466,465	1,429,367	1,293,956	1,006,734	39	39	42	17.7	15.7	12.2
17	Illinois	57,914	25	12,831,970	12,765,427	12,419,647	11,430,602	5	5	6	230.9	223.8	205.6
18	Indiana	36,418	38	6,313,520	6,266,019	6,080,517	5,544,156	15	14	14	176.0	169.9	154.6
19	Iowa	56,272	26	2,982,085	2,965,524	2,926,382	2,776,831	30	30	30	53.4	52.4	49.7
20	Kansas	82,277	15	2,764,075	2,748,172	2,688,824	2,477,588	33	32	32	33.8	32.9	30.3
21	Kentucky	40,409	37	4,206,074	4,172,608	4,042,285	3,686,892	26	25	23	105.9	101.9	92.8
22	Louisiana	51,840	31	4,287,768	4,507,331	4,468,958	4,221,826	25	22	21	98.4	102.6	96.9
23	Maine	35,385	39	1,321,574	1,318,220	1,274,923	1,227,928	40	40	38	42.8	41.4	39.8
24	Maryland	12,407	42	5,615,727	5,589,599	5,296,506	4,780,753	19	19	19	574.6	543.5	489.1
25	Massachusetts	10,555	44	6,437,193	6,433,367	6,349,105	6,016,425	13	13	13	821.1	811.6	767.6
26	Michigan	96,716	11	10,095,643	10,100,833	9,938,480	9,295,287	8	8	8	177.7	175.3	163.6
27	Minnesota	86,939	12	5,167,101	5,126,739	4,919,492	4,375,665	21	21	20	64.9	62.0	55.0
28	Mississippi	48,430	32	2,910,540	2,908,496	2,844,656	2,575,475	31	31	31	62.0	60.7	54.9
29	Missouri.	69,704	21	5,842,713	5,797,703	5,596,683	5,116,901	18	17	15	84.8	81.4	74.3
30	Montana	147,042	4	944,632	934,737	902,195	799,065	44	44	44	6.5	6.2	5.5
31	Nebraska.	77,354	16	1,768,331	1,758,163	1,711,265	1,578,417	38	38	36	23.0	22.3	20.5
32	Nevada	110,561	7	2,495,529	2,412,301	1,998,257	1,201,675	35	35	39	22.7	18.4	10.9
33	New Hampshire	9,350	46	1,314,895	1,306,819	1,235,786	1,109,252	41	41	40	146.6	138.3	123.7
34	New Jersey	8,721	47	8,724,560	8,703,150	8,414,347	7,747,750	11	9	9	1,176.2	1,137.1	1,044.3
35	New Mexico	121,589	5	1,954,599	1,925,985	1,819,046	1,515,069	36	36	37	16.1	15.0	12.5
36	New York	54,556	27	19,306,183	19,315,721	18,976,821	17,990,778	3	3	2	408.9	402.4	381.0
37	North Carolina	53,819	28	8,856,505	8,672,459	8,046,491	6,632,448	10	11	10	181.8	165.9	136.1
38	North Dakota	70,700	19	635,867	634,605	642,200	638,800	48	47	47	9.2	9.3	9.3
39	Ohio	44,825	34	11,478,006	11,470,685	11,353,145	10,847,115	7	7	7	280.3	277.5	264.9
40	Oklahoma	69,898	20	3,579,212	3,543,442	3,450,654	3,145,576	28	27	28	52.1	50.3	45.8
41	Oregon	98,381	9	3,700,758	3,638,871	3,421,436	2,842,337	27	28	29	38.6	35.7	29.6
42	Pennsylvania	46,055	33	12,440,621	12,405,348	12,281,054	11,882,842	6	6	5	277.6	274.2	265.1
44	Rhode Island	1,545	50	1,067,610	1,073,579	1,048,319	1,003,464	43	43	43	1,021.7	1,005.7	960.3
45	South Carolina	32,020	40	4,321,249	4,246,933	4,011,816	3,486,310	24	26	25	143.5	133.6	115.8
46	South Dakota	77,116	17	781,919	774,883	754,844	696,004	46	46	45	10.3	10.0	9.2
47	Tennessee	42,143	36	6,038,803	5,955,745	5,689,262	4,877,203	17	16	17	146.5	138.4	118.3
48	Texas	268,581	2	23,507,783	22,928,508	20,851,790	16,986,335	2	2	3	89.8	80.0	64.9
49	Utah	84,899	13	2,550,063	2,490,334	2,233,198	1,722,850	34	34	35	31.0	27.3	21.0
50	Vermont	9,614	45	623,908	622,387	608,827	562,758	49	49	48	67.5	65.9	60.8
51	Virginia	42,774	35	7,642,884	7,564,327	7,079,030	6,189,197	12	12	12	193.0	179.4	156.3
53	Washington	71,300	18	6,395,798	6,291,899	5,894,140	4,866,669	14	15	18	96.1	88.8	73.1
54	West Virginia	24,230	41	1,818,470	1,814,083	1,808,350	1,793,477	37	37	34	75.5	75.1	74.5
55	Wisconsin	65,498	23	5,556,506	5,527,644	5,363,715	4,891,954	20	18	16	102.3	99.0	90.1
56	Wyoming	97,814	10	515,004	508,798	493,782	453,589	50	50	50	5.3	5.1	4.7

X Not applicable.

[1] Federal Information Processing Standards (FIPS) codes for states and counties.

[2] Based on 50 states. When states share the same rank, the next lower rank is omitted.

[3] The Population Estimates base reflects modifications to the census population as documented in the Count Question Resolution program and geographic program revisions. 1990 also has adjustment for underenumeration in certain counties and cities.

[4] Persons per square mile was calculated on the basis of land area data from the 2000 census.

Survey, Census, or Data Collection Method: Based on population estimates and the "component of population change method"; for more information, see Appendix B, Limitations of the Data and Methodology, and also <http://www.census.gov/popest/topics/methodology/>.

Sources: Area—U.S. Census Bureau, 2000 Summary File 1 (SF1), GCT-PH1 Population, Housing Units, Area, and Density: 2000 (related Internet site <http://www.census.gov/Press-Release/www/2001/sumfile1.html>). Population, 2006, 2005, and 2000—U.S. Census Bureau, Population Estimates, Annual County Population Estimates and Components of Change: April 1, 2000 to July 1, 2006 (related Internet site <http://www.census.gov/popest/counties/files/CO-EST2006-alldata.txt>). Population, 1990—U.S. Census Bureau archive 1990 to 1999, "County Population Estimates for July 1,1999 and Population Change for April 1, 1990 to July 1, 1999" (related Internet site <http://www.census.gov/popest/archives/1990s/CO-99-02.html>).

State	Components of population change, April 1, 2000, to July 1, 2006						Population change, April 1, 1990, to April 1, 2000	
	Number							
	Total population change	Natural increase			Net international migration	Percent change	Number	Percent change
		Total	Births	Deaths				
UNITED STATES...	17,973,882	10,324,372	25,486,569	15,162,197	7,649,510	6.4	32,633,677	13.1
Alabama	151,679	87,818	375,808	287,990	30,537	3.4	406,962	10.1
Alaska	43,122	43,828	63,170	19,342	4,654	6.9	76,888	14.0
Arizona	1,035,686	297,928	564,062	266,134	204,661	20.2	1,465,293	40.0
Arkansas	137,474	62,519	237,755	175,236	26,467	5.1	322,774	13.7
California	2,585,896	1,909,368	3,375,297	1,465,929	1,724,790	7.6	4,060,226	13.6
Colorado	451,362	244,279	425,394	181,115	133,930	10.5	1,007,542	30.6
Connecticut	99,207	70,748	256,735	185,987	92,635	2.9	118,486	3.6
Delaware	69,876	25,673	69,846	44,173	13,394	8.9	117,432	17.6
District of Columbia	9,471	12,830	48,355	35,525	24,795	1.7	−34,841	−5.7
Florida	2,107,064	282,347	1,338,458	1,056,111	642,188	13.2	3,044,753	23.5
Georgia	1,177,125	438,939	849,414	410,475	228,415	14.4	1,708,667	26.4
Hawaii	73,961	56,251	110,926	54,675	31,092	6.1	103,308	9.3
Idaho	172,509	72,477	135,942	63,465	17,266	13.3	287,222	28.5
Illinois	412,323	481,799	1,138,398	656,599	402,257	3.3	989,045	8.7
Indiana	233,003	196,728	541,506	344,778	68,935	3.8	536,361	9.7
Iowa	55,703	65,553	239,348	173,795	36,142	1.9	149,551	5.4
Kansas	75,251	93,899	246,484	152,585	44,847	2.8	211,236	8.5
Kentucky	163,789	98,521	345,318	246,797	30,889	4.1	355,393	9.6
Louisiana	−181,190	145,355	410,364	265,009	22,244	−4.1	247,132	5.9
Maine	46,651	7,917	86,331	78,414	5,616	3.7	46,995	3.8
Maryland	319,221	189,158	464,251	275,093	129,730	6.0	515,753	10.8
Massachusetts	88,088	149,992	499,440	349,448	200,155	1.4	332,680	5.5
Michigan	157,163	272,304	816,225	543,921	151,435	1.6	643,193	6.9
Minnesota	247,609	196,095	432,306	236,211	86,925	5.0	543,827	12.4
Mississippi	65,884	89,504	266,971	177,467	10,896	2.3	269,181	10.5
Missouri	246,030	137,564	480,763	343,199	50,450	4.4	479,782	9.4
Montana	42,437	18,037	70,509	52,472	2,092	4.7	103,130	12.9
Nebraska	57,066	65,881	160,471	94,590	26,224	3.3	132,848	8.4
Nevada	497,272	103,155	210,950	107,795	80,482	24.9	796,582	66.3
New Hampshire	79,109	28,491	90,680	62,189	13,718	6.4	126,534	11.4
New Jersey	310,213	254,766	705,812	451,046	357,111	3.7	666,597	8.6
New Mexico	135,553	85,062	174,378	89,316	32,967	7.5	303,977	20.1
New York	329,362	601,779	1,576,125	974,346	820,388	1.7	986,043	5.5
North Carolina	810,014	293,761	749,959	456,198	180,986	10.1	1,414,043	21.3
North Dakota	−6,333	13,133	49,881	36,748	3,664	−1.0	3,400	0.5
Ohio	124,861	263,004	938,169	675,165	92,101	1.1	506,030	4.7
Oklahoma	128,558	97,602	317,771	220,169	41,665	3.7	305,078	9.7
Oregon	279,322	93,194	284,655	191,461	88,976	8.2	579,099	20.4
Pennsylvania	159,567	95,649	902,068	806,419	126,007	1.3	398,212	3.4
Rhode Island	19,291	18,543	79,147	60,604	23,086	1.8	44,855	4.5
South Carolina	309,433	115,324	349,748	234,424	40,168	7.7	525,506	15.1
South Dakota	27,075	24,750	68,615	43,865	4,333	3.6	58,840	8.5
Tennessee	349,541	142,266	493,881	351,615	59,385	6.1	812,059	16.7
Texas	2,655,993	1,389,275	2,351,909	962,634	801,576	12.7	3,865,455	22.8
Utah	316,865	226,268	308,460	82,192	60,944	14.2	510,348	29.6
Vermont	15,081	8,865	40,670	31,805	5,295	2.5	46,069	8.2
Virginia	563,854	276,039	633,794	357,755	151,748	8.0	889,833	14.4
Washington	501,658	221,958	503,819	281,861	157,950	8.5	1,027,471	21.1
West Virginia	10,120	−1,609	130,202	131,811	4,419	0.6	14,873	0.8
Wisconsin	192,791	144,051	434,966	290,915	56,557	3.6	471,761	9.6
Wyoming	21,222	15,734	41,063	25,329	2,323	4.3	40,193	8.9

Survey, Census, or Data Collection Method: Based on population estimates and the "component of populaton change method"; for more information, see Appendix B, Limitations of the Data and Methodology, and also <http://www.census.gov/popest/topics/methodology/>.

Sources: Population—U.S. Census Bureau, Components of Population Change, "Population Estimates, Cumulative Estimates of the Components of Population Change for Counties: April 1, 2000 to July 1, 2006" (related Internet site <http://www.census.gov/popest/counties/files/CO-EST2006-alldata.txt>). Population change—Census 2000, Demographic Profiles 1; 1990 census, 100 percent data, STF1 (related Internet site <http://www.census.gov/main/www/cen2000.html>). Net international migration—U.S. Census Bureau, "Cumulative Estimates of the Components of Population Change for Counties: April 1, 2000 to July 1, 2006" (related Internet site <http://www.census.gov/popest/counties/CO-EST2006-04.html>).

Table A-3. States — **Population by Age, Race, Hispanic Origin, and Sex**

	Population characteristics, 2005														
	Age (percent)								One race (percent)						
State	Under 5 years	5 to 14 years	15 to 24 years	25 to 34 years	35 to 44 years	45 to 54 years	55 to 64 years	65 to 74 years	75 years and over	White alone	Black or African American alone	Asian alone	American Indian and Alaska Native alone	Native Hawaiian and Other Pacific Islander alone	Hispanic or Latino origin[1] (percent)	Males per 100 females
UNITED STATES.........	6.8	13.6	14.2	13.5	14.8	14.3	10.2	6.3	6.1	80.2	12.8	4.3	1.0	0.2	14.4	97.1
Alabama	6.5	13.2	14.2	13.3	14.2	14.5	10.9	7.2	6.0	71.4	26.4	0.8	0.5	(Z)	2.3	94.3
Alaska	7.6	15.5	16.9	12.0	15.0	16.4	9.9	4.0	2.6	70.5	3.7	4.6	16.0	0.6	5.1	107.1
Arizona	7.7	14.6	14.2	14.5	13.8	12.7	9.8	6.9	5.9	87.4	3.6	2.2	5.1	0.2	28.5	100.2
Arkansas	6.7	13.3	14.3	13.2	13.9	13.8	11.0	7.5	6.3	81.3	15.7	1.0	0.7	0.1	4.7	96.2
California	7.4	14.9	14.5	14.3	15.2	13.7	9.3	5.4	5.3	77.0	6.7	12.2	1.2	0.4	35.2	99.8
Colorado	7.3	13.8	14.1	15.5	15.2	14.5	9.5	5.3	4.7	90.3	4.1	2.6	1.1	0.1	19.5	102.0
Connecticut	6.0	13.4	13.3	11.4	15.8	15.5	11.0	6.1	7.4	84.9	10.1	3.2	0.3	0.1	10.9	94.4
Delaware	6.6	12.6	13.9	13.3	15.1	14.5	10.8	7.0	6.3	74.9	20.7	2.7	0.4	0.1	6.0	95.2
District of Columbia	7.0	10.5	12.4	19.8	14.8	13.0	10.3	6.2	6.0	38.0	57.0	3.1	0.3	0.1	8.6	90.2
Florida................	6.3	12.6	13.0	12.2	14.3	13.9	11.0	8.5	8.3	80.4	15.7	2.1	0.4	0.1	19.5	96.2
Georgia...............	7.6	14.1	14.5	15.4	15.7	13.6	9.4	5.4	4.2	66.1	29.8	2.7	0.3	0.1	7.1	97.9
Hawaii................	7.1	12.5	14.0	12.4	14.0	14.8	11.5	6.1	7.6	26.8	2.3	41.5	0.3	9.0	8.0	99.4
Idaho.................	7.4	14.2	15.7	13.4	13.6	14.1	10.1	6.1	5.4	95.5	0.6	1.0	1.4	0.1	9.1	100.7
Illinois	7.0	14.0	14.1	14.0	14.8	14.2	9.8	6.0	6.0	79.4	15.1	4.1	0.3	0.1	14.3	96.6
Indiana	6.9	14.3	14.3	13.3	14.3	14.4	10.2	6.2	6.2	88.6	8.8	1.2	0.3	(Z)	4.5	97.0
Iowa	6.1	12.4	14.6	12.7	13.9	15.0	10.6	6.8	7.9	94.9	2.3	1.4	0.3	(Z)	3.7	97.0
Kansas	6.8	13.4	15.2	13.3	13.9	14.5	9.9	6.2	6.8	89.4	5.9	2.1	0.9	0.1	8.3	98.7
Kentucky	6.5	13.0	13.8	13.7	14.8	14.7	10.9	6.8	5.8	90.4	7.5	0.9	0.2	(Z)	2.0	96.6
Louisiana	7.1	13.8	15.5	13.4	14.0	14.4	10.2	6.2	5.5	64.1	33.1	1.4	0.6	(Z)	2.8	94.7
Maine	5.1	11.6	13.8	10.9	15.2	16.5	12.3	7.3	7.3	96.9	0.8	0.8	0.6	(Z)	1.0	95.5
Maryland	6.8	13.8	14.0	12.6	15.7	15.0	10.6	5.9	5.6	64.0	29.3	4.8	0.3	0.1	5.7	94.0
Massachusetts	6.2	12.5	13.3	13.6	15.8	14.8	10.5	6.1	7.2	86.7	6.9	4.7	0.3	0.1	7.9	94.0
Michigan	6.4	14.0	14.3	12.8	14.7	14.9	10.4	6.0	6.4	81.3	14.3	2.2	0.6	(Z)	3.8	96.7
Minnesota	6.5	13.1	14.8	13.3	15.2	15.0	9.9	5.9	6.2	89.6	4.3	3.4	1.2	0.1	3.6	98.6
Mississippi	7.3	13.9	15.2	13.6	13.8	13.9	10.1	6.7	5.6	61.2	36.9	0.7	0.4	(Z)	1.7	94.4
Missouri...............	6.5	13.0	14.5	13.1	14.4	14.6	10.6	6.8	6.5	85.4	11.5	1.3	0.4	0.1	2.7	95.7
Montana	5.7	11.9	15.0	11.6	13.3	16.6	12.1	7.2	6.6	91.1	0.4	0.5	6.5	0.1	2.4	99.6
Nebraska..............	7.0	13.2	15.2	13.2	13.7	14.4	10.0	6.3	7.0	92.0	4.3	1.6	0.9	0.1	7.1	97.8
Nevada................	7.2	14.4	13.2	15.0	15.1	13.4	10.4	6.6	4.7	82.0	7.7	5.7	1.4	0.5	23.5	103.7
New Hampshire..........	5.6	13.1	13.9	11.3	16.1	16.3	11.3	6.3	6.2	96.1	1.0	1.7	0.2	(Z)	2.2	97.2
New Jersey	6.7	13.8	13.0	12.2	16.0	14.9	10.5	6.2	6.8	76.6	14.5	7.2	0.3	0.1	15.2	95.1
New Mexico	7.0	13.8	15.4	12.4	13.6	14.6	11.0	6.7	5.5	84.5	2.4	1.3	10.2	0.1	43.4	96.8
New York	6.5	13.0	13.6	13.5	15.4	14.4	10.6	6.4	6.7	73.8	17.4	6.7	0.5	0.1	16.1	94.0
North Carolina..........	7.0	13.5	13.7	14.4	15.0	13.9	10.3	6.5	5.6	74.1	21.8	1.8	1.3	0.1	6.4	96.8
North Dakota	5.8	11.5	15.9	13.0	13.0	15.5	10.5	6.6	8.1	92.3	0.8	0.7	5.3	(Z)	1.6	99.6
Ohio	6.4	13.4	14.1	12.7	14.5	15.0	10.6	6.5	6.9	85.1	11.9	1.4	0.2	(Z)	2.3	95.1
Oklahoma	6.9	13.0	15.0	13.5	13.6	14.2	10.6	7.1	6.1	78.5	7.7	1.5	8.1	0.1	6.6	97.7
Oregon	6.2	13.0	13.8	14.1	14.1	14.8	11.0	6.4	6.5	90.8	1.8	3.4	1.4	0.3	9.9	98.9
Pennsylvania	5.8	12.6	13.8	11.8	14.4	15.3	11.1	6.8	8.4	86.0	10.6	2.2	0.2	(Z)	4.1	94.2
Rhode Island	6.0	12.7	14.1	13.0	15.0	14.8	10.5	5.8	8.1	88.9	6.2	2.7	0.6	0.1	10.7	93.4
South Carolina	6.6	13.2	14.3	13.6	14.4	14.3	11.1	6.9	5.6	68.4	29.2	1.1	0.4	0.1	3.3	95.1
South Dakota	6.7	13.1	15.6	12.2	13.4	14.7	10.0	6.7	7.5	88.5	0.8	0.7	8.8	(Z)	2.1	98.8
Tennessee	6.5	12.8	13.7	14.0	14.9	14.6	11.0	7.0	5.6	80.7	16.8	1.2	0.3	0.1	3.0	96.0
Texas	8.2	15.0	15.1	14.8	14.7	13.4	9.0	5.4	4.5	83.2	11.7	3.3	0.7	0.1	35.1	99.3
Utah	9.5	15.9	17.6	17.2	12.2	11.4	7.4	4.7	4.1	93.8	1.0	1.9	1.3	0.7	10.9	100.9
Vermont...............	5.1	11.8	14.6	11.5	14.9	16.7	12.3	6.6	6.6	96.9	0.6	1.0	0.4	(Z)	1.1	97.1
Virginia	6.8	13.2	14.2	13.4	15.5	14.8	10.8	6.1	5.3	73.6	19.9	4.6	0.3	0.1	6.0	96.9
Washington	6.3	13.1	14.5	13.8	15.2	15.1	10.6	5.8	5.6	85.0	3.5	6.4	1.7	0.5	8.8	99.7
West Virginia	5.6	11.6	13.1	12.6	13.7	15.7	12.4	7.9	7.4	95.2	3.2	0.6	0.2	(Z)	0.9	95.9
Wisconsin.............	6.1	12.9	14.7	12.7	14.9	15.2	10.4	6.3	6.7	90.1	6.0	2.0	0.9	(Z)	4.5	98.1
Wyoming	6.1	12.0	15.5	12.3	13.3	16.8	11.9	6.5	5.7	94.8	0.9	0.6	2.4	0.1	6.7	101.6

Z Less than .05 percent.

[1]Persons of Hispanic or Latino origin may be any race.

Survey, Census, or Data Collection Method: Based on population estimates and the "component of population change method"; for information, see Appendix B, Limitations of the Data and Methodology, and also <http://www.census.gov/popest/topics/methodology/>.

Source: U.S. Census Bureau, "County Population Estimates by Age, Sex, Race and Hispanic Origin: April 1, 2000 to July 1, 2005," released August 4, 2006 (related Internet site <http://www.census.gov/popest/datasets.html>).

Table A-4. States — **Population Characteristics**

State	Households, 2000 Total	With individuals under 18 years (percent of total)	Educational attainment[1] 2000 Total persons	High school graduate or higher (percent)	Bachelor's degree or higher (percent)	Foreign-born population, 2000 (percent)	Speaking language other than English at home, 2000 (percent)	Residing in same house in 1995 and 2000 (percent)	Workers who drove alone to work,[2] 2000 (percent)	Households with income of $75,000 or more in 1999 (percent)	Persons in poverty (percent) 2004	Persons in poverty (percent) 2000
UNITED STATES...	105,480,101	36.0	182,211,639	80.4	24.4	11.1	17.9	54.1	75.7	22.5	12.7	11.3
Alabama	1,737,080	36.1	2,887,400	75.3	19.0	2.0	3.9	57.4	83.0	15.4	16.1	14.6
Alaska	221,600	42.9	379,556	88.3	24.7	5.9	14.3	46.2	66.5	29.8	10.0	8.5
Arizona	1,901,327	35.4	3,256,184	81.0	23.5	12.8	25.9	44.3	74.1	20.5	14.6	12.5
Arkansas	1,042,696	35.6	1,731,200	75.3	16.7	2.8	5.0	53.3	79.9	12.4	15.6	15.0
California	11,502,870	39.7	21,298,900	76.8	26.6	26.2	39.5	50.2	71.8	28.8	13.2	12.7
Colorado	1,658,238	35.3	2,776,632	86.9	32.7	8.6	15.1	44.1	75.1	26.1	10.2	8.9
Connecticut	1,301,670	34.7	2,295,617	84.0	31.4	10.9	18.3	58.2	80.0	33.4	9.1	7.3
Delaware	298,736	35.4	514,658	82.6	25.0	5.7	9.5	56.0	79.2	26.1	9.6	8.7
District of Columbia	248,338	24.6	384,535	77.8	39.1	12.9	16.8	49.9	38.4	25.4	18.3	16.3
Florida	6,337,929	31.3	11,024,645	79.9	22.3	16.7	23.1	48.9	78.8	19.1	11.9	11.7
Georgia	3,006,369	39.1	5,185,965	78.6	24.3	7.1	9.9	49.2	77.5	22.7	13.7	12.3
Hawaii	403,240	37.9	802,477	84.6	26.2	17.5	26.6	56.8	63.9	29.3	9.0	9.9
Idaho	469,645	38.7	787,505	84.7	21.7	5.0	9.3	49.6	77.0	15.7	11.5	11.2
Illinois	4,591,779	36.2	7,973,671	81.4	26.1	12.3	19.2	56.8	73.2	26.0	11.9	10.0
Indiana	2,336,306	35.7	3,893,278	82.1	19.4	3.1	6.4	55.0	81.8	19.3	11.1	8.8
Iowa	1,149,276	33.3	1,895,856	86.1	21.2	3.1	5.8	56.9	78.6	16.1	10.5	8.3
Kansas	1,037,891	35.5	1,701,207	86.0	25.8	5.0	8.7	52.4	81.5	18.9	11.1	8.9
Kentucky	1,590,647	35.5	2,646,397	74.1	17.1	2.0	3.9	55.9	80.2	14.8	16.3	13.9
Louisiana	1,656,053	39.2	2,775,468	74.8	18.7	2.6	9.2	59.0	78.1	15.1	19.2	17.3
Maine	518,200	32.4	869,893	85.4	22.9	2.9	7.8	59.6	78.6	15.5	11.5	9.9
Maryland	1,980,859	37.3	3,495,595	83.8	31.4	9.8	12.6	55.7	73.7	31.7	9.2	7.9
Massachusetts	2,443,580	32.9	4,273,275	84.8	33.2	12.2	18.7	58.5	73.8	30.5	9.9	8.4
Michigan	3,785,661	35.6	6,415,941	83.4	21.8	5.3	8.4	57.3	83.2	24.1	12.5	9.7
Minnesota	1,895,127	34.8	3,164,345	87.9	27.4	5.3	8.5	57.0	77.6	24.7	8.1	6.9
Mississippi	1,046,434	39.6	1,757,517	72.9	16.9	1.4	3.6	58.5	79.4	12.8	19.3	17.6
Missouri.	2,194,594	34.7	3,634,906	81.3	21.6	2.7	5.1	53.6	80.5	17.6	13.0	10.6
Montana	358,667	33.3	586,621	87.2	24.4	1.8	5.2	53.6	73.9	12.0	13.6	13.3
Nebraska	666,184	34.5	1,087,241	86.6	23.7	4.4	7.9	54.7	80.0	16.9	10.0	8.9
Nevada	751,165	35.3	1,310,176	80.7	18.2	15.8	23.1	37.4	74.5	22.4	11.1	9.4
New Hampshire.	474,606	35.5	823,987	87.4	28.7	4.4	8.3	55.4	81.8	26.4	6.6	5.6
New Jersey	3,064,645	36.6	5,657,799	82.1	29.8	17.5	25.5	59.8	73.0	34.9	8.4	7.8
New Mexico	677,971	38.6	1,134,801	78.9	23.5	8.2	36.5	54.4	75.8	15.5	16.7	17.3
New York	7,056,860	35.0	12,542,536	79.1	27.4	20.4	28.0	61.8	63.6	25.8	14.5	13.2
North Carolina.	3,132,013	35.3	5,282,994	78.1	22.5	5.3	8.0	53.0	79.4	18.3	13.8	11.7
North Dakota	257,152	32.7	408,585	83.9	22.0	1.9	6.3	56.8	77.7	12.4	10.8	10.4
Ohio	4,445,773	34.5	7,411,740	83.0	21.1	3.0	6.1	57.5	82.8	19.8	11.7	9.8
Oklahoma	1,342,293	35.7	2,203,173	80.6	20.3	3.8	7.4	51.3	80.0	13.9	14.0	13.8
Oregon	1,333,723	33.4	2,250,998	85.1	25.1	8.5	12.1	46.8	73.2	19.7	12.9	10.6
Pennsylvania	4,777,003	32.6	8,266,284	81.9	22.4	4.1	8.4	63.5	76.5	19.9	11.2	9.5
Rhode Island	408,424	32.9	694,573	78.0	25.6	11.4	20.0	58.1	80.1	22.2	11.6	10.2
South Carolina	1,533,854	36.5	2,596,010	76.3	20.4	2.9	5.2	55.9	79.4	16.6	15.0	12.8
South Dakota	290,245	34.8	474,359	84.6	21.5	1.8	6.5	55.7	77.3	12.9	12.9	11.4
Tennessee	2,232,905	35.2	3,744,928	75.9	19.6	2.8	4.8	53.9	81.7	16.4	15.0	12.6
Texas	7,393,354	40.9	12,790,893	75.7	23.2	13.9	31.2	49.6	77.7	21.1	16.2	14.6
Utah	701,281	45.8	1,197,892	87.7	26.1	7.1	12.5	49.3	75.5	22.5	10.3	8.8
Vermont.	240,634	33.6	404,223	86.4	29.4	3.8	5.9	59.1	75.2	18.3	8.7	8.8
Virginia	2,699,173	35.9	4,666,574	81.5	29.5	8.1	11.1	52.2	77.1	26.5	9.5	8.9
Washington	2,271,398	35.2	3,827,507	87.1	27.7	10.4	14.0	48.6	73.3	24.2	11.6	9.6
West Virginia	736,481	31.8	1,233,581	75.2	14.8	1.1	2.7	63.3	80.3	11.1	16.2	15.5
Wisconsin.	2,084,544	33.9	3,475,878	85.1	22.4	3.6	7.3	56.5	79.5	20.3	10.9	8.1
Wyoming	193,608	35.0	315,663	87.9	21.9	2.3	6.4	51.3	75.4	15.7	10.3	10.4

[1]Persons 25 years and over.
[2]Workers 16 years and over.

Survey, Census, or Data Collection Method: Based on the Census of Population and Housing; for information, see Appendix B, Limitations of the Data and Methodology, and also 2000 Census of Population and Housing, Demographic Profile Technical Documentation, revised August 2002 (related Internet site <http://www.census.gov/prod/cen2000/doc/ProfileTD.pdf>). Census 2000 Summary File 1, Technical Documentation, SF1/13 (RV), issued March 2005 (related Internet site <http://www.census.gov/prod/cen2000/doc/sf1.pdf>). Census 2000 Summary File 3, Technical Documentation, SF3/15 (RV), issued March 2005 (related Internet site <http://www.census.gov/prod/cen2000/doc/sf3.pdf>).

Sources: Households—U.S. Census Bureau, 2000 Census of Population and Housing, "Census 2000 Profiles of General Demographic Characteristics" data files, (DP1) accessed June 14, 2002 (related Internet site <http://www.census.gov/Press-Release/www/2002/demoprofiles.html>). Educational attainment, foreign-born population, language, residence, commuting, and income—U.S. Census Bureau, "Census 2000 Profiles of General Demographic Characteristics" data files, (DP2) accessed June 14, 2002 (related Internet site <http://www.census.gov/Press-Release/www/2002/demoprofiles.html>). Poverty—U.S. Census Bureau, Small Area Income and Poverty Estimates, accessed December 4, 2006 (related Internet site <http://www.census.gov/hhes/www/saipe/index.html>).

Table A-5. States — **Births, Deaths, and Infant Deaths**

State	Births Number 2004	Births Number 2000	Births Rate per 1,000 population[1] 2004	Births Rate per 1,000 population[1] 2000	Deaths Number 2004	Deaths Number 2000	Deaths Rate per 1,000 population[1] 2004	Deaths Rate per 1,000 population[1] 2000	Infant deaths[2] Number 2004	Infant deaths[2] Number 2000	Infant deaths[2] Number 1990	Infant deaths[2] Rate per 1,000 live births[3] 2004	Infant deaths[2] Rate per 1,000 live births[3] 2000	Infant deaths[2] Rate per 1,000 live births[3] 1990
UNITED STATES...	4,112,052	4,058,814	14.0	14.4	2,397,615	2,403,351	8.2	8.5	27,936	28,035	38,351	6.8	6.9	9.2
Alabama	59,510	63,299	13.2	14.2	46,121	45,062	10.2	10.1	516	596	688	8.7	9.4	10.8
Alaska	10,338	9,974	15.7	15.9	3,051	2,914	4.6	4.6	69	68	125	6.7	6.8	10.5
Arizona	93,663	85,273	16.3	16.5	43,198	40,500	7.5	7.8	630	573	610	6.7	6.7	8.8
Arkansas	38,573	37,783	14.0	14.1	27,528	28,217	10.0	10.5	319	316	336	8.3	8.4	9.2
California	544,843	531,959	15.2	15.6	232,525	229,551	6.5	6.8	2,811	2,894	4,844	5.2	5.4	7.9
Colorado	68,503	65,438	14.9	15.1	28,309	27,288	6.2	6.3	434	404	472	6.3	6.2	8.8
Connecticut	42,095	43,026	12.0	12.6	29,314	30,129	8.4	8.8	233	282	398	5.5	6.6	7.9
Delaware	11,369	11,051	13.7	14.1	7,143	6,875	8.6	8.7	98	102	112	8.6	9.2	10.1
District of Columbia	7,933	7,666	14.3	13.4	5,454	6,001	9.8	10.5	95	92	245	12.0	12.0	20.7
Florida	218,053	204,125	12.5	12.7	169,008	164,395	9.7	10.2	1,537	1,425	1,918	7.0	7.0	9.6
Georgia	138,849	132,644	15.6	16.1	65,818	63,870	7.4	7.8	1,181	1,126	1,392	8.5	8.5	12.4
Hawaii	18,281	17,551	14.5	14.5	9,030	8,290	7.2	6.8	104	142	138	5.7	8.1	6.7
Idaho	22,532	20,366	16.2	15.7	10,028	9,563	7.2	7.4	139	153	143	6.2	7.5	8.7
Illinois	180,778	185,036	14.2	14.9	102,670	106,634	8.1	8.6	1,349	1,568	2,104	7.5	8.5	10.7
Indiana	87,142	87,699	14.0	14.4	54,211	55,469	8.7	9.1	700	685	831	8.0	7.8	9.6
Iowa	38,438	38,266	13.0	13.1	26,897	28,060	9.1	9.6	195	247	319	5.1	6.5	8.1
Kansas	39,669	39,666	14.5	14.7	23,818	24,717	8.7	9.2	284	268	329	7.2	6.8	8.4
Kentucky	55,720	56,029	13.5	13.8	38,646	39,504	9.3	9.8	378	401	461	6.8	7.2	8.5
Louisiana	65,369	67,898	14.5	15.2	42,215	41,138	9.4	9.2	684	608	799	10.5	9.0	11.1
Maine	13,944	13,603	10.6	10.6	12,443	12,354	9.5	9.7	79	66	108	5.7	4.9	6.2
Maryland	74,628	74,316	13.4	14.0	43,232	43,753	7.8	8.2	630	562	766	8.4	7.6	9.5
Massachusetts	78,484	81,614	12.2	12.8	54,511	56,681	8.5	8.9	380	376	650	4.8	4.6	7.0
Michigan	129,776	136,171	12.8	13.7	85,169	86,953	8.4	8.7	984	1,119	1,641	7.6	8.2	10.7
Minnesota	70,624	67,604	13.9	13.7	37,034	37,690	7.3	7.6	332	378	496	4.7	5.6	7.3
Mississippi	42,827	44,075	14.8	15.5	27,871	28,654	9.6	10.1	420	470	529	9.8	10.7	12.1
Missouri	77,765	76,463	13.5	13.6	53,950	54,865	9.4	9.8	584	547	748	7.5	7.2	9.4
Montana	11,519	10,957	12.4	12.1	8,094	8,096	8.7	9.0	52	67	105	4.5	6.1	9.0
Nebraska	26,332	24,646	15.1	14.4	14,657	14,992	8.4	8.8	173	180	202	6.6	7.3	8.3
Nevada	35,200	30,829	15.1	15.3	17,929	15,261	7.7	7.6	225	201	181	6.4	6.5	8.4
New Hampshire	14,565	14,609	11.2	11.8	10,111	9,697	7.8	7.8	81	84	125	5.6	5.7	7.1
New Jersey	115,253	115,632	13.3	13.7	71,371	74,800	8.2	8.9	651	733	1,102	5.6	6.3	9.0
New Mexico	28,384	27,223	14.9	14.9	14,298	13,425	7.5	7.4	179	180	246	6.3	6.6	9.0
New York	249,947	258,737	13.0	13.6	152,681	158,203	7.9	8.3	1,518	1,656	2,851	6.1	6.4	9.6
North Carolina	119,847	120,311	14.0	14.9	72,384	71,935	8.5	8.9	1,053	1,038	1,109	8.8	8.6	10.6
North Dakota	8,189	7,676	12.9	12.0	5,601	5,856	8.8	9.1	46	62	74	5.6	8.1	8.0
Ohio	148,954	155,472	13.0	13.7	106,288	108,125	9.3	9.5	1,143	1,187	1,640	7.7	7.6	9.8
Oklahoma	51,306	49,782	14.6	14.4	34,483	35,079	9.8	10.2	411	425	438	8.0	8.5	9.2
Oregon	45,678	45,804	12.7	13.3	30,313	29,552	8.4	8.6	251	255	354	5.5	5.6	8.3
Pennsylvania	144,744	146,281	11.7	11.9	127,640	130,813	10.3	10.6	1,049	1,039	1,643	7.2	7.1	9.6
Rhode Island	12,779	12,505	11.8	11.9	9,769	10,027	9.0	9.5	68	79	123	5.3	6.3	8.1
South Carolina	56,590	56,114	13.5	13.9	37,276	36,948	8.9	9.2	525	488	683	9.3	8.7	11.7
South Dakota	11,338	10,345	14.7	13.7	6,833	7,021	8.9	9.3	93	57	111	8.2	5.5	10.1
Tennessee	79,642	79,611	13.5	14.0	55,829	55,246	9.5	9.7	687	724	771	8.6	9.1	10.3
Texas	381,293	363,414	17.0	17.3	152,870	149,939	6.8	7.2	2,407	2,065	2,552	6.3	5.7	8.1
Utah	50,670	47,353	20.9	21.1	13,331	12,364	5.5	5.5	264	248	271	5.2	5.2	7.5
Vermont	6,599	6,500	10.6	10.7	4,995	5,127	8.0	8.4	30	39	53	4.5	6.0	6.4
Virginia	103,933	98,938	13.9	13.9	56,550	56,282	7.6	7.9	776	682	1,013	7.5	6.9	10.2
Washington	81,747	81,036	13.2	13.7	44,770	43,941	7.2	7.4	451	421	621	5.5	5.2	7.8
West Virginia	20,880	20,865	11.5	11.5	20,793	21,114	11.5	11.7	158	158	223	7.6	7.6	9.9
Wisconsin	70,146	69,326	12.7	12.9	45,600	46,461	8.3	8.6	420	457	598	6.0	6.6	8.2
Wyoming	6,807	6,253	13.5	12.7	3,955	3,920	7.8	7.9	60	42	60	8.8	6.7	8.6

[1] Per 1,000 resident population estimated as of July 1, 2004, and enumerated as of April 1, 2000.
[2] Deaths of infants under 1 year.
[3] Infant deaths per 1,000 live registered births.

Survey, Census, or Data Collection Method: For information about these data collections and surveys, see Appendix B, Limitations of the Data and Methodology, and also the following organization and Internet site: National Center for Health Statistics, <http://wonder.cdc.gov>.

Source: U.S. National Center for Health Statistics, Division of Vital Statistics, accessed January 25, 2007 (related Internet site <http://wonder.cdc.gov>), and unpublished data.

Physicians, Community Hospitals, Medicare, Social Security, and Supplemental Security Income

State	Physicians, 2004[1] Number	Physicians, 2004[1] Rate per 100,000 persons[2]	Community hospitals, 2004[3] Number	Community hospitals, 2004[3] Beds Number	Community hospitals, 2004[3] Beds Rate per 100,000 persons[2]	Medicare program enrollment, 2005[4] Total	Medicare program enrollment, 2005[4] Percent change, 2000–2005	Medicare program enrollment, 2005[4] Rate per 100,000 persons[2]	Social Security program beneficiaries, December 2005 Number	Social Security program beneficiaries, December 2005 Rate per 100,000 persons[2]	Social Security program beneficiaries, December 2005 Percent change, 2000–2005	Social Security program beneficiaries, December 2005 Retired workers, number	Supplemental Security Income program recipients, 2005 Number	Supplemental Security Income program recipients, 2005 Rate per 100,000 persons[2]
UNITED STATES...	872,250	297	4,919	808,127	275	[5]41,547,753	[5]7.2	[5]14,017	47,236,897	15,936	6.6	[5]29,839,453	[5]7,113,132	[5]2,400
Alabama	10,564	233	108	15,328	339	751,175	9.6	16,481	903,569	19,825	9.4	492,491	163,878	3,596
Alaska	1,580	240	19	1,427	217	52,179	24.2	7,862	64,843	9,771	19.3	38,643	11,064	1,667
Arizona	14,010	244	62	11,166	195	786,080	16.4	13,235	922,932	15,539	16.0	602,398	97,934	1,649
Arkansas	6,202	226	87	9,580	348	470,364	7.1	16,925	566,219	20,374	8.1	321,160	90,968	3,273
California	105,766	295	361	71,910	201	4,221,669	8.2	11,684	4,463,873	12,354	6.1	2,875,626	1,209,842	3,348
Colorado	13,455	292	70	9,250	201	519,698	11.2	11,140	584,556	12,530	9.4	378,990	55,532	1,190
Connecticut	14,043	401	35	7,826	224	527,058	2.3	15,015	585,199	16,671	1.3	407,045	52,260	1,489
Delaware	2,325	280	6	1,955	236	126,789	13.1	15,031	150,101	17,795	13.4	97,950	13,767	1,632
District of Columbia	4,723	852	11	3,453	623	73,879	-1.9	13,420	71,376	12,965	-3.2	46,064	21,108	3,834
Florida	51,024	293	203	49,962	287	3,043,361	8.5	17,107	3,430,205	19,282	7.3	2,331,733	423,209	2,379
Georgia	21,638	243	146	24,709	277	1,028,502	12.3	11,336	1,233,238	13,593	12.0	736,664	203,555	2,244
Hawaii	4,432	351	24	3,149	250	182,143	10.2	14,284	200,743	15,742	9.2	143,424	22,754	1,784
Idaho	2,693	193	39	3,434	246	190,494	15.4	13,330	226,250	15,832	15.6	144,936	22,261	1,558
Illinois	37,909	298	191	34,844	274	1,694,820	3.7	13,279	1,893,055	14,832	2.9	1,227,354	258,634	2,026
Indiana	14,696	236	113	18,796	302	904,108	6.1	14,415	1,063,854	16,962	6.5	672,315	98,614	1,572
Iowa	6,287	213	115	10,943	371	489,466	2.7	16,501	552,294	18,619	2.0	365,387	43,373	1,462
Kansas	6,869	251	134	10,362	379	401,243	2.8	14,619	452,119	16,473	2.6	296,145	39,162	1,427
Kentucky	10,464	253	105	15,276	369	676,648	8.6	16,213	797,660	19,113	7.9	415,727	179,955	4,312
Louisiana	12,999	288	131	17,199	382	639,225	6.3	14,131	715,127	15,809	0.5	368,496	152,698	3,376
Maine	4,052	308	37	3,549	270	235,324	8.7	17,807	270,706	20,485	8.0	163,965	31,990	2,421
Maryland	25,098	451	50	11,489	207	696,405	7.9	12,435	771,357	13,773	6.5	508,682	94,656	1,690
Massachusetts	31,215	487	78	16,215	253	974,377	1.4	15,228	1,066,962	16,675	0.6	693,001	171,137	2,675
Michigan	26,999	267	144	25,953	257	1,485,469	5.9	14,677	1,748,668	17,278	6.2	1,083,034	222,053	2,194
Minnesota	15,952	313	132	16,101	316	697,748	6.6	13,594	787,377	15,340	6.4	526,639	72,943	1,421
Mississippi	5,872	202	93	13,143	453	455,699	8.9	15,600	549,376	18,807	6.8	292,620	124,584	4,265
Missouri	15,026	261	119	19,131	332	910,638	5.8	15,700	1,063,174	18,330	5.4	653,609	117,760	2,030
Montana	2,425	262	54	4,337	468	147,634	8.0	15,778	169,375	18,102	7.6	109,049	14,793	1,581
Nebraska	4,672	267	85	7,336	420	261,326	3.0	14,858	291,980	16,601	2.3	191,931	22,331	1,270
Nevada	4,933	211	30	4,752	204	296,639	23.7	12,284	346,345	14,343	20.7	234,284	33,479	1,386
New Hampshire	3,884	299	28	2,807	216	190,783	12.2	14,564	220,796	16,855	10.5	145,126	13,689	1,045
New Jersey	29,247	337	80	21,952	253	1,232,802	2.5	14,141	1,375,796	15,781	2.0	942,992	152,142	1,745
New Mexico	5,169	272	37	3,678	193	265,823	13.4	13,785	311,468	16,152	12.3	186,639	53,865	2,793
New York	81,716	424	206	64,205	333	2,796,213	3.0	14,522	3,062,046	15,903	1.8	1,991,618	633,473	3,290
North Carolina	24,085	282	115	23,498	275	1,267,633	11.8	14,599	1,509,687	17,386	11.7	940,891	199,337	2,296
North Dakota	1,716	270	40	3,567	561	103,781	0.6	16,300	114,712	18,017	0.1	72,329	7,907	1,242
Ohio	33,103	289	166	33,398	292	1,754,413	3.1	15,304	1,960,946	17,105	2.6	1,207,381	250,364	2,184
Oklahoma	6,846	194	109	10,804	307	539,461	6.2	15,205	635,619	17,915	7.0	388,090	79,743	2,248
Oregon	10,957	305	58	6,505	181	536,992	9.7	14,748	618,624	16,990	10.0	414,216	60,701	1,667
Pennsylvania	40,832	329	197	40,079	323	2,133,435	1.8	17,164	2,419,005	19,462	2.7	1,561,281	317,808	2,557
Rhode Island	4,141	383	11	2,397	222	173,100	0.9	16,085	192,829	17,918	0.1	128,395	30,164	2,803
South Carolina	10,761	256	62	11,222	267	644,853	13.6	15,155	778,480	18,295	13.1	471,731	105,553	2,481
South Dakota	1,904	247	51	4,611	598	124,590	4.3	16,057	140,773	18,142	3.3	92,131	12,542	1,616
Tennessee	16,863	286	127	20,363	346	915,609	10.4	15,355	1,089,649	18,274	10.0	641,443	161,322	2,705
Texas	52,060	232	418	58,116	259	2,522,567	11.4	11,035	2,952,230	12,914	12.1	1,758,929	504,082	2,205
Utah	5,642	233	43	4,517	187	235,039	14.1	9,517	273,045	11,056	13.3	177,447	22,606	915
Vermont	2,589	417	14	1,473	237	96,352	8.2	15,465	112,251	18,016	7.4	72,248	13,110	2,104
Virginia	22,587	302	88	17,339	232	992,216	11.1	13,112	1,139,748	15,061	10.0	710,014	137,662	1,819
Washington	18,894	304	85	10,984	177	818,451	11.3	13,017	937,531	14,910	11.0	613,620	115,692	1,840
West Virginia	4,613	255	57	7,412	409	355,466	5.2	19,565	414,053	22,790	5.2	210,421	76,820	4,228
Wisconsin	15,625	284	121	14,577	265	825,876	5.5	14,918	953,581	17,224	5.8	639,221	92,288	1,667
Wyoming	1,093	216	24	2,048	405	71,005	8.5	13,942	81,495	16,002	7.1	53,912	5,786	1,136

[1]Active, nonfederal physicians as of December 31. Data subject to copyright; see below for source citation.
[2]Based on resident population estimated as of July 1 of the year shown.
[3]Nonfederal, short-term general, and other special hospitals except hospital units of institutions. Data subject to copyright; see below for source citation.
[4]Unduplicated count of persons enrolled in either hospital and/or supplemental medical insurance.
[5]Includes data not distrubuted by state.

Survey, Census, or Data Collection Method: For information about these data collections and surveys, see the following organizations and their Web sites: American Medical Association, *Physician Characteristics and Distribution in the U.S.*, <http://www.ama-assn.org/>; American Hospital Association (AHA), *Hospital Statistics*, <http://www.healthforum.com>; Centers for Medicare and Medicaid Services, CMS Statistics, Medicare Enrollment, <http://www.cms.hhs.gov/>; U.S. Social Security Administration, OASDI Beneficiaries by State and County, <http://www.ssa.gov/policy /docs/statcomps/oasdi_sc/2005/index.html>; SSI Monthly Statistics, Supplemental Security Income, <http://www.ssa.gov/policy/docs/statcomps/ssi_monthly>; and SSI Recipients by State and County, updated annually, <http://www.ssa.gov/policy/docs/statcomps/ssi_sc/>.

Sources: Physicians—American Medical Association, Chicago, IL, *Physician Characteristics and Distribution in the U.S.*, annual (copyright), accessed May 17, 2006. Community hospitals—Health Forum LLC, an American Hospital Association (AHA) Company, Chicago, IL, *Hospital Statistics*, and unpublished data (copyright), e-mail accessed May 4, 2006 (related Internet site <http://www.healthforum.com>). Medicare program enrollment—Centers for Medicare and Medicaid Services, CMS Statistics, Medicare Enrollment, accessed February 8, 2006 (related Internet site <http://www.cms.hhs.gov/>). Social Security program—U.S. Social Security Administration, Office of Research, Evaluation, and Statistics, OASDI Beneficiaries by State and County, accessed October 24, 2006 (related Internet site <http://www.ssa.gov/policy/docs/statcomps/oasdi_sc/2005/>). Supplemental Security Income program—U.S. Social Security Administration, Office of Research, Evaluation, and Statistics, *SSI Recipients by State and County, 2005*, accessed July 24, 2006 (related Internet site <http://www.ssa.gov/policy/docs/statcomps/ssi_sc/2005/>).

State	Housing units							Housing 2000, percent		New private housing units authorized by building permits		
	2005 (July 1)	2000[1] (April 1 estimates base)	1990 (April 1)	Net change, 2000–2005 Number	Percent	Units per square mile of land area 2005[2]	1990	Owner-occupied housing units[3]	Units in multi-unit structures	Cumulative, 2000–2005 period	2005	2004
United States......	124,521,886	115,904,474	102,263,678	8,617,412	7.4	35.2	28.9	66.2	26.4	11,091,316	2,155,316	2,070,077
Alabama...........	2,082,140	1,963,834	1,670,379	118,306	6.0	41.0	32.9	72.5	15.3	133,794	30,612	27,411
Alaska............	274,246	260,963	232,608	13,283	5.1	0.5	0.4	62.5	27.0	17,638	2,885	3,133
Arizona...........	2,544,806	2,189,189	1,659,430	355,617	16.2	22.4	14.6	68.0	22.1	446,503	90,851	90,644
Arkansas..........	1,249,116	1,173,042	1,000,667	76,074	6.5	24.0	19.2	69.4	13.9	80,672	17,932	15,855
California..........	12,989,254	12,214,550	11,182,882	774,704	6.3	83.3	71.7	56.9	31.4	1,056,245	205,020	207,390
Colorado..........	2,053,178	1,808,358	1,477,349	244,820	13.5	19.8	14.2	67.3	25.7	289,433	45,891	46,499
Connecticut........	1,423,343	1,385,997	1,320,850	37,346	2.7	293.8	272.6	66.8	35.1	62,554	11,885	11,837
Delaware..........	374,872	343,072	289,919	31,800	9.3	191.9	148.3	72.3	18.7	39,569	8,195	7,858
District of Columbia.....	277,775	274,845	278,489	2,930	1.1	4,524.0	4,534.9	40.8	60.2	9,516	2,860	1,936
Florida............	8,256,847	7,303,108	6,100,262	953,739	13.1	153.1	113.0	70.1	29.9	1,264,445	287,250	255,893
Georgia...........	3,771,466	3,281,866	2,638,418	489,600	14.9	65.1	45.6	67.5	20.8	596,798	109,336	108,356
Hawaii	491,071	460,542	389,810	30,529	6.6	76.5	60.7	56.5	39.4	41,743	9,828	9,034
Idaho............	595,572	527,825	413,327	67,747	12.8	7.2	5.0	72.4	14.4	91,000	21,578	18,108
Illinois............	5,144,623	4,885,744	4,506,275	258,879	5.3	92.6	81.1	67.3	34.0	356,660	66,942	59,753
Indiana...........	2,724,429	2,532,327	2,246,046	192,102	7.6	76.0	62.6	71.4	19.2	233,746	38,476	39,233
Iowa.............	1,306,943	1,232,530	1,143,669	74,413	6.0	23.4	20.5	72.3	18.4	89,570	16,766	16,345
Kansas...........	1,196,211	1,131,395	1,044,112	64,816	5.7	14.6	12.8	69.2	17.5	82,453	14,048	13,301
Kentucky..........	1,865,516	1,751,118	1,506,845	114,398	6.5	47.0	37.9	70.8	17.7	119,790	21,159	22,623
Louisiana.........	1,940,399	1,847,174	1,716,241	93,225	5.0	44.5	39.4	67.9	18.7	116,818	22,811	22,989
Maine............	683,799	651,901	587,045	31,898	4.9	22.2	19.0	71.6	20.3	45,549	8,969	8,771
Maryland..........	2,273,793	2,145,289	1,891,917	128,504	6.0	232.6	193.6	67.7	25.8	176,186	30,180	27,382
Massachusetts.......	2,688,014	2,621,993	2,472,711	66,021	2.5	342.9	315.5	61.7	42.7	119,782	24,549	22,477
Michigan..........	4,478,507	4,234,252	3,847,926	244,255	5.8	78.8	67.7	73.8	18.8	306,558	45,328	54,721
Minnesota.........	2,252,022	2,065,952	1,848,445	186,070	9.0	28.3	23.2	74.6	22.3	226,340	36,509	41,843
Mississippi.........	1,235,496	1,161,952	1,010,423	73,544	6.3	26.3	21.5	72.3	13.3	72,392	13,396	14,532
Missouri	2,592,809	2,442,003	2,199,129	150,806	6.2	37.6	31.9	70.3	20.0	172,529	33,114	32,791
Montana..........	428,357	412,633	361,155	15,724	3.8	2.9	2.5	69.1	15.7	22,295	4,803	4,975
Nebraska	766,951	722,669	660,621	44,282	6.1	10.0	8.6	67.4	20.0	57,769	9,929	10,920
Nevada...........	1,019,427	827,457	518,858	191,970	23.2	9.3	4.7	60.9	32.2	239,675	47,728	44,556
New Hampshire	583,324	547,024	503,904	36,300	6.6	65.0	56.2	69.7	26.5	46,892	7,586	8,653
New Jersey.........	3,443,981	3,310,274	3,075,310	133,707	4.0	464.3	414.5	65.6	36.1	200,801	38,588	35,936
New Mexico........	838,668	780,579	632,058	58,089	7.4	6.9	5.2	70.0	15.3	71,418	14,180	12,555
New York..........	7,853,020	7,679,307	7,226,891	173,713	2.3	166.3	153.0	53.0	50.6	303,950	61,949	53,497
North Carolina	3,940,554	3,522,334	2,818,193	418,220	11.9	80.9	57.8	69.4	16.1	510,443	97,910	93,077
North Dakota	304,458	289,679	276,340	14,779	5.1	4.4	4.0	66.6	24.8	19,872	4,038	4,033
Ohio.............	5,007,091	4,783,066	4,371,945	224,025	4.7	122.3	106.8	69.1	24.1	303,385	47,727	51,695
Oklahoma	1,588,749	1,514,399	1,406,499	74,350	4.9	23.1	20.5	68.4	15.2	86,877	18,362	17,068
Oregon...........	1,558,421	1,452,724	1,193,567	105,697	7.3	16.2	12.4	64.3	23.1	146,733	31,024	27,309
Pennsylvania	5,422,362	5,249,751	4,938,140	172,611	3.3	121.0	110.2	71.3	21.2	269,139	44,525	49,665
Rhode Island	447,810	439,837	414,572	7,973	1.8	428.6	396.7	60.0	41.2	15,505	2,836	2,532
South Carolina	1,927,864	1,753,586	1,424,155	174,278	9.9	64.0	47.3	72.2	15.8	232,627	54,157	43,230
South Dakota	347,931	323,207	292,436	24,724	7.6	4.6	3.9	68.2	18.9	29,977	5,685	5,839
Tennessee..........	2,637,441	2,439,433	2,026,067	198,008	8.1	64.0	49.2	69.9	18.7	227,782	46,615	44,791
Texas............	9,026,011	8,157,558	7,008,999	868,453	10.6	34.5	26.8	63.8	24.2	1,033,247	210,611	188,842
Utah.............	873,097	768,603	598,388	104,494	13.6	10.6	7.3	71.5	22.0	130,443	27,799	24,267
Vermont	307,345	294,382	271,214	12,963	4.4	33.2	29.3	70.6	23.0	17,673	2,917	3,588
Virginia...........	3,174,708	2,904,432	2,496,334	270,276	9.3	80.2	63.0	68.1	21.5	341,381	61,518	63,220
Washington	2,651,645	2,451,082	2,032,378	200,563	8.2	39.8	30.5	64.6	25.6	263,553	52,988	50,089
West Virginia	872,203	844,626	781,295	27,577	3.3	36.2	32.4	75.2	12.0	29,589	6,140	5,716
Wisconsin	2,498,500	2,321,157	2,055,774	177,343	7.6	46.0	37.9	68.4	26.2	226,345	35,334	39,992
Wyoming	235,721	223,854	203,411	11,867	5.3	2.4	2.1	70.0	15.2	15,662	3,997	3,317

[1]The April 1, 2000, housing estimates base reflects changes to the 2000 Census of Population and Housing as documented in the Count Question Resolution program and geographic program revisions.
[2]Based on land area data from the 2000 census.
[3]Owner-occupied housing units as a percent of all occupied housing.

Survey, Census, or Data Collection Method: Housing units and housing 2000—Based on the 2000 Census of Population and Housing; for information, see Appendix B, Limitations of the Data and Methodology, and also <http://www.census.gov/prod/cen2000/doc/sf1.pdf> and <http://www.census.gov/popest/topics/methodology>. Building permits—Based on a survey of local building permit officials using Form C-404; for information, see <http://www.census.gov/const/www/newresconstdoc.html>.

Sources: Housing units 2000 and 2005—U.S. Census Bureau, "Annual Estimates of Housing Units for Counties: April 1, 2000 to July 1, 2005," accessed November 14, 2005 (related Internet site <http://www.census.gov/popest/housing/HU-EST2005-4.html>). Housing units 1990—U.S. Census Bureau, 1990 Census of Population and Housing, Summary Tape File (STF) 1C on CD-ROM (archive). Housing 2000—U.S. Census Bureau, 2000 Census of Population and Housing, Census 2000 Profiles of General Demographic Characteristics data files, accessed July 19, 2005 (related Internet site <http://censtats.census.gov/pub/Profiles.shtml>). Building permits—U.S. Census Bureau, "New Residential Construction—Building Permits," May 24, 2006 e-mail from Manufacturing, Mining, and Construction Statistics Branch, subject: Annual Place Level Data 2000–2005 (related Internet site <http://www.census.gov/const/www/permitsindex.html>).

State	Violent crimes[1]						Property crimes[1]				
	2004					2000	2004				2000
	Total	Murder and non-negligent man-slaughter	Forcible rape	Robbery	Aggra-vated assault		Total	Burglary	Larceny-theft	Motor vehicle theft	
UNITED STATES[2] ..	1,313,779	15,607	88,248	390,437	819,487	1,349,339	9,812,534	2,033,649	6,578,616	1,200,269	9,403,713
Alabama	18,641	247	1,685	5,887	10,822	17,990	175,546	43,121	118,860	13,565	151,127
Alaska	4,082	36	549	444	3,053	3,151	21,605	3,704	15,708	2,193	21,074
Arizona	28,562	411	1,869	7,645	18,637	27,186	301,799	55,788	191,468	54,543	271,269
Arkansas	12,766	166	1,080	2,261	9,259	11,807	99,923	26,190	67,886	5,847	97,501
California	197,423	2,393	9,594	61,567	123,869	210,459	1,223,227	244,917	726,556	251,754	1,054,010
Colorado	16,582	198	1,872	3,642	10,870	13,508	172,467	31,836	117,540	23,091	145,469
Connecticut	9,169	97	732	3,808	4,532	11,166	89,898	15,220	64,205	10,473	99,162
Delaware	5,105	28	357	1,343	3,377	(NA)	27,256	5,669	19,285	2,302	29,553
District of Columbia	7,593	198	223	3,204	3,968	8,623	26,906	3,946	14,545	8,415	32,998
Florida	123,695	946	6,609	29,984	86,156	128,041	726,784	166,253	482,236	78,295	767,667
Georgia	36,900	554	2,205	12,805	21,336	39,423	337,563	74,004	223,127	40,432	325,603
Hawaii	3,274	33	361	963	1,917	2,954	60,391	10,719	41,045	8,627	60,033
Idaho	3,448	31	593	241	2,583	3,264	38,753	7,662	28,355	2,736	37,927
Illinois	(NA)	506	(NA)	17,390	22,217	50,655	177,867	32,649	119,639	25,579	199,349
Indiana	18,783	300	1,652	6,046	10,785	17,844	192,505	38,128	134,892	19,485	167,958
Iowa	8,272	44	757	1,138	6,333	7,697	83,253	17,435	60,304	5,514	84,001
Kansas	9,911	122	1,095	1,774	6,920	8,151	104,853	19,217	77,417	8,219	86,199
Kentucky	9,310	217	1,114	3,055	4,924	6,657	94,056	23,358	62,770	7,928	45,650
Louisiana	27,465	557	1,523	6,279	19,106	28,542	183,263	41,555	122,773	18,935	199,945
Maine	1,363	18	314	289	742	1,391	31,745	6,342	24,100	1,303	31,880
Maryland	38,938	521	1,317	12,761	24,339	41,847	202,326	36,682	129,786	35,858	214,440
Massachusetts	30,181	170	1,745	7,353	20,913	33,163	153,442	33,478	98,425	21,539	158,753
Michigan	49,272	643	5,400	11,242	31,987	54,015	305,434	63,430	191,885	50,119	343,233
Minnesota	13,671	113	2,107	4,053	7,398	13,678	154,552	27,747	113,401	13,404	155,293
Mississippi	6,579	178	885	2,154	3,362	7,397	80,936	21,304	53,110	6,522	84,888
Missouri	28,067	357	1,535	6,606	19,569	25,438	223,511	40,336	157,410	25,765	208,785
Montana	2,091	23	214	135	1,719	2,495	22,015	2,662	18,197	1,156	16,894
Nebraska	5,292	40	606	1,133	3,513	5,532	60,177	9,570	45,405	5,202	62,336
Nevada	14,379	172	954	4,905	8,348	10,474	98,214	23,142	52,437	22,635	74,823
New Hampshire	1,552	13	376	344	819	1,129	19,872	3,709	14,830	1,333	16,151
New Jersey	30,914	392	1,329	13,070	16,123	32,297	211,526	41,050	140,158	30,318	233,637
New Mexico	11,917	150	935	1,963	8,869	12,445	73,630	18,087	48,217	7,326	78,964
New York	84,274	894	3,543	33,366	46,471	99,934	414,862	69,479	304,675	40,708	427,466
North Carolina	36,579	511	2,221	11,430	22,417	38,909	336,105	95,134	215,229	25,742	343,174
North Dakota	525	8	167	43	307	502	11,678	1,897	8,911	870	13,522
Ohio	36,286	480	4,286	16,689	14,831	32,451	375,794	87,762	249,633	38,399	329,209
Oklahoma	17,632	186	1,556	3,090	12,800	17,176	149,452	35,234	101,263	12,955	140,125
Oregon	10,601	90	1,271	2,735	6,505	11,890	164,732	29,559	116,749	18,424	151,933
Pennsylvania	48,273	645	3,312	17,866	26,450	48,325	277,515	51,103	196,867	29,545	288,257
Rhode Island	2,673	26	320	731	1,596	3,119	31,166	5,465	21,623	4,078	33,323
South Carolina	33,112	285	1,769	5,457	25,601	32,671	190,203	43,665	130,831	15,707	178,319
South Dakota	1,222	16	321	111	774	1,138	13,654	2,895	9,981	778	14,808
Tennessee	41,084	356	2,281	8,861	29,586	40,213	254,865	60,370	169,739	24,756	237,893
Texas	121,148	1,361	8,347	35,743	75,697	113,270	1,007,982	219,434	694,567	93,981	915,304
Utah	5,583	51	951	1,229	3,352	5,349	95,961	14,866	73,562	7,533	87,056
Vermont	687	16	154	75	442	647	13,985	3,315	10,104	566	16,129
Virginia	20,287	389	1,787	6,838	11,273	19,771	197,034	28,266	151,543	17,225	188,954
Washington	21,190	189	2,824	5,852	12,325	21,445	298,447	59,955	195,448	43,044	273,851
West Virginia	4,716	66	319	709	3,622	5,448	42,170	10,138	28,563	3,469	39,134
Wisconsin	11,460	153	1,121	4,062	6,124	12,387	145,068	23,517	110,259	11,292	153,788
Wyoming	1,137	11	111	66	949	1,311	16,566	2,685	13,097	784	14,896

NA Not available.

[1]For individual crime data items, some data are incomplete. The U.S. and state totals are a summation of data for counties. The U.S. and state totals may differ from published Uniform Crime Reports (related Internet site <http://www.fbi.gov/ucr/cius_04/>).
[2]For individual crime data items, some data are not distributed by state.

Survey, Census, or Data Collection Method: Based on the Uniform Crime Reporting (UCR) Program; for information, see Appendix B, Limitations of the Data and Methodology.

Source: U.S. Department of Justice, Federal Bureau of Investigation, Uniform Crime Reporting Program, unpublished data, annual (related Internet site <http://www.fbi.gov/>).

Table A-9. States — Personal Income and Earnings by Industries

State	Total, by place of residence — 2005 (mil. dol.)	2004 (mil. dol.)	2000 (mil. dol.)	Percent change 2004–2005	2000–2005	Per capita (dol.) 2005	2000	Earnings — Total[2] (mil. dol.)	Construction	Retail trade	Professional and technical services	Health care and social assistance	Government
UNITED STATES...	10,220,942	9,716,351	8,422,074	5.2	21.4	34,471	29,845	7,983,652	6.4	6.5	9.4	9.4	16.5
Alabama	134,736	126,655	105,807	6.4	27.3	29,623	23,764	98,672	6.4	7.3	7.6	9.4	20.2
Alaska	23,588	22,259	18,741	6.0	25.9	35,564	29,867	20,147	8.6	6.5	5.6	9.0	31.9
Arizona	178,706	164,122	132,558	8.9	34.8	30,019	25,660	137,109	9.6	8.3	7.6	9.3	16.5
Arkansas	74,059	70,853	58,726	4.5	26.1	26,681	21,925	54,561	5.6	6.8	5.1	10.5	18.6
California	1,335,386	1,268,049	1,103,842	5.3	21.0	36,936	32,463	1,065,280	6.9	6.6	11.1	7.8	15.8
Colorado	174,919	164,673	144,394	6.2	21.1	37,510	33,371	144,091	8.6	5.9	11.4	7.4	15.6
Connecticut	165,890	158,567	141,570	4.6	17.2	47,388	41,489	128,707	5.6	6.0	9.7	9.8	12.2
Delaware	31,218	29,300	24,277	6.5	28.6	37,088	30,869	26,825	(NA)	6.3	11.6	9.6	14.2
District of Columbia	30,739	29,125	23,102	5.5	33.1	52,811	40,456	65,430	(NA)	1.0	22.5	4.9	41.5
Florida	604,131	564,997	457,539	6.9	32.0	34,001	28,509	407,351	8.3	8.1	8.8	10.2	16.0
Georgia	282,322	264,728	230,356	6.6	22.6	30,914	27,989	229,413	6.1	6.5	8.7	7.9	17.1
Hawaii	43,913	41,129	34,451	6.8	27.5	34,489	28,422	35,326	7.6	6.6	6.0	8.7	31.3
Idaho	40,706	38,229	31,290	6.5	30.1	28,478	24,075	30,059	8.4	8.6	9.0	8.9	18.4
Illinois	462,928	442,349	400,373	4.7	15.6	36,264	32,185	367,173	6.0	5.6	11.2	8.6	13.8
Indiana	195,332	187,533	165,285	4.2	18.2	31,173	27,132	149,311	6.5	6.4	5.0	10.0	14.3
Iowa	93,919	91,230	77,763	2.9	20.8	31,670	26,554	71,011	6.5	7.0	4.3	9.7	16.4
Kansas	90,320	85,520	74,570	5.6	21.1	32,866	27,694	69,918	5.4	6.2	6.4	9.2	19.8
Kentucky	117,967	111,873	98,845	5.4	19.3	28,272	24,412	90,811	5.7	6.9	5.3	10.6	19.4
Louisiana	111,167	121,781	103,151	-8.7	7.8	24,664	23,079	88,982	7.2	7.1	6.6	10.2	21.4
Maine	40,612	39,236	33,173	3.5	22.4	30,808	25,969	29,134	6.9	8.9	6.2	14.5	19.2
Maryland	234,609	220,603	181,957	6.3	28.9	41,972	34,257	163,980	8.0	6.3	13.2	9.6	22.8
Massachusetts	279,860	267,972	240,209	4.4	16.5	43,501	37,756	224,879	5.8	5.7	13.5	11.2	11.5
Michigan	331,349	320,261	294,227	3.5	12.6	32,804	29,552	257,610	5.7	6.1	9.9	9.6	14.0
Minnesota	191,175	184,225	157,964	3.8	21.0	37,290	32,017	152,818	6.2	6.0	7.8	10.5	13.8
Mississippi	72,862	69,450	59,837	4.9	21.8	25,051	21,005	51,278	5.7	7.6	4.6	9.6	24.1
Missouri	181,066	173,054	152,722	4.6	18.6	31,231	27,241	140,886	6.9	6.8	7.7	9.9	15.8
Montana	27,122	25,791	20,716	5.2	30.9	29,015	22,929	19,788	8.3	8.5	6.1	11.7	22.2
Nebraska	57,885	55,828	47,329	3.7	22.3	32,923	27,625	45,118	6.4	6.5	6.2	10.0	17.8
Nevada	86,224	79,353	61,428	8.7	40.4	35,744	30,437	67,329	12.6	7.3	6.8	6.8	14.2
New Hampshire	49,356	47,248	41,429	4.5	19.1	37,768	33,396	36,696	7.3	9.6	7.9	10.7	12.1
New Jersey	381,466	363,158	323,554	5.0	17.9	43,831	38,364	278,468	5.4	6.7	11.2	9.5	14.7
New Mexico	53,714	50,707	40,318	5.9	33.2	27,889	22,134	39,793	7.1	7.5	9.0	9.5	28.6
New York	771,990	742,209	663,005	4.0	16.4	39,967	34,897	630,690	4.1	5.0	11.3	10.2	14.5
North Carolina	269,203	252,253	218,668	6.7	23.1	31,041	27,068	206,623	6.5	6.9	6.6	8.9	19.4
North Dakota	19,899	18,509	16,097	7.5	23.6	31,357	25,106	16,282	6.2	7.1	4.3	11.9	22.0
Ohio	365,453	352,588	320,538	3.6	14.0	31,860	28,207	282,835	5.5	6.6	7.4	10.9	15.4
Oklahoma	106,119	100,027	84,310	6.1	25.9	29,948	24,407	79,336	4.8	6.7	5.6	8.8	20.9
Oregon	117,497	111,325	96,402	5.5	21.9	32,289	28,097	91,881	6.5	6.9	6.5	10.1	18.9
Pennsylvania	433,400	413,589	364,838	4.8	18.8	34,937	29,695	323,799	6.1	6.5	9.6	12.4	13.3
Rhode Island	37,923	36,679	30,697	3.4	23.5	35,324	29,214	27,049	5.9	6.4	7.3	13.0	18.1
South Carolina	120,123	113,632	98,270	5.7	22.2	28,285	24,424	89,011	7.2	8.0	6.0	7.9	20.9
South Dakota	25,201	24,053	19,438	4.8	29.6	32,523	25,720	18,157	6.2	7.6	3.5	12.9	19.3
Tennessee	184,443	174,452	148,833	5.7	23.9	30,969	26,097	147,894	5.8	7.6	6.7	11.7	13.9
Texas	744,270	690,480	593,139	7.8	25.5	32,460	28,313	618,504	6.5	6.3	8.7	8.2	14.8
Utah	68,039	63,478	53,561	7.2	27.0	27,321	23,878	57,047	8.1	7.5	8.6	7.7	18.9
Vermont	20,362	19,519	16,883	4.3	20.6	32,717	27,680	15,323	7.6	8.5	7.2	12.2	17.9
Virginia	283,685	266,751	220,845	6.3	28.5	37,503	31,087	228,461	6.8	5.7	15.0	6.9	23.7
Washington	223,232	216,921	187,853	2.9	18.8	35,479	31,779	175,684	7.2	7.0	8.2	8.8	19.1
West Virginia	47,926	45,819	39,582	4.6	21.1	26,419	21,899	33,284	6.3	7.5	5.5	13.1	22.6
Wisconsin	183,948	176,482	153,548	4.2	19.8	33,278	28,570	140,151	6.4	6.4	5.5	11.1	14.8
Wyoming	18,981	17,723	14,063	7.1	35.0	37,305	28,460	13,689	8.6	6.4	4.7	6.9	23.1

NA Not available.

[1] Based on resident population estimated as of July 1, 2000, and 2005.
[2] Includes other industries not shown separately.

Survey, Census, or Data Collection Method: Based on the Regional Economic Information System; for more information, see <http://www.bea.gov/regional/methods.cfm/>.

Source: U.S. Bureau of Economic Analysis, Regional Economic Information System (REIS), downloaded estimates and software, accessed June 5, 2007 (related Internet site <http://www.bea.gov/regional/docs/reis2005dvd.cfm>).

Labor Force and Private Business Establishments and Employment

State	Civilian labor force							Private nonfarm businesses					
	Total			Number of unemployed		Unemployment rate[1]		Establishments		Employment[2]		Annual payroll per employee, 2004	
	2006	2000	Net change, 2000–2006	2006	2000	2006	2000	2004	Net change, 2000–2004	2004	Net change, 2000–2004	Amount (dol.)	Percent of U.S. average
UNITED STATES...	151,428,000	142,583,000	8,845,000	7,001,000	5,692,000	4.6	4.0	7,387,724	317,676	115,074,924	1,009,948	36,967	100.0
Alabama	2,199,562	2,154,545	45,017	78,989	87,398	3.6	4.1	100,802	985	1,629,141	−23,933	30,552	82.6
Alaska	346,769	319,002	27,767	23,238	19,678	6.7	6.2	19,387	886	223,153	18,266	40,890	110.6
Arizona	2,977,094	2,505,306	471,788	122,713	100,390	4.1	4.0	125,693	10,889	2,044,134	124,781	33,834	91.5
Arkansas	1,364,646	1,260,256	104,390	71,760	52,904	5.3	4.2	65,291	2,106	1,007,512	16,682	28,457	77.0
California	17,901,874	16,857,578	1,044,296	872,567	833,237	4.9	4.9	841,774	41,911	13,264,918	380,226	41,820	113.1
Colorado	2,651,718	2,364,990	286,728	114,681	64,798	4.3	2.7	147,314	9,786	1,908,508	−4,794	37,505	101.5
Connecticut	1,844,235	1,736,831	107,404	79,160	39,161	4.3	2.3	93,011	575	1,537,461	−8,789	47,382	128.2
Delaware	440,322	416,503	23,819	15,816	13,726	3.6	3.3	25,391	1,620	391,682	14,405	41,040	111.0
District of Columbia	315,874	309,421	6,453	18,917	17,505	6.0	5.7	19,518	−137	436,865	21,882	55,587	150.4
Florida	8,988,611	7,869,690	1,118,921	295,850	300,284	3.3	3.8	484,938	56,500	6,864,987	647,601	32,017	86.6
Georgia	4,741,860	4,242,889	498,971	219,835	147,527	4.6	3.5	214,714	14,272	3,452,451	−31,049	35,147	95.1
Hawaii	643,486	609,018	34,468	15,209	24,160	2.4	4.0	31,605	1,752	473,500	41,408	31,837	86.1
Idaho	749,244	662,958	86,286	25,623	30,507	3.4	4.6	41,336	3,907	488,676	37,888	29,074	78.6
Illinois	6,613,346	6,467,692	145,654	297,631	290,855	4.5	4.5	315,854	7,787	5,217,160	−283,876	39,846	107.8
Indiana	3,271,496	3,144,379	127,117	162,690	91,660	5.0	2.9	149,381	3,060	2,586,799	−63,975	32,897	89.0
Iowa	1,664,339	1,601,920	62,419	61,490	44,839	3.7	2.8	81,565	675	1,241,864	−23,200	30,312	82.0
Kansas	1,466,004	1,405,104	60,900	65,835	53,116	4.5	3.8	75,827	888	1,116,277	−12,455	32,004	86.6
Kentucky	2,038,971	1,949,013	89,958	116,808	82,665	5.7	4.2	91,797	1,876	1,489,497	−24,225	30,992	83.8
Louisiana	1,990,120	2,031,292	−41,172	79,772	100,630	4.0	5.0	103,067	2,051	1,623,680	31,323	30,207	81.7
Maine	711,376	672,440	38,936	32,533	22,055	4.6	3.3	41,269	1,803	494,256	2,476	31,237	84.5
Maryland	3,009,143	2,811,657	197,486	116,523	100,275	3.9	3.6	136,062	7,595	2,151,474	93,170	39,204	106.1
Massachusetts	3,404,394	3,365,573	38,821	169,534	92,292	5.0	2.7	175,933	−289	2,979,690	−107,354	45,389	122.8
Michigan	5,081,336	5,143,916	−62,580	351,045	190,495	6.9	3.7	237,984	1,072	3,895,914	−176,872	37,917	102.6
Minnesota	2,939,304	2,807,668	131,636	117,007	87,176	4.0	3.1	148,626	9,546	2,393,126	−2,235	38,609	104.4
Mississippi	1,307,347	1,314,154	−6,807	88,683	74,295	6.8	5.7	60,534	746	928,313	−28,468	26,734	72.3
Missouri	3,032,434	2,973,092	59,342	146,577	97,756	4.8	3.3	153,985	9,230	2,421,450	22,471	32,690	88.4
Montana	493,842	468,865	24,977	15,680	22,313	3.2	4.8	34,686	2,837	314,865	18,645	26,288	71.1
Nebraska	974,476	949,762	24,714	29,206	26,564	3.0	2.8	50,928	1,305	774,311	23,235	30,584	82.7
Nevada	1,295,085	1,062,845	232,240	54,217	47,624	4.2	4.5	55,853	7,675	1,022,011	119,236	34,098	92.2
New Hampshire	736,780	694,254	42,526	25,268	18,713	3.4	2.7	38,843	1,429	551,001	4,601	36,307	98.2
New Jersey	4,518,035	4,287,783	230,252	209,014	157,473	4.6	3.7	240,539	6,980	3,609,640	61,211	44,392	120.1
New Mexico	935,350	852,293	83,057	39,727	42,269	4.2	5.0	44,205	1,423	580,576	31,224	28,957	78.3
New York	9,498,563	9,166,972	331,591	425,830	415,531	4.5	4.5	511,440	19,367	7,433,686	80,477	47,521	128.5
North Carolina	4,464,875	4,123,812	341,063	214,256	154,577	4.8	3.7	213,057	9,154	3,365,633	−19,859	32,556	88.1
North Dakota	357,960	345,881	12,079	11,601	10,101	3.2	2.9	20,822	683	265,663	10,485	27,531	74.5
Ohio	5,933,957	5,807,036	126,921	324,901	233,882	5.5	4.0	271,733	1,224	4,762,205	−239,775	34,135	92.3
Oklahoma	1,719,628	1,661,045	58,583	68,751	51,523	4.0	3.1	87,440	2,346	1,195,043	−6,563	29,788	80.6
Oregon	1,898,847	1,810,150	88,697	102,682	93,196	5.4	5.1	105,449	4,804	1,355,542	100	34,191	92.5
Pennsylvania	6,306,050	6,085,833	220,217	296,192	254,931	4.7	4.2	301,557	6,816	5,107,044	19,807	35,595	96.3
Rhode Island	577,338	543,404	33,934	29,720	22,646	5.1	4.2	30,011	1,477	434,706	19,538	34,564	93.5
South Carolina	2,126,439	1,972,850	153,589	138,061	70,821	6.5	3.6	101,165	4,019	1,560,573	−40,959	29,897	80.9
South Dakota	430,992	408,685	22,307	13,892	11,007	3.2	2.7	24,787	1,004	308,010	1,306	27,380	74.1
Tennessee	2,990,152	2,871,539	118,613	154,622	115,041	5.2	4.0	131,691	815	2,347,335	−42,987	32,770	88.6
Texas	11,487,496	10,347,847	1,139,649	565,823	451,845	4.9	4.4	491,092	19,583	8,118,483	92,045	36,161	97.8
Utah	1,311,073	1,136,036	175,037	38,272	38,121	2.9	3.4	62,834	7,455	935,126	18,037	30,587	82.7
Vermont	361,044	335,798	25,246	13,018	9,056	3.6	2.7	22,133	569	256,132	2,591	31,049	84.0
Virginia	3,998,569	3,584,037	414,532	119,581	81,513	3.0	2.3	188,989	13,407	3,054,816	151,268	37,610	101.7
Washington	3,326,524	3,050,021	276,503	166,174	151,344	5.0	5.0	171,529	7,511	2,268,913	1,428	39,735	107.5
West Virginia	806,996	808,861	−1,865	39,862	44,212	4.9	5.5	40,837	−210	568,619	10,448	27,449	74.3
Wisconsin	3,062,932	2,996,091	66,841	144,777	101,207	4.7	3.4	144,116	3,701	2,435,143	20,309	34,016	92.0
Wyoming	284,690	266,882	17,808	9,073	10,197	3.2	3.8	19,330	1,210	187,360	12,746	30,404	82.2

[1]Civilian unemployed as percent of total civilian labor force.
[2]For pay period including March 12 of the year shown.

Survey, Census, or Data Collection Method: Civilian labor force—Based on the Current Population Survey (CPS), the Current Employment Statistics (CES) survey, and the unemployment insurance (UI) system; for more information, see Appendix B, Limitations of the Data and Methodology, and also <http://www.bls.gov/lau/laumthd.htm>. Private nonfarm businesses—For data extracted from the Census Bureau's *County Business Patterns*, see Internet site <http://www.census.gov/epcd/cbp/view/cbpmethodology.htm>.

Sources: Civilian labor force—U.S. Bureau of Labor Statistics, *Local Area Unemployment Statistics, Annual Averages*, accessed April 17, 2007 (related Internet site <http://www.bls.gov/lau>). Private nonfarm businesses—U.S. Census Bureau, *County Business Patterns*, accessed July 12, 2006 (related Internet site <http://www.census.gov/epcd/cbp/view/cbpview.html>).

Banking, Retail Trade, and Accommodation and Food Services

State	Banking,[1] 2005 — Offices — Number	Banking,[1] 2005 — Offices — Rate per 10,000 people	Banking,[1] 2005 — Total deposits (mil. dol.)	Retail trade[2] (NAICS 44–45), 2002 — Estab-lishments	Retail trade[2] — Sales — Total ($1,000)	Retail trade[2] — Sales — Per capita[3] (dol.)	Retail trade[2] — Sales — General merchandise stores,[4] percent of total	Accommodation and food services[2] (NAICS 72), 2002 — Estab-lishments	Accommodation and food services[2] — Sales — Total ($1,000)	Accommodation — Sales — Per capita[3] (dol.)	Accommodation — Percent change, 1997–2002	Food services,[5] percent of total
UNITED STATES.	91,394	3.1	5,869,879	1,114,637	3,056,421,997	10,615	14.6	565,590	449,498,718	1,561	28.3	71.5
Alabama	1,454	3.2	65,307	19,608	43,784,342	9,771	17.6	7,075	4,692,297	1,047	20.9	85.1
Alaska.	134	2.0	6,435	2,661	7,437,071	11,605	25.2	1,849	1,393,225	2,174	30.8	65.7
Arizona	1,140	1.9	72,806	17,238	56,457,863	10,380	(NA)	9,944	8,612,730	1,583	29.8	69.2
Arkansas	1,370	4.9	40,996	12,141	25,611,630	9,459	20.5	4,659	2,766,905	1,022	26.9	82.1
California	6,620	1.8	753,579	108,941	359,120,365	10,264	13.0	66,568	55,559,669	1,588	31.3	74.4
Colorado	1,464	3.1	70,409	18,851	52,226,983	11,611	14.9	10,799	8,808,846	1,958	31.3	70.2
Connecticut	1,197	3.4	76,936	13,861	41,952,682	12,129	10.0	7,047	6,681,803	1,932	78.3	58.4
Delaware	263	3.1	138,758	3,727	10,912,971	13,538	14.0	1,576	1,231,595	1,528	22.1	83.7
District of Columbia	211	3.8	22,630	1,877	3,061,401	5,422	(NA)	1,799	2,943,078	5,212	30.0	55.1
Florida.	5,081	2.9	342,820	69,543	191,805,685	11,498	13.9	30,215	29,366,940	1,760	21.5	65.7
Georgia	2,643	2.9	149,442	34,050	90,098,578	10,551	15.1	15,463	12,740,423	1,492	31.5	78.6
Hawaii	285	2.2	24,783	4,924	13,008,182	10,537	19.7	3,138	5,551,380	4,497	10.9	42.0
Idaho.	489	3.4	15,125	5,874	13,540,952	10,081	17.1	3,088	1,653,671	1,231	34.1	72.0
Illinois	4,645	3.6	303,552	43,022	131,469,518	10,446	14.0	24,245	19,072,168	1,515	28.6	75.4
Indiana	2,345	3.7	84,543	24,322	67,261,298	10,922	17.4	11,788	9,409,270	1,528	41.6	70.8
Iowa	1,577	5.3	50,984	13,859	31,195,012	10,629	15.8	6,586	3,698,955	1,260	33.9	70.4
Kansas	1,505	5.5	48,304	11,890	26,505,396	9,770	17.9	5,584	3,196,947	1,178	19.0	82.6
Kentucky	1,750	4.2	57,241	16,847	40,062,561	9,795	19.0	6,660	4,908,331	1,200	21.0	84.1
Louisiana	1,547	3.4	57,069	17,613	41,885,192	9,356	18.7	7,535	7,411,702	1,655	40.9	62.6
Maine	507	3.8	18,105	7,050	16,053,515	12,370	12.2	3,726	2,045,841	1,576	35.5	66.3
Maryland	1,707	3.0	88,936	19,394	60,039,971	11,034	12.9	9,406	7,832,268	1,439	31.1	79.6
Massachusetts	2,131	3.3	172,205	25,761	73,903,837	11,525	9.7	15,175	11,789,582	1,839	27.0	79.0
Michigan	3,057	3.0	139,351	38,876	109,350,139	10,889	(NA)	19,084	12,248,269	1,220	20.6	84.3
Minnesota	1,763	3.4	96,053	21,129	60,015,531	11,943	14.3	10,232	7,959,590	1,584	34.1	72.6
Mississippi	1,136	3.9	35,047	12,561	25,017,531	8,724	20.7	4,329	5,486,105	1,913	79.0	40.0
Missouri.	2,225	3.8	92,765	23,837	61,861,163	10,891	16.7	11,280	8,607,025	1,515	26.9	73.5
Montana	370	4.0	12,566	5,145	10,122,625	11,116	16.2	3,260	1,537,986	1,689	28.2	71.9
Nebraska	1,021	5.8	33,415	8,157	20,249,200	11,729	14.0	3,992	2,088,710	1,210	21.0	84.8
Nevada	502	2.1	48,231	7,214	26,999,899	12,452	14.2	4,252	19,537,592	9,011	27.5	16.2
New Hampshire.	426	3.3	29,654	6,702	20,830,057	16,330	13.9	3,160	2,082,145	1,632	34.8	75.3
New Jersey	3,222	3.7	222,556	34,741	102,153,833	11,910	10.2	17,537	15,715,595	1,832	17.1	58.7
New Mexico	498	2.6	19,667	7,227	18,328,637	9,880	18.3	3,756	2,771,474	1,494	29.1	71.8
New York	4,931	2.6	689,775	76,425	178,067,530	9,298	11.1	39,428	27,835,952	1,453	28.4	75.5
North Carolina.	2,544	2.9	184,218	35,851	88,821,486	10,686	13.8	15,747	11,237,386	1,352	30.3	78.9
North Dakota	422	6.6	12,192	3,433	7,723,945	12,187	14.6	1,765	854,656	1,348	24.8	69.9
Ohio	3,994	3.5	201,186	42,280	119,778,409	10,497	15.0	22,663	14,875,890	1,304	19.9	87.0
Oklahoma	1,280	3.6	48,334	13,922	32,112,960	9,206	19.5	6,506	3,901,754	1,119	23.8	86.7
Oregon	1,044	2.9	42,285	14,277	37,896,022	10,756	18.5	8,816	5,527,223	1,569	26.0	75.2
Pennsylvania	4,643	3.7	225,238	48,041	130,713,197	10,603	12.9	24,778	15,305,402	1,241	25.2	79.8
Rhode Island	240	2.2	21,826	4,134	10,342,351	9,676	9.4	2,701	1,731,799	1,620	41.9	83.1
South Carolina	1,289	3.0	53,844	18,416	40,629,089	9,895	15.4	8,135	6,104,316	1,487	26.2	74.3
South Dakota	459	5.9	42,102	4,249	9,601,175	12,626	13.2	2,203	1,226,459	1,613	38.1	64.4
Tennessee	2,113	3.5	95,586	24,029	60,136,403	10,382	17.0	10,070	8,024,900	1,385	18.2	77.9
Texas	5,863	2.6	356,111	75,703	228,694,755	10,528	15.6	36,591	29,914,774	1,377	31.8	81.6
Utah	594	2.4	118,114	8,135	23,675,432	10,206	16.2	4,106	2,984,632	1,287	29.0	72.6
Vermont.	276	4.4	9,517	3,946	7,623,872	12,366	7.0	1,950	1,154,048	1,872	26.8	54.5
Virginia	2,438	3.2	155,264	28,914	80,509,062	11,069	15.6	13,305	10,929,429	1,503	32.0	73.4
Washington	1,832	2.9	91,469	22,564	65,262,333	10,757	15.9	13,699	8,642,681	1,425	23.4	79.5
West Virginia	639	3.5	23,340	7,454	16,747,900	9,277	18.9	3,310	1,974,851	1,094	20.9	77.4
Wisconsin.	2,298	4.2	100,643	21,360	59,978,700	11,025	14.7	13,268	6,885,765	1,266	21.9	80.1
Wyoming	210	4.1	8,563	2,861	5,783,756	11,586	15.3	1,742	984,684	1,973	21.7	58.2

NA Not available.

[1]As of June 30. Covers all FDIC-insured commercial banks and savings institutions.
[2]Includes only establishments with payroll.
[3]Based on resident population estimated as of July 1, 2002.
[4]Represents NAICS code 452.
[5]Represents NAICS code 722. Includes full-service restaurants, limited-service eating places, special food services, and drinking places (alcoholic beverages).

Survey, Census, or Data Collection Method: Banking—Based on surveys on every FDIC-insured bank and savings association as of June 30 each year conducted by the Federal Deposit Insurance Corporation (FDIC) and the Office of Thrift Supervision (OTS); for information, see Internet site <http://www2.fdic.gov/sod/sodPublications.asp?barItem=5>.   Retail trade and accommodation and food services—Based on the 2002 Economic Census; for more information, see Appendix B, Limitations of the Data and Methodology, and also <http://www.census.gov/econ/census02/>.

Sources: Banking—U.S. Federal Deposit Insurance Corporation (FDIC) and Office of Thrift Supervision (OTS), 2005 Bank and Thrift Branch Office Data Book: Summary of Deposits, accessed August 9, 2006 (related Internet site <http://www2.fdic.gov/sod/index.asp>).   Retail trade—U.S. Census Bureau, 2002 Economic Census, *Retail Trade, Geographic Area Series*, accessed June 21,2005 (related Internet site <http://www.census.gov/econ/census02/>).   Accommodation and food services—U.S. Census Bureau, 1997 and 2002 Economic Censuses, *Accommodation and Food Services, Geographic Area Series*, accessed June 21, 2005 (related Internet site <http://www.census.gov/econ/census02/>).

	Federal government expenditure					Federal, state, and local governments[1]							
						Earnings				Employment			
	2004					2005				2005			
State	Total (mil. dol.)	Percent change, 2000–2004	Per capita (dol.)	Direct payments to individuals, percent of total	2000 (mil. dol.)	Total (mil. dol.)	Percent of total	Percent change, 2000–2005	2000 (mil. dol.)	Total	Percent of total	Percent change, 2000–2005	2000
UNITED STATES...	[2]2,143,782	[2]31.9	[2]7,300	[2]50.2	[2]1,624,777	1,319,146	16.5	32.5	995,592	23,837,000	13.7	3.9	22,944,000
Alabama	39,047	33.5	8,619	51.9	29,250	19,935	20.2	30.9	15,232	400,711	16.0	3.9	385,840
Alaska	8,445	41.6	12,885	19.5	5,963	6,430	31.9	35.0	4,762	101,843	23.3	5.2	96,774
Arizona	41,979	43.4	7,309	46.7	29,282	22,687	16.5	44.8	15,664	432,718	13.4	11.3	388,894
Arkansas	19,489	31.3	7,080	59.5	14,847	10,149	18.6	40.0	7,251	222,969	14.3	8.1	206,332
California	232,387	32.1	6,474	48.3	175,967	168,589	15.8	36.5	123,531	2,656,123	12.9	3.7	2,560,477
Colorado	30,060	31.1	6,533	44.4	22,929	22,428	15.6	36.0	16,495	411,010	13.4	6.8	384,788
Connecticut	30,304	55.2	8,649	44.1	19,527	15,660	12.2	25.1	12,516	261,041	12.0	1.0	258,498
Delaware	5,253	32.6	6,326	59.8	3,962	3,805	14.2	38.3	2,752	68,313	12.9	3.1	66,249
District of Columbia	37,630	37.2	67,982	8.6	27,418	27,185	41.5	40.1	19,410	254,116	31.9	5.5	240,769
Florida	121,934	31.3	7,009	64.6	92,882	65,282	16.0	34.8	48,439	1,161,853	11.5	6.3	1,093,169
Georgia	55,153	29.7	6,247	51.0	42,525	39,149	17.1	37.2	28,527	752,395	14.5	8.2	695,234
Hawaii	12,187	34.9	9,651	37.8	9,036	11,046	31.3	44.0	7,670	172,708	20.7	3.9	166,273
Idaho	8,968	27.9	6,437	49.3	7,012	5,532	18.4	32.9	4,164	125,106	14.4	6.2	117,850
Illinois	76,828	27.9	6,043	57.6	60,046	50,586	13.8	26.0	40,144	893,899	12.0	-0.1	894,899
Indiana	37,918	31.9	6,079	58.3	28,743	21,423	14.3	29.7	16,517	439,733	11.9	1.9	431,482
Iowa	19,218	30.2	6,505	56.3	14,761	11,675	16.4	26.4	9,236	260,403	13.2	1.6	256,251
Kansas	19,131	33.9	6,993	52.5	14,282	13,834	19.8	43.6	9,634	289,010	16.1	3.6	279,003
Kentucky	31,714	29.6	7,649	52.3	24,472	17,595	19.4	35.8	12,957	356,173	15.0	2.9	346,110
Louisiana	32,954	26.8	7,298	55.1	25,995	19,035	21.4	34.5	14,158	408,868	16.6	-1.2	413,981
Maine	10,865	38.3	8,248	48.7	7,853	5,591	19.2	34.4	4,159	110,927	13.5	3.0	107,733
Maryland	64,726	42.7	11,645	32.8	45,365	37,401	22.8	33.9	27,935	530,082	15.9	2.6	516,474
Massachusetts	53,120	30.0	8,279	48.5	40,860	25,904	11.5	21.4	21,335	438,013	10.6	-3.7	454,616
Michigan	60,489	29.1	5,981	64.0	46,851	36,158	14.0	21.6	29,725	687,129	12.5	-1.6	698,242
Minnesota	28,791	25.1	5,644	54.2	23,013	21,034	13.8	26.8	16,594	415,134	11.9	2.1	406,659
Mississippi	22,338	21.5	7,695	53.3	18,389	12,340	24.1	32.1	9,339	277,407	18.4	1.3	273,722
Missouri	45,730	28.0	7,947	49.8	35,730	22,252	15.8	26.0	17,660	475,815	13.3	1.3	469,823
Montana	7,494	26.6	8,085	46.7	5,920	4,399	22.2	34.4	3,274	92,756	15.1	4.1	89,095
Nebraska	11,795	22.6	6,751	52.6	9,617	8,027	17.8	33.4	6,017	170,891	14.0	5.1	162,618
Nevada	12,769	47.9	5,469	57.5	8,633	9,588	14.2	46.2	6,559	155,942	10.2	19.4	130,585
New Hampshire	7,959	37.1	6,124	53.9	5,805	4,439	12.1	39.8	3,175	92,470	11.1	6.7	86,664
New Jersey	55,264	26.6	6,353	59.3	43,654	40,926	14.7	32.5	30,880	655,757	13.1	8.6	604,043
New Mexico	19,864	37.1	10,437	34.3	14,484	11,381	28.6	39.7	8,144	219,567	20.6	8.5	202,390
New York	143,903	30.3	7,484	51.1	110,459	91,727	14.5	24.8	73,526	1,499,714	13.9	1.1	1,483,872
North Carolina	55,233	33.4	6,467	55.3	41,414	40,012	19.4	35.9	29,436	803,802	15.7	8.6	740,400
North Dakota	6,035	15.0	9,513	38.1	5,246	3,583	22.0	37.6	2,605	80,693	17.1	5.1	76,779
Ohio	73,195	27.5	6,388	58.7	57,387	43,647	15.4	29.0	33,839	843,041	12.4	2.5	822,856
Oklahoma	26,644	28.4	7,562	53.7	20,758	16,603	20.9	30.5	12,727	347,025	16.7	5.0	330,563
Oregon	21,871	32.0	6,084	59.7	16,568	17,329	18.9	47.4	11,753	284,292	12.7	2.3	277,838
Pennsylvania	94,900	28.7	7,649	60.0	73,745	43,137	13.3	26.8	34,025	813,076	11.4	3.5	785,266
Rhode Island	8,245	19.9	7,630	53.3	6,879	4,894	18.1	28.6	3,806	75,375	12.4	-1.4	76,410
South Carolina	30,051	34.6	7,158	53.7	22,323	18,562	20.9	28.3	14,469	383,221	16.2	(Z)	383,222
South Dakota	6,602	28.4	8,564	45.7	5,141	3,495	19.3	33.0	2,628	80,055	14.9	2.7	77,984
Tennessee	45,441	35.3	7,701	51.3	33,588	20,546	13.9	30.3	15,765	438,664	12.1	4.3	420,670
Texas	141,858	33.0	6,308	48.7	106,671	91,458	14.8	34.9	67,784	1,828,003	14.0	6.3	1,720,427
Utah	13,684	36.3	5,728	43.8	10,043	10,783	18.9	36.5	7,901	220,758	14.6	8.4	203,739
Vermont	4,633	37.7	7,456	47.1	3,364	2,746	17.9	42.2	1,931	55,527	13.1	5.3	52,752
Virginia	90,638	44.3	12,150	32.2	62,808	54,200	23.7	36.4	39,726	847,623	17.9	4.9	807,976
Washington	44,841	32.2	7,228	48.5	33,923	33,585	19.1	33.3	25,204	598,542	16.0	6.2	563,358
West Virginia	15,183	29.2	8,364	58.5	11,751	7,510	22.6	26.3	5,947	151,623	16.7	(Z)	151,638
Wisconsin	31,554	29.8	5,728	58.8	24,308	20,698	14.8	26.0	16,425	426,577	12.1	2.1	417,767
Wyoming	4,393	36.4	8,673	39.4	3,221	3,163	23.1	41.3	2,239	68,507	19.0	5.5	64,946

Z Less than .05 percent.

[1]Government includes federal civilian and military and state and local.
[2]Includes data not distributed by state.

Survey, Census, or Data Collection Method: Federal government expenditure—Based on information systems in various federal government agencies; for information, see <http://ftp2.census.gov/govs/cffr/generictech.pdf>. Government earnings and employment—Based on the Regional Economic Information System; for more information, see Appendix B, Limitations of the Data and Methodology, and also <http://www.bea.gov/regional/methods.cfm>.

Sources: Federal government expenditure—U.S. Census Bureau, *Consolidated Federal Funds Report*, accessed February 28, 2006 (related Internet site <http://www.census.gov/govs/www /cffr.html>). Government earnings and employment—U.S. Bureau of Economic Analysis, Regional Economic Information System (REIS), downloaded estimates and software, accessed June 5, 2007 (related Internet site <http://www.bea.gov/regional/docs/reis2005dvd.cfm>).

Table A-13. States — **Local Government Finances and Elections**

State	Local government employment, March 2002		Local government finances, 2002							Elections, 2004[1]			
			General revenue				Total debt outstanding			Votes cast for President			
					Taxes							Republican candidate, percent of total	Democratic candidate, percent of total
	Total employment	Total payroll ($1,000)	Total ($1,000)	Per capita (dol.)	Total ($1,000)	Property, percent of total (taxes)	Amount ($1,000)	Per capita (dol.)		Total	Percent change, 2000–2004		
UNITED STATES...	13,277,647	37,483,436	995,855,965	3,458	369,730,209	72.9	1,043,904,090	3,625		122,295,345	16.0	48.3	50.7
Alabama	196,725	461,639	12,485,697	2,787	3,209,062	39.8	12,651,831	2,824		1,883,449	13.0	62.5	36.8
Alaska	31,883	96,526	2,678,056	4,180	980,404	79.6	3,337,621	5,209		312,598	9.5	61.1	35.5
Arizona	223,850	607,207	16,455,137	3,026	5,943,001	66.0	22,258,843	4,093		2,012,585	31.4	54.9	44.4
Arkansas	112,313	221,070	5,689,968	2,102	1,234,805	41.9	5,751,659	2,125		1,054,945	14.4	54.3	44.6
California	1,689,444	5,799,895	159,819,813	4,568	42,668,690	66.3	138,036,602	3,945		12,421,852	13.3	44.4	54.3
Colorado	201,382	559,644	16,153,765	3,591	6,976,853	59.7	21,299,122	4,735		2,130,330	22.3	51.7	47.0
Connecticut	128,740	427,008	10,679,196	3,088	6,092,141	98.4	6,983,652	2,019		1,578,769	8.2	44.0	54.3
Delaware	24,381	72,238	1,888,857	2,344	513,498	77.9	1,494,267	1,854		375,190	14.5	45.8	53.4
District of Columbia	46,408	190,598	6,922,336	12,260	3,227,909	24.9	5,436,087	9,628		227,586	12.7	9.3	89.2
Florida	685,418	1,851,207	54,956,082	3,295	19,488,212	78.6	70,010,245	4,198		7,609,810	27.6	52.1	47.1
Georgia	390,042	975,155	26,907,860	3,135	10,286,233	64.0	26,057,766	3,036		3,301,875	27.2	58.0	41.4
Hawaii	15,495	49,576	1,542,547	1,250	818,886	75.1	2,791,939	2,262		[2]429,013	[2]16.6	[2]45.3	[2]54.0
Idaho	67,536	140,405	3,698,592	2,752	1,020,020	94.0	1,440,447	1,072		598,447	19.3	68.4	30.3
Illinois	605,373	1,714,128	42,483,591	3,375	19,094,806	82.8	46,175,609	3,669		5,274,322	11.2	44.5	54.8
Indiana	276,500	674,315	18,538,509	3,012	6,786,047	88.0	14,614,998	2,375		2,468,002	12.2	59.9	39.3
Iowa	154,390	331,304	9,117,686	3,107	3,324,163	86.6	5,781,408	1,970		1,506,908	14.5	49.9	49.2
Kansas	164,726	347,345	8,469,363	3,122	3,166,614	78.0	10,024,660	3,696		1,187,756	10.8	62.0	36.6
Kentucky	168,339	365,852	8,731,629	2,136	2,806,067	54.9	19,954,998	4,881		1,795,882	16.3	59.6	39.7
Louisiana	206,183	458,667	12,648,133	2,826	4,825,129	39.5	11,752,840	2,626		1,943,106	10.1	56.7	42.2
Maine	65,421	133,870	3,531,360	2,723	1,914,316	97.4	2,024,883	1,561		740,752	13.6	44.6	53.6
Maryland	222,233	707,198	17,656,587	3,244	9,053,005	56.8	13,354,398	2,454		2,386,678	18.1	42.9	55.9
Massachusetts	264,423	838,996	20,912,683	3,262	9,072,844	96.1	20,106,252	3,136		2,912,388	7.7	36.8	61.9
Michigan	455,318	1,251,509	34,134,413	3,400	8,780,132	90.0	32,247,783	3,212		4,839,252	14.3	47.8	51.2
Minnesota	260,581	668,341	19,723,791	3,926	5,232,373	93.8	25,601,836	5,096		2,828,387	16.0	47.6	51.1
Mississippi	142,895	280,353	7,394,493	2,580	1,794,817	91.7	5,773,746	2,014		1,152,145	15.9	59.5	39.8
Missouri	259,747	601,701	15,182,868	2,673	6,394,500	60.4	11,551,697	2,033		[2]2,731,364	[2]15.7	[2]53.3	[2]46.1
Montana	43,133	86,449	2,219,274	2,438	692,451	96.9	1,210,984	1,330		450,445	9.6	59.1	38.6
Nebraska	100,486	228,892	5,392,362	3,123	2,323,819	75.0	5,690,799	3,296		778,186	11.6	65.9	32.7
Nevada	78,394	261,047	7,998,424	3,690	2,487,235	63.9	12,105,157	5,584		829,587	36.2	50.5	47.9
New Hampshire	55,489	131,378	3,440,977	2,700	1,701,841	98.0	1,824,741	1,432		677,738	19.1	48.9	50.2
New Jersey	391,066	1,373,633	31,721,374	3,699	16,299,990	98.4	25,497,303	2,973		3,611,691	13.3	46.6	52.9
New Mexico	81,800	193,774	5,162,757	2,783	1,249,559	56.3	4,109,904	2,215		756,304	26.3	49.8	49.1
New York	1,052,354	3,970,618	105,031,843	5,480	45,615,705	58.8	107,338,897	5,601		7,391,036	8.3	40.1	58.4
North Carolina	391,764	967,993	24,592,246	2,958	7,039,053	77.0	22,332,254	2,687		3,501,007	20.3	56.0	43.6
North Dakota	35,800	62,049	1,682,914	2,656	611,456	86.8	1,231,883	1,944		312,833	8.5	62.9	35.5
Ohio	548,000	1,478,129	40,285,092	3,532	16,034,775	66.3	31,335,000	2,748		5,627,908	19.7	50.8	48.7
Oklahoma	158,385	338,337	8,455,104	2,425	2,729,209	54.3	6,031,032	1,730		1,463,758	18.6	65.6	34.4
Oregon	161,419	422,669	12,118,367	3,440	3,839,550	81.1	11,159,367	3,168		1,836,782	19.7	47.2	51.4
Pennsylvania	459,188	1,332,171	38,501,369	3,124	15,491,083	70.1	62,826,518	5,098		[3]5,769,590	[3]17.4	[3]48.4	[3]50.9
Rhode Island	35,864	122,676	2,706,973	2,533	1,494,635	97.7	1,489,112	1,394		[3]437,134	[3]6.9	[3]38.7	[3]59.4
South Carolina	177,000	432,517	10,910,956	2,660	3,663,909	84.2	12,756,903	3,109		1,617,730	17.0	58.0	40.9
South Dakota	40,812	70,985	1,811,740	2,383	864,852	77.2	1,143,217	1,504		388,215	22.7	59.9	38.4
Tennessee	245,521	599,913	14,333,478	2,475	5,176,087	66.7	17,500,115	3,022		2,437,319	17.4	56.8	42.5
Texas	1,074,656	2,697,240	64,879,272	2,987	30,318,113	80.9	98,801,444	4,548		7,410,765	15.7	61.1	38.2
Utah	97,911	214,192	6,017,440	2,575	2,100,760	67.6	8,520,440	3,646		927,844	20.4	71.5	26.0
Vermont	29,346	61,704	1,510,640	2,451	446,653	96.9	743,968	1,207		312,309	6.1	38.8	58.9
Virginia	335,348	863,011	21,734,543	2,983	9,350,097	71.6	21,637,063	2,970		3,198,367	16.8	53.7	45.5
Washington	247,940	794,763	21,261,782	3,505	6,884,936	62.9	32,008,374	5,276		2,859,084	14.9	45.6	52.8
West Virginia	65,544	156,675	3,782,611	2,096	1,089,593	82.3	3,547,252	1,966		755,887	16.6	56.1	43.2
Wisconsin	273,406	716,314	19,507,188	3,586	6,796,085	93.8	15,457,196	2,842		2,997,007	15.3	49.3	49.7
Wyoming	37,275	80,496	2,394,227	4,798	723,966	75.7	1,089,978	2,184		243,428	11.5	68.9	29.1

[1]Data subject to copyright; see source citation.
[2]State total includes overseas ballots.
[3]State total includes write-in votes.

Survey, Census, or Data Collection Method: Local government employment and finances—For information about these data collections and surveys, see Appendix B, Limitations of the Data and Methodology, and Internet site <http://www.census.gov/govs/www/apesloc02.html>. Elections—For information, see CQ Press, 2005, *America Votes 2003–2004*, Washington, DC, and Internet site <http://www.cqpress.com>.

Sources: Local government employment and finances—U.S. Census Bureau, 2002 Census of Governments, Compendium of Government Employment, accessed November 20, 2006; Finances, accessed August 6, 2006 (related Internet site <http://www.census.gov/govs/www/cog2002.html>). Elections, 2004—CQ Press, 2005, *America Votes 2003–2004*, Washington, DC, (copyrighted and printed with permission of CQ Press) (related Internet site <http://www.cqpress.com>).

Table A-14. States — **Farm Earnings, Agriculture, and Water Use**

State	Farm earnings, 2005 Total ($1,000)	Farm earnings, 2005 Percent of total[1]	Farms Number	Farms Percent Less than 50 acres	Farms Percent 500 acres or more	Land in farms Total acres (1,000)	Land in farms Average size of farm (acres)	Value of farm products sold Total (mil. dol.)	Value of farm products sold Average per farm (dol.)	Percent from Crops[2]	Percent from Livestock and poultry[3]	Water use Total (mil. gal. per day)	Water use Ground water, percent of total	By selected major use (mil. gal. per day) Irrigation	By selected major use (mil. gal. per day) Public supply
UNITED STATES...	50,903,000	0.6	2,128,982	34.9	15.9	938,279	441	200,646	94,245	47.4	52.6	405,042	20.8	136,905	42,781
Alabama...........	1,324,547	1.3	45,126	37.1	8.3	8,904	197	3,265	72,352	18.1	81.9	9,990	4.4	43	834
Alaska...........	13,263	0.1	609	42.0	16.1	901	1,479	46	75,768	44.5	55.5	305	46.2	1	80
Arizona...........	836,378	0.6	7,294	58.0	17.6	26,587	3,645	2,395	328,413	66.3	33.7	6,730	51.0	5,400	1,080
Arkansas.........	1,005,559	1.8	47,483	27.3	14.5	14,503	305	4,950	104,256	32.7	67.3	10,900	63.5	7,910	421
California.........	9,315,861	0.9	79,631	61.7	10.5	27,589	346	25,737	323,205	74.4	25.6	51,200	30.1	30,500	6,120
Colorado.........	721,421	0.5	31,369	32.8	29.0	31,093	991	4,525	144,257	26.9	73.1	12,600	18.4	11,400	899
Connecticut.......	166,000	0.1	4,191	62.3	2.8	357	85	471	112,297	69.6	30.4	4,150	3.4	30	424
Delaware.........	283,786	1.1	2,391	52.3	11.0	540	226	619	258,826	24.3	75.7	1,320	8.7	44	95
District of Columbia....	–	0.4	(X)	(NA)	(NA)	(X)	(X)	(X)	(NA)	(NA)	(NA)	10	(NA)	(Z)	–
Florida...........	1,604,522	0.4	44,081	64.9	6.8	10,415	236	6,242	141,609	80.8	19.2	20,100	25.0	4,290	2,440
Georgia..........	1,839,814	0.8	49,311	39.2	9.9	10,744	218	4,912	99,608	32.2	67.8	6,500	22.3	1,140	1,250
Hawaii...........	217,252	0.6	5,398	88.0	3.1	1,300	241	533	98,819	83.5	16.5	641	67.7	364	250
Idaho............	969,612	3.2	25,017	49.2	18.0	11,767	470	3,908	156,224	45.7	54.3	19,500	21.2	17,100	244
Illinois...........	826,217	0.2	73,027	26.9	24.0	27,311	374	7,676	105,115	76.5	23.5	13,700	5.9	154	1,760
Indiana...........	700,191	0.5	60,296	39.9	13.8	15,059	250	4,783	79,328	62.6	37.4	10,100	6.5	101	670
Iowa............	2,237,042	3.2	90,655	23.3	22.7	31,729	350	12,274	135,388	49.5	50.5	3,360	20.2	22	383
Kansas..........	1,066,237	1.5	64,414	17.4	34.6	47,228	733	8,746	135,782	27.7	72.3	6,610	57.3	3,710	416
Kentucky.........	1,456,122	1.6	86,541	34.8	5.6	13,844	160	3,080	35,591	36.0	64.0	4,160	4.5	29	525
Louisiana.........	461,215	0.5	27,413	41.2	13.9	7,831	286	1,816	66,239	58.7	41.3	10,400	15.7	1,020	753
Maine...........	117,376	0.4	7,196	38.6	8.0	1,370	190	464	64,425	48.0	52.0	799	10.1	6	102
Maryland.........	352,785	0.2	12,198	47.8	7.8	2,078	170	1,293	106,026	34.8	65.2	7,910	2.8	42	824
Massachusetts.....	118,981	0.1	6,075	60.0	2.7	519	85	384	63,262	72.1	27.9	4,660	5.8	126	739
Michigan.........	820,687	0.3	53,315	41.1	9.0	10,143	190	3,772	70,757	62.6	37.4	10,000	7.3	201	1,140
Minnesota........	1,818,993	1.2	80,839	24.9	19.0	27,512	340	8,576	106,083	53.2	46.8	3,870	18.6	227	500
Mississippi........	1,231,711	2.4	42,186	30.0	9.9	11,098	263	3,116	73,870	32.9	67.1	2,960	73.6	1,410	359
Missouri..........	640,223	0.5	106,797	23.1	14.0	29,946	280	4,983	46,661	40.0	60.0	8,230	21.6	1,430	872
Montana.........	463,802	2.3	27,870	23.3	46.4	59,612	2,139	1,882	67,532	39.0	61.0	8,290	2.3	7,950	149
Nebraska........	1,500,483	3.3	49,355	14.8	41.6	45,903	930	9,704	196,609	34.9	65.1	12,300	63.9	8,790	330
Nevada..........	109,563	0.2	2,989	46.7	24.2	6,331	2,118	447	149,545	35.3	64.7	2,810	26.9	2,110	629
New Hampshire......	46,175	0.1	3,363	45.9	5.2	445	132	145	43,067	57.4	42.6	1,210	7.0	5	97
New Jersey........	264,521	0.1	9,924	70.5	3.5	806	81	750	75,561	87.7	12.3	5,560	9.0	140	1,050
New Mexico.......	659,356	1.7	15,170	44.7	28.8	44,810	2,954	1,700	112,065	23.4	76.6	3,260	47.2	2,860	296
New York.........	992,222	0.2	37,255	30.4	9.4	7,661	206	3,118	83,689	36.4	63.6	12,100	7.4	36	2,570
North Carolina......	2,464,936	1.2	53,930	45.6	7.2	9,079	168	6,962	129,087	28.9	71.1	11,400	5.1	287	945
North Dakota......	1,082,886	6.7	30,619	6.7	56.8	39,295	1,283	3,233	105,600	76.1	23.9	1,140	10.8	145	64
Ohio............	708,005	0.3	77,797	39.5	9.0	14,583	187	4,264	54,804	54.1	45.9	11,100	7.9	32	1,470
Oklahoma........	796,487	1.0	83,300	24.2	18.0	33,662	404	4,456	53,498	18.4	81.6	2,020	51.0	718	675
Oregon..........	1,172,970	1.3	40,033	62.5	10.2	17,080	427	3,195	79,822	68.7	31.3	6,930	14.3	6,080	566
Pennsylvania......	1,268,303	0.4	58,105	37.8	4.2	7,745	133	4,257	73,263	31.0	69.0	9,950	6.7	14	1,460
Rhode Island......	18,978	0.1	858	59.8	1.3	61	71	56	64,739	84.9	15.1	429	6.7	3	119
South Carolina.....	488,366	0.5	24,541	41.7	8.3	4,846	197	1,490	60,705	39.8	60.2	7,170	4.6	267	566
South Dakota......	1,254,104	6.9	31,736	13.6	49.0	43,785	1,380	3,835	120,829	41.1	58.9	528	42.0	373	93
Tennessee........	337,443	0.2	87,595	43.6	4.3	11,682	133	2,200	25,113	48.8	51.2	10,800	3.9	22	890
Texas...........	3,220,629	0.5	228,926	32.6	18.0	129,878	567	14,135	61,744	26.4	73.6	29,600	30.3	8,630	4,230
Utah............	244,518	0.4	15,282	54.8	14.0	11,731	768	1,116	73,020	23.1	76.9	4,970	21.1	3,860	638
Vermont.........	199,593	1.3	6,571	33.7	8.4	1,245	189	473	71,993	15.1	84.9	447	9.7	4	60
Virginia..........	548,230	0.2	47,606	35.9	7.5	8,625	181	2,361	49,593	30.4	69.6	8,830	3.6	26	720
Washington.......	1,596,733	0.9	35,939	57.5	12.8	15,318	426	5,331	148,327	67.2	32.8	5,310	27.7	3,040	1,020
West Virginia......	−29,891	(X)	20,812	27.3	6.3	3,585	172	483	23,199	14.4	85.6	5,150	1.8	(Z)	190
Wisconsin........	1,164,589	0.8	77,131	27.6	8.2	15,742	204	5,623	72,906	30.1	69.9	7,590	10.7	196	623
Wyoming.........	184,198	1.3	9,422	21.4	44.5	34,403	3,651	864	91,688	15.9	84.1	5,170	14.8	4,500	107

– Represents zero.   NA Not available.   X Not applicable.   Z Less than .5 of the unit presented.

[1]For total earnings, see Table B-9.
[2]Includes nursery and greenhouse crops.
[3]Includes related products.
[4]Withdrawals.

Survey, Census, or Data Collection Method: Farm earnings—Based on the Regional Economic Information System (REIS); for more information, see <http://www.bea.gov/regional/methods.cfm>. Agriculture—Based on the 2002 Census of Agriculture; for information, see Appendix B, Limitations of the Data and Methodology, and <http://www.agcensus.usda.gov/>.   Water use—For information, see <http://pubs.usgs.gov/chapter11/>.

Sources: Farm earnings—U.S. Bureau of Economic Analysis, Regional Economic Information System (REIS), downloaded estimates and software, accessed June 5, 2007 (related Internet site <http://www.bea.gov/regional/docs/reis2005dvd.cfm>).   Agriculture—U.S. Department of Agriculture, National Agricultural Statistics Service, 2002 Census of Agriculture, Volume 1, Geographic Area Series, accessed April 9, 2007 (related Internet site <http://www.agcensus.usda.gov/>).   Water use—U.S. Geological Survey (USGS), Water Use in the United States, individual state/county and United States by state, accessed May 19, 2006 (related Internet site <http://water.usgs.gov/watuse>).

State	Manufacturing (NAICS 31–33)											
	Establishments, 2002[1]		Employment, 2005[2]			Earnings, 2005[2]		Value added by manufactures, 2002[1]		Capital expenditures, 2002[1]		
	Total	Percent change, 1997–2002	Total	Percent of all employ-ees	Percent change, 2001–2005	Total ($1,000)	Percent of all earnings	Total ($1,000)	Percent change, 1997–2002	Total ($1,000)	Percent change, 1997–2002
UNITED STATES...	350,828	−3.6	14,860,900	8.5	−12.5	1,015,266,000	12.7	1,887,792,650	3.4	125,536,189	−16.8
Alabama	5,119	−6.0	307,616	12.2	−8.0	17,326,159	17.6	28,641,670	−2.0	3,070,882	0.4
Alaska	514	5.3	14,779	3.4	3.3	737,183	3.7	1,283,586	10.7	79,278	−39.1
Arizona	4,935	0.4	193,962	6.0	−8.3	13,652,988	10.0	25,976,992	−3.4	977,257	−61.0
Arkansas	3,185	−4.0	207,441	13.3	−10.9	9,472,372	17.4	21,965,415	13.5	1,209,902	−19.0
California	48,478	−1.9	1,605,418	7.8	−14.7	127,108,414	11.9	197,574,490	0.9	16,279,856	−0.9
Colorado	5,349	−2.4	162,694	5.3	−15.5	11,329,982	7.9	17,798,062	−13.9	1,975,737	19.1
Connecticut	5,384	−7.9	203,271	9.3	−13.1	18,409,179	14.3	27,673,466	1.4	1,448,543	−22.3
Delaware	705	4.4	34,273	6.5	−14.8	2,765,603	10.3	5,063,899	−6.0	481,872	−5.5
District of Columbia	146	−27.0	2,510	0.3	−35.4	223,184	0.3	163,118	−4.5	13,331	35.6
Florida	15,202	−4.9	423,934	4.2	−6.5	25,241,963	6.2	41,912,600	4.2	2,465,056	−17.3
Georgia	8,805	−3.1	465,899	9.0	−9.7	26,678,517	11.6	59,651,286	7.4	3,212,978	−22.9
Hawaii	929	0.9	18,941	2.3	−3.2	904,754	2.6	1,217,728	−3.5	82,960	−17.6
Idaho	1,814	10.1	68,151	7.8	−6.5	3,912,923	13.0	7,440,111	16.4	1,243,409	49.0
Illinois	16,860	−6.1	710,010	9.6	−14.9	50,284,578	13.7	91,825,126	−3.6	5,960,080	−19.2
Indiana	9,223	−0.9	585,556	15.9	−6.7	39,292,654	26.3	78,023,817	16.1	5,617,894	1.2
Iowa	3,804	1.5	236,301	12.0	−4.4	13,644,409	19.2	31,394,257	9.5	1,705,013	−13.8
Kansas	3,218	−2.8	186,457	10.4	−6.7	11,661,073	16.7	21,347,336	20.9	1,281,375	−12.2
Kentucky	4,283	1.5	270,289	11.4	−9.7	16,368,826	18.0	34,075,367	−11.1	2,562,414	−23.9
Louisiana	3,524	−0.6	158,696	6.4	−10.8	10,418,563	11.7	28,404,879	−2.3	3,488,400	1.6
Maine	1,880	3.8	66,627	8.1	−16.0	3,829,547	13.1	7,122,274	9.1	543,895	−8.5
Maryland	3,999	0.1	147,812	4.4	−15.6	10,887,094	6.6	19,265,920	2.9	1,594,941	8.6
Massachusetts	8,859	−7.3	318,080	7.7	−20.7	26,013,264	11.6	44,508,791	0.4	2,349,095	−32.6
Michigan	15,193	−5.3	700,904	12.7	−16.9	56,530,416	21.9	97,575,395	4.0	5,699,658	−38.3
Minnesota	8,139	0.6	362,545	10.4	−7.5	23,518,176	15.4	39,610,449	8.1	2,815,001	−11.3
Mississippi	2,796	−7.0	183,616	12.2	−10.6	8,526,643	16.6	16,126,629	−5.6	1,111,609	−21.5
Missouri	7,210	−3.8	321,452	9.0	−8.8	19,457,633	13.8	41,528,244	−3.8	2,280,359	−14.1
Montana	1,234	6.4	23,244	3.8	−5.4	1,125,661	5.7	1,673,980	−3.4	220,108	45.8
Nebraska	1,976	0.8	104,711	8.6	−7.6	5,193,739	11.5	11,469,004	6.0	799,333	−2.8
Nevada	1,764	9.2	51,662	3.4	11.0	2,984,083	4.4	4,654,748	41.1	340,170	7.6
New Hampshire	2,213	−4.9	84,617	10.1	−16.8	5,820,192	15.9	8,527,926	−24.7	539,919	−23.4
New Jersey	10,656	−9.8	341,916	6.8	−17.0	30,488,889	10.9	51,602,288	3.0	3,021,021	−3.0
New Mexico	1,587	−0.4	41,896	3.9	−9.1	2,317,315	5.8	5,990,566	−55.4	307,101	−46.4
New York	21,066	−11.9	613,482	5.7	−15.7	44,911,729	7.1	83,874,558	8.9	4,172,544	−27.1
North Carolina	10,762	−4.8	590,341	11.5	−18.1	34,269,266	16.6	87,355,207	11.1	4,428,770	−17.8
North Dakota	724	2.8	27,314	5.8	8.1	1,410,799	8.7	2,679,559	48.7	201,839	2.9
Ohio	17,494	−2.7	837,501	12.3	−14.1	55,005,108	19.4	113,243,351	0.7	7,427,634	−17.4
Oklahoma	4,027	−1.5	152,296	7.4	−13.8	12,178,517	15.4	17,005,404	−1.3	1,046,987	−6.0
Oregon	5,597	−3.0	217,267	9.7	−4.6	13,705,426	14.9	26,440,699	5.4	1,265,365	−53.4
Pennsylvania	16,665	−2.7	708,692	9.9	−16.6	47,879,355	14.8	92,319,195	7.1	4,922,598	−28.7
Rhode Island	2,131	−15.9	57,232	9.4	−18.5	3,310,118	12.2	6,148,634	12.1	306,180	−23.1
South Carolina	4,457	0.2	270,969	11.5	−15.4	15,766,873	17.7	38,611,266	14.7	2,911,246	−14.7
South Dakota	926	4.3	41,748	7.8	−2.1	1,982,618	10.9	5,176,605	33.4	193,948	−26.6
Tennessee	6,948	−6.2	424,041	11.7	−9.2	25,713,333	17.4	49,811,004	12.3	4,526,574	16.9
Texas	21,450	−1.6	951,778	7.3	−11.2	78,687,109	12.7	124,462,554	−3.8	9,916,978	−20.7
Utah	3,061	7.0	126,202	8.4	−1.0	6,860,384	12.0	12,158,925	7.2	786,006	−16.6
Vermont	1,176	−4.1	40,153	9.5	−16.9	2,378,975	15.5	5,163,905	27.7	450,230	−38.6
Virginia	5,909	−1.3	306,221	6.5	−13.0	17,918,413	7.8	48,261,833	10.8	2,384,729	−30.4
Washington	7,535	−3.4	288,975	7.7	−13.0	21,147,231	12.0	35,398,551	16.3	1,769,708	−33.0
West Virginia	1,480	−1.7	65,081	7.2	−13.0	3,932,819	11.8	7,983,845	−14.3	675,453	−26.2
Wisconsin	9,915	−0.2	524,975	14.8	−8.7	31,463,590	22.4	61,501,462	11.9	3,279,381	−19.9
Wyoming	560	11.3	11,352	3.1	−0.9	618,361	4.5	1,430,036	38.7	102,325	32.9

[1]Census Bureau, 2002 Economic Census.
[2]Bureau of Economic Analysis.

Survey, Census, or Data Collection Method: Manufacturing, general (U.S. Census Bureau)—Based on the 2002 Economic Census; for information, see Appendix B, Limitations of the Data and Methodology, and <http://www.census.gov/prod/ec02/ec0231sg1.pdf>.   Establishments—Based on the 2002 Economic Census; for information, see <http://www.census.gov/econ/census02/>. Employment and earnings—Based on the Regional Economic Information System; for information, see Appendix B, Limitations of the Data and Methodology, and <http://www.bea.gov/regional/methods .cfm/>.   Value added and capital expenditures—Based on the Annual Survey of Manufactures and the 2002 Economic Census; for information, see Appendix B, Limitations of the Data and Methodology, and <http://www.census.gov/econ/census02/>.

Sources: Establishments—U.S. Census Bureau, 2002 Economic Census (related Internet site <http://www.census.gov/econ/census02/>).   Employment and earnings—U.S. Bureau of Economic Analysis, Regional Economic Information System (REIS), downloaded estimates and software, accessed June 5, 2007 (related Internet site <http://www.bea.gov/regional/docs/reis2005dvd.cfm>). Value added and capital expenditures—U.S. Census Bureau, 2002 Economic Census, *Manufacturing, Geographic Area Series*, accessed December 2005 (related Internet site <http://www.census.gov /econ/census02/>).

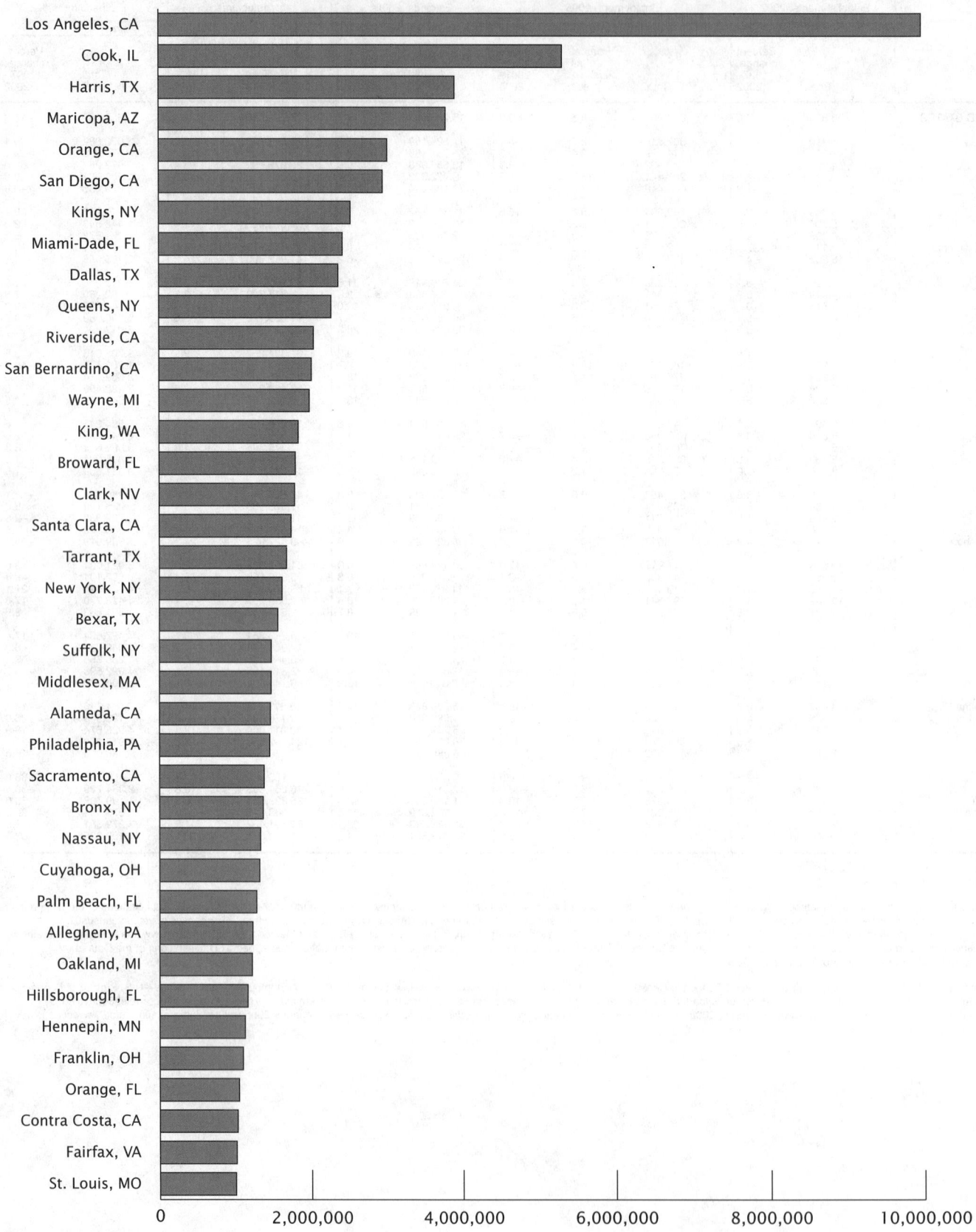

Figure 2.
Counties with 1 Million or More Population in the United States: 2006

County and City Data Book: 2007

U.S. Census Bureau

Counties

Table B

Page

You may visit us on the Web at
http://www.census.gov/compendia/ccdb

Counties

Table B

Table B-1. Counties — **Area and Population**

[Includes United States, states, and 3,141 counties/county equivalents defined as of February 22, 2005. For more information on these areas, see Appendix C, Geographic Information]

Metro-politan area code	FIPS state and county code[1]	County	Area, 2000 (square miles)		Population				Rank			Persons per square mile of land area		
			Total	Rank[2]	2006 (July 1)	2005 (July 1)	2000[3] (April 1 estimates base)	1990[3] (April 1 estimates base)	2006[2]	2000[2]	1990[4]	2006[5]	2000	1990
	00 000	UNITED STATES	3,794,083	(X)	299,398,484	296,507,061	281,424,602	248,790,925	(X)	(X)	(X)	84.6	79.8	70.4
	01 000	ALABAMA	52,419	(X)	4,599,030	4,548,327	4,447,351	4,040,389	(X)	(X)	(X)	90.6	87.7	79.6
33860	01 001	Autauga	604	1,724	49,730	48,454	43,671	34,222	959	1,021	1,160	83.4	73.7	57.4
19300	01 003	Baldwin	2,027	311	169,162	162,749	140,415	98,280	351	390	467	106.0	88.6	61.6
21640	01 005	Barbour	905	942	28,171	28,291	29,038	25,417	1,480	1,425	1,450	31.8	32.8	28.7
13820	01 007	Bibb	626	1,647	21,482	21,454	19,889	16,598	1,744	1,799	1,878	34.5	32.0	26.7
13820	01 009	Blount	651	1,572	56,436	55,572	51,034	39,248	879	908	1,019	87.4	79.4	60.8
...	01 011	Bullock	626	1,649	10,906	11,011	11,626	11,042	2,373	2,325	2,289	17.4	18.6	17.7
...	01 013	Butler	778	1,218	20,520	20,642	21,399	21,892	1,794	1,719	1,584	26.4	27.5	28.2
11500	01 015	Calhoun	612	1,701	112,903	112,242	112,243	116,032	510	478	396	185.6	183.1	190.7
46740	01 017	Chambers	603	1,728	35,176	35,373	36,583	36,876	1,290	1,201	1,079	58.9	61.2	61.7
...	01 019	Cherokee	600	1,742	24,863	24,592	23,988	19,543	1,590	1,594	1,696	45.0	43.5	35.3
13820	01 021	Chilton	701	1,436	41,953	41,648	39,593	32,458	1,102	1,124	1,202	60.5	57.4	46.8
...	01 023	Choctaw	921	889	14,656	14,727	15,922	16,018	2,125	2,027	1,922	16.0	17.4	17.5
...	01 025	Clarke	1,253	552	27,248	27,082	27,867	27,240	1,511	1,455	1,382	22.0	22.5	22.0
...	01 027	Clay	606	1,721	13,829	13,920	14,254	13,252	2,178	2,147	2,116	22.9	23.6	21.9
...	01 029	Cleburne	561	1,968	14,700	14,521	14,123	12,730	2,122	2,154	2,164	26.2	25.3	22.7
21460	01 031	Coffee	680	1,490	46,027	45,448	43,615	40,240	1,020	1,025	994	67.8	64.1	59.2
22520	01 033	Colbert	624	1,654	54,766	54,597	54,984	51,666	897	859	818	92.1	92.6	86.9
...	01 035	Conecuh	853	1,080	13,403	13,227	14,089	14,054	2,221	2,158	2,052	15.8	16.5	16.5
10760	01 037	Coosa	666	1,522	11,044	11,133	11,881	11,063	2,365	2,301	2,287	16.9	18.2	17.0
...	01 039	Covington	1,044	720	37,234	36,969	37,631	36,478	1,227	1,172	1,091	36.0	36.3	35.3
...	01 041	Crenshaw	611	1,704	13,719	13,598	13,665	13,635	2,189	2,190	2,089	22.5	22.5	22.4
18980	01 043	Cullman	755	1,268	80,187	79,747	77,481	67,613	671	654	657	108.6	105.1	91.6
21460	01 045	Dale	563	1,963	48,392	48,489	49,129	49,633	982	929	845	86.2	87.5	88.5
42820	01 047	Dallas	993	777	43,945	44,178	46,393	48,130	1,063	976	867	44.8	47.2	49.1
22840	01 049	DeKalb	779	1,213	68,014	67,365	64,452	54,651	759	753	788	87.4	83.1	70.2
33860	01 051	Elmore	657	1,548	75,688	73,746	65,876	49,210	694	741	854	121.8	106.7	79.2
...	01 053	Escambia	953	833	37,849	37,913	38,440	35,518	1,215	1,152	1,111	40.0	40.3	37.5
23460	01 055	Etowah	549	2,005	103,362	102,920	103,460	99,840	544	514	460	193.3	193.2	186.7
...	01 057	Fayette	629	1,641	18,005	18,200	18,495	17,962	1,914	1,870	1,790	28.7	29.4	28.6
...	01 059	Franklin	647	1,584	30,847	30,727	31,223	27,814	1,399	1,371	1,357	48.5	49.1	43.8
20020	01 061	Geneva	579	1,839	25,868	25,638	25,767	23,647	1,551	1,526	1,507	44.9	44.8	41.0
46220	01 063	Greene	660	1,535	9,374	9,663	9,974	10,153	2,490	2,449	2,373	14.5	15.4	15.7
46220	01 065	Hale	656	1,550	18,236	18,200	18,257	15,498	1,908	1,884	1,953	28.3	28.4	24.1
20020	01 067	Henry	568	1,939	16,706	16,565	16,310	15,374	1,992	2,005	1,966	29.7	29.1	27.4
20020	01 069	Houston	582	1,819	95,660	93,964	88,784	81,331	581	587	559	164.8	153.3	140.1
42460	01 071	Jackson	1,127	643	53,745	53,483	53,926	47,796	907	870	879	49.8	50.1	44.3
13820	01 073	Jefferson	1,124	645	656,700	656,014	662,041	651,520	90	77	71	590.2	595.0	585.5
...	01 075	Lamar	605	1,722	14,548	14,867	15,904	15,715	2,131	2,029	1,941	24.1	26.3	26.0
22520	01 077	Lauderdale	719	1,371	87,891	87,444	87,966	79,661	626	593	572	131.3	131.4	119.0
19460	01 079	Lawrence	718	1,384	34,312	34,496	34,803	31,513	1,309	1,259	1,230	49.5	50.3	45.4
12220	01 081	Lee	616	1,690	125,781	123,122	115,092	87,146	468	469	524	206.6	189.6	143.1
26620	01 083	Limestone	607	1,716	72,446	70,448	65,676	54,135	722	742	794	127.5	116.1	95.3
33860	01 085	Lowndes	725	1,338	12,759	12,954	13,473	12,658	2,260	2,198	2,171	17.8	18.8	17.6
46260	01 087	Macon	613	1,698	22,594	22,684	24,105	24,928	1,694	1,591	1,465	37.0	39.4	40.8
26620	01 089	Madison	813	1,148	304,307	298,193	276,951	238,912	199	204	209	378.1	345.2	296.8
...	01 091	Marengo	983	792	21,842	21,824	22,537	23,084	1,724	1,669	1,534	22.4	23.1	23.6
...	01 093	Marion	744	1,291	30,165	30,027	31,214	29,830	1,413	1,372	1,302	40.7	42.0	40.2
10700	01 095	Marshall	623	1,656	87,185	85,729	82,228	70,832	629	631	625	153.7	145.2	124.9
33660	01 097	Mobile	1,644	407	404,157	399,851	399,843	378,643	159	148	134	327.8	324.5	307.0
...	01 099	Monroe	1,035	732	23,342	23,545	24,324	23,968	1,660	1,583	1,493	22.8	23.7	23.4
33860	01 101	Montgomery	800	1,180	223,571	220,778	223,510	209,085	275	253	239	283.1	282.8	264.7
19460	01 103	Morgan	599	1,746	115,237	113,768	111,064	100,043	496	487	458	197.9	191.0	171.8
...	01 105	Perry	724	1,342	11,186	11,308	11,863	12,759	2,352	2,303	2,161	15.5	16.4	17.7
...	01 107	Pickens	890	999	20,133	20,135	20,949	20,699	1,815	1,740	1,645	22.8	23.7	23.5
45980	01 109	Pike	672	1,513	29,620	29,493	29,693	27,595	1,429	1,409	1,369	44.1	44.3	41.1
...	01 111	Randolph	584	1,806	22,673	22,576	22,380	19,881	1,688	1,675	1,684	39.0	38.6	34.2
17980	01 113	Russell	647	1,581	50,085	49,371	49,756	46,860	952	919	893	78.1	77.5	73.1
13820	01 115	St. Clair	654	1,562	75,232	72,177	64,742	49,811	699	751	843	118.7	102.8	78.6
13820	01 117	Shelby	810	1,150	178,182	171,373	143,293	99,363	331	380	462	224.2	181.9	125.0
...	01 119	Sumter	913	914	13,606	13,761	14,798	16,174	2,199	2,104	1,913	15.0	16.3	17.9
45180	01 121	Talladega	760	1,261	80,271	80,109	80,327	74,109	669	640	608	108.5	108.7	100.2
10760	01 123	Tallapoosa	766	1,244	41,010	40,718	41,794	38,826	1,134	1,059	1,028	57.1	58.1	54.1
46220	01 125	Tuscaloosa	1,351	500	171,159	168,396	164,875	150,500	346	326	310	129.2	124.6	113.6
13820	01 127	Walker	805	1,161	70,034	69,980	70,713	67,670	746	702	656	88.2	89.0	85.2
...	01 129	Washington	1,089	671	17,651	17,726	18,097	16,694	1,931	1,895	1,869	16.3	16.8	15.4
...	01 131	Wilcox	907	930	12,911	12,908	13,020	13,568	2,251	2,234	2,096	14.5	14.6	15.3
...	01 133	Winston	632	1,636	24,634	24,504	24,843	22,053	1,603	1,564	1,573	40.1	40.5	35.9

See footnotes at end of table.

[Includes United States, states, and 3,141 counties/county equivalents defined as of February 22, 2005. For more information on these areas, see Appendix C, Geographic Information]

Metropolitan area code	FIPS state and county code[1]	County	Area, 2000 (square miles)		Population									
							2000[3] (April 1 estimates base)	1990[3] (April 1 estimates base)	Rank			Persons per square mile of land area		
			Total	Rank[2]	2006 (July 1)	2005 (July 1)			2006[2]	2000[2]	1990[4]	2006[5]	2000	1990
	02 000	ALASKA	663,267	(X)	670,053	663,253	626,931	550,043	(X)	(X)	(X)	1.2	1.1	1.0
. . .	02 013	Aleutians East	15,012	17	2,647	2,696	2,697	2,464	3,002	3,014	3,023	0.4	0.4	0.4
. . .	02 016	Aleutians West	14,117	18	5,239	5,368	5,465	9,478	2,823	2,820	2,436	1.2	1.2	2.2
11260	02 020	Anchorage	1,961	321	278,700	275,474	260,283	226,338	217	212	218	164.2	153.5	133.3
. . .	02 050	Bethel	45,508	3	17,147	17,118	16,046	13,660	1,958	2,021	2,085	0.4	0.4	0.3
. . .	02 060	Bristol Bay	888	1,004	1,042	1,103	1,258	1,410	3,107	3,102	3,100	2.1	2.4	2.7
. . .	02 068	Denali	12,775	20	1,846	1,813	1,893	1,682	3,065	3,074	3,086	0.1	0.1	(NA)
. . .	02 070	Dillingham	20,928	11	4,970	4,966	4,922	4,010	2,843	2,855	2,918	0.3	0.3	0.2
21820	02 090	Fairbanks North Star	7,444	46	86,754	87,555	82,840	77,720	631	628	583	11.8	11.2	10.6
. . .	02 100	Haines	2,726	202	2,257	2,243	2,392	2,117	3,029	3,031	3,061	1.0	1.0	0.9
27940	02 110	Juneau	3,255	166	30,737	30,881	30,711	26,752	1,401	1,381	1,399	11.3	11.3	10.3
. . .	02 122	Kenai Peninsula	24,755	10	52,304	51,766	49,691	40,802	921	922	982	3.3	3.1	2.5
28540	02 130	Ketchikan Gateway	1,754	381	13,384	13,263	14,059	13,828	2,225	2,161	2,072	10.9	11.3	11.3
28980	02 150	Kodiak Island	12,024	22	13,072	13,073	13,913	13,309	2,237	2,170	2,113	2.0	2.1	2.1
. . .	02 164	Lake and Peninsula	30,907	6	1,548	1,578	1,823	1,666	3,082	3,078	3,088	0.1	0.1	0.1
11260	02 170	Matanuska-Susitna	25,260	8	80,480	76,112	59,322	39,683	667	810	1,008	3.3	2.4	1.6
. . .	02 180	Nome	28,283	7	9,245	9,355	9,196	8,288	2,505	2,515	2,538	0.4	0.4	0.4
. . .	02 185	North Slope	94,763	2	6,608	6,790	7,385	5,986	2,718	2,650	2,760	0.1	0.1	0.1
. . .	02 188	Northwest Arctic	40,762	4	7,511	7,435	7,208	6,106	2,638	2,667	2,743	0.2	0.2	0.2
. . .	02 201	Prince of Wales- Outer Ketchikan	12,706	21	5,688	5,657	6,157	6,278	2,788	2,768	2,726	0.8	0.8	0.9
. . .	02 220	Sitka	4,812	91	8,920	8,917	8,835	8,588	2,529	2,543	2,504	3.1	3.1	3.0
. . .	02 232	Skagway-Hoonah-Angoon	11,377	23	3,100	3,137	3,436	[6]4,404	2,969	2,960	[6]2,881	0.4	0.4	0.3
. . .	02 240	Southeast Fairbanks	25,061	9	6,773	6,488	6,174	5,925	2,699	2,766	2,766	0.3	0.2	0.2
. . .	02 261	Valdez-Cordova	40,199	5	9,872	9,923	10,195	9,920	2,454	2,429	2,392	0.3	0.3	0.3
. . .	02 270	Wade Hampton	19,669	13	7,580	7,493	7,028	5,789	2,634	2,682	2,779	0.4	0.4	0.3
. . .	02 280	Wrangell-Petersburg	9,021	36	6,096	6,230	6,684	7,042	2,760	2,720	2,654	1.0	1.1	1.2
. . .	02 282	Yakutat	9,459	32	689	715	808	(6)	3,127	3,124	(6)	(Z)	(Z)	(Z)
. . .	02 290	Yukon-Koyukuk	147,843	1	5,844	6,104	6,510	6,798	2,783	2,739	2,676	(Z)	(Z)	(Z)
	04 000	ARIZONA	113,998	(X)	6,166,318	5,953,007	5,130,632	3,665,339	(X)	(X)	(X)	54.3	45.5	32.3
. . .	04 001	Apache	11,218	24	71,118	69,600	69,423	61,591	731	714	709	6.3	6.2	5.5
43420	04 003	Cochise	6,219	59	127,757	126,153	117,755	97,624	457	458	471	20.7	19.1	15.8
22380	04 005	Coconino	18,661	14	124,953	123,826	116,320	96,591	470	463	477	6.7	6.3	5.2
37740	04 007	Gila	4,796	93	52,209	51,528	51,335	40,216	926	901	995	11.0	10.8	8.4
40940	04 009	Graham	4,641	101	33,660	33,089	33,489	26,554	1,321	1,301	1,405	7.3	7.2	5.7
40940	04 011	Greenlee	1,848	354	7,738	7,499	8,547	8,008	2,619	2,565	2,565	4.2	4.6	4.3
. . .	04 012	La Paz	4,513	107	20,256	20,225	19,715	13,844	1,808	1,812	2,068	4.5	4.4	3.1
38060	04 013	Maricopa	9,224	34	3,768,123	3,638,481	3,072,339	2,122,101	4	4	7	409.4	336.5	230.6
29420	04 015	Mohave	13,470	19	193,035	186,617	155,032	93,497	309	344	495	14.5	11.7	7.0
. . .	04 017	Navajo	9,959	29	111,399	108,494	97,470	77,674	516	532	586	11.2	9.8	7.8
46060	04 019	Pima	9,189	35	946,362	925,000	843,746	666,957	42	53	68	103.0	92.4	72.6
38060	04 021	Pinal	5,374	74	271,059	240,044	179,527	116,397	226	308	395	50.5	33.8	21.7
35700	04 023	Santa Cruz	1,238	561	43,080	42,012	38,381	29,676	1,079	1,155	1,309	34.8	31.2	24.0
39140	04 025	Yavapai	8,128	41	208,014	198,841	167,517	107,714	287	322	429	25.6	20.8	13.3
49740	04 027	Yuma	5,519	71	187,555	181,598	160,026	106,895	316	333	432	34.0	29.2	19.4
	05 000	ARKANSAS	53,179	(X)	2,810,872	2,775,708	2,673,398	2,350,624	(X)	(X)	(X)	54.0	51.4	45.1
. . .	05 001	Arkansas	1,034	734	19,884	20,043	20,745	21,653	1,824	1,750	1,595	20.1	20.9	21.9
. . .	05 003	Ashley	939	853	22,843	23,083	24,209	24,319	1,680	1,589	1,485	24.8	26.3	26.4
34260	05 005	Baxter	587	1,789	41,307	40,394	38,386	31,186	1,122	1,154	1,239	74.5	69.4	56.3
22220	05 007	Benton	880	1,021	196,045	187,381	153,346	97,530	303	346	472	231.7	183.0	115.7
25460	05 009	Boone	602	1,735	36,405	35,764	33,948	28,297	1,244	1,282	1,345	61.6	57.6	47.9
. . .	05 011	Bradley	654	1,561	12,111	12,195	12,600	11,793	2,290	2,257	2,229	18.6	19.4	18.1
15780	05 013	Calhoun	633	1,634	5,558	5,559	5,744	5,826	2,797	2,807	2,777	8.8	9.1	9.3
. . .	05 015	Carroll	639	1,615	27,339	26,983	25,357	18,623	1,509	1,551	1,758	43.4	40.3	29.4
. . .	05 017	Chicot	691	1,463	12,915	13,027	14,117	15,713	2,250	2,156	1,942	20.1	21.9	24.4
11660	05 019	Clark	883	1,012	22,913	22,906	23,546	21,437	1,673	1,615	1,606	26.5	27.2	24.8
. . .	05 021	Clay	641	1,601	16,497	16,598	17,611	18,107	2,007	1,923	1,785	25.8	27.4	28.3
. . .	05 023	Cleburne	592	1,767	25,485	25,324	24,046	19,411	1,564	1,593	1,710	46.1	43.6	35.1
38220	05 025	Cleveland	599	1,747	8,858	8,896	8,571	7,781	2,533	2,562	2,597	14.8	14.3	13.0
31620	05 027	Columbia	767	1,243	24,440	24,525	25,603	25,691	1,612	1,532	1,432	31.9	33.4	33.5
. . .	05 029	Conway	567	1,944	20,694	20,646	20,336	19,151	1,779	1,770	1,724	37.2	36.6	34.4
27860	05 031	Craighead	713	1,409	88,244	86,632	82,148	68,956	622	632	642	124.1	116.1	97.0
22900	05 033	Crawford	604	1,725	58,785	57,457	53,247	42,493	850	879	946	98.7	89.7	71.4
32820	05 035	Crittenden	637	1,621	52,083	51,605	50,866	49,939	927	912	842	85.4	83.6	81.8
. . .	05 037	Cross	622	1,658	19,056	19,244	19,526	19,225	1,870	1,819	1,718	30.9	31.6	31.2
. . .	05 039	Dallas	668	1,520	8,350	8,470	9,210	9,614	2,570	2,512	2,423	12.5	13.7	14.4
. . .	05 041	Desha	820	1,129	14,181	14,263	15,341	16,798	2,155	2,069	1,860	18.5	20.0	22.0
. . .	05 043	Drew	836	1,103	18,387	18,558	18,723	17,369	1,895	1,862	1,829	22.2	22.6	21.0
30780	05 045	Faulkner	664	1,528	100,685	97,739	86,014	60,006	557	605	724	155.5	133.5	92.7
22900	05 047	Franklin	620	1,672	18,276	18,169	17,771	14,897	1,902	1,914	1,995	30.0	29.1	24.4
. . .	05 049	Fulton	620	1,670	11,756	11,825	11,642	10,037	2,310	2,324	2,381	19.0	18.9	16.2

See footnotes at end of table.

[Includes United States, states, and 3,141 counties/county equivalents defined as of February 22, 2005. For more information on these areas, see Appendix C, Geographic Information]

Metro-politan area code	FIPS state and county code[1]	County	Area, 2000 (square miles) Total	Area, 2000 (square miles) Rank[2]	Population 2006 (July 1)	Population 2005 (July 1)	Population 2000[3] (April 1 estimates base)	Population 1990[3] (April 1 estimates base)	Rank 2006[2]	Rank 2000[2]	Rank 1990[4]	Persons per square mile of land area 2006[5]	Persons per square mile of land area 2000	Persons per square mile of land area 1990
		ARKANSAS—Con.												
26300	05 051	Garland	735	1,311	95,164	93,436	88,066	73,397	583	591	613	140.5	130.5	108.2
30780	05 053	Grant	633	1,631	17,493	17,308	16,464	13,948	1,941	1,994	2,061	27.7	26.1	22.1
37500	05 055	Greene	580	1,834	40,091	39,342	37,329	31,804	1,156	1,183	1,218	69.4	65.0	55.1
26260	05 057	Hempstead	741	1,296	23,347	23,289	23,587	21,621	1,659	1,609	1,597	32.0	32.4	29.7
...	05 059	Hot Spring	622	1,659	31,730	31,394	30,353	26,115	1,378	1,390	1,418	51.6	49.4	42.5
...	05 061	Howard	595	1,756	14,415	14,530	14,300	13,569	2,135	2,142	2,094	24.5	24.3	23.1
12900	05 063	Independence	772	1,233	34,909	34,673	34,233	31,192	1,297	1,275	1,238	45.7	44.9	40.8
...	05 065	Izard	584	1,807	13,356	13,328	13,249	11,364	2,227	2,210	2,264	23.0	22.9	19.6
...	05 067	Jackson	641	1,600	17,426	17,576	18,419	18,944	1,948	1,873	1,739	27.5	29.0	29.9
38220	05 069	Jefferson	914	912	80,655	81,103	84,282	85,487	666	617	537	91.2	95.2	96.6
...	05 071	Johnson	683	1,483	24,453	24,087	22,781	18,221	1,609	1,657	1,777	36.9	34.4	27.5
...	05 073	Lafayette	545	2,020	7,896	8,012	8,559	9,643	2,601	2,564	2,420	15.0	16.2	18.3
...	05 075	Lawrence	592	1,765	16,899	17,137	17,774	17,455	1,974	1,912	1,824	28.8	30.1	29.8
...	05 077	Lee	619	1,674	11,379	11,524	12,580	13,053	2,340	2,260	2,136	18.9	20.8	21.7
38220	05 079	Lincoln	572	1,907	14,125	14,202	14,492	13,690	2,161	2,123	2,082	25.2	25.8	24.4
...	05 081	Little River	565	1,954	13,074	13,088	13,628	13,966	2,236	2,191	2,059	24.6	25.6	26.3
...	05 083	Logan	732	1,317	22,903	22,827	22,486	20,557	1,674	1,673	1,651	32.3	31.7	29.0
30780	05 085	Lonoke	802	1,168	62,902	60,630	52,828	39,268	809	882	1,018	82.1	69.4	51.3
22220	05 087	Madison	837	1,097	15,361	14,989	14,243	11,618	2,081	2,148	2,247	18.4	17.1	13.9
...	05 089	Marion	640	1,609	16,931	16,693	16,140	12,001	1,971	2,015	2,219	28.3	27.1	20.1
45500	05 091	Miller	637	1,617	43,055	42,777	40,443	38,467	1,081	1,106	1,041	69.0	64.8	61.6
14180	05 093	Mississippi	920	894	47,517	47,763	51,979	57,525	991	893	756	52.9	57.7	64.0
...	05 095	Monroe	621	1,664	9,095	9,277	10,254	11,333	2,521	2,421	2,272	15.0	16.8	18.7
...	05 097	Montgomery	800	1,176	9,272	9,256	9,245	7,841	2,499	2,509	2,589	11.9	11.9	10.0
26260	05 099	Nevada	621	1,668	9,471	9,524	9,955	10,101	2,480	2,451	2,377	15.3	16.0	16.3
25460	05 101	Newton	823	1,122	8,411	8,387	8,608	7,666	2,567	2,558	2,605	10.2	10.5	9.3
15780	05 103	Ouachita	740	1,303	26,710	27,033	28,790	30,574	1,530	1,429	1,262	36.5	39.2	41.7
30780	05 105	Perry	560	1,971	10,411	10,453	10,209	7,969	2,409	2,427	2,574	18.9	18.6	14.5
48340	05 107	Phillips	727	1,329	23,331	23,823	26,445	28,830	1,662	1,506	1,336	33.7	37.9	41.6
...	05 109	Pike	614	1,695	10,859	10,926	11,303	10,086	2,376	2,350	2,379	18.0	18.8	16.7
27860	05 111	Poinsett	763	1,253	25,086	25,287	25,614	24,664	1,579	1,531	1,475	33.1	33.8	32.5
...	05 113	Polk	862	1,057	20,363	20,143	20,229	17,347	1,802	1,778	1,830	23.7	23.6	20.2
40780	05 115	Pope	831	1,112	57,671	56,778	54,469	45,883	861	865	906	71.0	67.1	56.5
...	05 117	Prairie	676	1,506	8,927	9,031	9,539	9,518	2,528	2,487	2,432	13.8	14.7	14.7
30780	05 119	Pulaski	808	1,154	367,319	365,274	361,475	349,569	173	162	147	476.5	469.2	453.4
...	05 121	Randolph	656	1,553	18,448	18,424	18,195	16,558	1,890	1,889	1,883	28.3	27.9	25.4
22620	05 123	St. Francis	642	1,597	27,535	27,725	29,329	28,497	1,502	1,420	1,343	43.4	46.2	45.0
30780	05 125	Saline	730	1,321	94,024	91,226	83,530	64,183	591	624	684	130.0	116.0	88.6
...	05 127	Scott	898	974	11,415	11,107	10,995	10,205	2,338	2,366	2,371	12.8	12.3	11.4
...	05 129	Searcy	669	1,517	8,075	8,022	8,261	7,841	2,584	2,586	2,589	12.1	12.4	11.8
22900	05 131	Sebastian	546	2,016	120,322	118,600	115,070	99,590	480	470	461	224.4	215.5	185.7
...	05 133	Sevier	581	1,821	16,297	16,327	15,757	13,637	2,026	2,036	2,088	28.9	27.9	24.2
...	05 135	Sharp	606	1,718	17,963	17,526	17,119	14,109	1,916	1,949	2,046	29.7	28.4	23.3
...	05 137	Stone	609	1,709	11,981	11,775	11,499	9,775	2,301	2,336	2,407	19.8	19.0	16.1
20980	05 139	Union	1,055	711	44,170	44,060	45,629	46,719	1,055	988	895	42.5	43.9	45.0
...	05 141	Van Buren	724	1,341	16,718	16,562	16,192	14,008	1,991	2,010	2,054	23.5	22.8	19.7
22220	05 143	Washington	956	829	186,521	181,366	157,775	113,409	317	338	405	196.4	167.1	119.3
42620	05 145	White	1,042	722	72,560	71,387	67,165	54,676	721	731	787	70.2	65.2	52.9
...	05 147	Woodruff	594	1,759	7,905	8,022	8,740	9,520	2,600	2,552	2,431	13.5	14.8	16.2
40780	05 149	Yell	949	840	21,834	21,393	21,139	17,759	1,725	1,728	1,800	23.5	22.8	19.1
	06 000	CALIFORNIA	163,696	(X)	36,457,549	36,154,147	33,871,653	29,811,427	(X)	(X)	(X)	233.8	218.1	191.1
41860	06 001	Alameda	821	1,128	1,457,426	1,451,065	1,443,741	1,304,347	23	21	21	1,976.0	1,966.9	1,768.6
...	06 003	Alpine	743	1,292	1,180	1,138	1,208	1,113	3,102	3,103	3,109	1.6	1.6	1.5
...	06 005	Amador	605	1,723	38,941	38,434	35,100	30,039	1,183	1,248	1,294	65.7	59.4	50.7
17020	06 007	Butte	1,677	399	215,881	214,153	203,171	182,120	283	270	266	131.7	124.3	111.1
...	06 009	Calaveras	1,037	729	47,722	46,779	40,554	31,998	990	1,100	1,211	46.8	39.9	31.4
...	06 011	Colusa	1,156	611	21,272	20,873	18,804	16,275	1,750	1,857	1,906	18.5	16.4	14.1
41860	06 013	Contra Costa	802	1,169	1,024,319	1,017,644	948,816	803,731	36	38	47	1,422.8	1,324.8	1,115.8
18860	06 015	Del Norte	1,230	569	28,893	28,719	27,507	23,460	1,450	1,467	1,517	28.7	27.3	23.3
40900	06 017	El Dorado	1,788	371	178,066	176,319	156,299	125,995	332	342	368	104.1	91.9	73.6
23420	06 019	Fresno	6,017	64	891,756	878,089	799,407	667,479	53	58	67	149.6	134.5	111.9
...	06 021	Glenn	1,327	510	28,061	27,683	26,453	24,798	1,486	1,504	1,471	21.3	20.1	18.9
21700	06 023	Humboldt	4,052	127	128,330	128,359	126,518	119,118	456	429	389	35.9	35.4	33.3
20940	06 025	Imperial	4,482	109	160,301	155,862	142,361	109,303	364	384	421	38.4	34.1	26.2
13860	06 027	Inyo	10,227	27	17,980	18,040	17,945	18,281	1,915	1,904	1,775	1.8	1.8	1.8
12540	06 029	Kern	8,161	40	780,117	756,981	661,655	544,981	68	78	88	95.8	81.5	66.9
25260	06 031	Kings	1,391	485	146,153	143,467	129,461	101,469	409	414	450	105.1	93.3	73.0
17340	06 033	Lake	1,329	509	65,933	65,157	58,309	50,631	778	820	832	52.4	46.6	40.2
45000	06 035	Lassen	4,720	100	34,715	34,603	33,828	27,598	1,302	1,287	1,368	7.6	7.4	6.1
31100	06 037	Los Angeles	4,752	96	9,948,081	9,941,197	9,519,330	8,863,052	1	1	1	2,449.7	2,351.2	2,183.0
31460	06 039	Madera	2,153	287	146,345	142,530	123,109	88,090	407	440	518	68.5	57.9	41.2

See footnotes at end of table.

[Includes United States, states, and 3,141 counties/county equivalents defined as of February 22, 2005. For more information on these areas, see Appendix C, Geographic Information]

Metro-politan area code	FIPS state and county code[1]	County	Area, 2000 (square miles) Total	Area, 2000 (square miles) Rank[2]	Population 2006 (July 1)	Population 2005 (July 1)	Population 2000[3] (April 1 estimates base)	Population 1990[3] (April 1 estimates base)	Rank 2006[2]	Rank 2000[2]	Rank 1990[4]	Persons per square mile of land area 2006[5]	Persons per square mile of land area 2000	Persons per square mile of land area 1990
		CALIFORNIA—Con.												
41860	06 041	Marin.	828	1,116	248,742	247,103	247,289	230,096	247	235	212	478.5	476.6	442.7
...	06 043	Mariposa	1,463	459	18,401	18,058	17,130	14,302	1,892	1,948	2,031	12.7	11.8	9.9
46380	06 045	Mendocino	3,878	131	88,109	88,276	86,265	80,345	625	603	568	25.1	24.6	22.9
32900	06 047	Merced	1,972	319	245,658	242,249	210,554	178,403	249	264	272	127.4	109.8	92.5
...	06 049	Modoc	4,203	120	9,597	9,503	9,449	9,678	2,471	2,492	2,414	2.4	2.4	2.5
...	06 051	Mono	3,132	176	12,754	12,712	12,853	9,956	2,261	2,245	2,390	4.2	4.2	3.3
41500	06 053	Monterey	3,771	140	410,206	412,340	401,764	355,660	156	147	144	123.5	121.4	107.1
34900	06 055	Napa	788	1,202	133,522	132,516	124,308	110,765	440	433	417	177.1	165.4	146.9
46020	06 057	Nevada	974	805	98,764	98,263	92,033	78,510	568	554	576	103.1	96.6	82.0
31100	06 059	Orange.	948	841	3,002,048	2,992,642	2,846,289	2,410,668	5	5	5	3,802.9	3,620.0	3,052.7
40900	06 061	Placer	1,503	444	326,242	316,868	248,399	172,796	189	233	280	232.3	179.0	123.0
...	06 063	Plumas.	2,613	217	21,263	21,409	20,824	19,739	1,752	1,745	1,689	8.3	8.1	7.7
40140	06 065	Riverside	7,303	47	2,026,803	1,945,392	1,545,387	1,170,413	11	16	26	281.2	216.5	162.4
40900	06 067	Sacramento	995	774	1,374,724	1,363,423	1,223,499	1,066,789	25	29	29	1,423.6	1,274.2	1,104.7
41940	06 069	San Benito	1,391	488	55,842	56,006	53,234	36,697	885	880	1,082	40.2	38.8	26.4
40140	06 071	San Bernardino	20,105	12	1,999,332	1,964,511	1,709,434	1,418,380	12	13	16	99.7	85.7	70.7
41740	06 073	San Diego.	4,526	106	2,941,454	2,936,609	2,813,833	2,498,016	6	6	4	700.4	672.6	594.1
41860	06 075	San Francisco	232	2,973	744,041	741,025	776,733	723,959	72	62	55	15,935.8	16,639.2	15,502.3
44700	06 077	San Joaquin	1,426	477	673,170	664,796	563,598	480,628	86	97	101	481.1	406.2	343.4
42020	06 079	San Luis Obispo	3,616	148	257,005	255,538	246,681	217,162	237	236	229	77.8	75.0	65.7
41860	06 081	San Mateo	741	1,299	705,499	701,175	707,163	649,623	78	70	72	1,571.0	1,578.0	1,446.5
42060	06 083	Santa Barbara	3,789	139	400,335	400,908	399,347	369,608	162	149	139	146.3	146.1	135.0
41940	06 085	Santa Clara.	1,304	520	1,731,281	1,705,158	1,682,585	1,497,577	17	14	14	1,341.4	1,307.0	1,159.8
42100	06 087	Santa Cruz	607	1,714	249,705	249,420	255,600	229,734	245	221	214	560.8	574.6	515.3
39820	06 089	Shasta	3,847	133	179,951	178,970	163,256	147,036	328	329	320	47.5	43.3	38.8
...	06 091	Sierra.	962	818	3,455	3,405	3,555	3,318	2,943	2,949	2,970	3.6	3.8	3.5
...	06 093	Siskiyou	6,347	58	45,091	45,066	44,301	43,531	1,037	1,009	931	7.2	7.0	6.9
46700	06 095	Solano	907	934	411,680	410,786	394,513	339,469	155	150	150	496.5	479.0	409.9
42220	06 097	Sonoma	1,768	377	466,891	466,970	458,614	388,222	135	125	130	296.3	292.2	246.3
33700	06 099	Stanislaus.	1,515	437	512,138	505,492	446,997	370,522	120	132	137	342.8	301.2	247.9
49700	06 101	Sutter.	609	1,712	91,410	89,005	78,930	64,409	612	649	677	151.7	131.5	106.9
39780	06 103	Tehama	2,962	187	61,686	60,932	56,039	49,625	827	842	846	20.9	19.0	16.8
...	06 105	Trinity	3,208	171	14,313	13,917	13,022	13,063	2,143	2,233	2,134	4.5	4.1	4.1
47300	06 107	Tulare	4,839	89	419,909	411,131	368,021	311,932	149	160	160	87.0	76.5	64.7
38020	06 109	Tuolumne	2,274	269	56,855	56,898	54,504	48,456	875	863	863	25.4	24.5	21.7
37100	06 111	Ventura	2,208	280	799,720	796,348	753,195	669,016	62	64	66	433.4	410.1	362.4
40900	06 113	Yolo	1,023	741	188,085	185,091	168,660	141,212	315	321	337	185.6	167.6	139.5
49700	06 115	Yuba	644	1,591	70,396	67,144	60,219	58,234	739	803	744	111.6	95.7	92.4
	08 000	COLORADO.	104,094	(X)	4,753,377	4,663,295	4,302,015	3,294,473	(X)	(X)	(X)	45.8	41.5	31.8
19740	08 001	Adams	1,198	585	414,338	402,219	347,963	265,038	152	168	186	347.6	294.7	222.3
...	08 003	Alamosa.	724	1,346	15,225	15,254	14,966	13,617	2,090	2,094	2,091	21.1	20.7	18.8
19740	08 005	Arapahoe	805	1,160	537,197	529,305	488,896	391,572	112	116	129	668.9	612.1	487.5
...	08 007	Archuleta	1,355	499	12,386	11,882	9,898	5,345	2,276	2,456	2,815	9.2	7.4	4.0
...	08 009	Baca	2,557	224	4,017	4,082	4,517	4,556	2,910	2,879	2,867	1.6	1.8	1.8
14500	08 011	Bent	1,541	432	5,551	5,563	5,998	5,048	2,798	2,782	2,836	3.7	3.9	3.3
14500	08 013	Boulder	751	1,277	282,304	279,508	269,787	225,339	214	205	221	380.2	365.5	303.5
19740	08 014	Broomfield	(X)	(X)	45,116	43,376	39,198	(X)	1,036	1,133	(X)	1,367.2	1,187.8	(NA)
...	08 015	Chaffee	1,015	751	16,918	16,879	16,242	12,684	1,973	2,007	2,167	16.7	16.1	12.5
...	08 017	Cheyenne	1,781	373	1,906	1,952	2,231	2,397	3,060	3,049	3,031	1.1	1.2	1.3
19740	08 019	Clear Creek.	396	2,613	9,130	9,196	9,322	7,619	2,518	2,504	2,608	23.1	23.6	19.3
...	08 021	Conejos	1,291	530	8,406	8,446	8,400	7,453	2,568	2,573	2,618	6.5	6.5	5.8
...	08 023	Costilla	1,230	568	3,378	3,409	3,663	3,190	2,949	2,942	2,984	2.8	3.0	2.6
...	08 025	Crowley	800	1,174	5,386	5,377	5,518	3,946	2,810	2,817	2,922	6.8	7.0	5.0
...	08 027	Custer	740	1,302	3,926	3,874	3,503	1,926	2,914	2,953	3,071	5.3	4.8	2.6
19740	08 029	Delta	1,149	621	30,401	29,991	27,834	20,980	1,403	1,456	1,631	26.6	24.4	18.4
19740	08 031	Denver.	155	3,069	566,974	558,663	553,693	467,549	105	101	106	3,697.3	3,622.7	3,050.3
...	08 033	Dolores	1,068	700	1,911	1,809	1,844	1,504	3,059	3,077	3,096	1.8	1.7	1.4
19740	08 035	Douglas	843	1,093	263,621	249,572	175,766	60,391	232	311	717	313.8	214.8	71.9
20780	08 037	Eagle.	1,692	396	49,085	47,684	41,672	21,928	972	1,065	1,581	29.1	24.9	13.0
19740	08 039	Elbert.	1,851	352	23,181	22,741	19,872	9,646	1,664	1,800	2,419	12.5	10.9	5.2
17820	08 041	El Paso	2,130	291	576,884	564,857	516,929	397,014	103	107	125	271.3	244.2	186.7
15860	08 043	Fremont	1,534	435	48,010	47,650	46,145	32,273	987	979	1,207	31.3	30.2	21.1
...	08 045	Garfield	2,956	188	51,908	49,772	43,794	29,974	930	1,020	1,299	17.6	15.0	10.2
19740	08 047	Gilpin	150	3,071	5,042	4,953	4,757	3,070	2,836	2,863	2,995	33.6	32.0	20.5
...	08 049	Grand	1,870	349	13,406	13,140	12,442	7,966	2,220	2,271	2,575	7.3	6.8	4.3
...	08 051	Gunnison	3,260	164	14,331	14,182	13,956	10,273	2,141	2,167	2,362	4.4	4.3	3.2
...	08 053	Hinsdale	1,123	646	819	786	790	467	3,119	3,125	3,135	0.7	0.7	0.4
...	08 055	Huerfano	1,593	419	7,808	7,741	7,862	6,009	2,612	2,618	2,756	4.9	4.9	3.8
...	08 057	Jackson	1,621	413	1,406	1,423	1,577	1,605	3,090	3,090	3,090	0.9	1.0	1.0

See footnotes at end of table.

[Includes United States, states, and 3,141 counties/county equivalents defined as of February 22, 2005. For more information on these areas, see Appendix C, Geographic Information]

Metro-politan area code	FIPS state and county code[1]	County	Area, 2000 (square miles)		Population				Rank			Persons per square mile of land area		
			Total	Rank[2]	2006 (July 1)	2005 (July 1)	2000[3] (April 1 estimates base)	1990[3] (April 1 estimates base)	2006[2]	2000[2]	1990[4]	2006[5]	2000	1990
		COLORADO—Con.												
19740	08 059	Jefferson	778	1,214	526,994	524,809	525,330	438,430	115	105	113	682.6	682.0	567.7
...	08 061	Kiowa	1,786	372	1,413	1,417	1,622	1,688	3,088	3,088	3,085	0.8	0.9	1.0
...	08 063	Kit Carson	2,162	286	7,590	7,664	8,011	7,140	2,633	2,606	2,639	3.5	3.7	3.3
20780	08 065	Lake	384	2,645	7,814	7,724	7,812	6,007	2,610	2,624	2,757	20.7	20.7	15.9
20420	08 067	La Plata	1,700	392	47,936	47,230	43,941	32,284	988	1,017	1,206	28.3	26.1	19.1
22660	08 069	Larimer	2,634	213	276,253	271,842	251,494	186,136	220	227	260	106.2	97.2	71.6
...	08 071	Las Animas	4,775	94	15,564	15,387	15,207	13,765	2,071	2,076	2,076	3.3	3.2	2.9
...	08 073	Lincoln	2,586	219	5,458	5,617	6,087	4,529	2,802	2,773	2,871	2.1	2.3	1.8
44540	08 075	Logan	1,845	355	20,780	20,687	20,574	17,567	1,770	1,757	1,817	11.3	11.2	9.6
24300	08 077	Mesa	3,341	160	134,189	129,746	116,935	93,145	439	462	498	40.3	35.3	28.0
...	08 079	Mineral	878	1,024	929	923	831	558	3,111	3,121	3,132	1.1	1.0	0.6
...	08 081	Moffat	4,751	97	13,680	13,397	13,184	11,357	2,191	2,214	2,266	2.9	2.8	2.4
...	08 083	Montezuma	2,040	309	25,217	24,767	23,830	18,672	1,576	1,599	1,752	12.4	11.7	9.2
33940	08 085	Montrose	2,243	274	38,559	37,554	33,432	24,423	1,197	1,302	1,480	17.2	15.0	10.9
22820	08 087	Morgan	1,294	528	28,109	27,997	27,171	21,939	1,482	1,477	1,580	21.9	21.2	17.1
...	08 089	Otero	1,270	544	19,452	19,507	20,311	20,185	1,847	1,772	1,665	15.4	16.0	16.0
...	08 091	Ouray	542	2,031	4,307	4,257	3,742	2,295	2,879	2,937	3,039	8.0	7.0	4.2
19740	08 093	Park	2,211	279	17,157	16,944	14,523	7,174	1,957	2,122	2,636	7.8	6.7	3.3
...	08 095	Phillips	688	1,473	4,601	4,577	4,480	4,189	2,860	2,884	2,899	6.7	6.5	6.1
...	08 097	Pitkin	973	808	14,798	14,822	14,872	12,661	2,118	2,102	2,170	15.2	15.2	13.0
...	08 099	Prowers	1,644	406	13,776	13,923	14,483	13,347	2,185	2,124	2,110	8.4	8.8	8.1
39380	08 101	Pueblo	2,398	245	152,912	150,974	141,472	123,051	386	388	374	64.0	59.4	51.5
...	08 103	Rio Blanco	3,223	170	6,180	6,000	5,986	6,051	2,750	2,784	2,751	1.9	1.9	1.9
...	08 105	Rio Grande	912	915	12,006	12,251	12,413	10,770	2,300	2,272	2,310	13.2	13.6	11.8
...	08 107	Routt	2,368	254	21,580	21,284	19,690	14,088	1,739	1,814	2,049	9.1	8.4	6.0
...	08 109	Saguache	3,170	172	7,006	7,032	5,917	4,619	2,676	2,793	2,865	2.2	1.9	1.5
...	08 111	San Juan	388	2,634	578	568	558	745	3,133	3,134	3,127	1.5	1.4	1.9
...	08 113	San Miguel	1,288	535	7,143	7,190	6,594	3,653	2,670	2,729	2,944	5.6	5.1	2.8
...	08 115	Sedgwick	550	2,004	2,467	2,523	2,747	2,690	3,017	3,011	3,014	4.5	5.0	4.9
43540	08 117	Summit	619	1,675	25,399	24,963	23,548	12,881	1,570	1,614	2,148	41.8	38.9	21.2
17820	08 119	Teller	559	1,972	22,243	21,862	20,555	12,468	1,713	1,758	2,183	39.9	37.1	22.4
...	08 121	Washington	2,524	229	4,630	4,628	4,926	4,812	2,859	2,854	2,855	1.8	2.0	1.9
24540	08 123	Weld	4,022	128	236,857	228,158	180,861	131,821	260	305	350	59.3	45.9	33.0
...	08 125	Yuma	2,369	253	9,829	9,785	9,841	8,954	2,457	2,462	2,475	4.2	4.2	3.8
	09 000	CONNECTICUT	5,543	(X)	3,504,809	3,500,701	3,405,602	3,287,116	(X)	(X)	(X)	723.4	704.4	678.4
14860	09 001	Fairfield	837	1,099	900,440	901,086	882,567	827,645	52	47	42	1,438.9	1,414.1	1,322.4
25540	09 003	Hartford	751	1,278	876,927	875,422	857,183	851,783	54	51	38	1,192.4	1,167.4	1,158.1
45860	09 005	Litchfield	945	847	190,119	189,358	182,212	174,092	313	301	278	206.7	198.6	189.2
25540	09 007	Middlesex	439	2,389	163,774	162,824	155,071	143,196	355	343	332	443.5	421.6	387.8
35300	09 009	New Haven	862	1,060	845,244	844,510	824,008	804,219	56	54	46	1,395.6	1,362.4	1,327.6
35980	09 011	New London	772	1,232	263,293	264,265	259,106	254,957	233	215	195	395.4	389.7	382.8
25540	09 013	Tolland	417	2,502	148,140	147,454	136,364	128,699	399	395	360	361.3	333.9	313.8
48740	09 015	Windham	521	2,096	116,872	115,782	109,091	102,525	493	495	449	227.9	213.0	199.9
	10 000	DELAWARE	2,489	(X)	853,476	841,741	783,600	666,168	(X)	(X)	(X)	436.9	402.6	340.8
20100	10 001	Kent	800	1,178	147,601	143,462	126,700	110,993	401	426	414	250.3	215.5	187.9
37980	10 003	New Castle	494	2,206	525,587	522,094	500,265	441,946	116	112	112	1,233.0	1,177.5	1,036.7
42580	10 005	Sussex	1,196	587	180,288	176,185	156,635	113,229	327	341	407	192.3	168.0	120.8
	11 000	DISTRICT OF COLUMBIA	68	(X)	581,530	582,049	572,059	606,900	(X)	(X)	(X)	9,471.2	9,300.4	9,882.8
47900	11 001	District of Columbia	68	3,101	581,530	582,049	572,059	606,900	100	94	76	9,471.2	9,300.4	9,882.8
	12 000	FLORIDA	65,755	(X)	18,089,888	17,768,191	15,982,824	12,938,071	(X)	(X)	(X)	335.5	297.6	239.6
23540	12 001	Alachua	969	814	227,120	223,709	217,955	181,596	270	259	268	259.8	249.6	207.7
27260	12 003	Baker	589	1,781	25,203	24,549	22,259	18,486	1,577	1,683	1,763	43.1	38.3	31.6
37460	12 005	Bay	1,033	735	163,505	161,322	148,218	126,994	356	366	365	214.1	194.1	166.3
...	12 007	Bradford	300	2,847	28,384	28,041	26,088	22,515	1,471	1,515	1,554	96.8	89.0	76.8
37340	12 009	Brevard	1,557	429	534,359	528,640	476,230	398,978	113	120	124	524.8	469.3	391.7
33100	12 011	Broward	1,320	512	1,787,636	1,782,016	1,623,018	1,255,531	15	15	23	1,483.0	1,354.6	1,038.6
...	12 013	Calhoun	574	1,888	13,410	13,315	13,017	11,011	2,219	2,235	2,291	23.6	23.0	19.4
39460	12 015	Charlotte	859	1,070	154,438	154,340	141,627	110,975	381	387	415	222.7	205.2	160.0
26140	12 017	Citrus	773	1,228	138,143	134,054	118,085	93,513	432	457	494	236.6	203.3	160.2
27260	12 019	Clay	644	1,592	178,899	170,609	140,814	105,986	329	389	437	297.6	235.7	176.3
34940	12 021	Collier	2,305	264	314,649	307,864	251,377	152,099	193	228	305	155.4	125.5	75.1
29380	12 023	Columbia	801	1,172	67,007	64,059	56,510	42,613	765	838	943	84.1	71.2	53.5
11580	12 027	DeSoto	640	1,612	35,315	35,060	32,209	23,865	1,280	1,342	1,497	55.4	50.7	37.4
...	12 029	Dixie	864	1,054	14,964	14,630	13,827	10,585	2,109	2,174	2,329	21.3	19.6	15.0
27260	12 031	Duval	918	898	837,964	826,791	778,866	672,971	58	61	63	1,083.1	1,007.8	869.6

See footnotes at end of table.

[Includes United States, states, and 3,141 counties/county equivalents defined as of February 22, 2005. For more information on these areas, see Appendix C, Geographic Information]

Metropolitan area code	FIPS state and county code[1]	County	Area, 2000 (square miles)		Population				Rank			Persons per square mile of land area		
			Total	Rank[2]	2006 (July 1)	2005 (July 1)	2000[3] (April 1 estimates base)	1990[3] (April 1 estimates base)	2006[2]	2000[2]	1990[4]	2006[5]	2000	1990
		FLORIDA—Con.												
37860	12 033	Escambia	876	1,029	295,426	295,624	294,410	262,445	206	192	191	446.0	444.4	395.5
37380	12 035	Flagler	571	1,921	83,084	76,045	49,835	28,701	649	918	1,338	171.3	104.3	59.2
...	12 037	Franklin	1,037	728	10,264	10,167	9,829	8,967	2,425	2,464	2,473	18.9	18.1	16.8
45220	12 039	Gadsden	528	2,072	46,658	46,207	45,087	41,116	1,008	996	978	90.4	87.3	79.7
23540	12 041	Gilchrist	355	2,716	16,865	16,480	14,437	9,667	1,977	2,128	2,417	48.3	41.7	27.7
...	12 043	Glades	986	784	11,230	11,265	10,576	7,591	2,349	2,391	2,610	14.5	13.7	9.8
...	12 045	Gulf	745	1,287	14,043	13,970	14,559	11,504	2,166	2,117	2,256	25.3	26.3	20.4
...	12 047	Hamilton	519	2,105	14,215	13,938	13,327	10,930	2,153	2,205	2,303	27.6	25.9	21.2
48100	12 049	Hardee	638	1,616	28,621	28,274	26,938	19,499	1,460	1,487	1,702	44.9	42.2	30.6
17500	12 051	Hendry	1,190	591	40,459	39,585	36,210	25,773	1,147	1,209	1,429	35.1	31.6	22.4
45300	12 053	Hernando	589	1,780	165,409	158,135	130,802	101,115	353	409	454	345.8	275.0	211.4
42700	12 055	Highlands	1,106	659	97,987	95,687	87,366	68,432	572	600	645	95.3	85.1	66.5
45300	12 057	Hillsborough	1,266	546	1,157,738	1,131,542	998,948	834,054	32	35	41	1,101.7	954.6	793.6
...	12 059	Holmes	489	2,216	19,285	19,095	18,564	15,778	1,853	1,868	1,936	40.0	38.4	32.7
42680	12 061	Indian River	617	1,685	130,100	127,357	112,947	90,208	454	476	507	258.5	225.3	179.3
...	12 063	Jackson	955	830	49,288	48,825	46,755	41,375	966	966	972	53.8	51.1	45.2
45220	12 065	Jefferson	637	1,622	14,677	14,458	12,902	11,296	2,124	2,243	2,275	24.6	21.6	18.9
...	12 067	Lafayette	548	2,008	8,045	7,919	7,022	5,578	2,590	2,684	2,792	14.8	13.0	10.3
36740	12 069	Lake	1,156	610	290,435	276,822	210,527	152,104	210	265	304	304.7	223.3	159.6
15980	12 071	Lee	1,212	580	571,344	544,196	440,888	335,113	104	136	154	711.0	552.4	417.0
45220	12 073	Leon	702	1,434	245,625	244,220	239,452	192,493	250	240	249	368.4	359.9	288.7
...	12 075	Levy	1,412	481	39,076	38,031	34,450	25,912	1,178	1,267	1,426	34.9	31.0	23.2
...	12 077	Liberty	843	1,092	7,782	7,727	7,021	5,569	2,616	2,685	2,793	9.3	8.4	6.7
...	12 079	Madison	716	1,392	19,210	18,981	18,733	16,569	1,861	1,861	1,882	27.8	27.1	23.9
42260	12 081	Manatee	893	991	313,298	306,254	264,002	211,707	194	209	237	422.8	358.6	285.6
36100	12 083	Marion	1,663	403	316,183	303,448	258,916	194,835	192	217	247	200.3	164.9	123.4
38940	12 085	Martin	753	1,273	139,393	139,282	126,731	100,900	429	425	455	250.9	228.8	181.6
33100	12 086	Miami-Dade	2,431	237	2,402,208	2,377,725	2,253,779	1,937,194	8	8	10	1,234.4	1,161.7	996.3
28580	12 087	Monroe	3,737	143	74,737	76,140	79,589	78,024	701	645	580	75.0	79.7	78.2
27260	12 089	Nassau	726	1,334	66,707	64,668	57,663	43,941	769	828	927	102.4	89.0	67.4
23020	12 091	Okaloosa	1,082	679	180,291	181,221	170,497	143,777	326	317	330	192.7	182.7	153.6
36380	12 093	Okeechobee	892	995	40,406	39,722	35,910	29,627	1,150	1,223	1,311	52.2	46.4	38.3
36740	12 095	Orange	1,004	763	1,043,500	1,021,884	896,346	677,491	35	45	62	1,149.9	994.4	746.4
36740	12 097	Osceola	1,506	441	244,045	231,482	172,493	107,728	251	315	428	184.6	131.8	81.5
33100	12 099	Palm Beach	2,386	248	1,274,013	1,264,956	1,131,191	863,503	29	31	37	645.4	575.4	424.5
45300	12 101	Pasco	868	1,040	450,171	430,053	344,768	281,131	142	170	176	604.4	466.4	377.4
45300	12 103	Pinellas	608	1,713	924,413	926,810	921,495	851,659	45	41	39	3,302.4	3,294.9	3,040.0
29460	12 105	Polk	2,010	313	561,606	541,910	483,924	405,382	107	119	122	299.6	259.0	216.2
37260	12 107	Putnam	827	1,118	74,083	73,343	70,423	65,070	703	705	673	102.6	97.6	90.1
27260	12 109	St. Johns	821	1,126	169,224	161,211	123,148	83,829	350	438	547	277.9	204.4	137.6
38940	12 111	St. Lucie	688	1,471	252,724	239,970	192,695	150,171	242	285	312	441.5	338.0	262.3
37860	12 113	Santa Rosa	1,174	600	144,561	142,442	117,743	81,961	415	459	554	142.2	116.5	80.7
42260	12 115	Sarasota	725	1,337	369,535	365,111	325,961	277,776	171	177	178	646.5	572.2	485.8
36740	12 117	Seminole	345	2,743	406,875	401,291	365,197	287,521	158	161	170	1,320.2	1,191.0	932.8
45540	12 119	Sumter	580	1,827	68,768	63,908	53,345	31,577	754	876	1,228	126.0	98.2	57.9
...	12 121	Suwannee	692	1,459	39,494	38,583	34,847	26,780	1,172	1,257	1,397	57.4	51.0	38.9
...	12 123	Taylor	1,232	566	19,842	19,623	19,256	17,111	1,827	1,832	1,845	19.0	18.4	16.4
...	12 125	Union	250	2,947	14,842	14,862	13,442	10,252	2,114	2,200	2,363	61.8	56.0	42.7
19660	12 127	Volusia	1,432	473	496,575	487,875	443,340	370,737	123	135	136	450.1	403.4	335.2
45220	12 129	Wakulla	736	1,309	29,542	28,227	22,863	14,202	1,432	1,652	2,037	48.7	37.9	23.4
...	12 131	Walton	1,238	562	52,270	50,403	40,602	27,759	923	1,098	1,360	49.4	38.6	26.2
...	12 133	Washington	616	1,689	22,720	22,232	20,973	16,919	1,684	1,739	1,855	39.2	36.2	29.2
	13 000	GEORGIA	59,425	(X)	9,363,941	9,132,553	8,186,816	6,478,149	(X)	(X)	(X)	161.7	142.1	111.8
...	13 001	Appling	512	2,127	17,860	17,892	17,415	15,744	1,921	1,929	1,937	35.1	34.3	30.9
20060	13 003	Atkinson	344	2,747	8,047	7,965	7,609	6,213	2,588	2,636	2,731	23.8	22.5	18.4
10500	13 005	Bacon	286	2,869	10,482	10,418	10,103	9,566	2,400	2,437	2,426	36.8	35.5	33.6
33300	13 007	Baker	349	2,729	4,098	4,137	4,074	3,615	2,901	2,913	2,949	11.9	11.8	10.5
	13 009	Baldwin	268	2,902	45,275	45,314	44,702	39,530	1,033	1,004	1,012	175.2	173.1	152.9
...	13 011	Banks	234	2,969	16,445	16,101	14,422	10,308	2,011	2,129	2,358	70.4	62.2	44.1
12060	13 013	Barrow	163	3,060	63,702	59,920	46,144	29,721	795	980	1,306	392.8	287.1	183.2
12060	13 015	Bartow	470	2,280	91,266	89,049	76,019	55,915	613	659	774	198.7	167.0	121.6
22340	13 017	Ben Hill	254	2,936	17,635	17,369	17,484	16,245	1,933	1,925	1,911	70.0	69.5	64.5
...	13 019	Berrien	458	2,314	16,756	16,735	16,235	14,153	1,989	2,008	2,041	37.0	36.0	31.3
31420	13 021	Bibb	255	2,935	154,903	154,381	153,887	150,137	379	345	313	619.7	615.4	600.5
...	13 023	Bleckley	219	2,990	12,353	12,210	11,666	10,430	2,279	2,322	2,346	56.8	53.8	48.0
15260	13 025	Brantley	447	2,348	15,735	15,474	14,629	11,077	2,059	2,112	2,285	35.4	33.1	24.9
46660	13 027	Brooks	498	2,189	16,464	16,269	16,450	15,398	2,010	1,995	1,964	33.4	33.4	31.2
42340	13 029	Bryan	454	2,323	29,648	28,575	23,417	15,438	1,427	1,622	1,959	67.1	53.3	34.9
44340	13 031	Bulloch	689	1,467	63,207	62,011	55,983	43,125	804	843	936	92.7	82.3	63.2
12260	13 033	Burke	835	1,104	22,986	23,154	22,243	20,579	1,669	1,684	1,650	27.7	26.8	24.8
12060	13 035	Butts	190	3,034	23,561	22,837	19,549	15,326	1,648	1,818	1,970	126.3	105.8	82.1
...	13 037	Calhoun	284	2,880	6,094	6,025	6,320	5,013	2,761	2,757	2,841	21.8	22.6	17.9
41220	13 039	Camden	783	1,210	45,118	45,751	43,664	30,167	1,035	1,023	1,291	71.6	69.4	47.9

See footnotes at end of table.

[Includes United States, states, and 3,141 counties/county equivalents defined as of February 22, 2005. For more information on these areas, see Appendix C, Geographic Information]

Metro-politan area code	FIPS state and county code[1]	County	Area, 2000 (square miles)		Population				Rank			Persons per square mile of land area		
			Total	Rank[2]	2006 (July 1)	2005 (July 1)	2000[3] (April 1 estimates base)	1990[3] (April 1 estimates base)	2006[2]	2000[2]	1990[4]	2006[5]	2000	1990
		GEORGIA—Con.												
...	13 043	Candler	249	2,948	10,674	10,352	9,577	7,744	2,388	2,483	2,599	43.2	38.8	31.4
12060	13 045	Carroll	504	2,164	107,325	104,386	87,268	71,422	530	601	620	215.1	176.5	143.1
16860	13 047	Catoosa	163	3,061	62,016	60,736	53,252	42,464	821	878	947	382.3	330.9	261.8
...	13 049	Charlton	783	1,208	10,882	10,714	10,282	8,496	2,374	2,419	2,513	13.9	13.2	10.9
42340	13 051	Chatham	632	1,635	241,411	238,039	232,347	216,774	253	248	230	551.0	530.2	492.2
17980	13 053	Chattahoochee	251	2,944	14,041	12,406	14,882	16,934	2,167	2,101	1,853	56.4	60.3	68.1
44900	13 055	Chattooga	314	2,814	26,442	26,499	25,470	22,236	1,537	1,542	1,569	84.4	81.4	70.9
12060	13 057	Cherokee	434	2,424	195,327	184,360	141,903	90,204	304	385	508	461.0	339.5	212.9
12020	13 059	Clarke	121	3,084	112,787	111,661	101,489	87,594	511	520	520	933.7	842.0	724.9
...	13 061	Clay.	217	2,991	3,180	3,232	3,357	3,364	2,962	2,967	2,966	16.3	17.2	17.2
12060	13 063	Clayton.	144	3,075	271,240	266,614	236,517	181,436	224	245	269	1,901.8	1,672.5	1,271.9
...	13 065	Clinch	824	1,121	6,897	6,992	6,878	6,160	2,690	2,700	2,736	8.5	8.5	7.6
12060	13 067	Cobb	345	2,745	679,325	663,528	607,751	447,745	85	89	111	1,997.1	1,800.8	1,316.0
20060	13 069	Coffee	603	1,729	40,242	39,588	37,412	29,592	1,154	1,180	1,314	67.2	62.7	49.4
34220	13 071	Colquitt	557	1,982	44,821	43,886	42,038	36,645	1,042	1,057	1,084	81.2	76.3	66.3
12260	13 073	Columbia	308	2,828	106,887	103,490	89,287	66,031	533	579	664	368.6	309.8	227.7
...	13 075	Cook	233	2,971	16,333	16,311	15,771	13,456	2,020	2,034	2,104	71.3	69.2	58.7
12060	13 077	Coweta	446	2,353	115,291	109,769	89,215	53,853	495	580	798	260.5	203.7	121.5
31420	13 079	Crawford.	326	2,790	12,823	12,837	12,495	8,991	2,256	2,267	2,471	39.5	38.3	27.7
18380	13 081	Crisp	281	2,887	22,051	21,884	21,996	20,011	1,719	1,695	1,677	80.5	80.3	73.1
16860	13 083	Dade	174	3,052	16,233	16,129	15,154	13,183	2,030	2,082	2,125	93.3	87.3	75.8
12060	13 085	Dawson	214	2,997	20,643	19,825	15,999	9,429	1,783	2,024	2,440	97.8	77.2	44.7
12460	13 087	Decatur	623	1,656	28,665	28,412	28,240	25,517	1,457	1,444	1,447	48.0	47.3	42.8
12060	13 089	DeKalb	271	2,897	723,602	713,679	666,057	546,174	76	76	87	2,697.9	2,492.3	2,035.8
...	13 091	Dodge	503	2,167	19,700	19,521	19,171	17,607	1,835	1,838	1,813	39.4	38.3	35.2
...	13 093	Dooly	397	2,610	11,748	11,703	11,525	9,901	2,313	2,333	2,398	29.9	29.3	25.2
10500	13 095	Dougherty	335	2,773	94,773	94,998	96,065	96,321	586	539	479	287.5	291.0	292.2
12060	13 097	Douglas	200	3,014	119,557	112,914	92,244	71,120	484	552	622	599.9	465.1	356.8
...	13 099	Early	516	2,115	12,065	12,068	12,354	11,854	2,296	2,279	2,227	23.6	24.1	23.2
46660	13 101	Echols	421	2,484	4,274	4,207	3,750	2,334	2,884	2,935	3,036	10.6	9.4	5.8
42340	13 103	Effingham	483	2,234	48,954	46,842	37,535	25,687	973	1,177	1,435	102.1	78.9	53.6
...	13 105	Elbert.	375	2,674	20,768	20,741	20,511	18,949	1,771	1,760	1,738	56.3	55.6	51.4
...	13 107	Emanuel	690	1,464	22,600	22,186	21,837	20,546	1,692	1,700	1,652	33.0	31.9	30.0
...	13 109	Evans	187	3,037	11,425	11,354	10,495	8,724	2,337	2,398	2,491	61.8	57.2	47.2
...	13 111	Fannin	391	2,628	22,319	21,812	19,798	15,992	1,709	1,803	1,923	57.9	51.7	41.5
12060	13 113	Fayette.	199	3,018	106,671	104,186	91,263	62,415	534	564	696	541.3	467.5	316.2
40660	13 115	Floyd	518	2,108	95,322	94,362	90,565	81,251	582	570	561	185.8	177.0	158.3
12060	13 117	Forsyth.	247	2,950	150,968	140,804	98,407	44,083	391	529	925	668.6	445.3	195.2
...	13 119	Franklin	266	2,907	21,691	21,560	20,287	16,650	1,735	1,775	1,873	82.4	77.2	63.2
12060	13 121	Fulton	535	2,056	960,009	934,242	815,821	648,776	40	55	73	1,815.9	1,544.8	1,227.1
...	13 123	Gilmer	432	2,433	28,175	27,349	23,456	13,368	1,479	1,619	2,108	66.0	55.7	31.3
...	13 125	Glascock	144	3,074	2,720	2,670	2,556	2,357	2,997	3,022	3,035	18.9	17.7	16.3
15260	13 127	Glynn	585	1,800	73,630	71,639	67,568	62,496	706	725	695	174.3	160.2	148.0
15660	13 129	Gordon.	358	2,715	51,419	50,227	44,104	35,067	936	1,014	1,130	144.6	124.8	98.7
...	13 131	Grady	460	2,312	25,082	24,508	23,659	20,279	1,580	1,605	1,662	54.7	51.6	44.3
...	13 133	Greene	406	2,568	15,534	15,570	14,406	11,793	2,075	2,132	2,229	40.0	37.2	30.4
12060	13 135	Gwinnett	437	2,401	757,104	726,790	588,448	352,910	71	92	146	1,749.6	1,378.8	815.3
18460	13 137	Habersham	279	2,890	41,112	39,621	35,898	27,622	1,129	1,224	1,367	147.8	129.9	99.3
23580	13 139	Hall	429	2,448	173,256	166,302	139,315	95,434	340	392	484	440.1	358.1	242.4
33300	13 141	Hancock	479	2,248	9,677	9,713	10,074	8,908	2,465	2,438	2,479	20.4	21.2	18.8
12060	13 143	Haralson.	283	2,881	28,616	28,335	25,690	21,966	1,461	1,529	1,578	101.4	91.5	77.8
17980	13 145	Harris	473	2,269	28,785	27,697	23,695	17,788	1,455	1,603	1,798	62.1	51.4	38.4
...	13 147	Hart	256	2,930	24,276	23,953	22,998	19,712	1,620	1,643	1,691	104.5	99.3	84.9
12060	13 149	Heard	301	2,844	11,472	11,336	11,012	8,628	2,331	2,364	2,500	38.8	37.5	29.1
12060	13 151	Henry	324	2,794	178,033	168,204	119,344	58,741	333	455	741	551.7	376.9	182.0
47580	13 153	Houston	380	2,655	127,530	125,576	110,765	89,208	460	489	514	338.5	295.3	236.8
22340	13 155	Irwin	363	2,701	10,403	10,227	9,931	8,649	2,411	2,455	2,498	29.2	27.9	24.2
...	13 157	Jackson	343	2,751	55,778	52,357	41,589	30,005	886	1,067	1,295	162.9	122.4	87.6
12060	13 159	Jasper	374	2,677	13,624	13,144	11,426	8,453	2,195	2,340	2,517	36.8	31.1	22.8
...	13 161	Jeff Davis	335	2,771	13,278	13,082	12,685	12,032	2,229	2,250	2,216	39.8	38.2	36.1
...	13 163	Jefferson	530	2,070	16,768	16,783	17,263	17,408	1,987	1,936	1,827	31.8	32.7	33.0
...	13 165	Jenkins	352	2,723	8,725	8,715	8,575	8,247	2,545	2,561	2,544	24.9	24.6	23.6
20140	13 167	Johnson	307	2,835	9,626	9,522	8,560	8,329	2,469	2,563	2,532	31.6	28.1	27.4
31420	13 169	Jones	395	2,618	26,973	26,744	23,639	20,739	1,519	1,606	1,643	68.5	60.2	52.7
12060	13 171	Lamar	186	3,040	16,679	16,605	15,912	13,038	1,996	2,028	2,138	90.2	86.5	70.5
46660	13 173	Lanier	200	3,015	7,723	7,521	7,241	5,531	2,623	2,662	2,798	41.3	38.9	29.6
20140	13 175	Laurens	819	1,135	47,316	46,939	44,874	39,988	995	1,000	1,000	58.3	55.4	49.2
10500	13 177	Lee	362	2,703	32,495	31,137	24,757	16,250	1,355	1,566	1,909	91.3	70.0	45.7
25980	13 179	Liberty	603	1,731	62,571	60,688	61,610	52,745	813	789	804	120.5	118.1	101.6
...	13 181	Lincoln	257	2,927	8,257	8,283	8,348	7,442	2,575	2,577	2,620	39.1	39.6	35.3

See footnotes at end of table.

County and City Data Book: 2007

U.S. Census Bureau

[Includes United States, states, and 3,141 counties/county equivalents defined as of February 22, 2005. For more information on these areas, see Appendix C, Geographic Information]

Metro-politan area code	FIPS state and county code[1]	County	Area, 2000 (square miles)		Population				Rank			Persons per square mile of land area		
			Total	Rank[2]	2006 (July 1)	2005 (July 1)	2000[3] (April 1 estimates base)	1990[3] (April 1 estimates base)	2006[2]	2000[2]	1990[4]	2006[5]	2000	1990
		GEORGIA—Con.												
25980	13 183	Long	403	2,585	11,452	11,122	10,304	6,202	2,333	2,415	2,732	28.6	25.8	15.5
46660	13 185	Lowndes	511	2,135	97,844	96,756	92,125	75,981	573	553	591	194.1	182.7	150.7
...	13 187	Lumpkin	285	2,876	25,462	24,529	20,986	14,573	1,566	1,736	2,015	89.5	74.4	51.2
12260	13 189	McDuffie	266	2,908	21,917	21,680	21,232	20,119	1,723	1,724	1,669	84.4	81.9	77.4
15260	13 191	McIntosh	575	1,887	11,248	11,000	10,847	8,634	2,347	2,377	2,499	25.9	25.2	19.9
	13 193	Macon	406	2,569	13,817	13,725	14,080	13,114	2,181	2,159	2,130	34.3	34.9	32.5
12020	13 195	Madison	286	2,873	27,837	27,442	25,730	21,050	1,493	1,527	1,626	98.1	91.1	74.0
17980	13 197	Marion	367	2,687	7,276	7,222	7,144	5,590	2,660	2,675	2,791	19.8	19.6	15.2
12060	13 199	Meriwether	505	2,157	22,881	22,754	22,528	22,411	1,677	1,670	1,559	45.5	44.8	44.5
...	13 201	Miller	284	2,878	6,239	6,161	6,383	6,280	2,747	2,751	2,725	22.0	22.6	22.2
...	13 205	Mitchell	514	2,121	23,852	23,710	23,934	20,275	1,633	1,596	1,663	46.6	46.8	39.6
31420	13 207	Monroe	398	2,607	24,443	23,734	21,774	17,113	1,610	1,707	1,844	61.8	55.2	43.3
47080	13 209	Montgomery	247	2,951	9,067	8,938	8,270	7,379	2,524	2,585	2,623	37.0	33.7	30.1
...	13 211	Morgan	355	2,718	17,908	17,524	15,457	12,883	1,919	2,054	2,147	51.2	44.4	36.8
19140	13 213	Murray	347	2,737	41,398	40,814	36,503	26,147	1,118	1,203	1,415	120.2	106.9	75.9
17980	13 215	Muscogee	221	2,987	188,660	185,799	186,291	179,280	314	295	271	872.4	862.1	828.8
12060	13 217	Newton	279	2,891	91,451	86,529	62,001	41,808	611	784	960	330.8	227.6	151.2
12020	13 219	Oconee	186	3,039	30,858	29,760	26,225	17,618	1,398	1,510	1,812	166.2	142.2	94.8
12020	13 221	Oglethorpe	442	2,377	13,997	13,601	12,635	9,763	2,171	2,255	2,408	31.7	28.8	22.1
12060	13 223	Paulding	315	2,810	121,530	112,566	81,608	41,611	477	637	967	387.7	265.0	132.7
22980	13 225	Peach	151	3,070	24,785	24,481	23,668	21,189	1,593	1,604	1,621	164.1	157.6	140.3
12060	13 227	Pickens	233	2,972	29,640	28,440	22,983	14,432	1,428	1,645	2,023	127.7	100.7	62.2
48180	13 229	Pierce	344	2,748	17,452	17,120	15,625	13,328	1,945	2,048	2,111	50.8	45.8	38.9
12060	13 231	Pike	219	2,989	16,801	16,073	13,688	10,224	1,984	2,188	2,368	76.9	63.2	46.8
16340	13 233	Polk	312	2,819	41,091	40,436	38,127	33,815	1,131	1,162	1,170	132.1	123.0	108.7
...	13 235	Pulaski	250	2,946	9,887	9,757	9,588	8,108	2,452	2,482	2,554	40.0	38.8	32.8
...	13 237	Putnam	361	2,708	19,930	19,703	18,812	14,137	1,822	1,855	2,043	57.8	54.7	41.0
21640	13 239	Quitman	161	3,063	2,486	2,461	2,598	2,210	3,016	3,020	3,054	16.4	17.2	14.6
...	13 241	Rabun	377	2,663	16,354	16,265	15,050	11,648	2,017	2,089	2,241	44.1	40.7	31.4
...	13 243	Randolph	431	2,440	7,357	7,282	7,791	8,023	2,650	2,627	2,562	17.1	18.1	18.7
12260	13 245	Richmond	328	2,786	194,398	194,135	199,775	189,719	306	277	253	599.9	615.8	585.4
12060	13 247	Rockdale	132	3,081	80,332	78,398	70,111	54,091	668	709	795	615.0	540.3	413.9
11140	13 249	Schley	168	3,056	4,198	4,101	3,766	3,590	2,890	2,932	2,951	25.0	22.6	21.4
...	13 251	Screven	656	1,555	15,190	15,288	15,374	13,842	2,093	2,062	2,069	23.4	23.7	21.3
...	13 253	Seminole	257	2,929	9,168	9,191	9,369	9,010	2,511	2,502	2,468	38.5	39.4	37.8
12060	13 255	Spalding	200	3,016	62,185	61,262	58,417	54,457	819	819	792	314.1	295.4	275.1
45740	13 257	Stephens	184	3,041	25,143	25,044	25,435	23,436	1,578	1,546	1,519	140.3	142.2	130.7
...	13 259	Stewart	463	2,305	4,754	4,878	5,259	5,654	2,851	2,836	2,788	10.4	11.4	12.3
11140	13 261	Sumter	493	2,209	32,490	32,507	33,200	30,232	1,356	1,309	1,285	67.0	68.5	62.3
...	13 263	Talbot	395	2,622	6,605	6,639	6,498	6,524	2,719	2,740	2,706	16.8	16.6	16.6
...	13 265	Taliaferro	195	3,026	1,877	1,835	2,077	1,915	3,062	3,061	3,073	9.6	10.6	9.8
...	13 267	Tattnall	488	2,217	23,492	23,181	22,305	17,722	1,652	1,679	1,802	48.6	46.2	36.6
...	13 269	Taylor	380	2,656	8,792	8,826	8,815	7,642	2,538	2,546	2,606	23.3	23.4	20.2
...	13 271	Telfair	444	2,363	13,268	13,341	11,794	11,000	2,230	2,308	2,293	30.1	26.8	24.9
10500	13 273	Terrell	338	2,764	10,657	10,684	10,970	10,653	2,389	2,369	2,322	31.8	32.7	31.8
45620	13 275	Thomas	552	1,997	45,135	44,643	42,734	38,943	1,034	1,042	1,024	82.3	78.1	71.0
45700	13 277	Tift	269	2,900	41,685	40,731	38,390	34,998	1,109	1,153	1,133	157.3	145.0	132.0
47080	13 279	Toombs	369	2,684	27,623	27,169	26,067	24,072	1,501	1,516	1,490	75.3	71.3	65.6
...	13 281	Towns	172	3,054	10,525	10,281	9,319	6,754	2,397	2,505	2,680	63.2	56.2	40.6
...	13 283	Treutlen	202	3,013	6,852	6,734	6,854	5,994	2,695	2,705	2,758	34.1	34.3	29.9
29300	13 285	Troup	446	2,354	63,245	62,632	58,779	55,532	803	816	779	152.8	142.4	134.2
...	13 287	Turner	290	2,859	9,322	9,436	9,504	8,703	2,495	2,490	2,492	32.6	33.3	30.4
31420	13 289	Twiggs	363	2,696	10,184	10,273	10,590	9,806	2,434	2,390	2,403	28.3	29.4	27.2
...	13 291	Union	329	2,783	20,652	20,079	17,289	11,993	1,781	1,934	2,220	64.0	54.0	37.2
45580	13 293	Upson	328	2,789	27,676	27,660	27,597	26,300	1,497	1,465	1,411	85.0	84.9	80.8
16860	13 295	Walker	447	2,349	64,606	63,812	61,053	58,310	788	797	743	144.7	136.9	130.7
12060	13 297	Walton	330	2,779	79,388	75,670	60,687	38,586	677	799	1,038	241.2	187.2	117.2
48180	13 299	Ware	906	935	35,748	35,353	35,494	35,471	1,265	1,234	1,112	39.6	39.3	39.3
...	13 301	Warren	287	2,866	5,949	6,067	6,336	6,078	2,776	2,755	2,748	20.8	22.1	21.3
...	13 303	Washington	684	1,479	20,723	19,998	21,176	19,112	1,776	1,727	1,726	30.5	31.1	28.1
27700	13 305	Wayne	649	1,579	28,895	28,536	26,569	22,356	1,449	1,497	1,561	44.8	41.3	34.7
...	13 307	Webster	210	3,002	2,252	2,254	2,383	2,263	3,031	3,033	3,046	10.7	11.4	10.8
...	13 309	Wheeler	300	2,846	6,908	6,703	6,179	4,903	2,687	2,765	2,844	23.2	20.7	16.5
...	13 311	White	242	2,960	24,738	24,024	19,944	13,006	1,596	1,795	2,141	102.4	83.3	53.8
19140	13 313	Whitfield	291	2,856	92,999	91,099	83,558	72,462	599	623	617	320.7	290.2	249.9
...	13 315	Wilcox	383	2,649	8,712	8,629	8,577	7,008	2,546	2,560	2,658	22.9	22.5	18.4
...	13 317	Wilkes	474	2,262	10,468	10,480	10,687	10,597	2,403	2,386	2,328	22.2	22.7	22.5
...	13 319	Wilkinson	452	2,335	9,995	10,094	10,220	10,228	2,443	2,425	2,367	22.4	22.9	22.9
10500	13 321	Worth	575	1,884	21,938	21,849	22,000	19,744	1,720	1,693	1,687	38.5	38.6	34.6

See footnotes at end of table.

[Includes United States, states, and 3,141 counties/county equivalents defined as of February 22, 2005. For more information on these areas, see Appendix C, Geographic Information]

Metropolitan area code	FIPS state and county code[1]	County	Area, 2000 (square miles) Total	Rank[2]	Population 2006 (July 1)	2005 (July 1)	2000[3] (April 1 estimates base)	1990[3] (April 1 estimates base)	Rank 2006[2]	2000[2]	1990[4]	Persons per square mile of land area 2006[5]	2000	1990
	15 000	HAWAII	10,931	(X)	1,285,498	1,273,278	1,211,537	1,108,229	(X)	(X)	(X)	200.2	188.7	172.5
25900	15 001	Hawaii	5,087	80	171,191	166,461	148,677	120,317	345	363	383	42.5	37.1	29.9
26180	15 003	Honolulu	2,127	292	909,863	904,645	876,156	836,231	50	48	40	1,517.0	1,459.6	1,393.3
...	15 005	Kalawao	52	3,106	120	120	147	130	3,140	3,140	3,139	9.1	11.1	9.8
28180	15 007	Kauai	1,266	545	63,004	62,365	58,463	51,177	807	818	823	101.2	94.0	82.2
27980	15 009	Maui	2,399	244	141,320	139,687	128,094	100,374	423	422	457	121.9	111.1	86.6
	16 000	IDAHO	83,570	(X)	1,466,465	1,429,367	1,293,956	1,006,734	(X)	(X)	(X)	17.7	15.7	12.2
14260	16 001	Ada	1,060	703	359,035	345,418	300,904	205,775	175	188	242	340.3	287.3	195.0
...	16 003	Adams	1,370	492	3,485	3,542	3,476	3,254	2,941	2,955	2,979	2.6	2.5	2.4
38540	16 005	Bannock	1,147	623	78,443	77,794	75,565	66,026	684	664	665	70.5	67.9	59.3
	16 007	Bear Lake	1,049	717	6,167	6,180	6,411	6,084	2,753	2,750	2,747	6.3	6.6	6.3
...	16 009	Benewah	784	1,205	9,347	9,165	9,171	7,937	2,492	2,517	2,579	12.0	11.8	10.2
13940	16 011	Bingham	2,120	294	44,051	43,775	41,735	37,583	1,060	1,062	1,056	21.0	20.0	17.9
	16 013	Blaine	2,661	209	21,501	21,173	18,991	13,552	1,743	1,848	2,097	8.1	7.2	5.1
14260	16 015	Boise	1,907	337	7,641	7,440	6,670	3,509	2,631	2,721	2,956	4.0	3.5	1.8
...	16 017	Bonner	1,920	331	41,275	40,736	36,835	26,622	1,125	1,194	1,402	23.8	21.3	15.3
26820	16 019	Bonneville	1,901	340	94,630	91,702	82,522	72,207	589	629	618	50.6	44.4	38.6
...	16 021	Boundary	1,278	539	10,831	10,563	9,871	8,332	2,379	2,459	2,531	8.5	7.8	6.6
...	16 023	Butte	2,234	275	2,781	2,782	2,899	2,918	2,993	2,999	3,004	1.2	1.3	1.3
...	16 025	Camas	1,079	684	1,088	1,064	991	727	3,104	3,111	3,128	1.0	0.9	0.7
14260	16 027	Canyon	604	1,727	173,302	164,981	131,441	90,076	339	406	510	293.9	225.7	152.7
...	16 029	Caribou	1,799	366	6,996	7,094	7,304	6,963	2,679	2,656	2,663	4.0	4.1	3.9
15420	16 031	Cassia	2,580	220	21,365	21,391	21,416	19,532	1,747	1,718	1,698	8.3	8.3	7.6
...	16 033	Clark	1,765	379	920	914	1,022	762	3,112	3,110	3,126	0.5	0.6	0.4
...	16 035	Clearwater	2,488	231	8,324	8,338	8,930	8,505	2,572	2,533	2,510	3.4	3.6	3.5
...	16 037	Custer	4,937	86	4,180	4,097	4,342	4,133	2,895	2,894	2,903	0.8	0.9	0.8
34300	16 039	Elmore	3,101	177	28,114	28,298	29,130	21,205	1,481	1,424	1,620	9.1	9.5	6.9
30860	16 041	Franklin	668	1,518	12,494	12,410	11,329	9,232	2,267	2,349	2,452	18.8	17.1	13.9
39940	16 043	Fremont	1,896	341	12,369	12,224	11,819	10,937	2,278	2,305	2,300	6.6	6.3	5.9
14260	16 045	Gem	566	1,952	16,558	16,265	15,181	11,844	2,002	2,077	2,228	29.4	27.1	21.1
...	16 047	Gooding	734	1,313	14,404	14,424	14,158	11,633	2,137	2,151	2,244	19.7	19.4	15.9
...	16 049	Idaho	8,502	38	15,762	15,659	15,511	13,768	2,056	2,053	2,074	1.9	1.8	1.6
26820	16 051	Jefferson	1,106	660	22,350	21,613	19,155	16,543	1,708	1,841	1,887	20.4	17.6	15.1
46300	16 053	Jerome	602	1,734	20,130	19,677	18,342	15,138	1,816	1,879	1,978	33.6	30.8	25.2
17660	16 055	Kootenai	1,316	513	131,507	127,722	108,685	69,795	443	496	635	105.6	88.0	56.1
34140	16 057	Latah	1,077	688	35,029	34,990	34,935	30,617	1,295	1,252	1,260	32.5	32.4	28.4
...	16 059	Lemhi	4,570	103	7,930	7,868	7,806	6,899	2,597	2,626	2,671	1.7	1.7	1.5
...	16 061	Lewis	480	2,244	3,756	3,739	3,747	3,516	2,925	2,936	2,955	7.8	7.8	7.3
...	16 063	Lincoln	1,206	583	4,522	4,532	4,044	3,308	2,869	2,917	2,975	3.8	3.4	2.7
39940	16 065	Madison	473	2,266	31,393	31,207	27,467	23,674	1,384	1,470	1,505	66.6	58.2	50.2
15420	16 067	Minidoka	763	1,256	19,041	18,996	20,174	19,361	1,871	1,782	1,712	25.1	26.5	25.5
30300	16 069	Nez Perce	856	1,074	38,324	38,008	37,410	33,754	1,200	1,181	1,172	45.1	44.0	39.8
...	16 071	Oneida	1,202	584	4,176	4,178	4,125	3,492	2,896	2,906	2,957	3.5	3.4	2.9
14260	16 073	Owyhee	7,697	45	11,104	11,037	10,644	8,392	2,361	2,388	2,521	1.4	1.4	1.1
36620	16 075	Payette	410	2,543	22,595	22,114	20,578	16,434	1,693	1,756	1,897	55.4	50.6	40.3
38540	16 077	Power	1,443	467	7,914	7,761	7,538	7,086	2,598	2,641	2,648	5.6	5.3	5.0
...	16 079	Shoshone	2,636	212	13,180	13,038	13,771	13,931	2,234	2,178	2,063	5.0	5.2	5.3
27220	16 081	Teton	451	2,340	7,838	7,494	5,999	3,439	2,605	2,781	2,960	17.4	13.6	7.6
46300	16 083	Twin Falls	1,928	329	71,575	69,540	64,284	53,580	729	758	801	37.2	33.4	27.8
...	16 085	Valley	3,734	144	8,836	8,310	7,651	6,109	2,534	2,634	2,741	2.4	2.1	1.7
...	16 087	Washington	1,474	455	10,202	10,114	9,977	8,550	2,433	2,448	2,509	7.0	6.9	5.9
	17 000	ILLINOIS	57,914	(X)	12,831,970	12,765,427	12,419,647	11,430,602	(X)	(X)	(X)	230.9	223.8	205.6
39500	17 001	Adams	871	1,037	67,221	67,053	68,277	66,090	764	721	662	78.5	79.6	77.1
16020	17 003	Alexander	253	2,942	8,635	8,840	9,590	10,626	2,555	2,481	2,324	36.5	40.6	44.9
41180	17 005	Bond	383	2,650	18,055	18,011	17,631	14,991	1,911	1,922	1,988	47.5	46.4	39.4
40420	17 007	Boone	282	2,884	52,617	50,419	41,784	30,806	919	1,060	1,249	187.1	149.6	109.5
...	17 009	Brown	307	2,829	6,701	6,750	6,950	5,836	2,706	2,692	2,776	21.9	22.8	19.1
36860	17 011	Bureau	873	1,032	35,257	35,172	35,503	35,688	1,285	1,233	1,107	40.6	40.9	41.1
41180	17 013	Calhoun	284	2,879	5,177	5,166	5,084	5,322	2,827	2,847	2,816	20.4	20.1	21.0
...	17 015	Carroll	466	2,298	16,035	16,090	16,674	16,805	2,044	1,978	1,859	36.1	37.4	37.8
...	17 017	Cass	384	2,647	13,766	13,841	13,695	13,437	2,187	2,187	2,105	36.4	36.4	35.7
16580	17 019	Champaign	998	772	185,682	184,704	179,669	173,025	319	307	279	186.3	180.4	173.5
45380	17 021	Christian	716	1,393	35,063	35,186	35,372	34,418	1,293	1,239	1,153	49.4	49.9	48.5
...	17 023	Clark	505	2,161	16,987	16,980	17,008	15,921	1,965	1,953	1,929	33.9	33.9	31.7
...	17 025	Clay	470	2,281	14,028	14,116	14,560	14,460	2,168	2,116	2,019	29.9	31.0	30.8
41180	17 027	Clinton	503	2,165	36,633	36,138	35,531	33,944	1,242	1,231	1,165	77.2	75.0	71.6
16660	17 029	Coles	510	2,136	50,949	51,053	53,196	51,644	942	881	819	100.2	104.4	101.6
16980	17 031	Cook	1,635	410	5,288,655	5,303,943	5,376,626	5,105,044	2	2	2	5,592.4	5,686.8	5,398.3
...	17 033	Crawford	446	2,356	19,825	19,909	20,452	19,464	1,830	1,763	1,704	44.7	46.0	43.9
16660	17 035	Cumberland	347	2,736	11,000	10,959	11,253	10,670	2,367	2,354	2,320	31.8	32.6	30.8
16980	17 037	DeKalb	635	1,624	100,139	97,770	88,969	77,932	560	585	582	157.9	140.8	122.9
...	17 039	De Witt	405	2,572	16,768	16,658	16,798	16,516	1,987	1,972	1,891	42.2	42.2	41.5

See footnotes at end of table.

[Includes United States, states, and 3,141 counties/county equivalents defined as of February 22, 2005. For more information on these areas, see Appendix C, Geographic Information]

Metro-politan area code	FIPS state and county code[1]	County	Area, 2000 (square miles) Total	Rank[2]	Population 2006 (July 1)	Population 2005 (July 1)	Population 2000[3] (April 1 estimates base)	Population 1990[3] (April 1 estimates base)	Rank 2006[2]	Rank 2000[2]	Rank 1990[4]	Persons per square mile 2006[5]	Persons per square mile 2000	Persons per square mile 1990
		ILLINOIS—Con.												
...	17 041	Douglas	417	2,501	19,791	19,818	19,922	19,464	1,832	1,797	1,704	47.5	47.8	46.7
16980	17 043	DuPage	337	2,767	932,670	931,219	904,349	781,689	43	42	49	2,795.7	2,719.1	2,337.3
...	17 045	Edgar	624	1,651	19,183	19,193	19,704	19,595	1,862	1,813	1,693	30.8	31.5	31.4
...	17 047	Edwards	223	2,985	6,617	6,718	6,971	7,440	2,715	2,689	2,621	29.8	31.3	33.5
20820	17 049	Effingham	480	2,243	34,429	34,505	34,264	31,704	1,307	1,274	1,222	71.9	71.6	66.2
...	17 051	Fayette	725	1,336	21,774	21,698	21,802	20,893	1,731	1,703	1,634	30.4	30.4	29.2
16580	17 053	Ford	486	2,222	14,211	14,163	14,241	14,275	2,154	2,149	2,032	29.2	29.3	29.4
...	17 055	Franklin	431	2,436	39,862	39,714	39,029	40,319	1,165	1,139	992	96.7	94.7	97.8
15900	17 057	Fulton	883	1,013	37,378	37,472	38,250	38,080	1,221	1,160	1,050	43.2	44.2	44.0
...	17 059	Gallatin	328	2,787	6,159	6,151	6,445	6,909	2,754	2,744	2,670	19.0	19.9	21.3
...	17 061	Greene	546	2,014	14,255	14,456	14,761	15,317	2,149	2,106	1,971	26.2	27.2	28.2
16980	17 063	Grundy	430	2,442	45,828	43,736	37,535	32,337	1,025	1,177	1,205	109.1	89.7	77.0
34500	17 065	Hamilton	436	2,408	8,335	8,319	8,621	8,499	2,571	2,557	2,511	19.2	19.8	19.5
...	17 067	Hancock	815	1,142	19,091	19,173	20,120	21,373	1,867	1,786	1,615	24.0	25.3	26.9
...	17 069	Hardin	182	3,043	4,585	4,670	4,800	5,189	2,864	2,860	2,826	25.7	26.9	29.1
15460	17 071	Henderson	395	2,619	7,819	7,949	8,213	8,096	2,608	2,591	2,555	20.6	21.7	21.4
19340	17 073	Henry	826	1,119	50,339	50,508	51,018	51,159	949	910	824	61.1	62.0	62.1
...	17 075	Iroquois	1,118	649	30,598	30,692	31,334	30,787	1,402	1,366	1,252	27.4	28.1	27.6
16060	17 077	Jackson	603	1,730	57,778	58,041	59,611	61,067	859	806	713	98.2	101.2	103.8
...	17 079	Jasper	498	2,188	9,880	9,954	10,117	10,609	2,453	2,435	2,327	20.0	20.4	21.5
34500	17 081	Jefferson	584	1,808	40,523	40,414	40,045	37,020	1,145	1,113	1,072	71.0	70.2	64.8
41180	17 083	Jersey	377	2,662	22,628	22,423	21,668	20,539	1,690	1,710	1,653	61.3	58.7	55.6
...	17 085	Jo Daviess	619	1,679	22,594	22,508	22,289	21,821	1,694	1,681	1,589	37.6	37.1	36.3
...	17 087	Johnson	349	2,730	13,360	13,170	12,880	11,347	2,226	2,244	2,268	38.8	37.5	32.8
16980	17 089	Kane	524	2,088	493,735	483,208	404,122	317,471	126	146	159	948.7	783.5	609.7
28100	17 091	Kankakee	681	1,488	109,090	107,824	103,833	96,255	526	511	480	161.2	153.5	142.1
16980	17 093	Kendall	323	2,796	88,158	79,597	54,520	39,413	624	862	1,014	275.0	172.2	122.9
23660	17 095	Knox	720	1,365	52,906	53,321	55,838	56,393	913	845	770	73.9	77.8	78.7
16980	17 097	Lake	1,368	494	713,076	704,086	644,586	516,418	77	84	90	1,593.3	1,449.8	1,153.3
36860	17 099	LaSalle	1,148	622	113,065	112,371	111,549	106,913	509	483	431	99.6	98.3	94.2
...	17 101	Lawrence	374	2,676	15,887	15,965	15,452	15,972	2,051	2,055	1,925	42.7	41.4	42.9
19940	17 103	Lee	729	1,324	35,701	35,637	36,062	34,392	1,266	1,214	1,154	49.2	49.7	47.4
38700	17 105	Livingston	1,045	719	38,658	38,951	39,676	39,301	1,194	1,120	1,017	37.0	38.0	37.7
30660	17 107	Logan	619	1,677	30,302	30,531	31,192	30,798	1,410	1,373	1,250	49.0	50.4	49.8
31380	17 109	McDonough	590	1,778	31,823	32,011	32,918	35,244	1,376	1,323	1,124	54.0	55.8	59.8
16980	17 111	McHenry	611	1,703	312,373	304,701	260,093	183,241	197	213	262	517.6	433.7	303.3
14060	17 113	McLean	1,186	593	161,202	158,977	150,435	129,180	361	357	358	136.2	127.5	109.1
19500	17 115	Macon	585	1,799	109,309	109,835	114,706	117,206	524	472	394	188.3	197.2	201.9
41180	17 117	Macoupin	868	1,041	48,841	49,016	49,019	47,679	976	931	880	56.6	56.8	55.2
41180	17 119	Madison	740	1,300	265,303	263,975	258,951	249,238	231	216	200	365.9	357.4	343.7
16460	17 121	Marion	576	1,867	40,088	40,068	41,691	41,561	1,157	1,064	969	70.1	72.9	72.6
37900	17 123	Marshall	399	2,605	13,003	13,122	13,150	12,846	2,241	2,216	2,151	33.7	34.0	33.3
...	17 125	Mason	563	1,960	15,503	15,733	16,037	16,269	2,078	2,022	1,907	28.8	29.7	30.2
37140	17 127	Massac	242	2,961	15,135	15,225	15,161	14,752	2,098	2,080	2,003	63.3	63.3	61.7
44100	17 129	Menard	315	2,809	12,588	12,587	12,486	11,164	2,265	2,268	2,280	40.1	39.8	35.5
19340	17 131	Mercer	569	1,938	16,780	16,840	16,957	17,290	1,986	1,956	1,834	29.9	30.2	30.8
41180	17 133	Monroe	398	2,608	31,876	31,289	27,619	22,422	1,372	1,462	1,557	82.1	71.5	57.7
...	17 135	Montgomery	710	1,418	30,367	30,304	30,644	30,728	1,405	1,384	1,256	43.1	43.5	43.7
27300	17 137	Morgan	572	1,905	35,666	35,734	36,619	36,397	1,268	1,199	1,093	62.7	64.4	64.0
...	17 139	Moultrie	344	2,746	14,383	14,426	14,287	13,930	2,139	2,143	2,064	42.9	42.7	41.5
40300	17 141	Ogle	763	1,255	54,826	54,057	51,032	45,957	896	909	904	72.3	67.4	60.6
37900	17 143	Peoria	631	1,639	182,495	182,056	183,439	182,827	325	298	263	294.6	295.8	295.1
...	17 145	Perry	447	2,350	22,865	22,789	23,094	21,412	1,678	1,639	1,610	51.9	52.3	48.6
16580	17 147	Piatt	440	2,383	16,688	16,602	16,369	15,548	1,994	2,001	1,950	37.9	37.2	35.3
...	17 149	Pike	849	1,084	16,840	17,035	17,379	17,577	1,981	1,930	1,816	20.3	20.9	21.2
...	17 151	Pope	375	2,673	4,184	4,194	4,413	4,373	2,894	2,887	2,886	11.3	11.9	11.8
...	17 153	Pulaski	203	3,011	6,726	6,815	7,348	7,523	2,704	2,653	2,614	33.5	36.5	37.5
36860	17 155	Putnam	172	3,053	6,005	6,063	6,086	5,730	2,768	2,774	2,784	37.6	38.1	35.9
...	17 157	Randolph	597	1,749	33,028	33,116	33,893	34,583	1,337	1,285	1,149	57.1	58.6	59.8
...	17 159	Richland	362	2,703	15,724	15,809	16,149	16,545	2,060	2,014	1,886	43.7	44.8	45.9
19340	17 161	Rock Island	451	2,338	147,545	147,454	149,388	148,723	402	361	318	345.7	349.5	348.5
41180	17 163	St. Clair	674	1,508	260,919	259,388	256,068	262,852	234	219	190	393.1	385.9	395.9
25380	17 165	Saline	387	2,639	26,062	26,054	26,733	26,551	1,547	1,494	1,406	68.0	69.5	69.3
44100	17 167	Sangamon	877	1,027	193,524	192,689	188,954	178,386	308	292	273	222.9	217.8	205.4
...	17 169	Schuyler	441	2,379	6,984	7,056	7,189	7,498	2,681	2,668	2,616	16.0	16.4	17.1
27300	17 171	Scott	253	2,940	5,377	5,439	5,534	5,644	2,811	2,816	2,789	21.4	22.1	22.5
...	17 173	Shelby	768	1,239	22,172	22,270	22,893	22,261	1,716	1,651	1,565	29.2	30.1	29.3
37900	17 175	Stark	288	2,863	6,233	6,159	6,332	6,534	2,748	2,756	2,704	21.6	21.9	22.7
23300	17 177	Stephenson	565	1,955	47,388	47,719	48,979	48,052	994	934	870	84.0	86.7	85.2
37900	17 179	Tazewell	658	1,543	130,559	129,603	128,485	123,692	450	420	372	201.2	198.0	190.6

See footnotes at end of table.

Table B-1. Counties — **Area and Population**—Con.

[Includes United States, states, and 3,141 counties/county equivalents defined as of February 22, 2005. For more information on these areas, see Appendix C, Geographic Information]

Metropolitan area code	FIPS state and county code[1]	County	Area, 2000 (square miles)		Population									
							2000[3] (April 1 estimates base)	1990[3] (April 1 estimates base)	Rank			Persons per square mile of land area		
			Total	Rank[2]	2006 (July 1)	2005 (July 1)			2006[2]	2000[2]	1990[4]	2006[5]	2000	1990
		ILLINOIS—Con.												
...	17 181	Union..................	422	2,479	18,261	18,219	18,293	17,619	1,904	1,882	1,811	43.9	43.9	42.3
19180	17 183	Vermilion...............	902	949	81,941	82,178	83,924	88,257	657	621	516	91.1	93.2	98.2
...	17 185	Wabash	228	2,979	12,457	12,542	12,937	13,111	2,270	2,240	2,131	55.7	57.7	58.7
23660	17 187	Warren	543	2,025	17,480	17,592	18,735	19,181	1,943	1,860	1,721	32.2	34.4	35.4
...	17 189	Washington............	564	1,958	14,927	14,946	15,148	14,965	2,113	2,083	1,990	26.5	27.0	26.6
...	17 191	Wayne	716	1,394	16,602	16,766	17,151	17,241	1,999	1,947	1,839	23.3	24.0	24.1
...	17 193	White..................	502	2,172	15,078	15,217	15,371	16,522	2,101	2,063	1,890	30.5	31.0	33.4
44580	17 195	Whiteside	697	1,447	59,880	59,745	60,651	60,186	841	800	721	87.4	88.6	87.9
16980	17 197	Will	849	1,083	668,217	642,625	502,267	357,313	88	111	143	798.4	607.4	426.8
32060	17 199	Williamson	444	2,362	63,740	63,411	61,310	57,733	793	794	753	150.5	144.7	136.1
40420	17 201	Winnebago	519	2,106	295,635	291,639	278,420	252,913	205	202	198	575.5	543.1	492.2
37900	17 203	Woodford	543	2,029	37,904	37,424	35,469	32,653	1,212	1,235	1,198	71.8	67.3	61.8
	18 000	INDIANA	36,418	(X)	6,313,520	6,266,019	6,080,517	5,544,156	(X)	(X)	(X)	176.0	169.9	154.6
19540	18 001	Adams	340	2,760	33,719	33,748	33,625	31,095	1,319	1,296	1,243	99.4	99.1	91.6
23060	18 003	Allen	660	1,534	347,316	343,946	331,849	300,836	180	176	164	528.4	506.3	457.7
18020	18 005	Bartholomew............	409	2,547	74,444	73,611	71,435	63,657	702	692	687	183.0	176.3	156.5
29140	18 007	Benton	406	2,567	9,050	9,023	9,421	9,441	2,525	2,494	2,439	22.3	23.1	23.2
...	18 009	Blackford	165	3,057	13,603	13,768	14,048	14,067	2,200	2,163	2,051	82.4	84.9	85.2
26900	18 011	Boone	423	2,474	53,526	51,918	46,107	38,147	910	982	1,049	126.6	109.7	90.2
26900	18 013	Brown	317	2,807	15,071	15,123	14,957	14,080	2,103	2,095	2,050	48.3	48.0	45.1
29140	18 015	Carroll	375	2,671	20,526	20,446	20,165	18,809	1,793	1,783	1,747	55.1	54.2	50.5
30900	18 017	Cass	415	2,512	39,902	40,179	40,930	38,413	1,164	1,082	1,042	96.6	99.3	93.0
31140	18 019	Clark	376	2,667	103,569	101,625	96,466	87,774	543	536	519	276.2	258.1	234.0
45460	18 021	Clay...................	360	2,711	27,021	27,118	26,567	24,705	1,516	1,498	1,473	75.6	74.3	69.1
23140	18 023	Clinton	405	2,570	34,217	34,073	33,866	30,974	1,311	1,286	1,246	84.5	83.9	76.5
...	18 025	Crawford...............	309	2,825	11,137	11,175	10,743	9,914	2,359	2,380	2,393	36.4	35.3	32.4
47780	18 027	Daviess	437	2,398	30,220	30,284	29,820	27,533	1,411	1,402	1,373	70.2	69.3	63.9
17140	18 029	Dearborn	307	2,832	49,663	48,930	46,130	38,835	960	981	1,027	162.7	151.9	127.2
24700	18 031	Decatur	373	2,678	24,948	25,016	24,555	23,645	1,586	1,574	1,508	67.0	66.0	63.5
12140	18 033	DeKalb................	364	2,693	41,902	41,638	40,285	35,324	1,104	1,108	1,120	115.5	111.3	97.3
34620	18 035	Delaware	396	2,615	114,879	116,203	118,769	119,659	497	456	386	292.1	301.8	304.2
27540	18 037	Dubois	435	2,413	41,212	40,922	39,674	36,616	1,126	1,121	1,086	95.8	92.3	85.1
21140	18 039	Elkhart	468	2,289	198,105	195,276	182,791	156,198	298	299	300	427.1	395.8	336.7
18220	18 041	Fayette................	215	2,996	24,648	24,804	25,588	26,015	1,601	1,535	1,420	114.7	118.9	121.0
31140	18 043	Floyd	148	3,073	72,570	72,025	70,823	64,404	719	701	678	490.3	479.1	435.1
...	18 045	Fountain...............	398	2,606	17,486	17,411	17,955	17,808	1,942	1,901	1,797	44.2	45.3	45.0
17140	18 047	Franklin	391	2,629	23,373	23,142	22,151	19,580	1,656	1,686	1,694	60.6	57.6	50.7
...	18 049	Fulton	371	2,680	20,622	20,597	20,511	18,840	1,785	1,760	1,744	56.0	55.8	51.1
21780	18 051	Gibson	499	2,183	33,396	33,347	32,500	31,913	1,327	1,334	1,215	68.3	66.6	65.3
31980	18 053	Grant	415	2,513	69,825	70,468	73,403	74,169	748	681	607	168.6	177.0	179.1
14020	18 055	Greene	546	2,018	33,360	33,408	33,157	30,410	1,328	1,312	1,274	61.6	61.3	56.1
26900	18 057	Hamilton...............	403	2,588	250,979	240,732	182,740	108,936	244	300	423	630.7	466.0	273.7
26900	18 059	Hancock	307	2,834	65,050	62,972	55,395	45,527	782	851	909	212.5	181.8	148.7
31140	18 061	Harrison	487	2,221	36,992	36,729	34,325	29,890	1,233	1,271	1,301	76.2	71.1	61.6
26900	18 063	Hendricks	409	2,550	131,204	127,261	104,093	75,717	445	508	594	321.3	258.1	185.4
35220	18 065	Henry..................	395	2,621	46,947	47,207	48,508	48,139	1,004	939	866	119.5	123.4	122.5
29020	18 067	Howard................	294	2,852	84,500	84,843	84,964	80,827	644	614	564	288.3	289.9	275.8
26540	18 069	Huntington	388	2,635	38,026	38,084	38,077	35,427	1,209	1,163	1,116	99.4	99.6	92.6
42980	18 071	Jackson	514	2,122	42,404	42,258	41,335	37,730	1,094	1,070	1,054	83.3	81.3	74.1
16980	18 073	Jasper	561	1,967	32,296	31,761	30,043	24,823	1,361	1,395	1,468	57.7	53.9	44.3
...	18 075	Jay	384	2,646	21,605	21,581	21,806	21,512	1,738	1,701	1,603	56.3	56.8	56.1
31500	18 077	Jefferson	363	2,697	32,668	32,379	31,705	29,797	1,347	1,353	1,304	90.4	87.8	82.5
35860	18 079	Jennings...............	378	2,659	28,473	28,471	27,554	23,661	1,464	1,466	1,506	75.5	73.4	62.1
26900	18 081	Johnson	322	2,801	133,316	129,823	115,209	88,109	441	468	517	416.4	362.3	275.2
47180	18 083	Knox	524	2,089	38,241	38,298	39,256	39,884	1,202	1,132	1,007	74.1	76.0	77.3
47700	18 085	Kosciusko	554	1,992	76,541	76,017	74,057	65,294	691	674	671	142.4	138.1	121.5
...	18 087	LaGrange	387	2,640	37,291	36,834	34,909	29,477	1,225	1,253	1,317	98.2	92.1	77.7
16980	18 089	Lake	626	1,646	494,202	491,706	484,564	475,594	125	118	103	994.4	975.3	956.9
33140	18 091	LaPorte	613	1,699	110,479	110,281	110,106	107,066	520	493	430	184.7	184.2	179.0
13260	18 093	Lawrence	452	2,334	46,143	46,342	45,922	42,836	1,012	986	940	103.4	102.4	95.4
11300	18 095	Madison	453	2,329	130,575	130,389	133,358	130,669	449	402	355	288.8	294.9	289.0
26900	18 097	Marion	403	2,586	865,504	861,760	860,454	797,159	55	50	48	2,184.2	2,171.6	2,010.9
38500	18 099	Marshall	450	2,342	47,295	46,997	45,128	42,182	996	994	955	106.5	101.9	94.9
...	18 101	Martin	341	2,757	10,340	10,320	10,369	10,369	2,419	2,407	2,351	30.8	30.8	30.8
37940	18 103	Miami.................	377	2,660	35,552	35,502	36,082	36,897	1,271	1,211	1,077	94.6	96.3	98.2
14020	18 105	Monroe	411	2,531	122,613	121,473	120,563	108,978	476	450	422	310.9	305.9	276.3
18820	18 107	Montgomery	505	2,157	38,173	38,189	37,629	34,436	1,204	1,173	1,152	75.7	74.6	68.2
26900	18 109	Morgan	409	2,546	70,290	69,751	66,689	55,920	742	733	773	172.9	164.6	137.6
16980	18 111	Newton................	404	2,584	14,293	14,423	14,566	13,551	2,146	2,115	2,098	35.6	36.2	33.7
28340	18 113	Noble	418	2,500	47,918	47,640	46,275	37,877	989	978	1,052	116.6	113.0	92.1
17140	18 115	Ohio	87	3,099	5,826	5,836	5,623	5,315	2,784	2,813	2,818	67.2	65.1	61.3
...	18 117	Orange................	408	2,555	19,659	19,716	19,306	18,409	1,836	1,830	1,769	49.2	48.4	46.1
14020	18 119	Owen..................	388	2,636	22,741	22,853	21,786	17,281	1,682	1,706	1,835	59.0	56.9	44.9

See footnotes at end of table.

Table B-1. Counties — **Area and Population**—Con.

[Includes United States, states, and 3,141 counties/county equivalents defined as of February 22, 2005. For more information on these areas, see Appendix C, Geographic Information]

Metro-politan area code	FIPS state and county code[1]	County	Area, 2000 (square miles) Total	Rank[2]	Population 2006 (July 1)	2005 (July 1)	2000[3] (April 1 estimates base)	1990[3] (April 1 estimates base)	Rank 2006[2]	2000[2]	1990[4]	Persons per square mile of land area 2006[5]	2000	1990
		INDIANA—Con.												
...	18 121	Parke	450	2,341	17,021	17,218	17,240	15,410	1,964	1,939	1,963	38.3	38.8	34.6
...	18 123	Perry	386	2,641	18,843	18,915	18,899	19,107	1,880	1,851	1,727	49.4	49.5	50.1
27540	18 125	Pike	341	2,756	12,855	12,766	12,836	12,509	2,255	2,246	2,181	38.2	38.1	37.2
16980	18 127	Porter	522	2,094	160,105	157,408	146,798	128,932	365	370	359	382.9	352.2	308.3
21780	18 129	Posey	419	2,491	26,765	26,834	27,061	25,968	1,525	1,481	1,422	65.5	66.3	63.6
...	18 131	Pulaski	435	2,418	13,861	13,786	13,755	12,780	2,176	2,179	2,157	32.0	31.7	29.5
26900	18 133	Putnam	483	2,236	36,978	36,914	36,019	30,315	1,234	1,216	1,279	77.0	75.2	63.1
...	18 135	Randolph	453	2,326	26,581	26,589	27,401	27,148	1,533	1,471	1,385	58.7	60.5	59.9
...	18 137	Ripley	448	2,347	27,748	27,647	26,523	24,616	1,495	1,502	1,476	62.2	59.7	55.1
...	18 139	Rush	409	2,553	17,684	17,785	18,261	18,129	1,926	1,883	1,781	43.3	44.6	44.4
43780	18 141	St. Joseph	461	2,311	266,678	266,019	265,559	247,052	230	208	203	583.1	581.4	540.2
42500	18 143	Scott	193	3,029	23,704	23,749	22,966	20,991	1,643	1,647	1,630	124.5	121.1	110.2
26900	18 145	Shelby	413	2,519	44,114	43,775	43,441	40,307	1,057	1,028	993	106.9	105.7	97.7
...	18 147	Spencer	401	2,597	20,596	20,476	20,391	19,490	1,786	1,767	1,703	51.7	51.2	48.9
...	18 149	Starke	312	2,817	23,069	22,953	23,556	22,747	1,666	1,613	1,546	74.6	76.1	73.5
11420	18 151	Steuben	322	2,798	33,683	33,673	33,214	27,446	1,320	1,307	1,378	109.1	107.9	88.9
45460	18 153	Sullivan	454	2,324	21,542	21,675	21,751	18,993	1,740	1,708	1,735	48.2	48.6	42.5
...	18 155	Switzerland	224	2,981	9,721	9,707	9,065	7,738	2,462	2,524	2,600	44.0	41.1	35.0
29140	18 157	Tippecanoe	503	2,168	156,169	154,024	148,955	130,598	373	362	356	312.5	298.5	261.3
29020	18 159	Tipton	260	2,920	16,377	16,425	16,577	16,119	2,016	1,987	1,916	62.9	63.6	61.9
...	18 161	Union	165	3,058	7,291	7,245	7,349	6,976	2,656	2,652	2,662	45.1	45.5	43.2
21780	18 163	Vanderburgh	236	2,964	173,356	172,774	171,922	165,058	338	316	289	739.0	732.7	703.6
45460	18 165	Vermillion	260	2,921	16,645	16,576	16,788	16,773	1,998	1,973	1,863	64.8	65.3	65.3
45460	18 167	Vigo	410	2,541	103,009	102,735	105,848	106,107	545	501	436	255.4	262.1	263.1
47340	18 169	Wabash	421	2,483	33,559	33,775	34,960	35,069	1,324	1,251	1,129	81.2	84.7	84.9
...	18 171	Warren	367	2,688	8,701	8,749	8,419	8,176	2,547	2,571	2,548	23.8	23.2	22.4
21780	18 173	Warrick	391	2,630	57,090	56,435	52,384	44,920	870	892	913	148.6	136.9	117.0
31140	18 175	Washington	517	2,111	28,062	27,817	27,223	23,717	1,485	1,475	1,502	54.6	53.0	46.1
39980	18 177	Wayne	404	2,578	68,846	69,192	71,097	71,951	752	699	619	170.6	176.1	178.3
23060	18 179	Wells	370	2,682	28,199	28,050	27,598	25,948	1,476	1,464	1,423	76.2	74.7	70.1
...	18 181	White	509	2,140	24,396	24,495	25,267	23,265	1,615	1,557	1,527	48.3	50.0	46.0
23060	18 183	Whitley	338	2,763	32,556	32,186	30,707	27,651	1,351	1,382	1,365	97.0	91.7	82.4
	19 000	IOWA	56,272	(X)	2,982,085	2,965,524	2,926,382	2,776,831	(X)	(X)	(X)	53.4	52.4	49.7
...	19 001	Adair	570	1,927	7,714	7,795	8,243	8,409	2,625	2,588	2,519	13.5	14.4	14.8
...	19 003	Adams	425	2,462	4,192	4,223	4,482	4,866	2,892	2,883	2,846	9.9	10.6	11.5
...	19 005	Allamakee	659	1,538	14,796	14,782	14,675	13,855	2,119	2,111	2,067	23.1	23.0	21.7
...	19 007	Appanoose	516	2,114	13,422	13,584	13,721	13,743	2,216	2,184	2,077	27.0	27.6	27.7
...	19 009	Audubon	444	2,370	6,278	6,363	6,830	7,334	2,742	2,708	2,627	14.2	15.4	16.5
16300	19 011	Benton	718	1,377	26,962	26,944	25,308	22,429	1,520	1,553	1,556	37.6	35.4	31.3
47940	19 013	Black Hawk	572	1,909	126,106	125,960	128,013	123,798	467	423	371	222.4	225.6	218.2
14340	19 015	Boone	574	1,894	26,584	26,495	26,224	25,186	1,532	1,511	1,455	46.5	45.9	44.1
47940	19 017	Bremer	440	2,387	23,837	23,590	23,325	22,813	1,635	1,629	1,541	54.4	53.2	52.1
...	19 019	Buchanan	573	1,896	21,045	21,021	21,093	20,844	1,761	1,733	1,638	36.8	36.9	36.5
44740	19 021	Buena Vista	580	1,831	20,091	20,103	20,409	19,965	1,818	1,766	1,679	35.0	35.4	34.7
...	19 023	Butler	582	1,820	15,073	15,045	15,305	15,731	2,102	2,072	1,939	26.0	26.4	27.1
...	19 025	Calhoun	572	1,904	10,437	10,482	11,115	11,508	2,405	2,358	2,255	18.3	19.4	20.2
...	19 027	Carroll	570	1,928	20,963	21,015	21,421	21,423	1,763	1,717	1,608	36.8	37.5	37.6
...	19 029	Cass	565	1,953	14,124	14,161	14,684	15,128	2,162	2,109	1,979	25.0	26.0	26.8
...	19 031	Cedar	582	1,817	18,326	18,240	18,187	17,444	1,898	1,891	1,825	31.6	31.4	30.1
32380	19 033	Cerro Gordo	575	1,875	44,384	44,594	46,447	46,733	1,054	975	894	78.1	81.5	82.2
...	19 035	Cherokee	577	1,848	12,094	12,245	13,037	14,098	2,293	2,232	2,048	21.0	22.6	24.4
...	19 037	Chickasaw	505	2,155	12,412	12,472	13,095	13,295	2,272	2,222	2,115	24.6	25.9	26.3
...	19 039	Clarke	432	2,434	9,156	9,118	9,133	8,287	2,513	2,520	2,539	21.2	21.3	19.2
43980	19 041	Clay	573	1,902	16,801	16,838	17,372	17,585	1,984	1,931	1,815	29.5	30.6	30.9
...	19 043	Clayton	793	1,193	18,251	18,224	18,678	19,054	1,905	1,864	1,730	23.4	23.9	24.5
17540	19 045	Clinton	710	1,415	49,782	49,744	50,149	51,040	958	914	827	71.6	72.1	73.4
...	19 047	Crawford	715	1,398	16,948	16,888	16,942	16,775	1,967	1,957	1,862	23.7	23.7	23.5
19780	19 049	Dallas	592	1,769	54,525	51,879	40,773	29,755	900	1,089	1,305	93.0	70.1	50.7
...	19 051	Davis	505	2,160	8,602	8,597	8,541	8,312	2,558	2,566	2,533	17.1	17.0	16.5
...	19 053	Decatur	533	2,062	8,656	8,645	8,689	8,338	2,550	2,553	2,530	16.3	16.3	15.7
...	19 055	Delaware	579	1,837	17,848	17,938	18,404	18,035	1,922	1,875	1,789	30.9	31.8	31.2
15460	19 057	Des Moines	430	2,444	40,885	40,975	42,351	42,614	1,137	1,047	942	98.2	101.6	102.4
44020	19 059	Dickinson	404	2,582	16,924	16,746	16,424	14,909	1,972	1,997	1,992	44.4	43.2	39.1
20220	19 061	Dubuque	617	1,686	92,384	91,603	89,156	86,403	601	582	528	151.9	146.8	142.1
...	19 063	Emmet	402	2,590	10,479	10,536	11,027	11,569	2,401	2,363	2,251	26.5	27.8	29.2
...	19 065	Fayette	731	1,318	20,996	21,195	22,008	21,843	1,762	1,692	1,587	28.7	30.1	29.9
...	19 067	Floyd	501	2,176	16,441	16,453	16,900	17,058	2,012	1,960	1,847	32.8	33.7	34.1
...	19 069	Franklin	583	1,813	10,708	10,759	10,704	11,364	2,385	2,383	2,264	18.4	18.4	19.5
...	19 071	Fremont	517	2,110	7,737	7,698	8,010	8,226	2,620	2,607	2,546	15.1	15.7	16.0
...	19 073	Greene	571	1,917	9,809	9,962	10,366	10,045	2,459	2,408	2,380	17.3	18.2	17.7
47940	19 075	Grundy	503	2,169	12,320	12,307	12,369	12,029	2,283	2,277	2,217	24.5	24.6	23.9
19780	19 077	Guthrie	593	1,762	11,344	11,419	11,353	10,935	2,344	2,347	2,301	19.2	19.2	18.5
...	19 079	Hamilton	577	1,847	16,087	16,223	16,438	16,071	2,041	1,996	1,919	27.9	28.5	27.9

See footnotes at end of table.

[Includes United States, states, and 3,141 counties/county equivalents defined as of February 22, 2005. For more information on these areas, see Appendix C, Geographic Information]

Metro-politan area code	FIPS state and county code[1]	County	Area, 2000 (square miles) Total	Rank[2]	Population 2006 (July 1)	2005 (July 1)	2000[3] (April 1 estimates base)	1990[3] (April 1 estimates base)	Rank 2006[2]	2000[2]	1990[4]	Persons per square mile of land area 2006[5]	2000	1990
		IOWA—Con.												
...	19 081	Hancock	573	1,899	11,680	11,758	12,100	12,638	2,317	2,291	2,174	20.5	21.2	22.1
...	19 083	Hardin	570	1,931	17,791	17,925	18,812	19,094	1,924	1,855	1,728	31.3	33.1	33.5
36540	19 085	Harrison	701	1,435	15,745	15,759	15,666	14,730	2,058	2,043	2,004	22.6	22.5	21.1
...	19 087	Henry	437	2,403	20,405	20,379	20,336	19,226	1,801	1,770	1,717	47.0	46.7	44.3
...	19 089	Howard	474	2,264	9,677	9,721	9,932	9,809	2,465	2,453	2,401	20.4	20.9	20.7
...	19 091	Humboldt	436	2,410	9,975	10,001	10,381	10,756	2,444	2,405	2,311	23.0	23.9	24.8
...	19 093	Ida	432	2,430	7,180	7,342	7,837	8,365	2,669	2,621	2,527	16.6	18.1	19.4
...	19 095	Iowa	587	1,787	16,140	16,054	15,671	14,630	2,038	2,042	2,010	27.5	26.8	24.9
...	19 097	Jackson	650	1,576	20,290	20,243	20,296	19,950	1,807	1,773	1,681	31.9	31.9	31.4
35500	19 099	Jasper	733	1,314	37,409	37,538	37,213	34,795	1,219	1,187	1,140	51.2	51.0	47.7
...	19 101	Jefferson	437	2,401	15,945	16,000	16,181	16,310	2,048	2,012	1,902	36.6	37.1	37.5
26980	19 103	Johnson	623	1,655	118,038	117,194	111,006	96,119	490	488	482	192.1	181.1	156.4
16300	19 105	Jones	577	1,852	20,505	20,495	20,221	19,444	1,795	1,779	1,706	35.6	35.1	33.8
...	19 107	Keokuk	580	1,832	11,081	11,121	11,400	11,624	2,363	2,342	2,246	19.1	19.7	20.1
...	19 109	Kossuth	974	806	16,011	16,181	17,163	18,591	2,046	1,945	1,759	16.5	17.6	19.1
22800	19 111	Lee	539	2,043	36,338	36,519	38,052	38,687	1,246	1,164	1,036	70.2	73.3	74.8
16300	19 113	Linn	725	1,340	201,853	199,553	191,701	168,767	294	286	284	281.4	268.0	235.2
34700	19 115	Louisa	418	2,499	11,858	11,813	12,183	11,592	2,305	2,285	2,249	29.5	30.3	28.8
...	19 117	Lucas	434	2,420	9,543	9,627	9,422	9,070	2,477	2,493	2,463	22.2	21.9	21.1
...	19 119	Lyon	588	1,786	11,636	11,690	11,763	11,952	2,322	2,314	2,223	19.8	20.0	20.3
19780	19 121	Madison	562	1,966	15,547	15,148	14,019	12,483	2,072	2,165	2,182	27.7	25.1	22.2
36820	19 123	Mahaska	573	1,895	22,298	22,309	22,335	21,532	1,711	1,677	1,602	39.1	39.1	37.7
37800	19 125	Marion	571	1,925	32,987	32,738	32,054	30,001	1,340	1,345	1,296	59.5	58.0	54.1
32260	19 127	Marshall	573	1,901	39,555	39,572	39,311	38,276	1,171	1,129	1,046	69.1	68.7	66.9
36540	19 129	Mills	440	2,385	15,595	15,255	14,547	13,202	2,068	2,120	2,122	35.7	33.4	30.2
...	19 131	Mitchell	469	2,282	10,856	10,872	10,874	10,928	2,377	2,376	2,304	23.2	23.2	23.3
...	19 133	Monona	699	1,443	9,343	9,504	10,020	10,034	2,493	2,443	2,383	13.5	14.4	14.5
...	19 135	Monroe	434	2,422	7,725	7,798	8,016	8,114	2,622	2,604	2,553	17.8	18.4	18.7
...	19 137	Montgomery	425	2,464	11,365	11,364	11,771	12,076	2,342	2,312	2,212	26.8	27.8	28.5
34700	19 139	Muscatine	449	2,344	42,883	42,567	41,722	39,907	1,086	1,063	1,006	97.8	95.3	91.0
...	19 141	O'Brien	573	1,897	14,409	14,410	15,102	15,444	2,136	2,085	1,958	25.1	26.3	26.9
...	19 143	Osceola	399	2,600	6,629	6,648	7,003	7,267	2,714	2,687	2,630	16.6	17.5	18.2
...	19 145	Page	535	2,052	16,263	16,291	16,976	16,870	2,028	1,955	1,858	30.4	31.6	31.5
...	19 147	Palo Alto	569	1,933	9,549	9,669	10,147	10,669	2,476	2,434	2,321	16.9	18.0	18.9
...	19 149	Plymouth	864	1,051	24,906	24,880	24,849	23,388	1,588	1,563	1,520	28.8	28.8	27.1
...	19 151	Pocahontas	579	1,836	7,794	7,931	8,662	9,525	2,614	2,555	2,430	13.5	14.9	16.5
19780	19 153	Polk	592	1,768	408,888	401,755	374,582	327,140	157	156	156	718.2	660.1	574.5
36540	19 155	Pottawattamie	960	820	90,218	89,673	87,803	82,628	616	596	550	94.5	92.2	86.6
...	19 157	Poweshiek	586	1,792	19,007	18,923	18,832	19,033	1,874	1,854	1,733	32.5	32.2	32.5
...	19 159	Ringgold	539	2,041	5,289	5,255	5,469	5,420	2,820	2,819	2,806	9.8	10.2	10.1
...	19 161	Sac	578	1,842	10,682	10,651	11,529	12,324	2,387	2,332	2,192	18.6	19.9	21.4
19340	19 163	Scott	468	2,287	162,621	161,170	158,689	150,973	358	335	309	355.1	346.7	329.7
...	19 165	Shelby	591	1,771	12,489	12,566	13,074	13,230	2,269	2,227	2,118	21.1	22.1	22.4
...	19 167	Sioux	769	1,236	32,525	32,332	31,589	29,903	1,353	1,357	1,300	42.4	41.1	38.9
11180	19 169	Story	574	1,891	80,145	79,787	79,981	74,252	672	643	606	139.9	139.7	129.6
...	19 171	Tama	722	1,352	17,890	17,937	18,103	17,419	1,920	1,894	1,826	24.8	25.1	24.1
...	19 173	Taylor	535	2,055	6,540	6,553	6,958	7,114	2,728	2,691	2,643	12.2	13.1	13.3
...	19 175	Union	426	2,459	12,093	11,978	12,309	12,750	2,294	2,281	2,163	28.5	28.9	30.0
...	19 177	Van Buren	491	2,214	7,836	7,732	7,809	7,676	2,606	2,625	2,603	16.2	16.1	15.8
36900	19 179	Wapello	436	2,406	36,010	35,976	36,051	35,696	1,258	1,215	1,106	83.4	83.4	82.7
19780	19 181	Warren	573	1,898	43,926	43,165	40,671	36,033	1,064	1,094	1,098	76.8	71.4	63.0
26980	19 183	Washington	571	1,920	21,529	21,372	20,670	19,612	1,742	1,753	1,692	37.9	36.4	34.5
...	19 185	Wayne	527	2,079	6,542	6,548	6,730	7,067	2,727	2,717	2,650	12.4	12.8	13.4
22700	19 187	Webster	718	1,386	38,960	38,963	40,235	40,342	1,181	1,109	991	54.5	56.2	56.4
...	19 189	Winnebago	402	2,595	11,216	11,360	11,723	12,122	2,350	2,318	2,206	28.0	29.4	30.3
...	19 191	Winneshiek	690	1,465	21,263	21,224	21,310	20,847	1,752	1,722	1,636	30.8	30.9	30.2
43580	19 193	Woodbury	877	1,025	102,970	102,518	103,877	98,276	546	510	468	118.0	119.0	112.6
32380	19 195	Worth	402	2,594	7,698	7,755	7,909	7,991	2,627	2,615	2,567	19.2	19.8	20.0
...	19 197	Wright	583	1,816	13,419	13,601	14,334	14,269	2,218	2,139	2,033	23.1	24.7	24.6
	20 000	KANSAS	82,277	(X)	2,764,075	2,748,172	2,688,824	2,477,588	(X)	(X)	(X)	33.8	32.9	30.3
...	20 001	Allen	505	2,159	13,677	13,739	14,385	14,638	2,192	2,136	2,008	27.2	28.6	29.1
...	20 003	Anderson	584	1,805	8,051	8,147	8,110	7,803	2,587	2,598	2,594	13.8	13.9	13.4
11860	20 005	Atchison	435	2,414	16,745	16,741	16,774	16,932	1,990	1,974	1,854	38.7	38.8	39.2
...	20 007	Barber	1,136	632	4,974	4,937	5,307	5,874	2,841	2,830	2,773	4.4	4.7	5.2
24460	20 009	Barton	900	964	27,511	27,553	28,205	29,382	1,503	1,446	1,318	30.8	31.5	32.9
...	20 011	Bourbon	639	1,614	14,950	14,947	15,379	14,966	2,110	2,061	1,989	23.5	24.2	23.5
...	20 013	Brown	572	1,906	10,236	10,222	10,724	11,128	2,430	2,381	2,281	17.9	18.8	19.5
48620	20 015	Butler	1,446	464	63,147	62,376	59,484	50,580	806	808	833	44.2	41.8	35.4
21380	20 017	Chase	778	1,216	3,070	3,070	3,030	3,021	2,972	2,992	2,998	4.0	3.9	3.9
...	20 019	Chautauqua	645	1,587	3,953	4,087	4,359	4,407	2,912	2,892	2,880	6.2	6.8	6.9

See footnotes at end of table.

[Includes United States, states, and 3,141 counties/county equivalents defined as of February 22, 2005. For more information on these areas, see Appendix C, Geographic Information]

Metro-politan area code	FIPS state and county code[1]	County	Area, 2000 (square miles)		Population				Rank			Persons per square mile of land area		
			Total	Rank[2]	2006 (July 1)	2005 (July 1)	2000[3] (April 1 estimates base)	1990[3] (April 1 estimates base)	2006[2]	2000[2]	1990[4]	2006[5]	2000	1990
		KANSAS—Con.												
...	20 021	Cherokee	591	1,773	21,451	21,462	22,603	21,374	1,746	1,667	1,614	36.5	38.4	36.4
...	20 023	Cheyenne	1,021	745	2,911	2,929	3,165	3,243	2,986	2,981	2,980	2.9	3.1	3.2
...	20 025	Clark	977	801	2,206	2,258	2,390	2,418	3,035	3,032	3,029	2.3	2.4	2.5
...	20 027	Clay	655	1,556	8,625	8,614	8,822	9,158	2,556	2,545	2,455	13.4	13.7	14.2
...	20 029	Cloud	718	1,376	9,594	9,730	10,268	11,023	2,472	2,420	2,290	13.4	14.3	15.4
...	20 031	Coffey	655	1,558	8,701	8,666	8,865	8,404	2,547	2,538	2,520	13.8	14.1	13.3
...	20 033	Comanche	790	1,200	1,884	1,945	1,967	2,313	3,061	3,066	3,038	2.4	2.5	2.9
49060	20 035	Cowley	1,133	639	34,931	35,104	36,291	36,915	1,296	1,206	1,076	31.0	32.2	32.8
38260	20 037	Crawford	595	1,757	38,059	38,106	38,245	35,582	1,207	1,161	1,109	64.2	64.5	60.0
...	20 039	Decatur	894	989	3,120	3,151	3,472	4,021	2,967	2,956	2,916	3.5	3.9	4.5
...	20 041	Dickinson	852	1,081	19,322	19,166	19,344	18,958	1,851	1,828	1,737	22.8	22.8	22.3
41140	20 043	Doniphan	397	2,610	7,865	7,823	8,249	8,134	2,604	2,587	2,551	20.1	21.0	20.7
29940	20 045	Douglas	474	2,258	112,123	111,519	99,965	81,798	513	525	556	245.4	219.2	179.0
...	20 047	Edwards	622	1,662	3,138	3,248	3,449	3,787	2,964	2,959	2,932	5.0	5.5	6.1
...	20 049	Elk	650	1,574	3,077	3,109	3,261	3,327	2,971	2,976	2,968	4.8	5.0	5.1
25700	20 051	Ellis	900	963	26,926	26,839	27,507	26,004	1,522	1,467	1,421	29.9	30.5	28.9
...	20 053	Ellsworth	723	1,347	6,332	6,294	6,525	6,586	2,739	2,737	2,700	8.8	9.1	9.2
23780	20 055	Finney	1,303	521	39,097	39,059	40,523	33,070	1,176	1,102	1,188	30.0	31.2	25.4
19980	20 057	Ford	1,099	663	33,783	33,716	32,459	27,463	1,318	1,335	1,377	30.8	29.7	25.0
28140	20 059	Franklin	577	1,854	26,513	26,179	24,784	21,994	1,535	1,565	1,576	46.2	43.3	38.3
31740	20 061	Geary	404	2,576	24,174	24,326	27,943	30,453	1,625	1,454	1,271	62.8	72.1	79.2
...	20 063	Gove	1,071	694	2,721	2,758	3,068	3,231	2,996	2,987	2,981	2.5	2.9	3.0
...	20 065	Graham	899	972	2,677	2,713	2,946	3,543	3,000	2,995	2,954	3.0	3.3	3.9
...	20 067	Grant	575	1,878	7,552	7,545	7,909	7,159	2,637	2,615	2,637	13.1	13.7	12.5
...	20 069	Gray	869	1,038	5,852	5,880	5,904	5,396	2,780	2,794	2,809	6.7	6.8	6.2
...	20 071	Greeley	778	1,216	1,331	1,361	1,534	1,774	3,095	3,093	3,079	1.7	2.0	2.3
...	20 073	Greenwood	1,153	615	7,067	7,335	7,673	7,847	2,673	2,633	2,587	6.2	6.7	6.9
...	20 075	Hamilton	998	771	2,594	2,591	2,670	2,388	3,006	3,017	3,032	2.6	2.7	2.4
...	20 077	Harper	803	1,167	5,952	6,045	6,536	7,124	2,775	2,736	2,641	7.4	8.1	8.9
48620	20 079	Harvey	541	2,037	33,643	33,711	32,869	31,028	1,322	1,324	1,245	62.4	61.0	57.5
...	20 081	Haskell	578	1,846	4,171	4,215	4,307	3,886	2,897	2,896	2,926	7.2	7.5	6.7
...	20 083	Hodgeman	860	1,064	2,071	2,065	2,084	2,177	3,046	3,059	3,055	2.4	2.4	2.5
45820	20 085	Jackson	658	1,544	13,500	13,448	12,657	11,525	2,206	2,253	2,254	20.6	19.3	17.5
45820	20 087	Jefferson	557	1,979	18,848	18,969	18,426	15,905	1,879	1,872	1,931	35.2	34.4	29.7
...	20 089	Jewell	914	907	3,324	3,324	3,791	4,251	2,954	2,928	2,894	3.7	4.1	4.7
28140	20 091	Johnson	480	2,241	516,731	506,172	451,476	355,021	118	131	145	1,083.8	953.6	744.6
...	20 093	Kearny	872	1,036	4,469	4,518	4,531	4,027	2,871	2,877	2,914	5.1	5.2	4.6
...	20 095	Kingman	867	1,044	7,975	8,132	8,673	8,292	2,594	2,554	2,536	9.2	10.1	9.6
...	20 097	Kiowa	723	1,350	2,969	2,983	3,278	3,660	2,980	2,975	2,942	4.1	4.5	5.1
37660	20 099	Labette	653	1,563	22,203	22,149	22,831	23,693	1,715	1,653	1,504	34.2	35.1	36.5
...	20 101	Lane	717	1,388	1,797	1,875	2,155	2,375	3,069	3,055	3,034	2.5	3.0	3.3
28140	20 103	Leavenworth	468	2,286	73,628	72,754	68,691	64,371	707	718	679	158.9	148.9	138.9
...	20 105	Lincoln	720	1,363	3,396	3,414	3,578	3,653	2,948	2,945	2,944	4.7	5.0	5.1
28140	20 107	Linn	606	1,720	9,962	9,954	9,570	8,254	2,445	2,484	2,543	16.6	16.0	13.8
...	20 109	Logan	1,073	693	2,675	2,764	3,046	3,081	3,001	2,991	2,994	2.5	2.8	2.9
21380	20 111	Lyon	855	1,076	35,369	35,579	35,935	34,732	1,277	1,221	1,144	41.6	42.3	40.8
32700	20 113	McPherson	901	958	29,380	29,492	29,554	27,268	1,436	1,413	1,381	32.7	32.9	30.3
...	20 115	Marion	954	832	12,760	12,918	13,361	12,888	2,259	2,203	2,146	13.5	14.2	13.7
...	20 117	Marshall	904	943	10,349	10,418	10,965	11,705	2,418	2,370	2,232	11.5	12.1	13.0
...	20 119	Meade	980	795	4,561	4,604	4,631	4,247	2,867	2,872	2,895	4.7	4.7	4.3
28140	20 121	Miami	590	1,777	30,900	30,385	28,351	23,466	1,397	1,437	1,516	53.6	49.4	40.7
...	20 123	Mitchell	719	1,373	6,299	6,405	6,932	7,203	2,740	2,693	2,632	9.0	9.6	10.3
17700	20 125	Montgomery	651	1,570	34,692	34,592	36,257	38,816	1,303	1,208	1,030	53.8	56.1	60.2
...	20 127	Morris	703	1,428	6,046	6,070	6,104	6,198	2,766	2,771	2,733	8.7	8.8	8.9
...	20 129	Morton	730	1,322	3,138	3,177	3,496	3,480	2,964	2,954	2,958	4.3	4.8	4.8
...	20 131	Nemaha	719	1,368	10,374	10,380	10,717	10,446	2,415	2,382	2,343	14.4	14.9	14.5
...	20 133	Neosho	578	1,843	16,298	16,496	16,997	17,035	2,024	1,954	1,848	28.5	29.6	29.8
...	20 135	Ness	1,075	690	2,946	3,003	3,454	4,033	2,982	2,958	2,913	2.7	3.2	3.8
...	20 137	Norton	881	1,017	5,584	5,643	5,953	5,947	2,794	2,789	2,765	6.4	6.8	6.8
45820	20 139	Osage	719	1,369	16,958	17,055	16,714	15,248	1,966	1,977	1,974	24.1	23.8	21.7
...	20 141	Osborne	894	988	3,978	4,033	4,452	4,867	2,911	2,886	2,845	4.5	5.0	5.5
41460	20 143	Ottawa	722	1,354	6,168	6,148	6,163	5,634	2,752	2,767	2,790	8.6	8.6	7.8
...	20 145	Pawnee	755	1,269	6,515	6,683	7,233	7,555	2,730	2,663	2,611	8.6	9.6	10.0
...	20 147	Phillips	895	986	5,444	5,484	6,001	6,590	2,804	2,780	2,699	6.1	6.8	7.4
31740	20 149	Pottawatomie	862	1,059	19,220	19,067	18,209	16,128	1,859	1,888	1,915	22.8	21.7	19.1
...	20 151	Pratt	736	1,308	9,436	9,485	9,647	9,702	2,484	2,475	2,412	12.8	13.1	13.2
...	20 153	Rawlins	1,070	697	2,643	2,667	2,966	3,404	3,003	2,994	2,964	2.5	2.8	3.2
26740	20 155	Reno	1,271	542	63,706	63,548	64,790	62,389	794	749	697	50.8	51.6	49.7
...	20 157	Republic	720	1,362	5,033	5,149	5,835	6,482	2,837	2,800	2,711	7.0	8.1	9.0
...	20 159	Rice	728	1,327	10,295	10,405	10,761	10,610	2,423	2,379	2,326	14.2	14.8	14.6

See footnotes at end of table.

Table B-1. Counties — **Area and Population**—Con.

[Includes United States, states, and 3,141 counties/county equivalents defined as of February 22, 2005. For more information on these areas, see Appendix C, Geographic Information]

Metro-politan area code	FIPS state and county code[1]	County	Area, 2000 (square miles)		Population				Rank			Persons per square mile of land area		
			Total	Rank[2]	2006 (July 1)	2005 (July 1)	2000[3] (April 1 estimates base)	1990[3] (April 1 estimates base)	2006[2]	2000[2]	1990[4]	2006[5]	2000	1990
		KANSAS—Con.												
31740	20 161	Riley	622	1,660	62,527	61,846	62,856	67,139	815	774	658	102.6	103.0	110.1
...	20 163	Rooks	895	984	5,290	5,308	5,685	6,039	2,819	2,810	2,752	6.0	6.4	6.8
...	20 165	Rush	718	1,379	3,317	3,394	3,551	3,842	2,957	2,950	2,929	4.6	4.9	5.3
...	20 167	Russell	899	968	6,740	6,812	7,370	7,835	2,701	2,651	2,591	7.6	8.3	8.9
41460	20 169	Saline	721	1,358	54,170	53,980	53,597	49,301	903	871	851	75.3	74.5	68.5
...	20 171	Scott	718	1,387	4,643	4,683	5,120	5,289	2,858	2,843	2,820	6.5	7.1	7.4
48620	20 173	Sedgwick	1,009	756	470,895	466,114	452,869	403,662	134	130	123	471.2	453.8	403.6
30580	20 175	Seward	641	1,606	23,404	23,263	22,510	18,743	1,655	1,671	1,748	36.6	35.3	29.3
45820	20 177	Shawnee	556	1,984	172,693	171,828	169,869	160,976	342	319	297	314.1	309.3	292.8
...	20 179	Sheridan	897	980	2,600	2,608	2,813	3,043	3,004	3,005	2,997	2.9	3.1	3.4
...	20 181	Sherman	1,056	710	5,981	6,120	6,760	6,926	2,770	2,715	2,667	5.7	6.4	6.6
...	20 183	Smith	897	981	4,024	4,113	4,536	5,078	2,909	2,876	2,834	4.5	5.1	5.7
...	20 185	Stafford	795	1,190	4,435	4,492	4,789	5,365	2,873	2,862	2,812	5.6	6.0	6.8
...	20 187	Stanton	680	1,491	2,232	2,258	2,406	2,333	3,032	3,029	3,037	3.3	3.5	3.4
...	20 189	Stevens	728	1,328	5,287	5,424	5,463	5,048	2,821	2,821	2,836	7.3	7.5	6.9
48620	20 191	Sumner	1,185	594	24,441	24,732	25,946	25,841	1,611	1,520	1,428	20.7	22.0	21.9
...	20 193	Thomas	1,075	691	7,468	7,599	8,180	8,258	2,640	2,596	2,542	6.9	7.6	7.7
...	20 195	Trego	899	967	2,993	3,029	3,319	3,694	2,977	2,971	2,941	3.4	3.7	4.2
45820	20 197	Wabaunsee	800	1,179	6,895	6,953	6,885	6,603	2,691	2,697	2,698	8.6	8.6	8.3
...	20 199	Wallace	914	908	1,557	1,556	1,749	1,821	3,080	3,083	3,076	1.7	1.9	2.0
...	20 201	Washington	899	969	5,944	5,999	6,483	7,073	2,777	2,741	2,649	6.6	7.2	7.9
...	20 203	Wichita	719	1,375	2,288	2,323	2,531	2,758	3,028	3,024	3,012	3.2	3.5	3.8
...	20 205	Wilson	575	1,880	9,889	9,850	10,332	10,289	2,451	2,411	2,360	17.2	18.0	17.9
...	20 207	Woodson	505	2,156	3,507	3,561	3,788	4,116	2,940	2,929	2,906	7.0	7.5	8.2
28140	20 209	Wyandotte	156	3,067	155,509	155,704	157,882	162,026	374	337	293	1,027.2	1,042.7	1,070.2
	21 000	KENTUCKY	40,409	(X)	4,206,074	4,172,608	4,042,285	3,686,892	(X)	(X)	(X)	105.9	101.9	92.8
...	21 001	Adair	412	2,527	17,650	17,515	17,244	15,360	1,932	1,937	1,967	43.4	42.5	37.8
...	21 003	Allen	352	2,724	18,788	18,604	17,800	14,628	1,882	1,911	2,011	54.3	51.5	42.3
23180	21 005	Anderson	204	3,008	20,885	20,391	19,111	14,571	1,765	1,844	2,016	103.0	94.7	71.9
37140	21 007	Ballard	274	2,896	8,245	8,262	8,286	7,902	2,577	2,582	2,581	32.8	33.1	31.5
23980	21 009	Barren	500	2,181	40,737	40,099	38,033	34,001	1,142	1,165	1,163	83.0	77.7	69.3
34460	21 011	Bath	284	2,877	11,707	11,581	11,085	9,692	2,315	2,360	2,413	41.9	39.8	34.7
33180	21 013	Bell	361	2,706	29,544	29,586	30,060	31,506	1,431	1,394	1,231	81.9	83.3	87.3
17140	21 015	Boone	257	2,928	110,080	106,278	85,989	57,589	521	607	755	447.0	353.3	233.8
30460	21 017	Bourbon	292	2,853	19,839	19,853	19,360	19,236	1,828	1,827	1,716	68.1	66.5	66.0
26580	21 019	Boyd	162	3,062	49,371	49,359	49,752	51,096	963	920	825	308.2	310.1	319.0
19220	21 021	Boyle	183	3,042	28,444	28,387	27,697	25,590	1,467	1,459	1,439	156.4	152.3	140.9
17140	21 023	Bracken	209	3,004	8,655	8,659	8,279	7,766	2,552	2,584	2,598	42.6	40.8	38.2
...	21 025	Breathitt	495	2,198	15,924	15,949	16,100	15,703	2,050	2,018	1,943	32.2	32.4	31.7
...	21 027	Breckinridge	586	1,796	19,225	19,217	18,648	16,312	1,858	1,865	1,901	33.6	32.7	28.5
31140	21 029	Bullitt	300	2,845	72,851	71,440	61,236	47,567	715	796	881	243.6	206.1	159.0
...	21 031	Butler	432	2,435	13,397	13,365	13,010	11,245	2,224	2,236	2,278	31.3	31.3	26.3
...	21 033	Caldwell	348	2,733	12,916	12,891	13,062	13,232	2,249	2,228	2,117	37.2	37.6	38.1
34660	21 035	Calloway	411	2,536	35,421	35,020	34,177	30,735	1,276	1,277	1,254	91.7	88.4	79.6
17140	21 037	Campbell	159	3,064	86,866	87,048	88,616	83,866	630	588	546	573.2	585.0	553.4
...	21 039	Carlisle	199	3,019	5,317	5,299	5,351	5,238	2,817	2,826	2,824	27.6	27.8	27.2
...	21 041	Carroll	137	3,077	10,521	10,458	10,155	9,292	2,398	2,431	2,445	80.9	78.2	71.4
...	21 043	Carter	412	2,528	27,365	27,253	26,889	24,340	1,507	1,489	1,484	66.6	65.5	59.3
...	21 045	Casey	446	2,357	16,326	16,238	15,447	14,211	2,021	2,056	2,035	36.6	34.7	31.9
17300	21 047	Christian	724	1,343	66,989	69,735	72,308	68,941	766	688	643	92.9	100.2	95.6
30460	21 049	Clark	255	2,934	35,275	34,830	33,144	29,496	1,284	1,314	1,316	138.7	130.7	116.0
...	21 051	Clay	471	2,274	24,052	24,140	24,556	21,746	1,628	1,573	1,591	51.1	52.0	46.2
...	21 053	Clinton	206	3,007	9,566	9,539	9,634	9,135	2,474	2,476	2,457	48.4	48.8	46.3
...	21 055	Crittenden	371	2,681	9,070	8,991	9,384	9,196	2,523	2,499	2,454	25.0	26.0	25.4
...	21 057	Cumberland	311	2,821	7,046	7,073	7,147	6,784	2,675	2,674	2,678	23.0	23.4	22.2
36980	21 059	Daviess	476	2,255	93,613	92,837	91,549	87,189	594	559	522	202.5	198.2	188.5
14540	21 061	Edmonson	308	2,827	12,054	12,015	11,644	10,357	2,297	2,323	2,353	39.8	38.6	34.2
...	21 063	Elliott	235	2,966	7,187	6,967	6,748	6,455	2,668	2,716	2,713	30.7	29.0	27.6
...	21 065	Estill	256	2,933	15,163	15,069	15,307	14,614	2,095	2,071	2,012	59.7	60.3	57.5
30460	21 067	Fayette	286	2,874	270,789	267,929	260,512	225,366	227	211	220	951.7	917.1	792.1
...	21 069	Fleming	351	2,725	14,576	14,581	13,792	12,292	2,128	2,176	2,197	41.5	39.5	35.0
...	21 071	Floyd	395	2,617	42,282	42,316	42,443	43,586	1,097	1,046	930	107.2	107.5	110.5
23180	21 073	Franklin	212	2,998	48,183	48,187	47,687	44,143	985	957	923	228.9	227.4	209.7
46460	21 075	Fulton	231	2,976	6,949	7,168	7,752	8,271	2,684	2,630	2,540	33.3	36.9	39.6
17140	21 077	Gallatin	105	3,091	8,153	8,163	7,873	5,393	2,581	2,617	2,810	82.5	79.6	54.6
...	21 079	Garrard	234	2,968	16,933	16,538	14,792	11,579	1,969	2,105	2,250	73.2	64.4	50.1
17140	21 081	Grant	261	2,918	24,769	24,589	22,384	15,737	1,594	1,674	1,938	95.3	86.8	60.6
32460	21 083	Graves	556	1,983	37,872	37,650	37,028	33,550	1,214	1,190	1,176	68.2	66.7	60.4
...	21 085	Grayson	511	2,132	25,425	25,234	24,053	21,050	1,569	1,592	1,626	50.5	47.9	41.8
...	21 087	Green	289	2,861	11,641	11,592	11,518	10,371	2,320	2,334	2,350	40.3	40.0	35.9
26580	21 089	Greenup	355	2,719	37,374	37,206	36,891	36,796	1,222	1,193	1,081	108.0	106.4	106.3

See footnotes at end of table.

Table B-1. Counties — **Area and Population**—Con.

[Includes United States, states, and 3,141 counties/county equivalents defined as of February 22, 2005. For more information on these areas, see Appendix C, Geographic Information]

Metro-politan area code	FIPS state and county code[1]	County	Area, 2000 (square miles)		Population									
							2000[3] (April 1 estimates base)	1990[3] (April 1 estimates base)	Rank			Persons per square mile of land area		
			Total	Rank[2]	2006 (July 1)	2005 (July 1)			2006[2]	2000[2]	1990[4]	2006[5]	2000	1990
		KENTUCKY—Con.												
36980	21 091	Hancock	199	3,020	8,636	8,614	8,392	7,864	2,554	2,574	2,585	45.7	44.6	41.7
21060	21 093	Hardin	630	1,640	97,087	96,825	94,170	89,240	577	545	513	154.6	150.2	142.1
...	21 095	Harlan	468	2,288	31,692	31,671	33,202	36,574	1,379	1,308	1,088	67.8	70.7	78.3
...	21 097	Harrison	310	2,823	18,592	18,415	17,983	16,248	1,887	1,900	1,910	60.0	58.2	52.5
...	21 099	Hart	418	2,496	18,547	18,368	17,449	14,890	1,889	1,927	1,996	44.6	42.2	35.8
21780	21 101	Henderson	467	2,291	45,666	45,563	44,829	43,044	1,029	1,002	937	103.8	101.8	97.8
31140	21 103	Henry	291	2,854	16,025	15,824	15,060	12,823	2,045	2,088	2,153	55.4	52.2	44.3
...	21 105	Hickman	253	2,939	4,974	5,072	5,262	5,566	2,841	2,835	2,794	20.3	21.5	22.8
31580	21 107	Hopkins	554	1,993	46,830	46,662	46,517	46,126	1,005	973	900	85.1	84.4	83.8
...	21 109	Jackson	347	2,739	13,810	13,705	13,495	11,955	2,182	2,197	2,222	39.9	39.0	34.5
31140	21 111	Jefferson	399	2,604	701,500	699,051	693,604	665,123	79	73	69	1,821.7	1,801.9	1,727.1
30460	21 113	Jessamine	174	3,051	44,790	43,402	39,041	30,508	1,043	1,138	1,268	258.7	226.5	176.2
...	21 115	Johnson	264	2,913	24,188	23,968	23,445	23,248	1,623	1,621	1,528	92.5	89.3	88.9
17140	21 117	Kenton	164	3,051	154,911	153,314	151,463	142,005	378	354	335	956.4	936.4	873.5
...	21 119	Knott	353	2,722	17,536	17,622	17,649	17,906	1,939	1,920	1,793	49.8	50.1	50.8
...	21 121	Knox	388	2,637	32,527	32,231	31,790	29,676	1,352	1,351	1,309	83.9	82.2	76.5
21060	21 123	Larue	264	2,915	13,791	13,663	13,373	11,679	2,184	2,202	2,239	52.4	50.9	44.3
30940	21 125	Laurel	444	2,369	56,979	56,316	52,715	43,438	873	884	932	130.8	121.5	99.7
...	21 127	Lawrence	420	2,487	16,321	16,162	15,569	13,998	2,022	2,050	2,057	39.0	37.3	33.4
...	21 129	Lee	211	3,000	7,648	7,667	7,916	7,422	2,630	2,614	2,622	36.4	37.3	35.4
...	21 131	Leslie	404	2,577	11,973	12,023	12,401	13,642	2,302	2,274	2,087	29.6	30.7	33.8
...	21 133	Letcher	339	2,762	24,520	24,504	25,277	27,000	1,605	1,555	1,389	72.3	74.4	79.6
32500	21 135	Lewis	496	2,196	14,012	13,879	14,092	13,029	2,169	2,157	2,139	28.9	29.2	26.9
19220	21 137	Lincoln	336	2,768	25,361	25,173	23,361	20,096	1,572	1,626	1,671	75.4	69.8	59.7
37140	21 139	Livingston	342	2,755	9,797	9,783	9,804	9,062	2,460	2,465	2,465	31.0	31.1	28.7
...	21 141	Logan	557	1,978	27,363	27,168	26,573	24,416	1,508	1,496	1,481	49.2	47.9	43.9
...	21 143	Lyon	256	2,930	8,273	8,145	8,080	6,624	2,573	2,600	2,693	38.4	37.6	30.7
37140	21 145	McCracken	268	2,901	64,950	64,690	65,514	62,879	784	746	693	258.7	260.7	250.4
...	21 147	McCreary	431	2,441	17,354	17,249	17,080	15,603	1,950	1,950	1,946	40.6	39.9	36.5
36980	21 149	McLean	256	2,932	9,844	9,945	9,934	9,628	2,456	2,452	2,422	38.7	39.2	37.9
40080	21 151	Madison	443	2,373	79,015	77,740	70,872	57,508	682	700	757	179.3	161.7	130.5
...	21 153	Magoffin	309	2,824	13,449	13,431	13,332	13,077	2,211	2,204	2,133	43.5	43.1	42.3
...	21 155	Marion	347	2,738	18,979	18,850	18,212	16,499	1,876	1,887	1,892	54.8	52.6	47.6
...	21 157	Marshall	340	2,758	31,278	30,942	30,125	27,205	1,390	1,393	1,383	102.6	98.9	89.2
...	21 159	Martin	231	2,975	12,093	12,200	12,578	12,526	2,294	2,261	2,180	52.4	54.5	54.3
32500	21 161	Mason	247	2,957	17,271	17,155	16,800	16,666	1,952	1,971	1,871	71.6	69.1	69.1
31140	21 163	Meade	324	2,795	27,994	28,257	26,349	24,170	1,487	1,507	1,488	90.7	86.1	78.3
34460	21 165	Menifee	206	3,006	6,788	6,776	6,556	5,092	2,697	2,733	2,832	33.3	32.4	25.0
...	21 167	Mercer	253	2,938	21,818	21,661	20,817	19,148	1,727	1,746	1,725	87.0	83.1	76.3
23980	21 169	Metcalfe	291	2,855	10,334	10,219	10,037	8,963	2,420	2,441	2,474	35.5	34.4	30.8
...	21 171	Monroe	332	2,776	11,771	11,723	11,756	11,401	2,308	2,315	2,261	35.6	35.5	34.5
34460	21 173	Montgomery	199	3,021	24,887	24,248	22,554	19,561	1,589	1,668	1,695	125.3	114.1	98.5
...	21 175	Morgan	384	2,647	14,306	14,302	13,948	11,648	2,144	2,168	2,241	37.5	36.6	30.5
16420	21 177	Muhlenberg	479	2,246	31,561	31,562	31,840	31,318	1,382	1,350	1,235	66.5	67.0	66.0
31140	21 179	Nelson	424	2,467	42,102	41,066	37,477	29,710	1,100	1,179	1,308	99.6	89.2	70.3
...	21 181	Nicholas	197	3,024	6,958	7,014	6,813	6,725	2,683	2,711	2,685	35.4	34.5	34.2
...	21 183	Ohio	597	1,751	23,844	23,731	22,916	21,105	1,634	1,649	1,625	40.2	38.6	35.5
31140	21 185	Oldham	197	3,025	55,285	53,459	46,618	33,263	893	968	1,185	292.2	248.6	175.8
...	21 187	Owen	354	2,720	11,428	11,383	10,547	9,035	2,335	2,394	2,466	32.5	30.0	25.7
...	21 189	Owsley	198	3,022	4,690	4,745	4,858	5,036	2,854	2,858	2,840	23.7	24.5	25.4
17140	21 191	Pendleton	282	2,885	15,334	15,179	14,390	12,062	2,082	2,134	2,213	54.7	51.7	43.1
...	21 193	Perry	343	2,753	29,753	29,505	29,422	30,283	1,425	1,417	1,280	87.0	85.7	88.5
...	21 195	Pike	789	1,201	66,860	66,754	68,734	72,584	767	716	616	84.9	87.0	92.1
...	21 197	Powell	180	3,044	13,825	13,719	13,237	11,686	2,179	2,212	2,236	76.7	73.7	64.9
43700	21 199	Pulaski	677	1,502	59,749	59,221	56,217	49,489	843	841	849	90.3	85.1	74.8
...	21 201	Robertson	100	3,093	2,332	2,263	2,266	2,124	3,024	3,044	3,060	23.3	22.6	21.2
40080	21 203	Rockcastle	318	2,805	16,857	16,781	16,582	14,803	1,978	1,986	2,000	53.1	52.4	46.6
...	21 205	Rowan	286	2,868	22,234	22,119	22,094	20,353	1,714	1,689	1,658	79.2	78.6	72.5
...	21 207	Russell	283	2,882	17,174	16,987	16,315	14,716	1,956	2,004	2,005	67.7	64.4	58.0
30460	21 209	Scott	285	2,875	41,605	39,530	33,061	23,867	1,112	1,319	1,496	146.1	117.4	83.7
31140	21 211	Shelby	386	2,642	39,717	38,216	33,337	24,824	1,168	1,305	1,467	103.4	87.4	64.6
...	21 213	Simpson	236	2,963	17,180	16,987	16,405	15,145	1,954	1,999	1,976	72.7	69.5	64.1
31140	21 215	Spencer	192	3,032	16,475	15,637	11,766	6,801	2,009	2,313	2,675	88.6	64.6	36.6
15820	21 217	Taylor	277	2,893	23,731	23,649	22,927	21,146	1,641	1,648	1,622	87.9	84.9	78.4
...	21 219	Todd	377	2,664	12,101	11,941	11,971	10,940	2,292	2,297	2,298	32.2	31.8	29.1
17300	21 221	Trigg	481	2,238	13,399	13,329	12,597	10,361	2,223	2,258	2,352	30.2	28.5	23.4
31140	21 223	Trimble	156	3,066	9,074	9,036	8,125	6,090	2,522	2,597	2,745	61.0	54.9	40.9
...	21 225	Union	363	2,695	15,371	15,553	15,637	16,557	2,080	2,047	1,884	44.5	45.2	48.0
14540	21 227	Warren	548	2,009	101,266	98,929	92,522	77,720	553	550	583	185.7	170.2	142.5
...	21 229	Washington	302	2,843	11,444	11,349	10,916	10,441	2,334	2,374	2,344	38.1	36.3	34.7

See footnotes at end of table.

U.S. Census Bureau

[Includes United States, states, and 3,141 counties/county equivalents defined as of February 22, 2005. For more information on these areas, see Appendix C, Geographic Information]

Metro-politan area code	FIPS state and county code[1]	County	Area, 2000 (square miles)		Population									
							2000[3] (April 1 estimates base)	1990[3] (April 1 estimates base)	Rank			Persons per square mile of land area		
			Total	Rank[2]	2006 (July 1)	2005 (July 1)			2006[2]	2000[2]	1990[4]	2006[5]	2000	1990
		KENTUCKY—Con.												
...	21 231	Wayne	484	2,229	20,504	20,411	19,923	17,468	1,796	1,796	1,823	44.6	43.5	38.0
21780	21 233	Webster	336	2,770	14,083	14,134	14,120	13,955	2,165	2,155	2,060	42.1	42.2	41.7
18340	21 235	Whitley	445	2,359	38,142	37,895	35,870	33,326	1,206	1,225	1,182	86.7	81.7	75.7
...	21 237	Wolfe	223	2,984	7,095	7,100	7,065	6,503	2,672	2,680	2,710	31.8	31.9	29.2
30460	21 239	Woodford	192	3,030	24,386	24,135	23,208	19,955	1,616	1,633	1,680	127.9	122.1	104.6
	22 000	LOUISIANA	51,840	(X)	4,287,768	4,507,331	4,468,958	4,221,826	(X)	(X)	(X)	98.4	102.6	96.9
18940	22 001	Acadia	658	1,546	60,457	59,247	58,864	55,882	836	813	775	92.3	89.8	85.3
...	22 003	Allen	766	1,248	25,447	25,241	25,440	21,226	1,567	1,545	1,619	33.3	33.3	27.8
12940	22 005	Ascension	303	2,839	97,335	90,447	76,627	58,214	576	656	745	333.9	265.4	199.7
38200	22 007	Assumption	365	2,692	23,472	23,108	23,388	22,753	1,653	1,625	1,545	69.3	69.1	67.2
...	22 009	Avoyelles	866	1,046	42,663	41,789	41,481	39,159	1,090	1,068	1,020	51.3	49.8	47.0
19760	22 011	Beauregard	1,166	606	35,130	34,542	32,986	30,083	1,291	1,321	1,293	30.3	28.5	25.9
...	22 013	Bienville	822	1,125	15,168	15,183	15,752	16,232	2,094	2,037	1,912	18.7	19.4	20.0
43340	22 015	Bossier	867	1,043	107,270	105,309	98,360	86,088	531	530	531	127.8	117.5	102.7
43340	22 017	Caddo	937	860	253,118	250,438	252,116	248,253	241	224	201	287.0	285.7	281.4
29340	22 019	Calcasieu	1,094	665	184,524	184,708	183,577	168,134	320	297	285	172.3	171.4	157.0
...	22 021	Caldwell	541	2,034	10,615	10,618	10,560	9,806	2,392	2,393	2,403	20.1	20.0	18.5
29340	22 023	Cameron	1,932	327	7,792	9,611	9,988	9,260	2,615	2,447	2,448	5.9	7.6	7.1
...	22 025	Catahoula	739	1,304	10,567	10,472	10,920	11,065	2,395	2,373	2,286	15.0	15.5	15.7
...	22 027	Claiborne	768	1,241	16,210	16,184	16,851	17,405	2,032	1,966	1,828	21.5	22.2	23.1
35020	22 029	Concordia	749	1,282	19,460	19,298	20,247	20,828	1,845	1,777	1,639	28.0	29.1	29.9
43340	22 031	De Soto	894	987	26,390	26,301	25,492	25,668	1,540	1,541	1,436	30.1	29.1	29.3
12940	22 033	East Baton Rouge	471	2,276	429,073	409,809	412,852	380,105	148	145	132	942.1	906.3	834.2
...	22 035	East Carroll	442	2,375	8,699	8,786	9,421	9,709	2,549	2,494	2,411	20.6	22.3	23.0
12940	22 037	East Feliciana	456	2,320	20,922	20,703	21,360	19,211	1,764	1,721	1,720	46.1	47.2	42.4
...	22 039	Evangeline	680	1,494	35,911	35,462	35,434	33,274	1,259	1,238	1,184	54.1	53.3	50.1
...	22 041	Franklin	635	1,623	20,455	20,390	21,263	22,387	1,797	1,723	1,560	32.8	34.1	35.9
10780	22 043	Grant	665	1,525	19,879	19,438	18,696	17,526	1,825	1,863	1,818	30.8	29.0	27.2
35340	22 045	Iberia	1,031	737	75,509	74,212	73,266	68,297	697	684	647	131.3	127.4	118.7
12940	22 047	Iberville	653	1,564	32,974	32,160	33,320	31,049	1,341	1,306	1,244	53.3	53.8	50.2
40820	22 049	Jackson	580	1,826	15,202	15,084	15,397	15,859	2,091	2,059	1,932	26.7	27.0	27.8
35380	22 051	Jefferson	642	1,596	431,361	451,049	455,466	448,306	147	128	110	1,407.3	1,483.7	1,465.4
27660	22 053	Jefferson Davis	659	1,539	31,418	31,194	31,435	30,722	1,383	1,363	1,257	48.2	48.2	47.1
29180	22 055	Lafayette	270	2,898	203,091	196,627	190,323	164,762	291	288	290	752.7	705.7	610.5
26380	22 057	Lafourche	1,472	456	93,554	91,910	89,983	85,860	595	575	535	86.3	83.0	79.1
...	22 059	La Salle	662	1,532	14,093	14,010	14,282	13,662	2,163	2,144	2,084	22.6	22.9	21.9
40820	22 061	Lincoln	472	2,271	41,857	41,907	42,509	41,745	1,106	1,045	963	88.8	90.1	88.6
12940	22 063	Livingston	703	1,428	114,805	108,958	91,808	70,523	498	558	629	177.2	142.9	108.8
45260	22 065	Madison	651	1,573	12,328	12,471	13,728	12,463	2,281	2,182	2,184	19.8	22.0	20.0
12820	22 067	Morehouse	805	1,162	29,761	29,919	31,021	31,938	1,423	1,378	1,214	37.5	39.0	40.2
35060	22 069	Natchitoches	1,299	524	38,719	38,320	39,080	37,254	1,188	1,136	1,065	30.8	31.1	29.7
35380	22 071	Orleans	350	2,728	223,388	452,170	484,674	496,938	276	117	98	1,237.2	2,677.8	2,750.8
33740	22 073	Ouachita	633	1,633	149,259	147,721	147,250	142,191	396	369	334	244.5	241.1	232.7
35380	22 075	Plaquemines	2,429	239	22,512	28,903	26,757	25,575	1,698	1,493	1,440	26.7	31.7	30.3
12940	22 077	Pointe Coupee	591	1,774	22,648	22,288	22,763	22,540	1,689	1,660	1,553	40.6	40.8	40.4
10780	22 079	Rapides	1,362	497	130,201	127,887	126,339	131,556	453	430	352	98.4	95.6	99.5
...	22 081	Red River	402	2,592	9,438	9,445	9,622	9,526	2,483	2,478	2,429	24.2	24.7	24.5
...	22 083	Richland	565	1,956	20,554	20,391	20,981	20,629	1,791	1,738	1,648	36.8	37.5	36.9
...	22 085	Sabine	1,012	754	23,934	23,715	23,459	22,646	1,631	1,618	1,551	27.7	27.2	26.2
35380	22 087	St. Bernard	1,794	368	15,514	65,147	67,229	66,631	2,077	728	660	33.4	144.1	143.2
35380	22 089	St. Charles	410	2,544	52,761	50,554	48,067	42,437	916	951	948	186.0	169.9	149.6
12940	22 091	St. Helena	409	2,545	10,759	10,138	10,525	9,874	2,382	2,395	2,399	26.3	25.7	24.2
...	22 093	St. James	258	2,926	21,721	21,031	21,195	20,879	1,734	1,726	1,635	88.3	86.1	84.8
35380	22 095	St. John the Baptist	348	2,734	48,537	46,150	43,049	39,996	978	1,035	998	221.7	197.1	182.7
36660	22 097	St. Landry	939	855	91,528	89,640	87,700	80,312	609	597	570	98.6	94.5	86.5
29180	22 099	St. Martin	816	1,137	51,341	50,228	48,583	44,007	937	938	924	69.4	65.8	59.6
34020	22 101	St. Mary	1,119	648	51,867	51,213	53,500	58,086	931	875	747	84.6	87.0	94.8
35380	22 103	St. Tammany	1,124	644	230,605	219,814	191,270	144,500	266	287	328	270.0	225.1	169.1
25220	22 105	Tangipahoa	823	1,123	113,137	106,152	100,592	85,709	508	521	536	143.2	127.6	108.4
...	22 107	Tensas	641	1,603	6,138	6,117	6,618	7,103	2,756	2,726	2,645	10.2	10.9	11.8
26380	22 109	Terrebonne	2,080	302	109,348	107,094	104,494	96,982	523	506	474	87.1	83.3	77.3
33740	22 111	Union	905	939	22,964	22,866	22,803	20,796	1,670	1,656	1,640	26.2	26.0	23.7
10020	22 113	Vermilion	1,538	434	56,021	55,267	53,990	50,055	882	869	841	47.7	46.0	42.6
22860	22 115	Vernon	1,342	502	46,748	48,511	52,531	61,961	1,006	888	704	35.2	39.5	46.6
14220	22 117	Washington	676	1,505	44,750	44,277	43,926	43,185	1,045	1,018	935	66.8	65.6	64.5
33380	22 119	Webster	615	1,693	41,301	41,144	41,828	41,989	1,124	1,058	956	69.4	70.1	70.5
12940	22 121	West Baton Rouge	204	3,010	22,463	21,634	21,601	19,419	1,700	1,715	1,709	117.5	112.8	101.6
...	22 123	West Carroll	360	2,712	11,732	11,815	12,314	12,093	2,314	2,280	2,209	32.6	34.2	33.6
12940	22 125	West Feliciana	426	2,458	15,535	15,185	15,111	12,915	2,074	2,084	2,145	38.3	37.3	31.8
...	22 127	Winn	957	826	15,835	15,929	16,894	16,498	2,052	1,962	1,893	16.7	17.7	17.4

See footnotes at end of table.

County and City Data Book: 2007

U.S. Census Bureau

[Includes United States, states, and 3,141 counties/county equivalents defined as of February 22, 2005. For more information on these areas, see Appendix C, Geographic Information]

Metro-politan area code	FIPS state and county code[1]	County	Area, 2000 (square miles) Total	Rank[2]	2006 (July 1)	2005 (July 1)	2000[3] (April 1 estimates base)	1990[3] (April 1 estimates base)	Rank 2006[2]	2000[2]	1990[4]	Persons per square mile of land area 2006[5]	2000	1990
	23 000	MAINE	35,385	(X)	1,321,574	1,318,220	1,274,923	1,227,928	(X)	(X)	(X)	42.8	41.4	39.8
30340	23 001	Androscoggin	497	2,193	107,552	107,061	103,793	105,259	529	512	438	228.7	220.9	223.8
...	23 003	Aroostook	6,829	52	73,008	73,030	73,938	86,936	712	676	525	10.9	11.1	13.0
38860	23 005	Cumberland	1,217	579	274,598	274,194	265,612	243,135	221	207	206	328.7	318.4	291.0
...	23 007	Franklin	1,744	384	30,017	29,861	29,467	29,008	1,418	1,415	1,329	17.7	17.4	17.1
...	23 009	Hancock	2,351	256	53,797	53,613	51,791	46,948	906	896	891	33.9	32.7	29.5
12300	23 011	Kennebec	951	836	121,068	120,782	117,114	115,904	479	461	397	139.5	135.1	133.6
40500	23 013	Knox	1,142	626	41,096	41,088	39,618	36,310	1,130	1,123	1,095	112.4	108.6	99.3
...	23 015	Lincoln	700	1,439	35,234	35,200	33,616	30,357	1,287	1,297	1,276	77.3	73.9	66.6
...	23 017	Oxford	2,175	285	57,118	56,766	54,755	52,602	868	860	806	27.5	26.4	25.3
12620	23 019	Penobscot	3,556	151	147,180	146,817	144,919	146,601	404	377	321	43.3	42.7	43.2
...	23 021	Piscataquis	4,377	112	17,585	17,596	17,235	18,653	1,935	1,940	1,755	4.4	4.4	4.7
38860	23 023	Sagadahoc	370	2,683	36,837	36,734	35,214	33,535	1,238	1,242	1,177	145.1	138.8	132.0
...	23 025	Somerset	4,095	125	52,249	51,649	50,888	49,767	925	911	844	13.3	13.0	12.7
...	23 027	Waldo	853	1,079	38,715	38,527	36,280	33,018	1,190	1,207	1,190	53.1	50.0	45.2
...	23 029	Washington	3,255	167	33,288	33,238	33,941	35,308	1,332	1,283	1,121	13.0	13.2	13.7
38860	23 031	York	1,271	541	202,232	202,064	186,742	164,587	292	294	291	204.1	189.9	166.1
	24 000	MARYLAND	12,407	(X)	5,615,727	5,589,599	5,296,506	4,780,753	(X)	(X)	(X)	574.6	543.5	489.1
19060	24 001	Allegany	430	2,443	72,831	73,245	74,930	74,946	716	667	600	171.2	175.9	176.2
12580	24 003	Anne Arundel	588	1,784	509,300	509,397	489,656	427,239	121	115	117	1,224.5	1,181.4	1,027.1
12580	24 005	Baltimore	682	1,485	787,384	783,405	754,292	692,134	63	63	60	1,315.4	1,263.0	1,156.3
47900	24 009	Calvert	345	2,741	88,804	87,622	74,563	51,372	620	672	822	412.7	349.4	238.7
...	24 011	Caroline	326	2,792	32,617	31,805	29,772	27,035	1,350	1,404	1,388	101.9	93.2	84.4
12580	24 013	Carroll	452	2,330	170,260	168,397	150,897	123,372	347	356	373	379.1	337.6	274.7
37980	24 015	Cecil	418	2,497	99,506	97,474	85,951	71,347	563	608	621	285.8	248.4	204.9
47900	24 017	Charles	643	1,594	140,416	138,106	120,546	101,154	426	451	453	304.6	263.1	219.4
15700	24 019	Dorchester	983	791	31,631	31,351	30,674	30,236	1,381	1,383	1,283	56.7	54.9	54.2
47900	24 021	Frederick	667	1,521	222,938	220,409	195,276	150,208	277	283	311	336.3	296.6	226.6
...	24 023	Garrett	656	1,554	29,859	29,863	29,846	28,138	1,420	1,401	1,347	46.1	46.0	43.4
12580	24 025	Harford	527	2,080	241,402	238,850	218,590	182,132	254	258	265	548.2	498.5	413.6
12580	24 027	Howard	254	2,937	272,452	269,174	247,842	187,328	222	234	258	1,081.0	990.3	742.8
...	24 029	Kent	414	2,516	19,983	19,908	19,197	17,842	1,821	1,835	1,796	71.5	69.0	63.8
47900	24 031	Montgomery	507	2,145	932,131	927,405	874,165	762,875	44	49	51	1,881.1	1,773.3	1,542.5
47900	24 033	Prince George's	498	2,186	841,315	842,764	800,691	722,705	57	57	56	1,733.1	1,653.6	1,485.8
12580	24 035	Queen Anne's	510	2,137	46,241	45,469	40,563	33,953	1,014	1,099	1,164	124.2	109.6	91.2
30500	24 037	St. Mary's	765	1,251	98,854	96,868	86,232	75,974	567	604	592	273.6	239.5	210.3
41540	24 039	Somerset	611	1,706	25,774	25,666	24,748	23,440	1,552	1,567	1,518	78.8	75.6	71.6
20660	24 041	Talbot	477	2,252	36,062	35,630	33,812	30,549	1,257	1,288	1,264	134.0	126.0	113.5
25180	24 043	Washington	468	2,290	143,748	141,563	131,923	121,393	417	404	379	313.8	288.4	265.0
41540	24 045	Wicomico	400	2,599	91,987	90,252	84,644	74,339	604	615	605	243.9	225.1	197.1
36180	24 047	Worcester	695	1,454	48,866	48,599	46,542	35,028	975	971	1,132	103.3	98.8	74.0
		Independent City												
12580	24 510	Baltimore city	92	3,097	631,366	636,377	651,154	736,014	94	82	53	7,813.9	8,025.8	9,108.0
	25 000	MASSACHUSETTS	10,555	(X)	6,437,193	6,433,367	6,349,105	6,016,425	(X)	(X)	(X)	821.1	811.6	767.6
12700	25 001	Barnstable	1,306	519	224,816	226,161	222,230	186,605	274	256	259	568.4	564.5	471.5
38340	25 003	Berkshire	946	844	131,117	131,783	134,953	139,352	446	399	342	140.8	144.8	149.6
39300	25 005	Bristol	691	1,462	545,379	545,861	534,678	506,325	110	104	94	980.9	964.3	910.6
...	25 007	Dukes	491	2,213	15,515	15,553	14,987	11,639	2,076	2,092	2,243	149.5	145.3	112.1
14460	25 009	Essex	829	1,115	735,958	734,261	723,419	670,080	74	69	65	1,469.9	1,449.0	1,345.4
44140	25 011	Franklin	725	1,339	72,183	72,310	71,535	70,086	723	691	632	102.8	101.9	99.8
44140	25 013	Hampden	634	1,628	460,520	460,828	456,226	456,310	138	127	109	744.7	738.4	737.7
44140	25 015	Hampshire	545	2,019	153,471	153,353	152,253	146,568	383	352	322	290.1	288.1	277.1
14460	25 017	Middlesex	848	1,086	1,467,016	1,464,985	1,466,394	1,398,468	22	19	18	1,781.5	1,784.0	1,698.1
...	25 019	Nantucket	304	2,838	10,240	10,139	9,520	6,012	2,427	2,489	2,755	214.2	200.1	125.8
14460	25 021	Norfolk	444	2,365	654,753	652,530	650,308	616,087	91	83	75	1,638.6	1,630.0	1,541.7
14460	25 023	Plymouth	1,093	666	493,623	491,934	472,822	435,276	127	121	114	747.0	718.1	658.9
14460	25 025	Suffolk	120	3,085	687,610	691,965	689,807	663,906	83	74	70	11,750.0	11,790.6	11,344.9
49340	25 027	Worcester	1,579	423	784,992	781,704	749,973	709,711	67	66	59	518.8	497.5	469.0
	26 000	MICHIGAN	96,716	(X)	10,095,643	10,100,833	9,938,480	9,295,287	(X)	(X)	(X)	177.7	175.3	163.6
...	26 001	Alcona	1,791	370	11,759	11,687	11,719	10,145	2,309	2,319	2,374	17.4	17.4	15.0
...	26 003	Alger	5,049	82	9,665	9,647	9,862	8,972	2,467	2,460	2,472	10.5	10.7	9.8
10880	26 005	Allegan	1,833	357	113,501	113,052	105,665	90,509	507	503	505	137.2	128.3	109.4
10980	26 007	Alpena	1,695	395	30,067	30,373	31,314	30,605	1,416	1,367	1,261	52.4	54.5	53.3
...	26 009	Antrim	602	1,733	24,463	24,404	23,110	18,185	1,607	1,637	1,779	51.3	48.8	38.1
...	26 011	Arenac	681	1,489	17,024	17,172	17,269	14,906	1,963	1,935	1,994	46.4	47.2	40.6
...	26 013	Baraga	1,069	698	8,742	8,732	8,746	7,954	2,544	2,551	2,577	9.7	9.7	8.8
24340	26 015	Barry	577	1,851	59,899	59,817	56,755	50,057	840	834	840	107.7	102.4	90.0
13020	26 017	Bay	631	1,638	108,390	108,896	110,157	111,723	528	492	411	244.0	247.9	251.5
45900	26 019	Benzie	860	1,067	17,652	17,574	15,998	12,200	1,930	2,025	2,201	54.9	50.1	38.0

See footnotes at end of table.

[Includes United States, states, and 3,141 counties/county equivalents defined as of February 22, 2005. For more information on these areas, see Appendix C, Geographic Information]

Metro-politan area code	FIPS state and county code[1]	County	Area, 2000 (square miles)		Population				Rank			Persons per square mile of land area		
			Total	Rank[2]	2006 (July 1)	2005 (July 1)	2000[3] (April 1 estimates base)	1990[3] (April 1 estimates base)	2006[2]	2000[2]	1990[4]	2006[5]	2000	1990
		MICHIGAN—Con.												
35660	26 021	Berrien............	1,581	422	161,705	162,090	162,455	161,378	360	330	294	283.2	284.8	282.6
17740	26 023	Branch............	519	2,103	45,875	46,275	45,787	41,502	1,024	987	970	90.4	90.4	81.8
12980	26 025	Calhoun...........	718	1,378	137,991	138,543	137,985	135,982	433	394	345	194.7	194.9	191.8
43780	26 027	Cass..............	508	2,143	51,329	51,553	51,102	49,477	938	907	850	104.3	104.0	100.5
...	26 029	Charlevoix.........	1,391	487	26,422	26,603	26,090	21,468	1,538	1,514	1,605	63.4	62.8	51.5
...	26 031	Cheboygan.........	885	1,009	27,282	27,335	26,448	21,398	1,510	1,505	1,611	38.1	37.1	29.9
42300	26 033	Chippewa..........	2,698	204	38,674	38,844	38,543	34,604	1,192	1,150	1,148	24.8	24.7	22.2
...	26 035	Clare.............	575	1,873	31,307	31,507	31,252	24,952	1,389	1,369	1,464	55.2	55.4	44.0
29620	26 037	Clinton............	575	1,885	69,909	69,359	64,753	57,893	747	750	749	122.3	113.7	101.3
...	26 039	Crawford...........	563	1,960	14,928	15,026	14,273	12,260	2,112	2,145	2,199	26.7	25.7	22.0
21540	26 041	Delta.............	1,992	317	38,156	38,189	38,520	37,780	1,205	1,151	1,053	32.6	33.0	32.3
27020	26 043	Dickinson..........	777	1,219	27,447	27,589	27,472	26,831	1,505	1,469	1,395	35.8	35.9	35.0
29620	26 045	Eaton.............	579	1,838	107,237	107,190	103,655	92,879	532	513	499	186.0	180.3	161.1
...	26 047	Emmet............	882	1,014	33,607	33,461	31,437	25,040	1,323	1,362	1,461	71.8	67.4	53.5
22420	26 049	Genesee...........	649	1,577	441,966	442,732	436,148	430,459	145	137	116	691.0	683.2	672.9
...	26 051	Gladwin...........	516	2,113	27,008	27,007	26,023	21,896	1,517	1,518	1,583	53.3	51.6	43.2
...	26 053	Gogebic...........	1,476	454	16,524	16,852	17,370	18,052	2,005	1,932	1,788	15.0	15.7	16.4
45900	26 055	Grand Traverse.....	601	1,737	84,952	83,954	77,654	64,273	641	653	682	182.7	167.7	138.2
10940	26 057	Gratiot............	572	1,912	42,107	42,257	42,285	38,982	1,099	1,049	1,022	73.9	74.2	68.4
...	26 059	Hillsdale..........	607	1,715	47,206	47,163	46,527	43,431	998	972	933	78.8	78.0	72.5
26340	26 061	Houghton..........	1,502	445	35,334	35,577	36,016	35,446	1,279	1,217	1,113	34.9	35.6	35.0
...	26 063	Huron.............	2,136	290	34,143	34,522	36,079	34,951	1,312	1,212	1,135	40.8	43.1	41.8
29620	26 065	Ingham............	561	1,969	276,898	278,119	279,414	281,912	218	201	175	495.2	499.8	504.1
24340	26 067	Ionia.............	580	1,828	64,821	64,468	61,518	57,024	785	791	764	113.1	107.6	99.5
...	26 069	Iosco.............	1,891	342	26,831	26,838	27,339	30,209	1,524	1,472	1,288	48.9	49.8	55.0
...	26 071	Iron..............	1,211	581	12,377	12,415	13,138	13,175	2,277	2,219	2,126	10.6	11.2	11.3
34380	26 073	Isabella...........	578	1,845	65,818	65,640	63,351	54,624	779	765	789	114.6	110.3	95.1
27100	26 075	Jackson...........	724	1,345	163,851	163,432	158,422	149,756	354	336	316	231.9	224.7	211.9
28020	26 077	Kalamazoo.........	580	1,829	240,720	240,112	238,603	223,411	255	242	223	428.4	425.1	397.6
45900	26 079	Kalkaska..........	571	1,921	17,330	17,199	16,571	13,497	1,951	1,988	2,102	30.9	29.6	24.1
24340	26 081	Kent..............	872	1,034	599,524	595,979	574,335	500,631	98	93	97	700.2	673.1	584.7
26340	26 083	Keweenaw.........	5,966	66	2,183	2,172	2,301	1,701	3,038	3,038	3,083	4.0	4.3	3.1
...	26 085	Lake.............	575	1,882	11,793	11,968	11,333	8,583	2,306	2,348	2,506	20.8	20.1	15.1
19820	26 087	Lapeer............	663	1,529	93,761	93,220	87,904	74,768	593	595	602	143.3	135.0	114.3
45900	26 089	Leelanau..........	2,532	226	22,112	22,030	21,119	16,527	1,718	1,732	1,888	63.5	61.0	47.4
10300	26 091	Lenawee..........	761	1,259	102,191	101,778	98,947	91,476	548	526	503	136.2	132.1	121.9
19820	26 093	Livingston.........	585	1,797	184,511	181,404	156,951	115,645	321	339	398	324.6	278.9	203.5
...	26 095	Luce..............	1,912	334	6,684	6,773	7,024	5,763	2,708	2,683	2,783	7.4	7.8	6.4
...	26 097	Mackinac..........	2,101	298	11,050	11,253	11,943	10,674	2,364	2,299	2,319	10.4	11.0	10.4
19820	26 099	Macomb...........	570	1,932	832,861	828,950	788,149	717,400	59	60	57	1,733.5	1,646.5	1,493.3
...	26 101	Manistee..........	1,281	537	25,067	25,131	24,527	21,265	1,581	1,577	1,617	46.1	45.3	39.1
32100	26 103	Marquette.........	3,425	155	64,675	64,677	64,634	70,887	787	752	624	35.5	35.5	38.9
...	26 105	Mason............	1,242	557	29,045	28,916	28,274	25,537	1,446	1,439	1,444	58.7	57.2	51.6
13660	26 107	Mecosta...........	571	1,918	42,252	42,180	40,553	37,308	1,098	1,101	1,064	76.0	73.2	67.1
31940	26 109	Menominee........	1,338	505	24,696	24,892	25,326	24,920	1,599	1,552	1,466	23.7	24.2	23.9
33220	26 111	Midland...........	528	2,075	83,792	83,984	82,874	75,651	646	627	595	160.8	159.3	145.1
15620	26 113	Missaukee.........	574	1,890	15,197	15,239	14,478	12,147	2,092	2,125	2,203	26.8	25.7	21.4
33780	26 115	Monroe...........	680	1,492	155,003	153,772	145,945	133,600	376	375	348	281.3	265.9	242.4
...	26 117	Montcalm..........	721	1,360	63,977	63,795	61,266	53,059	790	795	802	90.4	86.8	74.9
...	26 119	Montmorency.......	562	1,965	10,478	10,457	10,315	8,936	2,402	2,413	2,476	19.1	18.9	16.3
34740	26 121	Muskegon..........	1,459	460	175,231	174,971	170,200	158,983	337	318	298	344.2	335.0	312.2
24340	26 123	Newaygo..........	861	1,062	49,840	49,907	47,874	38,206	956	955	1,048	59.2	57.0	45.4
19820	26 125	Oakland...........	908	928	1,214,255	1,213,669	1,194,156	1,083,592	31	30	28	1,391.7	1,371.7	1,241.6
...	26 127	Oceana...........	1,307	518	28,639	28,516	26,873	22,455	1,459	1,490	1,555	53.0	49.9	41.5
...	26 129	Ogemaw...........	575	1,881	21,665	21,804	21,645	18,681	1,736	1,712	1,751	38.4	38.4	33.1
...	26 131	Ontonagon.........	3,741	142	7,202	7,330	7,818	8,854	2,666	2,623	2,484	5.5	6.0	6.8
...	26 133	Osceola...........	573	1,900	23,584	23,675	23,197	20,146	1,645	1,634	1,668	41.7	41.1	35.6
...	26 135	Oscoda...........	572	1,913	9,140	9,218	9,418	7,842	2,517	2,496	2,588	16.2	16.7	13.9
...	26 137	Otsego............	526	2,084	24,711	24,608	23,301	17,957	1,598	1,630	1,791	48.0	45.5	34.9
26100	26 139	Ottawa............	1,632	411	257,671	255,187	238,314	187,768	236	243	257	455.5	423.4	331.9
...	26 141	Presque Isle.......	2,573	223	14,144	14,219	14,411	13,743	2,159	2,131	2,077	21.4	21.8	20.8
...	26 143	Roscommon........	580	1,833	26,064	26,082	25,469	19,776	1,546	1,543	1,686	50.0	49.0	37.9
40980	26 145	Saginaw...........	816	1,139	206,300	207,846	210,042	211,946	290	266	236	255.0	259.5	262.0
19820	26 147	St. Clair..........	837	1,100	171,725	171,079	164,235	145,607	344	328	325	237.1	227.4	201.0
44780	26 149	St. Joseph.........	521	2,098	62,777	62,856	62,422	58,913	810	777	738	124.6	124.2	116.9
...	26 151	Sanilac...........	1,590	420	44,448	44,586	44,547	39,928	1,052	1,006	1,004	46.1	46.2	41.4
...	26 153	Schoolcraft........	1,884	343	8,744	8,779	8,903	8,302	2,542	2,534	2,535	7.4	7.6	7.0
37020	26 155	Shiawassee........	541	2,033	72,912	72,880	71,687	69,770	714	689	636	135.3	133.1	129.5
...	26 157	Tuscola...........	914	910	57,878	58,267	58,266	55,498	857	821	781	71.2	71.8	68.3

See footnotes at end of table.

Table B-1. Counties — **Area and Population**—Con.

[Includes United States, states, and 3,141 counties/county equivalents defined as of February 22, 2005. For more information on these areas, see Appendix C, Geographic Information]

Metro-politan area code	FIPS state and county code[1]	County	Area, 2000 (square miles) Total	Area, 2000 (square miles) Rank[2]	Population 2006 (July 1)	Population 2005 (July 1)	Population 2000[3] (April 1 estimates base)	Population 1990[3] (April 1 estimates base)	Rank 2006[2]	Rank 2000[2]	Rank 1990[4]	Persons per square mile of land area 2006[5]	Persons per square mile of land area 2000	Persons per square mile of land area 1990
		MICHIGAN—Con.												
28020	26 159	Van Buren............	1,090	669	79,018	78,724	76,263	70,060	681	658	633	129.4	125.0	114.7
11460	26 161	Washtenaw...........	723	1,351	344,047	342,124	322,770	282,937	182	179	173	484.6	456.8	398.5
19820	26 163	Wayne...............	672	1,512	1,971,853	1,990,932	2,061,162	2,111,687	13	11	8	3,210.7	3,353.0	3,438.4
15620	26 165	Wexford.............	576	1,862	31,994	31,799	30,484	26,360	1,368	1,387	1,410	56.6	54.0	46.6
	27 000	MINNESOTA..........	86,939	(X)	5,167,101	5,126,739	4,919,492	4,375,665	(X)	(X)	(X)	64.9	62.0	55.0
...	27 001	Aitkin...............	1,995	316	16,149	16,119	15,301	12,425	2,037	2,073	2,188	8.9	8.4	6.8
33460	27 003	Anoka...............	446	2,352	327,005	323,403	298,084	243,641	188	189	205	771.9	707.9	574.6
...	27 005	Becker...............	1,445	466	32,230	31,883	30,000	27,881	1,364	1,396	1,354	24.6	23.0	21.3
13420	27 007	Beltrami..............	3,056	179	43,169	42,741	39,650	34,384	1,078	1,122	1,155	17.2	15.9	13.7
41060	27 009	Benton...............	413	2,520	38,688	38,492	34,227	30,185	1,191	1,276	1,289	94.8	84.5	73.9
...	27 011	Big Stone............	528	2,076	5,510	5,523	5,820	6,285	2,799	2,803	2,723	11.1	11.7	12.6
31860	27 013	Blue Earth...........	766	1,245	58,254	57,565	55,937	54,044	853	844	797	77.4	74.3	71.8
35580	27 015	Brown...............	619	1,680	26,361	26,281	26,911	26,984	1,541	1,488	1,392	43.2	44.0	44.2
20260	27 017	Carlton..............	875	1,030	34,116	34,013	31,671	29,259	1,313	1,354	1,321	39.7	36.9	34.0
33460	27 019	Carver...............	376	2,668	87,545	84,930	70,205	47,915	627	707	874	245.2	198.5	134.2
14660	27 021	Cass................	2,414	241	29,036	28,917	27,153	21,791	1,447	1,478	1,590	14.4	13.5	10.8
...	27 023	Chippewa............	588	1,785	12,721	12,750	13,088	13,228	2,263	2,224	2,119	21.8	22.4	22.7
33460	27 025	Chisago.............	442	2,374	50,344	49,349	41,101	30,521	948	1,078	1,267	120.5	99.5	73.1
22020	27 027	Clay.................	1,053	713	54,476	53,716	51,229	50,422	901	903	837	52.1	49.1	48.2
...	27 029	Clearwater...........	1,030	739	8,440	8,457	8,423	8,309	2,566	2,570	2,534	8.5	8.4	8.4
...	27 031	Cook................	3,340	161	5,329	5,298	5,168	3,868	2,816	2,840	2,927	3.7	3.6	2.7
...	27 033	Cottonwood...........	649	1,578	11,659	11,810	12,167	12,694	2,318	2,287	2,166	18.2	19.0	19.8
14660	27 035	Crow Wing...........	1,157	609	61,009	60,018	55,099	44,249	834	857	921	61.2	55.5	44.4
33460	27 037	Dakota..............	586	1,790	388,001	383,368	355,904	275,210	165	164	180	681.2	628.4	483.1
40340	27 039	Dodge...............	440	2,386	19,770	19,530	17,731	15,731	1,833	1,916	1,939	45.0	40.6	35.8
10820	27 041	Douglas..............	720	1,363	35,467	35,133	32,821	28,674	1,274	1,325	1,339	55.9	51.9	45.2
...	27 043	Faribault.............	722	1,355	15,283	15,398	16,181	16,937	2,086	2,012	1,852	21.4	22.6	23.7
...	27 045	Fillmore.............	862	1,058	21,151	21,230	21,122	20,777	1,759	1,731	1,642	24.6	24.6	24.1
10660	27 047	Freeborn............	723	1,349	31,636	31,768	32,584	33,060	1,380	1,330	1,189	44.7	46.0	46.7
39860	27 049	Goodhue.............	780	1,211	45,807	45,529	44,127	40,690	1,026	1,013	984	60.4	58.2	53.6
...	27 051	Grant...............	575	1,874	6,078	6,099	6,289	6,246	2,762	2,759	2,729	11.1	11.5	11.4
33460	27 053	Hennepin............	606	1,717	1,122,093	1,118,746	1,116,039	1,032,431	33	32	30	2,015.9	2,008.2	1,854.8
29100	27 055	Houston.............	569	1,937	19,832	19,872	19,718	18,497	1,829	1,811	1,761	35.5	35.4	33.1
...	27 057	Hubbard.............	999	770	18,890	18,845	18,373	14,939	1,878	1,876	1,991	20.5	20.0	16.2
33460	27 059	Isanti...............	452	2,336	38,576	37,582	31,287	25,921	1,196	1,368	1,425	87.9	71.8	59.0
...	27 061	Itasca...............	2,928	189	44,729	44,460	43,992	40,844	1,046	1,015	981	16.8	16.5	15.3
...	27 063	Jackson..............	719	1,367	11,150	11,187	11,268	11,677	2,357	2,353	2,240	15.9	16.0	16.6
...	27 065	Kanabec.............	533	2,061	16,276	16,184	14,996	12,802	2,027	2,091	2,156	31.0	28.7	24.4
48820	27 067	Kandiyohi............	862	1,061	41,088	41,160	41,203	38,761	1,132	1,073	1,033	51.6	51.7	48.7
...	27 069	Kittson..............	1,104	662	4,691	4,793	5,285	5,767	2,853	2,831	2,782	4.3	4.8	5.3
...	27 071	Koochiching..........	3,154	174	13,658	13,811	14,355	16,299	2,193	2,138	1,904	4.4	4.6	5.3
...	27 073	Lac qui Parle.........	778	1,215	7,464	7,601	8,067	8,924	2,641	2,602	2,477	9.8	10.5	11.7
...	27 075	Lake................	2,991	184	10,966	11,058	11,058	10,415	2,369	2,362	2,348	5.2	5.3	5.0
...	27 077	Lake of the Woods........	1,775	376	4,327	4,377	4,522	4,076	2,878	2,878	2,910	3.3	3.5	3.1
...	27 079	Le Sueur.............	474	2,263	27,895	27,488	25,426	23,239	1,492	1,547	1,529	62.2	56.8	51.8
...	27 081	Lincoln..............	548	2,007	5,963	6,048	6,429	6,890	2,773	2,748	2,672	11.1	11.9	12.8
32140	27 083	Lyon................	721	1,357	24,640	24,659	25,425	24,789	1,602	1,548	1,472	34.5	35.6	34.7
26780	27 085	McLeod..............	506	2,154	37,279	36,593	34,898	32,030	1,226	1,254	1,210	75.8	70.9	65.1
...	27 087	Mahnomen...........	583	1,814	5,072	5,078	5,190	5,044	2,835	2,838	2,839	9.1	9.3	9.1
...	27 089	Marshall.............	1,813	361	9,951	9,959	10,155	10,993	2,446	2,431	2,296	5.6	5.7	6.2
21860	27 091	Martin...............	730	1,323	20,768	20,955	21,802	22,914	1,771	1,703	1,537	29.3	30.7	32.3
...	27 093	Meeker..............	645	1,586	23,405	23,249	22,642	20,846	1,654	1,665	1,637	38.5	37.3	34.3
...	27 095	Mille Lacs............	682	1,487	26,169	25,672	22,330	18,670	1,544	1,678	1,753	45.6	39.1	32.5
...	27 097	Morrison.............	1,153	614	32,919	32,758	31,712	29,604	1,343	1,352	1,313	29.3	28.3	26.3
12380	27 099	Mower..............	712	1,412	38,666	38,616	38,603	37,385	1,193	1,149	1,061	54.3	54.4	52.5
...	27 101	Murray..............	720	1,366	8,778	8,839	9,165	9,660	2,539	2,518	2,418	12.5	13.0	13.7
31860	27 103	Nicollet..............	467	2,293	31,313	30,930	29,771	28,076	1,387	1,405	1,348	69.2	66.1	62.1
49380	27 105	Nobles..............	722	1,353	20,445	20,503	20,832	20,098	1,800	1,743	1,670	28.6	29.1	28.1
...	27 107	Norman.............	877	1,028	6,850	7,003	7,442	7,975	2,696	2,646	2,572	7.8	8.5	9.1
40340	27 109	Olmsted.............	655	1,559	137,521	135,304	124,277	106,470	434	434	435	210.6	191.2	163.0
22260	27 111	Otter Tail............	2,225	277	57,817	57,582	57,159	50,714	858	833	831	29.2	28.9	25.6
...	27 113	Pennington...........	618	1,681	13,709	13,593	13,584	13,306	2,190	2,194	2,114	22.2	22.0	21.6
...	27 115	Pine................	1,435	471	28,419	28,316	26,530	21,264	1,470	1,501	1,618	20.1	18.9	15.1
...	27 117	Pipestone............	466	2,297	9,423	9,420	9,895	10,491	2,485	2,457	2,336	20.2	21.1	22.5
24220	27 119	Polk................	1,998	315	31,088	31,083	31,369	32,589	1,393	1,364	1,200	15.8	15.9	16.5
...	27 121	Pope................	717	1,389	11,212	11,197	11,236	10,745	2,351	2,355	2,314	16.7	16.8	16.0
33460	27 123	Ramsey..............	170	3,055	493,215	494,883	511,202	485,760	128	108	100	3,166.1	3,282.9	3,117.4
...	27 125	Red Lake............	433	2,427	4,168	4,260	4,299	4,525	2,898	2,897	2,872	9.6	9.9	10.5
...	27 127	Redwood.............	881	1,018	15,791	15,909	16,815	17,254	2,054	1,968	1,838	17.9	19.0	19.6
...	27 129	Renville.............	987	783	16,531	16,675	17,154	17,673	2,004	1,946	1,807	16.8	17.4	18.0

See footnotes at end of table.

Table B-1. Counties — **Area and Population**—Con.

[Includes United States, states, and 3,141 counties/county equivalents defined as of February 22, 2005. For more information on these areas, see Appendix C, Geographic Information]

Metro-politan area code	FIPS state and county code[1]	County	Area, 2000 (square miles) Total	Rank[2]	2006 (July 1)	2005 (July 1)	2000[3] (April 1 estimates base)	1990[3] (April 1 estimates base)	Rank 2006[2]	Rank 2000[2]	Rank 1990[4]	Persons per square mile of land area 2006[5]	2000	1990
		MINNESOTA—Con.												
22060	27 131	Rice.	516	2,117	61,980	61,054	56,665	49,183	822	836	855	124.6	114.2	98.8
...	27 133	Rock	483	2,233	9,535	9,552	9,721	9,806	2,478	2,469	2,403	19.8	20.1	20.3
...	27 135	Roseau	1,678	398	16,201	16,403	16,338	15,026	2,034	2,003	1,985	9.7	9.8	9.0
20260	27 137	St. Louis	6,860	51	196,067	196,824	200,528	198,232	302	275	245	31.5	32.2	31.8
33460	27 139	Scott	369	2,685	124,092	120,008	89,498	57,846	474	577	752	347.9	255.5	162.1
33460	27 141	Sherburne.	451	2,339	84,995	81,830	64,415	41,945	639	755	957	194.8	149.7	96.1
...	27 143	Sibley.	600	1,739	15,126	15,128	15,356	14,366	2,099	2,065	2,025	25.7	26.1	24.4
41060	27 145	Stearns.	1,390	489	144,096	142,481	133,169	119,324	416	403	388	107.2	99.3	88.7
36940	27 147	Steele.	432	2,432	36,221	35,687	33,680	30,729	1,248	1,292	1,255	84.3	78.7	71.5
...	27 149	Stevens.	575	1,872	9,827	9,793	10,053	10,634	2,458	2,439	2,323	17.5	17.8	18.9
...	27 151	Swift.	752	1,275	10,307	10,480	11,956	10,724	2,422	2,298	2,317	13.9	16.0	14.4
...	27 153	Todd.	979	796	24,375	24,490	24,426	23,363	1,617	1,579	1,523	25.9	25.9	24.8
...	27 155	Traverse.	586	1,794	3,799	3,825	4,134	4,463	2,923	2,905	2,877	6.6	7.2	7.8
40340	27 157	Wabasha.	550	2,003	22,282	22,160	21,610	19,744	1,712	1,713	1,687	42.4	41.3	37.6
...	27 159	Wadena.	543	2,027	13,445	13,553	13,713	13,154	2,213	2,185	2,127	25.1	25.6	24.6
...	27 161	Waseca.	433	2,426	19,469	19,358	19,526	18,079	1,843	1,819	1,787	46.0	46.1	42.7
33460	27 163	Washington.	423	2,475	225,000	220,167	201,130	145,860	273	272	324	574.4	517.4	372.3
...	27 165	Watonwan.	440	2,384	11,164	11,263	11,880	11,682	2,354	2,302	2,238	25.7	27.2	26.9
47420	27 167	Wilkin.	752	1,276	6,634	6,752	7,138	7,516	2,713	2,676	2,615	8.8	9.5	10.0
49100	27 169	Winona.	642	1,599	49,288	49,348	49,985	47,828	966	915	878	78.7	79.9	76.4
33460	27 171	Wright	714	1,400	114,787	110,562	89,993	68,710	499	574	644	173.7	137.4	104.0
...	27 173	Yellow Medicine	763	1,253	10,430	10,453	11,080	11,684	2,407	2,361	2,237	13.8	14.6	15.4
	28 000	MISSISSIPPI	48,430	(X)	2,910,540	2,908,496	2,844,656	2,575,475	(X)	(X)	(X)	62.0	60.7	54.9
35020	28 001	Adams.	486	2,223	32,626	32,059	34,340	35,356	1,349	1,270	1,119	70.9	74.4	76.8
18420	28 003	Alcorn.	401	2,596	35,589	35,211	34,558	31,722	1,269	1,264	1,220	89.0	86.6	79.3
32620	28 005	Amite.	732	1,316	13,466	13,395	13,599	13,328	2,209	2,193	2,112	18.5	18.6	18.3
...	28 007	Attala.	737	1,306	19,644	19,502	19,661	18,481	1,838	1,816	1,764	26.7	26.7	25.1
...	28 009	Benton.	409	2,552	7,873	7,803	8,026	8,046	2,603	2,603	2,560	19.4	19.7	19.8
17380	28 011	Bolivar.	906	938	38,352	38,342	40,633	41,875	1,199	1,096	958	43.8	46.2	47.8
...	28 013	Calhoun.	588	1,783	14,647	14,600	15,069	14,908	2,126	2,087	1,993	25.0	25.7	25.4
24900	28 015	Carroll.	635	1,627	10,326	10,405	10,769	9,237	2,421	2,378	2,451	16.4	17.2	14.7
...	28 017	Chickasaw.	504	2,162	18,998	19,052	19,440	18,085	1,875	1,823	1,786	37.9	38.7	36.1
...	28 019	Choctaw.	420	2,490	9,401	9,499	9,758	9,071	2,487	2,466	2,462	22.4	23.3	21.6
...	28 021	Claiborne.	501	2,175	11,487	11,496	11,831	11,370	2,330	2,304	2,262	23.6	24.3	23.4
32940	28 023	Clarke.	693	1,456	17,631	17,547	17,955	17,313	1,934	1,901	1,832	25.5	26.0	25.0
48500	28 025	Clay.	416	2,507	21,210	21,131	21,979	21,120	1,758	1,696	1,624	51.9	53.8	51.7
17260	28 027	Coahoma.	583	1,812	28,420	28,654	30,622	31,665	1,469	1,385	1,225	51.3	55.1	57.1
27140	28 029	Copiah.	779	1,212	29,223	28,932	28,757	27,592	1,441	1,430	1,370	37.6	37.0	35.5
...	28 031	Covington.	415	2,511	20,447	20,107	19,407	16,527	1,799	1,825	1,888	49.4	47.0	39.9
32820	28 033	DeSoto.	497	2,195	144,706	136,668	107,199	67,910	414	498	652	302.8	227.3	142.0
25620	28 035	Forrest.	470	2,279	76,372	74,915	72,604	68,314	693	686	646	163.7	156.0	146.4
...	28 037	Franklin.	567	1,943	8,269	8,293	8,448	8,377	2,574	2,568	2,525	14.6	15.0	14.8
37700	28 039	George.	484	2,232	21,828	21,171	19,144	16,673	1,726	1,842	1,870	45.6	40.2	34.9
24980	28 041	Greene.	719	1,372	13,103	13,145	13,299	10,220	2,235	2,206	2,370	18.4	18.7	14.3
25060	28 043	Grenada.	449	2,343	22,861	22,689	23,263	21,555	1,679	1,631	1,600	54.2	55.0	51.1
25060	28 045	Hancock.	553	1,994	40,421	46,546	42,967	31,760	1,149	1,036	1,219	84.8	90.8	66.6
25060	28 047	Harrison.	976	802	171,875	193,187	189,601	165,365	343	290	288	295.8	326.5	284.6
27140	28 049	Hinds.	877	1,026	249,012	248,124	250,800	254,441	246	229	197	286.5	288.3	292.7
...	28 051	Holmes.	764	1,252	20,866	20,921	21,609	21,604	1,766	1,714	1,598	27.6	28.6	28.6
...	28 053	Humphreys.	431	2,438	10,393	10,401	11,206	12,134	2,412	2,357	2,204	24.9	26.6	29.0
...	28 055	Issaquena.	441	2,380	1,805	1,899	2,274	1,909	3,068	3,043	3,074	4.4	5.5	4.6
46180	28 057	Itawamba.	540	2,038	23,352	23,285	22,770	20,017	1,658	1,659	1,676	43.9	42.9	37.6
37700	28 059	Jackson.	1,043	721	130,577	135,571	131,420	115,243	448	407	400	179.6	181.4	158.6
29860	28 061	Jasper.	677	1,501	18,197	17,964	18,149	17,114	1,909	1,892	1,843	26.9	26.8	25.3
...	28 063	Jefferson.	527	2,077	9,194	9,329	9,740	8,653	2,509	2,468	2,495	17.7	18.7	16.7
...	28 065	Jefferson Davis.	409	2,549	13,184	13,059	13,962	14,051	2,233	2,166	2,053	32.3	34.0	34.4
29860	28 067	Jones.	700	1,441	66,715	66,103	64,958	62,031	768	748	702	96.2	93.7	89.4
32940	28 069	Kemper.	767	1,242	10,108	10,214	10,453	10,356	2,437	2,401	2,354	13.2	13.6	13.5
37060	28 071	Lafayette.	679	1,495	40,865	40,262	38,738	31,826	1,140	1,147	1,217	64.8	61.4	50.4
25060	28 073	Lamar.	500	2,178	46,240	44,429	39,070	30,424	1,015	1,137	1,272	93.0	79.2	61.2
32940	28 075	Lauderdale.	715	1,397	76,724	76,935	78,161	75,555	688	650	596	109.1	111.0	107.4
...	28 077	Lawrence.	436	2,410	13,457	13,405	13,258	12,458	2,210	2,209	2,185	31.2	30.9	28.9
...	28 079	Leake.	585	1,798	22,769	22,528	20,940	18,436	1,681	1,741	1,766	39.1	35.9	31.6
46180	28 081	Lee.	453	2,327	79,714	78,495	75,755	65,579	676	662	668	177.3	169.0	145.8
24900	28 083	Leflore.	606	1,718	35,752	35,938	37,947	37,341	1,264	1,168	1,063	60.4	64.0	63.1
15020	28 085	Lincoln.	588	1,782	34,404	33,832	33,166	30,278	1,308	1,311	1,281	58.7	56.6	51.7
18060	28 087	Lowndes.	516	2,112	59,773	59,703	61,586	59,308	842	790	732	119.0	122.5	118.1
27140	28 089	Madison.	742	1,295	87,419	84,169	74,674	53,794	628	671	799	121.9	104.7	74.8
...	28 091	Marion.	549	2,006	25,730	25,274	25,595	25,544	1,556	1,533	1,443	47.4	47.2	47.1
32820	28 093	Marshall.	710	1,417	35,853	35,582	34,993	30,361	1,261	1,250	1,275	50.8	49.7	43.0
...	28 095	Monroe.	772	1,230	37,572	37,540	38,014	36,582	1,218	1,166	1,087	49.2	49.7	47.9
...	28 097	Montgomery.	408	2,556	11,754	11,722	12,189	12,387	2,311	2,284	2,190	28.9	29.8	30.4
...	28 099	Neshoba.	572	1,910	30,125	29,889	28,684	24,800	1,415	1,431	1,470	52.9	50.4	43.5

See footnotes at end of table.

Table B-1. Counties — **Area and Population**—Con.

[Includes United States, states, and 3,141 counties/county equivalents defined as of February 22, 2005. For more information on these areas, see Appendix C, Geographic Information]

Metro-politan area code	FIPS state and county code[1]	County	Area, 2000 (square miles) Total	Rank[2]	Population 2006 (July 1)	2005 (July 1)	2000[3] (April 1 estimates base)	1990[3] (April 1 estimates base)	Rank 2006[2]	2000[2]	1990[4]	Persons per square mile of land area 2006[5]	2000	1990
		MISSISSIPPI—Con.												
...	28 101	Newton	580	1,835	22,413	22,218	21,838	20,291	1,704	1,699	1,661	38.8	37.8	35.1
...	28 103	Noxubee	700	1,437	12,051	12,118	12,548	12,604	2,298	2,262	2,177	17.3	18.0	18.1
44260	28 105	Oktibbeha	462	2,308	41,633	41,288	42,902	38,375	1,111	1,039	1,043	91.0	93.8	83.8
...	28 107	Panola	705	1,427	35,427	35,217	34,280	29,996	1,275	1,272	1,297	51.8	50.3	43.8
38100	28 109	Pearl River	819	1,133	57,099	52,458	48,621	38,714	869	936	1,035	70.4	60.1	47.7
25620	28 111	Perry	650	1,575	12,132	12,058	12,138	10,865	2,288	2,289	2,307	18.7	18.8	16.8
32620	28 113	Pike	411	2,539	40,240	39,204	38,940	36,882	1,155	1,144	1,078	98.4	95.4	90.2
46180	28 115	Pontotoc	501	2,177	28,887	28,389	26,726	22,237	1,451	1,495	1,568	58.1	53.8	44.7
...	28 117	Prentiss	418	2,495	25,615	25,657	25,558	23,278	1,559	1,537	1,526	61.7	61.7	56.1
...	28 119	Quitman	406	2,566	9,289	9,476	10,115	10,490	2,498	2,436	2,337	22.9	24.8	25.9
27140	28 121	Rankin	806	1,157	135,830	131,521	115,327	87,161	437	467	523	175.4	150.0	112.5
...	28 123	Scott	610	1,707	28,790	28,627	28,423	24,137	1,453	1,435	1,489	47.3	46.6	39.6
...	28 125	Sharkey	435	2,415	5,851	5,967	6,580	7,066	2,781	2,731	2,651	13.7	15.3	16.5
27140	28 127	Simpson	591	1,775	27,972	27,934	27,639	23,953	1,488	1,461	1,495	47.5	47.0	40.7
...	28 129	Smith	637	1,619	15,970	15,920	16,182	14,798	2,047	2,011	2,001	25.1	25.5	23.3
25060	28 131	Stone	448	2,345	15,608	14,883	13,622	10,750	2,067	2,192	2,312	35.0	30.7	24.1
26940	28 133	Sunflower	707	1,423	31,833	31,885	34,369	35,129	1,374	1,269	1,127	45.9	49.4	50.6
...	28 135	Tallahatchie	652	1,566	13,798	14,069	14,903	15,210	2,183	2,099	1,975	21.4	23.1	23.6
32820	28 137	Tate	411	2,534	26,723	26,423	25,370	21,432	1,529	1,549	1,607	66.1	62.9	53.0
...	28 139	Tippah	460	2,313	21,248	21,192	20,826	19,523	1,754	1,744	1,699	46.4	45.6	42.6
...	28 141	Tishomingo	445	2,361	19,112	19,090	19,161	17,683	1,865	1,839	1,806	45.1	45.2	41.7
32820	28 143	Tunica	481	2,239	10,419	10,231	9,227	8,164	2,408	2,511	2,549	22.9	20.3	17.9
...	28 145	Union	417	2,503	27,008	26,757	25,362	22,085	1,517	1,550	1,572	65.0	61.6	53.2
...	28 147	Walthall	404	2,575	15,543	15,271	15,156	14,352	2,073	2,081	2,027	38.5	37.4	35.5
46980	28 149	Warren	619	1,678	49,308	48,745	49,644	47,880	965	923	876	84.1	84.5	81.6
24740	28 151	Washington	761	1,260	58,007	58,762	62,977	67,935	855	771	651	80.1	86.7	93.8
...	28 153	Wayne	814	1,147	21,087	21,109	21,216	19,517	1,760	1,725	1,700	26.0	26.2	24.1
...	28 155	Webster	423	2,473	10,041	10,031	10,294	10,222	2,440	2,416	2,369	23.8	24.4	24.2
...	28 157	Wilkinson	688	1,474	10,239	10,134	10,312	9,678	2,428	2,414	2,414	15.1	15.2	14.3
...	28 159	Winston	610	1,708	19,708	19,759	20,160	19,433	1,834	1,784	1,708	32.5	33.2	32.0
...	28 161	Yalobusha	495	2,200	13,401	13,363	13,051	12,033	2,222	2,230	2,215	28.7	28.1	25.8
49540	28 163	Yazoo	934	862	27,929	27,818	28,149	25,506	1,491	1,447	1,448	30.4	30.6	27.7
	29 000	MISSOURI	69,704	(X)	5,842,713	5,797,703	5,596,683	5,116,901	(X)	(X)	(X)	84.8	81.4	74.3
28860	29 001	Adair	569	1,935	24,461	24,452	24,977	24,577	1,608	1,561	1,478	43.1	44.0	43.3
41140	29 003	Andrew	437	2,404	17,177	16,824	16,492	14,632	1,955	1,991	2,009	39.5	38.0	33.6
...	29 005	Atchison	547	2,011	6,132	6,215	6,431	7,457	2,757	2,746	2,617	11.3	11.8	13.7
33020	29 007	Audrain	697	1,449	25,739	25,666	25,853	23,599	1,555	1,524	1,509	37.1	37.2	34.0
...	29 009	Barry	791	1,198	36,404	35,651	34,011	27,547	1,245	1,281	1,371	46.7	43.7	35.4
...	29 011	Barton	597	1,752	13,015	13,045	12,541	11,312	2,240	2,263	2,274	21.9	21.1	19.0
28140	29 013	Bates	851	1,082	17,116	16,989	16,653	15,025	1,960	1,983	1,986	20.2	19.7	17.7
...	29 015	Benton	752	1,274	18,728	18,740	17,180	13,859	1,884	1,943	2,066	26.5	24.5	19.6
16020	29 017	Bollinger	621	1,666	12,323	12,308	12,029	10,619	2,282	2,294	2,325	19.9	19.4	17.1
17860	29 019	Boone	691	1,461	146,048	143,343	135,454	112,379	410	398	409	213.1	198.1	164.0
41140	29 021	Buchanan	415	2,515	84,955	84,875	86,002	83,083	640	606	548	207.3	210.1	202.8
38740	29 023	Butler	699	1,442	41,582	41,338	40,867	38,765	1,113	1,087	1,032	59.6	58.5	55.6
28140	29 025	Caldwell	430	2,445	9,313	9,232	8,969	8,380	2,496	2,530	2,524	21.7	21.0	19.5
27620	29 027	Callaway	847	1,087	43,072	42,477	40,766	32,809	1,080	1,090	1,195	51.3	48.8	39.1
...	29 029	Camden	709	1,421	40,283	39,357	37,051	27,495	1,153	1,189	1,375	61.5	56.8	42.0
16020	29 031	Cape Girardeau	586	1,791	71,892	71,100	68,693	61,633	725	717	708	124.2	118.8	106.5
...	29 033	Carroll	702	1,432	10,058	10,160	10,285	10,748	2,439	2,418	2,313	14.5	14.8	15.5
...	29 035	Carter	509	2,138	5,956	5,909	5,941	5,515	2,774	2,790	2,801	11.7	11.7	10.9
28140	29 037	Cass	703	1,430	95,781	93,752	82,092	63,808	579	633	686	137.0	118.2	91.3
...	29 039	Cedar	499	2,185	13,998	14,093	13,733	12,093	2,170	2,181	2,210	29.4	28.9	25.4
...	29 041	Chariton	768	1,237	8,046	8,108	8,438	9,202	2,589	2,569	2,453	10.6	11.1	12.2
44180	29 043	Christian	564	1,959	70,514	67,306	54,285	32,644	736	867	1,199	125.2	97.6	58.0
22800	29 045	Clark	512	2,128	7,305	7,313	7,416	7,547	2,654	2,648	2,612	14.4	14.6	14.9
28140	29 047	Clay	409	2,551	206,957	201,681	183,975	153,411	288	296	302	522.2	466.2	387.0
28140	29 049	Clinton	423	2,471	20,671	20,673	18,975	16,595	1,780	1,849	1,879	49.4	45.5	39.6
27620	29 051	Cole	399	2,601	73,296	72,739	71,397	63,579	710	693	688	187.2	182.6	162.4
...	29 053	Cooper	570	1,929	17,441	17,285	16,670	14,835	1,947	1,980	1,998	30.9	29.6	26.3
...	29 055	Crawford	744	1,290	24,009	23,810	22,804	19,173	1,629	1,655	1,722	32.3	30.8	25.8
...	29 057	Dade	506	2,153	7,804	7,813	7,923	7,449	2,613	2,613	2,619	15.9	16.1	15.2
44180	29 059	Dallas	543	2,028	16,696	16,404	15,661	12,646	1,993	2,044	2,172	30.8	29.0	23.3
...	29 061	Daviess	569	1,936	8,072	8,059	8,016	7,865	2,585	2,604	2,584	14.2	14.1	13.9
41140	29 063	DeKalb	426	2,460	12,309	12,289	13,077	9,967	2,284	2,226	2,389	29.0	30.9	23.5
...	29 065	Dent	755	1,270	15,276	15,094	14,927	13,702	2,087	2,098	2,080	20.3	19.8	18.2
...	29 067	Douglas	815	1,141	13,658	13,574	13,084	11,876	2,193	2,225	2,225	16.8	16.1	14.6
28380	29 069	Dunklin	547	2,012	32,277	32,435	33,157	33,112	1,362	1,312	1,187	59.2	60.7	60.7

See footnotes at end of table.

[Includes United States, states, and 3,141 counties/county equivalents defined as of February 22, 2005. For more information on these areas, see Appendix C, Geographic Information]

Metro-politan area code	FIPS state and county code[1]	County	Area, 2000 (square miles)		Population									
			Total	Rank[2]	2006 (July 1)	2005 (July 1)	2000[3] (April 1 estimates base)	1990[3] (April 1 estimates base)	Rank			Persons per square mile of land area		
									2006[2]	2000[2]	1990[4]	2006[5]	2000	1990
		MISSOURI—Con.												
41180	29 071	Franklin	931	873	100,067	98,987	93,807	80,603	561	546	565	108.4	102.0	87.4
...	29 073	Gasconade	526	2,083	15,634	15,695	15,342	14,006	2,066	2,067	2,056	30.0	29.6	27.0
...	29 075	Gentry	492	2,210	6,389	6,510	6,861	6,854	2,737	2,703	2,673	13.0	14.0	13.9
44180	29 077	Greene	678	1,498	254,779	250,473	240,391	207,949	239	239	240	377.5	356.5	308.1
...	29 079	Grundy	438	2,392	10,239	10,293	10,432	10,536	2,428	2,403	2,332	23.5	23.9	24.2
...	29 081	Harrison	726	1,330	8,898	8,900	8,850	8,469	2,530	2,541	2,515	12.3	12.2	11.7
...	29 083	Henry	733	1,315	22,719	22,563	21,997	20,044	1,686	1,694	1,675	32.3	31.5	28.5
...	29 085	Hickory	412	2,530	9,243	9,221	8,940	7,335	2,506	2,532	2,626	23.2	22.4	18.4
...	29 087	Holt	469	2,283	4,997	5,062	5,351	6,034	2,840	2,826	2,753	10.8	11.5	13.1
17860	29 089	Howard	471	2,275	9,949	9,930	10,212	9,631	2,447	2,426	2,421	21.4	21.9	20.7
48460	29 091	Howell	928	875	38,734	38,415	37,238	31,447	1,187	1,185	1,232	41.8	40.1	33.9
...	29 093	Iron	552	1,998	10,279	10,266	10,697	10,726	2,424	2,384	2,316	18.6	19.3	19.5
28140	29 095	Jackson	616	1,687	664,078	662,133	654,880	633,234	89	81	74	1,097.9	1,084.0	1,047.0
27900	29 097	Jasper	641	1,602	112,505	110,533	104,686	90,465	512	504	506	175.9	164.1	141.4
41180	29 099	Jefferson	664	1,527	216,469	213,011	198,099	171,380	281	280	282	329.6	302.7	260.9
47660	29 101	Johnson	833	1,108	50,646	50,611	48,258	42,514	945	943	944	61.0	58.3	51.2
...	29 103	Knox	507	2,150	4,093	4,160	4,361	4,482	2,903	2,891	2,876	8.1	8.6	8.9
30060	29 105	Laclede	768	1,240	35,091	34,413	32,513	27,158	1,292	1,331	1,384	45.8	42.6	35.5
28140	29 107	Lafayette	639	1,613	33,186	33,104	32,960	31,107	1,333	1,322	1,241	52.7	52.5	49.4
...	29 109	Lawrence	613	1,697	37,400	37,072	35,203	30,236	1,220	1,243	1,283	61.0	57.6	49.3
39500	29 111	Lewis	511	2,132	10,152	10,140	10,494	10,233	2,435	2,399	2,365	20.1	20.8	20.3
41180	29 113	Lincoln	640	1,608	50,123	47,834	38,946	28,892	951	1,142	1,333	79.5	62.3	45.8
...	29 115	Linn	621	1,663	12,865	13,075	13,754	13,885	2,254	2,180	2,065	20.7	22.1	22.4
...	29 117	Livingston	538	2,046	14,291	14,266	14,558	14,592	2,147	2,118	2,013	26.7	27.1	27.3
22220	29 119	McDonald	540	2,040	22,949	22,785	21,681	16,938	1,671	1,709	1,851	42.5	40.2	31.4
...	29 121	Macon	813	1,149	15,651	15,603	15,762	15,345	2,064	2,035	1,968	19.5	19.6	19.1
...	29 123	Madison	498	2,190	12,109	12,079	11,800	11,127	2,291	2,307	2,283	24.4	23.8	22.4
...	29 125	Maries	530	2,069	9,099	8,985	8,903	7,976	2,520	2,534	2,570	17.2	16.9	15.1
25300	29 127	Marion	444	2,364	28,425	28,286	28,289	27,682	1,468	1,438	1,363	64.9	64.6	63.2
...	29 129	Mercer	455	2,322	3,584	3,581	3,757	3,723	2,937	2,934	2,937	7.9	8.3	8.2
...	29 131	Miller	600	1,743	24,989	24,730	23,564	20,700	1,585	1,611	1,644	42.2	39.9	35.0
...	29 133	Mississippi	429	2,450	13,770	13,647	13,427	14,442	2,186	2,201	2,021	33.3	32.3	35.0
27620	29 135	Moniteau	419	2,493	15,092	15,121	14,827	12,298	2,100	2,103	2,196	36.2	35.6	29.5
...	29 137	Monroe	670	1,516	9,396	9,351	9,311	9,104	2,488	2,506	2,460	14.5	14.4	14.1
...	29 139	Montgomery	540	2,039	12,170	12,136	12,136	11,355	2,286	2,290	2,267	22.6	22.6	21.1
...	29 141	Morgan	614	1,694	20,716	20,426	19,309	15,574	1,777	1,829	1,949	34.7	32.4	26.1
...	29 143	New Madrid	698	1,445	18,314	18,498	19,758	20,928	1,899	1,806	1,633	27.0	29.0	30.9
27900	29 145	Newton	627	1,644	56,047	55,435	52,636	44,445	881	886	920	89.5	84.2	70.9
32340	29 147	Nodaway	878	1,023	21,660	21,712	21,912	21,709	1,737	1,697	1,592	24.7	24.9	24.8
...	29 149	Oregon	792	1,197	10,407	10,350	10,344	9,470	2,410	2,409	2,437	13.2	13.0	12.0
27620	29 151	Osage	613	1,696	13,498	13,400	13,062	12,018	2,207	2,228	2,218	22.3	21.6	19.8
...	29 153	Ozark	755	1,267	9,393	9,418	9,542	8,598	2,489	2,486	2,503	12.7	12.9	11.5
...	29 155	Pemiscot	512	2,124	19,163	19,312	20,047	21,921	1,863	1,791	1,582	38.9	40.6	44.5
...	29 157	Perry	484	2,227	18,639	18,507	18,132	16,648	1,885	1,893	1,874	39.3	38.2	35.1
42740	29 159	Pettis	686	1,476	40,520	40,092	39,403	35,437	1,146	1,127	1,115	59.2	57.6	51.7
40620	29 161	Phelps	674	1,507	42,289	41,978	39,825	35,248	1,096	1,116	1,123	62.9	59.3	52.4
...	29 163	Pike	685	1,478	18,566	18,655	18,351	15,969	1,888	1,877	1,926	27.6	27.2	23.7
28140	29 165	Platte	427	2,452	83,061	82,089	73,808	57,867	650	680	750	197.6	176.6	137.7
44180	29 167	Polk	642	1,595	29,596	28,952	26,992	21,826	1,430	1,484	1,588	46.4	42.5	34.3
22780	29 169	Pulaski	551	2,000	44,022	44,050	41,165	41,307	1,061	1,076	975	80.5	76.3	75.5
...	29 171	Putnam	520	2,102	5,153	5,128	5,223	5,079	2,831	2,837	2,833	9.9	10.1	9.8
25300	29 173	Ralls	484	2,230	9,925	9,856	9,626	8,476	2,448	2,477	2,514	21.1	20.5	18.0
33620	29 175	Randolph	488	2,218	25,438	25,360	24,663	24,370	1,568	1,570	1,482	52.7	51.1	50.5
28140	29 177	Ray	574	1,892	23,999	23,889	23,354	21,968	1,630	1,627	1,577	42.1	41.1	38.6
...	29 179	Reynolds	814	1,143	6,547	6,550	6,689	6,661	2,726	2,719	2,688	8.1	8.3	8.2
...	29 181	Ripley	632	1,637	13,937	13,881	13,509	12,303	2,172	2,196	2,194	22.1	21.4	19.5
41180	29 183	St. Charles	592	1,764	338,719	329,606	283,893	212,751	183	197	234	604.4	510.8	378.9
...	29 185	St. Clair	702	1,433	9,589	9,626	9,652	8,457	2,473	2,474	2,516	14.2	14.3	12.5
...	29 186	Ste. Genevieve	509	2,139	18,248	18,138	17,842	16,037	1,906	1,909	1,921	36.3	35.7	31.9
22100	29 187	St. Francois	452	2,330	62,181	61,515	55,641	48,904	820	848	858	138.3	124.1	108.8
41180	29 189	St. Louis	524	2,091	1,000,510	1,002,258	1,016,300	993,508	38	34	31	1,970.2	2,001.7	1,956.6
32180	29 195	Saline	765	1,250	22,896	23,018	23,756	23,523	1,675	1,601	1,512	30.3	31.4	31.1
28860	29 197	Schuyler	308	2,826	4,271	4,288	4,170	4,236	2,885	2,901	2,897	13.9	13.6	13.8
...	29 199	Scotland	439	2,388	4,922	4,916	4,983	4,822	2,845	2,851	2,854	11.2	11.4	11.0
43460	29 201	Scott	426	2,457	41,068	40,985	40,422	39,376	1,133	1,107	1,015	97.5	95.9	93.5
...	29 203	Shannon	1,004	764	8,503	8,379	8,324	7,613	2,563	2,580	2,609	8.5	8.3	7.6
...	29 205	Shelby	502	2,170	6,645	6,751	6,799	6,942	2,711	2,713	2,665	13.3	13.5	13.9
...	29 207	Stoddard	829	1,114	29,754	29,734	29,705	28,895	1,424	1,408	1,332	36.0	35.9	34.9
14700	29 209	Stone	511	2,131	31,382	30,777	28,658	19,078	1,385	1,432	1,729	67.7	62.0	41.2
...	29 211	Sullivan	651	1,568	6,785	6,869	7,219	6,326	2,698	2,665	2,719	10.4	11.1	9.7

See footnotes at end of table.

Table B-1. Counties — **Area and Population**—Con.

[Includes United States, states, and 3,141 counties/county equivalents defined as of February 22, 2005. For more information on these areas, see Appendix C, Geographic Information]

Metro-politan area code	FIPS state and county code[1]	County	Area, 2000 (square miles) Total	Rank[2]	Population 2006 (July 1)	2005 (July 1)	2000[3] (April 1 estimates base)	1990[3] (April 1 estimates base)	Rank 2006[2]	2000[2]	1990[4]	Persons per square mile of land area 2006[5]	2000	1990
		MISSOURI—Con.												
14700	29 213	Taney.	651	1,567	43,770	42,849	39,703	25,561	1,069	1,118	1,441	69.2	63.1	40.4
...	29 215	Texas.	1,179	596	23,566	23,292	23,003	21,476	1,647	1,642	1,604	20.0	19.5	18.2
...	29 217	Vernon.	837	1,098	20,455	20,426	20,454	19,041	1,797	1,762	1,732	24.5	24.5	22.8
41180	29 219	Warren.	438	2,394	29,685	28,765	24,523	19,534	1,426	1,578	1,697	68.8	57.4	45.2
41180	29 221	Washington.	762	1,258	24,182	23,972	23,344	20,380	1,624	1,628	1,657	31.8	30.9	26.8
...	29 223	Wayne.	774	1,224	12,997	13,100	13,259	11,543	2,245	2,208	2,253	17.1	17.4	15.2
44180	29 225	Webster.	594	1,760	35,507	34,734	31,045	23,753	1,272	1,377	1,501	59.8	52.7	40.0
...	29 227	Worth.	267	2,906	2,186	2,205	2,382	2,440	3,036	3,034	3,026	8.2	8.9	9.2
...	29 229	Wright.	683	1,481	18,397	18,310	17,955	16,758	1,893	1,901	1,864	27.0	26.3	24.6
		Independent City												
41180	29 510	St. Louis city.	66	3,102	347,181	352,572	348,189	396,685	181	167	126	5,606.9	5,600.4	6,405.4
	30 000	**MONTANA.**	147,042	(X)	944,632	934,737	902,195	799,065	(X)	(X)	(X)	6.5	6.2	5.5
...	30 001	Beaverhead.	5,572	68	8,743	8,778	9,202	8,424	2,543	2,514	2,518	1.6	1.7	1.5
...	30 003	Big Horn.	5,015	85	13,035	13,076	12,671	11,337	2,238	2,251	2,270	2.6	2.5	2.3
...	30 005	Blaine.	4,239	117	6,615	6,634	7,009	6,728	2,716	2,686	2,684	1.6	1.7	1.6
...	30 007	Broadwater.	1,239	559	4,572	4,506	4,385	3,318	2,865	2,888	2,970	3.8	3.7	2.8
13740	30 009	Carbon.	2,062	304	9,903	9,895	9,552	8,080	2,449	2,485	2,556	4.8	4.7	3.9
...	30 011	Carter.	3,348	158	1,321	1,320	1,360	1,503	3,096	3,099	3,097	0.4	0.4	0.5
24500	30 013	Cascade.	2,712	203	79,385	79,490	80,357	77,691	678	639	585	29.4	29.7	28.8
...	30 015	Chouteau.	3,997	129	5,417	5,464	5,970	5,452	2,808	2,788	2,804	1.4	1.5	1.4
...	30 017	Custer.	3,793	138	11,151	11,256	11,696	11,697	2,356	2,320	2,234	2.9	3.1	3.1
...	30 019	Daniels.	1,427	476	1,774	1,825	2,017	2,266	3,072	3,064	3,044	1.2	1.4	1.6
...	30 021	Dawson	2,383	249	8,624	8,629	9,059	9,505	2,557	2,526	2,433	3.6	3.8	4.0
...	30 023	Deer Lodge.	741	1,298	8,888	8,986	9,417	10,356	2,531	2,497	2,354	12.1	12.7	14.1
...	30 025	Fallon.	1,623	412	2,717	2,709	2,837	3,103	2,998	3,003	2,992	1.7	1.7	1.9
...	30 027	Fergus.	4,350	113	11,496	11,503	11,893	12,083	2,329	2,300	2,211	2.6	2.7	2.8
28060	30 029	Flathead.	5,256	76	85,314	83,079	74,471	59,218	638	673	735	16.7	14.7	11.6
14580	30 031	Gallatin[7].	2,632	214	80,921	78,262	67,831	50,484	665	723	834	31.1	26.2	20.1
...	30 033	Garfield.	4,848	88	1,244	1,211	1,279	1,589	3,100	3,101	3,091	0.3	0.3	0.3
...	30 035	Glacier.	3,037	181	13,578	13,522	13,247	12,121	2,201	2,211	2,207	4.5	4.4	4.0
...	30 037	Golden Valley.	1,176	597	1,150	1,146	1,042	912	3,103	3,109	3,116	1.0	0.9	0.8
...	30 039	Granite.	1,733	386	2,909	2,932	2,830	2,548	2,987	3,004	3,020	1.7	1.6	1.5
25660	30 041	Hill.	2,916	190	16,403	16,276	16,673	17,654	2,013	1,979	1,808	5.7	5.7	6.1
25740	30 043	Jefferson.	1,659	404	11,256	11,136	10,049	7,939	2,346	2,440	2,578	6.8	6.1	4.8
...	30 045	Judith Basin.	1,871	348	2,142	2,170	2,329	2,282	3,039	3,036	3,041	1.1	1.2	1.2
25740	30 047	Lake.	1,654	405	28,606	28,275	26,507	21,041	1,462	1,503	1,628	19.2	17.8	14.1
25740	30 049	Lewis and Clark.	3,498	152	59,302	58,387	55,716	47,495	847	847	884	17.1	16.1	13.7
...	30 051	Liberty.	1,447	463	1,863	1,967	2,158	2,295	3,064	3,054	3,039	1.3	1.5	1.6
...	30 053	Lincoln.	3,675	147	19,226	19,182	18,837	17,481	1,856	1,853	1,821	5.3	5.2	4.8
...	30 055	McCone.	2,683	206	1,760	1,776	1,977	2,276	3,073	3,065	3,043	0.7	0.7	0.9
...	30 057	Madison.	3,603	149	7,404	7,252	6,851	5,989	2,647	2,706	2,759	2.1	1.9	1.7
...	30 059	Meagher.	2,395	247	1,968	1,961	1,932	1,819	3,053	3,069	3,077	0.8	0.8	0.8
...	30 061	Mineral.	1,223	575	4,057	4,033	3,884	3,315	2,906	2,924	2,974	3.3	3.2	2.7
33540	30 063	Missoula.	2,618	216	101,417	100,033	95,802	78,687	550	541	575	39.0	37.0	30.3
...	30 065	Musselshell.	1,871	347	4,586	4,474	4,497	4,106	2,863	2,881	2,908	2.5	2.4	2.2
...	30 067	Park[7].	2,814	196	16,084	15,965	15,694	14,515	2,042	2,039	2,018	5.7	5.6	5.5
...	30 069	Petroleum.	1,674	400	474	462	493	519	3,136	3,136	3,134	0.3	0.3	0.3
...	30 071	Phillips.	5,212	77	4,098	4,135	4,601	5,163	2,901	2,873	2,829	0.8	0.9	1.0
...	30 073	Pondera.	1,640	409	6,032	6,084	6,424	6,433	2,767	2,749	2,714	3.7	3.9	4.0
...	30 075	Powder River.	3,298	163	1,756	1,714	1,858	2,090	3,074	3,075	3,063	0.5	0.6	0.6
...	30 077	Powell.	2,333	260	6,997	6,968	7,180	6,620	2,677	2,669	2,695	3.0	3.1	2.8
...	30 079	Prairie.	1,743	385	1,074	1,090	1,199	1,383	3,105	3,104	3,103	0.6	0.7	0.8
...	30 081	Ravalli.	2,400	242	40,582	39,822	36,070	25,010	1,143	1,213	1,462	17.0	15.2	10.4
...	30 083	Richland.	2,103	297	9,295	9,163	9,667	10,716	2,497	2,473	2,318	4.5	4.6	5.1
...	30 085	Roosevelt.	2,370	252	10,496	10,601	10,620	10,999	2,399	2,389	2,294	4.5	4.5	4.7
...	30 087	Rosebud.	5,027	83	9,261	9,279	9,383	10,505	2,503	2,500	2,335	1.8	1.9	2.1
...	30 089	Sanders.	2,790	200	11,138	11,009	10,227	8,669	2,358	2,423	2,494	4.0	3.7	3.1
...	30 091	Sheridan.	1,706	391	3,447	3,517	4,105	4,732	2,944	2,907	2,860	2.1	2.4	2.8
15580	30 093	Silver Bow.	719	1,370	32,801	32,876	34,606	33,941	1,345	1,263	1,166	45.7	48.1	47.2
...	30 095	Stillwater.	1,805	365	8,646	8,468	8,195	6,536	2,553	2,595	2,703	4.8	4.6	3.6
...	30 097	Sweet Grass.	1,862	350	3,760	3,698	3,609	3,154	2,924	2,943	2,988	2.0	2.0	1.7
...	30 099	Teton.	2,293	268	6,115	6,174	6,445	6,271	2,758	2,744	2,727	2.7	2.8	2.8
...	30 101	Toole.	1,946	322	5,073	5,174	5,267	5,046	2,834	2,834	2,838	2.7	2.8	2.6
...	30 103	Treasure.	984	789	680	694	861	874	3,128	3,118	3,119	0.7	0.9	0.9
...	30 105	Valley.	5,062	81	6,995	7,144	7,675	8,239	2,680	2,632	2,545	1.4	1.6	1.7
...	30 107	Wheatland.	1,428	475	1,959	2,025	2,259	2,246	3,054	3,045	3,051	1.4	1.6	1.6
...	30 109	Wibaux.	890	998	909	944	1,068	1,191	3,114	3,107	3,108	1.0	1.2	1.3
13740	30 111	Yellowstone.	2,649	210	138,213	136,586	129,352	113,419	431	415	404	52.4	49.2	43.0
...	30 113	Yellowstone National Park[7].	(X)	(X)	(X)	(X)	(X)	(X)	(X)	(X)	(X)	(NA)	(NA)	(NA)

See footnotes at end of table.

[Includes United States, states, and 3,141 counties/county equivalents defined as of February 22, 2005. For more information on these areas, see Appendix C, Geographic Information]

Metropolitan area code	FIPS state and county code[1]	County	Area, 2000 (square miles)		Population				Rank			Persons per square mile of land area		
			Total	Rank[2]	2006 (July 1)	2005 (July 1)	2000[3] (April 1 estimates base)	1990[3] (April 1 estimates base)	2006[2]	2000[2]	1990[4]	2006[5]	2000	1990
	31 000	NEBRASKA	77,354	(X)	1,768,331	1,758,163	1,711,265	1,578,417	(X)	(X)	(X)	23.0	22.3	20.5
25580	31 001	Adams	564	1,957	33,185	33,123	31,151	29,625	1,334	1,374	1,312	58.9	55.3	52.6
...	31 003	Antelope	858	1,071	6,931	7,032	7,452	7,965	2,685	2,645	2,576	8.1	8.7	9.3
...	31 005	Arthur	718	1,381	372	374	444	462	3,138	3,137	3,136	0.5	0.6	0.6
42420	31 007	Banner	746	1,283	783	754	819	852	3,121	3,122	3,120	1.0	1.1	1.1
...	31 009	Blaine	714	1,401	492	482	583	675	3,135	3,133	3,131	0.7	0.8	0.9
...	31 011	Boone	687	1,475	5,668	5,777	6,259	6,667	2,790	2,761	2,687	8.3	9.1	9.7
...	31 013	Box Butte	1,078	687	11,132	11,302	12,158	13,130	2,360	2,288	2,128	10.4	11.3	12.2
...	31 015	Boyd	545	2,021	2,185	2,252	2,438	2,835	3,037	3,027	3,009	4.0	4.5	5.2
...	31 017	Brown	1,225	573	3,354	3,335	3,525	3,657	2,950	2,952	2,943	2.7	2.9	3.0
28260	31 019	Buffalo	975	804	43,954	43,640	42,259	37,447	1,062	1,051	1,060	45.4	43.7	38.7
...	31 021	Burt	497	2,194	7,341	7,405	7,791	7,868	2,651	2,627	2,583	14.9	15.8	16.0
...	31 023	Butler	584	1,804	8,595	8,666	8,861	8,601	2,559	2,539	2,502	14.7	15.2	14.7
36540	31 025	Cass	566	1,948	25,963	25,777	24,334	21,318	1,549	1,582	1,616	46.4	43.6	38.1
...	31 027	Cedar	746	1,284	8,819	9,017	9,615	10,131	2,535	2,479	2,375	11.9	12.9	13.7
...	31 029	Chase	898	977	3,811	3,861	4,068	4,381	2,920	2,914	2,884	4.3	4.5	4.9
...	31 031	Cherry	6,010	65	5,934	6,079	6,148	6,307	2,778	2,769	2,720	1.0	1.0	1.1
...	31 033	Cheyenne	1,196	586	9,865	10,011	9,830	9,494	2,455	2,463	2,434	8.2	8.2	7.9
25580	31 035	Clay	574	1,893	6,564	6,671	7,039	7,123	2,724	2,681	2,642	11.5	12.3	12.4
...	31 037	Colfax	419	2,494	10,113	10,292	10,441	9,139	2,436	2,402	2,456	24.5	25.3	22.1
...	31 039	Cuming	575	1,886	9,660	9,730	10,203	10,117	2,468	2,428	2,376	16.9	17.8	17.7
...	31 041	Custer	2,576	221	11,242	11,385	11,793	12,270	2,348	2,309	2,198	4.4	4.6	4.8
43580	31 043	Dakota	267	2,903	20,587	20,331	20,253	16,742	1,788	1,776	1,866	78.0	76.9	63.4
...	31 045	Dawes	1,401	484	8,466	8,592	9,060	9,021	2,565	2,525	2,467	6.1	6.5	6.5
30420	31 047	Dawson	1,019	746	25,018	24,642	24,365	19,940	1,584	1,581	1,683	24.7	24.1	19.7
...	31 049	Deuel	441	2,381	1,958	1,985	2,098	2,237	3,055	3,058	3,052	4.5	4.8	5.1
43580	31 051	Dixon	483	2,235	6,170	6,174	6,339	6,143	2,751	2,754	2,740	13.0	13.3	12.9
23340	31 053	Dodge	544	2,022	36,171	36,064	36,160	34,500	1,252	1,210	1,150	67.7	67.6	64.5
36540	31 055	Douglas	340	2,761	492,003	486,854	463,585	416,444	131	124	121	1,486.5	1,403.7	1,258.0
...	31 057	Dundy	921	890	2,109	2,138	2,292	2,582	3,042	3,040	3,017	2.3	2.5	2.8
...	31 059	Fillmore	577	1,855	6,259	6,338	6,634	7,103	2,744	2,723	2,645	10.9	11.5	12.3
...	31 061	Franklin	576	1,858	3,348	3,409	3,574	3,938	2,951	2,946	2,923	5.8	6.2	6.8
...	31 063	Frontier	980	794	2,729	2,776	3,099	3,101	2,995	2,985	2,993	2.8	3.2	3.2
...	31 065	Furnas	721	1,361	5,003	5,020	5,324	5,553	2,839	2,829	2,796	7.0	7.4	7.7
13100	31 067	Gage	860	1,066	23,365	23,273	22,993	22,794	1,657	1,644	1,544	27.3	26.9	26.6
...	31 069	Garden	1,731	388	1,995	2,005	2,292	2,460	3,050	3,040	3,024	1.2	1.3	1.4
...	31 071	Garfield	571	1,915	1,790	1,813	1,902	2,141	3,070	3,073	3,058	3.1	3.3	3.8
30420	31 073	Gosper	463	2,307	1,978	2,007	2,143	1,928	3,052	3,057	3,070	4.3	4.7	4.2
...	31 075	Grant	783	1,207	660	661	747	769	3,129	3,129	3,125	0.9	1.0	1.0
...	31 077	Greeley	571	1,923	2,454	2,475	2,714	3,006	3,019	3,013	2,999	4.3	4.7	5.3
24260	31 079	Hall	552	1,996	55,555	55,001	53,534	48,925	887	874	857	101.7	97.9	89.5
...	31 081	Hamilton	547	2,013	9,490	9,501	9,403	8,862	2,479	2,498	2,483	17.5	17.3	16.3
...	31 083	Harlan	574	1,889	3,446	3,486	3,786	3,810	2,945	2,930	2,930	6.2	6.8	6.9
...	31 085	Hayes	713	1,408	1,029	1,051	1,068	1,222	3,108	3,107	3,107	1.4	1.5	1.7
...	31 087	Hitchcock	719	1,374	2,926	2,953	3,111	3,750	2,985	2,984	2,935	4.1	4.4	5.3
...	31 089	Holt	2,418	240	10,610	10,796	11,551	12,599	2,394	2,330	2,178	4.4	4.8	5.2
...	31 091	Hooker	722	1,356	756	749	783	793	3,122	3,126	3,124	1.0	1.1	1.1
24260	31 093	Howard	576	1,864	6,736	6,678	6,567	6,057	2,703	2,732	2,750	11.8	11.5	10.6
...	31 095	Jefferson	576	1,869	7,874	7,932	8,333	8,759	2,602	2,579	2,489	13.7	14.5	15.3
...	31 097	Johnson	377	2,666	4,683	4,698	4,488	4,673	2,855	2,882	2,863	12.5	11.9	12.4
28260	31 099	Kearney	516	2,117	6,701	6,757	6,882	6,629	2,706	2,699	2,692	13.0	13.3	12.8
...	31 101	Keith	1,110	657	8,250	8,309	8,875	8,584	2,576	2,536	2,505	7.8	8.3	8.1
...	31 103	Keya Paha	774	1,222	892	907	983	1,029	3,115	3,112	3,111	1.2	1.3	1.3
...	31 105	Kimball	952	834	3,710	3,761	4,089	4,108	2,926	2,910	2,907	3.9	4.3	4.3
...	31 107	Knox	1,140	629	8,812	8,838	9,374	9,564	2,536	2,501	2,427	8.0	8.4	8.6
30700	31 109	Lancaster	847	1,088	267,135	264,704	250,291	213,641	229	230	233	318.4	299.4	254.7
35820	31 111	Lincoln	2,575	222	35,865	35,515	34,632	32,508	1,260	1,262	1,201	14.0	13.5	12.7
35820	31 113	Logan	571	1,916	749	736	774	878	3,123	3,127	3,118	1.3	1.4	1.5
...	31 115	Loup	571	1,919	656	674	712	683	3,130	3,132	3,130	1.2	1.3	1.2
35820	31 117	McPherson	860	1,065	497	502	533	546	3,134	3,135	3,133	0.6	0.6	0.6
35740	31 119	Madison	575	1,877	35,279	35,521	35,226	32,655	1,283	1,241	1,197	61.6	61.4	57.0
24260	31 121	Merrick	495	2,201	7,954	8,024	8,204	8,062	2,595	2,593	2,557	16.4	16.8	16.6
...	31 123	Morrill	1,430	474	5,171	5,159	5,440	5,423	2,828	2,822	2,805	3.6	3.8	3.8
...	31 125	Nance	448	2,346	3,705	3,710	4,038	4,275	2,927	2,919	2,891	8.4	9.2	9.7
...	31 127	Nemaha	412	2,529	7,247	7,120	7,576	7,980	2,663	2,639	2,569	17.7	18.5	19.5
...	31 129	Nuckolls	576	1,861	4,650	4,743	5,057	5,786	2,857	2,849	2,780	8.1	8.7	10.1
...	31 131	Otoe	619	1,676	15,747	15,507	15,396	14,252	2,057	2,060	2,034	25.6	25.1	23.1
...	31 133	Pawnee	433	2,425	2,804	2,867	3,087	3,317	2,992	2,986	2,972	6.5	7.1	7.7
...	31 135	Perkins	884	1,011	2,992	3,087	3,200	3,367	2,978	2,979	2,965	3.4	3.6	3.8
...	31 137	Phelps	541	2,036	9,442	9,460	9,747	9,715	2,482	2,467	2,409	17.5	18.0	18.0
35740	31 139	Pierce	575	1,871	7,564	7,658	7,857	7,827	2,635	2,619	2,592	13.2	13.7	13.6

See footnotes at end of table.

[Includes United States, states, and 3,141 counties/county equivalents defined as of February 22, 2005. For more information on these areas, see Appendix C, Geographic Information]

Metropolitan area code	FIPS state and county code[1]	County	Area, 2000 (square miles)		Population				Rank			Persons per square mile of land area		
			Total	Rank[2]	2006 (July 1)	2005 (July 1)	2000[3] (April 1 estimates base)	1990[3] (April 1 estimates base)	2006[2]	2000[2]	1990[4]	2006[5]	2000	1990
		NEBRASKA—Con.												
18100	31 141	Platte	689	1,466	31,962	31,590	31,568	29,820	1,370	1,360	1,303	47.1	46.5	44.0
...	31 143	Polk	441	2,382	5,349	5,394	5,639	5,655	2,812	2,812	2,787	12.2	12.8	12.9
...	31 145	Red Willow	718	1,385	10,865	11,044	11,450	11,705	2,375	2,339	2,232	15.2	16.0	16.3
...	31 147	Richardson	556	1,987	8,656	8,755	9,531	9,937	2,550	2,488	2,391	15.6	17.2	18.0
...	31 149	Rock	1,012	753	1,544	1,558	1,756	2,019	3,083	3,082	3,065	1.5	1.7	2.0
...	31 151	Saline	576	1,859	14,155	14,237	13,843	12,715	2,158	2,173	2,165	24.6	24.1	22.1
36540	31 153	Sarpy	247	2,953	142,637	139,245	122,595	102,583	419	443	448	593.0	512.3	426.2
36540	31 155	Saunders	759	1,264	20,344	20,439	19,830	18,285	1,805	1,801	1,774	27.0	26.3	24.2
42420	31 157	Scotts Bluff	746	1,285	36,546	36,641	36,951	36,025	1,243	1,192	1,100	49.4	50.0	48.7
30700	31 159	Seward	576	1,865	16,835	16,736	16,496	15,450	1,982	1,990	1,957	29.3	28.8	26.9
...	31 161	Sheridan	2,470	232	5,571	5,653	6,198	6,750	2,795	2,763	2,681	2.3	2.5	2.8
...	31 163	Sherman	572	1,911	3,083	3,106	3,318	3,718	2,970	2,972	2,939	5.4	5.8	6.6
...	31 165	Sioux	2,067	303	1,403	1,438	1,475	1,549	3,092	3,094	3,093	0.7	0.7	0.7
35740	31 167	Stanton	431	2,439	6,570	6,533	6,455	6,244	2,722	2,743	2,730	15.3	14.9	14.5
...	31 169	Thayer	575	1,870	5,317	5,441	6,055	6,635	2,817	2,776	2,691	9.3	10.5	11.5
...	31 171	Thomas	714	1,405	629	631	729	851	3,132	3,130	3,121	0.9	1.0	1.2
...	31 173	Thurston	396	2,614	7,273	7,296	7,171	6,936	2,661	2,671	2,666	18.5	18.2	17.6
...	31 175	Valley	571	1,926	4,373	4,404	4,647	5,169	2,876	2,871	2,827	7.7	8.2	9.1
36540	31 177	Washington	394	2,624	20,044	19,828	18,780	16,607	1,820	1,858	1,877	51.3	48.1	42.5
...	31 179	Wayne	443	2,371	9,196	9,330	9,851	9,364	2,508	2,461	2,441	20.7	22.1	21.1
...	31 181	Webster	575	1,879	3,701	3,774	4,061	4,279	2,929	2,916	2,890	6.4	7.1	7.4
...	31 183	Wheeler	576	1,868	823	818	886	948	3,118	3,117	3,115	1.4	1.5	1.6
...	31 185	York	576	1,860	14,502	14,346	14,598	14,428	2,133	2,113	2,024	25.2	25.3	25.1
	32 000	NEVADA	110,561	(X)	2,495,529	2,412,301	1,998,257	1,201,675	(X)	(X)	(X)	22.7	18.4	10.9
21980	32 001	Churchill	5,023	84	25,036	24,680	23,982	17,938	1,583	1,595	1,792	5.1	4.9	3.6
29820	32 003	Clark	8,091	42	1,777,539	1,709,364	1,375,738	741,368	16	25	52	224.7	176.1	93.7
23820	32 005	Douglas	738	1,305	45,909	46,046	41,259	27,637	1,021	1,072	1,366	64.7	58.4	38.9
21220	32 007	Elko	17,203	16	47,114	45,576	45,291	33,463	1,000	993	1,178	2.7	2.6	1.9
...	32 009	Esmeralda	3,589	150	790	805	971	1,344	3,120	3,113	3,104	0.2	0.3	0.4
21220	32 011	Eureka	4,180	122	1,480	1,412	1,651	1,547	3,086	3,087	3,094	0.4	0.4	0.4
...	32 013	Humboldt	9,658	31	17,446	17,155	16,106	12,844	1,946	2,017	2,152	1.8	1.7	1.3
...	32 015	Lander	5,519	70	5,272	5,105	5,794	6,266	2,822	2,805	2,728	1.0	1.0	1.1
...	32 017	Lincoln	10,637	25	4,738	4,517	4,165	3,775	2,852	2,902	2,933	0.4	0.4	0.4
22280	32 019	Lyon	2,016	312	51,231	47,344	34,501	20,001	940	1,265	1,678	25.7	17.5	10.0
...	32 021	Mineral	3,813	136	4,868	4,896	5,071	6,475	2,847	2,848	2,712	1.3	1.3	1.7
37220	32 023	Nye	18,159	15	42,693	40,395	32,512	17,781	1,089	1,332	1,799	2.4	1.8	1.0
...	32 027	Pershing	6,068	63	6,414	6,390	6,693	4,336	2,736	2,718	2,889	1.1	1.1	0.7
39900	32 029	Storey	264	2,914	4,132	4,045	3,399	2,526	2,899	2,963	3,021	15.7	12.9	9.6
39900	32 031	Washoe	6,551	57	396,428	389,775	339,486	254,667	164	172	196	62.5	53.8	40.2
...	32 033	White Pine	8,897	37	9,150	8,919	9,181	9,264	2,515	2,516	2,447	1.0	1.0	1.0
		Independent City												
16180	32 510	Carson City	156	3,068	55,289	55,877	52,457	40,443	892	891	988	385.7	366.6	281.8
	33 000	NEW HAMPSHIRE	9,350	(X)	1,314,895	1,306,819	1,235,786	1,109,252	(X)	(X)	(X)	146.6	138.3	123.7
29060	33 001	Belknap	469	2,285	61,562	61,422	56,325	49,216	829	839	853	153.4	141.0	122.6
...	33 003	Carroll	992	779	47,475	47,048	43,666	35,410	993	1,022	1,118	50.8	47.0	37.9
28300	33 005	Cheshire	729	1,325	77,393	77,053	73,825	70,121	687	678	631	109.4	104.6	99.1
13620	33 007	Coos	1,831	358	33,019	33,156	33,111	34,828	1,339	1,316	1,139	18.3	18.4	19.3
30100	33 009	Grafton	1,750	382	85,336	84,793	81,743	74,929	637	636	601	49.8	47.8	43.7
31700	33 011	Hillsborough	892	992	402,789	400,516	380,843	335,838	160	153	152	459.6	436.4	383.2
18180	33 013	Merrimack	956	827	148,085	146,823	136,225	120,240	400	396	385	158.5	146.3	128.7
14460	33 015	Rockingham	794	1,191	296,267	294,211	277,357	245,845	204	203	204	426.3	401.1	353.6
14460	33 017	Strafford	384	2,644	119,990	118,998	112,233	104,233	483	479	442	325.4	305.6	282.6
17200	33 019	Sullivan	552	1,999	42,979	42,799	40,458	38,592	1,083	1,104	1,037	80.0	75.5	71.8
	34 000	NEW JERSEY	8,721	(X)	8,724,560	8,703,150	8,414,347	7,747,750	(X)	(X)	(X)	1,176.2	1,137.1	1,044.3
12100	34 001	Atlantic	671	1,514	271,620	270,318	252,552	224,327	223	223	222	484.1	451.1	399.8
35620	34 003	Bergen	247	2,956	904,037	902,308	884,118	825,380	51	46	44	3,860.6	3,783.6	3,524.3
37980	34 005	Burlington	819	1,130	450,627	449,148	423,391	395,066	141	142	127	560.1	527.8	490.9
37980	34 007	Camden	228	2,980	517,001	515,381	507,907	502,824	117	110	96	2,325.7	2,284.3	2,261.5
36140	34 009	Cape May	620	1,671	97,724	98,805	102,326	95,089	574	519	488	382.9	400.9	372.6
47220	34 011	Cumberland	677	1,504	154,823	152,905	146,438	138,053	380	373	343	316.4	299.2	282.1
35620	34 013	Essex	130	3,083	786,147	789,166	792,305	777,964	66	59	50	6,225.9	6,277.4	6,160.1
37980	34 015	Gloucester	337	2,766	282,031	277,037	255,698	230,082	215	220	213	868.5	789.5	708.2
35620	34 017	Hudson	62	3,104	601,146	602,970	608,975	553,099	97	88	85	12,875.3	13,055.6	11,856.4
35620	34 019	Hunterdon	438	2,393	130,783	130,042	121,989	107,852	447	445	427	304.2	285.2	250.8
45940	34 021	Mercer	229	2,978	367,605	366,070	350,761	325,759	172	166	157	1,627.1	1,556.2	1,441.7
35620	34 023	Middlesex	323	2,797	786,971	789,283	750,162	671,712	64	65	64	2,540.9	2,431.9	2,162.4
35620	34 025	Monmouth	665	1,524	635,285	634,841	615,301	553,192	93	87	84	1,346.1	1,308.0	1,172.4
35620	34 027	Morris	481	2,237	493,160	490,084	470,212	421,330	130	123	120	1,051.5	1,005.5	898.2
35620	34 029	Ocean	916	901	562,335	558,170	510,916	433,203	106	109	115	883.8	807.4	680.8

See footnotes at end of table.

[Includes United States, states, and 3,141 counties/county equivalents defined as of February 22, 2005. For more information on these areas, see Appendix C, Geographic Information]

Metro-politan area code	FIPS state and county code[1]	County	Area, 2000 (square miles)		Population				Rank			Persons per square mile of land area		
			Total	Rank[2]	2006 (July 1)	2005 (July 1)	2000[3] (April 1 estimates base)	1990[3] (April 1 estimates base)	2006[2]	2000[2]	1990[4]	2006[5]	2000	1990
		NEW JERSEY—Con.												
35620	34 031	Passaic	197	3,023	497,093	496,985	490,377	470,872	122	114	104	2,682.8	2,650.0	2,544.6
37980	34 033	Salem	373	2,679	66,595	66,054	64,285	65,294	770	757	671	197.1	190.1	193.3
35620	34 035	Somerset	305	2,837	324,186	319,830	297,490	240,222	190	190	207	1,064.0	981.2	788.3
35620	34 037	Sussex	536	2,051	153,384	152,726	144,170	130,936	384	379	354	294.3	277.6	251.2
35620	34 039	Union	105	3,090	531,088	530,710	522,541	493,819	114	106	99	5,141.7	5,067.2	4,780.9
10900	34 041	Warren	363	2,700	110,919	110,317	102,433	91,675	518	518	501	309.9	287.8	256.1
	35 000	NEW MEXICO	121,589	(X)	1,954,599	1,925,985	1,819,046	1,515,069	(X)	(X)	(X)	16.1	15.0	12.5
10740	35 001	Bernalillo	1,169	602	615,099	603,783	556,002	480,577	96	100	102	527.5	477.6	412.1
...	35 003	Catron	6,929	50	3,476	3,395	3,543	2,563	2,942	2,951	3,019	0.5	0.5	0.4
40740	35 005	Chaves	6,075	62	62,474	61,861	61,382	57,849	816	792	751	10.3	10.1	9.5
24380	35 006	Cibola	4,542	104	27,481	27,598	25,595	23,794	1,504	1,533	1,500	6.1	5.7	5.2
...	35 007	Colfax	3,768	141	13,514	13,710	14,189	12,925	2,204	2,150	2,143	3.6	3.8	3.4
17580	35 009	Curry	1,408	482	45,513	45,677	45,044	42,207	1,032	997	954	32.4	31.9	30.0
...	35 011	De Baca	2,334	258	1,991	2,034	2,240	2,252	3,051	3,048	3,047	0.9	1.0	1.0
29740	35 013	Dona Ana	3,815	135	193,888	189,306	174,682	135,510	307	313	346	50.9	46.0	35.6
16100	35 015	Eddy	4,198	121	51,815	51,269	51,658	48,605	932	898	861	12.4	12.3	11.6
43500	35 017	Grant	3,968	130	29,792	29,609	31,002	27,676	1,421	1,379	1,364	7.5	7.8	7.0
...	35 019	Guadalupe	3,032	182	4,365	4,380	4,680	4,156	2,877	2,869	2,900	1.4	1.5	1.4
...	35 021	Harding	2,126	293	718	737	810	987	3,125	3,123	3,114	0.3	0.4	0.5
...	35 023	Hidalgo	3,446	154	5,087	5,115	5,932	5,958	2,833	2,791	2,763	1.5	1.7	1.7
26020	35 025	Lea	4,394	111	57,312	56,650	55,511	55,765	866	850	777	13.0	12.6	12.7
40760	35 027	Lincoln	4,831	90	21,223	20,976	19,411	12,219	1,757	1,824	2,200	4.4	4.0	2.5
31060	35 028	Los Alamos	109	3,088	19,022	18,858	18,343	18,115	1,873	1,878	1,783	174.0	167.2	165.7
19700	35 029	Luna	2,965	186	27,205	26,632	25,016	18,110	1,512	1,560	1,784	9.2	8.4	6.1
23700	35 031	McKinley	5,455	72	71,875	71,839	74,798	60,686	726	668	716	13.2	13.8	11.1
...	35 033	Mora	1,933	326	5,151	5,127	5,180	4,264	2,832	2,839	2,893	2.7	2.7	2.2
10460	35 035	Otero	6,627	56	62,744	63,128	62,298	51,928	811	781	814	9.5	9.4	7.8
...	35 037	Quay	2,882	192	9,155	9,259	10,155	10,823	2,514	2,431	2,309	3.2	3.5	3.8
21580	35 039	Rio Arriba	5,896	67	40,949	40,633	41,191	34,365	1,135	1,074	1,158	7.0	7.0	5.9
38780	35 041	Roosevelt	2,455	234	18,291	18,205	18,018	16,702	1,901	1,898	1,868	7.5	7.3	6.8
10740	35 043	Sandoval	3,714	145	113,772	107,146	90,584	63,319	506	569	689	30.7	24.6	17.1
22140	35 045	San Juan	5,538	69	126,473	125,820	113,801	91,605	465	473	502	22.9	20.7	16.6
29780	35 047	San Miguel	4,736	98	29,325	29,453	30,126	25,743	1,437	1,392	1,430	6.2	6.4	5.5
42140	35 049	Santa Fe	1,911	336	142,407	140,801	129,287	98,928	420	417	465	74.6	68.0	51.8
...	35 051	Sierra	4,236	118	12,669	12,777	13,270	9,912	2,264	2,207	2,395	3.0	3.2	2.4
...	35 053	Socorro	6,649	55	18,240	18,194	18,078	14,764	1,907	1,897	2,002	2.7	2.7	2.2
45340	35 055	Taos	2,205	281	31,832	31,610	29,979	23,118	1,375	1,397	1,532	14.4	13.7	10.5
10740	35 057	Torrance	3,346	159	17,551	17,456	16,915	10,285	1,937	1,959	2,361	5.2	5.1	3.1
...	35 059	Union	3,831	134	3,801	3,815	4,174	4,124	2,922	2,900	2,904	1.0	1.1	1.1
10740	35 061	Valencia	1,068	699	70,389	69,132	66,152	45,235	740	739	910	65.9	62.3	42.4
	36 000	NEW YORK	54,556	(X)	19,306,183	19,315,721	18,976,821	17,990,778	(X)	(X)	(X)	408.9	402.4	381.0
10580	36 001	Albany	533	2,064	297,556	297,598	294,570	292,812	202	191	166	568.5	562.8	559.1
...	36 003	Allegany	1,034	733	50,267	50,365	49,927	50,470	950	917	836	48.8	48.4	49.0
35620	36 005	Bronx	57	3,105	1,361,473	1,364,566	1,332,650	1,203,789	26	27	24	32,392.9	31,748.3	28,641.2
13780	36 007	Broome	715	1,396	196,269	196,547	200,536	212,160	300	274	235	277.7	283.3	300.1
36460	36 009	Cattaraugus	1,322	511	81,534	82,112	83,955	84,234	660	620	542	62.2	64.1	64.3
12180	36 011	Cayuga	864	1,055	81,243	81,365	81,963	82,313	663	634	551	117.2	118.2	118.7
27460	36 013	Chautauqua	1,500	448	135,357	136,102	139,750	141,895	438	391	336	127.4	131.4	133.6
21300	36 015	Chemung	411	2,536	88,641	89,005	91,070	95,195	621	565	486	217.2	223.1	233.2
...	36 017	Chenango	899	971	51,787	51,676	51,401	51,768	933	900	816	57.9	57.5	57.9
38460	36 019	Clinton	1,118	650	82,166	82,104	79,894	85,969	655	644	533	79.1	76.9	82.7
26460	36 021	Columbia	648	1,580	62,955	63,327	63,094	62,982	808	769	692	99.0	99.2	99.1
18660	36 023	Cortland	502	2,174	48,483	48,489	48,598	48,963	980	937	856	97.0	97.2	98.0
...	36 025	Delaware	1,468	457	46,977	47,360	48,057	47,352	1,003	952	886	32.5	33.2	32.7
39100	36 027	Dutchess	825	1,120	295,146	294,509	280,150	259,462	207	200	194	368.2	350.4	323.7
15380	36 029	Erie	1,227	572	921,390	928,215	950,265	968,584	46	37	32	882.4	909.2	927.2
...	36 031	Essex	1,917	333	38,649	38,543	38,851	37,152	1,195	1,146	1,069	21.5	21.6	20.7
31660	36 033	Franklin	1,697	394	50,968	50,910	51,134	46,540	941	904	896	31.2	31.3	28.5
24100	36 035	Fulton	533	2,065	55,435	55,425	55,073	54,191	891	858	793	111.7	110.9	109.2
12860	36 037	Genesee	495	2,197	58,830	59,173	60,370	60,060	849	801	723	119.1	122.1	121.5
...	36 039	Greene	658	1,542	49,822	49,559	48,195	44,739	957	944	915	76.9	74.5	69.1
...	36 041	Hamilton	1,808	362	5,162	5,196	5,379	5,279	2,830	2,823	2,822	3.0	3.1	3.1
46540	36 043	Herkimer	1,458	461	63,332	63,597	64,437	65,809	801	754	666	44.9	45.6	46.6
48060	36 045	Jefferson	1,857	351	114,264	115,536	111,738	110,943	503	482	416	89.8	87.6	87.2
35620	36 047	Kings	97	3,094	2,508,820	2,511,408	2,465,525	2,300,664	7	7	6	35,530.7	34,937.7	32,619.7
...	36 049	Lewis	1,290	534	26,685	26,506	26,944	26,796	1,531	1,486	1,396	20.9	21.2	21.0
40380	36 051	Livingston	640	1,607	64,173	64,192	64,328	62,372	789	756	698	101.5	101.9	98.7
45060	36 053	Madison	662	1,533	70,197	70,011	69,441	69,166	743	713	641	107.0	105.9	105.5
40380	36 055	Monroe	1,366	495	730,807	732,057	735,343	713,968	75	68	58	1,108.5	1,116.0	1,082.9
11220	36 057	Montgomery	410	2,542	49,112	49,006	49,708	51,981	971	921	813	121.3	122.7	128.4
35620	36 059	Nassau	453	2,328	1,325,662	1,331,620	1,334,539	1,287,873	27	26	22	4,624.0	4,662.1	4,491.0

See footnotes at end of table.

Table B-1. Counties — **Area and Population**—Con.

[Includes United States, states, and 3,141 counties/county equivalents defined as of February 22, 2005. For more information on these areas, see Appendix C, Geographic Information]

Metro-politan area code	FIPS state and county code[1]	County	Area, 2000 (square miles) Total	Rank[2]	2006 (July 1)	2005 (July 1)	2000[3] (April 1 estimates base)	1990[3] (April 1 estimates base)	Rank 2006[2]	Rank 2000[2]	Rank 1990[4]	Persons per square mile of land area 2006[5]	2000	1990
		NEW YORK—Con.												
35620	36 061	New York	34	3,112	1,611,581	1,606,275	1,537,372	1,487,536	19	17	15	70,190.8	67,056.2	52,414.9
15380	36 063	Niagara	1,140	628	216,130	216,581	219,844	220,756	282	257	225	413.3	420.0	422.1
46540	36 065	Oneida	1,257	549	233,954	233,969	235,459	250,836	262	246	199	192.9	194.0	206.8
45060	36 067	Onondaga	806	1,159	456,777	457,279	458,336	468,973	139	126	105	585.4	587.5	601.0
40380	36 069	Ontario	662	1,531	104,353	104,218	100,224	95,101	540	524	487	161.9	155.8	147.6
39100	36 071	Orange	839	1,096	376,392	372,750	341,367	307,571	169	171	162	461.1	420.3	376.7
40380	36 073	Orleans	817	1,136	43,213	43,265	44,173	41,846	1,075	1,012	959	110.4	112.9	106.9
45060	36 075	Oswego	1,312	514	123,077	123,144	122,377	121,785	475	444	378	129.1	128.6	127.7
36580	36 077	Otsego	1,015	750	62,583	62,750	61,676	60,390	812	788	718	62.4	61.5	60.2
35620	36 079	Putnam	246	2,958	100,603	100,528	95,843	83,941	558	540	545	435.0	416.1	362.5
35620	36 081	Queens	178	3,046	2,255,175	2,256,576	2,229,401	1,951,598	10	9	9	20,644.2	20,430.7	17,839.1
10580	36 083	Rensselaer	665	1,523	155,292	154,601	152,538	154,429	375	349	301	237.5	233.3	236.1
35620	36 085	Richmond	103	3,092	477,377	475,014	443,728	378,977	133	134	133	8,163.1	7,619.0	6,466.1
35620	36 087	Rockland	199	3,017	294,965	294,636	286,753	265,475	208	194	185	1,693.1	1,650.5	1,523.7
36300	36 089	St. Lawrence	2,821	195	111,284	111,258	111,919	111,974	517	481	410	41.4	41.7	41.7
10580	36 091	Saratoga	844	1,091	215,473	214,121	200,635	181,276	284	273	270	265.4	248.2	223.3
10580	36 093	Schenectady	210	3,003	150,440	148,975	146,550	149,285	393	372	317	729.9	710.6	724.3
10580	36 095	Schoharie	626	1,645	32,196	32,126	31,582	31,840	1,366	1,358	1,216	51.8	50.8	51.2
...	36 097	Schuyler	342	2,754	19,415	19,340	19,224	18,662	1,849	1,833	1,754	59.1	58.6	56.8
42900	36 099	Seneca	391	2,631	34,724	34,746	33,342	33,683	1,300	1,304	1,174	106.9	102.7	103.7
18500	36 101	Steuben	1,404	483	98,236	98,366	98,726	99,088	571	528	463	70.5	71.0	71.1
35620	36 103	Suffolk	2,373	250	1,469,715	1,472,086	1,419,352	1,321,339	21	22	20	1,611.2	1,561.4	1,450.1
...	36 105	Sullivan	997	773	76,588	76,155	73,964	69,277	690	675	640	79.0	76.4	71.4
13780	36 107	Tioga	523	2,092	51,285	51,349	51,784	52,337	939	897	809	98.9	99.8	100.9
27060	36 109	Tompkins	492	2,211	100,407	100,104	96,502	94,097	559	535	491	210.9	202.9	197.6
28740	36 111	Ulster	1,161	608	182,742	182,433	177,749	165,380	323	309	287	162.2	158.0	146.8
24020	36 113	Warren	932	870	66,087	65,571	63,303	59,209	776	766	736	76.0	72.9	68.1
24020	36 115	Washington	846	1,090	63,368	63,005	61,042	59,330	800	798	731	75.8	73.0	71.0
40380	36 117	Wayne	1,384	490	92,889	93,158	93,765	89,123	600	547	515	153.7	155.2	147.5
35620	36 119	Westchester	500	2,180	949,355	947,719	923,361	874,866	41	40	35	2,193.4	2,139.6	2,021.0
...	36 121	Wyoming	596	1,753	42,613	42,697	43,424	42,507	1,092	1,029	945	71.9	73.2	71.7
...	36 123	Yates	376	2,670	24,732	24,847	24,621	22,810	1,597	1,571	1,542	73.1	72.8	67.4
	37 000	NORTH CAROLINA	53,819	(X)	8,856,505	8,672,459	8,046,491	6,632,448	(X)	(X)	(X)	181.8	165.9	136.1
15500	37 001	Alamance	435	2,417	142,661	140,227	130,794	108,213	418	410	426	331.8	305.8	251.3
25860	37 003	Alexander	263	2,916	36,177	35,815	33,609	27,544	1,251	1,298	1,372	139.0	129.4	105.8
...	37 005	Alleghany	236	2,965	10,912	10,864	10,680	9,590	2,372	2,387	2,424	46.5	45.6	40.9
16740	37 007	Anson	537	2,049	25,472	25,689	25,275	23,474	1,565	1,556	1,515	47.9	47.5	44.2
...	37 009	Ashe	427	2,455	25,499	25,293	24,384	22,209	1,563	1,580	1,571	59.8	57.4	52.1
...	37 011	Avery	247	2,954	17,674	17,700	17,167	14,867	1,928	1,944	1,997	71.6	69.6	60.2
47820	37 013	Beaufort	959	822	46,355	45,878	44,958	42,283	1,013	999	953	56.0	54.3	51.1
...	37 015	Bertie	741	1,297	19,094	19,331	19,757	20,388	1,866	1,807	1,656	27.3	28.2	29.2
...	37 017	Bladen	887	1,005	32,921	32,885	32,279	28,663	1,342	1,341	1,341	37.6	36.9	32.8
48900	37 019	Brunswick	1,050	716	94,945	89,108	73,141	50,985	584	685	828	111.1	86.3	59.6
11700	37 021	Buncombe	660	1,536	222,174	218,380	206,299	174,357	278	269	276	338.7	315.6	265.7
25860	37 023	Burke	515	2,120	90,054	89,472	89,145	75,740	617	583	593	177.7	176.2	149.5
16740	37 025	Cabarrus	365	2,691	156,395	149,585	131,030	98,935	370	408	464	429.2	362.9	271.5
25860	37 027	Caldwell	474	2,260	79,841	79,334	77,388	70,709	675	655	627	169.3	164.6	149.9
21020	37 029	Camden	306	2,836	9,271	8,970	6,885	5,904	2,500	2,697	2,771	38.5	28.8	24.5
33980	37 031	Carteret	1,341	503	63,584	62,849	59,383	52,407	798	809	807	122.3	114.3	98.6
...	37 033	Caswell	428	2,451	23,546	23,490	23,501	20,662	1,649	1,616	1,646	55.4	55.5	48.5
25860	37 035	Catawba	414	2,518	153,784	151,345	141,677	118,412	382	386	393	384.5	356.3	296.0
20500	37 037	Chatham	709	1,420	60,052	58,089	49,334	38,979	839	927	1,023	87.9	72.8	57.1
...	37 039	Cherokee	467	2,295	26,309	25,723	24,298	20,170	1,543	1,585	1,666	57.8	53.6	44.3
...	37 041	Chowan	233	2,970	14,695	14,484	14,150	13,506	2,123	2,153	2,101	85.1	81.8	78.2
...	37 043	Clay	221	2,988	10,008	9,755	8,775	7,155	2,442	2,549	2,638	46.6	41.1	33.3
43140	37 045	Cleveland	469	2,284	98,373	97,999	96,284	84,958	570	538	540	211.7	207.9	183.0
...	37 047	Columbus	954	831	54,637	54,399	54,749	49,587	899	861	847	58.3	58.5	52.9
35100	37 049	Craven	774	1,223	94,875	93,829	91,523	81,812	585	560	555	133.9	129.4	117.6
22180	37 051	Cumberland	658	1,540	299,060	299,027	302,962	274,713	201	187	181	458.2	463.9	420.6
47260	37 053	Currituck	526	2,087	23,770	23,116	18,190	13,736	1,639	1,890	2,079	90.8	70.1	52.5
28620	37 055	Dare	1,562	425	33,935	33,720	29,967	22,746	1,316	1,398	1,547	88.5	78.7	59.6
45640	37 057	Davidson	567	1,942	156,236	154,533	147,269	126,688	372	368	366	283.0	267.5	229.4
49180	37 059	Davie	267	2,904	40,035	39,015	34,835	27,859	1,161	1,258	1,355	151.0	132.2	105.0
...	37 061	Duplin	819	1,132	52,790	51,838	49,063	39,995	914	930	999	64.6	60.2	48.9
20500	37 063	Durham	298	2,849	246,896	242,354	223,306	181,844	248	254	267	850.4	773.4	625.7
40580	37 065	Edgecombe	507	2,151	53,964	54,001	55,606	56,692	904	849	769	106.9	109.5	112.2
49180	37 067	Forsyth	413	2,521	332,355	325,726	306,044	265,855	186	186	184	811.4	749.3	649.0
39580	37 069	Franklin	495	2,202	55,886	54,620	47,260	36,414	884	963	1,092	113.6	96.8	74.1

See footnotes at end of table.

[Includes United States, states, and 3,141 counties/county equivalents defined as of February 22, 2005. For more information on these areas, see Appendix C, Geographic Information]

Metro-politan area code	FIPS state and county code[1]	County	Area, 2000 (square miles)		Population				Rank			Persons per square mile of land area		
			Total	Rank[2]	2006 (July 1)	2005 (July 1)	2000[3] (April 1 estimates base)	1990[3] (April 1 estimates base)	2006[2]	2000[2]	1990[4]	2006[5]	2000	1990
		NORTH CAROLINA—Con.												
16740	37 071	Gaston	364	2,694	199,397	196,237	190,310	174,769	296	289	275	559.8	535.4	490.2
...	37 073	Gates	346	2,740	11,527	11,180	10,516	9,305	2,325	2,396	2,443	33.8	30.8	27.3
...	37 075	Graham	302	2,842	7,995	8,004	7,993	7,196	2,593	2,608	2,634	27.4	27.4	24.6
...	37 077	Granville	537	2,050	54,473	53,424	48,498	38,341	902	941	1,044	102.6	91.8	72.2
24780	37 079	Greene	266	2,910	20,157	20,074	18,974	15,384	1,814	1,850	1,965	75.9	71.8	58.0
24660	37 081	Guilford	658	1,545	451,905	443,539	421,048	347,431	140	143	148	695.9	650.4	534.4
40260	37 083	Halifax	731	1,319	55,521	55,627	57,370	55,516	888	832	780	76.5	79.0	76.5
20380	37 085	Harnett	601	1,736	106,283	103,765	91,062	67,833	535	566	653	178.6	154.0	114.0
11700	37 087	Haywood	555	1,991	56,447	56,084	54,034	46,948	878	868	891	102.0	97.7	84.8
11700	37 089	Henderson	375	2,672	99,033	97,175	89,204	69,747	565	581	637	264.8	239.7	186.6
...	37 091	Hertford	360	2,709	23,581	23,536	22,977	22,317	1,646	1,646	1,562	66.8	65.0	63.1
22180	37 093	Hoke	392	2,626	42,303	40,675	33,646	22,856	1,095	1,294	1,539	108.1	86.7	58.4
...	37 095	Hyde	1,424	479	5,341	5,442	5,826	5,411	2,813	2,802	2,807	8.7	9.4	8.8
44380	37 097	Iredell	597	1,750	146,206	140,462	122,664	93,205	408	442	496	254.0	214.8	162.3
...	37 099	Jackson	495	2,204	35,562	35,224	33,120	26,835	1,270	1,315	1,394	72.5	67.8	54.7
39580	37 101	Johnston	796	1,185	152,143	146,324	121,900	81,306	389	446	560	192.1	155.7	102.7
35100	37 103	Jones	473	2,267	10,204	10,300	10,398	9,361	2,432	2,404	2,442	21.6	22.0	19.8
41820	37 105	Lee	259	2,922	56,908	55,747	49,172	41,370	874	928	973	221.2	192.0	160.8
28820	37 107	Lenoir	402	2,591	57,662	57,878	59,619	57,274	862	805	762	144.2	148.9	143.2
30740	37 109	Lincoln	307	2,833	71,894	69,748	63,780	50,319	724	761	838	240.6	214.4	168.4
...	37 111	McDowell	446	2,351	43,414	43,195	42,151	35,681	1,070	1,055	1,108	98.3	95.6	80.8
...	37 113	Macon	519	2,104	32,395	31,933	29,806	23,504	1,359	1,403	1,513	62.7	58.0	45.5
11700	37 115	Madison	452	2,337	20,355	20,211	19,635	16,953	1,803	1,817	1,850	45.3	43.8	37.7
...	37 117	Martin	461	2,310	24,342	24,469	25,546	25,078	1,619	1,538	1,458	55.3	55.3	54.2
16740	37 119	Mecklenburg	546	2,015	827,445	796,369	695,427	511,211	60	72	92	1,572.3	1,331.0	969.2
...	37 121	Mitchell	222	2,986	15,681	15,762	15,687	14,433	2,062	2,040	2,022	70.8	71.0	65.2
...	37 123	Montgomery	502	2,173	27,638	27,356	26,836	23,359	1,500	1,491	1,524	56.2	54.8	47.6
43860	37 125	Moore	706	1,426	83,162	81,342	74,770	59,000	648	669	737	119.2	107.7	84.4
40580	37 127	Nash	543	2,030	92,312	91,193	87,385	76,677	602	599	589	170.9	162.4	141.9
48900	37 129	New Hanover	328	2,788	182,591	179,043	160,327	120,284	324	332	384	917.9	807.7	604.6
40260	37 131	Northampton	551	2,002	21,247	21,401	22,086	21,004	1,755	1,690	1,629	39.6	41.2	39.2
27340	37 133	Onslow	909	924	150,673	150,508	150,355	149,838	392	358	315	196.5	195.7	195.4
20500	37 135	Orange	401	2,598	120,100	118,536	115,537	93,662	482	465	493	300.4	289.9	234.3
35100	37 137	Pamlico	566	1,947	12,785	12,779	12,934	11,368	2,258	2,241	2,263	37.9	38.4	33.7
21020	37 139	Pasquotank	289	2,860	39,591	38,260	34,897	31,298	1,170	1,255	1,236	174.5	153.7	137.9
48900	37 141	Pender	933	865	48,630	46,457	41,082	28,855	977	1,080	1,334	55.9	47.4	33.1
21020	37 143	Perquimans	329	2,785	12,337	12,046	11,368	10,447	2,280	2,345	2,342	49.9	46.2	42.3
20500	37 145	Person	404	2,581	37,341	37,201	35,623	30,180	1,223	1,229	1,290	95.2	91.1	76.9
24780	37 147	Pitt	655	1,557	145,619	142,285	133,719	108,480	412	401	424	223.5	205.8	166.5
...	37 149	Polk	239	2,962	19,226	19,062	18,324	14,458	1,856	1,880	2,020	80.8	77.4	60.8
24660	37 151	Randolph	790	1,199	140,410	138,176	130,470	106,546	427	411	434	178.3	166.5	135.3
40460	37 153	Richmond	480	2,245	46,555	46,706	46,551	44,511	1,011	970	918	98.2	98.2	93.9
31300	37 155	Robeson	951	837	129,021	127,752	123,241	105,170	455	437	439	136.0	130.1	110.8
24660	37 157	Rockingham	572	1,903	93,063	92,504	91,928	86,064	598	556	532	164.3	162.4	151.9
41580	37 159	Rowan	524	2,090	136,254	134,782	130,348	110,605	436	413	418	266.5	255.6	216.3
22580	37 161	Rutherford	566	1,951	63,867	63,654	62,901	56,956	791	773	765	113.2	111.7	100.9
...	37 163	Sampson	947	843	63,561	62,856	60,160	47,297	799	804	887	67.2	63.8	50.0
29900	37 165	Scotland	321	2,802	37,094	37,076	35,998	33,763	1,231	1,219	1,171	116.2	112.9	105.8
10620	37 167	Stanly	404	2,579	59,358	59,031	58,100	51,765	846	823	817	150.3	147.3	131.0
49180	37 169	Stokes	456	2,319	46,168	45,790	44,707	37,224	1,018	1,003	1,066	102.2	99.3	82.4
34340	37 171	Surry	538	2,048	72,687	72,422	71,227	61,704	717	697	707	135.5	132.8	115.0
...	37 173	Swain	541	2,035	13,445	13,249	12,973	11,268	2,213	2,238	2,277	25.5	24.7	21.3
14820	37 175	Transylvania	381	2,653	29,780	29,632	29,334	25,520	1,422	1,418	1,446	78.7	77.7	67.4
...	37 177	Tyrrell	600	1,740	4,187	4,146	4,149	3,856	2,893	2,903	2,928	10.7	10.6	9.9
16740	37 179	Union	640	1,611	175,272	163,483	123,738	84,210	336	435	543	275.0	197.1	132.1
25780	37 181	Vance	270	2,899	43,810	43,546	42,954	38,892	1,068	1,037	1,025	172.8	170.2	153.4
39580	37 183	Wake	857	1,072	786,522	750,865	627,865	426,311	65	85	118	945.4	761.3	511.2
...	37 185	Warren	444	2,368	19,605	19,760	19,972	17,265	1,840	1,794	1,837	45.7	46.5	40.3
...	37 187	Washington	424	2,465	13,227	13,283	13,723	13,997	2,231	2,183	2,058	38.0	39.4	40.2
14380	37 189	Watauga	313	2,816	42,700	42,434	42,693	36,952	1,088	1,043	1,074	136.6	136.8	118.2
24140	37 191	Wayne	557	1,981	113,847	113,827	113,329	104,666	505	475	441	206.0	205.1	189.4
35900	37 193	Wilkes	760	1,262	67,310	67,128	65,624	59,393	763	743	728	88.9	86.9	78.4
48980	37 195	Wilson	374	2,675	76,624	76,175	73,811	66,061	689	679	663	206.5	199.2	178.0
49180	37 197	Yadkin	337	2,765	38,056	37,689	36,348	30,488	1,208	1,205	1,269	113.4	108.8	90.8
...	37 199	Yancey	313	2,815	18,421	18,197	17,774	15,419	1,891	1,912	1,962	59.0	57.0	49.3
	38 000	NORTH DAKOTA	70,700	(X)	635,867	634,605	642,200	638,800	(X)	(X)	(X)	9.2	9.3	9.3
...	38 001	Adams	989	782	2,332	2,394	2,593	3,174	3,024	3,021	2,986	2.4	2.6	3.2
...	38 003	Barnes	1,513	438	10,955	11,006	11,775	12,545	2,370	2,311	2,179	7.3	7.9	8.4
...	38 005	Benson	1,439	470	6,997	7,023	6,964	7,198	2,677	2,690	2,633	5.1	5.0	5.2
19860	38 007	Billings	1,153	613	829	824	888	1,108	3,117	3,115	3,110	0.7	0.8	1.0
...	38 009	Bottineau	1,698	393	6,650	6,740	7,149	8,011	2,710	2,673	2,564	4.0	4.3	4.8

See footnotes at end of table.

[Includes United States, states, and 3,141 counties/county equivalents defined as of February 22, 2005. For more information on these areas, see Appendix C, Geographic Information]

Metro-politan area code	FIPS state and county code[1]	County	Area, 2000 (square miles)		Population				Rank			Persons per square mile of land area		
			Total	Rank[2]	2006 (July 1)	2005 (July 1)	2000[3] (April 1 estimates base)	1990[3] (April 1 estimates base)	2006[2]	2000[2]	1990[4]	2006[5]	2000	1990
		NORTH DAKOTA—Con.												
...	38 011	Bowman	1,167	603	2,991	3,029	3,242	3,596	2,979	2,977	2,950	2.6	2.8	3.1
...	38 013	Burke	1,129	640	1,947	2,022	2,242	3,002	3,056	3,047	3,000	1.8	2.0	2.7
13900	38 015	Burleigh	1,668	401	75,384	73,900	69,416	60,131	698	715	722	46.2	42.6	36.8
22020	38 017	Cass	1,768	378	132,525	130,455	123,138	102,874	442	439	447	75.1	69.9	58.3
...	38 019	Cavalier	1,510	439	4,099	4,274	4,831	6,064	2,900	2,859	2,749	2.8	3.2	4.1
...	38 021	Dickey	1,142	627	5,398	5,458	5,757	6,107	2,809	2,806	2,742	4.8	5.1	5.4
...	38 023	Divide	1,294	526	2,092	2,146	2,283	2,899	3,045	3,042	3,006	1.7	1.8	2.3
...	38 025	Dunn	2,082	301	3,443	3,433	3,600	4,005	2,946	2,944	2,919	1.7	1.8	2.0
...	38 027	Eddy	644	1,590	2,502	2,579	2,757	2,951	3,015	3,008	3,003	4.0	4.3	4.7
...	38 029	Emmons	1,555	430	3,645	3,759	4,331	4,830	2,934	2,895	2,853	2.4	2.9	3.2
...	38 031	Foster	647	1,583	3,583	3,548	3,759	3,983	2,938	2,933	2,920	5.6	5.9	6.3
...	38 033	Golden Valley	1,002	767	1,691	1,724	1,924	2,108	3,076	3,070	3,062	1.7	1.9	2.1
24220	38 035	Grand Forks	1,440	469	65,435	65,210	66,109	70,683	781	740	628	45.5	45.8	49.2
...	38 037	Grant	1,666	402	2,588	2,637	2,841	3,549	3,007	3,002	2,953	1.6	1.7	2.1
...	38 039	Griggs	716	1,391	2,456	2,492	2,754	3,303	3,018	3,009	2,976	3.5	3.9	4.7
...	38 041	Hettinger	1,134	637	2,564	2,549	2,715	3,445	3,009	3,012	2,959	2.3	2.4	3.0
...	38 043	Kidder	1,433	472	2,453	2,458	2,753	3,332	3,020	3,010	2,967	1.8	2.0	2.5
...	38 045	LaMoure	1,151	618	4,262	4,353	4,701	5,383	2,887	2,868	2,811	3.7	4.1	4.7
...	38 047	Logan	1,011	755	1,999	2,052	2,308	2,847	3,049	3,037	3,008	2.0	2.3	2.9
33500	38 049	McHenry	1,912	335	5,429	5,483	5,987	6,528	2,806	2,783	2,705	2.9	3.2	3.5
...	38 051	McIntosh	995	775	2,956	3,005	3,390	4,021	2,981	2,964	2,916	3.0	3.5	4.1
...	38 053	McKenzie	2,861	194	5,700	5,611	5,737	6,383	2,786	2,809	2,718	2.1	2.1	2.3
...	38 055	McLean	2,328	261	8,543	8,599	9,311	10,457	2,561	2,506	2,341	4.0	4.4	5.0
...	38 057	Mercer	1,112	653	8,234	8,323	8,644	9,808	2,578	2,556	2,402	7.9	8.2	9.4
13900	38 059	Morton	1,945	324	25,754	25,498	25,303	23,700	1,554	1,554	1,503	13.4	13.2	12.3
...	38 061	Mountrail	1,941	325	6,442	6,530	6,629	7,021	2,735	2,725	2,655	3.5	3.6	3.8
...	38 063	Nelson	1,009	758	3,289	3,412	3,715	4,410	2,959	2,941	2,879	3.4	3.8	4.5
...	38 065	Oliver	731	1,320	1,808	1,820	2,065	2,381	3,067	3,062	3,033	2.5	2.8	3.3
...	38 067	Pembina	1,122	647	7,906	7,981	8,585	9,238	2,599	2,559	2,450	7.1	7.6	8.3
...	38 069	Pierce	1,082	678	4,221	4,261	4,675	5,052	2,889	2,870	2,835	4.1	4.6	5.0
...	38 071	Ramsey	1,301	523	11,267	11,354	12,066	12,681	2,345	2,292	2,168	9.5	10.1	10.7
...	38 073	Ransom	864	1,050	5,695	5,776	5,890	5,921	2,787	2,795	2,768	6.6	6.8	6.9
33500	38 075	Renville	892	994	2,425	2,450	2,610	3,160	3,021	3,019	2,987	2.8	3.0	3.6
47420	38 077	Richland	1,446	465	16,888	17,287	17,998	18,148	1,975	1,899	1,780	11.8	12.5	12.6
...	38 079	Rolette	939	852	13,903	13,856	13,674	12,772	2,173	2,189	2,160	15.4	15.2	14.2
...	38 081	Sargent	867	1,042	4,198	4,156	4,366	4,549	2,890	2,890	2,868	4.9	5.1	5.3
...	38 083	Sheridan	1,006	760	1,408	1,444	1,710	2,148	3,089	3,084	3,057	1.4	1.7	2.2
...	38 085	Sioux	1,128	641	4,282	4,196	4,044	3,761	2,882	2,917	2,934	3.9	3.7	3.4
...	38 087	Slope	1,219	577	713	710	767	907	3,126	3,128	3,117	0.6	0.6	0.7
19860	38 089	Stark	1,340	504	22,167	22,119	22,636	22,832	1,717	1,666	1,540	16.6	16.8	17.1
...	38 091	Steele	715	1,395	1,943	2,016	2,258	2,420	3,057	3,046	3,028	2.7	3.1	3.4
27420	38 093	Stutsman	2,298	266	20,761	20,767	21,908	22,241	1,773	1,698	1,567	9.3	9.8	10.0
...	38 095	Towner	1,042	723	2,417	2,512	2,876	3,627	3,022	3,001	2,948	2.4	2.8	3.5
...	38 097	Traill	863	1,056	8,178	8,302	8,477	8,752	2,580	2,567	2,490	9.5	9.8	10.2
33500	38 099	Walsh	1,294	527	11,362	11,541	12,389	13,840	2,343	2,275	2,070	8.9	9.6	10.8
...	38 101	Ward	2,056	305	55,220	55,706	58,797	57,921	894	815	748	27.5	29.1	28.8
...	38 103	Wells	1,291	531	4,432	4,555	5,102	5,864	2,874	2,844	2,774	3.5	4.0	4.6
48780	38 105	Williams	2,148	288	19,456	19,270	19,761	21,129	1,846	1,805	1,623	9.4	9.5	10.2
	39 000	OHIO	44,825	(X)	11,478,006	11,470,685	11,353,145	10,847,115	(X)	(X)	(X)	280.3	277.5	264.9
...	39 001	Adams	586	1,795	28,516	28,454	27,330	25,371	1,463	1,473	1,452	48.8	46.8	43.4
30620	39 003	Allen	407	2,562	105,788	106,051	108,473	109,755	537	497	420	261.6	268.4	271.4
11740	39 005	Ashland	427	2,454	54,727	54,184	52,523	47,507	898	889	882	129.0	123.9	111.9
11780	39 007	Ashtabula	1,368	493	102,703	103,044	102,728	99,880	547	517	459	146.2	146.3	142.1
11900	39 009	Athens	509	2,142	61,860	62,028	62,223	59,549	825	782	727	122.1	123.0	117.5
47540	39 011	Auglaize	402	2,593	47,060	47,179	46,611	44,585	1,001	969	916	117.3	116.2	111.1
48540	39 013	Belmont	541	2,032	68,771	69,089	70,226	71,074	753	706	623	128.0	130.5	132.3
17140	39 015	Brown	495	2,199	44,423	44,255	42,285	34,966	1,053	1,049	1,134	90.3	86.6	71.1
17140	39 017	Butler	470	2,278	354,992	349,966	332,598	291,479	177	175	167	759.7	714.0	623.7
15940	39 019	Carroll	399	2,602	29,189	29,252	28,836	26,521	1,442	1,426	1,407	74.0	73.2	67.2
46500	39 021	Champaign	430	2,446	39,921	39,692	38,890	36,019	1,163	1,145	1,101	93.2	90.9	84.0
44220	39 023	Clark	404	2,583	141,872	141,908	144,741	147,538	422	378	319	354.8	361.8	368.8
17140	39 025	Clermont	458	2,315	192,706	190,329	177,450	150,094	311	310	314	426.4	394.2	332.0
48940	39 027	Clinton	412	2,525	43,399	42,561	40,520	35,444	1,072	1,103	1,114	105.6	99.0	86.3
20620	39 029	Columbiana	535	2,053	110,542	110,636	112,075	108,276	519	480	425	207.6	210.6	203.3
18740	39 031	Coshocton	568	1,940	36,976	36,969	36,655	35,427	1,235	1,198	1,117	65.6	65.1	62.8
15340	39 033	Crawford	403	2,587	45,047	45,616	46,966	47,870	1,039	964	877	112.0	116.6	119.0
17460	39 035	Cuyahoga	1,246	555	1,314,241	1,330,428	1,393,845	1,412,140	28	23	17	2,866.5	3,036.4	3,081.4
24820	39 037	Darke	600	1,741	52,780	52,967	53,309	53,617	915	877	800	88.0	88.9	89.4
19580	39 039	Defiance	414	2,517	39,091	38,934	39,500	39,350	1,177	1,126	1,016	95.1	96.0	95.7

See footnotes at end of table.

[Includes United States, states, and 3,141 counties/county equivalents defined as of February 22, 2005. For more information on these areas, see Appendix C, Geographic Information]

Metro-politan area code	FIPS state and county code[1]	County	Area, 2000 (square miles) Total	Rank[2]	Population 2006 (July 1)	2005 (July 1)	2000[3] (April 1 estimates base)	1990[3] (April 1 estimates base)	Rank 2006[2]	2000[2]	1990[4]	Persons per square mile of land area 2006[5]	2000	1990
		OHIO—Con.												
18140	39 041	Delaware	456	2,318	156,697	150,496	109,989	66,929	369	494	659	354.2	252.6	151.2
41780	39 043	Erie	626	1,648	78,116	78,374	79,551	76,781	686	646	588	306.5	312.3	301.7
18140	39 045	Fairfield	509	2,141	140,591	138,403	122,881	103,468	425	441	445	278.3	244.4	204.6
47860	39 047	Fayette	407	2,561	28,305	28,193	28,433	27,466	1,473	1,434	1,376	69.6	70.0	67.5
18140	39 049	Franklin	543	2,024	1,095,662	1,089,365	1,068,869	961,437	34	33	33	2,029.5	1,985.0	1,780.5
45780	39 051	Fulton	407	2,559	42,900	42,888	42,084	38,498	1,084	1,056	1,040	105.5	103.6	94.6
38580	39 053	Gallia	471	2,273	31,313	31,241	31,069	30,954	1,387	1,376	1,247	66.8	66.3	66.0
17460	39 055	Geauga	408	2,554	95,676	95,060	90,895	81,087	580	568	562	237.0	226.1	200.6
19380	39 057	Greene	416	2,506	152,298	151,823	147,886	136,731	387	367	344	367.1	357.2	329.5
15740	39 059	Guernsey	528	2,073	40,876	41,007	40,792	39,024	1,139	1,088	1,021	78.3	78.2	74.8
17140	39 061	Hamilton	413	2,522	822,596	828,487	845,273	866,228	61	52	36	2,019.3	2,071.9	2,126.3
22300	39 063	Hancock	534	2,059	73,824	73,508	71,295	65,536	704	696	670	138.9	134.2	123.3
...	39 065	Hardin	471	2,276	31,966	32,015	31,945	31,111	1,369	1,348	1,240	68.0	67.9	66.2
...	39 067	Harrison	411	2,537	15,799	15,881	15,856	16,085	2,053	2,031	1,917	39.2	39.3	39.9
...	39 069	Henry	420	2,489	29,520	29,431	29,210	29,108	1,433	1,423	1,326	70.9	70.2	69.9
...	39 071	Highland	558	1,975	42,833	42,528	40,875	35,728	1,087	1,086	1,105	77.4	74.2	64.6
...	39 073	Hocking	424	2,470	28,973	28,927	28,241	25,533	1,448	1,443	1,445	68.5	66.8	60.4
...	39 075	Holmes	424	2,468	41,574	41,424	38,943	32,849	1,114	1,143	1,194	98.3	92.3	77.7
35940	39 077	Huron	495	2,203	60,313	60,291	59,487	56,238	837	807	771	122.4	121.0	114.0
...	39 079	Jackson	422	2,481	33,543	33,576	32,641	30,230	1,325	1,328	1,286	79.8	77.7	71.9
48260	39 081	Jefferson	411	2,535	70,125	70,631	73,894	80,298	744	677	571	171.2	179.9	196.0
34540	39 083	Knox	530	2,071	58,561	58,207	54,503	47,473	851	864	885	111.1	103.7	90.1
17460	39 085	Lake	979	798	232,892	232,416	227,511	215,500	264	250	231	1,020.5	997.7	944.2
26580	39 087	Lawrence	457	2,317	63,179	62,946	62,319	61,834	805	779	706	138.9	136.9	135.8
18140	39 089	Licking	688	1,469	156,287	154,683	145,625	128,300	371	376	362	227.7	212.8	186.9
13340	39 091	Logan	467	2,294	46,189	46,392	46,005	42,310	1,017	983	951	100.8	100.4	92.3
17460	39 093	Lorain	923	882	301,993	300,266	284,664	271,126	200	196	183	613.2	579.2	550.4
45780	39 095	Lucas	596	1,755	445,281	447,410	455,054	462,361	144	129	108	1,307.9	1,336.0	1,358.3
18140	39 097	Madison	466	2,296	41,496	41,220	40,213	37,078	1,115	1,110	1,070	89.2	86.4	79.7
49660	39 099	Mahoning	423	2,472	251,026	253,181	257,555	264,806	243	218	187	604.5	619.1	637.7
32020	39 101	Marion	404	2,580	65,583	65,834	66,209	64,274	780	738	681	162.4	163.8	159.1
17460	39 103	Medina	423	2,476	169,353	166,968	151,095	122,354	349	355	376	401.7	360.3	290.2
...	39 105	Meigs	432	2,428	23,092	23,179	23,072	22,987	1,665	1,640	1,535	53.8	53.7	53.5
16380	39 107	Mercer	473	2,268	41,303	41,150	40,924	39,443	1,123	1,083	1,013	89.2	88.3	85.1
19380	39 109	Miami	409	2,548	101,914	101,414	98,868	93,184	549	527	497	250.4	243.2	228.9
...	39 111	Monroe	457	2,316	14,606	14,736	15,180	15,497	2,127	2,078	1,954	32.1	33.3	34.0
19380	39 113	Montgomery	464	2,303	542,237	545,603	559,062	573,809	111	99	83	1,174.5	1,209.7	1,242.8
...	39 115	Morgan	422	2,480	14,821	14,895	14,897	14,194	2,115	2,100	2,038	35.5	35.6	34.0
18140	39 117	Morrow	407	2,558	34,529	34,309	31,628	27,749	1,306	1,355	1,362	85.0	78.3	68.4
49780	39 119	Muskingum	673	1,511	86,125	85,606	84,585	82,068	635	616	553	129.6	127.5	123.5
...	39 121	Noble	405	2,574	14,165	14,097	14,058	11,336	2,157	2,162	2,271	35.5	35.3	28.4
45780	39 123	Ottawa	585	1,801	41,331	41,430	40,985	40,029	1,120	1,081	997	162.1	160.8	156.9
...	39 125	Paulding	419	2,492	19,432	19,483	20,293	20,488	1,848	1,774	1,654	46.7	48.6	49.2
...	39 127	Perry	413	2,523	35,313	35,106	34,074	31,557	1,281	1,279	1,229	86.2	83.3	77.0
18140	39 129	Pickaway	507	2,149	53,606	52,837	52,727	48,248	908	883	865	106.8	105.3	96.1
...	39 131	Pike	444	2,365	28,269	28,058	27,695	24,249	1,474	1,460	1,486	64.0	62.9	54.9
10420	39 133	Portage	507	2,147	155,012	155,150	152,061	142,585	377	353	333	314.8	309.5	289.6
19380	39 135	Preble	426	2,456	42,491	42,400	42,341	40,113	1,093	1,048	996	100.0	99.7	94.4
...	39 137	Putnam	484	2,228	34,744	34,807	34,726	33,819	1,299	1,261	1,169	71.8	71.8	69.9
31900	39 139	Richland	500	2,179	127,010	127,585	128,852	126,137	462	419	367	255.6	259.2	253.8
17060	39 141	Ross	693	1,457	75,556	75,135	73,345	69,330	696	682	639	109.8	106.7	100.7
23380	39 143	Sandusky	418	2,498	61,625	61,579	61,796	61,963	828	785	703	150.6	151.1	151.4
39020	39 145	Scioto	616	1,688	76,441	76,506	79,195	80,327	692	648	569	124.8	129.2	131.2
45660	39 147	Seneca	552	1,995	57,255	57,373	58,683	59,733	867	817	725	104.0	106.5	108.5
43380	39 149	Shelby	411	2,533	48,884	48,690	47,910	44,915	974	954	914	119.4	117.3	109.7
15940	39 151	Stark	581	1,823	380,575	380,275	378,132	367,585	168	155	140	660.6	656.4	638.0
10420	39 153	Summit	420	2,488	545,931	546,285	542,899	514,990	109	103	91	1,322.8	1,317.1	1,247.5
49660	39 155	Trumbull	635	1,625	217,362	218,672	225,116	227,795	280	252	216	352.6	365.0	369.9
35420	39 157	Tuscarawas	571	1,914	91,766	91,791	90,914	84,090	606	567	544	161.7	160.4	148.1
18140	39 159	Union	437	2,397	46,702	45,600	40,909	31,969	1,007	1,084	1,213	107.0	94.4	73.2
46780	39 161	Van Wert	410	2,540	29,303	29,213	29,659	30,464	1,438	1,411	1,270	71.5	72.3	74.3
...	39 163	Vinton	415	2,510	13,519	13,384	12,806	11,098	2,203	2,248	2,284	32.6	30.9	26.8
17140	39 165	Warren	407	2,560	201,871	196,793	159,169	113,973	293	334	402	505.1	404.0	285.0
37620	39 167	Washington	640	1,610	61,867	62,155	63,251	62,254	824	767	700	97.4	99.5	98.0
49300	39 169	Wayne	556	1,985	113,950	113,496	111,530	101,461	504	484	451	205.2	201.1	182.7
...	39 171	Williams	423	2,477	38,719	38,679	39,188	36,956	1,188	1,134	1,073	91.8	93.0	87.6
45780	39 173	Wood	621	1,669	124,183	123,889	121,061	113,269	473	448	406	201.2	196.3	183.5
...	39 175	Wyandot	408	2,557	22,553	22,711	22,908	22,254	1,696	1,650	1,566	55.6	56.5	54.9

See footnotes at end of table.

Table B-1. Counties — **Area and Population**—Con.

[Includes United States, states, and 3,141 counties/county equivalents defined as of February 22, 2005. For more information on these areas, see Appendix C, Geographic Information]

Metro-politan area code	FIPS state and county code[1]	County	Area, 2000 (square miles)		Population									
							2000[3] (April 1 estimates base)	1990[3] (April 1 estimates base)	Rank			Persons per square mile of land area		
			Total	Rank[2]	2006 (July 1)	2005 (July 1)			2006[2]	2000[2]	1990[4]	2006[5]	2000	1990
	40 000	OKLAHOMA	69,898	(X)	3,579,212	3,543,442	3,450,654	3,145,576	(X)	(X)	(X)	52.1	50.3	45.8
...	40 001	Adair	577	1,850	22,317	21,956	21,038	18,421	1,710	1,734	1,768	38.8	36.6	32.0
...	40 003	Alfalfa	881	1,016	5,673	5,719	6,105	6,416	2,789	2,770	2,715	6.5	7.0	7.4
...	40 005	Atoka	990	780	14,340	14,338	13,879	12,778	2,140	2,171	2,158	14.7	14.2	13.1
...	40 007	Beaver	1,818	360	5,336	5,401	5,857	6,023	2,814	2,799	2,754	2.9	3.2	3.3
21120	40 009	Beckham	904	945	19,271	18,810	19,799	18,812	1,854	1,802	1,746	21.4	21.9	20.9
...	40 011	Blaine	939	854	12,734	12,876	11,976	11,470	2,262	2,296	2,257	13.7	12.9	12.4
20460	40 013	Bryan	943	849	38,395	37,716	36,534	32,089	1,198	1,202	1,209	42.2	40.3	35.3
...	40 015	Caddo	1,290	532	30,063	30,089	30,150	29,550	1,417	1,391	1,315	23.5	23.6	23.1
36420	40 017	Canadian	905	941	101,335	98,451	87,697	74,409	552	598	603	112.6	98.0	82.7
11620	40 019	Carter	834	1,107	47,503	47,032	45,621	42,919	992	989	939	57.7	55.4	52.1
45140	40 021	Cherokee	776	1,220	44,910	44,416	42,521	34,049	1,041	1,044	1,162	59.8	56.8	45.3
...	40 023	Choctaw	801	1,173	15,334	15,315	15,342	15,302	2,082	2,067	1,973	19.8	19.8	19.8
...	40 025	Cimarron	1,841	356	2,807	2,809	3,148	3,301	2,991	2,982	2,977	1.5	1.7	1.8
36420	40 027	Cleveland	558	1,974	228,594	224,244	208,016	174,253	269	267	277	426.4	388.6	325.0
...	40 029	Coal	521	2,097	5,634	5,736	6,031	5,780	2,791	2,778	2,781	10.9	11.6	11.2
30020	40 031	Comanche	1,084	677	109,181	110,629	114,996	111,486	525	471	412	102.1	107.2	104.2
...	40 033	Cotton	642	1,598	6,491	6,526	6,614	6,651	2,733	2,727	2,689	10.2	10.4	10.4
...	40 035	Craig	763	1,257	15,046	15,047	14,950	14,104	2,105	2,096	2,047	19.8	19.6	18.5
46140	40 037	Creek	970	812	69,146	68,674	67,369	60,915	751	727	715	72.4	70.7	63.7
...	40 039	Custer	1,002	768	25,566	25,278	26,142	26,897	1,560	1,513	1,393	25.9	26.4	27.3
...	40 041	Delaware	792	1,195	40,061	39,221	37,077	28,070	1,158	1,188	1,350	54.1	50.2	37.9
...	40 043	Dewey	1,008	759	4,475	4,534	4,743	5,551	2,870	2,865	2,797	4.5	4.7	5.5
...	40 045	Ellis	1,232	567	3,912	3,958	4,075	4,497	2,915	2,912	2,875	3.2	3.3	3.7
21420	40 047	Garfield	1,060	705	57,068	56,885	57,813	56,735	871	826	768	53.9	54.5	53.6
...	40 049	Garvin	814	1,146	27,375	27,190	27,210	26,605	1,506	1,476	1,403	33.9	33.8	32.9
36420	40 051	Grady	1,105	661	50,490	49,364	45,514	41,747	946	991	962	45.9	41.4	37.9
...	40 053	Grant	1,004	765	4,653	4,779	5,144	5,689	2,856	2,842	2,785	4.7	5.1	5.7
...	40 055	Greer	644	1,593	5,864	5,870	6,061	6,559	2,779	2,775	2,702	9.2	9.4	10.3
...	40 057	Harmon	539	2,045	3,042	3,046	3,283	3,793	2,974	2,974	2,931	5.7	6.1	7.1
...	40 059	Harper	1,041	725	3,348	3,347	3,562	4,063	2,951	2,948	2,912	3.2	3.4	3.9
...	40 061	Haskell	625	1,650	12,155	12,084	11,792	10,940	2,287	2,310	2,298	21.1	20.5	19.0
...	40 063	Hughes	815	1,140	13,893	13,897	14,154	13,014	2,175	2,152	2,140	17.2	17.5	16.1
11060	40 065	Jackson	804	1,164	26,042	26,338	28,439	28,764	1,548	1,433	1,337	32.4	35.2	35.8
...	40 067	Jefferson	774	1,225	6,385	6,447	6,818	7,010	2,738	2,710	2,657	8.4	8.9	9.2
...	40 069	Johnston	658	1,541	10,436	10,295	10,513	10,032	2,406	2,397	2,384	16.2	16.3	15.6
38620	40 071	Kay	945	845	45,889	46,195	48,080	48,056	1,022	949	869	49.9	52.2	52.3
...	40 073	Kingfisher	906	937	14,316	14,230	13,926	13,212	2,142	2,169	2,121	15.9	15.4	14.6
...	40 075	Kiowa	1,031	738	9,778	9,882	10,227	11,347	2,461	2,423	2,268	9.6	10.1	11.2
...	40 077	Latimer	729	1,326	10,562	10,607	10,692	10,333	2,396	2,385	2,356	14.6	14.8	14.3
22900	40 079	Le Flore	1,608	416	50,079	49,412	48,111	43,270	953	947	934	31.6	30.4	27.3
36420	40 081	Lincoln	966	817	32,645	32,344	32,080	29,216	1,348	1,344	1,323	34.1	33.6	30.5
36420	40 083	Logan	749	1,281	36,971	36,414	33,924	29,011	1,236	1,284	1,328	49.7	45.6	39.0
11620	40 085	Love	532	2,068	9,162	9,148	8,831	7,788	2,512	2,544	2,596	17.8	17.1	15.1
36420	40 087	McClain	580	1,830	31,038	29,982	27,742	22,795	1,394	1,458	1,543	54.5	48.9	40.0
...	40 089	McCurtain	1,901	339	34,018	33,871	34,402	33,433	1,315	1,268	1,179	18.4	18.6	18.0
...	40 091	McIntosh	712	1,411	19,899	19,834	19,456	16,779	1,823	1,822	1,861	32.1	31.4	27.1
...	40 093	Major	958	824	7,329	7,309	7,545	8,055	2,652	2,640	2,558	7.7	7.9	8.4
...	40 095	Marshall	427	2,453	14,558	14,356	13,184	10,829	2,130	2,214	2,308	39.2	35.5	29.2
...	40 097	Mayes	684	1,480	39,774	39,416	38,369	33,366	1,167	1,156	1,180	60.6	58.6	50.8
...	40 099	Murray	425	2,463	12,945	12,809	12,623	12,042	2,248	2,256	2,214	31.0	30.2	28.8
34780	40 101	Muskogee	839	1,095	71,018	70,672	69,451	68,078	733	712	650	87.3	85.4	83.6
...	40 103	Noble	742	1,293	11,152	11,199	11,411	11,045	2,355	2,341	2,288	15.2	15.5	15.1
...	40 105	Nowata	581	1,824	10,785	10,799	10,569	9,992	2,381	2,392	2,386	19.1	18.7	17.7
...	40 107	Okfuskee	629	1,642	11,370	11,404	11,814	11,551	2,341	2,306	2,252	18.2	18.9	18.5
36420	40 109	Oklahoma	718	1,382	691,266	684,192	660,448	599,611	82	80	77	974.9	933.2	845.5
46140	40 111	Okmulgee	702	1,431	39,670	39,657	39,685	36,490	1,169	1,119	1,089	56.9	56.9	52.4
46140	40 113	Osage	2,304	265	45,549	45,342	44,434	41,645	1,031	1,008	965	20.2	19.8	18.5
33060	40 115	Ottawa	485	2,226	33,026	32,800	33,194	30,561	1,338	1,310	1,263	70.1	70.6	64.8
46140	40 117	Pawnee	595	1,758	16,844	16,792	16,612	15,575	1,980	1,985	1,948	29.6	29.3	27.3
44660	40 119	Payne	697	1,446	73,818	73,419	68,190	61,507	705	722	710	107.6	99.3	89.6
32540	40 121	Pittsburg	1,378	491	45,002	44,564	43,953	40,950	1,040	1,016	980	34.5	33.7	31.4
10220	40 123	Pontotoc	725	1,335	35,350	35,188	35,143	34,119	1,278	1,244	1,161	49.1	48.8	47.4
43060	40 125	Pottawatomie	793	1,192	68,638	68,076	65,519	58,760	756	745	739	87.1	83.4	74.6
...	40 127	Pushmataha	1,423	480	11,641	11,666	11,667	10,997	2,320	2,321	2,295	8.3	8.3	7.9
...	40 129	Roger Mills	1,146	624	3,293	3,309	3,436	4,147	2,958	2,960	2,901	2.9	3.0	3.6
46140	40 131	Rogers	711	1,414	82,435	80,509	70,638	55,170	654	703	782	122.1	105.8	81.7
...	40 133	Seminole	641	1,605	24,650	24,638	24,896	25,412	1,600	1,562	1,451	39.0	39.4	40.2
22900	40 135	Sequoyah	715	1,399	41,356	40,766	38,972	33,828	1,119	1,140	1,168	61.4	58.0	50.2
20340	40 137	Stephens	891	996	43,243	42,929	43,182	42,299	1,074	1,032	952	49.5	49.3	48.2
25100	40 139	Texas	2,049	306	20,238	20,136	20,107	16,419	1,810	1,789	1,898	9.9	9.9	8.1

See footnotes at end of table.

[Includes United States, states, and 3,141 counties/county equivalents defined as of February 22, 2005. For more information on these areas, see Appendix C, Geographic Information]

Metro-politan area code	FIPS state and county code[1]	County	Area, 2000 (square miles)		Population									
							2000[3] (April 1 estimates base)	1990[3] (April 1 estimates base)	Rank			Persons per square mile of land area		
			Total	Rank[2]	2006 (July 1)	2005 (July 1)			2006[2]	2000[2]	1990[4]	2006[5]	2000	1990
		OKLAHOMA—Con.												
...	40 141	Tillman	879	1,022	8,482	8,519	9,287	10,384	2,564	2,508	2,349	9.7	10.6	11.9
46140	40 143	Tulsa	587	1,788	577,795	570,627	563,301	503,341	102	98	95	1,013.1	988.7	882.5
46140	40 145	Wagoner	591	1,772	66,313	64,177	57,491	47,883	774	830	875	117.8	102.6	85.0
12780	40 147	Washington	424	2,466	49,241	48,997	48,996	48,066	968	933	868	118.1	117.6	115.3
...	40 149	Washita	1,009	757	11,583	11,449	11,508	11,441	2,324	2,335	2,259	11.5	11.5	11.4
...	40 151	Woods	1,290	533	8,385	8,481	9,089	9,103	2,569	2,523	2,461	6.5	7.0	7.1
49260	40 153	Woodward	1,246	554	19,231	19,009	18,486	18,976	1,855	1,871	1,736	15.5	14.8	15.3
	41 000	OREGON	98,381	(X)	3,700,758	3,638,871	3,421,436	2,842,337	(X)	(X)	(X)	38.6	35.7	29.6
18700	41 001	Baker	3,088	178	16,243	16,255	16,741	15,317	2,029	1,975	1,971	5.3	5.5	5.0
38900	41 003	Benton	679	1,497	79,061	78,597	78,139	70,811	680	651	626	116.9	115.5	104.7
38900	41 005	Clackamas	1,879	345	374,230	368,259	338,391	278,850	170	173	177	200.3	181.8	149.3
11820	41 007	Clatsop	1,085	675	37,315	36,842	35,630	33,301	1,224	1,228	1,183	45.1	43.0	40.3
38900	41 009	Columbia	688	1,470	49,163	47,899	43,560	37,557	970	1,027	1,058	74.9	66.5	57.2
18300	41 011	Coos	1,806	364	64,820	64,554	62,788	60,273	786	775	719	40.5	39.2	37.7
39260	41 013	Crook	2,987	185	22,941	21,999	19,184	14,111	1,672	1,836	2,045	7.7	6.5	4.7
15060	41 015	Curry	1,989	318	22,358	22,341	21,137	19,327	1,706	1,729	1,713	13.7	13.0	11.9
13460	41 017	Deschutes	3,055	180	149,140	141,288	115,367	74,976	397	466	599	49.4	38.6	24.8
40700	41 019	Douglas	5,134	79	105,117	104,139	100,399	94,649	538	523	490	20.9	20.0	18.8
...	41 021	Gilliam	1,223	576	1,775	1,792	1,915	1,717	3,071	3,071	3,082	1.5	1.6	1.4
...	41 023	Grant	4,529	105	7,250	7,319	7,935	7,853	2,662	2,612	2,586	1.6	1.7	1.7
...	41 025	Harney	10,226	28	6,888	6,910	7,609	7,060	2,692	2,636	2,653	0.7	0.8	0.7
26220	41 027	Hood River	534	2,060	21,533	21,321	20,411	16,903	1,741	1,765	1,856	41.2	39.2	32.4
32780	41 029	Jackson	2,802	198	197,071	195,151	181,323	146,387	299	304	323	70.8	65.3	52.6
...	41 031	Jefferson	1,791	369	20,352	20,007	19,009	13,676	1,804	1,847	2,083	11.4	10.7	7.7
24420	41 033	Josephine	1,642	408	81,688	80,667	75,676	62,649	659	663	694	49.8	46.3	38.2
28900	41 035	Klamath	6,136	61	66,438	65,803	63,775	57,702	773	762	754	11.2	10.8	9.7
...	41 037	Lake	8,358	39	7,473	7,269	7,422	7,186	2,639	2,647	2,635	0.9	0.9	0.9
21660	41 039	Lane	4,722	99	337,870	334,486	322,977	282,912	184	178	174	74.2	71.0	62.1
...	41 041	Lincoln	1,194	589	46,199	45,946	44,479	38,889	1,016	1,007	1,026	47.2	45.3	39.7
10540	41 043	Linn	2,310	262	111,489	108,942	103,083	91,227	514	515	504	48.6	45.0	39.8
36620	41 045	Malheur	9,930	30	31,247	31,292	31,615	26,038	1,391	1,356	1,419	3.2	3.2	2.6
41420	41 047	Marion	1,194	588	311,304	305,715	284,838	228,483	198	195	215	262.9	241.3	192.8
37820	41 049	Morrow	2,049	307	11,753	11,638	10,995	7,625	2,312	2,366	2,607	5.8	5.4	3.8
38900	41 051	Multnomah	466	2,299	681,454	672,947	660,486	583,887	84	79	81	1,565.7	1,520.1	1,341.4
41420	41 053	Polk	744	1,289	73,296	70,553	62,380	49,541	710	778	848	98.9	84.6	66.8
...	41 055	Sherman	831	1,111	1,699	1,729	1,934	1,918	3,075	3,068	3,072	2.1	2.3	2.3
...	41 057	Tillamook	1,333	508	25,380	25,226	24,262	21,570	1,571	1,586	1,599	23.0	22.0	19.6
37820	41 059	Umatilla	3,231	169	72,928	72,843	70,548	59,249	713	704	734	22.7	22.0	18.4
29260	41 061	Union	2,039	310	24,345	24,418	24,530	23,598	1,618	1,576	1,510	12.0	12.1	11.6
...	41 063	Wallowa	3,152	175	6,875	6,945	7,226	6,911	2,693	2,664	2,669	2.2	2.3	2.2
17180	41 065	Wasco	2,395	246	23,712	23,555	23,791	21,683	1,642	1,600	1,594	10.0	10.0	9.1
38900	41 067	Washington	726	1,331	514,269	500,714	445,342	311,554	119	133	161	710.6	619.8	430.4
...	41 069	Wheeler	1,715	389	1,404	1,430	1,547	1,396	3,091	3,092	3,102	0.8	0.9	0.8
38900	41 071	Yamhill	718	1,380	94,678	92,080	84,992	65,551	588	612	669	132.3	119.2	91.6
	42 000	PENNSYLVANIA	46,055	(X)	12,440,621	12,405,348	12,281,054	11,882,842	(X)	(X)	(X)	277.6	274.2	265.1
23900	42 001	Adams	522	2,095	101,105	99,746	91,292	78,274	555	563	577	194.4	176.2	150.5
38300	42 003	Allegheny	745	1,286	1,223,411	1,233,036	1,281,666	1,336,449	30	28	19	1,675.5	1,752.8	1,830.2
38300	42 005	Armstrong	664	1,526	70,096	70,527	72,392	73,478	745	687	612	107.2	110.6	112.4
38300	42 007	Beaver	444	2,367	175,736	176,825	181,412	186,093	335	303	261	404.7	417.2	427.5
...	42 009	Bedford	1,017	749	49,927	49,862	49,984	47,919	954	916	873	49.2	49.3	47.2
39740	42 011	Berks	866	1,046	401,149	396,236	373,661	336,523	161	157	151	467.1	436.2	391.7
11020	42 013	Blair	527	2,078	126,494	126,572	129,144	130,542	464	418	357	240.6	245.5	248.2
42380	42 015	Bradford	1,161	607	62,471	62,504	62,761	60,967	817	776	714	54.3	54.6	53.0
37980	42 017	Bucks	622	1,660	623,205	619,772	597,632	541,174	95	91	89	1,026.1	987.1	890.6
38300	42 019	Butler	795	1,189	182,901	181,526	174,081	152,013	322	314	306	232.0	221.4	192.8
27780	42 021	Cambria	693	1,455	146,967	147,804	152,598	163,062	406	348	292	213.6	221.3	237.0
...	42 023	Cameron	399	2,603	5,489	5,593	5,974	5,913	2,800	2,785	2,770	13.8	15.0	14.9
10900	42 025	Carbon	387	2,638	62,567	61,876	58,802	56,803	814	814	767	162.4	154.4	148.5
44300	42 027	Centre	1,112	654	140,953	140,313	135,758	124,812	424	397	369	127.3	122.7	112.7
37980	42 029	Chester	760	1,263	482,112	473,723	433,501	376,389	132	138	135	637.7	576.6	497.9
...	42 031	Clarion	609	1,711	40,385	40,388	41,765	41,699	1,151	1,061	964	67.0	69.3	69.2
20180	42 033	Clearfield	1,154	612	82,442	82,634	83,382	78,097	653	625	579	71.9	72.7	68.1
30820	42 035	Clinton	898	974	37,232	37,233	37,910	37,182	1,228	1,169	1,067	41.8	42.6	41.7
14100	42 037	Columbia	490	2,215	65,014	64,792	64,148	63,202	783	760	691	133.9	132.0	130.2
32740	42 039	Crawford	1,038	727	89,389	89,484	90,366	86,166	618	572	530	88.3	89.3	85.1
25420	42 041	Cumberland	551	2,001	226,117	223,017	213,674	195,257	272	261	246	411.0	388.9	354.9
25420	42 043	Dauphin	558	1,976	254,176	252,949	251,798	237,813	240	226	211	483.9	479.4	452.7
37980	42 045	Delaware	191	3,033	555,996	554,393	551,547	547,658	108	102	86	3,018.3	2,997.9	2,972.7
41260	42 047	Elk	832	1,110	33,179	33,473	35,112	34,878	1,335	1,247	1,137	40.0	42.3	42.1
21500	42 049	Erie	1,558	428	279,811	280,184	280,843	275,575	216	198	179	348.9	350.1	343.6

See footnotes at end of table.

County and City Data Book: 2007

U.S. Census Bureau

[Includes United States, states, and 3,141 counties/county equivalents defined as of February 22, 2005. For more information on these areas, see Appendix C, Geographic Information]

Metro-politan area code	FIPS state and county code[1]	County	Area, 2000 (square miles)		Population									
							2000[3] (April 1 estimates base)	1990[3] (April 1 estimates base)	Rank			Persons per square mile of land area		
			Total	Rank[2]	2006 (July 1)	2005 (July 1)			2006[2]	2000[2]	1990[4]	2006[5]	2000	1990
		PENNSYLVANIA—Con.												
38300	42 051	Fayette	798	1,183	145,760	146,206	148,644	145,351	411	364	326	184.5	188.0	184.0
...	42 053	Forest	431	2,436	6,506	6,507	4,946	4,802	2,731	2,852	2,857	15.2	11.5	11.2
16540	42 055	Franklin	773	1,229	139,991	137,273	129,313	121,082	428	416	380	181.4	167.8	156.8
...	42 057	Fulton	438	2,391	14,783	14,655	14,261	13,837	2,121	2,146	2,071	33.8	32.6	31.6
...	42 059	Greene	578	1,844	40,432	40,408	40,672	39,550	1,148	1,093	1,010	70.2	70.7	68.7
26500	42 061	Huntingdon	889	1,001	45,771	45,772	45,586	44,164	1,027	990	922	52.4	52.2	50.5
26860	42 063	Indiana	834	1,106	88,234	88,481	89,605	89,994	623	576	511	106.4	108.0	108.5
...	42 065	Jefferson	657	1,549	45,725	45,716	45,932	46,083	1,028	985	902	69.8	70.1	70.3
...	42 067	Juniata	394	2,625	23,512	23,412	22,821	20,625	1,651	1,654	1,649	60.0	58.4	52.7
42540	42 069	Lackawanna	465	2,301	209,728	209,622	213,295	219,097	286	263	226	457.3	464.3	477.6
29540	42 071	Lancaster	984	790	494,486	489,936	470,635	422,822	124	122	119	521.0	497.1	445.5
35260	42 073	Lawrence	363	2,698	91,795	92,412	94,645	96,246	605	543	481	254.7	262.5	267.0
30140	42 075	Lebanon	363	2,702	126,883	125,429	120,327	113,744	463	452	403	350.6	332.8	314.4
10900	42 077	Lehigh	348	2,732	335,544	330,168	312,090	291,130	185	183	169	967.9	902.0	839.8
42540	42 079	Luzerne	907	931	313,020	312,795	319,252	328,149	195	181	155	351.4	357.7	368.3
48700	42 081	Lycoming	1,244	556	117,668	118,102	120,048	118,710	491	454	391	95.3	97.1	96.1
14620	42 083	McKean	984	788	44,065	44,239	45,936	47,131	1,058	984	889	44.9	46.7	48.0
49660	42 085	Mercer	683	1,484	118,551	119,115	120,293	121,003	487	453	381	176.5	178.9	180.1
30380	42 087	Mifflin	415	2,514	46,057	46,085	46,486	46,197	1,019	974	899	111.8	112.9	112.5
20700	42 089	Monroe	617	1,684	165,685	162,415	138,687	95,681	352	393	483	272.3	229.8	157.5
37980	42 091	Montgomery	487	2,219	775,688	774,666	748,987	678,193	69	67	61	1,605.6	1,554.5	1,403.7
14100	42 093	Montour	132	3,080	17,934	17,983	18,239	17,735	1,918	1,886	1,801	137.2	139.6	135.6
10900	42 095	Northampton	377	2,660	291,306	287,334	267,069	247,110	209	206	202	779.3	715.7	661.0
44980	42 097	Northumberland	477	2,251	91,654	92,280	94,556	96,771	607	544	476	199.3	205.4	210.4
25420	42 099	Perry	556	1,988	45,087	44,724	43,602	41,172	1,038	1,026	976	81.5	78.8	74.4
37980	42 101	Philadelphia	143	3,076	1,448,394	1,456,350	1,517,550	1,585,577	24	18	12	10,721.7	11,204.8	11,733.7
35620	42 103	Pike	567	1,946	58,195	56,180	46,302	28,032	854	977	1,351	106.4	85.3	51.2
...	42 105	Potter	1,081	680	17,568	17,728	18,080	16,717	1,936	1,896	1,867	16.2	16.8	15.5
39060	42 107	Schuylkill	783	1,209	147,405	146,996	150,334	152,585	403	359	303	189.4	192.9	196.0
42780	42 109	Snyder	332	2,775	38,226	37,949	37,546	36,680	1,203	1,176	1,083	115.4	113.4	110.7
43740	42 111	Somerset	1,081	681	78,508	78,796	80,023	78,218	683	642	578	73.1	74.5	72.8
...	42 113	Sullivan	452	2,332	6,277	6,361	6,556	6,104	2,743	2,733	2,744	14.0	14.6	13.6
...	42 115	Susquehanna	832	1,109	41,889	41,943	42,238	40,380	1,105	1,052	989	50.9	51.4	49.1
...	42 117	Tioga	1,137	631	41,137	41,382	41,373	41,126	1,127	1,069	977	36.3	36.5	36.3
30260	42 119	Union	317	2,806	43,387	43,171	41,624	36,176	1,073	1,066	1,097	137.0	131.6	114.2
36340	42 121	Venango	683	1,482	55,488	55,938	57,565	59,381	889	829	729	82.2	85.1	88.0
47620	42 123	Warren	898	976	41,742	41,973	43,863	45,050	1,108	1,019	912	47.2	49.6	51.0
38300	42 125	Washington	861	1,063	206,432	206,418	202,897	204,584	289	271	243	240.9	236.9	238.7
...	42 127	Wayne	751	1,279	50,929	50,529	47,722	39,944	943	956	1,003	69.8	65.7	54.8
38300	42 129	Westmoreland	1,036	730	366,440	367,133	369,993	370,321	174	158	138	357.3	360.6	362.1
42540	42 131	Wyoming	405	2,573	28,093	28,122	28,080	28,076	1,483	1,450	1,348	70.7	70.6	70.7
49620	42 133	York	910	919	416,322	408,182	381,751	339,574	151	152	149	460.3	423.2	375.4
	44 000	RHODE ISLAND	1,545	(X)	1,067,610	1,073,579	1,048,319	1,003,464	(X)	(X)	(X)	1,021.7	1,005.7	960.3
39300	44 001	Bristol	45	3,109	52,256	52,601	50,648	48,859	924	913	859	2,117.3	2,055.9	1,979.7
39300	44 003	Kent	188	3,035	170,053	171,097	167,090	161,143	348	323	296	999.3	984.5	947.5
39300	44 005	Newport	314	2,813	82,144	83,233	85,433	87,194	656	611	521	789.5	823.3	837.9
39300	44 007	Providence	436	2,409	635,596	638,595	621,602	596,270	92	86	78	1,538.0	1,507.2	1,442.7
39300	44 009	Washington	563	1,962	127,561	128,053	123,546	109,998	459	436	419	383.4	372.7	330.4
	45 000	SOUTH CAROLINA	32,020	(X)	4,321,249	4,246,933	4,011,816	3,486,310	(X)	(X)	(X)	143.5	133.6	115.8
...	45 001	Abbeville	511	2,130	25,935	26,051	26,167	23,862	1,550	1,512	1,498	51.1	51.6	47.0
12260	45 003	Aiken	1,080	682	151,800	150,053	142,556	120,991	390	382	382	141.5	133.1	112.8
	45 005	Allendale	413	2,524	10,748	10,873	11,211	11,727	2,383	2,356	2,231	26.3	27.4	28.7
11340	45 007	Anderson	757	1,266	177,963	175,258	165,740	145,177	334	325	327	247.9	231.7	202.2
...	45 009	Bamberg	395	2,616	15,678	15,787	16,658	16,902	2,063	1,981	1,857	39.9	42.3	43.0
...	45 011	Barnwell	557	1,977	23,265	23,289	23,478	20,293	1,663	1,617	1,660	42.4	42.8	37.0
25940	45 013	Beaufort	923	883	142,045	138,037	120,948	86,425	421	449	527	242.0	207.9	147.2
16700	45 015	Berkeley	1,228	571	152,282	149,526	142,653	128,658	388	381	361	138.7	130.4	117.0
17900	45 017	Calhoun	392	2,626	15,026	15,059	15,180	12,753	2,106	2,078	2,162	39.5	40.1	33.5
16700	45 019	Charleston	1,358	498	331,917	329,482	309,978	295,159	187	184	165	361.4	338.3	321.7
23500	45 021	Cherokee	397	2,609	53,886	53,620	52,537	44,506	905	887	919	137.2	134.2	113.3
16900	45 023	Chester	586	1,793	32,875	33,093	34,068	32,170	1,344	1,280	1,208	56.6	58.8	55.4
...	45 025	Chesterfield	806	1,158	43,191	43,191	42,768	38,575	1,077	1,040	1,039	54.1	53.7	48.3
...	45 027	Clarendon	696	1,452	33,339	33,127	32,502	28,450	1,330	1,333	1,344	54.9	53.6	46.9
47500	45 029	Colleton	1,133	638	39,467	39,430	38,264	34,377	1,173	1,159	1,156	37.4	36.3	32.5
22500	45 031	Darlington	567	1,941	67,551	67,369	67,394	61,851	761	726	705	120.4	120.3	110.0
19900	45 033	Dillon	407	2,565	30,984	30,851	30,722	29,114	1,395	1,380	1,325	76.5	75.9	71.9
16700	45 035	Dorchester	577	1,853	118,979	112,784	96,341	83,060	486	537	549	207.0	168.3	144.5
12260	45 037	Edgefield	507	2,152	25,261	25,343	24,560	18,360	1,575	1,572	1,771	50.3	49.0	36.6
17900	45 039	Fairfield	710	1,416	23,810	23,844	23,454	22,295	1,637	1,620	1,563	34.7	34.3	32.5

See footnotes at end of table.

Table B-1. Counties — **Area and Population**—Con.

[Includes United States, states, and 3,141 counties/county equivalents defined as of February 22, 2005. For more information on these areas, see Appendix C, Geographic Information]

Metro-politan area code	FIPS state and county code[1]	County	Area, 2000 (square miles)		Population									
			Total	Rank[2]	2006 (July 1)	2005 (July 1)	2000[3] (April 1 estimates base)	1990[3] (April 1 estimates base)	Rank			Persons per square mile of land area		
									2006[2]	2000[2]	1990[4]	2006[5]	2000	1990
		SOUTH CAROLINA—Con.												
22500	45 041	Florence	804	1,166	131,297	130,259	125,761	114,344	444	432	401	164.2	157.3	143.1
23860	45 043	Georgetown	1,035	731	60,860	60,215	55,793	46,302	835	846	898	74.7	68.9	56.8
24860	45 045	Greenville	795	1,188	417,166	407,154	379,632	320,127	150	154	158	528.0	482.4	404.2
24940	45 047	Greenwood	463	2,306	68,213	67,860	66,272	59,567	758	736	726	149.7	145.6	130.8
...	45 049	Hampton	563	1,964	21,268	21,153	21,382	18,186	1,751	1,720	1,778	38.0	38.2	32.5
34820	45 051	Horry	1,255	551	238,493	227,520	196,629	144,053	259	281	329	210.4	174.7	127.1
25940	45 053	Jasper	700	1,440	21,809	21,409	20,671	15,487	1,728	1,752	1,955	33.2	31.6	23.7
17900	45 055	Kershaw	740	1,301	57,490	56,341	52,647	43,599	864	885	929	79.2	72.8	60.0
29580	45 057	Lancaster	555	1,990	63,628	63,060	61,351	54,516	797	793	791	115.9	111.8	99.3
24860	45 059	Laurens	724	1,344	70,374	70,247	69,533	58,132	741	710	746	98.4	97.4	81.5
...	45 061	Lee	411	2,532	20,559	20,589	20,119	18,437	1,789	1,787	1,765	50.1	49.1	44.9
17900	45 063	Lexington	758	1,265	240,160	234,934	216,010	167,526	258	260	286	343.5	310.2	239.0
...	45 065	McCormick	394	2,623	10,226	10,129	9,958	8,868	2,431	2,450	2,480	28.4	27.8	24.7
...	45 067	Marion	494	2,205	34,684	34,798	35,466	33,899	1,304	1,236	1,167	70.9	72.5	69.3
13500	45 069	Marlboro	485	2,225	29,152	27,722	28,818	29,716	1,444	1,427	1,307	60.8	60.1	61.9
35140	45 071	Newberry	647	1,582	37,762	37,315	36,004	33,172	1,217	1,218	1,186	59.9	57.1	52.6
42860	45 073	Oconee	674	1,510	70,567	69,676	66,215	57,494	735	737	758	112.8	106.2	92.0
36700	45 075	Orangeburg	1,128	642	90,845	90,916	91,514	84,804	614	561	541	82.1	82.7	76.7
24860	45 077	Pickens	512	2,129	114,446	113,221	110,757	93,896	501	490	492	230.3	223.4	189.0
17900	45 079	Richland	772	1,231	348,226	341,813	320,781	286,321	179	180	171	460.4	424.9	378.5
17900	45 081	Saluda	462	2,309	19,059	18,968	19,181	16,441	1,869	1,837	1,896	42.1	42.4	36.4
43900	45 083	Spartanburg	819	1,131	271,087	266,764	253,782	226,793	225	222	217	334.3	313.8	279.6
44940	45 085	Sumter	682	1,485	104,430	104,909	104,636	101,276	539	505	452	156.9	157.3	152.2
46420	45 087	Union	516	2,119	28,306	28,511	29,881	30,337	1,472	1,400	1,278	55.1	58.1	59.0
...	45 089	Williamsburg	937	859	36,105	35,272	37,221	36,815	1,254	1,186	1,080	38.7	39.8	39.4
16740	45 091	York	696	1,451	199,035	190,111	164,623	131,497	297	327	353	291.6	242.8	192.7
	46 000	**SOUTH DAKOTA**	77,116	(X)	781,919	774,883	754,844	696,004	(X)	(X)	(X)	10.3	10.0	9.2
...	46 003	Aurora	713	1,410	2,905	2,891	3,058	3,135	2,988	2,988	2,990	4.1	4.3	4.4
26700	46 005	Beadle	1,265	548	15,643	15,860	17,023	18,253	2,065	1,952	1,776	12.4	13.5	14.5
...	46 007	Bennett	1,191	590	3,543	3,561	3,574	3,206	2,939	2,946	2,983	3.0	3.0	2.7
...	46 009	Bon Homme	581	1,822	7,281	7,061	7,260	7,089	2,657	2,659	2,647	12.9	12.9	12.6
15100	46 011	Brookings	805	1,163	28,195	27,769	28,220	25,207	1,477	1,445	1,454	35.5	35.6	31.7
10100	46 013	Brown	1,731	387	34,645	34,684	35,460	35,580	1,305	1,237	1,110	20.2	20.7	20.8
...	46 015	Brule	846	1,089	5,167	5,150	5,364	5,485	2,829	2,825	2,802	6.3	6.5	6.7
...	46 017	Buffalo	487	2,220	2,109	2,087	2,032	1,759	3,042	3,063	3,080	4.5	4.3	3.7
...	46 019	Butte	2,266	270	9,374	9,347	9,094	7,914	2,490	2,522	2,580	4.2	4.1	3.5
...	46 021	Campbell	771	1,234	1,494	1,549	1,782	1,965	3,085	3,080	3,068	2.0	2.4	2.7
...	46 023	Charles Mix	1,150	619	9,224	9,221	9,350	9,131	2,507	2,503	2,458	8.4	8.5	8.3
...	46 025	Clark	968	815	3,683	3,802	4,143	4,403	2,931	2,904	2,882	3.8	4.3	4.6
46820	46 027	Clay	417	2,504	12,867	12,953	13,537	13,186	2,252	2,195	2,124	31.3	32.8	32.0
47980	46 029	Codington	717	1,390	26,347	26,037	25,897	22,698	1,542	1,522	1,548	38.3	37.7	33.0
...	46 031	Corson	2,529	227	4,288	4,327	4,176	4,195	2,881	2,899	2,898	1.7	1.7	1.7
...	46 033	Custer	1,559	426	7,944	7,825	7,275	6,179	2,596	2,658	2,734	5.1	4.7	4.0
33580	46 035	Davison	437	2,400	19,035	18,863	18,741	17,503	1,872	1,859	1,820	43.7	43.0	40.2
...	46 037	Day	1,091	667	5,778	5,791	6,267	6,978	2,785	2,760	2,661	5.6	6.1	6.8
...	46 039	Deuel	637	1,620	4,301	4,304	4,498	4,522	2,880	2,880	2,873	6.9	7.2	7.3
...	46 041	Dewey	2,446	235	6,112	6,137	5,972	5,523	2,759	2,787	2,800	2.7	2.6	2.4
...	46 043	Douglas	434	2,421	3,168	3,269	3,458	3,746	2,963	2,957	2,936	7.3	7.9	8.6
10100	46 045	Edmunds	1,151	617	4,062	4,105	4,367	4,356	2,905	2,889	2,888	3.5	3.8	3.8
...	46 047	Fall River	1,749	383	7,304	7,299	7,453	7,353	2,655	2,644	2,624	4.2	4.3	4.2
...	46 049	Faulk	1,006	761	2,339	2,370	2,640	2,744	3,023	3,018	3,013	2.3	2.6	2.7
...	46 051	Grant	688	1,472	7,278	7,376	7,852	8,372	2,659	2,620	2,526	10.7	11.5	12.3
...	46 053	Gregory	1,053	712	4,268	4,314	4,792	5,359	2,886	2,861	2,814	4.2	4.7	5.3
...	46 055	Haakon	1,827	359	1,864	1,915	2,196	2,624	3,063	3,051	3,016	1.0	1.2	1.4
47980	46 057	Hamlin	538	2,047	5,616	5,630	5,540	4,974	2,793	2,814	2,842	11.1	11.0	9.7
...	46 059	Hand	1,440	468	3,323	3,320	3,741	4,272	2,955	2,938	2,892	2.3	2.6	3.0
33580	46 061	Hanson	436	2,412	3,690	3,720	3,139	2,994	2,930	2,983	3,001	8.5	7.3	6.9
...	46 063	Harding	2,678	207	1,205	1,204	1,353	1,669	3,101	3,100	3,087	0.5	0.5	0.6
38180	46 065	Hughes	800	1,176	16,946	16,871	16,481	14,817	1,968	1,992	1,999	22.9	22.3	20.0
...	46 067	Hutchinson	814	1,144	7,426	7,555	8,075	8,262	2,645	2,601	2,541	9.1	9.9	10.2
...	46 069	Hyde	867	1,045	1,551	1,607	1,671	1,696	3,081	3,086	3,084	1.8	1.9	2.0
...	46 071	Jackson	1,871	346	2,900	2,891	2,930	2,811	2,989	2,997	3,011	1.6	1.6	1.5
...	46 073	Jerauld	533	2,066	2,071	2,112	2,295	2,425	3,046	3,039	3,027	3.9	4.3	4.6
...	46 075	Jones	972	809	1,067	1,050	1,193	1,324	3,106	3,105	3,105	1.1	1.2	1.4
...	46 077	Kingsbury	864	1,053	5,464	5,501	5,815	5,925	2,801	2,804	2,766	6.5	6.9	7.1
...	46 079	Lake	575	1,876	11,170	11,053	11,276	10,550	2,353	2,352	2,331	19.8	20.0	18.7
43940	46 081	Lawrence	800	1,175	22,685	22,510	21,802	20,655	1,687	1,703	1,647	28.4	27.2	25.8
43620	46 083	Lincoln	579	1,841	35,239	33,394	24,147	15,427	1,286	1,590	1,961	61.0	42.5	26.7
...	46 085	Lyman	1,707	390	3,929	3,930	3,895	3,638	2,913	2,923	2,946	2.4	2.4	2.2
43620	46 087	McCook	577	1,849	5,851	5,905	5,832	5,688	2,781	2,801	2,786	10.2	10.2	9.9
...	46 089	McPherson	1,152	616	2,565	2,638	2,904	3,228	3,008	2,998	2,982	2.3	2.5	2.8
...	46 091	Marshall	886	1,008	4,430	4,417	4,576	4,844	2,875	2,874	2,849	5.3	5.5	5.8

See footnotes at end of table.

Table B-1. Counties — **Area and Population**—Con.

[Includes United States, states, and 3,141 counties/county equivalents defined as of February 22, 2005. For more information on these areas, see Appendix C, Geographic Information]

Metro-politan area code	FIPS state and county code[1]	County	Area, 2000 (square miles) Total	Rank[2]	Population 2006 (July 1)	2005 (July 1)	2000[3] (April 1 estimates base)	1990[3] (April 1 estimates base)	Rank 2006[2]	2000[2]	1990[4]	Persons per square mile of land area 2006[5]	2000	1990
		SOUTH DAKOTA—Con.												
39660	46 093	Meade	3,482	153	24,425	24,551	24,245	21,878	1,613	1,587	1,585	7.0	7.0	6.3
...	46 095	Mellette	1,310	517	2,099	2,095	2,083	2,137	3,044	3,060	3,059	1.6	1.6	1.6
...	46 097	Miner	572	1,908	2,553	2,573	2,884	3,272	3,010	3,000	2,978	4.5	5.1	5.7
43620	46 099	Minnehaha	814	1,145	163,281	160,051	148,265	123,809	357	365	370	201.7	184.1	153.0
...	46 101	Moody	521	2,099	6,644	6,619	6,595	6,507	2,712	2,728	2,709	12.8	12.7	12.5
39660	46 103	Pennington	2,784	201	94,338	93,357	88,573	81,343	590	589	558	34.0	32.0	29.3
...	46 105	Perkins	2,891	191	3,025	3,047	3,368	3,932	2,975	2,966	2,924	1.1	1.2	1.4
...	46 107	Potter	898	973	2,321	2,371	2,693	3,190	3,026	3,015	2,984	2.7	3.1	3.7
...	46 109	Roberts	1,135	634	10,024	10,013	10,011	9,914	2,441	2,445	2,393	9.1	9.1	9.0
...	46 111	Sanborn	570	1,930	2,517	2,535	2,675	2,833	3,013	3,016	3,010	4.4	4.7	5.0
...	46 113	Shannon	2,097	299	13,824	13,552	12,466	9,902	2,180	2,270	2,397	6.6	6.0	4.7
...	46 115	Spink	1,510	440	6,923	6,930	7,454	7,981	2,686	2,643	2,568	4.6	4.9	5.3
38180	46 117	Stanley	1,517	436	2,815	2,787	2,772	2,453	2,990	3,006	3,025	2.0	1.9	1.7
...	46 119	Sully	1,070	695	1,435	1,432	1,556	1,589	3,087	3,091	3,091	1.4	1.5	1.6
...	46 121	Todd	1,391	486	10,088	9,892	9,050	8,352	2,438	2,527	2,528	7.3	6.5	6.0
43620	46 123	Tripp	1,617	414	6,066	6,069	6,430	6,924	2,765	2,747	2,668	3.8	4.0	4.3
43580	46 125	Turner	617	1,683	8,540	8,532	8,849	8,576	2,562	2,542	2,507	13.8	14.4	13.9
49460	46 127	Union	467	2,292	13,745	13,434	12,584	10,189	2,188	2,259	2,372	29.9	27.4	22.1
...	46 129	Walworth	744	1,288	5,425	5,474	5,974	6,087	2,807	2,785	2,746	7.7	8.4	8.6
49460	46 135	Yankton	533	2,067	21,779	21,753	21,652	19,252	1,730	1,711	1,715	41.8	41.4	36.9
...	46 137	Ziebach	1,971	320	2,706	2,641	2,519	2,220	2,999	3,025	3,053	1.4	1.3	1.1
	47 000	TENNESSEE	42,143	(X)	6,038,803	5,955,745	5,689,262	4,877,203	(X)	(X)	(X)	146.5	138.4	118.3
28940	47 001	Anderson	345	2,744	73,579	72,518	71,330	68,250	709	694	648	218.0	211.2	202.2
43180	47 003	Bedford	475	2,256	43,413	42,287	37,586	30,411	1,071	1,175	1,273	91.7	79.9	64.2
...	47 005	Benton	436	2,405	16,378	16,476	16,537	14,524	2,015	1,989	2,017	41.5	41.9	36.8
...	47 007	Bledsoe	407	2,563	13,030	12,902	12,364	9,669	2,239	2,278	2,416	32.1	30.5	23.8
28940	47 009	Blount	567	1,945	118,186	115,616	105,823	85,962	489	502	534	211.6	190.2	153.9
17420	47 011	Bradley	332	2,777	93,538	92,136	87,953	73,712	596	594	610	284.6	268.3	224.2
29220	47 013	Campbell	498	2,187	40,848	40,558	39,794	35,079	1,141	1,117	1,128	85.1	83.1	73.1
34980	47 015	Cannon	266	2,911	13,448	13,341	12,826	10,467	2,212	2,247	2,339	50.6	48.6	39.4
...	47 017	Carroll	600	1,744	29,096	29,014	29,486	27,514	1,445	1,414	1,374	48.6	49.2	45.9
27740	47 019	Carter	348	2,735	59,157	58,884	56,742	51,505	848	835	820	173.5	166.7	151.0
34980	47 021	Cheatham	307	2,831	39,018	38,525	35,912	27,140	1,179	1,222	1,387	128.9	119.3	89.7
27180	47 023	Chester	289	2,862	16,043	15,875	15,528	12,819	2,043	2,052	2,154	55.6	53.9	44.4
...	47 025	Claiborne	442	2,378	31,347	31,073	29,922	26,137	1,386	1,399	1,417	72.2	69.0	60.2
...	47 027	Clay	259	2,923	8,055	8,013	7,976	7,238	2,586	2,609	2,631	34.1	33.8	30.7
35460	47 029	Cocke	443	2,372	35,220	34,877	33,565	29,141	1,288	1,299	1,324	81.1	77.4	67.1
46100	47 031	Coffee	434	2,419	51,625	50,876	48,014	40,343	934	953	990	120.4	112.4	94.1
...	47 033	Crockett	265	2,912	14,392	14,499	14,532	13,378	2,138	2,121	2,107	54.3	54.8	50.4
18900	47 035	Cumberland	685	1,477	52,344	51,151	46,804	34,736	920	965	1,143	76.8	69.0	51.0
34980	47 037	Davidson	526	2,082	578,698	574,395	569,892	510,786	101	95	93	1,152.2	1,134.9	1,017.0
...	47 039	Decatur	345	2,742	11,426	11,586	11,731	10,472	2,336	2,317	2,338	34.2	35.1	31.4
...	47 041	DeKalb	329	2,784	18,360	18,299	17,421	14,360	1,896	1,928	2,026	60.3	57.3	47.1
34980	47 043	Dickson	491	2,212	46,583	45,822	43,156	35,061	1,010	1,033	1,131	95.1	88.5	71.6
20540	47 045	Dyer	526	2,081	37,886	37,773	37,279	34,854	1,213	1,184	1,138	74.2	73.1	68.3
32820	47 047	Fayette	706	1,425	36,102	34,418	28,796	25,559	1,255	1,428	1,442	51.2	41.3	36.3
...	47 049	Fentress	499	2,184	17,480	17,180	16,625	14,669	1,943	1,984	2,007	35.1	33.4	29.4
46100	47 051	Franklin	576	1,863	41,319	40,871	39,270	34,923	1,121	1,131	1,136	74.5	71.0	63.1
26480	47 053	Gibson	604	1,726	48,461	48,061	48,149	46,315	981	945	897	80.4	79.9	76.8
...	47 055	Giles	611	1,702	29,269	29,213	29,447	25,741	1,440	1,416	1,431	47.9	48.2	42.1
34100	47 057	Grainger	302	2,841	22,453	22,188	20,659	17,095	1,702	1,754	1,846	80.1	73.9	61.0
24620	47 059	Greene	624	1,652	65,945	65,248	62,909	55,832	777	772	776	106.1	101.4	89.8
...	47 061	Grundy	361	2,707	14,499	14,564	14,332	13,362	2,134	2,140	2,109	40.2	39.7	37.1
34100	47 063	Hamblen	176	3,048	61,026	60,191	58,128	50,480	833	822	835	379.0	361.7	313.5
16860	47 065	Hamilton	576	1,866	312,905	310,659	307,908	285,536	196	185	172	576.8	567.9	526.3
...	47 067	Hancock	224	2,982	6,713	6,730	6,780	6,739	2,705	2,714	2,683	30.2	30.5	30.3
...	47 069	Hardeman	670	1,515	28,176	28,091	28,105	23,377	1,478	1,449	1,521	42.2	42.1	35.0
...	47 071	Hardin	596	1,754	26,089	26,002	25,578	22,633	1,545	1,536	1,552	45.1	44.3	39.2
28700	47 073	Hawkins	500	2,182	56,850	56,203	53,563	44,565	876	873	917	116.8	110.4	91.6
15140	47 075	Haywood	534	2,058	19,405	19,423	19,797	19,437	1,850	1,804	1,707	36.4	37.2	36.5
...	47 077	Henderson	526	2,085	26,750	26,371	25,522	21,844	1,526	1,540	1,586	51.4	49.2	42.0
37540	47 079	Henry	593	1,761	31,837	31,475	31,102	27,888	1,373	1,375	1,353	56.7	55.4	49.6
34980	47 081	Hickman	613	1,700	23,812	23,726	22,295	16,754	1,636	1,680	1,865	38.9	36.6	27.3
...	47 083	Houston	207	3,005	8,076	8,027	8,088	7,018	2,583	2,599	2,656	40.3	40.1	35.0
...	47 085	Humphreys	557	1,980	18,394	18,208	17,929	15,813	1,894	1,906	1,935	34.6	33.7	29.7
18260	47 087	Jackson	320	2,804	10,918	11,072	10,984	9,297	2,371	2,368	2,444	35.3	35.7	30.1
34100	47 089	Jefferson	314	2,811	49,372	48,261	44,294	33,016	962	1,010	1,191	180.3	162.9	120.6
...	47 091	Johnson	303	2,840	18,043	18,077	17,499	13,766	1,912	1,924	2,075	60.5	58.7	46.1
28940	47 093	Knox	526	2,082	411,967	405,355	382,032	335,749	154	151	153	810.2	752.9	660.3
...	47 095	Lake	194	3,028	7,406	7,544	7,954	7,129	2,646	2,611	2,640	45.3	48.6	43.6
...	47 097	Lauderdale	507	2,145	26,732	26,672	27,101	23,491	1,527	1,479	1,514	56.8	57.5	49.9
29980	47 099	Lawrence	618	1,682	40,934	40,985	39,926	35,303	1,136	1,114	1,122	66.3	64.8	57.2

See footnotes at end of table.

Table B-1. Counties — **Area and Population**—Con.

[Includes United States, states, and 3,141 counties/county equivalents defined as of February 22, 2005. For more information on these areas, see Appendix C, Geographic Information]

Metro-politan area code	FIPS state and county code[1]	County	Area, 2000 (square miles)		Population				Rank			Persons per square mile of land area		
			Total	Rank[2]	2006 (July 1)	2005 (July 1)	2000[3] (April 1 estimates base)	1990[3] (April 1 estimates base)	2006[2]	2000[2]	1990[4]	2006[5]	2000	1990
		TENNESSEE—Con.												
...	47 101	Lewis	282	2,883	11,588	11,426	11,367	9,247	2,323	2,346	2,449	41.1	40.3	32.8
...	47 103	Lincoln	571	1,924	32,728	32,385	31,340	28,157	1,346	1,365	1,346	57.4	55.1	49.4
28940	47 105	Loudon	247	2,952	44,566	43,411	39,087	31,255	1,051	1,135	1,237	194.7	171.4	136.7
11940	47 107	McMinn	432	2,431	52,020	51,338	49,010	42,383	928	932	950	120.9	114.3	98.5
...	47 109	McNairy	561	1,970	25,722	25,323	24,665	22,422	1,557	1,569	1,557	45.9	44.1	40.0
34980	47 111	Macon	307	2,830	21,726	21,564	20,386	15,906	1,733	1,769	1,930	70.7	66.6	51.8
27180	47 113	Madison	559	1,973	95,894	94,673	91,837	77,982	578	557	581	172.2	165.2	140.0
16860	47 115	Marion	512	2,125	27,942	27,715	27,776	24,683	1,490	1,457	1,474	56.1	55.7	49.4
30280	47 117	Marshall	376	2,669	28,884	28,330	26,767	21,539	1,452	1,492	1,601	77.0	71.6	57.4
17940	47 119	Maury	616	1,691	78,309	76,228	69,498	54,812	685	711	784	127.8	113.8	89.4
...	47 121	Meigs	217	2,992	11,698	11,595	11,086	8,033	2,316	2,359	2,561	60.0	57.1	41.2
...	47 123	Monroe	653	1,565	44,163	43,184	38,965	30,541	1,056	1,141	1,265	69.6	61.7	48.1
17300	47 125	Montgomery	544	2,023	147,114	146,845	134,768	100,498	405	400	456	272.8	250.8	186.4
46100	47 127	Moore	130	3,082	6,070	6,037	5,740	4,696	2,764	2,808	2,861	47.0	44.7	36.4
...	47 129	Morgan	522	2,093	20,108	20,086	19,755	17,300	1,817	1,808	1,833	38.5	37.9	33.1
46460	47 131	Obion	555	1,989	32,184	32,177	32,450	31,717	1,367	1,336	1,221	59.1	59.6	58.2
18260	47 133	Overton	435	2,416	20,740	20,498	20,118	17,636	1,775	1,788	1,809	47.9	46.6	40.7
...	47 135	Perry	423	2,478	7,653	7,631	7,631	6,612	2,629	2,635	2,697	18.4	18.4	15.9
...	47 137	Pickett	175	3,050	4,855	4,867	4,945	4,548	2,848	2,853	2,869	29.8	30.3	27.9
17420	47 139	Polk	442	2,376	15,939	16,023	16,050	13,643	2,049	2,020	2,086	36.6	37.0	31.4
18260	47 141	Putnam	403	2,589	68,284	66,867	62,315	51,373	757	780	821	170.3	155.8	128.1
...	47 143	Rhea	336	2,769	30,347	29,872	28,403	24,344	1,408	1,436	1,483	96.1	90.1	77.1
25340	47 145	Roane	395	2,620	53,293	52,753	51,910	47,227	911	894	888	147.6	143.9	130.8
34980	47 147	Robertson	477	2,254	62,187	60,361	54,434	41,492	818	866	971	130.5	115.1	87.1
34980	47 149	Rutherford	624	1,653	228,829	218,478	182,023	118,570	268	302	392	369.7	296.5	191.6
...	47 151	Scott	533	2,063	21,926	21,855	21,127	18,358	1,721	1,730	1,772	41.2	39.8	34.5
16860	47 153	Sequatchie	266	2,909	13,002	12,707	11,370	8,863	2,242	2,344	2,482	48.9	42.9	33.3
42940	47 155	Sevier	598	1,748	81,382	79,339	71,170	51,050	662	698	826	137.4	121.1	86.2
32820	47 157	Shelby	784	1,206	911,438	905,705	897,472	826,330	49	44	43	1,208.0	1,190.4	1,094.7
34980	47 159	Smith	325	2,793	18,753	18,579	17,712	14,143	1,883	1,917	2,042	59.6	56.7	45.0
17300	47 161	Stewart	493	2,207	12,998	12,975	12,370	9,479	2,244	2,276	2,435	28.4	27.2	20.7
28700	47 163	Sullivan	430	2,447	153,239	152,535	153,048	143,596	385	347	331	371.0	370.3	347.6
34980	47 165	Sumner	543	2,026	149,416	144,769	130,448	103,281	395	412	446	282.3	247.8	195.1
32820	47 167	Tipton	475	2,257	57,380	55,999	51,271	37,568	865	902	1,057	124.9	112.2	81.8
34980	47 169	Trousdale	117	3,087	7,811	7,648	7,259	5,920	2,611	2,661	2,769	68.4	64.1	51.8
27740	47 171	Unicoi	186	3,038	17,663	17,599	17,667	16,549	1,929	1,919	1,885	94.9	94.9	88.9
28940	47 173	Union	247	2,955	19,086	19,005	17,808	13,694	1,868	1,910	2,081	85.4	79.9	61.3
...	47 175	Van Buren	275	2,895	5,448	5,436	5,508	4,846	2,803	2,818	2,848	19.9	20.2	17.7
32660	47 177	Warren	434	2,423	40,016	39,617	38,276	32,992	1,162	1,158	1,192	92.5	88.8	76.2
27740	47 179	Washington	330	2,780	114,316	112,422	107,198	92,336	502	499	500	350.3	329.4	283.0
...	47 181	Wayne	736	1,310	16,828	16,848	16,842	13,935	1,983	1,967	2,062	22.9	22.9	19.0
32280	47 183	Weakley	582	1,818	33,357	33,607	34,895	31,972	1,329	1,256	1,212	57.5	60.2	55.1
...	47 185	White	379	2,658	24,482	24,206	23,104	20,090	1,606	1,638	1,673	65.0	61.4	53.3
34980	47 187	Williamson	584	1,809	160,781	153,445	126,638	81,021	362	427	563	275.9	219.9	139.0
34980	47 189	Wilson	583	1,811	104,035	100,471	88,808	67,675	541	586	655	182.3	156.5	118.6
	48 000	TEXAS	268,581	(X)	23,507,783	22,928,508	20,851,790	16,986,335	(X)	(X)	(X)	89.8	80.0	64.9
37300	48 001	Anderson	1,078	686	57,064	56,470	55,109	48,024	872	856	871	53.3	51.5	44.8
11380	48 003	Andrews	1,501	447	12,952	12,751	13,004	14,338	2,246	2,237	2,029	8.6	8.6	9.6
31260	48 005	Angelina	864	1,049	82,524	81,581	80,130	69,884	652	641	634	103.0	100.1	87.2
18580	48 007	Aransas	528	2,074	24,831	24,684	22,497	17,892	1,591	1,672	1,794	98.6	89.5	71.0
48660	48 009	Archer	926	877	9,266	9,176	8,854	7,973	2,501	2,540	2,573	10.2	9.9	8.8
11100	48 011	Armstrong	914	911	2,120	2,176	2,148	2,021	3,041	3,056	3,064	2.3	2.4	2.2
41700	48 013	Atascosa	1,236	565	43,876	43,265	38,628	30,533	1,067	1,148	1,266	35.6	31.6	24.8
26420	48 015	Austin	656	1,551	26,407	26,018	23,590	19,832	1,539	1,607	1,685	40.5	36.4	30.4
...	48 017	Bailey	827	1,117	6,597	6,659	6,594	7,064	2,720	2,729	2,652	8.0	8.0	8.5
41700	48 019	Bandera	798	1,184	20,203	20,022	17,645	10,562	1,812	1,921	2,330	25.6	22.5	13.3
12420	48 021	Bastrop	896	983	71,684	69,810	57,716	38,263	727	827	1,047	80.7	65.6	43.1
...	48 023	Baylor	901	959	3,805	3,845	4,093	4,385	2,921	2,909	2,883	4.4	4.7	5.0
13300	48 025	Bee	880	1,020	33,176	32,900	32,359	25,135	1,336	1,339	1,457	37.7	36.7	28.6
28660	48 027	Bell	1,088	672	257,897	254,365	237,974	191,073	235	244	251	243.4	225.3	180.4
41700	48 029	Bexar	1,257	550	1,555,592	1,516,586	1,392,931	1,185,394	20	24	25	1,247.6	1,121.1	950.6
...	48 031	Blanco	713	1,407	9,250	9,159	8,418	5,972	2,504	2,572	2,762	13.0	11.9	8.4
...	48 033	Borden	906	936	648	651	729	799	3,131	3,130	3,123	0.7	0.8	0.9
...	48 035	Bosque	1,003	766	18,058	17,998	17,204	15,125	1,910	1,942	1,980	18.3	17.4	15.3
45500	48 037	Bowie	923	884	91,455	90,387	89,306	81,665	610	578	557	103.0	100.6	92.0
26420	48 039	Brazoria	1,597	418	287,898	277,821	241,767	191,707	211	238	250	207.7	175.5	138.2
17780	48 041	Brazos	590	1,776	159,006	156,640	152,419	121,862	368	350	377	271.4	260.5	208.0
...	48 043	Brewster	6,193	60	9,048	9,038	8,866	8,653	2,526	2,537	2,495	1.5	1.4	1.4
...	48 045	Briscoe	902	955	1,598	1,635	1,790	1,971	3,079	3,079	3,067	1.8	2.0	2.2
...	48 047	Brooks	944	848	7,731	7,688	7,976	8,204	2,621	2,609	2,547	8.2	8.4	8.7
15220	48 049	Brown	957	825	38,970	38,689	37,674	34,371	1,180	1,171	1,157	41.3	40.0	36.4

See footnotes at end of table.

Table B-1. Counties — **Area and Population**—Con.

[Includes United States, states, and 3,141 counties/county equivalents defined as of February 22, 2005. For more information on these areas, see Appendix C, Geographic Information]

Metro-politan area code	FIPS state and county code[1]	County	Area, 2000 (square miles) Total	Rank[2]	Population 2006 (July 1)	2005 (July 1)	2000[3] (April 1 estimates base)	1990[3] (April 1 estimates base)	Rank 2006[2]	2000[2]	1990[4]	Persons per square mile of land area 2006[5]	2000	1990
		TEXAS—Con.												
17780	48 051	Burleson.........	678	1,499	16,932	17,165	16,470	13,625	1,970	1,993	2,090	25.4	24.9	20.5
...	48 053	Burnet..........	1,021	744	42,896	41,489	34,120	22,677	1,085	1,278	1,549	43.1	34.7	22.8
12420	48 055	Caldwell........	547	2,010	36,720	36,542	32,192	26,392	1,240	1,343	1,409	67.3	59.5	48.4
47020	48 057	Calhoun.........	1,032	736	20,705	20,544	20,647	19,053	1,778	1,755	1,731	40.4	40.3	37.2
10180	48 059	Callahan........	901	957	13,491	13,437	12,905	11,859	2,208	2,242	2,226	15.0	14.4	13.2
15180	48 061	Cameron.........	1,276	540	387,717	378,905	335,227	260,120	166	174	193	428.1	371.9	287.2
...	48 063	Camp............	203	3,012	12,410	12,226	11,549	9,904	2,273	2,331	2,396	62.8	58.7	50.1
11100	48 065	Carson..........	924	879	6,595	6,577	6,516	6,576	2,721	2,738	2,701	7.1	7.1	7.1
...	48 067	Cass............	960	819	29,955	29,978	30,438	29,982	1,419	1,388	1,298	32.0	32.5	32.0
...	48 069	Castro..........	899	965	7,449	7,628	8,285	9,070	2,643	2,583	2,463	8.3	9.2	10.1
26420	48 071	Chambers........	872	1,035	28,779	28,491	26,031	20,088	1,456	1,517	1,674	48.0	43.7	33.5
27380	48 073	Cherokee........	1,062	701	48,513	48,217	46,659	41,049	979	967	979	46.1	44.4	39.0
...	48 075	Childress.......	714	1,406	7,717	7,669	7,688	5,953	2,624	2,631	2,764	10.9	10.8	8.4
48660	48 077	Clay............	1,116	652	11,104	11,208	11,006	10,024	2,361	2,365	2,385	10.1	10.1	9.1
...	48 079	Cochran.........	775	1,221	3,214	3,300	3,730	4,377	2,960	2,940	2,885	4.1	4.8	5.6
...	48 081	Coke............	928	876	3,623	3,629	3,864	3,424	2,936	2,925	2,961	4.0	4.3	3.8
...	48 083	Coleman.........	1,281	536	8,761	8,671	9,235	9,710	2,540	2,510	2,410	7.0	7.3	7.6
19100	48 085	Collin..........	886	1,007	698,851	660,926	491,772	264,036	81	113	188	824.5	590.2	311.5
...	48 087	Collingsworth...	919	895	2,930	2,968	3,206	3,573	2,984	2,978	2,952	3.2	3.5	3.9
...	48 089	Colorado........	974	807	20,824	20,701	20,390	18,383	1,769	1,768	1,770	21.6	21.1	19.1
41700	48 091	Comal...........	575	1,883	101,181	95,845	78,021	51,832	554	652	815	180.2	140.4	92.3
...	48 093	Comanche........	948	842	13,837	13,738	14,026	13,381	2,177	2,164	2,106	14.8	14.9	14.3
...	48 095	Concho..........	994	776	3,654	3,731	3,966	3,044	2,933	2,921	2,996	3.7	4.0	3.1
23620	48 097	Cooke...........	899	970	38,946	38,864	36,363	30,777	1,182	1,204	1,253	44.6	41.7	35.2
28660	48 099	Coryell.........	1,057	709	72,667	75,475	74,978	64,226	718	666	683	69.1	71.5	61.1
...	48 101	Cottle..........	902	955	1,679	1,720	1,904	2,247	3,077	3,072	3,050	1.9	2.1	2.5
...	48 103	Crane...........	786	1,203	3,845	3,825	3,996	4,652	2,919	2,920	2,864	4.9	5.0	5.9
...	48 105	Crockett........	2,807	197	3,879	3,933	4,099	4,078	2,917	2,908	2,909	1.4	1.4	1.5
31180	48 107	Crosby..........	902	953	6,549	6,636	7,072	7,304	2,725	2,679	2,628	7.3	7.8	8.1
...	48 109	Culberson.......	3,813	137	2,525	2,610	2,975	3,407	3,012	2,993	2,963	0.7	0.8	0.9
...	48 111	Dallam..........	1,505	442	6,143	6,177	6,224	5,461	2,755	2,762	2,803	4.1	4.1	3.6
19100	48 113	Dallas..........	909	924	2,345,815	2,308,527	2,218,843	1,852,691	9	10	11	2,666.9	2,530.6	2,105.6
29500	48 115	Dawson..........	902	950	14,174	14,240	14,985	14,349	2,156	2,093	2,028	15.7	16.6	15.9
25820	48 117	Deaf Smith......	1,498	449	18,623	18,498	18,561	19,153	1,886	1,869	1,723	12.4	12.4	12.8
19100	48 119	Delta...........	278	2,892	5,561	5,449	5,327	4,857	2,796	2,828	2,847	20.1	19.3	17.5
19100	48 121	Denton..........	958	823	584,238	554,994	432,966	273,644	99	139	182	657.5	493.9	308.0
...	48 123	DeWitt..........	910	918	20,167	20,376	20,010	18,840	1,813	1,793	1,744	22.2	22.0	20.7
...	48 125	Dickens.........	905	940	2,596	2,654	2,762	2,571	3,005	3,007	3,018	2.9	3.0	2.8
...	48 127	Dimmit..........	1,334	507	10,385	10,378	10,248	10,433	2,413	2,422	2,345	7.8	7.7	7.8
...	48 129	Donley..........	933	864	3,848	3,884	3,828	3,696	2,918	2,926	2,940	4.1	4.1	4.0
...	48 131	Duval...........	1,796	367	12,437	12,574	13,120	12,918	2,271	2,221	2,144	6.9	7.3	7.2
...	48 133	Eastland........	932	869	18,293	18,351	18,297	18,488	1,900	1,881	1,762	19.8	19.8	20.0
36220	48 135	Ector...........	902	954	127,462	125,267	121,123	118,934	461	447	390	141.5	134.0	132.0
...	48 137	Edwards.........	2,120	295	1,935	1,997	2,162	2,266	3,058	3,053	3,044	0.9	1.0	1.1
19100	48 139	Ellis...........	952	835	139,300	133,527	111,358	85,167	430	486	539	148.2	119.7	90.6
21340	48 141	El Paso.........	1,015	752	736,310	721,183	679,622	591,610	73	75	79	726.8	672.8	584.0
44500	48 143	Erath...........	1,090	670	34,289	33,869	33,001	27,991	1,310	1,320	1,352	31.6	30.4	25.8
...	48 145	Falls...........	774	1,226	17,547	17,600	18,576	17,712	1,938	1,867	1,803	22.8	24.1	23.0
14300	48 147	Fannin..........	899	966	33,337	33,109	31,242	24,804	1,331	1,370	1,469	37.4	35.2	27.8
...	48 149	Fayette.........	960	821	22,521	22,484	21,804	20,095	1,697	1,702	1,672	23.7	23.0	21.1
...	48 151	Fisher..........	902	952	4,027	4,049	4,344	4,842	2,907	2,893	2,851	4.5	4.8	5.4
...	48 153	Floyd...........	993	778	7,053	7,164	7,771	8,497	2,674	2,629	2,512	7.1	7.8	8.6
...	48 155	Foard...........	708	1,422	1,519	1,506	1,622	1,794	3,084	3,088	3,078	2.1	2.3	2.5
26420	48 157	Fort Bend.......	886	1,006	493,187	466,231	354,471	225,421	129	165	219	563.9	410.5	257.6
...	48 159	Franklin........	295	2,851	10,367	10,277	9,458	7,802	2,416	2,491	2,595	36.3	33.2	27.3
...	48 161	Freestone.......	892	993	18,803	18,675	17,867	15,818	1,881	1,908	1,934	21.4	20.4	17.9
...	48 163	Frio............	1,134	636	16,336	16,347	16,252	13,472	2,019	2,006	2,103	14.4	14.3	11.9
...	48 165	Gaines..........	1,503	443	15,008	14,746	14,467	14,123	2,107	2,126	2,044	10.0	9.6	9.4
26420	48 167	Galveston.......	873	1,033	283,551	277,330	250,158	217,396	213	231	228	711.6	629.3	545.3
...	48 169	Garza...........	896	982	4,877	4,891	4,872	5,143	2,846	2,857	2,830	5.4	5.4	5.7
...	48 171	Gillespie.......	1,061	702	23,527	23,001	20,814	17,204	1,650	1,747	1,842	22.2	19.7	16.2
...	48 173	Glasscock.......	901	960	1,248	1,301	1,406	1,447	3,098	3,097	3,098	1.4	1.6	1.6
47020	48 175	Goliad..........	859	1,069	7,192	7,117	6,928	5,980	2,667	2,694	2,761	8.4	8.2	7.0
37420	48 177	Gonzales........	1,070	696	19,566	19,529	18,628	17,205	1,842	1,866	1,841	18.3	17.5	16.1
37420	48 179	Gray............	929	874	21,919	21,512	22,744	23,967	1,722	1,663	1,494	23.6	24.3	25.8
43300	48 181	Grayson.........	979	797	118,478	116,763	110,595	95,019	488	491	489	126.9	119.0	101.8
30980	48 183	Gregg...........	276	2,894	117,090	115,502	111,379	104,948	492	485	440	427.3	406.2	382.9
...	48 185	Grimes..........	801	1,171	25,552	25,266	23,557	18,843	1,561	1,612	1,743	32.2	29.8	23.7
41700	48 187	Guadalupe.......	714	1,402	108,410	103,093	89,036	64,873	527	584	675	152.4	126.4	91.2
38380	48 189	Hale............	1,005	762	36,317	36,171	36,602	34,671	1,247	1,200	1,147	36.1	36.4	34.5

See footnotes at end of table.

[Includes United States, states, and 3,141 counties/county equivalents defined as of February 22, 2005. For more information on these areas, see Appendix C, Geographic Information]

Metropolitan area code	FIPS state and county code[1]	County	Area, 2000 (square miles)		Population				Rank			Persons per square mile of land area		
			Total	Rank[2]	2006 (July 1)	2005 (July 1)	2000[3] (April 1 estimates base)	1990[3] (April 1 estimates base)	2006[2]	2000[2]	1990[4]	2006[5]	2000	1990
		TEXAS—Con.												
...	48 191	Hall	904	946	3,668	3,666	3,782	3,905	2,932	2,931	2,925	4.1	4.2	4.3
...	48 193	Hamilton	836	1,101	8,186	8,130	8,229	7,733	2,579	2,590	2,601	9.8	9.8	9.3
...	48 195	Hansford	920	891	5,237	5,215	5,369	5,848	2,824	2,824	2,775	5.7	5.8	6.4
...	48 197	Hardeman	697	1,448	4,250	4,268	4,724	5,283	2,888	2,867	2,821	6.1	6.8	7.6
13140	48 199	Hardin	897	979	51,483	50,958	48,073	41,320	935	950	974	57.6	53.8	46.2
26420	48 201	Harris	1,778	375	3,886,207	3,762,844	3,400,554	2,818,101	3	3	3	2,247.9	1,975.6	1,629.9
32220	48 203	Harrison	915	906	63,819	63,075	62,110	57,483	792	783	759	71.0	69.1	64.0
...	48 205	Hartley	1,463	458	5,335	5,346	5,535	3,634	2,815	2,815	2,947	3.6	3.8	2.5
...	48 207	Haskell	910	919	5,438	5,561	6,093	6,820	2,805	2,772	2,674	6.0	6.7	7.6
12420	48 209	Hays	680	1,493	130,325	124,434	97,576	65,614	451	531	667	192.3	146.1	96.8
...	48 211	Hemphill	912	916	3,412	3,396	3,351	3,720	2,947	2,968	2,938	3.8	3.7	4.1
11980	48 213	Henderson	949	839	80,222	79,689	73,277	58,543	670	683	742	91.8	84.2	67.0
32580	48 215	Hidalgo	1,583	421	700,634	678,652	569,463	383,545	80	96	131	446.3	365.7	244.4
...	48 217	Hill	986	785	35,806	35,324	32,327	27,146	1,262	1,340	1,386	37.2	33.9	28.2
30220	48 219	Hockley	909	926	22,609	22,777	22,716	24,199	1,691	1,664	1,487	24.9	25.0	26.6
24180	48 221	Hood	437	2,399	49,238	47,772	41,100	28,981	969	1,079	1,331	116.8	98.5	68.7
44860	48 223	Hopkins	793	1,194	33,496	33,224	31,960	28,833	1,326	1,347	1,335	42.8	40.9	36.7
...	48 225	Houston	1,237	563	23,044	23,036	23,185	21,375	1,667	1,635	1,613	18.7	18.8	17.4
13700	48 227	Howard	904	944	32,463	32,540	33,627	32,343	1,357	1,295	1,204	36.0	37.1	35.8
...	48 229	Hudspeth	4,572	102	3,320	3,301	3,344	2,915	2,956	2,969	3,005	0.7	0.7	0.6
19100	48 231	Hunt	882	1,015	83,338	82,289	76,596	64,343	647	657	680	99.1	91.5	76.5
14420	48 233	Hutchinson	895	985	22,460	22,424	23,857	25,689	1,701	1,597	1,434	25.3	26.8	28.9
41660	48 235	Irion	1,052	714	1,814	1,748	1,771	1,629	3,066	3,081	3,089	1.7	1.7	1.5
...	48 237	Jack	920	893	9,110	9,069	8,763	6,981	2,519	2,550	2,660	9.9	9.6	7.6
...	48 239	Jackson	857	1,073	14,249	14,329	14,391	13,039	2,150	2,133	2,137	17.2	17.4	15.7
...	48 241	Jasper	970	813	35,293	35,510	35,604	31,102	1,282	1,230	1,242	37.6	38.0	33.2
...	48 243	Jeff Davis	2,265	271	2,315	2,274	2,207	1,946	3,027	3,050	3,069	1.0	1.0	0.9
13140	48 245	Jefferson	1,111	655	243,914	247,185	252,051	239,389	252	225	208	270.0	278.5	264.9
...	48 247	Jim Hogg	1,136	633	5,027	5,043	5,281	5,109	2,838	2,833	2,831	4.4	4.6	4.5
10860	48 249	Jim Wells	868	1,039	41,131	41,017	39,326	37,679	1,128	1,128	1,055	47.6	45.6	43.6
19100	48 251	Johnson	734	1,312	149,016	146,509	126,811	97,165	398	424	473	204.3	175.6	133.3
10180	48 253	Jones	937	858	19,645	19,756	20,785	16,490	1,837	1,749	1,895	21.1	22.3	17.7
...	48 255	Karnes	754	1,272	15,270	15,260	15,446	12,455	2,088	2,057	2,186	20.4	20.6	16.6
19100	48 257	Kaufman	807	1,156	93,241	88,901	71,310	52,220	597	695	811	118.6	91.8	66.4
41700	48 259	Kendall	663	1,530	30,213	28,684	23,743	14,589	1,412	1,602	2,014	45.6	36.2	22.0
28780	48 261	Kenedy	1,946	323	402	407	414	460	3,137	3,138	3,137	0.3	0.3	0.3
...	48 263	Kent	903	947	734	750	859	1,010	3,124	3,119	3,113	0.8	0.9	1.1
28500	48 265	Kerr	1,108	658	47,254	46,532	43,649	36,304	997	1,024	1,096	42.7	39.6	32.8
...	48 267	Kimble	1,251	553	4,570	4,586	4,468	4,122	2,866	2,885	2,905	3.7	3.6	3.3
...	48 269	King	913	913	287	300	356	354	3,139	3,139	3,138	0.3	0.4	0.4
...	48 271	Kinney	1,365	496	3,342	3,314	3,379	3,119	2,953	2,965	2,991	2.5	2.5	2.3
28780	48 273	Kleberg	1,090	668	30,353	30,606	31,549	30,274	1,407	1,361	1,282	34.8	36.2	34.8
...	48 275	Knox	855	1,075	3,702	3,745	4,253	4,837	2,928	2,898	2,852	4.4	5.0	5.7
37580	48 277	Lamar	932	866	49,863	49,598	48,499	43,949	955	940	926	54.4	53.0	47.9
...	48 279	Lamb	1,018	748	14,244	14,495	14,709	15,072	2,151	2,107	1,984	14.0	14.4	14.8
28660	48 281	Lampasas	714	1,404	20,758	19,824	17,760	13,521	1,774	1,915	2,100	29.2	25.2	19.0
...	48 283	La Salle	1,494	450	5,969	6,001	5,866	5,254	2,772	2,798	2,823	4.0	4.0	3.5
...	48 285	Lavaca	970	811	18,970	18,904	19,210	18,690	1,877	1,834	1,750	19.6	19.8	19.3
...	48 287	Lee	634	1,629	16,573	16,520	15,657	12,854	2,001	2,045	2,150	26.4	25.0	20.4
...	48 289	Leon	1,080	683	16,538	16,306	15,335	12,665	2,003	2,070	2,169	15.4	14.4	11.8
26420	48 291	Liberty	1,176	598	75,685	75,221	70,164	52,726	695	708	805	65.3	60.9	45.5
...	48 293	Limestone	933	863	22,720	22,627	22,051	20,946	1,684	1,691	1,632	25.0	24.3	23.0
...	48 295	Lipscomb	932	867	3,114	3,076	3,057	3,143	2,968	2,989	2,989	3.3	3.3	3.4
...	48 297	Live Oak	1,079	685	11,522	11,665	12,309	9,556	2,326	2,281	2,428	11.1	11.9	9.2
...	48 299	Llano	966	816	18,269	18,104	17,058	11,631	1,903	1,951	2,245	19.5	18.3	12.4
...	48 301	Loving	677	1,503	60	61	67	107	3,141	3,141	3,140	0.1	0.1	0.2
31180	48 303	Lubbock	901	961	254,862	252,338	242,628	222,636	238	237	224	283.3	270.0	247.5
...	48 305	Lynn	893	990	6,212	6,180	6,550	6,758	2,749	2,735	2,679	7.0	7.3	7.6
...	48 307	McCulloch	1,073	692	8,016	7,945	8,205	8,778	2,591	2,592	2,487	7.5	7.6	8.2
47380	48 309	McLennan	1,060	704	226,189	224,365	213,513	189,123	271	262	254	217.1	205.4	181.5
...	48 311	McMullen	1,143	625	913	890	851	817	3,113	3,120	3,122	0.8	0.8	0.7
...	48 313	Madison	472	2,270	13,310	13,158	12,940	10,931	2,228	2,239	2,302	28.3	27.6	23.3
...	48 315	Marion	420	2,486	10,970	10,958	10,941	9,984	2,368	2,372	2,387	28.8	28.7	26.2
...	48 317	Martin	916	902	4,441	4,391	4,746	4,956	2,872	2,864	2,843	4.9	5.2	5.4
...	48 319	Mason	932	868	3,902	3,849	3,738	3,423	2,916	2,939	2,962	4.2	4.0	3.7
13060	48 321	Matagorda	1,612	415	37,824	37,989	37,957	36,928	1,216	1,167	1,075	33.9	34.1	33.1
20580	48 323	Maverick	1,292	529	52,298	51,223	47,297	36,378	922	961	1,094	40.9	37.0	28.4
41700	48 325	Medina	1,335	506	43,913	42,935	39,304	27,312	1,065	1,130	1,380	33.1	29.7	20.6
...	48 327	Menard	902	948	2,210	2,208	2,360	2,252	3,034	3,035	3,047	2.5	2.6	2.5
33260	48 329	Midland	902	951	124,380	121,480	116,009	106,611	472	464	433	138.2	128.3	118.4

See footnotes at end of table.

Table B-1. Counties — **Area and Population**—Con.

[Includes United States, states, and 3,141 counties/county equivalents defined as of February 22, 2005. For more information on these areas, see Appendix C, Geographic Information]

Metro-politan area code	FIPS state and county code[1]	County	Area, 2000 (square miles)		Population									
							2000[3] (April 1 estimates base)	1990[3] (April 1 estimates base)	Rank			Persons per square mile of land area		
			Total	Rank[2]	2006 (July 1)	2005 (July 1)			2006[2]	2000[2]	1990[4]	2006[5]	2000	1990
		TEXAS—Con.												
...	48 331	Milam.............	1,022	743	25,286	25,198	24,238	22,946	1,573	1,588	1,536	24.9	23.9	22.6
...	48 333	Mills.............	750	1,280	5,184	5,267	5,151	4,531	2,825	2,841	2,870	6.9	6.9	6.1
...	48 335	Mitchell..........	916	900	9,327	9,406	9,698	8,016	2,494	2,471	2,563	10.2	10.6	8.8
...	48 337	Montague.........	938	857	19,810	19,622	19,117	17,274	1,831	1,843	1,836	21.3	20.6	18.6
26420	48 339	Montgomery.........	1,077	689	398,290	379,028	293,768	182,201	163	193	264	381.5	285.0	174.5
20300	48 341	Moore	910	922	20,591	20,294	20,121	17,865	1,787	1,785	1,795	22.9	22.4	19.9
...	48 343	Morris	259	2,925	13,002	12,934	13,048	13,200	2,242	2,231	2,123	51.1	51.3	51.9
...	48 345	Motley	990	781	1,276	1,281	1,426	1,532	3,097	3,096	3,095	1.3	1.5	1.5
34860	48 347	Nacogdoches	981	793	61,079	60,582	59,203	54,753	832	812	786	64.5	62.6	57.8
18620	48 349	Navarro	1,086	674	49,440	48,695	45,124	39,926	961	995	1,005	49.1	45.0	37.3
...	48 351	Newton.	940	851	14,090	14,290	15,072	13,569	2,164	2,086	2,094	15.1	16.1	14.5
45020	48 353	Nolan............	914	909	14,812	14,813	15,802	16,594	2,116	2,033	1,880	16.2	17.3	18.2
18580	48 355	Nueces	1,166	604	321,457	319,147	313,645	291,145	191	182	168	384.6	375.0	348.3
...	48 357	Ochiltree.........	918	899	9,550	9,436	9,006	9,128	2,475	2,529	2,459	10.4	9.8	9.9
...	48 359	Oldham	1,501	446	2,133	2,122	2,185	2,278	3,040	3,052	3,042	1.4	1.5	1.5
13140	48 361	Orange...........	380	2,657	84,243	84,997	84,966	80,509	645	613	566	236.4	238.5	225.9
33420	48 363	Palo Pinto........	986	786	27,797	27,512	27,026	25,055	1,494	1,482	1,459	29.2	28.4	26.3
...	48 365	Panola	821	1,127	22,989	22,791	22,756	22,035	1,668	1,662	1,574	28.7	28.4	27.5
19100	48 367	Parker	910	921	106,266	102,665	88,494	64,785	536	590	676	117.6	98.8	71.7
...	48 369	Parmer...........	885	1,010	9,714	9,801	10,016	9,863	2,463	2,444	2,400	11.0	11.3	11.2
...	48 371	Pecos	4,765	95	16,139	15,907	16,809	14,675	2,039	1,969	2,006	3.4	3.5	3.1
...	48 373	Polk.............	1,110	656	46,995	46,426	41,133	30,687	1,002	1,077	1,259	44.4	39.3	29.0
11100	48 375	Potter...........	922	887	121,328	120,033	113,546	97,841	478	474	470	133.4	125.1	107.6
...	48 377	Presidio	3,856	132	7,713	7,711	7,304	6,637	2,626	2,656	2,690	2.0	1.9	1.7
...	48 379	Rains............	259	2,924	11,514	11,265	9,139	6,715	2,328	2,519	2,686	49.6	39.7	28.9
11100	48 381	Randall.	922	886	111,472	110,021	104,312	89,673	515	507	512	121.9	114.5	98.1
...	48 383	Reagan	1,176	599	3,022	3,004	3,326	4,514	2,976	2,970	2,874	2.6	2.8	3.8
...	48 385	Real............	700	1,438	3,061	3,034	3,051	2,412	2,973	2,990	3,030	4.4	4.4	3.4
...	48 387	Red River.........	1,058	707	13,440	13,590	14,314	14,317	2,215	2,141	2,030	12.8	13.6	13.6
37780	48 389	Reeves	2,642	211	11,466	11,574	13,137	15,852	2,332	2,220	1,933	4.3	5.0	6.0
...	48 391	Refugio	819	1,134	7,596	7,644	7,828	7,976	2,632	2,622	2,570	9.9	10.2	10.4
37420	48 393	Roberts	924	878	835	841	887	1,025	3,116	3,116	3,112	0.9	1.0	1.1
17780	48 395	Robertson	866	1,047	16,214	16,155	15,996	15,511	2,031	2,026	1,952	19.0	18.7	18.1
19100	48 397	Rockwall.........	149	3,072	69,155	62,844	43,074	25,604	750	1,034	1,438	537.0	340.5	198.8
...	48 399	Runnels	1,057	708	10,724	10,961	11,495	11,294	2,384	2,337	2,276	10.2	10.9	10.7
30980	48 401	Rusk	939	856	48,354	47,906	47,372	43,735	983	960	928	52.4	51.3	47.4
...	48 403	Sabine	577	1,856	10,457	10,408	10,469	9,586	2,404	2,400	2,425	21.3	21.3	19.6
...	48 405	San Augustine	592	1,766	8,888	8,823	8,946	7,999	2,531	2,531	2,566	16.8	16.9	15.2
26420	48 407	San Jacinto	628	1,643	24,760	24,784	22,241	16,372	1,595	1,685	1,899	43.4	39.3	28.7
18580	48 409	San Patricio	707	1,424	69,522	69,276	67,138	58,749	749	732	740	100.5	97.3	84.9
...	48 411	San Saba	1,138	630	5,993	6,037	6,186	5,401	2,769	2,764	2,808	5.3	5.5	4.8
...	48 413	Schleicher.	1,311	515	2,776	2,766	2,935	2,990	2,994	2,996	3,002	2.1	2.2	2.3
43660	48 415	Scurry	908	929	16,202	16,176	16,361	18,634	2,033	2,002	1,757	18.0	18.0	20.6
...	48 417	Shackelford	916	903	3,194	3,189	3,302	3,316	2,961	2,973	2,973	3.5	3.6	3.6
...	48 419	Shelby	835	1,105	26,575	26,321	25,224	22,034	1,534	1,558	1,575	33.5	31.8	27.7
...	48 421	Sherman	923	881	2,936	2,959	3,186	3,007	2,983	2,980	3,007	3.2	3.5	3.1
46340	48 423	Smith............	949	838	194,635	190,501	174,706	151,309	305	312	308	209.7	189.0	163.0
24180	48 425	Somervell	192	3,031	7,773	7,604	6,809	5,360	2,617	2,712	2,813	41.5	36.5	28.6
40100	48 427	Starr	1,229	570	61,780	60,479	53,597	40,518	826	871	986	50.5	44.0	33.1
...	48 429	Stephens	921	888	9,610	9,524	9,674	9,010	2,470	2,472	2,468	10.7	10.8	10.1
...	48 431	Sterling.	923	880	1,246	1,295	1,393	1,438	3,099	3,098	3,099	1.3	1.5	1.6
...	48 433	Stonewall	920	892	1,402	1,372	1,693	2,013	3,093	3,085	3,066	1.5	1.8	2.2
...	48 435	Sutton	1,454	462	4,281	4,204	4,077	4,135	2,883	2,911	2,902	2.9	2.8	2.8
...	48 437	Swisher	901	962	7,830	7,827	8,378	8,133	2,607	2,576	2,552	8.7	9.3	9.0
19100	48 439	Tarrant	897	978	1,671,295	1,619,666	1,446,174	1,170,103	18	20	27	1,935.7	1,684.7	1,355.0
10180	48 441	Taylor............	919	896	124,927	124,962	126,551	119,655	471	428	387	136.4	138.1	130.7
...	48 443	Terrell...........	2,358	255	983	986	1,081	1,410	3,109	3,106	3,100	0.4	0.4	0.6
...	48 445	Terry	891	997	12,387	12,392	12,761	13,218	2,275	2,249	2,120	13.9	14.3	14.9
...	48 447	Throckmorton	915	904	1,678	1,642	1,850	1,880	3,078	3,076	3,075	1.8	2.0	2.1
34420	48 449	Titus............	426	2,461	30,306	29,579	28,118	24,009	1,409	1,448	1,492	73.8	68.5	58.5
41660	48 451	Tom Green	1,541	433	103,938	103,409	104,010	98,458	542	509	466	68.3	68.3	64.7
12420	48 453	Travis............	1,022	742	921,006	889,542	812,299	576,407	47	56	82	931.0	828.8	582.6
...	48 455	Trinity...........	714	1,403	14,296	14,302	13,779	11,445	2,145	2,177	2,258	20.6	20.0	16.5
...	48 457	Tyler	936	861	20,557	20,619	20,871	16,646	1,790	1,742	1,875	22.3	22.6	18.0
30980	48 459	Upshur...........	593	1,763	37,923	37,704	35,291	31,370	1,211	1,240	1,233	64.5	60.2	53.4
...	48 461	Upton............	1,242	558	3,134	3,075	3,404	4,447	2,966	2,962	2,878	2.5	2.7	3.6
46620	48 463	Uvalde	1,559	427	27,050	26,905	25,926	23,340	1,515	1,521	1,525	17.4	16.7	15.0
19620	48 465	Val Verde	3,232	168	48,145	47,651	44,856	38,721	986	1,001	1,034	15.2	14.2	12.2
...	48 467	Van Zandt	859	1,068	52,916	52,279	48,140	37,944	912	946	1,051	62.4	57.0	44.7
47020	48 469	Victoria..........	889	1,002	86,191	85,734	84,091	74,361	634	619	604	97.7	95.2	84.3

See footnotes at end of table.

[Includes United States, states, and 3,141 counties/county equivalents defined as of February 22, 2005. For more information on these areas, see Appendix C, Geographic Information]

Metro-politan area code	FIPS state and county code[1]	County	Area, 2000 (square miles)		Population				Rank			Persons per square mile of land area		
			Total	Rank[2]	2006 (July 1)	2005 (July 1)	2000[3] (April 1 estimates base)	1990[3] (April 1 estimates base)	2006[2]	2000[2]	1990[4]	2006[5]	2000	1990
		TEXAS—Con.												
26660	48 471	Walker	801	1,170	63,304	63,318	61,758	50,917	802	786	829	80.4	78.3	64.7
26420	48 473	Waller	518	2,107	35,185	34,801	32,658	23,374	1,289	1,327	1,522	68.5	63.9	45.5
...	48 475	Ward	836	1,102	10,352	10,258	10,909	13,115	2,417	2,375	2,129	12.4	13.0	15.7
14780	48 477	Washington	621	1,665	31,912	31,486	30,373	26,154	1,371	1,389	1,413	52.4	50.0	42.9
29700	48 479	Webb	3,376	157	231,470	224,874	193,117	133,239	265	284	349	69.0	58.0	39.7
20900	48 481	Wharton	1,094	664	41,475	41,403	41,188	39,955	1,116	1,075	1,002	38.0	37.8	36.6
...	48 483	Wheeler	915	905	4,854	4,801	5,284	5,879	2,849	2,832	2,772	5.3	5.7	6.4
48660	48 485	Wichita	633	1,631	125,158	125,732	131,664	122,378	469	405	375	199.4	209.3	195.0
46900	48 487	Wilbarger	978	800	14,218	14,104	14,676	15,121	2,152	2,110	1,981	14.6	15.1	15.6
39700	48 489	Willacy	784	1,204	20,645	20,412	20,082	17,705	1,782	1,790	1,805	34.6	33.6	29.7
12420	48 491	Williamson	1,135	635	353,830	334,378	249,980	139,551	178	232	340	315.1	227.2	124.1
41700	48 493	Wilson	809	1,152	38,829	37,617	32,408	22,650	1,185	1,337	1,550	48.1	40.5	28.1
...	48 495	Winkler	841	1,094	6,609	6,592	7,173	8,626	2,717	2,670	2,501	7.9	8.4	10.3
19100	48 497	Wise	923	884	57,891	56,746	48,793	34,679	856	935	1,146	64.0	54.7	38.3
...	48 499	Wood	696	1,450	41,776	40,797	36,752	29,380	1,107	1,197	1,319	64.2	56.7	45.2
...	48 501	Yoakum	800	1,180	7,438	7,396	7,322	8,786	2,644	2,654	2,486	9.3	9.1	11.0
...	48 503	Young	931	872	18,021	17,740	17,943	18,126	1,913	1,905	1,782	19.5	19.4	19.7
...	48 505	Zapata	1,058	706	13,615	13,433	12,182	9,279	2,196	2,286	2,446	13.7	12.3	9.3
...	48 507	Zavala	1,302	522	12,036	11,813	11,600	12,162	2,299	2,326	2,202	9.3	8.9	9.4
	49 000	**UTAH**	84,899	(X)	2,550,063	2,490,334	2,233,198	1,722,850	(X)	(X)	(X)	31.0	27.3	21.0
...	49 001	Beaver	2,592	218	6,294	6,202	6,005	4,765	2,741	2,779	2,859	2.4	2.3	1.8
14940	49 003	Box Elder	6,729	54	47,197	46,333	42,745	36,485	999	1,041	1,090	8.2	7.5	6.4
30860	49 005	Cache	1,173	601	98,662	98,358	91,391	70,183	569	562	630	84.7	78.7	60.3
39220	49 007	Carbon	1,485	452	19,469	19,459	20,425	20,228	1,843	1,764	1,664	13.2	13.8	13.7
...	49 009	Daggett	723	1,348	947	937	921	690	3,110	3,114	3,129	1.4	1.3	1.0
36260	49 011	Davis	634	1,630	276,259	268,084	238,994	187,941	219	241	256	907.3	789.3	617.2
...	49 013	Duchesne	3,256	165	15,701	15,328	14,371	12,645	2,061	2,137	2,173	4.8	4.4	3.9
...	49 015	Emery	4,462	110	10,698	10,711	10,962	10,332	2,386	2,371	2,357	2.4	2.5	2.3
...	49 017	Garfield	5,208	78	4,534	4,443	4,735	3,980	2,868	2,866	2,921	0.9	0.9	0.8
...	49 019	Grand	3,694	146	8,999	8,787	8,380	6,620	2,527	2,575	2,695	2.4	2.3	1.8
16260	49 021	Iron	3,302	162	40,544	38,438	33,779	20,789	1,144	1,289	1,641	12.3	10.3	6.3
39340	49 023	Juab	3,406	156	9,420	9,165	8,238	5,817	2,486	2,589	2,778	2.8	2.4	1.7
...	49 025	Kane	4,108	124	6,532	6,232	6,046	5,169	2,729	2,777	2,827	1.6	1.5	1.3
...	49 027	Millard	6,828	53	12,390	12,280	12,405	11,333	2,274	2,273	2,272	1.9	1.9	1.7
36260	49 029	Morgan	611	1,705	8,134	7,862	7,129	5,528	2,582	2,677	2,799	13.4	11.8	9.1
...	49 031	Piute	766	1,247	1,347	1,371	1,435	1,277	3,094	3,095	3,106	1.8	1.9	1.7
...	49 033	Rich	1,086	673	2,040	2,057	1,961	1,725	3,048	3,067	3,081	2.0	1.9	1.7
41620	49 035	Salt Lake	808	1,155	978,701	960,297	898,412	725,956	39	43	54	1,327.3	1,221.6	984.5
...	49 037	San Juan	7,933	44	14,265	14,117	14,413	12,621	2,148	2,130	2,176	1.8	1.6	1.6
...	49 039	Sanpete	1,603	417	24,196	23,995	22,763	16,259	1,622	1,660	1,908	15.2	14.4	10.2
...	49 041	Sevier	1,918	332	19,640	19,367	18,842	15,431	1,839	1,852	1,960	10.3	9.9	8.1
41620	49 043	Summit	1,882	344	35,466	35,119	29,736	15,518	1,273	1,406	1,951	19.0	16.0	8.3
41620	49 045	Tooele	7,287	48	53,552	51,269	40,735	26,601	909	1,092	1,404	7.7	6.0	3.8
46860	49 047	Uintah	4,499	108	27,955	27,129	25,224	22,211	1,489	1,558	1,570	6.2	5.6	5.0
39340	49 049	Utah	2,141	289	464,760	451,855	368,540	263,590	136	159	189	232.6	185.6	131.9
25720	49 051	Wasatch	1,209	582	20,255	19,015	15,215	10,089	1,809	2,075	2,378	17.2	13.1	8.5
41100	49 053	Washington	2,430	238	126,312	119,188	90,354	48,560	466	573	862	52.1	37.6	20.0
...	49 055	Wayne	2,466	233	2,544	2,454	2,509	2,177	3,011	3,026	3,055	1.0	1.0	0.9
36260	49 057	Weber	659	1,537	213,247	210,482	196,533	158,330	285	282	299	370.5	343.1	275.1
	50 000	**VERMONT**	9,614	(X)	623,908	622,387	608,827	562,758	(X)	(X)	(X)	67.5	65.9	60.8
13540	50 001	Addison	808	1,153	37,057	36,948	35,974	32,953	1,232	1,220	1,193	48.1	46.8	42.8
13540	50 003	Bennington	678	1,500	36,929	36,856	36,994	35,845	1,237	1,191	1,104	54.6	54.7	53.0
...	50 005	Caledonia	658	1,547	30,842	30,531	29,681	27,846	1,400	1,410	1,356	47.4	45.7	42.8
15540	50 007	Chittenden	620	1,673	150,069	149,550	146,571	131,761	394	371	351	278.4	272.7	244.5
13620	50 009	Essex	674	1,509	6,567	6,639	6,459	6,405	2,723	2,742	2,717	9.9	9.7	9.6
15540	50 011	Franklin	692	1,458	48,187	47,931	45,417	39,980	984	992	1,001	75.6	71.6	62.8
15540	50 013	Grand Isle	195	3,027	7,751	7,741	6,901	5,318	2,618	2,696	2,817	93.8	84.0	64.4
...	50 015	Lamoille	464	2,304	24,592	24,484	23,224	19,735	1,604	1,632	1,690	53.3	50.6	42.8
30100	50 017	Orange	692	1,460	29,440	29,306	28,252	26,149	1,435	1,442	1,414	42.8	41.2	38.0
...	50 019	Orleans	721	1,359	27,718	27,590	26,281	24,053	1,496	1,509	1,491	39.7	37.8	34.5
40860	50 021	Rutland	945	846	63,641	63,609	63,400	62,142	796	764	701	68.2	68.0	66.7
12740	50 023	Washington	695	1,453	59,564	59,428	58,039	54,928	845	824	783	86.4	84.3	79.7
...	50 025	Windham	798	1,182	43,898	43,985	44,216	41,588	1,066	1,011	968	55.7	56.0	52.7
30100	50 027	Windsor	976	803	57,653	57,789	57,418	54,055	863	831	796	59.4	59.2	55.7
	51 000	**VIRGINIA**	42,774	(X)	7,642,884	7,564,327	7,079,030	6,189,197	(X)	(X)	(X)	193.0	179.4	156.3
16820	51 001	Accomack	1,310	516	39,345	39,307	38,305	31,703	1,175	1,157	1,223	86.4	84.3	69.7
...	51 003	Albemarle	726	1,333	92,035	90,496	84,197	68,177	603	618	649	127.4	117.1	94.3
40060	51 005	Alleghany[8]	446	2,358	16,600	16,681	17,215	12,815	2,000	1,941	2,155	37.3	38.6	28.7
31340	51 007	Amelia	359	2,714	12,502	12,208	11,400	8,787	2,266	2,342	2,485	35.0	32.2	24.6
...	51 009	Amherst	479	2,247	32,239	32,004	31,894	28,578	1,363	1,349	1,342	67.8	67.1	60.1

See footnotes at end of table.

Table B-1. Counties — **Area and Population**—Con.

[Includes United States, states, and 3,141 counties/county equivalents defined as of February 22, 2005. For more information on these areas, see Appendix C, Geographic Information]

Metro-politan area code	FIPS state and county code[1]	County	Area, 2000 (square miles) Total	Rank[2]	Population 2006 (July 1)	2005 (July 1)	2000[3] (April 1 estimates base)	1990[3] (April 1 estimates base)	Rank 2006[2]	2000[2]	1990[4]	Persons per square mile of land area 2006[5]	2000	1990
		VIRGINIA—Con.												
31340	51 011	Appomattox	335	2,772	14,128	13,871	13,705	12,300	2,160	2,186	2,195	42.3	41.1	36.9
47900	51 013	Arlington	26	3,113	199,776	199,761	189,444	170,895	295	291	283	7,722.3	7,317.7	6,603.4
44420	51 015	Augusta	971	810	70,910	69,656	65,615	54,557	734	744	790	73.1	67.8	56.1
...	51 017	Bath	535	2,057	4,814	4,901	5,048	4,799	2,850	2,850	2,858	9.1	9.5	9.0
31340	51 019	Bedford	769	1,235	66,507	64,999	60,302	45,553	772	802	908	88.1	80.3	60.3
...	51 021	Bland	359	2,713	6,903	6,941	6,871	6,514	2,688	2,701	2,708	19.2	19.1	18.2
40220	51 023	Botetourt	546	2,017	32,228	31,909	30,530	24,992	1,365	1,386	1,463	59.4	56.4	46.1
...	51 025	Brunswick	569	1,934	17,938	17,857	18,419	15,987	1,917	1,873	1,924	31.7	32.5	28.2
...	51 027	Buchanan	504	2,163	24,409	24,690	26,978	31,333	1,614	1,485	1,234	48.4	53.2	62.2
...	51 029	Buckingham	584	1,810	16,099	16,036	15,623	12,873	2,040	2,049	2,149	27.7	26.9	22.2
31340	51 031	Campbell	507	2,144	52,667	52,187	51,105	47,499	918	905	883	104.4	101.4	94.2
40060	51 033	Caroline	539	2,042	26,731	25,437	22,121	19,217	1,528	1,687	1,719	50.2	41.6	36.1
...	51 035	Carroll	478	2,249	29,450	29,322	29,245	26,519	1,434	1,422	1,408	61.8	61.5	55.6
40060	51 036	Charles City	204	3,009	7,221	7,095	6,926	6,282	2,664	2,695	2,724	39.5	37.9	34.4
...	51 037	Charlotte	477	2,250	12,491	12,426	12,471	11,688	2,268	2,269	2,235	26.3	26.2	24.6
40060	51 041	Chesterfield	437	2,396	296,718	288,423	259,782	209,599	203	214	238	696.9	612.8	492.4
47900	51 043	Clarke	178	3,047	14,565	14,154	12,652	12,101	2,129	2,254	2,208	82.5	72.0	68.5
40220	51 045	Craig	331	2,778	5,179	5,132	5,091	4,372	2,826	2,845	2,887	15.7	15.4	13.2
19020	51 047	Culpeper	382	2,651	44,622	42,454	34,265	27,791	1,048	1,273	1,359	117.1	90.5	72.9
40060	51 049	Cumberland	300	2,848	9,465	9,359	9,017	7,825	2,481	2,528	2,593	31.7	30.2	26.2
...	51 051	Dickenson	334	2,774	16,182	16,260	16,395	17,620	2,035	2,000	1,810	48.8	49.3	53.0
40060	51 053	Dinwiddie	507	2,148	25,695	25,355	24,533	22,279	1,558	1,575	1,564	51.0	48.9	44.2
...	51 057	Essex	286	2,870	10,633	10,490	9,989	8,689	2,390	2,446	2,493	41.2	38.8	33.7
47900	51 059	Fairfax	407	2,564	1,010,443	1,010,015	969,677	818,310	37	36	45	2,557.8	2,468.9	2,068.7
47900	51 061	Fauquier	651	1,569	66,170	64,834	55,145	48,700	775	855	860	101.8	85.6	74.9
...	51 063	Floyd	381	2,652	14,789	14,652	13,874	11,965	2,120	2,172	2,221	38.8	36.6	31.4
16820	51 065	Fluvanna	290	2,857	25,058	24,714	20,047	12,429	1,582	1,791	2,187	87.2	70.4	43.2
40220	51 067	Franklin	712	1,413	50,784	50,172	47,283	39,549	944	962	1,011	73.4	68.6	57.1
49020	51 069	Frederick	416	2,509	71,187	68,984	59,209	45,723	730	811	907	171.7	143.7	110.3
13980	51 071	Giles	360	2,710	17,403	17,154	16,657	16,366	1,949	1,982	1,900	48.7	46.8	45.7
47260	51 073	Gloucester	288	2,865	38,293	37,750	34,780	30,131	1,201	1,260	1,292	176.8	161.0	139.1
40060	51 075	Goochland	290	2,858	20,085	19,275	16,863	14,163	1,819	1,965	2,040	70.6	59.5	49.8
...	51 077	Grayson	446	2,355	16,159	16,286	16,881	16,278	2,036	1,963	1,905	36.5	38.2	36.8
16820	51 079	Greene	157	3,065	17,709	17,354	15,244	10,297	1,925	2,074	2,359	113.1	98.1	65.7
...	51 081	Greensville	297	2,850	11,006	11,036	11,560	8,553	2,366	2,329	2,508	37.3	39.1	28.9
...	51 083	Halifax[9]	830	1,113	36,149	36,121	37,350	36,030	1,253	1,182	1,099	44.1	45.6	44.3
40060	51 085	Hanover	474	2,261	98,983	97,369	86,320	63,306	566	602	690	209.4	184.1	133.9
40060	51 087	Henrico	245	2,959	284,399	280,599	262,104	217,878	212	210	227	1,194.7	1,105.3	915.0
32300	51 089	Henry	384	2,643	56,208	56,367	57,964	56,942	880	825	766	147.0	151.6	148.9
...	51 091	Highland	416	2,508	2,510	2,481	2,536	2,635	3,014	3,023	3,015	6.0	6.1	6.3
47260	51 093	Isle of Wight	363	2,698	34,723	33,398	29,728	25,053	1,301	1,407	1,460	109.9	94.6	79.3
47260	51 095	James City	180	3,045	59,741	57,394	48,102	34,779	844	948	1,141	418.0	339.3	243.3
40060	51 097	King and Queen	326	2,791	6,903	6,795	6,630	6,289	2,688	2,724	2,722	21.8	20.9	19.9
...	51 099	King George	188	3,036	21,780	20,659	16,803	13,527	1,729	1,970	2,099	121.0	94.0	75.1
40060	51 101	King William	286	2,872	15,381	14,712	13,146	10,913	2,079	2,217	2,305	55.8	48.0	39.6
...	51 103	Lancaster	231	2,974	11,519	11,490	11,567	10,896	2,327	2,327	2,306	86.5	87.0	81.8
...	51 105	Lee	437	2,395	23,787	23,696	23,589	24,496	1,638	1,608	1,479	54.4	53.9	56.0
47900	51 107	Loudoun	521	2,099	268,817	256,417	169,599	86,185	228	320	529	517.1	334.7	165.8
40060	51 109	Louisa	511	2,134	31,226	30,034	25,627	20,325	1,392	1,530	1,659	62.8	51.8	40.9
...	51 111	Lunenburg	432	2,428	13,219	13,130	13,146	11,419	2,232	2,217	2,260	30.6	30.3	26.4
...	51 113	Madison	322	2,799	13,613	13,358	12,519	11,949	2,197	2,265	2,224	42.4	39.1	37.2
47260	51 115	Mathews	252	2,943	9,184	9,131	9,207	8,348	2,510	2,513	2,529	107.2	107.4	97.4
...	51 117	Mecklenburg	679	1,495	32,381	32,366	32,380	29,241	1,360	1,338	1,322	51.9	51.9	46.9
...	51 119	Middlesex	211	3,001	10,615	10,493	9,932	8,653	2,392	2,453	2,495	81.5	76.5	66.4
13980	51 121	Montgomery	389	2,633	84,541	84,263	83,681	73,913	643	622	609	217.8	215.4	190.4
16820	51 125	Nelson	474	2,259	15,161	15,094	14,445	12,778	2,096	2,127	2,158	32.1	30.7	27.0
40060	51 127	New Kent	223	2,983	16,852	16,126	13,462	10,466	1,979	2,199	2,340	80.4	64.6	49.9
...	51 131	Northampton	795	1,187	13,609	13,458	13,093	13,061	2,198	2,223	2,135	65.6	63.0	63.0
...	51 133	Northumberland	286	2,871	12,820	12,829	12,268	10,524	2,257	2,283	2,334	66.7	63.9	54.7
...	51 135	Nottoway	316	2,808	15,572	15,561	15,725	14,993	2,070	2,038	1,987	49.5	50.0	47.6
...	51 137	Orange	343	2,750	31,740	30,249	25,881	21,421	1,377	1,523	1,609	92.9	76.1	62.7
...	51 139	Page	314	2,812	24,104	23,836	23,175	21,690	1,627	1,636	1,593	77.5	74.6	69.7
...	51 141	Patrick	486	2,224	19,212	19,216	19,407	17,473	1,860	1,825	1,822	39.8	40.2	36.2
19260	51 143	Pittsylvania	978	799	61,501	61,583	61,745	55,672	830	787	778	63.4	63.6	57.3
40060	51 145	Powhatan	262	2,917	27,649	26,627	22,377	15,328	1,499	1,676	1,969	105.8	86.6	58.7
...	51 147	Prince Edward	354	2,721	20,530	20,441	19,720	17,320	1,792	1,810	1,831	58.2	55.8	49.1
40060	51 149	Prince George	282	2,886	36,184	36,497	33,108	27,390	1,250	1,317	1,379	136.2	124.9	103.1
47900	51 153	Prince William	348	2,731	357,503	349,155	280,813	214,954	176	199	232	1,058.4	840.3	635.2
13980	51 155	Pulaski	330	2,781	35,055	35,006	35,127	34,496	1,294	1,246	1,151	109.4	109.6	107.6
...	51 157	Rappahannock	267	2,905	7,203	7,275	6,983	6,622	2,665	2,688	2,694	27.0	26.1	24.8

See footnotes at end of table.

Table B-1. Counties — **Area and Population**—Con.

[Includes United States, states, and 3,141 counties/county equivalents defined as of February 22, 2005. For more information on these areas, see Appendix C, Geographic Information]

Metro-politan area code	FIPS state and county code[1]	County	Area, 2000 (square miles) Total	Rank[2]	2006 (July 1)	2005 (July 1)	2000[3] (April 1 estimates base)	1990[3] (April 1 estimates base)	Rank 2006[2]	2000[2]	1990[4]	Persons per square mile of land area 2006[5]	2000	1990
		VIRGINIA—Con.												
...	51 159	Richmond	216	2,993	9,142	9,049	8,800	7,273	2,516	2,548	2,629	47.7	45.9	38.0
40220	51 161	Roanoke	251	2,945	90,482	88,875	85,692	79,278	615	610	574	360.7	341.8	316.3
...	51 163	Rockbridge	601	1,738	21,337	21,271	20,808	18,350	1,748	1,748	1,773	35.6	34.8	30.6
25500	51 165	Rockingham	853	1,077	72,564	71,639	67,716	57,482	720	724	760	85.3	79.7	67.5
...	51 167	Russell	477	2,252	28,790	28,830	29,258	28,667	1,453	1,421	1,340	60.7	61.7	60.4
28700	51 169	Scott	539	2,044	22,882	22,899	23,403	23,204	1,676	1,624	1,530	42.6	43.6	43.2
...	51 171	Shenandoah	513	2,123	40,051	39,045	35,075	31,636	1,159	1,249	1,227	78.2	68.8	61.8
...	51 173	Smyth	452	2,333	32,506	32,440	33,081	32,370	1,354	1,318	1,203	71.9	73.2	71.6
...	51 175	Southampton	602	1,732	17,814	17,507	17,482	17,022	1,923	1,926	1,849	29.7	29.2	28.4
47900	51 177	Spotsylvania	412	2,526	119,529	116,312	90,393	57,397	485	571	761	298.2	228.5	143.2
47900	51 179	Stafford	280	2,889	120,170	117,968	92,446	62,255	481	551	699	444.5	346.1	230.6
47260	51 181	Surry	310	2,822	7,119	6,987	6,829	6,145	2,671	2,709	2,738	25.5	24.5	22.0
40060	51 183	Sussex	493	2,208	12,249	12,016	12,504	10,248	2,285	2,266	2,364	25.0	25.4	20.9
14140	51 185	Tazewell	520	2,101	44,608	44,532	44,598	45,960	1,049	1,005	903	85.8	85.5	88.4
47900	51 187	Warren	216	2,994	36,102	35,407	31,578	26,142	1,255	1,359	1,416	168.9	148.5	122.3
28700	51 191	Washington	566	1,949	51,984	51,918	51,103	45,887	929	906	905	92.4	90.9	81.3
...	51 193	Westmoreland	253	2,941	17,188	17,139	16,718	15,480	1,953	1,976	1,956	75.0	72.8	67.5
...	51 195	Wise	405	2,571	41,905	41,958	42,205	39,573	1,103	1,053	1,009	103.7	104.4	98.1
...	51 197	Wythe	465	2,300	28,640	28,363	27,599	25,471	1,458	1,463	1,449	61.8	59.7	55.0
47260	51 199	York	216	2,995	61,879	61,684	56,297	42,434	823	840	949	585.7	535.6	401.8
		Independent Cities												
47900	51 510	Alexandria	15	3,117	136,974	137,602	128,292	111,183	435	421	413	9,023.3	8,509.4	7,276.4
31340	51 515	Bedford	7	3,134	6,249	6,270	6,381	6,176	2,746	2,752	2,735	907.0	926.6	901.6
28700	51 520	Bristol	13	3,120	17,496	17,391	17,367	18,426	1,940	1,933	1,767	1,356.3	1,340.9	1,589.8
...	51 530	Buena Vista	7	3,135	6,457	6,412	6,349	6,406	2,734	2,753	2,716	945.4	931.3	937.9
16820	51 540	Charlottesville	10	3,124	40,315	40,358	40,088	40,470	1,152	1,111	987	3,929.3	3,900.6	3,944.4
47260	51 550	Chesapeake	351	2,726	220,560	218,219	199,184	151,982	279	278	307	647.3	588.1	446.1
...	51 560	Clifton Forge[6]	3	3,138	(X)	(X)	(X)	4,679	(X)	(X)	2,862	(NA)	(NA)	1,509.4
40060	51 570	Colonial Heights	8	3,131	17,676	17,502	16,897	16,064	1,927	1,961	1,920	2,363.1	2,261.0	2,150.5
...	51 580	Covington	6	3,137	6,073	6,145	6,303	7,352	2,763	2,758	2,625	1,071.1	1,111.8	1,655.9
19260	51 590	Danville	44	3,110	45,586	45,869	48,411	53,056	1,030	942	803	1,058.7	1,120.3	1,232.1
...	51 595	Emporia	7	3,133	5,625	5,546	5,665	5,556	2,792	2,811	2,795	816.4	822.2	806.4
47900	51 600	Fairfax	6	3,136	22,422	21,822	21,570	19,945	1,703	1,716	1,682	3,553.4	3,430.9	3,237.8
47900	51 610	Falls Church	2	3,141	10,799	10,764	10,377	9,464	2,380	2,406	2,438	5,426.6	5,230.2	4,732.0
...	51 620	Franklin	8	3,129	8,800	8,572	8,346	8,392	2,537	2,578	2,521	1,053.9	992.1	1,094.1
47900	51 630	Fredericksburg	11	3,123	21,273	20,672	19,279	19,033	1,749	1,831	1,733	2,022.1	1,835.6	1,810.9
...	51 640	Galax	8	3,130	6,682	6,657	6,837	6,745	2,709	2,707	2,682	811.9	832.8	835.8
47260	51 650	Hampton	136	3,078	145,017	145,154	146,437	133,773	413	374	347	2,800.6	2,826.6	2,581.5
25500	51 660	Harrisonburg	18	3,116	40,885	40,419	40,453	30,707	1,137	1,105	1,258	2,328.3	2,297.3	1,748.7
40060	51 670	Hopewell	11	3,122	22,731	22,513	22,277	23,101	1,683	1,682	1,533	2,219.8	2,177.2	2,253.8
...	51 678	Lexington	2	3,139	6,739	6,762	6,867	6,959	2,702	2,702	2,664	2,706.4	2,741.8	2,794.8
31340	51 680	Lynchburg	50	3,107	67,720	66,684	65,229	66,120	760	747	661	1,371.1	1,320.0	1,338.5
47900	51 683	Manassas	10	3,126	36,638	37,499	35,135	27,757	1,241	1,245	1,361	3,689.6	3,565.8	2,772.9
47900	51 685	Manassas Park	2	3,139	11,642	11,732	10,290	6,798	2,319	2,417	2,676	4,675.5	4,151.0	3,714.8
32300	51 690	Martinsville	11	3,121	14,945	14,900	15,365	16,162	2,111	2,064	1,914	1,363.6	1,398.4	1,474.6
47260	51 700	Newport News	119	3,086	178,281	178,869	180,697	171,477	330	306	281	2,610.6	2,643.7	2,509.5
47260	51 710	Norfolk	96	3,095	229,112	230,775	234,403	261,250	267	247	192	4,264.1	4,355.8	4,859.6
...	51 720	Norton	8	3,132	3,643	3,646	3,908	4,247	2,935	2,922	2,895	483.8	516.2	585.0
40060	51 730	Petersburg	23	3,114	32,445	32,282	33,756	37,071	1,358	1,290	1,071	1,418.1	1,468.1	1,620.2
47260	51 735	Poquoson	78	3,100	11,918	11,790	11,566	11,005	2,303	2,328	2,292	767.9	746.4	709.1
47260	51 740	Portsmouth	47	3,108	101,377	99,772	100,565	103,910	551	522	443	3,057.2	3,027.8	3,134.5
13980	51 750	Radford	10	3,125	14,525	14,504	15,859	15,940	2,132	2,030	1,927	1,479.1	1,610.8	1,623.2
40060	51 760	Richmond	63	3,103	192,913	193,186	198,107	202,713	310	279	244	3,211.5	3,292.1	3,371.2
40220	51 770	Roanoke	43	3,111	91,552	91,842	94,911	96,487	608	542	478	2,135.1	2,209.5	2,249.1
40220	51 775	Salem	15	3,119	24,825	24,560	24,747	23,835	1,592	1,568	1,499	1,701.5	1,698.6	1,638.1
...	51 780	South Boston[9]	(X)	(X)	(X)	(X)	(X)	(X)	(X)	(X)	(X)	(NA)	(NA)	(NA)
44420	51 790	Staunton	20	3,115	23,334	23,205	23,853	24,581	1,661	1,598	1,477	1,183.9	1,209.8	1,244.0
47260	51 800	Suffolk	429	2,449	81,071	78,787	63,677	52,143	664	763	812	202.7	160.5	130.3
47260	51 810	Virginia Beach	497	2,192	435,619	437,021	425,257	393,089	146	141	128	1,754.5	1,717.3	1,583.0
44420	51 820	Waynesboro	15	3,118	21,454	21,140	19,520	18,549	1,745	1,821	1,760	1,396.7	1,276.6	1,321.2
47260	51 830	Williamsburg	9	3,128	11,793	11,696	11,998	11,600	2,306	2,295	2,248	1,380.9	1,403.5	1,347.3
49020	51 840	Winchester	9	3,127	25,265	25,086	23,585	21,947	1,574	1,610	1,579	2,707.9	2,537.3	2,352.3
	53 000	WASHINGTON	71,300	(X)	6,395,798	6,291,899	5,894,140	4,866,669	(X)	(X)	(X)	96.1	88.8	73.1
...	53 001	Adams	1,930	328	16,887	16,849	16,424	13,603	1,976	1,997	2,092	8.8	8.6	7.1
30300	53 003	Asotin	641	1,604	21,247	21,050	20,551	17,605	1,755	1,759	1,814	33.4	32.4	27.7
28420	53 005	Benton	1,760	380	159,463	157,920	142,478	112,560	366	383	408	93.6	84.1	66.1
48300	53 007	Chelan	2,994	183	71,034	69,950	66,616	52,250	732	734	810	24.3	22.8	17.9
38820	53 009	Clallam	2,670	208	70,400	69,487	64,179	56,210	738	759	772	40.5	37.0	32.2

See footnotes at end of table.

[Includes United States, states, and 3,141 counties/county equivalents defined as of February 22, 2005. For more information on these areas, see Appendix C, Geographic Information]

Metro-politan area code	FIPS state and county code[1]	County	Area, 2000 (square miles)		Population				Rank			Persons per square mile of land area		
			Total	Rank[2]	2006 (July 1)	2005 (July 1)	2000[3] (April 1 estimates base)	1990[3] (April 1 estimates base)	2006[2]	2000[2]	1990[4]	2006[5]	2000	1990
		WASHINGTON—Con.												
38900	53 011	Clark	656	1,552	412,938	404,066	345,238	238,053	153	169	210	657.3	553.3	379.1
...	53 013	Columbia	874	1,031	4,087	4,140	4,064	4,024	2,904	2,915	2,915	4.7	4.7	4.6
31020	53 015	Cowlitz	1,166	605	99,905	97,178	92,948	82,119	562	549	552	87.7	81.7	72.1
48300	53 017	Douglas	1,849	353	35,772	34,904	32,603	26,205	1,263	1,329	1,412	19.6	17.9	14.4
...	53 019	Ferry	2,257	272	7,560	7,527	7,260	6,295	2,636	2,659	2,721	3.4	3.3	2.9
28420	53 021	Franklin	1,265	547	66,570	62,972	49,347	37,473	771	926	1,059	53.6	39.9	30.2
...	53 023	Garfield	718	1,383	2,223	2,293	2,397	2,248	3,033	3,030	3,049	3.1	3.4	3.2
34180	53 025	Grant	2,791	199	82,612	81,145	74,702	54,798	651	670	785	30.8	28.0	20.5
10140	53 027	Grays Harbor	2,224	278	71,587	70,904	67,194	64,175	728	729	685	37.3	35.1	33.5
36020	53 029	Island	517	2,109	81,489	79,983	71,558	60,195	661	690	720	391.0	344.9	288.6
...	53 031	Jefferson	2,184	283	29,279	28,676	26,299	20,406	1,439	1,508	1,655	16.1	14.6	11.3
42660	53 033	King	2,307	263	1,826,732	1,799,119	1,737,043	1,507,305	14	12	13	859.2	818.1	709.0
14740	53 035	Kitsap	566	1,949	240,604	241,525	231,969	189,731	256	249	252	607.6	586.9	479.1
21260	53 037	Kittitas	2,333	259	37,189	36,733	33,362	26,725	1,229	1,303	1,400	16.2	14.6	11.6
...	53 039	Klickitat	1,904	338	20,335	19,847	19,161	16,616	1,806	1,839	1,876	10.9	10.3	8.9
16500	53 041	Lewis	2,436	236	73,585	72,397	68,600	59,358	708	720	730	30.6	28.5	24.7
...	53 043	Lincoln	2,340	257	10,376	10,298	10,185	8,864	2,414	2,430	2,481	4.5	4.4	3.8
43220	53 045	Mason	1,051	715	55,951	54,169	49,405	38,341	883	925	1,044	58.2	51.6	39.9
...	53 047	Okanogan	5,315	75	40,040	39,779	39,564	33,350	1,160	1,125	1,181	7.6	7.5	6.3
...	53 049	Pacific	1,224	574	21,735	21,568	20,984	18,882	1,732	1,737	1,741	23.3	22.5	19.4
...	53 051	Pend Oreille	1,425	478	12,951	12,615	11,732	8,915	2,247	2,316	2,478	9.2	8.4	6.4
42660	53 053	Pierce	1,807	363	766,878	753,209	700,818	586,203	70	71	80	456.8	419.4	349.9
...	53 055	San Juan	621	1,667	15,298	15,215	14,077	10,035	2,085	2,160	2,382	87.5	80.9	57.4
34580	53 057	Skagit	1,920	330	115,700	113,181	102,982	79,545	494	516	573	66.7	59.6	45.8
38900	53 059	Skamania	1,684	397	10,833	10,606	9,872	8,289	2,378	2,458	2,537	6.5	6.0	5.0
42660	53 061	Snohomish	2,196	282	669,887	655,564	606,024	465,628	87	90	107	320.7	291.6	222.8
44060	53 063	Spokane	1,781	374	446,706	440,434	417,938	361,333	143	144	142	253.3	237.4	204.9
...	53 065	Stevens	2,541	225	42,632	41,934	40,066	30,948	1,091	1,112	1,248	17.2	16.2	12.5
36500	53 067	Thurston	774	1,227	234,670	228,881	207,355	161,238	261	268	295	322.8	286.6	221.8
...	53 069	Wahkiakum	287	2,867	4,026	3,885	3,824	3,327	2,908	2,927	2,968	15.2	14.5	12.6
47460	53 071	Walla Walla	1,299	525	57,721	57,461	55,180	48,439	860	854	864	45.4	43.5	38.1
13380	53 073	Whatcom	2,504	230	185,953	183,363	166,823	127,780	318	324	364	87.7	79.1	60.3
39420	53 075	Whitman	2,178	284	39,838	40,135	40,740	38,775	1,166	1,091	1,031	18.4	18.8	18.0
49420	53 077	Yakima	4,312	114	233,105	230,937	222,578	188,823	263	255	255	54.3	51.9	44.0
...	54 000	WEST VIRGINIA	24,230	(X)	1,818,470	1,814,083	1,808,350	1,793,477	(X)	(X)	(X)	75.5	75.1	74.5
...	54 001	Barbour	343	2,752	15,788	15,656	15,557	15,699	2,055	2,051	1,944	46.3	45.6	46.1
25180	54 003	Berkeley	322	2,800	97,534	93,286	75,905	59,253	575	660	733	303.7	238.0	184.5
16620	54 005	Boone	503	2,166	25,512	25,613	25,535	25,870	1,562	1,539	1,427	50.7	50.7	51.4
...	54 007	Braxton	516	2,116	14,810	14,856	14,702	12,998	2,117	2,108	2,142	28.8	28.7	25.3
48260	54 009	Brooke	92	3,096	24,132	24,474	25,447	26,992	1,626	1,544	1,391	271.6	285.6	303.8
26580	54 011	Cabell	288	2,864	93,904	93,988	96,785	96,827	592	534	475	333.5	343.3	343.8
...	54 013	Calhoun	281	2,888	7,381	7,367	7,582	7,885	2,648	2,638	2,582	26.3	27.0	28.1
16620	54 015	Clay	344	2,749	10,256	10,318	10,330	9,983	2,426	2,412	2,388	30.0	30.2	29.2
17220	54 017	Doddridge	320	2,803	7,459	7,474	7,403	6,994	2,642	2,649	2,659	23.3	23.1	21.8
36060	54 019	Fayette	668	1,518	46,610	46,558	47,579	47,952	1,009	958	872	70.2	71.6	72.2
...	54 021	Gilmer	340	2,759	6,965	6,962	7,160	7,669	2,682	2,672	2,604	20.5	21.1	22.6
...	54 023	Grant	480	2,240	11,915	11,688	11,299	10,428	2,304	2,351	2,347	25.0	23.7	21.9
...	54 025	Greenbrier	1,024	740	34,850	34,830	34,453	34,693	1,298	1,266	1,145	34.1	33.7	34.0
49020	54 027	Hampshire	645	1,588	22,480	22,011	20,203	16,498	1,699	1,780	1,893	35.0	31.7	25.7
48260	54 029	Hancock	88	3,098	30,911	31,191	32,667	35,233	1,396	1,326	1,125	373.2	394.0	424.3
...	54 031	Hardy	584	1,803	13,420	13,303	12,669	10,977	2,217	2,252	2,297	23.0	21.8	18.8
17220	54 033	Harrison	417	2,505	68,745	68,462	68,652	69,371	755	719	638	165.2	164.9	166.7
...	54 035	Jackson	472	2,272	28,451	28,306	28,000	25,938	1,466	1,452	1,424	61.1	60.2	55.7
47900	54 037	Jefferson	212	2,999	50,443	49,160	42,190	35,926	947	1,054	1,102	240.7	202.6	171.4
16620	54 039	Kanawha	911	917	192,419	193,413	200,073	207,619	312	276	241	213.1	221.1	229.9
...	54 041	Lewis	390	2,632	17,129	17,127	16,919	17,223	1,959	1,958	1,840	44.8	44.2	44.3
16620	54 043	Lincoln	439	2,390	22,357	22,446	22,108	21,382	1,707	1,688	1,612	51.1	50.6	48.9
...	54 045	Logan	456	2,321	36,218	36,216	37,710	43,032	1,249	1,170	938	79.7	82.8	94.7
...	54 047	McDowell	535	2,054	23,882	24,267	27,329	35,233	1,632	1,474	1,126	44.7	50.8	65.9
21900	54 049	Marion	311	2,820	56,706	56,662	56,598	57,249	877	837	763	183.1	182.5	184.9
48540	54 051	Marshall	312	2,818	33,896	34,250	35,519	37,356	1,317	1,232	1,062	110.4	115.3	121.7
38580	54 053	Mason	445	2,360	25,756	25,763	25,959	25,178	1,553	1,519	1,456	59.6	60.1	58.3
14140	54 055	Mercer	421	2,485	61,278	61,374	62,980	64,980	831	770	674	145.8	149.7	154.5
19060	54 057	Mineral	329	2,782	26,928	26,940	27,078	26,697	1,521	1,480	1,401	82.2	82.5	81.5
...	54 059	Mingo	424	2,469	27,100	27,165	28,253	33,739	1,513	1,441	1,173	64.1	66.3	79.8
34060	54 061	Monongalia	366	2,689	84,752	84,592	81,866	75,509	642	635	597	234.7	226.7	209.1
...	54 063	Monroe	474	2,265	13,510	13,539	13,194	12,406	2,205	2,213	2,189	28.5	27.9	26.2
25180	54 065	Morgan	230	2,977	16,337	15,987	14,943	12,128	2,018	2,097	2,205	71.3	65.6	53.0
...	54 067	Nicholas	654	1,560	26,446	26,369	26,562	26,775	1,536	1,499	1,398	40.8	40.9	41.3
48540	54 069	Ohio	109	3,089	44,662	44,958	47,433	50,871	1,047	959	830	420.6	445.9	479.1

See footnotes at end of table.

Table B-1. Counties — **Area and Population**—Con.

[Includes United States, states, and 3,141 counties/county equivalents defined as of February 22, 2005. For more information on these areas, see Appendix C, Geographic Information]

Metro-politan area code	FIPS state and county code[1]	County	Area, 2000 (square miles)		Population				Rank			Persons per square mile of land area		
			Total	Rank[2]	2006 (July 1)	2005 (July 1)	2000[3] (April 1 estimates base)	1990[3] (April 1 estimates base)	2006[2]	2000[2]	1990[4]	2006[5]	2000	1990
		WEST VIRGINIA—Con.												
...	54 071	Pendleton	698	1,444	7,679	7,764	8,196	8,054	2,628	2,594	2,559	11.0	11.7	11.5
37620	54 073	Pleasants	135	3,079	7,280	7,329	7,514	7,546	2,658	2,642	2,613	55.7	57.4	57.7
...	54 075	Pocahontas	942	850	8,755	8,829	9,131	9,008	2,541	2,521	2,470	9.3	9.7	9.6
34060	54 077	Preston	651	1,571	30,384	30,052	29,334	29,037	1,404	1,418	1,327	46.9	45.2	44.8
16620	54 079	Putnam	350	2,727	54,982	54,389	51,586	42,835	895	899	941	158.8	149.5	123.7
13220	54 081	Raleigh	609	1,710	79,302	79,186	79,220	76,819	679	647	587	130.7	130.3	126.6
...	54 083	Randolph	1,040	726	28,465	28,506	28,262	27,803	1,465	1,440	1,358	27.4	27.1	26.7
...	54 085	Ritchie	454	2,325	10,628	10,529	10,343	10,233	2,391	2,410	2,365	23.4	22.8	22.6
...	54 087	Roane	484	2,231	15,583	15,445	15,446	15,120	2,069	2,057	1,982	32.2	32.0	31.3
...	54 089	Summers	368	2,686	13,531	13,632	14,388	14,204	2,202	2,135	2,036	37.5	39.7	39.3
17220	54 091	Taylor	176	3,049	16,304	16,182	16,089	15,144	2,023	2,019	1,977	94.4	93.2	87.6
...	54 093	Tucker	421	2,482	6,856	6,948	7,321	7,728	2,694	2,655	2,602	16.4	17.4	18.4
...	54 095	Tyler	261	2,919	9,264	9,303	9,592	9,796	2,502	2,480	2,406	36.0	37.2	38.0
...	54 097	Upshur	355	2,717	23,685	23,586	23,404	22,867	1,644	1,623	1,538	66.8	66.0	64.5
26580	54 099	Wayne	512	2,126	41,647	41,959	42,903	41,636	1,110	1,038	966	82.3	84.8	82.3
...	54 101	Webster	556	1,986	9,696	9,739	9,719	10,729	2,464	2,470	2,315	17.4	17.4	19.3
...	54 103	Wetzel	361	2,705	16,685	16,974	17,693	19,258	1,995	1,918	1,714	46.4	49.2	53.6
37620	54 105	Wirt	235	2,967	5,980	5,882	5,873	5,192	2,771	2,797	2,825	25.7	25.2	22.3
37620	54 107	Wood	377	2,665	86,597	86,881	87,986	86,915	632	592	526	235.8	239.3	236.6
...	54 109	Wyoming	502	2,171	24,225	24,397	25,708	28,990	1,621	1,528	1,330	48.4	51.1	57.9
	55 000	**WISCONSIN**	65,498	(X)	5,556,506	5,527,644	5,363,715	4,891,954	(X)	(X)	(X)	102.3	99.0	90.1
...	55 001	Adams	689	1,468	20,843	20,834	19,920	15,682	1,767	1,798	1,945	32.2	30.9	24.2
...	55 003	Ashland	2,294	267	16,511	16,528	16,866	16,307	2,006	1,964	1,903	15.8	16.1	15.6
...	55 005	Barron	890	1,000	45,889	45,734	44,963	40,750	1,022	998	983	53.2	52.2	47.2
...	55 007	Bayfield	2,042	308	15,147	15,162	15,013	14,008	2,097	2,090	2,054	10.3	10.2	9.5
24580	55 009	Brown	615	1,692	240,213	238,610	226,658	194,594	257	251	248	454.4	429.9	368.1
...	55 011	Buffalo	710	1,419	13,897	13,956	13,804	13,584	2,174	2,175	2,093	20.3	20.2	19.8
...	55 013	Burnett	880	1,019	16,490	16,512	15,674	13,084	2,008	2,041	2,132	20.1	19.1	15.9
11540	55 015	Calumet	397	2,612	44,579	44,220	40,631	34,291	1,050	1,097	1,159	139.4	127.4	107.2
20740	55 017	Chippewa	1,041	724	60,300	59,696	55,205	52,360	838	853	808	59.7	54.8	51.8
...	55 019	Clark	1,219	578	34,094	34,074	33,557	31,647	1,314	1,300	1,226	28.0	27.7	26.0
31540	55 021	Columbia	796	1,186	55,440	55,122	52,467	45,088	890	890	911	71.6	68.0	58.3
...	55 023	Crawford	599	1,745	17,060	17,017	17,244	15,940	1,962	1,937	1,927	29.8	30.1	27.8
31540	55 025	Dane	1,238	560	463,826	458,333	426,526	367,085	137	140	141	385.9	356.4	305.3
13180	55 027	Dodge	907	933	88,983	87,970	85,898	76,559	619	609	590	100.9	97.5	86.8
...	55 029	Door	2,370	251	28,200	28,222	27,961	25,690	1,475	1,453	1,433	58.4	58.1	53.2
20260	55 031	Douglas	1,480	453	44,061	44,154	43,287	41,758	1,059	1,031	961	33.7	33.2	31.9
32860	55 033	Dunn	864	1,052	41,975	41,646	39,858	35,909	1,101	1,115	1,103	49.3	46.9	42.1
20740	55 035	Eau Claire	645	1,585	94,741	94,083	93,132	85,183	587	548	538	148.6	146.3	133.6
27020	55 037	Florence	497	2,191	4,941	4,949	5,088	4,590	2,844	2,846	2,866	10.1	10.5	9.4
22540	55 039	Fond du Lac	766	1,246	99,243	98,911	97,296	90,083	564	533	509	137.3	134.7	124.6
...	55 041	Forest	1,046	718	9,899	9,898	10,024	8,776	2,450	2,442	2,488	9.8	9.8	8.7
38420	55 043	Grant	1,183	595	49,362	49,473	49,597	49,266	964	924	852	43.0	43.2	42.9
33820	55 045	Green	585	1,802	35,688	35,086	33,647	30,339	1,267	1,293	1,277	61.1	57.8	51.9
...	55 047	Green Lake	380	2,654	19,147	19,158	19,105	18,651	1,864	1,845	1,756	54.0	53.9	52.6
31540	55 049	Iowa	768	1,238	23,756	23,535	22,780	20,150	1,640	1,658	1,667	31.1	29.9	26.4
...	55 051	Iron	919	897	6,502	6,608	6,861	6,153	2,732	2,703	2,737	8.6	9.1	8.1
...	55 053	Jackson	1,000	769	19,853	19,740	19,100	16,588	1,826	1,846	1,881	20.1	19.4	16.8
48020	55 055	Jefferson	583	1,815	80,025	79,277	75,767	67,783	673	661	654	143.7	136.4	121.7
...	55 057	Juneau	804	1,165	26,855	26,700	24,316	21,650	1,523	1,584	1,596	35.0	31.7	28.2
16980	55 059	Kenosha	754	1,271	162,001	160,382	149,577	128,181	359	360	363	593.8	550.1	469.8
24580	55 061	Kewaunee	1,085	676	20,832	20,746	20,187	18,878	1,768	1,781	1,742	60.8	59.0	55.1
29100	55 063	La Crosse	480	2,242	109,404	108,876	107,120	97,904	522	500	469	241.6	236.9	216.2
...	55 065	Lafayette	635	1,626	16,298	16,284	16,137	16,074	2,024	2,016	1,918	25.7	25.5	25.4
...	55 067	Langlade	888	1,003	20,631	20,690	20,740	19,505	1,784	1,751	1,701	23.6	23.8	22.3
32980	55 069	Lincoln	907	932	30,151	30,263	29,641	26,993	1,414	1,412	1,390	34.1	33.6	30.6
31820	55 071	Manitowoc	1,494	451	81,911	81,828	82,893	80,421	658	626	567	138.5	140.2	135.9
48140	55 073	Marathon	1,576	424	130,223	128,850	125,834	115,400	452	431	399	84.3	81.5	74.7
31940	55 075	Marinette	1,550	431	43,208	43,348	43,384	40,548	1,076	1,030	985	30.8	31.0	28.9
...	55 077	Marquette	464	2,302	15,227	15,202	14,555	12,321	2,089	2,119	2,193	33.4	32.1	27.0
...	55 078	Menominee	365	2,690	4,597	4,589	4,562	4,075	2,861	2,875	2,911	12.8	12.8	11.4
33340	55 079	Milwaukee	1,190	592	915,097	918,673	940,164	959,212	48	39	34	3,788.3	3,889.8	3,970.9
...	55 081	Monroe	908	927	43,028	42,544	40,896	36,633	1,082	1,085	1,085	47.8	45.5	40.7
24580	55 083	Oconto	1,149	620	37,958	37,727	35,652	30,226	1,210	1,227	1,287	38.0	35.9	30.3
...	55 085	Oneida	1,236	564	36,779	36,892	36,776	31,679	1,239	1,196	1,224	32.7	32.7	28.2
11540	55 087	Outagamie	644	1,589	172,734	170,930	161,091	140,510	341	331	338	269.8	252.7	219.4
33340	55 089	Ozaukee	1,116	651	86,321	85,983	82,317	72,894	633	630	615	372.2	356.0	314.3
...	55 091	Pepin	249	2,949	7,325	7,372	7,213	7,107	2,653	2,666	2,644	31.5	31.0	30.6
33460	55 093	Pierce	592	1,770	39,373	38,956	36,804	32,765	1,174	1,195	1,196	68.3	64.0	56.8
...	55 095	Polk	956	828	44,784	44,346	41,319	34,773	1,044	1,071	1,142	48.8	45.2	37.9
44620	55 097	Portage	823	1,124	67,484	67,279	67,182	61,405	762	730	711	83.7	83.4	76.1

See footnotes at end of table.

Table B-1. Counties — **Area and Population**—Con.

[Includes United States, states, and 3,141 counties/county equivalents defined as of February 22, 2005. For more information on these areas, see Appendix C, Geographic Information]

Metro-politan area code	FIPS state and county code[1]	County	Area, 2000 (square miles) Total	Area, 2000 Rank[2]	Population 2006 (July 1)	Population 2005 (July 1)	2000[3] (April 1) estimates base	1990[3] (April 1) estimates base	Rank 2006[2]	Rank 2000[2]	Rank 1990[4]	Persons per square mile of land area 2006[5]	2000	1990
		WISCONSIN—Con.												
...	55 099	Price	1,278	538	15,000	15,159	15,822	15,600	2,108	2,032	1,947	12.0	12.6	12.5
39540	55 101	Racine	792	1,196	196,096	195,219	188,831	175,034	301	293	274	588.7	567.4	525.4
...	55 103	Richland	589	1,779	18,341	18,380	17,924	17,521	1,897	1,907	1,819	31.3	30.7	29.9
27500	55 105	Rock	726	1,332	159,153	157,324	152,307	139,510	367	351	341	220.9	211.7	193.6
...	55 107	Rusk	931	871	15,054	15,147	15,347	15,079	2,104	2,066	1,983	16.5	16.8	16.5
33460	55 109	St. Croix	736	1,307	80,015	77,266	63,155	50,251	674	768	839	110.9	88.2	69.6
12660	55 111	Sauk	848	1,085	58,261	57,738	55,225	46,975	852	852	890	69.6	66.1	56.1
...	55 113	Sawyer	1,350	501	17,000	17,034	16,196	14,181	1,961	2,009	2,039	13.6	12.9	11.3
...	55 115	Shawano	909	923	41,401	41,223	40,664	37,157	1,117	1,095	1,068	46.4	45.7	41.6
43100	55 117	Sheboygan	1,271	543	114,756	114,406	112,656	103,877	500	477	444	223.4	219.6	202.2
...	55 119	Taylor	984	787	19,605	19,705	19,680	18,901	1,840	1,815	1,740	20.1	20.2	19.4
...	55 121	Trempealeau	742	1,294	28,078	27,822	27,010	25,263	1,484	1,483	1,453	38.2	36.9	34.4
...	55 123	Vernon	816	1,138	29,188	29,003	28,055	25,617	1,443	1,451	1,437	36.7	35.3	32.2
...	55 125	Vilas	1,018	747	22,379	22,312	21,033	17,707	1,705	1,735	1,804	25.6	24.2	20.3
48580	55 127	Walworth	577	1,857	101,007	99,755	92,013	75,000	556	555	598	181.9	166.5	135.0
...	55 129	Washburn	853	1,078	16,674	16,595	16,036	13,772	1,997	2,023	2,073	20.6	19.9	17.0
33340	55 131	Washington	436	2,407	127,578	125,928	117,496	95,328	458	460	485	296.1	273.9	221.3
33340	55 133	Waukesha	580	1,825	380,985	378,804	360,767	304,715	167	163	163	685.7	651.9	548.4
...	55 135	Waupaca	765	1,249	52,687	52,506	51,825	46,104	917	895	901	70.1	69.2	61.4
...	55 137	Waushara	637	1,618	24,915	24,764	23,066	19,385	1,587	1,641	1,711	39.8	36.9	31.0
36780	55 139	Winnebago	579	1,840	160,593	159,535	156,763	140,320	363	340	339	366.2	358.1	319.9
32270	55 141	Wood	809	1,151	74,774	75,051	75,555	73,605	700	665	611	94.3	95.3	92.8
	56 000	WYOMING	97,814	(X)	515,004	508,798	493,782	453,589	(X)	(X)	(X)	5.3	5.1	4.7
29660	56 001	Albany	4,309	115	30,360	30,837	32,014	30,797	1,406	1,346	1,251	7.1	7.5	7.2
...	56 003	Big Horn	3,159	173	11,390	11,325	11,461	10,525	2,339	2,338	2,333	3.6	3.6	3.4
23940	56 005	Campbell	4,802	92	38,934	37,420	33,698	29,370	1,184	1,291	1,320	8.1	7.1	6.1
...	56 007	Carbon	7,964	43	15,325	15,229	15,639	16,659	2,084	2,046	1,872	1.9	2.0	2.1
...	56 009	Converse	4,265	116	12,866	12,743	12,052	11,128	2,253	2,293	2,281	3.0	2.8	2.6
...	56 011	Crook	2,871	193	6,255	6,168	5,887	5,294	2,745	2,796	2,819	2.2	2.1	1.9
40180	56 013	Fremont	9,266	33	37,163	36,580	35,804	33,662	1,230	1,226	1,175	4.0	3.9	3.7
...	56 015	Goshen	2,232	276	12,119	12,112	12,538	12,373	2,289	2,264	2,191	5.5	5.6	5.6
...	56 017	Hot Springs	2,006	314	4,588	4,568	4,882	4,809	2,862	2,856	2,856	2.3	2.4	2.4
...	56 019	Johnson	4,175	123	8,014	7,785	7,075	6,145	2,592	2,678	2,738	1.9	1.7	1.5
16940	56 021	Laramie	2,688	205	85,384	85,031	81,607	73,142	636	638	614	31.8	30.4	27.2
...	56 023	Lincoln	4,089	126	16,383	15,940	14,573	12,625	2,014	2,114	2,175	4.0	3.6	3.1
16220	56 025	Natrona	5,376	73	70,401	69,655	66,533	61,226	737	735	712	13.2	12.5	11.5
...	56 027	Niobrara	2,628	215	2,253	2,296	2,407	2,499	3,030	3,028	3,022	0.9	0.9	1.0
...	56 029	Park	6,969	49	27,094	26,723	25,786	23,178	1,514	1,525	1,531	3.9	3.7	3.3
...	56 031	Platte	2,111	296	8,588	8,591	8,807	8,145	2,560	2,547	2,550	4.1	4.2	3.9
43260	56 033	Sheridan	2,527	228	27,673	27,341	26,560	23,562	1,498	1,500	1,511	11.0	10.5	9.3
...	56 035	Sublette	4,936	87	7,359	6,965	5,920	4,843	2,649	2,792	2,850	1.5	1.2	1.0
40540	56 037	Sweetwater	10,491	26	38,763	38,019	37,613	38,823	1,186	1,174	1,029	3.7	3.6	3.7
27220	56 039	Teton	4,222	119	19,288	19,021	18,251	11,173	1,852	1,885	2,279	4.8	4.6	2.8
21740	56 041	Uinta	2,088	300	20,213	19,873	19,742	18,705	1,811	1,809	1,749	9.7	9.5	9.0
...	56 043	Washakie	2,243	273	7,819	7,914	8,289	8,388	2,608	2,581	2,523	3.5	3.7	3.7
...	56 045	Weston	2,400	243	6,762	6,642	6,644	6,518	2,700	2,722	2,707	2.8	2.8	2.7

NA Not available.   X Not applicable.   Z Less than .05 persons per square mile.

[1]Federal Information Processing Standards (FIPS) codes for states and counties.
[2]Based on 3,141 counties/county equivalents. When counties share the same rank, the next lower rank is omitted.
[3]The Population Estimates base reflects modifications to the census population as documented in the Count Question Resolution program and geographic program revisions. 1990 also has adjustment for underenumeration in certain counties and cities.
[4]Based on 3,140 counties/county equivalents. When counties share the same rank, the next lower rank is omitted.
[5]Persons per square mile was calculated on the basis of land area data from the 2000 census.
[6]Yakutat City and Borough, AK, included with Skagway-Hoonah-Angoon Census Area.
[7]Yellowstone National Park County became incorporated with Gallatin and Park Counties, MT; effective November 7, 1997.
[8]Clifton Forge independent city became incorporated with Alleghany County, VA; effective July 1, 2001.
[9]South Boston independent city became incorporated with Halifax County, VA; effective June 30, 1995.

Survey, Census, or Data Collection Method: Based on population estimates and the "component of population change method"; for more information, see Appendix B, Limitations of the Data and Methodology, and also <http://www.census.gov/popest/topics/methodology/>.

Sources: Area—U.S. Census Bureau, 2000 Summary File 1 (SF1), GCT-PH1 Population, Housing Units, Area, and Density: 2000 (related Internet site <http://www.census.gov/Press-Release/www/2001/sumfile1.html>).   Population, 2006, 2005, and 2000—U.S. Census Bureau, Population Estimates, Annual County Population Estimates and Components of Change: April 1, 2000 to July 1, 2006 (related Internet site <http://www.census.gov/popest/counties/files/CO-EST2006-alldata.txt>).   Population, 1990—U.S. Census Bureau archive 1990 to 1999, "County Population Estimates for July 1,1999 and Population Change for April 1, 1990 to July 1, 1999" (related Internet site <http://www.census.gov/popest/archives/1990s/CO-99-02.html>).

[Includes United States, states, and 3,141 counties/county equivalents defined as of February 22, 2005. For more information on these areas, see Appendix C, Geographic Information]

County	Components of population change, April 1, 2000, to July 1, 2006						Population change, April 1, 1990, to April 1, 2000	
	Number					Percent change	Number	Percent change
	Total population change	Natural increase			Net international migration			
		Total	Births	Deaths				
UNITED STATES........	17,973,882	10,324,372	25,486,569	15,162,197	7,649,510	6.4	32,633,677	13.1
ALABAMA............	151,679	87,818	375,808	287,990	30,537	3.4	406,962	10.1
Autauga............	6,059	1,635	3,994	2,359	−17	13.9	9,449	27.6
Baldwin............	28,747	2,321	11,615	9,294	1,143	20.5	42,135	42.9
Barbour............	−867	375	2,249	1,874	273	−3.0	3,621	14.2
Bibb...............	1,593	301	1,653	1,352	42	8.0	3,291	19.8
Blount.............	5,402	949	4,197	3,248	607	10.6	11,786	30.0
Bullock............	−720	112	968	856	252	−6.2	584	5.3
Butler.............	−879	−132	1,699	1,831	21	−4.1	−493	−2.3
Calhoun............	660	1,257	9,446	8,189	424	0.6	−3,789	−3.3
Chambers...........	−1,407	−163	2,752	2,915	111	−3.8	−293	−0.8
Cherokee...........	875	−28	1,665	1,693	94	3.6	4,445	22.7
Chilton............	2,360	637	3,410	2,773	259	6.0	7,135	22.0
Choctaw............	−1,266	61	1,128	1,067	23	−8.0	−96	−0.6
Clarke.............	−619	548	2,311	1,763	−4	−2.2	627	2.3
Clay...............	−425	−155	947	1,102	19	−3.0	1,002	7.6
Cleburne...........	577	17	1,073	1,056	79	4.1	1,393	10.9
Coffee.............	2,412	665	3,531	2,866	153	5.5	3,375	8.4
Colbert............	−218	11	3,824	3,813	96	−0.4	3,318	6.4
Conecuh............	−686	−100	996	1,096	10	−4.9	35	0.2
Coosa..............	−837	−96	724	820	3	−7.0	818	7.4
Covington..........	−397	−306	2,792	3,098	97	−1.1	1,153	3.2
Crenshaw...........	54	−3	1,094	1,097	6	0.4	30	0.2
Cullman............	2,706	473	6,024	5,551	613	3.5	9,868	14.6
Dale...............	−737	1,944	4,741	2,797	−92	−1.5	−504	−1.0
Dallas.............	−2,448	959	4,441	3,482	58	−5.3	−1,737	−3.6
DeKalb.............	3,562	1,824	6,061	4,237	1,170	5.5	9,801	17.9
Elmore.............	9,812	2,276	5,962	3,686	12	14.9	16,666	33.9
Escambia...........	−591	334	3,128	2,794	67	−1.5	2,922	8.2
Etowah.............	−98	−284	7,891	8,175	603	−0.1	3,620	3.6
Fayette............	−490	−261	1,230	1,491	35	−2.6	533	3.0
Franklin...........	−376	259	2,632	2,373	768	−1.2	3,409	12.3
Geneva.............	101	−77	1,881	1,958	50	0.4	2,120	9.0
Greene.............	−600	146	861	715	−4	−6.0	−179	−1.8
Hale...............	−21	157	1,445	1,288	−4	−0.1	2,759	17.8
Henry..............	396	16	1,278	1,262	51	2.4	936	6.1
Houston............	6,876	2,404	7,990	5,586	355	7.7	7,453	9.2
Jackson............	−181	248	3,954	3,706	73	−0.3	6,130	12.8
Jefferson..........	−5,341	11,655	57,195	45,540	6,587	−0.8	10,521	1.6
Lamar..............	−1,356	−173	1,058	1,231	61	−8.5	189	1.2
Lauderdale.........	−75	179	5,989	5,810	337	−0.1	8,305	10.4
Lawrence...........	−491	418	2,535	2,117	66	−1.4	3,290	10.4
Lee................	10,689	3,937	8,845	4,908	1,122	9.3	27,946	32.1
Limestone..........	6,770	1,662	5,280	3,618	274	10.3	11,541	21.3
Lowndes............	−714	268	1,174	906	−2	−5.3	815	6.4
Macon..............	−1,511	−78	1,568	1,646	131	−6.3	−823	−3.3
Madison............	27,356	8,527	22,785	14,258	3,381	9.9	38,039	15.9
Marengo............	−695	324	1,890	1,566	123	−3.1	−547	−2.4
Marion.............	−1,049	−200	2,199	2,399	78	−3.4	1,384	4.6
Marshall...........	4,957	2,449	8,336	5,887	1,709	6.0	11,396	16.1
Mobile.............	4,314	12,096	36,683	24,587	3,109	1.1	21,200	5.6
Monroe.............	−982	323	1,940	1,617	3	−4.0	356	1.5
Montgomery.........	61	8,035	20,956	12,921	823	(Z)	14,425	6.9
Morgan.............	4,173	2,818	9,338	6,520	1,215	3.8	11,021	11.0
Perry..............	−677	218	1,169	951	−3	−5.7	−896	−7.0
Pickens............	−816	73	1,709	1,636	−2	−3.9	250	1.2
Pike...............	−73	600	2,530	1,930	318	−0.2	2,098	7.6
Randolph...........	293	28	1,747	1,719	38	1.3	2,499	12.6
Russell............	329	589	4,072	3,483	257	0.7	2,896	6.2
St. Clair..........	10,490	1,091	5,329	4,238	107	16.2	14,931	30.0
Shelby.............	34,889	9,298	15,463	6,165	1,184	24.3	43,930	44.2
Sumter.............	−1,192	123	1,128	1,005	−1	−8.1	−1,376	−8.5
Talladega..........	−56	821	6,427	5,606	138	−0.1	6,218	8.4
Tallapoosa.........	−784	−402	3,019	3,421	33	−1.9	2,968	7.6
Tuscaloosa.........	6,284	4,440	13,789	9,349	1,620	3.8	14,375	9.6
Walker.............	−679	−321	5,622	5,943	245	−1.0	3,043	4.5
Washington.........	−446	252	1,357	1,105	−1	−2.5	1,403	8.4
Wilcox.............	−109	406	1,309	903	1	−0.8	−548	−4.0
Winston............	−209	38	1,780	1,742	140	−0.8	2,790	12.7

See footnotes at end of table.

Table B-2. Counties — **Components of Population Change**—Con.

[Includes United States, states, and 3,141 counties/county equivalents defined as of February 22, 2005. For more information on these areas, see Appendix C, Geographic Information]

County	Components of population change, April 1, 2000, to July 1, 2006 — Number — Total population change	Natural increase Total	Births	Deaths	Net international migration	Percent change	Population change, April 1, 1990, to April 1, 2000 — Number	Percent change
ALASKA	43,122	43,828	63,170	19,342	4,654	6.9	76,888	14.0
Aleutians East.	−50	73	110	37	85	−1.9	233	9.5
Aleutians West	−226	146	222	76	105	−4.1	−4,013	−42.3
Anchorage	18,417	19,120	26,566	7,446	2,819	7.1	33,945	15.0
Bethel	1,101	2,074	2,646	572	51	6.9	2,386	17.5
Bristol Bay	−216	60	90	30	−4	−17.2	−152	−10.8
Denali	−47	82	124	42	−6	−2.5	211	12.5
Dillingham	48	375	554	179	−1	1.0	912	22.7
Fairbanks North Star	3,914	7,426	9,692	2,266	−96	4.7	5,120	6.6
Haines	−135	17	116	99	−4	−5.6	275	13.0
Juneau	26	1,634	2,449	815	298	0.1	3,959	14.8
Kenai Peninsula	2,613	1,836	3,787	1,951	118	5.3	8,889	21.8
Ketchikan Gateway	−675	619	1,147	528	93	−4.8	231	1.7
Kodiak Island	−841	1,047	1,342	295	474	−6.0	604	4.5
Lake and Peninsula	−275	90	164	74	−1	−15.1	157	9.4
Matanuska-Susitna	21,158	3,675	5,742	2,067	213	35.7	19,639	49.5
Nome	49	932	1,334	402	56	0.5	908	11.0
North Slope	−777	793	1,031	238	60	−10.5	1,399	23.4
Northwest Arctic	303	806	1,031	225	4	4.2	1,102	18.0
Prince of Wales-Outer Ketchikan	−469	214	388	174	−4	−7.6	−121	−1.9
Sitka	85	421	727	306	75	1.0	247	2.9
Skagway-Hoonah-Angoon	−336	81	186	105	−3	−9.8	[1]−968	[1]−22.0
Southeast Fairbanks	599	321	555	234	190	9.7	249	4.2
Valdez-Cordova.	−323	476	776	300	99	−3.2	275	2.8
Wade Hampton	552	1,131	1,387	256	−4	7.9	1,239	21.4
Wrangell-Petersburg.	−588	118	413	295	42	−8.8	−358	−5.1
Yakutat	−119	12	42	30	−4	−14.7	(¹)	(¹)
Yukon-Koyukuk	−666	249	549	300	−1	−10.2	−288	−4.2
ARIZONA	1,035,686	297,928	564,062	266,134	204,661	20.2	1,465,293	40.0
Apache	1,695	4,838	7,907	3,069	132	2.4	7,832	12.7
Cochise	10,002	4,109	11,028	6,919	1,606	8.5	20,131	20.6
Coconino	8,633	8,523	12,212	3,689	1,436	7.4	19,729	20.4
Gila	874	240	4,242	4,002	344	1.7	11,119	27.6
Graham	171	1,183	2,842	1,659	97	0.5	6,935	26.1
Greenlee	−809	281	617	336	46	−9.5	539	6.7
La Paz	541	−38	1,355	1,393	361	2.7	5,871	42.4
Maricopa	695,784	218,362	365,537	147,175	160,945	22.6	950,238	44.8
Mohave	38,003	−506	13,285	13,791	2,067	24.5	61,535	65.8
Navajo	13,929	6,050	10,721	4,671	441	14.3	19,796	25.5
Pima	102,616	31,782	79,589	47,807	21,694	12.2	176,789	26.5
Pinal	91,522	7,589	17,906	10,317	4,143	51.0	63,140	54.2
Santa Cruz.	4,699	3,552	4,933	1,381	1,868	12.2	8,705	29.3
Yavapai	40,497	−1,082	11,860	12,942	2,381	24.2	59,803	55.5
Yuma	27,529	13,045	20,028	6,983	7,100	17.2	53,131	49.7
ARKANSAS.	137,474	62,519	237,755	175,236	26,467	5.1	322,774	13.7
Arkansas	−861	2	1,665	1,663	7	−4.2	−908	−4.2
Ashley	−1,366	173	1,819	1,646	109	−5.6	−110	−0.5
Baxter	2,921	−1,789	2,234	4,023	21	7.6	7,200	23.1
Benton.	42,699	8,829	16,814	7,985	3,484	27.8	55,816	57.2
Boone	2,457	311	2,667	2,356	65	7.2	5,651	20.0
Bradley	−489	−1	1,053	1,054	118	−3.9	807	6.8
Calhoun	−186	−114	289	403	28	−3.2	−82	−1.4
Carroll	1,982	562	2,166	1,604	981	7.8	6,734	36.2
Chicot	−1,202	56	1,156	1,100	85	−8.5	−1,596	−10.2
Clark.	−633	121	1,739	1,618	301	−2.7	2,109	9.8
Clay	−1,114	−342	1,194	1,536	14	−6.3	−496	−2.7
Cleburne	1,439	−386	1,555	1,941	92	6.0	4,635	23.9
Cleveland.	287	147	688	541	29	3.3	790	10.2
Columbia	−1,163	52	1,940	1,888	132	−4.5	−88	−0.3
Conway	358	136	1,515	1,379	135	1.8	1,185	6.2
Craighead	6,096	2,761	7,764	5,003	790	7.4	13,192	19.1
Crawford	5,538	1,768	4,841	3,073	183	10.4	10,754	25.3
Crittenden	1,217	2,352	5,577	3,225	197	2.4	927	1.9
Cross	−470	355	1,653	1,298	18	−2.4	301	1.6
Dallas	−860	−135	622	757	18	−9.3	−404	−4.2
Desha	−1,160	301	1,377	1,076	54	−7.6	−1,457	−8.7
Drew	−336	265	1,418	1,153	29	−1.8	1,354	7.8
Faulkner.	14,671	4,096	8,256	4,160	611	17.1	26,008	43.3
Franklin	505	144	1,356	1,212	66	2.8	2,874	19.3
Fulton	114	−278	671	949	−	1.0	1,605	16.0

See footnotes at end of table.

[Includes United States, states, and 3,141 counties/county equivalents defined as of February 22, 2005. For more information on these areas, see Appendix C, Geographic Information]

County	Components of population change, April 1, 2000, to July 1, 2006						Population change, April 1, 1990, to April 1, 2000	
	Number							
	Total population change	Natural increase			Net international migration	Percent change	Number	Percent change
		Total	Births	Deaths				
ARKANSAS—Con.								
Garland	7,098	−1,257	6,694	7,951	444	8.1	14,669	20.0
Grant	1,029	76	1,162	1,086	10	6.3	2,516	18.0
Greene	2,762	820	3,421	2,601	68	7.4	5,525	17.4
Hempstead	−240	382	1,981	1,599	745	−1.0	1,966	9.1
Hot Spring	1,377	145	2,242	2,097	152	4.5	4,238	16.2
Howard	115	252	1,332	1,080	363	0.8	731	5.4
Independence	676	522	2,867	2,345	188	2.0	3,041	9.7
Izard	107	−309	867	1,176	8	0.8	1,885	16.6
Jackson	−993	−105	1,451	1,556	2	−5.4	−525	−2.8
Jefferson	−3,627	1,800	7,425	5,625	415	−4.3	−1,205	−1.4
Johnson	1,672	695	2,143	1,448	637	7.3	4,560	25.0
Lafayette	−663	−68	594	662	30	−7.7	−1,084	−11.2
Lawrence	−875	−49	1,377	1,426	60	−4.9	319	1.8
Lee	−1,201	26	896	870	20	−9.5	−473	−3.6
Lincoln	−367	94	916	822	−1	−2.5	802	5.9
Little River	−554	−118	862	980	21	−4.1	−338	−2.4
Logan	417	81	1,785	1,704	60	1.9	1,929	9.4
Lonoke	10,074	2,009	4,970	2,961	30	19.1	13,560	34.5
Madison	1,118	187	1,103	916	81	7.8	2,625	22.6
Marion	791	−227	843	1,070	–	4.9	4,139	34.5
Miller	2,612	950	3,409	2,459	179	6.5	1,976	5.1
Mississippi	−4,462	1,548	5,082	3,534	172	−8.6	−5,546	−9.6
Monroe	−1,159	−45	761	806	24	−11.3	−1,079	−9.5
Montgomery	27	−147	564	711	76	0.3	1,404	17.9
Nevada	−484	27	822	795	75	−4.9	−146	−1.4
Newton	−197	−25	544	569	1	−2.3	942	12.3
Ouachita	−2,080	−213	2,202	2,415	61	−7.2	−1,784	−5.8
Perry	202	60	717	657	−3	2.0	2,240	28.1
Phillips	−3,114	675	2,700	2,025	37	−11.8	−2,385	−8.3
Pike	−444	−228	718	946	90	−3.9	1,217	12.1
Poinsett	−528	175	2,193	2,018	96	−2.1	950	3.9
Polk	134	133	1,675	1,542	93	0.7	2,882	16.6
Pope	3,202	1,492	4,659	3,167	273	5.9	8,586	18.7
Prairie	−612	−126	626	752	3	−6.4	21	0.2
Pulaski	5,844	15,499	36,125	20,626	2,843	1.6	11,906	3.4
Randolph	253	10	1,319	1,309	106	1.4	1,637	9.9
St. Francis	−1,794	786	2,805	2,019	–	−6.1	832	2.9
Saline	10,494	1,580	6,201	4,621	219	12.6	19,347	30.1
Scott	420	84	890	806	206	3.8	790	7.7
Searcy	−186	−130	513	643	−4	−2.3	420	5.4
Sebastian	5,252	4,369	11,518	7,149	2,771	4.6	15,480	15.5
Sevier	540	703	1,709	1,006	778	3.4	2,120	15.5
Sharp	844	−397	1,166	1,563	5	4.9	3,010	21.3
Stone	482	−154	745	899	7	4.2	1,724	17.6
Union	−1,459	159	3,699	3,540	216	−3.2	−1,090	−2.3
Van Buren	526	−261	1,124	1,385	14	3.2	2,184	15.6
Washington	28,746	10,240	17,961	7,721	5,851	18.2	44,366	39.1
White	5,395	1,177	5,712	4,535	444	8.0	12,489	22.8
Woodruff	−835	−215	606	821	1	−9.6	−780	−8.2
Yell	695	451	2,030	1,579	933	3.3	3,380	19.0
CALIFORNIA	2,585,896	1,909,368	3,375,297	1,465,929	1,724,790	7.6	4,060,226	13.6
Alameda	13,685	74,798	134,827	60,029	95,737	0.9	139,394	10.7
Alpine	−28	13	64	51	−1	−2.3	95	8.5
Amador	3,841	−675	1,647	2,322	108	10.9	5,061	16.8
Butte	12,710	677	14,534	13,857	3,104	6.3	21,051	11.6
Calaveras	7,168	−500	2,033	2,533	105	17.7	8,556	26.7
Colusa	2,468	1,230	2,119	889	1,318	13.1	2,529	15.5
Contra Costa	75,503	40,214	83,243	43,029	36,615	8.0	145,085	18.1
Del Norte	1,386	148	1,813	1,665	418	5.0	4,047	17.3
El Dorado	21,767	3,683	11,182	7,499	2,063	13.9	30,304	24.1
Fresno	92,349	59,410	95,414	36,004	33,001	11.6	131,928	19.8
Glenn	1,608	1,057	2,549	1,492	839	6.1	1,655	6.7
Humboldt	1,812	1,366	9,213	7,847	986	1.4	7,400	6.2
Imperial	17,940	11,870	17,405	5,535	7,514	12.6	33,058	30.2
Inyo	35	−145	1,203	1,348	230	0.2	−336	−1.8
Kern	118,462	47,514	79,794	32,280	20,075	17.9	116,674	21.4
Kings	16,692	10,276	14,992	4,716	3,466	12.9	27,992	27.6
Lake	7,624	−859	4,117	4,976	691	13.1	7,678	15.2
Lassen	887	488	1,803	1,315	57	2.6	6,230	22.6
Los Angeles	428,751	584,235	958,675	374,440	624,081	4.5	656,278	7.4
Madera	23,236	8,421	14,172	5,751	5,858	18.9	35,019	39.8

See footnotes at end of table.

[Includes United States, states, and 3,141 counties/county equivalents defined as of February 22, 2005. For more information on these areas, see Appendix C, Geographic Information]

County	Components of population change, April 1, 2000, to July 1, 2006						Population change, April 1, 1990, to April 1, 2000	
	Number							
	Total population change	Natural increase			Net international migration	Percent change	Number	Percent change
		Total	Births	Deaths				
CALIFORNIA—Con.								
Marin	1,453	6,329	17,622	11,293	9,444	0.6	17,193	7.5
Mariposa	1,271	−107	904	1,011	34	7.4	2,828	19.8
Mendocino	1,844	1,573	6,869	5,296	2,283	2.1	5,920	7.4
Merced	35,104	17,094	26,090	8,996	8,941	16.7	32,151	18.0
Modoc	148	−144	496	640	86	1.6	−229	−2.4
Mono	−99	684	980	296	349	−0.8	2,897	29.1
Monterey	8,442	30,557	45,586	15,029	27,392	2.1	46,104	13.0
Napa	9,214	1,978	9,991	8,013	5,603	7.4	13,543	12.2
Nevada	6,731	−737	5,106	5,843	622	7.3	13,523	17.2
Orange	155,759	179,350	284,786	105,436	173,571	5.5	435,621	18.1
Placer	77,843	8,451	22,112	13,661	3,408	31.3	75,603	43.8
Plumas	439	−303	1,060	1,363	71	2.1	1,085	5.5
Riverside	481,416	90,780	173,801	83,021	48,767	31.2	374,974	32.0
Sacramento	151,225	64,958	124,936	59,978	46,453	12.4	156,710	14.7
San Benito	2,608	4,017	5,656	1,639	2,230	4.9	16,537	45.1
San Bernardino	289,898	118,413	192,182	73,769	46,516	17.0	291,054	20.5
San Diego	127,621	158,614	282,134	123,520	99,468	4.5	315,817	12.6
San Francisco	−32,692	14,726	53,399	38,673	55,105	−4.2	52,774	7.3
San Joaquin	109,572	37,337	65,602	28,265	21,200	19.4	82,970	17.3
San Luis Obispo	10,324	3,411	16,059	12,648	3,946	4.2	29,519	13.6
San Mateo	−1,664	34,492	63,882	29,390	47,851	−0.2	57,540	8.9
Santa Barbara	988	18,955	37,170	18,215	17,559	0.2	29,739	8.0
Santa Clara	48,696	114,691	168,859	54,168	156,989	2.9	185,008	12.4
Santa Cruz	−5,895	11,162	21,455	10,293	9,797	−2.3	25,866	11.3
Shasta	16,695	931	12,477	11,546	806	10.2	16,220	11.0
Sierra	−100	−104	134	238	18	−2.8	237	7.1
Siskiyou	790	−315	2,819	3,134	347	1.8	770	1.8
Solano	17,167	19,889	36,270	16,381	10,190	4.4	55,044	16.2
Sonoma	8,277	12,739	36,452	23,713	16,004	1.8	70,392	18.1
Stanislaus	65,141	27,090	49,464	22,374	14,476	14.6	76,475	20.6
Sutter	12,480	3,716	8,111	4,395	3,640	15.8	14,521	22.5
Tehama	5,647	543	4,391	3,848	609	10.1	6,414	12.9
Trinity	1,291	−241	670	911	24	9.9	−41	−0.3
Tulare	51,888	31,228	48,017	16,789	16,111	14.1	56,089	18.0
Tuolumne	2,351	−977	2,855	3,832	151	4.3	6,048	12.5
Ventura	46,525	43,768	74,042	30,274	26,796	6.2	84,179	12.6
Yolo	19,425	7,769	14,893	7,124	10,361	11.5	27,448	19.4
Yuba	10,177	3,830	7,166	3,336	1,307	16.9	1,985	3.4
COLORADO	²451,362	244,279	425,394	181,115	133,930	10.5	²1,007,542	²30.6
Adams	66,375	29,624	43,483	13,859	17,285	19.1	82,925	31.3
Alamosa	259	893	1,563	670	206	1.7	1,349	9.9
Arapahoe	48,301	30,501	48,901	18,400	18,159	9.9	97,324	24.9
Archuleta	2,488	369	727	358	8	25.1	4,553	85.2
Baca	−500	−137	235	372	–	−11.1	−39	−0.9
Bent	−447	12	394	382	26	−7.5	950	18.8
Boulder	12,517	13,598	22,258	8,660	10,588	4.6	44,448	19.7
Broomfield	5,918	2,537	3,825	1,288	828	15.1	(NA)	(NA)
Chaffee	676	26	930	904	52	4.2	3,558	28.1
Cheyenne	−325	20	141	121	18	−14.6	−166	−6.9
Clear Creek	−192	335	642	307	5	−2.1	1,703	22.4
Conejos	6	255	709	454	31	0.1	947	12.7
Costilla	−285	−22	234	256	9	−7.8	473	14.8
Crowley	−132	−28	286	314	−4	−2.4	1,572	39.8
Custer	423	29	178	149	−4	12.1	1,577	81.9
Delta	2,567	129	2,081	1,952	453	9.2	6,854	32.7
Denver	13,281	38,965	66,704	27,739	43,748	2.4	86,144	18.4
Dolores	67	4	129	125	−4	3.6	340	22.6
Douglas	87,855	20,950	24,365	3,415	2,725	50.0	115,375	191.0
Eagle	7,413	4,349	4,901	552	4,005	17.8	19,744	90.0
Elbert	3,309	772	1,368	596	46	16.7	10,226	106.0
El Paso	59,955	32,319	52,414	20,095	4,763	11.6	119,915	30.2
Fremont	1,865	−470	2,598	3,068	143	4.0	13,872	43.0
Garfield	8,114	3,395	5,169	1,774	1,980	18.5	13,820	46.1
Gilpin	285	212	358	146	10	6.0	1,687	55.0
Grand	964	503	902	399	107	7.7	4,476	56.2
Gunnison	375	644	1,079	435	139	2.7	3,683	35.9
Hinsdale	29	32	50	18	−4	3.7	323	69.2
Huerfano	−54	−174	454	628	32	−0.7	1,853	30.8
Jackson	−171	3	74	71	−1	−10.8	−28	−1.7

See footnotes at end of table.

Table B-2. Counties — **Components of Population Change**—Con.

[Includes United States, states, and 3,141 counties/county equivalents defined as of February 22, 2005. For more information on these areas, see Appendix C, Geographic Information]

County	Components of population change, April 1, 2000, to July 1, 2006						Population change, April 1, 1990, to April 1, 2000	
	Number							
	Total population change	Natural increase			Net international migration	Percent change	Number	Percent change
		Total	Births	Deaths				
COLORADO—Con.								
Jefferson	1,664	19,314	40,325	21,011	8,210	0.3	86,900	19.8
Kiowa	−209	−21	99	120	−4	−12.9	−66	−3.9
Kit Carson	−421	138	608	470	182	−5.3	871	12.2
Lake	2	508	749	241	643	(Z)	1,805	30.0
La Plata	3,995	1,441	3,013	1,572	220	9.1	11,657	36.1
Larimer	24,759	11,371	20,974	9,603	4,237	9.8	65,358	35.1
Las Animas	357	−68	1,085	1,153	126	2.3	1,442	10.5
Lincoln	−629	20	340	320	27	−10.3	1,558	34.4
Logan	206	355	1,594	1,239	284	1.0	3,007	17.1
Mesa	17,254	2,627	10,158	7,531	853	14.8	23,790	25.5
Mineral	98	−6	30	36	−4	11.8	273	48.9
Moffat	496	600	1,193	593	251	3.8	1,827	16.1
Montezuma	1,387	372	1,955	1,583	61	5.8	5,158	27.6
Montrose	5,127	858	2,992	2,134	375	15.3	9,009	36.9
Morgan	938	1,401	2,937	1,536	1,246	3.5	5,232	23.8
Otero	−859	485	1,939	1,454	234	−4.2	126	0.6
Ouray	565	69	208	139	16	15.1	1,447	63.1
Park	2,634	605	1,012	407	50	18.1	7,349	102.4
Phillips	121	57	391	334	152	2.7	291	6.9
Pitkin	−74	729	983	254	563	−0.5	2,211	17.5
Prowers	−707	665	1,472	807	570	−4.9	1,136	8.5
Pueblo	11,440	3,123	12,447	9,324	1,177	8.1	18,421	15.0
Rio Blanco	194	147	460	313	62	3.2	−65	−1.1
Rio Grande	−407	333	1,121	788	119	−3.3	1,643	15.3
Routt	1,890	1,013	1,450	437	353	9.6	5,602	39.8
Saguache	1,089	290	546	256	162	18.4	1,298	28.1
San Juan	20	19	37	18	−4	3.6	−187	−25.1
San Miguel	549	384	472	88	223	8.3	2,941	80.5
Sedgwick	−280	−65	188	253	25	−10.2	57	2.1
Summit	1,851	1,911	2,194	283	1,704	7.9	10,667	82.8
Teller	1,688	759	1,359	600	12	8.2	8,087	64.9
Washington	−296	−28	282	310	19	−6.0	114	2.4
Weld	55,996	14,999	22,736	7,737	6,158	31.0	49,040	37.2
Yuma	−12	229	893	664	279	−0.1	887	9.9
CONNECTICUT	99,207	70,748	256,735	185,987	92,635	2.9	118,486	3.6
Fairfield	17,873	29,633	72,788	43,155	43,811	2.0	54,922	6.6
Hartford	19,744	14,143	63,711	49,568	21,111	2.3	5,400	0.6
Litchfield	7,907	1,397	11,760	10,363	1,278	4.3	8,120	4.7
Middlesex	8,703	2,618	10,959	8,341	1,736	5.6	11,875	8.3
New Haven	21,236	13,080	61,852	48,772	19,566	2.6	19,789	2.5
New London	4,187	5,082	19,092	14,010	1,957	1.6	4,149	1.6
Tolland	11,776	3,086	8,653	5,567	1,968	8.6	7,665	6.0
Windham	7,781	1,709	7,920	6,211	1,208	7.1	6,566	6.4
DELAWARE	69,876	25,673	69,846	44,173	13,394	8.9	117,432	17.6
Kent	20,901	5,297	12,325	7,028	619	16.5	15,707	14.2
New Castle	25,322	18,325	44,205	25,880	10,512	5.1	58,319	13.2
Sussex	23,653	2,051	13,316	11,265	2,263	15.1	43,406	38.3
DISTRICT OF COLUMBIA	9,471	12,830	48,355	35,525	24,795	1.7	−34,841	−5.7
District of Columbia	9,471	12,830	48,355	35,525	24,795	1.7	−34,841	−5.7
FLORIDA	2,107,064	282,347	1,338,458	1,056,111	642,188	13.2	3,044,753	23.5
Alachua	9,165	6,159	15,998	9,839	5,606	4.2	36,359	20.0
Baker	2,944	1,086	2,263	1,177	31	13.2	3,773	20.4
Bay	15,287	4,149	13,220	9,071	289	10.3	21,224	16.7
Bradford	2,296	334	1,974	1,640	68	8.8	3,573	15.9
Brevard	58,129	−2,557	31,764	34,321	4,497	12.2	77,252	19.4
Broward	164,618	43,623	142,787	99,164	100,986	10.1	367,487	29.3
Calhoun	393	54	930	876	19	3.0	2,006	18.2
Charlotte	12,811	−7,393	6,627	14,020	1,194	9.0	30,652	27.6
Citrus	20,058	−7,439	5,618	13,057	453	17.0	24,572	26.3
Clay	38,085	5,228	12,702	7,474	754	27.0	34,828	32.9
Collier	63,272	8,202	23,219	15,017	16,876	25.2	99,278	65.3
Columbia	10,497	934	5,020	4,086	251	18.6	13,897	32.6
DeSoto	3,106	856	2,772	1,916	3,161	9.6	8,344	35.0
Dixie	1,137	−79	1,022	1,101	−3	8.2	3,242	30.6
Duval	59,098	33,689	78,430	44,741	9,603	7.6	105,895	15.7

See footnotes at end of table.

70

Table B-2. Counties — **Components of Population Change**—Con.

[Includes United States, states, and 3,141 counties/county equivalents defined as of February 22, 2005. For more information on these areas, see Appendix C, Geographic Information]

County	Components of population change, April 1, 2000, to July 1, 2006						Population change, April 1, 1990, to April 1, 2000	
	Number							
	Total population change	Natural increase			Net international migration	Percent change	Number	Percent change
		Total	Births	Deaths				
FLORIDA—Con.								
Escambia	1,016	6,739	24,970	18,231	744	0.3	31,965	12.2
Flagler	33,249	−1,089	3,360	4,449	492	66.7	21,134	73.6
Franklin	435	−5	708	713	18	4.4	862	9.6
Gadsden	1,571	1,523	4,369	2,846	488	3.5	3,971	9.7
Gilchrist	2,428	246	1,180	934	33	16.8	4,770	49.3
Glades	654	−142	524	666	154	6.2	2,985	39.3
Gulf	−516	−196	768	964	14	−3.5	3,055	26.6
Hamilton	888	276	1,107	831	132	6.7	2,397	21.9
Hardee	1,683	1,709	3,003	1,294	1,672	6.2	7,439	38.2
Hendry	4,249	2,400	4,204	1,804	3,234	11.7	10,437	40.5
Hernando	34,607	−5,530	8,234	13,764	581	26.5	29,687	29.4
Highlands	10,621	−2,558	5,789	8,347	2,365	12.2	18,934	27.7
Hillsborough	158,790	42,118	97,434	55,316	31,899	15.9	164,894	19.8
Holmes	721	76	1,392	1,316	14	3.9	2,786	17.7
Indian River	17,153	−3,777	7,419	11,196	2,025	15.2	22,739	25.2
Jackson	2,533	250	3,438	3,188	127	5.4	5,380	13.0
Jefferson	1,775	32	989	957	−3	13.8	1,606	14.2
Lafayette	1,023	127	588	461	156	14.6	1,444	25.9
Lake	79,908	−1,534	17,512	19,046	2,400	38.0	58,423	38.4
Lee	130,456	1,608	35,603	33,995	12,412	29.6	105,775	31.6
Leon	6,173	9,721	19,274	9,553	3,461	2.6	46,959	24.4
Levy	4,626	−213	2,641	2,854	176	13.4	8,538	32.9
Liberty	761	184	554	370	63	10.8	1,452	26.1
Madison	477	101	1,424	1,323	104	2.5	2,164	13.1
Manatee	49,296	573	21,376	20,803	5,976	18.7	52,295	24.7
Marion	57,267	−3,887	19,322	23,209	2,331	22.1	64,081	32.9
Martin	12,662	−2,626	7,852	10,478	2,334	10.0	25,831	25.6
Miami-Dade	148,429	87,668	204,079	116,411	257,492	6.6	316,585	16.3
Monroe	−4,852	195	4,642	4,447	2,612	−6.1	1,565	2.0
Nassau	9,044	906	4,448	3,542	233	15.7	13,722	31.2
Okaloosa	9,794	7,334	16,165	8,831	−442	5.7	26,720	18.6
Okeechobee	4,496	1,053	3,561	2,508	1,332	12.5	6,283	21.2
Orange	147,154	52,695	93,434	40,739	41,232	16.4	218,855	32.3
Osceola	71,552	10,315	19,272	8,957	9,945	41.5	64,765	60.1
Palm Beach	142,822	6,431	91,093	84,662	50,948	12.6	267,688	31.0
Pasco	105,403	−7,472	26,450	33,922	4,464	30.6	63,637	22.6
Pinellas	2,918	−19,170	58,064	77,234	20,235	0.3	69,836	8.2
Polk	77,682	10,630	44,513	33,883	8,464	16.1	78,542	19.4
Putnam	3,660	139	5,870	5,731	540	5.2	5,353	8.2
St. Johns	46,076	1,617	9,161	7,544	849	37.4	39,319	46.9
St. Lucie	60,029	1,064	16,060	14,996	3,964	31.2	42,524	28.3
Santa Rosa	26,818	3,859	10,082	6,223	112	22.8	35,782	43.7
Sarasota	43,574	−11,655	18,154	29,809	7,110	13.4	48,185	17.3
Seminole	41,678	12,422	29,326	16,904	8,552	11.4	77,676	27.0
Sumter	15,423	−1,554	3,039	4,593	490	28.9	21,768	68.9
Suwannee	4,647	152	3,093	2,941	714	13.3	8,067	30.1
Taylor	586	91	1,480	1,389	14	3.0	2,145	12.5
Union	1,400	−57	916	973	4	10.4	3,190	31.1
Volusia	53,235	−8,246	29,568	37,814	5,657	12.0	72,603	19.6
Wakulla	6,679	699	1,876	1,177	42	29.2	8,661	61.0
Walton	11,668	348	3,256	2,908	323	28.7	12,843	46.3
Washington	1,747	−89	1,476	1,565	115	8.3	4,054	24.0
GEORGIA	1,177,125	438,939	849,414	410,475	228,415	14.4	1,708,667	26.4
Appling	445	511	1,669	1,158	230	2.6	1,671	10.6
Atkinson	438	452	916	464	323	5.8	1,396	22.5
Bacon	379	235	980	745	73	3.8	537	5.6
Baker	24	8	224	216	19	0.6	459	12.7
Baldwin	573	961	3,418	2,457	148	1.3	5,172	13.1
Banks	2,023	633	1,407	774	133	14.0	4,114	39.9
Barrow	17,558	3,209	5,661	2,452	383	38.1	16,423	55.3
Bartow	15,247	4,884	9,008	4,124	835	20.1	20,104	36.0
Ben Hill	151	441	1,809	1,368	206	0.9	1,239	7.6
Berrien	521	442	1,532	1,090	45	3.2	2,082	14.7
Bibb	1,016	5,108	15,248	10,140	991	0.7	3,750	2.5
Bleckley	687	167	927	760	61	5.9	1,236	11.9
Brantley	1,106	178	1,026	848	3	7.6	3,552	32.1
Brooks	14	85	1,373	1,288	80	0.1	1,052	6.8
Bryan	6,231	1,387	2,473	1,086	7	26.6	7,979	51.7
Bulloch	7,224	2,099	4,733	2,634	664	12.9	12,858	29.8
Burke	743	998	2,516	1,518	40	3.3	1,664	8.1
Butts	4,012	625	1,813	1,188	24	20.5	4,223	27.6
Calhoun	−226	113	601	488	−1	−3.6	1,307	26.1
Camden	1,454	3,271	4,638	1,367	−609	3.3	13,497	44.7

See footnotes at end of table.

[Includes United States, states, and 3,141 counties/county equivalents defined as of February 22, 2005. For more information on these areas, see Appendix C, Geographic Information]

County	Components of population change, April 1, 2000, to July 1, 2006						Population change, April 1, 1990, to April 1, 2000	
	Number							
	Total population change	Natural increase			Net international migration	Percent change	Number	Percent change
		Total	Births	Deaths				
GEORGIA—Con.								
Candler	1,097	328	1,127	799	310	11.5	1,833	23.7
Carroll	20,057	4,297	9,294	4,997	1,383	23.0	15,846	22.2
Catoosa	8,764	1,666	4,771	3,105	189	16.5	10,788	25.4
Charlton	600	183	732	549	2	5.8	1,786	21.0
Chatham	9,064	8,506	22,746	14,240	2,495	3.9	15,573	7.2
Chattahoochee	−841	1,305	1,527	222	−743	−5.7	−2,052	−12.1
Chattooga	972	281	1,982	1,701	152	3.8	3,234	14.5
Cherokee	53,424	12,220	17,715	5,495	3,422	37.6	51,699	57.3
Clarke	11,298	4,702	8,563	3,861	4,636	11.1	13,895	15.9
Clay	−177	−14	276	290	−4	−5.3	−7	−0.2
Clayton	34,723	19,923	28,497	8,574	9,711	14.7	55,081	30.4
Clinch	19	249	734	485	47	0.3	718	11.7
Cobb	71,574	45,002	65,712	20,710	29,169	11.8	160,006	35.7
Coffee	2,830	1,844	3,991	2,147	879	7.6	7,820	26.4
Colquitt	2,783	1,673	4,436	2,763	1,418	6.6	5,393	14.7
Columbia	17,600	4,516	8,135	3,619	603	19.7	23,256	35.2
Cook	562	358	1,489	1,131	177	3.6	2,315	17.2
Coweta	26,076	5,590	9,838	4,248	1,694	29.2	35,362	65.7
Crawford	328	180	928	748	−4	2.6	3,504	39.0
Crisp	55	575	2,093	1,518	238	0.3	1,985	9.9
Dade	1,079	234	1,143	909	88	7.1	1,971	15.0
Dawson	4,644	775	1,594	819	67	29.0	6,570	69.7
Decatur	425	656	2,492	1,836	312	1.5	2,723	10.7
DeKalb	57,545	43,097	68,969	25,872	47,819	8.6	119,883	21.9
Dodge	529	180	1,547	1,367	117	2.8	1,564	8.9
Dooly	223	350	1,101	751	67	1.9	1,624	16.4
Dougherty	−1,292	3,956	9,417	5,461	419	−1.3	−256	−0.3
Douglas	27,313	5,590	9,777	4,187	1,112	29.6	21,124	29.7
Early	−289	323	1,212	889	35	−2.3	500	4.2
Echols	524	315	468	153	324	14.0	1,416	60.7
Effingham	11,419	2,049	3,835	1,786	70	30.4	11,848	46.1
Elbert	257	239	1,682	1,443	123	1.3	1,562	8.2
Emanuel	763	582	2,219	1,637	620	3.5	1,291	6.3
Evans	930	519	1,203	684	272	8.9	1,771	20.3
Fannin	2,521	−120	1,515	1,635	42	12.7	3,806	23.8
Fayette	15,408	2,164	5,872	3,708	1,356	16.9	28,848	46.2
Floyd	4,757	2,532	8,682	6,150	1,620	5.3	9,314	11.5
Forsyth	52,561	10,142	14,064	3,922	2,641	53.4	54,324	123.2
Franklin	1,404	180	1,676	1,496	43	6.9	3,637	21.8
Fulton	144,188	44,339	81,038	36,699	35,880	17.7	167,045	25.7
Gilmer	4,719	898	2,320	1,422	668	20.1	10,088	75.5
Glascock	164	−71	200	271	−2	6.4	199	8.4
Glynn	6,062	1,743	6,229	4,486	831	9.0	5,072	8.1
Gordon	7,315	2,498	5,025	2,527	1,370	16.6	9,037	25.8
Grady	1,423	943	2,518	1,575	759	6.0	3,380	16.7
Greene	1,128	157	1,246	1,089	130	7.8	2,613	22.2
Gwinnett	168,656	59,333	76,137	16,804	36,946	28.7	235,538	66.7
Habersham	5,214	1,429	3,511	2,082	956	14.5	8,276	30.0
Hall	33,941	11,990	18,582	6,592	11,269	24.4	43,881	46.0
Hancock	−397	53	724	671	—	−3.9	1,166	13.1
Haralson	2,926	621	2,375	1,754	73	11.4	3,724	17.0
Harris	5,090	542	1,878	1,336	66	21.5	5,907	33.2
Hart	1,278	20	1,756	1,736	82	5.6	3,286	16.7
Heard	460	272	940	668	9	4.2	2,384	27.6
Henry	58,689	9,730	14,786	5,056	621	49.2	60,603	103.2
Houston	16,765	5,753	11,109	5,356	203	15.1	21,557	24.2
Irwin	472	87	781	694	105	4.8	1,282	14.8
Jackson	14,189	2,012	4,625	2,613	399	34.1	11,584	38.6
Jasper	2,198	410	1,109	699	66	19.2	2,973	35.2
Jeff Davis	593	423	1,371	948	214	4.7	653	5.4
Jefferson	−495	405	1,648	1,243	22	−2.9	−145	−0.8
Jenkins	150	158	806	648	86	1.7	328	4.0
Johnson	1,066	46	697	651	9	12.5	231	2.8
Jones	3,334	758	2,063	1,305	67	14.1	2,900	14.0
Lamar	767	158	1,261	1,103	55	4.8	2,874	22.0
Lanier	482	239	686	447	29	6.7	1,710	30.9
Laurens	2,442	1,242	4,263	3,021	182	5.4	4,886	12.2
Lee	7,738	1,172	2,052	880	135	31.3	8,507	52.4
Liberty	961	7,158	8,940	1,782	−952	1.6	8,865	16.8
Lincoln	−91	−55	537	592	−4	−1.1	906	12.2

See footnotes at end of table.

Table B-2. Counties — **Components of Population Change**—Con.

[Includes United States, states, and 3,141 counties/county equivalents defined as of February 22, 2005. For more information on these areas, see Appendix C, Geographic Information]

County	Total population change	Natural increase Total	Births	Deaths	Net international migration	Percent change	Number	Percent change
GEORGIA—Con.								
Long	1,148	681	1,049	368	200	11.1	4,102	66.1
Lowndes	5,719	4,854	9,318	4,464	201	6.2	16,144	21.2
Lumpkin	4,476	865	1,957	1,092	248	21.3	6,413	44.0
McDuffie	685	515	2,052	1,537	36	3.2	1,113	5.5
McIntosh	401	196	908	712	6	3.7	2,213	25.6
Macon	−263	356	1,242	886	171	−1.9	966	7.4
Madison	2,107	706	2,190	1,484	168	8.2	4,680	22.2
Marion	132	211	674	463	158	1.8	1,554	27.8
Meriwether	353	334	1,977	1,643	5	1.6	117	0.5
Miller	−144	23	541	518	2	−2.3	103	1.6
Mitchell	−82	473	2,037	1,564	161	−0.3	3,659	18.0
Monroe	2,669	433	1,725	1,292	112	12.3	4,661	27.2
Montgomery	797	233	726	493	130	9.6	891	12.1
Morgan	2,451	461	1,353	892	73	15.9	2,574	20.0
Murray	4,895	2,151	3,921	1,770	426	13.4	10,356	39.6
Muscogee	2,369	7,512	18,883	11,371	964	1.3	7,011	3.9
Newton	29,450	4,738	8,225	3,487	475	47.5	20,193	48.3
Oconee	4,633	1,123	2,147	1,024	233	17.7	8,607	48.9
Oglethorpe	1,362	368	1,098	730	18	10.8	2,872	29.4
Paulding	39,922	7,800	11,086	3,286	339	48.9	39,997	96.1
Peach	1,117	734	2,072	1,338	445	4.7	2,479	11.7
Pickens	6,657	715	2,120	1,405	119	29.0	8,551	59.3
Pierce	1,827	474	1,545	1,071	133	11.7	2,297	17.2
Pike	3,113	382	1,128	746	27	22.7	3,464	33.9
Polk	2,964	1,327	4,205	2,878	937	7.8	4,312	12.8
Pulaski	299	64	733	669	140	3.1	1,480	18.3
Putnam	1,118	397	1,569	1,172	316	5.9	4,675	33.1
Quitman	−112	−27	209	236	6	−4.3	388	17.6
Rabun	1,304	107	1,178	1,071	325	8.7	3,402	29.2
Randolph	−434	−68	634	702	32	−5.6	−232	−2.9
Richmond	−5,377	7,795	19,792	11,997	90	−2.7	10,056	5.3
Rockdale	10,221	3,393	6,570	3,177	2,594	14.6	16,020	29.6
Schley	432	52	315	263	42	11.5	176	4.9
Screven	−184	120	1,180	1,060	47	−1.2	1,532	11.1
Seminole	−201	32	727	695	1	−2.1	359	4.0
Spalding	3,768	2,218	5,890	3,672	681	6.5	3,960	7.3
Stephens	−292	64	2,050	1,986	46	−1.1	1,999	8.5
Stewart	−505	−66	368	434	2	−9.6	−395	−7.0
Sumter	−710	939	3,138	2,199	221	−2.1	2,968	9.8
Talbot	107	3	506	503	2	1.6	−26	−0.4
Taliaferro	−200	−37	129	166	−4	−9.6	162	8.5
Tattnall	1,187	712	2,091	1,379	545	5.3	4,583	25.9
Taylor	−23	32	714	682	22	−0.3	1,173	15.3
Telfair	1,474	79	1,077	998	60	12.5	794	7.2
Terrell	−313	202	1,041	839	16	−2.9	317	3.0
Thomas	2,401	915	3,816	2,901	157	5.6	3,791	9.7
Tift	3,295	1,689	3,922	2,233	1,126	8.6	3,392	9.7
Toombs	1,556	949	2,691	1,742	676	6.0	1,995	8.3
Towns	1,206	−352	508	860	77	12.9	2,565	38.0
Treutlen	−2	64	548	484	64	(Z)	860	14.3
Troup	4,466	1,810	5,864	4,054	530	7.6	3,247	5.8
Turner	−182	247	907	660	69	−1.9	801	9.2
Twiggs	−406	96	781	685	−3	−3.8	784	8.0
Union	3,363	−314	1,106	1,420	6	19.5	5,296	44.2
Upson	79	−301	2,157	2,458	259	0.3	1,297	4.9
Walker	3,553	590	4,790	4,200	227	5.8	2,743	4.7
Walton	18,701	3,255	6,617	3,362	337	30.8	22,101	57.3
Ware	254	364	3,052	2,688	363	0.7	23	0.1
Warren	−387	13	526	513	−4	−6.1	258	4.2
Washington	−453	242	1,662	1,420	22	−2.1	2,064	10.8
Wayne	2,326	763	2,381	1,618	116	8.8	4,213	18.8
Webster	−131	3	164	161	32	−5.5	120	5.3
Wheeler	729	75	452	377	53	11.8	1,276	26.0
White	4,794	356	1,749	1,393	85	24.0	6,938	53.3
Whitfield	9,441	6,900	11,278	4,378	6,201	11.3	11,096	15.3
Wilcox	135	−51	631	682	14	1.6	1,569	22.4
Wilkes	−219	−115	780	895	58	−2.0	90	0.8
Wilkinson	−225	197	897	700	86	−2.2	−8	−0.1
Worth	−62	451	1,806	1,355	43	−0.3	2,256	11.4

See footnotes at end of table.

County and City Data Book: 2007

73

U.S. Census Bureau

[Includes United States, states, and 3,141 counties/county equivalents defined as of February 22, 2005. For more information on these areas, see Appendix C, Geographic Information]

County	Components of population change, April 1, 2000, to July 1, 2006 — Number						Population change, April 1, 1990, to April 1, 2000	
	Total population change	Natural increase — Total	Births	Deaths	Net international migration	Percent change	Number	Percent change
HAWAII..............	73,961	56,251	110,926	54,675	31,092	6.1	103,308	9.3
Hawaii................	22,514	5,446	13,101	7,655	3,119	15.1	28,360	23.6
Honolulu	33,707	42,472	81,260	38,788	23,254	3.8	39,925	4.8
Kalawao..............	−27	−13	—	13	−4	−18.4	17	13.1
Kauai................	4,541	2,162	4,955	2,793	905	7.8	7,286	14.2
Maui.................	13,226	6,184	11,610	5,426	3,818	10.3	27,720	27.6
IDAHO	172,509	72,477	135,942	63,465	17,266	13.3	287,222	28.5
Ada.................	58,131	19,501	31,766	12,265	4,998	19.3	95,129	46.2
Adams...............	9	−21	161	182	6	0.3	222	6.8
Bannock.............	2,878	5,201	8,878	3,677	481	3.8	9,539	14.4
Bear Lake	−244	124	525	401	2	−3.8	327	5.4
Benewah.............	176	84	706	622	2	1.9	1,234	15.5
Bingham	2,316	3,017	4,874	1,857	471	5.5	4,152	11.0
Blaine...............	2,510	1,177	1,692	515	683	13.2	5,439	40.1
Boise................	971	156	393	237	61	14.6	3,161	90.1
Bonner..............	4,440	312	2,424	2,112	90	12.1	10,213	38.4
Bonneville	12,108	6,196	10,055	3,859	678	14.7	10,315	14.3
Boundary	960	211	811	600	5	9.7	1,539	18.5
Butte................	−118	56	240	184	22	−4.1	−19	−0.7
Camas...............	97	28	71	43	−4	9.8	264	36.3
Canyon..............	41,861	12,096	18,615	6,519	2,642	31.8	41,365	45.9
Caribou.............	−308	234	619	385	14	−4.2	341	4.9
Cassia...............	−51	1,374	2,527	1,153	347	−0.2	1,884	9.6
Clark................	−102	61	102	41	72	−10.0	260	34.1
Clearwater	−606	−153	411	564	−3	−6.8	425	5.0
Custer...............	−162	—	199	199	6	−3.7	209	5.1
Elmore..............	−1,016	2,334	3,300	966	178	−3.5	7,925	37.4
Franklin	1,165	843	1,393	550	154	10.3	2,097	22.7
Fremont.............	550	781	1,386	605	260	4.7	882	8.1
Gem	1,377	129	1,214	1,085	158	9.1	3,337	28.2
Gooding.............	246	664	1,510	846	386	1.7	2,525	21.7
Idaho................	251	−23	986	1,009	33	1.6	1,743	12.7
Jefferson	3,195	1,691	2,509	818	296	16.7	2,612	15.8
Jerome	1,788	1,303	2,147	844	525	9.7	3,204	21.2
Kootenai............	22,822	3,978	9,781	5,803	330	21.0	38,890	55.7
Latah...............	94	1,189	2,550	1,361	751	0.3	4,318	14.1
Lemhi	124	−97	439	536	33	1.6	907	13.1
Lewis................	9	7	276	269	−4	0.2	231	6.6
Lincoln..............	478	202	444	242	103	11.8	736	22.2
Madison.............	3,926	3,496	4,222	726	256	14.3	3,793	16.0
Minidoka	−1,133	989	2,093	1,104	472	−5.6	813	4.2
Nez Perce	914	239	2,860	2,621	187	2.4	3,656	10.8
Oneida	51	63	343	280	11	1.2	633	18.1
Owyhee.............	460	610	1,145	535	346	4.3	2,252	26.8
Payette	2,017	816	1,966	1,150	129	9.8	4,144	25.2
Power	376	417	752	335	189	5.0	452	6.4
Shoshone............	−591	−279	799	1,078	33	−4.3	−160	−1.1
Teton................	1,839	693	871	178	286	30.7	2,560	74.4
Twin Falls...........	7,291	2,604	6,603	3,999	1,326	11.3	10,704	20.0
Valley	1,185	58	468	410	26	15.5	1,542	25.2
Washington	225	116	816	700	229	2.3	1,427	16.7
ILLINOIS............	412,323	481,799	1,138,398	656,599	402,257	3.3	989,045	8.7
Adams..............	−1,056	−218	5,060	5,278	129	−1.5	2,187	3.3
Alexander...........	−955	13	819	806	−4	−10.0	−1,036	−9.7
Bond................	424	131	1,266	1,135	37	2.4	2,640	17.6
Boone...............	10,833	2,020	4,001	1,981	927	25.9	10,978	35.6
Brown...............	−249	−8	387	395	40	−3.6	1,114	19.1
Bureau..............	−246	50	2,629	2,579	107	−0.7	−185	−0.5
Calhoun.............	93	−100	322	422	−4	1.8	−238	−4.5
Carroll..............	−639	−206	979	1,185	51	−3.8	−131	−0.8
Cass................	71	185	1,192	1,007	748	0.5	258	1.9
Champaign...........	6,013	6,839	14,290	7,451	7,105	3.3	6,644	3.8
Christian	−309	−72	2,535	2,607	117	−0.9	954	2.8
Clark................	−21	−112	1,179	1,291	8	−0.1	1,087	6.8
Clay.................	−532	−50	1,110	1,160	30	−3.7	100	0.7
Clinton..............	1,102	608	2,579	1,971	132	3.1	1,587	4.7
Coles................	−2,247	515	3,607	3,092	254	−4.2	1,552	3.0
Cook................	−87,971	236,443	512,042	275,599	274,026	−1.6	271,582	5.3
Crawford............	−627	−225	1,241	1,466	66	−3.1	988	5.1
Cumberland	−253	−37	772	809	9	−2.2	583	5.5
DeKalb	11,170	3,453	7,304	3,851	2,120	12.6	11,037	14.2
De Witt	−30	33	1,280	1,247	37	−0.2	282	1.7

See footnotes at end of table.

[Includes United States, states, and 3,141 counties/county equivalents defined as of February 22, 2005. For more information on these areas, see Appendix C, Geographic Information]

County	Components of population change, April 1, 2000, to July 1, 2006						Population change, April 1, 1990, to April 1, 2000	
	Number					Percent change	Number	Percent change
	Total population change	Natural increase			Net international migration			
		Total	Births	Deaths				
ILLINOIS—Con.								
Douglas	−131	622	1,865	1,243	176	−0.7	458	2.4
DuPage	28,321	45,641	80,758	35,117	36,593	3.1	122,660	15.7
Edgar	−521	−237	1,341	1,578	−2	−2.6	109	0.6
Edwards.	−354	−54	474	528	−4	−5.1	−469	−6.3
Effingham.	165	822	2,828	2,006	84	0.5	2,560	8.1
Fayette	−28	−9	1,560	1,569	10	−0.1	909	4.4
Ford	−30	−244	1,063	1,307	35	−0.2	−34	−0.2
Franklin	833	−508	3,052	3,560	23	2.1	−1,290	−3.2
Fulton	−872	−362	2,540	2,902	34	−2.3	170	0.4
Gallatin	−286	−117	406	523	6	−4.4	−464	−6.7
Greene	−506	−5	1,047	1,052	2	−3.4	−556	−3.6
Grundy	8,293	1,316	3,378	2,062	229	22.1	5,198	16.1
Hamilton	−286	−112	549	661	−4	−3.3	122	1.4
Hancock	−1,029	−20	1,345	1,365	13	−5.1	−1,253	−5.9
Hardin	−215	−178	265	443	59	−4.5	−389	−7.5
Henderson	−394	−127	414	541	−4	−4.8	117	1.4
Henry	−679	106	3,493	3,387	145	−1.3	−141	−0.3
Iroquois	−736	−229	2,199	2,428	214	−2.3	547	1.8
Jackson	−1,833	1,275	4,288	3,013	2,052	−3.1	−1,456	−2.4
Jasper	−237	75	718	643	−4	−2.3	−492	−4.6
Jefferson	478	351	3,014	2,663	78	1.2	3,025	8.2
Jersey	960	41	1,493	1,452	70	4.4	1,129	5.5
Jo Daviess	305	−19	1,398	1,417	150	1.4	468	2.1
Johnson	480	88	852	764	47	3.7	1,533	13.5
Kane	89,613	36,087	52,079	15,992	19,880	22.2	86,651	27.3
Kankakee.	5,257	2,600	9,497	6,897	967	5.1	7,578	7.9
Kendall	33,638	5,001	7,128	2,127	480	61.7	15,107	38.3
Knox	−2,932	−536	3,863	4,399	212	−5.3	−555	−1.0
Lake	68,490	41,189	65,261	24,072	24,102	10.6	128,168	24.8
LaSalle	1,516	814	8,777	7,963	636	1.4	4,636	4.3
Lawrence	435	−390	1,035	1,425	14	2.8	−520	−3.3
Lee	−361	11	2,392	2,381	136	−1.0	1,670	4.9
Livingston.	−1,018	562	3,242	2,680	154	−2.6	375	1.0
Logan	−890	11	2,081	2,070	112	−2.9	394	1.3
McDonough	−1,095	−60	1,800	1,860	522	−3.3	−2,326	−6.6
McHenry	52,280	16,428	26,437	10,009	5,146	20.1	76,852	41.9
McLean	10,767	6,925	13,291	6,366	2,095	7.2	21,255	16.5
Macon.	−5,397	1,312	8,749	7,437	337	−4.7	−2,500	−2.1
Macoupin.	−178	−38	3,597	3,635	27	−0.4	1,340	2.8
Madison	6,352	4,412	21,224	16,812	627	2.5	9,713	3.9
Marion.	−1,603	−78	3,124	3,202	22	−3.8	130	0.3
Marshall.	−147	−262	819	1,081	8	−1.1	304	2.4
Mason	−534	−13	1,180	1,193	−1	−3.3	−232	−1.4
Massac	−26	−81	1,175	1,256	−1	−0.2	409	2.8
Menard	102	12	827	815	25	0.8	1,322	11.8
Mercer.	−171	67	1,112	1,045	19	−1.0	−333	−1.9
Monroe	4,257	678	2,219	1,541	36	15.4	5,197	23.2
Montgomery	−277	−170	2,049	2,219	11	−0.9	−84	−0.3
Morgan	−953	124	2,650	2,526	123	−2.6	222	0.6
Moultrie	96	−79	1,149	1,228	17	0.7	357	2.6
Ogle	3,794	727	3,649	2,922	735	7.4	5,075	11.0
Peoria	−944	5,288	16,459	11,171	1,766	−0.5	612	0.3
Perry	−229	−82	1,587	1,669	42	−1.0	1,682	7.9
Piatt	319	208	1,119	911	24	1.9	821	5.3
Pike	−539	−242	1,138	1,380	44	−3.1	−198	−1.1
Pope.	−229	−98	191	289	4	−5.2	40	0.9
Pulaski.	−622	8	599	591	−1	−8.5	−175	−2.3
Putnam	−81	32	371	339	12	−1.3	356	6.2
Randolph	−865	−112	2,413	2,525	33	−2.6	−690	−2.0
Richland.	−425	−14	1,238	1,252	5	−2.6	−396	−2.4
Rock Island	−1,843	3,082	12,237	9,155	1,895	−1.2	665	0.4
St. Clair	4,851	6,993	23,177	16,184	386	1.9	−6,784	−2.6
Saline	−671	−597	1,939	2,536	61	−2.5	182	0.7
Sangamon	4,570	4,671	16,074	11,403	691	2.4	10,568	5.9
Schuyler.	−205	−106	451	557	9	−2.9	−309	−4.1
Scott	−157	52	421	369	−3	−2.8	−110	−1.9
Shelby	−721	−38	1,530	1,568	5	−3.1	632	2.8
Stark.	−99	−93	436	529	—	−1.6	−202	−3.1
Stephenson	−1,591	211	3,612	3,401	416	−3.2	927	1.9
Tazewell.	2,074	2,033	10,008	7,975	293	1.6	4,793	3.9

See footnotes at end of table.

[Includes United States, states, and 3,141 counties/county equivalents defined as of February 22, 2005. For more information on these areas, see Appendix C, Geographic Information]

County	Components of population change, April 1, 2000, to July 1, 2006						Population change, April 1, 1990, to April 1, 2000	
	Number							
	Total population change	Natural increase			Net international migration	Percent change	Number	Percent change
		Total	Births	Deaths				
ILLINOIS—Con.								
Union	−32	−181	1,356	1,537	101	−0.2	674	3.8
Vermilion	−1,983	783	6,893	6,110	344	−2.4	−4,333	−4.9
Wabash	−480	161	936	775	5	−3.7	−174	−1.3
Warren	−1,255	−27	1,243	1,270	55	−6.7	−446	−2.3
Washington	−221	40	1,074	1,034	15	−1.5	183	1.2
Wayne	−549	−89	1,213	1,302	8	−3.2	−90	−0.5
White	−293	−329	1,073	1,402	8	−1.9	−1,151	−7.0
Whiteside	−771	792	4,728	3,936	293	−1.3	465	0.8
Will	165,950	37,123	57,392	20,269	7,709	33.0	144,954	40.6
Williamson	2,430	−12	4,605	4,617	96	4.0	3,577	6.2
Winnebago	17,215	9,227	24,863	15,636	5,517	6.2	25,507	10.1
Woodford	2,435	484	2,682	2,198	46	6.9	2,816	8.6
INDIANA	233,003	196,728	541,506	344,778	68,935	3.8	536,361	9.7
Adams	94	1,918	3,818	1,900	60	0.3	2,530	8.1
Allen	15,467	16,892	33,041	16,149	5,235	4.7	31,013	10.3
Bartholomew	3,009	2,215	6,376	4,161	1,524	4.2	7,778	12.2
Benton	−371	176	764	588	4	−3.9	−20	−0.2
Blackford	−445	25	988	963	−4	−3.2	−19	−0.1
Boone	7,419	1,525	4,113	2,588	123	16.1	7,960	20.9
Brown	114	27	851	824	43	0.8	877	6.2
Carroll	361	451	1,480	1,029	138	1.8	1,356	7.2
Cass	−1,028	945	3,520	2,575	617	−2.5	2,517	6.6
Clark	7,103	2,191	8,217	6,026	610	7.4	8,692	9.9
Clay	454	256	2,164	1,908	68	1.7	1,862	7.5
Clinton	351	980	3,198	2,218	1,117	1.0	2,892	9.3
Crawford	394	131	871	740	−3	3.7	829	8.4
Daviess	400	1,161	3,027	1,866	308	1.3	2,287	8.3
Dearborn	3,533	1,580	3,813	2,233	72	7.7	7,295	18.8
Decatur	393	870	2,316	1,446	213	1.6	910	3.8
DeKalb	1,617	1,462	3,571	2,109	112	4.0	4,961	14.0
Delaware	−3,890	1,100	8,345	7,245	936	−3.3	−890	−0.7
Dubois	1,538	1,135	3,362	2,227	363	3.9	3,058	8.4
Elkhart	15,314	11,139	20,020	8,881	6,031	8.4	26,593	17.0
Fayette	−940	112	1,979	1,867	10	−3.7	−427	−1.6
Floyd	1,747	1,298	5,426	4,128	109	2.5	6,419	10.0
Fountain	−469	163	1,369	1,206	52	−2.6	147	0.8
Franklin	1,222	758	1,789	1,031	9	5.5	2,571	13.1
Fulton	111	164	1,573	1,409	117	0.5	1,671	8.9
Gibson	896	371	2,529	2,158	92	2.8	587	1.8
Grant	−3,578	144	5,196	5,052	168	−4.9	−766	−1.0
Greene	203	233	2,543	2,310	27	0.6	2,747	9.0
Hamilton	68,239	15,605	21,895	6,290	1,997	37.3	73,804	67.7
Hancock	9,655	2,004	4,922	2,918	37	17.4	9,868	21.7
Harrison	2,667	918	2,742	1,824	104	7.8	4,435	14.8
Hendricks	27,111	5,027	9,484	4,457	491	26.0	28,376	37.5
Henry	−1,561	−21	3,472	3,493	22	−3.2	369	0.8
Howard	−464	1,819	7,305	5,486	389	−0.5	4,137	5.1
Huntington	−51	604	3,044	2,440	63	−0.1	2,650	7.5
Jackson	1,069	1,309	3,786	2,477	623	2.6	3,605	9.6
Jasper	2,253	924	2,483	1,559	85	7.5	5,220	21.0
Jay	−201	541	1,873	1,332	158	−0.9	294	1.4
Jefferson	963	485	2,310	1,825	93	3.0	1,908	6.4
Jennings	919	1,019	2,482	1,463	40	3.3	3,893	16.5
Johnson	18,107	4,323	10,688	6,365	608	15.7	27,100	30.8
Knox	−1,015	−37	2,804	2,841	235	−2.6	−628	−1.6
Kosciusko	2,484	3,030	6,852	3,822	812	3.4	8,763	13.4
LaGrange	2,382	3,102	4,439	1,337	287	6.8	5,432	18.4
Lake	9,638	13,612	43,354	29,742	4,159	2.0	8,970	1.9
LaPorte	373	1,922	8,476	6,554	633	0.3	3,040	2.8
Lawrence	491	438	3,497	3,059	88	1.1	3,086	7.2
Madison	−2,783	940	10,182	9,242	589	−2.1	2,689	2.1
Marion	5,050	44,571	91,927	47,356	16,507	0.6	63,295	7.9
Marshall	2,167	1,713	4,216	2,503	905	4.8	2,946	7.0
Martin	−29	160	790	630	−2	−0.3	–	–
Miami	−530	815	2,827	2,012	25	−1.5	−815	−2.2
Monroe	2,050	3,167	7,831	4,664	3,782	1.7	11,585	10.6
Montgomery	544	730	3,020	2,290	369	1.4	3,193	9.3
Morgan	3,601	2,027	5,495	3,468	112	5.4	10,769	19.3
Newton	−273	14	946	932	71	−1.9	1,015	7.5
Noble	1,643	2,061	4,490	2,429	1,063	3.6	8,398	22.2
Ohio	203	56	407	351	−3	3.6	308	5.8
Orange	353	230	1,564	1,334	69	1.8	897	4.9
Owen	955	246	1,592	1,346	14	4.4	4,505	26.1

See footnotes at end of table.

Table B-2. Counties — **Components of Population Change**—Con.

[Includes United States, states, and 3,141 counties/county equivalents defined as of February 22, 2005. For more information on these areas, see Appendix C, Geographic Information]

County	Components of population change, April 1, 2000, to July 1, 2006						Population change, April 1, 1990, to April 1, 2000	
	Number					Percent change	Number	Percent change
	Total population change	Natural increase			Net international migration			
		Total	Births	Deaths				
INDIANA—Con.								
Parke	−219	95	1,087	992	−2	−1.3	1,830	11.9
Perry	−56	174	1,408	1,234	34	−0.3	−208	−1.1
Pike	19	63	960	897	9	0.1	327	2.6
Porter	13,307	4,125	11,454	7,329	1,017	9.1	17,866	13.9
Posey	−296	254	1,704	1,450	55	−1.1	1,093	4.2
Pulaski	106	89	1,018	929	13	0.8	975	7.6
Putnam	959	678	2,533	1,855	146	2.7	5,704	18.8
Randolph	−820	172	2,018	1,846	93	−3.0	253	0.9
Ripley	1,225	925	2,468	1,543	28	4.6	1,907	7.7
Rush	−577	250	1,427	1,177	20	−3.2	132	0.7
St. Joseph	1,119	8,737	23,868	15,131	4,281	0.4	18,507	7.5
Scott	738	390	1,895	1,505	–	3.2	1,975	9.4
Shelby	673	1,216	3,629	2,413	467	1.5	3,134	7.8
Spencer	205	330	1,489	1,159	66	1.0	901	4.6
Starke	−487	281	1,885	1,604	152	−2.1	809	3.6
Steuben	469	952	2,653	1,701	163	1.4	5,768	21.0
Sullivan	−209	−68	1,514	1,582	3	−1.0	2,758	14.5
Switzerland	656	137	693	556	−4	7.2	1,327	17.1
Tippecanoe	7,214	6,339	12,520	6,181	7,037	4.8	18,357	14.1
Tipton	−200	231	1,283	1,052	10	−1.2	458	2.8
Union	−58	113	545	432	4	−0.8	373	5.3
Vanderburgh	1,434	2,933	14,600	11,667	987	0.8	6,864	4.2
Vermillion	−143	−90	1,254	1,344	34	−0.9	15	0.1
Vigo	−2,839	910	8,162	7,252	832	−2.7	−259	−0.2
Wabash	−1,401	101	2,458	2,357	−2	−4.0	−109	−0.3
Warren	282	−29	570	599	−4	3.3	243	3.0
Warrick	4,706	1,380	4,199	2,819	100	9.0	7,464	16.6
Washington	839	640	2,250	1,610	30	3.1	3,506	14.8
Wayne	−2,251	703	5,609	4,906	323	−3.2	−854	−1.2
Wells	601	638	2,178	1,540	17	2.2	1,650	6.4
White	−871	496	2,132	1,636	368	−3.4	2,002	8.6
Whitley	1,849	787	2,589	1,802	82	6.0	3,056	11.1
IOWA	55,703	65,553	239,348	173,795	36,142	1.9	149,551	5.4
Adair	−529	−323	428	751	6	−6.4	−166	−2.0
Adams	−290	−101	249	350	−4	−6.5	−384	−7.9
Allamakee	121	159	1,160	1,001	597	0.8	820	5.9
Appanoose	−299	−217	951	1,168	30	−2.2	−22	−0.2
Audubon	−552	−332	328	660	−4	−8.1	−504	−6.9
Benton	1,654	501	1,977	1,476	21	6.5	2,879	12.8
Black Hawk	−1,907	2,992	10,234	7,242	2,728	−1.5	4,215	3.4
Boone	360	163	1,857	1,694	60	1.4	1,038	4.1
Bremer	512	146	1,514	1,368	39	2.2	512	2.2
Buchanan	−48	627	1,851	1,224	2	−0.2	249	1.2
Buena Vista	−318	450	1,609	1,159	984	−1.6	444	2.2
Butler	−232	−215	1,029	1,244	−4	−1.5	−426	−2.7
Calhoun	−678	−213	659	872	2	−6.1	−393	−3.4
Carroll	−458	211	1,609	1,398	40	−2.1	−2	(Z)
Cass	−560	−225	946	1,171	11	−3.8	−444	−2.9
Cedar	139	149	1,267	1,118	7	0.8	743	4.3
Cerro Gordo	−2,063	−147	3,103	3,250	142	−4.4	−286	−0.6
Cherokee	−943	−248	740	988	−3	−7.2	−1,061	−7.5
Chickasaw	−683	−57	881	938	49	−5.2	−200	−1.5
Clarke	23	180	773	593	45	0.3	846	10.2
Clay	−571	174	1,302	1,128	89	−3.3	−213	−1.2
Clayton	−427	−117	1,293	1,410	50	−2.3	−376	−1.7
Clinton	−367	389	3,681	3,292	224	−0.7	−891	−1.7
Crawford	6	396	1,452	1,056	541	(Z)	167	1.0
Dallas	13,752	1,833	3,807	1,974	517	33.7	11,018	37.0
Davis	61	184	777	593	2	0.7	229	2.8
Decatur	−33	46	594	548	135	−0.4	351	4.2
Delaware	−556	301	1,264	963	−4	−3.0	369	2.0
Des Moines	−1,466	492	3,212	2,720	167	−3.5	−263	−0.6
Dickinson	500	−19	1,069	1,088	12	3.0	1,515	10.2
Dubuque	3,228	2,338	7,538	5,200	807	3.6	2,753	3.2
Emmet	−548	43	833	790	54	−5.0	−542	−4.7
Fayette	−1,012	−221	1,351	1,572	69	−4.6	165	0.8
Floyd	−459	−63	1,186	1,249	84	−2.7	−158	−0.9
Franklin	4	−4	792	796	285	(Z)	−660	−5.8
Fremont	−273	−83	508	591	29	−3.4	−216	−2.6
Greene	−557	−189	644	833	25	−5.4	321	3.2
Grundy	−49	−130	751	881	2	−0.4	340	2.8
Guthrie	−9	−88	799	887	19	−0.1	418	3.8
Hamilton	−351	58	1,180	1,122	94	−2.1	367	2.3

See footnotes at end of table.

[Includes United States, states, and 3,141 counties/county equivalents defined as of February 22, 2005. For more information on these areas, see Appendix C, Geographic Information]

County	Total population change	Natural increase Total	Births	Deaths	Net international migration	Percent change	Number	Percent change
IOWA—Con.								
Hancock	−420	−29	746	775	64	−3.5	−538	−4.3
Hardin	−1,021	−253	1,318	1,571	90	−5.4	−282	−1.5
Harrison	79	−177	1,000	1,177	32	0.5	936	6.4
Henry	69	179	1,498	1,319	53	0.3	1,110	5.8
Howard	−255	−61	717	778	−	−2.6	123	1.3
Humboldt	−406	17	768	751	75	−3.9	−375	−3.5
Ida	−657	−142	506	648	−4	−8.4	−528	−6.3
Iowa	469	154	1,189	1,035	9	3.0	1,041	7.1
Jackson	−6	75	1,349	1,274	7	(Z)	346	1.7
Jasper	196	624	2,782	2,158	179	0.5	2,418	6.9
Jefferson	−236	14	950	936	236	−1.5	−129	−0.8
Johnson	7,032	5,948	9,258	3,310	3,627	6.3	14,887	15.5
Jones	284	123	1,346	1,223	17	1.4	777	4.0
Keokuk	−319	−4	852	856	6	−2.8	−224	−1.9
Kossuth	−1,152	−53	1,061	1,114	12	−6.7	−1,428	−7.7
Lee	−1,714	−259	2,487	2,746	109	−4.5	−635	−1.6
Linn	10,152	8,084	17,386	9,302	1,903	5.3	22,934	13.6
Louisa	−325	342	1,053	711	187	−2.7	591	5.1
Lucas	121	−67	627	694	−4	1.3	352	3.9
Lyon	−127	211	946	735	22	−1.1	−189	−1.6
Madison	1,528	371	1,206	835	−1	10.9	1,536	12.3
Mahaska	−37	406	1,714	1,308	141	−0.2	803	3.7
Marion	933	362	2,508	2,146	62	2.9	2,053	6.8
Marshall	244	679	3,699	3,020	902	0.6	1,035	2.7
Mills	1,048	274	1,101	827	29	7.2	1,345	10.2
Mitchell	−18	−99	779	878	−4	−0.2	−54	−0.5
Monona	−677	−459	629	1,088	−2	−6.8	−14	−0.1
Monroe	−291	−103	547	650	−4	−3.6	−98	−1.2
Montgomery	−406	−174	815	989	51	−3.4	−305	−2.5
Muscatine	1,161	1,388	3,874	2,486	510	2.8	1,815	4.5
O'Brien	−693	−67	1,062	1,129	58	−4.6	−342	−2.2
Osceola	−374	−25	496	521	23	−5.3	−264	−3.6
Page	−713	−259	1,044	1,303	33	−4.2	106	0.6
Palo Alto	−598	−157	684	841	34	−5.9	−522	−4.9
Plymouth	57	423	1,939	1,516	110	0.2	1,461	6.2
Pocahontas	−868	−264	442	706	27	−10.0	−863	−9.1
Polk	34,306	21,745	39,408	17,663	9,490	9.2	47,442	14.5
Pottawattamie	2,415	2,267	7,660	5,393	354	2.8	5,175	6.3
Poweshiek	175	−161	1,203	1,364	164	0.9	−201	−1.1
Ringgold	−180	−120	389	509	−4	−3.3	49	0.9
Sac	−847	−227	719	946	37	−7.3	−795	−6.5
Scott	3,932	6,145	14,329	8,184	1,515	2.5	7,716	5.1
Shelby	−585	−122	796	918	7	−4.5	−156	−1.2
Sioux	936	1,395	2,928	1,533	381	3.0	1,686	5.6
Story	164	2,818	5,738	2,920	3,691	0.2	5,729	7.7
Tama	−213	224	1,465	1,241	58	−1.2	684	3.9
Taylor	−418	−156	461	617	27	−6.0	−156	−2.2
Union	−216	−105	882	987	26	−1.8	−441	−3.5
Van Buren	27	−80	553	633	−4	0.3	133	1.7
Wapello	−41	318	2,903	2,585	218	−0.1	355	1.0
Warren	3,255	1,067	3,159	2,092	100	8.0	4,638	12.9
Washington	859	463	1,895	1,432	86	4.2	1,058	5.4
Wayne	−188	−114	513	627	2	−2.8	−337	−4.8
Webster	−1,275	184	3,066	2,882	217	−3.2	−107	−0.3
Winnebago	−507	−82	710	792	166	4.3	−399	−3.3
Winneshiek	−47	50	1,189	1,139	261	−0.2	463	2.2
Woodbury	−905	4,426	10,236	5,810	2,612	−0.9	5,601	5.7
Worth	−211	−194	473	667	11	−2.7	−82	−1.0
Wright	−915	−50	1,097	1,147	189	−6.4	65	0.5
KANSAS	75,251	93,899	246,484	152,585	44,847	2.8	211,236	8.5
Allen	−708	−74	1,053	1,127	38	−4.9	−253	−1.7
Anderson	−59	−13	624	637	8	−0.7	307	3.9
Atchison	−29	239	1,420	1,181	24	−0.2	−158	−0.9
Barber	−333	−188	266	454	2	−6.3	−567	−9.7
Barton	−694	145	2,124	1,979	500	−2.5	−1,177	−4.0
Bourbon	−429	74	1,328	1,254	22	−2.8	413	2.8
Brown	−488	−31	840	871	53	−4.6	−404	−3.6
Butler	3,663	1,295	4,695	3,400	263	6.2	8,904	17.6
Chase	40	112	319	207	17	1.3	9	0.3
Chautauqua	−406	−176	254	430	4	−9.3	−48	−1.1

See footnotes at end of table.

[Includes United States, states, and 3,141 counties/county equivalents defined as of February 22, 2005. For more information on these areas, see Appendix C, Geographic Information]

County	Components of population change, April 1, 2000, to July 1, 2006 — Number						Population change, April 1, 1990, to April 1, 2000	
	Total population change	Natural increase — Total	Births	Deaths	Net international migration	Percent change	Number	Percent change
KANSAS—Con.								
Cherokee	−1,152	20	1,632	1,612	28	−5.1	1,229	5.7
Cheyenne	−254	−77	168	245	40	−8.0	−78	−2.4
Clark	−184	−29	154	183	15	−7.7	−28	−1.2
Clay	−197	−82	567	649	−6	−2.2	−336	−3.7
Cloud	−674	−330	658	988	53	−6.6	−755	−6.8
Coffey	−164	2	663	661	16	−1.8	461	5.5
Comanche	−83	−78	124	202	−4	−4.2	−346	−15.0
Cowley	−1,360	195	2,858	2,663	390	−3.7	−624	−1.7
Crawford	−186	489	3,273	2,784	663	−0.5	2,663	7.5
Decatur	−352	−159	153	312	26	−10.1	−549	−13.7
Dickinson	−22	−122	1,323	1,445	59	−0.1	386	2.0
Doniphan	−384	−44	490	534	2	−4.7	115	1.4
Douglas	12,158	4,263	7,660	3,397	2,638	12.2	18,167	22.2
Edwards	−311	−30	253	283	69	−9.0	−338	−8.9
Elk	−184	−125	224	349	−	−5.6	−66	−2.0
Ellis	−581	676	2,205	1,529	239	−2.1	1,503	5.8
Ellsworth	−193	−266	281	547	−	−3.0	−61	−0.9
Finney	−1,426	3,820	5,080	1,260	2,806	−3.5	7,453	22.5
Ford	1,324	2,397	4,072	1,675	2,830	4.1	4,996	18.2
Franklin	1,729	809	2,282	1,473	124	7.0	2,790	12.7
Geary	−3,769	2,257	3,460	1,203	−8	−13.5	−2,510	−8.2
Gove	−347	−47	180	227	−4	−11.3	−163	−5.0
Graham	−269	−101	140	241	−4	−9.1	−597	−16.9
Grant	−357	534	870	336	274	−4.5	750	10.5
Gray	−52	274	613	339	241	−0.9	508	9.4
Greeley	−203	−12	120	132	39	−13.2	−240	−13.5
Greenwood	−606	−248	520	768	20	−7.9	−174	−2.2
Hamilton	−76	87	258	171	141	−2.8	282	11.8
Harper	−584	−270	391	661	2	−8.9	−588	−8.3
Harvey	774	369	2,594	2,225	417	2.4	1,841	5.9
Haskell	−136	279	484	205	159	−3.2	421	10.8
Hodgeman	−13	−47	126	173	−1	−0.6	−93	−4.3
Jackson	843	335	1,082	747	8	6.7	1,132	9.8
Jefferson	422	301	1,290	989	29	2.3	2,521	15.9
Jewell	−467	−211	131	342	−	−12.3	−460	−10.8
Johnson	65,255	28,417	46,182	17,765	8,765	14.5	96,455	27.2
Kearny	−62	236	450	214	136	−1.4	504	12.5
Kingman	−698	−205	525	730	−	−8.0	381	4.6
Kiowa	−309	12	235	223	11	−9.4	−382	−10.4
Labette	−628	−245	1,667	1,912	19	−2.8	−862	−3.6
Lane	−358	−80	96	176	−4	−16.6	−220	−9.3
Leavenworth	4,937	2,507	5,794	3,287	62	7.2	4,320	6.7
Lincoln	−182	−98	234	332	−4	−5.1	−75	−2.1
Linn	392	91	717	626	−2	4.1	1,316	15.9
Logan	−371	−41	189	230	−4	−12.2	−35	−1.1
Lyon	−566	1,482	3,303	1,821	1,251	−1.6	1,203	3.5
McPherson	−174	104	2,231	2,127	29	−0.6	2,286	8.4
Marion	−601	−280	842	1,122	9	−4.5	473	3.7
Marshall	−616	−177	732	909	24	−5.6	−740	−6.3
Meade	−70	93	383	290	110	−1.5	384	9.0
Miami	2,549	938	2,506	1,568	45	9.0	4,885	20.8
Mitchell	−633	−198	392	590	2	−9.1	−271	−3.8
Montgomery	−1,565	34	2,995	2,961	147	−4.3	−2,559	−6.6
Morris	−58	−101	373	474	28	−1.0	−94	−1.5
Morton	−358	115	336	221	119	−10.2	16	0.5
Nemaha	−343	−138	807	945	2	−3.2	271	2.6
Neosho	−699	88	1,331	1,243	20	−4.1	−38	−0.2
Ness	−508	−92	192	284	1	−14.7	−579	−14.4
Norton	−369	−134	336	470	2	−6.2	6	0.1
Osage	244	−15	1,141	1,156	20	1.5	1,466	9.6
Osborne	−474	−255	208	463	−4	−10.6	−415	−8.5
Ottawa	5	−33	446	479	5	0.1	529	9.4
Pawnee	−718	−161	392	553	9	−9.9	−322	−4.3
Phillips	−557	−142	383	525	−1	−9.3	−589	−8.9
Pottawatomie	1,011	693	1,748	1,055	3	5.6	2,081	12.9
Pratt	−211	−73	699	772	37	−2.2	−55	−0.6
Rawlins	−323	−153	119	272	−4	−10.9	−438	−12.9
Reno	−1,084	1,166	5,246	4,080	334	−1.7	2,401	3.8
Republic	−802	−310	292	602	−4	−13.7	−647	−10.0
Rice	−466	−18	814	832	136	−4.3	151	1.4

See footnotes at end of table.

Table B-2. Counties — **Components of Population Change**—Con.

[Includes United States, states, and 3,141 counties/county equivalents defined as of February 22, 2005. For more information on these areas, see Appendix C, Geographic Information]

County	Components of population change, April 1, 2000, to July 1, 2006 — Number						Population change, April 1, 1990, to April 1, 2000	
	Total population change	Natural increase — Total	Births	Deaths	Net international migration	Percent change	Number	Percent change
KANSAS—Con.								
Riley	−329	3,541	5,531	1,990	1,096	−0.5	−4,283	−6.4
Rooks	−395	−100	358	458	−4	−6.9	−354	−5.9
Rush	−234	−110	226	336	−4	−6.6	−291	−7.6
Russell	−630	−209	451	660	−4	−8.5	−465	−5.9
Saline	573	1,705	4,779	3,074	636	1.1	4,296	8.7
Scott	−477	106	403	297	21	−9.3	−169	−3.2
Sedgwick	18,026	24,435	47,887	23,452	8,884	4.0	49,207	12.2
Seward	894	2,410	3,302	892	2,306	4.0	3,767	20.1
Shawnee	2,824	4,967	15,456	10,489	1,400	1.7	8,893	5.5
Sheridan	−213	−22	187	209	−4	−7.6	−230	−7.6
Sherman	−779	16	476	460	15	−11.5	−166	−2.4
Smith	−512	−235	197	432	−2	−11.3	−542	−10.7
Stafford	−354	−124	283	407	38	−7.4	−576	−10.7
Stanton	−174	120	258	138	80	−7.2	73	3.1
Stevens	−176	239	540	301	203	−3.2	415	8.2
Sumner	−1,505	214	1,920	1,706	19	−5.8	105	0.4
Thomas	−712	101	621	520	−1	−8.7	−78	−0.9
Trego	−326	−102	195	297	−1	−9.8	−375	−10.2
Wabaunsee	10	110	507	397	3	0.1	282	4.3
Wallace	−192	5	113	108	6	−11.0	−72	−4.0
Washington	−539	−233	381	614	15	−8.3	−590	−8.3
Wichita	−243	63	235	172	20	−9.6	−227	−8.2
Wilson	−443	−148	725	873	5	−4.3	43	0.4
Woodson	−281	−169	207	376	−4	−7.4	−328	−8.0
Wyandotte	−2,373	8,080	17,608	9,528	6,593	−1.5	−4,144	−2.6
KENTUCKY	163,789	98,521	345,318	246,797	30,889	4.1	355,393	9.6
Adair	406	232	1,305	1,073	91	2.4	1,884	12.3
Allen	988	176	1,380	1,204	36	5.6	3,172	21.7
Anderson	1,774	459	1,475	1,016	42	9.3	4,540	31.2
Ballard	−41	−8	614	622	8	−0.5	384	4.9
Barren	2,704	554	3,203	2,649	152	7.1	4,032	11.9
Bath	622	180	977	797	−1	5.6	1,393	14.4
Bell	−516	102	2,347	2,245	92	−1.7	−1,446	−4.6
Boone	24,091	6,225	9,674	3,449	1,237	28.0	28,400	49.3
Bourbon	479	208	1,485	1,277	267	2.5	124	0.6
Boyd	−381	−132	3,645	3,777	130	−0.8	−1,344	−2.6
Boyle	747	15	1,929	1,914	286	2.7	2,107	8.2
Bracken	376	192	718	526	−4	4.5	513	6.6
Breathitt	−176	−50	1,085	1,135	17	−1.1	397	2.5
Breckinridge	577	152	1,474	1,322	25	3.1	2,336	14.3
Bullitt	11,615	2,283	4,599	2,316	5	19.0	13,669	28.7
Butler	387	233	1,049	816	110	3.0	1,765	15.7
Caldwell	−146	−234	827	1,061	−4	−1.1	−170	−1.3
Calloway	1,244	9	2,089	2,080	585	3.6	3,442	11.2
Campbell	−1,750	2,038	7,352	5,314	441	−2.0	4,750	5.7
Carlisle	−34	−25	390	415	−4	−0.6	113	2.2
Carroll	366	281	979	698	42	3.6	863	9.3
Carter	476	367	2,202	1,835	6	1.8	2,549	10.5
Casey	879	121	1,240	1,119	140	5.7	1,236	8.7
Christian	−5,319	5,678	9,317	3,639	−1,040	−7.4	3,367	4.9
Clark	2,131	721	2,679	1,958	102	6.4	3,648	12.4
Clay	−504	305	1,819	1,514	8	−2.1	2,810	12.9
Clinton	−68	31	781	750	36	0.7	499	5.5
Crittenden	−314	−164	592	756	6	−3.3	188	2.0
Cumberland	−101	−101	503	604	−4	−1.4	363	5.4
Daviess	2,064	2,738	8,297	5,559	261	2.3	4,360	5.0
Edmonson	410	137	805	668	16	3.5	1,287	12.4
Elliott	439	43	499	456	−4	6.5	293	4.5
Estill	−144	198	1,258	1,060	2	−0.9	693	4.7
Fayette	10,277	11,541	23,660	12,119	8,286	3.9	35,146	15.6
Fleming	784	216	1,156	940	–	5.7	1,500	12.2
Floyd	−161	367	3,435	3,068	22	−0.4	−1,143	−2.6
Franklin	496	957	3,841	2,884	425	1.0	3,544	8.0
Fulton	−803	−115	572	687	−2	−10.4	−519	−6.3
Gallatin	280	292	832	540	−2	3.6	2,480	46.0
Garrard	2,141	251	1,077	826	117	14.5	3,213	27.7
Grant	2,385	1,259	2,386	1,127	66	10.7	6,647	42.2
Graves	844	288	3,028	2,740	445	2.3	3,478	10.4
Grayson	1,372	347	2,018	1,671	30	5.7	3,003	14.3
Green	123	−58	803	861	17	1.1	1,147	11.1
Greenup	483	86	2,643	2,557	2	1.3	95	0.3

See footnotes at end of table.

[Includes United States, states, and 3,141 counties/county equivalents defined as of February 22, 2005. For more information on these areas, see Appendix C, Geographic Information]

County	Components of population change, April 1, 2000, to July 1, 2006 (Number)						Population change, April 1, 1990, to April 1, 2000	
	Total population change	Natural increase			Net international migration	Percent change	Number	Percent change
		Total	Births	Deaths				
KENTUCKY—Con.								
Hancock	244	303	746	443	2	2.9	528	6.7
Hardin	2,917	4,893	9,209	4,316	−34	3.1	4,930	5.5
Harlan	−1,510	−267	2,464	2,731	61	−4.5	−3,372	−9.2
Harrison	609	270	1,441	1,171	14	3.4	1,735	10.7
Hart	1,098	306	1,477	1,171	33	6.3	2,559	17.2
Henderson	837	1,115	3,794	2,679	141	1.9	1,785	4.1
Henry	965	376	1,323	947	90	6.4	2,237	17.4
Hickman	−288	−91	326	417	−4	−5.5	−304	−5.5
Hopkins	313	115	3,664	3,549	78	0.7	391	0.8
Jackson	315	231	1,146	915	2	2.3	1,540	12.9
Jefferson	7,896	17,782	61,417	43,635	9,638	1.1	28,481	4.3
Jessamine	5,749	1,584	3,518	1,934	268	14.7	8,533	28.0
Johnson	743	197	1,856	1,659	36	3.2	197	0.8
Kenton	3,448	6,417	14,635	8,218	788	2.3	9,458	6.7
Knott	−113	91	1,107	1,016	10	−0.6	−257	−1.4
Knox	737	864	3,031	2,167	44	2.3	2,114	7.1
Larue	418	18	949	931	−4	3.1	1,694	14.5
Laurel	4,264	1,549	4,773	3,224	188	8.1	9,277	21.4
Lawrence	752	92	1,217	1,125	2	4.8	1,571	11.2
Lee	−268	−119	515	634	2	−3.4	494	6.7
Leslie	−428	46	914	868	−4	−3.5	−1,241	−9.1
Letcher	−757	79	1,921	1,842	3	−3.0	−1,723	−6.4
Lewis	−80	110	1,057	947	9	−0.6	1,063	8.2
Lincoln	2,000	599	2,105	1,506	73	8.6	3,265	16.2
Livingston	−7	−141	589	730	−	−0.1	742	8.2
Logan	790	557	2,274	1,717	71	3.0	2,157	8.8
Lyon	193	−306	337	643	38	2.4	1,456	22.0
McCracken	−564	574	5,153	4,579	84	−0.9	2,635	4.2
McCreary	274	368	1,503	1,135	32	1.6	1,477	9.5
McLean	−90	94	790	696	44	−0.9	306	3.2
Madison	8,143	2,792	6,146	3,354	408	11.5	13,364	23.2
Magoffin	117	351	1,156	805	−	0.9	255	1.9
Marion	767	475	1,586	1,111	100	4.2	1,713	10.4
Marshall	1,153	−382	1,940	2,322	82	3.8	2,920	10.7
Martin	−485	309	1,056	747	−4	−3.9	52	0.4
Mason	471	62	1,283	1,221	84	2.8	134	0.8
Meade	1,645	619	1,725	1,106	−38	6.2	2,179	9.0
Menifee	232	123	495	372	4	3.5	1,464	28.8
Mercer	1,001	257	1,711	1,454	202	4.8	1,669	8.7
Metcalfe	297	−71	780	851	−4	3.0	1,074	12.0
Monroe	15	76	918	842	81	0.1	355	3.1
Montgomery	2,333	756	2,112	1,356	23	10.3	2,993	15.3
Morgan	358	265	993	728	20	2.6	2,300	19.7
Muhlenberg	−279	−18	2,357	2,375	8	−0.9	522	1.7
Nelson	4,625	1,533	3,466	1,933	206	12.3	7,767	26.1
Nicholas	145	30	606	576	−3	2.1	88	1.3
Ohio	928	345	1,945	1,600	83	4.0	1,811	8.6
Oldham	8,667	1,796	3,446	1,650	167	18.6	13,355	40.1
Owen	881	133	807	674	27	8.4	1,512	16.7
Owsley	−168	−57	382	439	−4	−3.5	−178	−3.5
Pendleton	944	469	1,197	728	39	6.6	2,328	19.3
Perry	331	496	2,606	2,110	90	1.1	−861	−2.8
Pike	−1,874	1	4,789	4,788	92	−2.7	−3,850	−5.3
Powell	588	372	1,204	832	−1	4.4	1,551	13.3
Pulaski	3,532	622	4,624	4,002	139	6.3	6,728	13.6
Robertson	66	−32	138	170	−4	2.9	142	6.7
Rockcastle	275	251	1,366	1,115	−1	1.7	1,779	12.0
Rowan	140	361	1,529	1,168	199	0.6	1,741	8.6
Russell	859	128	1,300	1,172	14	5.3	1,599	10.9
Scott	8,544	2,152	3,615	1,463	275	25.8	9,194	38.5
Shelby	6,380	1,514	3,256	1,742	858	19.1	8,513	34.3
Simpson	775	314	1,354	1,040	66	4.7	1,260	8.3
Spencer	4,709	585	1,179	594	28	40.0	4,965	73.0
Taylor	804	165	1,746	1,581	78	3.5	1,781	8.4
Todd	130	367	1,176	809	41	1.1	1,031	9.4
Trigg	802	−100	855	955	7	6.4	2,236	21.6
Trimble	949	186	681	495	−4	11.7	2,035	33.4
Union	−266	89	1,121	1,032	69	−1.7	−920	−5.6
Warren	8,744	3,375	8,144	4,769	2,439	9.5	14,802	19.0
Washington	528	183	897	714	26	4.8	475	4.5

See footnotes at end of table.

[Includes United States, states, and 3,141 counties/county equivalents defined as of February 22, 2005. For more information on these areas, see Appendix C, Geographic Information]

County	Components of population change, April 1, 2000, to July 1, 2006						Population change, April 1, 1990, to April 1, 2000	
	Number							
	Total population change	Natural increase			Net international migration	Percent change	Number	Percent change
		Total	Births	Deaths				
KENTUCKY—Con.								
Wayne.	581	178	1,562	1,384	174	2.9	2,455	14.1
Webster.	−37	226	1,226	1,000	145	−0.3	165	1.2
Whitley	2,272	334	2,936	2,602	69	6.3	2,544	7.6
Wolfe.	30	114	731	617	16	0.4	562	8.6
Woodford	1,178	676	1,886	1,210	400	5.1	3,253	16.3
LOUISIANA	−181,190	145,355	410,364	265,009	22,244	−4.1	247,132	5.9
Acadia.	1,593	1,929	5,769	3,840	64	2.7	2,982	5.3
Allen	7	630	2,117	1,487	4	(Z)	4,214	19.9
Ascension	20,708	5,471	8,842	3,371	568	27.0	18,413	31.6
Assumption	84	546	1,786	1,240	57	0.4	635	2.8
Avoyelles	1,182	821	3,875	3,054	2	2.8	2,322	5.9
Beauregard	2,144	767	2,761	1,994	30	6.5	2,903	9.6
Bienville.	−584	−237	1,216	1,453	5	−3.7	−480	−3.0
Bossier	8,910	4,732	9,859	5,127	−111	9.1	12,272	14.3
Caddo	1,002	6,613	23,160	16,547	644	0.4	3,863	1.6
Calcasieu	947	6,090	17,107	11,017	562	0.5	15,443	9.2
Caldwell.	55	105	859	754	–	0.5	754	7.7
Cameron	−2,196	163	623	460	56	−22.0	728	7.9
Catahoula	−353	64	864	800	–	−3.2	−145	−1.3
Claiborne	−641	−216	1,054	1,270	−4	−3.8	−554	−3.2
Concordia.	−787	325	1,635	1,310	16	−3.9	−581	−2.8
De Soto	898	475	2,267	1,792	48	3.5	−176	−0.7
East Baton Rouge	16,221	15,550	36,630	21,080	5,357	3.9	32,747	8.6
East Carroll	−722	329	974	645	9	−7.7	−288	−3.0
East Feliciana	−438	213	1,686	1,473	12	−2.1	2,149	11.2
Evangeline	477	812	3,276	2,464	31	1.3	2,160	6.5
Franklin	−808	236	1,943	1,707	23	−3.8	−1,124	−5.0
Grant.	1,183	313	1,549	1,236	4	6.3	1,170	6.7
Iberia.	2,243	3,051	7,146	4,095	231	3.1	4,969	7.3
Iberville	−346	879	2,935	2,056	21	−1.0	2,271	7.3
Jackson	−195	−37	1,252	1,289	–	−1.3	−462	−2.9
Jefferson	−24,105	13,369	39,395	26,026	5,394	−5.3	7,160	1.6
Jefferson Davis	−17	940	2,978	2,038	31	−0.1	713	2.3
Lafayette	12,768	9,509	18,392	8,883	1,664	6.7	25,561	15.5
Lafourche	3,571	3,029	7,580	4,551	392	4.0	4,123	4.8
La Salle	−189	36	1,111	1,075	15	−1.3	620	4.5
Lincoln.	−652	1,248	3,409	2,161	348	−1.5	764	1.8
Livingston.	22,997	5,190	9,690	4,500	159	25.0	21,285	30.2
Madison.	−1,400	312	1,300	988	30	−10.2	1,265	10.2
Morehouse	−1,260	381	2,736	2,355	2	−4.1	−917	−2.9
Natchitoches.	−361	1,352	3,722	2,370	227	−0.9	1,826	4.9
Orleans	−261,286	11,405	44,165	32,760	3,416	−53.9	−12,264	−2.5
Ouachita	2,009	6,053	14,415	8,362	289	1.4	5,059	3.6
Plaquemines.	−4,245	1,196	2,599	1,403	−38	−15.9	1,182	4.6
Pointe Coupee	−115	413	1,929	1,516	1	−0.5	223	1.0
Rapides	3,862	3,426	11,870	8,444	459	3.1	−5,217	−4.0
Red River.	−184	212	884	672	15	−1.9	96	1.0
Richland.	−427	310	1,881	1,571	12	−2.0	352	1.7
Sabine	475	419	2,089	1,670	71	2.0	813	3.6
St. Bernard.	−51,715	353	5,403	5,050	110	−76.9	598	0.9
St. Charles	4,694	2,264	4,362	2,098	298	9.8	5,630	13.3
St. Helena	234	98	701	603	–	2.2	651	6.6
St. James	526	802	1,981	1,179	6	2.5	316	1.5
St. John the Baptist	5,488	2,274	4,378	2,104	138	12.7	3,053	7.6
St. Landry	3,828	2,908	8,563	5,655	97	4.4	7,388	9.2
St. Martin	2,758	1,994	4,551	2,557	52	5.7	4,486	10.2
St. Mary.	−1,633	1,611	4,861	3,250	206	−3.1	−4,586	−7.9
St. Tammany.	39,335	8,013	17,822	9,809	644	20.6	46,770	32.4
Tangipahoa.	12,545	3,612	9,968	6,356	182	12.5	14,883	17.4
Tensas.	−480	96	549	453	28	−7.3	−485	−6.8
Terrebonne	4,854	5,537	10,772	5,235	371	4.6	7,512	7.7
Union	161	490	2,012	1,522	104	0.7	2,007	9.7
Vermilion	2,031	1,633	5,038	3,405	372	3.8	3,935	7.9
Vernon.	−5,783	3,874	5,992	2,118	−602	−11.0	−9,430	−15.2
Washington	824	492	3,952	3,460	8	1.9	741	1.7
Webster.	−527	−4	3,292	3,296	50	−1.3	−161	−0.4
West Baton Rouge.	862	860	1,937	1,077	36	4.0	2,182	11.2
West Carroll	−582	−34	897	931	4	−4.7	221	1.8
West Feliciana	424	136	739	603	18	2.8	2,196	17.0
Winn	−1,059	−78	1,264	1,342	6	−6.3	396	2.4

See footnotes at end of table.

[Includes United States, states, and 3,141 counties/county equivalents defined as of February 22, 2005. For more information on these areas, see Appendix C, Geographic Information]

County	Components of population change, April 1, 2000, to July 1, 2006 — Number					Percent change	Population change, April 1, 1990, to April 1, 2000	
	Total population change	Natural increase — Total	Births	Deaths	Net international migration		Number	Percent change
MAINE	46,651	7,917	86,331	78,414	5,616	3.7	46,995	3.8
Androscoggin	3,759	1,465	7,953	6,488	453	3.6	−1,466	−1.4
Aroostook.	−930	−964	4,303	5,267	471	−1.3	−12,998	−15.0
Cumberland	8,986	3,752	18,790	15,038	2,414	3.4	22,477	9.2
Franklin	550	–	1,699	1,699	50	1.9	459	1.6
Hancock	2,006	−465	3,168	3,633	173	3.9	4,843	10.3
Kennebec.	3,954	547	7,776	7,229	282	3.4	1,210	1.0
Knox	1,478	−217	2,537	2,754	83	3.7	3,308	9.1
Lincoln.	1,618	−463	1,928	2,391	24	4.8	3,259	10.7
Oxford	2,363	−380	3,434	3,814	74	4.3	2,153	4.1
Penobscot	2,261	1,059	9,707	8,648	847	1.6	−1,682	−1.1
Piscataquis.	350	−362	1,013	1,375	21	2.0	−1,418	−7.6
Sagadahoc.	1,623	560	2,562	2,002	9	4.6	1,679	5.0
Somerset	1,361	358	3,426	3,068	73	2.7	1,121	2.3
Waldo	2,435	350	2,467	2,117	23	6.7	3,262	9.9
Washington	−653	−540	2,200	2,740	119	−1.9	−1,367	−3.9
York	15,490	3,217	13,368	10,151	500	8.3	22,155	13.5
MARYLAND.	319,221	189,158	464,251	275,093	129,730	6.0	515,753	10.8
Allegany.	−2,099	−1,367	4,299	5,666	137	−2.8	−16	(Z)
Anne Arundel	19,644	20,282	42,629	22,347	2,644	4.0	62,417	14.6
Baltimore	33,092	10,595	58,234	47,639	12,782	4.4	62,158	9.0
Calvert.	14,241	2,898	6,332	3,434	243	19.1	23,191	45.1
Caroline.	2,845	723	2,687	1,964	343	9.6	2,737	10.1
Carroll	19,363	4,473	12,189	7,716	474	12.8	27,525	22.3
Cecil	13,555	2,916	7,467	4,551	328	15.8	14,604	20.5
Charles	19,870	6,013	11,267	5,254	200	16.5	19,392	19.2
Dorchester	957	−264	2,139	2,403	60	3.1	438	1.4
Frederick	27,662	9,913	18,622	8,709	1,832	14.2	45,068	30.0
Garrett.	13	38	2,017	1,979	29	(Z)	1,708	6.1
Harford	22,812	8,079	18,364	10,285	876	10.4	36,458	20.0
Howard	24,610	13,934	21,974	8,040	6,892	9.9	60,514	32.3
Kent	786	−403	1,137	1,540	180	4.1	1,355	7.6
Montgomery	57,966	49,076	83,692	34,616	62,627	6.6	111,290	14.6
Prince George's.	40,624	44,601	77,418	32,817	29,602	5.1	77,986	10.8
Queen Anne's.	5,678	846	3,138	2,292	280	14.0	6,610	19.5
St. Mary's.	12,622	4,747	8,533	3,786	−8	14.6	10,258	13.5
Somerset	1,026	−51	1,636	1,687	222	4.1	1,308	5.6
Talbot	2,250	−309	2,262	2,571	204	6.7	3,263	10.7
Washington	11,825	2,110	10,451	8,341	487	9.0	10,530	8.7
Wicomico.	7,343	2,212	7,301	5,089	983	8.7	10,305	13.9
Worcester.	2,324	−513	2,955	3,468	370	5.0	11,514	32.9
Independent City								
Baltimore city	−19,788	8,609	57,508	48,899	7,943	−3.0	−84,860	−11.5
MASSACHUSETTS.	88,088	149,992	499,440	349,448	200,155	1.4	332,680	5.5
Barnstable	2,586	−5,000	12,358	17,358	2,510	1.2	35,625	19.1
Berkshire	−3,836	−1,935	7,866	9,801	1,079	−2.8	−4,399	−3.2
Bristol	10,701	9,865	41,722	31,857	5,294	2.0	28,353	5.6
Dukes	528	137	957	820	314	3.5	3,348	28.8
Essex	12,539	18,544	59,358	40,814	18,451	1.7	53,339	8.0
Franklin	648	176	4,219	4,043	743	0.9	1,449	2.1
Hampden	4,294	7,415	35,977	28,562	8,527	0.9	−84	(Z)
Hampshire	1,218	531	7,911	7,380	3,128	0.8	5,685	3.9
Middlesex.	622	44,378	115,544	71,166	66,138	(Z)	67,926	4.9
Nantucket.	720	495	900	405	353	7.6	3,508	58.3
Norfolk.	4,445	15,795	51,450	35,655	16,840	0.7	34,221	5.6
Plymouth	20,801	13,888	39,502	25,614	5,656	4.4	37,546	8.6
Suffolk	−2,197	25,798	59,278	33,480	53,865	−0.3	25,901	3.9
Worcester.	35,019	19,905	62,398	42,493	17,257	4.7	40,262	5.7
MICHIGAN	157,163	272,304	816,225	543,921	151,435	1.6	643,193	6.9
Alcona.	40	−600	451	1,051	6	0.3	1,574	15.5
Alger.	−197	−251	490	741	3	−2.0	890	9.9
Allegan	7,836	3,913	9,221	5,308	833	7.4	15,156	16.7
Alpena.	−1,247	−325	1,867	2,192	72	−4.0	709	2.3
Antrim	1,353	3	1,497	1,494	32	5.9	4,925	27.1
Arenac.	−245	−203	1,086	1,289	9	−1.4	2,363	15.9
Baraga	−4	−54	614	668	8	(Z)	792	10.0
Barry	3,144	1,392	4,417	3,025	62	5.5	6,698	13.4
Bay	−1,767	1,016	7,943	6,927	196	−1.6	−1,566	−1.4
Benzie	1,654	160	1,188	1,028	36	10.3	3,798	31.1

See footnotes at end of table.

[Includes United States, states, and 3,141 counties/county equivalents defined as of February 22, 2005. For more information on these areas, see Appendix C, Geographic Information]

County	Components of population change, April 1, 2000, to July 1, 2006						Population change, April 1, 1990, to April 1, 2000	
	Number							
	Total population change	Natural increase			Net international migration	Percent change	Number	Percent change
		Total	Births	Deaths				
MICHIGAN—Con.								
Berrien	−750	3,096	13,087	9,991	2,837	−0.5	1,077	0.7
Branch	88	1,119	3,679	2,560	530	0.2	4,285	10.3
Calhoun	6	2,728	11,658	8,930	1,107	(Z)	2,003	1.5
Cass	227	316	3,210	2,894	161	0.4	1,625	3.3
Charlevoix	332	413	1,815	1,402	66	1.3	4,622	21.5
Cheboygan	834	−99	1,729	1,828	16	3.2	5,050	23.6
Chippewa	131	469	2,412	1,943	130	0.3	3,939	11.4
Clare	55	−263	2,106	2,369	3	0.2	6,300	25.2
Clinton	5,156	2,074	5,057	2,983	93	8.0	6,860	11.8
Crawford	655	−138	849	987	8	4.6	2,013	16.4
Delta	−364	−65	2,552	2,617	49	−0.9	740	2.0
Dickinson	−25	−258	1,725	1,983	26	−0.1	641	2.4
Eaton	3,582	2,576	7,687	5,111	636	3.5	10,776	11.6
Emmet	2,170	521	2,256	1,735	137	6.9	6,397	25.5
Genesee	5,818	14,051	38,943	24,892	1,334	1.3	5,689	1.3
Gladwin	985	−181	1,687	1,868	7	3.8	4,127	18.8
Gogebic	−846	−737	817	1,554	5	−4.9	−682	−3.8
Grand Traverse	7,298	1,954	6,036	4,082	446	9.4	13,381	20.8
Gratiot	−178	317	3,029	2,712	104	−0.4	3,303	8.5
Hillsdale	679	992	3,721	2,729	95	1.5	3,096	7.1
Houghton	−682	12	2,447	2,435	460	−1.9	570	1.6
Huron	−1,936	−786	2,086	2,872	73	−5.4	1,128	3.2
Ingham	−2,516	10,862	22,913	12,051	8,274	−0.9	−2,498	−0.9
Ionia	3,303	2,426	5,304	2,878	131	5.4	4,494	7.9
Iosco	−508	−892	1,502	2,394	17	−1.9	−2,870	−9.5
Iron	−761	−627	614	1,241	−4	−5.8	−37	−0.3
Isabella	2,467	1,899	4,499	2,600	744	3.9	8,727	16.0
Jackson	5,429	3,364	12,969	9,605	730	3.4	8,666	5.8
Kalamazoo	2,117	7,407	19,433	12,026	3,603	0.9	15,192	6.8
Kalkaska	759	435	1,380	945	8	4.6	3,074	22.8
Kent	25,189	32,195	58,142	25,947	14,898	4.4	73,704	14.7
Keweenaw	−118	−39	125	164	−4	−5.1	600	35.3
Lake	460	−278	677	955	−1	4.1	2,750	32.0
Lapeer	5,857	2,780	6,656	3,876	283	6.7	13,136	17.6
Leelanau	993	16	1,172	1,156	107	4.7	4,592	27.8
Lenawee	3,244	2,331	7,609	5,278	350	3.3	7,471	8.2
Livingston	27,560	6,352	12,574	6,222	1,067	17.6	41,306	35.7
Luce	−340	−147	391	538	−4	−4.8	1,261	21.9
Mackinac	−893	−241	641	882	5	−7.5	1,269	11.9
Macomb	44,712	17,515	63,173	45,658	13,525	5.7	70,749	9.9
Manistee	540	−251	1,562	1,813	27	2.2	3,262	15.3
Marquette	41	−133	3,837	3,970	161	0.1	−6,253	−8.8
Mason	771	−60	1,968	2,028	20	2.7	2,737	10.7
Mecosta	1,699	724	2,871	2,147	320	4.2	3,245	8.7
Menominee	−630	−192	1,498	1,690	44	−2.5	406	1.6
Midland	918	2,268	6,200	3,932	1,002	1.1	7,223	9.5
Missaukee	719	205	1,052	847	12	5.0	2,331	19.2
Monroe	9,090	3,228	10,827	7,599	751	6.2	12,345	9.2
Montcalm	2,711	1,934	5,357	3,423	125	4.4	8,207	15.5
Montmorency	163	−362	555	917	3	1.6	1,379	15.4
Muskegon	5,031	4,460	14,525	10,065	734	3.0	11,217	7.1
Newaygo	1,966	1,232	3,895	2,663	224	4.1	9,668	25.3
Oakland	20,099	40,124	96,338	56,214	33,103	1.7	110,564	10.2
Oceana	1,766	925	2,418	1,493	453	6.6	4,418	19.7
Ogemaw	20	−544	1,376	1,920	15	0.1	2,964	15.9
Ontonagon	−616	−422	294	716	1	−7.9	−1,036	−11.7
Osceola	387	548	1,904	1,356	20	1.7	3,051	15.1
Oscoda	−278	−147	549	696	−1	−3.0	1,576	20.1
Otsego	1,410	475	1,755	1,280	43	6.1	5,344	29.8
Ottawa	19,357	12,854	22,180	9,326	2,405	8.1	50,546	26.9
Presque Isle	−267	−328	773	1,101	6	−1.9	668	4.9
Roscommon	595	−1,028	1,310	2,338	11	2.3	5,693	28.8
Saginaw	−3,742	3,758	16,698	12,940	995	−1.8	−1,904	−0.9
St. Clair	7,490	3,688	12,934	9,246	588	4.6	18,628	12.8
St. Joseph	355	2,185	5,843	3,658	853	0.6	3,509	6.0
Sanilac	−99	368	3,282	2,914	25	−0.2	4,619	11.6
Schoolcraft	−159	−236	505	741	−4	−1.8	601	7.2
Shiawassee	1,225	1,722	5,622	3,900	60	1.7	1,917	2.7
Tuscola	−388	917	4,226	3,309	35	−0.7	2,768	5.0

See footnotes at end of table.

[Includes United States, states, and 3,141 counties/county equivalents defined as of February 22, 2005. For more information on these areas, see Appendix C, Geographic Information]

County	Components of population change, April 1, 2000, to July 1, 2006						Population change, April 1, 1990, to April 1, 2000	
	Number							
		Natural increase						
	Total population change	Total	Births	Deaths	Net international migration	Percent change	Number	Percent change
MICHIGAN—Con.								
Van Buren	2,755	2,186	6,468	4,282	599	3.6	6,203	8.9
Washtenaw.	21,277	14,479	26,131	11,652	14,697	6.6	39,833	14.1
Wayne.	−89,309	58,608	181,847	123,239	40,730	−4.3	−50,525	−2.4
Wexford.	1,510	599	2,489	1,890	69	5.0	4,124	15.6
MINNESOTA	247,609	196,095	432,306	236,211	86,925	5.0	543,827	12.4
Aitkin.	848	−155	947	1,102	6	5.5	2,876	23.1
Anoka	28,921	18,205	27,268	9,063	2,888	9.7	54,443	22.3
Becker.	2,230	495	2,530	2,035	53	7.4	2,119	7.6
Beltrami.	3,519	1,774	3,825	2,051	228	8.9	5,266	15.3
Benton	4,461	1,633	3,581	1,948	199	13.0	4,042	13.4
Big Stone.	−310	−223	336	559	−4	−5.3	−465	−7.4
Blue Earth	2,317	1,443	4,180	2,737	695	4.1	1,893	3.5
Brown	−550	34	1,799	1,765	50	−2.0	−73	−0.3
Carlton.	2,445	382	2,436	2,054	76	7.7	2,412	8.2
Carver	17,340	5,564	7,526	1,962	965	24.7	22,290	46.5
Cass	1,883	257	2,130	1,873	15	6.9	5,362	24.6
Chippewa.	−367	−100	875	975	7	−2.8	−140	−1.1
Chisago	9,243	2,425	4,348	1,923	32	22.5	10,580	34.7
Clay	3,247	1,396	3,725	2,329	399	6.3	807	1.6
Clearwater	17	76	736	660	–	0.2	114	1.4
Cook.	161	−58	235	293	32	3.1	1,300	33.6
Cottonwood	−508	−15	910	925	9	−4.2	−527	−4.2
Crow Wing	5,910	1,181	4,514	3,333	98	10.7	10,850	24.5
Dakota.	32,097	22,755	33,777	11,022	4,820	9.0	80,694	29.3
Dodge	2,039	1,022	1,772	750	116	11.5	2,000	12.7
Douglas	2,646	349	2,400	2,051	18	8.1	4,147	14.5
Faribault.	−898	−291	1,013	1,304	43	−5.5	−756	−4.5
Fillmore	29	98	1,646	1,548	2	0.1	345	1.7
Freeborn	−948	4	2,342	2,338	252	−2.9	−476	−1.4
Goodhue	1,680	676	3,426	2,750	129	3.8	3,437	8.4
Grant.	−211	−151	401	552	3	−3.4	43	0.7
Hennepin.	6,054	54,178	103,215	49,037	44,078	0.5	83,608	8.1
Houston	114	106	1,297	1,191	43	0.6	1,221	6.6
Hubbard.	517	138	1,240	1,102	7	2.8	3,434	23.0
Isanti.	7,289	1,183	2,744	1,561	73	23.3	5,366	20.7
Itasca	737	18	3,018	3,000	134	1.7	3,148	7.7
Jackson	−118	−106	699	805	8	−1.0	−409	−3.5
Kanabec	1,280	327	1,109	782	−1	8.5	2,194	17.1
Kandiyohi	−115	1,245	3,580	2,335	444	−0.3	2,442	6.3
Kittson	−594	−159	291	450	−4	−11.2	−482	−8.4
Koochiching	−697	−127	816	943	75	−4.9	−1,944	−11.9
Lac qui Parle	−603	−213	438	651	–	−7.5	−857	−9.6
Lake	−92	−272	561	833	6	−0.8	643	6.2
Lake of the Woods.	−195	−19	254	273	54	−4.3	446	10.9
Le Sueur	2,469	731	2,085	1,354	125	9.7	2,187	9.4
Lincoln.	−466	−226	417	643	−1	−7.2	−461	−6.7
Lyon	−785	559	2,008	1,449	394	−3.1	636	2.6
McLeod	2,381	1,411	3,284	1,873	182	6.8	2,868	9.0
Mahnomen	−118	194	510	316	3	−2.3	146	2.9
Marshall.	−204	128	690	562	23	−2.0	−838	−7.6
Martin	−1,034	−8	1,422	1,430	33	−4.7	−1,112	−4.9
Meeker	763	418	1,855	1,437	25	3.4	1,796	8.6
Mille Lacs.	3,839	431	1,947	1,516	24	17.2	3,660	19.6
Morrison.	1,207	681	2,623	1,942	14	3.8	2,108	7.1
Mower.	63	796	3,276	2,480	640	0.2	1,218	3.3
Murray.	−387	−81	576	657	18	−4.2	−495	−5.1
Nicollet	1,542	1,289	2,436	1,147	280	5.2	1,695	6.0
Nobles.	−387	851	1,991	1,140	485	−1.9	734	3.7
Norman	−592	−151	448	599	20	−8.0	−533	−6.7
Olmsted.	13,244	7,815	12,789	4,974	4,164	10.7	17,807	16.7
Otter Tail	658	−356	3,624	3,980	449	1.2	6,445	12.7
Pennington	125	187	1,114	927	74	0.9	278	2.1
Pine	1,889	429	1,961	1,532	17	7.1	5,266	24.8
Pipestone	−472	−64	742	806	6	−4.8	−596	−5.7
Polk	−281	68	2,217	2,149	179	−0.9	−1,220	−3.7
Pope.	−24	−178	703	881	3	−0.2	491	4.6
Ramsey.	−17,987	21,591	46,072	24,481	15,808	−3.5	25,442	5.2
Red Lake	−131	40	322	282	−1	−3.0	−226	−5.0
Redwood	−1,024	−115	1,194	1,309	5	−6.1	−439	−2.5
Renville	−623	−116	1,266	1,382	58	−3.6	−519	−2.9

See footnotes at end of table.

[Includes United States, states, and 3,141 counties/county equivalents defined as of February 22, 2005. For more information on these areas, see Appendix C, Geographic Information]

County	Components of population change, April 1, 2000, to July 1, 2006						Population change, April 1, 1990, to April 1, 2000	
	Number					Percent change	Number	Percent change
	Total population change	Natural increase			Net international migration			
		Total	Births	Deaths				
MINNESOTA—Con.								
Rice	5,315	1,896	4,629	2,733	1,125	9.4	7,482	15.2
Rock	-186	-39	783	822	9	-1.9	-85	-0.9
Roseau	-137	436	1,303	867	23	-0.8	1,312	8.7
St. Louis	-4,461	-773	12,804	13,577	544	-2.2	2,296	1.2
Scott	34,594	9,588	12,318	2,730	971	38.7	31,652	54.7
Sherburne	20,580	5,038	7,493	2,455	135	31.9	22,470	53.6
Sibley	-230	292	1,223	931	154	-1.5	990	6.9
Stearns	10,927	6,277	11,269	4,992	1,253	8.2	13,845	11.6
Steele	2,541	1,384	3,112	1,728	607	7.5	2,951	9.6
Stevens	-226	144	633	489	85	-2.2	-581	-5.5
Swift	-1,649	-17	734	751	21	-13.8	1,232	11.5
Todd	-51	334	1,756	1,422	177	-0.2	1,063	4.5
Traverse	-335	-134	219	353	–	-8.1	-329	-7.4
Wabasha	672	391	1,645	1,254	226	3.1	1,866	9.5
Wadena	-268	-214	1,022	1,236	-4	-2.0	559	4.2
Waseca	-57	456	1,587	1,131	44	-0.3	1,447	8.0
Washington	23,870	11,201	17,873	6,672	1,480	11.9	55,270	37.9
Watonwan	-716	202	941	739	194	-6.0	198	1.7
Wilkin	-504	18	490	472	8	-7.1	-378	-5.0
Winona	-697	787	3,298	2,511	516	-1.4	2,157	4.5
Wright	24,794	7,464	10,914	3,450	261	27.6	21,283	31.0
Yellow Medicine	-650	-35	748	783	21	-5.9	-604	-5.2
MISSISSIPPI	65,884	89,504	266,971	177,467	10,896	2.3	269,181	10.5
Adams	-1,714	202	2,716	2,514	51	-5.0	-1,016	-2.9
Alcorn	1,031	302	2,894	2,592	132	3.0	2,836	8.9
Amite	-133	135	1,038	903	4	-1.0	271	2.0
Attala	-17	100	1,762	1,662	67	-0.1	1,180	6.4
Benton	-153	138	699	561	-4	-1.9	-20	-0.2
Bolivar	-2,281	1,260	3,872	2,612	39	-5.6	-1,242	-3.0
Calhoun	-422	145	1,257	1,112	138	-2.8	161	1.1
Carroll	-443	28	673	645	18	-4.1	1,532	16.6
Chickasaw	-442	643	1,853	1,210	156	-2.3	1,355	7.5
Choctaw	-357	66	603	537	11	-3.7	687	7.6
Claiborne	-344	342	1,008	666	21	-2.9	461	4.1
Clarke	-324	304	1,483	1,179	4	-1.8	642	3.7
Clay	-769	570	1,934	1,364	35	-3.5	859	4.1
Coahoma	-2,202	1,209	3,352	2,143	76	-7.2	-1,043	-3.3
Copiah	466	932	2,736	1,804	4	1.6	1,165	4.2
Covington	1,040	492	1,846	1,354	33	5.4	2,880	17.4
DeSoto	37,507	6,431	11,741	5,310	806	35.0	39,289	57.9
Forrest	3,768	2,557	6,954	4,397	778	5.2	4,290	6.3
Franklin	-179	41	647	606	-4	-2.1	71	0.8
George	2,684	752	2,137	1,385	105	14.0	2,471	14.8
Greene	-196	191	941	750	3	-1.5	3,079	30.1
Grenada	-402	-117	1,842	1,959	82	-1.7	1,708	7.9
Hancock	-2,546	507	3,407	2,900	94	-5.9	11,207	35.3
Harrison	-17,726	7,218	18,548	11,330	269	-9.3	24,236	14.7
Hinds	-1,788	11,520	24,485	12,965	827	-0.7	-3,641	-1.4
Holmes	-743	702	2,402	1,700	-1	-3.4	5	(Z)
Humphreys	-813	489	1,247	758	44	-7.3	-928	-7.6
Issaquena	-469	42	111	69	-4	-20.6	365	19.1
Itawamba	582	-9	1,772	1,781	12	2.6	2,753	13.8
Jackson	-843	4,316	11,709	7,393	607	-0.6	16,177	14.0
Jasper	48	549	1,616	1,067	32	0.3	1,035	6.0
Jefferson	-546	262	864	602	-1	-5.6	1,087	12.6
Jefferson Davis	-778	113	1,029	916	-2	-5.6	-89	-0.6
Jones	1,757	1,793	6,360	4,567	986	2.7	2,927	4.7
Kemper	-345	166	826	660	2	-3.3	97	0.9
Lafayette	2,127	1,026	2,940	1,914	510	5.5	6,912	21.7
Lamar	7,170	2,127	4,060	1,933	36	18.4	8,646	28.4
Lauderdale	-1,437	1,359	7,347	5,988	-66	-1.8	2,606	3.4
Lawrence	199	240	1,126	886	6	1.5	800	6.4
Leake	1,829	763	2,303	1,540	80	8.7	2,504	13.6
Lee	3,959	3,102	7,672	4,570	272	5.2	10,176	15.5
Leflore	-2,195	1,136	3,638	2,502	141	-5.8	606	1.6
Lincoln	1,238	566	2,848	2,282	33	3.7	2,888	9.5
Lowndes	-1,813	2,376	5,701	3,325	39	-2.9	2,278	3.8
Madison	12,745	1,803	7,742	5,939	346	17.1	20,880	38.8
Marion	135	385	2,447	2,062	14	0.5	51	0.2
Marshall	860	974	3,171	2,197	76	2.5	4,632	15.3
Monroe	-442	658	3,193	2,535	17	-1.2	1,432	3.9
Montgomery	-435	209	1,042	833	-2	-3.6	-198	-1.6
Neshoba	1,441	1,166	3,140	1,974	32	5.0	3,884	15.7

See footnotes at end of table.

Table B-2. Counties — **Components of Population Change**—Con.

[Includes United States, states, and 3,141 counties/county equivalents defined as of February 22, 2005. For more information on these areas, see Appendix C, Geographic Information]

County	Components of population change, April 1, 2000, to July 1, 2006						Population change, April 1, 1990, to April 1, 2000	
	Number							
	Total population change	Natural increase			Net international migration	Percent change	Number	Percent change
		Total	Births	Deaths				
MISSISSIPPI—Con.								
Newton	575	695	2,145	1,450	−6	2.6	1,547	7.6
Noxubee	−497	557	1,281	724	52	−4.0	−56	−0.4
Oktibbeha	−1,269	1,807	3,550	1,743	944	−3.0	4,527	11.8
Panola	1,147	1,432	3,545	2,113	38	3.3	4,284	14.3
Pearl River	8,478	1,085	4,149	3,064	51	17.4	9,907	25.6
Perry	−6	258	1,017	759	–	(Z)	1,273	11.7
Pike	1,300	1,162	3,992	2,830	23	3.3	2,058	5.6
Pontotoc	2,161	1,043	2,571	1,528	121	8.1	4,489	20.2
Prentiss	57	472	2,014	1,542	4	0.2	2,280	9.8
Quitman	−826	180	906	726	3	−8.2	−375	−3.6
Rankin	20,503	6,150	11,291	5,141	644	17.8	28,166	32.3
Scott	367	1,217	2,936	1,719	585	1.3	4,286	17.8
Sharkey	−729	250	636	386	−4	−11.1	−486	−6.9
Simpson	333	667	2,554	1,887	110	1.2	3,686	15.4
Smith	−212	213	1,258	1,045	18	−1.3	1,384	9.4
Stone	1,986	337	1,253	916	53	14.6	2,872	26.7
Sunflower	−2,536	981	2,985	2,004	100	−7.4	−760	−2.2
Tallahatchie	−1,105	288	1,224	936	23	−7.4	−307	−2.0
Tate	1,353	912	2,444	1,532	11	5.3	3,938	18.4
Tippah	422	495	2,067	1,572	226	2.0	1,303	6.7
Tishomingo	−49	−196	1,426	1,622	65	−0.3	1,478	8.4
Tunica	1,192	528	1,177	649	42	12.9	1,063	13.0
Union	1,646	604	2,238	1,634	203	6.5	3,277	14.8
Walthall	387	334	1,361	1,027	6	2.6	804	5.6
Warren	−336	1,548	4,808	3,260	113	−0.7	1,764	3.7
Washington	−4,970	2,163	6,199	4,036	174	−7.9	−4,958	−7.3
Wayne	−129	556	1,840	1,284	18	−0.6	1,699	8.7
Webster	−253	−3	904	907	6	−2.5	72	0.7
Wilkinson	−73	−5	857	862	–	−0.7	634	6.6
Winston	−452	354	1,702	1,348	92	−2.2	727	3.7
Yalobusha	350	210	1,202	992	2	2.7	1,018	8.5
Yazoo	−220	929	2,705	1,776	225	−0.8	2,643	10.4
MISSOURI	246,030	137,564	480,763	343,199	50,450	4.4	479,782	9.4
Adair	−516	366	1,745	1,379	199	−2.1	400	1.6
Andrew	685	48	1,120	1,072	20	4.2	1,860	12.7
Atchison	−299	−149	390	539	6	−4.6	−1,026	−13.8
Audrain	−114	567	2,388	1,821	−4	−0.4	2,254	9.6
Barry	2,393	756	3,132	2,376	477	7.0	6,464	23.5
Barton	474	188	1,042	854	15	3.8	1,229	10.9
Bates	463	10	1,357	1,347	46	2.8	1,628	10.8
Benton	1,548	−555	1,013	1,568	−4	9.0	3,321	24.0
Bollinger	294	46	884	838	6	2.4	1,410	13.3
Boone	10,594	6,385	11,691	5,306	2,900	7.8	23,075	20.5
Buchanan	−1,047	1,249	7,070	5,821	198	−1.2	2,919	3.5
Butler	715	217	3,507	3,290	143	1.7	2,102	5.4
Caldwell	344	96	740	644	–	3.8	589	7.0
Callaway	2,306	991	3,205	2,214	201	5.7	7,957	24.3
Camden	3,232	−124	2,418	2,542	147	8.7	9,556	34.8
Cape Girardeau	3,199	1,275	5,536	4,261	402	4.7	7,060	11.5
Carroll	−227	−126	713	839	−4	−2.2	−463	−4.3
Carter	15	39	504	465	–	0.3	426	7.7
Cass	13,689	2,972	7,497	4,525	308	16.7	18,284	28.7
Cedar	265	−179	1,008	1,187	30	1.9	1,640	13.6
Chariton	−392	−228	525	753	–	−4.6	−764	−8.3
Christian	16,229	2,698	5,540	2,842	49	29.9	21,641	66.3
Clark	−111	−36	516	552	–	−1.5	−131	−1.7
Clay	22,982	9,071	17,898	8,827	1,722	12.5	30,564	19.9
Clinton	1,696	94	1,562	1,468	8	8.9	2,380	14.3
Cole	1,899	2,312	6,000	3,688	631	2.7	7,818	12.3
Cooper	771	57	1,172	1,115	8	4.6	1,835	12.4
Crawford	1,205	292	1,919	1,627	74	5.3	3,631	18.9
Dade	−119	−259	553	812	9	−1.5	474	6.4
Dallas	1,035	284	1,392	1,108	23	6.6	3,015	23.8
Daviess	56	184	740	556	–	0.7	151	1.9
DeKalb	−768	−25	695	720	32	−5.9	3,110	31.2
Dent	349	−98	1,115	1,213	2	2.3	1,225	8.9
Douglas	574	−53	877	930	34	4.4	1,208	10.2
Dunklin	−880	84	2,953	2,869	135	−2.7	45	0.1

See footnotes at end of table.

[Includes United States, states, and 3,141 counties/county equivalents defined as of February 22, 2005. For more information on these areas, see Appendix C, Geographic Information]

County	Components of population change, April 1, 2000, to July 1, 2006						Population change, April 1, 1990, to April 1, 2000	
	Number							
		Natural increase						
	Total population change	Total	Births	Deaths	Net international migration	Percent change	Number	Percent change
MISSOURI—Con.								
Franklin	6,260	2,728	8,191	5,463	48	6.7	13,204	16.4
Gasconade	292	−296	1,018	1,314	1	1.9	1,336	9.5
Gentry	−472	−164	470	634	14	−6.9	7	0.1
Greene	14,388	5,072	19,928	14,856	1,188	6.0	32,442	15.6
Grundy	−193	−49	840	889	59	−1.9	−104	−1.0
Harrison	48	−111	658	769	18	0.5	381	4.5
Henry	722	−82	1,778	1,860	44	3.3	1,953	9.7
Hickory	303	−409	453	862	12	3.4	1,605	21.9
Holt	−354	−62	352	414	–	−6.6	−683	−11.3
Howard	−263	34	723	689	27	−2.6	581	6.0
Howell	1,496	256	3,151	2,895	145	4.0	5,791	18.4
Iron	−418	−214	850	1,064	–	−3.9	−29	−0.3
Jackson	9,198	26,575	64,103	37,528	9,829	1.4	21,646	3.4
Jasper	7,819	3,899	10,743	6,844	1,051	7.5	14,221	15.7
Jefferson	18,370	7,536	17,187	9,651	455	9.3	26,719	15.6
Johnson	2,388	2,302	4,481	2,179	376	4.9	5,744	13.5
Knox	−268	−27	312	339	−4	−6.1	−121	−2.7
Laclede	2,578	781	2,933	2,152	43	7.9	5,355	19.7
Lafayette	226	266	2,598	2,332	43	0.7	1,853	6.0
Lawrence	2,197	500	3,054	2,554	285	6.2	4,967	16.4
Lewis	−342	−3	687	690	20	−3.3	261	2.6
Lincoln	11,177	1,767	3,968	2,201	66	28.7	10,054	34.8
Linn	−889	−163	1,009	1,172	25	−6.5	−131	−0.9
Livingston	−267	−152	1,039	1,191	26	−1.8	−34	−0.2
McDonald	1,268	1,005	2,246	1,241	541	5.8	4,743	28.0
Macon	−111	−122	1,220	1,342	12	−0.7	417	2.7
Madison	309	−27	931	958	24	2.6	673	6.0
Maries	196	59	642	583	15	2.2	927	11.6
Marion	136	254	2,437	2,183	58	0.5	607	2.2
Mercer	−173	−2	272	274	−4	−4.6	34	0.9
Miller	1,425	336	1,998	1,662	13	6.0	2,864	13.8
Mississippi	343	157	1,296	1,139	13	2.6	−1,015	−7.0
Moniteau	265	367	1,300	933	24	1.8	2,529	20.6
Monroe	85	9	665	656	9	0.9	207	2.3
Montgomery	34	52	1,018	966	18	0.3	781	6.9
Morgan	1,407	−128	1,483	1,611	42	7.3	3,735	24.0
New Madrid	−1,444	59	1,568	1,509	8	−7.3	−1,170	−5.6
Newton	3,411	1,254	4,564	3,310	208	6.5	8,191	18.4
Nodaway	−252	247	1,435	1,188	158	−1.2	203	0.9
Oregon	63	−174	695	869	−1	0.6	874	9.2
Osage	436	348	1,134	786	3	3.3	1,044	8.7
Ozark	−149	−161	633	794	12	−1.6	944	11.0
Pemiscot	−884	635	2,053	1,418	57	−4.4	−1,874	−8.5
Perry	507	442	1,601	1,159	30	2.8	1,484	8.9
Pettis	1,117	1,017	3,633	2,616	498	2.8	3,966	11.2
Phelps	2,464	655	3,222	2,567	712	6.2	4,577	13.0
Pike	215	106	1,409	1,303	156	1.2	2,382	14.9
Platte	9,253	3,427	6,522	3,095	948	12.5	15,941	27.5
Polk	2,604	485	2,315	1,830	194	9.6	5,166	23.7
Pulaski	2,857	2,282	3,984	1,702	−925	6.9	−142	−0.3
Putnam	−70	−71	388	459	−4	−1.3	144	2.8
Ralls	299	37	612	575	2	3.1	1,150	13.6
Randolph	775	438	2,184	1,746	139	3.1	293	1.2
Ray	645	223	1,773	1,550	−2	2.8	1,386	6.3
Reynolds	−142	−99	411	510	−4	−2.1	28	0.4
Ripley	428	76	1,143	1,067	2	3.2	1,206	9.8
St. Charles	54,826	16,291	27,575	11,284	1,422	19.3	71,142	33.4
St. Clair	−63	−296	580	876	–	−0.7	1,195	14.1
Ste. Genevieve	406	153	1,162	1,009	4	2.3	1,805	11.3
St. Francois	6,540	308	4,636	4,328	130	11.8	6,737	13.8
St. Louis	−15,790	16,600	76,956	60,356	12,237	−1.6	22,792	2.3
Saline	−860	−76	1,797	1,873	315	−3.6	233	1.0
Schuyler	101	−50	284	334	2	2.4	−66	−1.6
Scotland	−61	12	406	394	−1	−1.2	161	3.3
Scott	646	1,128	3,607	2,479	81	1.6	1,046	2.7
Shannon	179	77	639	562	2	2.2	711	9.3
Shelby	−154	−50	529	579	2	−2.3	−143	−2.1
Stoddard	49	−52	2,263	2,315	45	0.2	810	2.8
Stone	2,724	−85	1,830	1,915	62	9.5	9,580	50.2
Sullivan	−434	75	667	592	139	−6.0	893	14.1

See footnotes at end of table.

[Includes United States, states, and 3,141 counties/county equivalents defined as of February 22, 2005. For more information on these areas, see Appendix C, Geographic Information]

County	Components of population change, April 1, 2000, to July 1, 2006						Population change, April 1, 1990, to April 1, 2000	
	Number							
		Natural increase						
	Total population change	Total	Births	Deaths	Net international migration	Percent change	Number	Percent change
MISSOURI—Con.								
Taney	4,067	806	3,511	2,705	211	10.2	14,142	55.3
Texas	563	−37	1,793	1,830	25	2.4	1,527	7.1
Vernon	1	252	1,777	1,525	30	(Z)	1,413	7.4
Warren	5,162	768	2,264	1,496	63	21.0	4,989	25.5
Washington	838	441	1,973	1,532	30	3.6	2,964	14.5
Wayne	−262	−303	948	1,251	6	−2.0	1,716	14.9
Webster	4,462	1,436	3,100	1,664	35	14.4	7,292	30.7
Worth	−196	−50	147	197	−4	−8.2	−58	−2.4
Wright	442	318	1,626	1,308	24	2.5	1,197	7.1
Independent City								
St. Louis city	−1,008	8,279	32,963	24,684	11,050	−0.3	−48,496	−12.2
MONTANA	42,437	18,037	70,509	52,472	2,092	4.7	103,130	12.9
Beaverhead	−459	8	544	536	31	−5.0	778	9.2
Big Horn	364	997	1,642	645	20	2.9	1,334	11.8
Blaine	−394	294	709	415	6	−5.6	281	4.2
Broadwater	187	−56	212	268	10	4.3	1,067	32.2
Carbon	351	7	580	573	20	3.7	1,472	18.2
Carter	−39	−59	42	101	1	−2.9	−143	−9.5
Cascade	−972	2,080	6,923	4,843	−174	−1.2	2,666	3.4
Chouteau	−553	−114	276	390	11	−9.3	518	9.5
Custer	−545	−65	816	881	32	−4.7	−1	(Z)
Daniels	−243	−82	89	171	5	−12.0	−249	−11.0
Dawson	−435	−119	562	681	3	−4.8	−446	−4.7
Deer Lodge	−529	−239	548	787	−1	−5.6	−939	−9.1
Fallon	−120	1	170	169	–	−4.2	−266	−8.6
Fergus	−397	−337	625	962	3	−3.3	−190	−1.6
Flathead	10,843	1,825	6,313	4,488	210	14.6	15,253	25.8
Gallatin[3]	13,090	3,566	5,837	2,271	567	19.3	17,347	34.4
Garfield	−35	35	106	71	−3	−2.7	−310	−19.5
Glacier	331	918	1,618	700	33	2.5	1,126	9.3
Golden Valley	108	9	73	64	−3	10.4	130	14.3
Granite	79	−25	124	149	−3	2.8	282	11.1
Hill	−270	680	1,653	973	9	−1.6	−981	−5.6
Jefferson	1,207	54	595	541	5	12.0	2,110	26.6
Judith Basin	−187	−13	97	110	−3	−8.0	47	2.1
Lake	2,099	546	2,220	1,674	53	7.9	5,466	26.0
Lewis and Clark	3,586	1,253	4,246	2,993	190	6.4	8,221	17.3
Liberty	−295	−34	94	128	−3	−13.7	−137	−6.0
Lincoln	389	−102	1,102	1,204	24	2.1	1,356	7.8
McCone	−217	−13	82	95	–	−11.0	−299	−13.1
Madison	553	−160	302	462	–	8.1	862	14.4
Meagher	36	−6	132	138	4	1.9	113	6.2
Mineral	173	14	264	250	9	4.5	569	17.2
Missoula	5,615	3,051	7,293	4,242	576	5.9	17,115	21.8
Musselshell	89	−64	291	355	−2	2.0	391	9.5
Park[3]	390	55	976	921	52	2.5	1,179	8.1
Petroleum	−19	5	24	19	−2	−3.9	−26	−5.0
Phillips	−503	−68	249	317	6	−10.9	−562	−10.9
Pondera	−392	−93	453	546	3	−6.1	−9	−0.1
Powder River	−102	−46	79	125	–	−5.5	−232	−11.1
Powell	−183	−128	334	462	−2	−2.5	560	8.5
Prairie	−125	−76	50	126	−2	−10.4	−184	−13.3
Ravalli	4,512	355	2,562	2,207	50	12.5	11,060	44.2
Richland	−372	3	615	612	7	−3.8	−1,049	−9.8
Roosevelt	−124	611	1,347	736	12	−1.2	−379	−3.4
Rosebud	−122	593	1,047	454	20	−1.3	−1,122	−10.7
Sanders	911	−77	621	698	18	8.9	1,558	18.0
Sheridan	−658	−246	142	388	12	−16.0	−627	−13.3
Silver Bow	−1,805	−357	2,348	2,705	47	−5.2	665	2.0
Stillwater	451	156	596	440	10	5.5	1,659	25.4
Sweet Grass	151	6	226	220	15	4.2	455	14.4
Teton	−330	−45	369	414	6	−5.1	174	2.8
Toole	−194	−37	306	343	6	−3.7	221	4.4
Treasure	−181	−9	28	37	−2	−21.0	−13	−1.5
Valley	−680	−103	503	606	12	−8.9	−564	−6.8
Wheatland	−300	−57	132	189	−2	−13.3	13	0.6
Wibaux	−159	−88	43	131	1	−14.9	−123	−10.3
Yellowstone	8,861	3,833	11,279	7,446	195	6.9	15,933	14.0
Yellowstone National Park[3]	(NA)	(X)	(X)	(X)	(X)	(NA)	(NA)	(NA)

See footnotes at end of table.

[Includes United States, states, and 3,141 counties/county equivalents defined as of February 22, 2005. For more information on these areas, see Appendix C, Geographic Information]

County	Components of population change, April 1, 2000, to July 1, 2006						Population change, April 1, 1990, to April 1, 2000	
	Number							
	Total population change	Natural increase			Net international migration	Percent change	Number	Percent change
		Total	Births	Deaths				
NEBRASKA	57,066	65,881	160,471	94,590	26,224	3.3	132,848	8.4
Adams	2,034	794	2,651	1,857	742	6.5	1,526	5.2
Antelope	−521	−35	447	482	−2	−7.0	−513	−6.4
Arthur	−72	5	34	29	−2	−16.2	−18	−3.9
Banner	−36	9	29	20	−2	−4.4	−33	−3.9
Blaine	−91	7	32	25	−2	−15.6	−92	−13.6
Boone	−591	−73	355	428	1	−9.4	−408	−6.1
Box Butte	−1,026	129	917	788	101	−8.4	−972	−7.4
Boyd	−253	−111	117	228	−2	−10.4	−397	−14.0
Brown	−171	−37	229	266	−2	−4.9	−132	−3.6
Buffalo	1,695	1,795	3,874	2,079	337	4.0	4,812	12.9
Burt	−450	−175	485	660	–	−5.8	−77	−1.0
Butler	−266	6	638	632	31	−3.0	260	3.0
Cass	1,629	678	2,016	1,338	29	6.7	3,016	14.1
Cedar	−796	−46	630	676	−2	−8.3	−516	−5.1
Chase	−257	−66	293	359	−2	−6.3	−313	−7.1
Cherry	−214	35	463	428	11	−3.5	−159	−2.5
Cheyenne	35	147	837	690	24	0.4	336	3.5
Clay	−475	−10	465	475	24	−6.7	−84	−1.2
Colfax	−328	539	1,164	625	563	−3.1	1,302	14.2
Cuming	−543	111	826	715	127	−5.3	86	0.9
Custer	−551	−170	784	954	–	−4.7	−477	−3.9
Dakota	334	1,506	2,438	932	986	1.6	3,511	21.0
Dawes	−594	25	646	621	20	−6.6	39	0.4
Dawson	653	1,432	2,834	1,402	1,342	2.7	4,425	22.2
Deuel	−140	−78	108	186	−2	−6.7	−139	−6.2
Dixon	−169	−3	456	459	64	−2.7	196	3.2
Dodge	11	513	3,050	2,537	227	(Z)	1,660	4.8
Douglas	28,418	27,788	50,297	22,509	10,644	6.1	47,141	11.3
Dundy	−183	−65	127	192	12	−8.0	−290	−11.2
Fillmore	−375	−180	401	581	14	−5.7	−469	−6.6
Franklin	−226	−154	192	346	1	−6.3	−364	−9.2
Frontier	−370	6	169	163	1	−11.9	−2	−0.1
Furnas	−321	−207	316	523	−2	−6.0	−229	−4.1
Gage	372	−63	1,683	1,746	26	1.6	199	0.9
Garden	−297	−125	98	223	−2	−13.0	−168	−6.8
Garfield	−112	−111	111	222	1	−5.9	−239	−11.2
Gosper	−165	−38	156	194	−2	−7.7	215	11.2
Grant	−87	6	36	30	−2	−11.6	−22	−2.9
Greeley	−260	−41	192	233	−2	−9.6	−292	−9.7
Hall	2,021	2,611	5,673	3,062	1,695	3.8	4,609	9.4
Hamilton	87	76	686	610	−2	0.9	541	6.1
Harlan	−340	−106	204	310	−2	−9.0	−24	−0.6
Hayes	−39	15	62	47	−2	−3.7	−154	−12.6
Hitchcock	−185	−67	207	274	–	−5.9	−639	−17.0
Holt	−941	−23	764	787	16	−8.1	−1,048	−8.3
Hooker	−27	−27	47	74	−2	−3.4	−10	−1.3
Howard	169	82	478	396	1	2.6	510	8.4
Jefferson	−459	−96	554	650	−2	−5.5	−426	−4.9
Johnson	195	−16	310	326	19	4.3	−185	−4.0
Kearney	−181	13	470	457	−1	−2.6	253	3.8
Keith	−625	−15	570	585	30	−7.0	291	3.4
Keya Paha	−91	35	81	46	−2	−9.3	−46	−4.5
Kimball	−379	−108	244	352	4	−9.3	−19	−0.5
Knox	−562	−214	625	839	1	−6.0	−190	−2.0
Lancaster	16,844	14,093	24,721	10,628	6,483	6.7	36,650	17.2
Lincoln	1,233	861	2,981	2,120	128	3.6	2,124	6.5
Logan	−25	−1	65	66	−2	−3.2	−104	−11.8
Loup	−56	−12	35	47	−2	−7.9	29	4.2
McPherson	−36	19	31	12	−2	−6.8	−13	−2.4
Madison	53	1,460	3,611	2,151	525	0.2	2,571	7.9
Merrick	−250	30	556	526	10	−3.0	142	1.8
Morrill	−269	−1	362	363	9	−4.9	17	0.3
Nance	−333	−76	281	357	−2	−8.2	−237	−5.5
Nemaha	−329	−10	491	501	−2	−4.3	−404	−5.1
Nuckolls	−407	−149	340	489	18	−8.0	−729	−12.6
Otoe	351	71	1,147	1,076	19	2.3	1,144	8.0
Pawnee	−283	−123	161	284	−2	−9.2	−230	−6.9
Perkins	−208	−35	229	264	−2	−6.5	−167	−5.0
Phelps	−305	−13	719	732	4	−3.1	32	0.3
Pierce	−293	−14	550	564	4	−3.7	30	0.4

See footnotes at end of table.

[Includes United States, states, and 3,141 counties/county equivalents defined as of February 22, 2005. For more information on these areas, see Appendix C, Geographic Information]

County	Components of population change, April 1, 2000, to July 1, 2006						Population change, April 1, 1990, to April 1, 2000	
	Number							
	Total population change	Natural increase			Net international migration	Percent change	Number	Percent change
		Total	Births	Deaths				
NEBRASKA—Con.								
Platte	394	1,346	2,843	1,497	416	1.2	1,748	5.9
Polk	−290	11	401	390	10	−5.1	−16	−0.3
Red Willow	−585	71	882	811	28	−5.1	−255	−2.2
Richardson	−875	−378	565	943	1	−9.2	−406	−4.1
Rock	−212	−55	86	141	−2	−12.1	−263	−13.0
Saline	312	166	1,150	984	401	2.3	1,128	8.9
Sarpy	20,042	10,656	14,427	3,771	198	16.3	20,012	19.5
Saunders	514	368	1,498	1,130	71	2.6	1,545	8.4
Scotts Bluff	−405	640	3,355	2,715	394	−1.1	926	2.6
Seward	339	185	1,206	1,021	84	2.1	1,046	6.8
Sheridan	−627	−30	451	481	−2	−10.1	−552	−8.2
Sherman	−235	−67	213	280	−2	−7.1	−400	−10.8
Sioux	−72	4	58	54	−2	−4.9	−74	−4.8
Stanton	115	219	536	317	40	1.8	211	3.4
Thayer	−738	−262	316	578	−2	−12.2	−580	−8.7
Thomas	−100	−5	38	43	−2	−13.7	−122	−14.3
Thurston	102	513	976	463	39	1.4	235	3.4
Valley	−274	−98	281	379	−2	−5.9	−522	−10.1
Washington	1,264	369	1,393	1,024	129	6.7	2,173	13.1
Wayne	−655	188	592	404	67	−6.6	487	5.2
Webster	−360	−163	212	375	3	−8.9	−218	−5.1
Wheeler	−63	7	55	48	−2	−7.1	−62	−6.5
York	−96	193	1,086	893	120	−0.7	170	1.2
NEVADA	497,272	103,155	210,950	107,795	80,482	24.9	796,582	66.3
Churchill	1,054	1,174	2,545	1,371	133	4.4	6,044	33.7
Clark	401,801	82,373	155,344	72,971	64,365	29.2	634,370	85.6
Douglas	4,650	277	2,340	2,063	306	11.3	13,622	49.3
Elko	1,823	2,458	3,951	1,493	990	4.0	11,828	35.3
Esmeralda	−181	−27	36	63	7	−18.6	−373	−27.8
Eureka	−171	−2	95	97	45	−10.4	104	6.7
Humboldt	1,340	726	1,391	665	350	8.3	3,262	25.4
Lander	−522	196	446	250	38	−9.0	−472	−7.5
Lincoln	573	13	275	262	12	13.8	390	10.3
Lyon	16,730	562	3,063	2,501	358	48.5	14,500	72.5
Mineral	−203	−229	280	509	20	−4.0	−1,404	−21.7
Nye	10,181	−979	2,040	3,019	329	31.3	14,731	82.8
Pershing	−279	116	402	286	61	−4.2	2,357	54.4
Storey	733	−15	91	106	14	21.6	873	34.6
Washoe	56,942	16,080	33,624	17,544	12,076	16.8	84,819	33.3
White Pine	−31	−122	466	588	31	−0.3	−83	−0.9
Independent City								
Carson City	2,832	554	4,561	4,007	1,347	5.4	12,014	29.7
NEW HAMPSHIRE	79,109	28,491	90,680	62,189	13,718	6.4	126,534	11.4
Belknap	5,237	102	3,645	3,543	283	9.3	7,109	14.4
Carroll	3,809	−314	2,477	2,791	167	8.7	8,256	23.3
Cheshire	3,568	650	4,794	4,144	267	4.8	3,704	5.3
Coos	−92	−826	1,816	2,642	76	−0.3	−1,717	−4.9
Grafton	3,593	675	5,028	4,353	843	4.4	6,814	9.1
Hillsborough	21,946	13,876	31,225	17,349	8,326	5.8	45,005	13.4
Merrimack	11,860	2,194	9,628	7,434	1,015	8.7	15,985	13.3
Rockingham	18,910	8,468	20,486	12,018	1,649	6.8	31,512	12.8
Strafford	7,757	3,311	8,687	5,376	947	6.9	8,000	7.7
Sullivan	2,521	355	2,894	2,539	145	6.2	1,866	4.8
NEW JERSEY	310,213	254,766	705,812	451,046	357,111	3.7	666,597	8.6
Atlantic	19,068	4,698	21,497	16,799	8,409	7.6	28,225	12.6
Bergen	19,919	18,484	64,109	45,625	48,305	2.3	58,738	7.1
Burlington	27,236	9,997	32,780	22,783	3,960	6.4	28,325	7.2
Camden	9,094	12,707	42,092	29,385	7,245	1.8	5,083	1.0
Cape May	−4,602	−2,062	5,922	7,984	294	−4.5	7,237	7.6
Cumberland	8,385	3,834	13,278	9,444	3,142	5.7	8,385	6.1
Essex	−6,158	32,124	74,481	42,357	41,154	−0.8	14,341	1.8
Gloucester	26,333	4,825	19,242	14,417	1,051	10.3	25,616	11.1
Hudson	−7,829	26,276	53,847	27,571	60,520	−1.3	55,876	10.1
Hunterdon	8,794	3,749	8,636	4,887	1,514	7.2	14,137	13.1
Mercer	16,844	11,022	28,337	17,315	14,901	4.8	25,002	7.7
Middlesex	36,809	31,055	65,342	34,287	53,840	4.9	78,450	11.7
Monmouth	19,984	15,034	48,043	33,009	13,194	3.2	62,109	11.2
Morris	22,948	17,795	38,738	20,943	18,500	4.9	48,882	11.6
Ocean	51,419	1,612	44,593	42,981	4,606	10.1	77,713	17.9

See footnotes at end of table.

[Includes United States, states, and 3,141 counties/county equivalents defined as of February 22, 2005. For more information on these areas, see Appendix C, Geographic Information]

County	Components of population change, April 1, 2000, to July 1, 2006						Population change, April 1, 1990, to April 1, 2000	
	Number							
	Total population change	Natural increase			Net international migration	Percent change	Number	Percent change
		Total	Births	Deaths				
NEW JERSEY—Con.								
Passaic	6,716	22,680	47,729	25,049	29,390	1.4	19,505	4.1
Salem	2,310	421	4,697	4,276	444	3.6	−1,009	−1.5
Somerset	26,696	14,276	27,005	12,729	14,608	9.0	57,268	23.8
Sussex	9,214	4,067	10,370	6,303	998	6.4	13,234	10.1
Union	8,547	19,428	46,891	27,463	29,656	1.6	28,722	5.8
Warren	8,486	2,744	8,183	5,439	1,380	8.3	10,758	11.7
NEW MEXICO	135,553	85,062	174,378	89,316	32,967	7.5	303,977	20.1
Bernalillo	59,097	27,239	54,947	27,708	11,807	10.6	75,425	15.7
Catron	−67	−76	151	227	−	−1.9	980	38.2
Chaves	1,092	2,072	5,910	3,838	1,085	1.8	3,533	6.1
Cibola	1,886	1,310	2,596	1,286	86	7.4	1,801	7.6
Colfax	−675	86	995	909	38	−4.8	1,264	9.8
Curry	469	3,135	5,436	2,301	320	1.0	2,837	6.7
De Baca	−249	−34	124	158	−2	−11.1	−12	−0.5
Dona Ana	19,206	12,568	19,886	7,318	5,299	11.0	39,172	28.9
Eddy	157	1,247	4,599	3,352	269	0.3	3,053	6.3
Grant	−1,210	348	2,322	1,974	81	−3.9	3,326	12.0
Guadalupe	−315	33	345	312	44	−6.7	524	12.6
Harding	−92	−34	23	57	−2	−11.4	−177	−17.9
Hidalgo	−845	103	421	318	109	−14.2	−26	−0.4
Lea	1,801	2,797	5,736	2,939	639	3.2	−254	−0.5
Lincoln	1,812	392	1,392	1,000	232	9.3	7,192	58.9
Los Alamos	679	530	1,211	681	404	3.7	228	1.3
Luna	2,189	1,028	2,559	1,531	1,073	8.8	6,906	38.1
McKinley	−2,923	5,542	8,492	2,950	312	−3.9	14,112	23.3
Mora	−29	10	296	286	8	−0.6	916	21.5
Otero	446	2,327	5,363	3,036	2,125	0.7	10,370	20.0
Quay	−1,000	−109	690	799	77	−9.8	−668	−6.2
Rio Arriba	−242	2,169	4,241	2,072	587	−0.6	6,826	19.9
Roosevelt	273	1,027	1,927	900	113	1.5	1,316	7.9
Sandoval	23,188	4,073	7,985	3,912	486	25.6	27,265	43.1
San Juan	12,672	7,594	12,439	4,845	865	11.1	22,196	24.2
San Miguel	−801	725	2,338	1,613	255	−2.7	4,383	17.0
Santa Fe	13,120	4,886	10,017	5,131	4,790	10.1	30,359	30.7
Sierra	−601	−623	692	1,315	151	−4.5	3,358	33.9
Socorro	162	685	1,545	860	332	0.9	3,314	22.4
Taos	1,853	829	2,286	1,457	397	6.2	6,861	29.7
Torrance	636	449	1,181	732	121	3.8	6,630	64.5
Union	−373	−44	270	314	39	−8.9	50	1.2
Valencia	4,237	2,778	5,963	3,185	827	6.4	20,917	46.2
NEW YORK	329,362	601,779	1,576,125	974,346	820,388	1.7	986,043	5.5
Albany	2,986	1,963	19,780	17,817	4,402	1.0	1,758	0.6
Allegany	340	406	3,390	2,984	297	0.7	−543	−1.1
Bronx	28,823	78,303	140,902	62,599	85,005	2.2	128,861	10.7
Broome	−4,267	−277	12,962	13,239	2,486	−2.1	−11,624	−5.5
Cattaraugus	−2,421	720	6,100	5,380	111	−2.9	−279	−0.3
Cayuga	−720	843	5,368	4,525	220	−0.9	−350	−0.4
Chautauqua	−4,393	20	9,334	9,314	437	−3.1	−2,145	−1.5
Chemung	−2,429	741	6,519	5,778	347	−2.7	−4,125	−4.3
Chenango	386	−26	3,405	3,431	61	0.8	−367	−0.7
Clinton	2,272	735	4,771	4,036	467	2.8	−6,075	−7.1
Columbia	−139	−656	3,763	4,419	396	−0.2	112	0.2
Cortland	−115	596	3,312	2,716	220	−0.2	−365	−0.7
Delaware	−1,080	−674	2,703	3,377	103	−2.2	705	1.5
Dutchess	14,996	6,005	20,147	14,142	4,835	5.4	20,688	8.0
Erie	−28,875	3,533	65,809	62,276	8,526	−3.0	−18,319	−1.9
Essex	−202	−347	2,271	2,618	122	−0.5	1,699	4.6
Franklin	−166	305	3,046	2,741	128	−0.3	4,594	9.9
Fulton	362	−66	3,634	3,700	201	0.7	882	1.6
Genesee	−1,540	518	4,063	3,545	213	−2.6	310	0.5
Greene	1,627	−624	2,759	3,383	210	3.4	3,456	7.7
Hamilton	−217	−145	266	411	−	−4.0	100	1.9
Herkimer	−1,105	−250	4,305	4,555	114	−1.7	−1,372	−2.1
Jefferson	2,526	4,347	9,949	5,602	−599	2.3	795	0.7
Kings	43,295	136,168	248,737	112,569	197,175	1.8	164,861	7.2
Lewis	−259	511	1,908	1,397	−5	−1.0	148	0.6
Livingston	−155	920	3,988	3,068	192	−0.2	1,956	3.1
Madison	756	872	4,565	3,693	316	1.1	275	0.4
Monroe	−4,536	15,610	55,220	39,610	12,424	−0.6	21,375	3.0
Montgomery	−596	−252	3,714	3,966	112	−1.2	−2,273	−4.4
Nassau	−8,877	30,672	100,181	69,509	32,518	−0.7	46,666	3.6

See footnotes at end of table.

[Includes United States, states, and 3,141 counties/county equivalents defined as of February 22, 2005. For more information on these areas, see Appendix C, Geographic Information]

County	Components of population change, April 1, 2000, to July 1, 2006						Population change, April 1, 1990, to April 1, 2000	
	Number							
	Total population change	Natural increase			Net international migration	Percent change	Number	Percent change
		Total	Births	Deaths				
NEW YORK—Con.								
New York	74,209	57,481	127,349	69,868	111,695	4.8	49,836	3.4
Niagara	−3,714	286	14,922	14,636	1,079	−1.7	−912	−0.4
Oneida	−1,505	−43	15,928	15,971	5,124	−0.6	−15,377	−6.1
Onondaga	−1,559	10,052	35,435	25,383	6,843	−0.3	−10,637	−2.3
Ontario	4,129	1,093	6,956	5,863	453	4.1	5,123	5.4
Orange	35,025	16,283	32,121	15,838	4,863	10.3	33,796	11.0
Orleans	−960	547	2,947	2,400	175	−2.2	2,327	5.6
Oswego	700	2,122	8,673	6,551	247	0.6	592	0.5
Otsego	907	−296	3,443	3,739	117	1.5	1,286	2.1
Putnam	4,760	3,553	7,325	3,772	1,544	5.0	11,902	14.2
Queens	25,774	94,770	192,602	97,832	223,529	1.2	277,803	14.2
Rensselaer	2,754	1,574	10,810	9,236	1,725	1.8	−1,891	−1.2
Richmond	33,649	14,071	36,571	22,500	12,944	7.6	64,751	17.1
Rockland	8,212	16,023	28,862	12,839	10,222	2.9	21,278	8.0
St. Lawrence	−635	1,014	7,623	6,609	736	−0.6	−55	(Z)
Saratoga	14,838	5,846	15,194	9,348	867	7.4	19,359	10.7
Schenectady	3,890	1,354	11,144	9,790	1,602	2.7	−2,735	−1.8
Schoharie	614	−7	1,857	1,864	43	1.9	−258	−0.8
Schuyler	191	93	1,230	1,137	11	1.0	562	3.0
Seneca	1,382	212	2,241	2,029	183	4.1	−341	−1.0
Steuben	−490	630	7,103	6,473	317	−0.5	−362	−0.4
Suffolk	50,363	53,018	124,219	71,201	29,860	3.5	98,013	7.4
Sullivan	2,624	774	5,321	4,547	845	3.5	4,687	6.8
Tioga	−499	1,101	3,691	2,590	131	−1.0	−553	−1.1
Tompkins	3,905	1,916	5,586	3,670	5,302	4.0	2,405	2.6
Ulster	4,993	1,450	11,316	9,866	1,492	2.8	12,369	7.5
Warren	2,784	272	3,991	3,719	238	4.4	4,094	6.9
Washington	2,326	243	3,954	3,711	133	3.8	1,712	2.9
Wayne	−876	1,884	7,001	5,117	227	−0.9	4,642	5.2
Westchester	25,994	33,235	79,304	46,069	46,650	2.8	48,495	5.5
Wyoming	−811	406	2,698	2,292	75	−1.9	917	2.2
Yates	111	351	1,837	1,486	82	0.5	1,811	7.9
NORTH CAROLINA	810,014	293,761	749,959	456,198	180,986	10.1	1,414,043	21.3
Alamance	11,867	3,196	11,466	8,270	4,416	9.1	22,581	20.9
Alexander	2,568	723	2,578	1,855	290	7.6	6,065	22.0
Alleghany	232	−236	620	856	313	2.2	1,090	11.4
Anson	197	233	1,984	1,751	53	0.8	1,801	7.7
Ashe	1,115	−215	1,619	1,834	201	4.6	2,175	9.8
Avery	507	−170	1,040	1,210	156	3.0	2,300	15.5
Beaufort	1,397	522	3,877	3,355	450	3.1	2,675	6.3
Bertie	−663	−64	1,535	1,599	13	−3.4	−631	−3.1
Bladen	642	367	2,916	2,549	381	2.0	3,616	12.6
Brunswick	21,804	605	5,557	4,952	732	29.8	22,156	43.5
Buncombe	15,875	2,319	16,082	13,763	3,154	7.7	31,942	18.3
Burke	909	1,099	6,511	5,412	1,414	1.0	13,405	17.7
Cabarrus	25,365	6,618	14,058	7,440	2,763	19.4	32,095	32.4
Caldwell	2,453	1,299	6,030	4,731	651	3.2	6,679	9.4
Camden	2,386	187	595	408	−14	34.7	981	16.6
Carteret	4,201	−544	3,866	4,410	143	7.1	6,976	13.3
Caswell	45	−106	1,487	1,593	136	0.2	2,839	13.7
Catawba	12,107	4,416	12,751	8,335	4,184	8.5	23,265	19.6
Chatham	10,718	1,321	4,393	3,072	2,535	21.7	10,355	26.6
Cherokee	2,011	−332	1,669	2,001	45	8.3	4,128	20.5
Chowan	545	−34	1,143	1,177	27	3.9	644	4.8
Clay	1,233	−205	524	729	9	14.1	1,620	22.6
Cleveland	2,089	1,284	7,703	6,419	546	2.2	11,326	13.3
Columbus	−112	822	4,838	4,016	185	−0.2	5,162	10.4
Craven	3,352	4,431	9,946	5,515	−303	3.7	9,711	11.9
Cumberland	−3,902	20,888	33,623	12,735	−2,487	−1.3	28,249	10.3
Currituck	5,580	447	1,518	1,071	−4	30.7	4,454	32.4
Dare	3,968	977	2,648	1,671	239	13.2	7,221	31.7
Davidson	8,967	3,124	11,968	8,844	2,611	6.1	20,581	16.2
Davie	5,200	554	2,724	2,170	485	14.9	6,976	25.0
Duplin	3,727	1,805	4,992	3,187	2,942	7.6	9,068	22.7
Durham	23,590	13,713	24,281	10,568	13,769	10.6	41,462	22.8
Edgecombe	−1,642	1,130	4,895	3,765	588	−3.0	−1,086	−1.9
Forsyth	26,311	11,485	28,971	17,486	9,448	8.6	40,189	15.1
Franklin	8,626	1,565	4,273	2,708	935	18.3	10,846	29.8

See footnotes at end of table.

[Includes United States, states, and 3,141 counties/county equivalents defined as of February 22, 2005. For more information on these areas, see Appendix C, Geographic Information]

County	Components of population change, April 1, 2000, to July 1, 2006						Population change, April 1, 1990, to April 1, 2000	
	Number							
	Total population change	Natural increase			Net international migration	Percent change	Number	Percent change
		Total	Births	Deaths				
NORTH CAROLINA—Con.								
Gaston	9,087	3,873	16,203	12,330	3,577	4.8	15,541	8.9
Gates	1,011	−39	717	756	43	9.6	1,211	13.0
Graham	2	−26	607	633	36	(Z)	797	11.1
Granville	5,975	1,029	3,846	2,817	1,074	12.3	10,157	26.5
Greene	1,183	435	1,578	1,143	617	6.2	3,590	23.3
Guilford	30,857	14,860	37,103	22,243	13,483	7.3	73,617	21.2
Halifax	−1,849	533	4,669	4,136	190	−3.2	1,854	3.3
Harnett	15,221	4,201	9,153	4,952	1,418	16.7	23,229	34.2
Haywood	2,413	−652	3,494	4,146	227	4.5	7,086	15.1
Henderson	9,829	−359	6,919	7,278	2,165	11.0	19,457	27.9
Hertford	604	−46	1,846	1,892	144	2.6	660	3.0
Hoke	8,657	2,749	4,382	1,633	735	25.7	10,790	47.2
Hyde	−485	−56	375	431	22	−8.3	415	7.7
Iredell	23,542	4,253	11,347	7,094	2,165	19.2	29,459	31.6
Jackson	2,442	274	2,242	1,968	126	7.4	6,285	23.4
Johnston	30,243	7,428	13,873	6,445	3,521	24.8	40,594	49.9
Jones	−194	−138	569	707	56	−1.9	1,037	11.1
Lee	7,736	2,142	5,195	3,053	2,083	15.7	7,802	18.9
Lenoir	−1,957	580	4,972	4,392	518	−3.3	2,345	4.1
Lincoln	8,114	1,739	5,487	3,748	1,832	12.7	13,461	26.8
McDowell	1,263	457	3,238	2,781	496	3.0	6,470	18.1
Macon	2,589	−483	2,049	2,532	223	8.7	6,302	26.8
Madison	720	35	1,398	1,363	79	3.7	2,682	15.8
Martin	−1,204	−89	1,959	2,048	151	−4.7	468	1.9
Mecklenburg	132,018	49,849	79,326	29,477	30,199	19.0	184,216	36.0
Mitchell	−6	−214	1,026	1,240	111	(Z)	1,254	8.7
Montgomery	802	651	2,455	1,804	1,015	3.0	3,477	14.9
Moore	8,392	−22	5,814	5,836	1,132	11.2	15,770	26.7
Nash	4,927	2,017	7,736	5,719	789	5.6	10,708	14.0
New Hanover	22,264	4,188	13,265	9,077	1,646	13.9	40,043	33.3
Northampton	−839	−335	1,505	1,840	45	−3.8	1,082	5.2
Onslow	318	15,459	20,492	5,033	−4,181	0.2	517	0.3
Orange	4,563	3,910	8,290	4,380	5,113	3.9	21,875	23.4
Pamlico	−149	−229	693	922	50	−1.2	1,566	13.8
Pasquotank	4,694	800	3,109	2,309	138	13.5	3,599	11.5
Pender	7,548	646	3,043	2,397	602	18.4	12,227	42.4
Perquimans	969	−157	751	908	4	8.5	921	8.8
Person	1,718	500	2,858	2,358	134	4.8	5,443	18.0
Pitt	11,900	6,186	12,857	6,671	2,052	8.9	25,239	23.3
Polk	902	−665	1,071	1,736	212	4.9	3,866	26.7
Randolph	9,940	4,415	11,480	7,065	4,267	7.6	23,924	22.5
Richmond	4	654	3,937	3,283	388	(Z)	2,040	4.6
Robeson	5,780	5,514	12,902	7,388	3,110	4.7	18,071	17.2
Rockingham	1,135	495	6,973	6,478	1,370	1.2	5,864	6.8
Rowan	5,906	2,064	10,420	8,356	2,503	4.5	19,743	17.9
Rutherford	966	229	4,999	4,770	177	1.5	5,945	10.4
Sampson	3,401	1,608	5,615	4,007	2,222	5.7	12,863	27.2
Scotland	1,096	811	3,068	2,257	184	3.0	2,235	6.6
Stanly	1,258	1,043	4,722	3,679	622	2.2	6,335	12.2
Stokes	1,461	497	3,109	2,612	296	3.3	7,483	20.1
Surry	1,460	869	5,719	4,850	1,431	2.0	9,523	15.4
Swain	472	121	1,157	1,036	26	3.6	1,705	15.1
Transylvania	446	−631	1,667	2,298	220	1.5	3,814	14.9
Tyrrell	38	21	279	258	91	0.9	293	7.6
Union	51,534	9,404	15,096	5,692	3,700	41.6	39,528	46.9
Vance	856	1,290	4,364	3,074	731	2.0	4,062	10.4
Wake	158,657	48,804	70,615	21,811	28,962	25.3	201,554	47.3
Warren	−367	−181	1,269	1,450	126	−1.8	2,707	15.7
Washington	−496	58	1,092	1,034	60	−3.6	−274	−2.0
Watauga	7	371	2,214	1,843	391	(Z)	5,741	15.5
Wayne	518	4,164	10,933	6,769	1,257	0.5	8,663	8.3
Wilkes	1,686	1,032	5,205	4,173	1,116	2.6	6,231	10.5
Wilson	2,813	1,949	6,771	4,822	1,742	3.8	7,750	11.7
Yadkin	1,708	681	2,980	2,299	634	4.7	5,860	19.2
Yancey	647	−29	1,180	1,209	312	3.6	2,355	15.3
NORTH DAKOTA	−6,333	13,133	49,881	36,748	3,664	−1.0	3,400	0.5
Adams	−261	−140	111	251	−	−10.1	−581	−18.3
Barnes	−820	−270	709	979	45	−7.0	−770	−6.1
Benson	33	479	867	388	10	0.5	−234	−3.3
Billings	−59	18	47	29	4	−6.6	−220	−19.9
Bottineau	−499	−193	367	560	34	−7.0	−862	−10.8

See footnotes at end of table.

Table B-2. Counties — **Components of Population Change**—Con.

[Includes United States, states, and 3,141 counties/county equivalents defined as of February 22, 2005. For more information on these areas, see Appendix C, Geographic Information]

County	Components of population change, April 1, 2000, to July 1, 2006						Population change, April 1, 1990, to April 1, 2000	
	Number							
	Total population change	Natural increase			Net international migration	Percent change	Number	Percent change
		Total	Births	Deaths				
NORTH DAKOTA—Con.								
Bowman	−251	−100	181	281	—	−7.7	−354	−9.8
Burke	−295	−52	102	154	−2	−13.2	−760	−25.3
Burleigh	5,968	2,527	5,703	3,176	226	8.6	9,285	15.4
Cass	9,387	6,138	11,053	4,915	2,245	7.6	20,264	19.7
Cavalier	−732	−144	218	362	22	−15.2	−1,233	−20.3
Dickey	−359	−39	444	483	4	−6.2	−350	−5.7
Divide	−191	−143	96	239	−2	−8.4	−616	−21.2
Dunn	−157	−36	199	235	1	−4.4	−405	−10.1
Eddy	−255	−137	141	278	−2	−9.2	−194	−6.6
Emmons	−686	−141	199	340	—	−15.8	−499	−10.3
Foster	−176	−96	219	315	12	−4.7	−224	−5.6
Golden Valley	−233	−2	97	99	−2	−12.1	−184	−8.7
Grand Forks	−674	2,723	5,480	2,757	662	−1.0	−4,574	−6.5
Grant	−253	−147	110	257	4	−8.9	−708	−19.9
Griggs	−298	−161	109	270	—	−10.8	−549	−16.6
Hettinger	−151	−96	124	220	—	−5.6	−730	−21.2
Kidder	−300	−85	128	213	3	−10.9	−579	−17.4
LaMoure	−439	−91	283	374	—	−9.3	−682	−12.7
Logan	−309	−82	102	184	−2	−13.4	−539	−18.9
McHenry	−558	−68	347	415	−3	−9.3	−541	−8.3
McIntosh	−434	−249	173	422	−2	−12.8	−631	−15.7
McKenzie	−37	53	410	357	33	−0.6	−646	−10.1
McLean	−768	−302	470	772	—	−8.2	−1,146	−11.0
Mercer	−410	−34	449	483	31	−4.7	−1,164	−11.9
Morton	451	432	1,871	1,439	69	1.8	1,603	6.8
Mountrail	−187	31	623	592	2	−2.8	−392	−5.6
Nelson	−426	−246	177	423	6	−11.5	−695	−15.8
Oliver	−257	36	104	68	−2	−12.4	−316	−13.3
Pembina	−679	−85	474	559	17	−7.9	−653	−7.1
Pierce	−454	−148	271	419	4	−9.7	−377	−7.5
Ramsey	−799	−95	900	995	37	−6.6	−615	−4.8
Ransom	−195	−161	382	543	4	−3.3	−31	−0.5
Renville	−185	−55	152	207	−2	−7.1	−550	−17.4
Richland	−1,110	339	1,278	939	35	−6.2	−150	−0.8
Rolette	229	1,074	1,855	781	33	1.7	902	7.1
Sargent	−168	72	273	201	3	−3.8	−183	−4.0
Sheridan	−302	−51	45	96	−2	−17.7	−438	−20.4
Sioux	238	409	594	185	—	5.9	283	7.5
Slope	−54	14	36	22	−2	−7.0	−140	−15.4
Stark	−469	425	1,701	1,276	76	−2.1	−196	−0.9
Steele	−315	−51	89	140	—	−14.0	−162	−6.7
Stutsman	−1,147	−140	1,364	1,504	76	−5.2	−333	−1.5
Towner	−459	−138	108	246	—	−16.0	−751	−20.7
Traill	−299	−166	528	694	9	−3.5	−275	−3.1
Walsh	−1,027	−198	773	971	17	−8.3	−1,451	−10.5
Ward	−3,527	2,820	5,753	2,933	−93	−6.0	876	1.5
Wells	−670	−213	226	439	4	−13.1	−762	−13.0
Williams	−305	98	1,366	1,268	52	−1.5	−1,368	−6.5
OHIO	124,861	263,004	938,169	675,165	92,101	1.1	506,030	4.7
Adams	1,186	535	2,381	1,846	19	4.3	1,959	7.7
Allen	−2,685	2,620	9,268	6,648	227	−2.5	−1,282	−1.2
Ashland	2,204	1,341	4,326	2,985	151	4.2	5,016	10.6
Ashtabula	−25	1,021	7,889	6,868	277	(Z)	2,848	2.9
Athens	−363	1,124	3,954	2,830	1,248	−0.6	2,674	4.5
Auglaize	449	1,006	3,736	2,730	138	1.0	2,026	4.5
Belmont	−1,455	−1,388	4,382	5,770	77	−2.1	−848	−1.2
Brown	2,138	1,054	3,559	2,505	46	5.1	7,319	20.9
Butler	22,394	12,895	29,827	16,932	2,434	6.7	41,119	14.1
Carroll	353	365	1,987	1,622	10	1.2	2,315	8.7
Champaign	1,031	783	3,134	2,351	30	2.7	2,871	8.0
Clark	−2,869	1,054	11,247	10,193	188	−2.0	−2,797	−1.9
Clermont	15,256	8,844	17,098	8,254	756	8.6	27,356	18.2
Clinton	2,879	1,264	3,656	2,392	254	7.1	5,076	14.3
Columbiana	−1,533	96	7,715	7,619	203	−1.4	3,799	3.5
Coshocton	321	602	3,021	2,419	152	0.9	1,228	3.5
Crawford	−1,919	450	3,544	3,094	24	−4.1	−904	−1.9
Cuyahoga	−79,604	15,625	109,309	93,684	19,032	−5.7	−18,295	−1.3
Darke	−529	744	4,249	3,505	25	−1.0	−308	−0.6
Defiance	−409	1,095	3,180	2,085	104	−1.0	150	0.4

See footnotes at end of table.

Table B-2. Counties — **Components of Population Change**—Con.

[Includes United States, states, and 3,141 counties/county equivalents defined as of February 22, 2005. For more information on these areas, see Appendix C, Geographic Information]

County	Components of population change, April 1, 2000, to July 1, 2006						Population change, April 1, 1990, to April 1, 2000	
	Number					Percent change	Number	Percent change
	Total population change	Natural increase			Net international migration			
		Total	Births	Deaths				
OHIO—Con.								
Delaware	46,708	9,239	13,525	4,286	445	42.5	43,060	64.3
Erie	-1,435	562	5,683	5,121	158	-1.8	2,770	3.6
Fairfield	17,710	3,913	10,551	6,638	115	14.4	19,413	18.8
Fayette	-128	269	2,338	2,069	62	-0.5	967	3.5
Franklin	26,793	56,081	107,995	51,914	28,840	2.5	107,432	11.2
Fulton	816	1,018	3,282	2,264	64	1.9	3,586	9.3
Gallia	244	367	2,466	2,099	16	0.8	115	0.4
Geauga	4,781	2,698	6,930	4,232	184	5.3	9,808	12.1
Greene	4,412	3,455	10,837	7,382	1,247	3.0	11,155	8.2
Guernsey	84	492	3,187	2,695	30	0.2	1,768	4.5
Hamilton	-22,677	21,838	72,958	51,120	10,270	-2.7	-20,955	-2.4
Hancock	2,529	1,755	5,762	4,007	553	3.5	5,759	8.8
Hardin	21	477	2,448	1,971	69	0.1	834	2.7
Harrison	-57	-327	1,053	1,380	10	-0.4	-229	-1.4
Henry	310	815	2,393	1,578	121	1.1	102	0.4
Highland	1,958	939	3,673	2,734	62	4.8	5,147	14.4
Hocking	732	581	2,269	1,688	91	2.6	2,708	10.6
Holmes	2,631	3,557	5,274	1,717	8	6.8	6,094	18.6
Huron	826	2,103	5,417	3,314	353	1.4	3,249	5.8
Jackson	902	518	2,782	2,264	155	2.8	2,411	8.0
Jefferson	-3,769	-1,554	4,539	6,093	146	-5.1	-6,404	-8.0
Knox	4,058	957	4,426	3,469	61	7.4	7,030	14.8
Lake	5,381	3,014	16,205	13,191	2,825	2.4	12,011	5.6
Lawrence	860	79	4,721	4,642	77	1.4	485	0.8
Licking	10,662	4,585	12,759	8,174	377	7.3	17,325	13.5
Logan	184	959	3,869	2,910	152	0.4	3,695	8.7
Lorain	17,329	6,926	22,926	16,000	1,353	6.1	13,538	5.0
Lucas	-9,773	12,264	40,011	27,747	3,455	-2.1	-7,307	-1.6
Madison	1,283	827	3,036	2,209	199	3.2	3,135	8.5
Mahoning	-6,529	-2,022	17,020	19,042	721	-2.5	-7,251	-2.7
Marion	-626	782	4,909	4,127	136	-0.9	1,935	3.0
Medina	18,258	5,935	12,818	6,883	695	12.1	28,741	23.5
Meigs	20	167	1,797	1,630	28	0.1	85	0.4
Mercer	379	1,179	3,515	2,336	51	0.9	1,481	3.8
Miami	3,046	1,948	7,707	5,759	401	3.1	5,684	6.1
Monroe	-574	-30	1,013	1,043	7	-3.8	-317	-2.0
Montgomery	-16,825	11,730	46,063	34,333	2,591	-3.0	-14,747	-2.6
Morgan	-76	118	1,083	965	-1	-0.5	703	5.0
Morrow	2,901	1,021	2,697	1,676	28	9.2	3,879	14.0
Muskingum	1,540	1,524	6,793	5,269	111	1.8	2,517	3.1
Noble	107	73	814	741	25	0.8	2,722	24.0
Ottawa	346	-111	2,647	2,758	39	0.8	956	2.4
Paulding	-861	433	1,486	1,053	2	-4.2	-195	-1.0
Perry	1,239	855	2,866	2,011	54	3.6	2,517	8.0
Pickaway	879	1,038	3,752	2,714	42	1.7	4,479	9.3
Pike	574	484	2,382	1,898	58	2.1	3,446	14.2
Portage	2,951	3,010	10,315	7,305	874	1.9	9,476	6.6
Preble	150	715	3,163	2,448	80	0.4	2,228	5.6
Putnam	18	1,020	2,904	1,884	27	0.1	907	2.7
Richland	-1,842	2,243	9,879	7,636	354	-1.4	2,715	2.2
Ross	2,211	1,115	5,590	4,475	149	3.0	4,015	5.8
Sandusky	-171	1,205	5,086	3,881	83	-0.3	-167	-0.3
Scioto	-2,754	342	6,300	5,958	163	-3.5	-1,132	-1.4
Seneca	-1,428	1,186	4,706	3,520	135	-2.4	-1,050	-1.8
Shelby	974	2,079	4,586	2,507	320	2.0	2,995	6.7
Stark	2,443	4,448	28,380	23,932	800	0.6	10,547	2.9
Summit	3,032	8,660	42,463	33,803	3,837	0.6	27,909	5.4
Trumbull	-7,754	551	15,650	15,099	339	-3.4	-2,679	-1.2
Tuscarawas	852	1,730	7,426	5,696	202	0.9	6,824	8.1
Union	5,793	2,161	4,030	1,869	96	14.2	8,940	28.0
Van Wert	-356	436	2,316	1,880	39	-1.2	-805	-2.6
Vinton	713	304	1,075	771	–	5.6	1,708	15.4
Warren	42,702	9,333	16,567	7,234	1,055	26.8	45,196	39.7
Washington	-1,384	112	4,309	4,197	50	-2.2	997	1.6
Wayne	2,420	4,007	9,993	5,986	623	2.2	10,069	9.9
Williams	-469	610	2,947	2,337	90	-1.2	2,232	6.0
Wood	3,122	2,852	8,582	5,730	874	2.6	7,792	6.9
Wyandot	-355	224	1,763	1,539	30	-1.5	654	2.9

See footnotes at end of table.

Table B-2. Counties — **Components of Population Change**—Con.

[Includes United States, states, and 3,141 counties/county equivalents defined as of February 22, 2005. For more information on these areas, see Appendix C, Geographic Information]

County	Components of population change, April 1, 2000, to July 1, 2006						Population change, April 1, 1990, to April 1, 2000	
	Number							
	Total population change	Natural increase			Net international migration	Percent change	Number	Percent change
		Total	Births	Deaths				
OKLAHOMA	128,558	97,602	317,771	220,169	41,665	3.7	305,078	9.7
Adair	1,279	1,016	2,417	1,401	44	6.1	2,617	14.2
Alfalfa	-432	-169	281	450	3	-7.1	-311	-4.8
Atoka	461	9	979	970	-2	3.3	1,101	8.6
Beaver	-521	63	435	372	54	-8.9	-166	-2.8
Beckham	-528	206	1,750	1,544	58	-2.7	987	5.2
Blaine	758	-73	851	924	165	6.3	506	4.4
Bryan	1,861	347	3,111	2,764	290	5.1	4,445	13.9
Caddo	-87	391	2,664	2,273	160	-0.3	600	2.0
Canadian	13,638	3,461	7,677	4,216	542	15.6	13,288	17.9
Carter	1,882	280	4,111	3,831	167	4.1	2,702	6.3
Cherokee	2,389	1,204	3,793	2,589	646	5.6	8,472	24.9
Choctaw	-8	48	1,421	1,373	6	-0.1	40	0.3
Cimarron	-341	-27	206	233	131	-10.8	-153	-4.6
Cleveland	20,578	7,709	16,285	8,576	2,812	9.9	33,763	19.4
Coal	-397	-78	447	525	10	-6.6	251	4.3
Comanche	-5,815	6,551	12,025	5,474	-1,108	-5.1	3,510	3.1
Cotton	-123	-62	490	552	3	-1.9	-37	-0.6
Craig	96	-11	1,173	1,184	9	0.6	846	6.0
Creek	1,777	1,183	5,618	4,435	56	2.6	6,454	10.6
Custer	-576	499	2,249	1,750	216	-2.2	-755	-2.8
Delaware	2,984	-4	2,786	2,790	111	8.0	9,007	32.1
Dewey	-268	-180	343	523	18	-5.7	-808	-14.6
Ellis	-163	-60	283	343	-2	-4.0	-422	-9.4
Garfield	-745	1,106	5,470	4,364	204	-1.3	1,078	1.9
Garvin	165	-129	2,227	2,356	63	0.6	605	2.3
Grady	4,976	850	3,832	2,982	60	10.9	3,767	9.0
Grant	-491	-158	264	422	12	-9.5	-545	-9.6
Greer	-197	-108	409	517	6	-3.3	-498	-7.6
Harmon	-241	-96	237	333	18	-7.3	-510	-13.4
Harper	-214	-83	259	342	6	-6.0	-501	-12.3
Haskell	363	11	1,020	1,009	25	3.1	852	7.8
Hughes	-261	-163	1,109	1,272	53	-1.8	1,140	8.8
Jackson	-2,397	1,074	2,812	1,738	96	-8.4	-325	-1.1
Jefferson	-433	-131	520	651	30	-6.4	-192	-2.7
Johnston	-77	-79	817	896	16	-0.7	481	4.8
Kay	-2,191	390	4,199	3,809	306	-4.6	24	(Z)
Kingfisher	390	167	1,138	971	136	2.8	714	5.4
Kiowa	-449	-255	795	1,050	17	-4.4	-1,120	-9.9
Latimer	-130	-78	699	777	54	-1.2	359	3.5
Le Flore	1,968	1,288	4,622	3,334	644	4.1	4,841	11.2
Lincoln	565	343	2,539	2,196	37	1.8	2,864	9.8
Logan	3,047	708	2,666	1,958	117	9.0	4,913	16.9
Love	331	70	687	617	58	3.7	1,043	13.4
McClain	3,296	789	2,461	1,672	184	11.9	4,947	21.7
McCurtain	-384	371	3,010	2,639	175	-1.1	969	2.9
McIntosh	443	-376	1,367	1,743	56	2.3	2,677	16.0
Major	-216	-139	501	640	18	-2.9	-510	-6.3
Marshall	1,374	-42	1,103	1,145	274	10.4	2,355	21.7
Mayes	1,405	629	3,302	2,673	61	3.7	5,003	15.0
Murray	322	-169	976	1,145	141	2.6	581	4.8
Muskogee	1,567	1,010	6,197	5,187	479	2.3	1,373	2.0
Noble	-259	142	905	763	3	-2.3	366	3.3
Nowata	216	-22	793	815	4	2.0	577	5.8
Okfuskee	-444	-137	901	1,038	10	-3.8	263	2.3
Oklahoma	30,818	31,994	72,021	40,027	16,107	4.7	60,837	10.1
Okmulgee	-15	443	3,442	2,999	77	(Z)	3,195	8.8
Osage	1,115	572	2,903	2,331	126	2.5	2,789	6.7
Ottawa	-168	-4	2,643	2,647	147	-0.5	2,633	8.6
Pawnee	232	74	1,265	1,191	4	1.4	1,037	6.7
Payne	5,628	1,955	5,337	3,382	2,193	8.3	6,683	10.9
Pittsburg	1,049	-113	3,240	3,353	111	2.4	3,003	7.3
Pontotoc	207	432	3,057	2,625	146	0.6	1,024	3.0
Pottawatomie	3,119	960	5,582	4,622	260	4.8	6,759	11.5
Pushmataha	-26	-187	831	1,018	9	-0.2	670	6.1
Roger Mills	-143	24	275	251	2	-4.2	-711	-17.1
Rogers	11,797	2,050	5,860	3,810	209	16.7	15,468	28.0
Seminole	-246	246	2,331	2,085	78	-1.0	-516	-2.0
Sequoyah	2,384	907	3,454	2,547	99	6.1	5,144	15.2
Stephens	61	-262	3,389	3,651	10	0.1	883	2.1
Texas	131	1,618	2,482	864	1,544	0.7	3,688	22.5

See footnotes at end of table.

[Includes United States, states, and 3,141 counties/county equivalents defined as of February 22, 2005. For more information on these areas, see Appendix C, Geographic Information]

County	Components of population change, April 1, 2000, to July 1, 2006						Population change, April 1, 1990, to April 1, 2000	
	Number							
	Total population change	Natural increase			Net international migration	Percent change	Number	Percent change
		Total	Births	Deaths				
OKLAHOMA—Con.								
Tillman.	−805	−77	706	783	99	−8.7	−1,097	−10.6
Tulsa.	14,494	25,349	58,178	32,829	11,834	2.6	59,960	11.9
Wagoner	8,822	2,208	4,829	2,621	273	15.3	9,608	20.1
Washington	245	87	3,675	3,588	483	0.5	930	1.9
Washita	75	−95	813	908	24	0.7	67	0.6
Woods.	−704	−232	549	781	17	−7.7	−14	−0.2
Woodward	745	567	1,677	1,110	61	4.0	−490	−2.6
OREGON	279,322	93,194	284,655	191,461	88,976	8.2	579,099	20.4
Baker	−498	−294	984	1,278	77	−3.0	1,424	9.3
Benton.	922	1,830	4,824	2,994	2,433	1.2	7,328	10.3
Clackamas	35,839	8,606	25,581	16,975	6,403	10.6	59,541	21.4
Clatsop	1,685	49	2,457	2,408	509	4.7	2,329	7.0
Columbia	5,603	688	3,161	2,473	84	12.9	6,003	16.0
Coos	2,032	−1,452	3,923	5,375	302	3.2	2,515	4.2
Crook	3,757	278	1,470	1,192	181	19.6	5,073	36.0
Curry.	1,221	−955	995	1,950	86	5.8	1,810	9.4
Deschutes	33,773	3,661	9,759	6,098	599	29.3	40,391	53.9
Douglas	4,718	−794	6,769	7,563	262	4.7	5,750	6.1
Gilliam.	−140	−44	112	156	1	−7.3	198	11.5
Grant.	−685	−158	422	580	20	−8.6	82	1.0
Harney.	−721	42	485	443	14	−9.5	549	7.8
Hood River.	1,122	827	1,969	1,142	857	5.5	3,508	20.8
Jackson	15,748	1,152	13,176	12,024	1,839	8.7	34,936	23.9
Jefferson	1,343	863	1,933	1,070	261	7.1	5,333	39.0
Josephine	6,012	−1,578	4,845	6,423	145	7.9	13,027	20.8
Klamath.	2,663	507	4,890	4,383	455	4.2	6,073	10.5
Lake	51	−107	420	527	59	0.7	236	3.3
Lane	14,893	3,988	22,301	18,313	5,112	4.6	40,065	14.2
Lincoln.	1,720	−688	2,750	3,438	617	3.9	5,590	14.4
Linn	8,406	2,133	8,602	6,469	675	8.2	11,856	13.0
Malheur	−368	1,228	2,969	1,741	705	−1.2	5,577	21.4
Marion	26,466	12,987	28,575	15,588	11,662	9.3	56,355	24.7
Morrow	758	549	1,055	506	373	6.9	3,370	44.2
Multnomah	20,968	22,800	58,252	35,452	28,135	3.2	76,599	13.1
Polk	10,916	1,421	4,895	3,474	1,287	17.5	12,839	25.9
Sherman	−235	−25	93	118	13	−12.2	16	0.8
Tillamook	1,118	−128	1,601	1,729	373	4.6	2,692	12.5
Umatilla.	2,380	2,873	6,699	3,826	1,366	3.4	11,299	19.1
Union	−185	322	1,816	1,494	214	−0.8	932	3.9
Wallowa	−351	−82	383	465	−2	−4.9	315	4.6
Wasco	−79	−93	1,735	1,828	256	−0.3	2,108	9.7
Washington	68,927	30,003	47,355	17,352	21,414	15.5	133,788	42.9
Wheeler.	−143	−71	54	125	4	−9.2	151	10.8
Yamhill.	9,686	2,856	7,345	4,489	2,185	11.4	19,441	29.7
PENNSYLVANIA.	159,567	95,649	902,068	806,419	126,007	1.3	398,212	3.4
Adams.	9,813	1,270	6,725	5,455	982	10.7	13,018	16.6
Allegheny.	−58,255	−9,044	84,690	93,734	13,954	−4.5	−54,783	−4.1
Armstrong	−2,296	−958	4,429	5,387	20	−3.2	−1,086	−1.5
Beaver.	−5,676	−1,967	11,226	13,193	320	−3.1	−4,681	−2.5
Bedford	−57	216	3,273	3,057	28	−0.1	2,065	4.3
Berks.	27,488	7,868	30,123	22,255	4,364	7.4	37,138	11.0
Blair	−2,650	−907	9,151	10,058	196	−2.1	−1,398	−1.1
Bradford.	−290	445	4,627	4,182	40	−0.5	1,704	2.9
Bucks	25,573	12,131	43,698	31,567	6,551	4.3	56,458	10.4
Butler	8,820	1,670	12,956	11,286	568	5.1	22,068	14.5
Cambria.	−5,631	−2,593	9,416	12,009	351	−3.7	−10,464	−6.4
Cameron	−485	−129	356	485	4	−8.1	61	1.0
Carbon	3,765	−901	3,807	4,708	100	6.4	1,999	3.5
Centre	5,195	2,444	7,866	5,422	4,550	3.8	10,946	8.8
Chester	48,611	16,533	37,179	20,646	6,815	11.2	57,112	15.2
Clarion.	−1,380	−242	2,477	2,719	74	−3.3	66	0.2
Clearfield.	−940	−657	5,073	5,730	88	−1.1	5,285	6.8
Clinton.	−678	25	2,651	2,626	107	−1.8	728	2.0
Columbia	866	−329	3,803	4,132	123	1.4	946	1.5
Crawford	−977	633	6,533	5,900	89	−1.1	4,200	4.9
Cumberland	12,443	1,464	14,208	12,744	2,079	5.8	18,417	9.4
Dauphin.	2,378	4,702	20,044	15,342	3,111	0.9	13,985	5.9
Delaware	4,022	7,086	42,400	35,314	8,394	0.7	4,316	0.8
Elk	−1,933	−244	2,089	2,333	34	−5.5	234	0.7
Erie.	−1,032	3,995	20,870	16,875	2,861	−0.4	5,268	1.9

See footnotes at end of table.

Table B-2. Counties — **Components of Population Change**—Con.

[Includes United States, states, and 3,141 counties/county equivalents defined as of February 22, 2005. For more information on these areas, see Appendix C, Geographic Information]

County	Components of population change, April 1, 2000, to July 1, 2006 — Number						Population change, April 1, 1990, to April 1, 2000	
	Total population change	Natural increase Total	Births	Deaths	Net international migration	Percent change	Number	Percent change
PENNSYLVANIA—Con.								
Fayette	−2,884	−2,011	9,182	11,193	117	−1.9	3,293	2.3
Forest	1,560	−236	227	463	–	31.5	144	3.0
Franklin	10,678	2,339	10,336	7,997	941	8.3	8,231	6.8
Fulton	522	164	1,002	838	3	3.7	424	3.1
Greene	−240	−223	2,598	2,821	59	−0.6	1,122	2.8
Huntingdon	185	144	2,838	2,694	86	0.4	1,422	3.2
Indiana	−1,371	−158	5,389	5,547	502	−1.5	−389	−0.4
Jefferson	−207	−307	3,134	3,441	40	−0.5	−151	−0.3
Juniata	691	574	1,883	1,309	37	3.0	2,196	10.6
Lackawanna	−3,567	−4,038	13,693	17,731	850	−1.7	−5,802	−2.6
Lancaster	23,851	15,142	42,359	27,217	3,591	5.1	47,813	11.3
Lawrence	−2,850	−1,303	6,121	7,424	122	−3.0	−1,601	−1.7
Lebanon	6,556	1,154	9,283	8,129	788	5.4	6,583	5.8
Lehigh	23,454	5,191	24,861	19,670	5,350	7.5	20,960	7.2
Luzerne	−6,232	−8,117	19,127	27,244	1,120	−2.0	−8,897	−2.7
Lycoming	−2,380	494	8,268	7,774	143	−2.0	1,338	1.1
McKean	−1,871	−417	2,901	3,318	37	−4.1	−1,195	−2.5
Mercer	−1,742	−778	7,848	8,626	252	−1.4	−710	−0.6
Mifflin	−429	294	3,583	3,289	24	−0.9	289	0.6
Monroe	26,998	2,270	9,657	7,387	922	19.5	43,006	44.9
Montgomery	26,701	15,222	59,760	44,538	10,402	3.6	70,794	10.4
Montour	−305	−56	1,325	1,381	36	−1.7	504	2.8
Northampton	24,237	2,520	18,725	16,205	3,452	9.1	19,959	8.1
Northumberland	−2,902	−1,518	5,980	7,498	118	−3.1	−2,215	−2.3
Perry	1,485	868	3,340	2,472	24	3.4	2,430	5.9
Philadelphia	−69,156	31,811	135,243	103,432	37,187	−4.6	−68,027	−4.3
Pike	11,893	316	2,437	2,121	112	25.7	18,270	65.2
Potter	−512	−22	1,298	1,320	15	−2.8	1,363	8.2
Schuylkill	−2,929	−4,498	8,759	13,257	157	−1.9	−2,251	−1.5
Snyder	680	834	2,861	2,027	21	1.8	866	2.4
Somerset	−1,515	−945	4,791	5,736	103	−1.9	1,805	2.3
Sullivan	−279	−325	311	636	14	−4.3	452	7.4
Susquehanna	−349	−194	2,702	2,896	14	−0.8	1,858	4.6
Tioga	−236	107	2,647	2,540	81	−0.6	247	0.6
Union	1,763	340	2,566	2,226	444	4.2	5,448	15.1
Venango	−2,077	−512	3,683	4,195	28	−3.6	−1,816	−3.1
Warren	−2,121	−292	2,674	2,966	12	−4.8	−1,187	−2.6
Washington	3,535	−2,611	12,945	15,556	382	1.7	−1,687	−0.8
Wayne	3,207	−780	2,979	3,759	62	6.7	7,778	19.5
Westmoreland	−3,553	−6,124	21,438	27,562	579	−1.0	−328	−0.1
Wyoming	13	307	1,933	1,626	26	(Z)	4	(Z)
York	34,571	8,512	29,711	21,199	1,951	9.1	42,177	12.4
RHODE ISLAND	19,291	18,543	79,147	60,604	23,086	1.8	44,855	4.5
Bristol	1,608	−196	2,914	3,110	292	3.2	1,789	3.7
Kent	2,963	715	11,339	10,624	960	1.8	5,947	3.7
Newport	−3,289	1,152	5,498	4,346	649	−3.8	−1,761	−2.0
Providence	13,994	14,809	51,544	36,735	20,359	2.3	25,332	4.2
Washington	4,015	2,063	7,852	5,789	826	3.2	13,548	12.3
SOUTH CAROLINA	309,433	115,324	349,748	234,424	40,168	7.7	525,506	15.1
Abbeville	−232	414	1,996	1,582	95	−0.9	2,305	9.7
Aiken	9,244	2,754	11,597	8,843	1,146	6.5	21,565	17.8
Allendale	−463	310	1,034	724	51	−4.1	−516	−4.4
Anderson	12,223	2,553	13,797	11,244	810	7.4	20,563	14.2
Bamberg	−980	158	1,212	1,054	55	−5.9	−244	−1.4
Barnwell	−213	602	2,111	1,509	25	−0.9	3,185	15.7
Beaufort	21,097	6,317	12,669	6,352	2,112	17.4	34,523	39.9
Berkeley	9,629	7,441	13,403	5,962	96	6.7	13,995	10.9
Calhoun	−154	40	1,071	1,031	39	−1.0	2,427	19.0
Charleston	21,939	11,909	29,185	17,276	3,657	7.1	14,819	5.0
Cherokee	1,349	665	4,392	3,727	224	2.6	8,031	18.0
Chester	−1,193	667	2,805	2,138	77	−3.5	1,898	5.9
Chesterfield	423	759	3,457	2,698	339	1.0	4,193	10.9
Clarendon	837	570	2,690	2,120	153	2.6	4,052	14.2
Colleton	1,203	800	3,264	2,464	151	3.1	3,887	11.3
Darlington	157	1,123	5,633	4,510	184	0.2	5,543	9.0
Dillon	262	969	3,143	2,174	128	0.9	1,608	5.5
Dorchester	22,638	3,871	8,459	4,588	553	23.5	13,281	16.0
Edgefield	701	372	1,682	1,310	72	2.9	6,200	33.8
Fairfield	356	190	1,969	1,779	28	1.5	1,159	5.2

See footnotes at end of table.

[Includes United States, states, and 3,141 counties/county equivalents defined as of February 22, 2005. For more information on these areas, see Appendix C, Geographic Information]

County	Components of population change, April 1, 2000, to July 1, 2006 Number — Total population change	Natural increase Total	Natural increase Births	Natural increase Deaths	Net international migration	Percent change	Population change, April 1, 1990, to April 1, 2000 Number	Percent change
SOUTH CAROLINA—Con.								
Florence	5,536	3,374	11,695	8,321	530	4.4	11,417	10.0
Georgetown	5,067	981	4,599	3,618	369	9.1	9,491	20.5
Greenville	37,534	14,133	34,702	20,569	8,816	9.9	59,505	18.6
Greenwood	1,941	1,317	5,514	4,197	1,069	2.9	6,705	11.3
Hampton	−114	387	1,739	1,352	31	−0.5	3,196	17.6
Horry	41,864	4,364	16,749	12,385	2,798	21.3	52,576	36.5
Jasper	1,138	882	1,925	1,043	684	5.5	5,184	33.5
Kershaw	4,843	1,206	4,416	3,210	105	9.2	9,048	20.8
Lancaster	2,277	1,421	5,017	3,596	427	3.7	6,835	12.5
Laurens	841	522	5,098	4,576	577	1.2	11,401	19.6
Lee	440	268	1,641	1,373	355	2.2	1,682	9.1
Lexington	24,150	8,144	19,249	11,105	2,495	11.2	48,484	28.9
McCormick	268	−215	520	735	−2	2.7	1,090	12.3
Marion	−782	800	3,130	2,330	313	−2.2	1,567	4.6
Marlboro	334	286	2,337	2,051	23	1.2	−898	−3.0
Newberry	1,758	596	3,102	2,506	809	4.9	2,832	8.5
Oconee	4,352	875	5,038	4,163	490	6.6	8,721	15.2
Orangeburg	−669	1,970	7,972	6,002	238	−0.7	6,710	7.9
Pickens	3,689	2,469	8,047	5,578	1,542	3.3	16,861	18.0
Richland	27,445	12,182	28,106	15,924	3,052	8.6	34,460	12.0
Saluda	−122	287	1,546	1,259	800	−0.6	2,740	16.7
Spartanburg	17,305	5,190	21,445	16,255	3,178	6.8	26,989	11.9
Sumter	−206	4,545	10,389	5,844	−49	−0.2	3,360	3.3
Union	−1,575	−162	2,145	2,307	21	−5.3	−456	−1.5
Williamsburg	−1,116	685	3,174	2,489	46	−3.0	406	1.1
York	34,412	6,333	14,884	8,551	1,456	20.9	33,126	25.2
SOUTH DAKOTA	27,075	24,750	68,615	43,865	4,333	3.6	58,840	8.5
Aurora	−153	−55	187	242	4	−5.0	−77	−2.5
Beadle	−1,380	−79	1,176	1,255	42	−8.1	−1,230	−6.7
Bennett	−31	224	422	198	−2	−0.9	368	11.5
Bon Homme	21	−141	345	486	9	0.3	171	2.4
Brookings	−25	820	1,998	1,178	283	−0.1	3,013	12.0
Brown	−815	601	2,841	2,240	75	−2.3	−120	−0.3
Brule	−197	60	393	333	−1	−3.7	−121	−2.2
Buffalo	77	203	323	120	–	3.8	273	15.5
Butte	280	215	792	577	12	3.1	1,180	14.9
Campbell	−288	−19	69	88	4	−16.2	−183	−9.3
Charles Mix	−126	383	1,008	625	16	−1.3	219	2.4
Clark	−460	−5	278	283	4	−11.1	−260	−5.9
Clay	−670	348	969	621	189	−4.9	351	2.7
Codington	450	872	2,283	1,411	106	1.7	3,199	14.1
Corson	112	284	539	255	−2	2.7	−19	−0.5
Custer	669	−31	416	447	6	9.2	1,096	17.7
Davison	294	466	1,719	1,253	82	1.6	1,238	7.1
Day	−489	−194	409	603	17	−7.8	−711	−10.2
Deuel	−197	2	338	336	–	−4.4	−24	−0.5
Dewey	140	582	954	372	4	2.3	449	8.1
Douglas	−290	−46	219	265	–	−8.4	−288	−7.7
Edmunds	−305	−68	286	354	2	−7.0	11	0.3
Fall River	−149	−278	427	705	–	−2.0	100	1.4
Faulk	−301	−27	154	181	−2	−11.4	−104	−3.8
Grant	−574	−160	470	630	26	−7.3	−520	−6.2
Gregory	−524	−191	257	448	–	−10.9	−567	−10.6
Haakon	−332	−42	118	160	−2	−15.1	−428	−16.3
Hamlin	76	137	583	446	–	1.4	566	11.4
Hand	−418	−107	195	302	4	−11.2	−531	−12.4
Hanson	551	239	352	113	4	17.6	145	4.8
Harding	−148	35	82	47	7	−10.9	−316	−18.9
Hughes	465	370	1,244	874	85	2.8	1,664	11.2
Hutchinson	−649	−318	504	822	2	−8.0	−187	−2.3
Hyde	−120	−29	123	152	−2	−7.2	−25	−1.5
Jackson	−30	194	375	181	−2	−1.0	119	4.2
Jerauld	−224	−60	136	196	−2	−9.8	−130	−5.4
Jones	−126	15	68	53	−2	−10.6	−131	−9.9
Kingsbury	−351	−270	338	608	3	−6.0	−110	−1.9
Lake	−106	100	771	671	18	−0.9	726	6.9
Lawrence	883	300	1,548	1,248	12	4.1	1,147	5.6
Lincoln	11,092	1,985	3,154	1,169	124	45.9	8,720	56.5
Lyman	34	267	474	207	3	0.9	257	7.1
McCook	19	63	508	445	2	0.3	144	2.5
McPherson	−339	−98	150	248	−2	−11.7	−324	−10.0
Marshall	−146	−68	272	340	−2	−3.2	−268	−5.5

See footnotes at end of table.

[Includes United States, states, and 3,141 counties/county equivalents defined as of February 22, 2005. For more information on these areas, see Appendix C, Geographic Information]

County	Components of population change, April 1, 2000, to July 1, 2006						Population change, April 1, 1990, to April 1, 2000	
	Number							
		Natural increase						
	Total population change	Total	Births	Deaths	Net international migration	Percent change	Number	Percent change
SOUTH DAKOTA—Con.								
Meade	180	1,010	2,282	1,272	−98	0.7	2,367	10.8
Mellette	16	73	227	154	−2	0.8	−54	−2.5
Miner	−331	−59	170	229	−2	−11.5	−388	−11.9
Minnehaha	15,016	8,612	15,409	6,797	2,771	10.1	24,456	19.8
Moody	49	188	553	365	31	0.7	88	1.4
Pennington	5,765	4,949	9,148	4,199	281	6.5	7,230	8.9
Perkins	−343	−59	178	237	6	−10.2	−564	−14.3
Potter	−372	−89	160	249	−2	−13.8	−497	−15.6
Roberts	13	168	938	770	3	0.1	97	1.0
Sanborn	−158	−5	171	176	−	−5.9	−158	−5.6
Shannon	1,358	1,440	2,237	797	10	10.9	2,564	25.9
Spink	−531	37	517	480	−	−7.1	−527	−6.6
Stanley	43	135	238	103	2	1.6	319	13.0
Sully	−121	56	133	77	−2	−7.8	−33	−2.1
Todd	1,038	1,136	1,620	484	19	11.5	698	8.4
Tripp	−364	−2	489	491	−1	−5.7	−494	−7.1
Turner	−309	−164	517	681	5	−3.5	273	3.2
Union	1,161	441	1,065	624	126	9.2	2,395	23.5
Walworth	−549	−139	425	564	4	−9.2	−113	−1.9
Yankton	127	340	1,601	1,261	57	0.6	2,400	12.5
Ziebach	187	203	270	67	1	7.4	299	13.5
TENNESSEE	349,541	142,266	493,881	351,615	59,385	6.1	812,059	16.7
Anderson	2,249	4	5,138	5,134	552	3.2	3,080	4.5
Bedford	5,827	1,447	3,893	2,446	1,531	15.5	7,175	23.6
Benton	−159	−356	1,033	1,389	4	−1.0	2,013	13.9
Bledsoe	666	112	815	703	10	5.4	2,695	27.9
Blount	12,363	957	8,205	7,248	577	11.7	19,861	23.1
Bradley	5,585	2,372	7,389	5,017	805	6.3	14,241	19.3
Campbell	1,054	109	3,039	2,930	180	2.6	4,715	13.4
Cannon	622	−27	880	907	39	4.8	2,359	22.5
Carroll	−390	−453	2,171	2,624	57	−1.3	1,972	7.2
Carter	2,415	−261	3,788	4,049	148	4.3	5,237	10.2
Cheatham	3,106	1,294	3,027	1,733	62	8.6	8,772	32.3
Chester	515	235	1,146	911	39	3.3	2,709	21.1
Claiborne	1,425	43	2,229	2,186	147	4.8	3,785	14.5
Clay	79	−94	587	681	31	1.0	738	10.2
Cocke	1,655	−144	2,562	2,706	48	4.9	4,424	15.2
Coffee	3,611	708	4,228	3,520	393	7.5	7,671	19.0
Crockett	−140	−96	1,120	1,216	192	−1.0	1,154	8.6
Cumberland	5,540	−223	3,204	3,427	64	11.8	12,068	34.7
Davidson	8,806	24,192	55,744	31,552	18,161	1.5	59,106	11.6
Decatur	−305	−275	762	1,037	85	−2.6	1,259	12.0
DeKalb	939	135	1,423	1,288	278	5.4	3,061	21.3
Dickson	3,427	1,378	3,983	2,605	47	7.9	8,095	23.1
Dyer	607	520	3,143	2,623	240	1.6	2,425	7.0
Fayette	7,306	627	2,553	1,926	44	25.4	3,237	12.7
Fentress	855	−41	1,277	1,318	22	5.1	1,956	13.3
Franklin	2,049	157	2,839	2,682	185	5.2	4,347	12.4
Gibson	312	−420	3,841	4,261	146	0.6	1,834	4.0
Giles	−178	−278	2,055	2,333	72	−0.6	3,706	14.4
Grainger	1,794	178	1,589	1,411	97	8.7	3,564	20.8
Greene	3,036	11	4,563	4,552	349	4.8	7,077	12.7
Grundy	167	126	1,234	1,108	1	1.2	970	7.3
Hamblen	2,898	1,300	5,220	3,920	2,109	5.0	7,648	15.2
Hamilton	4,997	4,732	24,809	20,077	3,196	1.6	22,372	7.8
Hancock	−67	−5	505	510	−2	−1.0	41	0.6
Hardeman	71	287	2,093	1,806	26	0.3	4,728	20.2
Hardin	511	−446	1,717	2,163	36	2.0	2,945	13.0
Hawkins	3,287	572	4,066	3,494	117	6.1	8,998	20.2
Haywood	−392	387	1,785	1,398	129	−2.0	360	1.9
Henderson	1,228	179	2,160	1,981	18	4.8	3,678	16.8
Henry	735	−409	2,304	2,713	80	2.4	3,214	11.5
Hickman	1,517	295	1,732	1,437	4	6.8	5,541	33.1
Houston	−12	−18	654	672	56	−0.1	1,070	15.2
Humphreys	465	58	1,409	1,351	21	2.6	2,116	13.4
Jackson	−66	−222	689	911	16	−0.6	1,687	18.1
Jefferson	5,078	405	3,272	2,867	390	11.5	11,278	34.2
Johnson	544	−265	1,008	1,273	10	3.1	3,733	27.1
Knox	29,935	8,117	30,959	22,842	3,091	7.8	46,283	13.8
Lake	−548	−192	458	650	14	−6.9	825	11.6
Lauderdale	−369	588	2,414	1,826	85	−1.4	3,610	15.4
Lawrence	1,008	825	3,622	2,797	93	2.5	4,623	13.1

See footnotes at end of table.

[Includes United States, states, and 3,141 counties/county equivalents defined as of February 22, 2005. For more information on these areas, see Appendix C, Geographic Information]

County	Components of population change, April 1, 2000, to July 1, 2006						Population change, April 1, 1990, to April 1, 2000	
	Number							
	Total population change	Natural increase			Net international migration	Percent change	Number	Percent change
		Total	Births	Deaths				
TENNESSEE—Con.								
Lewis	221	130	970	840	22	1.9	2,120	22.9
Lincoln	1,388	178	2,541	2,363	100	4.4	3,183	11.3
Loudon	5,479	278	3,115	2,837	214	14.0	7,832	25.1
McMinn	3,010	358	3,833	3,475	211	6.1	6,627	15.6
McNairy	1,057	144	2,140	1,996	74	4.3	2,243	10.0
Macon	1,340	232	1,658	1,426	225	6.6	4,480	28.2
Madison	4,057	2,847	8,349	5,502	988	4.4	13,855	17.8
Marion	166	185	2,094	1,909	47	0.6	3,093	12.5
Marshall	2,117	582	2,274	1,692	259	7.9	5,228	24.3
Maury	8,811	1,865	6,272	4,407	729	12.7	14,686	26.8
Meigs	612	99	828	729	2	5.5	3,053	38.0
Monroe	5,198	876	3,362	2,486	214	13.3	8,424	27.6
Montgomery	12,346	9,414	14,951	5,537	-517	9.2	34,270	34.1
Moore	330	40	358	318	-2	5.7	1,044	22.2
Morgan	353	167	1,365	1,198	-2	1.8	2,455	14.2
Obion	-266	237	2,606	2,369	216	-0.8	733	2.3
Overton	622	-56	1,558	1,614	-1	3.1	2,482	14.1
Perry	22	-9	590	599	12	0.3	1,019	15.4
Pickett	-90	-62	342	404	-2	-1.8	397	8.7
Polk	-111	24	1,248	1,224	32	-0.7	2,407	17.6
Putnam	5,969	1,534	5,480	3,946	1,012	9.6	10,942	21.3
Rhea	1,944	569	2,489	1,920	73	6.8	4,059	16.7
Roane	1,383	-489	3,388	3,877	156	2.7	4,683	9.9
Robertson	7,753	2,458	5,670	3,212	865	14.2	12,942	31.2
Rutherford	46,806	11,963	19,594	7,631	2,308	25.7	63,453	53.5
Scott	799	603	1,992	1,389	23	3.8	2,769	15.1
Sequatchie	1,632	272	939	667	50	14.4	2,507	28.3
Sevier	10,212	1,695	5,977	4,282	335	14.3	20,120	39.4
Shelby	13,966	40,779	89,532	48,753	11,795	1.6	71,142	8.6
Smith	1,041	140	1,358	1,218	47	5.9	3,569	25.2
Stewart	628	59	929	870	-15	5.1	2,891	30.5
Sullivan	191	-1,081	10,088	11,169	656	0.1	9,452	6.6
Sumner	18,968	4,490	11,426	6,936	1,115	14.5	27,167	26.3
Tipton	6,109	1,589	4,496	2,907	69	11.9	13,703	36.5
Trousdale	552	-15	570	585	61	7.6	1,339	22.6
Unicoi	-4	-391	1,133	1,524	–	(Z)	1,118	6.8
Union	1,278	459	1,481	1,022	–	7.2	4,114	30.0
Van Buren	-60	3	346	343	–	-1.1	662	13.7
Warren	1,740	873	3,441	2,568	774	4.5	5,284	16.0
Washington	7,118	1,027	8,294	7,267	746	6.6	14,862	16.1
Wayne	-14	-48	1,037	1,085	35	-0.1	2,907	20.9
Weakley	-1,538	-88	2,243	2,331	415	-4.4	2,923	9.1
White	1,378	-63	1,854	1,917	30	6.0	3,014	15.0
Williamson	34,143	6,901	11,399	4,498	1,584	27.0	45,617	56.3
Wilson	15,227	3,373	7,935	4,562	335	17.1	21,133	31.2
TEXAS	2,655,993	1,389,275	2,351,909	962,634	801,576	12.7	3,865,455	22.8
Anderson	1,955	406	4,174	3,768	390	3.5	7,085	14.8
Andrews	-52	636	1,307	671	94	-0.4	-1,334	-9.3
Angelina	2,394	3,078	8,017	4,939	1,140	3.0	10,246	14.7
Aransas	2,334	-171	1,600	1,771	252	10.4	4,605	25.7
Archer	412	212	656	444	4	4.7	881	11.0
Armstrong	-28	-31	139	170	-2	-1.3	127	6.3
Atascosa	5,248	2,170	4,108	1,938	234	13.6	8,095	26.5
Austin	2,817	317	2,147	1,830	402	11.9	3,758	18.9
Bailey	3	387	795	408	66	(Z)	-470	-6.7
Bandera	2,558	240	1,198	958	117	14.5	7,083	67.1
Bastrop	13,968	2,610	5,633	3,023	1,098	24.2	19,453	50.8
Baylor	-288	-142	286	428	10	-7.0	-292	-6.7
Bee	817	937	2,366	1,429	41	2.5	7,224	28.7
Bell	19,923	23,029	33,257	10,228	-143	8.4	46,901	24.5
Bexar	162,661	90,834	155,701	64,867	26,623	11.7	207,537	17.5
Blanco	832	60	660	600	80	9.9	2,446	41.0
Borden	-81	1	19	18	1	-11.1	-70	-8.8
Bosque	854	-359	1,257	1,616	193	5.0	2,079	13.7
Bowie	2,149	959	7,113	6,154	337	2.4	7,641	9.4
Brazoria	46,131	15,843	26,547	10,704	4,931	19.1	50,060	26.1
Brazos	6,587	9,598	14,414	4,816	7,652	4.3	30,557	25.1
Brewster	182	257	753	496	224	2.1	213	2.5
Briscoe	-192	15	122	107	1	-10.7	-181	-9.2
Brooks	-245	461	854	393	20	-3.1	-228	-2.8
Brown	1,296	77	3,086	3,009	171	3.4	3,303	9.6

See footnotes at end of table.

[Includes United States, states, and 3,141 counties/county equivalents defined as of February 22, 2005. For more information on these areas, see Appendix C, Geographic Information]

County	Components of population change, April 1, 2000, to July 1, 2006						Population change, April 1, 1990, to April 1, 2000	
	Number							
	Total population change	Natural increase			Net international migration	Percent change	Number	Percent change
		Total	Births	Deaths				
TEXAS—Con.								
Burleson	462	445	1,427	982	69	2.8	2,845	20.9
Burnet	8,776	573	3,050	2,477	439	25.7	11,443	50.5
Caldwell.	4,528	1,648	3,409	1,761	317	14.1	5,800	22.0
Calhoun	58	847	1,956	1,109	577	0.3	1,594	8.4
Callahan	586	−79	822	901	28	4.5	1,046	8.8
Cameron	52,490	41,456	53,869	12,413	14,508	15.7	75,107	28.9
Camp	861	322	1,194	872	463	7.5	1,645	16.6
Carson.	79	90	470	380	33	1.2	−60	−0.9
Cass.	−483	−308	2,136	2,444	52	−1.6	456	1.5
Castro	−836	435	844	409	111	−10.1	−785	−8.7
Chambers	2,748	873	2,106	1,233	356	10.6	5,943	29.6
Cherokee.	1,854	1,186	4,574	3,388	1,357	4.0	5,610	13.7
Childress	29	21	516	495	73	0.4	1,735	29.1
Clay	98	−35	594	629	7	0.9	982	9.8
Cochran.	−516	112	362	250	43	−13.8	−647	−14.8
Coke.	−241	−145	194	339	4	−6.2	440	12.9
Coleman	−474	−269	658	927	40	−5.1	−475	−4.9
Collin.	207,079	48,522	61,779	13,257	22,805	42.1	227,736	86.3
Collingsworth	−276	−66	232	298	25	−8.6	−367	−10.3
Colorado	434	10	1,619	1,609	477	2.1	2,007	10.9
Comal	23,160	2,504	7,129	4,625	687	29.7	26,189	50.5
Comanche	−189	−49	1,092	1,141	213	−1.3	645	4.8
Concho	−312	−19	182	201	−2	−7.9	922	30.3
Cooke	2,583	875	3,308	2,433	824	7.1	5,586	18.1
Coryell.	−2,311	3,465	5,630	2,165	−1,598	−3.1	10,752	16.7
Cottle	−225	3	125	122	4	−11.8	−343	−15.3
Crane	−151	89	343	254	106	−3.8	−656	−14.1
Crockett.	−220	101	333	232	16	−5.4	21	0.5
Crosby	−523	208	702	494	21	−7.4	−232	−3.2
Culberson.	−450	96	239	143	12	−15.1	−432	−12.7
Dallam.	−81	322	638	316	74	−1.3	763	14.0
Dallas.	126,972	179,897	267,481	87,584	180,158	5.7	366,152	19.8
Dawson	−811	297	1,218	921	169	−5.4	636	4.4
Deaf Smith	62	1,266	2,228	962	375	0.3	−592	−3.1
Delta	234	−60	360	420	−	4.4	470	9.7
Denton	151,272	40,525	52,632	12,107	12,903	34.9	159,322	58.2
DeWitt.	157	−108	1,426	1,534	112	0.8	1,170	6.2
Dickens	−166	−76	155	231	7	−6.0	191	7.4
Dimmit.	137	639	1,133	494	14	1.3	−185	−1.8
Donley.	20	−103	217	320	10	0.5	132	3.6
Duval.	−683	511	1,278	767	25	−5.2	202	1.6
Eastland	−4	−482	1,376	1,858	216	(Z)	−191	−1.0
Ector.	6,339	7,473	14,152	6,679	1,416	5.2	2,189	1.8
Edwards.	−227	37	147	110	−2	−10.5	−104	−4.6
Ellis.	27,942	6,220	12,020	5,800	2,548	25.1	26,191	30.8
El Paso	56,688	63,257	89,424	26,167	29,630	8.3	88,012	14.9
Erath.	1,288	616	2,687	2,071	612	3.9	5,010	17.9
Falls.	−1,029	−118	1,282	1,400	153	−5.5	864	4.9
Fannin	2,095	−309	2,356	2,665	197	6.7	6,438	26.0
Fayette	717	−463	1,580	2,043	318	3.3	1,709	8.5
Fisher	−317	−159	210	369	27	−7.3	−498	−10.3
Floyd.	−718	208	714	506	28	−9.2	−726	−8.5
Foard	−103	−	91	91	−2	−6.4	−172	−9.6
Fort Bend	138,716	26,304	36,382	10,078	12,755	39.1	129,050	57.2
Franklin	909	67	706	639	141	9.6	1,656	21.2
Freestone.	936	−41	1,353	1,394	164	5.2	2,049	13.0
Frio.	84	839	1,597	758	80	0.5	2,780	20.6
Gaines.	541	1,159	1,788	629	424	3.7	344	2.4
Galveston.	33,393	10,105	24,383	14,278	5,472	13.3	32,762	15.1
Garza	5	92	424	332	4	0.1	−271	−5.3
Gillespie.	2,713	−291	1,478	1,769	249	13.0	3,610	21.0
Glasscock	−158	50	79	29	40	−11.2	−41	−2.8
Goliad	264	2	475	473	13	3.8	948	15.9
Gonzales	938	824	2,105	1,281	442	5.0	1,423	8.3
Gray	−825	−3	1,718	1,721	315	−3.6	−1,223	−5.1
Grayson.	7,883	2,269	10,027	7,758	1,548	7.1	15,576	16.4
Gregg.	5,711	4,083	11,621	7,538	1,823	5.1	6,431	6.1
Grimes.	1,995	570	2,081	1,511	192	8.5	4,714	25.0
Guadalupe	19,374	3,763	7,893	4,130	1,138	21.8	24,163	37.2
Hale	−285	2,019	3,953	1,934	593	−0.8	1,931	5.6

See footnotes at end of table.

[Includes United States, states, and 3,141 counties/county equivalents defined as of February 22, 2005. For more information on these areas, see Appendix C, Geographic Information]

County	Components of population change, April 1, 2000, to July 1, 2006						Population change, April 1, 1990, to April 1, 2000	
	Number							
	Total population change	Natural increase			Net international migration	Percent change	Number	Percent change
		Total	Births	Deaths				
TEXAS—Con.								
Hall	−114	−55	315	370	70	−3.0	−123	−3.1
Hamilton	−43	−334	537	871	35	−0.5	496	6.4
Hansford	−132	228	612	384	278	−2.5	−479	−8.2
Hardeman	−474	−1	347	348	21	−10.0	−559	−10.6
Hardin	3,410	1,088	4,154	3,066	72	7.1	6,753	16.3
Harris	485,653	285,154	413,741	128,587	225,869	14.3	582,453	20.7
Harrison	1,709	1,342	5,139	3,797	657	2.8	4,627	8.0
Hartley	−200	200	463	263	24	−3.6	1,901	52.3
Haskell	−655	−192	408	600	28	−10.8	−727	−10.7
Hays	32,749	6,669	10,167	3,498	1,318	33.6	31,962	48.7
Hemphill	61	78	289	211	10	1.8	−369	−9.9
Henderson	6,945	227	5,933	5,706	657	9.5	14,734	25.2
Hidalgo	131,171	81,813	100,663	18,850	32,768	23.0	185,918	48.5
Hill	3,479	422	2,982	2,560	841	10.8	5,181	19.1
Hockley	−107	881	2,189	1,308	168	−0.5	−1,483	−6.1
Hood	8,138	19	3,146	3,127	389	19.8	12,119	41.8
Hopkins	1,536	524	2,840	2,316	454	4.8	3,127	10.8
Houston	−141	−377	1,560	1,937	288	−0.6	1,810	8.5
Howard	−1,164	455	2,804	2,349	352	−3.5	1,284	4.0
Hudspeth	−24	196	303	107	158	−0.7	429	14.7
Hunt	6,742	2,153	6,813	4,660	1,456	8.8	12,253	19.0
Hutchinson	−1,397	374	1,982	1,608	295	−5.9	−1,832	−7.1
Irion	43	−13	69	82	2	2.4	142	8.7
Jack	347	23	587	564	67	4.0	1,782	25.5
Jackson	−142	295	1,270	975	192	−1.0	1,352	10.4
Jasper	−311	530	3,131	2,601	246	−0.9	4,502	14.5
Jeff Davis	108	−20	123	143	64	4.9	261	13.4
Jefferson	−8,137	5,364	21,482	16,118	3,514	−3.2	12,662	5.3
Jim Hogg	−254	197	499	302	16	−4.8	172	3.4
Jim Wells	1,805	1,871	3,974	2,103	94	4.6	1,647	4.4
Johnson	22,205	5,810	12,450	6,640	1,805	17.5	29,646	30.5
Jones	−1,140	−110	1,175	1,285	34	−5.5	4,295	26.0
Karnes	−176	103	1,085	982	104	−1.1	2,991	24.0
Kaufman	21,931	3,086	7,601	4,515	1,339	30.8	19,090	36.6
Kendall	6,470	511	2,057	1,546	276	27.3	9,154	62.7
Kenedy	−12	14	33	19	1	−2.9	−46	−10.0
Kent	−125	−74	38	112	−2	−14.6	−151	−15.0
Kerr	3,605	−824	3,179	4,003	576	8.3	7,345	20.2
Kimble	102	−78	305	383	100	2.3	346	8.4
King	−69	−	14	14	−2	−19.4	2	0.6
Kinney	−37	6	224	218	33	−1.1	260	8.3
Kleberg	−1,196	1,653	3,137	1,484	356	−3.8	1,275	4.2
Knox	−551	−96	306	402	54	−13.0	−584	−12.1
Lamar	1,364	604	4,195	3,591	462	2.8	4,550	10.4
Lamb	−465	415	1,490	1,075	114	−3.2	−363	−2.4
Lampasas	2,998	269	1,464	1,195	160	16.9	4,239	31.4
La Salle	103	292	577	285	6	1.8	612	11.6
Lavaca	−240	−228	1,496	1,724	86	−1.2	520	2.8
Lee	916	464	1,331	867	176	5.9	2,803	21.8
Leon	1,203	−74	1,202	1,276	129	7.8	2,670	21.1
Liberty	5,521	2,388	6,696	4,308	740	7.9	17,438	33.1
Limestone	669	−12	1,780	1,792	437	3.0	1,105	5.3
Lipscomb	57	19	249	230	70	1.9	−86	−2.7
Live Oak	−787	146	715	569	11	−6.4	2,753	28.8
Llano	1,211	−708	933	1,641	46	7.1	5,427	46.7
Loving	−7	1	2	1	−2	−10.4	−40	−37.4
Lubbock	12,234	12,624	24,849	12,225	1,940	5.0	19,992	9.0
Lynn	−338	192	578	386	14	−5.2	−208	−3.1
McCulloch	−189	−120	617	737	22	−2.3	−573	−6.5
McLennan	12,676	8,217	20,608	12,391	4,030	5.9	24,390	12.9
McMullen	62	−5	37	42	2	7.3	34	4.2
Madison	370	63	952	889	198	2.9	2,009	18.4
Marion	29	−107	747	854	24	0.3	957	9.6
Martin	−305	88	422	334	93	−6.4	−210	−4.2
Mason	164	−120	206	326	8	4.4	315	9.2
Matagorda	−133	1,287	3,516	2,229	1,068	−0.4	1,029	2.8
Maverick	5,001	5,045	6,620	1,575	2,046	10.6	10,919	30.0
Medina	4,609	1,432	3,502	2,070	109	11.7	11,992	43.9
Menard	−150	−56	143	199	−2	−6.4	108	4.8
Midland	8,371	5,985	11,716	5,731	1,186	7.2	9,398	8.8

See footnotes at end of table.

Table B-2. Counties — **Components of Population Change**—Con.

[Includes United States, states, and 3,141 counties/county equivalents defined as of February 22, 2005. For more information on these areas, see Appendix C, Geographic Information]

County	Components of population change, April 1, 2000, to July 1, 2006 — Number — Total population change	Natural increase Total	Births	Deaths	Net international migration	Percent change	Population change, April 1, 1990, to April 1, 2000 — Number	Percent change
TEXAS—Con.								
Milam	1,048	555	2,376	1,821	198	4.3	1,292	5.6
Mills	33	−148	277	425	23	0.6	620	13.7
Mitchell	−371	−144	587	731	14	−3.8	1,682	21.0
Montague	693	−198	1,559	1,757	78	3.6	1,843	10.7
Montgomery	104,522	17,903	31,515	13,612	8,054	35.6	111,567	61.2
Moore	470	1,862	2,678	816	983	2.3	2,256	12.6
Morris	−46	−133	970	1,103	51	−0.4	−152	−1.2
Motley	−150	−28	85	113	−2	−10.5	−106	−6.9
Nacogdoches	1,876	2,373	5,811	3,438	1,355	3.2	4,450	8.1
Navarro	4,316	989	4,190	3,201	1,692	9.6	5,198	13.0
Newton	−982	−41	913	954	41	−6.5	1,503	11.1
Nolan	−990	203	1,428	1,225	73	−6.3	−792	−4.8
Nueces	7,812	16,302	31,818	15,516	2,870	2.5	22,500	7.7
Ochiltree	544	630	1,057	427	532	6.0	−122	−1.3
Oldham	−52	63	168	105	14	−2.4	−93	−4.1
Orange	−723	1,265	6,814	5,549	327	−0.9	4,457	5.5
Palo Pinto	771	170	2,338	2,168	300	2.9	1,971	7.9
Panola	233	193	1,819	1,626	176	1.0	721	3.3
Parker	17,772	2,508	7,243	4,735	589	20.1	23,709	36.6
Parmer	−302	627	1,129	502	439	−3.0	153	1.6
Pecos	−670	672	1,458	786	201	−4.0	2,134	14.5
Polk	5,862	−414	3,192	3,606	278	14.3	10,446	34.0
Potter	7,782	6,702	14,208	7,506	2,649	6.9	15,705	16.1
Presidio	409	751	997	246	638	5.6	667	10.0
Rains	2,375	−22	682	704	106	26.0	2,424	36.1
Randall	7,160	3,703	8,409	4,706	835	6.9	14,639	16.3
Reagan	−304	144	300	156	22	−9.1	−1,188	−26.3
Real	10	−68	197	265	3	0.3	639	26.5
Red River	−874	−461	963	1,424	55	−6.1	−3	(Z)
Reeves	−1,671	495	1,184	689	155	−12.7	−2,715	−17.1
Refugio	−232	22	595	573	15	−3.0	−148	−1.9
Roberts	−52	−17	45	62	−2	−5.9	−138	−13.5
Robertson	218	162	1,423	1,261	141	1.4	485	3.1
Rockwall	26,081	2,906	5,010	2,104	667	60.5	17,470	68.2
Runnels	−771	−26	915	941	180	−6.7	201	1.8
Rusk	982	496	3,779	3,283	684	2.1	3,637	8.3
Sabine	−12	−349	673	1,022	15	−0.1	883	9.2
San Augustine	−58	−150	675	825	36	−0.6	947	11.8
San Jacinto	2,519	192	1,572	1,380	153	11.3	5,869	35.8
San Patricio	2,384	4,067	7,345	3,278	−121	3.6	8,389	14.3
San Saba	−193	−125	399	524	66	−3.1	785	14.5
Schleicher	−159	30	247	217	42	−5.4	−55	−1.8
Scurry	−159	319	1,388	1,069	92	−1.0	−2,273	−12.2
Shackelford	−108	−65	209	274	−	−3.3	−14	−0.4
Shelby	1,351	565	2,512	1,947	790	5.4	3,190	14.5
Sherman	−250	63	249	186	57	−7.8	328	11.5
Smith	19,929	7,031	17,592	10,561	3,810	11.4	23,397	15.5
Somervell	964	128	580	452	68	14.2	1,449	27.0
Starr	8,183	7,626	9,382	1,756	3,315	15.3	13,079	32.3
Stephens	−64	64	805	741	76	−0.7	664	7.4
Sterling	−147	−16	65	81	13	−10.6	−45	−3.1
Stonewall	−291	−22	105	127	−2	−17.2	−320	−15.9
Sutton	204	186	411	225	52	5.0	−58	−1.4
Swisher	−548	338	842	504	56	−6.5	245	3.0
Tarrant	225,121	108,386	169,193	60,807	61,212	15.6	276,071	23.6
Taylor	−1,624	5,347	12,778	7,431	428	−1.3	6,896	5.8
Terrell	−98	−13	53	66	23	−9.1	−329	−23.3
Terry	−374	437	1,191	754	332	−2.9	−457	−3.5
Throckmorton	−172	−67	85	152	10	−9.3	−30	−1.6
Titus	2,188	1,839	3,450	1,611	1,535	7.8	4,109	17.1
Tom Green	−72	3,679	9,967	6,288	432	−0.1	5,552	5.6
Travis	108,707	66,557	91,987	25,430	50,653	13.4	235,892	40.9
Trinity	517	−249	1,038	1,287	98	3.8	2,334	20.4
Tyler	−314	−166	1,466	1,632	100	−1.5	4,225	25.4
Upshur	2,632	332	2,928	2,596	145	7.5	3,921	12.5
Upton	−270	133	307	174	10	−7.9	−1,043	−23.5
Uvalde	1,124	1,433	2,925	1,492	305	4.3	2,586	11.1
Val Verde	3,289	4,013	5,885	1,872	1,389	7.3	6,135	15.8
Van Zandt	4,776	227	3,827	3,600	646	9.9	10,196	26.9
Victoria	2,100	4,220	8,571	4,351	740	2.5	9,730	13.1

See footnotes at end of table.

[Includes United States, states, and 3,141 counties/county equivalents defined as of February 22, 2005. For more information on these areas, see Appendix C, Geographic Information]

County	Components of population change, April 1, 2000, to July 1, 2006						Population change, April 1, 1990, to April 1, 2000	
	Number							
	Total population change	Natural increase			Net international migration	Percent change	Number	Percent change
		Total	Births	Deaths				
TEXAS—Con.								
Walker	1,546	1,118	3,798	2,680	706	2.5	10,841	21.3
Waller	2,527	1,691	3,229	1,538	696	7.7	9,284	39.7
Ward	−557	309	969	660	26	−5.1	−2,206	−16.8
Washington	1,539	371	2,578	2,207	452	5.1	4,219	16.1
Webb	38,353	31,465	37,548	6,083	11,396	19.9	59,878	44.9
Wharton	287	1,414	4,122	2,708	840	0.7	1,233	3.1
Wheeler	−430	−144	357	501	42	−8.1	−595	−10.1
Wichita	−6,506	3,836	11,958	8,122	370	−4.9	9,286	7.6
Wilbarger	−458	192	1,360	1,168	95	−3.1	−445	−2.9
Willacy	563	1,854	2,534	680	342	2.8	2,377	13.4
Williamson	103,850	23,670	32,000	8,330	4,808	41.5	110,429	79.1
Wilson	6,421	1,034	2,779	1,745	66	19.8	9,758	43.1
Winkler	−564	160	663	503	85	−7.9	−1,453	−16.8
Wise	9,098	1,573	4,271	2,698	689	18.6	14,114	40.7
Wood	5,024	−427	2,798	3,225	368	13.7	7,372	25.1
Yoakum	116	490	821	331	157	1.6	−1,464	−16.7
Young	78	−197	1,413	1,610	146	0.4	−183	−1.0
Zapata	1,433	1,286	1,768	482	431	11.8	2,903	31.3
Zavala	436	845	1,369	524	217	3.8	−562	−4.6
UTAH	316,865	226,268	308,460	82,192	60,944	14.2	510,348	29.6
Beaver	289	416	786	370	56	4.8	1,240	26.0
Box Elder	4,452	3,237	5,082	1,845	319	10.4	6,260	17.2
Cache	7,271	12,015	14,687	2,672	2,623	8.0	21,208	30.2
Carbon	−956	655	1,925	1,270	72	−4.7	197	1.0
Daggett	26	43	63	20	5	2.8	231	33.5
Davis	37,265	25,656	33,104	7,448	1,623	15.6	51,053	27.2
Duchesne	1,330	1,137	1,886	749	30	9.3	1,726	13.6
Emery	−264	577	1,036	459	54	−2.4	630	6.1
Garfield	−201	197	440	243	−1	−4.2	755	19.0
Grand	619	271	688	417	105	7.4	1,760	26.6
Iron	6,765	3,807	4,980	1,173	446	20.0	12,990	62.5
Juab	1,182	710	1,116	406	3	14.3	2,421	41.6
Kane	486	207	568	361	11	8.0	877	17.0
Millard	−15	540	1,235	695	312	−0.1	1,072	9.5
Morgan	1,005	441	671	230	20	14.1	1,601	29.0
Piute	−88	6	121	115	−1	−6.1	158	12.4
Rich	79	97	183	86	14	4.0	236	13.7
Salt Lake	80,289	81,345	114,326	32,981	37,406	8.9	172,456	23.8
San Juan	−148	1,026	1,524	498	12	−1.0	1,792	14.2
Sanpete	1,433	1,336	2,437	1,101	459	6.3	6,504	40.0
Sevier	798	1,060	2,110	1,050	69	4.2	3,411	22.1
Summit	5,733	2,673	3,301	628	1,047	19.3	14,218	91.6
Tooele	12,817	4,919	6,432	1,513	560	31.5	14,134	53.1
Uintah	2,731	2,064	3,212	1,148	63	10.8	3,013	13.6
Utah	96,220	55,697	66,202	10,505	9,906	26.1	104,950	39.8
Wasatch	5,040	1,694	2,253	559	293	33.1	5,126	50.8
Washington	35,958	8,184	12,906	4,722	1,154	39.8	41,794	86.1
Wayne	35	134	259	125	10	1.4	332	15.3
Weber	16,714	16,124	24,927	8,803	4,274	8.5	38,203	24.1
VERMONT	15,081	8,865	40,670	31,805	5,295	2.5	46,069	8.2
Addison	1,083	585	2,225	1,640	349	3.0	3,021	9.2
Bennington	−65	−172	2,326	2,498	217	−0.2	1,149	3.2
Caledonia	1,161	366	2,119	1,753	173	3.9	1,835	6.6
Chittenden	3,498	4,357	10,289	5,932	3,068	2.4	14,810	11.2
Essex	108	7	367	360	15	1.7	54	0.8
Franklin	2,770	1,574	3,760	2,186	171	6.1	5,437	13.6
Grand Isle	850	166	489	323	7	12.3	1,583	29.8
Lamoille	1,368	629	1,698	1,069	152	5.9	3,489	17.7
Orange	1,188	365	1,790	1,425	43	4.2	2,103	8.0
Orleans	1,437	72	1,793	1,721	76	5.5	2,228	9.3
Rutland	241	−36	3,843	3,879	94	0.4	1,258	2.0
Washington	1,525	816	3,860	3,044	533	2.6	3,111	5.7
Windham	−318	188	2,684	2,496	171	−0.7	2,628	6.3
Windsor	235	−52	3,427	3,479	226	0.4	3,363	6.2
VIRGINIA	563,854	276,039	633,794	357,755	151,748	8.0	889,833	14.4
Accomack	1,040	110	2,980	2,870	844	2.7	6,602	20.8
Albemarle	7,838	2,360	6,143	3,783	2,589	9.3	16,020	23.5
Alleghany[4]	−615	−339	1,155	1,494	18	−3.6	4,400	34.3
Amelia	1,102	122	904	782	−1	9.7	2,613	29.7
Amherst	345	47	1,956	1,909	124	1.1	3,316	11.6

See footnotes at end of table.

[Includes United States, states, and 3,141 counties/county equivalents defined as of February 22, 2005. For more information on these areas, see Appendix C, Geographic Information]

County	Components of population change, April 1, 2000, to July 1, 2006						Population change, April 1, 1990, to April 1, 2000	
	Number					Percent change	Number	Percent change
	Total population change	Natural increase			Net international migration			
		Total	Births	Deaths				
VIRGINIA—Con.								
Appomattox	423	64	921	857	55	3.1	1,405	11.4
Arlington	10,332	10,781	17,408	6,627	20,470	5.5	18,549	10.9
Augusta	5,295	1,039	4,508	3,469	201	8.1	11,058	20.3
Bath	−234	−137	205	342	127	−4.6	249	5.2
Bedford	6,205	838	3,801	2,963	169	10.3	14,749	32.4
Bland	32	−110	365	475	−1	0.5	357	5.5
Botetourt	1,698	128	1,739	1,611	11	5.6	5,538	22.2
Brunswick.	−481	−143	1,122	1,265	82	−2.6	2,432	15.2
Buchanan.	−2,569	−418	1,522	1,940	30	−9.5	−4,355	−13.9
Buckingham	476	−197	914	1,111	31	3.0	2,750	21.4
Campbell	1,562	938	3,754	2,816	126	3.1	3,606	7.6
Caroline	4,610	516	1,873	1,357	52	20.8	2,904	15.1
Carroll	205	−278	1,769	2,047	66	0.7	2,726	10.3
Charles City	295	4	439	435	11	4.3	644	10.3
Charlotte	20	−39	930	969	47	0.2	783	6.7
Chesterfield	36,936	11,984	21,972	9,988	3,131	14.2	50,183	23.9
Clarke	1,913	−11	798	809	66	15.1	551	4.6
Craig.	88	−3	318	321	−1	1.7	719	16.4
Culpeper	10,357	1,167	3,205	2,038	456	30.2	6,474	23.3
Cumberland	448	90	614	524	55	5.0	1,192	15.2
Dickenson	−213	−197	995	1,192	5	−1.3	−1,225	−7.0
Dinwiddie.	1,162	203	1,610	1,407	33	4.7	2,254	10.1
Essex	644	−81	771	852	22	6.4	1,300	15.0
Fairfax.	40,766	66,533	93,243	26,710	68,399	4.2	151,367	18.5
Fauquier	11,025	1,702	4,547	2,845	476	20.0	6,445	13.2
Floyd.	915	47	973	926	88	6.6	1,909	16.0
Fluvanna	5,011	942	1,876	934	35	25.0	7,618	61.3
Franklin	3,501	483	3,342	2,859	54	7.4	7,734	19.6
Frederick	11,978	2,347	5,314	2,967	297	20.2	13,486	29.5
Giles	746	−81	1,261	1,342	3	4.5	291	1.8
Gloucester	3,513	572	2,533	1,961	−32	10.1	4,649	15.4
Goochland	3,222	276	1,174	898	81	19.1	2,700	19.1
Grayson.	−722	−422	939	1,361	50	−4.3	603	3.7
Greene	2,465	824	1,577	753	42	16.2	4,947	48.0
Greensville	−554	167	735	568	6	−4.8	3,007	35.2
Halifax[5]	−1,201	−300	2,618	2,918	89	−3.2	1,320	3.7
Hanover	12,663	2,652	6,817	4,165	319	14.7	23,014	36.4
Henrico	22,295	9,098	23,673	14,575	6,012	8.5	44,226	20.3
Henry	−1,776	22	3,822	3,800	1,007	−3.1	1,042	1.8
Highland	−26	−97	96	193	−	−1.0	−99	−3.8
Isle of Wight	4,995	287	2,181	1,894	32	16.8	4,675	18.7
James City	11,639	448	3,110	2,662	336	24.2	13,323	38.3
King and Queen	273	−75	420	495	−1	4.1	341	5.4
King George	4,977	939	1,739	800	−20	29.6	3,276	24.2
King William	2,235	353	1,161	808	42	17.0	2,233	20.5
Lancaster.	−48	−609	654	1,263	13	−0.4	671	6.2
Lee.	198	−430	1,515	1,945	22	0.8	−907	−3.7
Loudoun	99,218	22,721	27,345	4,624	5,754	58.5	83,414	96.8
Louisa	5,599	450	2,096	1,646	30	21.8	5,302	26.1
Lunenburg	73	−157	771	928	89	0.6	1,727	15.1
Madison.	1,094	93	842	749	53	8.7	570	4.8
Mathews	−23	−388	431	819	6	−0.2	859	10.3
Mecklenburg	1	−421	2,146	2,567	187	(Z)	3,139	10.7
Middlesex	683	−396	489	885	92	6.9	1,279	14.8
Montgomery	860	1,838	5,112	3,274	2,734	1.0	9,768	13.2
Nelson.	716	−51	970	1,021	10	5.0	1,667	13.0
New Kent.	3,390	329	994	665	−	25.2	2,996	28.6
Northampton.	516	−266	1,005	1,271	250	3.9	32	0.2
Northumberland.	552	−388	680	1,068	23	4.5	1,744	16.6
Nottoway	−153	−105	1,133	1,238	132	−1.0	732	4.9
Orange	5,859	246	2,037	1,791	107	22.6	4,460	20.8
Page.	929	121	1,721	1,600	31	4.0	1,485	6.8
Patrick.	−195	−345	1,074	1,419	122	−1.0	1,934	11.1
Pittsylvania.	−244	355	4,240	3,885	283	−0.4	6,073	10.9
Powhatan.	5,272	734	1,657	923	−1	23.6	7,049	46.0
Prince Edward.	810	−32	1,280	1,312	22	4.1	2,400	13.9
Prince George.	3,076	1,275	2,360	1,085	−339	9.3	5,718	20.9
Prince William.	76,690	29,547	37,061	7,514	7,102	27.3	65,859	30.6
Pulaski.	−72	−367	2,193	2,560	41	−0.2	631	1.8
Rappahannock	220	39	481	442	5	3.2	361	5.5

See footnotes at end of table.

[Includes United States, states, and 3,141 counties/county equivalents defined as of February 22, 2005. For more information on these areas, see Appendix C, Geographic Information]

County	Components of population change, April 1, 2000, to July 1, 2006						Population change, April 1, 1990, to April 1, 2000	
	Number							
	Total population change	Natural increase			Net international migration	Percent change	Number	Percent change
		Total	Births	Deaths				
VIRGINIA—Con.								
Richmond	342	−154	554	708	56	3.9	1,527	21.0
Roanoke	4,790	1,684	7,021	5,337	723	5.6	6,414	8.1
Rockbridge	529	126	1,422	1,296	4	2.5	2,458	13.4
Rockingham	4,848	1,728	5,414	3,686	846	7.2	10,234	17.8
Russell	−468	−333	1,809	2,142	30	−1.6	591	2.1
Scott	−521	−498	1,400	1,898	19	−2.2	199	0.9
Shenandoah	4,976	253	2,796	2,543	325	14.2	3,439	10.9
Smyth	−575	−548	2,042	2,590	17	−1.7	711	2.2
Southampton	332	−70	1,064	1,134	−4	1.9	460	2.7
Spotsylvania	29,136	6,194	9,995	3,801	326	32.2	32,996	57.5
Stafford	27,724	6,682	9,647	2,965	−127	30.0	30,191	48.5
Surry	290	26	431	405	−	4.2	684	11.1
Sussex	−255	−80	758	838	56	−2.0	2,256	22.0
Tazewell	10	−612	2,922	3,534	76	(Z)	−1,362	−3.0
Warren	4,524	872	2,786	1,914	45	14.3	5,436	20.8
Washington	881	−210	3,227	3,437	81	1.7	5,216	11.4
Westmoreland	470	−191	1,132	1,323	92	2.8	1,238	8.0
Wise	−300	135	3,129	2,994	41	−0.7	2,632	6.7
Wythe	1,041	90	2,066	1,976	46	3.8	2,128	8.4
York	5,582	1,612	3,767	2,155	−51	9.9	13,863	32.7
Independent Cities								
Alexandria	8,682	10,123	15,115	4,992	12,733	6.8	17,109	15.4
Bedford	−132	−275	475	750	−2	−2.1	205	3.3
Bristol	129	−434	1,200	1,634	78	0.7	−1,059	−5.7
Buena Vista	108	−83	415	498	12	1.7	−57	−0.9
Charlottesville	227	1,111	3,111	2,000	1,246	0.6	−382	−0.9
Chesapeake[4]	21,376	9,073	17,955	8,882	−184	10.7	47,202	31.1
Clifton Forge[4]	(NA)	(X)	(X)	(X)	(X)	(NA)	(NA)	(NA)
Colonial Heights	779	−73	1,314	1,387	117	4.6	833	5.2
Covington	−230	−188	375	563	89	−3.6	−1,049	−14.3
Danville	−2,825	−775	3,604	4,379	279	−5.8	−4,645	−8.8
Emporia	−40	−161	473	634	111	−0.7	109	2.0
Fairfax	852	226	1,581	1,355	1,883	3.9	1,625	8.1
Falls Church	422	316	833	517	439	4.1	913	9.6
Franklin	454	56	879	823	23	5.4	−46	−0.5
Fredericksburg	1,994	1,046	2,386	1,340	295	10.3	246	1.3
Galax	−155	−1	611	612	183	−2.3	92	1.4
Hampton	−1,420	4,866	12,059	7,193	−94	−1.0	12,664	9.5
Harrisonburg	432	1,675	3,257	1,582	1,886	1.1	9,746	31.7
Hopewell	454	398	2,155	1,757	82	2.0	−824	−3.6
Lexington	−128	−167	257	424	76	−1.9	−92	−1.3
Lynchburg	2,491	232	5,263	5,031	948	3.8	−891	−1.3
Manassas	1,503	3,062	4,296	1,234	1,479	4.3	7,378	26.6
Manassas Park	1,352	1,348	1,563	215	468	13.1	3,492	51.4
Martinsville	−420	−496	1,090	1,586	270	−2.7	−797	−4.9
Newport News	−2,416	11,210	20,036	8,826	388	−1.3	9,220	5.4
Norfolk	−5,291	12,657	25,337	12,680	−1,672	−2.3	−26,847	−10.3
Norton	−265	−96	248	344	20	−6.8	−339	−8.0
Petersburg	−1,311	271	3,337	3,066	79	−3.9	−3,315	−8.9
Poquoson	352	70	596	526	5	3.0	561	5.1
Portsmouth	812	3,206	10,021	6,815	−525	0.8	−3,345	−3.2
Radford	−1,334	112	792	680	146	−8.4	−81	−0.5
Richmond	−5,194	5,011	19,232	14,221	2,940	−2.6	−4,606	−2.3
Roanoke	−3,359	−509	7,158	7,667	1,190	−3.5	−1,576	−1.6
Salem	78	−451	1,452	1,903	149	0.3	912	3.8
South Boston[5]	(NA)	(X)	(X)	(X)	(X)	(NA)	(NA)	(NA)
Staunton	−519	−269	1,597	1,866	30	−2.2	−728	−3.0
Suffolk	17,394	2,716	6,821	4,105	5	27.3	11,534	22.1
Virginia Beach	10,362	24,295	40,267	15,972	−191	2.4	32,168	8.2
Waynesboro	1,934	344	1,819	1,475	142	9.9	971	5.2
Williamsburg	−205	106	895	789	213	−1.7	398	3.4
Winchester	1,680	833	2,408	1,575	910	7.1	1,638	7.5
WASHINGTON	501,658	221,958	503,819	281,861	157,950	8.5	1,027,471	21.1
Adams	463	1,563	2,232	669	973	2.8	2,821	20.7
Asotin	696	309	1,600	1,291	11	3.4	2,946	16.7
Benton	16,985	7,228	13,573	6,345	3,429	11.9	29,918	26.6
Chelan	4,418	2,274	5,763	3,489	2,049	6.6	14,366	27.5
Clallam	6,221	−1,273	3,776	5,049	431	9.7	7,969	14.2

See footnotes at end of table.

Table B-2. Counties — **Components of Population Change**—Con.

[Includes United States, states, and 3,141 counties/county equivalents defined as of February 22, 2005. For more information on these areas, see Appendix C, Geographic Information]

County	Components of population change, April 1, 2000, to July 1, 2006						Population change, April 1, 1990, to April 1, 2000	
	Number							
	Total population change	Natural increase			Net international migration	Percent change	Number	Percent change
		Total	Births	Deaths				
WASHINGTON—Con.								
Clark	67,700	18,096	33,826	15,730	9,866	19.6	107,185	45.0
Columbia	23	−66	240	306	44	0.6	40	1.0
Cowlitz.	6,957	1,753	7,665	5,912	934	7.5	10,829	13.2
Douglas	3,169	1,149	2,766	1,617	978	9.7	6,398	24.4
Ferry	300	63	456	393	21	4.1	965	15.3
Franklin	17,223	6,033	7,839	1,806	3,996	34.9	11,874	31.7
Garfield	−174	−71	100	171	–	−7.3	149	6.6
Grant.	7,910	5,349	8,819	3,470	4,625	10.6	19,904	36.3
Grays Harbor	4,393	107	5,072	4,965	612	6.5	3,019	4.7
Island	9,931	2,301	5,954	3,653	−455	13.9	11,363	18.9
Jefferson	2,980	−515	1,260	1,775	147	11.3	5,893	28.9
King	89,689	68,476	140,177	71,701	78,631	5.2	229,738	15.2
Kitsap	8,635	7,569	18,745	11,176	−167	3.7	42,238	22.3
Kittitas	3,827	668	2,239	1,571	661	11.5	6,637	24.8
Klickitat	1,174	385	1,420	1,035	254	6.1	2,545	15.3
Lewis.	4,985	503	5,378	4,875	787	7.3	9,242	15.6
Lincoln.	191	−87	581	668	5	1.9	1,321	14.9
Mason	6,546	177	3,436	3,259	400	13.2	11,064	28.9
Okanogan	476	821	3,124	2,303	927	1.2	6,214	18.6
Pacific	751	−618	1,214	1,832	163	3.6	2,102	11.1
Pend Oreille	1,219	−90	726	816	8	10.4	2,817	31.6
Pierce	66,060	29,922	63,376	33,454	9,634	9.4	114,615	19.6
San Juan	1,221	−108	625	733	113	8.7	4,042	40.3
Skagit	12,718	2,662	8,771	6,109	2,659	12.3	23,437	29.5
Skamania.	961	147	592	445	38	9.7	1,583	19.1
Snohomish.	63,863	27,986	53,556	25,570	14,182	10.5	140,396	30.2
Spokane	28,768	11,170	34,352	23,182	5,247	6.9	56,605	15.7
Stevens	2,566	448	2,861	2,413	77	6.4	9,118	29.5
Thurston	27,315	5,872	16,078	10,206	1,947	13.2	46,117	28.6
Wahkiakum.	202	−138	174	312	−1	5.3	497	14.9
Walla Walla	2,541	1,070	4,375	3,305	1,297	4.6	6,741	13.9
Whatcom	19,130	4,526	12,665	8,139	4,217	11.5	39,043	30.6
Whitman	−902	1,083	2,427	1,344	1,765	−2.2	1,965	5.1
Yakima	10,527	15,214	25,986	10,772	7,445	4.7	33,755	17.9
WEST VIRGINIA	10,120	−1,609	130,202	131,811	4,419	0.6	14,873	0.8
Barbour	231	−163	1,031	1,194	6	1.5	−142	−0.9
Berkeley.	21,629	2,840	7,341	4,501	111	28.5	16,652	28.1
Boone	−23	201	2,056	1,855	36	−0.1	−335	−1.3
Braxton	108	−119	911	1,030	–	0.7	1,704	13.1
Brooke.	−1,315	−542	1,493	2,035	11	−5.2	−1,545	−5.7
Cabell	−2,881	−176	7,238	7,414	329	−3.0	−42	(Z)
Calhoun	−201	−127	452	579	−1	−2.7	−303	−3.8
Clay	−74	134	855	721	−1	−0.7	347	3.5
Doddridge	56	−80	462	542	–	0.8	409	5.8
Fayette	−969	−356	3,520	3,876	105	−2.0	−373	−0.8
Gilmer	−195	−106	388	494	33	−2.7	−509	−6.6
Grant.	616	73	818	745	−1	5.5	871	8.4
Greenbrier	397	−462	2,351	2,813	22	1.2	−240	−0.7
Hampshire	2,277	113	1,420	1,307	27	11.3	3,705	22.5
Hancock	−1,756	−521	2,194	2,715	5	−5.4	−2,566	−7.3
Hardy	751	−4	893	897	8	5.9	1,692	15.4
Harrison.	93	−312	5,111	5,423	313	0.1	−719	−1.0
Jackson	451	208	2,002	1,794	29	1.6	2,062	7.9
Jefferson	8,253	1,394	3,827	2,433	139	19.6	6,264	17.4
Kanawha	−7,654	−675	15,033	15,708	518	−3.8	−7,546	−3.6
Lewis.	210	−197	1,162	1,359	8	1.2	−304	−1.8
Lincoln.	249	135	1,812	1,677	−1	1.1	726	3.4
Logan	−1,492	−175	2,837	3,012	21	−4.0	−5,322	−12.4
McDowell	−3,447	−600	1,886	2,486	7	−12.6	−7,904	−22.4
Marion	108	−777	3,844	4,621	104	0.2	−651	−1.1
Marshall.	−1,623	−233	2,210	2,443	12	−4.6	−1,837	−4.9
Mason	−203	−22	1,831	1,853	−1	−0.8	781	3.1
Mercer	−1,702	−589	4,568	5,157	87	−2.7	−2,000	−3.1
Mineral	−150	–	1,940	1,940	46	−0.6	381	1.4
Mingo	−1,153	171	2,318	2,147	12	−4.1	−5,486	−16.3
Monongalia.	2,886	1,649	5,626	3,977	1,557	3.5	6,357	8.4
Monroe	316	−156	802	958	–	2.4	788	6.4
Morgan	1,394	−133	969	1,102	58	9.3	2,815	23.2
Nicholas	−116	−135	1,704	1,839	6	−0.4	−213	−0.8
Ohio	−2,771	−888	2,913	3,801	160	−5.8	−3,438	−6.8

See footnotes at end of table.

Table B-2. Counties — **Components of Population Change**—Con.

[Includes United States, states, and 3,141 counties/county equivalents defined as of February 22, 2005. For more information on these areas, see Appendix C, Geographic Information]

County	Components of population change, April 1, 2000, to July 1, 2006						Population change, April 1, 1990, to April 1, 2000	
	Number					Percent change	Number	Percent change
	Total population change	Natural increase			Net international migration			
		Total	Births	Deaths				
WEST VIRGINIA—Con.								
Pendleton	−517	−79	503	582	12	−6.3	142	1.8
Pleasants	−234	−97	449	546	8	−3.1	−32	−0.4
Pocahontas	−376	−240	551	791	−1	−4.1	123	1.4
Preston	1,050	−123	1,953	2,076	9	3.6	297	1.0
Putnam	3,396	1,190	4,030	2,840	34	6.6	8,751	20.4
Raleigh	82	−293	5,494	5,787	238	0.1	2,401	3.1
Randolph	203	−242	1,979	2,221	57	0.7	459	1.7
Ritchie	285	−29	768	797	−1	2.8	110	1.1
Roane	137	−23	1,105	1,128	30	0.9	326	2.2
Summers	−857	−353	722	1,075	6	−6.0	184	1.3
Taylor	215	−264	969	1,233	6	1.3	945	6.2
Tucker	−465	−152	389	541	−1	−6.4	−407	−5.3
Tyler	−328	−138	559	697	6	−3.4	−204	−2.1
Upshur	281	74	1,759	1,685	34	1.2	537	2.3
Wayne	−1,256	93	2,983	2,890	59	−2.9	1,267	3.0
Webster	−23	−154	581	735	13	−0.2	−1,010	−9.4
Wetzel	−1,008	−194	1,187	1,381	−1	−5.7	−1,565	−8.1
Wirt	107	26	373	347	−1	1.8	681	13.1
Wood	−1,389	234	6,333	6,099	134	−1.6	1,071	1.2
Wyoming	−1,483	−215	1,697	1,912	13	−5.8	−3,282	−11.3
WISCONSIN	192,791	144,051	434,966	290,915	56,557	3.6	471,761	9.6
Adams	923	−408	1,040	1,448	14	4.6	4,238	27.0
Ashland	−355	−45	1,244	1,289	18	−2.1	559	3.4
Barron	926	295	3,214	2,919	119	2.1	4,213	10.3
Bayfield	134	−103	838	941	21	0.9	1,005	7.2
Brown	13,555	10,395	20,318	9,923	3,222	6.0	32,064	16.5
Buffalo	93	172	958	786	3	0.7	220	1.6
Burnett	816	−251	940	1,191	35	5.2	2,590	19.8
Calumet	3,948	2,347	3,956	1,609	213	9.7	6,340	18.5
Chippewa	5,095	1,197	4,357	3,160	111	9.2	2,845	5.4
Clark	537	1,240	3,353	2,113	64	1.6	1,910	6.0
Columbia	2,973	704	3,925	3,221	147	5.7	7,379	16.4
Crawford	−184	89	1,186	1,097	3	−1.1	1,304	8.2
Dane	37,300	19,413	36,057	16,644	12,323	8.7	59,441	16.2
Dodge	3,085	648	6,070	5,422	236	3.6	9,339	12.2
Door	239	−386	1,519	1,905	37	0.9	2,271	8.8
Douglas	774	285	3,083	2,798	243	1.8	1,529	3.7
Dunn	2,117	1,153	2,878	1,725	241	5.3	3,949	11.0
Eau Claire	1,609	2,567	6,957	4,390	443	1.7	7,949	9.3
Florence	−147	−130	219	349	−1	−2.9	498	10.8
Fond du Lac	1,947	1,497	7,105	5,608	724	2.0	7,213	8.0
Forest	−125	−6	683	689	–	−1.2	1,248	14.2
Grant	−235	415	3,574	3,159	102	−0.5	331	0.7
Green	2,041	470	2,481	2,011	79	6.1	3,308	10.9
Green Lake	42	−43	1,431	1,474	39	0.2	454	2.4
Iowa	976	674	1,905	1,231	3	4.3	2,630	13.1
Iron	−359	−299	258	557	7	−5.2	708	11.5
Jackson	753	128	1,444	1,316	68	3.9	2,512	15.1
Jefferson	4,258	2,410	6,149	3,739	727	5.6	7,984	11.8
Juneau	2,539	21	1,791	1,770	36	10.4	2,666	12.3
Kenosha	12,424	5,322	13,349	8,027	1,517	8.3	21,396	16.7
Kewaunee	645	305	1,490	1,185	55	3.2	1,309	6.9
La Crosse	2,284	2,145	7,816	5,671	496	2.1	9,216	9.4
Lafayette	161	366	1,268	902	12	1.0	63	0.4
Langlade	−109	−143	1,359	1,502	9	−0.5	1,235	6.3
Lincoln	510	−3	1,940	1,943	117	1.7	2,648	9.8
Manitowoc	−982	521	5,497	4,976	584	−1.2	2,472	3.1
Marathon	4,389	3,619	9,569	5,950	690	3.5	10,434	9.0
Marinette	−176	−499	2,631	3,130	89	−0.4	2,836	7.0
Marquette	672	−96	970	1,066	7	4.6	2,234	18.1
Menominee	35	343	586	243	−1	0.8	487	12.0
Milwaukee	−25,067	36,773	91,818	55,045	19,571	−2.7	−19,048	−2.0
Monroe	2,132	1,133	3,727	2,594	196	5.2	4,263	11.6
Oconto	2,306	362	2,449	2,087	12	6.5	5,426	18.0
Oneida	3	−534	1,989	2,523	61	(Z)	5,097	16.1
Outagamie	11,643	7,262	14,294	7,032	1,322	7.2	20,581	14.6
Ozaukee	4,004	1,711	5,555	3,844	521	4.9	9,423	12.9
Pepin	112	43	529	486	2	1.6	106	1.5
Pierce	2,569	1,289	2,737	1,448	78	7.0	4,039	12.3
Polk	3,465	519	3,055	2,536	91	8.4	6,546	18.8
Portage	302	1,803	4,598	2,795	397	0.4	5,777	9.4

See footnotes at end of table.

[Includes United States, states, and 3,141 counties/county equivalents defined as of February 22, 2005. For more information on these areas, see Appendix C, Geographic Information]

County	Components of population change, April 1, 2000, to July 1, 2006						Population change, April 1, 1990, to April 1, 2000	
	Number					Percent change	Number	Percent change
	Total population change	Natural increase			Net international migration			
		Total	Births	Deaths				
WISCONSIN—Con.								
Price	−822	−439	854	1,293	6	−5.2	222	1.4
Racine	7,265	6,329	15,956	9,627	1,824	3.8	13,797	7.9
Richland	417	214	1,351	1,137	31	2.3	403	2.3
Rock	6,846	4,354	12,641	8,287	1,854	4.5	12,797	9.2
Rusk	−293	−132	1,005	1,137	61	−1.9	268	1.8
St. Croix	16,860	3,572	6,371	2,799	156	26.7	12,904	25.7
Sauk	3,036	1,177	4,401	3,224	208	5.5	8,250	17.6
Sawyer	884	−41	1,101	1,142	18	5.5	2,015	14.2
Shawano	737	195	2,928	2,733	82	1.8	3,507	9.4
Sheboygan	2,100	1,715	8,261	6,546	1,182	1.9	8,779	8.5
Taylor	−75	423	1,522	1,099	57	−0.4	779	4.1
Trempealeau	1,068	287	2,097	1,810	29	4.0	1,747	6.9
Vernon	1,133	679	2,551	1,872	−1	4.0	2,438	9.5
Vilas	1,346	−371	1,164	1,535	47	6.4	3,326	18.8
Walworth	8,994	1,921	7,165	5,244	1,335	9.8	17,013	22.7
Washburn	638	−92	1,043	1,135	3	4.0	2,264	16.4
Washington	10,082	3,782	9,185	5,403	492	8.6	22,168	23.3
Waukesha	20,218	9,930	27,217	17,287	2,296	5.6	56,052	18.4
Waupaca	862	−545	3,606	4,151	38	1.7	5,721	12.4
Waushara	1,849	−207	1,517	1,724	86	8.0	3,681	19.0
Winnebago	3,830	3,586	11,548	7,962	1,222	2.4	16,443	11.7
Wood	−781	1,024	5,323	4,299	428	−1.0	1,950	2.6
WYOMING	21,222	15,734	41,063	25,329	2,323	4.3	40,193	8.9
Albany	−1,654	1,254	2,375	1,121	503	−5.2	1,217	4.0
Big Horn	−71	117	894	777	51	−0.6	936	8.9
Campbell	5,236	2,438	3,455	1,017	106	15.5	4,328	14.7
Carbon	−314	292	1,180	888	46	−2.0	−1,020	−6.1
Converse	814	297	900	603	24	6.8	924	8.3
Crook	368	85	395	310	26	6.3	593	11.2
Fremont	1,359	959	3,200	2,241	47	3.8	2,142	6.4
Goshen	−409	−33	849	882	28	−3.3	165	1.3
Hot Springs	−294	−140	265	405	6	−6.0	73	1.5
Johnson	939	14	483	469	3	13.3	930	15.1
Laramie	3,777	3,335	7,526	4,191	16	4.6	8,465	11.6
Lincoln	1,810	574	1,305	731	−1	12.4	1,948	15.4
Natrona	3,868	2,163	5,799	3,636	281	5.8	5,307	8.7
Niobrara	−154	−39	104	143	−	−6.4	−92	−3.7
Park	1,308	175	1,639	1,464	66	5.1	2,608	11.3
Platte	−219	−52	541	593	47	−2.5	662	8.1
Sheridan	1,113	139	1,929	1,790	75	4.2	2,998	12.7
Sublette	1,439	158	462	304	5	24.3	1,077	22.2
Sweetwater	1,150	1,837	3,493	1,656	254	3.1	−1,210	−3.1
Teton	1,037	924	1,404	480	626	5.7	7,078	63.3
Uinta	471	1,164	1,871	707	75	2.4	1,037	5.5
Washakie	−470	35	580	545	36	−5.7	−99	−1.2
Weston	118	38	414	376	3	1.8	126	1.9

− Represents zero.   NA Not available.   X Not applicable.   Z Less than .05 percent.

[1]Yakutat City and Borough included with Skagway-Hoonah-Angoon Census Area.
[2]Colorado state total includes Broomfield city.
[3]Yellowstone National Park County became incorporated with Gallatin and Park Counties, MT; effective November 7, 1997.
[4]Clifton Forge independent city became incorporated with Alleghany County, VA; effective July 1, 2001.
[5]South Boston independent city became incorporated with Halifax County, VA; effective June 30, 1995.

Survey, Census, or Data Collection Method: Based on population estimates and the "component of populaton change method"; for more information, see Appendix B, Limitations of the Data and Methodology, and also <http://www.census.gov/popest/topics/methodology/>.

Sources: Population—U.S. Census Bureau, Components of Population Change, "Population Estimates, Cumulative Estimates of the Components of Population Change for Counties: April 1, 2000 to July 1, 2006" (related Internet site <http://www.census.gov/popest/counties/files/CO-EST2006-alldata.txt>).   Population change—Census 2000, Demographic Profiles 1; 1990 census, 100 percent data, STF1 (related Internet site <http://www.census.gov/main/www/cen2000.html>).   Net international migration—U.S. Census Bureau, "Cumulative Estimates of the Components of Population Change for Counties: April 1, 2000 to July 1, 2006" (related Internet site <http://www.census.gov/popest/counties/CO-EST2006-04.html>).

Table B-3. Counties — **Population by Age, Race, Hispanic Origin, and Sex**

[Includes United States, states, and 3,141 counties/county equivalents defined as of February 22, 2005. For more information on these areas, see Appendix C, Geographic Information]

County	Age (percent)									One race (percent)					Hispanic or Latino origin[1] (percent)	Males per 100 females
	Under 5 years	5 to 14 years	15 to 24 years	25 to 34 years	35 to 44 years	45 to 54 years	55 to 64 years	65 to 74 years	75 years and over	White alone	Black or African American alone	Asian alone	American Indian and Alaska Native alone	Native Hawaiian and Other Pacific Islander alone		
UNITED STATES.........	6.8	13.6	14.2	13.5	14.8	14.3	10.2	6.3	6.1	80.2	12.8	4.3	1.0	0.2	14.4	97.1
ALABAMA............	6.5	13.2	14.2	13.3	14.2	14.5	10.9	7.2	6.0	71.4	26.4	0.8	0.5	(Z)	2.3	94.3
Autauga..............	6.5	14.4	14.5	13.2	15.9	14.4	10.4	6.6	4.2	80.7	17.3	0.6	0.5	(Z)	1.7	95.2
Baldwin..............	5.8	12.4	12.6	13.3	14.0	14.3	11.4	8.8	7.5	88.4	9.9	0.4	0.5	(Z)	2.3	96.9
Barbour.............	6.0	12.7	14.2	13.7	14.9	13.8	11.4	6.9	6.3	52.2	46.8	0.3	0.4	(Z)	3.1	110.4
Bibb................	6.1	13.5	12.7	16.2	15.3	13.5	10.6	6.8	5.2	76.8	22.5	0.1	0.3	—	1.4	106.7
Blount..............	6.0	13.3	12.9	14.8	14.6	13.8	11.2	7.8	5.6	97.1	1.5	0.2	0.5	(Z)	6.4	99.8
Bullock.............	6.5	12.8	15.4	14.8	14.1	14.1	9.9	5.9	6.2	27.8	71.4	0.2	0.4	—	5.9	114.8
Butler..............	6.7	13.1	15.0	10.5	12.8	14.7	11.3	8.0	8.0	57.5	41.9	0.3	0.2	—	0.9	89.8
Calhoun.............	6.4	12.3	14.5	12.5	13.7	14.9	11.5	7.8	6.5	78.3	19.7	0.7	0.4	0.1	2.0	92.3
Chambers............	6.1	13.5	11.7	12.7	13.5	14.5	12.2	8.2	7.5	60.8	38.6	0.2	0.1	—	1.2	91.2
Cherokee............	5.3	12.0	11.2	13.4	13.7	14.4	13.3	9.8	6.9	93.3	5.5	0.3	0.3	—	1.1	95.5
Chilton.............	6.3	13.4	13.0	15.3	14.3	14.2	10.9	7.1	5.4	88.3	10.5	0.3	0.3	(Z)	3.7	97.4
Choctaw.............	6.1	13.3	13.1	10.6	13.1	14.8	13.4	8.8	6.9	55.7	43.9	0.1	0.1	—	0.8	89.3
Clarke..............	6.8	14.7	13.2	11.8	13.9	14.1	11.3	7.8	6.4	55.8	43.7	0.2	0.2	—	0.7	90.3
Clay................	5.3	12.2	12.3	12.4	14.0	14.1	12.3	9.0	8.4	84.2	15.0	0.1	0.3	(Z)	2.1	97.3
Cleburne............	5.4	12.8	12.9	13.1	14.8	14.4	12.3	8.5	5.6	95.3	3.8	0.2	0.3	(Z)	1.8	100.6
Coffee..............	6.1	12.8	12.9	13.6	13.8	14.3	11.9	8.0	6.4	77.9	18.5	1.1	0.9	0.1	3.3	96.7
Colbert.............	5.3	12.6	12.5	12.2	14.1	14.9	12.4	8.6	7.5	81.9	16.7	0.3	0.4	(Z)	1.3	92.1
Conecuh.............	6.3	13.4	13.2	10.8	13.1	14.9	12.9	7.9	7.6	55.3	44.1	0.1	0.2	(Z)	0.9	89.3
Coosa...............	5.3	12.6	11.4	12.1	15.2	15.2	12.6	8.5	7.1	67.6	31.6	0.1	0.3	(Z)	1.5	100.3
Covington...........	6.0	12.2	12.4	11.7	13.3	14.4	12.0	9.5	8.4	86.1	12.6	0.3	0.5	(Z)	0.9	92.7
Crenshaw............	6.4	12.5	12.6	12.3	13.0	14.3	11.8	8.7	8.4	74.6	24.6	0.1	0.4	—	0.8	91.1
Cullman.............	6.0	12.7	12.6	14.1	14.4	13.9	11.6	8.2	6.6	97.3	1.2	0.2	0.4	(Z)	3.1	98.0
Dale................	7.7	14.5	13.0	12.8	14.2	13.9	11.0	7.6	5.4	75.5	20.9	1.1	0.5	0.2	3.3	98.4
Dallas..............	8.2	14.5	15.0	10.9	12.6	14.7	10.5	7.4	6.2	32.4	66.9	0.3	0.1	(Z)	0.7	84.0
DeKalb..............	6.8	13.3	12.0	14.8	14.2	13.7	11.2	7.7	6.2	96.0	1.8	0.2	0.8	0.1	9.0	97.4
Elmore..............	6.5	13.1	14.2	15.4	15.7	14.1	10.2	6.2	4.7	77.3	20.7	0.5	0.4	(Z)	1.7	103.2
Escambia............	6.4	12.7	13.3	13.5	14.1	14.5	11.4	7.8	6.4	64.3	31.7	0.3	2.9	(Z)	1.0	103.5
Etowah..............	6.1	12.6	12.7	13.1	13.5	14.5	11.9	8.1	7.6	83.8	14.6	0.5	0.3	(Z)	2.4	92.7
Fayette.............	5.6	12.4	12.4	12.5	13.8	14.7	12.4	8.4	7.7	87.4	11.8	0.3	0.2	(Z)	0.9	95.0
Franklin............	6.7	12.8	12.5	14.0	13.7	13.7	11.3	8.6	6.6	94.1	4.2	0.2	0.4	0.4	10.9	98.7
Geneva..............	5.7	11.8	12.4	11.7	14.0	14.5	12.7	9.2	8.0	87.8	10.8	0.2	0.7	(Z)	2.0	95.2
Greene..............	7.1	15.3	14.3	10.9	12.3	15.8	10.2	6.8	7.3	19.9	79.7	0.1	0.1	(Z)	0.7	87.6
Hale................	6.2	14.6	15.2	13.8	14.3	13.6	9.7	6.6	6.1	40.3	59.2	0.1	0.1	(Z)	0.9	102.0
Henry...............	6.3	12.4	12.6	12.4	13.1	14.4	12.8	8.3	7.7	67.6	31.7	(Z)	0.2	(Z)	2.1	93.0
Houston.............	7.0	13.3	12.6	13.0	14.2	14.6	11.2	7.4	6.6	72.2	25.9	0.7	0.4	(Z)	1.6	91.6
Jackson.............	5.9	12.7	11.6	13.5	14.2	14.8	12.6	8.6	6.1	92.6	3.8	0.3	1.6	(Z)	1.6	95.4
Jefferson...........	6.8	12.9	13.6	13.2	14.2	15.3	10.5	6.7	6.7	56.8	41.2	1.0	0.2	(Z)	2.3	90.1
Lamar...............	5.4	11.9	11.7	12.5	14.3	14.5	12.6	9.4	7.7	88.1	11.4	0.1	0.2	(Z)	1.5	95.0
Lauderdale..........	5.5	11.9	14.3	12.4	13.8	14.5	11.7	8.6	7.4	88.9	9.7	0.4	0.3	(Z)	1.2	91.8
Lawrence............	5.8	13.2	12.8	12.9	16.1	14.4	12.1	7.5	5.3	79.5	12.1	0.1	5.4	(Z)	1.4	95.9
Lee.................	5.6	11.9	25.9	15.6	12.8	11.7	8.2	4.9	3.5	74.1	23.0	1.8	0.2	(Z)	1.6	96.8
Limestone...........	5.8	13.1	13.2	14.6	16.3	14.4	11.0	6.8	4.9	85.1	13.2	0.5	0.5	(Z)	3.3	103.5
Lowndes.............	7.7	14.4	15.0	11.4	14.1	14.4	10.2	7.3	5.6	27.9	71.7	0.1	0.1	(Z)	0.8	87.7
Macon...............	5.5	12.8	22.9	10.7	10.1	13.2	10.5	6.8	7.6	15.7	82.8	0.9	0.1	(Z)	1.0	86.1
Madison.............	6.1	13.5	14.6	12.6	15.9	14.9	10.6	7.2	4.8	71.7	23.5	2.0	0.8	0.1	2.2	96.2
Marengo.............	7.0	14.5	14.0	11.4	13.0	14.6	11.3	7.7	6.5	47.1	52.2	0.3	0.1	(Z)	1.8	91.0
Marion..............	5.7	11.7	11.2	13.4	14.2	14.0	12.8	9.1	7.9	95.0	3.9	0.2	0.3	0.1	1.5	99.0
Marshall............	7.5	13.3	12.1	14.0	14.2	13.8	11.2	7.9	6.0	96.6	1.6	0.3	0.5	0.1	8.7	95.7
Mobile..............	7.3	14.4	14.4	13.0	13.6	14.5	10.6	6.6	5.6	62.2	34.5	1.6	0.7	(Z)	1.3	92.1
Monroe..............	6.5	14.9	13.5	11.7	13.4	14.7	11.0	7.5	6.7	57.0	41.0	0.3	1.0	—	0.8	92.8
Montgomery..........	7.5	13.5	16.1	13.0	13.9	14.2	10.1	6.2	5.6	45.1	52.5	1.2	0.2	(Z)	1.4	91.5
Morgan..............	6.4	13.2	12.8	12.8	15.3	15.0	11.5	7.4	5.8	85.7	11.8	0.6	0.7	0.1	4.7	97.0
Perry...............	8.6	15.0	17.9	10.8	11.1	12.3	10.1	7.7	6.5	30.0	69.6	—	0.1	0.1	1.1	85.7
Pickens.............	6.5	13.9	13.8	11.0	13.3	14.3	11.1	8.6	7.4	57.2	42.4	0.1	0.1	0.1	0.8	89.1
Pike................	6.9	12.2	19.9	13.5	12.3	12.4	10.3	7.1	5.5	60.2	36.8	1.0	0.6	(Z)	1.6	92.8
Randolph............	6.0	13.5	13.0	12.3	13.4	13.7	11.5	8.8	7.7	76.8	22.1	0.4	0.3	—	1.3	94.0
Russell.............	6.2	14.5	12.7	13.4	14.1	14.4	11.2	7.7	6.0	56.1	42.1	0.5	0.3	0.1	2.2	91.1
St. Clair...........	5.9	13.0	13.1	15.0	15.4	14.3	11.2	7.2	4.9	90.3	8.2	0.2	0.4	(Z)	1.3	101.4
Shelby..............	7.3	13.7	13.4	15.0	16.1	15.3	10.5	5.2	3.4	88.2	9.4	1.4	0.3	(Z)	3.1	97.8
Sumter..............	6.6	14.9	18.1	11.8	11.4	13.9	9.1	6.5	7.7	24.9	74.7	0.1	0.1	(Z)	1.4	83.8
Talladega...........	6.5	12.9	13.3	13.5	14.1	14.4	11.5	7.5	6.0	67.5	31.4	0.3	0.2	(Z)	1.1	96.3
Tallapoosa..........	5.7	12.7	12.0	11.5	13.8	14.8	12.9	8.9	7.7	72.9	26.3	0.2	0.2	—	0.9	92.6
Tuscaloosa..........	6.4	12.3	19.1	15.1	12.8	13.8	9.5	5.9	5.1	67.7	30.1	1.1	0.2	(Z)	1.7	94.0
Walker..............	6.1	12.5	11.9	13.6	14.0	14.3	12.2	8.5	6.9	92.5	6.4	0.2	0.3	(Z)	1.2	93.5
Washington..........	6.1	15.0	13.2	12.4	13.9	14.2	11.8	7.6	5.8	66.0	26.4	0.1	6.7	(Z)	0.9	96.5
Wilcox..............	8.3	15.9	15.8	11.7	12.1	13.2	10.1	6.7	6.3	27.1	72.6	0.1	0.1	(Z)	0.8	84.8
Winston.............	5.3	12.5	12.1	12.6	15.2	14.0	13.3	8.6	6.4	98.3	0.6	0.1	0.4	(Z)	1.9	97.3

See footnotes at end of table.

County and City Data Book: 2007

U.S. Census Bureau

Table B-3. Counties — **Population by Age, Race, Hispanic Origin, and Sex**—Con.

[Includes United States, states, and 3,141 counties/county equivalents defined as of February 22, 2005. For more information on these areas, see Appendix C, Geographic Information]

County	Under 5 years	5 to 14 years	15 to 24 years	25 to 34 years	35 to 44 years	45 to 54 years	55 to 64 years	65 to 74 years	75 years and over	White alone	Black or African American alone	Asian alone	American Indian and Alaska Native alone	Native Hawaiian and Other Pacific Islander alone	Hispanic or Latino origin[1] (percent)	Males per 100 females
ALASKA	7.6	15.5	16.9	12.0	15.0	16.4	9.9	4.0	2.6	70.5	3.7	4.6	16.0	0.6	5.1	107.1
Aleutians East	3.3	6.5	13.7	17.7	24.9	21.7	8.7	1.9	1.5	33.4	1.9	32.4	29.6	1.1	14.8	199.8
Aleutians West	2.6	7.7	12.1	20.8	24.5	20.8	8.8	1.9	0.8	48.7	3.8	25.1	18.7	1.7	12.1	185.1
Anchorage	7.8	15.6	16.2	12.8	15.4	16.1	9.7	3.9	2.5	72.0	6.2	6.7	8.5	1.0	6.9	102.6
Bethel	12.6	19.9	18.0	10.6	13.8	12.5	7.5	3.1	1.9	13.4	0.6	1.3	82.0	–	1.1	113.7
Bristol Bay	5.7	13.9	15.3	8.1	15.8	24.1	11.2	4.0	1.9	57.6	0.6	0.1	41.4	0.2	1.0	122.4
Denali	6.4	10.0	14.4	11.7	15.1	24.8	13.0	3.7	1.0	89.6	1.3	2.1	4.7	0.2	2.8	140.8
Dillingham	8.5	19.3	18.1	8.6	14.9	15.1	9.0	3.7	2.9	23.5	0.5	0.5	71.3	–	2.6	107.6
Fairbanks North Star	8.7	15.4	18.5	15.0	14.4	14.0	8.3	3.3	2.2	79.1	5.3	2.3	7.8	0.3	5.5	110.0
Haines	4.0	11.3	14.2	6.3	13.8	21.8	16.8	6.6	5.2	87.5	0.3	0.7	9.6	–	1.4	100.5
Juneau	6.3	13.9	15.6	10.2	15.9	18.8	12.2	4.2	3.0	75.3	1.1	5.2	12.2	0.4	3.9	101.9
Kenai Peninsula	6.0	14.4	16.4	9.5	13.9	18.9	12.2	5.4	3.5	87.5	0.6	1.1	7.7	0.2	2.8	108.9
Ketchikan Gateway	6.4	14.7	14.8	9.4	15.8	17.7	12.6	4.9	3.8	74.1	1.0	5.3	15.8	(Z)	2.9	104.2
Kodiak Island	7.3	17.1	15.7	11.4	16.9	16.9	9.0	3.7	2.1	62.1	1.2	16.7	15.7	0.8	6.8	112.2
Lake and Peninsula	6.5	18.7	20.4	6.2	13.5	18.1	9.7	4.5	2.4	23.4	–	0.2	71.5	0.6	1.4	107.4
Matanuska-Susitna	6.3	15.3	17.9	11.2	15.0	17.9	9.7	4.3	2.5	88.3	1.1	0.8	5.7	0.2	3.0	107.8
Nome	10.8	18.3	18.1	11.1	13.5	13.8	8.5	3.2	2.7	20.0	0.5	1.1	75.7	–	1.1	112.9
North Slope	12.4	18.7	18.0	8.7	13.8	14.7	8.5	2.9	2.2	15.7	1.1	6.4	72.0	0.8	4.0	110.6
Northwest Arctic	12.3	20.3	19.2	11.8	13.0	11.4	6.8	3.1	2.1	13.1	0.1	1.0	83.6	–	5.7	111.3
Prince of Wales- Outer Ketchikan	5.3	15.0	15.8	9.4	13.9	19.8	12.6	5.6	2.7	53.5	0.2	0.4	40.9	–	2.4	120.7
Sitka	7.0	13.6	16.3	10.8	14.0	17.8	10.4	6.5	3.7	68.4	0.4	5.2	20.1	0.5	4.1	103.5
Skagway-Hoonah-Angoon	4.1	12.4	14.7	9.5	14.7	19.7	15.7	5.7	3.5	61.2	0.2	0.1	35.6	–	4.1	113.4
Southeast Fairbanks	7.2	15.9	19.2	10.9	12.5	15.5	11.0	5.3	2.5	81.8	2.8	0.7	11.5	(Z)	3.3	109.7
Valdez-Cordova	5.8	14.2	16.9	8.2	14.6	20.3	13.3	4.2	2.7	76.8	0.5	4.1	14.6	0.1	2.5	112.6
Wade Hampton	15.4	21.4	21.3	9.6	11.6	9.6	6.0	3.2	1.9	4.7	(Z)	0.1	93.4	–	0.4	108.9
Wrangell-Petersburg	5.3	14.2	16.3	7.6	13.5	19.2	13.1	5.5	5.3	75.7	0.2	2.2	16.2	(Z)	2.7	109.6
Yakutat	4.7	12.3	13.6	7.2	19.0	24.5	11.1	4.4	3.2	57.8	0.1	0.6	40.6	0.1	0.8	146.4
Yukon-Koyukuk	7.4	15.4	19.3	8.5	12.7	17.1	11.3	4.7	3.5	26.9	0.1	0.5	69.9	(Z)	1.3	117.1
ARIZONA	7.7	14.6	14.2	14.5	13.8	12.7	9.8	6.9	5.9	87.4	3.6	2.2	5.1	0.2	28.5	100.2
Apache	9.3	18.9	19.0	9.7	12.0	12.2	9.1	6.1	3.6	22.2	0.6	0.2	76.1	0.1	4.6	97.0
Cochise	6.9	13.7	15.0	10.8	12.1	13.5	11.9	9.3	6.8	90.1	4.4	1.8	1.3	0.3	31.2	99.6
Coconino	7.8	14.3	20.2	13.5	12.6	14.3	9.6	4.9	2.7	66.1	1.3	1.0	29.9	0.1	11.7	99.1
Gila	6.8	13.0	12.9	8.5	11.1	13.4	13.5	11.6	9.3	83.5	0.7	0.6	14.6	(Z)	16.3	95.8
Graham	6.7	15.9	18.3	13.3	12.9	11.6	8.7	6.9	5.8	80.4	2.2	0.7	16.3	0.1	27.8	113.6
Greenlee	5.7	17.6	15.0	7.4	14.2	17.1	11.7	6.8	4.4	96.2	0.8	0.3	1.9	0.2	46.5	108.7
La Paz	5.4	10.7	11.1	8.7	9.8	12.1	13.2	15.7	13.2	84.2	1.0	0.5	13.2	0.1	22.9	102.6
Maricopa	8.2	15.0	13.7	15.6	14.6	12.5	9.2	5.9	5.2	89.0	4.3	2.7	2.2	0.2	29.0	101.3
Mohave	5.9	12.7	11.5	11.6	11.8	12.8	12.9	12.0	8.8	94.2	1.0	0.9	2.5	0.2	12.9	97.4
Navajo	8.3	17.9	17.6	11.9	11.9	12.1	9.3	6.8	4.3	48.5	1.1	0.4	48.8	(Z)	8.8	98.0
Pima	6.9	13.3	15.0	13.4	13.2	13.5	10.4	7.5	6.9	88.7	3.4	2.4	3.6	0.2	31.9	95.8
Pinal	6.7	13.8	14.4	15.4	13.3	11.7	10.2	8.3	6.2	86.9	3.5	0.9	7.4	0.2	29.9	111.8
Santa Cruz	9.3	16.9	16.3	9.9	13.0	13.2	9.7	6.6	5.1	97.7	0.6	0.6	0.8	0.1	80.5	90.3
Yavapai	4.9	11.2	12.5	11.1	11.2	13.9	13.1	11.7	10.2	95.6	0.7	0.7	1.7	0.1	11.6	96.7
Yuma	8.8	15.7	15.0	11.9	12.2	10.6	8.5	9.3	8.1	93.0	2.7	1.1	1.9	0.3	55.1	99.8
ARKANSAS	6.7	13.3	14.3	13.2	13.9	13.8	11.0	7.5	6.3	81.3	15.7	1.0	0.7	0.1	4.7	96.2
Arkansas	6.5	12.8	12.9	11.8	12.9	15.4	11.9	8.3	7.4	74.6	24.5	0.4	0.1	–	1.1	91.8
Ashley	6.3	14.0	13.2	11.9	14.1	14.0	12.6	7.8	6.1	71.3	27.8	0.2	0.1	0.1	3.9	93.9
Baxter	4.3	10.1	10.9	9.9	11.6	13.0	13.7	13.7	12.7	98.0	0.3	0.4	0.5	(Z)	1.0	92.1
Benton	7.3	14.5	13.8	14.7	14.8	12.6	9.7	6.8	5.8	93.8	1.1	1.7	1.6	0.2	12.8	98.9
Boone	5.9	12.6	12.1	12.8	13.9	13.6	12.1	9.3	7.8	97.7	0.3	0.4	0.7	(Z)	1.5	94.5
Bradley	6.3	11.9	14.5	12.7	12.9	13.4	11.2	8.8	8.3	71.2	28.2	0.1	0.3	–	10.2	98.6
Calhoun	5.5	12.6	12.4	11.0	15.0	16.0	12.2	8.2	7.2	76.6	23.2	–	(Z)	0.1	2.1	94.1
Carroll	6.4	12.4	12.4	12.2	13.3	14.6	12.9	9.0	6.9	97.3	0.3	0.5	0.7	0.1	13.5	99.2
Chicot	6.4	13.8	14.5	11.3	12.8	14.2	11.2	8.7	6.9	45.2	53.9	0.6	(Z)	(Z)	4.0	95.6
Clark	5.7	11.1	23.4	12.4	11.1	12.1	10.0	7.4	6.9	75.3	22.3	1.0	0.5	0.1	3.9	95.0
Clay	5.5	12.5	11.9	10.8	13.5	13.7	12.9	9.8	9.3	98.2	0.3	0.2	0.7	–	1.0	93.2
Cleburne	4.7	11.1	12.0	11.3	12.7	13.4	13.2	12.2	9.4	98.2	0.5	0.2	0.3	(Z)	1.7	95.4
Cleveland	5.9	13.5	13.4	12.7	14.4	13.7	12.1	8.6	5.7	85.7	13.5	0.1	0.4	(Z)	1.8	96.1
Columbia	6.0	12.6	17.5	11.1	12.6	13.7	10.5	8.3	7.6	62.3	36.6	0.4	0.3	(Z)	1.6	93.6
Conway	6.3	13.3	13.4	12.0	13.9	13.9	11.7	8.2	7.4	85.5	12.5	0.5	0.5	(Z)	2.4	95.2
Craighead	7.0	13.0	16.2	15.4	13.6	12.9	10.2	6.5	5.3	88.3	9.7	0.7	0.4	(Z)	3.1	94.3
Crawford	6.6	14.6	13.8	13.0	14.9	14.3	10.9	7.2	4.8	93.4	1.1	1.4	2.1	(Z)	4.6	99.2
Crittenden	8.5	16.3	14.5	12.8	14.3	14.0	9.8	5.6	4.2	49.2	49.4	0.6	0.3	(Z)	1.9	91.6
Cross	6.5	14.2	14.1	12.2	14.0	14.0	11.9	6.8	6.3	75.5	23.4	0.4	0.3	–	1.2	94.9
Dallas	5.9	13.3	14.3	10.0	12.6	15.2	12.3	8.3	8.1	58.2	40.7	0.4	0.3	–	2.6	92.8
Desha	7.7	14.1	13.8	10.4	12.2	15.3	12.2	7.3	6.9	52.1	46.8	0.4	0.3	(Z)	3.8	87.8
Drew	5.8	13.3	18.1	12.6	13.1	13.7	10.3	7.3	5.8	71.2	27.5	0.5	0.2	–	2.6	97.6
Faulkner	6.6	13.0	19.6	15.6	14.0	12.7	8.8	5.4	4.3	88.3	9.3	0.8	0.5	(Z)	2.5	95.9
Franklin	5.8	13.0	13.9	12.5	13.6	13.7	11.2	8.6	7.6	96.7	0.7	0.7	0.8	0.2	2.0	98.9
Fulton	4.7	11.4	11.7	10.5	12.1	14.2	13.9	11.5	10.0	98.1	0.3	0.2	0.6	–	0.7	96.3

See footnotes at end of table.

U.S. Census Bureau

[Includes United States, states, and 3,141 counties/county equivalents defined as of February 22, 2005. For more information on these areas, see Appendix C, Geographic Information]

County	\	Population characteristics, 2005														
	\	Age (percent)									One race (percent)					
	Under 5 years	5 to 14 years	15 to 24 years	25 to 34 years	35 to 44 years	45 to 54 years	55 to 64 years	65 to 74 years	75 years and over	White alone	Black or African American alone	Asian alone	American Indian and Alaska Native alone	Native Hawaiian and Other Pacific Islander alone	Hispanic or Latino origin[1] (percent)	Males per 100 females
ARKANSAS—Con.																
Garland	5.7	11.4	12.0	11.7	12.9	13.6	12.0	10.6	10.1	89.3	7.9	0.6	0.7	(Z)	3.4	94.8
Grant	4.9	13.1	13.5	13.9	15.3	14.7	11.9	7.4	5.3	95.8	3.1	0.2	0.5	(Z)	1.7	98.5
Greene	6.7	13.4	13.0	14.2	14.4	13.5	11.1	7.5	6.3	97.8	0.3	0.2	0.4	(Z)	1.6	95.9
Hempstead	6.9	14.4	14.2	13.3	13.6	13.6	10.7	7.1	6.2	68.8	29.1	0.4	0.4	0.1	12.2	95.7
Hot Spring	5.8	13.1	12.9	12.7	13.6	14.6	12.1	8.2	7.1	87.9	10.2	0.3	0.5	0.1	1.7	97.6
Howard	7.2	13.6	13.4	13.0	14.7	13.1	10.7	7.3	6.8	77.8	20.7	0.5	0.5	–	8.8	97.0
Independence	6.4	12.4	14.2	11.9	13.7	14.8	11.7	8.4	6.4	95.5	2.1	1.0	0.4	(Z)	2.6	96.8
Izard	5.0	10.9	12.1	11.7	13.3	13.1	13.0	11.3	9.6	96.8	1.5	0.1	0.8	(Z)	1.2	105.1
Jackson	5.9	11.3	17.2	10.9	13.5	14.3	12.3	7.9	6.7	79.7	19.4	0.2	0.3	(Z)	1.4	92.9
Jefferson	7.1	13.5	15.2	12.4	13.6	14.7	10.8	6.6	6.2	46.2	51.9	0.9	0.3	0.1	1.2	96.2
Johnson	7.4	13.2	13.7	13.8	13.8	13.3	10.9	7.5	6.4	95.7	1.8	0.6	0.7	(Z)	9.3	98.8
Lafayette	6.0	12.7	13.1	10.6	12.8	14.6	13.0	8.7	8.6	63.1	36.1	0.3	0.4	–	1.6	94.9
Lawrence	6.1	12.4	14.3	11.4	13.0	13.2	12.1	8.8	8.7	97.8	0.7	0.1	0.6	(Z)	0.9	95.5
Lee	6.0	13.1	16.1	13.8	13.7	12.7	11.2	6.9	6.5	42.2	57.2	0.3	0.2	0.1	2.6	114.4
Lincoln	5.2	10.9	16.4	16.4	16.7	13.2	9.1	6.4	5.7	66.1	32.9	0.1	0.4	–	1.8	150.9
Little River	5.8	13.3	13.0	11.2	13.0	13.8	13.9	9.1	7.0	76.0	21.2	0.2	1.2	–	2.0	95.3
Logan	6.0	13.3	13.2	12.0	13.9	13.8	11.7	8.6	7.5	95.7	1.3	0.7	0.7	0.1	1.6	98.7
Lonoke	6.5	14.3	15.0	13.9	15.6	14.2	10.2	6.2	4.2	91.5	6.5	0.5	0.5	(Z)	2.3	99.2
Madison	5.7	13.4	13.6	12.1	13.9	14.9	12.1	8.0	6.3	97.2	0.2	0.1	1.2	0.2	4.0	99.7
Marion	3.7	10.9	12.1	9.8	13.2	14.7	14.8	12.2	9.2	97.7	0.3	0.2	0.7	(Z)	1.0	98.0
Miller	6.5	13.9	13.3	13.8	14.0	13.8	10.9	7.0	6.7	74.5	23.4	0.4	0.7	(Z)	1.9	96.1
Mississippi	8.2	15.8	14.0	11.9	13.4	14.0	10.3	6.9	5.4	63.9	34.1	0.4	0.3	(Z)	2.7	91.8
Monroe	6.5	14.3	14.0	9.2	11.7	14.6	12.0	9.1	8.5	59.3	39.3	0.2	0.2	0.1	1.7	86.5
Montgomery	4.7	12.5	12.4	9.1	13.9	14.1	13.1	10.9	8.6	97.1	0.6	0.4	0.9	–	3.7	98.1
Nevada	6.9	12.6	14.2	11.0	13.4	13.9	12.1	8.4	7.6	66.6	32.7	0.1	0.4	–	2.2	94.2
Newton	5.5	11.8	12.7	10.6	12.7	15.9	14.6	9.0	7.1	98.2	0.2	0.2	0.5	–	1.2	103.0
Ouachita	6.2	12.9	13.6	10.5	12.8	15.8	11.8	8.4	8.0	58.6	40.2	0.4	0.2	(Z)	1.1	90.2
Perry	5.5	13.1	13.3	12.0	14.4	14.4	12.2	8.3	6.9	96.3	2.0	0.1	0.9	(Z)	1.3	99.4
Phillips	8.8	17.0	15.3	9.8	11.0	13.2	10.9	7.7	6.4	37.3	61.4	0.5	0.2	(Z)	1.5	85.3
Pike	5.8	12.9	13.2	11.2	13.2	13.8	12.2	9.3	8.4	94.2	3.9	0.2	0.8	(Z)	5.0	97.8
Poinsett	6.8	13.7	13.1	13.1	13.6	13.8	11.8	7.9	6.2	91.8	7.4	0.2	0.2	(Z)	1.8	95.2
Polk	6.3	13.3	13.1	10.9	12.9	13.2	12.5	9.6	8.2	96.5	0.3	0.3	1.5	0.1	3.8	96.5
Pope	6.4	12.9	17.4	12.8	13.8	13.3	10.4	7.1	5.9	94.4	3.0	0.8	0.6	(Z)	3.8	97.8
Prairie	5.6	11.8	12.1	11.4	13.3	15.0	13.2	9.3	8.4	84.8	14.5	0.2	0.4	–	0.9	97.0
Pulaski	7.7	13.4	13.0	13.8	14.5	15.0	10.8	6.4	5.4	62.5	34.0	1.6	0.4	0.1	3.2	92.3
Randolph	5.6	12.4	14.0	12.1	13.1	13.7	12.0	9.0	8.3	97.4	1.2	0.1	0.6	(Z)	1.3	97.2
St. Francis	7.9	14.6	13.9	13.8	13.6	14.2	10.5	6.3	5.2	48.2	50.5	0.7	0.3	–	5.2	105.9
Saline	5.5	13.3	13.5	13.5	15.2	14.5	11.4	7.9	5.2	94.8	3.2	0.6	0.5	(Z)	2.0	99.3
Scott	6.5	13.8	12.8	12.5	13.6	13.2	12.5	8.9	6.3	95.4	0.5	0.2	2.0	–	7.0	100.4
Searcy	4.6	11.2	12.9	9.8	12.9	14.7	14.1	10.8	9.0	98.0	0.2	0.2	0.8	–	1.1	98.2
Sebastian	7.6	14.0	12.8	13.3	14.4	14.3	10.8	6.9	5.9	85.8	6.3	3.7	1.6	0.1	9.8	96.0
Sevier	9.0	15.4	13.5	13.8	13.6	12.0	10.1	7.0	5.6	92.4	4.4	0.2	2.0	0.1	26.6	99.3
Sharp	4.7	11.8	11.5	10.7	12.4	12.9	13.1	11.8	11.0	97.0	0.9	0.2	0.6	–	1.4	92.2
Stone	5.1	11.4	12.2	10.5	12.2	14.5	14.3	11.5	8.3	97.7	0.3	–	0.4	(Z)	1.2	96.9
Union	6.5	13.2	13.1	11.4	13.7	15.1	11.2	7.7	8.1	65.3	33.0	0.6	0.2	(Z)	1.7	91.9
Van Buren	5.1	11.2	12.0	10.8	11.6	13.5	12.7	11.6	11.5	97.1	0.5	0.3	0.8	(Z)	1.4	96.7
Washington	7.9	13.4	18.0	16.2	13.8	12.3	9.0	5.3	4.2	91.2	2.7	2.0	1.4	0.7	12.4	101.7
White	6.3	12.7	17.2	13.0	13.8	12.8	10.5	7.4	6.3	93.8	4.0	0.4	0.5	0.1	2.6	95.7
Woodruff	5.9	13.7	12.6	11.5	12.3	14.8	12.9	8.1	8.1	70.4	28.7	0.1	0.2	0.1	0.9	90.7
Yell	7.5	13.3	13.4	13.1	13.9	13.5	10.7	8.0	6.6	95.4	1.5	1.3	0.7	(Z)	17.2	101.7
CALIFORNIA	7.4	14.9	14.5	14.3	15.2	13.7	9.3	5.4	5.3	77.0	6.7	12.2	1.2	0.4	35.2	99.8
Alameda	7.4	13.7	12.7	14.1	16.4	15.0	10.3	5.4	5.1	56.9	13.8	24.2	0.7	0.7	20.8	96.9
Alpine	5.2	9.0	14.4	13.4	13.5	19.9	12.9	8.3	3.5	80.1	0.7	0.4	18.6	–	8.6	111.1
Amador	3.8	9.8	13.0	13.1	14.4	15.4	13.0	8.9	8.8	91.2	4.1	1.4	1.6	0.1	9.5	120.1
Butte	5.5	12.5	19.2	13.0	11.6	13.3	10.1	6.6	8.3	89.2	1.6	4.1	1.9	0.2	11.8	96.4
Calaveras	3.8	11.3	12.7	11.5	12.4	16.3	14.6	9.7	7.5	93.6	1.0	1.2	1.7	0.1	8.7	98.4
Colusa	8.0	15.7	16.4	12.7	12.7	12.8	8.7	6.6	6.5	93.5	1.0	1.7	2.4	0.7	49.1	103.7
Contra Costa	6.7	14.7	13.1	12.2	15.3	15.4	11.2	5.9	5.6	72.7	9.6	13.1	0.7	0.4	21.1	96.2
Del Norte	5.2	12.4	14.8	15.6	15.4	14.1	9.9	6.4	6.3	83.3	4.6	2.9	6.1	0.2	15.0	121.2
El Dorado	5.1	13.0	14.0	11.9	14.4	17.6	12.3	6.4	5.3	92.5	0.9	3.0	1.0	0.2	10.4	99.9
Fresno	8.6	17.0	16.6	14.2	13.5	12.2	8.2	4.8	4.8	81.4	5.7	8.8	1.9	0.2	46.9	101.1
Glenn	7.6	15.8	16.0	12.3	13.4	12.8	9.8	6.1	6.3	92.5	0.9	2.9	2.2	0.1	32.5	100.9
Humboldt	5.6	11.8	17.0	14.4	12.0	15.3	11.4	6.1	6.4	87.5	1.1	1.9	5.4	0.2	7.6	97.1
Imperial	9.1	15.8	17.5	13.4	14.2	11.2	7.6	5.2	5.1	90.6	4.2	2.3	1.9	0.3	75.3	107.5
Inyo	5.2	12.1	12.8	10.2	11.6	17.2	12.8	8.7	9.5	86.2	0.4	1.3	10.0	(Z)	15.9	95.3
Kern	8.5	17.0	16.2	15.2	14.1	12.3	7.8	4.7	4.1	85.8	6.2	3.9	1.7	0.3	44.1	106.1
Kings	8.2	15.5	16.6	18.4	16.2	11.2	6.5	4.0	3.4	84.3	8.5	3.3	2.0	0.3	47.0	134.8
Lake	5.3	12.7	13.4	11.8	13.0	15.1	12.7	8.0	8.1	90.9	2.2	1.1	3.1	0.2	14.7	97.1
Lassen	4.0	11.1	16.8	18.4	17.3	14.1	9.4	4.6	4.3	84.3	9.5	0.9	3.1	0.5	15.0	168.7
Los Angeles	7.6	15.4	14.4	14.6	15.6	13.4	8.9	5.2	4.9	74.1	9.7	13.1	1.1	0.3	46.8	97.8
Madera	8.0	15.4	15.5	15.4	13.9	12.3	8.7	5.6	5.1	88.6	4.4	1.7	3.1	0.4	48.4	93.2

See footnotes at end of table.

County and City Data Book: 2007

U.S. Census Bureau

[Includes United States, states, and 3,141 counties/county equivalents defined as of February 22, 2005. For more information on these areas, see Appendix C, Geographic Information]

County	Under 5 years	5 to 14 years	15 to 24 years	25 to 34 years	35 to 44 years	45 to 54 years	55 to 64 years	65 to 74 years	75 years and over	White alone	Black or African American alone	Asian alone	American Indian and Alaska Native alone	Native Hawaiian and Other Pacific Islander alone	Hispanic or Latino origin[1] (percent)	Males per 100 females
CALIFORNIA—Con.																
Marin	5.7	11.1	10.1	9.8	15.7	17.9	15.2	7.4	7.2	88.7	3.1	5.3	0.6	0.2	12.6	98.4
Mariposa	4.0	10.6	14.7	10.6	13.0	16.4	13.4	9.3	8.1	92.3	1.1	1.0	3.1	0.1	9.6	102.7
Mendocino	6.1	12.9	14.0	11.6	12.3	15.9	13.4	6.8	6.8	90.3	0.8	1.4	4.8	0.3	19.4	100.0
Merced	8.8	18.3	16.8	14.5	13.7	11.5	7.6	4.8	4.1	85.4	4.1	6.6	1.6	0.2	51.4	101.5
Modoc	4.2	12.6	14.1	9.9	12.3	14.8	13.9	9.8	8.5	92.9	0.8	0.7	4.0	–	12.0	102.0
Mono	5.6	12.1	13.0	15.8	15.5	18.4	11.5	5.5	2.6	94.6	0.6	1.4	2.5	(Z)	22.6	122.1
Monterey	8.7	15.2	15.5	15.1	14.1	12.9	8.6	4.9	5.0	85.5	3.8	6.5	1.3	0.6	50.8	108.4
Napa	6.2	13.0	13.3	12.9	13.9	14.7	11.5	6.9	7.6	89.3	2.0	5.2	1.0	0.4	27.6	100.5
Nevada	4.2	11.2	13.3	10.2	12.3	17.5	14.4	8.4	8.5	95.6	0.4	1.0	0.9	0.1	6.8	98.4
Orange	7.5	15.1	13.4	13.9	16.1	13.9	9.7	5.5	5.0	78.9	1.9	15.9	0.9	0.4	32.5	99.6
Placer	5.7	13.1	13.2	13.9	15.0	14.7	10.4	7.1	6.9	90.2	1.3	4.6	0.9	0.2	10.7	97.2
Plumas	4.0	10.9	13.1	9.8	11.5	16.9	15.3	9.9	8.5	94.1	0.8	0.7	2.4	(Z)	6.0	99.0
Riverside	7.4	16.1	15.3	15.5	14.6	12.0	7.7	5.5	6.0	84.5	6.5	4.8	1.4	0.4	41.0	100.0
Sacramento	7.5	15.3	14.0	14.9	14.9	13.6	9.1	5.5	5.4	70.0	10.5	13.2	1.1	0.7	18.7	96.4
San Benito	8.0	17.5	15.1	12.6	15.5	13.9	9.2	4.4	3.8	91.7	1.4	3.1	1.6	0.5	50.6	103.0
San Bernardino	8.0	17.4	16.3	15.1	14.7	12.7	7.8	4.4	3.7	80.6	9.5	5.6	1.4	0.4	44.8	100.6
San Diego	7.6	14.1	15.3	14.8	15.0	13.4	8.8	5.3	5.7	79.8	5.6	10.2	1.0	0.6	29.5	101.9
San Francisco	5.4	7.2	9.4	18.5	19.4	14.7	10.6	7.0	7.8	56.6	7.3	32.9	0.5	0.4	13.7	102.9
San Joaquin	8.0	16.5	15.7	14.8	14.2	12.6	8.5	4.9	4.8	73.0	7.9	13.8	1.3	0.5	34.7	100.4
San Luis Obispo	4.9	11.1	16.8	12.1	12.9	15.3	10.7	6.7	7.6	91.3	2.1	3.1	1.1	0.1	17.8	105.6
San Mateo	7.1	12.7	11.1	12.3	16.5	15.7	11.6	6.4	6.5	68.5	3.4	23.4	0.5	1.4	22.6	98.1
Santa Barbara	7.1	13.4	17.7	13.0	13.4	13.3	9.3	6.0	6.8	89.1	2.3	4.6	1.6	0.3	37.3	100.7
Santa Clara	7.8	13.6	12.2	14.5	17.1	14.5	9.9	5.6	4.8	63.2	2.8	30.2	0.8	0.4	24.9	103.8
Santa Cruz	6.7	12.2	16.3	12.0	14.5	16.5	11.5	5.0	5.2	90.9	1.2	4.0	1.2	0.2	27.8	100.3
Shasta	5.6	13.1	14.3	12.4	12.9	14.7	11.9	7.6	7.6	90.9	1.0	2.2	2.6	0.1	7.2	95.7
Sierra	3.8	11.7	13.9	8.4	12.3	17.7	15.1	9.3	7.7	96.9	0.3	0.1	1.8	(Z)	8.4	101.8
Siskiyou	5.1	11.6	14.1	9.3	11.2	16.4	14.2	9.0	9.1	90.7	1.4	1.3	3.7	0.1	9.0	96.7
Solano	7.2	15.5	14.4	13.2	14.9	14.7	9.7	5.4	4.8	64.0	15.3	14.1	0.9	0.9	21.2	101.3
Sonoma	6.2	13.1	14.1	11.7	14.3	16.1	12.0	5.9	6.7	90.2	1.6	3.8	1.4	0.3	21.1	97.7
Stanislaus	7.9	16.6	15.6	14.5	14.1	12.8	8.5	5.1	4.8	87.1	3.1	5.0	1.5	0.5	37.6	98.2
Sutter	7.4	15.1	14.7	14.3	13.9	12.8	9.6	6.7	5.5	80.9	2.3	12.5	1.6	0.2	25.7	99.3
Tehama	6.1	14.1	14.8	12.3	13.4	13.5	10.7	7.8	7.3	93.8	0.8	0.9	2.1	0.1	18.8	97.6
Trinity	4.1	11.0	13.2	9.0	11.7	17.6	16.1	9.7	7.6	90.4	0.5	0.8	4.5	0.1	4.8	104.9
Tulare	9.4	17.8	16.5	14.3	13.0	11.7	8.1	4.8	4.5	90.9	1.9	3.6	1.9	0.3	55.2	100.8
Tuolumne	3.9	10.0	13.7	12.9	13.6	15.7	12.6	9.0	8.7	91.8	3.1	0.9	1.8	0.2	10.1	119.8
Ventura	7.4	15.3	14.1	12.6	15.0	14.7	10.1	5.6	5.1	87.9	2.1	6.3	1.2	0.3	36.0	100.2
Yolo	6.5	13.3	22.9	14.7	12.7	12.1	8.2	4.8	4.7	80.7	2.6	11.7	1.4	0.4	27.5	95.2
Yuba	8.7	16.5	16.1	15.4	13.4	12.2	8.2	5.1	4.4	82.6	3.0	7.6	2.4	0.2	21.2	101.2
COLORADO	7.3	13.8	14.1	15.5	15.2	14.5	9.5	5.3	4.7	90.3	4.1	2.6	1.1	0.1	19.5	102.0
Adams	8.6	16.0	13.8	18.3	15.6	12.5	7.9	4.2	3.0	89.8	3.2	3.4	1.4	0.2	35.0	104.3
Alamosa	7.8	14.3	21.4	12.5	11.7	12.9	9.0	5.8	4.8	92.5	1.7	1.1	3.0	0.4	43.6	99.6
Arapahoe	7.4	14.4	13.4	15.0	15.3	15.2	9.8	5.1	4.3	82.4	9.6	4.7	0.8	0.1	16.2	98.1
Archuleta	5.3	11.9	13.3	13.3	12.9	16.5	13.5	8.2	5.0	96.5	0.4	0.5	1.6	(Z)	15.3	101.3
Baca	4.0	12.8	12.3	8.5	10.8	15.6	11.9	10.3	14.0	97.9	(Z)	0.3	0.8	0.1	9.3	95.5
Bent	5.5	12.3	15.4	14.1	14.6	13.2	10.5	7.7	6.7	91.8	4.1	1.0	2.8	–	30.8	126.0
Boulder	6.2	12.1	16.4	15.4	15.2	15.7	9.7	4.8	3.9	92.9	1.1	3.7	0.7	0.1	12.7	103.1
Broomfield	7.1	15.6	13.6	15.0	17.5	15.7	8.6	4.0	2.8	92.1	1.2	4.5	0.6	–	10.4	101.6
Chaffee	4.3	9.9	13.8	13.5	13.1	15.4	12.8	9.5	8.7	96.1	1.7	0.5	1.0	(Z)	8.6	112.4
Cheyenne	4.9	14.2	16.1	6.5	13.4	18.1	10.1	7.2	9.7	98.3	0.6	0.2	1.0	–	9.0	97.3
Clear Creek	5.5	12.0	10.4	12.9	16.0	21.5	14.7	4.8	2.2	97.3	0.4	0.7	0.9	–	4.2	107.0
Conejos	6.9	16.2	17.4	9.7	11.6	13.5	9.0	7.6	8.1	97.0	0.3	0.3	2.0	0.2	55.9	97.1
Costilla	5.5	11.8	13.5	8.6	12.0	15.9	13.8	10.1	8.8	93.3	1.1	1.1	3.4	0.6	63.0	96.3
Crowley	4.2	9.8	15.1	17.6	20.7	14.3	8.1	4.9	5.5	88.7	7.3	0.9	2.7	–	23.4	200.9
Custer	4.1	11.5	11.1	11.0	12.8	16.8	15.1	11.0	6.5	97.9	0.4	0.4	0.8	–	3.2	102.6
Delta	5.4	12.4	12.4	11.9	11.9	14.1	11.9	9.6	9.8	97.1	0.6	0.4	0.9	(Z)	12.6	99.6
Denver	9.2	12.1	11.5	18.6	16.0	12.8	8.9	5.0	5.9	82.9	10.6	3.1	1.4	0.2	34.7	103.4
Dolores	6.6	11.4	11.4	11.8	12.9	16.7	12.1	8.9	8.2	96.4	0.1	0.5	2.8	–	6.8	105.3
Douglas	8.1	16.7	12.6	16.6	18.5	14.5	8.3	3.0	1.8	92.8	1.5	3.5	0.5	0.1	6.5	100.2
Eagle	8.3	12.2	11.7	22.7	18.4	14.9	8.1	2.6	1.2	97.3	0.6	0.9	0.6	0.1	26.9	120.8
Elbert	5.3	14.9	14.2	11.2	16.4	19.8	11.1	4.6	2.5	96.4	0.7	0.6	0.8	0.1	5.2	101.0
El Paso	7.7	15.0	14.9	15.5	15.2	13.9	8.7	5.0	4.1	85.8	6.7	2.8	1.0	0.3	12.7	100.5
Fremont	4.4	10.8	12.9	15.8	16.5	14.3	10.0	7.7	7.5	91.3	5.3	0.6	1.3	0.1	10.5	132.1
Garfield	8.5	14.3	13.2	15.9	15.3	15.0	9.2	4.8	3.9	96.9	0.7	0.5	0.7	0.1	22.6	105.9
Gilpin	5.6	10.6	10.6	14.6	17.9	21.0	12.9	4.3	2.6	96.4	0.9	1.3	0.6	(Z)	4.6	108.9
Grand	5.9	11.0	11.5	17.1	15.9	18.3	11.6	5.5	3.2	97.5	0.6	0.8	0.6	0.1	5.0	112.5
Gunnison	5.9	9.0	22.1	19.1	13.9	13.5	8.9	4.5	3.1	96.8	0.6	0.7	1.0	(Z)	5.8	115.4
Hinsdale	4.1	11.5	7.7	8.2	13.3	19.9	18.6	10.6	6.1	97.9	–	0.5	1.6	–	1.6	100.8
Huerfano	5.0	10.2	13.0	11.8	13.3	15.5	12.7	9.2	9.5	91.9	3.0	0.5	3.3	(Z)	34.8	115.8
Jackson	4.9	12.4	13.0	7.0	14.4	17.4	14.4	8.8	7.7	98.8	0.3	0.1	0.8	–	8.1	95.9

See footnotes at end of table.

[Includes United States, states, and 3,141 counties/county equivalents defined as of February 22, 2005. For more information on these areas, see Appendix C, Geographic Information]

County	Under 5 years	5 to 14 years	15 to 24 years	25 to 34 years	35 to 44 years	45 to 54 years	55 to 64 years	65 to 74 years	75 years and over	White alone	Black or African American alone	Asian alone	American Indian and Alaska Native alone	Native Hawaiian and Other Pacific Islander alone	Hispanic or Latino origin[1] (percent)	Males per 100 females
COLORADO—Con.																
Jefferson	6.1	13.7	13.3	11.9	15.4	17.0	11.5	6.2	5.0	93.8	1.1	2.5	0.9	0.1	12.8	99.5
Kiowa	5.9	12.9	12.3	10.1	11.5	15.4	10.9	9.5	11.5	97.7	0.6	0.1	1.5	0.1	3.2	94.8
Kit Carson	5.4	14.3	14.1	11.1	14.6	14.1	10.6	7.7	8.1	97.0	1.9	0.4	0.5	(Z)	15.9	114.2
Lake	7.8	15.3	14.6	17.5	15.4	13.9	7.9	5.0	2.6	96.5	0.4	0.6	1.9	0.2	41.4	114.9
La Plata	5.2	11.2	18.2	14.7	13.1	16.2	10.8	5.7	4.8	91.4	0.6	0.6	5.8	0.1	10.4	103.6
Larimer	6.2	12.5	17.9	15.7	13.7	14.6	9.3	5.3	4.9	94.9	0.9	1.8	0.7	0.1	9.5	100.7
Las Animas	5.8	12.7	14.5	11.1	12.1	14.5	12.0	8.1	9.3	94.5	0.6	0.6	2.7	0.4	41.4	96.0
Lincoln	5.3	12.0	14.0	12.1	16.7	15.6	9.3	7.6	7.5	92.1	5.6	0.9	1.0	0.1	10.3	135.4
Logan	6.2	13.4	15.8	13.0	13.6	14.3	9.5	7.0	7.1	96.0	2.3	0.5	0.8	0.1	12.6	114.0
Mesa	6.2	12.9	14.7	14.0	12.7	14.2	9.9	7.4	7.9	96.3	0.7	0.6	0.9	0.1	11.0	96.7
Mineral	3.8	9.9	9.4	12.9	13.3	16.0	14.3	11.3	9.2	99.2	–	–	0.3	–	2.0	105.3
Moffat	7.4	14.2	14.3	13.4	14.2	16.8	10.5	5.0	4.1	97.3	0.4	0.4	0.9	(Z)	12.7	108.7
Montezuma	6.4	14.3	13.9	11.5	13.0	14.9	11.1	8.1	6.8	87.0	0.2	0.3	10.9	0.1	9.7	97.6
Montrose	6.4	14.0	13.2	12.9	12.9	13.9	10.8	8.2	7.7	96.3	0.6	0.6	1.3	0.1	16.8	97.2
Morgan	8.0	16.6	14.3	12.0	13.7	13.2	8.5	6.7	7.0	97.3	0.7	0.2	1.0	0.3	32.3	101.1
Otero	7.5	14.1	15.1	9.5	11.6	14.0	11.0	8.6	8.6	95.1	1.1	0.8	1.6	0.2	38.2	95.1
Ouray	4.1	11.7	11.9	10.1	13.3	19.1	16.5	8.1	5.1	97.9	0.1	0.4	0.8	–	3.8	99.2
Park	4.9	12.6	11.6	12.3	16.9	20.4	13.0	5.4	2.9	96.6	0.8	0.6	0.8	(Z)	5.8	106.1
Phillips	6.8	15.3	13.0	9.9	12.5	14.9	9.3	8.3	9.9	97.9	0.3	0.4	0.7	0.1	18.7	94.9
Pitkin	5.2	8.1	8.9	16.8	18.4	18.4	14.9	6.0	3.3	97.0	0.7	1.5	0.3	–	7.0	115.0
Prowers	8.2	16.5	15.5	12.7	12.3	12.8	9.1	6.2	6.7	96.8	0.6	0.5	1.5	0.2	37.4	104.0
Pueblo	6.6	14.1	14.4	13.8	13.3	13.5	9.5	7.1	7.7	93.7	2.2	0.7	1.9	0.2	39.0	96.5
Rio Blanco	6.3	12.1	17.5	10.1	13.0	17.1	11.4	7.0	5.5	97.8	0.2	0.4	0.9	–	5.8	101.9
Rio Grande	6.8	14.1	15.0	9.9	12.3	15.1	11.2	8.0	7.5	96.7	0.8	0.4	1.6	0.1	37.6	95.3
Routt	5.2	11.3	12.8	18.5	16.3	19.2	10.8	3.8	2.1	97.7	0.5	0.5	0.5	0.1	3.7	116.5
Saguache	6.6	14.7	15.2	12.7	13.3	15.6	11.9	5.4	4.5	96.4	0.2	0.5	2.2	0.1	45.7	102.1
San Juan	4.5	8.7	10.9	10.7	12.8	21.5	22.2	5.5	3.1	98.1	–	0.2	1.2	0.5	8.8	104.6
San Miguel	5.4	9.2	8.7	24.1	19.3	17.2	12.2	2.9	1.1	97.4	0.3	1.0	0.8	0.1	8.8	119.2
Sedgwick	5.7	13.0	10.6	10.0	11.8	14.7	11.1	11.3	11.7	98.0	0.6	0.9	(Z)	0.2	13.7	99.0
Summit	6.8	8.8	10.3	29.1	18.2	14.3	7.8	3.3	1.3	97.1	0.9	0.9	0.4	(Z)	13.1	138.7
Teller	5.2	12.8	13.5	10.0	15.3	20.5	13.5	6.3	2.9	95.8	1.0	0.7	1.0	(Z)	4.5	103.5
Washington	4.9	13.7	13.5	9.0	12.3	15.9	11.5	8.8	10.3	98.9	0.1	0.1	0.7	–	7.5	101.8
Weld	8.0	14.7	17.0	17.5	14.2	12.4	7.9	4.5	3.8	95.8	0.8	1.0	1.0	0.2	27.8	102.1
Yuma	6.9	14.8	14.0	11.4	12.4	14.1	10.3	7.7	8.4	99.1	0.2	0.1	0.3	0.1	18.5	96.7
CONNECTICUT	6.0	13.4	13.3	11.4	15.8	15.5	11.0	6.1	7.4	84.9	10.1	3.2	0.3	0.1	10.9	94.4
Fairfield	6.6	14.5	12.0	10.6	16.5	15.7	11.1	6.1	6.9	83.7	10.7	4.1	0.3	0.1	14.0	94.7
Hartford	6.0	13.3	13.1	11.5	15.4	15.3	11.2	6.3	8.0	81.6	13.3	3.3	0.3	0.1	12.8	93.0
Litchfield	5.0	12.8	12.2	10.0	15.9	17.2	12.4	6.5	7.9	96.0	1.4	1.4	0.2	(Z)	3.2	95.7
Middlesex	5.4	12.7	12.8	10.7	16.7	16.2	11.8	6.4	7.4	91.8	4.7	2.1	0.2	0.1	3.5	94.6
New Haven	6.0	13.2	13.9	12.3	15.2	14.9	10.7	5.9	7.9	82.4	12.6	3.2	0.3	0.1	12.0	92.8
New London	5.9	13.1	13.6	12.5	16.1	15.5	10.2	6.2	7.0	87.6	6.0	3.1	0.9	0.1	6.1	98.1
Tolland	4.9	11.7	19.7	11.6	15.4	15.4	10.8	5.2	5.3	92.6	3.4	2.7	0.2	(Z)	3.4	100.6
Windham	5.7	12.8	15.3	13.0	15.6	15.3	10.3	5.5	6.3	94.7	2.3	1.1	0.5	0.1	7.6	97.2
DELAWARE	6.6	12.6	13.9	13.3	15.1	14.5	10.8	7.0	6.3	74.9	20.7	2.7	0.4	0.1	6.0	95.2
Kent	7.0	13.4	15.1	13.8	14.7	13.5	10.0	6.8	5.5	73.7	22.0	1.9	0.6	0.1	3.8	93.6
New Castle	6.6	12.9	14.5	13.4	15.7	14.9	10.5	6.0	5.5	72.3	22.5	3.5	0.3	0.1	6.7	95.2
Sussex	5.9	11.1	11.3	12.5	13.6	13.9	12.2	10.4	9.0	83.5	14.1	0.8	0.6	0.1	5.8	96.3
DISTRICT OF COLUMBIA	7.0	10.5	12.4	19.8	14.8	13.0	10.3	6.2	6.0	38.0	57.0	3.1	0.3	0.1	8.6	90.2
District of Columbia	7.0	10.5	12.4	19.8	14.8	13.0	10.3	6.2	6.0	38.0	57.0	3.1	0.3	0.1	8.6	90.2
FLORIDA	6.3	12.6	13.0	12.2	14.3	13.9	11.0	8.5	8.3	80.4	15.7	2.1	0.4	0.1	19.5	96.2
Alachua	5.6	10.4	26.5	14.5	11.3	12.4	9.1	5.6	4.6	73.7	20.0	4.4	0.3	(Z)	6.4	95.2
Baker	7.4	13.8	15.8	13.8	15.0	14.3	10.2	6.3	3.3	85.3	13.3	0.5	0.3	(Z)	2.3	111.6
Bay	6.6	12.8	12.6	12.5	14.4	14.9	12.1	8.3	5.7	84.4	11.3	1.8	0.8	0.1	3.2	98.4
Bradford	5.6	11.4	13.5	16.0	15.7	14.4	10.7	7.4	5.4	76.3	21.9	0.7	0.4	0.1	2.9	131.1
Brevard	5.1	11.7	12.6	10.2	13.7	14.7	11.9	10.5	9.7	86.9	9.4	1.8	0.4	0.1	6.1	96.6
Broward	6.8	13.6	12.3	12.1	16.1	14.9	10.6	6.5	7.5	70.4	24.9	2.9	0.3	0.1	21.9	94.4
Calhoun	5.7	12.1	14.3	15.5	14.3	13.6	10.2	7.8	6.5	81.3	15.9	0.6	1.4	–	4.4	118.2
Charlotte	3.5	8.9	9.1	8.6	10.4	12.1	13.7	16.1	17.6	92.7	5.3	1.1	0.2	(Z)	4.2	92.0
Citrus	3.6	9.5	10.4	9.4	10.7	12.4	13.4	15.2	15.4	94.9	2.8	1.1	0.4	(Z)	3.4	92.4
Clay	6.3	14.1	14.5	12.6	15.2	15.2	11.9	6.3	3.9	86.6	8.7	2.4	0.5	0.1	5.5	97.8
Collier	6.4	11.1	10.6	11.8	12.7	12.0	11.7	12.2	11.5	92.0	5.9	0.9	0.4	0.2	24.4	102.2
Columbia	6.5	13.3	14.3	13.0	13.4	14.2	11.3	8.0	6.0	80.4	17.4	0.8	0.6	(Z)	3.5	103.3
DeSoto	6.7	11.7	15.5	16.7	11.8	10.6	9.5	9.0	8.5	84.4	11.8	0.6	2.9	0.1	31.4	137.1
Dixie	5.6	11.5	12.8	12.9	13.4	13.4	12.4	10.6	7.5	89.3	9.5	0.3	0.5	(Z)	2.1	114.5
Duval	7.8	14.6	13.6	13.4	15.4	14.6	10.2	5.9	4.4	64.7	30.0	3.3	0.4	0.1	5.4	94.7

See footnotes at end of table.

[Includes United States, states, and 3,141 counties/county equivalents defined as of February 22, 2005. For more information on these areas, see Appendix C, Geographic Information]

County	Population characteristics, 2005														
	Age (percent)									One race (percent)					His-panic or Latino origin[1] (per-cent)	Males per 100 females
	Under 5 years	5 to 14 years	15 to 24 years	25 to 34 years	35 to 44 years	45 to 54 years	55 to 64 years	65 to 74 years	75 years and over	White alone	Black or African Ameri-can alone	Asian alone	Ameri-can Indian and Alaska Native alone	Native Hawai-ian and Other Pacific Islander alone		
FLORIDA—Con.																
Escambia	6.8	12.7	16.0	11.7	13.0	13.8	11.4	8.3	6.3	71.4	23.0	2.4	0.9	0.1	2.9	98.1
Flagler	4.3	9.9	11.5	12.5	12.1	12.2	12.6	13.2	11.9	88.0	9.2	1.6	0.3	(Z)	6.6	94.7
Franklin	5.7	11.0	11.7	11.3	13.3	15.2	15.5	9.8	6.5	88.7	10.0	0.3	0.4	(Z)	1.5	105.3
Gadsden	7.8	13.6	14.2	13.2	13.9	14.6	10.4	7.0	5.2	42.6	56.4	0.3	0.3	(Z)	7.9	89.9
Gilchrist	5.7	12.5	19.9	10.7	12.3	13.6	11.1	8.3	6.0	91.9	6.6	0.3	0.4	–	3.7	109.9
Glades	3.5	12.1	12.4	13.7	13.6	12.3	11.7	11.8	8.9	83.6	10.5	0.4	4.9	0.1	17.6	121.0
Gulf	4.2	11.3	12.7	12.6	15.3	14.6	12.7	9.7	6.8	80.7	17.4	0.5	0.7	(Z)	2.4	119.0
Hamilton	6.4	12.0	15.2	15.1	15.9	14.1	10.1	6.9	4.2	62.5	36.5	0.3	0.5	0.1	8.3	144.2
Hardee	8.6	14.8	14.8	15.7	13.1	11.0	8.6	6.9	6.6	88.7	9.0	0.5	1.3	0.2	39.8	125.3
Hendry	8.9	15.7	18.0	15.0	13.4	10.5	8.2	6.1	4.1	84.2	13.5	0.5	1.4	0.1	45.8	128.8
Hernando	4.5	10.7	11.3	10.9	11.5	12.2	12.2	12.5	14.2	93.4	4.6	0.9	0.3	(Z)	7.4	91.7
Highlands	5.0	10.6	10.9	10.5	10.2	10.9	10.7	13.7	17.4	88.0	9.6	1.2	0.5	(Z)	15.1	96.3
Hillsborough	7.1	14.1	13.8	13.7	15.2	14.2	10.4	6.3	5.2	78.7	16.3	2.9	0.5	0.1	21.2	97.2
Holmes	5.9	11.9	13.8	13.7	14.2	12.7	11.9	9.0	6.9	90.7	6.6	0.5	1.0	(Z)	2.7	114.3
Indian River	4.9	10.4	11.2	10.3	11.7	13.0	11.5	12.0	15.1	89.8	8.4	0.9	0.3	(Z)	8.7	94.8
Jackson	5.6	11.5	14.5	13.6	14.4	14.1	11.2	8.3	6.6	70.5	27.3	0.5	0.7	(Z)	3.5	113.1
Jefferson	5.4	10.8	12.2	14.1	15.4	16.0	12.2	7.5	6.4	62.8	36.0	0.4	0.4	0.1	3.6	117.9
Lafayette	6.2	10.9	14.7	19.2	16.2	11.7	9.5	6.8	4.7	82.1	16.7	0.2	0.7	(Z)	12.0	162.1
Lake	5.4	11.0	10.6	11.8	12.5	11.6	10.6	13.1	13.6	88.4	8.8	1.4	0.4	0.1	9.1	94.6
Lee	5.7	11.2	10.9	11.9	12.7	12.7	12.2	11.3	11.4	90.0	7.5	1.1	0.4	0.1	14.3	97.3
Leon	6.4	11.5	22.8	14.5	12.5	13.6	10.0	5.0	3.7	65.8	30.2	2.5	0.3	(Z)	4.1	92.0
Levy	5.6	12.6	12.9	11.5	12.8	13.9	13.1	10.0	7.5	87.4	10.6	0.5	0.5	–	5.3	93.8
Liberty	6.0	10.9	13.5	20.0	17.5	13.1	8.9	5.9	4.1	79.0	19.0	0.2	1.7	–	6.5	151.2
Madison	6.3	12.5	14.8	14.1	13.1	13.6	10.5	8.1	7.0	58.6	40.4	0.4	0.3	(Z)	4.3	109.8
Manatee	5.9	11.8	11.2	11.3	12.7	13.0	11.6	10.4	12.1	88.8	8.7	1.3	0.3	0.1	11.8	95.0
Marion	5.3	11.4	12.0	11.2	12.5	12.6	11.4	11.7	11.9	85.9	11.6	1.0	0.5	(Z)	7.9	94.1
Martin	4.6	10.3	10.5	9.7	12.1	13.8	12.7	12.0	14.4	92.2	5.5	0.8	0.8	0.2	9.1	97.6
Miami-Dade	7.1	13.4	13.8	12.4	15.6	13.8	10.7	7.4	6.3	76.5	20.5	1.5	0.3	0.1	60.6	93.8
Monroe	4.7	9.2	8.4	9.6	15.7	20.1	17.2	9.3	5.9	92.3	5.4	1.1	0.4	(Z)	17.7	113.8
Nassau	5.7	12.8	12.8	11.6	14.2	15.4	13.2	8.9	5.3	90.5	7.5	0.7	0.4	(Z)	2.0	97.8
Okaloosa	7.1	13.2	13.1	12.5	14.8	14.5	11.7	8.3	4.7	84.2	9.7	2.7	0.6	0.1	5.3	102.2
Okeechobee	7.3	13.1	14.3	13.9	13.2	12.0	10.2	8.8	7.4	89.3	8.0	0.9	0.9	0.1	21.6	116.3
Orange	7.7	14.1	14.3	15.1	16.1	13.9	9.3	5.5	4.1	72.5	20.7	4.3	0.5	0.1	23.2	98.7
Osceola	7.3	14.4	13.8	15.4	15.0	13.1	9.6	6.5	4.2	84.4	10.1	2.8	0.6	0.2	37.8	99.0
Palm Beach	6.0	11.9	11.6	10.9	13.9	13.6	10.7	9.2	12.2	80.5	16.0	2.0	0.5	0.1	16.1	94.8
Pasco	5.3	11.7	11.6	12.0	13.5	12.8	11.5	9.8	11.8	93.5	3.4	1.5	0.4	0.1	8.4	93.8
Pinellas	5.2	11.1	10.7	10.1	14.0	15.4	12.8	9.6	11.2	85.6	10.1	2.7	0.4	0.1	6.2	92.2
Polk	6.9	13.4	13.2	12.3	13.0	12.8	10.8	9.0	8.5	82.9	14.2	1.3	0.5	0.1	13.3	97.0
Putnam	6.5	13.4	13.0	10.8	11.8	13.9	12.4	10.2	8.1	80.7	17.4	0.6	0.5	0.1	7.4	97.6
St. Johns	5.0	11.9	13.7	11.6	14.2	15.9	13.1	7.9	6.7	91.4	6.0	1.5	0.3	0.1	3.7	96.3
St. Lucie	5.6	12.3	12.5	12.1	13.0	12.9	10.6	10.3	10.8	80.8	16.5	1.3	0.3	0.1	12.4	96.3
Santa Rosa	5.9	13.4	13.8	12.2	15.4	15.5	11.9	7.5	4.5	90.9	4.9	1.5	0.9	0.1	3.2	100.5
Sarasota	4.3	9.2	9.5	9.4	11.6	13.3	13.1	13.1	16.4	93.4	4.5	1.1	0.2	(Z)	6.3	91.6
Seminole	6.0	13.7	13.6	12.4	15.7	16.2	11.7	6.3	4.5	83.9	10.9	3.3	0.4	0.1	13.8	96.9
Sumter	4.0	9.1	11.2	14.4	13.5	11.8	12.5	14.1	9.4	85.1	12.9	0.6	0.5	0.1	7.7	118.1
Suwannee	6.4	12.7	13.2	12.4	12.0	13.5	12.2	9.8	7.8	86.6	11.5	0.6	0.4	(Z)	7.1	96.6
Taylor	5.9	12.5	13.5	13.1	13.7	14.7	12.2	8.5	5.9	78.6	19.0	0.5	0.9	(Z)	1.9	107.6
Union	5.0	10.4	13.8	18.2	21.6	14.9	8.3	4.8	2.9	74.8	23.5	0.4	0.6	(Z)	4.0	190.1
Volusia	5.2	11.1	12.9	11.3	12.8	13.9	12.0	10.2	10.6	87.3	10.0	1.3	0.4	(Z)	9.1	95.6
Wakulla	5.5	12.3	14.3	13.0	15.8	15.7	11.5	7.3	4.7	86.5	11.7	0.4	0.6	(Z)	2.6	110.1
Walton	5.5	11.9	11.8	13.5	14.5	15.1	13.3	8.7	5.8	89.7	6.8	0.7	1.1	(Z)	2.8	104.4
Washington	5.3	12.8	13.0	12.9	14.8	14.1	12.6	8.4	6.2	82.5	13.9	0.6	1.4	(Z)	2.4	109.4
GEORGIA	7.6	14.1	14.5	15.4	15.7	13.6	9.4	5.4	4.2	66.1	29.8	2.7	0.3	0.1	7.1	97.9
Appling	7.4	14.2	13.2	14.4	13.8	14.2	11.2	6.6	5.2	80.4	18.5	0.4	0.3	(Z)	5.7	100.6
Atkinson	9.4	16.6	14.2	15.5	14.0	11.7	8.8	5.7	4.0	80.1	18.4	0.3	0.7	0.3	21.6	98.2
Bacon	7.4	13.8	13.3	14.6	14.4	13.0	10.2	7.4	6.0	82.3	16.3	0.7	0.1	–	4.1	97.7
Baker	4.7	15.0	15.4	15.1	14.4	13.2	10.4	6.4	5.5	48.4	51.2	–	0.3	(Z)	2.7	86.8
Baldwin	6.0	10.4	19.8	14.8	14.9	13.6	9.7	6.5	4.2	54.3	44.0	1.2	0.2	–	1.5	117.5
Banks	6.5	13.9	12.8	16.1	15.2	13.9	10.6	6.6	4.5	95.3	3.4	0.6	0.3	0.1	3.8	102.5
Barrow	7.9	15.0	13.2	19.0	17.0	11.8	7.8	4.6	3.7	85.1	10.8	2.7	0.3	(Z)	6.2	100.5
Bartow	8.2	14.6	13.1	16.6	16.1	13.0	9.0	5.4	4.0	88.6	9.3	0.8	0.3	(Z)	5.6	99.5
Ben Hill	8.0	14.5	14.4	13.6	12.8	13.9	10.3	6.4	6.2	65.2	33.7	0.4	0.3	(Z)	6.4	95.1
Berrien	6.8	14.2	13.7	13.8	14.5	12.9	10.8	7.6	5.6	87.9	11.0	0.4	0.2	(Z)	2.8	96.8
Bibb	7.9	14.5	14.5	13.0	13.6	13.9	9.9	6.5	6.2	47.5	50.3	1.4	0.2	(Z)	1.6	85.4
Bleckley	5.9	13.3	18.5	12.1	13.6	12.7	10.1	7.6	6.2	73.9	24.7	1.2	(Z)	–	1.4	93.9
Brantley	5.3	14.6	14.0	15.5	15.4	13.8	10.5	7.0	4.0	94.7	4.3	0.1	(Z)	(Z)	1.2	100.9
Brooks	6.9	13.9	14.6	12.8	13.2	13.4	11.1	7.4	6.7	60.9	38.1	0.3	0.1	(Z)	4.0	93.7
Bryan	6.9	15.2	15.9	15.2	16.0	14.9	8.9	4.0	3.0	82.2	15.0	1.0	0.4	0.1	2.4	98.6
Bulloch	6.3	11.2	28.8	14.6	11.5	10.8	7.6	5.1	4.0	69.5	28.6	1.1	0.2	(Z)	2.4	97.0
Burke	9.2	16.0	15.3	12.8	13.3	14.0	9.2	5.9	4.3	48.0	50.9	0.4	0.2	(Z)	1.8	90.9
Butts	7.4	13.5	13.5	16.5	14.5	13.5	10.2	6.6	4.3	73.9	24.5	0.4	0.5	(Z)	2.0	97.0
Calhoun	7.3	11.3	14.3	15.3	16.9	14.4	8.7	6.1	5.7	36.6	63.1	0.2	0.1	–	3.5	132.7
Camden	8.5	17.1	15.6	16.6	16.2	11.9	7.0	4.2	2.9	75.6	20.6	1.3	0.7	0.1	3.3	99.3

See footnotes at end of table.

Table B-3. Counties — **Population by Age, Race, Hispanic Origin, and Sex**—Con.

[Includes United States, states, and 3,141 counties/county equivalents defined as of February 22, 2005. For more information on these areas, see Appendix C, Geographic Information]

County	\multicolumn{9}{c}{Age (percent)}									\multicolumn{5}{c}{One race (percent)}					Hispanic or Latino origin[1] (percent)	Males per 100 females
	Under 5 years	5 to 14 years	15 to 24 years	25 to 34 years	35 to 44 years	45 to 54 years	55 to 64 years	65 to 74 years	75 years and over	White alone	Black or African American alone	Asian alone	American Indian and Alaska Native alone	Native Hawaiian and Other Pacific Islander alone		

GEORGIA—Con.

County	U5	5-14	15-24	25-34	35-44	45-54	55-64	65-74	75+	White	Black	Asian	AmInd	NHPI	Hisp	M/100F
Candler	8.4	13.4	14.1	14.8	12.5	12.0	10.6	6.6	7.5	73.8	25.2	0.3	0.6	(Z)	12.1	101.2
Carroll	7.5	13.5	16.6	17.3	14.5	12.1	8.9	5.6	4.1	81.3	16.7	0.8	0.3	(Z)	4.0	97.1
Catoosa	6.1	13.8	12.8	15.6	15.5	13.5	10.3	7.0	5.3	95.6	2.1	1.0	0.3	(Z)	1.7	94.7
Charlton	5.7	13.2	17.1	14.9	16.1	13.3	9.0	6.7	4.2	69.8	28.6	0.4	0.4	–	0.8	114.7
Chatham	7.6	13.4	15.5	14.3	13.6	13.2	9.8	6.5	6.1	55.1	41.3	2.1	0.3	0.1	2.7	92.9
Chattahoochee	7.3	15.8	33.4	19.3	14.9	5.0	1.9	1.4	0.8	65.3	28.8	2.1	0.8	0.9	10.7	176.0
Chattooga	6.2	12.6	13.2	16.1	14.4	13.3	10.5	7.2	6.6	88.3	10.7	0.3	(Z)	0.1	3.2	106.9
Cherokee	7.8	14.9	13.5	16.2	17.5	14.3	8.7	4.3	2.8	91.9	4.9	1.5	0.4	0.1	8.0	101.9
Clarke	6.1	8.8	33.3	18.6	10.0	8.6	6.3	4.4	4.1	69.1	26.0	3.4	0.3	0.1	8.3	95.1
Clay	7.1	13.4	13.5	9.9	10.7	14.6	13.2	8.0	9.5	39.2	60.3	0.3	–	–	0.9	83.1
Clayton	8.9	16.2	14.1	16.8	16.8	12.6	7.7	4.2	2.6	30.9	62.1	5.0	0.3	0.1	10.6	94.8
Clinch	8.6	14.6	13.4	14.3	14.3	13.8	10.1	6.3	4.6	67.2	31.0	0.6	0.7	–	1.1	100.0
Cobb	8.0	13.8	13.2	15.3	17.2	14.9	9.6	4.7	3.3	71.9	22.5	3.9	0.3	0.1	10.4	99.1
Coffee	8.0	15.0	14.6	15.4	14.8	13.0	9.0	5.7	4.5	71.4	27.0	0.7	0.4	0.1	8.7	100.1
Colquitt	7.8	14.4	14.4	14.8	13.8	12.3	9.9	6.7	5.9	75.3	23.4	0.4	0.3	0.1	14.0	101.0
Columbia	6.6	14.8	14.9	12.5	15.7	16.1	10.2	5.4	3.7	80.8	14.0	3.4	0.3	0.1	2.9	95.4
Cook	7.4	14.6	14.9	13.9	14.2	12.1	10.0	7.4	5.5	70.9	28.0	0.6	0.2	(Z)	4.9	94.3
Coweta	7.4	15.1	13.0	16.3	16.9	13.1	9.5	5.1	3.6	80.7	17.2	1.0	0.2	(Z)	5.1	99.9
Crawford	5.9	14.4	14.3	13.6	16.3	15.1	11.3	5.7	3.4	77.3	21.6	0.2	0.4	(Z)	2.5	101.8
Crisp	7.5	15.6	13.9	13.0	13.0	13.6	10.2	7.1	6.2	54.1	44.1	1.2	0.2	(Z)	2.5	89.4
Dade	5.7	12.4	16.9	13.7	13.0	14.7	11.1	7.3	5.3	97.5	1.2	0.4	0.4	–	1.1	97.1
Dawson	6.3	13.5	11.7	16.8	16.6	13.7	11.0	6.9	3.6	97.8	0.7	0.5	0.2	(Z)	2.8	101.8
Decatur	7.3	15.1	14.5	13.2	14.1	13.6	9.4	6.9	6.0	58.1	40.6	0.5	0.4	(Z)	3.6	92.9
DeKalb	8.2	13.0	13.6	16.3	17.5	14.1	9.1	4.6	3.6	38.9	55.6	4.0	0.3	0.1	9.0	94.8
Dodge	6.4	12.9	15.3	13.7	15.2	13.4	9.9	7.3	5.9	68.7	30.6	0.3	0.2	(Z)	1.8	110.4
Dooly	8.1	12.7	15.0	14.0	15.2	13.8	9.9	6.2	5.2	49.0	49.7	0.7	0.1	0.2	4.6	110.6
Dougherty	8.0	14.8	16.7	13.3	12.8	13.0	9.9	6.2	5.4	34.2	63.7	1.1	0.2	(Z)	1.5	87.9
Douglas	7.5	15.1	14.4	16.1	16.9	13.8	9.2	4.3	2.8	65.2	31.6	1.3	0.4	(Z)	4.9	97.3
Early	7.9	15.0	14.0	12.0	12.4	13.6	10.1	7.4	7.6	48.3	50.9	0.2	0.1	(Z)	1.4	88.0
Echols	8.3	13.8	15.2	20.3	15.6	10.8	7.4	5.5	3.1	90.0	8.8	0.1	1.0	(Z)	27.3	118.1
Effingham	6.9	14.8	14.9	16.2	16.0	14.1	8.9	4.9	3.1	85.0	13.3	0.6	0.3	(Z)	1.8	98.5
Elbert	6.3	13.1	13.4	13.6	13.6	13.9	11.0	8.3	6.9	68.9	30.2	0.3	0.2	–	3.6	93.2
Emanuel	8.1	13.4	15.8	13.4	12.8	12.8	10.7	7.1	5.9	66.5	32.6	0.4	0.2	(Z)	5.9	97.9
Evans	8.4	13.3	15.2	15.1	14.3	12.4	8.7	6.7	5.9	66.9	32.0	0.4	0.5	0.1	8.7	95.2
Fannin	5.6	10.9	11.6	13.3	13.0	13.5	12.8	10.8	8.5	97.8	0.6	0.3	0.4	–	1.2	93.8
Fayette	4.8	14.0	15.8	10.2	14.4	17.9	12.9	5.9	4.1	78.4	17.0	3.2	0.2	(Z)	3.7	96.0
Floyd	7.3	13.1	14.5	14.0	13.9	13.3	10.0	7.3	6.5	83.7	13.7	1.3	0.3	0.2	7.0	95.8
Forsyth	8.2	15.2	12.1	16.8	18.9	13.1	8.6	4.4	2.7	93.5	2.2	3.0	0.3	(Z)	7.6	103.7
Franklin	6.2	12.9	13.7	14.0	14.1	12.6	11.0	8.1	7.4	90.0	8.8	0.5	0.2	(Z)	1.5	94.1
Fulton	7.6	13.4	13.4	16.5	17.0	14.5	9.9	4.2	3.4	51.6	42.9	4.1	0.2	0.1	7.4	98.1
Gilmer	6.6	13.1	12.1	16.0	14.5	12.6	11.6	8.3	5.2	96.5	0.8	0.2	0.8	1.1	8.7	103.8
Glascock	6.2	12.6	11.9	13.9	13.9	13.5	10.6	7.7	9.7	89.8	9.8	–	0.1	–	0.4	93.9
Glynn	7.0	13.1	13.7	12.6	13.6	14.3	11.3	7.6	6.7	72.0	26.0	0.7	0.3	(Z)	4.1	93.5
Gordon	7.9	13.7	12.5	17.3	15.5	12.3	9.8	6.3	4.6	94.4	3.5	0.8	0.4	0.2	12.6	101.3
Grady	8.0	13.7	14.9	13.7	13.3	13.2	10.6	6.9	5.7	69.4	28.9	0.4	0.8	(Z)	8.8	93.9
Greene	6.8	12.5	13.9	13.2	12.1	12.8	12.6	9.7	6.4	58.8	40.3	0.4	0.3	0.1	3.5	94.7
Gwinnett	8.6	15.0	13.3	16.5	18.2	14.3	8.2	3.6	2.2	69.5	19.3	9.1	0.4	0.1	16.1	103.2
Habersham	7.0	12.3	14.7	14.7	13.7	13.1	10.3	7.6	6.5	92.6	3.8	2.2	0.6	0.2	10.7	104.5
Hall	8.8	14.5	13.7	17.4	15.3	12.0	8.9	5.4	3.9	90.1	7.0	1.5	0.4	0.4	25.0	104.9
Hancock	6.1	12.0	14.5	14.6	14.9	14.0	10.8	7.6	5.4	23.1	76.6	0.2	0.2	–	0.6	110.9
Haralson	6.7	13.7	13.1	14.7	15.0	12.9	10.5	7.5	5.9	93.5	5.5	0.4	0.1	–	1.0	97.1
Harris	5.6	13.1	13.2	14.0	15.2	15.3	11.9	6.4	5.3	79.9	18.4	0.7	0.4	–	1.7	99.5
Hart	6.1	12.6	12.6	12.6	14.4	13.5	11.8	9.3	7.1	79.2	19.6	0.7	0.1	–	1.4	99.2
Heard	6.2	16.1	13.5	13.8	15.6	13.2	10.6	6.3	4.8	89.0	10.3	0.1	0.2	0.1	1.4	97.0
Henry	7.6	15.5	14.2	17.9	17.5	12.8	7.9	4.0	2.7	68.5	27.2	2.7	0.3	0.1	4.0	98.2
Houston	7.4	14.5	15.0	14.4	15.8	14.0	9.0	6.0	3.9	69.2	26.9	1.9	0.4	0.1	3.7	96.6
Irwin	6.6	13.7	15.7	13.5	14.3	12.9	10.4	7.0	6.0	73.7	25.6	0.5	0.2	–	2.6	101.9
Jackson	7.2	13.8	13.4	17.1	15.8	12.6	9.6	6.1	4.5	90.6	7.1	1.4	0.1	–	3.8	100.7
Jasper	7.0	14.0	13.7	15.2	14.7	13.9	10.7	6.6	4.2	76.6	22.7	0.1	0.1	–	2.7	96.2
Jeff Davis	8.3	14.3	13.1	13.9	14.0	13.7	10.9	6.9	4.9	83.9	15.0	0.7	0.3	0.1	7.3	98.6
Jefferson	8.6	14.3	14.1	12.6	13.5	13.5	10.2	6.7	6.6	43.4	56.0	0.3	0.1	(Z)	1.8	89.4
Jenkins	7.2	14.7	15.6	11.6	13.5	13.6	10.7	6.9	6.2	58.1	41.1	0.3	0.3	0.1	4.2	93.7
Johnson	6.0	12.5	18.3	14.0	14.0	12.6	9.4	6.5	6.8	60.0	39.5	0.2	(Z)	(Z)	1.2	118.7
Jones	6.4	13.6	13.9	13.8	15.7	14.8	10.6	6.7	4.5	75.1	23.3	0.9	0.3	(Z)	0.9	98.4
Lamar	6.0	13.2	14.2	14.6	14.3	14.3	10.6	7.2	5.6	70.4	28.4	0.5	0.2	–	1.4	93.7
Lanier	7.2	14.6	14.4	15.4	15.2	13.7	9.0	6.0	4.6	72.9	25.2	0.4	0.7	0.1	2.4	103.1
Laurens	7.3	14.0	13.6	13.7	13.9	13.9	10.3	7.1	6.1	63.4	35.1	0.9	0.2	–	1.5	93.2
Lee	5.7	15.0	16.8	14.4	16.5	16.0	9.0	4.0	2.7	81.3	16.7	1.3	0.3	–	1.3	102.8
Liberty	11.3	18.8	18.3	17.4	14.6	9.9	4.8	2.9	2.0	49.4	44.5	1.9	0.5	0.5	7.2	108.1
Lincoln	4.8	12.5	12.8	12.9	14.3	15.9	12.2	8.8	5.7	66.9	32.5	0.1	0.4	(Z)	0.9	94.9

See footnotes at end of table.

[Includes United States, states, and 3,141 counties/county equivalents defined as of February 22, 2005. For more information on these areas, see Appendix C, Geographic Information]

County	Under 5 years	5 to 14 years	15 to 24 years	25 to 34 years	35 to 44 years	45 to 54 years	55 to 64 years	65 to 74 years	75 years and over	White alone	Black or African American alone	Asian alone	American Indian and Alaska Native alone	Native Hawaiian and Other Pacific Islander alone	Hispanic or Latino origin[1] (percent)	Males per 100 females
GEORGIA—Con.																
Long	7.2	19.0	14.4	20.9	14.9	10.6	6.3	4.2	2.5	72.6	24.0	1.0	0.7	0.4	9.1	99.9
Lowndes	7.6	13.8	18.7	16.2	14.3	12.0	7.9	5.3	4.2	63.0	34.1	1.3	0.4	(Z)	3.0	98.5
Lumpkin	6.3	12.4	19.7	15.5	14.3	12.4	9.3	6.1	4.0	96.0	1.7	0.4	0.7	(Z)	4.8	96.9
McDuffie	7.6	14.3	13.9	13.4	14.3	13.7	11.0	6.8	5.1	60.9	37.9	0.4	0.4	(Z)	1.8	90.9
McIntosh	6.4	14.6	12.1	12.5	13.8	15.0	11.6	8.4	5.7	64.3	34.3	0.4	0.4	(Z)	1.0	96.8
Macon	7.3	14.1	14.7	13.3	13.4	14.4	10.1	6.6	6.1	39.2	59.5	0.7	0.3	0.1	3.7	100.9
Madison	6.2	14.0	13.0	14.6	15.6	14.2	11.0	6.7	4.7	89.7	8.6	0.6	0.2	(Z)	2.4	98.6
Marion	7.1	14.8	13.7	13.6	14.2	14.9	11.3	6.3	4.3	64.0	33.9	0.5	0.3	0.5	6.9	99.6
Meriwether	7.0	13.7	14.0	13.2	13.6	13.5	11.3	7.5	6.2	57.9	41.0	0.2	0.4	0.1	1.3	93.4
Miller	7.1	12.8	14.2	10.2	13.2	13.7	11.6	9.1	8.3	71.9	27.7	(Z)	0.2	0.1	0.7	90.4
Mitchell	7.1	14.1	15.5	14.2	14.3	13.5	9.5	6.6	5.4	51.7	47.1	0.4	0.3	0.1	2.6	104.8
Monroe	6.1	13.1	15.5	12.7	15.0	15.8	11.0	6.4	4.4	73.0	25.6	0.5	0.4	(Z)	1.8	100.7
Montgomery	6.5	13.2	19.0	14.4	14.6	12.5	9.3	6.5	4.1	74.4	25.0	0.3	(Z)	(Z)	4.5	103.7
Morgan	6.0	14.1	13.2	14.2	14.1	14.7	10.8	7.2	5.6	73.5	25.4	0.5	0.1	–	2.0	96.7
Murray	7.3	15.1	13.3	17.6	15.9	12.6	9.4	5.4	3.3	97.1	1.3	0.3	0.4	(Z)	12.4	101.4
Muscogee	8.1	14.7	15.9	13.7	13.4	13.6	8.9	6.1	5.6	49.3	46.4	2.0	0.4	0.2	4.1	93.0
Newton	8.2	14.7	14.1	18.4	16.0	11.5	8.1	5.2	3.8	65.7	32.0	1.2	0.2	(Z)	3.2	96.6
Oconee	5.9	15.2	15.3	12.0	15.3	16.9	10.6	5.2	3.7	90.7	6.3	2.1	0.2	(Z)	3.3	98.2
Oglethorpe	6.2	14.0	12.3	15.2	15.5	13.8	11.2	7.0	5.0	80.3	18.8	0.2	0.1	(Z)	2.8	95.3
Paulding	8.3	16.4	13.3	18.9	18.9	11.7	6.8	3.5	2.1	84.8	12.9	0.7	0.3	(Z)	3.7	100.7
Peach	6.7	13.1	19.6	13.8	13.3	13.0	9.6	6.5	4.4	55.5	43.4	0.4	0.3	(Z)	4.8	95.0
Pickens	6.3	12.2	12.2	16.2	15.3	12.7	11.0	8.6	5.6	97.0	1.6	0.4	0.4	(Z)	2.7	97.5
Pierce	6.9	13.4	14.7	14.0	14.1	13.3	11.2	7.3	5.1	88.1	10.7	0.2	0.3	0.1	2.9	97.7
Pike	6.0	13.8	14.6	15.6	15.9	13.6	9.8	6.4	4.4	86.5	12.5	0.5	0.2	–	1.4	102.1
Polk	8.2	13.6	13.4	15.4	13.9	12.6	10.1	7.0	5.8	85.5	13.1	0.4	0.3	0.3	10.0	101.8
Pulaski	6.1	12.3	12.4	15.8	15.3	13.7	10.8	7.5	6.0	66.3	32.4	0.5	0.3	0.1	4.4	76.2
Putnam	6.5	11.8	12.6	12.6	13.6	13.8	13.1	10.2	5.8	71.0	27.8	0.7	0.2	(Z)	3.8	96.7
Quitman	7.1	12.8	12.2	9.9	12.2	14.5	14.0	9.2	8.2	54.6	45.1	(Z)	0.1	–	1.3	89.6
Rabun	5.5	11.8	11.9	13.4	12.8	12.9	13.4	10.4	8.0	97.2	1.3	0.4	0.4	0.1	7.2	99.1
Randolph	7.0	14.2	16.7	10.3	11.9	14.2	10.5	8.2	7.0	39.0	60.1	0.2	0.4	0.2	1.6	87.9
Richmond	8.2	14.3	16.2	14.0	13.5	13.5	9.2	6.1	5.0	43.7	52.7	1.6	0.3	0.1	2.7	91.8
Rockdale	7.1	14.4	15.1	13.1	15.4	15.0	10.5	5.5	3.8	62.2	34.4	2.0	0.3	0.1	8.6	99.9
Schley	6.4	15.6	14.2	13.9	15.9	11.9	11.5	5.8	4.8	72.8	26.6	–	–	0.3	2.4	94.0
Screven	6.4	14.3	15.6	11.4	13.2	14.5	10.5	7.2	7.0	54.8	44.4	0.4	0.3	0.1	1.2	94.8
Seminole	6.7	14.0	13.7	12.1	12.6	13.5	11.3	9.1	7.0	66.2	33.4	0.2	0.2	–	3.4	91.9
Spalding	7.7	14.8	13.4	14.6	14.3	13.5	10.1	6.5	5.0	65.8	32.4	0.8	0.2	(Z)	2.3	95.6
Stephens	6.3	12.7	14.4	13.0	12.8	13.5	11.1	8.2	7.9	86.2	12.0	0.7	0.3	0.1	1.5	92.9
Stewart	5.8	13.5	12.4	10.3	13.2	14.9	11.5	8.3	10.2	37.8	61.6	0.3	0.2	–	1.8	93.5
Sumter	7.5	15.1	16.0	13.5	12.9	12.3	9.8	6.3	6.7	49.0	49.8	0.6	0.3	–	3.5	89.7
Talbot	6.4	12.6	12.2	13.4	13.5	15.8	12.3	7.9	5.9	42.6	56.7	0.3	0.1	–	1.7	89.9
Taliaferro	5.6	11.5	13.1	10.8	12.8	14.2	12.8	8.9	10.3	38.6	61.2	–	–	–	1.0	90.6
Tattnall	7.2	11.7	15.3	18.3	15.9	11.9	8.7	6.0	4.9	69.2	29.6	0.4	0.3	0.2	11.8	133.7
Taylor	6.9	14.6	14.4	13.2	13.8	13.0	10.5	7.1	6.5	58.7	40.4	0.5	0.2	0.1	2.4	97.0
Telfair	6.7	10.2	14.9	17.7	15.7	13.4	8.7	6.6	6.1	57.4	42.1	0.3	(Z)	–	3.3	143.7
Terrell	7.8	15.1	14.9	11.4	13.5	13.9	11.0	6.9	5.5	38.0	61.2	0.5	0.2	(Z)	1.5	92.4
Thomas	6.8	13.8	14.3	12.5	14.0	14.0	10.4	7.1	7.0	60.4	38.2	0.5	0.2	(Z)	1.8	89.3
Tift	7.8	14.5	15.7	14.6	13.3	13.0	9.5	6.3	5.3	70.2	27.8	1.4	0.2	(Z)	10.1	96.2
Toombs	8.0	14.8	14.2	13.6	13.9	12.6	10.3	7.1	5.4	73.8	25.1	0.6	0.2	–	11.0	93.7
Towns	4.2	9.2	12.9	12.2	11.3	11.3	12.3	14.6	12.0	98.0	1.2	0.4	0.2	–	1.4	92.3
Treutlen	6.4	13.8	15.8	15.2	11.7	13.1	10.0	7.3	6.8	67.0	32.4	0.5	(Z)	–	1.6	102.1
Troup	7.6	14.7	14.5	14.3	14.0	13.7	9.6	6.0	5.8	65.5	32.8	0.8	0.1	0.1	2.3	93.9
Turner	7.8	15.4	15.0	13.4	12.7	12.5	10.1	6.9	6.3	58.2	41.0	0.5	0.2	–	3.2	93.9
Twiggs	5.9	13.9	14.6	13.4	14.4	14.4	10.9	7.3	5.1	58.0	41.4	0.2	0.1	(Z)	1.4	91.5
Union	4.7	10.5	12.2	12.8	12.4	12.8	12.0	12.7	9.9	98.0	1.2	0.3	0.2	–	1.0	97.4
Upson	6.2	13.8	13.7	13.5	14.5	14.0	10.8	7.4	6.2	70.1	28.8	0.4	0.3	–	1.7	92.9
Walker	5.8	13.2	12.8	14.9	14.4	14.0	11.1	7.6	6.2	94.6	4.1	0.4	0.2	(Z)	1.3	96.5
Walton	7.2	14.7	13.4	15.6	16.5	12.7	9.4	6.0	4.5	83.5	14.5	0.9	0.3	(Z)	2.5	96.5
Ware	7.2	13.5	14.0	12.6	13.1	13.5	10.9	7.6	7.8	71.6	27.3	0.5	0.2	–	2.7	94.0
Warren	7.1	13.7	13.8	11.9	12.2	14.5	11.2	7.7	7.9	41.0	58.5	0.2	0.2	–	1.1	87.7
Washington	6.5	14.1	14.4	12.2	14.6	14.7	10.1	7.1	6.4	46.1	53.3	0.3	0.2	(Z)	0.7	86.4
Wayne	7.2	13.4	13.1	16.0	15.2	13.7	10.1	6.7	4.5	78.4	20.2	0.6	0.2	(Z)	4.4	110.6
Webster	5.6	14.1	12.2	12.9	14.3	14.9	11.1	7.4	7.2	52.9	47.0	–	–	–	4.3	102.6
Wheeler	5.7	10.5	15.6	17.4	17.0	13.9	9.7	5.1	5.2	65.4	33.6	0.1	0.7	–	4.6	155.0
White	6.1	12.2	13.1	16.0	14.1	12.8	10.8	8.5	6.4	95.5	2.2	0.7	0.3	0.4	2.4	99.1
Whitfield	9.6	15.2	13.3	14.0	14.8	12.9	9.8	6.2	4.3	93.3	3.9	1.3	0.5	0.1	28.2	100.9
Wilcox	5.8	11.6	13.5	15.5	15.3	14.7	9.7	7.0	6.9	63.4	36.3	0.2	0.1	(Z)	1.5	131.6
Wilkes	6.0	12.4	12.9	11.6	14.0	13.6	12.3	8.9	8.3	56.8	42.2	0.4	0.2	–	2.5	94.0
Wilkinson	7.4	13.6	14.0	12.4	14.4	14.1	10.6	7.7	6.0	58.8	40.7	0.1	0.2	–	1.7	91.4
Worth	6.4	14.3	14.1	12.0	13.8	14.6	11.7	7.4	5.7	69.1	29.9	0.3	0.3	–	1.2	94.5

See footnotes at end of table.

[Includes United States, states, and 3,141 counties/county equivalents defined as of February 22, 2005. For more information on these areas, see Appendix C, Geographic Information]

County	Age (percent)									One race (percent)					His-panic or Latino origin[1] (per-cent)	Males per 100 females
	Under 5 years	5 to 14 years	15 to 24 years	25 to 34 years	35 to 44 years	45 to 54 years	55 to 64 years	65 to 74 years	75 years and over	White alone	Black or African American alone	Asian alone	American Indian and Alaska Native alone	Native Hawaiian and Other Pacific Islander alone		
HAWAII..............	7.1	12.5	14.0	12.4	14.0	14.8	11.5	6.1	7.6	26.8	2.3	41.5	0.3	9.0	8.0	99.4
Hawaii..............	6.7	13.8	15.0	11.4	12.1	15.7	11.9	6.3	7.0	35.9	0.7	25.4	0.5	10.6	11.6	100.0
Honolulu............	7.2	12.1	14.0	12.7	14.3	14.2	11.4	6.2	7.9	22.9	3.0	46.6	0.3	8.5	7.1	99.1
Kalawao............	–	–	1.8	2.7	15.3	27.9	36.0	9.0	7.2	41.4	–	25.2	–	30.6	8.1	76.2
Kauai..............	6.7	13.3	13.4	10.6	13.1	16.4	12.4	6.2	7.9	33.9	0.4	35.3	0.4	8.5	9.0	98.6
Maui...............	6.8	13.0	13.0	12.4	14.9	16.6	11.8	5.4	6.0	38.3	0.6	30.2	0.5	10.3	8.7	100.9
IDAHO..............	7.4	14.2	15.7	13.4	13.6	14.1	10.1	6.1	5.4	95.5	0.6	1.0	1.4	0.1	9.1	100.7
Ada................	7.2	14.0	14.0	15.3	15.7	14.6	9.7	5.0	4.5	94.6	0.8	1.9	0.7	0.2	5.5	101.4
Adams..............	4.0	10.0	14.2	7.2	12.3	17.9	16.0	11.2	7.3	97.6	0.1	0.4	1.5	0.1	2.1	103.1
Bannock............	8.9	14.2	17.8	14.0	11.7	13.4	9.4	5.6	4.9	93.5	0.7	1.1	3.1	0.2	5.3	97.0
Bear Lake..........	6.3	14.3	17.4	8.3	11.5	15.3	10.9	8.4	7.5	98.8	0.3	(Z)	0.6	0.1	2.3	98.0
Benewah............	6.3	12.9	13.2	8.6	13.1	16.1	13.7	9.5	6.6	90.2	0.2	0.2	8.0	(Z)	2.1	102.5
Bingham............	8.6	16.8	17.3	11.6	12.4	13.6	9.4	5.7	4.6	91.1	0.3	0.6	7.0	–	14.0	100.1
Blaine.............	6.2	11.6	11.8	13.0	16.3	18.3	13.5	5.6	3.5	97.2	0.5	1.0	0.4	(Z)	15.4	108.4
Boise..............	4.8	12.8	13.6	9.5	13.8	19.4	14.5	7.4	4.3	97.6	0.1	0.2	0.9	(Z)	3.6	106.6
Bonner.............	4.8	12.0	13.7	10.6	12.6	18.0	14.5	8.2	5.8	97.0	0.2	0.3	1.0	(Z)	1.9	99.8
Bonneville.........	8.6	15.5	15.9	13.2	12.9	14.0	9.6	5.5	4.8	96.6	0.7	0.8	0.7	0.1	8.2	98.8
Boundary...........	6.5	13.7	14.4	10.3	12.1	16.9	12.5	7.6	6.0	96.1	0.2	0.7	2.5	(Z)	3.3	99.3
Butte..............	7.1	14.6	13.8	6.6	12.4	16.5	12.4	9.3	7.2	98.1	0.4	0.2	0.6	–	4.8	98.7
Camas..............	5.7	9.4	14.6	11.0	17.7	15.2	14.1	7.3	5.0	98.3	1.0	0.2	0.1	–	5.9	101.9
Canyon.............	8.8	15.9	15.3	16.4	13.5	11.7	8.4	5.1	5.0	95.8	0.6	0.8	0.9	0.2	20.3	99.6
Caribou............	7.0	14.7	15.4	9.6	12.1	15.8	11.2	7.8	6.4	99.2	(Z)	(Z)	0.3	0.2	3.8	99.6
Cassia.............	8.5	16.9	16.5	10.1	12.2	13.2	9.6	6.4	6.5	97.6	0.3	0.4	0.9	(Z)	21.1	100.1
Clark..............	8.7	15.7	16.4	8.8	13.1	12.6	10.6	8.8	5.2	97.6	0.1	0.3	1.1	0.1	39.4	113.3
Clearwater.........	4.4	10.2	12.1	7.9	14.5	16.8	15.2	10.8	7.9	96.3	0.3	0.4	1.8	(Z)	1.7	118.5
Custer.............	3.6	11.7	12.6	6.7	14.4	19.1	15.7	8.7	7.5	98.7	(Z)	–	0.7	–	5.3	102.5
Elmore.............	8.9	14.5	15.4	16.4	18.1	11.3	7.3	4.8	3.3	91.4	3.5	1.8	1.0	0.2	12.9	123.7
Franklin...........	8.4	18.4	16.7	12.9	11.9	12.3	8.3	5.6	5.4	99.1	0.1	0.2	0.5	–	6.7	101.7
Fremont............	8.6	15.7	16.1	10.8	12.6	13.6	9.7	7.1	5.7	98.0	0.2	0.5	0.6	(Z)	12.4	107.0
Gem................	6.2	13.9	14.3	11.7	12.9	14.0	11.2	8.0	7.8	97.4	0.1	0.4	1.0	(Z)	7.1	99.0
Gooding............	8.2	14.7	14.3	11.5	12.8	13.5	10.4	7.2	7.5	98.0	0.3	0.3	0.9	(Z)	20.1	106.1
Idaho..............	4.9	11.3	14.8	7.8	12.1	17.2	14.1	9.8	8.1	95.1	0.1	0.4	3.2	(Z)	1.7	106.4
Jefferson..........	8.6	17.2	18.2	12.0	12.4	13.5	8.9	5.0	4.2	97.8	0.4	0.3	0.7	0.2	9.8	101.4
Jerome.............	8.2	16.0	14.8	12.6	13.5	14.0	9.3	6.0	5.7	97.4	0.5	0.4	0.9	(Z)	23.4	104.9
Kootenai...........	6.1	13.6	14.1	13.0	14.0	14.8	11.2	7.0	6.0	96.4	0.3	0.5	1.3	0.1	3.0	98.2
Latah..............	5.5	9.6	27.8	15.2	11.0	12.0	9.1	4.9	4.9	94.1	0.8	2.5	0.9	0.1	2.7	106.0
Lemhi..............	4.7	12.0	13.2	8.2	11.9	16.3	15.7	9.7	8.3	98.3	0.1	0.1	0.6	–	2.9	98.4
Lewis..............	5.8	11.8	12.7	7.8	11.9	15.7	13.1	11.0	10.0	94.2	0.4	0.6	4.5	(Z)	2.6	101.6
Lincoln............	8.1	15.2	15.7	13.4	12.8	13.2	9.8	5.8	6.0	96.3	1.1	0.4	1.4	–	17.5	103.3
Madison............	9.7	12.6	37.9	12.2	7.5	8.2	5.8	3.5	2.7	97.3	0.4	0.8	0.4	0.2	4.2	88.6
Minidoka...........	8.3	15.6	15.8	9.6	12.6	13.6	10.5	7.1	7.0	97.2	0.4	0.6	1.2	(Z)	27.5	99.7
Nez Perce..........	5.8	12.0	14.6	11.5	12.8	14.8	11.4	8.1	8.8	91.6	0.5	0.9	5.6	0.1	2.0	95.6
Oneida.............	7.0	14.4	17.4	9.6	11.5	14.1	10.5	7.4	8.0	99.4	0.1	0.1	0.4	–	2.4	102.1
Owyhee.............	7.7	15.4	14.9	11.7	13.7	13.0	10.5	6.9	6.3	95.0	0.2	0.6	2.9	0.2	22.7	110.2
Payette............	7.3	15.4	14.4	12.0	13.2	13.6	10.8	7.0	6.3	96.5	0.1	1.0	0.9	(Z)	13.6	98.7
Power..............	7.9	16.1	16.4	11.0	12.7	14.3	10.5	6.4	4.7	96.0	0.3	0.5	3.2	–	25.4	98.7
Shoshone...........	4.9	11.8	11.2	8.9	13.4	16.7	14.1	10.1	8.8	96.8	0.1	0.3	1.5	(Z)	2.4	99.8
Teton..............	9.4	15.7	13.5	14.2	17.7	15.1	8.6	3.3	2.5	98.3	0.3	0.2	0.6	0.4	13.9	115.5
Twin Falls.........	7.3	13.8	15.5	12.7	12.8	13.6	10.1	7.1	7.2	96.9	0.4	0.8	0.8	0.1	11.4	97.5
Valley.............	4.9	10.5	13.4	8.4	12.9	19.9	14.9	9.3	5.8	98.2	0.2	0.3	0.7	(Z)	2.9	106.8
Washington.........	6.3	13.7	13.3	10.4	11.5	14.5	11.6	9.4	9.3	97.1	0.2	1.1	0.8	0.2	16.2	97.0
ILLINOIS...........	7.0	14.0	14.1	14.0	14.8	14.2	9.8	6.0	6.0	79.4	15.1	4.1	0.3	0.1	14.3	96.6
Adams..............	5.9	13.1	14.0	11.8	13.3	13.9	10.6	7.7	9.6	95.2	3.3	0.5	0.2	(Z)	1.0	93.1
Alexander..........	7.5	12.9	12.3	12.5	12.5	14.1	10.4	8.6	9.1	63.9	34.8	0.5	0.2	–	1.7	95.7
Bond...............	5.7	11.5	15.4	15.2	14.3	14.0	9.8	6.7	7.4	91.7	7.1	0.4	0.5	(Z)	1.6	115.3
Boone..............	6.6	15.3	14.5	15.6	15.4	12.8	9.4	5.5	4.9	95.8	1.7	0.9	0.5	(Z)	17.0	101.4
Brown..............	4.6	8.9	15.8	20.0	17.1	12.9	8.2	6.3	6.3	80.9	18.7	0.2	–	0.1	4.4	180.7
Bureau.............	6.2	12.8	12.4	11.1	13.4	15.1	11.5	7.8	9.6	98.1	0.6	0.6	0.2	(Z)	6.1	95.3
Calhoun............	5.0	11.7	12.8	11.2	14.0	14.0	12.5	9.6	9.1	99.0	0.1	0.3	0.3	–	0.8	100.0
Carroll............	4.9	12.1	13.1	10.4	12.6	15.1	12.0	9.2	10.6	97.9	0.9	0.5	0.1	–	2.5	97.2
Cass...............	7.0	12.8	12.7	13.2	13.8	13.8	10.2	7.5	8.0	97.9	1.1	0.5	0.5	(Z)	15.1	102.3
Champaign..........	6.0	10.8	26.5	16.3	11.5	11.5	7.3	4.9	5.1	78.7	11.2	7.9	0.3	(Z)	3.8	102.4
Christian..........	5.5	12.8	12.6	13.0	14.3	14.6	10.7	7.9	8.7	96.4	2.5	0.6	0.2	(Z)	1.1	101.7
Clark..............	5.4	13.3	12.8	12.1	13.9	14.5	11.0	7.7	9.3	98.9	0.4	0.1	0.1	0.1	0.5	96.1
Clay...............	6.2	12.7	12.2	12.1	13.0	14.2	11.0	8.2	10.5	98.6	0.2	0.7	0.3	–	0.8	92.1
Clinton............	5.3	12.9	14.6	13.3	15.4	14.5	9.3	7.0	7.7	95.1	4.0	0.4	0.2	(Z)	2.0	106.6
Coles..............	5.2	10.2	25.8	13.3	10.6	12.4	8.8	6.5	7.2	95.5	2.4	1.1	0.3	(Z)	1.8	91.6
Cook...............	7.5	14.1	13.4	14.7	15.0	13.8	9.7	5.9	5.8	66.6	26.4	5.5	0.4	0.1	22.2	94.5
Crawford...........	5.0	11.7	13.7	13.4	14.3	14.6	10.8	8.1	8.4	94.1	4.8	0.4	0.3	–	2.0	109.7
Cumberland.........	5.5	13.7	13.5	11.5	14.3	14.6	11.4	7.3	8.4	99.0	0.3	0.2	0.2	–	0.6	96.9
DeKalb.............	5.8	11.7	26.1	15.8	12.3	11.4	7.3	4.6	5.0	90.8	5.0	2.7	0.2	0.1	8.5	99.2
De Witt............	6.2	13.2	12.3	12.1	14.2	15.3	10.9	7.9	7.9	98.2	0.7	0.3	0.2	(Z)	1.5	95.4

See footnotes at end of table.

[Includes United States, states, and 3,141 counties/county equivalents defined as of February 22, 2005. For more information on these areas, see Appendix C, Geographic Information]

County	Population characteristics, 2005															
	Age (percent)									One race (percent)					His-panic or Latino origin[1] (per-cent)	Males per 100 females
	Under 5 years	5 to 14 years	15 to 24 years	25 to 34 years	35 to 44 years	45 to 54 years	55 to 64 years	65 to 74 years	75 years and over	White alone	Black or African Ameri-can alone	Asian alone	Ameri-can Indian and Alaska Native alone	Native Hawai-ian and Other Pacific Islander alone		
ILLINOIS—Con.																
Douglas	7.5	13.7	13.2	11.9	12.9	14.7	10.0	7.8	8.2	98.4	0.5	0.5	0.2	(Z)	4.9	96.3
DuPage	6.8	14.5	12.9	12.7	16.1	16.0	10.7	5.3	4.9	84.8	4.1	9.7	0.2	(Z)	11.3	98.0
Edgar	4.9	12.3	12.8	13.3	13.0	14.8	11.1	8.0	9.7	97.3	2.0	0.3	0.2	(Z)	0.9	96.5
Edwards	5.8	12.2	11.8	11.7	12.4	15.6	11.7	8.9	9.7	99.1	0.2	0.5	(Z)	0.1	0.5	93.4
Effingham	6.5	14.9	13.8	12.1	14.0	14.4	9.9	6.8	7.5	98.8	0.3	0.4	0.2	(Z)	1.1	97.4
Fayette	5.4	12.3	14.0	14.0	14.6	14.0	10.3	7.7	7.8	94.7	4.8	0.2	(Z)	–	1.1	107.5
Ford	6.0	13.4	13.2	11.2	13.2	14.8	10.5	8.0	9.9	98.5	0.5	0.5	(Z)	–	1.5	92.1
Franklin	5.8	12.0	12.3	13.1	13.0	14.0	11.6	8.4	9.8	98.8	0.3	0.2	0.2	(Z)	1.0	92.7
Fulton	5.4	11.6	12.8	13.3	13.6	14.3	10.9	8.2	9.8	95.2	3.8	0.3	0.3	(Z)	1.4	106.5
Gallatin	5.6	12.0	11.6	12.6	12.5	13.5	13.8	9.2	9.3	99.2	0.3	–	0.4	–	0.8	91.8
Greene	6.1	13.1	13.2	12.8	12.7	14.5	10.5	7.8	9.3	98.3	0.9	0.1	0.2	0.1	0.7	95.8
Grundy	6.4	13.4	14.1	15.8	15.0	14.4	9.6	5.5	5.7	97.3	1.0	0.6	0.2	(Z)	6.2	100.1
Hamilton	5.2	12.8	11.3	11.8	13.3	14.6	12.2	8.3	10.6	98.7	0.6	0.2	0.3	–	1.1	93.3
Hancock	5.0	12.6	12.7	10.4	13.0	15.6	12.0	8.6	10.2	98.9	0.4	0.2	0.2	–	0.5	94.6
Hardin	4.9	11.0	12.0	11.8	13.3	15.0	13.8	9.2	9.0	97.1	2.2	0.6	–	–	1.2	99.1
Henderson	4.1	12.0	12.5	11.4	13.1	16.1	13.5	9.2	8.1	99.1	0.3	0.1	0.1	–	0.9	96.2
Henry	5.4	13.0	13.3	11.4	13.3	15.3	12.1	7.7	8.5	97.4	1.3	0.4	0.1	(Z)	3.4	97.4
Iroquois	5.5	13.1	13.4	10.6	13.0	14.6	11.6	8.4	9.8	97.7	1.0	0.5	0.3	(Z)	4.9	96.3
Jackson	5.5	9.2	29.8	16.9	9.8	10.0	7.6	5.3	6.0	81.2	12.6	4.3	0.3	0.1	2.9	104.9
Jasper	6.1	12.6	13.5	11.4	13.9	15.1	11.0	7.6	8.9	99.4	0.2	0.2	0.1	(Z)	0.6	96.1
Jefferson	5.7	12.6	13.5	13.8	14.0	14.5	10.8	7.1	8.0	89.8	8.4	0.7	0.1	–	1.5	104.9
Jersey	5.2	12.5	16.1	12.4	13.8	14.8	10.6	7.4	7.2	97.9	1.0	0.4	0.1	(Z)	0.9	95.9
Jo Daviess	5.1	11.9	11.8	11.9	12.7	14.8	12.6	9.6	9.5	98.8	0.4	0.2	0.2	–	2.5	102.2
Johnson	4.9	10.0	14.7	17.9	15.6	12.6	10.6	7.6	6.2	86.9	12.3	0.2	0.2	0.1	3.0	141.5
Kane	8.6	16.1	14.0	15.6	15.5	13.4	8.7	4.3	3.7	89.9	5.6	2.8	0.4	0.1	27.5	102.4
Kankakee	7.0	14.3	14.8	13.7	13.5	13.9	9.8	6.3	6.6	82.6	15.2	0.9	0.2	(Z)	6.5	95.2
Kendall	7.5	14.8	14.3	18.2	16.1	12.7	8.5	4.2	3.7	93.6	3.1	1.8	0.2	(Z)	12.8	100.3
Knox	5.5	12.0	13.5	12.4	12.8	14.6	11.5	8.6	9.0	90.6	7.2	0.8	0.2	–	3.8	99.9
Lake	7.4	16.1	14.2	13.0	15.8	15.1	9.4	4.9	4.1	85.9	6.8	5.5	0.3	0.1	18.2	101.3
LaSalle	6.1	13.2	13.2	12.3	14.3	14.7	10.3	7.2	8.7	96.8	1.7	0.6	0.2	–	6.5	97.3
Lawrence	4.9	11.6	13.0	13.7	13.8	14.7	10.1	8.2	10.0	95.2	4.1	0.1	(Z)	–	1.4	99.6
Lee	5.0	12.4	13.7	12.6	15.5	15.4	10.4	7.4	7.7	93.9	4.6	0.7	0.1	(Z)	4.0	103.9
Livingston	6.6	12.7	13.6	12.9	14.0	14.8	10.2	7.0	8.2	93.6	5.4	0.3	0.2	–	2.8	98.6
Logan	5.3	11.3	16.7	13.5	14.0	14.2	10.2	6.9	7.9	91.8	6.9	0.8	0.2	–	1.8	100.4
McDonough	4.1	8.3	33.9	12.1	8.8	10.6	8.3	6.2	7.6	92.0	4.3	2.8	0.1	(Z)	1.8	95.6
McHenry	6.9	15.8	13.4	13.7	17.1	15.0	9.1	4.8	4.2	95.5	0.9	2.4	0.2	0.1	10.1	100.6
McLean	6.4	12.2	23.4	14.6	13.1	12.5	8.0	4.8	5.0	89.3	6.5	2.7	0.1	(Z)	3.1	93.7
Macon	6.4	13.3	14.2	11.4	12.3	15.2	11.6	7.5	8.2	82.8	14.6	0.9	0.2	(Z)	1.2	91.4
Macoupin	5.6	12.4	13.9	11.9	13.7	14.8	10.9	7.8	9.0	98.0	1.0	0.2	0.2	(Z)	0.7	95.4
Madison	6.4	13.0	14.4	13.3	14.0	14.7	10.3	6.8	7.1	90.2	7.9	0.7	0.3	(Z)	1.9	93.4
Marion	6.1	13.6	12.5	12.0	13.1	14.2	11.3	8.0	9.2	94.1	4.0	0.6	0.2	(Z)	1.0	93.3
Marshall	5.3	13.0	12.4	11.0	13.1	15.0	12.2	8.6	9.4	98.5	0.5	0.3	0.2	(Z)	1.8	99.2
Mason	6.1	12.6	13.0	11.5	13.1	14.7	11.8	8.4	8.9	98.9	0.3	0.3	0.3	–	0.6	96.1
Massac	6.3	12.6	11.9	13.6	13.1	14.1	10.6	8.4	9.5	92.8	6.1	0.2	0.1	–	1.1	92.6
Menard	5.5	13.3	13.1	10.4	15.3	16.1	12.1	7.7	6.6	98.9	0.5	0.2	0.2	–	1.0	97.0
Mercer	5.5	12.4	12.5	11.3	13.5	15.5	12.7	8.4	8.1	98.9	0.5	0.2	0.1	–	1.4	98.6
Monroe	5.7	13.3	13.8	13.2	15.8	15.7	9.4	6.8	6.4	99.0	0.2	0.3	0.2	(Z)	1.3	98.8
Montgomery	5.4	12.3	13.1	13.4	14.4	14.5	9.9	7.5	9.5	95.3	3.9	0.2	0.2	(Z)	1.1	106.5
Morgan	5.6	11.7	16.0	11.9	13.6	14.2	11.2	7.3	8.4	93.0	5.5	0.6	0.2	(Z)	1.6	99.0
Moultrie	6.2	13.3	13.1	12.3	12.5	14.4	10.5	8.4	9.2	99.2	0.3	0.1	0.1	(Z)	0.6	94.7
Ogle	5.4	14.0	13.4	12.6	14.6	15.2	10.7	6.9	7.0	97.7	0.7	0.5	0.3	(Z)	7.7	97.4
Peoria	7.2	13.8	14.6	13.1	12.7	14.0	10.7	6.5	7.3	78.7	16.9	2.3	0.2	(Z)	2.6	93.1
Perry	5.4	11.6	14.4	14.4	14.0	14.3	10.6	7.3	8.0	90.4	8.5	0.3	0.3	0.1	2.1	116.2
Piatt	5.5	13.2	12.2	11.2	14.0	16.1	11.8	7.9	8.1	98.7	0.4	0.4	(Z)	(Z)	0.7	96.5
Pike	5.4	12.4	13.3	11.5	13.0	14.5	10.8	8.5	10.6	97.8	1.5	0.3	0.1	(Z)	0.6	98.2
Pope	3.7	10.1	15.9	10.8	12.6	13.5	13.6	10.2	9.5	93.5	4.9	0.3	0.7	–	1.1	103.5
Pulaski	6.9	14.1	15.4	10.5	13.1	14.6	10.2	7.0	8.3	67.6	30.9	1.0	–	–	1.5	90.7
Putnam	4.9	12.7	12.8	10.4	14.1	15.8	12.9	7.7	8.8	98.5	0.7	0.4	0.3	–	3.8	99.2
Randolph	5.5	11.4	14.5	14.2	14.6	14.5	10.3	6.7	8.2	89.9	9.2	0.3	0.1	(Z)	1.7	114.6
Richland	5.7	12.7	12.8	11.8	13.2	14.6	10.8	9.3	9.2	98.5	0.5	0.6	0.1	(Z)	0.8	95.1
Rock Island	6.6	12.6	13.8	12.9	12.9	14.6	11.1	7.3	8.2	89.1	7.8	1.2	0.3	(Z)	10.2	94.5
St. Clair	7.1	14.4	14.5	13.2	14.4	14.6	9.2	6.1	6.5	67.8	29.5	1.1	0.3	0.1	2.6	91.8
Saline	5.9	12.1	13.7	11.8	12.8	13.9	11.3	9.1	9.4	94.3	4.5	0.2	0.3	(Z)	1.1	94.3
Sangamon	6.6	13.2	12.6	13.0	14.4	15.6	10.9	6.6	7.0	86.8	10.4	1.3	0.2	(Z)	1.2	91.4
Schuyler	5.7	12.0	11.5	11.9	13.4	15.8	11.2	8.6	10.0	98.9	0.8	0.1	–	0.1	0.8	99.2
Scott	5.1	13.4	12.2	11.3	13.9	15.6	11.3	8.2	9.1	99.5	(Z)	0.2	0.2	–	0.2	94.4
Shelby	5.3	13.3	12.6	10.8	13.5	14.8	11.7	8.8	9.3	99.2	0.2	0.2	0.1	–	0.5	98.5
Stark	5.4	13.5	11.8	10.6	13.2	14.4	11.7	9.2	10.1	99.2	0.1	0.2	0.1	–	1.1	91.4
Stephenson	6.1	13.2	12.6	11.1	13.7	15.0	10.9	8.1	9.4	89.6	7.9	0.8	0.2	(Z)	2.1	93.5
Tazewell	6.0	12.8	12.7	12.9	13.9	15.0	11.3	7.7	7.7	97.5	1.1	0.6	0.2	(Z)	1.3	97.0

See footnotes at end of table.

[Includes United States, states, and 3,141 counties/county equivalents defined as of February 22, 2005. For more information on these areas, see Appendix C, Geographic Information]

County	Age (percent)									One race (percent)					Hispanic or Latino origin[1] (percent)	Males per 100 females
	Under 5 years	5 to 14 years	15 to 24 years	25 to 34 years	35 to 44 years	45 to 54 years	55 to 64 years	65 to 74 years	75 years and over	White alone	Black or African American alone	Asian alone	American Indian and Alaska Native alone	Native Hawaiian and Other Pacific Islander alone		
ILLINOIS—Con.																
Union	5.9	11.9	12.7	12.1	13.8	14.5	11.9	8.5	8.6	97.6	1.0	0.4	0.5	(Z)	3.5	94.4
Vermilion	6.6	13.6	12.4	13.0	13.1	14.2	11.0	7.8	8.3	87.1	11.2	0.6	0.2	(Z)	3.4	96.0
Wabash	5.4	12.5	13.0	12.0	13.4	15.4	11.5	7.6	9.3	98.1	0.5	0.5	0.1	(Z)	0.9	95.7
Warren	5.6	11.8	17.0	10.8	12.0	15.0	11.4	7.8	8.7	96.5	2.0	0.6	0.2	0.1	4.5	94.7
Washington	5.6	12.7	14.5	10.4	14.4	15.8	10.8	7.2	8.5	98.7	0.4	0.2	0.2	(Z)	1.0	98.6
Wayne	5.6	12.4	12.4	12.0	13.1	14.2	11.5	9.0	9.8	98.6	0.4	0.4	0.2	–	0.7	95.5
White	5.3	10.8	12.5	11.7	12.9	14.6	11.5	9.2	11.5	98.7	0.4	0.1	0.2	–	0.7	90.9
Whiteside	6.1	13.2	12.7	11.9	13.1	15.1	11.2	7.8	8.8	97.1	1.3	0.5	0.3	(Z)	9.5	94.9
Will	7.5	15.9	14.1	15.9	16.5	13.6	8.5	4.4	3.7	84.2	10.7	3.4	0.3	0.1	12.8	100.1
Williamson	5.8	12.1	12.7	14.5	13.8	13.7	11.1	7.9	8.5	95.0	3.1	0.6	0.3	(Z)	1.6	94.7
Winnebago	6.9	14.3	13.1	13.8	14.6	14.2	10.3	6.2	6.5	85.0	11.0	2.0	0.4	0.1	9.6	96.9
Woodford	5.6	13.8	15.3	11.2	13.3	15.7	10.9	6.7	7.4	98.3	0.5	0.5	0.1	(Z)	1.1	96.6
INDIANA	6.9	14.3	14.3	13.3	14.3	14.4	10.2	6.2	6.2	88.6	8.8	1.2	0.3	(Z)	4.5	97.0
Adams	8.9	16.8	14.2	11.8	12.7	13.1	9.2	5.9	7.5	99.0	0.2	0.3	0.1	(Z)	3.5	98.9
Allen	7.7	15.5	13.7	13.4	14.3	14.4	9.8	5.5	5.8	84.4	11.7	1.8	0.4	0.1	5.3	96.9
Bartholomew	6.8	14.9	12.0	12.9	14.6	14.6	11.3	7.1	5.9	94.4	2.0	2.6	0.2	(Z)	3.5	98.6
Benton	6.4	15.3	12.8	10.2	14.2	14.9	10.7	6.9	8.6	98.2	0.5	0.1	(Z)	–	2.8	99.3
Blackford	5.8	13.5	12.1	12.2	13.5	14.3	12.3	8.0	8.3	98.5	0.2	0.2	0.4	–	0.6	97.7
Boone	6.6	15.3	13.5	12.4	15.2	15.4	10.3	5.9	5.4	97.2	0.7	1.2	0.2	–	1.7	97.2
Brown	5.0	12.1	12.4	10.7	14.4	17.2	14.8	8.1	5.4	98.5	0.5	0.4	0.1	–	0.9	102.2
Carroll	5.7	14.4	12.8	12.7	14.0	15.3	11.3	6.6	7.1	99.2	0.3	0.1	0.1	(Z)	3.8	101.1
Cass	6.8	14.1	13.3	12.7	13.6	14.7	10.8	6.9	7.1	96.8	1.6	0.5	0.55	0.1	10.1	101.7
Clark	6.6	13.7	12.4	14.5	14.9	14.8	10.7	6.5	5.9	90.5	7.1	0.7	0.3	0.1	2.6	95.5
Clay	6.5	14.1	13.4	12.9	13.8	14.6	10.2	7.0	7.4	98.3	0.6	0.2	0.3	(Z)	0.7	94.9
Clinton	7.3	14.8	13.3	13.0	13.6	14.3	9.4	6.8	7.5	98.7	0.4	0.2	0.2	0.1	11.6	97.5
Crawford	6.0	13.7	12.6	14.0	14.0	15.2	11.5	7.2	5.8	98.9	0.2	(Z)	0.4	0.4	1.2	101.1
Daviess	7.9	15.8	12.9	12.5	12.8	13.6	10.1	6.6	7.7	98.5	0.6	0.3	0.2	(Z)	3.2	98.2
Dearborn	6.1	14.5	13.2	12.0	16.0	15.9	10.6	6.1	5.5	98.0	0.8	0.4	0.2	(Z)	0.7	99.5
Decatur	7.4	14.8	12.0	13.6	14.5	13.9	10.0	7.1	6.8	98.2	0.2	1.2	0.1	–	0.9	99.3
DeKalb	6.9	15.5	13.0	13.4	14.8	14.6	10.0	5.7	6.1	98.3	0.4	0.3	0.3	(Z)	1.9	100.0
Delaware	5.5	11.8	21.4	12.9	11.8	12.3	10.3	7.0	7.0	91.1	6.8	0.8	0.2	0.1	1.2	91.5
Dubois	6.4	14.9	13.1	11.9	15.2	15.1	10.0	6.7	6.6	99.0	0.2	0.3	0.1	0.1	4.5	97.6
Elkhart	8.2	15.8	13.7	14.5	14.3	13.2	9.3	5.4	5.5	91.6	5.5	1.0	0.3	0.1	12.6	99.9
Fayette	6.3	13.7	11.9	13.3	12.8	14.7	11.7	7.7	7.8	97.7	1.6	0.3	(Z)	(Z)	0.7	94.0
Floyd	6.0	14.3	12.8	12.2	14.9	16.1	11.2	6.3	6.2	93.1	4.9	0.7	0.2	(Z)	1.5	93.9
Fountain	6.1	14.5	11.9	11.2	14.3	14.4	10.9	8.4	8.2	99.0	0.2	0.3	0.2	–	1.8	98.7
Franklin	5.6	15.2	13.7	12.5	15.0	14.8	10.3	6.5	6.4	99.1	0.1	0.4	(Z)	(Z)	0.6	101.6
Fulton	6.0	14.4	11.7	12.5	14.1	14.7	11.1	7.6	7.7	98.0	0.7	0.4	0.3	–	2.9	96.3
Gibson	6.2	13.7	13.2	12.3	14.1	15.1	10.6	7.2	7.6	96.4	2.1	0.7	0.2	–	0.9	96.4
Grant	5.9	13.1	16.4	10.7	12.4	14.1	11.6	8.1	7.7	90.5	7.2	0.6	0.4	(Z)	2.7	91.6
Greene	6.1	13.3	12.7	12.1	14.7	14.5	11.6	7.2	7.8	98.8	0.1	0.2	0.3	(Z)	1.0	98.4
Hamilton	7.6	16.9	13.1	14.6	17.3	14.4	8.5	4.2	3.4	91.9	3.1	3.5	0.2	(Z)	2.5	97.6
Hancock	6.5	14.2	13.1	12.8	15.2	14.8	11.6	6.5	5.3	96.5	1.3	0.7	0.2	(Z)	1.2	96.6
Harrison	6.1	13.5	13.3	13.0	15.4	15.7	11.3	6.2	5.5	98.4	0.6	0.2	0.3	(Z)	1.4	99.9
Hendricks	6.1	15.0	13.9	15.0	16.2	14.4	9.6	5.3	4.6	93.9	3.7	1.1	0.2	0.1	2.0	101.3
Henry	5.8	13.5	11.6	11.8	14.2	14.9	12.2	8.0	8.1	98.2	1.0	0.3	0.2	(Z)	0.9	94.0
Howard	7.0	14.3	12.1	12.8	13.5	14.5	12.0	7.5	6.4	90.2	7.0	1.0	0.4	(Z)	2.1	93.7
Huntington	6.0	14.0	14.1	12.3	13.7	15.1	10.0	7.0	7.8	98.2	0.3	0.5	0.4	(Z)	1.0	96.1
Jackson	7.1	14.2	11.9	14.1	14.8	14.1	10.3	6.9	6.5	97.9	0.7	0.7	0.2	(Z)	4.3	98.6
Jasper	6.3	14.6	15.2	13.0	13.8	13.8	10.3	6.8	6.2	98.8	0.6	0.2	0.1	–	3.7	98.4
Jay	7.1	15.6	11.4	12.3	13.7	13.6	11.2	7.2	7.8	98.5	0.3	0.6	0.2	(Z)	2.4	98.3
Jefferson	5.5	13.5	14.4	12.7	14.4	14.4	11.3	7.1	6.6	96.6	1.6	0.7	0.3	(Z)	1.2	98.3
Jennings	6.6	15.9	12.3	14.2	15.2	14.3	10.6	6.2	4.8	98.0	0.9	0.3	0.2	–	0.9	99.8
Johnson	6.5	14.9	13.6	14.1	15.5	14.1	10.0	5.9	5.4	97.0	1.2	1.0	0.2	(Z)	1.9	97.3
Knox	5.8	12.5	15.8	11.9	13.0	14.4	11.0	7.6	8.1	96.6	2.1	0.8	0.1	(Z)	1.0	97.5
Kosciusko	7.1	15.1	13.2	13.3	14.0	14.3	10.4	6.4	6.1	97.7	0.7	0.6	0.3	(Z)	6.3	100.7
LaGrange	9.6	18.1	14.9	14.0	12.3	11.5	9.0	5.8	4.8	98.5	0.2	0.6	0.1	(Z)	3.4	103.8
Lake	7.1	14.9	13.6	12.1	13.8	15.1	10.5	6.4	6.5	71.3	26.2	0.6	0.3	0.1	13.7	93.0
LaPorte	6.1	13.6	12.9	13.1	14.5	15.1	11.0	6.5	7.1	87.7	10.3	0.4	0.3	(Z)	3.9	105.4
Lawrence	5.9	13.6	11.2	12.9	14.1	14.8	11.9	7.8	7.7	98.2	0.5	0.3	0.3	–	1.0	95.2
Madison	6.1	13.4	12.7	12.7	14.1	14.1	11.7	7.6	7.7	90.3	8.1	0.4	0.2	(Z)	2.0	97.7
Marion	8.4	14.6	12.6	14.9	15.5	14.1	9.0	5.4	5.5	70.7	25.8	1.5	0.3	0.1	5.9	94.4
Marshall	7.4	15.0	13.2	13.4	14.0	14.3	9.8	6.5	6.5	97.9	0.6	0.4	0.3	0.1	8.0	100.2
Martin	6.3	13.3	11.0	12.2	14.0	15.8	12.5	7.7	7.3	99.3	0.3	0.1	(Z)	–	0.4	104.5
Miami	6.3	14.0	12.5	12.7	14.9	15.2	11.0	6.7	6.7	94.6	3.0	0.3	1.0	(Z)	1.6	103.9
Monroe	4.8	9.3	29.7	16.8	11.0	10.8	7.5	4.9	5.1	90.5	3.2	4.5	0.2	0.1	2.1	96.7
Montgomery	6.1	14.3	13.7	12.4	14.3	14.0	10.7	7.3	7.1	97.8	1.0	0.5	0.2	(Z)	2.4	100.4
Morgan	6.4	14.9	12.7	12.6	15.7	15.4	11.4	6.3	4.7	98.4	0.3	0.3	0.2	(Z)	0.8	100.0
Newton	5.4	13.8	13.7	12.1	15.0	15.2	11.6	6.9	6.3	98.4	0.4	0.2	0.3	0.2	3.5	100.0
Noble	7.1	16.0	13.3	14.2	14.7	14.2	9.6	5.4	5.4	98.4	0.4	0.3	0.3	(Z)	9.5	103.2
Ohio	5.4	12.2	13.5	12.6	14.5	15.6	11.6	7.9	6.7	99.1	0.6	0.3	0.1	–	0.4	95.8
Orange	6.6	14.0	12.3	12.9	13.8	14.3	11.1	7.7	7.3	98.1	0.7	0.3	0.3	0.1	0.9	95.8
Owen	5.3	13.7	13.3	12.5	15.0	15.5	11.4	7.5	5.6	98.4	0.3	0.2	0.4	(Z)	0.9	98.4

See footnotes at end of table.

County and City Data Book: 2007

U.S. Census Bureau

Table B-3. Counties — **Population by Age, Race, Hispanic Origin, and Sex**—Con.

[Includes United States, states, and 3,141 counties/county equivalents defined as of February 22, 2005. For more information on these areas, see Appendix C, Geographic Information]

County	Age (percent) Under 5 years	5 to 14 years	15 to 24 years	25 to 34 years	35 to 44 years	45 to 54 years	55 to 64 years	65 to 74 years	75 years and over	One race (percent) White alone	Black or African American alone	Asian alone	American Indian and Alaska Native alone	Native Hawaiian and Other Pacific Islander alone	Hispanic or Latino origin[1] (percent)	Males per 100 females
INDIANA—Con.																
Parke	5.4	12.5	12.2	12.9	15.0	14.9	12.2	7.8	7.0	97.0	2.2	0.2	0.2	–	0.6	92.5
Perry	5.8	11.4	14.1	13.3	14.6	15.0	10.8	7.0	7.9	97.5	1.9	0.3	0.2	–	0.8	109.7
Pike	5.4	13.2	11.9	11.9	14.6	15.2	11.9	8.4	7.5	99.3	0.2	0.2	0.1	(Z)	0.7	100.2
Porter	6.0	13.6	15.2	12.9	13.8	16.0	11.2	5.9	5.4	95.6	2.1	1.0	0.3	(Z)	5.9	97.4
Posey	4.8	14.4	14.1	9.8	15.1	17.2	11.7	6.8	6.0	98.1	1.0	0.2	0.3	–	0.5	100.3
Pulaski	5.7	14.0	13.6	12.2	13.8	14.8	10.4	7.5	7.9	98.2	1.0	0.3	0.2	0.1	1.7	102.7
Putnam	5.4	12.8	18.1	12.8	14.8	13.4	10.0	7.0	5.7	95.2	3.1	0.7	0.4	(Z)	1.2	108.9
Randolph	6.0	14.1	12.4	11.5	13.6	14.7	11.6	8.0	8.1	98.6	0.4	0.2	0.1	(Z)	1.7	96.8
Ripley	7.0	15.3	12.9	12.5	14.5	13.9	10.3	6.8	6.8	98.9	0.1	0.4	0.3	–	1.2	98.5
Rush	6.6	15.1	11.6	11.7	14.7	15.0	10.5	7.1	7.7	98.1	0.8	0.6	0.1	–	0.6	98.4
St. Joseph	7.1	14.5	16.4	12.1	13.3	14.1	9.5	5.8	7.3	84.0	12.0	1.6	0.4	0.1	5.8	93.6
Scott	6.3	14.4	12.8	14.9	15.1	14.1	10.6	6.7	5.1	99.1	0.1	0.2	0.1	–	1.1	98.2
Shelby	6.4	14.3	12.8	12.5	15.3	15.5	10.6	6.6	6.0	97.3	1.0	0.9	0.2	(Z)	2.3	99.2
Spencer	5.8	14.0	13.2	11.2	14.7	15.5	12.0	7.3	6.3	98.6	0.7	0.2	0.2	–	2.1	101.1
Starke	6.6	14.8	13.5	9.6	13.6	15.5	11.3	8.0	7.1	98.4	0.4	0.2	0.2	(Z)	2.2	97.9
Steuben	6.1	14.0	14.8	12.5	14.1	14.5	11.3	6.8	5.8	98.2	0.7	0.4	0.2	(Z)	2.8	102.6
Sullivan	6.0	12.2	13.2	15.1	15.0	14.3	10.8	6.5	6.9	94.6	4.5	0.2	0.3	(Z)	0.9	117.4
Switzerland	6.0	13.9	12.4	14.7	14.7	14.2	11.6	6.9	5.6	99.4	0.2	0.1	0.1	–	1.0	102.1
Tippecanoe	6.2	11.2	27.3	16.2	11.2	10.8	7.5	4.6	4.8	90.5	3.0	5.1	0.3	(Z)	6.4	106.9
Tipton	6.0	13.4	12.7	10.8	14.3	15.6	12.7	7.1	7.4	99.0	0.2	0.4	0.3	–	1.3	97.1
Union	5.1	14.8	13.4	11.6	15.3	14.4	11.5	7.3	6.5	99.1	0.3	0.3	0.2	–	0.3	99.4
Vanderburgh	6.8	12.8	15.1	12.6	13.4	14.6	10.0	6.7	8.1	89.0	8.5	1.0	0.2	0.1	1.1	91.0
Vermillion	5.9	13.2	12.5	11.7	14.1	14.8	12.5	7.5	7.8	98.8	0.4	0.1	0.2	(Z)	0.9	94.9
Vigo	6.2	12.9	17.4	13.2	12.9	13.9	10.0	6.2	7.4	90.8	6.1	1.5	0.3	(Z)	1.3	97.3
Wabash	5.5	12.8	15.1	11.4	12.6	14.5	11.5	8.1	8.5	97.8	0.5	0.5	0.7	(Z)	1.2	94.4
Warren	5.4	14.2	12.3	11.9	14.8	15.3	12.7	7.2	6.2	99.3	0.1	0.2	0.1	–	0.6	103.9
Warrick	5.9	14.3	13.3	12.0	14.9	16.3	12.0	6.4	5.0	97.0	1.3	0.9	0.2	(Z)	1.3	98.3
Washington	6.3	14.3	12.9	13.8	14.7	14.9	10.9	6.6	5.7	99.0	0.3	0.2	(Z)	(Z)	0.8	100.7
Wayne	6.2	13.2	13.8	11.6	13.8	14.2	11.3	7.6	8.4	92.6	5.1	0.7	0.2	(Z)	1.9	92.8
Wells	6.2	14.4	13.9	11.6	13.5	15.5	10.3	6.9	7.6	98.6	0.3	0.2	0.2	(Z)	1.6	97.9
White	6.8	13.7	12.2	11.7	13.4	15.0	11.4	7.9	7.9	98.6	0.3	0.3	0.2	0.2	6.9	96.8
Whitley	6.6	14.1	13.6	12.7	13.8	15.7	10.5	6.5	6.5	98.5	0.2	0.4	0.3	0.1	1.0	99.4
IOWA	6.1	12.4	14.6	12.7	13.9	15.0	10.6	6.8	7.9	94.9	2.3	1.4	0.3	(Z)	3.7	97.0
Adair	4.5	11.2	11.8	10.2	13.1	16.2	11.0	9.3	12.6	99.2	0.1	0.5	(Z)	–	0.8	96.7
Adams	4.6	11.7	10.8	10.0	13.0	15.1	12.7	9.6	12.5	99.2	(Z)	0.2	0.5	–	0.6	96.8
Allamakee	5.5	12.0	12.7	11.3	14.0	15.3	11.5	8.5	9.2	99.0	0.2	0.2	0.3	–	6.9	104.5
Appanoose	5.8	11.5	12.7	12.0	12.9	14.5	11.8	8.7	10.2	98.5	0.7	0.4	0.1	(Z)	1.1	94.0
Audubon	4.6	12.8	12.4	7.6	12.8	15.3	12.1	9.2	13.3	99.3	0.2	0.2	0.1	–	0.6	94.7
Benton	5.7	13.1	13.6	12.7	15.8	15.0	9.9	6.6	7.7	99.1	0.2	0.2	0.1	–	0.6	98.4
Black Hawk	5.8	11.2	19.1	13.5	11.7	14.1	10.2	6.5	7.8	89.6	7.8	1.2	0.2	0.1	2.5	92.7
Boone	5.4	11.8	13.3	13.2	13.8	15.9	10.8	7.3	8.4	98.6	0.7	0.3	0.2	–	1.0	95.9
Bremer	4.9	11.3	18.1	10.3	12.3	14.6	12.0	7.7	8.8	98.4	0.5	0.6	0.1	(Z)	0.7	93.5
Buchanan	6.7	13.6	13.6	12.0	13.6	14.7	11.3	6.9	7.5	98.6	0.3	0.4	0.2	–	0.7	98.9
Buena Vista	5.8	13.1	17.1	9.2	13.6	16.1	9.4	6.4	9.2	94.0	1.3	3.9	0.2	(Z)	18.6	103.8
Butler	5.0	11.6	12.2	10.3	13.0	16.0	12.6	8.5	10.8	99.3	0.1	0.2	(Z)	–	0.7	97.9
Calhoun	4.2	10.7	12.1	9.3	13.3	17.1	11.1	9.3	12.9	98.5	1.0	0.2	0.2	–	1.1	102.9
Carroll	5.7	12.5	13.2	10.1	13.6	15.8	10.0	8.0	11.1	98.8	0.3	0.5	0.2	–	1.4	95.7
Cass	5.0	11.3	12.3	9.9	12.8	15.9	11.7	9.2	12.0	99.0	0.2	0.4	0.1	0.1	1.1	95.7
Cedar	5.1	12.4	12.4	11.3	14.5	16.9	11.8	6.8	8.8	98.6	0.4	0.4	0.2	(Z)	1.2	98.1
Cerro Gordo	5.3	12.0	11.6	11.9	13.8	16.4	11.3	7.9	9.7	97.0	1.0	0.8	0.2	(Z)	3.0	93.2
Cherokee	4.5	11.5	12.3	9.2	12.3	17.4	12.1	9.5	11.2	98.7	0.4	0.5	0.2	–	1.9	97.9
Chickasaw	5.6	12.3	13.3	8.8	13.8	16.6	11.5	8.6	9.5	99.3	0.1	0.4	(Z)	–	1.0	99.6
Clarke	6.4	12.4	12.7	10.9	13.8	15.9	11.0	7.3	9.6	98.7	0.1	0.4	0.4	(Z)	6.0	97.4
Clay	5.7	11.8	11.8	12.0	13.3	16.6	10.4	8.0	10.4	98.6	0.2	0.9	0.1	–	1.9	95.3
Clayton	5.3	11.9	12.7	10.0	13.4	16.4	11.5	8.8	10.0	99.2	0.2	0.1	0.3	–	0.9	99.2
Clinton	5.4	12.7	13.1	11.4	14.3	15.6	11.4	7.6	8.4	95.9	2.2	0.6	0.3	(Z)	1.6	96.0
Crawford	6.6	12.5	14.5	10.5	13.2	15.0	11.5	7.2	9.0	97.7	1.2	0.5	0.5	(Z)	16.7	102.6
Dallas	5.6	13.8	14.8	17.9	16.0	13.9	9.0	4.5	4.4	96.4	1.1	1.3	0.2	0.2	5.8	98.0
Davis	6.9	12.9	13.3	11.1	13.1	15.1	10.9	8.3	8.4	99.0	0.2	0.2	0.1	(Z)	0.9	99.8
Decatur	4.8	10.6	22.0	11.6	10.9	13.0	9.9	8.1	9.2	97.0	1.2	0.8	0.2	0.2	2.1	96.4
Delaware	5.5	13.5	13.8	9.9	14.8	16.1	10.5	7.4	8.5	99.4	0.1	0.2	0.1	–	0.8	98.1
Des Moines	5.9	12.6	11.5	11.4	13.7	15.5	12.7	7.5	9.1	94.1	3.8	0.7	0.3	(Z)	2.3	94.0
Dickinson	4.7	10.6	11.3	11.1	12.6	16.0	13.1	9.3	11.2	99.1	0.2	0.2	0.2	–	0.9	95.8
Dubuque	6.3	12.7	14.8	11.6	14.0	14.9	10.7	7.2	7.8	96.9	1.3	0.7	0.1	0.1	1.5	96.3
Emmet	6.1	11.0	15.9	9.9	12.0	15.5	10.9	8.0	10.7	98.7	0.3	0.4	0.4	–	5.0	97.9
Fayette	5.0	12.3	13.6	10.3	13.4	15.3	11.2	8.4	10.6	98.2	0.8	0.5	0.1	(Z)	1.5	97.1
Floyd	5.3	12.6	12.0	10.4	12.9	14.9	12.4	8.4	10.9	98.1	0.6	0.6	0.1	0.1	1.6	94.8
Franklin	5.5	12.1	11.5	10.9	12.8	15.7	12.3	8.2	10.9	98.9	0.1	0.4	0.2	0.2	10.5	99.7
Fremont	5.5	12.0	12.0	9.3	13.2	15.8	12.7	8.5	11.0	98.9	0.1	0.4	0.2	–	2.4	98.7
Greene	4.9	12.5	13.0	8.9	13.1	15.6	11.0	8.5	12.4	98.7	0.2	0.4	0.3	–	2.1	96.4
Grundy	4.7	11.8	13.2	10.1	13.4	16.2	11.8	8.3	10.4	99.3	0.1	0.3	(Z)	–	0.7	96.1
Guthrie	5.9	11.4	12.5	11.0	13.4	15.3	11.9	9.0	9.7	99.5	0.1	0.1	–	–	1.9	98.3
Hamilton	5.3	12.7	11.8	11.5	14.4	15.5	11.2	7.7	9.8	97.0	0.4	1.8	0.3	–	2.1	98.9

See footnotes at end of table.

Table B-3. Counties — **Population by Age, Race, Hispanic Origin, and Sex**—Con.

[Includes United States, states, and 3,141 counties/county equivalents defined as of February 22, 2005. For more information on these areas, see Appendix C, Geographic Information]

County	Age (percent)									One race (percent)					Hispanic or Latino origin[1] (percent)	Males per 100 females
	Under 5 years	5 to 14 years	15 to 24 years	25 to 34 years	35 to 44 years	45 to 54 years	55 to 64 years	65 to 74 years	75 years and over	White alone	Black or African American alone	Asian alone	American Indian and Alaska Native alone	Native Hawaiian and Other Pacific Islander alone		
IOWA—Con.																
Hancock	4.6	12.6	12.9	9.7	13.4	16.8	11.6	7.9	10.5	98.9	0.1	0.6	0.1	(Z)	3.5	96.7
Hardin	5.4	11.3	14.2	9.4	12.2	15.8	11.2	8.3	12.1	98.5	0.8	0.3	0.1	0.1	2.9	98.6
Harrison	5.3	12.8	12.2	11.5	14.6	15.7	11.0	8.0	9.0	99.0	0.1	0.3	0.1	(Z)	1.2	98.2
Henry	5.1	12.0	14.1	12.8	15.4	14.6	11.3	6.6	8.1	95.1	1.8	2.2	0.3	(Z)	1.9	105.0
Howard	5.2	12.6	12.0	10.5	13.8	15.6	10.7	7.8	11.6	99.2	0.2	0.2	0.2	–	0.7	99.8
Humboldt	5.1	11.2	13.1	9.3	12.4	16.8	11.7	8.7	11.7	98.7	0.4	0.4	0.1	0.1	2.3	97.6
Ida	4.9	11.5	12.7	9.4	12.3	16.4	11.3	8.8	12.8	99.2	0.3	0.2	0.1	–	0.7	96.0
Iowa	5.6	13.0	12.5	11.0	14.8	16.3	10.0	8.0	8.8	99.2	0.2	0.3	0.1	(Z)	1.2	95.7
Jackson	5.3	12.4	12.5	10.7	14.2	15.7	11.6	8.4	9.3	99.0	0.2	0.1	0.1	0.2	0.7	98.1
Jasper	5.7	12.3	11.7	12.8	14.9	15.3	11.4	7.4	8.5	97.3	1.2	0.6	0.3	0.1	1.3	102.6
Jefferson	4.4	10.8	13.9	10.8	11.9	20.5	14.2	6.0	7.5	96.6	1.0	1.8	0.2	(Z)	2.2	96.7
Johnson	5.7	9.5	26.0	18.2	12.7	12.2	7.6	4.0	4.1	90.5	3.3	4.4	0.3	(Z)	2.9	96.8
Jones	4.9	11.5	13.5	13.3	15.0	15.2	10.9	7.4	8.3	97.1	2.0	0.2	0.3	–	1.4	110.3
Keokuk	5.7	12.6	12.3	10.9	12.6	16.1	10.9	8.0	10.9	99.3	0.1	0.3	0.1	(Z)	0.7	94.0
Kossuth	4.7	12.0	12.7	7.9	12.8	17.2	12.0	9.5	11.2	99.1	0.2	0.4	0.2	–	1.0	98.2
Lee	5.3	12.1	11.6	10.8	14.3	16.7	12.8	7.6	8.9	95.1	3.1	0.6	0.2	0.1	2.6	98.9
Linn	6.7	13.2	12.8	14.3	15.1	14.8	10.5	6.2	6.4	93.7	3.0	1.6	0.2	0.1	1.6	96.1
Louisa	6.1	13.8	12.1	11.3	15.6	15.4	10.7	7.3	7.7	99.0	0.3	0.2	0.1	0.2	14.1	98.3
Lucas	5.3	12.5	12.6	12.2	13.6	14.5	11.1	8.5	9.6	99.0	0.2	0.5	0.1	–	0.9	93.7
Lyon	6.4	13.7	13.1	11.1	13.2	15.4	9.7	7.7	9.8	99.1	0.3	0.2	0.1	(Z)	0.5	98.7
Madison	6.2	13.2	12.8	13.3	14.2	15.8	10.7	6.8	6.9	98.9	0.2	0.2	0.3	–	0.9	97.9
Mahaska	6.0	12.7	14.5	11.9	14.1	15.0	10.2	6.7	8.8	96.9	0.9	1.2	0.2	–	1.3	99.2
Marion	5.6	12.2	15.4	12.7	13.2	14.8	10.2	7.0	8.7	97.9	0.5	1.0	0.2	(Z)	1.1	97.7
Marshall	6.9	12.6	12.5	11.1	13.4	14.6	11.9	7.9	8.2	96.4	1.2	1.0	0.5	0.1	12.7	96.5
Mills	5.4	13.5	13.5	11.7	15.2	16.7	12.2	6.1	5.8	98.7	0.4	0.3	0.2	–	2.2	102.5
Mitchell	5.6	13.0	12.5	8.8	12.9	15.2	11.0	8.5	12.4	99.5	0.0	0.2	0.1	(Z)	0.6	95.5
Monona	4.8	11.5	11.0	10.5	12.1	15.6	11.6	9.6	13.3	98.6	0.1	0.1	0.9	(Z)	0.8	95.1
Monroe	5.5	12.8	12.0	10.9	13.8	14.5	11.7	8.4	10.5	98.8	0.3	0.4	0.4	–	0.6	97.3
Montgomery	5.4	12.8	10.7	10.5	13.6	16.0	12.1	8.0	11.0	98.9	0.2	0.3	0.4	–	2.4	91.4
Muscatine	6.9	13.3	13.0	13.0	14.6	15.4	11.2	6.2	6.4	96.9	1.2	1.0	0.3	(Z)	13.2	99.2
O'Brien	5.2	11.6	12.8	9.2	12.3	16.3	10.5	9.6	12.5	98.8	0.3	0.6	0.4	–	1.8	96.8
Osceola	5.5	12.2	12.2	10.2	13.3	17.0	10.8	8.4	10.4	98.9	0.3	0.2	0.4	–	3.2	98.5
Page	4.8	11.2	12.8	12.7	13.2	15.3	10.9	8.2	11.0	96.1	2.0	0.8	0.5	(Z)	1.9	106.4
Palo Alto	5.5	11.3	15.0	9.6	11.3	15.7	10.4	9.3	11.9	99.2	0.1	0.3	0.1	–	0.9	99.2
Plymouth	5.7	13.5	13.8	10.9	13.4	16.5	10.6	6.9	8.6	98.5	0.3	0.4	0.2	(Z)	1.9	101.2
Pocahontas	4.0	11.5	12.5	6.5	12.5	17.7	12.7	9.1	13.4	99.0	0.3	0.3	0.2	(Z)	1.2	95.8
Polk	7.5	13.2	12.5	15.3	15.9	14.6	10.1	5.5	5.5	90.3	4.9	3.0	0.3	0.1	5.7	94.8
Pottawattamie	6.6	12.9	13.0	13.3	14.6	15.4	10.7	6.7	6.8	96.9	1.0	0.6	0.4	(Z)	4.2	96.2
Poweshiek	4.9	10.8	18.1	10.7	12.2	14.6	11.0	7.8	9.7	97.5	0.6	1.0	0.3	(Z)	1.5	92.8
Ringgold	5.7	11.5	12.0	9.4	12.3	14.1	11.7	10.8	12.6	99.3	0.1	0.3	0.2	–	0.6	93.6
Sac	4.9	11.6	12.7	8.2	12.2	16.5	11.2	9.3	13.5	98.8	0.4	0.3	0.1	(Z)	1.3	97.5
Scott	6.8	13.1	14.0	12.6	14.6	15.7	11.1	6.2	5.9	89.9	6.2	1.8	0.3	(Z)	4.5	96.6
Shelby	4.8	12.6	12.6	8.3	13.7	16.4	10.8	8.9	11.7	98.9	0.2	0.4	0.3	–	0.9	97.7
Sioux	6.8	12.6	21.0	10.9	11.6	13.7	8.7	6.4	8.3	98.4	0.4	0.7	0.1	(Z)	4.9	98.2
Story	5.0	8.2	32.0	16.7	9.9	10.6	7.2	4.9	5.7	91.2	1.9	5.6	0.2	(Z)	1.8	106.9
Tama	6.2	13.2	13.1	10.2	13.1	14.7	11.2	8.2	10.1	92.0	0.5	0.2	6.4	–	4.3	97.7
Taylor	5.1	11.7	11.3	9.8	12.5	15.3	12.1	9.0	13.1	99.3	(Z)	0.4	0.1	(Z)	3.9	93.3
Union	5.5	11.5	11.3	11.3	13.3	15.5	12.7	8.4	10.5	98.8	0.3	0.4	0.1	–	1.1	92.2
Van Buren	5.3	11.7	12.6	11.2	12.7	15.4	11.9	8.8	10.5	99.1	(Z)	0.3	0.1	0.1	0.9	99.1
Wapello	6.3	11.9	13.3	12.9	12.8	15.1	11.0	7.6	9.1	96.9	1.4	0.6	0.4	(Z)	7.2	96.0
Warren	5.5	13.0	15.7	12.3	14.8	15.4	11.1	6.7	5.6	98.1	0.4	0.5	0.2	(Z)	1.3	95.9
Washington	6.9	12.8	12.0	12.0	13.7	14.9	10.7	7.4	9.6	98.6	0.5	0.3	0.2	(Z)	3.8	95.5
Wayne	5.5	11.4	12.1	9.6	12.1	15.1	11.7	9.2	13.4	98.9	(Z)	0.2	0.1	0.3	0.9	88.7
Webster	5.9	12.3	15.1	11.4	12.9	15.1	10.6	7.4	9.2	93.8	3.8	1.0	0.4	(Z)	2.8	103.8
Winnebago	4.8	11.5	14.1	10.1	12.3	17.3	11.4	7.7	10.9	98.3	0.2	0.8	0.3	–	2.3	95.4
Winneshiek	4.2	10.3	22.7	9.7	12.4	14.8	9.8	7.1	8.9	98.1	0.7	0.9	0.1	–	1.0	98.4
Woodbury	7.6	14.4	13.7	12.8	14.1	14.5	10.0	6.0	6.9	91.6	2.3	2.4	1.9	0.1	11.2	95.9
Worth	4.9	12.3	11.1	11.2	13.9	17.0	11.3	8.2	10.2	99.3	0.3	0.2	(Z)	–	1.8	99.4
Wright	5.9	12.1	11.8	9.0	12.9	16.5	11.3	8.6	11.8	98.9	0.2	0.3	0.3	–	7.1	98.4
KANSAS	6.8	13.4	15.2	13.3	13.9	14.5	9.9	6.2	6.8	89.4	5.9	2.1	0.9	0.1	8.3	98.7
Allen	6.2	12.2	14.2	11.9	12.1	14.8	11.2	7.9	9.5	95.4	2.0	0.3	1.0	–	2.3	96.0
Anderson	6.0	13.1	12.9	11.7	13.0	13.4	10.6	8.3	11.0	98.0	0.3	0.3	0.8	–	1.1	95.4
Atchison	6.3	12.8	18.2	11.2	12.0	13.3	10.2	7.4	8.6	92.2	5.7	0.4	0.5	(Z)	2.0	95.6
Barber	3.9	11.5	14.2	7.0	12.5	17.1	12.5	9.4	11.8	98.3	0.5	0.1	0.7	–	2.1	93.0
Barton	6.1	13.1	14.2	10.3	12.6	15.8	10.3	8.0	9.5	96.5	1.6	0.3	0.5	0.2	10.5	97.0
Bourbon	6.7	12.7	14.6	11.9	11.8	13.9	11.4	7.3	9.6	94.4	3.4	0.4	0.7	(Z)	1.4	95.5
Brown	6.5	12.9	13.6	9.3	12.4	15.0	11.5	7.9	10.9	88.3	2.1	0.5	7.3	–	2.4	94.3
Butler	5.7	14.1	15.2	12.2	14.7	16.0	9.7	6.0	6.4	95.5	1.6	0.6	0.9	(Z)	2.6	102.6
Chase	7.8	11.4	13.7	10.1	13.6	14.4	11.4	8.2	9.5	97.6	1.3	0.2	0.6	–	3.0	101.9
Chautauqua	4.2	11.1	14.4	7.7	12.0	13.5	12.9	11.1	13.1	94.8	0.4	–	3.6	–	1.7	95.0

See footnotes at end of table.

Table B-3. Counties — **Population by Age, Race, Hispanic Origin, and Sex**—Con.

[Includes United States, states, and 3,141 counties/county equivalents defined as of February 22, 2005. For more information on these areas, see Appendix C, Geographic Information]

County	\multicolumn{9}{c}{Population characteristics, 2005 — Age (percent)}									One race (percent)					Hispanic or Latino origin (percent)	Males per 100 females
	Under 5 years	5 to 14 years	15 to 24 years	25 to 34 years	35 to 44 years	45 to 54 years	55 to 64 years	65 to 74 years	75 years and over	White alone	Black or African American alone	Asian alone	American Indian and Alaska Native alone	Native Hawaiian and Other Pacific Islander alone		
KANSAS—Con.																
Cherokee	6.1	13.7	12.6	12.0	14.1	14.3	11.7	7.4	8.0	92.7	0.8	0.4	3.4	(Z)	1.3	97.2
Cheyenne	4.0	11.7	12.1	6.3	12.8	16.0	11.7	9.0	16.5	99.2	0.1	0.3	(Z)	(Z)	4.3	99.2
Clark	4.6	13.5	12.5	8.0	12.0	15.0	11.9	9.3	13.1	98.0	0.3	0.4	1.2	–	5.3	96.3
Clay	4.8	11.6	13.6	10.5	12.2	15.6	11.4	8.0	12.3	97.9	0.8	0.2	0.5	–	1.0	98.8
Cloud	5.4	10.6	16.0	9.2	12.1	13.7	11.1	9.0	12.9	98.4	0.4	0.5	0.2	–	0.9	95.1
Coffey	5.7	12.7	13.9	10.5	13.8	16.6	11.6	6.8	8.5	97.9	0.3	0.6	0.4	–	1.8	96.9
Comanche	3.8	11.8	11.1	9.3	11.3	14.4	14.4	12.2	12.1	98.9	–	0.3	0.2	0.4	2.1	90.6
Cowley	6.4	13.2	15.8	11.4	13.1	14.4	10.6	7.2	8.1	91.6	3.3	1.7	1.8	–	5.9	97.7
Crawford	6.4	11.4	19.9	14.8	11.2	12.3	9.3	6.3	8.4	93.4	2.1	1.8	1.0	0.1	3.1	95.6
Decatur	4.4	10.6	12.7	5.8	12.1	16.6	11.6	11.0	15.3	98.8	0.7	0.1	–	0.2	1.7	98.0
Dickinson	5.4	12.5	13.3	10.3	13.8	15.4	11.0	8.6	9.6	97.3	0.9	0.3	0.4	–	3.3	96.1
Doniphan	5.0	13.2	15.9	11.1	12.6	15.9	10.7	6.8	8.8	94.8	2.6	0.4	1.4	–	2.0	97.2
Douglas	5.4	9.5	28.7	18.5	11.3	11.0	7.1	4.2	4.3	87.5	4.1	3.7	2.1	0.1	3.7	99.4
Edwards	6.1	12.2	12.8	8.9	13.5	15.8	10.7	9.4	10.6	98.4	0.4	0.5	0.6	–	14.0	95.8
Elk	4.3	10.0	12.8	10.0	11.3	14.3	13.6	10.9	12.9	97.1	0.2	0.2	1.0	0.1	2.6	92.1
Ellis	6.1	10.0	22.2	14.4	11.0	13.5	8.4	6.7	7.7	96.9	1.0	1.2	0.2	–	2.5	97.4
Ellsworth	3.5	9.5	14.6	10.8	13.5	16.8	11.7	8.6	11.0	94.9	4.0	0.3	0.5	–	3.9	115.5
Finney	9.5	18.6	14.6	12.0	15.7	13.5	8.3	4.1	3.6	93.9	1.3	2.6	1.1	0.1	42.0	100.8
Ford	9.6	16.7	14.7	15.3	14.3	11.8	7.7	4.9	5.2	94.3	2.1	1.9	0.6	0.2	46.2	108.8
Franklin	6.5	13.3	15.1	13.5	13.9	14.3	9.9	6.5	7.1	95.7	1.4	0.6	0.9	–	2.9	100.9
Geary	11.4	15.2	14.2	15.3	13.0	12.5	7.6	5.6	5.2	72.5	17.5	3.7	0.9	0.6	7.6	95.9
Gove	5.3	13.0	12.5	5.4	11.2	16.5	11.9	11.4	12.7	99.2	0.1	0.1	–	–	1.4	93.6
Graham	3.7	9.8	12.3	6.7	13.5	16.5	11.3	12.2	14.0	96.2	3.3	0.3	0.2	–	0.8	98.2
Grant	8.7	16.1	15.5	10.3	14.2	15.2	9.9	5.7	4.4	97.9	0.4	0.5	1.0	–	37.7	101.0
Gray	7.8	15.9	14.6	12.0	13.1	14.0	10.1	5.6	6.6	98.7	0.3	(Z)	0.6	–	12.8	101.4
Greeley	4.2	14.3	13.0	6.7	14.8	17.8	10.8	8.7	9.6	98.1	0.2	0.4	0.7	0.4	12.1	98.7
Greenwood	5.0	11.4	12.3	11.0	12.0	14.4	12.2	9.8	11.9	97.4	0.3	0.2	1.0	–	2.4	97.6
Hamilton	7.3	13.1	14.4	10.9	12.5	14.8	9.3	7.5	10.2	97.5	0.7	0.5	0.5	0.8	26.5	98.2
Harper	5.3	11.8	12.4	9.2	12.0	15.2	11.5	9.6	12.9	97.6	0.4	0.4	0.9	0.1	1.5	94.7
Harvey	6.2	12.9	14.8	11.8	13.1	14.7	9.8	7.2	9.5	95.5	1.8	0.7	0.7	(Z)	9.2	96.6
Haskell	7.9	17.0	15.4	12.8	12.2	14.7	9.1	5.8	5.2	97.8	0.2	0.7	0.7	–	27.1	102.6
Hodgeman	5.9	12.2	15.0	8.8	13.4	16.3	9.9	8.4	10.2	98.1	0.9	–	0.3	–	3.6	98.1
Jackson	6.7	13.5	15.0	11.3	13.8	14.5	10.9	6.7	7.6	90.7	1.0	0.3	6.3	(Z)	2.7	98.4
Jefferson	5.5	12.9	14.6	10.9	14.5	16.1	11.8	7.4	6.4	96.8	0.6	0.2	1.1	(Z)	1.9	101.8
Jewell	3.2	10.4	11.2	5.4	11.2	18.1	14.4	11.7	14.3	99.0	0.1	0.1	0.4	–	0.7	99.3
Johnson	7.0	13.8	12.9	14.5	16.1	15.4	10.1	5.1	5.1	90.7	3.7	3.7	0.4	(Z)	5.2	97.3
Kearny	7.5	17.4	15.8	11.3	13.6	14.1	9.1	5.9	5.3	97.3	0.6	0.4	1.2	–	27.9	102.5
Kingman	4.9	13.1	13.9	8.2	13.0	15.9	11.1	9.3	10.6	97.8	0.3	0.6	0.6	(Z)	1.7	98.1
Kiowa	6.1	11.6	12.9	8.9	10.1	16.4	12.2	9.1	12.7	98.4	0.3	0.4	0.9	–	3.1	94.9
Labette	5.9	13.0	14.1	11.5	13.8	13.8	11.6	7.1	9.2	90.5	5.0	0.4	2.0	–	3.1	97.3
Lane	5.2	11.7	12.2	6.3	14.1	16.6	12.7	10.7	10.5	98.8	–	–	0.1	0.1	2.1	100.2
Leavenworth	6.3	13.7	14.1	13.8	17.3	15.2	9.7	5.5	4.6	86.2	9.8	1.2	0.8	0.2	3.6	111.6
Lincoln	5.0	11.0	12.5	8.9	11.6	18.3	11.7	9.5	11.5	98.5	0.2	0.1	0.6	–	1.8	96.9
Linn	5.4	12.4	13.0	11.9	12.6	14.8	12.6	8.4	8.9	98.0	0.7	0.2	0.4	(Z)	1.0	101.5
Logan	5.5	12.6	10.4	10.2	12.0	17.1	10.5	9.0	12.6	98.5	0.6	0.1	0.1	–	2.0	96.8
Lyon	7.1	12.6	19.7	14.0	12.4	13.5	8.9	5.5	6.2	93.6	2.7	1.7	0.7	(Z)	19.4	97.4
McPherson	5.7	11.9	16.4	11.0	12.3	15.4	10.5	7.2	9.7	97.4	1.0	0.4	0.3	(Z)	2.3	97.4
Marion	4.8	12.2	14.7	9.1	12.3	15.0	11.2	8.7	12.1	98.1	0.4	0.2	0.7	–	2.1	97.5
Marshall	5.2	10.8	13.7	8.5	12.6	16.5	11.2	9.3	12.2	98.4	0.3	0.3	0.4	–	0.8	100.4
Meade	7.0	16.0	13.1	11.1	13.1	14.9	7.7	8.2	9.0	97.9	0.5	0.5	0.6	–	13.2	100.8
Miami	6.6	13.5	14.7	12.0	15.2	15.9	10.4	6.2	5.4	96.2	1.6	0.3	0.6	–	1.8	99.5
Mitchell	4.6	11.3	15.0	7.6	12.2	15.9	12.3	9.0	12.0	98.0	0.7	0.5	0.5	(Z)	1.0	96.7
Montgomery	6.1	12.5	13.7	10.9	12.8	14.4	11.9	7.8	10.0	87.0	6.2	0.6	3.3	(Z)	3.2	94.1
Morris	4.8	12.0	13.7	9.1	13.0	16.1	11.8	8.3	11.2	98.6	0.3	0.2	0.4	(Z)	3.6	98.8
Morton	7.3	15.9	12.7	8.7	12.9	15.7	11.1	8.2	7.7	96.7	0.3	1.2	1.4	–	14.1	92.3
Nemaha	6.1	14.4	13.8	8.5	13.2	13.9	9.2	8.4	12.5	98.4	0.5	0.1	0.5	(Z)	0.8	98.9
Neosho	6.2	12.4	14.2	11.4	13.1	14.6	11.0	8.1	9.1	96.2	1.1	0.4	0.8	–	2.8	95.7
Ness	4.7	10.8	10.2	5.3	12.7	17.5	12.2	12.0	14.6	99.2	0.1	0.1	0.2	–	2.7	99.7
Norton	4.2	10.6	14.2	11.8	14.9	14.8	11.1	7.4	11.0	94.4	4.3	0.7	0.5	–	2.5	124.1
Osage	5.1	13.2	14.1	11.6	13.9	15.4	11.2	7.8	7.7	97.7	0.3	0.2	0.7	0.1	1.5	96.7
Osborne	4.4	10.9	13.0	6.2	12.2	16.7	11.6	10.0	14.8	98.9	0.1	0.4	0.2	(Z)	0.4	100.1
Ottawa	5.3	12.3	13.1	10.4	14.1	16.4	11.9	8.2	8.3	98.1	0.6	0.2	0.5	–	2.0	101.2
Pawnee	4.7	11.4	15.0	10.0	13.2	16.3	11.8	7.8	9.9	92.7	5.3	0.7	1.1	–	4.6	114.4
Phillips	5.2	11.6	11.8	7.3	12.8	16.0	13.0	10.5	11.7	98.5	0.3	0.5	0.3	–	0.8	98.6
Pottawatomie	7.0	14.4	14.8	12.2	14.0	14.8	9.9	6.3	6.7	97.0	0.8	0.5	0.6	–	2.6	98.3
Pratt	5.6	11.7	16.5	9.4	12.1	16.9	9.7	7.8	10.4	97.4	1.2	0.5	0.3	0.1	4.6	95.6
Rawlins	3.3	10.6	13.4	4.2	11.8	17.4	13.5	11.0	14.7	98.9	0.4	0.1	0.3	–	1.1	98.5
Reno	6.3	12.2	13.7	12.2	13.1	15.1	10.8	7.5	9.1	94.6	2.9	0.6	0.7	(Z)	6.3	101.6
Republic	4.3	9.8	12.0	5.8	11.3	17.3	12.9	11.1	15.4	98.7	0.4	0.2	0.4	–	1.1	95.9
Rice	5.8	11.9	19.4	9.5	11.2	14.4	10.1	8.4	9.2	96.9	1.2	0.7	0.7	(Z)	7.0	93.3

See footnotes at end of table.

[Includes United States, states, and 3,141 counties/county equivalents defined as of February 22, 2005. For more information on these areas, see Appendix C, Geographic Information]

County	Population characteristics, 2005															
	Age (percent)									One race (percent)					His-panic or Latino origin[1] (per-cent)	Males per 100 females
	Under 5 years	5 to 14 years	15 to 24 years	25 to 34 years	35 to 44 years	45 to 54 years	55 to 64 years	65 to 74 years	75 years and over	White alone	Black or African American alone	Asian alone	American Indian and Alaska Native alone	Native Hawaiian and Other Pacific Islander alone		
KANSAS—Con.																
Riley	6.5	8.6	36.7	17.8	8.7	8.1	5.3	3.7	4.6	86.7	6.9	3.5	0.6	0.2	4.7	113.8
Rooks	5.3	12.0	13.9	9.0	13.1	14.8	10.7	9.6	11.6	98.0	1.3	0.2	0.5	–	1.2	98.4
Rush	5.3	10.5	12.3	8.5	11.9	15.8	11.9	9.8	13.8	98.8	0.3	0.2	0.5	–	1.5	95.6
Russell	5.1	10.8	12.0	8.0	12.4	15.5	12.6	9.8	13.7	98.2	0.7	0.4	0.4	–	1.2	95.0
Saline	6.7	13.5	13.9	12.9	13.9	14.7	10.3	6.7	7.4	92.3	3.3	1.9	0.6	(Z)	7.5	97.7
Scott	6.6	13.0	14.3	9.8	12.9	17.0	12.8	6.6	7.1	98.8	0.2	0.1	0.8	–	8.5	100.5
Sedgwick	7.7	14.8	13.8	14.3	14.3	14.5	9.3	5.6	5.7	83.4	9.3	3.7	1.1	0.1	9.8	98.6
Seward	10.7	16.7	14.6	14.6	14.7	12.5	7.6	4.4	4.3	91.5	3.9	2.9	0.8	0.2	50.4	106.1
Shawnee	7.0	12.9	13.4	13.1	13.5	15.1	11.0	6.9	7.0	86.0	9.1	1.1	1.4	0.1	8.4	95.2
Sheridan	5.1	11.4	14.5	5.7	12.6	18.2	11.3	10.3	10.8	99.3	0.2	(Z)	0.2	0.2	1.9	98.1
Sherman	5.7	11.9	15.5	9.4	11.6	15.3	11.8	8.5	10.4	98.5	0.5	0.1	0.3	0.3	8.5	104.4
Smith	3.9	10.1	11.6	6.2	12.6	15.7	12.3	11.6	16.1	99.0	0.2	(Z)	0.2	0.3	1.0	95.3
Stafford	4.9	12.7	13.6	7.3	13.9	16.5	11.1	9.2	10.9	98.6	0.2	0.2	0.3	–	7.2	97.0
Stanton	7.5	15.3	13.1	11.6	15.0	14.7	8.1	8.0	6.8	97.7	0.3	0.2	1.7	–	29.8	104.1
Stevens	7.8	16.2	14.6	11.8	13.3	14.0	9.4	5.7	7.1	97.1	1.1	0.4	1.1	(Z)	25.5	95.9
Sumner	6.0	13.9	14.5	9.7	12.9	16.9	10.7	7.0	8.4	96.6	1.0	0.2	0.8	(Z)	3.6	97.7
Thomas	5.9	13.4	16.6	10.9	11.9	16.0	9.6	7.3	8.4	97.9	0.7	0.5	0.4	–	2.2	94.1
Trego	4.9	10.9	12.3	7.6	11.2	18.1	10.8	10.2	14.0	98.3	0.4	0.7	0.2	(Z)	1.0	90.6
Wabaunsee	5.3	12.4	14.2	10.2	13.6	17.0	11.9	8.0	7.3	98.2	0.5	0.1	0.5	0.2	2.3	101.4
Wallace	6.0	14.1	14.9	7.1	10.9	17.2	10.8	9.6	9.2	98.0	0.9	0.2	0.9	–	6.2	98.4
Washington	4.8	11.9	11.4	8.1	12.4	15.2	12.6	9.9	13.6	99.2	0.1	–	0.5	–	1.1	106.6
Wichita	6.4	15.5	11.8	10.2	12.7	16.3	10.8	7.7	8.4	98.5	0.2	–	1.0	–	21.0	107.1
Wilson	5.2	12.6	13.1	11.1	12.0	15.4	11.4	8.3	10.9	97.3	0.6	0.3	1.0	0.1	2.0	95.0
Woodson	5.0	9.5	13.0	11.0	11.6	15.8	11.9	8.8	13.5	97.8	0.9	0.1	1.1	–	1.6	92.9
Wyandotte	8.5	14.9	13.9	14.9	13.9	13.8	9.3	5.3	5.3	68.3	27.0	1.7	0.8	0.1	21.4	96.2
KENTUCKY	6.5	13.0	13.8	13.7	14.8	14.7	10.9	6.8	5.8	90.4	7.5	0.9	0.2	(Z)	2.0	96.6
Adair	5.9	12.2	14.9	13.0	13.9	13.8	11.2	8.4	6.7	95.8	3.0	0.4	0.2	–	0.7	95.6
Allen	6.3	13.5	13.4	14.7	14.4	13.7	10.9	7.7	5.5	97.9	1.3	0.2	0.1	–	0.9	96.5
Anderson	5.7	14.6	12.2	14.3	16.7	14.9	10.5	6.3	4.9	96.8	2.4	0.3	(Z)	(Z)	1.0	97.7
Ballard	5.6	12.1	12.3	11.9	13.7	15.2	12.8	8.4	8.0	95.5	3.7	0.2	(Z)	(Z)	0.8	99.7
Barren	6.1	12.8	12.4	13.4	14.3	14.6	11.5	8.0	6.9	94.8	3.9	0.5	0.2	(Z)	1.2	94.3
Bath	6.6	13.1	11.8	14.5	14.5	14.3	11.1	7.8	6.4	97.5	1.7	–	0.3	–	0.9	97.7
Bell	6.2	12.4	13.4	13.2	14.6	14.2	12.0	7.6	6.4	96.2	2.6	0.4	0.2	(Z)	0.8	92.6
Boone	7.3	14.9	14.1	15.3	16.5	14.4	9.2	4.9	3.5	94.5	2.4	1.7	0.2	0.1	2.5	99.1
Bourbon	5.8	13.4	13.0	12.6	14.9	14.9	11.9	7.7	5.9	91.7	6.9	0.3	0.1	0.1	3.7	95.2
Boyd	5.9	11.3	12.2	12.7	14.1	15.9	12.2	8.5	7.1	95.9	2.9	0.4	0.1	(Z)	1.5	98.0
Boyle	5.5	12.2	15.8	12.5	14.2	14.5	11.6	7.2	6.6	88.6	9.1	0.9	0.4	(Z)	1.9	98.2
Bracken	5.9	13.0	13.5	13.7	14.7	15.1	10.7	7.6	5.7	98.9	0.6	0.1	0.3	(Z)	0.5	97.5
Breathitt	5.4	12.8	14.7	13.4	14.9	15.4	11.4	7.2	4.7	98.9	0.4	0.5	(Z)	–	0.7	99.3
Breckinridge	5.7	12.8	13.3	13.4	14.2	14.7	12.2	7.9	5.8	96.2	2.8	0.1	0.2	–	0.9	99.2
Bullitt	5.7	14.3	13.5	15.2	16.3	14.8	11.3	5.7	3.2	97.8	0.8	0.3	0.3	–	1.0	99.2
Butler	6.0	12.4	13.0	14.7	15.1	14.4	11.1	7.0	6.1	98.7	0.6	0.2	0.1	–	1.7	100.1
Caldwell	5.4	11.9	11.7	12.4	13.0	14.9	13.6	9.1	8.0	94.5	4.8	0.2	0.1	–	0.6	92.7
Calloway	4.9	9.3	23.8	13.6	11.3	11.7	10.5	7.6	7.3	93.0	4.0	2.1	0.2	(Z)	1.5	95.8
Campbell	6.4	13.5	14.4	12.2	15.4	15.1	10.2	6.7	6.1	96.2	2.1	0.7	0.2	(Z)	1.1	94.7
Carlisle	5.8	11.8	12.6	11.3	14.2	14.2	12.0	9.0	9.1	98.1	1.1	0.1	0.4	–	1.3	99.4
Carroll	7.2	13.1	12.8	14.1	15.0	13.8	11.6	6.6	5.7	96.3	1.9	0.5	0.3	0.1	3.9	100.2
Carter	6.0	13.0	14.2	13.9	14.4	13.6	11.7	7.8	5.5	98.9	0.2	0.2	0.3	(Z)	0.6	97.3
Casey	6.0	12.8	12.3	14.3	14.2	13.5	12.1	7.9	7.0	98.9	0.4	(Z)	0.3	0.1	2.0	95.7
Christian	10.6	16.7	16.0	15.6	12.6	10.5	8.0	5.4	4.6	73.5	22.4	0.9	0.4	0.4	4.7	105.8
Clark	6.0	13.0	12.3	14.1	15.1	14.8	12.0	6.9	5.8	94.2	4.8	0.3	0.2	–	1.3	94.0
Clay	6.0	14.2	13.8	15.6	16.4	14.6	10.2	6.4	4.4	94.3	5.0	0.1	0.2	(Z)	1.4	112.5
Clinton	6.4	11.9	10.5	14.1	13.7	13.9	13.1	9.5	6.9	98.9	0.1	–	0.2	0.6	2.5	94.8
Crittenden	4.7	11.8	13.1	10.6	13.9	14.8	14.0	9.1	8.1	98.8	0.6	0.1	(Z)	–	0.6	94.6
Cumberland	5.9	11.9	12.0	11.4	13.9	13.5	12.4	10.4	8.6	95.8	3.4	(Z)	0.1	0.2	0.7	94.3
Daviess	7.1	13.3	13.5	12.1	13.9	15.0	11.0	7.4	6.8	93.4	4.7	0.6	0.1	(Z)	1.2	94.3
Edmonson	5.3	12.1	12.4	15.0	13.6	14.2	13.0	8.3	6.1	98.6	0.6	0.2	0.4	–	0.9	97.7
Elliott	5.9	13.1	13.1	14.3	13.0	15.2	11.6	7.8	6.0	99.7	(Z)	–	–	–	0.6	96.4
Estill	6.3	12.7	12.1	13.8	15.6	14.0	12.3	7.7	5.6	99.2	0.2	0.1	0.2	–	0.7	95.3
Fayette	6.8	11.3	16.3	16.2	15.3	14.1	9.6	5.5	4.9	81.7	13.6	2.9	0.2	0.1	4.9	98.2
Fleming	6.2	13.4	12.8	14.0	14.5	14.4	11.4	7.6	5.7	97.7	1.5	0.2	0.1	–	0.8	96.9
Floyd	6.3	11.8	13.5	13.8	15.1	15.7	11.6	6.8	5.3	97.9	1.4	0.2	0.1	0.1	0.7	97.0
Franklin	6.2	11.9	13.3	13.0	15.1	15.8	12.2	6.8	5.7	88.0	9.5	1.0	0.1	(Z)	2.0	94.6
Fulton	5.7	12.6	13.1	11.0	12.8	14.8	12.0	8.3	9.7	75.5	23.4	0.3	0.1	–	0.8	88.7
Gallatin	7.4	15.2	12.7	12.9	15.8	14.8	10.7	6.1	4.4	97.2	1.7	0.3	0.1	–	2.3	99.9
Garrard	5.4	12.9	12.7	15.1	15.7	14.6	10.9	7.0	5.7	96.5	3.0	(Z)	0.1	–	1.7	97.4
Grant	7.4	15.0	13.2	15.8	15.8	13.3	9.8	5.6	4.0	98.5	0.4	0.4	0.2	0.1	1.3	98.5
Graves	6.3	13.2	12.7	12.6	14.0	14.1	11.6	7.8	7.8	93.7	4.6	0.3	0.3	(Z)	4.5	95.7
Grayson	6.2	13.0	12.5	14.0	13.9	14.5	11.7	8.3	5.9	98.5	0.6	0.2	0.1	–	1.0	98.9
Green	5.5	11.6	11.9	12.8	14.5	14.9	12.4	8.6	7.7	97.0	2.5	0.1	(Z)	–	1.1	98.1
Greenup	5.4	12.2	11.8	12.4	13.8	15.5	13.1	8.8	7.0	98.0	0.7	0.5	0.2	–	0.6	93.8

See footnotes at end of table.

County and City Data Book: 2007

U.S. Census Bureau

Table B-3. Counties — **Population by Age, Race, Hispanic Origin, and Sex**—Con.

[Includes United States, states, and 3,141 counties/county equivalents defined as of February 22, 2005. For more information on these areas, see Appendix C, Geographic Information]

County	Age (percent)									One race (percent)					His-panic or Latino origin[1] (per-cent)	Males per 100 females
	Under 5 years	5 to 14 years	15 to 24 years	25 to 34 years	35 to 44 years	45 to 54 years	55 to 64 years	65 to 74 years	75 years and over	White alone	Black or African American alone	Asian alone	American Indian and Alaska Native alone	Native Hawaiian and Other Pacific Islander alone		
KENTUCKY—Con.																
Hancock	6.4	14.2	12.8	12.9	14.8	14.3	12.8	6.7	5.0	98.4	1.0	0.2	0.3	–	1.3	98.5
Hardin	7.4	13.9	15.6	12.4	15.5	14.7	9.7	6.3	4.6	83.3	11.7	1.9	0.4	0.2	3.5	101.4
Harlan	6.0	13.0	13.5	12.0	13.9	15.9	12.5	7.3	6.0	95.8	2.5	0.5	0.4	(Z)	0.8	93.1
Harrison	6.1	12.9	12.6	12.7	15.1	15.4	11.7	7.0	6.5	96.6	2.3	0.2	0.3	(Z)	1.6	94.7
Hart	6.1	13.4	13.3	13.1	14.8	14.6	11.4	7.5	5.8	93.8	5.4	0.1	0.2	(Z)	1.2	98.7
Henderson	6.5	12.7	12.6	12.7	14.8	15.9	11.5	7.0	6.2	91.3	7.4	0.4	0.1	–	1.4	94.5
Henry	6.7	13.4	12.3	13.1	14.9	15.0	12.1	7.0	5.4	95.2	3.5	0.4	0.3	(Z)	2.7	99.0
Hickman	5.2	11.4	12.0	10.9	14.7	14.4	13.2	9.4	8.8	89.1	9.8	0.1	0.2	–	1.0	93.6
Hopkins	6.0	12.6	12.3	12.8	14.2	15.4	11.8	8.0	6.9	92.2	6.2	0.4	0.2	(Z)	1.2	92.6
Jackson	6.1	13.4	12.8	15.7	15.0	14.7	10.5	6.9	4.9	99.4	0.1	–	0.2	–	0.5	99.1
Jefferson	6.9	13.1	12.6	12.9	14.8	15.5	10.8	6.8	6.5	76.6	20.0	1.7	0.2	(Z)	2.4	92.7
Jessamine	6.5	14.0	15.4	15.5	14.6	14.5	9.4	5.7	4.4	94.4	3.4	0.9	0.2	(Z)	1.4	96.1
Johnson	6.3	12.2	13.2	13.3	14.5	15.4	12.5	7.4	5.3	99.0	0.3	0.3	0.1	(Z)	0.7	93.8
Kenton	7.4	14.1	13.2	13.5	15.7	15.2	10.3	5.8	5.2	93.6	4.2	0.8	0.1	0.1	1.4	97.5
Knott	5.0	12.6	15.1	12.2	15.1	16.1	12.0	6.5	5.4	98.7	0.8	0.2	0.1	(Z)	0.7	97.6
Knox	6.8	13.9	13.9	13.6	14.1	13.5	11.6	7.1	5.6	97.8	1.1	0.2	0.2	(Z)	0.7	93.6
Larue	5.7	12.7	12.6	12.3	14.9	14.9	11.5	8.2	7.4	95.6	3.4	0.2	0.2	–	1.1	95.5
Laurel	6.7	13.4	12.9	14.9	14.9	14.5	11.1	6.8	4.8	97.6	0.8	0.4	0.4	–	0.6	96.3
Lawrence	5.6	12.6	13.2	14.3	14.9	14.7	11.9	7.4	5.4	99.0	0.2	0.1	0.3	–	0.4	100.5
Lee	5.1	11.0	14.3	13.8	16.0	13.9	11.2	8.3	6.4	95.3	4.0	0.1	0.3	–	0.5	110.2
Leslie	5.3	12.2	13.0	13.4	15.5	16.9	11.1	7.6	5.1	99.5	0.1	0.2	(Z)	–	0.6	94.9
Letcher	5.6	11.9	12.4	13.3	14.8	16.4	12.6	7.6	5.5	98.9	0.6	0.3	(Z)	(Z)	0.5	96.6
Lewis	5.5	13.2	13.1	13.7	15.2	14.7	11.5	7.4	5.5	99.2	0.3	–	0.2	–	0.5	100.9
Lincoln	6.2	13.5	12.6	15.0	15.2	13.5	10.7	7.6	5.8	97.0	2.5	0.1	(Z)	–	1.4	97.0
Livingston	4.8	11.4	12.6	11.8	15.0	15.2	13.8	8.8	6.6	99.0	0.2	0.1	0.4	–	0.8	99.0
Logan	6.2	13.6	12.5	13.3	14.4	14.2	11.6	7.6	6.4	91.3	7.3	0.2	0.2	(Z)	1.6	93.5
Lyon	3.1	8.4	14.1	14.7	16.6	15.2	11.8	11.0	8.0	92.1	7.0	0.4	0.3	(Z)	0.8	135.8
McCracken	6.1	12.5	12.2	11.2	13.9	15.9	12.4	7.6	8.1	86.9	10.9	0.5	0.2	0.1	1.3	91.2
McCreary	6.7	13.7	15.2	13.6	14.1	13.6	11.9	6.6	4.6	98.0	0.8	(Z)	0.4	(Z)	0.7	98.3
McLean	6.1	12.6	11.8	13.0	14.1	14.7	13.1	8.0	6.5	99.2	0.4	0.1	(Z)	(Z)	1.3	96.4
Madison	6.2	11.9	20.3	16.4	13.6	12.3	9.3	5.6	4.5	93.3	4.2	0.9	0.3	(Z)	1.2	94.2
Magoffin	6.8	13.4	14.2	14.1	15.2	14.8	10.2	6.6	4.6	99.4	0.2	0.1	0.2	–	0.5	98.0
Marion	7.0	13.2	13.3	14.6	15.4	13.9	10.6	6.1	5.9	89.8	8.8	0.7	(Z)	(Z)	1.2	104.2
Marshall	4.6	11.1	12.7	11.5	14.2	15.1	12.6	10.1	8.0	98.7	0.2	0.2	0.1	–	0.8	96.9
Martin	6.5	14.3	13.5	13.6	14.8	15.5	11.0	6.2	4.6	99.5	0.1	0.1	(Z)	0.1	0.7	98.2
Mason	5.7	12.5	12.2	12.3	14.6	16.1	11.5	7.6	7.6	91.6	7.0	0.5	0.1	(Z)	1.1	93.5
Meade	5.5	16.2	13.8	16.0	16.4	14.1	9.5	5.3	3.3	92.8	4.5	0.5	0.7	0.2	2.4	100.2
Menifee	5.9	11.7	14.8	13.5	13.5	14.0	12.9	8.2	5.5	98.4	1.4	–	(Z)	–	1.1	101.0
Mercer	6.2	13.4	11.7	12.8	14.7	14.8	11.9	7.7	6.8	94.2	3.8	0.9	0.2	(Z)	1.7	95.4
Metcalfe	5.8	13.2	12.0	13.3	14.6	14.9	11.2	8.8	6.4	97.5	1.9	0.1	0.2	–	0.7	97.8
Monroe	5.6	13.0	12.1	13.3	14.1	14.4	11.8	8.7	6.9	96.5	2.8	0.1	0.1	0.1	2.3	96.3
Montgomery	6.8	13.3	11.9	15.3	14.4	14.2	11.3	6.5	6.3	95.8	3.3	0.1	0.1	(Z)	1.3	96.2
Morgan	5.1	11.2	14.2	16.2	16.0	14.9	10.0	7.1	5.3	95.2	4.5	0.1	0.1	(Z)	0.7	123.0
Muhlenberg	5.6	11.8	12.7	13.2	14.1	14.7	12.4	8.0	7.4	94.7	4.7	0.1	(Z)	–	0.9	98.4
Nelson	6.6	14.5	13.4	13.9	15.7	14.9	10.4	5.9	4.7	93.3	5.3	0.7	0.1	(Z)	1.1	96.7
Nicholas	6.2	12.3	11.8	13.1	14.8	14.5	11.8	8.6	7.0	98.8	0.8	0.2	0.2	–	0.6	96.3
Ohio	6.0	12.7	13.1	13.6	13.9	14.6	11.9	7.7	6.4	98.3	0.9	0.2	0.1	(Z)	1.3	98.1
Oldham	5.4	13.9	14.6	12.2	17.2	17.3	11.9	4.7	2.8	93.7	4.4	0.7	0.3	–	1.9	111.8
Owen	6.0	13.1	12.8	14.3	14.5	15.2	11.5	7.0	5.7	97.9	1.1	0.2	0.3	–	1.1	100.5
Owsley	5.8	11.9	13.3	12.4	13.9	15.1	11.8	8.6	7.2	99.5	0.1	0.1	0.1	(Z)	0.7	98.9
Pendleton	5.7	14.6	13.7	14.0	16.1	14.6	10.8	5.9	4.8	98.9	0.5	0.1	0.1	–	0.8	100.3
Perry	6.8	12.3	12.5	13.5	15.3	16.2	11.6	6.9	5.0	97.4	1.6	0.7	(Z)	(Z)	0.6	95.6
Pike	5.5	12.3	12.6	13.3	15.0	16.2	12.3	7.3	5.6	98.5	0.5	0.4	0.1	(Z)	0.8	95.7
Powell	6.5	12.8	13.0	14.0	14.7	14.5	10.8	8.3	5.4	99.1	0.7	(Z)	(Z)	(Z)	0.7	98.5
Pulaski	6.1	12.1	12.1	13.3	14.5	14.5	11.5	8.7	7.2	97.3	1.3	0.5	0.2	–	1.2	95.3
Robertson	4.8	12.7	12.7	10.7	15.6	14.2	12.7	8.9	7.8	99.0	0.3	–	–	0.7	1.0	97.7
Rockcastle	6.0	12.4	12.7	14.0	15.4	14.3	11.3	7.8	6.0	99.2	0.2	0.1	0.1	–	0.6	97.4
Rowan	5.7	10.5	25.8	13.3	12.1	11.8	9.1	6.5	5.0	96.3	1.6	1.2	0.2	–	1.3	95.8
Russell	5.8	11.7	11.7	12.8	14.3	14.6	12.6	9.2	7.2	98.9	0.7	0.2	0.1	(Z)	0.9	94.2
Scott	7.1	14.2	15.5	16.2	15.9	14.0	8.7	4.7	3.7	92.4	5.4	0.9	0.2	–	2.0	96.7
Shelby	6.9	13.1	13.2	15.3	15.7	14.2	11.1	6.0	4.6	89.3	8.2	0.6	0.4	0.4	8.0	98.1
Simpson	6.4	14.0	12.9	13.7	14.9	14.1	10.8	6.9	6.2	88.2	9.8	1.0	0.1	0.2	1.0	96.6
Spencer	6.0	14.3	13.5	16.4	17.1	14.7	9.2	5.2	3.6	97.1	1.6	0.1	0.2	–	1.1	103.1
Taylor	5.8	11.9	14.8	11.6	13.8	14.4	11.4	9.1	7.3	93.9	5.3	0.3	0.1	(Z)	1.4	92.3
Todd	7.3	14.3	12.2	13.3	14.2	14.1	11.5	7.0	6.2	90.7	8.6	0.2	0.2	–	2.0	96.7
Trigg	5.2	12.2	12.1	12.3	14.2	14.1	13.1	9.6	7.3	89.6	9.3	0.4	0.1	–	1.0	97.0
Trimble	5.7	13.7	13.5	14.4	15.9	14.5	11.2	6.1	4.9	98.8	0.3	0.1	0.4	(Z)	1.4	99.0
Union	6.1	11.9	19.9	11.7	12.3	14.5	10.8	6.8	5.8	85.1	13.6	0.3	0.2	(Z)	1.6	100.9
Warren	6.4	12.2	18.9	14.7	13.7	13.4	9.8	6.0	4.8	87.9	8.8	1.6	0.2	0.1	3.3	96.7
Washington	6.6	12.7	14.4	11.9	14.7	14.5	10.8	7.8	6.8	91.3	7.4	0.5	0.2	–	1.9	99.7

See footnotes at end of table.

[Includes United States, states, and 3,141 counties/county equivalents defined as of February 22, 2005. For more information on these areas, see Appendix C, Geographic Information]

County	Age (percent)									One race (percent)					Hispanic or Latino origin[1] (percent)	Males per 100 females
	Under 5 years	5 to 14 years	15 to 24 years	25 to 34 years	35 to 44 years	45 to 54 years	55 to 64 years	65 to 74 years	75 years and over	White alone	Black or African American alone	Asian alone	American Indian and Alaska Native alone	Native Hawaiian and Other Pacific Islander alone		
KENTUCKY—Con.																
Wayne	5.6	13.1	13.0	14.2	14.3	14.3	11.6	8.0	5.8	97.6	1.5	0.1	0.2	–	2.4	98.5
Webster	6.8	12.4	13.0	13.1	13.4	15.3	11.3	7.9	6.9	95.0	4.3	0.1	0.1	0.2	4.2	97.3
Whitley	6.8	13.2	15.0	13.7	13.8	13.2	11.1	7.3	5.9	98.3	0.4	0.3	0.3	(Z)	0.9	94.0
Wolfe	7.6	13.3	13.9	12.7	13.8	14.9	11.0	7.8	5.0	99.5	0.3	0.1	(Z)	(Z)	0.8	98.6
Woodford	6.5	12.7	13.6	11.5	15.4	17.2	11.8	6.5	4.9	93.3	5.5	0.4	0.1	(Z)	4.8	95.6
LOUISIANA	7.1	13.8	15.5	13.4	14.0	14.4	10.2	6.2	5.5	64.1	33.1	1.4	0.6	(Z)	2.8	94.7
Acadia	7.7	15.1	14.9	12.4	13.8	14.0	9.8	6.6	5.8	80.3	18.9	0.2	0.2	(Z)	1.0	94.8
Allen	6.4	12.8	14.0	16.2	16.1	12.8	9.4	6.7	5.6	72.6	24.5	0.6	1.6	(Z)	4.5	126.4
Ascension	7.8	15.0	15.3	15.7	16.0	14.0	8.8	4.4	3.1	78.6	19.8	0.7	0.3	0.1	3.4	98.2
Assumption	6.0	14.3	14.7	12.7	14.9	14.8	10.9	6.3	5.4	67.5	31.7	0.3	0.3	–	1.5	94.5
Avoyelles	7.6	13.4	14.5	14.0	14.1	13.4	9.9	6.8	6.4	67.8	30.5	0.3	1.0	(Z)	1.1	97.8
Beauregard	6.2	14.2	14.5	13.9	14.3	14.2	10.8	6.9	5.1	84.4	13.4	0.7	0.6	(Z)	2.2	101.8
Bienville	6.3	13.3	14.9	10.3	13.1	13.5	11.3	8.8	8.5	57.6	41.9	0.2	0.2	–	1.2	92.5
Bossier	7.4	14.3	14.7	14.2	14.8	14.0	9.4	6.6	4.6	75.2	21.3	1.4	0.6	0.1	3.9	97.3
Caddo	7.2	13.5	14.8	13.4	12.9	14.4	10.3	6.6	6.8	51.3	46.5	0.9	0.4	(Z)	1.9	90.8
Calcasieu	7.2	13.8	15.2	13.0	13.7	14.7	10.1	6.6	5.7	73.4	24.7	0.7	0.3	(Z)	1.6	95.5
Caldwell	5.7	12.5	14.4	14.9	13.5	14.2	10.6	7.9	6.3	81.6	17.7	0.2	0.4	–	1.6	103.8
Cameron	5.1	13.6	14.9	13.6	15.2	15.4	10.8	6.7	4.7	94.5	4.5	0.5	0.4	–	3.0	101.6
Catahoula	6.0	12.9	14.2	13.2	12.7	15.5	10.7	8.2	6.7	71.8	27.6	0.2	0.2	–	1.0	102.9
Claiborne	5.0	12.7	14.6	11.9	13.7	14.0	11.0	8.3	8.7	51.6	48.1	(Z)	0.1	(Z)	1.0	100.3
Concordia	5.9	14.2	14.1	11.3	12.8	15.4	11.0	7.7	7.5	60.5	38.6	0.4	0.2	–	1.7	97.0
De Soto	6.7	13.9	15.1	12.2	13.1	14.5	11.2	6.7	6.5	58.3	40.6	0.1	0.4	0.1	1.9	91.7
East Baton Rouge	7.0	13.4	18.5	13.6	13.1	14.0	9.9	5.4	5.0	53.3	43.3	2.4	0.2	(Z)	2.2	92.5
East Carroll	7.7	15.6	17.6	13.5	12.7	11.8	9.1	6.3	5.9	31.1	68.2	0.5	0.2	(Z)	1.3	104.7
East Feliciana	6.4	12.7	13.9	13.6	15.1	15.7	11.0	6.7	5.0	54.0	45.1	0.3	0.2	(Z)	1.0	113.6
Evangeline	6.9	15.4	15.6	12.4	14.2	13.4	9.8	6.5	5.8	70.2	29.1	0.3	0.2	(Z)	1.2	99.5
Franklin	7.1	13.8	14.2	11.8	13.1	14.0	10.2	8.4	7.4	67.9	31.3	0.2	0.3	–	0.9	91.6
Grant	6.6	14.8	13.8	13.4	13.9	14.1	11.1	6.9	5.5	86.5	11.2	0.3	0.8	(Z)	1.5	97.9
Iberia	7.6	15.2	14.6	13.2	14.1	14.2	9.5	6.3	5.3	65.0	31.6	2.2	0.3	(Z)	1.7	93.0
Iberville	7.0	13.0	15.2	13.4	15.5	14.8	9.8	6.2	5.0	49.5	49.8	0.3	0.2	(Z)	1.3	99.7
Jackson	6.7	12.4	13.3	12.9	12.8	13.8	12.0	8.2	7.9	72.2	27.1	0.3	0.3	–	0.9	91.9
Jefferson	6.9	13.0	13.4	12.9	14.6	15.3	11.4	6.4	6.1	68.2	26.8	3.4	0.4	(Z)	8.1	92.7
Jefferson Davis	7.5	15.0	14.3	12.7	13.3	13.8	9.9	7.1	6.3	81.2	17.5	0.3	0.4	(Z)	1.1	92.8
Lafayette	7.3	13.6	16.3	14.4	14.5	14.8	9.0	5.5	4.6	72.4	25.1	1.3	0.3	(Z)	2.2	95.6
Lafourche	6.4	13.7	15.1	13.4	15.2	14.3	10.1	6.5	5.3	82.6	13.3	0.7	2.5	(Z)	1.8	95.9
La Salle	6.2	12.6	15.1	12.8	13.6	13.9	11.1	7.8	6.8	86.5	12.2	0.2	0.7	–	0.9	101.8
Lincoln	6.2	10.9	29.8	12.2	10.4	10.6	8.4	5.6	6.0	58.0	39.9	1.4	0.3	(Z)	1.7	95.5
Livingston	6.9	14.3	14.9	16.3	15.5	13.7	9.5	5.1	3.7	94.3	4.4	0.4	0.4	(Z)	1.5	98.6
Madison	6.9	16.5	16.6	13.0	12.1	13.6	10.0	5.6	5.8	37.4	61.5	0.3	0.2	0.6	2.5	98.0
Morehouse	7.2	13.9	14.2	12.3	12.9	14.4	10.4	7.5	7.4	54.8	44.6	0.3	0.1	–	0.9	92.2
Natchitoches	7.6	12.9	21.2	12.7	11.5	12.1	9.7	6.2	6.1	57.9	39.7	0.7	1.1	(Z)	1.6	92.4
Orleans	7.6	13.5	15.6	13.5	13.6	14.5	10.2	5.6	5.9	28.8	67.5	2.4	0.2	(Z)	3.1	88.6
Ouachita	7.5	14.0	16.4	14.0	13.0	13.4	9.6	6.3	5.7	63.5	34.8	0.8	0.3	(Z)	1.4	90.8
Plaquemines	7.2	14.5	15.4	13.8	15.3	14.3	9.6	5.6	4.3	70.8	23.0	3.3	2.0	–	2.8	101.0
Pointe Coupee	6.8	13.6	14.0	11.0	13.8	15.5	11.3	7.5	6.6	62.1	37.2	0.3	0.2	–	1.4	95.7
Rapides	7.3	13.8	14.4	12.9	13.9	14.2	10.5	7.1	6.0	66.3	31.1	1.0	0.8	(Z)	1.9	92.6
Red River	7.9	15.0	16.0	11.8	12.3	13.1	10.6	6.6	6.6	56.0	43.3	0.1	0.4	(Z)	1.0	90.9
Richland	7.0	14.1	14.3	13.0	13.0	14.4	9.7	7.1	7.4	62.1	37.5	0.2	0.1	(Z)	1.4	88.7
Sabine	6.9	13.2	13.8	12.2	12.8	12.8	12.4	8.5	7.3	73.4	16.5	0.2	8.0	(Z)	3.4	97.3
St. Bernard	6.5	12.9	14.1	12.2	14.6	15.3	11.1	6.7	6.6	86.4	10.5	1.5	0.5	(Z)	5.5	93.9
St. Charles	6.6	14.7	16.0	11.4	16.1	16.3	9.6	5.1	4.3	71.9	26.2	0.9	0.3	(Z)	3.5	96.2
St. Helena	5.5	15.0	15.7	11.5	13.6	15.1	10.9	7.2	5.5	46.1	53.5	0.1	0.1	(Z)	1.2	94.4
St. James	7.3	14.2	15.8	11.2	14.2	15.5	9.9	6.8	5.2	49.9	49.9	0.1	0.1	–	0.9	93.5
St. John the Baptist	7.5	15.6	16.5	12.9	15.1	15.0	9.4	4.6	3.3	50.4	48.0	0.7	0.3	(Z)	4.1	94.9
St. Landry	7.6	14.8	14.9	12.2	13.3	13.7	10.1	7.0	6.3	56.4	42.5	0.3	0.2	(Z)	1.0	92.6
St. Martin	7.1	14.7	14.9	13.8	14.5	15.0	9.7	5.8	4.5	66.9	31.4	1.0	0.3	–	1.1	97.1
St. Mary	7.4	14.9	14.4	11.4	14.3	14.7	10.6	6.9	5.3	63.8	32.5	1.4	1.5	(Z)	2.8	94.9
St. Tammany	6.6	14.1	14.8	12.7	14.7	16.0	10.7	5.7	4.7	85.6	11.7	1.0	0.5	(Z)	3.2	97.5
Tangipahoa	7.4	13.9	17.1	14.6	13.2	13.7	9.7	5.9	4.6	69.8	29.0	0.5	0.2	(Z)	1.8	94.2
Tensas	7.0	12.7	17.2	10.1	11.7	15.9	11.3	6.7	7.3	42.8	56.7	0.2	–	(Z)	2.2	99.5
Terrebonne	7.8	14.3	14.8	13.7	14.8	14.1	9.9	6.0	4.7	74.5	18.1	0.8	5.3	(Z)	2.0	97.2
Union	6.8	13.0	12.9	13.3	13.1	14.2	11.4	8.5	6.9	72.2	27.0	0.3	0.2	(Z)	2.8	96.2
Vermilion	7.0	14.0	14.5	13.0	14.3	14.3	9.7	6.8	6.4	82.8	14.3	2.1	0.3	–	1.8	94.8
Vernon	9.8	17.2	15.8	16.1	13.8	10.3	7.9	5.4	3.7	77.1	15.4	1.9	1.5	0.4	7.2	112.1
Washington	7.2	13.9	14.3	13.4	12.8	13.7	10.8	7.2	6.9	67.6	31.6	0.2	0.3	(Z)	1.1	95.7
Webster	6.4	12.8	13.9	12.1	12.9	14.3	11.3	8.4	7.9	65.6	33.2	0.3	0.3	(Z)	1.0	93.0
West Baton Rouge	6.7	13.8	15.0	13.1	15.4	15.7	10.0	5.6	4.7	63.9	35.4	0.2	0.1	(Z)	1.9	97.5
West Carroll	6.1	12.8	15.5	12.0	13.1	14.0	11.1	8.6	7.1	80.8	18.7	0.2	0.3	–	1.4	103.5
West Feliciana	4.1	9.6	13.8	17.8	20.6	17.3	9.2	4.2	3.5	50.2	49.2	0.2	0.2	(Z)	1.1	187.0
Winn	5.9	12.5	13.9	14.2	14.8	13.6	11.1	7.2	6.7	67.3	31.6	0.2	0.6	(Z)	0.9	111.4

See footnotes at end of table.

County and City Data Book: 2007

U.S. Census Bureau

[Includes United States, states, and 3,141 counties/county equivalents defined as of February 22, 2005. For more information on these areas, see Appendix C, Geographic Information]

County	Age (percent)									One race (percent)					His-panic or Latino origin[1] (per-cent)	Males per 100 females
	Under 5 years	5 to 14 years	15 to 24 years	25 to 34 years	35 to 44 years	45 to 54 years	55 to 64 years	65 to 74 years	75 years and over	White alone	Black or African American alone	Asian alone	American Indian and Alaska Native alone	Native Hawaiian and Other Pacific Islander alone		
MAINE	5.1	11.6	13.8	10.9	15.2	16.5	12.3	7.3	7.3	96.9	0.8	0.8	0.6	(Z)	1.0	95.5
Androscoggin	5.9	12.0	14.0	12.0	15.5	15.0	11.1	7.0	7.4	96.2	1.4	0.7	0.3	0.1	1.2	95.2
Aroostook	4.5	10.9	13.5	9.8	14.0	16.5	13.3	8.8	8.6	96.9	0.5	0.6	1.3	(Z)	0.9	95.3
Cumberland	5.4	11.9	13.6	10.9	16.3	16.7	11.7	6.4	7.1	95.3	1.5	1.6	0.3	0.1	1.3	94.8
Franklin	4.3	11.1	17.9	10.8	13.8	16.0	12.7	6.9	6.4	98.1	0.4	0.5	0.4	–	0.7	94.3
Hancock	4.6	10.6	13.3	10.1	14.6	17.0	13.8	7.8	8.1	97.7	0.3	0.6	0.4	(Z)	0.8	96.7
Kennebec	5.0	11.5	14.1	10.9	15.1	16.6	12.4	7.2	7.2	97.6	0.5	0.7	0.4	(Z)	1.0	94.8
Knox	4.8	10.9	11.9	10.7	14.3	17.0	13.2	8.2	9.0	98.4	0.3	0.4	0.2	(Z)	0.8	97.2
Lincoln	4.0	10.8	12.3	9.4	13.7	16.7	14.6	9.0	9.5	98.8	0.2	0.3	0.3	(Z)	0.6	95.2
Oxford	4.7	11.6	13.3	10.6	14.9	17.3	12.5	7.7	7.5	98.4	0.3	0.4	0.3	(Z)	0.7	96.0
Penobscot	5.2	11.0	16.2	11.5	14.6	16.2	11.6	7.1	6.5	96.8	0.6	0.8	1.0	(Z)	0.8	96.2
Piscataquis	4.4	10.6	13.1	9.3	13.8	17.2	14.2	8.5	9.0	98.4	0.3	0.3	0.6	(Z)	0.5	95.5
Sagadahoc	5.5	12.5	12.7	10.8	15.7	17.2	12.3	7.0	6.4	96.9	1.1	0.6	0.4	0.1	1.6	97.8
Somerset	5.1	11.9	13.1	10.7	15.0	16.7	12.8	7.7	7.0	98.1	0.3	0.4	0.4	(Z)	0.5	96.0
Waldo	5.1	11.8	13.4	11.3	14.4	16.8	13.4	7.5	6.5	98.3	0.2	0.3	0.3	(Z)	0.7	96.5
Washington	5.2	11.2	12.9	10.3	13.6	16.1	13.0	8.9	8.9	93.8	0.4	0.4	4.6	(Z)	1.1	95.6
York	5.2	12.3	12.9	11.0	15.8	16.9	12.1	7.0	6.9	97.6	0.5	0.8	0.2	(Z)	1.0	95.4
MARYLAND	6.8	13.8	14.0	12.6	15.7	15.0	10.6	5.9	5.6	64.0	29.3	4.8	0.3	0.1	5.7	94.0
Allegany	4.6	10.7	16.2	12.3	13.4	13.4	11.2	8.3	9.8	92.7	6.0	0.6	0.1	(Z)	1.0	100.6
Anne Arundel	6.8	13.6	13.4	12.5	16.6	15.2	11.3	5.8	4.8	80.5	14.7	2.8	0.3	0.1	3.6	99.5
Baltimore	6.0	12.8	13.8	12.0	14.9	15.1	10.8	6.7	7.9	70.5	24.0	3.9	0.3	(Z)	2.4	90.7
Calvert	6.1	14.7	14.7	12.2	17.0	15.8	10.4	4.9	4.2	84.6	12.9	1.0	0.3	(Z)	2.0	97.2
Caroline	6.5	13.6	14.1	12.8	14.7	14.6	10.9	6.4	6.4	84.0	14.0	0.5	0.6	(Z)	4.0	95.6
Carroll	5.8	14.3	14.4	11.4	16.2	16.0	10.9	5.7	5.4	94.7	3.0	1.3	0.2	(Z)	1.5	98.1
Cecil	6.2	14.3	13.7	14.3	16.1	14.7	10.2	5.7	4.9	92.8	5.0	1.0	0.3	0.1	2.0	97.4
Charles	7.0	15.2	14.3	13.8	17.3	14.6	9.8	4.7	3.3	60.3	34.6	2.3	0.7	0.1	3.1	96.0
Dorchester	5.6	12.1	12.7	11.1	14.0	14.8	12.3	8.5	8.9	70.9	27.6	0.8	0.2	–	1.9	90.1
Frederick	7.1	14.6	13.7	12.8	17.0	15.3	9.8	5.1	4.7	87.2	7.8	2.9	0.3	0.1	4.6	97.8
Garrett	5.4	13.3	12.9	12.0	14.2	14.7	12.0	8.1	7.6	99.0	0.5	0.2	(Z)	(Z)	0.5	97.9
Harford	6.3	14.9	13.6	11.8	16.3	15.5	10.8	5.9	4.9	84.8	11.5	1.9	0.2	0.1	2.4	96.2
Howard	6.7	15.3	12.9	11.7	17.5	16.3	10.9	5.0	3.7	70.6	16.1	10.9	0.3	0.1	4.0	96.7
Kent	4.1	10.4	18.3	9.8	12.5	13.2	12.4	8.7	10.5	82.7	15.8	0.9	0.2	(Z)	3.3	92.4
Montgomery	7.3	13.7	12.3	11.7	16.1	16.0	11.1	5.8	5.9	67.9	16.4	13.2	0.3	0.1	13.6	92.9
Prince George's	7.8	14.6	15.0	13.8	16.0	14.4	10.0	5.0	3.4	27.7	66.1	3.9	0.4	0.1	10.7	92.7
Queen Anne's	5.7	13.4	12.8	11.0	16.1	15.7	12.4	7.1	5.9	90.3	7.9	0.9	0.2	(Z)	1.4	98.5
St. Mary's	7.0	14.5	15.3	13.8	16.8	13.9	9.3	5.1	4.3	81.7	14.3	2.0	0.4	0.1	2.3	100.0
Somerset	5.2	9.9	20.1	14.4	14.0	12.8	10.0	6.9	6.7	56.6	41.7	0.8	0.3	(Z)	1.8	114.2
Talbot	4.8	11.2	11.6	10.7	13.1	14.1	12.7	9.9	11.9	84.2	14.3	0.7	0.2	0.3	2.6	91.1
Washington	6.0	12.6	13.1	14.5	15.8	14.1	10.0	6.7	7.1	88.8	8.9	1.1	0.2	0.1	1.9	103.8
Wicomico	6.6	12.9	17.0	12.5	13.7	14.2	10.2	6.2	6.6	73.1	23.8	1.8	0.3	(Z)	2.8	91.0
Worcester	4.9	10.6	11.1	11.5	14.1	13.8	12.1	11.3	10.6	83.4	14.9	0.9	0.2	(Z)	1.8	94.5
Independent City																
Baltimore city	7.4	13.5	15.5	13.0	14.1	14.3	10.0	5.9	6.3	31.7	64.9	1.9	0.3	0.1	2.2	87.3
MASSACHUSETTS	6.2	12.5	13.3	13.6	15.8	14.8	10.5	6.1	7.2	86.7	6.9	4.7	0.3	0.1	7.9	94.0
Barnstable	4.3	10.3	10.6	10.7	13.7	14.9	12.5	10.0	13.0	95.6	2.1	0.9	0.5	(Z)	1.7	90.6
Berkshire	4.6	11.4	13.7	11.0	13.8	15.5	12.2	7.7	10.1	95.2	2.3	1.2	0.2	(Z)	2.3	92.9
Bristol	6.0	13.1	14.6	13.9	15.9	14.4	10.6	5.9	7.6	93.1	3.6	1.7	0.3	(Z)	4.7	93.1
Dukes	5.0	10.7	11.2	11.8	15.6	18.2	13.0	6.7	7.8	93.3	3.1	0.7	1.8	0.1	1.4	96.9
Essex	6.9	13.5	12.3	12.0	15.7	15.3	10.8	6.1	7.3	89.4	5.2	3.0	0.3	0.1	14.2	93.5
Franklin	4.7	11.2	13.6	12.9	14.2	17.3	12.4	5.9	7.8	95.9	1.2	1.4	0.3	(Z)	2.3	95.8
Hampden	6.1	13.7	14.3	12.8	14.4	14.3	10.3	6.1	7.8	86.7	9.5	1.6	0.4	0.4	17.6	93.1
Hampshire	4.0	9.4	24.5	12.6	12.7	14.5	10.2	5.2	6.8	92.4	2.4	3.7	0.2	(Z)	3.7	87.1
Middlesex	6.2	12.2	12.5	14.1	16.6	15.0	10.5	6.1	6.8	86.1	4.2	8.2	0.2	(Z)	5.1	95.4
Nantucket	7.0	9.6	10.3	17.3	19.9	15.2	9.5	5.8	5.4	89.2	9.5	1.1	–	0.1	4.4	104.3
Norfolk	6.2	12.9	11.5	11.9	16.3	15.8	11.2	6.5	7.7	86.7	4.7	7.4	0.1	(Z)	2.4	92.6
Plymouth	6.4	14.1	12.6	11.8	16.1	15.6	11.4	5.9	6.0	89.3	8.0	1.2	0.2	(Z)	2.7	95.7
Suffolk	6.9	10.1	16.7	19.5	15.6	11.7	8.2	5.3	6.0	65.1	24.9	7.7	0.5	0.1	17.6	93.0
Worcester	6.4	13.5	13.2	13.4	16.2	15.0	10.0	5.5	6.9	91.2	3.7	3.6	0.3	0.1	7.8	96.4
MICHIGAN	6.4	14.0	14.3	12.8	14.7	14.9	10.4	6.0	6.4	81.3	14.3	2.2	0.6	(Z)	3.8	96.7
Alcona	2.9	10.2	10.1	8.8	12.1	13.8	15.1	14.2	12.8	98.3	0.4	0.2	0.6	(Z)	1.0	100.8
Alger	3.7	10.2	13.4	11.7	14.3	16.5	12.4	8.4	9.3	88.0	6.4	0.4	3.6	(Z)	1.2	116.2
Allegan	6.4	14.7	14.1	13.0	15.3	15.4	9.9	5.7	5.5	96.4	1.5	0.7	0.5	0.1	6.3	99.9
Alpena	4.7	11.9	13.5	9.9	13.5	16.3	11.9	8.9	9.5	98.2	0.4	0.4	0.4	–	0.7	94.7
Antrim	4.8	12.4	12.5	11.9	13.3	14.6	12.1	9.7	8.8	97.3	0.4	0.2	1.0	0.1	1.3	99.1
Arenac	4.6	11.8	13.5	12.0	13.8	14.7	12.3	9.3	8.1	95.7	2.1	0.3	1.1	(Z)	1.5	105.7
Baraga	4.8	11.7	12.9	12.8	14.5	15.0	11.6	7.8	8.9	79.6	6.2	0.3	11.3	–	1.2	114.0
Barry	5.8	14.0	13.6	12.3	14.9	15.7	11.5	6.6	5.6	97.8	0.4	0.3	0.4	(Z)	1.9	99.7
Bay	5.7	12.9	13.2	11.5	14.0	15.8	11.8	7.0	8.1	96.4	1.4	0.5	0.5	–	4.1	95.0
Benzie	5.6	12.2	11.6	12.6	14.2	14.6	11.1	9.0	9.1	96.6	0.5	0.2	1.8	–	1.7	98.2

See footnotes at end of table.

Table B-3. Counties — **Population by Age, Race, Hispanic Origin, and Sex**—Con.

[Includes United States, states, and 3,141 counties/county equivalents defined as of February 22, 2005. For more information on these areas, see Appendix C, Geographic Information]

County	Under 5 years	5 to 14 years	15 to 24 years	25 to 34 years	35 to 44 years	45 to 54 years	55 to 64 years	65 to 74 years	75 years and over	White alone	Black or African American alone	Asian alone	American Indian and Alaska Native alone	Native Hawaiian and Other Pacific Islander alone	Hispanic or Latino origin[1] (percent)	Males per 100 females
MICHIGAN—Con.																
Berrien	6.7	13.8	13.7	10.9	14.0	14.9	11.3	7.0	7.8	81.4	15.3	1.4	0.4	0.1	3.7	94.3
Branch	6.3	13.1	12.9	13.5	15.3	14.8	10.4	7.0	6.7	94.8	3.4	0.5	0.5	(Z)	4.0	104.0
Calhoun	6.8	13.8	13.8	12.5	14.1	14.5	10.7	6.8	7.1	85.3	10.8	1.3	0.6	(Z)	3.6	94.6
Cass	5.3	13.4	13.2	10.9	14.5	15.9	12.5	7.3	7.1	90.9	5.8	0.7	0.9	.	2.8	100.0
Charlevoix	5.5	13.5	12.4	10.8	14.4	15.5	11.9	8.2	7.9	96.1	0.4	0.3	1.7	0.2	1.3	97.5
Cheboygan	5.0	12.4	11.7	11.7	13.6	14.7	12.4	9.3	9.1	95.6	0.3	0.2	2.2	–	0.9	98.8
Chippewa	4.6	10.8	17.2	14.7	15.5	14.3	9.8	6.5	6.6	78.0	5.9	0.5	12.1	(Z)	1.7	124.0
Clare	5.1	12.7	12.9	11.6	12.9	13.9	12.2	10.2	8.3	98.1	0.5	0.3	0.5	(Z)	1.1	96.5
Clinton	5.6	14.6	14.2	11.7	15.2	15.9	11.4	6.1	5.3	96.5	1.3	0.6	0.4	(Z)	2.6	98.9
Crawford	4.5	12.0	13.4	12.4	14.2	14.9	12.0	9.0	7.5	95.9	2.5	0.4	0.7	–	1.5	106.4
Delta	5.3	11.8	13.7	9.9	13.2	16.4	11.8	8.3	9.7	96.0	0.2	0.4	2.2	(Z)	0.8	98.5
Dickinson	4.8	12.7	12.5	9.0	14.0	16.2	10.6	8.1	12.1	98.1	0.2	0.5	0.5	(Z)	0.8	95.1
Eaton	5.8	13.3	14.8	12.3	14.2	15.9	11.7	6.1	6.1	90.3	6.3	1.5	0.5	(Z)	3.8	95.7
Emmet	5.8	12.9	12.5	12.2	13.8	16.4	11.2	7.4	7.8	94.6	0.6	0.5	3.2	(Z)	1.0	96.0
Genesee	7.0	14.9	13.5	13.1	14.3	14.8	10.4	6.2	5.8	76.6	20.0	0.9	0.5	(Z)	2.4	92.6
Gladwin	4.9	11.9	12.5	11.3	12.8	13.6	13.0	11.2	8.9	98.0	0.3	0.2	0.6	0.1	1.1	97.4
Gogebic	3.7	10.1	13.7	11.5	13.1	14.9	11.7	8.7	12.7	92.4	4.3	0.3	2.2	–	1.3	109.6
Grand Traverse	5.6	12.6	13.3	13.2	14.8	16.4	10.4	6.6	7.2	96.6	0.8	0.6	1.0	(Z)	1.8	97.7
Gratiot	5.5	12.2	16.3	13.8	14.6	13.8	10.0	6.7	7.2	94.2	4.1	0.5	0.5	(Z)	4.5	110.0
Hillsdale	6.0	13.4	14.8	12.7	13.4	14.9	11.1	7.2	6.5	98.0	0.6	0.4	0.3	(Z)	1.4	98.6
Houghton	5.4	10.7	24.9	11.8	10.5	12.5	9.4	6.4	8.4	95.6	1.4	1.7	0.6	(Z)	0.7	119.3
Huron	4.9	12.3	12.6	9.7	13.1	15.5	12.0	9.4	10.7	98.4	0.2	0.5	0.3	–	1.8	98.3
Ingham	6.5	12.3	22.6	14.0	12.6	13.1	9.0	4.8	5.1	81.5	11.0	4.3	0.6	0.1	5.9	93.9
Ionia	6.3	13.7	17.2	14.4	14.9	14.1	9.2	5.2	5.1	92.8	5.1	0.3	0.6	(Z)	2.9	117.1
Iosco	4.4	11.3	11.9	9.1	12.2	14.5	13.1	11.9	11.5	97.0	0.7	0.5	0.7	(Z)	1.2	95.5
Iron	3.7	10.6	12.4	8.8	12.7	16.2	12.8	8.9	14.0	96.8	1.4	0.2	1.0	–	0.6	98.6
Isabella	5.0	9.8	33.2	14.1	10.3	10.8	7.2	4.7	4.7	91.5	2.4	1.9	2.8	0.1	2.6	89.7
Jackson	6.3	13.7	13.5	13.2	15.2	15.1	10.3	6.1	6.6	89.4	7.9	0.4	0.4	0.1	2.6	104.3
Kalamazoo	6.5	12.9	19.2	13.4	13.0	13.9	9.5	5.6	6.1	85.3	9.9	2.3	0.4	0.1	3.0	93.7
Kalkaska	6.3	13.2	12.6	12.7	14.4	15.1	11.2	7.9	6.5	97.7	0.5	0.3	0.7	(Z)	1.0	101.2
Kent	7.8	15.2	14.6	14.1	15.1	14.2	8.7	4.9	5.5	85.9	9.5	2.1	0.5	0.1	8.9	97.9
Keweenaw	4.7	9.7	11.8	8.6	12.2	15.9	15.4	11.3	10.3	97.8	1.9	0.1	(Z)	–	0.5	109.6
Lake	4.5	10.9	15.0	11.6	11.8	13.5	12.7	10.7	9.3	85.3	11.6	0.1	1.3	(Z)	1.8	109.0
Lapeer	5.6	14.3	14.1	12.3	15.8	16.4	11.1	5.9	4.6	97.3	1.1	0.5	0.4	(Z)	3.6	103.3
Leelanau	4.3	12.0	12.6	9.1	12.2	17.7	13.0	9.6	9.4	95.0	0.4	0.3	3.7	(Z)	3.6	100.9
Lenawee	6.1	13.3	14.5	12.9	14.2	15.2	10.9	6.4	6.6	95.8	2.2	0.6	0.5	(Z)	7.3	100.6
Livingston	5.6	14.6	13.9	12.7	16.4	16.6	11.1	5.1	4.0	97.2	0.7	0.8	0.4	0.1	1.6	102.6
Luce	4.4	11.0	13.7	14.6	15.0	14.8	10.8	8.3	7.4	83.7	8.4	0.5	5.8	(Z)	1.8	125.8
Mackinac	4.6	11.0	11.7	9.0	13.2	16.1	13.7	10.9	9.7	81.3	1.0	0.3	13.1	(Z)	0.8	100.6
Macomb	6.1	13.3	12.2	13.9	15.7	14.8	10.5	6.3	7.1	89.6	5.6	2.9	0.3	(Z)	1.9	96.7
Manistee	5.2	11.5	12.4	11.4	13.5	15.4	12.1	9.1	9.4	95.1	2.3	0.4	1.2	(Z)	2.8	104.3
Marquette	4.7	10.6	18.7	12.2	12.8	16.1	10.9	6.7	7.4	95.3	1.6	0.5	1.6	(Z)	0.8	99.7
Mason	5.3	12.2	12.9	10.7	13.5	15.4	12.2	8.6	9.2	97.0	0.8	0.2	0.9	(Z)	3.4	96.5
Mecosta	5.3	11.6	23.9	13.2	10.9	11.4	9.5	7.4	6.7	92.8	4.1	1.0	0.6	(Z)	1.5	103.1
Menominee	5.1	12.4	12.4	10.0	13.9	17.1	11.7	8.1	9.3	96.6	0.3	0.2	2.2	–	0.9	98.6
Midland	5.8	14.1	14.5	10.8	15.1	15.9	10.8	6.4	6.7	95.8	1.2	1.8	0.4	(Z)	1.7	96.4
Missaukee	5.4	13.6	13.9	12.2	14.1	14.4	11.0	7.9	7.4	98.1	0.5	0.2	0.5	–	1.4	99.0
Monroe	5.6	14.1	14.1	12.7	15.3	15.8	10.9	5.8	5.6	95.7	2.2	0.6	0.3	(Z)	2.5	98.9
Montcalm	6.4	13.8	14.0	14.0	14.9	14.2	10.1	6.5	6.1	95.7	2.3	0.3	0.6	0.1	2.7	104.3
Montmorency	4.1	10.2	11.7	9.6	11.2	14.7	13.9	12.2	12.5	98.6	0.4	0.1	0.4	–	0.7	95.8
Muskegon	6.8	14.4	14.1	13.2	14.3	14.7	9.9	5.9	6.7	83.0	14.0	0.5	0.8	(Z)	4.0	98.4
Newaygo	6.2	14.8	14.8	11.6	14.1	14.7	10.6	7.1	6.2	96.5	1.3	0.3	0.8	(Z)	4.7	100.0
Oakland	6.3	13.9	12.1	11.8	16.4	16.4	11.5	5.6	6.0	81.2	11.8	5.3	0.3	(Z)	2.8	96.7
Oceana	6.6	13.7	14.8	11.9	13.5	14.1	11.1	7.2	7.1	97.2	0.6	0.3	1.0	0.1	13.9	101.1
Ogemaw	4.7	11.9	12.6	10.6	12.6	14.4	12.8	10.9	9.4	97.5	0.4	0.4	0.6	(Z)	1.4	98.1
Ontonagon	3.5	10.0	10.2	8.4	12.6	17.1	14.7	11.6	11.9	98.1	0.4	0.2	0.7	–	0.9	102.7
Osceola	6.3	13.4	14.1	11.9	13.4	14.5	11.3	8.1	7.1	97.9	0.5	0.2	0.5	(Z)	1.0	97.7
Oscoda	4.9	11.8	12.0	8.5	12.3	14.8	13.7	11.5	10.5	98.3	0.3	(Z)	0.8	(Z)	1.2	95.3
Otsego	5.7	13.6	13.0	12.2	15.0	14.9	10.7	7.9	6.9	97.7	0.4	0.5	0.5	–	0.7	99.1
Ottawa	6.9	14.9	17.4	13.0	14.6	13.7	9.0	5.1	5.5	94.8	1.3	2.3	0.4	(Z)	7.6	96.9
Presque Isle	4.5	10.5	11.2	9.3	12.2	15.2	13.4	11.1	12.4	98.2	0.6	0.2	0.6	(Z)	0.6	98.5
Roscommon	3.9	10.6	12.1	9.7	11.7	13.8	14.2	12.3	11.8	98.0	0.6	0.3	0.6	(Z)	1.0	96.9
Saginaw	6.4	14.3	14.3	11.7	13.4	14.8	11.3	6.6	7.2	77.8	19.3	1.0	0.5	(Z)	7.1	92.7
St. Clair	6.0	14.0	13.2	12.8	15.3	15.3	10.8	6.1	6.4	95.6	2.2	0.5	0.5	(Z)	2.6	97.9
St. Joseph	7.3	14.5	13.5	12.9	13.9	14.3	10.4	6.5	6.6	95.2	2.6	0.6	0.4	(Z)	6.0	99.0
Sanilac	5.8	13.7	13.5	11.7	13.7	14.9	10.7	7.7	8.3	98.1	0.5	0.3	0.3	(Z)	2.8	97.9
Schoolcraft	4.4	12.1	12.5	10.5	13.3	15.5	11.9	9.8	10.0	90.0	2.0	0.5	5.4	–	1.0	100.8
Shiawassee	5.9	14.2	13.4	12.2	14.9	15.4	11.3	6.5	6.2	98.0	0.3	0.3	0.4	(Z)	2.0	96.9
Tuscola	5.8	13.3	14.4	11.7	14.0	15.4	11.7	6.9	6.7	97.0	1.2	0.3	0.6	(Z)	2.4	98.3

See footnotes at end of table.

[Includes United States, states, and 3,141 counties/county equivalents defined as of February 22, 2005. For more information on these areas, see Appendix C, Geographic Information]

County				Age (percent)							One race (percent)					His-panic or Latino origin[1] (per-cent)	Males per 100 females
	Under 5 years	5 to 14 years	15 to 24 years	25 to 34 years	35 to 44 years	45 to 54 years	55 to 64 years	65 to 74 years	75 years and over	White alone	Black or African American alone	Asian alone	American Indian and Alaska Native alone	Native Hawaiian and Other Pacific Islander alone		
MICHIGAN—Con.																
Van Buren	6.6	14.4	14.3	11.5	14.0	15.8	10.9	6.4	6.1	92.3	4.8	0.4	0.9	(Z)	8.8	98.5
Washtenaw	6.1	11.9	20.1	15.9	14.7	13.5	9.1	4.4	4.2	77.3	12.2	7.8	0.4	0.1	3.1	99.6
Wayne	7.2	15.7	13.3	12.9	14.8	14.5	9.9	5.4	6.2	53.7	42.0	2.3	0.4	(Z)	4.6	92.5
Wexford	6.0	13.4	13.8	12.5	14.2	14.7	10.5	7.4	7.4	97.7	0.3	0.5	0.6	(Z)	1.3	98.4
MINNESOTA	6.5	13.1	14.8	13.3	15.2	15.0	9.9	5.9	6.2	89.6	4.3	3.4	1.2	0.1	3.6	98.6
Aitkin	4.5	10.1	11.8	10.0	11.6	14.1	13.8	12.6	11.6	96.9	0.3	0.2	2.1	(Z)	0.6	102.1
Anoka	6.7	14.8	14.0	14.1	17.2	15.2	9.8	4.8	3.4	90.7	3.1	3.4	0.8	0.1	2.4	101.7
Becker	6.0	12.2	14.2	12.2	12.9	14.8	11.4	8.2	8.0	89.8	0.4	0.4	7.5	(Z)	1.0	99.8
Beltrami	6.9	13.3	20.6	13.5	11.8	13.2	8.7	6.1	5.8	77.2	0.5	0.9	19.9	(Z)	1.2	97.5
Benton	7.1	12.8	15.8	18.6	14.8	12.6	7.9	5.1	5.3	95.4	1.4	1.6	0.6	(Z)	1.3	99.1
Big Stone	4.4	11.3	13.3	7.6	11.8	15.8	11.9	10.7	13.3	98.8	0.2	0.4	0.5	—	0.5	97.3
Blue Earth	5.6	9.9	24.7	15.9	11.5	12.3	8.2	5.3	6.7	94.5	2.1	2.2	0.3	0.1	1.9	101.3
Brown	5.0	11.5	16.9	9.8	12.9	15.5	10.8	7.6	10.0	98.9	0.3	0.4	0.1	(Z)	2.6	97.9
Carlton	5.5	11.8	15.4	12.5	14.6	15.3	10.4	7.1	7.6	91.8	1.2	0.4	5.4	(Z)	1.0	103.0
Carver	7.0	15.7	14.5	14.1	18.2	15.1	8.0	3.8	3.6	95.5	1.1	2.4	0.2	(Z)	3.4	99.6
Cass	5.4	11.3	13.9	11.9	12.4	13.9	12.8	10.3	8.1	87.6	0.2	0.3	10.8	(Z)	1.1	99.3
Chippewa	5.5	12.6	13.3	9.3	13.1	16.0	11.2	7.5	11.5	98.1	0.2	0.4	0.9	—	3.8	96.7
Chisago	7.0	14.0	14.8	15.8	16.8	13.9	8.5	4.9	4.4	96.1	1.1	1.3	0.6	(Z)	1.7	104.9
Clay	5.4	11.9	23.9	12.2	12.4	13.7	8.1	5.5	6.9	95.4	0.7	1.1	1.6	0.1	3.3	92.4
Clearwater	6.6	12.1	14.1	11.7	12.4	15.0	11.1	8.7	8.4	89.3	0.3	0.3	8.9	—	0.9	101.0
Cook	4.0	9.8	10.5	10.9	12.5	18.8	15.3	9.5	8.7	90.8	0.4	0.4	7.1	—	1.2	101.0
Cottonwood	5.7	12.5	12.7	9.3	12.1	14.6	11.5	8.6	13.0	96.1	0.9	2.3	0.3	0.1	3.8	95.8
Crow Wing	5.9	12.1	13.5	13.2	13.3	14.1	10.9	8.4	8.6	97.7	0.4	0.4	0.8	(Z)	0.9	96.8
Dakota	6.9	15.0	13.7	13.9	17.3	15.7	9.5	4.5	3.5	89.9	3.7	4.0	0.4	0.1	4.0	98.1
Dodge	7.2	14.7	14.5	13.5	15.4	14.8	8.8	5.4	5.8	98.4	0.3	0.5	0.2	—	3.6	99.8
Douglas	5.1	11.2	14.3	13.4	12.7	14.3	10.8	8.5	9.8	98.5	0.4	0.4	0.3	(Z)	0.9	99.3
Faribault	5.0	11.5	14.0	7.9	11.9	16.1	11.6	9.1	12.9	98.7	0.3	0.4	0.4	(Z)	3.9	98.8
Fillmore	6.0	12.4	13.2	11.1	12.7	15.0	10.9	8.1	10.5	99.3	0.2	0.2	0.1	—	0.7	98.3
Freeborn	5.6	11.5	12.7	10.5	13.2	15.2	11.9	8.8	10.7	98.0	0.6	0.6	0.3	(Z)	6.3	97.6
Goodhue	5.8	12.4	13.9	11.6	14.4	16.1	10.7	7.1	8.1	96.8	0.8	0.7	1.1	(Z)	1.6	99.0
Grant	5.4	10.9	13.6	9.2	12.4	14.6	11.2	9.2	13.5	99.0	0.2	0.2	0.3	—	0.6	96.1
Hennepin	7.1	12.4	12.9	14.5	16.4	15.6	10.1	5.3	5.7	81.0	10.3	5.4	1.1	0.1	5.5	98.0
Houston	5.0	12.9	13.7	10.9	13.9	16.7	10.6	7.2	9.2	98.4	0.6	0.4	0.2	—	0.7	98.0
Hubbard	5.1	11.4	13.7	10.2	12.2	15.2	12.8	10.3	9.2	96.6	0.2	0.3	2.0	—	0.9	98.7
Isanti	5.8	12.8	15.5	15.9	15.8	14.5	9.5	5.4	4.9	97.6	0.4	0.6	0.5	(Z)	1.2	100.4
Itasca	5.1	11.5	14.3	10.0	12.5	16.7	12.9	8.6	8.5	94.8	0.2	0.3	3.6	(Z)	0.7	99.6
Jackson	4.7	11.3	14.0	10.8	12.7	16.5	10.5	8.3	11.2	98.0	0.2	1.6	0.1	—	2.2	101.5
Kanabec	5.2	12.7	14.4	13.6	13.6	15.2	10.7	7.5	7.1	97.3	0.3	0.5	0.9	—	1.1	101.0
Kandiyohi	6.5	12.7	14.4	11.4	13.0	16.0	10.7	7.0	8.3	98.1	0.7	0.4	0.4	0.1	8.6	98.4
Kittson	4.0	13.0	13.0	6.3	12.2	17.2	11.6	9.6	13.0	98.7	0.2	0.4	0.4	—	1.5	97.1
Koochiching	4.4	11.9	12.4	9.0	13.0	17.2	12.5	9.4	10.3	96.0	0.4	0.2	2.4	0.1	0.8	97.8
Lac qui Parle	4.0	11.5	13.4	7.2	11.7	17.8	11.8	8.8	13.9	99.1	0.2	0.4	0.2	—	0.5	99.2
Lake	4.2	10.3	12.9	10.4	12.6	16.8	11.9	10.3	10.5	98.6	0.1	0.2	0.7	(Z)	0.6	97.9
Lake of the Woods	4.6	11.2	12.9	8.8	13.0	17.6	12.2	9.9	9.8	97.1	0.4	0.3	1.6	—	0.7	100.2
Le Sueur	5.8	12.7	14.2	12.9	14.8	14.9	10.9	6.6	7.3	98.6	0.2	0.4	0.3	(Z)	4.1	100.1
Lincoln	5.3	11.7	12.1	9.3	12.6	13.9	10.6	10.0	14.3	99.3	0.1	0.3	0.3	—	1.0	96.9
Lyon	5.9	12.8	18.5	11.8	12.9	14.5	9.1	6.2	8.2	96.1	0.9	2.2	0.4	(Z)	4.2	97.1
McLeod	6.8	13.4	13.3	13.7	14.8	14.0	10.1	6.3	7.6	98.1	0.3	0.7	0.2	0.1	4.3	98.7
Mahnomen	7.8	14.7	14.1	9.3	12.0	13.1	11.2	8.4	9.3	63.2	0.2	0.1	29.4	0.1	2.2	98.7
Marshall	5.1	11.8	13.4	9.3	13.4	16.1	11.7	8.4	10.7	98.9	0.1	0.3	0.4	—	3.8	102.8
Martin	5.3	11.9	13.0	8.7	12.3	16.7	11.9	8.3	11.9	98.6	0.4	0.5	0.2	(Z)	2.6	95.6
Meeker	6.2	12.8	13.7	11.6	13.7	15.3	10.6	7.5	8.7	98.8	0.3	0.5	0.2	(Z)	2.8	102.4
Mille Lacs	6.0	12.2	14.5	14.5	14.1	13.9	9.7	7.3	7.8	93.7	0.4	0.3	4.7	(Z)	1.4	96.7
Morrison	6.1	13.2	14.7	12.3	14.0	14.8	9.8	7.2	8.0	98.6	0.3	0.3	0.3	(Z)	1.8	101.0
Mower	6.7	12.8	13.0	11.2	13.4	14.1	10.3	7.4	11.1	96.1	1.3	1.5	0.3	(Z)	6.7	99.3
Murray	4.7	11.8	13.2	8.5	12.4	15.5	12.3	9.5	12.0	98.9	0.2	0.3	0.3	—	2.3	99.1
Nicollet	5.9	11.6	21.2	12.4	13.4	14.3	9.7	5.8	5.6	96.5	1.5	1.3	0.2	(Z)	2.4	100.4
Nobles	7.4	13.4	13.0	10.6	13.3	15.2	10.4	7.2	9.4	93.5	1.4	3.9	0.6	0.1	14.6	101.9
Norman	4.8	12.7	13.7	8.1	13.3	15.4	11.5	9.2	11.3	95.7	0.2	0.5	2.5	—	3.4	99.8
Olmsted	7.3	13.3	13.2	14.4	16.0	15.0	9.4	5.8	5.7	89.9	3.6	5.2	0.3	(Z)	2.8	97.6
Otter Tail	5.0	11.8	13.7	10.2	12.9	15.6	11.8	9.3	9.8	98.1	0.4	0.4	0.5	0.1	1.8	99.9
Pennington	6.4	11.9	13.6	13.4	12.9	15.2	11.0	6.8	8.5	96.7	0.4	0.8	1.4	(Z)	1.9	98.2
Pine	5.4	11.5	14.5	13.6	14.5	14.7	10.4	8.1	7.5	94.7	1.6	0.4	2.7	(Z)	1.8	107.0
Pipestone	5.7	12.2	13.8	8.8	12.8	14.8	10.0	9.0	12.9	97.1	0.2	0.7	1.5	(Z)	1.0	92.5
Polk	5.5	12.4	16.4	10.6	13.0	15.2	10.3	7.5	9.2	96.5	0.6	0.5	1.3	(Z)	4.6	98.0
Pope	5.3	11.0	13.9	10.0	12.2	15.5	11.7	9.0	11.4	99.0	0.3	0.1	0.2	0.3	0.8	100.9
Ramsey	7.1	13.2	14.8	13.2	14.6	14.8	9.8	5.7	6.7	78.3	9.3	9.1	0.9	0.1	6.0	93.3
Red Lake	5.6	11.0	14.3	11.2	12.0	16.3	11.1	8.3	10.1	98.1	0.2	0.1	1.5	—	0.9	99.8
Redwood	6.3	12.6	13.2	9.1	13.1	14.8	11.3	8.4	11.3	93.4	0.3	1.5	3.8	0.4	1.0	99.5
Renville	5.9	12.9	13.6	9.5	13.0	16.0	10.5	8.1	10.5	98.6	0.1	0.2	0.8	(Z)	6.5	101.3

See footnotes at end of table.

Table B-3. Counties — **Population by Age, Race, Hispanic Origin, and Sex**—Con.

[Includes United States, states, and 3,141 counties/county equivalents defined as of February 22, 2005. For more information on these areas, see Appendix C, Geographic Information]

County	Under 5 years	5 to 14 years	15 to 24 years	25 to 34 years	35 to 44 years	45 to 54 years	55 to 64 years	65 to 74 years	75 years and over	White alone	Black or African American alone	Asian alone	American Indian and Alaska Native alone	Native Hawaiian and Other Pacific Islander alone	Hispanic or Latino origin[1] (percent)	Males per 100 females
MINNESOTA—Con.																
Rice	5.6	12.0	21.5	13.0	13.6	13.8	9.0	5.9	5.6	95.2	1.7	1.6	0.5	0.1	7.0	101.4
Rock	6.3	12.5	14.2	10.4	12.5	14.5	10.9	7.6	11.3	97.7	0.8	0.9	0.5	(Z)	1.4	96.0
Roseau	6.5	14.4	14.1	11.7	16.0	15.1	9.9	5.7	6.6	95.6	0.2	1.9	1.8	(Z)	0.5	104.5
St. Louis	5.0	10.7	17.4	11.0	12.6	16.1	11.4	7.1	8.7	94.8	1.0	0.7	2.2	(Z)	0.9	97.3
Scott	8.2	15.6	13.7	17.2	18.7	13.1	7.4	3.4	2.6	91.0	1.7	4.9	0.7	0.1	3.5	100.6
Sherburne	7.3	14.6	16.4	17.0	16.9	13.1	7.6	3.9	3.2	96.4	1.2	1.1	0.4	(Z)	1.8	103.6
Sibley	6.3	13.6	13.5	11.0	14.4	14.8	10.0	7.5	8.8	98.6	0.2	0.2	0.4	—	6.0	101.4
Stearns	6.1	12.2	21.0	13.6	13.7	13.4	8.4	5.7	5.9	95.3	1.5	1.9	0.3	(Z)	1.7	101.0
Steele	6.9	13.5	14.7	12.5	15.0	15.2	9.3	6.2	6.8	96.3	2.2	0.8	0.1	(Z)	4.4	98.6
Stevens	4.9	9.6	27.2	9.3	10.1	13.6	8.8	6.3	10.3	95.2	1.4	1.6	1.1	—	1.3	94.3
Swift	5.1	11.1	12.5	11.7	15.8	15.1	10.0	7.2	11.4	92.5	3.6	2.6	0.6	0.4	2.9	126.0
Todd	5.7	12.8	14.7	10.9	13.0	15.4	11.3	7.8	8.3	98.0	0.2	0.5	0.7	(Z)	3.5	101.8
Traverse	4.0	11.9	14.2	7.3	11.0	13.9	10.3	11.1	16.2	95.1	—	0.4	4.3	0.1	1.4	94.6
Wabasha	5.7	12.5	14.2	11.1	14.6	15.5	11.3	7.1	8.1	98.6	0.3	0.6	0.3	—	2.0	99.8
Wadena	6.3	12.6	14.0	10.4	11.9	14.1	10.2	9.3	11.3	98.0	0.7	0.3	0.7	(Z)	0.8	97.9
Waseca	6.1	12.6	13.7	13.4	14.8	15.7	10.0	6.0	7.8	96.0	2.4	0.7	0.6	0.1	3.1	109.6
Washington	6.5	15.0	14.0	12.5	17.1	16.2	10.5	4.9	3.4	90.7	3.0	4.2	0.4	0.1	2.6	99.7
Watonwan	6.8	14.5	12.8	9.6	11.9	15.5	10.3	8.2	10.4	97.6	0.6	1.1	0.4	(Z)	17.9	95.7
Wilkin	5.6	13.4	14.2	9.3	14.4	16.7	10.1	7.6	8.7	97.9	0.3	0.2	0.8	(Z)	1.9	98.6
Winona	4.8	10.6	24.6	11.8	11.7	13.6	9.4	6.3	7.3	95.7	1.0	2.4	0.3	(Z)	1.2	95.4
Wright	7.8	14.8	14.9	15.8	16.6	13.3	8.4	4.5	3.9	96.9	0.6	1.0	0.4	(Z)	1.8	100.3
Yellow Medicine	6.0	12.4	12.9	8.9	12.8	15.9	10.9	8.2	11.9	96.9	0.2	0.2	2.5	(Z)	2.4	100.0
MISSISSIPPI	7.3	13.9	15.2	13.6	13.8	13.9	10.1	6.7	5.6	61.2	36.9	0.7	0.4	(Z)	1.7	94.4
Adams	6.6	13.6	13.2	10.1	12.6	16.6	11.3	8.5	7.5	43.5	55.7	0.3	0.1	(Z)	0.9	86.4
Alcorn	6.4	12.6	11.7	14.3	13.9	13.7	12.2	8.3	6.9	87.7	11.4	0.2	0.1	0.2	1.8	95.9
Amite	5.8	12.5	14.2	10.9	13.2	15.2	12.1	8.4	7.7	57.6	42.0	0.1	0.1	—	1.5	94.6
Attala	6.9	13.0	13.4	12.5	13.2	13.3	11.3	8.4	8.0	58.6	40.6	0.3	0.2	—	1.6	91.7
Benton	7.4	13.9	12.2	14.2	12.8	12.4	11.2	8.4	7.5	64.5	34.7	0.1	0.5	—	1.2	93.0
Bolivar	7.9	14.2	20.4	12.0	12.3	12.5	10.1	5.3	5.3	33.5	65.7	0.5	0.1	—	1.2	88.8
Calhoun	6.7	12.5	12.9	12.6	13.4	13.8	11.5	8.3	8.5	70.4	28.9	(Z)	0.2	0.1	3.5	92.3
Carroll	4.9	11.7	13.4	12.3	13.8	15.4	13.6	8.2	6.6	65.5	34.3	0.2	(Z)	—	1.0	100.5
Chickasaw	8.1	14.6	13.7	12.7	13.8	13.6	10.0	7.2	6.3	57.7	41.6	0.2	0.2	0.1	2.9	92.9
Choctaw	5.4	13.7	13.8	11.7	13.2	14.8	11.4	8.4	7.6	68.0	31.4	0.2	0.4	—	0.9	92.7
Claiborne	7.0	13.3	25.4	11.3	10.7	13.1	8.3	5.9	5.1	15.2	84.3	0.3	(Z)	(Z)	0.9	88.0
Clarke	6.8	13.7	12.0	12.3	13.4	14.6	11.7	8.0	7.5	66.0	33.7	0.1	0.1	—	0.7	93.9
Clay	7.1	14.6	15.1	12.5	12.2	15.0	10.0	7.2	6.3	42.4	57.2	0.2	(Z)	—	1.0	87.8
Coahoma	9.4	17.1	16.0	11.1	12.1	13.4	9.4	6.0	5.6	25.6	73.3	0.6	(Z)	(Z)	1.2	85.6
Copiah	7.4	12.9	17.4	12.1	12.9	14.5	9.9	6.7	6.2	48.6	50.7	0.3	(Z)	(Z)	1.4	93.2
Covington	7.2	14.8	14.1	13.5	13.2	13.5	9.9	7.8	5.8	63.1	36.2	0.1	0.1	(Z)	1.0	91.2
DeSoto	7.1	14.9	13.5	15.7	16.1	13.3	10.0	5.7	3.7	81.0	17.0	0.9	0.3	0.1	3.4	99.7
Forrest	7.1	12.4	21.3	15.6	11.9	11.6	8.5	6.0	5.7	63.3	34.5	1.1	0.3	(Z)	1.4	90.4
Franklin	6.6	12.4	14.8	12.2	12.6	15.8	10.0	8.1	7.3	63.3	36.2	0.1	0.1	—	0.6	93.4
George	8.0	15.0	13.7	15.9	14.0	12.1	10.3	6.6	4.3	89.7	9.2	0.2	0.3	—	2.5	104.2
Greene	5.4	12.6	16.1	17.8	15.2	12.7	9.8	6.0	4.3	73.0	26.5	0.1	0.3	(Z)	0.8	137.7
Grenada	6.6	13.9	13.8	12.7	13.9	13.9	10.7	7.6	6.8	57.1	42.0	0.5	0.2	(Z)	0.7	89.1
Hancock	5.8	12.8	12.5	12.5	14.3	14.8	12.3	8.4	6.5	90.6	7.0	0.8	0.6	(Z)	2.3	98.7
Harrison	7.5	13.8	14.3	13.4	14.7	14.2	10.1	6.9	5.1	72.3	22.6	2.6	0.5	0.1	2.7	98.5
Hinds	7.9	14.4	16.2	13.4	13.6	14.2	9.5	5.5	5.2	33.3	65.2	0.5	0.1	(Z)	0.9	89.6
Holmes	9.1	15.7	18.8	12.1	12.1	12.7	8.2	5.7	5.7	18.7	80.7	0.1	0.2	(Z)	0.9	89.5
Humphreys	9.8	15.7	16.1	11.6	12.5	13.7	8.9	6.2	5.5	25.9	73.6	0.3	0.1	—	2.1	88.4
Issaquena	4.6	12.5	18.3	13.3	16.1	13.4	9.5	7.9	4.3	37.3	62.4	—	—	—	0.5	116.9
Itawamba	6.1	12.8	14.7	14.0	14.1	13.3	11.3	7.8	6.1	92.8	6.6	0.2	0.1	—	1.1	95.1
Jackson	6.8	14.1	14.0	12.8	14.8	15.0	11.1	7.0	4.5	74.9	21.8	1.7	0.4	0.1	2.5	98.7
Jasper	7.4	13.9	13.5	12.9	13.2	14.2	10.6	7.7	6.6	47.0	52.5	0.1	(Z)	0.1	0.8	92.2
Jefferson	7.4	13.8	17.2	13.7	13.8	15.3	8.5	5.6	4.5	13.7	86.0	0.1	0.1	—	0.7	100.3
Jefferson Davis	6.6	14.4	14.7	11.8	12.4	14.3	11.5	7.2	7.0	41.6	57.8	0.2	0.1	(Z)	1.0	89.8
Jones	7.4	13.0	14.3	13.7	13.2	13.9	10.4	7.5	6.6	71.4	27.4	0.4	0.4	(Z)	3.6	96.2
Kemper	6.7	12.6	16.8	12.2	12.8	14.1	10.4	7.3	7.2	38.8	58.8	0.1	2.1	(Z)	1.0	97.5
Lafayette	5.3	9.4	29.5	16.7	10.8	10.3	7.4	5.9	4.7	73.3	24.1	1.8	0.2	(Z)	1.3	96.5
Lamar	7.4	14.3	15.8	15.4	14.5	13.9	9.3	5.5	3.9	84.2	14.2	0.9	0.2	—	1.5	95.8
Lauderdale	7.6	14.0	13.7	12.8	13.4	14.1	10.2	7.1	7.1	58.7	40.6	0.5	0.2	(Z)	1.2	91.5
Lawrence	6.9	13.7	14.2	12.8	13.6	14.8	10.2	8.0	5.7	67.5	31.8	0.5	0.1	(Z)	0.9	91.5
Leake	8.0	14.9	14.7	14.2	12.3	12.6	9.5	7.1	6.6	55.8	38.9	0.3	4.6	0.1	3.0	102.2
Lee	7.6	14.3	13.0	13.5	15.1	14.2	10.2	6.7	5.3	72.7	25.8	0.6	0.2	—	1.3	93.1
Leflore	8.2	15.2	18.1	13.3	12.3	12.8	8.6	5.7	5.8	28.5	70.6	0.5	0.1	(Z)	2.2	91.7
Lincoln	6.7	13.8	13.1	14.1	13.6	14.2	10.7	7.3	6.5	69.1	30.2	0.4	0.2	—	0.7	92.9
Lowndes	7.5	14.9	15.1	12.2	14.2	14.1	10.2	6.4	5.5	55.3	42.9	0.7	0.2	(Z)	1.2	90.5
Madison	7.4	14.7	14.6	14.2	15.8	14.6	8.7	5.7	4.4	59.8	38.0	1.6	0.1	(Z)	1.3	91.4
Marion	7.2	14.4	14.4	12.9	12.9	14.0	10.2	7.5	6.5	66.7	32.4	0.3	0.2	—	0.7	95.3
Marshall	7.1	13.5	15.0	14.2	13.9	14.3	10.6	6.7	4.8	49.6	49.6	0.1	0.2	(Z)	1.5	98.1
Monroe	6.4	13.6	13.8	12.9	13.6	13.8	11.1	7.7	7.2	68.4	31.0	0.2	0.1	(Z)	0.9	89.7
Montgomery	6.7	13.6	13.6	11.2	12.8	14.1	11.0	8.3	8.7	53.7	45.8	0.3	0.1	(Z)	0.9	88.9
Neshoba	8.4	14.9	13.9	13.6	13.3	13.0	9.9	6.5	6.6	63.6	20.5	0.4	14.4	(Z)	1.5	92.4

See footnotes at end of table.

Table B-3. Counties — **Population by Age, Race, Hispanic Origin, and Sex**—Con.

[Includes United States, states, and 3,141 counties/county equivalents defined as of February 22, 2005. For more information on these areas, see Appendix C, Geographic Information]

| County | \
Under 5 years | 5 to 14 years | 15 to 24 years | 25 to 34 years | 35 to 44 years | 45 to 54 years | 55 to 64 years | 65 to 74 years | 75 years and over | White alone | Black or African American alone | Asian alone | American Indian and Alaska Native alone | Native Hawaiian and Other Pacific Islander alone | Hispanic or Latino origin[1] (percent) | Males per 100 females |
|---|---|---|---|---|---|---|---|---|---|---|---|---|---|---|---|---|
| **MISSISSIPPI—Con.** | | | | | | | | | | | | | | | | |
| Newton | 7.5 | 13.8 | 14.9 | 13.0 | 12.4 | 12.8 | 10.3 | 7.8 | 7.5 | 65.2 | 30.1 | 0.2 | 4.3 | – | 1.2 | 93.7 |
| Noxubee | 8.4 | 15.3 | 15.4 | 12.6 | 12.3 | 13.9 | 9.4 | 6.4 | 6.4 | 28.9 | 70.4 | 0.1 | 0.3 | – | 1.4 | 91.1 |
| Oktibbeha | 6.1 | 9.6 | 33.1 | 15.2 | 9.6 | 9.9 | 7.0 | 5.1 | 4.5 | 60.2 | 36.2 | 2.8 | 0.2 | (Z) | 1.1 | 103.0 |
| Panola | 7.7 | 14.6 | 15.4 | 13.9 | 13.4 | 13.4 | 9.7 | 6.5 | 5.4 | 51.4 | 48.0 | 0.2 | 0.1 | (Z) | 1.4 | 93.3 |
| Pearl River | 6.4 | 13.9 | 14.1 | 13.2 | 13.7 | 14.1 | 11.7 | 7.7 | 5.3 | 85.8 | 12.3 | 0.3 | 0.5 | (Z) | 1.6 | 95.4 |
| Perry | 6.9 | 15.2 | 12.5 | 14.8 | 13.6 | 14.1 | 10.7 | 7.3 | 4.8 | 76.0 | 23.2 | 0.1 | 0.3 | (Z) | 1.2 | 95.4 |
| Pike | 8.1 | 14.5 | 13.5 | 12.4 | 12.6 | 14.1 | 10.5 | 7.4 | 6.9 | 49.6 | 49.4 | 0.5 | 0.2 | (Z) | 0.7 | 89.7 |
| Pontotoc | 6.5 | 14.1 | 14.0 | 14.3 | 14.8 | 13.6 | 10.1 | 6.5 | 6.1 | 84.7 | 14.6 | 0.1 | 0.3 | – | 2.8 | 96.1 |
| Prentiss | 5.9 | 13.3 | 14.1 | 14.0 | 13.8 | 13.2 | 11.1 | 7.8 | 6.9 | 85.1 | 14.0 | 0.2 | 0.2 | (Z) | 0.7 | 95.9 |
| Quitman | 7.5 | 16.4 | 15.5 | 12.6 | 12.6 | 13.3 | 9.4 | 6.6 | 6.1 | 30.5 | 69.0 | 0.2 | 0.1 | – | 0.6 | 90.2 |
| Rankin | 6.9 | 13.0 | 14.1 | 15.6 | 15.6 | 14.2 | 10.3 | 6.1 | 4.1 | 79.8 | 18.6 | 0.8 | 0.2 | (Z) | 1.7 | 96.2 |
| Scott | 7.9 | 14.4 | 14.0 | 13.7 | 13.5 | 13.6 | 10.3 | 6.7 | 5.9 | 59.9 | 38.7 | 0.2 | 0.5 | (Z) | 6.9 | 98.5 |
| Sharkey | 8.1 | 16.4 | 15.6 | 11.6 | 10.9 | 15.5 | 9.9 | 6.0 | 5.9 | 29.8 | 69.5 | 0.4 | 0.1 | (Z) | 1.5 | 89.1 |
| Simpson | 7.0 | 14.6 | 13.6 | 14.2 | 13.3 | 14.1 | 10.4 | 6.9 | 5.9 | 64.6 | 34.7 | 0.1 | 0.1 | (Z) | 1.5 | 94.9 |
| Smith | 6.5 | 14.1 | 13.7 | 13.2 | 13.6 | 13.9 | 11.0 | 7.9 | 6.1 | 76.4 | 23.2 | 0.1 | 0.1 | 0.1 | 0.8 | 96.5 |
| Stone | 6.6 | 13.4 | 16.2 | 14.8 | 13.6 | 13.5 | 10.2 | 7.1 | 4.5 | 79.1 | 20.0 | 0.2 | 0.3 | (Z) | 1.6 | 101.3 |
| Sunflower | 7.3 | 13.8 | 18.9 | 14.9 | 14.5 | 13.3 | 8.0 | 4.7 | 4.5 | 26.9 | 72.3 | 0.4 | 0.2 | (Z) | 1.7 | 117.4 |
| Tallahatchie | 7.5 | 14.7 | 15.9 | 12.3 | 12.6 | 13.7 | 10.1 | 6.8 | 6.4 | 38.8 | 60.5 | 0.4 | 0.1 | – | 1.0 | 86.9 |
| Tate | 7.5 | 13.3 | 16.8 | 12.6 | 13.6 | 13.7 | 10.7 | 6.7 | 5.1 | 68.8 | 30.5 | 0.1 | 0.2 | 0.1 | 1.3 | 95.7 |
| Tippah | 7.5 | 12.4 | 14.0 | 14.5 | 13.8 | 13.2 | 10.4 | 7.9 | 6.4 | 82.0 | 17.0 | 0.1 | 0.3 | (Z) | 3.3 | 93.3 |
| Tishomingo | 5.9 | 12.2 | 11.4 | 12.8 | 14.5 | 13.8 | 12.1 | 9.4 | 7.9 | 95.9 | 3.6 | 0.1 | 0.1 | (Z) | 2.6 | 93.6 |
| Tunica | 9.6 | 15.4 | 15.0 | 16.1 | 12.5 | 13.0 | 8.8 | 5.2 | 4.4 | 25.8 | 73.4 | 0.3 | 0.1 | 0.1 | 2.8 | 89.0 |
| Union | 6.7 | 13.9 | 12.4 | 15.6 | 14.0 | 13.2 | 10.6 | 7.3 | 6.3 | 83.8 | 15.1 | 0.3 | 0.2 | (Z) | 2.6 | 95.7 |
| Walthall | 7.2 | 14.1 | 14.6 | 13.3 | 12.4 | 13.1 | 10.6 | 7.6 | 7.1 | 55.1 | 44.3 | 0.2 | 0.1 | – | 1.3 | 92.3 |
| Warren | 8.0 | 14.9 | 13.6 | 11.9 | 13.7 | 15.5 | 10.8 | 6.5 | 5.2 | 52.5 | 46.0 | 0.7 | 0.2 | – | 1.2 | 88.8 |
| Washington | 8.5 | 16.4 | 15.3 | 11.7 | 12.2 | 14.5 | 9.9 | 6.1 | 5.3 | 31.7 | 67.2 | 0.6 | 0.1 | (Z) | 1.1 | 87.4 |
| Wayne | 7.2 | 14.7 | 13.9 | 13.7 | 13.4 | 13.9 | 10.6 | 7.4 | 5.2 | 61.4 | 38.2 | 0.2 | 0.1 | – | 0.7 | 91.3 |
| Webster | 6.8 | 13.0 | 13.2 | 11.8 | 13.9 | 14.2 | 10.6 | 8.9 | 7.6 | 79.8 | 19.8 | 0.2 | 0.2 | – | 1.9 | 95.0 |
| Wilkinson | 7.4 | 12.2 | 16.3 | 13.7 | 13.9 | 14.2 | 9.3 | 6.8 | 6.2 | 29.8 | 69.9 | – | 0.1 | – | 0.4 | 111.8 |
| Winston | 6.7 | 13.3 | 13.7 | 12.7 | 13.0 | 14.1 | 10.8 | 8.0 | 7.7 | 54.7 | 44.2 | 0.1 | 0.8 | – | 1.6 | 94.1 |
| Yalobusha | 7.2 | 13.1 | 13.0 | 12.9 | 13.4 | 13.7 | 11.3 | 8.1 | 7.2 | 60.2 | 39.2 | 0.1 | 0.2 | 0.1 | 1.0 | 90.9 |
| Yazoo | 7.6 | 14.4 | 13.9 | 15.2 | 14.0 | 14.1 | 9.1 | 6.0 | 5.7 | 44.2 | 54.9 | 0.4 | 0.2 | – | 5.2 | 106.8 |
| **MISSOURI** | 6.5 | 13.0 | 14.5 | 13.1 | 14.4 | 14.6 | 10.6 | 6.8 | 6.5 | 85.4 | 11.5 | 1.3 | 0.4 | 0.1 | 2.7 | 95.7 |
| Adair | 5.4 | 9.2 | 31.7 | 12.4 | 9.8 | 11.1 | 8.4 | 5.9 | 6.1 | 95.8 | 1.4 | 1.8 | 0.3 | 0.1 | 1.7 | 89.2 |
| Andrew | 5.2 | 13.2 | 14.3 | 12.0 | 14.4 | 15.8 | 11.6 | 6.7 | 7.0 | 98.5 | 0.6 | 0.3 | 0.4 | – | 1.2 | 96.9 |
| Atchison | 4.9 | 11.2 | 14.2 | 9.8 | 12.1 | 14.7 | 13.3 | 7.9 | 12.1 | 97.3 | 2.1 | 0.3 | 0.2 | – | 0.8 | 99.9 |
| Audrain | 7.4 | 12.5 | 12.1 | 12.9 | 14.1 | 14.0 | 10.9 | 7.4 | 8.7 | 90.8 | 7.7 | 0.4 | 0.3 | (Z) | 1.0 | 83.7 |
| Barry | 6.6 | 13.6 | 12.9 | 12.6 | 13.4 | 13.6 | 11.5 | 8.8 | 7.1 | 96.8 | 0.3 | 0.8 | 0.9 | 0.1 | 7.0 | 98.9 |
| Barton | 6.2 | 14.6 | 12.9 | 13.1 | 13.1 | 14.6 | 10.2 | 6.9 | 8.5 | 97.2 | 0.4 | 0.3 | 0.8 | 0.1 | 1.1 | 97.9 |
| Bates | 6.2 | 12.8 | 13.5 | 12.3 | 13.7 | 14.5 | 10.5 | 7.9 | 8.7 | 97.6 | 0.8 | 0.3 | 0.5 | (Z) | 1.4 | 96.1 |
| Benton | 4.3 | 10.1 | 11.6 | 11.4 | 11.9 | 13.9 | 13.9 | 13.3 | 9.7 | 98.4 | 0.1 | 0.1 | 0.5 | – | 1.1 | 97.9 |
| Bollinger | 5.4 | 12.7 | 13.6 | 12.9 | 13.9 | 14.8 | 11.8 | 7.9 | 6.9 | 98.2 | 0.3 | 0.2 | 0.6 | – | 0.5 | 98.7 |
| Boone | 6.3 | 11.5 | 23.3 | 15.8 | 13.2 | 12.7 | 8.3 | 4.8 | 4.2 | 85.9 | 8.6 | 3.0 | 0.4 | (Z) | 2.1 | 93.6 |
| Buchanan | 6.3 | 12.5 | 14.9 | 13.3 | 14.3 | 14.1 | 10.0 | 6.9 | 7.7 | 93.2 | 4.5 | 0.6 | 0.5 | (Z) | 2.5 | 97.7 |
| Butler | 6.5 | 12.4 | 12.8 | 13.4 | 13.0 | 14.2 | 11.5 | 8.4 | 7.8 | 92.6 | 5.1 | 0.7 | 0.6 | (Z) | 1.3 | 91.8 |
| Caldwell | 6.5 | 13.3 | 13.0 | 11.1 | 13.4 | 14.5 | 11.6 | 8.2 | 8.4 | 99.0 | 0.2 | 0.2 | 0.2 | – | 0.9 | 98.9 |
| Callaway | 5.8 | 12.9 | 16.6 | 13.8 | 15.5 | 14.7 | 10.0 | 5.8 | 5.0 | 92.4 | 4.9 | 0.8 | 0.5 | – | 1.1 | 104.7 |
| Camden | 5.3 | 10.1 | 11.7 | 11.3 | 12.2 | 14.8 | 15.3 | 11.8 | 7.4 | 98.0 | 0.4 | 0.4 | 0.3 | (Z) | 1.4 | 99.2 |
| Cape Girardeau | 6.0 | 11.7 | 17.5 | 13.5 | 13.1 | 14.3 | 10.0 | 6.8 | 7.1 | 91.6 | 5.9 | 1.0 | 0.4 | (Z) | 1.2 | 94.4 |
| Carroll | 5.6 | 13.2 | 13.1 | 11.6 | 12.5 | 14.3 | 11.5 | 8.3 | 10.0 | 97.1 | 1.9 | 0.1 | 0.3 | – | 1.0 | 93.5 |
| Carter | 6.0 | 12.8 | 13.2 | 11.6 | 13.2 | 14.5 | 12.6 | 9.0 | 7.2 | 96.9 | 0.1 | 0.1 | 1.5 | (Z) | 1.2 | 95.1 |
| Cass | 6.4 | 14.3 | 13.8 | 13.6 | 15.3 | 14.5 | 10.2 | 6.6 | 5.4 | 94.6 | 2.8 | 0.6 | 0.6 | (Z) | 3.0 | 97.5 |
| Cedar | 5.3 | 11.9 | 14.2 | 10.2 | 12.4 | 13.0 | 12.4 | 10.4 | 10.2 | 97.4 | 0.3 | 0.6 | 0.7 | – | 1.5 | 97.2 |
| Chariton | 4.7 | 11.0 | 13.4 | 9.0 | 11.9 | 15.8 | 12.5 | 10.0 | 11.7 | 96.3 | 3.2 | 0.1 | 0.2 | – | 0.7 | 92.1 |
| Christian | 6.4 | 13.9 | 13.7 | 16.8 | 15.0 | 13.7 | 9.7 | 5.8 | 4.9 | 97.5 | 0.5 | 0.4 | 0.5 | (Z) | 1.7 | 95.8 |
| Clark | 5.4 | 12.7 | 13.2 | 10.8 | 14.1 | 14.6 | 12.8 | 8.4 | 8.1 | 99.0 | 0.2 | 0.1 | 0.3 | – | 0.9 | 98.9 |
| Clay | 7.1 | 13.5 | 13.2 | 14.9 | 15.6 | 14.6 | 10.5 | 5.7 | 5.0 | 91.9 | 4.0 | 1.8 | 0.5 | 0.1 | 4.5 | 95.8 |
| Clinton | 6.1 | 12.8 | 14.5 | 12.4 | 14.6 | 14.6 | 11.2 | 7.5 | 6.3 | 96.8 | 1.5 | 0.4 | 0.3 | – | 1.4 | 97.5 |
| Cole | 6.3 | 12.4 | 14.2 | 14.3 | 15.5 | 15.3 | 10.5 | 5.9 | 5.6 | 87.3 | 10.2 | 1.0 | 0.4 | (Z) | 1.7 | 104.2 |
| Cooper | 5.5 | 11.8 | 18.9 | 13.6 | 12.3 | 14.1 | 9.5 | 6.7 | 7.6 | 89.6 | 8.9 | 0.3 | 0.4 | (Z) | 1.4 | 117.4 |
| Crawford | 6.3 | 13.0 | 13.5 | 12.7 | 13.9 | 14.0 | 10.8 | 8.8 | 7.2 | 98.5 | 0.2 | 0.1 | 0.4 | 0.1 | 1.5 | 98.7 |
| Dade | 5.2 | 11.7 | 13.2 | 10.6 | 12.4 | 15.2 | 11.9 | 9.7 | 10.1 | 98.1 | 0.4 | 0.2 | 0.6 | – | 1.2 | 98.8 |
| Dallas | 6.3 | 13.6 | 13.4 | 12.6 | 13.2 | 14.6 | 11.5 | 8.0 | 6.8 | 97.6 | 0.2 | 0.1 | 0.8 | 0.1 | 1.6 | 98.6 |
| Daviess | 7.4 | 13.7 | 13.1 | 12.0 | 12.2 | 13.1 | 12.3 | 8.3 | 7.8 | 99.2 | – | (Z) | 0.4 | 0.3 | 0.9 | 93.1 |
| DeKalb | 4.3 | 9.7 | 13.1 | 16.1 | 20.5 | 14.5 | 8.9 | 6.4 | 6.5 | 87.8 | 10.3 | 0.4 | 0.8 | (Z) | 1.3 | 172.7 |
| Dent | 5.6 | 12.7 | 12.9 | 11.9 | 13.2 | 14.5 | 11.6 | 9.4 | 8.2 | 97.4 | 0.4 | 0.3 | 0.9 | – | 0.8 | 95.0 |
| Douglas | 5.0 | 12.7 | 14.0 | 11.7 | 12.9 | 14.9 | 12.5 | 8.9 | 7.4 | 97.1 | 0.1 | 0.2 | 1.1 | – | 1.2 | 97.7 |
| Dunklin | 7.1 | 13.8 | 12.6 | 12.5 | 13.0 | 13.6 | 11.6 | 8.1 | 7.7 | 89.0 | 9.4 | 0.3 | 0.3 | – | 3.9 | 91.2 |

See footnotes at end of table.

[Includes United States, states, and 3,141 counties/county equivalents defined as of February 22, 2005. For more information on these areas, see Appendix C, Geographic Information]

County	Population characteristics, 2005														
	Age (percent)									One race (percent)					
	Under 5 years	5 to 14 years	15 to 24 years	25 to 34 years	35 to 44 years	45 to 54 years	55 to 64 years	65 to 74 years	75 years and over	White alone	Black or African American alone	Asian alone	American Indian and Alaska Native alone	Native Hawaiian and Other Pacific Islander alone	Hispanic or Latino origin[1] (percent)	Males per 100 females

MISSOURI—Con.																
Franklin	6.4	13.7	13.6	12.9	15.3	15.0	10.6	6.8	5.5	97.8	0.9	0.3	0.2	(Z)	1.0	98.6
Gasconade	5.3	12.1	13.1	11.4	13.6	14.9	11.3	9.3	9.0	98.9	0.2	0.3	0.1	–	0.8	96.8
Gentry	5.3	13.0	13.8	9.3	12.8	13.8	9.8	10.0	12.1	98.7	0.3	0.2	0.4	0.3	0.7	99.1
Greene	6.1	11.5	17.2	14.3	13.4	13.7	10.0	6.7	7.1	93.9	2.5	1.2	0.7	0.1	2.2	94.9
Grundy	5.9	12.1	12.7	10.3	12.5	13.7	12.1	9.8	10.7	98.4	0.5	0.2	0.5	–	2.3	92.2
Harrison	5.5	12.2	12.3	12.1	11.9	13.8	11.4	9.6	11.2	98.9	0.2	0.2	0.1	(Z)	1.5	96.2
Henry	5.8	11.9	12.5	12.7	13.3	13.5	11.8	9.1	9.4	97.1	1.1	0.3	0.6	(Z)	1.2	96.9
Hickory	4.0	9.8	11.5	10.0	10.4	12.4	15.2	14.3	12.3	98.6	0.1	0.1	0.3	–	1.2	93.6
Holt	5.7	11.0	13.4	8.4	13.1	15.1	12.2	8.9	12.2	98.9	0.2	0.1	0.5	–	0.5	100.0
Howard	5.6	11.7	18.6	10.8	12.5	14.4	10.8	6.6	8.9	92.6	6.3	0.1	0.3	0.1	0.9	95.1
Howell	6.3	13.2	13.2	12.4	13.2	13.6	11.1	8.8	8.2	96.8	0.4	0.3	1.0	(Z)	1.3	94.5
Iron	6.2	12.4	13.5	11.4	12.4	15.3	12.1	9.2	7.5	97.4	1.7	0.1	0.2	–	0.6	96.2
Jackson	7.6	13.4	12.9	13.7	15.1	14.8	10.3	6.2	6.1	72.6	23.4	1.3	0.5	0.2	6.8	94.2
Jasper	7.6	13.4	14.4	14.6	13.3	13.4	9.9	6.6	6.8	94.1	1.7	0.8	1.3	0.1	5.2	94.4
Jefferson	6.4	13.9	13.9	13.8	16.1	15.6	10.4	5.9	4.0	97.3	0.9	0.6	0.3	(Z)	1.2	98.8
Johnson	6.9	12.2	23.0	15.1	13.2	11.8	8.0	5.4	4.5	91.7	4.1	1.7	0.7	0.1	2.7	101.6
Knox	5.8	12.6	12.4	8.5	13.4	14.0	12.3	10.1	10.8	99.4	0.1	0.1	–	–	0.6	92.7
Laclede	6.7	13.4	13.3	13.5	14.1	13.8	10.7	7.9	6.7	97.2	0.6	0.3	0.5	(Z)	1.6	97.1
Lafayette	5.9	12.9	13.5	11.9	14.1	14.7	11.4	7.7	7.8	96.2	2.3	0.3	0.2	(Z)	1.3	97.6
Lawrence	6.6	14.1	13.5	12.9	13.7	13.6	10.5	7.8	7.3	97.4	0.4	0.3	0.8	(Z)	4.6	98.0
Lewis	5.1	13.4	17.4	10.5	12.8	12.9	10.8	8.3	8.7	96.0	2.7	0.4	0.3	–	0.8	97.2
Lincoln	6.5	14.5	15.4	15.2	15.5	14.1	9.2	5.3	4.4	96.4	1.9	0.2	0.4	(Z)	1.5	98.8
Linn	6.2	12.9	12.6	10.3	12.6	14.5	11.4	8.6	10.9	98.1	0.8	0.2	0.4	–	0.9	89.8
Livingston	5.6	12.3	12.2	11.7	13.1	14.3	11.6	8.3	10.8	96.1	2.7	0.4	0.4	(Z)	1.0	85.4
McDonald	7.8	14.9	13.9	13.4	14.6	13.5	10.8	6.4	4.7	93.6	0.3	0.4	2.5	0.5	12.1	102.7
Macon	5.9	12.8	12.0	11.0	12.8	14.4	12.2	8.8	10.0	96.1	2.5	0.2	0.4	–	0.9	97.4
Madison	5.9	12.0	13.2	12.6	13.7	14.1	11.1	8.7	8.9	99.0	0.2	0.3	0.1	–	0.9	92.2
Maries	5.5	13.3	13.1	11.9	14.2	14.2	12.2	8.4	7.1	98.2	0.4	0.1	0.6	–	1.3	101.9
Marion	6.9	13.3	13.8	12.3	13.3	14.5	10.3	7.3	8.4	93.2	4.9	0.4	0.3	0.1	1.2	90.8
Mercer	5.8	11.5	12.6	9.4	12.0	16.7	11.7	9.6	10.8	98.9	0.2	–	0.8	0.1	0.4	98.1
Miller	6.1	13.3	13.2	13.7	13.7	14.3	10.7	7.7	7.4	98.2	0.3	0.2	0.5	(Z)	1.1	95.7
Mississippi	7.0	12.6	13.8	12.7	13.8	13.5	12.0	7.1	7.6	77.9	20.7	0.4	0.4	(Z)	1.2	93.1
Moniteau	6.3	13.3	13.6	14.6	15.6	13.8	9.8	6.2	6.7	95.4	3.4	0.4	0.3	–	3.1	111.6
Monroe	5.7	13.0	13.3	11.2	13.3	14.0	12.1	8.8	8.6	95.3	3.7	0.1	0.5	–	0.8	99.2
Montgomery	6.3	12.1	13.6	11.2	12.9	15.2	11.4	8.8	8.6	96.3	2.1	0.6	0.1	–	0.9	100.1
Morgan	5.7	12.3	12.0	11.2	12.5	13.1	12.9	11.5	8.8	98.0	0.5	0.1	0.6	(Z)	0.9	96.8
New Madrid	6.3	13.5	12.4	11.9	13.2	14.5	12.3	7.8	8.1	84.4	14.7	0.2	0.1	–	0.9	92.9
Newton	6.3	13.6	13.6	12.9	13.6	14.4	11.7	7.5	6.4	94.0	0.8	0.6	2.1	0.5	2.8	96.9
Nodaway	4.7	9.7	29.9	11.9	11.1	11.6	8.4	6.3	7.5	96.3	1.8	1.2	0.3	(Z)	0.8	102.4
Oregon	5.4	12.4	12.5	10.6	13.0	14.0	13.7	9.7	8.7	95.3	0.1	0.2	2.5	–	1.2	95.6
Osage	6.7	13.2	14.3	12.1	14.7	14.0	10.4	7.6	7.0	99.1	0.2	0.1	0.1	(Z)	0.7	104.8
Ozark	5.2	11.0	12.2	10.5	11.6	14.6	14.0	12.4	8.5	98.5	0.2	(Z)	0.5	–	1.1	99.0
Pemiscot	8.3	16.0	13.8	11.8	12.2	13.8	10.2	6.8	7.2	73.7	25.3	0.4	0.2	–	1.8	88.7
Perry	6.5	13.0	12.3	13.3	14.5	14.6	10.3	7.4	8.2	98.4	0.2	0.8	0.3	–	0.8	99.8
Pettis	7.0	13.6	13.2	13.4	13.9	13.9	9.8	7.4	7.8	94.2	3.0	0.5	0.6	0.1	6.2	95.8
Phelps	6.1	11.4	19.6	14.0	12.1	13.1	10.1	7.0	6.7	94.0	1.9	2.1	0.5	(Z)	1.6	105.2
Pike	6.1	11.5	14.1	14.4	14.5	14.0	11.0	7.4	7.0	90.4	8.6	0.2	0.3	(Z)	2.5	122.4
Platte	6.2	13.1	13.2	14.3	16.0	16.1	11.6	5.4	4.1	91.9	4.4	1.7	0.4	0.3	3.9	98.5
Polk	6.0	13.0	17.6	13.5	12.7	12.2	9.8	7.5	7.8	97.4	0.5	0.5	0.7	(Z)	1.8	96.5
Pulaski	6.9	13.9	24.9	14.3	14.3	10.9	7.1	4.6	3.2	80.8	12.6	2.3	0.9	0.4	6.6	119.6
Putnam	5.5	12.3	11.6	10.4	13.4	13.5	12.7	10.1	10.4	99.7	(Z)	0.2	–	–	0.6	96.1
Ralls	4.6	12.3	13.6	11.5	14.2	16.5	13.4	7.3	6.7	98.4	1.1	0.1	0.1	–	0.6	99.5
Randolph	6.7	12.6	13.4	14.2	14.9	14.1	10.2	6.9	7.0	91.5	6.8	0.5	0.3	(Z)	1.5	108.7
Ray	6.3	13.5	14.6	11.3	14.7	15.0	11.8	7.0	5.8	97.0	1.5	0.2	0.3	–	1.4	100.3
Reynolds	4.7	12.0	12.7	10.7	12.7	14.7	14.2	10.7	7.6	96.9	0.7	0.1	0.8	–	0.9	102.4
Ripley	6.1	12.4	13.0	13.3	12.8	13.5	12.0	9.3	7.8	97.1	0.1	0.4	1.3	(Z)	1.3	94.8
St. Charles	6.7	14.4	14.7	13.8	16.3	15.0	9.5	5.5	4.2	93.5	3.5	1.5	0.2	(Z)	2.0	97.6
St. Clair	4.6	11.5	11.8	10.1	12.1	14.1	14.1	11.4	10.3	97.9	0.4	0.5	0.5	(Z)	1.0	100.5
Ste. Genevieve	5.0	12.9	14.5	11.3	14.7	15.9	11.1	7.7	6.9	98.2	1.0	0.2	0.3	–	0.7	101.3
St. Francois	5.9	11.5	14.0	15.8	15.3	13.7	9.8	7.3	6.7	95.2	3.2	0.4	0.4	(Z)	1.0	110.0
St. Louis	6.0	13.0	13.6	11.0	14.6	16.2	11.6	7.0	7.1	74.3	21.3	2.9	0.2	(Z)	1.7	91.0
Saline	5.9	12.4	16.7	11.2	12.9	14.1	11.3	7.0	8.6	92.5	5.4	0.4	0.4	0.3	5.8	99.6
Schuyler	4.9	12.5	12.1	10.8	12.7	15.0	11.8	9.9	10.4	98.8	(Z)	0.2	0.1	–	0.9	94.1
Scotland	6.2	14.4	14.6	10.6	13.4	13.3	10.0	8.0	9.4	99.4	0.2	(Z)	0.2	(Z)	0.8	96.5
Scott	6.9	14.0	13.2	12.9	13.8	14.3	11.1	6.9	6.9	87.2	11.6	0.3	0.2	–	1.3	92.7
Shannon	5.2	13.1	14.0	11.2	13.6	15.0	12.9	8.8	6.1	95.7	0.2	(Z)	1.6	(Z)	1.1	95.9
Shelby	5.6	12.2	14.0	10.2	12.6	14.7	11.7	8.6	10.4	98.3	1.1	0.2	0.3	–	0.7	94.5
Stoddard	5.6	11.8	13.0	12.7	13.9	13.8	11.9	8.8	8.5	97.5	1.2	0.1	0.3	–	1.0	93.2
Stone	4.9	11.3	10.8	11.3	12.3	14.0	14.6	12.5	8.1	97.7	0.3	0.3	0.7	(Z)	1.6	96.0
Sullivan	6.4	13.4	11.5	11.3	13.6	13.9	11.9	8.4	9.8	98.5	0.8	(Z)	0.3	0.2	11.8	101.2

See footnotes at end of table.

[Includes United States, states, and 3,141 counties/county equivalents defined as of February 22, 2005. For more information on these areas, see Appendix C, Geographic Information]

County	Age (percent)									One race (percent)					Hispanic or Latino origin[1] (percent)	Males per 100 females
	Under 5 years	5 to 14 years	15 to 24 years	25 to 34 years	35 to 44 years	45 to 54 years	55 to 64 years	65 to 74 years	75 years and over	White alone	Black or African American alone	Asian alone	American Indian and Alaska Native alone	Native Hawaiian and Other Pacific Islander alone		
MISSOURI—Con.																
Taney	6.5	11.6	14.0	13.2	12.9	13.3	11.8	9.2	7.5	96.7	0.9	0.5	0.7	0.1	3.1	93.5
Texas	5.6	11.7	13.5	11.8	13.9	14.3	11.8	9.2	8.2	94.5	2.4	0.3	1.0	–	1.1	102.0
Vernon	6.5	13.3	14.4	12.2	12.9	14.0	11.1	7.4	8.3	97.2	0.8	0.5	0.7	(Z)	1.4	95.1
Warren	6.3	13.0	14.5	13.7	14.6	14.8	10.4	7.4	5.3	96.3	2.3	0.2	0.3	–	2.1	99.2
Washington	6.6	13.0	14.6	14.8	14.6	13.8	10.7	7.1	4.9	95.5	2.7	0.2	0.7	–	1.0	106.9
Wayne	6.0	11.4	12.7	10.4	12.6	13.7	13.1	11.3	8.8	97.6	0.4	0.2	0.4	(Z)	0.5	98.3
Webster	6.9	14.5	14.1	14.1	15.2	13.7	9.8	6.7	5.1	96.9	1.2	0.3	0.7	(Z)	1.2	101.5
Worth	3.9	12.1	13.7	8.5	13.6	15.0	11.3	10.5	11.4	98.7	0.6	–	0.5	–	0.3	100.9
Wright	6.8	13.6	13.5	11.8	12.8	14.0	10.7	8.6	8.1	97.9	0.5	0.2	0.6	–	1.1	94.9
Independent City																
St. Louis city	7.6	13.4	14.2	14.2	14.9	14.5	9.0	5.6	6.6	45.6	50.7	2.0	0.3	(Z)	2.4	89.5
MONTANA	5.7	11.9	15.0	11.6	13.3	16.6	12.1	7.2	6.6	91.1	0.4	0.5	6.5	0.1	2.4	99.6
Beaverhead	4.6	11.0	19.0	8.6	11.8	16.9	12.6	8.4	7.2	97.4	0.2	0.2	1.6	(Z)	3.4	105.3
Big Horn	9.8	16.4	16.6	11.0	13.1	13.7	10.1	5.6	3.8	35.8	0.1	0.4	61.4	–	4.3	97.4
Blaine	7.8	15.4	16.5	8.7	12.8	15.2	11.0	6.5	6.1	50.4	0.3	0.2	48.0	(Z)	1.5	97.9
Broadwater	3.9	11.3	12.3	8.7	13.6	16.9	14.1	10.3	9.1	97.9	0.4	0.2	1.2	0.1	1.4	104.2
Carbon	3.9	11.1	12.8	9.1	13.8	19.0	13.9	8.1	8.2	98.4	0.2	0.3	0.6	–	2.0	100.8
Carter	2.6	10.4	14.9	7.7	14.2	17.2	13.6	10.1	9.4	99.2	0.1	0.3	0.4	–	0.7	97.0
Cascade	6.5	12.6	13.4	11.9	14.0	15.2	11.5	7.7	7.2	91.1	1.2	0.7	4.6	0.1	2.8	98.7
Chouteau	3.8	13.3	15.2	7.0	12.3	18.0	11.9	8.7	9.8	84.1	0.1	0.2	15.5	0.1	0.7	101.8
Custer	5.6	11.9	13.9	9.9	12.7	16.5	12.4	8.0	9.2	97.4	0.1	0.3	1.5	(Z)	1.7	94.9
Daniels	3.7	10.0	12.3	6.0	9.7	18.4	16.7	11.7	11.6	97.2	0.2	0.4	1.4	0.1	2.2	98.3
Dawson	4.8	10.5	15.1	8.6	11.4	18.3	13.0	9.2	9.1	98.0	0.3	0.1	1.4	–	1.4	98.6
Deer Lodge	4.1	9.9	14.8	9.0	12.2	17.7	13.9	8.8	9.5	95.5	0.3	0.4	2.4	–	2.0	100.6
Fallon	4.5	10.7	13.8	8.4	12.0	19.6	11.6	10.0	9.4	98.8	0.2	0.4	0.6	–	0.6	100.2
Fergus	4.7	11.1	12.9	8.5	11.8	17.2	13.4	9.8	10.7	96.8	0.1	0.3	1.7	–	1.0	95.9
Flathead	5.7	11.9	13.3	11.8	13.7	17.8	12.6	7.2	5.9	96.7	0.3	0.4	1.2	0.1	1.9	99.0
Gallatin[2]	5.8	10.4	19.8	17.5	13.2	15.1	9.6	4.6	4.0	96.6	0.4	0.8	1.0	0.1	2.2	108.6
Garfield	6.1	11.4	11.8	8.3	12.1	16.3	13.8	9.4	10.8	98.6	0.1	–	1.2	0.2	0.4	107.8
Glacier	9.4	14.9	18.3	10.1	12.9	15.1	9.2	5.5	4.5	34.5	0.1	(Z)	63.3	0.1	2.0	97.2
Golden Valley	8.0	10.8	13.8	9.9	11.6	16.5	13.4	8.8	7.2	98.2	–	0.2	1.4	–	1.4	103.7
Granite	3.7	10.3	13.6	9.8	11.9	16.7	16.4	10.3	7.4	97.3	–	0.1	1.2	(Z)	1.3	103.4
Hill	7.3	13.1	18.0	10.2	11.8	16.2	10.6	6.2	6.6	78.4	0.2	0.3	19.3	(Z)	1.8	98.4
Jefferson	4.1	11.8	15.5	9.1	14.0	20.2	14.7	6.6	4.1	96.7	0.2	0.4	1.4	(Z)	1.7	101.6
Judith Basin	3.5	11.8	14.1	5.6	12.8	18.7	14.4	9.4	9.7	99.1	(Z)	(Z)	0.4	–	0.8	105.4
Lake	6.4	12.7	15.3	10.3	12.5	15.6	12.4	7.8	7.1	73.1	0.3	0.2	23.5	(Z)	3.2	95.9
Lewis and Clark	5.4	11.9	14.1	10.9	14.2	17.8	13.2	6.7	5.7	95.6	0.3	0.5	2.1	(Z)	1.8	96.6
Liberty	3.8	9.6	14.7	5.5	12.1	18.2	12.5	11.4	12.1	99.5	–	0.4	0.1	–	0.2	96.6
Lincoln	4.6	11.0	13.5	7.6	12.8	18.0	14.9	10.4	7.1	96.2	0.2	0.4	1.5	–	1.9	101.7
McCone	3.4	11.5	12.3	5.2	13.2	18.7	14.2	10.8	10.7	97.1	0.6	0.4	1.3	–	1.2	100.3
Madison	3.6	10.1	12.4	9.6	12.5	18.6	15.6	9.5	8.0	98.3	(Z)	0.2	0.7	–	2.0	103.1
Meagher	5.2	11.6	12.2	8.4	11.4	17.6	14.4	11.5	7.8	98.5	–	0.2	1.1	0.1	1.6	99.7
Mineral	5.1	10.8	13.3	9.2	13.4	17.0	14.7	10.0	6.5	95.3	0.2	0.5	2.1	–	2.5	105.3
Missoula	5.3	10.7	17.9	15.5	13.6	15.4	11.1	5.4	5.0	94.4	0.3	1.1	2.5	0.1	1.9	99.8
Musselshell	5.8	10.3	12.2	7.6	11.9	20.3	15.3	8.5	8.1	97.6	0.1	0.2	1.5	(Z)	1.9	94.4
Park[2]	4.7	11.1	11.6	10.1	14.5	19.8	13.5	7.3	7.3	97.3	0.5	0.4	0.9	(Z)	2.6	98.8
Petroleum	4.9	13.4	12.8	7.0	13.8	15.7	14.5	8.9	8.9	98.9	–	–	1.1	–	1.5	108.9
Phillips	4.6	11.5	14.7	5.0	12.6	18.8	12.4	10.1	10.3	90.9	0.2	0.4	7.0	–	1.4	100.9
Pondera	5.8	12.6	16.6	7.5	12.6	16.6	12.4	7.6	8.1	82.7	0.2	0.1	16.2	(Z)	1.0	98.1
Powder River	3.3	12.5	13.0	6.7	11.8	19.4	14.3	9.1	9.9	98.1	–	0.1	1.9	–	1.4	98.7
Powell	3.9	9.6	14.4	10.9	16.5	18.0	11.9	8.1	6.8	93.6	0.6	0.4	3.8	–	2.3	143.5
Prairie	4.2	7.9	9.0	7.6	9.7	19.4	19.7	10.3	12.2	99.2	–	0.2	0.5	–	0.7	104.6
Ravalli	5.2	11.7	13.3	10.0	13.0	16.8	13.9	8.7	7.4	97.4	0.2	0.3	1.0	0.1	2.5	98.5
Richland	4.3	12.4	14.4	7.9	13.4	18.6	12.9	7.6	8.5	97.5	0.2	0.2	1.8	–	2.8	99.3
Roosevelt	9.1	16.3	16.9	9.5	12.6	15.7	9.2	5.7	4.9	38.2	0.2	0.6	59.2	(Z)	2.0	96.4
Rosebud	8.7	15.2	15.8	7.8	12.9	17.6	12.8	5.5	3.9	62.5	0.3	0.6	35.0	–	2.9	98.6
Sanders	4.7	10.1	13.2	9.1	11.3	17.1	16.2	10.4	8.0	93.1	0.2	0.3	4.5	–	2.2	100.5
Sheridan	2.5	9.6	12.9	3.6	10.7	20.7	14.6	11.5	13.9	97.2	0.3	0.3	1.6	–	1.6	97.3
Silver Bow	5.4	11.6	14.8	10.2	13.2	16.5	11.8	8.1	8.4	95.7	0.3	0.5	2.2	(Z)	3.1	98.4
Stillwater	5.2	11.8	12.3	9.0	13.6	19.1	14.2	8.4	6.5	97.7	0.2	0.3	1.0	–	2.1	105.1
Sweet Grass	4.7	12.7	12.1	9.4	12.7	16.9	14.9	8.2	8.3	97.9	0.1	0.3	0.5	0.1	1.9	101.9
Teton	5.1	12.6	14.2	7.5	12.8	16.3	13.2	9.5	8.9	96.8	0.2	0.3	1.6	–	1.4	98.8
Toole	4.4	11.8	14.9	11.3	14.7	18.2	12.0	6.3	6.4	93.0	0.2	0.3	4.8	–	2.2	112.7
Treasure	2.6	11.5	16.0	5.2	12.0	19.2	15.7	8.3	9.6	97.4	0.1	0.4	1.9	–	1.9	105.7
Valley	5.5	11.6	12.9	7.4	12.4	17.4	12.8	10.2	9.7	88.2	0.2	0.3	9.9	–	0.9	98.7
Wheatland	6.5	12.7	13.6	7.8	9.6	15.6	14.9	8.3	11.0	97.3	0.2	0.3	1.4	0.1	1.5	95.9
Wibaux	3.0	10.9	13.2	5.6	12.3	17.4	13.7	10.2	13.7	98.9	–	0.2	0.5	–	0.5	94.9
Yellowstone	6.2	12.4	13.9	12.7	13.9	16.0	11.3	6.8	6.7	93.6	0.5	0.5	3.5	0.1	4.1	96.0
Yellowstone National Park[2]	(NA)	(NA)	(NA)	(NA)	(NA)	(NA)	(NA)	(NA)	(NA)	(NA)	(NA)	(NA)	(NA)	(NA)	(NA)	(NA)

See footnotes at end of table.

[Includes United States, states, and 3,141 counties/county equivalents defined as of February 22, 2005. For more information on these areas, see Appendix C, Geographic Information]

County	\multicolumn{14}{c}{Population characteristics, 2005}

	\multicolumn{9}{c}{Age (percent)}	\multicolumn{5}{c}{One race (percent)}		
County	Under 5 years	5 to 14 years	15 to 24 years	25 to 34 years	35 to 44 years	45 to 54 years	55 to 64 years	65 to 74 years	75 years and over	White alone	Black or African American alone	Asian alone	American Indian and Alaska Native alone	Native Hawaiian and Other Pacific Islander alone	Hispanic or Latino origin[1] (percent)	Males per 100 females
NEBRASKA	7.0	13.2	15.2	13.2	13.7	14.4	10.0	6.3	7.0	92.0	4.3	1.6	0.9	0.1	7.1	97.8
Adams	6.0	12.5	16.7	12.2	12.6	14.6	10.4	6.4	8.8	95.5	0.9	2.4	0.5	(Z)	5.9	96.2
Antelope	4.7	12.6	14.4	8.1	11.8	16.7	12.0	8.8	10.9	99.4	0.1	(Z)	0.3	–	1.0	96.1
Arthur	7.1	9.3	13.2	8.7	13.5	17.5	11.1	12.4	7.1	98.4	–	0.8	–	0.5	1.9	104.3
Banner	2.5	12.6	16.0	7.9	15.6	17.3	13.0	9.0	6.3	99.6	0.1	–	0.1	–	6.1	108.2
Blaine	5.2	11.4	10.7	7.2	14.0	13.4	15.3	12.8	9.9	99.4	–	–	0.6	–	0.2	107.7
Boone	4.4	13.3	14.8	6.2	13.2	16.6	10.6	8.5	12.5	99.8	0.1	(Z)	(Z)	0.1	1.3	100.2
Box Butte	6.4	13.7	13.1	9.5	11.7	19.6	11.0	6.7	8.2	94.5	0.5	0.6	3.2	–	9.2	100.5
Boyd	4.2	11.3	13.5	6.0	10.7	16.9	13.4	9.4	14.7	99.2	–	0.2	0.6	–	0.1	93.9
Brown	4.8	11.4	11.9	7.7	12.2	16.1	12.3	10.7	12.8	99.0	–	0.4	0.2	–	1.0	96.7
Buffalo	6.7	12.1	21.4	15.3	11.8	12.8	8.7	5.3	6.0	97.6	0.7	0.6	0.4	(Z)	5.2	95.7
Burt	5.4	12.5	13.0	7.6	12.0	16.7	11.2	9.8	11.9	98.0	0.3	0.2	1.1	–	1.4	94.3
Butler	5.8	13.2	13.2	10.3	13.1	15.4	11.4	7.9	9.6	99.2	0.1	0.1	0.2	0.1	2.3	105.5
Cass	5.9	14.1	13.5	12.7	15.1	15.5	11.1	6.6	5.4	97.9	0.5	0.5	0.2	(Z)	1.8	97.0
Cedar	5.6	13.8	15.1	7.1	12.3	15.7	10.2	8.5	11.6	99.3	0.1	(Z)	0.2	(Z)	0.6	101.6
Chase	6.0	11.3	12.6	9.0	11.5	16.9	12.1	8.9	11.7	99.4	0.2	0.2	0.1	–	4.3	95.6
Cherry	5.4	12.8	13.5	11.5	12.0	15.3	11.8	8.4	9.1	93.4	0.1	0.4	4.3	0.3	1.0	100.7
Cheyenne	6.1	12.5	13.1	12.3	13.7	15.7	10.9	7.0	8.7	97.6	0.2	1.1	0.8	(Z)	4.7	97.0
Clay	5.3	12.8	14.1	7.9	12.6	16.5	12.0	8.7	10.0	98.8	0.3	0.3	0.4	–	4.2	95.0
Colfax	8.9	13.9	13.9	10.0	13.1	14.2	9.0	7.4	9.6	98.2	0.1	0.3	0.4	0.7	31.8	108.0
Cuming	6.3	13.1	13.5	8.4	13.3	15.0	10.2	8.7	11.4	99.0	0.2	0.2	0.5	(Z)	7.9	102.8
Custer	5.8	12.9	12.9	8.2	12.6	15.6	11.8	8.8	11.4	98.8	0.2	0.2	0.6	–	1.3	96.7
Dakota	9.0	16.1	13.7	13.9	14.0	13.4	9.2	5.7	5.1	91.5	1.5	3.3	2.4	(Z)	29.2	98.2
Dawes	5.6	9.5	28.1	12.0	9.0	11.4	9.0	6.8	8.6	93.5	1.2	0.3	3.9	(Z)	2.6	93.2
Dawson	8.7	15.5	13.3	11.3	13.9	14.1	10.3	6.0	7.0	97.1	1.0	0.7	0.7	0.1	29.9	101.9
Deuel	5.1	9.6	13.8	7.5	12.1	17.2	11.9	9.6	13.1	98.7	(Z)	0.5	0.5	–	2.9	95.5
Dixon	6.4	12.9	14.5	8.9	12.5	16.5	11.1	7.6	9.6	98.9	(Z)	0.3	0.6	0.1	7.5	100.2
Dodge	6.6	12.4	14.3	11.6	13.2	14.2	10.4	8.0	9.4	97.7	0.7	0.6	0.4	0.1	6.5	94.5
Douglas	7.9	13.7	14.5	15.0	14.6	14.2	9.5	5.3	5.3	83.8	11.7	2.2	0.6	0.1	8.7	96.8
Dundy	4.3	11.2	12.5	7.1	11.4	18.9	12.8	8.3	13.4	98.2	–	0.7	0.8	–	3.6	101.4
Fillmore	5.4	12.4	13.4	7.2	12.9	15.7	11.7	9.2	12.1	98.9	0.3	0.1	0.7	–	2.5	94.1
Franklin	4.1	12.1	12.9	8.4	12.7	15.1	10.7	10.3	13.7	99.3	–	0.1	0.4	–	0.7	91.8
Frontier	4.4	11.6	17.9	7.5	11.1	15.9	12.3	9.7	9.6	98.9	0.1	0.3	0.3	–	1.3	100.8
Furnas	4.9	12.6	11.4	8.1	11.6	16.2	12.2	9.7	13.3	98.8	0.1	0.3	0.4	–	1.3	91.1
Gage	5.7	11.8	12.6	12.4	13.3	15.1	10.5	8.2	10.5	98.0	0.4	0.4	0.4	0.1	1.3	94.9
Garden	3.1	9.1	11.0	5.9	12.7	17.2	13.2	13.0	15.0	99.3	0.1	0.3	0.2	–	1.8	93.7
Garfield	4.7	11.5	11.7	7.3	11.2	15.9	13.4	11.3	13.1	99.3	–	0.1	0.2	0.1	1.4	91.8
Gosper	5.5	11.0	11.5	8.0	12.1	15.5	13.4	12.5	10.3	99.4	–	0.4	0.1	–	1.3	102.2
Grant	5.4	9.7	15.7	5.8	12.7	21.0	12.2	9.3	8.2	99.7	–	0.1	0.1	–	1.5	110.0
Greeley	6.5	13.7	10.9	7.1	11.3	15.1	11.3	9.9	14.1	99.0	0.7	0.1	(Z)	–	1.1	95.8
Hall	8.2	14.2	12.6	13.3	13.8	13.9	10.4	6.5	7.1	96.4	1.2	1.1	0.4	0.2	18.3	99.6
Hamilton	6.0	14.5	13.5	9.9	13.7	16.4	11.0	7.2	7.8	99.2	0.2	0.2	0.1	–	1.3	100.1
Harlan	4.4	11.6	12.1	7.1	11.8	16.4	13.2	10.3	13.1	99.6	0.1	0.1	(Z)	–	0.9	100.5
Hayes	4.4	12.8	14.5	8.0	10.4	18.8	12.1	8.2	10.9	99.2	0.2	0.3	–	–	3.0	102.6
Hitchcock	5.4	10.3	12.7	7.3	12.4	15.8	12.8	10.3	13.1	99.1	0.1	0.2	0.3	–	1.8	93.5
Holt	5.1	12.8	13.1	7.0	12.9	16.7	11.6	8.8	11.9	99.2	0.1	0.1	0.3	(Z)	1.3	95.2
Hooker	4.0	9.9	13.7	5.5	11.7	16.9	10.9	9.8	17.5	99.2	–	0.1	0.3	–	1.1	84.2
Howard	5.8	12.9	14.0	10.8	13.5	14.2	11.8	7.6	9.3	98.8	0.5	0.3	0.2	0.1	1.4	102.2
Jefferson	4.9	10.9	12.8	8.8	11.7	16.3	11.9	9.4	13.2	98.5	0.1	0.4	0.7	(Z)	1.4	98.4
Johnson	5.1	11.4	12.5	8.3	12.9	15.2	10.6	8.4	15.7	95.8	0.4	0.1	3.1	–	5.7	90.0
Kearney	5.3	13.2	12.7	11.1	14.1	16.1	11.9	7.0	8.7	99.1	0.3	0.2	0.2	–	2.6	97.8
Keith	5.3	11.9	12.4	8.2	13.2	16.0	13.3	10.1	9.6	98.4	0.2	0.3	0.9	–	4.2	97.4
Keya Paha	7.2	12.6	9.8	10.1	10.8	14.4	13.4	9.0	12.7	99.8	–	–	0.2	–	4.7	99.6
Kimball	5.1	12.1	12.9	6.0	12.4	16.0	13.0	9.9	11.7	98.7	0.3	0.1	0.6	(Z)	4.2	96.4
Knox	5.4	12.0	12.8	7.7	11.2	15.5	12.0	10.1	13.4	91.6	0.1	0.2	8.0	(Z)	1.3	96.2
Lancaster	7.1	12.0	18.0	16.5	13.5	13.5	9.0	5.1	5.4	91.6	3.0	3.2	0.7	0.1	4.2	99.9
Lincoln	6.7	13.1	13.3	12.9	12.8	14.9	11.4	7.2	7.8	97.2	0.9	0.4	0.7	–	5.5	97.3
Logan	6.9	10.1	14.5	6.5	11.1	20.0	12.2	10.0	8.8	98.8	0.1	–	1.1	–	0.9	92.7
Loup	5.1	12.7	13.4	7.4	11.5	15.3	14.6	10.1	9.9	99.4	–	0.1	0.3	–	1.9	101.8
McPherson	4.1	13.6	14.6	8.3	11.4	17.8	10.1	9.1	11.0	99.6	–	0.4	–	–	1.6	98.8
Madison	7.5	13.4	15.0	12.5	13.2	14.7	9.5	6.2	8.0	95.3	1.9	0.7	1.4	0.1	12.3	100.1
Merrick	5.7	13.6	13.0	9.7	13.0	15.2	11.9	8.4	9.5	99.2	0.3	0.2	0.2	–	2.3	98.8
Morrill	5.8	12.2	14.5	10.0	12.0	16.5	12.1	8.5	8.4	98.6	0.1	0.4	0.8	–	10.1	97.1
Nance	5.2	13.4	13.4	9.0	11.4	17.3	10.4	9.4	10.4	99.4	–	(Z)	0.4	–	1.5	106.8
Nemaha	4.8	10.9	18.0	7.3	13.2	15.6	12.3	7.5	10.3	98.1	0.5	0.7	0.4	–	1.4	94.2
Nuckolls	5.5	10.5	12.3	8.4	11.1	16.1	12.7	9.7	13.8	99.5	0.1	0.3	(Z)	–	1.5	93.1
Otoe	5.8	13.1	12.5	11.6	13.0	15.1	11.2	7.9	9.9	98.4	0.4	0.3	0.3	–	3.2	98.0
Pawnee	4.1	11.8	11.5	8.0	10.7	15.3	12.7	10.1	15.7	99.3	–	0.2	0.2	–	0.9	92.3
Perkins	5.8	12.3	14.0	9.4	12.0	16.0	11.4	8.3	10.6	99.0	0.1	0.3	0.3	–	2.7	99.5
Phelps	5.7	13.3	12.6	9.4	13.4	15.6	11.6	8.5	9.9	98.8	0.2	0.2	0.3	0.1	3.0	97.2
Pierce	5.4	13.6	16.1	10.0	14.0	15.2	11.0	6.1	8.5	99.2	0.1	0.2	0.4	–	0.8	100.4

See footnotes at end of table.

[Includes United States, states, and 3,141 counties/county equivalents defined as of February 22, 2005. For more information on these areas, see Appendix C, Geographic Information]

County	Population characteristics, 2005															
	Age (percent)									One race (percent)					His-panic or Latino origin[1] (per-cent)	Males per 100 females
	Under 5 years	5 to 14 years	15 to 24 years	25 to 34 years	35 to 44 years	45 to 54 years	55 to 64 years	65 to 74 years	75 years and over	White alone	Black or African Ameri-can alone	Asian alone	Ameri-can Indian and Alaska Native alone	Native Hawai-ian and Other Pacific Islander alone		
NEBRASKA—Con.																
Platte	6.8	14.7	14.0	11.6	13.9	15.6	10.3	6.2	6.8	97.9	0.5	0.5	0.3	(Z)	9.6	99.7
Polk	6.3	12.7	11.9	9.6	12.0	15.8	11.3	8.5	12.0	99.4	0.1	(Z)	0.3	–	2.3	100.8
Red Willow	5.9	12.8	13.7	9.7	12.0	15.9	10.6	8.6	10.8	98.5	0.3	0.2	0.5	–	3.1	96.2
Richardson	4.6	12.4	13.1	8.1	13.0	15.0	12.3	9.3	12.2	95.8	0.3	0.3	2.3	–	1.2	93.8
Rock	4.5	10.4	11.9	8.3	10.7	19.0	12.8	9.3	13.1	99.0	–	–	0.3	0.6	0.6	96.9
Saline	6.2	13.0	17.6	11.7	13.0	13.3	9.8	6.7	8.7	96.4	1.0	1.6	0.4	–	15.3	102.1
Sarpy	8.2	15.2	15.3	16.0	15.9	13.5	8.4	4.7	2.9	91.5	4.0	2.1	0.4	0.1	5.4	99.0
Saunders	5.8	13.5	14.3	10.3	14.7	15.2	11.3	7.2	7.6	98.9	0.2	0.3	0.3	–	1.5	101.5
Scotts Bluff	7.0	13.1	13.0	11.9	12.2	14.8	11.1	7.8	9.2	95.8	0.5	0.6	2.2	(Z)	18.7	90.4
Seward	5.6	11.9	20.6	10.1	12.3	14.6	10.1	6.7	8.2	98.0	0.4	0.5	0.2	0.2	1.4	102.6
Sheridan	6.0	12.2	13.4	7.5	10.4	16.8	11.8	9.5	12.4	87.6	0.1	0.2	10.3	(Z)	1.5	95.5
Sherman	5.4	11.5	12.2	7.7	12.2	15.8	12.1	10.3	12.7	99.4	0.1	0.3	0.1	–	1.0	98.2
Sioux	3.3	11.7	13.4	11.1	11.7	18.3	12.7	10.5	7.3	99.6	–	0.2	0.1	–	2.5	109.8
Stanton	6.5	14.1	14.4	12.1	13.9	16.2	10.3	6.2	6.2	98.5	0.4	0.2	0.5	–	2.9	98.8
Thayer	4.7	12.0	11.4	6.1	11.8	15.9	13.5	10.0	14.7	99.4	–	0.1	0.3	–	1.2	96.1
Thomas	4.3	9.6	10.8	8.5	12.5	21.3	15.6	5.3	12.0	99.5	–	–	0.5	–	1.1	97.2
Thurston	11.2	18.6	17.2	9.5	12.5	10.8	8.0	5.7	6.6	44.8	0.6	0.1	53.4	–	3.3	99.1
Valley	5.2	12.1	13.0	7.9	11.9	15.1	12.1	9.4	13.3	98.9	0.2	0.1	0.4	0.1	1.8	93.0
Washington	5.3	13.2	16.0	12.2	13.3	15.6	11.2	6.8	6.4	98.5	0.5	0.4	0.2	0.1	1.1	101.2
Wayne	5.4	9.9	31.9	9.3	10.0	11.8	7.9	6.3	7.4	97.8	0.9	0.5	0.4	–	3.2	93.6
Webster	4.1	11.7	11.8	6.2	12.8	15.2	12.8	10.9	14.4	98.6	0.2	0.7	0.2	–	0.7	89.6
Wheeler	5.2	14.9	13.7	10.1	9.9	17.4	11.7	9.8	7.3	99.8	–	–	0.2	–	0.6	99.0
York	6.2	12.0	15.1	9.8	12.8	15.8	10.9	7.8	9.8	96.7	1.5	0.6	0.4	0.1	2.6	92.7
NEVADA	7.2	14.4	13.2	15.0	15.1	13.4	10.4	6.6	4.7	82.0	7.7	5.7	1.4	0.5	23.5	103.7
Churchill	8.4	15.5	13.6	11.7	13.1	13.6	11.0	6.9	6.1	87.9	1.6	3.0	5.0	0.2	9.8	99.1
Clark	7.5	14.6	12.9	15.9	15.5	12.8	10.1	6.4	4.3	78.9	10.1	6.7	1.0	0.6	26.1	103.5
Douglas	4.2	11.2	12.6	9.2	13.1	16.6	13.9	10.9	8.4	94.5	0.7	1.6	1.5	0.2	8.2	101.7
Elko	6.7	17.2	16.2	12.5	14.7	15.3	10.0	4.7	2.6	91.4	0.9	0.9	5.6	0.1	21.7	106.9
Esmeralda	2.5	9.7	11.4	9.7	12.1	16.9	14.6	14.6	8.5	93.1	0.1	–	5.7	0.3	11.7	115.6
Eureka	5.3	13.2	14.7	7.2	15.8	16.3	13.3	7.8	6.4	95.8	0.4	1.3	1.0	–	12.7	108.8
Humboldt	6.6	16.8	15.1	9.9	14.7	16.9	10.3	5.6	4.0	92.3	0.6	0.7	5.0	0.1	20.1	110.9
Lander	6.2	17.1	16.2	7.4	13.7	16.8	13.1	6.5	3.2	93.9	0.5	0.4	4.7	–	16.9	103.7
Lincoln	4.6	13.4	17.9	9.6	10.6	12.5	12.3	10.7	8.4	95.3	2.0	0.4	1.9	–	5.8	109.6
Lyon	5.7	13.7	14.3	13.4	13.9	13.9	11.2	8.0	5.8	92.8	1.2	1.0	2.4	0.3	12.6	103.4
Mineral	4.4	12.0	14.5	9.0	11.3	14.8	13.3	10.7	10.1	77.4	4.5	1.1	16.3	–	9.8	99.4
Nye	4.4	12.8	12.4	11.1	12.5	13.4	12.6	12.5	8.4	93.1	1.7	1.0	1.8	0.5	11.0	104.1
Pershing	4.1	13.5	15.6	15.2	18.0	14.1	10.6	5.4	3.5	89.5	5.8	0.8	3.0	0.2	19.9	159.5
Storey	2.7	10.7	12.6	14.0	14.0	18.0	16.6	7.2	4.2	95.5	0.3	1.9	1.3	(Z)	6.9	109.5
Washoe	6.9	13.7	14.1	13.7	14.7	14.6	11.0	6.5	4.9	87.8	2.4	5.0	2.0	0.5	19.9	102.8
White Pine	4.4	12.2	15.0	13.1	14.3	14.8	11.1	8.1	6.9	90.2	4.5	1.0	3.5	0.1	11.4	128.1
Independent City																
Carson City	6.5	12.8	12.9	12.4	14.2	14.0	11.5	8.2	7.5	92.0	2.2	2.2	2.1	0.2	18.5	106.6
NEW HAMPSHIRE	5.6	13.1	13.9	11.3	16.1	16.3	11.3	6.3	6.2	96.1	1.0	1.7	0.2	(Z)	2.2	97.2
Belknap	4.8	11.9	12.5	11.8	14.8	16.3	12.5	7.6	7.8	97.6	0.5	0.8	0.3	(Z)	0.8	96.3
Carroll	4.3	11.1	11.8	9.9	14.3	16.6	13.2	9.4	9.4	98.3	0.3	0.5	0.2	(Z)	0.8	97.2
Cheshire	4.8	11.5	17.6	10.9	14.1	15.6	11.4	7.0	7.1	97.7	0.6	0.7	0.3	(Z)	1.1	95.0
Coos	4.5	11.5	12.2	10.4	14.2	16.6	12.4	8.4	9.8	98.2	0.3	0.4	0.3	(Z)	0.9	98.2
Grafton	4.7	10.9	18.6	11.2	13.5	15.3	11.5	7.0	7.4	95.9	0.7	2.0	0.3	(Z)	1.3	96.4
Hillsborough	6.2	14.1	13.0	11.8	17.0	16.1	10.8	5.6	5.5	94.0	1.7	2.9	0.2	0.1	4.2	98.1
Merrimack	5.3	12.9	14.4	11.6	15.7	16.7	11.1	6.0	6.3	96.8	0.7	1.2	0.3	(Z)	1.3	97.2
Rockingham	5.7	14.0	12.1	10.2	17.6	17.6	11.8	5.9	5.1	96.8	0.8	1.4	0.2	0.1	1.8	98.5
Strafford	5.7	12.2	18.1	13.1	15.2	14.5	9.6	5.7	5.8	96.0	0.9	1.8	0.3	0.1	1.4	93.3
Sullivan	5.7	12.2	11.9	11.3	14.7	16.1	12.3	7.8	8.0	98.3	0.3	0.5	0.2	(Z)	0.9	97.3
NEW JERSEY	6.7	13.8	13.0	12.2	16.0	14.9	10.5	6.2	6.8	76.6	14.5	7.2	0.3	0.1	15.2	95.1
Atlantic	6.6	13.9	13.1	12.6	15.7	14.8	9.8	6.5	6.9	74.0	17.9	6.3	0.3	0.1	13.9	94.1
Bergen	5.8	13.3	11.6	10.8	16.3	15.7	11.7	6.9	7.9	79.2	5.9	13.5	0.2	(Z)	13.3	93.8
Burlington	6.1	13.6	13.1	12.4	16.4	15.1	10.5	6.4	6.4	77.6	16.6	3.7	0.2	(Z)	5.0	97.8
Camden	6.8	14.5	14.1	12.1	15.4	14.8	10.2	5.8	6.4	73.4	20.3	4.5	0.3	0.1	11.3	93.8
Cape May	5.0	11.9	12.1	9.8	13.5	15.0	12.2	9.4	11.1	93.3	5.0	0.8	0.2	(Z)	4.0	92.2
Cumberland	7.1	13.5	13.6	14.9	15.4	13.3	9.8	6.0	6.5	74.3	21.7	1.1	1.0	0.3	22.1	105.8
Essex	7.7	14.7	13.7	12.9	15.4	14.1	10.0	5.7	5.8	51.4	42.6	4.2	0.3	0.1	17.5	91.8
Gloucester	6.0	13.9	15.1	12.0	15.8	15.5	10.2	5.8	5.7	86.9	9.9	2.0	0.2	(Z)	3.1	94.2
Hudson	7.2	12.4	12.8	17.2	17.2	13.1	9.0	5.5	5.6	71.1	15.1	11.0	0.6	0.1	41.0	97.7
Hunterdon	5.6	14.0	12.5	9.4	16.5	18.4	12.7	5.7	5.3	93.4	2.8	3.0	0.2	(Z)	3.6	97.9
Mercer	6.4	13.3	15.0	12.9	15.4	14.7	10.2	5.6	6.4	70.0	20.6	7.6	0.2	0.2	11.8	96.1
Middlesex	6.8	13.2	13.7	13.8	16.4	14.4	9.7	5.6	6.2	69.5	10.4	18.2	0.3	0.1	16.2	97.3
Monmouth	6.3	14.5	13.0	10.2	15.8	16.3	11.4	6.1	6.4	85.8	8.1	4.9	0.2	(Z)	7.6	95.1
Morris	6.5	14.2	11.8	10.3	17.0	16.1	12.0	6.5	5.8	87.7	3.1	8.0	0.2	(Z)	9.7	96.6
Ocean	6.4	12.8	11.5	11.5	14.0	12.9	9.8	8.2	12.8	94.0	3.4	1.6	0.2	(Z)	6.3	91.1

See footnotes at end of table.

[Includes United States, states, and 3,141 counties/county equivalents defined as of February 22, 2005. For more information on these areas, see Appendix C, Geographic Information]

County	Under 5 years	5 to 14 years	15 to 24 years	25 to 34 years	35 to 44 years	45 to 54 years	55 to 64 years	65 to 74 years	75 years and over	White alone	Black or African American alone	Asian alone	American Indian and Alaska Native alone	Native Hawaiian and Other Pacific Islander alone	Hispanic or Latino origin[1] (percent)	Males per 100 females
NEW JERSEY—Con.																
Passaic	8.1	14.7	13.7	12.6	15.3	13.9	9.9	5.7	6.0	78.1	15.3	4.4	0.7	0.2	33.9	94.5
Salem	6.0	13.6	13.6	12.0	14.2	15.2	11.5	6.5	7.4	82.7	15.1	0.8	0.4	(Z)	4.8	94.3
Somerset	7.0	14.8	11.1	11.1	17.9	16.4	10.5	5.7	5.5	78.3	8.8	11.7	0.2	(Z)	11.1	96.5
Sussex	5.7	14.9	13.5	10.2	16.8	17.4	11.8	5.1	4.5	95.7	1.6	1.7	0.1	(Z)	5.1	98.4
Union	7.2	14.3	12.7	11.7	16.2	14.8	10.4	5.9	6.9	71.4	22.6	4.4	0.4	0.1	23.7	93.8
Warren	6.0	14.3	12.3	11.1	17.3	15.8	10.6	5.7	6.7	93.9	3.0	2.2	0.1	(Z)	5.6	95.1
NEW MEXICO	7.0	13.8	15.4	12.4	13.6	14.6	11.0	6.7	5.5	84.5	2.4	1.3	10.2	0.1	43.4	96.8
Bernalillo	7.0	13.0	14.5	13.5	14.3	15.0	11.0	6.2	5.5	87.6	3.3	2.1	4.9	0.1	44.0	95.5
Catron	3.1	9.4	11.1	6.9	9.2	17.4	19.0	14.4	9.5	95.4	0.5	0.8	2.6	–	19.3	99.6
Chaves	7.2	14.2	16.5	11.1	12.2	14.1	10.4	7.3	7.2	94.2	2.6	0.8	1.3	0.1	46.8	96.5
Cibola	7.5	14.4	15.6	12.9	13.8	13.7	10.1	7.1	5.0	55.7	1.5	0.4	41.5	0.1	33.4	95.8
Colfax	5.3	11.7	12.9	8.8	12.0	16.4	14.5	9.7	8.6	96.5	0.5	0.4	1.9	–	47.0	101.3
Curry	8.7	15.8	15.4	14.1	13.7	12.0	8.8	6.2	5.4	86.0	7.4	2.5	1.5	0.1	33.7	98.5
De Baca	4.5	10.3	13.7	7.5	11.4	13.4	13.5	11.0	14.7	98.3	0.2	0.2	1.1	–	34.9	96.7
Dona Ana	8.0	14.7	18.5	13.5	12.4	12.5	9.0	6.3	5.1	93.6	2.4	0.9	1.6	0.2	64.8	97.2
Eddy	6.9	14.4	14.8	10.5	12.3	15.5	11.4	7.2	6.9	95.0	1.9	0.6	1.5	0.2	41.0	95.7
Grant	5.6	12.6	14.0	9.4	11.5	14.0	14.0	9.8	9.2	95.9	1.1	0.5	1.5	0.1	48.1	94.0
Guadalupe	5.5	10.3	15.0	11.6	15.7	16.0	10.5	8.8	6.6	96.2	1.5	1.0	1.3	–	79.2	125.9
Harding	1.9	8.9	13.2	6.5	10.4	17.4	14.6	12.0	15.0	97.7	0.4	–	1.8	–	43.0	101.1
Hidalgo	6.0	15.6	14.8	8.5	12.6	14.3	12.3	8.0	7.9	97.7	0.6	0.6	0.9	0.1	55.8	97.6
Lea	7.9	14.8	16.3	12.3	13.1	14.0	9.7	6.5	5.4	92.1	5.1	0.6	1.2	0.1	44.5	100.3
Lincoln	5.3	11.0	12.5	9.5	11.5	16.1	15.6	10.9	7.7	95.4	1.2	0.3	2.3	0.1	27.5	95.7
Los Alamos	4.9	12.3	12.7	7.6	14.7	18.6	16.8	7.1	5.3	92.0	0.6	4.9	0.8	–	13.3	101.2
Luna	7.2	15.3	14.2	10.7	11.5	11.6	10.7	10.0	8.8	95.8	1.8	0.5	1.2	–	59.6	94.6
McKinley	9.4	18.6	18.5	10.6	13.2	13.0	8.5	5.0	3.2	20.6	0.6	0.5	76.8	(Z)	11.5	92.0
Mora	4.2	11.8	16.0	8.5	12.8	17.2	13.8	9.1	6.7	98.0	0.4	0.1	1.4	0.1	78.7	101.9
Otero	6.8	14.5	15.5	12.6	14.3	13.2	10.2	7.6	5.5	86.0	4.3	1.4	6.2	0.1	33.7	100.1
Quay	5.2	11.7	13.3	8.9	11.5	15.0	14.4	10.5	9.4	95.5	1.1	1.4	1.6	0.2	38.1	92.7
Rio Arriba	8.1	13.4	14.6	11.0	13.6	15.6	11.7	6.9	5.0	82.8	0.7	0.2	15.5	0.3	71.8	96.8
Roosevelt	7.8	14.1	22.3	12.5	11.3	11.4	8.8	6.2	5.5	94.9	2.3	0.8	1.4	(Z)	35.4	96.0
Sandoval	6.2	14.5	14.9	12.4	14.6	15.7	10.7	5.7	5.2	79.4	2.2	1.1	15.5	0.2	31.5	94.8
San Juan	7.8	15.9	17.3	12.9	13.2	14.1	9.1	5.6	4.0	56.1	0.8	0.4	40.9	0.1	16.2	98.2
San Miguel	5.8	12.8	17.1	10.9	13.4	15.0	12.1	7.1	5.8	94.9	1.2	0.7	2.2	0.2	77.5	95.6
Santa Fe	5.5	11.8	13.2	12.4	14.5	16.9	13.9	6.9	6.9	92.8	1.1	1.1	3.5	0.1	49.4	96.6
Sierra	4.1	10.2	11.3	7.7	10.0	14.2	14.4	13.9	14.2	96.7	0.5	0.3	1.9	0.1	28.8	95.9
Socorro	6.0	13.5	19.1	12.1	12.4	14.2	10.9	7.1	4.8	83.7	1.1	1.7	12.4	0.1	46.8	102.8
Taos	5.7	11.2	12.7	10.2	13.9	17.3	14.6	8.4	6.0	90.7	0.7	0.5	7.1	0.2	55.2	96.3
Torrance	4.9	14.0	15.4	12.0	15.4	16.0	11.6	6.5	4.3	92.7	3.0	0.4	2.5	0.1	38.4	113.9
Union	5.5	12.8	13.8	8.3	11.2	16.9	12.5	9.8	9.1	98.1	–	0.6	1.2	0.1	36.2	97.8
Valencia	6.8	14.7	15.2	11.8	15.0	14.9	10.9	6.3	4.5	92.2	1.8	0.6	3.9	0.2	55.4	101.0
NEW YORK	6.5	13.0	13.6	13.5	15.4	14.4	10.6	6.4	6.7	73.8	17.4	6.7	0.5	0.1	16.1	94.0
Albany	5.3	11.7	16.3	13.1	14.3	14.7	10.9	6.2	7.5	82.4	12.1	3.8	0.2	(Z)	3.5	92.8
Allegany	5.2	11.5	22.7	11.5	11.5	13.5	10.3	7.0	6.9	97.0	1.1	1.0	0.3	–	1.1	101.0
Bronx	8.7	15.9	14.8	14.8	14.9	12.1	8.6	5.2	5.0	49.6	42.5	3.4	1.2	0.5	51.3	88.2
Broome	5.2	11.8	16.6	11.6	13.2	14.5	10.8	7.4	9.0	90.9	4.1	3.4	0.2	(Z)	2.4	93.9
Cattaraugus	5.9	12.9	15.5	11.3	13.1	15.5	11.1	7.2	7.4	94.8	1.3	0.6	2.5	(Z)	1.2	96.6
Cayuga	5.2	12.6	13.6	12.7	15.0	15.6	10.8	6.6	7.8	94.4	4.1	0.4	0.3	(Z)	2.2	102.6
Chautauqua	5.3	12.4	16.0	11.6	13.0	14.9	10.9	7.3	8.6	95.8	2.4	0.4	0.5	(Z)	4.6	96.4
Chemung	5.9	12.5	13.9	12.4	13.7	15.2	10.9	6.9	8.6	91.5	6.1	1.0	0.3	(Z)	2.1	98.2
Chenango	5.2	13.0	13.6	11.8	14.3	15.0	12.1	7.4	7.7	97.9	1.0	0.4	0.2	(Z)	1.6	97.1
Clinton	4.7	11.1	17.4	14.6	15.3	14.4	10.0	6.7	5.9	94.4	3.8	0.8	0.4	(Z)	2.8	103.9
Columbia	4.9	12.0	12.7	11.4	14.2	15.5	13.2	7.8	8.2	92.6	4.9	1.3	0.3	(Z)	3.1	99.0
Cortland	5.3	11.8	21.1	12.7	12.9	13.6	10.1	6.1	6.5	97.0	1.3	0.6	0.2	–	1.7	92.6
Delaware	4.5	11.4	14.8	10.0	12.8	14.7	13.1	9.2	9.6	96.7	1.8	0.6	0.3	–	2.7	97.7
Dutchess	5.5	13.1	15.1	12.4	15.8	15.2	10.7	6.3	6.0	85.0	10.2	3.2	0.3	(Z)	8.1	100.3
Erie	5.6	12.8	14.1	11.6	14.1	15.2	11.0	7.0	8.5	83.0	13.6	1.8	0.6	(Z)	3.6	92.5
Essex	4.4	10.9	12.7	13.2	15.1	15.6	11.7	8.0	8.3	95.2	3.3	0.6	0.3	0.1	2.4	108.2
Franklin	4.3	11.0	15.1	14.9	16.6	14.7	10.4	6.4	6.6	86.2	7.2	0.4	5.7	–	4.0	121.8
Fulton	5.3	12.5	12.9	12.4	14.7	14.9	11.7	6.9	8.8	96.4	2.0	0.8	0.2	(Z)	1.9	97.0
Genesee	5.4	13.3	13.4	10.9	15.4	15.6	11.1	7.0	7.9	95.3	2.6	0.6	0.7	(Z)	1.9	98.2
Greene	4.6	11.9	15.1	12.5	14.0	14.7	12.0	7.6	7.6	92.0	6.2	0.7	0.3	(Z)	4.8	106.4
Hamilton	4.3	9.6	10.6	10.4	12.3	16.7	15.8	10.3	10.0	98.2	1.1	0.2	0.2	(Z)	1.4	97.1
Herkimer	5.3	12.4	13.5	11.8	13.9	15.1	11.8	7.3	8.9	97.6	0.9	0.6	0.2	(Z)	1.4	94.5
Jefferson	7.0	13.7	16.0	17.1	14.1	12.4	8.1	5.4	6.1	91.1	5.6	1.1	0.5	0.2	4.2	106.8
Kings	7.9	14.0	13.6	14.8	14.6	13.3	9.7	6.0	6.1	50.6	38.3	8.9	0.5	0.1	19.9	89.0
Lewis	5.7	13.2	14.5	11.8	14.3	15.7	10.6	7.2	7.1	98.3	0.9	0.3	0.3	(Z)	0.8	99.4
Livingston	4.7	11.4	20.5	11.5	14.6	15.0	10.3	6.1	5.9	95.0	3.1	0.9	0.3	(Z)	2.3	99.1
Madison	5.2	12.3	18.1	11.0	14.4	15.3	11.1	6.4	6.3	96.4	1.7	0.7	0.6	(Z)	1.3	97.0
Monroe	6.0	13.4	15.0	12.0	14.5	15.0	10.9	6.1	7.1	80.8	14.7	2.8	0.3	(Z)	5.7	94.2
Montgomery	5.7	12.7	12.4	11.9	13.6	14.9	11.2	7.1	10.5	96.3	1.8	0.8	0.3	(Z)	8.1	92.7
Nassau	6.0	13.5	12.6	9.9	15.2	16.1	12.0	6.9	7.9	80.8	11.3	6.6	0.2	(Z)	11.7	94.0

See footnotes at end of table.

County and City Data Book: 2007

U.S. Census Bureau

Table B-3. Counties — **Population by Age, Race, Hispanic Origin, and Sex**—Con.

[Includes United States, states, and 3,141 counties/county equivalents defined as of February 22, 2005. For more information on these areas, see Appendix C, Geographic Information]

County	Under 5 years	5 to 14 years	15 to 24 years	25 to 34 years	35 to 44 years	45 to 54 years	55 to 64 years	65 to 74 years	75 years and over	White alone	Black or African American alone	Asian alone	American Indian and Alaska Native alone	Native Hawaiian and Other Pacific Islander alone	Hispanic or Latino origin[1] (percent)	Males per 100 females
NEW YORK—Con.																
New York	6.3	8.3	11.0	19.8	18.2	13.4	10.2	6.3	6.4	66.5	19.8	10.7	0.7	0.1	25.9	90.5
Niagara	5.5	12.8	13.7	11.4	14.4	15.9	11.1	7.0	8.2	90.6	6.5	0.8	1.0	(Z)	1.4	93.6
Oneida	5.4	12.5	14.1	12.1	14.6	14.5	11.1	7.0	8.7	91.3	6.1	1.4	0.2	(Z)	3.6	99.8
Onondaga	6.1	13.5	15.1	12.1	14.3	14.9	10.3	6.3	7.4	84.7	10.2	2.5	0.9	(Z)	2.7	92.7
Ontario	5.4	12.8	14.0	11.5	14.8	15.7	11.8	6.8	7.1	95.7	2.3	0.9	0.2	(Z)	2.4	96.1
Orange	6.8	15.2	14.6	13.4	15.7	14.7	9.7	5.0	4.9	85.5	10.2	2.2	0.4	0.1	14.9	101.4
Orleans	5.3	13.3	14.1	13.0	15.6	15.0	10.6	6.5	6.6	91.2	7.2	0.4	0.5	(Z)	3.9	98.0
Oswego	5.4	13.3	17.6	11.9	14.8	14.9	10.5	5.9	5.7	97.5	0.8	0.5	0.4	(Z)	1.4	98.2
Otsego	4.2	10.5	21.7	11.4	11.9	14.2	11.3	7.0	7.9	96.1	2.0	0.9	0.2	(Z)	2.1	92.5
Putnam	5.8	14.2	12.2	11.1	17.0	17.5	11.9	5.7	4.5	94.4	2.6	1.9	0.2	(Z)	9.2	100.7
Queens	6.6	12.0	12.0	15.1	16.5	14.3	10.3	6.4	6.7	55.1	21.1	20.9	0.7	0.1	26.1	94.1
Rensselaer	5.5	12.5	13.0	14.6	15.1	11.0	6.3	6.9		90.9	5.6	2.2	0.2	(Z)	2.5	97.7
Richmond	6.2	13.6	12.9	13.7	15.8	14.9	11.1	6.0	5.7	80.3	10.8	7.2	0.3	0.1	14.6	94.4
Rockland	7.5	14.9	13.4	10.9	14.2	14.5	12.0	7.0	5.6	80.2	11.9	6.4	0.3	0.1	12.2	96.7
St. Lawrence	5.3	11.4	20.0	12.4	13.3	14.0	10.3	6.7	6.6	95.1	2.5	0.9	0.9	(Z)	1.9	103.0
Saratoga	5.6	12.8	12.8	13.7	16.4	15.3	11.4	5.9	6.1	95.8	1.5	1.6	0.2	(Z)	1.8	97.6
Schenectady	6.0	13.0	13.2	11.8	14.5	14.9	11.1	6.5	9.0	86.0	8.6	3.3	0.3	(Z)	3.9	93.7
Schoharie	4.6	11.9	16.3	11.2	13.9	15.3	12.0	7.2	7.6	97.2	1.4	0.4	0.4	(Z)	2.0	98.5
Schuyler	4.9	12.7	13.3	11.5	14.3	15.6	12.6	7.8	7.3	96.8	1.7	0.3	0.5	(Z)	1.4	100.4
Seneca	5.1	11.9	13.9	14.0	14.6	14.9	11.0	6.9	7.6	93.2	4.9	1.0	0.2	(Z)	2.8	108.2
Steuben	5.7	13.1	12.8	12.4	14.0	15.4	11.5	7.4	7.7	96.5	1.5	1.1	0.3	(Z)	1.1	96.1
Suffolk	6.6	14.1	12.7	11.7	16.4	15.0	11.1	6.5	5.9	87.4	7.8	3.2	0.3	0.1	12.6	97.3
Sullivan	5.7	12.6	13.4	12.3	15.2	15.0	11.9	7.0	7.0	87.7	9.5	1.5	0.2	0.1	11.0	103.2
Tioga	5.6	13.3	13.3	11.2	14.6	16.5	11.5	7.4	6.6	97.5	0.8	0.8	0.2	—	1.3	98.3
Tompkins	4.2	8.4	31.9	16.3	10.1	11.2	8.2	4.5	5.3	84.3	3.8	9.6	0.3	(Z)	3.5	99.4
Ulster	5.0	12.0	14.6	12.3	15.3	15.8	11.7	6.5	6.7	90.6	6.2	1.6	0.3	(Z)	6.9	99.4
Warren	4.9	11.9	12.6	12.8	14.9	15.2	12.1	7.5	8.1	97.6	0.8	0.7	0.2	(Z)	1.5	95.1
Washington	4.8	12.1	13.8	13.5	15.5	15.0	11.2	7.2	6.9	95.6	3.3	0.4	0.2	(Z)	2.5	106.7
Wayne	5.9	14.1	13.0	10.9	16.0	15.9	11.5	6.6	6.1	94.8	3.2	0.6	0.3	(Z)	3.0	97.4
Westchester	6.7	13.9	12.0	11.4	15.8	15.3	11.1	6.6	7.2	77.8	14.9	5.5	0.4	0.1	18.0	92.7
Wyoming	4.8	11.8	13.9	13.8	16.5	15.8	10.7	6.3	6.4	93.1	5.8	0.5	0.3	0.1	3.1	119.6
Yates	5.7	13.9	15.2	10.6	12.8	14.3	11.8	8.0	7.7	98.7	0.7	0.3	(Z)	(Z)	1.2	95.0
NORTH CAROLINA	7.0	13.5	13.7	14.4	15.0	13.9	10.3	6.5	5.6	74.1	21.8	1.8	1.3	0.1	6.4	96.8
Alamance	6.7	13.2	14.2	13.7	14.7	13.5	10.2	6.9	6.9	78.5	18.9	1.2	0.5	(Z)	9.9	93.2
Alexander	6.0	13.5	11.3	14.5	15.7	14.2	12.0	7.4	5.5	92.9	5.3	1.1	0.1	(Z)	3.2	103.2
Alleghany	4.3	11.0	10.6	13.1	13.1	14.5	13.7	10.8	8.9	97.9	1.5	0.3	0.3	—	7.9	100.1
Anson	6.7	13.4	12.6	14.1	14.9	13.5	11.0	6.6	7.2	49.8	48.6	0.8	0.6	—	1.2	101.9
Ashe	5.0	10.9	10.5	13.2	13.8	14.7	13.0	9.8	9.0	98.4	0.8	0.2	0.4	—	3.1	98.8
Avery	5.0	10.3	14.4	14.4	14.6	12.8	11.6	8.6	8.1	94.8	3.9	0.4	0.4	(Z)	3.3	113.4
Beaufort	6.7	12.7	11.9	11.9	12.5	14.7	13.0	9.2	7.4	71.1	28.0	0.3	0.2	(Z)	3.8	90.8
Bertie	6.7	13.7	13.1	11.1	13.0	15.5	10.9	8.2	7.9	36.4	62.7	0.2	0.5	(Z)	1.3	87.2
Bladen	7.1	13.8	12.7	13.1	13.2	14.5	11.8	7.6	6.2	60.3	36.8	0.2	2.3	0.1	5.0	93.0
Brunswick	5.3	11.7	11.7	14.3	13.2	13.0	12.9	10.8	7.2	85.4	12.6	0.4	0.8	0.1	3.4	97.2
Buncombe	5.9	12.0	12.7	13.4	14.2	14.9	11.6	7.5	7.7	90.2	7.3	0.9	0.4	0.1	3.7	93.0
Burke	5.6	13.2	13.0	13.0	15.2	14.1	11.6	7.8	6.5	88.5	6.7	3.5	0.5	0.2	4.7	101.0
Cabarrus	7.5	14.3	12.8	15.0	15.8	13.8	9.9	5.8	5.1	82.9	14.5	1.3	0.4	(Z)	7.6	97.6
Caldwell	5.9	13.3	11.2	13.9	15.2	14.5	11.9	7.9	6.1	93.3	5.4	0.5	0.2	(Z)	3.7	97.9
Camden	5.8	12.3	14.5	15.3	15.6	14.0	11.2	6.1	5.1	84.0	14.4	0.9	0.3	—	1.2	97.4
Carteret	4.9	11.1	11.3	12.3	13.8	15.5	13.7	9.7	7.8	90.8	7.0	0.7	0.5	0.1	2.0	97.0
Caswell	5.6	12.7	11.7	13.1	15.1	15.5	12.3	7.7	6.4	64.6	34.7	0.2	0.2	(Z)	2.6	102.9
Catawba	6.8	13.5	12.0	14.8	15.2	14.0	10.9	6.9	5.8	87.4	8.3	3.1	0.3	(Z)	8.1	98.4
Chatham	6.1	12.5	11.4	16.5	15.2	14.0	10.5	6.8	7.1	82.6	14.2	1.9	0.4	0.2	11.3	98.2
Cherokee	5.3	11.5	10.2	12.5	12.1	13.9	14.4	10.8	9.5	95.2	1.9	0.4	1.5	—	1.2	93.2
Chowan	6.2	13.2	12.6	11.6	12.0	14.7	11.6	9.1	8.9	62.7	36.4	0.3	0.3	—	2.1	88.9
Clay	4.7	9.9	11.6	11.4	11.1	14.9	14.2	11.0	11.1	98.2	1.0	0.1	0.4	(Z)	0.9	94.9
Cleveland	6.3	14.2	12.7	12.9	14.4	14.0	11.5	7.3	6.7	77.6	20.9	0.8	0.2	—	1.6	92.0
Columbus	7.1	13.8	13.1	12.3	13.7	13.9	11.5	8.1	6.5	64.9	31.1	0.2	3.2	(Z)	2.8	91.4
Craven	8.6	14.0	14.0	12.7	12.5	13.4	10.2	8.0	6.8	72.3	24.6	1.2	0.5	0.1	3.6	99.1
Cumberland	8.9	15.9	16.7	14.2	14.6	12.5	8.5	5.3	3.5	56.2	36.7	2.1	1.7	0.3	6.4	99.5
Currituck	5.5	13.2	13.3	14.2	15.9	15.3	11.4	6.4	4.8	91.1	7.0	0.7	0.4	(Z)	1.9	98.8
Dare	6.0	11.3	11.1	12.6	15.6	17.0	12.7	8.2	5.6	95.5	3.0	0.5	0.3	(Z)	3.1	101.4
Davidson	6.3	13.7	11.7	13.7	15.9	14.4	11.3	7.1	5.9	88.5	9.3	1.0	0.5	(Z)	5.2	96.7
Davie	5.7	13.5	11.7	13.8	14.9	14.6	11.5	7.8	6.5	91.6	6.8	0.5	0.3	(Z)	5.3	97.7
Duplin	7.4	14.5	12.2	15.4	14.3	13.3	9.7	7.2	5.8	71.5	27.5	0.2	0.4	0.2	18.9	99.1
Durham	8.1	12.7	14.7	17.6	15.7	12.9	8.8	4.8	4.7	56.2	38.0	4.0	0.4	0.1	11.0	95.0
Edgecombe	7.0	14.6	13.5	12.1	14.0	15.7	10.9	6.6	5.6	41.6	57.5	0.3	0.3	(Z)	3.7	87.7
Forsyth	7.2	13.5	13.2	13.9	15.0	14.3	10.4	6.6	6.0	71.3	25.9	1.3	0.4	0.1	9.5	92.8
Franklin	6.2	13.8	13.2	15.8	16.4	14.1	9.9	5.9	4.7	70.7	27.9	0.3	0.5	(Z)	6.6	97.9

See footnotes at end of table.

Table B-3. Counties — **Population by Age, Race, Hispanic Origin, and Sex**—Con.

[Includes United States, states, and 3,141 counties/county equivalents defined as of February 22, 2005. For more information on these areas, see Appendix C, Geographic Information]

County	Age (percent)									One race (percent)					Hispanic or Latino origin[1] (percent)	Males per 100 females
	Under 5 years	5 to 14 years	15 to 24 years	25 to 34 years	35 to 44 years	45 to 54 years	55 to 64 years	65 to 74 years	75 years and over	White alone	Black or African American alone	Asian alone	American Indian and Alaska Native alone	Native Hawaiian and Other Pacific Islander alone		
NORTH CAROLINA—Con.																
Gaston	6.5	13.9	11.9	14.5	15.1	14.4	11.1	6.9	5.8	83.1	14.7	1.1	0.3	(Z)	4.8	94.3
Gates	5.4	13.9	13.7	11.0	16.1	15.0	11.4	7.4	6.1	62.3	36.3	0.5	0.5	(Z)	0.8	97.9
Graham	6.2	12.0	10.5	12.5	13.2	13.8	13.4	10.1	8.2	91.6	0.5	0.4	7.2	–	0.9	94.9
Granville	5.9	13.3	13.5	15.2	16.6	14.4	10.1	6.1	4.8	63.8	34.2	0.6	0.7	(Z)	5.8	115.1
Greene	6.1	13.9	13.5	16.0	14.6	14.3	10.0	6.3	5.3	59.0	40.2	0.1	0.4	(Z)	10.8	106.5
Guilford	6.8	13.3	14.2	14.1	15.1	14.1	10.4	6.2	6.8	64.3	30.9	3.1	0.5	(Z)	5.3	93.0
Halifax	6.9	13.9	13.1	11.6	13.7	14.4	11.1	7.8	7.6	41.6	53.9	0.6	3.5	(Z)	1.1	90.7
Harnett	7.2	15.0	14.6	17.5	15.5	12.0	8.6	5.3	4.3	74.3	22.4	0.9	0.9	0.1	8.1	97.7
Haywood	5.1	11.5	10.4	12.3	14.1	13.7	13.0	10.4	9.5	97.1	1.4	0.3	0.6	(Z)	1.7	92.7
Henderson	5.8	11.7	10.5	12.2	13.2	13.3	11.8	10.0	11.5	95.2	3.1	0.7	0.3	(Z)	8.0	94.7
Hertford	6.3	12.0	15.9	10.7	13.2	16.0	11.2	7.9	6.8	35.5	62.3	0.6	1.3	(Z)	1.9	94.3
Hoke	9.2	16.6	14.5	18.2	15.1	12.0	7.0	4.4	3.0	50.6	36.3	1.0	10.1	0.2	9.8	101.1
Hyde	5.2	10.6	12.2	13.3	14.7	16.4	11.3	8.6	7.6	63.9	35.3	0.4	0.4	–	1.9	114.6
Iredell	6.8	14.2	11.9	14.4	15.6	14.2	10.5	6.7	5.7	84.7	12.8	1.5	0.3	(Z)	4.8	97.6
Jackson	5.1	10.1	22.7	12.7	11.3	12.4	11.9	7.7	6.2	85.6	2.3	0.6	10.5	(Z)	2.0	95.1
Johnston	7.6	14.9	12.1	16.7	17.0	13.0	9.4	5.2	4.1	82.1	16.2	0.5	0.5	0.2	10.1	99.7
Jones	4.5	13.8	12.3	11.5	14.3	15.3	12.0	8.6	7.8	64.8	34.1	0.3	0.4	0.1	3.5	92.9
Lee	8.1	14.2	12.5	11.1	14.6	14.9	11.1	7.2	6.4	78.0	20.2	0.7	0.6	0.1	14.2	97.2
Lenoir	6.7	14.0	12.5	11.2	13.5	15.0	11.6	8.2	7.2	57.8	41.2	0.4	0.2	0.1	4.2	90.1
Lincoln	6.6	13.8	12.1	14.0	16.0	14.5	11.2	6.7	5.1	92.3	6.3	0.4	0.3	(Z)	8.1	98.8
McDowell	6.0	12.6	11.0	15.3	14.3	14.5	11.4	8.1	6.8	94.2	4.0	1.0	0.3	–	4.2	99.1
Macon	5.1	10.9	11.2	11.0	11.9	13.6	13.4	11.7	11.1	96.9	1.6	0.6	0.4	(Z)	2.3	91.7
Madison	5.4	11.8	14.2	12.5	13.2	14.1	12.3	8.8	7.8	98.0	1.0	0.4	0.3	(Z)	1.6	98.0
Martin	6.3	13.6	12.3	10.8	13.4	15.5	12.0	8.7	7.5	54.3	44.8	0.3	0.4	(Z)	2.3	86.0
Mecklenburg	8.1	14.1	12.9	16.2	17.2	14.0	9.1	4.6	3.8	64.8	29.8	3.8	0.4	0.1	9.1	97.3
Mitchell	5.1	11.2	11.2	11.7	14.0	14.5	13.2	10.2	8.9	98.5	0.4	0.2	0.6	–	3.0	96.1
Montgomery	7.2	14.1	11.9	14.1	13.4	14.3	11.6	7.0	6.4	77.4	19.7	1.8	0.7	(Z)	14.1	102.3
Moore	5.6	12.2	11.7	12.0	13.2	13.0	11.0	9.9	11.4	82.8	14.9	0.6	0.8	0.1	5.1	93.9
Nash	6.8	14.0	12.8	12.7	14.7	14.9	10.9	7.0	6.3	61.7	36.4	0.6	0.6	–	4.2	92.3
New Hanover	6.0	11.5	14.9	15.5	14.2	13.7	10.9	7.0	6.2	81.2	16.3	1.1	0.4	0.1	2.7	94.7
Northampton	5.8	12.9	12.7	10.2	13.0	14.8	12.2	9.2	9.1	40.2	57.8	0.2	0.4	0.1	0.8	91.2
Onslow	10.1	14.1	25.8	15.0	11.3	9.5	6.7	4.5	2.9	75.8	17.8	2.0	0.9	0.2	6.6	131.0
Orange	5.5	10.6	23.0	14.6	13.0	14.5	9.5	4.9	4.5	79.0	13.3	5.7	0.5	(Z)	5.2	90.6
Pamlico	4.1	10.9	12.0	10.4	13.2	15.2	14.1	11.0	9.0	75.8	23.0	0.5	0.6	–	1.4	102.0
Pasquotank	6.9	13.0	16.7	12.8	13.9	13.7	10.1	6.3	6.6	57.9	39.5	1.2	0.4	–	1.8	94.1
Pender	5.3	12.6	12.6	13.7	14.9	14.6	12.0	8.1	6.3	78.0	20.7	0.3	0.5	(Z)	4.6	100.2
Perquimans	5.6	11.6	12.8	11.0	13.1	13.9	12.9	10.0	9.1	74.2	25.2	0.2	0.1	–	0.7	91.5
Person	6.3	13.4	11.5	13.7	15.2	15.3	11.4	7.1	6.1	70.4	28.3	0.2	0.6	(Z)	2.4	94.5
Pitt	7.2	12.6	20.3	16.1	13.1	12.6	8.4	5.2	4.5	63.4	34.1	1.1	0.3	(Z)	4.2	91.0
Polk	4.7	11.5	10.0	11.1	12.9	14.0	12.7	10.2	12.9	93.3	5.6	0.3	0.3	(Z)	3.2	90.9
Randolph	6.7	13.9	11.8	14.0	15.6	14.2	11.1	6.9	5.7	92.3	5.6	0.8	0.5	(Z)	9.3	98.5
Richmond	6.9	14.5	14.4	13.2	13.3	13.2	10.8	7.1	6.5	65.5	30.9	0.8	1.9	(Z)	3.9	97.3
Robeson	8.1	15.7	14.8	15.0	13.7	13.0	9.6	5.8	4.4	35.5	24.3	0.4	38.5	0.2	7.4	96.5
Rockingham	6.1	13.1	11.1	13.3	14.5	15.1	11.7	7.9	7.3	79.1	19.6	0.3	0.3	0.1	4.5	94.0
Rowan	6.3	13.7	13.2	13.6	14.8	14.0	10.6	6.9	7.0	82.2	15.8	0.9	0.4	(Z)	5.7	97.5
Rutherford	6.3	13.5	11.4	13.0	14.2	13.8	11.8	8.2	8.0	87.5	11.2	0.4	0.3	(Z)	2.2	93.5
Sampson	7.4	14.5	13.0	15.0	14.1	13.3	9.9	7.0	5.8	67.5	28.9	0.4	1.8	0.7	15.1	98.7
Scotland	6.7	14.9	15.4	12.8	13.5	14.4	11.1	6.1	5.1	50.2	38.2	0.6	9.8	(Z)	1.2	94.3
Stanly	6.1	13.6	12.9	12.9	14.8	14.0	11.2	7.5	6.9	86.0	11.6	1.7	0.3	(Z)	3.1	98.6
Stokes	5.5	13.6	11.3	12.8	15.9	15.4	11.8	7.7	6.0	94.2	4.9	0.2	0.3	0.1	2.1	95.3
Surry	6.3	13.4	11.1	13.1	14.7	13.8	11.5	8.1	7.8	94.8	4.0	0.5	0.3	(Z)	8.5	95.6
Swain	6.5	13.1	13.0	12.3	13.2	14.0	12.0	9.0	7.0	68.2	2.4	0.3	27.3	(Z)	1.8	95.9
Transylvania	4.7	10.8	13.0	10.2	11.2	13.6	13.2	11.9	11.3	93.7	4.6	0.5	0.3	(Z)	1.1	93.3
Tyrrell	5.3	10.6	12.4	14.8	16.8	15.2	9.8	7.6	7.5	59.5	38.6	1.4	0.2	–	6.6	125.6
Union	7.7	15.2	13.5	16.3	16.5	13.2	9.1	4.9	3.5	85.6	11.9	1.1	0.5	0.1	8.8	100.5
Vance	8.1	15.2	12.9	13.1	13.7	14.3	10.5	6.8	5.6	48.9	50.1	0.5	0.2	(Z)	5.6	90.1
Wake	7.7	14.0	14.2	16.3	17.2	14.2	8.8	4.3	3.3	73.2	20.6	4.4	0.4	(Z)	7.4	99.4
Warren	5.5	12.1	13.6	12.0	13.0	14.4	11.8	9.2	8.3	39.9	54.7	0.2	4.8	(Z)	2.2	98.1
Washington	6.4	13.9	12.5	10.4	12.1	15.6	12.9	8.5	7.7	48.8	50.2	0.6	–	(Z)	2.7	90.6
Watauga	3.9	7.8	31.5	12.9	9.9	12.0	9.8	6.6	5.5	96.4	1.9	0.8	0.3	(Z)	1.9	99.4
Wayne	7.6	14.3	13.4	13.7	14.8	14.1	9.9	7.0	5.2	64.4	33.3	0.8	0.5	0.1	6.6	98.2
Wilkes	6.3	12.7	10.5	13.9	14.5	14.8	12.2	8.4	6.8	94.3	4.2	0.7	0.2	0.1	4.5	98.7
Wilson	7.0	14.1	12.8	13.5	14.0	14.6	10.8	7.0	6.1	58.9	39.5	0.7	0.3	(Z)	8.0	92.3
Yadkin	6.1	13.8	10.9	13.5	15.5	14.0	11.6	8.1	6.6	95.6	3.6	0.3	0.2	0.1	8.5	97.4
Yancey	4.9	11.8	10.9	12.3	13.5	14.7	13.2	9.8	8.9	98.3	1.0	0.2	0.4	–	4.4	98.9
NORTH DAKOTA	5.8	11.5	15.9	13.0	13.0	15.5	10.5	6.6	8.1	92.3	0.8	0.7	5.3	(Z)	1.6	99.6
Adams	3.2	9.6	11.4	6.0	12.2	17.2	13.8	11.5	15.1	98.2	1.1	0.3	0.3	(Z)	0.3	91.4
Barnes	4.7	10.3	15.1	10.2	11.2	16.5	11.9	8.2	11.8	97.8	0.8	0.3	0.8	–	0.7	93.8
Benson	9.8	16.9	16.1	9.9	12.2	12.7	10.0	5.8	6.5	48.1	0.1	(Z)	51.2	0.1	2.5	98.9
Billings	4.7	8.5	13.7	8.2	14.1	22.9	14.6	5.5	7.7	99.5	–	–	0.1	–	0.5	106.9
Bottineau	4.1	9.6	14.3	6.7	12.2	17.6	14.8	8.6	12.1	96.9	0.3	0.5	1.8	–	0.7	103.1

See footnotes at end of table.

Table B-3. Counties — **Population by Age, Race, Hispanic Origin, and Sex**—Con.

[Includes United States, states, and 3,141 counties/county equivalents defined as of February 22, 2005. For more information on these areas, see Appendix C, Geographic Information]

County	Population characteristics, 2005															
	Age (percent)									One race (percent)					His-panic or Latino origin[1] (per-cent)	Males per 100 females
	Under 5 years	5 to 14 years	15 to 24 years	25 to 34 years	35 to 44 years	45 to 54 years	55 to 64 years	65 to 74 years	75 years and over	White alone	Black or African American alone	Asian alone	American Indian and Alaska Native alone	Native Hawaiian and Other Pacific Islander alone		
NORTH DAKOTA—Con.																
Bowman	4.3	10.1	11.9	7.0	12.5	18.8	12.8	9.7	12.9	99.5	–	(Z)	0.2	–	0.7	93.6
Burke	4.0	9.7	9.1	5.1	12.5	17.8	18.0	10.9	12.9	99.3	0.3	0.1	0.2	–	0.6	100.6
Burleigh	5.7	11.3	14.4	15.7	13.6	15.9	10.5	6.2	6.7	94.4	0.3	0.5	3.9	(Z)	0.9	95.8
Cass	6.3	11.1	18.0	18.9	13.6	13.9	8.5	4.6	5.1	95.2	1.3	1.2	1.2	(Z)	1.5	100.9
Cavalier	3.9	10.2	11.3	3.7	11.4	18.9	15.6	11.9	13.1	98.8	0.2	0.1	0.5	–	0.8	99.8
Dickey	6.2	11.7	14.9	8.7	10.8	15.1	11.6	9.1	11.9	97.8	0.1	0.9	0.6	–	2.3	100.2
Divide	3.1	8.5	10.9	5.9	12.1	16.2	15.9	11.3	16.2	99.1	–	0.7	0.2	–	0.8	101.8
Dunn	4.3	12.1	13.6	7.6	12.6	18.9	13.7	8.4	8.9	86.8	0.1	0.2	12.9	–	1.1	105.0
Eddy	4.5	10.9	10.5	9.4	11.2	16.9	11.0	10.3	15.2	95.8	0.1	0.2	3.7	(Z)	1.1	92.7
Emmons	4.2	11.9	9.7	4.6	12.5	15.4	13.5	11.5	16.8	99.4	0.1	0.2	0.1	0.3	1.5	97.7
Foster	5.1	12.1	11.8	9.3	13.6	15.5	10.7	10.5	11.5	99.1	0.1	–	0.5	–	0.9	98.8
Golden Valley	3.6	13.1	14.0	5.9	11.4	17.2	12.1	7.8	14.8	98.4	0.2	0.1	0.9	–	1.2	89.0
Grand Forks	5.9	10.8	24.8	15.7	12.3	12.6	8.2	4.6	5.2	93.1	1.3	1.2	2.7	0.1	2.4	104.3
Grant	2.8	9.7	11.9	6.8	11.2	17.5	15.2	10.6	14.4	97.9	–	0.3	1.6	–	1.1	105.3
Griggs	3.5	10.1	10.6	6.6	10.9	18.7	14.7	9.0	15.8	99.4	–	0.2	0.4	–	0.6	99.4
Hettinger	3.0	9.5	12.3	6.4	11.1	17.7	14.7	11.9	13.5	98.4	0.2	0.1	1.2	0.1	0.3	105.3
Kidder	4.5	9.8	10.7	5.7	12.9	19.3	13.5	10.0	13.6	99.5	0.2	0.1	0.2	–	1.5	103.9
LaMoure	4.6	10.4	11.2	7.4	11.5	17.8	12.6	10.4	14.1	99.5	0.1	0.1	0.2	–	0.6	102.8
Logan	4.2	10.8	10.2	5.6	12.2	14.9	13.8	11.9	16.4	98.9	0.1	0.4	0.1	–	0.8	98.0
McHenry	4.8	10.2	11.2	8.9	12.3	18.0	13.2	9.3	12.1	99.0	0.2	(Z)	0.5	–	0.9	101.7
McIntosh	3.3	8.7	10.0	5.2	10.9	15.1	12.1	13.7	21.0	99.2	–	0.4	0.1	–	1.0	91.1
McKenzie	5.0	13.7	15.0	6.8	12.2	18.6	13.4	7.2	8.0	76.9	0.3	0.1	22.0	0.1	1.1	100.1
McLean	4.0	10.4	11.7	6.6	11.6	20.0	15.5	8.8	11.4	92.6	(Z)	0.2	6.2	–	1.7	96.5
Mercer	4.1	11.5	14.2	6.0	14.3	22.2	12.8	7.0	8.1	95.9	(Z)	0.3	2.6	0.4	0.6	101.0
Morton	5.6	12.6	12.7	12.3	14.1	16.9	11.2	6.8	7.7	95.1	0.2	0.5	2.9	–	1.0	98.9
Mountrail	6.6	13.0	13.6	10.2	11.1	16.3	12.3	7.8	9.0	66.9	0.2	0.3	31.7	(Z)	2.6	97.5
Nelson	3.6	8.6	11.8	6.2	11.2	16.3	14.1	11.9	16.4	98.6	0.2	0.5	0.6	–	0.7	96.8
Oliver	4.6	11.0	13.3	4.1	12.0	23.0	18.2	6.5	7.4	97.2	0.2	0.1	2.1	–	0.8	108.2
Pembina	4.4	10.5	12.5	8.3	12.6	18.2	13.5	8.2	11.8	96.2	0.5	0.3	1.8	–	3.5	101.6
Pierce	5.4	11.1	9.7	7.3	13.5	16.9	11.6	10.0	14.6	97.7	0.3	0.4	1.4	–	0.8	95.3
Ramsey	5.9	11.9	12.4	8.9	13.8	16.9	12.0	7.5	10.8	90.2	0.4	0.5	7.5	(Z)	0.8	99.3
Ransom	5.1	11.8	11.0	12.0	13.6	15.9	11.1	7.9	11.6	98.8	0.2	0.3	0.3	–	1.4	104.5
Renville	4.3	10.4	10.6	9.1	13.2	18.8	13.1	9.5	11.1	97.9	0.8	0.6	0.6	–	0.8	103.5
Richland	5.4	11.7	18.5	10.7	12.7	16.5	9.5	6.2	8.7	95.9	0.5	0.4	2.5	(Z)	1.4	110.5
Rolette	9.8	16.2	16.5	11.5	13.6	13.5	9.0	5.2	4.7	25.1	0.1	0.5	72.8	–	0.9	95.5
Sargent	4.9	12.8	11.0	8.7	13.5	17.7	13.6	7.7	10.0	98.8	0.2	(Z)	0.5	–	0.9	109.7
Sheridan	2.7	9.0	10.0	4.0	10.3	19.4	16.9	11.7	16.1	99.3	0.1	–	0.5	–	0.3	102.8
Sioux	11.7	18.4	17.7	13.2	14.3	10.7	8.0	3.3	2.6	17.4	0.2	–	82.1	(Z)	1.7	102.9
Slope	4.8	11.1	11.8	5.6	13.4	24.5	12.1	9.9	6.6	99.9	–	–	0.1	–	–	120.9
Stark	5.3	11.5	16.8	11.4	12.3	15.9	10.5	7.3	9.0	97.9	0.2	0.3	1.0	(Z)	1.4	96.5
Steele	3.0	12.4	13.2	6.6	14.1	18.1	14.2	8.8	9.7	98.9	0.2	(Z)	0.8	–	0.2	105.4
Stutsman	4.7	10.4	14.4	10.2	13.2	17.6	11.8	7.4	10.2	97.5	0.4	0.5	1.3	(Z)	1.2	97.7
Towner	3.5	9.7	11.2	4.5	13.8	19.3	14.8	9.5	13.6	97.4	0.1	0.1	2.4	–	0.2	96.8
Traill	4.7	11.5	16.0	10.2	13.0	15.5	11.1	7.6	10.4	98.6	0.2	0.2	0.9	–	2.5	101.9
Walsh	5.3	11.4	11.8	8.3	13.5	17.3	12.7	8.1	11.5	97.7	0.4	0.2	1.3	(Z)	7.7	99.3
Ward	7.3	13.1	15.1	14.0	13.6	14.1	9.1	6.2	7.4	92.8	2.2	0.8	2.3	0.1	2.6	98.6
Wells	3.7	9.8	10.8	4.5	12.8	17.6	13.6	11.7	15.5	99.1	0.2	0.3	0.3	–	0.5	95.5
Williams	5.3	11.9	12.5	10.7	12.5	18.6	11.7	7.6	9.3	92.7	0.2	0.3	4.8	(Z)	1.3	93.9
OHIO	6.4	13.4	14.1	12.7	14.5	15.0	10.6	6.5	6.9	85.1	11.9	1.4	0.2	(Z)	2.3	95.1
Adams	6.5	13.3	13.4	14.7	13.7	14.3	10.7	7.1	6.2	98.0	0.3	0.1	0.6	(Z)	0.7	96.9
Allen	7.0	13.7	14.5	12.1	13.1	14.8	10.6	6.5	7.6	85.7	11.8	0.8	0.2	(Z)	1.6	98.0
Ashland	5.9	13.1	16.5	12.1	13.1	14.4	10.7	7.0	7.2	97.7	1.0	0.7	0.1	(Z)	0.7	95.9
Ashtabula	5.8	13.5	13.0	12.5	14.2	15.4	11.1	7.0	7.6	95.0	3.3	0.3	0.2	(Z)	2.7	96.2
Athens	4.8	8.8	34.3	13.9	10.1	10.5	7.9	4.9	4.7	93.8	2.3	2.3	0.3	(Z)	1.1	94.9
Auglaize	5.9	14.1	13.5	11.3	14.5	15.5	10.2	6.6	8.3	98.1	0.3	0.5	0.2	(Z)	0.8	96.4
Belmont	4.8	11.0	12.8	12.1	13.7	16.2	11.7	7.8	9.9	94.6	4.2	0.4	0.1	(Z)	0.5	98.0
Brown	6.2	14.2	13.2	13.7	15.4	14.7	10.4	6.7	5.7	98.0	1.1	0.2	0.2	(Z)	0.4	97.7
Butler	6.6	13.5	16.6	13.3	14.7	14.6	9.7	5.7	5.2	90.0	6.6	2.0	0.2	0.1	2.1	96.1
Carroll	5.3	12.6	12.6	12.3	13.9	15.8	12.5	7.6	7.3	98.5	0.6	0.1	0.3	(Z)	0.7	97.0
Champaign	6.2	13.6	13.2	12.2	14.8	14.7	12.2	6.7	6.3	95.8	2.5	0.4	0.3	(Z)	0.8	96.9
Clark	6.3	13.3	13.4	11.9	13.4	14.6	12.0	7.4	7.7	88.5	9.0	0.6	0.3	(Z)	1.5	93.0
Clermont	6.9	14.5	13.1	13.7	15.9	15.4	10.2	5.5	4.8	96.9	1.3	0.8	0.2	(Z)	1.1	97.1
Clinton	6.7	13.7	14.6	13.7	14.6	14.7	10.0	6.0	6.1	95.9	2.4	0.6	0.2	–	1.3	97.3
Columbiana	5.5	12.4	12.7	12.5	14.1	16.1	11.4	7.3	7.9	96.4	2.4	0.3	0.2	(Z)	1.3	99.8
Coshocton	6.1	13.3	13.3	12.2	13.9	15.2	11.3	7.4	7.3	97.5	1.2	0.4	0.2	(Z)	0.8	96.6
Crawford	6.1	13.0	12.3	12.1	13.7	15.0	11.9	7.9	8.1	98.3	0.7	0.4	0.2	(Z)	1.0	93.3
Cuyahoga	6.4	13.5	12.6	11.5	14.7	15.5	10.7	6.8	8.4	67.2	29.1	2.2	0.2	(Z)	3.8	90.0
Darke	6.0	13.6	13.1	11.6	14.1	14.6	11.4	7.2	8.3	98.4	0.5	0.3	0.2	(Z)	1.0	96.6
Defiance	6.3	13.4	13.8	12.1	13.1	15.7	11.5	6.8	7.4	96.9	1.7	0.4	0.3	(Z)	7.6	98.1

See footnotes at end of table.

Table B-3. Counties — **Population by Age, Race, Hispanic Origin, and Sex**—Con.

[Includes United States, states, and 3,141 counties/county equivalents defined as of February 22, 2005. For more information on these areas, see Appendix C, Geographic Information]

County	Under 5 years	5 to 14 years	15 to 24 years	25 to 34 years	35 to 44 years	45 to 54 years	55 to 64 years	65 to 74 years	75 years and over	White alone	Black or African American alone	Asian alone	American Indian and Alaska Native alone	Native Hawaiian and Other Pacific Islander alone	Hispanic or Latino origin[1] (percent)	Males per 100 females
OHIO—Con.																
Delaware	7.2	14.2	14.5	17.1	16.4	14.2	8.7	4.3	3.5	91.3	3.6	3.5	0.1	0.1	1.6	98.1
Erie	5.8	12.7	12.7	10.3	13.4	15.9	12.7	8.0	8.4	89.4	8.5	0.5	0.2	–	2.4	94.5
Fairfield	5.9	13.8	14.1	14.6	15.3	14.9	10.5	5.8	5.2	91.8	5.9	0.9	0.2	(Z)	1.2	99.4
Fayette	6.4	13.4	12.3	13.0	14.1	14.9	11.5	7.4	6.9	96.3	2.3	0.5	0.1	–	1.4	96.4
Franklin	7.7	13.6	14.5	15.8	15.6	14.0	9.0	5.0	4.8	74.2	19.8	3.6	0.3	0.1	3.3	95.9
Fulton	6.1	14.5	13.7	11.7	14.7	16.0	10.7	6.2	6.5	98.1	0.4	0.5	0.3	0.1	6.3	97.3
Gallia	6.1	12.7	14.3	12.4	13.6	15.2	11.3	7.9	6.6	95.5	2.8	0.4	0.4	–	0.8	95.7
Geauga	5.6	14.2	13.8	9.4	13.3	17.0	13.1	7.2	6.4	97.3	1.5	0.5	0.1	–	0.7	97.3
Greene	5.7	12.2	18.8	11.7	13.3	14.9	11.2	6.6	5.7	89.1	6.4	2.5	0.3	(Z)	1.6	96.3
Guernsey	6.1	13.6	12.8	12.5	14.1	14.9	11.3	7.7	7.1	96.5	1.7	0.3	0.3	–	0.8	95.2
Hamilton	7.0	13.4	14.2	11.9	14.6	15.1	10.2	6.3	7.2	71.9	24.8	1.8	0.2	(Z)	1.5	92.0
Hancock	6.0	13.4	14.8	13.1	13.9	14.8	10.6	6.4	7.1	96.0	1.4	1.6	0.2	–	3.3	95.4
Hardin	5.8	12.5	20.2	13.3	12.4	13.0	10.1	6.3	6.5	97.7	0.9	0.5	0.2	(Z)	1.0	96.8
Harrison	5.5	12.0	11.5	11.8	13.6	16.3	12.2	8.2	8.8	96.9	2.1	0.1	0.1	–	0.4	95.1
Henry	6.2	13.9	13.9	12.2	14.0	15.3	10.5	6.8	7.3	98.2	0.8	0.5	0.2	(Z)	5.9	98.5
Highland	6.9	14.0	12.8	14.2	13.8	13.8	10.7	7.2	6.6	97.1	1.5	0.5	0.2	(Z)	0.6	95.1
Hocking	6.1	13.1	13.0	13.1	14.1	15.1	12.0	7.3	6.1	97.5	1.1	0.2	0.2	–	0.6	99.8
Holmes	10.0	18.4	14.6	15.2	12.3	11.1	8.0	5.5	5.0	99.2	0.4	(Z)	(Z)	(Z)	0.8	100.2
Huron	6.9	14.8	13.4	13.3	14.2	14.5	10.3	6.3	6.4	97.6	1.0	0.3	0.2	(Z)	4.5	96.4
Jackson	6.0	13.2	13.8	14.0	14.3	14.6	10.5	6.8	6.8	98.0	0.7	0.2	0.4	(Z)	1.2	93.5
Jefferson	4.9	11.3	13.2	10.4	12.9	16.4	12.4	8.8	9.7	92.8	5.8	0.4	0.2	(Z)	0.7	91.4
Knox	6.0	12.6	17.0	12.4	13.4	14.4	10.3	6.9	6.9	97.8	0.9	0.4	0.1	(Z)	0.8	95.0
Lake	5.5	12.7	12.2	11.7	15.1	16.3	12.0	7.1	7.5	95.1	2.6	1.1	0.1	0.1	2.5	95.2
Lawrence	5.8	12.8	13.0	13.4	14.5	14.4	11.7	7.6	6.9	96.6	2.1	0.4	0.1	–	0.6	93.1
Licking	6.4	13.6	13.9	12.5	14.9	15.1	11.4	6.6	5.6	95.4	2.5	0.7	0.3	(Z)	0.9	95.7
Logan	6.5	14.0	13.1	12.5	14.0	15.0	10.9	7.0	7.0	96.4	1.7	0.5	0.2	(Z)	0.8	96.3
Lorain	6.2	14.0	13.9	12.5	14.6	15.1	10.8	6.3	6.5	88.3	8.6	0.8	0.3	0.1	7.3	96.5
Lucas	7.0	13.9	14.6	13.2	13.8	14.6	10.2	5.9	6.8	78.7	17.8	1.4	0.3	(Z)	5.1	93.9
Madison	5.9	12.8	14.0	14.1	16.6	15.0	10.2	6.1	5.5	91.7	6.7	0.7	0.2	(Z)	0.9	119.3
Mahoning	5.3	12.3	15.5	10.7	12.6	15.6	11.2	7.2	9.6	82.1	15.9	0.6	0.2	0.1	3.2	92.1
Marion	5.8	12.6	13.3	13.4	15.1	15.2	11.1	6.5	6.9	92.4	6.1	0.6	0.2	(Z)	1.3	108.2
Medina	6.0	14.1	13.4	12.6	15.8	15.9	11.3	5.9	5.2	97.0	1.1	0.9	0.2	(Z)	1.1	97.4
Meigs	5.9	11.9	12.8	12.5	14.4	15.4	12.0	7.6	7.5	98.1	0.9	0.2	0.1	–	0.6	95.9
Mercer	6.5	15.1	14.1	11.4	13.3	15.2	9.9	6.7	7.8	98.8	0.2	0.5	0.2	(Z)	1.4	101.1
Miami	6.1	13.2	13.3	12.0	14.5	15.2	12.0	7.1	6.7	95.7	2.0	1.1	0.2	–	1.1	96.6
Monroe	4.8	11.6	12.4	10.9	13.2	15.8	13.7	9.1	8.4	99.2	0.3	0.1	0.1	(Z)	0.5	98.4
Montgomery	6.6	13.1	13.9	12.3	14.2	14.6	11.0	7.0	7.3	76.1	20.7	1.5	0.2	(Z)	1.6	93.1
Morgan	5.9	13.0	12.7	11.8	13.9	14.3	12.1	8.9	7.4	94.2	3.3	0.1	0.2	(Z)	0.4	97.0
Morrow	6.0	13.6	13.8	13.6	14.8	15.6	11.1	6.4	5.1	98.4	0.5	0.2	0.3	–	0.9	99.5
Muskingum	6.1	13.7	13.9	12.5	14.0	14.4	10.7	7.1	7.6	93.9	4.1	0.3	0.2	(Z)	0.6	92.4
Noble	4.6	10.8	16.7	15.4	15.8	13.8	9.1	7.2	6.5	92.4	7.1	0.2	0.2	–	0.6	134.5
Ottawa	4.9	11.4	12.8	10.8	13.6	16.3	13.1	8.5	8.5	98.2	0.8	0.3	0.3	(Z)	3.8	98.1
Paulding	5.8	13.7	13.4	11.6	14.3	15.6	12.0	6.8	6.8	97.7	1.2	0.2	0.2	(Z)	3.4	97.4
Perry	6.3	14.9	13.7	12.7	14.9	14.6	10.6	6.4	5.9	98.7	0.3	0.1	0.2	(Z)	0.5	98.9
Pickaway	5.6	12.7	14.1	14.1	15.9	14.8	10.9	6.6	5.4	93.5	5.2	0.3	0.3	(Z)	0.8	113.6
Pike	6.5	13.9	13.2	14.4	14.5	13.8	9.8	6.8	7.1	96.9	1.0	0.3	0.7	(Z)	0.7	94.5
Portage	5.1	12.2	19.1	13.0	14.0	14.5	10.5	6.1	5.5	93.8	3.6	1.2	0.2	(Z)	0.8	95.0
Preble	5.8	13.1	13.0	12.2	14.8	15.7	11.7	7.0	6.8	98.4	0.5	0.4	0.2	(Z)	0.6	98.2
Putnam	6.5	14.9	15.2	10.6	14.0	15.3	9.5	6.4	7.5	99.1	0.3	0.2	0.2	(Z)	4.7	100.2
Richland	6.1	12.9	13.0	12.3	14.0	15.2	11.4	7.4	7.5	88.4	9.5	0.6	0.2	(Z)	1.1	101.3
Ross	5.8	12.5	12.8	14.4	15.9	15.3	10.7	6.7	5.9	91.9	6.4	0.4	0.3	(Z)	0.8	109.1
Sandusky	6.7	13.4	13.2	12.2	13.7	15.7	10.9	6.8	7.5	95.5	2.9	0.4	0.1	(Z)	7.6	96.6
Scioto	6.3	12.6	14.0	13.6	13.6	14.1	10.7	7.6	7.5	95.2	2.6	0.4	0.7	(Z)	0.8	94.9
Seneca	6.2	13.2	15.3	11.8	13.1	15.6	10.6	6.7	7.4	96.4	1.9	0.5	0.2	(Z)	3.8	98.5
Shelby	7.4	15.2	13.0	12.6	14.8	14.7	10.2	5.9	6.2	95.9	1.7	1.1	0.2	(Z)	1.1	99.2
Stark	5.9	13.1	13.3	11.4	13.7	15.5	11.6	7.2	8.2	90.2	7.5	0.6	0.2	(Z)	1.0	93.1
Summit	6.1	13.5	13.0	12.2	14.8	15.6	10.9	6.5	7.4	82.8	13.9	1.7	0.2	(Z)	1.1	93.3
Trumbull	5.5	12.8	12.5	11.4	13.6	15.6	12.4	7.6	8.6	90.3	8.2	0.4	0.2	(Z)	0.9	94.4
Tuscarawas	6.3	13.0	12.6	12.5	13.5	15.5	11.2	7.2	8.1	97.9	0.8	0.3	0.2	0.1	1.0	96.1
Union	6.9	14.6	12.7	14.9	17.2	14.9	9.4	5.0	4.3	95.1	3.1	0.9	0.1	(Z)	1.1	93.0
Van Wert	5.8	13.6	12.8	12.5	13.6	15.3	11.2	7.0	8.2	98.2	0.9	0.2	0.1	–	1.8	95.8
Vinton	6.6	14.0	13.0	14.4	14.0	14.9	10.8	6.8	5.4	98.5	0.4	0.1	0.5	–	0.6	99.2
Warren	6.6	14.5	13.4	15.2	17.2	14.6	9.0	5.2	4.2	92.9	3.2	2.7	0.1	0.1	1.5	102.0
Washington	5.4	12.2	13.6	11.0	13.8	16.1	12.0	8.0	7.9	97.5	1.1	0.4	0.2	(Z)	0.6	95.1
Wayne	6.8	14.0	14.7	12.2	13.8	14.8	10.6	6.6	6.4	96.8	1.5	0.8	0.2	(Z)	1.0	97.9
Williams	5.7	13.3	13.0	12.8	14.1	15.8	10.9	6.7	7.7	97.9	0.9	0.5	0.3	(Z)	3.0	99.3
Wood	5.2	11.6	22.5	12.9	12.6	14.0	9.8	5.6	5.8	96.1	1.6	1.2	0.3	(Z)	3.8	94.1
Wyandot	6.2	13.0	13.0	12.4	13.7	15.3	10.7	7.4	8.3	98.9	0.3	0.5	0.1	–	1.8	96.6

See footnotes at end of table.

Table B-3. Counties — **Population by Age, Race, Hispanic Origin, and Sex**—Con.

[Includes United States, states, and 3,141 counties/county equivalents defined as of February 22, 2005. For more information on these areas, see Appendix C, Geographic Information]

County	Age (percent) Under 5 years	5 to 14 years	15 to 24 years	25 to 34 years	35 to 44 years	45 to 54 years	55 to 64 years	65 to 74 years	75 years and over	One race (percent) White alone	Black or African American alone	Asian alone	American Indian and Alaska Native alone	Native Hawaiian and Other Pacific Islander alone	Hispanic or Latino origin[1] (percent)	Males per 100 females
OKLAHOMA	6.9	13.0	15.0	13.5	13.6	14.2	10.6	7.1	6.1	78.5	7.7	1.5	8.1	0.1	6.6	97.7
Adair	8.4	15.0	14.5	13.8	13.4	13.0	9.9	6.7	5.2	51.0	0.3	0.3	42.3	(Z)	3.6	97.3
Alfalfa	3.5	9.1	12.6	9.9	17.1	16.0	11.7	10.1	10.1	91.2	4.6	0.2	3.0	(Z)	3.1	135.6
Atoka	5.6	11.8	13.6	14.9	14.7	14.3	11.3	7.7	6.1	77.3	5.9	0.3	11.5	–	2.5	119.1
Beaver	5.8	13.5	13.7	8.2	13.7	16.0	12.8	8.1	8.2	97.6	0.5	0.1	1.3	0.1	14.0	101.5
Beckham	7.3	12.8	14.0	12.7	13.0	15.3	10.0	7.5	7.3	93.7	2.4	0.5	2.1	–	6.3	95.8
Blaine	5.1	10.6	15.6	15.4	14.8	14.0	9.5	7.1	7.8	77.4	8.6	1.7	9.2	0.8	7.8	137.0
Bryan	6.3	12.6	15.6	14.1	12.6	13.2	10.9	7.7	7.0	81.4	1.6	0.6	12.3	(Z)	3.7	97.0
Caddo	7.0	13.6	15.6	11.4	13.6	13.7	10.5	7.7	6.7	68.6	3.3	0.2	24.2	0.1	7.7	99.4
Canadian	5.9	13.3	15.2	13.6	15.1	15.8	10.8	6.1	4.2	88.1	2.5	2.4	4.5	(Z)	4.8	100.0
Carter	6.8	13.1	13.2	12.6	13.0	15.2	10.7	8.0	7.5	79.1	7.7	0.7	8.5	(Z)	3.7	93.6
Cherokee	6.7	12.7	20.6	13.3	12.1	12.2	10.0	7.1	5.3	58.5	1.6	0.4	32.7	(Z)	5.4	97.6
Choctaw	6.9	12.6	13.8	11.7	12.7	13.6	11.8	8.8	8.0	69.6	11.0	0.2	15.0	(Z)	2.2	91.1
Cimarron	5.9	13.8	13.2	8.0	12.5	14.7	12.1	9.7	10.0	97.3	0.8	0.2	1.2	–	19.2	96.7
Cleveland	5.6	12.0	19.2	15.7	14.3	14.2	9.9	5.4	3.7	84.0	4.3	3.3	4.4	0.1	4.9	101.4
Coal	6.3	13.8	12.3	12.0	13.0	14.1	10.8	8.8	8.9	76.6	0.6	0.3	17.6	–	2.3	98.9
Comanche	8.3	14.9	17.0	14.1	14.1	12.4	8.5	6.0	4.5	67.8	19.1	2.1	5.8	0.4	9.1	106.7
Cotton	5.7	13.6	12.8	11.4	14.1	14.1	12.0	8.0	8.3	86.6	3.5	0.1	7.8	0.1	5.4	97.6
Craig	6.4	11.8	13.1	11.9	14.5	14.8	11.8	8.1	7.5	70.4	3.1	0.3	16.3	(Z)	1.6	102.0
Creek	6.1	13.5	13.5	12.0	13.7	15.1	12.0	8.0	6.0	83.2	2.7	0.4	9.0	(Z)	2.3	96.4
Custer	6.9	11.1	22.5	11.6	11.8	12.8	9.4	7.2	6.8	87.8	3.0	1.3	5.7	0.1	10.9	95.2
Delaware	5.5	12.4	12.7	12.2	12.5	13.5	13.0	10.5	7.7	71.1	0.3	0.4	22.3	0.1	2.2	97.3
Dewey	5.2	10.6	13.4	8.6	12.0	15.3	14.0	9.9	11.0	93.0	0.2	0.1	5.3	–	3.2	97.9
Ellis	6.0	10.6	12.3	8.4	11.4	16.4	13.8	10.7	10.3	98.1	–	0.1	1.3	–	3.2	97.4
Garfield	7.2	12.8	12.9	12.4	13.2	15.0	10.6	8.0	7.8	90.5	3.4	1.0	2.3	0.5	5.9	95.4
Garvin	6.2	12.5	12.7	12.6	12.9	14.6	11.1	9.0	8.5	86.5	2.9	0.3	7.6	0.1	4.3	93.0
Grady	6.1	13.1	15.7	13.3	13.9	14.9	10.8	6.8	5.4	88.6	3.1	0.4	5.1	(Z)	3.6	96.8
Grant	4.0	12.1	13.8	8.5	12.6	16.4	12.3	10.0	10.3	96.0	0.1	0.3	2.9	(Z)	2.2	93.8
Greer	5.0	9.0	14.3	14.3	14.4	13.7	10.1	8.6	10.6	85.4	10.4	0.3	2.8	–	8.1	133.8
Harmon	5.5	12.3	14.8	9.2	12.3	16.0	11.2	9.2	9.4	87.4	10.4	0.5	1.6	(Z)	22.6	95.5
Harper	4.8	10.5	13.5	8.1	12.0	18.0	12.5	10.8	9.8	98.7	(Z)	0.1	1.1	0.1	10.1	96.9
Haskell	6.6	13.2	13.1	12.5	11.9	13.4	12.1	9.1	8.1	79.6	0.7	0.3	14.5	–	1.9	97.6
Hughes	5.7	11.8	13.5	13.2	13.8	13.6	11.5	8.7	8.1	74.6	4.6	0.3	16.3	–	3.0	107.0
Jackson	8.1	15.7	14.5	11.2	14.5	13.6	9.9	6.9	5.7	86.5	7.9	1.4	2.0	0.2	18.4	99.7
Jefferson	5.7	12.6	12.3	11.6	12.4	14.5	11.2	10.2	9.5	89.7	1.1	1.5	5.6	–	8.4	94.3
Johnston	5.9	13.1	14.1	11.9	12.3	14.7	12.0	9.0	6.9	77.7	2.0	0.3	15.5	–	3.1	96.3
Kay	7.1	13.4	13.4	10.2	12.7	14.9	11.4	8.1	8.7	85.8	1.9	0.7	8.3	(Z)	5.2	94.9
Kingfisher	6.5	12.8	14.7	10.9	13.5	16.1	10.4	7.7	7.4	93.5	1.6	0.2	2.8	–	9.4	97.0
Kiowa	5.8	11.7	13.8	10.3	12.7	14.9	11.9	9.0	10.0	85.8	4.9	0.4	7.0	0.1	8.5	97.9
Latimer	5.3	13.2	17.1	11.0	13.4	12.6	11.7	8.7	7.2	75.2	1.3	0.2	18.4	–	2.0	97.9
Le Flore	7.2	13.1	14.0	13.7	13.2	13.6	11.3	7.7	6.1	81.8	2.3	0.3	11.2	(Z)	5.6	101.2
Lincoln	5.9	13.4	14.2	11.9	13.6	15.1	11.9	8.0	5.9	87.4	2.6	0.3	6.5	(Z)	1.9	97.8
Logan	5.7	12.0	19.4	12.6	12.8	14.9	10.8	6.8	5.0	82.8	11.3	0.5	2.9	0.1	3.5	98.9
Love	5.6	12.6	13.3	12.5	12.8	14.5	12.9	8.8	7.2	88.7	1.9	0.3	6.7	–	9.0	98.0
McClain	6.3	12.9	14.0	12.4	14.6	15.2	11.5	7.9	5.2	89.6	0.8	0.2	6.0	(Z)	5.4	99.2
McCurtain	7.0	14.3	13.7	12.2	13.2	14.1	11.8	7.7	5.9	72.0	8.6	0.3	14.5	(Z)	3.7	93.7
McIntosh	5.7	11.2	12.5	10.6	11.9	13.3	13.1	11.9	9.7	74.1	4.4	0.2	15.4	(Z)	1.7	92.5
Major	4.6	11.3	13.3	9.0	12.4	16.9	12.2	10.5	9.9	97.8	0.1	0.1	1.1	(Z)	5.4	94.9
Marshall	6.1	12.0	13.6	12.1	12.3	12.9	12.0	10.6	8.5	85.3	1.9	0.3	9.0	(Z)	11.1	97.4
Mayes	6.2	13.2	13.7	13.2	13.0	14.0	11.4	8.5	6.7	72.3	0.4	0.3	20.2	(Z)	2.3	99.2
Murray	6.0	12.3	13.4	12.7	12.6	13.6	11.8	9.4	8.3	81.8	2.2	0.5	12.1	–	4.1	98.5
Muskogee	6.7	13.2	14.0	13.2	13.0	14.2	10.8	7.7	7.4	65.1	12.3	0.6	15.9	(Z)	3.5	94.4
Noble	6.8	12.6	13.0	11.0	13.5	16.1	11.4	8.6	7.0	86.8	2.0	0.4	8.1	(Z)	2.1	100.2
Nowata	5.6	13.2	13.0	11.8	13.0	14.8	11.5	9.1	8.0	73.9	2.5	0.1	16.4	–	1.4	96.6
Okfuskee	5.8	11.9	13.7	12.7	13.8	13.9	11.8	8.4	7.9	68.0	9.7	0.1	18.2	–	2.0	107.0
Oklahoma	8.0	13.1	14.0	15.0	13.8	14.0	9.9	6.4	5.8	74.3	15.4	3.2	3.6	0.1	11.2	95.5
Okmulgee	6.4	13.4	14.2	11.7	12.6	14.1	11.7	7.9	7.1	70.7	9.6	0.3	13.6	(Z)	2.0	95.0
Osage	4.8	12.9	14.4	11.7	14.0	16.5	12.4	7.5	5.8	68.0	11.0	0.3	14.4	(Z)	2.3	101.7
Ottawa	5.9	13.3	14.9	11.9	12.7	13.1	11.6	8.7	8.0	75.2	1.0	0.5	17.0	0.3	3.7	95.5
Pawnee	6.0	12.9	13.6	11.2	13.2	15.4	12.8	8.2	6.7	83.2	0.8	0.2	12.1	(Z)	1.3	98.8
Payne	5.5	8.9	29.9	16.0	10.5	10.8	7.6	5.4	5.4	85.1	3.6	3.2	4.7	0.1	2.4	105.7
Pittsburg	5.6	11.6	13.3	12.3	13.9	14.2	12.2	8.8	8.2	78.3	4.0	0.4	12.8	(Z)	2.6	103.7
Pontotoc	6.8	12.3	16.7	13.0	12.8	12.9	10.6	7.8	7.0	76.1	2.1	0.6	16.2	(Z)	2.9	94.8
Pottawatomie	6.3	13.0	15.8	13.6	13.5	13.4	10.8	7.6	6.0	79.7	3.3	0.8	11.9	0.1	3.0	94.0
Pushmataha	5.7	12.6	13.6	10.4	13.2	14.0	12.7	9.8	8.0	78.4	1.0	0.1	16.1	0.1	2.0	93.1
Roger Mills	6.7	10.8	12.2	8.9	12.8	16.9	13.0	9.5	9.4	92.4	0.3	0.2	6.9	–	3.4	103.0
Rogers	5.8	13.9	15.1	13.0	14.4	14.7	11.2	7.2	4.8	80.7	1.1	0.4	11.8	(Z)	2.7	97.7
Seminole	7.7	12.9	14.2	11.4	12.5	14.1	11.3	8.3	7.6	72.0	5.3	0.3	17.7	(Z)	2.3	94.3
Sequoyah	6.2	13.8	13.7	13.3	13.7	13.4	12.0	8.1	5.9	69.7	1.8	0.4	19.7	0.1	2.8	96.6
Stephens	5.9	12.3	13.5	11.1	12.8	15.3	11.9	8.8	8.3	89.5	2.5	0.3	5.4	(Z)	4.7	95.4
Texas	9.1	14.6	15.7	14.3	13.7	13.3	9.1	5.8	4.5	96.2	1.1	0.8	0.9	0.2	38.2	107.2

See footnotes at end of table.

Table B-3. Counties — **Population by Age, Race, Hispanic Origin, and Sex**—Con.

[Includes United States, states, and 3,141 counties/county equivalents defined as of February 22, 2005. For more information on these areas, see Appendix C, Geographic Information]

County	Age (percent) Under 5 years	5 to 14 years	15 to 24 years	25 to 34 years	35 to 44 years	45 to 54 years	55 to 64 years	65 to 74 years	75 years and over	One race (percent) White alone	Black or African American alone	Asian alone	American Indian and Alaska Native alone	Native Hawaiian and Other Pacific Islander alone	Hispanic or Latino origin[1] (percent)	Males per 100 females
OKLAHOMA—Con.																
Tillman	5.5	12.9	14.0	9.5	13.9	13.4	11.4	9.3	10.1	87.2	7.8	0.6	3.1	(Z)	18.7	95.4
Tulsa	7.8	13.5	13.4	14.0	14.4	14.6	10.2	6.3	5.7	77.6	11.3	1.7	5.4	0.1	8.2	95.7
Wagoner	5.8	14.1	14.7	13.5	14.6	15.1	12.2	6.3	3.8	80.9	4.2	0.7	9.2	(Z)	3.5	98.9
Washington	5.9	12.2	13.9	10.8	12.1	15.3	11.9	8.9	9.1	82.0	2.7	0.8	9.1	(Z)	3.8	93.3
Washita	5.6	12.2	14.3	10.8	13.1	15.0	10.9	8.7	9.4	95.0	0.6	0.4	2.8	–	5.0	94.4
Woods	4.8	9.0	19.2	13.3	11.0	12.9	10.3	9.1	10.4	94.3	2.4	0.6	2.0	(Z)	3.0	107.1
Woodward	6.7	11.9	14.5	12.6	13.6	15.6	10.7	7.8	6.8	94.2	1.7	0.4	2.6	(Z)	5.9	105.0
OREGON	6.2	13.0	13.8	14.1	14.1	14.8	11.0	6.4	6.5	90.8	1.8	3.4	1.4	0.3	9.9	98.9
Baker	4.5	11.6	13.3	8.2	12.3	16.2	13.5	10.3	10.0	96.8	0.4	0.5	1.3	–	2.8	99.4
Benton	4.8	10.3	24.4	13.3	11.6	14.3	10.1	5.4	5.7	90.4	1.2	5.2	0.9	0.3	5.5	100.2
Clackamas	5.5	13.5	13.5	13.0	14.1	16.4	12.2	6.1	5.6	92.6	0.9	3.3	0.8	0.2	6.5	98.2
Clatsop	5.1	11.6	14.3	11.7	12.5	16.5	12.3	8.0	7.9	95.3	0.8	1.3	1.1	0.1	6.1	97.8
Columbia	5.6	13.6	14.4	12.6	14.5	15.9	12.2	6.2	5.2	95.4	0.5	0.7	1.4	0.1	3.3	99.8
Coos	4.8	10.8	13.0	10.4	12.2	15.6	13.4	10.0	9.8	93.6	0.5	1.0	2.3	0.2	4.3	95.6
Crook	5.4	13.1	13.2	14.4	12.6	13.6	11.8	8.7	7.2	97.6	0.1	0.4	1.1	(Z)	6.6	98.7
Curry	3.7	9.7	10.6	9.7	10.7	14.9	14.4	12.6	13.6	95.0	0.2	1.0	2.0	0.1	4.3	95.3
Deschutes	5.7	12.4	13.2	15.0	14.0	15.1	11.4	7.0	6.1	95.6	0.4	0.9	1.2	0.1	5.2	98.7
Douglas	5.1	11.9	13.1	11.5	12.0	15.0	12.5	9.6	9.3	95.0	0.3	0.7	1.6	0.1	3.9	96.0
Gilliam	5.1	10.5	11.9	8.9	12.0	18.5	13.1	9.8	10.3	98.5	0.3	0.1	0.9	–	2.5	103.2
Grant	4.2	12.9	13.0	7.6	11.8	17.2	14.1	10.7	8.6	98.0	0.1	0.2	1.1	(Z)	2.7	99.4
Harney	4.9	13.1	12.6	7.5	13.7	17.5	13.0	9.8	7.9	94.1	0.2	0.7	3.9	(Z)	3.5	105.1
Hood River	7.4	14.3	13.1	12.6	14.3	15.9	9.9	6.0	6.5	95.5	0.9	1.6	1.2	(Z)	25.4	99.7
Jackson	5.4	12.6	13.8	12.7	12.5	14.8	12.0	7.6	8.5	94.8	0.6	1.1	1.1	0.2	8.1	94.9
Jefferson	7.7	15.1	14.2	12.1	13.5	12.9	10.7	8.1	5.6	81.4	0.4	0.2	16.3	0.2	18.9	101.3
Josephine	4.8	11.9	12.4	11.1	11.8	14.6	13.2	9.9	10.3	95.5	0.5	0.7	1.2	0.1	5.1	93.7
Klamath	6.0	13.5	14.6	11.6	12.1	14.6	12.0	8.2	7.4	91.7	0.8	0.9	4.1	0.2	8.7	101.0
Lake	4.7	11.8	12.3	9.4	12.1	16.8	13.7	10.4	8.8	95.0	0.2	0.8	2.5	–	6.3	102.6
Lane	5.4	11.7	16.0	14.0	12.9	14.8	11.4	6.7	7.2	92.3	0.9	2.6	1.2	0.2	5.6	96.9
Lincoln	4.7	10.8	12.1	10.7	12.1	16.4	14.1	10.0	9.2	93.2	0.5	0.9	3.1	0.1	6.5	93.9
Linn	6.2	13.6	13.4	13.2	13.3	14.2	11.4	7.1	7.6	95.1	0.5	1.0	1.3	0.2	5.3	97.9
Malheur	7.3	14.7	16.0	12.0	13.4	13.0	9.6	6.7	7.3	94.1	1.6	2.1	1.0	0.1	27.4	115.3
Marion	7.3	14.7	14.9	14.7	13.8	13.1	9.5	5.8	6.1	92.6	1.2	2.0	1.6	0.4	20.9	102.6
Morrow	7.3	17.0	14.2	13.0	12.8	14.7	10.4	6.2	4.4	96.4	0.5	0.6	1.8	0.1	27.7	107.0
Multnomah	6.7	12.3	12.0	16.4	16.2	15.3	10.4	5.2	5.6	83.5	5.8	6.1	1.1	0.4	9.6	98.6
Polk	5.5	12.6	17.6	13.0	11.9	13.7	10.5	6.7	8.3	93.6	0.7	1.4	1.9	0.3	10.0	94.5
Sherman	4.5	11.3	14.8	5.3	13.1	17.4	13.4	8.7	11.5	97.4	0.3	0.5	1.5	–	6.5	99.9
Tillamook	4.9	11.2	12.4	11.2	12.0	15.4	13.4	9.8	9.7	96.0	0.5	0.8	1.3	0.2	7.0	100.5
Umatilla	7.3	14.8	14.3	13.2	14.2	14.0	10.2	6.0	6.0	93.3	1.2	0.8	3.3	0.3	18.2	105.6
Union	6.1	12.2	17.4	11.4	10.7	15.2	11.9	7.8	7.4	95.4	0.6	1.0	1.0	0.8	3.2	95.8
Wallowa	4.5	10.7	12.9	6.6	10.8	19.0	14.5	10.7	10.4	98.2	–	0.3	0.7	–	1.8	102.2
Wasco	5.8	13.4	13.1	10.4	12.6	15.2	12.6	8.3	8.7	92.7	0.4	1.1	3.8	0.7	11.2	97.9
Washington	7.5	14.6	12.5	16.5	16.4	14.3	9.4	4.5	4.3	86.7	1.5	8.1	0.7	0.3	13.9	100.7
Wheeler	2.8	10.2	12.9	6.2	12.2	14.7	16.4	13.3	11.3	98.1	0.1	0.1	1.4	0.1	6.1	100.7
Yamhill	6.3	13.7	16.5	14.1	13.9	14.2	9.6	5.7	6.1	94.8	1.0	1.1	1.3	0.1	13.0	103.6
PENNSYLVANIA	5.8	12.6	13.8	11.8	14.4	15.3	11.1	6.8	8.4	86.0	10.6	2.2	0.2	(Z)	4.1	94.2
Adams	5.4	12.7	14.7	12.7	15.2	14.9	10.6	6.7	7.1	96.6	1.7	0.7	0.2	(Z)	4.9	97.9
Allegheny	5.5	11.8	13.1	10.9	14.1	16.1	11.3	7.2	10.0	83.6	13.1	2.1	0.1	(Z)	1.0	90.7
Armstrong	4.8	11.9	11.6	11.3	14.1	16.4	12.0	7.8	10.0	98.4	0.9	0.1	0.1	(Z)	0.5	95.3
Beaver	5.1	12.1	12.0	10.3	14.0	16.5	11.8	8.1	10.2	92.5	6.1	0.3	0.1	(Z)	0.9	92.3
Bedford	5.3	12.4	11.6	12.0	14.0	15.4	12.2	8.2	8.9	98.7	0.5	0.3	0.1	(Z)	0.6	97.2
Berks	6.2	13.1	14.0	12.5	14.8	14.6	10.7	6.4	7.7	92.6	4.7	1.2	0.2	0.1	12.4	96.6
Blair	5.6	11.9	12.6	11.9	13.5	15.4	11.9	7.7	9.6	97.5	1.3	0.5	0.1	(Z)	0.6	92.7
Bradford	5.6	13.1	12.5	10.7	14.1	15.3	12.3	7.9	8.4	98.1	0.5	0.4	0.3	–	0.7	95.7
Bucks	5.7	13.4	12.4	10.8	15.9	16.8	11.7	6.5	6.6	92.3	3.5	3.1	0.2	(Z)	3.0	97.5
Butler	5.7	13.0	13.8	11.4	15.3	15.8	10.7	6.5	7.8	97.6	1.0	0.8	0.1	(Z)	0.8	95.7
Cambria	5.0	11.0	13.3	11.1	13.0	15.9	11.8	7.7	11.2	95.7	3.2	0.5	0.1	(Z)	1.1	95.2
Cameron	5.2	12.1	12.8	9.3	12.8	15.1	13.4	8.0	11.3	98.7	0.6	0.1	0.2	0.2	0.9	97.4
Carbon	5.0	11.2	12.3	12.8	14.8	15.4	11.3	7.5	9.6	97.9	1.0	0.4	0.1	(Z)	2.1	93.9
Centre	4.2	8.4	32.4	15.0	10.9	10.5	7.6	5.3	5.6	91.3	3.0	4.6	0.2	0.1	1.9	104.8
Chester	6.4	13.7	13.9	11.4	15.6	16.1	11.0	5.9	6.0	89.6	6.2	3.0	0.2	0.1	4.2	96.9
Clarion	4.6	11.1	18.8	12.2	12.5	14.1	10.7	7.7	8.3	98.3	0.9	0.4	0.1	–	0.5	93.0
Clearfield	4.7	11.7	12.4	12.0	14.9	15.3	11.8	7.9	9.4	97.3	1.9	0.3	0.1	(Z)	0.7	101.8
Clinton	5.4	11.0	17.3	12.3	12.1	14.0	11.0	7.6	9.1	98.0	0.8	0.6	0.1	(Z)	0.7	93.9
Columbia	4.6	10.3	19.1	12.2	12.6	14.3	10.9	7.2	8.7	97.7	1.0	0.7	0.2	(Z)	1.4	91.1
Crawford	5.6	12.7	14.5	11.4	13.3	15.0	11.8	7.4	8.4	97.0	1.8	0.3	0.2	(Z)	0.7	94.9
Cumberland	5.1	11.5	15.1	12.2	14.4	15.2	11.4	7.0	8.1	94.0	2.9	2.1	0.1	(Z)	1.8	95.9
Dauphin	6.5	13.1	11.7	12.3	14.9	16.2	11.4	6.6	7.4	77.8	17.8	2.8	0.2	0.1	5.0	93.0
Delaware	6.2	13.4	14.5	10.7	14.8	15.4	10.4	6.1	8.3	76.7	18.0	4.1	0.1	(Z)	1.9	93.0
Elk	4.9	12.4	11.6	10.3	15.1	16.1	11.6	8.2	9.8	99.0	0.2	0.4	0.1	(Z)	0.5	99.3
Erie	6.0	13.2	15.6	11.9	13.4	15.2	10.5	6.3	8.0	91.4	6.5	0.8	0.2	(Z)	2.5	96.0

See footnotes at end of table.

[Includes United States, states, and 3,141 counties/county equivalents defined as of February 22, 2005. For more information on these areas, see Appendix C, Geographic Information]

County	Age (percent)									One race (percent)					Hispanic or Latino origin[1] (percent)	Males per 100 females
	Under 5 years	5 to 14 years	15 to 24 years	25 to 34 years	35 to 44 years	45 to 54 years	55 to 64 years	65 to 74 years	75 years and over	White alone	Black or African American alone	Asian alone	American Indian and Alaska Native alone	Native Hawaiian and Other Pacific Islander alone		
PENNSYLVANIA—Con.																
Fayette	5.1	12.0	12.0	12.1	13.7	15.8	11.8	7.5	10.0	94.9	4.0	0.3	0.1	(Z)	0.5	93.3
Forest	3.1	8.0	17.8	12.0	14.4	13.7	12.0	9.8	9.2	89.5	9.8	0.2	0.3	–	2.6	141.2
Franklin	6.1	12.7	12.0	13.2	14.4	14.2	11.2	7.5	8.7	95.6	2.7	0.7	0.2	0.1	2.7	95.1
Fulton	5.3	12.9	11.7	13.3	14.1	14.5	12.6	8.1	7.5	98.8	0.7	0.1	0.1	(Z)	0.5	98.8
Greene	4.7	11.6	14.1	13.5	14.0	16.0	11.6	6.6	8.1	95.4	3.8	0.2	0.1	(Z)	0.9	105.8
Huntingdon	4.9	11.0	14.4	13.4	14.7	14.4	11.7	7.4	7.9	93.7	5.5	0.3	0.1	(Z)	1.2	109.8
Indiana	4.8	10.3	21.0	11.8	12.0	14.2	10.7	6.8	8.4	96.8	1.8	0.9	0.1	–	0.7	94.0
Jefferson	5.5	11.9	12.3	11.7	13.7	15.6	11.5	8.0	9.8	98.8	0.3	0.3	0.2	(Z)	0.5	96.0
Juniata	6.1	13.0	11.5	13.4	13.8	14.3	11.5	8.0	8.3	98.3	0.5	0.2	0.2	0.7	2.4	98.0
Lackawanna	5.1	11.6	13.9	11.0	13.7	14.8	11.7	7.5	10.7	96.6	1.7	0.9	0.1	(Z)	2.2	90.1
Lancaster	6.8	14.1	13.8	12.4	13.9	14.5	10.3	6.5	7.7	93.5	3.4	1.6	0.2	0.1	6.7	95.7
Lawrence	5.3	12.2	13.1	10.8	12.8	15.9	11.4	7.8	10.7	95.0	3.9	0.3	0.1	(Z)	0.8	91.7
Lebanon	5.7	12.4	12.6	12.6	14.1	14.8	11.4	7.5	9.0	96.2	1.9	0.9	0.2	(Z)	5.9	95.3
Lehigh	6.2	12.9	12.6	12.3	14.8	15.2	10.7	6.6	8.5	90.3	5.1	2.7	0.3	0.1	13.8	94.5
Luzerne	4.9	11.2	12.6	11.6	14.3	15.0	12.1	7.7	10.7	96.3	2.3	0.7	0.1	(Z)	2.7	93.8
Lycoming	5.5	12.0	14.7	11.2	13.6	15.5	11.4	7.3	8.8	94.2	4.3	0.5	0.2	(Z)	0.8	95.1
McKean	5.4	12.5	12.2	12.2	14.4	15.4	11.3	7.5	9.0	96.7	2.3	0.4	0.3	(Z)	1.2	102.3
Mercer	5.3	12.2	14.3	10.6	13.0	15.3	11.3	7.7	10.2	93.2	5.4	0.5	0.1	–	0.8	94.6
Mifflin	6.1	12.9	11.5	11.8	14.1	13.9	11.9	8.2	9.6	98.6	0.7	0.3	0.1	–	0.6	93.8
Monroe	5.3	14.0	15.5	12.0	15.8	15.6	10.3	5.9	5.6	85.4	10.6	1.8	0.3	0.1	10.4	99.2
Montgomery	6.2	13.0	12.1	11.3	15.7	15.8	11.2	6.6	8.1	85.5	8.2	5.1	0.1	(Z)	2.7	94.8
Montour	5.7	12.4	11.8	10.0	14.8	16.0	11.0	8.7	9.5	96.3	1.8	1.5	0.1	–	1.2	92.4
Northampton	5.5	12.2	14.7	11.7	14.8	15.3	11.1	6.3	8.4	92.9	3.8	1.9	0.2	0.1	7.9	95.5
Northumberland	5.1	10.9	11.8	11.8	14.3	15.3	12.1	8.0	10.6	97.3	2.0	0.2	0.1	(Z)	1.4	97.6
Perry	5.8	12.9	12.6	12.3	15.2	16.6	12.3	6.4	5.9	98.6	0.7	0.2	0.1	(Z)	1.0	98.1
Philadelphia	7.5	13.5	15.1	13.7	14.1	13.4	9.7	5.9	7.1	47.4	45.4	5.2	0.3	0.1	10.2	87.1
Pike	4.1	13.9	13.4	11.6	16.0	15.7	11.0	7.4	6.9	92.8	5.2	0.8	0.3	(Z)	6.7	100.3
Potter	6.0	13.4	12.2	10.7	13.5	14.9	11.8	8.5	9.0	98.0	1.0	0.5	0.1	(Z)	0.6	99.7
Schuylkill	4.8	10.9	11.6	12.6	14.4	15.4	11.7	7.7	10.9	96.5	2.6	0.5	0.1	(Z)	1.5	100.8
Snyder	6.0	11.8	16.6	11.7	13.9	14.5	11.0	6.9	7.6	98.1	1.1	0.5	(Z)	–	1.3	95.5
Somerset	4.8	11.3	12.1	12.2	13.9	15.8	11.7	7.9	10.2	97.1	2.4	0.2	0.1	–	0.9	102.3
Sullivan	3.6	9.3	15.4	8.2	12.6	14.3	12.8	11.5	12.3	95.6	3.5	0.1	0.7	–	1.2	102.2
Susquehanna	5.3	12.9	12.9	10.5	14.1	16.1	12.5	7.9	7.8	98.5	0.6	0.3	0.2	(Z)	0.8	99.1
Tioga	5.3	11.7	16.2	10.7	12.9	14.5	11.8	8.3	8.6	97.9	1.0	0.4	0.2	(Z)	0.7	94.9
Union	4.7	9.8	18.5	14.7	14.9	13.5	9.9	6.3	7.6	90.2	7.7	1.2	0.1	(Z)	4.1	125.9
Venango	5.0	12.4	12.7	10.8	13.3	16.7	12.2	8.0	8.9	97.6	1.3	0.3	0.2	(Z)	0.6	95.4
Warren	4.9	12.4	11.9	9.8	13.7	16.7	13.0	8.4	9.0	98.8	0.4	0.3	0.1	(Z)	0.5	96.8
Washington	5.1	11.9	12.7	11.2	13.9	16.1	12.1	7.5	9.7	95.2	3.3	0.5	0.1	(Z)	0.7	92.6
Wayne	5.1	12.4	11.7	10.9	14.4	15.5	12.0	8.9	9.1	97.1	1.9	0.5	0.1	–	2.2	100.3
Westmoreland	4.7	11.5	11.9	10.4	14.2	16.6	12.6	8.0	10.2	96.4	2.2	0.6	0.1	(Z)	0.6	94.0
Wyoming	5.2	12.9	13.7	11.5	14.1	15.7	12.9	6.9	7.2	98.5	0.6	0.4	0.1	–	1.1	98.9
York	5.9	12.9	12.5	12.5	15.5	15.7	11.4	6.5	7.1	93.4	4.3	1.0	0.2	(Z)	3.9	97.2
RHODE ISLAND	6.0	12.7	14.1	13.0	15.0	14.8	10.5	5.8	8.1	88.9	6.2	2.7	0.6	0.1	10.7	93.4
Bristol	4.6	11.6	17.3	10.0	13.9	15.7	11.1	6.7	9.1	96.5	1.1	1.5	0.2	(Z)	1.6	93.5
Kent	5.5	12.5	10.9	12.5	15.9	16.4	11.9	6.2	8.3	95.2	1.5	1.9	0.3	(Z)	2.5	93.4
Newport	5.2	12.3	11.5	11.0	16.1	16.1	12.7	6.8	8.4	92.7	3.6	1.5	0.6	0.1	3.1	95.3
Providence	6.5	13.0	14.6	14.1	14.8	13.8	9.5	5.5	8.0	84.8	9.2	3.3	0.6	0.2	16.5	93.1
Washington	5.0	12.1	16.5	10.9	14.5	16.0	11.7	6.1	7.2	95.1	1.1	1.9	0.9	(Z)	1.8	94.1
SOUTH CAROLINA	6.6	13.2	14.3	13.6	14.4	14.3	11.1	6.9	5.6	68.4	29.2	1.1	0.4	0.1	3.3	95.1
Abbeville	6.2	13.4	13.4	12.4	13.5	14.8	11.7	7.5	7.1	69.7	29.6	0.3	(Z)	(Z)	1.1	93.3
Aiken	6.1	13.7	13.5	12.4	14.2	15.0	11.3	7.4	6.3	71.8	25.9	0.8	0.4	(Z)	3.0	93.2
Allendale	7.8	13.7	14.6	13.4	13.0	14.0	10.8	6.2	6.5	27.2	72.3	0.2	0.1	0.2	2.3	111.2
Anderson	6.3	13.3	12.4	13.7	14.2	14.4	11.8	7.6	6.3	81.5	16.9	0.6	0.2	(Z)	1.6	93.4
Bamberg	6.3	12.7	17.5	10.7	12.3	14.1	11.8	7.5	7.0	37.1	62.3	0.3	0.2	–	1.1	88.7
Barnwell	7.0	14.1	14.1	12.5	13.6	14.9	11.1	6.7	6.1	56.0	42.8	0.5	0.3	(Z)	1.5	92.4
Beaufort	7.5	12.6	14.1	12.8	13.0	11.7	11.0	9.6	7.8	75.7	21.9	0.9	0.3	0.1	8.6	100.9
Berkeley	7.1	14.5	15.4	13.9	15.0	14.2	10.6	5.7	3.6	68.2	27.6	2.0	0.5	0.1	3.1	101.3
Calhoun	5.9	12.9	12.9	11.4	13.7	16.2	13.7	7.2	6.2	53.9	45.4	0.2	0.2	(Z)	1.7	91.0
Charleston	7.1	12.4	15.1	14.3	14.1	14.1	10.8	6.4	5.6	64.5	32.7	1.3	0.3	0.1	3.1	94.1
Cherokee	6.8	14.0	12.9	14.3	14.3	14.1	11.2	6.7	5.7	78.1	20.5	0.5	0.2	(Z)	2.8	94.7
Chester	6.7	13.9	12.6	12.8	13.8	15.1	11.9	7.1	6.1	60.8	38.2	0.3	0.4	–	0.9	92.6
Chesterfield	6.4	14.1	13.0	12.9	14.7	14.6	11.9	7.2	5.4	65.1	33.6	0.4	0.3	(Z)	3.0	93.0
Clarendon	6.4	12.5	15.9	12.0	11.9	14.2	12.0	8.6	6.4	48.1	51.0	0.3	0.3	(Z)	2.2	98.6
Colleton	6.8	14.3	13.3	12.4	13.6	14.7	11.7	7.4	5.7	57.6	41.1	0.3	0.6	(Z)	1.9	93.5
Darlington	6.4	14.4	12.7	13.4	13.5	15.2	11.9	7.1	5.5	57.2	42.0	0.2	0.2	(Z)	1.1	89.2
Dillon	8.1	14.9	14.3	13.3	13.4	14.1	10.5	6.2	5.3	50.9	45.8	0.3	2.5	(Z)	2.6	88.1
Dorchester	6.2	14.4	14.8	13.8	16.2	14.6	10.4	5.7	3.9	71.4	25.2	1.3	0.7	0.1	2.5	96.4
Edgefield	5.4	12.3	14.4	14.8	15.9	15.3	11.2	5.9	4.8	57.9	41.0	0.4	0.4	(Z)	2.4	119.0
Fairfield	6.5	13.6	12.7	13.1	13.5	15.2	11.9	7.3	6.1	41.5	57.7	0.4	0.1		1.5	91.8

See footnotes at end of table.

[Includes United States, states, and 3,141 counties/county equivalents defined as of February 22, 2005. For more information on these areas, see Appendix C, Geographic Information]

County	Age (percent)									One race (percent)					Hispanic or Latino origin[1] (percent)	Males per 100 females
	Under 5 years	5 to 14 years	15 to 24 years	25 to 34 years	35 to 44 years	45 to 54 years	55 to 64 years	65 to 74 years	75 years and over	White alone	Black or African American alone	Asian alone	American Indian and Alaska Native alone	Native Hawaiian and Other Pacific Islander alone		
SOUTH CAROLINA—Con.																
Florence	7.4	13.2	14.1	13.2	13.9	14.7	11.2	6.8	5.5	57.7	40.5	0.9	0.3	(Z)	1.3	89.7
Georgetown	6.2	12.5	12.3	12.2	12.5	14.5	12.4	9.8	7.6	64.2	34.9	0.4	0.2	0.1	2.2	93.0
Greenville	6.8	13.3	13.1	13.9	15.3	14.5	11.0	6.5	5.5	78.5	18.5	1.6	0.2	0.1	5.7	96.4
Greenwood	6.5	13.7	14.4	13.6	13.6	13.5	10.7	7.2	6.7	66.1	32.1	1.0	0.3	0.1	4.1	88.7
Hampton	6.9	13.9	14.0	13.7	14.1	14.5	10.5	6.8	5.7	43.5	55.9	0.2	0.3	–	2.9	103.6
Horry	6.0	11.4	12.1	14.9	14.4	13.4	11.9	9.1	6.7	82.7	15.0	0.9	0.4	0.1	3.6	97.0
Jasper	7.0	14.2	13.6	15.5	15.3	13.1	10.2	6.0	5.1	48.2	50.6	0.6	0.4	0.1	10.0	115.3
Kershaw	6.4	13.5	12.9	12.8	14.3	15.3	11.8	7.1	5.8	72.7	26.0	0.4	0.3	(Z)	2.4	93.3
Lancaster	6.3	13.6	12.6	14.0	15.0	14.5	11.5	7.1	5.5	72.0	26.9	0.4	0.2	(Z)	2.8	99.5
Laurens	5.8	13.5	13.7	13.3	14.6	14.1	11.9	7.2	5.9	72.9	25.8	0.2	0.5	0.1	3.0	95.2
Lee	6.4	13.0	14.8	14.5	14.2	15.1	9.9	6.2	5.8	36.2	63.4	0.2	0.1	–	2.7	104.3
Lexington	6.7	13.8	12.9	13.4	15.4	15.4	11.4	6.4	4.7	83.3	14.3	1.1	0.4	(Z)	3.0	95.6
McCormick	4.2	9.3	12.6	12.6	13.6	13.6	13.9	11.8	8.3	48.0	51.4	0.4	(Z)	(Z)	1.0	115.3
Marion	7.0	14.0	14.4	12.9	12.3	15.1	11.6	6.8	5.9	43.0	56.2	0.4	0.2	–	2.4	86.1
Marlboro	6.5	13.5	13.8	13.5	14.3	14.6	11.3	6.5	5.9	43.8	51.6	0.3	3.4	–	0.8	99.0
Newberry	6.5	12.7	13.8	13.2	14.2	13.8	11.5	7.4	7.1	67.1	31.8	0.3	0.3	0.2	6.8	96.5
Oconee	5.7	12.3	11.7	13.1	13.4	14.2	12.8	9.9	6.9	90.6	8.2	0.4	0.2	(Z)	3.2	97.3
Orangeburg	6.9	13.0	18.1	11.4	12.5	13.7	10.9	7.3	6.3	35.5	62.9	0.5	0.4	(Z)	1.2	86.2
Pickens	5.4	11.6	21.1	13.9	12.9	12.6	10.0	6.8	5.7	90.8	6.7	1.6	0.2	(Z)	2.3	99.9
Richland	6.7	12.7	18.5	14.2	14.6	14.0	9.6	5.2	4.5	49.7	46.6	2.1	0.3	0.1	3.0	93.7
Saluda	5.9	13.3	13.0	14.2	13.7	14.1	11.6	7.6	6.6	71.1	28.1	(Z)	0.2	0.2	12.5	102.5
Spartanburg	6.4	13.5	13.2	13.9	14.9	14.4	11.2	6.9	5.8	76.2	20.9	1.7	0.3	(Z)	4.2	95.2
Sumter	7.9	14.7	15.0	11.9	14.3	14.0	10.0	6.7	5.4	50.0	47.5	1.0	0.3	0.1	2.0	93.0
Union	5.9	13.1	11.1	12.3	14.0	15.3	12.2	8.5	7.7	67.6	31.6	0.2	0.2	(Z)	0.8	88.6
Williamsburg	6.7	14.3	14.6	11.4	12.7	15.1	11.7	7.2	6.1	32.3	67.2	0.2	0.2	–	0.8	90.5
York	6.4	13.7	14.5	13.7	15.6	14.5	10.9	5.9	4.5	77.9	19.4	1.1	0.8	(Z)	2.9	94.9
SOUTH DAKOTA	6.7	13.1	15.6	12.2	13.4	14.7	10.0	6.7	7.5	88.5	0.8	0.7	8.8	(Z)	2.1	98.8
Aurora	5.4	13.4	14.7	8.0	11.6	14.4	11.4	10.7	10.4	96.7	0.3	0.1	2.8	–	3.3	106.2
Beadle	5.4	11.9	13.3	8.7	12.9	16.1	11.6	8.3	11.8	96.8	0.8	0.4	1.4	(Z)	2.0	95.9
Bennett	9.5	18.1	17.2	11.2	12.7	11.0	8.2	6.6	5.5	40.5	0.4	(Z)	52.7	0.1	2.9	99.5
Bon Homme	4.1	10.8	14.7	10.1	14.6	15.3	10.8	8.0	11.6	95.0	0.9	0.1	3.9	–	0.6	128.3
Brookings	5.0	9.3	31.1	14.6	9.9	11.6	7.6	4.8	6.1	95.7	0.5	2.0	1.0	0.1	1.0	102.1
Brown	6.0	11.8	15.3	11.5	12.9	14.4	10.7	7.6	9.4	95.1	0.4	0.5	3.1	0.1	1.0	92.7
Brule	5.9	15.1	15.0	8.6	12.8	15.5	9.9	7.5	9.5	88.9	0.4	0.5	9.8	(Z)	0.5	91.2
Buffalo	13.7	18.8	19.1	11.7	11.4	11.2	7.3	4.0	2.8	17.2	0.2	–	82.5	–	1.2	99.2
Butte	6.1	13.2	14.9	9.9	12.9	16.9	10.8	7.8	7.6	96.5	0.2	0.2	2.0	–	3.1	95.4
Campbell	3.2	12.8	12.2	3.6	14.8	17.0	11.9	11.8	12.7	98.9	–	0.4	0.7	–	0.3	100.6
Charles Mix	7.8	16.4	14.3	9.7	11.6	13.0	10.1	7.9	9.3	66.5	0.1	0.1	32.2	–	2.3	97.3
Clark	4.6	11.9	14.1	7.2	12.2	16.6	11.1	9.2	13.2	99.0	0.1	0.1	0.7	–	0.5	96.7
Clay	5.3	8.4	35.1	15.4	8.8	9.2	7.4	4.8	5.6	93.1	1.0	2.3	2.7	–	1.1	91.7
Codington	6.3	13.5	13.8	12.7	13.9	15.4	9.5	6.6	8.1	96.4	0.2	0.4	2.1	(Z)	1.2	99.7
Corson	9.9	18.8	17.6	11.3	12.1	11.4	8.2	5.9	4.8	33.2	0.2	(Z)	65.5	–	3.9	99.2
Custer	4.4	10.4	15.1	9.9	11.0	17.5	14.8	9.8	7.1	94.4	0.3	0.2	3.6	–	2.5	104.1
Davison	6.3	12.8	15.7	12.8	12.7	14.7	9.4	6.9	8.7	96.2	0.4	0.4	2.4	(Z)	1.7	96.5
Day	5.5	11.7	13.4	6.6	12.0	16.3	12.3	9.2	13.0	90.3	0.2	0.1	8.9	(Z)	0.9	97.4
Deuel	5.1	11.9	13.4	9.1	13.0	15.3	12.0	9.5	10.7	98.8	0.2	0.2	0.4	–	0.9	102.3
Dewey	11.8	18.1	18.8	10.7	13.0	12.0	7.0	4.6	4.1	24.8	0.3	0.2	73.8	0.1	2.3	94.4
Douglas	5.0	12.0	14.0	5.7	11.3	16.2	12.2	9.5	14.2	98.5	(Z)	0.2	1.1	–	0.5	95.7
Edmunds	4.7	13.6	12.0	7.2	13.3	15.1	12.1	10.5	11.6	99.2	0.1	0.1	0.3	(Z)	0.6	100.5
Fall River	4.5	10.8	13.2	7.7	10.3	16.2	14.2	11.6	11.6	91.0	0.5	0.3	6.0	(Z)	2.2	105.4
Faulk	5.0	12.0	13.4	5.9	13.2	16.0	11.5	9.9	13.0	99.6	0.1	(Z)	0.2	–	0.3	95.9
Grant	4.9	12.6	12.5	7.9	13.6	16.7	12.1	8.7	10.9	99.0	–	0.2	0.7	–	0.6	99.5
Gregory	4.2	11.0	12.8	6.1	11.4	17.4	12.5	10.6	14.0	92.8	0.1	0.3	6.7	–	1.0	95.4
Haakon	4.0	11.1	12.6	6.3	11.1	20.9	12.3	9.8	11.8	96.8	–	0.1	2.9	–	0.8	98.5
Hamlin	8.3	13.3	14.3	9.3	13.2	13.5	10.6	7.6	9.9	98.8	0.1	0.2	0.8	–	1.1	100.6
Hand	4.1	11.2	11.7	5.0	12.8	17.2	12.6	11.2	14.1	99.7	0.1	0.1	0.1	–	0.3	97.1
Hanson	7.7	13.9	13.7	13.7	13.8	14.3	9.7	6.4	6.8	99.8	–	0.1	0.1	–	0.1	101.7
Harding	4.6	12.0	14.4	7.3	13.7	20.0	12.2	7.3	8.5	98.2	–	0.3	1.5	–	1.1	104.7
Hughes	6.0	14.1	12.9	10.6	14.8	16.5	11.7	6.6	6.8	86.8	0.3	0.6	10.9	–	1.9	92.4
Hutchinson	5.3	12.3	12.0	7.9	11.5	14.5	10.9	10.4	15.1	99.1	0.1	0.1	0.7	–	0.6	95.7
Hyde	5.8	12.9	12.3	8.8	11.0	16.7	9.4	12.5	10.6	90.4	0.1	–	9.2	–	0.7	105.6
Jackson	9.4	16.3	18.4	9.9	12.4	12.5	9.2	5.9	6.0	45.2	(Z)	(Z)	53.9	(Z)	0.8	98.6
Jerauld	4.9	8.6	12.0	8.0	11.3	17.0	12.4	10.0	15.9	99.1	–	0.3	0.6	–	0.3	99.4
Jones	5.2	10.6	14.0	6.4	11.7	21.3	12.0	7.7	10.9	96.3	–	–	3.0	0.1	1.0	99.4
Kingsbury	4.7	11.3	13.4	7.2	12.1	16.8	11.1	10.1	13.3	98.6	(Z)	0.6	0.5	–	0.8	94.7
Lake	4.8	10.6	20.5	10.9	11.2	15.5	9.8	7.5	9.1	97.7	0.3	1.0	0.9	–	1.1	97.2
Lawrence	5.1	10.1	18.7	11.6	11.8	15.9	11.2	7.4	8.2	95.9	0.4	0.4	2.3	(Z)	2.3	97.7
Lincoln	7.1	13.8	15.6	18.8	14.9	13.5	8.5	3.9	3.9	96.8	0.6	0.9	0.6	(Z)	1.0	99.4
Lyman	8.9	16.5	14.3	10.1	13.1	14.8	9.8	6.8	5.8	61.1	0.1	0.6	37.3	–	0.7	104.3
McCook	6.7	14.2	13.6	8.6	13.6	15.0	10.4	7.2	10.7	99.2	0.1	0.3	0.4	–	1.0	98.7
McPherson	4.4	12.1	10.8	7.6	10.7	15.6	12.0	11.7	15.1	99.5	–	0.2	0.3	–	0.2	92.7
Marshall	4.1	13.3	13.8	7.3	12.8	15.9	12.0	9.1	11.7	91.9	0.1	0.1	7.8	–	1.1	100.0

See footnotes at end of table.

Table B-3. Counties — **Population by Age, Race, Hispanic Origin, and Sex**—Con.

[Includes United States, states, and 3,141 counties/county equivalents defined as of February 22, 2005. For more information on these areas, see Appendix C, Geographic Information]

County	Population characteristics, 2005															
	Age (percent)									One race (percent)					His-panic or Latino origin[1] (per-cent)	Males per 100 females
	Under 5 years	5 to 14 years	15 to 24 years	25 to 34 years	35 to 44 years	45 to 54 years	55 to 64 years	65 to 74 years	75 years and over	White alone	Black or African Ameri-can alone	Asian alone	Ameri-can Indian and Alaska Native alone	Native Hawai-ian and Other Pacific Islander alone		
SOUTH DAKOTA—Con.																
Meade	7.2	14.0	15.0	12.8	14.3	15.5	10.6	5.8	4.9	93.1	1.7	0.7	2.1	0.1	3.5	101.6
Mellette	7.8	18.0	16.1	10.0	12.3	13.6	8.9	6.1	7.2	43.8	–	0.2	54.6	–	1.9	101.5
Miner	4.6	11.5	13.2	6.7	12.3	16.6	11.6	8.7	14.9	98.7	0.6	0.2	0.3	–	1.0	98.9
Minnehaha	7.4	13.2	13.7	15.1	15.4	14.5	9.3	5.7	5.8	93.4	2.0	1.0	2.2	0.1	3.2	99.2
Moody	5.7	12.9	16.0	10.1	14.0	15.7	11.4	6.7	7.6	84.8	0.3	1.2	11.8	–	1.1	97.9
Pennington	7.6	13.0	14.6	13.5	13.5	15.1	10.1	6.6	6.1	87.3	1.0	0.7	8.2	0.1	3.1	98.2
Perkins	4.1	12.2	11.1	6.2	12.5	17.8	12.7	9.5	13.9	97.5	0.2	0.3	1.9	–	0.9	96.3
Potter	4.7	10.3	11.0	4.0	12.7	16.7	14.7	11.7	14.3	98.5	–	0.2	1.1	–	0.3	94.9
Roberts	7.2	14.8	14.7	9.9	12.1	14.4	10.8	8.0	8.3	65.7	0.1	0.2	32.4	–	1.0	99.8
Sanborn	5.1	11.9	13.6	9.1	12.0	18.5	11.3	9.1	9.5	98.8	–	0.4	0.6	–	1.3	104.9
Shannon	13.8	20.9	21.1	13.0	11.8	8.8	5.4	3.4	1.7	6.7	0.3	(Z)	91.8	0.1	2.7	98.5
Spink	5.5	12.2	14.1	7.8	13.5	16.5	11.1	8.9	10.4	97.9	0.3	0.1	1.7	–	0.5	105.9
Stanley	6.7	12.1	13.4	10.1	15.0	16.4	13.8	6.9	5.6	94.3	0.3	0.4	4.6	–	0.5	98.4
Sully	6.2	11.9	12.4	7.6	14.5	17.5	12.3	9.1	8.4	98.4	–	0.1	1.3	–	0.8	105.5
Todd	13.5	21.5	19.4	11.8	11.3	10.5	6.2	3.4	2.3	15.0	0.2	0.2	83.2	–	2.7	96.0
Tripp	5.2	13.5	13.5	8.2	12.8	15.2	11.0	8.7	11.9	87.7	(Z)	0.2	11.5	–	1.0	95.6
Turner	5.0	12.4	13.3	9.6	12.8	16.6	11.3	8.1	10.9	98.8	0.2	0.2	0.5	–	0.5	100.6
Union	6.2	13.8	12.6	11.4	14.6	16.4	12.0	6.3	6.8	96.6	0.4	1.7	0.6	(Z)	1.8	101.0
Walworth	7.1	12.5	11.3	7.2	11.8	15.5	12.7	10.3	11.7	84.4	(Z)	0.2	14.4	–	0.7	95.2
Yankton	5.5	12.7	14.1	11.7	14.8	15.7	10.6	6.6	8.2	95.8	1.5	0.5	1.6	–	2.6	105.9
Ziebach	8.4	19.7	19.5	13.5	12.2	12.0	7.6	4.3	3.0	25.5	–	0.3	74.0	–	1.1	96.6
TENNESSEE	6.5	12.8	13.7	14.0	14.9	14.6	11.0	7.0	5.6	80.7	16.8	1.2	0.3	0.1	3.0	96.0
Anderson	5.5	11.9	12.1	11.8	14.2	15.5	12.5	8.1	8.3	93.4	3.9	1.1	0.3	–	1.4	92.6
Bedford	7.2	13.5	13.2	16.7	14.4	13.1	10.2	6.4	5.3	89.7	8.0	0.9	0.4	0.1	11.7	99.8
Benton	4.8	11.4	11.1	12.3	13.8	14.4	13.6	10.0	8.6	96.8	2.2	0.3	0.4	–	1.3	93.1
Bledsoe	4.7	11.6	12.6	14.9	16.1	14.7	12.5	7.7	5.0	95.6	3.5	0.1	0.3	–	1.3	119.2
Blount	5.6	11.8	12.9	13.5	15.2	14.9	12.0	7.8	6.4	94.9	2.9	0.9	0.3	(Z)	1.4	95.1
Bradley	6.2	12.4	14.1	14.6	14.7	13.8	11.3	7.5	5.3	93.6	4.2	0.8	0.3	(Z)	3.0	96.3
Campbell	6.0	11.6	12.1	14.3	14.2	13.8	12.3	9.0	6.8	98.2	0.5	0.2	0.3	(Z)	1.0	93.8
Cannon	5.2	13.3	12.6	13.5	15.6	14.2	11.6	8.4	5.8	97.5	1.6	0.1	0.4	(Z)	2.1	96.0
Carroll	6.0	11.9	13.1	12.0	14.1	13.5	12.3	9.1	8.1	88.0	10.6	0.3	0.2	(Z)	1.3	94.0
Carter	4.9	10.7	13.1	14.6	15.2	14.5	12.2	8.2	6.7	97.2	1.6	0.3	0.2	–	1.2	100.2
Cheatham	6.1	13.9	13.1	13.2	17.5	16.1	10.5	5.8	3.8	96.5	2.1	0.3	0.4	(Z)	1.7	100.3
Chester	5.6	12.7	16.6	14.3	13.1	12.9	10.6	7.6	6.5	89.7	9.3	0.3	0.2	–	1.6	95.2
Claiborne	5.7	11.9	13.1	14.0	14.5	14.6	12.3	8.3	5.7	97.7	0.9	0.5	0.3	(Z)	0.8	94.0
Clay	4.5	11.2	11.9	13.1	15.2	14.3	13.8	9.6	6.5	96.6	1.8	0.2	0.7	0.4	2.3	97.1
Cocke	5.9	11.8	11.7	14.2	14.5	14.9	12.8	8.5	5.7	96.3	2.1	0.3	0.4	(Z)	1.3	94.9
Coffee	6.2	13.0	12.7	13.6	14.2	14.1	10.9	8.6	6.6	94.1	3.7	0.9	0.3	0.1	3.3	95.1
Crockett	6.5	13.1	12.9	12.6	14.6	13.8	11.1	8.2	7.2	85.9	13.4	0.2	0.2	–	7.5	92.8
Cumberland	4.9	11.0	11.2	12.5	13.0	12.4	11.9	12.8	10.3	98.4	0.4	0.3	0.2	(Z)	1.3	95.4
Davidson	7.6	11.9	13.3	15.9	15.9	14.5	9.7	5.9	5.3	67.8	27.5	2.8	0.3	0.1	6.6	95.1
Decatur	5.2	11.2	11.1	13.4	13.4	13.7	12.8	10.6	8.6	95.9	3.5	0.2	0.1	(Z)	2.6	96.9
DeKalb	6.1	12.0	12.3	14.6	15.4	14.1	11.5	7.7	6.3	97.1	1.7	0.4	0.3	(Z)	4.8	97.6
Dickson	6.7	13.6	13.1	13.7	15.5	14.4	10.7	7.2	5.1	93.6	4.4	0.4	0.5	(Z)	1.7	96.9
Dyer	6.5	13.5	13.2	13.1	14.6	14.2	11.6	7.3	5.9	84.6	13.9	0.6	0.2	(Z)	1.9	93.4
Fayette	5.9	12.6	14.0	16.3	14.2	14.2	10.8	6.8	5.3	69.6	28.2	1.2	0.2	–	1.9	98.0
Fentress	5.6	12.4	12.2	13.6	14.3	14.5	13.0	8.4	6.0	99.4	0.2	0.1	0.1	–	0.7	96.7
Franklin	5.5	11.6	15.7	12.3	13.2	14.6	11.7	8.5	6.8	92.9	5.5	0.6	0.2	(Z)	2.0	95.8
Gibson	6.1	12.5	12.0	13.0	13.8	14.0	11.4	8.5	8.6	79.3	19.5	0.3	0.2	(Z)	1.4	90.7
Giles	5.7	12.5	13.7	11.8	14.3	14.8	12.6	8.1	6.5	87.2	11.3	0.5	0.3	–	1.0	95.3
Grainger	5.9	11.9	11.6	14.6	15.4	14.6	12.3	8.4	5.3	98.7	0.6	0.1	0.1	(Z)	1.3	99.0
Greene	5.5	11.5	12.6	13.4	14.7	14.2	12.5	9.1	6.6	96.8	2.1	0.3	0.2	(Z)	1.6	95.7
Grundy	6.7	13.0	12.1	14.8	13.7	13.1	11.8	8.2	6.5	99.0	0.3	0.2	0.2	–	1.0	98.0
Hamblen	6.7	12.3	12.0	14.8	14.5	13.6	12.2	8.3	5.6	93.7	4.1	0.9	0.3	0.1	9.3	99.1
Hamilton	6.2	11.9	14.0	12.5	14.1	15.2	11.9	7.5	6.6	76.4	20.6	1.5	0.3	0.1	2.4	92.7
Hancock	5.2	11.2	12.8	13.6	13.9	15.6	12.6	8.4	6.6	99.0	0.5	0.1	0.1	–	0.4	98.2
Hardeman	5.8	11.9	13.9	15.3	15.9	14.3	10.4	6.6	5.9	58.1	40.6	0.5	0.2	(Z)	1.2	116.8
Hardin	5.3	12.2	12.1	12.8	13.7	14.8	12.8	9.1	7.1	95.2	3.7	0.3	0.3	(Z)	1.2	96.7
Hawkins	5.6	12.1	11.5	13.9	15.3	14.5	12.8	8.3	6.0	97.4	1.7	0.3	0.1	(Z)	0.9	95.3
Haywood	7.4	14.2	13.2	12.8	13.5	15.4	10.1	6.9	6.5	49.0	50.5	0.1	0.1	0.1	3.7	86.9
Henderson	6.7	12.7	12.0	14.2	14.7	14.1	11.8	7.7	6.0	91.0	8.0	0.2	0.1	–	1.1	93.4
Henry	5.4	11.5	11.9	12.4	13.3	14.6	12.7	9.9	8.5	90.0	8.6	0.3	0.2	(Z)	1.2	94.0
Hickman	5.8	12.7	12.9	14.9	15.9	14.3	10.6	7.3	5.5	94.4	4.4	0.1	0.5	(Z)	1.3	112.4
Houston	6.2	13.0	11.7	13.1	13.0	13.9	12.2	9.3	7.5	96.1	3.3	0.1	0.1	(Z)	2.1	98.5
Humphreys	5.7	12.3	11.8	13.4	13.8	14.6	12.7	8.8	7.0	95.8	3.2	0.4	0.2	–	1.2	96.5
Jackson	4.5	11.8	11.0	13.9	14.6	15.0	13.4	9.2	6.6	98.8	0.6	0.1	0.1	0.1	1.0	97.2
Jefferson	5.3	11.9	14.4	14.3	14.8	13.3	11.7	8.5	5.7	96.4	2.1	0.4	0.4	–	2.1	98.1
Johnson	4.2	9.9	11.1	15.3	16.2	14.6	12.9	8.9	7.2	96.4	2.9	0.1	0.3	–	0.8	116.3
Knox	6.0	11.7	15.3	13.8	14.8	14.8	10.9	6.7	5.9	88.2	8.7	1.6	0.3	(Z)	1.7	94.7
Lake	4.6	9.0	16.8	17.9	15.8	13.3	9.3	7.3	6.2	65.9	33.2	0.2	0.4	–	1.1	167.7
Lauderdale	7.2	12.9	13.9	15.1	15.1	13.7	10.2	6.3	5.6	63.9	34.7	0.3	0.6	(Z)	1.3	110.5
Lawrence	7.0	13.3	12.9	13.0	14.6	13.1	11.1	8.3	6.8	97.2	1.6	0.2	0.3	(Z)	1.3	94.7

See footnotes at end of table.

Table B-3. Counties — **Population by Age, Race, Hispanic Origin, and Sex**—Con.

[Includes United States, states, and 3,141 counties/county equivalents defined as of February 22, 2005. For more information on these areas, see Appendix C, Geographic Information]

County	Age (percent)									One race (percent)					Hispanic or Latino origin[1] (percent)	Males per 100 females
	Under 5 years	5 to 14 years	15 to 24 years	25 to 34 years	35 to 44 years	45 to 54 years	55 to 64 years	65 to 74 years	75 years and over	White alone	Black or African American alone	Asian alone	American Indian and Alaska Native alone	Native Hawaiian and Other Pacific Islander alone		
TENNESSEE—Con.																
Lewis	6.5	13.0	13.1	12.8	14.1	14.4	12.3	7.8	5.9	97.4	1.8	0.3	0.1	–	1.2	97.9
Lincoln	5.9	12.0	13.0	12.2	14.7	14.8	11.5	8.8	7.1	91.1	6.9	0.4	0.5	(Z)	1.8	95.0
Loudon	5.6	11.3	11.3	12.7	13.9	14.1	12.8	11.0	7.2	97.2	1.3	0.3	0.3	(Z)	3.5	97.3
McMinn	5.8	12.6	12.6	13.5	14.4	14.4	12.1	8.2	6.5	93.5	4.5	0.7	0.3	(Z)	2.3	94.9
McNairy	6.6	12.6	11.5	12.9	13.8	13.6	12.6	9.0	7.3	92.6	6.3	0.2	0.2	(Z)	1.1	95.4
Macon	5.9	13.5	12.5	15.4	15.5	13.5	11.3	7.0	5.4	98.6	0.6	0.3	0.3	0.1	2.8	100.5
Madison	7.0	13.4	15.0	13.5	14.3	14.6	10.2	6.2	5.9	63.9	34.3	0.8	0.2	(Z)	2.3	94.0
Marion	6.2	11.8	12.4	13.5	13.9	15.5	13.1	7.9	5.6	94.8	4.1	0.3	0.3	(Z)	0.8	96.5
Marshall	6.3	13.0	12.8	14.2	14.9	15.3	11.0	6.4	6.0	91.6	7.5	0.2	0.2	(Z)	3.6	97.2
Maury	6.7	13.0	13.4	14.3	14.5	15.7	10.5	6.4	5.5	84.8	13.3	0.5	0.3	(Z)	4.2	96.4
Meigs	5.9	13.0	11.9	14.5	14.9	13.4	13.5	7.8	5.1	97.4	1.8	0.2	0.3	–	0.7	99.2
Monroe	6.2	12.7	13.1	14.6	14.3	13.3	11.8	7.9	6.1	95.7	2.1	0.6	0.3	0.1	2.7	97.8
Montgomery	8.2	15.5	15.4	16.8	15.8	12.3	7.9	4.8	3.3	74.4	20.0	1.9	0.5	0.3	5.5	100.1
Moore	4.6	12.0	12.6	12.7	14.4	14.1	13.7	8.5	7.2	96.0	3.4	0.2	0.1	–	0.7	101.8
Morgan	5.3	11.8	12.5	15.2	15.9	14.6	11.6	7.6	5.4	96.8	2.5	0.2	0.2	–	0.8	115.5
Obion	6.1	12.5	11.8	13.2	13.1	15.2	12.4	8.7	7.0	88.9	10.2	0.3	0.1	0.1	3.2	93.9
Overton	5.6	12.0	11.8	13.4	14.1	14.3	12.7	9.3	6.9	98.3	0.8	0.1	0.3	0.1	0.8	95.9
Perry	5.9	12.5	13.1	12.3	12.6	14.2	13.0	9.3	7.1	96.0	2.8	0.1	0.2	0.4	1.1	98.5
Pickett	5.3	10.8	12.6	11.8	12.9	13.8	13.7	12.1	6.9	98.5	1.2	(Z)	(Z)	–	1.1	102.1
Polk	5.7	12.1	10.9	14.1	14.7	14.1	13.3	8.8	6.2	98.0	0.8	0.2	0.1	–	0.9	98.2
Putnam	6.1	11.5	18.2	14.6	13.3	12.4	10.3	7.3	6.3	95.9	1.9	1.0	0.3	0.1	4.4	101.0
Rhea	6.6	12.2	13.9	13.5	13.6	14.0	12.3	7.9	6.0	96.1	2.2	0.4	0.4	(Z)	2.2	94.8
Roane	5.1	11.5	11.7	12.2	13.7	15.5	13.5	9.1	7.6	95.2	2.9	0.5	0.2	(Z)	0.9	95.2
Robertson	7.2	13.3	13.3	14.5	16.1	14.7	9.9	6.5	4.6	90.3	8.3	0.4	0.3	(Z)	5.3	100.1
Rutherford	7.1	13.7	16.9	16.8	16.1	13.3	8.4	4.5	3.2	84.6	11.3	2.6	0.3	0.1	4.8	100.3
Scott	7.0	13.3	12.9	15.3	14.4	13.8	11.5	6.7	5.0	98.5	0.4	0.1	0.2	–	0.6	98.7
Sequatchie	6.1	13.1	11.7	16.2	14.3	13.9	11.6	7.7	5.4	98.4	0.7	0.3	0.3	(Z)	0.8	98.1
Sevier	5.9	11.8	11.9	14.4	14.9	14.9	12.3	8.2	5.6	97.5	0.8	0.6	0.3	(Z)	1.8	96.4
Shelby	7.7	14.7	14.6	13.6	14.9	14.9	9.8	5.3	4.5	45.6	51.3	2.0	0.2	(Z)	3.4	92.3
Smith	5.8	12.8	13.7	13.3	15.7	14.7	11.1	6.9	5.9	95.7	3.1	0.2	0.4	–	1.7	97.2
Stewart	5.5	12.4	12.8	12.9	15.1	14.6	12.1	8.7	5.9	94.8	2.6	1.5	0.6	–	1.3	98.5
Sullivan	5.3	11.4	11.4	12.2	14.5	15.3	13.4	9.1	7.6	96.5	2.1	0.5	0.2	(Z)	0.8	93.7
Sumner	6.4	13.2	13.5	13.4	15.6	15.3	11.4	6.5	4.7	91.3	6.5	0.8	0.3	0.1	2.5	97.6
Tipton	6.2	14.3	14.9	13.8	15.8	14.9	9.8	6.2	4.2	79.1	19.1	0.4	0.4	0.1	1.6	98.0
Trousdale	6.1	12.6	13.3	13.3	14.6	14.4	12.0	7.4	6.3	88.5	10.5	0.3	0.2	0.1	2.6	100.9
Unicoi	4.8	10.7	11.1	12.6	13.9	15.7	12.8	9.9	8.5	98.7	0.6	(Z)	0.3	(Z)	2.7	96.4
Union	6.2	12.7	13.1	14.4	16.3	14.6	11.1	7.2	4.6	98.4	0.6	0.2	0.1	(Z)	1.0	100.2
Van Buren	5.2	11.9	12.7	13.6	13.9	15.3	13.2	8.2	5.9	99.2	0.4	0.1	0.1	–	0.4	99.3
Warren	6.7	12.4	12.2	14.8	14.6	13.8	11.1	7.8	6.6	95.4	3.2	0.5	0.2	(Z)	6.7	99.0
Washington	5.7	11.3	14.0	14.4	14.6	14.3	11.3	7.7	6.6	93.8	4.0	0.9	0.3	(Z)	1.8	95.1
Wayne	4.6	10.7	13.2	15.8	16.2	13.5	11.6	8.3	6.2	91.7	7.5	0.4	0.2	(Z)	0.9	124.3
Weakley	5.2	11.3	18.5	13.2	13.0	13.4	10.9	7.5	7.2	90.4	7.0	1.9	0.1	(Z)	1.4	95.8
White	6.0	12.0	12.4	13.1	14.3	14.5	11.9	9.2	6.6	97.3	1.8	0.3	0.2	(Z)	1.1	97.0
Williamson	6.0	14.4	14.3	12.0	15.9	17.7	11.2	5.2	3.4	92.1	5.0	2.0	0.2	0.1	3.4	97.9
Wilson	6.4	13.2	13.8	13.1	16.2	15.6	11.5	6.2	3.9	91.4	6.8	0.6	0.3	0.1	2.1	98.0
TEXAS	8.2	15.0	15.1	14.8	14.7	13.4	9.0	5.4	4.5	83.2	11.7	3.3	0.7	0.1	35.1	99.3
Anderson	5.8	11.0	13.4	18.8	17.9	13.0	8.2	6.1	5.7	75.3	22.6	0.7	0.7	(Z)	13.2	151.6
Andrews	7.8	15.0	16.9	9.6	13.6	14.6	9.5	7.1	6.0	96.0	1.9	0.8	1.1	–	43.9	95.9
Angelina	7.8	14.9	13.9	13.3	13.7	13.3	10.0	7.0	6.1	83.3	14.9	0.7	0.4	(Z)	16.8	96.4
Aransas	5.5	12.2	12.8	10.9	12.0	13.4	12.6	11.2	9.4	93.7	2.0	2.6	0.6	(Z)	21.7	98.7
Archer	5.7	14.5	15.0	10.6	14.5	16.2	11.1	7.0	5.5	97.7	0.4	0.2	0.6	–	6.3	101.7
Armstrong	5.1	12.3	14.1	10.8	12.0	15.2	11.5	9.2	9.9	98.8	0.4	–	0.7	–	7.1	92.5
Atascosa	7.6	16.2	15.9	13.4	13.7	12.9	9.5	5.9	4.9	97.0	1.1	0.5	0.9	0.1	60.5	98.1
Austin	6.5	13.8	13.8	12.4	13.1	14.6	11.0	7.4	7.4	88.9	9.9	0.4	0.3	(Z)	19.6	99.0
Bailey	9.5	15.6	15.3	10.7	11.5	12.2	10.0	7.7	7.5	97.0	1.7	0.2	0.9	0.1	51.1	96.7
Bandera	4.9	12.4	13.5	11.4	13.6	15.5	12.8	9.1	6.8	97.2	0.5	0.4	0.9	(Z)	16.4	99.1
Bastrop	6.8	14.7	13.9	15.1	15.0	14.7	9.6	5.5	4.3	88.8	8.8	0.6	0.9	0.1	27.8	104.1
Baylor	6.2	11.4	12.9	7.7	11.7	14.2	13.0	10.4	12.4	94.9	3.4	0.8	0.8	0.2	9.7	89.3
Bee	5.5	11.9	17.9	20.5	14.8	11.5	7.8	5.3	4.9	87.7	10.7	0.7	0.6	(Z)	55.7	154.1
Bell	11.3	16.0	14.2	17.1	13.7	11.1	7.4	4.9	4.4	71.0	21.5	2.9	0.9	0.5	18.7	99.4
Bexar	8.1	15.3	15.3	14.5	14.5	13.0	8.9	5.4	4.9	88.2	7.4	1.9	1.1	0.2	56.8	95.3
Blanco	5.4	13.4	13.2	13.0	13.8	15.8	13.2	6.3	5.9	97.7	1.0	0.2	0.5	(Z)	17.5	97.5
Borden	2.5	10.5	18.4	9.7	15.0	16.7	12.5	8.8	6.0	98.8	0.2	–	–	–	14.7	94.6
Bosque	5.9	12.7	12.9	10.7	12.6	13.6	12.4	9.5	9.7	96.0	2.2	0.2	0.6	0.1	14.3	97.7
Bowie	6.3	13.4	13.8	14.4	14.0	14.0	10.8	6.7	6.5	73.2	24.3	0.6	0.6	(Z)	5.3	101.6
Brazoria	7.8	15.1	14.1	14.6	15.8	14.7	9.0	5.2	3.7	84.3	10.1	3.8	0.6	0.1	24.9	106.3
Brazos	6.9	10.9	34.2	15.7	10.1	8.9	5.9	4.0	3.4	83.0	10.8	4.6	0.5	0.1	19.7	103.1
Brewster	6.7	11.2	21.0	12.1	10.2	13.4	10.9	7.6	6.8	95.6	2.1	0.3	1.0	0.2	42.8	102.2
Briscoe	6.4	13.5	14.5	7.4	11.7	13.4	12.8	11.0	9.4	96.2	3.1	–	0.5	–	26.5	99.0
Brooks	8.5	16.3	16.0	9.4	10.6	12.9	10.6	8.5	7.2	98.6	0.5	0.1	0.8	(Z)	91.3	91.0
Brown	6.4	13.0	16.4	12.4	12.2	13.1	10.8	8.1	7.7	93.9	4.1	0.6	0.7	–	17.6	98.4

See footnotes at end of table.

County and City Data Book: 2007

U.S. Census Bureau

Table B-3. Counties — **Population by Age, Race, Hispanic Origin, and Sex**—Con.

[Includes United States, states, and 3,141 counties/county equivalents defined as of February 22, 2005. For more information on these areas, see Appendix C, Geographic Information]

County	Population characteristics, 2005															
	Age (percent)									One race (percent)					His-panic or Latino origin[1] (per-cent)	Males per 100 females
	Under 5 years	5 to 14 years	15 to 24 years	25 to 34 years	35 to 44 years	45 to 54 years	55 to 64 years	65 to 74 years	75 years and over	White alone	Black or African American alone	Asian alone	American Indian and Alaska Native alone	Native Hawaiian and Other Pacific Islander alone		
TEXAS—Con.																
Burleson	6.7	13.7	13.8	11.5	12.9	14.4	10.7	8.5	7.9	84.2	14.2	0.3	0.6	(Z)	16.2	95.3
Burnet	6.0	12.1	12.3	12.6	12.7	13.0	10.4	10.9	10.1	96.4	1.7	0.3	0.7	0.1	16.0	92.7
Caldwell	7.2	14.8	14.5	15.1	14.6	13.3	9.1	5.8	5.6	89.9	7.9	0.6	0.7	0.1	43.4	98.0
Calhoun	7.5	15.6	13.3	11.1	13.7	13.3	11.0	7.9	6.6	92.6	2.6	3.9	0.6	(Z)	43.9	100.5
Callahan	5.4	12.6	14.8	10.1	13.4	14.5	11.5	9.7	7.9	97.2	0.8	0.5	0.6	(Z)	8.0	93.8
Cameron	11.2	17.5	16.4	13.3	12.4	10.9	7.7	5.4	5.2	97.5	0.8	0.6	0.6	0.1	86.0	92.6
Camp	8.0	15.0	13.7	11.9	12.8	12.6	10.5	8.5	7.0	80.6	17.6	0.4	0.4	0.5	19.7	94.8
Carson	5.8	13.9	15.3	9.0	13.3	15.8	10.7	8.5	7.7	97.3	0.9	0.2	1.0	(Z)	8.6	97.7
Cass	5.8	12.9	13.1	10.6	12.2	14.0	13.1	9.5	8.9	79.6	18.8	0.2	0.5	(Z)	2.5	92.3
Castro	8.2	17.1	15.7	9.0	11.4	14.6	10.3	7.7	6.1	95.3	2.5	(Z)	1.8	0.3	53.4	101.7
Chambers	5.7	14.9	14.8	13.7	15.0	16.4	10.7	5.2	3.7	87.4	10.3	1.0	0.6	—	14.5	100.5
Cherokee	7.7	14.1	13.9	13.5	13.4	12.9	10.0	7.2	7.1	83.5	14.7	0.5	0.5	0.1	16.8	101.7
Childress	5.2	11.4	18.4	13.3	15.9	12.1	9.3	7.1	7.4	83.7	15.2	0.4	0.4	0.2	23.3	149.5
Clay	4.0	13.0	13.4	11.3	13.9	16.3	12.8	8.6	6.7	96.9	0.6	0.1	1.2	—	3.8	94.9
Cochran	8.0	14.4	18.3	7.6	13.1	13.4	9.6	8.5	7.1	92.3	6.1	0.3	1.1	0.1	48.3	87.1
Coke	4.2	11.4	14.6	6.7	11.7	12.8	11.8	12.7	11.8	96.5	2.2	0.1	0.9	0.1	18.9	102.0
Coleman	6.2	12.5	12.5	9.6	11.2	13.2	12.6	10.6	11.5	95.8	2.5	0.5	0.7	(Z)	14.6	92.9
Collin	7.8	15.5	12.7	16.9	18.3	14.1	8.7	3.7	2.3	81.3	6.9	9.5	0.5	0.1	12.8	100.8
Collingsworth	5.8	14.1	14.7	7.7	11.7	13.4	11.7	9.6	11.3	91.4	5.7	0.2	1.8	—	25.7	93.6
Colorado	6.3	12.9	16.0	9.9	11.8	14.1	10.8	9.1	9.1	84.6	14.2	0.3	0.5	0.1	22.5	95.5
Comal	6.4	12.9	14.0	13.6	13.7	14.7	10.9	7.4	6.4	96.4	1.5	0.6	0.6	(Z)	23.7	98.4
Comanche	5.8	13.5	13.9	9.9	12.4	11.9	12.6	10.5	9.7	97.8	0.6	0.3	0.8	0.1	23.4	96.3
Concho	3.7	8.0	14.9	21.6	16.0	12.2	10.2	6.9	6.5	98.0	1.2	0.1	0.6	(Z)	44.3	194.6
Cooke	6.7	13.9	15.3	12.6	12.9	13.6	10.7	7.7	6.7	94.1	3.2	0.6	1.0	(Z)	12.6	98.5
Coryell	6.4	15.2	20.1	20.0	16.5	9.6	5.7	3.7	2.9	72.0	21.5	2.0	1.0	0.6	13.9	104.7
Cottle	6.1	11.5	11.7	7.8	11.3	14.5	11.8	10.5	14.7	87.9	11.8	—	—	—	22.1	89.2
Crane	6.9	16.4	16.4	8.0	13.9	15.5	10.8	6.2	5.7	94.6	3.3	0.4	1.7	—	49.5	92.9
Crockett	6.4	13.7	15.3	9.3	12.2	16.2	12.5	7.9	6.5	97.3	0.9	0.3	1.1	0.3	56.3	96.5
Crosby	8.3	16.2	14.6	10.5	11.1	12.6	11.5	8.0	7.2	93.7	4.8	—	1.0	0.3	48.5	89.6
Culberson	7.8	16.3	16.3	8.4	13.1	13.6	12.1	7.4	5.1	97.5	1.0	1.1	0.4	—	71.5	97.2
Dallam	7.8	17.7	13.9	13.2	14.7	13.2	9.1	5.5	4.9	96.1	2.3	0.3	1.1	—	32.2	103.0
Dallas	9.1	15.2	13.5	16.4	16.0	13.1	8.4	4.6	3.7	72.9	20.9	4.4	0.6	0.1	36.4	101.8
Dawson	6.7	13.2	15.2	13.2	15.3	13.7	9.1	6.9	6.9	90.2	8.9	0.4	0.4	—	50.3	127.2
Deaf Smith	9.2	18.0	15.4	11.9	12.1	12.0	9.2	6.6	5.6	96.1	1.7	0.4	1.1	0.8	62.1	96.1
Delta	6.3	13.1	14.3	11.5	13.6	12.4	12.5	8.9	7.5	90.8	7.0	0.3	0.9	(Z)	4.1	95.3
Denton	7.8	14.8	15.4	17.6	17.2	13.7	8.1	3.3	2.0	85.1	7.1	5.5	0.6	0.1	15.3	99.9
DeWitt	5.9	12.0	12.8	12.0	14.8	14.4	10.7	8.5	8.9	88.2	10.7	0.3	0.6	0.1	29.4	106.7
Dickens	4.8	9.4	15.8	16.4	13.7	12.4	10.1	8.4	9.0	88.9	9.0	—	0.2	1.7	27.1	136.3
Dimmit	8.4	17.1	16.9	10.9	12.4	12.1	10.5	5.8	5.9	97.0	1.5	0.8	0.8	(Z)	83.5	94.9
Donley	5.0	11.5	17.5	9.7	10.6	12.9	11.8	10.6	10.5	93.5	4.9	0.3	1.0	—	7.1	94.9
Duval	7.1	14.9	16.4	11.0	13.3	12.3	10.5	7.2	7.3	98.4	0.7	0.2	0.7	0.1	88.0	103.6
Eastland	6.0	12.5	15.9	9.7	11.2	13.4	11.7	9.6	9.9	96.2	2.3	0.3	0.6	(Z)	13.6	94.0
Ector	8.9	15.9	15.6	13.0	12.9	13.8	8.9	6.0	5.0	92.4	4.9	0.7	1.1	0.1	47.9	95.1
Edwards	5.5	15.7	16.1	10.5	12.7	15.4	12.7	7.0	4.4	94.5	3.0	0.2	0.8	1.6	46.1	105.3
Ellis	7.4	15.1	15.8	14.5	14.5	14.2	9.4	5.1	4.0	89.2	8.7	0.5	0.7	(Z)	21.2	99.5
El Paso	9.7	16.7	16.5	12.8	13.5	12.5	8.1	5.5	4.7	93.5	3.3	1.1	1.1	0.2	81.2	92.5
Erath	6.5	12.6	21.8	13.1	12.1	11.6	8.9	6.7	6.7	96.5	1.1	0.9	0.7	0.1	16.4	99.1
Falls	5.8	14.0	16.4	11.2	13.0	13.4	10.2	7.8	8.1	71.8	26.9	0.2	0.7	0.1	17.8	85.9
Fannin	5.4	12.4	14.1	13.4	14.5	13.2	10.7	8.7	7.6	90.0	7.7	0.4	0.9	(Z)	7.2	113.1
Fayette	5.8	12.0	12.5	10.6	12.2	14.9	11.1	9.4	11.6	91.5	7.4	0.3	0.6	(Z)	15.6	94.9
Fisher	4.2	12.8	13.2	8.5	11.9	14.9	11.4	11.2	11.8	95.6	3.4	0.2	0.4	—	22.5	96.5
Floyd	7.1	16.8	14.7	9.5	12.1	13.4	10.1	8.0	8.4	94.3	4.1	0.2	1.1	0.4	48.3	93.9
Foard	5.1	14.5	12.6	9.0	12.0	13.1	11.4	11.2	11.1	94.7	3.6	0.3	1.1	—	18.4	92.4
Fort Bend	6.6	15.7	15.8	14.4	16.0	16.3	8.9	3.8	2.4	62.4	21.1	14.8	0.4	0.1	22.5	99.5
Franklin	5.4	12.5	13.5	13.0	12.6	13.8	11.0	10.2	8.0	93.4	5.0	0.5	0.8	—	10.2	95.2
Freestone	6.0	12.1	14.3	14.5	13.3	13.1	11.5	7.8	7.5	80.6	18.2	0.3	0.4	—	10.1	112.0
Frio	7.4	15.4	16.1	16.0	12.8	11.5	9.2	6.2	5.4	93.5	5.0	0.7	0.8	0.1	74.3	121.2
Gaines	9.1	16.8	17.9	11.5	12.8	12.7	8.4	6.3	4.5	95.8	2.7	0.2	1.1	0.1	38.6	97.6
Galveston	7.1	14.1	14.1	13.3	14.7	15.3	10.4	6.0	4.9	80.7	14.9	2.7	0.5	0.1	19.9	96.3
Garza	6.9	14.6	15.7	14.3	13.4	12.0	9.6	7.7	5.8	92.9	5.8	—	0.5	0.2	39.0	114.0
Gillespie	5.1	11.0	11.5	10.7	11.1	13.0	12.2	11.8	13.7	98.6	0.4	0.2	0.5	(Z)	16.9	92.3
Glasscock	5.9	16.7	17.0	6.1	14.1	16.6	11.9	7.8	4.0	98.0	0.8	—	0.2	1.1	30.7	113.7
Goliad	5.6	12.8	14.3	10.2	13.3	15.5	11.4	9.2	7.8	94.1	5.1	0.2	0.6	—	36.2	99.0
Gonzales	8.4	13.9	14.7	12.4	12.4	12.5	9.9	7.6	8.3	90.1	8.1	0.3	0.9	0.3	42.8	99.0
Gray	5.9	13.0	14.1	11.6	12.7	14.0	10.5	8.8	9.3	90.6	6.1	0.6	1.0	—	16.4	104.0
Grayson	6.7	13.4	14.2	12.7	13.4	14.0	10.8	7.5	7.2	90.1	5.9	0.7	1.4	(Z)	8.8	94.7
Gregg	8.0	14.1	14.7	13.1	13.0	14.2	9.6	7.0	6.3	76.9	20.4	1.0	0.6	(Z)	11.9	94.4
Grimes	6.4	12.8	12.6	13.8	15.8	14.8	10.5	7.3	6.1	80.4	18.3	0.4	0.4	0.1	17.5	113.7
Guadalupe	6.1	14.7	15.6	13.5	14.5	13.9	9.9	6.6	5.2	91.4	5.6	1.0	0.7	0.2	33.8	97.0
Hale	8.8	16.3	17.0	11.7	12.9	12.0	8.9	6.3	6.1	92.0	5.9	0.5	1.2	0.1	52.1	102.8

See footnotes at end of table.

Table B-3. Counties — **Population by Age, Race, Hispanic Origin, and Sex**—Con.

[Includes United States, states, and 3,141 counties/county equivalents defined as of February 22, 2005. For more information on these areas, see Appendix C, Geographic Information]

County	\multicolumn{9}{c}{Population characteristics, 2005}								
	\multicolumn{9}{c}{Age (percent)}								\multicolumn{5}{c}{One race (percent)}					His-panic or Latino origin[1] (percent)	Males per 100 females
	Under 5 years	5 to 14 years	15 to 24 years	25 to 34 years	35 to 44 years	45 to 54 years	55 to 64 years	65 to 74 years	75 years and over	White alone	Black or African American alone	Asian alone	American Indian and Alaska Native alone	Native Hawaiian and Other Pacific Islander alone		

TEXAS—Con.

County	Under 5	5 to 14	15 to 24	25 to 34	35 to 44	45 to 54	55 to 64	65 to 74	75+	White	Black	Asian	Amer Ind	Nat Haw	Hispanic	Males per 100 females
Hall	7.4	14.9	12.4	10.2	11.1	12.4	10.6	10.2	10.8	90.3	8.3	0.5	0.8		29.2	88.5
Hamilton	5.9	12.6	13.2	10.1	12.2	13.3	11.6	10.2	10.8	98.7	0.3	0.1	0.3	0.2	8.9	95.6
Hansford	8.9	14.7	14.4	9.1	12.6	14.2	10.4	8.4	7.3	98.2	0.3	0.4	0.9	–	38.8	98.2
Hardeman	5.6	13.0	14.1	9.2	11.1	15.1	12.2	9.4	10.5	92.9	5.4	0.3	1.0	–	15.3	88.1
Hardin	6.3	14.2	14.2	12.9	14.0	15.1	10.9	6.8	5.6	92.0	6.6	0.3	0.3	(Z)	3.0	96.9
Harris	8.8	15.6	14.1	15.5	15.4	14.0	8.8	4.4	3.3	74.4	18.4	5.5	0.6	0.1	37.5	100.0
Harrison	6.6	13.7	15.7	11.9	13.2	14.9	11.3	7.0	5.8	75.3	23.1	0.5	0.4	0.1	7.4	94.4
Hartley	7.9	11.2	8.6	12.4	19.4	16.0	11.4	6.8	6.2	91.0	8.1	0.3	0.5	0.1	17.0	156.0
Haskell	5.6	11.5	14.1	7.1	11.4	14.6	11.8	10.4	13.7	94.9	3.9	0.3	0.7	–	23.6	88.3
Hays	6.7	12.1	24.9	16.0	12.5	12.5	7.7	4.3	3.4	93.0	4.1	1.0	0.8	0.2	31.2	100.5
Hemphill	7.2	12.9	15.2	9.8	12.0	15.8	12.3	8.2	6.7	97.0	1.6	0.3	0.7	0.2	19.2	103.7
Henderson	6.1	13.0	13.2	13.0	12.4	13.3	11.3	9.7	7.9	91.8	6.4	0.4	0.5	(Z)	8.9	97.2
Hidalgo	11.7	18.4	16.7	14.7	12.5	10.1	6.7	4.7	4.6	97.4	0.9	0.8	0.6	0.1	89.4	95.1
Hill	6.9	13.6	14.1	12.6	12.4	12.9	10.9	8.6	8.0	91.2	6.9	0.4	0.4	(Z)	16.1	98.0
Hockley	7.6	14.9	17.6	11.3	12.9	13.4	9.7	6.8	5.9	94.5	3.7	0.3	1.0	0.1	41.2	96.1
Hood	5.3	12.4	12.9	12.1	13.0	14.0	11.8	10.5	8.0	97.0	0.8	0.4	0.8	(Z)	8.8	97.1
Hopkins	7.0	13.7	13.0	13.8	13.1	13.5	11.1	7.7	7.0	90.6	7.6	0.4	0.8	0.1	12.2	96.0
Houston	5.5	11.7	13.0	11.5	15.4	14.4	10.6	9.2	8.9	72.5	26.4	0.4	0.3	0.1	9.2	115.6
Howard	6.6	12.6	14.5	13.9	14.6	14.0	9.4	7.6	6.8	93.0	4.7	0.8	0.8	(Z)	40.5	119.3
Hudspeth	7.3	18.1	16.1	11.4	12.6	11.7	11.1	6.6	5.2	97.3	0.9	0.2	1.5	(Z)	75.4	96.8
Hunt	6.9	13.6	16.0	13.5	13.5	13.4	10.6	7.1	5.3	88.3	9.0	0.7	0.7	0.1	10.6	100.1
Hutchinson	6.9	14.7	14.4	10.2	11.3	16.4	10.4	7.7	8.0	93.9	2.9	0.5	1.3	–	17.5	96.7
Irion	4.4	12.5	15.0	10.9	14.3	14.6	13.2	8.2	6.9	97.4	1.7	–	0.9	–	27.1	97.3
Jack	5.3	12.1	16.1	13.1	15.1	13.2	9.9	8.4	6.9	92.6	5.5	0.5	0.7	0.2	9.9	121.3
Jackson	7.1	14.1	14.6	10.8	12.8	15.0	10.3	8.0	7.4	91.2	7.5	0.4	0.3	0.2	27.0	97.1
Jasper	7.0	13.9	13.4	11.7	13.4	13.9	11.3	8.5	7.0	81.0	17.2	0.4	0.4	(Z)	4.7	94.6
Jeff Davis	3.6	11.0	15.8	8.1	13.6	16.0	13.5	10.2	8.1	98.2	1.0	0.1	0.4	–	36.9	104.6
Jefferson	6.9	13.8	14.9	13.0	13.8	14.5	9.7	6.6	6.7	60.4	35.3	2.9	0.4	(Z)	12.6	101.4
Jim Hogg	7.2	15.8	16.9	8.3	13.1	11.7	11.4	7.9	7.7	98.4	0.6	0.2	0.8	–	89.2	97.5
Jim Wells	7.3	16.4	16.4	12.0	13.2	13.0	9.5	6.5	5.6	97.4	0.9	0.6	0.8	0.3	76.9	95.1
Johnson	6.8	14.8	14.9	14.6	15.0	14.1	9.9	5.8	4.0	94.1	3.2	0.7	0.7	0.2	14.8	100.3
Jones	4.2	10.8	18.5	13.7	16.0	13.0	9.9	7.0	6.8	86.5	12.2	0.5	0.4	(Z)	22.4	154.1
Karnes	5.5	10.9	17.2	17.9	14.4	12.0	7.8	6.8	7.6	87.5	11.1	0.4	0.9	0.1	49.4	145.5
Kaufman	7.2	14.7	15.3	15.0	14.6	14.0	9.5	5.5	4.2	87.4	10.1	0.7	0.6	0.1	14.4	98.4
Kendall	5.8	13.5	14.7	11.5	13.2	15.2	11.8	8.2	6.2	97.4	0.9	0.4	0.6	0.1	18.7	97.3
Kenedy	8.4	16.3	12.9	10.3	14.9	11.8	13.2	6.5	5.8	96.9	0.7	1.7	0.7	–	77.0	107.5
Kent	4.9	9.0	11.8	3.8	9.2	16.2	14.5	12.8	17.9	98.8	0.4	–	0.8	–	9.8	89.8
Kerr	5.6	11.7	13.4	9.9	11.4	13.0	10.6	11.1	13.4	95.9	2.0	0.6	0.6	(Z)	21.9	92.5
Kimble	5.6	12.3	12.6	10.0	12.2	14.5	13.2	10.6	9.0	98.3	0.5	0.6	0.4	–	23.3	98.4
King	4.9	15.0	17.9	6.2	16.0	18.9	12.7	4.2	4.2	98.7	–	–	1.3	–	15.3	130.8
Kinney	5.4	12.8	12.9	9.3	11.0	11.7	11.5	12.7	12.8	96.2	2.6	0.5	0.4	–	50.3	100.9
Kleberg	7.8	14.1	21.1	13.5	11.5	11.7	8.8	6.1	5.4	92.5	3.8	2.2	0.8	0.1	67.8	102.1
Knox	6.4	14.1	15.0	6.6	11.5	13.6	10.7	10.7	11.4	88.9	8.6	0.6	1.4	0.1	26.3	88.9
Lamar	6.6	14.3	13.4	12.2	13.5	13.2	11.1	7.9	7.8	83.7	13.3	0.6	1.1	(Z)	4.4	91.6
Lamb	7.9	15.2	14.9	10.1	12.5	13.1	9.5	8.5	8.3	94.1	4.3	0.2	1.1	0.2	47.5	94.9
Lampasas	5.7	14.1	14.1	13.2	13.9	14.0	10.6	7.7	6.7	93.7	3.3	0.9	0.7	0.1	15.7	97.9
La Salle	7.6	14.6	17.4	12.9	13.9	11.7	10.5	6.1	5.3	95.7	3.5	0.4	0.4	(Z)	78.2	115.7
Lavaca	6.4	12.3	13.2	9.3	11.9	14.2	11.3	9.5	11.9	92.2	7.0	0.3	0.2	(Z)	13.6	94.1
Lee	6.6	14.1	15.6	12.0	13.3	14.2	10.1	7.2	7.0	87.7	11.1	0.3	0.6	(Z)	20.6	100.9
Leon	5.9	12.2	13.3	11.0	11.6	14.2	11.8	10.6	9.4	89.5	9.7	0.2	0.3	–	10.5	95.9
Liberty	7.0	14.5	14.2	15.3	15.0	13.8	9.8	5.7	4.5	85.9	12.3	0.4	0.5	(Z)	13.4	95.5
Limestone	6.7	13.3	14.9	13.5	12.7	13.1	10.6	8.0	7.2	79.8	18.5	0.3	0.6	–	15.9	105.0
Lipscomb	6.9	14.6	13.4	9.0	13.6	14.5	10.9	7.4	8.8	97.5	0.6	0.1	1.6	–	27.7	99.8
Live Oak	4.8	11.2	15.1	10.9	13.2	15.2	12.1	9.1	8.4	96.6	2.6	0.3	0.3	–	40.6	122.7
Llano	4.3	8.7	9.3	9.5	9.7	12.9	15.2	15.2	15.1	98.0	0.5	0.4	0.4	–	7.3	95.8
Loving	8.1	6.5	8.1	3.2	9.7	27.4	12.9	14.5	9.7	100.0	–	–	–	–	17.7	100.0
Lubbock	7.7	13.5	19.9	14.5	12.3	12.5	8.4	6.0	5.3	89.1	7.7	1.4	0.7	0.1	29.6	96.2
Lynn	7.9	15.2	16.4	8.4	12.7	14.4	10.0	8.7	6.3	95.1	3.4	0.1	1.3	–	46.1	100.3
McCulloch	6.6	13.6	13.6	9.6	11.2	14.1	12.4	9.4	9.5	97.2	1.9	0.3	0.3	–	29.9	90.1
McLennan	7.4	14.0	19.3	13.2	12.3	12.6	8.8	6.2	6.2	81.7	15.2	1.3	0.6	0.1	20.6	94.7
McMullen	3.3	9.5	15.1	11.3	11.6	16.8	14.2	10.3	8.0	97.5	1.1	0.9	0.5	–	35.3	104.9
Madison	5.8	11.3	16.8	18.9	13.0	11.3	9.4	6.9	6.6	76.7	21.8	0.8	0.4	–	18.8	143.7
Marion	5.3	12.1	11.7	10.6	12.1	15.0	13.2	11.4	8.6	74.8	22.9	0.2	0.9	–	3.7	94.9
Martin	7.7	17.9	15.4	10.4	13.3	12.9	9.5	6.9	5.9	96.1	1.7	0.5	1.2	–	41.2	96.4
Mason	4.5	11.2	11.9	10.0	10.7	14.0	14.7	11.2	11.9	98.8	0.1	(Z)	0.7	0.1	22.2	92.0
Matagorda	7.1	15.7	15.2	11.4	12.9	14.9	10.0	7.2	5.7	83.7	12.4	2.3	0.9	(Z)	34.9	98.4
Maverick	10.0	19.4	16.5	11.8	12.7	11.4	8.1	5.1	4.9	96.7	0.8	0.4	1.6	0.5	95.3	91.9
Medina	6.4	14.9	14.7	14.0	13.8	13.3	10.2	6.7	6.0	95.3	2.7	0.4	0.8	0.2	46.8	104.4
Menard	4.5	10.2	13.6	7.2	12.0	14.2	14.4	11.2	12.8	97.2	1.1	0.4	0.7	0.6	31.5	101.4
Midland	7.6	15.4	15.7	12.1	13.0	15.6	8.8	6.2	5.6	90.3	7.1	1.0	0.8	0.1	34.1	94.0

See footnotes at end of table.

County and City Data Book: 2007

U.S. Census Bureau

[Includes United States, states, and 3,141 counties/county equivalents defined as of February 22, 2005. For more information on these areas, see Appendix C, Geographic Information]

County	Under 5 years	5 to 14 years	15 to 24 years	25 to 34 years	35 to 44 years	45 to 54 years	55 to 64 years	65 to 74 years	75 years and over	White alone	Black or African American alone	Asian alone	American Indian and Alaska Native alone	Native Hawaiian and Other Pacific Islander alone	Hispanic or Latino origin[1] (percent)	Males per 100 females
TEXAS—Con.																
Milam	7.2	14.2	13.4	11.9	11.9	13.7	11.0	8.1	8.5	88.0	10.5	0.3	0.6	(Z)	20.6	98.1
Mills	4.3	13.2	14.4	8.1	12.0	13.3	13.5	9.9	11.4	98.0	1.4	(Z)	0.1	0.2	15.9	102.9
Mitchell	5.2	10.0	16.8	14.5	15.8	14.7	9.7	6.5	6.7	84.9	13.9	0.4	0.7	–	32.7	166.9
Montague	6.4	12.4	12.9	11.2	12.2	13.2	12.1	10.2	9.3	97.5	0.4	0.4	0.7	(Z)	6.7	93.5
Montgomery	7.0	15.2	14.3	15.2	14.8	14.7	9.9	5.3	3.6	92.8	4.1	1.6	0.5	0.1	16.0	99.2
Moore	10.1	18.0	15.3	12.0	13.6	12.6	8.1	5.5	4.9	96.1	1.3	1.0	0.9	(Z)	50.8	101.8
Morris	5.7	13.0	13.4	11.6	11.3	15.2	11.1	9.7	8.8	74.8	23.6	0.3	0.5	(Z)	4.3	94.1
Motley	6.6	11.6	10.6	8.0	10.1	14.7	13.3	10.8	14.2	94.9	4.3	–	0.7	0.1	11.0	98.9
Nacogdoches	7.3	12.7	24.0	12.8	11.2	11.6	8.8	6.1	5.7	81.4	16.4	0.8	0.5	0.1	14.3	93.3
Navarro	7.3	14.4	15.6	13.5	13.5	12.5	10.0	6.8	6.4	81.9	15.6	0.7	0.6	0.6	20.7	98.8
Newton	5.0	13.9	14.0	12.5	13.6	14.3	12.5	7.9	6.4	77.4	20.9	0.5	0.6	(Z)	4.5	102.8
Nolan	7.5	14.3	15.0	9.5	11.9	14.6	10.7	8.2	8.3	92.9	5.4	0.4	0.7	0.1	31.1	94.5
Nueces	7.7	15.1	15.4	12.8	13.5	14.3	9.8	6.0	5.4	92.5	4.3	1.4	0.8	0.2	58.4	95.2
Ochiltree	8.7	15.9	14.7	12.7	13.6	13.8	9.6	6.2	4.8	97.5	0.4	0.6	1.0	–	39.2	101.1
Oldham	5.6	18.5	17.0	10.1	10.7	14.4	11.9	6.8	5.0	95.0	2.8	0.5	1.4	–	12.6	106.8
Orange	6.5	14.4	13.9	12.1	13.7	15.2	10.9	7.4	5.9	89.0	8.7	0.8	0.6	(Z)	4.4	95.5
Palo Pinto	6.4	13.9	13.3	12.5	12.8	13.7	11.7	8.1	7.5	95.2	2.3	0.7	0.7	–	15.1	96.5
Panola	6.6	13.1	13.9	11.5	12.0	15.2	11.7	8.4	7.6	81.1	17.4	0.4	0.4	(Z)	5.1	93.3
Parker	5.8	13.7	14.9	13.7	15.1	15.3	10.9	6.3	4.2	95.9	2.1	0.5	0.6	(Z)	8.4	103.1
Parmer	7.9	17.6	15.8	10.6	13.1	12.6	9.0	6.8	6.7	95.7	2.0	0.6	1.4	0.2	56.3	99.8
Pecos	6.3	13.5	20.1	12.3	12.6	13.8	9.7	6.6	5.0	93.4	5.1	0.6	0.6	(Z)	63.0	125.3
Polk	5.5	12.1	12.8	14.6	12.3	12.2	10.6	10.2	9.6	85.1	12.0	0.6	1.6	(Z)	10.0	105.3
Potter	9.1	15.4	14.4	15.0	14.0	12.4	8.1	5.9	5.8	84.6	10.4	2.6	1.0	0.1	32.2	102.1
Presidio	9.5	15.8	16.3	8.2	12.0	11.6	11.0	7.4	8.1	98.7	0.7	0.1	0.3	(Z)	83.8	89.4
Rains	4.8	11.6	13.0	14.8	12.8	13.5	12.3	10.0	7.3	95.1	3.0	0.5	0.9	0.1	7.8	100.6
Randall	6.2	14.0	16.2	13.6	13.6	15.2	10.2	6.1	4.8	94.9	2.0	1.4	0.7	(Z)	12.9	95.6
Reagan	8.0	16.1	17.0	7.3	14.7	16.0	9.2	6.7	5.0	95.0	3.8	0.3	0.7	0.2	50.4	96.4
Real	5.0	11.5	13.5	9.1	11.1	12.9	14.1	13.4	9.5	98.3	0.2	0.3	0.7	–	23.2	93.3
Red River	5.6	12.5	12.7	11.6	12.0	13.7	12.3	9.5	10.1	81.6	17.0	0.2	0.5	–	4.5	92.8
Reeves	8.1	14.1	19.0	8.1	12.0	13.4	11.0	8.0	6.3	96.3	2.5	0.5	0.7	(Z)	73.1	113.6
Refugio	6.0	13.0	14.2	9.1	13.8	14.4	12.3	9.3	7.9	91.8	6.7	0.5	0.7	0.2	44.7	96.5
Roberts	2.7	11.3	15.5	6.7	15.0	19.3	17.1	6.8	5.6	98.8	0.4	–	0.7	–	3.4	100.0
Robertson	6.9	15.3	13.5	11.2	12.2	13.4	11.3	8.3	8.0	76.4	22.5	0.2	0.3	(Z)	15.3	92.2
Rockwall	7.0	14.7	15.2	15.0	15.4	14.6	9.6	5.0	3.4	91.7	4.8	2.1	0.5	0.1	13.3	101.4
Runnels	6.7	14.3	14.2	9.1	11.7	13.5	11.7	9.0	9.8	96.8	1.6	0.4	0.9	(Z)	32.8	93.0
Rusk	6.1	12.8	13.8	12.6	14.0	14.5	11.2	7.6	7.3	80.2	18.5	0.3	0.3	–	10.5	105.1
Sabine	4.9	11.5	11.2	10.2	11.3	12.1	13.8	13.5	11.5	89.3	9.8	0.2	0.3	(Z)	2.4	93.1
San Augustine	5.7	12.0	12.0	10.3	11.5	12.9	12.5	11.5	11.6	72.5	26.9	0.2	0.2	–	4.6	92.0
San Jacinto	5.5	13.2	13.9	12.5	13.0	14.0	12.7	9.0	6.2	86.2	11.5	0.5	0.6	0.1	7.1	99.6
San Patricio	8.1	16.4	15.8	12.1	14.0	13.0	9.5	6.2	5.0	94.6	2.8	0.7	0.8	0.3	51.8	97.8
San Saba	5.8	12.5	19.0	8.9	11.0	13.5	11.6	8.6	9.0	95.6	3.0	0.2	1.2	(Z)	24.3	112.1
Schleicher	6.7	12.8	17.2	8.6	12.2	15.3	12.3	8.2	6.7	97.1	2.4	0.4	(Z)	–	46.5	96.3
Scurry	7.0	13.0	16.3	12.0	12.5	14.9	9.5	7.4	7.3	93.0	5.9	0.3	0.6	–	33.1	108.8
Shackelford	4.9	12.8	14.4	8.1	14.0	15.5	12.2	9.9	8.1	98.7	0.8	–	0.4	–	9.3	91.6
Shelby	7.3	14.2	13.5	14.3	12.6	12.7	10.1	8.0	7.3	77.1	18.1	0.3	0.4	3.7	15.6	94.6
Sherman	6.8	15.9	15.2	9.9	14.8	13.7	11.3	6.0	6.4	97.4	0.8	(Z)	1.0	0.8	30.5	102.3
Smith	7.5	14.1	14.5	13.4	13.0	13.4	10.0	7.4	6.7	78.9	18.6	0.9	0.5	0.1	14.3	92.8
Somervell	6.1	13.8	14.6	11.6	14.3	15.5	9.9	7.7	6.4	98.0	0.5	0.2	0.7	0.1	15.4	100.5
Starr	12.0	19.2	16.6	12.8	12.2	9.9	7.2	5.5	4.6	98.6	0.5	0.3	0.3	0.2	97.6	92.5
Stephens	6.9	12.3	14.9	11.0	12.7	13.4	11.5	8.7	8.6	95.5	3.3	0.6	0.4	–	16.9	107.4
Sterling	5.0	13.0	17.0	7.3	15.2	17.0	10.7	7.1	7.7	99.4	0.1	–	0.5	0.1	34.2	96.8
Stonewall	6.4	10.6	12.0	5.8	10.9	15.5	12.7	12.5	13.7	94.7	3.6	0.3	0.1	0.5	11.4	91.1
Sutton	7.6	14.6	13.9	11.4	13.1	16.8	10.7	6.1	5.7	98.6	0.5	0.3	0.5	–	54.4	100.7
Swisher	7.9	14.0	17.0	10.2	12.0	12.3	9.9	8.2	8.4	91.9	6.4	0.2	0.9	0.2	36.0	109.6
Tarrant	8.4	15.1	14.0	15.5	15.8	13.8	8.9	4.7	3.7	79.8	13.8	4.2	0.7	0.2	23.9	99.3
Taylor	8.0	14.1	17.7	13.1	12.9	12.7	8.5	6.8	6.1	89.0	6.9	1.5	0.8	0.1	20.0	93.9
Terrell	3.4	13.0	13.8	9.2	11.0	15.3	14.3	11.0	9.0	97.3	–	0.8	1.9	–	51.1	97.2
Terry	7.8	14.2	15.8	11.6	13.1	13.1	10.0	7.5	7.0	93.3	5.6	0.3	0.7	(Z)	46.7	107.2
Throckmorton	3.0	12.6	14.0	6.1	13.8	14.0	13.3	12.4	10.8	98.9	0.1	0.1	0.4	–	10.9	97.1
Titus	9.0	16.5	14.6	14.1	13.6	11.7	8.8	6.0	5.7	88.2	9.9	0.7	0.8	(Z)	34.7	99.9
Tom Green	7.5	13.6	17.4	12.2	12.7	13.2	9.5	7.1	6.8	92.7	4.3	1.0	0.8	0.1	33.6	93.4
Travis	8.1	12.9	15.6	19.1	16.1	13.4	7.8	3.9	3.1	83.4	8.8	5.4	0.7	0.1	31.7	106.4
Trinity	5.6	12.1	12.4	11.5	11.6	12.2	12.3	11.5	10.8	87.7	10.9	0.3	0.5	0.1	6.3	92.7
Tyler	5.4	12.3	13.3	13.8	13.2	12.7	11.6	9.5	8.2	86.8	11.3	0.3	0.5	–	4.7	106.9
Upshur	6.4	13.7	13.5	12.4	13.3	14.6	11.3	8.4	6.5	89.0	9.1	0.3	0.6	0.1	4.5	95.2
Upton	7.3	12.6	17.1	6.6	10.9	17.5	11.9	9.1	7.0	95.9	2.4	–	1.5	0.2	45.9	97.3
Uvalde	8.3	16.4	16.2	11.8	12.0	12.0	9.8	6.8	6.6	97.5	0.9	0.5	0.8	0.2	67.3	94.4
Val Verde	9.2	16.7	14.9	12.2	13.1	11.0	9.1	7.3	6.6	96.4	1.7	0.7	0.8	0.1	78.2	95.2
Van Zandt	6.1	13.2	13.2	12.1	13.0	13.8	11.7	9.3	7.6	94.9	3.2	0.3	0.7	0.1	8.5	98.2
Victoria	7.6	15.3	14.3	11.9	13.4	14.6	10.2	6.7	6.0	91.2	6.4	1.0	0.7	0.1	41.3	94.7

See footnotes at end of table.

Table B-3. Counties — **Population by Age, Race, Hispanic Origin, and Sex**—Con.

[Includes United States, states, and 3,141 counties/county equivalents defined as of February 22, 2005. For more information on these areas, see Appendix C, Geographic Information]

County	Age (percent) Under 5 years	5 to 14 years	15 to 24 years	25 to 34 years	35 to 44 years	45 to 54 years	55 to 64 years	65 to 74 years	75 years and over	One race (percent) White alone	Black or African American alone	Asian alone	American Indian and Alaska Native alone	Native Hawaiian and Other Pacific Islander alone	Hispanic or Latino origin[1] (percent)	Males per 100 females
TEXAS—Con.																
Walker	4.8	9.1	26.3	16.6	14.2	11.8	7.7	5.2	4.3	74.5	23.4	0.9	0.4	(Z)	15.1	148.2
Waller	7.2	13.3	22.2	12.9	12.4	13.0	9.4	5.4	4.2	71.7	26.5	0.5	0.6	0.1	22.0	99.0
Ward	6.7	14.1	17.8	8.3	12.5	14.4	11.2	7.6	7.3	93.4	5.0	0.4	0.9	–	44.6	99.6
Washington	6.6	12.5	15.8	11.6	12.3	14.4	10.1	7.9	8.9	79.7	18.3	1.4	0.3	–	11.6	96.5
Webb	13.0	18.9	16.5	13.9	13.0	10.3	6.6	4.1	3.6	98.0	0.6	0.5	0.6	0.1	94.9	93.3
Wharton	7.8	14.6	15.4	11.2	12.8	14.4	10.1	7.0	6.6	84.2	14.5	0.5	0.5	0.2	34.5	97.4
Wheeler	5.7	12.9	13.2	9.1	11.0	15.0	12.8	10.1	10.1	94.9	3.3	0.7	0.9	(Z)	17.4	94.1
Wichita	7.2	13.8	17.7	12.8	13.3	13.1	8.8	7.1	6.3	84.2	10.6	2.0	1.0	0.1	14.0	103.4
Wilbarger	7.7	14.0	15.6	11.4	12.5	13.6	10.6	7.3	7.3	88.6	9.2	0.8	0.9	–	23.4	99.7
Willacy	9.5	16.2	17.9	12.1	12.3	11.9	8.5	5.8	5.7	96.5	2.5	0.2	0.7	0.1	86.6	104.5
Williamson	7.9	15.7	13.8	16.1	17.3	13.7	7.9	4.3	3.4	87.8	6.3	3.7	0.5	0.1	19.8	100.4
Wilson	6.0	14.8	15.5	12.6	14.9	14.6	10.6	6.3	4.8	96.2	2.0	0.5	0.7	(Z)	37.7	100.4
Winkler	8.4	14.5	15.3	9.5	12.7	14.8	10.2	7.2	7.4	96.5	2.4	0.4	0.7	–	46.9	96.2
Wise	6.1	14.2	14.8	13.9	15.5	14.6	10.5	6.3	4.1	96.2	1.4	0.4	0.8	(Z)	12.8	101.5
Wood	5.6	11.4	13.2	12.0	11.9	12.8	12.2	11.6	9.3	92.6	5.9	0.3	0.5	(Z)	6.9	97.3
Yoakum	8.5	15.5	16.9	9.5	13.3	14.8	9.8	6.3	5.4	96.7	1.8	0.6	0.9	(Z)	50.5	95.1
Young	6.4	12.6	13.1	10.0	12.4	14.7	10.9	9.7	10.2	96.3	1.4	0.3	0.9	0.2	12.6	91.8
Zapata	10.4	17.4	15.9	13.4	11.9	10.6	8.3	5.7	6.4	98.4	0.5	0.3	0.4	0.3	87.7	95.7
Zavala	8.3	17.7	17.7	12.7	12.1	11.2	9.1	5.6	5.7	97.4	1.0	0.2	1.0	0.4	91.3	98.6
UTAH	9.5	15.9	17.6	17.2	12.2	11.4	7.4	4.7	4.1	93.8	1.0	1.9	1.3	0.7	10.9	100.9
Beaver	9.7	17.2	15.1	13.5	10.8	12.3	8.7	6.1	6.6	97.1	0.3	1.0	1.2	–	8.4	107.1
Box Elder	8.4	17.4	17.1	14.2	12.1	12.3	7.6	6.2	4.7	96.8	0.3	1.1	1.0	(Z)	7.2	102.0
Cache	10.8	14.9	24.2	18.2	9.6	9.1	5.6	3.8	3.8	95.4	0.5	2.3	0.6	0.3	8.1	95.8
Carbon	7.5	13.9	17.2	11.0	10.8	15.9	10.1	6.8	6.8	97.5	0.3	0.6	1.2	(Z)	10.8	97.8
Daggett	5.7	11.1	12.7	14.4	11.7	15.4	12.3	10.8	5.8	98.0	1.2	–	0.8	–	5.5	130.0
Davis	9.5	16.9	17.5	16.4	12.6	11.9	7.4	4.5	3.3	94.6	1.2	1.8	0.6	0.3	6.6	101.2
Duchesne	9.4	17.2	17.4	13.6	11.3	12.1	8.9	6.3	3.8	92.9	0.3	0.3	5.0	(Z)	4.2	103.5
Emery	7.3	16.5	17.9	10.3	11.4	14.9	10.3	6.3	5.2	97.9	0.3	0.4	0.8	(Z)	6.1	101.0
Garfield	7.6	16.1	14.5	9.7	10.8	14.0	11.1	9.1	7.2	97.4	0.2	0.3	2.0	–	3.1	105.7
Grand	5.8	12.9	14.0	14.3	13.0	16.2	11.1	7.1	5.6	93.4	0.3	0.3	5.3	–	6.6	99.4
Iron	9.6	15.2	22.4	16.9	9.6	9.9	7.0	5.1	4.3	94.5	0.4	1.3	2.2	0.5	5.1	97.5
Juab	9.0	19.4	16.1	16.5	11.3	10.6	7.4	5.0	4.6	98.0	0.2	0.6	1.2	(Z)	2.3	98.9
Kane	5.9	13.5	15.2	10.1	11.1	14.5	12.4	9.3	8.0	98.0	0.1	0.3	1.4	–	2.6	102.8
Millard	7.7	17.7	18.9	8.9	11.1	14.0	9.6	6.4	5.7	97.2	0.2	0.4	1.5	0.2	11.0	106.9
Morgan	6.9	16.6	19.8	12.8	11.7	13.4	9.3	5.9	3.8	98.5	0.1	0.3	0.2	–	1.7	103.0
Piute	6.2	14.7	14.3	8.6	10.0	13.1	13.0	11.0	9.1	98.5	0.1	0.1	1.2	–	5.3	105.0
Rich	7.5	14.7	18.3	10.5	10.3	13.5	11.8	7.1	6.2	99.6	–	0.4	–	–	2.0	104.5
Salt Lake	9.1	15.3	15.7	17.4	13.6	12.6	8.0	4.5	3.9	92.0	1.3	2.9	0.9	1.3	14.7	102.5
San Juan	8.5	18.6	19.6	11.3	12.3	11.7	8.6	5.3	4.1	43.2	0.1	0.2	55.9	(Z)	3.3	97.6
Sanpete	8.0	16.4	20.7	13.7	10.9	11.1	8.1	5.9	5.0	96.3	0.5	0.8	1.0	0.8	8.1	109.0
Sevier	8.4	16.4	17.4	12.8	10.6	12.0	9.2	7.1	6.0	97.3	0.3	0.3	1.7	0.1	3.0	99.5
Summit	7.1	13.7	15.0	15.6	15.5	17.2	10.1	3.7	2.2	97.3	0.5	1.2	0.4	(Z)	10.5	109.0
Tooele	9.8	17.3	15.9	20.3	13.0	10.1	6.7	4.0	3.0	94.4	1.6	0.9	1.5	0.2	9.3	98.0
Uintah	8.5	15.7	17.1	15.3	11.3	13.3	8.4	5.9	4.5	89.0	0.2	0.4	9.4	0.1	3.8	99.0
Utah	11.5	17.2	21.5	19.2	10.3	8.4	5.5	3.5	3.0	95.7	0.4	1.2	0.6	0.6	8.4	98.4
Wasatch	9.5	16.0	15.8	17.7	13.4	11.8	7.6	4.8	3.3	96.7	0.5	0.6	0.8	0.2	7.7	102.5
Washington	8.6	15.0	15.9	17.2	10.2	9.1	7.1	8.1	8.9	95.9	0.4	0.6	1.4	0.5	6.6	98.1
Wayne	7.8	16.6	13.6	11.3	10.1	13.4	11.8	8.0	7.4	98.9	0.2	–	0.4	0.4	2.7	107.1
Weber	9.1	15.5	15.7	16.8	12.5	12.1	8.1	5.3	4.9	94.7	1.5	1.4	0.9	0.2	15.2	101.5
VERMONT	5.1	11.8	14.6	11.5	14.9	16.7	12.3	6.6	6.6	96.9	0.6	1.0	0.4	(Z)	1.1	97.1
Addison	4.8	12.1	18.8	10.3	14.2	16.4	12.0	5.7	5.7	97.4	0.6	0.8	0.2	(Z)	1.2	98.1
Bennington	4.8	11.5	12.8	9.8	13.9	16.3	13.1	8.4	9.3	97.7	0.7	0.8	0.2	(Z)	1.3	94.1
Caledonia	5.2	11.8	15.3	11.3	13.7	16.3	12.5	6.4	7.5	97.8	0.4	0.5	0.5	(Z)	0.8	98.3
Chittenden	5.3	11.9	17.5	13.1	15.5	15.9	10.5	5.4	4.8	95.1	1.0	2.3	0.2	(Z)	1.2	95.9
Essex	4.1	12.3	13.2	11.3	15.1	16.0	13.0	7.6	7.4	97.1	0.4	0.5	0.5	–	0.6	98.2
Franklin	6.0	14.3	12.7	12.8	16.5	15.9	10.9	5.7	5.3	96.5	0.4	0.4	1.3	(Z)	0.7	98.7
Grand Isle	4.3	11.4	12.8	12.4	15.2	18.0	13.4	7.4	5.1	97.5	0.2	0.3	0.9	(Z)	0.5	100.7
Lamoille	5.3	11.9	14.6	13.4	14.9	15.9	11.9	6.5	5.7	97.2	0.6	0.5	0.5	(Z)	1.0	101.8
Orange	4.7	12.0	14.2	11.0	14.5	17.5	13.0	6.8	6.3	98.3	0.3	0.4	0.3	(Z)	0.9	100.0
Orleans	5.0	11.7	12.8	12.7	14.0	15.9	12.6	7.3	8.0	97.6	0.5	0.4	0.5	(Z)	1.0	98.3
Rutland	4.8	11.1	13.8	10.3	14.6	16.9	13.1	7.4	7.9	98.3	0.4	0.5	0.4	(Z)	0.8	95.9
Washington	5.1	11.3	13.8	11.4	15.0	17.3	12.8	6.8	6.4	97.0	0.5	0.8	0.3	(Z)	1.4	98.2
Windham	5.0	11.4	12.5	9.9	14.8	18.2	14.0	7.1	7.1	97.0	0.7	0.9	0.2	(Z)	1.3	96.1
Windsor	4.7	11.0	11.5	10.1	14.3	17.9	14.2	7.9	8.4	97.8	0.4	0.7	0.2	(Z)	1.1	95.8
VIRGINIA	6.8	13.2	14.2	13.4	15.5	14.8	10.8	6.1	5.3	73.6	19.9	4.6	0.3	0.1	6.0	96.9
Accomack	6.0	13.0	12.9	12.6	13.0	14.6	11.6	8.8	7.5	69.1	29.5	0.4	0.4	0.2	8.0	96.1
Albemarle	5.7	12.3	18.2	12.4	13.8	15.0	10.5	6.4	5.7	84.3	9.7	4.5	0.3	(Z)	3.6	92.9
Alleghany[3]	5.2	12.3	11.2	9.7	13.8	15.0	14.9	9.4	8.5	93.4	5.5	0.3	0.2	–	0.6	95.4
Amelia	6.1	12.6	12.7	11.9	14.6	15.3	12.5	8.1	6.1	74.8	24.5	0.1	0.3	–	0.8	99.5
Amherst	5.0	12.3	15.0	11.0	14.3	15.1	12.2	8.5	6.7	78.3	19.7	0.5	0.8	(Z)	1.2	92.4

See footnotes at end of table.

[Includes United States, states, and 3,141 counties/county equivalents defined as of February 22, 2005. For more information on these areas, see Appendix C, Geographic Information]

County	Age (percent)									One race (percent)					His-panic or Latino origin[1] (per-cent)	Males per 100 females
	Under 5 years	5 to 14 years	15 to 24 years	25 to 34 years	35 to 44 years	45 to 54 years	55 to 64 years	65 to 74 years	75 years and over	White alone	Black or African American alone	Asian alone	American Indian and Alaska Native alone	Native Hawaiian and Other Pacific Islander alone		
VIRGINIA—Con.																
Appomattox	5.4	13.0	12.5	11.2	13.9	14.7	13.3	8.9	7.1	77.7	21.6	0.2	0.2	(Z)	0.7	95.5
Arlington	6.8	8.8	9.7	20.7	19.3	14.5	10.9	4.5	4.8	80.0	8.8	8.9	0.4	0.1	16.1	101.3
Augusta	5.1	12.3	12.6	12.5	15.3	16.0	12.8	7.4	5.9	95.1	3.9	0.3	0.2	(Z)	1.6	100.8
Bath	3.6	10.5	11.1	11.4	14.7	14.7	14.5	11.6	7.8	91.9	7.1	0.6	0.1	(Z)	0.4	102.8
Bedford	4.9	12.7	12.5	11.6	15.4	16.8	13.3	7.6	5.3	92.2	6.4	0.6	0.2	(Z)	0.8	99.8
Bland	4.1	9.9	12.1	13.5	15.5	15.9	13.7	8.7	6.7	95.5	4.2	0.1	(Z)	–	0.5	122.3
Botetourt	4.7	12.1	12.3	10.5	15.0	17.6	14.1	7.9	5.8	94.3	4.3	0.7	0.2	–	0.9	99.7
Brunswick	5.0	10.3	14.7	14.2	14.9	14.9	11.2	7.9	6.7	43.3	56.3	0.2	(Z)	–	1.5	116.4
Buchanan	4.8	11.1	12.2	11.7	15.3	17.6	14.0	8.4	4.8	96.5	3.0	0.3	(Z)	–	0.6	104.2
Buckingham	4.5	11.2	13.8	14.1	16.8	14.8	11.5	7.1	6.1	61.4	37.6	0.2	0.2	–	1.0	122.5
Campbell	5.9	12.7	12.1	12.7	14.4	15.2	12.7	8.3	5.9	82.6	15.5	0.8	0.2	–	1.1	95.3
Caroline	6.4	13.0	13.2	14.6	15.1	14.1	11.4	6.5	5.6	67.3	30.3	0.6	0.7	(Z)	2.7	98.4
Carroll	4.8	11.6	10.9	12.8	14.2	14.9	13.1	9.2	8.5	99.0	0.6	0.1	0.1	–	2.0	97.5
Charles City	4.9	11.1	11.6	10.9	15.1	17.0	14.6	8.8	6.0	45.7	47.2	0.2	6.8	(Z)	0.8	97.4
Charlotte	5.9	12.6	12.4	11.1	13.5	14.6	12.2	9.2	8.4	68.0	31.6	0.2	(Z)	–	2.0	92.6
Chesterfield	6.3	14.6	15.3	12.0	15.7	17.0	11.7	4.5	3.0	74.8	20.8	2.8	0.4	0.1	4.6	96.5
Clarke	4.7	12.5	12.0	11.7	15.2	16.4	13.1	8.0	6.4	92.7	6.3	0.6	0.2	(Z)	2.6	99.4
Craig	5.4	12.2	11.8	10.6	15.5	16.6	13.8	8.3	5.8	98.9	0.5	0.2	0.2	–	0.3	104.0
Culpeper	6.6	13.2	13.6	16.1	15.8	13.8	9.9	6.0	5.0	80.9	16.2	1.1	0.5	(Z)	5.5	104.6
Cumberland	5.5	13.4	12.1	12.4	14.7	13.8	12.8	8.0	7.3	64.0	34.5	0.6	0.3	–	2.2	92.9
Dickenson	5.1	11.3	13.2	11.8	13.6	16.5	13.4	8.2	6.8	99.1	0.6	0.1	0.1	–	0.5	95.7
Dinwiddie	4.9	12.9	12.8	11.8	16.8	16.2	12.7	7.0	4.8	66.2	32.5	0.5	0.3	(Z)	1.4	97.5
Essex	5.6	12.1	12.0	11.4	13.9	15.1	12.4	8.7	8.8	58.4	39.4	1.0	0.6	–	1.4	89.9
Fairfax	7.2	13.9	12.3	11.5	16.6	16.9	12.8	5.2	3.6	72.5	9.3	15.4	0.3	0.1	12.5	98.3
Fauquier	6.0	13.7	13.8	12.2	15.6	16.3	12.0	6.1	4.4	88.5	8.8	1.1	0.3	0.1	4.4	99.3
Floyd	5.3	11.8	11.3	12.7	14.4	14.8	13.8	8.1	7.7	97.5	1.9	0.3	(Z)	(Z)	2.1	98.4
Fluvanna	6.2	12.9	11.7	14.6	16.8	14.2	10.1	7.7	5.8	81.3	17.0	0.5	0.1	(Z)	1.8	87.1
Franklin	5.3	11.7	12.9	11.9	14.4	15.1	13.4	8.7	6.6	90.2	8.7	0.4	0.2	(Z)	1.7	97.6
Frederick	6.2	13.7	13.4	14.1	16.2	14.9	10.5	6.2	4.7	94.2	3.6	0.9	0.2	(Z)	4.2	99.6
Giles	5.8	11.9	11.7	12.2	14.6	14.5	13.7	7.9	7.8	97.9	1.5	0.2	0.1	–	0.8	95.9
Gloucester	5.5	13.1	13.8	11.5	15.6	16.3	11.9	6.9	5.5	88.0	9.6	0.7	0.5	(Z)	1.9	96.9
Goochland	5.2	11.0	12.2	13.5	16.1	16.1	13.2	7.3	5.3	76.5	21.8	1.1	0.2	(Z)	1.4	100.2
Grayson	4.7	11.2	10.5	11.1	13.9	15.4	13.9	10.3	9.0	97.4	2.1	(Z)	0.1	0.2	2.2	96.7
Greene	7.4	14.8	11.7	13.1	17.6	14.5	10.7	6.1	4.2	91.5	6.8	0.6	0.2	(Z)	2.2	98.7
Greensville	5.3	8.7	12.1	16.3	18.9	16.0	11.3	6.2	5.3	40.6	58.8	0.4	0.1	–	1.4	154.2
Halifax[4]	6.0	12.7	11.5	10.2	12.8	15.3	13.3	9.1	9.0	61.0	38.0	0.2	0.3	–	1.4	91.2
Hanover	5.7	13.9	14.2	10.8	15.9	16.7	11.5	6.3	5.1	88.1	9.7	1.1	0.3	(Z)	1.2	98.0
Henrico	6.8	13.8	12.1	13.8	16.0	15.3	10.3	5.9	6.2	66.1	27.4	4.9	0.4	(Z)	3.1	89.7
Henry	5.5	11.7	11.9	11.7	14.8	14.9	13.4	8.9	7.3	76.0	22.6	0.6	0.3	0.1	5.5	97.0
Highland	3.5	9.8	10.4	7.3	13.0	17.2	15.7	12.4	10.8	99.4	0.2	0.1	0.2	–	0.5	97.7
Isle of Wight	5.3	13.0	13.4	11.9	15.3	16.5	12.0	7.3	5.3	73.8	24.8	0.4	0.3	(Z)	1.2	95.1
James City	4.7	11.8	13.2	13.3	14.0	14.3	10.9	9.2	8.5	83.9	13.0	1.7	0.3	(Z)	2.2	95.8
King and Queen	5.6	11.8	12.2	11.1	14.4	16.1	13.4	7.7	7.6	66.2	32.0	0.3	1.3	–	1.4	94.4
King George	6.8	14.5	14.7	14.9	16.1	14.1	10.0	5.1	3.8	79.3	17.4	1.3	0.6	(Z)	2.6	101.2
King William	6.6	13.8	12.3	12.9	16.1	15.4	11.6	6.3	4.9	77.0	20.4	0.4	1.4	0.1	1.5	96.6
Lancaster	4.7	9.3	10.6	7.8	10.4	13.5	13.5	14.4	15.9	72.1	27.2	0.4	0.1	(Z)	0.8	88.8
Lee	5.3	12.2	12.8	12.8	13.5	15.5	13.0	7.9	6.9	98.5	0.7	0.3	0.1	–	0.5	95.4
Loudoun	8.9	16.0	12.3	17.4	19.2	13.3	7.8	3.1	2.1	78.2	7.5	11.3	0.3	0.1	9.3	98.6
Louisa	5.6	12.6	12.6	12.9	15.8	15.2	11.9	7.7	5.6	79.1	19.4	0.3	0.4	–	1.2	96.3
Lunenburg	4.8	10.6	12.9	13.1	14.4	15.4	12.0	8.3	8.4	60.7	38.3	0.2	0.3	0.1	2.7	114.6
Madison	5.5	12.3	12.5	11.0	14.1	15.7	13.0	8.3	7.7	87.6	11.0	0.7	0.1	–	1.4	97.1
Mathews	4.2	10.2	11.4	9.3	11.9	14.7	15.9	12.0	10.4	88.7	10.8	0.2	0.2	–	0.8	94.6
Mecklenburg	5.7	11.3	11.4	11.8	14.1	14.2	12.7	9.9	8.9	60.9	38.0	0.5	0.3	(Z)	1.6	99.0
Middlesex	3.8	9.6	11.2	9.8	13.1	14.3	15.1	11.5	11.6	81.3	18.2	0.2	0.3	(Z)	1.3	93.0
Montgomery	4.6	8.6	34.9	14.9	10.5	9.8	7.6	5.0	4.1	89.8	4.0	4.7	0.2	(Z)	1.9	111.0
Nelson	5.4	10.9	11.8	10.5	12.8	16.5	14.7	9.8	7.5	84.7	14.2	0.3	0.1	(Z)	2.5	94.8
New Kent	5.0	12.6	13.6	13.1	16.6	17.1	12.6	5.6	3.9	83.2	14.6	0.6	1.0	–	1.6	101.8
Northampton	6.6	11.8	12.9	11.0	11.0	15.2	11.6	9.8	10.1	59.3	40.0	0.3	0.1	(Z)	5.8	91.0
Northumberland	4.4	9.7	10.4	8.8	11.1	12.9	15.1	14.9	12.8	74.0	25.1	0.4	0.2	–	1.1	92.4
Nottoway	5.6	11.9	13.4	12.9	14.4	14.6	10.9	8.1	8.2	58.7	40.4	0.4	0.1	(Z)	2.6	108.8
Orange	5.5	12.1	12.6	13.2	14.8	13.7	10.9	9.4	7.9	85.3	13.2	0.5	0.3	(Z)	2.1	95.2
Page	5.7	12.1	11.8	12.6	14.5	14.6	12.6	8.3	7.6	96.8	2.4	0.2	0.1	(Z)	1.3	97.5
Patrick	4.3	12.0	10.9	12.4	14.0	14.6	13.7	9.9	8.3	93.0	6.1	0.2	0.2	0.1	2.4	97.1
Pittsylvania	5.6	12.0	12.1	11.3	14.7	16.4	13.5	7.8	6.5	75.2	23.9	0.2	0.2	(Z)	1.6	95.7
Powhatan	5.3	12.3	13.9	14.5	18.2	15.4	11.5	5.3	3.7	84.0	15.2	0.2	0.2	(Z)	1.3	120.6
Prince Edward	5.1	10.5	28.1	10.5	11.4	12.0	8.9	6.7	6.9	62.8	35.8	0.7	0.2	0.1	1.2	98.0
Prince George	5.4	12.2	19.3	16.8	16.7	13.8	9.2	4.1	2.4	60.7	35.5	1.8	0.4	0.2	6.1	128.3
Prince William	8.9	16.1	14.2	16.0	17.0	13.8	8.5	3.6	2.0	70.1	19.4	6.4	0.5	0.2	18.0	100.7
Pulaski	5.0	11.3	11.4	12.7	14.3	14.9	14.3	8.7	7.5	92.6	6.1	0.4	0.1	(Z)	1.2	98.8
Rappahannock	5.1	11.0	11.5	10.8	13.2	17.3	15.8	8.8	6.3	93.4	5.4	0.2	0.2	–	1.9	97.7

See footnotes at end of table.

[Includes United States, states, and 3,141 counties/county equivalents defined as of February 22, 2005. For more information on these areas, see Appendix C, Geographic Information]

County	\	\	\	\	Age (percent)	\	\	\	\	\	\	One race (percent)	\	\	Hispanic or Latino origin[1] (percent)	Males per 100 females
	Under 5 years	5 to 14 years	15 to 24 years	25 to 34 years	35 to 44 years	45 to 54 years	55 to 64 years	65 to 74 years	75 years and over	White alone	Black or African American alone	Asian alone	American Indian and Alaska Native alone	Native Hawaiian and Other Pacific Islander alone		
VIRGINIA—Con.																
Richmond	4.7	8.4	12.2	14.3	16.6	14.5	10.4	9.1	9.8	66.1	33.1	0.5	(Z)	0.1	2.8	135.5
Roanoke	5.4	12.1	12.7	10.4	13.9	16.6	13.4	8.0	7.5	92.4	4.8	2.0	0.1	(Z)	1.6	91.5
Rockbridge	5.1	11.4	13.0	11.8	13.1	15.8	12.8	9.5	7.5	95.3	3.3	0.6	0.3	–	0.7	100.6
Rockingham	6.0	13.1	14.0	12.1	14.5	15.2	11.3	7.2	6.5	97.2	1.7	0.5	0.1	(Z)	4.3	98.7
Russell	5.3	11.7	11.9	12.7	13.9	16.4	13.3	8.5	6.3	98.7	0.9	0.1	0.1	–	0.7	95.4
Scott	4.7	11.1	11.3	11.6	13.9	15.2	13.6	9.7	9.0	98.6	0.8	0.1	0.1	(Z)	0.6	94.3
Shenandoah	5.9	11.9	11.6	12.6	14.1	14.4	12.1	9.1	8.3	97.1	1.5	0.5	0.1	(Z)	4.5	95.9
Smyth	5.4	11.9	10.9	12.6	14.1	15.1	12.8	9.3	7.8	97.1	2.2	0.2	0.1	–	1.0	94.6
Southampton	5.0	11.6	15.1	11.8	14.8	15.8	12.0	7.5	6.5	59.4	40.0	0.2	0.2	–	1.0	110.5
Spotsylvania	7.2	15.3	14.2	15.4	16.3	14.4	9.3	4.6	3.4	81.6	14.4	1.8	0.3	0.1	5.3	97.7
Stafford	7.1	16.1	15.2	15.0	17.3	14.8	8.8	3.5	2.2	78.4	16.1	2.3	0.4	0.2	6.4	101.2
Surry	5.5	12.4	13.7	10.2	14.5	17.3	12.7	7.6	6.1	49.6	49.7	0.3	0.1	0.1	0.9	92.3
Sussex	4.9	9.9	14.0	15.0	16.4	15.3	10.6	7.2	6.7	38.0	61.2	0.3	(Z)	(Z)	1.2	139.0
Tazewell	5.3	11.4	11.9	12.7	12.7	16.4	13.5	8.6	7.5	96.0	2.5	0.9	0.2	–	0.5	93.2
Warren	6.7	13.7	13.2	13.0	16.0	14.7	10.9	6.4	5.4	92.8	5.1	0.6	0.3	(Z)	2.7	98.1
Washington	5.1	11.0	12.8	12.3	13.9	15.7	13.2	8.8	7.2	97.4	1.6	0.4	0.1	(Z)	0.8	96.1
Westmoreland	5.5	11.5	12.6	10.2	12.6	14.7	13.7	10.5	8.8	68.4	30.2	0.4	0.4	–	3.6	93.5
Wise	5.9	11.6	14.3	14.2	13.7	15.5	11.4	7.0	6.4	93.5	5.5	0.4	0.2	–	0.9	103.8
Wythe	6.0	11.5	11.3	12.9	14.7	15.0	12.4	8.6	7.7	95.8	3.0	0.5	0.2	(Z)	0.8	92.5
York	5.1	14.4	15.1	10.8	16.4	16.1	11.4	6.3	4.2	79.8	13.5	4.2	0.4	0.2	3.6	97.5
Independent Cities																
Alexandria	8.9	8.9	7.9	19.2	19.9	14.0	10.8	5.1	5.4	70.7	21.7	5.3	0.4	0.1	13.7	93.0
Bedford	6.4	11.9	10.3	11.7	13.2	14.3	8.6	10.4	13.2	75.9	22.7	0.8	0.1	(Z)	0.9	90.9
Bristol	5.1	10.9	13.8	11.6	12.6	13.3	11.0	10.0	11.7	92.5	5.9	0.7	0.2	(Z)	1.3	82.4
Buena Vista	5.3	11.9	17.2	10.7	12.9	12.3	11.9	9.4	8.3	93.0	5.9	0.4	0.4	–	1.6	87.9
Charlottesville	6.2	8.2	28.3	15.7	10.7	9.9	7.1	6.3	7.5	71.9	21.4	4.7	0.1	(Z)	3.1	86.2
Chesapeake	6.7	14.9	15.2	12.4	16.1	15.7	9.7	5.3	4.1	65.8	30.1	2.1	0.4	0.1	2.6	94.9
Clifton Forge[3]	(NA)	(NA)	(NA)	(NA)	(NA)	(NA)	(NA)	(NA)	(NA)	(NA)	(NA)	(NA)	(NA)	(NA)	(NA)	(NA)
Colonial Heights	6.3	11.8	13.0	11.8	13.1	14.0	11.6	8.9	9.7	85.6	10.3	3.1	0.2	(Z)	2.8	91.2
Covington	5.9	12.6	10.4	13.2	13.0	12.8	11.9	8.7	11.7	83.2	14.5	1.0	0.4	–	1.0	93.9
Danville	6.3	12.3	12.2	10.5	12.0	14.5	11.8	9.2	11.2	52.9	45.7	0.8	0.2	(Z)	2.0	84.2
Emporia	7.0	13.2	13.8	10.8	13.2	12.8	9.8	8.6	10.7	41.2	58.2	0.6	–	–	2.8	83.8
Fairfax	6.8	11.0	11.4	14.1	16.5	14.2	11.8	7.2	7.0	77.3	6.5	14.3	0.4	(Z)	13.1	95.6
Falls Church	6.7	11.4	12.0	10.9	14.1	18.3	13.4	5.7	7.4	85.6	5.0	7.5	0.2	–	8.0	95.2
Franklin	8.5	12.3	14.3	10.1	12.2	13.9	11.4	8.0	9.3	43.2	55.7	0.8	0.2	–	1.1	81.1
Fredericksburg	8.9	9.4	24.1	14.7	10.6	9.7	8.0	6.3	8.3	75.7	20.7	1.7	0.4	0.1	7.0	80.1
Galax	7.6	12.2	11.4	11.9	12.6	12.9	11.4	9.3	10.8	91.0	7.4	0.8	0.5	–	13.7	92.3
Hampton	6.6	13.0	16.3	13.7	15.8	14.1	9.4	6.1	5.0	48.2	47.1	2.1	0.4	0.1	3.4	98.8
Harrisonburg	6.0	7.8	42.5	12.5	8.6	7.6	5.4	4.1	5.5	87.5	6.5	3.4	0.3	(Z)	11.9	88.9
Hopewell	8.0	15.1	12.7	13.6	13.5	12.5	10.1	7.0	7.5	60.1	37.2	1.0	0.4	0.1	4.1	89.2
Lexington	2.8	4.9	46.1	8.2	5.6	7.3	6.9	7.9	10.1	87.5	9.4	2.4	0.3	–	1.8	125.2
Lynchburg	6.5	11.3	21.8	11.2	11.0	12.1	9.3	7.4	9.5	66.9	29.8	1.6	0.2	(Z)	1.5	84.7
Manassas	9.4	16.1	13.5	14.6	17.2	13.6	8.5	4.4	2.7	80.5	13.3	3.8	0.5	0.1	25.6	107.3
Manassas Park	9.9	17.6	12.7	16.8	19.5	12.0	6.1	3.6	1.9	79.7	11.7	6.1	0.5	0.1	28.7	102.6
Martinsville	5.9	12.0	11.3	10.4	13.6	14.1	10.8	9.6	12.3	56.4	42.4	0.7	0.1	–	3.7	82.6
Newport News	9.1	15.7	13.3	14.2	15.3	13.3	8.7	5.5	5.0	52.0	42.2	2.6	0.4	0.2	4.6	91.9
Norfolk	8.7	13.3	20.1	15.6	12.8	11.8	7.5	4.6	5.5	49.2	44.9	3.0	0.4	0.1	4.2	106.6
Norton	5.3	12.2	12.6	12.1	12.9	16.2	12.5	8.1	8.1	92.1	6.0	1.5	–	0.1	1.1	79.4
Petersburg	8.5	13.0	12.9	11.2	13.1	13.9	11.1	8.0	8.3	19.7	78.6	0.9	0.1	(Z)	2.1	84.4
Poquoson	4.0	12.8	13.9	8.8	14.0	17.5	15.0	8.8	5.1	95.7	1.7	1.8	0.3	–	1.3	102.5
Portsmouth	8.1	14.1	15.1	12.8	14.0	13.5	9.3	6.1	7.1	44.7	52.3	0.9	0.5	0.1	2.0	94.5
Radford	4.0	5.3	49.5	11.7	6.2	6.8	5.9	4.8	5.9	88.2	7.7	2.6	0.3	0.1	1.5	81.6
Richmond	7.9	11.7	15.9	14.3	13.8	13.4	9.2	6.2	7.8	40.8	56.2	1.4	0.2	0.2	3.6	86.5
Roanoke	6.9	13.2	10.6	13.1	14.2	14.6	10.7	7.1	9.6	69.8	27.1	1.3	0.2	(Z)	2.2	87.7
Salem	4.9	10.9	17.1	10.8	13.0	14.9	11.7	8.4	8.4	91.5	6.7	1.2	0.1	–	1.2	90.4
South Boston[4]	(NA)	(NA)	(NA)	(NA)	(NA)	(NA)	(NA)	(NA)	(NA)	(NA)	(NA)	(NA)	(NA)	(NA)	(NA)	(NA)
Staunton	5.9	11.0	13.2	11.8	12.6	13.7	11.8	9.3	10.8	86.0	12.1	0.5	0.3	–	1.3	84.5
Suffolk	7.1	14.4	14.1	14.3	15.9	14.0	9.7	5.7	4.8	55.3	42.0	1.2	0.3	(Z)	1.9	93.3
Virginia Beach	7.3	14.7	14.2	14.3	16.6	14.3	9.0	5.3	4.3	71.5	20.0	5.3	0.4	0.1	4.9	97.8
Waynesboro	7.3	13.2	11.5	12.8	13.3	12.8	11.3	8.2	9.5	87.2	10.4	0.7	0.4	(Z)	4.4	89.8
Williamsburg	5.8	4.2	46.7	9.8	6.1	6.6	5.9	7.4	7.3	81.6	12.5	4.7	0.3	(Z)	3.0	79.5
Winchester	7.7	11.7	13.7	15.5	13.4	12.7	9.1	7.4	8.8	85.4	10.6	2.0	0.4	(Z)	10.3	95.5
WASHINGTON	6.3	13.1	14.5	13.8	15.2	15.1	10.6	5.8	5.6	85.0	3.5	6.4	1.7	0.5	8.8	99.7
Adams	9.9	17.3	16.4	11.3	12.5	12.5	9.2	5.7	5.1	96.5	0.7	0.7	1.2	0.2	50.9	105.2
Asotin	6.0	12.9	13.4	11.9	12.7	14.1	11.4	8.3	9.3	96.6	0.3	0.8	1.1	(Z)	2.3	92.4
Benton	6.8	14.7	15.0	13.2	14.2	15.0	10.5	5.6	5.0	93.4	1.2	2.5	1.0	0.1	14.6	99.5
Chelan	6.7	13.8	15.0	11.2	13.5	15.1	10.5	6.9	7.5	96.0	0.5	0.9	1.1	0.3	20.9	99.2
Clallam	4.4	10.6	13.3	11.1	11.5	14.5	12.5	10.1	11.9	90.9	0.9	1.3	5.0	0.2	4.0	97.8

See footnotes at end of table.

County and City Data Book: 2007

U.S. Census Bureau

Includes United States, states, and 3,141 counties/county equivalents defined as of February 22, 2005. For more information on these areas, see Appendix C, Geographic Information]

County	Population characteristics, 2005															
	Age (percent)									One race (percent)					His-panic or Latino origin[1] (per-cent)	Males per 100 females
	Under 5 years	5 to 14 years	15 to 24 years	25 to 34 years	35 to 44 years	45 to 54 years	55 to 64 years	65 to 74 years	75 years and over	White alone	Black or African American alone	Asian alone	American Indian and Alaska Native alone	Native Hawaiian and Other Pacific Islander alone		
WASHINGTON—Con.																
Clark	6.6	14.7	13.9	14.8	15.2	14.6	10.2	5.2	4.6	90.2	2.0	3.7	0.9	0.4	5.8	99.3
Columbia	4.3	11.6	12.8	10.7	12.6	15.7	14.4	8.7	9.2	97.6	0.4	0.6	1.0	–	6.2	97.2
Cowlitz	6.0	13.6	14.0	12.7	13.7	14.8	11.6	6.9	6.6	94.1	0.7	1.3	1.6	0.1	5.6	98.5
Douglas	6.2	14.8	15.5	11.7	13.6	14.8	10.3	6.8	6.3	80.5	0.2	0.8	1.3	0.2	22.2	98.7
Ferry	4.6	11.7	16.4	10.2	11.3	17.1	14.1	9.1	5.6	93.6	0.2	0.3	17.0	(Z)	2.8	106.3
Franklin	10.1	16.9	16.9	12.6	13.3	11.6	7.5	3.8	3.5	93.6	2.6	1.8	0.8	0.2	48.3	111.3
Garfield	3.8	10.9	13.8	7.0	12.2	17.6	11.8	11.0	11.9	98.8	–	0.5	0.3	–	3.0	97.6
Grant	8.4	16.2	16.1	13.5	13.1	12.4	8.9	5.9	5.6	95.1	1.1	1.1	1.4	0.1	33.8	105.2
Grays Harbor	5.5	12.4	14.3	12.6	13.7	14.8	11.9	7.4	7.3	90.9	0.5	1.3	4.8	0.1	6.3	102.2
Island	5.7	12.6	13.4	14.1	14.0	13.3	10.9	8.3	7.7	89.9	2.0	4.0	0.9	0.4	3.7	99.7
Jefferson	3.8	9.4	11.7	9.8	11.1	16.8	15.8	10.9	10.6	93.8	0.8	1.4	2.1	(Z)	2.4	97.6
King	6.0	11.7	12.6	14.7	17.3	16.2	11.0	5.3	5.3	76.2	5.9	12.9	1.0	0.6	6.7	99.7
Kitsap	6.1	13.5	14.7	12.7	14.7	15.5	11.4	6.0	5.5	86.0	2.8	4.6	1.6	0.8	4.7	103.8
Kittitas	4.8	9.4	28.3	13.4	10.5	12.2	9.6	6.2	5.5	93.2	0.9	3.1	1.1	0.2	5.7	97.8
Klickitat	5.7	13.0	13.9	10.5	12.7	16.3	13.2	8.0	6.9	94.2	0.4	0.7	3.1	0.1	8.5	98.7
Lewis	5.9	12.7	14.6	12.2	12.6	14.8	11.6	7.9	7.6	95.9	0.5	0.8	1.3	0.2	6.5	98.8
Lincoln	4.1	12.1	13.7	8.0	11.8	16.4	12.9	10.5	10.5	96.1	0.3	0.3	2.1	(Z)	2.1	98.2
Mason	5.2	11.5	14.1	12.6	13.1	14.9	11.7	8.9	8.1	91.5	1.2	1.2	3.6	0.5	6.3	104.6
Okanogan	6.2	13.0	15.1	10.3	12.1	15.7	12.4	8.4	7.0	86.0	0.4	0.6	11.1	0.1	14.3	98.4
Pacific	4.4	10.1	13.3	9.9	11.0	15.2	13.6	11.6	10.8	93.3	0.4	2.1	2.4	–	5.8	98.2
Pend Oreille	4.5	12.0	14.5	10.1	12.6	16.6	13.8	8.9	7.0	94.3	0.3	0.7	3.3	0.1	2.0	99.8
Pierce	6.7	14.0	15.1	14.2	15.4	14.5	9.7	5.5	4.8	80.1	7.1	5.7	1.5	0.9	6.8	99.4
San Juan	3.1	9.0	11.4	8.7	11.1	17.9	17.8	11.1	10.0	96.4	0.3	1.2	1.1	–	2.7	96.5
Skagit	6.0	12.9	14.9	13.0	13.5	14.3	10.9	6.9	7.6	93.7	0.7	1.7	2.0	0.2	13.0	98.4
Skamania	5.0	12.7	14.8	10.1	15.0	18.2	13.0	6.2	4.9	95.7	0.4	0.6	2.1	0.1	4.7	100.5
Snohomish	6.4	14.1	13.8	13.6	16.7	15.8	10.0	5.1	4.4	85.5	2.2	7.4	1.5	0.4	6.3	100.9
Spokane	6.1	13.0	15.9	13.5	13.9	14.8	10.3	6.0	6.4	92.0	1.7	2.1	1.5	0.2	3.3	96.9
Stevens	5.3	13.2	15.5	9.3	12.3	16.9	13.2	7.9	6.4	91.3	0.3	0.5	5.6	0.2	2.1	98.4
Thurston	5.6	12.5	14.8	13.9	14.5	15.5	11.4	6.0	5.8	86.9	2.7	4.9	1.6	0.6	5.2	96.8
Wahkiakum	3.5	11.3	13.3	8.4	12.7	14.7	15.9	10.9	9.3	96.1	0.3	0.5	1.7	–	2.6	99.0
Walla Walla	6.0	12.1	18.9	12.5	12.8	13.5	9.6	6.3	8.4	94.1	1.9	1.3	1.1	0.3	16.9	101.3
Whatcom	5.4	12.1	19.0	13.6	13.3	14.0	10.4	6.0	6.2	90.5	0.9	3.3	2.9	0.2	5.9	97.4
Whitman	4.6	8.4	37.5	14.5	9.0	9.5	7.0	4.3	5.1	87.4	2.1	7.2	0.7	0.4	3.4	102.3
Yakima	8.9	16.3	15.7	12.8	13.1	12.8	9.3	5.5	5.7	90.4	1.3	1.2	5.0	0.3	39.3	99.9
WEST VIRGINIA	5.6	11.6	13.1	12.6	13.7	15.7	12.4	7.9	7.4	95.2	3.2	0.6	0.2	(Z)	0.9	95.9
Barbour	5.1	11.7	13.9	12.5	13.8	15.0	12.6	8.1	7.4	97.2	0.8	0.4	0.7	(Z)	0.5	97.7
Berkeley	6.5	13.6	13.0	15.2	15.7	14.6	10.7	6.1	4.6	92.4	5.2	0.5	0.3	(Z)	2.5	100.0
Boone	6.3	12.3	10.7	14.4	12.9	17.0	12.9	7.1	6.3	98.8	0.6	0.2	0.1	(Z)	0.5	94.1
Braxton	5.0	11.4	12.2	13.1	14.5	15.7	12.7	8.0	7.5	98.5	0.7	0.1	0.2	0.1	0.5	103.1
Brooke	4.6	10.9	13.3	9.9	13.3	16.2	13.1	9.3	9.5	98.2	0.9	0.4	(Z)	(Z)	0.6	95.0
Cabell	6.0	10.8	15.5	13.2	12.4	14.2	11.7	8.0	8.1	93.7	4.3	0.7	0.2	(Z)	0.8	92.6
Calhoun	4.8	10.5	12.8	10.7	14.0	16.8	14.1	8.6	7.8	99.2	0.1	0.1	0.3	–	0.7	101.4
Clay	6.5	12.8	12.2	14.0	13.2	15.4	11.8	7.6	6.4	98.5	0.1	(Z)	0.7	–	0.4	100.0
Doddridge	4.6	12.0	14.3	13.1	14.2	15.8	11.6	8.1	6.3	99.0	0.3	0.2	0.2	(Z)	0.6	103.9
Fayette	6.0	11.2	13.2	12.6	12.8	16.0	12.1	7.8	8.3	93.4	5.0	0.4	0.3	(Z)	0.7	98.9
Gilmer	3.8	9.4	22.0	10.6	12.3	13.8	11.6	8.9	7.7	97.0	1.1	1.2	0.2	(Z)	0.8	105.8
Grant	5.5	12.0	10.3	13.1	14.2	14.2	13.4	9.6	7.8	98.5	0.8	0.2	0.2	–	0.6	100.0
Greenbrier	5.2	11.4	11.8	11.2	13.0	15.7	13.5	9.3	8.9	95.4	3.0	0.2	0.4	(Z)	0.7	94.7
Hampshire	5.3	13.3	12.4	13.0	14.7	14.8	12.5	8.0	6.1	97.8	1.1	0.3	0.2	(Z)	0.9	101.6
Hancock	5.3	11.1	10.5	10.8	13.6	17.0	12.8	9.6	9.3	96.8	2.4	0.3	0.1	–	1.0	93.4
Hardy	5.4	12.6	11.6	12.4	15.1	15.0	13.0	8.1	6.8	97.5	1.9	0.1	0.1	–	1.3	98.4
Harrison	5.7	12.2	12.6	11.6	14.0	15.4	12.7	7.8	8.1	96.7	1.6	0.8	0.1	(Z)	1.1	93.7
Jackson	5.4	12.3	12.5	12.2	13.7	15.2	11.6	9.8	7.3	98.7	0.1	0.3	0.2	(Z)	0.3	95.5
Jefferson	6.4	12.7	13.8	12.5	16.3	15.5	12.2	6.2	4.5	91.5	6.1	0.7	0.3	0.1	3.1	99.7
Kanawha	6.0	11.4	11.2	11.9	13.5	16.8	12.7	8.2	8.3	90.3	7.1	0.9	0.2	(Z)	0.6	92.3
Lewis	5.5	11.6	11.5	12.4	14.2	15.3	12.9	8.5	8.1	98.7	0.3	0.3	0.2	–	0.6	95.9
Lincoln	6.1	12.1	11.9	14.5	14.3	15.6	12.2	7.7	5.6	99.4	(Z)	0.1	0.1	–	0.5	97.3
Logan	5.9	11.5	11.2	13.9	12.9	17.6	12.7	7.7	6.5	96.7	2.5	0.3	0.1	(Z)	0.6	95.7
McDowell	5.6	11.3	11.2	12.2	12.9	18.4	13.6	7.8	7.8	88.7	10.6	(Z)	0.1	(Z)	0.5	91.9
Marion	5.4	10.8	14.3	12.4	13.0	14.9	12.5	7.8	9.0	95.3	3.3	0.4	0.2	(Z)	0.8	91.4
Marshall	4.9	11.9	12.1	10.5	13.7	16.8	13.4	8.2	8.4	98.4	0.5	0.3	0.1	(Z)	0.7	95.9
Mason	5.5	12.0	11.3	12.7	13.4	16.2	12.7	9.3	7.0	98.5	0.5	0.3	0.2	(Z)	0.6	95.4
Mercer	5.8	11.4	11.7	12.8	12.7	15.3	12.8	8.6	9.0	92.6	5.9	0.6	0.2	(Z)	0.6	92.2
Mineral	5.4	12.4	12.1	11.5	14.2	15.5	13.9	8.1	6.9	96.1	2.9	0.3	0.1	–	0.6	98.7
Mingo	6.6	12.2	12.4	12.5	14.3	16.9	12.3	7.0	5.7	96.5	2.4	0.2	0.3	(Z)	0.6	94.5
Monongalia	5.1	9.1	26.1	15.6	11.9	12.4	9.2	5.4	5.2	92.8	3.5	2.2	0.2	0.1	1.2	102.5
Monroe	4.6	11.4	12.1	12.3	13.6	14.7	14.4	8.6	8.2	98.4	0.9	0.1	0.2	(Z)	0.4	96.5
Morgan	4.8	12.5	10.3	12.4	14.7	15.6	13.0	9.1	7.7	98.8	0.7	0.1	0.2	–	0.8	98.7
Nicholas	5.2	11.4	12.3	12.2	13.7	16.3	12.9	8.8	7.2	99.0	0.1	0.2	0.2	(Z)	0.5	95.3
Ohio	5.2	11.1	14.7	9.1	12.6	16.4	12.1	8.4	10.4	94.5	3.6	0.9	0.1	(Z)	0.6	88.2

See footnotes at end of table.

Table B-3. Counties — **Population by Age, Race, Hispanic Origin, and Sex**—Con.

[Includes United States, states, and 3,141 counties/county equivalents defined as of February 22, 2005. For more information on these areas, see Appendix C, Geographic Information]

County	Age (percent)									One race (percent)					His-panic or Latino origin[1] (per-cent)	Males per 100 females
	Under 5 years	5 to 14 years	15 to 24 years	25 to 34 years	35 to 44 years	45 to 54 years	55 to 64 years	65 to 74 years	75 years and over	White alone	Black or African Ameri-can alone	Asian alone	Ameri-can Indian and Alaska Native alone	Native Hawai-ian and Other Pacific Islander alone		
WEST VIRGINIA—Con.																
Pendleton	5.8	11.0	10.8	9.6	13.5	16.0	13.2	10.2	10.0	97.0	1.9	0.3	0.3	0.1	1.2	102.5
Pleasants	5.1	12.6	11.3	12.0	14.6	16.5	12.8	7.5	7.5	98.4	0.6	0.4	0.5	–	0.4	100.4
Pocahontas	4.7	10.7	10.7	11.9	14.1	15.9	14.6	9.5	7.9	98.7	0.9	0.2	(Z)	–	0.5	107.6
Preston	5.1	11.6	12.6	12.9	14.0	15.9	12.7	8.0	7.1	99.1	0.3	0.1	(Z)	–	0.6	98.5
Putnam	5.8	13.0	12.2	12.4	15.1	16.6	12.4	7.1	5.4	97.6	0.9	0.7	0.2	(Z)	0.7	97.8
Raleigh	5.4	11.2	11.9	14.2	13.2	16.2	12.5	7.7	7.7	89.9	8.2	0.9	0.2	(Z)	1.1	97.5
Randolph	5.3	11.4	13.1	13.0	14.2	14.8	12.9	8.0	7.2	98.0	1.1	0.3	0.2	(Z)	0.7	103.1
Ritchie	5.8	11.7	11.8	12.5	13.8	15.9	13.2	8.4	7.0	99.0	0.2	0.1	0.3	–	0.5	97.4
Roane	5.5	11.5	12.6	13.4	13.0	16.1	13.0	8.5	6.3	98.9	0.3	0.3	0.1	–	0.9	98.3
Summers	4.2	9.5	10.8	13.2	14.7	16.2	12.6	9.6	9.2	91.6	7.4	0.1	0.2	(Z)	0.7	79.0
Taylor	4.9	11.3	13.3	12.2	14.7	16.0	12.0	7.9	7.8	98.3	0.8	0.2	0.2	0.1	0.6	97.4
Tucker	4.5	11.2	10.3	10.2	14.3	15.6	14.9	10.6	8.5	99.3	(Z)	–	0.1	0.1	0.3	96.0
Tyler	4.3	11.5	12.0	10.7	13.7	16.5	13.7	9.4	8.0	99.7	(Z)	0.1	–	–	0.4	96.6
Upshur	5.8	11.4	16.3	11.6	12.7	14.9	12.1	8.1	7.2	98.3	0.6	0.5	0.2	(Z)	0.6	94.6
Wayne	5.5	12.3	12.5	13.1	13.8	14.9	12.9	8.5	6.7	98.7	0.2	0.3	0.2	(Z)	0.5	96.2
Webster	5.0	11.5	12.2	12.8	12.8	16.6	13.6	8.2	7.2	99.5	–	0.1	(Z)	–	0.4	97.9
Wetzel	5.5	12.1	11.3	9.9	13.6	16.2	13.9	9.7	7.8	99.1	0.2	0.4	0.1	(Z)	0.5	94.5
Wirt	4.7	12.6	12.2	12.5	15.4	15.9	12.4	8.8	5.6	99.3	0.4	0.1	0.1	–	0.3	102.4
Wood	5.8	12.1	11.4	11.9	14.1	15.8	13.1	8.2	7.7	97.4	1.1	0.5	0.2	0.1	0.6	94.3
Wyoming	5.5	11.3	11.4	12.7	12.7	18.7	13.6	8.0	6.1	98.6	0.8	0.1	0.1	–	0.6	96.2
WISCONSIN	6.1	12.9	14.7	12.7	14.9	15.2	10.4	6.3	6.7	90.1	6.0	2.0	0.9	(Z)	4.5	98.1
Adams	3.9	9.9	11.2	13.9	14.8	14.8	12.1	10.8	8.8	94.9	3.4	0.4	1.0	(Z)	2.8	116.2
Ashland	6.0	12.5	17.0	10.5	13.4	15.1	10.1	6.9	8.6	87.0	0.3	0.4	11.0	(Z)	1.2	97.5
Barron	5.4	12.0	13.5	13.5	13.9	15.5	11.4	8.0	8.8	98.2	0.1	0.4	0.8	0.1	1.1	97.8
Bayfield	4.0	11.8	12.8	9.1	13.3	17.8	14.2	9.0	8.1	89.3	0.2	0.3	8.9	–	0.9	103.0
Brown	6.8	13.5	14.4	14.0	15.8	15.1	9.5	5.3	5.5	92.2	1.6	2.3	2.5	(Z)	5.4	98.8
Buffalo	5.5	12.4	12.3	10.5	14.7	16.5	11.4	8.3	8.5	98.9	0.2	0.4	0.3	(Z)	0.7	101.4
Burnett	4.4	10.9	12.1	10.8	12.5	15.3	12.9	11.7	9.4	93.8	0.5	0.3	4.3	0.1	0.8	100.2
Calumet	6.7	14.2	13.7	13.2	16.5	15.8	9.6	5.2	5.2	96.4	0.6	1.8	0.4	–	1.9	100.4
Chippewa	5.5	12.4	14.5	12.8	15.1	15.3	10.6	6.5	7.3	97.9	0.3	0.9	0.4	–	0.8	103.8
Clark	7.3	14.8	14.1	11.1	13.4	14.3	9.5	7.0	8.4	98.6	0.2	0.3	0.6	–	1.7	101.1
Columbia	5.6	12.4	12.7	12.4	15.8	15.6	11.2	7.0	7.4	97.6	1.1	0.4	0.4	(Z)	1.6	101.9
Crawford	5.9	12.5	15.2	8.7	12.9	16.0	12.0	8.1	8.7	97.5	1.7	0.3	0.3	–	0.9	103.4
Dane	6.1	11.6	17.3	16.0	15.3	14.7	9.6	4.7	4.8	89.2	4.3	4.4	0.4	(Z)	4.4	98.2
Dodge	5.3	12.0	13.5	13.6	16.1	15.8	9.9	6.8	7.0	96.0	2.8	0.4	0.5	(Z)	3.0	111.1
Door	4.3	10.5	11.7	9.9	13.1	16.8	13.4	9.7	10.5	98.1	0.3	0.4	0.8	–	1.1	98.1
Douglas	5.5	12.1	15.1	12.4	13.8	15.8	11.0	6.6	7.6	95.4	0.7	0.8	1.9	(Z)	0.9	97.2
Dunn	5.4	11.0	24.1	13.8	12.6	12.9	9.2	5.2	5.9	96.4	0.4	2.2	0.3	–	0.8	102.0
Eau Claire	5.6	11.7	20.8	13.7	12.8	13.4	9.8	5.5	6.8	95.2	0.7	2.5	0.5	(Z)	1.2	92.9
Florence	3.6	11.3	12.0	8.0	15.7	16.9	13.5	10.0	8.9	98.8	0.3	0.2	0.3	(Z)	0.5	104.2
Fond du Lac	5.7	12.4	14.4	12.4	14.5	15.6	10.7	6.5	7.8	97.0	1.1	0.8	0.5	(Z)	3.0	96.0
Forest	5.2	12.2	14.3	10.2	12.9	13.4	11.1	10.9	9.7	86.9	1.4	0.2	11.0	(Z)	1.5	99.6
Grant	5.5	11.0	19.9	11.2	12.2	14.3	10.0	7.7	8.3	97.7	1.0	0.7	0.2	(Z)	0.6	106.3
Green	5.6	13.4	13.1	11.5	15.0	16.2	10.7	6.6	7.8	98.6	0.4	0.3	0.1	–	1.0	97.4
Green Lake	5.9	11.5	12.3	10.2	13.5	16.2	12.1	8.3	10.1	98.9	0.2	0.4	0.2	(Z)	2.0	97.5
Iowa	6.3	13.5	12.8	11.2	15.9	16.3	10.8	6.3	6.8	98.9	0.3	0.3	0.1	–	0.8	99.5
Iron	2.9	9.5	10.8	9.1	14.0	16.5	12.9	11.0	13.2	98.0	0.1	0.2	0.9	0.1	0.8	97.4
Jackson	5.4	11.8	14.1	14.1	14.7	14.8	10.8	7.2	7.1	91.1	2.3	0.2	6.0	0.1	2.4	111.9
Jefferson	6.0	12.3	15.4	13.2	15.2	15.1	10.6	6.1	6.2	97.8	0.5	0.6	0.4	(Z)	5.2	99.1
Juneau	5.2	11.8	13.9	13.1	14.6	14.4	11.0	8.2	7.9	95.0	2.2	0.5	1.6	(Z)	1.9	105.8
Kenosha	6.8	14.3	14.3	12.9	16.4	14.9	9.4	5.4	5.6	90.8	5.7	1.3	0.4	0.1	8.9	98.6
Kewaunee	5.9	12.4	13.6	11.9	14.9	15.4	11.0	6.7	8.2	98.9	0.2	0.2	0.3	(Z)	1.6	100.5
La Crosse	5.5	11.9	19.3	13.4	13.4	14.2	9.6	6.0	6.7	94.2	1.1	3.3	0.4	(Z)	1.0	93.9
Lafayette	5.5	12.9	13.9	10.3	14.4	16.6	10.1	7.8	8.4	99.2	0.2	0.3	0.1	(Z)	0.8	100.4
Langlade	5.0	11.8	12.6	10.7	13.8	15.2	11.6	8.8	10.4	98.1	0.3	0.4	0.5	(Z)	1.1	98.9
Lincoln	4.8	12.3	13.2	11.5	14.4	15.6	11.0	8.6	8.6	98.1	0.5	0.5	0.5	(Z)	1.0	100.1
Manitowoc	5.2	12.7	13.1	10.7	15.0	16.3	11.4	7.2	8.5	96.1	0.5	2.3	0.5	(Z)	2.1	99.3
Marathon	5.8	13.6	13.2	12.0	15.4	15.9	10.8	6.2	7.1	93.7	0.4	4.8	0.4	(Z)	1.1	99.9
Marinette	4.8	11.4	14.1	9.7	13.9	16.2	12.2	8.7	9.1	98.1	0.3	0.4	0.6	(Z)	0.9	98.0
Marquette	5.1	10.8	12.4	11.6	13.6	15.2	11.3	9.9	10.1	98.3	0.7	0.2	0.4	0.1	1.8	101.7
Menominee	9.9	18.4	17.4	10.3	12.9	11.6	9.6	6.5	3.4	15.1	0.4	–	83.9	0.4	4.1	97.0
Milwaukee	7.8	14.0	14.4	13.6	14.6	14.2	9.3	5.5	6.5	68.0	26.3	3.0	0.8	0.1	10.8	92.8
Monroe	6.9	13.7	13.8	11.9	14.4	15.1	10.9	6.4	6.9	97.0	0.7	0.6	1.0	(Z)	2.3	100.9
Oconto	5.0	12.4	13.2	11.9	15.7	15.9	11.2	7.8	7.0	97.8	0.2	0.3	0.9	–	0.8	100.9
Oneida	4.0	10.8	12.1	9.2	14.6	16.5	12.7	10.5	9.5	97.7	0.5	0.4	0.8	(Z)	0.8	99.0
Outagamie	6.5	13.9	14.0	13.2	16.4	15.1	9.6	5.5	5.9	94.2	0.8	2.5	1.6	0.1	2.4	99.6
Ozaukee	5.1	13.2	13.9	9.2	14.6	17.8	12.6	6.9	6.7	96.4	1.3	1.4	0.2	(Z)	1.6	98.2
Pepin	5.4	12.7	13.4	10.8	14.2	15.5	11.4	8.1	8.5	98.9	0.3	0.2	0.2	(Z)	0.5	99.9
Pierce	5.6	11.9	21.5	13.0	14.1	14.8	9.6	5.0	4.7	97.9	0.3	0.7	0.3	(Z)	1.0	97.1
Polk	5.3	12.8	13.4	11.4	14.9	16.1	11.2	7.3	7.5	97.7	0.3	0.3	1.1	(Z)	0.9	100.2
Portage	5.3	11.5	21.1	12.8	13.4	14.5	9.7	5.7	5.9	96.0	0.5	2.4	0.4	(Z)	1.7	98.1

See footnotes at end of table.

[Includes United States, states, and 3,141 counties/county equivalents defined as of February 22, 2005. For more information on these areas, see Appendix C, Geographic Information]

County	Age (percent) Under 5 years	5 to 14 years	15 to 24 years	25 to 34 years	35 to 44 years	45 to 54 years	55 to 64 years	65 to 74 years	75 years and over	One race (percent) White alone	Black or African American alone	Asian alone	American Indian and Alaska Native alone	Native Hawaiian and Other Pacific Islander alone	Hispanic or Latino origin[1] (percent)	Males per 100 females
WISCONSIN—Con.																
Price	4.1	11.4	12.3	9.1	13.6	17.3	12.7	9.3	10.2	98.8	0.1	0.3	0.6	(Z)	0.8	101.6
Racine	6.5	13.9	13.9	12.1	15.4	15.4	10.6	5.9	6.2	86.3	10.9	0.9	0.4	0.1	9.4	98.5
Richland	5.6	12.0	14.4	11.3	13.0	16.1	11.0	7.4	9.2	98.7	0.3	0.3	0.2	(Z)	1.1	98.8
Rock	6.4	13.8	13.5	12.8	15.0	15.0	10.5	6.5	6.4	92.7	4.6	1.0	0.3	0.1	5.5	97.7
Rusk	5.3	12.2	14.6	9.7	13.4	15.4	11.7	8.3	9.5	98.0	0.7	0.4	0.5	0.2	0.8	97.7
St. Croix	6.4	13.8	13.7	15.0	16.5	15.5	9.8	4.7	4.4	97.3	0.5	1.1	0.4	(Z)	1.3	100.9
Sauk	5.9	12.9	12.9	12.6	14.8	15.5	10.8	6.7	8.0	97.8	0.3	0.4	0.9	(Z)	2.2	98.0
Sawyer	5.0	11.6	13.1	10.1	13.3	15.4	13.2	9.8	8.4	82.3	0.5	0.5	15.7	(Z)	1.4	101.8
Shawano	5.5	12.8	12.7	11.5	14.7	14.4	11.4	8.0	9.0	91.7	0.3	0.4	6.6	(Z)	1.5	100.2
Sheboygan	5.6	13.1	13.3	12.6	15.1	15.9	10.6	6.4	7.4	93.7	1.3	3.9	0.4	(Z)	4.5	101.5
Taylor	5.9	12.6	13.8	11.5	14.3	16.2	10.0	7.3	8.3	99.1	0.1	0.3	0.2	–	1.0	102.5
Trempealeau	5.8	13.0	12.5	11.7	14.9	15.4	11.0	7.1	8.8	99.3	0.2	0.1	0.2	(Z)	1.6	100.0
Vernon	6.7	13.4	13.5	10.2	12.9	15.4	11.4	7.7	8.7	99.2	0.1	0.2	0.2	–	0.8	98.4
Vilas	4.1	9.8	11.3	10.2	12.8	14.6	13.1	12.0	12.1	89.8	0.3	0.5	9.0	(Z)	1.0	98.6
Walworth	5.6	12.1	17.4	13.2	14.3	14.5	10.0	6.3	6.5	97.5	0.8	0.7	0.3	(Z)	8.3	99.7
Washburn	5.0	11.3	12.5	9.9	13.1	16.0	13.2	9.5	9.5	97.5	0.3	0.2	1.0	(Z)	1.0	101.0
Washington	5.8	13.4	13.0	12.1	16.6	16.1	11.0	6.1	5.8	97.5	0.7	0.8	0.3	0.1	1.6	99.7
Waukesha	5.6	13.2	13.4	10.3	15.4	17.3	12.0	6.8	6.1	95.6	1.1	2.2	0.2	(Z)	3.1	97.3
Waupaca	5.4	12.9	12.9	11.3	14.6	15.7	10.8	7.9	8.3	98.5	0.2	0.3	0.4	(Z)	1.9	99.2
Waushara	4.7	10.7	14.1	11.4	14.0	14.8	11.8	9.6	8.7	98.0	0.7	0.4	0.4	(Z)	4.6	109.1
Winnebago	5.4	12.0	16.0	13.8	15.2	15.0	10.0	6.0	6.6	95.5	1.3	1.9	0.5	(Z)	2.5	99.6
Wood	5.5	12.7	12.8	10.8	14.6	15.9	11.1	7.5	9.0	96.5	0.5	1.7	0.7	(Z)	1.1	96.0
WYOMING	6.1	12.0	15.5	12.3	13.3	16.8	11.9	6.5	5.7	94.8	0.9	0.6	2.4	0.1	6.7	101.6
Albany	5.6	8.4	31.6	15.1	9.5	12.0	9.0	4.8	4.0	94.1	1.2	2.0	1.0	0.1	6.8	105.5
Big Horn	5.7	13.6	14.8	8.7	11.7	15.1	13.1	8.6	8.6	98.0	0.2	0.3	0.9	0.1	6.3	100.4
Campbell	6.9	13.8	15.5	14.3	14.6	19.3	9.9	3.6	2.0	97.0	0.3	0.4	1.2	0.1	4.3	106.6
Carbon	5.5	10.8	12.9	10.8	14.3	18.5	13.9	7.4	5.9	96.3	1.0	0.9	1.2	(Z)	13.0	114.1
Converse	5.2	12.7	13.8	11.1	13.7	18.5	12.7	6.8	5.4	97.8	0.1	0.3	0.9	–	4.6	99.3
Crook	5.0	11.1	14.8	9.6	12.9	16.7	13.8	8.8	7.3	98.5	0.1	0.1	1.1	–	1.1	102.0
Fremont	6.6	12.7	14.8	10.6	12.7	16.2	12.2	7.9	6.3	77.5	0.3	0.3	20.6	(Z)	4.8	97.8
Goshen	5.3	11.4	15.4	9.0	11.7	15.7	13.1	8.7	9.6	98.1	0.2	0.2	1.0	0.1	9.1	99.4
Hot Springs	3.9	9.5	12.5	7.8	11.2	18.1	15.0	11.1	10.9	97.0	0.6	0.4	1.6	–	2.6	92.4
Johnson	4.1	11.2	13.0	10.7	11.4	18.0	14.1	8.9	8.6	98.2	0.1	0.2	0.7	–	2.3	97.2
Laramie	6.7	12.7	13.8	13.7	14.7	15.0	11.3	6.4	5.7	93.1	2.6	1.0	0.9	0.2	10.9	102.1
Lincoln	6.1	13.6	15.9	11.0	12.2	17.0	11.6	6.9	5.6	98.1	0.1	0.3	0.6	(Z)	2.7	102.7
Natrona	6.5	12.2	14.7	12.8	13.2	16.5	11.3	6.4	6.3	96.2	1.0	0.4	1.1	(Z)	5.0	98.0
Niobrara	4.1	10.1	12.8	8.6	13.4	18.7	13.4	10.3	8.7	99.0	0.2	0.1	0.5	–	1.6	94.9
Park	4.5	10.9	15.5	9.3	12.6	17.5	13.7	8.1	7.7	98.1	0.1	0.4	0.5	(Z)	4.1	95.8
Platte	4.9	11.0	14.0	9.2	12.0	17.0	14.5	9.4	8.0	98.5	0.2	0.2	0.6	–	5.7	97.6
Sheridan	5.5	10.9	13.9	10.8	12.2	17.5	13.8	7.6	7.8	96.9	0.3	0.3	1.5	0.1	2.6	96.7
Sublette	5.0	11.8	13.7	12.5	14.2	18.4	13.5	6.9	4.1	98.4	0.3	0.2	0.6	0.1	2.7	103.3
Sweetwater	7.1	13.1	15.5	12.2	13.7	18.4	11.8	4.6	3.6	95.5	1.1	0.9	1.1	0.1	10.5	103.6
Teton	5.4	9.4	9.6	19.7	16.8	19.0	12.2	5.4	2.5	97.9	0.2	0.8	0.4	(Z)	10.3	116.4
Uinta	7.4	14.9	16.9	11.2	13.1	18.2	10.4	4.2	3.6	97.5	0.1	0.3	1.1	0.1	6.0	102.6
Washakie	5.2	12.0	14.6	7.8	13.0	17.1	13.5	8.3	8.6	97.2	0.2	0.7	0.8	–	12.3	99.2
Weston	4.7	9.9	14.5	10.1	12.9	17.9	13.2	8.4	8.4	97.6	0.1	0.2	1.4	–	2.3	104.7

– Represents zero. NA Not available. Z Less than .05 percent.

[1]Persons of Hispanic or Latino origin may be any race.
[2]Yellowstone National Park County became incorporated with Gallatin and Park Counties, MT; effective November 7, 1997.
[3]Clifton Forge independent city became incorporated with Alleghany County, VA; effective July 1, 2001.
[4]South Boston independent city became incorporated with Halifax County, VA; effective June 30, 1995.

Survey, Census, or Data Collection Method: Based on population estimates and the "component of population change method"; for information, see Appendix B, Limitations of the Data and Methodology, and also <http://www.census.gov/popest/topics/methodology/>.

Source: U.S. Census Bureau, "County Population Estimates by Age, Sex, Race and Hispanic Origin: April 1, 2000 to July 1, 2005," released August 4, 2006 (related Internet site <http://www.census.gov/popest/datasets.html>).

Table B-4. Counties — **Population Characteristics**

[Includes United States, states, and 3,141 counties/county equivalents defined as of February 22, 2005. For more information on these areas, see Appendix C, Geographic Information]

County	Households, 2000 Total	With individuals under 18 years (percent of total)	Educational attainment,[1] 2000 Total persons	High school graduate or higher (percent)	Bachelor's degree or higher (percent)	Foreign-born population, 2000 (percent)	Persons 5 years and over Speaking language other than English at home, 2000 (percent)	Residing in same house in 1995 and 2000 (percent)	Workers who drove alone to work,[2] 2000 (percent)	Households with income of $75,000 or more in 1999 (percent)	Persons in poverty (percent) 2004	2000
UNITED STATES.......	105,480,101	36.0	182,211,639	80.4	24.4	11.1	17.9	54.1	75.7	22.5	12.7	11.3
ALABAMA............	1,737,080	36.1	2,887,400	75.3	19.0	2.0	3.9	57.4	83.0	15.4	16.1	14.6
Autauga..............	16,003	43.0	27,589	78.7	18.0	1.2	2.8	55.1	83.2	18.1	11.6	10.5
Baldwin..............	55,336	34.5	96,010	82.0	23.1	2.1	4.0	53.2	82.8	18.9	10.0	9.7
Barbour..............	10,409	38.1	18,896	64.7	10.9	1.5	3.6	60.5	78.7	10.6	23.9	22.2
Bibb.................	7,421	38.5	13,540	63.2	7.1	0.4	1.8	64.3	79.5	10.9	17.1	17.8
Blount...............	19,265	37.6	33,702	70.4	9.6	3.1	5.6	59.4	78.8	12.6	12.4	12.0
Bullock..............	3,986	39.4	7,570	60.5	7.7	3.1	6.1	59.4	71.3	6.8	30.3	28.6
Butler...............	8,398	37.1	13,767	67.8	10.4	0.4	2.2	62.2	78.9	9.3	21.0	20.7
Calhoun..............	45,307	33.5	74,015	73.9	15.2	1.7	3.5	57.1	85.1	12.2	16.9	15.1
Chambers............	14,522	34.9	24,497	64.2	9.5	0.8	2.3	63.6	82.1	8.2	17.2	15.4
Cherokee.............	9,719	32.2	16,825	63.5	9.7	1.1	2.1	63.4	81.5	9.5	16.1	15.6
Chilton..............	15,287	38.0	25,902	66.2	9.9	1.9	3.6	61.8	78.9	11.4	14.8	15.3
Choctaw..............	6,363	37.0	10,569	65.0	9.6	0.6	2.1	69.7	75.3	10.3	20.2	18.8
Clarke...............	10,578	39.8	17,702	70.8	12.1	0.5	2.1	69.8	80.4	12.2	20.9	19.1
Clay................	5,765	34.1	9,767	66.0	7.8	0.9	2.8	68.1	83.9	7.0	13.9	14.3
Cleburne.............	5,590	36.2	9,533	62.9	9.2	0.9	2.6	66.9	80.2	8.7	14.7	14.4
Coffee...............	17,421	35.2	28,885	73.2	19.3	2.7	5.1	55.3	83.2	14.8	14.2	14.4
Colbert..............	22,461	33.9	37,384	73.3	14.1	0.9	2.3	62.2	87.1	12.7	14.7	13.1
Conecuh.............	5,792	35.0	9,230	67.7	9.2	0.4	2.0	71.1	77.9	8.1	23.1	22.8
Coosa...............	4,682	34.8	8,255	65.7	8.0	0.3	1.8	66.2	83.1	8.4	14.0	14.5
Covington...........	15,640	32.7	25,705	68.4	12.2	0.6	2.0	63.1	80.3	8.8	18.7	17.6
Crenshaw............	5,577	34.5	9,268	60.1	11.2	0.3	1.8	65.4	72.5	8.1	18.6	19.1
Cullman.............	30,706	34.9	51,787	70.4	11.9	1.7	3.4	59.2	81.8	11.6	13.8	12.8
Dale................	18,878	39.0	31,390	77.8	14.0	3.1	6.2	51.8	82.7	9.7	16.7	15.3
Dallas...............	17,841	39.6	28,742	70.3	13.9	0.7	2.5	65.0	81.8	9.8	27.4	24.4
DeKalb..............	25,113	36.3	42,740	63.8	8.3	4.1	6.6	60.2	81.1	9.4	15.8	14.8
Elmore..............	22,737	40.9	43,177	77.6	16.6	1.1	3.1	53.3	84.4	17.8	12.5	12.1
Escambia............	14,297	36.5	25,510	68.5	10.6	0.6	2.4	61.3	81.1	10.0	20.1	18.6
Etowah..............	41,615	33.6	69,829	74.1	13.4	1.6	3.0	61.6	84.5	12.0	16.1	15.5
Fayette..............	7,493	34.0	12,579	66.1	9.2	0.7	1.5	66.6	84.3	8.0	17.4	15.5
Franklin.............	12,259	35.7	20,860	62.1	9.7	5.6	7.7	61.8	79.0	9.6	17.8	16.9
Geneva..............	10,477	34.0	17,588	65.6	8.7	0.8	2.1	64.2	82.7	8.1	18.1	18.4
Greene..............	3,931	38.8	6,204	64.8	10.5	0.7	1.8	71.1	75.9	7.0	26.5	26.8
Hale................	6,415	41.8	10,591	65.2	8.1	0.3	2.0	68.1	77.2	8.0	22.0	21.7
Henry...............	6,525	34.8	10,967	66.7	14.1	1.1	2.8	66.0	82.4	10.7	17.1	16.3
Houston.............	35,834	36.2	58,671	76.5	18.4	1.6	3.0	54.0	85.7	15.2	15.8	15.0
Jackson.............	21,615	34.9	36,435	67.0	10.4	0.7	2.1	61.6	83.4	10.9	15.3	13.3
Jefferson............	263,265	34.8	434,158	80.9	24.6	2.3	4.6	56.7	83.3	18.8	15.4	12.8
Lamar...............	6,468	34.1	10,758	65.1	7.8	0.8	1.9	65.3	85.3	7.0	16.8	16.1
Lauderdale...........	36,088	32.9	58,894	76.4	18.5	1.0	2.5	60.0	85.3	14.5	16.2	12.7
Lawrence............	13,538	38.4	22,894	65.6	7.5	0.5	2.5	65.4	84.4	11.9	14.7	14.0
Lee.................	45,702	32.8	62,170	81.4	27.9	2.7	5.1	44.1	84.1	15.2	16.0	14.2
Limestone...........	24,688	37.8	43,456	74.5	16.9	1.7	4.0	59.3	83.9	17.4	12.7	12.2
Lowndes............	4,909	43.0	8,183	64.3	11.0	0.3	1.7	75.7	76.1	8.8	25.5	24.3
Macon..............	8,950	34.9	13,955	70.0	18.8	1.5	4.7	59.2	74.2	8.2	28.3	27.6
Madison.............	109,955	35.9	180,389	85.4	34.3	4.0	5.5	50.4	83.9	24.9	11.7	10.1
Marengo............	8,767	39.3	14,326	71.9	12.1	0.7	2.5	68.4	78.9	12.7	21.3	20.5
Marion..............	12,697	33.2	21,611	63.2	8.0	0.5	2.4	61.9	84.6	9.0	17.9	16.9
Marshall............	32,547	35.8	54,961	69.4	13.9	4.0	5.8	56.2	82.3	12.8	15.8	14.3
Mobile..............	150,179	39.1	250,122	76.7	18.6	2.3	4.6	58.1	82.7	14.4	20.0	17.1
Monroe.............	9,383	40.3	15,378	67.9	11.8	0.3	2.0	69.0	82.1	10.8	18.5	18.8
Montgomery.........	86,068	36.2	141,342	80.3	28.5	2.0	4.0	51.9	82.7	17.8	19.4	16.0
Morgan.............	43,602	36.5	73,331	76.3	18.4	2.7	4.4	56.8	85.5	17.1	14.0	11.1
Perry...............	4,333	39.6	6,978	62.4	10.0	0.5	2.5	65.0	73.8	6.5	30.4	31.0
Pickens.............	8,086	37.6	13,536	69.7	9.8	0.4	1.9	67.3	82.3	8.4	20.8	20.1
Pike................	11,933	33.9	17,703	69.1	18.4	1.9	3.9	57.0	79.1	9.0	21.4	21.8
Randolph............	8,642	35.2	14,762	61.9	10.0	1.2	2.7	66.3	76.7	8.0	16.1	16.7
Russell.............	19,741	36.9	32,107	66.5	9.7	2.0	4.0	56.9	81.9	8.1	19.4	17.1
St. Clair.............	24,143	38.7	43,101	71.3	11.1	0.6	2.1	59.2	81.7	15.2	13.1	12.8
Shelby..............	54,631	39.0	94,185	86.8	36.8	2.4	4.2	48.9	86.2	33.5	7.0	6.4
Sumter..............	5,708	37.8	8,731	64.8	12.4	0.5	2.1	67.1	77.3	5.9	28.3	28.6
Talladega............	30,674	36.7	53,060	69.7	11.2	0.7	2.8	60.4	83.9	11.6	17.8	16.9
Tallapoosa...........	16,656	34.1	28,373	70.1	14.1	0.4	2.1	63.1	82.2	12.6	17.1	15.7
Tuscaloosa...........	64,517	33.6	99,039	78.8	24.0	2.1	4.4	51.0	84.0	16.3	17.2	15.1
Walker..............	28,364	34.8	47,919	67.2	9.1	0.7	2.2	63.9	83.7	10.8	16.2	14.9
Washington..........	6,705	42.4	11,240	72.3	8.6	0.5	2.0	74.5	74.7	9.6	18.1	17.0
Wilcox..............	4,776	42.3	7,979	59.5	10.1	0.3	2.8	69.1	76.2	5.8	30.4	30.6
Winston.............	10,107	34.5	17,078	62.6	8.3	1.0	2.6	62.9	80.9	9.1	17.2	17.6

See footnotes at end of table.

Table B-4. Counties — **Population Characteristics**—Con.

[Includes United States, states, and 3,141 counties/county equivalents defined as of February 22, 2005. For more information on these areas, see Appendix C, Geographic Information]

County	Households, 2000 Total	With individuals under 18 years (percent of total)	Educational attainment,[1] 2000 Total persons	High school graduate or higher (percent)	Bachelor's degree or higher (percent)	Foreign-born population, 2000 (percent)	Persons 5 years and over Speaking language other than English at home, 2000 (percent)	Residing in same house in 1995 and 2000 (percent)	Workers who drove alone to work,[2] 2000 (percent)	Households with income of $75,000 or more in 1999 (percent)	Persons in poverty (percent) 2004	2000
ALASKA	221,600	42.9	379,556	88.3	24.7	5.9	14.3	46.2	66.5	29.8	10.0	8.5
Aleutians East	526	41.4	2,007	74.7	4.9	18.3	41.3	56.5	26.7	26.8	12.7	12.6
Aleutians West	1,270	37.4	4,251	78.5	11.0	21.5	39.1	38.3	38.4	37.4	7.4	6.1
Anchorage	94,822	41.6	159,931	90.3	28.9	8.2	13.6	41.6	74.4	33.2	8.9	6.7
Bethel	4,226	58.5	8,026	71.0	13.1	1.4	65.6	63.3	18.7	19.5	20.7	22.2
Bristol Bay	490	39.6	782	88.9	21.1	0.6	4.2	56.1	63.6	28.6	7.6	5.9
Denali	785	32.0	1,316	91.7	22.7	2.9	7.7	54.5	56.7	31.6	6.0	4.8
Dillingham	1,529	50.9	2,655	76.6	16.4	1.0	36.3	65.3	33.4	22.5	17.6	17.9
Fairbanks North Star	29,777	43.6	47,974	91.8	27.0	4.0	7.8	39.4	72.8	26.8	8.0	7.0
Haines	991	33.5	1,660	88.9	23.8	4.1	3.9	52.2	56.8	19.8	10.7	10.2
Juneau	11,543	39.6	19,899	93.2	36.0	5.7	9.5	45.1	62.9	38.6	7.5	5.8
Kenai Peninsula	18,438	40.4	31,388	88.5	20.3	2.7	7.5	53.8	69.6	24.9	9.7	8.9
Ketchikan Gateway	5,399	39.4	8,999	89.6	20.2	5.7	8.2	48.7	60.7	29.0	8.4	7.2
Kodiak Island	4,424	49.2	8,187	85.4	18.7	16.7	24.5	39.1	62.8	34.2	8.5	7.2
Lake and Peninsula	588	51.5	981	72.2	12.4	0.7	13.6	73.4	15.7	20.9	16.6	17.3
Matanuska-Susitna	20,556	45.2	35,721	88.1	18.3	2.6	5.1	49.4	68.9	27.7	10.3	8.8
Nome	2,693	53.3	4,916	74.8	14.7	1.5	28.8	62.3	24.4	22.9	18.2	17.3
North Slope	2,109	54.6	3,883	77.4	17.0	5.8	49.9	51.6	23.9	40.5	12.4	7.8
Northwest Arctic	1,780	63.2	3,498	72.0	12.7	1.1	41.9	60.2	9.8	24.7	18.0	15.5
Prince of Wales- Outer Ketchikan	2,262	41.7	3,797	84.1	14.2	1.8	4.8	54.9	46.5	16.2	13.9	14.5
Sitka	3,278	39.5	5,608	90.6	29.5	5.1	9.6	43.0	56.6	30.2	7.7	6.8
Skagway-Hoonah-Angoon	1,369	34.4	2,273	84.4	21.6	2.0	8.1	59.7	43.7	18.0	11.2	7.8
Southeast Fairbanks	2,098	42.0	3,693	86.8	18.2	9.9	16.4	55.9	65.3	19.9	13.7	17.3
Valdez-Cordova	3,884	39.4	6,441	88.5	21.2	5.1	9.0	52.1	60.6	29.6	9.0	7.8
Wade Hampton	1,602	69.5	3,082	66.3	9.1	0.3	50.3	75.0	2.2	8.9	26.0	28.8
Wrangell-Petersburg	2,587	39.4	4,359	85.8	16.3	2.8	5.8	55.9	54.4	25.7	9.7	8.3
Yakutat	265	36.2	522	84.3	17.6	0.6	10.1	54.2	40.5	18.5	9.8	8.5
Yukon-Koyukuk	2,309	43.9	3,707	74.3	14.2	1.0	16.0	62.3	18.5	11.8	18.6	18.1
ARIZONA	1,901,327	35.4	3,256,184	81.0	23.5	12.8	25.9	44.3	74.1	20.5	14.6	12.5
Apache	19,971	52.4	36,217	63.6	11.3	0.9	61.7	70.6	65.6	7.2	29.8	30.8
Cochise	43,893	35.6	75,774	79.5	18.8	12.3	29.5	46.4	73.4	12.6	17.1	16.7
Coconino	40,448	39.0	65,976	83.8	29.9	4.3	28.2	46.2	68.1	18.2	16.5	15.6
Gila	20,140	30.7	35,150	78.2	13.9	3.6	18.2	54.5	75.5	11.1	18.2	17.8
Graham	10,116	44.1	19,302	75.6	11.8	2.6	23.7	57.5	71.1	8.6	22.3	21.3
Greenlee	3,117	43.2	5,207	82.5	12.2	3.4	26.0	57.1	74.6	10.9	12.5	9.7
La Paz	8,362	24.2	14,389	69.3	8.7	9.7	21.6	54.2	70.3	7.8	18.9	20.7
Maricopa	1,132,886	36.2	1,934,957	82.5	25.9	14.4	24.1	41.6	74.7	24.4	13.3	10.2
Mohave	62,809	28.5	109,347	77.5	9.9	5.9	10.7	46.2	74.0	10.9	15.4	15.4
Navajo	30,043	47.3	54,215	71.2	12.3	1.7	39.9	60.6	69.5	10.7	23.7	24.3
Pima	332,350	32.5	546,200	83.4	26.7	11.9	27.5	46.2	73.8	17.4	15.6	13.0
Pinal	61,364	34.2	119,102	72.7	11.9	9.0	25.2	47.2	73.8	13.6	15.1	15.8
Santa Cruz	11,809	51.8	22,445	60.7	15.2	37.7	80.5	55.2	74.2	12.9	19.1	21.7
Yavapai	70,171	26.3	120,223	84.7	21.1	5.9	9.7	44.1	75.1	14.4	12.6	12.0
Yuma	53,848	40.6	97,680	65.8	11.8	24.0	45.5	46.1	73.7	12.5	18.4	21.4
ARKANSAS	1,042,696	35.6	1,731,200	75.3	16.7	2.8	5.0	53.3	79.9	12.4	15.6	15.0
Arkansas	8,457	35.4	13,888	72.4	12.2	0.4	2.3	60.8	82.1	9.9	16.8	16.2
Ashley	9,384	38.4	15,722	72.5	10.1	2.2	4.0	61.6	83.7	10.7	18.0	16.5
Baxter	17,052	24.0	28,861	77.5	12.8	1.6	3.1	55.0	80.8	8.6	13.4	12.7
Benton	58,212	37.1	99,436	80.4	20.3	6.4	10.2	45.2	80.7	16.6	9.5	9.3
Boone	13,851	33.1	23,070	76.8	12.7	1.0	3.1	53.5	79.9	8.8	14.4	14.8
Bradley	4,834	34.1	8,368	66.6	11.9	4.3	7.5	62.8	72.2	8.5	20.4	20.6
Calhoun	2,317	34.8	3,906	68.7	7.3	0.9	2.2	65.0	80.2	8.2	14.8	14.5
Carroll	10,189	32.3	17,207	71.8	13.8	7.5	11.3	53.5	72.6	10.1	14.3	15.4
Chicot	5,205	38.6	9,062	64.2	11.7	2.3	4.8	61.8	71.4	7.7	28.0	27.8
Clark	8,912	33.0	13,735	75.3	19.8	2.0	4.1	50.5	76.3	10.1	17.1	16.6
Clay	7,417	31.3	12,175	60.6	7.4	0.3	1.8	59.6	81.6	6.5	16.2	16.0
Cleburne	10,190	28.8	17,299	74.8	13.9	1.1	2.6	56.7	78.0	10.3	13.7	14.2
Cleveland	3,273	39.2	5,659	73.1	10.0	1.4	2.3	64.4	77.3	9.8	14.4	14.1
Columbia	9,981	34.5	16,039	74.1	16.8	0.9	2.9	58.5	80.5	11.5	19.8	18.7
Conway	7,967	35.3	13,480	73.2	11.5	1.2	2.9	61.7	79.0	11.4	16.1	15.7
Craighead	32,301	35.1	50,725	77.3	20.9	2.0	3.8	47.2	83.1	13.6	15.4	14.0
Crawford	19,702	41.1	33,765	71.5	9.7	2.4	4.6	52.6	82.0	10.5	14.3	13.8
Crittenden	18,471	43.4	30,251	69.2	12.8	1.2	3.5	53.2	79.6	11.3	21.9	21.1
Cross	7,391	39.7	12,412	68.3	9.9	1.0	2.6	58.9	81.1	9.0	18.9	18.2
Dallas	3,519	35.3	5,989	66.8	9.6	0.9	3.5	61.1	75.2	6.3	18.5	19.4
Desha	5,922	39.9	9,574	65.0	11.1	2.1	3.7	61.3	75.6	9.6	23.3	22.1
Drew	7,337	37.3	11,553	73.1	17.3	1.5	3.2	55.8	78.6	11.3	18.7	17.3
Faulkner	31,882	38.4	50,849	83.3	25.2	1.7	4.0	45.6	78.7	16.5	12.8	10.7
Franklin	6,882	35.8	11,654	71.1	11.0	1.3	2.9	60.4	77.4	7.5	15.6	15.6
Fulton	4,810	29.9	8,243	72.2	10.5	0.4	1.5	59.8	78.2	6.8	17.6	19.6

See footnotes at end of table.

County and City Data Book: 2007

U.S. Census Bureau

[Includes United States, states, and 3,141 counties/county equivalents defined as of February 22, 2005. For more information on these areas, see Appendix C, Geographic Information]

County	Households, 2000 Total	Households, 2000 With individuals under 18 years (percent of total)	Educational attainment,[1] 2000 Total persons	High school graduate or higher (percent)	Bachelor's degree or higher (percent)	Foreign-born population, 2000 (percent)	Speaking language other than English at home, 2000 (percent)	Residing in same house in 1995 and 2000 (percent)	Workers who drove alone to work,[2] 2000 (percent)	Households with income of $75,000 or more in 1999 (percent)	Persons in poverty (percent) 2004	Persons in poverty (percent) 2000
ARKANSAS—Con.												
Garland	37,813	28.0	62,694	78.3	18.0	2.6	4.8	52.6	78.9	12.8	15.5	14.7
Grant	6,241	39.0	10,824	77.2	11.0	0.6	2.2	60.2	82.3	13.7	11.0	10.1
Greene	14,750	36.2	24,510	72.1	10.9	0.5	2.0	52.8	83.0	9.0	15.3	13.4
Hempstead	8,959	38.0	14,869	69.2	11.0	6.4	9.5	57.4	76.6	8.4	18.8	18.7
Hot Spring	12,004	35.5	20,260	73.3	11.2	1.2	2.6	57.3	81.1	7.8	14.9	13.9
Howard	5,471	37.7	9,271	70.7	11.6	3.5	7.3	57.9	76.5	9.5	15.1	15.5
Independence	13,467	35.2	22,705	75.5	13.7	1.2	3.0	57.5	80.4	9.1	14.7	14.2
Izard	5,440	28.1	9,524	73.3	11.7	0.8	2.3	55.3	78.6	6.6	17.5	18.3
Jackson	6,971	32.3	12,204	66.0	10.3	0.5	2.1	65.6	82.9	8.2	21.0	20.3
Jefferson	30,555	38.5	53,132	74.8	15.7	1.1	3.4	56.5	80.6	13.1	20.4	18.9
Johnson	8,738	35.9	14,901	67.6	13.1	4.5	6.2	53.5	76.0	7.5	16.4	16.4
Lafayette	3,434	33.5	5,692	65.3	9.5	1.0	2.8	68.6	72.5	9.0	22.1	22.4
Lawrence	7,108	33.7	11,824	63.3	8.5	0.6	1.5	56.2	79.5	6.5	18.5	18.0
Lee	4,182	38.2	7,924	56.2	7.3	0.3	3.8	55.3	74.7	5.7	30.3	30.0
Lincoln	4,265	39.9	9,533	65.0	7.6	0.7	1.9	54.4	76.5	10.1	23.3	24.1
Little River	5,465	35.9	9,009	73.4	9.9	1.7	3.4	59.4	83.0	11.3	15.2	15.9
Logan	8,693	36.5	15,004	69.8	9.4	0.9	2.6	56.6	77.0	7.4	16.4	15.7
Lonoke	19,262	44.1	33,468	77.6	14.6	1.4	2.6	51.3	82.0	16.3	10.6	10.3
Madison	5,463	36.9	9,327	67.8	10.1	1.8	3.7	63.7	69.3	7.4	16.0	16.7
Marion	6,776	28.6	11,593	76.0	10.4	1.1	2.7	55.6	74.2	6.6	16.6	17.2
Miller	15,637	38.1	25,790	74.3	12.5	1.1	3.0	54.9	84.8	12.1	17.1	18.0
Mississippi	19,349	41.4	31,612	64.7	11.3	1.2	3.2	54.1	80.2	10.6	22.1	20.0
Monroe	4,105	34.6	6,602	63.8	8.4	0.5	2.3	61.2	77.3	6.0	22.7	24.4
Montgomery	3,785	31.3	6,464	69.8	8.8	2.0	4.1	63.9	73.0	7.7	16.3	17.2
Nevada	3,893	35.7	6,575	69.1	10.7	1.1	3.1	63.0	79.5	7.3	18.7	18.5
Newton	3,500	34.3	5,814	70.2	11.8	0.5	1.6	62.2	69.8	5.2	19.4	21.4
Ouachita	11,613	35.3	18,975	73.5	12.7	0.7	2.3	62.3	81.0	8.4	18.1	18.0
Perry	3,989	35.5	6,859	73.8	11.1	0.8	2.9	60.4	76.7	10.3	14.4	14.2
Phillips	9,711	41.3	15,420	62.2	12.4	1.1	3.1	60.5	76.3	7.4	28.7	28.3
Pike	4,504	35.1	7,653	68.8	10.1	2.2	3.8	64.4	76.2	9.1	14.8	16.0
Poinsett	10,026	37.3	16,674	62.0	6.3	0.9	2.6	59.1	80.2	6.9	20.3	19.1
Polk	8,047	34.8	13,505	72.6	10.9	2.7	4.5	56.4	78.1	7.2	18.4	18.4
Pope	20,701	37.2	34,297	77.4	19.0	1.7	3.6	50.8	81.7	12.1	15.8	14.8
Prairie	3,894	34.7	6,550	68.2	9.0	0.4	2.4	64.3	80.7	8.7	15.1	15.2
Pulaski	147,942	33.8	235,921	84.4	28.1	3.0	5.5	50.4	81.6	18.6	14.8	12.4
Randolph	7,265	33.8	12,207	69.2	10.6	0.9	2.3	56.9	79.8	8.4	16.7	17.1
St. Francis	10,043	40.9	18,173	65.1	9.6	0.3	2.2	54.1	76.8	7.4	25.1	25.7
Saline	31,778	38.2	55,796	82.3	16.4	1.3	3.1	54.7	84.3	17.6	9.1	8.4
Scott	4,323	36.2	7,141	65.4	8.4	3.5	6.1	58.2	70.3	6.7	18.4	19.4
Searcy	3,523	29.8	5,792	68.0	8.4	0.6	1.9	63.9	72.5	4.2	20.6	23.7
Sebastian	45,300	35.9	74,601	76.6	16.6	6.9	9.4	49.9	81.1	14.3	15.2	13.4
Sevier	5,708	40.7	9,828	64.6	9.2	12.7	17.8	55.3	73.1	9.3	17.2	17.5
Sharp	7,211	28.4	12,294	72.9	10.3	0.8	2.3	56.6	76.6	6.6	18.2	19.9
Stone	4,768	29.6	8,119	68.0	9.8	0.8	2.3	62.5	71.3	6.4	17.8	18.9
Union	17,989	36.5	29,986	74.5	14.9	1.2	2.5	60.6	83.3	11.5	17.7	16.1
Van Buren	6,825	28.2	11,602	71.6	11.5	1.4	2.4	59.7	74.8	8.2	17.0	17.5
Washington	60,151	35.1	94,019	79.5	24.5	7.4	10.5	42.9	79.0	13.8	12.8	12.7
White	25,148	36.2	42,366	72.9	15.5	1.5	3.5	50.2	78.6	10.9	15.0	14.9
Woodruff	3,531	35.6	5,716	60.6	8.0	0.6	1.7	63.0	78.7	6.0	24.0	23.3
Yell	7,922	37.7	13,659	64.1	10.9	10.2	13.4	51.6	72.4	8.8	15.1	15.5
CALIFORNIA	11,502,870	39.7	21,298,900	76.8	26.6	26.2	39.5	50.2	71.8	28.8	13.2	12.7
Alameda	523,366	36.5	953,716	82.4	34.9	27.2	36.8	50.8	66.4	35.8	11.1	8.8
Alpine	483	31.3	797	88.3	28.2	3.2	8.2	57.9	51.9	19.5	13.2	17.7
Amador	12,759	28.9	25,549	84.0	16.6	3.4	7.6	53.4	76.8	22.9	8.8	0.9
Butte	79,566	31.2	126,736	82.3	21.8	7.7	12.5	47.9	74.3	13.8	15.2	17.2
Calaveras	16,469	29.9	29,201	85.7	17.1	3.0	6.2	55.0	73.9	20.4	9.3	10.8
Colusa	6,097	45.3	10,912	64.0	10.6	27.6	42.0	57.6	67.9	14.2	11.7	15.1
Contra Costa	344,129	38.8	625,641	86.9	35.0	19.0	26.0	53.2	70.2	41.6	7.8	6.7
Del Norte	9,170	37.3	18,459	71.6	11.0	5.7	9.8	45.5	73.9	13.1	19.2	21.8
El Dorado	58,939	36.8	105,034	89.1	26.5	7.2	10.1	52.7	75.8	30.5	6.9	7.3
Fresno	252,940	45.8	455,540	67.5	17.5	21.1	40.8	51.0	74.2	16.7	19.8	20.6
Glenn	9,172	41.5	16,099	68.5	10.7	17.8	31.2	57.3	71.3	11.5	14.4	17.8
Humboldt	51,238	31.4	81,501	84.9	23.0	4.5	8.3	51.3	71.6	12.6	15.4	15.9
Imperial	39,384	53.4	83,632	59.0	10.3	32.2	67.8	52.1	72.7	14.3	18.5	24.7
Inyo	7,703	30.3	12,566	82.3	17.1	7.6	11.8	54.3	70.4	16.3	10.5	11.9
Kern	208,652	46.8	383,667	68.5	13.5	16.9	33.4	47.2	73.8	17.2	17.8	18.6
Kings	34,418	51.0	77,095	68.8	10.4	16.0	36.7	42.3	73.5	15.8	17.6	20.5
Lake	23,974	30.0	40,717	77.3	12.1	6.6	10.2	51.9	72.2	12.7	15.6	15.8
Lassen	9,625	38.8	22,963	79.6	10.7	2.3	13.8	45.5	76.7	14.8	15.7	17.5
Los Angeles	3,133,774	41.3	5,882,948	69.9	24.9	36.2	54.1	52.0	70.4	25.3	16.7	15.9
Madera	36,155	45.2	74,830	65.4	12.0	20.1	37.0	52.8	73.1	15.6	17.9	20.9

See footnotes at end of table.

[Includes United States, states, and 3,141 counties/county equivalents defined as of February 22, 2005. For more information on these areas, see Appendix C, Geographic Information]

County	Households, 2000 Total	With individuals under 18 years (percent of total)	Educational attainment, 2000 Total persons	High school graduate or higher (percent)	Bachelor's degree or higher (percent)	Foreign-born population, 2000 (percent)	Speaking language other than English at home, 2000 (percent)	Residing in same house in 1995 and 2000 (percent)	Workers who drove alone to work,[2] 2000 (percent)	Households with income of $75,000 or more in 1999 (percent)	Persons in poverty (percent) 2004	2000
CALIFORNIA—Con.												
Marin	100,650	28.9	183,694	91.2	51.3	16.6	19.5	54.8	65.5	48.0	7.0	5.9
Mariposa	6,613	28.4	12,196	85.1	20.2	2.8	5.2	53.0	63.5	15.2	11.0	13.0
Mendocino	33,266	35.0	56,886	80.8	20.2	10.2	16.1	56.1	71.6	16.7	14.4	14.7
Merced	63,815	50.0	116,725	63.8	11.0	24.8	45.2	50.5	72.9	15.1	17.0	20.3
Modoc	3,784	32.0	6,464	77.1	12.4	5.9	11.3	59.8	72.8	12.4	15.5	19.7
Mono	5,137	30.9	8,674	87.9	28.9	12.4	17.4	38.0	62.4	20.0	8.2	9.0
Monterey	121,236	43.5	244,128	68.4	22.5	29.0	47.3	48.8	68.7	27.2	12.9	12.9
Napa	45,402	34.4	83,938	80.4	26.4	18.1	25.2	53.0	72.7	31.8	7.8	7.1
Nevada	36,894	31.3	65,148	90.3	26.1	4.4	6.4	52.3	75.4	24.3	7.9	8.0
Orange	935,287	40.5	1,813,456	79.5	30.8	29.9	41.4	48.0	76.5	37.5	10.2	9.3
Placer	93,382	37.7	165,894	90.5	30.3	7.1	10.6	47.4	80.1	35.5	5.6	5.6
Plumas	9,000	28.5	14,786	88.0	17.5	2.5	5.5	56.2	74.3	15.1	9.8	11.1
Riverside	506,218	43.2	936,024	75.0	16.6	19.0	32.9	46.7	73.4	23.2	11.9	12.5
Sacramento	453,602	37.3	772,488	83.3	24.8	16.1	24.4	47.5	75.4	23.3	13.6	12.9
San Benito	15,885	51.3	31,401	74.9	17.1	18.8	37.8	49.3	73.1	36.2	8.8	8.9
San Bernardino	528,594	48.8	983,273	74.2	15.9	18.6	34.0	48.2	73.6	21.7	15.4	15.0
San Diego	994,677	37.2	1,773,327	82.6	29.5	21.5	33.0	45.1	73.9	27.3	10.9	10.9
San Francisco	329,700	19.4	595,805	81.2	45.0	36.8	45.7	54.2	40.5	36.8	11.6	9.2
San Joaquin	181,629	45.3	333,572	71.2	14.5	19.5	33.7	51.2	74.6	21.6	14.0	15.1
San Luis Obispo	92,739	30.5	159,196	85.6	26.7	8.9	14.7	46.7	73.9	22.5	10.4	10.7
San Mateo	254,103	34.3	490,285	85.3	39.0	32.3	41.5	56.6	72.3	47.1	6.6	5.1
Santa Barbara	136,622	35.6	246,729	79.2	29.4	21.2	32.8	48.3	69.4	27.6	12.5	12.4
Santa Clara	565,863	38.6	1,113,058	83.4	40.5	34.1	45.4	51.2	77.3	49.7	8.4	6.7
Santa Cruz	91,139	34.7	164,999	83.2	34.2	18.2	27.8	50.6	69.5	34.7	10.8	10.6
Shasta	63,426	35.0	107,272	83.3	16.6	4.0	6.5	50.0	79.7	14.6	13.4	14.7
Sierra	1,520	29.5	2,540	85.2	17.2	3.0	6.3	61.1	68.6	13.8	9.1	10.6
Siskiyou	18,556	30.3	30,682	83.8	17.7	5.4	9.0	55.1	70.2	11.5	15.1	16.7
Solano	130,403	44.6	246,488	83.8	21.4	16.9	24.6	49.9	73.3	31.8	8.7	8.4
Sonoma	172,403	34.7	306,564	84.9	28.5	14.3	19.8	52.0	74.7	31.6	8.4	7.1
Stanislaus	145,146	45.8	264,578	70.4	14.1	18.3	32.4	50.8	76.9	19.0	13.6	14.6
Sutter	27,033	41.9	49,071	73.0	15.3	19.3	30.3	51.6	78.2	18.8	12.1	14.1
Tehama	21,013	36.5	36,261	75.7	11.3	7.9	14.4	52.5	75.4	11.8	14.5	17.2
Trinity	5,587	28.1	9,433	81.0	15.5	1.6	4.1	59.0	69.9	10.5	14.2	16.8
Tulare	110,385	50.0	204,888	61.7	11.5	22.6	43.8	53.1	72.2	14.9	20.9	23.2
Tuolumne	21,004	28.9	38,977	84.3	16.1	3.2	5.8	49.4	77.4	16.7	11.6	12.7
Ventura	243,234	43.6	471,756	80.1	26.9	20.7	33.0	51.7	75.9	37.8	9.3	8.9
Yolo	59,375	36.5	95,423	79.8	34.1	20.3	32.1	41.8	67.2	23.1	11.2	12.0
Yuba	20,535	42.7	35,218	71.8	10.3	13.2	21.9	47.2	73.2	10.8	15.6	19.3
COLORADO	1,658,238	35.3	2,776,632	86.9	32.7	8.6	15.1	44.1	75.1	26.1	10.2	8.9
Adams	128,156	42.0	223,094	78.8	17.4	12.5	21.6	43.8	76.0	22.4	10.8	8.9
Alamosa	5,467	38.0	8,567	82.6	27.0	4.7	28.3	51.8	69.2	10.9	19.2	20.3
Arapahoe	190,909	37.2	316,560	90.7	37.0	11.0	15.5	44.3	78.8	31.7	8.2	5.8
Archuleta	3,980	33.8	6,821	87.3	29.0	2.9	11.9	42.0	70.6	16.0	10.6	13.2
Baca	1,905	30.6	3,152	78.5	14.0	2.5	5.8	63.1	69.6	7.8	15.6	17.5
Bent	2,003	35.5	4,037	77.2	11.5	4.4	16.8	49.7	75.7	7.3	20.4	23.1
Boulder	114,680	32.3	186,126	92.8	52.4	9.4	13.6	40.8	70.8	35.3	9.8	7.8
Broomfield	(X)	(NA)	(X)	(NA)	(NA)	(NA)	(NA)	(NA)	(NA)	(NA)	5.2	(NA)
Chaffee	6,584	26.9	11,837	88.5	24.3	2.0	8.7	48.2	72.3	14.7	11.6	11.5
Cheyenne	880	35.2	1,431	84.1	14.2	4.1	7.6	62.3	69.3	12.0	11.6	12.6
Clear Creek	4,019	29.7	6,702	93.4	38.8	1.9	3.5	52.7	72.8	30.4	6.7	6.0
Conejos	2,980	42.4	4,979	72.1	14.4	3.0	42.1	68.8	72.3	8.1	19.1	23.9
Costilla	1,503	32.6	2,506	68.2	12.8	6.9	59.5	65.4	71.5	3.5	22.4	28.5
Crowley	1,358	37.3	3,897	77.5	11.9	1.1	14.7	42.2	72.1	8.3	27.8	34.1
Custer	1,480	27.7	2,548	90.3	26.7	1.7	3.6	45.4	64.4	15.1	10.7	13.6
Delta	11,058	31.1	19,330	80.1	17.6	4.2	10.3	52.0	69.8	11.5	12.5	14.2
Denver	239,235	26.3	374,478	78.9	34.5	17.4	27.0	42.7	68.3	20.7	15.2	13.1
Dolores	785	27.1	1,323	76.0	13.5	0.9	5.7	55.7	68.8	9.2	11.4	15.2
Douglas	60,924	48.5	112,436	97.0	51.9	5.2	7.2	34.3	81.0	57.3	3.7	1.7
Eagle	15,148	34.7	27,178	86.6	42.6	18.2	24.7	35.0	65.6	39.8	6.0	6.0
Elbert	6,770	45.2	12,814	92.5	26.6	1.9	4.8	44.1	76.2	38.8	5.4	5.1
El Paso	192,409	39.3	320,420	91.3	31.8	6.4	11.4	40.4	78.0	24.2	10.3	8.7
Fremont	15,232	32.7	33,214	80.5	13.5	1.5	7.4	41.1	75.5	11.9	14.2	15.2
Garfield	16,229	39.6	27,884	85.4	23.8	10.4	15.5	39.9	64.8	23.3	8.2	7.8
Gilpin	2,043	28.4	3,501	94.1	31.2	3.4	4.7	43.4	73.0	27.3	5.6	5.5
Grand	5,075	29.5	8,571	92.3	34.5	3.4	6.1	42.2	67.4	23.6	7.2	7.3
Gunnison	5,649	24.9	8,504	94.1	43.6	2.9	6.6	36.8	56.6	17.0	11.4	11.4
Hinsdale	359	24.0	593	93.1	34.9	2.0	4.9	50.0	50.8	12.3	7.8	10.6
Huerfano	3,082	27.7	5,647	77.8	16.1	1.6	18.2	51.1	67.2	7.9	19.7	21.9
Jackson	661	31.5	1,098	86.2	19.9	1.9	3.8	57.7	52.0	11.3	12.0	14.5

See footnotes at end of table.

[Includes United States, states, and 3,141 counties/county equivalents defined as of February 22, 2005. For more information on these areas, see Appendix C, Geographic Information]

County	Households, 2000 Total	With individuals under 18 years (percent of total)	Educational attainment,[1] 2000 Total persons	High school graduate or higher (percent)	Bachelor's degree or higher (percent)	Foreign-born population, 2000 (percent)	Speaking language other than English at home, 2000 (percent)	Residing in same house in 1995 and 2000 (percent)	Workers who drove alone to work,[2] 2000 (percent)	House-holds with income of $75,000 or more in 1999 (percent)	Persons in poverty (percent) 2004	2000
COLORADO—Con.												
Jefferson	206,067	35.5	351,579	91.8	36.5	5.4	9.2	50.9	79.6	34.5	7.1	5.1
Kiowa	665	32.0	1,085	86.3	16.1	1.4	3.5	64.4	70.6	10.5	11.1	12.8
Kit Carson	2,990	35.5	5,254	77.0	15.4	5.8	13.2	57.4	72.0	12.7	12.7	13.2
Lake	2,977	36.7	4,710	79.5	19.5	15.6	26.4	44.6	59.6	12.6	11.5	11.0
La Plata	17,342	31.6	27,973	91.4	36.4	2.7	9.4	45.4	69.5	21.0	10.3	10.7
Larimer	97,164	33.4	156,426	92.3	39.5	4.3	8.5	41.5	77.4	26.5	9.8	7.5
Las Animas	6,173	32.2	10,279	76.9	16.2	2.3	20.8	58.3	72.7	8.5	15.6	18.4
Lincoln	2,058	35.7	4,214	81.8	13.2	1.8	6.9	43.9	69.4	11.5	15.7	15.3
Logan	7,551	34.1	13,074	82.3	14.6	3.1	8.2	53.1	76.0	11.1	13.0	12.8
Mesa	45,823	33.9	76,358	85.0	22.0	3.0	8.0	45.1	77.1	14.3	10.8	11.0
Mineral	377	24.9	631	91.6	31.2	0.7	1.9	50.6	50.7	13.3	9.0	12.4
Moffat	4,983	40.4	8,404	79.6	12.5	4.1	8.4	49.5	70.1	14.8	9.5	9.9
Montezuma	9,201	36.5	15,512	81.1	21.0	2.2	13.3	52.5	73.0	11.4	14.5	16.2
Montrose	13,043	35.0	22,089	80.7	18.7	5.6	11.6	48.6	71.3	12.6	11.8	12.6
Morgan	9,539	41.5	16,661	71.4	13.5	14.6	25.6	50.0	76.6	10.9	12.6	12.9
Otero	7,920	35.4	13,172	75.7	15.4	4.9	21.9	56.2	74.5	9.3	17.8	19.1
Ouray	1,576	30.2	2,741	93.4	36.8	3.2	5.7	46.1	58.7	20.5	7.2	8.0
Park	5,894	31.7	10,371	93.3	30.3	2.2	4.2	41.5	66.0	27.2	7.5	6.2
Phillips	1,781	34.7	2,999	81.6	19.9	8.1	10.9	54.7	70.7	9.4	10.5	11.6
Pitkin	6,807	21.8	11,322	96.3	57.1	10.9	12.1	44.0	51.0	36.2	4.6	4.4
Prowers	5,307	40.8	8,545	72.0	11.9	10.6	24.4	51.7	75.2	8.8	17.4	18.5
Pueblo	54,579	35.2	92,080	81.3	18.3	3.0	16.1	51.5	79.4	13.0	16.3	14.6
Rio Blanco	2,306	37.3	3,857	88.4	19.5	3.2	6.6	51.3	70.6	11.7	9.1	10.1
Rio Grande	4,701	38.5	7,959	78.1	18.8	6.0	27.6	56.6	70.0	9.6	16.3	18.5
Routt	7,953	32.3	13,267	95.3	42.5	4.1	6.1	41.1	68.7	30.6	6.0	6.2
Saguache	2,300	36.7	3,760	70.0	19.6	14.5	36.5	50.8	61.8	7.7	22.7	21.7
San Juan	269	25.3	428	92.1	43.7	2.5	9.0	50.0	49.7	5.6	13.5	17.6
San Miguel	3,015	23.9	4,762	93.6	48.5	7.3	10.8	35.3	45.1	29.1	7.9	8.3
Sedgwick	1,165	28.4	1,938	79.3	13.4	2.7	9.3	64.1	68.0	7.6	11.3	12.9
Summit	9,120	25.3	15,795	93.3	48.3	11.6	13.6	29.1	65.7	33.8	5.9	6.1
Teller	7,993	36.2	14,240	94.0	31.7	1.8	4.0	41.4	74.5	27.0	7.2	6.2
Washington	1,989	33.1	3,314	81.7	14.3	2.5	5.2	64.2	63.1	12.1	10.3	11.9
Weld	63,247	40.5	106,245	79.6	21.6	9.3	20.3	42.5	78.5	20.1	9.9	10.0
Yuma	3,800	35.6	6,340	79.5	15.5	7.9	11.5	57.3	74.8	11.1	12.0	13.2
CONNECTICUT	1,301,670	34.7	2,295,617	84.0	31.4	10.9	18.3	58.2	80.0	33.4	9.1	7.3
Fairfield	324,232	36.8	596,371	84.4	39.9	16.9	23.9	57.3	74.7	43.6	8.5	6.2
Hartford	335,098	33.8	579,839	82.4	29.6	11.7	21.7	58.0	82.2	30.3	10.7	8.4
Litchfield	71,551	34.0	127,305	85.9	27.5	5.4	8.2	63.7	83.5	33.5	6.1	4.8
Middlesex	61,341	32.2	108,106	88.7	33.8	6.0	9.5	59.0	84.6	36.3	5.6	4.7
New Haven	319,040	33.8	551,642	83.0	27.6	9.0	17.7	58.5	80.7	28.7	10.7	8.8
New London	99,835	34.7	173,910	86.0	26.2	5.4	10.3	55.2	81.1	27.8	7.5	6.4
Tolland	49,431	34.9	87,202	89.2	32.8	5.9	10.0	59.3	82.5	35.9	5.8	4.6
Windham	41,142	36.2	71,242	79.6	19.0	4.3	11.7	58.9	80.8	21.6	9.4	8.2
DELAWARE	298,736	35.4	514,658	82.6	25.0	5.7	9.5	56.0	79.2	26.1	9.6	8.7
Kent	47,224	39.3	79,249	79.4	18.6	4.0	7.9	55.6	79.7	18.0	11.4	10.8
New Castle	188,935	36.0	324,810	85.5	29.5	6.6	10.7	55.3	79.0	31.3	8.9	7.4
Sussex	62,577	30.8	110,599	76.5	16.6	4.5	7.1	58.3	79.5	16.4	10.4	10.9
DISTRICT OF COLUMBIA	248,338	24.6	384,535	77.8	39.1	12.9	16.8	49.9	38.4	25.4	18.3	16.3
District of Columbia	248,338	24.6	384,535	77.8	39.1	12.9	16.8	49.9	38.4	25.4	18.3	16.3
FLORIDA	6,337,929	31.3	11,024,645	79.9	22.3	16.7	23.1	48.9	78.8	19.1	11.9	11.7
Alachua	87,509	27.8	123,524	88.1	38.7	7.3	11.5	39.9	74.7	16.2	14.5	14.7
Baker	7,043	46.2	13,953	71.9	8.2	1.1	3.9	59.0	79.8	12.7	12.7	13.6
Bay	59,597	33.8	99,771	81.0	17.7	3.6	6.4	49.4	81.0	14.2	11.9	12.7
Bradford	8,497	36.6	17,883	74.2	8.4	1.8	4.6	58.1	78.5	10.6	14.8	16.5
Brevard	198,195	29.2	339,738	86.3	23.6	6.5	8.7	51.6	83.4	18.9	9.2	9.2
Broward	654,445	32.2	1,126,502	82.0	24.5	25.3	28.8	47.1	80.0	22.9	11.6	9.8
Calhoun	4,468	36.5	8,884	69.1	7.7	2.2	5.6	67.1	77.4	8.3	17.2	21.1
Charlotte	63,864	19.5	113,071	82.1	17.6	8.0	8.2	52.5	81.7	14.3	8.1	9.0
Citrus	52,634	21.3	92,594	78.3	13.2	4.9	6.6	53.5	81.0	10.8	11.2	12.3
Clay	50,243	43.1	90,382	86.4	20.1	4.5	7.7	49.8	84.1	24.3	7.1	6.9
Collier	102,973	25.2	185,357	81.8	27.9	18.3	25.1	44.2	74.4	29.1	8.8	8.9
Columbia	20,925	36.5	36,880	74.7	10.9	2.3	5.1	53.0	80.5	10.7	14.1	16.2
DeSoto	10,746	31.4	21,222	63.5	8.4	18.7	24.1	48.3	52.3	9.3	16.7	19.4
Dixie	5,205	32.2	9,643	65.9	6.8	2.0	4.4	60.2	76.9	8.5	18.0	21.2
Duval	303,747	37.2	499,602	82.7	21.9	5.9	9.5	48.9	79.5	19.0	11.7	10.5

See footnotes at end of table.

[Includes United States, states, and 3,141 counties/county equivalents defined as of February 22, 2005. For more information on these areas, see Appendix C, Geographic Information]

County	Households, 2000		Educational attainment,[1] 2000			Foreign-born population, 2000 (percent)	Persons 5 years and over		Workers who drove alone to work,[2] 2000 (percent)	House-holds with income of $75,000 or more in 1999 (percent)	Persons in poverty (percent)	
	Total	With individuals under 18 years (percent of total)	Total persons	High school graduate or higher (percent)	Bachelor's degree or higher (percent)		Speaking language other than English at home, 2000 (percent)	Residing in same house in 1995 and 2000 (percent)			2004	2000
FLORIDA—Con.												
Escambia	111,049	33.8	189,710	82.1	21.0	3.7	6.8	47.7	76.9	14.5	14.2	14.8
Flagler	21,294	23.6	38,616	85.9	21.2	9.9	11.2	48.1	81.4	17.4	7.8	8.8
Franklin	4,096	27.8	8,202	68.3	12.4	1.9	5.1	59.5	73.6	8.4	13.5	16.3
Gadsden	15,867	39.8	28,932	70.7	12.9	4.1	7.4	64.7	74.2	10.3	15.8	18.7
Gilchrist	5,021	36.7	8,866	72.4	9.4	1.7	4.2	59.4	75.7	8.5	13.0	16.4
Glades	3,852	30.0	7,403	69.8	9.8	7.9	18.8	53.0	67.9	12.0	12.1	15.5
Gulf	4,931	33.0	9,527	72.6	10.1	2.1	4.5	57.9	77.3	8.9	14.5	18.6
Hamilton	4,161	39.2	8,758	62.9	7.3	2.3	6.4	54.0	76.8	5.9	20.9	24.2
Hardee	8,166	41.1	16,509	58.0	8.4	17.5	32.1	55.3	64.5	11.0	19.5	22.2
Hendry	10,850	46.5	20,551	54.2	8.2	24.0	38.0	51.2	63.7	12.2	16.7	19.5
Hernando	55,425	24.4	99,082	78.5	12.7	5.3	9.3	54.9	81.5	10.1	10.6	10.9
Highlands	37,471	23.0	65,087	74.5	13.6	9.1	13.9	52.9	74.1	10.0	13.1	14.2
Hillsborough	391,357	34.8	653,841	80.8	25.1	11.5	20.9	46.0	79.5	20.6	11.8	11.6
Holmes	6,921	34.1	12,659	65.2	8.8	1.7	4.5	57.2	80.0	8.3	17.6	20.6
Indian River	49,137	24.3	84,531	81.6	23.1	8.1	10.4	52.1	80.4	20.2	9.2	9.4
Jackson	16,620	34.6	31,771	69.1	12.8	1.5	4.4	61.8	81.6	10.3	15.7	17.1
Jefferson	4,695	34.5	8,911	73.2	16.9	1.2	3.1	60.4	75.3	14.0	14.5	17.7
Lafayette	2,142	38.7	4,745	68.2	7.2	6.6	11.3	53.7	73.2	9.2	18.6	20.6
Lake	88,413	26.1	155,572	79.8	16.6	5.1	8.4	49.5	80.6	15.2	9.5	10.4
Lee	188,599	24.8	327,672	82.3	21.1	9.2	13.5	47.7	78.7	18.8	8.9	9.4
Leon	96,521	30.3	137,537	89.1	41.7	4.7	7.6	41.0	79.4	19.9	12.7	12.1
Levy	13,867	31.5	24,030	73.9	10.6	2.6	6.1	54.6	74.7	8.4	15.0	17.5
Liberty	2,222	37.6	4,828	65.6	7.4	2.1	5.5	58.6	70.7	11.8	16.9	20.7
Madison	6,629	37.5	12,254	67.5	10.2	2.0	4.8	65.5	76.5	7.3	17.7	19.7
Manatee	112,460	25.6	192,789	81.4	20.8	8.4	12.3	47.3	79.7	18.2	9.7	9.4
Marion	106,755	27.8	187,187	78.2	13.7	5.2	8.8	50.3	80.6	11.1	12.2	13.6
Martin	55,288	23.3	96,467	85.3	26.3	8.1	11.3	50.0	79.2	24.9	8.1	8.7
Miami-Dade	776,774	39.0	1,491,789	67.9	21.7	50.9	67.9	50.2	73.8	19.0	17.1	17.4
Monroe	35,086	23.0	61,161	84.9	25.5	14.7	21.4	48.2	67.2	22.7	9.2	9.6
Nassau	21,980	36.7	38,972	81.0	18.9	2.7	3.9	55.0	80.1	22.6	8.3	8.4
Okaloosa	66,269	35.9	112,429	88.0	24.2	5.3	7.9	46.4	82.8	18.9	9.0	9.4
Okeechobee	12,593	34.9	23,388	65.1	8.9	11.5	19.2	51.5	67.8	10.3	13.7	16.7
Orange	336,286	36.2	574,101	81.8	26.1	14.4	25.4	42.3	79.9	20.2	12.6	10.9
Osceola	60,977	40.7	110,607	79.1	15.7	14.0	33.3	40.0	78.2	14.1	12.2	11.8
Palm Beach	474,175	27.3	817,899	83.6	27.7	17.4	21.7	49.5	79.6	26.3	10.1	9.5
Pasco	147,566	26.0	255,472	77.6	13.1	7.0	10.3	52.2	80.0	11.9	10.8	10.8
Pinellas	414,968	24.4	686,094	84.0	22.9	9.5	12.0	50.4	79.7	17.9	11.1	9.8
Polk	187,233	33.0	326,208	74.8	14.9	6.9	12.1	51.1	79.9	14.5	13.2	13.2
Putnam	27,839	32.2	47,761	70.4	9.4	3.4	7.3	60.6	78.0	10.2	17.3	19.1
St. Johns	49,614	31.7	86,199	87.2	33.1	4.9	6.7	45.9	81.2	30.0	7.5	7.3
St. Lucie	76,933	29.7	136,448	77.7	15.1	10.5	13.8	51.9	80.0	14.0	11.3	12.5
Santa Rosa	43,793	39.8	78,166	85.4	22.9	3.0	5.3	48.6	83.0	19.0	9.6	9.9
Sarasota	149,937	20.1	256,802	87.1	27.4	9.3	10.5	51.4	80.8	21.6	7.6	7.3
Seminole	139,572	37.0	243,216	88.7	31.0	9.1	15.6	46.9	83.1	28.2	8.5	7.4
Sumter	20,779	21.8	41,509	77.3	12.2	5.5	9.1	43.9	81.2	10.8	12.5	14.9
Suwannee	13,460	33.9	23,492	73.2	10.5	4.7	7.3	56.8	74.4	9.5	15.3	16.3
Taylor	7,176	36.6	12,914	70.0	8.9	1.7	4.3	61.0	76.8	11.0	15.9	17.8
Union	3,367	46.2	9,363	72.5	7.5	2.1	6.9	55.3	81.9	10.6	18.2	19.9
Volusia	184,723	27.0	317,225	82.0	17.6	6.4	10.8	51.7	78.7	14.2	11.2	11.1
Wakulla	8,450	39.1	15,211	78.4	15.7	1.5	4.3	55.8	78.7	14.3	10.4	12.2
Walton	16,548	29.7	28,838	76.0	16.2	3.2	5.1	52.5	77.1	12.3	11.5	14.9
Washington	7,931	33.8	14,338	71.2	9.2	2.5	5.5	56.4	78.2	9.5	15.5	18.3
GEORGIA	3,006,369	39.1	5,185,965	78.6	24.3	7.1	9.9	49.2	77.5	22.7	13.7	12.3
Appling	6,606	39.5	11,004	67.3	8.4	3.4	6.1	64.8	76.3	12.2	17.0	16.4
Atkinson	2,717	43.9	4,503	56.3	6.9	12.1	16.4	60.2	70.3	8.4	19.6	21.9
Bacon	3,833	38.3	6,525	67.7	6.6	1.6	3.5	61.0	79.0	6.9	18.2	18.2
Baker	1,514	39.0	2,543	66.0	10.7	1.9	4.9	68.3	78.3	11.4	21.4	23.5
Baldwin	14,758	35.4	28,445	72.6	16.2	1.9	5.3	55.0	81.2	16.1	18.8	17.0
Banks	5,364	39.3	9,401	65.4	8.6	2.1	3.7	60.9	78.7	12.9	12.3	12.2
Barrow	16,354	43.8	29,317	73.3	10.9	3.6	5.8	47.5	77.8	17.3	10.1	9.5
Bartow	27,176	42.6	48,709	71.8	14.1	2.5	5.5	51.3	80.4	18.1	11.4	9.5
Ben Hill	6,673	38.1	10,990	65.8	9.5	3.4	5.0	58.6	79.0	11.4	20.2	19.1
Berrien	6,261	39.1	10,451	66.0	9.4	1.4	4.0	59.9	79.8	9.0	17.2	17.3
Bibb	59,667	36.5	97,463	77.2	21.3	1.9	4.0	53.0	79.9	17.3	20.0	17.2
Bleckley	4,372	37.1	7,268	71.7	12.5	1.4	2.7	66.4	80.7	13.2	15.4	15.3
Brantley	5,436	42.3	9,282	72.5	6.2	0.9	2.6	65.8	76.1	8.0	16.3	16.4
Brooks	6,155	37.4	10,455	67.5	11.3	1.7	3.4	60.4	75.6	8.2	21.7	22.4
Bryan	8,089	48.8	14,333	79.0	19.3	2.5	4.2	47.5	82.7	26.7	9.9	9.8
Bulloch	20,743	32.9	28,740	77.9	25.4	3.1	5.5	44.7	78.3	14.1	19.9	18.6
Burke	7,934	44.7	13,338	64.9	9.5	0.8	3.5	63.4	79.0	10.5	21.7	21.0
Butts	6,455	40.2	13,055	69.8	8.6	0.9	2.8	49.4	80.4	15.3	12.5	12.9
Calhoun	1,962	37.3	4,277	65.5	11.7	1.9	2.1	59.9	72.4	7.6	26.3	27.1
Camden	14,705	49.9	24,073	83.3	16.0	2.3	6.2	39.8	76.9	15.0	11.1	9.8

See footnotes at end of table.

Table B-4. Counties — **Population Characteristics**—Con.

[Includes United States, states, and 3,141 counties/county equivalents defined as of February 22, 2005. For more information on these areas, see Appendix C, Geographic Information]

County	Households, 2000 Total	Households, 2000 With individuals under 18 years (percent of total)	Educational attainment,[1] 2000 Total persons	High school graduate or higher (percent)	Bachelor's degree or higher (percent)	Foreign-born population, 2000 (percent)	Persons 5 years and over Speaking language other than English at home, 2000 (percent)	Residing in same house in 1995 and 2000 (percent)	Workers who drove alone to work,[2] 2000 (percent)	Households with income of $75,000 or more in 1999 (percent)	Persons in poverty (percent) 2004	Persons in poverty (percent) 2000
GEORGIA—Con.												
Candler	3,375	39.9	6,166	56.9	10.2	6.1	9.5	57.7	69.0	8.5	21.6	22.2
Carroll	31,568	39.3	53,464	71.1	16.5	2.9	4.8	50.0	79.0	16.4	14.7	12.2
Catoosa	20,425	38.8	35,231	76.0	13.8	1.7	3.5	54.3	85.6	15.3	11.0	9.6
Charlton	3,342	42.9	6,404	65.1	6.4	0.9	2.2	62.1	77.7	8.6	20.1	19.2
Chatham	89,865	35.0	147,849	80.2	25.0	4.0	6.7	50.5	76.4	19.6	16.9	14.8
Chattahoochee	2,932	67.1	6,417	88.8	25.0	6.0	14.2	15.4	51.6	10.4	16.8	12.4
Chattooga	9,577	35.3	17,054	60.4	7.7	1.9	3.7	60.5	77.5	8.4	15.6	14.3
Cherokee	49,495	44.3	91,141	84.4	27.0	5.8	8.0	48.1	81.2	36.2	6.5	5.4
Clarke	39,706	25.4	51,845	81.0	39.8	8.4	11.8	33.9	75.1	13.9	19.7	17.5
Clay	1,347	32.1	2,215	64.3	10.1	0.7	1.9	60.9	69.7	8.7	26.3	28.6
Clayton	82,243	45.8	141,554	80.1	16.6	10.9	14.9	41.5	76.3	17.7	14.8	11.9
Clinch	2,512	42.3	4,380	58.9	10.4	1.4	3.1	57.9	75.0	6.8	20.9	21.6
Cobb	227,487	38.4	395,349	88.8	39.8	11.6	14.7	43.8	80.8	36.2	9.6	7.1
Coffee	13,354	42.5	22,798	64.8	10.0	5.4	7.8	54.6	79.1	11.2	19.3	19.8
Colquitt	15,495	39.4	26,127	64.9	11.4	6.5	10.8	54.5	71.8	9.8	20.1	19.4
Columbia	31,120	47.5	56,562	87.9	32.0	4.8	8.2	53.3	86.2	31.4	6.8	6.4
Cook	5,882	39.6	9,876	64.6	8.1	2.3	4.5	55.4	80.1	8.8	18.3	18.8
Coweta	31,442	44.3	56,821	81.6	20.6	3.7	5.6	47.7	81.1	28.7	9.5	8.1
Crawford	4,461	42.6	8,050	67.3	6.8	0.5	2.0	65.4	83.5	12.6	14.9	14.7
Crisp	8,337	39.5	13,709	65.9	12.8	2.1	4.6	58.0	78.0	11.9	24.1	23.8
Dade	5,633	36.1	9,728	67.0	10.9	1.4	3.3	59.8	76.6	12.2	12.3	11.8
Dawson	6,069	36.8	10,752	79.5	18.1	1.4	3.3	50.1	78.9	24.7	9.5	9.5
Decatur	10,380	40.6	17,633	69.7	12.1	2.3	4.7	57.7	75.9	10.4	21.5	21.1
DeKalb	249,339	35.7	429,981	85.1	36.3	15.2	17.4	43.8	70.5	27.4	14.7	11.0
Dodge	7,062	36.3	12,501	66.3	11.6	1.4	2.8	59.3	78.6	11.4	19.5	18.8
Dooly	3,909	38.9	7,309	68.5	9.6	1.5	4.7	57.7	79.2	9.6	21.6	22.6
Dougherty	35,552	38.2	58,024	73.7	17.8	1.7	4.4	52.1	78.1	14.3	22.3	21.0
Douglas	32,822	42.9	58,687	81.1	19.2	3.9	6.2	51.0	81.6	25.9	10.6	8.3
Early	4,695	37.8	7,872	68.4	12.6	0.7	2.6	59.9	72.1	11.8	23.9	24.3
Echols	1,264	43.7	2,167	60.5	8.4	12.6	22.4	57.9	70.3	8.5	19.9	20.7
Effingham	13,151	46.8	23,129	78.9	13.6	1.3	2.8	53.5	83.5	20.5	10.1	9.3
Elbert	8,004	36.6	13,617	67.2	9.8	1.9	3.4	63.1	77.5	8.7	16.5	15.3
Emanuel	8,045	39.1	13,465	61.4	10.1	4.1	5.9	65.1	72.2	10.4	22.3	23.1
Evans	3,778	40.4	6,540	65.7	9.0	4.3	7.1	50.9	70.6	7.0	21.2	22.5
Fannin	8,369	29.1	14,291	70.9	10.4	1.1	2.3	60.8	76.5	9.1	13.2	14.0
Fayette	31,524	45.6	59,016	92.4	36.2	5.0	7.0	51.3	84.5	46.8	5.3	3.8
Floyd	34,028	36.3	58,651	71.5	15.8	5.2	7.8	53.8	79.8	14.9	15.0	13.3
Forsyth	34,565	44.0	65,027	85.7	34.6	6.0	8.6	40.6	81.6	44.9	5.5	4.4
Franklin	7,888	34.9	13,448	67.0	10.3	1.2	2.4	59.9	80.4	8.9	15.0	13.9
Fulton	321,242	32.5	527,738	84.0	41.4	9.6	13.3	42.8	71.4	31.5	15.6	13.8
Gilmer	9,071	34.6	15,718	66.0	12.9	5.8	8.1	51.8	73.3	11.9	12.7	13.2
Glascock	1,004	36.7	1,764	66.1	6.5	–	0.4	60.0	73.2	9.8	14.0	14.1
Glynn	27,208	34.4	44,806	82.2	23.8	3.3	5.8	52.4	80.0	20.6	15.1	14.0
Gordon	16,173	40.5	28,490	65.9	10.6	6.4	8.9	52.9	78.4	14.1	12.1	11.1
Grady	8,797	39.4	14,988	69.4	10.6	3.9	5.3	56.5	73.8	10.8	18.8	19.0
Greene	5,477	34.8	9,508	70.1	17.6	2.6	3.6	56.4	71.9	18.8	18.2	17.3
Gwinnett	202,317	45.0	372,628	87.3	34.1	16.9	21.2	41.7	79.7	36.7	8.9	5.6
Habersham	13,259	35.4	23,501	70.9	15.8	7.8	11.7	55.4	79.2	13.7	11.7	11.2
Hall	47,381	41.5	86,821	70.5	18.7	16.2	20.7	47.8	76.4	22.3	12.0	10.5
Hancock	3,237	38.7	6,618	62.2	9.8	0.3	1.4	70.9	62.4	6.9	24.6	26.1
Haralson	9,826	37.7	16,814	63.0	9.0	0.9	2.1	58.5	75.8	10.8	15.1	14.7
Harris	8,822	38.6	16,231	79.0	21.1	1.9	4.1	56.0	84.9	27.3	8.5	8.9
Hart	9,106	33.0	15,838	71.1	13.5	1.3	2.6	61.4	78.9	12.7	14.3	13.1
Heard	4,043	43.0	7,020	66.0	7.3	0.7	2.3	62.5	72.7	9.3	15.3	14.8
Henry	41,373	46.9	75,501	84.2	19.5	3.4	5.6	45.2	83.0	31.3	7.0	5.3
Houston	40,911	42.0	69,038	84.3	19.8	3.4	6.1	47.3	83.3	19.9	11.8	10.1
Irwin	3,644	39.8	6,196	67.7	9.9	1.3	2.7	65.7	81.8	11.6	17.9	18.1
Jackson	15,057	40.4	26,849	68.1	11.7	2.5	5.0	50.6	79.3	16.7	11.8	11.9
Jasper	4,175	40.1	7,531	69.7	11.5	2.1	2.4	56.4	74.5	14.5	14.0	13.8
Jeff Davis	4,828	40.1	8,036	63.3	9.4	3.8	5.7	60.6	78.5	8.6	17.5	17.5
Jefferson	6,339	40.7	10,799	58.5	9.1	0.5	1.9	65.6	73.5	7.5	20.4	20.2
Jenkins	3,214	39.7	5,335	62.0	10.8	0.9	4.2	61.5	74.4	10.7	22.8	23.2
Johnson	3,130	36.3	5,206	62.4	7.8	0.2	1.2	70.1	79.7	9.7	22.9	22.8
Jones	8,659	41.8	15,383	77.9	15.0	1.0	3.3	63.5	85.7	20.0	10.7	9.8
Lamar	5,712	37.7	10,227	71.3	11.3	1.0	2.8	57.3	78.5	13.2	13.7	14.9
Lanier	2,593	42.0	4,487	67.0	8.8	1.1	2.6	52.3	77.8	8.9	18.8	19.6
Laurens	17,083	37.9	28,875	70.3	14.4	1.1	2.8	58.9	79.6	13.6	18.2	17.0
Lee	8,229	52.1	15,036	81.3	17.0	1.7	3.3	52.9	85.3	25.7	9.5	9.4
Liberty	19,383	54.1	30,797	86.8	14.5	5.7	12.9	32.7	72.1	9.8	15.6	15.3
Lincoln	3,251	35.8	5,701	71.0	10.1	0.7	1.9	67.4	77.2	10.4	15.6	16.2

See footnotes at end of table.

County and City Data Book: 2007

U.S. Census Bureau

[Includes United States, states, and 3,141 counties/county equivalents defined as of February 22, 2005. For more information on these areas, see Appendix C, Geographic Information]

County	Households, 2000 Total	With individuals under 18 years (percent of total)	Educational attainment,[1] 2000 Total persons	High school graduate or higher (percent)	Bachelor's degree or higher (percent)	Foreign-born population, 2000 (percent)	Persons 5 years and over: Speaking language other than English at home, 2000 (percent)	Residing in same house in 1995 and 2000 (percent)	Workers who drove alone to work,[2] 2000 (percent)	Households with income of $75,000 or more in 1999 (percent)	Persons in poverty (percent) 2004	2000
GEORGIA—Con.												
Long	3,574	50.1	5,527	74.3	5.8	5.4	9.4	47.0	74.3	7.2	18.3	19.5
Lowndes	32,654	39.3	54,237	77.7	19.7	2.7	4.9	45.7	79.9	13.8	18.0	16.8
Lumpkin	7,537	36.2	12,665	72.0	17.6	2.9	6.7	47.1	75.3	15.2	13.0	12.5
McDuffie	7,970	40.9	13,442	66.7	11.7	0.6	2.4	60.0	79.1	13.6	17.8	16.8
McIntosh	4,202	36.5	6,978	71.2	11.1	1.0	3.6	59.9	78.7	8.9	17.5	19.4
Macon	4,834	40.9	8,844	63.2	10.0	1.8	4.4	68.2	69.4	9.0	22.5	24.9
Madison	9,800	38.4	16,881	70.8	10.9	2.0	3.7	65.1	79.8	13.4	13.4	12.4
Marion	2,668	39.5	4,437	65.4	8.9	5.0	6.5	56.5	68.8	10.5	21.6	19.4
Meriwether	8,248	38.3	14,434	65.8	10.8	0.7	2.2	63.5	76.5	12.7	18.0	16.7
Miller	2,487	36.0	4,281	69.0	11.3	0.4	1.5	67.6	75.5	11.3	19.0	19.4
Mitchell	8,063	41.3	14,972	65.3	9.1	1.6	4.0	61.2	74.2	10.3	23.2	23.0
Monroe	7,719	40.7	14,185	77.7	17.1	1.0	3.0	65.0	83.0	21.3	11.6	11.9
Montgomery	2,919	38.3	5,108	71.4	13.5	3.9	4.2	57.2	71.3	11.1	19.1	20.4
Morgan	5,558	40.1	10,125	74.0	18.7	1.1	2.4	59.3	77.5	19.1	12.3	12.0
Murray	13,286	43.5	22,803	61.1	7.2	3.6	6.5	56.9	80.2	11.9	13.0	11.3
Muscogee	69,819	39.1	114,045	78.9	20.3	4.7	8.1	47.8	75.5	15.2	17.1	16.1
Newton	21,997	42.7	39,144	74.7	14.5	2.5	3.9	50.2	81.4	19.9	11.7	10.4
Oconee	9,051	47.1	16,470	86.7	39.8	4.4	6.4	51.3	82.5	33.2	7.0	6.5
Oglethorpe	4,849	38.0	8,436	72.1	15.6	0.8	2.4	66.3	82.1	14.1	12.8	12.0
Paulding	28,089	49.5	50,422	80.8	15.2	2.1	4.3	46.8	83.5	24.4	6.9	5.8
Peach	8,436	39.0	14,055	73.4	16.8	3.8	6.9	56.0	76.6	16.4	20.0	18.8
Pickens	8,960	34.2	15,868	70.2	15.6	2.0	3.6	56.7	78.7	17.1	10.4	9.9
Pierce	5,958	38.4	10,131	69.8	10.1	2.1	3.6	62.5	79.6	10.0	16.8	17.6
Pike	4,755	42.1	8,833	75.3	14.0	1.0	2.9	57.4	79.9	18.5	10.5	10.2
Polk	14,012	38.2	24,703	63.3	8.0	6.0	7.9	57.6	75.2	10.5	15.0	13.8
Pulaski	3,407	35.0	6,445	73.4	12.9	2.6	7.3	59.0	79.7	12.8	17.5	17.7
Putnam	7,402	32.6	12,931	75.5	14.4	2.5	4.7	58.2	73.5	18.3	14.1	13.6
Quitman	1,047	31.3	1,773	57.8	6.1	0.7	2.3	62.8	71.5	7.9	21.2	22.4
Rabun	6,279	29.3	10,675	75.4	17.6	4.1	7.2	59.8	74.7	13.5	12.1	11.7
Randolph	2,909	37.1	4,783	62.4	9.5	0.7	3.4	64.1	72.3	8.2	24.1	25.0
Richmond	73,920	38.7	122,592	78.0	18.7	3.4	6.6	50.7	76.5	13.4	20.0	18.7
Rockdale	24,052	43.3	44,794	82.4	23.4	7.6	9.7	52.0	79.7	29.7	11.8	8.5
Schley	1,435	40.8	2,364	70.0	13.7	1.8	3.8	58.3	76.0	11.6	15.6	17.9
Screven	5,797	39.2	9,685	66.9	10.2	1.7	3.7	65.1	76.8	8.3	19.5	18.5
Seminole	3,573	35.5	6,114	67.9	8.6	1.1	5.0	60.7	78.5	10.6	20.8	22.0
Spalding	21,519	39.7	37,110	67.8	12.5	2.2	4.1	53.4	76.1	15.2	17.0	14.6
Stephens	9,951	33.6	16,771	71.1	14.1	1.4	3.5	58.6	82.3	10.4	15.9	14.5
Stewart	2,007	35.7	3,495	63.2	9.3	1.6	2.6	65.6	65.1	8.5	23.9	22.6
Sumter	12,025	39.9	20,040	69.9	19.3	2.0	5.4	57.8	76.5	11.8	22.3	20.3
Talbot	2,538	34.8	4,403	64.8	7.9	0.7	1.9	71.8	73.9	9.6	18.9	18.3
Taliaferro	870	32.4	1,434	56.2	8.4	0.5	1.7	72.8	72.0	9.5	22.8	22.1
Tattnall	7,057	37.6	14,688	66.3	7.9	5.8	8.3	49.4	71.7	8.8	22.0	24.1
Taylor	3,281	36.8	5,594	63.6	8.5	1.0	2.5	67.0	76.2	9.4	20.8	22.5
Telfair	4,140	36.4	7,906	63.6	8.3	1.1	3.2	73.3	79.6	9.9	24.8	24.5
Terrell	4,002	39.6	6,741	64.5	10.7	1.7	3.6	62.2	72.0	8.2	23.5	23.4
Thomas	16,309	37.8	27,697	73.5	16.8	1.4	3.8	56.3	79.6	12.0	17.4	17.2
Tift	13,919	40.0	23,433	67.9	15.6	5.5	8.8	54.0	77.3	15.2	18.5	18.3
Toombs	9,877	39.6	16,212	67.3	12.7	5.9	10.2	58.6	78.1	11.2	21.2	21.7
Towns	3,998	22.1	6,935	75.1	17.4	2.7	4.1	56.1	73.8	12.2	11.9	12.3
Treutlen	2,531	38.0	4,292	61.8	8.5	1.9	4.5	65.5	75.7	7.3	22.7	24.4
Troup	21,920	39.7	36,815	73.0	18.0	2.0	3.8	53.1	78.7	15.7	15.8	13.8
Turner	3,435	42.0	5,707	67.7	10.5	2.4	6.2	63.6	73.6	10.1	23.1	23.6
Twiggs	3,832	39.9	6,702	63.2	5.4	0.8	2.2	71.2	77.9	12.4	17.7	18.2
Union	7,159	27.1	12,730	74.2	12.5	1.3	2.0	57.2	77.6	11.6	12.7	13.0
Upson	10,722	37.0	18,325	66.7	11.5	2.0	3.3	62.9	77.0	11.4	17.1	15.3
Walker	23,605	36.6	40,837	66.8	10.2	1.0	3.2	61.6	83.1	9.5	14.0	12.1
Walton	21,307	43.9	38,527	73.5	13.0	2.0	4.3	50.4	79.1	22.9	11.2	10.3
Ware	13,475	35.2	23,380	70.3	11.4	1.8	4.1	53.0	79.1	9.3	19.5	20.0
Warren	2,435	36.6	4,061	57.1	8.0	0.5	3.2	66.7	69.7	7.1	20.7	20.3
Washington	7,435	40.6	13,626	68.3	10.5	0.5	2.4	63.6	79.4	12.9	19.6	20.1
Wayne	9,324	39.9	17,531	70.1	11.6	1.5	5.6	53.1	80.5	13.5	17.7	18.6
Webster	911	37.9	1,588	61.3	9.1	2.0	5.8	69.5	75.9	9.5	18.1	17.3
Wheeler	2,011	36.8	4,144	67.9	7.1	1.9	3.5	57.7	69.9	9.0	25.6	27.2
White	7,731	34.0	13,473	76.0	15.4	2.0	4.4	51.4	79.8	11.2	12.0	11.7
Whitfield	29,385	41.3	52,570	63.0	12.8	16.6	22.2	52.4	77.0	17.6	11.9	10.3
Wilcox	2,785	37.3	5,761	68.2	7.0	0.8	2.0	61.6	78.0	9.9	23.7	23.1
Wilkes	4,314	34.0	7,265	65.0	12.0	1.3	2.6	67.0	74.0	9.8	17.2	15.9
Wilkinson	3,827	40.2	6,509	70.4	9.6	1.4	2.8	68.2	77.6	10.3	16.3	15.4
Worth	8,106	41.1	13,979	68.3	8.6	1.0	1.8	64.9	80.2	11.5	17.7	17.5

See footnotes at end of table.

U.S. Census Bureau

[Includes United States, states, and 3,141 counties/county equivalents defined as of February 22, 2005. For more information on these areas, see Appendix C, Geographic Information]

County	Households, 2000		Educational attainment,[1] 2000			Foreign-born population, 2000 (percent)	Persons 5 years and over		Workers who drove alone to work,[2] 2000 (percent)	Households with income of $75,000 or more in 1999 (percent)	Persons in poverty (percent)	
	Total	With individuals under 18 years (percent of total)	Total persons	High school graduate or higher (percent)	Bachelor's degree or higher (percent)		Speaking language other than English at home, 2000 (percent)	Residing in same house in 1995 and 2000 (percent)			2004	2000
HAWAII.	403,240	37.9	802,477	84.6	26.2	17.5	26.6	56.8	63.9	29.3	9.0	9.9
Hawaii	52,985	37.5	97,708	84.6	22.1	10.2	18.4	57.7	68.6	20.9	10.8	13.8
Honolulu	286,450	37.8	579,998	84.8	27.9	19.2	28.9	56.3	61.4	31.6	8.8	9.3
Kalawao.	115	1.7	147	39.5	10.2	20.4	40.1	90.5	75.9	–	–	(NA)
Kauai	20,183	39.8	38,872	83.3	19.4	13.0	19.5	62.8	74.9	23.1	8.6	10.3
Maui	43,507	38.8	85,752	83.4	22.4	16.5	24.1	55.8	71.1	27.3	8.3	9.4
IDAHO	469,645	38.7	787,505	84.7	21.7	5.0	9.3	49.6	77.0	15.7	11.5	11.2
Ada	113,408	38.2	188,662	90.8	31.2	4.3	7.8	43.7	80.9	23.8	9.1	7.3
Adams.	1,421	30.6	2,468	80.8	14.9	1.7	3.8	60.3	63.4	8.0	11.9	14.6
Bannock	27,192	39.0	43,285	87.5	24.9	2.2	6.3	49.4	78.6	15.8	13.0	12.9
Bear Lake	2,259	40.2	3,837	85.5	11.7	1.1	3.7	64.1	69.5	8.6	10.7	12.0
Benewah	3,580	34.4	6,051	79.8	11.4	0.6	3.4	61.2	78.0	9.1	12.7	13.8
Bingham	13,317	48.1	23,155	80.6	14.4	6.1	13.6	61.9	73.9	13.0	13.2	13.2
Blaine	7,780	33.1	13,021	90.2	43.1	10.6	12.5	47.6	69.1	29.0	5.9	6.2
Boise.	2,616	33.2	4,547	86.3	19.9	2.4	5.0	51.0	66.2	16.2	9.9	10.8
Bonner	14,693	33.1	25,043	85.6	16.9	2.0	3.4	56.2	73.4	10.8	12.9	13.7
Bonneville	28,753	42.9	48,502	87.8	26.1	3.9	7.9	53.0	77.6	19.4	11.4	10.5
Boundary	3,707	36.5	6,314	80.0	14.7	2.9	6.0	57.5	71.1	8.0	12.7	15.4
Butte.	1,089	34.7	1,873	82.6	13.0	3.9	6.3	63.4	60.6	10.4	13.4	15.2
Camas.	396	32.1	675	88.4	22.2	1.8	2.9	52.7	65.1	13.4	7.3	7.1
Canyon	45,018	43.0	76,619	76.0	14.9	8.6	17.6	45.3	77.0	12.0	13.2	12.7
Caribou	2,560	41.8	4,391	86.6	15.9	1.8	5.0	64.9	75.4	12.0	10.1	9.7
Cassia.	7,060	45.0	12,206	76.9	13.9	7.3	16.9	58.1	76.0	10.7	14.7	14.6
Clark	340	47.4	580	64.0	12.6	28.2	37.4	54.6	65.0	4.7	15.1	14.6
Clearwater	3,456	31.1	6,352	80.1	13.4	1.2	4.0	60.1	74.2	8.2	12.4	14.3
Custer	1,770	31.4	3,012	84.5	17.4	2.3	4.3	59.1	61.7	10.4	10.8	11.9
Elmore.	9,092	45.4	17,034	87.2	17.3	7.7	13.2	31.3	76.1	10.1	11.8	11.5
Franklin	3,476	50.2	6,069	88.2	13.6	3.4	7.1	59.1	72.7	11.8	9.1	10.4
Fremont.	3,885	42.2	6,790	80.4	12.0	7.3	10.7	64.9	76.6	9.7	12.6	14.2
Gem	5,539	37.3	9,663	79.4	11.4	4.9	7.2	55.7	76.6	13.2	11.9	12.4
Gooding	5,046	39.1	8,761	72.6	12.0	11.6	18.0	50.1	69.0	9.9	12.4	13.0
Idaho.	6,084	31.5	10,638	82.9	14.4	1.2	3.4	58.7	70.0	8.0	14.6	14.9
Jefferson	5,901	49.7	10,335	84.4	15.2	5.9	10.8	61.2	72.8	12.9	10.5	11.5
Jerome	6,298	42.5	10,946	75.1	14.0	10.5	16.9	54.2	76.5	11.8	13.2	13.1
Kootenai	41,308	37.4	69,872	87.3	19.1	2.4	3.7	46.8	80.8	14.8	9.7	10.6
Latah	13,059	29.1	19,493	91.0	41.0	4.3	6.8	41.0	66.1	13.6	13.5	13.6
Lemhi	3,275	30.7	5,373	82.5	17.9	1.5	3.4	59.9	69.0	9.3	12.6	14.5
Lewis.	1,554	30.1	2,596	84.2	14.8	1.1	3.1	66.8	70.8	9.8	11.9	13.7
Lincoln.	1,447	40.8	2,458	77.4	13.0	10.1	14.9	55.8	63.3	9.5	10.4	11.3
Madison	7,129	40.9	9,320	88.5	24.4	3.5	8.5	39.5	65.0	10.5	15.6	15.4
Minidoka	6,973	42.2	11,940	73.7	10.1	10.9	21.8	63.0	78.2	9.2	13.1	14.0
Nez Perce	15,286	31.7	24,759	85.5	18.9	1.9	3.9	54.5	83.5	14.1	11.9	11.4
Oneida	1,430	40.6	2,493	86.4	15.0	2.1	3.9	66.5	64.9	6.4	10.4	11.2
Owyhee	3,710	41.0	6,372	67.6	10.2	11.9	23.0	51.4	69.3	9.6	15.4	17.1
Payette	7,371	40.9	12,761	74.5	10.6	5.5	10.2	51.4	77.3	9.0	13.2	13.6
Power	2,560	44.6	4,344	74.7	14.3	10.5	21.1	61.1	72.8	12.1	14.4	14.6
Shoshone.	5,906	29.2	9,670	77.9	10.2	2.0	3.7	55.3	74.0	7.3	16.3	16.8
Teton.	2,078	41.8	3,614	87.3	28.1	9.9	12.6	52.1	61.4	13.9	9.0	9.3
Twin Falls.	23,853	37.4	39,544	81.3	16.0	6.4	11.5	51.5	80.1	11.9	12.5	12.2
Valley	3,208	30.0	5,525	88.9	26.3	1.4	3.3	57.3	75.1	13.0	9.1	10.0
Washington	3,762	35.8	6,542	76.6	12.7	7.1	13.1	53.3	68.5	9.6	14.0	15.2
ILLINOIS.	4,591,779	36.2	7,973,671	81.4	26.1	12.3	19.2	56.8	73.2	26.0	11.9	10.0
Adams.	26,860	33.4	45,101	83.7	17.6	0.8	2.5	59.0	83.8	11.9	11.3	11.2
Alexander.	3,808	34.0	6,395	67.0	6.9	0.9	3.1	63.5	76.7	7.6	23.8	25.2
Bond	6,155	34.7	11,731	72.8	15.0	0.8	3.1	55.7	75.9	15.3	11.2	11.0
Boone	14,597	42.9	26,061	80.8	14.5	7.5	12.7	53.7	80.9	27.6	7.9	6.5
Brown	2,108	31.2	4,844	63.3	9.2	1.6	4.5	54.5	80.5	9.7	12.3	14.2
Bureau	14,182	32.7	24,085	84.1	15.7	2.6	5.5	66.0	82.1	16.6	8.8	8.1
Calhoun	2,046	30.7	3,528	79.9	9.4	1.0	2.1	69.7	73.0	10.8	8.9	9.8
Carroll	6,794	31.2	11,516	83.3	13.1	1.9	3.5	63.7	76.1	12.6	10.1	9.6
Cass	5,347	34.9	9,056	80.0	12.6	7.8	9.1	59.0	72.3	10.7	10.7	10.5
Champaign.	70,597	29.1	100,559	91.0	38.0	8.0	11.8	42.5	69.4	18.1	13.4	11.7
Christian	13,921	33.0	24,202	81.0	10.5	1.3	2.7	63.2	78.3	12.5	11.1	10.4
Clark	6,971	33.4	11,569	80.0	13.6	0.6	1.9	65.0	82.6	11.0	10.6	10.6
Clay	5,839	32.7	9,898	75.9	9.7	0.7	2.0	66.7	81.6	8.7	12.1	12.0
Clinton	12,754	37.0	23,463	77.4	13.0	1.2	3.3	67.3	80.2	18.9	7.6	7.2
Coles.	21,043	27.9	30,326	82.9	20.8	1.6	4.1	48.4	77.1	12.9	14.4	13.4
Cook.	1,974,181	35.2	3,454,738	77.7	28.0	19.8	30.8	57.0	62.9	26.4	15.2	12.3
Crawford	7,842	32.9	13,995	79.3	10.3	1.3	3.6	62.8	84.0	11.3	11.9	11.5
Cumberland	4,368	35.7	7,352	80.2	10.1	0.6	1.4	65.0	83.1	10.3	10.3	10.7
DeKalb	31,674	34.4	48,912	87.5	26.8	5.8	10.0	45.7	77.6	22.5	9.6	8.1
De Witt	6,770	33.3	11,354	83.5	13.4	1.2	2.1	60.9	80.4	17.8	10.3	9.5

See footnotes at end of table.

[Includes United States, states, and 3,141 counties/county equivalents defined as of February 22, 2005. For more information on these areas, see Appendix C, Geographic Information]

County	Households, 2000 Total	With individuals under 18 years (percent of total)	Educational attainment,[1] 2000 Total persons	High school graduate or higher (percent)	Bachelor's degree or higher (percent)	Foreign-born population, 2000 (percent)	Speaking language other than English at home, 2000 (percent)	Residing in same house in 1995 and 2000 (percent)	Workers who drove alone to work,[2] 2000 (percent)	Households with income of $75,000 or more in 1999 (percent)	Persons in poverty (percent) 2004	2000
ILLINOIS—Con.												
Douglas	7,574	35.4	12,923	79.3	13.8	2.5	13.5	66.6	75.9	15.4	8.2	7.9
DuPage	325,601	38.9	589,120	90.0	41.7	15.3	20.8	57.3	79.6	44.3	6.0	3.8
Edgar	7,874	32.6	13,395	81.4	13.3	0.6	1.9	63.6	80.9	10.8	12.2	11.9
Edwards	2,905	31.6	4,815	82.3	9.8	0.4	1.4	69.2	77.6	8.0	9.4	9.9
Effingham	13,001	37.9	21,635	83.4	15.1	1.0	2.7	61.1	84.1	14.4	9.2	8.5
Fayette	8,146	34.5	14,611	72.2	9.0	0.4	2.2	60.2	81.3	9.0	13.6	13.4
Ford	5,639	33.9	9,557	86.0	13.9	1.1	2.7	64.2	78.2	15.4	8.1	8.0
Franklin	16,408	30.9	26,965	76.7	11.3	0.7	2.2	63.1	82.8	8.6	15.4	15.5
Fulton	14,877	31.1	26,529	78.3	11.4	0.8	2.1	61.4	78.9	12.0	12.1	11.1
Gallatin	2,726	30.3	4,481	73.6	7.7	0.4	2.2	65.7	79.3	7.9	16.1	17.6
Greene	5,757	35.4	9,688	78.9	10.1	0.3	2.0	63.0	76.1	9.0	12.5	12.4
Grundy	14,293	37.6	24,297	86.9	15.2	2.7	5.4	57.0	85.3	27.8	6.0	5.3
Hamilton	3,462	32.6	5,866	74.3	10.5	0.4	2.5	64.1	82.4	9.5	12.6	13.5
Hancock	8,069	32.4	13,724	85.7	15.6	0.5	1.8	67.4	81.4	10.8	9.8	9.8
Hardin	1,987	30.6	3,442	68.1	9.6	1.6	2.1	65.2	78.4	8.4	15.3	16.4
Henderson	3,365	31.3	5,680	82.4	10.0	0.4	2.1	68.5	77.8	11.4	10.4	9.8
Henry	20,056	34.0	34,183	84.5	15.7	1.7	3.9	63.8	82.4	16.8	8.2	7.9
Iroquois	12,220	33.7	21,111	80.3	11.8	2.4	5.1	65.2	80.0	13.0	10.2	9.3
Jackson	24,215	26.2	32,659	85.2	32.0	5.2	8.4	44.3	73.3	11.0	20.2	19.8
Jasper	3,930	34.9	6,579	82.6	11.2	0.2	1.5	71.6	78.0	10.2	10.0	10.8
Jefferson	15,374	33.6	26,841	77.0	13.7	0.8	2.9	59.7	83.7	12.0	13.9	14.2
Jersey	8,096	36.8	13,982	82.5	12.6	1.0	2.6	60.8	81.9	18.1	8.5	9.1
Jo Daviess	9,218	28.9	15,625	83.6	15.2	1.7	2.6	63.1	75.8	15.4	7.8	7.6
Johnson	4,183	33.0	9,057	67.1	11.7	1.5	2.7	59.5	83.0	12.6	13.5	15.0
Kane	133,901	44.6	245,486	80.2	27.7	15.7	25.1	54.0	79.8	35.9	7.9	5.9
Kankakee	38,182	37.8	65,844	79.8	15.0	3.5	6.4	57.3	81.1	18.8	11.9	11.4
Kendall	18,798	44.2	34,362	89.9	25.3	5.3	9.4	54.3	82.8	37.8	4.1	3.4
Knox	22,056	30.3	38,049	81.8	14.6	1.6	4.2	57.8	80.6	12.0	13.4	11.9
Lake	216,297	44.4	398,265	86.6	38.6	14.8	21.4	52.2	76.4	43.9	7.1	5.6
LaSalle	43,417	33.9	74,431	81.4	13.3	2.7	5.6	63.6	82.3	16.9	9.8	8.9
Lawrence	6,309	31.3	10,752	81.3	9.7	0.6	2.4	62.7	82.9	9.1	13.1	12.6
Lee	13,253	34.5	24,540	80.2	13.2	1.9	3.8	60.1	81.8	16.2	9.3	8.3
Livingston	14,374	35.1	26,496	78.1	12.6	1.3	3.6	60.1	80.2	16.4	10.1	9.0
Logan	11,113	33.5	20,714	80.4	14.2	1.4	4.0	56.1	81.0	15.1	10.7	10.5
McDonough	12,360	25.8	17,944	86.9	26.9	2.8	6.3	48.7	72.5	11.7	16.4	15.9
McHenry	89,403	44.9	163,780	89.2	27.7	7.2	10.9	55.9	82.4	40.0	4.5	3.4
McLean	56,746	33.1	87,220	90.7	36.2	3.3	6.0	46.4	79.7	25.2	10.1	8.1
Macon	46,561	32.4	75,195	83.2	16.9	1.4	3.3	55.8	84.4	16.7	14.3	12.7
Macoupin	19,253	34.0	32,878	82.1	11.8	0.5	2.3	62.7	81.1	12.5	10.6	10.0
Madison	101,953	34.9	170,432	84.3	19.2	1.3	3.3	58.6	83.9	19.3	11.2	9.8
Marion	16,619	34.2	27,710	79.1	12.1	0.8	2.7	61.0	83.8	11.4	13.6	13.6
Marshall	5,225	31.3	9,135	85.0	14.5	1.0	2.3	66.4	79.9	14.8	8.1	7.6
Mason	6,389	33.4	10,890	79.9	11.2	0.4	2.2	66.9	78.6	11.3	11.3	10.9
Massac	6,261	32.6	10,471	76.5	10.7	0.4	2.3	62.7	82.5	11.5	13.8	13.6
Menard	4,873	37.6	8,298	88.3	20.5	0.7	2.5	58.4	80.8	20.4	8.8	8.7
Mercer	6,624	34.8	11,529	84.9	12.6	0.6	2.0	64.8	82.9	14.0	8.6	8.3
Monroe	10,275	39.5	18,277	87.2	20.4	0.8	3.1	61.5	86.2	28.6	4.0	4.0
Montgomery	11,507	34.4	20,874	77.1	11.2	0.9	2.2	63.8	79.2	10.7	12.9	13.2
Morgan	14,039	32.3	24,276	79.9	19.9	1.1	3.3	58.6	78.6	14.0	12.4	11.1
Moultrie	5,405	35.2	9,515	78.8	14.7	0.6	6.9	61.3	79.8	15.1	8.3	8.1
Ogle	19,278	37.8	33,317	83.1	17.0	4.3	7.4	58.6	82.0	21.6	8.7	7.0
Peoria	72,733	32.7	118,498	83.8	23.3	3.2	6.0	54.9	82.9	19.7	13.2	12.4
Perry	8,504	32.8	15,727	72.3	10.1	1.0	2.7	63.1	80.8	9.9	13.8	13.3
Piatt	6,475	34.5	11,118	88.7	21.0	0.6	2.2	65.6	83.4	18.8	6.4	6.0
Pike	6,876	32.6	11,864	79.6	9.9	1.1	2.2	64.3	80.4	7.9	12.6	13.5
Pope	1,769	29.7	2,989	75.8	10.5	0.7	2.7	58.9	76.1	8.1	15.4	14.7
Pulaski	2,893	35.4	4,704	70.7	7.1	0.7	2.3	65.1	78.5	7.8	20.7	22.1
Putnam	2,415	32.7	4,136	83.8	12.1	1.8	5.9	67.0	82.0	16.2	6.4	6.6
Randolph	12,084	33.7	23,141	71.3	8.6	0.8	2.8	65.6	80.1	11.5	12.0	11.0
Richland	6,660	32.1	10,827	83.4	15.2	0.6	2.1	61.9	84.1	10.3	12.3	12.7
Rock Island	60,712	31.7	98,865	82.6	17.1	4.6	8.4	58.5	82.8	17.2	12.0	10.4
St. Clair	96,810	38.4	162,715	80.9	19.3	2.1	4.5	56.7	81.6	18.1	15.0	13.3
Saline	10,992	31.5	18,111	76.1	12.1	0.7	2.6	60.9	82.8	8.9	16.1	16.5
Sangamon	78,722	32.8	126,620	88.1	28.6	1.9	3.6	55.0	81.9	21.4	10.3	9.5
Schuyler	2,975	30.9	5,022	83.6	11.7	0.4	1.7	66.9	78.4	9.4	10.1	9.8
Scott	2,222	36.0	3,718	83.1	12.1	0.5	1.4	67.1	79.7	10.4	9.8	10.3
Shelby	9,056	33.1	15,448	82.9	11.5	0.4	1.8	66.7	78.7	12.1	9.5	9.4
Stark	2,525	32.4	4,312	83.4	13.4	0.4	2.3	67.3	77.3	10.5	9.3	8.6
Stephenson	19,785	32.8	32,851	84.1	15.6	1.9	4.0	59.7	81.7	16.2	10.8	9.4
Tazewell	50,327	34.2	86,666	85.0	18.1	1.1	2.6	60.5	85.3	20.9	8.6	7.0

See footnotes at end of table.

Table B-4. Counties — **Population Characteristics**—Con.

[Includes United States, states, and 3,141 counties/county equivalents defined as of February 22, 2005. For more information on these areas, see Appendix C, Geographic Information]

County	Households, 2000 Total	Households, 2000 With individuals under 18 years (percent of total)	Educational attainment,[1] 2000 Total persons	High school graduate or higher (percent)	Bachelor's degree or higher (percent)	Foreign-born population, 2000 (percent)	Speaking language other than English at home, 2000 (percent)	Residing in same house in 1995 and 2000 (percent)	Workers who drove alone to work,[2] 2000 (percent)	Households with income of $75,000 or more in 1999 (percent)	Persons in poverty (percent) 2004	Persons in poverty (percent) 2000
ILLINOIS—Con.												
Union	7,290	32.4	12,695	74.8	15.8	1.9	3.6	60.3	80.9	11.1	14.1	14.4
Vermilion	33,406	33.3	55,778	78.7	12.5	1.7	4.3	59.7	81.6	11.5	14.9	13.1
Wabash	5,192	33.5	8,627	82.2	12.5	0.7	3.0	62.9	76.6	10.6	11.8	11.7
Warren	7,166	32.1	12,131	82.3	15.8	1.4	4.0	63.5	78.8	12.7	11.3	11.0
Washington	5,848	35.3	10,168	79.1	13.4	0.6	3.8	66.3	80.2	14.8	7.2	6.9
Wayne	7,143	32.1	11,723	75.2	10.0	0.9	2.2	64.6	80.1	7.6	12.1	11.9
White	6,534	29.2	10,863	74.6	10.4	0.3	0.9	64.4	81.0	8.9	12.7	12.9
Whiteside	23,684	34.4	40,585	79.8	11.3	2.8	6.9	60.3	80.9	14.9	9.7	8.3
Will	167,542	45.6	310,918	86.9	25.5	7.1	12.0	54.2	82.9	38.0	6.6	5.3
Williamson	25,358	31.7	41,973	79.8	17.2	1.1	3.0	59.0	85.7	12.3	13.7	13.6
Winnebago	107,980	36.0	181,863	81.4	19.4	6.1	10.0	56.0	83.6	21.2	12.7	10.0
Woodford	12,797	37.2	22,945	87.8	21.1	1.0	3.2	63.2	82.9	24.9	6.0	5.2
INDIANA	2,336,306	35.7	3,893,278	82.1	19.4	3.1	6.4	55.0	81.8	19.3	11.1	8.8
Adams	11,818	39.2	20,158	80.0	10.7	1.1	14.3	66.0	78.3	16.2	10.1	9.0
Allen	128,745	36.6	208,769	85.7	22.7	4.0	7.5	52.7	84.1	20.5	11.3	8.2
Bartholomew	27,936	36.5	47,109	83.8	22.0	3.8	5.3	54.4	84.4	21.5	9.2	7.1
Benton	3,558	37.9	6,158	86.3	13.0	0.8	4.0	61.9	78.5	13.5	8.5	7.3
Blackford	5,690	33.5	9,550	81.3	10.3	0.1	2.2	60.4	82.6	9.5	11.0	9.5
Boone	17,081	40.1	30,048	88.3	27.6	1.5	2.8	57.1	83.9	27.4	6.0	5.3
Brown	5,897	32.2	10,530	83.6	18.5	1.0	2.5	63.7	81.4	18.8	9.3	7.9
Carroll	7,718	35.3	13,299	83.2	12.9	2.2	4.0	63.0	80.2	16.5	8.0	6.8
Cass	15,715	34.4	26,747	81.8	12.0	4.3	7.4	59.7	81.2	16.4	11.0	8.5
Clark	38,751	34.7	64,389	79.9	14.3	1.7	3.1	54.8	84.2	16.6	10.2	8.2
Clay	10,216	36.5	17,304	82.3	12.8	0.6	1.6	61.6	82.0	12.3	10.7	9.3
Clinton	12,545	37.8	21,744	80.1	10.1	4.8	7.8	57.9	79.4	15.9	10.3	8.3
Crawford	4,181	35.8	7,088	70.6	8.4	0.3	1.7	62.7	74.9	10.9	14.3	13.9
Daviess	10,894	37.8	18,655	71.8	9.7	1.9	13.7	67.1	72.4	11.2	13.1	12.4
Dearborn	16,832	40.3	29,712	82.0	15.4	0.8	2.6	60.7	83.0	23.4	7.4	6.3
Decatur	9,389	36.8	15,948	79.1	11.5	1.6	3.0	60.6	80.6	15.1	10.0	8.1
DeKalb	15,134	39.1	25,500	84.7	12.4	0.8	2.5	56.7	83.6	17.7	8.3	5.7
Delaware	47,131	30.4	72,444	81.6	20.4	1.5	3.5	52.0	81.2	15.6	15.3	11.9
Dubois	14,813	38.7	25,733	80.2	14.5	2.1	4.9	66.0	85.2	17.8	6.2	4.5
Elkhart	66,154	39.6	112,908	75.7	15.5	7.1	14.4	51.3	79.4	19.0	10.1	8.3
Fayette	10,199	34.0	17,125	73.7	7.8	0.5	1.6	58.0	79.3	14.3	11.6	9.6
Floyd	27,511	37.5	46,609	82.4	20.4	1.2	2.9	57.1	85.5	22.9	10.2	8.0
Fountain	7,041	35.4	11,914	80.7	10.1	1.0	2.9	61.2	78.6	12.4	10.1	8.3
Franklin	7,868	40.2	14,218	76.1	12.5	0.6	2.9	62.5	80.8	18.2	8.8	7.3
Fulton	8,082	34.4	13,613	80.2	10.3	2.0	3.7	60.8	82.0	13.3	10.2	8.7
Gibson	12,847	34.5	21,694	80.9	12.4	0.9	2.6	64.5	83.8	13.9	8.9	8.0
Grant	28,319	32.9	47,408	79.2	14.1	1.2	3.9	55.5	79.9	14.9	13.7	11.7
Greene	13,372	34.2	22,396	79.2	10.5	0.5	2.2	62.6	78.6	12.7	11.6	10.0
Hamilton	65,933	45.0	116,457	94.2	48.9	4.0	5.9	46.1	87.2	46.8	3.9	3.1
Hancock	20,718	39.0	37,073	87.8	22.2	0.9	3.0	56.9	86.1	32.2	5.4	4.4
Harrison	12,917	38.8	22,457	80.3	13.1	0.9	2.4	62.6	81.5	17.3	8.8	7.2
Hendricks	37,275	41.8	67,683	88.5	23.1	1.6	2.9	53.8	89.1	30.3	5.2	3.9
Henry	19,486	33.4	33,198	79.6	11.7	0.5	2.0	62.5	84.0	16.3	10.5	8.6
Howard	34,800	33.8	56,222	83.3	18.1	1.8	3.9	55.9	84.7	22.5	11.9	8.8
Huntington	14,242	36.8	24,386	85.0	14.2	0.8	3.2	58.5	81.4	15.8	8.4	6.6
Jackson	16,052	36.7	27,131	79.8	11.5	2.4	4.3	58.3	81.6	13.9	9.4	7.8
Jasper	10,686	39.4	18,751	82.4	13.0	1.5	3.8	60.3	81.7	18.1	8.1	6.9
Jay	8,405	34.9	14,280	78.5	9.9	1.5	5.8	63.7	80.8	10.1	11.4	9.8
Jefferson	12,148	35.0	20,605	81.0	16.4	1.2	3.4	55.5	81.2	14.6	11.4	10.0
Jennings	10,134	40.2	17,709	76.2	8.4	0.7	2.5	55.8	79.4	12.7	10.4	8.6
Johnson	42,434	39.8	73,966	85.7	23.1	1.7	3.5	51.8	86.2	28.5	7.7	5.7
Knox	15,552	32.1	24,865	81.7	14.4	1.1	3.2	56.1	82.6	11.2	15.2	13.9
Kosciusko	27,283	38.3	47,103	81.6	14.9	2.9	8.4	56.6	78.8	17.8	7.9	6.3
LaGrange	11,225	42.8	19,519	60.2	8.9	2.1	31.7	62.9	60.3	15.6	7.6	8.0
Lake	181,633	37.1	310,220	80.7	16.2	5.3	13.5	61.5	80.7	20.4	14.8	11.1
LaPorte	41,050	35.1	73,723	80.6	14.0	2.5	5.9	58.3	83.6	17.2	11.2	9.5
Lawrence	18,535	34.2	31,175	77.4	10.7	0.9	2.1	59.2	80.1	13.3	10.9	8.8
Madison	53,052	33.1	89,458	80.1	14.4	1.2	3.1	59.7	81.8	17.4	12.1	9.3
Marion	352,164	33.6	553,459	81.6	25.4	4.6	7.3	47.2	80.4	19.5	14.1	10.3
Marshall	16,519	38.3	28,555	79.8	14.9	4.4	9.8	59.8	78.7	16.7	8.1	7.5
Martin	4,183	33.9	7,066	74.2	8.8	0.3	1.4	66.3	77.9	10.8	11.1	10.2
Miami	13,716	36.3	23,741	81.9	10.4	1.0	3.6	58.0	81.4	14.1	11.1	9.1
Monroe	46,898	25.9	65,489	88.5	39.6	5.4	8.1	39.0	73.6	17.1	14.0	11.1
Montgomery	14,595	35.7	24,501	85.7	14.7	1.5	3.0	56.7	81.8	15.2	10.3	8.4
Morgan	24,437	40.2	43,397	80.7	12.6	0.9	2.3	58.5	82.8	21.8	8.9	7.1
Newton	5,340	37.4	9,576	78.7	9.6	2.3	5.0	63.5	80.7	13.2	9.0	8.0
Noble	16,696	40.5	28,554	77.3	11.1	4.9	9.6	56.8	80.5	16.2	8.7	6.8
Ohio	2,201	34.8	3,780	78.4	11.6	0.1	1.4	62.6	83.4	17.5	7.6	6.7
Orange	7,621	34.8	12,818	73.8	10.2	0.8	3.3	63.4	81.3	10.0	13.3	12.0
Owen	8,282	36.8	14,384	74.9	9.2	0.4	2.4	59.0	76.6	12.7	11.3	10.5

See footnotes at end of table.

168

County and City Data Book: 2007

U.S. Census Bureau

Table B-4. Counties — **Population Characteristics**—Con.

[Includes United States, states, and 3,141 counties/county equivalents defined as of February 22, 2005. For more information on these areas, see Appendix C, Geographic Information]

County	Households, 2000 Total	Households, 2000 With individuals under 18 years (percent of total)	Educational attainment,[1] 2000 Total persons	High school graduate or higher (percent)	Bachelor's degree or higher (percent)	Foreign-born population, 2000 (percent)	Persons 5 years and over Speaking language other than English at home, 2000 (percent)	Residing in same house in 1995 and 2000 (percent)	Workers who drove alone to work,[2] 2000 (percent)	House-holds with income of $75,000 or more in 1999 (percent)	Persons in poverty (percent) 2004	Persons in poverty (percent) 2000
INDIANA—Con.												
Parke	6,415	33.0	11,891	80.5	11.6	0.5	3.3	61.3	79.1	13.4	12.4	11.4
Perry	7,270	33.0	12,734	74.8	9.6	0.4	2.4	62.0	76.4	11.5	10.5	8.8
Pike	5,119	32.8	8,753	75.6	8.4	0.6	1.8	61.7	78.5	10.4	9.5	8.6
Porter	54,649	37.5	94,462	88.3	22.6	3.0	6.2	57.4	85.5	28.1	7.8	5.7
Posey	10,205	38.8	17,671	84.4	14.8	0.5	2.1	64.9	86.2	20.2	8.6	6.9
Pulaski	5,170	36.6	9,038	79.8	10.3	0.8	2.3	62.5	81.0	12.6	10.2	9.5
Putnam	12,374	36.5	22,740	81.2	13.1	1.1	2.9	53.7	79.4	15.3	9.9	8.5
Randolph	10,937	34.0	18,310	79.6	9.9	0.7	2.2	62.5	80.7	9.7	12.2	10.3
Ripley	9,842	39.3	17,027	78.9	11.5	0.7	1.8	61.6	79.4	15.3	8.8	7.3
Rush	6,923	37.0	12,020	79.6	10.3	0.3	2.9	59.7	78.1	14.2	9.3	8.1
St. Joseph	100,743	34.9	166,060	82.4	23.6	4.6	8.6	55.2	81.2	18.7	13.5	10.0
Scott	8,832	38.8	14,760	71.4	8.8	0.4	1.9	59.1	82.4	11.8	13.4	11.6
Shelby	16,561	37.9	28,351	79.8	12.7	1.6	2.6	58.6	84.0	20.6	9.7	7.2
Spencer	7,569	37.7	13,491	81.2	13.0	0.9	3.1	65.9	83.7	17.1	8.1	7.1
Starke	8,740	37.2	15,290	72.0	8.4	2.6	5.1	61.5	80.4	12.0	12.7	11.4
Steuben	12,738	35.2	21,170	84.3	15.5	1.4	4.4	53.6	82.3	17.3	9.0	7.1
Sullivan	7,819	34.9	14,782	80.8	9.4	0.3	3.2	60.6	84.4	10.8	13.0	12.7
Switzerland	3,435	36.3	5,889	71.4	7.6	0.5	3.0	59.8	78.5	12.0	12.0	11.4
Tippecanoe	55,226	30.4	79,911	87.8	33.2	8.2	11.4	38.3	77.3	19.1	13.4	10.0
Tipton	6,469	34.8	11,247	83.7	12.4	1.0	2.6	64.2	86.2	24.7	7.3	5.9
Union	2,793	38.0	4,784	79.9	11.1	0.4	3.9	65.4	82.6	14.2	9.7	9.0
Vanderburgh	70,623	31.2	112,193	83.1	19.3	1.6	3.8	54.3	83.9	15.9	12.9	10.6
Vermillion	6,762	33.0	11,410	81.2	11.2	0.8	2.7	64.1	84.8	12.9	10.3	9.1
Vigo	40,998	32.4	66,714	81.0	21.4	2.0	3.9	52.6	81.5	13.1	15.4	13.1
Wabash	13,215	33.9	22,744	81.7	13.7	0.7	2.5	60.6	80.7	14.5	9.4	7.7
Warren	3,219	36.1	5,648	85.0	14.0	0.3	1.7	66.0	82.7	14.7	7.8	7.3
Warrick	19,438	39.9	34,571	86.3	21.8	1.3	2.8	58.2	89.3	24.5	6.3	5.7
Washington	10,264	37.8	17,648	75.2	10.2	0.5	2.4	60.9	79.3	11.6	11.4	9.9
Wayne	28,469	33.2	47,322	78.1	13.7	1.5	4.0	56.9	81.4	12.5	13.2	10.8
Wells	10,402	37.1	17,767	87.3	14.3	0.8	3.4	62.1	84.8	17.2	7.6	5.9
White	9,727	35.1	16,829	82.1	10.5	3.5	7.2	59.3	78.2	12.6	9.3	7.5
Whitley	11,711	36.9	19,995	86.2	13.3	0.8	2.8	61.0	85.2	19.4	6.8	5.3
IOWA	1,149,276	33.3	1,895,856	86.1	21.2	3.1	5.8	56.9	78.6	16.1	10.5	8.3
Adair	3,398	30.5	5,695	87.8	11.2	0.7	2.0	66.0	74.9	8.6	9.7	8.4
Adams	1,867	29.7	3,131	84.5	12.0	0.2	1.6	65.4	76.5	7.8	10.6	10.9
Allamakee	5,722	32.0	9,946	81.4	14.4	5.5	8.2	64.1	67.1	10.7	10.8	9.2
Appanoose	5,779	30.6	9,401	81.4	12.2	1.0	2.5	60.2	79.7	6.6	14.9	14.2
Audubon	2,773	31.3	4,704	82.5	12.3	0.7	2.7	70.4	76.1	9.7	9.2	9.3
Benton	9,746	36.7	16,567	87.8	13.9	0.6	2.8	60.8	76.9	15.9	7.6	6.0
Black Hawk	49,683	31.7	78,401	86.5	23.0	3.7	6.5	54.5	82.8	15.6	13.7	10.1
Boone	10,374	32.8	17,529	89.0	18.8	0.8	2.6	60.6	79.0	14.2	8.8	6.8
Bremer	8,860	33.0	14,835	87.7	21.5	1.2	3.8	62.0	78.5	15.7	7.0	5.7
Buchanan	7,933	36.1	13,383	84.6	12.7	0.9	6.0	62.9	77.9	13.6	9.9	8.9
Buena Vista	7,499	33.6	12,736	81.3	18.7	12.4	16.6	55.9	72.2	11.1	10.7	9.5
Butler	6,175	32.1	10,563	82.2	12.4	0.9	3.8	69.0	76.9	10.9	8.9	7.4
Calhoun	4,513	29.2	7,877	85.4	15.4	0.5	2.5	62.9	78.4	9.1	10.5	9.9
Carroll	8,486	33.8	14,074	83.7	16.0	0.6	2.7	68.0	78.7	12.4	8.5	7.4
Cass	6,120	30.6	10,296	85.9	16.6	0.8	2.7	65.3	77.1	9.8	11.6	10.2
Cedar	7,147	34.8	12,291	87.7	16.3	0.7	3.1	60.9	77.4	14.0	6.8	5.8
Cerro Gordo	19,374	30.6	31,215	87.3	20.3	1.4	3.4	58.7	83.3	12.7	10.4	8.2
Cherokee	5,378	30.5	8,918	87.5	15.2	0.9	3.0	66.8	77.8	10.6	8.9	7.7
Chickasaw	5,192	33.2	8,797	83.4	12.2	0.9	2.9	67.8	74.3	10.8	8.5	7.9
Clarke	3,584	34.4	6,070	84.4	12.1	2.5	4.8	56.9	71.7	10.4	10.7	9.8
Clay	7,259	32.0	11,692	88.0	16.3	1.8	3.5	60.3	80.4	11.4	9.4	7.4
Clayton	7,375	32.2	12,743	82.6	12.8	1.2	2.9	67.3	69.1	9.0	9.7	8.4
Clinton	20,105	33.9	33,158	85.6	14.4	1.4	3.2	59.5	80.5	12.3	12.1	9.6
Crawford	6,441	33.7	11,068	78.5	12.4	6.1	10.5	62.5	75.8	8.9	11.2	10.1
Dallas	15,584	38.8	26,483	89.5	26.8	4.0	6.7	52.2	81.5	25.4	6.3	5.1
Davis	3,207	33.8	5,578	78.9	11.4	0.4	12.8	64.7	69.5	7.7	11.9	12.7
Decatur	3,337	29.8	5,283	81.7	15.1	2.0	5.6	53.8	67.1	7.3	16.8	15.2
Delaware	6,834	38.1	11,784	85.1	13.0	0.6	2.5	66.8	73.7	13.2	9.1	7.8
Des Moines	17,270	31.9	28,425	85.8	16.0	1.6	3.1	59.0	81.7	13.1	13.1	10.1
Dickinson	7,103	27.3	11,730	89.2	21.3	0.7	2.3	59.1	80.0	15.2	7.5	6.7
Dubuque	33,690	34.5	57,236	85.2	21.3	1.9	4.0	60.0	81.9	15.4	9.7	7.4
Emmet	4,450	29.3	7,265	82.2	13.0	2.3	5.3	61.3	76.8	10.8	9.8	9.3
Fayette	8,778	31.9	14,632	84.8	13.8	1.1	3.5	62.1	73.9	8.7	12.3	10.2
Floyd	6,828	32.0	11,451	85.9	14.8	1.1	3.3	61.4	81.4	9.2	10.5	9.8
Franklin	4,356	30.8	7,362	84.0	14.5	4.4	7.4	66.7	72.8	12.6	9.1	7.7
Fremont	3,199	32.2	5,557	85.0	14.0	1.7	4.1	61.5	80.3	11.3	10.8	9.8
Greene	4,205	32.0	7,048	85.6	14.6	1.2	4.0	64.8	77.4	9.6	10.1	9.7
Grundy	4,984	32.1	8,465	86.5	17.2	0.8	4.0	68.4	78.7	13.6	6.1	5.3
Guthrie	4,641	29.7	7,976	85.4	14.9	1.2	2.9	62.1	73.6	13.3	9.2	8.9
Hamilton	6,692	32.1	11,094	87.3	17.5	2.1	4.4	62.6	77.3	13.1	8.2	7.2

See footnotes at end of table.

County and City Data Book: 2007

U.S. Census Bureau

169

Table B-4. Counties — **Population Characteristics**—Con.

[Includes United States, states, and 3,141 counties/county equivalents defined as of February 22, 2005. For more information on these areas, see Appendix C, Geographic Information]

County	Households, 2000		Educational attainment,[1] 2000			Foreign-born population, 2000 (percent)	Persons 5 years and over		Workers who drove alone to work,[2] 2000 (percent)	House-holds with income of $75,000 or more in 1999 (percent)	Persons in poverty (percent)	
	Total	With individuals under 18 years (percent of total)	Total persons	High school graduate or higher (percent)	Bachelor's degree or higher (percent)		Speaking language other than English at home, 2000 (percent)	Residing in same house in 1995 and 2000 (percent)			2004	2000
IOWA—Con.												
Hancock	4,795	33.9	8,084	85.8	15.4	2.2	4.7	66.1	73.1	10.2	7.4	6.4
Hardin	7,628	30.9	12,615	85.7	17.1	1.7	4.3	60.8	78.1	10.5	10.0	8.3
Harrison	6,115	34.0	10,487	85.0	12.7	0.8	2.0	60.6	75.7	13.1	9.9	8.1
Henry	7,626	34.5	13,509	86.1	16.2	1.8	4.5	58.2	79.9	12.9	10.5	8.5
Howard	3,974	32.3	6,645	79.3	12.6	0.4	5.6	65.0	71.3	10.0	10.3	8.8
Humboldt	4,295	31.0	7,078	86.3	15.4	1.4	2.8	66.4	81.2	11.9	9.2	8.0
Ida	3,213	30.8	5,349	85.0	13.6	0.2	3.0	69.5	77.1	10.3	9.4	8.4
Iowa	6,163	34.2	10,565	87.0	15.8	0.8	4.8	65.9	71.3	12.4	6.8	5.6
Jackson	8,078	33.5	13,596	81.5	12.1	0.7	2.5	65.4	74.3	10.6	11.1	9.4
Jasper	14,689	33.3	25,291	86.8	15.9	1.5	3.1	59.6	78.7	15.0	8.4	6.3
Jefferson	6,649	32.9	10,893	88.1	31.2	4.0	5.3	56.4	74.2	15.3	13.1	11.5
Johnson	44,080	27.5	62,859	93.7	47.6	6.4	10.5	40.4	68.2	22.6	12.3	8.8
Jones	7,560	33.0	13,776	85.3	12.7	0.8	3.4	59.9	77.0	12.9	9.7	8.4
Keokuk	4,586	32.3	7,667	84.0	11.6	0.4	1.4	68.1	74.4	9.2	11.5	10.6
Kossuth	6,974	31.7	11,694	85.6	13.6	0.9	3.0	68.6	74.6	10.1	10.0	9.0
Lee	15,161	32.8	25,828	83.6	12.5	1.1	3.4	61.9	80.9	12.5	12.8	10.7
Linn	76,753	33.7	123,896	90.6	27.7	2.6	4.8	52.3	82.3	22.2	9.2	6.1
Louisa	4,519	37.9	7,828	79.7	12.7	6.8	13.0	63.9	78.3	13.6	10.5	8.4
Lucas	3,811	30.4	6,336	79.1	11.1	0.7	4.5	61.6	77.9	7.0	13.5	11.8
Lyon	4,428	35.8	7,539	78.7	14.2	0.9	4.6	68.7	73.0	11.3	8.1	7.5
Madison	5,326	36.6	9,254	87.6	14.4	0.6	1.7	59.9	78.2	15.5	7.8	6.5
Mahaska	8,880	34.2	14,504	82.6	16.5	1.6	3.4	57.8	77.4	11.6	12.0	9.4
Marion	12,017	34.6	20,684	84.0	18.9	1.7	4.4	56.2	75.1	16.6	8.8	6.8
Marshall	15,338	33.3	26,179	82.3	17.0	6.6	10.6	57.7	79.6	14.2	12.0	9.6
Mills	5,324	37.2	9,662	83.2	16.3	1.0	1.8	57.2	79.1	17.2	9.4	7.6
Mitchell	4,294	31.1	7,320	84.4	12.8	0.5	4.1	69.4	71.1	9.9	9.0	8.4
Monona	4,211	28.8	7,072	81.7	13.4	0.4	1.8	65.4	73.9	9.0	11.7	10.6
Monroe	3,228	32.8	5,400	82.2	12.6	0.6	3.3	63.7	82.5	10.5	11.8	10.5
Montgomery	4,886	31.5	8,124	81.8	12.9	1.2	2.6	59.1	79.5	9.2	11.6	10.1
Muscatine	15,847	37.4	26,877	80.3	17.2	5.9	11.7	58.4	79.8	18.3	11.2	8.7
O'Brien	6,001	31.3	10,174	80.7	14.7	2.0	4.2	66.4	74.2	9.1	8.7	7.4
Osceola	2,778	32.8	4,647	81.1	13.4	1.2	3.1	70.0	72.2	11.7	7.4	6.8
Page	6,708	29.9	11,655	85.5	16.6	1.0	2.7	58.0	80.5	11.4	12.8	11.2
Palo Alto	4,119	29.5	6,692	83.7	13.9	0.9	3.0	61.1	74.9	9.1	9.8	9.1
Plymouth	9,372	37.1	15,994	87.4	19.3	1.2	3.1	62.2	80.0	16.5	7.1	6.3
Pocahontas	3,617	30.7	6,002	86.6	15.0	0.9	2.7	70.1	72.7	9.5	10.5	9.0
Polk	149,112	34.5	243,458	88.3	29.7	5.9	8.9	49.8	82.0	23.4	9.8	7.1
Pottawattamie	33,844	35.5	57,013	84.0	15.0	2.0	4.5	56.5	81.6	16.4	11.4	8.7
Poweshiek	7,398	30.4	12,176	86.7	18.5	2.1	4.1	55.6	68.6	13.6	10.5	8.0
Ringgold	2,245	29.2	3,781	82.8	13.4	0.5	5.1	63.6	73.4	6.7	13.7	14.0
Sac	4,746	29.7	7,946	84.2	13.6	1.3	2.8	68.8	75.7	10.1	10.0	9.9
Scott	62,334	35.7	102,149	86.3	24.9	3.1	5.6	54.0	84.8	20.5	12.3	9.9
Shelby	5,173	33.6	8,957	86.6	15.3	0.6	3.0	67.8	75.0	11.7	8.8	7.5
Sioux	10,693	37.6	18,172	80.4	19.8	2.9	5.7	63.1	73.3	12.5	7.1	6.2
Story	29,383	28.2	42,148	93.5	44.5	6.9	9.4	39.3	71.3	19.9	11.7	8.2
Tama	7,018	33.9	12,011	84.2	12.9	2.0	8.2	61.9	76.9	11.2	9.7	8.4
Taylor	2,824	29.8	4,766	83.3	12.0	2.0	4.6	63.4	73.9	6.4	11.6	12.0
Union	5,242	29.2	8,342	87.3	14.7	0.9	2.7	61.4	80.3	8.8	12.3	10.1
Van Buren	3,181	30.4	5,322	82.7	11.8	0.6	5.2	65.1	70.3	6.9	12.6	12.1
Wapello	14,784	31.4	24,120	81.5	14.6	1.9	3.8	60.2	81.1	10.1	14.3	12.2
Warren	14,708	39.9	25,756	90.0	21.2	1.1	2.9	60.7	79.6	22.9	6.8	5.4
Washington	8,056	33.1	13,876	82.5	16.4	1.5	6.6	61.3	72.4	11.5	8.5	7.3
Wayne	2,821	29.0	4,722	83.9	12.1	0.6	2.4	60.3	70.2	9.1	13.6	14.1
Webster	15,878	32.1	25,981	84.2	16.9	2.0	4.5	58.4	83.7	12.6	12.4	10.4
Winnebago	4,749	31.6	7,772	87.3	16.5	1.8	4.9	60.8	71.7	12.0	9.2	7.5
Winneshiek	7,734	31.9	12,864	84.1	20.5	2.1	5.2	60.4	68.5	13.3	8.7	7.4
Woodbury	39,151	36.6	64,932	81.4	18.9	7.2	11.8	55.1	78.7	15.5	13.4	9.4
Worth	3,278	31.7	5,476	86.0	12.7	1.1	3.5	64.9	77.7	9.5	8.0	7.0
Wright	5,940	29.9	9,882	84.4	13.5	3.0	6.4	64.8	75.9	10.3	9.5	7.7
KANSAS	1,037,891	35.5	1,701,207	86.0	25.8	5.0	8.7	52.4	81.5	18.9	11.1	8.9
Allen	5,775	32.6	9,292	83.1	15.2	0.9	3.3	59.9	79.2	7.4	14.6	12.7
Anderson	3,221	32.9	5,459	81.9	11.7	0.6	3.9	58.3	76.8	8.8	12.4	12.0
Atchison	6,275	35.2	10,375	84.7	18.0	0.7	2.4	59.2	78.7	9.1	12.8	11.3
Barber	2,235	30.3	3,646	85.8	21.0	0.5	3.0	65.7	78.0	8.9	10.9	11.0
Barton	11,393	32.9	18,265	82.3	16.6	4.4	7.7	60.1	84.4	9.9	12.9	10.9
Bourbon	6,161	33.0	9,965	84.2	17.8	0.7	2.7	56.9	75.4	9.0	15.2	13.3
Brown	4,318	33.1	7,080	84.6	19.0	1.3	4.3	61.6	80.6	9.4	13.4	13.4
Butler	21,527	40.5	37,560	87.3	20.4	1.3	3.3	53.5	84.2	21.9	9.4	7.2
Chase	1,246	30.9	2,081	87.1	19.6	1.1	2.2	57.9	78.0	11.6	10.6	10.9
Chautauqua	1,796	28.0	3,058	81.0	12.3	0.8	2.8	63.0	73.7	8.5	14.4	14.9

See footnotes at end of table.

Table B-4. Counties — **Population Characteristics**—Con.

[Includes United States, states, and 3,141 counties/county equivalents defined as of February 22, 2005. For more information on these areas, see Appendix C, Geographic Information]

County	Households, 2000 Total	With individuals under 18 years (percent of total)	Educational attainment,[1] 2000 Total persons	High school graduate or higher (percent)	Bachelor's degree or higher (percent)	Foreign-born population, 2000 (percent)	Speaking language other than English at home, 2000 (percent)	Residing in same house in 1995 and 2000 (percent)	Workers who drove alone to work,[2] 2000 (percent)	House-holds with income of $75,000 or more in 1999 (percent)	Persons in poverty (percent) 2004	2000
KANSAS—Con.												
Cherokee	8,875	36.0	14,704	80.3	11.3	0.8	2.2	58.4	81.8	7.9	15.6	14.0
Cheyenne	1,360	28.6	2,257	85.5	16.0	2.5	5.0	62.2	71.0	11.2	10.0	11.5
Clark	979	32.3	1,640	87.4	22.1	2.8	4.7	57.5	76.9	11.1	11.1	9.9
Clay	3,617	31.9	6,026	87.0	16.5	1.0	3.8	65.4	74.3	9.3	10.5	9.5
Cloud	4,163	28.6	6,909	85.5	18.0	1.4	2.9	62.2	79.4	9.1	12.0	11.6
Coffey	3,489	35.1	5,932	86.9	20.1	0.8	3.5	61.8	80.0	16.0	9.2	8.4
Comanche	872	26.1	1,440	91.3	15.1	1.1	1.6	60.4	77.5	7.5	9.8	9.7
Cowley	14,039	34.8	22,982	85.4	18.3	2.5	4.7	55.3	82.0	11.9	14.4	11.3
Crawford	15,504	30.4	23,395	84.5	23.9	2.7	4.8	50.7	82.4	10.4	16.4	13.3
Decatur	1,494	26.6	2,479	86.4	15.4	1.2	3.6	64.1	74.6	6.4	10.4	11.9
Dickinson	7,903	33.2	13,156	86.4	15.2	1.7	3.6	60.8	79.9	10.9	9.3	8.1
Doniphan	3,173	34.7	5,176	80.2	14.8	0.8	2.3	63.3	79.7	8.5	12.3	11.1
Douglas	38,486	28.9	53,257	92.4	42.7	5.2	8.5	37.0	76.9	18.1	13.3	10.1
Edwards	1,455	30.0	2,378	81.2	16.3	6.7	10.0	66.1	77.1	8.5	10.7	11.5
Elk	1,412	26.5	2,354	80.0	10.6	0.7	2.7	67.0	72.6	8.4	15.6	16.5
Ellis	11,193	30.3	16,278	87.2	29.2	2.3	7.5	56.3	84.0	13.1	10.3	8.8
Ellsworth	2,481	29.5	4,660	84.8	16.4	1.3	5.9	62.7	75.7	11.4	9.5	8.8
Finney	12,948	49.3	22,196	67.4	14.3	22.7	39.2	45.3	74.0	14.4	13.9	10.8
Ford	10,852	44.1	18,632	69.9	16.4	22.5	35.1	49.6	75.7	13.7	12.3	11.3
Franklin	9,452	37.5	15,753	85.3	16.5	1.3	3.4	53.9	76.1	12.7	10.4	8.9
Geary	10,458	42.7	15,744	86.0	17.1	7.3	13.4	40.3	76.1	11.8	13.0	11.0
Gove	1,245	29.4	2,120	84.5	18.4	0.5	3.6	72.2	69.3	11.1	9.9	9.6
Graham	1,263	28.1	2,125	83.6	17.4	0.9	3.3	67.2	73.5	9.4	10.6	11.0
Grant	2,742	45.9	4,712	71.5	15.2	12.3	29.9	55.0	77.6	15.8	10.4	9.6
Gray	2,045	43.2	3,536	73.6	16.3	9.5	13.3	58.9	77.0	15.9	8.6	7.8
Greeley	602	36.5	983	83.7	17.4	8.5	11.8	63.7	69.5	15.9	8.8	9.2
Greenwood	3,234	29.2	5,343	80.9	14.5	1.0	2.6	57.3	68.2	7.5	13.2	13.0
Hamilton	1,054	36.1	1,727	76.7	17.4	13.5	18.7	52.0	72.7	11.6	10.1	12.4
Harper	2,773	29.8	4,462	83.8	14.0	0.4	2.6	62.1	76.2	9.1	11.9	11.5
Harvey	12,581	34.9	21,278	85.3	23.0	3.7	8.1	54.3	81.7	16.2	9.3	7.5
Haskell	1,481	45.4	2,505	74.8	17.5	13.4	24.5	59.5	74.7	15.7	10.7	9.8
Hodgeman	796	36.4	1,376	86.9	19.7	1.0	3.0	65.7	73.2	9.7	9.1	8.4
Jackson	4,727	37.4	8,228	87.7	15.4	0.5	2.5	62.7	75.5	15.0	9.9	8.5
Jefferson	6,830	38.3	12,127	88.9	17.9	0.6	2.4	60.1	77.7	16.9	7.9	6.6
Jewell	1,695	25.0	2,798	87.6	13.8	0.9	2.0	67.0	75.0	8.1	12.2	11.4
Johnson	174,570	37.5	295,829	94.9	47.7	5.7	8.2	50.0	86.7	38.1	5.4	3.5
Kearny	1,542	46.4	2,592	75.8	15.0	12.7	22.2	60.5	76.9	13.6	10.3	10.2
Kingman	3,371	34.4	5,809	84.7	17.8	0.3	2.9	63.6	76.6	14.5	10.5	9.6
Kiowa	1,365	28.8	2,227	85.2	18.9	1.9	4.0	57.5	75.5	10.5	11.6	10.9
Labette	9,194	33.4	15,007	83.0	15.9	1.0	3.0	57.3	81.5	8.5	14.6	12.9
Lane	910	31.9	1,491	88.5	18.5	0.5	2.1	66.4	75.1	11.8	8.2	9.4
Leavenworth	23,071	41.8	44,792	86.5	23.1	2.7	6.3	46.7	80.9	23.3	8.7	7.5
Lincoln	1,529	28.7	2,548	85.0	17.4	0.5	2.5	64.0	72.8	8.0	10.4	9.7
Linn	3,807	31.9	6,538	80.9	12.7	0.3	2.0	57.7	72.0	10.2	12.0	11.5
Logan	1,243	30.5	2,058	86.7	17.5	0.6	1.8	67.2	79.3	12.6	9.4	9.0
Lyon	13,691	34.9	20,559	81.8	23.0	9.0	15.4	46.5	76.4	12.0	14.1	11.4
McPherson	11,205	34.5	19,078	85.9	22.2	0.6	3.9	56.5	80.1	14.3	8.1	6.7
Marion	5,114	32.2	9,000	84.4	17.9	1.1	6.3	58.6	75.3	9.6	9.6	9.2
Marshall	4,458	31.4	7,460	85.1	13.2	1.1	3.4	66.1	76.6	11.3	9.9	9.6
Meade	1,728	37.8	2,946	80.3	19.6	8.9	14.4	58.0	77.6	14.1	9.5	8.2
Miami	10,365	39.3	18,444	87.5	19.4	0.6	2.4	55.7	81.3	23.2	8.0	7.2
Mitchell	2,850	28.7	4,645	88.1	16.9	0.3	2.7	63.3	77.6	11.6	10.1	8.7
Montgomery	14,903	32.5	24,090	81.2	16.0	1.3	3.7	55.3	80.7	9.3	14.5	12.2
Morris	2,539	31.7	4,224	84.7	16.0	1.5	3.5	61.8	79.5	10.3	10.0	9.2
Morton	1,306	38.5	2,165	81.9	17.6	9.5	14.6	58.8	77.9	14.6	10.5	9.7
Nemaha	3,959	35.0	7,038	83.7	14.6	0.4	2.5	68.8	79.0	9.3	8.6	9.5
Neosho	6,739	33.4	11,113	83.5	15.0	0.7	3.0	60.1	82.0	9.9	14.0	11.4
Ness	1,516	27.4	2,498	84.4	17.9	0.9	3.6	66.8	71.9	11.5	8.9	7.3
Norton	2,266	29.6	4,178	84.8	15.4	0.6	3.3	60.2	81.7	7.0	11.8	10.9
Osage	6,490	36.3	11,117	85.5	14.3	0.6	2.5	60.2	78.5	12.0	9.4	8.6
Osborne	1,940	26.6	3,115	84.8	15.5	0.7	2.0	68.9	74.9	8.9	11.4	10.8
Ottawa	2,430	33.6	4,228	86.2	16.3	0.7	2.5	59.1	79.8	11.3	8.2	7.7
Pawnee	2,739	30.8	4,875	84.8	21.8	1.4	2.7	64.3	81.2	13.4	11.5	10.1
Phillips	2,496	29.5	4,182	84.4	16.1	0.4	2.0	63.6	76.8	7.3	11.0	10.0
Pottawatomie	6,771	38.2	11,441	89.2	22.7	1.0	3.0	56.9	80.4	15.5	9.3	7.8
Pratt	3,963	31.4	6,365	86.3	21.0	1.2	3.6	59.7	79.2	13.3	10.8	9.8
Rawlins	1,269	28.2	2,152	84.7	15.9	0.4	3.8	69.2	68.3	12.3	10.9	10.4
Reno	25,498	32.4	43,082	82.7	17.3	2.0	5.9	54.9	82.6	12.8	13.4	10.6
Republic	2,557	26.2	4,256	88.6	14.9	0.8	3.3	65.0	78.4	8.0	10.9	10.8
Rice	4,050	33.1	6,701	83.4	17.5	2.2	4.9	57.1	77.7	10.7	12.2	10.8

See footnotes at end of table.

Table B-4. Counties — **Population Characteristics**—Con.

[Includes United States, states, and 3,141 counties/county equivalents defined as of February 22, 2005. For more information on these areas, see Appendix C, Geographic Information]

County	Households, 2000 Total	Households, 2000 With individuals under 18 years (percent of total)	Educational attainment,[1] 2000 Total persons	High school graduate or higher (percent)	Bachelor's degree or higher (percent)	Foreign-born population, 2000 (percent)	Persons 5 years and over Speaking language other than English at home, 2000 (percent)	Residing in same house in 1995 and 2000 (percent)	Workers who drove alone to work,[2] 2000 (percent)	Households with income of $75,000 or more in 1999 (percent)	Persons in poverty (percent) 2004	Persons in poverty (percent) 2000
KANSAS—Con.												
Riley	22,137	29.0	29,358	93.8	40.5	6.1	9.7	30.9	71.2	14.4	15.6	11.9
Rooks	2,362	30.4	3,901	87.1	15.4	0.2	3.0	64.8	78.9	6.4	11.5	11.4
Rush	1,548	27.5	2,568	82.8	16.4	0.5	6.5	65.0	75.4	9.6	11.1	10.6
Russell	3,207	26.9	5,323	83.1	16.7	0.7	3.6	67.6	79.7	12.1	12.7	10.6
Saline	21,436	34.4	34,680	87.0	20.4	4.0	7.0	51.6	84.2	13.1	11.0	8.6
Scott	2,045	35.2	3,376	84.5	23.0	2.6	5.8	55.1	79.9	19.0	7.3	7.0
Sedgwick	176,444	37.0	282,585	85.1	25.4	6.6	10.8	49.3	84.8	20.0	12.7	9.0
Seward	7,419	47.1	12,690	63.7	13.6	27.4	41.2	45.2	72.9	14.0	13.9	12.4
Shawnee	68,920	33.4	111,709	88.1	26.0	2.7	6.1	53.6	83.4	18.2	11.7	8.8
Sheridan	1,124	31.3	1,905	87.8	15.9	0.4	2.3	72.6	72.5	8.8	10.4	9.3
Sherman	2,758	30.3	4,319	86.6	15.0	1.8	9.3	57.7	80.1	11.5	13.8	12.6
Smith	1,953	26.8	3,338	84.6	16.7	0.6	1.9	70.4	74.2	6.2	10.5	10.2
Stafford	2,010	31.3	3,254	82.9	18.4	3.6	5.6	62.7	75.7	7.5	12.5	11.9
Stanton	858	43.0	1,468	78.0	16.9	12.7	18.8	54.2	71.4	16.4	9.9	10.7
Stevens	1,988	41.1	3,287	80.5	17.5	12.0	18.1	63.0	80.3	16.8	10.5	10.0
Sumner	9,888	37.1	16,662	86.3	15.7	0.8	3.4	60.2	80.5	14.9	11.2	9.0
Thomas	3,226	34.2	4,978	92.7	25.0	0.4	3.5	59.6	82.8	17.2	10.7	8.8
Trego	1,412	28.8	2,342	84.3	14.0	0.5	4.2	68.8	78.3	9.1	11.1	10.0
Wabaunsee	2,633	35.4	4,623	89.9	17.3	0.7	2.8	64.6	77.3	12.4	7.6	7.2
Wallace	674	35.8	1,133	84.0	17.2	2.2	5.1	68.4	70.7	13.4	11.9	11.6
Washington	2,673	27.8	4,572	81.2	15.2	0.5	2.8	70.6	72.0	7.0	10.0	10.1
Wichita	967	37.1	1,625	77.7	15.5	8.0	16.3	60.7	76.2	13.4	10.6	11.6
Wilson	4,203	31.8	6,944	81.1	10.9	0.6	2.2	58.5	79.6	8.0	13.7	12.5
Woodson	1,642	27.7	2,667	83.4	11.4	0.8	2.2	63.4	74.3	7.7	13.8	12.9
Wyandotte	59,700	37.6	96,608	74.0	12.0	9.5	15.6	53.9	78.1	12.7	17.6	14.1
KENTUCKY	1,590,647	35.5	2,646,397	74.1	17.1	2.0	3.9	55.9	80.2	14.8	16.3	13.9
Adair	6,747	34.0	11,270	60.1	10.9	0.6	5.0	58.5	77.6	7.3	21.5	21.5
Allen	6,910	36.7	11,643	64.5	9.1	0.8	3.6	57.1	77.1	7.2	17.2	13.3
Anderson	7,320	39.8	12,600	80.4	12.0	0.9	2.5	57.3	84.4	14.8	9.6	7.6
Ballard	3,395	33.5	5,766	76.3	10.6	0.8	2.0	61.4	87.0	13.6	14.5	13.1
Barren	15,346	34.3	25,751	69.5	11.1	1.2	3.4	56.0	81.9	10.9	16.6	14.4
Bath	4,445	35.3	7,451	59.0	10.1	0.7	1.7	61.7	77.0	9.0	20.1	18.8
Bell	12,004	35.9	20,042	56.6	9.0	0.7	2.2	63.1	79.1	4.5	28.8	26.8
Boone	31,258	42.4	54,166	85.1	22.8	3.0	5.2	48.1	84.6	29.4	7.7	5.5
Bourbon	7,681	36.1	13,015	75.4	13.5	2.0	4.1	55.5	78.2	15.8	14.3	11.9
Boyd	20,010	31.8	34,697	78.0	14.1	1.1	2.9	58.9	84.9	13.9	17.2	14.5
Boyle	10,574	34.2	18,491	76.6	19.3	1.8	4.3	51.7	78.0	16.0	14.8	12.2
Bracken	3,228	37.1	5,460	69.6	9.5	0.3	1.4	62.9	71.6	11.2	12.8	11.4
Breathitt	6,170	37.9	10,393	57.5	10.0	0.4	2.1	68.5	71.3	5.2	29.5	28.3
Breckinridge	7,324	34.3	12,501	68.9	7.4	0.5	2.2	62.6	74.4	9.5	16.3	15.5
Bullitt	22,171	43.0	39,307	76.0	9.2	0.6	1.9	58.6	84.9	18.0	10.4	7.6
Butler	5,059	37.6	8,489	60.7	6.4	1.8	3.1	64.4	78.4	6.6	17.5	15.9
Caldwell	5,431	31.3	9,265	73.1	10.0	0.5	2.0	62.7	80.5	8.9	15.6	14.5
Calloway	13,862	27.6	21,032	77.9	24.0	2.7	5.2	51.5	79.7	11.8	16.0	13.9
Campbell	34,742	35.4	57,184	80.8	20.5	1.4	3.2	58.9	79.1	20.0	10.9	8.6
Carlisle	2,208	32.5	3,690	73.4	10.6	0.2	0.7	63.8	81.2	9.0	13.4	12.6
Carroll	3,940	37.5	6,690	68.1	8.3	1.9	2.6	51.3	80.8	13.3	14.3	13.3
Carter	10,342	36.6	17,394	64.4	8.9	0.4	2.0	66.2	71.3	7.7	22.7	19.6
Casey	6,260	34.0	10,423	57.4	7.4	1.2	5.2	63.7	71.2	5.6	22.9	20.8
Christian	24,857	44.0	40,344	77.2	12.5	2.5	7.4	41.1	74.0	9.5	17.5	14.7
Clark	13,015	36.6	22,187	75.0	15.6	1.0	2.6	52.0	84.0	16.3	13.5	11.4
Clay	8,556	40.7	16,083	49.4	8.0	0.7	2.3	66.1	75.6	5.1	34.3	32.2
Clinton	4,086	31.8	6,594	53.5	8.0	0.4	3.2	67.3	80.5	7.4	23.6	22.8
Crittenden	3,829	32.0	6,460	67.0	7.3	0.4	6.1	64.9	78.0	9.3	17.1	16.1
Cumberland	2,976	33.0	4,972	56.0	7.1	0.3	1.7	66.5	76.9	6.6	22.1	22.6
Daviess	36,033	35.7	59,745	80.7	17.0	1.0	3.2	55.1	85.1	15.0	14.1	11.2
Edmonson	4,648	35.0	7,865	61.7	4.9	0.4	1.1	64.1	76.9	6.4	17.5	16.6
Elliott	2,638	35.9	4,422	52.6	7.8	0.2	0.9	69.1	66.1	7.2	25.3	24.7
Estill	6,108	35.7	10,189	58.5	6.9	0.3	1.6	58.3	77.1	6.7	23.6	20.9
Fayette	108,288	29.6	167,235	85.8	35.6	5.9	8.3	42.5	79.9	21.1	14.2	10.7
Fleming	5,367	37.7	9,154	66.5	8.8	0.2	2.4	61.3	77.4	9.5	17.8	16.9
Floyd	16,881	35.7	28,370	61.3	9.7	0.6	1.7	68.3	80.6	7.0	26.8	24.8
Franklin	19,907	32.4	32,388	78.8	23.8	1.9	3.6	51.1	79.7	20.0	12.3	9.2
Fulton	3,237	33.8	5,111	69.5	11.5	0.4	2.2	56.2	77.6	7.9	23.1	20.4
Gallatin	2,902	40.8	5,007	68.0	6.9	0.4	2.2	54.8	76.0	13.8	17.2	14.1
Garrard	5,741	36.5	9,951	69.4	10.5	1.6	3.2	52.0	75.9	11.9	14.6	13.5
Grant	8,175	43.3	13,861	72.4	9.4	1.0	2.5	51.4	78.7	14.1	13.3	11.2
Graves	14,841	34.2	24,932	73.4	12.6	2.1	4.3	60.2	81.0	11.3	16.5	13.7
Grayson	9,596	35.0	15,940	62.8	7.7	0.6	2.5	58.0	75.9	8.8	17.9	16.1
Green	4,706	32.6	7,983	61.4	9.1	0.7	2.2	68.4	79.3	8.2	18.3	18.0
Greenup	14,536	34.9	25,323	75.1	11.5	0.6	1.8	64.2	85.5	12.9	16.0	13.6

See footnotes at end of table.

Table B-4. Counties — **Population Characteristics**—Con.

[Includes United States, states, and 3,141 counties/county equivalents defined as of February 22, 2005. For more information on these areas, see Appendix C, Geographic Information]

County	Households, 2000 Total	Households, 2000 With individuals under 18 years (percent of total)	Educational attainment,[1] 2000 Total persons	Educational attainment,[1] 2000 High school graduate or higher (percent)	Educational attainment,[1] 2000 Bachelor's degree or higher (percent)	Foreign-born population, 2000 (percent)	Persons 5 years and over Speaking language other than English at home, 2000 (percent)	Persons 5 years and over Residing in same house in 1995 and 2000 (percent)	Workers who drove alone to work,[2] 2000 (percent)	Households with income of $75,000 or more in 1999 (percent)	Persons in poverty (percent) 2004	Persons in poverty (percent) 2000
KENTUCKY—Con.												
Hancock	3,215	38.7	5,427	77.2	8.1	0.8	2.0	57.4	87.5	13.4	12.1	10.2
Hardin	34,497	41.2	58,358	82.3	15.4	4.5	7.8	48.5	79.3	14.2	13.0	10.1
Harlan	13,291	35.9	22,041	58.7	8.9	0.6	1.6	70.3	80.6	5.0	29.3	27.6
Harrison	7,012	36.9	12,009	74.2	10.6	1.2	3.3	55.2	78.6	13.9	13.6	11.4
Hart	6,769	36.0	11,474	58.2	7.0	0.6	6.0	60.9	73.2	7.5	20.5	20.4
Henderson	18,095	35.5	29,960	78.3	13.8	1.1	3.0	55.5	82.8	13.6	14.3	11.9
Henry	5,844	37.7	10,032	73.4	9.8	1.4	2.6	57.6	76.6	15.0	13.7	12.8
Hickman	2,188	30.9	3,734	64.4	8.8	0.6	1.5	67.1	80.0	12.1	16.2	15.8
Hopkins	18,820	34.6	31,464	71.3	10.6	0.6	2.8	61.9	83.3	10.7	16.8	14.7
Jackson	5,307	38.7	8,611	52.9	6.8	0.4	1.9	66.3	74.0	3.2	25.2	24.2
Jefferson	287,012	32.8	464,284	81.8	24.8	3.4	5.5	53.6	80.8	20.2	14.8	10.5
Jessamine	13,867	42.0	24,182	79.1	21.5	1.8	3.2	47.4	78.5	19.0	13.2	11.3
Johnson	9,103	37.3	15,735	63.8	9.3	0.5	1.8	65.3	81.1	8.3	23.3	22.4
Kenton	59,444	36.3	97,727	82.1	22.9	1.6	3.5	55.3	80.8	21.5	11.3	8.6
Knott	6,717	37.9	11,427	58.7	10.2	0.4	1.8	71.9	76.1	5.8	27.0	25.4
Knox	12,416	38.2	20,401	54.1	8.8	0.4	1.8	62.6	80.1	6.1	29.1	27.4
Larue	5,275	35.4	9,017	71.0	10.9	0.4	2.0	60.1	80.8	11.8	15.4	14.2
Laurel	20,353	38.6	34,431	63.9	10.6	0.8	2.1	59.3	81.1	9.0	20.4	17.4
Lawrence	5,954	38.3	10,256	58.2	6.6	0.1	1.4	63.2	77.5	7.2	24.8	23.6
Lee	2,985	35.8	5,381	50.9	6.3	0.2	1.8	62.9	77.3	6.7	29.8	29.5
Leslie	4,885	38.8	8,214	52.5	6.3	0.2	0.9	75.1	79.2	4.8	28.6	24.8
Letcher	10,085	35.7	16,930	58.5	7.7	0.4	1.7	72.6	81.8	5.4	24.0	23.1
Lewis	5,422	37.9	9,256	57.4	6.4	0.1	1.4	68.6	73.9	5.7	26.9	23.8
Lincoln	9,206	36.5	15,440	64.6	8.4	0.7	2.7	56.3	78.1	6.7	18.8	17.0
Livingston	3,996	32.5	6,851	74.3	8.4	0.2	2.1	68.0	86.8	9.9	12.8	12.2
Logan	10,506	36.6	17,471	68.5	9.6	0.8	3.2	56.9	81.4	9.4	15.9	13.4
Lyon	2,898	27.2	6,185	68.0	10.1	0.8	2.3	67.2	86.7	11.1	14.3	13.8
McCracken	27,736	32.1	45,038	80.3	18.1	0.9	2.3	56.8	84.9	15.5	16.7	13.2
McCreary	6,520	39.6	10,668	52.6	6.7	0.5	1.6	61.0	77.0	3.6	30.1	29.7
McLean	3,984	35.1	6,737	70.8	8.7	0.7	1.5	63.2	83.5	8.5	14.9	13.4
Madison	27,152	34.1	42,125	75.2	21.8	1.5	3.5	44.0	77.1	12.6	16.3	14.1
Magoffin	5,024	40.6	8,410	50.1	6.3	0.2	1.0	71.8	72.2	5.4	29.9	28.6
Marion	6,613	38.5	11,772	70.5	9.1	1.2	2.4	63.0	76.3	10.0	16.4	16.4
Marshall	12,412	31.2	21,278	76.9	13.7	0.8	1.7	64.1	83.1	14.1	11.4	10.0
Martin	4,776	42.7	7,835	54.0	9.0	0.1	1.1	69.2	78.4	4.9	30.5	28.5
Mason	6,847	34.1	11,372	73.3	14.4	1.4	2.8	59.0	76.8	11.9	16.7	15.2
Meade	9,470	45.6	16,131	77.9	11.3	2.0	4.6	52.1	83.0	12.4	11.9	9.0
Menifee	2,537	35.7	4,213	57.6	8.4	0.4	2.7	64.0	68.8	5.0	24.2	23.4
Mercer	8,423	34.8	14,158	75.8	13.5	1.7	3.0	54.8	81.8	13.5	13.6	11.7
Metcalfe	4,016	35.2	6,729	58.0	6.6	0.2	2.0	61.8	79.3	6.8	20.6	20.3
Monroe	4,741	34.1	7,896	57.8	8.4	1.4	3.2	60.6	79.6	5.6	21.3	20.2
Montgomery	8,902	36.8	15,033	70.5	13.4	0.5	2.1	54.9	81.4	12.5	15.4	14.2
Morgan	4,752	37.4	9,321	56.4	7.7	0.7	2.9	64.4	73.8	6.9	27.0	26.0
Muhlenberg	12,357	34.1	21,676	65.8	8.1	0.3	2.1	67.0	80.9	9.3	19.0	15.3
Nelson	13,953	40.8	23,785	79.0	13.4	1.2	2.6	57.1	81.8	15.5	12.9	10.6
Nicholas	2,710	35.1	4,636	62.9	7.5	0.5	1.4	58.5	72.4	12.5	15.3	14.7
Ohio	8,899	35.9	15,237	67.0	7.4	0.7	1.8	62.8	77.7	9.0	17.7	15.6
Oldham	14,856	46.5	30,366	86.5	30.6	1.6	3.6	53.5	85.5	40.0	6.3	4.6
Owen	4,086	36.7	6,999	67.9	9.1	0.7	1.8	57.3	71.4	11.8	16.0	15.8
Owsley	1,894	37.2	3,242	49.2	7.7	0.1	1.0	70.9	71.8	3.4	35.5	36.9
Pendleton	5,170	42.4	9,081	72.8	9.7	0.5	2.0	57.2	76.2	13.8	13.6	11.1
Perry	11,460	38.1	19,596	58.3	8.9	0.6	2.0	72.2	79.5	6.4	26.0	24.4
Pike	27,612	36.6	46,153	61.8	9.9	0.4	1.5	67.5	82.7	7.9	22.9	20.5
Powell	5,044	40.3	8,485	56.1	6.5	0.2	0.7	56.6	75.9	7.3	23.3	20.5
Pulaski	22,719	33.9	38,430	65.6	10.5	0.8	2.1	58.2	82.5	8.5	18.7	16.5
Robertson	866	35.0	1,566	60.9	8.7	0.5	2.8	60.4	72.1	7.3	19.0	17.6
Rockcastle	6,544	36.6	11,109	57.7	8.3	(Z)	1.5	64.1	74.2	5.3	21.4	19.9
Rowan	7,927	32.7	12,455	70.9	21.9	1.4	3.7	50.3	74.4	9.8	20.7	19.4
Russell	6,941	32.0	11,437	61.8	9.6	1.0	3.0	64.4	82.8	6.4	21.5	21.2
Scott	12,110	41.3	20,459	80.5	20.3	1.9	3.9	44.9	80.3	25.1	10.5	9.3
Shelby	12,104	38.0	22,096	79.1	18.7	3.9	5.6	49.0	79.1	24.0	11.0	8.8
Simpson	6,415	37.1	10,680	73.6	11.9	1.2	2.9	53.5	79.1	12.5	13.9	11.1
Spencer	4,251	41.9	7,672	75.4	11.1	1.2	2.4	49.9	83.8	22.4	9.3	8.3
Taylor	9,233	33.7	15,253	68.0	12.2	1.3	2.8	58.5	79.9	8.7	17.8	15.7
Todd	4,569	36.8	7,758	63.5	9.2	1.3	7.7	60.7	73.9	8.0	16.9	14.9
Trigg	5,215	31.5	8,897	72.1	12.0	0.8	3.7	60.7	82.1	10.6	13.0	11.7
Trimble	3,137	38.8	5,340	70.7	7.6	1.1	3.2	54.6	76.8	12.1	14.1	11.8
Union	5,710	35.7	9,524	76.9	10.9	1.4	3.9	60.7	76.4	12.2	15.5	13.0
Warren	35,365	34.3	56,069	80.3	24.7	4.3	6.7	45.7	79.7	16.5	16.5	13.2
Washington	4,121	36.1	7,144	68.8	13.3	0.7	2.9	62.6	77.5	10.7	15.1	12.6

See footnotes at end of table.

Table B-4. Counties — **Population Characteristics**—Con.

[Includes United States, states, and 3,141 counties/county equivalents defined as of February 22, 2005. For more information on these areas, see Appendix C, Geographic Information]

County	Households, 2000 Total	With individuals under 18 years (percent of total)	Educational attainment,[1] 2000 Total persons	High school graduate or higher (percent)	Bachelor's degree or higher (percent)	Foreign-born population, 2000 (percent)	Speaking language other than English at home, 2000 (percent)	Residing in same house in 1995 and 2000 (percent)	Workers who drove alone to work,[2] 2000 (percent)	Households with income of $75,000 or more in 1999 (percent)	Persons in poverty (percent) 2004	200_
KENTUCKY—Con.												
Wayne	7,913	36.1	13,153	57.8	7.2	1.3	2.5	63.3	82.4	5.5	24.3	23._
Webster	5,560	35.3	9,424	70.9	7.1	1.9	4.2	60.2	77.2	9.9	14.9	13._
Whitley	13,780	37.2	22,708	61.3	13.4	0.7	2.0	61.6	76.6	7.5	25.3	23._
Wolfe	2,816	36.8	4,571	53.6	10.6	0.7	1.8	64.7	68.9	3.2	29.4	32._
Woodford	8,893	37.5	15,546	82.6	25.9	2.7	3.9	55.0	83.1	28.5	9.6	7._
LOUISIANA	1,656,053	39.2	2,775,468	74.8	18.7	2.6	9.2	59.0	78.1	15.1	19.2	17._
Acadia	21,142	42.6	35,573	64.7	9.4	0.4	20.0	64.3	79.3	8.9	21.0	19.6
Allen	8,102	41.4	16,817	63.2	9.3	0.6	12.3	57.0	78.5	10.1	22.0	21.4
Ascension	26,691	46.7	46,258	79.6	14.5	1.8	5.8	59.6	85.0	21.0	12.0	10.5
Assumption	8,239	43.7	14,411	59.4	7.4	0.8	19.0	72.0	76.9	11.7	19.3	18.4
Avoyelles	14,736	40.1	26,606	59.8	8.3	0.5	20.9	67.2	76.8	7.1	24.8	23.6
Beauregard	12,104	39.9	21,036	75.0	13.8	1.1	4.6	57.9	79.6	12.8	16.3	14.9
Bienville	6,108	36.6	10,172	71.9	11.5	0.4	2.0	66.4	75.4	6.8	22.5	22.1
Bossier	36,628	40.9	61,237	83.0	18.1	2.5	5.6	50.5	83.4	16.8	14.4	11.9
Caddo	97,974	36.1	159,011	78.7	20.6	1.5	3.8	55.1	79.9	15.0	20.5	18.9
Calcasieu	68,613	39.7	114,563	77.0	16.9	1.4	8.7	55.5	83.6	16.5	17.4	14.1
Caldwell	3,941	37.2	6,922	65.4	8.8	0.6	3.3	60.5	77.5	8.1	20.6	19.2
Cameron	3,592	43.2	6,257	68.1	7.9	1.6	14.4	68.7	79.9	12.1	12.9	11.3
Catahoula	4,082	37.5	6,904	61.4	9.4	0.1	1.8	67.4	76.9	8.5	24.5	24.9
Claiborne	6,270	35.0	11,169	65.7	12.4	0.4	1.8	59.9	77.8	9.5	23.9	23.8
Concordia	7,521	39.1	12,814	64.6	9.6	1.3	3.2	65.2	79.9	6.9	25.6	24.5
De Soto	9,691	39.2	16,118	70.3	10.2	1.0	3.9	65.5	78.3	8.6	19.5	20.4
East Baton Rouge	156,365	36.9	245,296	83.9	30.8	3.7	7.7	51.8	81.2	20.6	18.0	14.8
East Carroll	2,969	44.2	5,542	57.9	12.3	0.9	3.2	64.8	74.5	5.8	36.0	39.9
East Feliciana	6,699	42.6	13,877	70.7	11.3	0.6	5.4	63.1	81.1	14.9	19.3	18.6
Evangeline	12,736	41.6	21,511	55.5	9.5	0.6	27.7	64.3	80.5	8.2	26.0	25.4
Franklin	7,754	39.5	13,423	61.4	9.8	0.6	1.8	65.0	78.8	5.9	24.8	26.1
Grant	7,073	41.2	11,921	73.1	9.8	0.5	2.6	61.8	78.0	10.3	19.6	18.2
Iberia	25,381	44.8	43,965	66.9	11.2	2.0	15.8	64.8	80.4	12.1	21.1	18.9
Iberville	10,674	43.2	21,101	65.7	9.6	0.7	4.6	66.3	81.1	12.9	22.5	20.4
Jackson	6,086	35.8	10,062	73.6	12.9	0.4	2.1	64.3	82.2	11.0	17.8	16.9
Jefferson	176,234	36.2	298,761	79.3	21.5	7.5	13.0	61.4	78.5	18.2	16.5	13.5
Jefferson Davis	11,480	41.4	19,352	69.4	9.9	0.6	18.0	65.3	80.0	9.8	18.6	18.0
Lafayette	72,372	39.3	116,183	79.8	25.5	2.5	18.3	53.3	83.6	18.1	16.5	14.3
Lafourche	32,057	41.9	55,891	66.3	12.4	1.5	21.5	66.9	78.5	12.7	16.5	14.0
La Salle	5,291	38.0	9,219	68.5	11.2	0.6	3.9	60.7	79.7	8.6	18.1	16.4
Lincoln	15,235	33.6	22,059	80.4	31.8	2.1	5.2	49.8	78.8	12.4	22.6	20.5
Livingston	32,630	45.6	56,528	77.2	11.4	0.8	3.8	58.1	83.1	15.2	13.2	11.4
Madison	4,469	42.0	7,670	63.4	11.0	0.5	2.6	60.8	71.3	5.6	30.6	30.9
Morehouse	11,382	39.8	19,446	66.6	9.7	0.4	1.9	63.7	76.6	8.3	25.0	23.5
Natchitoches	14,263	37.5	22,033	72.7	18.4	1.5	3.8	56.2	74.7	10.4	23.6	22.0
Orleans	188,251	35.3	300,568	74.7	25.8	4.2	8.3	56.8	60.3	13.5	27.0	24.8
Ouachita	55,216	38.8	88,430	78.6	22.7	1.0	3.0	56.3	82.1	15.8	21.2	18.4
Plaquemines	9,021	45.3	16,448	68.7	10.8	2.8	8.0	65.5	76.8	17.6	16.2	15.4
Pointe Coupee	8,397	40.4	14,577	69.1	12.8	0.9	6.7	72.3	79.4	12.0	19.9	18.0
Rapides	47,120	39.2	79,811	74.6	16.5	1.6	4.9	59.9	78.7	12.4	20.2	18.5
Red River	3,414	41.4	5,792	67.4	8.7	0.4	1.7	66.4	77.5	7.2	23.7	24.4
Richland	7,490	40.2	13,060	61.9	12.8	0.5	1.8	64.4	77.1	8.5	24.7	25.6
Sabine	9,221	35.7	15,388	70.8	11.1	1.0	2.9	63.9	74.8	9.3	18.8	18.7
St. Bernard	25,123	38.2	44,127	73.1	8.9	3.0	7.3	65.1	78.7	14.0	15.1	13.0
St. Charles	16,422	47.9	29,551	80.0	17.5	2.5	6.7	66.5	84.1	23.1	13.3	11.6
St. Helena	3,873	41.1	6,489	67.5	11.2	0.3	2.2	74.1	78.9	9.0	22.0	22.8
St. James	6,992	46.0	12,840	73.9	10.1	0.2	6.5	78.8	80.5	16.5	17.7	16.3
St. John the Baptist	14,283	49.0	25,377	76.9	12.9	2.3	6.3	65.2	79.7	17.3	16.4	15.8
St. Landry	32,328	40.6	53,592	62.0	10.7	0.5	18.4	65.5	80.0	7.6	23.9	23.5
St. Martin	17,164	44.3	29,617	62.9	8.5	0.9	30.5	68.3	78.9	10.3	20.4	18.4
St. Mary	19,317	42.7	33,158	65.9	9.4	2.0	10.0	64.2	78.2	10.4	21.8	19.8
St. Tammany	69,253	42.7	122,959	83.9	28.3	2.4	5.3	54.7	80.2	28.0	11.2	10.1
Tangipahoa	36,558	40.1	59,909	71.5	16.3	0.8	3.7	61.5	78.7	11.3	22.2	21.1
Tensas	2,416	36.8	4,208	63.2	14.8	1.2	4.1	66.0	69.2	8.4	31.3	33.1
Terrebonne	35,997	44.6	63,271	67.1	12.3	1.5	13.2	62.4	79.6	14.8	18.4	15.9
Union	8,857	35.8	14,819	71.7	11.8	1.2	2.5	60.6	78.5	10.0	18.7	16.8
Vermilion	19,832	40.8	33,616	65.6	10.7	2.0	27.9	64.4	81.7	10.7	19.0	17.5
Vernon	18,260	45.4	29,329	80.1	13.5	4.1	9.0	44.6	73.2	9.4	16.4	12.7
Washington	16,467	38.4	27,954	68.2	10.9	0.4	2.4	64.3	75.7	8.0	25.5	23.0
Webster	16,501	35.2	27,687	70.8	12.6	0.7	2.1	63.3	79.7	9.8	19.0	17.1
West Baton Rouge	7,663	43.5	13,347	73.4	11.1	0.9	5.4	66.7	81.6	15.7	16.8	14.0
West Carroll	4,458	38.1	7,994	59.5	9.5	0.3	2.7	65.5	77.1	7.9	22.7	22.7
West Feliciana	3,645	43.1	10,749	53.3	10.6	0.5	3.1	47.9	83.1	19.9	20.4	19.3
Winn	5,930	38.0	11,093	65.4	9.4	0.5	1.9	60.5	80.3	8.3	22.8	22.5

See footnotes at end of table.

Table B-4. Counties — **Population Characteristics**—Con.

[Includes United States, states, and 3,141 counties/county equivalents defined as of February 22, 2005. For more information on these areas, see Appendix C, Geographic Information]

County	Households, 2000 Total	Households, 2000 With individuals under 18 years (percent of total)	Educational attainment,[1] 2000 Total persons	High school graduate or higher (percent)	Bachelor's degree or higher (percent)	Foreign-born population, 2000 (percent)	Speaking language other than English at home, 2000 (percent)	Residing in same house in 1995 and 2000 (percent)	Workers who drove alone to work,[2] 2000 (percent)	Households with income of $75,000 or more in 1999 (percent)	Persons in poverty (percent) 2004	Persons in poverty (percent) 2000
MAINE	518,200	32.4	869,893	85.4	22.9	2.9	7.8	59.6	78.6	15.5	11.5	9.9
Androscoggin	42,028	32.9	69,560	79.8	14.4	2.6	16.4	56.7	78.0	13.1	12.3	10.4
Aroostook.	30,356	30.3	51,439	76.9	14.6	5.8	24.1	67.8	79.7	7.8	15.1	13.4
Cumberland	107,989	31.8	181,276	90.1	34.2	3.8	5.9	54.2	78.9	22.6	9.2	7.3
Franklin	11,806	31.7	19,260	85.2	20.9	1.6	4.9	62.1	76.9	9.9	13.6	12.6
Hancock	21,864	30.1	36,416	87.8	27.1	2.3	3.6	61.7	74.5	14.6	9.9	9.8
Kennebec.	47,683	33.1	79,362	85.2	20.7	2.2	7.8	60.8	79.2	13.3	12.2	10.0
Knox	16,608	30.1	28,303	87.5	26.2	2.1	3.4	59.5	74.6	14.8	11.0	9.9
Lincoln.	14,158	30.2	24,094	87.9	26.6	2.0	2.8	64.9	76.5	16.0	10.2	9.4
Oxford	22,314	32.6	37,929	82.4	15.7	1.8	4.5	65.1	76.6	11.2	12.6	12.0
Penobscot	58,096	32.2	95,505	85.7	20.3	2.5	4.6	58.4	79.2	13.2	13.6	11.4
Piscataquis	7,278	30.8	12,240	80.3	13.3	1.9	3.4	67.1	77.0	7.0	13.5	13.3
Sagadahoc	14,117	35.3	23,862	88.0	25.0	2.4	4.4	57.5	78.1	17.5	8.8	8.1
Somerset	20,496	34.0	34,750	80.8	11.8	1.7	4.3	65.7	77.3	9.9	15.6	13.5
Waldo	14,726	32.9	24,818	84.6	22.3	1.7	3.3	63.4	76.9	13.0	12.7	12.2
Washington	14,118	30.4	23,488	79.9	14.7	4.1	5.4	66.7	76.0	7.8	17.4	16.8
York	74,563	34.3	127,591	86.5	22.9	2.8	9.4	58.0	81.3	19.4	8.9	7.1
MARYLAND.	1,980,859	37.3	3,495,595	83.8	31.4	9.8	12.6	55.7	73.7	31.7	9.2	7.9
Allegany.	29,322	29.0	51,205	79.9	14.1	1.2	2.8	64.4	80.6	10.2	14.2	13.8
Anne Arundel	178,670	38.3	326,999	86.4	30.6	4.7	7.3	55.7	80.3	38.0	6.5	5.2
Baltimore	299,877	33.4	511,434	84.3	30.6	7.1	9.6	58.1	79.7	28.2	8.2	6.7
Calvert.	25,447	45.6	47,768	86.9	22.5	2.2	4.2	58.6	77.6	41.6	5.4	5.1
Caroline.	11,097	39.2	19,550	75.0	12.1	2.5	4.8	59.8	77.0	15.7	10.5	10.4
Carroll	52,503	42.4	98,684	85.3	24.8	2.0	4.2	61.7	83.1	35.1	5.1	4.3
Cecil	31,223	40.9	55,809	81.2	16.4	1.8	4.1	55.9	83.2	26.1	8.1	7.1
Charles	41,668	45.5	76,987	85.8	20.0	2.9	5.1	55.6	77.5	38.2	7.2	6.1
Dorchester	12,706	31.7	21,435	74.2	12.0	2.0	3.5	64.6	76.9	13.6	13.9	13.4
Frederick	70,060	41.2	127,256	87.1	30.0	4.0	5.6	55.3	79.3	35.9	5.9	4.7
Garrett.	11,476	35.0	20,004	79.2	13.8	0.8	3.6	67.0	77.3	11.7	12.7	13.3
Harford	79,667	41.4	143,056	86.7	27.3	3.4	5.7	58.4	83.4	32.7	6.6	5.2
Howard	90,043	42.1	163,308	93.1	52.9	11.3	14.0	51.9	81.9	49.5	4.8	3.8
Kent	7,666	29.4	13,103	78.8	21.7	2.9	5.1	58.5	73.5	17.8	11.3	10.3
Montgomery	324,565	37.2	594,034	90.3	54.6	26.7	31.6	52.7	68.9	47.7	6.5	5.1
Prince George's.	286,610	41.0	503,698	84.9	27.2	13.8	15.9	52.7	66.8	32.3	9.3	7.4
Queen Anne's.	15,315	36.6	28,018	84.2	25.4	2.4	4.4	56.5	79.2	34.1	6.6	6.0
St. Mary's.	30,642	41.9	54,552	85.3	22.6	2.8	6.2	51.0	79.8	30.2	7.7	7.4
Somerset	8,361	30.7	16,321	69.5	11.6	2.5	4.2	61.9	75.8	10.4	19.7	20.8
Talbot	14,307	29.2	24,809	84.4	27.8	3.3	5.7	56.6	79.0	24.0	8.3	8.1
Washington	49,726	34.0	90,371	77.8	14.6	1.9	3.2	57.4	80.6	17.5	10.1	8.9
Wicomico	32,218	36.1	53,521	80.7	21.9	3.9	5.8	54.0	78.8	17.4	12.3	11.6
Worcester.	19,694	27.7	34,092	81.7	21.6	2.7	5.1	55.3	79.5	18.5	9.9	9.3
Independent City												
Baltimore city	257,996	32.7	419,581	68.4	19.1	4.6	7.8	57.1	54.7	12.9	21.5	19.1
MASSACHUSETTS.	2,443,580	32.9	4,273,275	84.8	33.2	12.2	18.7	58.5	73.8	30.5	9.9	8.4
Barnstable	94,822	26.1	165,115	91.8	33.6	4.9	6.8	57.6	81.3	24.3	7.3	6.7
Berkshire	56,006	29.4	93,339	85.1	26.0	3.7	6.4	61.5	79.2	18.7	10.5	9.4
Bristol	205,411	35.6	357,829	73.2	19.9	11.7	21.1	62.4	81.7	22.8	10.6	9.1
Dukes	6,421	30.2	10,693	90.4	38.4	6.3	8.2	61.2	72.2	23.9	6.2	6.2
Essex	275,419	35.2	487,103	84.6	31.3	11.3	19.4	58.7	78.7	32.1	10.3	8.4
Franklin	29,466	31.4	49,121	88.0	29.1	3.6	6.2	61.4	79.3	18.9	9.2	8.9
Hampden	175,288	34.8	295,837	79.2	20.5	7.2	22.3	58.7	81.4	19.1	15.1	13.7
Hampshire	55,991	29.9	93,193	89.4	37.9	6.6	11.7	53.9	74.1	24.1	9.7	7.5
Middlesex.	561,220	32.1	1,006,497	88.5	43.6	15.2	20.4	57.9	72.1	39.5	8.1	5.9
Nantucket	3,699	28.3	6,976	91.6	38.4	8.0	10.5	54.3	65.2	35.3	4.5	6.8
Norfolk.	248,827	33.0	452,517	91.3	42.9	11.8	14.5	62.2	72.9	41.5	5.4	5.0
Plymouth	168,361	39.1	312,683	87.6	27.8	6.3	10.1	63.5	80.9	33.7	7.8	6.6
Suffolk	278,722	26.5	446,504	78.1	32.5	25.5	33.8	49.3	43.7	22.2	16.7	15.3
Worcester.	283,927	35.9	495,868	83.5	26.9	7.9	15.0	59.0	82.6	27.4	9.8	8.3
MICHIGAN	3,785,661	35.6	6,415,941	83.4	21.8	5.3	8.4	57.3	83.2	24.1	12.5	9.7
Alcona.	5,132	22.8	8,958	79.7	10.9	1.5	2.5	64.7	79.0	9.4	12.9	12.4
Alger.	3,785	28.8	7,169	81.5	14.7	1.0	5.2	66.5	76.0	11.0	11.3	11.4
Allegan	38,165	40.1	66,925	82.3	15.8	2.9	6.8	57.9	82.8	20.5	9.4	7.1
Alpena	12,818	31.2	21,399	83.1	13.2	1.2	4.1	63.6	83.8	11.7	13.2	11.3
Antrim	9,222	31.9	16,025	84.6	19.4	1.5	3.2	57.7	78.3	14.7	10.0	8.8
Arenac.	6,710	31.4	11,868	76.8	9.1	1.1	3.8	64.7	82.5	13.1	15.0	14.2
Baraga	3,353	31.1	6,097	80.6	10.9	0.8	8.7	66.5	75.2	9.4	13.1	11.1
Barry	21,035	37.9	37,132	86.8	14.7	0.8	2.2	61.4	83.2	21.6	8.7	6.4
Bay	43,930	33.0	74,146	82.4	14.2	1.4	5.0	65.1	87.3	18.9	12.2	9.8
Benzie	6,500	31.0	11,283	85.4	20.0	1.7	3.9	57.7	80.2	12.4	9.0	8.4

See footnotes at end of table.

Table B-4. Counties — **Population Characteristics**—Con.

[Includes United States, states, and 3,141 counties/county equivalents defined as of February 22, 2005. For more information on these areas, see Appendix C, Geographic Information]

County	Households, 2000		Educational attainment,[1] 2000			Foreign-born population, 2000 (percent)	Persons 5 years and over		Workers who drove alone to work,[2] 2000 (percent)	Households with income of $75,000 or more in 1999 (percent)	Persons in poverty (percent)	
	Total	With individuals under 18 years (percent of total)	Total persons	High school graduate or higher (percent)	Bachelor's degree or higher (percent)		Speaking language other than English at home, 2000 (percent)	Residing in same house in 1995 and 2000 (percent)			2004	2000
MICHIGAN—Con.												
Berrien	63,569	34.5	106,690	81.9	19.6	4.9	7.1	57.7	81.6	17.9	13.8	12.2
Branch	16,349	36.2	30,300	80.0	10.6	2.6	6.5	58.3	78.3	14.5	12.4	11.0
Calhoun	54,100	35.0	90,137	83.2	16.0	2.4	4.8	57.1	82.3	16.9	13.4	10.8
Cass	19,676	34.6	34,286	80.4	12.1	1.9	4.2	61.2	82.7	17.5	12.0	10.5
Charlevoix	10,400	33.9	17,528	86.0	19.8	1.4	3.2	59.2	81.0	16.4	10.2	8.2
Cheboygan	10,835	30.8	18,562	81.9	13.9	1.2	2.7	61.3	78.8	10.9	13.1	11.2
Chippewa	13,474	32.3	25,683	82.4	15.0	3.0	5.2	53.5	74.5	10.6	14.8	13.8
Clare	12,686	30.8	21,333	76.1	8.8	1.1	3.5	58.9	79.9	9.2	16.7	14.9
Clinton	23,653	39.4	41,864	89.2	21.2	1.2	4.0	63.2	83.1	28.7	6.7	5.1
Crawford	5,625	32.5	9,871	80.8	12.9	1.3	3.1	57.8	83.2	10.8	14.1	13.3
Delta	15,836	31.5	26,362	86.1	17.1	1.0	2.5	66.5	83.4	13.1	11.7	9.8
Dickinson	11,386	32.5	18,831	88.8	16.7	1.1	3.4	65.0	81.5	13.0	10.3	8.6
Eaton	40,167	36.2	67,044	89.5	21.7	2.2	4.9	56.9	82.9	24.8	8.7	6.6
Emmet	12,577	33.5	21,258	89.0	26.2	1.7	3.6	56.7	77.5	18.8	9.6	7.5
Genesee	169,825	37.3	277,660	83.1	16.2	2.1	4.5	56.8	84.3	22.1	15.4	12.0
Gladwin	10,561	29.3	18,308	78.3	9.2	1.3	4.2	60.8	79.3	11.5	14.0	12.6
Gogebic	7,425	25.9	12,311	85.5	15.8	1.3	5.5	66.6	77.0	8.4	15.3	14.2
Grand Traverse	30,396	34.6	51,801	89.3	26.1	2.1	4.2	54.4	81.9	19.6	9.0	6.7
Gratiot	14,501	36.4	27,322	83.5	12.9	1.2	4.5	58.9	79.8	14.4	13.1	10.8
Hillsdale	17,335	35.6	29,595	83.1	12.0	1.1	3.5	58.0	81.2	15.7	11.4	9.4
Houghton	13,793	27.2	21,233	84.6	23.0	2.7	7.3	56.8	72.5	9.6	14.8	13.8
Huron	14,597	30.8	24,954	78.3	10.9	1.4	4.4	69.0	78.2	12.3	11.7	10.6
Ingham	108,593	32.2	162,909	88.1	33.0	6.3	10.3	46.5	78.8	21.1	14.6	11.4
Ionia	20,606	40.6	37,835	83.4	10.8	1.2	4.1	59.7	81.6	17.4	10.7	9.0
Iosco	11,727	27.1	19,764	77.9	11.3	1.3	3.2	57.4	83.4	9.5	14.5	12.5
Iron	5,748	25.1	9,670	84.8	13.7	1.1	4.5	67.2	77.8	7.3	12.9	12.4
Isabella	22,425	30.2	31,677	86.1	23.9	2.3	4.8	43.3	77.9	14.5	15.2	12.8
Jackson	58,168	36.6	104,880	84.2	16.3	1.7	4.4	59.0	83.5	20.2	12.7	10.1
Kalamazoo	93,479	32.5	144,995	88.8	31.2	4.0	6.7	49.8	83.0	21.5	13.8	10.0
Kalkaska	6,428	34.5	11,073	80.0	9.7	0.8	1.8	57.5	76.8	10.7	12.6	11.0
Kent	212,890	38.3	351,875	84.6	25.8	6.6	10.2	52.4	83.4	23.1	11.5	8.2
Keweenaw	998	21.6	1,634	83.7	19.1	1.0	4.4	66.8	75.5	9.1	12.8	10.4
Lake	4,704	25.8	7,964	72.2	7.8	1.0	2.9	55.9	74.9	7.2	19.7	19.0
Lapeer	30,729	41.0	56,454	84.5	12.7	2.2	4.3	60.5	83.6	28.6	8.5	5.9
Leelanau	8,436	31.3	14,785	90.7	31.4	2.2	5.5	61.2	79.0	21.4	7.2	6.8
Lenawee	35,930	37.0	64,311	83.4	16.3	1.6	5.7	58.1	83.3	21.4	9.2	7.5
Livingston	55,384	41.8	101,381	91.4	28.2	3.0	3.7	55.0	87.1	43.7	5.1	3.4
Luce	2,481	32.0	4,927	75.5	11.8	1.1	3.4	59.0	75.7	8.5	16.2	16.5
Mackinac	5,067	28.5	8,588	82.5	14.9	1.2	3.2	63.9	71.2	10.4	10.5	10.5
Macomb	309,203	33.2	535,836	82.9	17.6	8.8	12.4	58.3	89.0	29.8	8.2	5.6
Manistee	9,860	29.6	17,298	81.4	14.2	1.3	4.4	62.5	78.1	11.0	12.5	11.2
Marquette	25,767	30.2	41,934	88.5	23.7	1.4	4.4	58.3	80.3	13.9	12.1	9.7
Mason	11,406	31.9	19,449	82.7	15.9	1.6	4.5	60.2	81.4	13.3	12.6	10.9
Mecosta	14,915	31.2	23,314	83.8	19.1	1.9	5.0	51.6	74.1	12.8	15.3	14.0
Menominee	10,529	30.9	17,342	83.5	11.0	0.9	3.7	65.9	81.3	9.5	11.8	10.0
Midland	31,769	36.5	53,497	89.0	29.3	3.2	4.3	59.7	86.6	27.0	10.2	7.8
Missaukee	5,450	36.5	9,466	78.6	10.2	1.0	2.5	64.9	76.6	10.1	13.2	11.3
Monroe	53,772	39.1	94,281	83.1	14.3	1.9	4.0	61.0	88.1	29.0	8.7	6.4
Montcalm	22,079	38.2	39,560	81.2	10.8	1.1	4.0	58.6	77.8	12.8	11.3	11.0
Montmorency	4,455	24.7	7,604	74.8	8.2	1.3	2.8	60.0	79.8	8.4	13.7	12.9
Muskegon	63,330	37.8	108,661	83.1	13.9	1.9	4.4	58.6	84.0	15.3	15.5	11.7
Newaygo	17,599	38.1	30,329	78.7	11.4	1.8	4.8	60.5	78.9	13.3	13.1	10.9
Oakland	471,115	34.5	807,910	89.3	38.2	10.0	12.7	55.8	88.2	40.0	7.8	5.6
Oceana	9,778	36.8	17,134	79.8	12.6	4.4	11.5	62.6	77.0	12.3	15.4	13.7
Ogemaw	8,842	29.6	15,191	75.0	9.6	1.3	2.5	61.1	81.8	9.6	15.5	14.4
Ontonagon	3,456	24.7	5,899	83.8	13.0	1.4	7.0	71.2	73.4	8.7	11.8	12.1
Osceola	8,861	35.7	15,033	80.5	11.3	1.2	3.5	61.1	78.1	10.2	14.1	12.7
Oscoda	3,921	28.2	6,716	73.7	8.0	1.5	6.7	62.0	78.0	8.3	15.1	15.3
Otsego	8,995	36.2	15,468	85.5	17.4	1.6	3.8	55.6	81.8	17.3	9.8	8.4
Ottawa	81,662	41.2	141,870	86.6	26.0	4.9	8.9	55.0	85.9	27.0	7.5	4.8
Presque Isle	6,155	26.0	10,463	77.0	11.5	1.2	4.8	69.9	80.2	9.4	11.1	10.2
Roscommon	11,250	23.9	18,930	79.5	10.9	1.7	3.5	58.4	80.9	9.6	14.7	13.8
Saginaw	80,430	35.9	135,198	81.6	15.9	2.0	6.4	61.5	85.9	19.5	15.7	12.6
St. Clair	62,072	37.2	107,583	82.8	12.6	2.7	4.1	58.4	83.7	23.7	10.2	7.2
St. Joseph	23,381	37.4	39,807	78.6	12.7	3.4	7.6	57.8	79.6	15.1	12.5	10.4
Sanilac	16,871	35.0	29,197	79.7	10.0	1.6	4.7	63.5	77.2	13.0	13.0	10.8
Schoolcraft	3,606	30.0	6,272	79.4	11.3	1.0	3.0	62.2	74.4	11.3	13.4	12.8
Shiawassee	26,896	38.1	46,557	84.4	13.7	1.2	2.9	63.1	83.0	19.2	10.4	8.1
Tuscola	21,454	37.2	37,898	81.2	10.6	1.1	3.9	64.4	83.2	16.5	10.9	9.0

See footnotes at end of table.

County and City Data Book: 2007

U.S. Census Bureau

[Includes United States, states, and 3,141 counties/county equivalents defined as of February 22, 2005. For more information on these areas, see Appendix C, Geographic Information]

County	Households, 2000 Total	Households, 2000 With individuals under 18 years (percent of total)	Educational attainment,[1] 2000 Total persons	Educational attainment,[1] 2000 High school graduate or higher (percent)	Educational attainment,[1] 2000 Bachelor's degree or higher (percent)	Foreign-born population, 2000 (percent)	Persons 5 years and over Speaking language other than English at home, 2000 (percent)	Persons 5 years and over Residing in same house in 1995 and 2000 (percent)	Workers who drove alone to work,[2] 2000 (percent)	House-holds with income of $75,000 or more in 1999 (percent)	Persons in poverty (percent) 2004	Persons in poverty (percent) 2000
MICHIGAN—Con.												
Van Buren	27,982	38.3	48,920	78.9	14.3	3.5	8.9	61.1	82.6	16.5	14.1	11.7
Washtenaw	125,327	31.1	197,414	91.5	48.1	10.3	13.2	43.0	76.0	32.9	11.1	7.2
Wayne	768,440	37.7	1,305,288	77.0	17.2	6.7	10.8	60.0	80.1	22.2	18.8	14.4
Wexford	11,824	36.1	19,965	82.0	15.3	1.8	3.1	55.8	78.8	13.1	13.0	11.0
MINNESOTA	1,895,127	34.8	3,164,345	87.9	27.4	5.3	8.5	57.0	77.6	24.7	8.1	6.9
Aitkin	6,644	24.6	11,263	80.4	11.3	0.9	3.5	63.2	74.1	10.3	11.3	11.6
Anoka	106,428	42.3	187,122	91.0	21.3	3.6	5.7	59.2	82.4	31.3	5.5	4.2
Becker	11,844	33.1	19,834	82.9	16.7	1.0	4.4	61.8	76.2	13.0	10.9	11.1
Beltrami	14,337	38.2	22,748	83.4	23.5	1.8	5.9	56.4	72.3	12.2	15.8	15.6
Benton	13,065	37.0	20,789	84.9	17.2	2.1	5.0	55.7	81.3	15.8	7.3	6.7
Big Stone	2,377	29.4	4,050	79.0	11.4	0.8	4.7	74.9	72.0	7.0	9.7	10.8
Blue Earth	21,062	30.3	31,684	87.7	26.6	2.9	5.2	51.9	76.9	15.0	10.7	8.8
Brown	10,598	32.5	17,485	81.7	16.5	1.3	6.1	64.6	75.9	13.8	7.3	6.3
Carlton	12,064	34.7	21,238	84.3	14.9	1.6	5.0	65.9	82.1	15.9	8.2	8.1
Carver	24,356	46.6	43,218	91.4	34.3	3.4	6.2	55.4	82.6	41.5	3.9	3.2
Cass	10,893	30.2	18,721	83.9	16.6	0.8	4.7	62.8	74.3	11.8	11.6	12.3
Chippewa	5,361	32.1	8,819	81.6	13.7	1.4	3.7	65.5	76.9	11.4	8.2	7.8
Chisago	14,454	43.2	25,859	88.7	15.3	1.2	3.5	57.3	81.0	25.8	5.5	5.1
Clay	18,670	35.2	29,580	86.7	24.7	2.6	7.7	54.3	77.4	15.4	9.7	9.9
Clearwater	3,330	33.0	5,576	76.4	14.7	0.9	3.6	67.1	73.7	10.0	12.4	14.0
Cook	2,350	25.3	3,864	88.7	28.8	2.7	4.3	57.8	67.8	14.6	7.0	7.1
Cottonwood	4,917	30.0	8,344	80.4	14.2	2.2	7.1	68.9	73.1	8.8	9.3	9.6
Crow Wing	22,250	32.0	37,092	86.3	18.4	1.2	3.1	55.7	81.1	14.6	9.0	8.8
Dakota	131,151	41.6	224,313	93.2	34.9	5.1	7.6	54.3	83.5	37.6	5.0	3.5
Dodge	6,420	42.3	10,989	86.7	17.1	2.5	5.8	62.4	77.8	20.3	5.6	4.8
Douglas	13,276	30.9	21,961	85.6	17.3	0.9	3.2	60.7	79.0	13.6	7.5	7.7
Faribault	6,652	29.6	11,128	83.6	13.8	1.6	3.9	69.5	74.6	9.9	8.7	8.8
Fillmore	8,228	32.2	14,116	81.7	15.1	0.8	6.3	66.7	68.3	11.0	8.3	8.2
Freeborn	13,356	30.9	22,363	81.2	12.8	3.1	7.0	64.3	80.6	12.1	8.7	8.0
Goodhue	16,983	35.3	29,127	86.7	19.1	1.2	3.2	62.5	79.4	21.9	6.0	5.0
Grant	2,534	30.5	4,370	83.5	15.7	0.7	4.2	64.7	73.3	10.3	8.5	8.8
Hennepin	456,129	30.5	740,444	90.6	39.1	9.9	12.8	51.8	74.9	31.0	9.3	7.0
Houston	7,633	35.7	13,063	85.5	20.5	1.1	3.4	65.4	75.6	15.3	6.9	6.5
Hubbard	7,435	31.3	12,694	86.1	20.2	1.1	3.3	59.8	77.9	13.2	10.0	11.5
Isanti	11,236	40.7	19,915	86.6	14.5	1.3	3.4	61.8	80.0	22.0	6.3	5.6
Itasca	17,789	31.0	29,931	85.6	17.6	1.3	3.8	63.3	80.0	13.3	10.0	9.5
Jackson	4,556	30.9	7,768	84.1	14.2	1.5	3.8	68.3	76.6	9.8	7.6	7.8
Kanabec	5,759	36.2	9,797	80.6	10.5	0.9	3.0	61.2	76.8	12.9	8.9	9.1
Kandiyohi	15,936	34.4	26,419	83.5	18.3	3.8	9.9	60.4	78.5	16.4	9.3	8.9
Kittson	2,167	30.1	3,661	79.7	14.8	2.0	4.8	72.3	69.9	8.0	8.6	9.5
Koochiching	6,040	30.0	9,999	81.9	15.1	5.9	3.6	66.0	78.3	12.4	10.7	10.5
Lac qui Parle	3,316	29.0	5,644	80.8	13.0	1.0	3.6	72.4	72.0	9.9	7.6	7.6
Lake	4,646	28.4	7,847	86.4	19.5	1.7	4.1	68.2	75.4	13.6	7.7	7.3
Lake of the Woods	1,903	30.5	3,155	84.6	17.2	2.9	4.1	67.1	68.2	12.0	8.2	8.9
Le Sueur	9,630	36.1	16,499	84.6	16.9	1.8	6.6	65.3	78.2	19.4	6.6	5.8
Lincoln	2,653	27.6	4,516	79.8	14.1	0.7	4.1	67.7	72.1	7.6	8.4	9.3
Lyon	9,715	34.2	15,355	82.6	21.4	4.5	7.8	56.6	75.8	14.3	8.7	7.7
McLeod	13,449	36.4	22,495	84.7	15.4	2.2	6.3	61.0	78.4	18.4	5.9	5.2
Mahnomen	1,969	35.8	3,292	75.0	12.4	1.3	6.3	70.4	66.4	7.2	15.5	16.2
Marshall	4,101	31.0	6,914	79.1	12.0	1.9	6.7	71.8	73.2	9.0	8.7	8.9
Martin	9,067	30.9	14,935	83.7	16.1	1.4	3.8	64.7	79.1	11.0	9.8	8.9
Meeker	8,590	35.1	14,841	81.5	13.9	0.8	3.9	64.1	77.4	15.8	7.3	6.9
Mille Lacs	8,638	34.4	14,622	81.3	12.2	1.1	5.1	58.4	74.6	12.9	8.5	8.9
Morrison	11,816	36.1	20,347	79.7	12.6	1.0	3.9	67.4	73.6	12.6	9.0	9.6
Mower	15,582	31.3	25,749	82.3	14.7	3.6	7.2	60.9	79.1	13.8	9.3	8.0
Murray	3,722	30.0	6,320	79.1	11.9	1.4	4.3	72.4	69.7	8.2	7.5	7.7
Nicollet	10,642	36.4	17,496	90.1	29.3	2.7	5.8	55.0	76.6	21.2	7.5	6.5
Nobles	7,939	33.8	13,654	75.8	13.5	9.0	15.4	65.0	70.7	12.3	9.7	9.6
Norman	3,010	31.0	5,105	80.0	13.1	1.9	6.2	65.8	70.7	9.4	9.7	10.2
Olmsted	47,807	36.6	80,277	91.1	34.7	7.9	9.8	54.8	77.2	28.3	6.8	5.4
Otter Tail	22,671	31.5	38,739	81.4	17.2	2.0	5.3	63.2	75.9	12.6	9.0	9.1
Pennington	5,525	32.2	8,848	81.3	14.9	1.6	4.0	60.2	77.2	10.8	9.1	8.9
Pine	9,939	33.6	17,714	79.0	10.3	1.1	4.6	60.1	75.2	12.7	10.5	10.7
Pipestone	4,069	32.1	6,671	77.6	13.9	1.4	3.7	68.1	75.7	8.7	8.6	8.4
Polk	12,070	34.0	20,203	82.0	17.6	2.2	8.1	62.0	77.2	12.2	10.7	10.7
Pope	4,513	30.6	7,719	81.8	14.7	0.9	3.6	65.7	75.3	11.3	8.3	8.0
Ramsey	201,236	31.9	323,214	87.6	34.3	10.6	15.8	53.8	75.0	24.6	11.0	8.8
Red Lake	1,727	31.7	2,879	78.8	10.7	1.1	5.2	71.4	72.7	8.2	8.8	9.1
Redwood	6,674	32.6	11,269	80.2	13.4	0.7	2.9	69.3	72.2	13.4	8.0	7.5
Renville	6,779	32.8	11,464	80.9	12.6	2.1	7.4	69.5	73.4	11.7	9.1	8.0

See footnotes at end of table.

Table B-4. Counties — **Population Characteristics**—Con.

[Includes United States, states, and 3,141 counties/county equivalents defined as of February 22, 2005. For more information on these areas, see Appendix C, Geographic Information]

County	Households, 2000 Total	With individuals under 18 years (percent of total)	Educational attainment,[1] 2000 Total persons	High school graduate or higher (percent)	Bachelor's degree or higher (percent)	Foreign-born population, 2000 (percent)	Speaking language other than English at home, 2000 (percent)	Residing in same house in 1995 and 2000 (percent)	Workers who drove alone to work,[2] 2000 (percent)	Households with income of $75,000 or more in 1999 (percent)	Persons in poverty (percent) 2004	2000
MINNESOTA—Con.												
Rice	18,888	38.3	33,400	85.2	22.4	4.8	9.4	52.3	71.1	22.1	7.5	6.6
Rock	3,843	32.3	6,485	81.5	15.4	1.1	3.5	68.0	70.0	11.9	7.5	6.?
Roseau	6,190	39.6	10,366	82.5	14.9	2.8	5.1	67.1	68.0	11.4	5.9	6.1
St. Louis	82,619	29.3	132,801	87.2	21.9	1.9	5.0	60.8	78.3	14.6	10.6	9.4
Scott	30,692	47.0	55,564	91.0	29.4	4.0	6.9	52.8	83.5	41.6	4.0	3.3
Sherburne	21,581	46.8	38,349	89.9	19.4	1.5	4.3	54.1	81.2	29.1	4.7	4.1
Sibley	5,772	35.4	9,970	79.2	11.6	2.6	9.2	68.6	71.8	13.4	7.8	7.2
Stearns	47,604	36.3	77,519	86.2	22.0	2.4	6.3	57.1	77.2	18.6	8.7	6.2
Steele	12,846	37.0	21,550	86.6	20.1	3.5	7.0	57.5	79.7	18.4	7.0	6.1
Stevens	3,751	29.8	5,790	84.4	20.6	1.7	4.7	53.1	68.5	12.5	8.7	8.3
Swift	4,353	31.2	8,336	80.4	14.0	1.2	6.6	61.4	75.6	9.2	9.2	9.1
Todd	9,342	33.4	15,758	79.3	10.0	1.8	4.7	66.0	71.8	10.0	10.8	11.3
Traverse	1,717	29.0	2,850	82.2	10.7	0.7	2.9	70.2	68.7	9.4	10.7	10.1
Wabasha	8,277	35.3	14,189	85.6	16.9	2.0	3.8	63.6	73.1	17.0	6.2	5.6
Wadena	5,426	31.7	9,047	79.5	13.4	1.0	5.5	62.1	73.9	9.2	11.9	12.0
Waseca	7,059	36.3	12,818	84.8	16.2	1.3	3.8	60.4	77.9	15.3	8.0	7.2
Washington	71,462	43.2	128,215	94.0	33.9	3.4	5.7	58.3	83.7	41.9	4.6	3.3
Watonwan	4,627	34.1	7,745	75.9	13.7	8.0	15.9	68.3	72.4	9.9	8.9	9.0
Wilkin	2,752	36.7	4,673	84.5	14.0	0.7	4.6	64.0	77.1	12.0	8.3	8.2
Winona	18,744	31.6	29,165	84.0	23.2	2.7	6.0	54.8	75.4	15.5	9.7	8.5
Wright	31,465	43.7	55,234	88.1	17.9	1.1	3.2	58.4	80.3	27.7	5.1	4.4
Yellow Medicine	4,439	31.6	7,394	81.9	14.4	1.2	3.8	68.5	75.0	9.3	8.1	8.0
MISSISSIPPI	1,046,434	39.6	1,757,517	72.9	16.9	1.4	3.6	58.5	79.4	12.8	19.3	17.6
Adams	13,677	37.1	22,211	73.4	17.5	1.4	3.8	64.5	79.3	10.6	24.3	22.0
Alcorn	14,224	33.9	23,159	68.1	11.7	1.0	2.6	63.7	83.9	9.4	17.3	14.7
Amite	5,271	36.2	8,981	67.2	9.4	0.4	2.1	74.4	77.6	8.8	19.8	19.1
Attala	7,567	37.2	12,674	63.4	11.6	0.8	2.4	64.2	75.6	7.6	21.1	20.2
Benton	2,999	38.8	5,073	58.8	7.8	0.7	1.5	65.5	80.0	6.1	21.0	21.1
Bolivar	13,776	43.2	22,956	65.3	18.8	0.5	2.7	62.9	75.1	9.6	30.1	27.5
Calhoun	6,019	36.5	10,021	64.4	10.2	1.6	3.1	67.4	76.4	8.0	18.1	16.3
Carroll	4,071	37.1	7,121	66.6	10.9	0.8	2.3	71.4	77.7	10.5	16.8	16.8
Chickasaw	7,253	41.2	12,159	59.4	9.5	1.3	2.6	69.0	77.6	7.6	20.1	16.2
Choctaw	3,686	37.7	6,171	65.1	11.2	0.3	2.2	69.3	76.5	7.7	22.1	21.8
Claiborne	3,685	42.3	5,954	71.6	18.9	0.6	3.2	69.2	69.9	9.9	29.2	27.3
Clarke	6,978	37.6	11,541	68.8	9.6	0.3	1.7	69.6	79.9	8.6	19.7	16.9
Clay	8,152	40.9	13,441	68.6	14.6	0.5	2.2	63.6	77.3	10.8	22.4	19.0
Coahoma	10,553	44.9	17,403	62.2	16.2	0.9	2.7	60.8	69.4	9.9	30.6	27.7
Copiah	10,142	40.8	17,405	69.3	11.6	0.8	2.2	65.8	75.9	9.7	22.8	20.7
Covington	7,126	41.6	11,923	67.2	11.4	0.6	2.1	68.1	76.7	9.1	20.6	19.7
DeSoto	38,792	43.1	68,302	81.6	14.3	1.9	3.6	48.5	85.5	22.8	8.9	7.3
Forrest	27,183	35.2	41,526	79.3	22.8	2.0	4.1	48.6	80.1	10.4	21.8	20.2
Franklin	3,211	39.4	5,377	67.5	10.5	0.3	2.2	67.1	79.7	6.9	20.1	20.0
George	6,742	43.1	11,838	69.8	9.1	1.3	2.6	62.6	69.4	11.7	17.2	15.3
Greene	4,148	41.1	8,352	67.4	8.0	0.3	2.6	60.5	72.0	8.2	21.6	21.4
Grenada	8,820	39.3	14,675	63.8	13.5	1.0	2.7	59.5	79.6	8.9	19.2	18.0
Hancock	16,897	35.5	28,840	77.9	17.3	1.4	4.4	56.6	78.8	14.0	16.6	14.1
Harrison	71,538	37.7	119,169	80.3	18.4	3.6	6.7	49.0	79.1	14.5	16.9	14.5
Hinds	91,030	39.8	150,287	80.4	27.2	1.1	3.5	54.2	79.0	15.4	22.4	18.0
Holmes	7,314	44.5	12,071	59.7	11.2	0.3	2.1	68.9	67.3	6.5	33.7	34.8
Humphreys	3,765	46.0	6,379	53.7	11.6	0.8	2.6	67.7	65.7	6.5	32.7	30.8
Issaquena	726	41.7	1,380	58.8	7.1	0.2	0.7	61.0	71.2	8.3	34.7	33.4
Itawamba	8,773	36.4	14,833	65.9	8.8	0.6	2.4	66.2	81.0	10.3	14.0	12.7
Jackson	47,676	41.7	82,818	81.0	16.5	2.7	5.1	56.6	81.8	16.1	15.0	12.9
Jasper	6,708	40.7	11,263	66.7	9.8	0.3	2.5	72.8	76.7	6.8	21.3	18.7
Jefferson	3,308	44.1	5,785	59.7	10.6	0.3	2.2	71.0	76.4	5.7	29.6	29.2
Jefferson Davis	5,177	40.2	8,613	66.4	10.4	0.3	2.1	69.5	76.4	7.3	25.3	25.5
Jones	24,275	37.4	41,403	73.9	14.0	2.0	3.8	63.2	79.9	10.4	19.6	17.2
Kemper	3,909	37.0	6,498	60.5	10.3	0.4	3.0	72.1	73.0	6.8	21.5	21.5
Lafayette	14,373	29.7	20,628	78.5	31.1	2.4	4.7	43.9	78.3	13.0	16.2	15.4
Lamar	14,396	41.5	23,855	83.0	26.8	1.1	3.3	51.1	84.1	18.2	14.2	13.8
Lauderdale	29,990	37.5	49,511	74.9	16.2	0.7	2.8	57.3	81.1	12.3	20.1	18.1
Lawrence	5,040	40.2	8,394	72.9	12.0	0.6	2.0	68.2	75.0	11.3	17.9	17.7
Leake	7,611	39.6	13,160	64.1	11.6	1.4	6.2	66.9	73.6	8.8	20.8	20.7
Lee	29,200	39.7	48,382	74.7	18.1	1.1	3.2	55.2	83.9	15.4	14.7	12.4
Leflore	12,956	42.5	21,581	61.9	15.9	1.1	3.0	56.9	74.1	9.9	31.6	29.1
Lincoln	12,538	39.2	21,074	72.0	12.4	0.6	2.4	60.6	80.1	10.6	18.6	17.1
Lowndes	22,849	41.0	37,520	75.5	20.5	1.3	3.1	55.7	79.7	14.1	20.2	18.0
Madison	27,219	41.6	46,773	83.0	37.9	1.7	4.1	52.3	82.6	27.7	14.3	12.4
Marion	9,336	39.9	16,025	66.5	11.5	0.8	1.8	59.6	79.0	8.0	23.0	21.7
Marshall	12,163	41.0	21,519	61.0	9.0	1.0	2.9	67.5	77.3	9.2	19.9	17.5
Monroe	14,603	39.4	24,288	65.5	10.9	0.6	2.3	65.0	82.2	8.3	17.1	14.9
Montgomery	4,690	37.8	7,830	62.1	11.0	0.2	2.9	67.3	77.6	7.9	21.4	21.0
Neshoba	10,694	39.8	17,780	67.7	11.4	0.8	12.0	63.4	80.2	9.3	19.5	18.7

See footnotes at end of table.

Table B-4. Counties — **Population Characteristics**—Con.

[Includes United States, states, and 3,141 counties/county equivalents defined as of February 22, 2005. For more information on these areas, see Appendix C, Geographic Information]

County	Households, 2000		Educational attainment,[1] 2000			Foreign-born population, 2000 (percent)	Persons 5 years and over		Workers who drove alone to work,[2] 2000 (percent)	Households with income of $75,000 or more in 1999 (percent)	Persons in poverty (percent)	
	Total	With individuals under 18 years (percent of total)	Total persons	High school graduate or higher (percent)	Bachelor's degree or higher (percent)		Speaking language other than English at home, 2000 (percent)	Residing in same house in 1995 and 2000 (percent)			2004	2000
MISSISSIPPI—Con.												
Newton	8,221	38.4	13,663	72.9	12.1	0.5	4.3	63.2	80.0	8.5	17.7	16.4
Noxubee	4,470	42.3	7,456	58.4	10.9	1.0	2.8	71.5	75.2	8.1	28.6	28.1
Oktibbeha	15,945	31.3	21,250	80.0	34.8	3.3	5.3	42.2	79.1	13.7	22.3	19.5
Panola	12,232	42.2	20,668	63.5	10.8	0.6	2.6	65.8	78.0	9.1	22.2	20.5
Pearl River	18,078	39.2	30,940	74.6	13.9	1.2	3.6	56.4	78.4	10.9	19.0	18.1
Perry	4,420	43.0	7,400	72.0	7.7	0.5	2.3	65.4	76.7	6.5	19.1	19.0
Pike	14,792	39.4	24,139	70.3	12.5	0.9	3.4	62.8	80.5	9.2	23.9	22.9
Pontotoc	10,097	40.9	17,082	66.7	11.4	1.1	3.1	60.9	80.5	10.4	13.6	12.1
Prentiss	9,821	37.4	16,114	64.9	9.9	0.4	2.3	64.2	81.7	8.7	16.2	14.5
Quitman	3,565	43.6	5,906	55.1	10.6	0.2	1.4	67.0	67.9	6.5	30.0	28.2
Rankin	42,089	40.2	74,885	81.8	23.8	1.6	3.6	51.0	84.7	21.6	10.6	9.7
Scott	10,183	42.3	17,496	62.0	8.6	4.2	7.1	62.7	72.7	8.3	16.3	18.6
Sharkey	2,163	46.3	3,704	60.6	12.6	0.4	1.7	69.3	72.2	7.9	32.0	33.4
Simpson	10,076	39.9	17,269	68.8	10.9	0.9	1.9	65.5	74.9	8.9	20.6	19.7
Smith	6,046	40.2	10,274	70.8	9.1	0.5	2.0	69.3	74.6	9.1	17.3	15.7
Stone	4,747	41.8	8,258	74.8	12.4	1.0	3.8	55.7	78.3	12.3	18.2	18.7
Sunflower	9,637	48.1	19,976	59.3	12.0	0.6	3.4	62.5	74.7	9.4	34.3	31.6
Tallahatchie	5,263	42.0	8,979	54.4	10.9	0.5	2.4	70.6	70.7	6.4	27.1	26.5
Tate	8,850	41.4	15,460	71.7	12.3	0.2	2.0	60.8	77.2	13.8	15.6	13.6
Tippah	8,108	37.4	13,557	65.5	9.0	1.9	3.8	64.6	81.7	7.0	16.1	14.4
Tishomingo	7,917	33.0	13,276	64.6	8.7	1.0	2.5	67.5	83.6	8.9	15.2	13.9
Tunica	3,258	42.0	5,263	60.5	9.1	0.9	2.4	56.7	73.8	8.4	23.9	22.1
Union	9,786	38.1	16,499	68.5	13.2	1.8	3.5	63.5	82.8	9.2	13.1	12.0
Walthall	5,571	39.4	9,366	67.0	10.4	0.5	2.2	68.1	75.6	7.3	23.0	24.3
Warren	18,756	40.5	30,955	77.0	20.8	1.2	3.1	58.7	80.6	17.1	18.3	16.4
Washington	22,158	44.0	36,852	66.5	16.4	0.8	2.9	59.9	74.9	10.5	29.5	26.2
Wayne	7,857	42.7	12,933	64.7	9.5	0.3	1.3	67.3	78.4	8.7	21.8	20.9
Webster	3,905	37.7	6,717	67.7	13.0	0.5	2.0	63.2	81.7	8.8	18.9	16.9
Wilkinson	3,578	40.7	6,515	58.1	10.0	0.1	3.6	71.0	76.3	6.7	30.8	29.8
Winston	7,578	38.0	12,896	68.2	13.8	1.1	2.7	66.5	77.8	9.6	21.8	19.4
Yalobusha	5,260	35.0	8,539	69.0	9.6	0.4	1.7	63.9	78.1	7.5	20.1	18.8
Yazoo	9,178	42.3	17,308	65.0	11.8	3.9	5.9	57.8	76.2	10.7	29.1	28.7
MISSOURI	2,194,594	34.7	3,634,906	81.3	21.6	2.7	5.1	53.6	80.5	17.6	13.0	10.6
Adair	9,669	26.8	13,316	84.6	28.5	2.0	5.1	43.6	72.4	10.0	18.2	14.4
Andrew	6,273	37.1	10,847	84.7	18.8	0.6	2.2	59.2	80.9	16.7	9.1	7.8
Atchison	2,722	28.5	4,500	80.0	16.6	0.3	1.6	63.0	77.8	10.2	12.1	10.6
Audrain	9,844	33.6	17,476	75.1	12.7	0.7	6.0	57.5	77.2	11.8	15.1	12.5
Barry	13,398	34.1	22,381	75.7	10.7	3.5	6.0	52.4	73.6	7.4	16.6	14.5
Barton	4,895	36.6	8,070	77.3	10.6	0.7	2.8	57.7	75.0	7.0	14.3	12.3
Bates	6,511	35.0	10,977	76.9	10.1	0.9	2.4	56.8	74.6	8.8	14.3	13.2
Benton	7,420	25.8	12,669	71.8	8.8	0.7	2.7	56.1	72.8	6.8	16.5	15.7
Bollinger	4,576	37.0	7,956	70.7	6.9	0.4	1.6	61.0	75.8	7.2	14.9	13.8
Boone	53,094	32.2	77,919	89.2	41.7	4.5	7.1	39.7	77.4	18.4	12.7	10.2
Buchanan	33,557	33.6	55,583	81.5	16.9	1.1	3.2	55.1	82.6	12.7	13.8	12.0
Butler	16,718	32.9	27,596	70.5	11.6	1.4	3.1	55.8	81.3	9.1	19.3	17.0
Caldwell	3,523	34.7	5,890	81.5	11.7	0.4	1.4	55.4	74.4	9.7	12.7	11.5
Callaway	14,416	38.8	25,848	78.9	16.5	1.1	2.7	52.9	78.8	14.3	11.0	9.6
Camden	15,779	26.1	27,303	82.9	17.7	1.4	3.1	49.4	76.5	14.1	12.7	11.3
Cape Girardeau	26,980	33.3	43,840	81.1	24.2	1.3	3.3	51.7	82.7	14.9	12.9	9.7
Carroll	4,169	32.3	6,945	79.1	14.0	0.4	3.5	63.5	74.2	8.9	14.2	12.6
Carter	2,378	33.7	3,959	66.6	10.8	0.3	2.6	59.2	73.8	6.6	20.7	21.2
Cass	30,168	40.8	52,767	86.7	17.7	1.6	3.2	52.5	82.5	23.1	8.5	5.9
Cedar	5,685	30.1	9,473	74.0	10.0	1.3	3.0	58.2	73.0	5.6	17.9	16.2
Chariton	3,469	30.0	5,900	79.6	11.4	0.6	2.2	70.0	77.2	7.3	12.2	10.3
Christian	20,425	41.0	34,790	85.9	20.9	0.9	2.4	42.5	82.9	15.5	10.2	8.3
Clark	2,966	32.8	4,976	79.6	10.7	0.2	3.5	66.6	77.8	8.6	13.9	12.5
Clay	72,558	36.3	120,500	88.7	24.9	2.9	5.2	49.5	84.8	23.8	7.7	5.1
Clinton	7,152	37.4	12,496	86.1	14.5	0.5	2.4	53.7	80.1	17.7	9.6	8.1
Cole	27,040	35.4	47,339	85.3	27.4	2.2	4.6	52.5	79.8	19.6	10.2	7.4
Cooper	5,932	34.2	10,545	80.3	13.7	0.6	3.4	53.8	76.9	8.9	12.2	10.9
Crawford	8,858	35.7	15,057	69.4	8.4	1.2	2.5	56.7	77.4	8.1	16.0	15.0
Dade	3,202	30.9	5,451	78.5	9.9	1.0	2.1	61.2	72.1	5.8	14.4	12.6
Dallas	6,030	35.9	10,251	72.8	9.5	0.5	4.7	58.1	76.2	6.8	16.8	15.8
Daviess	3,178	33.5	5,213	79.1	12.0	0.2	7.7	56.8	67.2	8.8	15.1	14.4
DeKalb	3,528	34.4	8,252	77.0	10.7	1.0	3.9	51.7	76.0	8.2	14.9	13.5
Dent	5,982	33.2	10,098	66.3	10.1	0.6	2.1	54.0	79.6	7.5	17.4	16.4
Douglas	5,201	32.8	8,774	69.7	9.9	0.9	2.6	62.1	72.0	6.0	18.8	18.4
Dunklin	13,411	35.1	21,890	63.7	9.1	1.5	3.4	56.1	79.1	7.4	23.5	20.7

See footnotes at end of table.

[Includes United States, states, and 3,141 counties/county equivalents defined as of February 22, 2005. For more information on these areas, see Appendix C, Geographic Information]

County	Households, 2000		Educational attainment,[1] 2000			Foreign-born population, 2000 (percent)	Persons 5 years and over		Workers who drove alone to work,[2] 2000 (percent)	House-holds with income of $75,000 or more in 1999 (percent)	Persons in poverty (percent)	
	Total	With individuals under 18 years (percent of total)	Total persons	High school graduate or higher (percent)	Bachelor's degree or higher (percent)		Speaking language other than English at home, 2000 (percent)	Residing in same house in 1995 and 2000 (percent)			2004	2000
MISSOURI—Con.												
Franklin	34,945	38.9	60,467	77.7	12.8	0.8	2.6	57.5	81.6	18.1	9.4	6.9
Gasconade	6,171	33.2	10,530	74.0	10.4	0.5	2.9	61.8	77.2	10.2	10.9	9.2
Gentry	2,747	32.4	4,599	81.8	14.5	0.6	2.6	60.5	77.5	8.0	12.0	10.8
Greene	97,859	30.5	153,930	84.7	24.2	1.9	4.0	45.9	82.1	14.0	13.8	10.9
Grundy	4,382	29.5	7,149	79.0	12.5	1.4	5.0	59.1	75.8	7.0	15.6	13.4
Harrison	3,658	30.3	6,101	80.1	9.3	1.0	1.9	59.6	74.8	5.4	14.3	13.8
Henry	9,133	31.1	15,050	77.3	11.7	0.8	2.5	52.7	78.6	9.7	14.9	13.0
Hickory	3,911	24.7	6,712	73.4	7.7	1.0	2.2	58.7	73.1	5.5	17.8	17.6
Holt	2,237	30.0	3,736	81.9	11.7	0.4	2.1	66.5	79.1	8.5	12.7	11.4
Howard	3,836	33.8	6,420	81.3	17.9	1.0	2.8	58.9	73.5	10.2	13.3	12.4
Howell	14,762	35.2	24,600	73.4	10.9	1.3	2.6	53.3	80.4	6.8	18.7	17.0
Iron	4,197	34.7	7,204	65.2	8.4	0.4	2.1	58.8	76.3	7.1	19.5	17.3
Jackson	266,294	33.4	427,077	83.4	23.4	4.3	7.6	52.0	80.5	18.5	14.1	9.9
Jasper	41,412	35.0	66,206	79.5	16.5	2.6	5.2	48.2	82.6	9.8	17.0	13.0
Jefferson	71,499	42.4	125,956	79.4	12.1	1.0	2.9	57.7	84.3	20.6	8.6	6.6
Johnson	17,410	37.3	26,558	86.0	23.2	3.0	5.1	41.1	76.9	13.1	12.8	10.6
Knox	1,791	29.7	2,990	80.0	12.8	0.3	2.9	61.5	72.6	5.9	15.8	15.6
Laclede	12,760	37.1	21,120	72.9	11.3	0.9	2.7	54.1	78.1	9.9	15.5	13.3
Lafayette	12,569	36.6	21,863	79.9	13.8	0.7	2.5	56.7	78.4	14.5	11.5	9.0
Lawrence	13,568	36.4	22,882	77.4	12.1	2.3	4.7	54.9	79.3	9.0	15.0	13.2
Lewis	3,956	34.0	6,533	79.5	13.0	0.6	4.1	56.8	74.4	7.7	14.6	13.4
Lincoln	13,851	43.2	24,092	76.4	9.7	0.6	2.1	54.0	82.1	16.5	9.8	8.5
Linn	5,697	31.8	9,279	80.0	10.8	0.6	3.3	58.9	77.8	7.1	14.6	12.5
Livingston	5,736	32.4	9,954	80.6	13.1	0.4	2.3	56.1	74.9	10.4	14.1	11.8
McDonald	8,113	39.3	13,418	69.4	7.0	5.6	9.4	49.3	67.5	6.1	19.3	16.8
Macon	6,501	31.7	10,718	77.8	13.0	0.3	3.4	59.3	76.9	8.3	13.2	12.1
Madison	4,711	34.1	7,964	68.6	7.8	0.8	2.4	56.0	80.0	5.2	16.8	15.5
Maries	3,519	34.1	5,969	74.5	11.0	0.8	2.0	62.4	69.9	9.1	14.0	13.4
Marion	11,066	35.7	18,322	79.4	15.6	0.8	2.3	54.2	82.3	10.7	14.0	11.9
Mercer	1,600	29.4	2,647	82.5	12.2	0.4	1.6	59.9	74.2	7.3	12.6	12.6
Miller	9,284	35.5	15,369	73.9	11.4	0.7	2.4	56.5	74.9	8.4	15.0	13.6
Mississippi	5,383	36.0	8,702	61.1	9.6	0.5	0.9	60.1	74.8	7.9	23.3	21.1
Moniteau	5,259	37.5	9,751	77.6	13.0	1.6	6.9	56.6	73.8	10.8	11.8	9.9
Monroe	3,656	33.8	6,212	78.7	9.5	0.5	3.0	59.3	76.6	5.3	11.4	11.2
Montgomery	4,775	33.9	8,182	71.1	9.9	1.2	2.6	60.4	77.2	8.6	12.9	11.5
Morgan	7,850	29.1	13,466	74.5	10.7	1.0	6.9	55.9	69.9	9.6	15.7	15.0
New Madrid	7,824	36.8	12,868	63.6	9.6	0.3	1.4	58.8	83.7	8.5	21.5	18.1
Newton	20,140	36.0	34,211	79.8	16.1	1.4	3.6	51.7	79.5	12.0	13.2	11.9
Nodaway	8,138	28.3	12,169	87.1	23.6	1.4	4.0	50.4	74.7	9.4	13.0	10.3
Oregon	4,263	32.0	7,134	72.0	9.1	0.7	2.1	56.6	76.2	5.7	19.8	21.0
Osage	4,922	36.7	8,375	75.2	10.4	0.5	3.0	67.9	67.2	12.2	9.0	7.3
Ozark	3,950	29.3	6,795	73.0	8.3	1.0	2.1	62.1	73.2	5.5	20.0	20.0
Pemiscot	7,855	38.1	12,228	58.2	8.4	0.9	2.4	54.9	80.0	8.0	26.2	23.4
Perry	6,904	36.5	11,865	71.2	9.9	1.1	5.4	64.6	79.8	9.8	11.5	8.4
Pettis	15,568	35.4	25,355	78.3	15.0	2.9	5.9	52.7	79.8	9.5	14.3	12.0
Phelps	15,683	32.5	24,665	79.0	21.1	4.0	5.7	46.7	75.8	10.5	15.3	14.1
Pike	6,451	33.9	12,242	76.0	10.2	1.6	6.2	54.7	76.1	9.9	15.7	14.6
Platte	29,278	36.1	48,721	91.8	33.3	3.7	5.6	49.3	85.8	30.9	5.7	4.2
Polk	9,917	35.6	16,645	77.5	14.6	1.5	4.5	51.2	76.7	7.6	16.3	14.7
Pulaski	13,433	44.9	23,062	85.1	18.8	4.8	10.2	35.5	66.0	8.6	13.6	11.8
Putnam	2,228	29.7	3,649	80.0	11.2	0.5	2.8	64.5	74.3	5.0	14.8	15.0
Ralls	3,736	35.9	6,506	78.7	12.3	0.3	1.5	61.3	81.8	11.5	9.9	8.6
Randolph	9,199	34.2	16,452	77.1	11.7	1.3	3.7	53.1	78.1	9.5	15.3	13.0
Ray	8,743	38.2	15,165	79.3	10.8	0.4	2.2	60.9	79.4	17.8	9.5	7.5
Reynolds	2,721	31.1	4,639	65.2	7.5	0.4	2.0	59.1	75.1	5.4	18.3	20.1
Ripley	5,416	33.7	9,092	62.1	7.8	1.1	2.7	60.4	76.6	5.4	21.9	20.5
St. Charles	101,663	42.9	178,498	89.1	26.3	2.1	4.0	50.9	87.1	31.8	5.4	4.1
St. Clair	4,040	29.4	6,876	73.1	9.0	0.7	2.1	57.7	72.8	6.1	18.4	17.0
Ste. Genevieve	6,586	37.6	11,743	73.8	8.1	0.6	2.1	66.6	80.5	13.6	9.9	8.2
St. Francois	20,793	35.8	37,236	72.4	10.2	0.9	2.9	52.9	80.2	9.6	15.9	14.0
St. Louis	404,312	34.3	677,027	88.0	35.4	4.2	6.4	59.2	84.9	29.6	9.6	6.9
Saline	9,015	34.2	15,185	74.0	15.8	3.5	6.5	51.4	76.2	10.8	14.8	12.2
Schuyler	1,725	30.9	2,870	81.4	11.6	0.4	1.1	62.5	74.9	6.1	15.7	14.8
Scotland	1,902	34.0	3,172	76.8	11.2	0.3	7.9	66.0	70.4	9.1	13.8	15.5
Scott	15,626	38.8	25,749	72.9	10.6	0.6	1.9	56.0	82.9	10.9	16.3	14.7
Shannon	3,319	35.6	5,552	67.6	7.6	0.5	1.6	62.4	72.2	4.0	23.2	24.0
Shelby	2,745	32.2	4,589	81.0	12.5	0.8	2.4	59.5	76.6	8.5	14.1	13.8
Stoddard	12,064	33.3	20,121	66.9	10.1	0.5	2.3	56.5	81.1	8.3	16.4	14.5
Stone	11,822	28.5	20,799	80.4	14.2	1.1	2.1	53.1	75.5	11.0	14.3	12.6
Sullivan	2,925	31.7	4,870	72.4	8.4	5.8	8.7	58.1	72.1	5.6	15.8	15.0

See footnotes at end of table.

Table B-4. Counties — **Population Characteristics**—Con.

[Includes United States, states, and 3,141 counties/county equivalents defined as of February 22, 2005. For more information on these areas, see Appendix C, Geographic Information]

County	Households, 2000		Educational attainment,[1] 2000			Foreign-born population, 2000 (percent)	Persons 5 years and over		Workers who drove alone to work,[2] 2000 (percent)	Households with income of $75,000 or more in 1999 (percent)	Persons in poverty (percent)	
	Total	With individuals under 18 years (percent of total)	Total persons	High school graduate or higher (percent)	Bachelor's degree or higher (percent)		Speaking language other than English at home, 2000 (percent)	Residing in same house in 1995 and 2000 (percent)			2004	2000
MISSOURI—Con.												
Taney	16,158	30.5	26,814	81.4	14.9	2.0	3.6	45.9	75.4	9.8	14.2	12.9
Texas	9,378	33.2	15,641	71.4	10.8	0.8	2.4	58.5	75.3	6.6	20.2	19.4
Vernon	7,966	34.6	13,169	76.6	14.2	1.3	3.1	54.7	75.9	9.4	16.5	14.8
Warren	9,185	37.3	16,137	79.5	11.1	1.5	3.1	57.5	80.8	19.4	10.1	8.0
Washington	8,406	40.2	14,796	62.5	7.5	0.7	2.1	61.7	75.3	6.5	20.7	19.4
Wayne	5,551	31.1	9,301	59.7	6.8	0.3	1.7	62.2	75.7	6.1	21.7	21.8
Webster	11,073	40.4	19,515	74.8	11.0	0.8	5.6	51.9	77.3	9.5	14.6	14.1
Worth	1,009	30.3	1,644	80.2	11.3	0.2	2.0	64.2	75.4	5.5	13.8	14.5
Wright	7,081	35.4	11,638	71.1	9.8	0.9	2.7	53.1	72.7	6.7	20.3	19.1
Independent City												
St. Louis city	147,076	30.1	221,951	71.3	19.1	5.6	8.6	50.7	68.9	10.1	24.6	20.6
MONTANA	358,667	33.3	586,621	87.2	24.4	1.8	5.2	53.6	73.9	12.0	13.6	13.3
Beaverhead	3,684	32.0	5,825	89.3	26.4	1.6	4.3	53.8	69.5	9.1	14.6	15.1
Big Horn	3,924	51.5	7,051	76.4	14.3	0.8	33.7	61.1	64.9	7.3	23.1	23.8
Blaine	2,501	42.3	4,144	78.7	17.4	1.4	9.2	65.5	61.2	8.2	21.5	22.6
Broadwater	1,752	31.7	3,061	85.2	15.0	1.4	2.6	54.3	67.5	10.4	12.3	13.6
Carbon	4,065	29.8	6,701	88.1	23.3	1.6	3.7	57.3	66.0	11.1	10.2	11.4
Carter	543	32.2	946	83.3	13.6	1.0	2.8	73.8	33.3	7.2	10.7	16.3
Cascade	32,547	34.2	52,333	87.1	21.5	2.4	5.1	52.8	80.5	11.3	13.4	12.1
Chouteau	2,226	36.3	3,837	87.1	20.5	1.9	5.0	64.4	61.2	8.6	14.2	14.1
Custer	4,768	32.3	7,819	84.9	18.8	1.4	4.6	57.7	77.8	8.6	13.7	14.4
Daniels	892	24.9	1,467	85.3	14.1	4.7	3.2	69.2	59.8	9.5	10.7	13.6
Dawson	3,625	30.4	6,161	82.7	15.1	1.1	4.1	62.8	72.7	10.1	11.9	11.9
Deer Lodge	3,995	27.4	6,584	84.5	14.7	1.4	4.7	65.2	75.3	6.5	14.5	14.6
Fallon	1,140	33.6	1,935	85.7	14.4	1.0	3.1	67.0	73.2	7.5	9.0	10.7
Fergus	4,860	30.5	8,290	86.3	19.1	1.0	3.2	59.3	67.4	9.9	13.2	13.2
Flathead	29,588	34.5	49,648	87.4	22.4	2.1	3.5	52.4	77.0	12.8	12.1	11.6
Gallatin[3]	26,323	30.9	40,461	93.3	41.0	2.7	5.0	40.8	70.6	16.2	10.7	10.2
Garfield	532	29.3	871	84.7	16.8	1.1	2.4	66.4	60.2	4.5	10.7	15.0
Glacier	4,304	50.0	7,383	78.6	16.5	2.1	10.9	62.2	63.1	9.9	25.2	27.0
Golden Valley	365	27.9	704	70.5	16.2	2.6	15.2	65.7	39.5	7.7	17.9	21.9
Granite	1,200	29.3	1,988	87.8	22.1	1.0	3.8	61.5	65.1	10.6	13.6	15.9
Hill	6,457	37.1	10,031	86.8	20.0	2.0	7.1	55.4	78.0	9.1	17.3	16.8
Jefferson	3,747	37.4	6,717	90.2	27.7	1.0	3.5	55.4	75.2	17.4	9.4	9.5
Judith Basin	951	30.9	1,595	87.6	23.6	1.4	8.6	68.2	55.7	7.9	13.6	15.0
Lake	10,192	36.0	16,971	84.2	22.2	1.6	6.6	53.9	71.2	9.7	18.7	18.2
Lewis and Clark.	22,850	34.0	36,690	91.4	31.6	1.6	4.0	53.2	75.9	14.0	11.3	10.3
Liberty	833	31.3	1,470	75.0	17.6	1.4	16.8	74.2	52.9	8.5	11.9	15.0
Lincoln	7,764	31.6	13,008	80.2	13.7	1.4	4.4	55.6	74.3	6.7	17.9	17.0
McCone	810	31.6	1,374	86.1	16.4	0.7	2.0	72.6	60.4	7.9	10.4	14.4
Madison	2,956	27.3	4,945	89.8	25.5	1.4	3.7	56.6	62.7	9.6	10.9	12.2
Meagher	803	28.8	1,334	83.4	18.7	1.8	6.5	64.7	61.7	7.1	14.9	18.1
Mineral	1,584	30.4	2,691	83.2	12.3	1.5	3.7	52.3	68.0	8.8	16.6	17.7
Missoula	38,439	31.0	59,298	91.0	32.8	2.3	4.8	45.4	73.3	13.7	14.5	13.0
Musselshell.	1,878	28.9	3,181	82.6	16.7	2.0	5.4	59.8	68.3	7.6	15.4	17.4
Park[3].	6,828	29.4	11,013	87.6	23.1	2.7	3.3	51.9	68.5	10.0	11.5	11.8
Petroleum.	211	32.7	333	82.9	17.4	0.6	6.1	65.8	35.1	8.1	10.8	17.8
Phillips.	1,848	34.7	3,102	82.4	17.1	1.0	3.9	64.8	62.3	7.0	15.5	16.7
Pondera.	2,410	37.8	4,108	81.6	19.8	1.6	9.0	66.4	65.0	10.0	16.8	17.5
Powder River	737	32.6	1,272	83.4	16.0	0.6	1.3	66.9	58.1	6.1	9.9	14.0
Powell	2,422	31.3	5,098	81.9	13.1	0.6	3.7	53.4	66.9	7.8	15.8	15.6
Prairie	537	24.0	913	78.8	14.8	1.2	3.2	67.2	51.5	6.9	11.1	13.6
Ravalli.	14,289	32.3	24,565	87.4	22.5	1.7	3.5	48.1	69.7	11.7	12.9	13.5
Richland.	3,878	35.2	6,398	83.5	17.2	1.4	2.9	64.5	75.3	8.1	12.2	12.6
Roosevelt.	3,581	47.1	6,107	80.6	15.6	0.9	6.7	68.8	69.4	8.3	26.8	26.4
Rosebud	3,307	44.1	5,543	84.4	17.6	1.1	13.1	58.8	69.4	11.9	17.7	17.0
Sanders	4,273	28.1	7,242	81.2	15.5	2.0	4.0	56.7	65.0	7.0	15.6	18.2
Sheridan	1,741	28.0	2,931	81.2	18.4	1.9	3.3	72.6	65.7	8.8	12.3	11.7
Silver Bow	14,432	30.1	23,097	85.1	21.7	1.6	4.0	59.0	81.2	10.3	15.1	14.4
Stillwater	3,234	34.5	5,632	87.5	17.8	1.5	3.2	55.0	63.0	13.4	8.6	9.2
Sweet Grass.	1,476	32.0	2,487	88.9	23.6	1.7	3.0	55.3	57.2	11.7	9.4	10.9
Teton.	2,538	33.1	4,295	83.4	20.8	1.5	8.1	61.8	64.2	8.6	11.8	13.7
Toole.	1,962	34.0	3,570	81.0	16.8	3.6	7.7	60.6	67.8	6.7	13.4	15.4
Treasure	357	33.1	577	86.3	18.2	0.8	2.2	63.7	62.2	6.2	12.1	12.9
Valley	3,150	31.6	5,345	83.9	15.7	1.1	3.3	69.7	74.5	8.9	13.8	15.2
Wheatland	853	27.2	1,508	69.0	13.5	2.9	16.0	69.0	45.9	5.2	18.8	22.7
Wibaux	421	29.7	738	76.8	16.0	1.4	3.9	69.8	63.8	8.8	10.6	15.2
Yellowstone	52,084	33.7	84,233	88.5	26.4	1.4	4.8	52.3	81.4	15.2	12.0	10.8
Yellowstone National Park[3]	(X)	(NA)	(X)	(NA)	(NA)	(NA)	(NA)	(NA)	(NA)	(NA)	(NA)	(NA)

See footnotes at end of table.

[Includes United States, states, and 3,141 counties/county equivalents defined as of February 22, 2005. For more information on these areas, see Appendix C, Geographic Information]

County	Households, 2000		Educational attainment,[1] 2000			Foreign-born population, 2000 (percent)	Persons 5 years and over		Workers who drove alone to work,[2] 2000 (percent)	House-holds with income of $75,000 or more in 1999 (percent)	Persons in poverty (percent)	
	Total	With individuals under 18 years (percent of total)	Total persons	High school graduate or higher (percent)	Bachelor's degree or higher (percent)		Speaking language other than English at home, 2000 (percent)	Residing in same house in 1995 and 2000 (percent)			2004	2000
NEBRASKA............	666,184	34.5	1,087,241	86.6	23.7	4.4	7.9	54.7	80.0	16.9	10.0	8.9
Adams..............	12,141	32.6	19,814	86.3	19.9	4.4	7.1	54.2	80.9	12.7	10.1	9.0
Antelope............	2,953	33.2	4,939	85.5	14.3	0.4	2.6	69.4	72.8	7.2	11.3	12.4
Arthur..............	185	30.3	306	89.5	15.7	0.7	2.1	64.8	58.2	9.7	9.4	10.5
Banner.............	311	33.1	551	94.2	19.6	0.9	3.7	68.0	56.6	10.3	9.6	10.6
Blaine.............	238	30.7	407	93.4	12.3	0.3	4.2	74.3	47.2	4.6	13.6	18.6
Boone..............	2,454	34.6	4,134	84.4	13.1	0.9	3.1	68.2	73.3	8.7	9.7	11.0
Box Butte..........	4,780	37.4	7,864	88.1	15.3	3.1	7.2	58.4	79.5	15.0	11.4	10.3
Boyd..............	1,014	30.2	1,698	83.0	12.8	0.4	3.3	75.0	62.9	6.4	11.2	14.1
Brown.............	1,530	28.1	2,478	83.3	17.2	0.7	2.3	66.7	73.5	7.4	10.9	13.0
Buffalo............	15,930	34.1	24,177	89.2	30.2	2.6	6.7	47.8	84.4	13.2	10.6	9.4
Burt..............	3,155	31.3	5,382	84.1	14.2	1.1	2.6	63.5	75.4	10.2	9.6	9.5
Butler.............	3,426	34.3	5,741	83.4	13.6	0.9	7.3	69.0	75.2	10.5	8.7	8.1
Cass..............	9,161	38.0	15,887	89.4	18.7	1.2	3.4	57.9	81.4	19.5	6.2	6.5
Cedar.............	3,623	35.7	6,208	83.5	13.0	0.4	2.5	72.7	70.7	7.6	8.0	8.5
Chase.............	1,662	31.6	2,791	86.4	16.6	1.4	2.9	61.8	75.3	11.3	9.5	10.6
Cherry.............	2,508	33.1	4,115	85.2	19.4	0.7	2.6	60.0	62.2	9.6	11.8	13.2
Cheyenne...........	4,071	32.6	6,543	86.7	16.8	0.9	3.5	59.3	78.9	10.9	9.4	9.2
Clay..............	2,756	34.3	4,685	86.7	16.2	2.6	6.4	65.4	77.0	10.4	10.0	9.6
Colfax.............	3,682	37.8	6,562	72.0	11.5	18.2	28.6	61.3	67.1	11.3	9.5	8.8
Cuming............	3,945	33.6	6,755	78.7	12.3	3.8	7.3	67.5	73.2	9.4	8.3	8.8
Custer.............	4,826	32.0	8,026	87.5	16.1	0.4	2.9	63.8	71.4	8.1	11.8	13.1
Dakota.............	7,095	43.1	12,103	73.5	12.4	15.6	24.7	51.8	76.9	15.0	11.1	10.2
Dawes.............	3,512	27.7	5,018	86.9	28.4	2.2	4.8	47.7	72.2	12.1	15.8	15.7
Dawson............	8,824	38.0	15,175	73.6	14.4	15.9	22.9	52.6	74.6	11.4	10.9	10.3
Deuel.............	908	27.2	1,515	85.3	17.4	0.9	3.1	56.6	77.2	9.8	9.1	9.9
Dixon.............	2,413	34.7	4,147	82.1	14.1	3.4	7.3	67.7	72.6	7.9	8.3	9.1
Dodge.............	14,433	32.7	23,787	83.5	15.0	2.8	5.6	57.3	82.7	11.9	9.7	7.9
Douglas............	182,194	34.4	293,076	87.3	30.6	5.9	9.5	52.6	82.4	22.9	11.1	8.6
Dundy.............	961	29.6	1,630	82.4	16.7	1.9	4.2	68.6	72.0	9.6	12.0	11.8
Fillmore............	2,689	31.4	4,561	88.2	15.7	0.8	4.3	64.7	74.7	10.5	9.3	8.7
Franklin............	1,485	29.5	2,533	85.7	15.8	0.6	2.6	71.0	77.1	7.4	11.2	11.9
Frontier............	1,192	32.7	1,941	88.3	17.9	1.0	3.0	61.3	66.3	10.6	10.5	12.1
Furnas.............	2,278	29.1	3,764	84.2	16.1	0.3	2.8	65.1	77.1	8.5	11.5	11.6
Gage..............	9,316	31.6	15,689	82.0	15.4	0.7	3.3	60.2	81.5	10.6	9.3	9.0
Garden.............	1,020	25.9	1,685	85.2	14.2	0.9	3.0	60.4	64.8	6.2	12.3	14.8
Garfield............	813	27.3	1,374	81.1	13.4	0.7	1.4	68.6	69.9	6.5	10.6	12.1
Gosper.............	863	30.4	1,517	88.9	17.6	0.5	1.7	64.1	76.0	11.9	6.9	8.0
Grant.............	292	37.7	493	90.3	24.7	1.1	1.1	64.3	58.8	5.8	7.9	9.9
Greeley............	1,077	30.6	1,813	83.2	13.5	0.7	2.7	73.2	62.2	6.3	11.1	13.0
Hall...............	20,356	37.1	34,369	82.2	15.9	8.3	13.6	54.4	82.5	12.7	12.2	10.3
Hamilton...........	3,503	38.8	6,126	89.6	18.6	0.4	2.9	65.5	80.3	12.9	7.9	7.5
Harlan.............	1,597	27.5	2,675	85.8	15.3	0.3	1.8	64.6	75.2	6.8	10.5	10.9
Hayes.............	430	28.8	727	89.1	11.6	2.0	5.0	66.2	60.5	7.4	9.3	12.2
Hitchcock..........	1,287	29.1	2,180	85.6	13.8	1.2	3.7	64.2	71.4	8.2	12.5	13.7
Holt..............	4,608	32.6	7,748	84.5	14.5	0.8	3.1	69.9	72.5	8.1	11.6	12.8
Hooker.............	335	27.5	562	89.7	15.7	–	0.5	69.3	68.8	6.0	6.9	11.4
Howard............	2,546	35.3	4,327	87.2	14.2	0.8	2.6	63.5	75.8	8.7	10.2	10.3
Jefferson...........	3,527	29.3	5,878	84.2	14.4	0.4	2.7	66.2	75.9	8.4	8.8	9.8
Johnson............	1,887	31.0	3,143	80.4	14.7	4.3	6.8	66.0	75.3	9.0	8.9	9.6
Kearney............	2,643	35.9	4,594	88.5	21.3	1.6	4.1	58.6	79.4	12.1	8.2	7.4
Keith..............	3,707	32.0	6,103	86.6	16.8	1.7	4.9	55.8	78.0	9.7	10.0	10.7
Keya Paha..........	409	26.2	681	82.2	15.7	2.2	4.1	76.2	51.9	4.6	13.1	17.4
Kimball............	1,727	28.5	2,849	84.6	13.5	0.7	3.2	62.8	74.3	9.4	11.4	12.2
Knox..............	3,811	30.6	6,462	82.0	14.4	1.0	3.5	68.9	68.1	6.0	13.4	14.2
Lancaster..........	99,187	31.8	152,747	90.5	32.6	5.4	8.8	46.6	80.6	19.2	9.6	8.3
Lincoln............	14,076	33.9	22,736	86.3	16.2	1.2	4.3	52.9	83.4	14.7	10.5	10.2
Logan.............	316	31.3	524	90.8	10.5	0.3	4.6	63.9	61.9	6.6	7.3	11.6
Loup..............	289	32.2	487	91.8	13.3	1.0	2.9	72.8	54.4	5.2	8.5	15.1
McPherson..........	202	36.1	360	88.6	22.2	–	1.2	70.6	43.4	8.9	11.5	13.0
Madison............	13,436	34.8	21,724	82.6	17.0	5.5	9.8	54.3	80.7	12.8	11.7	9.5
Merrick............	3,209	35.2	5,432	85.3	14.9	1.0	3.2	63.2	77.8	8.7	9.1	8.6
Morrill............	2,138	34.2	3,575	79.4	14.3	3.8	9.4	59.5	72.9	7.9	13.9	14.4
Nance.............	1,577	33.8	2,651	80.6	11.4	0.8	4.5	66.8	73.0	8.6	10.5	12.6
Nemaha............	3,047	30.7	4,907	85.5	22.9	0.8	2.7	57.8	76.5	13.1	11.4	10.3
Nuckolls...........	2,218	27.5	3,567	84.5	13.1	0.6	2.3	69.4	73.2	6.0	10.3	10.7
Otoe..............	6,060	34.4	10,373	85.6	18.1	1.4	3.5	58.3	76.8	12.8	8.4	7.9
Pawnee............	1,339	26.1	2,228	83.7	14.4	0.4	2.9	67.9	70.2	7.5	11.4	12.1
Perkins............	1,275	34.0	2,159	87.1	17.6	1.4	3.8	63.8	74.8	11.9	10.4	11.1
Phelps.............	3,844	34.2	6,565	89.1	20.4	0.8	3.2	62.9	78.6	13.0	9.7	8.8
Pierce.............	2,979	36.6	5,019	84.6	13.3	0.8	2.4	65.9	76.5	10.5	9.3	9.6

See footnotes at end of table.

[Includes United States, states, and 3,141 counties/county equivalents defined as of February 22, 2005. For more information on these areas, see Appendix C, Geographic Information]

County	Households, 2000 Total	With individuals under 18 years (percent of total)	Educational attainment, 2000 Total persons	High school graduate or higher (percent)	Bachelor's degree or higher (percent)	Foreign-born population, 2000 (percent)	Persons 5 years and over Speaking language other than English at home, 2000 (percent)	Residing in same house in 1995 and 2000 (percent)	Workers who drove alone to work, 2000 (percent)	Households with income of $75,000 or more in 1999 (percent)	Persons in poverty (percent) 2004	2000
NEBRASKA—Con.												
Platte	12,076	37.4	19,988	84.7	17.2	4.1	7.8	60.1	80.9	13.7	8.6	7.3
Polk	2,259	31.3	3,886	86.6	13.5	0.8	2.7	66.8	76.2	9.3	7.4	7.3
Red Willow	4,710	31.4	7,490	87.9	15.2	1.2	2.4	61.2	80.6	8.8	10.4	10.2
Richardson	3,993	31.5	6,543	81.8	13.6	1.2	3.2	63.1	78.5	8.0	11.7	11.4
Rock	763	27.7	1,242	87.4	12.2	0.3	2.8	69.0	63.9	5.5	13.9	15.7
Saline	5,188	34.4	8,691	81.2	14.0	6.0	12.8	58.7	70.7	10.6	8.4	7.8
Sarpy	43,426	45.0	73,804	93.3	30.2	3.7	6.2	46.4	86.1	26.9	5.4	4.3
Saunders	7,498	35.7	13,047	86.8	16.9	1.2	4.5	64.2	80.1	15.4	7.2	6.7
Scotts Bluff	14,887	34.0	24,314	79.6	17.3	4.1	13.7	57.1	80.5	12.1	14.5	13.6
Seward	6,013	33.8	10,009	87.5	22.6	1.7	4.0	55.2	73.6	16.5	7.0	6.4
Sheridan	2,549	31.6	4,232	86.1	17.2	0.7	4.1	62.0	65.1	7.2	13.5	14.9
Sherman	1,394	29.3	2,355	82.0	10.8	0.4	3.5	70.7	70.3	5.2	11.1	12.0
Sioux	605	31.1	1,009	86.4	21.5	1.3	2.3	60.5	53.9	9.9	9.1	12.7
Stanton	2,297	40.6	4,065	86.2	13.7	1.2	4.8	66.2	75.0	10.2	7.4	8.4
Thayer	2,541	28.8	4,301	80.9	15.0	0.8	3.8	68.3	75.5	9.8	9.8	10.9
Thomas	325	26.8	528	83.7	17.2	1.6	2.9	71.5	59.6	8.3	9.1	12.1
Thurston	2,255	47.4	3,953	80.4	12.0	1.6	6.9	60.9	69.6	6.8	20.5	22.2
Valley	1,965	29.1	3,285	84.7	16.4	1.1	3.8	66.7	73.3	5.8	11.2	12.4
Washington	6,940	38.1	11,956	89.7	22.7	1.6	3.2	56.6	83.3	23.6	6.2	5.5
Wayne	3,437	31.6	5,115	87.0	28.0	1.7	4.1	50.7	73.5	10.1	10.7	10.8
Webster	1,708	27.9	2,910	83.6	13.7	1.3	2.9	66.2	73.6	6.9	9.9	10.1
Wheeler	352	33.5	577	90.8	14.9	–	2.1	77.3	65.3	7.7	10.3	15.1
York	5,722	32.0	9,579	87.2	17.0	1.7	5.3	59.2	76.9	11.0	8.6	7.8
NEVADA	751,165	35.3	1,310,176	80.7	18.2	15.8	23.1	37.4	74.5	22.4	11.1	9.4
Churchill	8,912	40.4	15,167	85.1	16.7	6.0	10.9	45.4	74.0	16.4	10.2	9.8
Clark	512,253	35.4	900,400	79.5	17.3	18.0	26.0	34.5	74.6	22.7	11.6	9.7
Douglas	16,401	33.2	29,279	91.6	23.2	5.7	8.8	48.9	79.0	27.9	7.0	6.6
Elko	15,638	46.2	26,798	79.1	14.8	10.2	20.0	47.6	64.2	20.4	8.7	7.7
Esmeralda	455	23.7	711	78.9	9.6	6.5	9.1	53.1	63.9	12.7	12.4	12.1
Eureka	666	35.1	1,104	76.7	13.6	7.8	10.7	59.4	64.0	15.8	9.0	10.4
Humboldt	5,733	44.1	9,846	78.3	14.2	10.4	19.2	45.8	60.5	22.0	9.8	9.4
Lander	2,093	42.8	3,581	79.2	10.8	9.6	18.6	56.0	66.1	16.4	9.5	9.5
Lincoln	1,540	31.8	2,654	83.0	15.1	3.5	6.1	55.8	66.3	11.1	13.0	15.0
Lyon	13,007	36.5	22,863	81.5	11.3	6.0	10.9	44.1	75.7	13.8	9.0	10.3
Mineral	2,197	29.2	3,527	77.1	10.1	2.4	7.0	56.0	72.4	9.8	14.8	16.3
Nye	13,309	29.4	23,234	79.2	10.1	5.0	9.0	41.1	70.4	14.7	11.9	12.3
Pershing	1,962	41.4	4,498	75.9	8.7	7.0	16.2	48.4	69.9	13.0	13.0	14.2
Storey	1,462	25.2	2,540	86.7	18.0	2.2	9.0	49.1	77.8	23.1	5.1	5.0
Washoe	132,084	34.0	221,837	83.9	23.7	14.1	19.9	41.2	75.3	24.2	10.1	8.4
White Pine	3,282	33.9	6,184	82.0	11.8	2.9	9.7	52.5	71.3	12.5	12.4	13.9
Independent City												
Carson City	20,171	32.7	35,953	82.5	18.5	9.9	14.9	46.1	77.7	19.9	10.2	9.5
NEW HAMPSHIRE	474,606	35.5	823,987	87.4	28.7	4.4	8.3	55.4	81.8	26.4	6.6	5.6
Belknap	22,459	32.5	39,260	85.7	23.3	2.5	5.8	55.9	80.8	19.6	7.0	6.5
Carroll	18,351	29.3	31,534	88.2	26.5	2.4	4.1	58.8	79.6	17.4	7.0	7.9
Cheshire	28,299	32.7	48,032	86.2	26.6	2.2	5.0	57.5	78.8	18.5	7.0	6.7
Coos	13,961	30.1	23,490	76.9	11.9	4.0	17.6	64.1	78.8	9.7	10.2	9.5
Grafton	31,598	31.4	52,795	87.7	32.7	3.9	5.6	54.5	72.8	19.5	8.2	6.5
Hillsborough	144,455	37.2	251,908	87.0	30.1	6.8	12.7	53.6	83.3	30.5	6.6	5.1
Merrimack	51,843	36.0	91,278	88.2	29.1	3.2	6.4	55.6	81.2	25.3	6.3	5.8
Rockingham	104,529	38.1	187,172	90.5	31.7	3.7	6.0	57.1	84.8	34.7	4.6	4.0
Strafford	42,581	34.8	70,319	86.4	26.4	3.4	7.0	50.3	80.3	20.7	8.8	7.1
Sullivan	16,530	31.9	28,199	83.0	19.7	2.9	4.4	59.6	79.4	16.7	7.9	7.6
NEW JERSEY	3,064,645	36.6	5,657,799	82.1	29.8	17.5	25.5	59.8	73.0	34.9	8.4	7.8
Atlantic	95,024	35.7	168,546	78.2	18.7	11.8	20.3	57.6	73.1	22.0	10.0	9.5
Bergen	330,817	34.2	623,469	86.6	38.2	25.1	32.4	62.8	72.8	43.3	5.7	5.0
Burlington	154,371	37.5	285,553	87.2	28.4	6.3	10.3	60.0	82.7	35.7	5.5	5.1
Camden	185,744	38.5	331,765	80.3	24.0	6.9	15.6	63.0	74.0	27.1	10.6	10.0
Cape May	42,148	28.6	72,878	81.9	22.0	3.2	6.6	61.1	80.1	23.1	8.5	9.3
Cumberland	49,143	39.3	96,899	68.5	11.7	6.2	20.4	60.9	78.3	17.8	14.2	13.7
Essex	283,736	38.9	513,570	75.6	27.5	21.2	29.7	57.9	61.5	29.0	13.9	13.6
Gloucester	90,717	39.9	164,801	84.3	22.0	3.4	6.5	65.4	82.0	31.4	6.2	5.9
Hudson	230,546	33.3	408,799	70.5	25.3	38.5	56.1	53.8	42.0	22.9	14.4	13.6
Hunterdon	43,678	38.5	83,548	91.5	41.8	6.3	8.6	61.8	82.5	53.6	3.1	2.6
Mercer	125,807	36.2	231,139	81.8	34.0	13.9	20.2	57.4	73.3	36.1	8.1	7.8
Middlesex	265,815	37.0	501,552	84.4	33.0	24.2	33.4	57.5	74.4	38.9	6.9	5.8
Monmouth	224,236	38.0	413,058	87.9	34.6	10.4	14.7	61.1	75.7	42.3	5.9	5.3
Morris	169,711	37.3	323,881	90.6	44.1	15.4	19.7	61.1	81.2	51.8	4.1	3.2
Ocean	200,402	30.3	358,354	83.0	19.5	6.5	10.9	60.4	82.7	25.7	7.6	6.7

See footnotes at end of table.

Table B-4. Counties — **Population Characteristics**—Con.

[Includes United States, states, and 3,141 counties/county equivalents defined as of February 22, 2005. For more information on these areas, see Appendix C, Geographic Information]

County	Households, 2000		Educational attainment,[1] 2000			Foreign-born population, 2000 (percent)	Persons 5 years and over		Workers who drove alone to work,[2] 2000 (percent)	House-holds with income of $75,000 or more in 1999 (percent)	Persons in poverty (percent)	
	Total	With individuals under 18 years (percent of total)	Total persons	High school graduate or higher (percent)	Bachelor's degree or higher (percent)		Speaking language other than English at home, 2000 (percent)	Residing in same house in 1995 and 2000 (percent)			2004	2000
NEW JERSEY—Con.												
Passaic	163,856	40.1	316,401	73.3	21.2	26.6	41.9	59.4	71.2	30.1	12.0	11.2
Salem	24,295	36.2	42,789	79.4	15.2	2.5	6.3	67.2	83.8	23.8	9.2	8.4
Somerset	108,984	38.0	204,343	89.6	46.5	18.1	22.9	55.5	81.7	51.3	4.3	3.6
Sussex	50,831	42.0	95,094	89.8	27.2	5.7	8.3	64.0	83.9	41.3	4.4	3.8
Union	186,124	37.8	351,903	79.3	28.5	25.1	35.2	60.8	71.0	35.2	9.1	7.8
Warren	38,660	36.9	69,457	84.9	24.4	5.8	8.4	60.0	81.4	33.5	5.4	5.5
NEW MEXICO	677,971	38.6	1,134,801	78.9	23.5	8.2	36.5	54.4	75.8	15.5	16.7	17.3
Bernalillo	220,936	34.8	358,680	84.4	30.5	8.6	29.5	48.9	77.4	19.8	14.1	13.0
Catron	1,584	24.6	2,657	78.4	18.4	1.6	16.9	57.7	56.0	6.8	18.0	22.3
Chaves	22,561	39.8	37,811	72.6	16.2	11.2	33.4	55.6	77.7	10.3	20.0	21.3
Cibola	8,327	45.5	15,273	75.0	12.0	2.3	43.9	67.4	73.7	7.6	20.8	22.1
Colfax	5,821	33.2	9,518	80.8	18.5	2.2	26.6	56.4	70.9	9.3	14.4	15.8
Curry	16,766	41.3	26,403	78.4	15.3	5.9	23.1	44.5	78.7	9.6	17.3	19.0
De Baca	922	29.8	1,584	72.3	16.2	3.7	31.1	67.3	75.4	7.3	16.1	20.6
Dona Ana	59,556	43.0	99,893	70.0	22.3	18.7	54.4	53.1	77.2	12.1	23.0	23.6
Eddy	19,379	39.7	32,572	75.0	13.5	5.3	30.4	59.0	77.1	11.4	16.4	18.0
Grant	12,146	35.1	20,350	79.4	20.5	3.3	36.7	58.5	73.1	8.5	17.9	18.3
Guadalupe	1,655	37.9	3,099	68.3	10.3	4.0	66.9	62.2	74.3	4.8	19.5	21.8
Harding	371	24.8	609	72.2	18.1	2.5	40.6	73.0	60.6	6.5	12.7	14.7
Hidalgo	2,152	41.5	3,596	68.8	9.9	11.1	43.6	64.4	70.7	8.1	21.2	25.2
Lea	19,699	43.1	33,291	67.1	11.6	11.3	32.8	56.5	78.8	9.8	17.6	18.2
Lincoln	8,202	29.3	13,849	84.5	22.8	6.1	20.7	50.2	73.6	15.0	14.5	17.5
Los Alamos	7,497	34.5	12,822	96.3	60.5	6.7	11.5	59.6	81.6	52.9	3.2	2.7
Luna	9,397	37.9	15,777	59.8	10.4	19.5	49.5	57.3	73.8	5.2	24.3	28.2
McKinley	21,476	54.9	38,988	65.2	12.0	1.8	61.3	69.8	63.1	8.7	27.4	29.1
Mora	2,017	35.0	3,348	69.8	15.5	1.7	68.6	69.3	61.5	7.6	19.6	24.2
Otero	22,984	40.5	38,061	81.0	15.4	11.1	29.7	48.1	74.3	8.8	15.2	16.6
Quay	4,201	32.4	6,970	73.8	13.7	3.4	27.3	62.3	72.5	8.3	20.1	22.4
Rio Arriba	15,044	41.7	25,930	73.0	15.4	3.7	65.9	71.3	69.9	10.3	18.1	18.3
Roosevelt	6,639	38.7	10,245	75.2	22.6	6.2	26.4	49.6	77.0	8.5	20.0	22.7
Sandoval	31,411	43.4	56,479	86.0	24.8	4.3	31.8	56.6	79.9	20.1	11.5	11.8
San Juan	37,711	47.1	65,262	76.8	13.5	2.4	32.7	57.2	78.7	13.6	16.5	18.7
San Miguel	11,134	38.9	18,531	74.5	21.2	2.5	60.8	63.2	71.3	8.3	21.4	23.7
Santa Fe	52,482	33.2	87,870	84.5	36.9	10.1	36.9	53.4	71.4	24.0	12.0	12.3
Sierra	6,113	22.7	9,906	76.1	13.1	6.6	21.6	50.6	68.0	6.3	20.4	22.2
Socorro	6,675	38.3	10,642	72.1	19.4	6.4	42.3	58.5	68.5	11.0	23.6	27.9
Taos	12,675	32.8	20,526	79.1	25.9	4.1	52.4	64.4	71.7	9.5	17.5	21.5
Torrance	6,024	41.7	10,556	77.1	14.4	4.2	26.2	53.6	69.9	9.1	22.4	22.5
Union	1,733	33.8	2,786	79.9	13.0	2.2	23.0	60.4	73.3	8.3	15.0	17.0
Valencia	22,681	44.2	40,917	76.1	14.8	6.4	33.9	56.3	77.3	12.8	16.3	15.9
NEW YORK	7,056,860	35.0	12,542,536	79.1	27.4	20.4	28.0	61.8	56.3	25.8	14.5	13.2
Albany	120,512	29.9	195,381	86.3	33.3	6.5	9.9	56.7	76.8	23.5	10.8	9.6
Allegany	18,009	34.0	30,010	83.2	17.2	1.8	4.1	60.4	71.0	10.7	15.1	15.4
Bronx	463,212	43.8	794,792	62.3	14.6	29.0	52.7	60.5	27.0	12.6	28.2	25.4
Broome	80,749	30.3	132,541	83.8	22.7	5.3	8.9	59.4	79.5	15.9	12.4	11.6
Cattaraugus	32,023	34.8	54,154	81.2	14.9	1.4	5.1	63.8	76.6	10.9	13.2	12.8
Cayuga	30,558	35.1	54,649	79.1	15.5	2.3	5.5	64.6	80.2	14.3	11.7	11.3
Chautauqua	54,515	32.8	91,261	81.2	16.9	1.9	7.2	60.9	78.5	11.9	14.9	13.5
Chemung	35,049	33.9	60,796	82.1	18.6	2.2	4.3	60.0	81.1	14.7	14.0	11.9
Chenango	19,926	35.2	34,363	80.6	14.4	1.7	3.8	63.3	76.6	12.1	13.4	13.4
Clinton	29,423	34.5	51,598	76.4	17.8	4.5	6.3	57.9	77.2	15.3	13.0	12.6
Columbia	24,796	32.2	43,990	81.0	22.6	4.4	6.7	62.9	75.7	20.1	9.7	9.7
Cortland	18,210	33.5	29,527	82.8	18.8	2.2	4.4	54.6	74.1	12.9	13.6	12.9
Delaware	19,270	30.2	33,070	79.9	16.6	3.4	6.0	65.1	73.7	11.7	12.4	13.1
Dutchess	99,536	37.1	183,725	84.0	27.6	8.4	11.9	59.5	78.5	32.0	7.7	6.9
Erie	380,873	31.9	637,676	82.9	24.5	4.5	9.0	62.9	80.9	19.2	13.4	11.2
Essex	15,028	31.5	27,337	80.4	18.3	3.4	5.3	61.9	75.2	12.9	11.6	11.8
Franklin	17,931	34.6	34,482	69.7	13.0	3.7	5.8	55.8	76.9	10.0	14.7	15.3
Fulton	21,884	33.3	37,483	77.8	13.5	1.9	4.6	62.7	79.6	11.9	13.0	12.2
Genesee	22,770	35.8	40,125	84.4	16.3	2.2	4.0	65.8	82.8	15.5	9.4	8.6
Greene	18,256	31.4	32,570	78.6	16.4	6.4	8.4	64.9	78.1	15.7	12.4	12.6
Hamilton	2,362	25.7	4,022	83.4	18.4	1.5	3.9	69.7	78.4	11.7	9.1	9.4
Herkimer	25,734	32.8	43,455	79.4	15.7	2.0	5.2	66.4	77.3	10.7	12.6	11.7
Jefferson	40,068	39.4	68,965	82.9	16.0	3.7	7.2	51.6	75.3	11.8	13.9	13.1
Kings	880,727	38.2	1,552,870	68.8	21.8	37.8	46.7	62.9	22.4	17.2	23.8	21.4
Lewis	10,040	37.7	17,367	81.0	11.7	1.1	3.0	71.2	75.0	10.0	12.8	12.5
Livingston	22,150	36.3	40,081	82.3	19.2	2.6	4.7	59.0	77.8	18.0	10.8	9.9
Madison	25,368	36.0	43,762	83.3	21.6	2.2	5.0	61.4	78.5	18.5	10.6	9.6
Monroe	286,512	34.3	477,957	84.9	31.2	7.3	12.1	57.4	82.0	25.0	13.1	10.8
Montgomery	20,038	31.9	33,900	78.1	13.6	3.2	10.9	64.4	76.9	11.8	13.1	12.7
Nassau	447,387	38.6	908,693	86.7	35.4	17.9	23.2	69.9	69.4	48.0	6.2	5.2

See footnotes at end of table.

County and City Data Book: 2007

U.S. Census Bureau

[Includes United States, states, and 3,141 counties/county equivalents defined as of February 22, 2005. For more information on these areas, see Appendix C, Geographic Information]

County	Households, 2000		Educational attainment,[1] 2000			Foreign-born population, 2000 (percent)	Persons 5 years and over		Workers who drove alone to work,[2] 2000 (percent)	Households with income of $75,000 or more in 1999 (percent)	Persons in poverty (percent)	
	Total	With individuals under 18 years (percent of total)	Total persons	High school graduate or higher (percent)	Bachelor's degree or higher (percent)		Speaking language other than English at home, 2000 (percent)	Residing in same house in 1995 and 2000 (percent)			2004	2000
NEW YORK—Con.												
New York	738,644	19.7	1,125,987	78.7	49.4	29.4	41.9	56.9	7.6	33.0	18.8	17.2
Niagara	87,846	33.3	147,153	83.3	17.4	3.9	5.9	65.7	85.2	17.4	11.7	10.4
Oneida	90,496	32.7	158,846	79.0	18.3	5.2	9.6	63.5	80.2	14.9	13.6	12.6
Onondaga	181,153	34.2	296,914	85.7	28.5	5.7	8.9	57.7	80.1	21.3	12.2	10.8
Ontario	38,370	35.2	66,539	87.4	24.7	2.7	4.9	60.2	81.8	21.8	8.4	7.8
Orange	114,788	42.5	212,816	81.8	22.5	8.4	18.2	58.9	76.6	30.5	10.2	9.6
Orleans	15,363	38.4	29,043	76.4	13.0	2.7	4.6	60.1	80.2	13.6	12.5	11.6
Oswego	45,522	37.7	76,165	80.4	14.4	1.6	4.2	60.7	80.7	15.0	13.6	12.6
Otsego	23,291	31.7	38,808	83.0	22.0	2.3	5.1	58.5	73.2	12.7	12.6	12.3
Putnam	32,703	41.4	64,624	90.2	33.9	8.8	13.2	64.3	79.1	48.3	4.5	4.0
Queens	782,664	35.9	1,509,502	74.4	24.3	46.1	53.6	61.8	34.3	23.1	15.0	14.6
Rensselaer	59,894	33.6	100,233	84.9	23.7	3.7	7.1	62.8	78.9	20.9	10.3	9.3
Richmond	156,341	38.5	293,795	82.6	23.2	16.4	26.0	63.2	54.3	33.9	10.2	8.9
Rockland	92,675	40.5	184,012	85.3	37.5	19.1	29.9	64.5	73.7	45.8	9.5	9.3
St. Lawrence	40,506	34.1	70,201	79.2	16.4	3.4	5.4	59.0	75.9	11.4	15.5	14.9
Saratoga	78,165	35.7	135,015	88.2	30.9	3.1	5.3	58.5	83.4	26.7	6.4	6.0
Schenectady	59,684	32.1	99,568	84.8	26.3	5.3	9.9	61.1	80.7	21.4	11.7	9.5
Schoharie	11,991	33.5	20,695	81.7	17.3	2.4	4.7	63.8	77.6	14.4	11.6	11.8
Schuyler	7,374	35.3	12,842	82.4	15.5	1.2	3.6	63.7	76.9	12.2	11.7	11.4
Seneca	12,630	34.4	22,585	79.1	17.5	2.4	5.4	62.3	81.3	15.4	11.4	11.5
Steuben	39,071	34.5	65,765	82.8	17.9	1.9	4.0	62.4	77.4	14.4	13.6	12.3
Suffolk	469,299	40.5	942,401	86.2	27.5	11.2	17.1	64.7	78.1	42.1	7.0	6.2
Sullivan	27,661	34.2	50,228	76.2	16.7	7.9	14.2	59.7	76.7	17.4	13.3	13.9
Tioga	19,725	37.3	34,223	84.8	19.7	1.7	3.8	65.1	80.2	17.4	9.4	8.7
Tompkins	36,420	27.4	53,075	91.4	47.5	10.5	13.9	41.9	59.8	18.7	13.5	12.0
Ulster	67,499	33.3	120,670	81.7	25.0	5.9	10.1	61.6	78.1	21.5	10.7	10.5
Warren	25,726	32.8	43,364	84.6	23.2	2.4	4.3	61.5	80.8	16.7	9.8	10.0
Washington	22,458	36.2	40,957	79.2	14.3	1.9	3.4	62.9	78.9	14.3	10.8	11.0
Wayne	34,908	38.8	61,731	82.3	17.0	2.3	4.7	63.4	82.5	20.3	10.1	8.9
Westchester	337,142	36.6	628,941	83.6	40.9	22.2	28.4	61.2	61.6	43.4	8.9	7.6
Wyoming	14,906	36.6	29,522	75.6	11.5	2.3	3.3	67.6	79.7	12.8	9.9	9.2
Yates	9,029	34.2	15,714	80.0	18.2	2.3	8.5	60.6	71.2	12.4	12.3	13.3
NORTH CAROLINA	3,132,013	35.3	5,282,994	78.1	22.5	5.3	8.0	53.0	79.4	18.3	13.8	11.7
Alamance	51,584	34.4	86,635	76.5	19.2	6.3	9.3	54.5	81.5	16.3	11.8	9.4
Alexander	13,137	35.9	22,729	68.7	9.3	2.4	4.0	63.5	82.0	12.9	11.5	9.4
Alleghany	4,593	26.9	7,829	68.0	11.7	4.1	6.1	64.9	73.8	10.7	16.5	13.6
Anson	9,204	37.4	16,824	70.2	9.2	0.7	2.8	67.7	76.6	9.4	19.7	16.8
Ashe	10,411	28.4	17,722	68.6	12.1	1.9	3.3	64.6	76.2	8.3	14.1	13.9
Avery	6,532	29.7	12,058	70.6	14.5	2.6	4.7	61.2	72.7	8.1	15.5	14.9
Beaufort	18,319	32.7	30,868	75.0	16.0	2.6	4.7	62.1	78.6	13.0	17.7	17.1
Bertie	7,743	36.2	13,135	63.8	8.8	0.7	2.3	68.0	74.9	8.4	21.3	20.8
Bladen	12,897	35.3	21,409	70.6	11.3	2.3	5.1	69.9	80.2	9.0	20.2	18.5
Brunswick	30,438	29.2	52,605	78.3	16.1	2.9	4.8	53.9	78.5	14.7	13.2	13.2
Buncombe	85,776	30.2	143,649	81.9	25.3	3.9	5.9	53.0	79.6	15.3	13.8	11.4
Burke	34,528	34.4	59,922	67.6	12.8	4.8	8.1	59.6	81.8	11.7	14.0	11.0
Cabarrus	49,519	38.2	86,732	78.2	19.1	4.7	7.2	53.4	83.3	22.3	10.8	7.8
Caldwell	30,768	35.0	53,539	66.2	10.4	1.9	3.5	60.9	79.9	12.0	13.6	11.0
Camden	2,662	35.8	4,770	82.1	16.2	0.7	2.6	55.0	79.0	19.2	8.7	10.0
Carteret	25,204	29.1	43,457	82.1	19.8	2.0	3.9	54.5	78.1	16.9	11.8	11.4
Caswell	8,670	35.8	16,212	69.2	8.3	1.6	3.8	66.8	76.4	11.4	16.2	13.1
Catawba	55,533	35.0	94,747	74.8	17.0	6.5	9.5	56.2	81.6	16.7	11.4	8.9
Chatham	19,741	31.9	34,920	77.9	27.6	8.7	10.7	59.5	76.9	22.1	10.2	8.7
Cherokee	10,336	28.4	17,709	73.3	11.0	1.2	3.0	64.9	77.5	8.9	15.1	15.0
Chowan	5,580	34.8	9,583	73.1	16.4	0.9	3.1	65.6	70.0	10.6	16.9	16.9
Clay	3,847	25.9	6,578	76.5	15.4	1.2	2.5	58.3	78.5	13.1	12.7	13.5
Cleveland	37,046	36.7	63,396	72.2	13.3	1.7	3.9	60.2	81.7	13.0	15.4	13.5
Columbus	21,308	36.5	35,921	68.6	10.1	1.4	3.5	69.6	80.1	9.0	21.1	19.9
Craven	34,582	36.7	57,027	82.1	19.3	3.4	6.4	48.5	77.8	14.3	13.7	12.6
Cumberland	107,358	43.5	176,714	85.0	19.1	5.3	10.9	45.5	77.2	14.3	16.2	13.1
Currituck	6,902	37.4	12,361	77.6	13.3	1.4	3.1	58.4	79.8	16.6	9.6	10.3
Dare	12,690	29.5	21,713	88.6	27.7	2.5	4.1	49.8	76.8	20.6	7.8	8.0
Davidson	58,156	36.0	100,128	72.0	12.8	3.6	5.6	60.2	81.9	15.1	13.2	9.9
Davie	13,750	35.3	23,840	78.1	17.6	3.4	5.4	59.7	83.2	20.1	9.3	8.1
Duplin	18,267	38.0	31,700	65.8	10.5	11.3	15.3	61.3	73.4	9.4	17.9	18.5
Durham	89,015	32.6	143,804	83.0	40.1	10.9	13.9	44.2	74.8	23.4	14.9	11.4
Edgecombe	20,392	39.8	35,748	65.6	8.5	2.1	4.6	58.0	77.4	9.8	21.5	19.6
Forsyth	123,851	33.6	204,081	82.0	28.7	6.5	9.2	52.5	80.5	21.6	13.6	10.6
Franklin	17,843	37.6	31,467	73.6	13.2	3.6	6.4	58.1	78.4	14.5	13.6	12.4

See footnotes at end of table.

[Includes United States, states, and 3,141 counties/county equivalents defined as of February 22, 2005. For more information on these areas, see Appendix C, Geographic Information]

County	Households, 2000		Educational attainment,[1] 2000			Foreign-born population, 2000 (percent)	Persons 5 years and over		Workers who drove alone to work,[2] 2000 (percent)	House-holds with income of $75,000 or more in 1999 (percent)	Persons in poverty (percent)	
	Total	With individuals under 18 years (percent of total)	Total persons	High school graduate or higher (percent)	Bachelor's degree or higher (percent)		Speaking language other than English at home, 2000 (percent)	Residing in same house in 1995 and 2000 (percent)			2004	2000
NORTH CAROLINA—Con.												
Gaston	73,936	36.5	127,748	71.4	14.2	3.3	5.7	58.3	83.7	16.8	14.2	11.5
Gates	3,901	39.6	7,095	71.4	10.5	1.1	2.6	66.9	77.1	12.8	14.1	14.1
Graham	3,354	30.1	5,622	68.4	11.2	1.3	3.9	67.6	67.8	7.9	16.7	16.3
Granville	16,654	38.2	32,641	73.0	13.0	4.0	6.2	57.7	81.0	16.4	14.5	11.6
Greene	6,696	39.6	12,380	65.4	8.2	4.9	8.5	60.9	78.1	9.4	19.1	17.5
Guilford	168,667	33.5	275,494	83.0	30.3	6.5	9.2	49.4	81.2	22.5	14.7	10.4
Halifax	22,122	36.9	37,719	65.4	11.1	1.1	2.8	65.5	78.0	9.0	23.2	21.1
Harnett	33,800	40.2	57,138	75.0	12.8	4.6	7.8	51.3	79.1	12.8	15.8	14.6
Haywood	23,100	28.8	39,552	77.7	16.0	1.6	3.3	60.5	81.3	11.5	13.8	12.5
Henderson	37,414	28.3	65,039	83.2	24.1	5.9	8.0	54.1	80.8	16.2	11.2	10.7
Hertford	8,953	35.9	14,976	65.6	11.1	1.2	3.2	67.9	71.7	9.7	20.8	20.0
Hoke	11,373	47.7	19,934	73.5	10.9	5.8	10.4	51.2	75.8	10.1	16.1	16.2
Hyde	2,185	30.8	4,190	68.4	10.6	2.3	4.6	65.7	73.2	7.4	19.3	21.6
Iredell	47,360	36.9	82,036	78.4	17.4	3.6	5.5	55.1	82.7	19.5	10.1	8.3
Jackson	13,191	28.3	20,881	78.8	25.5	1.7	5.7	54.8	76.3	12.7	15.8	14.2
Johnston	46,595	38.8	80,268	75.9	15.9	5.9	9.1	52.1	79.9	16.7	12.9	11.5
Jones	4,061	36.4	6,998	72.2	9.5	2.1	4.6	67.2	78.0	9.3	16.9	16.8
Lee	18,466	37.6	32,043	76.3	17.2	9.5	12.3	56.6	78.3	19.0	13.1	11.8
Lenoir	23,862	35.5	39,833	71.9	13.3	2.7	5.3	58.8	80.1	11.1	17.8	16.3
Lincoln	24,041	37.7	43,259	71.7	13.0	4.8	6.8	58.8	82.1	16.8	11.1	9.3
McDowell	16,604	33.9	29,157	70.2	9.0	2.7	4.4	60.2	77.4	9.3	13.1	12.0
Macon	12,828	27.1	21,908	77.3	16.2	2.6	3.5	58.1	80.2	11.0	13.3	12.5
Madison	8,000	30.8	13,409	69.3	16.1	1.7	3.4	59.7	79.0	9.3	15.4	14.6
Martin	10,020	36.3	17,014	70.7	11.6	1.5	3.1	67.0	78.8	10.6	18.8	18.2
Mecklenburg	273,416	35.2	455,163	86.2	37.1	9.8	13.1	43.6	79.2	29.5	12.8	8.8
Mitchell	6,551	29.7	11,315	68.6	12.2	1.5	3.9	66.0	76.0	8.9	14.6	12.4
Montgomery	9,848	35.7	17,713	64.2	10.0	8.0	12.2	61.2	74.4	11.5	15.9	14.6
Moore	30,713	29.7	53,347	82.6	26.8	4.2	6.0	56.0	80.5	19.7	12.1	10.2
Nash	33,644	36.9	57,522	75.6	17.2	3.0	6.0	56.0	82.5	16.6	14.7	12.8
New Hanover	68,183	28.6	107,671	86.3	31.0	3.2	5.4	45.4	82.4	19.8	13.9	12.0
Northampton	8,691	33.7	15,199	62.5	10.8	0.7	2.6	68.3	78.6	10.1	20.9	20.6
Onslow	48,122	45.7	75,286	84.3	14.8	4.1	9.4	35.8	66.7	10.1	15.8	13.5
Orange	45,863	30.3	69,530	87.6	51.5	9.1	11.9	41.2	70.1	26.9	12.6	9.8
Pamlico	5,178	30.2	9,332	75.2	14.7	1.8	4.9	67.6	74.3	13.3	15.5	16.0
Pasquotank	12,907	37.6	22,223	76.8	16.4	2.3	4.0	53.3	75.1	11.2	16.8	16.9
Pender	16,054	33.5	28,566	76.8	13.6	3.6	5.4	55.8	80.2	14.6	14.2	13.9
Perquimans	4,645	31.9	7,970	71.9	12.3	0.7	2.3	61.3	76.2	9.6	16.0	16.0
Person	14,085	35.4	24,473	74.9	10.3	1.3	3.7	63.0	79.2	12.8	13.6	10.4
Pitt	52,539	33.4	79,040	79.9	26.4	3.6	6.0	44.7	80.5	15.6	17.8	16.9
Polk	7,908	26.2	13,653	80.6	25.7	3.7	5.9	62.1	78.1	14.3	11.2	9.8
Randolph	50,659	37.0	87,450	70.0	11.1	5.7	7.8	59.5	81.4	13.5	11.5	8.9
Richmond	17,873	36.9	29,870	69.2	10.1	2.2	4.5	59.2	76.5	9.4	19.7	17.5
Robeson	43,677	43.8	74,458	64.9	11.4	4.2	6.8	61.9	75.3	9.1	23.8	23.6
Rockingham	36,989	34.2	63,470	68.9	10.8	2.7	4.7	62.5	80.6	12.4	13.5	11.7
Rowan	49,940	36.1	86,345	74.2	14.2	3.7	5.8	57.7	81.2	14.5	13.0	10.7
Rutherford	25,191	33.7	42,889	70.4	12.5	1.4	3.3	60.9	82.1	10.3	16.1	13.7
Sampson	22,273	38.2	38,796	69.1	11.1	7.1	11.2	60.2	78.4	10.5	17.5	16.2
Scotland	13,399	40.4	22,563	71.4	15.9	1.3	3.0	58.8	81.7	12.5	20.5	18.6
Stanly	22,223	35.8	38,702	73.4	12.7	2.6	4.7	61.1	82.0	13.6	12.8	10.6
Stokes	17,579	36.8	30,598	73.2	9.3	1.5	3.6	63.1	81.6	13.6	11.1	9.5
Surry	28,408	33.7	49,018	67.0	12.0	5.3	8.1	62.5	78.4	12.2	14.6	12.1
Swain	5,137	33.9	8,739	70.5	13.9	1.0	5.3	67.0	77.1	9.4	15.4	15.7
Transylvania	12,320	27.3	20,973	82.5	23.7	2.3	4.0	57.5	79.7	16.5	12.6	10.8
Tyrrell	1,537	34.0	2,828	66.3	10.6	4.0	5.7	63.1	65.1	9.4	23.5	24.9
Union	43,390	43.0	78,878	80.2	21.3	5.7	8.3	53.2	81.4	25.9	9.7	8.1
Vance	16,199	38.9	27,360	68.1	10.7	3.4	5.8	58.5	76.8	11.1	20.7	17.7
Wake	242,040	36.2	403,481	89.3	43.9	9.7	12.2	41.7	81.1	33.7	9.2	6.6
Warren	7,708	33.5	13,599	67.5	11.6	2.3	4.7	62.8	75.2	9.3	21.8	19.3
Washington	5,367	36.2	9,091	69.9	11.6	1.4	3.4	67.9	76.0	11.6	20.6	20.4
Watauga	16,540	24.7	23,939	81.6	33.2	1.9	4.6	46.5	74.5	13.2	14.7	14.0
Wayne	42,612	38.7	72,894	77.2	15.0	4.2	7.2	53.0	80.5	12.7	15.4	14.2
Wilkes	26,650	33.0	45,498	66.0	11.3	3.0	5.0	64.7	79.7	11.4	13.9	12.2
Wilson	28,613	36.5	48,061	69.4	15.1	4.9	8.1	55.6	78.8	13.4	17.5	15.9
Yadkin	14,505	34.8	24,916	72.0	10.3	4.4	7.3	64.5	80.0	13.9	11.6	9.8
Yancey	7,472	29.5	12,709	71.1	13.1	2.8	3.9	66.4	73.2	8.1	16.4	14.5
NORTH DAKOTA	257,152	32.7	408,585	83.9	22.0	1.9	6.3	56.8	77.7	12.4	10.8	10.4
Adams	1,121	27.5	1,885	83.1	16.6	1.5	3.6	66.1	69.1	8.5	10.1	11.2
Barnes	4,884	28.4	7,792	85.0	22.1	0.9	3.2	62.1	72.1	9.1	10.7	10.9
Benson	2,328	44.0	3,902	73.8	10.9	0.5	8.2	66.5	63.2	7.8	22.4	25.0
Billings	366	30.3	644	77.8	18.8	1.0	6.0	72.9	50.6	10.1	9.3	13.8
Bottineau	2,962	28.3	4,973	81.3	14.9	2.1	3.9	67.4	72.6	9.4	11.0	10.8

See footnotes at end of table.

Table B-4. Counties — **Population Characteristics**—Con.

[Includes United States, states, and 3,141 counties/county equivalents defined as of February 22, 2005. For more information on these areas, see Appendix C, Geographic Information]

County	Households, 2000 Total	Households, 2000 With individuals under 18 years (percent of total)	Educational attainment,[1] 2000 Total persons	High school graduate or higher (percent)	Bachelor's degree or higher (percent)	Foreign-born population, 2000 (percent)	Persons 5 years and over Speaking language other than English at home, 2000 (percent)	Residing in same house in 1995 and 2000 (percent)	Workers who drove alone to work,[2] 2000 (percent)	Households with income of $75,000 or more in 1999 (percent)	Persons in poverty (percent) 2004	Persons in poverty (percent) 2000
NORTH DAKOTA—Con.												
Bowman	1,358	30.3	2,290	82.2	17.9	0.4	1.6	64.0	72.3	9.6	7.8	9.9
Burke	1,013	23.6	1,687	78.8	12.0	1.5	2.8	75.2	66.8	5.0	10.2	11.4
Burleigh	27,670	33.8	44,636	87.9	28.7	1.5	7.1	54.8	83.4	17.4	8.8	7.7
Cass	51,315	30.9	74,668	90.9	31.3	3.2	5.5	44.8	83.5	16.4	9.2	7.8
Cavalier	2,017	28.1	3,462	78.8	13.1	2.5	2.4	76.8	74.5	8.0	9.8	9.9
Dickey	2,283	29.0	3,815	79.6	16.6	1.6	8.7	64.0	63.5	8.2	12.2	12.1
Divide	1,005	23.5	1,741	80.4	13.3	2.4	4.1	73.6	67.4	9.3	10.1	11.4
Dunn	1,378	33.5	2,393	77.5	16.3	0.7	7.8	70.1	65.1	8.1	11.5	13.3
Eddy	1,164	28.1	1,933	75.5	15.9	0.4	3.6	72.0	68.7	9.1	10.1	10.0
Emmons	1,786	28.3	3,125	65.9	12.3	0.5	16.3	71.6	57.5	7.6	12.6	13.5
Foster	1,540	32.1	2,569	78.0	19.8	1.5	4.1	61.0	71.8	9.7	8.2	8.9
Golden Valley	761	30.5	1,278	87.4	19.8	0.5	2.0	68.9	67.2	6.8	11.4	14.3
Grand Forks	25,435	33.5	37,366	89.2	27.8	3.2	6.1	42.9	80.3	13.4	11.3	10.3
Grant	1,195	26.0	2,044	73.4	11.2	1.3	13.9	75.2	51.4	5.7	15.5	17.3
Griggs	1,178	27.4	1,993	78.7	15.7	1.0	2.7	74.6	66.9	8.3	9.9	11.2
Hettinger	1,152	27.2	1,978	74.8	14.4	0.1	6.7	77.3	65.0	8.3	11.3	11.6
Kidder	1,158	28.0	1,982	72.0	11.0	0.9	7.2	75.3	58.4	7.7	11.4	14.0
LaMoure	1,942	28.6	3,297	75.3	13.9	0.8	9.2	72.0	62.9	8.6	9.8	10.2
Logan	963	26.3	1,693	66.0	12.9	0.6	25.5	76.4	57.6	10.1	10.4	14.4
McHenry	2,526	29.8	4,192	76.9	13.2	1.0	5.1	71.6	65.9	7.4	12.8	14.4
McIntosh	1,467	22.6	2,580	59.3	9.9	0.8	35.9	71.7	61.7	6.6	13.4	13.0
McKenzie	2,151	37.7	3,644	79.1	15.7	1.4	7.3	70.1	67.4	8.5	13.7	15.7
McLean	3,815	30.6	6,620	79.0	15.1	0.9	5.4	71.0	67.8	10.4	11.3	12.3
Mercer	3,346	38.3	5,780	79.0	14.4	1.5	12.7	73.6	72.2	15.6	7.4	6.9
Morton	9,889	36.3	16,520	80.2	17.0	0.9	7.9	62.3	78.7	11.9	9.9	9.6
Mountrail	2,560	35.4	4,309	77.9	15.6	1.2	6.6	66.2	69.0	6.7	14.2	15.7
Nelson	1,628	25.3	2,753	81.4	17.5	1.7	5.0	70.6	70.6	8.0	9.5	10.1
Oliver	791	36.4	1,402	79.9	12.0	0.3	4.9	76.9	62.0	14.3	8.9	9.9
Pembina	3,535	30.6	5,908	79.8	16.4	3.8	5.6	68.9	73.9	12.2	8.7	9.0
Pierce	1,964	29.2	3,300	76.7	14.7	1.2	10.3	65.0	65.2	6.1	11.4	12.2
Ramsey	4,957	31.5	8,123	80.1	18.8	1.5	3.5	55.8	76.5	10.7	13.5	12.3
Ransom	2,350	31.9	4,065	81.3	15.8	0.9	6.1	64.6	73.1	11.7	8.9	8.5
Renville	1,085	29.3	1,872	84.1	16.1	1.5	2.4	70.1	67.2	7.6	9.4	9.4
Richland	6,885	33.6	10,991	83.2	15.2	1.1	4.1	60.2	74.4	10.5	10.0	9.1
Rolette	4,556	50.0	7,406	73.7	14.7	1.3	6.8	64.4	71.4	7.1	25.9	26.3
Sargent	1,786	31.2	2,989	81.1	12.7	0.5	2.4	66.1	63.6	12.2	7.1	7.4
Sheridan	731	26.0	1,280	67.8	9.7	1.1	12.9	80.6	57.6	7.3	16.9	17.6
Sioux	1,095	61.1	1,919	78.5	11.2	0.8	12.1	53.8	65.5	4.2	28.1	31.3
Slope	313	31.6	538	82.5	16.0	0.3	3.7	77.1	50.0	5.4	9.6	13.7
Stark	8,932	33.6	14,252	79.9	22.3	0.8	7.5	61.8	78.3	10.1	11.4	10.8
Steele	923	31.0	1,529	86.1	19.8	0.3	3.5	71.7	71.0	10.9	8.0	7.6
Stutsman	8,954	29.8	14,618	81.1	19.7	1.0	6.3	58.6	77.4	10.6	11.4	10.8
Towner	1,218	28.7	2,057	81.9	16.1	0.8	2.1	71.4	64.8	9.4	9.6	9.9
Traill	3,341	32.0	5,542	83.7	21.8	1.4	5.1	60.9	76.3	12.8	9.1	8.9
Walsh	5,029	31.6	8,530	76.6	13.3	1.9	10.3	69.9	75.8	8.8	11.1	10.2
Ward	23,041	35.7	35,957	87.4	22.1	2.1	4.7	50.9	81.7	11.8	10.7	9.9
Wells	2,215	26.5	3,715	72.6	13.7	0.8	6.7	70.9	68.7	9.1	11.7	10.6
Williams	8,095	33.0	13,048	82.5	16.5	1.2	3.9	61.0	79.5	10.2	11.1	11.4
OHIO	4,445,773	34.5	7,411,740	83.0	21.1	3.0	6.1	57.5	82.8	19.8	11.7	9.8
Adams	10,501	37.1	17,775	68.6	7.2	0.2	2.7	60.8	75.9	9.5	16.1	16.4
Allen	40,646	35.8	69,669	82.5	13.4	1.0	3.4	58.8	84.9	15.0	12.2	10.6
Ashland	19,524	35.0	33,339	83.3	15.9	1.1	4.4	60.7	82.6	15.0	9.7	8.1
Ashtabula	39,397	35.6	67,994	79.9	11.1	1.6	5.1	61.8	81.0	12.7	12.7	11.9
Athens	22,501	28.5	31,563	82.9	25.7	3.3	5.4	44.4	70.0	12.0	20.2	19.3
Auglaize	17,376	37.1	30,093	85.7	13.4	1.1	2.5	62.9	84.5	19.0	7.0	5.9
Belmont	28,309	30.7	49,616	80.9	11.1	1.0	3.8	67.4	84.1	9.5	14.8	14.6
Brown	15,555	40.7	27,209	74.8	8.8	0.4	1.9	59.1	79.0	13.5	11.9	10.4
Butler	123,082	38.3	207,213	83.3	23.5	2.7	5.0	51.0	84.2	25.9	9.8	7.2
Carroll	11,126	34.7	19,460	80.1	9.1	0.6	2.9	66.0	83.7	10.3	10.9	10.5
Champaign	14,952	36.4	25,644	82.3	10.6	0.7	2.1	60.6	82.3	17.8	8.9	7.8
Clark	56,648	34.6	95,298	81.2	14.9	1.2	3.0	57.7	82.6	17.8	12.8	10.6
Clermont	66,013	40.9	113,513	82.0	20.8	1.6	3.1	54.3	84.5	26.2	7.8	6.5
Clinton	15,416	37.5	25,720	83.1	14.1	1.0	2.9	53.2	81.9	16.4	9.8	8.4
Columbiana	42,973	34.5	76,022	80.6	10.8	1.4	3.5	63.8	83.5	11.6	12.2	11.9
Coshocton	14,356	34.8	24,172	78.7	9.8	1.0	6.7	64.4	79.2	11.9	11.3	10.0
Crawford	18,957	33.7	31,379	80.2	9.7	0.5	2.8	64.0	83.2	12.2	11.4	9.5
Cuyahoga	571,457	31.7	936,148	81.6	25.1	6.4	11.1	59.6	78.8	20.3	15.0	12.0
Darke	20,419	35.5	35,206	82.8	10.1	0.7	1.9	65.6	83.6	14.8	8.3	7.2
Defiance	15,138	36.9	25,426	84.7	14.3	1.5	6.6	63.3	84.6	18.5	7.9	6.2

See footnotes at end of table.

[Includes United States, states, and 3,141 counties/county equivalents defined as of February 22, 2005. For more information on these areas, see Appendix C, Geographic Information]

County	Households, 2000 Total	With individuals under 18 years (percent of total)	Educational attainment,[1] 2000 Total persons	High school graduate or higher (percent)	Bachelor's degree or higher (percent)	Foreign-born population, 2000 (percent)	Speaking language other than English at home, 2000 (percent)	Residing in same house in 1995 and 2000 (percent)	Workers who drove alone to work,[2] 2000 (percent)	Households with income of $75,000 or more in 1999 (percent)	Persons in poverty (percent) 2004	Persons in poverty (percent) 2000
OHIO—Con.												
Delaware	39,674	41.8	70,617	92.9	41.0	2.6	4.7	46.6	86.1	43.9	5.0	4.2
Erie	31,727	33.3	54,232	84.0	16.6	1.5	3.8	61.7	88.1	20.0	9.6	8.6
Fairfield	45,425	39.4	79,948	87.6	20.8	1.3	3.3	56.7	85.4	25.0	7.7	6.5
Fayette	11,054	36.0	18,954	78.7	10.7	0.9	2.7	56.5	81.3	12.1	12.0	10.0
Franklin	438,778	33.1	676,318	85.7	31.8	6.0	9.0	46.4	80.9	22.0	13.1	9.9
Fulton	15,480	39.5	26,887	85.3	13.2	1.3	5.6	63.2	84.7	18.3	7.1	5.7
Gallia	12,060	35.8	20,207	73.7	11.6	0.8	3.0	61.8	84.0	10.9	17.4	16.8
Geauga	31,630	39.0	59,216	86.3	31.7	2.8	11.0	67.6	82.3	37.6	5.5	5.2
Greene	55,312	35.0	92,414	87.8	31.1	3.4	5.5	52.9	84.4	26.8	9.4	7.1
Guernsey	16,094	35.4	26,839	78.4	10.0	1.1	4.0	59.9	81.0	8.2	15.2	14.4
Hamilton	346,790	33.0	546,048	82.7	29.2	3.4	5.6	55.4	78.9	22.4	13.1	10.3
Hancock	27,898	34.9	45,871	88.4	21.7	2.0	4.4	56.3	84.3	19.8	7.9	7.0
Hardin	11,963	34.1	19,220	80.6	11.4	1.0	4.0	57.5	76.9	11.0	11.6	10.3
Harrison	6,398	31.5	11,097	79.6	9.0	0.5	2.2	67.5	80.9	9.1	13.0	12.3
Henry	10,935	37.3	18,833	83.5	11.1	1.3	6.0	66.7	84.9	15.9	7.3	6.1
Highland	15,587	37.5	26,372	76.3	9.7	0.6	2.1	56.4	79.1	12.4	12.2	11.2
Hocking	10,843	36.3	18,720	78.0	9.8	0.6	2.4	60.5	80.6	10.1	13.3	12.4
Holmes	11,337	46.0	21,016	51.5	8.3	0.7	44.1	68.3	53.7	12.2	9.7	10.7
Huron	22,307	38.9	37,576	81.0	10.9	1.9	4.5	58.4	84.9	14.3	9.5	8.1
Jackson	12,619	38.2	21,306	73.5	11.0	1.1	2.6	59.1	83.4	9.6	15.5	15.0
Jefferson	30,417	29.3	51,819	81.7	11.8	1.3	3.8	69.3	84.8	10.1	14.7	13.4
Knox	19,975	34.7	34,485	81.8	16.7	1.0	4.9	56.0	77.5	15.2	10.6	9.5
Lake	89,700	33.2	156,177	86.4	21.5	4.3	6.7	62.4	87.4	24.5	6.6	5.6
Lawrence	24,732	35.3	41,685	75.6	10.3	0.5	1.9	65.2	86.7	9.2	17.4	18.0
Licking	55,609	37.1	95,009	84.7	18.4	1.1	3.0	55.9	83.5	20.9	9.5	7.5
Logan	17,956	36.0	29,962	83.6	11.5	1.1	3.8	58.6	82.0	17.3	10.0	8.6
Lorain	105,836	37.1	185,491	82.8	16.6	2.6	8.1	59.4	84.4	22.3	10.9	8.9
Lucas	182,847	34.1	291,022	82.9	21.3	3.2	6.8	56.6	84.5	18.7	14.7	11.9
Madison	13,672	38.4	26,615	79.0	13.0	1.1	5.0	56.2	83.5	19.8	9.6	8.8
Mahoning	102,587	31.5	174,803	82.4	17.5	2.4	7.0	64.2	86.6	15.2	14.3	12.3
Marion	24,578	35.5	44,466	80.3	11.1	1.1	3.1	59.5	83.6	14.2	12.0	10.5
Medina	54,542	39.9	99,005	88.8	24.8	3.0	5.3	60.1	87.0	31.0	5.9	4.6
Meigs	9,234	34.2	15,602	73.2	7.4	0.2	1.7	66.3	80.8	7.2	18.1	18.0
Mercer	14,756	38.7	25,614	84.0	12.7	0.8	2.7	66.2	83.2	16.4	6.4	6.5
Miami	38,437	35.8	65,765	82.7	16.3	1.5	2.9	56.4	86.4	20.4	8.2	6.8
Monroe	6,021	31.8	10,544	78.8	8.4	0.3	3.3	68.9	77.2	6.4	12.4	14.9
Montgomery	229,229	32.7	367,099	83.5	22.8	2.5	4.6	54.3	83.7	19.7	12.5	9.9
Morgan	5,890	33.8	9,934	80.6	9.1	0.5	2.0	62.7	77.4	6.3	14.8	15.5
Morrow	11,499	39.3	20,591	78.6	9.5	0.5	3.0	59.3	82.2	14.1	9.8	9.5
Muskingum	32,518	36.3	54,616	80.6	12.6	0.7	2.7	60.5	81.4	12.3	14.2	12.7
Noble	4,546	35.9	9,210	78.6	8.1	0.6	4.4	60.4	80.5	8.1	13.2	14.5
Ottawa	16,474	31.4	28,829	84.2	16.0	1.1	4.5	64.1	85.3	21.4	7.5	6.4
Paulding	7,773	36.8	13,108	81.6	7.8	0.6	3.1	66.9	84.1	13.6	8.7	7.4
Perry	12,500	39.9	21,626	78.9	6.9	0.6	2.3	65.0	78.9	10.5	13.2	12.9
Pickaway	17,599	38.5	35,258	77.2	11.4	0.7	3.1	57.5	84.2	18.9	11.1	9.8
Pike	10,444	38.9	17,710	70.1	9.7	0.6	2.7	57.6	80.7	11.6	17.2	16.7
Portage	56,449	34.8	94,073	85.9	21.0	2.0	4.3	55.6	84.0	21.1	9.7	8.2
Preble	16,001	37.0	28,079	81.7	10.1	0.6	2.0	61.0	83.5	15.3	8.1	7.2
Putnam	12,200	41.0	21,524	86.1	12.9	0.7	4.5	71.8	84.1	19.3	6.5	5.3
Richland	49,534	33.9	86,184	80.2	12.6	1.8	4.5	59.4	84.7	15.6	12.0	10.4
Ross	27,136	35.9	49,443	76.1	11.3	0.7	2.8	58.1	83.1	14.8	13.1	12.8
Sandusky	23,717	36.3	40,565	82.1	11.9	1.3	6.3	63.6	84.8	16.2	8.9	7.6
Scioto	30,871	35.3	52,236	74.1	10.1	0.6	2.2	62.3	83.3	9.8	18.9	18.5
Seneca	22,292	35.9	37,271	83.1	12.5	1.2	3.8	62.6	82.5	12.3	9.8	8.3
Shelby	17,636	39.3	30,280	81.5	12.8	1.4	3.3	59.8	86.3	19.6	7.8	6.5
Stark	148,316	33.8	252,971	83.4	17.9	1.8	4.3	61.8	86.2	17.6	10.7	9.1
Summit	217,788	33.3	362,645	85.7	25.1	3.3	5.6	58.4	85.9	21.8	12.3	9.6
Trumbull	89,020	33.0	153,044	82.5	14.5	1.8	5.7	64.1	87.1	16.6	12.1	9.9
Tuscarawas	35,653	34.8	60,653	80.3	12.2	0.9	4.9	62.3	84.5	11.6	10.1	9.2
Union	14,346	41.0	26,534	86.0	15.9	1.0	3.1	51.8	83.6	26.0	6.7	5.6
Van Wert	11,587	34.9	19,453	86.6	12.0	0.7	2.8	64.5	84.7	13.0	7.0	6.2
Vinton	4,892	37.8	8,223	70.7	6.0	0.3	1.9	62.7	79.1	7.6	16.8	17.1
Warren	55,966	42.1	103,306	86.2	28.4	2.3	4.3	48.9	86.0	34.9	5.3	4.7
Washington	25,137	33.3	42,770	84.5	15.0	0.6	2.5	64.3	84.2	13.4	12.2	11.2
Wayne	40,445	37.2	69,953	80.0	17.2	1.7	9.0	60.1	79.5	16.6	9.1	8.0
Williams	15,105	35.8	25,690	83.1	10.7	1.0	3.6	59.2	83.4	13.6	8.3	6.7
Wood	45,172	33.9	71,551	88.6	26.2	2.4	5.8	53.4	84.6	22.7	8.0	6.8
Wyandot	8,882	35.6	15,097	82.5	9.8	0.8	3.1	64.6	83.6	11.1	6.6	6.0

See footnotes at end of table.

[Includes United States, states, and 3,141 counties/county equivalents defined as of February 22, 2005. For more information on these areas, see Appendix C, Geographic Information]

County	Households, 2000 Total	Households, 2000 With individuals under 18 years (percent of total)	Educational attainment,[1] 2000 Total persons	High school graduate or higher (percent)	Bachelor's degree or higher (percent)	Foreign-born population, 2000 (percent)	Persons 5 years and over Speaking language other than English at home, 2000 (percent)	Residing in same house in 1995 and 2000 (percent)	Workers who drove alone to work,[2] 2000 (percent)	House-holds with income of $75,000 or more in 1999 (percent)	Persons in poverty (percent) 2004	Persons in poverty (percent) 2000
OKLAHOMA	1,342,293	35.7	2,203,173	80.6	20.3	3.8	7.4	51.3	80.0	13.9	14.0	13.8
Adair	7,471	42.6	12,764	66.7	9.8	1.4	11.7	60.2	71.2	5.3	18.7	20.9
Alfalfa	2,199	28.4	4,543	81.4	14.9	0.7	4.2	63.3	79.0	7.8	13.5	15.8
Atoka	4,964	35.3	9,377	69.4	10.1	0.3	2.9	58.2	76.5	6.9	18.7	22.8
Beaver	2,245	35.8	3,898	81.2	17.6	5.5	10.0	64.0	80.8	12.9	10.2	10.0
Beckham	7,356	35.0	12,968	75.9	15.5	1.6	6.6	49.6	79.4	9.4	14.5	17.7
Blaine	4,159	34.0	8,118	75.5	14.0	3.5	9.3	55.8	80.7	8.2	17.4	18.6
Bryan	14,422	34.3	23,175	74.9	17.9	1.4	3.5	52.0	80.1	8.3	16.6	17.8
Caddo	10,957	38.5	19,020	75.9	14.2	2.2	7.0	58.0	77.6	7.0	18.3	20.2
Canadian	31,484	42.8	56,207	87.3	20.9	3.2	6.4	53.1	85.6	20.2	8.3	7.8
Carter	17,992	36.3	30,195	77.0	15.1	1.3	4.2	55.3	81.4	10.2	14.7	15.5
Cherokee	16,175	36.4	25,237	76.7	22.1	2.6	7.9	51.4	73.2	8.3	18.3	20.8
Choctaw	6,220	34.6	10,210	69.0	9.9	0.5	3.3	59.7	77.9	4.7	21.1	24.2
Cimarron	1,257	33.5	2,077	76.6	17.7	10.3	16.0	63.8	74.3	9.9	13.2	15.0
Cleveland	79,186	36.2	126,569	88.1	28.0	4.4	7.6	45.9	84.0	19.8	9.3	9.2
Coal	2,373	34.7	3,964	68.6	12.4	1.6	6.0	62.6	71.9	4.8	18.6	21.7
Comanche	39,808	42.8	67,220	85.2	19.1	5.4	11.3	42.6	73.3	12.0	15.4	15.6
Cotton	2,614	34.7	4,436	77.0	14.0	1.5	4.9	60.1	81.3	10.6	13.8	15.8
Craig	5,620	34.4	10,197	76.9	10.5	0.5	2.3	56.1	77.3	8.7	15.2	14.4
Creek	25,289	38.8	43,523	77.6	11.7	0.7	3.4	58.3	80.9	12.0	13.0	12.0
Custer	10,136	33.2	15,156	81.2	22.8	3.4	9.0	50.0	80.5	10.2	15.6	15.4
Delaware	14,838	32.7	25,549	75.4	13.3	1.3	6.4	52.0	75.6	9.1	15.9	17.2
Dewey	1,962	29.2	3,310	79.8	16.6	1.3	3.5	66.2	78.3	9.6	11.4	14.4
Ellis	1,769	27.1	2,918	81.2	19.2	0.8	3.6	67.6	76.1	10.0	11.0	13.9
Garfield	23,175	34.1	38,067	82.2	19.6	2.7	5.7	51.7	81.6	11.5	13.4	13.4
Garvin	10,865	34.0	18,263	73.0	12.0	1.6	3.9	56.4	78.7	8.0	15.0	15.5
Grady	17,341	38.2	29,172	79.5	14.4	1.1	3.3	56.6	80.8	11.7	12.5	13.2
Grant	2,089	32.3	3,500	85.7	16.2	0.9	3.0	62.3	74.6	9.0	12.3	14.3
Greer	2,237	29.1	4,302	76.7	12.6	1.5	7.9	55.5	84.9	7.9	20.5	23.6
Harmon	1,266	33.3	2,192	63.2	12.1	3.0	18.7	62.1	78.3	6.3	20.8	25.9
Harper	1,509	29.8	2,507	82.1	19.2	3.5	5.4	63.4	78.1	12.1	9.2	10.1
Haskell	4,624	35.4	7,762	66.9	10.3	0.8	2.5	56.6	72.4	6.4	17.0	19.8
Hughes	5,319	32.8	9,762	70.8	9.7	1.1	6.4	57.4	77.4	6.8	19.7	22.0
Jackson	10,590	41.3	17,270	79.1	18.5	4.7	14.0	44.2	81.8	10.8	14.7	15.0
Jefferson	2,716	32.1	4,710	69.3	10.6	3.6	7.3	58.5	74.5	5.4	18.0	19.3
Johnston	4,057	35.9	6,759	69.1	13.3	0.8	3.4	56.5	74.8	7.5	16.1	19.9
Kay	19,157	34.6	31,106	80.9	18.3	2.3	4.8	55.7	81.0	11.9	15.5	14.4
Kingfisher	5,247	38.3	8,984	81.2	16.1	4.1	7.8	60.9	81.5	16.0	9.6	10.5
Kiowa	4,208	31.1	6,963	77.4	14.8	1.0	6.9	60.1	79.0	8.1	17.1	19.6
Latimer	3,951	36.6	6,716	73.8	12.0	1.3	3.9	57.1	75.6	6.9	17.2	20.2
Le Flore	17,861	38.2	30,966	70.4	11.3	2.5	5.7	55.4	77.3	7.7	18.0	19.0
Lincoln	12,178	37.8	20,746	77.5	11.1	0.8	3.0	58.0	77.0	9.6	13.4	13.6
Logan	12,389	36.9	21,195	81.5	19.1	1.5	4.4	54.7	78.0	15.4	12.9	13.0
Love	3,442	35.3	5,931	73.6	10.8	3.2	7.1	60.9	77.9	10.3	12.9	14.1
McClain	10,331	39.1	18,069	79.3	15.7	2.6	5.2	54.5	80.6	16.0	9.8	11.1
McCurtain	13,216	38.9	21,875	69.2	10.8	1.8	6.0	61.6	77.6	8.8	20.5	23.7
McIntosh	8,085	29.4	13,787	71.6	13.1	0.5	4.5	58.1	74.7	9.9	17.1	19.0
Major	3,046	32.9	5,191	78.6	14.4	2.1	5.7	67.6	76.9	8.9	10.1	11.8
Marshall	5,371	31.3	9,078	71.0	11.4	5.0	8.4	55.6	76.3	7.8	14.2	16.6
Mayes	14,823	36.2	24,849	76.1	12.1	1.0	5.8	54.8	79.7	10.1	14.8	14.6
Murray	5,003	34.3	8,566	74.3	14.9	2.8	5.4	57.5	79.1	8.7	13.8	15.1
Muskogee	26,458	36.0	44,890	75.1	15.4	1.8	4.7	53.9	78.2	9.8	17.2	16.9
Noble	4,504	35.2	7,635	81.5	15.8	1.1	3.1	58.1	83.3	12.6	12.5	12.1
Nowata	4,147	35.2	7,092	76.2	9.5	0.2	2.3	59.3	74.1	7.6	13.6	14.5
Okfuskee	4,270	34.1	7,904	69.4	9.2	1.7	8.0	59.4	70.7	6.4	19.9	23.0
Oklahoma	266,834	34.2	420,823	82.5	25.4	7.2	11.6	47.7	80.8	15.8	15.2	13.4
Okmulgee	15,300	36.7	25,225	74.7	11.4	0.7	4.0	55.6	76.8	9.1	17.8	18.7
Osage	16,617	37.1	29,417	80.2	14.6	1.0	3.4	61.1	79.9	13.6	12.6	12.7
Ottawa	12,984	34.5	21,510	75.7	12.2	1.7	4.3	53.2	78.2	6.5	15.1	17.1
Pawnee	6,383	36.0	10,997	78.8	12.1	0.6	2.7	57.4	77.3	10.4	13.4	13.1
Payne	26,680	27.8	37,237	86.7	34.2	4.6	7.1	39.2	75.6	13.0	16.3	15.3
Pittsburg	17,157	33.0	30,162	76.2	12.9	1.1	3.6	55.4	81.1	8.8	15.6	17.0
Pontotoc	13,978	34.0	22,031	78.2	21.8	1.2	4.2	52.1	81.0	8.7	16.6	17.7
Pottawatomie	24,540	36.8	41,142	79.3	15.5	1.1	4.1	54.4	80.9	11.0	15.4	16.3
Pushmataha	4,739	34.2	7,861	69.0	12.4	0.5	4.1	60.7	74.0	6.2	19.1	23.9
Roger Mills	1,428	32.2	2,396	79.3	15.8	0.7	3.1	65.9	74.2	11.1	9.6	14.5
Rogers	25,724	41.6	45,152	83.4	16.9	1.3	3.1	54.6	82.8	19.3	9.1	8.3
Seminole	9,575	36.1	15,988	73.2	12.1	1.0	5.8	58.2	77.2	7.2	20.5	21.2
Sequoyah	14,761	38.9	24,980	70.2	10.9	0.7	4.6	55.7	78.6	7.6	17.6	18.2
Stephens	17,463	33.7	29,111	77.0	16.6	1.8	4.6	60.0	82.1	11.1	13.5	14.1
Texas	7,153	41.6	11,776	71.9	17.7	16.9	26.3	48.1	74.6	12.7	11.1	11.1

See footnotes at end of table.

[Includes United States, states, and 3,141 counties/county equivalents defined as of February 22, 2005. For more information on these areas, see Appendix C, Geographic Information]

County	Households, 2000 Total	Households, 2000 With individuals under 18 years (percent of total)	Educational attainment,[1] 2000 Total persons	Educational attainment,[1] 2000 High school graduate or higher (percent)	Educational attainment,[1] 2000 Bachelor's degree or higher (percent)	Foreign-born population, 2000 (percent)	Persons 5 years and over Speaking language other than English at home, 2000 (percent)	Persons 5 years and over Residing in same house in 1995 and 2000 (percent)	Workers who drove alone to work,[2] 2000 (percent)	Households with income of $75,000 or more in 1999 (percent)	Persons in poverty (percent) 2004	Persons in poverty (percent) 2000
OKLAHOMA—Con.												
Tillman	3,594	34.4	6,141	67.4	12.5	4.3	13.9	60.9	80.8	8.4	18.7	20.4
Tulsa	226,892	35.0	359,386	85.1	26.9	5.4	8.4	46.5	80.8	18.9	12.5	11.0
Wagoner	21,010	41.0	36,895	81.3	15.4	1.8	4.0	56.4	83.1	17.6	10.2	10.3
Washington	20,179	32.9	32,905	85.2	25.8	2.0	4.9	54.0	78.8	18.1	11.8	10.8
Washita	4,506	36.2	7,613	79.7	15.1	1.6	5.0	59.4	78.2	9.6	13.7	15.5
Woods	3,684	25.8	5,993	82.7	23.7	0.9	3.2	52.5	80.9	9.3	13.5	15.1
Woodward	7,141	36.0	11,992	79.9	15.2	2.5	4.8	55.0	80.7	12.0	11.6	12.8
OREGON	1,333,723	33.4	2,250,998	85.1	25.1	8.5	12.1	46.8	73.2	19.7	12.9	10.6
Baker	6,883	30.1	11,712	80.3	16.4	1.8	4.0	53.9	67.7	8.6	15.2	14.4
Benton	30,145	29.9	45,758	93.1	47.4	7.6	10.0	42.3	70.7	23.3	12.5	9.3
Clackamas	128,201	36.8	223,211	88.9	28.4	7.1	9.6	51.8	78.2	30.9	9.0	6.7
Clatsop	14,703	30.8	24,069	85.6	19.1	4.2	7.1	47.9	74.1	14.1	13.0	11.9
Columbia	16,375	37.3	28,725	85.6	14.0	1.8	3.9	53.4	78.7	19.5	9.5	8.5
Coos	26,213	28.9	44,667	81.6	15.0	2.7	4.5	53.6	77.1	10.7	16.0	14.9
Crook	7,354	35.2	12,692	80.5	12.6	3.3	6.3	46.1	70.9	10.6	12.5	12.0
Curry	9,543	23.0	16,168	81.7	16.4	3.7	5.4	52.3	74.4	9.6	13.0	12.9
Deschutes	45,595	34.3	77,981	88.4	25.0	2.8	5.4	40.6	75.2	19.9	10.7	9.6
Douglas	39,821	32.4	68,783	81.0	13.3	2.1	3.9	52.2	78.2	11.2	15.0	12.9
Gilliam	819	30.0	1,368	89.3	13.4	1.7	3.2	56.3	73.3	11.8	9.7	10.5
Grant	3,246	32.8	5,428	84.5	15.7	1.4	2.8	56.1	74.0	10.0	13.0	13.2
Harney	3,036	32.0	5,130	81.2	11.9	2.1	6.0	46.2	68.3	12.7	14.1	14.3
Hood River	7,248	38.3	12,972	78.2	23.1	16.4	24.7	52.0	72.2	14.4	13.0	12.3
Jackson	71,532	33.0	121,155	85.0	22.3	4.9	7.7	46.5	77.4	16.4	14.0	12.8
Jefferson	6,727	39.6	11,972	76.5	13.7	9.9	19.0	45.5	71.3	12.2	15.2	13.9
Josephine	31,000	29.8	53,427	81.8	14.1	3.1	4.8	51.1	77.6	11.5	16.1	15.8
Klamath	25,205	33.4	41,833	81.5	15.9	4.8	8.1	48.5	78.2	11.2	16.6	14.3
Lake	3,084	31.4	5,199	79.6	15.5	3.4	4.8	55.1	68.9	9.2	15.9	15.2
Lane	130,453	31.0	210,601	87.5	25.5	4.9	7.9	46.8	71.6	15.9	14.9	12.0
Lincoln	19,296	27.2	32,000	84.9	20.8	4.2	5.7	46.8	72.5	12.4	15.3	13.9
Linn	39,541	35.1	67,605	81.9	13.4	3.5	5.9	51.0	79.3	14.3	13.7	11.1
Malheur	10,221	39.3	19,587	71.0	11.1	8.2	21.1	51.0	72.8	10.0	19.5	19.1
Marion	101,641	37.6	177,683	79.3	19.8	12.6	19.5	44.9	72.8	17.1	15.1	12.5
Morrow	3,776	42.5	6,627	74.1	11.0	14.5	23.3	46.5	72.9	12.6	13.7	10.6
Multnomah	272,098	29.1	446,322	85.6	30.7	12.7	16.6	44.9	65.6	20.5	14.2	10.5
Polk	23,058	34.6	39,357	85.5	25.3	6.5	10.0	47.7	74.5	19.3	11.3	9.6
Sherman	797	31.6	1,316	84.3	19.0	2.5	8.0	62.6	71.6	12.0	14.4	13.6
Tillamook	10,200	27.0	17,145	84.1	17.6	4.2	6.3	53.7	70.8	11.2	12.9	11.8
Umatilla	25,195	38.4	44,515	77.8	16.0	8.4	16.2	50.9	79.3	13.8	14.9	13.6
Union	9,740	32.5	15,562	85.6	21.8	2.7	4.5	50.1	74.0	13.1	13.8	12.6
Wallowa	3,029	30.4	5,099	87.5	20.3	0.8	2.5	57.2	70.6	11.6	12.6	12.2
Wasco	9,401	33.1	16,023	82.1	15.7	6.2	10.5	50.2	75.6	13.4	14.1	12.4
Washington	169,162	37.7	285,518	88.9	34.5	14.2	18.6	41.2	75.1	29.7	9.3	6.6
Wheeler	653	24.3	1,143	79.4	14.3	2.1	4.2	56.4	54.6	8.3	13.3	10.8
Yamhill	28,732	40.4	52,645	82.8	20.6	7.6	11.2	47.6	75.3	19.2	11.2	9.2
PENNSYLVANIA	4,777,003	32.6	8,266,284	81.9	22.4	4.1	8.4	63.5	76.5	19.9	11.2	9.5
Adams	33,652	36.2	60,173	79.7	16.7	3.4	5.5	60.4	80.9	16.7	7.7	6.2
Allegheny	537,150	28.5	891,171	86.3	28.3	3.8	6.6	64.6	72.1	19.6	11.4	9.1
Armstrong	29,005	31.6	50,638	80.0	10.4	0.7	2.5	70.9	82.0	9.5	12.3	10.8
Beaver	72,576	31.1	126,933	83.6	15.8	1.7	4.3	68.5	83.6	14.9	11.4	9.1
Bedford	19,768	33.1	34,582	78.3	10.2	0.6	2.5	70.6	79.1	9.4	10.8	9.9
Berks	141,570	34.3	248,864	78.0	18.5	4.3	12.7	61.1	81.1	21.8	10.5	8.1
Blair	51,518	31.9	88,366	83.8	13.9	1.0	3.1	66.7	82.2	10.8	13.4	11.6
Bradford	24,453	34.4	42,428	81.7	14.8	1.0	2.8	66.4	77.5	12.4	11.8	11.0
Bucks	218,725	37.7	402,575	88.6	31.2	5.9	8.7	63.2	83.0	36.7	5.9	4.5
Butler	65,862	34.7	116,072	86.8	23.5	1.4	3.1	63.3	84.9	21.2	8.3	7.0
Cambria	60,531	29.2	106,780	80.0	13.7	1.3	4.1	71.7	81.7	9.7	12.4	11.8
Cameron	2,465	30.2	4,150	79.8	12.1	0.6	2.2	70.2	77.4	8.1	10.5	9.6
Carbon	23,701	31.2	41,690	79.0	11.0	1.8	5.7	69.2	81.8	11.3	10.0	8.5
Centre	49,323	27.0	74,785	88.2	36.3	5.8	8.6	46.9	66.7	16.9	12.1	9.7
Chester	157,905	37.1	285,816	89.3	42.5	5.5	8.8	58.6	80.7	42.6	5.5	4.5
Clarion	16,052	30.5	26,334	81.8	15.3	1.0	2.6	63.0	79.0	9.6	12.7	12.5
Clearfield	32,785	32.1	58,138	79.1	11.1	0.7	2.5	70.1	81.9	9.5	13.6	11.9
Clinton	14,773	30.3	24,701	80.4	13.4	0.9	4.7	63.7	77.2	9.7	13.0	11.8
Columbia	24,915	29.8	41,658	80.6	15.8	1.4	3.2	62.6	79.4	12.2	11.5	10.6
Crawford	34,678	32.9	59,684	81.6	14.7	1.1	5.4	62.9	77.8	12.3	13.2	11.9
Cumberland	83,015	31.3	144,215	86.1	27.9	3.2	5.7	57.3	82.1	24.0	6.7	5.1
Dauphin	102,670	32.5	171,783	83.4	23.5	4.1	8.5	59.0	78.5	20.1	10.3	8.2
Delaware	206,320	34.4	365,174	86.5	30.0	6.7	9.3	64.4	75.4	29.4	9.9	7.5
Elk	14,124	33.0	24,337	82.7	12.3	1.1	3.6	74.4	84.2	12.8	8.8	7.1
Erie	106,507	34.3	180,106	84.6	20.9	2.7	5.9	60.2	79.9	14.6	13.7	11.1

See footnotes at end of table.

County and City Data Book: 2007

U.S. Census Bureau

[Includes United States, states, and 3,141 counties/county equivalents defined as of February 22, 2005. For more information on these areas, see Appendix C, Geographic Information]

County	Households, 2000		Educational attainment,[1] 2000			Foreign-born population, 2000 (percent)	Persons 5 years and over		Workers who drove alone to work,[2] 2000 (percent)	House-holds with income of $75,000 or more in 1999 (percent)	Persons in poverty (percent)	
	Total	With individuals under 18 years (percent of total)	Total persons	High school graduate or higher (percent)	Bachelor's degree or higher (percent)		Speaking language other than English at home, 2000 (percent)	Residing in same house in 1995 and 2000 (percent)			2004	2000
PENNSYLVANIA—Con.												
Fayette	59,969	31.6	103,227	76.0	11.5	0.6	3.1	70.9	83.1	9.7	16.9	15.1
Forest	2,000	25.5	3,540	79.4	8.9	0.6	3.1	68.6	74.0	6.6	14.8	13.8
Franklin	50,633	33.2	87,959	78.9	14.8	2.0	4.5	62.8	81.7	15.8	8.2	7.1
Fulton	5,660	34.4	9,687	73.2	9.3	0.7	1.7	70.5	78.4	10.3	9.7	8.9
Greene	15,060	33.6	27,758	75.7	12.2	0.7	3.7	67.0	81.5	10.8	15.7	15.1
Huntingdon	16,759	32.5	31,152	74.6	11.9	0.7	3.2	68.2	73.6	10.3	12.4	11.4
Indiana	34,123	29.8	55,995	81.0	17.0	1.6	4.8	64.3	77.2	10.6	14.6	13.8
Jefferson	18,375	32.3	31,583	81.0	11.7	0.6	3.2	69.5	81.3	9.5	12.1	11.3
Juniata	8,584	35.1	15,225	74.5	8.8	1.0	6.2	67.9	71.6	10.3	8.8	7.9
Lackawanna	86,218	29.1	148,116	82.0	19.6	2.3	5.6	69.2	80.5	15.0	11.2	9.8
Lancaster	172,560	35.9	302,503	77.4	20.5	3.2	13.1	60.2	78.2	20.7	8.8	6.8
Lawrence	37,091	31.4	64,767	81.6	15.1	1.3	5.0	67.9	84.4	12.3	13.1	11.5
Lebanon	46,551	32.8	82,008	78.6	15.4	2.4	8.0	62.6	81.0	17.1	9.0	7.6
Lehigh	121,906	32.9	212,665	81.1	23.3	6.2	15.3	58.9	81.7	22.6	9.9	8.0
Luzerne	130,687	28.6	226,374	81.1	16.4	1.9	5.1	69.1	81.9	13.6	11.5	9.4
Lycoming	47,003	32.3	80,500	80.6	15.1	1.2	3.3	61.0	80.3	12.1	12.0	10.3
McKean	18,024	32.7	31,529	82.2	14.0	1.4	3.5	64.1	79.0	10.2	13.6	11.9
Mercer	46,712	31.9	81,499	82.9	17.3	1.6	4.8	65.3	83.2	12.4	13.0	11.5
Mifflin	18,413	32.6	31,722	77.2	10.9	0.8	7.3	68.5	77.1	9.3	12.4	11.4
Monroe	49,454	38.8	89,793	83.8	20.5	5.8	10.0	57.2	77.5	23.3	9.3	7.7
Montgomery	286,098	34.0	515,871	88.5	38.7	7.0	9.6	61.2	80.5	38.4	5.8	4.4
Montour	7,085	31.9	12,573	82.3	22.1	2.2	6.3	65.2	82.7	15.9	9.5	8.6
Northampton	101,541	33.6	180,018	80.7	21.2	4.6	11.0	61.7	82.3	22.8	8.2	6.4
Northumberland	38,835	29.3	67,112	77.8	11.1	1.1	4.4	67.9	79.9	9.0	10.6	10.7
Perry	16,695	35.8	29,250	79.9	11.3	0.9	3.6	67.3	77.8	16.1	8.2	7.3
Philadelphia	590,071	33.1	966,197	71.2	17.9	9.0	17.7	61.9	49.2	13.5	21.6	18.5
Pike	17,433	36.7	31,525	86.8	19.0	5.0	8.6	60.4	78.7	20.4	7.4	7.2
Potter	7,005	34.0	12,144	80.6	12.3	1.1	3.6	64.9	73.4	9.8	11.9	11.2
Schuylkill	60,530	29.2	108,010	77.2	10.7	1.0	4.5	69.5	79.7	10.6	10.8	9.4
Snyder	13,654	34.2	24,217	73.2	12.5	0.9	8.0	67.8	75.9	11.8	8.8	9.3
Somerset	31,222	31.5	55,956	77.5	10.8	0.7	3.8	70.6	79.2	7.8	12.6	11.9
Sullivan	2,660	26.6	4,659	78.0	12.8	0.8	2.9	70.1	70.7	11.7	11.3	12.0
Susquehanna	16,529	34.3	28,581	82.5	13.2	1.3	3.0	70.0	78.3	11.2	11.5	10.8
Tioga	15,925	33.0	27,176	80.5	14.2	1.1	3.0	62.5	75.0	10.0	12.3	11.7
Union	13,178	32.7	27,521	73.1	18.0	3.7	10.4	57.3	76.9	17.0	10.0	10.2
Venango	22,747	32.8	39,366	81.0	13.1	0.6	3.0	67.2	80.4	10.4	14.0	12.3
Warren	17,696	32.1	30,535	84.8	14.2	0.9	3.3	67.7	78.4	11.8	11.2	9.7
Washington	81,130	30.8	142,118	82.6	18.8	1.2	3.6	68.9	82.5	17.2	10.6	9.0
Wayne	18,350	32.8	33,326	80.7	14.6	3.0	5.5	67.0	80.1	11.5	11.0	10.8
Westmoreland	149,813	30.3	263,593	85.6	20.2	1.4	3.7	70.0	84.7	16.4	9.6	8.4
Wyoming	10,762	35.7	18,741	83.7	15.4	1.2	2.7	65.5	81.3	14.5	10.3	9.5
York	148,219	34.9	259,040	80.7	18.4	2.2	5.3	60.2	84.3	19.5	8.1	6.2
RHODE ISLAND	408,424	32.9	694,573	78.0	25.6	11.4	20.0	58.1	80.1	22.2	11.6	10.2
Bristol	19,033	33.7	34,218	80.7	34.3	10.0	15.4	63.5	82.0	31.7	7.2	6.2
Kent	67,320	32.1	116,628	83.9	24.8	4.9	8.5	63.6	86.6	24.4	7.1	6.5
Newport	35,228	30.4	59,084	87.7	38.3	4.9	8.6	55.4	80.1	27.8	7.7	6.7
Providence	239,936	33.2	403,779	72.5	21.3	15.6	27.4	56.6	77.4	18.3	14.8	13.0
Washington	46,907	33.9	80,864	88.6	35.5	4.2	7.9	57.5	82.8	30.8	6.5	5.9
SOUTH CAROLINA	1,533,854	36.5	2,596,010	76.3	20.4	2.9	5.2	55.9	79.4	16.6	15.0	12.8
Abbeville	10,131	36.5	17,068	70.1	12.8	1.0	3.8	64.0	79.9	9.4	15.1	12.1
Aiken	55,587	37.0	92,922	77.7	19.9	2.3	4.3	59.7	81.6	18.2	14.5	12.1
Allendale	3,915	38.5	7,094	60.0	9.3	1.4	2.7	72.2	72.1	6.9	32.1	28.8
Anderson	65,649	35.3	111,037	73.4	15.9	1.5	3.3	58.8	83.3	14.9	13.6	10.5
Bamberg	6,123	37.3	10,213	64.7	15.4	0.9	2.0	65.6	71.7	8.2	23.1	21.2
Barnwell	9,021	39.5	14,770	67.5	11.6	0.6	2.1	67.8	77.8	11.7	19.2	17.5
Beaufort	45,532	33.4	78,502	87.8	33.2	6.3	9.9	43.9	71.2	26.4	11.4	10.3
Berkeley	49,922	43.8	86,015	80.2	14.4	3.1	5.9	52.9	78.6	15.7	12.7	11.3
Calhoun	5,917	35.4	10,266	72.8	14.2	1.0	2.4	70.8	78.1	13.3	15.8	15.1
Charleston	123,326	32.7	199,361	81.5	30.7	3.6	6.4	49.6	76.6	19.8	15.0	13.7
Cherokee	20,495	37.7	34,283	66.7	11.8	1.3	3.0	61.2	79.0	11.5	16.4	12.9
Chester	12,880	38.8	22,043	67.1	9.6	0.8	2.7	66.0	79.0	10.1	16.5	14.2
Chesterfield	16,557	38.4	27,769	65.2	9.7	1.6	3.4	65.2	80.0	9.1	19.3	16.4
Clarendon	11,812	37.7	20,698	65.3	11.4	1.3	3.4	64.4	77.2	9.9	23.2	20.6
Colleton	14,470	39.1	24,716	69.6	11.5	1.2	2.9	64.2	72.0	9.1	20.0	19.3
Darlington	25,793	38.0	43,512	69.3	13.5	0.9	3.0	64.2	80.0	12.5	19.9	17.9
Dillon	11,199	41.8	18,867	60.7	9.2	1.0	3.4	64.6	76.0	8.1	22.2	21.9
Dorchester	34,709	44.0	61,334	82.2	21.4	2.8	5.0	52.4	82.0	19.7	11.8	10.1
Edgefield	8,270	39.4	16,227	71.4	12.5	1.3	4.4	62.6	80.6	13.4	17.2	15.7
Fairfield	8,774	38.8	15,244	67.0	11.7	0.5	2.4	70.5	77.2	12.1	17.8	15.8

See footnotes at end of table.

Table B-4. Counties — **Population Characteristics**—Con.

[Includes United States, states, and 3,141 counties/county equivalents defined as of February 22, 2005. For more information on these areas, see Appendix C, Geographic Information]

County	Households, 2000		Educational attainment,[1] 2000			Foreign-born population, 2000 (percent)	Persons 5 years and over		Workers who drove alone to work,[2] 2000 (percent)	Households with income of $75,000 or more in 1999 (percent)	Persons in poverty (percent)	
	Total	With individuals under 18 years (percent of total)	Total persons	High school graduate or higher (percent)	Bachelor's degree or higher (percent)		Speaking language other than English at home, 2000 (percent)	Residing in same house in 1995 and 2000 (percent)			2004	2000
SOUTH CAROLINA—Con.												
Florence.	47,147	38.7	80,904	73.1	18.7	1.8	4.1	59.6	80.6	14.9	17.8	15.9
Georgetown	21,659	35.3	37,340	75.2	20.0	2.2	3.5	62.0	76.3	16.8	16.2	14.8
Greenville	149,556	35.1	250,258	79.5	26.2	4.9	7.1	51.5	81.6	21.4	13.0	9.8
Greenwood	25,729	36.2	42,412	73.1	18.9	2.8	4.8	54.6	81.5	13.4	15.1	12.5
Hampton	7,444	41.0	13,668	66.9	10.1	0.7	2.6	68.8	73.2	9.6	21.6	20.0
Horry	81,800	29.5	136,551	81.1	18.7	4.0	6.3	49.3	79.0	14.2	13.9	12.6
Jasper	7,042	41.7	13,112	65.2	8.7	5.4	7.7	60.5	68.4	11.0	21.6	22.2
Kershaw	20,188	38.4	34,863	75.4	16.3	1.7	3.3	60.5	79.6	15.1	13.3	10.9
Lancaster	23,178	38.2	40,520	69.8	10.2	1.3	3.5	62.7	78.9	11.9	14.9	12.9
Laurens	26,290	37.5	45,470	67.7	11.7	1.6	3.6	61.4	79.9	10.8	16.3	13.2
Lee	6,886	40.1	12,918	61.4	9.2	2.1	5.4	67.6	71.3	10.1	22.7	22.7
Lexington	83,240	38.4	142,083	83.0	24.6	2.9	5.3	55.2	83.1	22.2	11.3	9.0
McCormick	3,558	29.8	7,192	66.1	16.0	0.6	3.2	59.1	73.3	11.7	18.0	16.5
Marion	13,301	39.8	22,224	68.0	10.2	1.4	3.9	63.6	74.2	8.6	22.5	21.5
Marlboro	10,478	39.3	18,482	60.9	8.3	0.6	1.8	67.6	76.4	7.9	22.0	20.0
Newberry	14,026	34.6	23,881	69.1	14.8	3.5	5.4	63.9	80.3	12.4	16.3	13.5
Oconee	27,283	31.6	45,896	73.9	18.2	2.4	3.8	59.4	80.7	14.6	12.7	10.1
Orangeburg	34,118	38.1	57,037	71.5	16.3	1.0	3.0	65.0	77.6	10.9	21.6	19.3
Pickens	41,306	34.1	66,787	73.7	19.1	2.9	4.8	52.6	80.7	13.6	13.7	10.2
Richland	120,101	35.3	198,703	85.2	32.5	3.9	7.3	49.0	76.7	20.2	15.1	11.9
Saluda	7,127	36.7	12,654	69.3	11.9	5.9	8.0	67.7	76.4	12.5	15.7	15.2
Spartanburg	97,735	36.4	167,802	73.1	18.2	3.7	6.3	56.3	82.2	16.1	13.5	11.0
Sumter	37,728	41.7	64,144	74.3	15.8	2.1	4.6	55.0	80.4	12.0	17.7	15.2
Union	12,087	34.6	20,222	66.9	9.8	0.6	2.0	68.3	79.6	9.2	16.0	12.8
Williamsburg	13,714	41.3	23,189	65.5	11.5	0.5	2.6	74.9	71.4	8.1	25.8	24.0
York	61,051	39.5	105,757	77.2	20.9	2.4	4.6	52.3	82.1	21.6	12.0	9.1
SOUTH DAKOTA	290,245	34.8	474,359	84.6	21.5	1.8	6.5	55.7	77.3	12.9	12.9	11.4
Aurora	1,165	30.9	2,020	79.5	12.7	1.5	3.5	66.9	67.5	6.5	11.3	12.7
Beadle	7,210	29.6	11,368	83.0	18.3	1.2	5.5	61.0	77.5	9.6	12.3	10.4
Bennett	1,123	45.5	1,972	71.3	12.7	0.4	13.7	61.1	60.8	6.9	29.3	30.6
Bon Homme	2,635	29.7	5,026	79.0	15.3	0.7	8.4	61.7	68.6	6.5	13.7	11.2
Brookings.	10,665	29.4	14,819	90.2	32.2	2.3	5.2	45.5	76.4	13.6	12.9	9.6
Brown	14,638	31.0	22,959	85.8	23.6	0.6	5.3	55.3	82.2	11.4	10.5	8.6
Brule	1,998	32.4	3,371	81.1	20.6	0.4	7.4	63.0	71.5	8.7	13.2	11.8
Buffalo	526	59.9	948	63.9	5.4	0.4	12.6	68.6	67.8	1.5	31.6	35.3
Butte	3,516	37.1	5,859	79.8	12.2	1.2	3.0	54.9	70.7	8.1	13.2	13.9
Campbell	725	30.9	1,251	79.2	14.8	0.4	8.6	80.0	56.2	7.6	11.0	11.7
Charles Mix	3,343	38.1	5,676	74.7	14.1	0.8	11.0	67.0	68.4	5.5	22.4	20.4
Clark.	1,598	30.3	2,781	76.6	11.4	0.8	10.1	68.9	60.8	6.9	12.9	12.1
Clay	4,878	28.7	6,719	89.5	38.7	2.6	5.1	39.4	69.9	10.7	19.8	16.0
Codington	10,357	34.8	16,377	85.3	18.8	1.2	3.8	56.4	82.7	11.8	10.3	8.1
Corson.	1,271	47.9	2,238	76.0	11.3	0.3	15.3	65.7	55.9	4.4	32.4	31.5
Custer	2,970	29.1	5,099	88.9	24.4	1.1	3.0	55.7	72.1	11.2	10.2	11.0
Davison	7,585	32.6	11,719	83.9	20.2	1.0	3.1	52.5	78.0	12.4	11.6	10.4
Day	2,586	29.2	4,354	80.0	15.4	0.9	3.9	69.3	69.8	7.5	13.6	14.3
Deuel	1,843	30.1	3,094	81.9	13.3	0.7	3.9	68.5	71.6	7.2	9.1	9.9
Dewey	1,863	52.2	3,107	77.4	12.2	0.6	16.2	54.8	55.1	5.0	25.7	27.3
Douglas	1,321	33.0	2,332	68.8	14.5	0.4	6.9	73.1	60.5	6.8	10.9	11.0
Edmunds	1,681	32.5	2,975	73.6	15.5	1.0	13.6	68.8	64.9	9.9	9.8	10.6
Fall River	3,127	25.9	5,313	82.5	19.2	0.6	4.4	60.3	71.7	10.0	13.2	14.4
Faulk.	1,014	29.9	1,803	73.7	13.1	2.0	16.3	73.9	57.3	8.6	10.0	10.8
Grant.	3,116	34.3	5,303	79.5	14.8	1.1	3.0	67.0	74.8	10.2	9.8	8.6
Gregory	2,022	28.0	3,367	77.7	12.0	0.7	2.1	71.2	65.5	6.4	16.0	17.3
Haakon	870	33.7	1,477	86.3	15.4	1.0	3.2	67.0	64.2	10.9	9.9	11.1
Hamlin.	2,048	34.7	3,507	79.9	12.8	0.8	5.7	65.5	71.9	9.5	9.7	10.4
Hand.	1,543	28.8	2,627	80.1	15.6	1.0	5.8	73.1	64.2	11.2	9.7	10.3
Hanson	1,115	35.2	1,962	75.1	14.0	0.5	11.8	72.8	70.2	10.0	8.3	10.0
Harding	525	35.8	850	87.8	17.8	0.5	1.8	69.5	44.2	6.7	11.5	13.7
Hughes	6,512	35.3	10,853	89.5	32.0	1.3	4.5	57.6	77.9	16.5	10.5	9.0
Hutchinson.	3,190	29.1	5,629	71.7	14.1	0.7	15.6	69.9	66.0	8.2	12.0	10.5
Hyde	679	31.5	1,147	80.5	16.0	0.3	9.0	69.7	60.5	12.8	10.9	12.7
Jackson	945	45.2	1,662	82.7	16.2	0.9	13.4	68.1	63.1	5.9	27.3	27.2
Jerauld	987	25.5	1,661	79.6	12.3	0.3	8.0	75.0	68.0	7.9	12.3	11.7
Jones	509	31.4	811	86.2	17.8	–	1.2	67.4	66.0	10.2	13.3	11.6
Kingsbury	2,406	29.2	4,015	82.3	16.2	0.6	2.7	65.9	68.0	8.9	9.0	8.7
Lake	4,372	31.0	6,917	85.7	21.1	0.9	4.8	58.1	76.1	9.4	10.9	9.3
Lawrence	8,881	30.4	13,746	87.5	24.0	1.2	4.3	48.6	77.7	10.8	12.6	10.6
Lincoln	8,782	42.3	15,093	89.4	25.5	1.1	3.3	53.1	83.8	22.4	4.8	4.1
Lyman	1,400	39.9	2,344	81.1	15.9	0.6	4.9	65.3	66.7	8.4	19.0	20.4
McCook	2,204	35.3	3,827	82.9	16.3	0.7	4.1	62.2	69.5	9.4	9.3	8.9
McPherson	1,227	24.2	2,128	58.8	10.7	0.8	32.7	73.2	54.7	5.6	13.4	12.2
Marshall.	1,844	31.5	3,111	75.6	16.2	0.7	8.8	73.3	69.1	7.0	10.3	11.6

See footnotes at end of table.

County and City Data Book: 2007

U.S. Census Bureau

[Includes United States, states, and 3,141 counties/county equivalents defined as of February 22, 2005. For more information on these areas, see Appendix C, Geographic Information]

County	Households, 2000 Total	Households, 2000 With individuals under 18 years (percent of total)	Educational attainment, 2000 Total persons	High school graduate or higher (percent)	Bachelor's degree or higher (percent)	Foreign-born population, 2000 (percent)	Persons 5 years and over Speaking language other than English at home, 2000 (percent)	Residing in same house in 1995 and 2000 (percent)	Workers who drove alone to work,[2] 2000 (percent)	Households with income of $75,000 or more in 1999 (percent)	Persons in poverty (percent) 2004	Persons in poverty (percent) 2000
SOUTH DAKOTA—Con.												
Meade	8,805	42.1	14,816	87.7	16.8	1.4	4.3	50.2	79.2	12.7	9.3	9.3
Mellette	694	45.0	1,199	78.1	16.6	0.4	15.8	67.2	54.1	7.6	28.6	30.2
Miner	1,212	29.2	1,982	79.6	13.5	0.4	4.7	71.1	67.7	6.8	11.4	10.8
Minnehaha	57,996	35.4	93,400	88.5	26.0	4.1	6.7	49.0	83.7	18.2	10.4	7.0
Moody	2,526	37.7	4,193	84.7	17.4	1.4	5.8	63.0	73.1	11.1	9.5	8.9
Pennington	34,641	35.8	55,535	87.8	25.0	2.1	5.1	47.7	82.9	14.9	14.0	11.6
Perkins	1,429	27.9	2,367	80.3	14.6	1.3	2.4	74.3	56.7	7.3	13.9	14.9
Potter	1,145	27.2	1,969	80.8	16.2	0.5	2.3	67.9	70.1	10.1	9.5	11.1
Roberts	3,683	37.7	6,301	75.8	13.4	0.8	6.8	65.4	69.4	8.5	18.4	18.8
Sanborn	1,043	32.4	1,788	82.7	14.8	0.6	6.0	69.1	71.5	10.8	12.9	10.8
Shannon	2,785	68.8	5,524	70.0	12.1	0.6	26.2	67.7	61.7	5.6	38.4	37.9
Spink	2,847	31.9	5,024	81.4	14.4	0.6	8.2	67.5	69.3	11.0	12.1	12.9
Stanley	1,111	35.4	1,823	87.7	22.1	0.7	3.7	59.9	80.3	15.8	8.8	8.7
Sully	630	32.9	1,065	84.9	16.4	0.8	3.3	65.3	68.1	10.0	8.3	8.2
Todd	2,462	60.7	4,173	74.1	12.1	0.6	22.0	59.3	61.5	6.4	36.4	38.0
Tripp	2,550	32.8	4,218	80.2	13.5	0.4	3.8	69.7	68.0	7.4	17.3	16.9
Turner	3,510	33.1	6,019	83.2	17.0	0.5	3.7	65.5	70.9	11.2	8.9	7.9
Union	4,927	36.3	8,262	87.2	26.3	2.4	4.1	54.4	79.4	21.1	6.9	6.4
Walworth	2,506	28.9	4,083	78.1	15.8	0.7	9.6	57.9	76.1	7.6	16.0	15.5
Yankton	8,187	34.3	14,178	86.1	23.0	1.5	5.6	54.9	80.4	11.0	12.8	9.5
Ziebach	741	55.6	1,223	71.4	12.0	0.4	23.8	64.8	45.2	4.2	39.4	42.0
TENNESSEE	2,232,905	35.2	3,744,928	75.9	19.6	2.8	4.8	53.9	81.7	16.4	15.0	12.6
Anderson	29,780	32.4	49,499	78.9	20.8	1.9	3.6	61.5	86.4	15.1	14.6	12.2
Bedford	13,905	38.2	24,232	69.7	11.1	6.4	8.4	51.4	78.2	12.6	14.3	12.5
Benton	6,863	30.9	11,798	65.8	6.3	0.7	1.9	61.9	80.2	7.4	18.0	16.3
Bledsoe	4,430	35.5	8,455	66.0	7.1	0.4	2.1	56.9	76.2	8.6	19.0	19.2
Blount	42,667	33.3	72,938	78.4	17.9	1.5	3.2	55.6	84.9	15.3	11.3	10.0
Bradley	34,281	35.4	57,163	73.3	15.9	2.2	4.4	53.6	83.6	14.4	13.9	11.7
Campbell	16,125	33.2	27,359	58.7	7.0	0.8	2.3	61.6	80.9	6.2	21.7	20.4
Cannon	4,998	36.3	8,486	67.2	8.4	0.8	2.2	63.5	76.3	9.8	14.1	13.4
Carroll	11,779	33.6	20,238	67.9	11.1	1.1	2.6	59.5	82.0	9.6	17.0	14.1
Carter	23,486	31.4	39,450	69.1	12.8	0.8	2.7	59.5	82.4	7.5	18.3	15.6
Cheatham	12,878	43.6	23,341	75.4	15.1	1.1	3.1	57.4	79.1	17.7	9.9	8.1
Chester	5,660	37.1	9,531	67.8	11.2	0.5	2.1	57.4	79.8	11.5	15.3	14.3
Claiborne	11,799	35.1	20,200	60.3	8.9	0.9	2.1	62.6	80.4	6.3	19.9	19.5
Clay	3,379	30.5	5,623	58.4	6.8	1.1	1.8	64.6	79.0	6.4	21.4	19.8
Cocke	13,762	33.7	23,070	61.2	6.2	0.8	2.4	62.8	78.5	6.1	21.4	19.4
Coffee	18,885	35.8	32,079	73.7	17.5	2.3	3.7	56.1	82.4	13.8	14.5	12.6
Crockett	5,632	36.7	9,690	65.1	9.1	3.9	6.1	66.8	82.0	8.8	16.4	14.6
Cumberland	19,508	29.4	33,595	72.5	13.7	1.9	3.7	55.9	82.5	10.6	14.7	14.0
Davidson	237,405	30.0	377,734	81.5	30.5	6.9	9.8	45.5	78.6	19.5	15.7	11.8
Decatur	4,908	30.6	8,247	63.6	7.3	1.7	3.1	65.0	79.8	8.5	17.0	15.4
DeKalb	6,984	33.6	11,870	64.6	11.3	2.7	3.6	58.8	76.3	10.3	16.4	15.5
Dickson	16,473	39.1	28,108	72.6	11.3	0.7	2.5	56.1	79.3	14.9	12.8	11.0
Dyer	14,751	36.8	24,356	66.3	12.0	1.3	3.0	51.8	84.0	11.4	17.0	14.7
Fayette	10,467	37.1	18,991	70.6	12.8	0.7	2.1	61.9	80.3	17.7	12.9	12.4
Fentress	6,693	34.5	11,275	57.3	8.3	0.4	1.6	59.1	78.9	5.8	21.9	21.8
Franklin	15,003	34.6	25,963	73.8	15.3	1.4	3.4	57.8	80.0	13.8	13.5	12.4
Gibson	19,518	33.9	32,751	70.9	10.1	0.8	2.3	58.9	84.6	10.1	15.3	13.1
Giles	11,713	35.0	19,829	72.5	10.6	0.9	2.6	62.6	82.5	12.8	14.5	12.1
Grainger	8,270	34.3	14,210	60.1	7.8	1.1	2.5	65.8	81.5	6.9	17.0	16.4
Greene	25,756	32.6	43,752	69.6	12.8	1.3	3.0	59.1	83.9	9.0	15.3	13.9
Grundy	5,562	37.8	9,441	55.2	7.1	0.7	1.8	67.6	73.0	5.4	22.2	22.7
Hamblen	23,211	34.3	39,340	69.3	13.3	5.3	7.1	55.5	84.6	11.9	15.2	12.9
Hamilton	124,444	32.4	207,180	80.7	23.9	3.0	5.1	54.8	82.4	18.7	14.6	11.7
Hancock	2,769	33.4	4,617	55.9	10.2	0.3	1.5	71.0	71.4	4.3	28.5	27.0
Hardeman	9,412	38.4	18,595	66.7	7.8	0.7	4.4	58.0	78.9	8.3	21.1	20.2
Hardin	10,426	32.8	17,644	66.9	9.8	0.7	1.9	58.4	80.7	10.1	19.2	17.9
Hawkins	21,936	34.1	37,146	70.4	10.0	0.7	1.9	61.3	85.9	9.3	15.7	14.2
Haywood	7,558	39.1	12,421	65.6	11.1	1.7	3.8	60.6	78.5	9.0	19.0	17.3
Henderson	10,306	35.8	17,140	69.3	9.3	0.7	1.9	58.8	84.7	9.8	14.3	13.0
Henry	13,019	30.7	21,791	70.5	12.1	1.0	2.8	55.5	82.5	8.4	15.9	13.9
Hickman	8,081	37.1	14,899	64.3	6.7	0.8	2.5	55.8	76.5	8.3	16.5	14.5
Houston	3,216	34.5	5,539	70.1	10.3	1.6	2.7	64.6	81.1	10.4	16.6	15.1
Humphreys	7,238	33.7	12,270	72.0	9.3	0.9	2.4	61.4	80.3	12.5	13.1	11.9
Jackson	4,466	32.1	7,671	61.6	8.4	1.6	3.1	64.2	79.0	7.1	19.1	17.2
Jefferson	17,155	34.2	29,455	71.0	12.8	1.5	3.0	55.9	82.4	10.2	15.2	13.7
Johnson	6,827	30.4	12,755	58.4	6.9	0.6	1.9	63.3	76.2	6.2	21.8	21.5
Knox	157,872	31.0	252,530	82.5	29.0	2.5	4.4	52.0	84.5	19.4	13.8	10.8
Lake	2,410	33.6	5,492	56.0	5.4	0.5	3.6	58.2	81.0	5.2	31.4	29.0
Lauderdale	9,567	38.6	17,507	62.3	7.7	0.7	3.2	56.6	83.3	6.8	20.7	17.9
Lawrence	15,480	36.7	26,145	65.5	8.7	0.9	3.8	60.9	80.8	8.6	15.9	14.2

See footnotes at end of table.

Table B-4. Counties — **Population Characteristics**—Con.

[Includes United States, states, and 3,141 counties/county equivalents defined as of February 22, 2005. For more information on these areas, see Appendix C, Geographic Information]

County	Households, 2000 Total	With individuals under 18 years (percent of total)	Educational attainment,[1] 2000 Total persons	High school graduate or higher (percent)	Bachelor's degree or higher (percent)	Foreign-born population, 2000 (percent)	Speaking language other than English at home, 2000 (percent)	Residing in same house in 1995 and 2000 (percent)	Workers who drove alone to work,[2] 2000 (percent)	Households with income of $75,000 or more in 1999 (percent)	Persons in poverty (percent) 2004	Persons in poverty (percent) 2000
TENNESSEE—Con.												
Lewis.	4,381	37.0	7,466	69.5	8.5	1.0	2.8	59.2	77.1	7.6	16.7	15.3
Lincoln.	12,503	34.4	21,361	69.6	11.9	0.9	2.9	57.7	80.6	14.7	14.4	12.9
Loudon.	15,944	31.3	27,899	75.6	17.0	1.8	3.2	57.9	83.7	18.0	11.1	9.6
McMinn.	19,721	34.7	33,110	69.3	10.8	1.3	3.1	58.7	83.0	11.2	15.1	13.2
McNairy.	9,980	33.4	16,787	68.5	8.8	0.9	2.3	61.5	81.7	8.6	17.5	15.8
Macon.	7,916	37.9	13,331	60.2	5.6	1.8	3.0	57.6	73.7	9.6	16.3	15.1
Madison.	35,552	37.1	58,038	78.8	21.5	2.3	3.9	50.8	84.1	16.7	15.7	12.9
Marion.	11,037	35.3	18,815	64.6	9.5	0.5	2.1	64.7	81.9	11.3	15.0	13.6
Marshall.	10,307	37.6	17,615	73.6	10.6	1.4	2.9	54.5	80.8	15.0	12.4	10.2
Maury.	26,444	38.7	45,288	77.9	13.6	2.1	3.9	54.8	82.9	19.4	12.6	11.0
Meigs.	4,304	36.6	7,405	63.5	7.0	0.6	3.0	58.3	79.3	8.4	17.5	16.9
Monroe.	15,329	35.7	25,955	66.7	10.1	1.2	2.8	58.0	82.3	8.2	16.2	15.6
Montgomery.	48,330	43.9	79,823	84.3	19.3	4.4	8.4	42.1	81.6	14.4	11.6	10.1
Moore.	2,211	34.5	3,939	76.6	11.8	1.0	0.8	66.8	88.8	15.3	10.6	10.7
Morgan.	6,990	37.6	13,371	63.8	6.0	0.4	1.4	67.4	79.6	6.6	18.7	17.6
Obion.	13,182	34.3	22,119	71.0	10.3	1.3	3.1	59.6	83.5	11.5	14.5	12.5
Overton.	8,110	32.6	13,751	59.0	8.3	0.5	2.7	65.9	82.9	4.5	16.7	16.0
Perry.	3,023	33.8	5,209	63.8	7.1	0.5	2.4	66.4	74.5	10.8	17.0	15.0
Pickett.	2,091	29.3	3,466	62.9	9.1	0.3	2.1	66.5	80.1	6.1	17.1	17.5
Polk.	6,448	33.8	11,113	62.2	7.5	0.8	2.4	65.9	75.5	10.2	15.1	13.4
Putnam.	24,865	31.8	39,403	72.6	20.2	3.4	5.3	48.3	80.6	11.7	15.2	13.8
Rhea.	11,184	34.6	18,894	65.3	9.1	1.3	2.7	58.4	77.7	10.1	16.2	14.5
Roane.	21,200	32.0	36,455	74.8	14.8	1.2	2.0	62.3	86.1	14.2	14.7	12.8
Robertson.	19,906	41.3	35,252	74.8	11.9	2.5	4.4	56.6	79.9	18.6	10.7	9.2
Rutherford.	66,443	40.9	109,913	81.8	22.9	3.6	5.9	44.4	83.1	21.2	10.0	8.2
Scott.	8,203	39.1	13,480	60.7	7.5	0.4	1.5	65.3	82.6	5.3	21.1	20.7
Sequatchie.	4,463	36.7	7,610	66.7	10.2	1.2	2.3	57.9	83.4	10.8	15.7	14.8
Sevier.	28,467	33.9	48,843	74.6	13.5	1.6	2.9	54.3	80.6	11.4	13.4	12.5
Shelby.	338,366	39.0	558,056	80.8	25.3	3.8	6.5	51.2	80.2	21.0	19.1	14.3
Smith.	6,878	37.3	11,798	67.5	9.3	0.9	2.0	57.3	82.3	11.5	13.0	11.9
Stewart.	4,930	34.5	8,486	74.3	10.2	1.7	3.6	56.7	78.3	8.5	13.7	12.6
Sullivan.	63,556	31.2	108,605	75.8	18.1	1.3	2.3	60.2	86.1	14.0	14.0	12.0
Sumner.	48,941	39.8	85,651	79.7	18.6	2.4	4.0	51.8	82.9	22.4	9.6	8.4
Tipton.	18,106	44.3	31,856	74.6	10.8	0.8	2.3	52.9	82.9	17.1	12.9	11.8
Trousdale.	2,780	36.0	4,852	61.4	8.9	1.7	4.4	62.7	76.1	10.7	14.5	13.2
Unicoi.	7,516	29.6	12,744	67.7	10.6	1.4	2.6	64.9	85.6	8.6	14.8	13.2
Union.	6,742	39.4	11,632	56.3	5.8	0.3	1.2	62.2	81.0	7.6	18.7	17.5
Van Buren.	2,180	34.0	3,738	62.0	7.8	0.2	1.3	69.8	72.2	5.3	16.5	15.2
Warren.	15,181	35.4	25,691	67.2	9.1	3.7	6.3	54.6	78.5	9.9	16.6	14.9
Washington.	44,195	30.8	72,947	77.2	22.9	1.9	3.4	54.4	85.0	13.9	14.9	12.6
Wayne.	5,936	34.1	11,733	61.3	8.0	0.4	1.6	58.9	79.3	5.2	18.9	19.9
Weakley.	13,599	32.2	21,908	70.3	15.3	2.0	3.6	53.5	82.2	8.6	16.6	14.1
White.	9,229	33.8	15,806	64.8	7.9	0.8	2.2	62.6	81.8	8.5	16.2	15.0
Williamson.	44,725	45.1	81,620	90.1	44.4	3.9	5.4	48.2	83.6	45.7	5.4	4.5
Wilson.	32,798	40.7	58,683	80.9	19.6	1.4	2.9	53.8	83.3	26.1	8.5	7.6
TEXAS.	7,393,354	40.9	12,790,893	75.7	23.2	13.9	31.2	49.6	77.7	21.1	16.2	14.6
Anderson.	15,678	38.3	38,506	64.4	11.1	3.2	6.8	61.3	79.3	11.3	21.0	20.5
Andrews.	4,601	44.5	7,815	68.0	12.4	10.6	33.6	63.3	83.8	9.7	14.8	14.9
Angelina.	28,685	40.7	50,290	71.2	14.7	6.9	14.1	57.0	80.0	12.7	17.3	16.3
Aransas.	9,132	30.2	15,728	74.6	16.7	5.7	18.3	48.9	75.1	14.4	18.9	20.6
Archer.	3,345	39.9	5,729	81.1	15.9	2.3	5.0	60.5	80.3	16.3	9.7	10.0
Armstrong.	802	36.3	1,458	82.4	20.5	0.9	4.0	60.0	79.6	16.0	9.7	12.2
Atascosa.	12,816	46.6	22,751	65.2	10.5	5.1	45.3	60.9	73.7	11.3	18.9	19.1
Austin.	8,747	37.9	15,280	74.5	17.3	7.3	17.1	58.1	79.8	17.3	11.2	10.7
Bailey.	2,348	40.8	3,960	61.5	9.3	13.1	41.7	57.1	79.3	9.5	17.6	19.7
Bandera.	7,010	32.4	12,287	84.8	19.4	3.9	13.5	49.5	75.1	18.7	12.3	13.3
Bastrop.	20,097	40.2	37,249	76.9	17.0	8.1	22.3	52.0	74.6	19.4	12.7	11.9
Baylor.	1,791	27.9	2,939	70.1	12.1	2.0	9.4	57.2	84.4	7.4	17.2	18.3
Bee.	9,061	42.5	20,568	73.7	12.2	2.0	42.3	43.8	74.9	8.1	24.9	28.2
Bell.	85,507	43.4	137,430	84.7	19.8	7.3	17.7	39.5	78.9	14.7	13.2	12.4
Bexar.	488,942	41.4	849,004	76.9	22.7	10.9	43.2	51.2	75.7	18.6	17.3	15.7
Blanco.	3,303	32.9	5,895	80.6	22.2	5.0	16.5	54.3	75.1	18.3	10.3	9.7
Borden.	292	31.5	490	83.9	21.4	4.5	16.5	69.3	85.6	15.4	6.3	10.0
Bosque.	6,726	32.5	11,910	75.9	15.4	4.4	10.7	55.3	74.0	12.8	13.8	14.3
Bowie.	33,058	37.3	58,767	77.3	16.1	1.5	5.5	52.8	82.4	14.1	17.4	17.0
Brazoria.	81,954	44.7	152,244	79.5	19.6	8.5	21.3	53.1	82.8	27.1	10.9	10.3
Brazos.	55,202	30.3	70,708	81.3	37.0	10.3	19.9	32.1	76.5	15.9	19.0	17.6
Brewster.	3,669	29.8	5,519	78.6	27.7	6.9	42.7	48.9	68.3	9.4	16.9	19.7
Briscoe.	724	33.0	1,181	74.8	17.5	4.9	16.5	65.8	78.0	7.9	14.6	19.0
Brooks.	2,711	44.7	4,717	49.9	6.8	6.1	77.7	71.9	71.2	4.8	28.8	36.0
Brown.	14,306	34.9	24,016	74.6	15.0	3.1	12.4	50.1	82.6	11.0	18.0	18.3

See footnotes at end of table.

County and City Data Book: 2007

U.S. Census Bureau

Table B-4. Counties — **Population Characteristics**—Con.

[Includes United States, states, and 3,141 counties/county equivalents defined as of February 22, 2005. For more information on these areas, see Appendix C, Geographic Information]

County	Households, 2000		Educational attainment,[1] 2000			Foreign-born population, 2000 (percent)	Persons 5 years and over		Workers who drove alone to work,[2] 2000 (percent)	Households with income of $75,000 or more in 1999 (percent)	Persons in poverty (percent)	
	Total	With individuals under 18 years (percent of total)	Total persons	High school graduate or higher (percent)	Bachelor's degree or higher (percent)		Speaking language other than English at home, 2000 (percent)	Residing in same house in 1995 and 2000 (percent)			2004	2000
TEXAS—Con.												
Burleson	6,363	35.6	10,787	71.1	13.2	3.0	14.1	63.3	76.5	12.8	15.4	15.2
Burnet	13,133	33.3	23,436	77.8	17.4	5.4	13.5	51.3	76.2	17.1	11.8	11.6
Caldwell	10,816	42.1	20,337	71.3	13.3	5.1	32.3	55.2	74.7	13.7	14.7	14.9
Calhoun	7,442	40.2	13,012	69.0	12.1	8.5	32.8	59.6	78.5	14.8	16.6	16.2
Callahan	5,061	35.4	8,658	79.3	12.3	1.4	5.9	57.2	77.6	9.2	14.0	15.4
Cameron	97,267	52.7	187,064	55.2	13.4	25.6	79.0	58.5	73.2	10.1	29.4	30.2
Camp	4,336	36.2	7,474	69.5	12.2	9.9	15.9	54.1	77.6	11.0	17.1	18.5
Carson	2,470	38.4	4,305	82.6	15.5	2.7	7.3	64.6	84.1	16.4	8.2	9.0
Cass	12,190	34.4	20,546	75.0	12.0	1.1	3.2	62.2	80.8	9.9	17.3	17.7
Castro	2,761	45.3	4,871	65.4	14.7	12.1	44.9	63.7	75.9	10.9	19.2	21.7
Chambers	9,139	44.9	16,348	76.9	12.1	5.1	11.7	57.7	84.4	26.6	10.7	10.1
Cherokee	16,651	37.5	30,008	68.4	11.4	7.9	12.9	56.5	75.6	9.4	18.2	19.1
Childress	2,474	34.4	5,173	65.0	8.6	4.7	17.7	63.7	79.5	6.6	22.7	24.5
Clay	4,323	34.6	7,549	80.4	13.9	1.4	3.3	61.0	79.5	11.9	10.6	11.5
Cochran	1,309	42.4	2,236	62.7	10.2	9.8	42.3	63.6	76.3	8.9	21.9	25.3
Coke	1,544	29.6	2,620	74.2	14.7	2.8	14.4	57.1	82.4	12.4	13.0	15.8
Coleman	3,889	30.4	6,373	71.0	11.7	3.4	10.2	59.6	79.9	8.5	20.1	21.8
Collin	181,970	42.5	315,665	91.8	47.3	13.3	18.5	38.1	83.5	46.8	5.5	4.3
Collingsworth	1,294	32.6	2,159	71.3	15.3	4.3	18.2	63.4	83.3	10.3	17.5	20.9
Colorado	7,641	34.9	13,383	69.1	14.4	7.9	19.9	65.9	75.0	13.3	14.7	16.1
Comal	29,066	36.6	52,549	83.9	26.2	4.8	19.6	51.5	80.6	23.8	9.3	9.0
Comanche	5,522	32.6	9,411	70.2	13.0	7.1	19.0	59.3	74.2	7.9	17.7	19.2
Concho	1,058	32.8	2,921	59.3	14.1	2.8	29.2	48.8	73.4	11.4	19.4	25.4
Cooke	13,643	37.2	23,148	79.2	15.7	5.5	9.7	53.2	77.5	16.4	13.4	12.4
Coryell	19,950	50.7	41,764	81.1	12.4	5.3	15.3	39.4	68.1	11.4	13.7	13.9
Cottle	820	30.2	1,342	66.1	15.3	3.6	15.9	63.3	72.7	7.3	18.8	23.8
Crane	1,360	46.5	2,394	68.7	12.8	14.4	40.6	67.5	71.7	11.5	10.8	13.9
Crockett	1,524	41.7	2,659	62.1	10.4	10.5	48.0	68.2	79.5	10.0	15.9	18.0
Crosby	2,512	41.0	4,299	61.8	10.5	3.9	41.8	58.0	79.1	9.5	23.2	25.5
Culberson	1,052	44.8	1,781	56.1	13.9	15.6	73.4	68.0	74.7	5.4	22.0	27.8
Dallam	2,317	42.9	3,703	65.0	9.6	7.9	19.6	53.7	74.8	7.2	14.0	16.0
Dallas	807,621	39.4	1,365,848	75.0	27.0	20.9	32.5	45.3	74.8	23.9	17.0	12.0
Dawson	4,726	39.8	9,949	65.2	10.5	4.2	44.3	58.1	79.0	10.5	22.6	25.7
Deaf Smith	6,180	46.1	10,539	60.9	11.8	11.6	48.9	57.4	79.1	9.6	16.5	21.2
Delta	2,094	33.9	3,618	75.5	13.9	0.5	2.2	56.6	78.1	10.5	15.9	18.4
Denton	158,903	41.4	265,220	89.4	36.6	9.4	15.5	37.7	82.0	36.4	8.0	5.7
DeWitt	7,207	35.2	13,969	67.9	11.8	2.6	23.2	61.7	77.2	10.8	19.4	19.8
Dickens	980	27.1	1,940	70.6	8.4	2.0	21.8	61.2	80.6	6.5	18.9	24.4
Dimmit	3,308	48.0	5,982	54.3	10.1	7.6	76.5	68.5	76.5	5.2	28.2	34.0
Donley	1,578	27.5	2,586	78.2	15.8	1.6	6.4	57.9	82.5	10.0	16.5	19.5
Duval	4,350	43.7	8,042	59.7	8.9	3.4	78.4	70.7	71.0	6.5	25.3	27.5
Eastland	7,321	30.8	12,171	72.6	12.7	4.0	10.4	57.7	76.7	9.1	18.4	19.6
Ector	43,846	43.4	71,756	68.0	12.0	10.6	37.1	57.1	81.7	11.1	19.3	18.4
Edwards	801	36.6	1,418	67.1	17.3	10.8	46.7	71.1	67.3	9.0	21.9	28.0
Ellis	37,020	46.7	67,470	77.8	17.1	7.1	16.8	50.9	80.8	25.8	10.6	9.4
El Paso	210,022	51.3	391,540	65.8	16.6	27.4	73.3	55.2	75.9	12.8	24.6	25.3
Erath	12,568	33.6	19,350	77.1	25.0	7.3	14.8	47.5	78.9	13.3	15.3	15.4
Falls	6,496	35.2	12,013	66.2	9.6	4.6	13.9	62.3	78.6	9.2	21.7	23.8
Fannin	11,105	34.8	21,120	72.5	12.6	3.1	6.4	50.9	78.2	13.0	15.4	15.3
Fayette	8,722	31.0	15,183	71.3	14.6	5.6	20.3	62.5	79.4	14.3	12.3	12.0
Fisher	1,785	30.3	3,036	73.3	12.4	2.3	19.6	63.6	77.3	7.7	13.9	17.5
Floyd	2,730	42.5	4,773	63.5	12.3	5.9	40.4	60.7	81.9	12.9	20.5	21.5
Foard	664	31.0	1,116	70.0	10.5	1.6	12.5	63.4	68.6	6.9	15.8	17.0
Fort Bend	110,915	53.5	214,461	84.3	36.9	18.3	30.7	52.0	81.6	41.2	8.1	7.1
Franklin	3,754	33.3	6,421	77.4	16.2	5.4	10.1	56.6	78.7	12.9	13.6	14.4
Freestone	6,588	33.8	12,085	76.8	10.9	3.1	6.9	63.6	78.1	12.0	15.2	16.1
Frio	4,743	46.8	9,807	57.7	8.4	5.8	61.2	64.7	69.2	7.3	28.0	32.2
Gaines	4,681	49.2	8,006	56.2	10.5	18.9	47.7	59.6	76.6	10.4	18.1	21.1
Galveston	94,782	37.9	161,503	80.9	22.7	8.3	17.2	52.4	78.2	24.9	13.4	11.9
Garza	1,663	39.4	3,131	70.1	10.0	6.3	30.1	58.1	79.0	9.4	20.5	21.9
Gillespie	8,521	27.9	15,255	80.1	22.9	7.0	26.5	60.1	73.6	15.5	10.2	11.1
Glasscock	483	43.7	836	69.9	18.7	14.1	27.0	71.8	69.9	15.7	7.3	11.0
Goliad	2,644	36.6	4,603	72.4	12.3	2.8	29.2	60.9	74.9	14.0	15.3	16.0
Gonzales	6,782	38.7	11,797	62.0	10.7	11.0	34.1	61.3	71.1	10.3	18.3	21.1
Gray	8,793	33.2	15,420	75.3	11.9	4.3	13.0	59.0	82.7	12.7	14.4	15.3
Grayson	42,849	35.7	72,382	80.2	17.2	3.9	7.1	51.3	80.8	16.6	13.6	12.2
Gregg	42,687	37.5	70,006	79.1	19.5	5.4	9.3	52.0	83.2	15.9	16.3	14.9
Grimes	7,753	38.9	16,080	67.3	10.3	5.0	14.1	58.2	75.7	11.6	16.9	17.3
Guadalupe	30,900	42.6	55,679	78.1	19.1	6.5	26.8	51.1	79.7	20.0	11.4	12.1
Hale	11,975	45.2	21,498	65.9	14.4	8.2	39.3	51.0	79.6	11.1	19.7	20.1

See footnotes at end of table.

Table B-4. Counties — **Population Characteristics**—Con.

[Includes United States, states, and 3,141 counties/county equivalents defined as of February 22, 2005. For more information on these areas, see Appendix C, Geographic Information]

County	Households, 2000 Total	With individuals under 18 years (percent of total)	Educational attainment,[1] 2000 Total persons	High school graduate or higher (percent)	Bachelor's degree or higher (percent)	Foreign-born population, 2000 (percent)	Speaking language other than English at home, 2000 (percent)	Residing in same house in 1995 and 2000 (percent)	Workers who drove alone to work,[2] 2000 (percent)	Households with income of $75,000 or more in 1999 (percent)	Persons in poverty (percent) 2004	2000
TEXAS—Con.												
Hall	1,548	31.4	2,527	61.7	10.3	9.1	25.6	57.7	79.1	5.0	22.1	26.4
Hamilton	3,374	30.4	5,792	73.8	16.8	3.7	9.0	56.8	73.1	11.9	15.3	17.3
Hansford	2,005	40.2	3,420	69.9	18.6	15.6	29.5	58.4	76.7	12.7	13.5	12.9
Hardeman	1,943	32.9	3,135	70.7	12.8	2.5	11.9	59.9	80.4	10.8	16.7	17.2
Hardin	17,805	40.9	30,747	79.5	13.0	1.3	3.4	62.1	84.6	17.4	12.7	11.8
Harris	1,205,516	41.9	2,067,399	74.6	26.9	22.2	36.2	47.8	75.7	24.7	16.8	13.4
Harrison	23,087	38.8	39,130	78.3	15.4	3.3	6.5	57.8	81.7	13.5	15.8	16.4
Hartley	1,604	37.4	4,136	77.3	17.6	2.6	11.2	52.9	86.6	20.5	9.1	9.0
Haskell	2,569	29.8	4,314	71.1	14.4	3.6	17.3	63.2	85.5	10.5	20.5	22.0
Hays	33,410	37.1	53,635	84.7	31.3	5.6	23.1	41.4	76.5	24.8	12.6	10.3
Hemphill	1,280	34.8	2,190	79.9	17.9	6.5	13.3	60.4	75.4	14.9	7.7	9.8
Henderson	28,804	33.3	49,886	73.5	12.1	3.8	7.5	55.4	77.8	13.6	16.7	15.9
Hidalgo	156,824	56.5	304,670	50.5	12.9	29.5	83.1	61.1	73.7	9.3	30.5	31.7
Hill	12,204	35.1	21,209	71.8	12.5	5.9	12.9	55.0	77.3	11.8	16.2	16.2
Hockley	7,994	42.5	13,466	68.2	13.6	5.2	29.3	58.2	77.8	11.6	17.4	18.0
Hood	16,176	32.3	28,621	83.5	20.5	3.3	7.5	48.6	79.9	21.6	11.1	9.7
Hopkins	12,286	36.3	21,003	73.6	15.1	5.6	9.8	52.3	77.0	12.6	14.5	14.9
Houston	8,259	32.9	16,244	70.0	12.2	3.0	7.5	54.1	76.8	9.2	21.7	23.4
Howard	11,389	36.8	22,544	70.6	11.1	6.0	31.1	53.2	80.6	10.8	19.9	21.2
Hudspeth	1,092	51.0	1,910	46.1	9.7	33.2	74.1	66.6	72.8	4.5	26.6	32.7
Hunt	28,742	37.2	48,548	76.9	16.8	4.7	8.8	51.2	77.0	15.5	15.3	14.0
Hutchinson	9,283	37.6	15,282	79.6	14.3	5.8	13.0	59.1	83.0	14.3	12.6	12.2
Irion	694	36.2	1,217	78.8	21.5	3.5	22.8	60.9	81.9	16.1	8.3	10.3
Jack	3,047	35.7	5,830	75.8	12.8	2.8	6.6	50.3	73.6	9.4	11.9	16.8
Jackson	5,336	38.6	9,278	72.7	12.8	4.8	19.0	61.6	77.1	12.7	14.3	13.8
Jasper	13,450	37.9	23,420	73.0	10.5	2.2	5.0	62.0	79.5	10.0	18.7	17.8
Jeff Davis	896	30.4	1,560	74.7	35.1	10.9	36.9	52.8	67.8	13.8	11.0	16.6
Jefferson	92,880	37.2	161,261	78.5	16.3	6.2	13.2	57.3	82.3	16.6	18.7	17.0
Jim Hogg	1,815	43.6	3,203	58.0	9.5	5.1	81.8	60.2	81.2	9.0	22.0	26.5
Jim Wells	12,961	46.6	23,525	64.8	10.9	3.6	62.6	66.1	76.8	9.9	21.4	23.7
Johnson	43,636	44.0	79,417	77.6	13.8	5.2	12.0	50.3	80.4	20.7	11.6	10.2
Jones	6,140	37.4	13,780	64.3	8.2	1.6	16.4	47.9	80.7	9.8	20.5	23.9
Karnes	4,454	38.4	10,352	59.1	9.4	3.7	43.2	59.5	72.2	10.4	24.9	26.5
Kaufman	24,367	44.5	44,859	74.5	12.3	5.7	11.0	53.4	77.9	21.9	11.5	11.3
Kendall	8,613	38.7	15,827	85.4	31.4	5.6	17.0	50.3	78.3	28.8	8.8	8.5
Kenedy	138	45.7	261	57.9	20.3	13.3	85.4	72.8	47.6	5.8	14.2	19.7
Kent	353	27.8	643	78.1	15.1	1.7	11.4	62.7	87.5	12.2	9.5	15.3
Kerr	17,813	28.5	31,006	81.2	23.3	6.6	18.2	51.6	77.3	15.0	13.2	14.2
Kimble	1,866	30.9	3,146	72.1	17.3	5.5	18.0	59.8	75.6	9.8	16.3	18.8
King	108	41.7	228	78.1	24.6	2.2	4.8	67.4	58.1	1.9	9.1	12.0
Kinney	1,314	30.5	2,335	66.9	17.7	11.7	47.2	58.5	76.7	10.8	18.8	23.4
Kleberg	10,896	39.8	17,896	68.2	20.4	6.5	55.3	53.2	75.5	11.9	22.7	24.6
Knox	1,690	33.8	2,819	66.8	11.8	6.7	23.3	63.9	81.7	7.9	20.6	24.8
Lamar	19,077	36.3	31,612	76.3	14.5	2.1	4.7	49.6	81.3	11.7	17.7	17.8
Lamb	5,360	39.8	9,202	63.7	11.1	6.3	35.3	63.9	77.7	10.2	19.3	20.3
Lampasas	6,554	38.9	11,491	78.8	16.2	6.0	15.9	52.3	78.7	13.0	14.1	14.5
La Salle	1,819	43.4	3,602	50.1	6.4	4.0	70.2	70.1	64.9	7.0	26.3	32.8
Lavaca	7,669	32.3	13,214	68.6	11.4	2.5	14.0	68.1	74.4	10.7	12.8	13.2
Lee	5,663	38.7	9,804	71.7	13.1	6.1	20.1	59.0	73.4	14.8	11.7	11.6
Leon	6,189	31.6	10,652	73.8	12.1	4.2	8.6	57.2	78.1	13.9	13.9	15.7
Liberty	23,242	43.0	44,206	69.6	8.1	5.1	12.3	55.0	78.5	14.5	16.0	16.1
Limestone	7,906	36.0	14,564	67.4	11.1	5.5	12.0	58.3	79.2	10.5	17.8	19.7
Lipscomb	1,205	35.0	2,047	74.5	18.9	11.7	35.8	58.6	72.5	11.5	12.3	14.0
Live Oak	4,230	34.9	8,399	67.1	12.0	2.3	30.4	62.7	74.1	12.6	18.0	19.2
Llano	7,879	18.8	13,571	83.5	21.0	2.0	6.7	53.8	76.9	15.7	12.3	12.3
Loving	31	19.4	51	86.3	5.9	–	32.8	65.7	68.4	22.6	15.0	18.1
Lubbock	92,516	35.5	141,363	78.4	24.4	3.3	22.3	47.4	80.7	14.2	17.8	17.2
Lynn	2,354	42.6	4,037	61.9	13.4	5.0	37.4	63.2	78.1	13.1	19.0	20.5
McCulloch	3,277	34.5	5,550	70.5	14.0	3.2	21.0	58.5	83.4	6.9	20.2	22.0
McLennan	78,859	37.0	125,961	76.6	19.1	6.1	15.6	48.2	79.1	15.0	18.3	16.1
McMullen	355	28.7	613	74.7	16.2	4.2	27.4	71.6	73.5	14.9	11.2	12.9
Madison	3,914	35.9	8,907	72.8	11.5	4.8	16.2	51.2	74.1	10.4	20.2	22.6
Marion	4,610	29.0	7,792	67.5	8.5	0.9	3.6	60.0	76.4	8.9	21.6	22.9
Martin	1,624	46.3	2,785	65.8	11.8	8.1	39.3	66.2	80.6	13.2	17.5	18.6
Mason	1,607	27.6	2,701	78.1	18.7	4.7	18.7	65.1	70.1	13.4	12.3	17.5
Matagorda	13,901	40.9	23,509	70.3	12.5	9.9	26.6	58.8	74.9	14.9	18.3	16.1
Maverick	13,089	59.5	25,468	42.1	9.1	37.8	92.1	64.7	70.2	6.5	27.9	32.4
Medina	12,880	43.8	24,629	72.2	13.3	4.1	36.8	57.4	75.1	13.7	15.9	16.5
Menard	990	31.5	1,660	69.4	17.2	4.8	27.1	57.0	72.9	10.7	21.0	24.2
Midland	42,745	42.4	71,008	79.2	24.8	7.6	25.8	54.0	83.3	20.9	14.6	14.3

See footnotes at end of table.

Table B-4. Counties — **Population Characteristics**—Con.

[Includes United States, states, and 3,141 counties/county equivalents defined as of February 22, 2005. For more information on these areas, see Appendix C, Geographic Information]

County	Households, 2000		Educational attainment,[1] 2000			Foreign-born population, 2000 (percent)	Persons 5 years and over		Workers who drove alone to work,[2] 2000 (percent)	House-holds with income of $75,000 or more in 1999 (percent)	Persons in poverty (percent)	
	Total	With individuals under 18 years (percent of total)	Total persons	High school graduate or higher (percent)	Bachelor's degree or higher (percent)		Speaking language other than English at home, 2000 (percent)	Residing in same house in 1995 and 2000 (percent)			2004	2000
TEXAS—Con.												
Milam	9,199	36.2	15,641	70.9	11.6	5.6	17.3	59.2	78.5	12.0	16.6	16.2
Mills	2,001	30.2	3,582	76.7	20.2	4.4	12.3	63.0	74.0	11.5	16.0	18.6
Mitchell	2,837	34.2	6,634	71.7	10.4	2.8	27.6	45.6	81.5	8.1	23.0	26.0
Montague	7,770	32.1	13,208	73.0	11.3	2.4	5.9	58.0	76.8	11.8	13.6	15.7
Montgomery	103,296	44.1	183,743	81.6	25.3	8.6	13.8	46.7	80.0	31.4	10.2	9.4
Moore	6,774	48.3	11,460	62.1	11.0	20.9	40.7	49.0	74.8	12.0	13.9	13.5
Morris	5,215	34.0	8,776	73.7	11.2	2.0	3.9	61.6	85.0	10.3	16.4	17.6
Motley	606	29.9	987	73.5	14.7	3.3	11.2	61.8	74.1	9.1	14.7	19.0
Nacogdoches	22,006	33.9	33,175	73.7	22.8	6.2	11.6	49.6	79.0	12.8	20.1	20.0
Navarro	16,491	38.5	28,324	71.7	12.2	9.1	15.4	55.4	77.9	12.0	17.1	17.2
Newton	5,583	37.4	9,738	68.7	5.5	0.9	3.6	67.2	74.7	6.5	21.1	20.8
Nolan	6,170	35.8	10,203	69.9	13.2	4.2	24.1	58.6	80.5	9.0	19.9	21.3
Nueces	110,365	41.8	191,848	74.4	18.8	6.5	42.9	53.2	76.4	16.6	19.4	18.9
Ochiltree	3,261	43.6	5,441	69.2	16.1	16.1	29.0	58.2	75.8	14.4	12.2	12.5
Oldham	735	37.0	1,250	80.5	19.4	5.4	12.9	47.5	70.6	9.7	12.4	13.9
Orange	31,642	39.5	54,229	79.0	11.0	2.1	5.8	59.3	84.3	17.2	15.0	14.0
Palo Pinto	10,594	34.7	17,764	71.2	12.1	4.4	11.4	52.7	78.7	10.4	16.1	15.8
Panola	8,821	36.0	14,848	75.9	13.4	2.9	4.6	62.9	81.4	13.0	14.2	15.0
Parker	31,131	41.8	57,072	80.5	18.6	2.6	7.1	50.8	79.9	23.4	10.3	8.6
Parmer	3,322	46.4	5,868	60.7	13.4	20.1	44.1	59.9	75.3	9.7	13.4	16.2
Pecos	5,153	46.2	9,870	62.5	12.9	13.5	55.9	56.8	75.8	9.5	20.9	23.0
Polk	15,119	32.9	28,453	70.0	10.4	4.3	12.0	53.7	75.7	11.8	16.5	15.8
Potter	40,760	39.3	69,427	71.1	13.5	9.4	24.7	46.7	79.0	10.5	21.2	20.0
Presidio	2,530	45.3	4,303	44.7	11.7	35.8	84.4	56.6	68.8	5.5	26.4	30.8
Rains	3,617	32.4	6,298	73.0	11.5	2.5	5.5	47.5	73.9	12.6	14.4	15.4
Randall	41,240	36.3	65,628	89.5	28.9	2.6	8.4	49.6	84.6	20.4	8.0	7.7
Reagan	1,107	51.9	1,955	63.0	9.2	16.4	47.6	67.2	74.9	11.1	12.9	14.1
Real	1,245	30.0	2,150	73.0	17.3	4.0	20.3	58.8	65.8	6.6	20.9	22.9
Red River	5,827	32.4	9,801	65.7	9.0	2.5	5.8	62.1	75.4	8.3	18.4	20.3
Reeves	4,091	45.4	7,692	46.6	8.0	14.7	67.5	65.2	77.1	5.3	25.9	28.3
Refugio	2,985	36.3	5,178	68.1	11.6	2.6	32.2	63.6	76.9	10.9	14.7	17.7
Roberts	362	33.7	623	90.0	25.4	0.5	1.7	53.1	80.4	17.7	6.7	9.2
Robertson	6,179	36.9	10,218	68.1	12.7	3.3	12.7	59.5	74.0	11.3	18.8	20.1
Rockwall	14,530	47.1	27,113	86.7	32.7	7.8	12.6	46.6	83.1	41.6	6.5	5.7
Runnels	4,428	34.8	7,723	68.9	13.1	4.5	23.3	57.7	77.5	7.2	17.6	19.1
Rusk	17,364	36.6	31,843	74.1	12.8	4.4	8.4	62.9	82.5	12.4	15.2	15.6
Sabine	4,485	26.9	7,676	72.5	10.6	1.1	3.2	62.3	75.9	8.7	16.4	17.4
San Augustine	3,575	31.4	6,221	69.9	11.8	2.0	4.0	66.9	77.3	10.1	20.2	22.1
San Jacinto	8,651	34.2	15,040	72.6	9.6	2.5	6.4	59.5	75.2	11.2	17.9	18.5
San Patricio	22,093	46.8	39,551	71.4	13.0	3.3	39.1	54.6	76.1	14.8	18.6	18.6
San Saba	2,289	32.3	3,997	70.0	15.8	5.5	19.6	56.0	79.7	10.1	18.2	20.5
Schleicher	1,115	37.5	1,913	60.4	17.6	13.9	40.6	65.0	74.7	13.2	13.4	19.2
Scurry	5,756	37.4	10,632	72.3	11.8	3.1	22.8	56.2	80.5	11.4	17.2	18.5
Shackelford	1,300	35.1	2,221	79.2	20.8	2.9	9.5	59.6	78.3	12.2	12.1	14.8
Shelby	9,595	36.8	16,266	68.9	12.2	6.6	9.3	63.8	74.2	10.8	18.3	20.4
Sherman	1,124	43.0	1,968	73.1	20.4	12.4	25.8	56.4	82.4	12.0	12.2	13.7
Smith	65,692	37.0	111,020	80.2	22.5	6.6	12.0	51.0	81.8	17.9	14.5	13.3
Somervell	2,438	41.3	4,372	78.0	17.2	5.7	12.4	51.7	82.6	17.7	10.2	11.1
Starr	14,410	62.7	27,716	34.7	6.9	36.9	90.7	72.4	69.2	4.9	34.8	42.2
Stephens	3,661	34.7	6,471	72.3	13.4	6.6	13.2	57.7	77.9	10.1	18.8	19.6
Sterling	513	40.2	916	70.4	17.1	9.2	26.9	68.1	75.9	13.8	11.2	13.8
Stonewall	713	30.6	1,211	71.0	12.6	2.0	12.5	67.7	75.6	10.2	15.6	18.3
Sutton	1,515	42.4	2,632	64.4	13.0	13.0	48.3	63.9	79.3	12.1	12.9	16.7
Swisher	2,925	38.9	5,200	69.7	16.2	4.9	27.4	57.0	82.3	10.8	20.1	21.2
Tarrant	533,864	40.4	898,850	81.3	26.6	12.7	21.9	44.9	81.3	25.5	12.8	10.1
Taylor	47,274	38.0	75,496	81.2	22.5	4.0	14.2	46.5	81.1	13.4	16.1	15.3
Terrell	443	33.0	736	70.9	19.0	9.9	52.7	67.0	70.9	9.9	15.1	22.2
Terry	4,278	40.3	8,008	62.5	9.5	7.2	38.8	59.4	78.8	11.2	21.6	24.3
Throckmorton	765	30.5	1,272	77.4	18.2	1.6	6.9	65.1	77.6	12.5	12.5	15.0
Titus	9,552	43.4	16,899	65.5	13.2	17.4	26.9	51.6	79.2	13.7	16.0	16.0
Tom Green	39,503	36.6	63,430	76.2	19.5	5.9	26.5	48.4	79.4	12.4	16.0	16.1
Travis	320,766	32.1	501,361	84.7	40.6	15.1	28.7	37.6	74.9	27.4	14.3	9.9
Trinity	5,723	29.6	9,623	73.1	9.4	2.7	5.1	56.3	72.6	8.3	18.1	19.2
Tyler	7,775	33.8	14,433	71.9	9.7	1.2	4.7	58.3	75.7	9.8	18.1	18.9
Upshur	13,290	38.2	22,977	76.3	11.1	2.0	4.5	57.8	79.2	11.6	15.7	16.3
Upton	1,256	40.9	2,165	67.1	11.8	11.2	38.1	64.7	77.8	9.9	15.2	17.5
Uvalde	8,559	45.5	15,280	59.6	13.8	11.2	60.0	59.2	71.4	10.2	22.2	24.7
Val Verde	14,151	49.3	26,281	58.7	14.1	23.4	69.9	55.1	75.1	9.8	22.1	24.3
Van Zandt	18,195	35.7	32,427	72.0	11.6	3.6	7.4	57.3	76.3	13.1	13.7	14.1
Victoria	30,071	41.6	51,985	76.2	16.2	4.3	27.0	52.0	77.8	18.2	16.1	14.1

See footnotes at end of table.

Table B-4. Counties — **Population Characteristics**—Con.

[Includes United States, states, and 3,141 counties/county equivalents defined as of February 22, 2005. For more information on these areas, see Appendix C, Geographic Information]

County	Households, 2000 Total	Households, 2000 With individuals under 18 years (percent of total)	Educational attainment,[1] 2000 Total persons	High school graduate or higher (percent)	Bachelor's degree or higher (percent)	Foreign-born population, 2000 (percent)	Persons 5 years and over Speaking language other than English at home, 2000 (percent)	Residing in same house in 1995 and 2000 (percent)	Workers who drove alone to work,[2] 2000 (percent)	Households with income of $75,000 or more in 1999 (percent)	Persons in poverty (percent) 2004	Persons in poverty (percent) 2000
TEXAS—Con.												
Walker	18,303	31.9	36,678	73.1	18.3	4.5	14.3	41.7	78.9	13.0	20.9	19.5
Waller	10,557	39.8	18,395	73.9	16.8	9.4	18.1	48.4	74.0	20.1	17.3	16.0
Ward	3,964	41.1	6,765	70.1	12.4	6.6	36.1	59.9	78.3	10.7	17.1	18.6
Washington	11,322	34.6	19,451	72.1	19.0	5.4	13.0	57.1	78.8	15.2	13.6	13.4
Webb	50,740	60.8	101,182	53.0	13.9	29.0	91.9	58.8	71.5	11.9	26.8	27.7
Wharton	14,799	40.0	25,567	69.8	14.3	6.6	26.7	62.1	78.0	14.1	15.4	14.8
Wheeler	2,152	32.4	3,601	72.0	13.0	5.4	10.4	58.7	76.4	9.9	11.9	16.3
Wichita	48,441	37.0	80,740	79.9	20.0	5.1	12.3	45.9	77.9	12.3	15.9	14.8
Wilbarger	5,537	35.9	9,313	72.2	17.1	4.2	16.7	54.1	83.8	11.5	16.0	16.0
Willacy	5,584	50.6	11,332	48.7	7.5	13.3	78.1	70.2	74.3	6.3	29.6	35.6
Williamson	86,766	46.5	155,565	88.8	33.6	7.4	17.2	39.6	82.2	35.8	7.1	5.1
Wilson	11,038	44.0	20,590	73.8	12.8	3.3	29.6	57.7	76.4	18.6	11.9	12.0
Winkler	2,584	42.7	4,380	60.3	10.5	14.3	39.8	64.1	73.5	8.4	15.7	16.6
Wise	17,178	41.9	31,130	76.1	13.0	5.1	10.9	49.7	77.5	18.5	10.5	10.2
Wood	14,583	29.9	25,895	76.3	14.5	3.8	5.5	54.4	77.1	12.1	14.5	15.7
Yoakum	2,469	46.9	4,322	59.4	10.2	16.6	39.6	64.3	77.1	13.7	14.2	17.2
Young	7,167	34.1	12,265	72.1	14.4	3.7	9.6	57.2	77.2	11.7	16.8	17.2
Zapata	3,921	48.2	6,945	53.1	8.7	24.1	78.7	65.1	75.2	6.8	27.2	32.3
Zavala	3,428	52.2	6,371	43.4	7.6	13.8	84.8	66.8	67.6	4.8	31.6	40.4
UTAH	701,281	45.8	1,197,892	87.7	26.1	7.1	12.5	49.3	75.5	22.5	10.3	8.8
Beaver	1,982	43.6	3,442	83.2	12.1	4.4	8.3	58.4	73.4	10.2	9.9	10.5
Box Elder	13,144	49.8	22,766	87.8	19.5	3.0	8.3	58.9	72.0	17.8	8.6	7.4
Cache	27,543	45.6	42,544	90.4	31.9	6.7	10.9	44.1	73.2	15.6	12.4	9.5
Carbon	7,413	39.8	12,090	81.1	12.3	2.0	7.8	59.2	77.9	14.4	14.5	13.4
Daggett	340	30.0	632	83.7	11.9	2.7	7.1	54.7	69.8	11.2	6.5	8.9
Davis	71,201	52.3	125,532	92.2	28.8	3.6	7.6	51.9	78.9	28.8	7.5	5.8
Duchesne	4,559	49.6	7,752	81.0	12.7	1.3	4.3	63.0	74.1	8.0	14.0	16.0
Emery	3,468	48.5	5,980	84.2	11.6	2.5	5.5	65.9	73.6	13.0	12.0	11.3
Garfield	1,576	40.9	2,829	85.8	20.3	0.8	3.5	61.7	65.8	10.2	9.8	12.0
Grand	3,434	32.8	5,486	82.5	22.9	3.0	8.7	51.2	67.7	11.0	14.3	15.2
Iron	10,627	43.4	16,318	88.6	23.8	2.9	7.5	42.1	74.2	11.7	14.7	15.1
Juab	2,456	51.9	4,290	82.9	12.2	1.4	4.0	58.8	67.6	11.8	10.6	10.7
Kane	2,237	34.7	3,842	86.4	21.1	2.9	6.1	57.4	71.5	9.3	9.3	11.5
Millard	3,840	48.5	6,769	86.7	16.8	5.1	8.6	62.7	68.5	11.4	11.8	12.6
Morgan	2,046	52.2	3,805	92.6	23.3	2.7	5.1	60.8	74.8	26.3	4.6	4.4
Piute	509	37.3	893	85.7	14.4	2.0	4.9	66.9	68.8	6.5	13.9	17.0
Rich	645	43.7	1,144	91.5	22.0	1.9	3.3	64.7	65.7	14.9	9.0	9.9
Salt Lake	295,141	43.4	509,453	86.8	27.4	10.4	16.2	50.0	76.4	25.3	10.2	8.2
San Juan	4,089	53.1	7,290	69.6	13.9	0.9	47.2	68.5	67.0	9.0	25.5	24.6
Sanpete	6,547	46.1	11,522	84.6	17.3	4.8	9.2	51.1	67.6	10.2	13.8	14.8
Sevier	6,081	45.4	10,480	85.8	15.2	1.3	4.5	58.8	76.1	12.0	12.4	12.5
Summit	10,332	42.6	18,366	92.5	45.5	7.7	10.2	43.0	74.4	42.8	5.3	5.3
Tooele	12,677	51.0	21,752	85.6	15.9	3.7	8.5	41.7	67.1	17.7	8.2	7.3
Uintah	8,187	48.1	13,736	79.8	13.2	1.4	6.5	59.8	73.2	11.5	12.7	13.9
Utah	99,937	51.3	166,240	90.9	31.5	6.3	11.5	43.2	72.5	22.5	10.7	9.2
Wasatch	4,743	48.6	8,448	89.3	26.3	4.2	8.0	49.5	74.7	23.4	6.8	6.6
Washington	29,939	39.5	51,842	87.6	21.0	4.1	7.6	42.5	75.8	13.9	10.9	11.7
Wayne	890	37.6	1,493	88.5	20.9	1.7	3.2	62.7	70.6	11.3	11.1	12.6
Weber	65,698	43.6	111,156	85.0	19.9	6.4	12.6	51.7	78.7	20.2	10.9	9.0
VERMONT	240,634	33.6	404,223	86.4	29.4	3.8	5.9	59.1	75.2	18.3	8.7	8.8
Addison	13,068	36.4	22,468	86.4	29.8	3.5	5.1	60.3	71.3	18.4	7.6	8.5
Bennington	14,846	32.5	25,311	84.9	27.1	2.7	4.4	61.6	76.0	18.3	9.4	10.2
Caledonia	11,663	34.4	19,596	82.6	22.5	2.5	4.5	61.9	75.7	11.9	11.0	11.0
Chittenden	56,452	33.7	92,651	90.6	41.2	5.9	8.0	51.5	76.1	26.1	7.5	6.6
Essex	2,602	34.0	4,384	75.0	10.8	5.5	10.1	68.0	75.8	6.3	11.3	12.6
Franklin	16,765	40.1	29,485	82.6	16.6	3.7	6.5	62.1	73.3	15.1	8.8	9.4
Grand Isle	2,761	33.6	4,796	84.2	25.0	4.2	5.7	61.1	73.8	20.0	7.0	7.3
Lamoille	9,221	33.8	15,281	87.0	31.2	3.8	4.8	56.8	74.8	17.6	8.6	9.8
Orange	10,936	35.6	18,821	84.1	23.9	1.8	3.1	67.2	74.5	14.9	8.9	8.8
Orleans	10,446	34.1	17,814	78.2	16.1	5.5	9.8	64.1	72.7	9.2	12.2	13.9
Rutland	25,678	31.7	43,289	84.3	23.2	2.0	4.6	62.0	77.9	13.4	9.9	9.9
Washington	23,659	32.6	39,167	88.4	32.2	3.6	6.1	59.5	74.1	18.8	7.6	8.1
Windham	18,375	31.9	30,542	87.3	30.5	3.1	4.7	59.9	74.0	16.2	9.0	8.9
Windsor	24,162	30.9	40,618	88.1	30.2	3.0	4.3	61.2	76.4	18.8	8.1	8.9
VIRGINIA	2,699,173	35.9	4,666,574	81.5	29.5	8.1	11.1	52.2	77.1	26.5	9.5	8.9
Accomack	15,299	34.4	25,894	67.9	13.5	4.2	6.7	60.3	76.7	9.9	14.9	17.1
Albemarle	31,876	34.1	53,847	87.4	47.7	7.3	8.6	49.8	78.8	30.6	7.3	6.1
Alleghany[4]	5,149	33.0	9,168	77.5	13.6	0.9	2.1	71.3	85.3	13.6	10.8	9.9
Amelia	4,240	38.1	7,789	68.3	9.8	0.7	2.6	63.2	78.2	16.3	9.1	9.3
Amherst	11,941	35.6	21,293	70.6	13.1	1.2	3.0	63.7	79.5	12.9	11.2	10.5

See footnotes at end of table.

Table B-4. Counties — **Population Characteristics**—Con.

[Includes United States, states, and 3,141 counties/county equivalents defined as of February 22, 2005. For more information on these areas, see Appendix C, Geographic Information]

County	Households, 2000 Total	With individuals under 18 years (percent of total)	Educational attainment,[1] 2000 Total persons	High school graduate or higher (percent)	Bachelor's degree or higher (percent)	Foreign-born population, 2000 (percent)	Persons 5 years and over Speaking language other than English at home, 2000 (percent)	Residing in same house in 1995 and 2000 (percent)	Workers who drove alone to work,[2] 2000 (percent)	House-holds with income of $75,000 or more in 1999 (percent)	Persons in poverty (percent) 2004	2000
VIRGINIA—Con.												
Appomattox	5,322	36.2	9,421	70.7	10.5	1.4	2.9	63.9	81.9	13.2	11.8	11.1
Arlington	86,352	20.9	138,844	87.8	60.2	27.8	33.1	39.3	54.9	41.0	7.1	5.8
Augusta	24,818	36.1	45,609	78.2	15.4	1.4	2.6	62.0	84.1	17.5	7.1	7.4
Bath	2,053	29.9	3,705	74.0	11.1	4.3	4.6	65.6	78.4	13.0	7.3	7.5
Bedford	23,838	35.0	42,413	80.1	20.9	1.8	2.8	60.4	85.2	20.1	7.7	6.7
Bland	2,568	30.8	4,989	70.9	9.2	0.8	3.0	69.4	85.4	10.2	11.9	11.3
Botetourt	11,700	35.3	21,621	81.4	19.6	0.9	2.2	63.1	86.8	23.3	6.0	5.2
Brunswick	6,277	32.7	12,777	63.2	10.8	0.7	2.1	58.6	75.6	9.6	18.1	16.9
Buchanan	10,464	33.9	18,851	52.9	8.0	0.3	1.4	76.4	82.2	6.4	21.1	21.5
Buckingham	5,324	35.0	10,893	62.8	8.5	0.8	2.2	56.9	73.5	10.0	17.3	16.9
Campbell	20,639	34.2	35,018	73.4	14.6	1.1	2.8	62.9	85.0	13.6	11.1	9.6
Caroline	8,021	38.0	15,082	71.3	12.1	1.7	2.7	67.3	77.5	17.0	9.5	10.4
Carroll	12,186	30.4	21,006	64.3	9.5	0.9	2.8	69.5	78.8	7.4	13.3	12.3
Charles City	2,670	34.4	4,845	65.7	10.5	1.3	2.6	74.3	79.9	17.9	9.9	9.5
Charlotte	4,951	33.4	8,570	63.2	10.3	0.8	4.1	66.5	75.3	7.8	15.2	14.7
Chesterfield	93,772	43.6	167,037	88.1	32.6	5.2	7.8	54.8	85.8	33.9	6.5	4.8
Clarke	4,942	32.9	9,015	82.1	23.9	2.5	3.4	59.8	77.3	27.6	6.1	6.5
Craig	2,060	33.6	3,561	76.6	10.8	0.3	1.8	65.8	78.9	10.2	9.1	8.4
Culpeper	12,141	39.4	22,628	73.7	15.7	3.5	5.8	51.7	74.8	22.4	8.8	9.0
Cumberland	3,528	35.3	6,183	63.8	11.8	1.3	4.9	64.3	77.1	10.8	13.9	13.5
Dickenson	6,732	33.6	11,308	58.9	6.7	0.2	1.5	72.5	80.7	5.0	18.3	19.3
Dinwiddie	9,107	37.7	17,199	70.0	11.0	1.4	3.3	64.1	85.1	16.8	10.1	9.4
Essex	3,995	32.3	7,052	73.5	17.4	1.4	3.1	62.7	77.0	13.6	11.7	12.2
Fairfax	350,714	38.4	653,237	90.7	54.8	24.5	30.0	49.2	73.4	54.6	5.3	4.1
Fauquier	19,842	39.7	36,792	84.5	27.1	3.6	5.2	57.1	77.6	38.5	5.8	5.4
Floyd	5,791	31.0	9,836	70.1	12.5	1.5	2.9	64.8	73.4	8.7	10.9	10.6
Fluvanna	7,387	35.8	14,125	80.0	24.5	2.3	3.4	56.6	77.5	21.3	6.2	6.5
Franklin	18,963	32.2	33,037	72.2	14.8	1.4	3.1	61.7	80.3	15.4	10.9	10.0
Frederick	22,097	39.5	39,271	78.6	18.6	2.4	4.5	56.5	83.4	21.4	5.8	6.1
Giles	6,994	31.0	11,856	75.9	12.4	0.8	2.0	68.0	79.1	11.0	10.3	9.5
Gloucester	13,127	38.7	23,273	81.7	17.6	1.9	4.6	59.7	79.3	19.7	8.7	8.3
Goochland	6,158	33.0	12,248	78.8	29.4	2.0	3.5	61.8	83.1	35.1	6.9	6.7
Grayson	7,259	28.8	13,086	64.1	8.0	1.2	2.9	68.5	73.8	8.1	14.3	13.5
Greene	5,574	41.8	10,120	78.4	19.8	1.6	2.9	56.9	78.8	17.6	7.8	7.1
Greensville	3,375	35.7	8,610	62.1	11.0	0.3	1.0	63.4	81.1	10.3	16.5	17.7
Halifax[5]	15,018	33.1	26,073	63.9	9.5	1.0	2.6	67.2	81.1	10.2	16.0	14.6
Hanover	31,121	42.1	56,892	86.6	28.7	1.8	3.6	57.0	86.2	34.8	5.1	4.1
Henrico	108,121	34.6	177,191	86.6	34.9	6.7	9.0	50.1	84.8	26.6	7.8	6.2
Henry	23,910	32.7	40,518	64.9	9.4	2.7	4.6	66.2	79.8	9.2	13.4	11.1
Highland	1,131	26.3	1,929	72.8	13.2	0.4	2.8	76.0	70.3	7.3	10.8	11.9
Isle of Wight	11,319	38.3	20,121	76.2	17.5	1.1	3.0	63.4	84.3	22.0	9.2	8.7
James City	19,003	32.9	34,042	89.3	41.5	4.1	5.9	49.7	82.0	34.8	6.6	5.8
King and Queen	2,673	32.7	4,663	68.2	10.3	0.9	1.8	69.2	77.0	13.9	11.2	11.9
King George	6,091	41.4	10,803	80.4	23.6	1.3	4.3	57.1	79.6	27.3	6.6	7.0
King William	4,846	40.6	8,960	79.1	14.8	1.2	4.1	64.1	82.6	22.5	6.8	6.6
Lancaster	5,004	24.4	8,841	74.4	24.5	1.7	3.3	63.8	79.1	19.6	12.3	12.9
Lee	9,706	32.5	16,314	60.6	9.5	0.5	2.3	64.8	80.9	8.0	21.1	22.3
Loudoun	59,900	45.1	109,567	92.5	47.2	11.3	15.0	40.4	81.6	55.0	3.4	2.8
Louisa	9,945	36.0	17,697	71.7	14.0	1.3	2.6	61.2	75.8	16.1	9.7	9.2
Lunenburg	4,998	31.5	9,305	63.4	9.2	1.2	3.2	68.6	75.4	8.5	17.1	16.3
Madison	4,739	34.5	8,644	75.0	19.4	2.2	3.4	64.1	76.9	15.6	9.1	9.8
Mathews	3,932	26.6	6,926	80.8	19.2	2.2	3.4	62.7	75.6	18.9	8.3	8.7
Mecklenburg	12,951	30.7	22,981	67.8	12.1	1.6	4.0	64.9	77.9	11.9	14.8	13.4
Middlesex	4,253	25.7	7,436	73.7	18.9	2.1	4.2	58.7	79.0	16.2	11.6	11.5
Montgomery	30,997	27.1	43,106	82.8	35.9	5.8	7.4	38.7	77.4	15.1	14.9	12.5
Nelson	5,887	30.4	10,403	69.0	20.8	1.9	3.6	66.9	70.8	18.2	10.4	10.3
New Kent	4,925	38.4	9,285	80.6	16.3	0.9	2.2	61.6	85.0	28.9	5.5	5.1
Northampton	5,321	31.3	9,133	67.4	15.7	3.4	5.7	64.7	71.1	10.9	17.6	18.6
Northumberland	5,470	23.5	9,476	75.9	21.7	1.6	2.5	64.6	81.2	17.8	11.8	11.8
Nottoway	5,664	34.8	10,841	64.4	11.1	1.4	3.6	61.4	75.9	10.0	16.8	16.4
Orange	10,150	33.2	18,202	75.2	18.5	1.9	3.1	58.2	78.6	18.8	8.0	8.9
Page	9,305	33.2	16,085	64.8	9.8	1.5	2.9	64.2	74.3	10.1	11.6	10.6
Patrick	8,141	30.9	13,815	62.2	8.6	1.5	3.7	66.9	76.8	7.8	14.0	12.5
Pittsylvania	24,684	34.3	43,120	67.3	9.3	1.0	2.7	66.2	82.1	11.1	12.1	10.1
Powhatan	7,258	41.0	15,411	78.9	19.1	1.5	2.8	59.2	85.3	31.6	5.7	5.4
Prince Edward	6,561	33.9	11,089	69.9	19.2	1.4	5.2	54.6	69.5	11.1	18.7	18.6
Prince George	10,159	45.7	20,272	81.6	19.4	4.5	9.9	49.8	76.3	24.3	8.6	7.6
Prince William	94,570	47.6	171,058	88.8	31.5	11.5	16.3	45.6	72.7	41.8	5.6	4.8
Pulaski	14,643	30.2	25,362	74.2	12.5	0.6	2.1	62.5	85.0	11.6	13.1	11.2
Rappahannock	2,788	30.7	5,059	76.0	22.9	3.2	3.0	66.1	74.8	25.6	6.6	7.9

See footnotes at end of table.

[Includes United States, states, and 3,141 counties/county equivalents defined as of February 22, 2005. For more information on these areas, see Appendix C, Geographic Information]

County	Households, 2000		Educational attainment,[1] 2000			Foreign-born population, 2000 (percent)	Persons 5 years and over		Workers who drove alone to work,[2] 2000 (percent)	House-holds with income of $75,000 or more in 1999 (percent)	Persons in poverty (percent)	
	Total	With individuals under 18 years (percent of total)	Total persons	High school graduate or higher (percent)	Bachelor's degree or higher (percent)		Speaking language other than English at home, 2000 (percent)	Residing in same house in 1995 and 2000 (percent)			2004	2000
VIRGINIA—Con.												
Richmond.	2,937	30.9	6,552	60.0	9.9	1.9	5.1	59.2	78.6	13.1	15.8	15.7
Roanoke	34,686	32.7	60,771	85.8	28.2	3.1	5.1	58.0	87.7	24.6	6.6	4.8
Rockbridge.	8,486	32.0	14,556	71.0	18.7	2.0	3.0	64.7	79.0	11.4	9.3	8.9
Rockingham	25,355	36.0	45,123	72.4	17.6	3.3	5.6	62.6	79.5	16.0	8.5	7.7
Russell	11,789	34.1	21,362	62.5	9.4	0.4	1.8	67.5	82.1	7.7	16.5	16.7
Scott	9,795	30.2	16,846	64.4	8.3	0.3	1.2	69.5	80.9	6.8	14.9	14.1
Shenandoah.	14,296	30.9	24,926	75.3	14.7	3.1	4.9	59.0	79.4	14.4	8.6	8.0
Smyth.	13,493	32.3	23,255	67.5	10.6	0.5	2.3	63.9	81.2	8.7	14.0	13.1
Southampton	6,279	35.6	12,070	63.2	11.7	0.3	2.2	63.0	81.6	13.0	13.5	14.0
Spotsylvania	31,308	46.0	56,633	83.8	22.8	3.2	5.5	53.4	79.1	32.1	5.7	5.3
Stafford	30,187	50.4	56,029	88.6	29.6	4.0	7.3	50.2	74.1	41.5	4.9	4.4
Surry	2,619	36.8	4,569	70.4	12.8	0.5	1.7	67.3	75.1	12.5	10.7	11.6
Sussex	4,126	33.4	8,899	57.6	10.0	1.0	2.2	62.3	80.6	11.1	17.7	17.2
Tazewell.	18,277	31.9	31,291	67.5	11.0	1.0	2.4	66.7	84.1	8.8	15.7	15.5
Warren.	12,087	36.3	21,127	75.5	15.0	2.1	3.5	56.7	72.4	19.8	8.9	8.6
Washington	21,056	30.9	35,958	72.3	16.1	0.9	2.3	61.6	84.9	12.2	12.3	11.4
Westmoreland	6,846	30.4	11,808	69.3	13.3	3.1	5.0	68.0	77.4	14.5	13.3	13.4
Wise	16,013	34.3	26,731	62.5	10.8	0.5	2.1	64.9	82.6	7.9	19.2	19.3
Wythe	11,511	31.8	19,528	70.2	12.1	0.5	2.5	65.1	78.7	10.3	11.9	11.8
York	20,000	44.9	36,168	91.7	37.4	5.2	7.2	47.8	85.5	35.5	4.8	4.3
Independent Cities												
Alexandria	61,889	20.5	95,730	86.8	54.3	25.4	30.0	36.7	62.8	35.1	8.3	7.5
Bedford	2,519	30.5	4,494	70.9	15.2	1.6	3.4	57.5	73.9	8.3	15.1	15.0
Bristol	7,678	27.5	12,366	72.4	17.0	1.4	2.5	58.3	84.7	9.0	16.8	15.4
Buena Vista	2,547	33.3	4,250	69.0	10.5	0.5	2.7	59.7	77.2	8.7	11.4	10.5
Charlottesville	16,851	23.0	22,868	80.8	40.8	6.9	10.7	35.1	60.4	14.7	17.2	16.8
Chesapeake[4]	69,900	45.3	125,498	85.1	24.7	3.0	5.6	51.9	83.9	25.6	8.7	7.7
Clifton Forge[4]	1,841	29.4	3,110	75.0	9.6	0.3	2.5	60.1	74.4	7.5	(NA)	(NA)
Colonial Heights	7,027	32.0	11,675	83.7	19.0	4.9	7.5	58.7	88.5	20.8	7.3	6.2
Covington	2,835	27.9	4,485	71.4	6.4	2.3	3.0	62.5	76.2	6.2	12.9	13.0
Danville	20,607	30.6	33,196	68.5	13.9	1.4	3.6	60.0	79.9	9.9	19.4	17.1
Emporia.	2,226	34.1	3,775	58.5	14.2	3.2	3.6	54.8	76.7	9.7	16.5	15.9
Fairfax.	8,035	30.5	15,222	88.6	45.7	25.4	30.6	47.7	73.5	44.4	5.0	4.5
Falls Church	4,471	31.5	7,464	95.9	63.7	16.1	18.7	47.2	63.0	50.0	2.6	2.9
Franklin	3,384	34.5	5,642	71.0	16.4	0.7	2.9	57.5	76.3	16.5	16.6	17.5
Fredericksburg	8,102	24.1	11,211	80.2	30.5	5.2	9.6	39.5	70.6	17.0	14.4	12.8
Galax	2,950	30.2	4,782	60.4	11.1	8.6	11.0	53.5	76.5	7.3	17.0	18.4
Hampton	53,887	36.8	92,477	85.5	21.8	3.9	6.7	47.7	79.7	16.6	12.5	12.2
Harrisonburg.	13,133	25.3	17,448	76.8	31.2	9.2	13.9	33.2	70.7	13.2	17.9	19.7
Hopewell	9,055	36.5	14,323	71.8	10.2	1.9	5.0	54.0	82.7	10.0	15.5	14.5
Lexington	2,232	20.0	3,285	77.1	42.6	4.0	7.7	42.0	55.7	20.7	15.8	16.9
Lynchburg	25,477	30.9	40,806	78.0	25.2	3.2	5.6	51.6	76.8	14.4	17.8	15.0
Manassas	11,757	45.5	21,188	81.3	28.1	14.2	18.5	48.4	75.1	36.9	7.5	5.9
Manassas Park	3,254	50.2	6,224	76.4	20.3	15.0	20.0	39.8	72.8	34.2	6.0	5.9
Martinsville	6,498	30.8	10,843	68.5	16.6	2.7	4.7	58.0	78.2	10.4	18.5	16.4
Newport News.	69,686	39.3	110,083	84.5	19.9	4.8	8.3	45.5	78.7	14.1	13.4	12.4
Norfolk.	86,210	34.9	135,258	78.4	19.6	5.0	8.9	42.7	66.8	12.4	18.8	18.6
Norton.	1,730	29.8	2,665	66.5	14.0	1.1	3.1	49.5	77.6	8.9	18.0	18.6
Petersburg	13,799	33.8	22,289	68.6	14.8	2.3	4.4	55.6	73.4	10.3	18.3	17.8
Poquoson.	4,166	41.8	7,759	88.5	31.6	2.9	3.8	59.4	87.8	36.0	4.6	4.2
Portsmouth.	38,170	36.6	63,685	75.2	13.8	1.6	4.6	51.4	72.8	11.7	15.9	15.7
Radford	5,809	20.7	6,766	83.4	34.1	2.5	5.2	31.6	75.0	9.5	19.1	17.2
Richmond.	84,549	27.7	128,555	75.2	29.5	3.9	6.7	48.0	70.6	14.8	19.8	18.1
Roanoke	42,003	29.1	65,593	76.0	18.7	3.1	5.3	53.4	79.7	11.0	16.3	15.0
Salem	9,954	30.4	16,657	82.0	19.8	2.1	4.0	56.3	84.2	16.6	7.9	7.1
South Boston[5].	(X)	(NA)	(X)	(NA)	(NA)	(NA)	(NA)	(NA)	(NA)	(NA)	(NA)	(NA)
Staunton	9,676	27.5	16,703	75.6	20.4	2.0	4.4	55.1	80.1	13.4	12.5	11.9
Suffolk.	23,283	41.7	41,662	76.8	17.3	1.9	4.0	53.4	80.4	18.7	10.8	11.6
Virginia Beach.	154,455	42.1	266,627	90.4	28.1	6.6	10.3	45.8	82.0	24.0	7.8	6.8
Waynesboro	8,332	32.4	13,303	77.9	20.6	2.4	5.0	52.0	81.9	11.2	12.7	11.6
Williamsburg.	3,619	18.4	5,360	89.6	45.0	5.2	7.7	28.0	66.6	19.9	17.3	17.7
Winchester	10,001	28.7	15,316	75.4	23.7	6.8	10.0	44.1	72.2	15.2	11.5	11.0
WASHINGTON.	2,271,398	35.2	3,827,507	87.1	27.7	10.4	14.0	48.6	73.3	24.2	11.6	9.6
Adams.	5,229	47.3	9,242	63.3	12.2	22.9	43.3	56.4	69.0	8.5	16.0	15.9
Asotin	8,364	33.7	13,619	85.8	18.0	1.8	3.0	51.7	82.3	13.6	15.4	14.7
Benton.	52,866	40.7	88,217	85.1	26.3	8.5	14.2	51.2	80.2	25.1	10.7	9.5
Chelan.	25,021	36.9	42,425	79.1	21.9	12.9	19.6	51.9	73.5	17.5	13.0	12.5
Clallam	27,164	27.8	45,711	85.5	20.8	4.5	6.3	54.3	74.0	13.4	12.3	12.1

See footnotes at end of table.

[Includes United States, states, and 3,141 counties/county equivalents defined as of February 22, 2005. For more information on these areas, see Appendix C, Geographic Information]

County	Households, 2000 Total	Households, 2000 With individuals under 18 years (percent of total)	Educational attainment,[1] 2000 Total persons	Educational attainment,[1] 2000 High school graduate or higher (percent)	Educational attainment,[1] 2000 Bachelor's degree or higher (percent)	Foreign-born population, 2000 (percent)	Persons 5 years and over Speaking language other than English at home, 2000 (percent)	Persons 5 years and over Residing in same house in 1995 and 2000 (percent)	Workers who drove alone to work,[2] 2000 (percent)	Households with income of $75,000 or more in 1999 (percent)	Persons in poverty (percent) 2004	Persons in poverty (percent) 2000
WASHINGTON—Con.												
Clark	127,208	40.0	217,293	87.8	22.1	8.5	11.5	44.2	79.3	24.2	11.2	8.9
Columbia	1,687	30.1	2,827	82.7	17.5	3.2	6.2	58.1	76.0	11.7	12.0	12.2
Cowlitz	35,850	36.0	60,355	83.2	13.3	3.7	6.0	52.6	81.6	16.4	14.3	12.5
Douglas	11,726	41.2	20,435	78.4	16.2	13.5	19.5	54.4	75.4	15.4	12.1	11.7
Ferry	2,823	33.6	4,748	82.7	13.5	2.5	3.7	54.9	68.9	8.2	17.8	20.2
Franklin	14,840	49.1	26,779	63.5	13.6	25.2	44.6	49.0	69.6	18.3	15.2	16.7
Garfield	987	32.1	1,655	84.4	17.0	1.0	2.0	62.9	78.5	11.1	12.3	12.6
Grant	25,204	43.2	43,309	72.2	13.7	17.1	28.3	50.0	73.0	13.1	16.2	15.6
Grays Harbor	26,808	33.9	44,588	81.1	12.7	4.2	6.4	56.7	75.8	12.3	15.8	15.0
Island	27,784	35.2	47,112	92.1	27.0	6.4	8.2	46.5	73.6	20.3	8.3	7.6
Jefferson	11,645	24.8	19,551	91.6	28.4	4.0	4.0	52.9	68.8	16.8	10.9	10.7
King	710,916	30.4	1,188,740	90.3	40.0	15.4	18.4	47.6	68.7	32.4	10.0	7.2
Kitsap	86,416	38.5	148,704	90.8	25.3	5.7	8.3	48.7	66.3	24.1	9.3	8.1
Kittitas	13,382	27.9	19,303	87.2	26.2	5.3	7.7	44.0	68.4	14.7	14.4	14.0
Klickitat	7,473	35.3	12,806	81.7	16.4	6.0	10.6	53.3	71.8	11.6	15.1	15.0
Lewis	26,306	34.8	44,857	80.5	12.9	4.1	6.4	55.3	78.8	12.2	14.6	13.6
Lincoln	4,151	31.1	7,117	86.5	18.8	1.2	2.9	59.0	71.1	12.6	11.8	12.4
Mason	18,912	32.3	33,936	83.7	15.6	4.4	6.3	53.8	74.2	14.2	12.2	12.2
Okanogan	15,027	36.3	25,826	76.6	15.9	10.2	15.1	54.4	70.3	9.8	18.8	19.8
Pacific	9,096	25.8	15,298	78.9	15.2	6.0	8.2	57.0	73.7	10.2	14.5	14.8
Pend Oreille	4,639	32.3	7,995	81.0	12.3	2.0	3.5	59.0	72.1	11.7	15.9	16.9
Pierce	260,800	38.9	442,665	86.9	20.6	8.1	11.8	46.9	76.4	22.3	11.8	9.5
San Juan	6,466	24.1	10,691	94.4	40.2	5.9	4.9	50.1	61.9	22.6	8.4	8.7
Skagit	38,852	35.6	66,959	84.0	20.8	8.8	11.7	50.2	77.1	20.0	12.2	10.5
Skamania	3,755	37.0	6,557	85.9	16.8	3.5	4.9	53.0	76.0	14.7	11.5	11.4
Snohomish	224,852	39.7	388,997	89.2	24.4	9.7	12.2	47.0	75.2	29.2	9.5	7.1
Spokane	163,611	34.7	266,829	89.1	25.0	4.5	6.6	50.8	76.7	16.4	13.3	11.6
Stevens	15,017	37.5	25,984	85.4	15.3	2.4	2.7	56.5	74.6	11.9	15.1	15.2
Thurston	81,625	35.4	135,686	89.5	29.8	6.1	9.2	48.1	77.2	22.6	9.4	8.6
Wahkiakum	1,553	29.3	2,715	84.2	14.8	1.3	4.3	62.2	67.9	11.9	9.8	10.8
Walla Walla	19,647	34.6	34,372	81.1	23.3	9.4	16.2	51.1	73.0	14.4	14.7	13.7
Whatcom	64,446	32.5	102,787	87.5	27.2	9.8	9.2	45.4	75.9	18.2	13.2	11.4
Whitman	15,257	25.5	20,070	92.8	44.0	7.7	11.0	38.0	58.1	13.1	16.6	15.1
Yakima	73,993	43.9	130,747	68.7	15.3	16.9	31.8	53.8	77.5	14.3	18.6	17.4
WEST VIRGINIA	736,481	31.8	1,233,581	75.2	14.8	1.1	2.7	63.3	80.3	11.1	16.2	15.5
Barbour	6,123	32.9	10,510	72.7	11.8	0.5	1.9	67.0	77.6	5.7	19.0	19.4
Berkeley	29,569	36.8	50,092	77.6	15.1	1.7	3.6	54.7	80.8	14.3	11.2	10.4
Boone	10,291	34.4	17,282	64.0	7.2	0.4	1.4	66.4	83.5	7.8	18.2	18.4
Braxton	5,771	33.4	10,273	67.3	9.2	0.2	1.4	66.5	76.3	7.4	20.1	20.4
Brooke	10,396	29.5	17,855	79.7	13.4	1.1	3.8	68.8	85.7	10.9	12.0	10.4
Cabell	41,180	27.8	64,444	80.0	20.9	1.3	2.7	56.2	80.9	12.0	18.4	15.4
Calhoun	3,071	32.0	5,283	62.4	9.3	0.6	1.8	70.1	67.1	4.4	21.6	21.2
Clay	4,020	36.3	6,766	63.7	7.3	0.1	2.2	66.0	77.2	5.2	22.4	24.2
Doddridge	2,845	35.8	4,897	69.4	10.2	0.6	2.8	68.8	74.6	6.6	17.6	16.6
Fayette	18,945	32.7	32,721	68.6	10.7	0.8	2.0	63.7	81.9	7.3	20.5	20.6
Gilmer	2,768	31.0	4,515	70.0	17.1	1.0	1.9	57.0	73.1	7.8	19.7	22.2
Grant	4,591	32.4	7,859	70.8	11.4	0.5	2.2	69.5	75.3	7.3	14.1	13.3
Greenbrier	14,571	30.3	24,373	73.4	13.6	0.6	2.0	64.3	80.6	8.8	15.8	15.9
Hampshire	7,955	34.1	13,690	71.3	11.3	0.6	2.1	66.7	69.4	7.0	14.0	13.8
Hancock	13,678	29.2	23,502	82.9	11.5	1.8	5.8	67.8	86.1	11.3	11.2	9.7
Hardy	5,204	32.8	8,759	70.3	9.4	0.5	1.6	64.6	73.5	9.1	12.5	12.1
Harrison	27,867	32.5	46,870	78.4	16.3	1.4	3.0	65.1	82.8	11.6	16.5	15.3
Jackson	11,061	34.6	19,074	77.4	12.4	0.5	1.7	63.0	80.7	9.9	15.0	14.1
Jefferson	16,165	35.5	27,920	79.0	21.6	2.1	4.1	56.3	72.1	22.2	9.0	8.8
Kanawha	86,226	29.3	140,588	80.0	20.6	1.4	3.1	62.7	79.6	15.3	14.5	13.0
Lewis	6,946	31.3	11,872	73.7	11.2	0.5	1.5	62.6	79.2	6.5	16.5	17.2
Lincoln	8,664	36.2	14,864	62.7	5.9	(Z)	1.5	69.8	79.5	7.2	21.8	22.2
Logan	14,880	34.8	25,824	63.1	8.8	0.5	1.4	69.0	80.2	9.1	20.4	21.8
McDowell	11,169	33.7	18,802	50.0	5.6	0.5	1.4	75.7	83.4	3.3	33.0	32.1
Marion	23,652	28.6	38,957	79.5	16.0	1.0	2.7	65.4	82.9	10.1	15.8	14.4
Marshall	14,207	32.1	24,707	79.7	10.7	0.7	2.4	69.4	82.3	11.4	14.9	13.4
Mason	10,587	33.2	17,947	72.4	8.8	0.5	1.7	66.6	83.5	8.5	17.3	16.3
Mercer	26,509	29.9	43,673	72.1	13.8	0.8	2.2	63.5	83.7	8.7	18.9	17.8
Mineral	10,784	33.2	18,443	80.3	11.7	0.6	1.8	66.9	79.1	9.7	14.0	13.8
Mingo	11,303	37.1	18,793	59.6	7.3	0.3	1.6	72.1	83.2	6.4	25.4	24.4
Monongalia	33,446	25.9	47,943	83.6	32.4	3.8	6.8	49.8	75.9	13.9	15.7	14.2
Monroe	5,447	31.3	10,474	73.7	8.2	0.5	1.7	63.3	79.4	8.8	14.3	16.3
Morgan	6,145	31.1	10,591	75.8	11.2	1.4	2.4	62.1	76.4	10.6	10.6	10.8
Nicholas	10,722	33.3	18,149	70.0	9.8	0.6	2.2	68.3	79.3	8.3	18.2	18.7
Ohio	19,733	28.1	32,263	83.0	23.1	1.3	3.6	62.1	78.2	12.7	14.9	13.2

See footnotes at end of table.

Table B-4. Counties — **Population Characteristics**—Con.

[Includes United States, states, and 3,141 counties/county equivalents defined as of February 22, 2005. For more information on these areas, see Appendix C, Geographic Information]

County	Households, 2000		Educational attainment,[1] 2000			Persons 5 years and over					Persons in poverty (percent)	
	Total	With individuals under 18 years (percent of total)	Total persons	High school graduate or higher (percent)	Bachelor's degree or higher (percent)	Foreign-born population, 2000 (percent)	Speaking language other than English at home, 2000 (percent)	Residing in same house in 1995 and 2000 (percent)	Workers who drove alone to work,[2] 2000 (percent)	House-holds with income of $75,000 or more in 1999 (percent)	2004	2000
WEST VIRGINIA—Con.												
Pendleton	3,350	30.4	5,813	72.0	10.8	0.7	2.6	69.7	70.7	6.7	12.1	12.2
Pleasants	2,887	35.5	5,121	79.4	9.7	0.5	1.4	64.3	85.3	12.2	12.3	12.0
Pocahontas	3,835	28.5	6,556	70.9	11.8	0.6	1.9	64.3	72.1	7.0	15.8	16.5
Preston	11,544	34.4	20,050	74.0	10.8	0.6	1.7	69.9	76.7	6.9	15.8	15.2
Putnam	20,028	37.7	34,854	83.8	19.7	1.0	2.2	59.5	85.2	20.6	9.9	8.6
Raleigh	31,793	31.6	55,201	72.0	12.7	1.2	3.6	62.4	83.1	10.5	17.8	17.2
Randolph	11,072	32.6	19,498	73.5	13.6	0.7	2.2	63.6	76.8	8.3	17.2	16.7
Ritchie	4,184	32.9	7,177	73.4	7.1	0.3	1.1	68.8	80.0	7.6	15.5	16.3
Roane	6,161	33.6	10,442	66.8	9.0	0.6	1.8	62.4	74.6	7.7	19.4	19.5
Summers	5,530	28.6	9,302	65.4	10.1	0.4	1.4	67.2	79.3	5.0	22.8	22.3
Taylor	6,320	33.3	11,146	74.7	11.3	0.6	2.3	67.4	82.9	7.8	16.7	17.8
Tucker	3,052	29.1	5,301	75.5	10.6	0.2	2.6	73.6	79.6	7.2	14.5	14.3
Tyler	3,836	32.8	6,749	75.4	8.5	0.3	1.3	66.6	78.7	9.9	15.7	15.0
Upshur	8,972	33.4	15,222	74.6	13.8	0.4	2.1	62.3	76.2	7.6	18.6	18.9
Wayne	17,239	34.0	29,223	70.5	11.9	0.6	1.5	66.9	85.2	8.9	17.4	16.9
Webster	4,010	32.5	6,701	58.2	8.7	0.4	1.5	69.5	69.0	4.2	23.7	26.7
Wetzel	7,164	33.0	12,287	77.6	10.4	0.4	1.6	67.5	81.8	11.6	16.6	15.9
Wirt	2,284	37.8	3,944	72.4	9.9	0.3	1.0	61.9	76.9	8.1	17.1	17.6
Wood	36,275	31.9	60,697	81.4	15.2	1.1	1.9	59.7	84.3	14.0	13.8	13.2
Wyoming	10,454	34.2	17,722	64.3	7.1	0.2	1.5	75.2	79.4	8.1	22.3	22.2
WISCONSIN	2,084,544	33.9	3,475,878	85.1	22.4	3.6	7.3	56.5	79.5	20.3	10.9	8.1
Adams	7,900	26.0	13,730	76.7	10.0	2.3	4.8	59.4	78.1	10.3	13.3	12.3
Ashland	6,718	32.5	10,668	84.1	16.5	1.0	4.4	62.3	73.1	8.0	14.4	12.5
Barron	17,851	33.4	29,942	82.4	14.9	1.2	3.8	58.1	78.5	12.9	11.1	9.3
Bayfield	6,207	30.8	10,526	86.9	21.6	1.2	3.7	66.5	73.8	10.4	10.9	11.4
Brown	87,295	35.6	144,172	86.3	22.5	3.9	7.1	53.3	84.7	21.6	10.0	6.6
Buffalo	5,511	32.5	9,384	84.1	14.0	0.6	3.3	66.4	72.9	11.9	9.3	8.5
Burnett	6,613	27.1	11,273	82.8	14.0	1.2	3.3	62.6	75.4	10.2	11.0	10.1
Calumet	14,910	39.9	26,068	87.3	20.8	2.1	4.9	61.3	82.7	23.8	5.7	4.1
Chippewa	21,356	35.5	36,330	84.3	14.7	0.9	3.0	62.7	81.2	13.1	11.0	8.2
Clark	12,047	36.6	20,991	75.4	10.3	1.2	9.1	66.3	68.7	9.9	11.1	10.9
Columbia	20,439	34.0	35,529	86.2	16.7	1.3	4.6	59.1	79.7	18.1	7.2	5.8
Crawford	6,677	33.3	11,301	81.3	13.2	0.7	2.9	62.0	73.0	11.1	11.6	10.5
Dane	173,484	30.3	269,998	92.2	40.6	6.3	9.3	46.1	74.1	25.9	9.8	6.9
Dodge	31,417	35.5	57,453	82.3	13.2	1.6	4.6	58.2	80.1	17.4	8.1	5.9
Door	11,828	28.2	20,062	87.8	21.4	1.5	4.2	64.1	76.0	15.9	8.1	6.7
Douglas	17,808	31.2	28,653	85.9	18.3	1.6	4.0	61.0	80.3	12.8	13.6	10.8
Dunn	14,337	32.9	22,644	86.6	21.1	2.1	4.7	53.2	74.9	14.2	11.4	10.0
Eau Claire	35,822	31.4	55,290	88.9	27.0	2.2	6.1	50.8	80.3	16.4	11.7	8.7
Florence	2,133	29.1	3,641	83.7	12.4	0.6	4.0	69.2	85.6	9.6	9.9	9.2
Fond du Lac	36,931	34.5	63,548	84.2	16.9	2.0	4.8	59.5	80.8	17.4	8.2	6.1
Forest	4,043	31.0	6,694	78.5	10.0	1.1	5.2	62.1	73.6	10.2	12.3	11.5
Grant	18,465	31.9	30,625	83.5	17.2	1.0	3.7	59.4	72.4	11.6	11.0	9.2
Green	13,212	35.3	22,523	84.1	16.7	1.3	4.0	58.5	76.3	16.8	8.2	6.4
Green Lake	7,703	31.0	13,229	81.9	14.5	1.8	6.1	64.1	74.5	12.2	8.7	7.5
Iowa	8,764	36.4	15,100	88.5	18.5	0.6	3.1	63.3	74.6	16.9	8.1	7.5
Iron	3,083	24.0	5,124	83.7	13.2	1.8	3.9	62.9	76.1	8.7	11.4	10.9
Jackson	7,070	33.7	12,779	79.0	11.3	1.9	5.9	60.4	74.3	11.9	11.3	10.2
Jefferson	28,205	35.0	49,057	84.7	17.4	2.8	6.1	57.5	80.7	20.0	7.6	5.3
Juneau	9,696	32.8	16,457	78.5	10.0	1.5	4.3	61.1	77.8	11.0	11.6	9.7
Kenosha	56,057	37.6	95,038	83.5	19.2	4.8	9.7	55.7	82.8	24.1	10.9	8.2
Kewaunee	7,623	35.0	13,336	84.0	11.4	0.9	3.9	65.4	76.6	16.1	7.2	5.7
La Crosse	41,599	31.4	65,263	89.7	25.4	2.5	5.6	51.0	81.0	16.9	11.9	8.7
Lafayette	6,211	34.9	10,528	85.5	13.3	0.8	2.9	66.7	70.2	11.0	9.0	8.3
Langlade	8,452	31.3	14,372	80.9	11.7	1.0	2.7	65.5	78.2	9.7	12.1	10.1
Lincoln	11,721	33.2	20,120	81.6	13.6	1.6	3.7	63.5	78.4	13.3	8.8	7.0
Manitowoc	32,721	33.0	55,452	84.6	15.5	2.3	5.3	64.6	80.9	16.1	8.1	5.9
Marathon	47,702	35.5	81,925	83.8	18.3	3.5	7.4	61.7	81.1	18.7	8.8	6.8
Marinette	17,585	30.4	29,575	82.5	12.9	1.2	3.9	64.2	78.2	12.0	10.5	8.4
Marquette	5,986	29.0	11,428	78.8	10.1	1.5	6.2	57.9	75.5	9.4	10.1	8.9
Menominee	1,345	52.6	2,399	78.2	12.9	2.7	11.9	69.2	70.0	6.4	22.8	24.1
Milwaukee	377,729	32.6	594,387	80.2	23.6	6.8	13.1	52.3	75.0	17.5	20.2	14.0
Monroe	15,399	36.7	26,323	81.1	13.2	1.8	7.6	58.4	75.6	12.2	11.7	10.4
Oconto	13,979	34.1	24,186	80.6	10.6	0.7	2.9	63.0	77.9	14.6	8.6	7.2
Oneida	15,333	28.7	26,449	85.1	20.0	1.0	3.3	61.1	81.4	14.7	9.6	7.8
Outagamie	60,530	37.4	102,218	88.1	22.5	3.1	6.0	57.4	84.6	22.7	7.0	4.6
Ozaukee	30,857	37.1	54,912	91.9	38.6	3.3	5.7	58.9	84.7	39.5	4.5	3.0
Pepin	2,759	33.5	4,733	82.6	13.3	0.6	5.7	65.8	73.9	13.1	9.4	8.8
Pierce	13,015	36.7	21,542	89.6	24.6	1.0	3.5	56.1	75.1	21.9	7.3	6.0
Polk	16,254	34.1	27,725	85.9	15.6	1.0	3.0	61.4	76.9	16.6	8.4	7.1
Portage	25,040	33.5	40,143	86.5	23.4	2.2	6.4	56.1	78.5	19.5	10.3	7.8

See footnotes at end of table.

County and City Data Book: 2007

U.S. Census Bureau

Table B-4. Counties — **Population Characteristics**—Con.

[Includes United States, states, and 3,141 counties/county equivalents defined as of February 22, 2005. For more information on these areas, see Appendix C, Geographic Information]

County	Households, 2000 Total	Households, 2000 With individuals under 18 years (percent of total)	Educational attainment,[1] 2000 Total persons	High school graduate or higher (percent)	Bachelor's degree or higher (percent)	Foreign-born population, 2000 (percent)	Persons 5 years and over — Speaking language other than English at home, 2000 (percent)	Persons 5 years and over — Residing in same house in 1995 and 2000 (percent)	Workers who drove alone to work,[2] 2000 (percent)	Households with income of $75,000 or more in 1999 (percent)	Persons in poverty (percent) 2004	Persons in poverty (percent) 2000
WISCONSIN—Con.												
Price	6,564	30.4	11,122	82.4	13.0	0.6	3.6	65.9	75.1	11.5	10.6	9.5
Racine	70,819	37.3	122,356	82.9	20.3	4.1	8.4	57.3	83.6	23.8	11.3	8.3
Richland	7,118	32.2	11,896	82.1	14.1	1.0	3.5	62.0	72.0	10.5	11.3	10.2
Rock	58,617	36.3	98,770	83.9	16.7	3.3	6.1	55.3	83.1	20.8	9.9	8.2
Rusk	6,095	30.7	10,296	79.1	11.2	1.7	4.1	64.4	71.6	8.6	12.9	12.2
St. Croix	23,410	39.6	40,357	91.6	26.3	1.1	3.1	56.9	80.7	31.4	5.1	3.9
Sauk	21,644	34.5	36,701	83.5	17.6	1.9	5.0	59.1	77.4	16.1	8.4	7.1
Sawyer	6,640	29.7	11,343	84.7	16.5	1.6	5.2	62.2	73.7	11.4	12.9	12.6
Shawano	15,876	33.4	27,503	81.5	12.6	1.0	3.4	62.3	76.1	13.4	9.6	8.3
Sheboygan	43,545	33.8	74,561	84.4	17.9	4.3	8.7	59.3	81.0	19.0	7.9	5.4
Taylor	7,529	35.6	12,872	78.3	11.0	0.9	4.2	67.5	71.9	13.3	9.9	9.6
Trempealeau	10,747	33.5	18,317	80.9	13.3	0.8	5.3	63.9	74.7	11.5	9.4	8.1
Vernon	10,825	33.2	18,473	78.9	14.0	0.8	9.3	64.1	71.3	10.1	12.4	12.3
Vilas	9,066	25.2	15,667	85.4	17.6	2.4	5.0	64.7	80.2	11.7	9.2	9.0
Walworth	34,522	33.9	58,153	84.2	21.8	5.4	9.0	51.6	80.3	21.6	9.5	6.9
Washburn	6,604	29.6	11,248	83.7	15.2	1.0	3.1	61.9	75.7	10.7	11.4	10.4
Washington	43,842	38.0	77,709	88.8	21.9	1.9	5.0	59.9	85.5	30.4	5.6	3.8
Waukesha	135,229	36.8	241,299	92.0	34.1	3.6	5.9	58.6	87.0	38.7	4.8	3.2
Waupaca	19,863	34.5	34,726	82.7	14.8	1.0	3.7	61.4	80.6	15.0	8.7	6.8
Waushara	9,336	29.5	16,310	78.8	11.7	2.0	5.9	62.9	78.8	11.6	11.4	10.7
Winnebago	61,157	32.4	101,095	86.3	22.8	2.8	5.7	53.7	84.5	18.9	9.1	6.0
Wood	30,135	33.7	50,259	84.8	16.9	2.1	4.5	63.7	82.2	16.3	9.5	7.3
WYOMING	193,608	35.0	315,663	87.9	21.9	2.3	6.4	51.3	75.4	15.7	10.3	10.4
Albany	13,269	25.3	17,016	93.5	44.1	3.8	8.0	35.6	70.7	11.9	14.7	13.2
Big Horn	4,312	35.3	7,343	83.2	15.9	2.2	5.7	58.1	72.8	9.9	12.0	14.1
Campbell	12,207	45.4	20,107	88.3	15.7	1.7	4.9	52.4	77.3	23.2	7.9	6.5
Carbon	6,129	33.5	10,508	83.5	17.2	2.9	10.5	53.6	73.6	13.0	11.8	11.6
Converse	4,694	38.5	7,818	86.4	14.7	1.9	5.6	56.4	68.3	14.7	9.8	10.3
Crook	2,308	33.8	3,888	85.8	17.5	0.9	3.1	64.1	69.3	15.0	7.9	8.6
Fremont	13,545	36.2	23,053	84.8	19.7	0.8	8.1	59.2	73.4	11.0	12.9	15.8
Goshen	5,061	31.0	8,406	84.7	18.6	1.9	7.4	57.0	76.9	9.7	13.9	14.9
Hot Springs	2,108	27.7	3,515	84.2	17.9	1.3	3.4	54.2	69.3	11.9	10.5	12.1
Johnson	2,959	30.4	4,981	90.1	22.2	0.8	3.5	52.6	70.4	11.7	8.7	10.5
Laramie	31,927	35.6	53,041	89.1	23.4	2.9	8.0	46.3	80.4	16.5	10.1	9.4
Lincoln	5,266	38.7	9,049	87.9	17.2	1.4	3.8	59.1	68.7	15.6	8.3	9.0
Natrona	26,819	34.8	42,656	88.3	20.0	1.8	5.1	51.0	82.7	14.9	11.1	11.1
Niobrara	1,011	28.7	1,731	87.3	15.3	0.7	3.3	63.5	66.3	10.7	12.9	14.7
Park	10,312	31.7	17,145	87.6	23.7	1.8	4.2	51.1	74.4	13.0	10.4	11.1
Platte	3,625	32.0	6,034	84.9	15.2	1.5	4.7	61.8	74.0	12.7	11.3	12.3
Sheridan	11,167	30.3	17,980	88.4	22.4	1.6	5.2	50.1	78.9	14.7	11.0	10.7
Sublette	2,371	34.5	4,044	89.0	21.6	1.6	3.6	55.7	71.9	15.4	6.9	8.7
Sweetwater	14,105	41.1	23,053	87.4	17.0	2.7	7.5	54.9	71.6	20.8	8.1	7.7
Teton	7,688	27.1	12,838	94.7	45.8	5.9	8.2	39.5	66.2	29.8	4.9	4.6
Uinta	6,823	46.9	11,443	84.8	15.0	2.5	5.6	51.4	71.1	16.0	9.8	9.9
Washakie	3,278	34.3	5,460	85.6	18.7	2.4	7.0	58.5	77.9	14.9	10.8	11.1
Weston	2,624	33.0	4,554	85.2	14.5	0.8	1.8	62.7	69.3	12.4	9.8	10.2

- Represents zero. NA Not available. X Not applicable. Z Less than .05 percent.

[1]Persons 25 years and over.
[2]Workers 16 years and over.
[3]Yellowstone National Park County became incorporated with Gallatin and Park Counties, MT; effective November 7, 1997.
[4]Clifton Forge independent city became incorporated with Alleghany County, VA; effective July 1, 2001.
[5]South Boston independent city became incorporated with Halifax County, VA; effective June 30, 1995.

Survey, Census, or Data Collection Method: Based on the Census of Population and Housing; for information, see Appendix B, Limitations of the Data and Methodology, and also 2000 Census of Population and Housing, Demographic Profile Technical Documentation, revised August 2002 (related Internet site <http://www.census.gov/prod/cen2000/doc/ProfileTD.pdf>). Census 2000 Summary File 1, Technical Documentation, SF1/13 (RV), issued March 2005 (related Internet site <http://www.census.gov/prod/cen2000/doc/sf1.pdf>). Census 2000 Summary File 3, Technical Documentation, SF3/15 (RV), issued March 2005 (related Internet site <http://www.census.gov/prod/cen2000/doc/sf3.pdf>).

Sources: Households—U.S. Census Bureau, 2000 Census of Population and Housing, "Census 2000 Profiles of General Demographic Characteristics" data files, (DP1) accessed June 14, 2002 (related Internet site <http://www.census.gov/Press-Release/www/2002/demoprofiles.html>). Educational attainment, foreign-born population, language, residence, commuting, and income—U.S. Census Bureau, "Census 2000 Profiles of General Demographic Characteristics" data files, (DP2) accessed June 14, 2002 (related Internet site <http://www.census.gov/Press-Release/www/2002/demoprofiles.html>). Poverty—U.S. Census Bureau, Small Area Income and Poverty Estimates, accessed December 4, 2006 (related Internet site <http://www.census.gov/hhes/www/saipe/index.html>).

Table B-5. Counties — **Births, Deaths, and Infant Deaths**

[Includes United States, states, and 3,141 counties/county equivalents defined as of February 22, 2005. For more information on these areas, see Appendix C, Geographic Information]

County	Births Number 2004	2000	Births Rate per 1,000 population[1] 2004	2000	Deaths Number 2004	2000	Deaths Rate per 1,000 population[1] 2004	2000	Infant deaths[2] Number 2004	2000	1990	Infant deaths[2] Rate per 1,000 live births[3] 2004	2000	1990
UNITED STATES	4,112,052	4,058,814	14.0	14.4	2,397,615	2,403,351	8.2	8.5	27,936	28,035	38,351	6.8	6.9	9.2
ALABAMA	59,510	63,299	13.2	14.2	46,121	45,062	10.2	10.1	516	596	688	8.7	9.4	10.8
Autauga	657	586	13.8	13.3	377	356	7.9	8.1	5	2	7	7.6	3.4	12.2
Baldwin.	1,872	1,813	11.9	12.8	1,549	1,322	9.9	9.3	12	11	8	6.4	6.1	5.8
Barbour	343	400	12.0	13.8	278	303	9.7	10.4	4	5	8	11.7	12.5	19.1
Bibb	251	284	11.8	14.2	220	191	10.3	9.6	3	2	3	12.0	7.0	12.8
Blount.	660	677	12.0	13.2	529	450	9.6	8.8	9	6	7	13.6	8.9	13.5
Bullock	158	165	14.1	14.2	135	146	12.1	12.6	2	4	–	12.7	24.2	–
Butler	262	306	12.7	14.3	287	263	13.9	12.3	3	2	2	11.5	6.5	6.6
Calhoun	1,542	1,528	13.8	13.7	1,284	1,365	11.5	12.3	7	19	24	4.5	12.4	14.1
Chambers	435	493	12.2	13.5	441	506	12.4	13.8	4	3	7	9.2	6.1	12.0
Cherokee	265	303	10.8	12.6	265	266	10.8	11.1	3	3	–	11.3	9.9	–
Chilton	544	589	13.1	14.8	485	412	11.7	10.4	6	7	6	11.0	11.9	12.4
Choctaw	158	201	10.4	12.7	172	175	11.4	11.0	1	4	5	6.3	19.9	20.7
Clarke	339	434	12.4	15.6	281	293	10.3	10.5	2	3	9	5.9	6.9	19.1
Clay.	140	191	10.0	13.4	183	179	13.0	12.5	2	2	1	14.3	10.5	6.4
Cleburne	179	191	12.4	13.5	174	144	12.0	10.2	1	1	1	5.6	5.2	5.6
Coffee	589	576	13.1	13.2	476	454	10.6	10.4	6	3	7	10.2	5.2	10.9
Colbert	607	667	11.1	12.1	595	598	10.9	10.9	9	6	4	14.8	9.0	5.4
Conecuh	135	181	10.1	12.9	181	187	13.5	13.3	–	2	3	–	11.0	11.7
Coosa	112	117	9.9	9.8	145	108	12.8	9.1	2	2	1	17.9	17.1	6.2
Covington	450	451	12.2	12.0	489	495	13.3	13.2	3	2	6	6.7	4.4	11.7
Crenshaw	172	170	12.6	12.4	163	171	11.9	12.5	–	–	–	–	–	–
Cullman	956	991	12.1	12.8	866	879	10.9	11.3	5	4	10	5.2	4.0	10.9
Dale.	745	794	15.2	16.2	434	448	8.9	9.1	5	8	9	6.7	10.1	10.1
Dallas	664	811	14.8	17.5	573	541	12.8	11.7	6	2	10	9.0	2.5	11.1
DeKalb	1,017	911	15.2	14.1	682	660	10.2	10.2	12	9	5	11.8	9.9	6.4
Elmore	958	982	13.3	14.8	640	549	8.9	8.3	7	10	10	7.3	10.2	11.9
Escambia	489	542	12.8	14.1	471	429	12.3	11.2	5	5	6	10.2	9.2	11.4
Etowah	1,197	1,384	11.6	13.4	1,258	1,320	12.2	12.8	6	11	19	5.0	7.9	14.1
Fayette	179	234	9.8	12.7	262	232	14.4	12.6	3	1	8	16.8	4.3	31.0
Franklin.	399	446	13.0	14.3	392	359	12.8	11.5	2	4	4	5.0	9.0	10.4
Geneva.	303	297	11.9	11.5	309	317	12.1	12.3	2	3	2	6.6	10.1	5.9
Greene	135	145	13.9	14.6	116	106	12.0	10.6	3	2	3	22.2	13.8	16.2
Hale.	216	270	11.8	14.7	211	202	11.6	11.0	6	5	3	27.8	18.5	12.8
Henry	194	214	11.7	13.1	197	181	11.9	11.1	1	3	2	5.2	14.0	9.3
Houston	1,247	1,392	13.4	15.7	931	891	10.0	10.0	11	12	12	8.8	8.6	9.3
Jackson	603	659	11.2	12.2	597	518	11.1	9.6	5	5	2	8.3	7.6	2.8
Jefferson.	9,152	9,567	13.9	14.5	7,197	7,186	10.9	10.9	91	115	119	9.9	12.0	11.7
Lamar.	162	203	10.8	12.8	187	221	12.5	13.9	1	1	4	6.2	4.9	19.7
Lauderdale	923	995	10.6	11.3	919	913	10.5	10.4	4	4	7	4.3	4.0	6.6
Lawrence	390	434	11.3	12.4	331	375	9.6	10.8	7	2	4	17.9	4.6	7.8
Lee	1,458	1,457	12.1	12.6	780	771	6.5	6.7	9	15	14	6.2	10.3	10.7
Limestone	824	953	11.9	14.5	576	548	8.3	8.3	4	4	7	4.9	4.2	8.8
Lowndes	161	225	12.2	16.7	149	118	11.3	8.8	2	2	6	12.4	8.9	21.8
Macon	226	315	9.8	13.1	238	296	10.3	12.3	3	3	8	13.3	9.5	18.6
Madison	3,705	3,757	12.6	13.5	2,368	2,213	8.1	8.0	31	21	38	8.4	5.6	9.4
Marengo	280	353	12.7	15.6	246	244	11.2	10.8	3	6	9	10.7	17.0	20.9
Marion	339	379	11.2	12.2	399	377	13.2	12.1	4	4	5	11.8	10.6	14.2
Marshall	1,405	1,168	16.6	14.2	936	890	11.0	10.8	14	10	12	10.0	8.6	11.9
Mobile	5,707	6,359	14.3	15.9	3,904	3,995	9.8	10.0	49	68	72	8.6	10.7	10.9
Monroe	289	352	12.2	14.5	256	276	10.8	11.4	1	3	8	3.5	8.5	19.1
Montgomery	3,279	3,656	14.8	16.4	2,065	1,980	9.3	8.9	23	22	45	7.0	6.0	11.7
Morgan	1,497	1,585	13.3	14.3	1,036	1,025	9.2	9.2	14	14	11	9.4	8.8	7.4
Perry	173	212	15.0	17.9	138	159	12.0	13.5	2	3	1	11.6	14.2	4.5
Pickens.	262	298	12.9	14.2	250	282	12.3	13.5	–	2	12	–	6.7	35.7
Pike	387	458	13.2	15.4	285	320	9.7	10.8	7	5	3	18.1	10.9	6.7
Randolph	277	298	12.3	13.3	273	267	12.1	11.9	2	2	6	7.2	6.7	19.3
Russell	685	701	13.9	14.1	550	627	11.2	12.6	1	15	8	1.5	21.4	11.3
St. Clair	856	876	12.2	13.5	728	552	10.4	8.5	11	8	6	12.9	9.1	7.7
Shelby	2,562	2,225	15.5	15.4	1,038	878	6.3	6.1	13	21	9	5.1	9.4	5.0
Sumter	170	221	12.1	15.0	175	149	12.4	10.1	6	5	2	35.3	22.6	7.2
Talladega	961	1,139	12.0	14.2	886	852	11.1	10.6	7	8	10	7.3	7.0	9.1
Tallapoosa.	472	542	11.6	13.0	527	518	12.9	12.4	2	6	5	4.2	11.1	8.3
Tuscaloosa	2,166	2,331	13.0	14.1	1,485	1,476	8.9	8.9	26	33	22	12.0	14.2	10.1
Walker	878	976	12.6	13.8	977	940	14.0	13.3	8	13	13	9.1	13.3	14.1
Washington	194	260	10.9	14.4	185	172	10.4	9.5	2	1	2	10.3	3.8	6.9
Wilcox	204	263	15.8	20.2	137	139	10.6	10.7	3	5	1	14.7	19.0	4.0
Winston	294	346	12.0	13.9	252	287	10.3	11.5	3	2	5	10.2	5.8	17.1

See footnotes at end of table.

204

Table B-5. Counties — **Births, Deaths, and Infant Deaths**—Con.

[Includes United States, states, and 3,141 counties/county equivalents defined as of February 22, 2005. For more information on these areas, see Appendix C, Geographic Information]

County	Births Number 2004	Births Number 2000	Births Rate per 1,000 population[1] 2004	Births Rate per 1,000 population[1] 2000	Deaths Number 2004	Deaths Number 2000	Deaths Rate per 1,000 population[1] 2004	Deaths Rate per 1,000 population[1] 2000	Infant deaths[2] Number 2004	Infant deaths[2] Number 2000	Infant deaths[2] Number 1990	Infant deaths Rate per 1,000 live births[3] 2004	Infant deaths Rate per 1,000 live births[3] 2000	Infant deaths Rate per 1,000 live births[3] 1990
ALASKA	10,338	9,974	15.7	15.9	3,051	2,914	4.6	4.6	69	68	125	6.7	6.8	10.5
Aleutians East	16	27	6.0	10.1	6	6	2.2	2.2	–	–	–	–	–	–
Aleutians West	40	37	7.3	6.8	12	14	2.2	2.6	–	1	4	–	27.0	21.6
Anchorage	4,392	4,122	16.0	15.8	1,142	1,064	4.2	4.1	24	16	43	5.5	3.9	8.8
Bethel	423	420	24.9	26.1	86	77	5.1	4.8	4	8	8	9.5	19.0	19.5
Bristol Bay	16	16	14.6	13.0	4	10	3.7	8.1	–	–	1	–	–	31.3
Denali	12	–	6.3	–	9	–	4.7	–	–	–	–	–	–	–
Dillingham	94	91	19.0	18.5	25	20	5.1	4.1	–	1	–	–	11.0	–
Fairbanks North Star	1,589	1,538	18.3	18.6	383	330	4.4	4.0	10	12	14	6.3	7.8	8.1
Haines	14	19	6.2	7.9	16	18	7.1	7.5	–	–	–	–	–	–
Juneau	378	409	12.2	13.3	132	131	4.2	4.3	3	2	6	7.9	4.9	10.8
Kenai Peninsula	583	597	11.3	12.0	318	304	6.2	6.1	3	6	7	5.1	10.1	9.4
Ketchikan Gateway	183	192	13.8	13.7	77	97	5.8	6.9	2	2	–	10.9	10.4	–
Kodiak Island	210	233	15.9	16.7	46	44	3.5	3.1	1	–	3	4.8	–	9.0
Lake and Peninsula	32	23	20.2	12.7	8	25	5.1	13.8	–	3	–	–	130.4	–
Matanuska-Susitna	1,007	864	14.0	14.4	332	304	4.6	5.1	3	7	12	3.0	8.1	17.4
Nome	229	191	24.5	20.8	56	58	6.0	6.3	4	3	7	17.5	15.7	27.3
North Slope	169	157	24.1	21.3	46	35	6.6	4.7	2	1	5	11.8	6.4	22.9
Northwest Arctic	177	157	23.4	21.8	32	35	4.2	4.9	4	2	3	22.6	12.7	12.8
Prince of Wales-Outer Ketchikan	57	85	9.9	13.8	29	27	5.0	4.4	–	–	2	–	–	18.3
Sitka	108	130	12.2	14.7	49	54	5.5	6.1	–	1	2	–	7.7	12.6
Skagway-Hoonah-Angoon	30	22	9.6	6.4	16	23	5.1	6.7	–	–	–	–	–	–
Southeast Fairbanks	87	91	14.2	14.8	39	27	6.4	4.4	–	–	1	–	–	8.4
Valdez-Cordova	127	114	12.8	11.1	48	66	4.8	6.4	1	1	3	7.9	8.8	20.3
Wade Hampton	222	214	29.6	30.4	46	39	6.1	5.5	4	2	1	18.0	9.3	3.8
Wrangell-Petersburg	63	83	10.0	12.4	48	35	7.6	5.2	–	–	1	–	–	8.5
Yakutat	6	8	8.5	10.0	4	5	5.7	6.3	–	–	–	–	–	–
Yukon-Koyukuk	74	134	11.8	20.7	42	66	6.7	10.2	4	–	2	54.1	–	12.0
ARIZONA	93,663	85,273	16.3	16.5	43,198	40,500	7.5	7.8	630	573	610	6.7	6.7	8.8
Apache	1,352	1,329	19.6	19.2	513	470	7.5	6.8	12	18	15	8.9	13.5	8.3
Cochise	1,816	1,743	14.7	14.8	1,109	1,072	9.0	9.1	13	11	13	7.2	6.3	7.5
Coconino	2,032	1,876	16.6	16.1	606	507	4.9	4.3	14	16	22	6.9	8.5	11.2
Gila	671	677	13.1	13.2	648	579	12.6	11.3	6	6	3	8.9	8.9	4.0
Graham	452	460	13.8	13.7	274	245	8.3	7.3	1	1	4	2.2	2.2	9.4
Greenlee	102	111	13.6	13.0	46	73	6.1	8.5	1	–	–	9.8	–	–
La Paz	235	188	11.8	9.6	252	192	12.7	9.8	3	3	–	12.8	16.0	–
Maricopa	60,636	54,506	17.3	17.6	23,742	22,725	6.8	7.3	400	358	363	6.6	6.6	9.0
Mohave	2,305	1,986	12.8	12.7	2,344	1,973	13.1	12.6	17	16	21	7.4	8.1	13.7
Navajo	1,793	1,685	16.9	17.2	776	666	7.3	6.8	12	11	23	6.7	6.5	11.7
Pima	13,055	12,516	14.4	14.7	7,691	7,364	8.5	8.7	100	76	93	7.7	6.1	8.1
Pinal	3,072	2,613	14.3	14.4	1,684	1,547	7.8	8.5	21	25	17	6.8	9.6	8.0
Santa Cruz	808	798	19.8	20.7	226	205	5.5	5.3	7	3	8	8.7	3.8	10.2
Yavapai	2,008	1,755	10.5	10.4	2,114	1,914	11.1	11.3	6	13	8	3.0	7.4	6.5
Yuma	3,326	3,030	18.9	18.8	1,173	968	6.7	6.0	17	16	20	5.1	5.3	7.4
ARKANSAS	38,573	37,783	14.0	14.1	27,528	28,217	10.0	10.5	319	316	336	8.3	8.4	9.2
Arkansas	265	255	13.2	12.3	239	258	11.9	12.5	3	3	2	11.3	11.8	6.7
Ashley	258	313	11.0	12.9	255	301	10.9	12.4	2	2	4	7.8	6.4	9.8
Baxter	381	352	9.6	9.2	644	619	16.2	16.1	1	3	6	2.6	8.5	19.9
Benton	2,893	2,247	16.1	14.5	1,243	1,248	6.9	8.1	26	9	16	9.0	4.0	11.0
Boone	419	393	11.9	11.5	366	378	10.4	11.1	1	1	8	2.4	2.5	20.2
Bradley	177	162	14.4	12.9	149	178	12.1	14.1	2	–	3	11.3	–	16.1
Calhoun	32	48	5.8	8.4	57	79	10.3	13.8	–	2	–	–	41.7	–
Carroll	349	370	13.1	14.6	264	232	9.9	9.1	3	3	–	8.6	8.1	–
Chicot	182	208	13.8	14.8	170	181	12.9	12.8	1	1	2	5.5	4.8	7.5
Clark	294	286	12.8	12.2	258	257	11.2	10.9	3	3	5	10.2	10.5	19.3
Clay	188	195	11.2	11.1	228	270	13.6	15.4	1	3	2	5.3	15.4	7.7
Cleburne	255	251	10.2	10.4	312	296	12.5	12.3	1	3	–	3.9	12.0	–
Cleveland	112	104	12.8	12.2	89	114	10.1	13.3	1	–	3	8.9	–	28.8
Columbia	321	308	12.9	12.0	296	312	11.9	12.2	4	2	7	12.5	6.5	18.7
Conway	233	250	11.3	12.3	212	217	10.3	10.7	3	2	3	12.9	8.0	11.1
Craighead	1,265	1,264	14.7	15.3	777	724	9.1	8.8	7	11	6	5.5	8.7	5.7
Crawford	772	804	13.6	15.1	484	489	8.5	9.2	5	9	3	6.5	11.2	4.0
Crittenden	885	928	17.2	18.2	493	501	9.6	9.8	11	7	14	12.4	7.5	13.8
Cross	286	256	15.0	13.1	175	225	9.2	11.5	4	4	3	14.0	15.6	9.6
Dallas	97	109	11.2	11.9	98	169	11.3	18.5	–	1	2	–	9.2	15.3
Desha	202	242	13.9	15.8	160	184	11.0	12.0	1	2	4	5.0	8.3	13.2
Drew	223	267	12.0	14.3	163	181	8.8	9.7	1	2	5	4.5	7.5	17.7
Faulkner	1,367	1,277	14.4	14.8	685	569	7.2	6.6	5	10	13	3.7	7.8	15.3
Franklin	208	220	11.5	12.4	198	196	11.0	11.1	1	–	2	–	4.5	9.9
Fulton	103	117	8.7	10.0	164	165	13.8	14.1	1	–	1	9.7	–	8.1

See footnotes at end of table.

[Includes United States, states, and 3,141 counties/county equivalents defined as of February 22, 2005. For more information on these areas, see Appendix C, Geographic Information]

County	Births Number		Births Rate per 1,000 population[1]		Deaths Number		Deaths Rate per 1,000 population[1]		Infant deaths[2] Number			Infant deaths[2] Rate per 1,000 live births[3]		
	2004	2000	2004	2000	2004	2000	2004	2000	2004	2000	1990	2004	2000	1990
ARKANSAS—Con.														
Garland	1,103	1,016	12.0	11.5	1,222	1,229	13.3	13.9	13	7	6	11.8	6.9	6.5
Grant	189	212	11.0	12.8	191	167	11.1	10.1	2	2	–	10.6	9.4	–
Greene	534	562	13.7	15.0	423	405	10.9	10.8	5	4	3	9.4	7.1	6.8
Hempstead	320	345	13.7	14.6	253	275	10.8	11.7	3	2	1	9.4	5.8	3.0
Hot Spring	355	383	11.5	12.6	329	360	10.6	11.9	2	4	3	5.6	10.4	9.3
Howard	237	232	16.4	16.3	175	190	12.1	13.3	2	1	3	8.4	4.3	14.6
Independence	475	428	13.7	12.5	352	384	10.2	11.2	3	2	3	6.3	4.7	8.0
Izard	152	118	11.4	8.9	181	192	13.6	14.5	3	3	–	19.7	25.4	–
Jackson	255	215	14.4	11.7	241	248	13.6	13.5	1	1	2	3.9	4.7	7.5
Jefferson	1,164	1,289	14.2	15.3	890	874	10.8	10.4	14	10	14	12.0	7.8	9.6
Johnson	330	314	13.9	13.8	211	251	8.9	11.0	3	2	1	9.1	6.4	3.5
Lafayette	98	126	12.0	14.7	108	128	13.3	15.0	–	2	1	–	15.9	6.9
Lawrence	219	222	12.6	12.6	222	249	12.8	14.1	2	1	4	9.1	4.5	18.6
Lee	129	157	11.1	12.5	137	158	11.7	12.6	3	4	2	23.3	25.5	7.6
Lincoln	136	161	9.5	11.1	133	146	9.3	10.1	–	3	1	–	18.6	6.2
Little River	146	152	11.0	11.2	153	163	11.6	12.0	1	3	–	6.8	19.7	–
Logan	281	279	12.3	12.4	289	280	12.6	12.4	1	–	1	3.6	–	3.5
Lonoke	868	690	14.8	13.0	487	470	8.3	8.8	5	4	6	5.8	5.8	11.6
Madison	185	159	12.6	11.1	140	156	9.5	10.9	1	4	1	5.4	25.2	6.7
Marion	144	138	8.7	8.5	153	183	9.3	11.3	2	1	1	13.9	7.2	6.2
Miller	606	593	14.3	14.7	424	381	10.0	9.4	8	6	6	13.2	10.1	9.8
Mississippi	774	939	16.0	18.1	534	585	11.0	11.3	9	8	14	11.6	8.5	11.8
Monroe	122	127	13.0	12.5	113	146	12.0	14.3	2	1	1	16.4	7.9	5.0
Montgomery	95	94	10.3	10.1	119	135	12.9	14.5	–	2	–	–	21.3	–
Nevada	143	133	14.9	13.4	117	161	12.2	16.2	2	2	–	14.0	15.0	–
Newton	79	94	9.3	10.9	96	97	11.3	11.2	–	–	–	–	–	–
Ouachita	350	366	12.8	12.8	375	395	13.7	13.8	6	–	2	17.1	–	3.8
Perry	101	120	9.7	11.7	96	108	9.2	10.5	–	2	1	–	16.7	10.5
Phillips	426	480	17.5	18.3	327	363	13.4	13.8	8	7	8	18.8	14.6	13.5
Pike	99	127	9.0	11.2	162	162	14.7	14.3	1	1	1	10.1	7.9	8.4
Poinsett	340	382	13.5	14.9	330	316	13.1	12.3	2	5	8	5.9	13.1	21.4
Polk	262	275	13.0	13.6	241	246	12.0	12.1	2	2	3	7.6	7.3	11.6
Pope	770	728	13.7	13.4	482	498	8.6	9.1	3	5	6	3.9	6.9	8.2
Prairie	89	112	9.7	11.8	127	126	13.9	13.2	2	1	1	22.5	8.9	7.3
Pulaski	5,893	5,856	16.1	16.2	3,240	3,296	8.9	9.1	47	66	65	8.0	11.3	10.3
Randolph	218	183	11.8	10.1	205	204	11.1	11.2	–	2	2	–	10.9	10.0
St. Francis	423	448	15.0	15.3	290	338	10.3	11.5	8	4	5	18.9	8.9	9.3
Saline	1,014	947	11.4	11.3	728	707	8.2	8.4	8	4	3	7.9	4.2	3.3
Scott	137	139	12.5	12.6	129	123	11.7	11.2	–	4	2	–	–	13.0
Searcy	87	88	10.9	10.6	97	108	12.2	13.0	–	1	–	–	11.4	–
Sebastian	1,822	1,857	15.5	16.1	1,171	1,136	10.0	9.8	12	8	9	6.6	4.3	5.5
Sevier	238	277	14.8	17.6	162	173	10.1	11.0	1	4	1	4.2	14.4	5.0
Sharp	208	184	11.9	10.7	236	267	13.5	15.5	1	1	2	4.8	5.4	14.9
Stone	120	134	10.3	11.6	142	128	12.2	11.1	–	1	1	–	7.5	8.6
Union	582	597	13.1	13.1	530	639	11.9	14.0	4	10	7	6.9	16.8	9.5
Van Buren	185	161	11.2	9.9	214	252	13.0	15.5	1	2	2	5.4	12.4	13.0
Washington	2,981	2,595	17.1	16.4	1,260	1,188	7.2	7.5	30	15	16	10.1	5.8	8.8
White	913	895	12.9	13.3	725	715	10.3	10.6	6	11	2	6.6	12.3	2.5
Woodruff	94	93	11.6	10.7	132	131	16.2	15.1	2	–	1	21.3	–	7.0
Yell	315	335	14.8	15.8	255	242	12.0	11.4	1	1	–	3.2	3.0	–
CALIFORNIA	544,843	531,959	15.2	15.6	232,525	229,551	6.5	6.8	2,811	2,894	4,844	5.2	5.4	7.9
Alameda	20,924	22,176	14.4	15.3	9,271	9,888	6.4	6.8	111	104	205	5.3	4.7	8.8
Alpine	11	10	9.2	8.3	9	11	7.5	9.1	–	–	–	–	–	–
Amador	262	233	6.9	6.6	359	374	9.5	10.6	3	1	2	11.5	4.3	6.2
Butte	2,355	2,197	11.1	10.8	2,178	2,141	10.2	10.5	14	14	21	5.9	6.4	7.9
Calaveras	322	307	7.0	7.5	420	383	9.2	9.4	2	1	4	6.2	3.3	9.8
Colusa	345	331	16.9	17.6	141	144	6.9	7.6	1	2	3	2.9	6.0	10.8
Contra Costa	13,281	13,209	13.2	13.9	6,791	6,677	6.7	7.0	51	64	87	3.8	4.8	6.4
Del Norte	287	316	10.1	11.5	261	274	9.2	10.0	–	2	3	–	6.3	7.9
El Dorado	1,901	1,630	11.0	10.4	1,235	1,116	7.2	7.1	10	4	18	5.3	2.5	8.9
Fresno	15,898	14,265	18.4	17.8	5,812	5,379	6.7	6.7	128	102	132	8.1	7.2	8.5
Glenn	399	385	14.5	14.6	246	260	9.0	9.8	–	1	5	–	2.6	10.6
Humboldt	1,509	1,372	11.8	10.9	1,253	1,204	9.8	9.5	7	10	15	4.6	7.3	8.3
Imperial	2,856	2,640	18.7	18.5	869	862	5.7	6.0	16	12	24	5.6	4.5	8.3
Inyo	215	172	11.8	9.6	219	201	12.0	11.2	1	1	4	4.7	5.8	15.6
Kern	13,456	11,689	18.3	17.6	5,251	4,643	7.2	7.0	95	86	129	7.1	7.4	10.3
Kings	2,551	2,180	17.9	16.8	760	714	5.3	5.5	19	13	28	7.4	6.0	12.3
Lake	686	583	10.7	9.9	780	826	12.1	14.1	3	2	5	4.4	3.4	6.8
Lassen	308	305	8.9	9.0	227	205	6.6	6.1	–	4	2	–	13.1	4.8
Los Angeles	151,579	157,508	15.3	16.5	59,174	59,352	6.0	6.2	757	780	1,634	5.0	5.0	8.0
Madera	2,346	2,109	16.9	17.1	914	883	6.6	7.1	6	12	6	2.6	5.7	3.3

See footnotes at end of table.

County and City Data Book: 2007

U.S. Census Bureau

Table B-5. Counties — **Births, Deaths, and Infant Deaths**—Con.

[Includes United States, states, and 3,141 counties/county equivalents defined as of February 22, 2005. For more information on these areas, see Appendix C, Geographic Information]

County	Births Number 2004	2000	Births Rate per 1,000 population[1] 2004	2000	Deaths Number 2004	2000	Deaths Rate per 1,000 population[1] 2004	2000	Infant deaths[2] Number 2004	2000	1990	Infant deaths Rate per 1,000 live births[3] 2004	2000	1990
CALIFORNIA—Con.														
Marin	2,792	2,826	11.4	11.4	1,722	1,844	7.0	7.4	4	10	18	1.4	3.5	5.9
Mariposa	150	127	8.4	7.4	156	153	8.7	8.9	1	2	–	6.7	15.7	–
Mendocino	1,125	1,084	12.7	12.5	853	821	9.6	9.5	10	9	11	8.9	8.3	9.0
Merced	4,297	3,875	18.1	18.3	1,383	1,320	5.8	6.2	19	19	33	4.4	4.9	7.6
Modoc	91	96	9.5	10.2	102	93	10.6	9.9	–	–	2	–	–	13.8
Mono	174	137	13.7	10.6	45	55	3.5	4.3	1	1	2	5.7	7.3	10.8
Monterey	7,395	6,717	17.8	16.7	2,372	2,364	5.7	5.9	32	39	61	4.3	5.8	7.7
Napa	1,603	1,496	12.1	12.0	1,264	1,300	9.5	10.4	5	6	10	3.1	4.0	6.7
Nevada	819	768	8.4	8.3	916	867	9.4	9.4	6	1	12	7.3	1.3	11.7
Orange	45,065	47,022	15.1	16.5	16,752	16,605	5.6	5.8	179	232	397	4.0	4.9	7.7
Placer	3,798	3,072	12.4	12.2	2,284	1,938	7.5	7.7	18	22	14	4.7	7.2	5.4
Plumas	175	178	8.2	8.6	224	214	10.5	10.3	–	2	2	–	11.2	8.6
Riverside	29,551	24,855	15.8	15.9	13,644	12,137	7.3	7.8	160	167	221	5.4	6.7	8.8
Sacramento	20,837	18,221	15.4	14.8	9,637	9,023	7.1	7.3	114	106	176	5.5	5.8	9.0
San Benito	887	876	15.8	16.3	251	285	4.5	5.3	2	4	5	2.3	4.6	6.8
San Bernardino	31,921	28,713	16.7	16.7	11,912	11,196	6.2	6.5	219	201	329	6.9	7.0	9.8
San Diego	45,770	44,337	15.6	15.7	19,712	19,741	6.7	7.0	246	263	367	5.4	5.9	7.2
San Francisco	8,581	8,665	11.5	11.2	5,908	6,506	7.9	8.4	31	35	73	3.6	4.0	7.2
San Joaquin	11,011	9,606	17.0	16.9	4,433	4,221	6.8	7.4	74	66	86	6.7	6.9	8.7
San Luis Obispo	2,696	2,436	10.6	9.8	1,996	1,987	7.8	8.0	17	11	26	6.3	4.5	8.6
San Mateo	10,090	10,421	14.5	14.7	4,573	4,727	6.6	6.7	36	55	66	3.6	5.3	6.1
Santa Barbara	6,209	5,685	15.5	14.2	2,899	2,932	7.2	7.3	28	33	45	4.5	5.8	6.7
Santa Clara	26,540	27,686	15.8	16.4	8,472	8,845	5.0	5.2	119	124	154	4.5	4.5	5.5
Santa Cruz	3,399	3,675	13.6	14.4	1,579	1,698	6.3	6.6	17	16	20	5.0	4.4	4.6
Shasta	2,047	1,831	11.5	11.2	1,887	1,651	10.6	10.1	10	11	20	4.9	6.0	8.7
Sierra	19	29	5.5	8.1	37	31	10.6	8.7	–	–	–	–	–	–
Siskiyou	465	407	10.4	9.2	500	485	11.1	11.0	3	2	4	6.5	4.9	6.6
Solano	5,692	5,902	13.8	14.9	2,591	2,590	6.3	6.5	19	27	57	3.3	4.6	8.5
Sonoma	5,963	5,652	12.7	12.3	3,621	3,843	7.7	8.3	15	27	29	2.5	4.8	4.7
Stanislaus	8,059	7,249	16.2	16.1	3,474	3,412	7.0	7.6	52	51	64	6.5	7.0	8.1
Sutter	1,343	1,166	15.5	14.7	687	712	7.9	9.0	7	7	11	5.2	6.0	9.0
Tehama	700	686	11.7	12.2	593	619	9.9	11.0	7	3	8	10.0	4.4	10.1
Trinity	109	85	8.0	6.5	157	140	11.5	10.8	1	–	1	9.2	–	5.6
Tulare	7,958	7,261	19.8	19.7	2,637	2,646	6.6	7.2	32	49	57	4.0	6.7	7.9
Tuolumne	477	427	8.4	7.8	607	588	10.7	10.8	–	6	6	–	14.1	10.6
Ventura	11,956	11,768	15.0	15.6	4,852	4,802	6.1	6.3	90	48	99	7.5	4.1	7.8
Yolo	2,404	2,246	13.1	13.2	1,105	1,068	6.0	6.3	7	14	17	2.9	6.2	7.1
Yuba	1,184	1,059	18.4	17.6	518	555	8.0	9.2	6	10	14	5.1	9.4	9.9
COLORADO	68,503	65,438	14.9	15.1	28,309	27,288	6.2	6.3	434	404	472	6.3	6.2	8.8
Adams	6,489	6,143	16.7	17.5	2,122	2,048	5.5	5.8	53	36	46	8.2	5.9	9.6
Alamosa	268	252	17.7	16.8	86	104	5.7	6.9	–	1	3	–	4.0	11.3
Arapahoe	7,852	7,167	15.0	14.6	2,901	2,693	5.6	5.5	52	52	39	6.6	7.3	6.3
Archuleta	117	112	10.1	11.2	58	56	5.0	5.6	1	1	–	8.5	8.9	–
Baca	38	47	9.2	10.4	50	62	12.1	13.8	–	–	1	–	–	15.9
Bent	58	62	10.3	10.4	54	64	9.6	10.7	–	–	1	–	–	16.7
Boulder	3,562	3,878	12.7	14.3	1,379	1,420	4.9	5.2	15	20	23	4.2	5.2	6.9
Broomfield	660	(X)	15.5	(NA)	204	(X)	4.8	(NA)	–	(X)	(X)	–	(NA)	(NA)
Chaffee	147	156	8.7	9.6	134	146	7.9	9.0	–	–	2	–	–	15.0
Cheyenne	23	20	11.5	9.0	13	12	6.5	5.4	–	–	–	–	–	–
Clear Creek	100	95	10.9	10.2	50	36	5.5	3.9	1	–	2	10.0	–	19.0
Conejos	111	140	13.2	16.6	67	90	8.0	10.7	1	1	3	9.0	7.1	23.4
Costilla	27	41	7.6	11.2	41	42	11.5	11.4	1	–	–	37.0	–	–
Crowley	48	50	8.8	9.0	54	34	9.9	6.1	–	–	–	–	–	–
Custer	30	31	7.9	8.8	25	15	6.6	4.3	–	1	1	–	32.3	76.9
Delta	359	287	12.1	10.3	282	317	9.5	11.4	3	1	2	8.4	3.5	8.7
Denver	11,710	10,992	21.1	19.8	4,365	4,567	7.9	8.2	77	66	100	6.6	6.0	11.6
Dolores	20	26	11.0	14.1	19	19	10.5	10.3	–	–	–	–	–	–
Douglas	3,972	3,468	16.7	19.2	579	448	2.4	2.5	10	5	4	2.5	1.4	3.3
Eagle	771	778	16.7	18.5	89	67	1.9	1.6	1	4	1	1.3	5.1	2.4
Elbert	200	233	8.9	11.6	96	82	4.3	4.1	–	1	1	–	4.3	6.4
El Paso	8,118	8,301	14.6	16.0	3,179	2,925	5.7	5.6	70	71	68	8.6	8.6	9.3
Fremont	396	456	8.3	9.8	482	462	10.2	10.0	5	4	4	12.6	8.8	12.8
Garfield	815	792	16.8	17.9	276	265	5.7	6.0	8	4	4	9.8	5.1	8.1
Gilpin	56	67	11.5	14.0	20	17	4.1	3.5	–	–	–	–	–	–
Grand	131	148	9.9	11.9	60	69	4.5	5.5	–	–	2	–	–	16.7
Gunnison	160	190	11.3	13.6	64	54	4.5	3.9	3	2	4	18.8	10.5	31.3
Hinsdale	9	8	11.4	10.2	2	2	2.5	2.5	–	–	–	–	–	–
Huerfano	67	71	8.6	9.1	106	81	13.6	10.4	–	–	1	–	–	–
Jackson	8	12	5.4	7.6	12	14	8.1	8.9	–	–	1	–	–	43.5

See footnotes at end of table.

Table B-5. Counties — **Births, Deaths, and Infant Deaths**—Con.

[Includes United States, states, and 3,141 counties/county equivalents defined as of February 22, 2005. For more information on these areas, see Appendix C, Geographic Information]

County	Births Number 2004	Births Number 2000	Births Rate per 1,000 population[1] 2004	Births Rate per 1,000 population[1] 2000	Deaths Number 2004	Deaths Number 2000	Deaths Rate per 1,000 population[1] 2004	Deaths Rate per 1,000 population[1] 2000	Infant deaths[2] Number 2004	Infant deaths[2] Number 2000	Infant deaths[2] Number 1990	Infant deaths[2] Rate per 1,000 live births[3] 2004	Infant deaths[2] Rate per 1,000 live births[3] 2000	Infant deaths[2] Rate per 1,000 live births[3] 1990
COLORADO—Con.														
Jefferson	6,226	6,700	11.8	12.7	3,288	3,127	6.2	5.9	26	44	65	4.2	6.6	9.7
Kiowa	16	12	11.2	7.4	18	17	12.6	10.6	–	–	–	–	–	–
Kit Carson	105	117	13.6	14.6	74	81	9.6	10.1	–	1	1	–	8.5	9.1
Lake	107	140	13.8	17.9	36	40	4.7	5.1	1	3	–	9.3	21.4	–
La Plata	500	440	10.7	10.0	249	242	5.3	5.5	2	4	1	4.0	9.1	2.2
Larimer	3,353	3,254	12.5	12.9	1,475	1,498	5.5	5.9	13	16	17	3.9	4.9	6.1
Las Animas	179	173	11.6	11.3	174	181	11.3	11.8	1	3	–	5.6	17.3	–
Lincoln	52	48	9.1	7.9	37	51	6.5	8.4	1	–	–	19.2	–	–
Logan	241	256	11.5	12.4	194	189	9.3	9.1	1	3	4	4.1	11.7	17.0
Mesa	1,710	1,473	13.4	12.5	1,164	1,136	9.1	9.7	12	8	12	7.0	5.4	9.4
Mineral	4	8	4.3	9.5	6	6	6.4	7.2	–	–	–	–	–	–
Moffat	182	178	13.5	13.5	79	106	5.8	8.0	–	–	3	–	–	18.6
Montezuma	300	308	12.2	12.9	253	231	10.3	9.7	1	4	4	3.3	13.0	14.4
Montrose	492	452	13.4	13.5	327	285	8.9	8.5	2	1	2	4.1	2.2	5.8
Morgan	460	452	16.4	16.6	226	257	8.1	9.4	5	3	–	10.9	6.6	–
Otero	321	281	16.4	13.9	220	235	11.2	11.6	4	3	3	12.5	10.7	10.1
Ouray	33	28	8.0	7.4	25	17	6.0	4.5	1	–	–	30.3	–	–
Park	155	156	9.2	10.6	66	60	3.9	4.1	1	5	2	6.5	32.1	21.7
Phillips	67	69	14.6	15.5	56	58	12.2	13.0	1	–	–	14.9	–	–
Pitkin	137	156	9.3	10.6	42	38	2.8	2.6	–	1	–	–	6.4	–
Prowers	217	252	15.5	17.4	114	127	8.1	8.8	–	2	3	–	7.9	13.5
Pueblo	1,976	1,945	13.2	13.7	1,456	1,387	9.7	9.8	13	8	17	6.6	4.1	9.6
Rio Blanco	78	69	13.0	11.5	56	49	9.3	8.2	1	1	1	12.8	14.5	13.2
Rio Grande	186	170	15.0	13.7	115	111	9.3	8.9	–	1	–	–	5.9	–
Routt	247	215	11.7	10.8	67	66	3.2	3.3	–	2	2	–	9.3	10.1
Saguache	93	80	13.3	13.4	30	47	4.3	7.9	2	1	1	21.5	12.5	11.5
San Juan	6	4	10.3	7.2	4	5	6.9	9.0	–	–	–	–	–	–
San Miguel	74	64	10.4	9.7	12	17	1.7	2.6	–	–	–	–	–	–
Sedgwick	32	30	12.5	10.9	38	31	14.9	11.3	1	–	–	31.3	–	–
Summit	372	333	15.0	14.1	55	38	2.2	1.6	4	1	1	10.8	3.0	4.8
Teller	206	201	9.5	9.7	98	85	4.5	4.1	1	1	2	4.9	5.0	10.9
Washington	43	60	9.2	12.1	45	48	9.6	9.7	–	–	1	–	–	17.2
Weld	3,859	3,171	17.5	17.3	1,242	1,112	5.6	6.1	39	18	17	10.1	5.7	7.7
Yuma	152	120	15.5	12.2	99	99	10.1	10.1	–	–	1	–	–	7.2
CONNECTICUT	42,095	43,026	12.0	12.6	29,314	30,129	8.4	8.8	233	282	398	5.5	6.6	7.9
Fairfield	11,878	12,430	13.2	14.0	6,680	7,072	7.4	8.0	39	55	95	3.3	4.4	7.3
Hartford	10,495	11,262	12.0	13.1	7,800	8,290	8.9	9.7	72	98	124	6.9	8.7	9.7
Litchfield	1,944	2,035	10.3	11.1	1,648	1,585	8.7	8.7	7	8	12	3.6	3.9	4.9
Middlesex	1,821	1,847	11.2	11.9	1,286	1,407	7.9	9.0	10	16	16	5.5	8.7	7.5
New Haven	10,158	10,139	12.0	12.3	7,842	7,973	9.3	9.7	71	65	98	7.0	6.4	7.9
New London	3,183	2,455	12.0	9.5	2,216	1,957	8.3	7.5	19	18	37	6.0	7.3	9.1
Tolland	1,365	1,537	9.3	11.2	890	871	6.1	6.4	6	10	7	4.4	6.5	4.1
Windham	1,251	1,321	10.9	12.1	952	974	8.3	8.9	9	12	9	7.2	9.1	6.0
DELAWARE	11,369	11,051	13.7	14.1	7,143	6,875	8.6	8.7	98	102	112	8.6	9.2	10.1
Kent	2,006	1,942	14.4	15.3	1,156	1,024	8.3	8.1	17	21	29	8.5	10.8	14.2
New Castle	7,112	7,115	13.7	14.2	4,156	4,103	8.0	8.2	61	66	70	8.6	9.3	9.6
Sussex	2,251	1,994	13.1	12.7	1,831	1,748	10.6	11.1	20	15	13	8.9	7.5	7.4
DISTRICT OF COLUMBIA	7,933	7,666	14.3	13.4	5,454	6,001	9.8	10.5	95	92	245	12.0	12.0	20.7
District of Columbia	7,933	7,666	14.3	13.4	5,454	6,001	9.8	10.5	95	92	245	12.0	12.0	20.7
FLORIDA	218,053	204,125	12.5	12.7	169,008	164,395	9.7	10.2	1,537	1,425	1,918	7.0	7.0	9.6
Alachua	2,718	2,602	12.2	11.9	1,557	1,545	7.0	7.1	32	28	32	11.8	10.8	11.7
Baker	372	356	15.5	15.9	184	187	7.7	8.4	2	1	3	5.4	2.8	10.4
Bay	2,248	2,012	14.2	13.6	1,450	1,433	9.2	9.7	12	10	22	5.3	5.0	10.7
Bradford	323	320	11.7	12.3	260	262	9.4	10.0	2	4	3	6.2	12.5	8.8
Brevard	5,221	5,015	10.1	10.5	5,590	5,282	10.8	11.1	32	26	32	6.1	5.2	5.6
Broward	22,911	22,093	13.1	13.5	15,515	16,023	8.9	9.8	135	129	174	5.9	5.8	9.3
Calhoun	143	157	11.0	12.0	141	133	10.8	10.2	1	–	5	7.0	–	31.4
Charlotte	1,072	1,034	6.8	7.3	2,333	2,206	14.8	15.5	6	8	9	5.6	7.7	8.5
Citrus	924	870	7.1	7.3	2,070	1,982	15.9	16.7	7	7	14	7.6	8.0	15.5
Clay	2,099	1,830	12.8	12.9	1,226	1,072	7.5	7.6	12	14	16	5.7	7.7	9.6
Collier	3,893	3,067	13.1	12.1	2,382	2,363	8.0	9.3	25	17	19	6.4	5.5	7.6
Columbia	794	765	12.9	13.5	657	640	10.6	11.3	9	7	6	11.3	9.2	8.7
DeSoto	430	424	12.3	13.1	311	319	8.9	9.9	3	3	6	7.0	7.1	14.8
Dixie	153	159	10.7	11.5	183	157	12.8	11.4	1	3	1	6.5	18.9	7.2
Duval	12,726	12,180	15.5	15.6	7,094	6,671	8.7	8.6	139	118	153	10.9	9.7	11.8

See footnotes at end of table.

208

County and City Data Book: 2007

U.S. Census Bureau

[Includes United States, states, and 3,141 counties/county equivalents defined as of February 22, 2005. For more information on these areas, see Appendix C, Geographic Information]

County	Births				Deaths				Infant deaths[2]					
	Number		Rate per 1,000 population[1]		Number		Rate per 1,000 population[1]		Number			Rate per 1,000 live births[3]		
	2004	2000	2004	2000	2004	2000	2004	2000	2004	2000	1990	2004	2000	1990
FLORIDA—Con.														
Escambia	4,063	3,845	13.7	13.1	2,885	2,829	9.7	9.6	43	47	43	10.6	12.2	9.5
Flagler	593	414	8.6	8.2	772	596	11.2	11.8	1	2	5	1.7	4.8	16.6
Franklin	122	106	12.1	10.8	98	116	9.7	11.8	1	1	1	8.2	9.4	9.5
Gadsden	666	706	14.5	15.7	442	463	9.6	10.3	9	12	9	13.5	17.0	11.3
Gilchrist	192	182	12.1	12.5	149	161	9.4	11.1	2	3	1	10.4	16.5	7.9
Glades	79	89	7.1	8.4	113	108	10.1	10.2	2	1	–	25.3	11.2	–
Gulf	128	127	9.3	8.7	151	150	11.0	10.3	–	3	1	–	23.6	6.8
Hamilton	180	173	12.8	13.0	130	128	9.2	9.6	1	–	3	5.6	–	16.4
Hardee	493	451	17.6	16.8	205	213	7.3	7.9	2	1	4	4.1	2.2	8.8
Hendry	660	643	17.3	17.7	295	269	7.7	7.4	6	2	4	9.1	3.1	6.6
Hernando	1,404	1,176	9.3	8.9	2,238	1,971	14.9	15.0	14	6	6	10.0	5.1	6.0
Highlands	974	841	10.5	9.5	1,381	1,238	14.8	14.2	6	10	10	6.2	11.9	11.7
Hillsborough	16,047	14,673	14.6	14.6	8,856	8,681	8.0	8.7	142	116	162	8.8	7.9	11.2
Holmes	213	219	11.2	11.8	205	219	10.8	11.8	3	2	2	14.1	9.1	9.3
Indian River	1,234	1,129	9.9	10.0	1,638	1,497	13.1	13.2	7	10	9	5.7	8.9	8.1
Jackson	558	575	11.7	12.3	505	523	10.6	11.2	3	3	4	5.4	5.2	7.3
Jefferson	159	137	11.0	10.6	141	165	9.8	12.8	2	–	2	12.6	–	9.9
Lafayette	77	91	10.3	12.9	85	66	11.3	9.4	1	–	2	13.0	–	28.6
Lake	3,041	2,363	11.6	11.1	3,037	2,855	11.6	13.4	17	7	15	5.6	3.0	7.5
Lee	5,929	5,200	11.5	11.7	5,560	5,087	10.8	11.5	38	36	31	6.4	6.9	6.8
Leon	3,132	2,993	12.9	12.5	1,435	1,557	5.9	6.5	32	29	41	10.2	9.7	14.8
Levy	407	431	10.9	12.4	470	435	12.6	12.6	9	4	3	22.1	9.3	8.4
Liberty	90	78	12.1	11.2	64	66	8.6	9.4	–	1	–	–	12.8	–
Madison	222	218	11.6	11.6	220	204	11.5	10.9	4	3	2	18.0	13.8	7.1
Manatee	3,491	3,239	11.8	12.2	3,276	3,394	11.1	12.8	20	24	36	5.7	7.4	12.5
Marion	3,182	2,902	10.9	11.1	3,853	3,389	13.2	13.0	27	19	26	8.5	6.5	9.4
Martin	1,284	1,240	9.3	9.8	1,738	1,590	12.6	12.5	7	10	16	5.5	8.1	12.0
Miami-Dade	32,066	32,306	13.6	14.3	18,384	18,540	7.8	8.2	167	186	337	5.2	5.8	9.8
Monroe	739	795	9.5	10.0	704	673	9.0	8.5	5	7	5	6.8	8.8	4.9
Nassau	706	744	11.2	12.8	604	523	9.6	9.0	1	7	4	1.4	9.4	5.7
Okaloosa	2,712	2,363	15.0	13.8	1,411	1,327	7.8	7.8	9	15	22	3.3	6.3	8.8
Okeechobee	592	527	15.2	14.7	425	378	10.9	10.5	2	8	7	3.4	15.2	12.2
Orange	15,351	14,078	15.5	15.6	6,472	6,293	6.5	7.0	117	93	87	7.6	6.6	7.2
Osceola	3,351	2,616	15.2	15.0	1,490	1,265	6.8	7.3	19	9	18	5.7	3.4	9.5
Palm Beach	15,034	13,326	12.1	11.7	13,663	13,069	11.0	11.5	97	95	135	6.5	7.1	10.4
Pasco	4,597	3,761	11.3	10.8	5,558	5,263	13.6	15.2	35	25	17	7.6	6.6	5.6
Pinellas	9,051	9,598	9.8	10.4	11,931	12,662	12.9	13.7	54	62	111	6.0	6.5	10.6
Polk	7,206	6,877	13.7	14.2	5,565	5,316	10.6	10.9	63	48	67	8.7	7.0	10.3
Putnam	966	899	13.3	12.8	938	912	12.9	12.9	13	11	8	13.5	12.2	7.7
St. Johns	1,552	1,328	10.2	10.7	1,249	1,126	8.2	9.0	13	7	8	8.4	5.3	6.9
St. Lucie	2,863	2,251	12.6	11.6	2,440	2,372	10.7	12.3	17	16	26	5.9	7.1	10.6
Santa Rosa	1,684	1,501	12.2	12.7	1,085	896	7.9	7.6	10	7	8	5.9	4.7	6.1
Sarasota	2,942	2,718	8.3	8.3	4,751	4,892	13.4	15.0	8	22	29	2.7	8.1	10.3
Seminole	4,747	4,586	12.1	12.5	2,703	2,619	6.9	7.1	29	22	35	6.1	4.8	8.0
Sumter	508	477	8.4	8.9	761	622	12.6	11.6	5	3	7	9.8	6.3	16.2
Suwannee	509	465	13.5	13.3	486	431	12.9	12.3	4	10	6	7.9	21.5	16.3
Taylor	229	249	11.9	13.0	215	247	11.2	12.9	4	–	3	17.5	–	10.3
Union	146	133	10.0	9.9	167	152	11.4	11.3	1	1	1	6.8	7.5	7.5
Volusia	4,746	4,456	9.9	10.0	6,182	5,694	12.9	12.8	35	39	39	7.4	8.8	8.2
Wakulla	308	287	11.4	12.5	181	190	6.7	8.3	4	1	–	13.0	3.5	–
Walton	553	440	11.4	10.8	487	434	10.1	10.6	5	–	3	9.0	–	8.1
Washington	248	219	11.3	10.4	261	254	11.9	12.1	3	4	2	12.1	18.3	8.1
GEORGIA	138,849	132,644	15.6	16.1	65,818	63,870	7.4	7.8	1,181	1,126	1,392	8.5	8.5	12.4
Appling	256	265	14.3	15.2	187	197	10.4	11.3	4	2	1	15.6	7.5	3.9
Atkinson	161	172	20.3	22.6	80	67	10.1	8.8	1	3	1	6.2	17.4	8.3
Bacon	154	147	14.9	14.5	119	114	11.5	11.3	1	1	3	6.5	6.8	19.6
Baker	30	37	7.1	9.1	33	38	7.8	9.4	–	1	–	–	27.0	–
Baldwin	558	536	12.3	12.0	370	340	8.2	7.6	4	5	11	7.2	9.3	20.2
Banks	245	156	15.6	10.7	87	102	5.5	7.0	1	2	2	4.1	12.8	17.9
Barrow	1,016	792	17.9	17.0	400	397	7.1	8.5	5	5	4	4.9	6.3	6.9
Bartow	1,476	1,405	17.0	18.3	654	624	7.5	8.1	9	11	14	6.1	7.8	13.4
Ben Hill	300	327	17.4	18.7	219	208	12.7	11.9	4	5	8	13.3	15.3	27.4
Berrien	290	259	17.5	15.9	183	150	11.1	9.2	2	–	5	6.9	–	21.9
Bibb	2,573	2,577	16.6	16.8	1,607	1,654	10.4	10.8	32	31	45	12.4	12.0	16.8
Bleckley	160	157	13.3	13.4	120	126	10.0	10.8	2	3	1	12.5	19.1	6.1
Brantley	133	119	8.6	8.1	153	119	9.9	8.1	2	1	–	15.0	8.4	–
Brooks	182	188	11.1	11.4	201	218	12.3	13.2	1	1	4	5.5	5.3	16.3
Bryan	480	401	17.5	17.0	198	134	7.2	5.7	1	3	3	2.1	7.5	10.5
Bulloch	750	662	12.5	11.8	437	391	7.3	7.0	10	9	4	13.3	13.6	6.4
Burke	354	414	15.3	18.6	226	216	9.8	9.7	3	3	10	8.5	7.2	26.1
Butts	301	310	14.6	15.8	191	187	9.3	9.5	2	3	2	6.6	9.7	8.9
Calhoun	103	90	16.9	14.2	72	56	11.8	8.9	–	1	–	–	11.1	–
Camden	834	695	18.5	15.9	265	188	5.9	4.3	5	7	3	6.0	10.1	4.6

See footnotes at end of table.

[Includes United States, states, and 3,141 counties/county equivalents defined as of February 22, 2005. For more information on these areas, see Appendix C, Geographic Information]

County	Births				Deaths				Infant deaths[2]					
	Number		Rate per 1,000 population[1]		Number		Rate per 1,000 population[1]		Number			Rate per 1,000 live births[3]		
	2004	2000	2004	2000	2004	2000	2004	2000	2004	2000	1990	2004	2000	1990
GEORGIA—Con.														
Candler	195	170	19.1	17.7	141	142	13.8	14.8	2	4	–	10.3	23.5	–
Carroll	1,549	1,406	15.2	16.0	808	771	7.9	8.8	9	12	8	5.8	8.5	6.7
Catoosa	802	726	13.4	13.5	487	444	8.2	8.3	6	3	7	7.5	4.1	11.6
Charlton	141	139	13.2	13.5	94	71	8.8	6.9	–	1	1	–	7.2	6.5
Chatham	3,761	3,534	15.8	15.2	2,293	2,245	9.6	9.7	37	26	48	9.8	7.4	11.7
Chattahoochee	292	256	18.7	17.1	36	31	2.3	2.1	1	1	3	3.4	3.9	12.0
Chattooga	303	331	11.4	13.0	265	309	10.0	12.1	2	3	4	6.6	9.1	12.3
Cherokee	2,988	2,439	17.1	17.0	905	787	5.2	5.5	14	20	15	4.7	8.2	8.2
Clarke	1,509	1,335	14.3	13.1	621	651	5.9	6.4	13	11	17	8.6	8.2	14.2
Clay	52	76	15.6	22.6	53	47	15.9	14.0	–	1	2	–	13.2	34.5
Clayton	4,547	4,298	17.2	18.0	1,331	1,358	5.0	5.7	50	41	49	11.0	9.5	14.2
Clinch	116	125	16.7	18.2	80	80	11.5	11.7	–	2	2	–	16.0	18.3
Cobb	10,676	10,379	16.3	16.9	3,351	3,203	5.1	5.2	70	61	72	6.6	5.9	9.3
Coffee	631	673	16.1	17.9	351	329	9.0	8.8	2	9	11	3.2	13.4	18.7
Colquitt	730	709	16.7	16.8	447	441	10.2	10.5	7	9	8	9.6	12.7	13.8
Columbia	1,316	1,213	13.1	13.5	591	498	5.9	5.5	7	10	11	5.3	8.2	9.7
Cook	234	244	14.5	15.4	187	178	11.6	11.2	2	2	3	8.5	8.2	13.2
Coweta	1,627	1,507	15.4	16.7	688	665	6.5	7.4	14	12	15	8.6	8.0	15.2
Crawford	128	137	9.9	11.0	125	102	9.7	8.2	–	1	2	–	7.3	15.6
Crisp	334	344	15.2	15.6	240	268	10.9	12.2	2	7	4	6.0	20.3	10.5
Dade	180	175	11.3	11.5	146	132	9.2	8.7	1	–	1	5.6	–	5.3
Dawson	321	262	16.9	16.1	148	107	7.8	6.6	1	1	1	3.1	3.8	6.0
Decatur	381	442	13.3	15.7	290	316	10.2	11.2	2	5	6	5.2	11.3	13.5
DeKalb	10,588	10,930	15.7	16.4	3,952	3,943	5.9	5.9	101	101	119	9.5	9.2	12.8
Dodge	252	238	13.0	12.4	201	213	10.3	11.1	–	3	8	–	12.6	28.1
Dooly	155	191	13.3	16.6	120	121	10.3	10.5	4	–	2	25.8	–	14.0
Dougherty	1,570	1,625	16.5	16.9	915	841	9.6	8.8	24	22	23	15.3	13.5	12.5
Douglas	1,667	1,384	15.6	14.9	685	580	6.4	6.3	15	4	12	9.0	2.9	9.4
Early	200	169	16.6	13.7	145	138	12.0	11.2	3	1	3	15.0	5.9	14.5
Echols	29	16	7.1	4.2	21	25	5.1	6.6	–	–	–	–	–	–
Effingham	599	532	13.5	14.1	265	263	6.0	7.0	6	6	6	10.0	11.3	15.2
Elbert	295	283	14.2	13.8	229	249	11.0	12.1	3	–	5	10.2	–	16.2
Emanuel	342	316	15.5	14.4	242	240	11.0	11.0	4	6	9	11.7	19.0	25.0
Evans	187	205	16.5	19.4	98	124	8.6	11.7	4	3	3	21.4	14.6	22.7
Fannin	249	232	11.5	11.6	287	255	13.3	12.8	–	4	3	–	17.2	15.9
Fayette	951	936	9.4	10.2	637	494	6.3	5.4	4	6	5	4.2	6.4	6.7
Floyd	1,385	1,329	14.7	14.6	966	1,019	10.3	11.2	19	11	21	13.7	8.3	15.7
Forsyth	2,223	1,938	16.8	19.3	622	544	4.7	5.4	12	14	6	5.4	7.2	8.4
Franklin	277	232	12.9	11.4	236	241	11.0	11.9	4	1	3	14.4	4.3	11.5
Fulton	13,282	14,085	14.7	17.2	5,837	6,361	6.4	7.8	95	114	174	7.2	8.1	14.6
Gilmer	384	348	14.4	14.6	220	228	8.2	9.6	12	5	1	31.3	14.4	4.9
Glascock	33	28	12.4	11.0	49	32	18.4	12.5	–	–	2	–	–	90.9
Glynn	1,022	1,011	14.4	14.9	723	692	10.2	10.2	10	6	12	9.8	5.9	11.7
Gordon	817	800	16.7	18.0	420	400	8.6	9.0	10	8	6	12.2	10.0	9.6
Grady	425	375	17.5	15.8	246	270	10.1	11.4	6	4	5	14.1	10.7	15.8
Greene	181	194	11.7	13.4	179	182	11.5	12.6	2	3	2	11.0	15.5	8.4
Gwinnett	12,744	10,369	18.2	17.4	2,781	2,374	4.0	4.0	90	58	53	7.1	5.6	8.2
Habersham	626	548	16.1	15.2	306	316	7.9	8.7	3	5	5	4.8	9.1	14.2
Hall	3,038	2,887	18.9	20.5	1,091	1,021	6.8	7.2	18	16	13	5.9	5.5	7.5
Hancock	113	119	11.5	11.8	107	99	10.9	9.8	4	3	3	35.4	25.2	22.6
Haralson	379	382	13.6	14.8	273	267	9.8	10.3	2	2	4	5.3	5.2	14.1
Harris	324	297	12.1	12.5	210	182	7.8	7.6	3	2	1	9.3	6.7	3.6
Hart	261	264	11.0	11.5	283	284	11.9	12.3	3	–	4	11.5	–	13.2
Heard	141	143	12.5	12.9	105	105	9.3	9.5	1	2	1	7.1	14.0	8.8
Henry	2,820	2,093	17.7	17.2	815	747	5.1	6.1	18	17	7	6.4	8.1	6.3
Houston	1,807	1,596	14.6	14.3	843	761	6.8	6.8	22	14	18	12.2	8.8	11.9
Irwin	103	109	10.5	10.9	102	116	10.4	11.6	1	3	1	9.7	27.5	9.4
Jackson	873	724	17.6	17.3	454	411	9.2	9.8	6	3	7	6.9	4.1	14.0
Jasper	157	129	12.3	11.2	114	103	8.9	9.0	2	2	–	12.7	15.5	–
Jeff Davis	239	232	18.6	18.2	153	151	11.9	11.9	2	7	3	8.4	30.2	15.4
Jefferson	237	285	14.0	16.5	185	210	10.9	12.2	4	4	3	16.9	14.0	9.4
Jenkins	123	136	14.2	15.8	109	97	12.6	11.3	1	1	–	8.1	7.4	–
Johnson	119	129	12.4	15.1	112	105	11.6	12.3	1	–	4	8.4	–	26.8
Jones	233	251	8.8	10.6	190	174	7.2	7.3	1	–	7	4.3	–	26.0
Lamar	204	199	12.5	12.4	183	162	11.2	10.1	3	1	1	14.7	5.0	4.9
Lanier	118	85	15.9	11.7	75	84	10.1	11.6	–	1	2	–	11.8	21.7
Laurens	679	689	14.6	15.3	488	444	10.5	9.9	5	5	12	7.4	7.3	18.5
Lee	321	331	10.7	13.3	144	123	4.8	4.9	2	1	5	6.2	3.0	20.7
Liberty	1,485	1,436	24.5	23.4	284	284	4.7	4.6	14	21	16	9.4	14.6	11.0
Lincoln	92	98	11.0	11.7	86	87	10.3	10.4	–	2	–	–	20.4	–

See footnotes at end of table.

County and City Data Book: 2007

U.S. Census Bureau

[Includes United States, states, and 3,141 counties/county equivalents defined as of February 22, 2005. For more information on these areas, see Appendix C, Geographic Information]

County	Births				Deaths				Infant deaths[2]					
	Number		Rate per 1,000 population[1]		Number		Rate per 1,000 population[1]		Number			Rate per 1,000 live births[3]		
	2004	2000	2004	2000	2004	2000	2004	2000	2004	2000	1990	2004	2000	1990
GEORGIA—Con.														
Long	166	184	15.2	17.8	57	62	5.2	6.0	1	1	1	6.0	5.4	6.4
Lowndes	1,673	1,522	17.5	16.5	725	695	7.6	7.5	26	18	22	15.5	11.8	16.3
Lumpkin	281	306	11.8	14.5	183	185	7.7	8.7	2	1	1	7.1	3.3	4.8
McDuffie	332	373	15.4	17.5	248	227	11.5	10.7	8	5	–	24.1	13.4	–
McIntosh	138	174	12.4	16.0	123	97	11.1	8.9	2	3	3	14.5	17.2	21.4
Macon	191	241	13.7	17.1	132	163	9.4	11.6	2	4	3	10.5	16.6	12.1
Madison	358	348	13.2	13.5	233	233	8.6	9.0	2	2	6	5.6	5.7	15.5
Marion	115	98	16.1	13.6	75	60	10.5	8.4	2	1	–	17.4	10.2	–
Meriwether	295	288	12.9	12.8	265	240	11.6	10.7	1	4	3	3.4	13.9	8.2
Miller	76	97	12.2	15.2	81	77	13.0	12.1	–	–	4	–	–	50.6
Mitchell	300	360	12.6	15.0	246	246	10.3	10.3	3	6	1	10.0	16.7	2.6
Monroe	231	269	9.9	12.3	205	222	8.8	10.2	1	3	5	4.3	11.2	18.9
Montgomery	121	114	13.6	13.8	83	76	9.3	9.2	1	1	–	8.3	8.8	–
Morgan	226	225	13.3	14.5	136	143	8.0	9.2	1	3	–	4.4	13.3	–
Murray	640	536	15.9	14.6	306	262	7.6	7.1	6	2	3	9.4	3.7	6.6
Muscogee	2,998	3,197	16.1	17.1	1,791	1,799	9.6	9.6	42	49	59	14.0	15.3	16.5
Newton	1,412	1,146	17.3	18.2	559	499	6.8	7.9	4	6	8	2.8	5.2	10.6
Oconee	344	298	11.9	11.3	167	154	5.8	5.8	1	3	4	2.9	10.1	14.4
Oglethorpe	165	153	12.2	12.0	104	124	7.7	9.7	4	–	2	24.2	–	14.2
Paulding	1,761	1,511	16.6	18.2	544	426	5.1	5.1	14	8	4	8.0	5.3	5.0
Peach	385	411	15.7	17.3	222	221	9.0	9.3	3	3	9	7.8	7.3	23.6
Pickens	318	327	11.4	14.0	206	206	7.4	8.8	4	3	7	12.6	9.2	34.7
Pierce	274	241	16.4	15.3	181	168	10.8	10.7	2	2	–	7.3	8.3	–
Pike	193	175	12.3	12.7	144	119	9.2	8.6	2	1	–	10.4	5.7	–
Polk	686	652	17.1	17.0	498	422	12.4	11.0	6	7	7	8.7	10.7	13.1
Pulaski	125	125	12.8	13.0	107	101	10.9	10.5	–	1	1	–	8.0	7.4
Putnam	234	271	11.9	14.4	198	156	10.0	8.3	4	1	5	17.1	3.7	23.9
Quitman	28	52	11.3	19.9	36	30	14.6	11.5	3	1	1	107.1	19.2	28.6
Rabun	202	186	12.7	12.3	176	178	11.0	11.8	1	1	5	5.0	5.4	30.9
Randolph	103	90	14.0	11.6	99	113	13.4	14.6	1	1	1	9.7	11.1	7.1
Richmond	3,183	3,329	16.2	16.7	1,906	1,912	9.7	9.6	33	42	58	10.4	12.6	15.7
Rockdale	1,090	991	14.2	14.0	505	498	6.6	7.1	12	3	9	11.0	3.0	11.0
Schley	52	57	12.9	15.1	43	38	10.7	10.0	1	–	1	19.2	–	22.2
Screven	176	198	11.4	12.9	164	166	10.6	10.8	3	5	4	17.0	25.3	16.3
Seminole	113	136	12.2	14.5	104	110	11.2	11.7	1	2	3	8.8	14.7	21.4
Spalding	922	886	15.2	15.1	567	585	9.3	10.0	9	9	8	9.8	10.2	8.1
Stephens	347	370	13.8	14.5	324	322	12.9	12.6	2	4	4	5.8	10.8	11.2
Stewart	61	57	12.3	10.9	65	71	13.1	13.6	1	–	2	16.4	–	25.0
Sumter	497	524	15.0	15.8	355	347	10.7	10.4	10	4	11	20.1	7.6	18.0
Talbot	71	89	10.7	13.6	73	96	11.0	14.7	1	2	2	14.1	22.5	20.0
Taliaferro	24	23	12.7	11.1	31	33	16.4	15.9	–	–	–	–	–	–
Tattnall	333	321	14.5	14.4	214	216	9.3	9.7	3	2	1	9.0	6.2	3.7
Taylor	112	125	12.5	14.2	104	113	11.6	12.8	1	1	3	8.9	8.0	23.3
Telfair	168	196	12.9	16.6	151	135	11.6	11.4	3	1	4	17.9	5.1	22.3
Terrell	159	190	14.5	17.3	136	113	12.4	10.3	2	1	2	12.6	5.3	10.8
Thomas	674	653	15.4	15.2	450	486	10.3	11.3	6	2	10	8.9	3.1	14.0
Tift	675	649	16.8	16.9	351	386	8.7	10.0	3	9	7	4.4	13.9	11.6
Toombs	437	462	16.3	17.7	267	288	10.0	11.0	6	2	4	13.7	4.3	9.1
Towns	85	94	8.4	10.0	142	135	14.0	14.4	1	1	1	11.8	10.6	18.9
Treutlen	92	87	13.0	12.6	79	74	11.2	10.7	1	1	2	10.9	11.5	21.1
Troup	970	930	15.9	15.8	638	713	10.4	12.1	8	13	14	8.2	14.0	13.9
Turner	144	160	15.2	16.8	103	105	10.9	11.0	1	2	2	6.9	12.5	12.7
Twiggs	112	129	10.7	12.2	114	104	10.9	9.8	2	1	1	17.9	7.8	6.5
Union	172	195	8.8	11.2	243	217	12.5	12.5	–	2	–	–	10.3	–
Upson	329	360	11.8	13.0	406	354	14.6	12.8	3	2	2	9.1	5.6	5.3
Walker	781	792	12.4	13.0	665	722	10.5	11.8	4	8	16	5.1	10.1	19.0
Walton	1,115	1,024	15.5	16.6	562	461	7.8	7.5	12	5	11	10.8	4.9	15.5
Ware	480	523	14.0	14.7	438	406	12.7	11.4	6	4	9	12.5	7.6	16.7
Warren	74	85	12.0	13.5	79	98	12.8	15.6	–	3	2	–	35.3	20.0
Washington	269	270	12.8	12.8	232	213	11.0	10.1	2	2	3	7.4	7.4	9.3
Wayne	374	356	13.3	13.4	245	237	8.7	8.9	2	2	–	5.3	5.6	–
Webster	27	32	11.6	13.4	26	33	11.2	13.8	1	–	–	37.0	–	–
Wheeler	78	68	12.0	11.0	68	66	10.4	10.7	2	–	–	25.6	–	–
White	284	269	12.0	13.4	253	190	10.7	9.4	2	3	1	7.0	11.2	5.5
Whitfield	1,873	1,805	21.0	21.5	697	712	7.8	8.5	7	9	8	3.7	5.0	6.2
Wilcox	100	110	11.4	12.8	129	93	14.7	10.9	1	3	1	10.0	27.3	11.8
Wilkes	120	129	11.4	12.1	148	142	14.0	13.3	1	1	2	8.3	7.8	15.5
Wilkinson	146	159	14.3	15.5	104	107	10.2	10.5	2	2	1	13.7	12.6	6.0
Worth	236	284	10.7	12.9	239	206	10.9	9.4	2	1	7	8.5	3.5	19.5

See footnotes at end of table.

Table B-5. Counties — **Births, Deaths, and Infant Deaths**—Con.

[Includes United States, states, and 3,141 counties/county equivalents defined as of February 22, 2005. For more information on these areas, see Appendix C, Geographic Information]

County	Births				Deaths				Infant deaths[2]					
	Number		Rate per 1,000 population[1]		Number		Rate per 1,000 population[1]		Number			Rate per 1,000 live births[3]		
	2004	2000	2004	2000	2004	2000	2004	2000	2004	2000	1990	2004	2000	1990
HAWAII	18,281	17,551	14.5	14.5	9,030	8,290	7.2	6.8	104	142	138	5.7	8.1	6.7
Hawaii	2,233	2,389	13.7	16.0	1,252	1,158	7.7	7.8	16	20	20	7.2	8.4	9.0
Honolulu	13,321	12,651	14.8	14.5	6,393	5,835	7.1	6.7	74	105	103	5.6	8.3	6.7
Kalawao	–	18	–	123.3	–	1	–	6.8	–	–	–	–	–	–
Kauai	828	728	13.4	12.4	483	454	7.8	7.8	4	2	4	4.8	2.7	4.2
Maui	1,899	1,765	13.8	13.7	902	842	6.5	6.5	10	15	11	5.3	8.5	5.8
IDAHO	22,532	20,366	16.2	15.7	10,028	9,563	7.2	7.4	139	153	143	6.2	7.5	8.7
Ada	5,213	4,868	15.7	16.1	1,963	1,822	5.9	6.0	36	34	32	6.9	7.0	9.6
Adams	27	23	7.7	6.6	30	36	8.6	10.4	–	–	–	–	–	–
Bannock	1,410	1,379	18.1	18.2	562	554	7.2	7.3	8	9	11	5.7	6.5	9.6
Bear Lake	86	95	13.8	14.8	68	62	10.9	9.6	–	–	–	–	–	–
Benewah	111	117	12.3	12.7	93	95	10.3	10.3	2	2	2	18.0	17.1	13.7
Bingham	787	798	18.2	19.1	291	285	6.7	6.8	5	4	3	6.4	5.0	4.8
Blaine	266	244	12.7	12.8	80	76	3.8	4.0	1	2	1	3.8	8.2	5.2
Boise	54	70	7.3	10.4	39	24	5.3	3.6	–	–	1	–	–	20.8
Bonner	388	371	9.7	10.0	341	295	8.6	8.0	3	2	5	7.7	5.4	13.0
Bonneville	1,677	1,417	18.7	17.1	616	521	6.9	6.3	9	9	11	5.4	6.4	8.2
Boundary	115	136	11.0	13.7	100	78	9.6	7.9	3	–	1	26.1	–	9.4
Butte	36	33	12.7	11.4	33	27	11.7	9.3	–	–	–	–	–	–
Camas	13	9	12.8	9.2	9	4	8.9	4.1	–	–	–	–	–	–
Canyon	3,197	2,516	20.2	18.9	1,051	1,005	6.7	7.6	24	15	14	7.5	6.0	8.4
Caribou	92	104	12.7	14.2	57	65	7.9	8.9	2	2	1	21.7	19.2	8.7
Cassia	423	408	19.8	19.1	177	171	8.3	8.0	1	4	5	2.4	9.8	13.8
Clark	15	21	16.0	20.4	4	9	4.3	8.8	1	–	1	66.7	–	76.9
Clearwater	55	72	6.6	8.1	83	90	9.9	10.1	1	–	1	18.2	–	10.1
Custer	32	38	7.8	8.8	32	25	7.8	5.8	–	–	–	–	–	–
Elmore	515	528	17.9	18.2	160	126	5.5	4.3	3	3	3	5.8	5.7	6.3
Franklin	240	233	19.7	20.5	82	83	6.7	7.3	–	1	1	–	4.3	6.2
Fremont	235	195	19.1	16.5	89	110	7.2	9.3	1	1	2	4.3	5.1	10.0
Gem	188	179	11.8	11.8	169	177	10.6	11.6	–	–	5	–	–	29.4
Gooding	256	235	17.8	16.5	124	122	8.6	8.6	1	2	–	3.9	8.5	–
Idaho	166	154	10.6	10.0	163	160	10.4	10.3	2	2	2	12.0	13.0	12.4
Jefferson	444	372	21.3	19.3	134	114	6.4	5.9	4	3	3	9.0	8.1	8.5
Jerome	367	329	19.0	17.8	122	135	6.3	7.3	1	3	2	2.7	9.1	8.3
Kootenai	1,633	1,507	13.3	13.8	938	873	7.7	8.0	7	10	7	4.3	6.6	7.0
Latah	393	413	11.2	11.8	213	207	6.1	5.9	1	–	3	2.5	–	6.8
Lemhi	71	56	9.1	7.2	75	90	9.6	11.6	–	2	1	–	35.7	11.1
Lewis	47	42	12.7	11.2	47	39	12.7	10.4	–	–	–	–	–	–
Lincoln	73	76	16.9	18.7	47	39	10.9	9.6	–	–	1	–	–	20.4
Madison	823	462	27.2	16.8	118	97	3.9	3.5	–	3	3	–	6.5	7.0
Minidoka	333	344	17.4	17.1	162	175	8.4	8.7	3	5	3	9.0	14.5	9.4
Nez Perce	469	418	12.4	11.2	401	397	10.6	10.6	6	3	3	12.8	7.2	7.0
Oneida	52	74	12.5	17.9	42	39	10.1	9.4	–	–	–	–	–	–
Owyhee	189	171	17.2	16.0	83	88	7.5	8.2	1	4	3	5.3	23.4	20.1
Payette	320	303	14.8	14.7	180	189	8.3	9.2	1	5	3	3.1	16.5	11.2
Power	127	115	16.5	15.3	55	52	7.1	6.9	1	–	–	7.9	–	–
Shoshone	118	155	9.2	11.3	163	198	12.7	14.4	–	3	1	–	19.4	6.1
Teton	147	122	20.4	20.0	26	33	3.6	5.4	1	2	–	6.8	16.4	–
Twin Falls	1,121	951	16.5	14.8	629	591	9.2	9.2	8	13	7	7.1	13.7	8.5
Valley	78	60	9.8	7.9	68	67	8.6	8.8	–	1	–	–	16.7	–
Washington	130	153	12.9	15.3	109	118	10.9	11.8	2	4	1	15.4	26.1	7.9
ILLINOIS	180,778	185,036	14.2	14.9	102,670	106,634	8.1	8.6	1,349	1,568	2,104	7.5	8.5	10.7
Adams	801	827	12.0	12.1	833	847	12.4	12.4	5	6	7	6.2	7.3	7.3
Alexander	126	132	13.7	13.8	138	125	15.0	13.0	–	3	3	–	22.7	15.5
Bond	208	184	11.5	10.4	183	167	10.1	9.5	3	2	4	14.4	10.9	20.8
Boone	648	590	13.4	14.0	343	309	7.1	7.3	3	3	5	4.6	5.1	10.8
Brown	58	63	8.4	9.1	71	60	10.3	8.6	–	–	–	–	–	–
Bureau	396	434	11.3	12.2	398	424	11.3	11.9	3	4	5	7.6	9.2	11.1
Calhoun	52	52	10.1	10.2	67	57	13.0	11.2	1	–	–	19.2	–	–
Carroll	150	170	9.3	10.2	180	196	11.1	11.8	–	3	3	–	17.6	13.6
Cass	181	181	13.1	13.2	164	161	11.9	11.8	3	1	1	16.6	5.5	5.3
Champaign	2,292	2,320	12.4	12.9	1,196	1,110	6.5	6.2	20	23	20	8.7	9.9	7.7
Christian	424	406	12.0	11.5	392	448	11.1	12.7	3	7	5	7.1	17.2	10.5
Clark	189	189	11.1	11.1	190	195	11.2	11.5	2	–	1	10.6	–	5.2
Clay	170	187	12.0	12.9	184	172	13.0	11.8	2	–	3	11.8	–	14.2
Clinton	442	439	12.2	12.3	302	325	8.4	9.1	3	2	2	6.8	4.6	4.8
Coles	584	615	11.3	11.6	476	552	9.2	10.4	2	5	8	3.4	8.1	13.7
Cook	80,014	85,397	15.0	15.9	42,210	46,185	7.9	8.6	640	846	1,295	8.0	9.9	13.3
Crawford	190	237	9.5	11.6	231	234	11.6	11.5	1	–	2	5.3	–	9.0
Cumberland	122	120	11.0	10.7	124	113	11.2	10.0	–	–	–	–	–	–
DeKalb	1,196	1,123	12.5	12.6	637	633	6.7	7.1	8	8	8	6.7	7.1	7.8
De Witt	203	206	12.3	12.3	179	195	10.8	11.6	1	1	–	4.9	4.9	–

See footnotes at end of table.

[Includes United States, states, and 3,141 counties/county equivalents defined as of February 22, 2005. For more information on these areas, see Appendix C, Geographic Information]

County	Births Number 2004	2000	Births Rate per 1,000 population[1] 2004	2000	Deaths Number 2004	2000	Deaths Rate per 1,000 population[1] 2004	2000	Infant deaths[2] Number 2004	2000	1990	Infant deaths Rate per 1,000 live births[3] 2004	2000	1990
ILLINOIS—Con.														
Douglas	281	287	14.1	14.4	192	198	9.6	9.9	5	3	1	17.8	10.5	4.0
DuPage	12,619	13,551	13.6	14.9	5,459	5,596	5.9	6.2	85	85	91	6.7	6.3	6.6
Edgar	234	199	12.2	10.1	258	238	13.4	12.1	1	3	1	4.3	15.1	4.2
Edwards	74	86	10.9	12.3	88	102	13.0	14.6	6	–	4	81.1	–	43.0
Effingham	451	441	13.0	12.9	302	319	8.7	9.3	1	5	4	2.2	11.3	7.2
Fayette	266	268	12.3	12.3	241	260	11.1	11.9	1	2	–	3.8	7.5	–
Ford	168	192	11.8	13.5	197	221	13.8	15.5	3	2	2	17.9	10.4	12.4
Franklin	506	495	12.8	12.7	565	595	14.3	15.2	4	4	5	7.9	8.1	10.4
Fulton	388	431	10.3	11.3	445	516	11.8	13.5	2	1	4	5.2	2.3	9.3
Gallatin	58	74	9.4	11.5	77	89	12.5	13.8	1	1	–	17.2	13.5	–
Greene	150	169	10.3	11.5	165	200	11.3	13.6	1	1	1	6.7	5.9	5.1
Grundy	577	492	14.0	13.1	347	321	8.4	8.5	6	4	3	10.4	8.1	6.0
Hamilton	86	99	10.2	11.5	112	106	13.3	12.3	1	1	–	11.6	10.1	–
Hancock	223	258	11.5	12.8	207	259	10.7	12.9	2	1	–	9.0	3.9	–
Hardin	40	35	8.5	7.3	77	71	16.3	14.8	–	–	–	–	–	–
Henderson	63	78	7.8	9.5	81	90	10.0	11.0	–	–	–	–	–	–
Henry	556	597	11.0	11.7	539	530	10.7	10.4	1	7	2	1.8	11.7	3.3
Iroquois	354	367	11.6	11.7	380	371	12.4	11.8	3	2	5	8.5	5.4	12.4
Jackson	711	668	12.2	11.2	498	504	8.6	8.5	4	8	9	5.6	12.0	13.1
Jasper	109	110	10.8	10.9	93	117	9.3	11.6	–	3	–	–	27.3	–
Jefferson	486	477	12.1	11.9	434	422	10.8	10.5	1	3	1	2.1	6.3	1.7
Jersey	244	211	10.9	9.7	246	209	11.0	9.6	1	–	4	4.1	–	16.0
Jo Daviess	213	247	9.5	11.1	226	236	10.0	10.6	3	2	1	14.1	8.1	3.7
Johnson	140	150	10.7	11.6	126	133	9.7	10.3	–	1	–	–	6.7	–
Kane	8,562	7,852	18.1	19.3	2,536	2,499	5.4	6.1	52	56	57	6.1	7.1	9.2
Kankakee	1,487	1,562	13.9	15.0	1,100	1,120	10.3	10.8	19	21	19	12.8	13.4	11.1
Kendall	1,293	881	17.8	16.0	367	350	5.0	6.3	9	7	3	7.0	7.9	4.9
Knox	626	625	11.6	11.2	687	701	12.8	12.6	4	4	12	6.4	6.4	17.0
Lake	10,275	10,571	14.8	16.3	3,883	3,673	5.6	5.7	68	48	69	6.6	4.5	7.1
LaSalle	1,367	1,488	12.2	13.3	1,306	1,203	11.6	10.8	11	8	8	8.0	5.4	5.3
Lawrence	165	137	10.3	8.9	217	259	13.6	16.8	2	1	3	12.1	7.3	15.6
Lee	398	409	11.2	11.3	364	407	10.2	11.3	2	4	2	5.0	9.8	4.6
Livingston	509	524	13.0	13.2	454	412	11.6	10.4	5	3	3	9.8	5.7	5.7
Logan	334	349	10.9	11.2	313	329	10.2	10.6	3	2	3	9.0	5.7	8.3
McDonough	286	327	8.9	10.0	291	315	9.0	9.6	2	–	4	7.0	–	12.5
McHenry	4,378	4,062	14.8	15.5	1,662	1,521	5.6	5.8	20	22	22	4.6	5.4	6.5
McLean	2,215	1,991	14.0	13.2	1,018	986	6.4	6.5	22	7	8	9.9	3.5	4.4
Macon	1,347	1,445	12.2	12.6	1,223	1,153	11.1	10.1	17	11	20	12.6	7.6	11.6
Macoupin	596	519	12.1	10.6	539	586	11.0	12.0	7	2	5	11.7	3.9	8.3
Madison	3,350	3,378	12.7	13.0	2,666	2,685	10.1	10.4	31	26	30	9.3	7.7	7.8
Marion	467	532	11.6	12.8	483	503	11.9	12.1	4	3	2	8.6	5.6	3.1
Marshall	143	132	10.8	10.0	170	167	12.9	12.7	–	–	1	–	–	5.9
Mason	190	166	12.0	10.4	178	192	11.2	12.0	1	–	2	5.3	–	9.8
Massac	197	184	12.9	12.2	187	232	12.2	15.3	–	1	3	–	5.4	15.8
Menard	116	150	9.1	12.0	133	130	10.4	10.4	2	–	1	17.2	–	7.3
Mercer	158	180	9.3	10.6	147	209	8.7	12.3	–	–	1	–	–	4.6
Monroe	344	351	11.3	12.6	246	245	8.1	8.8	1	3	2	2.9	8.5	6.2
Montgomery	312	363	10.2	11.8	343	387	11.3	12.6	2	–	–	6.4	–	–
Morgan	442	430	12.3	11.7	383	414	10.7	11.3	3	5	2	6.8	11.6	4.2
Moultrie	176	204	12.2	14.2	195	191	13.5	13.3	–	1	1	–	4.9	4.9
Ogle	570	600	10.6	11.7	466	453	8.7	8.9	4	6	5	7.0	10.0	6.9
Peoria	2,660	2,687	14.6	14.7	1,777	1,738	9.8	9.5	34	22	37	12.8	8.2	13.0
Perry	262	242	11.5	10.5	265	250	11.7	10.8	–	1	1	–	4.1	3.1
Piatt	179	193	10.8	11.8	139	149	8.4	9.1	1	4	1	5.6	20.7	5.0
Pike	166	192	9.7	11.1	214	229	12.5	13.2	1	1	1	6.0	5.2	4.8
Pope	31	35	7.2	7.9	51	64	11.9	14.5	1	–	–	32.3	–	–
Pulaski	88	102	12.7	13.9	90	105	12.9	14.3	–	1	–	–	9.8	–
Putnam	53	61	8.7	10.0	53	52	8.7	8.5	–	–	–	–	–	–
Randolph	385	379	11.6	11.2	407	372	12.2	11.0	–	5	4	–	13.2	10.3
Richland	213	198	13.4	12.3	209	192	13.2	11.9	1	1	2	4.7	5.1	10.4
Rock Island	1,962	1,922	13.3	12.9	1,399	1,538	9.5	10.3	10	22	24	5.1	11.4	11.3
St. Clair	3,724	3,775	14.4	14.7	2,540	2,565	9.8	10.0	29	41	65	7.8	10.9	13.8
Saline	310	294	11.8	11.0	380	417	14.5	15.6	2	6	2	6.5	20.4	5.8
Sangamon	2,591	2,646	13.5	14.0	1,814	1,791	9.4	9.5	29	21	21	11.2	7.9	7.7
Schuyler	69	79	9.8	11.0	76	94	10.8	13.1	–	2	1	–	25.3	11.1
Scott	82	72	15.1	13.0	52	68	9.6	12.3	–	1	1	–	13.9	14.1
Shelby	259	244	11.6	10.7	240	247	10.7	10.8	–	2	1	–	8.2	3.3
Stark	80	75	12.9	11.9	74	86	12.0	13.6	–	–	2	–	–	28.2
Stephenson	568	595	11.8	12.2	562	508	11.7	10.4	8	2	8	14.1	3.4	11.9
Tazewell	1,609	1,586	12.5	12.3	1,271	1,288	9.9	10.0	12	20	17	7.5	12.6	9.7

See footnotes at end of table.

[Includes United States, states, and 3,141 counties/county equivalents defined as of February 22, 2005. For more information on these areas, see Appendix C, Geographic Information]

County	Births Number		Births Rate per 1,000 population[1]		Deaths Number		Deaths Rate per 1,000 population[1]		Infant deaths[2] Number			Infant deaths Rate per 1,000 live births[3]		
	2004	2000	2004	2000	2004	2000	2004	2000	2004	2000	1990	2004	2000	1990
ILLINOIS—Con.														
Union	221	205	12.1	11.2	222	263	12.2	14.4	1	–	5	4.5	–	20.7
Vermilion	1,075	1,208	13.0	14.4	989	939	12.0	11.2	6	11	12	5.6	9.1	9.5
Wabash	180	130	14.3	10.1	107	146	8.5	11.3	–	–	4	–	–	20.8
Warren	193	213	10.9	11.4	203	220	11.5	11.8	3	1	1	15.5	4.7	4.4
Washington	170	182	11.2	12.0	164	168	10.8	11.1	–	1	–	–	5.5	–
Wayne	185	182	11.0	10.6	220	187	13.1	10.9	–	2	6	–	11.0	28.4
White	174	159	11.4	10.4	214	262	14.1	17.1	–	–	1	–	–	5.7
Whiteside	758	772	12.6	12.7	627	598	10.5	9.9	5	2	2	6.6	2.6	2.4
Will	9,629	8,216	15.6	16.2	3,309	3,014	5.4	5.9	61	56	45	6.3	6.8	7.5
Williamson	740	673	11.7	11.0	735	738	11.6	12.1	2	6	2	2.7	8.9	2.8
Winnebago	3,998	4,020	13.9	14.4	2,504	2,481	8.7	8.9	19	40	36	4.8	10.0	8.6
Woodford	428	433	11.6	12.2	353	332	9.6	9.3	1	3	4	2.3	6.9	9.8
INDIANA	87,142	87,699	14.0	14.4	54,211	55,469	8.7	9.1	700	685	831	8.0	7.8	9.6
Adams	607	582	18.0	17.3	300	328	8.9	9.8	9	3	8	14.8	5.2	12.8
Allen	5,324	5,207	15.6	15.6	2,479	2,586	7.3	7.8	41	34	50	7.7	6.5	9.4
Bartholomew	1,047	1,069	14.4	14.9	707	628	9.7	8.8	8	9	5	7.6	8.4	5.0
Benton	135	138	14.8	14.7	95	95	10.4	10.1	1	2	–	7.4	14.5	–
Blackford	151	147	10.9	10.5	154	146	11.1	10.4	–	–	2	–	–	9.0
Boone	657	627	12.9	13.5	386	450	7.6	9.7	1	6	5	1.5	9.6	8.4
Brown	114	124	7.5	8.3	123	126	8.1	8.4	–	–	2	–	–	11.9
Carroll	250	227	12.3	11.3	167	179	8.2	8.9	1	1	2	4.0	4.4	8.3
Cass	570	603	14.1	14.7	389	429	9.6	10.5	6	4	3	10.5	6.6	5.4
Clark	1,325	1,359	13.2	14.0	938	944	9.3	9.8	11	8	13	8.3	5.9	10.8
Clay	337	324	12.5	12.2	293	324	10.8	12.2	3	3	1	8.9	9.3	2.7
Clinton	494	553	14.5	16.3	361	398	10.6	11.7	1	4	7	2.0	7.2	13.9
Crawford	140	157	12.6	14.5	126	114	11.3	10.6	–	–	–	–	–	–
Daviess	483	475	15.9	15.9	278	313	9.2	10.5	5	3	2	10.4	6.3	4.4
Dearborn	639	676	13.1	14.6	368	396	7.6	8.5	4	4	5	6.3	5.9	9.7
Decatur	362	380	14.5	15.5	234	225	9.4	9.2	1	3	3	2.8	7.9	8.2
DeKalb	555	556	13.4	13.8	329	343	7.9	8.5	5	6	3	9.0	10.8	5.3
Delaware	1,310	1,435	11.1	12.1	1,119	1,188	9.5	10.0	8	21	17	6.1	14.6	10.9
Dubois	550	541	13.5	13.6	349	377	8.6	9.5	4	7	3	7.3	12.9	5.1
Elkhart	3,246	3,305	16.9	18.0	1,399	1,468	7.3	8.0	22	31	27	6.8	9.4	9.9
Fayette	305	356	12.2	13.9	289	291	11.6	11.4	–	5	8	–	14.0	21.3
Floyd	885	893	12.4	12.6	617	677	8.6	9.5	4	4	6	4.5	4.5	6.4
Fountain	215	222	12.2	12.4	186	217	10.6	12.1	5	2	2	23.3	9.0	9.0
Franklin	329	288	14.4	13.0	162	168	7.1	7.6	4	1	2	12.2	3.5	7.2
Fulton	245	270	11.9	13.1	225	193	10.9	9.4	1	4	1	4.1	14.8	3.7
Gibson	416	359	12.5	11.0	351	353	10.6	10.8	–	1	2	–	2.8	4.7
Grant	801	947	11.2	12.9	794	822	11.1	11.2	4	5	20	5.0	5.3	18.2
Greene	395	411	11.8	12.4	377	334	11.3	10.1	3	3	5	7.6	7.3	12.0
Hamilton	3,650	3,169	15.9	17.1	1,044	925	4.5	5.0	22	20	11	6.0	6.3	6.0
Hancock	826	724	13.5	13.0	500	453	8.2	8.1	2	2	12	2.4	2.8	19.9
Harrison	439	444	12.1	12.9	274	279	7.5	8.1	3	3	3	6.8	6.8	7.2
Hendricks	1,547	1,407	12.5	13.3	704	648	5.7	6.1	8	5	6	5.2	3.6	5.7
Henry	539	560	11.3	11.6	552	539	11.6	11.1	5	6	4	9.3	10.7	6.4
Howard	1,143	1,170	13.5	13.8	824	861	9.7	10.1	6	8	16	5.2	6.8	12.7
Huntington	499	514	13.1	13.5	389	370	10.2	9.7	3	2	3	6.0	3.9	5.7
Jackson	591	621	14.1	15.0	355	423	8.5	10.2	3	3	2	5.1	4.8	3.8
Jasper	397	401	12.6	13.3	242	254	7.7	8.4	2	2	1	5.0	5.0	2.6
Jay	287	307	13.2	14.1	194	242	9.0	11.1	2	2	1	7.0	6.5	2.9
Jefferson	382	364	11.9	11.5	265	321	8.2	10.1	1	3	3	2.6	8.2	7.7
Jennings	415	396	14.7	14.3	211	233	7.5	8.4	1	3	3	2.4	7.6	8.3
Johnson	1,772	1,669	14.1	14.4	1,039	966	8.3	8.3	7	7	10	4.0	4.2	7.8
Knox	461	429	12.0	10.9	451	492	11.7	12.6	5	3	4	10.8	7.0	8.0
Kosciusko	1,086	1,198	14.4	16.1	625	619	8.3	8.3	12	5	8	11.0	4.2	7.0
LaGrange	698	607	19.1	19.7	208	232	5.7	6.6	7	6	2	10.0	8.7	3.5
Lake	6,966	7,056	14.2	14.6	4,670	4,915	9.5	10.1	69	61	77	9.9	8.6	10.1
LaPorte	1,329	1,442	12.1	13.1	1,041	1,069	9.5	9.7	14	10	12	10.5	6.9	7.7
Lawrence	537	617	11.6	13.4	486	513	10.5	11.2	5	6	2	9.3	9.7	3.5
Madison	1,633	1,648	12.5	12.4	1,459	1,449	11.2	10.9	15	15	19	9.2	9.1	10.5
Marion	14,897	14,691	17.3	17.1	7,470	7,666	8.7	8.9	149	145	187	10.0	9.9	12.3
Marshall	655	689	14.1	15.2	381	440	8.2	9.7	2	3	7	3.1	4.4	11.1
Martin	113	144	10.9	13.9	92	80	8.8	7.7	2	2	1	17.7	13.9	6.3
Miami	437	482	12.2	13.3	319	310	8.9	8.6	2	3	1	4.6	6.2	1.6
Monroe	1,274	1,246	10.5	10.3	738	735	6.1	6.1	8	12	8	6.3	9.6	6.3
Montgomery	486	478	12.8	12.7	365	372	9.6	9.9	3	4	5	6.2	8.4	9.5
Morgan	859	967	12.4	14.5	544	547	7.9	8.2	10	5	10	11.6	5.2	11.4
Newton	140	175	9.7	12.0	161	127	11.2	8.7	–	–	–	–	–	–
Noble	740	723	15.7	15.6	406	376	8.6	8.1	7	4	12	9.5	5.5	18.3
Ohio	64	63	11.0	11.2	64	48	11.0	8.5	–	–	1	–	–	13.0
Orange	238	273	12.1	14.1	204	209	10.4	10.8	2	2	–	8.4	7.3	–
Owen	262	263	11.4	12.0	222	175	9.7	8.0	6	2	3	22.9	7.6	11.6

See footnotes at end of table.

Table B-5. Counties — **Births, Deaths, and Infant Deaths**—Con.

[Includes United States, states, and 3,141 counties/county equivalents defined as of February 22, 2005. For more information on these areas, see Appendix C, Geographic Information]

County	Births Number 2004	Births Number 2000	Births Rate per 1,000 population[1] 2004	Births Rate per 1,000 population[1] 2000	Deaths Number 2004	Deaths Number 2000	Deaths Rate per 1,000 population[1] 2004	Deaths Rate per 1,000 population[1] 2000	Infant deaths[2] Number 2004	Infant deaths[2] Number 2000	Infant deaths[2] Number 1990	Infant deaths Rate per 1,000 live births[3] 2004	Rate per 1,000 live births[3] 2000	Rate per 1,000 live births[3] 1990
INDIANA—Con.														
Parke	157	200	9.1	11.6	150	171	8.7	9.9	2	1	1	12.7	5.0	4.8
Perry	220	240	11.6	12.7	200	204	10.5	10.8	–	5	1	–	20.8	4.3
Pike	168	147	13.0	11.5	142	122	11.0	9.5	1	6	1	6.0	40.8	6.3
Porter	1,824	1,839	11.8	12.5	1,206	1,118	7.8	7.6	14	11	15	7.7	6.0	9.1
Posey	292	288	10.9	10.6	232	246	8.6	9.1	3	8	2	10.3	27.8	5.4
Pulaski	172	179	12.5	13.0	157	119	11.4	8.7	1	1	2	5.8	5.6	9.1
Putnam	407	426	11.1	11.8	280	315	7.6	8.7	4	3	3	9.8	7.0	7.6
Randolph	317	346	11.9	12.6	279	280	10.5	10.2	3	3	2	9.5	8.7	5.9
Ripley	388	438	14.1	16.4	266	219	9.7	8.2	3	2	1	7.7	4.6	2.5
Rush	195	244	10.9	13.4	202	189	11.3	10.4	2	–	4	10.3	–	16.2
St. Joseph	3,841	3,969	14.5	14.9	2,390	2,403	9.0	9.0	30	29	43	7.8	7.3	11.0
Scott	290	348	12.3	15.1	243	231	10.3	10.0	1	2	2	3.4	5.7	6.1
Shelby	581	628	13.3	14.4	370	396	8.5	9.1	7	7	7	12.0	11.1	12.8
Spencer	234	268	11.5	13.1	186	161	9.2	7.9	2	1	3	8.5	3.7	11.2
Starke	288	314	12.6	13.3	249	275	10.9	11.7	1	3	2	3.5	9.6	5.5
Steuben	404	423	12.0	12.7	269	260	8.0	7.8	4	4	1	9.9	9.5	2.7
Sullivan	214	255	9.8	11.7	241	268	11.0	12.3	3	3	1	14.0	11.8	4.4
Switzerland	109	110	11.4	12.1	81	100	8.5	11.0	2	2	1	18.3	18.2	10.2
Tippecanoe	2,073	1,931	13.6	12.9	960	1,040	6.3	7.0	22	19	15	10.6	9.8	8.2
Tipton	215	193	13.0	11.7	170	158	10.3	9.5	3	2	2	14.0	10.4	9.5
Union	101	111	14.0	15.1	83	60	11.5	8.2	–	1	–	–	9.0	–
Vanderburgh	2,350	2,340	13.6	13.6	1,824	1,903	10.5	11.1	21	16	38	8.9	6.8	14.8
Vermillion	206	209	12.5	12.5	187	231	11.3	13.8	1	–	–	4.9	–	–
Vigo	1,308	1,384	12.7	13.1	1,091	1,251	10.6	11.8	11	10	24	8.4	7.2	16.1
Wabash	378	429	11.1	12.3	346	369	10.1	10.5	6	3	–	15.9	7.0	–
Warren	85	107	9.7	12.7	95	95	10.9	11.2	1	1	2	11.8	9.3	20.0
Warrick	703	684	12.7	13.0	426	424	7.7	8.1	1	2	3	1.4	2.9	4.7
Washington	359	358	12.9	13.1	249	234	8.9	8.6	1	2	2	2.8	5.6	6.6
Wayne	942	901	13.5	12.7	778	841	11.2	11.8	9	3	9	9.6	3.3	9.4
Wells	353	373	12.6	13.5	229	248	8.2	9.0	2	3	2	5.7	8.0	5.1
White	323	351	13.1	13.9	250	277	10.1	11.0	3	1	3	9.3	2.8	9.7
Whitley	396	418	12.4	13.6	286	261	9.0	8.5	1	3	1	2.5	7.2	2.3
IOWA	38,438	38,266	13.0	13.1	26,897	28,060	9.1	9.6	195	247	319	5.1	6.5	8.1
Adair	60	68	7.6	8.3	126	109	16.0	13.3	–	–	–	–	–	–
Adams	38	35	8.8	7.8	55	55	12.8	12.3	–	–	–	–	–	–
Allamakee	206	158	14.0	10.8	152	173	10.3	11.8	1	–	–	4.9	–	–
Appanoose	145	142	10.6	10.4	197	174	14.5	12.7	–	–	3	–	–	18.0
Audubon	46	47	7.1	6.9	114	114	17.6	16.7	–	1	1	–	21.3	11.0
Benton	315	325	11.8	12.8	227	229	8.5	9.0	3	2	–	9.5	6.2	–
Black Hawk	1,716	1,553	13.7	12.1	1,145	1,157	9.1	9.0	6	11	17	3.5	7.1	10.0
Boone	287	317	10.9	12.1	248	319	9.4	12.2	4	4	–	13.9	12.6	–
Bremer	232	250	9.9	10.7	210	218	8.9	9.4	1	2	–	4.3	8.0	–
Buchanan	290	302	13.8	14.3	185	183	8.8	8.7	2	–	1	6.9	–	3.3
Buena Vista	268	233	13.3	11.4	168	202	8.3	9.9	1	–	–	3.7	–	–
Butler	179	170	11.9	11.1	190	200	12.7	13.1	1	1	1	5.6	5.9	5.4
Calhoun	115	107	10.9	9.7	128	161	12.2	14.5	–	–	–	–	–	–
Carroll	260	262	12.4	12.3	210	238	10.0	11.1	–	–	2	–	–	6.3
Cass	152	158	10.6	10.8	174	190	12.2	12.9	–	1	1	–	6.3	5.2
Cedar	205	206	11.2	11.3	176	167	9.6	9.2	1	–	3	4.9	–	13.6
Cerro Gordo	501	531	11.2	11.5	498	533	11.1	11.5	3	4	6	6.0	7.5	8.8
Cherokee	115	146	9.3	11.2	151	161	12.2	12.4	–	–	5	–	–	25.0
Chickasaw	131	169	10.4	12.9	148	128	11.7	9.8	2	–	–	15.3	–	–
Clarke	124	97	13.4	10.5	91	97	9.8	10.5	–	1	–	–	10.3	–
Clay	213	204	12.6	11.7	171	181	10.1	10.4	–	1	–	–	4.9	–
Clayton	207	194	11.3	10.4	226	228	12.3	12.2	–	1	–	–	5.2	–
Clinton	599	592	12.0	11.8	496	513	10.0	10.2	9	4	8	15.0	6.8	11.6
Crawford	244	189	14.4	11.2	169	182	10.0	10.7	1	1	1	–	5.3	4.4
Dallas	655	566	13.2	13.8	320	302	6.5	7.4	4	4	1	6.1	7.1	2.4
Davis	118	129	13.6	15.1	92	91	10.6	10.6	1	1	–	8.5	7.8	–
Decatur	103	101	11.9	11.6	73	114	8.5	13.1	1	1	–	9.7	9.9	–
Delaware	189	227	10.5	12.3	141	154	7.8	8.4	–	1	2	–	4.4	7.0
Des Moines	526	555	12.9	13.1	429	428	10.5	10.1	2	4	6	3.8	7.2	10.6
Dickinson	182	159	11.0	9.7	161	193	9.7	11.7	–	–	1	–	–	6.3
Dubuque	1,204	1,221	13.2	13.7	823	855	9.0	9.6	5	9	16	4.2	7.4	12.7
Emmet	132	126	12.4	11.5	110	149	10.4	13.6	1	2	1	7.6	15.9	7.5
Fayette	209	233	9.8	10.6	234	261	11.0	11.9	1	–	1	4.8	–	3.5
Floyd	197	199	11.9	11.8	197	205	11.9	12.2	–	–	–	–	–	–
Franklin	133	113	12.4	10.6	115	131	10.7	12.3	–	1	1	–	8.8	8.0
Fremont	75	82	9.7	10.2	90	101	11.6	12.6	–	1	–	–	12.2	–
Greene	100	92	10.0	8.9	123	132	12.3	12.8	–	1	1	–	10.9	9.2
Grundy	112	133	9.1	10.7	156	132	12.6	10.7	1	2	1	8.9	15.0	6.8
Guthrie	106	134	9.2	11.8	134	158	11.6	13.9	1	–	–	9.4	–	–
Hamilton	201	192	12.4	11.7	182	172	11.2	10.5	1	2	3	5.0	10.4	14.4

See footnotes at end of table.

[Includes United States, states, and 3,141 counties/county equivalents defined as of February 22, 2005. For more information on these areas, see Appendix C, Geographic Information]

County	Births				Deaths				Infant deaths[2]					
	Number		Rate per 1,000 population[1]		Number		Rate per 1,000 population[1]		Number			Rate per 1,000 live births[3]		
	2004	2000	2004	2000	2004	2000	2004	2000	2004	2000	1990	2004	2000	1990
IOWA—Con.														
Hancock	117	131	9.9	10.8	126	149	10.7	12.3	–	1	2	–	7.6	12.2
Hardin	200	209	11.0	11.1	251	280	13.8	14.9	3	3	2	15.0	14.4	9.4
Harrison	136	192	8.6	12.2	178	187	11.3	11.9	–	1	1	–	5.2	5.4
Henry	255	264	12.6	13.0	208	204	10.3	10.0	2	2	–	7.8	7.6	–
Howard	119	109	12.1	11.0	125	135	12.8	13.6	–	1	1	–	9.2	7.4
Humboldt	143	99	14.2	9.5	117	119	11.7	11.5	–	–	2	–	–	17.9
Ida	80	70	10.8	9.0	100	102	13.5	13.1	–	1	–	–	14.3	–
Iowa	192	184	12.0	11.7	161	159	10.1	10.1	2	1	–	10.4	5.4	–
Jackson	193	239	9.5	11.8	201	219	9.9	10.8	–	3	1	–	12.6	4.0
Jasper	421	458	11.2	12.3	338	357	9.0	9.6	1	2	–	2.4	4.4	–
Jefferson	152	145	9.5	9.0	143	138	8.9	8.5	–	–	3	–	–	15.6
Johnson	1,560	1,382	13.4	12.4	523	492	4.5	4.4	3	8	13	1.9	5.8	9.2
Jones	219	227	10.7	11.2	193	181	9.4	9.0	–	–	4	–	–	15.9
Keokuk	133	154	11.8	13.5	135	155	12.0	13.6	–	–	1	–	–	6.7
Kossuth	175	166	10.7	9.7	165	205	10.1	12.0	–	1	4	–	6.0	15.9
Lee	385	410	10.5	10.8	432	456	11.8	12.0	3	4	2	7.8	9.8	4.0
Linn	2,760	2,717	14.0	14.1	1,480	1,435	7.5	7.5	22	12	26	8.0	4.4	9.8
Louisa	164	164	13.6	13.5	113	105	9.4	8.6	1	1	4	6.1	6.1	24.5
Lucas	89	119	9.2	12.6	105	109	10.9	11.6	–	3	–	–	25.2	–
Lyon	167	159	14.2	13.5	114	132	9.7	11.2	–	1	1	–	6.3	5.6
Madison	196	196	13.1	13.9	118	159	7.9	11.3	–	2	1	–	10.2	6.3
Mahaska	268	284	12.1	12.7	196	221	8.9	9.9	3	9	1	11.2	31.7	3.5
Marion	398	383	12.2	11.9	342	317	10.5	9.9	3	1	1	7.5	2.6	2.7
Marshall	642	556	16.3	14.1	450	506	11.4	12.9	3	3	4	4.7	5.4	8.0
Mills	183	156	12.2	10.7	131	145	8.7	9.9	2	–	–	10.9	–	–
Mitchell	111	131	10.1	12.1	139	140	12.7	12.9	–	1	1	–	7.6	7.6
Monona	103	98	10.7	9.8	177	168	18.3	16.8	–	–	1	–	–	8.8
Monroe	82	102	10.4	12.8	100	109	12.7	13.6	–	1	–	–	9.8	–
Montgomery	125	139	11.1	11.8	151	175	13.4	14.8	–	2	1	–	14.4	6.3
Muscatine	588	638	13.9	15.3	396	352	9.3	8.4	2	1	2	3.4	1.6	3.0
O'Brien	173	187	12.0	12.4	160	198	11.1	13.1	–	1	2	–	5.3	10.9
Osceola	83	73	12.2	10.5	81	79	11.9	11.3	1	–	–	12.0	–	–
Page	168	168	10.3	9.9	189	215	11.6	12.7	–	1	–	–	6.0	–
Palo Alto	107	110	11.0	10.8	127	124	13.0	12.2	–	1	1	–	9.1	10.5
Plymouth	326	309	13.1	12.4	237	275	9.5	11.1	2	7	2	6.1	22.7	5.8
Pocahontas	74	73	9.2	8.5	108	107	13.4	12.4	–	–	–	–	–	–
Polk	6,322	6,221	16.0	16.6	2,761	2,774	7.0	7.4	34	46	57	5.4	7.4	10.6
Pottawattamie	1,222	1,185	13.7	13.5	842	868	9.4	9.9	11	10	5	9.0	8.4	3.7
Poweshiek	183	212	9.6	11.3	205	209	10.8	11.1	1	–	–	5.5	–	–
Ringgold	57	69	10.6	12.6	72	99	13.4	18.1	–	–	–	–	–	–
Sac	123	136	11.4	11.8	139	166	12.9	14.5	–	–	1	–	–	6.8
Scott	2,299	2,348	14.4	14.8	1,279	1,244	8.0	7.8	11	20	27	4.8	8.5	10.9
Shelby	114	150	8.9	11.5	136	156	10.6	11.9	1	2	3	8.8	13.3	16.5
Sioux	477	457	14.8	14.5	216	238	6.7	7.5	2	1	3	4.2	2.2	6.9
Story	902	940	11.2	11.7	449	474	5.6	5.9	6	6	10	6.7	6.4	10.8
Tama	237	251	13.2	13.9	180	220	10.0	12.2	1	1	2	4.2	4.0	9.3
Taylor	68	88	10.2	12.6	97	86	14.6	12.3	1	–	–	14.7	–	–
Union	143	127	11.9	10.3	154	160	12.8	13.0	–	2	1	–	15.7	6.8
Van Buren	87	97	11.2	12.4	100	101	12.9	12.9	2	–	1	23.0	–	11.2
Wapello	476	424	13.3	11.8	399	451	11.1	12.5	1	2	4	2.1	4.7	8.2
Warren	507	513	12.0	12.6	313	338	7.4	8.3	1	3	–	2.0	5.8	–
Washington	290	290	13.6	14.0	215	217	10.1	10.5	2	–	1	6.9	–	3.3
Wayne	81	79	12.3	11.7	97	110	14.7	16.3	–	1	1	–	12.7	12.0
Webster	491	492	12.5	12.2	448	499	11.4	12.4	5	2	5	10.2	4.1	8.4
Winnebago	103	134	9.0	11.4	107	123	9.4	10.5	1	–	–	9.7	–	–
Winneshiek	185	191	8.7	9.0	171	190	8.1	8.9	–	1	2	–	5.2	7.7
Woodbury	1,634	1,692	15.8	16.3	900	950	8.7	9.1	6	9	26	3.7	5.3	16.0
Worth	73	84	9.4	10.6	109	91	14.1	11.5	2	2	–	27.4	23.8	–
Wright	187	168	13.7	11.7	163	197	11.9	13.8	2	1	3	10.7	6.0	14.0
KANSAS	39,669	39,666	14.5	14.7	23,818	24,717	8.7	9.2	284	268	329	7.2	6.8	8.4
Allen	158	199	11.4	13.8	176	169	12.6	11.8	2	–	2	12.7	–	12.7
Anderson	92	111	11.3	13.7	97	104	11.9	12.8	2	1	–	21.7	9.0	–
Atchison	244	209	14.5	12.5	191	184	11.3	11.0	5	4	1	20.5	19.1	4.5
Barber	48	40	9.6	7.6	76	73	15.2	13.8	1	–	–	20.8	–	–
Barton	321	343	11.5	12.2	320	351	11.4	12.5	3	–	4	9.3	–	9.0
Bourbon	236	206	15.6	13.4	194	222	12.9	14.4	2	2	5	8.5	9.7	23.4
Brown	132	147	12.8	13.7	142	135	13.7	12.6	–	2	–	–	13.6	–
Butler	778	776	12.6	13.0	551	581	8.9	9.7	9	4	9	11.6	5.2	12.2
Chase	46	29	14.9	9.6	22	37	7.1	12.2	–	–	–	–	–	–
Chautauqua	55	40	13.1	9.2	63	65	15.0	14.9	–	–	1	–	–	23.8

See footnotes at end of table.

[Includes United States, states, and 3,141 counties/county equivalents defined as of February 22, 2005. For more information on these areas, see Appendix C, Geographic Information]

County	Births				Deaths				Infant deaths[2]					
	Number		Rate per 1,000 population[1]		Number		Rate per 1,000 population[1]		Number			Rate per 1,000 live births[3]		
	2004	2000	2004	2000	2004	2000	2004	2000	2004	2000	1990	2004	2000	1990
KANSAS—Con.														
Cherokee	226	279	10.4	12.4	262	277	12.0	12.3	2	2	2	8.8	7.2	7.1
Cheyenne	27	38	9.1	12.0	36	43	12.1	13.6	1	–	2	37.0	–	58.8
Clark	25	30	10.7	12.6	33	28	14.1	11.7	–	–	–	–	–	–
Clay	91	97	10.6	11.0	106	107	12.4	12.1	–	–	1	–	–	11.8
Cloud	100	102	10.3	10.0	153	175	15.7	17.1	2	1	1	20.0	9.8	8.8
Coffey	101	109	11.6	12.3	101	95	11.6	10.7	–	1	–	–	9.2	–
Comanche	24	26	12.6	13.3	31	31	16.2	15.9	–	–	–	–	–	–
Cowley	428	458	12.0	12.6	417	440	11.7	12.1	5	1	3	11.7	2.2	5.8
Crawford	524	580	13.7	15.2	424	484	11.1	12.7	9	4	–	17.2	6.9	–
Decatur	16	36	4.9	10.4	43	47	13.2	13.6	–	–	–	–	–	–
Dickinson	209	232	10.9	12.0	212	228	11.1	11.8	2	4	5	9.6	17.2	20.2
Doniphan	72	96	9.0	11.6	78	108	9.8	13.1	–	–	1	–	–	10.1
Douglas	1,256	1,182	12.2	11.8	528	540	5.1	5.4	5	7	5	4.0	5.9	4.7
Edwards	38	53	11.5	15.5	49	45	14.8	13.1	–	2	–	–	37.7	–
Elk	44	32	14.2	9.9	51	72	16.4	22.3	–	3	–	–	93.8	–
Ellis	364	334	13.5	12.2	240	229	8.9	8.4	1	2	2	2.7	6.0	6.5
Ellsworth	42	43	6.6	6.6	78	103	12.3	15.8	–	2	1	–	46.5	14.3
Finney	803	921	20.5	22.7	176	226	4.5	5.6	3	11	5	3.7	11.9	6.8
Ford	635	655	19.0	20.1	254	265	7.6	8.1	3	7	3	4.7	10.7	5.2
Franklin	374	354	14.3	14.2	231	245	8.8	9.9	4	1	5	10.7	2.8	14.6
Geary	498	566	19.8	20.4	182	196	7.2	7.1	1	4	9	2.0	7.1	7.2
Gove	25	37	8.8	12.1	31	32	11.0	10.4	–	–	–	–	–	–
Graham	26	23	9.5	7.9	38	43	13.8	14.7	1	1	–	38.5	43.5	–
Grant	128	138	16.7	17.5	53	64	6.9	8.1	1	2	–	7.8	14.5	–
Gray	102	98	17.1	16.6	45	56	7.5	9.5	1	1	–	9.8	10.2	–
Greeley	23	19	16.3	12.3	27	19	19.1	12.3	–	–	–	–	–	–
Greenwood	80	94	10.7	12.3	109	114	14.5	14.9	–	–	1	–	–	10.9
Hamilton	39	45	14.8	16.9	26	31	9.8	11.7	1	–	–	25.6	–	–
Harper	57	69	9.2	10.6	105	107	16.9	16.5	1	–	1	17.5	–	11.2
Harvey	386	447	11.5	13.6	368	368	10.9	11.2	1	1	6	2.6	2.2	13.7
Haskell	84	81	19.7	18.8	35	30	8.2	7.0	1	–	–	11.9	–	–
Hodgeman	18	15	8.5	7.2	35	14	16.5	6.7	–	–	–	–	–	–
Jackson	178	164	13.5	12.9	103	130	7.8	10.2	–	1	–	–	6.1	–
Jefferson	196	190	10.3	10.3	161	160	8.5	8.7	1	2	1	5.1	10.5	5.1
Jewell	22	19	6.4	5.0	50	67	14.6	17.8	–	1	1	–	52.6	28.6
Johnson	7,655	6,992	15.4	15.4	2,834	2,663	5.7	5.9	46	42	33	6.0	6.0	5.7
Kearny	71	70	15.7	15.5	25	38	5.5	8.4	–	–	–	–	–	–
Kingman	77	101	9.2	11.6	121	100	14.5	11.5	–	2	–	–	19.8	–
Kiowa	36	34	11.7	10.4	31	42	10.1	12.9	–	–	–	–	–	–
Labette	259	255	11.7	11.2	306	328	13.8	14.4	1	4	4	3.9	15.7	11.1
Lane	14	16	7.2	7.5	26	20	13.5	9.3	–	–	–	–	–	–
Leavenworth	915	891	12.6	12.9	524	443	7.2	6.4	7	6	10	7.7	6.7	11.2
Lincoln	35	48	10.3	13.4	39	53	11.4	14.8	–	1	–	–	20.8	–
Linn	122	126	12.5	13.1	86	114	8.8	11.9	–	2	–	–	15.9	–
Logan	25	38	8.9	12.5	32	50	11.4	16.4	–	–	–	–	–	–
Lyon	508	539	14.2	15.0	292	325	8.1	9.0	1	2	4	2.0	3.7	7.6
McPherson	364	346	12.4	11.7	329	344	11.2	11.6	4	2	2	11.0	5.8	5.2
Marion	138	141	10.6	10.5	181	210	13.9	15.7	1	1	1	7.2	7.1	7.6
Marshall	126	106	12.1	9.7	136	140	13.1	12.8	–	–	1	–	–	8.3
Meade	55	77	12.0	16.6	45	52	9.8	11.2	–	–	–	–	–	–
Miami	428	377	14.4	13.2	239	265	8.0	9.3	1	5	2	2.3	13.3	5.7
Mitchell	63	61	9.7	8.8	97	111	14.9	16.1	–	–	–	–	–	–
Montgomery	498	486	14.3	13.4	478	490	13.7	13.5	6	1	6	12.0	2.1	10.8
Morris	59	68	9.9	11.1	69	83	11.5	13.6	–	1	–	–	–	12.7
Morton	49	63	15.2	18.1	43	33	13.3	9.5	–	–	–	–	–	–
Nemaha	122	136	11.7	12.7	153	159	14.7	14.9	1	–	–	8.2	–	–
Neosho	224	216	13.5	12.7	192	208	11.6	12.3	1	3	2	4.5	13.9	7.9
Ness	30	31	9.8	9.0	41	61	13.4	17.7	–	–	–	–	–	–
Norton	51	72	8.9	12.1	86	81	15.0	13.6	–	–	1	–	–	17.9
Osage	180	192	10.6	11.5	184	172	10.8	10.3	1	2	–	5.6	10.4	–
Osborne	31	35	7.6	7.9	74	74	18.0	16.7	1	–	–	32.3	–	–
Ottawa	72	80	11.7	12.9	68	68	11.1	11.0	–	–	1	–	–	16.7
Pawnee	57	77	8.4	10.7	82	102	12.1	14.1	1	–	–	17.5	–	–
Phillips	55	88	9.8	14.7	63	84	11.2	14.0	–	–	–	–	–	–
Pottawatomie	296	264	15.7	14.4	171	174	9.1	9.5	1	2	–	3.4	7.6	–
Pratt	113	118	12.1	12.3	128	128	13.7	13.3	–	–	–	–	–	–
Rawlins	16	26	5.8	8.8	49	49	17.7	16.6	–	–	–	–	–	–
Reno	836	886	13.2	13.7	600	700	9.4	10.8	2	4	6	2.4	4.5	7.2
Republic	45	47	8.6	8.1	83	109	15.9	18.8	1	–	–	22.2	–	–
Rice	138	127	13.2	11.8	140	135	13.4	12.6	1	–	3	7.2	–	21.6

See footnotes at end of table.

[Includes United States, states, and 3,141 counties/county equivalents defined as of February 22, 2005. For more information on these areas, see Appendix C, Geographic Information]

County	Births Number 2004	2000	Births Rate per 1,000 population[1] 2004	2000	Deaths Number 2004	2000	Deaths Rate per 1,000 population[1] 2004	2000	Infant deaths[2] Number 2004	2000	1990	Infant deaths[2] Rate per 1,000 live births[3] 2004	2000	1990
KANSAS—Con.														
Riley	822	901	13.0	14.4	317	297	5.0	4.7	8	1	7	9.7	1.1	8.5
Rooks	55	53	10.2	9.4	75	71	14.0	12.5	1	–	–	18.2	–	–
Rush	34	46	9.9	13.0	50	54	14.5	15.2	–	–	–	–	–	–
Russell	76	80	10.9	10.9	110	106	15.8	14.4	1	1	–	13.2	12.5	–
Saline	783	752	14.5	14.0	495	493	9.2	9.2	9	4	6	11.5	5.3	8.1
Scott	65	61	14.0	12.0	39	58	8.4	11.4	–	–	–	–	–	–
Sedgwick	7,803	7,837	16.8	17.3	3,702	3,629	8.0	8.0	61	58	88	7.8	7.4	11.7
Seward	527	536	22.7	23.8	139	161	6.0	7.1	3	5	3	5.7	9.3	7.5
Shawnee	2,498	2,464	14.6	14.5	1,564	1,758	9.1	10.3	21	24	25	8.4	9.7	10.0
Sheridan	34	23	13.1	8.2	27	27	10.4	9.6	–	–	–	–	–	–
Sherman	73	82	11.8	12.2	78	73	12.6	10.8	–	2	2	–	24.4	19.6
Smith	31	34	7.5	7.5	65	76	15.6	16.8	–	–	–	–	–	–
Stafford	40	46	8.8	9.7	63	74	13.9	15.5	–	–	2	–	–	34.5
Stanton	45	44	19.0	18.3	25	26	10.6	10.8	–	1	–	–	22.7	–
Stevens	84	98	15.3	18.0	47	52	8.6	9.5	1	–	–	11.9	–	–
Sumner	287	324	11.4	12.5	277	309	11.0	11.9	4	1	–	13.9	3.1	–
Thomas	99	106	12.7	13.0	96	79	12.3	9.7	–	–	–	–	–	–
Trego	30	32	9.6	9.7	54	49	17.2	14.9	–	–	–	–	–	–
Wabaunsee	89	79	13.0	11.5	60	75	8.7	10.9	1	–	2	11.2	–	24.7
Wallace	14	22	8.8	12.7	9	19	5.7	10.9	1	–	1	71.4	–	30.3
Washington	60	62	9.9	9.6	92	100	15.1	15.5	–	–	–	–	–	–
Wichita	47	27	20.1	10.7	35	26	14.9	10.3	–	–	–	–	–	–
Wilson	119	124	12.0	12.0	132	169	13.3	16.4	–	–	2	–	–	16.1
Woodson	32	31	9.0	8.2	59	55	16.6	14.6	–	–	–	–	–	–
Wyandotte	2,788	2,810	17.9	17.8	1,458	1,533	9.3	9.7	26	18	37	9.3	6.4	11.8
KENTUCKY	55,720	56,029	13.5	13.8	38,646	39,504	9.3	9.8	378	401	461	6.8	7.2	8.5
Adair	198	214	11.3	12.4	168	179	9.6	10.4	–	2	1	–	9.3	5.8
Allen	202	233	10.9	13.1	187	181	10.1	10.2	–	–	–	–	–	–
Anderson	244	262	12.2	13.7	156	154	7.8	8.0	1	–	1	4.1	–	4.1
Ballard	101	93	12.3	11.2	89	121	10.8	14.6	2	–	–	19.8	–	–
Barren	554	492	14.0	12.9	406	422	10.3	11.1	1	2	1	1.8	4.1	2.2
Bath	152	162	13.2	14.6	122	133	10.6	11.9	1	1	2	6.6	6.2	13.2
Bell	379	372	12.8	12.4	335	354	11.3	11.8	4	2	1	10.6	5.4	2.1
Boone	1,660	1,437	16.4	16.5	563	505	5.6	5.8	13	5	2	7.8	3.5	2.0
Bourbon	247	229	12.5	11.8	202	202	10.3	10.4	1	2	2	4.0	8.7	8.0
Boyd	595	535	12.0	10.8	621	632	12.5	12.7	5	7	5	8.4	13.1	8.4
Boyle	305	345	10.8	12.5	299	285	10.6	10.3	2	1	2	6.6	2.9	6.1
Bracken	129	112	14.8	13.5	83	92	9.5	11.1	–	3	1	–	26.8	10.4
Breathitt	170	144	10.7	9.0	174	165	10.9	10.3	1	3	2	5.9	20.8	8.8
Breckinridge	249	222	13.0	11.9	226	195	11.8	10.4	3	1	4	12.0	4.5	22.0
Bullitt	704	730	10.5	11.8	350	350	5.2	5.7	7	5	3	9.9	6.8	4.0
Butler	174	159	13.0	12.2	133	134	9.9	10.3	5	3	2	28.7	18.9	13.5
Caldwell	123	128	9.6	9.8	171	154	13.3	11.8	3	–	4	24.4	–	23.0
Calloway	317	329	9.1	9.6	297	367	8.5	10.7	2	1	4	6.3	3.0	12.9
Campbell	1,160	1,251	13.3	14.1	829	831	9.5	9.4	12	7	18	10.3	5.6	13.7
Carlisle	62	71	11.6	13.3	63	76	11.8	14.2	–	–	–	–	–	–
Carroll	164	153	15.9	15.0	100	137	9.7	13.5	–	1	–	–	6.5	–
Carter	346	363	12.7	13.5	299	298	11.0	11.1	3	–	2	8.7	–	5.4
Casey	198	196	12.3	12.7	175	167	10.9	10.8	4	1	1	20.2	5.1	5.5
Christian	1,348	1,673	19.2	23.1	573	606	8.1	8.4	10	16	7	7.4	9.6	5.1
Clark	447	428	13.0	12.9	310	312	9.0	9.4	6	2	1	13.4	4.7	2.4
Clay	275	278	11.3	11.3	243	238	10.0	9.7	3	2	1	10.9	7.2	2.8
Clinton	127	131	13.3	13.6	125	104	13.1	10.8	–	1	–	–	7.6	–
Crittenden	96	105	10.6	11.2	107	133	11.8	14.1	–	–	1	–	–	9.5
Cumberland	71	90	9.9	12.6	89	103	12.4	14.4	1	1	1	14.1	11.1	10.5
Daviess	1,331	1,294	14.4	14.1	874	950	9.4	10.4	12	11	11	9.0	8.5	8.6
Edmonson	122	134	10.3	11.5	99	98	8.3	8.4	1	–	1	8.2	–	10.1
Elliott	77	79	11.2	11.7	80	72	11.6	10.6	1	1	1	13.0	12.7	14.3
Estill	203	184	13.4	12.0	161	164	10.6	10.7	3	2	4	14.8	10.9	18.4
Fayette	3,899	3,702	14.6	14.2	1,839	1,975	6.9	7.6	19	36	17	4.9	9.7	4.9
Fleming	190	159	13.1	11.5	146	149	10.1	10.8	1	–	–	5.3	–	–
Floyd	565	539	13.4	12.7	499	493	11.8	11.6	2	2	6	3.5	3.7	9.3
Franklin	621	617	12.9	12.9	434	449	9.0	9.4	4	4	6	6.4	6.5	10.7
Fulton	89	105	12.1	13.6	99	115	13.5	14.9	1	1	1	11.2	9.5	8.2
Gallatin	153	115	19.2	14.6	85	86	10.6	10.9	–	1	2	–	8.7	24.1
Garrard	166	178	10.2	12.0	130	130	8.0	8.7	1	2	–	6.0	11.2	–
Grant	388	401	15.9	17.8	160	184	6.6	8.2	1	–	5	2.6	–	19.5
Graves	478	501	12.8	13.5	423	457	11.3	12.3	5	–	–	10.5	–	–
Grayson	336	362	13.4	15.0	246	280	9.8	11.6	4	3	–	11.9	8.3	–
Green	121	127	10.4	11.0	145	113	12.5	9.8	3	1	–	24.8	7.9	–
Greenup	436	443	11.7	12.0	410	421	11.0	11.4	2	2	3	4.6	4.5	6.9

See footnotes at end of table.

Table B-5. Counties — Births, Deaths, and Infant Deaths—Con.

[Includes United States, states, and 3,141 counties/county equivalents defined as of February 22, 2005. For more information on these areas, see Appendix C, Geographic Information]

County	Births Number		Births Rate per 1,000 population[1]		Deaths Number		Deaths Rate per 1,000 population[1]		Infant deaths[2] Number			Infant deaths[2] Rate per 1,000 live births[3]		
	2004	2000	2004	2000	2004	2000	2004	2000	2004	2000	1990	2004	2000	1990
KENTUCKY—Con.														
Hancock	123	158	14.6	18.8	70	61	8.3	7.2	2	1	1	16.3	6.3	9.1
Hardin	1,490	1,478	15.6	15.7	686	697	7.2	7.4	10	12	9	6.7	8.1	5.1
Harlan	386	416	12.1	12.6	428	421	13.5	12.7	–	2	11	–	4.8	20.1
Harrison	225	235	12.3	13.0	183	186	10.0	10.3	5	1	3	22.2	4.3	14.4
Hart	244	240	13.5	13.7	196	201	10.8	11.5	1	2	1	4.1	8.3	4.7
Henderson	635	618	14.0	13.8	420	460	9.3	10.3	5	4	7	7.9	6.5	11.3
Henry	201	238	12.7	15.8	146	166	9.2	11.0	2	1	–	10.0	4.2	–
Hickman	50	46	9.8	8.8	62	58	12.1	11.1	1	–	–	20.0	–	–
Hopkins	604	624	12.9	13.4	569	549	12.2	11.8	7	1	9	11.6	1.6	13.8
Jackson	192	192	14.1	14.2	134	140	9.9	10.4	2	–	2	10.4	–	10.9
Jefferson	9,833	10,130	14.1	14.6	6,766	7,181	9.7	10.3	57	73	101	5.8	7.2	9.7
Jessamine	588	557	13.9	14.2	319	290	7.5	7.4	3	2	4	5.1	3.6	7.7
Johnson	285	324	12.0	13.9	266	268	11.2	11.5	1	2	5	3.5	6.2	15.8
Kenton	2,365	2,447	15.5	16.1	1,294	1,216	8.5	8.0	18	15	26	7.6	6.1	10.7
Knott	180	185	10.3	10.5	144	163	8.2	9.2	3	1	2	16.7	5.4	8.2
Knox	538	466	16.9	14.6	349	332	10.9	10.4	3	6	5	5.6	12.9	10.4
Larue	143	174	10.6	13.0	147	148	10.9	11.0	–	2	3	–	11.5	19.6
Laurel	734	774	13.2	14.6	509	520	9.1	9.8	6	7	5	8.2	9.0	8.2
Lawrence	203	198	12.7	12.7	186	170	11.6	10.9	1	–	2	4.9	–	8.8
Lee	77	89	9.9	11.2	101	74	12.9	9.3	1	2	1	13.0	22.5	12.5
Leslie	151	150	12.6	12.1	144	136	12.0	11.0	2	1	4	13.2	6.7	20.5
Letcher	337	286	13.7	11.3	279	302	11.3	12.0	2	4	5	5.9	14.0	13.4
Lewis	185	194	13.4	13.7	157	147	11.3	10.4	–	–	1	–	–	5.9
Lincoln	358	320	14.5	13.6	241	218	9.7	9.3	2	1	1	5.6	3.1	3.4
Livingston	90	111	9.3	11.3	124	100	12.8	10.2	–	1	3	–	9.0	28.3
Logan	371	420	13.7	15.8	272	259	10.1	9.7	1	2	5	2.7	4.8	13.9
Lyon	53	58	6.5	7.1	106	117	13.0	14.4	–	1	1	–	17.2	17.5
McCracken	832	848	12.9	13.0	691	799	10.7	12.2	3	6	8	3.6	7.1	9.5
McCreary	259	226	15.2	13.2	201	166	11.8	9.7	3	–	1	11.6	–	4.0
McLean	119	155	12.0	15.5	104	108	10.5	10.8	1	1	–	8.4	6.5	–
Madison	1,000	958	13.1	13.4	524	509	6.9	7.1	1	8	6	1.0	8.4	7.5
Magoffin	182	204	13.6	15.3	132	142	9.8	10.7	1	1	3	5.5	4.9	14.3
Marion	246	249	13.1	13.7	177	182	9.5	10.0	1	3	2	4.1	12.0	8.2
Marshall	330	296	10.7	9.8	385	357	12.5	11.8	1	1	1	3.0	3.4	3.1
Martin	165	176	13.4	14.0	118	113	9.6	9.0	2	3	3	12.1	17.0	14.1
Mason	203	253	12.0	15.1	178	221	10.5	13.2	1	4	4	4.9	15.8	17.4
Meade	227	293	8.0	11.0	197	158	7.0	5.9	2	3	1	8.8	10.2	3.2
Menifee	75	89	11.1	13.5	58	51	8.5	7.7	–	–	1	–	–	16.9
Mercer	281	282	13.1	13.5	241	257	11.2	12.3	1	2	2	3.6	7.1	7.8
Metcalfe	125	151	12.3	15.1	144	96	14.2	9.6	2	–	2	16.0	–	15.9
Monroe	160	164	13.8	14.0	128	132	11.0	11.2	–	1	2	–	6.1	12.4
Montgomery	347	351	14.7	15.5	201	218	8.5	9.6	3	5	4	8.6	14.2	13.4
Morgan	168	137	11.7	9.8	115	126	8.0	9.0	1	2	3	6.0	14.6	20.8
Muhlenberg	380	398	12.0	12.5	359	389	11.3	12.2	2	3	2	5.3	7.5	5.1
Nelson	582	557	14.4	14.8	304	338	7.5	9.0	3	3	2	5.2	5.4	4.2
Nicholas	105	99	14.9	14.6	98	80	13.9	11.8	1	–	–	9.5	–	–
Ohio	339	313	14.4	13.6	228	269	9.7	11.7	2	4	1	5.9	12.8	3.7
Oldham	555	533	10.7	11.3	252	268	4.8	5.7	3	5	3	5.4	9.4	7.2
Owen	126	127	11.2	12.0	98	105	8.7	9.9	1	–	–	7.9	–	–
Owsley	68	52	14.2	10.7	67	64	14.0	13.2	–	–	1	–	–	14.5
Pendleton	194	203	12.9	14.0	119	122	7.9	8.4	1	2	3	5.2	9.9	16.2
Perry	415	439	14.0	15.0	326	294	11.0	10.0	4	3	2	9.6	6.8	3.9
Pike	771	767	11.5	11.2	730	776	10.9	11.3	3	12	7	3.9	15.6	7.1
Powell	193	185	14.2	13.9	142	119	10.4	9.0	–	1	2	–	5.4	10.8
Pulaski	753	708	12.8	12.6	649	622	11.1	11.0	4	3	2	5.3	4.2	3.0
Robertson	17	24	7.4	10.6	20	26	8.7	11.5	–	–	–	–	–	–
Rockcastle	226	213	13.5	12.8	182	156	10.9	9.4	–	2	4	–	9.4	19.7
Rowan	216	277	9.8	12.5	211	158	9.5	7.2	2	1	3	9.3	3.6	10.5
Russell	215	214	12.8	13.1	181	204	10.8	12.5	–	2	1	–	9.3	5.2
Scott	635	533	16.8	15.9	234	253	6.2	7.6	3	5	1	4.7	9.4	3.0
Shelby	534	525	14.4	15.6	278	284	7.5	8.5	4	5	1	7.5	9.5	2.6
Simpson	205	238	12.2	14.5	164	171	9.7	10.4	5	2	6	24.4	8.4	26.0
Spencer	203	175	13.7	14.6	96	103	6.5	8.6	1	–	2	4.9	–	20.0
Taylor	273	292	11.6	12.7	243	266	10.4	11.6	1	1	4	3.7	3.4	13.1
Todd	198	178	16.6	14.9	136	111	11.4	9.3	–	4	1	–	22.5	5.5
Trigg	146	143	11.0	11.3	154	152	11.6	12.0	1	2	1	6.8	14.0	9.2
Trimble	121	106	13.4	13.0	84	87	9.3	10.6	1	–	2	8.3	–	24.1
Union	156	197	10.0	12.6	153	159	9.8	10.2	1	1	3	6.4	5.1	14.0
Warren	1,353	1,211	13.9	13.1	725	735	7.5	7.9	15	10	9	11.1	8.3	8.2
Washington	141	135	12.5	12.4	113	145	10.0	13.3	–	–	–	–	–	–

See footnotes at end of table.

Table B-5. Counties — **Births, Deaths, and Infant Deaths**—Con.

[Includes United States, states, and 3,141 counties/county equivalents defined as of February 22, 2005. For more information on these areas, see Appendix C, Geographic Information]

County	Births Number 2004	2000	Births Rate per 1,000 population[1] 2004	2000	Deaths Number 2004	2000	Deaths Rate per 1,000 population[1] 2004	2000	Infant deaths[2] Number 2004	2000	1990	Infant deaths Rate per 1,000 live births[3] 2004	2000	1990
KENTUCKY—Con.														
Wayne	270	249	13.3	12.5	227	199	11.2	10.0	2	1	3	7.4	4.0	13.0
Webster	197	194	14.0	13.7	156	158	11.1	11.2	1	3	–	5.1	15.5	–
Whitley	405	496	10.8	13.8	411	401	10.9	11.2	9	3	4	22.2	6.0	7.5
Wolfe	121	105	17.3	14.8	101	97	14.4	13.7	–	1	–	–	9.5	–
Woodford	275	306	11.5	13.1	188	212	7.9	9.1	–	3	5	–	9.8	18.5
LOUISIANA	65,369	67,898	14.5	15.2	42,215	41,138	9.4	9.2	684	608	799	10.5	9.0	11.1
Acadia	917	947	15.5	16.1	605	599	10.2	10.2	8	5	13	8.7	5.3	12.5
Allen.	345	327	13.7	12.9	247	246	9.8	9.7	4	2	1	11.6	6.1	2.7
Ascension	1,470	1,336	16.9	17.3	543	478	6.2	6.2	11	11	13	7.5	8.2	13.0
Assumption	266	344	11.5	14.7	194	189	8.4	8.1	4	4	6	15.0	11.6	18.2
Avoyelles	594	632	14.2	15.2	502	481	12.0	11.6	7	8	1	11.8	12.7	1.7
Beauregard	461	459	13.6	13.9	330	300	9.7	9.1	6	4	2	13.0	8.7	3.7
Bienville	192	221	12.6	14.1	232	233	15.2	14.8	1	1	5	5.2	4.5	19.9
Bossier	1,633	1,534	15.7	15.6	860	776	8.3	7.9	16	17	13	9.8	11.1	8.8
Caddo	3,683	3,839	14.7	15.2	2,614	2,631	10.4	10.4	50	55	51	13.6	14.3	11.7
Calcasieu	2,705	2,803	14.7	15.3	1,833	1,684	9.9	9.2	15	27	30	5.5	9.6	10.9
Caldwell	139	143	13.0	13.5	126	112	11.8	10.6	–	2	2	–	14.0	14.8
Cameron.	96	118	10.0	11.9	79	65	8.2	6.5	1	1	2	10.4	8.5	14.7
Catahoula	148	145	14.0	13.3	130	106	12.3	9.7	3	3	3	20.3	20.7	18.5
Claiborne	168	172	10.3	10.3	185	245	11.3	14.6	2	3	3	11.9	17.4	13.7
Concordia	269	291	13.8	14.4	215	198	11.0	9.8	5	1	5	18.6	3.4	15.3
De Soto	367	415	14.0	16.3	274	300	10.5	11.8	3	4	4	8.2	9.6	9.5
East Baton Rouge	5,722	6,213	13.9	15.1	3,361	3,204	8.2	7.8	64	57	78	11.2	9.2	11.8
East Carroll	173	162	19.5	17.2	106	122	12.0	13.0	2	4	3	11.6	24.7	14.7
East Feliciana	259	314	12.4	14.7	243	211	11.6	9.9	4	2	6	15.4	6.4	18.6
Evangeline	536	557	15.2	15.7	403	408	11.4	11.5	4	3	10	7.5	5.4	16.7
Franklin.	309	317	14.9	14.9	266	285	12.9	13.4	–	6	2	–	18.9	5.5
Grant	234	265	12.2	14.2	196	214	10.2	11.4	5	2	2	21.4	7.5	9.0
Iberia	1,109	1,262	15.0	17.2	646	602	8.7	8.2	8	11	12	7.2	8.7	9.6
Iberville.	458	510	14.1	15.3	343	319	10.6	9.6	4	4	4	8.7	7.8	7.1
Jackson	189	196	12.4	12.7	192	192	12.6	12.5	1	1	1	5.3	5.1	4.7
Jefferson.	6,285	6,474	13.9	14.2	4,122	4,083	9.1	9.0	70	48	53	11.1	7.4	7.3
Jefferson Davis	462	547	14.8	17.4	321	343	10.3	10.9	3	4	7	6.5	7.3	13.9
Lafayette.	2,974	2,836	15.2	14.9	1,424	1,370	7.3	7.2	28	25	26	9.4	8.8	9.1
Lafourche	1,205	1,242	13.1	13.8	705	711	7.7	7.9	9	16	14	7.5	12.9	9.9
La Salle	166	179	11.8	12.5	180	184	12.8	12.9	2	1	2	12.0	5.6	10.2
Lincoln	537	535	12.7	12.6	365	356	8.6	8.4	7	4	7	13.0	7.5	13.6
Livingston	1,625	1,506	15.4	16.3	730	650	6.9	7.0	18	4	10	11.1	2.7	8.9
Madison	224	253	17.7	18.4	168	155	13.3	11.3	6	5	6	26.8	19.8	27.3
Morehouse	416	479	13.7	15.5	391	353	12.9	11.4	9	3	5	21.6	6.3	9.1
Natchitoches	584	626	15.2	16.0	381	409	9.9	10.5	5	8	3	8.6	12.8	5.3
Orleans.	6,860	7,586	14.9	15.7	5,037	5,057	10.9	10.5	67	53	153	9.8	7.0	16.5
Ouachita.	2,343	2,372	15.8	16.1	1,272	1,386	8.6	9.4	26	34	32	11.1	14.3	13.2
Plaquemines	442	382	15.3	14.3	225	203	7.8	7.6	2	3	6	4.5	7.9	13.5
Pointe Coupee.	297	360	13.2	15.8	250	242	11.1	10.6	4	4	5	13.5	11.1	13.9
Rapides	1,879	1,989	14.7	15.7	1,304	1,341	10.2	10.6	22	21	16	11.7	10.6	7.8
Red River	140	139	14.6	14.5	96	121	10.0	12.6	2	1	4	14.3	7.2	23.3
Richland	296	344	14.4	16.4	242	274	11.8	13.1	7	4	8	23.6	11.6	20.1
Sabine	337	343	14.3	14.6	258	275	10.9	11.7	3	1	3	8.9	2.9	8.8
St. Bernard	887	781	13.5	11.7	806	717	12.3	10.7	7	5	6	7.9	6.4	5.9
St. Charles	719	733	14.4	15.2	326	336	6.5	7.0	12	4	8	16.7	5.5	10.1
St. Helena.	102	127	9.9	12.1	98	94	9.5	8.9	–	1	–	–	7.9	–
St. James	309	374	14.7	17.6	189	191	9.0	9.0	6	6	4	19.4	16.0	10.2
St. John the Baptist.	713	727	15.7	16.8	364	300	8.0	7.0	9	5	6	12.6	6.9	7.2
St. Landry	1,381	1,396	15.5	15.9	901	859	10.1	9.8	17	17	17	12.3	12.2	12.3
St. Martin	701	795	13.9	16.3	391	411	7.8	8.4	11	6	8	15.7	7.5	10.5
St. Mary	758	838	14.6	15.7	563	461	10.8	8.6	6	7	13	7.9	8.4	12.8
St. Tammany	2,962	2,728	13.9	14.2	1,630	1,441	7.6	7.5	30	15	18	10.1	5.5	7.6
Tangipahoa	1,611	1,632	15.3	16.2	1,046	946	10.0	9.4	24	12	23	14.9	7.4	14.0
Tensas	85	113	13.8	17.2	69	79	11.2	12.0	2	1	2	23.5	8.8	18.2
Terrebonne	1,719	1,774	16.1	17.0	841	766	7.9	7.3	12	22	19	7.0	12.4	10.2
Union	322	328	14.1	14.4	227	285	9.9	12.5	1	1	1	3.1	3.0	3.2
Vermilion.	805	814	14.7	15.1	545	516	10.0	9.6	5	6	8	6.2	7.4	10.1
Vernon	884	1,009	17.9	19.2	317	341	6.4	6.5	4	8	11	4.5	7.9	6.8
Washington	609	655	13.8	14.9	565	559	12.8	12.7	5	7	10	8.2	10.7	16.2
Webster	509	568	12.3	13.6	500	518	12.1	12.4	8	5	8	15.7	8.8	13.7
West Baton Rouge	331	318	15.1	14.7	179	157	8.2	7.3	5	2	2	15.1	6.3	5.8
West Carroll.	132	141	11.1	11.5	149	146	12.5	11.9	–	–	2	–	–	14.3
West Feliciana	113	128	7.5	8.5	91	97	6.0	6.4	–	–	–	–	–	–
Winn	203	205	12.6	12.2	222	205	13.8	12.2	2	1	1	9.9	4.9	4.0

See footnotes at end of table.

Table B-5. Counties — **Births, Deaths, and Infant Deaths**—Con.

[Includes United States, states, and 3,141 counties/county equivalents defined as of February 22, 2005. For more information on these areas, see Appendix C, Geographic Information]

County	Births Number 2004	Births Number 2000	Births Rate per 1,000 population[1] 2004	Births Rate per 1,000 population[1] 2000	Deaths Number 2004	Deaths Number 2000	Deaths Rate per 1,000 population[1] 2004	Deaths Rate per 1,000 population[1] 2000	Infant deaths[2] Number 2004	Infant deaths[2] Number 2000	Infant deaths[2] Number 1990	Infant deaths Rate per 1,000 live births[3] 2004	Infant deaths Rate per 1,000 live births[3] 2000	Infant deaths Rate per 1,000 live births[3] 1990
MAINE	13,944	13,603	10.6	10.6	12,443	12,354	9.5	9.7	79	66	108	5.7	4.9	6.2
Androscoggin	1,290	1,136	12.0	10.9	1,008	1,023	9.4	9.8	7	9	8	5.4	7.9	5.3
Aroostook	681	730	9.3	9.9	828	813	11.3	11.0	2	1	10	2.9	1.4	8.0
Cumberland	3,015	2,987	11.0	11.2	2,384	2,344	8.7	8.8	16	18	29	5.3	6.0	8.2
Franklin	275	281	9.2	9.5	272	278	9.1	9.4	4	1	–	14.5	3.6	–
Hancock	520	491	9.7	9.5	592	513	11.1	9.9	2	2	4	3.8	4.1	6.5
Kennebec	1,267	1,247	10.5	10.6	1,151	1,079	9.6	9.2	7	6	13	5.5	4.8	8.2
Knox	408	411	9.9	10.4	409	455	10.0	11.5	–	2	3	–	4.9	6.0
Lincoln	329	291	9.4	8.6	392	375	11.2	11.1	2	2	4	6.1	6.9	10.2
Oxford	583	516	10.3	9.4	623	557	11.0	10.2	4	1	6	6.9	1.9	7.9
Penobscot	1,558	1,541	10.6	10.6	1,387	1,403	9.5	9.7	8	5	10	5.1	3.2	5.1
Piscataquis	170	167	9.7	9.7	219	190	12.5	11.0	–	1	2	–	6.0	8.3
Sagadahoc	417	386	11.3	11.0	343	275	9.3	7.8	5	–	3	12.0	–	5.4
Somerset	545	544	10.6	10.7	458	551	8.9	10.8	6	2	2	11.0	3.7	3.2
Waldo	380	416	9.9	11.4	329	384	8.6	10.5	3	4	4	7.9	9.6	8.6
Washington	336	354	10.0	10.4	440	438	13.1	12.9	1	1	1	3.0	2.8	2.3
York	2,170	2,105	10.8	11.2	1,608	1,676	8.0	8.9	12	11	9	5.5	5.2	3.5
MARYLAND	74,628	74,316	13.4	14.0	43,232	43,753	7.8	8.2	630	562	766	8.4	7.6	9.5
Allegany	659	824	8.9	11.0	913	921	12.3	12.3	6	4	6	9.1	4.9	6.7
Anne Arundel	6,573	6,527	12.9	13.3	3,551	3,554	7.0	7.2	53	44	41	8.1	6.7	6.0
Baltimore	9,263	9,063	11.9	12.0	7,368	7,657	9.4	10.1	66	65	64	7.1	7.2	6.3
Calvert	1,005	1,035	11.6	13.8	579	494	6.7	6.6	4	5	1	4.0	4.8	1.2
Caroline	471	411	15.2	13.8	303	329	9.7	11.0	1	8	3	2.1	19.5	7.0
Carroll	2,062	2,059	12.4	13.6	1,237	1,163	7.4	7.7	5	7	7	2.4	3.4	3.6
Cecil	1,229	1,144	12.9	13.2	721	689	7.5	8.0	4	11	12	3.3	9.6	10.0
Charles	1,778	1,693	13.1	14.0	853	739	6.3	6.1	17	15	13	9.6	8.9	7.5
Dorchester	360	331	11.6	10.8	359	403	11.6	13.2	5	3	7	13.9	9.1	14.7
Frederick	2,889	2,802	13.3	14.3	1,376	1,289	6.3	6.6	15	8	11	5.2	2.9	4.3
Garrett	307	315	10.2	10.6	310	283	10.3	9.5	2	2	3	6.5	6.3	7.0
Harford	2,940	2,918	12.5	13.3	1,708	1,479	7.3	6.7	18	15	27	6.1	5.1	9.2
Howard	3,474	3,540	13.0	14.2	1,151	1,234	4.3	4.9	26	22	17	7.5	6.2	5.4
Kent	236	236	11.9	12.2	274	227	13.9	11.8	1	3	1	4.2	12.7	4.1
Montgomery	13,663	13,268	14.8	15.1	5,312	5,235	5.8	6.0	87	47	100	6.4	3.5	7.8
Prince George's	12,203	12,313	14.5	15.3	5,427	5,209	6.4	6.5	155	135	184	12.7	11.0	13.7
Queen Anne's	482	461	10.7	11.3	360	327	8.0	8.0	4	2	4	8.3	4.3	8.1
St. Mary's	1,485	1,254	15.6	14.5	595	612	6.3	7.1	9	12	12	6.1	9.6	8.9
Somerset	263	263	10.2	10.6	262	270	10.2	10.9	8	2	6	30.4	7.6	22.2
Talbot	397	379	11.3	11.2	404	394	11.5	11.6	1	3	4	2.5	7.9	9.6
Washington	1,703	1,591	12.2	12.0	1,352	1,283	9.7	9.7	5	9	12	2.9	5.7	7.2
Wicomico	1,170	1,180	13.2	13.9	819	830	9.2	9.8	15	17	11	12.8	14.4	9.5
Worcester	452	496	9.3	10.6	531	552	10.9	11.8	3	4	4	6.6	8.1	8.4
Independent City														
Baltimore city	9,564	10,213	14.9	15.7	7,467	8,580	11.6	13.2	120	119	216	12.5	11.7	15.0
MASSACHUSETTS	78,484	81,614	12.2	12.8	54,511	56,681	8.5	8.9	380	376	650	4.8	4.6	7.0
Barnstable	1,934	1,996	8.5	8.9	2,777	2,769	12.2	12.4	9	13	25	4.7	6.5	10.1
Berkshire	1,300	1,205	9.8	8.9	1,527	1,560	11.5	11.6	9	3	12	6.9	2.5	6.6
Bristol	6,658	6,753	12.2	12.6	4,953	5,110	9.1	9.5	24	30	34	3.6	4.4	4.3
Dukes	148	143	9.5	9.5	127	125	8.2	8.3	–	–	–	–	–	–
Essex	9,351	9,563	12.7	13.2	6,407	6,540	8.7	9.0	43	53	90	4.6	5.5	8.2
Franklin	671	706	9.3	9.9	656	700	9.1	9.8	5	1	7	7.5	1.4	6.8
Hampden	5,746	5,879	12.5	12.9	4,433	4,734	9.6	10.4	42	25	53	7.3	4.3	7.3
Hampshire	1,225	1,272	8.0	8.3	1,132	1,288	7.4	8.5	2	5	9	1.6	3.9	5.6
Middlesex	17,915	19,393	12.2	13.2	10,998	11,859	7.5	8.1	69	81	133	3.9	4.2	6.5
Nantucket	150	141	14.8	14.7	65	54	6.4	5.6	–	1	–	–	7.1	–
Norfolk	8,038	8,567	12.3	13.2	5,517	5,841	8.4	9.0	34	24	48	4.2	2.8	5.7
Plymouth	6,233	6,423	12.7	13.5	4,112	3,902	8.4	8.2	33	33	40	5.3	5.1	5.7
Suffolk	9,326	9,561	14.0	13.9	5,155	5,484	7.8	7.9	59	57	113	6.3	6.0	9.4
Worcester	9,789	10,012	12.6	13.3	6,652	6,715	8.5	8.9	51	50	86	5.2	5.0	7.6
MICHIGAN	129,776	136,171	12.8	13.7	85,169	86,953	8.4	8.7	984	1,119	1,641	7.6	8.2	10.7
Alcona	73	78	6.3	6.7	154	179	13.2	15.3	–	1	1	–	12.8	10.4
Alger	75	77	7.7	7.8	119	118	12.2	12.0	–	–	–	–	–	–
Allegan	1,507	1,527	13.4	14.4	829	858	7.4	8.1	8	9	13	5.3	5.9	8.8
Alpena	284	351	9.3	11.2	342	375	11.1	12.0	1	2	1	3.5	5.7	2.7
Antrim	249	255	10.2	11.0	249	221	10.2	9.5	3	2	2	12.0	7.8	8.1
Arenac	191	165	11.1	9.5	228	196	13.2	11.3	1	1	1	5.2	6.1	4.9
Baraga	109	90	12.4	10.3	101	118	11.5	13.5	–	1	2	–	11.1	18.3
Barry	714	716	12.1	12.6	498	462	8.4	8.1	4	6	8	5.6	8.4	10.9
Bay	1,272	1,289	11.7	11.7	1,073	1,135	9.8	10.3	2	6	12	1.6	4.7	7.1
Benzie	177	201	10.2	12.5	155	156	8.9	9.7	–	–	4	–	–	23.0

See footnotes at end of table.

Table B-5. Counties — **Births, Deaths, and Infant Deaths**—Con.

[Includes United States, states, and 3,141 counties/county equivalents defined as of February 22, 2005. For more information on these areas, see Appendix C, Geographic Information]

County	Births Number		Births Rate per 1,000 population[1]		Deaths Number		Deaths Rate per 1,000 population[1]		Infant deaths[2] Number			Infant deaths[2] Rate per 1,000 live births[3]		
	2004	2000	2004	2000	2004	2000	2004	2000	2004	2000	1990	2004	2000	1990
MICHIGAN—Con.														
Berrien	2,037	2,235	12.5	13.7	1,595	1,604	9.8	9.9	8	19	41	3.9	8.5	15.6
Branch	592	622	12.7	13.6	406	388	8.7	8.5	8	4	10	13.5	6.4	15.5
Calhoun	1,840	1,874	13.2	13.6	1,364	1,427	9.8	10.3	18	15	26	9.8	8.0	11.6
Cass	513	587	9.9	11.5	454	470	8.8	9.2	3	4	6	5.8	6.8	8.8
Charlevoix	282	287	10.6	11.0	206	232	7.7	8.9	–	2	3	–	7.0	8.8
Cheboygan	276	264	10.1	9.9	299	295	11.0	11.1	1	1	6	3.6	3.8	20.5
Chippewa	402	425	10.4	11.0	314	312	8.1	8.1	–	4	3	–	9.4	7.2
Clare	332	348	10.5	11.1	386	361	12.2	11.5	5	4	4	15.1	11.5	9.5
Clinton	856	795	12.5	12.2	476	471	6.9	7.2	3	5	7	3.5	6.3	8.1
Crawford	131	156	8.8	10.9	164	168	11.1	11.7	–	2	5	–	12.8	26.2
Delta	394	423	10.3	11.0	407	420	10.6	10.9	4	5	3	10.2	11.8	6.3
Dickinson	282	267	10.2	9.7	307	306	11.1	11.1	1	–	1	3.5	–	2.9
Eaton	1,186	1,291	11.1	12.4	842	774	7.9	7.4	5	7	9	4.2	5.4	7.3
Emmet	343	377	10.3	12.0	249	296	7.5	9.4	1	3	–	2.9	8.0	–
Genesee	6,223	6,360	14.0	14.6	3,942	3,920	8.9	9.0	77	78	93	12.4	12.3	12.1
Gladwin	252	300	9.3	11.5	293	291	10.8	11.1	3	1	5	11.9	3.3	16.8
Gogebic	148	137	8.7	7.9	237	251	13.9	14.5	–	1	–	–	7.3	–
Grand Traverse	994	1,026	12.0	13.2	658	620	7.9	7.9	6	6	5	6.0	5.8	5.3
Gratiot	501	534	11.8	12.6	427	427	10.1	10.1	5	5	1	10.0	9.4	1.8
Hillsdale	591	642	12.5	13.8	417	400	8.8	8.6	–	5	7	–	7.8	11.2
Houghton	390	389	10.9	10.8	374	404	10.5	11.2	3	1	4	7.7	2.6	8.4
Huron	303	398	8.7	11.0	447	463	12.8	12.8	–	4	3	–	10.1	6.1
Ingham	3,661	3,781	13.1	13.5	1,927	1,923	6.9	6.9	29	29	56	7.9	7.7	12.2
Ionia	884	856	13.8	13.9	459	492	7.1	8.0	3	8	9	3.4	9.3	10.9
Iosco	230	266	8.6	9.7	385	340	14.4	12.4	1	1	2	4.3	3.8	3.4
Iron	107	87	8.6	6.6	184	208	14.7	15.9	1	2	2	9.3	23.0	14.5
Isabella	753	707	11.5	11.2	409	370	6.3	5.8	3	5	5	4.0	7.1	6.6
Jackson	2,161	2,122	13.3	13.4	1,581	1,442	9.7	9.1	14	21	25	6.5	9.9	10.4
Kalamazoo	3,123	3,189	13.0	13.4	1,866	1,919	7.8	8.0	21	28	29	6.7	8.8	8.2
Kalkaska	228	227	13.2	13.7	144	159	8.4	9.6	1	2	2	4.4	8.8	10.0
Kent	9,386	9,598	15.8	16.7	4,194	4,112	7.1	7.1	75	87	86	8.0	9.1	8.8
Keweenaw	16	26	7.2	11.3	28	21	12.6	9.1	–	–	–	–	–	–
Lake	111	133	9.3	11.7	156	149	13.1	13.1	1	1	5	9.0	7.5	46.3
Lapeer	1,056	1,075	11.4	12.2	605	645	6.5	7.3	1	5	4	0.9	4.7	3.5
Leelanau	174	207	7.9	9.7	190	176	8.6	8.3	2	–	–	11.5	–	–
Lenawee	1,199	1,246	11.8	12.6	784	906	7.7	9.1	5	6	11	4.2	4.8	7.8
Livingston	2,038	2,063	11.5	13.0	1,033	911	5.8	5.7	6	11	12	2.9	5.3	7.2
Luce	61	77	8.9	11.0	86	77	12.5	11.0	–	2	–	–	26.0	–
Mackinac	95	96	8.3	8.1	139	165	12.2	13.8	1	2	–	10.5	20.8	–
Macomb	10,041	10,336	12.2	13.1	7,182	7,177	8.7	9.1	58	64	66	5.8	6.2	6.3
Manistee	232	269	9.2	10.9	267	284	10.6	11.5	2	–	–	8.6	–	–
Marquette	618	604	9.5	9.3	615	635	9.5	9.8	–	3	6	–	5.0	5.8
Mason	318	364	11.0	12.8	310	302	10.7	10.7	–	5	2	–	13.7	5.4
Mecosta	422	488	10.0	12.0	334	356	7.9	8.8	5	4	8	11.8	8.2	16.8
Menominee	252	267	10.0	10.6	248	288	9.9	11.4	–	–	2	–	–	6.8
Midland	960	1,042	11.4	12.6	612	608	7.3	7.3	8	6	9	8.3	5.8	7.4
Missaukee	162	180	10.6	12.4	130	142	8.5	9.8	–	3	2	–	16.7	11.8
Monroe	1,759	1,859	11.5	12.7	1,213	1,172	8.0	8.0	13	9	9	7.4	4.8	4.8
Montcalm	877	833	13.8	13.6	532	539	8.4	8.8	4	1	7	4.6	1.2	8.0
Montmorency	91	106	8.7	10.2	136	143	12.9	13.8	–	–	1	–	–	12.8
Muskegon	2,294	2,393	13.2	14.0	1,600	1,623	9.2	9.5	21	18	24	9.2	7.5	8.7
Newaygo	621	633	12.5	13.2	401	418	8.1	8.7	3	5	3	4.8	7.9	4.4
Oakland	15,264	16,266	12.6	13.6	8,753	8,910	7.2	7.4	95	106	119	6.2	6.5	7.0
Oceana	420	372	14.8	13.8	240	245	8.5	9.1	4	1	3	9.5	2.7	7.5
Ogemaw	229	237	10.5	10.9	326	304	14.9	14.0	2	1	4	8.7	4.2	13.8
Ontonagon	41	50	5.4	6.4	118	108	15.7	13.8	1	–	–	24.4	–	–
Osceola	309	286	13.0	12.3	205	221	8.6	9.5	2	3	3	6.5	10.5	10.1
Oscoda	83	94	8.8	10.0	109	114	11.6	12.1	–	2	–	–	21.3	–
Otsego	272	277	11.1	11.8	198	192	8.1	8.2	3	–	3	11.0	–	10.0
Ottawa	3,550	3,667	14.0	15.3	1,476	1,466	5.8	6.1	18	26	21	5.1	7.1	6.6
Presque Isle	111	127	7.7	8.8	157	221	11.0	15.4	1	2	2	9.0	15.7	13.9
Roscommon	217	205	8.3	8.0	367	348	14.0	13.6	4	2	1	18.4	9.8	4.0
Saginaw	2,651	2,831	12.7	13.5	2,011	2,031	9.6	9.7	21	28	46	7.9	9.9	12.4
St. Clair	2,088	2,181	12.2	13.2	1,444	1,465	8.4	8.9	20	17	22	9.6	7.8	10.0
St. Joseph	933	962	14.8	15.4	610	631	9.7	10.1	8	6	13	8.6	6.2	14.0
Sanilac	518	531	11.6	11.9	466	487	10.4	10.9	3	3	8	5.8	5.6	14.3
Schoolcraft	79	89	8.9	10.0	124	114	14.0	12.8	1	1	–	12.7	11.2	–
Shiawassee	929	933	12.7	13.0	596	620	8.2	8.6	8	5	6	8.6	5.4	5.6
Tuscola	659	706	11.3	12.1	521	519	8.9	8.9	5	6	5	7.6	8.5	6.8

See footnotes at end of table.

Table B-5. Counties — **Births, Deaths, and Infant Deaths**—Con.

[Includes United States, states, and 3,141 counties/county equivalents defined as of February 22, 2005. For more information on these areas, see Appendix C, Geographic Information]

County	Births				Deaths				Infant deaths[2]					
	Number		Rate per 1,000 population[1]		Number		Rate per 1,000 population[1]		Number			Rate per 1,000 live births[3]		
	2004	2000	2004	2000	2004	2000	2004	2000	2004	2000	1990	2004	2000	1990
MICHIGAN—Con.														
Van Buren	1,050	1,071	13.4	14.0	676	629	8.6	8.2	9	3	17	8.6	2.8	14.7
Washtenaw	4,229	4,137	12.5	12.8	1,812	1,895	5.3	5.8	29	33	33	6.9	8.0	7.9
Wayne	28,283	31,149	14.0	15.1	18,899	20,299	9.4	9.9	301	338	661	10.6	10.9	16.2
Wexford	412	384	13.1	12.6	299	314	9.5	10.3	1	4	1	2.4	10.4	2.5
MINNESOTA	70,624	67,604	13.9	13.7	37,034	37,690	7.3	7.6	332	378	496	4.7	5.6	7.3
Aitkin	168	137	10.5	8.9	164	189	10.3	12.3	–	–	1	–	–	7.0
Anoka	4,423	4,325	13.8	14.4	1,428	1,409	4.5	4.7	20	22	20	4.5	5.1	4.8
Becker	443	378	14.0	12.6	324	347	10.2	11.5	–	6	2	–	15.9	4.8
Beltrami	632	585	14.9	14.7	317	304	7.5	7.6	3	4	6	4.7	6.8	10.0
Benton	577	578	15.1	16.8	311	294	8.2	8.5	3	4	4	5.2	6.9	7.7
Big Stone	53	49	9.6	8.5	89	108	16.1	18.6	–	–	1	–	–	13.0
Blue Earth	666	674	11.6	12.1	425	457	7.4	8.2	3	3	1	4.5	4.5	1.5
Brown	302	316	11.3	11.8	306	255	11.5	9.5	2	2	3	6.6	6.3	8.1
Carlton	407	368	12.1	11.6	330	317	9.8	10.0	1	1	1	2.5	2.7	2.7
Carver	1,254	1,140	15.3	16.1	337	295	4.1	4.2	2	2	4	1.6	1.8	4.3
Cass	366	304	12.9	11.1	289	285	10.2	10.4	3	3	2	8.2	9.9	6.0
Chippewa	145	135	11.4	10.3	164	152	12.9	11.6	–	1	1	–	7.4	6.3
Chisago	689	676	14.3	16.3	302	298	6.3	7.2	1	4	4	1.5	5.9	8.8
Clay	654	573	12.3	11.2	351	379	6.6	7.4	1	8	3	1.5	14.0	4.5
Clearwater	126	103	14.9	12.3	98	111	11.6	13.2	2	1	1	15.9	9.7	8.9
Cook	33	34	6.2	6.5	43	58	8.1	11.2	–	1	–	–	29.4	–
Cottonwood	158	149	13.2	12.3	144	137	12.0	11.3	–	–	1	–	–	6.7
Crow Wing	749	649	12.7	11.7	538	507	9.1	9.2	4	3	3	5.3	4.6	4.6
Dakota	5,542	5,312	14.6	14.8	1,792	1,687	4.7	4.7	29	23	23	5.2	4.3	4.5
Dodge	285	244	14.7	13.7	118	121	6.1	6.8	2	3	3	7.0	12.3	11.2
Douglas	412	359	11.9	10.9	310	341	9.0	10.4	4	1	5	9.7	2.8	13.5
Faribault	169	160	10.8	9.9	189	208	12.1	12.9	–	1	–	–	6.3	–
Fillmore	260	253	12.2	12.0	241	237	11.3	11.2	1	4	1	3.8	15.8	3.5
Freeborn	386	402	12.1	12.3	372	355	11.6	10.9	2	–	2	5.2	–	4.9
Goodhue	579	513	12.7	11.6	430	446	9.5	10.1	3	2	6	5.2	3.9	11.1
Grant	62	62	10.1	9.9	91	84	14.8	13.4	–	–	2	–	–	24.7
Hennepin	16,721	16,558	14.9	14.8	7,592	7,952	6.8	7.1	91	91	151	5.4	5.5	8.8
Houston	203	219	10.2	11.1	204	195	10.3	9.9	1	3	2	4.9	13.7	7.4
Hubbard	209	179	11.1	9.7	174	172	9.2	9.3	–	1	1	–	5.6	5.8
Isanti	468	381	12.8	12.1	267	206	7.3	6.5	–	–	3	–	–	8.1
Itasca	515	468	11.6	10.6	480	458	10.8	10.4	2	2	1	3.9	4.3	2.0
Jackson	113	122	10.1	10.9	126	138	11.2	12.3	1	2	1	8.8	16.4	7.6
Kanabec	186	151	11.6	10.0	128	124	8.0	8.2	1	–	5	5.4	–	28.2
Kandiyohi	603	523	14.6	12.7	373	373	9.1	9.1	2	1	3	3.3	1.9	5.2
Kittson	51	64	10.5	12.1	72	68	14.9	12.9	–	–	–	–	–	–
Koochiching	128	137	9.2	9.6	142	173	10.2	12.1	–	3	5	–	21.9	25.0
Lac qui Parle	75	82	9.7	10.2	99	107	12.8	13.3	1	–	–	13.3	–	–
Lake	73	104	6.5	9.4	135	115	12.1	10.4	1	2	–	13.7	19.2	–
Lake of the Woods	42	40	9.5	8.9	36	48	8.2	10.6	–	1	1	–	25.0	14.5
Le Sueur	353	301	13.0	11.8	189	223	7.0	8.7	2	2	3	5.7	6.6	8.8
Lincoln	72	67	11.8	10.5	115	93	18.8	14.5	–	–	–	–	–	–
Lyon	318	350	12.9	13.8	227	240	9.2	9.4	1	5	2	3.1	14.3	5.5
McLeod	552	473	15.2	13.6	307	284	8.5	8.1	1	5	5	1.8	10.6	10.7
Mahnomen	81	74	15.9	14.3	45	51	8.8	9.9	1	–	–	12.3	–	–
Marshall	121	103	12.1	10.2	80	107	8.0	10.6	1	–	–	8.3	–	–
Martin	226	218	10.7	10.0	197	233	9.4	10.7	–	–	2	–	–	6.8
Meeker	295	282	12.7	12.4	221	232	9.5	10.2	3	1	3	10.2	3.5	9.8
Mille Lacs	326	286	13.0	12.7	227	253	9.1	11.3	1	–	3	3.1	–	10.7
Morrison	431	393	13.2	12.4	309	305	9.5	9.6	2	3	3	4.6	7.6	7.2
Mower	509	525	13.1	13.6	392	418	10.1	10.8	3	2	3	5.9	3.8	6.1
Murray	95	80	10.6	8.7	107	111	12.0	12.1	1	–	–	10.5	–	–
Nicollet	404	393	13.1	13.1	185	159	6.0	5.3	3	2	3	7.4	5.1	7.7
Nobles	336	271	16.4	13.0	176	183	8.6	8.8	1	2	–	3.0	7.4	–
Norman	75	79	10.5	10.6	88	100	12.4	13.4	–	–	3	–	–	34.1
Olmsted	2,153	1,899	16.2	15.2	800	775	6.0	6.2	7	10	12	3.3	5.3	6.4
Otter Tail	577	555	10.0	9.7	613	644	10.6	11.3	2	4	6	3.5	7.2	9.9
Pennington	186	170	13.7	12.5	141	151	10.4	11.1	2	2	–	10.8	11.8	–
Pine	317	325	11.3	12.2	236	265	8.4	9.9	3	4	–	9.5	12.3	–
Pipestone	126	113	13.2	11.5	127	128	13.3	13.0	–	1	2	–	8.8	15.5
Polk	379	368	12.2	11.7	306	353	9.9	11.2	2	–	1	5.3	–	2.2
Pope	107	101	9.5	9.0	131	154	11.7	13.7	–	1	1	–	9.9	6.7
Ramsey	7,269	7,586	14.6	14.8	3,821	4,160	7.7	8.1	40	50	81	5.5	6.6	9.7
Red Lake	54	58	12.4	13.5	44	47	10.1	11.0	–	1	–	–	17.2	–
Redwood	175	186	10.8	11.1	200	209	12.4	12.5	–	–	–	–	–	–
Renville	206	219	12.3	12.8	235	225	14.1	13.1	3	1	–	14.6	4.6	–

See footnotes at end of table.

Table B-5. Counties — **Births, Deaths, and Infant Deaths**—Con.

[Includes United States, states, and 3,141 counties/county equivalents defined as of February 22, 2005. For more information on these areas, see Appendix C, Geographic Information]

County	Births Number 2004	Number 2000	Rate per 1,000 population[1] 2004	2000	Deaths Number 2004	Number 2000	Rate per 1,000 population[1] 2004	2000	Infant deaths[2] Number 2004	Number 2000	Number 1990	Rate per 1,000 live births[3] 2004	2000	1990
MINNESOTA—Con.														
Rice	796	667	13.2	11.7	414	393	6.9	6.9	4	5	2	5.0	7.5	3.0
Rock	126	130	13.2	13.4	119	118	12.5	12.1	–	–	–	–	–	–
Roseau	201	210	12.3	12.9	135	146	8.3	9.0	2	4	3	10.0	19.0	10.9
St. Louis	2,103	2,046	10.6	10.2	2,116	2,177	10.7	10.9	10	14	18	4.8	6.8	7.7
Scott	2,115	1,685	18.4	18.5	458	377	4.0	4.1	5	7	8	2.4	4.2	7.3
Sherburne	1,229	1,073	15.6	16.4	411	320	5.2	4.9	6	4	2	4.9	3.7	2.9
Sibley	198	211	13.0	13.7	148	165	9.7	10.7	–	1	–	–	4.7	–
Stearns	1,839	1,746	13.0	13.1	802	832	5.7	6.2	6	11	15	3.3	6.3	8.8
Steele	507	459	14.4	13.6	253	250	7.2	7.4	2	4	4	3.9	8.7	8.8
Stevens	100	117	10.2	11.7	64	103	6.5	10.3	–	–	2	–	–	23.3
Swift	116	129	10.1	10.8	115	136	10.0	11.4	1	1	–	8.6	7.8	–
Todd	277	268	11.2	11.0	224	217	9.1	8.9	–	4	1	–	14.9	3.7
Traverse	37	42	9.5	10.2	55	60	14.2	14.6	–	1	–	–	23.8	–
Wabasha	261	256	11.8	11.8	206	169	9.3	7.8	1	2	5	3.8	7.8	17.1
Wadena	153	159	11.2	11.6	192	193	14.1	14.1	2	–	2	13.1	–	11.0
Waseca	270	245	14.0	12.5	191	187	9.9	9.6	4	–	1	14.8	–	4.3
Washington	2,855	2,810	13.2	13.9	1,065	983	4.9	4.9	12	8	15	4.2	2.8	6.4
Watonwan	137	177	12.0	15.0	106	138	9.3	11.7	1	–	–	7.3	–	–
Wilkin	82	85	12.0	11.9	73	74	10.7	10.4	1	2	–	12.2	23.5	–
Winona	560	544	11.4	10.9	380	427	7.7	8.5	2	2	5	3.6	3.7	8.5
Wright	1,885	1,419	17.6	15.6	547	479	5.1	5.3	8	6	7	4.2	4.2	5.8
Yellow Medicine	107	145	10.1	13.1	110	133	10.4	12.0	–	1	–	–	6.9	–
MISSISSIPPI	42,827	44,075	14.8	15.5	27,871	28,654	9.6	10.1	420	470	529	9.8	10.7	12.1
Adams	413	488	12.7	14.2	379	410	11.7	12.0	6	5	5	14.5	10.2	8.4
Alcorn	446	454	12.7	13.1	400	495	11.4	14.3	4	5	3	9.0	11.0	6.8
Amite	174	173	13.0	12.7	141	153	10.5	11.3	2	1	–	11.5	5.8	–
Attala	291	288	14.8	14.7	278	242	14.2	12.3	2	1	3	6.9	3.5	10.0
Benton	96	133	12.3	16.6	87	97	11.1	12.1	2	3	1	20.8	22.6	7.4
Bolivar	608	671	15.6	16.6	409	458	10.5	11.3	6	6	15	9.9	8.9	18.9
Calhoun	197	220	13.3	14.6	174	198	11.8	13.2	2	1	3	10.2	4.5	11.5
Carroll	108	118	10.3	10.9	101	105	9.6	9.7	1	2	2	9.3	16.9	19.8
Chickasaw	281	314	14.6	16.2	182	214	9.5	11.0	2	4	6	7.1	12.7	17.7
Choctaw	82	121	8.6	12.4	78	90	8.1	9.2	2	3	1	24.4	24.8	7.4
Claiborne	154	195	13.4	16.5	100	116	8.7	9.8	2	1	3	13.0	5.1	14.1
Clarke	232	259	13.1	14.4	186	201	10.5	11.2	–	2	3	–	7.7	12.4
Clay	296	325	13.7	14.8	209	228	9.7	10.4	6	2	8	20.3	6.2	19.0
Coahoma	506	654	17.3	21.4	327	358	11.2	11.7	10	6	8	19.8	9.2	12.6
Copiah	443	461	15.2	16.0	280	284	9.6	9.9	3	6	7	6.8	13.0	14.3
Covington	282	305	13.9	15.7	205	200	10.1	10.3	2	4	3	7.1	13.1	9.6
DeSoto	1,978	1,814	15.1	16.7	897	794	6.9	7.3	9	14	15	4.6	7.7	13.5
Forrest	1,148	1,092	15.4	15.0	671	733	9.0	10.1	20	10	13	17.4	9.2	11.6
Franklin	93	110	11.1	13.0	98	116	11.6	13.7	1	1	2	10.8	9.1	15.9
George	316	327	15.2	17.0	238	206	11.5	10.7	2	4	1	6.3	12.2	3.4
Greene	157	155	11.9	11.6	115	101	8.7	7.6	3	2	3	19.1	12.9	20.8
Grenada	278	331	12.2	14.3	310	334	13.6	14.4	4	7	3	14.4	21.1	7.0
Hancock	547	577	11.9	13.3	456	483	9.9	11.2	7	4	3	12.8	6.9	6.5
Harrison	3,009	2,990	15.6	15.8	1,810	1,806	9.4	9.5	33	36	30	11.0	12.0	10.5
Hinds	3,929	4,013	15.7	16.0	2,005	2,149	8.0	8.6	51	62	60	13.0	15.4	13.4
Holmes	390	420	18.4	19.4	293	250	13.8	11.6	3	5	4	7.7	11.9	9.5
Humphreys	185	202	17.4	18.1	105	141	9.9	12.7	4	2	7	21.6	9.9	27.2
Issaquena	14	30	7.1	13.3	8	19	4.0	8.4	1	–	–	71.4	–	–
Itawamba	297	282	12.8	12.3	280	267	12.1	11.7	3	4	1	10.1	14.2	3.3
Jackson	1,897	1,930	14.0	14.6	1,169	1,186	8.7	9.0	11	13	10	5.8	6.7	5.6
Jasper	246	289	13.6	15.9	153	237	8.4	13.1	5	3	5	20.3	10.4	18.0
Jefferson	140	150	14.7	15.4	101	82	10.6	8.4	2	4	1	14.3	26.7	7.3
Jefferson Davis	150	203	11.4	14.6	139	166	10.6	12.0	1	4	4	6.7	19.7	19.2
Jones	1,044	1,047	15.9	16.1	746	703	11.4	10.8	8	12	5	7.7	11.5	5.9
Kemper	127	133	12.2	12.8	97	100	9.4	9.6	3	1	1	23.6	7.5	6.6
Lafayette	488	425	12.1	11.0	294	271	7.3	7.0	1	1	1	2.0	2.4	2.6
Lamar	667	600	15.4	15.2	323	291	7.5	7.4	3	6	6	4.5	10.0	12.1
Lauderdale	1,191	1,157	15.4	14.8	936	978	12.1	12.5	21	15	16	17.6	13.0	12.6
Lawrence	171	189	12.7	14.2	139	151	10.3	11.4	2	–	2	11.7	–	10.4
Leake	377	375	16.8	17.9	233	233	10.4	11.1	–	4	3	–	10.7	9.4
Lee	1,237	1,289	15.8	17.0	723	778	9.3	10.2	12	13	24	9.7	10.1	20.2
Leflore	544	635	14.9	16.8	372	418	10.2	11.0	8	11	12	14.7	17.3	15.9
Lincoln	455	462	13.5	13.9	329	447	9.8	13.5	1	5	6	2.2	10.8	12.7
Lowndes	911	946	15.1	15.4	533	469	8.8	7.6	11	8	13	12.1	8.5	11.4
Madison	1,261	1,290	15.4	17.2	984	801	12.0	10.7	8	12	17	6.3	9.3	16.2
Marion	422	387	16.7	15.1	326	353	12.9	13.8	4	3	6	9.5	7.8	15.6
Marshall	487	558	13.7	15.9	368	333	10.4	9.5	2	1	11	4.1	1.8	18.4
Monroe	526	509	13.9	13.4	418	418	11.0	11.0	3	6	12	5.7	11.8	20.8
Montgomery	174	164	14.8	13.5	130	154	11.1	12.7	–	5	2	–	30.5	9.7
Neshoba	523	479	17.7	16.7	303	319	10.2	11.1	5	5	6	9.6	10.4	14.4

See footnotes at end of table.

224

County and City Data Book: 2007

U.S. Census Bureau

[Includes United States, states, and 3,141 counties/county equivalents defined as of February 22, 2005. For more information on these areas, see Appendix C, Geographic Information]

County	Births				Deaths				Infant deaths[2]					
	Number		Rate per 1,000 population[1]		Number		Rate per 1,000 population[1]		Number			Rate per 1,000 live births[3]		
	2004	2000	2004	2000	2004	2000	2004	2000	2004	2000	1990	2004	2000	1990
MISSISSIPPI—Con.														
Newton	346	365	15.6	16.7	221	237	10.0	10.8	5	2	4	14.5	5.5	11.3
Noxubee	197	218	16.1	17.4	113	115	9.2	9.2	3	7	4	15.2	32.1	15.7
Oktibbeha	594	568	14.4	13.2	276	286	6.7	6.7	3	5	8	5.1	8.8	14.3
Panola	578	583	16.3	17.0	327	369	9.2	10.7	3	13	2	5.2	22.3	3.6
Pearl River	663	662	12.8	13.6	497	482	9.6	9.9	3	2	4	4.5	3.0	6.5
Perry	144	178	11.8	14.6	110	151	9.0	12.4	2	2	3	13.9	11.2	15.4
Pike	644	634	16.5	16.3	448	424	11.5	10.9	1	4	5	1.6	6.3	8.8
Pontotoc	457	402	16.3	15.0	228	256	8.2	9.6	3	3	4	6.6	7.5	12.5
Prentiss	329	346	12.8	13.5	261	227	10.2	8.9	4	3	6	12.2	8.7	17.4
Quitman	136	166	14.0	16.5	122	132	12.5	13.1	2	3	4	14.7	18.1	18.1
Rankin	1,878	1,698	14.6	14.6	827	780	6.4	6.7	17	12	15	9.1	7.1	11.2
Scott	489	458	17.1	16.1	265	244	9.3	8.6	5	5	2	10.2	10.9	4.0
Sharkey	103	107	17.1	16.3	58	59	9.6	9.0	–	1	3	–	9.3	22.6
Simpson	423	389	15.3	14.1	279	321	10.1	11.6	6	1	4	14.2	2.6	10.4
Smith	197	178	12.4	11.0	172	154	10.8	9.5	3	–	2	15.2	–	9.2
Stone	206	216	14.2	15.8	141	139	9.7	10.2	3	–	1	14.6	–	5.6
Sunflower	461	556	14.2	16.2	301	339	9.2	9.9	5	10	11	10.8	18.0	16.8
Tallahatchie	179	213	12.5	14.3	139	153	9.7	10.3	3	3	5	16.8	14.1	16.3
Tate	392	415	14.9	16.3	231	241	8.8	9.5	3	4	2	7.7	9.6	5.7
Tippah	334	349	15.9	16.7	225	246	10.7	11.8	2	1	2	6.0	2.9	7.4
Tishomingo	223	239	11.7	12.5	253	276	13.3	14.4	1	1	3	4.5	4.2	12.2
Tunica	189	181	18.8	19.6	102	91	10.1	9.9	2	3	–	10.6	16.6	–
Union	345	426	13.1	16.6	244	275	9.2	10.7	3	2	7	8.7	4.7	20.5
Walthall	216	222	14.2	14.7	158	178	10.4	11.8	2	–	3	9.3	–	12.3
Warren	755	817	15.3	16.5	507	502	10.3	10.1	6	8	10	7.9	9.8	12.4
Washington	913	1,137	15.3	18.1	610	681	10.2	10.8	14	17	17	15.3	15.0	12.8
Wayne	273	317	12.9	15.0	200	192	9.5	9.1	1	3	6	3.7	9.5	17.7
Webster	145	161	14.3	15.6	136	146	13.4	14.2	2	4	3	13.8	24.8	20.8
Wilkinson	131	137	12.8	13.3	133	123	13.0	11.9	2	2	1	15.3	14.6	6.9
Winston	278	312	14.0	15.5	222	235	11.2	11.7	2	3	1	7.2	9.6	3.4
Yalobusha	199	197	15.0	15.0	164	149	12.3	11.3	2	2	5	10.1	10.2	24.2
Yazoo	422	489	14.9	17.4	263	315	9.3	11.2	3	9	6	7.1	18.4	12.1
MISSOURI	77,765	76,463	13.5	13.6	53,950	54,865	9.4	9.8	584	547	748	7.5	7.2	9.4
Adair	268	261	10.9	10.5	209	219	8.5	8.8	5	–	4	18.7	–	14.0
Andrew	177	201	10.5	12.2	179	173	10.6	10.5	1	–	1	5.6	–	5.6
Atchison	59	56	9.3	8.7	86	93	13.6	14.5	–	–	–	–	–	–
Audrain	375	389	14.6	15.1	276	274	10.8	10.6	2	3	4	5.3	7.7	12.2
Barry	521	465	14.8	13.7	372	377	10.6	11.1	3	–	3	5.8	–	7.9
Barton	158	187	12.1	14.9	144	130	11.1	10.4	–	–	–	–	–	–
Bates	222	230	13.1	13.8	211	221	12.4	13.2	–	2	2	–	8.7	9.3
Benton	171	151	9.3	8.8	253	251	13.7	14.5	–	1	3	–	6.6	18.3
Bollinger	140	154	11.4	12.8	159	114	12.9	9.4	1	2	1	7.1	13.0	6.5
Boone	1,942	1,786	13.8	13.2	814	848	5.8	6.2	12	18	20	6.2	10.1	11.9
Buchanan	1,157	1,151	13.6	13.4	928	929	10.9	10.8	11	9	11	9.5	7.8	9.0
Butler	573	576	14.0	14.1	505	495	12.3	12.1	2	4	4	3.5	6.9	7.6
Caldwell	112	128	12.1	14.2	100	100	10.8	11.1	2	1	1	17.9	7.8	8.3
Callaway	529	491	12.6	12.0	379	345	9.0	8.4	3	2	5	5.7	4.1	10.8
Camden	394	368	10.2	9.9	420	391	10.9	10.5	2	4	6	5.1	10.9	18.7
Cape Girardeau	909	849	12.9	12.3	687	692	9.7	10.1	5	7	13	5.5	8.2	14.9
Carroll	103	125	10.2	12.2	132	134	13.0	13.0	–	–	3	–	–	20.4
Carter	87	68	14.7	11.4	72	88	12.2	14.8	1	–	–	11.5	–	–
Cass	1,243	1,159	13.5	14.0	697	713	7.6	8.6	9	3	8	7.2	2.6	8.0
Cedar	173	171	12.4	12.5	179	198	12.9	14.4	1	–	1	5.8	–	6.6
Chariton	95	81	11.6	9.6	115	129	14.1	15.3	–	–	–	–	–	–
Christian	952	859	14.8	15.6	468	416	7.3	7.6	7	3	1	7.4	3.5	2.0
Clark	88	89	12.0	12.0	95	90	12.9	12.2	2	–	2	22.7	–	21.5
Clay	2,890	2,681	14.6	14.5	1,382	1,387	7.0	7.5	18	13	18	6.2	4.8	8.1
Clinton	248	251	12.0	13.2	242	224	11.7	11.8	–	1	1	–	4.0	4.9
Cole	1,019	862	14.1	12.1	586	586	8.1	8.2	4	12	8	3.9	13.9	8.5
Cooper	187	181	10.9	10.8	179	179	10.4	10.7	1	1	3	5.3	5.5	15.2
Crawford	313	301	13.2	13.2	247	260	10.4	11.4	1	–	2	3.2	–	7.1
Dade	95	101	12.1	12.8	137	120	17.5	15.2	1	2	–	10.5	19.8	–
Dallas	235	212	14.4	13.5	179	176	11.0	11.2	4	1	1	17.0	4.7	5.3
Daviess	115	129	14.2	16.1	92	97	11.4	12.1	–	2	1	–	15.5	7.7
DeKalb	109	119	8.8	9.1	118	106	9.6	8.1	–	–	–	–	–	–
Dent	177	190	11.8	12.7	174	191	11.6	12.8	1	–	1	5.6	–	7.2
Douglas	151	122	11.2	9.3	153	148	11.3	11.3	–	–	4	–	–	22.2
Dunklin	461	481	14.2	14.5	444	470	13.7	14.2	4	5	3	8.7	10.4	5.7

See footnotes at end of table.

Table B-5. Counties — **Births, Deaths, and Infant Deaths**—Con.

[Includes United States, states, and 3,141 counties/county equivalents defined as of February 22, 2005. For more information on these areas, see Appendix C, Geographic Information]

County	Births Number 2004	Births Number 2000	Births Rate per 1,000 population[1] 2004	Births Rate per 1,000 population[1] 2000	Deaths Number 2004	Deaths Number 2000	Deaths Rate per 1,000 population[1] 2004	Deaths Rate per 1,000 population[1] 2000	Infant deaths[2] Number 2004	Infant deaths[2] Number 2000	Infant deaths[2] Number 1990	Infant deaths Rate per 1,000 live births[3] 2004	Infant deaths Rate per 1,000 live births[3] 2000	Infant deaths Rate per 1,000 live births[3] 1990
MISSOURI—Con.														
Franklin	1,314	1,249	13.4	13.3	852	805	8.7	8.6	5	7	13	3.8	5.6	9.8
Gasconade	162	178	10.4	11.6	208	208	13.3	13.5	–	2	–	–	11.2	–
Gentry	87	75	13.3	10.9	101	123	15.4	17.9	2	–	1	23.0	–	12.3
Greene	3,270	3,102	13.2	12.9	2,309	2,347	9.3	9.8	27	26	25	8.3	8.4	8.8
Grundy	140	122	13.7	11.7	124	139	12.1	13.4	–	1	–	–	8.2	–
Harrison	113	112	12.8	12.6	122	139	13.9	15.7	–	–	–	–	–	–
Henry	287	309	12.7	14.0	293	302	13.0	13.7	1	2	2	3.5	6.5	8.2
Hickory	73	73	8.0	8.2	141	119	15.4	13.3	1	–	2	13.7	–	27.8
Holt	59	43	11.5	8.1	60	62	11.7	11.6	–	2	–	–	46.5	–
Howard	113	127	11.4	12.5	112	108	11.3	10.6	3	–	3	26.5	–	24.8
Howell	528	455	13.9	12.2	468	484	12.4	13.0	4	2	4	7.6	4.4	8.9
Iron	142	118	13.8	11.1	159	176	15.4	16.6	–	–	1	–	–	7.5
Jackson	10,310	10,124	15.6	15.4	5,931	6,084	9.0	9.3	91	60	112	8.8	5.9	10.2
Jasper	1,710	1,727	15.6	16.5	1,093	1,063	10.0	10.1	4	13	10	2.3	7.5	7.5
Jefferson	2,764	2,755	13.1	13.9	1,529	1,462	7.3	7.4	18	11	15	6.5	4.0	5.3
Johnson	730	735	14.4	15.2	356	306	7.0	6.3	6	1	9	8.2	1.4	13.1
Knox	48	47	11.4	10.8	43	56	10.2	12.8	–	–	–	–	–	–
Laclede	485	443	14.4	13.6	342	337	10.2	10.3	6	2	6	12.4	4.5	14.5
Lafayette	412	382	12.5	11.6	339	391	10.3	11.8	2	2	1	4.9	5.2	2.5
Lawrence	477	485	13.0	13.7	398	425	10.8	12.0	5	4	2	10.5	8.2	4.6
Lewis	109	119	10.7	11.3	114	138	11.2	13.1	2	–	2	18.3	–	16.3
Lincoln	689	540	15.1	13.8	366	302	8.0	7.7	3	4	1	4.4	7.4	2.2
Linn	152	171	11.5	12.5	175	201	13.2	14.6	3	–	3	19.7	–	14.6
Livingston	171	146	12.0	10.1	187	196	13.1	13.5	1	–	1	5.8	–	5.3
McDonald	367	377	16.4	17.4	206	201	9.2	9.3	5	4	–	13.6	10.6	–
Macon	203	193	13.1	12.3	203	223	13.1	14.2	1	2	–	4.9	10.4	–
Madison	158	134	13.2	11.3	147	157	12.2	13.3	2	1	1	12.7	7.5	6.7
Maries	104	100	11.7	11.2	85	105	9.5	11.8	1	–	3	9.6	–	28.6
Marion	376	423	13.3	15.0	350	334	12.4	11.8	1	1	3	2.7	2.4	7.6
Mercer	44	39	12.1	10.4	43	53	11.8	14.1	–	–	–	–	–	–
Miller	342	310	13.9	13.1	263	304	10.7	12.9	1	3	3	2.9	9.7	9.9
Mississippi	216	221	15.9	16.5	194	179	14.3	13.4	–	3	4	–	13.6	18.2
Moniteau	223	218	14.9	14.7	153	163	10.2	11.0	1	2	1	4.5	9.2	5.3
Monroe	99	96	10.5	10.3	91	127	9.7	13.6	–	1	4	–	10.4	32.8
Montgomery	168	157	13.9	12.9	139	156	11.5	12.9	1	1	2	6.0	6.4	12.7
Morgan	241	236	11.9	12.2	250	257	12.3	13.3	1	1	3	4.1	4.2	13.8
New Madrid	255	252	13.5	12.8	231	239	12.2	12.1	3	2	8	11.8	7.9	23.7
Newton	733	696	13.4	13.2	502	577	9.2	10.9	4	5	4	5.5	7.2	6.7
Nodaway	249	214	11.5	9.8	193	209	8.9	9.6	2	–	4	8.0	–	16.2
Oregon	113	125	10.9	12.1	146	151	14.0	14.6	–	2	–	–	16.0	–
Osage	181	157	13.6	12.0	107	145	8.0	11.1	–	3	3	–	19.1	19.2
Ozark	104	96	11.0	10.1	136	148	14.4	15.5	–	2	1	–	20.8	9.3
Pemiscot	302	360	15.5	18.0	219	227	11.2	11.3	3	6	4	9.9	16.7	8.9
Perry	265	262	14.4	14.4	170	211	9.3	11.6	5	1	1	18.9	3.8	4.4
Pettis	586	605	14.8	15.3	406	421	10.2	10.7	3	5	4	5.1	8.3	8.0
Phelps	520	442	12.5	11.1	409	416	9.8	10.4	3	6	4	5.8	13.6	8.5
Pike	234	201	12.7	11.0	212	204	11.5	11.1	3	1	3	12.8	5.0	12.8
Platte	1,073	1,003	13.3	13.5	488	487	6.0	6.6	5	12	7	4.7	12.0	8.3
Polk	394	389	13.9	14.4	283	277	10.0	10.2	1	4	–	2.5	10.3	–
Pulaski	648	622	14.6	14.9	263	255	5.9	6.1	8	7	9	12.3	11.3	10.7
Putnam	64	58	12.6	11.1	71	61	14.0	11.6	–	–	4	–	–	61.5
Ralls	118	92	12.2	9.5	88	91	9.1	9.4	1	–	–	8.5	–	–
Randolph	353	357	14.0	14.5	246	299	9.8	12.1	3	6	3	8.5	16.8	8.4
Ray	266	303	11.1	13.0	275	223	11.5	9.5	3	1	4	11.3	3.3	11.9
Reynolds	61	64	9.3	9.5	81	83	12.3	12.3	2	–	2	32.8	–	24.7
Ripley	193	160	14.0	11.9	172	186	12.5	13.8	2	–	1	10.4	–	5.9
St. Charles	4,512	4,248	14.1	14.8	1,863	1,653	5.8	5.8	31	27	15	6.9	6.4	3.9
St. Clair	95	97	9.9	10.0	143	116	14.9	12.0	–	1	–	–	–	9.5
Ste. Genevieve	178	197	9.8	11.0	142	156	7.8	8.7	–	–	4	–	–	19.4
St. Francois	761	713	12.5	12.8	666	702	11.0	12.6	2	8	8	2.6	11.2	12.2
St. Louis	12,181	12,876	12.1	12.7	9,381	9,650	9.3	9.5	99	90	139	8.1	7.0	9.5
Saline	298	282	12.9	11.9	327	298	14.2	12.6	6	1	–	20.1	3.5	–
Schuyler	49	53	11.4	12.7	56	55	13.0	13.2	–	1	–	–	18.9	–
Scotland	68	64	13.8	12.9	50	78	10.2	15.7	2	–	–	29.4	–	–
Scott	576	522	14.1	12.9	368	445	9.0	11.0	1	5	6	1.7	9.6	9.1
Shannon	109	98	13.1	11.8	95	77	11.4	9.3	4	1	–	36.7	10.2	–
Shelby	94	84	14.0	12.4	93	90	13.9	13.3	1	1	–	10.6	11.9	–
Stoddard	388	388	13.1	13.1	361	369	12.2	12.4	6	2	3	15.5	5.2	8.1
Stone	283	341	9.2	11.9	310	278	10.1	9.7	2	3	1	7.1	8.8	5.0
Sullivan	113	116	16.2	16.1	95	112	13.6	15.5	2	1	–	17.7	8.6	–

See footnotes at end of table.

County and City Data Book: 2007

U.S. Census Bureau

Table B-5. Counties — **Births, Deaths, and Infant Deaths**—Con.

[Includes United States, states, and 3,141 counties/county equivalents defined as of February 22, 2005. For more information on these areas, see Appendix C, Geographic Information]

County	Births				Deaths				Infant deaths[2]					
	Number		Rate per 1,000 population[1]		Number		Rate per 1,000 population[1]		Number			Rate per 1,000 live births[3]		
	2004	2000	2004	2000	2004	2000	2004	2000	2004	2000	1990	2004	2000	1990
MISSOURI—Con.														
Taney	565	570	13.5	14.3	438	425	10.4	10.6	4	2	5	7.1	3.5	16.1
Texas	298	264	12.2	11.5	310	286	12.7	12.4	4	2	2	13.4	7.6	7.7
Vernon	287	319	14.1	15.6	231	232	11.4	11.4	3	2	2	10.5	6.3	7.6
Warren	387	345	13.9	13.9	262	202	9.4	8.2	3	–	2	7.8	–	6.6
Washington	297	304	12.4	13.0	259	238	10.8	10.2	4	2	7	13.5	6.6	23.2
Wayne	134	154	10.3	11.6	210	164	16.1	12.4	1	3	2	7.5	19.5	13.4
Webster	505	513	14.8	16.4	268	267	7.9	8.5	4	5	4	7.9	9.7	11.8
Worth	31	21	13.8	8.8	28	37	12.5	15.6	–	–	–	–	–	–
Wright	267	236	14.7	13.1	201	223	11.1	12.4	3	4	1	11.2	16.9	4.2
Independent City														
St. Louis city	5,243	5,434	14.9	15.7	3,736	4,206	10.7	12.1	50	70	108	9.5	12.9	12.7
MONTANA	11,519	10,957	12.4	12.1	8,094	8,096	8.7	9.0	52	67	105	4.5	6.1	9.0
Beaverhead	82	95	9.3	10.3	77	73	8.7	7.9	–	1	–	–	10.5	–
Big Horn	266	234	20.3	18.5	103	103	7.9	8.1	1	1	2	3.8	4.3	7.3
Blaine	123	97	18.4	13.9	56	66	8.4	9.4	1	1	–	8.1	10.3	–
Broadwater	32	31	7.1	7.1	39	49	8.6	11.2	–	–	–	–	–	–
Carbon	110	81	11.3	8.5	85	108	8.7	11.3	–	1	1	–	12.3	12.3
Carter	7	6	5.2	4.4	13	18	9.7	13.3	–	–	–	–	–	–
Cascade	1,157	1,008	14.5	12.6	745	792	9.3	9.9	6	10	12	5.2	9.9	8.9
Chouteau	42	38	7.6	6.4	58	78	10.5	13.0	1	–	1	23.8	–	5.7
Custer	125	148	10.9	12.7	134	135	11.7	11.6	1	–	1	8.0	–	5.7
Daniels	14	14	7.6	7.0	24	21	13.0	10.4	–	–	–	–	–	–
Dawson	88	103	10.2	11.4	108	93	12.5	10.3	1	–	–	11.4	–	–
Deer Lodge	94	84	10.5	8.9	119	131	13.3	14.0	1	–	2	10.6	–	16.9
Fallon	31	24	11.2	8.5	24	24	8.7	8.5	–	–	–	–	–	–
Fergus	88	117	7.6	9.8	131	160	11.3	13.4	–	3	2	–	25.6	12.0
Flathead	1,045	965	12.9	12.9	715	655	8.8	8.8	7	5	9	6.7	5.2	11.0
Gallatin[4]	985	835	13.0	12.2	336	360	4.4	5.3	4	8	1	4.1	9.6	1.5
Garfield	20	17	16.3	13.4	5	9	4.1	7.1	–	–	–	–	–	–
Glacier	268	253	19.8	19.2	107	114	7.9	8.6	1	1	1	3.7	4.0	3.9
Golden Valley	12	9	10.9	8.8	11	9	10.0	8.8	–	–	–	–	–	–
Granite	20	21	6.9	7.4	15	33	5.2	11.6	–	–	–	–	–	–
Hill	271	263	16.6	15.8	157	144	9.6	8.7	2	2	7	7.4	7.6	24.6
Jefferson	104	88	9.6	8.7	85	63	7.8	6.2	2	–	–	19.2	–	–
Judith Basin	12	18	5.4	7.7	14	16	6.4	6.8	–	–	–	–	–	–
Lake	349	368	12.5	13.8	271	274	9.7	10.3	1	4	5	2.9	10.9	15.4
Lewis and Clark	694	687	12.0	12.3	486	440	8.4	7.9	4	2	2	5.8	2.9	3.0
Liberty	11	20	5.4	9.3	16	17	7.9	7.9	–	–	–	–	–	–
Lincoln	158	190	8.3	10.1	186	205	9.8	10.9	1	1	2	6.3	5.3	9.3
McCone	11	12	6.1	6.1	11	21	6.1	10.7	–	–	–	–	–	–
Madison	40	50	5.6	7.3	70	76	9.9	11.1	–	1	–	–	43.5	–
Meagher	19	23	9.5	11.9	19	22	9.5	11.4	–	–	–	–	–	–
Mineral	48	46	12.4	11.8	39	29	10.1	7.5	1	–	–	20.8	–	–
Missoula	1,206	1,142	12.2	11.9	680	642	6.9	6.7	5	7	14	4.1	6.1	12.8
Musselshell	42	40	9.3	8.9	54	61	12.0	13.6	1	1	1	23.8	25.0	24.4
Park[4]	146	174	9.3	11.1	140	157	8.9	10.0	–	1	4	–	5.7	22.6
Petroleum	3	5	6.0	10.2	3	2	6.0	4.1	–	–	–	–	–	–
Phillips	36	41	8.5	9.0	38	58	9.0	12.7	–	–	–	–	–	–
Pondera	71	80	11.6	12.5	97	86	15.9	13.5	–	1	1	–	12.5	9.0
Powder River	11	13	6.2	7.0	16	29	9.1	15.6	–	–	1	–	–	41.7
Powell	49	55	7.1	7.7	72	62	10.4	8.6	–	–	–	–	–	–
Prairie	7	12	6.1	10.1	18	15	15.8	12.6	–	–	–	–	–	–
Ravalli	397	391	10.1	10.8	334	295	8.5	8.1	–	1	2	–	2.6	6.4
Richland	110	101	12.1	10.5	88	98	9.7	10.2	–	1	2	–	9.9	15.6
Roosevelt	240	186	22.7	17.5	109	106	10.3	10.0	3	–	4	12.5	–	15.0
Rosebud	180	170	19.5	18.1	72	63	7.8	6.7	2	4	3	11.1	23.5	14.4
Sanders	94	92	8.6	9.0	109	111	10.0	10.8	–	2	4	–	21.7	35.4
Sheridan	28	32	7.7	7.8	62	55	17.0	13.5	–	–	–	–	–	–
Silver Bow	375	397	11.3	11.5	429	432	13.0	12.5	2	1	4	5.3	2.5	8.7
Stillwater	101	89	12.0	10.8	66	67	7.8	8.1	–	1	–	–	11.2	–
Sweet Grass	34	31	9.2	8.5	27	41	7.3	11.3	–	–	–	–	–	–
Teton	50	70	8.0	10.9	55	69	8.8	10.7	–	–	1	–	–	15.6
Toole	45	61	8.7	11.6	54	56	10.5	10.6	–	–	–	–	–	–
Treasure	6	5	8.2	5.8	5	9	6.8	10.5	–	–	–	–	–	–
Valley	71	91	9.8	11.9	90	80	12.4	10.5	–	–	3	–	–	27.8
Wheatland	16	26	7.8	11.5	27	29	13.1	12.9	–	–	–	–	–	–
Wibaux	8	10	8.2	9.3	23	13	23.6	12.1	–	–	–	–	–	–
Yellowstone	1,867	1,698	13.8	13.1	1,167	1,122	8.7	8.7	4	6	14	2.1	3.5	8.3
Yellowstone National Park[4]	(X)	(X)	(NA)	(NA)	(X)	(X)	(NA)	(NA)	(X)	(X)	–	(NA)	(NA)	–

See footnotes at end of table.

[Includes United States, states, and 3,141 counties/county equivalents defined as of February 22, 2005. For more information on these areas, see Appendix C, Geographic Information]

County	Births				Deaths				Infant deaths[2]					
	Number		Rate per 1,000 population[1]		Number		Rate per 1,000 population[1]		Number			Rate per 1,000 live births[3]		
	2004	2000	2004	2000	2004	2000	2004	2000	2004	2000	1990	2004	2000	1990
NEBRASKA	26,332	24,646	15.1	14.4	14,657	14,992	8.4	8.8	173	180	202	6.6	7.3	8.3
Adams	455	422	13.9	13.5	288	258	8.8	8.3	1	3	7	2.2	7.1	16.2
Antelope	76	72	10.7	9.7	74	89	10.4	12.0	1	–	–	13.2	–	–
Arthur	7	6	17.9	13.6	6	1	15.3	2.3	–	–	–	–	–	–
Banner	6	3	7.9	3.6	2	1	2.6	1.2	–	–	1	–	–	–
Blaine	5	9	9.8	15.5	5	5	9.8	8.6	–	–	–	–	–	166.7
Boone	60	57	10.3	9.2	69	58	11.8	9.3	–	–	–	–	–	–
Box Butte	133	152	11.6	12.5	116	137	10.1	11.3	–	1	3	–	6.6	14.8
Boyd	19	13	8.3	5.4	41	28	18.0	11.5	–	–	–	–	–	–
Brown	40	42	11.6	11.9	34	47	9.9	13.3	–	–	–	–	–	–
Buffalo	639	600	14.7	14.2	329	323	7.6	7.6	6	3	4	9.4	5.0	6.9
Burt	70	85	9.3	10.9	89	109	11.8	14.0	–	–	–	–	–	–
Butler	95	116	10.8	13.1	90	111	10.2	12.5	–	1	1	–	8.6	9.3
Cass	335	324	13.1	13.3	209	203	8.2	8.3	3	1	4	9.0	3.1	11.8
Cedar	102	100	11.2	10.4	95	106	10.5	11.1	–	1	2	–	10.0	13.3
Chase	46	42	11.7	10.4	62	53	15.7	13.1	1	–	–	21.7	–	–
Cherry	80	77	13.2	12.5	67	74	11.0	12.0	–	–	–	–	–	–
Cheyenne	145	133	14.7	13.5	90	122	9.1	12.4	–	4	–	–	30.1	–
Clay	67	88	9.8	12.5	68	84	10.0	11.9	–	–	1	–	–	11.6
Colfax	186	166	17.7	15.9	99	110	9.4	10.5	1	2	–	5.4	12.0	–
Cuming	138	137	14.1	13.5	103	127	10.5	12.5	–	2	2	–	14.6	13.4
Custer	116	130	10.1	11.0	141	147	12.3	12.5	1	–	3	8.6	–	16.7
Dakota	402	375	19.6	18.5	144	164	7.0	8.1	1	1	3	2.5	2.7	9.0
Dawes	104	100	11.9	11.1	106	86	12.1	9.5	1	–	–	9.6	–	–
Dawson	478	466	19.5	19.1	220	240	9.0	9.8	6	4	3	12.6	8.6	10.8
Deuel	15	19	7.4	9.0	26	20	12.8	9.5	–	–	–	–	–	–
Dixon	62	73	10.1	11.6	78	70	12.7	11.1	–	–	–	–	–	–
Dodge	499	469	13.9	12.9	393	388	10.9	10.7	6	2	6	12.0	4.3	12.2
Douglas	8,352	7,564	17.4	16.3	3,512	3,536	7.3	7.6	52	66	63	6.2	8.7	8.5
Dundy	18	29	8.2	12.6	32	28	14.7	12.2	–	–	–	–	–	–
Fillmore	52	80	8.1	12.1	88	101	13.7	15.3	2	–	3	38.5	–	37.0
Franklin	30	36	8.8	10.1	48	63	14.2	17.8	–	–	–	–	–	–
Frontier	25	27	8.7	8.7	20	31	6.9	10.0	–	1	–	–	37.0	–
Furnas	49	59	9.6	11.1	83	101	16.3	19.0	–	–	1	–	–	14.7
Gage	265	260	11.3	11.3	270	316	11.5	13.7	–	3	3	–	11.5	11.2
Garden	18	17	8.5	7.5	32	39	15.0	17.1	–	–	–	–	–	–
Garfield	19	19	10.3	10.0	34	28	18.4	14.8	–	–	–	–	–	–
Gosper	23	24	11.2	11.2	31	26	15.1	12.1	1	1	–	43.5	41.7	–
Grant	4	10	5.9	13.4	4	3	5.9	4.0	–	–	–	–	–	–
Greeley	28	32	11.0	11.8	37	41	14.6	15.2	1	–	–	35.7	–	–
Hall	884	858	16.1	16.0	479	524	8.7	9.8	12	6	3	13.6	7.0	3.7
Hamilton	103	96	10.8	10.2	101	93	10.6	9.9	–	1	1	–	10.4	9.1
Harlan	36	29	10.0	7.7	55	43	15.3	11.4	1	–	–	27.8	–	–
Hayes	9	10	8.4	9.3	6	8	5.6	7.5	–	–	–	–	–	–
Hitchcock	35	29	11.6	9.3	42	52	13.9	16.8	–	–	–	–	–	–
Holt	126	121	11.6	10.5	119	126	11.0	11.0	1	–	1	7.9	–	5.2
Hooker	9	9	12.1	11.5	11	11	14.7	14.1	–	–	–	–	–	–
Howard	77	73	11.4	11.1	65	82	9.7	12.5	–	–	1	–	–	11.4
Jefferson	91	104	11.3	12.5	97	125	12.1	15.0	–	1	3	–	9.6	28.3
Johnson	54	45	11.2	10.0	45	57	9.3	12.7	–	–	1	–	–	18.2
Kearney	77	74	11.2	10.7	78	71	11.4	10.3	–	2	2	–	27.0	19.0
Keith	88	90	10.5	10.2	86	108	10.3	12.2	–	1	2	–	11.1	19.0
Keya Paha	15	14	16.1	14.3	7	10	7.5	10.2	–	–	–	–	–	–
Kimball	35	44	9.2	10.8	58	43	15.3	10.6	–	–	1	–	–	17.2
Knox	98	95	10.9	10.2	133	127	14.8	13.6	3	–	4	30.6	–	37.0
Lancaster	4,126	3,758	15.8	15.0	1,691	1,652	6.5	6.6	26	22	23	6.3	5.9	7.4
Lincoln	483	450	13.8	13.0	322	305	9.2	8.8	2	4	7	4.1	8.9	16.4
Logan	9	13	12.5	16.9	8	7	11.1	9.1	–	–	–	–	–	–
Loup	2	8	2.9	11.2	9	7	13.0	9.8	–	–	–	–	–	–
McPherson	5	4	9.5	7.5	1	1	1.9	1.9	–	–	–	–	–	–
Madison	604	529	16.9	15.0	338	323	9.5	9.2	6	3	7	9.9	5.7	12.2
Merrick	83	81	10.2	9.9	84	81	10.3	9.9	–	1	–	–	12.3	–
Morrill	50	65	9.6	11.9	59	56	11.3	10.3	–	1	–	–	15.4	–
Nance	51	50	13.8	12.4	56	45	15.1	11.1	2	–	–	39.2	–	–
Nemaha	90	80	12.8	10.6	59	96	8.4	12.7	–	–	–	–	–	–
Nuckolls	56	43	11.6	8.6	81	80	16.8	15.9	1	–	–	17.9	–	–
Otoe	172	183	11.1	11.9	158	174	10.2	11.3	–	2	1	–	10.9	5.6
Pawnee	28	29	9.7	9.4	36	56	12.5	18.2	–	1	–	–	34.5	–
Perkins	42	36	13.7	11.3	43	39	14.0	12.3	–	–	–	–	–	–
Phelps	115	112	12.0	11.5	117	126	12.2	12.9	–	2	–	–	17.9	–
Pierce	90	98	11.8	12.5	96	95	12.6	12.1	1	–	–	11.1	–	–

See footnotes at end of table.

Table B-5. Counties — **Births, Deaths, and Infant Deaths**—Con.

[Includes United States, states, and 3,141 counties/county equivalents defined as of February 22, 2005. For more information on these areas, see Appendix C, Geographic Information]

County	Births Number 2004	2000	Births Rate per 1,000 population[1] 2004	2000	Deaths Number 2004	2000	Deaths Rate per 1,000 population[1] 2004	2000	Infant deaths[2] Number 2004	2000	1990	Infant deaths Rate per 1,000 live births[3] 2004	2000	1990
NEBRASKA—Con.														
Platte	482	466	15.4	14.8	212	268	6.8	8.5	5	8	4	10.4	17.2	8.7
Polk	60	68	11.1	12.1	55	59	10.1	10.5	–	–	–	–	–	–
Red Willow	145	153	13.1	13.4	127	128	11.5	11.2	–	1	3	–	6.5	19.1
Richardson	101	78	11.4	8.2	149	150	16.8	15.8	1	–	2	9.9	–	14.8
Rock	15	13	9.4	7.4	22	20	13.8	11.4	–	–	–	–	–	–
Saline	197	171	13.9	12.3	147	178	10.3	12.8	1	2	–	5.1	11.7	–
Sarpy	2,373	2,099	17.5	17.0	594	502	4.4	4.1	15	11	11	6.3	5.2	5.6
Saunders	235	227	11.6	11.4	187	145	9.2	7.3	2	1	1	8.5	4.4	3.7
Scotts Bluff	538	529	14.7	14.3	424	423	11.6	11.4	4	1	6	7.4	1.9	10.3
Seward	203	208	12.1	12.6	168	146	10.0	8.8	1	1	–	4.9	4.8	–
Sheridan	71	75	12.2	12.1	64	85	11.0	13.7	–	2	1	–	26.7	12.2
Sherman	35	36	11.1	10.9	46	45	14.6	13.7	–	–	1	–	–	19.2
Sioux	11	9	7.6	6.1	13	10	9.0	6.8	–	–	–	–	–	–
Stanton	85	70	13.0	10.9	41	52	6.3	8.1	–	–	–	–	–	–
Thayer	47	57	8.6	9.4	92	89	16.8	14.7	–	–	–	–	–	–
Thomas	7	6	10.9	8.2	6	7	9.3	9.5	–	–	–	–	–	–
Thurston	148	155	20.6	21.6	64	67	8.9	9.3	2	3	4	13.5	19.4	24.8
Valley	43	38	9.6	8.2	55	63	12.2	13.6	–	–	–	–	–	–
Washington	231	217	11.8	11.5	161	171	8.2	9.1	–	1	–	–	4.6	–
Wayne	91	88	9.7	9.0	54	65	5.8	6.6	2	–	1	22.0	–	8.5
Webster	31	48	8.1	11.8	61	55	15.9	13.6	–	3	1	–	62.5	18.2
Wheeler	6	13	7.4	14.7	5	9	6.1	10.2	–	1	–	–	76.9	–
York	171	159	12.0	10.9	135	158	9.5	10.8	1	2	–	5.8	12.6	–
NEVADA	35,200	30,829	15.1	15.3	17,929	15,261	7.7	7.6	225	201	181	6.4	6.5	8.4
Churchill	344	358	14.2	14.9	229	228	9.4	9.5	2	2	4	5.8	5.6	12.4
Clark	26,152	22,304	15.9	16.0	12,131	10,320	7.4	7.4	184	143	117	7.0	6.4	8.6
Douglas	377	336	8.2	8.1	385	290	8.4	7.0	–	2	2	–	6.0	4.9
Elko	654	717	14.7	15.8	235	213	5.3	4.7	3	6	7	4.6	8.4	10.1
Esmeralda	6	8	7.3	8.2	7	7	8.6	7.2	–	–	–	–	–	–
Eureka	13	14	9.2	8.6	21	13	14.8	8.0	1	–	–	76.9	–	–
Humboldt	225	262	13.3	16.5	109	93	6.5	5.8	–	2	1	–	7.6	4.0
Lander	64	99	12.6	17.3	39	39	7.7	6.8	1	–	1	15.6	–	6.9
Lincoln	53	55	12.3	13.2	40	38	9.3	9.1	–	1	2	–	18.2	40.0
Lyon	543	443	12.5	12.7	433	334	10.0	9.6	7	3	5	12.9	6.8	15.6
Mineral	46	58	9.3	11.6	82	76	16.6	15.2	–	2	–	–	34.5	–
Nye	348	296	9.2	9.0	552	377	14.6	11.5	3	2	1	8.6	6.8	3.9
Pershing	61	69	9.5	10.4	49	37	7.7	5.6	–	–	–	–	–	–
Storey	19	4	5.1	1.2	16	21	4.3	6.2	–	–	–	–	–	–
Washoe	5,508	5,010	14.5	14.7	2,853	2,536	7.5	7.4	22	34	39	4.0	6.8	8.6
White Pine	69	77	8.1	8.5	104	90	12.1	10.0	–	–	–	–	–	–
Independent City														
Carson City	718	719	12.8	13.7	644	549	11.5	10.4	2	4	2	2.8	5.6	3.3
NEW HAMPSHIRE	14,565	14,609	11.2	11.8	10,111	9,697	7.8	7.8	81	84	125	5.6	5.7	7.1
Belknap	623	576	10.2	10.2	566	537	9.3	9.5	2	3	5	3.2	5.2	6.7
Carroll	393	412	8.4	9.4	442	426	9.4	9.7	5	4	1	12.7	9.7	2.2
Cheshire	780	802	10.2	10.8	641	675	8.3	9.1	8	4	10	10.3	5.0	10.2
Coos	275	334	8.2	10.1	444	410	13.3	12.4	1	4	4	3.6	12.0	9.0
Grafton	823	837	9.8	10.2	716	674	8.5	8.2	3	4	12	3.6	4.8	11.7
Hillsborough	5,000	5,016	12.6	13.1	2,801	2,788	7.0	7.3	31	27	43	6.2	5.4	7.4
Merrimack	1,562	1,485	10.7	10.9	1,223	1,156	8.4	8.5	7	11	10	4.5	7.4	5.5
Rockingham	3,227	3,379	11.0	12.1	1,978	1,804	6.8	6.5	15	12	24	4.6	3.6	5.8
Strafford	1,415	1,336	12.0	11.9	891	820	7.5	7.3	9	6	11	6.4	4.5	6.8
Sullivan	467	432	11.0	10.7	409	407	9.6	10.0	–	9	5	–	20.8	8.9
NEW JERSEY	115,253	115,632	13.3	13.7	71,371	74,800	8.2	8.9	651	733	1,102	5.6	6.3	9.0
Atlantic	3,541	3,403	13.2	13.4	2,732	2,537	10.2	10.0	38	35	53	10.7	10.3	13.0
Bergen	10,483	10,928	11.6	12.3	7,297	7,703	8.1	8.7	43	49	72	4.1	4.5	6.8
Burlington	5,524	5,116	12.3	12.0	3,637	3,559	8.1	8.4	26	25	38	4.7	4.9	6.4
Camden	7,003	7,105	13.6	14.0	4,672	4,825	9.1	9.5	64	59	91	9.1	8.3	10.2
Cape May	896	1,047	8.9	10.2	1,275	1,361	12.7	13.3	7	8	10	7.8	7.6	7.3
Cumberland	2,278	2,032	15.1	13.9	1,541	1,531	10.2	10.5	24	27	20	10.5	13.3	8.6
Essex	12,089	12,179	15.2	15.4	6,545	7,294	8.2	9.2	94	114	197	7.8	9.4	14.4
Gloucester	3,344	3,216	12.3	12.6	2,346	2,160	8.6	8.5	20	16	30	6.0	5.0	8.5
Hudson	8,916	8,873	14.7	14.6	4,281	4,796	7.1	7.9	54	70	112	6.1	7.9	11.5
Hunterdon	1,323	1,428	10.2	11.6	764	802	5.9	6.5	2	4	9	1.5	2.8	6.0
Mercer	4,657	4,705	12.8	13.4	2,646	3,091	7.3	8.8	41	39	56	8.8	8.3	11.1
Middlesex	10,479	10,478	13.4	13.9	5,421	5,883	6.9	7.8	48	69	90	4.6	6.6	8.7
Monmouth	7,680	8,127	12.1	13.2	5,215	5,425	8.2	8.8	27	38	69	3.5	4.7	8.2
Morris	6,136	6,465	12.6	13.7	3,272	3,527	6.7	7.5	14	21	32	2.3	3.2	5.4
Ocean	7,676	6,556	13.9	12.8	6,898	6,874	12.5	13.4	36	32	36	4.7	4.9	5.7

See footnotes at end of table.

[Includes United States, states, and 3,141 counties/county equivalents defined as of February 22, 2005. For more information on these areas, see Appendix C, Geographic Information]

County	Births Number 2004	2000	Births Rate per 1,000 population[1] 2004	2000	Deaths Number 2004	2000	Deaths Rate per 1,000 population[1] 2004	2000	Infant deaths[2] Number 2004	2000	1990	Infant deaths[2] Rate per 1,000 live births[3] 2004	2000	1990
NEW JERSEY—Con.														
Passaic	7,658	7,903	15.3	16.1	3,956	4,028	7.9	8.2	44	43	74	5.7	5.4	8.9
Salem	764	814	11.7	12.7	699	707	10.7	11.0	5	6	14	6.5	7.4	15.2
Somerset	4,235	4,397	13.4	14.7	2,045	2,072	6.5	6.9	17	16	24	4.0	3.6	6.0
Sussex	1,639	1,771	10.8	12.2	1,012	1,029	6.7	7.1	3	7	16	1.8	4.0	7.0
Union	7,577	7,712	14.3	14.7	4,197	4,686	7.9	9.0	42	48	51	5.5	6.2	6.7
Warren	1,355	1,377	12.3	13.4	920	910	8.4	8.8	2	7	8	1.5	5.1	5.4
NEW MEXICO	28,384	27,223	14.9	14.9	14,298	13,425	7.5	7.4	179	180	246	6.3	6.6	9.0
Bernalillo	9,125	8,305	15.4	14.9	4,507	4,032	7.6	7.2	63	52	66	6.9	6.3	8.1
Catron	28	17	8.2	4.8	37	27	10.8	7.6	–	–	1	–	–	40.0
Chaves	964	959	15.7	15.6	614	620	10.0	10.1	5	9	12	5.2	9.4	12.8
Cibola	433	441	15.7	17.2	202	197	7.3	7.7	3	3	2	6.9	6.8	4.1
Colfax	164	161	11.8	11.3	136	141	9.8	9.9	–	–	3	–	–	18.2
Curry	946	782	20.7	17.4	368	351	8.0	7.8	5	4	7	5.3	5.1	7.3
De Baca	20	22	9.9	9.9	22	29	10.8	13.1	–	–	–	–	–	–
Dona Ana	3,264	3,034	17.6	17.3	1,206	1,057	6.5	6.0	15	14	27	4.6	4.6	9.3
Eddy	727	735	14.1	14.3	488	555	9.4	10.8	3	8	9	4.1	10.9	11.3
Grant	354	420	12.1	13.6	317	335	10.8	10.8	3	5	3	8.5	11.9	7.5
Guadalupe	53	67	11.9	14.3	55	48	12.3	10.3	1	1	2	18.9	14.9	27.0
Harding	4	6	5.2	7.5	9	11	11.6	13.7	1	–	–	250.0	–	–
Hidalgo	69	77	13.3	13.4	56	47	10.8	8.2	2	1	2	29.0	13.0	23.3
Lea	928	873	16.5	15.8	435	465	7.8	8.4	7	8	7	7.5	9.2	7.1
Lincoln	232	209	11.2	10.7	140	166	6.8	8.5	–	2	1	–	9.6	5.4
Los Alamos	201	194	10.7	10.6	102	112	5.4	6.1	1	2	2	5.0	10.3	11.1
Luna	430	381	16.5	15.2	241	248	9.2	9.9	3	8	3	7.0	21.0	9.7
McKinley	1,364	1,351	18.8	18.0	471	433	6.5	5.8	14	11	14	10.3	8.1	7.6
Mora	48	53	9.2	10.2	47	49	9.1	9.4	1	–	–	20.8	–	–
Otero	834	863	13.1	13.9	505	447	7.9	7.2	3	3	9	3.6	3.5	8.9
Quay	113	111	12.0	11.0	127	115	13.5	11.4	1	–	3	8.8	–	21.1
Rio Arriba	662	695	16.2	16.8	322	337	7.9	8.2	2	1	7	3.0	1.4	9.7
Roosevelt	310	303	17.0	16.8	132	145	7.3	8.1	–	1	2	–	3.3	7.9
Sandoval	1,254	1,248	12.2	13.8	670	536	6.5	5.9	10	7	12	8.0	5.6	9.5
San Juan	2,000	1,953	16.1	17.1	775	709	6.2	6.2	15	13	23	7.5	6.7	11.8
San Miguel	378	385	12.8	12.8	241	286	8.2	9.5	2	1	4	5.3	2.6	9.9
Santa Fe	1,592	1,640	11.4	12.6	830	764	6.0	6.0	7	13	11	4.4	7.9	7.6
Sierra	117	100	9.0	7.5	195	210	15.1	15.9	1	2	3	8.5	20.0	30.0
Socorro	261	270	14.4	15.0	132	131	7.3	7.3	–	–	2	–	–	7.5
Taos	362	350	11.5	11.6	220	209	7.0	6.9	2	3	2	5.5	8.6	5.3
Torrance	197	188	11.2	11.1	108	112	6.2	6.6	5	2	1	25.4	10.6	7.1
Union	41	38	10.7	9.1	44	51	11.5	12.2	–	2	–	–	52.6	–
Valencia	909	992	13.3	14.9	544	450	7.9	6.8	4	4	6	4.4	4.0	8.1
NEW YORK	249,947	258,737	13.0	13.6	152,681	158,203	7.9	8.3	1,518	1,656	2,851	6.1	6.4	9.6
Albany	3,064	3,292	10.3	11.2	2,808	2,960	9.4	10.0	22	28	31	7.2	8.5	7.6
Allegany	536	542	10.6	10.9	457	499	9.0	10.0	5	6	3	9.3	11.1	4.3
Bronx	22,299	22,747	16.4	17.0	9,734	10,238	7.1	7.7	156	172	361	7.0	7.6	13.3
Broome	2,029	2,230	10.3	11.1	2,073	2,220	10.5	11.1	12	19	16	5.9	8.5	5.2
Cattaraugus	948	1,008	11.4	12.0	911	834	11.0	9.9	6	6	9	6.3	6.0	7.0
Cayuga	843	947	10.4	11.6	698	735	8.6	9.0	8	8	17	9.5	8.4	14.2
Chautauqua	1,448	1,544	10.6	11.1	1,431	1,542	10.4	11.0	9	6	11	6.2	3.9	5.5
Chemung	977	1,089	10.9	12.0	903	962	10.0	10.6	5	3	15	5.1	2.8	10.8
Chenango	525	577	10.1	11.2	551	528	10.6	10.3	7	6	9	13.3	10.4	11.7
Clinton	757	784	9.3	9.8	626	617	7.7	7.7	7	5	13	9.2	6.4	9.8
Columbia	575	651	9.0	10.3	718	716	11.3	11.4	3	4	2	5.2	6.1	2.5
Cortland	508	564	10.4	11.6	428	426	8.7	8.8	4	5	5	7.9	8.9	7.1
Delaware	437	462	9.2	9.6	531	566	11.2	11.8	4	6	5	9.2	13.0	7.8
Dutchess	3,164	3,342	10.8	11.9	2,255	2,210	7.7	7.9	19	16	24	6.0	4.8	6.2
Erie	10,197	11,280	10.9	11.9	9,698	10,083	10.4	10.6	76	86	124	7.5	7.6	8.5
Essex	376	348	9.7	8.9	427	397	11.0	10.2	3	5	4	8.0	14.4	7.1
Franklin	525	467	10.3	9.1	438	465	8.6	9.1	3	1	6	5.7	2.1	9.6
Fulton	549	662	9.9	12.0	568	585	10.3	10.6	3	1	5	5.5	1.5	6.7
Genesee	627	685	10.5	11.4	539	583	9.0	9.7	6	5	7	9.6	7.3	7.7
Greene	441	479	9.0	9.9	529	547	10.8	11.3	4	4	3	9.1	8.4	4.7
Hamilton	38	48	7.2	8.9	61	72	11.6	13.4	–	–	1	–	–	18.2
Herkimer	700	658	11.0	10.2	718	745	11.2	11.6	4	5	3	5.7	7.6	3.4
Jefferson	1,518	1,654	13.3	14.8	929	870	8.1	7.8	16	6	12	10.5	3.6	5.6
Kings	39,808	39,899	15.9	16.2	17,625	18,670	7.1	7.6	269	281	623	6.8	7.0	13.4
Lewis	276	336	10.4	12.4	221	234	8.3	8.7	–	3	1	–	8.9	2.2
Livingston	633	664	9.8	10.3	468	534	7.3	8.3	1	3	7	1.6	4.5	8.5
Madison	705	780	10.0	11.2	609	579	8.7	8.3	5	9	7	7.1	11.5	6.8
Monroe	8,543	9,526	11.6	12.9	6,266	6,371	8.5	8.7	54	87	119	6.3	9.1	9.9
Montgomery	611	614	12.4	12.4	622	624	12.7	12.6	5	4	6	8.2	6.5	7.7
Nassau	15,643	17,057	11.7	12.8	10,787	11,234	8.1	8.4	62	95	141	4.0	5.6	7.8

See footnotes at end of table.

Table B-5. Counties — **Births, Deaths, and Infant Deaths**—Con.

[Includes United States, states, and 3,141 counties/county equivalents defined as of February 22, 2005. For more information on these areas, see Appendix C, Geographic Information]

County	Births Number 2004	Births Number 2000	Births Rate per 1,000 population[1] 2004	Births Rate per 1,000 population[1] 2000	Deaths Number 2004	Deaths Number 2000	Deaths Rate per 1,000 population[1] 2004	Deaths Rate per 1,000 population[1] 2000	Infant deaths[2] Number 2004	Infant deaths[2] Number 2000	Infant deaths[2] Number 1990	Infant deaths[2] Rate per 1,000 live births[3] 2004	Infant deaths[2] Rate per 1,000 live births[3] 2000	Infant deaths[2] Rate per 1,000 live births[3] 1990
NEW YORK—Con.														
New York	20,643	20,172	13.0	13.1	10,809	11,632	6.8	7.6	94	113	234	4.6	5.6	10.4
Niagara	2,306	2,508	10.6	11.4	2,307	2,319	10.6	10.6	21	19	25	9.1	7.6	7.5
Oneida	2,581	2,505	11.0	10.6	2,486	2,558	10.6	10.9	22	27	30	8.5	10.8	8.1
Onondaga	5,567	6,013	12.1	13.1	3,969	4,155	8.6	9.1	43	48	67	7.7	8.0	8.8
Ontario	1,073	1,147	10.4	11.4	962	865	9.3	8.6	4	9	11	3.7	7.8	7.9
Orange	5,315	5,022	14.4	14.6	2,549	2,479	6.9	7.2	32	28	40	6.0	5.6	7.3
Orleans	453	528	10.4	12.0	362	398	8.3	9.0	2	3	4	4.4	5.7	6.1
Oswego	1,356	1,479	10.9	12.1	1,040	1,028	8.4	8.4	15	10	16	11.1	6.8	7.9
Otsego	549	575	8.8	9.3	596	604	9.5	9.8	3	2	9	5.5	3.5	11.7
Putnam	1,159	1,168	11.5	12.2	623	582	6.2	6.1	12	5	6	10.4	4.3	4.1
Queens	30,415	32,279	13.5	14.5	15,119	16,342	6.7	7.3	178	178	291	5.9	5.5	9.0
Rensselaer	1,739	1,714	11.3	11.2	1,473	1,478	9.5	9.7	15	16	20	8.6	9.3	8.8
Richmond	5,903	5,944	12.8	13.3	3,590	3,516	7.8	7.9	30	36	52	5.1	6.1	8.0
Rockland	4,734	4,650	16.2	16.2	1,986	2,117	6.8	7.4	23	18	39	4.9	3.9	9.2
St. Lawrence	1,224	1,225	11.0	11.0	1,039	1,057	9.3	9.5	7	8	11	5.7	6.5	7.1
Saratoga	2,409	2,619	11.3	13.0	1,508	1,402	7.1	7.0	15	10	10	6.2	3.8	3.5
Schenectady	1,837	1,743	12.4	11.9	1,559	1,544	10.5	10.5	11	12	30	6.0	6.9	13.3
Schoharie	290	321	9.1	10.2	295	304	9.2	9.6	2	–	2	6.9	–	5.6
Schuyler	188	215	9.7	11.2	164	194	8.4	10.1	2	–	1	10.6	–	3.8
Seneca	337	360	9.6	10.8	308	334	8.8	10.0	1	2	4	3.0	5.6	8.4
Steuben	1,094	1,183	11.1	12.0	1,031	1,005	10.4	10.2	7	11	13	6.4	9.3	8.9
Suffolk	19,668	20,238	13.3	14.2	11,244	11,197	7.6	7.9	91	95	179	4.6	4.7	8.4
Sullivan	851	831	11.2	11.2	724	800	9.5	10.8	5	12	9	5.9	14.4	7.9
Tioga	583	595	11.3	11.5	415	387	8.1	7.5	4	1	10	6.9	1.7	12.7
Tompkins	913	839	9.1	8.7	575	573	5.7	5.9	9	11	8	9.9	13.1	7.0
Ulster	1,839	1,781	10.1	10.0	1,533	1,553	8.4	8.7	13	10	11	7.1	5.6	4.3
Warren	624	622	9.6	9.8	582	641	8.9	10.1	3	5	7	4.8	8.0	7.9
Washington	666	617	10.6	10.1	575	587	9.2	9.6	7	1	6	10.5	1.6	7.0
Wayne	1,118	1,172	11.9	12.5	821	813	8.8	8.7	9	7	15	8.1	6.0	10.2
Westchester	12,486	13,032	13.3	14.1	7,235	7,444	7.7	8.0	54	69	95	4.3	5.3	7.2
Wyoming	429	429	10.0	9.9	365	373	8.5	8.6	2	2	3	4.7	4.7	5.6
Yates	298	275	12.0	11.2	208	276	8.4	11.2	4	3	3	13.4	10.9	9.0
NORTH CAROLINA	119,847	120,311	14.0	14.9	72,384	71,935	8.5	8.9	1,053	1,038	1,109	8.8	8.6	10.6
Alamance	1,769	1,903	12.8	14.5	1,276	1,342	9.2	10.2	15	30	16	8.5	15.8	10.6
Alexander	393	468	11.1	13.9	308	304	8.7	9.0	6	1	4	15.3	2.1	11.5
Alleghany	98	126	9.0	11.8	133	130	12.2	12.1	2	1	1	20.4	7.9	9.1
Anson	285	353	11.1	14.0	253	287	9.8	11.4	3	9	4	10.5	25.5	9.7
Ashe	261	257	10.3	10.5	289	278	11.4	11.4	1	–	7	3.8	–	31.4
Avery	144	183	8.1	10.6	191	188	10.8	10.9	–	–	3	–	–	15.5
Beaufort	594	641	13.0	14.2	523	552	11.5	12.3	1	6	5	1.7	9.4	8.0
Bertie	231	249	11.8	12.6	244	280	12.5	14.2	2	1	3	8.7	4.0	9.9
Bladen	467	482	14.2	14.9	410	368	12.4	11.4	6	4	5	12.8	8.3	12.0
Brunswick	897	856	10.6	11.6	855	725	10.1	9.8	6	4	7	6.7	4.7	9.8
Buncombe	2,578	2,599	12.0	12.6	2,124	2,207	9.8	10.7	14	23	28	5.4	8.8	11.6
Burke	1,007	1,168	11.3	13.1	890	851	10.0	9.5	5	12	14	5.0	10.3	13.4
Cabarrus	2,268	2,162	15.5	16.3	1,197	1,122	8.2	8.5	20	20	17	8.8	9.3	11.3
Caldwell	957	1,052	12.1	13.6	717	741	9.1	9.5	11	9	11	11.5	8.6	10.8
Camden	107	76	12.6	11.0	69	63	8.1	9.1	–	–	1	–	–	14.1
Carteret	649	637	10.5	10.7	687	640	11.1	10.8	6	6	8	9.2	9.4	11.3
Caswell	212	262	9.0	11.1	260	217	11.0	9.2	1	4	4	4.7	15.3	14.9
Catawba	1,945	2,140	13.0	15.0	1,333	1,291	8.9	9.1	10	19	16	5.1	8.9	9.0
Chatham	724	666	12.7	13.4	483	487	8.5	9.8	8	4	5	11.0	6.0	8.4
Cherokee	260	268	10.2	11.0	313	302	12.3	12.4	2	2	2	7.7	7.5	9.2
Chowan	182	188	12.6	13.3	198	194	13.7	13.7	1	1	6	5.5	5.3	29.7
Clay	86	80	9.1	9.1	113	122	11.9	13.8	1	–	–	11.6	–	–
Cleveland	1,182	1,336	12.0	13.8	1,024	1,025	10.4	10.6	14	13	11	11.8	9.7	8.1
Columbus	757	809	13.8	14.8	635	640	11.6	11.7	9	7	10	11.9	8.7	12.4
Craven	1,584	1,652	17.4	18.0	901	831	9.9	9.1	12	11	19	7.6	6.7	11.7
Cumberland	5,232	5,666	17.0	18.7	1,993	2,016	6.5	6.7	56	60	52	10.7	10.6	9.0
Currituck	265	236	12.0	12.9	176	164	8.0	8.9	–	2	3	–	8.5	13.5
Dare	490	352	14.6	11.7	277	271	8.2	9.0	3	2	1	6.1	5.7	2.9
Davidson	1,883	1,973	12.3	13.4	1,378	1,383	9.0	9.4	14	21	17	7.4	10.6	9.0
Davie	419	482	11.0	13.7	342	348	9.0	9.9	3	11	1	7.2	22.8	2.7
Duplin	795	833	15.4	16.9	505	523	9.8	10.6	6	6	6	7.5	7.2	9.5
Durham	3,842	3,808	16.0	17.0	1,650	1,736	6.9	7.7	26	29	39	6.8	7.6	12.4
Edgecombe	783	856	14.4	15.5	572	648	10.5	11.7	11	11	6	14.0	12.9	6.2
Forsyth	4,599	4,589	14.3	15.0	2,800	2,777	8.7	9.0	47	48	52	10.2	10.5	12.5
Franklin	713	675	13.3	14.2	424	446	7.9	9.4	5	9	10	7.0	13.3	18.9

See footnotes at end of table.

[Includes United States, states, and 3,141 counties/county equivalents defined as of February 22, 2005. For more information on these areas, see Appendix C, Geographic Information]

County	Births Number 2004	Births Number 2000	Births Rate per 1,000 population[1] 2004	Births Rate per 1,000 population[1] 2000	Deaths Number 2004	Deaths Number 2000	Deaths Rate per 1,000 population[1] 2004	Deaths Rate per 1,000 population[1] 2000	Infant deaths[2] Number 2004	Infant deaths[2] Number 2000	Infant deaths[2] Number 1990	Infant deaths[2] Rate per 1,000 live births[3] 2004	Infant deaths[2] Rate per 1,000 live births[3] 2000	Infant deaths[2] Rate per 1,000 live births[3] 1990
NORTH CAROLINA—Con.														
Gaston	2,582	2,751	13.3	14.4	1,938	2,021	10.0	10.6	20	28	25	7.7	10.2	8.8
Gates	114	107	10.5	10.2	109	135	10.0	12.8	1	–	–	8.8	–	–
Graham	92	106	11.4	13.3	99	118	12.3	14.8	1	–	2	10.9	–	27.8
Granville	616	599	11.6	12.3	454	443	8.6	9.1	5	4	7	8.1	6.7	12.9
Greene	264	259	13.1	13.6	187	174	9.3	9.1	6	2	2	22.7	7.7	9.4
Guilford	5,862	6,095	13.4	14.4	3,538	3,567	8.1	8.4	60	45	55	10.2	7.4	10.6
Halifax	723	797	12.9	13.9	645	653	11.5	11.4	16	6	16	22.1	7.5	16.8
Harnett	1,456	1,435	14.4	15.7	824	746	8.1	8.1	14	13	13	9.6	9.1	11.1
Haywood	530	564	9.4	10.4	665	624	11.8	11.5	4	3	4	7.5	5.3	7.3
Henderson	1,119	1,034	11.7	11.5	1,193	1,126	12.5	12.6	6	7	10	5.4	6.8	11.5
Hertford	311	280	13.2	12.2	298	307	12.7	13.4	3	6	7	9.6	21.4	20.0
Hoke	710	668	18.1	19.7	274	246	7.0	7.3	7	4	5	9.9	6.0	11.7
Hyde	56	62	10.2	10.7	68	77	12.4	13.3	–	1	–	–	16.1	–
Iredell	1,733	1,985	12.7	16.1	1,113	1,153	8.1	9.3	8	19	15	4.6	9.6	10.5
Jackson	345	367	9.8	11.0	318	302	9.0	9.1	1	5	3	2.9	13.6	9.1
Johnston	2,310	2,122	16.3	17.2	1,073	967	7.6	7.8	18	14	7	7.8	6.6	5.3
Jones	93	87	8.9	8.4	94	133	9.0	12.8	–	–	3	–	–	20.1
Lee	822	876	15.1	17.7	491	524	9.0	10.6	11	3	6	13.4	3.4	8.6
Lenoir	779	861	13.4	14.5	663	710	11.4	11.9	8	7	11	10.3	8.1	12.8
Lincoln	860	906	12.6	14.1	620	571	9.1	8.9	3	11	4	3.5	12.1	5.3
McDowell	490	445	11.4	10.5	441	395	10.2	9.4	4	2	–	8.2	4.5	–
Macon	331	307	10.5	10.2	422	372	13.4	12.4	3	4	–	9.1	13.0	–
Madison	227	231	11.3	11.7	209	230	10.4	11.7	–	2	–	–	8.7	–
Martin	314	443	12.6	17.4	333	419	13.4	16.4	1	5	7	3.2	11.3	18.4
Mecklenburg	12,962	11,992	16.8	17.1	4,691	4,594	6.1	6.6	119	104	101	9.2	8.7	11.2
Mitchell	164	155	10.4	9.9	185	224	11.7	14.2	1	1	–	6.1	6.5	–
Montgomery	367	416	13.5	15.4	306	278	11.2	10.3	2	2	6	5.4	4.8	16.0
Moore	962	928	12.0	12.3	968	865	12.1	11.5	6	4	4	6.2	4.3	4.7
Nash	1,225	1,302	13.5	14.8	918	887	10.1	10.1	14	16	16	11.4	12.3	12.7
New Hanover	2,185	2,019	12.6	12.6	1,429	1,339	8.2	8.3	10	11	11	4.6	5.4	6.1
Northampton	227	260	10.6	11.8	293	283	13.6	12.8	3	3	2	13.2	11.5	6.3
Onslow	3,373	3,331	21.8	22.2	819	751	5.3	5.0	24	29	42	7.1	8.7	12.2
Orange	1,331	1,289	11.4	11.1	696	699	5.9	6.0	16	5	12	12.0	3.9	10.8
Pamlico	123	108	9.7	8.3	146	126	11.5	9.7	2	–	3	16.3	–	20.8
Pasquotank	519	454	14.0	13.0	358	372	9.7	10.7	3	2	5	5.8	4.4	10.1
Pender	479	491	10.6	11.9	379	372	8.4	9.0	3	4	2	6.3	8.1	4.7
Perquimans	112	124	9.5	10.9	142	143	12.1	12.5	2	4	4	17.9	32.3	29.4
Person	447	433	12.2	12.1	356	386	9.7	10.8	4	7	1	8.9	16.2	2.1
Pitt	2,102	2,031	15.0	15.1	1,048	1,060	7.5	7.9	15	17	28	7.1	8.4	16.6
Polk	164	193	8.7	10.5	276	288	14.6	15.6	2	3	1	12.2	15.5	6.3
Randolph	1,777	1,949	13.0	14.9	1,111	1,119	8.2	8.5	6	18	13	3.4	9.2	8.4
Richmond	608	714	13.0	15.3	501	523	10.7	11.2	14	3	8	23.0	4.2	11.1
Robeson	2,029	2,154	16.1	17.5	1,129	1,183	8.9	9.6	26	26	29	12.8	12.1	14.6
Rockingham	1,057	1,206	11.5	13.1	1,002	1,084	10.9	11.8	4	8	9	3.8	6.6	7.5
Rowan	1,611	1,705	12.0	13.0	1,288	1,364	9.6	10.4	23	11	16	14.3	6.5	10.5
Rutherford	783	872	12.3	13.8	761	760	12.0	12.1	6	8	10	7.7	9.2	11.8
Sampson	863	925	13.9	15.3	631	633	10.1	10.5	9	10	4	10.4	10.8	6.0
Scotland	482	543	13.0	15.1	351	415	9.5	11.5	10	3	11	20.7	5.5	18.2
Stanly	770	754	13.1	13.0	563	613	9.6	10.5	13	6	5	16.9	8.0	6.6
Stokes	490	526	10.8	11.7	393	420	8.6	9.4	4	6	6	8.2	11.4	12.7
Surry	866	973	12.0	13.7	775	762	10.7	10.7	5	7	7	5.8	7.2	8.0
Swain	197	183	15.0	14.1	156	172	11.9	13.2	1	1	2	5.1	5.5	10.1
Transylvania	253	298	8.6	10.1	361	326	12.3	11.1	2	2	2	7.9	6.7	7.1
Tyrrell	44	46	10.6	11.1	33	40	7.9	9.6	2	–	–	45.5	–	–
Union	2,497	2,243	16.2	17.8	950	829	6.2	6.6	24	11	19	9.6	4.9	13.6
Vance	659	754	15.1	17.5	487	452	11.1	10.5	13	8	6	19.7	10.6	8.8
Wake	11,751	10,198	16.3	16.1	3,518	3,249	4.9	5.1	82	74	69	7.0	7.3	9.9
Warren	190	193	9.6	9.7	217	209	10.9	10.5	1	3	4	5.3	15.5	16.4
Washington	184	201	13.8	14.7	157	203	11.8	14.8	–	1	6	–	5.0	25.1
Watauga	347	363	8.2	8.5	285	276	6.7	6.5	8	3	3	23.1	8.3	7.9
Wayne	1,759	1,764	15.4	15.6	1,105	1,098	9.7	9.7	19	20	20	10.8	11.3	11.7
Wilkes	750	927	11.2	14.1	647	684	9.7	10.4	9	2	12	12.0	2.2	16.4
Wilson	1,082	1,081	14.3	14.6	796	742	10.5	10.0	18	11	8	16.6	10.2	7.7
Yadkin	471	525	12.6	14.4	350	382	9.4	10.5	1	7	2	2.1	13.3	5.2
Yancey	188	218	10.4	12.2	195	218	10.8	12.2	–	–	4	–	–	19.2
NORTH DAKOTA	8,189	7,676	12.9	12.0	5,601	5,856	8.8	9.1	46	62	74	5.6	8.1	8.0
Adams	18	23	7.3	8.9	40	47	16.3	18.2	–	–	–	–	–	–
Barnes	113	105	10.2	9.0	167	130	15.0	11.1	2	–	3	17.7	–	21.3
Benson	147	129	21.0	18.5	61	54	8.7	7.8	2	–	3	13.6	–	25.9
Billings	6	6	7.3	6.9	3	8	3.6	9.2	–	–	–	–	–	–
Bottineau	62	51	9.1	7.2	81	84	11.9	11.8	–	1	1	–	19.6	12.5

See footnotes at end of table.

County and City Data Book: 2007

U.S. Census Bureau

Table B-5. Counties — **Births, Deaths, and Infant Deaths**—Con.

[Includes United States, states, and 3,141 counties/county equivalents defined as of February 22, 2005. For more information on these areas, see Appendix C, Geographic Information]

County	Births				Deaths				Infant deaths[2]					
	Number		Rate per 1,000 population[1]		Number		Rate per 1,000 population[1]		Number			Rate per 1,000 live births[3]		
	2004	2000	2004	2000	2004	2000	2004	2000	2004	2000	1990	2004	2000	1990
NORTH DAKOTA—Con.														
Bowman	30	34	9.7	10.5	44	43	14.2	13.3	–	–	–	–	–	–
Burke	15	15	7.2	6.7	22	25	10.6	11.2	–	–	1	–	–	47.6
Burleigh	947	881	13.1	12.7	460	550	6.3	7.9	4	3	3	4.2	3.4	3.4
Cass	1,798	1,635	13.9	13.3	767	753	5.9	6.1	8	18	15	4.4	11.0	9.6
Cavalier	30	35	6.8	7.3	52	79	11.8	16.4	–	–	–	–	–	–
Dickey	73	75	13.1	13.0	76	86	13.6	15.0	1	–	1	13.7	–	12.5
Divide	18	11	8.2	4.9	30	45	13.7	19.9	–	–	1	–	–	38.5
Dunn	32	31	9.3	8.6	35	27	10.1	7.5	–	–	1	–	–	19.2
Eddy	21	26	8.0	9.5	44	52	16.8	19.0	–	1	1	–	38.5	23.3
Emmons	27	29	6.9	6.7	52	68	13.2	15.8	–	–	–	–	–	–
Foster	34	29	9.6	7.8	33	62	9.4	16.6	–	–	1	–	–	20.4
Golden Valley	17	15	9.6	7.8	16	21	9.1	10.9	–	–	–	–	–	–
Grand Forks	905	889	13.7	13.5	438	433	6.6	6.6	4	6	13	4.4	6.7	10.6
Grant	17	18	6.5	6.3	36	48	13.7	16.9	–	–	–	–	–	–
Griggs	17	20	6.7	7.3	40	37	15.8	13.5	–	1	1	–	50.0	23.8
Hettinger	23	18	9.1	6.7	29	39	11.4	14.5	–	1	–	–	55.6	–
Kidder	14	27	5.5	9.9	33	33	12.9	12.1	–	–	–	–	–	–
LaMoure	51	41	11.4	8.8	69	44	15.4	9.4	1	–	1	19.6	–	17.5
Logan	14	17	6.7	7.4	27	34	12.9	14.8	–	–	–	–	–	17.2
McHenry	57	56	10.2	9.4	64	68	11.4	11.4	–	–	1	–	–	–
McIntosh	29	32	9.4	9.5	78	60	25.2	17.8	–	–	1	–	–	31.3
McKenzie	69	67	12.5	11.7	55	63	10.0	11.0	1	1	–	14.5	14.9	–
McLean	74	76	8.4	8.2	116	129	13.2	13.9	1	1	–	13.5	13.2	–
Mercer	67	74	8.0	8.6	69	74	8.2	8.6	–	1	–	–	13.5	–
Morton	307	287	12.1	11.3	213	244	8.4	9.6	4	3	–	13.0	10.5	–
Mountrail	117	88	17.9	13.3	84	81	12.9	12.3	–	2	1	–	22.7	10.9
Nelson	31	34	9.0	9.2	64	84	18.6	22.7	–	–	–	–	–	–
Oliver	16	14	8.5	6.8	8	10	4.3	4.9	–	–	–	–	–	–
Pembina	68	90	8.3	10.5	90	83	11.0	9.7	–	–	1	–	–	–
Pierce	38	39	8.7	8.4	59	64	13.5	13.7	–	–	1	–	–	15.6
Ramsey	136	144	11.9	12.0	156	138	13.6	11.5	2	3	4	14.7	20.8	24.1
Ransom	62	55	10.6	9.3	86	92	14.8	15.6	–	–	–	–	–	–
Renville	28	14	11.4	5.4	34	33	13.8	12.7	–	–	–	–	–	–
Richland	207	198	11.9	11.0	142	148	8.1	8.2	–	–	1	–	–	4.4
Rolette	316	276	22.9	20.2	133	104	9.6	7.6	1	5	4	3.2	18.1	13.1
Sargent	41	47	9.9	10.8	24	45	5.8	10.3	–	–	–	–	–	–
Sheridan	3	10	2.1	5.9	11	18	7.5	10.6	–	–	–	–	–	–
Sioux	95	99	23.0	24.4	26	25	6.3	6.2	–	–	3	–	–	26.5
Slope	4	6	5.5	7.9	4	2	5.5	2.6	–	–	–	–	–	–
Stark	303	249	13.7	11.0	199	201	9.0	8.9	1	2	2	3.3	8.0	5.8
Steele	17	11	8.2	4.9	21	23	10.2	10.3	–	–	–	–	–	–
Stutsman	225	192	10.8	8.8	253	230	12.1	10.5	5	–	–	22.2	–	–
Towner	16	13	6.2	4.6	39	32	15.1	11.2	–	–	–	–	–	–
Traill	83	78	10.0	9.2	110	102	13.2	12.0	–	3	2	–	38.5	18.0
Walsh	109	147	9.4	11.9	145	144	12.5	11.6	1	1	1	9.2	6.8	5.7
Ward	985	857	17.5	14.6	412	503	7.3	8.6	7	7	6	7.1	8.2	5.9
Wells	33	45	7.1	8.9	56	91	12.1	17.9	–	–	–	–	–	–
Williams	224	218	11.6	11.1	195	163	10.1	8.3	1	2	1	4.5	9.2	3.4
OHIO	148,954	155,472	13.0	13.7	106,288	108,125	9.3	9.5	1,143	1,187	1,640	7.7	7.6	9.8
Adams	380	389	13.4	14.2	294	302	10.4	11.0	3	1	2	7.9	2.6	5.5
Allen	1,444	1,582	13.6	14.6	987	1,116	9.3	10.3	14	14	18	9.7	8.8	9.9
Ashland	695	725	12.9	13.8	467	463	8.7	8.8	4	6	1	5.8	8.3	1.6
Ashtabula	1,265	1,320	12.3	12.8	1,053	1,177	10.2	11.5	12	8	16	9.5	6.1	10.9
Athens	608	672	9.8	10.8	409	476	6.6	7.6	3	5	3	4.9	7.4	4.8
Auglaize	632	579	13.5	12.4	414	446	8.8	9.6	5	4	8	7.9	6.9	11.1
Belmont	728	732	10.5	10.4	929	916	13.4	13.1	5	4	9	6.9	5.5	10.6
Brown	567	591	12.8	13.9	418	368	9.5	8.6	5	7	4	8.8	11.8	7.8
Butler	4,804	4,887	13.9	14.6	2,664	2,637	7.7	7.9	43	34	44	9.0	7.0	9.9
Carroll	302	324	10.3	11.2	252	259	8.6	9.0	1	1	2	3.3	3.1	5.4
Champaign	504	507	12.7	13.0	366	376	9.2	9.7	2	3	1	4.0	5.9	2.1
Clark	1,714	1,928	12.0	13.3	1,584	1,628	11.1	11.3	13	9	20	7.6	4.7	9.4
Clermont	2,771	2,773	14.7	15.5	1,281	1,305	6.8	7.3	17	17	16	6.1	6.1	6.1
Clinton	601	591	14.2	14.5	392	387	9.3	9.5	2	3	1	3.3	5.1	2.0
Columbiana	1,183	1,312	10.6	11.7	1,177	1,248	10.6	11.1	10	12	14	8.5	9.1	9.5
Coshocton	510	482	13.8	13.1	383	373	10.3	10.2	5	–	7	9.8	–	14.2
Crawford	547	602	11.9	12.8	465	509	10.1	10.9	3	11	6	5.5	18.3	8.8
Cuyahoga	16,949	18,798	12.6	13.5	14,698	15,303	10.9	11.0	165	191	326	9.7	10.2	14.1
Darke	708	640	13.3	12.0	571	528	10.8	9.9	1	1	7	1.4	1.6	9.0
Defiance	501	536	12.8	13.6	345	316	8.8	8.0	4	2	8	8.0	3.7	14.2

See footnotes at end of table.

Table B-5. Counties — **Births, Deaths, and Infant Deaths**—Con.

[Includes United States, states, and 3,141 counties/county equivalents defined as of February 22, 2005. For more information on these areas, see Appendix C, Geographic Information]

County	Births				Deaths				Infant deaths[2]					
	Number		Rate per 1,000 population[1]		Number		Rate per 1,000 population[1]		Number			Rate per 1,000 live births[3]		
	2004	2000	2004	2000	2004	2000	2004	2000	2004	2000	1990	2004	2000	1990
OHIO—Con.														
Delaware	2,349	1,677	16.5	15.0	707	633	5.0	5.7	11	13	9	4.7	7.8	9.4
Erie	889	951	11.3	11.9	828	811	10.5	10.2	3	8	10	3.4	8.4	9.3
Fairfield	1,729	1,738	12.7	14.1	1,084	1,053	8.0	8.5	17	8	9	9.8	4.6	6.0
Fayette	377	359	13.4	12.6	311	342	11.1	12.0	2	–	3	5.3	–	7.2
Franklin	17,408	17,491	16.0	16.3	8,290	8,119	7.6	7.6	139	143	179	8.0	8.2	10.8
Fulton	494	631	11.5	15.0	359	372	8.4	8.8	4	5	6	8.1	7.9	10.0
Gallia	383	410	12.2	13.2	342	327	10.9	10.5	6	7	10	15.7	17.1	23.1
Geauga	1,110	1,143	11.7	12.5	700	631	7.4	6.9	5	6	7	4.5	5.2	5.8
Greene	1,724	1,740	11.3	11.7	1,152	1,182	7.6	8.0	9	6	11	5.2	3.4	6.1
Guernsey	502	500	12.2	12.3	430	418	10.4	10.2	5	1	3	10.0	2.0	5.5
Hamilton	11,458	12,411	14.1	14.7	7,955	8,322	9.8	9.9	126	123	155	11.0	9.9	10.7
Hancock	940	902	12.8	12.6	670	609	9.1	8.5	6	8	5	6.4	8.9	5.0
Hardin	394	410	12.2	12.8	323	284	10.0	8.9	2	2	2	5.1	4.9	5.0
Harrison	151	169	9.5	10.7	219	217	13.8	13.7	1	4	2	6.6	23.7	9.8
Henry	377	375	12.8	12.8	219	270	7.5	9.2	–	2	3	–	5.3	6.5
Highland	567	576	13.3	14.0	435	448	10.2	10.9	5	7	6	8.8	12.2	10.6
Hocking	360	349	12.5	12.4	245	301	8.5	10.7	2	2	3	5.6	5.7	8.0
Holmes	797	918	19.3	23.5	275	256	6.7	6.6	2	6	3	2.5	6.5	4.0
Huron	843	853	14.0	14.3	533	536	8.9	9.0	4	4	9	4.7	4.7	9.4
Jackson	476	433	14.3	13.3	350	373	10.5	11.4	4	2	3	8.4	4.6	7.1
Jefferson	726	808	10.2	11.0	907	1,039	12.7	14.1	2	6	7	2.8	7.4	8.5
Knox	694	736	12.0	13.5	569	532	9.9	9.7	4	3	3	5.8	4.1	4.9
Lake	2,553	2,651	11.0	11.6	2,105	2,042	9.1	9.0	14	11	18	5.5	4.1	5.9
Lawrence	752	806	12.0	12.9	738	738	11.8	11.8	7	7	6	9.3	8.7	7.0
Licking	2,081	1,998	13.6	13.7	1,299	1,280	8.5	8.8	16	14	13	7.7	7.0	7.4
Logan	614	633	13.2	13.8	478	442	10.3	9.6	8	7	7	13.0	11.1	10.3
Lorain	3,664	3,859	12.5	13.5	2,591	2,394	8.8	8.4	28	29	53	7.6	7.5	12.6
Lucas	6,428	6,559	14.3	14.4	4,248	4,660	9.4	10.2	55	49	75	8.6	7.5	9.2
Madison	454	518	11.1	12.9	345	365	8.4	9.1	1	9	4	2.2	17.4	7.6
Mahoning	2,644	2,987	10.3	11.6	3,016	3,160	11.8	12.3	26	16	42	9.8	5.4	11.5
Marion	766	802	11.6	12.1	694	613	10.5	9.3	5	10	12	6.5	12.5	12.1
Medina	2,072	2,000	12.6	13.2	1,101	1,031	6.7	6.8	7	9	16	3.4	4.5	9.4
Meigs	285	302	12.3	13.1	255	278	11.0	12.1	3	1	2	10.5	3.3	6.4
Mercer	583	560	14.2	13.7	372	366	9.1	8.9	2	4	5	3.4	7.1	6.8
Miami	1,186	1,333	11.8	13.5	895	984	8.9	9.9	6	12	11	5.1	9.0	8.6
Monroe	170	171	11.4	11.3	159	176	10.7	11.6	–	–	–	–	–	–
Montgomery	7,195	7,796	13.1	14.0	5,363	5,588	9.8	10.0	50	64	84	6.9	8.2	9.1
Morgan	165	176	11.0	11.8	136	167	9.1	11.2	–	1	2	–	5.7	10.5
Morrow	434	413	12.7	13.0	275	248	8.1	7.8	4	2	5	9.2	4.8	12.2
Muskingum	1,111	1,146	13.0	13.5	831	819	9.7	9.7	7	11	8	6.3	9.6	6.4
Noble	120	147	8.5	10.4	109	115	7.7	8.2	–	–	–	–	–	–
Ottawa	422	449	10.2	10.9	450	412	10.9	10.0	1	1	4	2.4	2.2	8.4
Paulding	258	233	13.2	11.5	180	170	9.2	8.4	–	2	5	–	8.6	15.5
Perry	443	479	12.6	14.0	303	316	8.6	9.3	2	6	1	4.5	12.5	2.0
Pickaway	597	646	11.5	12.2	391	448	7.5	8.5	1	5	2	1.7	7.7	3.1
Pike	381	366	13.5	13.2	293	297	10.4	10.7	3	2	–	7.9	5.5	–
Portage	1,634	1,727	10.5	11.3	1,212	1,062	7.8	7.0	8	8	16	4.9	4.6	8.1
Preble	500	526	11.8	12.4	407	387	9.6	9.1	5	–	5	10.0	–	8.9
Putnam	462	485	13.3	14.0	314	278	9.0	8.0	2	4	3	4.3	8.2	5.1
Richland	1,565	1,598	12.2	12.4	1,229	1,211	9.6	9.4	9	10	25	5.8	6.3	13.3
Ross	884	949	11.8	12.9	669	709	8.9	9.7	6	4	13	6.8	4.2	14.1
Sandusky	756	892	12.2	14.4	631	589	10.2	9.5	8	6	7	10.6	6.7	7.9
Scioto	1,007	1,080	13.1	13.7	926	970	12.1	12.3	8	6	10	7.9	5.6	8.9
Seneca	775	730	13.4	12.5	559	589	9.7	10.0	6	2	7	7.7	2.7	11.4
Shelby	714	808	14.7	16.8	366	420	7.5	8.8	6	8	11	8.4	9.9	15.4
Stark	4,446	4,952	11.7	13.1	3,688	3,883	9.7	10.3	26	35	34	5.8	7.1	6.3
Summit	6,657	7,095	12.2	13.1	5,336	5,368	9.8	9.9	56	57	59	8.4	8.0	7.5
Trumbull	2,423	2,732	11.0	12.1	2,385	2,401	10.8	10.7	18	25	35	7.4	9.2	11.4
Tuscarawas	1,156	1,210	12.6	13.3	868	942	9.4	10.3	3	5	10	2.6	4.1	8.7
Union	661	631	14.8	15.3	315	288	7.0	7.0	4	5	9	6.1	7.9	19.6
Van Wert	404	334	13.8	11.3	276	314	9.4	10.6	1	–	3	2.5	–	6.6
Vinton	162	165	12.2	12.9	114	127	8.6	9.9	1	–	3	6.2	–	17.9
Warren	2,785	2,475	14.7	15.4	1,198	1,067	6.3	6.6	19	9	10	6.8	3.6	5.8
Washington	683	686	10.9	10.9	641	693	10.2	11.0	4	3	11	5.9	4.4	13.2
Wayne	1,578	1,621	13.9	14.5	946	959	8.4	8.6	12	12	10	7.6	7.4	6.1
Williams	485	480	12.5	12.2	389	384	10.0	9.8	6	7	9	12.4	14.6	15.1
Wood	1,406	1,428	11.4	11.8	890	922	7.2	7.6	10	8	11	7.1	5.6	7.4
Wyandot	272	288	11.9	12.6	250	245	11.0	10.7	3	2	3	11.0	6.9	9.1

See footnotes at end of table.

Table B-5. Counties — **Births, Deaths, and Infant Deaths**—Con.

[Includes United States, states, and 3,141 counties/county equivalents defined as of February 22, 2005. For more information on these areas, see Appendix C, Geographic Information]

County	Births								Deaths								Infant deaths[2]					
	Number		Rate per 1,000 population[1]		Number		Rate per 1,000 population[1]		Number			Rate per 1,000 live births[3]										
	2004	2000	2004	2000	2004	2000	2004	2000	2004	2000	1990	2004	2000	1990								
OKLAHOMA	51,306	49,782	14.6	14.4	34,483	35,079	9.8	10.2	411	425	438	8.0	8.5	9.2								
Adair	408	379	18.8	18.0	218	233	10.0	11.1	5	4	5	12.3	10.6	13.4								
Alfalfa	51	40	8.7	6.6	74	75	12.7	12.3	–	–	–	–	–	–								
Atoka	150	145	10.5	10.5	147	165	10.3	11.9	1	2	–	6.7	13.8	–								
Beaver	84	52	15.4	9.0	58	73	10.6	12.6	1	–	–	11.9	–	–								
Beckham	276	238	15.0	12.0	230	263	12.5	13.3	2	3	1	7.2	12.6	3.6								
Blaine	143	127	11.1	10.6	138	163	10.7	13.6	–	1	1	–	7.9	5.5								
Bryan	489	527	13.0	14.4	466	474	12.4	12.9	8	4	3	16.4	7.6	6.8								
Caddo	430	407	14.2	13.5	337	372	11.1	12.4	3	4	7	7.0	9.8	15.0								
Canadian	1,319	1,113	13.8	12.6	699	657	7.3	7.4	11	10	7	8.3	9.0	6.5								
Carter	656	636	14.0	13.9	642	629	13.7	13.8	4	3	4	6.1	4.7	6.8								
Cherokee	583	618	13.2	14.5	431	374	9.8	8.8	7	5	3	12.0	8.1	5.4								
Choctaw	236	207	15.3	13.5	226	202	14.7	13.2	2	–	1	8.5	–	4.0								
Cimarron	33	33	11.4	10.5	31	34	10.7	10.8	–	2	–	–	60.6	–								
Cleveland	2,693	2,472	12.2	11.9	1,419	1,260	6.4	6.0	13	18	21	4.8	7.3	9.7								
Coal	66	77	11.2	12.8	85	93	14.4	15.5	3	1	–	45.5	13.0	–								
Comanche	1,930	1,934	17.1	16.9	874	808	7.7	7.0	9	7	15	4.7	3.6	7.0								
Cotton	80	66	12.2	9.9	98	96	15.0	14.4	–	–	–	–	–	–								
Craig	173	200	11.6	13.4	205	196	13.7	13.1	2	2	4	11.6	10.0	22.6								
Creek	909	878	13.2	13.0	673	698	9.8	10.3	6	6	3	6.6	6.8	3.5								
Custer	361	312	14.4	12.0	260	303	10.3	11.6	–	3	2	–	9.6	5.2								
Delaware	450	439	11.5	11.8	439	417	11.2	11.2	1	3	1	2.2	6.8	2.8								
Dewey	58	53	12.5	11.2	85	111	18.3	23.5	1	–	–	17.2	–	–								
Ellis	50	37	12.6	9.1	41	63	10.3	15.5	–	–	–	–	–	–								
Garfield	895	815	15.6	14.1	685	687	11.9	11.9	8	13	7	8.9	16.0	8.3								
Garvin	350	400	12.9	14.7	372	382	13.7	14.0	4	4	2	11.4	10.0	5.7								
Grady	640	573	13.3	12.6	466	509	9.7	11.2	4	3	4	6.3	5.2	6.8								
Grant	41	56	8.6	10.9	61	79	12.7	15.4	–	1	1	–	17.9	12.8								
Greer	67	66	11.4	10.9	73	93	12.4	15.4	–	–	1	–	–	15.6								
Harmon	40	34	13.3	10.4	45	53	15.0	16.1	–	–	–	–	–	–								
Harper	49	42	14.5	11.9	48	47	14.2	13.3	–	–	–	–	–	–								
Haskell	153	160	12.7	13.5	151	159	12.5	13.4	–	3	1	–	18.8	9.6								
Hughes	186	171	13.3	12.1	192	196	13.8	13.9	1	5	–	5.4	29.2	–								
Jackson	441	479	16.3	17.0	281	274	10.4	9.7	3	2	6	6.8	4.2	10.6								
Jefferson	93	74	14.3	10.9	83	122	12.8	18.0	1	–	–	10.8	–	–								
Johnston	138	118	13.3	11.2	140	134	13.5	12.7	–	–	2	–	–	17.1								
Kay	648	682	13.8	14.2	594	590	12.7	12.3	7	4	9	10.8	5.9	12.9								
Kingfisher	165	173	11.7	12.4	153	163	10.8	11.7	1	1	2	6.1	5.8	10.6								
Kiowa	133	131	13.6	12.8	157	199	16.0	19.5	1	1	–	7.5	7.6	–								
Latimer	135	127	12.7	11.9	121	142	11.4	13.3	2	1	1	14.8	7.9	7.0								
Le Flore	698	746	14.2	15.5	552	537	11.2	11.1	9	7	5	12.9	9.4	7.7								
Lincoln	417	385	12.9	12.0	350	355	10.8	11.0	3	–	4	7.2	–	10.9								
Logan	446	370	12.2	10.9	293	317	8.0	9.3	5	1	1	11.2	2.7	2.8								
Love	118	95	13.0	10.8	91	106	10.0	12.0	–	–	2	–	–	15.7								
McClain	405	393	13.9	14.1	268	249	9.2	8.9	5	1	5	12.3	2.5	15.5								
McCurtain	460	555	13.6	16.1	429	430	12.6	12.5	–	4	10	–	7.2	17.3								
McIntosh	196	219	9.8	11.2	279	281	14.0	14.4	3	–	2	15.3	–	11.6								
Major	90	73	12.2	9.7	103	105	14.0	13.9	1	1	3	11.1	13.7	37.0								
Marshall	187	163	13.4	12.4	189	181	13.5	13.7	1	2	1	5.3	12.3	7.9								
Mayes	529	564	13.5	14.7	418	401	10.7	10.4	2	5	6	3.8	8.9	13.4								
Murray	151	149	11.9	11.8	172	152	13.5	12.0	1	–	1	6.6	–	6.8								
Muskogee	1,000	968	14.2	13.9	831	818	11.8	11.8	5	7	15	5.0	7.2	14.0								
Noble	135	141	12.0	12.4	108	109	9.6	9.6	2	–	1	14.8	–	7.0								
Nowata	126	138	11.8	13.0	127	136	11.8	12.8	2	–	1	15.9	–	9.0								
Okfuskee	145	143	12.5	12.1	186	163	16.0	13.8	2	1	1	13.8	7.0	6.8								
Oklahoma	11,776	10,960	17.3	16.6	6,147	6,372	9.0	9.6	121	125	127	10.3	11.4	12.6								
Okmulgee	564	550	14.2	13.9	486	458	12.2	11.6	7	8	5	12.4	14.5	9.7								
Osage	456	523	10.1	11.7	377	380	8.4	8.5	2	3	5	4.4	5.7	10.1								
Ottawa	417	460	12.7	13.8	407	444	12.4	13.4	4	2	2	9.6	4.3	4.6								
Pawnee	190	212	11.3	12.7	180	210	10.7	12.6	1	1	3	5.3	4.7	15.2								
Payne	880	793	12.7	11.6	532	507	7.7	7.4	5	4	–	5.7	5.0	–								
Pittsburg	532	495	12.0	11.3	500	580	11.3	13.2	7	4	5	13.2	8.1	9.7								
Pontotoc	478	541	13.6	15.4	390	487	11.1	13.9	4	6	2	8.4	11.1	4.3								
Pottawatomie	870	912	12.8	13.9	721	737	10.6	11.2	5	5	8	5.7	5.5	9.5								
Pushmataha	136	130	11.6	11.2	171	184	14.6	15.8	–	3	–	–	23.1	–								
Roger Mills	45	42	13.8	12.3	37	46	11.4	13.4	1	–	2	22.2	–	48.8								
Rogers	938	925	11.9	13.0	615	543	7.8	7.6	8	5	5	8.5	5.4	6.0								
Seminole	356	378	14.4	15.2	319	348	12.9	14.0	3	4	5	8.4	10.6	14.1								
Sequoyah	568	538	14.0	13.8	429	399	10.6	10.2	3	6	3	5.3	11.2	5.8								
Stephens	574	512	13.4	11.9	557	618	13.0	14.3	6	2	4	10.5	3.9	7.0								
Texas	420	392	20.8	19.4	130	144	6.4	7.1	5	8	1	11.9	20.4	4.0								

See footnotes at end of table.

County and City Data Book: 2007

235

U.S. Census Bureau

Table B-5. Counties — **Births, Deaths, and Infant Deaths**—Con.

[Includes United States, states, and 3,141 counties/county equivalents defined as of February 22, 2005. For more information on these areas, see Appendix C, Geographic Information]

County	Births				Deaths				Infant deaths[2]					
	Number		Rate per 1,000 population[1]		Number		Rate per 1,000 population[1]		Number			Rate per 1,000 live births[3]		
	2004	2000	2004	2000	2004	2000	2004	2000	2004	2000	1990	2004	2000	1990
OKLAHOMA—Con.														
Tillman	124	109	14.2	11.8	121	123	13.9	13.3	1	2	1	8.1	18.3	7.1
Tulsa	9,193	9,343	16.2	16.6	5,055	5,161	8.9	9.2	61	84	82	6.6	9.0	9.3
Wagoner	804	720	12.8	12.5	445	382	7.1	6.6	5	3	2	6.2	4.2	3.4
Washington	578	594	11.8	12.1	542	578	11.0	11.8	4	2	4	6.9	3.4	6.5
Washita	132	125	11.5	10.9	143	123	12.5	10.7	1	1	–	7.6	8.0	–
Woods	90	82	10.6	9.1	116	132	13.6	14.6	–	1	–	–	12.2	–
Woodward	280	253	14.8	13.7	169	195	8.9	10.6	5	1	–	17.9	4.0	–
OREGON	45,678	45,804	12.7	13.3	30,313	29,552	8.4	8.6	251	255	354	5.5	5.6	8.3
Baker	151	170	9.2	10.2	207	186	12.6	11.1	2	–	1	13.2	–	5.2
Benton	759	760	9.7	9.7	485	440	6.2	5.6	2	1	6	2.6	1.3	6.8
Clackamas	4,006	4,184	11.0	12.3	2,729	2,635	7.5	7.8	17	24	38	4.2	5.7	9.4
Clatsop	396	386	10.9	10.8	360	376	9.9	10.6	2	4	3	5.1	10.4	6.8
Columbia	480	527	10.2	12.1	404	384	8.6	8.8	2	–	7	4.2	–	13.1
Coos	639	619	10.0	9.9	829	813	13.0	13.0	4	2	8	6.3	3.2	10.9
Crook	248	213	11.6	11.0	172	205	8.0	10.6	–	3	5	–	14.1	24.0
Curry	162	161	7.3	7.6	320	349	14.4	16.5	2	1	4	12.3	6.2	16.1
Deschutes	1,667	1,439	12.4	12.3	969	916	7.2	7.9	10	10	5	6.0	6.9	4.7
Douglas	1,103	1,054	10.7	10.5	1,213	1,157	11.8	11.5	6	6	9	5.4	5.7	7.2
Gilliam	18	17	9.9	8.9	27	21	14.8	11.0	–	–	–	–	–	–
Grant	68	69	9.2	8.7	77	101	10.5	12.8	1	–	1	14.7	–	8.9
Harney	76	95	10.7	12.5	66	80	9.3	10.5	1	1	–	13.2	10.5	–
Hood River	315	361	14.9	17.6	181	177	8.6	8.6	4	4	–	12.7	11.1	–
Jackson	2,112	2,051	10.9	11.3	1,893	1,878	9.8	10.3	13	6	18	6.2	2.9	8.6
Jefferson	310	316	15.6	16.5	160	168	8.1	8.8	1	3	6	3.2	9.5	20.5
Josephine	803	762	10.1	10.0	1,030	965	12.9	12.7	5	4	4	6.2	5.2	4.8
Klamath	735	831	11.3	13.0	706	648	10.8	10.1	5	7	10	6.8	8.4	11.6
Lake	57	83	7.7	11.2	87	90	11.8	12.1	1	–	–	17.5	–	–
Lane	3,491	3,705	10.5	11.5	2,970	2,845	9.0	8.8	18	28	25	5.2	7.6	6.4
Lincoln	462	438	10.2	9.9	529	542	11.7	12.2	5	7	2	10.8	16.0	4.1
Linn	1,396	1,398	13.0	13.6	1,069	927	10.0	9.0	8	6	9	5.7	4.3	6.6
Malheur	457	523	14.6	16.6	277	291	8.8	9.2	2	2	6	4.4	3.8	12.7
Marion	4,674	4,542	15.5	15.9	2,438	2,430	8.1	8.5	22	28	31	4.7	6.2	8.0
Morrow	178	149	15.2	13.5	83	72	7.1	6.5	1	1	1	5.6	6.7	8.1
Multnomah	9,417	9,467	14.0	14.3	5,435	5,718	8.1	8.6	54	60	76	5.7	6.3	8.1
Polk	805	739	11.9	11.8	549	487	8.1	7.8	10	5	5	12.4	6.8	7.4
Sherman	15	16	8.7	8.3	20	19	11.6	9.9	–	–	–	–	–	–
Tillamook	275	240	11.0	9.9	262	261	10.5	10.8	–	1	4	–	4.2	13.7
Umatilla	1,077	1,039	14.6	14.7	613	572	8.3	8.1	4	3	15	3.7	2.9	15.4
Union	268	300	11.0	12.2	233	217	9.5	8.8	–	5	1	–	16.7	2.9
Wallowa	57	70	8.2	9.7	70	82	10.0	11.4	–	1	2	–	14.3	24.1
Wasco	265	307	11.3	12.9	285	280	12.1	11.8	3	2	2	11.3	6.5	6.6
Washington	7,576	7,559	15.5	16.9	2,802	2,573	5.7	5.7	43	23	39	5.7	3.0	7.3
Wheeler	8	11	5.5	7.1	22	23	15.0	14.9	–	–	–	–	–	–
Yamhill	1,152	1,203	12.7	14.1	741	624	8.2	7.3	3	7	11	2.6	5.8	11.0
PENNSYLVANIA	144,748	146,281	11.7	11.9	127,640	130,813	10.3	10.6	1,049	1,039	1,643	7.2	7.1	9.6
Adams	1,088	1,048	11.1	11.4	864	811	8.8	8.9	9	1	9	8.3	1.0	7.6
Allegheny	13,231	14,293	10.6	11.2	14,572	15,120	11.7	11.8	97	120	173	7.3	8.4	9.6
Armstrong	721	739	10.1	10.2	838	867	11.7	12.0	1	8	9	1.4	10.8	10.1
Beaver	1,781	1,893	10.0	10.4	2,090	2,070	11.7	11.4	13	11	23	7.3	5.8	9.4
Bedford	481	591	9.6	11.8	485	537	9.7	10.7	2	4	4	4.2	6.8	6.7
Berks	4,938	4,711	12.6	12.6	3,457	3,624	8.8	9.7	33	31	44	6.7	6.6	8.9
Blair	1,476	1,500	11.6	11.6	1,552	1,590	12.2	12.3	8	6	16	5.4	4.0	10.0
Bradford	776	718	12.4	11.4	636	654	10.2	10.4	5	5	3	6.4	7.0	3.3
Bucks	6,919	7,338	11.2	12.2	5,141	5,031	8.3	8.4	53	27	53	7.7	3.7	6.6
Butler	2,063	2,070	11.4	11.9	1,874	1,640	10.4	9.4	15	10	17	7.3	4.8	8.3
Cambria	1,512	1,570	10.2	10.3	1,869	2,014	12.6	13.2	6	16	15	4.0	10.2	7.9
Cameron	52	70	9.2	11.8	81	70	14.3	11.8	–	–	1	–	–	11.4
Carbon	619	571	10.1	9.7	729	790	11.9	13.4	3	3	4	4.8	5.3	6.2
Centre	1,257	1,278	9.0	9.4	833	864	6.0	6.4	8	3	15	6.4	2.3	9.8
Chester	6,076	5,850	13.0	13.4	3,298	3,319	7.1	7.6	39	37	48	6.4	6.3	8.1
Clarion	404	419	10.0	10.0	432	437	10.7	10.5	–	2	3	–	4.8	6.0
Clearfield	813	819	9.8	9.8	906	909	10.9	10.9	7	5	11	8.6	6.1	11.0
Clinton	420	445	11.3	11.7	419	429	11.2	11.3	4	3	6	9.5	6.7	12.8
Columbia	598	614	9.2	9.6	670	630	10.3	9.8	3	–	9	5.0	–	11.9
Crawford	1,051	1,109	11.7	12.3	936	977	10.4	10.8	6	10	13	5.7	9.0	11.4
Cumberland	2,299	2,224	10.4	10.4	2,041	1,987	9.2	9.3	13	8	21	5.7	3.6	8.6
Dauphin	3,230	3,141	12.8	12.5	2,433	2,453	9.6	9.7	25	25	33	7.7	8.0	8.9
Delaware	6,738	6,913	12.2	12.5	5,531	5,886	10.0	10.7	55	41	71	8.2	5.9	8.4
Elk	309	394	9.1	11.2	373	361	11.0	10.3	–	2	6	–	5.1	12.7
Erie	3,286	3,479	11.7	12.4	2,697	2,745	9.6	9.8	19	23	58	5.8	6.6	13.8

See footnotes at end of table.

Table B-5. Counties — **Births, Deaths, and Infant Deaths**—Con.

[Includes United States, states, and 3,141 counties/county equivalents defined as of February 22, 2005. For more information on these areas, see Appendix C, Geographic Information]

County	Births Number 2004	2000	Births Rate per 1,000 population[1] 2004	2000	Deaths Number 2004	2000	Deaths Rate per 1,000 population[1] 2004	2000	Infant deaths[2] Number 2004	2000	1990	Infant deaths[2] Rate per 1,000 live births[3] 2004	2000	1990
PENNSYLVANIA—Con.														
Fayette	1,416	1,537	9.6	10.3	1,756	1,815	12.0	12.2	11	19	21	7.8	12.4	11.2
Forest	37	40	6.4	8.1	74	77	12.8	15.6	1	–	–	27.0	–	–
Franklin	1,688	1,667	12.5	12.9	1,280	1,289	9.5	10.0	13	12	12	7.7	7.2	7.2
Fulton	160	154	11.0	10.8	136	135	9.3	9.5	1	–	3	6.3	–	18.0
Greene	441	371	11.0	9.1	427	449	10.7	11.0	4	5	1	9.1	13.5	2.2
Huntingdon	413	515	9.0	11.3	450	437	9.8	9.6	1	2	5	2.4	3.9	9.5
Indiana	856	857	9.6	9.6	853	895	9.6	10.0	3	3	7	3.5	3.5	6.7
Jefferson	483	525	10.5	11.4	547	539	11.9	11.7	2	3	3	4.1	5.7	5.1
Juniata	311	313	13.3	13.7	198	239	8.5	10.5	5	3	2	16.1	9.6	7.6
Lackawanna	2,254	2,151	10.7	10.1	2,755	2,951	13.1	13.9	13	14	15	5.8	6.5	5.6
Lancaster	6,871	6,871	14.1	14.6	4,422	4,265	9.1	9.0	57	45	72	8.3	6.5	9.9
Lawrence	965	1,055	10.4	11.1	1,198	1,178	12.9	12.4	14	10	7	14.5	9.5	5.9
Lebanon	1,531	1,447	12.3	12.0	1,329	1,285	10.7	10.7	7	8	14	4.6	5.5	9.2
Lehigh	4,100	3,780	12.6	12.1	3,067	3,259	9.4	10.4	15	29	29	3.7	7.7	7.0
Luzerne	3,128	3,012	10.0	9.5	4,208	4,491	13.4	14.1	14	20	25	4.5	6.6	6.6
Lycoming	1,344	1,342	11.3	11.2	1,229	1,267	10.4	10.6	3	8	14	2.2	6.0	8.2
McKean	440	481	9.8	10.5	521	584	11.6	12.8	6	4	9	13.6	8.3	14.2
Mercer	1,280	1,338	10.7	11.1	1,354	1,543	11.3	12.8	13	15	11	10.2	11.2	7.5
Mifflin	568	598	12.3	12.9	535	527	11.6	11.3	3	4	6	5.3	6.7	8.9
Monroe	1,590	1,456	10.0	10.4	1,174	1,154	7.4	8.3	17	6	16	10.7	4.1	10.7
Montgomery	9,587	9,573	12.4	12.7	7,178	7,256	9.3	9.7	57	55	70	5.9	5.7	7.1
Montour	208	214	11.6	11.7	213	239	11.8	13.1	1	2	1	4.8	9.3	4.0
Northampton	3,234	2,866	11.4	10.7	2,661	2,454	9.4	9.2	17	13	24	5.3	4.5	7.1
Northumberland	923	923	9.9	9.8	1,212	1,203	13.1	12.7	8	6	11	8.7	6.5	9.4
Perry	542	513	12.2	11.8	416	360	9.3	8.3	5	2	3	9.2	3.9	4.9
Philadelphia	21,821	21,895	14.8	14.5	16,293	17,717	11.1	11.7	244	230	461	11.2	10.5	15.5
Pike	327	411	6.1	8.8	291	385	5.4	8.3	2	–	1	6.1	–	2.2
Potter	188	217	10.5	12.0	195	197	10.9	10.9	2	3	2	10.6	13.8	7.9
Schuylkill	1,341	1,437	9.1	9.6	2,144	2,108	14.5	14.0	4	11	10	3.0	7.7	5.6
Snyder	458	439	12.0	11.7	315	361	8.3	9.6	–	3	6	–	6.8	11.2
Somerset	719	868	9.1	11.5	875	924	11.0	11.5	2	8	10	2.8	9.2	10.6
Sullivan	53	50	8.2	7.6	99	101	15.4	15.4	–	1	1	–	20.0	18.2
Susquehanna	410	495	9.8	11.7	437	459	10.4	10.9	2	5	5	4.9	10.1	7.8
Tioga	390	473	9.4	11.4	360	463	8.6	11.2	2	3	7	5.1	6.3	13.1
Union	414	395	9.7	9.5	341	358	8.0	8.6	4	3	3	9.7	7.6	7.2
Venango	595	630	10.6	11.0	688	650	12.3	11.3	3	2	7	5.0	3.2	8.9
Warren	403	493	9.5	11.3	447	482	10.5	11.0	4	6	3	9.9	12.2	5.2
Washington	2,031	2,112	9.9	10.4	2,501	2,448	12.2	12.1	11	22	16	5.4	10.4	6.6
Wayne	449	541	9.0	11.3	602	572	12.1	11.9	2	–	2	4.5	–	3.6
Westmoreland	3,387	3,591	9.2	9.7	4,362	4,269	11.9	11.5	22	25	30	6.5	7.0	6.8
Wyoming	313	312	11.1	11.1	251	260	8.9	9.3	–	2	1	–	6.4	2.6
York	4,941	4,526	12.3	11.8	3,489	3,353	8.7	8.8	30	26	32	6.1	5.7	6.5
RHODE ISLAND	12,779	12,505	11.8	11.9	9,769	10,027	9.0	9.5	68	79	123	5.3	6.3	8.1
Bristol	448	502	8.5	9.9	515	529	9.7	10.4	1	4	2	2.2	8.0	3.1
Kent	1,737	1,929	10.1	11.5	1,693	1,688	9.9	10.1	11	11	19	6.3	5.7	8.7
Newport	907	946	10.7	11.0	804	751	9.5	8.8	2	4	11	2.2	4.2	9.3
Providence	8,464	7,879	13.2	12.7	5,786	6,123	9.0	9.8	48	57	79	5.7	7.2	8.2
Washington	1,223	1,249	9.5	10.1	971	936	7.6	7.5	6	3	12	4.9	2.4	7.7
SOUTH CAROLINA	56,590	56,114	13.5	13.9	37,276	36,948	8.9	9.2	525	488	683	9.3	8.7	11.7
Abbeville	303	336	11.5	12.8	245	229	9.3	8.7	7	3	1	23.1	8.9	2.9
Aiken	1,893	1,943	12.7	13.6	1,407	1,321	9.5	9.2	22	17	23	11.6	8.7	11.0
Allendale	150	178	13.6	15.9	119	109	10.8	9.7	3	3	1	20.0	16.9	5.0
Anderson	2,206	2,218	12.7	13.3	1,826	1,700	10.5	10.2	20	21	25	9.1	9.5	11.7
Bamberg	176	233	11.0	14.0	156	210	9.8	12.6	2	3	5	11.4	12.9	17.1
Barnwell	341	335	14.6	14.3	224	223	9.6	9.5	1	7	6	2.9	20.9	17.4
Beaufort	2,152	1,896	16.1	15.5	1,046	921	7.8	7.5	13	7	15	6.0	3.7	8.3
Berkeley	2,221	2,115	14.9	14.8	934	879	6.3	6.1	21	15	36	9.5	7.1	13.8
Calhoun	157	193	10.3	12.7	167	158	11.0	10.4	1	2	3	6.4	10.4	16.3
Charleston	4,762	4,588	14.5	14.8	2,692	2,905	8.2	9.3	55	30	69	11.5	6.5	12.0
Cherokee	639	784	11.9	14.9	622	529	11.6	10.0	11	4	7	17.2	5.1	10.1
Chester	419	514	12.5	15.1	345	341	10.3	10.0	6	5	4	14.3	9.7	7.6
Chesterfield	529	620	12.2	14.4	440	425	10.2	9.9	6	7	2	11.3	11.3	3.2
Clarendon	432	440	13.1	13.5	337	331	10.2	10.2	3	6	10	6.9	13.6	19.5
Colleton	499	590	12.6	15.4	387	386	9.8	10.1	6	1	7	12.0	1.7	13.2
Darlington	901	953	13.3	14.1	696	742	10.3	11.0	7	11	22	7.8	11.5	22.4
Dillon	480	519	15.4	16.9	358	316	11.5	10.3	1	7	8	2.1	13.5	14.3
Dorchester	1,476	1,228	13.8	12.7	728	715	6.8	7.4	12	13	12	8.1	10.6	7.5
Edgefield	252	299	10.0	12.2	207	198	8.2	8.1	–	5	2	–	16.7	6.4
Fairfield	306	342	12.7	14.5	282	322	11.7	13.7	8	2	3	26.1	5.8	7.9

See footnotes at end of table.

[Includes United States, states, and 3,141 counties/county equivalents defined as of February 22, 2005. For more information on these areas, see Appendix C, Geographic Information]

County	Births				Deaths				Infant deaths[2]					
	Number		Rate per 1,000 population[1]		Number		Rate per 1,000 population[1]		Number			Rate per 1,000 live births[3]		
	2004	2000	2004	2000	2004	2000	2004	2000	2004	2000	1990	2004	2000	1990
SOUTH CAROLINA—Con.														
Florence	1,844	1,867	14.2	14.8	1,364	1,327	10.5	10.5	21	23	28	11.4	12.3	14.3
Georgetown	704	770	11.8	13.7	597	532	10.0	9.5	9	12	12	12.8	15.6	14.7
Greenville	5,739	5,390	14.3	14.1	3,171	3,355	7.9	8.8	41	28	60	7.1	5.2	11.9
Greenwood	848	954	12.5	14.4	660	702	9.8	10.6	15	11	17	17.7	11.5	18.1
Hampton	266	297	12.5	13.9	224	226	10.5	10.6	7	5	2	26.3	16.8	6.0
Horry	2,806	2,570	12.9	13.0	2,009	1,941	9.2	9.8	27	23	24	9.6	8.9	10.3
Jasper	321	286	15.1	13.8	174	150	8.2	7.2	1	2	4	3.1	7.0	12.9
Kershaw	706	729	12.7	13.8	514	516	9.3	9.8	2	3	10	2.8	4.1	15.2
Lancaster	787	831	12.5	13.5	573	624	9.1	10.2	7	12	9	8.9	14.4	10.3
Laurens	804	823	11.5	11.8	723	711	10.3	10.2	10	6	6	12.4	7.3	6.7
Lee	263	264	12.7	13.1	227	188	11.0	9.3	2	4	7	7.6	15.2	23.3
Lexington	3,116	3,003	13.5	13.8	1,793	1,694	7.8	7.8	14	26	31	4.5	8.7	11.0
McCormick	76	99	7.5	9.9	114	99	11.3	9.9	1	1	1	13.2	10.1	8.5
Marion	493	527	14.1	14.9	350	417	10.0	11.8	4	5	8	8.1	9.5	14.1
Marlboro	352	434	12.4	15.1	304	356	10.7	12.4	3	7	6	8.5	16.1	12.4
Newberry	513	497	13.8	13.8	387	356	10.4	9.8	1	2	5	1.9	4.0	10.4
Oconee	846	768	12.3	11.6	684	639	9.9	9.6	5	7	14	5.9	9.1	17.3
Orangeburg	1,270	1,312	13.8	14.3	954	935	10.4	10.2	13	21	15	10.2	16.0	10.3
Pickens	1,269	1,330	11.2	12.0	875	902	7.8	8.1	11	7	10	8.7	5.3	7.9
Richland	4,608	4,464	13.7	13.9	2,464	2,607	7.3	8.1	40	39	54	8.7	8.7	11.3
Saluda	254	260	13.5	13.6	193	202	10.3	10.5	2	2	4	7.9	7.7	17.2
Spartanburg	3,490	3,344	13.2	13.1	2,615	2,602	9.9	10.2	49	22	34	14.0	6.6	9.9
Sumter	1,631	1,742	15.4	16.6	926	948	8.8	9.1	14	15	23	8.6	8.6	12.1
Union	323	376	11.3	12.6	378	357	13.2	11.9	4	6	3	12.4	16.0	6.6
Williamsburg	515	543	14.4	14.6	393	361	11.0	9.7	5	8	8	9.7	14.7	12.6
York	2,452	2,310	13.4	13.9	1,392	1,241	7.6	7.5	12	22	27	4.9	9.5	12.2
SOUTH DAKOTA	11,338	10,345	14.7	13.7	6,833	7,021	8.9	9.3	93	57	111	8.2	5.5	10.1
Aurora	32	33	10.9	10.8	32	38	10.9	12.4	1	–	–	31.3	–	–
Beadle	195	172	12.2	10.1	199	216	12.4	12.7	2	1	3	10.3	5.8	12.2
Bennett	69	59	19.4	16.5	31	27	8.7	7.6	1	–	–	14.5	–	–
Bon Homme	53	50	7.4	6.9	69	87	9.7	12.0	1	–	–	18.9	–	–
Brookings	320	323	11.4	11.4	186	191	6.6	6.8	2	1	1	6.3	3.1	3.1
Brown	465	486	13.4	13.7	336	368	9.7	10.4	–	3	4	–	6.2	8.9
Brule	60	54	11.6	10.1	50	48	9.6	9.0	–	–	–	–	–	–
Buffalo	55	29	26.5	14.5	18	30	8.7	15.0	1	–	1	18.2	–	23.8
Butte	133	127	14.4	13.9	82	92	8.9	10.1	–	1	–	–	7.9	–
Campbell	8	15	5.0	8.4	12	14	7.5	7.9	–	–	1	–	–	45.5
Charles Mix	177	142	19.5	15.2	96	112	10.6	12.0	2	1	3	11.3	7.0	18.5
Clark	49	40	12.5	9.7	44	38	11.3	9.2	–	–	–	–	–	–
Clay	147	175	11.3	13.0	100	114	7.7	8.5	1	–	3	6.8	–	21.9
Codington	393	370	15.1	14.3	222	217	8.6	8.4	5	2	–	12.7	5.4	–
Corson	82	97	18.8	23.0	45	46	10.3	10.9	1	1	2	12.2	10.3	24.1
Custer	66	51	8.4	7.0	67	72	8.5	9.9	–	–	4	–	–	61.5
Davison	309	246	16.4	13.1	210	189	11.1	10.1	5	–	1	16.2	–	3.9
Day	64	68	11.0	10.9	91	88	15.6	14.1	1	–	1	15.6	–	11.6
Deuel	63	44	14.7	9.8	61	48	14.2	10.7	1	–	–	15.9	–	–
Dewey	159	129	25.9	21.5	70	58	11.4	9.7	3	–	2	18.9	–	14.7
Douglas	35	36	10.6	10.5	38	47	11.5	13.7	–	–	1	–	–	19.2
Edmunds	52	36	12.7	8.3	58	72	14.2	16.5	–	–	–	–	–	–
Fall River	76	63	10.4	8.5	112	113	15.3	15.2	–	–	1	–	–	12.0
Faulk	24	19	9.9	7.2	29	26	11.9	9.9	–	–	–	–	–	–
Grant	70	74	9.3	9.5	103	105	13.7	13.4	–	2	1	–	27.0	8.1
Gregory	46	39	10.5	8.2	66	94	15.1	19.7	–	–	1	–	–	14.5
Haakon	19	22	9.6	10.1	26	43	13.2	19.8	–	–	–	–	–	–
Hamlin	91	83	16.2	15.0	74	61	13.2	11.0	4	–	–	44.0	–	–
Hand	32	24	9.4	6.5	50	46	14.7	12.4	–	–	–	–	–	–
Hanson	50	59	13.5	18.7	16	19	4.3	6.0	–	–	2	–	–	40.8
Harding	13	15	10.5	11.2	6	7	4.8	5.2	–	–	–	–	–	–
Hughes	195	196	11.6	11.9	119	142	7.1	8.6	2	–	–	10.3	–	–
Hutchinson	72	89	9.4	11.0	129	110	16.9	13.6	1	–	1	13.9	–	11.0
Hyde	24	18	14.8	10.8	25	21	15.4	12.6	–	–	–	–	–	–
Jackson	62	54	21.6	18.4	33	21	11.5	7.1	2	1	–	32.3	18.5	–
Jerauld	23	17	10.8	7.4	32	31	15.0	13.6	–	–	1	–	–	33.3
Jones	12	4	11.1	3.4	12	10	11.1	8.5	–	–	–	–	–	–
Kingsbury	52	57	9.5	9.8	93	97	16.9	16.7	2	–	–	38.5	–	–
Lake	135	110	12.3	9.8	103	102	9.4	9.1	–	–	4	–	–	31.3
Lawrence	264	214	11.8	9.8	197	191	8.8	8.8	1	–	3	3.8	–	10.8
Lincoln	582	367	18.5	14.9	209	157	6.6	6.4	3	1	–	5.2	2.7	–
Lyman	80	69	20.3	17.6	30	36	7.6	9.2	–	2	–	–	29.0	–
McCook	86	71	14.6	12.1	75	53	12.7	9.1	–	–	–	–	–	–
McPherson	20	26	7.5	9.0	37	50	13.8	17.3	–	–	–	–	–	–
Marshall	53	34	12.1	7.4	49	48	11.2	10.5	1	–	–	18.9	–	–

See footnotes at end of table.

County and City Data Book: 2007

U.S. Census Bureau

Table B-5. Counties — **Births, Deaths, and Infant Deaths**—Con.

[Includes United States, states, and 3,141 counties/county equivalents defined as of February 22, 2005. For more information on these areas, see Appendix C, Geographic Information]

County	Births Number 2004	2000	Rate per 1,000 population[1] 2004	2000	Deaths Number 2004	2000	Rate per 1,000 population[1] 2004	2000	Infant deaths[2] Number 2004	2000	1990	Rate per 1,000 live births[3] 2004	2000	1990
SOUTH DAKOTA—Con.														
Meade	330	311	13.4	12.8	211	173	8.6	7.1	2	3	3	6.1	9.6	8.6
Mellette	43	29	20.8	13.9	33	25	15.9	12.0	4	–	2	93.0	–	45.5
Miner	28	34	10.6	11.8	32	40	12.1	13.9	–	–	–	–	–	–
Minnehaha	2,548	2,310	16.2	15.5	1,024	1,084	6.5	7.3	13	12	24	5.1	5.2	11.4
Moody	97	74	14.7	11.2	57	70	8.7	10.6	2	1	–	20.6	13.5	–
Pennington	1,536	1,415	16.5	15.9	639	655	6.9	7.4	20	14	13	13.0	9.9	7.7
Perkins	26	28	8.4	8.4	38	48	12.2	14.4	–	2	–	–	–	44.4
Potter	26	28	10.6	10.5	33	42	13.4	15.7	1	–	–	38.5	–	–
Roberts	159	141	15.7	14.1	125	127	12.4	12.7	–	–	1	–	–	6.2
Sanborn	29	30	11.1	11.2	24	26	9.2	9.7	–	–	–	–	–	–
Shannon	350	343	26.2	27.3	135	111	10.1	8.9	4	4	10	11.4	11.7	30.6
Spink	84	88	12.1	11.8	66	89	9.5	12.0	–	–	3	–	–	28.3
Stanley	39	39	13.7	14.0	14	19	4.9	6.8	–	–	1	–	–	27.0
Sully	25	15	17.6	9.7	18	11	12.7	7.1	–	–	–	–	–	–
Todd	252	244	25.9	26.8	79	81	8.1	8.9	–	1	2	–	4.1	7.1
Tripp	83	79	13.6	12.4	65	80	10.6	12.5	–	2	1	–	25.3	9.9
Turner	81	87	9.4	9.8	100	118	11.6	13.3	3	–	2	37.0	–	22.5
Union	163	184	12.3	14.6	95	116	7.2	9.2	–	–	2	–	–	14.5
Walworth	64	69	11.6	11.6	98	87	17.7	14.7	–	1	–	–	14.5	–
Yankton	266	240	12.2	11.1	200	204	9.2	9.4	1	2	1	3.8	8.3	3.4
Ziebach	42	51	15.9	20.5	5	20	1.9	8.0	–	1	3	–	19.6	68.2
TENNESSEE	79,642	79,611	13.5	14.0	55,829	55,246	9.5	9.7	687	724	771	8.6	9.1	10.3
Anderson	845	797	11.7	11.2	826	790	11.5	11.1	6	1	9	7.1	1.3	10.4
Bedford	656	614	15.9	16.2	392	388	9.5	10.3	8	6	5	12.2	9.8	11.4
Benton	162	178	9.8	10.8	216	225	13.1	13.6	1	2	3	6.2	11.2	16.9
Bledsoe	133	138	10.4	11.1	107	120	8.4	9.7	1	–	–	7.5	–	–
Blount	1,333	1,314	11.8	12.4	1,160	1,047	10.2	9.9	9	8	11	6.8	6.1	9.6
Bradley	1,203	1,188	13.2	13.5	791	823	8.7	9.3	17	9	8	14.1	7.6	7.4
Campbell	483	478	11.9	12.0	460	437	11.3	10.9	3	5	6	6.2	10.5	12.8
Cannon	135	130	10.2	10.1	148	147	11.1	11.4	1	1	1	7.4	7.7	6.7
Carroll	330	359	11.2	12.2	396	457	13.5	15.5	3	9	7	9.1	25.1	19.1
Carter	637	596	10.9	10.5	645	617	11.0	10.9	11	5	4	17.3	8.4	6.8
Cheatham	491	488	12.9	13.5	276	258	7.3	7.1	6	3	1	12.2	6.1	2.4
Chester	185	175	11.7	11.3	132	165	8.3	10.6	–	3	–	–	17.1	–
Claiborne	354	365	11.5	12.2	330	357	10.7	11.9	1	5	6	2.8	13.7	17.2
Clay	114	96	14.3	12.0	116	86	14.5	10.8	1	1	1	8.8	10.4	11.1
Cocke	402	414	11.6	12.3	445	380	12.8	11.3	2	2	2	5.0	4.8	4.9
Coffee	710	660	14.2	13.7	581	508	11.6	10.5	8	6	6	11.3	9.1	9.0
Crockett	158	198	10.8	13.6	189	180	13.0	12.4	2	–	4	12.7	–	22.9
Cumberland	515	479	10.3	10.2	539	552	10.7	11.7	3	7	2	5.8	14.6	4.7
Davidson	9,011	8,983	15.8	15.8	4,854	5,060	8.5	8.9	59	90	82	6.5	10.0	9.4
Decatur	116	144	9.9	12.3	168	149	14.4	12.7	–	1	1	–	6.9	8.1
DeKalb	246	200	13.5	11.5	226	206	12.4	11.8	4	2	2	16.3	10.0	11.5
Dickson	643	634	14.2	14.6	405	367	8.9	8.5	4	1	11	6.2	1.6	19.3
Dyer	503	516	13.4	13.8	403	464	10.7	12.4	4	8	7	8.0	15.5	12.7
Fayette	407	394	12.1	13.5	334	276	10.0	9.5	2	2	4	4.9	5.1	10.7
Fentress	208	209	12.3	12.6	202	180	11.9	10.8	3	3	3	14.4	14.4	17.4
Franklin	447	464	11.0	11.8	436	428	10.7	10.9	2	1	5	4.5	2.2	11.9
Gibson	604	666	12.6	13.8	653	699	13.6	14.5	2	9	10	3.3	13.5	14.5
Giles	311	353	10.6	12.0	398	314	13.6	10.7	2	3	1	6.4	8.5	2.6
Grainger	234	238	10.7	11.5	236	203	10.8	9.8	4	2	3	17.1	8.4	14.3
Greene	716	782	11.1	12.4	709	692	11.0	11.0	8	10	12	11.2	12.8	17.8
Grundy	195	187	13.5	13.0	166	207	11.5	14.4	2	1	4	10.3	5.3	21.7
Hamblen	837	869	14.1	14.9	625	625	10.5	10.7	5	4	10	6.0	4.6	13.5
Hamilton	3,979	4,034	12.8	13.1	3,227	3,210	10.4	10.4	30	51	35	7.5	12.6	8.0
Hancock	94	79	14.1	11.7	71	89	10.6	13.1	1	1	1	10.6	12.7	11.8
Hardeman	331	365	11.8	13.0	276	302	9.8	10.7	7	7	7	21.1	19.2	18.4
Hardin	274	281	10.6	11.0	355	330	13.8	12.9	–	4	1	–	14.2	3.1
Hawkins	655	656	11.8	12.2	572	520	10.3	9.7	7	3	1	10.7	4.6	1.8
Haywood	264	301	13.4	15.2	214	221	10.9	11.1	3	2	2	11.4	6.6	6.3
Henderson	336	344	12.8	13.4	321	315	12.3	12.3	7	2	2	20.8	5.8	7.1
Henry	373	375	11.9	12.0	433	441	13.8	14.2	4	7	5	10.7	18.7	14.8
Hickman	265	300	11.2	13.4	215	247	9.1	11.0	1	–	3	3.8	–	15.2
Houston	109	94	13.7	11.7	107	88	13.5	11.0	1	–	1	9.2	–	13.7
Humphreys	235	219	13.0	12.2	227	193	12.5	10.8	–	3	1	–	13.7	4.7
Jackson	124	126	11.1	11.4	146	156	13.1	14.1	–	1	2	–	7.9	17.1
Jefferson	524	535	11.0	12.0	477	420	10.0	9.4	4	3	2	7.6	5.6	5.0
Johnson	171	164	9.5	9.4	208	176	11.5	10.0	4	–	4	23.4	–	28.4
Knox	5,086	4,797	12.7	12.5	3,617	3,618	9.0	9.5	23	23	33	4.5	4.8	7.0
Lake	70	76	9.2	9.6	101	107	13.2	13.5	1	–	2	14.3	–	24.7
Lauderdale	362	421	13.5	15.6	286	306	10.7	11.3	5	8	5	13.8	19.0	13.2
Lawrence	554	595	13.6	14.9	485	401	11.9	10.0	5	5	7	9.0	8.4	11.7

See footnotes at end of table.

[Includes United States, states, and 3,141 counties/county equivalents defined as of February 22, 2005. For more information on these areas, see Appendix C, Geographic Information]

County	Births Number 2004	Births Number 2000	Births Rate per 1,000 population[1] 2004	Births Rate 2000	Deaths Number 2004	Deaths Number 2000	Deaths Rate per 1,000 population[1] 2004	Deaths Rate 2000	Infant deaths[2] Number 2004	Infant Number 2000	Infant Number 1990	Infant deaths Rate per 1,000 live births[3] 2004	Infant Rate 2000	Infant Rate 1990
TENNESSEE—Con.														
Lewis	170	142	14.8	12.5	146	123	12.7	10.8	1	2	3	5.9	14.1	23.6
Lincoln	435	378	13.6	12.0	373	394	11.7	12.5	3	4	2	6.9	10.6	4.8
Loudon	510	479	12.1	12.2	455	429	10.8	10.9	3	5	7	5.9	10.4	16.4
McMinn	615	585	12.1	11.9	579	513	11.4	10.4	4	1	3	6.5	1.7	5.6
McNairy	344	351	13.7	14.2	313	341	12.5	13.8	2	4	3	5.8	11.4	10.6
Macon	270	268	12.6	13.1	235	195	11.0	9.5	2	1	–	7.4	3.7	–
Madison	1,339	1,394	14.2	15.1	870	909	9.2	9.9	21	13	17	15.7	9.3	13.4
Marion	325	371	11.7	13.4	296	287	10.7	10.3	4	4	4	12.3	10.8	11.9
Marshall	358	351	12.8	13.1	278	260	9.9	9.7	3	2	4	8.4	5.7	13.4
Maury	1,000	1,020	13.4	14.6	716	670	9.6	9.6	6	5	4	6.0	4.9	4.7
Meigs	117	154	10.2	13.8	116	95	10.1	8.5	–	1	1	–	6.5	9.3
Monroe	555	517	13.2	13.2	376	382	8.9	9.7	6	10	–	10.8	19.3	–
Montgomery	2,367	2,517	16.7	18.6	912	840	6.4	6.2	18	21	18	7.6	8.3	8.8
Moore	61	64	10.2	11.1	50	49	8.4	8.5	–	–	1	–	–	17.5
Morgan	215	221	10.7	11.2	199	189	9.9	9.6	3	2	2	14.0	9.0	8.8
Obion	412	416	12.7	12.8	358	369	11.1	11.4	7	6	4	17.0	14.4	9.2
Overton	268	247	13.1	12.2	254	248	12.4	12.3	3	4	1	11.2	16.2	4.6
Perry	98	92	12.9	12.0	96	95	12.6	12.4	2	–	1	20.4	–	11.9
Pickett	63	55	13.0	11.1	52	69	10.7	14.0	–	–	–	–	–	–
Polk	201	226	12.6	14.0	186	176	11.7	10.9	1	–	–	5.0	–	–
Putnam	924	860	14.1	13.8	615	642	9.4	10.3	9	6	5	9.7	7.0	6.8
Rhea	393	393	13.3	13.8	318	308	10.7	10.8	3	2	–	7.6	5.1	–
Roane	499	611	9.5	11.8	630	610	11.9	11.7	–	1	4	–	1.6	7.9
Robertson	956	868	16.1	15.8	525	504	8.9	9.2	6	3	2	6.3	3.5	3.0
Rutherford	3,335	2,794	15.9	15.2	1,265	1,141	6.0	6.2	17	16	11	5.1	5.7	5.5
Scott	317	288	14.6	13.6	242	201	11.1	9.5	4	–	–	12.6	–	–
Sequatchie	159	144	12.9	12.6	101	122	8.2	10.7	2	–	–	12.6	–	–
Sevier	977	967	12.7	13.5	680	650	8.8	9.1	3	2	10	3.1	2.1	13.6
Shelby	14,277	14,752	15.8	16.4	7,564	8,199	8.3	9.1	183	202	229	12.8	13.7	14.4
Smith	213	236	11.6	13.2	194	208	10.5	11.7	3	1	4	14.1	4.2	20.2
Stewart	147	139	11.5	11.2	120	154	9.4	12.4	4	1	1	27.2	7.2	7.9
Sullivan	1,533	1,814	10.1	11.9	1,770	1,708	11.6	11.2	15	21	15	9.8	11.6	8.3
Sumner	1,845	1,782	13.0	13.6	1,137	1,065	8.0	8.1	8	6	11	4.3	3.4	7.5
Tipton	743	742	13.6	14.4	459	469	8.4	9.1	16	11	9	21.5	14.8	13.2
Trousdale	90	93	12.0	12.7	101	94	13.5	12.8	–	–	3	–	–	36.1
Unicoi	190	176	10.8	10.0	243	227	13.8	12.9	1	2	4	5.3	11.4	24.0
Union	230	219	12.2	12.3	159	153	8.4	8.6	1	–	1	4.3	–	5.3
Van Buren	49	47	9.0	8.5	56	55	10.3	10.0	–	–	–	–	–	–
Warren	523	581	13.2	15.1	422	372	10.7	9.7	–	3	5	–	5.2	10.7
Washington	1,353	1,341	12.2	12.5	1,162	1,108	10.5	10.3	14	10	10	10.3	7.5	8.3
Wayne	177	181	10.5	10.8	180	150	10.7	8.9	–	2	1	–	11.0	5.2
Weakley	326	417	9.7	12.0	371	374	11.0	10.7	2	4	5	6.1	9.6	12.7
White	294	305	12.3	13.2	304	294	12.7	12.7	1	2	3	3.4	6.6	10.9
Williamson	1,945	1,701	13.2	13.3	737	625	5.0	4.9	8	11	9	4.1	6.5	8.0
Wilson	1,294	1,244	13.2	13.9	712	633	7.3	7.1	11	3	9	8.5	2.4	8.9
TEXAS	381,293	363,414	17.0	17.3	152,870	149,939	6.8	7.2	2,407	2,065	2,552	6.3	5.7	8.1
Anderson	670	673	12.0	12.2	597	626	10.7	11.4	3	3	3	4.5	4.5	4.9
Andrews	211	210	16.4	16.2	111	94	8.6	7.3	3	3	3	14.2	14.3	11.9
Angelina	1,296	1,311	15.9	16.3	777	824	9.6	10.3	6	8	13	4.6	6.1	11.3
Aransas	258	266	10.8	11.8	299	298	12.5	13.2	–	5	3	–	18.8	12.9
Archer	120	75	13.0	8.4	66	71	7.1	7.9	–	2	–	–	26.7	–
Armstrong	27	25	12.7	11.5	31	24	14.5	11.1	–	–	–	–	–	–
Atascosa	656	615	15.4	15.8	300	306	7.0	7.9	8	2	7	12.2	3.3	14.3
Austin	343	336	13.4	14.1	311	274	12.1	11.5	4	3	2	11.7	8.9	6.6
Bailey	127	115	19.0	17.5	68	55	10.2	8.3	–	–	–	–	–	–
Bandera	195	193	9.9	10.8	141	144	7.2	8.1	1	1	1	5.1	5.2	8.8
Bastrop	867	860	12.7	14.7	487	446	7.1	7.6	5	3	4	5.8	3.5	6.7
Baylor	47	37	11.9	9.1	66	64	16.8	15.7	–	–	1	–	–	15.4
Bee	370	409	11.2	12.7	223	227	6.8	7.0	2	3	3	5.4	7.3	6.5
Bell	4,923	5,389	19.7	22.6	1,657	1,555	6.6	6.5	46	40	47	9.3	7.4	10.0
Bexar	25,422	24,038	17.0	17.2	10,456	10,190	7.0	7.3	157	118	154	6.2	4.9	7.0
Blanco	111	111	12.3	13.1	93	104	10.3	12.3	3	1	–	27.0	9.0	–
Borden	2	6	2.9	8.4	1	3	1.5	4.2	–	–	–	–	–	–
Bosque	186	219	10.4	12.7	247	278	13.8	16.1	2	2	1	10.8	9.1	5.8
Bowie	1,133	1,220	12.6	13.7	975	992	10.8	11.1	11	6	12	9.7	4.9	9.8
Brazoria	4,291	3,992	15.8	16.4	1,688	1,610	6.2	6.6	25	19	26	5.8	4.8	7.9
Brazos	2,384	2,227	15.3	14.6	744	742	4.8	4.9	9	8	9	3.8	3.6	4.8
Brewster	104	115	11.3	13.0	82	79	8.9	8.9	1	4	–	–	8.7	33.1
Briscoe	17	29	10.1	16.3	14	19	8.3	10.7	–	1	–	–	34.5	–
Brooks	140	135	18.1	17.0	47	69	6.1	8.7	–	–	2	–	–	13.1
Brown	491	524	12.8	13.9	474	466	12.4	12.4	4	8	2	8.1	15.3	4.6

See footnotes at end of table.

Table B-5. Counties — **Births, Deaths, and Infant Deaths**—Con.

[Includes United States, states, and 3,141 counties/county equivalents defined as of February 22, 2005. For more information on these areas, see Appendix C, Geographic Information]

County	Births Number 2004	2000	Births Rate per 1,000 population[1] 2004	2000	Deaths Number 2004	2000	Deaths Rate per 1,000 population[1] 2004	2000	Infant deaths[2] Number 2004	2000	1990	Infant deaths Rate per 1,000 live births[3] 2004	2000	1990
TEXAS—Con.														
Burleson	231	252	13.5	15.2	152	162	8.9	9.8	1	2	1	4.3	7.9	4.7
Burnet	487	463	12.1	13.4	397	376	9.9	10.9	4	4	–	8.2	8.6	–
Caldwell	573	516	15.7	15.9	276	269	7.6	8.3	4	3	5	7.0	5.8	12.9
Calhoun	293	357	14.3	17.3	174	152	8.5	7.4	1	–	4	3.4	–	12.2
Callahan	133	129	10.0	10.0	150	150	11.3	11.6	1	–	1	7.5	–	8.0
Cameron	8,619	8,318	23.2	24.7	1,937	1,808	5.2	5.4	58	30	40	6.7	3.6	6.0
Camp	193	161	16.1	13.9	135	171	11.3	14.7	–	2	1	–	12.4	7.4
Carson	76	68	11.7	10.4	55	62	8.5	9.5	–	–	1	–	–	11.6
Cass	338	339	11.3	11.1	381	395	12.7	13.0	2	6	6	5.9	17.7	14.9
Castro	142	150	18.5	18.2	59	59	7.7	7.2	–	1	2	–	6.7	12.3
Chambers	360	294	12.8	11.2	198	192	7.0	7.3	4	2	1	11.1	6.8	4.0
Cherokee	695	718	14.5	15.4	549	503	11.4	10.8	7	4	6	10.1	5.6	10.0
Childress	82	84	10.7	10.9	60	92	7.8	12.0	–	–	1	–	–	16.1
Clay	100	97	8.9	8.7	100	110	8.9	9.9	1	1	1	10.0	10.3	10.3
Cochran	67	34	20.1	9.2	39	42	11.7	11.3	–	2	–	–	58.8	–
Coke	30	44	8.2	11.4	54	43	14.7	11.2	2	–	–	66.7	–	–
Coleman	107	120	12.3	13.1	136	157	15.6	17.1	–	1	1	–	8.3	9.3
Collin	10,415	8,678	16.6	17.4	2,248	1,814	3.6	3.6	54	30	32	5.2	3.5	6.9
Collingsworth	45	30	14.9	9.4	54	47	17.9	14.7	1	–	2	22.2	–	45.5
Colorado	247	276	11.9	13.6	247	266	11.9	13.1	2	2	2	8.1	7.2	7.8
Comal	1,145	1,081	12.5	13.7	767	642	8.4	8.1	7	5	6	6.1	4.6	8.4
Comanche	200	159	14.7	11.4	160	209	11.7	14.9	1	–	–	5.0	–	–
Concho	37	31	9.9	7.8	29	36	7.7	9.1	–	–	1	–	–	23.8
Cooke	545	499	14.2	13.7	382	381	9.9	10.4	2	6	5	3.7	12.0	10.3
Coryell	801	1,040	10.7	13.8	360	356	4.8	4.7	8	6	6	10.0	5.8	6.5
Cottle	14	28	8.0	14.9	10	38	5.7	20.2	–	1	–	–	35.7	–
Crane	61	52	15.8	13.2	43	36	11.1	9.1	–	1	1	–	19.2	12.7
Crockett	60	40	15.2	9.9	36	40	9.1	9.9	–	–	–	–	–	–
Crosby	115	120	17.3	17.0	86	84	12.9	11.9	2	–	1	17.4	–	7.6
Culberson	25	48	9.3	16.3	27	23	10.1	7.8	–	–	1	–	–	16.7
Dallam	107	101	17.3	16.2	49	48	7.9	7.7	2	1	2	18.7	9.9	22.0
Dallas	42,530	42,451	18.6	19.1	13,784	13,983	6.0	6.3	285	235	321	6.7	5.5	8.7
Dawson	186	242	13.0	16.2	152	147	10.7	9.8	–	2	1	–	8.3	3.9
Deaf Smith	355	375	19.2	20.3	157	153	8.5	8.3	5	4	5	14.1	10.7	11.7
Delta	50	55	9.0	10.3	55	78	9.9	14.6	–	–	1	–	–	17.5
Denton	8,860	7,434	16.7	16.9	1,975	1,752	3.7	4.0	50	30	37	5.6	4.0	7.4
DeWitt	217	245	10.7	12.3	228	280	11.2	14.0	1	–	3	4.6	–	13.8
Dickens	25	22	9.3	8.1	30	41	11.1	15.0	–	1	–	–	45.5	–
Dimmit	190	166	18.6	16.2	70	104	6.8	10.2	–	1	1	–	6.0	4.9
Donley	31	46	7.8	12.0	55	54	13.9	14.1	–	1	1	–	21.7	29.4
Duval	226	188	17.8	14.4	110	133	8.7	10.2	1	–	4	4.4	–	16.3
Eastland	227	206	12.3	11.2	320	291	17.4	15.9	6	5	1	26.4	24.3	4.8
Ector	2,313	2,147	18.6	17.8	1,113	1,015	9.0	8.4	12	22	17	5.2	10.2	7.5
Edwards	28	18	14.0	8.4	18	14	9.0	6.5	–	–	–	–	–	–
Ellis	2,000	1,771	15.5	15.7	964	862	7.5	7.7	10	11	18	5.0	6.2	12.3
El Paso	14,425	14,293	20.2	21.0	4,162	3,948	5.8	5.8	56	63	90	3.9	4.4	6.0
Erath	406	434	12.0	13.1	349	320	10.3	9.7	1	2	5	2.5	4.6	13.0
Falls	208	203	11.7	11.0	225	227	12.7	12.3	5	–	8	24.0	–	28.9
Fannin	409	350	12.6	11.2	415	449	12.7	14.3	3	1	2	7.3	2.9	6.6
Fayette	238	263	10.6	12.1	338	316	15.1	14.5	–	–	3	–	–	14.2
Fisher	32	39	7.9	9.0	65	67	16.0	15.5	–	–	1	–	–	19.2
Floyd	114	122	15.6	15.8	77	94	10.5	12.1	1	3	2	8.8	24.6	12.2
Foard	13	14	8.4	8.7	10	22	6.5	13.7	–	–	1	–	71.4	50.0
Fort Bend	6,167	5,246	13.9	14.6	1,683	1,374	3.8	3.8	32	18	24	5.2	3.4	5.9
Franklin	123	106	12.2	11.2	93	90	9.2	9.5	–	1	2	–	9.4	18.9
Freestone	213	211	11.4	11.8	227	216	12.2	12.1	1	2	8	4.7	9.5	43.2
Frio	236	288	14.4	17.8	119	125	7.3	7.7	1	–	1	4.2	–	3.8
Gaines	313	300	21.5	20.8	104	103	7.2	7.1	6	–	–	19.2	–	–
Galveston	3,957	3,806	14.5	15.2	2,269	2,155	8.3	8.6	26	28	28	6.6	7.4	7.5
Garza	65	74	12.7	15.2	46	62	9.0	12.7	–	–	–	–	–	–
Gillespie	247	215	11.0	10.3	279	320	12.4	15.3	1	–	1	4.0	–	6.3
Glasscock	7	16	5.3	11.4	5	4	3.8	2.9	–	–	–	–	–	–
Goliad	73	74	10.3	10.6	76	87	10.7	12.5	–	–	–	–	–	–
Gonzales	357	293	18.5	15.7	197	233	10.2	12.5	5	1	3	14.0	3.4	10.6
Gray	288	266	13.5	11.8	270	294	12.6	13.0	4	2	4	13.9	7.5	11.6
Grayson	1,662	1,550	14.3	14.0	1,228	1,306	10.6	11.8	7	8	12	4.2	5.2	8.3
Gregg	1,880	1,782	16.4	16.0	1,189	1,210	10.4	10.9	15	16	17	8.0	9.0	9.6
Grimes	343	351	13.6	14.9	229	255	9.1	10.8	4	3	1	11.7	8.5	3.3
Guadalupe	1,352	1,221	13.6	13.6	667	603	6.7	6.7	6	10	8	4.4	8.2	8.4
Hale	628	666	17.3	18.2	306	318	8.4	8.7	3	10	5	4.8	15.0	7.1

See footnotes at end of table.

[Includes United States, states, and 3,141 counties/county equivalents defined as of February 22, 2005. For more information on these areas, see Appendix C, Geographic Information]

County	Births				Deaths				Infant deaths[2]					
	Number		Rate per 1,000 population[1]		Number		Rate per 1,000 population[1]		Number			Rate per 1,000 live births[3]		
	2004	2000	2004	2000	2004	2000	2004	2000	2004	2000	1990	2004	2000	1990
TEXAS—Con.														
Hall	41	50	10.9	13.3	53	59	14.0	15.7	1	1	1	24.4	20.0	16.1
Hamilton	76	89	9.4	10.8	143	150	17.7	18.2	–	–	–	–	–	–
Hansford	112	100	21.5	18.7	61	64	11.7	12.0	–	1	–	–	10.0	–
Hardeman	62	52	14.2	11.0	44	66	10.1	14.0	2	3	2	32.3	57.7	32.8
Hardin	705	644	14.0	13.4	502	489	10.0	10.2	6	3	2	8.5	4.7	3.5
Harris	67,179	63,327	18.5	18.5	20,269	19,632	5.6	5.7	439	313	498	6.5	4.9	8.7
Harrison	809	801	12.9	12.9	594	628	9.4	10.1	4	7	5	4.9	8.7	6.4
Hartley	65	67	11.8	12.1	54	26	9.8	4.7	–	–	1	–	–	21.3
Haskell	65	57	11.6	9.4	103	109	18.4	18.0	–	–	–	–	–	–
Hays	1,697	1,478	14.2	14.9	566	505	4.7	5.1	5	3	8	2.9	2.0	9.0
Hemphill	45	47	13.4	14.1	39	26	11.6	7.8	1	–	–	22.2	–	–
Henderson	937	958	11.8	13.0	889	912	11.2	12.4	6	6	2	6.4	6.3	2.6
Hidalgo	16,530	15,361	25.1	26.8	3,068	2,729	4.7	4.8	67	77	58	4.1	5.0	5.4
Hill	451	472	12.9	14.5	402	360	11.5	11.0	4	2	2	8.9	4.2	5.5
Hockley	363	354	15.9	15.6	211	179	9.3	7.9	5	1	3	13.8	2.8	7.6
Hood	537	469	11.6	11.3	528	482	11.4	11.6	6	1	5	11.2	2.1	13.2
Hopkins	431	457	13.0	14.3	363	373	11.0	11.6	3	7	1	7.0	15.3	2.7
Houston	249	255	10.7	11.0	304	341	13.0	14.7	1	3	2	4.0	11.8	6.8
Howard	465	482	14.2	14.4	378	398	11.5	11.9	2	1	8	4.3	2.1	16.1
Hudspeth	51	31	15.5	9.3	18	16	5.5	4.8	1	1	–	19.6	32.3	–
Hunt	1,052	1,019	12.9	13.2	736	705	9.0	9.2	9	2	9	8.6	2.0	8.9
Hutchinson	316	317	14.0	13.3	252	268	11.1	11.3	1	4	5	3.2	12.6	14.3
Irion	9	10	5.2	5.6	14	12	8.1	6.8	–	–	–	–	–	–
Jack	90	114	10.0	13.0	81	90	9.0	10.3	3	2	–	33.3	17.5	–
Jackson	194	223	13.5	15.4	147	172	10.2	11.9	–	1	2	–	4.5	10.2
Jasper	488	515	13.7	14.5	421	424	11.8	11.9	7	3	6	14.3	5.8	12.8
Jeff Davis	19	19	8.4	8.5	23	23	10.1	10.3	–	–	–	–	–	–
Jefferson	3,446	3,555	13.9	14.1	2,522	2,620	10.2	10.4	22	31	35	6.4	8.7	9.5
Jim Hogg	84	75	16.6	14.2	45	42	8.9	8.0	–	2	1	–	26.7	13.9
Jim Wells	665	671	16.3	17.0	306	335	7.5	8.5	3	2	4	4.5	3.0	5.9
Johnson	2,059	1,908	14.4	14.9	1,046	1,041	7.3	8.1	10	12	16	4.9	6.3	11.2
Jones	191	193	9.5	9.3	185	235	9.2	11.3	3	1	2	15.7	5.2	9.1
Karnes	171	204	11.1	13.2	148	159	9.6	10.3	–	1	2	–	4.9	9.5
Kaufman	1,259	1,118	14.7	15.5	716	674	8.4	9.3	3	5	8	2.4	4.5	10.3
Kendall	352	311	12.9	13.0	238	239	8.7	10.0	1	2	3	2.8	6.4	13.7
Kenedy	3	7	7.4	16.9	2	5	4.9	12.0	–	–	–	–	–	–
Kent	5	5	6.5	5.9	20	18	25.8	21.2	–	–	–	–	–	–
Kerr	514	479	11.2	10.9	654	612	14.2	14.0	3	2	6	5.8	4.2	12.2
Kimble	43	43	9.5	9.6	61	59	13.4	13.1	–	–	1	–	–	23.3
King	1	5	3.1	13.9	3	2	9.3	5.6	–	–	–	–	–	–
Kinney	33	37	10.0	10.9	33	40	10.0	11.8	–	1	–	–	27.0	–
Kleberg	495	532	16.0	16.9	250	236	8.1	7.5	7	2	5	14.1	3.8	8.9
Knox	46	50	11.8	11.8	58	65	14.9	15.3	1	–	–	21.7	–	–
Lamar	689	725	13.9	14.9	587	584	11.8	12.0	4	4	7	5.8	5.5	9.7
Lamb	248	212	17.1	14.5	142	197	9.8	13.4	1	2	–	4.0	9.4	–
Lampasas	240	208	11.6	11.6	189	182	9.2	10.2	3	2	2	12.5	9.6	8.9
La Salle	87	96	14.7	16.3	44	48	7.4	8.2	–	–	1	–	–	11.1
Lavaca	234	228	12.4	11.9	269	279	14.2	14.5	–	4	3	–	17.5	12.6
Lee	198	220	12.0	14.0	130	148	7.9	9.4	–	1	3	–	4.5	19.0
Leon	198	202	12.3	13.1	207	174	12.9	11.3	2	–	–	10.1	–	–
Liberty	1,098	997	14.6	14.1	673	622	9.0	8.8	11	12	4	10.0	12.0	5.0
Limestone	270	285	11.8	12.9	291	295	12.8	13.4	3	2	–	11.1	7.0	–
Lipscomb	43	35	14.0	11.5	43	44	14.0	14.5	1	–	–	23.3	–	–
Live Oak	110	127	9.4	10.3	78	120	6.6	9.8	1	2	–	9.1	15.7	–
Llano	144	136	8.0	7.9	274	266	15.2	15.5	–	2	–	–	14.7	–
Loving	–	–	–	–	–	–	–	–	–	–	–	–	–	–
Lubbock	4,049	3,855	16.1	15.9	1,904	1,927	7.6	7.9	25	31	35	6.2	8.0	8.8
Lynn	86	88	13.9	13.5	51	72	8.2	11.1	–	–	–	–	–	–
McCulloch	93	107	11.5	13.1	118	130	14.6	15.9	1	1	–	10.8	9.3	–
McLennan	3,262	3,288	14.6	15.4	1,959	1,990	8.8	9.3	36	25	22	11.0	7.6	7.2
McMullen	7	5	8.4	5.9	6	9	7.2	10.5	–	–	–	–	–	–
Madison	145	154	11.0	11.9	143	159	10.8	12.2	3	–	1	20.7	–	7.8
Marion	121	122	11.0	11.1	129	152	11.7	13.9	1	–	–	8.3	–	–
Martin	66	73	14.9	15.5	57	64	12.9	13.6	–	1	1	–	13.7	12.0
Mason	33	29	8.6	7.7	53	47	13.8	12.5	–	2	–	–	69.0	–
Matagorda	587	534	15.4	14.1	317	384	8.3	10.1	3	5	7	5.1	9.4	10.9
Maverick	1,093	996	21.6	21.0	242	263	4.8	5.6	9	6	9	8.2	6.0	10.0
Medina	574	539	13.6	13.7	342	347	8.1	8.8	2	3	2	3.5	5.6	4.4
Menard	26	21	11.4	8.9	31	35	13.6	14.9	–	–	–	–	–	–
Midland	1,916	1,844	16.0	16.0	908	894	7.6	7.7	16	12	18	8.4	6.5	8.4

See footnotes at end of table.

Table B-5. Counties — **Births, Deaths, and Infant Deaths**—Con.

[Includes United States, states, and 3,141 counties/county equivalents defined as of February 22, 2005. For more information on these areas, see Appendix C, Geographic Information]

County	Births Number		Births Rate per 1,000 population[1]		Deaths Number		Deaths Rate per 1,000 population[1]		Infant deaths[2] Number			Infant deaths Rate per 1,000 live births[3]		
	2004	2000	2004	2000	2004	2000	2004	2000	2004	2000	1990	2004	2000	1990
TEXAS—Con.														
Milam	395	362	15.6	14.9	284	306	11.2	12.6	6	3	4	15.2	8.3	13.2
Mills	54	45	10.5	8.8	57	65	11.1	12.6	–	–	1	–	–	21.7
Mitchell	96	96	10.3	10.0	107	134	11.4	13.9	2	1	1	20.8	10.4	8.3
Montague	252	258	12.9	13.5	271	288	13.9	15.1	1	1	2	4.0	3.9	9.7
Montgomery	5,152	4,662	14.2	15.7	2,176	2,040	6.0	6.9	31	35	21	6.0	7.5	6.8
Moore	438	416	21.4	20.7	123	141	6.0	7.0	1	3	3	2.3	7.2	8.2
Morris	162	160	12.5	12.3	164	205	12.6	15.7	2	1	3	12.3	6.3	18.6
Motley	12	12	9.3	8.3	18	21	13.9	14.6	–	–	1	–	–	58.8
Nacogdoches	994	867	16.6	14.6	575	581	9.6	9.8	8	6	9	8.0	6.9	11.5
Navarro	619	685	12.8	15.1	501	554	10.4	12.2	7	7	2	11.3	10.2	3.3
Newton	141	160	9.9	10.6	156	137	10.9	9.1	2	1	–	14.2	6.3	–
Nolan	227	246	15.1	15.6	209	207	13.9	13.1	1	1	2	4.4	4.1	8.6
Nueces	5,023	5,250	15.8	16.8	2,411	2,535	7.6	8.1	38	38	46	7.6	7.2	8.7
Ochiltree	188	150	20.6	16.7	56	73	6.1	8.1	–	–	3	–	–	20.3
Oldham	34	25	15.9	11.4	19	14	8.9	6.4	1	–	–	29.4	–	–
Orange	1,080	1,093	12.7	12.9	869	831	10.3	9.8	6	4	8	5.6	3.7	6.4
Palo Pinto	389	373	14.3	13.8	332	340	12.2	12.6	3	5	1	7.7	13.4	2.6
Panola	285	284	12.6	12.5	282	238	12.4	10.5	6	3	4	21.1	10.6	15.1
Parker	1,165	1,054	11.6	11.8	755	720	7.5	8.1	11	5	3	9.4	4.7	3.1
Parmer	200	172	20.2	17.2	73	89	7.4	8.9	2	1	–	10.0	5.8	–
Pecos	270	212	16.8	12.7	120	98	7.5	5.9	3	–	5	11.1	–	18.0
Polk	508	534	11.0	12.8	600	558	13.0	13.4	4	4	6	7.9	7.5	15.0
Potter	2,405	2,244	20.3	19.7	1,167	1,151	9.9	10.1	29	28	13	12.1	12.5	6.3
Presidio	135	166	17.8	22.6	37	48	4.9	6.5	–	–	1	–	–	9.8
Rains	115	104	10.4	11.3	119	100	10.8	10.8	1	–	1	8.7	–	13.5
Randall	1,365	1,201	12.6	11.5	737	711	6.8	6.8	12	11	7	8.8	9.2	5.5
Reagan	47	57	15.3	17.3	20	29	6.5	8.8	–	–	–	–	–	–
Real	34	32	11.2	10.5	52	28	17.1	9.1	–	–	–	–	–	–
Red River	146	165	10.7	11.6	217	237	15.9	16.6	2	1	1	13.7	6.1	5.6
Reeves	160	206	13.5	15.8	108	107	9.1	8.2	–	–	2	–	–	8.0
Refugio	94	120	12.3	15.3	93	93	12.2	11.9	1	2	–	10.6	16.7	–
Roberts	9	9	10.9	10.2	10	9	12.1	10.2	–	–	–	–	–	–
Robertson	217	288	13.6	18.0	192	213	12.0	13.3	4	2	3	18.4	6.9	10.3
Rockwall	855	682	14.6	15.5	358	309	6.1	7.0	5	1	2	5.8	1.5	5.4
Runnels	145	144	13.3	12.5	140	157	12.8	13.7	2	2	3	13.8	13.9	18.2
Rusk	618	614	12.9	13.0	507	531	10.6	11.2	7	8	7	11.3	13.0	10.9
Sabine	118	109	11.4	10.4	156	169	15.1	16.2	1	–	1	8.5	–	10.5
San Augustine	106	124	11.9	13.9	140	121	15.7	13.5	–	1	1	–	8.1	10.0
San Jacinto	237	264	9.6	11.8	225	196	9.2	8.7	1	1	–	4.2	3.8	–
San Patricio	1,215	1,204	17.8	17.9	521	525	7.6	7.8	11	6	5	9.1	5.0	4.8
San Saba	58	67	9.5	10.8	72	73	11.8	11.8	–	–	–	–	–	–
Schleicher	39	41	14.1	14.0	36	30	13.1	10.3	–	–	–	–	–	–
Scurry	220	203	13.6	12.5	166	171	10.3	10.5	1	1	1	4.5	4.9	4.4
Shackelford	35	31	10.9	9.4	48	41	15.0	12.4	–	–	–	–	–	–
Shelby	405	408	15.5	16.1	314	320	12.1	12.7	3	1	–	7.4	2.5	–
Sherman	34	41	11.0	12.9	29	24	9.4	7.5	–	–	–	–	–	–
Smith	2,877	2,653	15.4	15.1	1,578	1,703	8.4	9.7	19	25	18	6.6	9.4	7.7
Somervell	93	84	12.5	12.3	61	72	8.2	10.5	1	1	–	10.8	11.9	–
Starr	1,492	1,459	25.0	27.1	282	249	4.7	4.6	5	9	5	3.4	6.2	4.3
Stephens	123	137	12.9	14.2	123	105	12.9	10.9	–	–	1	–	–	7.8
Sterling	6	10	4.5	7.3	14	5	10.6	3.6	–	–	1	–	–	40.0
Stonewall	17	11	12.0	6.6	16	21	11.3	12.5	–	–	–	–	–	–
Sutton	71	60	17.2	14.9	35	40	8.5	9.9	–	–	–	–	–	–
Swisher	141	140	17.9	16.7	72	81	9.1	9.7	2	–	–	14.2	–	–
Tarrant	27,600	25,432	17.4	17.5	9,707	9,362	6.1	6.4	177	160	228	6.4	6.3	10.0
Taylor	2,054	2,049	16.4	16.2	1,203	1,142	9.6	9.0	14	7	23	6.8	3.4	10.7
Terrell	11	7	11.3	6.6	13	11	13.4	10.4	–	–	–	–	–	–
Terry	182	211	14.5	16.6	122	117	9.7	9.2	1	–	–	5.5	–	–
Throckmorton	14	15	8.6	8.2	25	22	15.3	12.0	–	–	1	–	–	37.0
Titus	588	540	20.2	19.2	249	267	8.5	9.5	5	4	6	8.5	7.4	14.1
Tom Green	1,590	1,615	15.3	15.5	1,001	1,024	9.6	9.8	14	18	9	8.8	11.1	5.4
Travis	14,816	14,476	17.1	17.7	3,993	4,001	4.6	4.9	87	69	67	5.9	4.8	6.4
Trinity	166	173	11.6	12.5	228	195	16.0	14.1	2	2	3	12.0	11.6	23.6
Tyler	252	241	12.1	11.6	279	238	13.4	11.4	2	2	3	7.9	8.3	13.5
Upshur	457	435	12.3	12.3	386	467	10.4	13.2	2	4	4	4.4	9.2	9.9
Upton	51	56	16.3	16.6	18	33	5.7	9.8	–	1	1	–	17.9	10.5
Uvalde	471	475	17.7	18.3	228	223	8.6	8.6	7	–	5	14.9	–	10.5
Val Verde	998	889	21.0	19.7	282	312	5.9	6.9	4	4	6	4.0	4.5	6.2
Van Zandt	598	615	11.5	12.7	567	577	10.9	11.9	2	5	7	3.3	8.1	15.5
Victoria	1,410	1,323	16.5	15.7	692	661	8.1	7.9	7	10	16	5.0	7.6	12.4

See footnotes at end of table.

U.S. Census Bureau

[Includes United States, states, and 3,141 counties/county equivalents defined as of February 22, 2005. For more information on these areas, see Appendix C, Geographic Information]

County	Births				Deaths				Infant deaths[2]					
	Number		Rate per 1,000 population[1]		Number		Rate per 1,000 population[1]		Number			Rate per 1,000 live births[3]		
	2004	2000	2004	2000	2004	2000	2004	2000	2004	2000	1990	2004	2000	1990
TEXAS—Con.														
Walker	587	631	9.4	10.2	433	435	6.9	7.1	5	5	7	8.5	7.9	11.8
Waller	528	522	15.2	15.9	247	224	7.1	6.8	3	–	1	5.7	–	3.1
Ward	156	164	15.2	15.2	109	115	10.6	10.6	–	1	3	–	6.1	14.8
Washington	429	381	13.8	12.5	347	355	11.1	11.7	2	4	1	4.7	10.5	3.0
Webb	6,038	5,777	27.6	29.7	946	904	4.3	4.6	28	35	23	4.6	6.1	5.9
Wharton	663	622	16.0	15.1	451	345	10.9	8.4	5	2	6	7.5	3.2	9.7
Wheeler	60	55	12.4	10.5	72	66	14.9	12.6	–	1	1	–	18.2	15.6
Wichita	1,963	1,896	15.4	14.4	1,293	1,263	10.2	9.6	17	22	17	8.7	11.6	8.4
Wilbarger	228	201	16.4	13.7	182	186	13.1	12.7	1	4	1	4.4	19.9	5.3
Willacy	410	406	20.3	20.2	117	101	5.8	5.0	1	2	2	2.4	4.9	5.3
Williamson	5,323	4,450	16.7	17.5	1,413	1,187	4.4	4.7	20	22	14	3.8	4.9	5.9
Wilson	458	451	12.5	13.8	301	250	8.2	7.6	3	4	–	6.6	8.9	–
Winkler	101	99	15.0	14.0	87	82	12.9	11.6	–	1	1	–	10.1	6.3
Wise	683	708	12.3	14.3	431	437	7.8	8.8	5	3	6	7.3	4.2	11.2
Wood	454	409	11.3	11.1	496	493	12.3	13.4	1	4	3	2.2	9.8	9.2
Yoakum	137	133	18.6	18.3	50	54	6.8	7.4	1	–	3	7.3	–	22.4
Young	213	224	11.9	12.5	255	280	14.2	15.6	1	1	4	4.7	4.5	15.6
Zapata	297	244	22.7	20.0	66	79	5.0	6.5	–	–	1	–	–	5.5
Zavala	241	202	20.6	17.4	77	107	6.6	9.2	–	1	–	–	5.0	–
UTAH	50,670	47,353	20.9	21.1	13,331	12,364	5.5	5.5	264	248	271	5.2	5.2	7.5
Beaver	132	114	21.7	18.9	61	62	10.0	10.3	–	2	–	–	17.5	–
Box Elder	818	777	17.8	18.1	297	279	6.5	6.5	3	3	7	3.7	3.9	9.8
Cache	2,475	2,172	25.5	23.7	419	447	4.3	4.9	5	11	10	2.0	5.1	5.9
Carbon	321	300	16.4	14.7	202	185	10.3	9.1	2	2	–	6.2	6.7	–
Daggett	8	16	8.6	17.2	1	–	1.1	–	–	–	–	–	–	–
Davis	5,590	4,836	21.4	20.1	1,211	1,094	4.6	4.6	25	26	28	4.5	5.4	7.2
Duchesne	304	279	20.2	19.4	125	101	8.3	7.0	2	–	1	6.6	–	3.9
Emery	166	172	15.5	15.7	72	60	6.7	5.5	1	–	–	6.0	–	–
Garfield	71	55	15.9	11.6	33	50	7.4	10.5	–	–	–	–	–	–
Grand	109	111	12.5	13.2	59	57	6.8	6.8	1	–	3	9.2	–	27.5
Iron	846	771	23.2	22.7	196	147	5.4	4.3	6	4	–	7.1	5.2	–
Juab	193	177	21.5	21.4	75	56	8.3	6.8	3	1	1	15.5	5.6	9.4
Kane	103	102	16.8	16.8	62	71	10.1	11.7	2	–	1	19.4	–	10.5
Millard	197	183	15.9	14.7	111	90	9.0	7.3	3	1	3	15.2	5.5	13.0
Morgan	114	98	14.9	13.7	41	26	5.4	3.6	2	2	2	17.5	20.4	21.5
Piute	24	17	17.3	11.8	19	15	13.7	10.4	–	1	–	–	58.8	–
Rich	34	27	16.4	13.7	16	11	7.7	5.6	1	–	–	29.4	–	–
Salt Lake	18,394	18,337	19.7	20.4	5,314	5,026	5.7	5.6	103	106	116	5.6	5.8	7.8
San Juan	249	235	17.7	16.4	79	74	5.6	5.1	2	–	3	8.0	–	9.1
Sanpete	399	367	16.8	16.1	181	166	7.6	7.3	2	2	5	5.0	5.4	16.8
Sevier	343	334	17.7	17.7	174	164	9.0	8.7	–	–	1	–	–	4.0
Summit	578	473	17.0	15.8	103	86	3.0	2.9	3	1	2	5.2	2.1	7.4
Tooele	1,056	956	21.2	22.9	259	230	5.2	5.5	7	2	1	6.6	2.1	2.0
Uintah	570	459	21.5	18.2	189	171	7.1	6.8	3	3	3	5.3	6.5	6.9
Utah	10,959	9,873	25.2	26.6	1,700	1,551	3.9	4.2	55	50	46	5.0	5.1	6.8
Wasatch	372	310	20.5	20.1	87	82	4.8	5.3	–	1	1	–	3.2	5.5
Washington	2,259	1,814	20.5	19.9	807	670	7.3	7.3	14	9	6	6.2	5.0	6.4
Wayne	42	45	17.0	17.7	20	19	8.1	7.5	–	–	1	–	–	33.3
Weber	3,944	3,943	18.9	20.0	1,418	1,374	6.8	7.0	19	21	30	4.8	5.3	9.6
VERMONT	6,599	6,500	10.6	10.7	4,995	5,127	8.0	8.4	30	39	53	4.5	6.0	6.4
Addison	356	387	9.7	10.7	257	249	7.0	6.9	2	2	5	5.6	5.2	9.7
Bennington	380	369	10.3	10.0	397	430	10.7	11.6	2	3	–	5.3	8.1	–
Caledonia	368	342	12.1	11.5	265	285	8.7	9.6	1	1	3	2.7	2.9	8.4
Chittenden	1,663	1,677	11.1	11.4	907	932	6.1	6.3	4	14	15	2.4	8.3	7.6
Essex	56	62	8.4	9.6	60	64	9.0	9.9	–	–	1	–	–	9.3
Franklin	628	582	13.2	12.8	310	367	6.5	8.0	1	4	4	1.6	6.9	5.6
Grand Isle	94	73	12.3	10.5	55	46	7.2	6.6	1	2	–	10.6	27.4	–
Lamoille	278	283	11.4	12.1	165	179	6.8	7.7	4	3	3	14.4	10.6	9.5
Orange	306	273	10.5	9.6	220	209	7.5	7.4	4	–	1	13.1	–	2.6
Orleans	289	272	10.6	10.3	275	262	10.0	9.9	–	1	3	–	3.7	9.2
Rutland	587	660	9.2	10.4	614	631	9.7	9.9	4	3	3	6.8	4.5	3.5
Washington	618	568	10.5	9.8	467	511	7.9	8.8	2	2	10	3.2	3.5	12.5
Windham	407	435	9.2	9.8	380	459	8.6	10.4	1	1	1	2.5	2.3	1.6
Windsor	569	517	9.8	9.0	623	503	10.7	8.7	4	3	4	7.0	5.8	5.5
VIRGINIA	103,933	98,938	13.9	13.9	56,550	56,282	7.6	7.9	776	682	1,013	7.5	6.9	10.2
Accomack	490	463	12.5	12.1	443	439	11.3	11.4	3	3	4	6.1	6.5	8.1
Albemarle	960	1,057	10.8	12.5	603	636	6.8	7.5	2	6	9	2.1	5.7	9.8
Alleghany[5]	198	122	11.8	7.1	246	127	14.7	7.4	1	–	3	5.1	–	19.1
Amelia	140	153	11.7	13.3	114	138	9.5	12.0	2	2	1	14.3	13.1	6.8
Amherst	295	339	9.2	10.6	295	291	9.2	9.1	1	3	–	3.4	8.8	–

See footnotes at end of table.

Table B-5. Counties — **Births, Deaths, and Infant Deaths**—Con.

[Includes United States, states, and 3,141 counties/county equivalents defined as of February 22, 2005. For more information on these areas, see Appendix C, Geographic Information]

County	Births Number 2004	Births Number 2000	Births Rate per 1,000 population[1] 2004	Births Rate 2000	Deaths Number 2004	Deaths Number 2000	Deaths Rate per 1,000 population[1] 2004	Deaths Rate 2000	Infant deaths[2] Number 2004	Number 2000	Number 1990	Infant deaths Rate per 1,000 live births[3] 2004	Rate 2000	Rate 1990
VIRGINIA—Con.														
Appomattox	145	162	10.4	11.8	132	159	9.5	11.6	–	–	2	–	–	12.8
Arlington	2,814	2,710	14.2	14.3	1,009	1,108	5.1	5.9	7	6	16	2.5	2.2	5.8
Augusta	766	682	11.1	10.4	570	468	8.3	7.1	9	6	3	11.7	8.8	4.3
Bath	26	44	5.2	8.7	47	74	9.5	14.7	–	–	–	–	–	–
Bedford	622	608	9.7	10.0	473	403	7.4	6.6	1	3	8	1.6	4.9	13.4
Bland	55	66	7.8	9.6	80	82	11.4	12.0	–	1	–	–	15.2	–
Botetourt	258	313	8.1	10.2	268	242	8.4	7.9	2	1	2	7.8	3.2	7.7
Brunswick	173	180	9.6	9.8	193	211	10.7	11.5	2	1	6	11.6	5.6	29.6
Buchanan	239	263	9.5	9.8	320	267	12.7	10.0	2	–	4	8.4	–	10.9
Buckingham	162	92	10.2	5.9	200	126	12.6	8.1	2	2	2	12.3	21.7	10.2
Campbell	574	665	11.1	13.0	455	439	8.8	8.6	2	3	5	3.5	4.5	7.6
Caroline	318	267	13.3	12.1	206	201	8.6	9.1	5	2	4	15.7	7.5	12.5
Carroll	285	260	9.7	8.9	348	298	11.8	10.2	2	1	1	7.0	3.8	3.2
Charles City	68	73	9.6	10.5	70	68	9.8	9.8	3	–	–	44.1	–	–
Charlotte	150	159	12.1	12.8	144	154	11.7	12.4	1	–	4	6.7	–	20.8
Chesterfield	3,657	3,404	12.9	13.0	1,654	1,450	5.9	5.6	29	19	22	7.9	5.6	6.4
Clarke	132	112	9.5	8.8	128	128	9.2	10.1	1	–	2	7.6	–	12.3
Craig	43	58	8.3	11.4	52	40	10.1	7.8	–	2	1	–	34.5	16.1
Culpeper	538	480	13.4	13.9	326	327	8.1	9.5	6	2	2	11.2	4.2	4.1
Cumberland	99	89	10.8	9.9	80	90	8.7	10.0	–	1	–	–	11.2	–
Dickenson	163	146	10.1	8.9	178	167	11.0	10.2	1	–	1	6.1	–	5.4
Dinwiddie	284	245	11.3	10.0	233	187	9.3	7.6	1	1	2	3.5	4.1	7.4
Essex	136	119	13.2	11.9	138	143	13.4	14.3	1	5	3	7.4	42.0	22.2
Fairfax	14,995	14,315	15.0	14.7	4,138	4,203	4.1	4.3	62	60	84	4.1	4.2	6.9
Fauquier	741	702	11.8	12.6	488	369	7.7	6.6	3	3	6	4.0	4.3	7.9
Floyd	169	159	11.7	11.4	139	132	9.6	9.5	–	1	1	–	6.3	7.6
Fluvanna	349	218	14.6	10.8	142	146	6.0	7.2	3	3	2	8.6	13.8	8.8
Franklin	530	535	10.7	11.3	467	420	9.4	8.8	6	7	9	11.3	13.1	18.1
Frederick	923	837	13.8	14.0	534	370	8.0	6.2	4	5	4	4.3	6.0	5.9
Giles	189	256	11.2	15.3	224	201	13.2	12.0	2	–	2	10.6	–	10.3
Gloucester	417	404	11.2	11.6	323	309	8.7	8.9	1	6	4	2.4	14.9	8.4
Goochland	181	204	9.7	12.0	127	149	6.8	8.8	1	3	–	5.5	14.7	–
Grayson	132	174	8.0	10.3	218	230	13.3	13.6	–	1	3	–	5.7	17.0
Greene	263	224	15.5	14.6	124	129	7.3	8.4	1	2	3	3.8	8.9	16.9
Greensville	124	108	11.3	9.3	82	128	7.4	11.1	–	–	–	–	–	–
Halifax[6]	397	475	10.9	12.7	456	452	12.5	12.1	8	3	4	20.2	6.3	11.0
Hanover	1,133	1,060	11.8	12.2	692	684	7.2	7.9	7	4	12	6.2	3.8	12.6
Henrico	3,954	3,693	14.3	14.0	2,287	2,348	8.3	8.9	36	31	36	9.1	8.4	10.6
Henry	606	657	10.7	11.3	625	557	11.0	9.6	7	6	6	11.6	9.1	7.1
Highland	15	14	6.1	5.5	26	28	10.6	11.0	–	–	–	–	–	–
Isle of Wight	355	363	10.9	12.1	323	239	9.9	8.0	4	1	5	11.3	2.8	13.4
James City	501	486	9.0	10.0	450	340	8.1	7.0	2	2	4	4.0	4.1	8.1
King and Queen	68	63	10.1	9.5	71	69	10.5	10.4	–	1	1	–	15.9	10.9
King George	322	243	16.6	14.4	127	129	6.6	7.6	2	4	–	6.2	16.5	–
King William	184	197	12.8	14.9	124	121	8.7	9.2	2	–	–	10.9	–	–
Lancaster	96	111	8.3	9.6	188	229	16.3	19.8	2	1	4	20.8	9.0	27.8
Lee	235	239	9.9	10.2	324	301	13.6	12.8	1	2	2	4.3	8.4	6.8
Loudoun	4,792	3,636	20.0	20.9	743	699	3.1	4.0	26	17	12	5.4	4.7	7.2
Louisa	358	331	12.4	12.9	251	262	8.7	10.2	3	4	4	8.4	12.1	12.9
Lunenburg	131	96	10.0	7.3	153	157	11.7	12.0	1	1	2	7.6	10.4	15.2
Madison	134	113	10.2	9.0	110	135	8.4	10.7	1	–	–	7.5	–	–
Mathews	56	75	6.1	8.1	128	131	14.0	14.2	–	–	–	–	–	–
Mecklenburg	325	333	10.0	10.3	401	402	12.4	12.4	1	2	4	3.1	6.0	10.5
Middlesex	82	83	7.9	8.3	135	160	12.9	16.1	–	–	2	–	–	23.5
Montgomery	841	823	10.0	9.8	518	484	6.2	5.8	3	4	8	3.6	4.9	8.9
Nelson	154	159	10.3	11.0	150	177	10.0	12.2	1	2	1	6.5	12.6	6.3
New Kent	175	157	11.3	11.6	111	101	7.2	7.5	–	2	1	–	12.7	6.1
Northampton	162	151	12.1	11.6	196	208	14.7	15.9	1	1	1	6.2	6.6	4.9
Northumberland	109	99	8.5	8.1	164	187	12.8	15.2	–	–	–	–	–	–
Nottoway	184	186	11.8	11.8	178	226	11.4	14.4	1	4	3	5.4	21.5	15.0
Orange	355	326	12.3	12.5	258	314	8.9	12.1	3	3	1	8.5	9.2	3.3
Page	275	266	11.6	11.5	269	232	11.4	10.0	–	2	–	–	7.5	–
Patrick	186	171	9.7	8.8	251	190	13.1	9.8	3	–	2	16.1	–	10.6
Pittsylvania	652	779	10.6	12.6	630	606	10.2	9.8	4	7	6	6.1	9.0	10.2
Powhatan	259	259	10.0	11.5	160	124	6.2	5.5	1	1	3	3.9	3.9	14.7
Prince Edward	203	217	10.0	11.0	196	215	9.7	10.9	–	2	3	–	9.2	13.6
Prince George	369	407	10.1	12.3	184	149	5.0	4.5	3	4	4	8.1	9.8	9.5
Prince William	6,433	5,029	19.1	17.7	1,224	1,138	3.6	4.0	50	31	27	7.8	6.2	6.1
Pulaski	348	412	9.9	11.7	407	426	11.6	12.1	3	–	4	8.6	–	9.4
Rappahannock	79	98	11.0	14.1	67	69	9.4	9.9	–	1	–	–	10.2	–

See footnotes at end of table.

[Includes United States, states, and 3,141 counties/county equivalents defined as of February 22, 2005. For more information on these areas, see Appendix C, Geographic Information]

County	Births				Deaths				Infant deaths[2]					
	Number		Rate per 1,000 population[1]		Number		Rate per 1,000 population[1]		Number			Rate per 1,000 live births[3]		
	2004	2000	2004	2000	2004	2000	2004	2000	2004	2000	1990	2004	2000	1990
VIRGINIA—Con.														
Richmond	96	86	10.6	9.8	114	122	12.5	13.9	4	1	–	41.7	11.6	–
Roanoke	1,402	891	16.0	10.4	818	941	9.3	11.0	4	6	10	2.9	6.7	13.6
Rockbridge	265	170	12.6	8.2	208	177	9.9	8.5	4	2	1	15.1	11.8	5.0
Rockingham	870	860	12.4	12.7	599	540	8.5	8.0	10	4	3	11.5	4.7	3.8
Russell	262	273	9.1	9.3	351	304	12.2	10.4	1	3	2	3.8	11.0	6.3
Scott	227	252	9.9	10.8	312	328	13.6	14.0	1	2	1	4.4	7.9	4.0
Shenandoah	462	398	12.1	11.3	415	367	10.9	10.4	3	1	6	6.5	2.5	13.9
Smyth	297	360	9.1	10.9	409	394	12.6	11.9	–	1	4	–	2.8	9.6
Southampton	172	160	9.9	9.2	184	191	10.6	10.9	4	2	1	23.3	12.5	5.0
Spotsylvania	1,700	1,302	15.2	14.2	613	522	5.5	5.7	13	8	7	7.6	6.1	7.8
Stafford	1,617	1,370	14.1	14.6	477	429	4.2	4.6	11	7	13	6.8	5.1	12.8
Surry	64	79	9.2	11.5	47	46	6.7	6.7	–	–	2	–	–	22.0
Sussex	123	138	10.1	11.1	125	123	10.3	9.8	1	2	4	8.1	14.5	25.5
Tazewell	479	435	10.7	9.8	585	495	13.1	11.1	1	4	1	2.1	9.2	1.8
Warren	446	424	12.9	13.4	306	305	8.9	9.6	2	1	4	4.5	2.4	9.3
Washington	490	531	9.5	10.4	585	492	11.3	9.6	1	1	3	2.0	1.9	5.7
Westmoreland	179	169	10.5	10.1	199	230	11.7	13.8	–	5	3	–	29.6	12.1
Wise	494	515	11.8	12.2	480	466	11.5	11.0	5	6	7	10.1	11.7	11.9
Wythe	332	337	11.8	12.2	278	313	9.9	11.3	3	4	–	9.0	11.9	–
York	580	722	9.5	12.8	344	361	5.7	6.4	4	5	8	6.9	6.9	18.2
Independent Cities														
Alexandria	2,585	2,569	18.9	19.9	765	839	5.6	6.5	9	14	17	3.5	5.4	7.4
Bedford	53	110	8.5	17.5	102	148	16.4	23.5	1	1	1	18.9	9.1	11.8
Bristol	220	176	12.7	10.2	264	261	15.2	15.1	–	–	4	–	–	18.6
Buena Vista	53	97	8.1	15.2	85	89	13.1	14.0	–	–	1	–	–	11.5
Charlottesville	474	548	11.6	13.7	292	333	7.2	8.3	5	4	6	10.5	7.3	10.1
Chesapeake[5]	2,973	2,830	13.8	14.1	1,427	1,360	6.6	6.8	31	29	32	10.4	10.2	12.4
Clifton Forge[5]	(X)	68	(NA)	15.9	(X)	90	(NA)	21.0	(X)	–	1	(NA)	–	24.4
Colonial Heights	216	195	12.4	11.5	229	212	13.1	12.5	2	1	–	9.3	5.1	–
Covington	43	90	6.9	14.3	82	110	13.1	17.5	–	–	–	–	–	–
Danville	567	554	12.2	11.5	642	724	13.8	15.0	3	5	14	5.3	9.0	15.3
Emporia	64	82	11.5	14.5	90	120	16.1	21.2	2	–	5	31.3	–	44.2
Fairfax	275	354	12.5	16.4	267	163	12.1	7.6	8	2	1	29.1	5.6	2.6
Falls Church	113	296	10.7	28.4	95	85	9.0	8.2	–	1	2	–	3.4	6.3
Franklin	155	113	18.3	13.6	112	155	13.3	18.7	3	–	4	19.4	–	21.3
Fredericksburg	406	408	19.5	21.1	195	240	9.4	12.4	7	4	6	17.2	9.8	10.2
Galax	83	124	12.5	18.1	86	138	13.0	20.1	1	2	1	12.0	16.1	11.6
Hampton	1,979	2,014	13.6	13.8	1,150	1,150	7.9	7.9	28	17	26	14.1	8.4	10.8
Harrisonburg	556	451	13.7	11.2	242	295	6.0	7.3	7	1	–	12.6	2.2	–
Hopewell	337	370	15.0	16.6	281	264	12.5	11.8	7	1	8	20.8	2.7	18.7
Lexington	30	82	4.4	12.0	55	123	8.1	18.0	–	–	–	–	–	–
Lynchburg	831	846	12.5	13.0	793	851	12.0	13.0	12	9	4	14.4	10.6	3.8
Manassas	662	783	17.6	22.1	197	214	5.2	6.0	7	8	8	10.6	10.2	13.9
Manassas Park	294	207	25.6	20.0	37	51	3.2	4.9	–	–	–	–	–	–
Martinsville	154	213	10.3	13.8	237	273	15.9	17.7	3	1	3	19.5	4.7	17.0
Newport News	3,211	3,145	17.7	17.4	1,379	1,477	7.6	8.2	34	36	54	10.6	11.4	15.2
Norfolk	4,109	4,001	17.3	17.1	1,968	2,029	8.3	8.7	43	48	110	10.5	12.0	19.7
Norton	45	58	11.9	14.9	56	59	14.7	15.2	–	–	–	–	–	–
Petersburg	528	525	16.1	15.6	472	520	14.4	15.5	7	6	13	13.3	11.4	17.0
Poquoson	98	104	8.4	9.0	76	81	6.5	7.0	2	1	–	20.4	9.6	–
Portsmouth	1,647	1,547	16.6	15.4	1,071	1,124	10.8	11.2	21	15	40	12.8	9.7	18.7
Radford	111	161	7.6	10.2	105	122	7.2	7.7	3	2	2	27.0	12.4	14.1
Richmond	3,006	3,054	15.5	15.5	2,107	2,471	10.9	12.5	33	39	61	11.0	12.8	16.5
Roanoke	951	1,355	10.3	14.3	1,173	1,168	12.7	12.3	8	13	20	8.4	9.6	11.4
Salem	219	240	8.9	9.7	289	330	11.8	13.3	–	1	–	–	4.2	–
South Boston[6]	(X)	(X)	(NA)	(NA)	(X)	(X)	(NA)	(NA)	(X)	(X)	1	(NA)	(NA)	8.6
Staunton	253	264	11.0	11.1	290	313	12.6	13.1	–	–	3	–	–	9.3
Suffolk	1,186	1,008	15.5	15.7	669	592	8.7	9.2	12	8	21	10.1	7.9	24.7
Virginia Beach	6,670	6,459	15.2	15.1	2,552	2,360	5.8	5.5	52	39	74	7.8	6.0	9.7
Waynesboro	298	296	14.3	15.1	225	266	10.8	13.6	3	2	–	10.1	6.8	–
Williamsburg	176	60	15.3	5.0	113	132	9.8	11.0	1	1	1	5.7	16.7	6.1
Winchester	414	335	16.7	14.2	243	266	9.8	11.2	4	2	2	9.7	6.0	4.5
WASHINGTON	81,747	81,036	13.2	13.7	44,770	43,941	7.2	7.4	451	421	621	5.5	5.2	7.8
Adams	395	334	23.7	20.3	109	97	6.5	5.9	4	4	4	10.1	12.0	14.5
Asotin	259	255	12.4	12.4	214	198	10.2	9.6	4	3	5	15.4	11.8	18.0
Benton	2,186	2,080	14.0	14.5	996	944	6.4	6.6	9	19	22	4.1	9.1	11.4
Chelan	903	983	13.1	14.7	538	562	7.8	8.4	2	3	10	2.2	3.1	10.0
Clallam	602	622	8.9	9.7	828	753	12.2	11.7	4	5	7	6.6	8.0	9.2

See footnotes at end of table.

[Includes United States, states, and 3,141 counties/county equivalents defined as of February 22, 2005. For more information on these areas, see Appendix C, Geographic Information]

County	Births				Deaths				Infant deaths[2]					
	Number		Rate per 1,000 population[1]		Number		Rate per 1,000 population[1]		Number			Rate per 1,000 live births[3]		
	2004	2000	2004	2000	2004	2000	2004	2000	2004	2000	1990	2004	2000	1990
WASHINGTON—Con.														
Clark	5,560	5,420	14.2	15.6	2,623	2,344	6.7	6.7	28	18	22	5.0	3.3	5.4
Columbia	40	34	9.6	8.3	49	49	11.8	12.0	–	–	–	–	–	–
Cowlitz	1,227	1,290	12.8	13.9	956	953	9.9	10.2	8	11	14	6.5	8.5	10.3
Douglas	453	454	13.2	13.9	269	252	7.8	7.7	2	1	3	4.4	2.2	6.8
Ferry	73	69	9.7	9.5	72	45	9.6	6.2	–	–	3	–	–	35.3
Franklin	1,325	1,096	22.2	22.1	291	311	4.9	6.3	6	4	8	4.5	3.6	8.8
Garfield	14	22	6.1	9.2	30	30	13.0	12.5	–	–	–	–	–	–
Grant	1,441	1,431	18.0	19.1	569	498	7.1	6.6	13	8	12	9.0	5.6	12.0
Grays Harbor	835	794	11.9	11.8	779	814	11.1	12.1	3	2	7	3.6	2.5	7.4
Island	990	958	12.4	13.3	592	534	7.4	7.4	9	3	6	9.1	3.1	5.7
Jefferson	195	211	6.9	8.0	292	263	10.4	9.9	–	1	1	–	4.7	4.6
King	22,939	22,499	12.9	12.9	11,213	11,563	6.3	6.6	101	102	156	4.4	4.5	6.8
Kitsap	3,010	3,109	12.5	13.4	1,773	1,723	7.3	7.4	14	19	24	4.7	6.1	7.0
Kittitas	341	368	9.4	11.0	244	237	6.7	7.1	4	5	2	11.7	13.6	6.2
Klickitat	219	255	11.1	13.3	163	180	8.2	9.4	–	1	2	–	3.9	8.6
Lewis	862	869	12.1	12.7	792	765	11.1	11.1	8	8	8	9.3	9.2	8.9
Lincoln	91	99	8.7	9.7	104	133	10.0	13.1	–	1	1	–	10.1	10.3
Mason	551	560	10.4	11.3	533	517	10.0	10.4	7	3	7	12.7	5.4	13.8
Okanogan	500	507	12.7	12.8	361	319	9.1	8.1	6	5	5	12.0	9.9	9.0
Pacific	199	195	9.4	9.3	274	315	12.9	15.0	2	2	2	10.1	10.3	8.7
Pend Oreille	116	109	9.3	9.3	141	108	11.3	9.2	–	1	3	–	9.2	21.9
Pierce	10,243	10,177	13.7	14.5	5,233	5,177	7.0	7.4	59	63	98	5.8	6.2	9.3
San Juan	107	92	7.1	6.5	107	113	7.1	8.0	–	–	–	–	–	–
Skagit	1,422	1,396	12.8	13.5	957	940	8.6	9.1	11	11	10	7.7	7.9	8.1
Skamania	73	107	6.9	10.8	76	71	7.2	7.2	1	2	1	13.7	18.7	9.7
Snohomish	8,630	8,550	13.4	14.0	4,113	3,830	6.4	6.3	40	36	49	4.6	4.2	5.9
Spokane	5,487	5,667	12.6	13.5	3,695	3,670	8.5	8.8	37	27	37	6.7	4.8	6.6
Stevens	480	445	11.6	11.1	391	354	9.5	8.8	4	1	6	8.3	2.2	15.1
Thurston	2,592	2,549	11.5	12.2	1,601	1,550	7.1	7.4	18	10	16	6.9	3.9	6.8
Wahkiakum	26	29	6.9	7.6	44	45	11.7	11.7	–	–	–	–	–	–
Walla Walla	716	660	12.5	11.9	507	518	8.9	9.4	2	2	6	2.8	3.0	9.1
Whatcom	2,057	2,077	11.4	12.4	1,328	1,228	7.4	7.3	9	7	14	4.4	3.4	7.9
Whitman	379	411	9.4	10.1	202	244	5.0	6.0	2	2	5	5.3	4.9	12.4
Yakima	4,209	4,253	18.3	19.1	1,711	1,694	7.5	7.6	34	31	45	8.1	7.3	11.2
WEST VIRGINIA	20,880	20,865	11.5	11.5	20,793	21,114	11.5	11.7	158	158	223	7.6	7.6	9.9
Barbour	170	139	11.0	8.9	190	207	12.2	13.3	1	3	2	5.9	21.6	10.5
Berkeley	1,280	1,072	14.3	14.0	775	627	8.7	8.2	11	8	7	8.6	7.5	7.6
Boone	316	371	12.3	14.5	289	307	11.3	12.0	3	3	–	9.5	8.1	–
Braxton	136	157	9.1	10.7	150	143	10.1	9.7	–	1	3	–	6.4	15.6
Brooke	236	238	9.5	9.4	332	306	13.4	12.1	4	2	2	16.9	8.4	6.6
Cabell	1,137	1,191	12.0	12.3	1,163	1,162	12.3	12.0	9	6	11	7.9	5.0	9.2
Calhoun	60	81	8.2	10.7	90	92	12.3	12.1	1	–	–	16.7	–	–
Clay	134	115	12.8	11.1	113	123	10.8	11.9	2	1	–	14.9	8.7	–
Doddridge	79	69	10.7	9.3	88	97	11.9	13.1	–	1	–	–	14.5	–
Fayette	550	572	11.7	12.0	603	658	12.8	13.8	3	5	5	5.5	8.7	8.8
Gilmer	72	52	10.3	7.3	78	87	11.2	12.1	1	–	–	13.9	–	–
Grant	130	147	11.2	13.0	119	138	10.3	12.2	–	4	1	–	27.2	7.8
Greenbrier	376	382	10.8	11.1	453	441	13.0	12.8	1	3	–	2.7	7.9	–
Hampshire	225	232	10.4	11.4	217	199	10.1	9.8	2	1	4	8.9	4.3	17.2
Hancock	348	364	11.1	11.2	427	404	13.6	12.4	4	2	3	11.5	5.5	7.8
Hardy	144	149	10.9	11.7	141	126	10.7	9.9	–	1	2	–	6.7	13.5
Harrison	847	783	12.4	11.4	843	905	12.3	13.2	5	4	10	5.9	5.1	11.1
Jackson	312	368	11.0	13.1	259	309	9.1	11.0	5	5	2	16.0	13.6	6.7
Jefferson	632	584	13.3	13.8	388	378	8.2	8.9	5	2	5	7.9	3.4	9.1
Kanawha	2,449	2,420	12.6	12.1	2,469	2,503	12.7	12.5	14	18	29	5.7	7.4	11.1
Lewis	172	192	10.0	11.4	208	217	12.1	12.9	1	4	1	5.8	20.8	5.3
Lincoln	294	272	13.1	12.3	276	280	12.3	12.7	3	8	6	10.2	29.4	19.5
Logan	437	504	12.0	13.4	474	481	13.0	12.8	4	3	7	9.2	6.0	14.1
McDowell	310	316	12.6	11.6	397	437	16.1	16.1	1	5	5	3.2	15.8	9.7
Marion	623	597	11.0	10.6	694	703	12.3	12.4	5	4	6	8.0	6.7	9.1
Marshall	355	367	10.3	10.4	397	395	11.5	11.2	3	3	3	8.5	8.2	6.8
Mason	296	308	11.5	11.9	289	313	11.2	12.1	1	3	4	3.4	9.7	14.5
Mercer	708	790	11.4	12.6	814	799	13.1	12.7	7	3	10	9.9	3.8	12.3
Mineral	321	305	11.9	11.3	306	325	11.3	12.0	1	2	5	3.1	6.6	14.7
Mingo	370	361	13.6	12.9	336	333	12.3	11.9	1	2	5	2.7	5.5	10.0
Monongalia	925	863	11.0	10.5	613	663	7.3	8.1	3	2	15	3.2	2.3	15.8
Monroe	123	132	9.1	10.0	163	156	12.1	11.8	–	–	1	–	–	7.2
Morgan	147	157	9.3	10.5	171	154	10.9	10.3	1	1	1	6.8	6.4	7.1
Nicholas	263	284	10.0	10.7	284	317	10.8	11.9	–	2	3	–	7.0	8.5
Ohio	455	480	10.0	10.1	600	601	13.2	12.7	5	6	4	11.0	12.5	6.3

See footnotes at end of table.

[Includes United States, states, and 3,141 counties/county equivalents defined as of February 22, 2005. For more information on these areas, see Appendix C, Geographic Information]

County	Births				Deaths				Infant deaths[2]					
	Number		Rate per 1,000 population[1]		Number		Rate per 1,000 population[1]		Number			Rate per 1,000 live births[3]		
	2004	2000	2004	2000	2004	2000	2004	2000	2004	2000	1990	2004	2000	1990
WEST VIRGINIA—Con.														
Pendleton	66	76	8.4	9.3	99	92	12.5	11.3	–	1	1	–	13.2	10.8
Pleasants	62	82	8.3	10.9	84	82	11.3	10.9	–	–	2	–	–	19.4
Pocahontas	91	80	10.2	8.8	139	111	15.6	12.2	4	1	–	44.0	12.5	–
Preston	320	270	10.7	9.2	318	369	10.7	12.6	3	4	3	9.4	14.8	8.7
Putnam	665	585	12.4	11.3	464	445	8.6	8.6	8	3	2	12.0	5.1	3.7
Raleigh	900	879	11.4	11.1	886	962	11.2	12.2	8	6	12	8.9	6.8	13.5
Randolph	316	322	11.1	11.4	353	343	12.4	12.2	2	4	3	6.3	12.4	8.7
Ritchie	125	112	11.9	10.8	126	125	12.0	12.1	3	–	–	24.0	–	–
Roane	188	171	12.3	11.1	180	180	11.8	11.6	–	2	2	–	11.7	10.9
Summers	110	136	8.0	9.5	164	168	11.9	11.7	1	1	1	9.1	7.4	8.1
Taylor	145	159	9.0	9.9	196	212	12.1	13.2	–	2	3	–	12.6	16.2
Tucker	58	67	8.2	9.2	85	87	12.1	11.9	–	–	6	–	–	64.5
Tyler	90	96	9.6	10.0	103	113	11.0	11.8	1	–	–	11.1	–	–
Upshur	284	248	11.9	10.6	267	268	11.2	11.4	2	1	6	7.0	4.0	18.6
Wayne	450	496	10.6	11.6	447	442	10.5	10.3	5	3	3	11.1	6.0	6.0
Webster	90	106	9.1	10.9	120	114	12.2	11.8	–	1	3	–	9.4	21.9
Wetzel	190	203	11.1	11.5	231	225	13.5	12.7	2	1	1	10.5	4.9	3.6
Wirt	61	56	10.4	9.5	58	46	9.9	7.8	–	–	1	–	–	17.5
Wood	987	1,034	11.3	11.8	937	1,042	10.8	11.9	11	6	10	11.1	5.8	8.6
Wyoming	250	273	10.2	10.7	327	302	13.3	11.8	1	4	2	4.0	14.7	6.0
WISCONSIN	70,146	69,326	12.7	12.9	45,600	46,461	8.3	8.6	420	457	598	6.0	6.6	8.2
Adams	163	158	8.0	7.9	222	231	10.9	11.5	–	2	2	–	12.7	11.4
Ashland	184	224	11.0	13.3	210	208	12.6	12.3	1	4	3	5.4	17.9	14.9
Barron	526	466	11.5	10.3	431	444	9.4	9.9	4	3	9	7.6	6.4	15.6
Bayfield	140	143	9.2	9.5	145	151	9.6	10.0	4	1	–	28.6	7.0	–
Brown	3,211	3,212	13.6	14.1	1,561	1,591	6.6	7.0	25	20	22	7.8	6.2	6.9
Buffalo	157	165	11.4	11.9	112	124	8.1	9.0	–	1	2	–	6.1	11.4
Burnett	145	135	8.8	8.6	174	183	10.5	11.6	2	–	1	13.8	–	6.9
Calumet	701	514	16.0	12.6	273	253	6.2	6.2	2	2	4	2.9	3.9	8.1
Chippewa	719	673	12.2	12.2	464	536	7.9	9.7	3	3	–	4.2	4.5	–
Clark	564	497	16.5	14.8	353	306	10.4	9.1	5	1	5	8.9	2.0	8.6
Columbia	637	617	11.6	11.7	497	509	9.1	9.7	4	4	6	6.3	6.5	9.8
Crawford	176	183	10.3	10.6	165	178	9.7	10.3	–	–	–	–	–	–
Dane	5,994	5,558	13.2	13.0	2,640	2,514	5.8	5.9	22	27	35	3.7	4.9	6.6
Dodge	981	993	11.2	11.5	829	848	9.4	9.9	–	9	4	–	9.1	4.1
Door	233	232	8.2	8.3	289	315	10.2	11.2	1	2	2	4.3	8.6	6.2
Douglas	486	513	11.0	11.8	450	455	10.2	10.5	3	4	6	6.2	7.8	11.2
Dunn	455	486	11.0	12.2	271	279	6.5	7.0	2	2	3	4.4	4.1	7.2
Eau Claire	1,105	1,117	11.7	12.0	705	641	7.5	6.9	3	1	9	2.7	0.9	7.5
Florence	33	37	6.6	7.3	56	62	11.2	12.2	–	–	–	–	–	–
Fond du Lac	1,116	1,151	11.3	11.8	888	908	9.0	9.3	5	8	9	4.5	7.0	7.1
Forest	107	114	10.6	11.3	103	132	10.2	13.1	–	3	2	–	26.3	14.6
Grant	593	539	12.0	10.9	508	499	10.2	10.1	7	2	5	11.8	3.7	7.5
Green	404	402	11.6	11.9	306	322	8.8	9.5	1	–	6	2.5	–	14.4
Green Lake	229	219	12.0	11.5	222	243	11.6	12.7	–	–	3	–	–	12.4
Iowa	312	264	13.3	11.6	201	196	8.6	8.6	2	–	1	6.4	–	3.1
Iron	42	39	6.3	5.7	89	85	13.3	12.4	–	3	–	–	76.9	–
Jackson	244	234	12.5	12.2	215	219	11.0	11.4	2	2	3	8.2	8.5	13.9
Jefferson	1,020	931	13.0	12.3	590	610	7.5	8.0	4	3	3	3.9	3.2	3.4
Juneau	293	275	11.5	11.3	279	264	11.0	10.8	–	1	2	–	3.6	7.2
Kenosha	2,126	2,151	13.4	14.3	1,292	1,226	8.2	8.2	14	12	15	6.6	5.6	7.2
Kewaunee	235	224	11.4	11.1	184	190	8.9	9.4	–	1	4	–	4.5	16.9
La Crosse	1,259	1,233	11.6	11.5	891	888	8.2	8.3	2	7	5	1.6	5.7	3.5
Lafayette	224	175	13.7	10.8	141	144	8.7	8.9	2	–	3	8.9	–	13.0
Langlade	216	210	10.4	10.1	244	221	11.7	10.7	1	1	2	4.6	4.8	8.6
Lincoln	315	281	10.4	9.5	287	333	9.5	11.2	1	2	4	3.2	7.1	11.6
Manitowoc	889	894	10.9	10.8	764	855	9.3	10.3	5	5	10	5.6	5.6	9.3
Marathon	1,532	1,521	12.0	12.1	928	923	7.3	7.3	8	9	16	5.2	5.9	9.5
Marinette	421	455	9.7	10.5	472	470	10.9	10.8	4	3	3	9.5	6.6	5.8
Marquette	156	147	10.4	10.1	168	172	11.2	11.8	1	1	2	6.4	6.8	13.5
Menominee	102	93	22.3	20.3	44	36	9.6	7.9	–	–	–	–	–	–
Milwaukee	14,645	14,856	15.8	15.8	8,515	9,075	9.2	9.7	149	151	188	10.2	10.2	11.0
Monroe	587	602	13.9	14.7	408	415	9.7	10.1	5	7	4	8.5	11.6	6.8
Oconto	400	383	10.7	10.7	327	358	8.7	10.0	1	3	–	2.5	7.8	–
Oneida	333	317	9.0	8.6	421	432	11.4	11.7	2	–	3	6.0	–	8.0
Outagamie	2,295	2,289	13.6	14.1	1,118	1,107	6.6	6.8	6	9	20	2.6	3.9	8.8
Ozaukee	883	869	10.3	10.5	636	583	7.4	7.1	3	3	7	3.4	3.5	7.4
Pepin	89	78	12.0	10.8	69	72	9.3	10.0	1	3	3	11.2	38.5	33.3
Pierce	464	414	12.1	11.2	234	245	6.1	6.6	2	1	6	4.3	2.4	12.8
Polk	511	455	11.6	11.0	398	378	9.1	9.1	–	3	4	–	6.6	7.5
Portage	710	806	10.5	12.0	456	406	6.8	6.0	2	1	4	2.8	1.2	4.4

See footnotes at end of table.

County and City Data Book: 2007

U.S. Census Bureau

[Includes United States, states, and 3,141 counties/county equivalents defined as of February 22, 2005. For more information on these areas, see Appendix C, Geographic Information]

County	Births Number 2004	2000	Births Rate per 1,000 population[1] 2004	2000	Deaths Number 2004	2000	Deaths Rate per 1,000 population[1] 2004	2000	Infant deaths[2] Number 2004	2000	1990	Infant deaths Rate per 1,000 live births[3] 2004	2000	1990
WISCONSIN—Con.														
Price	137	125	8.9	7.9	215	206	14.0	13.0	1	–	3	7.3	–	16.2
Racine	2,501	2,651	12.9	14.0	1,504	1,614	7.8	8.5	25	17	26	10.0	6.4	9.6
Richland	231	201	12.5	11.2	166	185	9.0	10.3	3	–	–	13.0	–	–
Rock	2,005	2,077	12.8	13.6	1,312	1,335	8.4	8.8	10	20	20	5.0	9.6	9.2
Rusk	151	148	9.9	9.6	176	168	11.5	10.9	–	1	–	–	6.8	–
St. Croix	1,135	909	15.3	14.3	415	445	5.6	7.0	2	3	8	1.8	3.3	9.5
Sauk	764	755	13.4	13.6	512	487	9.0	8.8	3	4	7	3.9	5.3	10.4
Sawyer	184	183	10.9	11.3	152	183	9.0	11.3	3	–	3	16.3	–	17.0
Shawano	473	471	11.5	11.5	421	476	10.2	11.7	1	2	3	2.1	4.2	5.7
Sheboygan	1,383	1,439	12.1	12.8	1,038	1,084	9.1	9.6	17	14	9	12.3	9.7	6.4
Taylor	240	247	12.2	12.5	159	176	8.1	8.9	–	2	3	–	8.1	10.4
Trempealeau	357	320	13.0	11.8	260	297	9.5	11.0	1	2	3	2.8	6.3	8.1
Vernon	428	389	14.9	13.9	272	331	9.5	11.8	2	1	2	4.7	2.6	6.0
Vilas	188	155	8.5	7.3	222	254	10.0	12.0	–	1	1	–	6.5	5.0
Walworth	1,145	1,103	11.7	11.9	873	825	8.9	8.9	–	6	7	–	5.4	7.0
Washburn	168	163	10.1	10.1	174	198	10.5	12.3	–	1	2	–	6.1	12.6
Washington	1,432	1,491	11.5	12.6	873	795	7.0	6.7	7	8	7	4.9	5.4	5.2
Waukesha	4,363	4,358	11.6	12.0	2,725	2,798	7.2	7.7	18	18	20	4.1	4.1	4.9
Waupaca	556	567	10.6	10.9	657	634	12.5	12.2	3	4	4	5.4	7.1	6.0
Waushara	259	225	10.5	9.7	297	243	12.0	10.5	1	1	2	3.9	4.4	8.2
Winnebago	1,838	1,926	11.6	12.3	1,256	1,196	7.9	7.6	9	16	10	4.9	8.3	5.2
Wood	846	879	11.2	11.6	676	696	9.0	9.2	3	6	9	3.5	6.8	8.7
WYOMING	6,807	6,253	13.5	12.7	3,955	3,920	7.8	7.9	60	42	60	8.8	6.7	8.6
Albany	371	359	11.8	11.3	169	197	5.4	6.2	7	1	3	18.9	2.8	6.9
Big Horn	150	147	13.2	12.9	122	134	10.7	11.7	1	1	2	6.7	6.8	12.7
Campbell	591	494	16.1	14.5	147	154	4.0	4.5	3	2	2	5.1	4.0	3.8
Carbon	204	190	13.3	12.2	139	145	9.1	9.3	2	–	–	9.8	–	–
Converse	146	151	11.7	12.5	101	94	8.1	7.8	2	3	1	13.7	19.9	6.6
Crook	67	60	11.1	10.2	44	58	7.3	9.8	–	–	–	–	–	–
Fremont	542	483	15.0	13.5	320	320	8.8	8.9	8	3	5	14.8	6.2	8.6
Goshen	127	139	10.3	11.1	146	132	11.9	10.5	3	2	3	23.6	14.4	18.5
Hot Springs	43	41	9.4	8.4	62	65	13.5	13.4	–	–	1	–	–	20.4
Johnson	99	59	13.0	8.3	81	86	10.6	12.1	–	–	–	–	–	–
Laramie	1,257	1,162	14.8	14.2	655	660	7.7	8.1	10	7	12	8.0	6.0	10.0
Lincoln	228	183	14.6	12.5	118	102	7.5	7.0	2	3	4	8.8	16.4	15.7
Natrona	941	906	13.6	13.6	543	567	7.9	8.5	11	4	10	11.7	4.4	10.7
Niobrara	17	25	7.4	10.5	19	34	8.3	14.2	–	1	–	–	40.0	–
Park	275	262	10.4	10.1	256	203	9.7	7.9	1	–	3	3.6	–	9.1
Platte	86	80	9.9	9.1	90	100	10.4	11.4	1	–	–	11.6	–	–
Sheridan	328	264	12.0	9.9	274	283	10.1	10.6	1	1	3	3.0	3.8	10.5
Sublette	86	54	12.9	9.1	54	44	8.1	7.4	–	–	2	–	–	27.8
Sweetwater	566	517	15.1	13.8	276	232	7.3	6.2	4	7	5	7.1	13.5	8.9
Teton	238	198	12.5	10.8	75	71	3.9	3.9	3	2	1	12.6	10.1	4.7
Uinta	292	302	14.8	15.3	115	100	5.8	5.1	1	5	2	3.4	16.6	5.5
Washakie	86	106	10.9	12.8	92	77	11.7	9.3	–	–	–	–	–	–
Weston	67	71	10.0	10.7	57	62	8.5	9.3	–	–	1	–	–	13.0

– Represents zero.   NA Not available.   X Not applicable.

[1]Per 1,000 resident population estimated as of July 1, 2004, and enumerated as of April 1, 2000.
[2]Deaths of infants under 1 year.
[3]Infant deaths per 1,000 live registered births.
[4]Yellowstone National Park County became incorporated with Gallatin and Park Counties, MT; effective November 7, 1997.
[5]Clifton Forge independent city became incorporated with Alleghany County, VA; effective July 1, 2001.
[6]South Boston independent city became incorporated with Halifax County, VA; effective June 30, 1995.

Survey, Census, or Data Collection Method: For information about these data collections and surveys, see Appendix B, Limitations of the Data and Methodology, and also the following organization and Internet site: National Center for Health Statistics, <http://wonder.cdc.gov>.

Source: U.S. National Center for Health Statistics, Division of Vital Statistics, accessed January 25, 2007 (related Internet site <http://wonder.cdc.gov>), and unpublished data.

Table B-6. Counties — Physicians, Community Hospitals, Medicare, Social Security, and Supplemental Security Income

[Includes United States, states, and 3,141 counties/county equivalents defined as of February 22, 2005. For more information on these areas, see Appendix C, Geographic Information]

County	Physicians, 2004[1] Number	Physicians, 2004[1] Rate per 100,000 persons[2]	Community hospitals, 2004[3] Number	Beds Number	Beds Rate per 100,000 persons[2]	Medicare program enrollment, 2005[4] Total	Medicare Percent change, 2000–2005	Medicare Rate per 100,000 persons[2]	Social Security program beneficiaries, December 2005 Number	SS Rate per 100,000 persons[2]	SS Percent change, 2000–2005	Retired workers, number	Supplemental Security Income program recipients, 2005 Number	SSI Rate per 100,000 persons[2]
UNITED STATES........	872,250	297	4,919	808,127	275	[5]41,547,753	[5]7.2	[5]14,017	47,236,897	15,936	6.6	[5]29,839,453	[5]7,113,132	[5]2,400
ALABAMA...............	10,564	233	108	15,328	339	[6]751,175	[6]9.6	[6]16,481	[7]903,569	[7]19,825	[7]9.4	[7]492,491	163,878	3,596
Autauga...............	32	67	1	47	99	6,523	20.9	13,418	8,400	17,280	22.9	4,550	1,366	2,810
Baldwin...............	355	227	4	502	320	29,108	24.8	17,903	35,160	21,625	24.2	22,530	2,787	1,714
Barbour...............	21	74	1	74	259	4,521	4.0	15,911	5,970	21,011	10.1	2,990	1,747	6,148
Bibb..................	12	56	1	160	752	3,647	16.6	16,950	4,440	20,636	16.0	2,015	1,020	4,741
Blount................	19	35	1	40	73	6,860	19.7	12,310	10,415	18,690	19.2	5,635	1,345	2,414
Bullock...............	9	80	1	41	366	1,862	−5.6	16,843	2,095	18,951	−10.8	995	813	7,354
Butler................	17	82	2	100	483	4,101	1.6	19,749	4,970	23,933	1.5	2,615	1,302	6,270
Calhoun...............	221	197	3	416	371	22,496	8.7	20,060	25,640	22,864	5.8	13,555	4,332	3,863
Chambers..............	35	98	1	192	540	7,118	3.0	20,073	8,385	23,646	5.4	4,825	1,527	4,306
Cherokee..............	11	45	1	45	184	4,245	14.1	17,311	5,960	24,305	18.6	3,340	876	3,572
Chilton...............	20	48	1	60	145	6,037	9.1	14,462	7,995	19,152	11.4	3,995	1,352	3,239
Choctaw...............	6	40	–	–	–	3,066	10.9	20,706	3,965	26,778	12.4	1,810	981	6,625
Clarke................	22	80	3	94	343	5,236	9.1	19,201	6,225	22,828	3.8	3,100	1,597	5,856
Clay..................	8	57	1	46	327	2,903	8.0	20,789	3,585	25,673	7.9	2,010	617	4,419
Cleburne..............	1	7	–	–	–	2,646	11.2	18,299	3,335	23,064	12.6	1,820	473	3,271
Coffee................	58	129	2	248	550	7,823	12.4	17,168	9,330	20,475	10.3	5,440	1,517	3,329
Colbert...............	94	172	2	192	351	10,972	8.5	20,073	13,580	24,844	8.8	7,110	2,015	3,686
Conecuh...............	10	75	1	42	313	2,735	2.7	20,631	3,495	26,363	4.1	1,710	859	6,480
Coosa.................	2	18	–	–	–	2,273	10.6	20,364	2,895	25,936	9.2	1,485	586	5,250
Covington.............	45	122	3	179	486	8,161	4.2	22,055	9,515	25,714	4.9	5,690	1,550	4,189
Crenshaw..............	8	59	1	65	476	2,915	4.6	21,236	3,385	24,659	6.2	1,890	769	5,602
Cullman...............	104	131	2	185	234	14,229	9.7	17,812	17,290	21,643	10.2	9,850	2,496	3,124
Dale..................	38	78	1	69	141	10,442	12.8	21,420	9,165	18,801	9.3	4,905	1,840	3,775
Dallas................	91	204	1	149	333	8,965	4.3	20,207	10,340	23,306	3.2	4,910	4,496	10,134
DeKalb................	47	70	1	103	154	11,258	10.9	16,735	14,100	20,960	3.1	7,695	2,417	3,593
Elmore................	44	61	2	109	152	10,649	19.5	14,403	12,710	17,190	20.2	7,180	2,039	2,758
Escambia..............	35	91	2	118	308	6,729	9.1	17,670	8,355	21,939	7.6	4,380	1,401	3,679
Etowah................	214	208	2	439	426	20,174	4.5	19,551	24,895	24,126	5.2	12,740	4,431	4,294
Fayette...............	14	77	1	183	1,006	3,395	8.5	18,625	4,695	25,757	8.6	2,610	847	4,647
Franklin..............	29	95	2	125	407	6,321	5.8	20,565	7,135	23,213	5.7	3,795	1,125	3,660
Geneva................	13	51	1	161	630	5,453	8.9	21,189	6,495	25,238	6.4	3,710	1,210	4,702
Greene................	4	41	1	20	206	1,826	4.3	18,901	2,275	23,548	7.0	1,020	952	9,854
Hale..................	10	55	1	23	126	3,364	11.1	18,366	3,625	19,791	11.2	1,645	1,119	6,109
Henry.................	8	48	–	–	–	3,290	9.4	19,807	3,945	23,751	6.3	2,225	731	4,401
Houston...............	332	357	3	606	652	13,299	15.4	14,110	19,275	20,451	12.4	11,120	3,562	3,779
Jackson...............	59	110	1	92	171	10,216	11.8	19,042	11,765	21,929	11.6	6,590	1,707	3,182
Jefferson.............	3,700	562	13	3,803	578	113,075	2.5	17,205	124,540	18,949	−0.2	67,010	22,670	3,449
Lamar.................	3	20	–	–	–	3,447	5.2	23,038	3,960	26,467	6.1	2,325	632	4,224
Lauderdale............	183	209	1	322	368	17,070	10.7	19,466	20,480	23,355	12.0	11,365	2,716	3,097
Lawrence..............	11	32	1	37	107	4,818	10.7	13,923	7,275	21,023	16.0	3,670	1,411	4,077
Lee...................	203	168	1	273	226	12,396	17.6	10,057	16,250	13,184	14.8	9,245	2,777	2,253
Limestone.............	51	74	1	101	146	9,401	16.5	13,341	12,495	17,731	18.2	7,000	1,908	2,708
Lowndes...............	5	38	–	–	–	1,905	9.3	14,569	2,705	20,687	5.8	1,225	1,066	8,152
Macon.................	20	86	–	–	–	3,714	3.7	16,282	4,290	18,808	4.7	2,285	1,344	5,892
Madison...............	824	281	3	885	301	41,002	20.2	13,750	45,880	15,386	18.8	28,545	5,960	1,999
Marengo...............	16	73	1	99	449	3,752	4.8	17,149	5,355	24,476	14.5	2,615	1,642	7,505
Marion................	23	76	2	177	587	6,147	9.6	20,385	7,390	24,508	10.5	4,200	1,105	3,665
Marshall..............	97	114	2	192	227	16,518	7.1	19,289	18,460	21,557	17.7	10,160	2,792	3,260
Mobile................	1,158	289	6	1,450	362	61,299	7.2	15,270	75,155	18,722	7.7	39,295	13,655	3,402
Monroe................	23	97	1	62	262	4,032	5.2	16,989	5,120	21,573	6.8	2,665	1,101	4,639
Montgomery............	683	308	5	877	395	32,610	5.0	14,714	38,265	17,266	5.1	21,335	9,251	4,174
Morgan................	218	193	3	483	428	19,270	13.7	16,942	22,370	19,668	13.5	12,875	3,008	2,645
Perry.................	5	43	–	–	–	2,064	2.1	18,151	2,830	24,888	1.7	1,375	1,320	11,608
Pickens...............	11	54	1	52	256	4,237	7.9	20,998	5,040	24,978	6.2	2,605	1,383	6,854
Pike..................	33	112	1	78	265	5,257	7.2	17,737	5,885	19,856	4.9	3,215	1,618	5,459
Randolph..............	8	35	2	63	279	4,363	7.7	19,206	5,265	23,176	7.6	3,200	865	3,808
Russell...............	27	55	1	38	77	9,010	8.2	18,266	10,085	20,446	7.7	5,665	1,973	4,000
St. Clair.............	28	40	1	40	57	9,382	21.9	12,971	13,435	18,575	23.2	7,015	1,806	2,497
Shelby................	451	273	1	187	113	14,384	23.9	8,389	23,005	13,417	28.2	13,740	2,026	1,182
Sumter................	5	36	–	–	–	2,648	8.1	19,162	3,125	22,614	7.1	1,420	1,299	9,400
Talladega.............	69	86	2	207	258	14,953	8.5	18,585	18,285	22,726	7.7	8,795	3,997	4,968
Tallapoosa............	60	147	2	79	194	7,913	8.6	19,434	10,220	25,100	9.4	5,700	1,737	4,266
Tuscaloosa............	501	300	2	610	365	24,369	8.7	14,427	30,750	18,205	10.9	16,030	6,173	3,655
Walker................	72	103	2	195	279	15,507	8.6	22,116	17,645	25,165	8.2	8,215	3,179	4,534
Washington............	7	39	1	19	107	3,162	13.8	17,791	4,100	23,069	12.6	1,925	870	4,895
Wilcox................	7	54	1	32	248	2,610	6.6	20,175	3,230	24,967	7.1	1,275	1,727	13,349
Winston...............	14	57	1	42	172	4,995	10.4	20,389	5,870	23,961	10.4	3,010	1,063	4,339

See footnotes at end of table.

[Includes United States, states, and 3,141 counties/county equivalents defined as of February 22, 2005. For more information on these areas, see Appendix C, Geographic Information]

County	Physicians, 2004[1] Number	Rate per 100,000 persons[2]	Community hospitals, 2004[3] Number	Beds Number	Beds Rate per 100,000 persons[2]	Medicare program enrollment, 2005[4] Total	Percent change, 2000–2005	Rate per 100,000 persons[2]	Social Security program beneficiaries, December 2005 Number	Rate per 100,000 persons[2]	Percent change, 2000–2005	Retired workers, number	Supplemental Security Income program recipients, 2005 Number	Rate per 100,000 persons[2]
ALASKA	1,580	240	19	1,427	217	[6]52,179	[6]24.2	[6]7,862	[7]64,843	[7]9,771	[7]19.3	[7]38,643	11,064	1,667
Aleutians East	2	75	–	–	–	[8]([8])	[8](NA)	(NA)	120	4,423	20.0	75	8	295
Aleutians West	1	18	–	–	–	[8]236	[8]18.0	[8]4,385	150	2,787	–1.3	85	15	279
Anchorage	956	349	3	692	252	21,140	25.0	7,686	24,735	8,993	18.2	14,735	4,858	1,766
Bethel	19	112	–	–	–	732	2.5	4,274	1,430	8,349	15.2	580	544	3,176
Bristol Bay	–	–	–	–	–	603	169.2	54,227	130	11,691	12.1	85	12	1,079
Denali	–	–	–	–	–	[9]([9])	[9](NA)	(NA)	170	9,038	54.5	105	9	478
Dillingham	11	223	1	14	284	[10]405	[10]6.3	[10]8,222	490	9,947	4.9	240	131	2,659
Fairbanks North Star	208	239	1	217	250	5,552	15.3	6,341	7,155	8,172	16.7	4,445	1,013	1,157
Haines	6	267	–	–	–	350	18.6	15,405	395	17,386	17.6	285	49	2,157
Juneau	84	270	1	72	231	3,109	25.0	10,033	3,180	10,262	13.0	2,010	491	1,585
Kenai Peninsula	81	157	3	96	186	5,697	28.5	10,964	7,290	14,030	26.7	4,500	888	1,709
Ketchikan Gateway	36	272	1	64	484	1,462	15.6	11,024	1,735	13,082	11.6	1,160	229	1,727
Kodiak Island	22	166	1	44	333	433	–1.4	3,318	1,095	8,390	17.2	680	153	1,172
Lake and Peninsula	–	–	–	–	–	[10]([10])	(NA)	(NA)	160	10,191	2.6	80	30	1,911
Matanuska-Susitna	74	103	1	36	50	5,726	41.3	7,534	7,965	10,479	38.1	4,615	1,106	1,455
Nome	8	86	1	34	364	585	18.9	6,271	910	9,756	5.4	410	243	2,605
North Slope	5	71	–	–	–	358	12.2	5,170	555	8,016	0.2	270	61	881
Northwest Arctic	5	66	–	–	–	413	10.1	5,419	665	8,726	2.8	260	124	1,627
Prince of Wales-Outer Ketchikan	4	69	–	–	–	497	22.1	8,781	665	11,749	25.7	410	102	1,802
Sitka	35	394	2	76	855	910	20.7	10,127	1,025	11,407	12.9	730	88	979
Skagway-Hoonah-Angoon	1	32	–	–	–	[11]408	[11]18.3	[11]13,052	355	11,356	5.3	245	41	1,312
Southeast Fairbanks	4	65	–	–	–	581	26.6	8,784	880	13,305	32.7	525	174	2,631
Valdez-Cordova	7	70	2	33	332	855	22.7	8,637	1,085	10,961	16.2	695	128	1,293
Wade Hampton	–	–	–	–	–	433	11.3	5,742	710	9,415	0.1	260	271	3,594
Wrangell-Petersburg	10	159	2	49	779	750	10.3	12,010	950	15,212	6.9	665	67	1,073
Yakutat	–	–	–	–	–	[11]([11])	(NA)	(NA)	70	9,695	18.6	45	6	831
Yukon-Koyukuk	1	16	–	–	–	[9]820	[9]17.3	[9]13,349	715	11,639	7.7	410	223	3,630
ARIZONA	14,010	244	62	11,166	195	[6]786,080	[6]16.4	[6]13,235	[7]922,932	[7]15,539	[7]16.0	[7]602,398	97,934	1,649
Apache	81	118	1	12	17	7,812	21.0	11,266	9,485	13,678	16.2	4,540	4,466	6,440
Cochise	126	102	5	180	145	21,381	18.3	16,955	25,045	19,860	15.2	16,165	2,639	2,093
Coconino	336	274	2	292	238	15,269	19.0	12,327	14,300	11,545	15.3	8,185	2,972	2,399
Gila	88	172	2	82	160	12,149	9.5	23,516	14,575	28,212	8.9	9,365	1,334	2,582
Graham	19	58	1	55	167	4,619	10.3	13,966	5,510	16,660	9.2	3,100	773	2,337
Greenlee	5	67	–	–	–	1,096	7.1	14,573	1,305	17,351	–0.1	685	127	1,689
La Paz	18	90	1	39	196	4,140	16.5	20,457	4,900	24,212	14.6	3,425	448	2,214
Maricopa	8,698	249	29	7,022	201	419,003	15.2	11,525	491,305	13,514	14.9	323,040	48,151	1,324
Mohave	221	123	3	386	215	41,099	23.5	21,955	49,390	26,384	22.8	33,995	3,410	1,822
Navajo	128	120	2	91	86	13,756	24.8	12,686	17,020	15,696	24.1	9,405	4,953	4,568
Pima	3,421	377	10	2,171	239	143,477	13.7	15,515	161,325	17,445	12.3	104,460	16,945	1,832
Pinal	125	58	2	245	114	30,055	19.4	13,093	41,810	18,214	30.1	26,850	4,293	1,870
Santa Cruz	49	120	1	79	194	5,569	17.7	13,257	6,360	15,140	18.2	4,020	1,213	2,887
Yavapai	470	246	2	235	123	42,932	21.5	21,606	54,300	27,327	21.3	37,980	3,008	1,514
Yuma	225	128	1	277	158	22,271	19.9	12,286	26,290	14,503	19.5	17,180	3,202	1,766
ARKANSAS	6,202	226	87	9,580	348	[6]470,364	[6]7.1	[6]16,925	[7]566,219	[7]20,374	[7]8.1	[7]321,160	90,968	3,273
Arkansas	23	114	2	122	607	3,848	–1.7	19,170	4,315	21,497	–0.4	2,450	672	3,348
Ashley	20	85	1	36	153	4,249	1.4	18,332	5,260	22,694	4.7	2,675	955	4,120
Baxter	100	251	1	266	668	12,072	7.6	29,933	14,340	35,557	9.7	9,845	884	2,192
Benton	253	141	4	333	185	26,053	9.2	13,937	31,280	16,733	10.0	20,435	2,157	1,154
Boone	72	205	1	125	355	7,971	11.0	22,270	9,190	25,675	9.7	5,255	969	2,707
Bradley	10	81	1	49	398	2,419	–1.8	19,841	2,825	23,171	–3.0	1,555	499	4,093
Calhoun	1	18	–	–	–	910	0.7	16,282	1,310	23,439	–0.5	705	209	3,739
Carroll	31	117	2	60	226	4,831	11.3	17,893	6,160	22,816	13.0	3,915	489	1,811
Chicot	16	121	1	35	265	2,626	–2.7	20,158	2,990	22,952	–0.8	1,580	1,010	7,753
Clark	22	95	1	25	108	4,066	0.3	17,743	4,485	19,571	0.3	2,705	628	2,740
Clay	9	54	1	35	209	3,959	–0.9	23,881	4,685	28,260	2.4	2,650	722	4,355
Cleburne	37	148	1	18	72	6,115	9.8	24,083	7,415	29,203	10.2	4,710	678	2,670
Cleveland	1	11	–	–	–	1,515	12.8	17,017	1,825	20,499	10.7	1,000	240	2,696
Columbia	23	92	1	62	249	4,924	0.8	19,939	5,825	23,588	–0.7	3,070	1,181	4,782
Conway	19	92	–	–	–	4,857	4.8	23,420	5,135	24,760	6.3	2,840	871	4,200
Craighead	291	339	3	476	555	12,728	11.9	14,675	15,575	17,957	17.5	8,665	2,826	3,258
Crawford	49	87	1	103	182	9,319	16.0	16,170	11,775	20,432	15.9	5,895	1,844	3,200
Crittenden	51	99	1	121	235	6,529	7.1	12,584	8,500	16,383	8.9	4,140	2,973	5,730
Cross	12	63	1	15	79	3,124	1.1	16,240	3,855	20,040	5.9	2,040	857	4,455
Dallas	4	46	1	25	288	1,691	–9.2	19,838	2,020	23,698	–4.8	1,045	477	5,596
Desha	11	76	2	75	516	2,527	–1.0	17,600	3,005	20,929	5.8	1,540	795	5,537
Drew	9	48	1	58	312	2,757	5.3	14,749	3,620	19,366	9.0	1,975	670	3,584
Faulkner	138	145	1	149	157	11,498	19.6	11,836	14,195	14,612	20.0	8,225	1,751	1,802
Franklin	7	39	1	25	139	3,412	8.0	18,729	4,235	23,246	9.8	2,270	574	3,151
Fulton	9	76	1	40	337	3,029	10.7	25,381	3,495	29,286	2.5	1,955	489	4,098

See footnotes at end of table.

Table B-6. Counties — **Physicians, Community Hospitals, Medicare, Social Security, and Supplemental Security Income**—Con.

[Includes United States, states, and 3,141 counties/county equivalents defined as of February 22, 2005. For more information on these areas, see Appendix C, Geographic Information]

County	Physicians, 2004[1]		Community hospitals, 2004[3]			Medicare program enrollment, 2005[4]			Social Security program beneficiaries, December 2005				Supplemental Security Income program recipients, 2005	
				Beds										
	Number	Rate per 100,000 persons[2]	Number	Number	Rate per 100,000 persons[2]	Total	Percent change, 2000–2005	Rate per 100,000 persons[2]	Number	Rate per 100,000 persons[2]	Percent change, 2000–2005	Retired workers, number	Number	Rate per 100,000 persons[2]
ARKANSAS—Con.														
Garland	285	309	3	469	509	24,105	7.0	25,767	25,620	27,386	6.6	16,895	2,784	2,976
Grant	11	64	–	–	–	2,491	9.4	14,359	3,220	18,561	12.0	1,785	328	1,891
Greene	41	105	1	129	332	6,862	11.4	17,416	8,640	21,928	9.8	4,630	1,441	3,657
Hempstead	19	81	2	104	444	3,553	-0.4	15,195	4,550	19,459	3.6	2,600	898	3,840
Hot Spring	17	55	1	81	262	5,558	4.8	17,778	7,100	22,710	9.8	3,875	917	2,933
Howard	11	76	–	–	–	2,635	-0.7	18,107	2,955	20,306	0.5	1,655	423	2,907
Independence	71	205	1	174	503	6,629	7.5	19,083	8,205	23,620	10.0	4,490	1,236	3,558
Izard	10	75	1	25	188	3,354	1.1	24,974	4,175	31,087	7.0	2,485	507	3,775
Jackson	34	192	2	169	956	4,319	-13.5	24,538	4,075	23,152	-1.0	2,165	907	5,153
Jefferson	174	212	1	373	454	12,866	0.2	15,748	14,855	18,182	1.9	7,725	3,681	4,506
Johnson	27	114	1	80	337	4,178	5.5	17,378	5,300	22,045	8.6	2,790	906	3,768
Lafayette	4	49	–	–	–	1,573	-3.4	19,596	1,975	24,604	4.4	1,045	518	6,453
Lawrence	9	52	1	214	1,232	4,164	3.2	24,276	4,555	26,555	2.2	2,435	841	4,903
Lee	9	77	–	–	–	1,880	-5.4	16,284	2,345	20,312	-5.9	1,155	985	8,532
Lincoln	1	7	–	–	–	1,854	1.8	13,000	2,350	16,477	0.4	1,250	519	3,639
Little River	7	53	1	25	189	2,478	6.6	18,734	3,015	22,794	10.5	1,700	438	3,311
Logan	13	57	2	41	179	4,673	4.9	20,367	5,630	24,538	5.7	2,965	783	3,413
Lonoke	30	51	–	–	–	7,750	19.5	12,777	9,615	15,851	21.0	5,200	1,319	2,174
Madison	9	61	–	–	–	2,688	10.4	17,966	3,385	22,624	8.2	1,850	418	2,794
Marion	8	49	–	–	–	3,694	12.0	22,073	4,940	29,519	14.2	2,990	522	3,119
Miller	52	122	–	–	–	6,792	15.9	15,736	7,810	18,095	10.8	4,245	1,514	3,508
Mississippi	38	79	2	136	281	7,790	1.2	16,259	9,705	20,256	1.5	4,850	3,195	6,669
Monroe	5	53	–	–	–	1,926	-3.7	20,705	2,295	24,672	-1.7	1,260	651	6,998
Montgomery	6	65	–	–	–	1,905	5.0	20,541	2,515	27,119	9.8	1,520	299	3,224
Nevada	3	31	–	–	–	1,880	0.6	19,686	2,230	23,351	0.4	1,195	527	5,518
Newton	3	35	–	–	–	1,757	10.9	20,788	2,350	27,804	10.6	1,130	480	5,679
Ouachita	24	88	1	98	359	5,805	-2.3	21,419	6,595	24,334	-2.8	3,525	1,386	5,114
Perry	2	19	–	–	–	2,038	5.5	19,469	2,475	23,643	13.1	1,350	371	3,544
Phillips	25	103	1	100	411	4,421	-5.5	18,339	5,275	21,882	-7.4	2,620	2,217	9,196
Pike	7	64	1	32	291	2,124	4.5	19,243	2,685	24,325	5.3	1,535	323	2,926
Poinsett	9	36	–	–	–	4,843	4.9	19,105	5,920	23,354	5.4	2,965	1,435	5,661
Polk	28	139	1	58	289	4,341	9.4	21,516	5,300	26,269	11.0	3,170	651	3,227
Pope	97	173	1	154	275	8,949	11.3	15,817	11,630	20,555	11.4	6,220	1,781	3,148
Prairie	4	44	–	–	–	1,718	-0.7	18,852	2,175	23,867	0.6	1,195	343	3,764
Pulaski	2,578	706	11	2,504	686	54,980	8.6	15,003	62,695	17,108	7.1	35,770	11,072	3,021
Randolph	20	109	1	45	244	3,733	6.4	20,217	4,865	26,347	11.2	2,670	722	3,910
St. Francis	24	85	1	70	249	4,551	-0.4	16,311	5,095	18,260	-1.0	2,625	1,951	6,992
Saline	92	103	1	106	119	9,645	18.1	10,577	17,635	19,339	20.9	10,940	1,615	1,771
Scott	4	36	1	24	218	2,342	8.4	21,004	2,820	25,291	1.2	1,445	408	3,659
Searcy	5	63	–	–	–	2,126	3.6	26,678	2,455	30,807	2.5	1,295	457	5,735
Sebastian	418	355	4	750	638	18,463	6.7	15,548	22,760	19,166	9.1	12,375	3,403	2,866
Sevier	17	106	1	44	273	2,431	3.1	14,773	2,880	17,501	3.3	1,610	386	2,346
Sharp	11	63	–	–	–	4,999	4.5	28,735	6,075	34,920	13.2	3,590	790	4,541
Stone	11	94	1	25	215	2,841	13.5	24,249	3,690	31,495	14.8	2,085	617	5,266
Union	99	222	1	140	314	8,724	-0.5	19,744	10,585	23,956	2.1	5,490	1,911	4,325
Van Buren	12	73	2	192	1,164	4,172	6.3	25,240	5,200	31,460	9.5	3,140	589	3,563
Washington	464	266	5	585	336	21,292	11.7	11,805	25,280	14,017	11.9	14,685	2,880	1,597
White	111	157	2	318	451	12,490	11.4	17,510	14,650	20,538	14.1	8,305	1,957	2,744
Woodruff	4	49	–	–	–	1,699	-5.1	20,980	1,930	23,833	-3.2	995	485	5,989
Yell	21	99	2	62	291	4,193	3.1	19,602	4,820	22,533	1.2	2,530	761	3,558
CALIFORNIA	105,766	295	361	71,910	201	[6]4,221,669	[6]8.2	[6]11,684	[7]4,463,873	[7]12,354	[7]6.1	[7]2,875,626	1,209,842	3,348
Alameda	4,720	325	13	4,419	304	162,595	3.2	11,222	166,775	11,510	1.7	106,345	50,793	3,506
Alpine	2	167	–	–	–	147	13.1	12,683	155	13,374	9.9	110	24	2,071
Amador	78	206	1	66	175	7,595	11.2	19,742	8,560	22,251	7.7	6,000	587	1,526
Butte	503	236	4	524	246	38,107	5.1	17,792	43,350	20,240	4.3	26,680	10,569	4,935
Calaveras	54	118	1	30	66	8,914	12.6	19,018	10,515	22,434	10.2	7,125	1,041	2,221
Colusa	15	73	1	48	235	3,034	21.6	14,383	3,085	14,624	8.5	1,800	575	2,726
Contra Costa	2,981	296	7	1,462	145	126,919	8.6	12,470	136,110	13,373	6.2	88,960	23,379	2,297
Del Norte	53	187	1	59	208	4,762	12.6	16,589	5,520	19,230	9.6	3,075	2,013	7,013
El Dorado	364	211	2	219	127	26,484	6.5	14,976	29,250	16,540	12.0	19,650	2,844	1,608
Fresno	1,902	220	12	2,155	249	97,658	8.5	11,128	107,890	12,294	6.9	65,525	40,180	4,578
Glenn	11	40	1	10	36	4,105	2.3	14,788	5,000	18,012	5.9	3,005	1,141	4,110
Humboldt	329	256	4	250	195	20,713	7.6	16,135	23,900	18,617	6.5	13,240	6,960	5,422
Imperial	143	94	2	270	177	19,983	13.9	12,824	22,905	14,699	5.7	12,970	10,071	6,463
Inyo	49	269	2	67	367	3,598	-4.7	19,817	4,125	22,720	-1.4	2,850	494	2,721
Kern	1,174	160	9	1,389	189	82,572	11.6	10,910	97,735	12,914	10.6	54,525	31,693	4,188
Kings	141	99	3	108	76	12,042	13.2	8,396	14,440	10,068	10.7	8,065	4,680	3,263
Lake	92	143	2	85	132	12,804	-0.5	19,654	15,220	23,363	1.8	9,130	3,697	5,675
Lassen	47	136	1	38	110	4,071	7.2	11,715	4,540	13,064	7.5	2,545	1,078	3,102
Los Angeles	30,102	304	92	21,514	217	1,059,297	7.3	10,662	1,047,590	10,544	4.8	681,035	400,125	4,027
Madera	159	114	2	361	260	19,736	10.5	13,822	20,235	14,171	10.3	12,695	4,714	3,301

See footnotes at end of table.

Table B-6. Counties — **Physicians, Community Hospitals, Medicare, Social Security, and Supplemental Security Income**—Con.

[Includes United States, states, and 3,141 counties/county equivalents defined as of February 22, 2005. For more information on these areas, see Appendix C, Geographic Information]

County	Physicians, 2004[1] Number	Physicians, 2004[1] Rate per 100,000 persons[2]	Community hospitals, 2004[3] Number	Beds Number	Beds Rate per 100,000 persons[2]	Medicare program enrollment, 2005[4] Total	Medicare Percent change, 2000–2005	Medicare Rate per 100,000 persons[2]	Social Security program beneficiaries, December 2005 Number	SS Rate per 100,000 persons[2]	SS Percent change, 2000–2005	Retired workers, number	Supplemental Security Income program recipients, 2005 Number	SSI Rate per 100,000 persons[2]
CALIFORNIA—Con.														
Marin	1,700	691	4	449	183	37,688	8.7	15,261	39,965	16,183	6.9	28,965	3,738	1,514
Mariposa	18	100	1	34	190	3,378	10.6	18,695	4,345	24,047	11.2	2,875	568	3,144
Mendocino	242	274	3	133	150	15,050	8.7	17,071	16,980	19,260	5.4	10,215	3,945	4,475
Merced	257	109	2	289	122	22,541	13.2	9,326	29,080	12,031	8.3	16,630	10,618	4,393
Modoc	11	115	2	113	1,179	1,885	8.6	19,792	2,410	25,304	12.9	1,495	432	4,536
Mono	33	260	1	15	118	1,062	24.4	8,490	1,115	8,914	7.1	820	109	871
Monterey	967	233	4	646	156	44,298	3.0	10,749	49,520	12,016	1.0	31,480	9,274	2,250
Napa	556	420	2	421	318	22,209	1.5	16,728	22,600	17,023	3.8	15,105	2,287	1,723
Nevada	292	300	2	151	155	17,469	6.5	17,754	21,500	21,851	5.7	14,880	1,822	1,852
Orange	9,663	324	29	5,334	179	322,546	11.2	10,794	332,710	11,135	7.3	229,755	65,133	2,180
Placer	919	300	2	224	73	44,878	36.4	14,156	52,760	16,642	30.5	36,745	4,555	1,437
Plumas	39	183	4	154	722	4,253	8.0	19,803	5,015	23,351	7.6	3,310	772	3,595
Riverside	2,809	150	17	3,139	168	233,020	15.0	11,972	266,775	13,706	13.3	176,595	49,630	2,550
Sacramento	3,942	292	9	2,972	220	167,048	10.2	12,252	175,420	12,866	6.7	105,285	57,343	4,206
San Benito	49	88	1	125	223	5,003	10.0	8,944	6,045	10,807	9.9	3,900	844	1,509
San Bernardino	3,601	188	15	3,096	162	186,737	10.8	9,510	214,445	10,921	9.5	124,825	64,558	3,288
San Diego	10,262	350	18	5,663	193	355,045	4.0	12,103	377,110	12,855	1.7	248,325	80,811	2,755
San Francisco	6,231	838	8	2,816	379	119,645	1.9	16,181	104,470	14,129	-0.5	71,865	45,882	6,205
San Joaquin	1,049	162	7	1,048	161	74,248	9.4	11,180	83,720	12,606	7.8	49,240	27,854	4,194
San Luis Obispo	844	332	4	350	138	40,887	4.3	16,004	45,495	17,808	3.2	30,575	5,259	2,058
San Mateo	3,040	435	7	1,504	215	94,245	2.6	13,471	94,645	13,528	1.1	67,555	12,909	1,845
Santa Barbara	1,338	333	6	864	215	56,922	3.4	14,203	61,505	15,347	0.7	40,255	9,850	2,458
Santa Clara	6,690	398	11	2,937	175	181,986	8.8	10,711	181,285	10,670	6.8	123,360	44,757	2,634
Santa Cruz	756	301	3	371	148	29,009	2.5	11,619	31,970	12,805	2.7	20,730	5,562	2,228
Shasta	516	290	3	504	283	35,150	12.0	19,538	40,040	22,256	10.8	23,230	9,123	5,071
Sierra	–	–	1	40	1,147	682	-2.0	19,860	765	22,277	1.1	505	76	2,213
Siskiyou	90	200	2	110	245	10,034	5.3	22,170	11,325	25,023	5.6	7,095	2,576	5,692
Solano	875	212	4	543	132	44,955	13.9	10,922	51,225	12,446	10.4	31,135	10,845	2,635
Sonoma	1,487	318	7	777	166	65,588	3.5	14,060	72,635	15,571	2.8	48,040	9,691	2,077
Stanislaus	904	182	4	1,131	227	60,553	10.3	11,979	68,940	13,638	7.9	40,250	20,286	4,013
Sutter	195	225	1	90	104	12,163	11.1	13,685	13,730	15,448	8.0	8,170	3,457	3,890
Tehama	74	123	1	64	107	10,016	7.5	16,367	13,055	21,333	11.0	7,880	3,101	5,067
Trinity	15	110	1	40	294	3,286	27.6	24,123	3,475	25,510	10.4	2,070	735	5,396
Tulare	520	130	3	722	180	44,538	8.7	10,840	52,525	12,784	7.6	30,705	18,573	4,520
Tuolumne	138	243	2	226	398	11,651	7.1	19,621	13,675	23,030	6.2	9,255	1,669	2,811
Ventura	1,926	242	7	1,297	163	94,794	11.5	11,907	103,415	12,990	8.0	68,415	15,541	1,952
Yolo	725	394	2	163	89	19,707	12.3	10,656	21,020	11,366	5.4	13,135	5,042	2,726
Yuba	74	115	1	281	436	8,528	5.3	12,699	9,775	14,556	3.6	5,300	3,957	5,893
COLORADO	13,455	292	70	9,250	201	[6]519,698	[6]11.2	[6]11,140	[7]584,556	[7]12,530	[7]9.4	[7]378,990	[6]55,532	[6]1,190
Adams	363	94	4	431	111	38,587	(NA)	9,661	41,915	10,494	(NA)	25,905	4,643	1,162
Alamosa	35	231	1	57	376	1,899	11.2	12,426	2,190	14,331	10.4	1,215	522	3,416
Arapahoe	1,682	322	3	781	150	51,337	19.3	9,703	57,415	10,852	11.5	38,135	4,850	917
Archuleta	20	172	–	–	–	1,782	35.0	14,992	2,230	18,762	36.6	1,565	101	850
Baca	6	145	1	81	1,962	1,033	-2.3	25,387	1,095	26,911	-5.9	655	97	2,384
Bent	2	36	–	–	–	894	-7.5	16,085	960	17,272	-6.0	555	189	3,401
Boulder	1,067	382	3	459	164	32,521	(NA)	11,596	33,280	11,867	(NA)	22,480	2,091	746
Broomfield	66	155	–	–	–	–	(NA)	–	660	1,518	(NA)	405	241	554
Chaffee	38	225	1	34	201	3,323	9.6	19,584	3,760	22,159	8.4	2,645	220	1,297
Cheyenne	3	149	1	12	598	331	-9.6	16,948	370	18,945	-10.8	215	17	870
Clear Creek	5	55	–	–	–	608	8.8	6,611	1,045	11,362	6.6	735	68	739
Conejos	6	71	1	47	558	1,480	5.2	17,387	1,675	19,678	4.6	910	405	4,758
Costilla	3	84	–	–	–	870	6.5	25,409	1,040	30,374	2.3	560	273	7,973
Crowley	2	36	–	–	–	626	-4.0	11,590	705	13,053	-5.5	385	133	2,463
Custer	7	184	–	–	–	787	32.5	20,389	925	23,964	28.3	655	49	1,269
Delta	48	161	1	48	161	6,347	5.6	21,194	7,090	23,675	4.1	4,780	444	1,483
Denver	3,912	704	9	2,679	482	69,480	-1.9	12,453	71,220	12,765	-5.8	45,890	12,235	2,193
Dolores	2	110	–	–	–	385	1.3	21,073	450	24,631	1.6	265	34	1,861
Douglas	423	178	1	106	45	8,152	59.9	3,268	16,610	6,660	54.5	11,380	541	217
Eagle	158	342	1	58	126	1,855	45.3	3,903	2,400	5,049	40.8	1,670	63	133
Elbert	2	9	–	–	–	1,583	33.9	6,947	2,205	9,676	24.7	1,460	64	281
El Paso	1,360	244	3	840	151	58,832	13.2	10,402	68,050	12,032	12.0	42,450	5,805	1,026
Fremont	51	108	1	55	116	8,204	10.2	17,175	9,480	19,847	10.2	5,950	865	1,811
Garfield	97	200	2	142	293	4,848	12.4	9,733	5,350	10,741	6.8	3,580	270	542
Gilpin	2	41	–	–	–	224	23.1	4,542	480	9,732	3.0	305	18	365
Grand	18	136	1	19	144	1,206	15.2	9,129	1,455	11,014	16.5	1,080	41	310
Gunnison	28	198	1	24	169	1,113	9.9	7,824	1,405	9,876	14.8	965	53	373
Hinsdale	4	506	–	–	–	123	50.0	16,078	145	18,954	36.8	110	(D)	(NA)
Huerfano	11	142	1	25	322	1,654	10.3	21,284	1,875	24,128	11.6	1,180	272	3,500
Jackson	2	136	–	–	–	250	5.9	17,265	290	20,028	5.1	210	10	691

See footnotes at end of table.

[Includes United States, states, and 3,141 counties/county equivalents defined as of February 22, 2005. For more information on these areas, see Appendix C, Geographic Information]

County	Physicians, 2004[1] Number	Rate per 100,000 persons[2]	Community hospitals, 2004[3] Number	Beds Number	Beds Rate per 100,000 persons[2]	Medicare program enrollment, 2005[4] Total	Percent change, 2000–2005	Rate per 100,000 persons[2]	Social Security program beneficiaries, December 2005 Number	Rate per 100,000 persons[2]	Percent change, 2000–2005	Retired workers, number	Supplemental Security Income program recipients, 2005 Number	Rate per 100,000 persons[2]
COLORADO—Con.														
Jefferson	1,339	254	2	626	119	62,219	(NA)	11,811	68,865	13,072	(NA)	47,335	4,017	763
Kiowa	1	70	1	42	2,947	336	5.0	23,629	345	24,262	−0.9	225	17	1,195
Kit Carson	4	52	1	22	284	1,281	3.0	16,763	1,490	19,498	1.6	925	100	1,309
Lake	5	65	1	25	323	647	12.3	8,361	765	9,886	6.1	450	55	711
La Plata	201	431	1	75	161	5,380	17.2	11,338	6,305	13,287	15.5	4,270	376	792
Larimer	694	258	3	451	168	30,838	15.8	11,341	35,525	13,064	16.3	24,075	1,942	714
Las Animas	19	123	1	25	162	3,129	0.2	20,258	3,350	21,688	1.1	1,915	584	3,781
Lincoln	5	87	1	50	874	850	0.2	15,130	990	17,622	0.1	630	60	1,068
Logan	25	119	1	36	172	3,448	1.8	16,642	3,785	18,268	0.7	2,320	381	1,839
Mesa	377	296	3	466	366	22,649	13.0	17,439	25,130	19,350	10.8	16,755	2,105	1,621
Mineral	2	215	–	–	–	145	21.8	15,558	210	22,532	34.6	155	8	858
Moffat	16	118	1	25	185	1,532	−0.3	11,418	1,840	13,714	8.3	1,095	124	924
Montezuma	53	215	1	61	247	4,172	12.3	16,838	4,950	19,977	10.6	3,120	431	1,739
Montrose	83	226	1	51	139	6,552	16.8	17,480	7,560	20,170	13.8	5,080	554	1,478
Morgan	32	114	2	65	232	3,978	7.2	14,210	4,445	15,878	4.5	2,765	355	1,268
Otero	30	153	1	176	898	4,085	0.3	20,954	4,165	21,364	−1.5	2,435	808	4,145
Ouray	18	434	–	–	–	532	20.9	12,488	720	16,901	26.3	540	15	352
Park	10	60	–	–	–	1,377	30.2	8,124	1,890	11,151	28.2	1,290	77	454
Phillips	7	153	2	57	1,244	960	1.2	20,933	975	21,260	14.4	630	56	1,221
Pitkin	83	562	1	25	169	1,099	26.8	7,369	1,525	10,225	29.6	1,185	24	161
Prowers	16	114	1	25	179	2,090	1.1	15,045	2,210	15,908	−5.2	1,355	332	2,390
Pueblo	416	277	2	541	361	26,757	6.7	17,682	28,930	19,118	4.4	16,185	4,972	3,286
Rio Blanco	7	116	1	48	798	840	9.9	14,063	995	16,658	6.2	635	45	753
Rio Grande	13	105	1	6	48	2,094	4.9	17,126	2,640	21,592	−2.1	1,615	408	3,337
Routt	78	370	1	88	417	1,422	24.2	6,672	1,800	8,446	26.1	1,210	72	338
Saguache	2	29	–	–	–	852	13.3	12,118	780	11,094	41.3	505	79	1,124
San Juan	–	–	–	–	–	65	4.8	11,265	85	14,731	2.4	55	(D)	(NA)
San Miguel	20	281	–	–	–	343	27.0	4,755	435	6,031	17.9	285	17	236
Sedgwick	3	118	1	64	2,509	642	−3.9	25,386	685	27,086	−8.3	475	43	1,700
Summit	79	318	–	–	–	1,309	48.4	5,259	1,670	6,709	44.8	1,285	31	125
Teller	36	166	–	–	–	2,542	29.5	11,598	3,255	14,851	27.8	2,105	147	671
Washington	–	–	–	–	–	868	−2.9	18,735	975	21,045	−0.4	605	45	971
Weld	341	155	1	276	125	20,909	(NA)	9,133	24,995	10,918	(NA)	15,595	2,502	1,093
Yuma	17	174	2	26	266	1,634	−1.1	16,692	1,840	18,797	−9.1	1,180	130	1,328
CONNECTICUT	14,043	401	35	7,826	224	[6]527,058	[6]2.3	[6]15,015	[7]585,199	[7]16,671	[7]1.3	407,045	52,260	1,489
Fairfield	3,686	409	6	1,715	190	125,000	0.5	13,846	135,835	15,046	−1.3	97,450	10,501	1,163
Hartford	3,765	431	9	2,271	260	141,055	1.2	16,077	155,120	17,680	(Z)	108,025	17,520	1,997
Litchfield	448	237	3	244	129	30,105	6.2	15,839	34,530	18,167	6.5	24,440	1,421	748
Middlesex	515	318	1	168	104	24,747	8.6	15,162	28,130	17,235	8.0	20,110	1,267	776
New Haven	4,497	533	10	2,707	321	132,068	0.6	15,597	146,165	17,262	(Z)	99,550	15,775	1,863
New London	732	275	2	428	161	40,099	4.9	15,040	45,310	16,994	4.5	30,465	3,131	1,174
Tolland	240	164	2	146	99	16,928	12.8	11,466	20,515	13,896	10.2	14,515	817	553
Windham	160	140	2	147	128	16,733	5.8	14,447	19,590	16,913	5.0	12,490	1,828	1,578
DELAWARE	2,325	280	6	1,955	236	[6]126,789	[6]13.1	[6]15,031	[7]150,101	[7]17,795	[7]13.4	97,950	13,767	1,632
Kent	241	173	1	352	253	20,195	24.4	14,027	25,415	17,653	26.3	15,865	2,910	2,021
New Castle	1,708	329	3	1,166	225	69,083	7.3	13,209	81,140	15,514	7.4	51,220	8,245	1,576
Sussex	376	218	2	437	254	37,256	18.7	21,102	43,545	24,665	18.8	30,865	2,612	1,479
DISTRICT OF COLUMBIA	4,723	852	11	3,453	623	73,879	−1.9	13,420	71,376	12,965	−3.2	46,064	21,108	3,834
District of Columbia	4,723	852	11	3,453	623	73,879	−1.9	13,420	71,376	12,965	−3.2	46,064	21,108	3,834
FLORIDA	51,024	293	203	49,962	287	[6]3,043,361	[6]8.5	[6]17,107	[7]3,430,205	[7]19,282	[7]7.3	[7]2,331,733	423,209	2,379
Alachua	1,981	890	4	1,171	526	28,592	11.7	12,773	31,420	14,036	10.8	19,620	4,694	2,097
Baker	16	67	1	68	284	3,026	19.8	12,316	3,835	15,609	19.3	1,935	555	2,259
Bay	351	222	3	605	383	26,764	16.0	16,566	30,680	18,990	10.8	18,390	3,701	2,291
Bradford	14	51	1	25	91	3,623	8.7	12,885	4,600	16,360	39.1	2,735	746	2,653
Brevard	1,268	244	6	1,428	275	108,034	12.8	20,336	123,475	23,242	9.3	84,340	8,507	1,601
Broward	4,698	268	17	4,900	280	243,953	−2.4	13,723	269,990	15,188	−3.2	184,765	32,520	1,829
Calhoun	8	61	1	25	192	2,234	10.0	16,810	2,660	20,015	6.1	1,440	517	3,890
Charlotte	423	269	3	722	459	40,614	4.0	25,781	50,785	32,237	1.2	38,100	1,694	1,075
Citrus	292	224	2	299	230	39,116	10.0	29,111	49,015	36,478	12.0	35,490	2,218	1,651
Clay	362	220	1	230	140	19,442	26.9	11,363	25,730	15,038	23.9	16,060	1,897	1,109
Collier	1,155	389	1	548	185	58,377	18.5	19,000	65,420	21,293	14.9	49,040	2,326	757
Columbia	109	177	2	154	250	10,708	18.0	16,721	12,525	19,558	15.1	7,435	2,304	3,598
DeSoto	30	86	1	49	141	5,026	−0.8	14,195	5,990	16,918	2.7	3,905	771	2,178
Dixie	5	35	–	–	–	2,967	15.4	20,257	3,655	24,954	9.6	2,125	700	4,779
Duval	2,851	348	7	2,450	299	102,227	8.4	12,370	116,730	14,125	7.4	70,160	18,925	2,290

See footnotes at end of table.

[Includes United States, states, and 3,141 counties/county equivalents defined as of February 22, 2005. For more information on these areas, see Appendix C, Geographic Information]

County	Physicians, 2004[1] Number	Rate per 100,000 persons[2]	Community hospitals, 2004[3] Number	Beds Number	Beds Rate per 100,000 persons[2]	Medicare program enrollment, 2005[4] Total	Percent change, 2000–2005	Rate per 100,000 persons[2]	Social Security program beneficiaries, December 2005 Number	Rate per 100,000 persons[2]	Percent change, 2000–2005	Retired workers, number	Supplemental Security Income program recipients, 2005 Number	Rate per 100,000 persons[2]
FLORIDA—Con.														
Escambia	973	328	3	1,280	431	49,281	12.9	16,606	57,155	19,259	10.2	34,175	8,380	2,824
Flagler	115	167	1	81	117	19,133	34.2	25,040	23,715	31,037	35.2	17,445	1,036	1,356
Franklin	9	89	1	25	248	1,869	-0.6	18,365	2,260	22,207	-2.0	1,495	350	3,439
Gadsden	46	100	1	25	54	7,356	6.9	15,844	8,780	18,911	3.8	5,085	2,499	5,383
Gilchrist	1	6	–	–	–	2,680	24.1	16,339	3,095	18,870	18.3	1,815	414	2,524
Glades	5	45	–	–	–	1,066	16.5	9,474	2,195	19,508	20.1	1,545	190	1,689
Gulf	17	124	1	30	219	2,758	8.2	19,735	3,160	22,612	3.8	1,820	376	2,691
Hamilton	11	78	1	42	298	2,076	10.5	14,847	2,570	18,379	14.4	1,350	562	4,019
Hardee	11	39	–	–	–	3,469	2.7	12,264	4,060	14,353	1.1	2,440	844	2,984
Hendry	23	60	1	25	66	4,246	15.3	10,733	5,110	12,917	3.1	3,060	1,051	2,657
Hernando	240	159	3	380	252	44,726	8.2	28,235	51,345	32,413	7.9	36,045	2,686	1,696
Highlands	200	215	2	250	268	27,045	6.1	28,321	30,510	31,949	5.6	22,505	2,098	2,197
Hillsborough	3,749	341	11	3,279	298	149,400	10.7	13,196	171,555	15,153	9.3	106,210	30,386	2,684
Holmes	12	63	1	25	131	3,894	11.0	20,214	4,590	23,827	3.3	2,595	782	4,059
Indian River	449	360	3	554	444	33,323	4.5	25,913	36,700	28,539	6.5	26,725	1,375	1,069
Jackson	52	109	2	101	212	9,338	10.8	19,063	10,695	21,833	9.2	5,960	1,925	3,930
Jefferson	8	56	–	–	–	2,323	11.7	16,032	2,750	18,979	6.2	1,715	653	4,507
Lafayette	3	40	–	–	–	760	8.6	9,556	1,000	12,574	-11.8	585	138	1,735
Lake	535	204	3	713	272	81,457	33.0	29,403	77,260	27,888	20.9	56,960	4,382	1,582
Lee	1,404	273	5	1,601	311	112,754	11.8	20,698	128,230	23,539	11.2	93,620	7,364	1,352
Leon	752	309	3	813	334	23,980	10.3	9,758	28,775	11,709	13.3	18,935	4,145	1,687
Levy	23	62	1	40	107	7,506	11.8	19,754	9,920	26,107	13.6	6,130	1,287	3,387
Liberty	–	–	–	–	–	984	8.4	12,659	1,190	15,309	7.5	645	269	3,461
Madison	9	47	1	31	163	3,413	9.2	17,877	3,855	20,192	4.1	2,170	1,066	5,583
Manatee	863	292	2	810	274	57,503	6.4	18,744	72,040	23,483	6.8	52,440	3,998	1,303
Marion	539	185	2	678	232	78,638	15.5	25,915	91,590	30,184	17.2	64,990	6,598	2,174
Martin	486	353	1	308	224	34,880	2.6	24,963	40,095	28,695	6.9	30,140	1,460	1,045
Miami-Dade	9,253	392	26	8,309	352	335,441	8.7	14,118	338,210	14,234	5.7	229,765	126,636	5,330
Monroe	247	317	3	215	276	11,117	1.1	14,565	12,840	16,822	-1.8	9,085	1,126	1,475
Nassau	111	176	1	32	51	10,277	27.0	15,873	12,580	19,430	23.7	7,895	927	1,432
Okaloosa	502	277	3	422	233	27,730	13.9	15,222	30,550	16,770	9.6	19,420	2,278	1,250
Okeechobee	50	128	1	101	259	7,449	10.0	18,699	7,775	19,518	5.5	4,885	937	2,352
Orange	2,784	281	3	3,511	355	117,017	11.4	11,438	131,385	12,843	9.7	79,230	25,036	2,447
Osceola	251	114	2	299	136	29,458	35.2	12,721	34,605	14,943	26.0	19,860	5,914	2,554
Palm Beach	4,376	352	15	3,048	245	251,014	4.1	19,788	273,180	21,535	2.8	201,945	16,165	1,274
Pasco	627	154	5	1,053	258	89,997	5.8	20,975	109,080	25,423	5.7	73,705	7,796	1,817
Pinellas	2,998	323	14	3,494	377	196,628	-3.5	21,188	214,925	23,159	-3.1	147,690	17,014	1,833
Polk	985	188	4	1,297	247	98,412	10.4	18,127	118,300	21,790	11.6	77,335	14,675	2,703
Putnam	81	112	1	141	194	14,784	7.3	20,096	18,170	24,698	5.7	10,735	2,854	3,879
St. Johns	540	354	1	300	196	25,538	22.0	15,811	29,955	18,545	22.2	20,430	1,870	1,158
St. Lucie	352	155	2	539	237	47,022	15.6	19,487	54,750	22,689	7.6	37,680	5,215	2,161
Santa Rosa	280	203	3	192	139	19,521	29.1	13,641	24,115	16,851	25.1	14,630	1,979	1,383
Sarasota	1,492	419	5	1,073	302	109,729	5.9	29,960	109,040	29,772	5.3	82,095	3,603	984
Seminole	765	196	2	432	110	43,956	13.5	10,945	57,300	14,267	10.5	36,790	5,457	1,359
Sumter	53	88	1	60	99	8,798	4.3	13,708	26,920	41,943	57.1	20,935	1,366	2,128
Suwannee	17	45	1	15	40	8,117	16.7	21,015	9,910	25,658	16.8	6,080	1,271	3,291
Taylor	18	93	1	48	249	3,464	8.3	17,654	4,290	21,863	7.8	2,460	714	3,639
Union	15	102	1	52	355	1,392	15.5	9,332	1,720	11,531	12.3	910	335	2,246
Volusia	1,034	216	6	1,405	293	107,324	6.0	21,900	121,245	24,741	5.2	82,795	9,230	1,883
Wakulla	14	52	–	–	–	3,854	50.0	13,661	3,910	13,859	23.0	2,495	551	1,953
Walton	65	134	2	100	207	6,443	16.8	12,803	9,515	18,907	14.8	5,920	934	1,856
Washington	16	73	1	59	268	3,979	5.5	17,844	5,220	23,409	10.1	2,820	937	4,202
GEORGIA	21,638	243	146	24,709	277	[6]1,028,502	[6]12.3	[6]11,336	[7]1,233,238	[7]13,593	[7]12.0	[7]736,664	203,555	2,244
Appling	13	73	1	140	782	2,597	8.4	14,465	3,310	18,436	8.8	1,730	723	4,027
Atkinson	1	13	–	–	–	1,137	10.0	14,159	1,270	15,816	6.5	630	382	4,757
Bacon	15	145	1	113	1,093	1,547	4.9	14,905	2,035	19,607	3.8	1,085	436	4,201
Baker	–	–	–	–	–	393	-11.1	9,461	730	17,573	3.5	400	220	5,296
Baldwin	126	279	1	109	241	6,487	8.8	14,342	7,400	16,361	8.1	4,075	1,256	2,777
Banks	3	19	–	–	–	1,764	20.8	10,987	2,870	17,876	20.6	1,680	397	2,473
Barrow	31	55	1	56	99	6,323	23.7	10,546	7,740	12,910	28.5	4,515	1,197	1,997
Bartow	106	122	1	112	129	10,675	21.6	11,964	13,495	15,124	20.0	7,855	1,702	1,907
Ben Hill	12	70	1	67	388	2,985	0.7	17,238	3,295	19,029	1.1	1,840	766	4,424
Berrien	10	60	1	171	1,034	2,793	13.1	16,717	3,325	19,901	12.1	1,845	673	4,028
Bibb	769	497	5	976	630	26,998	3.4	17,427	28,250	18,235	0.1	15,735	6,205	4,005
Bleckley	11	91	1	25	207	2,010	3.1	16,555	2,470	20,344	12.5	1,415	440	3,624
Brantley	2	13	–	–	–	2,135	17.4	13,782	2,910	18,785	16.4	1,385	556	3,589
Brooks	7	43	1	35	214	2,315	1.4	14,179	3,190	19,538	-1.5	1,775	789	4,832
Bryan	45	164	–	–	–	2,950	19.4	10,333	3,395	11,892	17.8	1,890	497	1,741
Bulloch	98	163	1	114	189	6,098	11.7	9,923	7,760	12,627	10.3	4,665	1,519	2,472
Burke	17	74	1	40	173	3,040	3.5	13,048	4,160	17,855	13.9	2,150	1,172	5,030
Butts	11	53	1	21	102	3,430	23.5	16,298	3,740	17,771	20.7	2,160	536	2,547
Calhoun	8	131	1	25	410	1,149	-1.4	19,240	1,110	18,587	-0.8	595	351	5,877
Camden	54	120	1	40	89	3,931	41.8	8,591	5,300	11,582	34.2	2,900	727	1,589

See footnotes at end of table.

[Includes United States, states, and 3,141 counties/county equivalents defined as of February 22, 2005. For more information on these areas, see Appendix C, Geographic Information]

County	Physicians, 2004[1] Number	Physicians, 2004[1] Rate per 100,000 persons[2]	Community hospitals, 2004[3] Number	Beds Number	Beds Rate per 100,000 persons[2]	Medicare program enrollment, 2005[4] Total	Medicare Percent change, 2000–2005	Medicare Rate per 100,000 persons[2]	Social Security beneficiaries, Dec. 2005 Number	Social Security Rate per 100,000 persons[2]	Social Security Percent change, 2000–2005	Retired workers, number	Supplemental Security Income recipients, 2005 Number	SSI Rate per 100,000 persons[2]
GEORGIA—Con.														
Candler	8	79	1	42	412	1,601	6.2	15,512	2,005	19,426	7.7	1,135	524	5,077
Carroll	161	158	2	215	210	13,889	19.9	13,171	16,125	15,291	17.2	9,500	2,347	2,226
Catoosa	64	107	1	294	492	5,982	17.7	9,837	10,090	16,592	16.9	6,215	972	1,598
Charlton	7	66	1	25	234	1,535	17.3	14,226	1,865	17,285	13.2	970	360	3,336
Chatham	952	399	3	983	412	34,080	2.0	14,295	38,460	16,132	0.5	23,800	5,863	2,459
Chattahoochee	–	–	–	–	–	439	32.2	2,991	570	3,883	42.5	260	120	817
Chattooga	11	42	–	–	–	4,682	6.7	17,621	5,335	20,079	7.3	3,160	827	3,113
Cherokee	166	95	1	84	48	13,483	37.0	7,319	19,010	10,320	38.1	12,520	1,212	658
Clarke	343	324	2	617	583	11,287	10.7	10,807	12,385	11,859	10.0	7,585	2,353	2,253
Clay	3	90	–	–	–	587	-7.4	18,106	760	23,442	-9.2	435	236	7,279
Clayton	271	103	1	336	127	23,904	36.7	8,921	24,250	9,050	10.8	12,360	5,412	2,020
Clinch	4	58	1	25	360	1,059	3.4	15,137	1,355	19,368	2.0	595	445	6,361
Cobb	1,285	196	3	898	137	61,501	23.3	9,265	64,805	9,762	15.3	42,770	6,144	926
Coffee	61	156	1	88	225	5,275	14.5	13,296	6,335	15,968	12.4	3,195	1,510	3,806
Colquitt	56	128	1	73	167	6,488	5.9	14,774	7,665	17,454	3.5	4,340	1,849	4,210
Columbia	654	650	–	–	–	10,905	28.6	10,505	13,260	12,773	28.1	8,185	1,048	1,010
Cook	13	80	1	155	958	2,528	6.0	15,447	3,015	18,422	1.3	1,695	630	3,849
Coweta	118	112	1	271	257	11,338	26.0	10,316	14,330	13,039	26.5	8,925	1,488	1,354
Crawford	9	70	–	–	–	936	10.0	7,270	2,015	15,652	40.3	1,025	379	2,944
Crisp	34	155	1	208	946	3,560	8.0	16,169	4,100	18,622	5.8	2,330	1,124	5,105
Dade	13	82	1	13	82	2,676	16.7	16,683	3,050	19,015	18.3	1,680	367	2,288
Dawson	15	79	–	–	–	2,431	36.6	12,321	2,750	13,937	37.3	1,785	235	1,191
Decatur	36	126	1	211	739	4,446	5.9	15,536	5,360	18,729	5.2	2,915	1,358	4,745
DeKalb	3,500	519	5	1,577	234	62,301	5.9	9,189	72,705	10,724	5.3	44,235	12,747	1,880
Dodge	28	144	1	87	447	3,098	9.4	15,827	3,445	17,600	-3.6	1,825	822	4,199
Dooly	4	34	–	–	–	1,726	3.9	14,691	2,415	20,555	6.1	1,330	690	5,873
Dougherty	299	314	2	613	644	14,504	5.5	15,286	16,200	17,074	2.8	9,180	4,749	5,005
Douglas	102	95	1	71	66	9,940	19.2	8,815	13,040	11,564	23.9	7,690	1,600	1,419
Early	7	58	1	152	1,259	2,011	-1.2	16,680	2,460	20,405	-1.9	1,370	742	6,155
Echols	–	–	–	–	–	164	11.6	3,856	480	11,286	31.9	250	81	1,905
Effingham	21	47	1	130	292	4,158	27.1	8,861	5,840	12,446	24.7	3,065	716	1,526
Elbert	15	72	1	52	249	4,084	6.3	19,636	4,675	22,477	4.3	2,670	862	4,144
Emanuel	18	82	1	91	414	3,910	1.9	17,686	4,590	20,762	-5.1	2,575	1,319	5,966
Evans	10	88	1	195	1,718	1,742	9.9	15,223	2,030	17,740	3.2	1,160	510	4,457
Fannin	23	106	1	34	157	4,835	13.9	22,091	5,845	26,705	13.7	3,500	654	2,988
Fayette	251	248	–	–	–	10,873	29.2	10,430	13,780	13,218	28.4	9,350	610	585
Floyd	365	388	2	500	532	15,751	7.0	16,721	18,780	19,937	5.6	11,170	2,728	2,896
Forsyth	98	74	1	78	59	8,929	42.0	6,360	12,145	8,651	35.1	8,370	658	469
Franklin	18	84	1	331	1,545	4,450	9.0	20,611	4,960	22,974	9.0	3,075	719	3,330
Fulton	4,797	530	10	3,951	436	74,586	-6.9	8,146	92,555	10,108	3.3	56,665	20,380	2,226
Gilmer	25	94	1	150	562	4,535	18.7	16,590	5,305	19,407	23.3	3,405	580	2,122
Glascock	1	37	–	–	–	563	3.1	20,813	585	21,627	5.8	360	81	2,994
Glynn	257	362	1	247	348	11,883	8.1	16,533	14,105	19,625	6.5	8,675	1,652	2,298
Gordon	52	106	1	65	133	6,903	17.5	13,729	8,235	16,379	14.1	5,005	1,046	2,080
Grady	15	62	1	48	198	3,611	6.1	14,759	4,680	19,129	5.8	2,595	1,038	4,243
Greene	24	155	1	54	348	2,938	19.4	18,722	3,655	23,291	16.4	2,335	535	3,409
Gwinnett	888	127	2	561	80	42,163	30.2	5,805	56,100	7,724	29.2	36,010	6,325	871
Habersham	39	100	1	159	408	6,492	14.5	16,393	7,475	18,875	13.8	4,945	673	1,699
Hall	364	226	1	418	260	18,715	19.1	11,290	22,845	13,781	19.5	14,995	2,101	1,267
Hancock	5	51	–	–	–	1,559	2.7	16,167	1,940	20,118	1.9	1,020	470	4,874
Haralson	19	68	1	25	89	4,687	16.7	16,540	5,620	19,832	12.0	3,365	911	3,215
Harris	29	108	–	–	–	3,151	12.5	11,343	4,360	15,695	18.2	2,780	475	1,710
Hart	23	97	1	174	734	3,633	8.3	15,115	5,320	22,133	11.3	3,465	684	2,846
Heard	–	–	–	–	–	1,279	2.2	11,273	1,875	16,526	7.0	1,050	335	2,953
Henry	238	150	1	196	123	13,899	33.2	8,281	19,245	11,466	43.8	11,535	1,920	1,144
Houston	190	154	2	231	187	14,281	22.1	11,319	16,630	13,181	21.2	9,670	2,499	1,981
Irwin	3	30	1	34	346	1,320	0.8	13,078	1,910	18,924	-0.5	1,070	416	4,122
Jackson	31	63	1	209	422	7,064	27.5	13,509	8,095	15,480	23.3	4,945	1,062	2,031
Jasper	9	70	1	67	524	1,559	12.1	11,858	2,320	17,647	15.9	1,370	321	2,442
Jeff Davis	8	62	1	25	194	2,149	7.5	16,426	2,690	20,561	5.4	1,370	480	3,669
Jefferson	15	88	1	37	218	3,136	0.1	18,528	3,600	21,269	-0.5	1,960	1,101	6,505
Jenkins	5	58	1	25	289	1,422	0.9	16,291	1,670	19,132	1.6	925	473	5,419
Johnson	3	31	–	–	–	1,486	4.4	15,580	1,795	18,819	3.0	985	495	5,190
Jones	14	53	–	–	–	2,207	23.1	8,224	4,425	16,489	32.8	2,405	589	2,195
Lamar	14	86	–	–	–	2,527	7.4	15,429	3,155	19,264	8.5	1,885	427	2,607
Lanier	5	67	1	87	1,172	917	13.5	12,141	1,375	18,205	19.7	700	311	4,118
Laurens	138	297	1	190	409	7,751	9.6	16,528	9,135	19,479	8.8	5,135	1,879	4,007
Lee	19	63	–	–	–	2,031	24.4	6,531	2,900	9,325	23.6	1,715	417	1,341
Liberty	58	96	1	91	150	3,781	24.1	6,571	4,915	8,541	20.6	2,520	1,052	1,828
Lincoln	8	96	–	–	–	1,455	4.6	17,729	1,825	22,237	5.2	1,100	276	3,363

See footnotes at end of table.

Table B-6. Counties — Physicians, Community Hospitals, Medicare, Social Security, and Supplemental Security Income—Con.

[Includes United States, states, and 3,141 counties/county equivalents defined as of February 22, 2005. For more information on these areas, see Appendix C, Geographic Information]

County	Physicians, 2004[1] Number	Physicians, 2004[1] Rate per 100,000 persons[2]	Community hospitals, 2004[3] Number	Beds Number	Beds Rate per 100,000 persons[2]	Medicare program enrollment, 2005[4] Total	Medicare Percent change, 2000–2005	Medicare Rate per 100,000 persons[2]	Social Security beneficiaries, Dec 2005 Number	Social Security Rate per 100,000 persons[2]	Social Security Percent change, 2000–2005	Retired workers, number	Supplemental Security Income recipients, 2005 Number	Supplemental Security Income Rate per 100,000 persons[2]
GEORGIA—Con.														
Long	1	9	–	–	–	744	28.1	6,713	1,115	10,060	18.6	575	243	2,193
Lowndes	212	221	2	364	380	11,942	13.2	12,349	13,820	14,291	13.5	7,930	2,723	2,816
Lumpkin	24	101	1	49	205	2,736	25.8	11,248	3,845	15,807	28.8	2,460	470	1,932
McDuffie	19	88	1	35	162	3,225	5.8	14,832	3,910	17,983	4.6	2,200	925	4,254
McIntosh	7	63	–	–	–	1,885	20.4	17,031	2,420	21,865	17.6	1,355	412	3,722
Macon	11	79	1	39	279	1,966	6.4	14,303	2,070	15,060	4.0	1,080	688	5,005
Madison	7	26	–	–	–	4,207	13.1	15,416	5,040	18,469	14.5	2,940	788	2,888
Marion	4	56	–	–	–	763	4.1	10,533	1,215	16,773	23.7	615	315	4,348
Meriwether	20	88	2	89	391	3,503	5.4	15,284	4,355	19,002	5.4	2,605	985	4,298
Miller	8	129	1	135	2,170	1,128	2.1	18,112	1,275	20,472	-1.8	760	272	4,367
Mitchell	16	67	1	181	759	3,428	5.4	14,409	4,265	17,927	5.1	2,335	1,174	4,935
Monroe	17	73	1	25	107	2,856	18.1	12,008	4,195	17,637	20.9	2,500	537	2,258
Montgomery	1	11	–	–	–	1,333	10.4	14,962	1,520	17,061	6.4	840	326	3,659
Morgan	13	77	1	46	271	2,572	16.5	14,704	3,275	18,723	17.4	2,110	377	2,155
Murray	13	32	1	33	82	4,465	21.2	10,940	5,775	14,150	18.1	3,075	907	2,222
Muscogee	617	332	4	1,025	552	26,534	4.2	14,322	30,095	16,244	1.2	17,450	5,841	3,153
Newton	63	77	1	90	110	10,015	29.6	11,550	11,925	13,752	28.2	7,105	1,804	2,080
Oconee	77	266	–	–	–	3,031	21.7	10,189	3,650	12,270	20.2	2,355	307	1,032
Oglethorpe	4	29	–	–	–	1,236	7.1	9,082	2,385	17,525	15.3	1,405	396	2,910
Paulding	12	11	1	216	204	6,186	36.1	5,503	11,010	9,794	46.6	6,295	1,105	983
Peach	21	86	1	25	102	4,240	19.6	17,101	4,165	16,798	3.9	2,290	871	3,513
Pickens	41	147	1	40	144	4,147	35.0	14,581	5,500	19,338	27.5	3,770	432	1,519
Pierce	14	84	–	–	–	2,952	15.4	17,244	3,305	19,306	11.0	1,715	697	4,071
Pike	3	19	–	–	–	2,206	20.0	13,678	2,680	16,617	18.8	1,715	279	1,730
Polk	25	62	1	22	55	7,008	6.7	17,313	7,830	19,343	2.9	4,415	1,306	3,226
Pulaski	18	184	1	55	561	1,689	9.7	17,346	2,065	21,208	16.7	1,195	398	4,088
Putnam	16	81	1	25	127	3,254	20.1	16,410	4,190	21,131	17.8	2,755	420	2,118
Quitman	32	1,297	–	–	–	439	-29.0	17,795	595	24,118	-3.7	355	151	6,121
Rabun	3	19	1	25	157	3,161	9.8	19,649	3,780	23,497	11.8	2,535	412	2,561
Randolph	1,199	16,280	1	105	1,426	1,340	-2.6	18,331	1,625	22,230	-0.4	835	500	6,840
Richmond	144	73	5	1,385	703	27,465	5.4	14,029	32,565	16,634	3.7	17,715	6,944	3,547
Rockdale	1	1	–	–	–	8,281	13.7	10,543	10,320	13,139	15.7	6,460	1,140	1,451
Schley	–	–	–	–	–	520	3.0	12,615	650	15,769	5.2	375	158	3,833
Screven	9	58	1	25	162	2,508	2.9	16,254	2,995	19,410	3.2	1,685	773	5,010
Seminole	13	140	1	140	1,509	1,847	5.3	20,020	2,300	24,930	11.0	1,260	515	5,582
Spalding	93	153	1	160	263	9,267	8.0	15,120	11,230	18,323	7.1	6,680	2,023	3,301
Stephens	45	179	1	178	710	5,686	5.8	22,690	5,890	23,504	0.9	3,630	897	3,579
Stewart	5	101	1	25	504	957	–	19,603	1,070	21,917	-1.0	580	320	6,555
Sumter	52	157	1	232	701	4,661	1.7	14,162	5,565	16,909	5.2	3,210	1,462	4,442
Talbot	2	30	–	–	–	1,118	1.8	16,664	1,290	19,228	-4.7	710	317	4,725
Taliaferro	–	–	–	–	–	411	-2.6	22,508	430	23,549	-5.7	255	121	6,627
Tattnall	13	56	–	–	–	3,378	8.3	14,553	3,805	16,393	9.2	2,085	936	4,033
Taylor	3	34	–	–	–	1,629	7.7	18,330	1,760	19,804	6.3	970	475	5,345
Telfair	7	54	1	25	192	2,341	4.1	17,728	2,635	19,955	1.3	1,410	654	4,953
Terrell	8	73	–	–	–	1,722	1.7	16,077	2,105	19,653	0.3	1,130	631	5,891
Thomas	167	381	1	328	748	8,512	10.9	19,046	9,175	20,529	7.8	5,190	2,131	4,768
Tift	104	259	1	191	475	5,936	8.2	14,552	6,920	16,964	9.9	4,010	1,443	3,537
Toombs	57	213	1	89	332	4,665	12.1	17,104	5,270	19,322	7.0	2,940	1,360	4,986
Towns	14	138	1	137	1,354	2,938	15.4	28,483	3,355	32,525	16.8	2,360	218	2,113
Treutlen	3	42	–	–	–	1,083	8.6	16,037	1,360	20,139	5.2	740	381	5,642
Troup	117	191	1	448	733	9,669	3.3	15,591	11,140	17,963	4.8	6,715	1,997	3,220
Turner	10	105	–	–	–	1,633	2.8	17,237	1,860	19,633	8.0	1,045	486	5,130
Twiggs	–	–	–	–	–	1,517	9.2	14,730	2,170	21,070	9.4	1,030	517	5,020
Union	32	164	1	195	1,001	4,850	23.4	24,517	5,865	29,648	21.2	4,135	451	2,280
Upson	40	144	1	115	413	4,647	-2.3	16,789	6,000	21,677	1.1	3,630	941	3,400
Walker	30	47	–	–	–	12,142	8.0	19,005	13,055	20,434	4.9	7,590	1,595	2,496
Walton	65	90	1	115	160	9,923	34.1	13,118	10,570	13,973	34.2	6,720	1,354	1,790
Ware	105	305	1	181	526	7,249	2.4	21,016	7,315	21,208	4.4	3,875	1,788	5,184
Warren	2	32	–	–	–	1,073	0.9	17,587	1,345	22,046	2.5	740	332	5,442
Washington	24	114	1	116	552	3,256	4.8	16,185	3,965	19,709	5.7	2,150	937	4,658
Wayne	34	121	1	84	299	4,240	11.8	14,935	5,200	18,316	11.8	2,880	1,001	3,526
Webster	–	–	–	–	–	297	-6.6	12,975	415	18,130	0.2	255	100	4,369
Wheeler	1	15	1	73	1,121	906	-1.4	13,510	1,110	16,552	2.4	600	274	4,086
White	22	93	–	–	–	4,115	25.6	17,107	5,015	20,848	26.0	3,390	438	1,821
Whitfield	192	215	1	256	287	12,192	11.1	13,414	14,085	15,497	8.5	8,805	1,761	1,938
Wilcox	2	23	–	–	–	1,474	6.9	16,902	1,515	17,372	0.6	815	413	4,736
Wilkes	12	114	1	25	237	2,301	4.7	22,004	2,595	24,816	6.1	1,535	517	4,944
Wilkinson	2	20	–	–	–	1,933	10.5	19,057	2,175	21,443	8.8	1,080	336	3,313
Worth	12	55	1	25	114	2,774	12.4	12,611	3,875	17,617	5.5	2,225	799	3,632

See footnotes at end of table.

[Includes United States, states, and 3,141 counties/county equivalents defined as of February 22, 2005. For more information on these areas, see Appendix C, Geographic Information]

County	Physicians, 2004[1]		Community hospitals, 2004[3]			Medicare program enrollment, 2005[4]			Social Security program beneficiaries, December 2005				Supplemental Security Income program recipients, 2005	
				Beds										
	Number	Rate per 100,000 persons[2]	Number	Number	Rate per 100,000 persons[2]	Total	Percent change, 2000–2005	Rate per 100,000 persons[2]	Number	Rate per 100,000 persons[2]	Percent change, 2000–2005	Retired workers, number	Number	Rate per 100,000 persons[2]
HAWAII	4,432	351	24	3,149	250	[6]182,143	[6]10.2	[6]14,284	[7]200,743	[7]15,742	[7]9.2	[7]143,424	22,754	1,784
Hawaii	383	236	5	474	292	24,383	14.0	14,575	29,120	17,407	12.7	19,245	3,796	2,269
Honolulu	3,548	394	13	2,097	233	131,700	9.3	14,548	140,960	15,571	8.0	102,660	16,523	1,825
Kalawao	–	–	–	–	–	44	-31.3	39,640	–	–	–	–	–	–
Kauai	154	249	2	226	365	9,193	11.4	14,676	10,690	17,066	11.3	7,665	865	1,381
Maui	347	251	4	352	255	16,718	11.7	11,951	19,970	14,276	12.0	13,855	1,570	1,122
IDAHO	2,693	193	39	3,434	246	[6]190,494	[6]15.4	[6]13,330	226,250	15,832	15.6	[7]144,936	22,261	1,558
Ada	1,040	313	3	945	284	37,705	22.6	10,938	44,660	12,955	23.7	29,490	4,132	1,199
Adams	3	86	–	–	–	827	13.8	23,030	985	27,430	12.1	650	49	1,365
Bannock	177	227	1	274	352	9,785	8.2	12,520	10,580	13,537	9.1	6,310	1,473	1,885
Bear Lake	5	80	1	82	1,311	1,121	2.4	18,151	1,280	20,725	4.0	845	101	1,635
Benewah	8	89	1	20	222	1,790	13.1	19,419	2,115	22,944	12.1	1,245	232	2,517
Bingham	26	60	1	100	232	5,446	8.0	12,451	6,630	15,158	5.5	4,095	771	1,763
Blaine	109	518	1	25	119	1,944	29.9	9,185	2,380	11,244	27.3	1,720	53	250
Boise	2	27	–	–	–	827	21.6	10,975	1,210	16,058	23.1	795	102	1,354
Bonner	74	186	1	41	103	6,415	17.0	15,682	8,155	19,935	16.5	5,105	708	1,731
Bonneville	217	242	2	301	335	11,311	15.5	12,314	13,680	14,893	15.6	8,560	1,499	1,632
Boundary	12	115	1	60	576	1,797	11.8	16,922	2,200	20,718	15.4	1,370	235	2,213
Butte	3	106	1	43	1,522	542	5.9	19,302	640	22,792	7.4	405	68	2,422
Camas	–	–	–	–	–	146	9.8	13,905	165	15,714	3.8	110	6	571
Canyon	174	110	2	207	131	19,636	20.0	11,930	23,380	14,205	24.8	14,665	3,030	1,841
Caribou	5	69	2	62	858	1,130	3.6	15,846	1,310	18,370	2.5	840	65	912
Cassia	29	136	1	25	117	3,021	3.4	14,167	3,680	17,258	5.5	2,415	424	1,988
Clark	–	–	–	–	–	128	25.5	13,574	125	13,256	1.6	95	9	954
Clearwater	17	203	1	23	274	1,837	14.1	21,940	2,420	28,902	13.8	1,460	233	2,783
Custer	2	49	–	–	–	754	8.8	18,494	900	22,075	7.9	605	69	1,692
Elmore	28	97	1	72	250	2,564	13.0	8,954	3,120	10,896	12.8	2,010	300	1,048
Franklin	5	41	1	65	535	1,572	9.0	12,707	1,875	15,156	6.4	1,225	125	1,010
Fremont	6	49	–	–	–	1,802	5.1	14,720	2,125	17,358	4.1	1,425	135	1,103
Gem	10	63	1	16	100	2,925	15.6	17,975	3,635	22,338	18.9	2,415	331	2,034
Gooding	8	56	1	14	97	2,302	-2.3	15,919	2,730	18,878	1.1	1,855	272	1,881
Idaho	19	122	2	43	275	2,956	8.1	18,832	3,985	25,387	10.2	2,425	428	2,727
Jefferson	3	14	–	–	–	2,447	14.0	11,339	3,010	13,948	12.6	1,875	218	1,010
Jerome	13	67	1	65	337	2,563	4.3	13,051	3,025	15,404	2.2	2,005	314	1,599
Kootenai	287	234	1	246	201	19,881	27.9	15,572	23,835	18,670	26.2	15,145	1,862	1,458
Latah	49	140	1	25	71	3,920	5.9	11,292	4,535	13,064	8.0	2,945	341	982
Lemhi	7	89	1	18	230	1,670	10.8	21,115	2,015	25,477	10.4	1,325	158	1,998
Lewis	1	27	–	–	–	1,394	17.7	37,173	1,225	32,667	8.2	705	143	3,813
Lincoln	1	23	–	–	–	557	2.6	12,255	895	19,692	12.2	605	50	1,100
Madison	34	112	1	49	162	2,050	13.5	6,618	2,470	7,974	10.3	1,575	181	584
Minidoka	9	47	1	79	412	3,114	3.2	16,377	3,335	17,540	2.2	2,160	339	1,783
Nez Perce	95	252	1	156	413	7,574	10.7	19,968	8,610	22,699	8.1	5,360	879	2,317
Oneida	1	24	1	52	1,254	702	2.9	16,679	805	19,126	2.3	530	54	1,283
Owyhee	1	9	–	–	–	1,404	11.2	12,679	1,880	16,978	14.0	1,165	230	2,077
Payette	10	46	–	–	–	3,317	8.5	14,943	4,185	18,854	8.9	2,785	450	2,027
Power	1	13	1	41	531	901	13.6	11,621	1,180	15,220	14.6	735	108	1,393
Shoshone	12	93	1	25	194	3,051	4.1	23,189	3,635	27,628	4.7	2,045	435	3,306
Teton	9	125	1	13	180	603	6.9	8,076	795	10,647	12.4	535	51	683
Twin Falls	152	223	1	204	300	10,921	10.9	15,732	12,615	18,172	11.5	8,425	1,281	1,845
Valley	25	315	2	25	315	1,523	10.1	18,279	1,825	21,904	6.5	1,300	77	924
Washington	4	40	1	18	179	2,104	9.3	20,836	2,410	23,866	5.2	1,580	240	2,377
ILLINOIS	37,909	298	191	34,844	274	[6]1,694,820	[6]3.7	[6]13,279	[7]1,893,055	[7]14,832	[7]2.9	[7]1,227,354	258,634	2,026
Adams	167	250	1	319	477	12,716	0.4	18,968	14,210	21,196	0.1	9,580	1,196	1,784
Alexander	3	33	–	–	–	1,945	0.5	21,788	2,075	23,244	-7.5	1,130	585	6,553
Bond	12	67	1	150	831	2,894	3.2	16,054	3,345	18,556	3.7	2,065	290	1,609
Boone	68	140	1	69	142	5,592	20.9	11,077	7,120	14,104	20.7	4,855	320	634
Brown	3	44	–	–	–	944	-2.6	13,811	1,045	15,289	-2.9	655	109	1,595
Bureau	43	122	2	152	432	6,652	-0.7	18,828	7,475	21,158	2.0	5,105	319	903
Calhoun	4	78	–	–	–	1,081	4.8	20,937	1,265	24,501	7.0	770	88	1,704
Carroll	10	62	–	–	–	3,600	1.8	22,380	3,855	23,965	3.0	2,605	208	1,293
Cass	4	29	–	–	–	2,460	0.2	17,700	2,630	18,924	-2.0	1,680	226	1,626
Champaign	643	349	2	546	296	20,335	7.2	10,998	22,275	12,047	5.8	14,320	2,445	1,322
Christian	29	82	2	100	284	6,625	-1.0	18,834	7,895	22,444	-3.5	4,875	627	1,782
Clark	7	41	–	–	–	3,239	-2.4	19,080	3,690	21,737	-1.5	2,330	263	1,549
Clay	10	71	1	24	169	2,924	-2.0	20,705	3,320	23,509	-1.9	2,025	334	2,365
Clinton	32	89	1	60	166	5,131	4.8	14,215	6,675	18,493	3.8	4,220	427	1,183
Coles	87	169	1	132	257	7,867	0.4	15,406	8,620	16,880	1.3	5,590	1,030	2,017
Cook	21,189	398	58	16,982	319	667,017	-0.7	12,576	722,160	13,616	-2.6	468,230	154,868	2,920
Crawford	18	90	1	64	320	3,903	0.6	19,615	4,370	21,962	-1.2	2,780	285	1,432
Cumberland	2	18	–	–	–	1,828	0.2	16,659	2,215	20,186	2.3	1,400	172	1,567
DeKalb	95	100	2	127	133	10,901	9.5	11,162	11,805	12,087	9.0	7,985	552	565
De Witt	15	91	1	25	151	3,022	1.6	18,186	3,325	20,010	2.0	2,155	218	1,312

See footnotes at end of table.

[Includes United States, states, and 3,141 counties/county equivalents defined as of February 22, 2005. For more information on these areas, see Appendix C, Geographic Information]

County	Physicians, 2004[1] Number	Physicians, 2004[1] Rate per 100,000 persons[2]	Community hospitals, 2004[3] Number	Beds Number	Beds Rate per 100,000 persons[2]	Medicare program enrollment, 2005[4] Total	Medicare Percent change, 2000–2005	Medicare Rate per 100,000 persons[2]	Social Security program beneficiaries, December 2005 Number	Social Security Rate per 100,000 persons[2]	Social Security Percent change, 2000–2005	Retired workers, number	Supplemental Security Income program recipients, 2005 Number	SSI Rate per 100,000 persons[2]
ILLINOIS—Con.														
Douglas	12	60	–	–	–	2,880	0.6	14,436	3,860	19,348	–4.0	2,580	217	1,088
DuPage	4,179	450	8	1,940	209	101,779	7.3	10,954	113,505	12,216	0.8	80,920	6,401	689
Edgar	13	68	1	25	130	3,724	0.5	19,439	4,275	22,316	1.7	2,650	451	2,354
Edwards	1	15	–	–	–	1,298	–	19,133	1,580	23,290	–2.2	1,035	95	1,400
Effingham	84	242	1	146	421	5,863	6.6	16,954	6,385	18,464	4.7	4,040	412	1,191
Fayette	11	51	1	145	670	3,727	0.2	17,165	4,620	21,278	3.2	2,805	498	2,294
Ford	18	127	1	80	562	2,621	–3.9	18,514	3,015	21,297	–3.4	1,990	142	1,003
Franklin	25	63	1	25	63	8,823	2.6	22,211	9,900	24,923	2.2	5,610	1,338	3,368
Fulton	31	82	1	124	329	7,477	–2.4	19,829	8,460	22,436	–1.4	5,365	688	1,825
Gallatin	3	49	–	–	–	1,410	1.5	22,919	1,590	25,845	–0.4	885	228	3,706
Greene	7	48	1	65	446	2,982	–0.2	20,451	3,250	22,289	–1.6	1,920	363	2,490
Grundy	50	121	1	83	202	5,703	10.2	13,009	6,705	15,295	13.6	4,355	273	623
Hamilton	6	71	1	85	1,013	1,811	0.5	21,817	2,055	24,756	–0.7	1,260	235	2,831
Hancock	11	57	1	15	77	4,187	0.8	21,861	4,360	22,764	–2.1	2,860	264	1,378
Hardin	4	85	1	25	529	926	–1.9	19,627	1,180	25,011	–0.1	640	186	3,942
Henderson	6	74	–	–	–	1,400	1.3	17,561	1,705	21,387	5.1	1,205	101	1,267
Henry	33	65	2	99	196	8,897	0.5	17,586	10,425	20,606	2.6	6,960	549	1,085
Iroquois	28	92	1	112	366	6,286	1.4	20,491	7,010	22,851	–0.8	4,555	454	1,480
Jackson	196	337	2	167	287	7,832	2.9	13,514	8,155	14,072	2.8	4,940	1,270	2,191
Jasper	2	20	–	–	–	1,789	3.2	17,854	2,255	22,505	5.4	1,405	173	1,727
Jefferson	81	201	2	190	471	6,814	3.1	16,852	7,820	19,340	3.4	4,800	970	2,399
Jersey	19	85	1	67	300	3,184	8.7	14,179	4,475	19,928	6.4	2,705	303	1,349
Jo Daviess	19	84	1	82	364	4,663	9.2	20,651	5,410	23,959	7.7	3,890	182	806
Johnson	2	15	–	–	–	2,392	9.2	18,164	2,690	20,427	8.9	1,650	275	2,088
Kane	716	151	4	820	173	46,523	15.5	9,650	50,465	10,467	31.8	33,960	3,676	762
Kankakee	187	175	2	416	389	17,159	5.5	15,892	19,655	18,204	5.6	11,480	2,607	2,415
Kendall	38	52	–	–	–	5,395	33.8	6,785	8,515	10,709	34.7	5,815	322	405
Knox	112	208	2	234	435	10,693	–1.3	20,059	11,535	21,638	1.0	7,540	1,237	2,320
Lake	2,445	353	6	872	126	68,567	13.9	9,758	78,605	11,186	13.2	53,350	5,913	841
LaSalle	134	119	4	339	302	20,189	0.4	17,929	23,485	20,856	1.8	15,640	1,234	1,096
Lawrence	12	75	1	54	338	3,228	–2.3	20,264	3,735	23,446	–2.7	2,195	322	2,021
Lee	49	137	1	99	277	6,368	4.9	17,853	7,190	20,158	4.2	4,595	478	1,340
Livingston	30	77	1	42	108	6,199	0.5	15,819	7,700	19,650	3.7	4,810	476	1,215
Logan	19	62	1	25	81	5,054	–4.4	16,515	5,610	18,332	–4.1	3,680	358	1,170
McDonough	51	158	1	91	282	4,897	–1.9	15,319	5,575	17,440	–6.2	3,720	510	1,595
McHenry	407	137	3	355	120	31,613	29.1	10,399	34,990	11,510	23.4	23,965	1,254	413
McLean	351	222	2	390	247	17,758	8.3	11,168	20,085	12,631	8.5	13,330	1,401	881
Macon	276	250	2	567	513	20,352	1.8	18,474	22,865	20,755	2.4	14,395	3,038	2,758
Macoupin	31	63	2	58	118	9,581	–1.4	19,509	10,485	21,350	0.1	6,405	808	1,645
Madison	339	129	4	640	243	43,255	2.2	16,365	49,245	18,632	1.7	29,935	4,980	1,884
Marion	71	176	2	156	386	9,097	3.3	22,661	8,795	21,909	2.6	5,355	965	2,404
Marshall	10	76	–	–	–	2,338	–1.9	17,689	2,855	21,601	–3.3	1,900	120	908
Mason	10	63	1	25	157	3,360	1.7	21,346	3,875	24,617	–0.8	2,380	290	1,842
Massac	8	52	1	25	163	3,067	2.5	19,983	3,660	23,847	3.9	2,165	471	3,069
Menard	10	78	–	–	–	1,936	8.0	15,199	2,300	18,056	5.1	1,525	138	1,083
Mercer	7	41	1	39	230	2,882	4.7	17,041	3,735	22,085	4.7	2,450	184	1,088
Monroe	25	82	–	–	–	4,341	11.1	13,985	5,070	16,334	12.0	3,320	145	467
Montgomery	25	82	2	151	496	5,974	1.3	19,654	6,670	21,944	1.2	4,175	604	1,987
Morgan	56	156	1	112	311	6,584	2.0	18,431	7,485	20,953	2.0	4,635	906	2,536
Moultrie	5	35	–	–	–	3,087	2.6	21,275	3,000	20,675	2.6	2,015	129	889
Ogle	43	80	1	54	101	7,904	10.1	14,559	9,445	17,397	8.7	6,390	435	801
Peoria	920	505	3	1,068	586	29,466	0.2	16,161	33,320	18,275	1.0	21,340	4,629	2,539
Perry	22	97	2	102	450	4,061	–2.2	17,800	4,505	19,746	–0.3	2,750	405	1,775
Piatt	11	67	1	16	97	3,100	5.7	18,585	3,150	18,885	6.3	2,140	98	588
Pike	14	82	1	25	146	3,628	(Z)	21,218	3,915	22,896	–1.6	2,490	330	1,930
Pope	2	47	–	–	–	827	11.0	19,639	1,105	26,241	10.4	630	124	2,945
Pulaski	–	–	–	–	–	1,300	–11.9	19,135	1,600	23,550	–6.1	925	330	4,857
Putnam	1	16	–	–	–	1,121	4.2	18,395	1,290	21,168	7.0	890	47	771
Randolph	35	105	3	264	794	5,797	–2.5	17,502	6,395	19,307	–3.2	3,965	469	1,416
Richland	39	246	1	112	706	3,401	5.0	21,528	3,875	24,528	1.8	2,470	350	2,215
Rock Island	312	211	2	437	296	25,860	2.8	17,496	29,000	19,620	2.2	19,285	2,832	1,916
St. Clair	510	197	4	841	325	38,348	0.4	14,745	43,085	16,567	–0.1	25,225	8,375	3,220
Saline	30	114	2	96	366	5,679	–0.6	21,782	6,330	24,279	–2.3	3,510	1,133	4,346
Sangamon	1,035	538	2	982	511	30,181	4.2	15,655	35,180	18,248	4.7	22,385	4,287	2,224
Schuyler	5	71	1	55	781	1,373	–1.8	19,412	1,625	22,975	1.2	1,050	93	1,315
Scott	2	37	–	–	–	955	3.1	17,646	1,090	20,140	–4.3	710	66	1,220
Shelby	10	45	1	45	201	4,282	0.6	19,183	4,895	21,929	11.5	3,130	318	1,425
Stark	2	32	–	–	–	1,283	–0.1	20,798	1,375	22,289	–12.3	885	62	1,005
Stephenson	74	154	1	189	393	9,576	5.0	19,965	10,620	22,141	5.3	7,370	849	1,770
Tazewell	165	128	2	184	143	22,430	5.1	17,254	25,325	19,481	5.5	16,830	1,655	1,273

See footnotes at end of table.

[Includes United States, states, and 3,141 counties/county equivalents defined as of February 22, 2005. For more information on these areas, see Appendix C, Geographic Information]

County	Physicians, 2004[1] Number	Rate per 100,000 persons[2]	Community hospitals, 2004[3] Number	Beds Number	Beds Rate per 100,000 persons[2]	Medicare program enrollment, 2005[4] Total	Percent change, 2000–2005	Rate per 100,000 persons[2]	Social Security program beneficiaries, December 2005 Number	Rate per 100,000 persons[2]	Percent change, 2000–2005	Retired workers, number	Supplemental Security Income program recipients, 2005 Number	Rate per 100,000 persons[2]
ILLINOIS—Con.														
Union	27	148	1	47	258	3,620	1.0	19,888	4,150	22,800	2.3	2,405	707	3,884
Vermilion	162	196	2	267	323	15,851	1.4	19,250	17,870	21,702	1.1	10,845	2,586	3,140
Wabash	10	79	1	25	198	2,282	-1.6	18,154	2,635	20,963	-1.2	1,660	190	1,512
Warren	14	79	1	68	384	3,281	0.3	18,687	3,375	19,222	6.6	2,210	290	1,652
Washington	7	46	1	58	384	2,563	-3.2	17,176	3,045	20,406	-0.7	1,895	156	1,045
Wayne	9	54	1	163	969	3,423	0.9	20,380	4,015	23,905	1.9	2,540	297	1,768
White	9	59	1	98	644	3,688	-0.4	24,130	3,940	25,779	-4.3	2,455	362	2,368
Whiteside	75	125	2	188	314	11,684	4.6	19,518	13,185	22,025	4.1	8,295	957	1,599
Will	689	112	2	685	111	55,387	24.8	8,616	71,545	11,110	33.3	45,165	5,386	838
Williamson	138	219	2	181	287	11,436	4.8	17,976	13,610	21,394	4.6	8,280	1,446	2,273
Winnebago	800	279	4	859	300	43,176	7.7	14,956	51,010	17,669	8.9	32,760	5,920	2,051
Woodford	31	84	–	–	–	5,011	3.1	13,381	6,265	16,730	7.8	4,330	254	678
INDIANA	14,696	236	113	18,796	302	[6]904,108	[6]6.1	[6]14,415	[7]1,063,854	[7]16,962	[7]6.5	672,315	98,614	1,572
Adams	19	56	1	87	258	4,654	2.1	13,749	5,465	16,145	3.1	3,770	278	821
Allen	941	275	5	1,353	396	45,005	5.8	13,083	53,125	15,443	6.4	34,640	5,274	1,533
Bartholomew	199	273	1	235	323	11,257	14.6	15,307	13,560	18,439	15.2	8,590	1,080	1,469
Benton	7	77	–	–	–	1,697	-0.4	18,774	1,860	20,577	3.6	1,175	121	1,339
Blackford	11	79	1	25	181	2,539	5.2	18,333	3,200	23,106	8.1	2,020	218	1,574
Boone	292	575	1	48	94	6,064	10.1	11,648	7,565	14,531	10.9	5,200	314	603
Brown	12	79	–	–	–	1,410	7.8	9,304	3,000	19,797	4.9	2,050	154	1,016
Carroll	11	54	–	–	–	2,711	4.3	13,272	3,910	19,142	5.0	2,635	128	627
Cass	56	139	1	104	258	6,658	-0.9	16,591	7,500	18,689	0.9	4,730	657	1,637
Clark	172	171	2	318	317	16,094	12.2	15,842	18,870	18,574	12.8	10,690	1,946	1,916
Clay	20	74	1	25	92	5,030	2.2	18,532	5,545	20,430	1.3	3,335	512	1,886
Clinton	19	56	1	25	73	5,215	0.2	15,297	5,920	17,365	3.7	3,830	395	1,159
Crawford	2	18	–	–	–	1,990	7.1	17,743	2,320	20,685	6.0	1,210	299	2,666
Daviess	23	76	1	70	231	4,551	2.0	14,938	5,285	17,347	2.2	3,260	527	1,730
Dearborn	56	115	1	87	179	6,793	10.6	13,840	8,220	16,747	7.3	5,115	459	935
Decatur	22	88	1	71	285	4,110	6.9	16,320	4,775	18,960	7.0	3,055	328	1,302
DeKalb	40	97	1	45	109	5,788	12.3	13,894	7,000	16,803	16.2	4,440	464	1,114
Delaware	341	290	1	393	334	19,025	4.1	16,350	22,510	19,345	4.0	14,000	2,450	2,105
Dubois	74	182	2	149	367	6,096	9.3	14,920	7,340	17,965	12.4	4,885	347	849
Elkhart	274	143	2	421	220	24,098	9.1	12,335	27,920	14,291	8.8	18,920	2,295	1,175
Fayette	24	96	1	111	445	4,834	3.6	19,425	5,690	22,865	3.6	3,340	605	2,431
Floyd	179	250	2	258	361	10,832	6.0	15,045	12,660	17,584	6.5	7,550	1,439	1,999
Fountain	8	46	–	–	–	3,709	4.6	21,240	3,835	21,962	0.3	2,430	259	1,483
Franklin	7	31	–	–	–	3,050	9.8	13,212	4,745	20,554	12.9	2,970	316	1,369
Fulton	21	102	1	35	170	3,548	1.9	17,169	4,320	20,905	4.7	2,925	254	1,229
Gibson	26	78	1	70	211	5,650	0.1	16,912	6,435	19,262	0.8	4,070	437	1,308
Grant	126	177	1	201	282	13,229	3.9	18,749	15,500	21,968	2.1	9,675	1,637	2,320
Greene	23	69	1	25	75	5,741	1.3	17,148	6,775	20,237	4.7	4,080	641	1,915
Hamilton	1,215	529	2	219	95	17,989	31.0	7,474	23,530	9,776	31.0	16,250	1,002	416
Hancock	102	167	1	100	164	8,105	19.3	12,837	10,120	16,028	20.6	6,920	395	626
Harrison	35	96	1	47	129	5,472	12.4	14,859	6,680	18,139	12.7	3,785	526	1,428
Hendricks	200	162	1	141	114	12,986	23.0	10,186	16,075	12,610	23.6	11,090	534	419
Henry	50	105	1	107	224	9,014	2.0	19,080	10,765	22,786	2.1	6,830	830	1,757
Howard	168	199	3	370	437	14,420	7.5	16,969	17,405	20,482	10.1	11,365	1,782	2,097
Huntington	40	105	1	36	94	6,593	6.8	17,243	7,145	18,687	6.4	4,860	384	1,004
Jackson	53	127	1	108	258	7,034	6.7	16,654	8,150	19,296	7.4	5,040	646	1,529
Jasper	24	76	1	66	209	4,878	12.6	15,303	5,720	17,945	12.0	3,600	282	885
Jay	19	88	1	65	300	4,016	4.8	18,587	4,590	21,244	5.3	2,950	326	1,509
Jefferson	61	189	1	112	348	5,389	8.7	16,617	6,590	20,321	10.1	3,980	610	1,881
Jennings	12	42	1	25	88	3,984	4.4	14,015	5,205	18,310	10.3	2,810	528	1,857
Johnson	253	201	1	153	122	16,547	17.3	12,883	19,445	15,140	18.8	13,320	926	721
Knox	86	223	1	232	602	7,258	3.4	18,918	8,160	21,269	0.9	4,935	1,026	2,674
Kosciusko	78	103	1	72	95	10,577	8.4	13,904	12,680	16,668	7.9	8,610	609	801
LaGrange	11	30	1	50	137	3,932	14.8	10,663	4,835	13,112	12.6	3,240	241	654
Lake	983	201	7	2,309	471	73,747	2.5	14,950	85,975	17,429	1.5	50,660	11,279	2,286
LaPorte	195	178	2	444	405	16,989	4.0	15,373	20,235	18,310	5.9	12,900	1,793	1,622
Lawrence	63	136	2	154	333	8,170	7.9	17,607	9,470	20,408	5.6	5,880	863	1,860
Madison	197	151	2	231	177	23,495	4.0	18,016	27,435	21,037	3.7	17,480	2,666	2,044
Marion	4,104	476	8	4,248	493	114,170	2.0	13,227	129,355	14,987	1.7	79,170	18,136	2,101
Marshall	46	99	2	69	148	6,914	5.4	14,728	8,075	17,201	5.9	5,445	505	1,076
Martin	4	38	–	–	–	1,952	5.3	18,795	2,095	20,171	2.6	1,295	209	2,012
Miami	31	86	1	27	75	5,621	6.7	15,780	5,995	16,830	4.8	3,745	607	1,704
Monroe	355	294	1	840	695	14,031	11.0	11,557	16,335	13,455	10.8	10,995	1,349	1,111
Montgomery	48	127	1	86	227	6,294	8.3	16,640	7,365	19,260	7.0	4,820	447	1,169
Morgan	67	97	2	140	202	9,011	11.5	12,914	11,130	15,951	13.5	6,980	737	1,056
Newton	5	35	–	–	–	1,963	5.5	13,579	2,700	18,677	10.8	1,680	162	1,121
Noble	28	59	1	30	64	5,999	6.2	12,643	7,510	15,828	8.8	4,710	478	1,007
Ohio	–	–	–	–	–	844	8.8	14,368	1,040	17,705	13.8	635	55	936
Orange	16	81	1	24	122	3,446	5.7	17,430	4,265	21,573	6.7	2,470	480	2,428
Owen	8	35	–	–	–	3,094	10.7	13,557	4,195	18,381	14.9	2,520	317	1,389

See footnotes at end of table.

[Includes United States, states, and 3,141 counties/county equivalents defined as of February 22, 2005. For more information on these areas, see Appendix C, Geographic Information]

County	Physicians, 2004[1] Number	Rate per 100,000 persons[2]	Community hospitals, 2004[3] Number	Beds Number	Beds Rate per 100,000 persons[2]	Medicare program enrollment, 2005[4] Total	Percent change, 2000–2005	Rate per 100,000 persons[2]	Social Security program beneficiaries, December 2005 Number	Rate per 100,000 persons[2]	Percent change, 2000–2005	Retired workers, number	Supplemental Security Income program recipients, 2005 Number	Rate per 100,000 persons[2]
INDIANA—Con.														
Parke	9	52	–	–	–	2,902	4.1	16,715	3,485	20,073	5.6	2,135	318	1,832
Perry	11	58	1	25	131	3,231	1.6	16,977	3,740	19,651	1.5	2,425	317	1,666
Pike	4	31	–	–	–	2,321	6.3	18,181	2,830	22,168	8.1	1,630	238	1,864
Porter	310	200	1	276	178	19,492	13.4	12,355	24,780	15,706	15.3	15,355	1,436	910
Posey	10	37	–	–	–	3,714	2.4	13,831	4,850	18,062	7.9	2,990	339	1,262
Pulaski	7	51	1	25	182	2,458	5.5	17,834	2,840	20,605	4.2	1,735	212	1,538
Putnam	27	74	1	55	150	5,133	8.8	13,889	6,335	17,142	9.2	4,140	358	969
Randolph	19	71	1	25	94	4,963	0.6	18,599	5,805	21,755	1.0	3,750	428	1,604
Ripley	36	131	1	79	287	4,831	7.5	17,434	4,850	17,503	7.1	2,940	355	1,281
Rush	13	73	1	25	140	2,902	0.9	16,282	3,530	19,806	3.2	2,255	233	1,307
St. Joseph	734	276	3	726	273	40,517	-0.8	15,223	44,915	16,875	0.1	30,365	4,215	1,584
Scott	16	68	1	56	237	4,090	12.1	17,170	4,840	20,319	10.9	2,480	754	3,165
Shelby	31	71	1	68	156	6,030	6.9	13,778	7,490	17,114	6.3	4,835	553	1,264
Spencer	8	39	–	–	–	3,321	9.3	16,178	3,905	19,023	8.2	2,460	261	1,271
Starke	12	53	1	57	250	4,074	13.5	17,765	5,405	23,569	11.3	2,925	538	2,346
Steuben	35	104	1	25	74	5,224	9.4	15,468	6,055	17,929	10.9	4,115	324	959
Sullivan	9	41	1	37	169	3,633	-0.7	16,693	4,355	20,011	1.5	2,525	400	1,838
Switzerland	3	31	–	–	–	1,381	12.2	14,211	1,745	17,956	12.0	1,005	184	1,893
Tippecanoe	386	254	1	440	289	16,585	10.6	10,778	19,445	12,637	12.1	12,665	1,530	994
Tipton	14	85	1	75	453	2,528	2.1	15,429	3,290	20,079	8.9	2,240	174	1,062
Union	5	69	–	–	–	1,221	11.4	16,940	1,365	18,937	19.0	790	90	1,249
Vanderburgh	614	355	4	918	531	30,542	1.1	17,635	34,385	19,854	0.9	21,425	3,955	2,284
Vermillion	8	48	1	35	212	2,920	1.6	17,631	3,515	21,223	2.5	2,075	270	1,630
Vigo	311	302	3	534	518	17,050	-1.4	16,619	19,870	19,368	0.1	12,080	2,618	2,552
Wabash	36	106	1	50	147	6,452	4.6	19,065	7,560	22,338	4.7	5,050	496	1,466
Warren	2	23	1	16	183	1,038	2.9	11,816	1,680	19,124	5.9	1,060	94	1,070
Warrick	193	349	2	118	213	7,255	17.4	12,872	9,285	16,474	19.8	5,780	535	949
Washington	21	75	1	15	54	4,063	6.8	14,571	5,225	18,738	7.4	2,975	578	2,073
Wayne	161	231	1	233	335	13,374	1.6	19,329	15,460	22,344	2.5	9,665	1,575	2,276
Wells	47	168	1	79	282	4,080	7.4	14,527	5,010	17,839	8.2	3,480	225	801
White	20	81	1	25	101	4,971	5.9	20,320	5,340	21,829	8.4	3,490	244	997
Whitley	22	69	1	118	370	4,989	6.5	15,435	5,550	17,170	7.7	3,915	203	628
IOWA	6,287	213	115	10,943	371	[6]489,466	[6]2.7	[6]16,501	[7]552,294	[7]18,619	[7]2.0	[7]365,387	43,373	1,462
Adair	3	38	1	22	279	1,551	-1.7	19,735	1,825	23,222	-2.8	1,230	90	1,145
Adams	5	116	1	22	512	978	-2.0	22,936	1,110	26,032	-5.5	720	78	1,829
Allamakee	12	82	1	25	170	2,838	-1.0	19,294	3,270	22,231	2.6	2,245	186	1,265
Appanoose	10	73	1	51	374	3,072	-0.1	22,479	3,415	24,989	-1.0	2,050	453	3,315
Audubon	2	31	1	25	386	1,472	-9.4	22,797	1,740	26,947	-6.8	1,150	79	1,223
Benton	9	34	1	83	310	4,055	0.5	15,019	4,825	17,870	1.7	3,105	269	996
Black Hawk	309	246	3	570	453	20,362	2.3	16,174	23,100	18,349	0.4	14,960	2,835	2,252
Boone	20	76	1	48	182	4,431	0.6	16,657	5,370	20,186	2.1	3,490	359	1,350
Bremer	24	102	2	50	213	4,356	5.5	18,398	4,840	20,442	8.9	3,280	170	718
Buchanan	14	67	1	84	400	3,523	2.1	16,761	3,885	18,483	0.9	2,485	277	1,318
Buena Vista	18	89	1	42	208	3,532	-6.5	17,528	3,785	18,783	-6.8	2,530	221	1,097
Butler	3	20	–	–	–	3,294	-2.1	21,885	3,595	23,852	-1.6	2,285	162	1,075
Calhoun	10	95	1	25	237	2,500	-3.9	23,939	2,795	26,764	-6.1	1,825	127	1,216
Carroll	35	167	2	215	1,024	4,454	2.2	21,175	4,770	22,678	1.5	3,055	239	1,136
Cass	14	98	1	49	343	3,382	2.2	23,785	3,645	25,635	-0.8	2,425	307	2,159
Cedar	8	44	–	–	–	2,887	-1.6	15,816	3,525	19,311	(Z)	2,400	142	778
Cerro Gordo	173	386	1	238	531	9,137	(Z)	20,466	10,075	22,567	-2.1	6,705	728	1,631
Cherokee	16	129	1	25	201	2,756	-2.6	22,522	3,090	25,251	-3.3	2,060	134	1,095
Chickasaw	5	40	1	53	420	2,521	-0.5	20,067	2,890	23,004	-4.2	1,865	147	1,170
Clarke	5	54	1	55	594	1,556	-1.5	16,985	1,940	21,177	4.4	1,295	155	1,692
Clay	30	177	1	85	501	3,362	3.7	19,897	3,860	22,844	2.7	2,580	229	1,355
Clayton	13	71	2	40	218	3,794	1.2	20,690	4,385	23,913	0.8	2,835	252	1,374
Clinton	70	141	2	439	882	9,156	2.9	18,416	10,500	21,120	2.9	6,805	1,000	2,011
Crawford	10	59	1	28	166	3,080	-2.4	18,237	3,490	20,664	-2.5	2,135	184	1,089
Dallas	35	71	1	25	51	5,403	5.7	10,438	6,445	12,451	13.8	4,435	345	667
Davis	5	58	1	57	657	1,503	-1.1	17,358	1,715	19,806	0.2	1,100	156	1,802
Decatur	5	58	1	25	290	1,738	0.9	20,198	1,835	21,325	-3.8	1,225	206	2,394
Delaware	10	55	1	25	138	2,843	2.0	15,773	3,420	18,974	2.2	2,205	215	1,193
Des Moines	89	218	1	378	926	7,779	0.6	19,062	8,855	21,698	2.6	5,985	864	2,117
Dickinson	24	145	1	49	296	3,850	4.8	23,072	4,325	25,918	2.7	3,080	165	989
Dubuque	236	259	2	444	487	15,551	7.4	16,971	17,445	19,038	5.2	11,655	1,393	1,520
Emmet	10	94	1	25	235	2,234	-3.2	21,208	2,340	22,214	-6.6	1,545	116	1,101
Fayette	8	38	2	89	419	4,289	-1.3	20,138	4,930	23,148	-0.6	3,140	402	1,888
Floyd	13	79	1	25	151	3,575	1.7	21,742	4,050	24,631	-1.5	2,560	325	1,977
Franklin	2	19	1	77	718	1,985	-5.0	18,496	2,475	23,062	-4.1	1,660	123	1,146
Fremont	5	64	1	25	322	1,603	-1.9	20,660	1,840	23,714	-4.0	1,215	124	1,598
Greene	8	80	1	101	1,007	2,211	-5.7	22,192	2,455	24,641	-7.2	1,635	154	1,546
Grundy	8	65	1	80	647	2,365	-1.5	19,182	2,840	23,035	-0.9	1,980	76	616
Guthrie	6	52	1	25	216	2,448	-4.2	21,200	2,770	23,989	-4.3	1,915	141	1,221
Hamilton	11	68	1	25	154	3,056	-2.2	18,854	3,475	21,439	-2.0	2,390	196	1,209

See footnotes at end of table.

[Includes United States, states, and 3,141 counties/county equivalents defined as of February 22, 2005. For more information on these areas, see Appendix C, Geographic Information]

County	Physicians, 2004[1] Number	Physicians, 2004 Rate per 100,000 persons[2]	Community hospitals, 2004[3] Number	Beds Number	Beds Rate per 100,000 persons[2]	Medicare program enrollment, 2005[4] Total	Medicare Percent change, 2000–2005	Medicare Rate per 100,000 persons[2]	Social Security program beneficiaries, December 2005 Number	Social Security Rate per 100,000 persons[2]	Social Security Percent change, 2000–2005	Retired workers, number	Supplemental Security Income program recipients, 2005 Number	SSI Rate per 100,000 persons[2]
IOWA—Con.														
Hancock	6	51	1	25	212	2,250	0.4	19,090	2,540	21,551	−2.5	1,635	101	857
Hardin	12	66	1	40	220	4,153	−3.1	23,068	4,365	24,246	−3.2	2,945	199	1,105
Harrison	9	57	1	25	158	2,989	0.7	18,818	3,315	20,870	0.4	2,085	234	1,473
Henry	24	119	1	74	367	3,454	3.4	17,060	3,870	19,115	4.4	2,580	291	1,437
Howard	8	82	1	25	255	1,937	−2.9	19,969	2,240	23,093	−6.3	1,450	114	1,175
Humboldt	6	60	1	49	488	2,129	−5.8	21,348	2,415	24,215	−7.0	1,600	143	1,434
Ida	1	13	1	25	337	1,612	−7.2	21,846	1,810	24,529	−6.4	1,170	68	922
Iowa	9	56	1	25	156	2,888	3.6	17,988	3,320	20,679	2.6	2,355	119	741
Jackson	19	94	1	43	212	3,922	4.6	19,287	4,480	22,031	3.2	2,945	343	1,687
Jasper	19	50	1	52	138	6,403	2.7	16,996	7,485	19,868	1.6	5,160	404	1,072
Jefferson	22	137	1	67	418	2,416	3.1	15,126	2,895	18,125	5.8	1,860	295	1,847
Johnson	1,778	1,530	2	886	762	10,570	14.5	9,029	12,490	10,669	14.7	8,460	1,117	954
Jones	7	34	1	25	122	3,431	2.1	16,729	4,115	20,064	2.9	2,755	224	1,092
Keokuk	1	9	1	25	222	2,522	−4.1	22,605	2,525	22,632	−7.7	1,575	173	1,551
Kossuth	9	55	1	22	135	3,591	−0.5	22,246	4,280	26,515	−1.2	2,840	203	1,258
Lee	57	155	2	155	422	6,710	−0.3	18,281	7,720	21,033	1.5	4,975	811	2,210
Linn	453	230	2	805	409	28,805	8.9	14,482	33,080	16,631	8.6	22,895	2,537	1,275
Louisa	1	8	−	−	−	1,875	1.6	15,833	2,140	18,071	−2.8	1,385	157	1,326
Lucas	2	21	1	25	259	1,952	−3.7	20,182	2,105	21,764	−3.7	1,410	213	2,202
Lyon	3	26	1	16	136	2,117	−6.4	18,017	2,345	19,957	−6.5	1,550	67	570
Madison	2	13	1	25	168	2,292	3.9	15,121	2,690	17,746	4.7	1,785	134	884
Mahaska	23	104	1	49	222	3,925	1.5	17,551	4,525	20,233	0.2	2,970	442	1,976
Marion	41	125	2	178	544	5,632	3.0	17,075	6,360	19,282	2.1	4,125	377	1,143
Marshall	61	155	1	105	266	7,327	2.9	18,588	8,260	20,955	3.3	5,590	567	1,438
Mills	14	93	−	−	−	2,412	2.9	15,781	2,690	17,600	0.3	1,530	291	1,904
Mitchell	5	46	1	25	228	2,483	−2.3	22,740	2,555	23,400	−0.6	1,735	99	907
Monona	9	93	1	38	394	2,246	−6.6	23,592	2,565	26,943	−3.1	1,625	161	1,691
Monroe	1	13	1	25	319	1,594	−2.6	20,345	1,820	23,229	−5.1	1,190	142	1,812
Montgomery	9	80	1	40	354	2,478	−4.3	21,904	2,740	24,220	−4.7	1,800	228	2,015
Muscatine	32	76	1	66	156	6,446	3.4	15,076	7,360	17,214	4.4	4,805	631	1,476
O'Brien	10	69	2	108	749	3,442	(Z)	23,880	3,685	25,565	−1.9	2,325	202	1,401
Osceola	2	29	1	25	369	1,356	−3.7	20,257	1,525	22,782	−3.4	975	56	837
Page	20	123	2	113	696	3,597	−3.2	22,131	3,990	24,549	−3.0	2,675	348	2,141
Palo Alto	9	92	1	47	482	2,262	−3.7	23,327	2,320	23,905	−7.4	1,480	150	1,547
Plymouth	18	72	1	44	176	4,187	−0.8	16,776	4,850	19,433	0.1	3,160	203	813
Pocahontas	2	25	1	20	248	2,017	−2.9	25,435	2,135	26,923	−2.9	1,385	93	1,173
Polk	1,052	267	4	1,328	337	50,397	7.7	12,568	56,980	14,209	5.7	38,460	5,839	1,456
Pottawattamie	122	137	2	299	335	14,456	3.9	16,109	16,160	18,008	6.0	10,060	1,666	1,857
Poweshiek	37	195	1	51	268	3,614	4.4	19,096	3,950	20,872	1.6	2,755	197	1,041
Ringgold	3	56	1	23	430	1,246	−2.4	23,630	1,425	27,024	1.7	965	120	2,276
Sac	8	74	1	44	407	2,586	−5.3	24,348	2,730	25,704	−7.4	1,865	132	1,243
Scott	399	249	2	520	325	22,900	7.9	14,224	26,525	16,475	7.8	17,260	3,083	1,915
Shelby	9	70	1	40	313	2,710	−1.8	21,450	3,000	23,745	−3.4	1,985	153	1,211
Sioux	27	84	4	336	1,046	5,107	0.5	15,822	5,605	17,365	−1.7	3,655	219	679
Story	168	209	2	292	364	9,321	7.8	11,658	10,160	12,708	6.3	7,315	552	690
Tama	8	45	−	−	−	3,575	−0.9	19,951	3,975	22,183	0.3	2,610	161	898
Taylor	−	−	−	−	−	1,569	−6.0	23,722	1,740	26,308	−3.9	1,145	123	1,860
Union	8	67	1	34	284	2,744	3.4	22,920	2,855	23,847	1.0	1,800	300	2,506
Van Buren	2	26	1	25	323	1,821	2.3	23,388	1,895	24,339	−3.1	1,240	131	1,683
Wapello	78	218	1	83	232	7,331	−1.5	20,384	8,025	22,313	−2.7	4,895	1,072	2,981
Warren	18	42	−	−	−	5,516	13.2	12,834	6,780	15,774	13.2	4,685	306	712
Washington	16	75	1	68	319	4,171	2.7	19,439	4,545	21,182	1.9	3,140	270	1,258
Wayne	3	45	1	28	424	1,628	−4.9	24,663	1,865	28,253	−2.3	1,215	149	2,257
Webster	77	196	1	154	393	7,667	−1.6	19,657	8,560	21,947	−3.1	5,460	743	1,905
Winnebago	6	53	−	−	−	2,474	−0.8	21,795	2,550	22,465	−5.4	1,795	112	987
Winneshiek	33	156	1	75	354	3,548	3.7	16,709	4,020	18,932	2.9	2,770	174	819
Woodbury	205	199	2	430	417	15,885	−0.2	15,482	17,495	17,051	−0.9	11,040	1,863	1,816
Worth	3	39	−	−	−	1,469	−3.9	18,911	1,600	20,597	−7.7	1,095	75	965
Wright	8	58	2	47	343	3,089	−5.1	22,635	3,305	24,218	−5.1	2,150	172	1,260
KANSAS	6,869	251	134	10,362	379	[6]401,243	[6]2.8	[6]14,619	[7]452,119	[7]16,473	[7]2.6	296,145	39,162	1,427
Allen	6	43	1	25	180	2,713	−4.0	19,678	3,205	23,247	−2.4	2,005	321	2,328
Anderson	8	98	1	47	575	1,721	−3.6	21,034	1,965	24,016	−0.9	1,350	100	1,222
Atchison	17	101	1	67	397	2,922	0.2	17,389	3,215	19,132	−2.1	2,070	299	1,779
Barber	3	60	2	89	1,784	1,183	−6.0	23,860	1,335	26,926	−2.1	870	91	1,835
Barton	42	150	3	111	396	5,315	−1.3	18,911	5,825	20,726	−1.1	3,850	426	1,516
Bourbon	26	172	1	94	623	2,956	−4.6	19,711	3,490	23,271	−2.3	2,235	369	2,460
Brown	14	135	2	50	483	2,153	−3.7	21,027	2,410	23,537	−3.1	1,565	221	2,158
Butler	66	107	1	82	133	8,352	7.4	13,394	10,120	16,230	7.0	6,595	613	983
Chase	−	−	−	−	−	541	−4.4	17,559	650	21,097	−1.4	415	41	1,331
Chautauqua	2	48	2	65	1,551	988	−5.5	24,045	1,195	29,083	−6.6	775	106	2,580

See footnotes at end of table.

[Includes United States, states, and 3,141 counties/county equivalents defined as of February 22, 2005. For more information on these areas, see Appendix C, Geographic Information]

County	Physicians, 2004[1]		Community hospitals, 2004[3]			Medicare program enrollment, 2005[4]			Social Security program beneficiaries, December 2005				Supplemental Security Income program recipients, 2005	
				Beds										
	Number	Rate per 100,000 persons[2]	Number	Number	Rate per 100,000 persons[2]	Total	Percent change, 2000–2005	Rate per 100,000 persons[2]	Number	Rate per 100,000 persons[2]	Percent change, 2000–2005	Retired workers, number	Number	Rate per 100,000 persons[2]
KANSAS—Con.														
Cherokee	5	23	1	18	83	3,827	0.1	17,755	4,685	21,735	1.2	2,720	651	3,020
Cheyenne	3	101	1	16	539	765	−9.0	25,967	860	29,192	−7.9	555	18	611
Clark	3	128	2	101	4,324	525	−4.2	22,996	545	23,872	−3.4	375	22	964
Clay	9	105	1	25	292	1,870	−2.2	21,671	2,055	23,815	−2.6	1,345	126	1,460
Cloud	14	144	1	25	257	2,359	−6.9	24,173	2,540	26,027	−7.7	1,755	179	1,834
Coffey	6	69	1	78	892	1,538	−1.1	17,713	1,910	21,997	−0.6	1,240	182	2,096
Comanche	1	52	1	14	732	497	−4.2	25,685	505	26,098	−7.7	355	24	1,240
Cowley	36	101	2	79	221	6,084	−6.1	17,236	7,125	20,185	−2.3	4,580	722	2,045
Crawford	56	147	2	179	469	6,616	−0.4	17,309	7,125	18,641	−2.6	4,290	877	2,294
Decatur	5	153	1	60	1,840	879	−5.8	27,546	960	30,085	−8.3	660	27	846
Dickinson	16	84	2	134	700	3,881	−0.9	20,204	4,165	21,683	−0.5	2,860	245	1,275
Doniphan	3	38	–	–	–	1,337	−5.0	17,106	1,550	19,831	−5.3	995	125	1,599
Douglas	219	213	1	141	137	10,241	12.9	9,951	11,480	11,155	11.4	7,625	930	904
Edwards	2	60	–	–	–	692	−10.5	21,021	725	22,023	−13.0	490	41	1,245
Elk	–	–	–	–	–	771	−7.6	25,073	915	29,756	−3.5	595	69	2,244
Ellis	84	311	1	158	584	4,292	1.8	16,035	4,695	17,540	0.3	3,125	320	1,196
Ellsworth	4	63	1	20	315	1,246	−6.3	19,644	1,480	23,333	−0.5	1,040	64	1,009
Finney	43	110	1	101	258	3,694	5.3	9,475	3,835	9,836	3.0	2,260	479	1,229
Ford	52	155	1	99	296	3,645	−2.4	10,800	4,000	11,852	−4.8	2,655	389	1,153
Franklin	19	73	1	47	180	4,027	1.8	15,343	4,745	18,078	4.2	3,055	425	1,619
Geary	30	119	1	69	274	2,993	2.8	12,174	3,575	14,541	1.2	2,165	481	1,956
Gove	7	247	1	76	2,686	729	–	26,384	750	27,144	−0.8	490	25	905
Graham	3	109	1	25	909	723	4.2	26,571	885	32,525	−0.9	585	41	1,507
Grant	6	78	1	44	576	864	3.7	11,474	1,015	13,479	2.8	640	70	930
Gray	2	34	–	–	–	797	−4.8	13,598	865	14,759	−5.5	550	19	324
Greeley	1	71	1	50	3,541	275	−8.0	20,385	305	22,609	−6.2	190	5	371
Greenwood	4	53	1	25	334	1,810	−7.0	24,666	1,955	26,642	−6.8	1,290	146	1,990
Hamilton	2	76	1	73	2,762	479	−4.4	18,395	505	19,393	−5.3	340	23	883
Harper	9	145	2	50	807	1,405	−6.8	23,105	1,570	25,818	−6.2	1,065	99	1,628
Harvey	89	264	1	79	234	6,260	4.4	18,497	6,490	19,177	11.6	4,555	366	1,081
Haskell	2	47	1	57	1,336	475	1.7	11,224	580	13,705	2.1	355	37	874
Hodgeman	–	–	1	32	1,509	387	−1.0	18,341	440	20,853	−4.8	295	10	474
Jackson	11	83	1	12	91	2,096	4.5	15,486	2,690	19,874	4.2	1,705	170	1,256
Jefferson	10	53	1	75	396	3,002	11.6	15,712	3,450	18,057	7.7	2,250	179	937
Jewell	3	88	1	49	1,431	919	−7.8	27,416	1,070	31,921	−4.9	700	52	1,551
Johnson	2,388	481	9	1,255	253	54,550	14.2	10,769	61,300	12,101	14.2	43,390	2,645	522
Kearny	2	44	1	90	1,986	550	3.6	12,179	630	13,950	−0.8	395	53	1,174
Kingman	2	24	1	34	408	1,652	−2.6	20,233	1,865	22,841	−6.0	1,225	73	894
Kiowa	3	97	1	25	812	766	−2.4	25,670	800	26,810	−5.5	570	57	1,910
Labette	39	176	2	82	370	4,294	−2.9	19,369	4,850	21,877	−1.3	2,920	631	2,846
Lane	2	103	1	31	1,604	441	−9.3	23,284	465	24,551	−13.7	310	15	792
Leavenworth	87	120	2	130	179	7,661	11.1	10,478	9,665	13,219	9.6	6,190	725	992
Lincoln	2	59	1	14	411	756	−11.7	22,164	840	24,626	−12.3	565	38	1,114
Linn	3	31	–	–	–	1,959	1.3	19,760	2,290	23,099	6.6	1,490	152	1,533
Logan	1	35	1	60	2,130	670	−5.8	23,980	675	24,159	−6.3	450	24	859
Lyon	48	134	1	122	340	4,851	3.4	13,623	5,095	14,308	2.7	3,320	528	1,483
McPherson	36	122	3	86	292	5,484	1.3	18,575	5,955	20,171	−4.5	4,255	237	803
Marion	9	69	2	129	991	2,774	−4.6	21,418	3,025	23,355	−5.8	2,060	129	996
Marshall	7	67	1	25	240	2,402	−5.6	23,085	2,550	24,507	−4.5	1,685	167	1,605
Meade	4	87	1	20	436	847	−0.6	18,314	915	19,784	−2.5	590	35	757
Miami	35	117	1	20	67	3,709	3.3	12,162	4,775	15,658	10.6	3,105	446	1,462
Mitchell	7	107	1	99	1,519	1,475	−6.9	22,975	1,525	23,754	−8.5	1,065	79	1,231
Montgomery	42	121	2	145	416	7,476	−1.9	21,626	8,455	24,458	−1.4	5,220	987	2,855
Morris	6	100	1	28	468	1,296	−2.5	21,425	1,445	23,888	−5.0	1,000	82	1,356
Morton	7	217	1	120	3,716	545	2.1	17,053	620	19,399	1.6	380	35	1,095
Nemaha	4	38	2	55	527	2,164	−5.2	20,722	2,365	22,647	−4.0	1,590	115	1,101
Neosho	14	85	1	59	357	3,286	−1.1	19,880	3,620	21,901	−2.1	2,295	372	2,251
Ness	1	33	2	112	3,652	884	−3.9	29,379	920	30,575	−2.6	655	21	698
Norton	6	105	1	25	436	1,131	−10.5	19,968	1,265	22,334	−5.4	860	47	830
Osage	7	41	–	–	–	2,937	–	17,125	3,395	19,796	3.8	2,230	256	1,493
Osborne	2	49	1	25	610	1,086	−8.7	26,815	1,190	29,383	−7.1	800	43	1,062
Ottawa	6	98	1	52	846	1,077	−3.1	17,589	1,270	20,741	−1.6	890	68	1,111
Pawnee	18	267	1	55	815	1,200	−14.7	17,807	1,460	21,665	−7.8	1,030	69	1,024
Phillips	5	89	1	58	1,034	1,362	−3.8	24,746	1,505	27,344	−5.6	940	70	1,272
Pottawatomie	16	85	2	194	1,027	2,594	2.4	13,561	3,130	16,363	2.4	2,065	163	852
Pratt	13	139	1	85	907	1,825	−3.5	19,219	2,090	22,009	−1.5	1,410	112	1,179
Rawlins	4	144	1	24	866	733	−6.6	27,433	805	30,127	−5.7	525	42	1,572
Reno	141	222	1	154	242	11,717	1.9	18,435	13,190	20,753	0.5	8,865	1,083	1,704
Republic	7	134	1	63	1,206	1,412	−9.3	27,343	1,530	29,628	−9.3	1,080	73	1,414
Rice	4	38	1	25	238	2,060	−5.8	19,709	2,310	22,101	−5.1	1,540	128	1,225

See footnotes at end of table.

[Includes United States, states, and 3,141 counties/county equivalents defined as of February 22, 2005. For more information on these areas, see Appendix C, Geographic Information]

County	Physicians, 2004[1] Number	Rate per 100,000 persons[2]	Community hospitals, 2004[3] Number	Beds Number	Beds Rate per 100,000 persons[2]	Medicare program enrollment, 2005[4] Total	Percent change, 2000–2005	Rate per 100,000 persons[2]	Social Security program beneficiaries, December 2005 Number	Rate per 100,000 persons[2]	Percent change, 2000–2005	Retired workers, number	Supplemental Security Income program recipients, 2005 Number	Rate per 100,000 persons[2]
KANSAS—Con.														
Riley	136	216	1	121	192	5,559	7.8	8,848	5,895	9,383	6.5	4,025	445	708
Rooks	4	74	1	19	353	1,255	–4.4	23,454	1,405	26,257	–4.1	920	69	1,289
Rush	4	116	1	46	1,333	925	–6.5	27,158	975	28,626	–9.3	645	62	1,820
Russell	8	115	1	58	831	1,821	–6.8	26,603	1,995	29,145	–5.5	1,335	114	1,665
Saline	154	286	1	227	421	8,829	5.9	16,375	9,820	18,213	4.1	6,525	846	1,569
Scott	5	108	1	25	540	414	–15.3	9,000	985	21,413	0.2	650	42	913
Sedgwick	1,387	299	7	1,607	347	60,970	5.4	13,082	70,815	15,194	5.8	45,605	8,026	1,722
Seward	38	163	1	89	383	2,090	–0.3	8,980	2,425	10,419	–1.9	1,485	284	1,220
Shawnee	538	314	3	661	385	28,618	4.7	16,603	31,300	18,159	4.9	19,885	3,706	2,150
Sheridan	2	77	1	60	2,309	538	–0.4	20,764	660	25,473	1.1	440	10	386
Sherman	6	97	1	25	404	1,282	4.1	20,835	1,435	23,322	6.5	910	121	1,967
Smith	4	96	1	54	1,299	1,172	–7.9	28,440	1,300	31,546	–6.2	875	45	1,092
Stafford	1	22	1	25	551	1,048	–3.3	23,351	1,125	25,067	–7.6	745	53	1,181
Stanton	2	85	1	43	1,817	365	7.0	16,258	380	16,927	–0.3	245	11	490
Stevens	2	36	1	17	310	776	–1.8	14,339	880	16,260	–7.8	560	37	684
Sumner	10	40	2	86	343	4,494	–4.0	18,123	4,705	18,974	–1.5	2,970	332	1,339
Thomas	8	103	1	93	1,193	1,269	0.6	16,612	1,425	18,654	–1.6	940	80	1,047
Trego	4	128	1	62	1,978	725	–6.7	23,770	830	27,213	–4.8	560	51	1,672
Wabaunsee	3	44	–	–	–	1,158	2.5	16,737	1,370	19,801	–2.8	925	71	1,026
Wallace	1	63	–	–	–	333	–4.9	21,170	340	21,615	–5.6	230	10	636
Washington	3	49	2	59	971	1,577	–10.0	26,244	1,710	28,457	–9.7	1,175	81	1,348
Wichita	2	85	1	35	1,494	399	–5.5	17,280	465	20,139	–5.5	305	19	823
Wilson	7	71	2	76	768	2,064	–2.6	20,988	2,490	25,320	–0.3	1,540	230	2,339
Woodson	1	28	–	–	–	920	–10.7	25,756	940	26,316	–12.1	605	82	2,296
Wyandotte	618	396	2	732	469	20,984	–6.3	13,473	23,210	14,902	–6.5	13,605	4,310	2,767
KENTUCKY	10,464	253	105	15,276	369	[6]676,648	[6]8.6	[6]16,213	[7]797,660	[7]19,113	[7]7.9	[7]415,727	179,955	4,312
Adair	17	97	1	25	143	3,224	8.4	18,346	3,970	22,591	5.8	2,040	1,143	6,504
Allen	5	27	–	–	–	3,094	9.9	16,540	3,885	20,769	10.2	2,170	879	4,699
Anderson	18	90	–	–	–	2,696	15.1	13,220	3,355	16,451	11.6	1,940	379	1,858
Ballard	2	24	–	–	–	2,011	6.2	24,296	1,950	23,559	6.6	1,090	276	3,335
Barren	95	240	1	196	495	7,096	9.0	17,708	8,840	22,060	10.5	4,950	1,870	4,666
Bath	7	61	–	–	–	2,124	5.3	18,269	2,550	21,934	8.6	1,225	953	8,197
Bell	54	182	2	246	828	6,365	3.3	21,456	7,370	24,844	(Z)	2,585	3,329	11,222
Boone	157	155	1	177	175	11,068	29.8	10,415	13,585	12,783	29.0	7,880	1,226	1,154
Bourbon	25	127	1	58	295	3,209	8.1	16,180	3,985	20,093	10.1	2,355	699	3,524
Boyd	216	436	2	761	1,535	10,520	4.4	21,212	11,405	22,997	4.1	5,660	2,408	4,855
Boyle	106	376	1	177	627	5,140	8.8	18,122	5,905	20,819	7.9	3,405	1,102	3,885
Bracken	4	46	–	–	–	1,494	7.9	17,232	1,840	21,223	12.5	865	322	3,714
Breathitt	27	170	1	55	345	2,903	5.0	18,193	3,615	22,655	0.6	1,095	2,319	14,533
Breckinridge	8	42	1	43	225	3,359	5.4	17,410	4,190	21,718	14.2	2,145	988	5,121
Bullitt	28	42	–	–	–	6,713	29.2	9,804	10,855	15,853	32.3	5,735	1,390	2,030
Butler	3	22	–	–	–	2,072	9.5	15,447	2,900	21,619	15.5	1,400	676	5,040
Caldwell	12	93	1	48	373	2,738	0.3	21,105	3,200	24,667	1.7	1,835	567	4,371
Calloway	70	201	1	323	928	5,993	5.3	17,063	7,145	20,343	8.4	4,450	735	2,093
Campbell	153	175	1	222	254	12,863	1.8	14,743	14,740	16,894	1.3	8,805	1,889	2,165
Carlisle	1	19	–	–	–	1,143	1.8	21,449	1,290	24,207	–1.2	760	162	3,040
Carroll	6	58	1	25	242	1,720	5.4	16,453	2,105	20,136	5.9	1,155	506	4,840
Carter	11	40	–	–	–	4,891	9.5	17,912	5,895	21,589	13.5	2,530	1,793	6,566
Casey	7	43	–	–	–	2,727	6.8	16,740	3,500	21,486	5.4	1,700	1,275	7,827
Christian	124	176	1	139	198	8,599	6.1	12,259	10,130	14,442	4.3	5,720	2,309	3,292
Clark	59	171	1	112	326	5,528	11.9	15,845	6,700	19,205	13.2	3,605	1,278	3,663
Clay	14	58	1	63	260	4,015	10.8	16,628	4,785	19,817	6.5	1,540	3,678	15,232
Clinton	5	52	1	42	439	2,234	8.8	23,371	2,540	26,572	5.2	1,235	1,036	10,838
Crittenden	5	55	1	228	2,524	1,820	3.9	20,258	2,315	25,768	5.8	1,225	348	3,874
Cumberland	4	56	1	25	348	1,594	3.8	22,303	1,800	25,185	2.3	980	608	8,507
Daviess	227	245	1	345	372	16,367	9.1	17,588	19,355	20,798	9.8	11,260	3,233	3,474
Edmonson	3	25	–	–	–	1,743	6.3	14,489	2,710	22,527	9.9	1,350	660	5,486
Elliott	1	15	–	–	–	1,030	22.9	14,923	1,525	22,095	11.9	580	698	10,113
Estill	8	53	1	25	165	3,275	–3.4	21,705	3,190	21,141	5.4	1,465	1,286	8,523
Fayette	2,022	759	7	1,643	617	32,729	9.1	12,209	37,125	13,848	8.3	22,810	5,827	2,174
Fleming	13	90	1	32	221	2,568	11.6	17,577	3,075	21,047	8.3	1,575	727	4,976
Floyd	72	171	3	210	497	8,805	9.4	20,856	10,950	25,937	4.4	3,245	4,247	10,060
Franklin	84	174	1	146	303	9,272	5.6	19,234	10,805	22,414	8.8	6,075	1,365	2,832
Fulton	15	204	1	56	763	1,805	–2.9	25,010	1,845	25,565	–5.0	955	507	7,025
Gallatin	2	25	–	–	–	1,017	10.5	12,503	1,035	12,724	–5.0	535	190	2,336
Garrard	10	62	–	–	–	2,596	15.0	15,658	3,225	19,452	12.4	1,770	644	3,884
Grant	12	49	1	15	62	3,506	17.5	14,246	4,170	16,944	15.0	2,000	711	2,889
Graves	47	126	1	107	286	7,532	3.3	20,019	8,635	22,950	3.7	4,985	1,453	3,862
Grayson	27	108	1	75	300	4,806	12.3	19,080	5,590	22,192	9.9	2,880	1,289	5,117
Green	6	52	1	64	550	2,180	2.6	18,813	2,755	23,775	1.4	1,475	724	6,248
Greenup	43	116	–	–	–	7,246	13.3	19,487	7,655	20,587	16.3	3,430	1,614	4,341

See footnotes at end of table.

Table B-6. Counties — **Physicians, Community Hospitals, Medicare, Social Security, and Supplemental Security Income**—Con.

[Includes United States, states, and 3,141 counties/county equivalents defined as of February 22, 2005. For more information on these areas, see Appendix C, Geographic Information]

County	Physicians, 2004[1] Number	Physicians, 2004 Rate per 100,000 persons[2]	Community hospitals, 2004[3] Number	Beds Number	Beds Rate per 100,000 persons[2]	Medicare program enrollment, 2005[4] Total	Percent change, 2000–2005	Rate per 100,000 persons[2]	Social Security program beneficiaries, December 2005 Number	Rate per 100,000 persons[2]	Percent change, 2000–2005	Retired workers, number	Supplemental Security Income program recipients, 2005 Number	Rate per 100,000 persons[2]
KENTUCKY—Con.														
Hancock	2	24	–	–	–	1,295	14.3	15,035	1,665	19,331	16.5	890	238	2,763
Hardin	225	235	2	308	322	13,313	18.9	13,732	15,090	15,565	15.3	8,115	2,603	2,685
Harlan	42	132	1	150	472	7,027	-1.7	22,227	8,495	26,871	-6.4	2,580	3,027	9,575
Harrison	24	131	1	49	267	3,170	11.1	17,110	3,690	19,917	5.7	2,050	727	3,924
Hart	9	50	1	25	138	3,075	10.8	16,786	3,810	20,798	10.1	1,870	1,142	6,234
Henderson	71	157	1	209	461	7,593	8.7	16,661	9,040	19,836	9.1	5,100	1,513	3,320
Henry	10	63	–	–	–	2,662	7.8	16,739	2,950	18,550	8.4	1,685	533	3,352
Hickman	2	39	–	–	–	840	-2.8	16,552	1,300	25,616	3.7	765	224	4,414
Hopkins	139	297	1	271	580	8,954	6.1	19,171	10,400	22,267	5.9	5,170	1,921	4,113
Jackson	5	37	–	–	–	2,427	10.3	17,822	2,870	21,075	7.7	1,125	1,445	10,611
Jefferson	3,478	498	10	3,308	473	113,400	2.6	16,204	126,270	18,043	2.0	75,780	20,003	2,858
Jessamine	82	194	–	–	–	5,171	22.3	11,897	6,455	14,852	19.5	3,650	1,142	2,628
Johnson	40	168	1	72	302	4,770	8.5	19,874	5,640	23,499	8.5	2,080	2,019	8,412
Kenton	444	290	2	496	324	19,982	2.8	13,004	22,765	14,815	3.2	13,295	3,510	2,284
Knott	6	34	–	–	–	2,822	7.1	16,070	3,785	21,553	3.1	1,150	1,797	10,233
Knox	18	56	1	39	122	4,762	5.4	14,849	7,170	22,358	7.2	2,750	4,138	12,903
Larue	5	37	–	–	–	2,417	8.6	17,644	2,890	21,096	5.9	1,605	490	3,577
Laurel	81	145	1	87	156	8,453	14.8	15,004	11,430	20,288	13.9	4,895	3,340	5,929
Lawrence	14	87	1	74	462	2,991	12.0	18,502	3,515	21,743	7.9	1,305	1,518	9,390
Lee	3	38	–	–	–	1,530	1.9	19,847	1,735	22,506	-1.3	685	929	12,051
Leslie	7	58	1	25	208	2,519	5.9	21,002	3,180	26,513	0.1	885	1,342	11,189
Letcher	40	162	2	142	576	5,188	5.4	21,233	6,400	26,193	0.9	1,965	2,405	9,843
Lewis	5	36	–	–	–	2,443	7.2	17,611	2,825	20,365	8.3	1,285	1,056	7,612
Lincoln	14	57	1	55	222	4,677	14.6	18,617	5,225	20,799	14.9	2,610	1,530	6,090
Livingston	9	93	1	25	257	2,080	8.0	21,311	2,505	25,666	9.6	1,290	296	3,033
Logan	17	63	1	92	340	4,831	7.8	17,781	5,685	20,925	5.9	3,185	992	3,651
Lyon	3	37	–	–	–	1,757	16.5	21,532	2,150	26,348	11.9	1,315	203	2,488
McCracken	227	352	2	577	894	12,223	2.8	18,892	14,430	22,304	5.7	8,260	2,246	3,472
McCreary	5	29	–	–	–	3,117	15.1	18,087	3,770	21,877	9.8	1,330	2,127	12,343
McLean	2	20	–	–	–	1,908	5.6	19,222	2,200	22,164	6.5	1,210	322	3,244
Madison	120	158	2	117	154	10,254	17.5	13,189	12,140	15,614	18.1	6,545	2,613	3,361
Magoffin	5	37	–	–	–	2,322	13.7	17,236	2,885	21,415	9.7	890	1,707	12,671
Marion	22	117	–	–	–	3,165	2.9	16,712	3,735	19,721	7.8	1,930	1,103	5,824
Marshall	23	75	1	80	260	6,534	9.1	21,100	7,850	25,350	9.3	4,695	737	2,380
Martin	6	49	–	–	–	2,270	8.6	18,584	2,985	24,437	2.1	760	1,482	12,133
Mason	40	236	1	101	597	3,069	5.5	17,905	3,665	21,383	7.5	2,135	690	4,026
Meade	9	32	–	–	–	2,734	18.8	9,611	4,210	14,799	21.7	2,025	587	2,063
Menifee	–	–	–	–	–	1,300	24.9	19,092	1,540	22,617	16.4	650	603	8,856
Mercer	17	79	1	59	275	3,938	9.8	18,223	4,675	21,634	9.2	2,735	722	3,341
Metcalfe	3	30	–	–	–	2,158	9.2	21,163	2,385	23,389	3.2	1,230	685	6,718
Monroe	9	77	1	49	421	2,666	7.2	22,864	2,970	25,472	5.6	1,455	956	8,199
Montgomery	33	139	1	63	266	3,947	11.3	16,272	4,845	19,974	14.2	2,455	1,231	5,075
Morgan	7	49	1	40	279	2,352	9.4	16,409	2,730	19,046	14.6	1,150	1,190	8,302
Muhlenberg	32	101	1	135	427	6,213	4.3	19,694	7,620	24,154	4.4	3,475	1,556	4,932
Nelson	43	106	1	52	129	6,106	15.6	14,861	7,220	17,572	13.4	3,950	1,221	2,972
Nicholas	5	71	1	122	1,735	1,381	5.8	19,653	1,645	23,410	10.5	920	359	5,109
Ohio	13	55	1	25	106	4,148	7.4	17,520	5,235	22,111	8.9	2,615	1,127	4,760
Oldham	96	184	1	82	157	4,351	23.8	8,128	5,905	11,031	28.1	3,710	375	701
Owen	6	53	1	45	399	1,302	3.1	11,447	1,975	17,364	14.5	1,080	460	4,044
Owsley	2	42	–	–	–	1,132	4.4	23,852	1,215	25,601	0.3	465	958	20,185
Pendleton	5	33	–	–	–	2,014	12.4	13,316	2,545	16,826	11.6	1,290	464	3,068
Perry	95	321	1	308	1,040	6,304	9.3	21,404	7,250	24,616	1.8	2,280	3,077	10,448
Pike	147	219	2	389	580	14,330	8.2	21,413	17,720	26,479	4.5	4,950	5,161	7,712
Powell	6	44	–	–	–	1,898	47.4	13,867	2,980	21,772	12.4	1,195	1,117	8,161
Pulaski	139	237	1	234	399	13,135	15.7	22,188	15,165	25,617	12.5	7,350	3,797	6,414
Robertson	1	44	–	–	–	400	5.0	17,552	480	21,062	10.1	240	122	5,353
Rockcastle	14	84	1	86	515	2,813	11.8	16,832	3,640	21,781	14.4	1,625	1,307	7,821
Rowan	68	307	1	133	601	3,319	13.9	14,933	4,060	18,267	12.3	2,065	1,195	5,377
Russell	17	101	1	45	267	3,643	6.3	21,404	4,420	25,969	6.1	2,135	1,439	8,455
Scott	56	148	2	120	317	4,231	21.1	10,744	5,170	13,128	24.0	2,950	848	2,153
Shelby	45	121	1	70	189	4,379	14.2	11,462	5,695	14,906	14.6	3,540	688	1,801
Simpson	12	71	1	25	148	2,637	9.5	15,493	3,250	19,094	10.8	1,935	474	2,785
Spencer	8	54	–	–	–	1,623	26.4	10,370	2,190	13,993	30.0	1,200	297	1,898
Taylor	39	166	1	90	384	5,197	14.8	21,878	5,910	24,880	8.9	3,215	1,322	5,565
Todd	2	17	–	–	–	1,854	1.4	15,522	2,385	19,968	6.1	1,265	492	4,119
Trigg	10	75	1	25	189	2,833	12.5	21,223	3,380	25,320	14.1	2,070	423	3,169
Trimble	1	11	–	–	–	1,248	14.7	13,831	1,615	17,899	12.8	825	257	2,848
Union	8	51	1	41	262	2,611	5.2	16,746	3,135	20,106	3.9	1,580	407	2,610
Warren	272	280	3	758	780	14,052	13.3	14,200	15,840	16,006	11.2	9,125	3,048	3,080
Washington	8	71	–	–	–	2,025	6.8	17,765	2,475	21,712	7.1	1,375	518	4,544

See footnotes at end of table.

County and City Data Book: 2007

265

U.S. Census Bureau

[Includes United States, states, and 3,141 counties/county equivalents defined as of February 22, 2005. For more information on these areas, see Appendix C, Geographic Information]

County	Physicians, 2004[1] Number	Physicians, 2004[1] Rate per 100,000 persons[2]	Community hospitals, 2004[3] Number	Beds Number	Beds Rate per 100,000 persons[2]	Medicare program enrollment, 2005[4] Total	Medicare Percent change, 2000–2005	Medicare Rate per 100,000 persons[2]	Social Security program beneficiaries, December 2005 Number	SS Rate per 100,000 persons[2]	SS Percent change, 2000–2005	Retired workers, number	Supplemental Security Income program recipients, 2005 Number	SSI Rate per 100,000 persons[2]
KENTUCKY—Con.														
Wayne.	11	54	1	30	147	3,686	8.4	18,111	4,610	22,651	6.3	2,110	1,980	9,729
Webster.	2	14	–	–	–	2,703	5.6	19,088	3,155	22,280	4.5	1,580	492	3,474
Whitley.	95	253	1	240	639	9,467	16.3	24,894	8,070	21,221	11.1	3,435	2,979	7,833
Wolfe.	4	57	–	–	–	1,518	13.6	21,471	1,900	26,874	2.2	695	1,229	17,383
Woodford.	44	184	1	25	104	3,203	16.2	13,210	3,855	15,900	11.4	2,470	364	1,501
LOUISIANA.	12,999	288	131	17,199	382	[6]639,225	[6]6.3	[6]14,131	[7]715,127	[7]15,809	[7]0.5	[7]368,496	152,698	3,376
Acadia.	55	93	3	237	401	8,923	3.1	14,984	10,885	18,278	1.8	4,850	2,820	4,735
Allen.	21	83	1	59	234	3,513	6.1	13,902	4,475	17,709	6.4	2,030	957	3,787
Ascension.	76	87	3	140	161	8,428	20.7	9,313	11,580	12,795	28.2	5,560	2,056	2,272
Assumption.	10	43	1	6	26	3,244	7.7	13,985	4,410	19,012	12.7	1,870	1,173	5,057
Avoyelles.	26	62	2	72	172	7,038	2.3	16,718	8,660	20,571	7.4	3,830	2,939	6,981
Beauregard.	30	88	1	60	176	5,100	8.2	14,756	5,790	16,753	11.5	2,935	983	2,844
Bienville.	6	39	–	–	–	2,991	-3.0	19,709	3,355	22,107	0.5	1,790	844	5,561
Bossier.	170	164	–	–	–	12,899	16.1	12,222	15,725	14,899	15.4	9,275	2,496	2,365
Caddo.	1,533	611	8	2,224	886	39,308	2.1	15,641	44,475	17,697	2.9	25,625	10,620	4,226
Calcasieu.	409	222	7	896	485	27,619	7.9	14,895	31,935	17,223	5.0	16,225	4,920	2,653
Caldwell.	7	65	1	25	234	1,864	3.0	17,647	2,040	19,313	7.3	1,025	470	4,449
Cameron.	3	31	1	33	343	928	8.9	9,709	1,305	13,653	-4.0	645	129	1,350
Catahoula.	5	47	–	–	–	2,015	0.6	19,288	2,280	21,824	-2.0	1,065	641	6,136
Claiborne.	15	92	1	60	367	2,807	-2.8	17,211	3,395	20,817	(Z)	1,935	904	5,543
Concordia.	20	103	2	65	333	3,542	1.9	18,378	4,345	22,544	9.1	2,180	1,303	6,761
De Soto.	9	34	1	57	218	4,343	1.9	16,461	5,195	19,691	5.0	2,740	1,368	5,185
East Baton Rouge.	1,461	355	7	1,740	423	48,926	8.2	11,892	59,670	14,504	12.4	31,975	13,025	3,166
East Carroll.	8	90	1	11	124	1,372	-3.8	15,669	1,520	17,360	-0.8	735	672	7,675
East Feliciana.	21	101	–	–	–	2,979	7.8	14,306	3,280	15,752	9.9	1,640	943	4,529
Evangeline.	52	147	2	261	740	5,929	0.3	16,683	7,065	19,879	1.4	2,795	2,587	7,279
Franklin.	8	39	1	57	275	3,688	1.0	18,096	4,275	20,976	1.6	2,270	1,347	6,609
Grant.	6	31	–	–	–	3,007	6.6	15,418	3,695	18,946	9.3	1,680	769	3,943
Iberia.	123	166	2	166	224	10,777	8.2	14,488	13,120	17,637	7.5	6,015	3,003	4,037
Iberville.	29	89	1	75	231	4,621	6.2	14,269	5,615	17,338	8.8	2,735	1,514	4,675
Jackson.	4	26	1	18	118	2,955	1.7	19,524	3,315	21,903	1.5	1,800	600	3,964
Jefferson.	2,063	455	6	1,616	357	66,488	6.7	14,683	70,645	15,601	-2.9	40,475	10,593	2,339
Jefferson Davis.	31	99	1	60	192	5,059	3.2	16,177	6,000	19,186	2.3	2,840	1,149	3,674
Lafayette.	693	355	7	1,069	547	23,679	12.4	11,996	28,545	14,461	13.8	14,955	5,352	2,711
Lafourche.	137	149	3	234	254	12,455	7.4	13,512	16,205	17,580	7.9	7,115	2,990	3,244
La Salle.	10	71	2	95	674	2,510	0.4	17,877	2,945	20,976	0.8	1,360	482	3,433
Lincoln.	69	163	1	124	293	5,536	4.1	13,147	6,035	14,332	7.2	3,415	1,246	2,959
Livingston.	28	26	–	–	–	11,342	24.4	10,386	15,270	13,983	28.6	7,300	2,412	2,209
Madison.	7	55	1	25	198	1,709	-5.5	13,719	2,070	16,617	-4.5	1,020	810	6,502
Morehouse.	27	89	1	60	197	5,611	0.5	18,710	6,185	20,624	1.3	3,145	1,722	5,742
Natchitoches.	37	96	1	190	495	5,687	4.4	14,756	6,470	16,787	7.1	3,245	1,972	5,117
Orleans.	3,107	674	9	2,712	588	64,807	-2.7	14,248	40,755	8,960	-47.1	23,610	8,310	1,827
Ouachita.	451	304	7	1,061	716	20,707	5.2	13,969	24,265	16,369	7.6	13,490	5,511	3,718
Plaquemines.	21	72	–	–	–	3,506	12.6	12,092	3,175	10,950	-16.8	1,605	491	1,693
Pointe Coupee.	13	58	1	25	111	3,448	3.5	15,409	4,185	18,702	10.5	2,085	1,132	5,059
Rapides.	448	351	5	721	564	21,351	6.5	16,620	24,520	19,087	7.2	12,095	6,595	5,134
Red River.	3	31	1	25	261	1,478	-5.2	15,615	1,770	18,700	-3.6	935	514	5,431
Richland.	27	131	2	83	404	3,609	-3.9	17,583	3,945	19,220	-1.4	2,090	1,130	5,505
Sabine.	13	55	1	44	187	4,282	1.4	18,002	5,200	21,862	2.9	2,700	1,011	4,250
St. Bernard.	58	88	1	194	296	10,584	-1.2	16,192	6,690	10,235	-46.6	3,695	544	832
St. Charles.	41	82	1	56	112	5,584	11.8	11,028	7,135	14,092	12.9	3,515	1,146	2,263
St. Helena.	6	58	1	25	243	1,007	3.2	9,816	2,665	25,977	8.6	1,190	1,023	9,972
St. James.	18	85	1	16	76	3,168	10.8	14,979	3,815	18,038	9.4	1,765	710	3,357
St. John the Baptist.	46	101	1	60	132	4,921	17.4	10,607	6,935	14,948	21.1	3,025	1,686	3,634
St. Landry.	147	165	3	354	396	14,863	4.4	16,526	17,525	19,486	4.4	7,510	5,911	6,572
St. Martin.	23	46	1	25	50	6,232	8.3	12,357	8,640	17,131	9.6	3,825	1,883	3,734
St. Mary.	60	115	2	75	144	8,383	10.9	16,304	10,650	20,713	8.0	4,795	2,538	4,936
St. Tammany.	744	348	5	714	334	27,360	21.9	12,420	33,320	15,125	20.4	18,815	3,759	1,706
Tangipahoa.	122	116	3	252	240	15,141	9.8	14,217	17,065	16,023	13.6	7,885	5,124	4,811
Tensas.	3	49	–	–	–	1,058	-9.8	17,273	1,210	19,755	-3.7	590	479	7,820
Terrebonne.	211	198	2	404	380	15,372	12.0	14,301	19,055	17,727	8.6	7,940	4,482	4,170
Union.	12	53	2	36	158	4,018	6.7	17,545	4,675	20,414	8.5	2,525	840	3,668
Vermilion.	44	81	4	109	200	8,513	4.1	15,423	10,370	18,788	4.1	4,780	1,857	3,364
Vernon.	60	121	1	60	121	5,269	10.6	10,809	6,325	12,976	9.2	3,045	1,168	2,396
Washington.	41	93	2	91	206	8,154	4.2	18,273	9,725	21,794	4.9	4,465	2,906	6,512
Webster.	36	87	2	219	531	8,154	1.9	19,717	9,085	21,968	1.8	5,030	1,817	4,394
West Baton Rouge.	8	37	–	–	–	2,747	8.7	12,698	3,440	15,901	10.6	1,710	741	3,425
West Carroll.	5	42	1	21	176	2,287	-0.4	19,372	2,625	22,234	2.3	1,410	584	4,947
West Feliciana.	10	66	1	22	146	1,186	15.3	7,803	1,525	10,034	19.7	785	357	2,349
Winn.	12	74	1	60	372	2,407	-2.2	15,074	3,060	19,163	0.7	1,490	638	3,995

See footnotes at end of table.

County and City Data Book: 2007

U.S. Census Bureau

[Includes United States, states, and 3,141 counties/county equivalents defined as of February 22, 2005. For more information on these areas, see Appendix C, Geographic Information]

County	Physicians, 2004[1] Number	Physicians, 2004[1] Rate per 100,000 persons[2]	Community hospitals, 2004[3] Number	Beds Number	Beds Rate per 100,000 persons[2]	Medicare program enrollment, 2005[4] Total	Medicare Percent change, 2000–2005	Medicare Rate per 100,000 persons[2]	Social Security program beneficiaries, December 2005 Number	Social Security Rate per 100,000 persons[2]	Social Security Percent change, 2000–2005	Retired workers, number	Supplemental Security Income program recipients, 2005 Number	SSI Rate per 100,000 persons[2]
MAINE	4,052	308	37	3,549	270	[6]235,324	[6]8.7	[6]17,807	[7]270,706	[7]20,485	[7]8.0	[7]163,965	31,990	2,421
Androscoggin	285	266	2	360	336	19,388	8.0	17,945	21,830	20,206	5.1	12,965	3,318	3,071
Aroostook	171	234	4	328	448	16,386	5.5	22,373	18,840	25,724	5.9	10,355	2,809	3,835
Cumberland	1,500	548	6	951	348	43,837	7.5	15,944	48,460	17,625	5.8	30,685	4,851	1,764
Franklin	68	228	1	56	188	5,030	0.5	16,934	6,625	22,303	9.6	4,145	850	2,862
Hancock	161	301	3	98	183	9,851	6.7	18,358	11,560	21,543	7.8	7,645	889	1,657
Kennebec	379	315	2	295	246	22,374	10.2	18,493	26,870	22,209	9.0	15,140	3,899	3,223
Knox	156	380	1	171	417	8,080	7.2	19,603	9,105	22,089	6.6	5,945	756	1,834
Lincoln	116	330	2	106	302	7,251	8.1	20,576	8,405	23,851	8.7	5,660	594	1,686
Oxford	71	126	2	75	133	10,614	4.4	18,743	13,230	23,363	9.2	7,865	1,589	2,806
Penobscot	504	344	4	463	316	26,395	10.6	17,947	29,930	20,351	8.5	16,340	4,464	3,035
Piscataquis	28	160	2	82	468	4,068	6.0	23,017	4,390	24,839	8.4	2,560	551	3,118
Sagadahoc	67	182	–	–	–	5,573	15.6	15,078	6,675	18,059	13.5	4,195	579	1,566
Somerset	75	146	2	90	175	9,777	10.8	18,923	10,920	21,135	10.1	6,165	1,753	3,393
Waldo	84	219	1	45	117	6,729	14.1	17,385	8,035	20,760	12.4	4,810	1,058	2,733
Washington	62	185	2	59	176	7,501	4.1	22,426	8,570	25,622	3.4	5,270	1,270	3,797
York	325	162	3	370	185	32,135	12.1	15,884	37,260	18,417	10.6	24,215	2,760	1,364
MARYLAND	25,098	451	50	11,489	207	[6]696,405	[6]7.9	[6]12,435	[7]771,357	[7]13,773	[7]6.5	[7]508,682	94,656	1,690
Allegany	214	289	2	403	545	15,475	1.0	21,015	16,395	22,264	1.3	10,025	1,973	2,679
Anne Arundel	1,426	281	3	706	139	61,243	12.1	11,988	68,540	13,416	10.6	46,170	4,668	914
Baltimore	3,848	493	5	1,299	166	122,101	5.5	15,532	136,270	17,335	2.5	91,875	12,241	1,557
Calvert	146	169	1	118	137	8,918	22.6	10,143	10,390	11,817	22.2	6,825	709	806
Caroline	17	55	–	–	–	4,831	5.8	15,181	5,875	18,462	7.8	3,770	712	2,237
Carroll	249	150	1	192	115	23,037	16.1	13,668	24,035	14,261	12.3	16,555	1,099	652
Cecil	131	137	1	122	128	11,967	17.9	12,237	14,560	14,888	18.8	8,555	1,306	1,335
Charles	149	110	1	105	77	11,962	18.7	8,617	14,570	10,495	18.6	8,930	1,556	1,121
Dorchester	55	177	1	64	206	5,967	5.0	19,003	6,900	21,974	5.7	4,815	884	2,815
Frederick	483	222	1	200	92	22,777	16.3	10,320	27,595	12,503	15.5	18,455	1,574	713
Garrett	34	113	1	56	186	4,932	8.3	16,490	6,180	20,663	9.7	3,640	706	2,360
Harford	440	187	2	254	108	28,208	18.3	11,790	33,730	14,098	17.4	22,270	2,251	941
Howard	1,765	662	1	204	77	19,573	23.6	7,264	26,095	9,684	18.4	18,150	2,159	801
Kent	83	420	1	50	253	4,805	5.2	24,147	5,365	26,961	2.8	3,825	329	1,653
Montgomery	8,390	910	6	1,406	153	105,894	9.5	11,416	104,195	11,233	6.8	75,435	11,439	1,233
Prince George's	1,656	197	5	1,031	122	78,463	14.8	9,273	83,720	9,895	9.6	53,295	11,275	1,333
Queen Anne's	35	78	–	–	–	5,415	12.6	11,872	6,860	15,040	16.7	4,850	337	739
St. Mary's	130	137	1	113	119	9,713	18.0	10,063	10,900	11,293	17.1	6,925	1,163	1,205
Somerset	26	101	1	101	392	4,054	3.5	15,686	4,635	17,934	4.6	3,045	616	2,383
Talbot	211	601	1	111	316	8,199	13.7	22,977	9,145	25,628	14.5	6,770	494	1,384
Washington	317	228	1	340	244	21,797	7.9	15,361	24,855	17,516	9.5	16,060	2,284	1,610
Wicomico	323	365	2	394	445	13,263	12.4	14,671	15,660	17,323	12.7	10,450	1,734	1,918
Worcester	77	158	1	62	127	11,214	13.5	23,003	13,180	27,036	12.4	10,055	654	1,342
Independent City														
Baltimore city	4,893	762	11	4,158	648	91,662	–10.5	14,416	101,705	15,996	–8.8	57,935	32,493	5,110
MASSACHUSETTS	31,215	487	78	16,215	253	[6]974,377	[6]1.4	[6]15,228	[7]1,066,962	[7]16,675	[7]0.6	[7]693,001	171,137	2,675
Barnstable	829	364	2	318	139	57,799	3.0	25,517	63,105	27,859	2.0	46,040	3,318	1,465
Berkshire	552	417	3	361	273	26,987	1.3	20,465	30,455	23,095	1.5	19,735	3,767	2,857
Bristol	913	167	4	1,181	216	89,904	2.4	16,456	101,370	18,555	2.7	63,275	18,419	3,371
Dukes	64	411	1	25	161	2,591	5.7	16,617	2,940	18,856	6.9	2,100	159	1,020
Essex	1,856	252	8	1,639	222	112,517	1.2	15,240	123,485	16,726	0.3	80,380	20,784	2,815
Franklin	136	188	1	95	132	11,894	3.9	16,443	13,540	18,719	4.3	8,235	2,052	2,837
Hampden	1,370	297	8	1,626	352	77,188	1.9	16,722	87,145	18,879	1.5	52,220	23,403	5,070
Hampshire	651	424	2	156	102	21,271	4.9	13,872	23,685	15,446	4.2	15,435	2,787	1,818
Middlesex	8,305	568	14	2,900	198	207,129	0.7	14,197	218,765	14,994	–1.7	149,610	24,519	1,681
Nantucket	22	218	1	15	148	1,189	10.5	11,694	1,325	13,031	6.8	980	33	325
Norfolk	4,175	639	4	758	116	97,863	–0.5	14,973	107,210	16,403	–0.3	73,185	9,444	1,445
Plymouth	942	192	3	620	127	68,758	7.1	13,964	79,205	16,085	7.0	49,970	8,428	1,712
Suffolk	8,545	1,286	17	4,761	717	85,739	–2.1	13,101	87,430	13,360	–3.2	50,995	34,812	5,319
Worcester	2,855	367	10	1,760	226	113,021	0.9	14,430	127,300	16,253	0.2	80,840	19,212	2,453
MICHIGAN	26,999	267	144	25,953	257	[6]1,485,469	[6]5.9	[6]14,677	[7]1,748,668	[7]17,278	[7]6.2	[7]1,083,034	222,053	2,194
Alcona	7	60	–	–	–	3,432	12.0	29,452	4,365	37,458	12.5	2,955	239	2,051
Alger	11	113	1	25	257	2,063	2.2	21,352	2,425	25,098	6.8	1,605	186	1,925
Allegan	77	69	1	63	56	13,059	12.3	11,539	18,010	15,914	16.0	11,340	1,548	1,368
Alpena	77	251	1	130	424	7,023	6.2	23,081	7,990	26,259	6.4	4,750	935	3,073
Antrim	26	107	–	–	–	4,809	14.3	19,691	6,275	25,694	13.6	4,405	384	1,572
Arenac	10	58	1	68	395	3,957	6.5	23,068	4,390	25,592	9.2	2,710	493	2,874
Baraga	8	91	1	52	594	1,737	5.9	19,861	2,000	22,868	5.3	1,150	185	2,115
Barry	57	96	1	88	149	7,320	11.3	12,222	10,260	17,131	11.2	6,810	706	1,179
Bay	163	149	2	339	311	19,117	5.9	17,534	23,295	21,366	7.6	13,950	2,463	2,259
Benzie	35	201	1	48	276	3,479	14.3	19,718	4,195	23,776	15.3	2,875	256	1,451

See footnotes at end of table.

[Includes United States, states, and 3,141 counties/county equivalents defined as of February 22, 2005. For more information on these areas, see Appendix C, Geographic Information]

County	Physicians, 2004[1]		Community hospitals, 2004[3]			Medicare program enrollment, 2005[4]			Social Security program beneficiaries, December 2005				Supplemental Security Income program recipients, 2005	
				Beds										
	Number	Rate per 100,000 per-sons[2]	Number	Number	Rate per 100,000 per-sons[2]	Total	Percent change, 2000–2005	Rate per 100,000 per-sons[2]	Number	Rate per 100,000 per-sons[2]	Percent change, 2000–2005	Retired workers, number	Number	Rate per 100,000 per-sons[2]
MICHIGAN—Con.														
Berrien	328	201	2	633	389	29,827	5.8	18,343	32,725	20,125	4.3	20,940	4,719	2,902
Branch	47	101	1	96	206	7,015	5.1	15,099	8,840	19,027	7.5	5,770	832	1,791
Calhoun	252	181	3	497	356	23,513	4.8	16,893	27,795	19,969	5.4	16,955	3,990	2,867
Cass	16	31	1	15	29	7,244	6.2	13,932	10,410	20,021	10.0	6,755	1,019	1,960
Charlevoix	56	210	1	33	124	4,923	10.8	18,423	5,620	21,031	10.8	3,895	370	1,385
Cheboygan	25	92	1	92	337	5,192	8.7	18,905	7,040	25,634	10.2	4,730	602	2,192
Chippewa	51	132	1	133	343	6,287	10.1	16,212	7,475	19,275	12.7	4,595	849	2,189
Clare	16	50	1	64	202	7,380	8.3	23,315	8,610	27,201	7.6	5,315	1,115	3,523
Clinton	52	76	1	28	41	7,057	14.6	10,179	10,770	15,535	13.4	7,260	611	881
Crawford	19	128	1	89	601	2,534	9.0	16,810	3,510	23,285	13.0	2,205	320	2,123
Delta	61	159	1	64	167	8,271	7.9	21,569	9,455	24,656	9.4	5,675	884	2,305
Dickinson	76	275	1	96	347	6,053	11.5	21,593	6,455	23,027	2.0	4,045	452	1,612
Eaton	78	73	2	52	49	11,413	13.2	10,627	15,070	14,032	-6.1	10,015	1,353	1,260
Emmet	190	570	1	192	576	5,878	14.7	17,504	6,475	19,282	15.4	4,455	403	1,200
Genesee	1,020	230	3	1,234	278	67,966	9.2	15,312	80,670	18,174	7.1	46,250	13,281	2,992
Gladwin	16	59	1	36	133	6,375	14.1	23,430	7,735	28,428	13.1	4,955	669	2,459
Gogebic	27	158	1	54	317	4,346	-7.2	25,775	4,625	27,430	-6.1	2,960	406	2,408
Grand Traverse	369	445	1	368	444	14,907	15.5	17,753	15,490	18,447	13.3	10,630	1,029	1,225
Gratiot	61	144	1	127	300	6,818	4.2	16,101	7,810	18,444	4.4	4,900	921	2,175
Hillsdale	36	76	1	68	144	7,584	9.0	16,114	9,105	19,345	7.3	5,720	1,006	2,137
Houghton	61	171	2	91	255	6,059	-2.3	16,970	7,240	20,277	1.1	4,430	714	2,000
Huron	45	129	3	173	495	7,958	1.6	22,973	9,255	26,718	2.6	6,020	750	2,165
Ingham	952	340	2	887	317	38,944	6.8	13,979	42,070	15,101	13.6	25,600	5,921	2,125
Ionia	29	45	1	56	87	7,724	8.9	11,955	9,600	14,859	12.8	5,880	1,043	1,614
Iosco	28	104	1	49	183	7,357	8.0	27,256	8,755	32,436	6.8	5,770	621	2,301
Iron	12	96	1	25	200	3,362	-9.0	27,336	3,940	32,035	-1.9	2,565	303	2,464
Isabella	73	112	1	62	95	6,995	11.1	10,660	8,835	13,464	10.4	5,410	1,176	1,792
Jackson	210	129	2	476	293	25,137	5.5	15,362	29,735	18,172	7.2	18,695	3,579	2,187
Kalamazoo	990	413	3	709	296	33,315	7.3	13,850	39,695	16,503	8.6	25,680	4,805	1,998
Kalkaska	7	41	1	96	558	2,484	10.6	14,409	3,755	21,782	16.3	2,260	404	2,344
Kent	1,752	295	5	1,887	318	73,649	7.2	12,343	84,950	14,237	8.9	53,610	11,882	1,991
Keweenaw	2	90	–	–	–	539	6.7	24,556	630	28,702	5.5	415	32	1,458
Lake	3	25	–	–	–	2,749	10.9	22,777	3,435	28,461	7.1	2,120	571	4,731
Lapeer	55	60	1	145	157	10,677	18.7	11,436	14,430	15,156	20.4	9,340	934	1,000
Leelanau	45	203	1	95	429	3,597	14.8	16,234	5,405	24,394	16.9	4,000	154	695
Lenawee	113	111	2	161	158	16,398	8.9	16,071	19,405	19,018	9.8	12,380	1,664	1,631
Livingston	176	99	1	50	28	15,840	26.9	8,726	23,925	13,181	29.8	16,130	805	443
Luce	11	160	1	73	1,064	1,332	0.9	19,620	1,580	23,273	8.1	1,000	206	3,034
Mackinac	13	114	1	106	929	2,480	7.8	21,887	3,075	27,138	2.2	2,000	207	1,827
Macomb	1,113	135	6	1,264	154	124,880	5.1	15,056	144,120	17,375	5.6	93,015	10,783	1,300
Manistee	37	147	1	54	215	5,455	7.2	21,625	6,630	26,282	9.3	4,360	569	2,256
Marquette	241	371	2	308	475	10,796	7.1	16,671	12,435	19,202	7.0	7,740	1,009	1,558
Mason	37	128	1	85	293	5,876	12.2	20,272	6,960	24,012	12.2	4,555	648	2,236
Mecosta	44	104	1	64	152	6,758	13.1	15,942	8,215	19,379	11.9	5,515	900	2,123
Menominee	20	80	–	–	–	4,807	1.8	19,231	5,665	22,664	5.0	3,590	433	1,732
Midland	227	269	1	250	297	12,417	12.3	14,771	15,310	18,212	10.8	9,655	1,293	1,538
Missaukee	5	33	–	–	–	2,488	10.4	16,263	3,345	21,864	12.2	2,105	301	1,967
Monroe	151	99	1	177	116	20,778	11.0	13,498	25,430	16,520	5.2	15,345	2,098	1,363
Montcalm	41	65	3	172	271	10,537	10.0	16,492	11,905	18,633	9.0	7,505	1,441	2,255
Montmorency	7	67	–	–	–	3,470	8.1	33,222	3,670	35,136	4.1	2,340	263	2,518
Muskegon	278	160	2	382	219	28,829	6.5	16,422	34,450	19,624	7.1	19,515	5,404	3,078
Newaygo	44	89	1	83	167	7,307	10.8	14,608	10,015	20,022	10.6	6,150	1,149	2,297
Oakland	6,654	549	12	3,356	277	159,482	6.3	13,133	182,290	15,011	6.5	119,725	16,130	1,328
Oceana	14	49	1	24	85	5,155	10.0	18,105	5,935	20,844	10.4	3,735	638	2,241
Ogemaw	28	128	1	88	402	5,026	12.2	22,945	6,375	29,103	9.8	3,910	648	2,958
Ontonagon	8	106	1	71	943	2,039	4.1	27,693	2,385	32,392	3.3	1,525	176	2,390
Osceola	12	51	1	82	345	4,898	11.3	20,623	5,425	22,842	8.4	3,410	722	3,040
Oscoda	3	32	–	–	–	1,890	9.4	20,327	2,850	30,652	12.0	1,735	255	2,743
Otsego	37	151	1	87	356	4,503	16.7	18,257	5,200	21,083	13.7	3,460	417	1,691
Ottawa	355	140	3	280	111	31,253	14.6	12,237	36,155	14,156	14.5	24,705	2,064	808
Presque Isle	6	42	1	18	126	3,999	6.3	27,906	4,445	31,019	5.7	2,830	293	2,045
Roscommon	23	88	–	–	–	7,931	7.2	30,411	9,140	35,047	7.5	6,140	683	2,619
Saginaw	577	276	3	1,108	530	35,056	5.2	16,825	41,165	19,757	5.3	24,135	7,211	3,461
St. Clair	237	139	3	373	218	25,430	10.0	14,834	30,195	17,614	11.8	18,725	2,610	1,523
St. Joseph	66	105	2	109	173	9,854	6.6	15,645	11,855	18,822	6.9	7,580	1,149	1,824
Sanilac	28	62	3	131	292	8,173	7.0	18,263	9,770	21,831	5.7	6,160	839	1,875
Schoolcraft	9	101	1	25	282	2,090	6.3	23,699	2,290	25,967	3.1	1,445	225	2,551
Shiawassee	58	79	1	131	179	11,583	10.1	15,879	13,395	18,363	10.9	8,265	1,263	1,731
Tuscola	26	44	2	43	74	9,987	10.6	17,093	11,810	20,213	10.1	7,120	1,133	1,939

See footnotes at end of table.

[Includes United States, states, and 3,141 counties/county equivalents defined as of February 22, 2005. For more information on these areas, see Appendix C, Geographic Information]

County	Physicians, 2004[1] Number	Physicians, 2004[1] Rate per 100,000 persons[2]	Community hospitals, 2004[3] Number	Beds Number	Beds Rate per 100,000 persons[2]	Medicare program enrollment, 2005[4] Total	Medicare program enrollment, 2005[4] Percent change, 2000–2005	Medicare program enrollment, 2005[4] Rate per 100,000 persons[2]	Social Security program beneficiaries, December 2005 Number	Social Security program beneficiaries, December 2005 Rate per 100,000 persons[2]	Social Security program beneficiaries, December 2005 Percent change, 2000–2005	Social Security program beneficiaries, December 2005 Retired workers, number	Supplemental Security Income program recipients, 2005 Number	Supplemental Security Income program recipients, 2005 Rate per 100,000 persons[2]
MICHIGAN—Con.														
Van Buren	87	111	2	207	264	12,343	8.8	15,661	14,715	18,671	8.7	9,070	1,957	2,483
Washtenaw	3,560	1,051	5	1,567	463	34,362	13.1	10,052	40,100	11,730	17.4	26,030	3,831	1,121
Wayne	5,054	251	17	5,410	269	285,435	-3.1	14,284	329,515	16,490	-3.0	184,080	74,729	3,740
Wexford	68	216	1	79	251	5,982	13.4	18,766	6,900	21,646	13.0	4,295	792	2,485
MINNESOTA	15,952	313	132	16,101	316	[6]697,748	[6]6.6	[6]13,594	[7]787,377	[7]15,340	[7]6.4	[7]526,639	72,943	1,421
Aitkin	14	88	1	72	451	4,138	10.3	25,584	4,245	26,246	-1.6	3,020	258	1,595
Anoka	403	126	2	494	155	27,693	23.1	8,547	36,525	11,273	18.8	24,085	2,899	895
Becker	56	177	1	154	486	5,662	7.5	17,767	6,980	21,903	12.0	4,625	597	1,873
Beltrami	78	184	1	194	459	6,279	15.0	14,646	6,810	15,885	8.0	4,160	1,037	2,419
Benton	38	100	–	–	–	3,447	9.5	8,952	4,875	12,661	6.1	2,925	445	1,156
Big Stone	9	162	2	211	3,808	1,494	-1.0	27,258	1,585	28,918	-3.6	1,045	107	1,952
Blue Earth	166	289	1	174	303	8,958	4.4	15,437	8,705	15,001	1.8	5,615	866	1,492
Brown	40	150	3	96	360	5,406	1.5	20,374	5,900	22,236	2.6	3,945	246	927
Carlton	39	116	2	239	711	5,965	6.7	17,531	6,675	19,617	7.8	4,140	507	1,490
Carver	140	171	1	109	133	6,511	22.8	7,672	7,860	9,262	16.3	5,395	334	394
Cass	21	74	–	–	–	5,865	9.2	20,287	7,780	26,911	14.1	5,410	661	2,286
Chippewa	14	110	1	25	197	2,459	-3.5	19,208	2,755	21,520	-1.6	1,805	171	1,336
Chisago	40	83	1	50	104	6,168	18.6	12,486	7,245	14,666	22.4	4,810	404	818
Clay	28	53	–	–	–	7,381	3.7	13,710	8,195	15,222	4.1	5,260	821	1,525
Clearwater	10	118	1	77	908	1,598	2.6	18,853	1,900	22,416	8.9	1,240	192	2,265
Cook	13	245	1	56	1,054	1,000	9.9	18,632	1,200	22,359	13.7	895	38	708
Cottonwood	14	117	2	38	318	2,697	-5.0	22,790	3,080	26,027	-2.1	2,015	204	1,724
Crow Wing	156	264	2	322	544	12,029	12.4	20,076	13,590	22,681	15.6	9,415	913	1,524
Dakota	647	171	3	341	90	28,353	19.3	7,391	42,680	11,126	20.5	28,795	2,882	751
Dodge	14	72	–	–	–	2,377	4.9	12,131	2,705	13,805	5.3	1,860	130	663
Douglas	76	220	1	99	286	7,237	11.6	20,596	8,265	23,522	13.4	5,690	469	1,335
Faribault	11	70	1	48	306	3,674	-5.1	23,694	3,945	25,442	-4.3	2,695	199	1,283
Fillmore	14	66	–	–	–	4,394	-2.6	20,563	4,615	21,598	-2.3	3,195	226	1,058
Freeborn	54	169	1	129	403	6,582	0.7	20,604	7,630	23,884	0.6	5,135	431	1,349
Goodhue	87	191	3	265	582	7,369	5.8	16,165	8,085	17,736	3.3	5,720	364	799
Grant	2	33	1	20	326	1,555	-0.6	25,433	1,725	28,214	3.7	1,145	74	1,210
Hennepin	5,338	477	9	3,261	291	139,354	1.6	12,449	149,060	13,316	1.3	102,820	20,164	1,801
Houston	25	126	–	–	–	3,487	3.3	17,487	3,875	19,432	3.3	2,705	182	913
Hubbard	38	202	1	43	228	3,927	12.0	20,821	4,820	25,555	12.0	3,365	322	1,707
Isanti	49	134	1	81	222	4,024	17.2	10,684	5,170	13,727	14.6	3,395	293	778
Itasca	71	160	3	228	515	9,013	7.5	20,307	10,685	24,074	10.2	6,715	821	1,850
Jackson	6	53	1	20	178	2,081	-2.8	18,610	2,355	21,061	-2.3	1,565	93	832
Kanabec	15	94	1	25	156	2,550	12.1	15,726	3,105	19,149	15.3	2,075	223	1,375
Kandiyohi	131	318	1	199	483	6,994	3.7	16,976	7,860	19,078	4.5	5,160	599	1,454
Kittson	3	62	1	92	1,902	1,142	-5.5	23,831	1,250	26,085	-1.8	815	56	1,169
Koochiching	20	144	1	25	180	3,148	5.0	22,636	3,470	24,951	3.8	2,110	278	1,999
Lac qui Parle	9	117	1	95	1,232	1,738	-6.6	22,856	1,960	25,776	-6.1	1,275	89	1,170
Lake	23	206	1	68	609	2,359	5.4	21,146	2,635	23,620	6.0	1,745	118	1,058
Lake of the Woods	5	113	1	65	1,475	913	9.1	20,651	1,055	23,863	6.6	735	46	1,040
Le Sueur	5	18	1	109	401	4,773	8.7	17,363	4,460	16,224	-0.1	3,180	208	757
Lincoln	8	131	3	210	3,429	1,489	-4.3	24,612	1,610	26,612	-8.2	1,100	67	1,107
Lyon	28	114	2	131	533	4,327	0.1	17,681	4,540	18,552	0.1	2,830	353	1,442
McLeod	44	122	2	325	898	5,627	6.6	15,359	6,260	17,087	5.8	4,395	247	674
Mahnomen	3	59	1	48	943	1,051	6.1	20,555	935	18,287	-15.8	560	130	2,543
Marshall	4	40	1	20	200	2,109	2.2	21,164	2,305	23,131	-2.5	1,505	121	1,214
Martin	44	209	1	97	460	4,717	0.8	22,460	5,385	25,640	1.4	3,520	336	1,600
Meeker	16	69	1	38	163	3,814	3.5	16,319	4,545	19,447	6.5	3,065	209	894
Mille Lacs	34	136	2	124	496	5,129	12.0	19,973	5,325	20,736	7.8	3,595	335	1,305
Morrison	34	104	1	199	611	5,587	3.4	17,040	6,585	20,084	2.2	4,170	469	1,430
Mower	69	177	1	73	187	7,976	-4.3	20,557	8,635	22,256	-3.8	5,755	610	1,572
Murray	6	67	1	25	280	1,940	-0.6	21,916	2,245	25,362	-4.2	1,460	91	1,028
Nicollet	56	182	1	17	55	3,107	13.4	10,072	4,480	14,523	10.6	3,100	233	755
Nobles	31	151	1	66	322	3,808	-3.3	18,568	4,175	20,358	-3.6	2,690	295	1,438
Norman	5	70	1	14	196	1,572	-4.1	22,448	1,845	26,346	-1.2	1,125	129	1,842
Olmsted	3,034	2,277	3	1,195	897	16,517	17.0	12,218	19,450	14,387	14.2	13,970	1,671	1,236
Otter Tail	85	147	2	248	429	11,639	4.5	20,186	13,675	23,717	4.1	9,330	806	1,398
Pennington	22	162	1	158	1,165	2,368	2.0	17,402	2,550	18,739	(Z)	1,660	213	1,565
Pine	15	53	1	94	334	4,942	11.6	17,349	5,905	20,730	8.5	3,905	449	1,576
Pipestone	8	84	1	76	796	2,198	-1.2	23,331	2,170	23,034	-6.5	1,415	135	1,433
Polk	25	81	2	270	871	5,734	-0.7	18,418	6,445	20,702	1.4	4,230	598	1,921
Pope	15	134	2	53	472	2,377	-1.0	21,125	2,585	22,974	-4.4	1,830	126	1,120
Ramsey	2,095	420	6	1,463	293	80,688	5.3	16,303	70,690	14,283	0.1	47,005	12,881	2,603
Red Lake	1	23	–	–	–	791	-6.3	18,323	825	19,110	-9.0	550	36	834
Redwood	11	68	1	30	185	3,456	-1.5	21,570	3,690	23,031	-3.9	2,365	217	1,354
Renville	8	48	1	25	150	3,239	-6.1	19,321	3,680	21,952	-3.2	2,365	206	1,229

See footnotes at end of table.

U.S. Census Bureau

[Includes United States, states, and 3,141 counties/county equivalents defined as of February 22, 2005. For more information on these areas, see Appendix C, Geographic Information]

County	Physicians, 2004[1] Number	Rate per 100,000 persons[2]	Community hospitals, 2004[3] Number	Beds Number	Beds Rate per 100,000 persons[2]	Medicare program enrollment, 2005[4] Total	Percent change, 2000–2005	Rate per 100,000 persons[2]	Social Security program beneficiaries, December 2005 Number	Rate per 100,000 persons[2]	Percent change, 2000–2005	Retired workers, number	Supplemental Security Income program recipients, 2005 Number	Rate per 100,000 persons[2]
MINNESOTA—Con.														
Rice	92	153	1	54	90	7,490	8.0	12,289	8,785	14,414	9.8	6,120	559	917
Rock	14	147	1	28	294	1,930	−5.3	20,273	2,160	22,689	−9.5	1,375	77	809
Roseau	14	86	1	149	912	2,300	1.5	13,944	2,640	16,005	4.0	1,740	141	855
St. Louis	755	381	8	1,230	621	36,359	0.6	18,440	41,360	20,976	2.8	25,295	4,659	2,363
Scott	123	107	2	89	78	7,248	30.9	6,049	10,035	8,375	32.5	6,805	620	517
Sherburne	39	50	–	–	–	6,253	31.1	7,649	8,475	10,367	33.4	5,505	423	517
Sibley	6	39	1	17	111	2,544	−2.9	16,696	2,995	19,656	−2.3	1,975	94	617
Stearns	426	302	4	627	444	20,429	12.5	14,321	21,235	14,886	11.7	13,595	1,600	1,122
Steele	62	176	1	48	136	5,220	6.1	14,599	5,840	16,333	5.3	4,020	331	926
Stevens	12	122	1	25	254	1,782	−1.8	18,136	1,840	18,726	−2.4	1,170	118	1,201
Swift	8	70	2	149	1,297	2,335	−2.7	20,620	2,405	21,238	−4.7	1,545	156	1,378
Todd	20	81	2	245	995	4,249	2.8	17,270	5,075	20,628	4.5	3,225	472	1,918
Traverse	1	26	1	15	387	1,072	−1.2	28,136	1,160	30,446	−9.7	740	50	1,312
Wabasha	34	153	1	179	806	4,009	5.8	18,059	4,355	19,617	4.7	2,965	175	788
Wadena	14	103	1	25	184	3,201	6.0	23,451	3,565	26,117	9.7	2,250	380	2,784
Waseca	18	93	1	25	130	2,970	−1.8	15,365	3,545	18,339	0.1	2,445	188	973
Washington	535	248	2	105	49	14,678	20.2	6,659	26,275	11,920	26.4	18,215	1,416	642
Watonwan	6	53	2	33	290	2,349	−1.1	20,910	2,450	21,809	−4.8	1,615	121	1,077
Wilkin	3	44	1	145	2,128	1,256	−2.7	18,465	1,380	20,288	−1.1	865	79	1,161
Winona	57	116	1	68	138	7,285	4.8	14,784	8,155	16,550	1.3	5,525	588	1,193
Wright	80	75	2	145	135	10,880	19.7	9,826	13,205	11,925	18.9	8,795	623	563
Yellow Medicine	10	95	2	177	1,677	2,483	−3.8	23,763	2,590	24,787	−4.3	1,660	143	1,369
MISSISSIPPI	5,872	202	93	13,143	453	[6]455,699	[6]8.9	[6]15,600	[7]549,376	[7]18,807	[7]6.8	292,620	124,584	4,265
Adams	86	265	2	210	647	6,513	5.3	20,290	8,000	24,923	4.9	4,255	2,010	6,262
Alcorn	52	148	1	157	446	7,320	10.6	20,733	9,170	25,973	11.1	4,625	1,872	5,302
Amite	2	15	–	–	–	2,364	3.5	17,596	3,250	24,191	17.2	1,670	810	6,029
Attala	20	102	1	71	362	3,976	1.5	20,336	4,415	22,581	−4.7	2,350	1,067	5,457
Benton	3	38	–	–	–	1,664	9.0	21,192	1,840	23,434	18.3	985	524	6,673
Bolivar	39	100	1	143	366	6,071	−0.3	15,711	7,050	18,245	0.2	3,380	3,422	8,856
Calhoun	6	41	1	150	1,016	3,050	3.0	20,816	3,825	26,106	1.1	2,015	885	6,040
Carroll	7	67	–	–	–	1,651	7.6	15,880	2,270	21,833	3.6	1,205	654	6,290
Chickasaw	14	73	1	84	436	3,878	5.3	20,215	4,160	21,685	−6.6	2,165	957	4,989
Choctaw	5	52	1	72	752	1,525	12.0	15,932	2,050	21,417	13.8	1,055	521	5,443
Claiborne	3	26	1	32	279	1,520	3.9	13,227	1,940	16,881	3.7	930	727	6,326
Clarke	6	34	1	40	226	3,416	5.6	19,332	4,145	23,458	2.0	2,240	940	5,320
Clay	24	111	1	60	279	3,470	4.2	16,350	4,340	20,450	3.6	2,260	1,121	5,282
Coahoma	56	192	1	175	599	4,569	−5.2	15,754	5,555	19,154	−5.8	2,675	2,471	8,520
Copiah	21	72	1	49	168	5,704	8.4	19,558	6,100	20,916	5.0	3,095	1,645	5,641
Covington	8	40	1	50	247	3,547	13.1	17,496	4,075	20,101	5.3	2,060	1,062	5,238
DeSoto	98	75	1	199	152	14,845	33.5	10,835	18,880	13,771	34.0	11,220	1,880	1,372
Forrest	401	539	2	563	756	12,710	10.4	16,925	12,810	17,058	3.4	6,785	2,640	3,516
Franklin	4	48	1	36	428	1,464	4.7	17,406	1,780	21,163	2.5	895	393	4,672
George	17	82	1	53	255	3,556	16.9	16,727	4,180	19,662	15.6	2,005	625	2,940
Greene	7	53	–	–	–	1,478	3.2	11,211	1,645	12,478	2.0	775	430	3,262
Grenada	29	127	1	142	624	4,245	6.0	18,569	5,230	22,877	11.2	2,670	1,284	5,617
Hancock	71	155	1	104	227	7,271	18.3	15,566	7,760	16,613	−2.2	4,515	913	1,955
Harrison	586	304	4	917	476	30,079	14.9	15,520	31,255	16,127	0.8	17,540	4,836	2,495
Hinds	1,291	517	7	2,767	1,108	33,671	2.3	13,504	40,455	16,225	1.3	22,280	10,198	4,090
Holmes	18	85	1	42	198	3,656	−4.4	17,328	4,235	20,072	10.4	1,905	2,036	9,650
Humphreys	6	56	1	25	235	1,727	−1.8	16,405	2,015	19,141	−9.8	935	1,039	9,870
Issaquena	–	–	–	–	–	165	5.1	8,643	215	11,262	−29.7	105	74	3,876
Itawamba	10	43	–	–	–	3,429	7.7	14,680	5,500	23,546	5.1	3,050	712	3,048
Jackson	325	241	1	388	287	18,182	16.1	13,375	24,245	17,835	12.2	13,345	2,896	2,130
Jasper	3	17	1	126	694	3,339	6.1	18,385	3,695	20,345	3.9	1,740	1,025	5,644
Jefferson	3	32	1	30	315	1,311	−4.9	13,899	1,790	18,978	−4.6	665	815	8,641
Jefferson Davis	3	23	1	101	768	2,136	2.5	16,233	2,820	21,432	−6.9	1,350	719	5,464
Jones	108	165	1	349	532	12,051	4.4	18,215	14,745	22,287	8.4	7,655	2,972	4,492
Kemper	1	10	–	–	–	1,700	−2.4	16,592	1,705	16,641	−21.4	910	554	5,407
Lafayette	105	261	1	217	539	4,427	14.8	10,839	5,655	13,846	12.0	3,285	1,011	2,475
Lamar	10	23	1	211	488	4,337	14.4	9,721	7,175	16,082	25.4	3,995	976	2,188
Lauderdale	252	325	5	648	836	13,295	3.6	17,217	15,020	19,451	3.2	8,625	3,470	4,494
Lawrence	6	44	1	25	185	3,211	10.3	23,782	3,395	25,144	−5.1	1,665	616	4,562
Leake	9	40	1	69	308	4,057	6.6	18,069	4,760	21,200	6.5	2,415	1,070	4,766
Lee	316	405	1	757	969	13,330	14.6	16,918	15,480	19,646	10.6	8,600	2,542	3,226
Leflore	59	162	1	175	480	5,597	−1.1	15,363	6,555	17,993	0.5	3,395	2,784	7,642
Lincoln	40	119	1	109	323	5,706	7.7	16,829	7,455	21,987	5.7	3,880	1,478	4,359
Lowndes	116	192	1	328	544	9,113	9.9	15,215	10,650	17,781	13.2	5,960	2,436	4,067
Madison	448	547	1	34	41	9,691	20.4	11,498	12,030	14,273	16.4	6,940	2,253	2,673
Marion	24	95	1	79	313	4,898	2.1	19,410	6,015	23,836	1.4	2,955	1,437	5,694
Marshall	10	28	1	40	113	5,539	10.3	15,533	6,530	18,312	8.4	3,420	1,723	4,832
Monroe	41	108	2	120	316	6,546	9.2	17,362	8,435	22,372	(Z)	4,650	1,583	4,198
Montgomery	11	94	2	44	374	2,571	2.7	21,735	2,775	23,459	−4.5	1,525	699	5,909
Neshoba	21	71	1	204	689	4,041	2.2	13,513	6,175	20,649	11.5	3,340	1,346	4,501

See footnotes at end of table.

County and City Data Book: 2007

U.S. Census Bureau

[Includes United States, states, and 3,141 counties/county equivalents defined as of February 22, 2005. For more information on these areas, see Appendix C, Geographic Information]

County	Physicians, 2004[1] Number	Physicians, 2004[1] Rate per 100,000 persons[2]	Community hospitals, 2004[3] Number	Beds Number	Beds Rate per 100,000 persons[2]	Medicare program enrollment, 2005[4] Total	Medicare Percent change, 2000–2005	Medicare Rate per 100,000 persons[2]	Social Security beneficiaries Number	Social Security Rate per 100,000 persons[2]	Social Security Percent change, 2000–2005	Retired workers, number	Supplemental Security Income recipients, 2005 Number	Supplemental Security Income Rate per 100,000 persons[2]
MISSISSIPPI—Con.														
Newton	9	41	1	49	221	4,882	6.6	21,828	4,930	22,042	−5.2	2,770	943	4,216
Noxubee	7	57	1	85	693	2,188	4.8	17,931	2,695	22,087	3.8	1,230	1,207	9,892
Oktibbeha	52	126	1	96	233	5,210	10.3	12,631	5,750	13,940	11.6	3,210	1,584	3,840
Panola	22	62	1	53	150	5,877	8.3	16,634	7,075	20,025	1.4	3,460	2,083	5,896
Pearl River	34	66	2	211	407	8,475	15.0	16,094	11,550	21,934	16.1	6,040	1,809	3,435
Perry	5	41	–	–	–	1,837	16.3	15,107	2,985	24,548	9.3	1,410	663	5,452
Pike	73	187	2	193	494	7,466	6.5	18,937	8,575	21,750	8.2	4,340	2,280	5,783
Pontotoc	9	32	1	73	261	4,324	11.8	15,329	5,810	20,597	19.4	3,085	896	3,176
Prentiss	20	78	1	66	258	5,491	11.2	21,455	5,905	23,073	17.9	3,205	949	3,708
Quitman	4	41	1	33	339	1,801	−1.6	18,934	1,930	20,290	−5.0	880	913	9,598
Rankin	409	318	1	134	104	15,904	23.0	12,063	20,410	15,481	21.2	11,845	2,596	1,969
Scott	8	28	1	55	192	4,812	7.9	16,744	5,500	19,138	11.2	2,880	1,342	4,670
Sharkey	1	17	–	–	–	1,007	2.8	16,876	1,265	21,200	10.8	620	550	9,217
Simpson	14	51	2	105	381	4,486	4.4	16,054	5,450	19,503	8.5	2,830	1,223	4,377
Smith	5	31	–	–	–	2,408	2.1	14,996	3,790	23,602	−5.0	1,950	789	4,913
Stone	14	97	1	25	173	2,655	15.7	17,864	3,095	20,825	12.2	1,560	528	3,553
Sunflower	24	74	2	145	445	4,008	−0.8	12,404	5,080	15,722	−0.2	2,400	2,232	6,908
Tallahatchie	5	35	1	77	539	2,387	−0.2	16,821	3,000	21,140	−9.0	1,345	1,339	9,436
Tate	15	57	1	52	198	3,960	10.5	14,916	4,840	18,231	16.9	2,610	891	3,356
Tippah	9	43	1	110	524	4,783	8.0	22,549	5,520	26,023	11.0	2,640	1,158	5,459
Tishomingo	13	68	1	48	252	4,946	10.5	25,758	5,300	27,601	7.9	2,825	805	4,192
Tunica	5	50	–	–	–	1,304	10.3	12,634	1,735	16,810	20.3	750	801	7,761
Union	32	121	1	153	580	4,610	7.5	17,212	6,010	22,439	12.0	3,225	900	3,360
Walthall	15	98	1	49	322	2,349	6.0	15,194	3,475	22,477	21.8	1,795	934	6,041
Warren	104	211	1	374	760	7,168	5.5	14,590	8,620	17,545	5.7	4,680	1,939	3,947
Washington	101	170	2	270	454	9,298	2.1	15,701	11,100	18,744	−0.9	5,505	4,681	7,904
Wayne	11	52	1	80	378	3,006	7.9	14,119	4,100	19,257	0.9	1,935	1,119	5,256
Webster	7	69	1	74	730	2,162	6.4	21,423	3,130	31,015	3.8	1,575	730	7,233
Wilkinson	10	98	1	25	244	1,662	−0.2	16,185	2,155	20,985	8.9	1,030	819	7,975
Winston	12	60	1	185	929	3,583	5.1	18,032	4,540	22,849	8.5	2,500	1,000	5,033
Yalobusha	6	45	1	103	775	3,211	6.4	23,932	3,550	26,459	4.3	1,845	863	6,432
Yazoo	16	56	1	25	88	4,253	1.5	15,084	5,255	18,638	−1.0	2,685	1,865	6,615
MISSOURI	15,026	261	119	19,131	332	[6]910,638	[6]5.8	[6]15,700	[7]1,063,174	[7]18,330	[7]5.4	[7]653,609	117,760	2,030
Adair	14	57	1	109	443	3,423	0.5	13,966	3,930	16,035	−5.3	2,420	573	2,338
Andrew	4	24	1	488	2,891	2,043	(Z)	12,089	2,945	17,427	2.2	1,830	179	1,059
Atchison	6	95	1	25	396	1,365	−3.9	21,854	1,515	24,256	−3.4	910	97	1,553
Audrain	45	175	1	107	417	4,647	1.1	18,040	5,360	20,808	−0.4	3,305	484	1,879
Barry	34	97	2	65	185	7,185	5.8	20,183	8,040	22,585	7.8	4,840	814	2,287
Barton	3	23	1	40	308	2,213	2.1	16,949	2,825	21,636	4.7	1,700	279	2,137
Bates	8	47	1	60	354	3,248	2.2	19,076	3,950	23,198	0.9	2,360	320	1,879
Benton	4	22	–	–	–	5,123	14.2	27,172	5,960	31,611	12.5	3,790	437	2,318
Bollinger	1	8	–	–	–	2,174	10.0	17,639	2,905	23,570	9.3	1,595	419	3,400
Boone	1,144	810	4	910	644	16,155	15.0	11,272	18,620	12,991	13.2	11,455	1,971	1,375
Buchanan	182	215	–	–	–	15,217	0.4	17,923	16,545	19,487	0.2	10,315	2,007	2,364
Butler	130	317	1	257	627	8,601	5.5	20,807	10,510	25,425	7.3	5,475	2,241	5,421
Caldwell	3	32	–	–	–	1,792	3.0	19,254	1,930	20,737	−1.1	1,210	157	1,687
Callaway	31	74	1	31	74	5,818	8.9	13,676	7,255	17,054	10.1	4,245	663	1,558
Camden	66	171	1	140	362	7,267	11.5	18,429	10,145	25,728	9.9	7,100	458	1,161
Cape Girardeau	255	361	2	456	646	11,210	9.6	15,753	12,850	18,058	8.5	8,015	1,361	1,913
Carroll	4	39	1	56	553	2,113	−4.6	20,730	2,260	22,172	−7.1	1,370	206	2,021
Carter	1	17	–	–	–	1,380	6.5	23,350	1,670	28,257	8.9	835	370	6,261
Cass	50	54	2	76	83	11,963	15.4	12,695	14,940	15,854	18.8	9,765	745	791
Cedar	9	65	1	34	245	3,419	4.2	24,145	3,855	27,225	3.2	2,395	372	2,627
Chariton	1	12	–	–	–	1,689	−4.3	20,790	2,050	25,234	−2.9	1,300	179	2,203
Christian	55	86	–	–	–	8,588	27.4	12,767	10,870	16,160	28.7	6,780	842	1,252
Clark	–	–	–	–	–	1,320	1.9	18,025	1,660	22,668	7.2	980	132	1,803
Clay	334	169	4	725	367	25,647	12.0	12,692	29,890	14,791	13.4	19,570	1,610	797
Clinton	10	48	1	54	262	3,370	11.3	16,268	3,390	16,365	9.7	2,150	189	912
Cole	159	221	2	301	418	10,301	9.0	14,158	12,235	16,816	8.1	7,585	1,087	1,494
Cooper	14	81	1	49	285	2,862	3.9	16,549	3,360	19,429	6.1	2,125	225	1,301
Crawford	4	17	–	–	–	4,233	9.0	17,688	5,540	23,149	7.7	3,130	615	2,570
Dade	3	38	–	–	–	1,786	−0.4	22,810	2,025	25,862	−1.4	1,280	175	2,235
Dallas	2	12	–	–	–	2,885	8.9	17,552	3,885	23,636	8.9	2,125	499	3,036
Daviess	–	–	–	–	–	1,455	−5.5	17,917	1,805	22,226	−0.9	1,150	125	1,539
DeKalb	–	–	–	–	–	1,406	−1.7	11,392	2,125	17,218	0.4	1,375	134	1,086
Dent	10	66	1	43	286	3,278	6.2	21,733	3,865	25,625	3.1	2,195	533	3,534
Douglas	4	30	–	–	–	2,383	3.6	17,530	3,340	24,570	6.6	1,900	480	3,531
Dunklin	35	108	1	116	358	6,839	1.2	21,014	8,200	25,196	1.9	4,070	2,447	7,519

See footnotes at end of table.

[Includes United States, states, and 3,141 counties/county equivalents defined as of February 22, 2005. For more information on these areas, see Appendix C, Geographic Information]

County	Physicians, 2004[1] Number	Rate per 100,000 persons[2]	Community hospitals, 2004[3] Number	Beds Number	Beds Rate per 100,000 persons[2]	Medicare program enrollment, 2005[4] Total	Percent change, 2000–2005	Rate per 100,000 persons[2]	Social Security program beneficiaries, December 2005 Number	Rate per 100,000 persons[2]	Percent change, 2000–2005	Retired workers, number	Supplemental Security Income program recipients, 2005 Number	Rate per 100,000 persons[2]
MISSOURI—Con.														
Franklin	107	109	2	168	171	15,737	12.2	15,882	18,300	18,468	10.9	11,170	1,302	1,314
Gasconade	9	58	1	25	160	3,398	4.6	21,581	3,745	23,785	5.6	2,485	229	1,454
Gentry	4	61	1	35	534	1,748	-3.2	26,667	1,910	29,138	-3.9	1,145	126	1,922
Greene	888	358	3	1,355	546	40,739	10.6	16,245	46,615	18,588	10.5	28,535	5,150	2,054
Grundy	6	59	1	25	244	2,365	0.6	22,901	2,555	24,741	-1.4	1,580	235	2,276
Harrison	4	45	1	20	227	2,116	-0.1	23,840	2,300	25,913	0.6	1,465	182	2,050
Henry	19	84	1	106	469	5,265	6.7	23,320	5,940	26,310	5.5	3,625	602	2,666
Hickory	3	33	–	–	–	2,495	7.9	26,912	3,365	36,296	9.5	2,165	251	2,707
Holt	2	39	–	–	–	1,169	-5.6	23,007	1,340	26,373	-5.4	765	82	1,614
Howard	10	101	–	–	–	1,753	0.7	17,606	2,025	20,337	4.0	1,320	227	2,280
Howell	63	166	2	133	351	8,368	9.7	21,792	10,550	27,474	10.0	5,910	1,554	4,047
Iron	9	87	–	–	–	2,337	2.2	22,749	2,890	28,132	3.5	1,435	543	5,286
Jackson	1,801	272	11	2,760	417	96,725	2.2	14,590	110,450	16,660	1.7	69,405	13,272	2,002
Jasper	279	255	2	421	385	20,842	8.0	18,840	21,585	19,512	6.3	12,420	2,819	2,548
Jefferson	105	50	1	228	108	24,095	19.0	11,277	33,205	15,540	17.9	18,605	2,438	1,141
Johnson	47	93	1	75	148	5,502	11.7	10,834	6,670	13,134	7.8	4,145	538	1,059
Knox	–	–	–	–	–	936	-4.8	22,441	1,080	25,893	-5.7	680	103	2,469
Laclede	26	77	1	48	143	6,281	14.0	18,210	7,615	22,078	14.9	4,325	949	2,751
Lafayette	12	36	1	25	76	5,986	5.3	18,080	7,045	21,279	3.8	4,500	463	1,398
Lawrence	30	82	1	25	68	6,227	7.1	16,772	8,185	22,046	7.0	4,920	780	2,101
Lewis	1	10	–	–	–	1,974	4.3	19,380	2,085	20,469	1.4	1,300	148	1,453
Lincoln	14	31	1	25	55	5,535	19.4	11,597	7,330	15,358	23.0	4,195	613	1,284
Linn	6	45	1	25	188	3,034	-6.0	23,102	3,125	23,795	-4.8	2,010	298	2,269
Livingston	12	84	1	30	210	3,030	2.7	21,202	3,395	23,756	2.4	2,155	349	2,442
McDonald	3	13	–	–	–	3,105	8.1	13,592	3,860	16,897	2.7	2,090	554	2,425
Macon	6	39	1	20	129	3,339	1.7	21,404	3,850	24,679	4.8	2,430	312	2,000
Madison	10	83	1	119	992	2,568	4.2	21,134	3,130	25,759	5.0	1,750	436	3,588
Maries	4	45	–	–	–	1,337	5.1	14,874	1,870	20,803	10.6	1,125	157	1,747
Marion	56	198	1	105	371	5,482	0.8	19,320	6,025	21,233	-0.4	3,555	908	3,200
Mercer	1	28	–	–	–	758	-7.9	21,085	920	25,591	-6.3	580	83	2,309
Miller	8	32	–	–	–	4,766	7.8	19,286	4,945	20,011	9.0	2,965	527	2,133
Mississippi	4	29	–	–	–	2,752	2.7	20,237	3,250	23,899	3.2	1,660	706	5,192
Moniteau	4	27	–	–	–	2,274	0.7	15,076	2,680	17,767	4.6	1,695	192	1,273
Monroe	1	11	–	–	–	1,877	3.3	20,013	2,125	22,657	2.8	1,285	165	1,759
Montgomery	4	33	–	–	–	2,496	5.1	20,516	2,800	23,015	4.9	1,615	244	2,006
Morgan	7	35	–	–	–	4,753	12.5	23,258	5,710	27,941	12.4	3,780	450	2,202
New Madrid	3	16	–	–	–	3,455	1.5	18,609	4,300	23,161	2.1	2,025	1,073	5,779
Newton	24	44	2	383	700	6,721	8.2	12,098	10,970	19,747	12.4	6,615	956	1,721
Nodaway	26	120	1	55	253	3,309	2.6	15,242	3,690	16,997	3.6	2,375	253	1,165
Oregon	2	19	–	–	–	2,350	5.9	22,590	2,825	27,156	7.7	1,470	633	6,085
Osage	2	15	–	–	–	1,965	7.1	14,572	2,400	17,798	4.9	1,555	124	920
Ozark	2	21	–	–	–	2,291	5.4	24,141	2,855	30,084	2.9	1,710	374	3,941
Pemiscot	18	92	1	169	867	3,707	-1.0	19,096	4,655	23,980	0.3	2,095	1,729	8,907
Perry	13	71	1	25	136	3,058	5.3	16,467	3,600	19,385	6.7	2,315	354	1,906
Pettis	51	128	1	153	385	7,106	5.0	17,711	8,230	20,513	5.3	5,070	924	2,303
Phelps	77	185	1	198	475	7,156	8.4	16,988	8,285	19,668	7.4	4,735	1,044	2,478
Pike	8	43	1	24	130	3,134	3.2	16,704	3,730	19,881	3.7	2,255	387	2,063
Platte	134	166	1	79	98	8,479	21.0	10,330	10,130	12,341	15.9	6,750	459	559
Polk	32	113	1	74	261	5,619	12.3	19,448	6,055	20,957	15.7	3,610	695	2,406
Pulaski	37	83	–	–	–	4,760	9.4	10,772	5,355	12,119	5.5	2,950	732	1,657
Putnam	1	20	1	35	691	1,143	-2.4	22,117	1,450	28,057	5.8	875	164	3,173
Ralls	2	21	–	–	–	1,253	9.2	12,837	1,970	20,182	12.1	1,235	169	1,731
Randolph	18	72	1	96	381	4,408	3.5	17,398	4,480	17,682	1.7	2,570	677	2,672
Ray	10	42	1	37	154	3,150	6.9	13,070	4,425	18,360	9.0	2,665	276	1,145
Reynolds	4	61	–	–	–	1,424	10.9	21,625	1,875	28,474	8.8	960	312	4,738
Ripley	9	65	1	27	196	3,096	5.9	22,352	3,850	27,796	7.0	2,040	828	5,978
St. Charles	340	106	4	522	163	36,614	29.4	11,097	44,405	13,459	25.8	29,305	1,736	526
St. Clair	12	125	2	72	750	2,213	3.5	22,847	2,730	28,185	0.3	1,585	286	2,953
Ste. Genevieve	13	71	1	35	192	2,953	5.8	16,227	3,660	20,112	6.7	2,240	246	1,352
St. Francois	60	99	2	203	334	11,523	10.1	18,688	13,745	22,291	10.8	7,315	1,928	3,127
St. Louis	5,353	531	13	4,107	408	160,045	0.8	15,930	177,510	17,669	-0.2	119,430	13,234	1,317
Saline	25	109	1	52	226	4,370	-3.4	18,938	4,890	21,192	-0.7	2,930	544	2,358
Schuyler	–	–	–	–	–	1,130	6.5	26,230	1,045	24,257	5.2	640	107	2,484
Scotland	1	20	1	25	509	935	-7.2	18,973	1,070	21,713	-3.4	650	71	1,441
Scott	62	152	1	158	387	7,701	6.6	18,718	8,940	21,729	6.1	4,650	1,675	4,071
Shannon	2	24	–	–	–	1,478	6.3	17,665	2,100	25,099	7.3	1,085	370	4,422
Shelby	3	45	–	–	–	1,497	-2.7	22,198	1,595	23,651	-4.5	955	128	1,898
Stoddard	14	47	1	41	138	6,524	6.0	21,956	7,705	25,931	6.1	4,270	1,124	3,783
Stone	19	62	–	–	–	6,388	18.8	20,652	8,435	27,270	17.1	5,935	472	1,526
Sullivan	1	14	1	39	560	1,347	-7.0	19,502	1,565	22,658	3.4	960	185	2,678

See footnotes at end of table.

County and City Data Book: 2007

U.S. Census Bureau

[Includes United States, states, and 3,141 counties/county equivalents defined as of February 22, 2005. For more information on these areas, see Appendix C, Geographic Information]

County	Physicians, 2004[1] Number	Physicians, 2004[1] Rate per 100,000 persons[2]	Community hospitals, 2004[3] Number	Beds Number	Beds Rate per 100,000 persons[2]	Medicare program enrollment, 2005[4] Total	Medicare Percent change, 2000–2005	Medicare Rate per 100,000 persons[2]	Social Security beneficiaries, Dec 2005 Number	Social Security Rate per 100,000 persons[2]	Social Security Percent change, 2000–2005	Retired workers, number	Supplemental Security Income recipients, 2005 Number	SSI Rate per 100,000 persons[2]
MISSOURI—Con.														
Taney	67	160	1	132	315	8,506	14.3	19,788	10,230	23,799	13.7	6,840	645	1,501
Texas	12	49	1	66	269	4,914	6.5	19,964	5,115	20,781	4.6	2,980	701	2,848
Vernon	26	128	1	53	261	3,833	2.3	18,752	4,570	22,357	2.9	2,695	619	3,028
Warren	6	22	–	–	–	4,172	20.5	14,504	5,540	19,260	20.8	3,515	309	1,074
Washington	5	21	1	25	104	3,567	14.0	14,843	4,735	19,703	8.5	2,230	1,064	4,427
Wayne	7	54	–	–	–	3,846	8.0	29,366	4,240	32,374	4.9	2,195	727	5,551
Webster	23	68	–	–	–	5,948	18.8	17,119	6,465	18,607	15.5	3,645	713	2,052
Worth	1	45	–	–	–	545	–4.4	25,069	595	27,369	–7.0	385	41	1,886
Wright	5	27	–	–	–	4,339	10.2	23,703	4,940	26,986	6.3	2,725	809	4,419
Independent City														
St. Louis city	2,306	658	7	2,331	665	49,201	–13.1	14,288	55,495	16,115	–13.3	31,135	16,451	4,777
MONTANA	2,425	262	54	4,337	468	[6]147,634	[6]8.0	[6]15,778	169,375	18,102	7.6	[7]109,049	14,793	1,581
Beaverhead	14	159	1	20	227	1,477	8.1	16,836	1,725	19,663	9.1	1,170	103	1,174
Big Horn	19	145	1	89	681	1,328	12.9	10,100	1,665	12,663	8.5	930	318	2,418
Blaine	6	90	–	–	–	910	–2.6	13,728	1,075	16,217	–3.6	640	179	2,700
Broadwater	6	133	1	42	928	982	24.0	21,740	1,100	24,352	15.9	740	63	1,395
Carbon	18	184	1	52	532	1,706	1.4	17,229	1,995	20,147	2.0	1,355	100	1,010
Carter	1	75	–	–	–	270	3.1	20,455	305	23,106	5.2	205	9	682
Cascade	235	294	1	470	588	13,624	6.5	17,122	15,385	19,335	5.0	9,965	1,517	1,907
Chouteau	5	90	2	82	1,479	1,032	–0.1	18,891	1,135	20,776	0.4	725	53	970
Custer	24	210	1	136	1,190	2,267	1.5	20,121	2,530	22,455	2.2	1,630	251	2,228
Daniels	1	54	1	54	2,924	454	–9.7	24,728	485	26,416	–13.5	325	14	763
Dawson	10	116	1	100	1,155	1,662	–2.4	19,130	1,780	20,488	0.5	1,145	102	1,174
Deer Lodge	19	212	1	87	970	2,047	–4.4	22,877	2,315	25,872	–1.5	1,395	248	2,772
Fallon	1	36	1	52	1,877	555	2.2	20,427	615	22,635	–0.8	410	17	626
Fergus	18	155	1	124	1,067	2,576	1.6	22,301	2,840	24,587	2.3	1,905	185	1,602
Flathead	264	325	2	174	215	13,144	12.2	15,803	15,090	18,143	11.2	9,630	1,097	1,319
Gallatin[12]	230	304	1	69	91	7,621	19.3	9,744	8,905	11,386	18.4	6,115	399	510
Garfield	–	–	–	–	–	237	–4.8	19,766	275	22,936	–1.1	175	9	751
Glacier	15	111	1	20	148	1,465	8.8	10,810	1,745	12,876	6.0	1,025	454	3,350
Golden Valley	–	–	–	–	–	221	2.8	19,068	260	22,433	19.3	165	17	1,467
Granite	1	35	1	33	1,140	500	13.6	16,863	715	24,115	23.5	480	37	1,248
Hill	24	147	1	185	1,132	2,408	–0.8	14,769	2,455	15,058	–0.6	1,395	353	2,165
Jefferson	26	239	–	–	–	1,493	13.5	13,366	1,840	16,473	12.4	1,150	127	1,137
Judith Basin	1	45	–	–	–	431	3.9	19,609	505	22,975	7.0	320	21	955
Lake	53	190	2	121	433	4,515	11.1	15,956	5,615	19,843	9.6	3,610	570	2,014
Lewis and Clark	171	295	1	99	171	8,591	12.0	14,698	10,335	17,682	11.1	6,770	998	1,707
Liberty	3	147	1	76	3,735	683	6.6	34,099	420	20,969	5.5	255	11	549
Lincoln	32	168	1	24	126	4,092	16.1	21,320	5,080	26,468	16.4	2,955	472	2,459
McCone	2	112	1	38	2,124	359	–2.2	19,889	385	21,330	3.2	250	12	665
Madison	16	226	2	16	226	1,312	8.7	18,037	1,600	21,996	9.6	1,185	39	536
Meagher	3	150	1	37	1,846	398	3.9	19,910	480	24,012	–0.6	330	27	1,351
Mineral	3	77	1	41	1,057	946	20.1	23,568	1,060	26,408	21.0	655	103	2,566
Missoula	398	402	2	346	349	12,263	10.0	12,252	14,065	14,053	10.0	8,890	1,590	1,589
Musselshell	5	111	1	48	1,063	905	1.8	20,125	1,075	23,905	3.5	650	94	2,090
Park[12]	33	209	1	28	178	2,654	3.9	16,621	2,665	16,690	7.5	1,760	214	1,340
Petroleum	–	–	–	–	–	83	2.5	17,660	90	19,149	1.1	60	4	851
Phillips	1	24	1	12	283	920	2.8	22,015	1,055	25,245	5.3	685	97	2,321
Pondera	5	82	1	79	1,293	1,144	–3.6	18,794	1,245	20,453	–7.0	810	115	1,889
Powder River	–	–	–	–	–	288	–4.0	16,891	340	19,941	–4.5	230	12	704
Powell	10	145	1	35	506	1,169	3.2	16,702	1,260	18,003	3.7	830	87	1,243
Prairie	1	88	1	21	1,842	272	–9.9	24,615	315	28,507	–2.8	210	14	1,267
Ravalli	76	193	1	48	122	7,277	14.9	18,220	8,600	21,532	13.4	5,695	528	1,322
Richland	16	176	1	130	1,432	1,720	2.4	18,909	1,875	20,613	–3.7	1,130	122	1,341
Roosevelt	8	76	3	141	1,333	1,365	–7.6	12,970	1,670	15,868	–7.4	925	332	3,155
Rosebud	10	108	1	71	769	1,128	9.1	12,245	1,400	15,198	6.0	835	188	2,041
Sanders	12	110	1	44	404	2,373	15.8	21,462	2,860	25,866	15.6	1,815	224	2,026
Sheridan	1	27	1	110	3,024	957	–8.2	27,157	1,035	29,370	–5.9	670	59	1,674
Silver Bow	79	239	1	69	209	6,445	1.4	19,541	7,485	22,694	3.4	4,615	820	2,486
Stillwater	7	83	1	23	273	1,402	8.9	16,508	1,640	19,310	11.4	1,095	65	765
Sweet Grass	4	108	1	60	1,623	637	1.0	17,347	755	20,561	7.5	525	17	463
Teton	3	48	1	46	735	1,166	3.2	18,686	1,365	21,875	–0.3	880	75	1,202
Toole	8	156	1	88	1,711	478	–15.8	9,501	880	17,492	–8.0	570	69	1,371
Treasure	1	136	–	–	–	168	–4.0	24,383	185	26,851	–2.1	130	4	581
Valley	10	138	1	25	345	1,659	–0.1	23,226	1,740	24,360	–5.4	1,175	139	1,946
Wheatland	2	97	1	54	2,618	422	–10.4	20,717	435	21,355	–5.4	300	19	933
Wibaux	–	–	1	–	–	217	–5.2	22,818	255	26,814	–1.9	155	10	1,052
Yellowstone	514	381	2	618	458	20,721	7.9	15,159	23,370	17,097	8.4	15,400	1,990	1,456
Yellowstone National Park[12]	(X)	(NA)	(X)	(X)	(NA)	(X)	(NA)	(NA)	(X)	(NA)	(NA)	(X)	(X)	(NA)

See footnotes at end of table.

[Includes United States, states, and 3,141 counties/county equivalents defined as of February 22, 2005. For more information on these areas, see Appendix C, Geographic Information]

County	Physicians, 2004[1] Number	Rate per 100,000 persons[2]	Community hospitals, 2004[3] Number	Beds Number	Beds Rate per 100,000 persons[2]	Medicare program enrollment, 2005[4] Total	Percent change, 2000–2005	Rate per 100,000 persons[2]	Social Security program beneficiaries, December 2005 Number	Rate per 100,000 persons[2]	Percent change, 2000–2005	Retired workers, number	Supplemental Security Income program recipients, 2005 Number	Rate per 100,000 persons[2]
NEBRASKA	4,672	267	85	7,336	420	[6]261,326	[6]3.0	[6]14,858	291,980	16,601	2.3	[7]191,931	[6]22,331	[6]1,270
Adams	86	262	1	165	504	5,220	0.3	15,785	5,890	17,811	1.4	3,880	454	1,373
Antelope	5	71	3	66	932	1,383	–4.0	19,746	1,630	23,272	–3.6	1,075	85	1,214
Arthur	–	–	–	–	–	99	–7.5	26,190	110	29,101	2.8	70	7	1,852
Banner	–	–	–	–	–	92	1.1	12,551	140	19,100	–0.7	85	(D)	(NA)
Blaine	–	–	–	–	–	100	13.6	20,661	95	19,628	–7.8	70	(D)	(NA)
Boone	7	120	1	25	428	1,300	–5.9	22,523	1,385	23,995	–6.7	895	62	1,074
Box Butte	8	70	1	29	254	1,898	–2.6	16,687	1,910	16,793	–0.7	1,205	149	1,310
Boyd	7	307	1	20	878	634	–7.6	28,041	675	29,854	–7.8	405	40	1,769
Brown	5	145	1	20	581	828	–1.8	24,880	900	27,043	–3.9	445	43	1,292
Buffalo	133	306	1	185	426	5,695	5.2	13,070	6,430	14,757	6.8	4,210	370	849
Burt	2	27	1	23	305	1,759	–4.5	23,595	1,950	26,157	–3.5	1,290	124	1,663
Butler	5	57	1	25	284	1,657	–2.1	19,002	1,875	21,502	–2.4	1,230	101	1,158
Cass	17	67	–	–	–	3,454	5.2	13,422	4,020	15,621	6.3	2,685	169	657
Cedar	4	44	–	–	–	1,805	–4.9	19,910	2,020	22,281	–6.7	1,315	62	684
Chase	5	127	1	25	633	884	–4.1	22,866	965	24,961	–4.6	660	44	1,138
Cherry	6	99	1	25	411	1,243	–0.3	20,384	1,350	22,138	2.7	865	92	1,509
Cheyenne	8	81	1	117	1,182	1,817	–4.8	18,183	1,970	19,714	–5.2	1,290	117	1,171
Clay	2	29	–	–	–	1,458	–1.0	21,655	1,505	22,353	–2.7	940	49	728
Colfax	5	48	1	15	143	3,689	–0.1	35,359	1,695	16,247	–6.1	1,100	69	661
Cuming	6	61	1	95	971	1,916	–3.5	19,777	2,285	23,586	–4.0	1,530	70	723
Custer	9	78	2	130	1,132	2,477	–3.5	21,709	2,730	23,926	–6.7	1,785	155	1,358
Dakota	5	24	–	–	–	2,473	3.4	12,153	2,960	14,546	4.0	1,880	246	1,209
Dawes	13	149	1	25	286	1,533	0.7	17,751	1,665	19,280	–2.7	1,100	132	1,528
Dawson	19	77	3	111	452	3,495	–3.1	14,198	4,050	16,452	–1.5	2,615	289	1,174
Deuel	2	99	–	–	–	509	–4.7	25,399	555	27,695	–2.3	385	15	749
Dixon	2	33	–	–	–	1,238	2.0	20,114	1,140	18,522	–11.1	750	40	650
Dodge	56	156	1	262	728	6,939	2.7	19,233	7,850	21,758	0.9	5,255	446	1,236
Douglas	2,537	527	7	2,095	435	61,795	4.6	12,691	67,315	13,824	4.0	43,940	7,365	1,513
Dundy	2	92	1	14	641	479	–5.3	22,457	550	25,785	–7.9	360	21	985
Fillmore	6	93	1	25	388	1,386	–2.9	21,707	1,590	24,902	–0.9	1,050	65	1,018
Franklin	3	88	1	12	354	891	–2.3	26,045	970	28,354	–7.3	635	44	1,286
Frontier	–	–	–	–	–	543	2.6	19,428	600	21,467	–4.0	390	28	1,002
Furnas	4	78	1	51	999	1,396	–5.9	27,814	1,445	28,791	–2.8	920	91	1,813
Gage	21	90	1	118	504	5,081	1.8	21,801	5,660	24,286	1.7	3,550	375	1,609
Garden	4	188	1	50	2,351	637	1.4	31,898	620	31,047	–10.9	445	24	1,202
Garfield	3	163	–	–	–	531	–3.5	29,240	550	30,286	–5.8	385	29	1,597
Gosper	–	–	–	–	–	504	0.4	24,950	550	27,228	–11.0	400	17	842
Grant	–	–	–	–	–	168	13.5	25,075	190	28,358	–3.1	125	5	746
Greeley	–	–	–	–	–	621	–4.2	24,721	670	26,672	–3.6	415	25	995
Hall	128	234	1	200	365	8,389	3.9	15,224	9,290	16,859	4.0	6,105	737	1,337
Hamilton	11	116	1	75	790	1,515	1.1	15,834	1,835	19,179	0.5	1,200	69	721
Harlan	2	56	1	25	695	808	–4.4	23,339	910	26,285	–5.0	665	40	1,155
Hayes	–	–	–	–	–	116	–7.2	11,295	205	19,961	5.1	130	11	1,071
Hitchcock	–	–	–	–	–	767	0.8	25,825	840	28,283	–4.0	565	48	1,616
Holt	16	148	2	45	416	2,368	–1.8	21,958	2,640	24,481	–2.8	1,645	198	1,836
Hooker	2	268	–	–	–	215	–2.3	28,898	235	31,586	–5.6	170	5	672
Howard	2	30	1	25	372	1,272	6.7	18,962	1,425	21,243	7.5	930	59	880
Jefferson	7	87	1	64	796	1,988	–2.5	25,085	2,100	26,498	–3.3	1,360	138	1,741
Johnson	4	83	1	25	518	989	–7.1	21,065	1,040	22,151	–11.2	730	48	1,022
Kearney	4	58	1	59	861	1,139	–4.4	16,814	1,240	18,305	–3.8	810	75	1,107
Keith	10	119	1	18	215	1,709	0.8	20,516	2,060	24,730	1.6	1,440	102	1,224
Keya Paha	–	–	–	–	–	196	–1.0	21,729	245	27,162	–6.5	145	13	1,441
Kimball	–	–	1	20	526	896	–2.9	23,691	1,000	26,441	–6.1	675	53	1,401
Knox	8	89	1	69	766	2,224	–4.2	24,944	2,365	26,525	–4.2	1,495	144	1,615
Lancaster	741	283	3	932	356	31,436	7.3	11,871	35,125	13,264	6.5	23,675	3,429	1,295
Lincoln	85	242	1	98	279	6,074	4.1	17,045	5,835	16,374	3.5	3,590	616	1,729
Logan	–	–	–	–	–	164	2.5	22,162	180	24,324	–3.7	110	15	2,027
Loup	–	–	–	–	–	86	–9.5	12,536	150	21,866	–10.7	90	7	1,020
McPherson	–	–	–	–	–	124	–	24,458	105	20,710	–3.7	55	6	1,183
Madison	86	241	1	222	622	6,059	3.1	17,073	6,475	18,246	2.1	4,190	491	1,384
Merrick	3	37	1	71	874	1,550	4.2	19,216	1,875	23,246	–0.3	1,185	136	1,686
Morrill	4	77	1	20	383	1,032	–0.1	19,981	1,195	23,136	4.6	750	103	1,994
Nance	1	27	1	60	1,622	807	–3.1	22,013	945	25,777	–4.7	595	83	2,264
Nemaha	7	100	1	20	284	1,394	–4.1	20,014	1,605	23,044	–3.4	1,030	115	1,651
Nuckolls	5	104	1	25	519	1,268	–7.0	26,757	1,360	28,698	–9.3	920	65	1,372
Otoe	14	90	2	36	233	2,889	0.3	18,628	3,355	21,633	0.3	2,335	181	1,167
Pawnee	2	70	1	17	592	780	–10.9	27,102	845	29,361	–12.0	590	39	1,355
Perkins	2	65	1	70	2,279	624	0.6	20,412	720	23,553	–0.1	490	23	752
Phelps	13	136	1	30	314	1,854	2.9	19,621	2,120	22,436	1.6	1,435	110	1,164
Pierce	6	79	1	25	328	1,232	–11.2	16,211	1,450	19,079	–8.2	915	58	763

See footnotes at end of table.

Table B-6. Counties — Physicians, Community Hospitals, Medicare, Social Security, and Supplemental Security Income—Con.

[Includes United States, states, and 3,141 counties/county equivalents defined as of February 22, 2005. For more information on these areas, see Appendix C, Geographic Information]

| County | Physicians, 2004[1] | | Community hospitals, 2004[3] | | | Medicare program enrollment, 2005[4] | | | Social Security program beneficiaries, December 2005 | | | | Supplemental Security Income program recipients, 2005 | |
| | | | Number | Beds | | | | | | | | | | |
	Number	Rate per 100,000 persons[2]	Number	Number	Rate per 100,000 persons[2]	Total	Percent change, 2000–2005	Rate per 100,000 persons[2]	Number	Rate per 100,000 persons[2]	Percent change, 2000–2005	Retired workers, number	Number	Rate per 100,000 persons[2]
NEBRASKA—Con.														
Platte	33	105	1	54	173	3,156	3.7	10,095	5,580	17,849	1.7	3,775	266	851
Polk	3	55	1	21	388	1,063	-5.6	19,609	1,260	23,243	-3.6	885	39	719
Red Willow	16	144	1	44	397	2,389	-1.8	21,600	2,540	22,966	-0.9	1,705	162	1,465
Richardson	4	45	1	25	282	2,169	-3.7	24,840	2,385	27,313	-2.3	1,485	153	1,752
Rock	2	126	1	45	2,827	367	-10.5	23,421	375	23,931	-4.3	260	15	957
Saline	11	77	2	119	838	2,426	-5.1	17,091	2,625	18,492	-3.8	1,735	110	775
Sarpy	251	185	2	130	96	9,798	30.3	7,030	14,605	10,479	26.2	9,630	832	597
Saunders	11	54	1	87	430	3,226	1.8	15,769	3,675	17,964	5.4	2,445	156	763
Scotts Bluff	101	275	1	95	259	7,360	1.6	20,026	8,210	22,339	-0.5	5,110	801	2,179
Seward	13	78	1	154	918	2,541	1.0	15,180	2,925	17,474	1.0	2,025	128	765
Sheridan	6	104	1	65	1,121	1,310	-7.6	23,112	1,410	24,876	-9.1	985	68	1,200
Sherman	1	32	–	–	–	755	-4.8	24,261	840	26,992	-7.3	575	37	1,189
Sioux	1	69	–	–	–	135	4.7	9,259	270	18,519	13.0	175	9	617
Stanton	1	15	–	–	–	584	-4.1	8,938	990	15,152	3.2	615	38	582
Thayer	4	73	1	14	255	1,487	-5.0	27,355	1,570	28,882	-9.0	1,045	81	1,490
Thomas	–	–	–	–	–	114	-20.8	18,299	145	23,274	-31.3	90	6	963
Thurston	5	70	1	133	1,851	968	-3.6	13,143	1,165	15,818	-1.7	660	188	2,553
Valley	7	156	1	95	2,111	1,077	-5.4	24,466	1,170	26,579	-7.1	800	72	1,636
Washington	18	92	1	25	128	2,593	8.3	13,115	3,145	15,906	7.9	2,190	121	612
Wayne	6	64	1	25	268	1,319	-4.8	14,320	1,550	16,828	-3.1	1,050	90	977
Webster	2	52	1	16	417	1,058	-2.1	28,123	1,105	29,373	-5.8	725	70	1,861
Wheeler	–	–	–	–	–	147	-3.3	17,927	185	22,561	-6.6	115	4	488
York	16	112	2	210	1,476	2,713	1.8	18,844	3,025	21,011	-0.9	2,045	145	1,007
NEVADA	4,933	211	30	4,752	204	[6]296,639	[6]23.7	[6]12,284	[7]346,345	[7]14,343	[7]20.7	[7]234,284	33,479	1,386
Churchill	33	136	1	40	165	3,710	17.1	15,108	4,360	17,755	15.0	2,845	383	1,560
Clark	3,308	201	15	3,239	196	195,730	23.1	11,443	230,760	13,490	20.6	155,390	24,895	1,455
Douglas	101	220	–	–	–	7,571	30.7	16,103	9,900	21,056	28.7	7,475	288	613
Elko	49	110	1	50	112	3,886	29.6	8,528	4,805	10,544	28.5	2,955	455	998
Esmeralda	–	–	–	–	–	174	20.0	22,109	250	31,766	1.6	175	19	2,414
Eureka	1	70	–	–	–	244	5.2	17,087	275	19,258	9.1	185	14	980
Humboldt	8	47	1	52	308	1,790	19.3	10,450	2,130	12,435	17.9	1,330	213	1,244
Lander	3	59	1	25	492	559	20.0	10,931	725	14,177	21.2	435	73	1,427
Lincoln	1	23	–	–	–	1,150	47.2	26,190	1,025	23,343	15.2	660	86	1,959
Lyon	18	42	1	63	145	7,754	37.5	16,319	9,215	19,394	32.5	6,150	555	1,168
Mineral	3	61	1	11	223	1,183	5.8	24,094	1,380	28,106	9.9	865	139	2,831
Nye	29	77	1	44	117	9,544	39.1	23,579	11,820	29,202	33.6	8,280	741	1,831
Pershing	3	47	1	37	578	603	16.2	9,481	820	12,893	24.1	505	79	1,242
Storey	–	–	–	–	–	174	5.5	4,271	655	16,078	-2.8	455	28	687
Washoe	1,204	316	5	1,031	271	49,383	23.3	12,666	55,925	14,344	19.6	37,950	4,695	1,204
White Pine	15	175	1	29	339	1,570	13.0	17,456	1,790	19,902	8.9	1,155	153	1,701
Independent City														
Carson City	157	281	1	131	234	10,947	12.0	19,527	10,505	18,738	6.3	7,470	663	1,183
NEW HAMPSHIRE	3,884	299	28	2,807	216	[6]190,783	[6]12.2	[6]14,564	[7]220,796	[7]16,855	[7]10.5	[7]145,126	13,689	1,045
Belknap	152	249	1	106	174	11,871	11.6	19,288	13,110	21,301	8.4	8,875	808	1,313
Carroll	113	241	2	156	333	9,505	10.9	20,036	11,405	24,041	14.6	7,965	525	1,107
Cheshire	176	229	1	146	190	12,260	8.3	15,863	14,445	18,690	9.3	9,700	845	1,093
Coos	83	248	3	100	298	7,589	4.3	22,549	9,035	26,846	6.9	5,500	755	2,243
Grafton	979	1,163	5	486	577	13,924	11.6	16,438	15,870	18,735	9.8	10,815	800	944
Hillsborough	944	237	5	827	208	50,340	8.7	12,545	59,050	14,715	8.9	38,335	4,332	1,080
Merrimack	461	317	4	358	246	20,695	8.6	14,090	25,140	17,116	11.1	16,210	1,687	1,149
Rockingham	610	209	4	415	142	37,302	14.0	12,641	44,625	15,123	14.0	29,865	1,739	589
Strafford	246	208	2	185	156	15,945	9.5	13,397	19,045	16,002	10.4	12,090	1,455	1,223
Sullivan	120	283	1	28	66	7,476	7.6	17,369	8,960	20,817	7.4	5,720	743	1,726
NEW JERSEY	29,247	337	80	21,952	253	[6]1,232,802	[6]2.5	[6]14,141	[7]1,375,796	[7]15,781	[7]2.0	[7]942,992	152,142	1,745
Atlantic	655	244	4	816	304	40,996	8.3	15,127	46,575	17,185	8.4	31,345	5,221	1,926
Bergen	4,952	549	5	1,876	208	138,516	-1.3	15,347	148,530	16,457	-2.3	109,890	10,064	1,115
Burlington	1,280	285	4	787	175	63,176	9.5	14,016	73,425	16,290	8.3	49,440	4,743	1,052
Camden	1,758	341	5	1,516	294	73,715	1.6	14,224	82,205	15,862	1.8	51,425	13,238	2,554
Cape May	154	153	1	208	207	22,030	0.4	22,188	25,255	25,437	0.6	17,640	1,520	1,531
Cumberland	217	144	1	409	271	23,125	4.2	15,090	26,405	17,230	2.9	16,245	4,674	3,050
Essex	3,692	464	11	3,386	426	99,570	-2.8	12,587	109,350	13,823	-4.4	71,085	25,358	3,206
Gloucester	321	118	1	240	88	34,815	10.2	12,573	43,975	15,881	10.9	27,730	3,497	1,263
Hudson	1,261	208	7	1,580	261	69,515	-3.8	11,518	73,960	12,255	-4.9	48,025	21,493	3,561
Hunterdon	437	338	1	182	141	16,008	17.2	12,276	17,995	13,799	12.3	12,770	685	525
Mercer	1,529	420	6	1,309	359	52,849	2.2	14,430	57,455	15,687	1.0	38,000	6,952	1,898
Middlesex	2,907	371	5	1,781	227	98,771	1.9	12,510	111,185	14,083	1.6	76,760	10,371	1,314
Monmouth	2,459	387	6	1,463	230	90,844	4.4	14,285	100,325	15,776	4.0	68,370	6,808	1,071
Morris	2,052	421	3	1,511	310	64,135	9.9	13,073	70,550	14,381	9.3	51,590	3,614	737
Ocean	921	167	5	1,273	230	124,310	4.8	22,264	141,320	25,311	5.4	104,145	5,354	959

See footnotes at end of table.

[Includes United States, states, and 3,141 counties/county equivalents defined as of February 22, 2005. For more information on these areas, see Appendix C, Geographic Information]

County	Physicians, 2004[1] Number	Physicians, 2004[1] Rate per 100,000 persons[2]	Community hospitals, 2004[3] Number	Beds Number	Beds Rate per 100,000 persons[2]	Medicare program enrollment, 2005[4] Total	Medicare Percent change, 2000–2005	Medicare Rate per 100,000 persons[2]	Social Security beneficiaries, Dec 2005 Number	SS Rate per 100,000 persons[2]	SS Percent change, 2000–2005	Retired workers, number	Supplemental Security Income recipients, 2005 Number	SSI Rate per 100,000 persons[2]
NEW JERSEY—Con.														
Passaic	1,145	229	5	1,403	281	64,965	−0.1	13,017	72,105	14,448	−1.5	47,840	13,479	2,701
Salem	75	115	1	110	168	10,869	3.6	16,382	13,155	19,828	4.8	8,290	1,289	1,943
Somerset	1,465	463	2	587	186	34,525	6.5	10,792	42,060	13,148	7.9	30,320	2,280	713
Sussex	220	145	1	146	96	17,481	13.3	11,416	21,120	13,792	14.5	13,780	1,437	938
Union	1,558	293	4	1,129	213	75,054	−5.1	14,122	80,430	15,134	−5.2	55,735	8,939	1,682
Warren	189	172	2	240	219	16,518	6.8	14,965	18,415	16,684	7.1	12,565	1,126	1,020
NEW MEXICO	5,169	272	37	3,678	193	[6]265,823	[6]13.4	[6]13,785	[7]311,468	[7]16,152	[7]12.3	[7]186,639	53,865	2,793
Bernalillo	2,797	472	11	1,435	242	80,347	13.8	13,312	91,945	15,234	11.9	56,785	13,092	2,169
Catron	3	88	–	–	–	853	24.9	25,022	1,045	30,654	20.0	700	66	1,936
Chaves	124	202	2	190	309	10,438	4.1	16,874	12,145	19,633	3.8	7,160	2,165	3,500
Cibola	24	87	1	25	91	2,956	22.0	10,702	4,145	15,007	12.3	2,115	859	3,110
Colfax	27	195	1	80	577	2,734	6.9	19,876	3,280	23,846	9.7	2,095	400	2,908
Curry	72	157	1	106	232	6,242	5.8	13,615	6,805	14,843	2.6	3,860	1,465	3,195
De Baca	3	148	–	–	–	530	−7.2	26,290	565	28,026	−7.4	385	90	4,464
Dona Ana	320	172	2	350	189	23,930	18.5	12,632	27,400	14,463	16.0	16,900	6,008	3,171
Eddy	74	143	2	147	285	8,568	−0.7	16,657	10,160	19,752	−0.3	5,670	1,512	2,940
Grant	81	276	1	68	232	6,225	12.5	20,926	7,570	25,448	13.4	4,635	899	3,022
Guadalupe	3	67	–	–	–	839	7.0	19,203	975	22,316	6.1	525	294	6,729
Harding	–	–	–	–	–	223	−10.1	30,135	225	30,405	−11.8	155	21	2,838
Hidalgo	2	39	–	–	–	841	0.8	16,365	1,050	20,432	8.6	640	180	3,503
Lea	55	98	2	226	403	7,913	2.7	13,951	9,335	16,458	0.1	5,155	1,647	2,904
Lincoln	33	160	1	25	121	3,995	15.1	19,017	4,790	22,802	15.2	3,295	342	1,628
Los Alamos	66	352	1	36	192	2,322	8.4	12,337	2,505	13,309	12.0	1,825	47	250
Luna	21	80	1	119	456	5,353	13.5	20,202	6,320	23,851	12.0	4,115	1,124	4,242
McKinley	168	232	1	89	123	6,965	18.1	9,685	8,160	11,346	13.5	3,950	4,106	5,709
Mora	1	19	–	–	–	997	9.3	19,522	1,240	24,280	11.0	635	351	6,873
Otero	74	116	1	99	156	8,595	14.4	13,527	10,435	16,423	10.9	6,530	1,386	2,181
Quay	10	106	1	25	265	2,083	−1.6	22,497	2,435	26,299	−0.5	1,490	416	4,493
Rio Arriba	40	98	1	80	196	5,958	11.0	14,593	7,625	18,676	8.0	3,860	1,607	3,936
Roosevelt	11	60	–	–	–	2,640	1.8	14,475	2,985	16,367	−1.1	1,775	643	3,526
Sandoval	185	180	–	–	–	12,897	22.7	12,002	16,375	15,238	28.6	10,185	2,113	1,966
San Juan	197	159	1	168	135	13,882	17.9	10,999	16,680	13,216	13.0	9,085	3,736	2,960
San Miguel	52	176	1	54	183	4,824	10.8	16,336	5,575	18,879	14.0	2,860	1,784	6,041
Santa Fe	568	408	1	246	177	18,523	21.7	13,150	21,615	15,346	19.7	14,095	2,199	1,561
Sierra	17	131	1	25	193	3,547	0.2	27,679	4,015	31,330	2.1	2,675	517	4,034
Socorro	14	77	1	15	83	2,309	13.9	12,723	2,780	15,318	11.6	1,565	935	5,152
Taos	83	263	1	49	156	5,035	20.7	15,872	6,125	19,308	19.4	3,665	1,119	3,528
Torrance	1	6	–	–	–	2,085	17.3	11,914	2,770	15,828	19.6	1,445	548	3,131
Union	3	78	1	21	549	884	1.8	22,961	980	25,455	−1.8	610	130	3,377
Valencia	40	58	–	–	–	9,713	14.7	13,992	11,405	16,430	25.7	6,195	2,064	2,973
NEW YORK	81,716	424	206	64,205	333	[6]2,796,213	[6]3.0	[6]14,522	[7]3,062,046	[7]15,903	[7]1.8	[7]1,991,618	633,473	3,290
Albany	1,696	569	3	1,191	400	44,839	−0.4	15,076	52,110	17,521	−0.5	34,905	6,573	2,210
Allegany	55	108	1	70	138	8,308	4.6	16,418	10,055	19,871	4.9	6,205	1,468	2,901
Bronx	3,522	258	9	4,325	317	151,909	4.1	11,190	161,580	11,902	0.8	95,030	92,614	6,822
Broome	645	326	2	584	295	38,756	1.4	19,678	43,735	22,206	1.0	28,605	5,823	2,957
Cattaraugus	130	157	2	206	248	14,890	1.9	18,048	17,080	20,703	2.1	10,660	2,512	3,045
Cayuga	107	131	1	243	298	13,099	2.6	16,081	15,035	18,458	3.1	9,935	1,861	2,285
Chautauqua	223	163	4	608	443	25,847	0.1	18,948	29,895	21,916	1.2	19,210	4,105	3,009
Chemung	201	290	2	506	563	16,781	1.2	18,747	19,745	22,058	2.5	12,320	2,938	3,282
Chenango	66	128	1	138	267	9,422	5.8	18,205	11,375	21,979	7.2	7,050	1,613	3,117
Clinton	209	256	1	405	496	12,322	13.1	15,018	15,470	18,855	9.8	8,945	2,740	3,340
Columbia	123	193	1	245	385	11,495	2.7	18,068	13,610	21,392	3.3	8,955	1,661	2,611
Cortland	67	137	1	202	413	7,298	3.7	15,010	8,715	17,924	3.5	5,565	1,268	2,608
Delaware	58	122	3	64	135	9,299	2.1	19,563	11,045	23,236	0.6	7,055	1,234	2,596
Dutchess	841	287	3	702	239	43,278	7.5	14,678	49,695	16,854	5.9	31,310	4,835	1,640
Erie	3,802	406	10	4,551	486	166,682	−1.3	17,909	189,735	20,386	−0.3	118,285	26,018	2,796
Essex	49	126	2	40	103	7,675	3.9	19,844	8,385	21,680	6.6	5,320	991	2,562
Franklin	105	206	2	228	448	8,099	4.7	15,870	10,225	20,036	3.8	5,750	1,819	3,564
Fulton	79	143	1	170	307	9,341	1.1	16,793	12,055	21,672	2.4	7,705	1,858	3,340
Genesee	90	151	1	126	211	10,411	5.0	17,569	12,035	20,310	5.1	7,890	1,038	1,752
Greene	45	91	–	–	–	8,887	3.3	17,888	10,820	21,779	6.5	6,870	1,176	2,367
Hamilton	4	76	–	–	–	1,270	2.0	24,292	1,500	28,692	6.2	1,115	102	1,951
Herkimer	54	85	2	273	428	11,640	−2.1	18,250	13,895	21,786	0.3	9,040	1,619	2,538
Jefferson	240	210	3	350	306	15,886	4.3	13,650	18,890	16,231	6.3	11,265	2,923	2,512
Kings	7,336	294	15	7,361	295	299,100	2.1	12,030	285,315	11,476	−2.8	178,855	142,379	5,727
Lewis	28	105	–	–	–	4,310	6.1	16,221	4,965	18,686	−0.6	3,000	622	2,341
Livingston	66	102	1	72	112	9,675	8.4	15,069	11,270	17,553	6.8	7,470	1,040	1,620
Madison	110	156	2	345	490	10,830	6.3	15,397	12,265	17,447	5.7	7,760	1,233	1,753
Monroe	3,629	493	5	1,930	262	113,316	4.0	15,451	132,615	18,083	4.9	87,885	19,753	2,693
Montgomery	91	185	2	342	696	10,788	−5.2	22,031	12,205	24,924	−5.6	8,095	1,625	3,318
Nassau	8,908	666	13	5,034	376	218,185	−1.5	16,366	236,660	17,752	−2.3	164,395	16,560	1,242

See footnotes at end of table.

U.S. Census Bureau

Physicians, Community Hospitals, Medicare, Social Security, and Supplemental Security Income—Con.

[Includes United States, states, and 3,141 counties/county equivalents defined as of February 22, 2005. For more information on these areas, see Appendix C, Geographic Information]

County	Physicians, 2004[1] Number	Physicians, 2004[1] Rate per 100,000 persons[2]	Community hospitals, 2004[3] Number	Beds Number	Beds Rate per 100,000 persons[2]	Medicare program enrollment, 2005[4] Total	Medicare Percent change, 2000–2005	Medicare Rate per 100,000 persons[2]	Social Security program beneficiaries, December 2005 Number	SS Rate per 100,000 persons[2]	SS Percent change, 2000–2005	Retired workers, number	Supplemental Security Income program recipients, 2005 Number	SSI Rate per 100,000 persons[2]
NEW YORK—Con.														
New York	19,849	1,248	20	9,737	612	223,982	5.8	14,059	221,520	13,904	3.2	156,755	80,527	5,054
Niagara	318	146	4	646	297	40,300	1.7	18,571	47,370	21,829	3.0	28,870	5,144	2,370
Oneida	611	260	3	815	347	44,744	-0.4	19,113	51,240	21,888	0.8	31,295	7,794	3,329
Onondaga	2,297	501	4	1,522	332	73,755	1.9	16,102	85,430	18,651	2.4	55,160	12,376	2,702
Ontario	278	269	3	672	650	16,892	11.0	16,171	20,125	19,266	11.2	13,570	1,740	1,666
Orange	807	218	4	859	232	44,695	7.0	11,986	52,895	14,185	6.5	31,685	6,124	1,642
Orleans	35	80	1	101	232	6,639	7.3	15,302	8,330	19,199	8.7	5,175	931	2,146
Oswego	119	96	2	141	114	18,828	7.0	15,261	23,125	18,744	6.6	13,065	3,101	2,514
Otsego	319	509	2	395	630	11,032	3.9	17,582	12,795	20,392	5.6	8,330	1,449	2,309
Putnam	216	215	1	144	143	11,755	13.4	11,696	14,140	14,069	12.0	9,305	802	798
Queens	6,224	277	11	4,918	219	284,190	0.2	12,678	286,830	12,796	-3.1	197,410	72,549	3,236
Rensselaer	293	190	2	417	270	24,153	1.5	15,557	27,620	17,791	1.3	17,925	3,300	2,126
Richmond	1,791	387	3	1,252	271	62,177	6.1	13,384	72,525	15,611	5.9	42,510	12,392	2,667
Rockland	1,297	443	4	1,163	397	42,520	7.2	14,516	47,235	16,126	5.4	32,580	5,245	1,791
St. Lawrence	179	161	5	410	368	19,291	6.1	17,320	22,390	20,102	7.1	12,415	3,869	3,474
Saratoga	403	190	1	211	99	29,630	11.2	13,790	35,750	16,639	15.8	23,670	2,646	1,232
Schenectady	549	371	4	710	480	29,266	0.5	19,631	31,110	20,868	1.6	20,110	4,182	2,805
Schoharie	22	69	1	40	125	5,502	5.3	17,046	6,030	18,682	0.3	3,860	674	2,088
Schuyler	20	103	1	166	854	3,202	6.4	16,555	4,200	21,714	6.5	2,640	469	2,425
Seneca	22	63	–	–	–	5,643	2.6	16,190	7,085	20,327	4.5	4,590	731	2,097
Steuben	163	165	3	510	516	17,800	3.3	18,047	20,795	21,083	4.4	12,785	3,012	3,054
Suffolk	4,758	323	12	3,599	244	212,154	7.4	14,384	247,200	16,760	6.3	158,385	20,713	1,404
Sullivan	118	155	1	274	361	13,377	5.2	17,477	15,925	20,806	3.3	9,525	2,816	3,679
Tioga	38	74	–	–	–	8,083	7.8	15,703	10,245	19,903	7.6	6,600	1,058	2,055
Tompkins	265	265	1	166	166	11,274	6.5	11,272	13,085	13,083	6.4	8,790	1,604	1,604
Ulster	384	211	3	375	206	28,511	5.5	15,606	34,025	18,624	5.5	21,160	4,338	2,374
Warren	247	380	1	304	467	12,364	10.5	18,863	14,640	22,335	10.8	9,415	1,564	2,386
Washington	39	62	–	–	–	10,478	9.4	16,625	11,990	19,024	9.5	7,375	1,425	2,261
Wayne	88	94	1	275	293	15,893	5.6	16,978	18,855	20,142	6.8	11,715	2,107	2,251
Westchester	7,244	770	13	3,661	389	140,927	1.1	14,979	152,335	16,192	0.2	109,935	15,598	1,658
Wyoming	49	114	1	206	481	6,431	4.5	15,063	7,880	18,457	7.5	4,940	634	1,485
Yates	35	141	1	205	828	4,712	3.9	19,034	5,335	21,550	3.4	3,615	558	2,254
NORTH CAROLINA	24,085	282	115	23,498	275	[6]1,267,633	[6]11.8	[6]14,599	[7]1,509,687	[7]17,386	[7]11.7	[7]940,891	199,337	2,296
Alamance	241	174	1	210	152	23,462	7.9	16,695	27,195	19,351	9.2	18,340	2,487	1,770
Alexander	20	57	–	–	–	5,279	17.3	14,874	6,345	17,877	17.1	4,090	557	1,569
Alleghany	25	230	1	46	423	2,595	6.0	23,807	2,915	26,743	10.0	1,910	338	3,101
Anson	15	58	1	125	486	4,398	2.4	17,248	5,185	20,334	1.6	2,910	1,089	4,271
Ashe	40	158	1	115	455	5,480	10.1	21,620	6,375	25,151	9.4	4,130	841	3,318
Avery	49	276	1	70	394	3,692	10.3	20,929	3,735	21,172	4.7	2,435	396	2,245
Beaufort	95	208	2	134	294	9,487	10.3	20,616	11,475	24,936	10.6	6,755	1,865	4,053
Bertie	6	31	1	6	31	4,469	4.5	22,941	5,395	27,695	3.3	2,755	1,512	7,762
Bladen	28	85	1	35	106	5,657	4.3	17,175	7,460	22,649	5.4	3,730	1,926	5,847
Brunswick	108	128	2	160	189	18,107	29.9	20,308	23,185	26,003	31.6	15,595	1,941	2,177
Buncombe	1,053	488	2	828	384	39,544	8.4	18,067	45,330	20,710	7.8	29,045	4,647	2,123
Burke	188	210	2	468	523	14,756	10.8	16,506	18,145	20,297	13.6	11,460	1,886	2,110
Cabarrus	351	240	1	357	244	21,572	10.6	14,358	23,965	15,951	13.8	16,195	1,948	1,297
Caldwell	99	126	1	72	91	13,382	13.0	16,913	16,490	20,841	13.5	10,415	1,496	1,891
Camden	4	47	–	–	–	1,219	16.0	13,594	1,630	18,178	16.4	1,010	143	1,595
Carteret	129	209	1	221	358	11,270	9.2	18,025	14,320	22,903	11.1	9,440	1,158	1,852
Caswell	10	42	–	–	–	3,693	12.0	15,643	4,825	20,438	9.9	2,780	830	3,516
Catawba	391	262	2	568	380	23,310	13.2	15,372	28,115	18,541	12.0	19,160	2,338	1,542
Chatham	75	132	1	25	44	7,441	10.1	12,829	10,845	18,698	10.7	7,560	726	1,252
Cherokee	43	169	1	184	724	6,286	11.8	24,368	7,510	29,113	14.7	4,630	866	3,357
Chowan	31	215	1	76	527	3,022	2.9	20,801	3,535	24,332	3.0	2,255	536	3,689
Clay	11	116	–	–	–	2,431	11.3	24,895	2,905	29,749	14.4	1,890	298	3,052
Cleveland	173	176	2	378	385	18,078	10.6	18,393	21,595	21,971	10.2	13,115	2,713	2,760
Columbus	55	101	1	113	207	10,976	9.0	20,049	13,240	24,184	7.0	6,470	3,517	6,424
Craven	282	310	1	284	313	16,723	12.1	18,418	18,725	20,623	10.3	12,095	2,345	2,583
Cumberland	741	241	1	581	189	34,303	17.3	11,265	41,015	13,469	13.2	21,725	8,114	2,665
Currituck	11	50	–	–	–	2,925	18.7	12,656	3,540	15,317	18.8	2,225	270	1,168
Dare	48	143	1	19	57	4,833	10.8	14,255	5,750	16,960	9.1	4,015	237	699
Davidson	123	80	2	168	109	21,506	10.4	13,909	29,280	18,936	13.4	19,115	2,551	1,650
Davie	65	171	1	25	66	6,280	17.6	16,047	7,555	19,304	16.9	5,160	518	1,324
Duplin	34	66	1	89	172	7,826	8.9	15,054	9,575	18,419	4.0	5,430	2,027	3,899
Durham	2,849	1,190	3	1,036	433	27,461	8.7	11,320	31,365	12,930	7.1	19,930	4,697	1,936
Edgecombe	48	88	1	127	234	9,223	-2.8	17,039	11,060	20,433	-1.6	6,015	2,894	5,346
Forsyth	1,946	607	3	1,753	546	49,844	9.2	15,291	55,645	17,071	9.1	37,165	5,789	1,776
Franklin	26	49	1	56	105	6,596	15.5	12,119	8,405	15,442	15.5	4,785	1,394	2,561

See footnotes at end of table.

[Includes United States, states, and 3,141 counties/county equivalents defined as of February 22, 2005. For more information on these areas, see Appendix C, Geographic Information]

County	Physicians, 2004[1] Number	Physicians, 2004[1] Rate per 100,000 persons[2]	Community hospitals, 2004[3] Number	Beds Number	Beds Rate per 100,000 persons[2]	Medicare program enrollment, 2005[4] Total	Medicare Percent change, 2000–2005	Medicare Rate per 100,000 persons[2]	Social Security program beneficiaries, December 2005 Number	SS Rate per 100,000 persons[2]	SS Percent change, 2000–2005	Retired workers, number	Supplemental Security Income program recipients, 2005 Number	SSI Rate per 100,000 persons[2]
NORTH CAROLINA—Con.														
Gaston	366	189	1	378	195	31,149	8.3	15,881	37,075	18,903	7.4	23,065	4,266	2,175
Gates	4	37	–	–	–	1,862	4.7	16,589	2,260	20,135	4.2	1,270	340	3,029
Graham	4	50	–	–	–	1,731	6.3	21,410	2,100	25,974	7.3	1,165	299	3,698
Granville	59	111	1	142	268	7,237	8.0	13,483	9,260	17,252	11.4	5,235	1,496	2,787
Greene	3	15	–	–	–	2,413	6.1	12,049	3,040	15,180	–1.2	1,765	723	3,610
Guilford	1,267	289	2	1,669	381	62,500	10.6	14,092	72,010	16,236	10.3	48,265	7,811	1,761
Halifax	83	148	2	208	371	12,143	3.7	21,675	14,195	25,338	1.4	7,200	4,303	7,681
Harnett	67	66	2	125	123	10,887	10.6	10,499	14,970	14,437	21.2	8,455	2,561	2,470
Haywood	134	239	1	125	223	12,713	10.2	22,508	15,205	26,920	10.9	9,565	1,493	2,643
Henderson	296	310	2	279	292	23,299	10.4	23,966	26,405	27,161	13.2	18,460	1,689	1,737
Hertford	35	149	1	105	447	4,327	2.3	18,355	5,060	21,464	0.3	2,685	1,391	5,901
Hoke	12	31	–	–	–	2,965	17.1	7,229	4,960	12,093	13.3	2,455	1,212	2,955
Hyde	1	18	–	–	–	955	–3.3	17,643	1,050	19,398	–9.8	625	214	3,953
Iredell	269	197	3	455	333	20,455	17.6	14,515	24,775	17,580	19.3	16,375	2,106	1,494
Jackson	108	307	1	201	571	5,401	8.5	15,271	6,570	18,576	10.4	4,265	674	1,906
Johnston	100	71	1	160	113	16,154	13.7	11,031	21,450	14,648	18.4	12,025	3,473	2,372
Jones	14	135	–	–	–	1,970	9.0	19,106	2,270	22,015	1.0	1,290	384	3,724
Lee	100	184	1	137	252	9,569	12.0	17,178	10,055	18,051	7.3	6,205	1,139	2,045
Lenoir	114	196	1	219	377	12,068	5.4	20,821	13,630	23,516	4.8	7,920	2,733	4,715
Lincoln	55	81	1	87	128	10,285	15.8	14,724	12,030	17,222	19.6	7,710	1,084	1,552
McDowell	36	84	1	65	151	8,142	12.7	18,847	9,675	22,395	13.0	5,865	1,108	2,565
Macon	101	320	2	163	516	7,958	11.0	24,754	9,285	28,882	11.0	6,420	736	2,289
Madison	17	85	–	–	–	4,020	11.3	19,846	4,615	22,783	9.6	2,675	816	4,028
Martin	18	72	1	49	197	5,057	5.4	20,521	5,600	22,725	0.4	3,175	1,180	4,788
Mecklenburg	2,508	325	8	2,152	279	79,067	14.4	9,928	91,675	11,512	14.6	59,065	11,571	1,453
Mitchell	24	151	1	40	252	3,572	7.5	22,631	4,055	25,691	10.1	2,450	536	3,396
Montgomery	17	62	1	55	202	4,403	3.5	16,115	5,025	18,392	10.8	3,090	730	2,672
Moore	344	430	1	356	445	19,141	8.1	23,433	21,775	26,657	9.0	15,315	1,489	1,823
Nash	185	204	2	343	378	15,048	14.8	16,468	17,300	18,932	11.4	9,945	3,215	3,518
New Hanover	782	450	1	655	377	28,030	16.2	15,611	32,665	18,192	16.7	20,955	3,697	2,059
Northampton	6	28	–	–	–	4,880	6.4	22,716	5,595	26,044	–0.4	3,025	1,410	6,563
Onslow	253	164	1	133	86	14,092	18.7	9,244	17,155	11,254	17.8	9,960	2,630	1,725
Orange	2,074	1,771	1	688	587	13,179	14.1	11,132	14,310	12,088	12.3	9,595	1,407	1,188
Pamlico	11	86	–	–	–	2,616	7.1	20,542	3,430	26,934	9.3	2,265	363	2,850
Pasquotank	110	297	1	150	405	5,882	6.1	15,370	6,945	18,147	7.5	4,185	1,149	3,002
Pender	32	71	1	68	151	7,466	18.7	16,080	9,340	20,117	14.7	5,650	1,109	2,389
Perquimans	9	77	–	–	–	2,711	10.6	22,442	3,220	26,656	8.7	2,075	356	2,947
Person	39	106	1	110	299	5,750	4.2	15,450	7,675	20,622	12.0	4,685	989	2,657
Pitt	960	685	1	745	531	18,215	13.2	12,776	21,900	15,361	12.6	12,255	5,035	3,532
Polk	52	274	1	63	332	4,751	4.8	24,830	5,360	28,013	4.1	3,760	302	1,578
Randolph	141	103	1	107	79	20,986	14.1	15,167	25,050	18,104	12.0	16,510	2,213	1,599
Richmond	50	107	2	205	439	8,910	5.0	19,046	10,460	22,360	5.6	5,420	2,077	4,440
Robeson	139	110	1	403	319	19,697	12.6	15,438	22,865	17,921	8.3	10,945	6,927	5,429
Rockingham	101	109	2	394	427	17,417	7.6	18,806	20,800	22,459	8.5	12,925	2,813	3,037
Rowan	228	170	1	188	140	20,083	9.2	14,865	26,065	19,293	9.5	16,450	2,382	1,763
Rutherford	105	165	1	143	225	12,147	6.6	19,048	15,065	23,624	11.8	9,470	1,708	2,678
Sampson	50	80	1	146	234	9,393	8.4	14,895	12,315	19,528	3.9	6,835	2,272	3,603
Scotland	68	183	1	159	429	5,879	12.1	15,812	7,975	21,450	11.1	3,970	1,959	5,269
Stanly	72	123	1	119	203	10,506	6.3	17,818	12,025	20,394	4.0	7,990	1,074	1,821
Stokes	22	48	1	65	143	6,792	22.0	14,811	8,875	19,353	18.6	5,405	886	1,932
Surry	94	130	2	333	461	14,620	9.3	20,137	15,670	21,584	4.2	9,830	1,897	2,613
Swain	19	145	1	25	191	2,732	11.9	20,749	3,355	25,480	8.7	2,005	366	2,780
Transylvania	80	272	1	54	183	7,617	11.1	25,711	8,830	29,805	11.3	6,135	561	1,894
Tyrrell	–	–	–	–	–	713	–2.5	17,152	830	19,966	–6.8	505	139	3,344
Union	161	105	1	215	140	14,252	24.3	8,747	20,190	12,392	27.6	13,240	1,584	972
Vance	67	153	1	102	233	7,789	6.5	17,795	9,455	21,601	5.1	5,025	2,260	5,163
Wake	2,032	282	4	1,523	212	70,353	24.1	9,395	81,080	10,828	24.1	52,245	8,799	1,175
Warren	4	20	–	–	–	3,632	5.0	18,409	4,350	22,049	7.2	2,360	1,044	5,292
Washington	6	45	1	25	188	2,705	5.0	20,366	3,230	24,319	4.8	1,740	664	4,999
Watauga	117	276	2	195	459	5,562	11.0	13,096	7,130	16,788	14.1	4,875	669	1,575
Wayne	201	176	1	270	236	18,315	8.6	16,003	21,465	18,755	7.5	12,080	4,454	3,892
Wilkes	68	101	1	131	196	11,806	12.9	17,519	15,355	22,785	16.8	9,415	2,002	2,971
Wilson	133	175	1	220	290	12,576	9.0	16,486	16,035	21,021	10.7	9,380	3,007	3,942
Yadkin	19	51	–	–	–	6,726	11.6	17,856	7,805	20,721	8.3	5,020	760	2,018
Yancey	26	143	–	–	–	4,022	9.5	22,098	4,805	26,400	9.5	2,960	711	3,906
NORTH DAKOTA	1,716	270	40	3,567	561	[6]103,781	[6]0.6	[6]16,300	[7]114,712	[7]18,017	[7]0.1	[7]72,329	7,907	1,242
Adams	17	694	1	40	1,633	587	1.6	24,127	690	28,360	–1.3	430	17	699
Barnes	14	126	1	25	225	2,407	–5.7	21,734	2,685	24,244	–4.4	1,720	134	1,210
Benson	1	14	–	–	–	1,014	–1.8	14,488	1,215	17,360	–2.6	690	188	2,686
Billings	–	–	–	–	–	70	–9.1	8,610	160	19,680	7.4	90	5	615
Bottineau	6	88	1	25	368	1,504	–5.5	22,311	1,720	25,516	–2.2	1,145	66	979

See footnotes at end of table.

Table B-6. Counties — Physicians, Community Hospitals, Medicare, Social Security, and Supplemental Security Income—Con.

[Includes United States, states, and 3,141 counties/county equivalents defined as of February 22, 2005. For more information on these areas, see Appendix C, Geographic Information]

County	Physicians, 2004[1] Number	Physicians, 2004[1] Rate per 100,000 persons[2]	Community hospitals, 2004[3] Number	Community hospitals, 2004[3] Beds Number	Community hospitals, 2004[3] Beds Rate per 100,000 persons[2]	Medicare program enrollment, 2005[4] Total	Medicare program enrollment, 2005[4] Percent change, 2000–2005	Medicare program enrollment, 2005[4] Rate per 100,000 persons[2]	Social Security program beneficiaries, December 2005 Number	Social Security program beneficiaries, December 2005 Rate per 100,000 persons[2]	Social Security program beneficiaries, December 2005 Percent change, 2000–2005	Social Security program beneficiaries, December 2005 Retired workers, number	Supplemental Security Income program recipients, 2005 Number	Supplemental Security Income program recipients, 2005 Rate per 100,000 persons[2]
NORTH DAKOTA—Con.														
Bowman	4	129	1	90	2,912	725	-4.9	23,786	760	24,934	-6.1	505	33	1,083
Burke	1	48	–	–	–	560	-12.4	27,559	600	29,528	-14.2	380	15	738
Burleigh	317	437	2	470	648	10,792	11.4	14,620	12,260	16,608	10.4	7,960	905	1,226
Cass	613	473	2	596	460	14,621	7.6	11,159	16,340	12,471	7.6	10,420	1,272	971
Cavalier	7	159	1	25	569	1,096	-4.4	25,312	1,255	28,984	-4.1	775	38	878
Dickey	5	90	1	25	449	1,142	-5.5	20,813	1,250	22,781	-6.6	865	71	1,294
Divide	1	46	1	12	547	505	-10.3	23,499	600	27,920	-5.4	400	14	651
Dunn	–	–	–	–	–	533	-7.3	15,485	685	19,901	-6.4	435	33	959
Eddy	1	38	–	–	–	655	-6.0	24,943	705	26,847	-6.0	450	38	1,447
Emmons	–	–	1	20	509	1,047	-6.2	27,230	1,170	30,429	-4.3	730	50	1,300
Foster	6	170	1	49	1,389	839	-1.9	23,436	885	24,721	-3.3	580	41	1,145
Golden Valley	2	113	–	–	–	427	-6.2	24,554	460	26,452	-3.2	310	13	748
Grand Forks	246	373	2	353	535	7,351	4.0	11,148	8,100	12,284	3.6	5,250	554	840
Grant	5	190	1	46	1,752	664	-6.1	25,392	740	28,298	-6.8	450	34	1,300
Griggs	6	237	1	10	396	629	-8.7	25,190	695	27,833	-8.4	450	31	1,241
Hettinger	–	–	–	–	–	732	-4.2	29,445	775	31,175	-8.4	470	27	1,086
Kidder	2	78	–	–	–	576	-10.1	23,216	675	27,207	-4.4	385	33	1,330
LaMoure	1	22	–	–	–	1,133	-3.2	25,844	1,180	26,916	-8.5	725	47	1,072
Logan	–	–	–	–	–	562	-5.7	27,295	635	30,840	-10.2	375	23	1,117
McHenry	2	36	–	–	–	1,370	-9.2	24,859	1,420	25,767	-8.5	860	69	1,252
McIntosh	6	194	2	109	3,521	1,096	-8.4	36,376	1,150	38,168	-9.7	720	47	1,560
McKenzie	3	54	1	24	436	796	-2.5	14,230	1,035	18,502	7.0	645	64	1,144
McLean	6	68	1	25	284	2,055	-4.6	23,884	2,190	25,453	-4.7	1,375	122	1,418
Mercer	8	95	1	25	297	1,379	0.8	16,487	1,580	18,890	2.0	955	68	813
Morton	21	83	–	–	–	4,361	3.2	17,083	4,755	18,627	3.0	2,890	329	1,289
Mountrail	8	123	1	11	169	1,214	-6.1	18,640	1,390	21,342	-5.2	845	126	1,935
Nelson	4	116	1	19	552	1,040	-5.5	30,374	1,035	30,228	-4.6	705	26	759
Oliver	–	–	–	–	–	225	-3.4	12,410	370	20,408	-4.4	245	16	883
Pembina	6	73	1	85	1,040	1,693	-4.5	21,062	1,815	22,580	-5.5	1,190	66	821
Pierce	10	230	1	180	4,132	1,008	-4.7	23,491	1,140	26,567	-5.3	730	50	1,165
Ramsey	24	209	1	35	305	2,347	-6.5	20,535	2,565	22,443	-4.9	1,620	187	1,636
Ransom	10	172	1	65	1,116	1,139	-6.6	19,604	1,220	20,998	-5.5	795	59	1,015
Renville	2	81	–	–	–	517	-9.5	21,346	605	24,979	-4.6	375	12	495
Richland	23	132	1	–	–	2,610	-5.9	15,052	2,925	16,869	-6.5	1,780	114	657
Rolette	18	130	1	25	181	1,670	6.9	12,046	2,010	14,498	2.2	1,085	712	5,136
Sargent	–	–	–	–	–	839	1.8	20,217	925	22,289	4.5	565	25	602
Sheridan	–	–	–	–	–	418	-8.1	29,231	470	32,867	-8.4	275	36	2,517
Sioux	3	72	–	–	–	310	11.9	7,413	420	10,043	13.2	185	177	4,232
Slope	–	–	–	–	–	90	-2.2	12,694	145	20,451	-12.7	100	3	423
Stark	36	163	1	83	375	4,166	3.6	18,874	4,520	20,478	0.1	2,710	331	1,500
Steele	–	–	–	–	–	403	-10.6	20,080	480	23,916	-13.0	315	9	448
Stutsman	37	177	1	56	268	4,178	-3.6	20,053	4,435	21,286	-3.3	2,820	427	2,049
Towner	5	194	1	98	3,797	587	-12.6	23,074	670	26,336	-9.3	420	11	432
Traill	9	108	2	93	1,117	1,572	-6.0	18,892	1,715	20,611	-5.6	1,135	43	517
Walsh	17	146	2	31	267	2,549	-5.1	21,961	2,790	24,037	-5.6	1,795	118	1,017
Ward	152	269	1	586	1,038	8,516	2.7	15,271	9,160	16,425	1.5	5,745	637	1,142
Wells	3	65	1	131	2,829	1,339	-5.8	29,274	1,385	30,280	-3.6	870	69	1,509
Williams	48	249	2	100	520	3,795	0.7	19,682	4,145	21,497	-2.9	2,585	272	1,411
OHIO	33,103	289	166	33,398	292	[6]1,754,413	[6]3.1	[6]15,304	[7]1,960,946	[7]17,105	[7]2.6	[7]1,207,381	250,364	2,184
Adams	19	67	1	25	88	5,356	7.8	18,823	5,760	20,243	4.7	2,815	1,736	6,101
Allen	290	273	3	637	599	17,063	0.7	16,062	19,885	18,718	1.0	12,380	2,489	2,343
Ashland	63	117	1	70	130	8,113	7.3	14,990	9,585	17,710	8.5	6,295	541	1,000
Ashtabula	80	78	3	242	235	17,916	3.4	17,357	19,675	19,061	4.8	11,605	2,500	2,422
Athens	56	90	2	128	206	7,985	7.1	12,866	8,035	12,947	1.6	4,355	1,992	3,210
Auglaize	55	117	1	90	192	8,530	4.7	18,056	7,915	16,754	1.7	5,120	410	868
Belmont	97	140	3	269	387	13,815	-1.9	19,956	15,900	22,968	-2.2	9,135	2,108	3,045
Brown	38	86	1	59	134	6,342	13.9	14,284	8,170	18,402	18.6	4,430	1,019	2,295
Butler	485	140	4	704	203	44,898	9.0	12,813	52,945	15,109	8.0	31,305	5,505	1,571
Carroll	15	51	–	–	–	3,567	6.5	12,138	5,585	19,004	7.0	3,425	505	1,718
Champaign	20	51	1	12	30	5,707	4.8	14,376	6,850	17,255	5.6	4,200	501	1,262
Clark	242	170	2	362	254	24,825	2.4	17,436	27,390	19,238	2.1	16,620	3,470	2,437
Clermont	287	153	1	124	66	19,143	18.3	10,044	27,335	14,342	4.4	15,940	2,455	1,288
Clinton	83	197	1	87	206	6,564	9.1	15,419	7,110	16,702	-1.3	4,065	701	1,647
Columbiana	113	101	2	283	254	20,099	2.1	18,119	22,350	20,148	2.4	13,120	2,742	2,472
Coshocton	28	76	1	135	364	6,151	2.0	16,649	7,310	19,786	2.3	4,330	725	1,962
Crawford	44	96	2	151	329	8,588	3.2	18,762	9,450	20,645	1.3	6,015	939	2,051
Cuyahoga	8,270	613	19	6,190	459	225,581	-5.0	16,893	241,140	18,059	-5.9	156,185	41,450	3,104
Darke	44	83	1	73	137	8,800	3.7	16,609	10,595	19,997	6.7	6,765	684	1,291
Defiance	63	161	2	86	220	6,417	11.1	16,407	7,455	19,061	10.8	4,475	609	1,557

See footnotes at end of table.

[Includes United States, states, and 3,141 counties/county equivalents defined as of February 22, 2005. For more information on these areas, see Appendix C, Geographic Information]

County	Physicians, 2004[1]		Community hospitals, 2004[3]			Medicare program enrollment, 2005[4]			Social Security program beneficiaries, December 2005				Supplemental Security Income program recipients, 2005	
				Beds										
	Number	Rate per 100,000 persons[2]	Number	Number	Rate per 100,000 persons[2]	Total	Percent change, 2000–2005	Rate per 100,000 persons[2]	Number	Rate per 100,000 persons[2]	Percent change, 2000–2005	Retired workers, number	Number	Rate per 100,000 persons[2]
OHIO—Con.														
Delaware	455	319	1	75	53	11,287	28.7	7,511	15,760	10,488	27.5	10,630	784	522
Erie	144	182	1	269	341	14,316	6.1	18,199	15,465	19,659	3.9	10,095	1,230	1,564
Fairfield	211	155	1	222	163	17,234	12.7	12,450	20,960	15,142	12.6	12,850	1,879	1,357
Fayette	23	82	1	34	121	4,460	3.1	15,816	5,310	18,830	9.5	3,100	807	2,862
Franklin	4,206	387	9	3,860	355	128,032	4.5	11,738	138,390	12,687	4.2	83,510	24,378	2,235
Fulton	45	105	1	172	402	6,846	5.4	15,938	7,350	17,111	6.4	4,695	383	892
Gallia	104	332	1	173	553	5,882	10.1	18,755	6,360	20,279	3.0	3,175	1,625	5,181
Geauga	210	222	2	445	471	11,316	18.3	11,884	14,680	15,417	11.4	10,380	515	541
Greene	398	262	1	111	73	16,292	8.0	10,719	23,450	15,428	10.1	14,765	1,703	1,120
Guernsey	62	150	1	140	340	7,604	5.0	18,491	8,555	20,803	2.5	4,970	1,315	3,198
Hamilton	4,485	551	12	3,351	412	131,181	-2.4	16,262	136,155	16,879	-3.0	85,260	20,668	2,562
Hancock	137	187	1	104	142	9,978	6.8	13,575	12,105	16,469	5.7	8,080	802	1,091
Hardin	21	65	1	25	78	4,856	2.2	15,160	5,555	17,342	3.5	3,275	587	1,833
Harrison	12	75	1	25	157	3,307	1.4	20,773	3,530	22,173	0.5	1,975	491	3,084
Henry	19	65	1	25	85	4,795	4.0	16,280	5,370	18,232	2.2	3,350	292	991
Highland	36	84	2	80	188	6,851	5.1	16,000	8,170	19,081	6.7	4,600	1,092	2,550
Hocking	23	80	1	92	319	4,352	7.2	15,002	5,365	18,494	7.6	2,970	838	2,889
Holmes	37	90	1	40	97	3,218	7.3	7,742	3,930	9,455	5.8	2,490	316	760
Huron	89	148	3	213	354	10,343	6.3	17,128	9,940	16,641	4.0	6,100	891	1,476
Jackson	22	66	–	–	–	5,534	6.0	16,507	6,520	19,448	6.9	3,085	1,560	4,653
Jefferson	106	149	1	338	474	15,874	-1.8	22,485	17,300	24,505	-1.6	9,500	2,389	3,384
Knox	78	135	1	82	142	9,157	9.5	15,680	10,510	17,997	8.4	6,380	970	1,661
Lake	370	159	1	318	137	37,718	5.6	16,225	42,175	18,142	5.5	28,580	1,956	841
Lawrence	52	83	–	–	–	11,984	6.9	18,988	13,700	21,707	7.1	6,255	3,787	6,000
Licking	162	106	1	233	152	21,087	11.9	13,622	25,650	16,569	12.6	15,750	2,430	1,570
Logan	44	95	1	110	236	7,464	3.3	16,024	8,215	17,636	6.5	5,125	629	1,350
Lorain	509	173	4	640	218	42,778	8.6	14,437	50,135	16,920	8.8	31,015	5,248	1,771
Lucas	1,907	423	9	2,524	561	66,714	-1.1	14,884	74,475	16,615	-1.2	44,600	14,444	3,222
Madison	37	90	1	43	105	6,111	11.9	14,798	6,255	15,147	9.2	3,880	541	1,310
Mahoning	802	313	2	855	334	49,117	-4.8	19,317	54,150	21,296	-4.2	32,825	7,320	2,879
Marion	121	183	1	131	198	10,929	2.7	16,576	11,930	18,094	1.7	6,735	1,792	2,718
Medina	261	158	3	218	132	20,408	16.7	12,220	24,020	14,382	15.4	15,950	951	569
Meigs	7	30	–	–	–	3,941	4.3	16,964	4,745	20,424	9.2	2,285	1,100	4,735
Mercer	41	100	1	60	146	6,699	2.2	16,259	7,535	18,288	0.2	4,935	397	964
Miami	128	127	1	178	177	16,379	9.2	16,118	18,525	18,230	7.6	11,965	1,277	1,257
Monroe	6	40	–	–	–	2,866	4.4	19,499	3,515	23,915	9.1	1,880	490	3,334
Montgomery	1,983	361	6	2,029	369	95,903	3.0	17,519	99,960	18,260	1.1	61,430	13,355	2,440
Morgan	1	7	–	–	–	2,396	5.6	16,018	2,985	19,956	3.4	1,675	509	3,403
Morrow	9	26	1	53	156	3,879	10.1	11,302	5,345	15,573	9.3	3,085	474	1,381
Muskingum	168	197	1	405	474	15,589	6.4	18,216	17,245	20,151	4.3	9,970	2,499	2,920
Noble	3	21	–	–	–	1,744	2.8	12,320	2,370	16,742	3.3	1,365	265	1,872
Ottawa	57	138	1	25	60	8,239	4.1	19,813	9,125	21,944	4.5	5,995	386	928
Paulding	5	26	1	25	128	3,050	6.4	15,611	3,765	19,271	6.7	2,110	318	1,628
Perry	9	26	–	–	–	5,679	6.6	16,112	6,230	17,676	4.6	3,170	1,020	2,894
Pickaway	42	81	1	85	163	7,113	11.6	13,424	8,705	16,428	14.3	5,115	1,054	1,989
Pike	33	117	1	33	117	4,518	5.9	16,052	5,695	20,234	6.5	2,765	1,728	6,139
Portage	180	116	1	118	76	19,942	8.1	12,814	23,480	15,087	8.2	14,795	1,945	1,250
Preble	15	35	–	–	–	6,597	6.3	15,512	7,650	17,989	3.7	4,585	509	1,197
Putnam	17	49	–	–	–	5,366	5.7	15,363	5,920	16,949	4.2	3,820	295	845
Richland	243	190	1	328	256	22,364	5.5	17,479	25,305	19,777	6.6	16,060	2,669	2,086
Ross	135	180	1	190	254	11,796	8.2	15,687	13,150	17,487	8.8	7,170	2,471	3,286
Sandusky	55	89	2	304	492	8,998	2.0	14,589	11,430	18,532	2.8	7,015	898	1,456
Scioto	126	164	1	222	290	15,068	1.4	19,681	15,795	20,631	-1.0	7,735	5,314	6,941
Seneca	71	123	2	90	156	10,934	-0.7	19,021	10,965	19,075	-0.1	6,600	908	1,580
Shelby	48	99	1	90	186	6,458	3.6	13,251	7,705	15,810	2.4	4,795	626	1,284
Stark	937	246	5	1,415	372	68,645	3.4	18,036	73,325	19,265	3.1	46,500	6,866	1,804
Summit	1,761	322	6	1,684	308	84,924	0.9	15,537	95,055	17,390	-0.4	60,220	11,213	2,051
Trumbull	306	139	3	497	225	39,158	1.5	17,856	46,315	21,120	1.3	28,625	4,788	2,183
Tuscarawas	116	126	2	164	178	15,924	5.8	17,319	17,680	19,229	5.2	10,925	1,527	1,661
Union	37	83	1	81	181	4,236	9.3	9,259	5,775	12,623	14.3	3,560	404	883
Van Wert	27	92	1	80	273	4,457	(Z)	15,288	5,755	19,740	-1.0	3,690	407	1,396
Vinton	–	–	–	–	–	1,940	9.1	14,446	2,325	17,313	12.3	1,085	522	3,887
Warren	404	213				19,627	22.7	9,982	24,945	12,687	25.7	15,750	1,554	790
Washington	89	142	2	193	308	11,635	6.9	18,703	13,035	20,953	5.4	7,580	1,608	2,585
Wayne	164	145	2	139	123	17,275	9.3	15,194	18,820	16,553	8.2	12,040	1,452	1,277
Williams	45	116	1	113	291	6,393	5.3	16,525	7,020	18,145	5.4	4,675	459	1,186
Wood	237	192	1	97	79	15,629	8.0	12,611	17,580	14,186	7.0	11,120	1,116	901
Wyandot	18	79	1	25	110	3,976	1.8	17,429	4,290	18,805	1.9	2,755	247	1,083

See footnotes at end of table.

Table B-6. Counties — Physicians, Community Hospitals, Medicare, Social Security, and Supplemental Security Income—Con.

[Includes United States, states, and 3,141 counties/county equivalents defined as of February 22, 2005. For more information on these areas, see Appendix C, Geographic Information]

County	Physicians, 2004[1] Number	Physicians, 2004[1] Rate per 100,000 persons[2]	Community hospitals, 2004[3] Number	Community hospitals, 2004[3] Beds Number	Community hospitals, 2004[3] Beds Rate per 100,000 persons[2]	Medicare program enrollment, 2005[4] Total	Medicare program enrollment, 2005[4] Percent change, 2000–2005	Medicare program enrollment, 2005[4] Rate per 100,000 persons[2]	Social Security program beneficiaries, December 2005 Number	Social Security program beneficiaries, December 2005 Rate per 100,000 persons[2]	Social Security program beneficiaries, December 2005 Percent change, 2000–2005	Social Security program beneficiaries, December 2005 Retired workers, number	Supplemental Security Income program recipients, 2005 Number	Supplemental Security Income program recipients, 2005 Rate per 100,000 persons[2]
OKLAHOMA	6,846	194	109	10,804	307	[6]539,461	[6]6.2	[6]15,205	[7]635,619	[7]17,915	[7]7.0	[7]388,090	79,743	2,248
Adair	13	60	1	31	143	3,405	8.0	15,486	4,130	18,783	10.5	2,110	924	4,202
Alfalfa	–	–	–	–	–	1,296	-4.1	22,638	1,385	24,192	-2.3	930	55	961
Atoka	–	–	1	25	175	2,204	2.0	15,246	3,265	22,586	18.9	1,830	622	4,303
Beaver	2	37	1	15	275	920	-8.6	17,104	1,115	20,729	-0.1	700	51	948
Beckham	35	190	2	101	549	3,111	-4.2	16,478	3,780	20,021	-0.8	2,260	565	2,993
Blaine	8	62	2	56	435	2,019	-1.1	15,701	2,330	18,120	-2.8	1,410	238	1,851
Bryan	30	80	1	120	319	6,811	3.9	18,011	7,780	20,574	4.3	4,500	1,324	3,501
Caddo	12	40	2	40	132	5,318	-0.9	17,592	5,960	19,716	-2.2	3,445	876	2,898
Canadian	76	80	2	94	98	10,350	21.7	10,486	13,090	13,262	21.7	8,565	935	947
Carter	71	151	1	199	424	9,190	4.3	19,501	9,925	21,061	4.2	5,860	1,321	2,803
Cherokee	57	129	1	75	170	6,138	11.1	13,740	7,605	17,024	11.9	4,335	1,270	2,843
Choctaw	7	45	1	34	221	3,347	1.5	21,880	3,780	24,711	2.2	2,025	935	6,112
Cimarron	4	138	1	20	688	589	-5.2	20,791	700	24,709	-5.3	435	47	1,659
Cleveland	375	170	1	324	147	19,667	17.8	8,745	28,880	12,841	23.3	18,375	2,468	1,097
Coal	2	34	1	95	1,611	1,178	-2.1	20,512	1,300	22,636	-1.7	735	255	4,440
Comanche	231	204	2	445	394	13,701	9.1	12,186	16,390	14,578	9.1	9,360	2,473	2,200
Cotton	3	46	–	–	–	1,126	-8.4	17,089	1,360	20,640	-1.8	840	155	2,352
Craig	19	127	1	58	388	3,392	5.3	22,496	3,460	22,947	3.4	2,035	549	3,641
Creek	37	54	2	42	61	10,306	13.4	15,000	13,295	19,350	9.9	7,890	1,350	1,965
Custer	27	107	2	74	294	3,893	2.9	15,444	4,445	17,633	2.5	2,840	543	2,154
Delaware	31	79	1	50	128	6,610	13.3	16,886	8,845	22,595	14.1	5,605	977	2,496
Dewey	2	43	1	18	387	1,031	-3.7	22,570	1,115	24,409	-2.8	690	67	1,467
Ellis	6	151	1	27	679	911	-3.7	22,988	985	24,855	-5.8	655	50	1,262
Garfield	130	227	2	311	543	10,378	1.3	18,220	11,815	20,743	2.5	7,420	1,206	2,117
Garvin	17	63	1	50	184	6,024	1.2	22,124	6,775	24,882	1.3	3,980	901	3,309
Grady	40	83	1	99	205	6,483	5.1	13,132	8,555	17,329	9.0	5,120	1,067	2,161
Grant	2	42	–	–	–	1,057	-8.0	22,118	1,230	25,738	-3.5	760	58	1,214
Greer	5	85	1	17	288	1,347	-4.1	22,827	1,465	24,826	-6.0	910	189	3,203
Harmon	2	67	1	20	667	614	-14.7	20,264	725	23,927	-10.9	430	154	5,083
Harper	2	59	1	25	739	786	-9.0	23,725	790	23,845	-22.2	525	34	1,026
Haskell	3	25	1	31	256	2,595	4.1	21,300	3,040	24,953	5.1	1,690	481	3,948
Hughes	4	29	1	25	179	2,888	-5.4	20,875	3,290	23,780	-2.7	1,910	490	3,542
Jackson	44	162	1	101	373	3,711	-0.3	13,994	4,315	16,272	-0.3	2,640	675	2,545
Jefferson	1	15	1	25	386	1,535	-5.2	23,758	1,650	25,538	-6.4	970	185	2,863
Johnston	6	58	1	25	241	2,029	4.5	19,778	2,505	24,418	4.2	1,380	439	4,279
Kay	64	137	2	131	280	9,187	-0.5	19,765	10,515	22,623	1.0	6,390	885	1,904
Kingfisher	9	64	1	25	177	2,415	3.5	16,886	2,630	18,389	(Z)	1,680	180	1,259
Kiowa	7	71	1	38	387	2,194	-3.9	22,279	2,510	25,487	-2.9	1,485	386	3,920
Latimer	20	188	1	26	245	1,505	3.9	14,151	2,745	25,811	5.1	1,525	445	4,184
Le Flore	15	31	1	72	146	8,981	7.9	18,133	10,290	20,776	7.9	5,380	1,964	3,965
Lincoln	10	31	1	19	59	5,071	6.1	15,694	6,615	20,473	10.6	3,825	692	2,142
Logan	13	36	1	25	68	4,051	6.4	10,980	6,050	16,398	15.4	3,885	577	1,564
Love	2	22	1	25	275	1,634	6.2	17,905	2,025	22,189	10.1	1,270	198	2,170
McClain	17	58	1	30	103	4,587	17.5	15,241	5,250	17,444	17.2	3,285	427	1,419
McCurtain	12	35	1	73	215	5,925	2.0	17,431	7,210	21,211	5.5	3,755	1,593	4,686
McIntosh	8	40	1	33	166	4,925	3.9	24,668	5,565	27,874	4.8	3,480	684	3,426
Major	3	41	1	25	339	1,473	1.3	20,003	1,800	24,443	1.2	1,155	89	1,209
Marshall	4	29	1	20	143	2,970	7.0	20,538	3,545	24,514	8.1	2,330	406	2,808
Mayes	21	54	1	52	133	6,749	10.5	17,099	8,510	21,560	7.4	4,950	1,021	2,587
Murray	12	94	1	25	197	2,429	0.6	18,859	2,900	22,516	1.0	1,770	294	2,283
Muskogee	139	197	2	254	360	13,307	6.1	18,847	15,090	21,372	8.0	8,685	2,431	3,443
Noble	7	62	1	26	231	2,034	7.5	18,143	2,440	21,764	7.6	1,450	259	2,310
Nowata	1	9	1	10	93	2,106	1.7	19,385	2,545	23,426	3.0	1,550	233	2,145
Okfuskee	4	34	–	–	–	2,276	0.8	19,906	2,695	23,570	6.0	1,530	533	4,662
Oklahoma	2,764	407	14	3,168	466	97,221	7.4	14,202	105,055	15,347	4.5	67,225	15,212	2,222
Okmulgee	21	53	3	143	360	6,945	2.3	17,480	8,755	22,035	7.8	5,005	1,353	3,405
Osage	9	20	4	342	759	3,948	6.1	8,693	8,745	19,255	11.8	5,210	812	1,788
Ottawa	31	94	1	100	305	7,356	2.1	22,382	8,295	25,239	3.2	4,960	1,080	3,286
Pawnee	5	30	2	37	220	2,924	5.9	17,343	3,810	22,598	6.6	2,255	355	2,106
Payne	102	147	2	184	265	8,679	7.5	12,551	9,930	14,360	7.1	6,190	1,041	1,505
Pittsburg	67	151	1	163	368	8,385	5.5	18,783	10,605	23,756	8.0	6,275	1,413	3,165
Pontotoc	75	214	1	156	445	6,525	3.2	18,460	7,625	21,572	2.8	4,410	1,156	3,271
Pottawatomie	77	114	1	104	154	10,653	8.0	15,604	12,895	18,888	9.5	7,660	1,679	2,459
Pushmataha	4	34	1	37	315	2,535	3.6	21,680	3,055	26,127	5.8	1,710	588	5,029
Roger Mills	3	92	1	15	461	699	-1.7	21,111	810	24,464	-1.2	515	54	1,631
Rogers	64	81	1	46	58	9,636	22.9	11,932	13,280	16,444	22.4	8,250	949	1,175
Seminole	10	40	1	29	117	4,876	-1.1	19,685	5,545	22,386	-1.2	3,110	971	3,920
Sequoyah	13	32	1	41	101	7,078	10.9	17,319	9,020	22,071	13.7	4,735	1,719	4,206
Stephens	40	94	1	98	229	8,017	-2.4	18,668	10,270	23,914	0.5	6,330	942	2,193
Texas	11	54	1	47	232	2,186	-0.1	10,869	2,635	13,102	-0.5	1,660	171	850

See footnotes at end of table.

[Includes United States, states, and 3,141 counties/county equivalents defined as of February 22, 2005. For more information on these areas, see Appendix C, Geographic Information]

County	Physicians, 2004[1] Number	Physicians, 2004[1] Rate per 100,000 persons[2]	Community hospitals, 2004[3] Number	Beds Number	Beds Rate per 100,000 persons[2]	Medicare program enrollment, 2005[4] Total	Medicare Percent change, 2000–2005	Medicare Rate per 100,000 persons[2]	Social Security program beneficiaries, December 2005 Number	SS Rate per 100,000 persons[2]	SS Percent change, 2000–2005	Retired workers, number	Supplemental Security Income program recipients, 2005 Number	SSI Rate per 100,000 persons[2]
OKLAHOMA—Con.														
Tillman	5	57	1	55	630	1,759	−7.6	20,663	2,020	23,728	−7.9	1,210	319	3,747
Tulsa	1,744	307	8	2,016	355	87,218	6.1	15,246	91,495	15,994	6.7	57,900	10,235	1,789
Wagoner	19	30	1	100	159	5,263	13.6	8,200	10,325	16,087	20.6	6,335	992	1,546
Washington	80	163	1	132	269	10,167	4.3	20,686	11,490	23,378	4.2	7,510	868	1,766
Washita	2	17	1	25	218	2,297	−1.0	20,024	2,510	21,881	−5.5	1,550	248	2,162
Woods	6	71	1	117	1,375	1,682	−8.4	19,682	1,830	21,414	−6.1	1,225	94	1,100
Woodward	22	116	1	68	360	3,061	6.3	16,036	3,610	18,912	3.6	2,310	266	1,394
OREGON	10,957	305	58	6,505	181	[6]536,992	[6]9.7	[6]14,748	[7]618,624	[7]16,990	[7]10.0	[7]414,216	60,701	1,667
Baker	23	140	1	75	456	3,698	5.6	22,705	4,205	25,818	5.0	2,765	359	2,204
Benton	282	360	1	134	171	9,090	11.7	11,559	11,210	14,255	12.9	7,850	772	982
Clackamas	929	256	4	465	128	46,306	17.0	12,567	55,450	15,049	14.4	38,255	3,579	971
Clatsop	65	179	2	72	198	6,735	8.3	18,303	7,705	20,939	7.9	5,125	660	1,794
Columbia	25	53	–	–	–	6,671	11.7	13,879	8,455	17,591	14.5	5,420	626	1,302
Coos	170	266	3	160	251	14,627	9.7	22,604	17,110	26,441	8.8	10,915	1,822	2,816
Crook	17	79	1	25	117	3,903	24.3	17,687	4,735	21,457	24.7	3,230	295	1,337
Curry	43	194	1	24	108	6,669	7.0	29,736	7,565	33,732	4.2	5,470	500	2,229
Deschutes	441	328	2	220	163	21,254	26.1	15,033	25,940	18,347	24.7	18,085	1,413	999
Douglas	224	217	2	202	196	22,966	12.8	22,040	27,160	26,065	13.4	17,750	2,086	2,002
Gilliam	–	–	–	–	–	438	7.9	24,415	450	25,084	−3.0	320	32	1,784
Grant	6	81	1	68	924	1,617	8.5	22,160	1,820	24,942	7.3	1,265	138	1,891
Harney	8	113	1	20	282	1,399	9.9	20,281	1,645	23,847	8.8	1,265	163	2,363
Hood River	84	398	1	25	119	2,865	3.1	13,461	3,315	15,575	4.0	2,360	221	1,038
Jackson	600	311	3	418	217	35,666	11.4	18,260	41,195	21,091	9.9	28,040	3,074	1,574
Jefferson	23	116	1	78	393	3,371	11.8	16,771	3,815	18,980	14.5	2,660	382	1,900
Josephine	146	183	1	98	123	18,820	9.5	23,303	21,655	26,814	9.8	14,525	1,871	2,317
Klamath	157	241	1	133	204	11,720	9.9	17,706	14,000	21,151	10.2	8,940	1,584	2,393
Lake	6	81	1	68	922	1,702	10.9	23,274	1,975	27,007	10.3	1,325	191	2,612
Lane	926	279	4	603	182	53,725	11.1	16,029	62,270	18,578	11.8	40,795	5,972	1,782
Lincoln	91	201	2	67	148	10,197	4.6	22,170	12,245	26,623	9.0	8,410	962	2,092
Linn	159	148	2	112	104	19,176	11.7	17,607	22,080	20,273	11.1	13,995	2,313	2,124
Malheur	54	172	1	49	156	4,920	3.7	15,704	5,700	18,193	4.1	3,695	684	2,183
Marion	643	213	3	505	167	42,595	5.8	13,953	48,945	16,034	7.5	32,920	5,475	1,794
Morrow	5	43	1	10	86	1,389	9.1	11,906	1,735	14,872	9.9	1,125	171	1,466
Multnomah	3,807	567	7	1,875	279	89,180	0.6	13,253	91,920	13,660	1.2	59,675	15,611	2,320
Polk	86	127	1	6	9	10,595	20.0	15,072	12,585	17,903	14.5	8,600	1,039	1,478
Sherman	–	–	–	–	–	424	4.2	24,242	475	27,158	23.7	325	33	1,887
Tillamook	49	197	1	25	100	5,610	4.8	22,194	6,635	26,249	5.0	4,570	418	1,654
Umatilla	99	135	2	70	95	10,256	4.4	13,882	11,755	15,911	5.9	7,685	1,286	1,741
Union	51	209	1	63	258	4,363	5.4	17,779	4,985	20,314	7.0	3,255	493	2,009
Wallowa	10	143	1	57	817	1,663	9.8	23,710	1,955	27,873	8.9	1,370	116	1,654
Wasco	58	246	1	49	208	4,626	5.4	19,608	5,195	22,019	2.8	3,525	537	2,276
Washington	1,510	310	2	626	128	45,111	14.4	9,026	55,695	11,144	15.4	38,590	4,723	945
Wheeler	1	68	–	–	–	352	−6.1	24,192	455	31,271	0.4	330	23	1,581
Yamhill	159	175	2	103	114	12,272	11.5	13,311	14,590	15,825	13.8	9,940	1,077	1,168
PENNSYLVANIA	40,832	329	197	40,079	323	[6]2,133,435	[6]1.8	[6]17,164	[7]2,419,005	[7]19,462	[7]2.7	[7]1,561,281	317,808	2,557
Adams	108	110	1	95	97	14,373	11.6	14,409	18,255	18,301	13.4	12,830	908	910
Allegheny	7,323	587	22	6,048	485	232,506	−4.5	18,814	257,525	20,838	−3.4	164,925	31,591	2,556
Armstrong	66	92	1	147	206	15,842	0.3	22,444	16,740	23,716	0.7	9,470	2,098	2,972
Beaver	260	146	2	567	318	35,727	−0.6	20,142	41,805	23,568	0.1	25,440	4,234	2,387
Bedford	35	70	1	27	54	9,721	6.4	19,407	11,420	22,799	8.9	7,090	1,227	2,450
Berks	779	199	3	960	245	62,741	3.5	15,831	72,910	18,397	5.9	50,490	7,387	1,864
Blair	331	260	5	474	373	25,294	1.7	19,949	26,375	20,801	7.3	16,380	4,552	3,590
Bradford	258	413	3	414	662	11,848	5.2	18,946	14,145	22,619	8.8	8,860	1,959	3,133
Bucks	1,572	255	6	1,155	187	88,714	11.0	14,278	103,965	16,732	10.0	70,995	5,883	947
Butler	303	168	2	433	240	29,189	8.1	16,030	34,105	18,730	9.1	20,845	3,106	1,706
Cambria	429	289	3	605	407	32,424	−3.6	21,897	36,130	24,400	−1.8	21,215	4,683	3,163
Cameron	4	70	–	–	–	1,235	−5.2	21,901	1,425	25,270	−2.9	960	130	2,305
Carbon	58	95	2	272	446	12,628	3.6	20,381	14,795	23,879	8.0	9,330	1,165	1,880
Centre	317	227	2	257	184	17,012	10.3	12,103	19,495	13,869	11.0	13,270	1,666	1,185
Chester	1,357	291	6	878	188	57,399	12.4	12,109	69,315	14,623	11.2	48,135	3,384	714
Clarion	20	49	1	83	205	7,242	5.2	17,842	8,935	22,013	5.0	5,270	1,160	2,858
Clearfield	143	173	2	286	345	15,657	4.2	18,913	18,545	22,402	5.0	11,325	2,497	3,016
Clinton	42	113	2	245	657	6,871	1.3	18,353	8,030	21,448	2.6	5,230	1,014	2,708
Columbia	101	156	2	409	630	12,477	5.4	19,213	13,550	20,866	3.9	9,045	1,331	2,050
Crawford	137	153	2	304	339	16,699	5.1	18,670	19,090	21,343	5.2	11,770	2,710	3,030
Cumberland	682	308	3	547	247	37,656	8.3	16,879	39,855	17,865	10.5	28,780	1,858	833
Dauphin	1,256	496	2	1,111	439	39,579	2.4	15,583	44,885	17,672	3.6	30,250	5,529	2,177
Delaware	2,720	491	4	1,474	266	88,354	−3.4	15,901	98,050	17,646	−3.3	64,545	9,766	1,758
Elk	48	141	1	221	651	6,803	3.2	20,261	8,005	23,841	4.3	5,300	646	1,924
Erie	624	222	6	1,136	404	46,206	2.2	16,476	53,415	19,046	3.7	33,520	9,057	3,229

See footnotes at end of table.

Table B-6. Counties — **Physicians, Community Hospitals, Medicare, Social Security, and Supplemental Security Income**—Con.

[Includes United States, states, and 3,141 counties/county equivalents defined as of February 22, 2005. For more information on these areas, see Appendix C, Geographic Information]

County	Physicians, 2004[1] Number	Physicians, 2004[1] Rate per 100,000 persons[2]	Community hospitals, 2004[3] Number	Beds Number	Beds Rate per 100,000 persons[2]	Medicare program enrollment, 2005[4] Total	Medicare Percent change, 2000–2005	Medicare Rate per 100,000 persons[2]	Social Security beneficiaries Dec 2005 Number	Social Security Rate per 100,000 persons[2]	Social Security Percent change, 2000–2005	Retired workers, number	Supplemental Security Income recipients, 2005 Number	Supplemental Security Income Rate per 100,000 persons[2]
PENNSYLVANIA—Con.														
Fayette	177	121	3	344	234	30,903	−0.9	21,146	34,455	23,576	1.3	18,170	8,507	5,821
Forest	–	–	–	–	–	1,482	10.5	25,823	1,650	28,751	5.2	1,055	141	2,457
Franklin	221	164	2	293	217	23,801	11.9	17,321	28,230	20,545	13.8	19,310	2,071	1,507
Fulton	4	27	1	82	563	2,639	14.7	17,985	3,155	21,502	15.4	1,925	342	2,331
Greene	35	87	1	45	112	7,179	−0.2	18,034	8,075	20,285	−2.8	4,200	1,904	4,783
Huntingdon	54	118	1	71	155	8,089	7.4	17,605	9,295	20,230	8.8	5,875	1,112	2,420
Indiana	127	143	1	162	182	15,498	4.7	17,472	17,565	19,802	2.5	10,350	2,532	2,854
Jefferson	51	111	2	106	231	9,490	3.4	20,739	10,525	23,001	3.7	6,590	1,412	3,086
Juniata	6	26	–	–	–	3,963	12.7	16,859	4,590	19,526	10.2	2,980	437	1,859
Lackawanna	575	274	6	989	471	43,661	−2.6	20,838	49,950	23,840	0.3	32,015	5,851	2,793
Lancaster	936	192	4	1,034	213	75,993	9.1	15,491	86,915	17,717	10.0	60,880	7,640	1,557
Lawrence	129	138	2	356	382	20,965	−2.7	22,589	22,160	23,877	−2.3	13,300	2,925	3,152
Lebanon	302	243	1	176	142	22,589	8.0	17,988	26,030	20,728	8.7	18,465	1,813	1,444
Lehigh	1,042	320	4	1,091	335	54,949	5.0	16,629	65,290	19,759	8.2	43,510	7,654	2,316
Luzerne	789	252	7	974	311	65,874	−3.9	21,055	75,710	24,199	−1.7	49,125	8,609	2,752
Lycoming	252	213	2	439	370	22,014	2.7	18,594	25,035	21,145	4.5	16,395	3,175	2,682
McKean	67	150	2	211	472	8,683	0.6	19,570	10,210	23,011	0.7	6,445	1,581	3,563
Mercer	217	181	3	550	459	24,527	1.5	20,508	28,235	23,608	2.9	16,985	3,949	3,302
Mifflin	72	156	1	123	266	8,939	3.4	19,334	10,615	22,959	6.7	6,675	1,447	3,130
Monroe	234	147	1	192	121	22,202	14.5	13,601	27,755	17,003	14.3	16,930	2,210	1,354
Montgomery	5,101	660	10	2,281	295	129,606	3.5	16,704	134,240	17,302	2.6	95,550	6,531	842
Montour	458	2,545	2	408	2,267	3,666	5.4	20,331	4,060	22,516	6.2	2,720	467	2,590
Northampton	787	278	2	666	235	48,289	3.2	16,781	54,395	18,902	4.3	37,305	4,488	1,560
Northumberland	91	98	2	175	189	19,834	−1.0	21,417	22,780	24,598	0.1	14,540	2,525	2,726
Perry	21	47	–	–	–	6,614	8.6	14,787	7,615	17,025	16.1	4,795	602	1,346
Philadelphia	7,332	498	25	7,172	487	223,649	−6.2	15,284	245,920	16,806	−6.6	144,810	94,548	6,461
Pike	56	104	–	–	–	7,504	21.4	13,320	11,100	19,703	22.0	7,105	538	955
Potter	29	162	1	124	691	3,532	4.8	19,805	4,260	23,887	8.0	2,720	514	2,882
Schuylkill	191	130	4	563	382	31,243	−3.6	21,189	35,820	24,293	−1.5	22,845	3,208	2,176
Snyder	42	110	–	–	–	6,241	3.4	16,335	7,405	19,381	6.4	4,825	544	1,424
Somerset	103	130	3	256	323	15,928	1.7	20,186	18,175	23,033	3.0	11,035	2,225	2,820
Sullivan	3	47	–	–	–	1,549	3.5	24,237	1,825	28,556	−7.2	1,245	128	2,003
Susquehanna	37	88	2	121	288	7,670	3.6	18,208	9,735	23,110	8.0	6,225	931	2,210
Tioga	54	129	1	83	199	8,204	8.4	19,698	9,720	23,338	7.4	6,100	1,235	2,965
Union	128	299	1	136	317	6,510	9.8	15,094	7,335	17,006	9.9	5,150	537	1,245
Venango	98	175	1	209	372	11,332	1.7	20,262	13,750	24,585	2.8	7,810	2,007	3,589
Warren	80	188	1	105	247	8,268	2.5	19,670	10,030	23,862	4.3	6,525	896	2,132
Washington	395	192	3	622	303	41,149	0.3	19,936	47,755	23,136	2.0	28,585	5,330	2,582
Wayne	64	129	1	90	181	12,239	9.3	24,423	12,555	25,053	5.5	8,240	909	1,814
Westmoreland	695	189	5	855	232	72,802	1.1	19,803	85,345	23,215	2.6	53,150	7,907	2,151
Wyoming	19	67	1	58	206	5,027	11.3	17,852	5,875	20,863	11.3	3,615	628	2,230
York	785	196	4	769	192	61,760	11.2	15,108	73,090	17,879	12.4	49,930	6,257	1,531
RHODE ISLAND	4,141	383	11	2,397	222	[6]173,100	[6]0.9	[6]16,085	[7]192,829	[7]17,918	[7]0.1	128,395	30,164	2,803
Bristol	275	520	–	–	–	9,005	0.8	17,073	10,175	19,292	−1.0	7,275	702	1,331
Kent	531	309	1	320	186	29,760	2.2	17,344	33,680	19,628	1.4	22,395	3,070	1,789
Newport	262	309	1	130	153	14,404	5.1	17,201	15,960	19,059	4.9	11,115	1,272	1,519
Providence	2,691	419	7	1,739	271	100,732	−1.8	15,748	110,975	17,349	−2.5	72,190	23,716	3,708
Washington	382	297	2	208	162	19,076	10.7	14,849	22,035	17,153	9.5	15,420	1,404	1,093
SOUTH CAROLINA	10,761	256	62	11,222	267	[6]644,853	[6]13.6	[6]15,155	778,480	18,295	13.1	[7]471,731	105,553	2,481
Abbeville	24	91	1	40	152	3,986	2.9	15,253	5,505	21,065	6.9	3,370	658	2,518
Aiken	233	157	1	269	181	23,761	15.6	15,822	29,025	19,327	14.7	18,105	3,634	2,420
Allendale	8	73	1	69	627	1,653	3.2	15,142	1,950	17,862	−0.5	1,055	751	6,879
Anderson	369	213	1	412	237	30,123	11.9	17,163	37,775	21,522	12.0	22,920	3,622	2,064
Bamberg	14	88	1	128	803	2,648	4.8	16,675	3,305	20,812	5.8	1,895	814	5,126
Barnwell	15	64	1	33	141	3,691	5.8	15,811	4,140	17,734	6.5	2,345	1,058	4,532
Beaufort	565	422	2	286	214	24,258	27.4	17,598	28,895	20,961	23.8	21,015	1,749	1,269
Berkeley	123	83	–	–	–	14,502	22.6	9,561	21,900	14,439	20.8	11,610	2,920	1,925
Calhoun	6	39	–	–	–	1,845	2.8	12,219	2,970	19,669	15.8	1,730	510	3,377
Charleston	2,494	762	6	1,481	452	47,078	9.7	14,250	51,260	15,516	7.8	31,715	7,408	2,242
Cherokee	51	95	1	125	233	8,197	10.5	15,224	11,040	20,504	11.4	6,015	1,370	2,544
Chester	31	92	1	154	459	5,837	6.1	17,567	7,045	21,202	4.4	4,055	927	2,790
Chesterfield	34	79	1	59	137	6,832	8.1	15,729	8,690	20,007	8.2	4,820	1,655	3,810
Clarendon	35	106	1	56	169	5,696	13.6	17,073	7,275	21,806	13.5	4,145	1,778	5,329
Colleton	52	132	1	131	332	6,399	9.6	16,157	8,275	20,894	5.8	4,445	1,824	4,605
Darlington	78	115	1	120	178	10,345	7.9	15,361	13,390	19,882	8.6	7,610	2,853	4,236
Dillon	26	83	1	86	276	4,857	6.6	15,681	5,875	18,968	4.6	3,070	1,788	5,773
Dorchester	110	103	1	80	75	13,541	23.7	11,998	16,710	14,806	22.3	9,265	2,141	1,897
Edgefield	14	55	1	40	158	2,683	4.9	10,510	4,160	16,296	14.3	2,480	682	2,672
Fairfield	18	75	1	25	104	3,771	7.0	15,682	4,650	19,337	9.2	2,685	858	3,568

See footnotes at end of table.

County and City Data Book: 2007

283

U.S. Census Bureau

[Includes United States, states, and 3,141 counties/county equivalents defined as of February 22, 2005. For more information on these areas, see Appendix C, Geographic Information]

County	Physicians, 2004[1]		Community hospitals, 2004[3]			Medicare program enrollment, 2005[4]			Social Security program beneficiaries, December 2005				Supplemental Security Income program recipients, 2005	
				Beds										
	Number	Rate per 100,000 persons[2]	Number	Number	Rate per 100,000 persons[2]	Total	Percent change, 2000–2005	Rate per 100,000 persons[2]	Number	Rate per 100,000 persons[2]	Percent change, 2000–2005	Retired workers, number	Number	Rate per 100,000 persons[2]
SOUTH CAROLINA—Con.														
Florence	410	316	4	654	504	21,116	12.8	16,107	23,440	17,880	11.7	13,145	5,238	3,996
Georgetown	125	209	2	218	364	14,746	23.1	24,181	15,440	25,319	26.1	9,315	1,562	2,561
Greenville	1,327	331	5	1,204	300	60,299	12.7	14,802	70,135	17,216	13.5	44,440	7,519	1,846
Greenwood	233	345	1	351	519	12,094	9.1	17,791	13,925	20,484	8.4	8,825	1,580	2,324
Hampton	16	75	1	25	117	3,980	8.2	18,660	4,155	19,481	3.0	2,085	1,003	4,703
Horry	445	204	3	656	301	38,030	26.8	16,754	50,710	22,340	26.4	33,650	4,571	2,014
Jasper	22	103	–	–	–	2,512	11.0	11,739	3,455	16,146	36.9	1,860	669	3,126
Kershaw	77	139	1	195	352	9,261	11.6	16,395	11,155	19,748	13.1	6,690	1,310	2,319
Lancaster	66	105	1	194	308	9,654	11.8	15,296	12,310	19,505	14.7	7,440	1,349	2,137
Laurens	62	88	1	90	128	10,727	7.2	15,260	14,780	21,026	10.9	8,125	2,060	2,931
Lee	4	19	–	–	–	2,909	3.7	14,095	3,735	18,098	3.5	1,960	1,118	5,417
Lexington	400	173	1	312	135	29,653	20.6	12,604	36,385	15,465	18.4	23,455	3,290	1,398
McCormick	8	79	–	–	–	2,293	20.9	22,685	2,645	26,167	10.9	1,815	316	3,126
Marion	42	120	1	124	354	6,184	7.4	17,717	6,905	19,783	6.6	3,755	1,746	5,002
Marlboro	23	81	1	98	346	4,902	3.1	17,494	6,055	21,609	3.7	3,100	1,573	5,614
Newberry	38	102	1	77	208	6,738	5.7	18,089	7,710	20,698	5.5	4,845	979	2,628
Oconee	147	213	1	201	291	14,379	17.0	20,666	17,405	25,015	16.8	11,290	1,272	1,828
Orangeburg	164	178	1	286	310	15,579	7.1	16,903	18,330	19,888	6.1	10,540	4,092	4,440
Pickens	170	151	2	121	107	18,189	15.8	16,015	20,900	18,402	14.6	12,975	1,751	1,542
Richland	1,540	459	4	1,389	414	40,628	7.7	11,947	47,190	13,876	8.2	28,340	7,090	2,085
Saluda	6	32	–	–	–	2,516	1.0	13,316	3,730	19,741	9.3	2,395	518	2,741
Spartanburg	639	242	2	633	240	44,117	12.5	16,535	51,855	19,435	11.1	30,045	6,045	2,266
Sumter	158	149	1	246	233	15,214	11.8	14,419	18,240	17,286	8.4	10,600	3,910	3,706
Union	32	112	1	220	768	6,155	5.1	21,567	7,660	26,840	6.2	4,215	1,016	3,560
Williamsburg	18	50	1	34	95	5,878	4.0	16,607	6,735	19,028	-6.7	3,315	2,185	6,173
York	289	157	2	300	163	24,623	20.3	12,953	29,660	15,603	17.5	19,160	2,791	1,468
SOUTH DAKOTA	1,904	247	51	4,611	598	[6]124,590	[6]4.3	[6]16,057	[7]140,773	[7]18,142	[7]3.3	[7]92,131	12,542	1,616
Aurora	–	–	–	–	–	597	-6.3	20,579	680	23,440	-8.6	445	37	1,275
Beadle	29	181	1	61	381	3,540	-2.3	22,270	3,670	23,088	-6.4	2,355	352	2,214
Bennett	1	28	1	62	1,746	442	2.8	12,329	515	14,365	-6.5	290	153	4,268
Bon Homme	6	84	2	53	744	1,490	-6.3	21,024	1,625	22,929	-8.3	1,100	66	931
Brookings	29	103	1	140	499	3,308	3.0	11,763	3,695	13,140	0.3	2,515	217	772
Brown	99	285	1	269	774	6,477	2.5	18,662	6,955	20,040	0.4	4,695	489	1,409
Brule	10	193	1	70	1,350	1,015	1.9	19,568	975	18,797	-12.4	645	69	1,330
Buffalo	1	48	–	–	–	141	9.3	6,714	240	11,429	1.7	105	114	5,429
Butte	5	54	–	–	–	1,699	5.7	18,218	1,845	19,783	-1.4	1,145	162	1,737
Campbell	–	–	–	–	–	670	-3.9	42,812	455	29,073	-9.0	260	17	1,086
Charles Mix	8	88	2	83	914	1,673	-1.4	18,197	1,885	20,503	0.4	1,195	241	2,621
Clark	–	–	–	–	–	892	-8.3	23,480	970	25,533	-10.3	650	76	2,001
Clay	20	154	1	116	891	1,499	0.7	11,535	1,685	12,967	0.8	1,145	131	1,008
Codington	59	227	1	119	458	4,435	6.5	17,051	4,940	18,993	4.3	3,235	329	1,265
Corson	–	–	–	–	–	965	2.3	22,103	550	12,597	-12.7	305	212	4,856
Custer	11	140	1	87	1,110	1,507	11.8	19,066	1,790	22,647	8.2	1,225	112	1,417
Davison	46	243	1	213	1,127	3,517	0.9	18,730	3,845	20,477	0.2	2,490	346	1,843
Day	5	86	1	25	428	1,409	-10.9	24,475	1,590	27,619	-8.9	1,070	120	2,084
Deuel	3	70	1	20	467	933	-3.9	21,718	1,110	25,838	1.6	740	53	1,234
Dewey	5	82	–	–	–	660	8.0	10,713	790	12,823	3.7	435	328	5,324
Douglas	3	90	1	11	332	782	-2.7	23,633	820	24,781	-6.1	505	49	1,481
Edmunds	4	98	1	54	1,318	926	-5.3	22,519	1,010	24,562	-5.2	680	34	827
Fall River	26	354	1	70	954	2,031	4.0	27,614	2,135	29,028	2.4	1,360	179	2,434
Faulk	–	–	1	19	783	629	-10.9	26,362	605	25,356	-13.8	405	44	1,844
Grant	7	93	1	25	333	1,594	-2.0	21,587	1,700	23,023	-3.5	1,125	90	1,210
Gregory	4	92	2	110	2,521	1,208	-7.9	28,159	1,245	29,021	-10.5	790	105	2,448
Haakon	5	253	1	48	2,432	456	8.6	23,849	450	23,536	-1.5	290	15	785
Hamlin	–	–	–	–	–	1,025	-5.9	17,960	1,120	19,625	-6.6	755	60	1,051
Hand	3	88	1	44	1,298	751	-5.7	22,709	930	28,122	-6.1	645	50	1,512
Hanson	–	–	–	–	–	762	58.8	20,336	1,050	28,022	75.6	805	52	1,388
Harding	–	–	–	–	–	202	–	16,585	235	19,294	-2.1	135	10	821
Hughes	29	173	1	165	983	2,405	3.2	14,252	2,795	16,563	2.5	1,880	239	1,416
Hutchinson	13	170	2	184	2,407	1,948	-7.8	25,696	2,130	28,097	-7.6	1,360	106	1,398
Hyde	–	–	–	–	–	356	-4.3	22,057	360	22,305	-15.9	250	20	1,239
Jackson	–	–	–	–	–	379	7.4	13,261	455	15,920	-2.4	290	131	4,584
Jerauld	3	141	1	25	1,175	570	-4.7	26,685	705	33,004	4.3	480	41	1,919
Jones	–	–	–	–	–	221	-1.8	21,394	250	24,201	-1.6	170	5	484
Kingsbury	7	128	1	14	255	1,475	-5.8	26,663	1,430	25,850	-9.7	985	56	1,012
Lake	9	82	1	25	228	2,039	1.1	18,471	2,250	20,382	-0.8	1,545	133	1,205
Lawrence	52	233	2	58	260	3,926	11.5	17,531	4,600	20,540	11.8	2,995	268	1,197
Lincoln	142	450	1	18	57	1,950	2.4	5,842	2,605	7,804	-19.0	1,730	149	446
Lyman	–	–	–	–	–	554	-3.8	14,136	685	17,479	-4.7	425	73	1,863
McCook	4	68	–	–	–	1,095	-5.9	18,465	1,210	20,405	-5.4	780	68	1,147
McPherson	3	112	1	6	224	505	-15.7	19,297	800	30,569	-15.1	520	66	2,522
Marshall	2	46	1	20	457	991	-4.6	22,431	1,105	25,011	-2.7	725	64	1,449

See footnotes at end of table.

Table B-6. Counties — **Physicians, Community Hospitals, Medicare, Social Security, and Supplemental Security Income**—Con.

[Includes United States, states, and 3,141 counties/county equivalents defined as of February 22, 2005. For more information on these areas, see Appendix C, Geographic Information]

County	Physicians, 2004[1] Number	Physicians Rate per 100,000 persons[2]	Community hospitals, 2004[3] Number	Beds Number	Beds Rate per 100,000 persons[2]	Medicare program enrollment, 2005[4] Total	Medicare Percent change, 2000–2005	Medicare Rate per 100,000 persons[2]	Social Security program beneficiaries, December 2005 Number	Social Security Rate per 100,000 persons[2]	Social Security Percent change, 2000–2005	Social Security Retired workers, number	Supplemental Security Income program recipients, 2005 Number	Supplemental Security Income Rate per 100,000 persons[2]
SOUTH DAKOTA—Con.														
Meade	40	162	1	109	442	3,455	6.4	14,032	3,955	16,062	13.7	2,450	279	1,133
Mellette	–	–	–	–	–	271	3.8	12,979	310	14,847	–2.8	175	107	5,125
Miner	–	–	–	–	–	637	–9.1	24,652	675	26,122	–8.0	440	38	1,471
Minnehaha	644	410	4	1,218	775	22,191	14.7	13,862	25,520	15,941	18.2	17,300	2,023	1,264
Moody	2	30	1	18	273	907	–3.5	13,666	1,185	17,854	4.6	755	54	814
Pennington	341	367	1	371	399	13,867	13.9	14,818	16,440	17,568	10.9	10,515	1,588	1,697
Perkins	–	–	1	47	1,514	787	–8.6	26,034	795	26,298	–16.3	505	72	2,382
Potter	4	162	2	84	3,409	713	–5.8	30,328	725	30,838	–9.7	485	16	681
Roberts	9	89	1	27	267	1,723	–3.4	17,155	2,050	20,410	–1.8	1,305	237	2,360
Sanborn	1	38	–	–	–	572	–9.1	22,511	570	22,432	–8.1	385	29	1,141
Shannon	11	82	–	–	–	902	13.2	6,605	1,235	9,043	6.7	465	902	6,605
Spink	9	129	1	25	359	1,673	–3.8	24,250	1,705	24,714	–6.9	1,065	157	2,276
Stanley	1	35	–	–	–	407	5.4	14,387	480	16,967	6.9	335	26	919
Sully	–	–	–	–	–	235	–4.5	16,434	320	22,378	–2.4	215	6	420
Todd	10	103	–	–	–	602	12.3	6,092	795	8,045	10.9	380	466	4,716
Tripp	7	115	1	106	1,736	1,302	–0.9	21,467	1,425	23,495	–4.0	910	138	2,275
Turner	7	81	1	64	743	1,730	–6.2	20,305	1,885	22,124	–7.3	1,210	73	857
Union	65	490	–	–	–	2,172	4.8	16,134	2,365	17,568	10.1	1,615	76	565
Walworth	7	127	1	31	561	855	–5.7	15,562	1,475	26,847	–3.2	1,000	133	2,421
Yankton	93	427	1	297	1,364	3,641	4.9	16,765	4,190	19,293	5.8	2,845	317	1,460
Ziebach	–	–	–	–	–	147	–2.0	5,587	180	6,842	4.7	100	74	2,813
TENNESSEE	16,863	286	127	20,363	346	[6]915,609	[6]10.4	[6]15,355	[7]1,089,649	[7]18,274	[7]10.0	[7]641,443	161,322	2,705
Anderson	206	286	1	161	223	13,969	4.9	19,286	16,790	23,181	5.5	9,495	2,280	3,148
Bedford	31	75	1	176	428	6,081	10.1	14,409	7,455	17,664	13.5	4,620	822	1,948
Benton	7	43	1	30	182	3,798	10.7	23,064	4,550	27,631	9.9	2,700	509	3,091
Bledsoe	5	39	1	28	219	1,668	16.2	12,902	2,490	19,261	24.6	1,430	445	3,442
Blount	225	198	1	258	227	18,901	13.4	16,360	23,720	20,531	17.7	14,355	2,294	1,986
Bradley	158	174	2	234	257	14,380	17.9	15,615	18,155	19,714	19.7	10,865	2,197	2,386
Campbell	40	99	2	210	518	8,823	9.2	21,686	10,425	25,623	6.1	4,800	2,804	6,892
Cannon	8	60	1	55	414	2,245	12.7	16,833	2,785	20,882	8.4	1,730	359	2,692
Carroll	28	95	2	59	201	6,642	3.8	22,808	7,260	24,930	0.3	4,465	831	2,854
Carter	57	97	1	121	206	9,569	10.2	16,256	13,435	22,823	10.4	7,145	2,099	3,566
Cheatham	22	58	1	8	21	4,225	22.3	10,945	5,765	14,934	22.6	3,325	534	1,383
Chester	5	32	–	–	–	2,239	7.1	14,046	3,210	20,137	8.3	1,960	395	2,478
Claiborne	25	81	1	45	146	6,667	13.5	21,484	8,005	25,795	12.0	3,485	2,088	6,728
Clay	4	50	1	34	425	1,258	6.4	15,741	1,990	24,900	7.4	1,090	449	5,618
Cocke	22	63	1	103	297	6,795	13.6	19,454	8,165	23,376	11.8	4,230	1,852	5,302
Coffee	106	211	3	285	569	9,634	14.6	18,939	10,915	21,457	11.9	6,585	1,295	2,546
Crockett	7	48	–	–	–	2,744	0.9	18,801	3,240	22,199	–0.4	1,965	487	3,337
Cumberland	114	227	1	156	311	12,687	21.9	24,709	16,250	31,648	22.8	11,165	1,478	2,879
Davidson	3,503	612	11	3,300	577	75,626	3.8	13,146	82,850	14,402	1.3	52,005	11,735	2,040
Decatur	9	77	1	40	342	2,235	4.8	19,125	3,215	27,512	5.9	2,005	393	3,363
DeKalb	17	94	1	51	281	3,278	8.3	17,958	3,830	20,982	8.5	2,285	610	3,342
Dickson	56	123	1	116	256	6,918	13.8	15,074	8,290	18,063	13.3	4,970	974	2,122
Dyer	66	176	1	105	280	6,582	6.9	17,399	8,065	21,320	7.3	4,450	1,403	3,709
Fayette	13	39	1	10	30	3,828	16.3	11,109	5,920	17,180	8.1	3,460	1,365	3,961
Fentress	13	77	1	71	419	3,707	13.8	21,604	4,485	26,138	12.6	2,270	1,106	6,446
Franklin	55	135	1	198	486	7,011	7.7	17,099	8,900	21,706	8.5	5,575	975	2,378
Gibson	43	90	3	117	244	9,942	1.0	20,649	11,580	24,051	1.6	7,145	1,496	3,107
Giles	30	103	1	95	325	5,302	7.2	18,097	6,420	21,914	8.9	3,855	797	2,720
Grainger	6	27	–	–	–	4,280	20.3	19,207	4,925	22,102	25.8	2,430	932	4,183
Greene	110	170	2	330	511	13,406	13.7	20,524	16,110	24,664	13.0	9,120	2,257	3,455
Grundy	8	55	–	–	–	2,896	9.4	19,825	3,510	24,028	7.9	1,725	843	5,771
Hamblen	145	244	2	278	468	10,159	12.4	16,960	11,980	20,001	2.2	6,780	1,779	2,970
Hamilton	1,310	423	5	1,578	509	52,493	6.2	16,882	59,400	19,104	5.4	37,585	7,396	2,379
Hancock	4	60	–	–	–	1,177	2.3	17,557	1,355	20,212	0.6	600	563	8,398
Hardeman	14	50	1	37	131	4,725	5.1	16,773	5,615	19,933	8.5	2,940	1,491	5,293
Hardin	18	70	1	119	462	4,899	7.0	18,893	6,610	25,492	8.7	3,760	1,139	4,393
Hawkins	38	68	1	50	90	10,106	20.8	17,983	13,150	23,400	20.1	6,390	2,028	3,609
Haywood	15	76	1	62	315	2,870	–0.5	14,601	3,710	18,875	0.2	2,075	1,133	5,764
Henderson	14	53	1	36	137	4,948	7.8	18,725	5,395	20,416	10.1	3,060	735	2,781
Henry	53	169	1	271	865	6,952	6.2	22,062	8,290	26,308	6.2	5,175	869	2,758
Hickman	10	42	1	65	275	3,760	15.5	15,803	4,575	19,228	14.6	2,580	609	2,560
Houston	3	38	1	31	390	1,610	7.0	20,155	1,805	22,596	4.6	1,030	279	3,493
Humphreys	11	61	1	25	138	3,393	9.7	18,631	4,140	22,732	9.4	2,490	447	2,454
Jackson	5	45	–	–	–	1,800	11.8	16,257	2,730	24,657	10.4	1,475	521	4,706
Jefferson	47	99	1	58	122	9,923	21.6	20,505	11,570	23,908	32.8	6,795	1,237	2,556
Johnson	12	67	1	6	33	3,970	15.8	21,914	4,505	24,868	13.3	2,390	850	4,692
Knox	1,865	466	6	1,927	481	60,884	7.8	15,034	68,920	17,018	6.3	42,470	8,692	2,146
Lake	4	52	–	–	–	1,251	–1.4	16,497	1,430	18,858	–1.7	765	338	4,457
Lauderdale	10	37	1	14	52	4,441	3.9	16,574	4,990	18,623	2.6	2,670	1,153	4,303
Lawrence	32	79	1	98	241	8,373	12.9	20,372	9,415	22,907	11.2	5,250	1,221	2,971

See footnotes at end of table.

[Includes United States, states, and 3,141 counties/county equivalents defined as of February 22, 2005. For more information on these areas, see Appendix C, Geographic Information]

County	Physicians, 2004[1]		Community hospitals, 2004[3]			Medicare program enrollment, 2005[4]			Social Security program beneficiaries, December 2005				Supplemental Security Income program recipients, 2005	
	Number	Rate per 100,000 persons[2]	Number	Beds Number	Beds Rate per 100,000 persons[2]	Total	Percent change, 2000-2005	Rate per 100,000 persons[2]	Number	Rate per 100,000 persons[2]	Percent change, 2000-2005	Retired workers, number	Number	Rate per 100,000 persons[2]
TENNESSEE—Con.														
Lewis	6	52	–	–	–	1,854	7.9	16,213	2,470	21,600	6.7	1,370	350	3,061
Lincoln	28	87	1	327	1,022	5,890	8.1	18,184	6,945	21,440	8.1	4,425	802	2,476
Loudon	55	130	1	30	71	9,952	25.1	22,938	11,230	25,883	22.8	7,635	820	1,890
McMinn	67	132	2	143	281	9,189	12.2	17,903	11,390	22,191	13.1	6,585	1,572	3,063
McNairy	17	68	1	38	151	5,815	10.5	22,998	6,450	25,509	10.1	3,640	1,081	4,275
Macon	8	37	1	25	117	3,154	9.7	14,636	4,395	20,395	13.3	2,410	744	3,453
Madison	422	448	2	733	778	14,157	7.2	14,915	16,585	17,473	8.3	9,790	2,820	2,971
Marion	23	83	1	68	246	4,637	9.8	16,706	6,005	21,634	10.4	3,055	977	3,520
Marshall	17	61	1	77	275	4,230	9.8	14,909	5,275	18,592	12.2	3,095	533	1,879
Maury	188	252	1	267	357	11,415	12.1	14,962	13,035	17,086	11.3	7,705	1,505	1,973
Meigs	5	43	–	–	–	2,012	17.0	17,260	2,465	21,146	10.5	1,240	485	4,161
Monroe	31	74	1	59	140	7,532	20.7	17,441	9,545	22,103	16.1	5,290	1,639	3,795
Montgomery	217	153	1	206	145	14,066	18.5	9,556	17,800	12,092	17.7	10,070	2,446	1,662
Moore	2	33	–	–	–	616	9.0	10,226	1,145	19,007	26.0	780	85	1,411
Morgan	4	20	–	–	–	2,926	16.9	14,516	4,490	22,275	-2.6	2,135	852	4,227
Obion	45	139	1	85	262	6,504	6.2	20,191	7,165	22,243	5.0	4,295	905	2,809
Overton	22	108	1	67	328	3,976	12.3	19,373	5,055	24,631	11.2	2,880	824	4,015
Perry	3	39	1	53	696	1,520	5.3	20,069	1,925	25,416	3.3	1,120	215	2,839
Pickett	1	21	–	–	–	915	10.6	18,979	1,395	28,936	3.9	815	215	4,460
Polk	18	113	1	44	276	3,518	11.6	22,065	3,855	24,178	2.5	2,045	593	3,719
Putnam	164	249	1	207	315	12,948	15.4	19,447	13,600	20,427	12.4	8,100	1,584	2,379
Rhea	12	40	1	131	442	5,564	12.0	18,597	6,320	21,124	9.3	3,760	967	3,232
Roane	42	80	1	66	125	11,267	8.9	21,303	13,040	24,655	12.8	7,615	1,751	3,311
Robertson	54	91	1	90	152	8,200	15.4	13,581	10,015	16,587	13.3	5,975	1,121	1,857
Rutherford	349	166	1	199	95	19,922	29.0	9,126	25,190	11,540	28.2	14,775	2,570	1,177
Scott	19	87	1	77	354	3,865	11.8	17,674	4,845	22,156	9.3	1,880	1,582	7,234
Sequatchie	8	65	–	–	–	1,819	22.3	14,333	2,635	20,763	27.4	1,440	443	3,491
Sevier	83	108	1	108	140	13,418	23.6	16,924	16,385	20,667	23.1	10,105	1,549	1,954
Shelby	3,490	385	11	3,447	380	108,625	2.7	11,949	127,370	14,012	3.7	72,590	30,398	3,344
Smith	15	82	2	88	478	2,961	4.9	15,879	3,590	19,252	9.2	2,050	482	2,585
Stewart	3	23	–	–	–	2,357	5.0	18,174	2,975	22,939	7.8	1,690	410	3,161
Sullivan	649	426	4	959	630	32,457	10.0	21,253	38,215	25,024	10.4	21,985	4,347	2,846
Sumner	209	147	2	185	131	18,411	19.5	12,696	23,550	16,240	19.7	14,820	2,310	1,593
Tipton	43	79	1	54	99	6,991	16.7	12,484	8,910	15,911	14.1	4,875	1,555	2,777
Trousdale	4	53	1	25	333	1,138	7.1	14,823	1,590	20,711	9.6	885	273	3,556
Unicoi	16	91	1	94	532	4,230	7.3	24,072	4,495	25,580	12.9	2,430	630	3,585
Union	5	26	–	–	–	2,541	18.0	13,320	3,885	20,366	4.5	1,875	876	4,592
Van Buren	1	18	–	–	–	758	7.2	13,857	1,160	21,207	15.1	690	198	3,620
Warren	44	111	1	127	322	7,382	11.3	18,570	8,325	20,942	7.6	4,965	1,331	3,348
Washington	831	749	4	670	604	21,005	14.0	18,670	23,200	20,621	12.7	13,610	2,736	2,432
Wayne	10	59	1	78	462	2,731	9.0	16,151	3,630	21,468	9.2	2,055	495	2,927
Weakley	34	101	1	65	193	5,561	2.6	16,486	6,970	20,663	3.6	4,420	774	2,295
White	25	105	1	44	184	4,980	11.5	20,534	5,840	24,079	10.2	3,550	804	3,315
Williamson	849	578	1	131	89	14,842	31.1	9,663	17,585	11,449	29.9	12,095	860	560
Wilson	116	119	1	245	251	11,456	21.3	11,398	15,415	15,337	20.8	9,840	1,229	1,223
TEXAS	52,060	232	418	58,116	259	[6]2,522,567	[6]11.4	[6]11,035	[7]2,952,230	[7]12,914	[7]12.1	[7]1,758,929	[6]504,082	[6]2,205
Anderson	75	134	2	146	261	8,023	6.9	14,223	8,595	15,237	9.3	4,985	1,235	2,189
Andrews	11	86	1	88	684	1,901	6.1	14,912	2,215	17,375	1.5	1,185	284	2,358
Angelina	143	176	2	326	401	13,299	9.1	16,306	15,775	19,342	11.7	8,465	2,630	3,225
Aransas	40	167	–	–	–	4,704	17.5	19,091	5,980	24,269	16.7	3,955	581	2,358
Archer	4	43	–	–	–	1,094	3.1	12,029	1,670	18,362	9.2	1,030	121	1,330
Armstrong	1	47	–	–	–	391	3.2	17,994	445	20,479	1.6	305	14	644
Atascosa	29	68	1	47	110	4,949	15.7	11,449	6,750	15,616	14.0	3,415	1,498	3,466
Austin	16	62	1	25	97	4,350	10.2	16,652	4,870	18,643	13.8	3,105	397	1,520
Bailey	6	90	1	25	374	1,098	-0.6	16,325	1,210	17,990	-1.9	730	173	2,572
Bandera	17	86	–	–	–	3,224	15.9	16,130	3,925	19,637	15.7	2,525	282	1,411
Bastrop	37	54	1	150	219	8,004	20.6	11,445	9,280	13,270	38.2	5,665	1,231	1,760
Baylor	2	51	1	38	966	1,007	-7.3	26,203	1,110	28,884	-8.6	720	131	3,409
Bee	22	67	1	63	191	3,684	6.4	11,207	4,290	13,050	2.7	2,275	1,063	3,234
Bell	1,094	437	3	810	323	25,993	16.6	10,151	31,055	12,128	19.8	17,780	4,764	1,861
Bexar	5,592	375	18	4,467	299	178,957	10.9	11,786	206,780	13,619	11.7	117,825	42,869	2,823
Blanco	6	66	–	–	–	2,718	-22.6	29,835	1,840	20,198	16.2	1,260	91	999
Borden	–	–	–	–	–	38	-19.1	5,864	120	18,519	26.3	75	(D)	(NA)
Bosque	18	101	1	40	224	3,779	3.4	20,933	4,215	23,348	5.6	2,815	309	1,712
Bowie	290	322	5	635	704	14,061	1.2	15,513	16,455	18,154	7.2	9,340	3,253	3,589
Brazoria	679	251	3	213	79	27,840	16.9	9,997	33,170	11,911	22.8	19,745	3,650	1,311
Brazos	398	256	2	400	257	12,782	15.7	8,178	14,800	9,469	14.1	9,165	2,164	1,384
Brewster	17	185	1	35	381	1,436	4.3	15,817	1,630	17,954	6.2	1,115	185	2,038
Briscoe	–	–	–	–	–	376	-4.1	22,871	420	25,547	0.5	255	45	2,737
Brooks	2	26	–	–	–	1,423	6.1	18,512	1,640	21,335	4.1	840	641	8,339
Brown	68	178	1	174	455	7,095	3.6	18,350	8,265	21,376	7.7	5,025	1,093	2,827

See footnotes at end of table.

Table B-6. Counties — **Physicians, Community Hospitals, Medicare, Social Security, and Supplemental Security Income**—Con.

[Includes United States, states, and 3,141 counties/county equivalents defined as of February 22, 2005. For more information on these areas, see Appendix C, Geographic Information]

County	Physicians, 2004[1] Number	Physicians, 2004[1] Rate per 100,000 persons[2]	Community hospitals, 2004[3] Number	Beds Number	Beds Rate per 100,000 persons[2]	Medicare program enrollment, 2005[4] Total	Medicare Percent change, 2000–2005	Medicare Rate per 100,000 persons[2]	Social Security program beneficiaries, December 2005 Number	SS Rate per 100,000 persons[2]	SS Percent change, 2000–2005	Retired workers, number	Supplemental Security Income program recipients, 2005 Number	SSI Rate per 100,000 persons[2]
TEXAS—Con.														
Burleson	7	41	1	25	146	3,058	6.8	17,740	3,440	19,956	4.1	2,160	480	2,785
Burnet	57	141	1	28	69	7,098	43.3	17,031	9,150	21,955	18.8	6,240	574	1,377
Caldwell	23	63	2	63	173	4,528	8.2	12,398	5,320	14,566	9.1	3,140	873	2,390
Calhoun	22	107	1	25	122	3,147	7.2	15,272	3,815	18,514	8.6	2,300	429	2,082
Callahan	3	23	–	–	–	2,515	10.0	18,608	3,030	22,418	6.3	1,985	292	2,160
Cameron	577	156	5	1,002	270	39,964	10.8	10,564	46,850	12,384	12.1	26,245	17,968	4,750
Camp	13	109	1	42	351	2,422	6.3	19,791	2,570	21,000	7.8	1,550	395	3,228
Carson	–	–	–	–	–	1,077	3.4	16,353	1,210	18,372	5.6	780	70	1,063
Cass	14	47	2	84	280	6,445	5.5	21,373	7,740	25,667	10.0	4,290	1,124	3,727
Castro	4	52	1	25	325	1,059	1.0	13,861	1,245	16,296	–5.2	720	162	2,120
Chambers	5	18	1	14	50	2,300	10.7	8,095	4,065	14,308	18.7	2,230	465	1,637
Cherokee	72	150	2	68	141	6,876	2.1	14,188	9,455	19,509	5.6	5,660	1,356	2,798
Childress	10	131	1	38	496	1,167	–6.1	15,203	1,275	16,610	–2.8	775	155	2,019
Clay	6	54	1	25	223	1,500	–1.4	13,290	2,265	20,067	3.8	1,410	189	1,674
Cochran	2	60	1	18	541	569	–4.0	17,300	645	19,611	–7.6	340	130	3,953
Coke	3	82	–	–	–	788	–1.4	21,816	935	25,886	1.5	635	52	1,440
Coleman	7	80	1	25	287	2,197	–6.1	25,355	2,450	28,275	–10.9	1,570	280	3,231
Collin	1,545	246	7	962	153	37,734	53.7	5,722	50,540	7,664	49.7	33,365	4,582	695
Collingsworth	1	33	1	16	529	623	–11.1	20,991	710	23,922	–7.7	435	99	3,336
Colorado	31	150	3	99	478	3,866	2.7	18,644	4,525	21,822	4.1	2,910	460	2,218
Comal	191	208	1	132	144	14,991	17.8	15,613	17,230	17,945	22.8	11,535	1,001	1,043
Comanche	13	95	2	33	242	2,809	–0.9	20,490	3,330	24,291	–5.7	2,175	356	2,597
Concho	1	27	1	16	426	533	–6.3	14,270	610	16,332	1.2	380	71	1,901
Cooke	25	65	2	78	203	5,702	5.1	14,678	6,910	17,788	7.5	4,520	591	1,521
Coryell	22	29	1	138	184	5,554	13.8	7,327	7,210	9,512	18.8	4,025	848	1,119
Cottle	–	–	–	–	–	459	–6.9	26,289	510	29,210	–6.9	325	63	3,608
Crane	3	77	1	25	646	497	4.0	12,953	590	15,377	1.2	315	78	2,033
Crockett	–	–	–	–	–	562	4.9	14,286	655	16,650	1.9	385	82	2,084
Crosby	2	30	1	25	376	1,103	–3.1	16,497	1,310	19,593	–3.9	745	218	3,261
Culberson	–	–	1	14	523	356	13.4	13,552	465	17,701	4.5	265	114	4,340
Dallam	5	81	1	102	1,651	1,275	3.9	20,651	915	14,820	0.3	550	107	1,733
Dallas	7,091	310	29	6,455	282	222,201	8.2	9,638	244,740	10,616	7.7	150,370	42,024	1,823
Dawson	9	63	1	38	267	2,207	–4.8	15,481	2,495	17,501	–8.2	1,430	485	3,402
Deaf Smith	12	65	1	35	189	2,477	3.9	13,362	2,760	14,888	0.8	1,615	511	2,757
Delta	–	–	–	–	–	1,026	2.1	18,723	1,240	22,628	3.9	770	187	3,412
Denton	762	144	4	705	133	29,211	35.1	5,267	42,840	7,724	43.1	26,720	3,852	695
DeWitt	8	39	1	60	296	3,359	–2.7	16,380	4,285	20,895	–2.3	2,530	685	3,340
Dickens	–	–	–	–	–	545	–9.2	20,597	575	21,731	–12.5	375	69	2,608
Dimmit	9	88	1	35	342	1,432	–3.8	13,776	1,780	17,124	–1.1	885	695	6,686
Donley	1	25	–	–	–	882	2.8	22,679	1,025	26,356	5.8	655	84	2,160
Duval	–	–	–	–	–	2,080	1.5	16,537	2,435	19,359	0.8	1,095	807	6,416
Eastland	11	60	1	40	217	4,085	–3.6	22,210	4,630	25,173	0.4	2,915	523	2,843
Ector	274	220	4	521	419	16,393	7.2	13,079	18,835	15,027	4.0	10,040	3,517	2,806
Edwards	2	100	–	–	–	1,209	–33.8	60,845	510	25,667	27.2	285	86	4,328
Ellis	117	91	2	95	74	14,693	21.2	11,008	16,825	12,605	20.1	10,265	1,817	1,361
El Paso	1,339	188	8	1,675	235	83,334	12.1	11,549	93,535	12,962	11.5	51,475	24,705	3,424
Erath	41	121	1	55	162	5,048	3.2	14,814	5,410	15,876	7.7	3,460	450	1,321
Falls	14	79	1	32	180	2,822	–5.3	15,992	3,290	18,644	–5.2	1,910	776	4,398
Fannin	20	61	1	39	120	5,821	7.2	17,564	6,835	20,623	10.5	4,370	750	2,263
Fayette	21	94	1	40	178	5,167	2.4	22,927	5,670	25,159	–4.0	3,735	442	1,961
Fisher	2	49	1	10	246	896	–6.2	21,912	1,060	25,923	–4.3	655	94	2,299
Floyd	6	82	1	25	342	1,183	–7.4	16,490	1,370	19,097	–5.7	835	172	2,398
Foard	–	–	–	–	–	369	–2.9	24,308	385	25,362	–13.9	240	38	2,503
Fort Bend	929	210	4	331	75	25,219	36.7	5,439	36,510	7,874	39.5	21,365	6,404	1,381
Franklin	8	79	1	30	298	1,528	10.8	14,980	2,375	23,284	6.4	1,565	209	2,049
Freestone	8	43	1	44	236	2,965	1.8	15,771	3,675	19,548	2.5	2,255	395	2,101
Frio	7	43	1	22	135	1,980	11.8	12,083	2,380	14,524	5.7	1,180	785	4,790
Gaines	4	28	1	37	255	1,641	6.4	11,154	1,915	13,017	1.1	1,055	332	2,257
Galveston	1,399	514	3	1,000	368	34,525	11.2	12,439	40,155	14,467	13.8	24,165	5,047	1,818
Garza	–	–	–	–	–	773	0.5	15,454	895	17,893	–1.5	540	112	2,239
Gillespie	100	444	1	84	373	5,527	9.9	23,939	5,985	25,923	3.2	4,320	205	888
Glasscock	–	–	–	–	–	115	19.8	8,666	160	12,057	16.8	110	11	829
Goliad	2	28	–	–	–	1,169	4.0	16,460	1,445	20,346	3.6	850	181	2,549
Gonzales	15	78	1	34	176	3,381	0.8	17,261	3,785	19,324	–1.2	2,250	683	3,487
Gray	22	103	1	91	425	4,299	–1.3	20,015	4,700	21,882	–4.2	2,940	435	2,025
Grayson	245	211	2	479	413	19,739	6.3	16,895	22,330	19,113	7.7	14,195	2,226	1,905
Gregg	318	277	3	599	522	20,814	8.0	17,998	21,310	18,426	3.5	12,365	3,285	2,840
Grimes	15	60	1	25	99	3,442	8.6	13,663	4,010	15,918	18.0	2,340	610	2,421
Guadalupe	113	114	1	97	97	12,307	23.6	11,945	16,275	15,796	23.1	10,035	1,756	1,704
Hale	34	94	1	31	85	5,231	–1.4	14,437	5,655	15,607	–3.2	3,265	861	2,376

See footnotes at end of table.

[Includes United States, states, and 3,141 counties/county equivalents defined as of February 22, 2005. For more information on these areas, see Appendix C, Geographic Information]

County	Physicians, 2004[1]		Community hospitals, 2004[3]			Medicare program enrollment, 2005[4]			Social Security program beneficiaries, December 2005				Supplemental Security Income program recipients, 2005	
				Beds										
	Number	Rate per 100,000 persons[2]	Number	Number	Rate per 100,000 persons[2]	Total	Percent change, 2000–2005	Rate per 100,000 persons[2]	Number	Rate per 100,000 persons[2]	Percent change, 2000–2005	Retired workers, number	Number	Rate per 100,000 persons[2]
TEXAS—Con.														
Hall	3	79	–	–	–	807	-3.8	21,811	905	24,459	-6.7	535	114	3,081
Hamilton	9	111	1	24	297	1,562	-5.3	19,272	2,185	26,959	0.4	1,505	168	2,073
Hansford	1	19	1	20	384	834	-2.5	15,946	915	17,495	-4.5	540	71	1,358
Hardeman	4	91	2	45	1,028	954	-6.4	22,233	1,100	25,635	-5.0	675	142	3,309
Hardin	24	48	–	–	–	7,453	12.4	14,621	9,070	17,793	14.8	5,050	1,022	2,005
Harris	11,419	314	43	11,037	303	314,989	12.5	8,529	365,550	9,898	13.8	212,745	76,754	2,078
Harrison	54	86	1	122	194	8,254	2.0	13,007	11,110	17,507	11.7	6,400	2,000	3,152
Hartley	–	–	–	–	–	148	-2.0	2,716	580	10,642	7.6	380	30	550
Haskell	3	54	1	25	447	1,409	-10.8	25,429	1,590	28,695	-9.4	985	184	3,321
Hays	165	138	1	113	95	10,836	29.9	8,708	13,010	10,456	29.7	8,215	1,208	971
Hemphill	4	119	1	19	564	486	1.9	14,202	550	16,072	-3.3	350	32	935
Henderson	72	91	1	117	148	10,612	5.8	13,262	17,930	22,408	11.9	11,560	1,833	2,291
Hidalgo	784	119	8	1,527	232	62,544	16.6	9,221	73,495	10,836	16.6	40,545	31,547	4,651
Hill	28	80	2	104	297	6,500	7.2	18,349	7,525	21,243	7.5	4,720	801	2,261
Hockley	14	61	1	22	97	3,120	1.6	13,692	3,780	16,588	0.8	2,035	543	2,383
Hood	47	101	1	38	82	9,587	18.1	20,002	11,060	23,075	17.5	7,785	505	1,054
Hopkins	34	103	1	54	163	5,406	3.0	16,195	6,485	19,427	5.4	3,970	811	2,430
Houston	15	64	1	54	231	4,656	2.9	20,053	5,260	22,655	2.5	3,230	905	3,898
Howard	72	219	1	122	372	5,235	-1.5	16,097	5,835	17,942	-2.2	3,415	892	2,743
Hudspeth	1	30	–	–	–	400	17.3	12,140	500	15,175	7.8	285	146	4,431
Hunt	64	78	2	186	228	11,855	9.5	14,362	15,035	18,215	12.1	9,135	1,959	2,373
Hutchinson	20	88	1	38	168	3,985	-3.1	17,724	4,560	20,281	-4.6	2,675	393	1,748
Irion	–	–	–	–	–	258	-3.0	14,692	370	21,071	15.6	205	24	1,367
Jack	4	44	1	17	189	1,339	4.3	14,773	1,695	18,700	3.2	1,070	131	1,445
Jackson	5	35	1	54	376	2,249	-1.6	15,684	2,740	19,109	4.1	1,560	315	2,197
Jasper	31	87	1	50	140	6,052	5.9	17,006	7,760	21,806	5.7	4,200	1,233	3,465
Jeff Davis	3	132	–	–	–	428	15.7	18,560	485	21,032	21.9	340	46	1,995
Jefferson	620	250	8	1,413	569	38,335	0.2	15,484	44,005	17,775	-0.9	24,490	7,462	3,014
Jim Hogg	2	40	–	–	–	841	2.9	16,723	980	19,487	0.4	515	280	5,568
Jim Wells	36	88	1	73	179	6,251	6.4	15,265	7,230	17,655	6.7	3,640	2,003	4,891
Johnson	132	92	1	125	87	17,733	15.4	12,115	19,675	13,441	17.4	11,895	1,967	1,344
Jones	8	40	3	79	394	2,682	-5.1	13,589	3,390	17,177	-2.8	2,055	452	2,290
Karnes	6	39	1	30	195	2,523	(Z)	16,435	2,695	17,556	-5.7	1,490	608	3,961
Kaufman	61	71	2	198	232	14,765	15.5	16,566	13,435	15,074	15.4	8,250	1,592	1,786
Kendall	162	592	–	–	–	5,077	27.7	17,747	5,665	19,803	28.1	3,885	265	926
Kenedy	–	–	–	–	–	63	14.5	15,108	50	11,990	-3.8	30	5	1,199
Kent	–	–	–	–	–	202	-4.7	25,831	220	28,133	-8.7	145	17	2,174
Kerr	189	411	1	105	229	12,103	6.9	26,030	13,100	28,174	8.6	9,080	766	1,647
Kimble	4	88	1	15	330	891	2.3	19,408	1,110	24,178	7.4	715	110	2,396
King	–	–	–	–	–	28	-24.3	9,121	30	9,772	-21.1	20	–	–
Kinney	1	30	–	–	–	768	3.5	23,084	880	26,450	1.6	615	143	4,298
Kleberg	24	78	1	100	324	3,787	6.2	12,313	4,400	14,306	4.2	2,440	1,071	3,482
Knox	3	77	–	–	–	897	-8.1	23,724	985	26,051	-8.8	590	142	3,756
Lamar	120	242	2	266	536	8,952	6.4	18,032	10,575	21,302	7.4	6,405	1,736	3,497
Lamb	7	48	1	41	283	2,592	-3.3	17,917	2,945	20,357	-4.1	1,685	445	3,076
Lampasas	18	87	1	25	121	3,296	19.7	16,757	3,650	18,557	12.4	2,210	401	2,039
La Salle	–	–	–	–	–	825	6.6	13,713	1,015	16,872	-0.4	545	347	5,768
Lavaca	21	111	2	61	322	4,945	-0.5	26,129	5,250	27,741	0.7	3,345	469	2,478
Lee	2	12	–	–	–	2,332	10.5	14,111	2,910	17,609	5.4	1,780	291	1,761
Leon	6	37	–	–	–	4,125	8.5	25,239	4,320	26,432	13.2	2,745	423	2,588
Liberty	46	61	2	136	181	10,205	11.7	13,581	11,140	14,825	9.4	5,670	1,806	2,403
Limestone	10	44	2	75	329	4,229	1.3	18,570	5,060	22,229	3.4	2,830	783	3,440
Lipscomb	–	–	–	–	–	551	-10.7	17,768	585	18,865	-10.1	335	31	1,000
Live Oak	2	17	–	–	–	1,404	3.5	11,983	1,770	15,106	-10.7	1,010	272	2,321
Llano	31	172	1	30	166	4,821	6.6	26,437	5,300	29,063	-0.5	3,730	293	1,607
Loving	–	–	–	–	–	21	10.5	33,871	20	32,258	11.1	15	(D)	(NA)
Lubbock	1,046	416	5	1,393	555	31,776	7.6	12,595	36,405	14,430	6.8	22,060	5,136	2,036
Lynn	3	49	1	24	388	1,043	4.4	16,723	1,195	19,160	-6.6	680	161	2,581
McCulloch	5	62	1	25	310	1,768	-1.4	22,222	2,025	25,452	-0.8	1,255	306	3,846
McLennan	508	228	2	823	369	31,796	4.7	14,152	36,225	16,124	5.0	21,835	5,552	2,471
McMullen	–	–	–	–	–	148	9.6	16,761	180	20,385	11.1	110	15	1,699
Madison	6	45	1	25	189	1,840	5.9	13,974	2,290	17,392	2.5	1,440	284	2,157
Marion	6	54	–	–	–	1,958	8.1	17,878	2,390	21,822	-5.3	1,395	447	4,081
Martin	2	45	1	20	453	615	-5.4	14,006	730	16,625	-6.9	400	97	2,209
Mason	2	52	–	–	–	894	-0.7	23,041	1,020	26,289	4.4	680	73	1,881
Matagorda	36	95	2	84	221	5,474	4.8	14,463	6,610	17,464	-7.7	3,880	951	2,513
Maverick	35	69	2	73	145	6,615	15.1	12,925	7,630	14,908	15.0	3,890	3,733	7,294
Medina	25	59	1	25	59	5,338	12.3	12,406	6,705	15,583	12.6	3,850	1,140	2,649
Menard	–	–	–	–	–	557	3.3	25,307	625	28,396	4.0	400	83	3,771
Midland	229	191	3	362	302	15,145	8.8	12,478	17,900	14,748	6.8	10,995	2,245	1,850

See footnotes at end of table.

Physicians, Community Hospitals, Medicare, Social Security, and Supplemental Security Income—Con.

[Includes United States, states, and 3,141 counties/county equivalents defined as of February 22, 2005. For more information on these areas, see Appendix C, Geographic Information]

County	Physicians, 2004[1]		Community hospitals, 2004[3]			Medicare program enrollment, 2005[4]			Social Security program beneficiaries, December 2005				Supplemental Security Income program recipients, 2005	
				Beds										
	Number	Rate per 100,000 persons[2]	Number	Number	Rate per 100,000 persons[2]	Total	Percent change, 2000–2005	Rate per 100,000 persons[2]	Number	Rate per 100,000 persons[2]	Percent change, 2000–2005	Retired workers, number	Number	Rate per 100,000 persons[2]
TEXAS—Con.														
Milam	14	55	2	59	233	4,603	3.8	18,155	5,280	20,825	4.3	3,120	707	2,789
Mills	4	78	–	–	–	1,100	–5.8	21,004	1,280	24,441	–4.8	835	145	2,769
Mitchell	5	53	1	25	267	1,415	–11.3	15,032	1,630	17,316	–7.0	975	223	2,369
Montague	14	72	2	77	396	4,390	4.7	22,310	4,970	25,258	4.1	3,095	469	2,383
Montgomery	627	173	2	339	94	36,264	31.3	9,593	46,920	12,412	33.6	28,865	4,811	1,273
Moore	12	59	1	100	489	2,163	(Z)	10,630	2,550	12,532	–0.2	1,490	246	1,209
Morris	4	31	–	–	–	2,984	4.6	23,067	3,375	26,090	7.6	1,965	494	3,819
Motley	–	–	–	–	–	324	–6.6	24,942	355	27,329	–2.5	230	32	2,463
Nacogdoches	136	227	2	287	478	8,530	5.0	14,107	9,550	15,793	4.5	5,375	1,711	2,830
Navarro	59	122	1	144	299	7,674	3.9	15,762	9,190	18,876	9.5	5,465	1,441	2,960
Newton	9	63	–	–	–	2,200	4.1	15,375	2,610	18,240	5.3	1,265	566	3,956
Nolan	6	40	1	54	359	2,949	–3.5	19,821	3,200	21,508	–4.3	1,925	493	3,314
Nueces	923	291	6	1,549	488	41,623	6.5	13,019	48,885	15,291	8.0	26,920	10,503	3,285
Ochiltree	5	55	1	25	274	1,106	1.0	11,785	1,295	13,799	0.1	770	112	1,193
Oldham	–	–	–	–	–	357	–0.3	16,856	365	17,233	–0.3	230	32	1,511
Orange	47	55	1	154	182	13,847	11.1	16,294	16,430	19,333	7.6	8,585	2,091	2,460
Palo Pinto	22	81	1	42	154	4,489	–1.2	16,337	5,435	19,779	–1.4	3,375	594	2,162
Panola	10	44	1	37	163	3,790	3.2	16,480	4,615	20,068	3.3	2,575	649	2,822
Parker	86	86	1	78	78	11,415	18.4	11,104	15,260	14,844	16.2	9,830	1,030	1,002
Parmer	4	40	1	25	253	1,271	0.4	13,031	1,455	14,917	–4.8	840	155	1,589
Pecos	9	56	2	36	225	1,919	3.1	12,100	2,205	13,904	2.4	1,255	444	2,800
Polk	47	102	1	35	76	15,192	23.8	32,573	18,220	39,065	15.4	13,095	1,421	3,047
Potter	450	380	2	871	736	24,371	8.1	20,334	16,920	14,117	2.6	9,820	2,816	2,350
Presidio	3	39	–	–	–	1,494	14.6	19,347	1,555	20,137	14.7	890	766	9,920
Rains	2	18	–	–	–	1,804	35.2	15,958	2,260	19,991	13.7	1,455	213	1,884
Randall	226	208	1	62	57	4,885	–0.9	4,439	15,815	14,370	8.7	10,460	869	790
Reagan	3	98	1	14	457	392	6.8	13,088	455	15,192	–3.0	245	46	1,536
Real	2	66	–	–	–	828	8.5	27,318	980	32,333	4.0	640	135	4,454
Red River	7	51	1	36	263	2,986	–2.5	21,996	3,410	25,120	0.5	2,010	576	4,243
Reeves	9	76	1	44	372	1,874	1.5	16,102	2,170	18,646	1.2	1,195	586	5,035
Refugio	2	26	1	20	261	1,512	2.2	19,793	1,735	22,712	3.1	1,015	227	2,972
Roberts	–	–	–	–	–	112	–9.7	13,659	140	17,073	–34.9	90	9	1,098
Robertson	3	19	–	–	–	2,845	–0.4	17,570	3,370	20,813	3.1	1,975	693	4,280
Rockwall	101	173	–	–	–	5,393	46.7	8,568	6,885	10,938	46.8	4,530	478	759
Runnels	6	55	2	37	339	2,344	–3.9	21,360	2,625	23,920	–4.9	1,590	322	2,934
Rusk	39	81	1	76	159	6,755	0.1	14,081	9,125	19,022	3.1	5,380	1,242	2,589
Sabine	5	48	1	29	280	3,331	4.1	31,980	3,495	33,554	0.7	2,120	357	3,427
San Augustine	5	56	1	18	202	1,992	4.0	22,364	2,470	27,731	5.9	1,385	491	5,513
San Jacinto	4	16	–	–	–	3,206	11.4	12,927	5,085	20,503	15.9	3,000	765	3,085
San Patricio	33	48	1	64	94	9,775	13.1	14,124	10,980	15,865	9.1	5,855	2,252	3,254
San Saba	1	16	–	–	–	1,107	–10.3	18,219	1,325	21,807	–4.3	860	170	2,798
Schleicher	2	73	1	14	508	458	–5.2	16,703	540	19,694	–4.1	300	65	2,371
Scurry	12	74	1	73	451	2,665	–4.0	16,433	2,965	18,283	–4.4	1,790	350	2,158
Shackelford	3	94	–	–	–	625	–1.0	19,735	710	22,419	–6.7	440	63	1,989
Shelby	17	65	1	46	177	4,660	1.3	17,688	5,410	20,534	2.6	2,980	1,010	3,834
Sherman	1	32	–	–	–	399	–14.2	13,291	355	11,825	–9.9	210	18	600
Smith	759	406	5	998	534	30,757	12.0	16,137	34,880	18,301	12.0	21,755	4,227	2,218
Somervell	8	107	1	16	214	1,033	20.8	13,632	1,275	16,825	22.4	820	122	1,610
Starr	20	34	1	49	82	7,031	34.4	11,537	7,590	12,455	18.4	3,565	4,607	7,560
Stephens	6	63	1	33	347	1,753	–0.6	18,335	2,095	21,912	0.4	1,310	233	2,437
Sterling	–	–	–	–	–	177	–0.6	13,584	210	16,117	1.4	130	23	1,765
Stonewall	1	71	1	12	849	371	–10.2	27,041	415	30,248	–13.4	250	35	2,551
Sutton	3	73	1	12	290	540	–1.2	12,821	625	14,839	–3.3	395	92	2,184
Swisher	5	64	1	29	368	1,510	–1.4	19,290	1,665	21,270	–3.4	995	165	2,108
Tarrant	2,833	179	21	3,643	230	149,727	13.2	9,240	177,410	10,948	15.1	108,765	22,381	1,381
Taylor	309	247	2	568	454	19,341	5.2	15,468	21,505	17,199	3.5	13,195	2,939	2,350
Terrell	–	–	–	–	–	225	6.1	22,590	220	22,088	–2.2	140	25	2,510
Terry	7	56	1	42	336	2,043	–0.1	16,451	2,335	18,802	–1.5	1,300	373	3,003
Throckmorton	1	61	1	14	855	382	2.1	23,609	450	27,812	5.4	275	33	2,040
Titus	44	151	1	144	494	3,879	3.3	13,174	4,440	15,079	5.5	2,660	629	2,136
Tom Green	233	224	2	385	371	16,398	4.3	15,827	18,575	17,928	3.3	11,475	2,452	2,367
Travis	2,687	309	12	1,865	215	69,685	13.5	7,846	81,325	9,156	15.1	49,690	12,216	1,375
Trinity	5	35	1	22	154	3,472	9.8	24,173	4,110	28,615	10.5	2,550	516	3,593
Tyler	13	63	1	25	120	3,932	2.4	19,072	4,855	23,549	3.6	2,740	599	2,905
Upshur	20	54	1	37	99	6,698	11.6	17,682	7,915	20,894	6.4	4,575	1,002	2,645
Upton	3	96	2	50	1,596	553	6.3	18,096	655	21,433	1.2	355	72	2,356
Uvalde	23	86	1	54	203	3,977	3.7	14,754	4,670	17,325	5.3	2,745	1,149	4,263
Val Verde	49	103	1	72	152	5,335	33.2	11,209	6,805	14,297	7.3	3,900	2,343	4,923
Van Zandt	20	39	1	24	46	9,000	9.0	17,146	10,860	20,689	9.2	7,110	999	1,903
Victoria	218	255	2	608	710	12,445	9.9	14,530	14,480	16,906	9.0	8,305	2,203	2,572

See footnotes at end of table.

[Includes United States, states, and 3,141 counties/county equivalents defined as of February 22, 2005. For more information on these areas, see Appendix C, Geographic Information]

County	Physicians, 2004[1] Number	Rate per 100,000 persons[2]	Community hospitals, 2004[3] Number	Beds Number	Beds Rate per 100,000 persons[2]	Medicare program enrollment, 2005[4] Total	Percent change, 2000–2005	Rate per 100,000 persons[2]	Social Security program beneficiaries, December 2005 Number	Rate per 100,000 persons[2]	Percent change, 2000–2005	Retired workers, number	Supplemental Security Income program recipients, 2005 Number	Rate per 100,000 persons[2]
TEXAS—Con.														
Walker	57	91	1	127	202	6,403	9.7	10,206	7,440	11,859	14.3	4,700	971	1,548
Waller	8	23	–	–	–	3,420	13.0	9,822	4,470	12,837	18.3	2,685	604	1,735
Ward	4	39	1	25	244	1,767	1.3	17,261	2,060	20,123	-1.7	1,105	320	3,126
Washington	49	157	1	60	193	5,822	4.1	18,470	6,560	20,812	5.0	4,170	799	2,535
Webb	239	109	2	492	225	19,763	17.8	8,795	22,800	10,147	18.5	11,975	9,382	4,175
Wharton	58	140	2	158	382	6,357	0.9	15,298	7,305	17,580	-0.6	4,320	1,041	2,505
Wheeler	6	124	2	41	850	1,117	-8.9	23,276	1,190	24,797	-12.4	725	92	1,917
Wichita	365	287	4	458	360	19,803	2.7	15,730	21,565	17,129	2.7	13,040	2,943	2,338
Wilbarger	20	144	1	47	337	2,542	-4.7	18,293	2,910	20,941	-2.1	1,750	408	2,936
Willacy	5	25	–			2,765	7.0	13,566	3,200	15,700	6.4	1,685	1,372	6,731
Williamson	409	129	3	263	83	26,640	44.7	7,989	33,950	10,181	48.6	22,030	2,478	743
Wilson	21	57	1	31	84	4,173	14.3	11,119	5,390	14,362	17.1	3,080	690	1,839
Winkler	3	44	1	15	222	1,040	-5.9	15,546	1,255	18,759	-7.5	630	205	3,064
Wise	29	52	1	85	153	6,274	16.9	11,066	7,890	13,916	15.6	4,835	673	1,187
Wood	26	65	2	74	184	9,155	14.1	22,409	10,860	26,582	22.9	7,420	847	2,073
Yoakum	4	54	1	24	325	993	2.7	13,404	1,185	15,996	2.4	685	135	1,822
Young	16	89	2	62	345	3,860	1.3	21,444	4,355	24,194	1.3	2,725	445	2,472
Zapata	7	53	–	–	–	1,394	2.3	10,424	1,665	12,450	2.9	860	588	4,397
Zavala	5	43	–	–	–	1,672	4.9	14,174	1,980	16,785	1.4	1,060	874	7,409
UTAH	5,642	233	43	4,517	187	[6]235,039	[6]14.1	[6]9,517	[7]273,045	[7]11,056	[7]13.3	[7]177,447	22,606	915
Beaver	7	115	2	114	1,872	913	-0.7	14,716	1,020	16,441	7.3	650	43	693
Box Elder	38	83	2	107	233	5,453	12.0	11,742	6,275	13,512	7.7	4,185	339	730
Cache	161	166	2	142	146	7,968	14.1	8,126	9,420	9,607	11.8	6,280	513	523
Carbon	26	133	1	84	428	3,299	1.4	16,973	3,920	20,168	3.7	2,145	408	2,099
Daggett	–	–	–	–	–	161	27.8	17,073	195	20,679	31.8	145	4	424
Davis	403	154	2	252	96	22,077	19.7	8,232	26,035	9,708	18.8	17,355	1,636	610
Duchesne	23	153	1	97	646	2,072	13.8	13,495	2,510	16,348	9.8	1,470	262	1,706
Emery	1	9	–	–	–	1,405	10.1	13,117	1,800	16,805	12.6	1,070	122	1,139
Garfield	1	22	1	44	987	836	7.5	18,702	900	20,134	0.7	665	30	671
Grand	20	230	1	25	288	1,287	9.8	14,720	1,490	17,042	3.3	985	133	1,521
Iron	39	107	1	42	115	4,468	29.9	11,662	5,255	13,717	30.9	3,320	450	1,175
Juab	6	67	1	19	211	1,013	15.0	11,116	1,255	13,772	11.7	780	108	1,185
Kane	7	114	1	38	620	1,211	8.3	19,526	1,455	23,460	11.2	1,060	57	919
Millard	10	81	2	40	323	1,656	3.1	13,481	1,915	15,589	2.5	1,255	119	969
Morgan	10	131	–	–	–	809	19.0	10,233	925	11,700	19.5	650	15	190
Piute	–	–	–	–	–	318	13.2	23,297	380	27,839	11.8	250	13	952
Rich	–	–	–	–	–	301	9.5	14,676	350	17,065	12.5	255	8	390
Salt Lake	3,367	360	11	2,031	217	87,707	10.2	9,250	101,510	10,706	9.2	66,005	9,733	1,027
San Juan	7	50	1	22	157	1,362	12.1	9,657	1,595	11,309	7.6	890	588	4,169
Sanpete	25	105	2	49	207	2,954	10.0	12,286	3,645	15,160	9.0	2,375	257	1,069
Sevier	10	52	1	27	139	2,937	5.8	15,150	3,555	18,338	3.3	2,360	239	1,233
Summit	181	533	–	–	–	2,113	35.9	6,037	2,805	8,014	35.9	1,945	85	243
Tooele	27	54	1	35	70	3,838	22.9	7,480	4,660	9,082	28.0	2,795	405	789
Uintah	24	90	1	31	117	2,996	10.5	11,098	3,710	13,743	5.4	2,230	353	1,308
Utah	612	141	5	621	143	30,361	15.5	6,842	36,860	8,307	16.4	22,515	3,190	719
Wasatch	20	110	1	19	105	1,823	33.6	9,608	2,090	11,015	23.4	1,365	87	459
Washington	220	199	1	212	192	18,724	33.4	15,750	22,345	18,795	32.2	15,995	821	691
Wayne	3	121	–	–	–	408	5.2	16,653	470	19,184	2.0	330	16	653
Weber	394	189	2	466	224	23,917	7.5	11,349	24,695	11,718	7.6	16,120	2,572	1,220
VERMONT	2,589	417	14	1,473	237	[6]96,352	[6]8.2	[6]15,465	[7]112,251	[7]18,016	[7]7.4	[7]72,248	13,110	2,104
Addison	99	269	1	45	122	4,694	5.4	12,698	5,670	15,339	6.1	3,730	569	1,539
Bennington	157	424	1	99	267	7,188	7.4	19,428	8,365	22,609	6.2	5,670	944	2,551
Caledonia	59	194	1	25	82	5,112	4.9	16,794	6,010	19,744	5.9	3,745	836	2,746
Chittenden	1,237	828	1	519	347	18,048	12.1	12,063	21,475	14,354	11.7	14,000	2,260	1,511
Essex	4	60	–	–	–	1,383	9.1	20,948	1,665	25,220	13.3	970	180	2,726
Franklin	69	145	1	52	109	6,036	7.1	12,598	6,740	14,067	7.9	3,965	1,079	2,252
Grand Isle	17	223	–	–	–	1,139	14.2	14,786	1,365	17,720	18.1	915	122	1,584
Lamoille	73	300	1	42	172	3,474	13.3	14,182	3,960	16,167	9.1	2,555	432	1,764
Orange	68	233	1	45	154	4,407	9.9	15,048	5,200	17,755	8.9	3,400	564	1,926
Orleans	61	223	1	48	175	5,090	9.7	18,415	6,045	21,870	10.4	3,610	936	3,386
Rutland	168	264	1	120	189	12,067	7.0	18,931	13,795	21,642	5.2	8,685	1,781	2,794
Washington	160	271	1	238	403	9,675	7.5	16,267	11,120	18,696	5.7	7,095	1,358	2,283
Windham	131	296	2	80	181	7,301	5.4	16,539	8,590	19,459	4.1	5,635	961	2,177
Windsor	286	493	2	160	276	10,634	5.7	18,326	12,245	21,102	4.5	8,270	1,088	1,875
VIRGINIA	22,587	302	88	17,339	232	[6]992,216	[6]11.1	[6]13,112	[7]1,139,748	[7]15,061	[7]10.0	[7]710,014	137,662	1,819
Accomack	28	71	–	–	–	7,009	4.3	17,779	8,165	20,711	1.8	5,360	1,203	3,051
Albemarle	722	811	–	–	–	9,090	10.2	10,020	13,635	15,030	15.0	9,540	778	858
Alleghany[13]	29	173	1	89	532	1,918	353.4	11,475	3,715	22,226	56.4	2,050	485	2,902
Amelia	3	25	–	–	–	1,896	16.0	15,449	2,695	21,959	28.6	1,655	343	2,795
Amherst	17	53	–	–	–	5,538	11.9	17,234	6,780	21,099	14.3	4,220	740	2,303

See footnotes at end of table.

Physicians, Community Hospitals, Medicare, Social Security, and Supplemental Security Income—Con.

[Includes United States, states, and 3,141 counties/county equivalents defined as of February 22, 2005. For more information on these areas, see Appendix C, Geographic Information]

County	Physicians, 2004[1] Number	Physicians, 2004[1] Rate per 100,000 persons[2]	Community hospitals, 2004[3] Number	Community hospitals, 2004[3] Beds Number	Community hospitals, 2004[3] Beds Rate per 100,000 persons[2]	Medicare program enrollment, 2005[4] Total	Medicare program enrollment, 2005[4] Percent change, 2000–2005	Medicare program enrollment, 2005[4] Rate per 100,000 persons[2]	Social Security program beneficiaries, December 2005 Number	Social Security program beneficiaries, December 2005 Rate per 100,000 persons[2]	Social Security program beneficiaries, December 2005 Percent change, 2000–2005	Social Security program beneficiaries, December 2005 Retired workers, number	Supplemental Security Income program recipients, 2005 Number	Supplemental Security Income program recipients, 2005 Rate per 100,000 persons[2]
VIRGINIA—Con.														
Appomattox	4	29	–	–	–	2,332	9.5	16,696	3,230	23,126	12.0	2,005	418	2,993
Arlington	850	429	2	398	201	17,320	-2.0	8,838	16,310	8,323	-4.2	11,970	1,885	962
Augusta	104	151	2	197	287	7,328	12.0	10,510	14,270	20,466	20.5	9,330	915	1,312
Bath	8	161	1	25	504	1,175	10.7	23,800	1,260	25,522	12.7	825	80	1,620
Bedford	93	145	–	–	–	10,671	19.7	16,345	12,775	19,568	24.1	8,220	858	1,314
Bland	3	43	–	–	–	1,432	15.7	20,625	1,690	24,341	14.1	865	166	2,391
Botetourt	35	110	–	–	–	4,913	9.6	15,340	6,015	18,781	11.0	3,880	331	1,034
Brunswick	6	33	–	–	–	3,161	2.8	17,640	3,845	21,456	2.3	2,300	712	3,973
Buchanan	22	87	1	134	533	6,900	4.7	27,873	9,125	36,861	-3.0	2,265	1,999	8,075
Buckingham	7	44	–	–	–	2,104	4.6	13,103	3,010	18,745	4.0	1,780	488	3,039
Campbell	13	25	–	–	–	7,331	15.8	14,007	11,290	21,571	13.0	6,985	1,094	2,090
Caroline	5	21	–	–	–	3,396	10.5	13,285	4,385	17,154	13.0	2,680	399	1,561
Carroll	14	48	–	–	–	5,011	11.3	17,022	7,455	25,324	12.4	4,495	834	2,833
Charles City	2	28	–	–	–	1,017	25.2	14,286	1,460	20,508	13.2	880	163	2,290
Charlotte	7	57	–	–	–	3,334	8.4	26,878	3,330	26,846	6.3	1,995	598	4,821
Chesterfield	836	296	1	60	21	26,739	24.9	9,256	38,285	13,253	24.4	23,870	2,724	943
Clarke	27	195	–	–	–	1,956	9.6	13,770	2,295	16,156	9.5	1,630	131	922
Craig	–	–	–	–	–	835	9.0	16,201	1,180	22,895	15.0	635	120	2,328
Culpeper	57	142	1	60	149	5,571	16.5	13,099	6,535	15,366	16.6	4,150	658	1,547
Cumberland	5	55	–	–	–	1,077	11.4	11,484	1,970	21,007	17.2	1,175	319	3,402
Dickenson	13	80	1	15	93	4,069	8.4	25,051	5,425	33,399	5.3	1,525	1,098	6,760
Dinwiddie	12	48	–	–	–	3,288	14.0	12,949	4,880	19,219	10.5	2,830	721	2,840
Essex	20	194	1	28	271	1,953	11.7	18,614	2,415	23,018	5.5	1,535	281	2,678
Fairfax	3,956	395	5	1,509	151	73,070	23.1	7,260	90,125	8,954	10.6	64,835	9,483	942
Fauquier	98	155	1	83	132	6,962	15.6	10,711	8,195	12,608	14.5	5,580	450	692
Floyd	8	55	–	–	–	2,465	8.5	16,827	3,240	22,118	12.8	1,985	271	1,850
Fluvanna	44	185	–	–	–	3,685	18.0	14,888	4,305	17,393	19.3	3,090	232	937
Franklin	56	113	1	37	74	8,081	15.5	16,051	11,390	22,624	20.3	7,080	934	1,855
Frederick	88	132	1	411	616	7,178	17.4	10,384	10,495	15,183	21.1	7,090	688	995
Giles	18	106	1	32	189	3,796	5.1	22,201	4,385	25,646	7.2	2,320	539	3,152
Gloucester	56	151	1	27	73	5,179	16.4	13,706	6,310	16,699	17.1	4,020	549	1,453
Goochland	51	273	–	–	–	2,293	15.0	11,844	3,480	17,975	22.5	2,355	231	1,193
Grayson	7	43	–	–	–	3,088	3.5	18,868	4,640	28,351	3.4	2,800	574	3,507
Greene	14	82	–	–	–	1,935	18.3	11,109	2,465	14,152	18.6	1,585	231	1,326
Greensville	20	182	–	–	–	804	0.4	7,251	2,125	19,165	4.4	1,265	403	3,635
Halifax[14]	68	187	1	144	396	7,888	23.4	21,740	9,570	26,375	7.6	5,485	1,756	4,840
Hanover	168	175	2	265	276	14,699	21.2	15,087	14,580	14,965	20.3	10,145	662	679
Henrico	1,680	609	3	856	310	31,257	9.1	11,140	42,775	15,245	6.6	28,465	3,708	1,322
Henry	11	19	–	–	–	9,891	17.7	17,506	15,130	26,778	16.2	9,305	1,202	2,127
Highland	4	162	–	–	–	584	7.6	23,596	685	27,677	3.6	455	36	1,455
Isle of Wight	40	123	–	–	–	4,749	15.6	14,211	6,000	17,955	14.5	3,725	596	1,784
James City	334	602	–	–	–	3,197	57.5	5,558	11,790	20,495	29.1	8,755	398	692
King and Queen	6	89	–	–	–	1,140	5.9	16,775	1,395	20,527	16.2	820	138	2,031
King George	10	52	–	–	–	2,060	16.3	9,982	2,370	11,484	18.1	1,510	179	867
King William	8	56	–	–	–	2,094	13.4	14,214	2,630	17,852	17.4	1,650	225	1,527
Lancaster	66	571	1	63	545	3,825	5.8	32,994	3,950	34,072	4.4	2,895	246	2,122
Lee	27	114	1	52	219	5,361	4.8	22,634	6,920	29,216	3.3	2,570	1,961	8,279
Loudoun	456	191	1	92	38	13,993	40.6	5,476	16,215	6,346	34.3	11,080	1,144	448
Louisa	22	76	–	–	–	4,593	22.9	15,300	5,550	18,488	21.1	3,405	583	1,942
Lunenburg	6	46	–	–	–	1,987	-2.7	15,060	2,730	20,691	1.2	1,645	529	4,009
Madison	14	107	–	–	–	1,932	7.0	14,420	2,385	17,801	5.4	1,580	207	1,545
Mathews	13	142	–	–	–	2,212	4.9	24,059	2,490	27,083	4.7	1,730	116	1,262
Mecklenburg	55	169	1	284	875	7,283	9.0	22,389	8,595	26,423	9.3	5,400	1,310	4,027
Middlesex	18	172	–	–	–	2,659	10.6	25,341	2,980	28,400	7.2	2,085	215	2,049
Montgomery	160	191	2	186	222	9,303	10.3	11,035	10,930	12,965	14.1	6,765	1,082	1,283
Nelson	39	261	–	–	–	3,408	11.8	22,568	3,375	22,350	6.0	2,235	349	2,311
New Kent	11	71	–	–	–	2,217	22.7	13,764	2,500	15,521	29.4	1,590	142	882
Northampton	56	420	1	256	1,919	2,986	1.1	22,040	3,425	25,280	2.6	2,275	714	5,270
Northumberland	22	172	–	–	–	3,175	9.8	24,662	3,970	30,837	10.9	2,940	229	1,779
Nottoway	34	219	–	–	–	3,147	1.3	20,225	3,450	22,172	3.7	2,100	580	3,728
Orange	47	163	–	–	–	6,454	17.5	21,338	6,890	22,780	17.9	4,825	486	1,607
Page	18	76	1	15	63	4,436	9.9	18,614	5,435	22,806	10.2	3,350	565	2,371
Patrick	13	68	1	50	260	4,080	13.2	21,240	4,775	24,858	13.1	3,055	484	2,520
Pittsylvania	11	18	–	–	–	8,760	8.5	14,162	14,585	23,580	2.5	8,735	1,937	3,132
Powhatan	18	70	–	–	–	3,022	31.3	11,362	3,670	13,798	31.1	2,450	240	902
Prince Edward	43	213	1	116	574	3,827	5.7	18,709	3,795	18,553	6.3	2,310	751	3,671
Prince George	14	38	–	–	–	2,614	27.6	7,118	4,335	11,804	24.6	2,575	399	1,086
Prince William	350	104	1	153	45	16,619	41.0	4,768	24,410	7,003	30.4	15,585	2,524	724
Pulaski	48	137	1	72	205	6,663	7.9	18,993	8,395	23,930	9.1	4,785	937	2,671
Rappahannock	8	112	–	–	–	1,552	19.4	21,345	1,485	20,424	13.5	1,035	95	1,307

See footnotes at end of table.

Physicians, Community Hospitals, Medicare, Social Security, and Supplemental Security Income—Con.

[Includes United States, states, and 3,141 counties/county equivalents defined as of February 22, 2005. For more information on these areas, see Appendix C, Geographic Information]

County	Physicians, 2004[1] Number	Physicians, 2004[1] Rate per 100,000 persons[2]	Community hospitals, 2004[3] Number	Beds Number	Beds Rate per 100,000 persons[2]	Medicare program enrollment, 2005[4] Total	Medicare Percent change, 2000–2005	Medicare Rate per 100,000 persons[2]	Social Security program beneficiaries, December 2005 Number	Social Security Rate per 100,000 persons[2]	Social Security Percent change, 2000–2005	Social Security Retired workers, number	Supplemental Security Income program recipients, 2005 Number	SSI Rate per 100,000 persons[2]
VIRGINIA—Con.														
Richmond.	2	22	–	–	–	1,718	11.2	18,850	1,900	20,847	6.1	1,260	223	2,447
Roanoke	328	375	1	723	826	6,915	19.6	7,843	17,435	19,774	8.7	11,820	948	1,075
Rockbridge	5	24	–	–	–	2,497	11.0	11,755	4,930	23,209	22.7	3,185	387	1,822
Rockingham	49	70	–	–	–	9,760	11.4	13,698	13,705	19,235	13.8	9,305	928	1,302
Russell	17	59	1	78	270	5,957	13.2	20,578	8,125	28,067	-2.4	2,730	1,649	5,696
Scott	10	43	–	–	–	5,558	8.7	24,205	6,740	29,353	10.1	3,095	1,453	6,328
Shenandoah	48	126	1	23	60	7,421	12.9	18,939	8,655	22,088	15.1	6,040	553	1,411
Smyth	62	191	1	285	876	7,403	9.2	22,681	8,905	27,282	10.7	4,735	1,330	4,075
Southampton	6	34	–	–	–	2,333	1.6	13,267	3,665	20,842	5.5	2,130	573	3,258
Spotsylvania	132	118	1	408	365	5,935	38.6	5,092	12,715	10,910	22.4	7,720	901	773
Stafford	85	74	–	–	–	6,030	41.5	5,116	9,730	8,255	30.8	6,160	677	574
Surry	2	29	–	–	–	1,060	7.0	15,115	1,310	18,680	11.4	760	158	2,253
Sussex	1	8	–	–	–	2,301	2.4	19,062	2,440	20,214	4.1	1,410	440	3,645
Tazewell	129	289	2	174	390	11,147	6.9	24,884	12,380	27,637	14.7	5,040	2,059	4,596
Warren	33	96	1	166	481	4,538	10.9	12,763	5,570	15,665	9.7	3,585	473	1,330
Washington	127	245	1	135	261	9,318	19.8	17,890	13,170	25,286	12.6	7,165	1,709	3,281
Westmoreland	8	47	–	–	–	3,483	4.5	20,218	4,030	23,394	4.9	2,775	400	2,322
Wise	59	141	2	189	452	9,110	7.3	21,692	11,010	26,216	8.0	3,790	2,535	6,036
Wythe	45	160	1	90	320	6,397	11.6	22,508	7,080	24,911	10.6	3,990	798	2,808
York	188	309	1	110	181	10,056	41.9	16,283	8,705	14,095	20.2	5,970	364	589
Independent Cities														
Alexandria	546	400	1	330	242	18,559	-6.6	13,713	11,350	8,386	-0.3	8,020	1,547	1,143
Bedford	–	–	1	161	2,588	3,645	10.1	58,686	1,830	29,464	-5.6	1,200	228	3,671
Bristol	7	40	–	–	–	5,741	0.8	33,118	4,850	27,978	5.6	2,840	833	4,805
Buena Vista	4	61	–	–	–	1,606	12.5	24,950	1,480	22,992	5.0	865	191	2,967
Charlottesville	1,121	2,751	3	750	1,841	8,320	13.6	20,575	5,770	14,269	-2.6	3,680	950	2,349
Chesapeake	653	304	1	310	144	23,082	15.5	10,541	27,715	12,657	13.5	16,950	3,168	1,447
Clifton Forge[13]	(X)	(NA)	(X)	(X)	(NA)	(X)	(NA)	(NA)	(X)	(NA)	(NA)	(X)	(X)	(NA)
Colonial Heights	58	332	–	–	–	4,069	9.3	23,163	4,010	22,827	6.0	2,675	234	1,332
Covington	12	191	–	–	–	3,155	5.3	50,846	1,770	28,525	-2.1	945	278	4,480
Danville	179	385	1	201	433	13,340	0.4	28,910	12,275	26,602	8.8	7,745	2,168	4,698
Emporia	–	–	1	154	2,757	2,030	-0.2	36,334	1,400	25,058	-5.9	785	424	7,589
Fairfax	143	650	–	–	–	11,150	19.1	50,767	2,600	11,838	4.8	1,880	228	1,038
Falls Church	83	785	–	–	–	2,691	-25.6	24,961	1,350	12,522	0.1	985	98	909
Franklin	33	391	1	193	2,284	2,525	7.0	29,381	2,015	23,447	3.4	1,105	507	5,899
Fredericksburg	167	804	–	–	–	9,115	8.3	43,966	3,470	16,737	5.9	2,245	398	1,920
Galax	50	754	1	76	1,147	3,541	7.5	53,041	2,115	31,681	7.9	1,245	353	5,288
Hampton	230	159	1	194	134	19,268	9.2	13,235	21,485	14,758	6.4	13,015	2,667	1,832
Harrisonburg	204	502	1	270	664	4,422	-2.6	10,930	4,420	10,930	2.1	2,965	512	1,266
Hopewell	44	196	1	264	1,179	4,227	4.6	18,629	4,540	20,009	2.8	2,605	817	3,601
Lexington	48	706	1	45	662	2,941	13.2	43,403	1,540	22,727	-16.6	1,060	120	1,771
Lynchburg	364	549	1	823	1,242	15,074	2.7	22,508	13,875	20,717	(Z)	8,550	2,016	3,010
Manassas	132	351	1	163	433	7,752	35.0	20,634	3,100	8,251	14.0	1,930	315	838
Manassas Park	–	–	–	–	–	7	-41.7	60	895	7,701	28.6	515	109	938
Martinsville	101	677	1	152	1,019	6,590	-1.8	44,154	4,395	29,447	-12.4	2,600	553	3,705
Newport News	464	255	3	503	276	22,083	6.0	12,275	25,305	14,066	4.8	14,800	4,217	2,344
Norfolk	1,108	467	4	1,079	455	27,645	-3.9	11,918	31,060	13,391	-3.6	17,940	7,132	3,075
Norton	41	1,080	1	133	3,503	1,373	0.9	37,340	1,210	32,907	-19.0	460	301	8,186
Petersburg	92	281	1	283	864	7,709	-6.6	23,644	7,435	22,804	-4.5	4,145	2,217	6,800
Poquoson	33	283	–	–	–	839	9.8	7,104	1,860	15,748	16.1	1,315	51	432
Portsmouth	304	306	1	466	469	15,887	-0.4	15,860	17,410	17,381	-1.9	10,155	3,834	3,828
Radford	62	423	–	–	–	2,333	5.0	16,007	2,010	13,791	-2.1	1,295	215	1,475
Richmond	1,076	555	5	1,701	877	36,822	-1.8	19,002	32,430	16,736	-4.1	19,490	8,357	4,313
Roanoke	565	610	–	–	–	24,302	0.1	26,235	19,520	21,073	4.7	11,100	3,518	3,798
Salem	189	771	1	521	2,126	6,777	8.6	27,488	5,400	21,903	5.7	3,530	338	1,371
South Boston[14]	(X)	(NA)	(X)	(X)	(NA)	(X)	(NA)	(NA)	(X)	(NA)	(NA)	(X)	(X)	(NA)
Staunton	89	386	–	–	–	7,107	11.0	30,454	5,520	23,653	0.5	3,615	486	2,083
Suffolk	255	333	1	138	180	10,337	15.8	13,086	12,485	15,805	15.2	7,240	2,210	2,798
Virginia Beach	1,219	278	2	339	77	45,429	16.0	10,362	52,705	12,022	12.1	33,805	4,528	1,033
Waynesboro	63	303	–	–	–	5,857	13.9	27,538	4,900	23,038	4.2	3,095	489	2,299
Williamsburg	11	96	–	–	–	6,229	-3.3	53,008	2,415	20,551	22.2	1,745	109	928
Winchester	245	985	–	–	–	5,990	21.3	23,846	4,850	19,308	8.1	3,230	537	2,138
WASHINGTON.	18,894	304	85	10,984	177	[6]818,451	[6]11.3	[6]13,017	[7]937,531	[7]14,910	[7]11.0	[7]613,620	115,692	1,840
Adams	16	96	2	34	204	1,614	6.6	9,605	2,295	13,658	2.3	1,485	290	1,726
Asotin	41	196	1	25	120	4,334	13.6	20,465	5,245	24,766	15.5	3,230	636	3,003
Benton	333	214	3	329	211	19,109	16.7	12,098	22,690	14,365	14.6	14,505	2,320	1,469
Chelan	257	373	2	193	280	8,616	14.1	12,345	12,990	18,613	11.3	9,200	1,189	1,704
Clallam	207	304	2	256	377	17,573	13.3	25,216	19,900	28,555	12.7	13,860	1,557	2,234

See footnotes at end of table.

Table B-6. Counties — Physicians, Community Hospitals, Medicare, Social Security, and Supplemental Security Income—Con.

[Includes United States, states, and 3,141 counties/county equivalents defined as of February 22, 2005. For more information on these areas, see Appendix C, Geographic Information]

County	Physicians, 2004[1] Number	Physicians, 2004[1] Rate per 100,000 persons[2]	Community hospitals, 2004[3] Number	Beds Number	Beds Rate per 100,000 persons[2]	Medicare program enrollment, 2005[4] Total	Medicare Percent change, 2000–2005	Medicare Rate per 100,000 persons[2]	Social Security program beneficiaries, December 2005 Number	Social Security Rate per 100,000 persons[2]	Social Security Percent change, 2000–2005	Retired workers, number	Supplemental Security Income program recipients, 2005 Number	SSI Rate per 100,000 persons[2]
WASHINGTON—Con.														
Clark	702	179	1	356	91	45,701	24.0	11,319	53,515	13,254	23.7	34,465	6,451	1,598
Columbia	3	72	1	61	1,467	869	5.1	21,046	1,055	25,551	7.9	670	117	2,834
Cowlitz	206	214	1	202	210	16,185	11.0	16,630	19,975	20,524	16.7	11,975	2,712	2,787
Douglas	27	78	–	–	–	7,612	11.2	21,763	5,815	16,625	16.1	3,940	427	1,221
Ferry	4	53	1	25	332	1,224	22.5	16,229	1,590	21,082	19.0	955	247	3,275
Franklin	58	97	1	132	221	5,199	11.6	8,251	6,165	9,784	15.0	3,840	1,171	1,858
Garfield	2	86	–	–	–	554	5.5	23,635	600	25,597	-2.1	360	32	1,365
Grant	81	101	2	98	123	11,063	9.4	13,620	12,605	15,518	10.4	8,115	1,735	2,136
Grays Harbor	75	107	2	118	168	13,217	5.5	18,642	15,445	21,770	5.8	9,490	2,230	3,145
Island	176	221	1	49	61	11,297	30.3	14,255	15,105	19,059	19.9	10,965	744	939
Jefferson	91	324	1	25	89	6,816	15.7	23,777	8,245	28,762	18.3	6,130	442	1,542
King	8,935	503	17	3,623	204	208,752	5.2	11,639	223,865	12,481	4.1	153,960	30,335	1,691
Kitsap	617	256	1	255	106	31,222	15.1	12,973	35,815	14,882	16.1	23,245	4,064	1,689
Kittitas	46	127	1	38	105	4,764	10.9	12,931	5,705	15,485	12.1	4,020	401	1,088
Klickitat	25	126	2	50	253	3,568	16.1	17,985	4,250	21,422	14.5	2,725	496	2,500
Lewis	101	142	2	145	203	13,792	10.3	19,037	16,220	22,388	11.8	9,875	1,875	2,588
Lincoln	9	86	1	36	346	2,347	11.9	22,609	2,575	24,805	12.0	1,675	172	1,657
Mason	56	105	1	49	92	10,685	15.0	19,656	13,055	23,979	15.7	8,780	1,204	2,215
Okanogan	65	165	3	147	372	7,179	11.8	18,046	8,660	21,769	11.4	5,655	1,173	2,949
Pacific	17	80	2	27	127	5,405	4.9	25,047	6,515	30,191	9.2	4,395	587	2,720
Pend Oreille	11	88	3	164	1,317	2,417	16.4	19,072	2,545	20,082	10.5	1,495	393	3,101
Pierce	1,925	258	5	1,040	139	91,338	11.9	12,117	106,230	14,093	11.8	64,910	15,430	2,047
San Juan	62	409	–	–	–	2,973	17.7	19,464	3,430	22,456	16.3	2,670	110	720
Skagit	310	279	3	178	160	18,576	11.5	16,414	21,360	18,874	10.8	14,545	1,830	1,617
Skamania	4	38	–	–	–	1,094	13.3	10,259	1,730	16,223	23.5	1,105	192	1,800
Snohomish	1,076	167	4	585	91	69,230	13.0	10,554	81,540	12,431	12.8	52,910	8,991	1,371
Spokane	1,395	321	6	1,304	300	64,740	9.8	14,690	73,415	16,658	10.2	45,895	10,524	2,388
Stevens	52	126	2	117	283	6,747	16.8	16,059	9,075	21,600	20.3	5,605	1,080	2,571
Thurston	647	288	2	422	188	31,917	18.3	13,946	38,105	16,649	17.4	24,440	3,930	1,717
Wahkiakum	4	106	–	–	–	884	18.2	22,967	1,065	27,670	15.4	715	67	1,741
Walla Walla	219	383	2	145	253	9,098	4.9	15,807	10,005	17,382	3.3	6,820	1,071	1,861
Whatcom	528	293	1	235	130	25,485	18.4	13,890	29,870	16,281	17.9	19,490	3,342	1,822
Whitman	63	157	2	59	147	4,227	3.5	10,523	4,815	11,987	7.1	3,120	358	891
Yakima	448	195	4	462	201	29,647	6.6	12,802	34,465	14,882	6.8	22,375	5,767	2,490
WEST VIRGINIA	4,613	255	57	7,412	409	[6]355,466	[6]5.2	[6]19,565	[7]414,053	[7]22,790	[7]5.2	[7]210,421	76,820	4,228
Barbour	9	58	1	72	464	3,021	4.7	19,256	3,685	23,488	6.3	1,795	885	5,641
Berkeley	146	164	1	143	160	12,280	19.9	13,149	14,795	15,841	23.0	8,785	1,667	1,785
Boone	8	31	1	25	97	5,064	7.7	19,702	6,265	24,375	6.2	2,170	1,500	5,836
Braxton	4	27	1	25	168	2,778	5.5	18,706	3,305	22,254	5.0	1,590	860	5,791
Brooke	6	24	1	238	963	4,372	1.7	17,834	5,910	24,108	2.0	3,325	553	2,256
Cabell	591	625	3	689	729	20,534	2.8	21,837	20,570	21,876	1.9	11,410	3,967	4,219
Calhoun	3	41	1	43	586	1,599	-0.1	21,646	1,990	26,939	5.3	900	692	9,368
Clay	4	38	–	–	–	2,074	7.5	20,027	2,440	23,561	5.9	955	801	7,735
Doddridge	2	27	–	–	–	970	1.9	12,975	1,190	15,918	-25.2	635	241	3,224
Fayette	58	123	2	124	264	10,369	1.2	22,145	12,315	26,301	2.3	5,365	2,765	5,905
Gilmer	3	43	–	–	–	1,389	4.0	19,986	1,605	23,094	-2.5	835	380	5,468
Grant	14	121	1	57	492	2,500	28.8	21,417	2,665	22,830	14.0	1,475	412	3,530
Greenbrier	78	224	1	101	290	7,874	5.5	22,480	8,575	24,481	5.4	4,515	1,348	3,848
Hampshire	10	46	1	44	204	3,607	9.2	16,377	4,580	20,795	11.5	2,680	721	3,274
Hancock	69	220	–	–	–	7,501	-0.9	23,927	7,855	25,056	-2.6	4,515	681	2,172
Hardy	9	68	–	–	–	2,343	10.8	17,634	2,880	21,675	14.5	1,660	413	3,108
Harrison	179	262	1	369	540	14,110	0.8	20,638	16,195	23,688	3.2	8,730	2,964	4,335
Jackson	18	63	1	60	211	5,812	14.9	20,463	6,785	23,888	11.5	3,475	1,128	3,971
Jefferson	71	149	1	60	126	6,252	14.4	12,706	7,300	14,836	12.3	4,565	737	1,498
Kanawha	897	460	4	1,144	587	40,700	2.1	21,027	45,780	23,652	1.5	25,020	6,769	3,497
Lewis	23	134	1	70	408	3,900	7.6	22,676	4,370	25,408	7.1	2,340	977	5,681
Lincoln	5	22	–	–	–	4,316	9.9	19,290	5,180	23,152	5.8	1,920	1,825	8,157
Logan	52	143	2	144	396	8,549	3.8	23,592	9,995	27,582	3.3	3,435	2,418	6,673
McDowell	20	81	–	–	–	6,706	-7.0	27,627	7,900	32,546	-10.8	2,245	3,433	14,143
Marion	101	179	1	167	296	11,850	-0.2	20,970	13,230	23,412	-0.2	7,530	1,941	3,435
Marshall	34	98	1	127	367	5,985	2.3	17,430	7,250	21,114	3.7	4,090	955	2,781
Mason	28	108	1	201	778	5,176	11.1	20,092	6,140	23,834	10.1	3,035	1,218	4,728
Mercer	176	284	4	537	867	14,452	3.5	23,465	16,300	26,466	5.1	7,545	3,583	5,818
Mineral	25	93	1	30	111	4,761	-0.1	17,615	5,700	21,089	11.4	3,250	759	2,808
Mingo	25	92	1	76	278	6,533	8.8	24,010	7,890	28,997	4.1	2,205	2,807	10,316
Monongalia	822	978	3	711	846	9,910	3.8	11,744	11,780	13,960	5.4	6,885	1,580	1,872
Monroe	6	44	–	–	–	3,181	7.6	23,551	3,420	25,320	9.4	1,780	540	3,998
Morgan	14	89	1	41	260	2,932	10.4	18,300	3,620	22,594	14.7	2,320	323	2,016
Nicholas	29	110	2	143	543	5,727	8.4	21,641	6,865	25,941	6.8	3,055	1,303	4,924
Ohio	268	591	2	447	985	10,297	-1.7	22,825	11,475	25,437	-3.0	7,405	1,385	3,070

See footnotes at end of table.

[Includes United States, states, and 3,141 counties/county equivalents defined as of February 22, 2005. For more information on these areas, see Appendix C, Geographic Information]

County	Physicians, 2004[1] Number	Physicians, 2004[1] Rate per 100,000 persons[2]	Community hospitals, 2004[3] Number	Beds Number	Beds Rate per 100,000 persons[2]	Medicare program enrollment, 2005[4] Total	Medicare Percent change, 2000–2005	Medicare Rate per 100,000 persons[2]	Social Security program beneficiaries, December 2005 Number	Social Security Rate per 100,000 persons[2]	Social Security Percent change, 2000–2005	Retired workers, number	Supplemental Security Income program recipients, 2005 Number	SSI Rate per 100,000 persons[2]
WEST VIRGINIA—Con.														
Pendleton	6	76	–	–	–	1,743	7.8	22,221	1,980	25,242	7.6	1,195	256	3,264
Pleasants	2	27	–	–	–	1,398	5.2	18,953	1,645	22,302	6.3	850	257	3,484
Pocahontas	8	90	1	25	280	1,896	0.2	21,421	2,260	25,534	2.1	1,245	319	3,604
Preston	34	114	1	25	84	5,478	5.6	18,190	6,630	22,016	8.2	3,430	1,267	4,207
Putnam	82	152	1	68	126	7,722	18.1	14,184	9,965	18,304	18.8	5,385	1,085	1,993
Raleigh	214	270	2	398	503	16,354	5.1	20,658	19,640	24,808	5.2	8,470	3,417	4,316
Randolph	63	221	1	90	316	5,852	7.4	20,482	6,670	23,345	10.5	3,460	1,372	4,802
Ritchie	3	29	–	–	–	2,063	8.9	19,573	2,750	26,091	12.1	1,435	567	5,380
Roane	20	131	1	60	392	3,021	9.5	19,608	3,970	25,768	8.6	1,865	1,028	6,672
Summers	13	94	1	61	442	2,832	1.2	20,611	3,090	22,489	6.7	1,465	934	6,798
Taylor	12	74	1	101	624	2,728	3.1	16,745	3,310	20,318	9.5	1,735	699	4,291
Tucker	8	114	–	–	–	1,524	3.5	21,950	1,905	27,438	3.5	1,095	240	3,457
Tyler	5	53	1	12	128	1,685	8.1	18,041	2,325	24,893	8.6	1,215	331	3,544
Upshur	31	130	1	69	290	4,352	8.9	18,354	5,155	21,740	8.7	2,705	1,091	4,601
Wayne	53	125	–	–	–	6,520	3.3	15,490	9,485	22,535	7.4	4,310	2,529	6,008
Webster	4	41	1	15	152	2,150	4.0	21,930	2,595	26,469	5.3	990	828	8,446
Wetzel	18	105	1	53	310	4,085	6.0	23,865	4,320	25,238	3.6	2,270	754	4,405
Wirt	4	68	–	–	–	1,149	16.1	19,488	1,290	21,879	6.6	640	315	5,343
Wood	219	252	3	547	629	17,117	8.9	19,664	20,085	23,074	8.7	11,230	3,048	3,502
Wyoming	7	29	–	–	–	5,700	3.6	23,285	7,185	29,352	1.4	1,990	1,952	7,974
WISCONSIN	15,625	284	121	14,577	265	[6]825,876	[6]5.5	[6]14,918	[7]953,581	[7]17,224	[7]5.8	[7]639,221	92,288	1,667
Adams	7	34	1	43	210	3,138	9.0	15,066	5,850	28,087	16.3	4,085	440	2,113
Ashland	60	360	1	100	599	3,317	0.1	19,949	3,615	21,742	2.3	2,275	373	2,243
Barron	91	199	3	234	513	8,717	6.1	19,019	10,050	21,927	5.4	6,695	821	1,791
Bayfield	20	132	–	–	–	2,770	6.7	18,290	3,705	24,464	8.8	2,570	257	1,697
Brown	637	269	4	662	279	29,780	10.6	12,461	34,715	14,526	11.0	22,210	3,422	1,432
Buffalo	5	36	–	–	–	2,745	5.4	19,652	3,080	22,050	4.9	2,050	204	1,460
Burnett	8	48	1	70	424	3,521	10.5	21,303	4,545	27,499	8.9	3,265	262	1,585
Calumet	15	34	1	25	57	3,904	6.2	8,845	6,400	14,500	13.8	4,310	354	802
Chippewa	86	146	3	221	375	9,486	4.2	15,823	11,125	18,557	5.0	7,215	989	1,650
Clark	21	62	1	141	414	6,018	0.5	17,649	6,575	19,283	-0.6	4,265	516	1,513
Columbia	72	131	2	201	367	10,010	7.0	18,080	10,155	18,342	3.6	7,155	479	865
Crawford	23	135	1	24	140	3,128	5.1	18,256	3,755	21,915	8.7	2,485	354	2,066
Dane	2,670	589	4	1,166	257	49,841	10.5	10,880	57,530	12,558	10.6	39,465	5,847	1,276
Dodge	107	122	2	267	304	10,132	3.5	11,500	15,290	17,355	5.5	10,685	679	771
Door	71	251	1	73	258	6,179	9.8	21,796	7,330	25,856	11.3	5,425	237	836
Douglas	39	89	1	24	55	7,636	6.3	17,273	8,205	18,560	6.6	5,055	1,096	2,479
Dunn	34	82	1	43	104	5,608	11.9	13,446	6,705	16,076	13.2	4,025	638	1,530
Eau Claire	415	441	2	366	389	13,689	5.9	14,549	15,810	16,803	7.4	10,190	1,721	1,829
Florence	3	60	–	–	–	728	-12.6	14,636	1,240	24,930	7.7	840	93	1,870
Fond du Lac	178	180	3	220	223	16,469	4.0	16,579	17,535	17,652	4.8	12,070	1,106	1,113
Forest	6	60	–	–	–	2,192	5.9	22,006	2,550	25,600	9.2	1,780	209	2,098
Grant	46	93	3	271	546	9,563	4.8	19,253	10,230	20,596	0.8	7,000	711	1,431
Green	76	219	1	100	288	5,589	4.8	15,894	6,405	18,214	6.3	4,410	351	998
Green Lake	30	157	1	135	705	4,030	1.0	21,025	4,525	23,607	1.7	3,160	225	1,174
Iowa	17	73	1	84	359	3,184	3.6	13,509	3,800	16,123	2.1	2,595	287	1,218
Iron	7	105	–	–	–	1,587	-0.4	23,868	1,900	28,576	-2.9	1,315	117	1,760
Jackson	27	139	1	25	128	3,183	4.5	16,110	3,920	19,840	8.4	2,575	365	1,847
Jefferson	71	91	1	100	128	12,905	7.0	16,268	13,720	17,295	7.5	9,020	821	1,035
Juneau	25	98	1	157	616	5,162	7.7	19,315	6,015	22,507	8.7	3,940	481	1,800
Kenosha	241	152	2	220	139	19,652	5.4	12,241	24,385	15,189	6.7	15,310	2,504	1,560
Kewaunee	16	77	–	–	–	3,451	4.0	16,560	3,865	18,546	4.7	2,545	167	801
La Crosse	565	521	2	482	444	15,905	6.3	14,597	18,060	16,575	6.3	12,270	1,963	1,802
Lafayette	10	61	1	25	153	2,754	2.6	16,885	3,215	19,712	1.6	2,145	207	1,269
Langlade	28	134	1	42	201	4,340	3.8	20,931	5,070	24,451	3.0	3,420	424	2,045
Lincoln	35	116	1	14	46	6,174	7.4	20,363	6,635	21,884	4.1	4,575	384	1,267
Manitowoc	157	192	2	217	265	14,682	1.5	17,916	17,005	20,751	2.8	11,820	1,101	1,344
Marathon	348	272	1	253	198	18,109	6.9	14,044	21,825	16,926	7.7	14,645	1,881	1,459
Marinette	70	162	1	99	229	9,369	4.6	21,585	10,540	24,282	5.9	6,965	725	1,670
Marquette	5	33	–	–	–	4,106	7.8	26,948	4,265	27,991	5.8	3,030	220	1,444
Menominee	4	87	–	–	–	578	17.0	12,620	805	17,576	11.3	475	187	4,083
Milwaukee	3,525	380	13	3,254	351	132,594	-4.6	14,387	148,850	16,150	-4.3	93,140	33,320	3,615
Monroe	55	130	2	80	189	6,361	4.3	14,917	7,380	17,306	4.5	4,800	727	1,705
Oconto	25	67	1	25	67	5,894	7.9	15,648	7,840	20,815	10.1	5,195	455	1,208
Oneida	169	456	2	113	305	8,931	8.9	24,142	10,190	27,545	7.9	7,335	530	1,433
Outagamie	394	233	3	362	214	22,556	12.1	13,190	25,060	14,654	9.0	16,620	1,672	978
Ozaukee	417	487	1	106	124	12,877	14.1	14,961	14,640	17,009	11.9	10,725	373	433
Pepin	7	94	1	83	1,118	1,420	3.0	19,241	1,565	21,206	4.6	1,050	115	1,558
Pierce	39	101	1	27	70	5,042	8.3	12,894	5,230	13,375	8.8	3,550	270	691
Polk	67	153	3	93	212	7,115	8.5	16,050	8,585	19,367	9.9	5,835	484	1,092
Portage	126	187	1	122	181	8,950	7.9	13,243	10,790	15,965	11.1	7,250	855	1,265

See footnotes at end of table.

[Includes United States, states, and 3,141 counties/county equivalents defined as of February 22, 2005. For more information on these areas, see Appendix C, Geographic Information]

| County | Physicians, 2004[1] | | Community hospitals, 2004[3] | | | Medicare program enrollment, 2005[4] | | | Social Security program beneficiaries, December 2005 | | | | Supplemental Security Income program recipients, 2005 | |
| | | | | Beds | | | | | | | | | | |
	Number	Rate per 100,000 persons[2]	Number	Number	Rate per 100,000 persons[2]	Total	Percent change, 2000-2005	Rate per 100,000 persons[2]	Number	Rate per 100,000 persons[2]	Percent change, 2000-2005	Retired workers, number	Number	Rate per 100,000 persons[2]
WISCONSIN—Con.														
Price	15	98	1	25	163	3,320	2.3	21,813	3,860	25,361	2.6	2,545	265	1,741
Racine	371	191	3	438	226	29,380	6.0	15,012	33,535	17,135	6.4	21,760	3,645	1,862
Richland	27	147	1	25	136	3,052	3.0	16,584	3,815	20,730	4.1	2,475	392	2,130
Rock	349	223	3	401	257	23,575	7.9	14,965	27,800	17,647	8.0	18,190	2,963	1,881
Rusk	14	92	1	122	800	3,025	-0.9	19,904	3,595	23,654	1.3	2,305	361	2,375
St. Croix	81	109	3	75	101	7,249	18.6	9,397	9,355	12,127	21.7	6,320	451	585
Sauk	96	168	3	208	364	9,495	7.1	16,443	11,035	19,110	7.7	7,625	675	1,169
Sawyer	30	178	1	117	695	3,390	7.7	19,971	4,395	25,891	13.7	3,120	349	2,056
Shawano	30	73	1	39	95	7,322	3.0	17,714	8,770	21,217	3.9	5,955	571	1,381
Sheboygan	205	180	2	311	273	17,927	3.2	15,642	20,430	17,826	4.4	14,325	1,327	1,158
Taylor	12	61	1	122	619	3,173	3.7	16,053	3,795	19,200	5.7	2,500	270	1,366
Trempealeau	30	109	3	272	990	5,318	2.9	19,121	5,760	20,710	1.6	3,820	422	1,517
Vernon	41	143	2	88	307	5,333	2.5	18,355	6,025	20,737	2.3	3,930	491	1,690
Vilas	31	140	1	8	36	5,735	13.0	25,683	7,215	32,311	12.2	5,390	229	1,026
Walworth	112	114	1	75	76	13,662	9.4	13,683	16,290	16,315	10.5	11,200	834	835
Washburn	20	121	2	164	988	4,514	10.5	27,191	4,390	26,444	4.1	3,020	373	2,247
Washington	169	136	2	158	127	16,802	15.4	13,318	19,745	15,651	14.1	14,110	622	493
Waukesha	1,721	457	4	668	177	53,976	13.5	14,243	61,330	16,183	11.6	44,705	1,955	516
Waupaca	61	116	1	25	48	10,828	4.0	20,600	11,550	21,974	8.1	7,945	634	1,206
Waushara	23	93	1	27	109	4,680	6.5	18,879	5,835	23,539	5.3	4,055	391	1,577
Winnebago	468	295	2	338	213	23,043	4.8	14,449	27,375	17,165	7.2	18,500	1,954	1,225
Wood	549	730	2	502	667	15,020	8.2	19,964	15,595	20,729	5.2	10,590	1,095	1,455
WYOMING	1,093	216	24	2,048	405	[6]71,005	[6]8.5	[6]13,942	81,495	16,002	7.1	[7]53,912	5,786	1,136
Albany	76	242	1	99	315	3,123	2.4	10,110	3,450	11,169	4.3	2,385	261	845
Big Horn	10	88	1	100	880	2,095	3.2	18,486	2,400	21,177	2.8	1,615	166	1,465
Campbell	58	158	1	201	548	2,584	19.5	6,908	3,245	8,675	15.3	1,925	227	607
Carbon	18	117	1	45	293	2,218	2.0	14,467	2,520	16,437	4.5	1,705	151	985
Converse	17	136	1	25	200	1,730	15.4	13,552	2,075	16,254	11.3	1,365	118	924
Crook	4	66	1	48	796	992	10.8	16,047	1,190	19,249	12.6	815	30	485
Fremont	91	251	2	159	439	6,002	9.0	16,448	7,090	19,429	5.1	4,640	793	2,173
Goshen	16	130	1	25	203	2,421	3.4	19,775	2,790	22,789	4.3	1,890	210	1,715
Hot Springs	8	175	1	25	546	1,149	7.3	25,325	1,350	29,755	8.3	895	88	1,940
Johnson	11	145	1	75	986	1,527	8.9	19,777	1,745	22,601	4.9	1,245	39	505
Laramie	235	276	1	210	247	11,858	10.7	13,924	13,120	15,406	10.5	8,470	1,088	1,278
Lincoln	14	89	2	80	511	2,130	11.7	13,313	2,575	16,095	12.2	1,805	102	638
Natrona	182	264	1	205	297	10,135	5.3	14,520	11,640	16,676	2.7	7,540	1,081	1,549
Niobrara	1	44	–	–	–	508	1.2	22,222	605	26,465	6.1	395	32	1,400
Park	69	261	2	278	1,053	4,726	15.8	17,724	5,640	21,152	14.1	3,865	256	960
Platte	7	81	1	68	784	1,757	4.5	20,385	1,985	23,031	2.0	1,360	106	1,230
Sheridan	73	268	1	62	228	4,698	2.9	17,153	5,260	19,205	2.9	3,565	302	1,103
Sublette	12	180	–	–	–	879	10.4	12,691	1,045	15,088	9.2	745	27	390
Sweetwater	41	109	1	99	264	3,841	6.2	10,115	4,515	11,889	5.3	2,825	303	798
Teton	102	537	1	108	568	1,619	18.7	8,507	1,855	9,747	19.4	1,400	39	205
Uinta	30	152	1	42	212	1,930	15.8	9,680	2,300	11,535	14.1	1,325	225	1,128
Washakie	10	127	1	25	317	1,494	1.8	18,833	1,725	21,745	1.5	1,220	82	1,034
Weston	8	120	1	69	1,033	1,262	6.5	18,918	1,375	20,612	-2.1	915	60	899

– Represents zero.   D Data withheld to avoid disclosure.   NA Not available.   X Not applicable.   Z Less than .05 percent.

[1]Active, nonfederal physicians as of December 31. Data subject to copyright; see below for source citation.
[2]Based on resident population estimated as of July 1 of the year shown.
[3]Nonfederal, short-term general, and other special hospitals except hospital units of institutions. Data subject to copyright; see below for source citation.
[4]Unduplicated count of persons enrolled in either hospital and/or supplemental medical insurance.
[5]Includes data not distributed by state.
[6]Includes data not distributed by county.
[7]Includes data not distributed by county. Counties do not add to the state total due to use of rounding procedure to avoid disclosure and/or presence of unknowns.
[8]Aleutians East Borough included with Aleutians West Census Area; data not available separately.
[9]Denali Borough included with Yukon-Koyukuk Census Area; data not available separately.
[10]Lake and Peninsula Borough included with Dillingham Census Area; data not available separately.
[11]Yakutat City and Borough included with Skagway-Hoonah-Angoon Census Area; data not available separately.
[12]Yellowstone National Park County became incorporated with Gallatin and Park Counties, MT; effective November 7, 1997.
[13]Clifton Forge independent city became incorporated with Alleghany County, VA; effective July 1, 2001.
[14]South Boston independent city became incorporated with Halifax County, VA; effective June 30, 1995.

Survey, Census, or Data Collection Method: For information about these data collections and surveys, see the following organizations and their Web sites: American Medical Association, *Physician Characteristics and Distribution in the U.S.*, <http://www.ama-assn.org/>;   American Hospital Association (AHA), *Hospital Statistics*, <http://www.healthforum.com>;   Centers for Medicare and Medicaid Services, CMS Statistics, Medicare Enrollment, <http://www.cms.hhs.gov/>;   U.S. Social Security Administration, OASDI Beneficiaries by State and County, <http://www.ssa.gov/policy /docs/statcomps/oasdi_sc/2005/index.html>; SSI Monthly Statistics, Supplemental Security Income, <http://www.ssa.gov/policy/docs/statcomps/ssi_monthly/>; and SSI Recipients by State and County, updated annually, <http://www.ssa.gov/policy/docs/statcomps/ssi_sc/>.

Sources: Physicians—American Medical Association, Chicago, IL, *Physician Characteristics and Distribution in the U.S.*, annual (copyright), accessed May 17, 2006.   Community hospitals—Health Forum LLC, an American Hospital Association (AHA) Company, Chicago, IL, *Hospital Statistics*, and unpublished data (copyright), e-mail accessed May 4, 2006 (related Internet site <http://www.healthforum.com>).   Medicare program enrollment—Centers for Medicare and Medicaid Services, CMS Statistics, Medicare Enrollment, accessed February 8, 2006 (related Internet site <http://www.cms.hhs.gov/>).   Social Security program—U.S. Social Security Administration, Office of Research, Evaluation, and Statistics, OASDI Beneficiaries by State and County, accessed October 24, 2006 (related Internet site <http://www.ssa.gov/policy/docs/statcomps/oasdi_sc/2005/>).   Supplemental Security Income program—U.S. Social Security Administration, Office of Research, Evaluation, and Statistics, *SSI Recipients by State and County, 2005*, accessed July 24, 2006 (related Internet site <http://www.ssa.gov/policy/docs/statcomps/ssi_sc/2005/>).

[Includes United States, states, and 3,141 counties/county equivalents defined as of February 22, 2005. For more information on these areas, see Appendix C, Geographic Information]

County	Housing units							Housing 2000, percent		New private housing units authorized by building permits		
	2005 (July 1)	2000[1] (April 1 esti-mates base)	1990 (April 1)	Net change, 2000–2005 Number	Percent	Units per square mile of land area 2005[2]	1990	Owner-occupied housing units[3]	Units in multi-unit structures	Cumu-lative, 2000–2005 period	2005	2004
UNITED STATES.........	124,521,886	115,904,474	102,263,678	8,617,412	7.4	35.2	28.9	66.2	26.4	11,091,316	2,155,316	2,070,077
ALABAMA..............	2,082,140	1,963,834	1,670,379	118,306	6.0	41.0	32.9	72.5	15.3	133,794	30,612	27,411
Autauga.................	19,263	17,663	12,732	1,600	9.1	32.3	21.4	80.8	4.6	1,820	313	367
Baldwin.................	89,900	74,285	50,933	15,615	21.0	56.3	31.9	79.5	18.9	22,157	6,715	4,759
Barbour.................	12,770	12,461	10,705	309	2.5	14.4	12.1	73.1	10.6	169	24	19
Bibb...................	8,576	8,345	6,404	231	2.8	13.8	10.3	80.2	6.3	19	3	4
Blount.................	21,681	21,162	15,790	519	2.5	33.6	24.5	83.4	4.2	347	49	78
Bullock.................	4,788	4,683	4,458	105	2.2	7.7	7.1	74.5	7.9	19	–	1
Butler.................	10,277	9,958	8,745	319	3.2	13.2	11.3	76.2	9.2	209	52	18
Calhoun.................	52,897	51,321	46,753	1,576	3.1	86.9	76.8	72.5	11.5	1,479	266	222
Chambers.................	16,471	16,256	14,910	215	1.3	27.6	25.0	75.7	7.7	109	14	17
Cherokee.................	14,473	14,025	9,379	448	3.2	26.2	17.0	81.7	3.9	139	27	22
Chilton.................	18,341	17,651	13,883	690	3.9	26.4	20.0	82.3	3.2	437	141	96
Choctaw.................	8,036	7,839	6,789	197	2.5	8.8	7.4	86.3	3.4	13	5	2
Clarke.................	12,951	12,631	10,853	320	2.5	10.5	8.8	81.2	6.4	135	13	20
Clay...................	6,784	6,612	5,608	172	2.6	11.2	9.3	77.2	7.5	67	7	40
Cleburne.................	6,372	6,189	5,232	183	3.0	11.4	9.3	80.4	3.7	81	34	6
Coffee.................	20,953	19,837	16,951	1,116	5.6	30.9	25.0	71.4	12.8	1,500	525	369
Colbert.................	25,903	24,980	21,812	923	3.7	43.6	36.7	75.7	11.6	907	148	135
Conecuh.................	7,421	7,265	6,207	156	2.1	8.7	7.3	81.0	5.7	15	–	1
Coosa.................	6,291	6,140	5,113	151	2.5	9.6	7.8	84.8	2.5	44	44	–
Covington.................	18,925	18,578	16,178	347	1.9	18.3	15.6	77.7	6.3	145	13	54
Crenshaw.................	6,797	6,644	5,938	153	2.3	11.2	9.7	76.7	7.4	69	39	3
Cullman.................	36,300	35,232	28,369	1,068	3.0	49.2	38.4	78.0	7.5	471	92	86
Dale.................	22,394	21,779	19,432	615	2.8	39.9	34.6	64.3	12.7	364	80	75
Dallas.................	20,825	20,450	19,045	375	1.8	21.2	19.4	65.7	13.2	143	4	4
DeKalb.................	28,917	28,051	22,939	866	3.1	37.2	29.5	78.7	5.9	460	84	87
Elmore.................	28,046	25,734	19,497	2,312	9.0	45.1	31.4	81.3	5.6	2,275	522	474
Escambia.................	16,839	16,544	14,356	295	1.8	17.8	15.2	77.1	7.5	173	82	17
Etowah.................	47,604	45,959	41,787	1,645	3.6	89.0	78.1	74.4	10.9	1,940	399	309
Fayette.................	8,684	8,472	7,555	212	2.5	13.8	12.0	77.3	8.5	42	9	8
Franklin.................	14,025	13,749	11,772	276	2.0	22.1	18.5	74.3	9.6	139	30	19
Geneva.................	12,368	12,117	10,416	251	2.1	21.5	18.1	80.6	4.9	113	22	19
Greene.................	5,256	5,117	4,162	139	2.7	8.1	6.4	75.6	5.7	19	1	1
Hale.................	8,086	7,756	6,370	330	4.3	12.6	9.9	80.2	6.3	265	76	44
Henry.................	8,293	8,037	7,056	256	3.2	14.8	12.6	80.9	4.7	180	50	31
Houston.................	42,220	39,569	33,196	2,651	6.7	72.7	57.2	69.5	15.0	3,077	629	681
Jackson.................	24,903	24,168	19,768	735	3.0	23.1	18.3	77.9	7.1	409	83	59
Jefferson.................	301,672	288,160	273,097	13,512	4.7	271.1	245.4	66.5	25.4	20,466	3,861	4,269
Lamar.................	7,677	7,517	6,617	160	2.1	12.7	10.9	76.8	9.2	10	–	3
Lauderdale.................	41,752	40,424	33,522	1,328	3.3	62.4	50.1	73.2	15.0	1,065	178	170
Lawrence.................	15,447	15,009	12,212	438	2.9	22.3	17.6	83.0	4.3	71	7	6
Lee.................	56,954	50,329	36,636	6,625	13.2	93.6	60.2	62.1	24.3	7,286	1,766	1,500
Limestone.................	28,487	26,897	21,455	1,590	5.9	50.1	37.8	77.3	9.8	1,046	284	155
Lowndes.................	5,852	5,800	4,792	52	0.9	8.2	6.7	83.3	5.4	20	3	4
Macon.................	10,800	10,627	9,818	272	2.6	17.9	16.1	67.3	18.3	223	21	18
Madison.................	131,859	120,411	97,855	11,448	9.5	163.8	121.6	69.9	22.7	12,070	3,157	3,534
Marengo.................	10,333	10,127	9,144	206	2.0	10.6	9.4	79.2	9.6	90	30	17
Marion.................	14,824	14,416	12,597	408	2.8	20.0	17.0	77.8	9.5	230	25	29
Marshall.................	37,664	36,330	30,225	1,334	3.7	66.4	53.3	74.7	9.7	1,263	343	184
Mobile.................	174,745	165,101	151,220	9,644	5.8	141.7	122.6	68.8	17.7	12,482	2,183	2,370
Monroe.................	11,664	11,343	9,633	321	2.8	11.4	9.4	80.4	5.5	119	8	13
Montgomery.................	99,880	95,437	84,525	4,443	4.7	126.5	107.0	64.1	23.6	6,513	1,558	1,215
Morgan.................	49,514	47,388	40,419	2,126	4.5	85.0	69.4	73.1	15.8	2,253	393	368
Perry.................	5,510	5,406	4,807	104	1.9	7.7	6.7	74.0	8.3	10	–	2
Pickens.................	9,736	9,520	8,379	216	2.3	11.0	9.5	79.3	6.9	46	8	8
Pike.................	14,540	14,025	11,506	515	3.7	21.7	17.1	67.2	14.1	471	123	85
Randolph.................	10,543	10,285	8,728	258	2.5	18.1	15.0	79.2	4.7	10	–	2
Russell.................	24,589	22,831	19,633	1,758	7.7	38.3	30.6	62.5	20.5	2,245	512	533
St. Clair.................	29,726	27,303	20,382	2,423	8.9	46.9	32.1	83.7	4.6	2,655	810	546
Shelby.................	71,457	59,302	39,201	12,155	20.5	89.9	49.3	81.0	12.7	13,550	2,734	2,688
Sumter.................	7,109	6,953	6,545	156	2.2	7.9	7.2	72.3	13.3	39	2	3
Talladega.................	35,625	34,470	29,861	1,155	3.4	48.2	40.4	76.3	10.0	808	186	144
Tallapoosa.................	21,025	20,510	17,312	515	2.5	29.3	24.1	76.3	9.4	332	91	43
Tuscaloosa.................	77,583	71,429	58,740	6,154	8.6	58.6	44.3	63.5	24.9	7,127	1,650	1,223
Walker.................	33,322	32,417	28,427	905	2.8	41.9	35.8	80.0	6.3	386	70	119
Washington.................	8,353	8,123	6,625	230	2.8	7.7	6.1	88.1	1.8	21	3	3
Wilcox.................	6,362	6,183	5,119	179	2.9	7.2	5.8	83.3	4.7	–	3	–
Winston.................	12,807	12,502	10,254	305	2.4	20.8	16.7	80.1	5.5	28	11	10

See footnotes at end of table.

[Includes United States, states, and 3,141 counties/county equivalents defined as of February 22, 2005. For more information on these areas, see Appendix C, Geographic Information]

County	Housing units								Housing 2000, percent		New private housing units authorized by building permits		
	2005 (July 1)	2000[1] (April 1 estimates base)	1990 (April 1)	Net change, 2000–2005		Units per square mile of land area			Owner-occupied housing units[3]	Units in multi-unit structures	Cumulative, 2000–2005 period	2005	2004
				Number	Percent	2005[2]	1990						
ALASKA	274,246	260,963	232,608	13,283	5.1	0.5	0.4		62.5	27.0	[4]17,638	[4]2,885	[4]3,133
Aleutians East.	742	724	693	18	2.5	0.1	0.1		58.2	17.5	17	–	4
Aleutians West	2,343	2,234	2,051	109	4.9	0.5	0.5		27.8	36.5	113	8	11
Anchorage.	108,787	100,368	94,153	8,419	8.4	64.1	55.5		60.1	36.9	10,971	1,666	1,775
Bethel	5,446	5,188	4,362	258	5.0	0.1	0.1		61.1	12.2	309	69	69
Bristol Bay	969	979	596	–10	–1.0	1.9	1.1		50.0	14.9	4	3	1
Denali	1,405	1,351	([5])	54	4.0	0.1	([5])		65.1	13.1	(NA)	–	–
Dillingham	2,433	2,332	1,691	101	4.3	0.1	0.1		60.4	13.7	(NA)	–	–
Fairbanks North Star	34,046	33,291	31,823	755	2.3	4.6	4.3		54.0	33.8	1,253	182	337
Haines	1,462	1,419	1,112	43	3.0	0.6	0.5		70.0	15.1	43	3	4
Juneau	12,673	12,282	10,638	391	3.2	4.7	4.1		63.7	30.4	664	125	122
Kenai Peninsula	25,228	24,871	19,364	357	1.4	1.6	1.2		73.7	13.3	655	128	101
Ketchikan Gateway	6,533	6,218	5,463	315	5.1	5.3	4.5		60.7	40.0	227	29	42
Kodiak Island	5,559	5,159	4,885	400	7.8	0.8	0.8		54.8	32.8	368	60	74
Lake and Peninsula	1,575	1,557	991	18	1.2	0.1	(Z)		68.2	2.9	(NA)	–	–
Matanuska-Susitna	28,153	27,329	20,953	824	3.0	1.1	0.8		78.9	9.9	1,169	233	267
Nome	3,674	3,649	3,684	25	0.7	0.2	0.2		58.1	18.0	26	2	7
North Slope	2,716	2,538	2,153	178	7.0	(Z)	(Z)		48.9	25.1	87	9	16
Northwest Arctic	2,564	2,540	1,998	24	0.9	0.1	0.1		56.0	18.0	(NA)	–	–
Prince of Wales- Outer Ketchikan	3,180	3,055	2,543	125	4.1	0.4	0.3		69.8	9.2	13	3	7
Sitka	3,828	3,650	3,222	178	4.9	1.3	1.1		58.1	30.0	306	71	46
Skagway-Hoonah-Angoon	2,308	2,108	[6]2,102	200	9.5	0.3	[6]0.2		62.9	10.9	106	19	6
Southeast Fairbanks	3,354	3,225	3,149	129	4.0	0.1	0.1		68.5	17.1	(NA)	–	–
Valdez-Cordova	5,223	5,148	5,196	75	1.5	0.2	0.1		67.9	20.2	153	26	21
Wade Hampton	2,075	2,063	1,882	12	0.6	0.1	0.1		66.7	4.2	(NA)	–	–
Wrangell-Petersburg.	3,393	3,284	3,005	109	3.3	0.6	0.5		70.4	16.0	83	11	16
Yakutat	513	499	([6])	14	2.8	0.1	([6])		59.6	7.4	24	4	5
Yukon-Koyukuk	4,064	3,902	[5]4,899	162	4.2	(Z)	(Z)		67.3	2.9	(NA)	–	–
ARIZONA	2,544,806	2,189,189	1,659,430	355,617	16.2	22.4	14.6		68.0	22.1	446,503	90,851	90,644
Apache	32,103	31,621	26,731	482	1.5	2.9	2.4		74.3	5.4	682	143	134
Cochise	54,911	51,126	40,238	3,785	7.4	8.9	6.5		67.3	12.6	5,246	1,381	956
Coconino	58,104	53,443	42,914	4,661	8.7	3.1	2.3		61.4	18.4	5,604	1,080	910
Gila	29,661	28,189	22,961	1,472	5.2	6.2	4.8		78.7	5.3	1,967	493	283
Graham	11,775	11,430	9,112	345	3.0	2.5	2.0		73.2	6.8	569	208	93
Greenlee	3,742	3,744	3,582	–2	–0.1	2.0	1.9		50.6	4.9	22	9	2
La Paz	15,443	15,133	10,182	310	2.0	3.4	2.3		78.0	3.4	390	138	82
Maricopa	1,481,431	1,250,357	952,041	231,074	18.5	161.0	103.4		67.5	26.6	282,725	50,823	54,892
Mohave	94,768	80,062	50,822	14,706	18.4	7.1	3.8		73.6	10.9	18,483	4,011	4,121
Navajo	51,128	47,413	38,967	3,715	7.8	5.1	3.9		75.4	5.7	5,274	1,535	950
Pima	407,048	366,737	298,207	40,311	11.0	44.3	32.5		64.3	25.1	52,473	11,644	10,521
Pinal	108,777	81,028	52,732	27,749	34.2	20.3	9.8		77.4	9.0	39,320	11,794	10,367
Santa Cruz	15,459	13,036	9,595	2,423	18.6	12.5	7.8		68.0	16.4	3,272	845	630
Yavapai	97,270	81,730	54,805	15,540	19.0	12.0	6.7		73.4	10.7	19,229	4,439	4,003
Yuma	83,186	74,140	46,541	9,046	12.2	15.1	8.4		72.3	12.0	11,247	2,308	2,700
ARKANSAS	1,249,116	1,173,042	1,000,667	76,074	6.5	24.0	19.2		69.4	13.9	80,672	17,932	15,855
Arkansas	9,811	9,671	9,575	140	1.4	9.9	9.7		67.9	9.0	118	36	23
Ashley	10,905	10,615	9,820	290	2.7	11.8	10.7		76.0	5.6	116	11	11
Baxter	20,759	19,891	15,549	868	4.4	37.4	28.0		79.7	7.8	794	168	105
Benton	76,074	64,281	41,444	11,793	18.3	89.9	49.1		72.2	13.8	15,071	4,663	3,090
Boone	15,962	15,426	12,380	536	3.5	27.0	20.9		73.3	11.3	568	76	58
Bradley	5,949	5,930	5,092	19	0.3	9.1	7.8		72.7	8.2	42	9	10
Calhoun	3,090	3,012	2,437	78	2.6	4.9	3.9		82.3	2.3	6	2	1
Carroll	12,254	11,828	8,740	426	3.6	19.4	13.8		73.0	9.8	286	78	78
Chicot	6,107	5,974	6,191	133	2.2	9.5	9.6		69.8	9.2	85	15	10
Clark	10,593	10,166	8,807	427	4.2	12.2	10.2		65.7	16.1	326	19	27
Clay	8,648	8,498	8,362	150	1.8	13.5	13.1		74.9	7.5	93	10	13
Cleburne	14,369	13,732	10,802	637	4.6	26.0	19.5		80.4	6.0	344	63	59
Cleveland	3,952	3,834	3,322	118	3.1	6.6	5.6		82.2	2.8	3	–	3
Columbia	11,848	11,566	10,690	282	2.4	15.5	14.0		71.4	8.5	136	6	9
Conway	9,255	9,028	8,009	227	2.5	16.6	14.4		78.1	6.7	72	15	16
Craighead	37,711	35,133	28,434	2,578	7.3	53.1	40.0		63.9	18.6	3,002	571	521
Crawford	22,636	21,315	16,711	1,321	6.2	38.0	28.1		75.9	9.6	1,231	251	213
Crittenden	21,934	20,507	18,875	1,427	7.0	35.9	30.9		60.3	21.3	1,816	412	303
Cross	8,336	8,030	7,254	306	3.8	13.5	11.8		70.8	9.4	235	41	38
Dallas	4,474	4,401	4,049	73	1.7	6.7	6.1		73.8	6.9	22	6	2
Desha	6,824	6,663	6,706	161	2.4	8.9	8.8		63.5	12.6	126	6	9
Drew	8,702	8,287	7,159	415	5.0	10.5	8.6		69.0	9.5	284	20	27
Faulkner	39,174	34,546	23,397	4,628	13.4	60.5	36.1		68.6	15.7	5,926	1,800	946
Franklin	7,880	7,673	6,228	207	2.7	12.9	10.2		78.1	6.6	93	13	15
Fulton	6,147	5,973	4,839	174	2.9	9.9	7.8		81.1	3.8	11	1	–

See footnotes at end of table.

[Includes United States, states, and 3,141 counties/county equivalents defined as of February 22, 2005. For more information on these areas, see Appendix C, Geographic Information]

County	Housing units 2005 (July 1)	2000[1] (April 1) estimates base	1990 (April 1)	Net change, 2000–2005 Number	Net change, 2000–2005 Percent	Units per square mile of land area 2005[2]	Units per square mile of land area 1990	Housing 2000, percent Owner-occupied housing units[3]	Housing 2000, percent Units in multi-unit structures	New private housing units authorized by building permits Cumulative, 2000–2005 period	2005	2004
ARKANSAS—Con.												
Garland	46,282	44,953	37,966	1,329	3.0	68.3	56.0	71.1	15.5	771	159	140
Grant.	7,297	6,960	5,540	337	4.8	11.5	8.8	80.4	2.5	199	49	60
Greene	17,288	16,161	13,216	1,127	7.0	29.9	22.9	71.3	11.1	1,179	227	209
Hempstead.	10,460	10,166	9,690	294	2.9	14.4	13.3	69.3	6.5	196	68	54
Hot Spring	13,723	13,384	11,378	339	2.5	22.3	18.5	77.9	5.5	66	3	1
Howard	6,479	6,297	5,600	182	2.9	11.0	9.5	72.2	8.3	97	20	16
Independence.	15,307	14,841	12,838	466	3.1	20.0	16.8	74.4	6.2	169	27	24
Izard	6,786	6,591	5,535	195	3.0	11.7	9.5	80.2	5.1	91	22	13
Jackson	8,087	7,960	8,086	127	1.6	12.8	12.8	69.6	11.2	76	19	7
Jefferson	35,290	34,351	33,311	939	2.7	39.9	37.6	66.2	13.6	936	160	135
Johnson	10,329	9,926	7,984	403	4.1	15.6	12.1	73.1	9.8	249	48	42
Lafayette	4,715	4,560	4,523	155	3.4	9.0	8.6	78.6	4.3	22	–	4
Lawrence	8,237	8,085	7,692	152	1.9	14.0	13.1	71.1	7.9	77	8	14
Lee	4,992	4,768	5,085	224	4.7	8.3	8.5	63.7	12.6	160	5	14
Lincoln.	5,090	4,955	4,295	135	2.7	9.1	7.7	76.1	4.5	27	9	2
Little River	6,588	6,435	6,171	153	2.4	12.4	11.6	76.5	7.1	52	16	3
Logan	10,175	9,942	8,539	233	2.3	14.3	12.0	77.1	5.1	98	13	19
Lonoke	23,762	20,749	15,009	3,013	14.5	31.0	19.6	75.9	6.9	3,350	677	672
Madison.	6,820	6,537	5,182	283	4.3	8.1	6.2	79.1	3.8	127	9	37
Marion.	8,687	8,235	6,139	452	5.5	14.5	10.3	80.1	5.2	334	47	32
Miller	18,801	17,727	16,172	1,074	6.1	30.1	25.9	68.0	15.3	1,047	92	111
Mississippi	22,589	22,310	22,232	279	1.3	25.1	24.7	58.9	18.3	205	29	28
Monroe	5,204	5,067	5,063	137	2.7	8.6	8.3	65.0	11.3	80	1	2
Montgomery	5,221	5,048	4,269	173	3.4	6.7	5.5	82.9	1.9	(NA)	–	–
Nevada	5,600	4,751	4,287	849	17.9	9.0	6.9	74.8	6.0	1,124	342	298
Newton	4,445	4,316	3,439	129	3.0	5.4	4.2	81.5	3.7	11	1	2
Ouachita	13,604	13,450	13,204	154	1.1	18.6	18.0	71.4	11.6	39	8	10
Perry.	4,848	4,702	3,702	146	3.1	8.8	6.7	82.2	2.8	12	–	2
Phillips.	10,975	10,859	11,094	116	1.1	15.8	16.0	56.2	15.3	42	3	2
Pike	5,712	5,536	4,550	176	3.2	9.5	7.5	78.9	4.4	(NA)	–	–
Poinsett	11,377	11,051	10,271	326	2.9	15.0	13.6	66.8	13.2	254	39	39
Polk	9,513	9,236	7,732	277	3.0	11.1	9.0	78.4	4.6	111	19	13
Pope	24,029	22,851	18,430	1,178	5.2	29.6	22.7	71.2	14.8	1,009	189	169
Prairie	4,904	4,790	4,340	114	2.4	7.6	6.7	73.1	6.1	43	7	2
Pulaski.	170,520	161,135	151,538	9,385	5.8	221.2	196.6	60.9	25.1	11,799	2,387	3,197
Randolph.	8,625	8,268	7,343	357	4.3	13.2	11.3	74.4	8.3	321	105	50
St. Francis	11,550	11,242	10,958	308	2.7	18.2	17.3	63.2	14.4	219	40	41
Saline	38,092	33,825	24,602	4,267	12.6	52.7	33.9	80.7	5.4	4,413	835	648
Scott	5,070	4,923	4,485	147	3.0	5.7	5.0	74.3	7.2	48	5	7
Searcy	4,409	4,292	3,739	117	2.7	6.6	5.6	77.7	4.4	20	5	4
Sebastian.	51,782	49,311	43,621	2,471	5.0	96.6	81.3	63.5	23.1	3,011	634	548
Sevier	6,579	6,434	5,880	145	2.3	11.7	10.4	74.1	5.8	50	11	8
Sharp	9,580	9,342	7,617	238	2.5	15.9	12.6	80.3	3.8	68	40	28
Stone	5,927	5,715	4,548	212	3.7	9.8	7.5	78.1	3.4	82	13	19
Union	20,994	20,676	20,276	318	1.5	20.2	19.5	72.9	8.7	111	20	24
Van Buren	9,475	9,164	7,580	311	3.4	13.3	10.7	81.1	7.5	20	9	14
Washington	77,035	64,330	47,349	12,705	19.7	81.1	49.8	59.5	25.0	15,849	2,896	3,276
White.	29,203	27,613	21,658	1,590	5.8	28.2	20.9	72.9	11.5	1,409	303	205
Woodruff	4,162	4,085	4,169	77	1.9	7.1	7.1	65.4	11.5	29	6	4
Yell	9,503	9,157	7,868	346	3.8	10.2	8.5	72.9	8.0	156	15	19
CALIFORNIA	12,989,254	12,214,550	11,182,882	774,704	6.3	83.3	71.7	56.9	31.4	1,056,245	205,020	207,390
Alameda	556,474	540,183	504,109	16,291	3.0	754.5	683.5	54.7	37.6	25,081	4,376	5,378
Alpine	1,694	1,514	1,319	180	11.9	2.3	1.8	68.3	37.3	207	16	22
Amador	16,732	15,035	12,814	1,697	11.3	28.2	21.6	75.5	6.4	2,027	412	448
Butte	92,187	85,523	76,115	6,664	7.8	56.2	46.4	60.7	20.2	8,864	1,693	1,989
Calaveras.	25,864	22,946	19,153	2,918	12.7	25.4	18.8	78.7	3.7	3,874	862	830
Colusa.	7,251	6,774	6,295	477	7.0	6.3	5.5	63.2	11.6	453	134	170
Contra Costa	383,328	354,577	316,170	28,751	8.1	532.4	438.9	69.3	24.0	35,098	6,464	5,588
Del Norte	10,869	10,434	9,091	435	4.2	10.8	9.0	63.8	13.2	612	106	200
El Dorado.	80,279	71,278	61,451	9,001	12.6	46.9	35.9	74.7	11.5	10,884	1,604	2,041
Fresno.	292,733	270,767	235,563	21,966	8.1	49.1	39.5	56.5	26.6	31,071	7,400	7,157
Glenn	10,372	9,982	9,329	390	3.9	7.9	7.1	63.8	14.3	686	214	150
Humboldt	58,160	55,912	51,134	2,248	4.0	16.3	14.3	57.6	18.1	3,153	510	612
Imperial	49,491	43,891	36,559	5,600	12.8	11.9	8.8	58.3	20.8	8,021	2,191	1,778
Inyo	9,071	9,042	8,712	29	0.3	0.9	0.9	65.9	9.6	107	12	21
Kern	254,226	231,567	198,636	22,659	9.8	31.2	24.4	62.1	18.9	32,537	8,857	6,794
Kings.	40,021	36,563	30,843	3,458	9.5	28.8	22.2	55.9	19.0	4,793	1,103	867
Lake.	34,031	32,528	28,822	1,503	4.6	27.1	22.9	70.6	5.2	2,221	514	632
Lassen	12,576	12,000	10,358	576	4.8	2.8	2.3	68.3	8.5	817	156	160
Los Angeles	3,339,763	3,270,906	3,163,343	68,857	2.1	822.4	779.2	47.9	42.2	122,646	23,498	26,529
Madera	45,498	40,387	30,831	5,111	12.7	21.3	14.4	66.2	12.0	7,589	2,268	1,676

See footnotes at end of table.

[Includes United States, states, and 3,141 counties/county equivalents defined as of February 22, 2005. For more information on these areas, see Appendix C, Geographic Information]

County	Housing units							Housing 2000, percent		New private housing units authorized by building permits		
	2005 (July 1)	2000[1] (April 1 estimates base)	1990 (April 1)	Net change, 2000–2005 Number	Percent	Units per square mile of land area 2005[2]	1990	Owner-occupied housing units[3]	Units in multi-unit structures	Cumulative, 2000–2005 period	2005	2004
CALIFORNIA—Con.												
Marin	107,423	104,990	99,757	2,433	2.3	206.7	191.9	63.6	29.3	3,922	781	1,039
Mariposa	9,478	8,826	7,700	652	7.4	6.5	5.3	69.8	6.8	919	217	178
Mendocino	38,418	36,937	33,649	1,481	4.0	10.9	9.6	61.3	12.9	2,050	300	378
Merced	77,571	68,373	58,410	9,198	13.5	40.2	30.3	58.7	18.4	13,230	3,665	2,598
Modoc	4,809	4,807	4,672	2	(Z)	1.2	1.2	70.7	5.6	71	24	14
Mono	12,860	11,757	10,664	1,103	9.4	4.2	3.5	60.0	42.9	1,673	539	221
Monterey	137,533	131,708	121,224	5,825	4.4	41.4	36.5	54.6	26.1	7,975	1,430	1,198
Napa	52,167	48,568	44,199	3,599	7.4	69.2	58.6	65.1	18.2	4,667	687	917
Nevada	48,499	44,282	37,352	4,217	9.5	50.6	39.0	75.8	8.4	5,191	822	954
Orange	1,017,219	969,484	875,072	47,735	4.9	1,288.6	1,108.1	61.4	33.2	58,574	7,143	9,256
Placer	137,086	107,302	77,879	29,784	27.8	97.6	55.5	73.2	15.9	35,046	5,331	4,884
Plumas	14,431	13,386	11,942	1,045	7.8	5.7	4.7	70.0	5.8	1,461	337	266
Riverside	699,474	584,673	483,847	114,801	19.6	97.0	67.1	68.9	17.6	154,464	34,373	33,446
Sacramento	528,035	474,814	417,574	53,221	11.2	546.8	432.4	58.2	27.4	66,891	11,545	12,879
San Benito	17,723	16,499	12,230	1,224	7.4	12.8	8.8	68.2	11.9	1,351	123	112
San Bernardino	652,802	601,370	542,332	51,432	8.6	32.6	27.0	64.5	19.4	71,646	16,635	18,017
San Diego	1,113,207	1,040,149	946,240	73,058	7.0	265.1	225.1	55.4	35.1	92,605	14,306	15,587
San Francisco	354,963	346,527	328,471	8,436	2.4	7,602.5	7,033.6	35.0	67.7	11,219	2,538	2,051
San Joaquin	217,991	189,160	166,274	28,831	15.2	155.8	118.8	60.4	20.9	35,508	5,869	6,724
San Luis Obispo	112,099	102,275	90,200	9,824	9.6	33.9	27.3	61.5	18.6	12,635	2,316	2,450
San Mateo	266,154	260,578	251,782	5,576	2.1	592.7	560.6	61.4	32.3	8,385	724	1,183
Santa Barbara	150,053	142,901	138,149	7,152	5.0	54.8	50.4	56.1	29.2	7,599	1,050	1,499
Santa Clara	605,121	579,329	540,240	25,792	4.5	468.8	418.4	59.8	31.6	35,079	5,613	5,380
Santa Cruz	101,686	98,873	91,878	2,813	2.8	228.4	206.1	60.0	20.4	4,481	861	801
Shasta	74,219	68,810	60,552	5,409	7.9	19.6	16.0	66.1	15.4	7,297	1,566	1,038
Sierra	2,268	2,202	2,166	66	3.0	2.4	2.3	70.7	5.0	99	13	18
Siskiyou	22,975	21,947	20,141	1,028	4.7	3.7	3.2	67.2	10.7	1,492	465	306
Solano	146,724	134,499	119,533	12,225	9.1	176.9	144.3	65.2	20.7	15,232	2,354	2,961
Sonoma	193,353	183,153	161,062	10,200	5.6	122.7	102.2	64.1	17.7	14,016	2,819	1,929
Stanislaus	167,079	150,807	132,027	16,272	10.8	111.8	88.3	61.9	17.0	22,576	4,525	4,521
Sutter	31,733	28,319	24,163	3,414	12.1	52.7	40.1	61.5	20.0	4,935	1,291	1,300
Tehama	25,216	23,547	20,403	1,669	7.1	8.5	6.9	67.6	11.9	2,509	685	715
Trinity	8,192	7,980	7,540	212	2.7	2.6	2.4	71.3	2.8	327	66	78
Tulare	129,128	119,639	105,013	9,489	7.9	26.8	21.8	61.5	13.6	13,471	3,317	2,492
Tuolumne	29,848	28,336	25,175	1,512	5.3	13.4	11.3	71.3	7.9	2,044	384	400
Ventura	266,554	251,711	228,478	14,843	5.9	144.5	123.8	67.6	20.5	20,633	4,511	2,617
Yolo	69,106	61,587	53,000	7,519	12.2	68.2	52.3	53.1	31.0	9,558	1,702	2,195
Yuba	25,437	22,636	21,245	2,801	12.4	40.3	33.7	54.1	17.5	4,713	1,703	1,746
COLORADO	2,053,178	[7]1,808,358	1,477,349	244,820	13.5	19.8	14.2	67.3	25.7	[8]289,433	45,891	46,499
Adams	154,442	127,089	106,947	27,353	21.5	131.1	89.7	70.6	23.2	31,748	4,572	5,058
Alamosa	6,393	6,088	5,254	305	5.0	8.8	7.3	64.0	16.1	354	66	54
Arapahoe	223,141	197,192	168,665	25,949	13.2	277.8	210.0	68.0	31.2	32,004	4,007	3,848
Archuleta	7,774	6,212	3,951	1,562	25.1	5.8	2.9	76.8	17.4	1,744	257	240
Baca	2,455	2,364	2,434	91	3.8	1.0	1.0	76.1	5.2	41	1	9
Bent	2,410	2,366	2,332	44	1.9	1.6	1.5	68.0	8.4	59	9	10
Boulder	121,500	111,441	94,621	10,059	9.0	166.0	127.4	64.7	28.6	11,759	1,141	1,372
Broomfield	18,475	14,652	(X)	3,823	26.1	559.8	(NA)	(NA)	(NA)	(NA)	771	734
Chaffee	9,501	8,392	6,547	1,109	13.2	9.4	6.5	73.4	8.6	1,223	157	168
Cheyenne	1,148	1,105	1,083	43	3.9	0.6	0.6	74.3	4.0	14	3	3
Clear Creek	5,407	5,128	4,811	279	5.4	13.7	12.2	76.1	10.5	335	41	41
Conejos	4,252	3,886	3,574	366	9.4	3.3	2.8	78.8	5.3	695	37	47
Costilla	2,281	2,202	1,743	79	3.6	1.9	1.4	78.2	4.5	(NA)	24	26
Crowley	1,586	1,542	1,415	44	2.9	2.0	1.8	72.5	4.7	35	5	4
Custer	3,672	2,989	2,216	683	22.9	5.0	3.0	79.2	2.9	770	104	109
Delta	13,065	12,374	10,082	691	5.6	11.4	8.8	77.5	5.5	432	117	94
Denver	268,540	251,069	239,636	17,471	7.0	1,751.2	1,563.4	52.5	44.8	23,031	3,164	4,098
Dolores	1,288	1,193	947	95	8.0	1.2	0.9	76.8	1.2	43	6	6
Douglas	90,010	63,333	22,291	26,677	42.1	107.1	26.5	87.9	9.6	31,303	5,563	5,097
Eagle	25,395	22,118	15,226	3,277	14.8	15.0	9.0	63.7	42.2	4,012	784	755
Elbert	8,358	7,113	3,997	1,245	17.5	4.5	2.2	89.6	1.7	1,462	258	219
El Paso	233,380	202,428	165,056	30,952	15.3	109.8	77.6	64.7	25.5	38,712	6,782	6,485
Fremont	18,785	17,145	13,683	1,640	9.6	12.3	8.9	75.9	9.9	1,799	273	221
Garfield	20,116	17,337	12,517	2,779	16.0	6.8	4.2	65.2	21.1	3,212	591	498
Gilpin	3,268	2,929	2,438	339	11.6	21.8	16.3	78.4	6.9	437	87	76
Grand	13,065	10,894	9,985	2,425	22.3	7.2	5.4	68.2	30.8	2,980	629	527
Gunnison	10,301	9,135	7,294	1,166	12.8	3.2	2.3	58.3	26.6	1,395	273	197
Hinsdale	1,372	1,304	1,254	68	5.2	1.2	1.1	64.9	3.2	86	18	15
Huerfano	4,975	4,599	3,913	376	8.2	3.1	2.5	70.7	9.6	398	44	52
Jackson	1,221	1,145	1,326	76	6.6	0.8	0.8	67.6	3.8	87	14	10

See footnotes at end of table.

Table B-7. Counties — **Housing Units and Building Permits**—Con.

[Includes United States, states, and 3,141 counties/county equivalents defined as of February 22, 2005. For more information on these areas, see Appendix C, Geographic Information]

County	Housing units 2005 (July 1)	2000[1] (April 1 esti- mates base)	1990 (April 1)	Net change, 2000–2005 Number	Percent	Units per square mile of land area 2005[2]	1990	Housing 2000, percent Owner- occupied housing units[3]	Units in multi- unit structures	New private housing units authorized by building permits Cumu- lative, 2000–2005 period	2005	2004
COLORADO—Con.												
Jefferson	224,332	211,828	178,611	12,504	5.9	291.9	231.3	72.5	23.8	13,113	2,094	2,344
Kiowa	825	817	878	8	1.0	0.5	0.5	71.3	5.6	4	1	2
Kit Carson	3,562	3,430	3,224	132	3.8	1.6	1.5	71.9	8.1	86	11	6
Lake	4,251	3,913	3,527	338	8.6	11.3	9.4	68.2	14.2	399	57	67
La Plata	23,870	20,765	15,412	3,105	15.0	14.1	9.1	68.4	14.0	3,915	907	751
Larimer	122,541	105,392	77,811	17,149	16.3	47.1	29.9	67.7	21.5	19,366	2,887	3,252
Las Animas	8,006	7,629	6,975	377	4.9	1.7	1.5	70.6	11.1	444	56	46
Lincoln	2,455	2,406	2,204	49	2.0	0.9	0.9	69.0	7.6	44	6	5
Logan	8,709	8,454	7,824	255	3.0	4.7	4.3	69.9	12.5	330	56	46
Mesa	55,942	48,718	39,208	7,224	14.8	16.8	11.8	72.7	16.9	8,584	1,505	1,551
Mineral	1,199	1,119	1,201	80	7.1	1.4	1.4	74.0	1.6	106	25	19
Moffat	5,950	5,635	5,235	315	5.6	1.3	1.1	72.1	16.4	355	76	71
Montezuma	11,104	10,497	8,050	607	5.8	5.5	4.0	74.8	7.1	271	61	42
Montrose	16,201	14,202	10,353	1,999	14.1	7.2	4.6	74.9	9.1	2,468	605	499
Morgan	11,040	10,410	9,230	630	6.1	8.6	7.2	68.4	12.9	754	134	143
Otero	8,925	8,813	8,739	112	1.3	7.1	6.9	69.1	11.9	181	14	22
Ouray	2,606	2,146	1,507	460	21.4	4.8	2.8	73.4	9.5	545	91	103
Park	12,543	10,697	7,247	1,846	17.3	5.7	3.3	87.6	1.3	2,085	292	321
Phillips	2,057	2,014	1,960	43	2.1	3.0	2.9	75.6	5.5	62	9	13
Pitkin	10,914	10,096	9,837	818	8.1	11.2	10.1	59.2	40.9	862	142	112
Prowers	6,118	5,977	5,855	141	2.4	3.7	3.6	66.2	11.2	73	11	8
Pueblo	65,018	58,926	50,872	6,092	10.3	27.2	21.3	70.4	16.7	7,472	1,179	1,220
Rio Blanco	2,979	2,855	2,803	124	4.3	0.9	0.9	70.6	12.4	171	49	39
Rio Grande	6,556	6,003	5,277	553	9.2	7.2	5.8	70.7	10.3	574	71	100
Routt	13,398	11,217	9,252	2,181	19.4	5.7	3.9	69.2	32.8	2,192	477	356
Saguache	3,634	3,087	2,306	547	17.7	1.1	0.7	69.3	6.8	586	80	106
San Juan	695	632	481	63	10.0	1.8	1.2	67.7	8.4	89	21	20
San Miguel	5,807	5,197	2,635	610	11.7	4.5	2.0	51.6	41.7	814	213	129
Sedgwick	1,393	1,387	1,414	6	0.4	2.5	2.6	73.0	7.8	11	2	2
Summit	27,456	24,201	17,091	3,255	13.4	45.1	28.1	58.9	58.8	2,883	474	330
Teller	11,734	10,362	7,565	1,372	13.2	21.1	13.6	80.9	6.4	1,503	201	281
Washington	2,369	2,307	2,307	62	2.7	0.9	0.9	73.6	6.0	62	6	4
Weld	86,749	66,167	51,138	20,582	31.1	21.8	12.8	68.6	18.4	25,737	4,279	4,414
Yuma	4,410	4,295	4,082	115	2.7	1.9	1.7	70.8	7.9	48	1	2
CONNECTICUT	1,423,343	1,385,997	1,320,850	37,346	2.7	293.8	272.6	66.8	35.1	62,554	11,885	11,837
Fairfield	346,942	339,466	324,355	7,476	2.2	554.4	518.3	69.2	34.5	13,955	3,119	2,495
Hartford	360,450	353,022	341,812	7,428	2.1	490.1	464.7	64.2	39.0	13,476	2,487	2,389
Litchfield	82,375	79,281	74,274	3,094	3.9	89.5	80.7	75.2	22.8	4,516	678	810
Middlesex	71,037	67,285	61,593	3,752	5.6	192.4	166.8	72.1	24.7	5,065	795	963
New Haven	346,893	340,732	327,079	6,161	1.8	572.8	539.9	63.1	40.7	11,816	2,251	2,534
New London	114,805	110,682	104,461	4,123	3.7	172.4	156.8	66.7	28.7	6,330	1,208	1,348
Tolland	54,764	51,570	46,677	3,194	6.2	133.5	113.8	73.5	24.7	4,305	754	706
Windham	46,077	43,959	40,599	2,118	4.8	89.9	79.2	67.4	29.9	3,091	593	592
DELAWARE	374,872	343,072	289,919	31,800	9.3	191.9	148.0	72.3	18.7	39,569	8,195	7,858
Kent	58,161	50,483	42,106	7,678	15.2	98.6	71.3	70.0	14.5	9,855	2,182	2,178
New Castle	209,592	199,521	173,560	10,071	5.0	491.7	407.1	70.1	24.0	12,815	1,751	2,203
Sussex	107,119	93,068	74,253	14,051	15.1	114.3	79.2	80.7	9.7	16,899	4,262	3,477
DISTRICT OF COLUMBIA	277,775	274,845	278,489	2,930	1.1	4,524.0	4,534.9	40.8	60.2	9,516	2,860	1,936
District of Columbia	277,775	274,845	278,489	2,930	1.1	4,524.0	4,534.9	40.8	60.2	9,516	2,860	1,936
FLORIDA	8,256,847	7,303,108	6,100,262	953,739	13.1	153.1	113.0	70.1	29.9	1,264,445	287,250	255,893
Alachua	104,613	95,113	79,022	9,500	10.0	119.7	90.4	54.9	36.3	12,085	2,293	2,009
Baker	8,288	7,592	5,975	696	9.2	14.2	10.2	81.2	3.1	1,001	279	206
Bay	89,761	78,435	65,999	11,326	14.4	117.5	86.4	68.6	24.9	17,197	5,538	3,844
Bradford	9,938	9,605	8,099	333	3.5	33.9	27.6	79.0	5.1	490	108	84
Brevard	252,273	222,072	185,150	30,201	13.6	247.8	181.8	74.6	22.5	39,831	8,787	8,925
Broward	790,308	741,043	628,660	49,265	6.6	655.6	520.0	69.5	47.5	58,637	6,951	8,709
Calhoun	5,376	5,250	4,468	126	2.4	9.5	7.9	80.2	3.4	212	58	34
Charlotte	91,522	79,758	64,641	11,764	14.7	132.0	93.2	83.7	15.7	16,656	4,694	3,652
Citrus	70,149	62,204	49,854	7,945	12.8	120.2	85.4	85.6	5.7	11,668	3,581	2,531
Clay	65,570	53,748	40,249	11,822	22.0	109.1	67.0	77.9	11.9	16,092	4,113	3,148
Collier	181,261	144,536	94,165	36,725	25.4	89.5	46.5	75.6	46.6	42,773	6,622	6,921
Columbia	24,974	23,578	17,818	1,396	5.9	31.3	22.4	77.2	7.9	2,061	580	380
DeSoto	14,194	13,608	10,310	586	4.3	22.3	16.2	74.7	9.6	811	166	149
Dixie	7,633	7,362	6,445	271	3.7	10.8	9.2	86.4	1.5	476	180	64
Duval	366,817	329,778	284,673	37,039	11.2	474.1	367.9	63.1	27.7	52,396	13,507	9,661

See footnotes at end of table.

[Includes United States, states, and 3,141 counties/county equivalents defined as of February 22, 2005. For more information on these areas, see Appendix C, Geographic Information]

County	Housing units 2005 (July 1)	2000[1] (April 1 esti- mates base)	1990 (April 1)	Net change, 2000–2005 Number	Net change, 2000–2005 Percent	Units per square mile of land area 2005[2]	Units per square mile of land area 1990	Housing 2000, percent Owner- occupied housing units[3]	Housing 2000, percent Units in multi- unit structures	New private housing units authorized by building permits Cumu- lative, 2000– 2005 period	2005	2004
FLORIDA—Con.												
Escambia	134,473	124,647	112,230	9,826	7.9	203.0	169.1	67.3	20.4	13,154	2,602	2,613
Flagler	39,309	24,452	15,215	14,857	60.8	81.0	31.4	84.0	9.7	18,939	3,985	5,208
Franklin	8,056	7,180	5,891	876	12.2	14.8	11.0	79.2	8.5	1,166	252	248
Gadsden	18,248	17,703	14,859	545	3.1	35.4	28.8	78.0	5.9	903	255	204
Gilchrist	6,307	5,906	4,071	401	6.8	18.1	11.7	86.3	1.8	517	102	107
Glades	5,940	5,790	4,624	150	2.6	7.7	6.0	81.7	4.3	254	85	48
Gulf	8,498	7,587	6,339	911	12.0	15.3	11.2	81.0	8.5	975	38	183
Hamilton	5,133	4,966	4,119	167	3.4	10.0	8.0	77.4	5.4	232	41	34
Hardee	10,198	9,820	7,941	378	3.8	16.0	12.5	73.4	5.8	558	119	82
Hendry	12,677	12,294	9,945	383	3.1	11.0	8.6	72.4	8.2	836	410	133
Hernando	72,953	62,727	50,018	10,226	16.3	152.5	104.6	86.5	4.3	14,970	4,600	3,012
Highlands	51,893	48,846	40,114	3,047	6.2	50.5	39.0	79.7	11.2	4,513	1,278	959
Hillsborough	490,712	425,962	367,740	64,750	15.2	466.9	349.9	64.1	28.8	81,858	15,827	13,713
Holmes	8,219	7,998	6,785	221	2.8	17.0	14.1	81.5	3.4	318	54	49
Indian River	70,487	57,902	47,128	12,585	21.7	140.1	93.6	77.6	25.5	16,231	3,819	4,185
Jackson	20,300	19,490	16,320	810	4.2	22.2	17.8	77.9	6.5	1,095	195	158
Jefferson	5,589	5,251	4,395	338	6.4	9.4	7.4	80.9	3.1	485	122	86
Lafayette	2,776	2,660	2,266	116	4.4	5.1	4.2	80.6	2.8	155	29	27
Lake	127,656	102,829	75,707	24,827	24.1	133.9	79.4	81.5	9.8	31,508	6,769	6,213
Lee	312,724	245,405	189,051	67,319	27.4	389.1	235.3	76.5	28.9	96,625	29,330	20,395
Leon	116,357	103,974	81,325	12,383	11.9	174.5	122.0	57.0	30.9	15,898	3,231	2,912
Levy	17,384	16,570	12,307	814	4.9	15.5	11.0	83.6	3.8	1,253	386	225
Liberty	3,226	3,156	2,157	70	2.2	3.9	2.6	81.8	0.9	103	17	18
Madison	8,098	7,836	6,275	262	3.3	11.7	9.1	78.4	6.1	384	76	66
Manatee	160,869	138,128	115,245	22,741	16.5	217.1	155.5	73.8	26.9	28,881	5,735	6,590
Marion	145,693	122,663	94,567	23,030	18.8	92.3	59.9	79.8	9.4	31,040	7,453	5,426
Martin	72,983	65,471	54,199	7,512	11.5	131.4	97.5	79.8	29.1	9,638	2,006	1,459
Miami-Dade	928,715	852,414	771,288	76,301	9.0	477.2	396.7	57.8	45.5	105,586	26,120	22,856
Monroe	52,911	51,617	46,215	1,294	2.5	53.1	46.3	62.4	24.4	2,121	538	383
Nassau	30,294	25,917	18,726	4,377	16.9	46.5	28.7	80.6	16.4	5,903	1,471	1,287
Okaloosa	87,674	78,593	62,569	9,081	11.6	93.7	66.9	66.4	24.6	13,044	3,720	2,711
Okeechobee	16,209	15,504	13,266	705	4.5	20.9	17.1	74.8	5.4	931	181	185
Orange	423,688	361,349	282,686	62,339	17.3	466.9	311.5	60.7	31.5	80,442	17,220	14,628
Osceola	102,187	72,293	47,959	29,894	41.4	77.3	36.3	67.7	20.0	37,696	7,996	9,070
Palm Beach	619,427	556,433	461,665	62,994	11.3	313.8	226.9	74.7	41.1	77,093	12,491	14,519
Pasco	203,449	173,719	148,965	29,730	17.1	273.1	200.0	82.4	10.7	40,284	9,876	9,263
Pinellas	495,191	481,587	458,341	13,604	2.8	1,769.0	1,636.1	70.8	35.1	20,500	3,871	3,569
Polk	256,762	226,376	186,225	30,386	13.4	137.0	99.3	73.4	13.9	44,483	13,179	10,242
Putnam	34,985	33,870	31,840	1,115	3.3	48.5	44.1	80.0	6.0	1,563	294	232
St. Johns	74,850	58,008	40,712	16,842	29.0	122.9	66.8	76.4	20.8	22,636	5,718	5,024
St. Lucie	117,020	91,262	73,843	25,758	28.2	204.4	129.0	78.0	20.3	34,975	8,776	9,097
Santa Rosa	56,761	49,119	32,831	7,642	15.6	55.8	32.3	80.4	9.2	9,144	1,354	2,022
Sarasota	209,010	182,471	157,055	26,539	14.5	365.7	274.7	79.1	25.2	35,629	8,310	7,906
Seminole	166,066	147,080	117,845	18,986	12.9	538.8	382.3	69.5	25.5	23,167	4,152	4,081
Sumter	35,786	25,195	15,298	10,591	42.0	65.6	28.0	86.5	2.5	15,577	5,047	4,153
Suwannee	16,356	15,680	11,699	676	4.3	23.8	17.0	80.9	4.4	951	210	199
Taylor	9,917	9,646	7,908	271	2.8	9.5	7.6	79.8	4.5	430	105	85
Union	3,882	3,736	2,975	146	3.9	16.2	12.4	74.6	5.5	207	46	32
Volusia	236,900	211,938	180,972	24,962	11.8	214.7	163.6	75.3	21.7	32,779	6,884	6,436
Wakulla	12,005	9,820	6,587	2,185	22.3	19.8	10.9	84.2	1.9	2,874	675	525
Walton	37,422	29,083	18,728	8,339	28.7	35.4	17.7	79.0	23.9	11,043	2,719	2,592
Washington	9,945	9,503	7,703	442	4.7	17.1	13.3	81.9	3.1	512	24	126
GEORGIA	3,771,466	3,281,866	2,638,418	489,600	14.9	65.1	45.6	67.5	20.8	596,798	109,336	108,356
Appling	8,001	7,853	6,629	148	1.9	15.7	13.0	79.1	5.0	35	8	7
Atkinson	3,234	3,171	2,449	63	2.0	9.6	7.2	74.4	5.9	(NA)	3	1
Bacon	4,530	4,464	3,859	66	1.5	15.9	13.5	74.9	8.3	16	5	2
Baker	1,776	1,740	1,499	36	2.1	5.2	4.4	77.7	2.8	(NA)	–	–
Baldwin	18,325	17,173	14,200	1,152	6.7	70.9	54.9	66.5	14.7	1,627	460	374
Banks	6,479	5,808	4,193	671	11.6	27.7	17.9	80.9	1.9	734	143	139
Barrow	23,141	17,304	11,812	5,837	33.7	142.7	72.8	75.5	9.5	7,154	1,416	1,358
Bartow	35,075	28,751	21,757	6,324	22.0	76.3	47.3	75.3	9.1	7,292	1,085	1,099
Ben Hill	7,870	7,623	6,875	247	3.2	31.3	27.3	66.7	12.4	346	78	86
Berrien	7,407	7,100	5,858	307	4.3	16.4	12.9	75.4	4.9	243	92	61
Bibb	70,608	67,194	61,462	3,414	5.1	282.5	245.8	58.8	28.6	4,446	606	731
Bleckley	5,072	4,866	4,268	206	4.2	23.3	19.6	76.1	7.2	262	49	37
Brantley	6,661	6,490	4,404	171	2.6	15.0	9.9	86.9	1.2	23	1	4
Brooks	7,299	7,118	5,972	181	2.5	14.8	12.1	76.9	6.0	268	89	57
Bryan	10,743	8,675	5,549	2,068	23.8	24.3	12.6	77.9	9.4	2,736	699	499
Bulloch	25,580	22,742	16,541	2,838	12.5	37.5	24.2	58.1	24.0	3,342	543	566
Burke	9,178	8,842	8,329	336	3.8	11.1	10.0	76.0	9.7	370	68	96
Butts	8,821	7,377	5,536	1,444	19.6	47.3	29.7	76.6	9.4	1,684	253	289
Calhoun	2,342	2,305	2,061	37	1.6	8.4	7.4	71.8	7.8	9	1	2
Camden	19,608	16,958	10,885	2,650	15.6	31.1	17.3	63.3	17.7	3,318	718	514

See footnotes at end of table.

Table B-7. Counties — **Housing Units and Building Permits**—Con.

[Includes United States, states, and 3,141 counties/county equivalents defined as of February 22, 2005. For more information on these areas, see Appendix C, Geographic Information]

County	Housing units 2005 (July 1)	Housing units 2000[1] (April 1 estimates base)	Housing units 1990 (April 1)	Net change, 2000–2005 Number	Net change, 2000–2005 Percent	Units per square mile of land area 2005[2]	Units per square mile of land area 1990	Housing 2000, percent Owner-occupied housing units[3]	Housing 2000, percent Units in multi-unit structures	New private housing Cumulative, 2000–2005 period	New private housing 2005	New private housing 2004
GEORGIA—Con.												
Candler	3,960	3,893	3,203	67	1.7	16.0	13.0	73.1	4.4	32	14	5
Carroll	42,982	34,067	27,736	8,915	26.2	86.1	55.6	70.5	13.0	11,432	1,655	1,920
Catoosa	24,744	21,774	16,762	2,970	13.6	152.5	103.3	77.1	10.2	3,972	892	785
Charlton	3,992	3,859	3,222	133	3.4	5.1	4.1	80.8	5.0	159	53	30
Chatham	107,922	99,780	91,178	8,142	8.2	246.3	207.0	60.4	26.7	11,094	2,490	1,752
Chattahoochee	3,336	3,316	3,108	20	0.6	13.4	12.5	27.0	22.3	50	18	16
Chattooga	10,883	10,677	9,142	206	1.9	34.7	29.1	75.3	6.6	158	62	63
Cherokee	71,370	51,938	33,840	19,432	37.4	168.5	79.9	83.9	6.2	23,232	4,162	4,084
Clarke	48,212	42,126	35,971	6,086	14.4	399.1	297.7	42.0	43.6	7,239	1,014	1,287
Clay	1,959	1,925	1,586	34	1.8	10.0	8.1	74.5	4.1	14	1	–
Clayton	101,944	86,461	71,926	15,483	17.9	714.8	504.2	60.6	30.8	17,464	2,114	3,014
Clinch	2,895	2,837	2,423	58	2.0	3.6	3.0	72.6	7.8	76	15	13
Cobb	268,152	237,522	189,872	30,630	12.9	788.3	558.1	68.2	26.4	36,849	6,142	6,889
Coffee	16,475	15,609	11,650	866	5.5	27.5	19.4	74.4	7.6	966	171	156
Colquitt	17,999	17,549	14,350	450	2.6	32.6	26.0	66.7	12.5	522	250	149
Columbia	39,919	33,321	23,745	6,598	19.8	137.6	81.9	82.1	6.5	8,366	1,794	1,650
Cook	6,795	6,558	5,340	237	3.6	29.7	23.3	74.9	4.9	291	56	35
Coweta	42,277	33,182	20,413	9,095	27.4	95.5	46.1	78.0	10.1	11,137	2,057	1,984
Crawford	5,545	4,872	3,279	673	13.8	17.1	10.1	84.6	2.3	783	124	110
Crisp	9,965	9,559	8,318	406	4.2	36.4	30.4	60.5	16.5	546	127	75
Dade	6,395	6,224	4,998	171	2.7	36.8	28.7	80.3	3.8	148	74	13
Dawson	9,080	7,163	4,321	1,917	26.8	43.0	20.5	81.4	5.0	2,332	429	392
Decatur	13,254	11,968	10,120	1,286	10.7	22.2	17.0	72.5	10.4	1,014	320	247
DeKalb	295,252	261,231	231,520	34,021	13.0	1,100.8	862.9	58.5	36.3	39,118	6,336	6,719
Dodge	8,408	8,186	7,094	222	2.7	16.8	14.2	73.7	7.4	272	54	55
Dooly	4,560	4,499	4,003	61	1.4	11.6	10.2	71.3	8.2	34	19	13
Dougherty	41,268	39,656	37,373	1,612	4.1	125.2	113.4	53.5	29.2	2,025	238	407
Douglas	44,733	34,866	26,495	9,867	28.3	224.5	132.9	74.8	15.4	11,236	1,915	1,874
Early	5,451	5,338	4,714	113	2.1	10.7	9.2	72.4	5.5	46	18	14
Echols	1,521	1,481	942	40	2.7	3.8	2.3	75.7	0.7	(NA)	2	2
Effingham	17,108	14,169	9,492	2,939	20.7	35.7	19.8	82.6	5.5	3,845	957	831
Elbert	9,291	9,136	7,891	155	1.7	25.2	21.4	75.9	8.0	176	122	4
Emanuel	9,599	9,419	8,344	180	1.9	14.0	12.2	71.1	8.6	134	47	53
Evans	4,538	4,381	3,512	157	3.6	24.5	19.0	71.5	8.1	194	39	37
Fannin	15,848	11,134	8,363	4,714	42.3	41.1	21.7	82.6	4.2	5,489	814	1,103
Fayette	37,486	32,726	22,428	4,760	14.5	190.2	113.6	86.4	8.1	5,633	911	955
Floyd	39,020	36,615	32,821	2,405	6.6	76.0	63.9	66.8	16.7	3,243	613	573
Forsyth	51,536	36,505	17,869	15,031	41.2	228.2	79.1	88.0	2.2	18,781	4,173	3,085
Franklin	9,543	9,304	7,613	239	2.6	36.2	28.9	79.3	5.6	158	36	23
Fulton	405,173	348,634	297,503	56,539	16.2	766.4	562.7	52.0	46.0	76,629	16,114	16,919
Gilmer	15,082	11,924	6,986	3,158	26.5	35.3	16.4	78.1	4.7	3,913	703	794
Glascock	1,219	1,192	1,036	27	2.3	8.5	7.2	80.0	3.2	–	–	–
Glynn	36,325	32,636	27,724	3,689	11.3	86.0	65.6	65.5	22.2	4,843	1,063	946
Gordon	19,912	17,145	13,777	2,767	16.1	56.0	38.8	71.8	12.2	3,328	577	551
Grady	10,337	9,991	8,129	346	3.5	22.6	17.7	73.4	6.3	450	108	90
Greene	7,634	6,653	4,699	981	14.7	19.7	12.1	76.4	0.0	1,272	295	298
Gwinnett	265,462	209,682	137,608	55,780	26.6	613.5	317.9	72.4	22.4	64,026	9,938	10,463
Habersham	16,753	14,633	11,076	2,120	14.5	60.2	39.8	76.2	6.9	2,595	444	441
Hall	59,048	51,057	38,315	7,991	15.7	150.0	97.3	71.1	12.4	11,531	2,204	1,758
Hancock	4,565	4,287	3,396	278	6.5	9.6	7.2	76.4	4.5	342	63	69
Haralson	11,626	10,719	9,016	907	8.5	41.2	32.0	75.1	7.3	838	209	130
Harris	12,142	10,288	7,814	1,854	18.0	26.2	16.8	86.1	3.5	2,288	449	436
Hart	11,635	11,114	8,942	521	4.7	50.1	38.5	80.8	4.5	454	238	165
Heard	4,815	4,512	3,536	303	6.7	16.3	11.9	77.4	4.4	330	43	41
Henry	64,533	43,182	21,275	21,351	49.4	200.0	65.9	85.2	8.5	24,824	3,903	3,855
Houston	53,021	44,509	34,785	8,512	19.1	140.7	92.3	68.5	16.4	10,407	1,825	1,968
Irwin	4,207	4,149	3,479	58	1.4	11.8	9.7	76.8	6.1	12	12	–
Jackson	21,072	16,226	11,775	4,846	29.9	61.5	34.4	74.9	5.4	6,369	1,457	1,523
Jasper	5,759	4,806	3,637	953	19.8	15.5	9.8	79.0	2.9	1,194	242	263
Jeff Davis	5,672	5,582	4,792	90	1.6	17.0	14.4	77.4	8.2	14	–	4
Jefferson	7,369	7,221	7,065	148	2.0	14.0	13.4	72.2	9.3	191	31	40
Jenkins	3,931	3,907	3,365	24	0.6	11.2	9.6	73.3	5.6	40	13	12
Johnson	3,678	3,634	3,389	44	1.2	12.1	11.1	79.8	5.5	3	–	1
Jones	10,661	9,272	7,722	1,389	15.0	27.1	19.6	85.8	2.2	1,606	246	352
Lamar	6,914	6,145	5,066	769	12.5	37.4	27.4	72.4	11.0	973	188	182
Lanier	3,219	3,011	2,202	208	6.9	17.2	11.8	76.2	5.6	289	91	100
Laurens	20,177	19,687	16,504	490	2.5	24.8	20.3	71.3	9.0	326	45	111
Lee	10,802	8,813	5,537	1,989	22.6	30.4	15.6	78.3	12.2	2,048	415	384
Liberty	23,621	21,977	16,776	1,644	7.5	45.5	32.3	50.7	20.3	1,954	337	321
Lincoln	4,719	4,514	3,870	205	4.5	22.4	18.3	81.7	1.9	245	49	35

See footnotes at end of table.

Table B-7. Counties — **Housing Units and Building Permits**—Con.

[Includes United States, states, and 3,141 counties/county equivalents defined as of February 22, 2005. For more information on these areas, see Appendix C, Geographic Information]

County	Housing units							Housing 2000, percent		New private housing units authorized by building permits		
	2005 (July 1)	2000[1] (April 1 estimates base)	1990 (April 1)	Net change, 2000–2005 Number	Net change, 2000–2005 Percent	Units per square mile of land area 2005[2]	Units per square mile of land area 1990	Owner-occupied housing units[3]	Units in multi-unit structures	Cumulative, 2000–2005 period	2005	2004
GEORGIA—Con.												
Long	4,350	4,232	2,638	118	2.8	10.9	6.6	66.2	1.5	(NA)	–	–
Lowndes	40,983	36,555	28,906	4,428	12.1	81.3	57.3	60.8	19.9	5,458	1,044	1,278
Lumpkin	10,162	8,254	5,729	1,908	23.1	35.7	20.1	72.3	7.0	2,396	519	473
McDuffie	9,246	8,916	8,043	330	3.7	35.6	31.0	71.3	9.0	378	49	71
McIntosh	6,315	5,735	4,276	580	10.1	14.6	9.9	83.6	3.1	771	213	154
Macon	5,611	5,495	4,848	116	2.1	13.9	12.0	73.0	8.5	146	27	33
Madison	11,329	10,520	8,428	809	7.7	39.9	29.6	80.2	2.1	989	224	167
Marion	3,210	3,130	2,152	80	2.6	8.7	5.9	78.1	4.8	(NA)	–	–
Meriwether	10,156	9,211	8,409	945	10.3	20.2	16.7	74.2	6.2	1,107	143	172
Miller	2,811	2,770	2,602	41	1.5	9.9	9.2	77.0	5.7	19	7	3
Mitchell	9,246	8,881	7,443	365	4.1	18.1	14.5	72.0	10.0	403	35	54
Monroe	9,306	8,434	6,401	872	10.3	23.5	16.2	79.5	7.0	1,127	263	337
Montgomery	3,749	3,492	2,885	257	7.4	15.3	11.8	77.9	4.8	290	37	66
Morgan	7,088	6,128	4,814	960	15.7	20.3	13.8	77.5	4.7	1,242	283	249
Murray	15,483	14,319	10,207	1,164	8.1	45.0	29.6	73.7	6.7	1,433	324	203
Muscogee	81,008	76,182	70,902	4,826	6.3	374.6	327.8	56.4	27.6	6,563	1,266	1,093
Newton	33,365	23,033	15,494	10,332	44.9	120.7	56.0	77.7	9.2	12,308	2,115	1,929
Oconee	11,481	9,528	6,561	1,953	20.5	61.8	35.3	80.2	5.3	2,504	537	500
Oglethorpe	5,880	5,368	3,936	512	9.5	13.3	8.9	82.6	1.9	(NA)	221	159
Paulding	43,769	29,233	15,237	14,536	49.7	139.6	48.6	86.8	4.7	17,702	3,454	3,103
Peach	9,962	9,093	7,537	869	9.6	65.9	49.9	68.4	14.5	1,135	335	237
Pickens	13,073	10,686	6,403	2,387	22.3	56.3	27.6	82.1	6.1	2,817	445	484
Pierce	7,195	6,713	5,271	482	7.2	21.0	15.4	80.6	4.7	588	110	138
Pike	6,228	5,068	3,797	1,160	22.9	28.5	17.4	81.6	4.1	1,442	289	269
Polk	16,547	15,059	13,585	1,488	9.9	53.2	43.7	71.3	11.2	1,807	255	226
Pulaski	4,189	3,944	3,470	245	6.2	16.9	14.0	73.6	7.8	288	38	44
Putnam	11,611	10,319	7,113	1,292	12.5	33.7	20.6	79.3	3.5	1,602	340	322
Quitman	1,808	1,773	1,346	35	2.0	11.9	8.9	81.1	0.4	2	–	–
Rabun	11,937	10,210	7,883	1,727	16.9	32.2	21.2	79.5	7.1	2,174	450	414
Randolph	3,419	3,402	3,225	17	0.5	8.0	7.5	68.9	5.5	5	2	1
Richmond	85,759	82,312	77,288	3,447	4.2	264.7	238.5	58.0	25.6	4,595	693	831
Rockdale	29,222	25,082	19,963	4,140	16.5	223.7	152.7	74.5	15.9	5,163	1,021	633
Schley	1,648	1,612	1,447	36	2.2	9.8	8.6	76.4	5.3	18	2	2
Screven	7,082	6,853	5,861	229	3.3	10.9	9.0	77.9	5.0	103	42	53
Seminole	4,858	4,742	3,962	116	2.4	20.4	16.6	80.5	2.4	108	59	26
Spalding	25,404	23,001	20,702	2,403	10.4	128.3	104.6	62.8	17.6	2,927	445	549
Stephens	12,169	11,652	10,254	517	4.4	67.9	57.2	72.7	9.7	542	111	85
Stewart	2,361	2,355	2,156	6	0.3	5.1	4.7	72.9	5.9	8	–	–
Sumter	14,165	13,700	11,726	465	3.4	29.2	24.2	64.0	18.7	497	60	118
Talbot	3,053	2,871	2,645	182	6.3	7.8	6.7	82.6	3.9	72	21	51
Taliaferro	1,114	1,085	886	29	2.7	5.7	4.5	76.9	3.7	(NA)	3	3
Tattnall	8,734	8,578	6,756	156	1.8	18.1	14.0	70.6	6.7	214	56	62
Taylor	4,117	3,978	3,162	139	3.5	10.9	8.4	76.9	5.3	200	64	36
Telfair	5,150	5,083	4,756	67	1.3	11.7	10.8	78.4	6.3	11	3	2
Terrell	4,635	4,460	4,069	175	3.9	13.8	12.1	66.3	10.5	220	35	31
Thomas	19,344	18,283	15,936	1,061	5.8	35.3	29.1	70.0	10.9	1,459	376	244
Tift	16,055	15,405	13,359	650	4.2	60.6	50.4	67.3	13.5	812	151	135
Toombs	11,742	11,371	9,952	371	3.3	32.0	27.1	65.5	10.2	388	85	93
Towns	7,580	6,282	4,577	1,298	20.7	45.5	27.5	85.2	2.7	1,628	380	321
Treutlen	2,895	2,865	2,437	30	1.0	14.4	12.1	74.8	6.8	2	2	–
Troup	26,180	23,824	22,426	2,356	9.9	63.3	54.2	64.5	13.7	2,871	444	545
Turner	3,970	3,916	3,426	54	1.4	13.9	12.0	71.6	13.1	39	7	5
Twiggs	4,424	4,291	3,648	133	3.1	12.3	10.1	82.6	3.2	147	20	25
Union	12,393	10,001	6,624	2,392	23.9	38.4	20.5	82.3	3.7	2,936	564	543
Upson	12,165	11,616	10,667	549	4.7	37.4	32.8	69.8	9.9	705	121	116
Walker	27,667	25,577	23,347	2,090	8.2	62.0	52.3	76.9	8.4	2,594	490	522
Walton	29,050	22,500	14,514	6,550	29.1	88.2	44.1	76.5	8.9	8,443	1,664	1,353
Ware	16,291	15,837	14,628	454	2.9	18.1	16.2	70.3	13.1	647	126	112
Warren	2,804	2,767	2,443	37	1.3	9.8	8.6	77.0	8.1	4	1	1
Washington	8,476	8,327	7,416	149	1.8	12.5	10.9	74.0	6.5	148	85	16
Wayne	11,050	10,828	8,812	222	2.1	17.1	13.7	76.5	8.3	100	21	19
Webster	1,138	1,114	898	24	2.2	5.4	4.3	81.7	2.4	(NA)	–	–
Wheeler	2,489	2,447	2,148	42	1.7	8.4	7.2	77.5	7.3	1	–	–
White	11,232	9,454	6,082	1,778	18.8	46.5	25.2	79.2	5.2	2,151	398	366
Whitfield	34,047	30,743	28,832	3,304	10.7	117.4	99.4	67.6	16.6	3,976	713	610
Wilcox	3,383	3,320	2,865	63	1.9	8.9	7.5	79.9	2.9	–	–	–
Wilkes	5,141	5,022	4,548	119	2.4	10.9	9.6	75.5	8.4	158	35	21
Wilkinson	4,550	4,449	4,151	101	2.3	10.2	9.3	82.5	3.2	(NA)	3	6
Worth	9,362	9,098	7,597	264	2.9	16.4	13.3	76.2	7.1	313	63	51

See footnotes at end of table.

Table B-7. Counties — Housing Units and Building Permits—Con.

[Includes United States, states, and 3,141 counties/county equivalents defined as of February 22, 2005. For more information on these areas, see Appendix C, Geographic Information]

County	Housing units 2005 (July 1)	Housing units 2000¹ (April 1 esti-mates base)	Housing units 1990 (April 1)	Net change, 2000–2005 Number	Net change, 2000–2005 Percent	Units per square mile of land area 2005²	Units per square mile of land area 1990	Housing 2000, percent Owner-occupied housing units³	Housing 2000, percent Units in multi-unit structures	New private housing units authorized by building permits Cumulative, 2000–2005 period	New private housing 2005	New private housing 2004
HAWAII	491,071	460,542	389,810	30,529	6.6	76.5	60.7	56.5	39.4	41,743	9,828	9,034
Hawaii	71,984	62,674	48,253	9,310	14.9	17.9	12.0	64.5	19.1	12,904	3,358	3,035
Honolulu	329,300	315,988	281,683	13,312	4.2	549.0	469.3	54.6	45.0	18,162	3,988	4,084
Kalawao	178	172	101	6	3.5	13.5	7.6	-	27.3	(NA)	-	-
Kauai	27,447	25,331	17,613	2,116	8.4	44.1	28.3	61.4	23.2	3,165	923	432
Maui	62,162	56,377	42,160	5,785	10.3	53.6	36.4	57.6	37.5	7,512	1,559	1,483
IDAHO	595,572	527,825	413,327	67,747	12.8	7.2	5.0	72.4	14.4	91,000	21,578	18,108
Ada	141,202	118,516	80,849	22,686	19.1	133.8	76.6	70.7	18.8	30,475	7,854	5,788
Adams	2,282	1,982	1,778	300	15.1	1.7	1.3	79.1	4.3	387	81	83
Bannock	30,635	29,102	25,694	1,533	5.3	27.5	23.1	70.7	19.9	2,476	649	560
Bear Lake	3,581	3,268	2,934	313	9.6	3.7	3.0	83.1	5.6	351	13	71
Benewah	4,312	4,238	3,731	74	1.7	5.6	4.8	78.5	5.6	129	31	23
Bingham	15,024	14,303	12,664	721	5.0	7.2	6.0	79.3	9.1	1,076	265	240
Blaine	13,857	12,186	9,500	1,671	13.7	5.2	3.6	68.9	27.8	1,980	307	385
Boise	4,792	4,349	2,894	443	10.2	2.5	1.5	83.4	1.4	600	151	103
Bonner	19,879	19,646	15,152	233	1.2	11.4	8.7	77.9	9.4	339	13	157
Bonneville	34,663	30,484	26,049	4,179	13.7	18.6	13.9	74.7	18.1	5,928	1,553	1,392
Boundary	4,303	4,095	3,242	208	5.1	3.4	2.6	78.3	5.1	371	142	57
Butte	1,289	1,290	1,265	-1	-0.1	0.6	0.6	77.0	9.5	15	5	5
Camas	705	601	481	104	17.3	0.7	0.4	77.5	2.2	140	34	28
Canyon	60,524	47,965	33,137	12,559	26.2	102.6	56.2	73.3	11.8	15,913	3,245	2,817
Caribou	3,245	3,188	2,867	57	1.8	1.8	1.6	79.5	8.3	98	19	10
Cassia	8,047	7,862	7,212	185	2.4	3.1	2.8	72.6	9.1	313	65	53
Clark	542	521	502	21	4.0	0.3	0.3	67.9	8.8	31	6	8
Clearwater	4,268	4,144	3,805	124	3.0	1.7	1.5	78.0	4.9	166	33	19
Custer	3,042	2,983	2,437	59	2.0	0.6	0.5	74.9	4.7	24	8	5
Elmore	11,372	10,527	8,430	845	8.0	3.7	2.7	57.4	12.8	1,185	305	280
Franklin	4,215	3,872	3,240	343	8.9	6.3	4.9	80.8	5.6	455	89	77
Fremont	7,490	6,890	5,961	600	8.7	4.0	3.2	84.4	4.9	828	188	206
Gem	6,426	5,888	4,725	538	9.1	11.4	8.4	79.8	5.6	781	215	131
Gooding	5,834	5,506	4,800	328	6.0	8.0	6.6	72.3	5.8	450	91	89
Idaho	7,775	7,537	6,346	238	3.2	0.9	0.7	77.2	5.2	34	5	4
Jefferson	7,189	6,287	5,353	902	14.3	6.6	4.9	84.9	4.3	1,271	361	348
Jerome	7,029	6,713	5,886	316	4.7	11.7	9.8	70.0	7.5	502	143	95
Kootenai	54,650	46,607	31,964	8,043	17.3	43.9	25.7	74.5	13.6	10,822	2,688	2,365
Latah	14,669	13,838	11,870	831	6.0	13.6	11.0	58.7	28.9	1,261	339	290
Lemhi	4,367	4,154	3,752	213	5.1	1.0	0.8	76.2	5.9	300	65	58
Lewis	1,814	1,795	1,681	19	1.1	3.8	3.5	74.6	8.1	38	4	10
Lincoln	1,749	1,651	1,386	98	5.9	1.5	1.1	74.8	5.3	127	19	34
Madison	10,412	7,630	6,133	2,782	36.5	22.1	13.0	59.1	32.3	3,163	293	551
Minidoka	7,566	7,498	7,044	68	0.9	10.0	9.3	76.9	8.3	148	31	25
Nez Perce	16,610	16,203	14,463	407	2.5	19.6	17.0	68.8	18.5	693	171	106
Oneida	1,841	1,755	1,496	86	4.9	1.5	1.2	82.4	4.4	111	12	14
Owyhee	4,678	4,452	3,332	226	5.1	0.6	0.4	69.6	4.0	330	84	56
Payette	8,562	7,949	6,520	613	7.7	21.0	16.0	74.1	10.2	812	156	135
Power	2,973	2,844	2,701	129	4.5	2.1	1.9	74.6	9.2	88	27	21
Shoshone	7,089	7,057	6,923	32	0.5	2.7	2.6	72.6	11.5	115	17	08
Teton	3,693	2,632	1,645	1,061	40.3	8.2	3.7	73.5	3.8	1,319	270	245
Twin Falls	28,025	25,595	21,158	2,430	9.5	14.6	11.0	68.3	14.3	3,672	1,036	690
Valley	9,132	8,084	6,640	1,048	13.0	2.5	1.8	78.9	10.7	1,510	438	375
Washington	4,220	4,138	3,685	82	2.0	2.9	2.5	73.7	8.0	173	57	31
ILLINOIS	5,144,623	4,885,744	4,506,275	258,879	5.3	92.6	81.1	67.3	34.0	356,660	66,942	59,753
Adams	30,190	29,386	28,021	804	2.7	35.2	32.7	73.7	17.4	779	125	126
Alexander	4,630	4,591	4,902	39	0.8	19.6	20.7	71.8	14.0	15	5	4
Bond	7,035	6,689	6,136	346	5.2	18.5	16.1	79.7	7.2	493	112	76
Boone	17,759	15,414	11,477	2,345	15.2	63.1	40.8	78.6	14.5	2,953	537	593
Brown	2,533	2,456	2,357	77	3.1	8.3	7.7	74.1	8.9	37	1	13
Bureau	15,525	15,331	14,762	194	1.3	17.9	17.0	76.0	11.4	413	72	69
Calhoun	2,798	2,681	2,951	117	4.4	11.0	11.6	80.7	4.0	165	23	35
Carroll	8,193	7,945	7,481	248	3.1	18.4	16.8	76.7	9.5	424	83	67
Cass	5,888	5,784	5,698	104	1.8	15.7	15.2	74.9	7.9	246	86	100
Champaign	80,549	75,280	68,416	5,269	7.0	80.8	68.6	55.7	35.6	7,770	2,032	1,070
Christian	15,341	14,992	14,640	349	2.3	21.6	20.6	76.2	11.6	585	75	79
Clark	8,061	7,816	7,115	245	3.1	16.1	14.2	77.5	7.7	47	6	8
Clay	6,568	6,394	6,270	174	2.7	14.0	13.4	79.9	7.6	56	9	10
Clinton	14,666	13,802	12,746	864	6.3	30.9	26.9	80.2	9.3	872	249	192
Coles	23,312	22,768	20,329	544	2.4	45.9	40.0	61.9	25.2	562	49	174
Cook	2,143,737	2,096,154	2,021,833	47,583	2.3	2,266.9	2,138.0	57.9	54.4	88,789	18,725	13,907
Crawford	8,980	8,785	8,464	195	2.2	20.2	19.1	80.3	7.6	44	8	8
Cumberland	5,059	4,876	4,448	183	3.8	14.6	12.9	82.1	4.9	61	1	13
DeKalb	36,428	32,988	27,351	3,440	10.4	57.4	43.1	59.5	33.1	5,157	1,459	856
De Witt	7,480	7,282	6,942	198	2.7	18.8	17.5	75.0	12.8	318	44	48

See footnotes at end of table.

[Includes United States, states, and 3,141 counties/county equivalents defined as of February 22, 2005. For more information on these areas, see Appendix C, Geographic Information]

County	Housing units 2005 (July 1)	Housing units 2000[1] (April 1 estimates base)	Housing units 1990 (April 1)	Net change, 2000–2005 Number	Net change, 2000–2005 Percent	Units per square mile of land area 2005[2]	Units per square mile of land area 1990	Housing 2000, percent Owner-occupied housing units[3]	Housing 2000, percent Units in multi-unit structures	New private housing units authorized by building permits Cumulative, 2000–2005 period	New private housing units authorized by building permits 2005	New private housing units authorized by building permits 2004
ILLINOIS—Con.												
Douglas	8,256	8,005	7,607	251	3.1	19.8	18.2	76.9	10.3	340	63	59
DuPage	353,126	335,619	292,537	17,507	5.2	1,058.5	874.7	76.4	27.8	21,574	3,589	3,221
Edgar	8,825	8,611	8,733	214	2.5	14.2	14.0	74.6	8.8	146	11	14
Edwards	3,308	3,199	3,260	109	3.4	14.9	14.7	81.2	5.7	(NA)	–	–
Effingham	14,474	13,959	12,189	515	3.7	30.2	25.5	76.0	12.9	365	76	69
Fayette	9,324	9,053	8,551	271	3.0	13.0	11.9	79.8	5.4	76	13	25
Ford	6,196	6,060	6,118	136	2.2	12.8	12.6	76.2	8.5	211	44	33
Franklin	18,425	18,109	18,430	316	1.7	44.7	44.7	77.7	7.9	197	29	18
Fulton	16,399	16,240	16,480	159	1.0	18.9	19.0	76.4	9.9	445	97	70
Gallatin	3,196	3,071	3,197	125	4.1	9.9	9.9	81.1	5.6	–	–	–
Greene	6,515	6,332	6,575	183	2.9	12.0	12.1	76.2	7.4	41	6	10
Grundy	17,369	15,040	12,652	2,329	15.5	41.4	30.1	72.4	16.0	3,434	687	955
Hamilton	4,098	3,983	4,013	115	2.9	9.4	9.2	81.4	5.0	(NA)	–	–
Hancock	9,217	8,911	9,692	306	3.4	11.6	12.2	80.4	7.6	181	14	23
Hardin	2,544	2,494	2,403	50	2.0	14.3	13.5	80.4	7.2	1	–	–
Henderson	4,238	4,126	4,089	112	2.7	11.2	10.8	78.8	2.8	172	32	33
Henry	21,599	21,270	20,881	329	1.5	26.2	25.4	78.7	9.9	670	126	104
Iroquois	13,580	13,362	12,819	218	1.6	12.2	11.5	76.4	8.4	437	71	90
Jackson	27,817	26,847	25,539	970	3.6	47.3	43.4	53.3	27.8	789	122	120
Jasper	4,460	4,294	4,297	166	3.9	9.0	8.7	83.2	6.0	7	1	1
Jefferson	17,535	16,990	16,075	545	3.2	30.7	28.1	74.6	11.7	290	37	60
Jersey	9,490	8,918	8,216	572	6.4	25.7	22.3	77.7	8.4	839	217	183
Jo Daviess	12,855	12,003	10,757	852	7.1	21.4	17.9	77.3	11.8	1,117	202	233
Johnson	5,265	5,046	4,671	219	4.3	15.3	13.5	84.7	4.0	(NA)	7	1
Kane	163,546	138,995	111,496	24,551	17.7	314.2	214.1	76.0	21.9	33,407	5,499	4,807
Kankakee	42,900	40,610	37,001	2,290	5.6	63.4	54.6	69.4	19.8	3,459	827	651
Kendall	28,149	19,507	13,747	8,642	44.3	87.8	42.9	84.1	11.1	8,417	2,332	1,864
Knox	23,975	23,717	23,722	258	1.1	33.5	33.1	71.6	17.9	604	70	67
Lake	246,761	226,022	183,283	20,739	9.2	551.3	409.3	77.8	20.3	25,678	4,206	4,557
LaSalle	48,545	46,462	43,827	2,083	4.5	42.8	38.6	75.0	15.2	2,575	524	604
Lawrence	7,181	7,014	6,980	167	2.4	19.3	18.8	77.0	8.4	10	–	3
Lee	14,668	14,310	13,314	358	2.5	20.2	18.4	73.9	15.4	616	104	89
Livingston	15,571	15,297	14,365	274	1.8	14.9	13.8	74.1	13.8	526	99	83
Logan	12,011	11,873	11,638	138	1.2	19.4	18.8	71.3	14.0	300	43	46
McDonough	14,110	13,289	13,257	821	6.2	23.9	22.5	63.1	21.3	683	43	64
McHenry	109,477	92,900	65,985	16,577	17.8	181.4	109.2	83.2	12.8	22,696	3,519	3,655
McLean	66,521	59,972	49,164	6,549	10.9	56.2	41.5	66.5	28.3	7,850	885	1,165
Macon	51,619	50,241	50,049	1,378	2.7	88.9	86.2	71.6	17.2	2,168	306	357
Macoupin	21,965	21,097	20,068	868	4.1	25.4	23.2	79.0	7.6	490	156	137
Madison	115,179	108,949	101,098	6,230	5.7	158.9	139.4	73.8	17.4	8,789	1,519	1,553
Marion	18,441	18,022	18,123	419	2.3	32.2	31.7	76.6	10.0	247	45	12
Marshall	6,112	5,896	5,317	216	3.7	15.8	13.8	80.1	6.9	212	18	36
Mason	7,102	7,032	7,684	70	1.0	13.2	14.3	76.8	5.7	165	19	23
Massac	7,121	6,951	6,446	170	2.4	29.8	27.0	78.6	7.1	97	38	44
Menard	5,614	5,285	4,650	329	6.2	17.9	14.8	78.9	8.8	431	65	58
Mercer	7,238	7,109	7,244	129	1.8	12.9	12.9	79.7	6.0	287	103	38
Monroe	12,228	10,749	8,774	1,479	13.8	31.5	22.6	80.2	12.1	1,908	357	332
Montgomery	12,687	12,525	12,456	162	1.3	18.0	17.7	78.4	8.7	173	41	58
Morgan	15,622	15,291	14,724	331	2.2	27.5	25.9	70.4	18.8	297	20	21
Moultrie	5,942	5,743	5,384	199	3.5	17.7	16.0	78.5	8.3	337	93	43
Ogle	21,557	20,420	18,052	1,137	5.6	28.4	23.8	74.5	15.9	1,619	289	291
Peoria	81,128	78,204	75,211	2,924	3.7	131.0	121.4	67.7	22.8	4,463	945	768
Perry	9,782	9,457	9,235	325	3.4	22.2	20.9	78.6	10.0	(NA)	–	–
Piatt	7,118	6,799	6,227	319	4.7	16.2	14.2	80.2	7.6	483	102	88
Pike	8,181	8,010	8,057	171	2.1	9.9	9.7	77.1	6.7	335	83	47
Pope	2,433	2,351	2,154	82	3.5	6.6	5.8	82.2	7.4	3	–	–
Pulaski	3,422	3,353	3,410	69	2.1	17.0	17.0	75.6	7.6	12	6	–
Putnam	3,063	2,888	2,600	175	6.1	19.2	16.3	82.6	6.4	243	46	35
Randolph	13,586	13,328	13,179	258	1.9	23.5	22.8	79.4	8.7	477	106	76
Richland	7,730	7,468	7,142	262	3.5	21.5	19.8	76.5	8.6	199	13	31
Rock Island	65,034	64,493	63,327	541	0.8	152.4	148.4	69.7	23.3	1,716	435	307
St. Clair	111,496	104,437	103,432	7,059	6.8	168.0	155.8	67.0	18.9	9,683	1,917	2,058
Saline	12,837	12,360	12,350	477	3.9	33.5	32.2	76.5	7.2	–	–	–
Sangamon	89,328	85,461	76,873	3,867	4.5	102.9	88.5	70.0	21.1	5,411	935	931
Schuyler	3,430	3,304	3,329	126	3.8	7.8	7.6	78.8	7.4	(NA)	–	–
Scott	2,556	2,464	2,442	92	3.7	10.2	9.7	77.6	7.3	–	–	–
Shelby	10,291	10,060	9,329	231	2.3	13.6	12.3	81.0	5.6	310	17	81
Stark	2,816	2,725	2,716	91	3.3	9.8	9.4	77.2	9.3	48	6	7
Stephenson	22,098	21,713	20,378	385	1.8	39.2	36.1	74.8	18.8	721	110	108
Tazewell	55,346	52,974	49,315	2,372	4.5	85.3	76.0	76.1	14.7	3,629	774	712

See footnotes at end of table.

[Includes United States, states, and 3,141 counties/county equivalents defined as of February 22, 2005. For more information on these areas, see Appendix C, Geographic Information]

County	Housing units							Housing 2000, percent		New private housing units authorized by building permits		
	2005 (July 1)	2000[1] (April 1) esti-mates base	1990 (April 1)	Net change, 2000–2005 Number	Percent	Units per square mile of land area 2005[2]	1990	Owner-occupied housing units[3]	Units in multi-unit structures	Cumu-lative, 2000–2005 period	2005	2004
ILLINOIS—Con.												
Union	8,079	7,894	7,408	185	2.3	19.4	17.8	75.4	10.5	274	43	37
Vermilion	36,828	36,350	37,061	478	1.3	41.0	41.2	71.7	15.1	429	45	122
Wabash	5,863	5,758	5,572	105	1.8	26.2	24.9	75.3	10.5	86	16	24
Warren	7,870	7,787	8,229	83	1.1	14.5	15.2	74.6	11.6	197	23	25
Washington	6,670	6,385	6,261	285	4.5	11.9	11.1	81.1	4.9	379	54	64
Wayne	8,211	7,950	7,622	261	3.3	11.5	10.7	79.4	6.0	67	3	–
White	7,639	7,393	7,797	246	3.3	15.4	15.8	78.0	7.3	6	2	–
Whiteside	25,464	25,023	24,000	441	1.8	37.2	35.0	74.5	15.4	867	166	181
Will	216,289	175,527	122,870	40,762	23.2	258.4	146.8	83.1	13.9	48,228	8,166	7,997
Williamson	29,121	27,704	25,183	1,417	5.1	68.8	59.4	73.6	13.8	1,547	341	349
Winnebago	121,710	114,404	101,666	7,306	6.4	236.9	197.9	70.0	25.6	10,340	2,029	1,980
Woodford	14,519	13,486	11,932	1,033	7.7	27.5	22.6	82.8	8.7	1,340	194	297
INDIANA	2,724,429	2,532,327	2,246,046	192,102	7.6	76.0	62.6	71.4	19.2	233,746	38,476	39,233
Adams	12,935	12,404	10,931	531	4.3	38.1	32.2	77.0	15.2	742	159	128
Allen	149,351	138,905	122,923	10,446	7.5	227.2	187.0	71.0	22.0	13,398	2,259	2,270
Bartholomew	30,950	29,853	25,432	1,097	3.7	76.1	62.5	74.3	14.8	1,419	292	278
Benton	3,886	3,818	3,833	68	1.8	9.6	9.4	75.8	7.5	126	19	20
Blackford	6,402	6,155	5,856	247	4.0	38.8	35.5	78.7	10.3	286	23	64
Boone	20,582	17,929	14,516	2,653	14.8	48.7	34.3	78.7	12.8	3,413	751	572
Brown	7,772	7,163	6,997	609	8.5	24.9	22.4	85.0	3.1	683	104	32
Carroll	9,205	8,675	8,431	530	6.1	24.7	22.6	79.7	6.9	693	121	126
Cass	17,241	16,620	15,633	621	3.7	41.8	37.9	73.7	13.9	405	54	65
Clark	45,982	41,176	35,313	4,806	11.7	122.6	94.1	70.0	21.5	5,832	981	1,021
Clay	11,633	11,099	10,606	534	4.8	32.5	29.7	79.1	8.2	243	30	32
Clinton	13,619	13,267	12,100	352	2.7	33.6	29.9	72.9	14.3	450	54	54
Crawford	5,410	5,138	4,374	272	5.3	17.7	14.3	82.9	3.6	18	2	2
Daviess	12,274	11,898	10,985	376	3.2	28.5	25.5	78.6	9.3	109	18	21
Dearborn	19,546	17,797	14,532	1,749	9.8	64.0	47.6	78.6	14.5	2,094	313	329
Decatur	10,635	9,992	9,098	643	6.4	28.5	24.4	73.2	12.4	783	90	110
DeKalb	17,137	16,144	13,601	993	6.2	47.2	37.5	81.5	12.2	1,231	196	205
Delaware	52,679	51,032	48,793	1,647	3.2	133.9	124.1	67.2	21.3	2,240	267	359
Dubois	16,581	15,511	13,964	1,070	6.9	38.6	32.5	78.0	14.9	1,290	204	265
Elkhart	75,807	69,791	60,182	6,016	8.6	163.4	129.7	72.2	19.3	7,318	1,024	1,163
Fayette	11,309	10,981	10,525	328	3.0	52.6	49.0	71.5	14.3	432	25	71
Floyd	30,930	29,087	25,238	1,843	6.3	209.0	170.5	72.5	19.9	2,333	344	373
Fountain	7,916	7,692	7,344	224	2.9	20.0	18.6	77.9	7.5	57	11	6
Franklin	9,188	8,596	7,176	592	6.9	23.8	18.6	81.4	6.4	620	97	120
Fulton	9,491	9,123	8,656	368	4.0	25.8	23.5	78.4	8.8	259	78	68
Gibson	14,943	14,125	13,454	818	5.8	30.6	27.5	77.9	9.9	652	133	225
Grant	31,641	30,560	29,904	1,081	3.5	76.4	72.2	73.2	15.7	1,086	96	122
Greene	15,833	15,053	13,337	780	5.2	29.2	24.6	80.0	6.4	–	–	–
Hamilton	91,613	69,478	41,074	22,135	31.9	230.2	103.2	80.9	15.8	25,990	4,276	4,252
Hancock	26,248	21,750	16,495	4,498	20.7	85.7	53.9	81.4	10.8	5,367	762	890
Harrison	14,748	13,699	11,456	1,049	7.7	30.4	23.6	84.1	6.3	1,171	181	215
Hendricks	51,172	39,229	26,962	11,943	30.4	125.3	66.0	83.0	11.1	14,298	2,387	2,007
Henry	21,385	20,592	19,835	793	3.9	54.4	50.5	77.0	11.9	1,070	144	168
Howard	39,225	37,604	33,820	1,621	4.3	133.8	115.4	71.7	18.5	2,098	239	268
Huntington	15,978	15,269	13,629	709	4.6	41.8	35.6	77.1	12.8	937	139	153
Jackson	18,117	17,137	14,820	980	5.7	35.6	29.1	74.3	12.4	1,070	175	175
Jasper	12,529	11,236	8,984	1,293	11.5	22.4	16.0	77.5	9.9	1,552	248	232
Jay	9,386	9,074	8,905	312	3.4	24.5	23.2	77.7	8.5	313	34	41
Jefferson	14,099	13,386	11,921	713	5.3	39.0	33.0	74.6	14.1	844	130	142
Jennings	12,556	11,469	9,129	1,087	9.5	33.3	24.2	79.1	7.2	943	119	134
Johnson	52,197	45,095	33,289	7,102	15.7	163.0	104.0	76.5	17.9	9,109	1,882	1,662
Knox	17,659	17,305	16,730	354	2.0	34.2	32.4	69.0	16.1	343	52	54
Kosciusko	34,957	32,188	30,516	2,769	8.6	65.0	56.8	79.0	9.7	3,268	547	499
LaGrange	13,975	12,938	12,218	1,037	8.0	36.8	32.2	81.5	6.9	1,221	272	187
Lake	205,293	194,992	183,014	10,301	5.3	413.1	368.2	69.0	24.2	14,912	2,916	2,855
LaPorte	47,555	45,621	42,268	1,934	4.2	79.5	70.6	75.2	17.3	2,801	577	512
Lawrence	21,279	20,560	17,587	719	3.5	47.4	39.2	78.9	9.7	227	36	36
Madison	58,837	56,939	53,353	1,898	3.3	130.1	118.0	74.2	14.5	2,875	569	555
Marion	412,299	387,183	349,403	25,116	6.5	1,040.5	881.4	59.3	32.4	32,118	4,618	5,135
Marshall	19,096	18,099	16,820	997	5.5	43.0	37.9	76.8	11.2	1,232	201	174
Martin	4,943	4,729	4,116	214	4.5	14.7	12.2	81.2	6.4	25	3	3
Miami	15,827	15,299	14,639	528	3.5	42.1	39.0	76.0	10.2	633	61	48
Monroe	55,601	50,846	41,948	4,755	9.4	141.0	106.4	54.0	35.7	5,717	868	1,135
Montgomery	16,440	15,678	13,957	762	4.9	32.6	27.7	73.4	15.5	964	102	179
Morgan	28,206	25,908	20,500	2,298	8.9	69.4	50.4	79.7	10.6	2,597	306	345
Newton	6,015	5,726	5,276	289	5.0	15.0	13.1	79.9	6.5	364	51	43
Noble	19,365	18,233	15,516	1,132	6.2	47.1	37.7	78.0	11.9	1,425	258	208
Ohio	2,631	2,424	2,161	207	8.5	30.3	24.9	77.6	11.7	254	45	42
Orange	8,730	8,348	7,732	382	4.6	21.9	19.4	79.1	7.8	23	12	4
Owen	10,264	9,853	8,011	411	4.2	26.6	20.8	81.6	3.9	174	160	3

See footnotes at end of table.

[Includes United States, states, and 3,141 counties/county equivalents defined as of February 22, 2005. For more information on these areas, see Appendix C, Geographic Information]

County	Housing units								Housing 2000, percent		New private housing units authorized by building permits		
	2005 (July 1)	2000[1] (April 1 esti- mates base)	1990 (April 1)	Net change, 2000–2005		Units per square mile of land area		Owner- occupied housing units[3]	Units in multi- unit structures	Cumu- lative, 2000– 2005 period	2005	2004
				Number	Percent	2005[2]	1990					
INDIANA—Con.												
Parke	7,804	7,539	7,189	265	3.5	17.5	16.2	80.2	5.3	262	45	42
Perry	8,458	8,223	7,404	235	2.9	22.2	19.4	79.3	9.6	277	44	46
Pike	5,992	5,611	5,487	381	6.8	17.8	16.3	82.5	5.2	313	46	53
Porter	63,347	57,616	47,240	5,731	9.9	151.5	113.0	76.7	17.8	7,174	1,411	1,286
Posey	11,561	11,076	10,401	485	4.4	28.3	25.5	81.8	7.3	597	96	102
Pulaski	6,228	5,918	5,541	310	5.2	14.4	12.8	80.6	3.6	326	25	38
Putnam	14,147	13,505	10,981	642	4.8	29.5	22.9	78.6	10.9	586	261	157
Randolph	12,005	11,775	11,327	230	2.0	26.5	25.0	75.9	9.9	349	42	54
Ripley	11,517	10,482	9,587	1,035	9.9	25.8	21.5	76.8	11.9	1,325	225	218
Rush	7,671	7,337	7,014	334	4.6	18.8	17.2	74.1	9.9	436	45	114
St. Joseph	112,224	107,013	97,956	5,211	4.9	245.4	214.2	71.7	19.1	7,054	1,072	1,140
Scott	10,617	9,737	8,078	880	9.0	55.8	42.4	75.9	9.6	974	142	146
Shelby	18,475	17,633	15,654	842	4.8	44.8	37.9	73.4	14.5	1,222	272	303
Spencer	8,955	8,333	7,636	622	7.5	22.5	19.2	83.2	6.5	692	97	96
Starke	10,654	10,201	9,888	453	4.4	34.4	32.0	80.9	5.2	580	108	38
Steuben	18,837	17,337	15,768	1,500	8.7	61.0	51.1	78.1	8.9	1,763	302	307
Sullivan	9,173	8,804	8,487	369	4.2	20.5	19.0	79.8	8.0	77	10	7
Switzerland	4,942	4,226	3,732	716	16.9	22.3	16.9	77.9	6.6	777	140	138
Tippecanoe	65,496	58,343	48,134	7,153	12.3	131.0	96.3	55.9	34.5	8,152	939	1,365
Tipton	7,067	6,848	6,427	219	3.2	27.1	24.7	79.9	9.1	358	119	38
Union	3,333	3,077	2,813	256	8.3	20.6	17.4	75.3	7.4	227	25	32
Vanderburgh	80,423	76,300	72,637	4,123	5.4	342.9	309.6	66.8	26.1	5,525	862	1,024
Vermillion	7,601	7,405	7,288	196	2.6	29.6	28.4	79.5	6.2	207	28	32
Vigo	46,733	45,203	44,203	1,530	3.4	115.9	109.6	67.5	20.5	2,289	435	518
Wabash	14,425	14,034	13,394	391	2.8	34.9	32.4	75.9	11.7	529	55	76
Warren	3,794	3,477	3,275	317	9.1	10.4	9.0	81.1	4.3	296	29	37
Warrick	22,971	20,546	16,926	2,425	11.8	59.8	44.1	83.3	9.6	3,288	873	591
Washington	11,878	11,191	9,520	687	6.1	23.1	18.5	81.1	5.5	383	93	120
Wayne	31,004	30,468	29,586	536	1.8	76.8	73.3	68.7	20.1	930	159	211
Wells	11,545	10,970	9,928	575	5.2	31.2	26.8	80.9	9.6	741	108	102
White	12,807	12,083	11,875	724	6.0	25.3	23.5	76.6	6.5	576	79	80
Whitley	13,642	12,545	10,852	1,097	8.7	40.7	32.3	83.3	8.8	1,314	174	265
IOWA	1,306,943	1,232,530	1,143,669	74,413	6.0	23.4	20.5	72.3	18.4	89,570	16,766	16,345
Adair	3,801	3,690	3,714	111	3.0	6.7	6.5	75.0	9.0	133	14	14
Adams	2,117	2,109	2,234	8	0.4	5.0	5.3	74.7	6.9	32	3	7
Allamakee	7,520	7,142	6,603	378	5.3	11.8	10.3	76.4	10.6	502	86	86
Appanoose	6,758	6,697	6,402	61	0.9	13.6	12.9	74.0	11.8	90	19	20
Audubon	3,009	2,995	3,247	14	0.5	6.8	7.3	79.2	5.1	41	7	7
Benton	10,922	10,377	9,125	545	5.3	15.2	12.7	79.4	10.3	561	94	105
Black Hawk	53,910	51,760	49,688	2,150	4.2	95.1	87.6	68.9	21.7	2,905	571	490
Boone	11,477	10,968	10,371	509	4.6	20.1	18.1	75.8	14.2	601	111	120
Bremer	9,938	9,337	8,847	601	6.4	22.7	20.2	78.2	13.5	737	115	138
Buchanan	9,129	8,697	8,272	432	5.0	16.0	14.5	78.2	9.8	229	20	57
Buena Vista	8,180	8,144	8,140	36	0.4	14.2	14.2	70.4	14.7	141	17	25
Butler	6,642	6,578	6,483	64	1.0	11.4	11.2	80.4	5.9	204	39	42
Calhoun	5,208	5,219	5,362	−11	−0.2	9.1	9.4	77.4	10.3	81	20	20
Carroll	9,245	9,019	8,356	226	2.5	16.2	14.7	74.4	15.0	379	72	66
Cass	6,722	6,590	6,788	132	2.0	11.9	12.0	74.6	13.8	130	17	16
Cedar	7,930	7,570	7,146	360	4.8	13.7	12.3	76.8	8.5	511	87	87
Cerro Gordo	21,840	21,488	20,954	352	1.6	38.4	36.9	71.5	18.6	698	150	155
Cherokee	5,907	5,851	5,973	56	1.0	10.2	10.3	73.7	12.0	115	17	25
Chickasaw	5,735	5,593	5,486	142	2.5	11.4	10.9	80.2	8.6	94	18	23
Clarke	4,138	3,934	3,599	204	5.2	9.6	8.3	72.4	11.3	170	17	44
Clay	8,057	7,828	7,659	229	2.9	14.2	13.5	69.1	18.3	304	36	70
Clayton	9,105	8,619	8,344	486	5.6	11.7	10.7	76.5	10.3	505	69	60
Clinton	22,130	21,585	21,296	545	2.5	31.8	30.6	72.9	18.7	861	194	174
Crawford	7,040	6,958	6,920	82	1.2	9.9	9.7	73.0	12.1	202	46	32
Dallas	19,480	16,529	11,812	2,951	17.9	33.2	20.1	76.3	15.7	3,256	969	504
Davis	3,656	3,530	3,365	126	3.6	7.3	6.7	79.7	7.7	52	9	9
Decatur	3,885	3,833	3,692	52	1.4	7.3	6.9	71.1	12.9	48	7	9
Delaware	7,905	7,682	7,408	223	2.9	13.7	12.8	77.8	9.3	117	26	16
Des Moines	18,879	18,643	18,248	236	1.3	45.4	43.8	74.2	17.8	419	104	84
Dickinson	12,558	11,375	9,723	1,183	10.4	33.0	25.5	78.0	13.5	1,357	345	282
Dubuque	38,105	35,508	32,053	2,597	7.3	62.7	52.7	73.5	24.0	3,252	560	872
Emmet	4,944	4,889	4,914	55	1.1	12.5	12.4	75.1	10.6	118	14	18
Fayette	9,687	9,505	9,262	182	1.9	13.3	12.7	75.7	10.9	170	10	20
Floyd	7,426	7,317	7,233	109	1.5	14.8	14.4	74.1	12.3	225	33	38
Franklin	4,786	4,763	5,018	23	0.5	8.2	8.6	75.0	11.2	57	11	20
Fremont	3,557	3,514	3,607	43	1.2	7.0	7.1	74.5	8.1	133	25	23
Greene	4,668	4,623	4,707	45	1.0	8.2	8.3	75.6	9.4	105	20	17
Grundy	5,594	5,304	5,158	290	5.5	11.1	10.3	79.9	8.5	338	49	57
Guthrie	5,719	5,467	5,179	252	4.6	9.7	8.8	79.6	9.5	275	26	50
Hamilton	7,299	7,082	6,879	217	3.1	12.7	11.9	72.8	12.9	139	11	28

See footnotes at end of table.

[Includes United States, states, and 3,141 counties/county equivalents defined as of February 22, 2005. For more information on these areas, see Appendix C, Geographic Information]

County	Housing units							Housing 2000, percent		New private housing units authorized by building permits		
	2005 (July 1)	2000[1] (April 1 estimates base)	1990 (April 1)	Net change, 2000–2005		Units per square mile of land area		Owner-occupied housing units[3]	Units in multi-unit structures	Cumulative, 2000–2005 period	2005	2004
				Number	Percent	2005[2]	1990					
IOWA—Con.												
Hancock	5,270	5,164	5,236	106	2.1	9.2	9.2	78.2	8.3	180	39	29
Hardin	8,434	8,318	8,419	116	1.4	14.8	14.8	74.6	12.6	223	32	31
Harrison	6,811	6,602	6,175	209	3.2	9.8	8.9	76.6	8.8	396	67	54
Henry	8,470	8,246	7,507	224	2.7	19.5	17.3	73.0	16.2	277	44	36
Howard	4,424	4,327	4,155	97	2.2	9.3	8.8	79.2	8.6	79	20	12
Humboldt	4,795	4,645	4,670	150	3.2	11.0	10.7	76.0	11.6	193	19	46
Ida	3,529	3,506	3,473	23	0.7	8.2	8.0	73.2	12.0	81	41	8
Iowa	6,811	6,545	6,003	266	4.1	11.6	10.2	77.9	13.6	158	22	29
Jackson	9,295	8,949	8,426	346	3.9	14.6	13.2	76.0	11.3	465	82	95
Jasper	16,105	15,659	14,338	446	2.8	22.1	19.6	75.7	15.8	678	137	109
Jefferson	7,477	7,241	6,739	236	3.3	17.2	15.5	67.2	16.7	194	39	23
Johnson	52,640	45,831	37,210	6,809	14.9	85.7	60.5	56.6	37.5	7,717	1,244	1,323
Jones	8,379	8,126	7,366	253	3.1	14.6	12.8	75.9	11.0	188	40	46
Keokuk	5,064	5,013	5,024	51	1.0	8.7	8.7	78.7	7.0	59	15	3
Kossuth	7,645	7,605	7,765	40	0.5	7.9	8.0	77.8	9.8	117	19	20
Lee	16,791	16,612	16,443	179	1.1	32.5	31.8	75.5	15.7	197	15	21
Linn	89,570	80,551	68,357	9,019	11.2	124.8	95.3	72.7	22.7	10,113	1,598	1,905
Louisa	5,186	5,133	5,044	53	1.0	12.9	12.5	77.3	7.5	142	34	20
Lucas	4,290	4,239	4,179	51	1.2	10.0	9.7	78.3	12.5	19	5	3
Lyon	4,855	4,758	4,561	97	2.0	8.3	7.8	81.8	5.8	143	21	24
Madison	6,246	5,661	4,995	585	10.3	11.1	8.9	78.0	9.6	747	151	164
Mahaska	9,804	9,551	8,977	253	2.6	17.2	15.7	71.1	14.4	218	36	27
Marion	13,619	12,757	11,420	862	6.8	24.6	20.6	75.6	14.7	1,133	179	144
Marshall	16,885	16,324	15,862	561	3.4	29.5	27.7	73.7	17.5	662	94	134
Mills	5,894	5,671	5,004	223	3.9	13.5	11.5	79.5	8.0	106	16	11
Mitchell	4,676	4,594	4,514	82	1.8	10.0	9.6	81.6	8.6	104	18	28
Monona	4,755	4,660	4,555	95	2.0	6.9	6.6	76.0	8.2	171	33	29
Monroe	3,609	3,588	3,740	21	0.6	8.3	8.6	78.4	10.9	94	22	22
Montgomery	5,392	5,399	5,363	-7	-0.1	12.7	12.7	73.1	14.6	78	19	11
Muscatine	17,524	16,786	16,044	738	4.4	39.9	36.6	75.4	15.0	1,084	216	167
O'Brien	6,661	6,509	6,476	152	2.3	11.6	11.3	76.9	9.8	151	21	18
Osceola	3,015	3,012	2,998	3	0.1	7.6	7.5	77.5	7.4	37	8	7
Page	7,307	7,302	7,339	5	0.1	13.7	13.7	71.6	14.9	113	23	17
Palo Alto	4,731	4,631	4,826	100	2.2	8.4	8.6	74.1	10.5	69	11	8
Plymouth	10,365	9,880	8,806	485	4.9	12.0	10.2	77.5	11.6	625	103	108
Pocahontas	4,021	3,988	4,193	33	0.8	7.0	7.3	79.3	7.3	26	3	7
Polk	176,730	156,448	135,979	20,282	13.0	310.4	238.8	68.8	26.9	23,278	4,782	4,386
Pottawattamie	38,218	35,808	32,831	2,410	6.7	40.0	34.4	71.1	19.0	2,991	498	452
Poweshiek	9,013	8,561	8,199	452	5.3	15.4	14.0	71.9	16.1	435	60	112
Ringgold	2,922	2,789	2,713	133	4.8	5.4	5.0	75.7	5.7	23	3	2
Sac	5,557	5,460	5,648	97	1.8	9.7	9.8	76.8	7.9	65	16	11
Scott	69,148	65,656	61,379	3,492	5.3	151.0	134.0	70.6	23.9	4,801	813	821
Shelby	5,463	5,412	5,430	51	0.9	9.2	9.2	77.0	8.8	115	22	12
Sioux	11,769	11,260	10,333	509	4.5	15.3	13.5	80.5	10.4	654	122	101
Story	34,348	30,630	26,847	3,718	12.1	60.0	46.9	58.3	33.8	4,478	946	736
Tama	7,801	7,583	7,417	218	2.9	10.8	10.3	77.5	9.1	250	45	37
Taylor	3,245	3,199	3,307	46	1.4	6.1	6.2	76.4	6.2	29	1	7
Union	5,788	5,657	5,622	131	2.3	13.6	13.2	72.1	14.6	133	5	11
Van Buren	3,669	3,581	3,529	88	2.5	7.6	7.3	79.7	7.1	30	3	1
Wapello	16,254	15,873	15,640	381	2.4	37.6	36.2	75.6	13.0	502	127	74
Warren	16,723	15,289	13,157	1,434	9.4	29.3	23.0	79.9	14.6	1,772	372	357
Washington	8,850	8,543	7,866	307	3.6	15.6	13.8	75.3	14.0	270	44	39
Wayne	3,411	3,357	3,334	54	1.6	6.5	6.3	79.3	5.6	12	1	2
Webster	17,285	16,969	17,063	316	1.9	24.2	23.9	71.3	17.4	463	66	65
Winnebago	5,194	5,065	5,030	129	2.5	13.0	12.6	76.1	13.4	93	9	25
Winneshiek	8,563	8,208	7,726	355	4.3	12.4	11.2	73.5	14.7	341	83	105
Woodbury	41,882	41,394	39,071	488	1.2	48.0	44.8	68.6	20.8	1,331	162	273
Worth	3,558	3,534	3,443	24	0.7	8.9	8.6	79.0	9.6	69	23	15
Wright	6,599	6,559	6,636	40	0.6	11.4	11.4	74.2	12.6	111	19	32
KANSAS	1,196,211	1,131,395	1,044,112	64,816	5.7	14.6	12.8	69.2	17.5	82,453	14,048	13,301
Allen	6,487	6,449	6,454	38	0.6	12.9	12.8	75.0	8.6	114	21	17
Anderson	3,684	3,596	3,514	88	2.4	6.3	6.0	80.0	5.6	73	24	33
Atchison	6,961	6,818	6,691	143	2.1	16.1	15.5	73.3	12.0	132	25	27
Barber	2,778	2,740	3,120	38	1.4	2.4	2.8	75.3	7.6	20	1	8
Barton	12,976	12,888	13,144	88	0.7	14.5	14.7	72.1	9.8	255	52	41
Bourbon	7,313	7,135	6,920	178	2.5	11.5	10.9	74.0	11.0	109	11	3
Brown	4,918	4,815	4,890	103	2.1	8.6	8.6	71.4	10.4	61	6	3
Butler	25,164	23,177	20,072	1,987	8.6	17.6	14.1	77.7	8.6	2,346	296	384
Chase	1,553	1,529	1,547	24	1.6	2.0	2.0	73.3	2.2	1	–	–
Chautauqua	2,241	2,169	2,249	72	3.3	3.5	3.5	82.1	1.4	(NA)	1	–

See footnotes at end of table.

[Includes United States, states, and 3,141 counties/county equivalents defined as of February 22, 2005. For more information on these areas, see Appendix C, Geographic Information]

County	Housing units								Housing 2000, percent		New private housing units authorized by building permits		
	2005 (July 1)	2000[1] (April 1 esti- mates base)	1990 (April 1)	Net change, 2000–2005		Units per square mile of land area		Owner- occupied housing units[3]	Units in multi- unit structures	Cumu- lative, 2000– 2005 period	2005	2004
				Number	Percent	2005[2]	1990					
KANSAS—Con.												
Cherokee	10,352	10,031	9,428	321	3.2	17.6	16.1	76.1	4.4	113	19	19
Cheyenne	1,648	1,636	1,687	12	0.7	1.6	1.7	77.2	4.0	5	–	–
Clark	1,146	1,111	1,327	35	3.2	1.2	1.4	76.4	3.5	11	1	2
Clay	4,167	4,084	4,138	83	2.0	6.5	6.4	76.7	8.0	153	29	28
Cloud	4,854	4,838	5,198	16	0.3	6.8	7.3	74.3	9.8	9	–	2
Coffey	4,039	3,876	3,712	163	4.2	6.4	5.9	78.3	5.3	170	23	28
Comanche	1,090	1,088	1,256	2	0.2	1.4	1.6	73.9	4.1	1	–	–
Cowley	16,106	15,673	15,569	433	2.8	14.3	13.8	70.8	10.2	497	79	81
Crawford	17,968	17,222	16,526	746	4.3	30.3	27.9	64.4	13.6	984	141	107
Decatur	1,839	1,821	2,063	18	1.0	2.1	2.3	76.0	7.7	9	–	–
Dickinson	8,867	8,686	8,415	181	2.1	10.5	9.9	74.8	10.5	322	58	51
Doniphan	3,554	3,489	3,337	65	1.9	9.1	8.5	74.5	7.4	92	15	24
Douglas	44,817	40,251	31,782	4,566	11.3	98.1	69.6	51.9	33.6	5,424	697	879
Edwards	1,776	1,754	1,867	22	1.3	2.9	3.0	77.7	5.2	3	–	1
Elk	1,928	1,860	1,743	68	3.7	3.0	2.7	81.1	3.7	(NA)	–	–
Ellis	12,361	12,078	11,115	283	2.3	13.7	12.3	63.3	22.5	428	55	45
Ellsworth	3,320	3,228	3,317	92	2.9	4.6	4.6	79.6	6.5	56	4	19
Finney	13,971	13,763	11,696	208	1.5	10.7	9.0	64.8	20.0	268	13	30
Ford	12,017	11,651	10,842	366	3.1	10.9	9.9	64.8	17.2	465	30	68
Franklin	10,951	10,229	8,926	722	7.1	19.1	15.6	73.5	10.0	967	221	140
Geary	12,125	11,959	11,952	166	1.4	31.5	31.1	50.5	23.9	293	61	64
Gove	1,457	1,423	1,494	34	2.4	1.4	1.4	79.8	2.7	3	–	–
Graham	1,573	1,553	1,753	20	1.3	1.8	2.0	79.5	4.2	10	10	–
Grant	3,089	3,027	2,599	62	2.0	5.4	4.5	74.6	6.1	35	2	10
Gray	2,298	2,181	2,114	117	5.4	2.6	2.4	72.7	4.5	108	7	27
Greeley	723	712	801	11	1.5	0.9	1.0	74.4	1.7	3	–	1
Greenwood	4,355	4,274	4,243	81	1.9	3.8	3.7	75.2	5.8	12	1	1
Hamilton	1,237	1,211	1,214	26	2.1	1.2	1.2	69.4	7.8	12	1	3
Harper	3,287	3,270	3,481	17	0.5	4.1	4.3	74.3	6.3	31	10	4
Harvey	13,988	13,378	12,290	610	4.6	25.9	22.8	71.9	14.0	861	133	111
Haskell	1,689	1,639	1,586	50	3.1	2.9	2.7	72.2	4.3	2	–	–
Hodgeman	978	944	1,022	34	3.6	1.1	1.2	78.5	3.8	(NA)	–	–
Jackson	5,379	5,094	4,564	285	5.6	8.2	6.9	80.6	5.9	385	72	76
Jefferson	8,019	7,491	6,314	528	7.0	15.0	11.8	84.8	3.3	694	132	110
Jewell	2,141	2,103	2,409	38	1.8	2.4	2.6	79.4	5.1	2	1	–
Johnson	207,249	181,800	144,155	25,449	14.0	434.7	302.4	72.3	22.9	30,403	4,456	4,398
Kearny	1,724	1,657	1,561	67	4.0	2.0	1.8	73.3	5.9	50	4	10
Kingman	3,920	3,852	3,645	68	1.8	4.5	4.2	77.8	5.1	88	1	6
Kiowa	1,662	1,643	1,738	19	1.2	2.3	2.4	71.8	6.8	2	–	–
Labette	10,404	10,304	10,641	100	1.0	16.0	16.4	73.2	9.8	184	22	9
Lane	1,060	1,065	1,117	–5	–0.5	1.5	1.6	77.3	3.2	7	1	1
Leavenworth	26,979	24,401	21,264	2,578	10.6	58.2	45.9	67.0	17.1	3,408	675	590
Lincoln	1,879	1,853	1,864	26	1.4	2.6	2.6	78.3	4.8	6	–	1
Linn	4,975	4,720	4,811	255	5.4	8.3	8.0	82.6	2.5	317	60	89
Logan	1,435	1,423	1,466	12	0.8	1.3	1.4	76.3	6.0	14	2	8
Lyon	15,057	14,757	14,346	300	2.0	17.7	16.9	61.0	23.0	558	172	176
McPherson	12,364	11,830	10,941	534	4.5	13.7	12.2	74.0	12.4	763	131	128
Marion	6,099	5,882	5,659	217	3.7	6.5	6.0	79.9	7.6	294	50	64
Marshall	5,088	4,999	5,269	89	1.8	5.6	5.8	79.5	6.3	40	9	11
Meade	1,994	1,968	2,049	26	1.3	2.0	2.1	74.4	4.4	12	2	2
Miami	12,038	10,984	8,971	1,054	9.6	20.9	15.6	78.6	8.0	1,234	252	302
Mitchell	3,362	3,340	3,359	22	0.7	4.8	4.8	74.6	9.4	25	2	11
Montgomery	17,317	17,209	17,920	108	0.6	26.8	27.8	71.6	10.3	84	14	11
Morris	3,241	3,160	3,149	81	2.6	4.6	4.5	78.0	4.1	36	10	7
Morton	1,562	1,519	1,515	43	2.8	2.1	2.1	71.3	4.3	29	1	–
Nemaha	4,456	4,340	4,319	116	2.7	6.2	6.0	80.8	7.0	98	25	8
Neosho	7,550	7,461	7,726	89	1.2	13.2	13.5	74.6	8.4	64	12	7
Ness	1,856	1,835	2,048	21	1.1	1.7	1.9	76.0	4.4	11	1	1
Norton	2,698	2,673	2,798	25	0.9	3.1	3.2	77.8	8.0	11	–	1
Osage	7,378	7,019	6,324	359	5.1	10.5	9.0	79.8	7.0	450	59	84
Osborne	2,432	2,419	2,496	13	0.5	2.7	2.8	78.8	6.1	5	–	–
Ottawa	2,829	2,755	2,591	74	2.7	3.9	3.6	82.1	5.4	68	18	25
Pawnee	3,145	3,114	3,412	31	1.0	4.2	4.5	74.2	8.8	28	6	3
Phillips	3,134	3,088	3,264	46	1.5	3.5	3.7	77.9	7.2	20	–	1
Pottawatomie	7,905	7,311	6,472	594	8.1	9.4	7.7	78.4	5.2	856	266	142
Pratt	4,775	4,633	4,620	142	3.1	6.5	6.3	73.4	10.5	132	4	16
Rawlins	1,586	1,565	1,744	21	1.3	1.5	1.6	76.8	5.6	5	–	2
Reno	27,987	27,625	26,607	362	1.3	22.3	21.2	70.7	13.9	791	187	100
Republic	3,152	3,113	3,283	39	1.3	4.4	4.6	79.0	6.9	50	39	–
Rice	4,628	4,609	4,868	19	0.4	6.4	6.7	76.6	6.1	34	8	8

See footnotes at end of table.

Table B-7. Counties — **Housing Units and Building Permits**—Con.

[Includes United States, states, and 3,141 counties/county equivalents defined as of February 22, 2005. For more information on these areas, see Appendix C, Geographic Information]

County	Housing units 2005 (July 1)	Housing units 2000[1] (April 1 esti-mates base)	Housing units 1990 (April 1)	Net change, 2000–2005 Number	Net change, 2000–2005 Percent	Units per square mile of land area 2005[2]	Units per square mile of land area 1990	Housing 2000, percent Owner-occupied housing units[3]	Housing 2000, percent Units in multi-unit structures	New private housing units authorized by building permits Cumulative, 2000–2005 period	New private housing units authorized by building permits 2005	New private housing units authorized by building permits 2004
KANSAS—Con.												
Riley	24,854	23,400	22,868	1,454	6.2	40.8	37.5	47.2	37.1	2,049	407	439
Rooks	2,777	2,758	2,979	19	0.7	3.1	3.4	77.1	5.0	4	2	1
Rush	1,944	1,928	1,999	16	0.8	2.7	2.8	82.0	2.1	5	1	–
Russell	3,850	3,871	4,079	–21	–0.5	4.4	4.6	75.2	6.3	21	11	4
Saline	23,372	22,695	21,129	677	3.0	32.5	29.4	69.0	16.4	1,055	173	190
Scott	2,322	2,291	2,305	31	1.4	3.2	3.2	74.4	8.2	45	1	9
Sedgwick	202,166	191,133	170,159	11,033	5.8	202.3	170.1	66.2	23.0	15,313	2,870	2,556
Seward	8,095	8,027	7,572	68	0.8	12.7	11.8	64.1	15.6	105	33	26
Shawnee	77,521	73,767	68,991	3,754	5.1	141.0	125.5	67.4	21.8	5,241	897	866
Sheridan	1,310	1,263	1,324	47	3.7	1.5	1.5	82.3	3.7	(NA)	–	–
Sherman	3,263	3,184	3,177	79	2.5	3.1	3.0	68.9	10.0	70	2	15
Smith	2,367	2,326	2,615	41	1.8	2.6	2.9	79.6	5.1	10	–	–
Stafford	2,474	2,458	2,666	16	0.7	3.1	3.4	77.8	3.8	2	–	1
Stanton	1,029	1,007	956	22	2.2	1.5	1.4	67.8	3.4	8	1	–
Stevens	2,305	2,265	2,116	40	1.8	3.2	2.9	75.6	4.8	25	–	4
Sumner	11,121	10,877	10,769	244	2.2	9.4	9.1	76.6	7.4	309	50	55
Thomas	3,595	3,562	3,534	33	0.9	3.3	3.3	69.0	13.6	17	3	3
Trego	1,737	1,723	1,851	14	0.8	2.0	2.1	81.1	4.1	32	1	25
Wabaunsee	3,179	3,033	2,853	146	4.8	4.0	3.6	83.1	3.2	201	31	31
Wallace	803	791	840	12	1.5	0.9	0.9	77.3	3.8	–	–	–
Washington	3,216	3,142	3,355	74	2.4	3.6	3.7	79.5	5.1	3	–	2
Wichita	1,135	1,119	1,190	16	1.4	1.6	1.7	74.0	4.9	6	–	1
Wilson	5,020	4,937	5,091	83	1.7	8.7	8.9	78.1	6.4	20	3	3
Woodson	2,092	2,076	2,199	16	0.8	4.2	4.4	81.4	5.3	40	8	7
Wyandotte	66,560	65,892	69,102	668	1.0	439.7	456.4	62.9	22.9	2,155	813	394
KENTUCKY	1,865,516	1,751,118	1,506,845	114,398	6.5	47.0	37.9	70.8	17.7	119,790	21,159	22,623
Adair	7,869	7,792	6,434	77	1.0	19.3	15.8	80.2	6.6	–	–	–
Allen	8,371	8,057	6,381	314	3.9	24.2	18.4	79.0	5.7	(NA)	–	–
Anderson	8,653	7,752	5,804	901	11.6	42.7	28.6	79.7	11.2	1,117	220	201
Ballard	3,966	3,837	3,553	129	3.4	15.8	14.1	81.9	5.5	(NA)	–	–
Barren	17,510	17,095	14,202	415	2.4	35.7	28.9	72.3	10.7	712	356	55
Bath	5,218	4,994	4,021	224	4.5	18.7	14.4	79.8	4.9	49	11	10
Bell	13,751	13,341	12,568	410	3.1	38.1	34.8	67.6	14.7	378	54	60
Boone	41,781	33,352	21,476	8,429	25.3	169.7	87.2	74.3	22.2	9,878	1,554	1,711
Bourbon	8,809	8,349	7,781	460	5.5	30.2	26.7	65.5	16.8	581	99	72
Boyd	22,301	21,976	21,365	325	1.5	139.2	133.4	72.9	13.5	320	225	23
Boyle	12,133	11,418	10,191	715	6.3	66.7	56.1	69.3	17.6	886	128	163
Bracken	3,844	3,715	3,166	129	3.5	18.9	15.6	76.9	6.1	(NA)	–	–
Breathitt	7,090	6,812	6,127	278	4.1	14.3	12.4	76.5	5.0	6	2	–
Breckinridge	10,273	9,890	8,261	383	3.9	17.9	14.4	81.7	4.9	152	42	44
Bullitt	27,249	23,160	16,629	4,089	17.7	91.1	55.6	83.9	8.4	4,771	788	954
Butler	6,008	5,815	4,698	193	3.3	14.0	11.0	79.6	6.6	4	–	–
Caldwell	6,288	6,126	5,794	162	2.6	18.1	16.7	77.4	7.0	81	8	7
Calloway	16,825	16,069	13,242	756	4.7	43.6	34.3	68.4	16.9	538	121	114
Campbell	38,393	36,898	32,910	1,495	4.1	253.3	217.1	69.0	30.2	2,130	317	384
Carlisle	2,573	2,490	2,295	83	3.3	13.4	11.9	83.8	2.7	(NA)	–	–
Carroll	4,554	4,439	3,870	115	2.6	35.0	29.7	66.7	15.9	24	4	4
Carter	12,071	11,534	9,290	537	4.7	29.4	22.6	81.0	5.2	105	4	15
Casey	7,499	7,242	6,046	257	3.5	16.8	13.6	80.9	3.7	12	2	2
Christian	28,554	27,207	23,429	1,347	5.0	39.6	32.5	55.3	21.0	1,098	103	203
Clark	15,384	13,749	11,635	1,635	11.9	60.5	45.7	68.7	15.5	1,989	265	316
Clay	9,807	9,439	7,930	368	3.9	20.8	16.8	74.7	6.8	–	–	–
Clinton	5,024	4,888	4,189	136	2.8	25.4	21.2	77.1	5.3	99	25	23
Crittenden	4,555	4,410	4,039	145	3.3	12.6	11.2	80.5	5.4	(NA)	–	1
Cumberland	3,603	3,567	3,051	36	1.0	11.8	10.0	77.6	5.9	10	3	3
Daviess	42,070	38,432	35,041	3,638	9.5	91.0	75.8	70.3	19.4	4,091	444	413
Edmonson	6,360	6,104	5,009	256	4.2	21.0	16.6	85.6	3.4	(NA)	–	–
Elliott	3,244	3,107	2,639	137	4.4	13.9	11.3	82.3	4.6	(NA)	–	–
Estill	7,037	6,824	5,863	213	3.1	27.7	23.1	74.0	8.9	8	4	1
Fayette	127,634	116,167	97,742	11,467	9.9	448.6	343.5	55.3	36.5	14,655	2,763	2,960
Fleming	6,310	6,120	5,163	190	3.1	18.0	14.7	78.9	5.3	9	3	1
Floyd	19,304	18,551	17,169	753	4.1	49.0	43.5	76.3	7.4	81	14	13
Franklin	22,595	21,409	18,543	1,186	5.5	107.4	88.1	64.8	27.2	1,540	285	272
Fulton	3,741	3,697	3,684	44	1.2	17.9	17.6	64.3	18.1	43	8	18
Gallatin	3,539	3,362	2,290	177	5.3	35.8	23.2	76.8	9.3	106	35	66
Garrard	6,648	6,414	4,929	234	3.6	28.8	21.3	76.4	8.8	104	15	18
Grant	10,226	9,306	6,543	920	9.9	39.3	25.2	74.2	13.6	962	157	154
Graves	16,756	16,340	14,528	416	2.5	30.2	26.1	77.9	8.6	77	19	12
Grayson	12,907	12,802	10,446	105	0.8	25.6	20.7	77.3	7.3	20	3	3
Green	5,453	5,420	4,523	33	0.6	18.9	15.7	78.2	5.4	–	–	–
Greenup	16,284	15,977	14,657	307	1.9	47.0	42.3	81.6	6.2	302	51	36

See footnotes at end of table.

310

County and City Data Book: 2007

U.S. Census Bureau

[Includes United States, states, and 3,141 counties/county equivalents defined as of February 22, 2005. For more information on these areas, see Appendix C, Geographic Information]

County	Housing units			Net change, 2000–2005		Units per square mile of land area		Housing 2000, percent		New private housing units authorized by building permits		
	2005 (July 1)	2000[1] (April 1 estimates base)	1990 (April 1)	Number	Percent	2005[2]	1990	Owner-occupied housing units[3]	Units in multi-unit structures	Cumulative, 2000–2005 period	2005	2004
KENTUCKY—Con.												
Hancock	3,669	3,600	3,080	69	1.9	19.4	16.3	82.4	8.6	55	11	—
Hardin	41,555	37,671	32,375	3,884	10.3	66.2	51.6	66.9	19.5	5,029	1,221	1,067
Harlan	15,477	15,017	14,735	460	3.1	33.1	31.5	73.5	9.3	–	–	–
Harrison	8,006	7,660	6,488	346	4.5	25.9	20.9	70.5	12.8	442	84	75
Hart	8,264	8,046	6,501	218	2.7	19.9	15.6	77.3	7.5	241	52	41
Henderson	20,326	19,466	17,932	860	4.4	46.2	40.7	67.3	20.8	1,052	174	233
Henry	6,863	6,381	5,447	482	7.6	23.7	18.8	77.6	6.1	537	86	84
Hickman	2,516	2,436	2,374	80	3.3	10.3	9.7	81.4	4.5	(NA)	–	–
Hopkins	21,364	20,668	19,325	696	3.4	38.8	35.1	74.7	10.6	706	169	161
Jackson	6,291	6,065	4,895	226	3.7	18.2	14.1	80.1	4.7	–	–	–
Jefferson	322,329	305,835	282,578	16,494	5.4	837.0	733.8	64.9	29.5	21,177	2,400	3,886
Jessamine	17,505	14,646	11,209	2,859	19.5	101.1	64.7	67.1	15.8	3,472	640	804
Johnson	10,410	10,236	9,381	174	1.7	39.8	35.9	76.5	10.4	56	3	18
Kenton	68,315	63,570	56,086	4,745	7.5	421.8	345.0	66.4	29.0	6,514	1,305	1,401
Knott	7,905	7,579	6,718	326	4.3	22.4	19.1	79.6	4.7	(NA)	–	–
Knox	14,541	13,999	11,731	542	3.9	37.5	30.3	71.4	9.2	29	13	3
Larue	6,356	5,860	4,824	496	8.5	24.1	18.3	80.2	7.4	531	104	93
Laurel	23,229	22,317	16,923	912	4.1	53.3	38.8	77.0	9.6	110	23	7
Lawrence	7,326	7,040	5,684	286	4.1	17.5	13.6	78.1	5.6	–	–	–
Lee	3,455	3,321	3,025	134	4.0	16.5	14.4	76.6	7.1	(NA)	–	–
Leslie	5,744	5,502	5,038	242	4.4	14.2	12.5	82.3	2.6	(NA)	–	–
Letcher	11,840	11,405	10,808	435	3.8	34.9	31.9	80.9	4.5	–	–	–
Lewis	6,417	6,173	5,328	244	4.0	13.2	11.0	81.2	4.1	–	–	–
Lincoln	11,181	10,127	7,985	1,054	10.4	33.3	23.7	78.9	6.4	1,141	159	223
Livingston	4,959	4,772	4,177	187	3.9	15.7	13.2	85.2	1.3	(NA)	–	–
Logan	12,087	11,875	10,303	212	1.8	21.8	18.5	75.2	9.1	224	37	35
Lyon	4,386	4,189	3,460	197	4.7	20.3	16.0	81.8	7.1	83	12	10
McCracken	31,485	30,361	27,581	1,124	3.7	125.4	109.8	68.7	18.4	1,517	330	415
McCreary	7,513	7,405	6,039	108	1.5	17.6	14.1	75.7	6.3	(NA)	–	–
McLean	4,548	4,392	4,042	156	3.6	17.9	15.9	80.3	5.3	22	2	2
Madison	32,059	29,595	21,456	2,464	8.3	72.7	48.7	59.7	28.0	2,756	562	544
Magoffin	5,712	5,447	4,800	265	4.9	18.5	15.5	82.0	4.2	(NA)	–	–
Marion	7,469	7,277	6,115	192	2.6	21.6	17.6	78.1	8.6	56	6	20
Marshall	15,340	14,730	12,528	610	4.1	50.3	41.1	82.6	6.2	583	47	26
Martin	5,810	5,551	4,697	259	4.7	25.2	20.4	79.4	6.3	(NA)	–	–
Mason	7,968	7,754	7,089	214	2.8	33.0	29.4	67.4	16.9	145	–	45
Meade	10,892	10,294	8,907	598	5.8	35.3	28.9	73.8	12.6	365	171	149
Menifee	3,855	3,710	2,421	145	3.9	18.9	11.9	81.4	3.0	(NA)	–	–
Mercer	9,894	9,289	8,212	605	6.5	39.4	32.7	74.6	13.7	755	133	112
Metcalfe	4,763	4,592	3,793	171	3.7	16.4	13.0	79.3	4.1	(NA)	–	–
Monroe	5,468	5,288	4,882	180	3.4	16.5	14.8	75.2	6.1	(NA)	–	–
Montgomery	10,629	9,682	7,759	947	9.8	53.5	39.1	71.4	16.8	1,129	213	248
Morgan	5,739	5,487	4,562	252	4.6	15.1	12.0	79.8	4.3	(NA)	9	3
Muhlenberg	14,106	13,676	12,754	430	3.1	29.7	26.9	82.8	6.3	97	13	12
Nelson	17,308	14,934	11,078	2,374	15.9	41.0	26.2	78.0	10.9	2,825	489	436
Nicholas	3,132	3,051	2,930	81	2.7	15.9	14.9	74.7	10.6	14	–	5
Ohio	10,292	9,909	8,680	383	3.9	17.3	14.6	80.3	5.9	112	16	14
Oldham	19,299	15,691	11,202	3,608	23.0	102.0	59.2	86.9	6.2	4,198	610	742
Owen	5,554	5,345	4,723	209	3.9	15.8	13.4	78.3	6.0	25	1	1
Owsley	2,335	2,247	2,137	88	3.9	11.8	10.8	78.5	5.1	(NA)	–	–
Pendleton	5,937	5,756	4,782	181	3.1	21.2	17.1	77.9	7.0	10	3	–
Perry	13,272	12,757	11,565	515	4.0	38.8	33.8	77.4	8.6	86	16	14
Pike	32,393	30,923	28,760	1,470	4.8	41.1	36.5	78.7	6.7	228	37	31
Powell	5,758	5,526	4,458	232	4.2	32.0	24.7	74.0	9.1	(NA)	–	–
Pulaski	27,676	27,181	22,328	495	1.8	41.8	33.7	76.0	11.6	261	29	70
Robertson	1,069	1,034	955	35	3.4	10.7	9.5	78.1	4.2	(NA)	–	–
Rockcastle	7,649	7,353	5,958	296	4.0	24.1	18.8	79.5	5.4	(NA)	–	–
Rowan	9,349	8,985	7,375	364	4.1	33.3	26.3	69.8	10.2	83	3	7
Russell	9,222	9,064	7,375	158	1.7	36.4	29.1	79.5	5.7	37	10	1
Scott	15,248	12,977	9,173	2,271	17.5	53.6	32.2	69.8	18.2	3,382	1,090	766
Shelby	15,154	12,857	9,617	2,297	17.9	39.4	25.0	72.8	16.2	2,878	559	590
Simpson	7,609	7,016	6,172	593	8.5	32.2	26.1	71.8	12.7	685	91	110
Spencer	5,844	4,555	2,640	1,289	28.3	31.4	14.2	82.6	7.5	1,669	432	119
Taylor	10,269	10,180	8,798	89	0.9	38.1	32.6	72.3	13.3	147	36	68
Todd	5,255	5,120	4,415	135	2.6	14.0	11.7	76.6	5.1	9	2	2
Trigg	6,982	6,698	5,284	284	4.2	15.8	11.9	81.5	5.0	90	17	16
Trimble	3,573	3,437	2,510	136	4.0	24.0	16.9	80.7	3.3	(NA)	–	–
Union	6,337	6,234	6,091	103	1.7	18.4	17.6	77.9	9.4	93	7	8
Warren	42,940	38,350	31,065	4,590	12.0	78.8	57.0	64.0	24.8	5,933	1,385	1,324
Washington	4,660	4,542	4,009	118	2.6	15.5	13.3	80.0	7.8	44	19	5

See footnotes at end of table.

Table B-7. Counties — **Housing Units and Building Permits**—Con.

[Includes United States, states, and 3,141 counties/county equivalents defined as of February 22, 2005. For more information on these areas, see Appendix C, Geographic Information]

County	Housing units							Housing 2000, percent		New private housing units authorized by building permits		
	2005 (July 1)	2000¹ (April 1 esti- mates base)	1990 (April 1)	Net change, 2000–2005 Number	Net change, 2000–2005 Percent	Units per square mile of land area 2005²	Units per square mile of land area 1990	Owner- occupied housing units³	Units in multi- unit structures	Cumu- lative, 2000– 2005 period	2005	2004
KENTUCKY—Con.												
Wayne	9,901	9,789	7,791	112	1.1	21.6	17.0	76.5	6.3	–	–	–
Webster	6,409	6,250	5,914	159	2.5	19.1	17.7	78.1	5.4	18	–	2
Whitley	15,884	15,288	13,399	596	3.9	36.1	30.4	72.6	10.6	214	46	40
Wolfe	3,411	3,264	2,779	147	4.5	15.3	12.5	73.9	6.1	(NA)	–	–
Woodford	10,165	9,374	7,689	791	8.4	53.3	40.3	72.4	14.4	966	150	203
LOUISIANA	1,940,399	1,847,174	1,716,241	93,225	5.0	44.5	39.4	67.9	18.7	116,818	22,811	22,989
Acadia	23,982	23,211	21,441	771	3.3	36.6	32.7	72.2	7.9	1,066	185	170
Allen	9,397	9,157	8,275	240	2.6	12.3	10.8	76.1	6.5	110	7	15
Ascension	34,865	29,172	21,165	5,693	19.5	119.6	72.6	82.3	5.6	7,151	1,674	1,498
Assumption	10,174	9,635	8,644	539	5.6	30.0	25.5	84.0	2.0	547	104	94
Avoyelles	17,435	16,576	15,428	859	5.2	20.9	18.5	74.4	8.0	911	127	110
Beauregard	14,925	14,501	12,666	424	2.9	12.9	10.9	79.8	6.5	132	70	29
Bienville	8,060	7,830	7,085	230	2.9	9.9	8.7	77.9	5.9	–	–	–
Bossier	44,823	40,283	34,994	4,540	11.3	53.4	41.7	69.5	16.0	5,204	1,164	958
Caddo	111,341	108,300	107,615	3,041	2.8	126.2	122.0	63.8	21.3	4,952	1,375	999
Calcasieu	81,857	75,995	66,426	5,862	7.7	76.4	62.0	71.6	13.4	6,297	757	1,188
Caldwell	5,140	5,035	4,533	105	2.1	9.7	8.6	79.2	3.0	82	12	27
Cameron	5,725	5,336	5,031	389	7.3	4.4	3.8	85.1	1.7	515	161	159
Catahoula	5,554	5,351	5,138	203	3.8	7.9	7.3	83.1	3.2	181	24	39
Claiborne	8,008	7,815	7,513	193	2.5	10.6	10.0	75.8	4.6	7	4	3
Concordia	9,446	9,148	9,043	298	3.3	13.6	13.0	76.1	4.5	306	39	54
De Soto	11,566	11,203	10,919	363	3.2	13.2	12.4	76.7	7.4	3	1	1
East Baton Rouge	178,346	169,073	156,767	9,273	5.5	391.6	344.0	61.6	28.9	12,849	2,805	2,150
East Carroll	3,267	3,303	3,563	−36	−1.1	7.8	8.5	62.1	10.6	2	–	–
East Feliciana	8,166	7,915	6,476	251	3.2	18.0	14.3	82.4	3.6	11	3	1
Evangeline	14,855	14,258	13,311	597	4.2	22.4	20.0	69.4	6.6	663	76	101
Franklin	8,845	8,623	8,719	222	2.6	14.2	14.0	76.3	4.8	269	53	39
Grant	8,831	8,531	7,494	300	3.5	13.7	11.6	81.7	2.4	126	86	38
Iberia	28,842	27,844	25,472	998	3.6	50.1	44.3	73.4	9.4	1,163	174	262
Iberville	12,403	11,953	11,352	450	3.8	20.0	18.3	77.4	5.8	537	87	124
Jackson	7,522	7,338	7,041	184	2.5	13.2	12.4	77.2	6.7	7	1	1
Jefferson	192,373	187,907	185,072	4,466	2.4	627.6	605.0	63.9	30.4	6,713	944	1,217
Jefferson Davis	13,220	12,824	11,963	396	3.1	20.3	18.3	74.9	5.7	478	76	89
Lafayette	84,909	78,063	67,431	6,846	8.8	314.7	249.9	66.0	22.4	8,241	1,633	2,047
Lafourche	36,679	35,045	31,332	1,634	4.7	33.8	28.9	78.0	9.1	1,962	388	356
La Salle	6,450	6,273	5,969	177	2.8	10.3	9.6	83.3	3.8	11	2	2
Lincoln	18,033	17,001	15,286	1,032	6.1	38.3	32.4	60.0	21.2	947	168	361
Livingston	41,392	36,211	26,848	5,181	14.3	63.9	41.4	83.7	3.6	6,020	1,256	1,121
Madison	5,037	4,979	4,823	58	1.2	8.1	7.7	61.9	14.0	75	14	10
Morehouse	13,076	12,711	12,314	365	2.9	16.5	15.5	71.5	7.9	191	59	38
Natchitoches	17,701	16,890	15,210	811	4.8	14.1	12.1	64.5	12.4	942	114	135
Orleans	213,137	215,091	225,573	−1,954	−0.9	1,180.4	1,248.7	46.5	42.7	4,343	617	887
Ouachita	62,317	60,154	56,300	2,163	3.6	102.1	92.1	64.1	18.2	3,122	799	432
Plaquemines	11,290	10,481	9,432	809	7.7	13.4	11.2	78.9	9.2	790	75	157
Pointe Coupee	10,792	10,297	9,695	495	4.8	19.4	17.4	77.7	3.8	593	94	78
Rapides	54,533	52,038	51,239	2,495	4.8	41.2	38.7	68.0	14.8	3,273	624	647
Red River	4,113	3,988	3,839	125	3.1	10.6	9.9	76.3	5.8	11	1	1
Richland	8,604	8,335	8,031	269	3.2	15.4	14.4	72.2	7.0	358	106	77
Sabine	14,179	13,671	12,789	508	3.7	16.4	14.8	81.0	4.8	7	–	–
St. Bernard	27,292	26,790	25,147	502	1.9	58.7	54.1	74.6	14.8	634	46	97
St. Charles	18,673	17,429	16,016	1,244	7.1	65.8	56.5	81.4	10.8	1,572	323	335
St. Helena	5,189	5,034	3,840	155	3.1	12.7	9.4	84.9	2.1	112	14	46
St. James	7,935	7,596	6,934	339	4.5	32.2	28.2	85.6	7.2	361	172	94
St. John the Baptist	16,879	15,533	14,255	1,346	8.7	77.1	65.1	81.0	9.1	1,587	267	267
St. Landry	37,667	36,216	31,137	1,451	4.0	40.6	33.5	70.7	8.9	1,864	363	350
St. Martin	21,308	20,245	17,592	1,063	5.3	28.8	23.8	81.7	5.1	1,081	184	200
St. Mary	22,241	21,650	21,884	591	2.7	36.3	35.7	73.9	10.4	646	92	116
St. Tammany	88,791	75,399	57,993	13,392	17.8	104.0	67.9	80.5	10.1	15,659	2,509	3,440
Tangipahoa	44,490	40,794	33,640	3,696	9.1	56.3	42.6	73.3	12.3	4,671	1,231	830
Tensas	3,446	3,359	3,334	87	2.6	5.7	5.5	69.1	3.0	115	15	30
Terrebonne	42,581	39,928	35,416	2,653	6.6	33.9	28.2	75.6	11.1	3,134	559	539
Union	11,597	10,872	9,304	725	6.7	13.2	10.6	81.2	4.5	587	297	268
Vermilion	23,585	22,520	20,361	1,065	4.7	20.1	17.3	77.1	4.8	1,335	272	286
Vernon	21,679	21,030	21,622	649	3.1	16.3	16.3	56.7	21.1	102	20	23
Washington	19,750	19,106	17,617	644	3.4	29.5	26.3	76.4	5.7	846	147	157
Webster	19,596	18,991	18,365	605	3.2	32.9	30.8	74.5	7.5	308	57	33
West Baton Rouge	8,870	8,370	7,298	500	6.0	46.4	38.2	78.8	7.3	657	205	102
West Carroll	5,129	4,980	4,831	149	3.0	14.3	13.4	78.9	2.8	6	1	1
West Feliciana	4,812	4,485	3,392	327	7.3	11.9	8.4	74.5	8.2	370	76	60
Winn	7,679	7,502	7,006	177	2.4	8.1	7.4	74.8	5.2	3	2	1

See footnotes at end of table.

County and City Data Book: 2007

U.S. Census Bureau

Table B-7. Counties — **Housing Units and Building Permits**—Con.

[Includes United States, states, and 3,141 counties/county equivalents defined as of February 22, 2005. For more information on these areas, see Appendix C, Geographic Information]

County	Housing units 2005 (July 1)	2000¹ (April 1 esti- mates base)	1990 (April 1)	Net change, 2000–2005 Number	Net change, 2000–2005 Percent	Units per square mile of land area 2005²	Units per square mile of land area 1990	Housing 2000, percent Owner- occupied housing units³	Housing 2000, percent Units in multi- unit structures	New private housing units authorized by building permits Cumu- lative, 2000– 2005 period	2005	2004
MAINE	683,799	651,901	587,045	31,898	4.9	22.2	19.0	71.6	20.3	⁴45,549	⁴8,969	⁴8,771
Androscoggin	47,633	45,960	43,815	1,673	3.6	101.3	93.2	63.4	35.6	2,575	521	545
Aroostook	39,181	38,719	38,421	462	1.2	5.9	5.8	73.0	18.2	873	169	183
Cumberland	130,156	122,600	109,890	7,556	6.2	155.8	131.5	66.8	28.2	10,262	1,909	1,698
Franklin	19,895	19,159	17,280	736	3.8	11.7	10.2	76.1	14.9	1,097	271	247
Hancock	36,134	33,945	30,396	2,189	6.4	22.8	19.1	75.7	8.7	2,865	484	565
Kennebec	58,707	56,364	51,648	2,343	4.2	67.7	59.5	71.2	23.1	3,567	806	715
Knox	22,980	21,612	19,009	1,368	6.3	62.8	52.0	74.0	14.1	1,813	268	345
Lincoln	22,101	20,849	17,538	1,252	6.0	48.5	38.5	83.0	6.9	1,584	302	385
Oxford	33,783	32,295	29,689	1,488	4.6	16.3	14.3	77.0	14.5	2,161	477	456
Penobscot	69,331	66,848	61,359	2,483	3.7	20.4	18.1	69.8	22.7	3,823	996	741
Piscataquis	14,052	13,782	13,194	270	2.0	3.5	3.3	79.5	8.3	439	102	90
Sagadahoc	17,348	16,489	14,633	859	5.2	68.3	57.6	72.1	18.1	1,189	257	237
Somerset	28,657	28,222	24,927	435	1.5	7.3	6.3	77.8	11.3	641	155	128
Waldo	19,981	18,904	16,181	1,077	5.7	27.4	22.2	79.8	8.5	1,270	192	196
Washington	22,589	21,919	19,124	670	3.1	8.8	7.4	77.7	8.8	1,009	215	237
York	101,271	94,234	79,941	7,037	7.5	102.2	80.7	72.6	21.6	9,252	1,614	1,742
MARYLAND	2,273,793	2,145,289	1,891,917	128,504	6.0	232.6	193.6	67.7	25.8	176,186	30,180	27,382
Allegany	33,083	32,984	32,513	99	0.3	77.8	76.4	70.2	19.4	603	114	120
Anne Arundel	199,398	186,937	157,194	12,461	6.7	479.4	377.9	75.5	16.6	15,789	2,495	2,364
Baltimore	324,596	313,734	281,553	10,862	3.5	542.3	470.4	67.6	27.7	15,204	1,936	2,103
Calvert	31,652	27,576	18,974	4,076	14.8	147.1	88.2	85.2	4.6	4,549	488	525
Caroline	13,035	12,028	10,745	1,007	8.4	40.7	33.6	74.1	10.2	1,442	362	316
Carroll	60,405	54,260	43,553	6,145	11.3	134.5	97.0	82.0	12.1	7,417	809	1,040
Cecil	39,048	34,461	27,656	4,587	13.3	112.2	79.4	75.0	12.9	5,319	743	811
Charles	50,154	43,903	34,487	6,251	14.2	108.8	74.8	78.2	9.0	7,624	1,309	1,000
Dorchester	15,671	14,681	14,269	990	6.7	28.1	25.6	70.1	15.0	1,605	490	423
Frederick	83,173	73,016	54,872	10,157	13.9	125.5	82.8	75.9	16.2	11,790	1,872	1,773
Garrett	18,253	16,761	14,119	1,492	8.9	28.2	21.8	77.9	8.4	1,895	334	355
Harford	92,122	83,146	66,446	8,976	10.8	209.2	150.9	78.0	16.4	11,900	2,659	1,836
Howard	101,136	92,818	72,583	8,318	9.0	401.3	287.8	73.8	23.3	10,150	1,778	1,837
Kent	11,089	9,410	8,181	1,679	17.8	39.7	29.3	70.4	14.9	1,931	206	221
Montgomery	356,603	334,935	295,723	21,668	6.5	719.7	597.9	68.7	30.7	27,052	3,591	3,821
Prince George's	314,221	302,075	270,090	12,146	4.0	647.3	555.3	61.8	34.2	17,379	3,425	1,948
Queen Anne's	18,790	16,674	13,944	2,116	12.7	50.5	37.5	83.4	6.2	2,549	394	362
St. Mary's	39,193	34,088	27,863	5,105	15.0	108.5	77.1	71.8	13.5	6,097	993	1,384
Somerset	10,588	10,092	9,393	496	4.9	32.4	28.7	69.6	12.5	770	209	185
Talbot	18,638	16,500	14,697	2,138	13.0	69.3	54.6	71.6	14.3	2,886	648	625
Washington	57,935	52,972	47,448	4,963	9.4	126.5	103.6	65.6	22.7	7,360	1,945	1,368
Wicomico	38,450	34,401	30,108	4,049	11.8	101.9	79.8	66.5	16.3	5,263	1,003	1,000
Worcester	52,298	47,360	41,800	4,938	10.4	110.5	88.3	75.0	47.5	6,176	1,121	1,225
Independent City												
Baltimore city	294,262	300,477	303,706	−6,215	−2.1	3,641.9	3,758.3	50.3	34.8	3,436	1,256	740
MASSACHUSETTS	2,688,014	2,621,993	2,472,711	66,021	2.5	342.9	315.5	61.7	42.7	119,782	24,549	22,477
Barnstable	153,798	147,083	135,192	6,715	4.6	388.9	341.6	77.8	13.0	8,985	1,388	1,475
Berkshire	67,450	66,301	64,324	1,149	1.7	72.4	69.1	66.9	33.1	2,513	486	480
Bristol	223,028	216,918	201,235	6,110	2.8	401.1	361.9	61.6	44.2	10,292	1,817	1,878
Dukes	15,896	14,836	11,604	1,060	7.1	153.2	111.8	71.3	6.3	1,382	237	255
Essex	294,198	287,144	271,977	7,054	2.5	587.6	546.1	63.5	42.4	12,944	2,554	2,820
Franklin	32,718	31,939	30,394	779	2.4	46.6	43.3	66.9	29.8	1,400	251	265
Hampden	187,904	185,875	180,025	2,029	1.1	303.9	291.1	61.9	38.9	5,057	866	923
Hampshire	60,390	58,645	53,068	1,745	3.0	114.2	100.3	65.0	34.3	2,886	539	521
Middlesex	586,233	576,681	543,796	9,552	1.7	711.9	660.3	61.7	46.2	22,313	6,129	3,806
Nantucket	10,296	9,210	7,021	1,086	11.8	215.4	146.9	63.1	9.4	1,395	260	275
Norfolk	261,606	255,154	236,816	6,452	2.5	654.7	592.6	69.7	36.2	11,676	2,393	2,621
Plymouth	189,216	181,524	168,555	7,692	4.2	286.3	255.2	75.6	22.9	11,984	2,566	2,066
Suffolk	293,948	292,520	289,276	1,428	0.5	5,023.0	4,943.2	33.9	81.6	7,073	1,465	1,400
Worcester	311,333	298,163	279,428	13,170	4.4	205.8	184.7	64.1	39.2	19,882	3,598	3,692
MICHIGAN	4,478,507	4,234,252	3,847,926	244,255	5.8	78.8	67.7	73.8	18.8	⁴306,558	⁴45,328	⁴54,721
Alcona	11,103	10,584	10,414	519	4.9	16.5	15.4	89.9	1.1	591	62	67
Alger	6,458	5,964	5,775	494	8.3	7.0	6.3	82.5	6.2	599	82	210
Allegan	47,349	43,292	36,395	4,057	9.4	57.2	44.0	82.9	9.6	4,628	713	926
Alpena	15,551	15,289	14,431	262	1.7	27.1	25.1	79.1	12.3	364	53	44
Antrim	16,364	15,090	13,145	1,274	8.4	34.3	27.6	84.9	5.6	1,447	142	148
Arenac	10,003	9,563	8,891	440	4.6	27.3	24.2	84.6	5.0	499	78	97
Baraga	4,821	4,631	4,684	190	4.1	5.3	5.2	77.7	8.9	242	37	37
Barry	25,602	23,876	20,887	1,726	7.2	46.0	37.6	85.8	5.8	2,149	341	371
Bay	47,897	46,423	44,234	1,474	3.2	107.8	99.6	79.3	15.8	2,143	300	405
Benzie	11,565	10,312	8,557	1,253	12.2	36.0	26.6	85.7	5.0	1,467	222	211

See footnotes at end of table.

[Includes United States, states, and 3,141 counties/county equivalents defined as of February 22, 2005. For more information on these areas, see Appendix C, Geographic Information]

County	Housing units								Housing 2000, percent		New private housing units authorized by building permits		
	2005 (July 1)	2000[1] (April 1) esti-mates base)	1990 (April 1)	Net change, 2000–2005		Units per square mile of land area			Owner-occupied housing units[3]	Units in multi-unit structures	Cumu-lative, 2000–2005 period	2005	2004
				Number	Percent	2005[2]	1990						
MICHIGAN—Con.													
Berrien.	76,004	73,446	69,532	2,558	3.5	133.1	121.8		72.3	17.5	3,820	816	731
Branch.	20,630	19,822	18,449	808	4.1	40.7	36.4		78.9	9.5	1,005	127	136
Calhoun.	60,430	58,691	55,619	1,739	3.0	85.3	78.5		73.0	20.0	2,527	406	370
Cass.	25,242	23,883	22,644	1,359	5.7	51.3	46.0		81.9	5.8	1,694	310	221
Charlevoix.	17,001	15,370	13,119	1,631	10.6	40.8	31.5		81.1	11.4	1,873	277	267
Cheboygan.	17,662	16,583	14,090	1,079	6.5	24.7	19.7		82.8	5.2	1,268	202	203
Chippewa.	20,530	19,430	18,023	1,100	5.7	13.2	11.5		74.0	10.9	1,270	115	350
Clare.	22,998	22,229	19,135	769	3.5	40.6	33.8		82.3	4.3	886	134	162
Clinton.	28,899	24,630	20,959	4,269	17.3	50.6	36.7		85.3	9.2	4,756	600	666
Crawford.	10,558	10,042	8,727	516	5.1	18.9	15.6		82.8	4.0	685	166	115
Delta.	20,045	19,223	17,928	822	4.3	17.1	15.3		79.6	13.1	1,065	149	209
Dickinson.	14,038	13,702	12,902	336	2.5	18.3	16.8		80.2	11.5	531	97	73
Eaton.	45,112	42,118	35,517	2,994	7.1	78.3	61.6		74.2	21.1	3,633	498	535
Emmet.	20,430	18,554	14,731	1,876	10.1	43.7	31.5		75.6	15.2	2,340	470	339
Genesee.	195,545	183,635	170,808	11,910	6.5	305.7	267.0		73.2	16.9	14,672	1,854	2,398
Gladwin.	18,136	16,828	14,885	1,308	7.8	35.8	29.4		85.7	3.1	1,449	187	225
Gogebic.	11,025	10,839	10,997	186	1.7	10.0	10.0		78.8	14.3	299	46	40
Grand Traverse.	38,942	34,842	28,740	4,100	11.8	83.7	61.8		77.4	13.9	5,210	1,163	968
Gratiot.	15,900	15,516	14,699	384	2.5	27.9	25.8		77.7	11.5	542	85	108
Hillsdale.	21,560	20,189	18,547	1,371	6.8	36.0	31.0		79.9	9.5	1,632	205	255
Houghton.	18,287	17,748	17,296	539	3.0	18.1	17.1		71.4	15.8	843	137	134
Huron.	21,217	20,430	19,755	787	3.9	25.4	23.6		83.4	6.5	1,012	117	158
Ingham.	120,041	115,096	108,542	4,945	4.3	214.7	194.1		60.8	30.7	6,285	1,023	1,005
Ionia.	23,648	22,006	19,674	1,642	7.5	41.3	34.3		80.0	11.0	2,038	368	290
Iosco.	21,102	20,432	19,517	670	3.3	38.4	35.5		82.0	7.3	889	123	145
Iron.	8,999	8,772	9,039	227	2.6	7.7	7.7		82.4	6.6	375	76	50
Isabella.	28,185	24,528	19,950	3,657	14.9	49.1	34.7		63.2	25.5	3,890	410	713
Jackson.	66,883	62,906	57,979	3,977	6.3	94.7	82.0		76.5	15.4	5,224	897	704
Kalamazoo.	106,084	99,250	88,955	6,834	6.9	188.8	158.3		65.7	29.0	8,509	1,156	1,373
Kalkaska.	11,566	10,822	9,151	744	6.9	20.6	16.3		85.1	3.1	810	111	152
Kent.	239,558	224,000	192,698	15,558	6.9	279.8	225.1		70.3	26.9	19,758	2,941	3,586
Keweenaw.	2,431	2,327	2,257	104	4.5	4.5	4.2		88.8	3.1	154	26	28
Lake.	14,174	13,498	12,114	676	5.0	25.0	21.3		83.0	2.0	723	132	131
Lapeer.	35,247	32,732	26,445	2,515	7.7	53.9	40.4		84.9	9.4	3,091	502	569
Leelanau.	14,594	13,297	11,171	1,297	9.8	41.9	32.1		84.6	8.2	1,525	209	246
Lenawee.	42,267	39,790	35,104	2,477	6.2	56.3	46.8		78.2	15.0	3,200	532	537
Livingston.	70,449	58,919	41,863	11,530	19.6	123.9	73.7		88.0	7.9	12,209	1,537	2,127
Luce.	4,250	4,008	3,594	242	6.0	4.7	4.0		80.3	5.2	309	56	59
Mackinac.	10,135	9,413	9,254	722	7.7	9.9	9.1		79.2	6.8	890	184	202
Macomb.	346,503	320,276	274,843	26,227	8.2	721.2	572.1		78.9	19.3	30,736	4,343	5,450
Manistee.	14,860	14,272	13,330	588	4.1	27.3	24.5		81.3	8.4	393	41	65
Marquette.	34,080	32,877	31,049	1,203	3.7	18.7	17.0		69.8	21.8	1,743	333	337
Mason.	16,844	16,063	14,119	781	4.9	34.0	28.5		78.4	10.0	1,141	316	178
Mecosta.	21,051	19,593	17,274	1,458	7.4	37.9	31.1		73.7	10.8	1,845	459	337
Menominee.	14,226	13,639	12,509	587	4.3	13.6	12.0		79.5	11.3	766	116	126
Midland.	35,113	33,796	29,343	1,317	3.9	67.4	56.3		78.4	14.0	1,561	198	224
Missaukee.	9,080	8,621	7,112	459	5.3	16.0	12.5		83.7	2.2	517	84	79
Monroe.	62,179	56,471	48,312	5,708	10.1	112.8	87.7		81.0	13.2	6,253	934	1,182
Montcalm.	27,285	25,900	22,817	1,385	5.3	38.5	32.2		81.6	8.2	1,650	248	293
Montmorency.	9,683	9,238	8,791	445	4.8	17.7	16.1		86.1	1.9	520	69	79
Muskegon.	72,652	68,556	61,962	4,096	6.0	142.7	121.7		77.7	14.7	5,118	657	766
Newaygo.	24,603	23,202	20,105	1,401	6.0	29.2	23.9		84.4	4.6	1,553	237	284
Oakland.	519,056	492,006	432,684	27,050	5.5	594.9	495.8		74.7	22.4	32,778	4,638	6,365
Oceana.	15,715	15,009	12,857	706	4.7	29.1	23.8		82.7	5.1	878	216	230
Ogemaw.	16,028	15,404	13,977	624	4.1	28.4	24.8		84.6	2.8	799	150	98
Ontonagon.	5,590	5,404	5,332	186	3.4	4.3	4.1		85.0	5.3	147	22	34
Osceola.	13,423	12,853	11,444	570	4.4	23.7	20.2		81.4	5.3	690	80	110
Oscoda.	9,052	8,690	8,112	362	4.2	16.0	14.4		85.8	2.1	406	53	67
Otsego.	14,664	13,375	10,669	1,289	9.6	28.5	20.7		81.7	7.2	1,374	106	187
Ottawa.	97,636	86,856	66,624	10,780	12.4	172.6	117.8		80.7	16.6	13,009	1,939	2,355
Presque Isle.	10,527	9,910	8,917	617	6.2	15.9	13.5		85.6	5.0	737	83	117
Roscommon.	24,813	23,109	19,881	1,704	7.4	47.6	38.1		85.9	2.8	1,943	206	290
Saginaw.	88,392	85,507	81,931	2,885	3.4	109.3	101.3		73.8	18.7	4,031	582	618
St. Clair.	72,921	67,107	57,494	5,814	8.7	100.7	79.4		79.6	14.2	5,485	798	980
St. Joseph.	27,418	26,503	24,242	915	3.5	54.4	48.1		76.9	12.1	1,177	171	208
Sanilac.	22,074	21,314	19,465	760	3.6	22.9	20.2		81.9	6.9	920	91	156
Schoolcraft.	5,995	5,700	5,487	295	5.2	5.1	4.7		82.0	6.7	373	50	67
Shiawassee.	30,253	29,087	25,833	1,166	4.0	56.2	47.9		80.1	12.6	1,497	207	220
Tuscola.	24,099	23,378	21,231	721	3.1	29.7	26.1		84.1	6.8	948	151	116

See footnotes at end of table.

County and City Data Book: 2007

U.S. Census Bureau

Table B-7. Counties — **Housing Units and Building Permits**—Con.

[Includes United States, states, and 3,141 counties/county equivalents defined as of February 22, 2005. For more information on these areas, see Appendix C, Geographic Information]

County	Housing units							Housing 2000, percent		New private housing units authorized by building permits		
	2005 (July 1)	2000[1] (April 1 esti- mates base)	1990 (April 1)	Net change, 2000–2005 Number	Percent	Units per square mile of land area 2005[2]	1990	Owner- occupied housing units[3]	Units in multi- unit structures	Cumu- lative, 2000– 2005 period	2005	2004
MICHIGAN—Con.												
Van Buren	36,223	33,975	31,530	2,248	6.6	59.3	51.6	79.6	9.7	2,697	454	494
Washtenaw	144,754	130,974	111,256	13,780	10.5	203.9	156.7	59.7	34.7	13,329	1,676	2,708
Wayne	839,238	826,145	832,710	13,093	1.6	1,366.5	1,355.9	66.6	24.6	29,714	4,574	6,317
Wexford	15,960	14,872	12,862	1,088	7.3	28.2	22.7	79.3	8.0	1,392	299	216
MINNESOTA	2,252,022	2,065,952	1,848,445	186,070	9.0	28.3	23.2	74.6	22.3	226,340	36,509	41,843
Aitkin	15,728	14,168	12,934	1,560	11.0	8.6	7.1	85.4	4.8	1,887	357	347
Anoka	121,187	108,091	85,519	13,096	12.1	286.1	201.7	83.4	15.5	15,623	2,341	3,380
Becker	17,969	16,612	15,563	1,357	8.2	13.7	11.9	80.5	8.7	1,658	298	343
Beltrami	18,237	16,989	14,670	1,248	7.3	7.3	5.9	74.5	12.1	890	184	254
Benton	15,706	13,461	11,521	2,245	16.7	38.5	28.2	67.3	29.7	1,994	277	278
Big Stone	3,253	3,171	3,192	82	2.6	6.5	6.4	85.1	9.3	127	24	24
Blue Earth	24,580	21,971	20,358	2,609	11.9	32.7	27.1	66.4	27.9	3,257	515	453
Brown	11,568	11,163	10,814	405	3.6	18.9	17.7	80.0	15.3	572	65	117
Carlton	15,007	13,721	12,342	1,286	9.4	17.4	14.3	82.1	9.9	1,661	356	245
Carver	31,686	24,883	17,449	6,803	27.3	88.7	48.9	83.5	14.0	7,728	996	1,244
Cass	23,816	21,287	18,863	2,529	11.9	11.8	9.3	85.9	3.8	3,940	1,441	384
Chippewa	5,976	5,855	5,755	121	2.1	10.3	9.9	76.6	13.6	154	22	26
Chisago	18,692	15,533	11,946	3,159	20.3	44.8	28.6	87.1	9.0	3,463	349	494
Clay	21,891	19,746	18,546	2,145	10.9	20.9	17.7	71.6	24.9	2,929	673	746
Clearwater	4,278	4,114	4,008	164	4.0	4.3	4.0	81.6	6.3	23	7	2
Cook	5,305	4,708	4,312	597	12.7	3.7	3.0	78.3	6.8	720	114	141
Cottonwood	5,425	5,376	5,495	49	0.9	8.5	8.6	80.4	12.3	134	23	20
Crow Wing	38,201	33,483	29,916	4,718	14.1	38.3	30.0	79.7	9.9	5,766	981	1,119
Dakota	151,318	133,750	102,707	17,568	13.1	265.7	180.3	78.2	22.3	20,170	2,495	3,561
Dodge	7,592	6,642	5,771	950	14.3	17.3	13.1	84.0	9.8	1,136	176	162
Douglas	19,249	16,694	14,590	2,555	15.3	30.3	23.0	77.2	14.7	3,096	489	566
Faribault	7,284	7,247	7,416	37	0.5	10.2	10.4	80.7	11.5	153	33	28
Fillmore	9,556	8,908	8,356	648	7.3	11.1	9.7	80.9	10.6	907	147	153
Freeborn	14,182	13,996	13,783	186	1.3	20.0	19.5	78.7	15.5	250	1	1
Goodhue	19,564	17,879	15,936	1,685	9.4	25.8	21.0	79.0	17.9	2,087	349	381
Grant	3,174	3,098	3,178	76	2.5	5.8	5.8	82.1	9.2	40	10	5
Hennepin	492,083	468,826	443,583	23,257	5.0	884.1	796.9	66.2	36.2	32,157	4,970	5,156
Houston	8,554	8,168	7,257	386	4.7	15.3	13.0	81.0	11.7	526	89	121
Hubbard	12,912	12,228	10,042	684	5.6	14.0	10.9	83.3	6.0	340	89	74
Isanti	14,871	12,061	9,693	2,810	23.3	33.9	22.1	85.7	10.6	3,400	545	714
Itasca	26,368	24,528	22,494	1,840	7.5	9.9	8.4	83.0	8.2	2,299	485	424
Jackson	5,162	5,092	5,121	70	1.4	7.4	7.3	79.0	9.7	155	28	25
Kanabec	7,469	6,847	6,098	622	9.1	14.2	11.6	84.6	7.2	640	114	102
Kandiyohi	19,525	18,415	16,669	1,110	6.0	24.5	20.9	75.6	18.2	1,420	235	265
Kittson	2,750	2,719	2,865	31	1.1	2.5	2.6	82.8	8.7	47	5	9
Koochiching	7,993	7,719	7,825	274	3.5	2.6	2.5	80.4	11.0	375	87	51
Lac qui Parle	3,788	3,774	3,955	14	0.4	5.0	5.2	80.9	9.1	58	7	10
Lake	7,335	6,840	6,776	495	7.2	3.5	3.2	84.0	7.8	615	94	112
Lake of the Woods	3,472	3,238	3,050	234	7.2	2.7	2.4	85.3	4.9	102	22	72
Le Sueur	12,074	10,858	9,785	1,216	11.2	26.9	21.8	83.3	10.6	1,261	235	281
Lincoln	3,107	3,043	3,050	64	2.1	5.8	5.7	80.3	8.4	86	46	20
Lyon	10,843	10,298	9,675	545	5.3	15.2	13.5	68.4	24.5	756	153	104
McLeod	15,334	14,087	12,391	1,247	8.9	31.2	25.2	78.2	18.9	1,581	263	328
Mahnomen	2,815	2,700	2,505	115	4.3	5.1	4.5	77.2	7.5	16	–	1
Marshall	4,949	4,791	5,049	158	3.3	2.8	2.8	83.6	8.2	45	1	5
Martin	9,996	9,800	9,847	196	2.0	14.1	13.9	77.4	13.9	342	90	32
Meeker	10,614	9,820	9,139	794	8.1	17.4	15.0	81.7	10.5	1,012	151	208
Mille Lacs	11,826	10,467	9,065	1,359	13.0	20.6	15.8	80.1	11.8	1,624	258	319
Morrison	15,467	13,870	12,434	1,597	11.5	13.8	11.1	81.9	9.6	1,931	311	305
Mower	16,894	16,251	15,831	643	4.0	23.7	22.2	78.2	17.6	903	101	156
Murray	4,525	4,357	4,611	168	3.9	6.4	6.5	84.2	7.2	238	39	34
Nicollet	12,431	11,240	9,963	1,191	10.6	27.5	22.0	75.8	20.6	1,427	193	263
Nobles	8,544	8,465	8,094	79	0.9	11.9	11.3	75.0	16.4	198	35	40
Norman	3,508	3,455	3,648	53	1.5	4.0	4.2	81.0	8.3	89	13	30
Olmsted	57,307	49,422	41,603	7,885	16.0	87.8	63.7	75.9	23.8	8,670	1,144	1,277
Otter Tail	35,357	33,862	29,295	1,495	4.4	17.9	14.8	80.0	9.6	1,028	194	217
Pennington	6,251	6,033	5,682	218	3.6	10.1	9.2	74.4	19.3	209	35	28
Pine	16,403	15,353	12,738	1,050	6.8	11.6	9.0	83.7	5.6	885	183	244
Pipestone	4,496	4,434	4,387	62	1.4	9.7	9.4	78.0	11.2	124	21	18
Polk	14,519	14,008	14,275	511	3.6	7.4	7.2	74.1	16.6	717	146	118
Pope	6,312	5,827	5,836	485	8.3	9.4	8.7	81.0	9.5	545	89	106
Ramsey	213,126	206,448	201,016	6,678	3.2	1,368.1	1,290.1	63.5	37.4	9,848	1,135	2,793
Red Lake	1,942	1,883	1,899	59	3.1	4.5	4.4	80.1	11.9	25	1	5
Redwood	7,316	7,230	7,144	86	1.2	8.3	8.1	79.8	12.0	179	37	17
Renville	7,477	7,413	7,442	64	0.9	7.6	7.6	80.9	8.5	153	24	24

See footnotes at end of table.

Table B-7. Counties — **Housing Units and Building Permits**—Con.

[Includes United States, states, and 3,141 counties/county equivalents defined as of February 22, 2005. For more information on these areas, see Appendix C, Geographic Information]

County	Housing units							Housing 2000, percent		New private housing units authorized by building permits		
	2005 (July 1)	2000[1] (April 1 esti-mates base)	1990 (April 1)	Net change, 2000–2005 Number	Percent	Units per square mile of land area 2005[2]	1990	Owner-occupied housing units[3]	Units in multi-unit structures	Cumu-lative, 2000–2005 period	2005	2004
MINNESOTA—Con.												
Rice	22,720	20,061	17,520	2,659	13.3	45.7	35.2	77.9	18.0	3,385	600	665
Rock	4,229	4,137	3,963	92	2.2	8.8	8.2	77.9	15.0	165	38	29
Roseau	7,464	7,101	6,236	363	5.1	4.5	3.8	83.8	9.9	198	42	31
St. Louis	98,760	95,800	95,403	2,960	3.1	15.9	15.3	74.7	19.7	4,683	917	1,185
Scott	42,578	31,609	20,302	10,969	34.7	119.4	56.9	86.5	11.0	12,797	1,730	2,087
Sherburne	29,896	22,827	14,964	7,069	31.0	68.5	34.3	84.1	12.7	7,826	1,168	1,537
Sibley	6,365	6,024	5,625	341	5.7	10.8	9.6	80.9	11.4	452	89	97
Stearns	57,654	50,293	43,806	7,361	14.6	42.9	32.6	73.8	22.1	8,131	1,437	1,428
Steele	14,512	13,306	11,840	1,206	9.1	33.8	27.6	80.1	16.5	1,545	254	280
Stevens	4,184	4,074	4,108	110	2.7	7.4	7.3	70.4	19.3	175	33	49
Swift	4,902	4,821	4,795	81	1.7	6.6	6.4	77.0	12.9	147	27	18
Todd	12,649	11,900	11,234	749	6.3	13.4	11.9	83.2	8.2	961	184	218
Traverse	2,249	2,199	2,220	50	2.3	3.9	3.9	80.5	11.2	56	13	15
Wabasha	9,970	9,066	8,205	904	10.0	19.0	15.6	82.4	11.3	1,200	222	223
Wadena	6,711	6,334	5,801	377	6.0	12.5	10.8	77.6	12.3	429	68	67
Waseca	7,779	7,427	7,011	352	4.7	18.4	16.6	80.1	14.9	478	76	82
Washington	84,554	73,635	51,648	10,919	14.8	215.9	131.8	85.7	12.5	13,624	2,677	2,708
Watonwan	5,113	5,036	4,886	77	1.5	11.8	11.2	77.1	16.8	147	35	31
Wilkin	3,189	3,105	3,140	84	2.7	4.2	4.2	80.8	13.9	172	73	30
Winona	20,769	19,551	17,630	1,218	6.2	33.2	28.1	70.8	23.6	1,547	193	265
Wright	44,673	34,357	26,353	10,316	30.0	67.6	39.9	84.4	10.8	11,639	2,221	2,193
Yellow Medicine	4,963	4,873	4,983	90	1.8	6.5	6.6	79.5	9.9	192	21	23
MISSISSIPPI	1,235,496	1,161,952	1,010,423	73,544	6.3	26.3	21.5	72.3	13.3	72,392	13,396	14,532
Adams	15,349	15,175	14,715	174	1.1	33.3	32.0	70.3	13.1	40	5	1
Alcorn	16,272	15,817	13,704	455	2.9	40.7	34.3	73.5	10.4	211	5	44
Amite	6,673	6,446	5,695	227	3.5	9.1	7.8	86.0	2.1	29	1	2
Attala	8,949	8,639	7,674	310	3.6	12.2	10.4	77.7	7.0	153	19	25
Benton	3,559	3,456	3,379	103	3.0	8.7	8.3	84.3	1.2	9	2	1
Bolivar	15,305	14,939	14,514	366	2.4	17.5	16.6	61.1	17.3	279	52	36
Calhoun	7,094	6,902	6,260	192	2.8	12.1	10.7	76.3	7.3	8	2	2
Carroll	5,063	4,888	3,948	175	3.6	8.1	6.3	84.8	2.3	(NA)	–	–
Chickasaw	8,208	7,981	6,997	227	2.8	16.4	13.9	77.9	7.2	53	5	11
Choctaw	4,369	4,249	3,539	120	2.8	10.4	8.4	81.3	6.0	12	1	–
Claiborne	4,383	4,252	4,099	131	3.1	9.0	8.4	80.2	5.1	4	1	1
Clarke	8,349	8,100	7,065	249	3.1	12.1	10.2	84.3	2.5	52	17	6
Clay	9,026	8,810	7,737	216	2.5	22.1	18.9	73.6	11.3	108	13	20
Coahoma	11,587	11,490	11,495	97	0.8	20.9	20.7	57.3	18.7	199	44	28
Copiah	11,385	11,101	10,260	284	2.6	14.7	13.2	79.9	6.9	66	15	11
Covington	8,358	8,083	6,535	275	3.4	20.2	15.8	84.9	3.8	31	7	4
DeSoto	52,979	40,795	24,472	12,184	29.9	110.9	51.2	79.2	12.0	14,721	2,815	2,618
Forrest	31,703	29,913	27,740	1,790	6.0	67.9	59.4	60.2	26.3	1,933	232	603
Franklin	4,259	4,119	3,555	140	3.4	7.5	6.3	86.1	3.0	4	–	–
George	7,750	7,513	6,663	237	3.2	16.2	13.9	86.2	3.3	8	–	–
Greene	5,145	4,947	3,864	198	4.0	7.2	5.4	87.1	2.8	33	–	–
Grenada	10,272	9,973	8,712	299	3.0	24.4	20.6	69.2	12.5	223	29	36
Hancock	23,531	21,072	16,561	2,459	11.7	49.3	34.7	79.6	8.6	1,468	416	581
Harrison	88,138	79,636	67,813	8,502	10.7	151.7	116.7	62.7	22.3	9,921	1,570	1,754
Hinds	104,535	100,287	99,860	4,248	4.2	120.3	114.9	63.9	24.1	5,430	629	1,148
Holmes	8,725	8,439	7,972	286	3.4	11.5	10.5	73.3	8.4	119	15	13
Humphreys	4,169	4,138	4,231	31	0.7	10.0	10.1	61.4	9.6	37	9	–
Issaquena	885	877	698	8	0.9	2.1	1.7	66.9	9.8	–	–	–
Itawamba	10,159	9,804	8,116	355	3.6	19.1	15.2	82.4	3.6	104	15	10
Jackson	56,732	51,678	45,542	5,054	9.8	78.0	62.7	74.6	13.1	5,956	918	1,295
Jasper	7,982	7,670	6,700	312	4.1	11.8	9.9	86.7	2.9	80	4	3
Jefferson	3,958	3,819	3,167	139	3.6	7.6	6.1	80.4	8.0	21	–	–
Jefferson Davis	6,065	5,891	5,336	174	3.0	14.9	13.1	84.5	3.8	–	–	–
Jones	27,624	26,921	25,044	703	2.6	39.8	36.1	76.8	9.1	186	37	48
Kemper	4,689	4,533	4,151	156	3.4	6.1	5.4	83.8	5.3	–	–	–
Lafayette	18,125	16,587	12,478	1,538	9.3	28.7	19.8	60.6	23.0	1,463	310	149
Lamar	15,970	15,433	11,849	537	3.5	32.1	23.8	75.8	12.7	65	3	7
Lauderdale	34,351	33,418	31,232	933	2.8	48.8	44.4	67.8	19.1	856	367	240
Lawrence	5,874	5,688	5,160	186	3.3	13.6	12.0	84.2	3.6	17	2	5
Leake	8,867	8,585	7,614	282	3.3	15.2	13.1	82.0	4.4	69	13	12
Lee	32,800	31,887	25,971	913	2.9	73.0	57.8	69.2	16.8	974	224	208
Leflore	14,612	14,097	13,799	515	3.7	24.7	23.3	53.4	20.6	851	280	302
Lincoln	14,456	14,052	12,133	404	2.9	24.7	20.7	78.1	8.0	77	5	18
Lowndes	26,120	25,104	23,117	1,016	4.0	52.0	46.0	66.5	14.9	1,176	157	257
Madison	34,109	28,781	20,761	5,328	18.5	47.6	28.9	70.9	20.9	6,527	1,182	1,790
Marion	10,654	10,394	10,132	260	2.5	19.6	18.7	80.4	5.6	27	5	7
Marshall	13,956	13,252	10,984	704	5.3	19.8	15.5	80.5	4.5	866	226	175
Monroe	16,594	16,236	14,285	358	2.2	21.7	18.7	79.0	6.9	92	34	17
Montgomery	5,902	5,402	4,987	500	9.3	14.5	12.3	77.0	7.1	516	85	92
Neshoba	12,347	11,980	9,770	367	3.1	21.7	17.1	79.5	5.7	119	46	41

See footnotes at end of table.

[Includes United States, states, and 3,141 counties/county equivalents defined as of February 22, 2005. For more information on these areas, see Appendix C, Geographic Information]

County	Housing units							Housing 2000, percent		New private housing units authorized by building permits		
	2005 (July 1)	2000[1] (April 1 esti- mates base)	1990 (April 1)	Net change, 2000–2005 Number	Net change, 2000–2005 Percent	Units per square mile of land area 2005[2]	Units per square mile of land area 1990	Owner- occupied housing units[3]	Units in multi- unit structures	Cumu- lative, 2000– 2005 period	2005	2004
MISSISSIPPI—Con.												
Newton	9,538	9,260	8,095	278	3.0	16.5	14.0	81.9	5.6	52	2	2
Noxubee	5,388	5,228	4,645	160	3.1	7.8	6.7	79.5	6.9	19	4	3
Oktibbeha	18,972	17,344	13,861	1,628	9.4	41.4	30.3	55.6	30.7	1,947	595	180
Panola	14,276	13,736	11,482	540	3.9	20.9	16.8	77.9	7.0	200	41	40
Pearl River	22,521	20,610	15,793	1,911	9.3	27.8	19.5	79.8	5.7	2,201	388	392
Perry	5,282	5,107	4,292	175	3.4	8.2	6.6	84.5	4.5	27	6	6
Pike	17,080	16,720	14,995	360	2.2	41.8	36.7	74.4	10.8	217	137	22
Pontotoc	11,291	10,816	9,001	475	4.4	22.7	18.1	77.9	5.6	216	16	16
Prentiss	11,050	10,682	9,155	368	3.4	26.6	22.1	77.9	9.3	257	57	28
Quitman	3,957	3,922	3,880	35	0.9	9.8	9.6	68.5	8.9	32	–	8
Rankin	51,411	45,070	31,872	6,341	14.1	66.4	41.1	77.1	12.5	7,808	1,667	1,519
Scott	11,472	11,116	9,488	356	3.2	18.8	15.6	78.3	6.0	84	7	13
Sharkey	2,466	2,416	2,290	50	2.1	5.8	5.4	65.5	5.5	12	1	1
Simpson	11,531	11,307	9,374	224	2.0	19.6	15.9	81.1	6.3	211	38	38
Smith	7,205	7,005	5,850	200	2.9	11.3	9.2	86.9	2.2	33	8	7
Stone	5,603	5,343	4,148	260	4.9	12.6	9.3	81.2	5.4	168	38	33
Sunflower	10,629	10,338	10,167	291	2.8	15.3	14.7	61.8	12.3	306	57	79
Tallahatchie	5,892	5,711	5,492	181	3.2	9.2	8.5	76.2	4.8	62	16	13
Tate	10,320	9,354	7,474	966	10.3	25.5	18.5	78.3	6.5	1,164	232	196
Tippah	9,192	8,868	7,846	324	3.7	20.1	17.1	78.2	5.0	148	31	28
Tishomingo	9,815	9,553	8,455	262	2.7	23.1	19.9	78.9	5.7	22	6	4
Tunica	4,377	3,705	2,990	672	18.1	9.6	6.6	51.7	21.1	681	57	42
Union	11,017	10,693	9,104	324	3.0	26.5	21.9	77.6	7.0	124	33	14
Walthall	6,619	6,419	5,643	200	3.1	16.4	14.0	83.3	3.6	4	–	–
Warren	21,190	20,789	19,512	401	1.9	36.1	33.3	68.2	17.9	170	32	29
Washington	24,958	24,381	24,567	577	2.4	34.5	33.9	59.5	19.0	720	55	134
Wayne	9,356	9,049	7,723	307	3.4	11.5	9.5	85.0	4.2	53	8	10
Webster	4,475	4,344	4,326	131	3.0	10.6	10.2	78.4	7.5	51	10	14
Wilkinson	5,282	5,106	4,242	176	3.4	7.8	6.3	83.3	4.2	–	–	–
Winston	8,686	8,472	7,613	214	2.5	14.3	12.5	79.7	6.6	48	2	10
Yalobusha	6,490	6,224	5,414	266	4.3	13.9	11.6	79.0	6.0	146	31	27
Yazoo	10,189	10,015	9,549	174	1.7	11.1	10.4	68.8	12.7	16	4	3
MISSOURI	2,592,809	2,442,003	2,199,129	150,806	6.2	37.6	31.9	70.3	20.0	172,529	33,114	32,791
Adair	11,226	10,826	10,097	400	3.7	19.8	17.8	60.3	24.0	357	63	58
Andrew	6,935	6,662	5,841	273	4.1	15.9	13.4	80.0	7.9	204	67	19
Atchison	3,140	3,104	3,298	36	1.2	5.8	6.1	69.0	10.8	22	4	4
Audrain	11,098	10,881	10,039	217	2.0	16.0	14.5	74.1	10.0	153	17	32
Barry	16,790	15,965	12,908	825	5.2	21.6	16.6	75.7	7.5	546	103	76
Barton	5,630	5,409	5,014	221	4.1	9.5	8.4	73.5	6.8	111	15	14
Bates	7,537	7,247	6,782	290	4.0	8.9	8.0	75.1	6.2	111	20	53
Benton	13,174	12,691	10,280	483	3.8	18.7	14.6	82.2	3.1	52	8	12
Bollinger	5,677	5,522	4,542	155	2.8	9.1	7.3	81.3	3.4	15	2	1
Boone	65,283	56,678	44,695	8,605	15.2	95.2	65.2	57.5	31.9	10,986	2,324	2,330
Buchanan	37,496	36,579	35,652	917	2.5	91.5	87.0	67.6	20.4	1,441	204	287
Butler	19,274	18,707	17,046	567	3.0	27.6	24.4	68.9	11.7	222	34	43
Caldwell	4,659	4,493	3,649	166	3.7	10.9	8.5	77.3	6.8	108	50	56
Callaway	17,147	16,167	13,003	980	6.1	20.4	15.5	76.8	10.1	653	139	137
Camden	35,273	33,470	25,662	1,803	5.4	53.8	39.2	82.2	23.2	871	179	169
Cape Girardeau	30,872	29,434	25,315	1,438	4.9	53.4	43.7	68.4	21.5	1,440	247	233
Carroll	4,982	4,897	5,001	85	1.7	7.2	7.2	74.0	7.8	51	36	4
Carter	3,148	3,028	2,693	120	4.0	6.2	5.3	76.8	3.1	6	–	–
Cass	36,791	31,677	24,337	5,114	16.1	52.6	34.8	79.5	11.5	6,148	1,142	1,090
Cedar	7,057	6,813	6,035	244	3.6	14.8	12.7	78.3	5.5	138	44	23
Chariton	4,396	4,250	4,479	146	3.4	5.8	5.9	80.6	6.8	23	–	6
Christian	26,591	21,826	12,812	4,765	21.8	47.2	22.7	75.9	10.7	5,836	1,719	1,299
Clark	3,586	3,483	3,398	103	3.0	7.1	6.7	78.5	5.7	29	4	9
Clay	82,638	76,230	63,000	6,408	8.4	208.5	158.9	70.7	21.7	4,518	580	1,046
Clinton	8,698	7,876	6,559	822	10.4	20.8	15.7	78.9	9.3	1,188	206	193
Cole	31,423	28,915	24,939	2,508	8.7	80.3	63.7	67.8	25.3	2,987	434	406
Cooper	7,092	6,676	6,002	416	6.2	12.6	10.6	74.1	11.4	310	13	47
Crawford	11,313	10,850	9,030	463	4.3	15.2	12.2	76.6	6.7	175	52	21
Dade	3,869	3,758	3,543	111	3.0	7.9	7.2	78.5	4.3	4	–	4
Dallas	7,243	6,914	5,484	329	4.8	13.4	10.1	79.2	5.0	(NA)	29	41
Daviess	3,979	3,853	3,613	126	3.3	7.0	6.4	76.6	6.5	34	13	9
DeKalb	4,079	3,840	3,358	239	6.2	9.6	7.9	73.6	12.7	30	11	9
Dent	7,203	6,994	6,115	209	3.0	9.6	8.1	74.2	7.6	47	18	6
Douglas	6,125	5,919	5,105	206	3.5	7.5	6.3	79.0	5.3	46	16	3
Dunklin	15,117	14,684	14,102	433	2.9	27.7	25.8	66.0	8.5	228	18	25

See footnotes at end of table.

Table B-7. Counties — **Housing Units and Building Permits**—Con.

[Includes United States, states, and 3,141 counties/county equivalents defined as of February 22, 2005. For more information on these areas, see Appendix C, Geographic Information]

County	Housing units							Housing 2000, percent		New private housing units authorized by building permits		
	2005 (July 1)	2000¹ (April 1 estimates base)	1990 (April 1)	Net change, 2000–2005 Number	Net change, 2000–2005 Percent	Units per square mile of land area 2005²	Units per square mile of land area 1990	Owner-occupied housing units³	Units in multi-unit structures	Cumulative, 2000–2005 period	2005	2004
MISSOURI—Con.												
Franklin	41,583	38,295	32,451	3,288	8.6	45.1	35.2	78.1	10.7	4,287	958	828
Gasconade	8,090	7,813	7,158	277	3.5	15.5	13.8	80.4	7.9	90	35	19
Gentry	3,277	3,214	3,232	63	2.0	6.7	6.6	75.5	9.8	20	1	4
Greene	115,592	104,517	87,910	11,075	10.6	171.3	130.2	63.6	20.9	14,224	3,089	2,659
Grundy	5,256	5,102	5,113	154	3.0	12.1	11.7	71.8	11.1	128	25	23
Harrison	4,448	4,316	4,245	132	3.1	6.1	5.9	74.8	8.2	42	7	7
Henry	10,621	10,261	9,317	360	3.5	15.1	13.3	72.9	10.7	255	38	35
Hickory	6,488	6,184	5,482	304	4.9	16.3	13.8	84.5	1.7	–	–	–
Holt	3,009	2,931	3,190	78	2.7	6.5	6.9	74.5	6.8	25	–	1
Howard	4,464	4,346	4,025	118	2.7	9.6	8.6	75.3	7.3	55	5	9
Howell	17,116	16,340	13,326	776	4.7	18.4	14.4	73.6	8.5	543	134	116
Iron	5,073	4,908	4,700	165	3.4	9.2	8.5	75.9	6.4	29	9	11
Jackson	307,700	288,231	280,729	19,469	6.8	508.7	464.2	62.9	27.3	32,703	6,068	5,990
Jasper	48,363	45,571	39,554	2,792	6.1	75.6	61.8	67.0	13.8	3,087	641	645
Jefferson	83,572	75,586	63,423	7,986	10.6	127.2	96.6	83.4	8.6	9,533	1,648	1,788
Johnson	20,136	18,886	16,010	1,250	6.6	24.2	19.3	61.7	18.9	1,053	199	233
Knox	2,383	2,317	2,254	66	2.8	4.7	4.5	77.4	7.2	18	3	4
Laclede	15,275	14,320	11,564	955	6.7	19.9	15.1	72.8	10.7	720	140	141
Lafayette	14,319	13,707	12,820	612	4.5	22.8	20.4	75.4	10.9	622	126	149
Lawrence	15,454	14,788	12,788	666	4.5	25.2	20.9	74.3	8.0	359	49	118
Lewis	4,780	4,602	4,244	178	3.9	9.5	8.4	76.5	10.1	54	5	15
Lincoln	16,968	15,511	12,284	1,457	9.4	26.9	19.5	80.7	5.9	1,201	325	290
Linn	6,683	6,554	6,566	129	2.0	10.8	10.6	76.9	8.0	56	8	8
Livingston	6,682	6,467	6,294	215	3.3	12.5	11.8	70.7	15.9	274	44	34
McDonald	9,655	9,287	7,327	368	4.0	17.9	13.6	71.4	6.8	76	25	11
Macon	7,680	7,502	6,955	178	2.4	9.6	8.7	76.2	9.0	81	26	20
Madison	5,882	5,655	5,282	227	4.0	11.8	10.6	76.2	6.4	102	18	32
Maries	4,314	4,149	3,715	165	4.0	8.2	7.0	81.7	5.4	(NA)	5	5
Marion	12,727	12,443	12,026	284	2.3	29.1	27.5	70.3	19.8	443	69	73
Mercer	2,190	2,125	2,225	65	3.1	4.8	4.9	76.8	7.1	3	–	–
Miller	12,008	11,263	9,766	745	6.6	20.3	16.5	75.0	11.9	403	15	85
Mississippi	5,944	5,840	5,757	104	1.8	14.4	13.9	63.6	10.7	67	2	7
Moniteau	5,945	5,742	5,043	203	3.5	14.3	12.1	77.7	9.6	22	1	3
Monroe	4,813	4,565	4,114	248	5.4	7.5	6.4	78.7	4.4	305	55	59
Montgomery	6,091	5,726	5,241	365	6.4	11.3	9.7	78.5	5.4	268	65	77
Morgan	14,472	13,898	12,642	574	4.1	24.2	21.2	82.8	3.8	(NA)	–	3
New Madrid	8,907	8,598	8,557	309	3.6	13.1	12.6	66.0	11.9	146	24	36
Newton	22,953	21,897	18,384	1,056	4.8	36.6	29.3	76.6	7.4	394	65	70
Nodaway	9,422	8,909	8,349	513	5.8	10.7	9.5	63.7	20.0	324	39	67
Oregon	5,145	4,997	4,484	148	3.0	6.5	5.7	78.2	4.1	14	2	3
Osage	6,114	5,905	5,414	209	3.5	10.1	8.9	82.9	6.9	(NA)	–	–
Ozark	5,331	5,114	4,451	217	4.2	7.2	6.0	81.3	1.9	24	6	6
Pemiscot	8,977	8,793	8,806	184	2.1	18.2	17.9	58.3	12.7	107	15	17
Perry	8,119	7,815	6,867	304	3.9	17.1	14.5	80.1	7.3	387	58	66
Pettis	17,328	16,963	15,443	365	2.2	25.3	22.5	72.5	12.9	261	62	76
Phelps	18,779	17,501	14,715	1,278	7.3	27.9	21.9	65.5	17.2	1,110	157	170
Pike	7,709	7,493	7,128	216	2.9	11.5	10.6	74.0	10.2	70	12	14
Platte	34,931	30,897	24,362	4,034	13.1	83.1	58.0	67.5	28.1	2,639	375	412
Polk	11,965	11,183	8,979	782	7.0	18.8	14.1	72.8	8.5	576	110	159
Pulaski	16,169	15,408	13,838	761	4.9	29.6	25.3	58.1	16.5	369	176	138
Putnam	3,004	2,914	2,590	90	3.1	5.8	5.0	77.0	7.5	36	8	17
Ralls	4,716	4,564	3,766	152	3.3	10.0	8.0	82.2	6.2	13	4	1
Randolph	11,064	10,740	10,131	324	3.0	22.9	21.0	72.1	12.7	199	34	80
Ray	9,989	9,371	8,611	618	6.6	17.5	15.1	79.5	8.2	826	174	156
Reynolds	3,905	3,759	3,537	146	3.9	4.8	4.4	77.3	3.6	(NA)	–	–
Ripley	6,635	6,392	5,597	243	3.8	10.5	8.9	77.9	3.5	16	1	1
St. Charles	127,309	105,517	79,113	21,792	20.7	227.2	140.9	82.0	14.6	25,716	4,112	4,698
St. Clair	5,423	5,205	4,645	218	4.2	8.0	6.9	79.4	4.9	(NA)	11	14
Ste. Genevieve	8,277	8,018	6,766	259	3.2	16.5	13.5	82.3	5.4	50	12	15
St. Francois	25,833	24,449	20,321	1,384	5.7	57.5	45.2	73.1	12.2	1,717	330	326
St. Louis	432,486	423,730	401,839	8,756	2.1	851.7	791.4	74.1	23.1	14,748	2,541	2,625
Saline	10,296	10,019	10,033	277	2.8	13.6	13.3	69.1	10.4	251	27	16
Schuyler	2,150	2,027	1,986	123	6.1	7.0	6.5	75.5	9.1	93	14	15
Scotland	2,340	2,292	2,302	48	2.1	5.3	5.2	76.6	8.6	16	5	1
Scott	17,557	16,951	15,881	606	3.6	41.7	37.7	69.4	10.1	559	82	88
Shannon	4,020	3,862	3,312	158	4.1	4.0	3.3	79.2	4.4	48	1	1
Shelby	3,323	3,245	3,277	78	2.4	6.6	6.5	74.7	7.5	11	3	–
Stoddard	13,698	13,221	12,288	477	3.6	16.6	14.9	72.4	7.9	291	60	42
Stone	17,194	16,242	11,294	952	5.9	37.1	24.4	81.2	8.2	810	359	362
Sullivan	3,463	3,364	3,093	99	2.9	5.3	4.8	71.5	9.7	18	2	1

See footnotes at end of table.

Table B-7. Counties — **Housing Units and Building Permits**—Con.

[Includes United States, states, and 3,141 counties/county equivalents defined as of February 22, 2005. For more information on these areas, see Appendix C, Geographic Information]

County	Housing units 2005 (July 1)	Housing units 2000[1] (April 1 esti-mates base)	Housing units 1990 (April 1)	Net change, 2000–2005 Number	Net change, 2000–2005 Percent	Units per square mile of land area 2005[2]	Units per square mile of land area 1990	Housing 2000, percent Owner-occupied housing units[3]	Housing 2000, percent Units in multi-unit structures	New private housing units authorized by building permits Cumu-lative, 2000–2005 period	New private housing units authorized by building permits 2005	New private housing units authorized by building permits 2004
MISSOURI—Con.												
Taney	22,441	19,688	13,273	2,753	14.0	35.5	21.0	68.9	19.7	3,604	1,010	748
Texas	11,196	10,764	9,525	432	4.0	9.5	8.1	76.6	7.2	60	4	5
Vernon	9,123	8,872	8,181	251	2.8	10.9	9.8	72.2	10.4	95	21	14
Warren	13,071	11,046	8,841	2,025	18.3	30.3	20.5	83.1	6.1	2,311	503	463
Washington	10,312	9,894	8,075	418	4.2	13.6	10.6	80.0	4.7	15	4	7
Wayne	7,842	7,496	6,406	346	4.6	10.3	8.4	78.2	3.0	(NA)	–	–
Webster	13,015	12,052	9,067	963	8.0	21.9	15.3	77.9	7.5	796	168	131
Worth	1,265	1,245	1,269	20	1.6	4.7	4.8	76.6	7.0	–	–	–
Wright	8,152	7,957	7,214	195	2.5	12.0	10.6	73.1	7.8	62	9	8
Independent City												
St. Louis city	176,267	176,354	194,919	−87	(Z)	2,846.7	3,147.4	46.9	56.2	3,401	865	455
MONTANA	428,357	412,633	361,155	15,724	3.8	2.9	2.5	69.1	15.7	22,295	4,803	4,975
Beaverhead	4,615	4,571	4,128	44	1.0	0.8	0.7	63.4	12.6	55	2	26
Big Horn	4,679	4,655	4,304	24	0.5	0.9	0.9	64.6	7.2	35	7	6
Blaine	2,947	2,947	2,930	–	–	0.7	0.7	61.1	12.9	3	–	–
Broadwater	2,030	2,002	1,593	28	1.4	1.7	1.3	79.4	7.0	37	7	6
Carbon	5,650	5,494	4,828	156	2.8	2.8	2.4	74.4	6.5	237	65	63
Carter	808	811	816	−3	−0.4	0.2	0.2	74.8	3.0	–	–	–
Cascade	35,707	35,225	33,063	482	1.4	13.2	12.3	64.9	23.4	1,127	316	224
Chouteau	2,782	2,776	2,668	6	0.2	0.7	0.7	68.8	5.2	22	5	6
Custer	5,343	5,360	5,405	−17	−0.3	1.4	1.4	70.2	17.6	30	7	5
Daniels	1,146	1,154	1,220	−8	−0.7	0.8	0.9	78.4	6.3	7	1	–
Dawson	4,152	4,168	4,487	−16	−0.4	1.7	1.9	74.0	10.1	14	4	3
Deer Lodge	5,027	4,958	4,830	69	1.4	6.8	6.6	73.6	13.1	167	33	28
Fallon	1,416	1,410	1,525	6	0.4	0.9	0.9	77.4	7.2	15	1	4
Fergus	5,558	5,558	5,732	–	–	1.3	1.3	73.5	11.2	43	6	8
Flathead	36,674	34,773	26,979	1,901	5.5	7.2	5.3	73.3	12.5	2,819	724	684
Gallatin[9]	34,097	29,489	21,350	4,608	15.6	13.1	8.5	62.4	24.4	6,394	1,681	1,930
Garfield	959	961	924	−2	−0.2	0.2	0.2	73.7	2.5	1	1	–
Glacier	5,252	5,243	4,797	9	0.2	1.8	1.6	62.0	11.7	1	–	–
Golden Valley	449	450	432	−1	−0.2	0.4	0.4	77.3	0.9	–	–	–
Granite	2,080	2,074	1,924	6	0.3	1.2	1.1	74.4	3.4	3	–	–
Hill	7,445	7,453	7,345	−8	−0.1	2.6	2.5	64.3	18.3	35	2	9
Jefferson	4,213	4,199	3,302	14	0.3	2.5	2.0	83.2	3.7	3	–	–
Judith Basin	1,324	1,325	1,346	−1	−0.1	0.7	0.7	77.1	2.7	–	–	–
Lake	13,929	13,605	10,972	324	2.4	9.3	7.3	71.4	8.0	516	119	121
Lewis and Clark	26,166	25,672	21,412	494	1.9	7.6	6.2	70.1	18.8	800	252	145
Liberty	1,070	1,070	1,007	–	–	0.7	0.7	71.3	16.1	–	–	–
Lincoln	9,392	9,319	8,002	73	0.8	2.6	2.2	76.6	5.2	58	10	2
McCone	1,082	1,087	1,161	−5	−0.5	0.4	0.4	78.0	5.1	–	–	–
Madison	4,734	4,671	3,902	63	1.3	1.3	1.1	70.4	12.4	65	9	20
Meagher	1,363	1,363	1,259	–	–	0.6	0.5	73.2	5.6	–	–	–
Mineral	1,988	1,961	1,635	27	1.4	1.6	1.3	73.4	3.8	26	6	4
Missoula	44,834	41,319	33,466	3,515	8.5	17.3	12.9	61.9	23.3	4,394	638	588
Musselshell	2,311	2,317	2,183	−6	−0.3	1.2	1.2	76.9	5.3	2	–	1
Park[9]	8,387	8,247	6,926	140	1.7	3.0	2.6	66.4	12.7	245	76	53
Petroleum	292	292	293	–	–	0.2	0.2	74.4	2.1	–	–	–
Phillips	2,498	2,502	2,765	−4	−0.2	0.5	0.5	70.6	10.0	7	1	1
Pondera	2,822	2,834	2,618	−12	−0.4	1.7	1.6	70.5	11.4	7	2	–
Powder River	1,009	1,007	1,096	2	0.2	0.3	0.3	73.8	3.9	–	–	–
Powell	2,931	2,930	2,835	1	(Z)	1.3	1.2	71.3	7.6	2	–	–
Prairie	715	718	749	−3	−0.4	0.4	0.4	77.5	6.1	4	1	–
Ravalli	16,374	15,946	11,099	428	2.7	6.8	4.6	75.7	7.8	485	100	62
Richland	4,562	4,557	4,825	5	0.1	2.2	2.3	72.4	16.1	69	27	10
Roosevelt	4,038	4,044	4,265	−6	−0.1	1.7	1.8	65.1	8.1	15	9	–
Rosebud	3,930	3,912	4,251	18	0.5	0.8	0.8	67.1	10.8	7	2	2
Sanders	5,330	5,271	4,335	59	1.1	1.9	1.6	76.4	4.7	21	–	–
Sheridan	2,154	2,167	2,417	−13	−0.6	1.3	1.4	80.2	9.3	2	–	–
Silver Bow	16,228	16,176	15,474	52	0.3	22.6	21.5	70.4	18.8	294	67	74
Stillwater	4,028	3,947	3,291	81	2.1	2.2	1.8	76.0	4.9	82	5	4
Sweet Grass	1,907	1,860	1,639	47	2.5	1.0	0.9	74.1	5.7	52	2	1
Teton	2,914	2,910	2,725	4	0.1	1.3	1.2	75.4	9.0	25	5	2
Toole	2,291	2,300	2,354	−9	−0.4	1.2	1.2	71.2	13.3	15	3	4
Treasure	420	422	448	−2	−0.5	0.4	0.5	71.4	3.3	–	–	–
Valley	4,830	4,847	5,304	−17	−0.4	1.0	1.1	75.8	20.0	6	2	2
Wheatland	1,151	1,154	1,129	−3	−0.3	0.8	0.8	72.6	6.2	–	–	–
Wibaux	584	587	563	−3	−0.5	0.7	0.6	73.4	11.8	2	1	1
Yellowstone	57,740	54,563	48,781	3,177	5.8	21.9	18.5	69.2	19.9	4,046	604	876
Yellowstone National Park[9]	(X)	(X)	46	(NA)	(NA)	(NA)	0.2	(NA)	(NA)	(NA)	(X)	(X)

See footnotes at end of table.

County and City Data Book: 2007

U.S. Census Bureau

319

Table B-7. Counties — **Housing Units and Building Permits**—Con.

[Includes United States, states, and 3,141 counties/county equivalents defined as of February 22, 2005. For more information on these areas, see Appendix C, Geographic Information]

County	Housing units			Net change, 2000–2005		Units per square mile of land area		Housing 2000, percent		New private housing units authorized by building permits		
	2005 (July 1)	2000[1] (April 1 estimates base)	1990 (April 1)	Number	Percent	2005[2]	1990	Owner-occupied housing units[3]	Units in multi-unit structures	Cumulative, 2000–2005 period	2005	2004
NEBRASKA	766,951	722,669	660,621	44,282	6.1	10.0	8.6	67.4	20.0	57,769	9,929	10,920
Adams	13,611	13,014	12,491	597	4.6	24.2	22.2	66.8	18.8	933	181	276
Antelope	3,371	3,346	3,478	25	0.7	3.9	4.1	76.4	4.3	90	29	16
Arthur	282	273	242	9	3.3	0.4	0.3	63.2	1.1	(NA)	–	–
Banner	387	375	366	12	3.2	0.5	0.5	64.6	2.4	(NA)	–	–
Blaine	344	333	381	11	3.3	0.5	0.5	65.5	0.6	(NA)	–	–
Boone	2,789	2,733	2,878	56	2.0	4.1	4.2	75.1	6.4	57	12	10
Box Butte	5,505	5,488	5,534	17	0.3	5.1	5.1	70.1	15.9	36	2	1
Boyd	1,445	1,406	1,538	39	2.8	2.7	2.8	80.2	1.8	–	–	–
Brown	1,949	1,916	1,950	33	1.7	1.6	1.6	74.2	5.7	26	4	4
Buffalo	18,227	16,830	14,538	1,397	8.3	18.8	15.0	63.6	21.1	1,680	295	419
Burt	3,757	3,723	3,740	34	0.9	7.6	7.6	75.8	7.5	52	15	11
Butler	4,139	4,015	3,801	124	3.1	7.1	6.5	75.8	5.9	67	13	12
Cass	10,946	10,179	8,951	767	7.5	19.6	16.0	79.5	7.1	972	146	175
Cedar	4,296	4,200	4,149	96	2.3	5.8	5.6	80.6	6.0	98	19	20
Chase	1,962	1,927	2,011	35	1.8	2.2	2.2	76.9	3.3	61	6	5
Cherry	3,300	3,220	3,023	80	2.5	0.6	0.5	62.4	8.1	84	21	22
Cheyenne	4,755	4,569	4,345	186	4.1	4.0	3.6	72.8	16.3	276	38	37
Clay	3,092	3,066	3,173	26	0.8	5.4	5.5	77.8	7.0	78	18	12
Colfax	4,124	4,087	3,971	37	0.9	10.0	9.6	75.2	10.1	59	18	11
Cuming	4,343	4,283	4,132	60	1.4	7.6	7.2	71.4	10.1	72	14	13
Custer	5,678	5,585	5,728	93	1.7	2.2	2.2	73.0	8.0	25	3	5
Dakota	7,729	7,528	6,486	201	2.7	29.3	24.6	67.4	18.2	285	31	32
Dawes	4,045	4,004	3,909	41	1.0	2.9	2.8	62.7	15.1	51	6	9
Dawson	9,846	9,805	9,021	41	0.4	9.7	8.9	69.2	11.1	180	37	28
Deuel	1,024	1,032	1,075	–8	–0.8	2.3	2.4	78.0	4.9	7	1	1
Dixon	2,743	2,673	2,613	70	2.6	5.8	5.5	76.3	6.7	59	3	14
Dodge	15,950	15,468	14,601	482	3.1	29.8	27.3	67.8	17.0	746	112	127
Douglas	206,273	192,672	172,335	13,601	7.1	623.2	520.6	63.3	29.6	18,750	3,626	3,135
Dundy	1,210	1,196	1,326	14	1.2	1.3	1.4	72.7	6.4	1	–	–
Fillmore	2,997	2,990	3,102	7	0.2	5.2	5.4	74.5	6.6	51	6	4
Franklin	1,733	1,746	1,950	–13	–0.7	3.0	3.4	81.3	1.1	14	2	2
Frontier	1,572	1,543	1,565	29	1.9	1.6	1.6	72.5	4.3	23	7	11
Furnas	2,749	2,730	2,905	19	0.7	3.8	4.0	76.6	6.9	12	2	1
Gage	10,478	10,030	9,735	448	4.5	12.3	11.4	71.2	14.2	451	42	44
Garden	1,310	1,298	1,343	12	0.9	0.8	0.8	70.1	3.9	14	7	3
Garfield	1,032	1,021	1,021	11	1.1	1.8	1.8	72.6	5.2	6	1	1
Gosper	1,296	1,281	1,212	15	1.2	2.8	2.6	75.9	1.2	35	5	6
Grant	464	449	425	15	3.3	0.6	0.5	68.8	4.5	(NA)	–	–
Greeley	1,228	1,199	1,284	29	2.4	2.2	2.3	78.6	4.8	1	–	–
Hall	22,323	21,574	19,528	749	3.5	40.9	35.7	65.9	20.4	1,135	183	232
Hamilton	3,939	3,850	3,589	89	2.3	7.2	6.6	75.1	6.8	165	37	23
Harlan	2,371	2,327	2,409	44	1.9	4.3	4.4	80.3	3.1	35	2	12
Hayes	540	526	583	14	2.7	0.8	0.8	71.9	0.8	2	–	–
Hitchcock	1,685	1,675	1,873	10	0.6	2.4	2.6	78.2	2.2	5	1	–
Holt	5,435	5,281	5,472	154	2.9	2.3	2.3	73.6	6.9	114	16	12
Hooker	442	440	433	2	0.5	0.6	0.6	74.3	5.5	4	2	2
Howard	2,947	2,782	2,598	165	5.9	5.2	4.6	76.9	5.8	224	34	27
Jefferson	3,977	3,942	4,082	35	0.9	6.9	7.1	76.1	8.1	51	20	11
Johnson	2,169	2,116	2,153	53	2.5	5.8	5.7	75.3	9.3	46	5	7
Kearney	2,855	2,846	2,756	9	0.3	5.5	5.3	74.3	4.4	40	9	2
Keith	5,465	5,178	4,938	287	5.5	5.1	4.7	72.9	8.1	339	18	20
Keya Paha	572	548	584	24	4.4	0.7	0.8	72.1	3.6	(NA)	2	6
Kimball	1,983	1,972	1,967	11	0.6	2.1	2.1	76.3	6.3	12	2	2
Knox	4,867	4,773	4,799	94	2.0	4.4	4.3	75.0	5.5	109	43	45
Lancaster	113,873	104,217	86,734	9,656	9.3	135.7	103.4	60.5	31.7	12,084	1,699	2,616
Lincoln	16,065	15,438	14,210	627	4.1	6.3	5.5	69.2	14.0	908	134	172
Logan	399	386	387	13	3.4	0.7	0.7	71.5	1.3	(NA)	–	–
Loup	387	377	399	10	2.7	0.7	0.7	78.2	0.5	2	–	1
McPherson	293	283	257	10	3.5	0.3	0.3	67.3	2.1	(NA)	–	–
Madison	14,909	14,432	13,069	477	3.3	26.0	22.8	65.6	23.1	757	137	154
Merrick	3,737	3,649	3,533	88	2.4	7.7	7.3	74.1	6.1	165	33	30
Morrill	2,493	2,460	2,530	33	1.3	1.8	1.8	71.4	4.1	5	2	–
Nance	1,780	1,787	1,807	–7	–0.4	4.0	4.1	74.7	4.6	18	6	6
Nemaha	3,517	3,439	3,432	78	2.3	8.6	8.4	72.5	11.7	90	34	12
Nuckolls	2,571	2,530	2,699	41	1.6	4.5	4.7	80.0	6.0	24	–	18
Otoe	6,873	6,567	6,137	306	4.7	11.2	10.0	74.0	11.6	436	71	68
Pawnee	1,620	1,587	1,674	33	2.1	3.8	3.9	80.7	4.9	7	–	1
Perkins	1,463	1,444	1,537	19	1.3	1.7	1.7	75.7	5.4	8	1	1
Phelps	4,260	4,191	4,084	69	1.6	7.9	7.6	73.4	8.2	99	27	25
Pierce	3,332	3,247	3,177	85	2.6	5.8	5.5	77.6	3.3	147	25	33

See footnotes at end of table.

Table B-7. Counties — **Housing Units and Building Permits**—Con.

[Includes United States, states, and 3,141 counties/county equivalents defined as of February 22, 2005. For more information on these areas, see Appendix C, Geographic Information]

County	Housing units 2005 (July 1)	2000[1] (April 1 esti-mates base)	1990 (April 1)	Net change, 2000–2005 Number	Net change, 2000–2005 Percent	Units per square mile of land area 2005[2]	Units per square mile of land area 1990	Housing 2000, percent Owner-occupied housing units[3]	Housing 2000, percent Units in multi-unit structures	New private housing units authorized by building permits Cumulative, 2000–2005 period	2005	2004
NEBRASKA—Con.												
Platte	13,213	12,803	11,716	410	3.2	19.5	17.3	73.3	15.7	443	69	55
Polk	2,780	2,717	2,742	63	2.3	6.3	6.2	77.2	4.9	39	7	2
Red Willow	5,361	5,279	5,279	82	1.6	7.5	7.4	70.6	12.9	89	5	13
Richardson	4,585	4,560	4,704	25	0.5	8.3	8.5	74.9	8.6	15	1	4
Rock	950	935	1,001	15	1.6	0.9	1.0	73.0	4.2	11	1	1
Saline	5,717	5,611	5,299	106	1.9	9.9	9.2	70.7	11.9	219	47	26
Sarpy	54,560	44,981	35,994	9,579	21.3	226.8	149.6	69.2	19.2	11,607	1,993	2,307
Saunders	8,856	8,266	7,594	590	7.1	11.7	10.1	79.7	7.3	833	166	141
Scotts Bluff	16,348	16,119	15,514	229	1.4	22.1	21.0	66.2	16.0	437	39	50
Seward	6,756	6,428	5,908	328	5.1	11.8	10.3	72.0	14.0	463	81	90
Sheridan	3,019	3,013	3,211	6	0.2	1.2	1.3	70.2	5.3	9	3	3
Sherman	1,846	1,839	1,874	7	0.4	3.3	3.3	80.0	3.0	34	6	6
Sioux	803	780	869	23	2.9	0.4	0.4	66.6	1.8	(NA)	8	4
Stanton	2,497	2,452	2,355	45	1.8	5.8	5.5	80.0	3.0	94	22	14
Thayer	2,863	2,828	3,017	35	1.2	5.0	5.3	80.0	4.8	38	5	10
Thomas	462	446	404	16	3.6	0.6	0.6	73.2	2.0	(NA)	–	–
Thurston	2,483	2,467	2,548	16	0.6	6.3	6.5	60.8	10.3	73	34	5
Valley	2,279	2,273	2,469	6	0.3	4.0	4.3	75.7	7.7	24	9	7
Washington	7,918	7,408	6,378	510	6.9	20.3	16.3	77.2	13.3	690	119	125
Wayne	3,737	3,662	3,517	75	2.0	8.4	7.9	64.9	15.9	71	12	13
Webster	1,988	1,972	2,048	16	0.8	3.5	3.6	78.6	7.4	16	3	7
Wheeler	578	561	561	17	3.0	1.0	1.0	69.3	3.0	–	–	–
York	6,229	6,172	5,861	57	0.9	10.8	10.2	69.5	16.4	161	34	32
NEVADA	1,019,427	827,457	518,858	191,970	23.2	9.3	4.7	60.9	32.2	239,675	47,728	44,556
Churchill	10,332	9,732	7,290	600	6.2	2.1	1.5	65.8	11.7	979	312	277
Clark	718,358	559,784	317,188	158,574	28.3	90.8	40.1	59.1	36.3	197,451	39,237	36,395
Douglas	22,114	19,006	14,121	3,108	16.4	31.2	19.9	74.3	12.5	3,739	613	553
Elko	19,066	18,456	13,461	610	3.3	1.1	0.8	69.9	16.1	941	198	309
Esmeralda	865	833	966	32	3.8	0.2	0.3	67.0	14.5	(NA)	–	–
Eureka	1,064	1,025	817	39	3.8	0.3	0.2	73.7	3.6	(NA)	–	–
Humboldt	7,030	6,954	5,044	76	1.1	0.7	0.5	72.9	9.2	193	58	47
Lander	2,765	2,780	2,586	-15	-0.5	0.5	0.5	77.2	3.8	16	4	2
Lincoln	2,231	2,178	1,800	53	2.4	0.2	0.2	75.1	9.0	103	27	24
Lyon	16,647	14,279	8,722	2,368	16.6	8.3	4.4	75.8	8.1	3,144	733	931
Mineral	2,870	2,866	2,994	4	0.1	0.8	0.8	72.5	10.7	34	2	10
Nye	16,548	15,949	8,073	599	3.8	0.9	0.4	76.4	6.4	–	–	–
Pershing	2,380	2,389	1,908	-9	-0.4	0.4	0.3	69.5	9.3	21	5	5
Storey	1,755	1,596	1,085	159	10.0	6.7	4.1	79.8	8.3	217	47	51
Washoe	168,342	143,908	112,193	24,434	17.0	26.5	17.7	59.3	32.5	31,132	6,282	5,692
White Pine	4,451	4,439	3,982	12	0.3	0.5	0.4	76.6	8.7	84	20	28
Independent City												
Carson City	22,609	21,283	16,628	1,326	6.2	157.7	115.8	63.1	25.2	1,621	190	232
NEW HAMPSHIRE	583,324	547,024	503,904	36,300	6.6	65.0	56.2	69.7	26.5	46,892	7,586	8,653
Belknap	34,667	32,121	30,306	2,546	7.9	86.4	75.5	74.1	17.7	3,330	648	507
Carroll	37,565	34,750	32,146	2,815	8.1	40.2	34.4	77.8	12.1	3,585	641	730
Cheshire	33,326	31,876	30,350	1,450	4.5	47.1	42.9	70.8	22.3	2,000	331	421
Coos	19,967	19,623	18,712	344	1.8	11.1	10.4	71.2	23.9	584	126	133
Grafton	46,173	43,729	42,206	2,444	5.6	26.9	24.6	68.6	24.4	3,222	566	666
Hillsborough	159,315	149,961	135,622	9,354	6.2	181.8	154.7	64.9	36.0	12,220	1,862	2,160
Merrimack	60,571	56,245	50,870	4,326	7.7	64.8	54.4	69.5	26.6	5,707	831	1,023
Rockingham	121,382	113,022	101,773	8,360	7.4	174.7	146.4	75.6	23.0	10,401	1,667	1,888
Strafford	49,131	45,539	42,387	3,592	7.9	133.2	114.9	64.5	30.4	4,435	668	822
Sullivan	21,227	20,158	19,532	1,069	5.3	39.5	36.3	72.0	20.4	1,408	246	303
NEW JERSEY	3,443,981	3,310,274	3,075,310	133,707	4.0	464.3	414.5	65.6	36.1	200,801	38,588	35,936
Atlantic	123,025	114,090	106,877	8,935	7.8	219.3	190.5	66.4	33.4	11,692	2,002	2,075
Bergen	346,033	339,820	324,817	6,213	1.8	1,477.7	1,386.9	67.2	40.4	12,805	2,972	2,142
Burlington	171,133	161,310	143,236	9,823	6.1	212.7	178.0	77.4	20.1	12,114	1,475	1,516
Camden	203,760	199,679	190,145	4,081	2.0	916.6	855.2	70.0	24.7	7,766	1,706	1,413
Cape May	98,354	91,047	85,537	7,307	8.0	385.4	335.2	74.2	36.2	10,342	2,433	2,149
Cumberland	54,192	52,863	50,294	1,329	2.5	110.8	102.8	67.9	21.8	2,391	630	566
Essex	306,412	301,011	298,710	5,401	1.8	2,426.6	2,365.3	45.6	61.7	12,333	3,128	2,343
Gloucester	103,137	95,054	82,459	8,083	8.5	317.6	253.8	79.9	16.8	10,758	2,075	2,050
Hudson	247,446	240,618	229,682	6,828	2.8	5,299.8	4,923.5	30.7	84.2	14,410	4,498	3,808
Hunterdon	48,085	45,032	39,987	3,053	6.8	111.8	93.0	83.6	13.8	3,871	506	648
Mercer	138,901	133,280	123,666	5,621	4.2	614.8	547.3	67.0	29.0	8,191	1,296	1,641
Middlesex	282,858	273,637	250,174	9,221	3.4	913.3	805.4	66.7	34.4	14,477	3,206	2,622
Monmouth	252,569	240,884	218,408	11,685	4.9	535.2	462.9	74.6	23.6	15,446	2,584	2,628
Morris	182,328	174,379	155,745	7,949	4.6	388.8	332.0	76.0	23.5	11,660	2,503	1,427
Ocean	268,843	248,711	219,863	20,132	8.1	422.5	345.5	83.2	13.5	23,728	2,904	3,818

See footnotes at end of table.

Table B-7. Counties — **Housing Units and Building Permits**—Con.

[Includes United States, states, and 3,141 counties/county equivalents defined as of February 22, 2005. For more information on these areas, see Appendix C, Geographic Information]

County	Housing units							Housing 2000, percent		New private housing units authorized by building permits		
	2005 (July 1)	2000[1] (April 1 estimates base)	1990 (April 1)	Net change, 2000–2005 Number	Percent	Units per square mile of land area 2005[2]	1990	Owner-occupied housing units[3]	Units in multi-unit structures	Cumulative, 2000–2005 period	2005	2004
NEW JERSEY—Con.												
Passaic	171,315	170,048	162,512	1,267	0.7	924.6	878.2	55.6	52.1	4,016	647	763
Salem	27,063	26,158	25,349	905	3.5	80.1	75.0	73.0	17.6	1,449	297	334
Somerset	119,260	112,023	92,653	7,237	6.5	391.4	304.0	77.2	24.7	9,093	1,220	1,362
Sussex	59,546	56,529	51,574	3,017	5.3	114.2	98.9	82.7	13.6	4,073	668	612
Union	195,112	192,945	187,033	2,167	1.1	1,889.0	1,810.8	61.6	42.5	5,883	1,278	1,399
Warren	44,609	41,156	36,589	3,453	8.4	124.7	102.2	72.7	21.5	4,303	560	620
NEW MEXICO	838,668	780,579	632,058	58,089	7.4	6.9	5.2	70.0	15.3	[4]71,418	[4]14,180	[4]12,555
Bernalillo	266,266	238,801	201,235	27,465	11.5	228.4	172.6	63.7	27.2	32,227	5,416	5,884
Catron	2,873	2,548	1,552	325	12.8	0.4	0.2	80.6	0.5	(NA)	–	–
Chaves	25,938	25,647	23,386	291	1.1	4.3	3.9	70.9	10.6	271	78	52
Cibola	10,688	10,328	9,692	360	3.5	2.4	2.1	77.0	9.5	(NA)	–	–
Colfax	9,410	8,959	8,265	451	5.0	2.5	2.2	72.6	12.7	(NA)	72	65
Curry	19,988	19,212	16,906	776	4.0	14.2	12.0	59.4	12.5	783	144	228
De Baca	1,418	1,307	1,329	111	8.5	0.6	0.6	78.0	4.4	(NA)	–	–
Dona Ana	72,372	65,210	49,148	7,162	11.0	19.0	12.9	67.5	16.3	9,142	2,511	1,675
Eddy	22,646	22,249	20,134	397	1.8	5.4	4.8	74.3	9.4	341	85	65
Grant	14,457	14,066	11,349	391	2.8	3.6	2.9	74.4	7.3	(NA)	–	–
Guadalupe	2,309	2,160	2,149	149	6.9	0.8	0.7	73.8	8.8	(NA)	–	–
Harding	636	545	614	91	16.7	0.3	0.3	75.2	1.3	(NA)	–	–
Hidalgo	3,033	2,848	2,413	185	6.5	0.9	0.7	67.9	6.1	(NA)	–	–
Lea	23,859	23,405	23,333	454	1.9	5.4	5.3	72.6	8.4	214	45	107
Lincoln	16,279	15,298	12,622	981	6.4	3.4	2.6	77.2	8.6	1,231	278	239
Los Alamos	8,607	7,937	7,565	670	8.4	78.7	69.2	78.6	23.9	766	65	105
Luna	11,737	11,291	7,766	446	4.0	4.0	2.6	74.9	9.0	321	87	62
McKinley	27,475	26,718	20,933	757	2.8	5.0	3.8	72.4	8.3	305	21	21
Mora	3,096	2,973	2,486	123	4.1	1.6	1.3	82.4	0.9	(NA)	–	–
Otero	30,340	29,272	23,177	1,068	3.6	4.6	3.5	66.9	7.6	1,008	290	223
Quay	5,859	5,664	5,576	195	3.4	2.0	1.9	70.6	7.7	(NA)	–	–
Rio Arriba	18,571	18,017	14,357	554	3.1	3.2	2.5	81.6	2.1	63	13	14
Roosevelt	8,049	7,746	6,902	303	3.9	3.3	2.8	62.7	9.8	211	35	45
Sandoval	40,761	35,139	23,667	5,622	16.0	11.0	6.4	83.6	7.1	5,793	1,214	1,225
San Juan	44,630	43,221	34,248	1,409	3.3	8.1	6.2	75.4	8.9	1,779	439	351
San Miguel	14,681	14,254	11,066	427	3.0	3.1	2.3	73.1	8.0	(NA)	–	–
Santa Fe	61,051	57,699	41,464	3,352	5.8	32.0	21.7	68.6	15.7	3,238	580	561
Sierra	9,082	8,727	6,457	355	4.1	2.2	1.5	74.9	9.6	(NA)	7	30
Socorro	8,182	7,808	6,289	374	4.8	1.2	0.9	71.1	8.6	75	23	4
Taos	18,406	17,404	12,200	1,002	5.8	8.4	5.5	75.5	9.7	1,359	308	272
Torrance	7,557	7,258	4,878	299	4.1	2.3	1.5	83.9	1.5	(NA)	–	–
Union	2,403	2,225	2,299	178	8.0	0.6	0.6	73.0	3.8	(NA)	–	–
Valencia	26,009	24,643	16,781	1,366	5.5	24.4	15.7	83.9	4.6	2,129	408	346
NEW YORK	7,853,020	7,679,307	7,226,891	173,713	2.3	166.3	153.0	53.0	50.6	303,950	61,949	53,497
Albany	132,706	129,972	124,255	2,734	2.1	253.5	237.2	57.7	44.5	5,018	850	912
Allegany	24,856	24,505	21,951	351	1.4	23.8	21.3	73.8	12.5	680	91	112
Bronx	502,211	490,659	440,955	11,552	2.4	11,948.9	10,491.4	19.6	88.7	19,284	4,937	4,924
Broome	88,915	88,817	87,969	98	0.1	125.8	124.5	65.1	33.3	1,375	210	211
Cattaraugus	40,270	39,839	36,839	431	1.1	30.7	28.1	74.4	16.8	1,048	204	203
Cayuga	35,890	35,477	33,280	413	1.2	51.8	48.0	72.1	22.5	979	161	173
Chautauqua	65,515	64,900	62,682	615	0.9	61.7	59.0	69.2	25.6	1,885	446	265
Chemung	38,026	37,745	37,290	281	0.7	93.2	91.4	68.9	27.0	845	107	95
Chenango	24,109	23,890	22,164	219	0.9	27.0	24.8	75.3	15.8	571	124	126
Clinton	34,125	33,091	32,190	1,034	3.1	32.8	31.0	68.5	22.1	1,638	325	275
Columbia	31,377	30,207	29,139	1,170	3.9	49.4	45.8	70.6	18.6	1,815	335	360
Cortland	20,289	20,116	18,681	173	0.9	40.6	37.4	64.3	30.3	461	57	110
Delaware	29,456	28,952	27,361	504	1.7	20.4	18.9	75.7	12.0	929	168	180
Dutchess	110,712	106,103	97,632	4,609	4.3	138.1	121.8	69.0	26.6	6,534	1,012	1,049
Erie	421,954	415,868	402,131	6,086	1.5	404.1	384.9	65.3	40.0	12,690	1,623	1,932
Essex	24,054	23,115	21,493	939	4.1	13.4	12.0	73.8	14.3	1,471	292	292
Franklin	24,314	23,936	21,962	378	1.6	14.9	13.5	70.5	15.6	790	165	176
Fulton	27,993	27,787	26,260	206	0.7	56.4	52.9	72.1	24.7	640	110	105
Genesee	24,438	24,190	22,596	248	1.0	49.5	45.7	73.0	23.7	620	92	110
Greene	27,646	26,544	25,000	1,102	4.2	42.7	38.6	72.1	17.2	1,718	375	446
Hamilton	8,195	7,965	8,234	230	2.9	4.8	4.8	79.3	3.2	373	73	84
Herkimer	32,367	32,026	30,799	341	1.1	22.9	21.8	71.2	21.7	851	162	162
Jefferson	54,627	54,070	50,519	557	1.0	42.9	39.7	59.7	25.6	1,454	395	228
Kings	947,632	930,867	873,671	16,765	1.8	13,420.6	12,387.2	27.1	86.2	33,031	9,028	6,825
Lewis	15,898	15,134	13,182	764	5.0	12.5	10.3	77.2	11.3	1,030	137	151
Livingston	24,823	24,023	23,084	800	3.3	39.3	36.5	74.5	17.9	1,209	208	176
Madison	29,245	28,646	26,641	599	2.1	44.6	40.6	75.0	18.3	1,093	214	222
Monroe	311,917	304,388	285,524	7,529	2.5	473.1	433.1	65.1	31.6	12,385	1,743	2,009
Montgomery	22,565	22,522	21,851	43	0.2	55.7	54.0	67.3	36.9	423	82	79
Nassau	458,011	458,151	446,292	–140	(Z)	1,597.6	1,556.3	80.3	19.7	7,070	1,435	1,177

See footnotes at end of table.

322

County and City Data Book: 2007

U.S. Census Bureau

[Includes United States, states, and 3,141 counties/county equivalents defined as of February 22, 2005. For more information on these areas, see Appendix C, Geographic Information]

County	Housing units 2005 (July 1)	2000[1] (April 1 esti-mates base)	1990 (April 1)	Net change, 2000–2005 Number	Percent	Units per square mile of land area 2005[2]	1990	Housing 2000, percent Owner-occupied housing units[3]	Units in multi-unit structures	New private housing units authorized by building permits Cumu-lative, 2000–2005 period	2005	2004
NEW YORK—Con.												
New York	819,796	798,144	785,127	21,652	2.7	35,705.4	27,664.8	20.1	99.1	34,906	8,493	4,555
Niagara	97,423	95,715	90,385	1,708	1.8	186.3	172.8	69.9	29.8	3,257	473	578
Oneida	103,174	102,803	101,251	371	0.4	85.1	83.5	67.2	33.7	2,036	434	350
Onondaga	200,736	196,633	190,878	4,103	2.1	257.3	244.6	64.5	33.7	7,370	1,200	1,157
Ontario	44,708	42,647	38,947	2,061	4.8	69.4	60.4	73.6	20.6	2,863	429	531
Orange	131,436	122,754	110,814	8,682	7.1	161.0	135.7	67.0	28.2	11,450	1,830	1,714
Orleans	17,510	17,347	16,345	163	0.9	44.7	41.8	75.6	18.4	421	56	96
Oswego	53,730	52,831	48,548	899	1.7	56.4	50.9	72.8	17.3	1,615	232	254
Otsego	30,425	28,481	26,385	1,944	6.8	30.3	26.3	73.0	16.2	2,360	167	168
Putnam	36,379	35,070	31,898	1,309	3.7	157.3	137.8	82.2	13.3	1,743	141	196
Queens	831,819	817,250	752,690	14,569	1.8	7,614.6	6,880.2	42.8	69.1	27,972	7,269	6,853
Rensselaer	67,967	66,120	62,591	1,847	2.8	103.9	95.7	64.9	37.7	3,504	896	596
Richmond	173,954	163,993	139,726	9,961	6.1	2,974.6	2,384.0	63.8	41.8	13,238	1,872	2,051
Rockland	96,720	94,973	88,264	1,747	1.8	555.2	506.6	71.7	29.9	2,712	476	481
St. Lawrence	50,478	49,720	47,521	758	1.5	18.8	17.7	70.6	16.5	1,500	235	260
Saratoga	92,540	86,701	75,105	5,839	6.7	114.0	92.5	72.0	24.0	7,671	1,379	1,279
Schenectady	65,796	65,032	62,769	764	1.2	319.2	304.5	65.4	37.4	1,982	363	367
Schoharie	16,281	15,915	14,431	366	2.3	26.2	23.2	75.2	14.6	648	151	114
Schuyler	9,332	9,181	8,472	151	1.6	28.4	25.8	77.1	10.4	286	46	48
Seneca	14,838	14,794	14,314	44	0.3	45.7	44.1	73.8	15.4	242	38	42
Steuben	46,782	46,132	43,019	650	1.4	33.6	30.9	73.2	17.9	1,318	197	177
Suffolk	538,826	522,323	481,317	16,503	3.2	590.7	528.2	79.8	13.2	25,704	5,183	3,397
Sullivan	46,998	44,730	41,814	2,268	5.1	48.5	43.1	68.1	18.2	3,665	975	823
Tioga	21,668	21,410	20,254	258	1.2	41.8	39.0	77.8	14.8	528	73	78
Tompkins	40,164	38,625	35,338	1,539	4.0	84.4	74.2	53.7	37.7	2,171	340	241
Ulster	80,509	77,656	71,716	2,853	3.7	71.5	63.7	68.0	21.5	4,547	910	864
Warren	36,713	34,852	31,737	1,861	5.3	42.2	36.5	69.8	19.2	2,688	534	530
Washington	27,695	26,794	24,216	901	3.4	33.2	29.0	74.4	17.2	1,812	648	279
Wayne	39,708	38,767	35,188	941	2.4	65.7	58.2	77.6	16.5	1,599	294	233
Westchester	355,224	349,405	336,727	5,819	1.7	820.7	777.9	60.1	49.8	11,155	1,226	1,790
Wyoming	17,211	16,940	15,848	271	1.6	29.0	26.7	76.7	16.0	540	96	101
Yates	12,344	12,064	11,629	280	2.3	36.5	34.4	77.1	11.3	537	132	125
NORTH CAROLINA	3,940,554	3,522,334	2,818,193	418,220	11.9	80.9	57.8	69.4	16.1	510,443	97,910	93,077
Alamance	61,039	55,461	45,312	5,578	10.1	142.0	105.2	70.1	15.3	7,319	1,484	1,366
Alexander	15,014	14,104	11,197	910	6.5	57.7	43.0	80.5	3.2	1,007	157	189
Alleghany	6,956	6,421	5,344	535	8.3	29.6	22.8	78.9	5.7	643	113	107
Anson	10,479	10,221	9,255	258	2.5	19.7	17.4	75.9	5.5	327	60	72
Ashe	14,657	13,268	11,119	1,389	10.5	34.4	26.1	81.0	5.6	1,719	340	291
Avery	12,926	11,911	8,923	1,015	8.5	52.3	36.1	80.6	16.9	1,231	288	267
Beaufort	23,273	22,139	19,598	1,134	5.1	28.1	23.7	75.0	6.8	1,410	316	255
Bertie	9,307	9,043	8,331	264	2.9	13.3	11.9	74.9	1.7	283	36	63
Bladen	15,838	15,316	12,685	522	3.4	18.1	14.5	77.8	4.8	572	88	118
Brunswick	64,647	51,430	37,114	13,217	25.7	75.6	43.4	82.2	6.9	17,604	4,710	3,829
Buncombe	103,252	93,954	77,951	9,298	9.9	157.4	118.8	70.3	15.5	11,995	2,549	2,073
Burke	38,922	37,429	31,575	1,493	4.0	76.8	62.3	74.1	8.7	1,666	266	243
Cabarrus	62,620	52,848	39,713	9,772	18.5	171.8	109.0	74.7	12.1	12,449	2,659	2,153
Caldwell	35,462	33,420	29,454	2,042	6.1	75.2	62.4	74.9	9.4	2,355	362	394
Camden	3,586	2,973	2,466	613	20.6	14.9	10.2	83.4	1.8	761	141	132
Carteret	44,109	40,947	34,576	3,162	7.7	84.9	65.1	76.6	14.5	4,062	1,035	744
Caswell	10,108	9,601	8,254	507	5.3	23.8	19.4	79.3	3.0	557	80	104
Catawba	65,724	59,913	49,192	5,811	9.7	164.3	123.0	72.5	15.1	6,599	841	1,059
Chatham	24,339	21,358	16,642	2,981	14.0	35.6	24.4	77.2	7.7	3,628	709	663
Cherokee	15,328	13,499	10,319	1,829	13.5	33.7	22.7	82.2	3.7	2,332	531	485
Chowan	6,697	6,443	5,910	254	3.9	38.8	34.2	72.2	9.7	484	225	77
Clay	6,255	5,425	4,158	830	15.3	29.1	19.4	84.5	2.9	1,058	242	192
Cleveland	42,390	40,313	34,232	2,077	5.2	91.2	73.7	72.8	8.9	2,615	492	472
Columbus	24,685	24,060	20,513	625	2.6	26.4	21.9	76.4	4.1	659	97	104
Craven	42,221	38,194	32,293	4,027	10.5	59.6	46.4	66.7	13.9	4,872	1,285	1,032
Cumberland	128,305	118,426	98,360	9,879	8.3	196.6	150.6	59.4	17.4	13,623	3,665	3,005
Currituck	13,119	10,687	7,367	2,432	22.8	50.1	28.1	81.6	2.2	2,881	485	574
Dare	31,279	26,671	21,567	4,608	17.3	81.5	56.5	74.5	8.9	5,506	726	858
Davidson	66,909	62,433	53,266	4,476	7.2	121.2	96.5	74.2	9.4	5,424	1,104	864
Davie	16,665	14,953	11,496	1,712	11.4	62.8	43.3	83.3	5.0	2,126	449	395
Duplin	21,300	20,520	16,395	780	3.8	26.0	20.0	74.9	4.6	854	142	149
Durham	110,792	95,452	77,710	15,340	16.1	381.6	267.4	54.3	36.0	17,612	2,431	2,919
Edgecombe	25,038	24,006	21,827	1,032	4.3	49.6	43.2	64.1	12.6	687	74	95
Forsyth	146,751	133,092	115,715	13,659	10.3	358.3	282.5	65.6	24.3	17,194	3,138	3,235
Franklin	22,746	20,364	14,957	2,382	11.7	46.2	30.4	77.8	3.0	2,782	539	488

See footnotes at end of table.

[Includes United States, states, and 3,141 counties/county equivalents defined as of February 22, 2005. For more information on these areas, see Appendix C, Geographic Information]

County	Housing units							Housing 2000, percent		New private housing units authorized by building permits		
	2005 (July 1)	2000[1] (April 1 esti- mates base)	1990 (April 1)	Net change, 2000–2005 Number	Percent	Units per square mile of land area 2005[2]	1990	Owner- occupied housing units[3]	Units in multi- unit structures	Cumu- lative, 2000– 2005 period	2005	2004
NORTH CAROLINA—Con.												
Gaston	84,759	78,820	69,133	5,939	7.5	237.9	193.9	68.8	13.7	7,543	1,427	1,310
Gates	4,506	4,389	3,696	117	2.7	13.2	10.9	82.1	0.8	144	42	29
Graham	5,424	5,084	4,132	340	6.7	18.6	14.1	82.7	2.2	424	95	75
Granville	20,399	17,896	14,164	2,503	14.0	38.4	26.7	75.0	8.2	3,106	665	652
Greene	7,548	7,368	5,944	180	2.4	28.4	22.4	74.7	4.3	174	29	10
Guilford	200,648	180,391	146,812	20,257	11.2	309.0	225.8	62.7	26.4	26,998	4,995	4,978
Halifax	25,898	25,309	22,480	589	2.3	35.7	31.0	67.0	8.6	691	90	181
Harnett	42,932	38,605	27,896	4,327	11.2	72.2	46.9	70.3	7.4	5,336	1,190	993
Haywood	30,889	28,641	23,975	2,248	7.8	55.8	43.3	77.4	7.0	2,792	512	454
Henderson	47,781	43,015	34,131	4,766	11.1	127.8	91.3	78.8	8.3	5,714	1,035	1,066
Hertford	9,931	9,724	8,870	207	2.1	28.1	25.1	70.0	9.2	252	45	24
Hoke	14,674	12,518	7,999	2,156	17.2	37.5	20.4	75.0	5.3	2,752	660	523
Hyde	3,405	3,302	2,905	103	3.1	5.6	4.7	78.4	3.5	138	35	24
Iredell	62,092	51,918	39,191	10,174	19.6	107.9	68.2	75.4	9.2	12,609	2,546	2,387
Jackson	22,303	19,290	14,052	3,013	15.6	45.5	28.6	72.5	9.3	3,683	769	678
Johnston	58,660	50,163	34,172	8,497	16.9	74.1	43.1	73.4	6.6	10,240	1,956	1,545
Jones	4,736	4,697	3,829	39	0.8	10.0	8.1	79.8	2.2	47	25	7
Lee	21,565	19,983	16,954	1,582	7.9	83.8	65.9	71.7	12.9	2,147	557	402
Lenoir	27,972	27,160	23,739	812	3.0	70.0	59.4	67.0	13.3	869	77	121
Lincoln	29,518	25,717	20,189	3,801	14.8	98.8	67.6	78.5	7.0	4,417	734	708
McDowell	19,319	18,377	15,091	942	5.1	43.7	34.2	77.2	5.8	1,155	246	271
Macon	22,550	20,746	17,174	1,804	8.7	43.7	33.3	81.3	4.9	2,157	363	390
Madison	10,453	9,722	7,667	731	7.5	23.3	17.1	76.6	4.9	853	143	161
Martin	11,124	10,910	10,104	214	2.0	24.1	21.8	71.8	6.7	251	31	36
Mecklenburg	357,016	292,755	216,416	64,261	22.0	678.4	410.3	62.3	32.4	69,791	10,828	11,906
Mitchell	8,218	7,919	6,983	299	3.8	37.1	31.5	80.8	5.6	368	68	61
Montgomery	14,685	14,145	10,421	540	3.8	29.9	21.2	76.7	3.9	616	108	94
Moore	38,895	35,145	27,358	3,750	10.7	55.7	39.2	78.7	10.1	4,775	1,075	857
Nash	40,030	37,047	31,024	2,983	8.1	74.1	57.4	67.7	13.4	4,105	692	660
New Hanover	92,685	79,634	57,076	13,051	16.4	465.9	286.9	64.7	27.3	16,650	3,401	3,594
Northampton	10,727	10,455	8,974	272	2.6	20.0	16.7	77.0	3.8	425	177	53
Onslow	62,017	55,726	47,526	6,291	11.3	80.9	62.0	58.1	12.5	7,850	1,818	1,860
Orange	53,494	47,708	38,683	5,786	12.1	133.8	96.8	57.6	31.5	6,895	1,018	1,118
Pamlico	7,144	6,781	6,050	363	5.4	21.2	18.0	82.2	2.7	444	107	108
Pasquotank	15,353	14,289	12,298	1,064	7.4	67.7	54.2	65.7	16.0	1,661	548	429
Pender	23,509	20,798	15,437	2,711	13.0	27.0	17.7	82.6	4.5	3,786	1,095	909
Perquimans	6,472	6,043	4,972	429	7.1	26.2	20.1	78.6	3.8	578	161	132
Person	16,622	15,504	12,548	1,118	7.2	42.4	32.0	74.6	6.3	1,341	235	277
Pitt	67,726	58,364	43,070	9,362	16.0	103.9	66.1	58.1	29.7	11,889	2,548	2,191
Polk	10,014	9,192	7,273	822	8.9	42.1	30.6	78.7	8.9	992	165	155
Randolph	58,418	54,428	43,634	3,990	7.3	74.2	55.4	76.6	9.3	4,672	855	702
Richmond	21,336	19,886	18,218	1,450	7.3	45.0	38.4	71.9	8.7	1,846	392	331
Robeson	49,638	47,748	39,045	1,890	4.0	52.3	41.1	72.8	8.2	2,019	391	328
Rockingham	42,116	40,208	35,667	1,908	4.7	74.4	62.9	73.7	8.1	2,422	440	459
Rowan	57,840	53,980	46,264	3,860	7.2	113.1	90.5	73.6	10.3	4,625	870	766
Rutherford	31,110	29,536	25,220	1,574	5.3	55.1	44.7	74.5	8.4	2,017	437	344
Sampson	25,985	25,142	19,183	843	3.4	27.5	20.3	73.5	5.4	987	224	176
Scotland	15,219	14,693	12,759	526	3.6	47.7	40.0	69.2	11.5	567	69	78
Stanly	26,423	24,582	21,808	1,841	7.5	66.9	55.2	76.3	6.5	2,420	516	476
Stokes	20,175	19,262	15,160	913	4.7	44.7	33.6	82.1	3.6	1,140	266	192
Surry	32,158	31,024	26,022	1,134	3.7	59.9	48.5	76.3	7.7	1,306	188	228
Swain	7,823	7,105	5,664	718	10.1	14.8	10.7	76.8	5.0	832	136	148
Transylvania	16,788	15,553	12,893	1,235	7.9	44.4	34.1	79.4	6.2	1,559	323	241
Tyrrell	2,132	2,032	1,907	100	4.9	5.5	4.9	74.9	5.1	118	23	33
Union	59,917	45,723	30,760	14,194	31.0	94.0	48.3	80.5	6.2	17,915	3,972	3,312
Vance	18,885	18,196	15,743	689	3.8	74.5	62.1	66.3	9.9	769	118	124
Wake	314,400	258,961	177,146	55,439	21.4	377.9	212.4	65.9	27.1	68,318	12,119	12,371
Warren	11,145	10,548	8,714	597	5.7	26.0	20.3	77.4	3.2	706	155	139
Washington	6,236	6,174	5,644	62	1.0	17.9	16.2	73.6	7.5	84	19	10
Watauga	25,995	23,156	19,538	2,839	12.3	83.2	62.5	62.9	20.9	3,594	650	536
Wayne	49,883	47,313	39,483	2,570	5.4	90.3	71.4	65.4	12.1	3,119	607	540
Wilkes	30,478	29,261	24,960	1,217	4.2	40.3	33.0	77.9	5.8	1,396	231	289
Wilson	33,175	30,728	26,662	2,447	8.0	89.4	71.8	61.2	19.5	2,900	442	486
Yadkin	16,541	15,821	12,921	720	4.6	49.3	38.5	80.3	2.9	827	141	127
Yancey	10,307	9,729	7,994	578	5.9	33.0	25.6	80.2	4.4	731	156	146
NORTH DAKOTA	304,458	289,679	276,340	14,779	5.1	4.4	4.0	66.6	24.8	19,872	4,038	4,033
Adams	1,420	1,417	1,504	3	0.2	1.4	1.5	71.1	19.8	22	3	4
Barnes	5,694	5,599	5,801	95	1.7	3.8	3.9	71.2	20.2	203	50	49
Benson	2,999	2,932	3,163	67	2.3	2.2	2.3	68.3	8.4	–	–	–
Billings	528	529	533	–1	–0.2	0.5	0.5	76.8	8.5	6	1	1
Bottineau	4,526	4,409	4,661	117	2.7	2.7	2.8	80.0	6.8	29	6	8

See footnotes at end of table.

[Includes United States, states, and 3,141 counties/county equivalents defined as of February 22, 2005. For more information on these areas, see Appendix C, Geographic Information]

County	Housing units							Housing 2000, percent		New private housing units authorized by building permits		
	2005 (July 1)	2000[1] (April 1 esti- mates base)	1990 (April 1)	Net change, 2000–2005		Units per square mile of land area		Owner- occupied housing units[3]	Units in multi- unit structures	Cumu- lative, 2000– 2005 period	2005	2004
				Number	Percent	2005[2]	1990					
NORTH DAKOTA—Con.												
Bowman	1,594	1,596	1,691	−2	−0.1	1.4	1.5	79.4	7.0	17	1	5
Burke	1,428	1,412	1,691	16	1.1	1.3	1.5	84.4	5.1	10	3	1
Burleigh	31,951	29,004	23,803	2,947	10.2	19.6	14.6	68.0	30.4	3,706	557	657
Cass	61,356	53,790	42,407	7,566	14.1	34.8	24.0	54.3	44.4	9,870	2,047	2,075
Cavalier	2,751	2,725	3,038	26	1.0	1.8	2.0	81.5	11.3	11	2	–
Dickey	2,678	2,656	2,763	22	0.8	2.4	2.4	71.5	15.4	9	1	1
Divide	1,472	1,469	1,667	3	0.2	1.2	1.3	82.1	9.5	1	–	–
Dunn	1,960	1,965	2,057	−5	−0.3	1.0	1.0	80.0	5.1	18	4	4
Eddy	1,436	1,418	1,470	18	1.3	2.3	2.3	75.4	14.2	7	1	–
Emmons	2,177	2,168	2,200	9	0.4	1.4	1.5	83.4	6.1	34	1	4
Foster	1,795	1,793	1,876	2	0.1	2.8	3.0	74.4	15.6	21	5	4
Golden Valley	968	973	1,035	−5	−0.5	1.0	1.0	78.1	8.3	10	2	–
Grand Forks	28,538	27,373	27,085	1,165	4.3	19.8	18.8	53.9	39.6	1,922	501	472
Grant	1,755	1,722	2,011	33	1.9	1.1	1.2	79.3	5.5	7	–	3
Griggs	1,542	1,521	1,660	21	1.4	2.2	2.3	78.3	9.1	–	–	–
Hettinger	1,434	1,419	1,637	15	1.1	1.3	1.4	83.6	7.5	6	1	–
Kidder	1,669	1,610	1,672	59	3.7	1.2	1.2	81.7	3.9	25	4	4
LaMoure	2,327	2,271	2,434	56	2.5	2.0	2.1	80.6	8.1	29	3	1
Logan	1,209	1,193	1,335	16	1.3	1.2	1.3	85.8	3.3	3	–	2
McHenry	3,030	2,983	3,320	47	1.6	1.6	1.8	81.4	6.5	24	5	9
McIntosh	1,866	1,853	2,031	13	0.7	1.9	2.1	83.1	6.2	27	10	7
McKenzie	2,785	2,719	3,178	66	2.4	1.0	1.2	73.9	7.8	4	1	1
McLean	5,340	5,264	5,515	76	1.4	2.5	2.6	82.2	7.0	135	20	31
Mercer	4,462	4,402	4,496	60	1.4	4.3	4.3	84.5	14.4	47	8	6
Morton	11,280	10,587	9,467	693	6.5	5.9	4.9	75.5	15.7	976	185	195
Mountrail	3,495	3,436	3,675	59	1.7	1.9	2.0	72.6	9.2	113	19	48
Nelson	2,027	2,014	2,261	13	0.6	2.1	2.3	80.2	10.8	31	2	1
Oliver	898	903	968	−5	−0.6	1.2	1.3	85.7	4.4	5	–	1
Pembina	4,111	4,115	4,294	−4	−0.1	3.7	3.8	78.4	11.4	20	1	3
Pierce	2,280	2,269	2,355	11	0.5	2.2	2.3	72.9	14.9	17	3	–
Ramsey	5,799	5,729	5,616	70	1.2	4.9	4.7	65.0	26.4	73	12	13
Ransom	2,745	2,604	2,569	141	5.4	3.2	3.0	75.3	15.6	165	5	4
Renville	1,440	1,413	1,558	27	1.9	1.6	1.8	77.8	8.9	13	2	2
Richland	7,652	7,575	7,394	77	1.0	5.3	5.1	69.6	23.1	167	36	23
Rolette	5,025	5,027	4,742	−2	(Z)	5.6	5.3	67.4	10.0	8	–	1
Sargent	2,057	2,016	2,057	41	2.0	2.4	2.4	79.8	10.8	71	26	10
Sheridan	930	924	1,061	6	0.6	1.0	1.1	84.5	3.9	5	1	4
Sioux	1,260	1,216	1,175	44	3.6	1.2	1.1	46.3	8.9	–	–	–
Slope	462	451	481	11	2.4	0.4	0.4	86.9	–	–	–	–
Stark	10,023	9,722	9,585	301	3.1	7.5	7.2	70.3	22.9	447	144	80
Steele	1,246	1,231	1,311	15	1.2	1.7	1.8	77.2	6.6	14	11	3
Stutsman	9,901	9,817	9,770	84	0.9	4.5	4.4	67.2	22.5	209	38	48
Towner	1,578	1,558	1,770	20	1.3	1.5	1.7	73.9	14.2	–	–	–
Traill	3,740	3,708	3,770	32	0.9	4.3	4.4	72.6	18.2	67	20	13
Walsh	5,739	5,757	6,093	−18	−0.3	4.5	4.8	76.8	14.1	38	6	4
Ward	25,668	25,099	23,585	569	2.3	12.8	11.7	62.6	24.8	1,023	234	195
Wells	2,668	2,643	2,869	25	0.9	2.1	2.3	76.5	12.6	5	1	1
Williams	9,744	9,680	10,180	64	0.7	4.7	4.9	71.4	18.6	202	55	35
OHIO	5,007,091	4,783,066	4,371,945	224,025	4.7	122.3	106.8	69.1	24.1	303,385	47,727	51,695
Adams	12,092	11,822	10,237	270	2.3	20.7	17.5	73.9	6.2	10	–	4
Allen	45,118	44,245	42,758	873	2.0	111.6	105.7	72.1	18.2	1,614	320	369
Ashland	21,653	20,832	18,139	821	3.9	51.0	42.7	75.6	14.1	1,284	358	214
Ashtabula	45,465	43,792	41,214	1,673	3.8	64.7	58.7	74.1	15.0	2,222	214	375
Athens	25,226	24,901	21,737	325	1.3	49.8	42.9	60.5	22.4	210	26	43
Auglaize	19,233	18,470	16,907	763	4.1	47.9	42.1	77.9	12.9	1,091	190	209
Belmont	31,393	31,236	30,575	157	0.5	58.4	56.9	75.0	15.7	222	41	96
Brown	18,059	17,193	13,720	866	5.0	36.7	27.9	79.6	7.8	826	202	225
Butler	139,840	129,749	110,353	10,091	7.8	299.3	236.1	71.6	22.5	15,656	2,777	3,060
Carroll	13,102	13,016	11,536	86	0.7	33.2	29.2	80.0	6.6	89	5	33
Champaign	16,714	15,890	14,030	824	5.2	39.0	32.7	75.9	14.3	1,043	114	212
Clark	61,925	61,055	58,377	870	1.4	154.9	145.9	71.5	19.8	1,669	287	258
Clermont	76,707	69,026	55,315	7,681	11.1	169.7	122.4	74.7	20.1	9,055	1,528	1,311
Clinton	17,655	16,576	13,740	1,079	6.5	43.0	33.4	68.9	16.9	1,340	264	249
Columbiana	46,984	46,083	44,035	901	2.0	88.2	82.7	76.0	12.7	815	193	142
Coshocton	16,247	16,107	14,964	140	0.9	28.8	26.5	76.0	10.2	45	5	7
Crawford	20,445	20,178	19,514	267	1.3	50.8	48.5	72.6	18.0	632	60	148
Cuyahoga	620,564	616,876	604,538	3,688	0.6	1,353.5	1,319.1	63.2	35.8	12,749	1,993	2,248
Darke	22,181	21,583	20,338	598	2.8	37.0	33.9	76.6	12.4	921	169	127
Defiance	16,634	16,040	14,737	594	3.7	40.5	35.8	79.6	11.8	895	201	140

See footnotes at end of table.

[Includes United States, states, and 3,141 counties/county equivalents defined as of February 22, 2005. For more information on these areas, see Appendix C, Geographic Information]

County	Housing units								Housing 2000, percent		New private housing units authorized by building permits		
	2005 (July 1)	2000[1] (April 1 esti-mates base)	1990 (April 1)	Net change, 2000–2005		Units per square mile of land area			Owner-occupied housing units[3]	Units in multi-unit structures	Cumu-lative, 2000–2005 period	2005	2004
				Number	Percent	2005[2]	1990						
OHIO—Con.													
Delaware	57,012	42,374	24,377	14,638	34.5	128.9	55.1		80.4	16.1	16,210	1,957	2,437
Erie	37,082	35,909	32,827	1,173	3.3	145.5	129.0		72.0	20.9	1,874	423	356
Fairfield	54,637	47,934	39,014	6,703	14.0	108.2	77.1		76.3	14.6	6,826	992	1,265
Fayette	12,403	11,904	10,816	499	4.2	30.5	26.6		66.6	17.3	775	181	162
Franklin	512,706	471,007	405,418	41,699	8.9	949.7	750.8		56.9	37.5	53,271	7,284	7,086
Fulton	17,057	16,232	14,095	825	5.1	41.9	34.6		80.1	11.2	1,061	171	222
Gallia	13,477	13,498	12,564	−21	−0.2	28.7	26.8		74.9	8.3	24	1	6
Geauga	34,940	32,805	27,922	2,135	6.5	86.6	69.1		87.2	6.8	2,632	365	435
Greene	63,707	58,224	50,238	5,483	9.4	153.6	121.1		69.7	20.2	6,431	1,367	1,192
Guernsey	19,540	18,771	17,262	769	4.1	37.4	33.1		73.4	13.2	460	74	61
Hamilton	382,982	373,381	361,421	9,601	2.6	940.2	887.2		59.9	39.7	11,828	2,107	1,582
Hancock	31,846	29,785	26,107	2,061	6.9	59.9	49.1		73.1	18.9	3,043	981	991
Hardin	13,154	12,907	11,976	247	1.9	28.0	25.5		73.0	15.4	293	39	53
Harrison	7,785	7,680	7,301	105	1.4	19.3	18.1		77.6	7.1	10	3	3
Henry	12,040	11,622	11,000	418	3.6	28.9	26.4		80.5	10.1	509	81	84
Highland	18,134	17,583	14,842	551	3.1	32.8	26.8		75.3	10.1	514	144	62
Hocking	12,425	12,141	10,481	284	2.3	29.4	24.8		75.7	8.7	341	156	46
Holmes	12,574	12,280	10,007	294	2.4	29.7	23.7		77.0	7.8	354	142	135
Huron	24,484	23,594	21,382	890	3.8	49.7	43.4		72.2	18.3	1,087	166	197
Jackson	14,550	13,909	12,452	641	4.6	34.6	29.6		73.9	9.8	740	89	114
Jefferson	33,614	33,291	33,911	323	1.0	82.1	82.8		74.3	14.4	484	11	94
Knox	23,515	21,794	18,508	1,721	7.9	44.6	35.1		75.7	13.2	2,132	373	376
Lake	97,103	93,487	83,194	3,616	3.9	425.5	364.5		77.5	18.4	5,253	933	1,046
Lawrence	27,451	27,189	24,788	262	1.0	60.3	54.4		74.8	10.1	322	35	29
Licking	64,277	58,800	50,032	5,477	9.3	93.6	72.9		74.4	17.4	7,709	1,087	1,169
Logan	22,822	21,571	19,473	1,251	5.8	49.8	42.5		75.6	12.0	1,390	191	285
Lorain	120,052	111,368	99,937	8,684	7.8	243.8	202.9		74.2	18.5	11,797	1,958	2,041
Lucas	202,426	196,259	191,388	6,167	3.1	594.6	562.3		65.4	27.4	9,343	1,507	1,947
Madison	15,298	14,399	12,621	899	6.2	32.9	27.1		72.3	14.9	1,134	163	135
Mahoning	113,677	111,762	107,915	1,915	1.7	273.8	259.9		72.8	19.7	3,868	511	773
Marion	27,194	26,295	25,149	899	3.4	67.3	62.3		72.9	15.5	1,248	242	415
Medina	64,202	56,793	43,330	7,409	13.0	152.3	102.8		81.3	14.3	8,970	1,189	1,639
Meigs	10,869	10,782	9,795	87	0.8	25.3	22.8		79.4	5.0	80	12	17
Mercer	16,605	15,875	14,969	730	4.6	35.8	32.3		80.1	10.8	875	145	182
Miami	41,805	40,554	35,985	1,251	3.1	102.7	88.4		72.3	17.9	1,924	307	376
Monroe	7,265	7,212	6,567	53	0.7	15.9	14.4		80.8	4.9	41	–	36
Montgomery	253,475	248,443	240,820	5,032	2.0	549.0	521.6		64.7	27.4	9,839	1,372	1,467
Morgan	7,939	7,771	6,681	168	2.2	19.0	16.0		78.3	5.7	126	63	57
Morrow	12,878	12,132	10,312	746	6.1	31.7	25.4		82.2	6.7	833	171	432
Muskingum	35,568	35,163	33,029	405	1.2	53.5	49.7		73.5	15.9	683	82	121
Noble	5,626	5,480	4,998	146	2.7	14.1	12.5		79.8	5.3	193	27	38
Ottawa	26,633	25,532	23,340	1,101	4.3	104.5	91.5		80.6	12.4	1,596	336	255
Paulding	8,785	8,478	7,951	307	3.6	21.1	19.1		83.8	6.5	369	43	24
Perry	14,059	13,655	12,260	404	3.0	34.3	29.9		79.4	7.2	396	117	77
Pickaway	19,611	18,596	16,385	1,015	5.5	39.1	32.6		74.6	12.6	1,180	169	249
Pike	12,214	11,602	9,722	612	5.3	27.7	22.0		70.0	7.5	745	155	233
Portage	64,131	60,096	52,299	4,035	6.7	130.2	106.2		71.3	22.7	4,328	756	711
Preble	17,915	17,186	15,174	729	4.2	42.2	35.7		78.9	9.3	944	109	125
Putnam	13,323	12,753	11,600	570	4.5	27.5	24.0		84.1	8.1	586	102	139
Richland	54,769	53,062	50,350	1,707	3.2	110.2	101.3		71.5	19.9	2,840	430	446
Ross	30,310	29,461	26,173	849	2.9	44.0	38.0		73.5	12.7	312	39	47
Sandusky	26,019	25,253	23,753	766	3.0	63.6	58.0		75.3	15.3	1,117	132	198
Scioto	34,813	34,054	32,408	759	2.2	56.9	52.9		70.1	13.3	287	59	43
Seneca	24,362	23,692	22,473	670	2.8	44.2	40.8		75.1	14.8	986	122	132
Shelby	19,613	18,682	16,509	931	5.0	47.9	40.3		74.3	15.5	1,348	295	218
Stark	162,337	157,024	146,910	5,313	3.4	281.8	255.0		72.4	20.9	8,213	1,404	1,493
Summit	240,329	230,880	211,477	9,449	4.1	582.3	512.3		70.2	23.5	13,726	1,968	2,223
Trumbull	96,682	95,117	90,533	1,565	1.6	156.8	147.0		74.3	18.0	2,829	449	520
Tuscarawas	38,868	38,113	33,982	755	2.0	68.5	59.9		74.9	14.3	1,106	164	229
Union	18,015	15,217	11,599	2,798	18.4	41.3	26.6		77.5	14.7	3,012	440	517
Van Wert	12,700	12,363	11,998	337	2.7	31.0	29.3		81.7	8.7	469	67	74
Vinton	5,735	5,653	4,856	82	1.5	13.8	11.7		77.8	4.3	4	4	–
Warren	71,965	58,951	40,636	13,014	22.1	180.1	101.6		78.5	17.0	16,766	2,477	2,664
Washington	28,047	27,760	25,752	287	1.0	44.2	40.5		76.3	12.4	203	39	36
Wayne	45,136	42,324	37,036	2,812	6.6	81.3	66.7		73.3	17.7	3,234	466	496
Williams	16,827	16,140	14,745	687	4.3	39.9	35.0		76.8	11.7	917	121	133
Wood	50,823	47,468	41,760	3,355	7.1	82.3	67.6		70.7	22.3	6,499	1,152	1,705
Wyandot	9,637	9,324	8,596	313	3.4	23.8	21.2		74.7	13.3	458	63	74

See footnotes at end of table.

[Includes United States, states, and 3,141 counties/county equivalents defined as of February 22, 2005. For more information on these areas, see Appendix C, Geographic Information]

County	Housing units								Housing 2000, percent		New private housing units authorized by building permits		
	2005 (July 1)	2000[1] (April 1 esti- mates base)	1990 (April 1)	Net change, 2000–2005		Units per square mile of land area		Owner- occupied housing units[3]	Units in multi- unit structures	Cumu- lative, 2000– 2005 period	2005	2004
				Number	Percent	2005[2]	1990					
OKLAHOMA	1,588,749	1,514,399	1,406,499	74,350	4.9	23.1	20.5	68.4	15.2	86,877	18,362	17,068
Adair	8,639	8,348	7,124	291	3.5	15.0	12.4	73.4	5.6	85	5	10
Alfalfa	2,849	2,832	3,357	17	0.6	3.3	3.9	81.6	2.1	2	–	–
Atoka	5,818	5,673	5,110	145	2.6	5.9	5.2	76.2	4.7	29	9	3
Beaver	2,771	2,719	2,923	52	1.9	1.5	1.6	79.1	2.4	2	–	–
Beckham	9,035	8,796	9,117	239	2.7	10.0	10.1	71.0	12.6	273	72	26
Blaine	5,255	5,208	5,729	47	0.9	5.7	6.2	76.8	3.5	7	3	2
Bryan	17,410	16,715	14,875	695	4.2	19.2	16.4	69.4	9.2	512	108	73
Caddo	13,373	13,096	13,191	277	2.1	10.5	10.3	73.4	5.3	111	23	19
Canadian	38,271	33,969	28,560	4,302	12.7	42.5	31.7	79.0	9.3	2,637	620	525
Carter	21,294	20,577	19,201	717	3.5	25.8	23.3	71.2	8.2	898	292	107
Cherokee	20,695	19,499	15,935	1,196	6.1	27.6	21.2	66.8	12.8	848	108	131
Choctaw	7,733	7,539	6,844	194	2.6	10.0	8.8	70.9	7.2	125	52	21
Cimarron	1,595	1,583	1,690	12	0.8	0.9	0.9	72.2	3.3	–	–	–
Cleveland	94,485	84,844	71,038	9,641	11.4	176.2	132.5	67.0	21.0	9,113	1,982	2,431
Coal	2,802	2,744	2,725	58	2.1	5.4	5.3	75.1	5.0	24	7	7
Comanche	46,096	45,416	43,589	680	1.5	43.1	40.8	60.3	17.2	1,405	635	166
Cotton	3,134	3,085	3,152	49	1.6	4.9	5.0	76.6	4.5	14	1	4
Craig	6,563	6,459	6,041	104	1.6	8.6	7.9	75.1	5.5	27	6	8
Creek	29,093	27,987	25,143	1,106	4.0	30.4	26.3	78.0	5.0	851	200	199
Custer	11,903	11,675	11,636	228	2.0	12.1	11.8	63.6	15.7	271	68	57
Delaware	23,479	22,290	16,808	1,189	5.3	31.7	22.7	79.2	3.4	645	144	109
Dewey	2,471	2,425	2,733	46	1.9	2.5	2.7	79.2	2.9	–	–	–
Ellis	2,167	2,146	2,449	21	1.0	1.8	2.0	80.7	1.6	13	1	–
Garfield	26,685	26,047	26,502	638	2.4	25.2	25.0	70.3	10.1	937	148	229
Garvin	12,854	12,641	11,932	213	1.7	15.9	14.7	73.8	6.8	96	15	16
Grady	20,210	19,444	17,788	766	3.9	18.4	16.2	75.7	6.8	703	137	113
Grant	2,652	2,622	2,955	30	1.1	2.7	3.0	78.7	2.4	6	–	2
Greer	2,807	2,788	3,126	19	0.7	4.4	4.9	75.0	6.7	5	2	–
Harmon	1,673	1,647	1,793	26	1.6	3.1	3.3	77.0	5.2	(NA)	–	–
Harper	1,879	1,863	2,077	16	0.9	1.8	2.0	79.2	3.1	12	–	–
Haskell	5,754	5,573	5,138	181	3.2	10.0	8.9	77.5	4.1	52	7	11
Hughes	6,339	6,237	6,021	102	1.6	7.9	7.5	75.8	5.0	27	5	3
Jackson	12,464	12,377	12,125	87	0.7	15.5	15.1	60.2	9.4	134	38	26
Jefferson	3,423	3,373	3,522	50	1.5	4.5	4.6	74.2	6.2	4	1	–
Johnston	4,967	4,782	4,478	185	3.9	7.7	6.9	73.9	5.3	131	29	26
Kay	21,959	21,804	22,456	155	0.7	23.9	24.4	71.7	10.0	242	12	35
Kingfisher	6,044	5,879	5,791	165	2.8	6.7	6.4	78.2	3.6	162	38	30
Kiowa	5,330	5,304	5,645	26	0.5	5.3	5.6	75.3	6.9	16	–	4
Latimer	4,837	4,709	4,303	128	2.7	6.7	6.0	74.6	5.2	23	–	1
Le Flore	20,810	20,143	18,029	667	3.3	13.1	11.4	75.2	5.2	400	95	55
Lincoln	14,126	13,712	12,302	414	3.0	14.7	12.8	80.0	3.5	180	29	38
Logan	14,330	13,906	12,277	424	3.0	19.2	16.5	78.4	3.4	194	36	91
Love	4,202	4,066	3,583	136	3.3	8.2	7.0	81.6	3.7	63	17	12
McClain	12,216	11,189	9,300	1,027	9.2	21.4	16.3	81.4	3.3	1,251	352	281
McCurtain	15,877	15,427	13,828	450	2.9	8.6	7.5	73.3	6.1	229	60	38
McIntosh	13,182	12,640	10,708	542	4.3	21.3	17.3	79.0	3.0	180	15	26
Major	3,602	3,540	3,855	62	1.8	3.8	4.0	81.1	4.4	17	3	2
Marshall	8,796	8,517	7,389	279	3.3	23.7	19.9	79.3	3.0	16	2	3
Mayes	18,086	17,423	15,470	663	3.8	27.6	23.6	77.0	5.8	319	29	36
Murray	6,655	6,479	5,742	176	2.7	15.9	13.7	74.2	4.4	134	31	38
Muskogee	30,545	29,575	28,882	970	3.3	37.5	35.5	69.6	13.1	1,070	235	239
Noble	5,162	5,082	4,894	80	1.6	7.1	6.7	75.3	3.5	38	8	3
Nowata	4,801	4,705	4,534	96	2.0	8.5	8.0	77.8	6.5	40	11	7
Okfuskee	5,265	5,114	4,894	151	3.0	8.4	7.8	76.2	5.7	107	25	22
Oklahoma	312,515	295,020	279,340	17,495	5.9	440.7	393.9	60.4	25.0	30,031	5,893	5,852
Okmulgee	17,692	17,316	16,431	376	2.2	25.4	23.6	72.5	7.7	235	10	99
Osage	19,696	18,824	18,196	872	4.6	8.8	8.1	80.6	4.9	739	157	232
Ottawa	15,155	14,842	14,064	313	2.1	32.2	29.8	73.9	8.4	186	39	24
Pawnee	7,629	7,464	7,407	165	2.2	13.4	13.0	80.1	4.1	24	20	2
Payne	31,214	29,326	27,381	1,888	6.4	45.5	39.9	55.9	22.5	2,072	338	957
Pittsburg	22,174	21,520	19,433	654	3.0	17.0	14.9	76.0	6.4	419	117	54
Pontotoc	15,895	15,575	15,094	320	2.1	22.1	21.0	67.0	12.3	184	22	33
Pottawatomie	28,146	27,302	24,528	844	3.1	35.7	31.1	72.1	8.6	963	347	147
Pushmataha	5,943	5,795	5,190	148	2.6	4.3	3.7	77.7	4.2	18	2	2
Roger Mills	1,781	1,749	2,048	32	1.8	1.6	1.8	78.7	1.8	1	–	–
Rogers	29,996	27,474	21,455	2,522	9.2	44.4	31.8	81.1	5.9	2,977	643	560
Seminole	11,407	11,146	11,404	261	2.3	18.0	18.0	72.5	5.6	207	66	14
Sequoyah	17,777	16,940	14,314	837	4.9	26.4	21.2	75.2	9.0	534	58	56
Stephens	20,191	19,854	19,675	337	1.7	23.1	22.4	75.5	6.6	351	83	71
Texas	8,296	8,013	7,328	283	3.5	4.1	3.6	66.8	7.4	221	15	10

See footnotes at end of table.

Table B-7. Counties — **Housing Units and Building Permits**—Con.

[Includes United States, states, and 3,141 counties/county equivalents defined as of February 22, 2005. For more information on these areas, see Appendix C, Geographic Information]

County	Housing units 2005 (July 1)	2000[1] (April 1 esti- mates base)	1990 (April 1)	Net change, 2000–2005 Number	Net change, 2000–2005 Percent	Units per square mile of land area 2005[2]	Units per square mile of land area 1990	Housing 2000, percent Owner- occupied housing units[3]	Housing 2000, percent Units in multi- unit structures	New private housing units authorized by building permits Cumu- lative, 2000–2005 period	2005	2004
OKLAHOMA—Con.												
Tillman	4,335	4,342	4,704	−7	−0.2	5.0	5.4	77.3	5.4	–	–	–
Tulsa	256,321	243,955	227,834	12,366	5.1	449.4	399.5	61.8	26.6	18,862	3,924	2,895
Wagoner	27,063	23,174	19,262	3,889	16.8	48.1	34.2	81.1	5.4	3,470	690	668
Washington	22,581	22,250	21,707	331	1.5	54.2	52.1	74.0	12.8	548	194	93
Washita	5,527	5,452	6,101	75	1.4	5.5	6.1	74.7	3.6	35	2	–
Woods	4,515	4,492	4,782	23	0.5	3.5	3.7	69.8	7.5	28	2	–
Woodward	8,437	8,341	8,512	96	1.2	6.8	6.9	72.0	11.3	92	24	14
OREGON	1,558,421	1,452,724	1,193,567	105,697	7.3	16.2	12.4	64.3	23.1	[4]146,733	[4]31,024	[4]27,309
Baker	8,661	8,402	7,525	259	3.1	2.8	2.5	70.1	8.4	257	56	57
Benton	34,361	31,977	27,024	2,384	7.5	50.8	39.9	57.3	29.8	2,729	496	366
Clackamas	146,886	136,959	109,003	9,927	7.2	78.6	58.3	71.1	21.4	12,811	2,680	2,200
Clatsop	20,473	19,685	17,367	788	4.0	24.7	21.0	64.2	22.0	1,230	280	270
Columbia	19,105	17,572	14,576	1,533	8.7	29.1	22.2	76.1	11.5	1,969	365	328
Coos	29,505	29,250	26,668	255	0.9	18.4	16.7	68.1	14.1	376	159	65
Crook	9,408	8,265	6,066	1,143	13.8	3.2	2.0	74.3	8.2	1,499	351	299
Curry	11,968	11,406	9,885	562	4.9	7.4	6.1	73.0	11.3	886	185	153
Deschutes	68,602	54,583	35,928	14,019	25.7	22.7	11.9	72.3	12.1	18,457	4,460	3,892
Douglas	44,961	43,284	38,298	1,677	3.9	8.9	7.6	71.7	11.9	2,333	497	360
Gilliam	1,040	1,043	932	−3	−0.3	0.9	0.8	70.2	3.3	1	–	–
Grant	4,161	4,004	3,774	157	3.9	0.9	0.8	73.5	5.6	(NA)	–	–
Harney	3,571	3,533	3,305	38	1.1	0.4	0.3	72.7	9.3	69	14	17
Hood River	8,477	7,818	7,569	659	8.4	16.2	14.5	64.9	15.6	869	166	159
Jackson	84,243	75,739	60,376	8,504	11.2	30.2	21.7	66.5	18.0	10,774	2,036	2,099
Jefferson	9,056	8,319	6,311	737	8.9	5.1	3.5	71.3	10.3	950	235	122
Josephine	35,895	33,238	26,912	2,657	8.0	21.9	16.4	70.1	10.1	3,588	849	760
Klamath	29,974	28,883	25,954	1,091	3.8	5.0	4.4	68.0	12.8	1,823	560	366
Lake	4,098	3,999	3,434	99	2.5	0.5	0.4	68.9	4.4	122	33	19
Lane	145,876	138,954	116,676	6,922	5.0	32.0	25.6	62.3	22.4	9,980	2,356	1,750
Lincoln	28,162	26,889	22,389	1,273	4.7	28.7	22.9	65.7	16.5	1,795	443	380
Linn	45,191	42,524	36,482	2,667	6.3	19.7	15.9	67.9	16.7	4,236	1,015	905
Malheur	11,398	11,233	10,649	165	1.5	1.2	1.1	63.8	13.7	263	40	34
Marion	115,500	108,176	86,869	7,324	6.8	97.6	73.3	62.9	23.5	10,325	1,984	2,059
Morrow	4,389	4,276	3,412	113	2.6	2.2	1.7	73.1	9.4	(NA)	10	24
Multnomah	303,086	288,556	255,751	14,530	5.0	696.4	587.6	56.9	34.8	22,055	4,573	3,842
Polk	26,541	24,461	18,978	2,080	8.5	35.8	25.6	68.4	18.0	2,086	454	501
Sherman	945	935	900	10	1.1	1.1	1.1	70.5	4.5	11	–	–
Tillamook	17,007	15,906	13,324	1,101	6.9	15.4	12.1	71.8	8.0	1,583	400	294
Umatilla	28,761	27,676	24,333	1,085	3.9	8.9	7.6	64.9	17.0	1,221	220	174
Union	10,695	10,603	9,974	92	0.9	5.3	4.9	66.5	15.3	230	56	32
Wallowa	4,008	3,900	3,755	108	2.8	1.3	1.2	71.8	7.5	(NA)	–	–
Wasco	10,705	10,651	10,476	54	0.5	4.5	4.4	68.4	13.8	102	–	4
Washington	196,957	178,913	124,716	18,044	10.1	272.1	172.3	60.6	32.8	25,795	4,673	4,769
Wheeler	850	842	782	8	1.0	0.5	0.5	72.1	1.2	7	–	–
Yamhill	33,905	30,270	23,194	3,635	12.0	47.4	32.4	69.6	15.8	4,773	1,069	749
PENNSYLVANIA	5,422,362	5,249,751	4,938,140	172,611	3.3	121.0	110.2	71.3	21.2	269,139	44,525	49,665
Adams	38,693	35,831	30,141	2,862	8.0	74.4	58.0	76.8	12.4	3,682	606	675
Allegheny	590,376	583,646	580,738	6,730	1.2	808.5	795.3	67.0	28.3	15,824	2,004	2,511
Armstrong	32,938	32,387	31,757	551	1.7	50.4	48.6	77.3	9.7	1,005	162	211
Beaver	79,204	77,765	76,336	1,439	1.9	182.4	175.4	74.9	17.8	2,665	387	581
Bedford	24,212	23,529	21,738	683	2.9	23.9	21.4	80.1	8.4	966	118	188
Berks	158,423	150,222	134,482	8,201	5.5	184.5	156.5	74.0	18.7	10,960	1,368	1,640
Blair	56,101	55,061	54,349	1,040	1.9	106.7	103.4	72.9	19.1	1,840	180	496
Bradford	29,274	28,664	27,058	610	2.1	25.4	23.5	75.5	12.2	919	104	169
Bucks	237,546	225,497	199,934	12,049	5.3	391.1	329.0	77.4	19.4	15,633	2,104	2,560
Butler	74,909	69,868	59,061	5,041	7.2	95.0	74.9	77.9	14.3	6,609	1,160	1,040
Cambria	66,215	65,796	67,374	419	0.6	96.2	97.9	74.8	16.8	1,441	246	320
Cameron	4,609	4,592	4,399	17	0.4	11.6	11.1	74.8	11.3	64	4	11
Carbon	31,933	30,492	27,380	1,441	4.7	83.8	71.6	78.2	11.2	2,324	571	521
Centre	56,954	53,161	46,195	3,793	7.1	51.4	41.7	60.2	30.3	4,843	701	694
Chester	178,778	163,773	139,597	15,005	9.2	236.5	184.6	76.3	18.1	18,992	3,081	3,661
Clarion	19,916	19,426	18,022	490	2.5	33.1	29.9	72.3	11.8	746	97	186
Clearfield	38,641	37,855	34,300	786	2.1	33.7	29.9	79.2	10.6	1,275	176	303
Clinton	18,754	18,166	16,478	588	3.2	21.1	18.5	72.9	14.7	850	100	150
Columbia	28,701	27,732	25,598	969	3.5	59.1	52.7	72.4	16.1	1,414	211	358
Crawford	43,393	42,416	40,462	977	2.3	42.8	39.9	75.5	13.3	1,499	162	300
Cumberland	92,328	86,951	77,108	5,377	6.2	167.8	140.2	73.1	19.0	7,364	1,348	1,266
Dauphin	114,955	111,133	102,684	3,822	3.4	218.8	195.5	65.4	26.8	6,056	1,204	1,062
Delaware	220,114	216,978	211,024	3,136	1.4	1,194.9	1,145.4	71.9	24.1	6,540	836	911
Elk	18,343	18,116	17,249	227	1.3	22.1	20.8	79.4	11.3	436	42	88
Erie	116,922	114,322	108,585	2,600	2.3	145.8	135.4	69.2	26.1	4,453	724	898

See footnotes at end of table.

County and City Data Book: 2007

Table B-7. Counties — **Housing Units and Building Permits**—Con.

[Includes United States, states, and 3,141 counties/county equivalents defined as of February 22, 2005. For more information on these areas, see Appendix C, Geographic Information]

County	Housing units — 2005 (July 1)	Housing units — 2000[1] (April 1 estimates base)	Housing units — 1990 (April 1)	Net change, 2000–2005 — Number	Net change, 2000–2005 — Percent	Units per square mile of land area — 2005[2]	Units per square mile of land area — 1990	Housing 2000, percent — Owner-occupied housing units[3]	Housing 2000, percent — Units in multi-unit structures	New private housing units authorized by building permits — Cumulative, 2000–2005 period	New private housing units authorized by building permits — 2005	New private housing units authorized by building permits — 2004
PENNSYLVANIA—Con.												
Fayette	67,248	66,490	61,406	758	1.1	85.1	77.7	73.2	14.4	1,510	99	273
Forest	8,899	8,701	8,445	198	2.3	20.8	19.7	82.7	1.5	284	21	32
Franklin	57,988	53,803	48,629	4,185	7.8	75.1	63.0	74.0	14.4	5,639	1,082	1,199
Fulton	7,171	6,790	6,184	381	5.6	16.4	14.1	78.8	5.5	487	89	96
Greene	17,068	16,678	15,982	390	2.3	29.6	27.8	74.1	10.4	639	132	144
Huntingdon	21,834	21,058	19,286	776	3.7	25.0	22.0	77.5	9.7	1,113	174	213
Indiana	38,251	37,250	34,770	1,001	2.7	46.1	41.9	71.7	16.1	1,297	61	240
Jefferson	22,774	22,104	21,242	670	3.0	34.7	32.4	77.1	11.2	922	107	284
Juniata	10,365	10,031	8,505	334	3.3	26.5	21.7	77.7	8.1	495	86	122
Lackawanna	96,717	95,362	91,707	1,355	1.4	210.9	199.9	67.6	32.9	3,000	469	572
Lancaster	190,744	179,990	156,462	10,754	6.0	201.0	164.8	70.8	20.3	14,236	2,040	2,675
Lawrence	40,368	39,635	38,844	733	1.8	112.0	107.8	77.3	14.4	1,324	169	228
Lebanon	52,299	49,320	44,634	2,979	6.0	144.5	123.4	72.7	18.3	4,329	845	807
Lehigh	135,188	128,910	118,335	6,278	4.9	390.0	341.3	68.8	25.6	9,035	1,731	1,650
Luzerne	146,911	144,686	138,724	2,225	1.5	164.9	155.7	70.3	22.7	4,776	814	884
Lycoming	53,594	52,464	49,580	1,130	2.2	43.4	40.1	69.4	19.7	1,993	299	349
McKean	21,755	21,644	21,454	111	0.5	22.2	21.9	74.7	13.6	394	39	59
Mercer	51,305	49,859	48,689	1,446	2.9	76.4	72.5	76.3	15.3	2,186	268	363
Mifflin	21,192	20,745	19,641	447	2.2	51.5	47.8	74.0	13.8	714	77	122
Monroe	75,650	67,581	54,823	8,069	11.9	124.3	90.3	78.3	8.8	9,909	1,660	1,753
Montgomery	308,738	297,434	265,856	11,304	3.8	639.1	550.3	73.5	24.4	17,538	3,668	2,687
Montour	7,903	7,628	6,885	275	3.6	60.4	52.7	73.0	15.9	402	64	64
Northampton	114,125	106,711	95,345	7,414	6.9	305.3	255.0	73.3	19.1	10,635	1,986	1,821
Northumberland	43,718	43,164	41,900	554	1.3	95.1	91.1	73.5	15.9	1,248	164	254
Perry	19,610	18,941	17,063	669	3.5	35.4	30.8	79.8	9.2	946	152	70
Philadelphia	659,769	661,958	674,899	-2,189	-0.3	4,883.9	4,994.4	59.3	31.6	9,783	2,506	2,864
Pike	38,224	34,681	30,852	3,543	10.2	69.9	56.4	84.8	2.5	4,692	1,033	1,052
Potter	12,622	12,159	11,334	463	3.8	11.7	10.5	77.3	6.3	623	69	146
Schuylkill	69,176	67,806	66,457	1,370	2.0	88.9	85.4	78.0	13.7	2,789	543	639
Snyder	15,445	14,890	13,629	555	3.7	46.6	41.1	76.5	10.9	795	120	126
Somerset	38,003	37,163	35,713	840	2.3	35.4	33.2	78.1	11.9	1,302	141	233
Sullivan	6,201	6,017	5,458	184	3.1	13.8	12.1	80.8	5.0	282	43	83
Susquehanna	22,434	21,829	20,308	605	2.8	27.3	24.7	79.5	9.6	899	136	170
Tioga	20,590	19,893	18,202	697	3.5	18.2	16.1	76.2	10.2	948	113	148
Union	15,299	14,684	12,886	615	4.2	48.3	40.7	73.3	14.6	910	177	163
Venango	27,286	26,904	26,961	382	1.4	40.4	39.9	76.4	12.8	781	121	151
Warren	23,371	23,058	22,236	313	1.4	26.5	25.2	78.2	12.3	600	67	169
Washington	91,027	87,267	84,113	3,760	4.3	106.2	98.1	77.1	15.1	5,420	817	1,004
Wayne	32,205	30,593	28,480	1,612	5.3	44.2	39.0	80.4	7.0	2,273	460	491
Westmoreland	165,007	161,058	153,554	3,949	2.5	160.9	150.2	78.0	14.6	6,439	972	1,236
Wyoming	13,181	12,713	11,857	468	3.7	33.2	29.8	78.9	9.5	651	99	142
York	168,875	156,720	134,761	12,155	7.8	186.7	149.0	76.1	16.0	16,501	3,116	3,087
RHODE ISLAND	447,810	439,837	414,572	7,973	1.8	428.6	396.7	60.0	41.2	15,505	2,836	2,532
Bristol	20,163	19,881	18,567	282	1.4	817.0	752.3	71.3	28.0	623	109	91
Kent	71,725	70,365	65,450	1,360	1.9	421.5	384.8	71.5	26.9	2,645	623	363
Newport	40,575	39,561	37,475	1,014	2.6	390.0	360.1	61.6	31.1	1,707	286	296
Providence	255,444	253,214	243,224	2,230	0.9	618.1	588.5	53.2	53.0	6,403	1,169	1,238
Washington	59,903	56,816	49,856	3,087	5.4	180.0	149.8	72.8	17.9	4,127	649	544
SOUTH CAROLINA	1,927,864	1,753,586	1,424,155	174,278	9.9	64.0	47.3	72.2	15.8	232,627	54,157	43,230
Abbeville	11,880	11,656	9,846	224	1.9	23.4	19.4	80.5	7.9	332	64	57
Aiken	66,114	61,987	49,266	4,127	6.7	61.6	45.9	75.6	9.4	5,524	1,159	966
Allendale	4,631	4,568	4,242	63	1.4	11.3	10.4	72.7	8.2	34	4	4
Anderson	79,350	73,213	60,745	6,137	8.4	110.5	84.6	76.3	9.9	8,344	1,931	1,248
Bamberg	7,208	7,130	6,408	78	1.1	18.3	16.3	74.7	8.9	128	24	24
Barnwell	10,283	10,191	7,854	92	0.9	18.8	14.3	75.5	6.1	161	36	31
Beaufort	73,812	60,516	45,981	13,296	22.0	125.8	78.3	73.2	21.9	17,824	4,650	2,942
Berkeley	61,273	54,717	45,697	6,556	12.0	55.8	41.6	74.2	12.0	7,045	1,869	1,609
Calhoun	7,262	6,862	5,225	400	5.8	19.1	13.7	84.4	2.0	483	68	66
Charleston	159,680	141,025	123,550	18,655	13.2	173.8	134.7	61.0	27.9	26,953	6,388	4,844
Cherokee	23,123	22,400	17,610	723	3.2	58.9	44.8	73.9	10.7	912	108	181
Chester	14,748	14,374	12,293	374	2.6	25.4	21.2	78.4	6.5	524	79	79
Chesterfield	19,533	18,818	15,101	715	3.8	24.5	18.9	76.3	6.8	827	99	123
Clarendon	15,858	15,303	12,101	555	3.6	26.1	19.9	79.1	5.9	797	228	126
Colleton	18,813	18,129	14,926	684	3.8	17.8	14.1	80.3	6.0	891	170	135
Darlington	29,831	28,942	23,601	889	3.1	53.2	42.0	77.0	7.2	1,140	181	225
Dillon	12,879	12,679	10,590	200	1.6	31.8	26.2	72.0	8.1	306	61	57
Dorchester	43,150	37,215	30,632	5,935	15.9	75.1	53.3	75.0	13.9	8,572	2,561	1,853
Edgefield	9,698	9,206	7,290	492	5.3	19.3	14.5	80.5	7.7	659	129	94
Fairfield	10,760	10,383	8,730	377	3.6	15.7	12.7	77.4	7.3	518	106	104

See footnotes at end of table.

Table B-7. Counties — **Housing Units and Building Permits**—Con.

[Includes United States, states, and 3,141 counties/county equivalents defined as of February 22, 2005. For more information on these areas, see Appendix C, Geographic Information]

County	Housing units							Housing 2000, percent		New private housing units authorized by building permits		
	2005 (July 1)	2000[1] (April 1 estimates base)	1990 (April 1)	Net change, 2000–2005 Number	Percent	Units per square mile of land area 2005[2]	1990	Owner-occupied housing units[3]	Units in multi-unit structures	Cumulative, 2000–2005 period	2005	2004
SOUTH CAROLINA—Con.												
Florence	53,182	51,836	43,209	1,346	2.6	66.5	54.1	73.0	13.3	2,171	725	182
Georgetown	31,617	28,281	21,134	3,336	11.8	38.8	25.9	81.4	12.8	4,409	1,053	787
Greenville	178,686	162,804	131,645	15,882	9.8	226.2	166.2	68.2	20.3	21,580	4,290	3,770
Greenwood	29,623	28,244	24,735	1,379	4.9	65.0	54.3	69.2	15.8	1,777	258	436
Hampton	8,700	8,581	7,058	119	1.4	15.5	12.6	78.1	4.7	195	46	34
Horry	147,207	122,085	89,960	25,122	20.6	129.8	79.4	73.0	32.1	36,803	11,828	7,068
Jasper	8,326	7,922	6,070	404	5.1	12.7	9.3	77.7	5.2	616	198	116
Kershaw	24,606	22,683	17,479	1,923	8.5	33.9	24.1	82.0	4.1	2,610	624	550
Lancaster	26,649	24,962	20,929	1,687	6.8	48.5	38.1	75.0	7.6	2,177	405	373
Laurens	31,239	30,233	23,201	1,006	3.3	43.7	32.5	77.5	6.7	1,159	173	168
Lee	7,865	7,670	6,537	195	2.5	19.2	15.9	79.4	5.8	302	89	91
Lexington	99,697	90,979	67,556	8,718	9.6	142.6	96.4	77.2	10.9	11,298	2,259	2,255
McCormick	4,777	4,459	3,347	318	7.1	13.3	9.3	81.0	5.9	380	57	51
Marion	15,408	15,143	12,777	265	1.7	31.5	26.1	73.5	7.3	346	40	54
Marlboro	11,996	11,894	10,955	102	0.9	25.0	22.8	70.8	10.5	151	24	24
Newberry	17,389	16,805	14,455	584	3.5	27.6	22.9	76.8	7.3	785	118	137
Oconee	35,585	32,383	25,983	3,202	9.9	56.9	41.6	78.4	7.8	4,139	861	839
Orangeburg	40,840	39,274	32,340	1,566	4.0	36.9	29.2	75.6	7.6	1,922	281	365
Pickens	49,923	46,000	35,865	3,923	8.5	100.5	72.2	73.5	13.6	4,675	599	1,065
Richland	145,840	129,793	109,564	16,047	12.4	192.8	144.8	61.4	28.3	20,741	4,324	4,226
Saluda	8,770	8,543	6,792	227	2.7	19.4	15.0	80.6	2.6	305	49	48
Spartanburg	116,789	106,986	89,927	9,803	9.2	144.0	110.9	72.0	13.6	11,556	2,131	2,219
Sumter	43,977	41,747	35,016	2,230	5.3	66.1	52.6	69.5	10.2	3,010	627	674
Union	13,529	13,351	12,230	178	1.3	26.3	23.8	76.7	8.3	300	41	83
Williamsburg	15,800	15,553	13,265	247	1.6	16.9	14.2	80.5	4.7	344	61	49
York	79,958	66,061	50,438	13,897	21.0	117.2	73.9	73.1	13.9	16,902	3,081	2,798
SOUTH DAKOTA	347,931	323,207	292,436	24,724	7.6	4.6	3.9	68.2	18.9	29,977	5,685	5,839
Aurora	1,334	1,298	1,342	36	2.8	1.9	1.9	76.7	5.6	35	16	10
Beadle	8,291	8,206	8,093	85	1.0	6.6	6.4	67.8	20.6	219	57	31
Bennett	1,316	1,278	1,292	38	3.0	1.1	1.1	59.1	9.2	2	–	–
Bon Homme	3,061	3,007	3,087	54	1.8	5.4	5.5	75.9	10.0	16	11	16
Brookings	12,440	11,576	9,824	864	7.5	15.7	12.4	58.2	29.8	1,142	239	192
Brown	16,317	15,861	15,101	456	2.9	9.5	8.8	66.3	26.1	695	130	114
Brule	2,347	2,272	2,275	75	3.3	2.9	2.8	71.2	14.5	93	14	22
Buffalo	628	602	535	26	4.3	1.3	1.1	42.8	9.3	(NA)	–	–
Butte	4,223	4,059	3,502	164	4.0	1.9	1.6	73.2	13.6	218	99	62
Campbell	983	962	944	21	2.2	1.3	1.3	82.2	2.7	2	–	–
Charles Mix	3,941	3,853	3,751	88	2.3	3.6	3.4	68.4	10.5	36	8	3
Clark	1,897	1,880	2,026	17	0.9	2.0	2.1	80.3	6.3	53	15	14
Clay	5,688	5,438	4,892	250	4.6	13.8	11.9	54.4	28.2	308	46	97
Codington	11,947	11,324	9,539	623	5.5	17.4	13.9	70.2	21.2	815	146	156
Corson	1,582	1,535	1,557	47	3.1	0.6	0.6	59.4	4.2	–	–	–
Custer	4,120	3,624	3,003	496	13.7	2.6	1.9	77.0	7.2	589	114	143
Davison	8,529	8,093	7,490	436	5.4	19.6	17.2	61.9	25.8	612	115	95
Day	3,716	3,618	3,914	98	2.7	3.6	3.8	76.0	9.0	158	30	36
Deuel	2,283	2,172	2,208	111	5.1	3.7	3.5	80.1	8.8	138	19	26
Dewey	2,208	2,133	2,123	75	3.5	1.0	0.9	55.2	11.6	16	–	–
Douglas	1,474	1,453	1,517	21	1.4	3.4	3.5	80.8	5.1	16	4	4
Edmunds	2,085	2,022	2,004	63	3.1	1.8	1.7	81.9	6.3	54	18	22
Fall River	3,942	3,812	3,692	130	3.4	2.3	2.1	69.7	14.9	146	74	8
Faulk	1,293	1,235	1,286	58	4.7	1.3	1.3	81.9	8.2	45	4	8
Grant	3,577	3,458	3,549	119	3.4	5.2	5.2	77.6	13.4	160	24	29
Gregory	2,464	2,405	2,595	59	2.5	2.4	2.6	75.0	6.4	35	16	11
Haakon	1,030	1,002	1,071	28	2.8	0.6	0.6	76.8	6.5	12	8	2
Hamlin	2,747	2,626	2,500	121	4.6	5.4	4.9	81.9	5.3	183	43	36
Hand	1,880	1,840	2,053	40	2.2	1.3	1.4	73.8	10.8	39	16	1
Hanson	1,255	1,218	1,232	37	3.0	2.9	2.8	79.1	8.6	(NA)	6	–
Harding	807	804	776	3	0.4	0.3	0.3	73.5	3.6	2	–	–
Hughes	7,337	7,055	6,255	282	4.0	9.9	8.4	66.1	26.6	373	81	47
Hutchinson	3,576	3,517	3,657	59	1.7	4.4	4.5	78.8	7.4	75	11	15
Hyde	785	769	816	16	2.1	0.9	0.9	71.7	4.3	12	5	7
Jackson	1,215	1,173	1,147	42	3.6	0.7	0.6	63.4	8.0	–	–	–
Jerauld	1,203	1,167	1,182	36	3.1	2.3	2.2	72.2	8.4	34	11	14
Jones	624	614	699	10	1.6	0.6	0.7	72.5	9.3	6	–	–
Kingsbury	2,806	2,724	2,765	82	3.0	3.3	3.3	75.6	11.5	127	19	16
Lake	5,586	5,282	5,148	304	5.8	9.9	9.1	70.5	13.6	386	62	49
Lawrence	11,446	10,427	9,092	1,019	9.8	14.3	11.4	64.8	23.2	1,328	287	321
Lincoln	12,917	9,131	5,823	3,786	41.5	22.3	10.1	79.7	13.8	1,576	391	290
Lyman	1,679	1,636	1,523	43	2.6	1.0	0.9	69.4	6.0	48	13	12
McCook	2,523	2,383	2,371	140	5.9	4.4	4.1	78.9	9.4	186	30	22
McPherson	1,460	1,465	1,566	–5	–0.3	1.3	1.4	83.1	8.3	15	4	1
Marshall	2,639	2,562	2,640	77	3.0	3.2	3.1	77.8	7.7	113	26	17

See footnotes at end of table.

County and City Data Book: 2007

U.S. Census Bureau

[Includes United States, states, and 3,141 counties/county equivalents defined as of February 22, 2005. For more information on these areas, see Appendix C, Geographic Information]

County	Housing units								Housing 2000, percent		New private housing units authorized by building permits		
	2005 (July 1)	2000[1] (April 1 esti- mates base)	1990 (April 1)	Net change, 2000–2005		Units per square mile of land area		Owner- occupied housing units[3]	Units in multi- unit structures	Cumu- lative, 2000– 2005 period	2005	2004
				Number	Percent	2005[2]	1990					

County	2005	2000	1990	Number	Percent	2005	1990	Owner	Multi	Cumul	2005	2004
SOUTH DAKOTA—Con.												
Meade.	11,126	10,146	7,592	980	9.7	3.2	2.2	68.2	13.4	1,242	273	315
Mellette	845	824	910	21	2.5	0.6	0.7	64.7	4.6	–	–	–
Miner.	1,430	1,408	1,474	22	1.6	2.5	2.6	76.7	7.2	40	9	8
Minnehaha.	67,853	60,237	49,780	7,616	12.6	83.8	61.5	64.7	29.4	12,151	1,837	2,106
Moody.	2,822	2,745	2,666	77	2.8	5.4	5.1	72.6	13.6	75	35	30
Pennington	40,673	37,252	33,741	3,421	9.2	14.7	12.2	66.2	21.6	4,370	903	1,060
Perkins	1,899	1,854	2,007	45	2.4	0.7	0.7	76.6	7.6	2	–	1
Potter	1,823	1,760	1,664	63	3.6	2.1	1.9	79.5	8.4	23	1	2
Roberts	4,894	4,732	4,728	162	3.4	4.4	4.3	69.1	6.8	222	41	35
Sanborn.	1,240	1,220	1,326	20	1.6	2.2	2.3	77.9	5.4	46	16	9
Shannon	3,290	3,123	2,699	167	5.3	1.6	1.3	49.6	4.5	(NA)	–	–
Spink.	3,374	3,352	3,545	22	0.7	2.2	2.4	73.8	13.1	65	13	23
Stanley	1,377	1,277	1,056	100	7.8	1.0	0.7	76.4	9.6	119	25	19
Sully	883	844	811	39	4.6	0.9	0.8	75.9	5.9	43	6	11
Todd	2,880	2,766	2,572	114	4.1	2.1	1.9	45.1	12.9	2	2	–
Tripp	3,109	3,036	3,023	73	2.4	1.9	1.9	74.7	8.7	21	3	1
Turner	3,959	3,852	3,800	107	2.8	6.4	6.2	77.5	7.9	177	37	30
Union	5,915	5,345	4,286	570	10.7	12.8	9.3	74.4	15.8	730	129	126
Walworth	3,179	3,144	2,928	35	1.1	4.5	4.1	71.3	12.9	33	8	11
Yankton	9,233	8,840	7,571	393	4.4	17.7	14.5	69.1	19.5	465	135	103
Ziebach	926	879	800	47	5.3	0.5	0.4	59.4	7.4	(NA)	–	–
TENNESSEE.	2,637,441	2,439,433	2,026,067	198,008	8.1	64.0	49.2	69.9	18.7	227,782	46,615	44,791
Anderson	33,663	32,451	29,323	1,212	3.7	99.7	86.9	72.5	16.2	1,650	304	276
Bedford	16,505	14,990	12,638	1,515	10.1	34.8	26.7	73.5	7.6	1,552	459	584
Benton.	8,934	8,595	7,107	339	3.9	22.6	18.0	80.5	3.7	35	5	9
Bledsoe	5,360	5,141	3,771	219	4.3	13.2	9.3	81.8	3.8	(NA)	–	–
Blount	50,671	47,059	36,532	3,612	7.7	90.7	65.4	75.9	11.7	3,192	1,007	1,042
Bradley	39,803	36,820	29,562	2,983	8.1	121.1	89.9	68.6	20.2	3,565	666	746
Campbell	18,956	18,527	14,817	429	2.3	39.5	30.9	73.4	9.9	302	47	25
Cannon	5,638	5,420	4,368	218	4.0	21.2	16.4	78.6	6.8	60	5	7
Carroll	13,484	13,057	11,783	427	3.3	22.5	19.7	78.9	5.8	152	24	13
Carter	26,872	25,920	21,779	952	3.7	78.8	63.9	74.9	12.2	691	287	300
Cheatham	15,095	13,508	10,297	1,587	11.7	49.9	34.0	83.7	3.8	1,588	258	291
Chester	6,569	6,174	4,944	395	6.4	22.8	17.1	77.3	8.1	331	115	40
Claiborne	14,604	13,262	10,711	1,342	10.1	33.6	24.7	78.6	5.7	1,314	175	192
Clay	4,131	3,959	3,340	172	4.3	17.5	14.1	80.1	4.6	(NA)	–	–
Cocke	16,427	15,844	12,282	583	3.7	37.8	28.3	75.5	7.8	18	4	4
Coffee	21,896	20,746	16,786	1,150	5.5	51.1	39.1	71.5	12.1	1,418	545	197
Crockett.	6,307	6,138	5,521	169	2.8	23.8	20.8	74.9	5.9	38	10	2
Cumberland	23,721	22,443	15,864	1,278	5.7	34.8	23.3	80.6	8.2	664	124	166
Davidson	270,516	252,978	229,064	17,538	6.9	538.6	456.1	55.3	38.7	24,245	5,020	4,808
Decatur	6,711	6,448	5,346	263	4.1	20.1	16.0	80.1	4.2	52	2	8
DeKalb	8,706	8,408	6,694	298	3.5	28.6	22.0	74.9	6.8	100	25	25
Dickson	19,353	17,615	14,149	1,738	9.9	39.5	28.9	76.1	10.7	1,897	266	297
Dyer	16,934	16,123	14,384	811	5.0	33.2	28.2	65.7	15.2	887	90	140
Fayette	12,750	11,210	9,115	1,540	13.7	18.1	12.9	80.3	5.9	2,185	708	664
Fentress	7,888	7,598	6,120	290	3.8	15.8	12.3	79.1	5.8	24	4	4
Franklin	18,333	16,813	13,717	1,520	9.0	33.1	24.8	78.5	7.1	1,664	252	294
Gibson.	21,918	21,058	19,635	860	4.1	36.4	32.6	72.2	11.2	1,124	285	246
Giles	13,656	13,113	10,828	543	4.1	22.4	17.7	75.3	9.4	252	14	58
Grainger	10,157	9,732	7,501	425	4.4	36.2	26.8	83.7	2.4	10	5	5
Greene	29,915	28,116	23,270	1,799	6.4	48.1	37.4	76.6	8.1	2,088	489	393
Grundy	6,523	6,282	5,155	241	3.8	18.1	14.3	82.2	4.7	(NA)	–	–
Hamblen	25,952	24,693	20,514	1,259	5.1	161.2	127.4	72.6	16.1	1,492	284	238
Hamilton	143,020	134,692	122,588	8,328	6.2	263.7	226.0	65.9	25.4	11,149	2,200	2,074
Hancock	3,379	3,277	2,890	102	3.1	15.2	13.0	78.9	7.9	8	–	1
Hardeman	11,200	10,694	9,174	506	4.7	16.8	13.7	74.2	6.4	506	85	77
Hardin	13,376	12,807	10,275	569	4.4	23.1	17.8	77.2	5.2	225	25	19
Hawkins.	25,660	24,416	18,779	1,244	5.1	52.7	38.6	78.8	9.8	656	129	119
Haywood	8,429	8,086	7,475	343	4.2	15.8	14.0	65.9	15.2	301	55	44
Henderson	11,964	11,446	9,278	518	4.5	23.0	17.8	79.3	6.0	174	33	29
Henry	16,496	15,781	13,774	715	4.5	29.4	24.5	77.4	7.2	285	45	39
Hickman.	9,258	8,904	6,662	354	4.0	15.1	10.9	80.2	4.3	49	4	5
Houston	4,052	3,900	3,085	152	3.9	20.2	15.4	77.0	4.8	14	4	3
Humphreys.	8,868	8,482	7,136	386	4.6	16.7	13.4	77.9	6.4	191	32	29
Jackson	5,362	5,163	4,219	199	3.9	17.4	13.7	80.7	4.0	–	–	–
Jefferson	21,379	19,319	14,170	2,060	10.7	78.1	51.7	77.9	8.5	2,303	463	468
Johnson	8,454	7,879	6,090	575	7.3	28.3	20.4	79.7	6.5	387	3	1
Knox	186,871	171,439	143,582	15,432	9.0	367.5	282.4	66.9	24.4	19,678	3,836	4,183
Lake	2,745	2,716	2,610	29	1.1	16.8	16.0	60.0	20.7	40	10	8
Lauderdale	11,300	10,563	9,343	737	7.0	24.0	19.9	64.8	13.2	829	132	149
Lawrence	17,282	16,821	14,229	461	2.7	28.0	23.1	77.1	8.4	94	11	16

See footnotes at end of table.

Table B-7. Counties — **Housing Units and Building Permits**—Con.

[Includes United States, states, and 3,141 counties/county equivalents defined as of February 22, 2005. For more information on these areas, see Appendix C, Geographic Information]

County	Housing units — 2005 (July 1)	Housing units — 2000¹ (April 1 esti-mates base)	Housing units — 1990 (April 1)	Net change, 2000–2005 Number	Net change, 2000–2005 Percent	Units per square mile of land area 2005²	Units per square mile of land area 1990	Housing 2000, percent — Owner-occupied housing units³	Housing 2000, percent — Units in multi-unit structures	New private housing units — Cumulative, 2000–2005 period	New private housing units — 2005	New private housing units — 2004
TENNESSEE—Con.												
Lewis	4,998	4,821	3,943	177	3.7	17.7	14.0	79.6	4.8	40	5	8
Lincoln	14,409	13,999	11,902	410	2.9	25.3	20.9	76.3	8.5	45	14	–
Loudon	18,592	17,277	12,995	1,315	7.6	81.2	56.8	79.1	7.7	1,710	455	331
McMinn	22,422	21,625	17,616	797	3.7	52.1	40.9	75.7	11.6	388	69	98
McNairy	11,647	11,223	9,734	424	3.8	20.8	17.4	80.0	4.4	153	31	28
Macon	9,338	8,894	6,879	444	5.0	30.4	22.4	78.6	5.8	160	28	47
Madison	41,583	38,205	31,809	3,378	8.8	74.7	57.1	67.0	21.6	4,034	624	688
Marion	13,183	12,140	10,011	1,043	8.6	26.5	20.0	80.7	6.3	1,013	129	140
Marshall	12,322	11,181	8,909	1,141	10.2	32.8	23.7	73.1	10.3	1,338	264	232
Maury	32,891	28,674	22,286	4,217	14.7	53.7	36.4	72.8	13.7	7,918	1,936	1,702
Meigs	5,509	5,188	3,689	321	6.2	28.3	18.9	81.9	4.3	123	60	40
Monroe	18,351	17,288	12,803	1,063	6.1	28.9	20.2	78.3	7.9	1,131	276	236
Montgomery	61,146	52,167	37,233	8,979	17.2	113.4	69.1	63.5	18.8	11,535	2,622	2,500
Moore	2,781	2,515	1,912	266	10.6	21.5	14.8	83.7	3.5	312	66	47
Morgan	8,034	7,713	6,378	321	4.2	15.4	12.2	82.9	2.4	21	1	–
Obion	14,866	14,489	13,359	377	2.6	27.3	24.5	71.5	13.1	385	47	67
Overton	9,513	9,168	7,388	345	3.8	22.0	17.0	80.9	4.1	33	6	11
Perry	4,286	4,115	3,225	171	4.2	10.3	7.8	86.0	2.3	1	–	–
Pickett	3,072	2,956	2,253	116	3.9	18.9	13.8	84.3	4.6	(NA)	–	–
Polk	7,817	7,369	5,659	448	6.1	18.0	13.0	80.8	3.3	384	160	113
Putnam	29,082	26,916	21,417	2,166	8.0	72.5	53.4	65.6	19.6	2,665	715	512
Rhea	13,475	12,566	10,361	909	7.2	42.7	32.8	75.5	8.5	904	129	178
Roane	24,238	23,369	20,334	869	3.7	67.1	56.3	77.6	10.6	293	55	62
Robertson	23,968	20,995	15,823	2,973	14.2	50.3	33.2	76.5	9.8	3,760	668	533
Rutherford	90,147	70,616	45,755	19,531	27.7	145.7	73.9	69.8	21.8	24,182	5,011	5,590
Scott	9,257	8,909	7,122	348	3.9	17.4	13.4	76.4	6.5	50	13	19
Sequatchie	5,151	4,916	3,570	235	4.8	19.4	13.4	76.4	5.1	93	13	24
Sevier	40,982	37,252	24,166	3,730	10.0	69.2	40.8	73.4	15.3	3,533	838	570
Shelby	389,208	362,954	327,796	26,254	7.2	515.8	434.2	63.1	28.4	33,582	5,716	5,526
Smith	8,001	7,665	6,049	336	4.4	25.4	19.2	78.7	6.6	460	163	26
Stewart	6,222	5,977	4,384	245	4.1	13.6	9.6	79.2	3.0	50	26	10
Sullivan	72,240	69,052	60,623	3,188	4.6	174.9	146.8	75.7	13.6	3,946	776	700
Sumner	58,504	51,657	39,807	6,847	13.3	110.5	75.2	75.6	15.5	8,121	1,818	1,600
Tipton	21,964	19,064	14,071	2,900	15.2	47.8	30.6	76.1	6.7	3,390	626	606
Trousdale	3,277	3,095	2,537	182	5.9	28.7	22.2	76.4	8.7	205	44	41
Unicoi	8,527	8,214	7,076	313	3.8	45.8	38.0	76.4	7.7	121	8	12
Union	8,688	7,916	5,696	772	9.8	38.9	25.5	81.0	4.1	727	155	133
Van Buren	2,553	2,453	2,001	100	4.1	9.3	7.3	85.3	2.9	(NA)	–	–
Warren	17,275	16,689	13,802	586	3.5	39.9	31.9	72.8	13.1	247	29	78
Washington	50,936	47,779	38,378	3,157	6.6	156.1	117.6	68.2	21.5	4,133	970	773
Wayne	7,013	6,701	5,741	312	4.7	9.6	7.8	82.9	3.6	75	9	26
Weakley	15,538	14,928	12,857	610	4.1	26.8	22.2	69.0	14.5	669	111	102
White	10,573	10,192	8,369	381	3.7	28.1	22.2	79.8	5.8	80	14	8
Williamson	56,686	47,005	29,875	9,681	20.6	97.3	51.3	81.5	13.2	9,771	1,941	1,947
Wilson	40,133	34,920	26,198	5,213	14.9	70.3	45.9	81.4	9.2	6,522	1,428	1,089
TEXAS	9,026,011	8,157,558	7,008,999	868,453	10.6	34.5	26.8	63.8	24.2	1,033,247	210,611	188,842
Anderson	19,044	18,436	16,909	608	3.3	17.8	15.8	74.0	9.6	248	23	21
Andrews	5,521	5,400	5,462	121	2.2	3.7	3.6	79.7	6.7	95	24	12
Angelina	33,772	32,435	28,796	1,337	4.1	42.1	35.9	72.4	10.5	854	104	107
Aransas	13,967	12,848	10,889	1,119	8.7	55.5	43.2	75.2	12.7	887	256	220
Archer	3,961	3,871	3,680	90	2.3	4.4	4.0	81.3	3.5	56	16	10
Armstrong	941	920	916	21	2.3	1.0	1.0	78.9	1.6	15	1	4
Atascosa	15,587	14,877	11,614	710	4.8	12.7	9.4	78.4	4.0	409	68	72
Austin	10,695	10,205	8,885	490	4.8	16.4	13.6	77.2	8.4	325	49	28
Bailey	2,754	2,738	3,109	16	0.6	3.3	3.8	71.4	8.4	14	6	2
Bandera	9,886	9,503	6,485	383	4.0	12.5	8.2	82.9	1.0	61	52	2
Bastrop	24,273	22,250	16,301	2,023	9.1	27.3	18.3	80.4	4.9	1,658	269	342
Baylor	2,842	2,820	3,006	22	0.8	3.3	3.5	72.4	7.6	–	–	–
Bee	11,142	10,939	10,208	203	1.9	12.7	11.6	65.5	13.4	65	11	16
Bell	105,980	92,782	75,957	13,198	14.2	100.0	71.7	55.7	25.0	16,228	3,669	3,409
Bexar	573,153	521,359	455,832	51,794	9.9	459.7	365.6	61.2	26.9	71,204	17,808	13,320
Blanco	4,225	4,031	3,135	194	4.8	5.9	4.4	78.8	3.4	122	26	22
Borden	448	435	478	13	3.0	0.5	0.5	74.0	–	(NA)	–	–
Bosque	8,867	8,644	8,074	223	2.6	9.0	8.2	77.7	3.4	36	5	8
Bowie	38,084	36,463	34,234	1,621	4.4	42.9	38.6	71.0	13.6	1,232	156	220
Brazoria	105,408	90,628	74,504	14,780	16.3	76.0	53.7	74.0	15.4	19,817	4,688	4,367
Brazos	66,955	59,023	48,799	7,932	13.4	114.3	83.3	45.6	39.8	9,203	1,610	1,159
Brewster	4,808	4,614	4,486	194	4.2	0.8	0.7	59.5	15.6	129	7	15
Briscoe	1,031	1,006	1,074	25	2.5	1.1	1.2	77.1	1.4	(NA)	–	–
Brooks	3,247	3,203	3,104	44	1.4	3.4	3.3	73.0	7.8	17	3	2
Brown	18,311	17,889	16,909	422	2.4	19.4	17.9	72.2	9.9	313	127	20

See footnotes at end of table.

Table B-7. Counties — **Housing Units and Building Permits**—Con.

[Includes United States, states, and 3,141 counties/county equivalents defined as of February 22, 2005. For more information on these areas, see Appendix C, Geographic Information]

County	Housing units							Housing 2000, percent		New private housing units authorized by building permits		
	2005 (July 1)	2000[1] (April 1 estimates base)	1990 (April 1)	Net change, 2000–2005 Number	Percent	Units per square mile of land area 2005[2]	1990	Owner-occupied housing units[3]	Units in multi-unit structures	Cumulative, 2000–2005 period	2005	2004

TEXAS—Con.

County	2005	2000	1990	Number	Percent	2005[2]	1990	Owner	Multi	Cumulative	2005	2004
Burleson	8,538	8,197	7,044	341	4.2	12.8	10.6	79.7	3.7	85	9	18
Burnet	18,748	15,912	12,801	2,836	17.8	18.8	12.9	78.3	6.2	3,280	561	686
Caldwell	12,978	11,904	10,123	1,074	9.0	23.8	18.5	69.7	11.6	695	84	103
Calhoun	10,783	10,238	9,559	545	5.3	21.0	18.7	72.8	9.9	659	118	155
Callahan	6,109	5,925	5,503	184	3.1	6.8	6.1	80.7	2.4	66	31	15
Cameron	137,240	119,654	88,759	17,586	14.7	151.5	98.0	67.7	20.1	20,852	3,694	3,592
Camp	5,390	5,228	4,530	162	3.1	27.3	22.9	74.7	5.6	51	8	17
Carson	2,884	2,815	2,856	69	2.5	3.1	3.1	83.7	1.1	43	7	7
Cass	14,370	13,890	13,191	480	3.5	15.3	14.1	78.6	7.4	153	23	34
Castro	3,221	3,198	3,357	23	0.7	3.6	3.7	71.1	8.3	1	–	–
Chambers	12,475	10,336	8,061	2,139	20.7	20.8	13.4	83.6	4.2	2,412	517	571
Cherokee	19,839	19,173	17,629	666	3.5	18.9	16.8	73.8	7.2	277	32	35
Childress	3,098	3,059	3,046	39	1.3	4.4	4.3	70.5	14.9	52	1	–
Clay	5,131	4,992	4,708	139	2.8	4.7	4.3	83.0	2.0	37	9	–
Cochran	1,596	1,587	1,763	9	0.6	2.1	2.3	73.6	3.3	–	–	–
Coke	2,919	2,843	2,793	76	2.7	3.2	3.1	78.9	3.8	4	–	6
Coleman	5,322	5,248	5,382	74	1.4	4.2	4.2	74.4	7.9	22	2	2
Collin	250,452	194,947	103,827	55,505	28.5	295.5	122.5	68.6	27.8	68,963	13,844	12,090
Collingsworth	1,721	1,723	1,952	–2	–0.1	1.9	2.1	78.8	4.6	–	–	–
Colorado	9,647	9,431	8,537	216	2.3	10.0	8.9	76.7	6.1	83	20	9
Comal	40,240	32,718	22,987	7,522	23.0	71.7	40.9	77.2	10.9	9,620	2,205	1,840
Comanche	7,278	7,105	6,724	173	2.4	7.8	7.2	76.2	4.1	19	5	4
Concho	1,529	1,488	1,514	41	2.8	1.5	1.5	75.0	2.6	(NA)	–	–
Cooke	15,629	15,061	13,315	568	3.8	17.9	15.2	72.1	6.9	388	46	125
Coryell	22,737	21,775	18,970	962	4.4	21.6	18.0	54.9	21.3	1,396	533	229
Cottle	1,085	1,088	1,286	–3	–0.3	1.2	1.4	71.6	8.0	1	–	–
Crane	1,600	1,596	1,795	4	0.3	2.0	2.3	85.1	3.2	–	–	–
Crockett	2,110	2,049	1,897	61	3.0	0.8	0.7	71.3	6.9	(NA)	–	–
Crosby	3,218	3,202	3,312	16	0.5	3.6	3.7	69.3	7.6	5	1	2
Culberson	1,350	1,321	1,286	29	2.2	0.4	0.3	70.8	5.5	32	18	1
Dallam	2,744	2,697	2,577	47	1.7	1.8	1.7	63.1	3.9	49	5	2
Dallas	914,267	854,075	795,513	60,192	7.0	1,039.4	904.1	52.6	39.9	86,063	14,404	13,297
Dawson	5,510	5,500	5,969	10	0.2	6.1	6.6	73.5	7.1	10	1	1
Deaf Smith	6,942	6,914	7,152	28	0.4	4.6	4.8	67.4	12.1	34	19	6
Delta	2,472	2,410	2,305	62	2.6	8.9	8.3	77.3	4.6	24	–	9
Denton	207,862	168,065	112,263	39,797	23.7	233.9	126.4	64.4	27.2	35,331	5,265	5,239
DeWitt	8,932	8,756	8,568	176	2.0	9.8	9.4	76.5	5.1	72	5	5
Dickens	1,399	1,368	1,564	31	2.3	1.5	1.7	77.7	2.0	(NA)	–	–
Dimmit	4,216	4,112	3,991	104	2.5	3.2	3.0	73.9	5.9	81	15	15
Donley	2,436	2,378	2,304	58	2.4	2.6	2.5	74.7	4.5	19	4	3
Duval	5,724	5,543	5,127	181	3.3	3.2	2.9	80.9	6.3	(NA)	–	–
Eastland	9,727	9,547	9,768	180	1.9	10.5	10.5	76.7	6.8	2	–	–
Ector	50,721	49,500	48,789	1,221	2.5	56.3	54.1	68.6	20.7	1,161	255	194
Edwards	1,255	1,217	1,550	38	3.1	0.6	0.7	79.9	1.7	(NA)	–	–
Ellis	46,574	39,071	31,314	7,503	19.2	49.6	33.3	76.2	9.4	7,709	1,832	1,900
El Paso	244,193	224,447	187,473	19,746	8.8	241.0	185.1	63.6	24.3	24,969	5,405	3,942
Erath	15,154	14,422	12,758	732	5.1	13.9	11.7	63.2	14.4	589	67	239
Falls	7,796	7,658	7,733	138	1.8	10.1	10.1	71.5	8.6	67	18	9
Fannin	13,409	12,887	11,504	522	4.1	15.0	12.9	74.8	8.8	387	85	66
Fayette	11,387	11,113	10,756	274	2.5	12.0	11.3	78.3	5.7	124	33	37
Fisher	2,305	2,277	2,413	28	1.2	2.6	2.7	76.8	6.0	–	–	–
Floyd	3,235	3,221	3,535	14	0.4	3.3	3.6	73.9	5.7	36	24	2
Foard	868	850	890	18	2.1	1.2	1.3	75.2	5.5	–	–	–
Fort Bend	136,003	115,989	77,075	20,014	17.3	155.5	88.1	80.8	9.3	13,990	4,097	4,152
Franklin	5,374	5,132	4,219	242	4.7	18.8	14.8	79.0	4.3	124	6	4
Freestone	8,552	8,138	7,812	414	5.1	9.7	8.8	78.8	4.8	273	42	43
Frio	5,857	5,660	4,879	197	3.5	5.2	4.3	69.0	10.2	142	19	81
Gaines	5,524	5,410	5,221	114	2.1	3.7	3.5	78.6	5.1	48	17	13
Galveston	125,465	111,733	99,451	13,732	12.3	314.9	249.5	66.2	22.1	17,794	3,318	3,059
Garza	1,943	1,928	2,184	15	0.8	2.2	2.4	70.7	9.6	10	–	–
Gillespie	10,528	9,902	8,265	626	6.3	9.9	7.8	77.5	6.5	603	144	79
Glasscock	680	660	600	20	3.0	0.8	0.7	67.3	3.0	(NA)	–	–
Goliad	3,542	3,426	2,835	116	3.4	4.1	3.3	80.0	3.2	(NA)	–	–
Gonzales	8,391	8,194	7,810	197	2.4	7.9	7.3	69.1	8.1	49	9	4
Gray	10,554	10,567	11,532	–13	–0.1	11.4	12.4	77.4	8.0	27	3	1
Grayson	50,506	48,315	44,223	2,191	4.5	54.1	47.4	70.6	14.5	2,427	744	521
Gregg	47,757	46,349	44,689	1,408	3.0	174.3	163.1	64.1	22.1	1,752	367	390
Grimes	9,821	9,490	7,744	331	3.5	12.4	9.8	77.7	5.0	87	28	7
Guadalupe	38,433	33,591	25,592	4,842	14.4	54.0	36.0	77.0	8.4	5,977	1,533	1,552
Hale	13,765	13,526	13,168	239	1.8	13.7	13.1	64.8	11.0	278	86	19

See footnotes at end of table.

[Includes United States, states, and 3,141 counties/county equivalents defined as of February 22, 2005. For more information on these areas, see Appendix C, Geographic Information]

County	Housing units							Housing 2000, percent		New private housing units authorized by building permits		
	2005 (July 1)	2000¹ (April 1 esti-mates base)	1990 (April 1)	Net change, 2000–2005		Units per square mile of land area		Owner-occupied housing units³	Units in multi-unit structures	Cumu-lative, 2000–2005 period	2005	2004
				Number	Percent	2005²	1990					
TEXAS—Con.												
Hall	1,991	1,988	2,189	3	0.2	2.2	2.4	74.1	5.6	–	–	–
Hamilton	4,544	4,455	4,266	89	2.0	5.4	5.1	78.1	3.9	18	3	2
Hansford	2,336	2,329	2,525	7	0.3	2.5	2.7	74.7	5.5	2	–	–
Hardeman	2,366	2,358	2,678	8	0.3	3.4	3.9	73.3	7.1	2	–	–
Hardin	20,781	19,836	16,486	945	4.8	23.2	18.4	82.7	4.5	295	98	115
Harris	1,456,218	1,298,131	1,173,808	158,087	12.2	842.3	678.9	55.3	37.1	204,207	41,506	36,395
Harrison	27,027	26,271	23,481	756	2.9	30.1	26.1	77.2	7.4	233	40	44
Hartley	1,793	1,760	1,541	33	1.9	1.2	1.1	76.4	6.9	(NA)	–	–
Haskell	3,600	3,555	3,843	45	1.3	4.0	4.3	78.9	3.4	7	6	–
Hays	44,427	35,633	25,247	8,794	24.7	65.5	37.2	64.8	23.1	11,171	2,655	2,578
Hemphill	1,557	1,548	1,712	9	0.6	1.7	1.9	77.0	4.8	4	4	–
Henderson	37,657	35,935	31,779	1,722	4.8	43.1	36.3	80.0	5.0	806	177	145
Hidalgo	231,571	192,658	128,241	38,913	20.2	147.5	81.7	73.1	12.0	46,265	8,889	9,314
Hill	15,024	14,626	12,899	398	2.7	15.6	13.4	74.9	6.9	122	15	24
Hockley	9,315	9,148	9,279	167	1.8	10.3	10.2	74.4	7.1	96	20	13
Hood	20,136	19,105	14,958	1,031	5.4	47.8	35.5	81.2	6.9	461	140	104
Hopkins	14,571	14,020	12,676	551	3.9	18.6	16.2	71.3	11.8	346	29	93
Houston	11,006	10,730	10,265	276	2.6	8.9	8.3	76.1	6.6	40	7	7
Howard	13,713	13,589	13,651	124	0.9	15.2	15.1	69.4	11.7	163	66	–
Hudspeth	1,531	1,471	1,288	60	4.1	0.3	0.3	81.0	1.6	(NA)	–	–
Hunt	33,887	32,490	28,959	1,397	4.3	40.3	34.4	71.5	14.1	1,174	435	447
Hutchinson	10,941	10,871	11,419	70	0.6	12.3	12.9	78.9	7.7	6	1	3
Irion	942	914	842	28	3.1	0.9	0.8	77.7	1.5	(NA)	–	–
Jack	3,729	3,668	3,497	61	1.7	4.1	3.8	76.7	3.5	9	1	3
Jackson	6,648	6,545	5,841	103	1.6	8.0	7.0	73.8	9.7	124	20	20
Jasper	17,089	16,576	13,824	513	3.1	18.2	14.7	80.7	6.5	41	8	7
Jeff Davis	1,463	1,420	1,348	43	3.0	0.6	0.6	70.1	1.6	(NA)	–	–
Jefferson	105,378	102,080	101,289	3,298	3.2	116.6	112.1	66.0	19.3	4,842	819	759
Jim Hogg	2,378	2,308	2,103	70	3.0	2.1	1.9	77.6	4.9	(NA)	–	–
Jim Wells	15,190	14,819	13,948	371	2.5	17.6	16.1	76.5	8.0	328	154	47
Johnson	50,539	46,269	37,029	4,270	9.2	69.3	50.8	78.9	7.4	5,011	1,151	911
Jones	7,429	7,236	7,639	193	2.7	8.0	8.2	79.3	4.6	29	17	3
Karnes	5,580	5,479	5,117	101	1.8	7.4	6.8	74.2	8.7	62	8	26
Kaufman	29,754	26,132	20,097	3,622	13.9	37.9	25.6	79.2	7.1	3,918	918	799
Kendall	11,860	9,609	6,137	2,251	23.4	17.9	9.3	79.5	6.3	2,695	552	599
Kenedy	289	281	213	8	2.8	0.2	0.1	34.8	17.8	(NA)	–	–
Kent	567	551	603	16	2.9	0.6	0.7	79.3	–	(NA)	–	–
Kerr	21,192	20,226	17,161	966	4.8	19.2	15.5	73.3	13.0	641	88	104
Kimble	3,059	2,996	2,593	63	2.1	2.4	2.1	73.5	5.9	21	13	5
King	179	174	191	5	2.9	0.2	0.2	34.3	1.1	(NA)	–	–
Kinney	1,959	1,907	1,821	52	2.7	1.4	1.3	77.4	9.6	11	–	2
Kleberg	12,845	12,743	12,008	102	0.8	14.7	13.8	58.6	20.3	52	7	6
Knox	2,177	2,129	2,459	48	2.3	2.6	2.9	75.4	7.0	(NA)	–	–
Lamar	21,971	21,113	18,964	858	4.1	24.0	20.7	67.2	13.8	751	60	129
Lamb	6,315	6,294	6,531	21	0.3	6.2	6.4	75.6	4.8	12	–	–
Lampasas	7,919	7,601	6,193	318	4.2	11.1	8.7	73.9	7.2	121	30	10
La Salle	2,471	2,436	2,244	35	1.4	1.7	1.5	74.7	5.3	7	3	2
Lavaca	9,877	9,657	9,549	220	2.3	10.2	9.8	78.5	3.6	89	20	18
Lee	7,139	6,851	5,773	288	4.2	11.4	9.2	79.3	5.7	116	23	15
Leon	8,622	8,299	7,019	323	3.9	8.0	6.5	82.8	3.9	(NA)	–	–
Liberty	27,820	26,360	22,243	1,460	5.5	24.0	19.2	79.0	6.7	1,468	287	263
Limestone	9,988	9,725	9,922	263	2.7	11.0	10.9	74.9	5.6	100	11	23
Lipscomb	1,551	1,541	1,683	10	0.6	1.7	1.8	77.8	6.7	–	–	–
Live Oak	6,374	6,196	5,519	178	2.9	6.2	5.3	81.4	3.7	16	4	1
Llano	13,155	11,848	9,773	1,307	11.0	14.1	10.5	80.9	6.2	1,625	320	256
Loving	72	70	59	2	2.9	0.1	0.1	83.9	–	(NA)	–	–
Lubbock	111,752	100,595	91,770	11,157	11.1	124.2	102.0	59.2	24.6	13,038	1,781	3,774
Lynn	2,702	2,671	2,978	31	1.2	3.0	3.3	74.3	4.5	12	2	3
McCulloch	4,305	4,184	4,424	121	2.9	4.0	4.1	72.8	8.3	113	11	21
McLennan	89,797	84,794	78,857	5,003	5.9	86.2	75.7	60.2	23.2	6,184	1,322	1,541
McMullen	615	593	565	22	3.7	0.6	0.5	80.6	–	(NA)	–	–
Madison	4,985	4,797	4,326	188	3.9	10.6	9.2	77.0	4.4	87	20	19
Marion	6,612	6,384	5,729	228	3.6	17.3	15.0	82.1	3.1	9	–	1
Martin	2,015	1,898	2,039	117	6.2	2.2	2.2	74.1	7.0	23	10	3
Mason	2,426	2,372	2,356	54	2.3	2.6	2.5	80.2	4.1	43	14	14
Matagorda	19,247	18,611	18,540	636	3.4	17.3	16.6	66.8	15.0	724	97	201
Maverick	16,176	14,889	11,143	1,287	8.6	12.6	8.7	69.6	14.0	1,249	227	226
Medina	15,532	14,826	10,860	706	4.8	11.7	8.2	79.8	5.4	347	43	111
Menard	1,656	1,607	1,562	49	3.0	1.8	1.7	74.6	2.4	(NA)	–	–
Midland	49,247	48,060	45,181	1,187	2.5	54.7	50.2	69.6	22.3	1,478	390	289

See footnotes at end of table.

Table B-7. Counties — **Housing Units and Building Permits**—Con.

[Includes United States, states, and 3,141 counties/county equivalents defined as of February 22, 2005. For more information on these areas, see Appendix C, Geographic Information]

County	Housing units							Housing 2000, percent		New private housing units authorized by building permits		
	2005 (July 1)	2000[1] (April 1 estimates base)	1990 (April 1)	Net change, 2000–2005 Number	Percent	Units per square mile of land area 2005[2]	1990	Owner-occupied housing units[3]	Units in multi-unit structures	Cumulative, 2000–2005 period	2005	2004
TEXAS—Con.												
Milam	11,168	10,866	10,511	302	2.8	11.0	10.3	73.0	6.1	161	15	17
Mills	2,767	2,691	2,582	76	2.8	3.7	3.5	80.5	2.5	(NA)	–	–
Mitchell	4,215	4,168	4,559	47	1.1	4.6	5.0	75.9	6.5	1	1	–
Montague	10,168	9,862	9,262	306	3.1	10.9	10.0	78.8	4.3	45	–	3
Montgomery	140,596	112,770	73,871	27,826	24.7	134.7	70.7	78.1	12.3	34,078	7,441	6,977
Moore	7,642	7,478	6,837	164	2.2	8.5	7.6	70.5	13.6	151	26	33
Morris	6,156	6,017	5,800	139	2.3	24.2	22.8	77.9	6.7	43	7	4
Motley	858	839	1,026	19	2.3	0.9	1.0	76.7	2.6	–	–	–
Nacogdoches	26,315	25,051	22,768	1,264	5.0	27.8	24.0	61.6	17.7	892	103	102
Navarro	18,881	18,449	17,219	432	2.3	18.7	16.1	70.8	11.7	255	68	41
Newton	7,613	7,331	6,378	282	3.8	8.2	6.8	84.5	1.8	–	–	–
Nolan	7,112	7,112	7,462	–	–	7.8	8.2	67.4	13.3	20	4	3
Nueces	129,818	123,041	114,326	6,777	5.5	155.3	136.8	61.3	26.5	9,253	2,019	2,356
Ochiltree	3,830	3,769	3,996	61	1.6	4.2	4.4	72.5	5.6	62	7	6
Oldham	835	815	861	20	2.5	0.6	0.6	66.4	3.3	12	3	4
Orange	36,009	34,781	32,032	1,228	3.5	101.0	89.9	77.2	9.7	1,384	283	251
Palo Pinto	14,382	14,102	13,349	280	2.0	15.1	14.0	72.0	9.2	45	15	7
Panola	10,875	10,524	9,700	351	3.3	13.6	12.1	80.8	3.2	65	16	7
Parker	37,057	34,083	26,044	2,974	8.7	41.0	28.8	80.6	5.5	2,331	541	426
Parmer	3,772	3,732	3,685	40	1.1	4.3	4.2	72.3	4.7	20	1	4
Pecos	6,455	6,338	5,841	117	1.8	1.4	1.2	74.1	8.2	34	16	1
Polk	22,055	21,177	18,662	878	4.1	20.9	17.6	81.7	4.4	846	187	187
Potter	47,176	44,598	42,927	2,578	5.8	51.9	47.2	60.1	19.5	5,427	1,112	953
Presidio	3,702	3,299	2,890	403	12.2	1.0	0.7	70.3	8.1	472	103	89
Rains	4,753	4,523	3,533	230	5.1	20.5	15.2	82.8	2.4	107	14	32
Randall	45,124	43,261	37,807	1,863	4.3	49.3	41.3	70.3	18.5	245	57	46
Reagan	1,483	1,452	1,685	31	2.1	1.3	1.4	78.4	3.0	18	3	1
Real	2,133	2,009	2,049	124	6.2	3.0	2.9	76.9	1.0	69	–	8
Red River	7,071	6,916	6,650	155	2.2	6.7	6.3	74.9	5.9	29	4	4
Reeves	5,072	5,043	6,044	29	0.6	1.9	2.3	77.7	6.2	7	2	1
Refugio	3,718	3,669	3,739	49	1.3	4.8	4.9	74.9	3.5	71	12	12
Roberts	459	449	492	10	2.2	0.5	0.5	79.0	3.1	(NA)	–	–
Robertson	8,110	7,874	7,338	236	3.0	9.5	8.6	71.5	7.5	93	17	15
Rockwall	22,103	15,349	9,816	6,754	44.0	171.6	76.2	82.7	9.6	8,264	2,001	1,598
Runnels	5,425	5,400	5,345	25	0.5	5.2	5.1	77.4	5.1	7	1	–
Rusk	20,474	19,867	19,092	607	3.1	22.2	20.7	79.9	5.3	178	22	89
Sabine	7,965	7,659	6,996	306	4.0	16.2	14.3	86.2	2.3	3	–	1
San Augustine	5,530	5,356	4,168	174	3.2	10.5	7.9	81.4	4.6	5	–	–
San Jacinto	11,943	11,520	9,823	423	3.7	20.9	17.2	87.7	2.6	44	3	11
San Patricio	26,848	24,864	22,126	1,984	8.0	38.8	32.0	68.2	14.6	2,450	338	479
San Saba	3,050	2,951	3,078	99	3.4	2.7	2.7	75.8	5.0	52	1	5
Schleicher	1,395	1,371	1,288	24	1.8	1.1	1.0	75.7	6.3	8	–	1
Scurry	7,155	7,112	7,702	43	0.6	7.9	8.5	73.8	9.5	23	7	4
Shackelford	1,656	1,613	1,755	43	2.7	1.8	1.9	79.0	4.3	(NA)	–	–
Shelby	12,361	11,955	10,616	406	3.4	15.6	13.4	78.3	4.9	38	3	30
Sherman	1,378	1,276	1,293	102	8.0	1.5	1.4	73.6	3.1	112	23	21
Smith	75,779	71,701	64,369	4,078	5.7	81.6	69.3	69.7	16.2	3,837	745	724
Somervell	2,979	2,750	2,429	229	8.3	15.9	13.0	74.9	4.1	170	24	18
Starr	18,141	17,589	12,209	552	3.1	14.8	10.0	79.5	6.0	–	–	–
Stephens	4,950	4,893	4,982	57	1.2	5.5	5.6	72.4	9.9	5	1	2
Sterling	652	633	623	19	3.0	0.7	0.7	75.6	1.6	(NA)	–	–
Stonewall	961	936	1,085	25	2.7	1.0	1.2	78.7	4.4	(NA)	–	–
Sutton	2,024	1,998	1,924	26	1.3	1.4	1.3	72.3	7.3	2	–	–
Swisher	3,333	3,315	3,497	18	0.5	3.7	3.9	70.4	5.4	–	–	–
Tarrant	639,226	565,810	491,152	73,416	13.0	740.3	568.8	60.8	30.0	93,348	19,312	17,288
Taylor	53,497	52,055	49,988	1,442	2.8	58.4	54.6	61.6	18.9	1,922	298	273
Terrell	1,017	991	810	26	2.6	0.4	0.3	77.0	0.7	(NA)	–	–
Terry	5,110	5,087	5,296	23	0.5	5.7	6.0	71.2	4.7	12	5	–
Throckmorton	1,091	1,066	1,106	25	2.3	1.2	1.2	77.0	3.6	(NA)	–	–
Titus	11,046	10,675	9,357	371	3.5	26.9	22.8	72.4	10.3	241	46	51
Tom Green	45,161	43,916	40,135	1,245	2.8	29.7	26.4	64.1	21.0	1,517	270	235
Travis	391,425	335,888	264,173	55,537	16.5	395.7	267.0	51.4	40.0	68,876	14,234	10,658
Trinity	8,450	8,141	7,200	309	3.8	12.2	10.4	80.8	3.4	1	1	–
Tyler	10,764	10,419	9,047	345	3.3	11.7	9.8	84.1	2.7	11	3	4
Upshur	15,436	14,930	12,887	506	3.4	26.3	21.9	81.8	5.0	83	7	9
Upton	1,632	1,609	1,868	23	1.4	1.3	1.5	75.2	2.3	–	–	–
Uvalde	10,474	10,166	9,692	308	3.0	6.7	6.2	72.2	8.4	201	39	24
Val Verde	17,106	16,288	13,905	818	5.0	5.4	4.4	66.0	12.0	815	156	130
Van Zandt	21,735	20,896	17,013	839	4.0	25.6	20.0	80.8	3.9	294	55	59
Victoria	34,191	32,945	29,162	1,246	3.8	38.7	33.0	67.4	18.5	1,161	123	398

See footnotes at end of table.

[Includes United States, states, and 3,141 counties/county equivalents defined as of February 22, 2005. For more information on these areas, see Appendix C, Geographic Information]

County	Housing units 2005 (July 1)	Housing units 2000[1] (April 1) estimates base	Housing units 1990 (April 1)	Net change, 2000–2005 Number	Net change, 2000–2005 Percent	Units per square mile of land area 2005[2]	Units per square mile of land area 1990	Housing 2000, percent Owner-occupied housing units[3]	Housing 2000, percent Units in multi-unit structures	New private housing units authorized by building permits Cumulative, 2000–2005 period	New private housing units authorized by building permits 2005	New private housing units authorized by building permits 2004
TEXAS—Con.												
Walker	22,295	21,099	18,349	1,196	5.7	28.3	23.3	59.8	24.0	1,300	282	356
Waller	13,494	11,955	8,824	1,539	12.9	26.3	17.2	72.5	10.5	1,323	219	213
Ward	4,884	4,832	5,365	52	1.1	5.8	6.4	78.1	9.4	19	3	4
Washington	13,791	13,241	11,717	550	4.2	22.6	19.2	73.5	9.4	460	140	39
Webb	64,901	55,206	37,197	9,695	17.6	19.3	11.1	65.7	16.8	11,467	2,176	2,193
Wharton	17,137	16,606	16,277	531	3.2	15.7	14.9	68.8	11.3	283	34	30
Wheeler	2,707	2,687	3,071	20	0.7	3.0	3.4	78.0	2.1	2	–	–
Wichita	54,973	53,304	51,413	1,669	3.1	87.6	81.9	62.3	19.1	2,455	540	317
Wilbarger	6,432	6,371	6,812	61	1.0	6.6	7.0	66.3	11.7	77	–	63
Willacy	7,131	6,727	6,072	404	6.0	12.0	10.2	77.3	6.6	456	36	35
Williamson	117,797	90,325	54,466	27,472	30.4	104.9	48.4	74.2	16.5	30,962	5,999	4,334
Wilson	12,719	12,110	8,516	609	5.0	15.8	10.6	85.0	2.8	259	44	45
Winkler	3,230	3,214	3,708	16	0.5	3.8	4.4	83.2	4.7	26	8	6
Wise	20,449	19,242	14,219	1,207	6.3	22.6	15.7	81.4	3.9	743	192	175
Wood	18,482	17,939	14,541	543	3.0	28.4	22.4	81.4	4.6	102	16	19
Yoakum	3,015	2,974	3,372	41	1.4	3.8	4.2	78.1	3.1	8	–	–
Young	8,603	8,504	8,523	99	1.2	9.3	9.2	73.9	8.5	59	6	7
Zapata	6,435	6,167	4,225	268	4.3	6.5	4.2	81.9	3.5	(NA)	–	–
Zavala	4,152	4,075	4,180	77	1.9	3.2	3.2	73.1	9.6	24	3	3
UTAH	873,097	768,603	598,388	104,494	13.6	10.6	7.3	71.5	22.0	130,443	27,799	24,267
Beaver	2,791	2,660	2,200	131	4.9	1.1	0.8	79.0	11.2	177	36	20
Box Elder	15,698	14,209	11,890	1,489	10.5	2.7	2.1	80.2	11.3	2,020	483	277
Cache	33,575	29,035	22,053	4,540	15.6	28.8	18.9	64.6	27.4	5,375	1,015	1,327
Carbon	8,994	8,742	8,713	252	2.9	6.1	5.9	77.3	9.7	331	51	35
Daggett	1,158	1,084	825	74	6.8	1.7	1.2	70.9	0.4	84	19	14
Davis	86,469	74,114	55,777	12,355	16.7	284.0	183.2	77.5	16.8	15,713	3,186	3,007
Duchesne	7,594	6,988	5,860	606	8.7	2.3	1.8	80.8	4.4	735	162	114
Emery	4,271	4,140	3,928	131	3.2	1.0	0.9	82.0	6.6	138	15	14
Garfield	3,146	2,767	2,488	379	13.7	0.6	0.5	79.1	1.4	470	103	95
Grand	4,437	4,014	2,992	423	10.5	1.2	0.8	71.0	9.6	542	144	68
Iron	16,137	13,618	8,499	2,519	18.5	4.9	2.6	66.2	24.2	3,237	1,013	631
Juab	3,195	2,810	2,311	385	13.7	0.9	0.7	79.8	5.8	529	147	69
Kane	4,374	3,767	3,237	607	16.1	1.1	0.8	77.9	3.2	827	247	153
Millard	4,758	4,522	4,125	236	5.2	0.7	0.6	79.7	6.9	276	49	48
Morgan	2,529	2,158	1,681	371	17.2	4.2	2.8	88.3	3.6	565	185	120
Piute	776	745	704	31	4.2	1.0	0.9	87.0	0.3	51	15	9
Rich	2,896	2,408	1,859	488	20.3	2.8	1.8	83.9	13.1	565	87	68
Salt Lake	337,601	310,996	257,339	26,605	8.6	457.8	349.0	69.0	27.7	36,633	7,660	6,409
San Juan	5,639	5,449	4,650	190	3.5	0.7	0.6	79.3	5.8	236	61	56
Sanpete	8,457	7,879	6,570	578	7.3	5.3	4.1	78.8	7.4	467	56	55
Sevier	7,492	7,016	6,059	476	6.8	3.9	3.2	82.0	6.1	610	102	97
Summit	20,471	17,489	11,256	2,982	17.1	10.9	6.0	75.6	25.9	3,853	908	699
Tooele	16,973	13,812	9,510	3,161	22.9	2.4	1.4	78.4	10.6	3,689	675	551
Uintah	9,636	9,040	8,142	596	6.6	2.2	1.8	77.0	11.2	819	229	137
Utah	127,340	104,316	72,820	23,024	22.1	63.7	36.4	66.8	25.8	25,297	5,249	4,492
Wasatch	8,183	6,564	4,465	1,619	24.7	7.0	3.8	80.7	7.5	2,102	493	346
Washington	48,777	36,478	19,523	12,299	33.7	20.1	8.0	73.9	13.2	15,825	3,848	3,792
Wayne	1,411	1,329	1,061	82	6.2	0.6	0.4	77.8	4.2	99	14	16
Weber	78,319	70,454	57,851	7,865	11.2	136.1	100.5	74.9	19.7	9,178	1,547	1,548
VERMONT	307,345	294,382	271,214	12,963	4.4	33.2	29.3	70.6	23.0	17,673	2,917	3,588
Addison	16,121	15,312	14,022	809	5.3	20.9	18.2	74.9	13.8	1,092	192	187
Bennington	20,342	19,403	18,501	939	4.8	30.1	27.4	71.4	19.9	1,289	219	296
Caledonia	15,116	14,507	13,449	609	4.2	23.2	20.7	72.0	19.9	856	152	186
Chittenden	62,118	58,864	52,095	3,254	5.5	115.2	96.7	66.1	32.9	4,132	501	854
Essex	4,851	4,762	4,403	89	1.9	7.3	6.6	79.5	9.2	145	38	36
Franklin	20,475	19,191	17,250	1,284	6.7	32.1	27.1	75.0	16.4	1,729	330	336
Grand Isle	4,880	4,663	4,135	217	4.7	59.1	50.0	81.4	4.3	260	33	37
Lamoille	11,777	11,005	9,872	772	7.0	25.5	21.4	70.9	19.3	948	152	179
Orange	13,735	13,386	12,336	349	2.6	19.9	17.9	78.3	11.0	494	87	100
Orleans	15,299	14,674	12,997	625	4.3	21.9	18.7	74.1	14.9	971	294	265
Rutland	32,796	32,311	31,181	485	1.5	35.2	33.4	69.7	27.0	892	169	165
Washington	28,787	27,644	25,328	1,143	4.1	41.8	36.7	68.5	29.4	1,624	255	279
Windham	28,054	27,039	25,796	1,015	3.8	35.6	32.7	67.9	22.7	1,382	207	266
Windsor	32,994	31,621	29,849	1,373	4.3	34.0	30.7	71.5	22.1	1,859	288	402
VIRGINIA	3,174,708	2,904,432	2,496,334	270,276	9.3	80.2	63.0	68.1	21.5	341,381	61,518	63,220
Accomack	20,578	19,550	15,840	1,028	5.3	45.2	34.8	75.1	3.7	1,450	424	251
Albemarle	39,065	33,740	25,958	5,325	15.8	54.1	35.9	65.9	21.3	6,521	1,073	1,294
Alleghany[10]	8,023	7,881	5,481	142	1.8	18.0	12.3	84.9	3.2	223	31	32
Amelia	5,069	4,609	3,439	460	10.0	14.2	9.6	81.9	1.9	617	169	114
Amherst	13,533	12,958	10,598	575	4.4	28.5	22.3	78.1	7.4	727	124	131

See footnotes at end of table.

Includes United States, states, and 3,141 counties/county equivalents defined as of February 22, 2005. For more information on these areas, see Appendix C, Geographic Information]

County	Housing units							Housing 2000, percent		New private housing units authorized by building permits		
	2005 (July 1)	2000[1] (April 1 esti- mates base)	1990 (April 1)	Net change, 2000–2005		Units per square mile of land area		Owner- occupied housing units[3]	Units in multi- unit structures	Cumu- lative, 2000– 2005 period	2005	2004
				Number	Percent	2005[2]	1990					
VIRGINIA—Con.												
Appomattox	6,219	5,828	4,913	391	6.7	18.6	14.7	81.1	4.0	516	133	121
Arlington	92,622	90,426	84,847	2,196	2.4	3,580.3	3,278.5	43.3	59.1	4,304	1,275	1,274
Augusta	29,452	26,738	21,202	2,714	10.2	30.4	21.8	83.1	5.0	3,296	557	653
Bath	3,072	2,896	2,596	176	6.1	5.8	4.9	79.9	3.8	219	31	33
Bedford	29,683	26,849	19,641	2,834	10.6	39.3	26.0	86.6	4.1	3,507	744	695
Bland	3,432	3,161	2,706	271	8.6	9.6	7.5	86.1	1.6	301	41	68
Botetourt	13,745	12,571	9,785	1,174	9.3	25.3	18.0	87.8	3.3	1,476	273	364
Brunswick	7,785	7,541	6,456	244	3.2	13.8	11.4	77.6	3.1	272	47	42
Buchanan	12,090	11,887	12,222	203	1.7	24.0	24.3	82.9	2.3	161	35	34
Buckingham	6,629	6,290	5,013	339	5.4	11.4	8.6	77.8	3.5	420	102	79
Campbell	23,491	22,098	19,008	1,393	6.3	46.6	37.7	77.3	9.4	1,706	339	285
Caroline	10,369	8,889	7,292	1,480	16.6	19.5	13.7	81.9	2.7	2,158	646	577
Carroll	15,545	14,680	12,209	865	5.9	32.6	25.6	81.7	3.5	1,025	185	151
Charles City	3,095	2,895	2,314	200	6.9	16.9	12.7	84.9	1.9	236	41	44
Charlotte	6,142	5,733	4,947	409	7.1	12.9	10.4	77.6	3.0	457	59	69
Chesterfield	111,750	97,687	77,329	14,063	14.4	262.5	181.6	80.9	11.9	17,006	2,717	3,138
Clarke	5,979	5,388	4,531	591	11.0	33.9	25.7	75.6	7.6	849	221	130
Craig	2,738	2,554	1,993	184	7.2	8.3	6.0	81.2	3.6	211	34	30
Culpeper	16,154	12,871	10,471	3,283	25.5	42.4	27.5	70.5	13.8	4,889	1,502	1,428
Cumberland	4,355	4,085	3,170	270	6.6	14.6	10.6	77.2	2.8	317	63	53
Dickenson	7,840	7,684	7,112	156	2.0	23.6	21.4	82.1	3.2	134	18	23
Dinwiddie	10,654	9,707	8,023	947	9.8	21.2	15.9	79.2	3.4	1,123	174	227
Essex	5,353	4,926	4,073	427	8.7	20.8	15.8	77.3	6.9	612	172	112
Fairfax	386,856	359,411	307,966	27,445	7.6	979.3	778.5	70.9	26.1	33,069	4,353	6,780
Fauquier	24,537	21,047	17,716	3,490	16.6	37.8	27.2	76.2	6.7	4,288	706	703
Floyd	7,260	6,763	5,505	497	7.3	19.0	14.4	81.9	2.3	596	102	94
Fluvanna	9,876	8,018	5,035	1,858	23.2	34.4	17.5	85.2	1.6	2,097	248	325
Franklin	25,106	22,716	17,526	2,390	10.5	36.3	25.3	81.1	7.3	2,952	628	473
Frederick	27,202	23,319	17,864	3,883	16.7	65.6	43.1	80.3	6.2	5,181	1,271	1,069
Giles	8,068	7,732	7,098	336	4.3	22.6	19.8	79.1	7.0	383	67	67
Gloucester	15,663	14,494	12,451	1,169	8.1	72.3	57.5	81.4	7.4	1,456	288	257
Goochland	7,886	6,555	5,203	1,331	20.3	27.7	18.3	86.6	1.2	1,712	380	310
Grayson	9,590	9,123	7,529	467	5.1	21.7	17.0	81.4	3.3	517	59	64
Greene	6,967	5,986	4,154	981	16.4	44.5	26.5	81.4	4.3	1,172	207	166
Greensville	4,009	3,765	3,393	244	6.5	13.6	11.5	78.3	1.5	288	60	62
Halifax[11]	17,348	16,951	11,790	397	2.3	21.2	14.5	76.1	5.5	518	104	93
Hanover	36,459	32,196	23,727	4,263	13.2	77.1	50.2	84.3	7.7	4,903	619	566
Henrico	122,746	112,518	94,539	10,228	9.1	515.6	397.0	65.7	27.5	12,927	2,082	1,956
Henry	26,463	25,942	23,169	521	2.0	69.2	60.6	76.9	8.2	583	84	115
Highland	1,917	1,822	1,759	95	5.2	4.6	4.2	83.8	3.0	128	23	23
Isle of Wight	13,660	12,066	9,753	1,594	13.2	43.2	30.9	80.8	5.6	2,051	534	366
James City	25,820	20,772	14,330	5,048	24.3	180.7	100.3	77.0	14.0	6,118	1,178	1,111
King and Queen	3,197	3,010	2,698	187	6.2	10.1	8.5	82.5	0.6	246	60	45
King George	8,283	6,820	5,280	1,463	21.5	46.0	29.3	71.8	9.4	2,009	529	443
King William	5,880	5,189	4,193	691	13.3	21.3	15.2	85.0	3.3	905	199	236
Lancaster	6,960	6,498	5,918	462	7.1	52.3	44.4	83.0	3.2	617	132	118
Lee	11,450	11,086	10,263	364	3.3	26.2	23.5	74.4	4.3	415	57	66
Loudoun	93,374	62,160	32,932	31,214	50.2	179.6	63.3	79.4	14.6	35,794	5,199	6,664
Louisa	13,994	11,855	9,080	2,139	18.0	28.1	18.3	81.5	4.1	2,878	728	596
Lunenburg	5,863	5,736	5,065	127	2.2	13.6	11.7	77.7	2.7	164	30	27
Madison	5,791	5,239	4,547	552	10.5	18.0	14.1	76.8	2.9	696	123	112
Mathews	5,639	5,333	4,725	306	5.7	65.8	55.1	84.7	2.7	426	91	98
Mecklenburg	18,324	17,403	14,589	921	5.3	29.4	23.4	74.4	4.8	1,080	195	207
Middlesex	6,915	6,362	5,486	553	8.7	53.1	42.1	83.1	2.6	696	132	168
Montgomery	35,119	32,561	27,770	2,558	7.9	90.5	71.5	55.1	31.0	2,931	373	650
Nelson	9,254	8,554	7,063	700	8.2	19.6	15.0	80.8	11.7	934	216	201
New Kent	6,293	5,203	3,968	1,090	20.9	30.0	18.9	88.7	0.6	1,435	340	276
Northampton	7,271	6,547	6,183	724	11.1	35.1	29.8	68.6	5.6	889	135	305
Northumberland	8,863	8,065	6,841	798	9.9	46.1	35.6	87.4	1.1	1,051	232	207
Nottoway	6,661	6,373	5,732	288	4.5	21.2	18.2	70.9	6.9	386	74	76
Orange	13,196	11,354	9,038	1,842	16.2	38.6	26.4	77.1	6.9	2,594	718	526
Page	11,075	10,557	8,948	518	4.9	35.6	28.8	73.9	7.3	785	224	158
Patrick	10,252	9,823	8,125	429	4.4	21.2	16.8	80.3	3.9	506	100	61
Pittsylvania	29,339	28,011	22,861	1,328	4.7	30.2	23.5	80.1	3.6	1,531	280	254
Powhatan	9,056	7,509	4,910	1,547	20.6	34.7	18.8	88.8	2.1	1,909	360	347
Prince Edward	8,186	7,527	6,075	659	8.8	23.2	17.2	68.4	10.4	810	130	87
Prince George	11,804	10,711	8,640	1,093	10.2	44.4	32.5	73.0	10.5	1,332	238	245
Prince William	125,667	98,052	74,759	27,615	28.2	372.0	220.9	71.7	17.5	32,894	5,427	5,822
Pulaski	16,902	16,325	14,740	577	3.5	52.7	46.0	73.7	12.9	807	174	131
Rappahannock	3,572	3,304	2,964	268	8.1	13.4	11.1	75.2	2.6	352	60	58

See footnotes at end of table.

[Includes United States, states, and 3,141 counties/county equivalents defined as of February 22, 2005. For more information on these areas, see Appendix C, Geographic Information]

County	Housing units 2005 (July 1)	2000[1] (April 1 esti- mates base)	1990 (April 1)	Net change, 2000–2005 Number	Percent	Units per square mile of land area 2005[2]	1990	Housing 2000, percent Owner- occupied housing units[3]	Units in multi- unit structures	New private housing units authorized by building permits Cumu- lative, 2000– 2005 period	2005	2004
VIRGINIA—Con.												
Richmond.	3,694	3,504	3,179	190	5.4	19.3	16.6	77.4	6.4	251	51	55
Roanoke.	38,731	36,087	31,689	2,644	7.3	154.4	126.4	77.2	17.6	3,200	407	592
Rockbridge.	10,514	9,550	7,975	964	10.1	17.5	13.3	77.7	5.4	1,178	208	161
Rockingham.	29,868	27,325	22,614	2,543	9.3	35.1	26.6	78.0	8.8	3,394	812	802
Russell.	13,581	13,191	11,558	390	3.0	28.6	24.3	81.1	4.5	423	79	81
Scott.	11,722	11,355	10,003	367	3.2	21.8	18.6	78.2	4.1	418	51	67
Shenandoah.	18,584	16,709	15,160	1,875	11.2	36.3	29.6	73.2	12.0	2,534	561	458
Smyth.	15,421	15,111	13,132	310	2.1	34.1	29.0	74.1	7.8	372	51	69
Southampton	7,424	7,058	6,560	366	5.2	12.4	10.9	74.3	4.4	483	103	93
Spotsylvania.	41,941	33,329	20,483	8,612	25.8	104.6	51.1	82.2	6.3	10,164	1,665	1,419
Stafford.	40,220	31,405	20,529	8,815	28.1	148.8	76.0	80.6	7.9	10,326	1,639	1,864
Surry.	3,599	3,294	2,982	305	9.3	12.9	10.7	77.2	4.6	381	82	72
Sussex.	4,724	4,653	4,252	71	1.5	9.6	8.7	69.5	6.8	104	35	20
Tazewell.	20,845	20,390	18,901	455	2.2	40.1	36.4	77.3	6.7	517	85	82
Warren.	14,774	13,297	11,223	1,477	11.1	69.1	52.5	74.2	10.7	1,950	398	416
Washington	24,583	22,985	19,183	1,598	7.0	43.7	34.0	77.2	9.8	1,991	342	483
Westmoreland	10,110	9,286	8,378	824	8.9	44.1	36.6	79.2	3.5	1,022	152	358
Wise.	18,208	17,789	15,927	419	2.4	45.1	39.5	75.3	7.9	366	63	60
Wythe	13,221	12,744	10,659	477	3.7	28.5	23.0	77.3	8.2	609	145	113
York	23,894	20,701	15,284	3,193	15.4	226.2	144.7	75.8	11.6	3,533	360	474
Independent Cities												
Alexandria	68,406	64,251	58,252	4,155	6.5	4,506.3	3,812.3	40.0	63.8	5,605	1,017	843
Bedford	2,751	2,702	2,625	49	1.8	399.3	383.2	60.3	28.6	79	6	5
Bristol	8,725	8,469	8,174	256	3.0	676.4	705.3	65.1	25.7	434	97	76
Buena Vista	2,814	2,716	2,494	98	3.6	412.0	365.2	70.7	13.5	136	15	21
Charlottesville	18,268	17,571	16,785	697	4.0	1,780.5	1,636.0	40.8	44.6	1,169	285	271
Chesapeake	79,291	72,672	55,742	6,619	9.1	232.7	163.6	74.9	16.8	8,931	2,089	1,463
Clifton Forge[10]	(X)	(X)	2,131	(NA)	(NA)	(NA)	687.4	62.6	23.5	(NA)	(X)	(X)
Colonial Heights	7,619	7,340	6,592	279	3.8	1,018.6	882.5	69.3	18.4	398	54	46
Covington.	3,233	3,195	3,269	38	1.2	570.2	736.3	69.7	10.3	55	6	3
Danville.	23,277	23,108	23,297	169	0.7	540.6	541.0	58.1	24.2	411	30	124
Emporia.	2,607	2,412	2,178	195	8.1	378.4	316.1	52.2	16.9	220	16	10
Fairfax.	8,608	8,204	7,677	404	4.9	1,364.2	1,246.3	69.1	27.6	475	28	47
Falls Church	4,694	4,725	4,668	−31	−0.7	2,358.8	2,334.0	60.6	38.3	45	24	13
Franklin	3,888	3,767	3,166	121	3.2	465.6	412.8	53.7	35.7	216	62	45
Fredericksburg	9,234	8,888	8,063	346	3.9	877.8	767.2	35.6	50.3	842	410	170
Galax	3,266	3,217	2,943	49	1.5	396.8	364.7	66.2	21.3	86	22	12
Hampton	58,810	57,311	53,623	1,499	2.6	1,135.8	1,034.8	58.6	26.8	2,779	879	321
Harrisonburg.	14,871	13,685	10,900	1,186	8.7	846.9	620.7	39.0	47.4	1,637	386	280
Hopewell	9,938	9,749	9,625	189	1.9	970.5	939.0	56.0	24.2	419	152	48
Lexington	2,411	2,376	2,311	35	1.5	968.3	928.1	54.9	28.7	70	9	12
Lynchburg	28,981	27,622	27,233	1,359	4.9	586.8	551.3	58.5	29.9	2,082	496	218
Manassas	12,688	12,114	10,232	574	4.7	1,277.7	1,022.2	69.8	22.3	784	154	147
Manassas Park	4,175	3,365	2,252	810	24.1	1,676.7	1,230.6	78.7	1.1	989	188	189
Martinsville	7,254	7,229	7,310	25	0.3	661.9	667.0	60.2	25.4	104	9	5
Newport News.	77,426	74,367	69,728	3,059	4.1	1,133.8	1,020.5	52.4	38.5	4,159	650	743
Norfolk.	96,280	94,416	98,762	1,864	2.0	1,791.9	1,837.1	45.5	44.4	4,035	1,183	769
Norton	1,973	1,949	1,845	24	1.2	262.0	254.1	55.9	27.5	29	1	6
Petersburg	15,917	15,970	16,196	−53	−0.3	695.7	707.9	51.5	30.0	122	21	56
Poquoson	4,549	4,300	3,890	249	5.8	293.1	250.6	84.1	6.5	363	90	97
Portsmouth	42,538	41,605	42,283	933	2.2	1,282.8	1,275.5	58.6	28.4	1,574	227	379
Radford	6,335	6,137	5,496	198	3.2	645.1	559.7	44.6	46.4	318	72	56
Richmond.	93,220	92,354	94,141	866	0.9	1,551.9	1,565.6	46.1	42.1	2,716	754	398
Roanoke	46,235	45,257	44,384	978	2.2	1,078.2	1,034.6	56.3	35.3	1,646	191	234
Salem	10,650	10,403	9,609	247	2.4	730.0	660.4	67.6	24.5	390	71	65
South Boston[11]	(X)	(X)	2,997	(NA)	(NA)	(NA)	541.0	(NA)	(NA)	(NA)	(X)	(X)
Staunton	10,883	10,427	10,003	456	4.4	552.2	506.2	61.4	26.0	770	197	328
Suffolk.	30,552	24,704	20,011	5,848	23.7	76.4	50.0	72.2	13.3	7,039	1,090	1,135
Virginia Beach.	171,423	162,277	147,037	9,146	5.6	690.4	592.1	65.6	24.0	11,901	2,103	2,218
Waynesboro	9,291	8,863	7,902	428	4.8	604.9	562.8	61.2	26.8	613	116	123
Williamsburg	4,575	3,880	3,960	695	17.9	535.7	459.9	44.3	41.6	728	31	109
Winchester	11,319	10,587	9,808	732	6.9	1,213.2	1,051.2	45.7	34.2	1,051	219	160
WASHINGTON.	2,651,645	2,451,082	2,032,378	200,563	8.2	39.8	30.5	64.6	25.6	263,553	52,988	50,089
Adams.	5,918	5,772	5,263	146	2.5	3.1	2.7	68.4	13.6	233	37	27
Asotin	9,345	9,111	7,519	234	2.6	14.7	11.8	67.1	15.9	419	106	120
Benton.	61,410	55,963	44,877	5,447	9.7	36.1	26.3	68.7	22.6	7,030	1,219	1,436
Chelan.	31,888	30,407	25,048	1,481	4.9	10.9	8.6	64.7	17.7	2,221	507	446
Clallam	32,773	30,683	25,225	2,090	6.8	18.8	14.5	72.7	11.4	3,089	819	589

See footnotes at end of table.

Table B-7. Counties — **Housing Units and Building Permits**—Con.

[Includes United States, states, and 3,141 counties/county equivalents defined as of February 22, 2005. For more information on these areas, see Appendix C, Geographic Information]

County	Housing units			Net change, 2000–2005		Units per square mile of land area		Housing 2000, percent		New private housing units authorized by building permits		
	2005 (July 1)	2000[1] (April 1 esti-mates base)	1990 (April 1)	Number	Percent	2005[2]	1990	Owner-occupied housing units[3]	Units in multi-unit structures	Cumu-lative, 2000–2005 period	2005	2004
WASHINGTON—Con.												
Clark	152,584	134,030	92,849	18,554	13.8	242.9	147.9	67.3	22.5	22,536	3,771	3,855
Columbia	2,065	2,018	2,046	47	2.3	2.4	2.4	69.4	7.6	75	10	6
Cowlitz	40,577	38,624	33,304	1,953	5.1	35.6	29.2	67.6	18.7	2,766	515	409
Douglas	13,906	12,944	10,640	962	7.4	7.6	5.8	70.9	14.0	1,411	395	247
Ferry	3,905	3,775	3,239	130	3.4	1.8	1.5	73.0	4.3	180	32	33
Franklin	20,433	16,084	13,664	4,349	27.0	16.4	11.0	65.6	21.8	5,743	1,231	1,828
Garfield	1,277	1,288	1,209	−11	−0.9	1.8	1.7	74.0	5.0	10	6	2
Grant	30,605	29,082	22,809	1,523	5.2	11.4	8.5	66.7	12.5	2,079	639	397
Grays Harbor	33,550	32,489	29,932	1,061	3.3	17.5	15.6	69.0	14.5	1,783	420	370
Island	35,515	32,378	25,860	3,137	9.7	170.4	124.0	70.1	11.5	4,038	768	890
Jefferson	15,526	14,144	11,014	1,382	9.8	8.6	6.1	76.2	7.9	1,771	326	375
King	792,682	742,240	647,343	50,442	6.8	372.8	304.5	59.8	37.0	65,787	12,034	11,945
Kitsap	98,431	92,644	74,038	5,787	6.2	248.6	187.0	67.4	19.9	7,915	1,611	1,366
Kittitas	18,304	16,475	13,215	1,829	11.1	8.0	5.8	58.3	24.4	2,458	559	467
Klickitat	9,074	8,633	7,213	441	5.1	4.8	3.9	68.8	9.6	635	129	126
Lewis	30,685	29,585	25,487	1,100	3.7	12.7	10.6	71.4	11.2	1,880	529	396
Lincoln	5,425	5,298	4,607	127	2.4	2.3	2.0	76.8	4.3	226	47	42
Mason	27,648	25,515	22,292	2,133	8.4	28.8	23.2	79.0	4.5	2,883	633	542
Okanogan	19,868	19,085	16,629	783	4.1	3.8	3.2	68.6	8.2	1,124	244	179
Pacific	14,302	13,991	12,404	311	2.2	15.3	12.7	74.8	7.5	637	209	125
Pend Oreille	6,901	6,608	5,404	293	4.4	4.9	3.9	77.4	5.2	419	88	67
Pierce	303,051	277,060	228,842	25,991	9.4	180.5	136.6	63.5	24.6	33,893	6,826	6,026
San Juan	10,867	9,752	6,075	1,115	11.4	62.1	34.7	73.5	7.5	1,313	212	190
Skagit	46,476	42,681	33,580	3,795	8.9	26.8	19.4	69.7	15.6	5,056	1,018	851
Skamania	4,847	4,576	3,922	271	5.9	2.9	2.4	73.8	5.9	424	120	116
Snohomish	264,287	236,205	183,942	28,082	11.9	126.5	88.0	67.8	26.5	34,895	6,659	6,164
Spokane	187,865	175,005	150,105	12,860	7.3	106.5	85.1	65.5	24.1	17,249	4,396	3,920
Stevens	18,263	17,599	14,601	664	3.8	7.4	5.9	78.1	5.8	979	223	189
Thurston	95,102	86,652	66,464	8,450	9.8	130.8	91.4	66.6	20.0	11,450	2,570	2,253
Wahkiakum	1,861	1,792	1,496	69	3.9	7.0	5.7	79.7	4.7	134	49	23
Walla Walla	22,118	21,147	19,029	971	4.6	17.4	15.0	65.2	20.0	1,420	257	320
Whatcom	82,934	73,897	55,742	9,037	12.2	39.1	26.3	63.4	23.2	11,970	2,556	2,488
Whitman	17,734	16,676	14,598	1,058	6.3	8.2	6.8	47.9	37.8	1,625	438	325
Yakima	81,643	79,174	70,852	2,469	3.1	19.0	16.5	64.4	17.9	3,797	780	939
WEST VIRGINIA	872,203	844,626	781,295	27,577	3.3	36.2	32.4	75.2	12.0	29,589	6,140	5,716
Barbour	7,535	7,348	6,956	187	2.5	22.1	20.4	78.6	5.8	54	4	8
Berkeley	39,522	32,913	25,385	6,609	20.1	123.1	79.0	74.2	13.8	8,562	1,935	1,811
Boone	11,827	11,575	10,705	252	2.2	23.5	21.3	78.9	4.4	235	16	158
Braxton	7,572	7,374	5,708	198	2.7	14.7	11.1	78.2	4.7	5	1	1
Brooke	11,194	11,149	10,838	45	0.4	126.0	122.0	76.7	13.6	121	23	24
Cabell	46,068	45,615	43,596	453	1.0	163.6	154.8	64.6	23.8	654	241	218
Calhoun	3,961	3,848	3,446	113	2.9	14.1	12.3	78.9	3.1	(NA)	–	–
Clay	4,960	4,836	4,359	124	2.6	14.5	12.7	79.2	2.7	134	22	26
Doddridge	3,761	3,661	3,251	100	2.7	11.7	10.1	81.2	1.8	(NA)	–	–
Fayette	22,204	21,616	20,841	588	2.7	33.4	31.4	77.2	7.5	802	119	134
Gilmer	3,707	3,621	3,243	86	2.4	10.9	9.5	72.4	5.7	–	–	–
Grant	6,508	6,105	4,746	403	6.6	13.6	9.9	80.9	5.7	493	92	69
Greenbrier	18,258	17,644	16,757	614	3.5	17.9	16.4	76.6	8.3	858	193	143
Hampshire	11,938	11,185	8,817	753	6.7	18.6	13.7	81.1	3.5	1,035	293	165
Hancock	14,824	14,729	14,697	95	0.6	179.0	177.0	77.1	13.4	283	25	38
Hardy	7,671	7,115	5,573	556	7.8	13.1	9.6	80.5	3.5	716	166	117
Harrison	31,657	31,112	29,988	545	1.8	76.1	72.1	74.8	11.8	985	223	150
Jackson	12,558	12,245	10,571	313	2.6	27.0	22.7	79.6	7.6	232	15	13
Jefferson	20,644	17,623	14,606	3,021	17.1	98.5	69.7	75.8	10.9	3,572	527	540
Kanawha	94,787	93,788	92,747	999	1.1	105.0	102.7	70.3	17.9	1,134	329	367
Lewis	8,094	7,944	7,454	150	1.9	21.2	19.2	73.0	9.1	4	–	–
Lincoln	10,083	9,846	8,429	237	2.4	23.1	19.3	79.1	3.0	225	24	42
Logan	17,292	16,807	16,848	485	2.9	38.1	37.1	76.8	8.3	44	1	9
McDowell	13,615	13,582	15,330	33	0.2	25.5	28.7	80.1	5.4	64	3	3
Marion	27,023	26,660	25,491	363	1.4	87.3	82.3	74.8	13.7	131	28	25
Marshall	15,978	15,814	15,630	164	1.0	52.0	50.9	77.6	11.0	48	11	11
Mason	12,356	12,056	10,932	300	2.5	28.6	25.3	81.0	6.2	52	5	7
Mercer	30,196	30,143	28,426	53	0.2	71.8	67.6	76.8	11.2	120	24	17
Mineral	12,819	12,094	10,930	725	6.0	39.1	33.3	78.0	11.8	856	131	111
Mingo	13,293	12,898	13,087	395	3.1	31.5	31.0	77.7	9.4	41	4	2
Monongalia	37,705	36,695	31,563	1,010	2.8	104.4	87.4	61.0	27.1	568	117	120
Monroe	7,476	7,261	5,994	215	3.0	15.8	12.7	84.5	1.4	7	1	2
Morgan	9,055	8,076	6,757	979	12.1	39.5	29.5	83.3	4.5	1,237	257	238
Nicholas	12,822	12,406	11,235	416	3.4	19.8	17.3	82.8	4.9	104	2	3
Ohio	22,161	22,169	23,229	−8	(Z)	208.7	218.8	68.6	27.5	146	39	34

See footnotes at end of table.

[Includes United States, states, and 3,141 counties/county equivalents defined as of February 22, 2005. For more information on these areas, see Appendix C, Geographic Information]

County	Housing units								Housing 2000, percent		New private housing units authorized by building permits		
	2005 (July 1)	2000[1] (April 1 esti-mates base)	1990 (April 1)	Net change, 2000–2005		Units per square mile of land area		Owner-occupied housing units[3]	Units in multi-unit structures	Cumu-lative, 2000–2005 period	2005	2004
				Number	Percent	2005[2]	1990					
WEST VIRGINIA—Con.												
Pendleton	5,314	5,102	4,516	212	4.2	7.6	6.5	79.4	2.7	247	27	40
Pleasants	3,252	3,214	3,134	38	1.2	24.9	24.0	80.4	7.9	50	7	15
Pocahontas	7,837	7,594	5,579	243	3.2	8.3	5.9	80.3	14.6	91	10	1
Preston	13,769	13,444	12,137	325	2.4	21.2	18.7	83.0	5.9	12	1	2
Putnam	22,935	21,621	16,884	1,314	6.1	66.2	48.8	84.0	7.9	1,544	274	252
Raleigh	36,439	35,678	33,278	761	2.1	60.0	54.8	76.5	9.2	1,253	391	262
Randolph	13,863	13,478	12,548	385	2.9	13.3	12.1	75.7	10.2	141	10	20
Ritchie	5,628	5,513	4,936	115	2.1	12.4	10.9	81.7	4.4	21	4	10
Roane	7,580	7,360	6,611	220	3.0	15.7	13.7	79.6	5.8	190	99	90
Summers	7,450	7,337	6,769	113	1.5	20.6	18.7	79.1	6.8	168	31	34
Taylor	7,251	7,125	6,528	126	1.8	42.0	37.8	79.6	9.5	20	5	1
Tucker	4,770	4,634	3,900	136	2.9	11.4	9.3	82.6	7.2	81	20	22
Tyler	4,871	4,780	4,441	91	1.9	18.9	17.2	83.7	3.5	5	–	–
Upshur	11,223	10,751	9,506	472	4.4	31.6	26.8	76.7	8.1	544	60	118
Wayne	19,395	19,107	16,991	288	1.5	38.3	33.6	78.1	6.9	330	64	46
Webster	5,411	5,273	5,072	138	2.6	9.7	9.1	79.0	5.1	–	–	–
Wetzel	8,373	8,313	8,129	60	0.7	23.3	22.6	78.5	8.7	42	5	8
Wirt	3,371	3,266	2,795	105	3.2	14.5	12.0	83.1	2.8	55	38	15
Wood	40,580	39,785	37,620	795	2.0	110.5	102.4	73.4	15.6	1,266	222	171
Wyoming	11,767	11,698	11,756	69	0.6	23.5	23.5	83.3	4.7	7	1	3
WISCONSIN	2,498,500	2,321,157	2,055,774	177,343	7.6	46.0	37.9	68.4	26.2	226,345	35,334	39,992
Adams	15,672	14,123	12,418	1,549	11.0	24.2	19.2	85.3	3.0	1,881	423	361
Ashland	9,195	8,883	8,371	312	3.5	8.8	8.0	70.7	16.3	368	61	59
Barron	22,991	20,969	19,363	2,022	9.6	26.6	22.4	75.8	13.4	2,245	322	391
Bayfield	12,336	11,640	10,918	696	6.0	8.4	7.4	82.6	4.4	937	195	157
Brown	100,137	90,199	74,740	9,938	11.0	189.4	141.4	65.4	30.1	12,213	1,722	2,080
Buffalo	6,553	6,098	5,586	455	7.5	9.6	8.2	76.5	13.8	559	61	104
Burnett	13,686	12,582	11,743	1,104	8.8	16.7	14.3	84.5	3.3	1,327	196	232
Calumet	18,219	15,758	12,465	2,461	15.6	57.0	39.0	80.4	16.6	2,465	269	293
Chippewa	25,593	22,825	21,024	2,768	12.1	25.3	20.8	75.7	16.7	3,147	529	514
Clark	14,101	13,531	12,904	570	4.2	11.6	10.6	81.2	8.4	754	121	152
Columbia	24,590	22,685	19,258	1,905	8.4	31.8	24.9	74.8	17.6	2,349	302	393
Crawford	8,836	8,481	7,315	355	4.2	15.4	12.8	76.8	9.9	297	49	60
Dane	202,425	180,398	147,851	22,027	12.2	168.4	123.0	57.6	40.0	27,871	4,614	4,709
Dodge	35,997	33,672	28,720	2,325	6.9	40.8	32.5	73.4	22.0	2,618	362	642
Door	21,793	19,587	18,037	2,206	11.3	45.1	37.4	79.4	11.9	2,670	395	505
Douglas	21,446	20,356	20,610	1,090	5.4	16.4	15.7	71.3	19.9	1,432	204	285
Dunn	16,978	15,277	13,252	1,701	11.1	19.9	15.6	69.1	19.1	2,077	352	423
Eau Claire	40,717	37,470	32,741	3,247	8.7	63.9	51.3	65.0	28.1	4,048	441	588
Florence	4,278	4,239	3,775	39	0.9	8.8	7.7	85.7	3.7	74	34	40
Fond du Lac	41,523	39,271	34,548	2,252	5.7	57.4	47.8	72.9	22.2	3,115	618	504
Forest	8,873	8,322	7,203	551	6.6	8.8	7.1	78.9	4.7	659	100	120
Grant	20,500	19,940	18,450	560	2.8	17.9	16.1	72.3	16.4	820	149	139
Green	15,093	13,878	12,087	1,215	8.8	25.8	20.7	73.8	17.1	1,531	277	270
Green Lake	10,221	9,831	9,202	390	4.0	28.9	26.0	77.2	12.3	551	95	105
Iowa	10,644	9,579	8,220	1,065	11.1	14.0	10.8	75.9	12.2	1,319	198	204
Iron	6,053	5,706	5,243	347	6.1	8.0	6.9	80.7	10.2	465	79	93
Jackson	8,635	8,029	7,627	606	7.5	8.7	7.7	74.9	12.0	753	149	171
Jefferson	32,739	30,109	25,719	2,630	8.7	58.8	46.2	71.7	22.2	3,676	620	785
Juneau	13,443	12,370	11,422	1,073	8.7	17.5	14.9	77.0	9.5	1,180	151	198
Kenosha	65,568	59,989	51,262	5,579	9.3	240.3	187.9	69.1	27.3	7,080	1,100	1,306
Kewaunee	8,865	8,221	7,544	644	7.8	25.9	22.0	81.8	12.5	804	106	127
La Crosse	46,250	43,479	38,239	2,771	6.4	102.2	84.5	65.1	30.7	3,526	521	727
Lafayette	6,987	6,674	6,313	313	4.7	11.0	10.0	77.5	9.4	445	76	105
Langlade	11,982	11,187	10,825	795	7.1	13.7	12.4	79.0	11.6	944	89	214
Lincoln	15,728	14,681	13,256	1,047	7.1	17.8	15.0	78.2	13.2	1,321	218	227
Manitowoc	36,291	34,653	31,843	1,638	4.7	61.4	53.8	76.0	22.2	2,210	281	284
Marathon	55,511	50,360	43,774	5,151	10.2	35.9	28.3	75.7	19.0	6,563	1,178	1,192
Marinette	27,631	26,260	25,650	1,371	5.2	19.7	18.3	79.3	8.8	1,650	276	287
Marquette	9,372	8,664	8,035	708	8.2	20.6	17.6	82.3	5.0	818	115	218
Menominee	2,225	2,098	1,742	127	6.1	6.2	4.9	73.8	4.1	138	15	37
Milwaukee	404,974	400,093	390,715	4,881	1.2	1,676.5	1,617.5	52.6	48.5	11,287	1,697	2,117
Monroe	17,777	16,671	14,135	1,106	6.6	19.7	15.7	73.7	16.1	1,347	262	262
Oconto	22,488	19,818	18,832	2,670	13.5	22.5	18.9	83.0	6.7	3,438	779	862
Oneida	28,790	26,625	25,173	2,165	8.1	25.6	22.4	79.7	7.7	2,686	431	464
Outagamie	69,404	62,614	51,923	6,790	10.8	108.4	81.1	72.4	23.7	8,491	1,215	1,235
Ozaukee	34,556	32,034	26,482	2,522	7.9	149.0	114.2	76.3	22.9	3,123	406	380
Pepin	3,263	3,036	2,919	227	7.5	14.0	12.6	79.7	12.9	289	41	53
Pierce	15,248	13,493	11,536	1,755	13.0	26.4	20.0	73.1	19.3	2,406	401	500
Polk	23,458	21,129	18,562	2,329	11.0	25.6	20.2	80.2	9.7	2,812	431	569
Portage	28,811	26,589	22,910	2,222	8.4	35.7	28.4	70.9	21.1	2,686	377	421

See footnotes at end of table.

Table B-7. Counties — **Housing Units and Building Permits**—Con.

[Includes United States, states, and 3,141 counties/county equivalents defined as of February 22, 2005. For more information on these areas, see Appendix C, Geographic Information]

County	Housing units							Housing 2000, percent		New private housing units authorized by building permits		
	2005 (July 1)	2000[1] (April 1 estimates base)	1990 (April 1)	Net change, 2000–2005 Number	Net change, 2000–2005 Percent	Units per square mile of land area 2005[2]	Units per square mile of land area 1990	Owner-occupied housing units[3]	Units in multi-unit structures	Cumulative, 2000–2005 period	2005	2004
WISCONSIN—Con.												
Price	10,482	9,574	9,052	908	9.5	8.4	7.2	80.7	7.5	1,153	217	229
Racine	79,121	74,718	66,945	4,403	5.9	237.5	201.0	70.6	28.0	6,088	1,006	1,278
Richland	8,544	8,163	7,325	381	4.7	14.6	12.5	74.2	13.4	493	70	80
Rock	66,647	62,187	54,840	4,460	7.2	92.5	76.1	71.1	21.0	5,736	996	1,096
Rusk	8,160	7,609	7,904	551	7.2	8.9	8.7	78.7	7.6	678	102	117
St. Croix	31,140	24,265	18,519	6,875	28.3	43.1	25.7	76.4	18.6	7,761	1,041	1,347
Sauk	27,281	24,297	20,439	2,984	12.3	32.6	24.4	73.3	18.6	3,683	644	360
Sawyer	15,203	13,722	13,025	1,481	10.8	12.1	10.4	77.1	4.6	1,806	289	329
Shawano	19,534	18,317	16,737	1,217	6.6	21.9	18.8	78.2	11.4	1,703	393	241
Sheboygan	48,819	45,951	40,695	2,868	6.2	95.0	79.2	71.4	27.7	3,742	506	657
Taylor	9,013	8,595	7,710	418	4.9	9.2	7.9	80.6	10.9	361	77	69
Trempealeau	12,159	11,482	10,097	677	5.9	16.6	13.8	74.1	15.9	910	172	177
Vernon	13,136	12,416	10,830	720	5.8	16.5	13.6	79.1	9.8	700	133	180
Vilas	24,016	22,399	20,225	1,617	7.2	27.5	23.2	81.8	4.3	1,916	223	397
Walworth	48,461	43,766	36,937	4,695	10.7	87.3	66.5	69.1	22.7	5,972	987	1,113
Washburn	12,177	10,814	9,829	1,363	12.6	15.0	12.1	80.8	6.3	1,626	283	364
Washington	50,815	45,809	34,382	5,006	10.9	117.9	79.8	76.0	23.6	6,629	1,371	1,205
Waukesha	151,812	140,309	110,452	11,503	8.2	273.2	198.8	76.4	23.2	14,220	1,970	2,200
Waupaca	24,503	22,509	20,141	1,994	8.9	32.6	26.8	77.0	15.8	2,592	368	481
Waushara	14,884	13,667	12,246	1,217	8.9	23.8	19.6	83.5	4.4	1,401	183	227
Winnebago	70,207	64,721	56,123	5,486	8.5	160.1	128.0	68.0	28.3	6,838	777	1,114
Wood	33,940	31,691	28,839	2,249	7.1	42.8	36.4	74.3	17.7	2,872	423	567
WYOMING	235,721	223,854	203,411	11,867	5.3	2.4	2.1	70.0	15.2	15,662	3,997	3,317
Albany	16,329	15,215	13,844	1,114	7.3	3.8	3.2	51.5	30.1	1,828	594	410
Big Horn	5,221	5,105	5,048	116	2.3	1.7	1.6	74.7	6.5	61	8	17
Campbell	14,085	13,288	11,538	797	6.0	2.9	2.4	73.6	17.1	871	273	129
Carbon	8,455	8,307	8,190	148	1.8	1.1	1.0	71.0	11.9	256	65	60
Converse	5,852	5,669	5,234	183	3.2	1.4	1.2	74.0	13.8	170	58	18
Crook	3,132	2,935	2,605	197	6.7	1.1	0.9	79.9	5.5	141	21	24
Fremont	16,150	15,541	14,437	609	3.9	1.8	1.6	72.9	9.7	411	85	66
Goshen	5,997	5,881	5,551	116	2.0	2.7	2.5	70.7	8.4	41	11	17
Hot Springs	2,572	2,536	2,429	36	1.4	1.3	1.2	68.4	12.1	19	5	5
Johnson	3,694	3,503	3,112	191	5.5	0.9	0.7	73.7	8.5	172	25	15
Laramie	36,747	34,213	30,507	2,534	7.4	13.7	11.4	69.1	18.3	3,569	872	876
Lincoln	7,763	6,831	5,409	932	13.6	1.9	1.3	81.3	6.4	1,220	261	212
Natrona	30,668	29,882	29,082	786	2.6	5.7	5.4	69.9	16.3	1,337	444	284
Niobrara	1,354	1,338	1,456	16	1.2	0.5	0.6	72.9	7.8	9	4	4
Park	12,684	11,869	10,306	815	6.9	1.8	1.5	71.4	11.0	1,073	187	242
Platte	4,628	4,528	4,026	100	2.2	2.2	1.9	76.0	8.1	135	47	42
Sheridan	13,283	12,577	11,154	706	5.6	5.3	4.4	68.9	13.8	975	175	200
Sublette	3,944	3,552	2,911	392	11.0	0.8	0.6	73.3	4.2	591	185	93
Sweetwater	16,254	15,921	15,444	333	2.1	1.6	1.5	75.1	15.0	666	260	216
Teton	11,597	10,267	7,060	1,330	13.0	2.9	1.8	54.8	28.0	1,635	308	301
Uinta	8,307	8,011	7,246	296	3.7	4.0	3.5	75.3	15.8	402	95	63
Washakie	3,688	3,654	3,732	34	0.9	1.6	1.7	73.1	9.4	39	9	7
Weston	3,317	3,231	3,090	86	2.7	1.4	1.3	77.9	6.3	41	5	16

– Represents zero.   NA Not available.   X Not applicable.   Z Less than .05 units or .05 percent.

[1]The April 1, 2000, housing estimates base reflects changes to the 2000 Census of Population and Housing as documented in the Count Question Resolution program and geographic program revisions.

[2]Based on land area data from the 2000 census.

[3]Owner-occupied housing units as a percent of all occupied housing.

[4]Includes data not distributed by county.

[5]Denali Borough, AK, included with Yukon-Koyukuk Census Area.

[6]Yakutat City and Borough, AK, included with Skagway-Hoonah-Angoon Census Area.

[7]Colorado state total includes Broomfield city.

[8]Colorado state total includes Broomfield County (Broomfield County exists as of November 15, 2001).

[9]Yellowstone National Park County became incorporated with Gallatin and Park Counties, MT; effective November 7, 1997.

[10]Clifton Forge independent city became incorporated with Alleghany County, VA; effective July 1, 2001.

[11]South Boston independent city became incorporated with Halifax County, VA; effective June 30, 1995.

Survey, Census, or Data Collection Method: Housing units and housing 2000—Based on the 2000 Census of Population and Housing; for information, see Appendix B, Limitations of the Data and Methodology, and also <http://www.census.gov/prod/cen2000/doc/sf1.pdf> and <http://www.census.gov/popest/topics/methodology>.   Building permits—Based on a survey of local building permit officials using Form C-404; for information, see <http://www.census.gov/const/www/newresconstdoc.html>.

Sources: Housing units 2000 and 2005—U.S. Census Bureau, "Annual Estimates of Housing Units for Counties: April 1, 2000 to July 1, 2005," accessed November 14, 2005 (related Internet site <http://www.census.gov/popest/housing/HU-EST2005-4.html>).   Housing units 1990—U.S. Census Bureau, 1990 Census of Population and Housing, Summary Tape File (STF) 1C on CD-ROM (archive).   Housing 2000—U.S. Census Bureau, 2000 Census of Population and Housing, Census 2000 Profiles of General Demographic Characteristics data files, accessed July 19, 2005 (related Internet site <http://censtats.census.gov/pub/Profiles.shtml>).   Building permits—U.S. Census Bureau, "New Residential Construction—Building Permits," May 24, 2006 e-mail from Manufacturing, Mining, and Construction Statistics Branch, subject: Annual Place Level Data 2000–2005 (related Internet site <http://www.census.gov/const/www/permitsindex.html>).

Table B-8. Counties — **Crime—Number of Offenses**

[Includes United States, states, and 3,141 counties/county equivalents defined as of February 22, 2005. For more information on these areas, see Appendix C, Geographic Information]

County	Violent crimes[1]						Property crimes[1]				
	2004					2000	2004				2000
	Total	Murder and non-negligent man-slaughter	Forcible rape	Robbery	Aggra-vated assault		Total	Burglary	Larceny-theft	Motor vehicle theft	
UNITED STATES[2]	1,313,779	15,607	88,248	390,437	819,487	1,349,339	9,812,534	2,033,649	6,578,616	1,200,269	9,403,713
ALABAMA	18,641	247	1,685	5,887	10,822	17,990	175,546	43,121	118,860	13,565	151,127
Autauga	152	–	11	38	103	191	1,606	358	1,162	86	1,540
Baldwin	255	1	43	39	172	264	3,007	730	2,145	132	3,817
Barbour	74	1	8	20	45	30	784	127	610	47	64
Bibb	49	–	2	8	39	(NA)	349	101	212	36	(NA)
Blount	120	2	14	6	98	87	1,440	434	868	138	1,102
Bullock	23	–	1	1	21	(NA)	67	39	28	–	(NA)
Butler	77	1	5	12	59	1	683	129	530	24	6
Calhoun	657	8	57	191	401	682	5,483	1,434	3,748	301	4,738
Chambers	97	–	5	14	78	150	590	162	404	24	670
Cherokee	7	–	2	–	5	3	130	34	87	9	156
Chilton	433	1	12	8	412	49	851	249	563	39	198
Choctaw	3	–	–	2	1	3	29	16	11	2	26
Clarke	39	–	6	3	30	52	422	68	345	9	316
Clay	19	1	1	1	16	4	233	83	146	4	66
Cleburne	13	–	8	2	3	7	332	95	168	69	209
Coffee	48	1	5	8	34	105	693	209	433	51	726
Colbert	196	1	15	32	148	77	2,111	483	1,555	73	1,556
Conecuh	15	–	1	2	12	22	200	36	155	9	147
Coosa	47	–	5	3	39	25	217	69	136	12	195
Covington	135	1	15	12	107	(NA)	926	235	650	41	(NA)
Crenshaw	31	2	3	5	21	97	272	82	168	22	270
Cullman	124	2	27	6	89	91	2,647	679	1,784	184	1,828
Dale	153	2	16	14	121	191	1,017	214	717	86	1,075
Dallas	361	6	24	93	238	563	2,673	724	1,715	234	2,804
DeKalb	59	–	1	4	54	22	1,069	263	709	97	665
Elmore	99	2	12	28	57	95	1,476	397	1,024	55	1,238
Escambia	245	4	12	41	188	180	1,393	354	967	72	992
Etowah	446	4	55	121	266	144	4,716	1,073	3,265	378	1,094
Fayette	70	–	7	1	62	31	392	116	233	43	341
Franklin	57	–	4	9	44	29	438	114	281	43	186
Geneva	93	–	9	6	78	58	520	166	315	39	299
Greene	43	1	3	4	35	24	218	80	128	10	98
Hale	69	–	5	3	61	3	412	125	251	36	65
Henry	39	1	3	5	30	54	327	87	201	39	345
Houston	301	10	59	124	108	353	3,595	861	2,551	183	3,155
Jackson	124	3	13	11	97	93	1,705	422	1,090	193	1,146
Jefferson	4,926	64	369	2,093	2,400	4,396	36,991	9,092	24,057	3,842	32,586
Lamar	12	–	–	2	10	7	133	40	76	17	55
Lauderdale	211	2	11	41	157	168	2,576	612	1,887	77	1,956
Lawrence	28	–	4	1	23	7	524	151	338	35	209
Lee	553	10	62	111	370	910	5,218	1,239	3,785	194	5,596
Limestone	63	–	12	14	37	107	1,071	208	754	109	1,093
Lowndes	88	–	4	20	64	52	288	203	60	25	228
Macon	76	2	8	22	44	83	915	364	513	38	1,009
Madison	1,371	6	130	417	818	1,517	13,434	2,737	9,542	1,155	13,375
Marengo	127	1	9	18	99	126	574	141	415	18	403
Marion	56	–	3	4	49	34	707	215	450	42	448
Marshall	190	1	31	31	127	189	3,068	677	2,244	147	1,345
Mobile	1,818	34	171	857	756	2,430	22,728	5,804	15,037	1,887	23,165
Monroe	192	4	4	11	173	211	467	103	326	38	565
Montgomery	1,406	26	118	645	617	1,683	14,799	3,974	9,513	1,312	15,923
Morgan	298	3	23	147	125	3	4,763	1,011	3,549	203	69
Perry	94	–	3	12	79	5	385	95	248	42	64
Pickens	67	–	7	4	56	29	247	74	160	13	135
Pike	58	1	–	16	41	153	1,204	197	966	41	1,094
Randolph	73	1	13	9	50	63	596	116	436	44	541
Russell	155	5	20	40	90	182	1,481	443	859	179	1,389
St. Clair	195	2	31	19	143	70	1,708	360	1,241	107	633
Shelby	303	7	42	94	160	102	3,097	762	2,122	213	1,477
Sumter	65	1	1	8	55	14	227	67	146	14	196
Talladega	185	–	28	63	94	81	2,532	445	2,011	76	925
Tallapoosa	202	1	22	34	145	139	1,556	312	1,173	71	1,178
Tuscaloosa	793	16	70	219	488	1,319	7,873	1,981	5,375	517	13,330
Walker	143	1	16	51	75	52	2,584	610	1,742	232	578
Washington	18	–	–	2	16	13	183	59	117	7	121
Wilcox	33	1	1	2	29	30	144	40	89	15	97
Winston	69	3	3	3	60	35	450	141	274	35	211

See footnotes at end of table.

[Includes United States, states, and 3,141 counties/county equivalents defined as of February 22, 2005. For more information on these areas, see Appendix C, Geographic Information]

| County | Violent crimes[1] | | | | | | Property crimes[1] | | | | |
| | 2004 | | | | | 2000 | 2004 | | | | 2000 |
	Total	Murder and non-negligent man-slaughter	Forcible rape	Robbery	Aggra-vated assault		Total	Burglary	Larceny-theft	Motor vehicle theft	
ALASKA[3]	4,082	36	549	444	3,053	3,151	21,605	3,704	15,708	2,193	21,074
Aleutians East	(NA)	(NA)	(NA)	(NA)	(NA)	(NA)	(NA)	(NA)	(NA)	(NA)	(NA)
Aleutians West	17	–	1	2	14	39	85	8	63	14	51
Anchorage	2,176	15	263	332	1,566	1,525	10,098	1,525	7,529	1,044	11,449
Bethel	65	1	–	8	56	31	198	29	87	82	182
Bristol Bay	16	–	–	–	16	16	65	6	48	11	54
Denali	(NA)	(NA)	(NA)	(NA)	(NA)	(NA)	(NA)	(NA)	(NA)	(NA)	(NA)
Dillingham	14	1	3	–	10	94	38	4	17	17	54
Fairbanks North Star	247	2	55	47	143	214	1,735	238	1,349	148	1,773
Haines	1	–	–	–	1	7	61	7	54	–	80
Juneau	133	–	39	7	87	(NA)	1,382	163	1,181	38	(NA)
Kenai Peninsula	95	–	12	2	81	128	877	99	736	42	808
Ketchikan Gateway	41	1	9	3	28	(NA)	536	56	437	43	(NA)
Kodiak Island	41	–	1	–	40	59	208	15	174	19	361
Lake and Peninsula	(NA)	(NA)	(NA)	(NA)	(NA)	(NA)	(NA)	(NA)	(NA)	(NA)	(NA)
Matanuska-Susitna	135	–	2	7	126	101	849	72	713	64	823
Nome	(NA)	(NA)	(NA)	(NA)	(NA)	(NA)	(NA)	(NA)	(NA)	(NA)	(NA)
North Slope	55	1	11	4	39	54	195	94	75	26	216
Northwest Arctic	22	1	3	1	17	159	135	26	92	17	181
Prince of Wales-Outer Ketchikan	24	–	–	2	22	16	39	5	33	1	106
Sitka	21	–	9	2	10	18	390	31	331	28	254
Skagway-Hoonah-Angoon	1	–	–	–	1	(NA)	47	1	46	–	(NA)
Southeast Fairbanks	(NA)	(NA)	(NA)	(NA)	(NA)	(NA)	(NA)	(NA)	(NA)	(NA)	(NA)
Valdez-Cordova	15	–	–	–	15	22	50	5	43	2	136
Wade Hampton	(NA)	(NA)	(NA)	(NA)	(NA)	4	(NA)	(NA)	(NA)	(NA)	1
Wrangell-Petersburg	7	–	–	–	7	56	261	52	189	20	249
Yakutat	(NA)	(NA)	(NA)	(NA)	(NA)	(NA)	(NA)	(NA)	(NA)	(NA)	(NA)
Yukon-Koyukuk	(NA)	(NA)	(NA)	(NA)	(NA)	–	(NA)	(NA)	(NA)	(NA)	21
ARIZONA	28,562	411	1,869	7,645	18,637	27,186	301,799	55,788	191,468	54,543	271,269
Apache	75	–	3	1	71	90	453	128	308	17	529
Cochise	928	7	46	50	825	460	4,383	848	3,065	470	4,423
Coconino	629	7	65	70	487	486	5,909	879	4,704	326	6,154
Gila	242	–	16	10	216	242	1,608	507	993	108	1,619
Graham	35	–	–	1	34	62	649	156	463	30	676
Greenlee	6	–	–	–	6	4	93	32	61	–	63
La Paz	111	–	–	2	109	35	801	167	559	75	649
Maricopa	17,075	281	1,064	5,374	10,356	17,002	188,920	35,088	112,386	41,446	175,297
Mohave	614	10	26	65	513	495	9,255	2,135	6,198	922	6,354
Navajo	353	5	24	20	304	283	2,813	781	1,873	159	2,510
Pima	5,883	81	481	1,784	3,537	5,555	63,731	9,109	46,525	8,097	53,484
Pinal	920	13	58	140	709	1,081	10,562	3,009	6,059	1,494	7,051
Santa Cruz	86	–	1	11	74	129	877	208	511	158	1,095
Yavapai	650	4	44	50	552	588	6,286	1,436	4,396	454	6,584
Yuma	955	3	41	67	844	674	5,459	1,305	3,367	787	4,781
ARKANSAS	12,766	166	1,080	2,261	9,259	11,807	99,923	26,190	67,886	5,847	97,501
Arkansas	96	1	4	8	83	103	701	241	446	14	552
Ashley	130	1	7	7	115	86	582	203	344	35	567
Baxter	55	–	13	1	41	72	979	126	810	43	613
Benton	295	5	94	25	171	211	4,775	687	3,909	179	3,457
Boone	78	–	13	2	63	49	695	164	495	36	523
Bradley	24	–	2	8	14	16	199	155	41	3	251
Calhoun	10	1	–	1	8	9	45	17	26	2	49
Carroll	29	1	4	2	22	66	452	112	302	38	550
Chicot	67	3	1	3	60	55	150	39	106	5	526
Clark	69	2	7	8	52	28	555	215	319	21	441
Clay	7	–	1	–	6	23	57	22	33	2	298
Cleburne	40	–	9	1	30	77	524	182	304	38	724
Cleveland	4	1	1	–	2	8	131	77	49	5	62
Columbia	193	3	10	13	167	156	826	262	537	27	899
Conway	22	–	2	5	15	21	194	35	148	11	287
Craighead	284	3	26	49	206	244	2,644	1,026	1,483	135	3,402
Crawford	92	–	11	6	75	141	939	265	626	48	1,321
Crittenden	699	6	34	124	535	613	3,122	1,248	1,647	227	2,115
Cross	59	–	4	5	50	81	314	97	199	18	402
Dallas	34	–	–	7	27	78	254	90	156	8	286
Desha	113	3	5	7	98	112	359	155	189	15	672
Drew	41	–	4	8	29	45	588	131	427	30	263
Faulkner	202	5	50	32	115	203	3,494	641	2,605	248	2,972
Franklin	22	–	2	1	19	29	125	33	87	5	165
Fulton	11	–	3	–	8	13	135	46	74	15	150

See footnotes at end of table.

Table B-8. Counties — **Crime—Number of Offenses**—Con.

[Includes United States, states, and 3,141 counties/county equivalents defined as of February 22, 2005. For more information on these areas, see Appendix C, Geographic Information]

County	Violent crimes[1]						Property crimes[1]				
	2004					2000	2004				2000
	Total	Murder and non-negligent man-slaughter	Forcible rape	Robbery	Aggra-vated assault		Total	Burglary	Larceny-theft	Motor vehicle theft	
ARKANSAS—Con.											
Garland	505	8	25	95	377	416	6,305	1,876	4,016	413	3,915
Grant	10	–	2	–	8	8	92	21	69	2	135
Greene	55	–	15	2	38	53	1,064	312	691	61	965
Hempstead	98	–	13	17	68	100	764	246	475	43	751
Hot Spring	131	1	24	17	89	90	774	324	411	39	842
Howard	44	2	4	5	33	6	344	129	214	1	273
Independence	35	2	8	4	21	58	1,150	332	753	65	1,347
Izard	13	1	2	1	9	20	125	52	65	8	177
Jackson	77	–	8	10	59	87	596	163	380	53	528
Jefferson	698	11	46	170	471	1,222	5,494	1,826	3,222	446	5,657
Johnson	5	–	1	–	4	9	416	29	373	14	490
Lafayette	6	1	2	1	2	7	32	8	20	4	61
Lawrence	2	–	1	–	1	41	148	25	113	10	217
Lee	33	1	5	7	20	60	271	114	148	9	578
Lincoln	15	2	–	3	10	30	122	55	66	1	115
Little River	10	–	2	2	6	20	163	39	108	16	264
Logan	48	3	5	1	39	11	390	163	202	25	246
Lonoke	190	2	18	12	158	115	1,738	505	1,162	71	1,328
Madison	35	–	2	4	29	63	100	38	58	4	122
Marion	11	–	1	–	10	48	119	33	83	3	197
Miller	453	3	22	49	379	323	2,002	470	1,425	107	2,035
Mississippi	392	3	32	58	299	384	2,800	842	1,818	140	2,633
Monroe	1	–	–	–	1	27	69	12	47	10	84
Montgomery	9	–	–	–	9	46	17	7	8	2	108
Nevada	57	1	5	6	45	15	136	51	76	9	100
Newton	14	–	–	1	13	16	70	26	42	2	59
Ouachita	90	2	8	18	62	149	728	258	437	33	914
Perry	29	–	2	1	26	14	87	60	25	2	138
Phillips	102	1	12	25	64	113	724	444	260	20	820
Pike	24	–	5	–	19	–	111	39	64	8	35
Poinsett	96	–	9	7	80	184	918	368	514	36	1,029
Polk	32	–	–	2	30	30	289	118	166	5	214
Pope	20	1	2	1	16	104	471	170	284	17	1,926
Prairie	24	2	2	–	20	28	106	40	52	14	125
Pulaski	4,426	58	206	1,166	2,996	2,816	27,208	6,079	19,343	1,786	26,035
Randolph	7	–	–	–	7	82	53	15	33	5	429
St. Francis	179	3	6	42	128	332	1,501	383	1,066	52	1,568
Saline	90	–	10	5	75	204	1,657	292	1,299	66	2,604
Scott	32	–	2	1	29	17	225	119	90	16	202
Searcy	(NA)	(NA)	(NA)	(NA)	(NA)	9	(NA)	(NA)	(NA)	(NA)	41
Sebastian	841	4	101	95	641	665	6,787	1,270	5,178	339	7,008
Sevier	25	3	2	2	18	46	189	52	129	8	335
Sharp	34	–	5	3	26	18	201	70	113	18	223
Stone	1	–	–	1	–	16	28	16	11	1	131
Union	210	3	7	36	164	375	1,803	657	1,036	110	1,585
Van Buren	15	1	4	–	10	31	200	49	130	21	114
Washington	574	9	112	46	407	491	5,731	933	4,482	316	4,928
White	207	3	24	20	160	197	2,502	637	1,672	193	2,017
Woodruff	6	–	–	–	6	–	19	9	7	3	43
Yell	79	–	11	2	66	72	245	145	88	12	263
CALIFORNIA	197,423	2,393	9,594	61,567	123,869	210,459	1,223,227	244,917	726,556	251,754	1,054,010
Alameda	9,114	117	472	3,904	4,621	9,503	65,798	11,824	38,618	15,356	58,320
Alpine	11	–	3	–	8	10	82	25	57	–	77
Amador	121	2	19	7	93	179	1,148	362	657	129	674
Butte	752	6	92	129	525	699	8,265	2,452	4,393	1,420	6,514
Calaveras	127	3	11	10	103	118	1,002	338	533	131	914
Colusa	59	–	2	5	52	57	576	207	314	55	396
Contra Costa	4,021	76	205	1,466	2,274	4,532	41,495	7,053	24,925	9,517	31,095
Del Norte	181	1	24	10	146	118	924	345	507	72	818
El Dorado	467	2	45	59	361	702	4,106	1,149	2,441	516	2,858
Fresno	5,169	69	272	1,541	3,287	6,041	42,199	7,418	27,150	7,631	42,210
Glenn	71	–	3	6	62	80	1,042	290	619	133	699
Humboldt	428	5	52	106	265	427	5,145	1,310	3,205	630	5,084
Imperial	687	4	34	123	526	707	5,619	1,913	2,714	992	5,449
Inyo	52	–	4	6	42	55	428	106	280	42	406
Kern	4,421	51	217	931	3,222	3,237	31,782	8,227	18,651	4,904	22,296
Kings	462	6	44	75	337	364	3,870	756	2,519	595	2,812
Lake	301	1	18	24	258	234	1,940	580	1,139	221	1,520
Lassen	100	–	8	3	89	73	530	148	327	55	423
Los Angeles	76,652	1,038	2,483	26,565	46,566	89,986	297,521	59,425	165,971	72,125	289,465
Madera	723	7	35	158	523	804	3,946	1,139	2,031	776	3,792

See footnotes at end of table.

County and City Data Book: 2007

U.S. Census Bureau

Table B-8. Counties — **Crime—Number of Offenses**—Con.

[Includes United States, states, and 3,141 counties/county equivalents defined as of February 22, 2005. For more information on these areas, see Appendix C, Geographic Information]

County	Violent crimes[1] 2004 Total	Murder and non-negligent man-slaughter	Forcible rape	Robbery	Aggra-vated assault	2000	Property crimes[1] 2004 Total	Burglary	Larceny-theft	Motor vehicle theft	2000
CALIFORNIA—Con.											
Marin	495	3	44	132	316	642	6,129	1,275	4,025	829	5,232
Mariposa	82	1	7	–	74	130	408	118	268	22	367
Mendocino	472	6	28	32	406	318	1,924	688	1,091	145	1,912
Merced	1,612	16	83	232	1,281	1,307	10,459	2,358	6,507	1,594	7,686
Modoc	15	–	2	1	12	38	147	48	81	18	156
Mono	44	–	8	3	33	30	573	147	403	23	547
Monterey	2,097	33	129	721	1,214	2,311	14,143	2,622	9,472	2,049	10,649
Napa	451	3	50	58	340	322	3,722	596	2,690	436	2,342
Nevada	236	1	23	19	193	159	1,840	508	1,141	191	1,635
Orange	8,308	81	522	2,511	5,194	8,600	74,159	13,155	48,439	12,565	65,698
Placer	623	3	41	113	466	533	9,262	1,941	6,097	1,224	6,706
Plumas	56	2	7	4	43	63	459	155	280	24	548
Riverside	8,495	93	466	2,248	5,688	9,591	70,309	17,042	40,103	13,164	51,062
Sacramento	9,164	92	449	3,326	5,297	7,206	67,681	12,952	38,140	16,589	53,302
San Benito	237	–	25	32	180	337	1,281	317	808	156	1,114
San Bernardino	9,813	165	551	3,348	5,749	9,169	65,949	14,388	35,680	15,881	56,006
San Diego	13,886	127	797	3,588	9,374	13,746	97,390	17,547	55,671	24,172	80,662
San Francisco	5,782	88	154	3,058	2,482	6,562	36,910	6,199	22,606	8,105	36,600
San Joaquin	5,431	55	192	1,558	3,626	4,596	36,314	6,494	21,652	8,168	25,048
San Luis Obispo	777	2	97	81	597	697	6,875	1,582	4,810	483	6,459
San Mateo	2,168	26	156	685	1,301	1,991	19,302	2,935	13,424	2,943	16,609
Santa Barbara	1,804	7	128	321	1,348	1,312	9,981	2,350	6,553	1,078	8,883
Santa Clara	5,090	37	454	1,169	3,430	7,226	43,957	7,103	30,140	6,714	37,281
Santa Cruz	1,198	5	124	205	864	1,186	9,397	1,697	6,849	851	7,504
Shasta	909	4	114	92	699	825	5,793	1,539	3,572	682	4,516
Sierra	13	–	–	–	13	4	61	20	36	5	41
Siskiyou	139	1	9	6	123	140	1,012	277	659	76	971
Solano	2,005	19	120	520	1,346	2,504	12,815	2,704	8,068	2,043	13,443
Sonoma	2,242	17	214	272	1,739	1,356	13,303	2,552	9,169	1,582	12,156
Stanislaus	2,874	41	159	719	1,955	3,088	30,200	5,304	18,548	6,348	20,752
Sutter	354	3	36	56	259	263	3,342	815	2,121	406	2,702
Tehama	429	3	31	21	374	272	1,786	484	1,090	212	1,558
Trinity	57	1	4	4	48	23	205	103	49	53	270
Tulare	2,614	25	105	445	2,039	2,377	19,835	4,885	11,465	3,485	13,712
Tuolumne	186	2	7	13	164	202	2,191	759	1,199	233	1,166
Ventura	1,898	33	101	621	1,143	2,112	17,526	3,641	11,496	2,389	15,400
Yolo	1,053	5	85	167	796	953	6,565	1,790	3,765	1,010	5,028
Yuba	395	5	29	58	303	342	2,604	760	1,338	506	2,465
COLORADO	16,582	198	1,872	3,642	10,870	13,508	172,467	31,836	117,540	23,091	145,469
Adams	1,468	20	196	315	937	1,407	18,124	2,961	11,965	3,198	15,455
Alamosa	98	1	3	4	90	55	487	83	382	22	439
Arapahoe	2,196	21	257	635	1,283	1,716	22,307	3,893	14,994	3,420	16,765
Archuleta	21	–	9	1	11	3	300	98	188	14	314
Baca	8	–	–	–	8	5	10	–	10	–	14
Bent	15	–	2	–	13	24	58	14	42	2	112
Boulder	364	4	49	53	258	780	6,331	1,095	4,920	316	8,366
Broomfield	40	1	7	12	20	(X)	1,556	151	1,298	107	(X)
Chaffee	44	–	12	–	32	35	475	60	400	15	420
Cheyenne	–	–	–	–	–	3	17	2	14	1	27
Clear Creek	40	–	3	1	36	40	302	41	243	18	230
Conejos	(NA)	(NA)	(NA)	(NA)	(NA)	(NA)	1	(NA)	1	(NA)	(NA)
Costilla	7	–	–	–	7	24	1	–	1	–	62
Crowley	7	–	–	–	7	9	1	1	–	–	7
Custer	1	–	–	–	1	3	48	8	33	7	52
Delta	61	–	10	6	45	39	437	88	333	16	389
Denver	4,517	87	244	1,443	2,743	2,945	30,873	7,350	15,934	7,589	23,868
Dolores	1	–	–	–	1	2	22	7	14	1	32
Douglas	287	2	66	27	192	80	4,635	791	3,555	289	2,026
Eagle	70	–	6	9	55	67	1,274	98	1,149	27	1,581
Elbert	19	–	1	2	16	60	194	56	121	17	158
El Paso	2,480	17	341	376	1,746	1,994	23,939	4,592	16,956	2,391	19,445
Fremont	136	2	30	7	97	68	836	119	668	49	894
Garfield	130	–	9	8	113	77	1,375	263	1,014	98	1,139
Gilpin	8	–	–	1	7	36	46	11	32	3	283
Grand	7	–	–	1	6	18	331	43	267	21	538
Gunnison	47	–	13	–	34	27	370	38	317	15	508
Hinsdale	1	–	–	–	1	1	11	–	9	2	33
Huerfano	18	1	–	1	16	21	137	24	107	6	146
Jackson	3	–	–	–	3	1	10	1	7	2	25

See footnotes at end of table.

[Includes United States, states, and 3,141 counties/county equivalents defined as of February 22, 2005. For more information on these areas, see Appendix C, Geographic Information]

County	Violent crimes[1] 2004						Property crimes[1] 2004				
	Total	Murder and non-negligent man-slaughter	Forcible rape	Robbery	Aggra-vated assault	2000	Total	Burglary	Larceny-theft	Motor vehicle theft	2000
COLORADO—Con.											
Jefferson	1,369	9	161	333	866	899	19,861	3,016	13,991	2,854	16,978
Kiowa	(NA)	(NA)	(NA)	(NA)	(NA)	4	(NA)	(NA)	(NA)	(NA)	2
Kit Carson	12	–	1	–	11	18	128	21	102	5	174
Lake	22	–	–	–	22	13	134	29	90	15	104
La Plata	71	1	12	6	52	119	1,298	228	992	78	1,446
Larimer	578	2	177	44	355	585	8,790	1,328	6,944	518	8,435
Las Animas	20	–	2	1	17	55	241	41	189	11	253
Lincoln	2	–	1	–	1	5	17	–	15	2	37
Logan	38	1	6	4	27	61	438	92	315	31	647
Mesa	344	3	50	26	265	235	4,757	927	3,489	341	4,306
Mineral	1	–	–	–	1	2	3	2	1	–	2
Moffat	30	1	1	1	27	26	370	60	294	16	362
Montezuma	92	3	1	3	85	18	710	140	528	42	591
Montrose	55	–	14	3	38	53	742	113	584	45	874
Morgan	19	–	–	3	16	29	633	89	521	23	736
Otero	58	–	7	6	45	60	613	77	526	10	352
Ouray	–	–	–	–	–	1	25	3	22	–	9
Park	30	1	–	–	29	3	83	52	16	15	193
Phillips	4	1	2	–	1	4	25	7	15	3	12
Pitkin	28	–	11	1	16	36	643	80	528	35	969
Prowers	20	–	5	5	10	10	494	105	368	21	473
Pueblo	713	8	37	212	456	1,019	7,183	1,625	5,053	505	5,319
Rio Blanco	17	–	1	–	16	22	109	16	89	4	121
Rio Grande	35	–	4	3	28	24	209	53	155	1	391
Routt	25	–	3	–	22	35	287	40	229	18	477
Saguache	30	1	2	1	26	11	63	26	33	4	89
San Juan	3	–	–	–	3	3	15	3	12	–	28
San Miguel	12	–	–	1	11	5	171	20	148	3	176
Sedgwick	5	–	–	–	5	6	43	15	26	2	42
Summit	21	–	2	2	17	46	1,016	79	917	20	1,985
Teller	47	2	5	1	39	28	406	60	327	19	267
Washington	5	–	1	–	4	5	71	16	47	8	16
Weld	770	9	106	84	571	524	8,236	1,551	5,896	789	6,138
Yuma	12	–	2	–	10	4	146	34	105	7	137
CONNECTICUT[3]	9,169	97	732	3,808	4,532	11,166	89,898	15,220	64,205	10,473	99,162
Fairfield	2,535	25	137	983	1,390	3,076	20,316	3,446	14,726	2,144	21,914
Hartford	2,996	26	201	1,493	1,276	3,049	30,557	5,018	21,026	4,513	29,778
Litchfield	148	4	10	22	112	167	2,128	393	1,588	147	2,180
Middlesex	85	2	3	39	41	104	2,346	265	1,920	161	2,408
New Haven	2,323	15	166	994	1,148	2,966	24,193	4,012	17,547	2,634	29,309
New London	541	11	106	146	278	501	3,788	633	2,919	236	4,065
Tolland	47	–	10	18	19	48	732	143	525	64	1,360
Windham	98	1	14	36	47	164	1,043	173	791	79	1,309
DELAWARE	5,105	28	357	1,343	3,377	(NA)	27,256	5,669	19,285	2,302	29,553
Kent	938	4	77	136	721	(NA)	4,629	914	3,379	336	4,415
New Castle	3,241	23	201	1,068	1,949	(NA)	17,610	3,321	12,545	1,744	20,637
Sussex	926	1	79	139	707	(NA)	5,017	1,434	3,361	222	4,501
DISTRICT OF COLUMBIA	7,593	198	223	3,204	3,968	8,623	26,906	3,946	14,545	8,415	32,998
District of Columbia	7,593	198	223	3,204	3,968	8,623	26,906	3,946	14,545	8,415	32,998
FLORIDA	123,695	946	6,609	29,984	86,156	128,041	726,784	166,253	482,236	78,295	767,667
Alachua	1,896	8	157	310	1,421	2,095	9,341	2,533	6,064	744	12,646
Baker	106	1	2	11	92	92	414	89	293	32	464
Bay	1,095	11	97	163	824	914	7,642	1,632	5,493	517	7,072
Bradford	146	–	13	8	125	148	535	140	347	48	740
Brevard	3,344	14	204	502	2,624	2,819	15,374	4,261	9,935	1,178	14,385
Broward	10,513	63	506	3,520	6,424	9,792	64,006	13,013	43,933	7,060	67,449
Calhoun	25	–	–	2	23	(NA)	110	30	72	8	(NA)
Charlotte	632	5	41	82	504	312	4,657	1,267	3,118	272	2,985
Citrus	390	2	28	22	338	329	2,496	607	1,710	179	2,366
Clay	655	6	46	61	542	498	3,606	833	2,481	292	4,602
Collier	1,317	14	94	218	991	1,378	6,834	1,550	4,868	416	8,576
Columbia	418	2	29	55	332	175	2,240	569	1,550	121	1,139
DeSoto	228	4	6	24	194	268	898	280	583	35	976
Dixie	84	1	16	8	59	58	421	160	243	18	387
Duval	6,810	105	232	2,292	4,181	8,507	45,748	9,497	31,357	4,894	45,608

See footnotes at end of table.

County and City Data Book: 2007

U.S. Census Bureau

[Includes United States, states, and 3,141 counties/county equivalents defined as of February 22, 2005. For more information on these areas, see Appendix C, Geographic Information]

County	Violent crimes[1] 2004					2000	Property crimes[1] 2004				2000
	Total	Murder and non-negligent manslaughter	Forcible rape	Robbery	Aggravated assault		Total	Burglary	Larceny-theft	Motor vehicle theft	
FLORIDA—Con.											
Escambia	2,057	19	134	370	1,534	1,825	11,149	2,852	7,513	784	9,448
Flagler	198	–	12	19	167	150	1,430	347	981	102	1,244
Franklin	38	1	7	7	23	20	319	54	247	18	243
Gadsden	361	6	23	38	294	332	1,351	390	880	81	1,649
Gilchrist	30	–	2	2	26	76	327	114	185	28	343
Glades	45	1	1	2	41	32	230	76	134	20	321
Gulf	57	–	4	1	52	61	246	88	139	19	249
Hamilton	96	–	1	14	81	101	378	106	229	43	307
Hardee	165	–	10	19	136	102	885	244	578	63	919
Hendry	295	2	12	63	218	271	1,244	336	802	106	1,274
Hernando	899	4	81	70	744	846	4,563	1,320	2,976	267	4,514
Highlands	426	4	22	72	328	443	2,837	928	1,735	174	2,886
Hillsborough	10,343	58	449	2,496	7,340	11,263	57,736	13,035	36,836	7,865	60,185
Holmes	53	–	3	5	45	58	229	73	135	21	177
Indian River	496	1	56	65	374	436	3,995	869	2,906	220	4,589
Jackson	258	4	19	13	222	323	1,009	296	637	76	985
Jefferson	99	–	10	3	86	90	148	53	86	9	300
Lafayette	40	1	9	2	28	(NA)	96	34	56	6	(NA)
Lake	1,615	9	82	135	1,389	1,838	6,649	2,134	3,960	555	6,849
Lee	2,908	31	175	757	1,945	2,600	18,259	4,618	11,432	2,209	18,732
Leon	1,996	13	205	391	1,387	2,525	10,852	3,611	6,217	1,024	14,159
Levy	278	1	35	15	227	284	1,198	353	764	81	1,368
Liberty	17	–	1	2	14	18	42	16	22	4	78
Madison	155	–	13	12	130	133	613	180	410	23	1,110
Manatee	2,491	13	98	511	1,869	2,379	14,559	3,522	9,908	1,129	11,481
Marion	2,018	17	167	208	1,626	2,021	8,794	2,405	5,730	659	9,832
Martin	542	7	28	107	400	481	3,937	806	2,907	224	3,890
Miami-Dade	24,424	218	901	7,774	15,531	27,784	136,030	24,627	92,351	19,052	157,756
Monroe	460	1	44	91	324	577	4,142	791	2,984	367	4,988
Nassau	784	2	34	25	723	739	1,433	435	876	122	1,128
Okaloosa	587	3	39	102	443	572	5,230	1,197	3,712	321	4,202
Okeechobee	282	1	20	12	249	213	1,128	482	555	91	1,351
Orange	9,617	61	507	2,407	6,642	9,570	51,677	11,820	33,464	6,393	54,457
Osceola	1,190	5	102	221	862	1,194	8,916	2,960	5,323	633	9,224
Palm Beach	8,963	89	487	2,570	5,817	8,152	58,810	13,239	38,658	6,913	63,810
Pasco	1,622	17	139	242	1,224	1,808	13,610	3,793	8,736	1,081	12,282
Pinellas	7,472	37	415	1,676	5,344	7,451	42,187	9,295	28,344	4,548	41,908
Polk	2,482	15	137	511	1,819	2,916	21,073	5,442	13,917	1,714	25,224
Putnam	804	5	44	80	675	726	3,358	1,147	1,969	242	3,663
St. Johns	632	2	11	68	551	586	4,038	999	2,780	259	3,590
St. Lucie	1,329	8	94	244	983	1,449	7,800	2,324	4,880	596	7,411
Santa Rosa	414	5	46	32	331	390	2,218	605	1,501	112	2,154
Sarasota	1,447	5	87	254	1,101	1,482	13,406	3,074	9,526	806	12,101
Seminole	1,486	18	114	282	1,072	1,875	10,859	2,412	7,578	869	12,540
Sumter	304	3	33	22	246	273	1,129	297	745	87	1,041
Suwannee	189	–	15	17	157	213	1,082	405	596	81	1,333
Taylor	139	1	12	13	113	145	659	292	340	27	576
Union	72	–	5	2	65	78	289	111	156	22	122
Volusia	3,000	19	166	649	2,166	3,347	18,143	4,626	11,344	2,173	18,187
Wakulla	102	–	17	2	83	104	545	168	344	33	605
Walton	224	3	8	5	208	283	1,291	326	869	96	1,209
Washington	35	–	2	6	27	21	334	65	236	33	278
GEORGIA	36,900	554	2,205	12,805	21,336	39,423	337,563	74,004	223,127	40,432	325,603
Appling	72	–	3	3	66	68	228	56	156	16	227
Atkinson	17	–	–	3	14	13	75	19	54	2	79
Bacon	5	–	–	2	3	5	254	76	158	20	121
Baker	2	–	–	–	2	4	3	3	–	–	11
Baldwin	87	1	7	17	62	147	1,100	268	790	42	1,595
Banks	18	1	1	4	12	25	557	110	411	36	447
Barrow	406	1	14	15	376	134	1,882	476	1,192	214	1,750
Bartow	278	1	9	57	211	127	4,574	1,135	2,985	454	1,888
Ben Hill	76	1	1	10	64	209	910	250	620	40	1,036
Berrien	90	–	4	13	73	45	295	74	204	17	242
Bibb	770	18	68	269	415	882	11,063	2,352	7,496	1,215	12,441
Bleckley	25	2	–	4	19	18	332	55	263	14	137
Brantley	32	1	–	6	25	30	453	148	261	44	299
Brooks	144	1	2	6	135	109	452	91	322	39	377
Bryan	44	–	2	19	23	23	635	92	509	34	379
Bulloch	117	1	9	40	67	44	2,046	375	1,560	111	1,385
Burke	463	–	3	19	441	304	949	176	689	84	1,025
Butts	21	–	–	6	15	30	544	82	401	61	657
Calhoun	25	–	–	3	22	20	110	32	72	6	118
Camden	120	3	11	12	94	208	1,282	263	953	66	1,417

See footnotes at end of table.

[Includes United States, states, and 3,141 counties/county equivalents defined as of February 22, 2005. For more information on these areas, see Appendix C, Geographic Information]

| County | Violent crimes[1] | | | | | | Property crimes[1] | | | | |
| | 2004 | | | | | | 2004 | | | | |
	Total	Murder and non-negligent man-slaughter	Forcible rape	Robbery	Aggra-vated assault	2000	Total	Burglary	Larceny-theft	Motor vehicle theft	2000
GEORGIA—Con.											
Candler	52	–	–	18	34	54	280	47	212	21	327
Carroll	807	5	30	48	724	318	4,792	1,229	3,196	367	3,203
Catoosa	117	5	5	18	89	105	1,793	280	1,353	160	1,843
Charlton	17	–	–	2	15	19	57	13	40	4	155
Chatham	1,576	26	81	741	728	1,948	13,375	2,809	8,987	1,579	13,941
Chattahoochee	10	–	–	–	10	9	87	32	43	12	72
Chattooga	10	–	–	–	10	2	41	7	32	2	118
Cherokee	113	3	15	19	76	175	1,436	151	1,188	97	2,829
Clarke	473	5	50	167	251	424	6,593	1,221	5,003	369	7,086
Clay	17	–	2	–	15	11	7	1	5	1	10
Clayton	1,478	21	65	714	678	1,239	13,650	3,242	7,669	2,739	14,322
Clinch	11	–	–	–	11	125	42	15	22	5	195
Cobb	1,801	20	155	716	910	1,533	18,791	3,905	12,394	2,492	19,003
Coffee	175	1	11	30	133	276	2,787	517	2,139	131	2,290
Colquitt	241	10	15	60	156	351	2,311	574	1,591	146	1,821
Columbia	64	1	15	17	31	106	1,683	211	1,378	94	2,091
Cook	62	2	1	8	51	19	264	63	193	8	164
Coweta	159	3	6	46	104	230	2,517	500	1,743	274	2,600
Crawford	23	1	1	5	16	13	352	91	234	27	266
Crisp	92	1	6	26	59	181	1,364	232	1,100	32	1,536
Dade	8	–	–	–	8	12	46	9	28	9	249
Dawson	19	–	1	2	16	9	502	100	337	65	350
Decatur	118	1	8	24	85	146	1,328	258	1,028	42	1,192
DeKalb	3,792	88	299	2,093	1,312	3,448	32,128	8,778	16,157	7,193	33,891
Dodge	76	–	–	–	76	80	280	85	168	27	538
Dooly	24	–	–	3	21	31	157	52	97	8	289
Dougherty	544	5	51	225	263	570	5,703	1,674	3,655	374	5,576
Douglas	345	5	27	77	236	283	4,631	790	3,436	405	3,854
Early	39	1	6	1	31	20	150	50	90	10	158
Echols	(NA)	(NA)	(NA)	(NA)	(NA)	(NA)	(NA)	(NA)	(NA)	(NA)	(NA)
Effingham	79	–	4	13	62	153	758	152	549	57	1,567
Elbert	55	–	3	11	41	19	616	180	412	24	271
Emanuel	9	1	–	2	6	177	256	111	112	33	738
Evans	(NA)	(NA)	(NA)	(NA)	(NA)	(NA)	(NA)	(NA)	(NA)	(NA)	(NA)
Fannin	4	–	–	–	4	2	34	8	26	–	214
Fayette	56	6	8	16	26	53	1,758	213	1,390	155	1,487
Floyd	420	8	16	94	302	710	4,256	958	3,002	296	4,455
Forsyth	254	1	11	22	220	286	2,733	535	1,922	276	2,426
Franklin	44	–	1	4	39	109	347	77	235	35	800
Fulton	9,724	138	351	3,920	5,315	12,755	52,719	10,901	33,845	7,973	57,086
Gilmer	6	–	2	1	3	3	273	64	163	46	256
Glascock	(NA)	(NA)	(NA)	(NA)	(NA)	4	(NA)	(NA)	(NA)	(NA)	9
Glynn	273	4	25	134	110	649	4,889	911	3,748	230	4,945
Gordon	51	–	8	7	36	73	1,216	237	902	77	1,508
Grady	108	1	1	21	85	112	635	185	430	20	643
Greene	44	–	2	6	36	18	375	74	269	32	311
Gwinnett	2,049	31	177	916	925	1,261	21,574	5,377	13,345	2,852	16,328
Habersham	63	–	8	3	52	61	892	275	535	82	604
Hall	415	9	35	84	287	239	6,255	1,205	4,383	667	2,508
Hancock	23	2	4	1	16	36	56	24	28	4	85
Haralson	73	–	3	5	65	42	1,231	315	745	171	357
Harris	37	3	1	10	23	31	405	76	287	42	155
Hart	53	–	–	8	45	44	463	167	253	43	420
Heard	13	1	–	1	11	22	205	65	103	37	130
Henry	217	3	4	37	173	291	2,384	428	1,706	250	3,698
Houston	371	4	39	93	235	390	5,171	1,145	3,700	326	4,555
Irwin	24	–	4	7	13	22	269	63	179	27	276
Jackson	142	3	4	4	131	92	1,107	277	749	81	1,398
Jasper	10	–	–	1	9	13	241	92	128	21	128
Jeff Davis	36	2	–	4	30	57	514	79	392	43	550
Jefferson	72	–	1	3	68	51	307	77	204	26	351
Jenkins	53	2	–	5	46	108	77	28	44	5	174
Johnson	20	–	–	1	19	5	35	18	14	3	67
Jones	30	1	–	3	26	103	599	152	388	59	611
Lamar	31	1	3	1	26	70	137	43	82	12	256
Lanier	2	–	1	–	1	9	3	2	–	1	14
Laurens	144	1	12	35	96	191	1,721	353	1,262	106	1,753
Lee	42	–	4	8	30	45	674	134	501	39	571
Liberty	247	3	19	56	169	265	2,678	555	2,022	101	2,618
Lincoln	6	–	–	–	6	10	72	25	46	1	113

See footnotes at end of table.

Table B-8. Counties — **Crime—Number of Offenses**—Con.

[Includes United States, states, and 3,141 counties/county equivalents defined as of February 22, 2005. For more information on these areas, see Appendix C, Geographic Information]

| County | Violent crimes[1] | | | | | | Property crimes[1] | | | | |
| | 2004 | | | | | 2000 | 2004 | | | | 2000 |
	Total	Murder and non-negligent man-slaughter	Forcible rape	Robbery	Aggra-vated assault		Total	Burglary	Larceny-theft	Motor vehicle theft	
GEORGIA—Con.											
Long	16	–	–	5	11	14	173	80	74	19	183
Lowndes	415	5	50	124	236	20	4,703	805	3,654	244	340
Lumpkin	26	1	2	1	22	25	627	142	446	39	437
McDuffie	31	–	7	10	14	49	506	109	356	41	789
McIntosh	33	–	2	2	29	28	328	53	250	25	408
Macon	50	–	2	7	41	47	244	65	162	17	280
Madison	61	–	6	5	50	36	556	59	470	27	341
Marion	9	–	–	2	7	35	25	11	11	3	126
Meriwether	65	–	1	11	53	80	665	145	436	84	700
Miller	11	–	3	2	6	11	104	18	84	2	133
Mitchell	29	–	2	8	19	43	387	78	293	16	588
Monroe	1	–	–	1	–	39	386	128	212	46	541
Montgomery	1	–	–	–	1	1	10	2	8	–	11
Morgan	26	–	1	10	15	26	190	39	141	10	224
Murray	59	–	–	4	55	23	702	207	446	49	871
Muscogee	905	25	31	395	454	1,074	12,575	2,303	8,788	1,484	10,848
Newton	116	3	8	22	83	172	1,998	530	1,270	198	1,714
Oconee	16	–	3	4	9	19	334	68	235	31	660
Oglethorpe	5	–	–	–	5	76	78	17	52	9	175
Paulding	259	–	15	13	231	181	2,234	483	1,479	272	1,503
Peach	106	–	2	18	86	270	679	156	476	47	682
Pickens	8	–	–	2	6	13	405	100	272	33	269
Pierce	15	–	–	3	12	47	359	45	305	9	197
Pike	26	–	–	6	20	17	165	39	107	19	194
Polk	145	4	14	23	104	85	1,360	359	915	86	1,233
Pulaski	5	–	–	1	4	15	76	28	41	7	77
Putnam	41	1	2	3	35	80	262	83	164	15	501
Quitman	8	–	–	1	7	11	64	19	44	1	92
Rabun	21	–	–	1	20	29	338	75	228	35	187
Randolph	15	–	1	1	13	19	71	35	34	2	118
Richmond	838	14	155	467	202	768	13,407	2,624	9,046	1,737	11,947
Rockdale	389	5	16	72	296	222	3,536	642	2,536	358	2,286
Schley	7	–	1	–	6	13	40	9	25	6	34
Screven	29	–	1	6	22	62	181	60	119	2	206
Seminole	25	–	–	7	18	93	149	36	102	11	164
Spalding	327	2	25	63	237	418	2,580	584	1,769	227	3,597
Stephens	31	–	6	3	22	75	440	127	248	65	595
Stewart	14	–	–	1	13	31	32	20	9	3	47
Sumter	93	1	–	16	76	162	1,177	408	730	39	1,318
Talbot	3	–	1	1	1	7	26	12	12	2	76
Taliaferro	2	–	–	1	1	8	40	15	20	5	16
Tattnall	78	3	2	5	68	83	526	114	379	33	324
Taylor	2	–	1	–	1	33	12	7	3	2	79
Telfair	51	1	–	2	48	47	173	44	123	6	226
Terrell	41	–	3	15	23	48	215	60	147	8	278
Thomas	123	–	7	24	92	182	1,647	386	1,168	93	2,049
Tift	506	3	13	60	430	286	2,604	461	1,989	154	1,859
Toombs	77	2	3	24	48	107	670	158	481	31	840
Towns	11	1	–	–	10	6	223	53	159	11	144
Treutlen	7	–	–	4	3	20	147	56	78	13	52
Troup	228	1	25	65	137	199	3,077	457	2,419	201	3,352
Turner	8	–	1	–	7	98	81	16	56	9	341
Twiggs	14	1	3	–	10	22	18	3	11	4	69
Union	4	–	1	1	2	13	102	50	35	17	196
Upson	139	3	4	16	116	159	916	179	687	50	705
Walker	87	3	–	14	70	74	2,470	497	1,808	165	1,612
Walton	86	5	6	14	61	118	1,332	318	838	176	1,447
Ware	123	2	7	41	73	159	1,686	342	1,245	99	1,690
Warren	4	–	1	1	2	22	39	11	27	1	113
Washington	88	–	3	23	62	84	648	114	492	42	613
Wayne	32	–	–	2	30	–	54	13	40	1	6
Webster	–	–	–	–	–	(NA)	11	6	4	1	(NA)
Wheeler	–	–	–	–	–	1	17	8	5	4	19
White	51	2	4	3	42	48	724	164	464	96	460
Whitfield	375	6	25	54	290	286	4,471	808	3,281	382	3,736
Wilcox	12	–	–	1	11	11	26	11	15	–	25
Wilkes	44	–	4	6	34	23	195	77	102	16	203
Wilkinson	22	–	–	2	20	73	161	53	92	16	196
Worth	30	–	–	1	29	14	280	70	195	15	225

See footnotes at end of table.

[Includes United States, states, and 3,141 counties/county equivalents defined as of February 22, 2005. For more information on these areas, see Appendix C, Geographic Information]

County	Violent crimes[1]						Property crimes[1]				
	2004						2004				
	Total	Murder and non-negligent man-slaughter	Forcible rape	Robbery	Aggra-vated assault	2000	Total	Burglary	Larceny-theft	Motor vehicle theft	2000
HAWAII	3,274	33	361	963	1,917	2,954	60,391	10,719	41,045	8,627	60,033
Hawaii	290	3	86	53	148	237	5,929	1,162	4,335	432	6,188
Honolulu	2,507	26	222	818	1,441	2,302	44,121	7,240	29,512	7,369	44,357
Kalawao	(NA)	(NA)	(NA)	(NA)	(NA)	(NA)	(NA)	(NA)	(NA)	(NA)	(NA)
Kauai	208	2	37	22	147	144	2,493	526	1,865	102	2,434
Maui	269	2	16	70	181	271	7,848	1,791	5,333	724	7,054
IDAHO	3,448	31	593	241	2,583	3,264	38,753	7,662	28,355	2,736	37,927
Ada	1,091	4	196	93	798	858	9,478	1,603	7,183	692	11,043
Adams	4	–	–	–	4	4	43	8	34	1	51
Bannock	226	1	22	16	187	213	2,891	402	2,337	152	2,349
Bear Lake	4	–	2	–	2	7	25	2	22	1	31
Benewah	20	–	2	–	18	12	66	17	45	4	143
Bingham	40	–	6	2	32	87	881	189	641	51	850
Blaine	26	–	2	–	24	33	382	109	254	19	381
Boise	12	–	1	–	11	14	129	34	91	4	80
Bonner	58	1	8	1	48	62	927	185	678	64	928
Bonneville	188	4	44	11	129	196	2,946	474	2,309	163	2,866
Boundary	24	–	2	–	22	13	139	34	99	6	141
Butte	4	–	–	–	4	12	35	6	26	3	27
Camas	2	–	–	–	2	–	2	1	1	–	3
Canyon	533	12	126	50	345	433	5,521	1,136	3,777	608	4,891
Caribou	8	–	–	–	8	9	73	20	49	4	113
Cassia	87	–	6	2	79	75	730	189	506	35	671
Clark	1	–	–	–	1	1	27	2	23	2	18
Clearwater	15	–	3	–	12	14	171	40	121	10	129
Custer	5	–	–	–	5	8	63	6	53	4	44
Elmore	46	1	12	1	32	91	657	134	467	56	664
Franklin	4	–	1	–	3	3	109	27	79	3	83
Fremont	17	–	5	–	12	12	124	19	102	3	96
Gem	18	–	7	–	11	19	182	27	139	16	172
Gooding	18	–	4	2	12	16	155	33	116	6	170
Idaho	33	–	2	–	31	21	225	39	170	16	198
Jefferson	22	2	2	1	17	32	185	12	166	7	238
Jerome	45	1	7	6	31	56	484	116	329	39	523
Kootenai	337	1	51	18	267	421	4,185	985	2,937	263	3,850
Latah	31	1	3	2	25	26	774	158	592	24	713
Lemhi	10	–	1	–	9	(NA)	71	17	52	2	(NA)
Lewis	11	–	3	–	8	3	71	35	33	3	40
Lincoln	6	–	1	–	5	1	13	11	2	–	4
Madison	9	–	2	1	6	14	283	29	245	9	377
Minidoka	37	–	8	1	28	38	386	99	261	26	352
Nez Perce	33	1	5	4	23	61	1,469	221	1,169	79	1,314
Oneida	3	–	–	–	3	6	46	20	18	8	65
Owyhee	20	–	1	–	19	32	203	79	103	21	246
Payette	46	–	7	5	34	41	546	128	389	29	548
Power	14	–	3	–	11	19	218	35	170	13	181
Shoshone	55	1	9	1	44	38	285	92	176	17	301
Teton	18	–	5	1	12	10	119	27	87	5	218
Twin Falls	228	1	28	23	176	193	2,990	742	2,016	232	2,463
Valley	20	–	4	–	16	42	260	68	165	27	191
Washington	19	–	2	–	17	18	184	52	123	9	161
ILLINOIS	(NA)	506	(NA)	17,390	22,217	[3]50,655	177,867	32,649	119,639	25,579	199,349
Adams	(NA)	(NA)	(NA)	(NA)	(NA)	(NA)	(NA)	(NA)	(NA)	(NA)	(NA)
Alexander	(NA)	(NA)	(NA)	(NA)	(NA)	(NA)	(NA)	(NA)	(NA)	(NA)	(NA)
Bond	(NA)	(NA)	(NA)	(NA)	(NA)	(NA)	(NA)	(NA)	(NA)	(NA)	(NA)
Boone	(NA)	(NA)	(NA)	(NA)	(NA)	(NA)	(NA)	(NA)	(NA)	(NA)	(NA)
Brown	(NA)	(NA)	(NA)	(NA)	(NA)	(NA)	(NA)	(NA)	(NA)	(NA)	(NA)
Bureau	(NA)	(NA)	(NA)	(NA)	(NA)	(NA)	(NA)	(NA)	(NA)	(NA)	(NA)
Calhoun	(NA)	(NA)	(NA)	(NA)	(NA)	(NA)	(NA)	(NA)	(NA)	(NA)	(NA)
Carroll	(NA)	(NA)	(NA)	(NA)	(NA)	(NA)	(NA)	(NA)	(NA)	(NA)	(NA)
Cass	(NA)	(NA)	(NA)	(NA)	(NA)	(NA)	(NA)	(NA)	(NA)	(NA)	(NA)
Champaign	(NA)	(NA)	(NA)	(NA)	(NA)	(NA)	(NA)	(NA)	(NA)	(NA)	(NA)
Christian	(NA)	(NA)	(NA)	(NA)	(NA)	(NA)	(NA)	(NA)	(NA)	(NA)	(NA)
Clark	(NA)	(NA)	(NA)	(NA)	(NA)	(NA)	(NA)	(NA)	(NA)	(NA)	(NA)
Clay	(NA)	(NA)	(NA)	(NA)	(NA)	(NA)	(NA)	(NA)	(NA)	(NA)	(NA)
Clinton	(NA)	(NA)	(NA)	(NA)	(NA)	(NA)	(NA)	(NA)	(NA)	(NA)	(NA)
Coles	(NA)	(NA)	(NA)	(NA)	(NA)	(NA)	(NA)	(NA)	(NA)	(NA)	(NA)
Cook	(NA)	448	(NA)	15,912	18,746	(NA)	140,602	24,428	93,375	22,799	164,181
Crawford	(NA)	(NA)	(NA)	(NA)	(NA)	(NA)	(NA)	(NA)	(NA)	(NA)	(NA)
Cumberland	(NA)	(NA)	(NA)	(NA)	(NA)	(NA)	(NA)	(NA)	(NA)	(NA)	(NA)
DeKalb	(NA)	(NA)	(NA)	(NA)	(NA)	(NA)	(NA)	(NA)	(NA)	(NA)	(NA)
De Witt	(NA)	(NA)	(NA)	(NA)	(NA)	(NA)	(NA)	(NA)	(NA)	(NA)	(NA)

See footnotes at end of table.

County and City Data Book: 2007

U.S. Census Bureau

[Includes United States, states, and 3,141 counties/county equivalents defined as of February 22, 2005. For more information on these areas, see Appendix C, Geographic Information]

County	Violent crimes[1]						Property crimes[1]				
	2004					2000	2004				2000
	Total	Murder and non-negligent man-slaughter	Forcible rape	Robbery	Aggra-vated assault		Total	Burglary	Larceny-theft	Motor vehicle theft	
ILLINOIS—Con.											
Douglas	(NA)	(NA)	(NA)	(NA)	(NA)	(NA)	(NA)	(NA)	(NA)	(NA)	(NA)
DuPage	(NA)	5	–	56	195	(NA)	2,963	458	2,359	146	2,962
Edgar	(NA)	(NA)	(NA)	(NA)	(NA)	(NA)	(NA)	(NA)	(NA)	(NA)	(NA)
Edwards	(NA)	(NA)	(NA)	(NA)	(NA)	(NA)	(NA)	(NA)	(NA)	(NA)	(NA)
Effingham	(NA)	(NA)	(NA)	(NA)	(NA)	(NA)	(NA)	(NA)	(NA)	(NA)	(NA)
Fayette	(NA)	(NA)	(NA)	(NA)	(NA)	(NA)	(NA)	(NA)	(NA)	(NA)	(NA)
Ford	(NA)	(NA)	(NA)	(NA)	(NA)	(NA)	(NA)	(NA)	(NA)	(NA)	(NA)
Franklin	(NA)	(NA)	(NA)	(NA)	(NA)	(NA)	(NA)	(NA)	(NA)	(NA)	(NA)
Fulton	(NA)	(NA)	(NA)	(NA)	(NA)	(NA)	(NA)	(NA)	(NA)	(NA)	(NA)
Gallatin	(NA)	(NA)	(NA)	(NA)	(NA)	(NA)	(NA)	(NA)	(NA)	(NA)	(NA)
Greene	(NA)	(NA)	(NA)	(NA)	(NA)	(NA)	(NA)	(NA)	(NA)	(NA)	(NA)
Grundy	(NA)	(NA)	(NA)	(NA)	(NA)	(NA)	(NA)	(NA)	(NA)	(NA)	(NA)
Hamilton	(NA)	(NA)	(NA)	(NA)	(NA)	(NA)	(NA)	(NA)	(NA)	(NA)	(NA)
Hancock	(NA)	(NA)	(NA)	(NA)	(NA)	(NA)	(NA)	(NA)	(NA)	(NA)	(NA)
Hardin	(NA)	(NA)	(NA)	(NA)	(NA)	(NA)	(NA)	(NA)	(NA)	(NA)	(NA)
Henderson	(NA)	(NA)	(NA)	(NA)	(NA)	(NA)	(NA)	(NA)	(NA)	(NA)	(NA)
Henry	(NA)	(NA)	(NA)	(NA)	(NA)	(NA)	(NA)	(NA)	(NA)	(NA)	(NA)
Iroquois	(NA)	(NA)	(NA)	(NA)	(NA)	(NA)	(NA)	(NA)	(NA)	(NA)	(NA)
Jackson	(NA)	(NA)	(NA)	(NA)	(NA)	(NA)	(NA)	(NA)	(NA)	(NA)	(NA)
Jasper	(NA)	(NA)	(NA)	(NA)	(NA)	(NA)	(NA)	(NA)	(NA)	(NA)	(NA)
Jefferson	(NA)	(NA)	(NA)	(NA)	(NA)	(NA)	(NA)	(NA)	(NA)	(NA)	(NA)
Jersey	(NA)	(NA)	(NA)	(NA)	(NA)	(NA)	(NA)	(NA)	(NA)	(NA)	(NA)
Jo Daviess	(NA)	(NA)	(NA)	(NA)	(NA)	(NA)	(NA)	(NA)	(NA)	(NA)	(NA)
Johnson	(NA)	(NA)	(NA)	(NA)	(NA)	(NA)	(NA)	(NA)	(NA)	(NA)	(NA)
Kane	(NA)	12	(NA)	108	346	(NA)	3,607	625	2,751	231	3,753
Kankakee	(NA)	(NA)	(NA)	(NA)	(NA)	(NA)	(NA)	(NA)	(NA)	(NA)	(NA)
Kendall	(NA)	–	(NA)	4	8	(NA)	92	19	68	5	(NA)
Knox	(NA)	(NA)	(NA)	(NA)	(NA)	(NA)	(NA)	(NA)	(NA)	(NA)	(NA)
Lake	(NA)	(NA)	(NA)	(NA)	(NA)	(NA)	(NA)	(NA)	(NA)	(NA)	(NA)
LaSalle	(NA)	(NA)	(NA)	(NA)	(NA)	(NA)	(NA)	(NA)	(NA)	(NA)	(NA)
Lawrence	(NA)	(NA)	(NA)	(NA)	(NA)	(NA)	(NA)	(NA)	(NA)	(NA)	(NA)
Lee	(NA)	(NA)	(NA)	(NA)	(NA)	(NA)	(NA)	(NA)	(NA)	(NA)	(NA)
Livingston	(NA)	(NA)	(NA)	(NA)	(NA)	(NA)	(NA)	(NA)	(NA)	(NA)	(NA)
Logan	(NA)	(NA)	(NA)	(NA)	(NA)	(NA)	(NA)	(NA)	(NA)	(NA)	(NA)
McDonough	(NA)	(NA)	(NA)	(NA)	(NA)	(NA)	(NA)	(NA)	(NA)	(NA)	(NA)
McHenry	(NA)	(NA)	(NA)	(NA)	(NA)	(NA)	(NA)	(NA)	(NA)	(NA)	(NA)
McLean	(NA)	(NA)	(NA)	(NA)	(NA)	(NA)	(NA)	(NA)	(NA)	(NA)	(NA)
Macon	(NA)	(NA)	(NA)	(NA)	(NA)	(NA)	(NA)	(NA)	(NA)	(NA)	(NA)
Macoupin	(NA)	(NA)	(NA)	(NA)	(NA)	(NA)	(NA)	(NA)	(NA)	(NA)	(NA)
Madison	(NA)	(NA)	(NA)	(NA)	(NA)	(NA)	(NA)	(NA)	(NA)	(NA)	(NA)
Marion	(NA)	(NA)	(NA)	(NA)	(NA)	(NA)	(NA)	(NA)	(NA)	(NA)	(NA)
Marshall	(NA)	(NA)	(NA)	(NA)	(NA)	(NA)	(NA)	(NA)	(NA)	(NA)	(NA)
Mason	(NA)	(NA)	(NA)	(NA)	(NA)	(NA)	(NA)	(NA)	(NA)	(NA)	(NA)
Massac	(NA)	(NA)	(NA)	(NA)	(NA)	(NA)	(NA)	(NA)	(NA)	(NA)	(NA)
Menard	(NA)	(NA)	(NA)	(NA)	(NA)	(NA)	(NA)	(NA)	(NA)	(NA)	(NA)
Mercer	(NA)	(NA)	(NA)	(NA)	(NA)	(NA)	(NA)	(NA)	(NA)	(NA)	(NA)
Monroe	(NA)	(NA)	(NA)	(NA)	(NA)	(NA)	(NA)	(NA)	(NA)	(NA)	(NA)
Montgomery	(NA)	(NA)	(NA)	(NA)	(NA)	(NA)	(NA)	(NA)	(NA)	(NA)	(NA)
Morgan	(NA)	(NA)	(NA)	(NA)	(NA)	(NA)	(NA)	(NA)	(NA)	(NA)	(NA)
Moultrie	(NA)	(NA)	(NA)	(NA)	(NA)	(NA)	(NA)	(NA)	(NA)	(NA)	(NA)
Ogle	(NA)	(NA)	(NA)	(NA)	(NA)	(NA)	(NA)	(NA)	(NA)	(NA)	(NA)
Peoria	(NA)	14	(NA)	343	523	(NA)	6,928	1,760	4,508	660	9,334
Perry	(NA)	(NA)	(NA)	(NA)	(NA)	(NA)	(NA)	(NA)	(NA)	(NA)	(NA)
Piatt	(NA)	(NA)	(NA)	(NA)	(NA)	(NA)	(NA)	(NA)	(NA)	(NA)	(NA)
Pike	(NA)	(NA)	(NA)	(NA)	(NA)	(NA)	(NA)	(NA)	(NA)	(NA)	(NA)
Pope	(NA)	(NA)	(NA)	(NA)	(NA)	(NA)	(NA)	(NA)	(NA)	(NA)	(NA)
Pulaski	(NA)	(NA)	(NA)	(NA)	(NA)	(NA)	(NA)	(NA)	(NA)	(NA)	(NA)
Putnam	(NA)	(NA)	(NA)	(NA)	(NA)	(NA)	(NA)	(NA)	(NA)	(NA)	(NA)
Randolph	(NA)	(NA)	(NA)	(NA)	(NA)	(NA)	(NA)	(NA)	(NA)	(NA)	(NA)
Richland	(NA)	(NA)	(NA)	(NA)	(NA)	(NA)	(NA)	(NA)	(NA)	(NA)	(NA)
Rock Island	(NA)	(NA)	(NA)	(NA)	(NA)	(NA)	(NA)	(NA)	(NA)	(NA)	(NA)
St. Clair	(NA)	(NA)	(NA)	(NA)	(NA)	(NA)	(NA)	(NA)	(NA)	(NA)	(NA)
Saline	(NA)	(NA)	(NA)	(NA)	(NA)	(NA)	(NA)	(NA)	(NA)	(NA)	(NA)
Sangamon	(NA)	10	(NA)	285	1,309	(NA)	8,133	1,831	5,898	404	7,272
Schuyler	(NA)	(NA)	(NA)	(NA)	(NA)	(NA)	(NA)	(NA)	(NA)	(NA)	(NA)
Scott	(NA)	(NA)	(NA)	(NA)	(NA)	(NA)	(NA)	(NA)	(NA)	(NA)	(NA)
Shelby	(NA)	(NA)	(NA)	(NA)	(NA)	(NA)	(NA)	(NA)	(NA)	(NA)	(NA)
Stark	(NA)	(NA)	(NA)	(NA)	(NA)	(NA)	(NA)	(NA)	(NA)	(NA)	(NA)
Stephenson	(NA)	(NA)	(NA)	(NA)	(NA)	(NA)	(NA)	(NA)	(NA)	(NA)	(NA)
Tazewell	(NA)	(NA)	(NA)	(NA)	(NA)	(NA)	(NA)	(NA)	(NA)	(NA)	(NA)

See footnotes at end of table.

Table B-8. Counties — **Crime—Number of Offenses**—Con.

[Includes United States, states, and 3,141 counties/county equivalents defined as of February 22, 2005. For more information on these areas, see Appendix C, Geographic Information]

County	Violent crimes[1] 2004 Total	Murder and non-negligent man-slaughter	Forcible rape	Robbery	Aggra-vated assault	2000	Property crimes[1] 2004 Total	Burglary	Larceny-theft	Motor vehicle theft	2000
ILLINOIS—Con.											
Union	(NA)	(NA)	(NA)	(NA)	(NA)	(NA)	(NA)	(NA)	(NA)	(NA)	(NA)
Vermilion	(NA)	(NA)	(NA)	(NA)	(NA)	(NA)	(NA)	(NA)	(NA)	(NA)	(NA)
Wabash	(NA)	(NA)	(NA)	(NA)	(NA)	(NA)	(NA)	(NA)	(NA)	(NA)	(NA)
Warren	(NA)	(NA)	(NA)	(NA)	(NA)	(NA)	(NA)	(NA)	(NA)	(NA)	(NA)
Washington	(NA)	(NA)	(NA)	(NA)	(NA)	(NA)	(NA)	(NA)	(NA)	(NA)	(NA)
Wayne	(NA)	(NA)	(NA)	(NA)	(NA)	(NA)	(NA)	(NA)	(NA)	(NA)	(NA)
White	(NA)	(NA)	(NA)	(NA)	(NA)	(NA)	(NA)	(NA)	(NA)	(NA)	(NA)
Whiteside	(NA)	(NA)	(NA)	(NA)	(NA)	(NA)	(NA)	(NA)	(NA)	(NA)	(NA)
Will	(NA)	9	(NA)	173	376	(NA)	4,724	921	3,568	235	641
Williamson	(NA)	(NA)	(NA)	(NA)	(NA)	(NA)	(NA)	(NA)	(NA)	(NA)	(NA)
Winnebago	(NA)	8	(NA)	509	714	(NA)	10,818	2,607	7,112	1,099	11,206
Woodford	(NA)	(NA)	(NA)	(NA)	(NA)	(NA)	(NA)	(NA)	(NA)	(NA)	(NA)
INDIANA	18,783	300	1,652	6,046	10,785	17,844	192,505	38,128	134,892	19,485	167,958
Adams	15	–	–	2	13	17	226	30	175	21	248
Allen	765	23	109	331	302	956	12,758	2,474	9,313	971	13,770
Bartholomew	108	–	10	15	83	92	2,729	252	2,382	95	2,696
Benton	–	–	–	–	–	3–	–	–	–	2	
Blackford	11	1	–	1	9	10	306	48	242	16	252
Boone	3	–	1	–	2	2	6	–	4	2	18
Brown	4	1	–	1	2	13	68	28	38	2	212
Carroll	8	–	–	1	7	24	27	7	17	3	63
Cass	62	1	9	5	47	29	1,058	182	823	53	796
Clark	250	3	39	76	132	356	4,027	765	2,791	471	4,882
Clay	35	1	2	3	29	39	334	76	226	32	413
Clinton	28	–	6	9	13	49	1,079	184	848	47	872
Crawford	14	1	–	3	10	10	39	16	22	1	30
Daviess	11	–	–	1	10	4	167	49	103	15	227
Dearborn	191	–	1	3	187	46	445	113	257	75	549
Decatur	15	–	1	2	12	10	370	62	299	9	12
DeKalb	26	–	3	10	13	13	432	96	310	26	28
Delaware	412	7	139	88	178	110	4,117	691	3,168	258	1,183
Dubois	22	–	4	7	11	35	390	51	321	18	441
Elkhart	350	2	62	183	103	746	7,579	1,552	5,477	550	8,972
Fayette	43	–	5	9	29	21	1,284	216	1,013	55	875
Floyd	218	5	17	80	116	258	3,185	584	2,380	221	3,298
Fountain	22	–	–	3	19	5	49	15	31	3	9
Franklin	23	–	–	3	20	14	238	91	129	18	45
Fulton	1	–	–	–	–	1	10	2	7	1	10
Gibson	12	–	5	2	5	62	49	1	36	12	270
Grant	135	–	20	67	48	109	2,487	524	1,836	127	1,221
Greene	21	–	2	6	13	14	285	76	193	16	39
Hamilton	110	1	22	24	63	72	3,004	460	2,403	141	2,192
Hancock	27	1	6	7	13	24	738	180	521	37	567
Harrison	49	4	9	4	32	30	893	344	451	98	697
Hendricks	135	3	12	22	98	36	2,372	484	1,717	171	796
Henry	39	2	12	11	14	24	2,514	565	1,842	107	2,438
Howard	259	5	28	54	172	275	3,482	633	2,660	189	3,035
Huntington	34	–	4	6	24	35	453	68	365	20	591
Jackson	111	–	10	3	98	117	1,247	122	1,047	78	1,172
Jasper	18	–	1	–	17	29	194	30	157	7	279
Jay	2	–	–	–	2	7	241	40	198	3	245
Jefferson	47	–	13	4	30	34	474	143	302	29	448
Jennings	80	–	5	1	74	36	347	82	242	23	316
Johnson	361	2	29	31	299	192	4,038	341	3,576	121	2,826
Knox	54	1	11	8	34	41	1,680	393	1,215	72	1,298
Kosciusko	50	–	13	11	26	82	1,484	250	1,160	74	1,412
LaGrange	21	–	1	4	16	14	220	65	144	11	50
Lake	2,732	83	117	828	1,704	2,376	17,978	3,532	11,024	3,422	16,093
LaPorte	215	6	20	76	113	267	3,895	515	3,097	283	4,972
Lawrence	31	1	3	6	21	33	719	131	543	45	911
Madison	219	7	36	70	106	38	3,421	687	2,560	174	1,015
Marion	7,372	110	503	2,892	3,867	7,072	49,844	11,362	30,385	8,097	33,439
Marshall	25	–	3	3	19	37	612	56	522	34	594
Martin	8	–	1	1	6	17	66	20	37	9	133
Miami	22	–	–	1	21	8	60	13	43	4	24
Monroe	218	2	40	56	120	208	3,621	734	2,717	170	4,108
Montgomery	17	–	2	6	9	18	782	131	635	16	886
Morgan	54	–	5	11	38	64	1,256	119	1,064	73	1,132
Newton	6	–	–	1	5	25	156	56	76	24	148
Noble	35	–	4	10	21	34	402	71	286	45	694
Ohio	2	–	–	–	2	4	12	–	9	3	9
Orange	9	–	3	1	5	20	25	8	17	–	150
Owen	4	–	2	–	2	8	13	4	7	2	21

See footnotes at end of table.

Table B-8. Counties — **Crime—Number of Offenses**—Con.

[Includes United States, states, and 3,141 counties/county equivalents defined as of February 22, 2005. For more information on these areas, see Appendix C, Geographic Information]

County	Violent crimes[1] 2004					Violent crimes[1] 2000	Property crimes[1] 2004				Property crimes[1] 2000
	Total	Murder and non-negligent man-slaughter	Forcible rape	Robbery	Aggra-vated assault	2000	Total	Burglary	Larceny-theft	Motor vehicle theft	2000
INDIANA—Con.											
Parke	3	–	1	–	2	12	18	4	12	2	25
Perry	28	–	3	4	21	26	364	138	197	29	256
Pike	5	–	–	4	1	4	11	6	5	–	16
Porter	223	–	11	33	179	140	3,624	542	2,803	279	3,848
Posey	9	–	3	1	5	12	156	60	75	21	129
Pulaski	1	1	–	–	–	21	17	4	11	2	68
Putnam	160	–	7	1	152	132	554	232	267	55	519
Randolph	21	3	8	–	10	25	453	85	348	20	309
Ripley	56	–	2	11	43	33	306	73	220	13	147
Rush	15	–	1	1	13	9	116	25	90	1	152
St. Joseph	1,273	11	109	435	718	1,173	12,187	2,312	9,045	830	14,319
Scott	59	1	3	11	44	62	511	76	419	16	374
Shelby	19	1	1	2	15	2	281	81	170	30	8
Spencer	11	–	1	3	7	9	33	5	25	3	42
Starke	15	–	3	–	12	45	465	120	282	63	398
Steuben	29	–	6	2	21	60	1,112	189	882	41	1,144
Sullivan	18	1	1	3	13	20	185	66	108	11	38
Switzerland	4	1	–	–	3	14	13	1	10	2	15
Tippecanoe	310	6	33	80	191	256	5,258	1,137	3,870	251	4,936
Tipton	32	–	–	–	32	31	143	28	112	3	240
Union	10	–	1	–	9	3	56	9	39	8	17
Vanderburgh	511	1	40	178	292	769	7,146	1,281	5,546	319	6,833
Vermillion	10	–	–	5	5	5	128	20	89	19	17
Vigo	401	–	32	117	252	206	5,718	1,038	4,184	496	5,510
Wabash	18	–	5	7	6	10	393	74	294	25	314
Warren	2	–	1	–	1	1	3	–	2	1	6
Warrick	95	–	2	6	87	155	661	122	515	24	651
Washington	11	–	1	3	7	10	43	11	25	7	80
Wayne	188	1	20	58	109	222	1,872	433	1,268	171	2,895
Wells	18	–	2	12	4	12	329	75	238	16	331
White	19	–	3	2	14	29	193	35	144	14	185
Whitley	38	–	2	4	32	5	169	22	134	13	12
IOWA	8,272	44	757	1,138	6,333	7,697	83,253	17,435	60,304	5,514	84,001
Adair	–	–	–	–	–	3	30	1	24	5	50
Adams	6	–	–	–	6	4	94	29	60	5	68
Allamakee	(NA)	(NA)	(NA)	(NA)	(NA)	(NA)	(NA)	(NA)	(NA)	(NA)	(NA)
Appanoose	17	–	3	1	13	47	467	79	348	40	536
Audubon	1	–	–	–	1	1	29	5	24	–	30
Benton	17	–	–	–	17	5	169	56	104	9	136
Black Hawk	449	3	67	67	312	479	4,532	1,072	3,219	241	5,022
Boone	31	–	–	2	29	13	347	56	267	24	358
Bremer	28	–	3	–	25	17	213	40	164	9	218
Buchanan	4	–	–	–	4	5	346	119	205	22	443
Buena Vista	28	–	7	2	19	25	419	69	327	23	357
Butler	7	–	1	–	6	8	55	18	34	3	43
Calhoun	5	–	–	1	4	12	101	24	69	8	115
Carroll	8	–	–	2	6	3	186	32	142	12	363
Cass	5	–	–	–	5	10	243	64	168	11	327
Cedar	8	–	1	–	7	7	159	25	123	11	227
Cerro Gordo	83	–	11	10	62	78	1,825	298	1,470	57	2,515
Cherokee	10	–	2	–	8	6	171	28	138	5	209
Chickasaw	13	–	1	–	12	4	75	31	36	8	60
Clarke	7	–	–	1	6	18	241	55	174	12	344
Clay	3	–	–	–	3	5	359	66	271	22	410
Clayton	12	–	1	–	11	–	76	29	37	10	9
Clinton	120	–	8	18	94	2	1,327	278	996	53	74
Crawford	1	–	–	–	1	4	87	10	68	9	153
Dallas	61	–	6	4	51	23	938	150	730	58	638
Davis	5	–	–	–	5	–	38	9	28	1	7
Decatur	4	–	3	–	1	–	24	–	22	2	5
Delaware	12	–	–	–	12	25	148	53	87	8	140
Des Moines	200	2	12	22	164	161	1,506	317	1,132	57	1,766
Dickinson	9	–	2	–	7	(NA)	206	47	156	3	(NA)
Dubuque	270	1	9	13	247	147	2,250	533	1,577	140	2,151
Emmet	12	–	2	1	9	18	192	65	120	7	191
Fayette	36	–	9	–	27	2	196	59	130	7	117
Floyd	22	–	2	–	20	14	195	43	145	7	207
Franklin	10	–	–	–	10	2	92	21	66	5	115
Fremont	(NA)	(NA)	(NA)	(NA)	(NA)	(NA)	(NA)	(NA)	(NA)	(NA)	(NA)
Greene	–	–	–	–	–	2	109	37	68	4	64
Grundy	4	–	–	–	4	4	146	43	97	6	92
Guthrie	–	–	–	–	–	–	25	6	18	1	67
Hamilton	18	–	5	1	12	13	318	63	225	30	336

See footnotes at end of table.

[Includes United States, states, and 3,141 counties/county equivalents defined as of February 22, 2005. For more information on these areas, see Appendix C, Geographic Information]

County	Violent crimes[1] 2004 Total	Murder and non-negligent man-slaughter	Forcible rape	Robbery	Aggra-vated assault	2000	Property crimes[1] 2004 Total	Burglary	Larceny-theft	Motor vehicle theft	2000
IOWA—Con.											
Hancock	7	–	–	–	7	17	64	13	44	7	117
Hardin	18	–	4	–	14	28	350	61	277	12	346
Harrison	6	1	1	1	3	8	174	51	109	14	237
Henry	28	1	3	–	24	12	358	89	245	24	171
Howard	13	–	–	4	9	13	161	39	115	7	220
Humboldt	3	–	–	–	3	3	74	16	47	11	158
Ida	3	–	–	–	3	–	65	1	61	3	32
Iowa	15	–	1	–	14	17	131	32	89	10	70
Jackson	11	–	3	1	7	2	229	49	164	16	235
Jasper	29	1	–	1	27	16	607	120	437	50	717
Jefferson	34	1	3	1	29	42	312	76	214	22	487
Johnson	362	2	47	60	253	447	3,192	627	2,455	110	3,013
Jones	10	–	–	–	10	9	213	41	162	10	209
Keokuk	1	–	–	–	1	–	24	5	18	1	1
Kossuth	14	–	5	1	8	12	154	65	78	11	181
Lee	175	–	5	2	168	130	888	143	689	56	1,071
Linn	495	1	54	84	356	409	7,664	1,651	5,634	379	6,831
Louisa	30	–	3	–	27	1	150	68	75	7	172
Lucas	9	–	1	–	8	12	247	60	174	13	243
Lyon	8	–	5	–	3	27	69	22	41	6	95
Madison	7	–	–	–	7	(NA)	104	25	68	11	(NA)
Mahaska	41	–	7	3	31	40	570	123	424	23	470
Marion	54	–	5	2	47	58	392	92	273	27	568
Marshall	196	–	10	15	171	244	1,321	325	928	68	1,217
Mills	35	–	5	2	28	36	350	77	242	31	336
Mitchell	2	–	–	–	2	6	79	21	56	2	81
Monona	1	–	–	–	1	22	13	4	9	–	211
Monroe	1	–	–	–	1	26	18	8	8	2	78
Montgomery	11	–	–	–	11	20	272	64	198	10	334
Muscatine	149	1	26	3	119	238	905	212	655	38	1,163
O'Brien	3	–	1	–	2	7	84	21	56	7	194
Osceola	3	–	1	–	2	–	87	21	62	4	82
Page	10	–	1	1	8	20	298	87	186	25	377
Palo Alto	10	–	–	–	10	3	31	8	19	4	44
Plymouth	33	–	8	1	24	8	314	62	232	20	332
Pocahontas	–	–	–	–	–	3	18	2	13	3	27
Polk	1,520	16	97	354	1,053	1,058	17,761	3,044	13,333	1,384	18,824
Pottawattamie	631	2	108	71	450	502	6,208	1,311	4,045	852	5,434
Poweshiek	17	–	1	–	16	31	291	84	185	22	513
Ringgold	–	–	–	–	–	–	2	–	2	–	44
Sac	3	–	–	–	3	7	76	19	56	1	77
Scott	1,475	7	59	290	1,119	1,713	8,715	1,746	6,461	508	7,603
Shelby	9	–	–	–	9	(NA)	42	7	32	3	(NA)
Sioux	11	–	2	–	9	7	154	39	102	13	157
Story	167	–	31	16	120	109	2,353	559	1,664	130	2,230
Tama	47	–	1	–	46	75	155	53	84	18	205
Taylor	2	–	–	–	2	1	27	6	16	5	64
Union	31	–	1	1	29	(NA)	262	94	146	22	(NA)
Van Buren	8	–	2	–	6	6	72	25	37	10	84
Wapello	206	–	13	6	187	204	1,398	320	1,003	75	1,588
Warren	62	1	7	1	53	35	648	136	468	44	884
Washington	55	–	11	–	44	(NA)	174	68	95	11	(NA)
Wayne	4	–	–	–	4	6	50	12	35	3	119
Webster	195	2	17	27	149	184	2,204	547	1,528	129	2,143
Winnebago	6	–	1	–	5	17	20	9	8	3	59
Winneshiek	18	–	2	–	16	8	136	23	105	8	177
Woodbury	443	2	49	45	347	616	4,415	979	3,155	281	5,455
Worth	3	–	–	–	3	8	78	11	57	10	81
Wright	6	–	1	–	5	7	96	32	61	3	177
KANSAS	9,911	122	1,095	1,774	6,920	8,151	104,853	19,217	77,417	8,219	86,199
Allen	–	–	–	–	–	44	5	–	5	–	454
Anderson	18	–	1	–	17	25	175	64	103	8	189
Atchison	44	–	7	8	29	36	473	117	327	29	454
Barber	10	1	–	–	9	4	41	16	22	3	48
Barton	22	1	3	2	16	114	297	101	187	9	978
Bourbon	59	1	3	6	49	68	588	205	357	26	544
Brown	18	–	7	1	10	13	198	52	140	6	208
Butler	95	1	15	4	75	109	1,732	331	1,314	87	1,532
Chase	3	–	2	–	1	5	36	22	13	1	32
Chautauqua	23	1	2	–	20	18	106	37	64	5	92

See footnotes at end of table.

[Includes United States, states, and 3,141 counties/county equivalents defined as of February 22, 2005. For more information on these areas, see Appendix C, Geographic Information]

County	Violent crimes[1]						Property crimes[1]				
	2004					2000	2004				2000
	Total	Murder and non-negligent man-slaughter	Forcible rape	Robbery	Aggra-vated assault		Total	Burglary	Larceny-theft	Motor vehicle theft	
KANSAS—Con.											
Cherokee	44	–	2	2	40	53	666	134	476	56	748
Cheyenne	–	–	–	–	–	3	17	4	12	1	27
Clark	1	–	–	–	1	1	8	3	5	–	2
Clay	26	2	4	–	20	16	182	59	110	13	178
Cloud	20	1	2	–	17	13	203	66	120	17	158
Coffey	6	1	1	2	2	11	109	23	82	4	158
Comanche	1	–	–	–	1	(NA)	1	–	1	–	(NA)
Cowley	141	1	19	5	116	98	1,303	280	971	52	817
Crawford	163	–	17	19	127	94	2,167	453	1,593	121	765
Decatur	9	–	–	–	9	7	40	21	13	6	44
Dickinson	50	1	12	1	36	43	385	78	295	12	547
Doniphan	19	1	3	–	15	6	167	47	103	17	86
Douglas	427	2	58	67	300	35	4,941	871	3,826	244	708
Edwards	1	–	–	1	–	4	18	4	13	1	49
Elk	6	–	2	–	4	6	63	17	46	–	78
Ellis	46	2	2	6	36	48	792	114	651	27	847
Ellsworth	6	–	2	–	4	9	103	21	75	7	128
Finney	152	2	18	17	115	243	1,688	288	1,327	73	2,613
Ford	159	1	21	22	115	191	1,615	275	1,233	107	2,109
Franklin	77	–	17	–	60	72	1,081	245	788	48	743
Geary	179	–	12	17	150	252	1,144	181	915	48	2,027
Gove	4	–	–	–	4	–	39	12	25	2	42
Graham	4	–	2	–	2	2	34	6	28	–	28
Grant	17	–	2	–	15	29	137	28	104	5	147
Gray	–	–	–	–	–	1	22	11	10	1	21
Greeley	1	–	–	–	1	1	18	4	11	3	6
Greenwood	9	–	2	–	7	9	120	51	56	13	139
Hamilton	3	–	–	–	3	5	34	6	25	3	79
Harper	15	–	–	–	15	5	87	30	51	6	81
Harvey	89	–	11	4	74	61	838	130	680	28	1,020
Haskell	9	–	–	–	9	7	44	16	24	4	65
Hodgeman	4	–	–	–	4	–	67	14	53	–	66
Jackson	43	–	2	2	39	23	331	65	248	18	242
Jefferson	34	–	4	–	30	63	392	115	253	24	526
Jewell	(NA)	(NA)	(NA)	(NA)	(NA)	1	(NA)	(NA)	(NA)	(NA)	6
Johnson	978	5	122	160	691	703	11,768	1,351	9,262	1,155	9,085
Kearny	12	–	5	–	7	6	118	25	89	4	145
Kingman	18	–	5	–	13	14	140	38	98	4	155
Kiowa	3	–	–	–	3	1	26	7	16	3	56
Labette	80	1	4	4	71	63	729	182	522	25	563
Lane	3	–	–	–	3	2	39	7	32	–	49
Leavenworth	284	1	24	46	213	227	2,091	424	1,520	147	1,932
Lincoln	8	–	2	–	6	8	63	14	47	2	22
Linn	25	–	3	–	22	17	230	94	118	18	221
Logan	5	–	1	1	3	3	47	11	32	4	82
Lyon	72	2	16	9	45	107	1,581	291	1,226	64	2,033
McPherson	26	–	10	2	14	35	455	137	302	16	499
Marion	12	–	4	–	8	12	179	63	110	6	139
Marshall	13	–	2	–	11	9	81	13	60	8	89
Meade	4	–	1	–	3	–	39	18	18	3	3
Miami	76	–	7	2	67	63	826	223	547	56	712
Mitchell	8	–	5	–	3	6	93	34	57	2	160
Montgomery	153	1	10	29	113	82	1,577	471	1,037	69	945
Morris	3	–	1	1	1	10	90	31	57	2	120
Morton	12	1	–	–	11	9	56	19	35	2	46
Nemaha	10	–	1	–	9	5	108	36	66	6	162
Neosho	50	–	7	2	41	54	528	137	368	23	617
Ness	1	–	–	–	1	(NA)	24	12	12	–	(NA)
Norton	2	–	1	–	1	8	27	11	14	2	68
Osage	42	1	4	3	34	32	335	132	184	19	330
Osborne	2	–	–	–	2	–	32	17	13	2	1
Ottawa	6	–	–	–	6	10	102	44	52	6	88
Pawnee	39	–	2	–	37	48	228	46	175	7	236
Phillips	–	–	–	–	–	(NA)	28	7	19	2	(NA)
Pottawatomie	26	–	3	1	22	29	341	89	234	18	415
Pratt	23	–	2	1	20	27	211	28	176	7	331
Rawlins	7	–	4	–	3	1	23	8	14	1	10
Reno	273	–	44	24	205	245	3,191	689	2,422	80	3,340
Republic	4	–	1	–	3	6	117	56	52	9	82
Rice	18	–	3	1	14	35	162	29	122	11	191

See footnotes at end of table.

Table B-8. Counties — **Crime—Number of Offenses**—Con.

[Includes United States, states, and 3,141 counties/county equivalents defined as of February 22, 2005. For more information on these areas, see Appendix C, Geographic Information]

County	Violent crimes[1] 2004						Property crimes[1] 2004				
	Total	Murder and non-negligent man-slaughter	Forcible rape	Robbery	Aggra-vated assault	2000	Total	Burglary	Larceny-theft	Motor vehicle theft	2000
KANSAS—Con.											
Riley	173	3	29	19	122	197	1,764	288	1,421	55	2,109
Rooks	5	–	–	–	5	7	37	21	15	1	58
Rush	2	–	–	–	2	–	27	16	10	1	9
Russell	25	3	3	1	18	15	152	38	99	15	158
Saline	187	1	44	12	130	186	2,925	396	2,398	131	3,148
Scott	16	1	–	–	15	10	114	28	82	4	112
Sedgwick	3,070	31	273	636	2,130	2,180	24,370	4,685	17,792	1,893	21,063
Seward	95	3	11	12	69	157	1,307	268	976	63	1,100
Shawnee	736	8	57	258	413	1,463	10,245	1,636	7,870	739	13,196
Sheridan	–	–	–	–	–	–	11	2	7	2	6
Sherman	22	1	3	1	17	37	188	37	143	8	247
Smith	1	–	–	–	1	(NA)	37	13	22	2	(NA)
Stafford	4	–	1	–	3	8	90	24	62	4	95
Stanton	–	–	–	–	–	4	25	14	8	3	7
Stevens	20	–	1	–	19	13	128	45	79	4	134
Sumner	63	–	5	1	57	37	672	144	493	35	655
Thomas	30	–	2	3	25	12	251	36	210	5	238
Trego	3	–	–	2	1	2	22	7	14	1	40
Wabaunsee	7	–	1	–	6	16	147	52	85	10	164
Wallace	2	–	–	–	2	–	2	1	1	–	3
Washington	2	–	1	–	1	2	19	10	9	–	55
Wichita	9	–	–	–	9	9	39	15	19	5	30
Wilson	15	–	1	1	13	19	210	82	118	10	114
Woodson	6	–	–	1	5	3	73	30	38	5	56
Wyandotte	1,063	40	114	355	554	49	13,806	1,918	9,583	2,305	644
KENTUCKY	[3]9,310	[3]217	[3]1,114	[3]3,055	[3]4,924	6,657	[3]94,056	[3]23,358	[3]62,770	[3]7,928	45,650
Adair	6	–	1	–	5	(NA)	56	14	37	5	(NA)
Allen	12	1	1	1	9	(NA)	101	27	64	10	(NA)
Anderson	12	–	2	2	8	(NA)	293	82	201	10	(NA)
Ballard	8	–	1	–	7	(NA)	100	23	66	11	(NA)
Barren	20	–	2	6	12	(NA)	526	140	348	38	(NA)
Bath	2	–	–	–	2	(NA)	45	14	24	7	(NA)
Bell	10	1	–	–	9	(NA)	163	40	103	20	(NA)
Boone	200	2	27	44	127	146	2,771	431	2,124	216	2,352
Bourbon	20	–	1	6	13	(NA)	306	75	201	30	(NA)
Boyd	127	–	9	26	92	79	1,568	268	1,215	85	1,070
Boyle	27	–	5	7	15	(NA)	599	160	401	38	(NA)
Bracken	1	–	–	–	1	(NA)	5	2	2	1	(NA)
Breathitt	5	–	–	–	5	(NA)	74	14	52	8	(NA)
Breckinridge	3	–	1	1	1	(NA)	72	34	30	8	(NA)
Bullitt	59	1	8	12	38	(NA)	971	296	610	65	(NA)
Butler	4	–	–	–	4	(NA)	33	13	15	5	(NA)
Caldwell	15	–	2	3	10	(NA)	213	46	160	7	(NA)
Calloway	49	1	11	8	29	24	1,014	278	679	57	491
Campbell	54	3	27	7	17	59	654	109	509	36	288
Carlisle	–	–	–	–	–	(NA)	5	2	3	–	(NA)
Carroll	12	–	1	1	10	9	125	30	87	8	131
Carter	11	–	2	1	8	(NA)	210	78	110	22	(NA)
Casey	–	–	–	–	–	(NA)	47	16	31	–	(NA)
Christian	156	2	18	64	72	(NA)	2,166	576	1,485	105	(NA)
Clark	58	–	2	22	34	(NA)	1,078	221	793	64	(NA)
Clay	29	–	6	1	22	(NA)	248	73	142	33	(NA)
Clinton	2	–	–	–	2	(NA)	20	8	11	1	(NA)
Crittenden	5	–	1	–	4	(NA)	110	36	71	3	(NA)
Cumberland	–	–	–	–	–	(NA)	3	–	3	–	(NA)
Daviess	194	1	17	42	134	172	2,863	667	2,069	127	3,196
Edmonson	5	–	2	1	2	(NA)	66	22	39	5	(NA)
Elliott	(NA)	(NA)	(NA)	(NA)	(NA)	(NA)	(NA)	(NA)	(NA)	(NA)	(NA)
Estill	10	–	1	3	6	(NA)	127	46	76	5	(NA)
Fayette	1,317	24	146	577	570	1,888	10,886	2,265	7,830	791	11,769
Fleming	3	–	–	–	3	(NA)	65	25	33	7	(NA)
Floyd	14	–	–	1	13	(NA)	211	30	170	11	(NA)
Franklin	96	1	12	15	68	(NA)	1,411	308	1,019	84	(NA)
Fulton	18	–	2	2	14	(NA)	215	36	160	19	(NA)
Gallatin	5	–	–	–	5	(NA)	66	18	37	11	(NA)
Garrard	10	–	2	2	6	(NA)	227	48	172	7	(NA)
Grant	2	–	–	1	1	(NA)	74	15	54	5	(NA)
Graves	56	2	4	17	33	(NA)	437	157	241	39	(NA)
Grayson	13	–	4	1	8	(NA)	289	98	157	34	(NA)
Green	–	–	–	–	–	(NA)	1	1	–	–	(NA)
Greenup	5	–	–	3	2	(NA)	153	30	108	15	(NA)

See footnotes at end of table.

[Includes United States, states, and 3,141 counties/county equivalents defined as of February 22, 2005. For more information on these areas, see Appendix C, Geographic Information]

| County | Violent crimes[1] | | | | | | Property crimes[1] | | | | |
| | 2004 | | | | | 2000 | 2004 | | | | 2000 |
	Total	Murder and non-negligent man-slaughter	Forcible rape	Robbery	Aggra-vated assault		Total	Burglary	Larceny-theft	Motor vehicle theft	
KENTUCKY—Con.											
Hancock	–	–	–	–	–	(NA)	26	5	19	2	(NA)
Hardin	157	2	25	44	86	76	2,125	428	1,621	76	696
Harlan	22	–	1	4	17	(NA)	258	37	213	8	(NA)
Harrison	9	–	1	2	6	(NA)	230	29	183	18	(NA)
Hart	6	–	1	–	5	(NA)	179	51	121	7	(NA)
Henderson	–	–	–	–	–	(NA)	(NA)	(NA)	(NA)	(NA)	(NA)
Henry	15	1	5	1	8	(NA)	29	15	12	2	(NA)
Hickman	1	–	–	–	1	(NA)	48	24	24	(NA)	(NA)
Hopkins	90	1	15	7	67	141	1,280	249	940	91	1,018
Jackson	–	–	–	–	–	(NA)	18	8	8	2	(NA)
Jefferson	3,542	66	228	1,582	1,666	3,323	28,745	7,374	18,086	3,285	18,158
Jessamine	14	–	5	1	8	(NA)	271	85	160	26	(NA)
Johnson	7	–	1	1	5	(NA)	192	22	145	25	(NA)
Kenton	147	1	15	44	87	(NA)	1,934	343	1,458	133	(NA)
Knott	1	–	–	–	1	(NA)	68	15	52	1	(NA)
Knox	9	–	1	3	5	(NA)	190	41	117	32	(NA)
Larue	18	–	2	2	14	(NA)	144	49	78	17	(NA)
Laurel	32	1	3	6	22	(NA)	1,012	205	690	117	(NA)
Lawrence	–	–	–	–	–	(NA)	33	9	21	3	(NA)
Lee	1	–	–	–	1	(NA)	20	3	12	5	(NA)
Leslie	–	–	–	–	–	(NA)	(NA)	(NA)	(NA)	(NA)	(NA)
Letcher	6	–	–	–	6	(NA)	129	35	77	17	(NA)
Lewis	3	1	1	–	1	(NA)	124	45	73	6	(NA)
Lincoln	2	–	–	–	2	(NA)	75	28	43	4	(NA)
Livingston	4	–	–	1	3	(NA)	160	77	76	7	(NA)
Logan	53	–	7	3	43	(NA)	539	162	361	16	(NA)
Lyon	6	–	–	–	6	(NA)	45	12	33	(NA)	(NA)
McCracken	260	9	31	66	154	170	1,957	273	1,535	149	1,798
McCreary	2	–	–	2	–	(NA)	79	25	45	9	(NA)
McLean	–	–	–	–	–	(NA)	34	22	10	2	(NA)
Madison	59	–	7	13	39	251	1,559	298	1,168	93	1,752
Magoffin	1	–	–	–	1	(NA)	34	9	16	9	(NA)
Marion	–	–	–	–	–	(NA)	(NA)	(NA)	(NA)	(NA)	(NA)
Marshall	33	5	5	2	21	(NA)	508	184	289	35	(NA)
Martin	1	–	–	–	1	(NA)	62	10	25	27	(NA)
Mason	49	–	3	13	33	(NA)	632	176	412	44	(NA)
Meade	10	–	1	1	8	(NA)	218	95	101	22	(NA)
Menifee	1	–	–	–	1	(NA)	29	9	19	1	(NA)
Mercer	28	–	2	3	23	(NA)	225	92	116	17	(NA)
Metcalfe	4	–	–	3	1	(NA)	56	15	35	6	(NA)
Monroe	–	–	–	–	–	(NA)	(NA)	(NA)	(NA)	(NA)	(NA)
Montgomery	11	–	–	1	10	(NA)	585	87	460	38	(NA)
Morgan	–	–	–	–	–	(NA)	(NA)	(NA)	(NA)	(NA)	(NA)
Muhlenberg	5	–	–	–	5	(NA)	65	15	44	6	(NA)
Nelson	26	2	5	2	17	(NA)	253	66	170	17	(NA)
Nicholas	4	–	–	–	4	(NA)	31	11	17	3	(NA)
Ohio	7	–	1	–	6	(NA)	202	76	109	17	(NA)
Oldham	17	1	3	4	9	(NA)	425	88	292	45	(NA)
Owen	4	–	1	–	3	(NA)	76	52	23	1	(NA)
Owsley	–	–	–	–	–	(NA)	16	4	11	1	(NA)
Pendleton	1	–	–	–	1	(NA)	83	22	59	2	(NA)
Perry	41	1	4	17	19	(NA)	468	106	331	31	(NA)
Pike	13	–	–	3	10	(NA)	451	57	372	22	(NA)
Powell	6	–	–	1	5	(NA)	182	42	134	6	(NA)
Pulaski	51	–	9	15	27	(NA)	1,582	351	1,115	116	(NA)
Robertson	–	–	–	–	–	(NA)	(NA)	(NA)	(NA)	(NA)	(NA)
Rockcastle	16	–	2	4	10	(NA)	171	64	89	18	(NA)
Rowan	17	–	2	3	12	(NA)	236	26	199	11	(NA)
Russell	1	–	–	–	1	(NA)	41	18	23	(NA)	(NA)
Scott	46	–	6	11	29	(NA)	1,072	182	839	51	(NA)
Shelby	39	–	2	13	24	(NA)	588	146	372	70	(NA)
Simpson	28	–	4	11	13	(NA)	483	108	338	37	(NA)
Spencer	3	–	–	–	3	(NA)	40	12	23	5	(NA)
Taylor	46	1	9	14	22	(NA)	484	137	329	18	(NA)
Todd	8	–	–	1	7	(NA)	66	26	38	2	(NA)
Trigg	7	–	–	–	7	(NA)	150	37	99	14	(NA)
Trimble	1	–	–	1	–	(NA)	12	2	5	5	(NA)
Union	9	–	1	–	8	(NA)	115	39	68	8	(NA)
Warren	291	1	33	74	183	279	3,116	561	2,425	130	2,682
Washington	–	–	–	–	–	(NA)	(NA)	(NA)	(NA)	(NA)	(NA)

See footnotes at end of table.

Table B-8. Counties — **Crime—Number of Offenses**—Con.

[Includes United States, states, and 3,141 counties/county equivalents defined as of February 22, 2005. For more information on these areas, see Appendix C, Geographic Information]

| County | Violent crimes[1] | | | | | | Property crimes[1] | | | | |
| | 2004 | | | | | 2000 | 2004 | | | | 2000 |
	Total	Murder and non-negligent man-slaughter	Forcible rape	Robbery	Aggra-vated assault		Total	Burglary	Larceny-theft	Motor vehicle theft	
KENTUCKY—Con.											
Wayne	7	–	2	2	3	(NA)	126	48	70	8	(NA)
Webster	8	–	1	3	4	(NA)	34	7	22	5	(NA)
Whitley	22	1	4	8	9	(NA)	311	81	202	28	(NA)
Wolfe	1	–	–	–	1	(NA)	34	10	20	4	(NA)
Woodford	90	–	4	8	78	40	464	84	358	22	249
LOUISIANA	27,465	557	1,523	6,279	19,106	28,542	183,263	41,555	122,773	18,935	199,945
Acadia	110	1	10	15	84	258	1,330	273	982	75	1,761
Allen	23	–	–	1	22	81	34	2	32	–	387
Ascension	446	10	39	34	363	252	3,297	583	2,405	309	2,418
Assumption	225	–	5	5	215	76	449	91	332	26	326
Avoyelles	38	–	11	8	19	73	519	203	306	10	727
Beauregard	105	2	13	6	84	113	550	184	340	26	568
Bienville	42	1	5	7	29	29	118	42	73	3	106
Bossier	1,325	4	39	70	1,212	610	3,994	669	2,968	357	4,467
Caddo	2,396	35	160	700	1,501	2,075	16,005	3,671	10,745	1,589	16,637
Calcasieu	966	12	117	217	620	1,169	9,010	2,799	5,745	466	9,282
Caldwell	34	–	–	–	34	33	95	41	45	9	119
Cameron	42	–	1	1	40	34	219	34	164	21	218
Catahoula	6	–	–	–	6	45	136	68	60	8	146
Claiborne	54	–	2	6	46	36	279	112	162	5	257
Concordia	71	2	3	12	54	78	585	126	432	27	431
De Soto	103	1	6	4	92	181	779	159	551	69	709
East Baton Rouge	3,158	60	129	1,106	1,863	3,297	27,674	5,854	19,632	2,188	33,450
East Carroll	51	5	2	6	38	38	182	55	111	16	180
East Feliciana	75	1	2	1	71	277	249	89	139	21	420
Evangeline	78	–	9	5	64	57	688	194	432	62	583
Franklin	25	2	–	–	23	83	222	60	150	12	320
Grant	60	1	3	–	56	101	507	132	334	41	389
Iberia	33	–	1	8	24	117	253	37	196	20	1,168
Iberville	221	1	10	5	205	245	762	142	596	24	862
Jackson	3	–	–	1	2	18	94	26	67	1	99
Jefferson	3,041	52	215	872	1,902	3,297	21,935	4,029	14,948	2,958	24,980
Jefferson Davis	263	3	16	23	221	303	1,181	283	828	70	1,028
Lafayette	1,301	7	114	195	985	1,190	9,224	1,930	6,729	565	9,431
Lafourche	297	4	29	40	224	246	2,759	480	2,155	124	2,670
La Salle	20	1	1	1	17	29	140	15	122	3	90
Lincoln	134	2	4	37	91	210	1,451	383	1,015	53	1,798
Livingston	301	2	15	27	257	356	2,251	751	1,387	113	2,144
Madison	38	–	–	–	38	96	130	22	86	22	203
Morehouse	80	1	6	11	62	109	984	249	693	42	663
Natchitoches	295	2	8	31	254	346	1,969	730	1,166	73	1,571
Orleans	4,477	264	189	1,843	2,181	5,174	24,942	5,325	13,051	6,566	29,249
Ouachita	1,275	8	57	162	1,048	1,241	8,698	1,920	6,393	385	8,327
Plaquemines	79	2	2	8	67	78	415	111	242	62	362
Pointe Coupee	74	–	2	2	70	127	341	65	253	23	401
Rapides	1,248	11	35	205	997	871	6,561	1,855	4,295	411	7,871
Red River	41	1	1	2	37	38	158	50	99	9	209
Richland	9	–	1	1	7	3	214	60	141	13	137
Sabine	76	–	1	4	71	90	340	92	230	18	330
St. Bernard	210	3	9	45	153	(NA)	2,118	368	1,556	194	(NA)
St. Charles	228	2	5	32	189	386	1,631	392	1,073	166	1,651
St. Helena	42	1	3	3	35	41	162	47	102	13	163
St. James	208	–	2	9	197	208	706	171	498	37	677
St. John the Baptist	110	10	9	38	61	89	1,230	276	834	120	1,475
St. Landry	196	4	14	25	153	655	1,867	621	1,113	133	3,162
St. Martin	3	–	–	3	–	135	291	49	211	31	464
St. Mary	394	1	25	53	315	438	1,928	360	1,472	96	2,635
St. Tammany	745	5	54	102	584	592	6,159	1,112	4,607	440	6,137
Tangipahoa	884	3	33	56	792	732	4,168	1,466	2,561	141	3,750
Tensas	29	2	2	–	25	27	76	20	53	3	65
Terrebonne	776	12	63	126	575	801	5,700	1,383	3,931	386	5,389
Union	82	1	3	3	75	77	271	81	187	3	562
Vermilion	108	–	–	7	101	167	536	116	398	22	1,096
Vernon	159	6	7	6	140	235	933	140	766	27	1,083
Washington	216	1	20	48	147	289	1,662	466	1,088	108	1,489
Webster	121	3	3	9	106	227	770	249	477	44	645
West Baton Rouge	133	2	7	26	98	134	878	109	731	38	1,274
West Carroll	29	1	1	3	24	47	259	89	143	27	199
West Feliciana	33	2	–	–	31	28	164	26	128	10	210
Winn	12	–	–	3	9	54	31	18	12	1	325

See footnotes at end of table.

[Includes United States, states, and 3,141 counties/county equivalents defined as of February 22, 2005. For more information on these areas, see Appendix C, Geographic Information]

County	Violent crimes[1]						Property crimes[1]				
	2004					2000	2004				2000
	Total	Murder and non-negligent man-slaughter	Forcible rape	Robbery	Aggra-vated assault		Total	Burglary	Larceny-theft	Motor vehicle theft	
MAINE	1,363	18	314	289	742	1,391	31,745	6,342	24,100	1,303	31,880
Androscoggin	123	3	35	35	50	179	2,865	547	2,203	115	3,483
Aroostook	45	2	15	13	15	64	1,420	388	970	62	1,521
Cumberland	403	3	74	118	208	358	7,434	1,361	5,703	370	7,492
Franklin	39	–	12	3	24	15	736	142	563	31	913
Hancock	38	1	–	4	33	47	1,168	238	875	55	1,155
Kennebec	101	1	31	23	46	99	3,094	609	2,384	101	2,659
Knox	34	–	8	1	25	26	953	128	797	28	712
Lincoln	11	3	4	2	2	21	526	85	414	27	479
Oxford	61	1	19	3	38	43	1,205	307	844	54	1,160
Penobscot	105	1	20	29	55	154	4,630	929	3,561	140	4,076
Piscataquis	24	–	4	1	19	33	323	81	224	18	445
Sagadahoc	12	–	5	3	4	20	760	114	623	23	858
Somerset	59	1	18	8	32	46	1,518	396	1,063	59	1,491
Waldo	39	1	2	3	33	16	720	161	531	28	302
Washington	55	–	8	–	47	65	678	171	481	26	743
York	214	1	59	43	111	205	3,715	685	2,864	166	4,391
MARYLAND	38,938	521	1,317	12,761	24,339	41,847	202,326	36,682	129,786	35,858	214,440
Allegany	325	–	23	27	275	271	2,024	488	1,481	55	2,107
Anne Arundel	3,462	19	110	767	2,566	3,429	17,141	2,986	12,524	1,631	18,141
Baltimore	6,180	29	198	1,565	4,388	6,199	26,897	4,942	19,019	2,936	30,278
Calvert	228	1	10	13	204	314	1,317	289	954	74	1,338
Caroline	146	–	12	10	124	217	839	204	558	77	761
Carroll	415	–	47	48	320	433	2,485	456	1,878	151	3,072
Cecil	431	2	18	60	351	455	2,957	753	1,940	264	2,531
Charles	736	5	32	159	540	690	4,205	778	2,903	524	3,806
Dorchester	137	3	10	15	109	182	1,152	261	799	92	1,023
Frederick	873	1	39	177	656	908	3,739	657	2,861	221	4,040
Garrett	55	1	–	2	52	46	436	100	320	16	508
Harford	885	3	45	214	623	619	5,361	1,112	3,836	413	4,869
Howard	609	1	40	224	344	503	6,856	1,167	5,091	598	7,331
Kent	58	–	3	8	47	58	380	140	211	29	350
Montgomery	2,060	18	149	856	1,037	1,873	22,706	3,893	16,083	2,730	25,671
Prince George's	8,189	146	294	4,100	3,649	7,409	53,432	7,460	27,490	18,482	43,483
Queen Anne's	78	1	5	13	59	113	875	187	668	20	911
St. Mary's	308	3	12	32	261	292	1,909	488	1,314	107	1,883
Somerset	135	1	9	21	104	124	673	192	455	26	630
Talbot	139	1	9	30	99	89	878	173	669	36	963
Washington	536	5	17	88	426	439	3,107	699	2,138	270	3,161
Wicomico	792	5	32	205	550	772	3,814	914	2,715	185	3,683
Worcester	401	–	21	42	338	351	2,138	321	1,725	92	2,367
Independent City											
Baltimore city	11,760	276	182	4,085	7,217	16,061	37,005	8,022	22,154	6,829	51,533
MASSACHUSETTS	30,181	170	1,745	7,353	20,913	33,163	153,442	33,478	98,425	21,539	158,753
Barnstable	1,006	7	57	80	862	1,169	5,300	1,700	3,305	295	5,485
Berkshire	326	–	46	19	261	468	1,704	550	1,040	114	2,483
Bristol	3,197	11	198	640	2,348	2,985	14,319	3,814	8,812	1,693	13,768
Dukes	31	–	2	1	28	17	233	29	195	9	283
Essex	2,591	12	128	507	1,944	3,198	15,300	3,648	9,623	2,029	17,900
Franklin	350	2	17	20	311	525	1,212	516	607	89	1,387
Hampden	4,161	22	261	885	2,993	5,044	19,146	4,322	11,494	3,330	18,177
Hampshire	409	2	48	42	317	441	2,847	844	1,785	218	2,616
Middlesex	3,713	19	203	1,050	2,441	3,536	27,465	5,367	18,879	3,219	27,340
Nantucket	45	1	3	2	39	51	210	50	137	23	554
Norfol	1,295	3	90	298	904	1,089	9,564	1,989	6,710	865	9,784
Plymouth	2,016	11	105	333	1,567	2,092	8,809	1,668	5,759	1,382	9,267
Suffolk	8,106	67	313	2,854	4,872	8,356	32,327	5,366	20,723	6,238	32,632
Worcester	2,935	13	274	622	2,026	4,192	15,006	3,615	9,356	2,035	17,077
MICHIGAN	49,272	643	5,400	11,242	31,987	54,015	305,434	63,430	191,885	50,119	343,233
Alcona	10	–	3	–	7	8	245	100	139	6	194
Alger	9	–	2	1	6	33	104	40	49	15	147
Allegan	251	2	52	14	183	248	1,729	404	1,225	100	1,812
Alpena	62	1	25	3	33	74	646	188	441	17	707
Antrim	33	–	5	1	27	29	409	115	272	22	253
Arenac	46	2	18	–	26	49	296	99	179	18	321
Baraga	16	–	4	–	12	12	59	19	35	5	54
Barry	107	3	27	2	75	107	907	248	599	60	1,017
Bay	312	2	79	47	184	291	2,768	580	1,980	208	3,366
Benzie	34	–	12	–	22	25	278	77	181	20	294

See footnotes at end of table.

[Includes United States, states, and 3,141 counties/county equivalents defined as of February 22, 2005. For more information on these areas, see Appendix C, Geographic Information]

County	Violent crimes[1]						Property crimes[1]				
	2004					2000	2004				2000
	Total	Murder and non-negligent man-slaughter	Forcible rape	Robbery	Aggra-vated assault		Total	Burglary	Larceny-theft	Motor vehicle theft	
MICHIGAN—Con.											
Berrien	859	5	128	107	619	698	4,966	1,064	3,582	320	5,509
Branch	116	–	25	4	87	135	1,086	225	806	55	1,060
Calhoun	944	9	143	128	664	1,354	6,126	1,304	4,489	333	7,141
Cass	102	1	30	14	57	99	1,232	345	825	62	1,304
Charlevoix	36	1	13	–	22	45	451	80	356	15	289
Cheboygan	45	–	23	2	20	40	597	142	418	37	505
Chippewa	77	–	19	3	55	55	771	181	539	51	675
Clare	79	1	12	8	58	62	1,185	467	656	62	726
Clinton	73	–	13	2	58	74	813	193	567	53	777
Crawford	41	1	14	–	26	23	267	82	159	26	319
Delta	39	–	15	–	24	20	287	97	175	15	216
Dickinson	43	3	21	3	16	25	536	69	448	19	577
Eaton	247	1	53	45	148	212	2,430	458	1,820	152	2,375
Emmet	57	–	21	8	28	49	668	147	502	19	678
Genesee	3,410	51	277	723	2,359	2,860	17,901	4,880	10,349	2,672	21,203
Gladwin	59	–	16	1	42	69	385	134	226	25	466
Gogebic	21	–	7	–	14	19	104	30	69	5	380
Grand Traverse	190	–	66	9	115	145	1,669	304	1,297	68	2,239
Gratio	76	–	37	3	36	50	605	123	456	26	810
Hillsdale	102	–	29	11	62	97	1,012	274	684	54	1,006
Houghton	51	–	19	2	30	34	542	81	434	27	521
Huron	40	–	16	–	24	41	619	125	479	15	609
Ingham	1,634	18	215	315	1,086	1,583	9,923	2,150	7,086	687	11,212
Ionia	182	1	55	8	118	160	1,422	326	1,027	69	1,231
Iosco	48	–	13	–	35	50	669	215	422	32	668
Iron	26	–	4	2	20	25	195	59	125	11	230
Isabella	160	1	49	22	88	117	1,549	318	1,148	83	1,648
Jackson	681	4	174	94	409	709	4,482	985	3,193	304	5,717
Kalamazoo	889	4	110	204	571	1,139	9,718	1,856	7,302	560	10,589
Kalkaska	41	–	25	–	16	37	448	147	292	9	473
Kent	3,018	20	266	713	2,019	2,991	20,098	4,670	14,149	1,279	21,749
Keweenaw	2	–	–	–	2	9	49	14	32	3	56
Lake	56	–	12	2	42	116	276	119	147	10	497
Lapeer	151	1	34	9	107	82	1,498	280	1,129	89	1,161
Leelanau	19	3	5	1	10	16	232	56	165	11	228
Lenawee	303	1	72	29	201	200	1,829	383	1,338	108	2,076
Livingston	214	2	39	26	147	182	2,536	504	1,848	184	2,356
Luce	16	–	10	–	6	34	68	23	35	10	124
Mackinac	26	–	9	–	17	37	398	67	317	14	586
Macomb	2,421	16	231	488	1,686	2,617	19,546	2,791	13,405	3,350	19,666
Manistee	52	1	20	1	30	73	448	133	289	26	577
Marquette	92	–	38	4	50	110	1,335	241	1,026	68	1,564
Mason	95	3	26	4	62	73	849	178	651	20	862
Mecosta	99	1	31	6	61	145	1,227	258	909	60	1,302
Menominee	36	–	12	–	24	40	518	151	353	14	494
Midland	149	1	42	12	94	135	1,338	195	1,097	46	1,407
Missaukee	28	–	6	–	22	21	239	98	129	12	315
Monroe	305	–	69	36	200	406	3,388	787	2,322	279	3,953
Montcalm	137	–	59	4	74	168	1,493	444	952	97	1,316
Montmorency	15	–	6	–	9	14	92	37	44	11	140
Muskegon	994	4	141	150	699	724	8,716	1,543	6,506	667	7,434
Newaygo	166	2	45	2	117	143	1,235	358	789	88	1,377
Oakland	4,091	15	418	821	2,837	3,725	28,947	5,081	20,446	3,420	32,650
Oceana	63	4	15	2	42	48	476	126	329	21	473
Ogemaw	49	–	13	1	35	75	513	166	329	18	447
Ontonagon	13	–	2	–	11	11	84	26	51	7	83
Osceola	62	1	25	–	36	54	445	136	285	24	346
Oscoda	16	3	6	–	7	28	249	83	156	10	232
Otsego	57	–	13	1	43	41	547	162	354	31	534
Ottawa	475	2	176	31	266	409	4,999	1,014	3,775	210	5,077
Presque Isle	5	–	2	–	3	24	91	38	47	6	167
Roscommon	69	–	22	5	42	77	825	242	525	58	923
Saginaw	2,211	24	142	265	1,780	1,650	7,487	2,033	4,834	620	8,622
St. Clair	450	1	91	35	323	421	3,567	656	2,628	283	4,120
St. Joseph	244	–	66	15	163	209	1,837	383	1,360	94	1,915
Sanilac	64	–	16	1	47	71	588	172	387	29	666
Schoolcraft	18	1	6	–	11	11	122	58	55	9	93
Shiawassee	197	1	45	14	137	124	1,352	297	954	101	1,336
Tuscola	73	–	29	1	43	83	668	196	429	43	957

See footnotes at end of table.

County and City Data Book: 2007

U.S. Census Bureau

Table B-8. Counties — **Crime—Number of Offenses**—Con.

[Includes United States, states, and 3,141 counties/county equivalents defined as of February 22, 2005. For more information on these areas, see Appendix C, Geographic Information]

County	Violent crimes[1]						Property crimes[1]				
	2004					2000	2004				2000
	Total	Murder and non-negligent man-slaughter	Forcible rape	Robbery	Aggra-vated assault		Total	Burglary	Larceny-theft	Motor vehicle theft	
MICHIGAN—Con.											
Van Buren	270	1	46	18	205	303	2,466	595	1,602	269	2,563
Washtenaw	1,091	9	125	268	689	1,045	9,844	1,995	6,834	1,015	10,893
Wayne	20,021	414	1,067	6,488	12,052	26,255	91,838	17,738	43,065	31,035	111,309
Wexford	91	1	33	3	54	113	982	172	777	33	1,269
MINNESOTA	13,671	113	2,107	4,053	7,398	13,678	154,552	27,747	113,401	13,404	155,293
Aitkin	31	–	12	–	19	22	544	228	269	47	466
Anoka	516	4	93	97	322	570	12,447	1,577	10,082	788	10,392
Becker	48	–	10	4	34	19	599	97	428	74	495
Beltrami	140	–	30	8	102	61	1,614	256	1,228	130	1,552
Benton	70	–	24	9	37	64	991	145	787	59	664
Big Stone	7	–	2	–	5	11	84	31	40	13	88
Blue Earth	97	1	43	7	46	106	2,198	410	1,675	113	2,053
Brown	15	–	5	1	9	20	330	57	258	15	426
Carlton	41	–	14	1	26	33	895	150	692	53	516
Carver	61	–	9	8	44	78	1,116	151	912	53	1,270
Cass	122	–	58	11	53	98	1,140	277	768	95	1,361
Chippewa	10	–	2	–	8	3	215	31	171	13	156
Chisago	36	–	7	8	21	40	1,354	220	1,005	129	1,062
Clay	80	1	27	14	38	81	1,156	159	914	83	1,118
Clearwater	10	–	4	–	6	21	178	50	112	16	153
Cook	4	–	–	–	4	4	137	35	96	6	157
Cottonwood	13	1	5	1	6	13	172	35	128	9	246
Crow Wing	118	1	30	6	81	117	2,188	395	1,658	135	2,227
Dakota	438	4	86	112	236	460	10,015	1,296	8,144	575	10,041
Dodge	3	–	1	–	2	13	250	53	178	19	173
Douglas	37	2	17	3	15	43	713	134	547	32	944
Faribault	10	–	1	–	9	15	300	65	209	26	225
Fillmore	12	–	3	–	9	10	143	45	87	11	161
Freeborn	24	–	3	1	20	44	525	44	449	32	700
Goodhue	58	–	20	7	31	84	1,236	210	951	75	1,363
Grant	4	–	3	–	1	2	105	37	62	6	164
Hennepin	6,065	61	633	2,670	2,701	5,949	43,132	8,382	29,565	5,185	48,818
Houston	15	–	4	1	10	15	293	31	231	31	227
Hubbard	35	1	5	2	27	34	632	188	382	62	720
Isanti	32	–	7	5	20	21	826	184	542	100	658
Itasca	32	–	4	2	26	26	541	170	315	56	329
Jackson	15	–	2	–	13	11	189	50	132	7	160
Kanabec	29	1	7	–	21	33	458	102	311	45	378
Kandiyohi	64	–	26	7	31	99	1,156	209	900	47	1,102
Kittson	6	–	–	–	6	2	72	13	58	1	53
Koochiching	16	–	8	–	8	34	356	90	242	24	408
Lac qui Parle	4	–	2	–	2	5	83	20	56	7	87
Lake	1	–	1	–	–	11	109	40	65	4	165
Lake of the Woods	5	–	2	–	3	2	102	30	69	3	74
Le Sueur	12	–	4	–	8	14	289	49	215	25	262
Lincoln	10	–	–	–	10	8	79	11	68	–	(NA)
Lyon	38	–	17	2	19	21	543	106	412	25	257
McLeod	63	1	21	1	40	81	866	158	656	52	1,018
Mahnomen	22	–	2	2	18	33	209	68	124	17	170
Marshall	13	–	–	1	12	10	87	19	64	4	173
Martin	16	–	4	1	11	44	503	90	395	18	298
Meeker	35	–	27	3	5	34	577	129	402	46	623
Mille Lacs	41	1	11	2	27	44	834	165	598	71	781
Morrison	33	1	6	1	25	46	675	102	537	36	720
Mower	89	1	21	11	56	105	1,232	200	964	68	1,276
Murray	10	–	3	–	7	5	117	14	95	8	100
Nicollet	27	–	14	–	13	43	644	54	559	31	722
Nobles	16	–	1	2	13	28	349	108	227	14	375
Norman	11	–	3	1	7	7	63	31	29	3	74
Olmsted	263	–	54	69	140	288	2,991	496	2,312	183	2,777
Otter Tail	72	–	20	2	50	49	1,017	233	720	64	1,123
Pennington	24	1	12	1	10	19	342	64	265	13	368
Pine	41	1	16	3	21	43	1,216	371	752	93	866
Pipestone	–	–	–	–	–	10	74	17	55	2	194
Polk	52	–	9	2	41	67	510	137	350	23	766
Pope	10	–	4	–	6	5	95	27	60	8	176
Ramsey	2,731	21	270	765	1,675	2,756	21,342	4,180	14,538	2,624	23,920
Red Lake	–	–	–	–	–	3	11	4	7	–	70
Redwood	23	1	6	–	16	34	376	81	265	30	262
Renville	24	–	8	1	15	41	323	63	230	30	317

See footnotes at end of table.

Table B-8. Counties — **Crime—Number of Offenses**—Con.

[Includes United States, states, and 3,141 counties/county equivalents defined as of February 22, 2005. For more information on these areas, see Appendix C, Geographic Information]

County	Violent crimes[1] 2004 Total	Murder and non-negligent man-slaughter	Forcible rape	Robbery	Aggra-vated assault	2000	Property crimes[1] 2004 Total	Burglary	Larceny-theft	Motor vehicle theft	2000
MINNESOTA—Con.											
Rice	95	–	22	8	65	120	1,659	422	1,154	83	1,799
Rock	16	–	–	–	16	6	48	13	30	5	75
Roseau	4	–	1	–	3	12	286	32	246	8	324
St. Louis	425	–	90	65	270	470	7,250	1,463	5,361	426	6,189
Scott	127	1	25	13	88	143	2,566	411	2,002	153	2,406
Sherburne	101	1	26	8	66	59	1,923	237	1,583	103	1,119
Sibley	–	–	–	–	–	–	52	29	20	3	52
Stearns	285	–	67	36	182	142	3,676	499	3,021	156	1,968
Steele	63	–	11	12	40	55	974	207	728	39	933
Stevens	14	–	4	1	9	10	128	39	82	7	161
Swift	12	–	5	–	7	6	187	57	114	16	139
Todd	34	1	16	–	17	27	510	105	375	30	496
Traverse	8	–	2	–	6	4	86	13	68	5	53
Wabasha	14	–	5	3	6	21	280	34	232	14	367
Wadena	24	–	5	–	19	31	271	67	191	13	352
Waseca	32	–	5	2	25	27	397	87	301	9	311
Washington	246	–	49	30	167	245	6,327	843	5,088	396	5,441
Watonwan	13	–	3	1	9	14	235	40	184	11	220
Wilkin	13	–	3	–	10	15	204	30	157	17	148
Winona	41	3	5	6	27	69	777	129	610	38	1,304
Wright	96	2	19	12	63	84	2,659	283	2,181	195	2,305
Yellow Medicine	8	–	1	1	6	6	99	33	56	10	91
MISSISSIPPI	6,579	178	885	2,154	3,362	7,397	80,936	21,304	53,110	6,522	84,888
Adams	78	1	16	23	38	107	1,852	380	1,429	43	2,036
Alcorn	60	2	14	22	22	56	1,092	185	872	35	811
Amite	1	–	–	–	1	8	9	6	–	3	2
Attala	35	3	7	–	25	26	404	221	174	9	338
Benton	(NA)	(NA)	(NA)	(NA)	(NA)	(NA)	(NA)	(NA)	(NA)	(NA)	(NA)
Bolivar	39	1	4	18	16	19	884	230	630	24	290
Calhoun	2	–	–	–	2	1	8	3	4	1	7
Carroll	–	–	–	–	–	(NA)	1	–	1	–	(NA)
Chickasaw	31	1	2	6	22	32	75	47	27	1	102
Choctaw	(NA)	(NA)	(NA)	(NA)	(NA)	(NA)	(NA)	(NA)	(NA)	(NA)	(NA)
Claiborne	39	1	–	4	34	45	136	77	59	–	143
Clarke	(NA)	(NA)	(NA)	(NA)	(NA)	(NA)	(NA)	(NA)	(NA)	(NA)	(NA)
Clay	47	1	10	9	27	(NA)	535	191	343	1	(NA)
Coahoma	12	5	1	3	3	14	173	74	56	43	245
Copiah	(NA)	(NA)	(NA)	(NA)	(NA)	(NA)	(NA)	(NA)	(NA)	(NA)	(NA)
Covington	9	–	1	7	1	54	197	53	129	15	235
DeSoto	233	3	47	97	86	259	4,696	885	3,302	509	4,428
Forrest	145	3	15	68	59	152	3,006	723	2,139	144	3,276
Franklin	(NA)	(NA)	(NA)	(NA)	(NA)	(NA)	(NA)	(NA)	(NA)	(NA)	(NA)
George	112	2	2	1	107	10	332	96	179	57	60
Greene	(NA)	(NA)	(NA)	(NA)	(NA)	(NA)	(NA)	(NA)	(NA)	(NA)	(NA)
Grenada	108	2	13	24	69	109	941	259	610	72	963
Hancock	22	–	3	10	9	36	848	110	698	40	918
Harrison	634	10	96	305	223	686	10,296	2,690	7,004	602	12,595
Hinds	1,334	56	183	693	402	1,931	13,494	3,692	7,633	2,169	18,298
Holmes	2	–	–	–	2	59	29	12	16	1	93
Humphreys	16	1	3	5	7	21	149	58	90	1	167
Issaquena	(NA)	(NA)	(NA)	(NA)	(NA)	(NA)	(NA)	(NA)	(NA)	(NA)	(NA)
Itawamba	11	2	4	2	3	2	233	95	111	27	136
Jackson	340	13	68	114	145	463	5,863	1,854	3,477	532	6,096
Jasper	2	–	–	2	–	2	22	11	11	–	10
Jefferson	35	1	–	4	30	(NA)	32	10	22	–	(NA)
Jefferson Davis	(NA)	(NA)	(NA)	(NA)	(NA)	(NA)	(NA)	(NA)	(NA)	(NA)	(NA)
Jones	105	7	15	41	42	221	2,003	225	1,714	64	2,767
Kemper	(NA)	(NA)	(NA)	(NA)	(NA)	3	(NA)	(NA)	(NA)	(NA)	5
Lafayette	27	–	4	4	19	25	492	67	401	24	565
Lamar	45	–	22	6	17	11	840	270	510	60	279
Lauderdale	203	5	39	89	70	228	2,719	1,173	1,363	183	2,496
Lawrence	(NA)	(NA)	(NA)	(NA)	(NA)	(NA)	(NA)	(NA)	(NA)	(NA)	(NA)
Leake	(NA)	(NA)	(NA)	(NA)	(NA)	(NA)	(NA)	(NA)	(NA)	(NA)	(NA)
Lee	207	4	39	66	98	219	2,816	563	2,040	213	3,074
Leflore	248	9	10	55	174	403	2,032	604	1,335	93	1,993
Lincoln	80	1	3	11	65	138	837	180	589	68	879
Lowndes	166	2	21	41	102	181	1,928	353	1,489	86	2,477
Madison	220	8	23	52	137	133	1,880	360	1,413	107	1,909
Marion	23	–	2	3	18	32	394	131	242	21	286
Marshall	167	–	3	7	157	(NA)	356	80	246	30	(NA)
Monroe	43	1	9	8	25	52	615	124	482	9	681
Montgomery	2	–	1	–	1	6	23	15	7	1	33
Neshoba	(NA)	(NA)	(NA)	(NA)	(NA)	(NA)	(NA)	(NA)	(NA)	(NA)	(NA)

See footnotes at end of table.

County and City Data Book: 2007

U.S. Census Bureau

Table B-8. Counties — **Crime—Number of Offenses**—Con.

[Includes United States, states, and 3,141 counties/county equivalents defined as of February 22, 2005. For more information on these areas, see Appendix C, Geographic Information]

County	Violent crimes[1] 2004					Violent crimes[1] 2000	Property crimes[1] 2004				Property crimes[1] 2000
	Total	Murder and non-negligent man-slaughter	Forcible rape	Robbery	Aggra-vated assault	2000	Total	Burglary	Larceny-theft	Motor vehicle theft	2000
MISSISSIPPI—Con.											
Newton	11	–	–	3	8	24	91	26	57	8	97
Noxubee	(NA)	(NA)	(NA)	(NA)	(NA)	51	(NA)	(NA)	(NA)	(NA)	32
Oktibbeha	42	–	1	12	29	83	1,123	153	947	23	1,497
Panola	111	–	7	16	88	100	714	326	341	47	850
Pearl River	75	3	19	12	41	52	1,561	413	1,033	115	741
Perry	(NA)	(NA)	(NA)	(NA)	(NA)	(NA)	(NA)	(NA)	(NA)	(NA)	(NA)
Pike	94	3	7	24	60	81	1,327	365	886	76	708
Pontotoc	–	–	–	–	–	58	98	44	48	6	181
Prentiss	11	–	–	3	8	39	346	112	231	3	439
Quitman	(NA)	(NA)	(NA)	(NA)	(NA)	(NA)	(NA)	(NA)	(NA)	(NA)	(NA)
Rankin	174	4	36	41	93	173	3,026	815	2,019	192	2,056
Scott	89	–	23	14	52	–	346	141	178	27	59
Sharkey	10	–	–	3	7	(NA)	38	38	–	–	(NA)
Simpson	35	1	7	3	24	15	420	110	283	27	240
Smith	(NA)	(NA)	(NA)	(NA)	(NA)	(NA)	(NA)	(NA)	(NA)	(NA)	(NA)
Stone	79	1	13	11	54	13	610	164	429	17	24
Sunflower	75	2	16	14	43	138	692	249	414	29	1,127
Tallahatchie	(NA)	(NA)	(NA)	(NA)	(NA)	(NA)	(NA)	(NA)	(NA)	(NA)	(NA)
Tate	25	–	1	6	18	11	642	190	384	68	391
Tippah	39	1	1	4	33	48	96	57	29	10	90
Tishomingo	23	–	2	11	10	4	127	85	35	7	18
Tunica	141	1	7	32	101	(NA)	686	141	391	154	(NA)
Union	9	1	–	1	7	18	436	166	239	31	462
Walthall	24	1	3	1	19	–	56	41	10	5	2
Warren	269	3	29	40	197	289	2,547	592	1,821	134	2,010
Washington	323	10	31	102	180	432	3,580	879	2,448	253	4,988
Wayne	3	–	–	1	2	7	44	27	15	2	134
Webster	25	–	–	–	25	14	11	9	2	–	36
Wilkinson	(NA)	(NA)	(NA)	(NA)	(NA)	(NA)	(NA)	(NA)	(NA)	(NA)	(NA)
Winston	3	1	–	–	2	(NA)	51	44	7	–	(NA)
Yalobusha	6	1	2	–	3	3	26	10	16	–	13
Yazoo	(NA)	(NA)	(NA)	(NA)	(NA)	(NA)	(NA)	(NA)	(NA)	(NA)	(NA)
MISSOURI	28,067	357	1,535	6,606	19,569	25,438	223,511	40,336	157,410	25,765	208,785
Adair	72	–	2	5	65	30	658	105	533	20	634
Andrew	4	–	1	–	3	3	187	51	117	19	125
Atchison	15	–	–	–	15	3	35	24	9	2	38
Audrain	49	1	4	3	41	24	405	123	263	19	442
Barry	53	–	6	–	47	8	963	300	607	56	229
Barton	69	–	10	–	59	33	335	84	243	8	234
Bates	77	1	1	–	75	15	479	137	331	11	212
Benton	46	–	1	1	44	9	463	168	275	20	304
Bollinger	33	–	4	–	29	(NA)	93	28	64	1	(NA)
Boone	525	1	26	120	378	450	4,380	663	3,514	203	4,359
Buchanan	178	6	30	65	77	224	4,915	969	3,580	366	3,703
Butler	140	2	6	35	97	174	1,801	368	1,343	90	1,377
Caldwell	22	–	–	1	21	6	92	33	49	10	48
Callaway	71	–	8	14	49	23	1,053	193	809	51	306
Camden	59	4	4	8	43	94	1,244	272	922	50	853
Cape Girardeau	311	1	18	48	244	164	2,858	455	2,297	106	2,995
Carroll	21	–	–	2	19	(NA)	108	31	72	5	(NA)
Carter	9	–	1	–	8	16	62	14	44	4	75
Cass	193	–	37	18	138	150	2,670	392	2,090	188	1,446
Cedar	28	–	1	1	26	7	405	106	280	19	187
Chariton	14	1	1	–	12	1	159	12	142	5	17
Christian	77	–	6	7	64	17	1,291	257	927	107	545
Clark	24	–	2	–	22	1	98	42	46	10	37
Clay	1,619	21	86	437	1,075	1,587	10,396	1,898	7,127	1,371	10,793
Clinton	98	–	4	–	94	71	338	95	217	26	235
Cole	296	–	18	45	233	238	1,965	363	1,510	92	1,983
Cooper	44	–	–	3	41	17	539	31	503	5	322
Crawford	99	1	4	8	86	34	786	130	595	61	295
Dade	11	–	3	–	8	(NA)	58	31	22	5	(NA)
Dallas	29	3	–	–	26	(NA)	257	68	167	22	(NA)
Daviess	15	1	–	3	11	12	85	32	37	16	77
DeKalb	21	–	1	1	19	10	225	64	149	12	147
Dent	42	1	5	–	36	10	286	71	189	26	199
Douglas	57	–	2	1	54	(NA)	186	45	122	19	(NA)
Dunklin	103	2	4	14	83	107	831	222	563	46	662

See footnotes at end of table.

[Includes United States, states, and 3,141 counties/county equivalents defined as of February 22, 2005. For more information on these areas, see Appendix C, Geographic Information]

County	Violent crimes[1]						Property crimes[1]				
	2004					2000	2004				2000
	Total	Murder and non-negligent man-slaughter	Forcible rape	Robbery	Aggra-vated assault		Total	Burglary	Larceny-theft	Motor vehicle theft	
MISSOURI—Con.											
Franklin	256	3	11	10	232	153	2,497	374	1,987	136	2,249
Gasconade	37	–	–	1	36	(NA)	357	91	233	33	(NA)
Gentry	10	–	2	–	8	–	50	18	32	–	15
Greene	955	10	88	189	668	982	14,047	2,276	10,853	918	14,359
Grundy	9	–	1	–	8	41	303	60	235	8	213
Harrison	11	1	–	1	9	(NA)	139	43	86	10	(NA)
Henry	88	–	2	3	83	55	1,022	255	707	60	865
Hickory	6	1	–	1	4	9	116	44	62	10	34
Holt	17	–	–	1	16	(NA)	91	24	61	6	(NA)
Howard	27	–	4	–	23	6	89	49	37	3	106
Howell	84	6	6	11	61	120	1,287	283	935	69	874
Iron	14	1	3	–	10	22	99	32	56	11	53
Jackson	6,053	75	326	1,614	4,038	6,224	41,564	7,860	28,252	5,452	42,389
Jasper	341	2	51	92	196	256	5,487	1,048	3,991	448	5,218
Jefferson	791	1	53	23	714	631	4,880	535	3,949	396	3,787
Johnson	112	–	17	6	89	44	1,289	337	887	65	656
Knox	4	–	–	–	4	(NA)	124	24	99	1	(NA)
Laclede	114	–	9	7	98	54	1,151	249	864	38	898
Lafayette	82	3	4	5	70	35	724	183	500	41	433
Lawrence	68	3	10	4	51	4	863	222	606	35	98
Lewis	23	–	3	–	20	8	134	35	94	5	72
Lincoln	97	1	2	4	90	(NA)	694	119	533	42	(NA)
Linn	19	–	2	–	17	15	206	70	118	18	162
Livingston	35	–	5	3	27	17	316	63	224	29	243
McDonald	60	2	5	3	50	5	460	132	275	53	12
Macon	53	2	4	4	43	37	276	91	181	4	163
Madison	19	2	3	–	14	(NA)	177	46	119	12	(NA)
Maries	28	–	1	1	26	(NA)	71	24	44	3	(NA)
Marion	119	–	15	25	79	125	1,573	218	1,347	8	776
Mercer	6	–	–	–	6	11	18	15	1	2	36
Miller	89	2	7	5	75	119	489	125	320	44	557
Mississippi	63	4	2	6	51	58	361	65	275	21	193
Moniteau	21	–	–	1	20	(NA)	189	54	120	15	(NA)
Monroe	16	–	1	1	14	11	134	37	87	10	36
Montgomery	19	–	1	2	16	3	229	60	151	18	184
Morgan	109	–	–	1	108	24	646	218	409	19	269
New Madrid	54	–	2	7	45	11	300	132	145	23	62
Newton	168	2	12	15	139	55	2,194	450	1,552	192	1,219
Nodaway	31	1	–	1	29	43	440	72	348	20	273
Oregon	8	1	–	–	7	(NA)	30	14	12	4	(NA)
Osage	15	–	–	–	15	(NA)	142	58	73	11	(NA)
Ozark	24	1	3	–	20	12	95	51	36	8	73
Pemiscot	78	3	6	8	61	28	758	208	515	35	163
Perry	18	–	4	–	14	4	298	60	220	18	99
Pettis	232	1	7	17	207	168	1,908	372	1,458	78	1,451
Phelps	171	2	14	18	137	68	1,567	308	1,183	76	956
Pike	53	4	2	2	45	4	192	60	120	12	86
Platte	613	7	34	170	402	662	3,947	724	2,690	533	3,989
Polk	58	–	9	1	48	30	808	194	566	48	597
Pulaski	136	1	8	19	108	19	571	171	373	27	210
Putnam	8	–	–	–	8	1	32	11	20	1	9
Ralls	36	1	2	1	32	(NA)	174	63	105	6	(NA)
Randolph	43	–	9	6	28	58	683	150	505	28	884
Ray	39	–	5	1	33	30	544	122	364	58	273
Reynolds	11	–	3	–	8	(NA)	68	52	13	3	(NA)
Ripley	14	–	–	1	13	19	296	108	171	17	67
St. Charles	560	3	41	79	437	501	7,039	979	5,690	370	7,096
St. Clair	19	1	3	–	15	(NA)	295	120	171	4	(NA)
Ste. Genevieve	19	–	–	3	16	6	211	55	142	14	218
St. Francois	146	4	18	11	113	13	1,426	204	1,121	101	89
St. Louis	2,762	31	179	675	1,877	2,505	29,787	4,197	22,057	3,533	35,397
Saline	37	–	3	8	26	9	546	121	404	21	443
Schuyler	6	–	1	–	5	–	22	8	8	6	40
Scotland	4	–	–	–	4	(NA)	47	15	30	2	(NA)
Scott	150	2	13	23	112	173	922	233	633	56	968
Shannon	28	–	–	–	28	14	56	15	32	9	43
Shelby	2	–	2	–	–	1	81	24	50	7	44
Stoddard	80	1	5	5	69	24	512	153	336	23	120
Stone	393	1	12	3	377	130	812	264	485	63	623
Sullivan	23	–	–	1	22	(NA)	56	14	34	8	(NA)

See footnotes at end of table.

Table B-8. Counties — **Crime—Number of Offenses**—Con.

[Includes United States, states, and 3,141 counties/county equivalents defined as of February 22, 2005. For more information on these areas, see Appendix C, Geographic Information]

County	Violent crimes[1] 2004					2000	Property crimes[1] 2004				2000
	Total	Murder and non-negligent man-slaughter	Forcible rape	Robbery	Aggra-vated assault		Total	Burglary	Larceny-theft	Motor vehicle theft	
MISSOURI—Con.											
Taney	255	3	15	10	227	92	1,638	247	1,310	81	827
Texas	23	–	2	1	20	(NA)	295	92	182	21	(NA)
Vernon	102	2	9	7	84	37	896	203	607	86	764
Warren	93	3	1	10	79	28	628	103	494	31	569
Washington	46	1	3	–	42	67	308	43	232	33	346
Wayne	38	2	1	–	35	(NA)	240	78	145	17	(NA)
Webster	114	1	2	3	108	76	669	169	469	31	188
Worth	6	–	–	4	2	7	11	6	4	1	32
Wright	15	–	–	–	15	(NA)	305	57	225	23	(NA)
Independent City											
St. Louis city	6,957	113	171	2,632	4,041	7,936	38,804	6,300	23,592	8,912	42,738
MONTANA	2,091	23	214	135	1,719	2,495	22,015	2,662	18,197	1,156	16,894
Beaverhead	16	–	2	1	13	13	108	7	86	15	106
Big Horn	25	1	–	–	24	(NA)	178	19	146	13	(NA)
Blaine	12	–	2	1	9	4	81	17	58	6	16
Broadwater	43	–	3	–	40	20	244	3	237	4	35
Carbon	4	1	1	–	2	13	62	5	50	7	36
Carter	–	–	–	–	–	(NA)	6	–	6	–	(NA)
Cascade	262	3	19	19	221	655	4,221	318	3,743	160	4,284
Chouteau	14	1	5	1	7	36	44	8	34	2	91
Custer	(NA)	(NA)	(NA)	(NA)	(NA)	(NA)	(NA)	(NA)	(NA)	(NA)	(NA)
Daniels	(NA)	(NA)	(NA)	(NA)	(NA)	(NA)	(NA)	(NA)	(NA)	(NA)	(NA)
Dawson	25	–	–	–	25	34	187	20	164	3	183
Deer Lodge	55	–	–	2	53	224	185	26	143	16	279
Fallon	2	1	–	–	1	5	12	2	10	–	23
Fergus	19	–	6	–	13	58	131	14	111	6	128
Flathead	91	–	3	7	81	77	1,370	102	1,204	64	1,232
Gallatin[4]	204	4	34	11	155	29	2,378	318	1,888	172	297
Garfield	(NA)	(NA)	(NA)	(NA)	(NA)	(NA)	(NA)	(NA)	(NA)	(NA)	(NA)
Glacier	57	–	1	2	54	92	222	31	183	8	194
Golden Valley	1	–	–	–	1	13	9	5	4	–	20
Granite	3	–	–	–	3	25	57	6	51	–	54
Hill	83	–	14	1	68	285	564	49	490	25	776
Jefferson	13	–	2	–	11	(NA)	59	9	44	6	(NA)
Judith Basin	2	–	–	–	2	(NA)	14	1	12	1	(NA)
Lake	117	1	18	3	95	67	636	97	482	57	405
Lewis and Clark	185	1	31	13	140	(NA)	1,386	234	1,089	63	(NA)
Liberty	(NA)	(NA)	(NA)	(NA)	(NA)	(NA)	(NA)	(NA)	(NA)	(NA)	(NA)
Lincoln	86	–	1	1	84	22	570	110	434	26	303
McCone	4	–	–	–	4	(NA)	–	–	–	–	(NA)
Madison	8	–	–	–	8	4	68	17	45	6	38
Meagher	8	–	–	–	8	9	30	6	22	2	54
Mineral	24	–	–	–	24	5	33	11	16	6	7
Missoula	(NA)	(NA)	(NA)	(NA)	(NA)	(NA)	(NA)	(NA)	(NA)	(NA)	(NA)
Musselshell	19	1	3	–	15	(NA)	168	12	152	4	(NA)
Park[4]	89	–	9	–	80	(NA)	267	34	210	23	(NA)
Petroleum	–	–	–	–	–	(NA)	2	2	–	–	(NA)
Phillips	16	–	1	–	15	12	47	7	39	1	55
Pondera	–	–	–	–	–	10	43	6	34	3	80
Powder River	(NA)	(NA)	(NA)	(NA)	(NA)	(NA)	(NA)	(NA)	(NA)	(NA)	(NA)
Powell	39	–	3	1	35	49	175	22	141	12	172
Prairie	–	–	–	–	–	(NA)	4	1	2	1	(NA)
Ravalli	82	1	8	1	72	144	403	48	345	10	368
Richland	(NA)	(NA)	(NA)	(NA)	(NA)	(NA)	(NA)	(NA)	(NA)	(NA)	(NA)
Roosevelt	1	–	–	–	1	12	15	4	11	–	43
Rosebud	27	–	3	1	23	54	71	26	38	7	75
Sanders	43	1	1	–	41	73	214	52	153	9	177
Sheridan	1	–	–	–	1	4	22	6	15	1	26
Silver Bow	83	2	7	10	64	(NA)	1,528	201	1,204	123	(NA)
Stillwater	10	–	–	1	9	20	101	19	80	2	107
Sweet Grass	8	–	–	–	8	13	38	7	27	4	65
Teton	10	–	2	–	8	11	54	12	41	1	139
Toole	7	–	–	–	7	(NA)	76	15	55	6	(NA)
Treasure	(NA)	(NA)	(NA)	(NA)	(NA)	(NA)	(NA)	(NA)	(NA)	(NA)	(NA)
Valley	12	–	2	–	10	6	135	14	114	7	46
Wheatland	–	–	–	–	–	6	2	1	1	–	22
Wibaux	–	–	–	–	–	(NA)	2	–	1	1	(NA)
Yellowstone	281	5	33	59	184	391	5,793	738	4,782	273	6,958
Yellowstone National Park[4]	(NA)	(X)	(X)	(X)	(X)	(X)	(NA)	(X)	(X)	(X)	(X)

See footnotes at end of table.

[Includes United States, states, and 3,141 counties/county equivalents defined as of February 22, 2005. For more information on these areas, see Appendix C, Geographic Information]

County	Violent crimes[1]						Property crimes[1]				
	2004					2000	2004				2000
	Total	Murder and non-negligent man-slaughter	Forcible rape	Robbery	Aggra-vated assault		Total	Burglary	Larceny-theft	Motor vehicle theft	
NEBRASKA............	5,292	40	606	1,133	3,513	5,532	60,177	9,570	45,405	5,202	62,336
Adams................	65	1	18	3	43	19	1,082	188	852	42	1,136
Antelope.............	1	–	–	–	1	1	37	16	18	3	65
Arthur...............	(NA)	(NA)	(NA)	(NA)	(NA)	–	(NA)	(NA)	(NA)	(NA)	3
Banner...............	(NA)	(NA)	(NA)	(NA)	(NA)	1	(NA)	(NA)	(NA)	(NA)	(NA)
Blaine...............	(NA)	(NA)	(NA)	(NA)	(NA)	(NA)	(NA)	(NA)	(NA)	(NA)	(NA)
Boone................	–	–	–	–	–	3	33	10	19	4	45
Box Butte............	38	–	1	1	36	23	215	28	179	8	239
Boyd.................	–	–	–	–	–	5	10	2	7	1	15
Brown................	1	–	–	–	1	2	55	16	36	3	47
Buffalo..............	95	–	16	3	76	103	1,166	185	930	51	1,872
Burt.................	8	–	1	–	7	6	36	7	28	1	108
Butler...............	2	–	–	–	2	3	72	11	61	–	81
Cass.................	11	–	4	1	6	27	193	23	148	22	440
Cedar................	(NA)	(NA)	(NA)	(NA)	(NA)	–	(NA)	(NA)	(NA)	(NA)	32
Chase................	3	–	–	–	3	4	29	8	18	3	20
Cherry...............	–	–	–	–	–	23	15	1	12	2	158
Cheyenne.............	9	1	2	–	6	5	189	34	148	7	217
Clay.................	3	–	–	1	2	1	62	18	44	–	8
Colfax...............	18	–	1	1	16	5	129	21	102	6	167
Cuming...............	6	–	1	1	4	5	49	8	31	10	69
Custer...............	8	–	2	–	6	–	135	26	100	9	116
Dakota...............	9	–	3	1	5	22	264	47	200	17	448
Dawes................	5	–	4	–	1	3	60	9	41	10	147
Dawson...............	61	–	20	4	37	29	677	97	525	55	762
Deuel................	–	–	–	–	–	1	20	7	12	1	32
Dixon................	5	–	2	–	3	4	58	18	37	3	70
Dodge................	47	1	10	8	28	31	1,109	175	871	63	1,054
Douglas..............	2,797	20	199	837	1,741	3,301	24,182	3,975	16,653	3,554	25,004
Dundy................	–	–	–	–	–	1	19	2	15	2	29
Fillmore.............	2	–	1	–	1	6	38	15	17	6	94
Franklin.............	1	–	–	–	1	–	21	9	9	3	41
Frontier.............	3	–	1	–	2	3	28	3	24	1	70
Furnas...............	3	–	–	–	3	5	45	17	27	1	75
Gage.................	49	–	18	2	29	19	916	145	734	37	614
Garden...............	1	–	–	–	1	2	11	1	9	1	41
Garfield.............	1	–	1	–	–	1	–	–	–	–	1
Gosper...............	–	–	–	–	–	–	16	2	14	–	24
Grant................	(NA)	(NA)	(NA)	(NA)	(NA)	4	(NA)	(NA)	(NA)	(NA)	14
Greeley..............	(NA)	(NA)	(NA)	(NA)	(NA)	1	(NA)	(NA)	(NA)	(NA)	30
Hall.................	146	–	25	24	97	174	2,947	405	2,409	133	3,245
Hamilton.............	9	–	1	–	8	7	155	22	128	5	220
Harlan...............	1	–	–	–	1	–	2	–	1	1	1
Hayes................	(NA)	(NA)	(NA)	(NA)	(NA)	–	(NA)	(NA)	(NA)	(NA)	1
Hitchcock............	–	–	–	–	–	2	7	2	5	–	17
Holt.................	3	–	1	–	2	5	50	13	35	2	135
Hooker...............	(NA)	(NA)	(NA)	(NA)	(NA)	–	(NA)	(NA)	(NA)	(NA)	1
Howard...............	6	–	3	–	3	12	94	25	60	9	215
Jefferson............	10	–	1	–	9	6	135	28	100	7	189
Johnson..............	1	–	–	–	1	3	12	5	5	2	41
Kearney..............	8	–	2	1	5	2	110	25	78	7	156
Keith................	4	–	–	1	3	6	337	40	284	13	186
Keya Paha............	–	–	–	–	–	–	1	1	–	–	1
Kimball..............	3	–	–	–	3	1	22	11	11	–	92
Knox.................	6	–	–	–	6	7	36	5	27	4	64
Lancaster............	1,267	7	143	200	917	1,226	14,129	2,119	11,544	466	14,028
Lincoln..............	102	–	7	8	87	43	1,673	268	1,351	54	282
Logan................	1	–	1	–	–	–	2	–	–	2	1
Loup.................	(NA)	(NA)	(NA)	(NA)	(NA)	1	(NA)	(NA)	(NA)	(NA)	1
McPherson............	1	–	–	–	1	–	6	2	4	–	3
Madison..............	67	2	25	9	31	47	1,220	186	958	76	1,087
Merrick..............	9	–	1	2	6	6	169	19	139	11	111
Morrill..............	3	–	–	–	3	6	95	13	79	3	98
Nance................	–	–	–	–	–	2	31	9	21	1	30
Nemaha...............	3	–	1	–	2	3	116	18	89	9	111
Nuckolls.............	8	–	1	–	7	–	8	3	3	2	5
Otoe.................	14	2	4	–	8	10	344	70	257	17	352
Pawnee...............	2	–	–	–	2	1	59	9	48	2	18
Perkins..............	–	–	–	–	–	2	41	10	29	2	31
Phelps...............	9	–	2	–	7	9	225	42	172	11	237
Pierce...............	6	–	2	–	4	4	31	15	15	1	88

See footnotes at end of table.

[Includes United States, states, and 3,141 counties/county equivalents defined as of February 22, 2005. For more information on these areas, see Appendix C, Geographic Information]

County	Violent crimes[1] 2004						Property crimes[1] 2004				
	Total	Murder and non-negligent man-slaughter	Forcible rape	Robbery	Aggra-vated assault	2000	Total	Burglary	Larceny-theft	Motor vehicle theft	2000
NEBRASKA—Con.											
Platte	33	1	10	1	21	20	651	85	542	24	1,038
Polk	–	–	–	–	–	3	33	5	27	1	75
Red Willow	19	1	5	2	11	26	317	46	246	25	321
Richardson	3	–	1	–	2	5	88	21	63	4	135
Rock	1	–	1	–	–	1	15	5	10	–	20
Saline	30	–	5	1	24	11	295	68	215	12	242
Sarpy	142	4	29	14	95	74	2,938	374	2,343	221	3,073
Saunders	9	–	1	–	8	9	226	68	139	19	219
Scotts Bluff	50	–	6	4	40	66	1,426	209	1,161	56	1,180
Seward	8	–	3	1	4	4	200	25	170	5	312
Sheridan	11	–	3	–	8	22	74	16	54	4	195
Sherman	4	–	3	–	1	1	34	3	31	–	53
Sioux	(NA)	(NA)	(NA)	(NA)	(NA)	–	(NA)	(NA)	(NA)	(NA)	5
Stanton	10	–	2	–	8	1	72	18	49	5	65
Thayer	2	–	–	–	2	3	54	17	35	2	67
Thomas	(NA)	(NA)	(NA)	(NA)	(NA)	(NA)	(NA)	(NA)	(NA)	(NA)	(NA)
Thurston	2	–	–	–	2	3	2	–	1	1	2
Valley	1	–	–	–	1	1	19	–	15	4	29
Washington	12	–	7	2	3	15	234	52	154	28	313
Wayne	5	–	3	–	2	7	140	20	114	6	111
Webster	3	–	–	–	3	3	51	13	36	2	66
Wheeler	–	–	–	–	–	–	10	6	3	1	18
York	6	–	2	–	4	3	270	30	224	16	362
NEVADA	14,379	172	954	4,905	8,348	10,474	98,214	23,142	52,437	22,635	74,823
Churchill	96	–	22	6	68	79	840	190	604	46	585
Clark	11,390	152	734	4,263	6,241	8,129	74,730	17,935	37,083	19,712	54,033
Douglas	71	–	–	12	59	70	1,217	238	878	101	801
Elko	81	1	13	12	55	188	1,039	317	640	82	1,282
Esmeralda	5	–	–	–	5	1	7	2	5	–	5
Eureka	9	–	–	1	8	10	22	5	15	2	19
Humboldt	49	–	4	3	42	53	255	83	143	29	317
Lander	42	1	1	1	39	36	78	28	37	13	85
Lincoln	7	–	–	–	7	4	38	13	17	8	48
Lyon	96	1	7	7	81	97	891	286	519	86	747
Mineral	5	–	1	1	3	10	52	29	18	5	126
Nye	102	–	2	4	96	107	1,220	465	647	108	894
Pershing	58	–	7	1	50	30	161	77	73	11	127
Storey	5	1	–	1	3	41	60	22	36	2	51
Washoe	2,045	14	161	568	1,302	1,401	15,762	3,043	10,512	2,207	13,934
White Pine	25	1	2	1	21	11	178	35	134	9	209
Independent City											
Carson City	293	1	–	24	268	207	1,664	374	1,076	214	1,560
NEW HAMPSHIRE	1,552	13	376	344	819	1,129	19,872	3,709	14,830	1,333	16,151
Belknap	94	1	18	21	54	42	1,370	272	1,016	82	851
Carroll	65	1	23	6	35	58	972	262	640	70	859
Cheshire	79	–	25	10	44	103	739	179	505	55	1,184
Coos	44	–	10	2	32	38	465	114	324	27	436
Grafton	89	–	28	9	52	94	1,525	283	1,190	52	1,647
Hillsborough	495	7	94	203	191	321	6,021	1,131	4,427	463	4,791
Merrimack	154	1	38	17	98	31	2,055	426	1,495	134	419
Rockingham	347	2	79	53	213	258	3,989	610	3,045	334	3,683
Strafford	127	–	47	17	63	133	2,030	253	1,689	88	1,655
Sullivan	58	1	14	6	37	51	706	179	499	28	626
NEW JERSEY	30,914	392	1,329	13,070	16,123	32,297	211,526	41,050	140,158	30,318	233,637
Atlantic	1,408	11	86	550	761	1,125	10,752	1,825	8,464	463	13,003
Bergen	1,110	5	60	391	654	1,125	14,150	2,126	10,794	1,230	15,454
Burlington	846	4	105	291	446	854	8,275	1,607	6,030	638	9,634
Camden	3,150	55	145	1,232	1,718	2,972	17,234	3,482	11,440	2,312	17,391
Cape May	373	3	27	78	265	380	4,544	975	3,414	155	4,938
Cumberland	1,167	9	50	404	704	1,050	6,352	1,502	4,420	430	5,533
Essex	6,805	136	192	3,349	3,128	8,324	31,881	5,979	15,155	10,747	34,939
Gloucester	649	7	46	196	400	563	7,483	1,742	5,229	512	7,581
Hudson	4,102	36	106	2,023	1,937	4,048	17,991	3,979	10,653	3,359	21,178
Hunterdon	64	2	3	8	51	69	1,228	295	869	64	1,273
Mercer	1,782	23	79	744	936	1,812	9,679	1,950	6,387	1,342	12,257
Middlesex	1,653	17	83	593	960	1,831	15,948	2,969	11,449	1,530	18,026
Monmouth	1,365	9	92	495	769	1,215	12,690	2,287	9,781	622	12,528
Morris	510	4	36	129	341	559	6,657	1,174	5,069	414	7,342
Ocean	894	11	51	189	643	919	10,408	2,095	7,789	524	11,619

See footnotes at end of table.

[Includes United States, states, and 3,141 counties/county equivalents defined as of February 22, 2005. For more information on these areas, see Appendix C, Geographic Information]

County	Violent crimes[1]						Property crimes[1]				
	2004					2000	2004				2000
	Total	Murder and non-negligent man-slaughter	Forcible rape	Robbery	Aggra-vated assault		Total	Burglary	Larceny-theft	Motor vehicle theft	
NEW JERSEY—Con.											
Passaic	2,318	18	55	1,094	1,151	2,463	12,461	2,693	7,457	2,311	13,641
Salem	184	1	7	39	137	175	1,478	398	968	112	1,462
Somerset	311	14	24	141	132	302	4,395	754	3,334	307	4,913
Sussex	116	1	6	11	98	120	1,657	300	1,283	74	1,770
Union	1,988	22	71	1,092	803	2,299	14,825	2,642	9,087	3,096	17,612
Warren	119	4	5	21	89	92	1,438	276	1,086	76	1,543
NEW MEXICO	[3]11,917	[3]150	[3]935	[3]1,963	[3]8,869	12,445	[3]73,630	[3]18,087	48,217	7,326	78,964
Bernalillo	5,576	53	279	1,350	3,894	5,986	33,067	6,028	22,702	4,337	38,976
Catron	3	–	–	–	3	5	3	1	–	2	15
Chaves	513	8	51	43	411	555	3,552	950	2,421	181	3,403
Cibola	103	–	1	18	84	189	591	209	316	66	667
Colfax	40	–	–	–	40	66	204	73	122	9	226
Curry	208	10	16	26	156	485	2,119	699	1,304	116	2,173
De Baca	(NA)	(NA)	(NA)	(NA)	(NA)	141	(NA)	(NA)	(NA)	(NA)	352
Dona Ana	391	3	86	113	189	534	4,743	795	3,715	233	6,822
Eddy	185	3	30	23	129	221	2,286	737	1,445	104	2,644
Grant	39	–	6	5	28	35	781	270	484	27	154
Guadalupe	5	–	–	2	3	(NA)	13	5	7	1	(NA)
Harding	14	1	–	1	12	2	10	6	2	2	4
Hidalgo	13	–	–	1	12	5	49	17	14	18	1
Lea	442	3	37	30	372	319	2,706	568	2,052	86	1,702
Lincoln	133	1	5	6	121	172	580	199	340	41	469
Los Alamos	1	–	–	–	1	14	45	17	26	2	182
Luna	98	2	4	9	83	140	1,194	433	639	122	1,009
McKinley	434	3	25	56	350	520	2,378	376	1,842	160	3,251
Mora	6	–	–	–	6	10	36	36	–	–	8
Otero	150	3	8	10	129	246	1,218	218	957	43	1,392
Quay	74	1	–	1	72	90	244	125	103	16	242
Rio Arriba	12	2	1	–	9	45	11	9	2	–	131
Roosevelt	76	2	11	3	60	49	584	224	332	28	660
Sandoval	251	2	19	16	214	298	1,538	455	928	155	1,717
San Juan	847	2	137	65	643	696	3,273	693	2,282	298	3,287
San Miguel	157	1	13	17	126	212	662	161	448	53	931
Santa Fe	807	8	73	78	648	672	5,294	2,362	2,491	441	5,628
Sierra	52	–	4	5	43	23	291	60	204	27	99
Socorro	215	–	2	5	208	242	550	132	400	18	538
Taos	74	1	4	11	58	183	539	186	346	7	597
Torrance	27	–	5	3	19	7	159	83	62	14	72
Union	17	–	–	2	15	10	44	32	10	2	68
Valencia	642	10	55	28	549	273	2,401	818	1,148	435	1,544
NEW YORK	84,274	894	3,543	33,366	46,471	99,934	414,862	69,479	304,675	40,708	427,466
Albany	1,426	13	76	480	857	1,354	10,997	1,972	8,353	672	12,639
Allegany	97	–	19	2	76	140	845	202	612	31	732
Bronx[5]	(NA)	(NA)	(NA)	(NA)	(NA)	(NA)	(NA)	(NA)	(NA)	(NA)	(NA)
Broome	328	2	52	89	185	414	5,431	698	4,588	145	5,573
Cattaraugus	212	1	22	13	176	187	2,334	381	1,904	49	1,640
Cayuga	131	2	14	20	95	165	1,639	318	1,291	30	1,601
Chautauqua	344	1	42	70	231	287	3,434	749	2,579	106	3,513
Chemung	253	2	36	54	161	259	2,817	429	2,316	72	2,465
Chenango	119	–	18	11	90	103	976	234	722	20	1,057
Clinton	187	–	27	9	151	239	1,401	424	941	36	1,176
Columbia	53	1	6	5	41	145	795	135	627	33	979
Cortland	107	–	24	10	73	105	1,267	217	1,009	41	1,528
Delaware	86	1	5	2	78	104	758	226	513	19	605
Dutchess	721	4	42	169	506	540	4,388	625	3,499	264	5,365
Erie	4,693	57	297	1,684	2,655	4,421	27,844	5,621	19,375	2,848	29,094
Essex	66	–	7	1	58	93	436	166	259	11	556
Franklin	160	2	9	3	146	192	837	320	491	26	760
Fulton	96	1	8	12	75	133	1,406	240	1,105	61	1,131
Genesee	108	1	22	18	67	76	1,719	289	1,399	31	1,308
Greene	140	2	9	8	121	153	655	194	446	15	721
Hamilton	4	–	1	–	3	7	53	18	35	–	116
Herkimer	133	2	16	11	104	161	851	212	624	15	1,182
Jefferson	231	4	39	25	163	157	2,051	404	1,604	43	1,977
Kings[5]	55,905	570	1,432	24,446	29,457	75,946	173,135	26,178	125,869	21,088	215,863
Lewis	26	–	1	–	25	14	291	94	190	7	248
Livingston	86	1	19	13	53	86	1,638	210	1,405	23	1,464
Madison	71	–	14	15	41	87	1,318	316	978	24	1,206
Monroe	2,331	47	156	1,105	1,023	2,069	28,615	4,614	19,899	4,102	29,787
Montgomery	56	1	6	2	47	100	607	134	461	12	741
Nassau	2,502	23	108	1,039	1,332	844	19,830	2,881	14,576	2,373	4,340

See footnotes at end of table.

[Includes United States, states, and 3,141 counties/county equivalents defined as of February 22, 2005. For more information on these areas, see Appendix C, Geographic Information]

County	Violent crimes[1]						Property crimes[1]				
	2004					2000	2004				2000
	Total	Murder and non-negligent man-slaughter	Forcible rape	Robbery	Aggra-vated assault		Total	Burglary	Larceny-theft	Motor vehicle theft	
NEW YORK—Con.											
New York[5]	(NA)	(NA)	(NA)	(NA)	(NA)	(NA)	(NA)	(NA)	(NA)	(NA)	(NA)
Niagara	894	8	65	250	571	654	6,937	1,541	4,856	540	5,700
Oneida	545	7	63	168	307	571	5,666	1,264	4,127	275	5,828
Onondaga	1,665	22	110	521	1,012	2,001	12,507	2,721	8,476	1,310	14,125
Ontario	86	5	8	16	57	106	1,691	360	1,260	71	1,869
Orang	932	13	80	219	620	988	6,429	962	5,078	389	7,527
Orleans	68	1	5	4	58	54	513	133	354	26	611
Oswego	136	1	18	18	99	87	2,496	604	1,822	70	1,904
Otsego	129	1	17	10	101	134	1,077	278	771	28	898
Putnam	77	—	10	8	59	47	1,012	197	778	37	999
Queens[5]	(NA)	(NA)	(NA)	(NA)	(NA)	(NA)	(NA)	(NA)	(NA)	(NA)	(NA)
Rensselaer	488	2	48	113	325	478	3,830	975	2,584	271	4,396
Richmond[5]	(NA)	(NA)	(NA)	(NA)	(NA)	(NA)	(NA)	(NA)	(NA)	(NA)	(NA)
Rockland	570	5	27	177	361	622	4,701	558	3,926	217	5,314
St. Lawrence	143	—	24	11	108	227	2,491	560	1,844	87	2,398
Saratoga	248	4	32	28	184	263	2,600	471	2,021	108	2,762
Schenectady	613	10	48	196	359	556	4,796	908	3,579	309	4,684
Schoharie	45	—	8	2	35	26	478	87	373	18	529
Schuyler	4	—	—	—	4	20	191	18	169	4	400
Seneca	35	—	6	1	28	19	502	53	429	20	342
Steuben	188	5	37	15	131	129	1,905	362	1,496	47	1,863
Suffolk	2,845	28	131	958	1,728	466	29,148	4,305	22,080	2,763	3,945
Sullivan	273	2	31	31	209	304	1,607	515	1,017	75	1,917
Tioga	29	—	6	3	20	34	517	152	343	22	471
Tompkins	64	1	13	7	43	112	1,352	188	1,137	27	2,371
Ulster	468	6	36	94	332	372	3,440	575	2,739	126	3,475
Warren	85	—	13	4	68	110	1,014	124	868	22	1,662
Washington	86	—	14	5	67	203	687	143	526	18	851
Wayne	197	4	46	15	132	121	1,977	429	1,482	66	2,022
Westchester	2,600	28	105	1,170	1,297	2,516	16,012	2,298	12,179	1,535	17,974
Wyoming	59	2	7	3	47	113	622	110	489	23	999
Yates	30	—	8	3	19	20	296	87	202	7	263
NORTH CAROLINA	36,579	511	2,221	11,430	22,417	38,909	336,105	95,134	215,229	25,742	343,174
Alamance	520	2	21	127	370	458	4,870	1,236	3,396	238	5,038
Alexander	42	—	6	6	30	61	778	309	425	44	850
Alleghany	2	—	—	—	2	11	26	7	16	3	96
Anson	90	3	7	21	59	91	1,066	422	586	58	965
Ashe	32	5	5	2	20	21	482	265	193	24	342
Avery	11	1	2	1	7	7	207	53	140	14	118
Beaufort	181	2	17	58	104	204	1,432	411	957	64	1,355
Bertie	33	1	3	6	23	68	570	246	289	35	462
Bladen	338	2	4	37	295	279	1,239	412	768	59	1,200
Brunswick	174	3	29	32	110	214	3,283	1,299	1,739	245	2,755
Buncombe	578	7	43	273	255	809	6,780	1,708	4,350	722	7,676
Burke	163	—	16	43	104	120	2,219	742	1,359	118	2,357
Cabarrus	311	7	23	130	151	237	4,588	1,114	3,208	266	2,751
Caldwell	149	4	12	14	119	249	2,158	659	1,374	125	2,299
Camden	14	—	—	—	14	4	81	46	35	—	50
Carteret	161	3	23	24	111	134	1,897	516	1,297	84	1,935
Caswell	57	—	5	1	51	67	393	154	208	31	386
Catawba	495	8	51	147	289	452	6,398	1,821	4,287	290	6,285
Chatham	118	6	12	23	77	114	1,372	443	835	94	1,399
Cherokee	108	2	8	5	93	18	664	217	412	35	283
Chowan	40	2	3	12	23	41	395	164	221	10	469
Clay	6	1	—	—	5	11	120	71	40	9	93
Cleveland	287	7	14	73	193	459	2,623	749	1,799	75	4,742
Columbus	373	6	11	61	295	276	3,077	1,078	1,804	195	2,715
Craven	302	6	21	59	216	302	3,625	987	2,491	147	2,462
Cumberland	1,965	31	83	560	1,291	1,649	17,566	4,669	11,849	1,048	16,726
Currituck	46	—	6	2	38	56	630	209	393	28	403
Dare	88	1	17	7	63	60	1,574	468	1,049	57	1,848
Davidson	444	5	22	97	320	315	4,336	777	3,211	348	3,594
Davie	83	1	5	14	63	44	963	275	624	64	679
Duplin	179	3	6	33	137	194	1,708	708	891	109	1,527
Durham	1,680	33	95	848	704	1,964	14,071	3,565	9,481	1,025	16,608
Edgecombe	271	5	15	77	174	306	2,736	838	1,749	149	2,762
Forsyth	1,682	21	110	567	984	2,847	14,602	3,984	9,453	1,165	19,044
Franklin	83	5	2	23	53	54	1,231	501	651	79	1,307

See footnotes at end of table.

[Includes United States, states, and 3,141 counties/county equivalents defined as of February 22, 2005. For more information on these areas, see Appendix C, Geographic Information]

| County | Violent crimes[1] | | | | | | Property crimes[1] | | | | |
| | 2004 | | | | | 2000 | 2004 | | | | 2000 |
	Total	Murder and non-negligent man-slaughter	Forcible rape	Robbery	Aggra-vated assault		Total	Burglary	Larceny-theft	Motor vehicle theft	
NORTH CAROLINA—Con.											
Gaston	1,102	9	74	337	682	1,043	9,590	2,351	6,427	812	6,903
Gates	17	–	–	1	16	17	147	60	85	2	127
Graham	(NA)	(NA)	(NA)	(NA)	(NA)	21	(NA)	(NA)	(NA)	(NA)	93
Granville	212	2	14	40	156	202	1,708	634	975	99	1,742
Greene	73	4	8	11	50	66	567	144	378	45	626
Guilford	2,598	27	168	1,085	1,318	2,866	22,181	6,029	14,396	1,756	22,193
Halifax	240	8	12	64	156	267	2,589	835	1,548	206	2,448
Harnett	400	8	16	74	302	443	3,682	1,336	2,053	293	3,397
Haywood	150	1	29	20	100	133	1,541	521	897	123	1,374
Henderson	151	1	38	39	73	154	2,379	651	1,555	173	2,247
Hertford	95	3	8	20	64	118	1,081	301	736	44	1,029
Hoke	152	10	11	34	97	96	1,615	868	657	90	1,276
Hyde	–	–	–	–	–	1	51	1	49	1	43
Iredell	455	7	32	92	324	476	4,490	1,324	2,863	303	4,313
Jackson	112	–	21	7	84	44	1,142	383	682	77	508
Johnston	373	9	31	102	231	503	4,456	1,229	2,814	413	5,118
Jones	17	–	1	4	12	12	200	70	115	15	100
Lee	206	3	13	75	115	156	2,387	749	1,473	165	2,040
Lenoir	383	6	11	60	306	366	3,450	1,055	2,239	156	2,729
Lincoln	20	–	–	8	12	102	852	122	687	43	2,023
McDowell	83	2	5	25	51	60	1,059	375	604	80	932
Macon	37	5	3	4	25	29	633	248	352	33	575
Madison	11	1	2	–	8	6	180	68	95	17	64
Martin	122	–	4	17	101	132	831	264	530	37	1,109
Mecklenburg	7,492	64	330	2,847	4,251	7,675	50,521	12,623	30,900	6,998	44,679
Mitchell	3	–	1	1	1	–	45	9	31	5	14
Montgomery	81	–	12	11	58	57	849	271	535	43	840
Moore	188	5	8	34	141	161	1,962	682	1,160	120	2,107
Nash	466	6	19	152	289	478	4,493	1,376	2,850	267	4,610
New Hanover	1,123	9	100	313	701	929	10,488	2,912	6,887	689	10,317
Northampton	83	–	5	16	62	68	595	260	304	31	400
Onslow	114	–	7	28	79	447	1,044	211	778	55	5,393
Orange	398	4	22	140	232	379	5,049	1,289	3,553	207	5,015
Pamlico	18	–	1	3	14	17	212	74	132	6	193
Pasquotank	165	2	11	45	107	178	1,502	426	1,004	72	1,094
Pender	68	2	5	12	49	59	915	296	531	88	800
Perquimans	18	3	1	9	5	22	286	133	126	27	230
Person	154	–	10	19	125	147	1,151	404	709	38	932
Pitt	858	6	45	231	576	877	7,167	2,139	4,696	332	8,425
Polk	41	1	4	8	28	32	358	137	186	35	262
Randolph	169	2	12	40	115	184	4,672	1,092	3,318	262	4,921
Richmond	166	2	11	46	107	199	2,248	714	1,437	97	2,410
Robeson	929	24	40	307	558	828	7,805	3,119	4,037	649	8,028
Rockingham	250	8	6	88	148	287	3,832	1,079	2,589	164	3,266
Rowan	447	3	31	143	270	477	4,381	1,111	2,999	271	3,992
Rutherford	223	2	21	42	158	183	2,329	757	1,400	172	2,026
Sampson	165	7	22	36	100	154	1,652	746	797	109	2,162
Scotland	140	4	9	38	89	155	1,786	809	907	70	1,757
Stanly	162	–	25	29	108	132	1,625	537	1,013	75	2,334
Stokes	122	2	11	3	106	75	1,250	408	739	103	920
Surry	267	3	8	34	222	426	2,422	748	1,485	189	2,203
Swain	34	–	5	1	28	13	291	53	218	20	139
Transylvania	73	–	7	4	62	36	610	205	373	32	582
Tyrrell	5	2	1	–	2	7	69	23	36	10	51
Union	153	2	14	46	91	338	1,550	217	1,232	101	3,879
Vance	219	4	8	96	111	326	3,022	1,157	1,755	110	2,721
Wake	2,493	23	151	841	1,478	2,545	20,835	4,656	14,646	1,533	26,358
Warren	38	–	8	8	22	33	515	231	252	32	456
Washington	52	2	2	4	44	53	268	69	196	3	301
Watauga	55	1	7	6	41	62	1,223	328	836	59	1,464
Wayne	564	12	11	126	415	671	5,001	1,584	3,110	307	5,171
Wilkes	134	2	6	15	111	161	1,686	473	1,121	92	1,614
Wilson	254	11	15	96	132	452	2,817	707	1,928	182	3,676
Yadkin	70	4	10	10	46	66	866	253	573	40	770
Yancey	10	–	1	–	9	11	142	75	60	7	78
NORTH DAKOTA	525	8	167	43	307	502	11,678	1,897	8,911	870	13,522
Adams	2	1	1	–	–	1	17	2	11	4	22
Barnes	1	–	–	–	1	1	116	26	74	16	156
Benson	(NA)	(NA)	(NA)	(NA)	(NA)	(NA)	(NA)	(NA)	(NA)	(NA)	(NA)
Billings	(NA)	(NA)	(NA)	(NA)	(NA)	(NA)	(NA)	(NA)	(NA)	(NA)	(NA)
Bottineau	–	–	–	–	–	–	81	12	59	10	32

See footnotes at end of table.

[Includes United States, states, and 3,141 counties/county equivalents defined as of February 22, 2005. For more information on these areas, see Appendix C, Geographic Information]

| | Violent crimes[1] | | | | | | Property crimes[1] | | | | |
| | 2004 | | | | | 2000 | 2004 | | | | 2000 |
County	Total	Murder and non-negligent man-slaughter	Forcible rape	Robbery	Aggra-vated assault		Total	Burglary	Larceny-theft	Motor vehicle theft	
NORTH DAKOTA—Con.											
Bowman	(NA)	(NA)	(NA)	(NA)	(NA)	–	(NA)	(NA)	(NA)	(NA)	15
Burke	–	–	–	–	–	–	25	10	13	2	9
Burleigh	65	1	14	5	45	40	1,652	233	1,313	106	1,943
Cass	105	1	38	8	58	132	2,834	530	2,092	212	3,442
Cavalier	–	–	–	–	–	–	17	3	11	3	82
Dickey	2	1	–	–	1	1	49	5	39	5	43
Divide	(NA)	(NA)	(NA)	(NA)	(NA)	(NA)	(NA)	(NA)	(NA)	(NA)	(NA)
Dunn	(NA)	(NA)	(NA)	(NA)	(NA)	(NA)	(NA)	(NA)	(NA)	(NA)	(NA)
Eddy	–	–	–	–	–	–	35	13	20	2	24
Emmons	1	–	1	–	–	–	20	2	17	1	31
Foster	–	–	–	–	–	(NA)	5	2	2	1	(NA)
Golden Valley	(NA)	(NA)	(NA)	(NA)	(NA)	(NA)	(NA)	(NA)	(NA)	(NA)	(NA)
Grand Forks	81	–	27	4	50	101	2,237	309	1,788	140	2,421
Grant	1	–	–	–	1	1	8	1	7	–	7
Griggs	–	–	–	–	–	–	1	–	–	1	2
Hettinger	–	–	–	–	–	–	9	2	7	–	2
Kidder	2	–	–	–	2	1	20	8	10	2	22
LaMoure	–	–	–	–	–	–	3	1	1	1	11
Logan	–	–	–	–	–	–	6	3	3	–	12
McHenry	1	–	–	–	1	–	36	14	17	5	51
McIntosh	(NA)	(NA)	(NA)	(NA)	(NA)	–	(NA)	(NA)	(NA)	(NA)	16
McKenzie	3	–	–	–	3	6	43	4	39	–	41
McLean	–	–	2	–	–	–	92	25	64	3	139
Mercer	6	–	2	–	4	1	75	15	54	6	104
Morton	34	–	15	3	16	33	434	56	350	28	612
Mountrail	1	–	1	–	–	1	34	3	28	3	36
Nelson	(NA)	(NA)	(NA)	(NA)	(NA)	(NA)	(NA)	(NA)	(NA)	(NA)	(NA)
Oliver	–	–	–	–	–	–	1	–	1	–	13
Pembina	1	–	–	–	1	7	38	7	19	12	81
Pierce	–	–	–	–	–	2	36	1	32	3	70
Ramsey	25	1	1	1	22	22	344	62	254	28	452
Ransom	6	–	5	–	1	1	57	20	32	5	58
Renville	–	–	–	–	–	3	16	6	8	2	26
Richland	11	–	2	3	6	13	396	71	303	22	463
Rolette	2	–	–	–	2	2	46	5	40	1	66
Sargent	1	–	1	–	–	1	36	1	34	1	63
Sheridan	–	–	–	–	–	–	27	10	16	1	32
Sioux	(NA)	(NA)	(NA)	(NA)	(NA)	(NA)	(NA)	(NA)	(NA)	(NA)	(NA)
Slope	(NA)	(NA)	(NA)	(NA)	(NA)	(NA)	(NA)	(NA)	(NA)	(NA)	(NA)
Stark	19	–	3	8	8	19	486	70	388	28	421
Steele	(NA)	(NA)	(NA)	(NA)	(NA)	(NA)	(NA)	(NA)	(NA)	(NA)	(NA)
Stutsman	28	–	14	4	10	14	343	46	272	25	432
Towner	2	1	1	–	–	2	21	12	8	1	5
Traill	9	–	–	–	9	7	40	12	21	7	57
Walsh	8	1	–	–	7	16	291	55	206	30	279
Ward	89	1	38	7	43	57	1,290	182	992	116	1,387
Wells	–	–	–	–	–	3	64	20	41	3	28
Williams	19	–	3	–	16	14	297	38	225	34	314
OHIO	36,286	480	4,286	16,689	14,831	32,451	375,794	87,762	249,633	38,399	329,209
Adams	18	–	3	4	11	(NA)	225	74	132	19	(NA)
Allen	526	6	102	167	251	453	4,298	1,102	2,994	202	4,603
Ashland	34	–	14	10	10	6	873	173	675	25	104
Ashtabula	22	1	5	3	13	33	660	127	481	52	512
Athens	94	–	23	11	60	52	1,055	182	850	23	1,110
Auglaize	12	–	3	2	7	37	224	54	158	12	188
Belmont	34	2	6	9	17	31	808	178	583	47	425
Brown	29	–	9	11	9	1	751	227	480	44	16
Butler	1,388	8	174	350	856	1,043	15,307	3,148	11,092	1,067	13,514
Carroll	21	–	12	2	7	29	266	93	150	23	484
Champaign	27	1	4	4	18	91	823	201	580	42	942
Clark	583	8	80	292	203	889	8,619	2,155	5,780	684	6,649
Clermont	188	–	75	45	68	250	4,542	836	3,506	200	4,196
Clinton	90	–	11	15	64	45	863	153	689	21	947
Columbiana	51	–	14	6	31	29	630	165	405	60	453
Coshocton	–	–	–	–	–	19	565	93	450	22	826
Crawford	35	–	6	4	25	17	803	163	628	12	515
Cuyahoga	7,212	84	659	3,765	2,704	6,967	39,631	10,409	22,185	7,037	39,873
Darke	67	–	13	9	45	71	881	234	596	51	781
Defiance	22	–	4	8	10	5	748	165	557	26	389

See footnotes at end of table.

[Includes United States, states, and 3,141 counties/county equivalents defined as of February 22, 2005. For more information on these areas, see Appendix C, Geographic Information]

County	Violent crimes[1] 2004						Property crimes[1] 2004				
	Total	Murder and non-negligent man-slaughter	Forcible rape	Robbery	Aggra-vated assault	2000	Total	Burglary	Larceny-theft	Motor vehicle theft	2000
OHIO—Con.											
Delaware	141	–	50	46	45	96	2,944	736	2,065	143	2,273
Erie	188	2	22	44	120	245	3,054	610	2,321	123	3,221
Fairfield	209	2	46	81	80	68	3,835	899	2,679	257	709
Fayette	37	–	6	11	20	37	1,252	334	859	59	1,179
Franklin	6,883	101	725	3,755	2,302	6,711	70,982	17,011	44,270	9,701	70,959
Fulton	39	–	9	4	26	30	732	124	569	39	724
Gallia	40	3	10	13	14	(NA)	904	335	507	62	(NA)
Geauga	26	–	5	5	16	9	733	113	595	25	426
Greene	189	1	56	78	54	194	5,203	881	4,016	306	5,575
Guernsey	46	–	7	8	31	37	932	91	814	27	884
Hamilton	4,599	82	481	2,852	1,184	3,589	39,264	7,856	27,564	3,844	33,742
Hancock	96	1	22	17	56	(NA)	1,920	399	1,483	38	(NA)
Hardin	4	–	–	1	3	3	206	49	130	27	173
Harrison	12	–	3	1	8	7	255	109	128	18	146
Henr	11	–	2	1	8	38	277	81	187	9	772
Highland	51	–	5	12	34	89	1,155	280	825	50	449
Hocking	31	1	10	4	16	23	919	257	601	61	528
Holmes	13	–	2	1	10	23	160	52	85	23	236
Huron	21	–	–	4	17	29	886	274	555	57	1,194
Jackson	46	2	7	5	32	(NA)	812	166	405	241	(NA)
Jefferson	190	4	14	52	120	86	1,548	274	1,178	96	215
Knox	4	–	2	–	2	1	47	11	36	–	22
Lake	184	1	28	58	97	195	3,638	475	2,902	261	3,180
Lawrence	16	–	–	–	16	(NA)	105	12	77	16	(NA)
Licking	219	3	52	72	92	168	4,661	1,011	3,294	356	3,755
Logan	152	2	21	5	124	86	781	196	547	38	882
Lorain	462	7	53	134	268	340	4,849	1,608	3,021	220	3,649
Lucas	3,359	22	163	1,228	1,946	2,536	25,202	6,108	16,152	2,942	26,099
Madison	21	–	7	9	5	69	543	113	397	33	557
Mahoning	822	24	76	314	408	1,011	6,601	2,115	3,924	562	6,329
Marion	122	2	22	49	49	69	2,652	587	1,975	90	2,643
Medina	48	1	20	14	13	19	723	159	526	38	462
Meigs	23	–	4	3	16	(NA)	288	107	153	28	(NA)
Mercer	37	–	11	3	23	2	707	114	565	28	57
Miami	97	1	36	30	30	77	2,202	452	1,653	97	1,718
Monroe	(NA)	(NA)	(NA)	(NA)	(NA)	–	(NA)	(NA)	(NA)	(NA)	28
Montgomer	2,033	39	212	1,102	680	2,685	21,378	5,300	12,835	3,243	25,256
Morgan	8	–	2	–	6	16	104	22	60	22	189
Morrow	13	2	3	1	7	11	490	213	254	23	154
Muskingum	144	3	34	66	41	30	3,007	628	2,193	186	1,513
Noble	(NA)	(NA)	(NA)	(NA)	(NA)	3	(NA)	(NA)	(NA)	(NA)	69
Ottawa	5	–	1	2	2	5	298	49	238	11	311
Paulding	21	–	3	–	18	–	220	71	149	–	12
Perry	16	–	6	2	8	22	494	156	303	35	684
Pickaway	68	1	13	16	38	–	1,966	647	1,255	64	2
Pike	6	1	2	3	–	1	571	92	463	16	206
Portage	161	3	31	36	91	123	2,759	379	2,267	113	2,519
Preble	32	–	10	7	15	67	777	197	539	41	908
Putnam	8	–	2	–	6	(NA)	190	63	122	5	(NA)
Richland	221	4	42	117	58	231	5,765	1,413	4,091	261	5,317
Ross	115	2	27	52	34	74	3,900	827	2,860	213	3,177
Sandusky	52	–	5	13	34	100	1,530	231	1,251	48	1,931
Scioto	267	7	40	100	120	200	5,448	1,568	3,516	364	3,564
Seneca	21	–	9	6	6	15	789	111	648	30	813
Shelby	(NA)	(NA)	(NA)	(NA)	(NA)	6	(NA)	(NA)	(NA)	(NA)	322
Stark	1,428	9	169	471	779	1,307	13,257	3,136	9,123	998	9,367
Summit	1,650	22	276	718	634	1,030	21,384	4,673	14,709	2,002	13,869
Trumbull	613	8	67	226	312	206	5,956	1,603	3,787	566	2,147
Tuscarawas	53	–	6	19	28	30	1,070	219	779	72	717
Union	25	1	9	5	10	8	930	212	679	39	392
Van Wert	28	–	10	5	13	38	734	173	515	46	625
Vinton	3	1	–	1	1	(NA)	427	176	205	46	(NA)
Warren	104	–	22	23	59	85	2,280	441	1,722	117	1,470
Washington	89	2	32	21	34	74	1,216	276	880	60	1,126
Wayne	52	–	16	10	26	25	826	285	505	36	253
Williams	52	–	23	8	21	12	739	149	569	21	358
Wood	107	3	20	28	56	83	3,730	512	3,082	136	2,283
Wyandot	–	–	–	–	–	9	15	9	5	1	342

See footnotes at end of table.

Table B-8. Counties — **Crime—Number of Offenses**—Con.

[Includes United States, states, and 3,141 counties/county equivalents defined as of February 22, 2005. For more information on these areas, see Appendix C, Geographic Information]

County	Violent crimes[1]						Property crimes[1]				
	2004						2004				
	Total	Murder and non-negligent man-slaughter	Forcible rape	Robbery	Aggra-vated assault	2000	Total	Burglary	Larceny-theft	Motor vehicle theft	2000
OKLAHOMA	17,632	186	1,556	3,090	12,800	17,176	149,452	35,234	101,263	12,955	140,125
Adair	100	1	3	2	94	119	450	134	271	45	446
Alfalfa	20	–	2	–	18	5	69	21	44	4	71
Atoka	33	–	–	–	33	45	255	88	151	16	250
Beaver	6	–	2	–	4	4	115	25	84	6	93
Beckham	45	–	5	2	38	38	434	80	328	26	577
Blaine	48	–	2	2	44	53	196	48	141	7	190
Bryan	178	–	25	11	142	113	1,389	439	834	116	1,084
Caddo	142	3	5	2	132	77	878	253	541	84	597
Canadian	431	4	39	83	305	385	4,379	792	3,276	311	3,886
Carter	329	2	27	29	271	285	1,965	476	1,386	103	1,996
Cherokee	133	2	13	7	111	201	1,113	258	766	89	1,011
Choctaw	105	1	7	16	81	110	563	204	348	11	366
Cimarron	2	–	–	–	2	7	15	7	6	2	10
Cleveland	785	7	103	171	504	783	10,402	2,183	7,289	930	9,888
Coal	28	–	3	–	25	45	128	42	74	12	135
Comanche	784	5	61	155	563	659	5,577	1,478	3,841	258	4,904
Cotton	14	–	–	1	13	35	75	19	47	9	81
Craig	47	–	5	1	41	30	301	91	189	21	307
Creek	150	–	10	13	127	212	1,882	565	1,120	197	1,526
Custer	71	–	6	8	57	79	748	164	550	34	773
Delaware	147	2	13	1	131	107	727	227	429	71	647
Dewey	7	–	1	–	6	11	22	8	7	7	93
Ellis	1	–	–	1	–	–	15	8	4	3	33
Garfield	232	1	38	18	175	226	2,759	633	2,017	109	2,699
Garvin	79	1	13	5	60	102	778	222	514	42	755
Grady	199	3	10	24	162	272	1,587	476	1,008	103	1,177
Grant	2	–	1	–	1	1	55	15	36	4	84
Greer	6	–	1	1	4	4	81	22	54	5	138
Harmon	4	–	1	1	2	12	95	20	70	5	135
Harper	5	–	–	–	5	3	56	15	35	6	47
Haskell	66	–	6	–	60	16	167	41	114	12	193
Hughes	32	1	4	–	27	40	344	138	169	37	369
Jackson	77	3	15	14	45	105	1,141	346	757	38	1,286
Jefferson	41	–	–	1	40	20	104	41	53	10	92
Johnston	57	2	2	–	53	45	144	45	86	13	117
Kay	223	1	41	17	164	232	1,948	538	1,323	87	1,987
Kingfisher	4	–	2	–	2	7	195	45	129	21	240
Kiowa	12	–	–	3	9	38	168	66	87	15	237
Latimer	33	–	6	2	25	42	126	61	53	12	132
Le Flore	135	–	4	10	121	122	728	199	484	45	789
Lincoln	86	1	10	4	71	70	474	135	297	42	410
Logan	98	3	13	6	76	109	684	256	400	28	640
Love	34	–	4	–	30	20	187	43	130	14	170
McClain	58	–	5	9	44	103	698	256	390	52	636
McCurtain	137	3	15	8	111	216	1,228	316	827	85	940
McIntosh	52	4	4	4	40	58	699	236	423	40	739
Major	23	–	2	–	21	6	121	47	68	6	132
Marshall	26	–	5	2	19	34	271	91	157	23	238
Mayes	126	5	8	6	107	117	887	259	576	52	892
Murray	20	–	2	1	17	41	368	121	235	12	226
Muskogee	428	6	30	52	340	459	2,196	797	1,191	208	2,729
Noble	6	–	3	1	2	17	241	53	168	20	118
Nowata	11	–	–	–	11	33	190	65	113	12	300
Okfuskee	30	1	3	–	26	36	226	63	144	19	344
Oklahoma	4,295	38	389	1,129	2,739	4,037	46,729	8,820	34,084	3,825	45,304
Okmulgee	107	5	11	7	84	202	1,072	342	639	91	1,292
Osage	166	3	9	21	133	146	1,121	350	654	117	1,188
Ottawa	118	–	17	3	98	107	1,061	296	716	49	1,261
Pawnee	88	2	10	1	75	19	380	120	228	32	395
Payne	197	–	38	23	136	228	2,276	483	1,703	90	1,842
Pittsburg	114	2	13	9	90	125	1,333	420	803	110	1,427
Pontotoc	130	3	14	5	108	150	1,040	268	724	48	942
Pottawatomie	285	2	31	34	218	193	2,502	740	1,485	277	2,317
Pushmataha	47	–	7	3	37	59	233	84	120	29	219
Roger Mills	3	–	–	–	3	4	28	12	13	3	12
Rogers	92	2	10	10	70	113	1,402	368	909	125	1,219
Seminole	81	5	6	5	65	98	796	248	495	53	598
Sequoyah	270	–	13	6	251	281	909	247	583	79	1,144
Stephens	111	2	11	9	89	87	1,344	278	991	75	1,356
Texas	59	1	12	9	37	72	534	121	385	28	477

See footnotes at end of table.

Table B-8. Counties — **Crime—Number of Offenses**—Con.

[Includes United States, states, and 3,141 counties/county equivalents defined as of February 22, 2005. For more information on these areas, see Appendix C, Geographic Information]

County	Violent crimes[1] 2004						Property crimes[1] 2004				
	Total	Murder and non-negligent man-slaughter	Forcible rape	Robbery	Aggra-vated assault	2000	Total	Burglary	Larceny-theft	Motor vehicle theft	2000
OKLAHOMA—Con.											
Tillman	20	2	–	3	15	24	220	58	149	13	195
Tulsa	5,183	55	346	1,092	3,690	4,803	32,182	7,756	20,278	4,148	27,116
Wagoner	119	2	16	14	87	79	1,301	332	848	121	1,229
Washington	123	–	14	11	98	203	1,609	400	1,133	76	1,646
Washita	9	–	–	–	9	7	112	32	75	5	112
Woods	22	–	3	2	17	39	153	43	100	10	232
Woodward	45	–	6	–	39	91	471	145	314	12	647
OREGON	10,601	90	1,271	2,735	6,505	11,890	164,732	29,559	116,749	18,424	151,933
Baker	21	–	7	3	11	34	474	84	348	42	584
Bento	145	1	28	29	87	190	3,113	522	2,412	179	3,411
Clackamas	465	3	94	158	210	510	14,201	2,257	10,390	1,554	14,612
Clatsop	62	–	11	12	39	96	1,585	288	1,201	96	1,619
Columbia	36	–	3	8	25	30	767	131	589	47	1,188
Coos	68	–	5	17	46	48	1,679	419	1,128	132	1,752
Crook	126	–	3	4	119	57	713	179	499	35	462
Curry	15	–	3	1	11	26	462	100	328	34	384
Deschutes	225	2	51	43	129	196	5,799	1,182	4,209	408	4,599
Douglas	116	4	23	32	57	103	3,274	644	2,380	250	3,112
Gilliam	1	–	–	–	1	1	28	8	16	4	24
Grant	6	–	3	–	3	9	133	34	96	3	109
Harney	13	–	2	2	9	22	127	36	79	12	191
Hood River	16	1	–	1	14	18	365	84	235	46	523
Jackson	612	5	63	66	478	444	7,896	1,317	6,054	525	7,693
Jefferson	72	1	9	4	58	19	562	121	364	77	595
Josephine	129	6	20	42	61	114	3,012	560	2,163	289	2,861
Klamath	213	3	24	45	141	233	1,878	489	1,217	172	1,748
Lake	14	–	4	2	8	27	207	54	138	15	154
Lane	860	5	129	243	483	1,014	16,374	3,655	10,691	2,028	17,210
Lincoln	226	1	21	18	186	149	2,277	501	1,613	163	2,168
Linn	186	3	19	59	105	192	6,741	1,289	4,915	537	4,874
Malheur	81	1	11	10	59	79	939	181	702	56	1,109
Marion	1,002	6	90	204	702	824	15,574	2,451	11,192	1,931	14,897
Morrow	16	–	3	–	13	48	70	21	45	4	309
Multnomah	4,591	33	397	1,421	2,740	6,164	49,506	8,573	33,499	7,434	42,328
Polk	190	–	29	28	133	122	2,566	416	1,936	214	2,436
Sherman	3	1	1	–	1	1	33	6	24	3	54
Tillamook	20	–	3	3	14	24	944	137	745	62	692
Umatilla	89	3	14	28	44	98	2,355	581	1,577	197	2,540
Union	30	2	7	4	17	27	544	120	389	35	490
Wallowa	5	–	–	–	5	3	81	21	56	4	40
Wasco	38	–	7	2	29	47	1,031	239	737	55	880
Washington	771	9	153	227	382	704	16,656	2,401	12,690	1,565	13,467
Wheeler	–	–	–	–	–	7	28	10	15	3	14
Yamhill	138	–	34	19	85	210	2,738	448	2,077	213	2,804
PENNSYLVANIA	48,273	645	3,312	17,866	26,450	48,325	277,515	51,103	196,867	29,545	288,257
Adams	139	1	22	19	97	99	1,152	233	834	85	935
Allegheny	5,879	72	198	2,222	3,387	5,452	30,254	5,472	21,250	3,532	32,440
Armstrong	85	3	11	18	53	67	786	220	518	48	586
Beaver	429	2	18	96	313	394	3,400	561	2,602	237	1,811
Bedford	47	–	6	9	32	51	688	235	420	33	863
Berks	1,528	19	72	477	960	1,376	10,078	2,109	6,427	1,542	9,887
Blair	271	4	36	83	148	316	2,551	644	1,742	165	3,223
Bradford	60	5	21	6	28	56	555	154	366	35	728
Bucks	931	6	63	323	539	845	12,779	1,685	10,073	1,021	12,667
Butler	322	3	41	45	233	176	2,999	457	2,419	123	3,135
Cambria	362	5	15	70	272	340	2,225	566	1,533	126	2,168
Cameron	8	–	2	1	5	10	147	61	84	2	110
Carbon	123	2	10	6	105	96	984	211	724	49	1,141
Centre	158	3	33	27	95	182	2,745	366	2,308	71	3,294
Chester	711	3	71	145	492	974	6,773	1,074	5,322	377	7,404
Clarion	54	3	15	5	31	37	651	169	444	38	566
Clearfield	146	1	22	15	108	168	1,345	264	1,007	74	1,313
Clinton	38	2	6	7	23	42	726	107	565	54	943
Columbia	80	1	20	6	53	51	1,019	145	835	39	1,139
Crawford	90	–	15	14	61	102	1,477	401	964	112	1,617
Cumberland	287	1	45	69	172	284	3,681	625	2,910	146	4,165
Dauphin	1,135	14	91	503	527	784	7,024	1,277	5,379	368	6,645
Delaware	2,428	33	100	603	1,692	2,568	10,659	1,688	7,769	1,202	11,938
Elk	66	–	5	4	57	91	696	182	482	32	740
Erie	712	1	106	260	345	732	6,417	1,452	4,683	282	6,802

See footnotes at end of table.

County and City Data Book: 2007

U.S. Census Bureau

[Includes United States, states, and 3,141 counties/county equivalents defined as of February 22, 2005. For more information on these areas, see Appendix C, Geographic Information]

| County | Violent crimes[1] | | | | | | Property crimes[1] | | | | |
| | 2004 | | | | | | 2004 | | | | |
	Total	Murder and non-negligent man-slaughter	Forcible rape	Robbery	Aggra-vated assault	2000	Total	Burglary	Larceny-theft	Motor vehicle theft	2000
PENNSYLVANIA—Con.											
Fayette	310	5	36	108	161	271	3,195	761	2,118	316	2,452
Forest	10	–	1	1	8	9	161	100	60	1	201
Franklin	383	2	37	42	302	432	2,526	498	1,853	175	2,455
Fulton	33	–	7	3	23	16	181	69	102	10	196
Greene	37	1	15	9	12	70	519	135	344	40	574
Huntingdon	83	4	17	13	49	108	473	143	310	20	492
Indiana	176	1	38	15	122	132	1,382	251	1,046	85	1,132
Jefferson	89	–	9	6	74	75	589	132	422	35	549
Juniata	17	–	4	4	9	27	289	148	126	15	145
Lackawanna	534	4	66	128	336	248	3,719	692	2,739	288	1,972
Lancaster	830	7	97	317	409	1,115	10,780	1,829	8,221	730	10,874
Lawrence	310	4	22	106	178	330	2,417	699	1,551	167	2,017
Lebanon	346	3	60	78	205	277	2,426	465	1,831	130	2,681
Lehigh	1,051	17	92	433	509	1,032	10,758	1,991	8,041	726	9,812
Luzerne	771	9	61	229	472	494	6,179	1,079	4,648	452	3,458
Lycoming	200	2	13	63	122	116	2,457	479	1,844	134	1,610
McKean	82	–	17	7	58	59	552	120	406	26	714
Mercer	230	3	31	44	152	185	2,400	447	1,802	151	2,126
Mifflin	115	–	10	28	77	94	1,069	296	716	57	824
Monroe	271	9	43	73	146	322	2,760	652	1,918	190	3,488
Montgomery	1,518	9	124	500	885	1,467	15,382	2,302	11,939	1,141	16,695
Montour	73	–	3	2	68	25	385	163	211	11	207
Northampton	506	3	60	142	301	539	5,366	816	4,162	388	5,052
Northumberland	169	2	22	12	133	270	1,033	221	760	52	1,410
Perry	86	–	14	9	63	74	588	147	403	38	533
Philadelphia	20,908	330	1,001	9,757	9,820	22,812	60,937	10,536	37,814	12,587	75,192
Pike	49	3	14	10	22	60	721	319	352	50	896
Potter	17	1	5	–	11	32	189	89	90	10	289
Schuylkill	309	7	21	30	251	335	1,646	323	1,187	136	2,071
Snyder	58	1	14	3	40	79	599	129	432	38	575
Somerset	90	3	18	7	62	81	801	284	456	61	925
Sullivan	13	1	9	–	3	5	139	71	59	9	122
Susquehanna	38	1	10	5	22	52	454	118	306	30	561
Tioga	14	–	7	1	6	43	399	130	246	23	480
Union	37	–	18	2	17	20	358	119	232	7	294
Venango	94	–	16	12	66	77	1,034	219	758	57	1,256
Warren	123	–	13	4	106	37	533	134	380	19	637
Washington	440	3	48	99	290	348	3,723	610	2,818	295	3,328
Wayne	43	1	12	6	24	104	643	175	421	47	873
Westmorelan	671	5	53	146	467	563	6,166	1,214	4,506	446	5,188
Wyoming	45	2	12	3	28	31	369	100	247	22	387
York	1,005	18	98	376	513	566	9,407	1,540	7,330	537	7,224
RHODE ISLAND[3]	2,673	26	320	731	1,596	3,119	31,166	5,465	21,623	4,078	33,323
Bristol	53	–	6	3	44	64	931	155	730	46	947
Kent	267	–	42	43	182	303	4,006	560	3,132	314	4,263
Newport	206	–	31	35	140	226	2,334	569	1,664	101	2,618
Providence	2,014	26	212	640	1,136	2,333	21,548	3,796	14,240	3,512	22,796
Washington	120	–	26	10	84	169	2,313	384	1,826	103	2,658
SOUTH CAROLINA	33,112	285	1,769	5,457	25,601	32,671	190,203	43,665	130,831	15,707	178,319
Abbeville	186	1	6	11	168	164	800	211	540	49	841
Aiken	497	5	60	94	338	791	5,074	1,208	3,382	484	4,791
Allendale	73	–	2	5	66	124	313	145	153	15	232
Anderson	1,263	14	56	161	1,032	937	8,202	1,986	5,523	693	6,524
Bamberg	168	3	6	10	149	135	457	157	274	26	473
Barnwell	171	1	4	21	145	171	858	186	643	29	736
Beaufort	1,018	4	47	153	814	945	5,742	1,592	3,741	409	5,266
Berkeley	787	2	62	110	613	988	4,864	1,206	3,204	454	5,356
Calhoun	69	2	5	6	56	103	299	70	191	38	313
Charleston	3,404	19	162	735	2,488	2,646	16,685	3,094	11,852	1,739	19,689
Cherokee	375	5	36	59	275	442	3,038	635	2,249	154	1,976
Chester	442	5	10	42	385	358	1,619	389	1,117	113	1,405
Chesterfield	223	3	13	13	194	338	1,287	345	852	90	1,418
Clarendon	245	3	10	49	183	270	913	264	578	71	969
Colleton	351	3	17	33	298	422	1,377	332	920	125	1,698
Darlington	965	6	27	100	832	446	3,682	1,104	2,304	274	3,372
Dillon	306	3	18	54	231	353	1,709	507	1,040	162	1,883
Dorchester	547	4	43	103	397	549	3,383	719	2,394	270	3,354
Edgefield	92	–	6	9	77	115	499	117	344	38	489
Fairfield	291	2	12	27	250	330	935	253	626	56	881

See footnotes at end of table.

[Includes United States, states, and 3,141 counties/county equivalents defined as of February 22, 2005. For more information on these areas, see Appendix C, Geographic Information]

County	Violent crimes[1]						Property crimes[1]				
	2004					2000	2004				2000
	Total	Murder and non-negligent man-slaughter	Forcible rape	Robbery	Aggra-vated assault		Total	Burglary	Larceny-theft	Motor vehicle theft	
SOUTH CAROLINA—Con.											
Florence............	1,287	11	54	304	918	1,235	8,488	2,124	5,849	515	7,652
Georgetown	426	–	17	56	353	481	2,294	487	1,650	157	2,346
Greenville............	3,076	31	175	544	2,326	3,004	17,097	4,038	11,524	1,535	15,942
Greenwood............	673	3	35	46	589	869	3,113	582	2,401	130	2,978
Hampton	130	–	7	12	111	174	552	169	332	51	570
Horry...............	1,911	13	144	419	1,335	1,981	16,411	3,162	11,769	1,480	14,148
Jasper.............	163	1	18	23	121	263	1,258	315	914	29	1,437
Kershaw.............	319	4	17	28	270	327	1,618	385	1,117	116	1,617
Lancaster............	409	3	29	49	328	528	2,576	774	1,675	127	3,105
Laurens.............	608	5	24	60	519	703	2,738	680	1,844	214	2,674
Lee...............	173	3	6	23	141	227	945	265	599	81	549
Lexington............	1,116	9	67	247	793	1,158	8,206	1,607	5,882	717	7,841
McCormick............	45	–	1	5	39	67	142	52	81	9	173
Marion.............	309	7	18	51	233	287	2,110	559	1,405	146	1,432
Marlboro............	425	4	12	37	372	486	1,422	429	905	88	1,658
Newberry............	200	2	12	18	168	204	1,120	133	961	26	603
Oconee.............	364	4	33	29	298	303	2,211	613	1,457	141	1,605
Orangeburg...........	741	20	36	111	574	1,384	5,129	1,501	3,135	493	5,248
Pickens.............	371	1	43	29	298	322	3,487	739	2,462	286	2,852
Richland............	3,515	40	185	819	2,471	2,791	20,397	3,804	14,846	1,747	16,385
Saluda.............	173	1	1	5	166	97	250	50	194	6	383
Spartanburg...........	1,868	17	104	324	1,423	2,385	12,022	2,683	8,216	1,123	12,101
Sumter.............	1,255	13	33	179	1,030	999	5,747	1,930	3,340	477	4,794
Union.............	227	–	11	21	195	219	877	199	603	75	911
Williamsburg...........	232	4	18	31	179	214	1,210	421	658	131	717
York...............	1,623	4	67	192	1,360	1,336	7,047	1,444	5,085	518	6,932
SOUTH DAKOTA	1,222	16	321	111	774	1,138	13,654	2,895	9,981	778	14,808
Aurora.............	1	–	1	–	–	1	12	4	5	3	(NA)
Beadle..............	–	–	–	–	–	10	13	6	6	1	415
Bennett.............	4	–	–	1	3	(NA)	16	7	8	1	(NA)
Bon Homme	–	–	–	–	–	1	1	–	–	1	5
Brookings............	14	–	2	3	9	16	381	40	326	15	473
Brown.............	43	–	16	–	27	37	527	95	406	26	624
Brule..............	–	–	–	–	–	(NA)	12	2	8	2	(NA)
Buffalo.............	(NA)	(NA)	(NA)	(NA)	(NA)	(NA)	(NA)	(NA)	(NA)	(NA)	(NA)
Butte..............	11	–	1	–	10	9	86	12	70	4	81
Campbell............	1	–	–	–	1	(NA)	1	1	–	–	(NA)
Charles Mix	20	1	5	1	13	35	55	30	19	6	106
Clark.............	1	–	1	–	–	(NA)	8	5	3	–	(NA)
Clay..............	15	–	4	1	10	17	249	33	206	10	334
Codington............	47	–	13	1	33	33	829	164	620	45	723
Corson.............	4	–	–	1	3	7	30	15	15	–	17
Custer.............	–	–	–	–	–	(NA)	34	8	22	4	(NA)
Davison............	12	–	2	–	10	19	299	52	240	7	555
Day..............	–	–	–	–	–	1	24	10	14	–	16
Deuel.............	4	–	2	–	2	4	36	8	26	2	57
Dewey.............	2	–	–	–	2	11	9	2	4	3	23
Douglas.............	(NA)	(NA)	(NA)	(NA)	(NA)	–	(NA)	(NA)	(NA)	(NA)	3
Edmunds............	–	–	–	–	–	–	2	–	2	–	5
Fall River	6	–	–	–	6	7	8	2	6	–	35
Faulk..............	1	–	1	–	–	–	6	1	4	1	11
Grant..............	(NA)	(NA)	(NA)	(NA)	(NA)	2	(NA)	(NA)	(NA)	(NA)	36
Gregory.............	(NA)	(NA)	(NA)	(NA)	(NA)	–	(NA)	(NA)	(NA)	(NA)	4
Haakon.............	(NA)	(NA)	(NA)	(NA)	(NA)	(NA)	(NA)	(NA)	(NA)	(NA)	(NA)
Hamlin.............	3	–	2	–	1	3	5	1	4	–	4
Hand..............	1	–	–	–	1	2	29	8	20	1	45
Hanson.............	2	–	–	–	2	(NA)	12	1	9	2	(NA)
Harding.............	(NA)	(NA)	(NA)	(NA)	(NA)	(NA)	(NA)	(NA)	(NA)	(NA)	(NA)
Hughes.............	76	6	14	–	56	25	587	66	503	18	494
Hutchinson...........	5	1	1	–	3	3	17	4	7	6	20
Hyde..............	2	–	–	2	–	–	21	3	17	1	1
Jackson.............	1	–	–	1	–	3	13	9	4	–	20
Jerauld.............	2	–	–	–	2	(NA)	4	–	4	–	(NA)
Jones..............	(NA)	(NA)	(NA)	(NA)	(NA)	(NA)	(NA)	(NA)	(NA)	(NA)	(NA)
Kingsbury............	1	–	–	–	1	(NA)	32	6	24	2	(NA)
Lake..............	6	–	2	1	3	2	203	49	147	7	154
Lawrence............	35	–	6	2	27	49	456	76	362	18	510
Lincoln.............	42	–	10	5	27	23	583	163	376	44	251
Lyman.............	(NA)	(NA)	(NA)	(NA)	(NA)	2	(NA)	(NA)	(NA)	(NA)	17
McCook.............	6	–	–	–	6	1	31	1	26	4	42
McPherson...........	(NA)	(NA)	(NA)	(NA)	(NA)	1	(NA)	(NA)	(NA)	(NA)	2
Marshall............	3	–	–	–	3	–	51	11	36	4	40

See footnotes at end of table.

[Includes United States, states, and 3,141 counties/county equivalents defined as of February 22, 2005. For more information on these areas, see Appendix C, Geographic Information]

County	Violent crimes[1]						Property crimes[1]				
	2004						2004				
	Total	Murder and non-negligent man-slaughter	Forcible rape	Robbery	Aggra-vated assault	2000	Total	Burglary	Larceny-theft	Motor vehicle theft	2000
SOUTH DAKOTA—Con.											
Meade	32	–	12	1	19	23	396	88	276	32	415
Mellette	6	–	–	–	6	(NA)	5	1	3	1	(NA)
Miner	–	–	–	–	–	4	3	2	1	–	35
Minnehaha	422	3	106	41	272	406	4,433	1,030	3,100	303	4,025
Moody	4	–	–	–	4	(NA)	6	1	3	2	(NA)
Pennington	314	3	107	48	156	311	3,261	682	2,419	160	4,048
Perkins	1	–	–	–	1	–	56	25	30	1	42
Potter	1	–	–	–	1	2	20	2	15	3	35
Roberts	23	–	3	–	20	5	94	35	53	6	113
Sanborn	1	1	–	–	–	7	20	–	17	3	39
Shannon	(NA)	(NA)	(NA)	(NA)	(NA)	(NA)	(NA)	(NA)	(NA)	(NA)	(NA)
Spink	5	–	2	–	3	3	71	24	46	1	27
Stanley	5	–	1	–	4	2	31	2	29	–	46
Sully	–	–	–	–	–	–	5	–	5	–	2
Todd	–	–	–	–	–	(NA)	5	3	2	–	(NA)
Tripp	4	–	–	–	4	2	60	13	41	6	90
Turner	3	–	2	1	–	(NA)	59	29	27	3	(NA)
Union	7	–	–	–	7	9	53	9	36	8	50
Walworth	1	–	–	–	1	3	27	5	19	3	246
Yankton	20	1	5	1	13	30	364	49	308	7	462
Ziebach	2	–	–	–	2	7	3	–	2	1	10
TENNESSEE	41,084	356	2,281	8,861	29,586	40,213	254,865	60,370	169,739	24,756	237,893
Anderson	293	2	18	61	212	255	3,230	766	2,207	257	2,549
Bedford	161	4	8	22	127	156	865	256	533	76	926
Benton	39	1	2	2	34	25	311	101	188	22	259
Bledsoe	34	–	–	–	34	12	161	47	104	10	142
Blount	446	5	59	29	353	485	3,101	800	2,033	268	2,847
Bradley	666	1	31	49	585	391	3,826	979	2,562	285	2,888
Campbell	312	3	13	13	283	156	1,507	454	933	120	1,007
Cannon	22	–	–	–	22	32	142	64	63	15	181
Carroll	72	2	4	6	60	63	602	193	357	52	561
Carter	139	2	6	16	115	159	1,732	437	1,197	98	1,794
Cheatham	95	2	2	8	83	83	828	185	543	100	698
Chester	62	–	4	10	48	57	437	110	306	21	281
Claiborne	120	3	4	2	111	62	777	225	491	61	596
Clay	13	1	–	–	12	25	78	32	43	3	103
Cocke	148	5	3	12	128	221	1,263	455	626	182	1,316
Coffee	178	1	5	22	150	82	1,995	459	1,392	144	1,607
Crockett	43	–	2	4	37	41	240	90	132	18	199
Cumberland	138	–	10	6	122	82	1,868	501	1,202	165	1,399
Davidson	8,846	59	412	2,170	6,205	9,203	38,169	7,145	26,749	4,275	42,299
Decatur	20	–	–	–	20	22	300	140	138	22	173
DeKalb	98	3	5	6	84	117	558	144	376	38	471
Dickson	262	–	61	15	186	158	1,392	329	973	90	1,226
Dyer	218	1	16	28	173	210	1,702	328	1,164	210	1,247
Fayette	149	–	7	21	121	156	724	219	424	81	681
Fentress	50	1	1	–	48	53	417	156	233	28	335
Franklin	154	2	4	6	142	136	1,110	363	655	92	1,124
Gibson	280	1	17	18	244	250	1,439	374	968	97	1,351
Giles	128	1	8	13	106	136	768	244	487	37	641
Grainger	60	–	5	4	51	82	548	135	371	42	409
Greene	287	2	13	27	245	193	2,405	726	1,478	201	1,974
Grundy	30	2	2	3	23	77	175	53	71	51	290
Hamblen	286	3	14	48	221	299	2,540	375	1,944	221	2,114
Hamilton	2,616	15	165	536	1,900	3,284	18,839	3,692	13,356	1,791	19,893
Hancock	5	–	–	–	5	11	135	63	69	3	116
Hardeman	179	3	9	14	153	174	848	290	459	99	738
Hardin	138	–	6	4	128	35	826	250	509	67	565
Hawkins	162	2	8	11	141	129	1,650	508	1,010	132	982
Haywood	196	–	13	13	170	289	795	261	471	63	862
Henderson	143	3	11	19	110	115	861	243	544	74	719
Henry	126	2	7	16	101	172	1,099	318	725	56	947
Hickman	85	2	7	6	70	72	552	210	290	52	284
Houston	26	1	1	2	22	25	184	48	113	23	124
Humphreys	44	–	3	1	40	45	357	103	230	24	276
Jackson	16	–	–	–	16	13	218	65	140	13	133
Jefferson	129	1	12	10	106	173	1,515	362	1,013	140	1,570
Johnson	52	–	3	–	49	54	189	93	84	12	174
Knox	2,244	26	110	611	1,497	2,550	17,483	4,061	11,601	1,821	14,646
Lake	33	–	–	1	32	12	83	30	50	3	51
Lauderdale	187	1	8	22	156	221	1,187	352	728	107	978
Lawrence	391	–	24	12	355	184	1,649	512	1,036	101	1,238

See footnotes at end of table.

[Includes United States, states, and 3,141 counties/county equivalents defined as of February 22, 2005. For more information on these areas, see Appendix C, Geographic Information]

County	Violent crimes[1]						Property crimes[1]				
	2004						2004				
	Total	Murder and non-negligent man-slaughter	Forcible rape	Robbery	Aggra-vated assault	2000	Total	Burglary	Larceny-theft	Motor vehicle theft	2000
TENNESSEE—Con.											
Lewis	19	2	1	–	16	24	248	62	172	14	199
Lincoln	165	2	3	11	149	124	846	279	523	44	694
Loudon	127	3	12	6	106	139	1,362	269	975	118	1,231
McMinn	354	4	17	18	315	247	2,017	545	1,339	133	2,022
McNairy	103	1	6	5	91	91	659	140	456	63	646
Macon	103	–	6	1	96	43	396	94	269	33	305
Madison	927	7	51	199	670	1,060	5,858	1,360	3,972	526	4,705
Marion	95	–	7	2	86	170	789	166	488	135	711
Marshall	68	–	6	13	49	139	659	155	474	30	662
Maury	514	4	30	65	415	562	3,312	605	2,528	179	2,955
Meigs	52	1	4	1	46	10	245	90	135	20	205
Monroe	296	6	11	9	270	234	1,560	387	1,041	132	1,151
Montgomery	886	5	73	150	658	691	5,917	1,247	4,429	241	4,985
Moore	6	–	1	1	4	11	66	25	41	–	93
Morgan	35	–	1	1	33	23	232	102	98	32	141
Obion	110	1	5	9	95	109	1,140	245	828	67	1,066
Overton	35	–	–	5	30	33	367	137	201	29	199
Perry	21	–	2	–	19	5	176	79	79	18	119
Pickett	1	–	–	–	1	8	21	9	10	2	3
Polk	47	–	3	5	39	22	277	85	161	31	179
Putnam	184	4	20	24	136	211	2,128	416	1,570	142	2,016
Rhea	87	2	2	3	80	53	708	81	591	36	677
Roane	192	2	15	20	155	141	2,130	556	1,389	185	1,394
Robertson	363	8	24	32	299	386	1,597	270	1,223	104	1,903
Rutherford	1,054	4	80	139	831	910	6,738	1,298	4,974	466	6,608
Scott	121	1	5	–	115	69	632	220	372	40	427
Sequatchie	44	–	2	2	40	40	207	48	121	38	270
Sevier	238	1	29	22	186	173	3,552	893	2,398	261	3,084
Shelby	10,719	110	492	3,891	6,226	10,280	61,287	16,410	37,008	7,869	57,432
Smith	59	2	4	4	49	43	286	64	203	19	293
Stewart	51	–	4	–	47	30	271	111	136	24	102
Sullivan	931	8	75	104	744	727	6,734	1,471	4,837	426	4,312
Sumner	601	3	55	42	501	535	3,107	610	2,273	224	3,623
Tipton	329	2	18	40	269	222	1,764	508	1,061	195	1,619
Trousdale	21	–	6	1	14	33	113	46	61	6	189
Unicoi	19	–	–	1	18	41	672	77	575	20	340
Union	43	–	1	2	40	49	432	148	244	40	275
Van Buren	5	1	–	–	4	10	69	11	45	13	63
Warren	120	1	14	8	97	126	954	217	641	96	1,265
Washington	521	4	19	70	428	529	5,176	1,044	3,845	287	4,500
Wayne	40	–	2	1	37	24	274	122	114	38	168
Weakley	88	–	10	3	75	84	708	167	506	35	789
White	77	–	7	3	67	54	818	272	464	82	804
Williamson	236	1	18	26	191	244	2,232	326	1,781	125	2,549
Wilson	356	3	17	23	313	417	2,449	557	1,717	175	2,936
TEXAS	121,148	1,361	8,347	35,743	75,697	113,270	1,007,982	219,434	694,567	93,981	915,304
Anderson	141	2	5	21	113	244	1,315	410	813	92	1,348
Andrews	46	2	13	1	30	12	380	89	281	10	382
Angelina	537	3	47	63	424	539	2,906	855	1,860	191	3,112
Aransas	128	3	5	14	106	39	1,612	425	1,135	52	1,247
Archer	8	–	2	–	6	15	93	43	36	14	101
Armstrong	4	–	–	–	4	–	30	8	20	2	29
Atascosa	69	8	14	5	42	73	928	278	600	50	576
Austin	101	–	9	5	87	81	582	197	341	44	529
Bailey	13	–	–	–	13	7	168	37	118	13	108
Bandera	34	–	5	1	28	24	407	110	275	22	392
Bastrop	201	1	9	11	180	163	2,088	677	1,280	131	1,482
Baylor	10	–	–	1	9	15	99	32	66	1	88
Bee	65	–	6	4	55	53	737	216	488	33	587
Bell	1,145	20	108	232	785	970	10,255	3,042	6,726	487	9,424
Bexar	8,622	104	756	2,278	5,484	8,700	92,493	17,061	69,250	6,182	87,361
Blanco	5	–	–	–	5	14	196	61	129	6	118
Borden	–	–	–	–	–	1	9	6	3	–	11
Bosque	39	–	3	1	35	23	177	93	75	9	189
Bowie	592	5	39	85	463	436	3,793	854	2,707	232	3,057
Brazoria	564	7	99	100	358	619	6,698	1,848	4,507	343	6,213
Brazos	941	–	107	128	706	610	8,505	1,653	6,512	340	7,667
Brewster	22	–	2	1	19	23	174	50	121	3	135
Briscoe	–	–	–	–	–	–	21	8	8	5	13
Brooks	14	–	–	1	13	23	263	106	156	1	283
Brown	113	3	16	11	83	246	1,961	378	1,507	76	1,755

See footnotes at end of table.

Table B-8. Counties — **Crime—Number of Offenses**—Con.

[Includes United States, states, and 3,141 counties/county equivalents defined as of February 22, 2005. For more information on these areas, see Appendix C, Geographic Information]

County	Violent crimes[1]						Property crimes[1]				
	2004					2000	2004				2000
	Total	Murder and non-negligent man-slaughter	Forcible rape	Robbery	Aggra-vated assault		Total	Burglary	Larceny-theft	Motor vehicle theft	
TEXAS—Con.											
Burleson	38	5	3	4	26	63	200	85	101	14	326
Burnet	73	—	6	4	63	74	847	224	564	59	619
Caldwell	133	—	12	9	112	96	963	217	708	38	626
Calhoun	64	3	6	6	49	87	667	197	430	40	719
Callahan	24	4	—	1	19	3	126	51	61	14	78
Cameron	1,724	7	126	301	1,290	1,574	20,018	3,737	15,376	905	19,146
Camp	32	—	10	2	20	30	314	100	195	19	257
Carson	9	—	—	—	9	5	27	11	15	1	26
Cass	68	2	18	6	42	84	664	176	446	42	556
Castro	23	—	1	1	21	24	228	61	154	13	132
Chambers	75	2	4	14	55	43	942	300	574	68	853
Cherokee	207	1	27	21	158	255	1,478	440	939	99	1,234
Childress	17	—	2	1	14	23	143	55	82	6	205
Clay	15	—	3	2	10	18	217	79	124	14	163
Cochran	3	—	—	—	3	6	68	10	51	7	65
Coke	4	—	—	—	4	2	12	7	4	1	50
Coleman	11	—	1	2	8	8	242	103	131	8	124
Collin	1,764	22	174	521	1,047	1,692	19,930	4,037	14,249	1,644	15,649
Collingsworth	3	—	—	—	3	3	46	31	15	—	81
Colorado	54	1	5	2	46	76	378	100	253	25	474
Comal	258	1	42	18	197	276	3,176	657	2,405	114	3,502
Comanche	27	—	9	—	18	16	306	104	186	16	202
Concho	5	—	—	—	5	6	21	8	10	3	40
Cooke	73	1	4	25	43	43	1,637	392	1,127	118	997
Coryell	158	—	27	21	110	184	1,382	360	973	49	1,334
Cottle	1	—	—	—	1	2	12	8	2	2	30
Crane	18	1	—	—	17	7	93	25	65	3	67
Crockett	7	—	1	1	5	9	65	22	42	1	44
Crosby	16	—	4	2	10	5	66	28	32	6	23
Culberson	2	—	—	—	2	8	9	2	4	3	29
Dallam	25	—	2	1	22	16	145	45	95	5	117
Dallas	18,945	278	802	8,126	9,739	18,695	140,121	31,722	87,656	20,743	128,215
Dawson	41	—	1	3	37	64	371	116	241	14	360
Deaf Smith	79	—	4	3	72	118	592	141	433	18	468
Delta	11	—	—	1	10	19	190	72	112	6	70
Denton	1,319	16	140	390	773	1,123	16,419	3,004	11,946	1,469	13,402
DeWitt	61	—	7	5	49	51	524	144	364	16	340
Dickens	1	—	1	—	—	4	13	8	5	—	16
Dimmit	45	—	—	3	42	37	310	85	194	31	202
Donley	14	—	—	1	13	8	58	27	27	4	80
Duval	52	1	2	—	49	57	259	95	154	10	204
Eastland	22	1	3	3	15	18	531	142	366	23	427
Ector	639	3	19	94	523	620	5,363	1,145	3,929	289	5,843
Edwards	7	—	—	—	7	4	46	25	15	6	51
Ellis	306	3	36	46	221	305	4,093	965	2,840	288	3,489
El Paso	3,632	17	229	606	2,780	4,789	23,624	2,720	18,833	2,071	33,124
Erath	78	2	27	9	40	35	939	196	711	32	784
Falls	56	2	1	6	47	85	282	93	159	30	440
Fannin	99	1	14	7	77	90	658	178	444	36	597
Fayette	17	—	2	1	14	16	223	60	153	10	211
Fisher	8	—	—	1	7	7	60	18	40	2	64
Floyd	13	—	4	2	7	14	164	70	89	5	113
Foard	4	—	—	—	4	1	19	14	5	—	11
Fort Bend	1,786	21	163	549	1,053	1,352	11,107	2,644	7,432	1,031	9,691
Franklin	9	1	1	—	7	29	103	40	59	4	170
Freestone	33	2	5	—	26	24	232	89	112	31	272
Frio	52	1	—	8	43	46	364	128	226	10	378
Gaines	7	—	1	—	6	10	167	30	130	7	205
Galveston	1,376	14	175	319	868	1,236	10,743	2,674	7,218	851	11,671
Garza	3	1	1	—	1	3	78	11	61	6	31
Gillespie	15	—	2	—	13	9	371	60	302	9	296
Glasscock	(NA)	(NA)	(NA)	(NA)	(NA)	—	(NA)	(NA)	(NA)	(NA)	10
Goliad	5	1	—	2	2	3	33	15	18	—	51
Gonzales	108	3	2	7	96	94	470	98	365	7	241
Gray	85	—	8	7	70	103	909	233	638	38	831
Grayson	331	7	20	55	249	339	4,138	990	2,948	200	4,324
Gregg	931	7	69	179	676	602	6,573	1,388	4,685	500	6,363
Grimes	58	2	1	13	42	68	667	203	428	36	581
Guadalupe	267	1	39	27	200	245	2,899	667	2,116	116	3,049
Hale	76	1	5	18	52	108	1,830	405	1,384	41	1,724

See footnotes at end of table.

[Includes United States, states, and 3,141 counties/county equivalents defined as of February 22, 2005. For more information on these areas, see Appendix C, Geographic Information]

County	Violent crimes[1]						Property crimes[1]				
	2004					2000	2004				2000
	Total	Murder and non-negligent man-slaughter	Forcible rape	Robbery	Aggra-vated assault		Total	Burglary	Larceny-theft	Motor vehicle theft	
TEXAS—Con.											
Hall	8	–	–	1	7	5	43	22	14	7	44
Hamilton	14	2	2	–	10	9	100	44	51	5	73
Hansford	3	–	–	–	3	9	41	7	30	4	72
Hardeman	11	–	2	–	9	9	110	29	76	5	45
Hardin	80	1	2	12	65	95	1,013	247	691	75	902
Harris	31,741	346	1,459	12,385	17,551	27,150	181,370	40,156	113,652	27,562	158,236
Harrison	306	5	19	46	236	132	2,467	827	1,478	162	1,990
Hartley	10	–	2	–	8	11	97	35	59	3	85
Haskell	16	–	–	–	16	7	96	35	59	2	58
Hays	224	1	29	40	154	396	2,755	510	2,047	198	3,329
Hemphill	7	–	–	1	6	7	43	18	21	4	48
Henderson	393	5	13	23	352	288	2,393	750	1,406	237	2,199
Hidalgo	3,320	30	196	662	2,432	2,748	36,399	6,774	27,237	2,388	29,558
Hill	64	1	4	14	45	36	962	258	652	52	891
Hockley	72	1	4	2	65	82	544	150	383	11	455
Hood	66	1	2	3	60	56	1,279	288	917	74	1,073
Hopkins	85	2	7	6	70	88	763	228	485	50	631
Houston	59	1	6	8	44	63	500	126	347	27	459
Howard	81	1	18	11	51	111	1,067	434	591	42	1,267
Hudspeth	5	–	–	–	5	9	42	21	19	2	24
Hunt	357	9	10	72	266	419	4,003	1,100	2,546	357	3,270
Hutchinson	61	–	11	8	42	51	980	187	749	44	951
Irion	5	–	–	–	5	1	21	11	8	2	36
Jack	6	–	–	–	6	7	83	23	54	6	144
Jackson	24	–	6	2	16	13	230	56	166	8	211
Jasper	133	1	13	7	112	140	876	242	604	30	914
Jeff Davis	3	–	1	–	2	3	11	5	5	1	17
Jefferson	1,485	14	109	479	883	1,589	13,805	3,223	9,676	906	12,325
Jim Hogg	7	–	–	1	6	20	80	21	58	1	75
Jim Wells	390	2	24	8	356	156	2,679	745	1,839	95	1,647
Johnson	442	1	43	44	354	287	4,749	1,173	3,222	354	4,017
Jones	67	2	10	9	46	51	528	200	307	21	412
Karnes	16	1	–	–	15	6	109	48	58	3	23
Kaufman	527	5	50	56	416	352	3,382	1,073	2,000	309	2,390
Kendall	35	1	5	2	27	18	389	76	295	18	357
Kenedy	2	–	–	2	–		–	–	–	–	5
Kent	2	–	–	–	2	1	11	9	2	–	3
Kerr	94	–	10	13	71	90	1,218	247	928	43	1,166
Kimble	21	–	–	1	20	8	162	32	127	3	77
King	(NA)	(NA)	(NA)	(NA)	(NA)	(NA)	(NA)	(NA)	(NA)	(NA)	(NA)
Kinney	–	–	–	–	–	3	2	–	1	1	4
Kleberg	201	–	15	12	174	135	1,885	483	1,370	32	1,457
Knox	10	–	2	–	8	11	78	25	44	9	68
Lamar	405	6	91	41	267	581	2,974	577	2,304	93	2,931
Lamb	53	–	6	–	47	47	369	123	231	15	221
Lampasas	32	–	8	4	20	11	368	55	305	8	291
La Salle	17	–	2	–	15	16	106	39	56	11	85
Lavaca	10	–	1	–	9	18	218	49	164	5	205
Lee	45	–	4	3	38	37	326	89	214	23	202
Leon	56	–	3	1	52	41	183	75	96	12	188
Liberty	255	8	18	29	200	155	2,133	587	1,356	190	1,774
Limestone	80	3	12	17	48	96	916	205	662	49	607
Lipscomb	3	–	–	–	3	1	13	6	4	3	17
Live Oak	5	–	–	–	5	6	115	32	77	6	79
Llano	27	1	8	–	18	21	400	141	243	16	338
Loving	1	–	–	–	1	–	1	1	–	–	4
Lubbock	2,328	19	113	325	1,871	2,590	14,618	3,079	10,734	805	13,467
Lynn	8	–	2	–	6	5	101	29	68	4	87
McCulloch	19	–	1	2	16	57	198	43	145	10	269
McLennan	1,244	19	89	287	849	1,206	12,757	2,977	9,015	765	11,677
McMullen	–	–	–	–	–	1	7	6	1	–	5
Madison	39	1	4	4	30	24	364	112	228	24	209
Marion	33	–	9	3	21	51	319	145	147	27	255
Martin	2	–	1	–	1	2	42	25	17	–	55
Mason	8	–	–	–	8	2	44	16	27	1	11
Matagorda	204	4	6	32	162	206	1,610	365	1,182	63	1,998
Maverick	161	–	2	16	143	66	1,575	362	1,165	48	1,518
Medina	90	3	21	12	54	105	784	252	496	36	759
Menard	12	–	–	–	12	2	26	9	16	1	31
Midland	263	2	26	50	185	449	2,004	514	1,422	68	3,464

See footnotes at end of table.

Table B-8. Counties — **Crime—Number of Offenses**—Con.

[Includes United States, states, and 3,141 counties/county equivalents defined as of February 22, 2005. For more information on these areas, see Appendix C, Geographic Information]

County	Violent crimes[1]						Property crimes[1]				
	2004						2004				
	Total	Murder and non-negligent man-slaughter	Forcible rape	Robbery	Aggra-vated assault	2000	Total	Burglary	Larceny-theft	Motor vehicle theft	2000
TEXAS—Con.											
Milam	71	2	9	6	54	72	668	177	456	35	453
Mills	2	–	–	–	2	1	24	13	11	–	17
Mitchell	9	–	–	1	8	12	169	38	124	7	205
Montague	35	2	12	4	17	43	629	158	420	51	618
Montgomery	1,313	10	90	219	994	1,118	10,216	2,387	7,082	747	8,913
Moore	67	–	11	5	51	38	511	93	395	23	389
Morris	27	–	3	2	22	43	253	84	152	17	381
Motley	–	–	–	–	–	1	3	–	–	3	4
Nacogdoches	202	1	13	34	154	290	1,961	554	1,308	99	1,908
Navarro	99	4	14	26	55	101	1,962	532	1,327	103	1,893
Newton	16	–	2	1	13	12	156	73	76	7	124
Nolan	30	–	4	3	23	6	381	152	210	19	81
Nueces	2,188	26	235	557	1,370	2,223	21,883	4,482	16,281	1,120	20,304
Ochiltree	23	–	1	–	22	38	176	31	138	7	231
Oldham	10	1	6	–	3	2	30	13	16	1	24
Orange	477	2	37	75	363	411	3,073	944	1,883	246	3,151
Palo Pinto	64	1	11	13	39	84	1,094	289	743	62	944
Panola	76	–	2	5	69	59	537	118	367	52	569
Parker	140	1	17	26	96	131	2,460	695	1,593	172	1,860
Parmer	27	–	2	5	20	18	133	51	71	11	90
Pecos	14	1	1	–	12	42	332	122	201	9	370
Polk	110	5	20	13	72	84	1,103	371	650	82	870
Potter	834	6	44	218	566	855	6,932	1,396	4,957	579	7,400
Presidio	9	–	–	–	9	12	63	19	40	4	35
Rains	10	–	2	–	8	16	201	75	110	16	173
Randall	684	6	42	164	472	661	5,497	1,126	3,917	454	5,852
Reagan	2	–	–	–	2	3	20	4	15	1	29
Real	3	1	–	–	2	1	23	14	9	–	27
Red River	37	–	4	1	32	51	245	111	123	11	242
Reeves	13	–	–	–	13	18	299	73	220	6	390
Refugio	27	–	1	1	25	24	113	46	57	10	124
Roberts	1	–	–	–	1	1	23	7	16	–	16
Robertson	106	–	8	9	89	22	376	143	213	20	143
Rockwall	118	–	9	17	92	63	1,309	321	884	104	954
Runnels	23	–	–	3	20	32	275	86	179	10	222
Rusk	340	4	41	17	278	231	1,819	390	1,298	131	1,515
Sabine	5	1	–	1	3	14	255	116	129	10	110
San Augustine	37	–	2	2	33	21	217	93	109	15	163
San Jacinto	41	3	1	6	31	44	448	173	223	52	454
San Patricio	166	2	22	23	119	143	2,275	634	1,549	92	2,004
San Saba	7	1	–	–	6	10	72	34	33	5	73
Schleicher	2	–	–	–	2	1	22	5	17	–	37
Scurry	46	–	1	3	42	33	322	97	205	20	383
Shackelford	–	–	–	–	–	–	17	6	9	2	17
Shelby	74	–	4	8	62	73	565	191	334	40	449
Sherman	2	–	–	–	2	1	45	19	25	1	18
Smith	881	9	97	167	608	832	7,393	1,848	5,105	440	7,659
Somervell	7	–	1	–	6	40	151	81	64	6	181
Starr	159	4	8	22	125	142	1,242	385	682	175	1,032
Stephens	8	–	1	–	7	11	138	60	73	5	169
Sterling	–	–	–	–	–	2	3	3	–	–	7
Stonewall	–	–	–	–	–	3	7	3	3	1	14
Sutton	8	–	1	1	6	9	41	8	31	2	87
Swisher	27	–	–	1	26	26	154	48	99	7	136
Tarrant	7,441	79	690	2,447	4,225	7,506	83,872	16,886	59,888	7,098	73,382
Taylor	493	6	55	172	260	420	5,912	1,751	3,881	280	4,503
Terrell	7	–	–	–	7	7	15	9	6	–	(NA)
Terry	36	–	3	4	29	31	258	73	162	23	251
Throckmorton	–	–	–	–	–	–	28	5	23	–	6
Titus	114	2	7	21	84	122	930	213	660	57	907
Tom Green	421	1	68	60	292	409	6,226	1,167	4,803	256	4,794
Travis	3,982	29	367	1,426	2,160	3,494	47,111	8,141	36,069	2,901	40,822
Trinity	33	–	1	7	25	57	292	116	142	34	351
Tyler	32	1	4	3	24	47	199	87	102	10	223
Upshur	85	4	4	6	71	73	1,061	305	691	65	798
Upton	1	–	–	–	1	8	32	5	25	2	31
Uvalde	84	1	1	7	75	125	1,236	407	785	44	1,275
Val Verde	68	1	1	9	57	151	1,299	339	881	79	1,504
Van Zandt	151	4	2	15	130	115	1,360	468	725	167	1,117
Victoria	466	7	39	97	323	469	4,960	1,062	3,674	224	3,612

See footnotes at end of table.

[Includes United States, states, and 3,141 counties/county equivalents defined as of February 22, 2005. For more information on these areas, see Appendix C, Geographic Information]

County	Violent crimes[1]						Property crimes[1]				
	2004					2000	2004				2000
	Total	Murder and non-negligent man-slaughter	Forcible rape	Robbery	Aggra-vated assault		Total	Burglary	Larceny-theft	Motor vehicle theft	
TEXAS—Con.											
Walker	272	3	18	33	218	260	1,812	436	1,275	101	1,848
Waller	95	3	6	6	80	89	1,241	372	758	111	879
Ward	31	–	3	2	26	20	180	43	133	4	189
Washington	105	1	10	10	84	162	793	235	521	37	1,061
Webb	1,157	19	55	229	854	1,020	13,780	2,195	10,524	1,061	12,758
Wharton	182	–	12	29	141	234	1,576	493	992	91	1,862
Wheeler	12	–	1	2	9	3	63	35	21	7	38
Wichita	1,248	9	78	220	941	646	8,426	2,022	5,793	611	6,304
Wilbarger	66	–	2	8	56	54	560	112	418	30	645
Willacy	117	–	3	3	111	74	848	289	538	21	407
Williamson	567	4	92	83	388	459	6,062	1,153	4,597	312	5,329
Wilson	90	–	5	2	83	43	545	177	350	18	304
Winkler	11	1	2	1	7	16	81	30	45	6	86
Wise	172	–	14	2	156	80	1,163	326	790	47	721
Wood	31	–	–	2	29	158	741	306	423	12	818
Yoakum	14	–	–	1	13	22	85	12	70	3	110
Young	24	–	5	–	19	47	435	93	317	25	434
Zapata	54	–	3	2	49	5	448	243	169	36	69
Zavala	20	–	–	–	20	60	245	61	170	14	223
UTAH	5,583	51	951	1,229	3,352	5,349	95,961	14,866	73,562	7,533	87,056
Beaver	7	–	–	–	7	6	76	15	55	6	92
Box Elder	69	–	22	4	43	60	1,220	284	892	44	1,188
Cache	67	–	26	4	37	76	1,859	326	1,463	70	2,196
Carbon	30	–	6	3	21	43	557	130	401	26	642
Daggett	2	–	–	–	2	1	24	7	16	1	14
Davis	314	1	86	51	176	347	6,300	930	4,984	386	6,414
Duchesne	23	1	7	1	14	34	341	72	248	21	446
Emery	5	–	–	–	5	5	146	39	105	2	296
Garfield	(NA)	(NA)	(NA)	(NA)	(NA)	(NA)	(NA)	(NA)	(NA)	(NA)	(NA)
Grand	37	2	2	2	31	33	335	58	262	15	448
Iron	49	2	9	6	32	34	828	148	640	40	1,090
Juab	13	–	3	–	10	7	246	48	185	13	219
Kane	1	–	–	–	1	7	67	16	49	2	71
Millard	21	1	6	–	14	15	384	63	288	33	364
Morgan	8	–	5	–	3	–	76	25	49	2	88
Piute	(NA)	(NA)	(NA)	(NA)	(NA)	7	(NA)	(NA)	(NA)	(NA)	31
Rich	6	–	–	–	6	–	53	16	36	1	38
Salt Lake	3,563	31	498	941	2,093	3,228	53,635	7,351	41,203	5,081	45,943
San Juan	11	–	6	1	4	12	74	16	53	5	87
Sanpete	18	–	3	–	15	26	286	82	189	15	531
Sevier	29	1	7	1	20	48	679	99	549	31	745
Summit	24	–	12	7	5	29	1,159	180	923	56	1,208
Tooele	108	–	29	14	65	54	1,327	273	948	106	879
Uintah	63	1	13	2	47	40	1,017	406	553	58	654
Utah	417	5	127	52	233	348	14,407	2,390	11,311	706	12,201
Wasatch	14	–	1	–	13	7	229	73	143	13	240
Washington	171	–	24	2	145	240	2,023	431	1,400	192	1,918
Wayne	2	–	–	–	2	5	33	7	24	2	58
Weber	511	6	59	138	308	637	8,580	1,381	6,593	606	8,955
VERMONT	687	16	154	75	442	647	13,985	3,315	10,104	566	16,129
Addison	6	–	1	–	5	19	252	86	150	16	650
Bennington	38	–	9	1	28	34	824	180	606	38	790
Caledonia	30	–	7	4	19	31	551	153	364	34	668
Chittenden	255	7	48	41	159	243	4,845	971	3,731	143	5,533
Essex	(NA)	(NA)	(NA)	(NA)	(NA)	(NA)	(NA)	(NA)	(NA)	(NA)	(NA)
Franklin	73	–	20	3	50	51	1,317	442	802	73	1,096
Grand Isle	1	–	–	–	1	5	49	16	27	6	49
Lamoille	17	–	2	–	15	25	512	96	392	24	596
Orange	30	–	9	2	19	22	338	111	206	21	332
Orleans	5	–	3	2	–	23	413	151	236	26	554
Rutland	51	–	7	13	31	52	1,459	253	1,147	59	2,011
Washington	51	–	19	2	30	63	1,340	306	1,008	26	1,745
Windham	87	4	21	4	58	56	1,086	260	769	57	1,252
Windsor	43	5	8	3	27	23	999	290	666	43	853
VIRGINIA	20,287	389	1,787	6,838	11,273	19,771	197,034	28,266	151,543	17,225	188,954
Accomack	59	1	11	21	26	93	630	85	495	50	816
Albemarle	128	1	29	20	78	128	1,765	212	1,473	80	2,035
Alleghany[6]	28	–	3	4	21	57	231	59	159	13	126
Amelia	11	–	1	1	9	8	104	11	79	14	98
Amherst	38	1	10	10	17	33	370	56	281	33	340

See footnotes at end of table.

[Includes United States, states, and 3,141 counties/county equivalents defined as of February 22, 2005. For more information on these areas, see Appendix C, Geographic Information]

County	Violent crimes[1]						Property crimes[1]				
	2004						2004				
	Total	Murder and non-negligent man-slaughter	Forcible rape	Robbery	Aggra-vated assault	2000	Total	Burglary	Larceny-theft	Motor vehicle theft	2000
VIRGINIA—Con.											
Appomattox	18	–	2	4	12	7	100	23	75	2	124
Arlington	418	1	27	179	211	198	4,972	364	4,059	549	2,527
Augusta	94	4	8	10	72	77	870	184	615	71	787
Bath	1	–	1	–	–	1	8	3	5	–	31
Bedford	61	–	14	2	45	60	692	145	510	37	490
Bland	3	–	1	2	–	4	86	44	38	4	64
Botetourt	32	–	2	2	28	33	381	40	323	18	351
Brunswick	14	1	3	3	7	13	308	86	188	34	129
Buchanan	61	6	11	8	36	60	623	201	372	50	300
Buckingham	19	–	2	2	15	27	188	41	134	13	178
Campbell	75	1	14	11	49	77	749	154	538	57	817
Caroline	89	1	7	5	76	82	228	28	168	32	261
Carroll	51	1	3	5	42	45	433	116	261	56	414
Charles City	3	–	–	–	3	–	33	14	17	2	4
Charlotte	17	–	1	1	15	29	24	10	11	3	108
Chesterfield	534	9	51	203	271	561	7,778	1,393	5,908	477	7,122
Clarke	41	3	7	–	31	44	255	32	206	17	212
Craig	8	2	–	–	6	7	29	11	16	2	15
Culpeper	72	–	13	12	47	16	731	76	622	33	18
Cumberland	12	–	1	–	11	16	101	38	57	6	81
Dickenson	13	–	2	1	10	8	199	71	121	7	163
Dinwiddie	40	4	6	5	25	51	598	48	492	58	564
Essex	13	1	–	2	10	14	220	17	194	9	199
Fairfax	663	4	36	361	262	249	16,070	166	14,502	1,402	11,288
Fauquier	95	–	9	7	79	91	918	93	781	44	846
Floyd	6	–	1	–	5	9	204	32	151	21	139
Fluvanna	32	–	6	2	24	19	233	44	167	22	187
Franklin	58	2	12	3	41	96	783	107	600	76	724
Frederick	77	1	23	15	38	45	1,178	215	859	104	1,230
Giles	31	–	3	–	28	20	65	13	52	–	162
Gloucester	31	1	10	6	14	41	418	45	357	16	588
Goochland	48	2	2	3	41	26	193	42	125	26	144
Grayson	25	–	4	–	21	15	157	67	74	16	109
Greene	15	–	3	2	10	14	142	30	101	11	195
Greensville	24	–	3	6	15	43	258	72	168	18	86
Halifax[7]	70	3	7	18	42	103	909	204	669	36	558
Hanover	68	3	15	24	26	92	1,448	137	1,226	85	1,511
Henrico	668	17	28	293	330	597	10,785	1,628	8,393	764	10,438
Henry	178	8	12	39	119	227	1,338	303	919	116	1,361
Highland	–	–	–	–	–	3	2	–	1	1	21
Isle of Wight	38	1	4	12	21	42	646	22	586	38	649
James City	85	–	20	12	53	71	892	124	715	53	857
King and Queen	–	–	–	–	–	2	1	–	–	1	3
King George	22	2	4	3	13	27	386	40	319	27	393
King William	6	–	2	1	3	18	124	20	91	13	199
Lancaster	7	–	1	1	5	15	131	49	78	4	134
Lee	36	3	4	4	25	38	384	59	297	28	446
Loudoun	207	1	39	47	120	301	3,615	327	3,074	214	3,425
Louisa	34	–	10	5	19	29	475	63	384	28	300
Lunenburg	13	–	–	–	13	22	131	36	88	7	109
Madison	8	–	2	1	5	14	79	7	70	2	100
Mathews	7	1	2	1	3	9	135	43	86	6	85
Mecklenburg	71	1	13	10	47	89	689	131	527	31	727
Middlesex	4	–	1	2	1	11	98	13	78	7	127
Montgomery	144	4	35	16	89	128	2,005	374	1,541	90	1,712
Nelson	14	1	1	2	10	21	234	52	162	20	222
New Kent	9	–	–	3	6	21	234	42	182	10	214
Northampton	34	1	2	8	23	33	299	98	183	18	305
Northumberland	9	1	–	1	7	5	195	34	149	12	87
Nottoway	27	–	2	9	16	29	317	32	258	27	327
Orange	30	–	7	3	20	21	330	49	252	29	191
Page	20	1	4	1	14	25	188	34	148	6	197
Patrick	23	2	4	7	10	22	359	106	224	29	375
Pittsylvania	72	1	10	8	53	94	519	190	260	69	440
Powhatan	12	–	1	2	9	27	237	48	163	26	231
Prince Edward	19	1	7	–	11	20	85	5	79	1	52
Prince George	52	1	12	13	26	42	367	21	310	36	421
Prince William	573	5	31	218	319	578	8,084	1,105	6,104	875	7,295
Pulaski	50	–	7	5	38	76	998	128	843	27	884
Rappahannock	4	–	1	–	3	1	60	17	36	7	87

See footnotes at end of table.

[Includes United States, states, and 3,141 counties/county equivalents defined as of February 22, 2005. For more information on these areas, see Appendix C, Geographic Information]

County	Violent crimes[1]						Property crimes[1]				
	2004					2000	2004				2000
	Total	Murder and non-negligent man-slaughter	Forcible rape	Robbery	Aggra-vated assault		Total	Burglary	Larceny-theft	Motor vehicle theft	
VIRGINIA—Con.											
Richmond	12	2	–	–	10	10	74	13	54	7	52
Roanoke	213	1	18	10	184	193	1,424	241	1,065	118	1,229
Rockbridge	15	–	9	–	6	30	367	63	289	15	301
Rockingham	34	1	10	3	20	19	487	147	305	35	420
Russell	61	1	10	8	42	21	570	95	434	41	213
Scott	42	–	6	8	28	34	448	86	325	37	207
Shenandoah	39	1	6	3	29	56	421	46	351	24	422
Smyth	55	2	13	2	38	48	678	113	527	38	472
Southampton	21	–	3	3	15	23	310	40	246	24	279
Spotsylvania	176	5	11	20	140	118	1,627	100	1,441	86	2,254
Stafford	116	5	26	17	68	132	1,620	160	1,354	106	1,762
Surry	25	1	2	3	19	19	86	26	57	3	106
Sussex	29	2	2	3	22	37	198	35	151	12	169
Tazewell	86	–	22	8	56	353	1,305	279	963	63	1,107
Warren	47	–	12	10	25	39	793	77	656	60	790
Washington	116	6	16	6	88	58	1,301	243	980	78	742
Westmoreland	38	3	1	3	31	31	232	54	161	17	214
Wise	111	3	22	6	80	94	946	213	667	66	473
Wythe	48	–	10	4	34	60	575	50	493	32	714
York	56	1	9	11	35	158	1,168	96	1,033	39	1,073
Independent Cities											
Alexandria	379	2	30	161	186	315	3,445	351	2,523	571	4,990
Bedford	23	–	4	4	15	19	216	24	188	4	171
Bristol	94	1	7	24	62	61	672	108	528	36	444
Buena Vista	28	–	3	2	23	4	80	12	61	7	31
Charlottesville	329	4	35	68	222	417	1,919	230	1,534	155	2,313
Chesapeake[6]	1,111	12	61	295	743	1,070	7,724	1,296	5,804	624	5,836
Clifton Forge[6]	(NA)	(X)	(X)	(X)	(X)	15	(NA)	(X)	(X)	(X)	72
Colonial Heights	52	4	4	20	24	38	780	73	672	35	1,189
Covington	19	1	3	6	9	7	259	86	163	10	174
Danville	299	3	16	92	188	240	2,228	270	1,840	118	1,957
Emporia	42	–	2	15	25	67	458	60	385	13	385
Fairfax	10	–	7	1	2	41	537	22	494	21	1,081
Falls Church	25	1	2	8	14	–	401	35	316	50	2
Franklin	30	2	1	8	19	20	313	22	268	23	239
Fredericksburg	95	2	12	24	57	105	1,011	78	855	78	1,118
Galax	29	–	2	1	26	40	323	53	253	17	256
Hampton	592	14	51	226	301	491	5,072	798	3,727	547	5,307
Harrisonburg	121	1	20	27	73	157	1,290	302	907	81	1,657
Hopewell	177	1	12	55	109	185	1,135	275	738	122	1,097
Lexington	5	–	–	2	3	10	153	41	104	8	87
Lynchburg	244	4	19	64	157	301	2,510	386	1,944	180	2,482
Manassas	162	3	22	48	89	136	1,143	126	878	139	1,296
Manassas Park	30	–	5	5	20	17	291	23	228	40	292
Martinsville	57	1	6	19	31	86	530	90	415	25	692
Newport News	1,396	18	111	524	743	1,355	7,897	1,442	5,521	934	8,724
Norfolk	1,388	35	88	697	568	1,690	13,022	1,600	10,177	1,245	14,552
Norton	16	1	–	2	13	28	211	19	184	8	208
Petersburg	316	4	26	113	173	414	2,564	564	1,605	395	2,417
Poquoson	9	–	–	2	7	8	183	38	136	9	91
Portsmouth	892	8	31	344	509	987	5,414	1,245	3,587	582	5,560
Radford	4	–	1	–	3	5	70	2	67	1	139
Richmond	2,745	96	107	1,355	1,187	2,538	13,915	2,763	8,735	2,417	15,591
Roanoke	856	8	62	187	599	539	5,993	995	4,503	495	4,231
Salem	34	–	5	8	21	14	624	66	515	43	572
South Boston[7]	(NA)	(X)	(X)	(X)	(X)	(X)	(NA)	(X)	(X)	(X)	(X)
Staunton	61	1	6	10	44	42	670	68	576	26	683
Suffolk	427	5	31	94	297	353	2,849	496	2,205	148	2,553
Virginia Beach	1,014	15	141	478	380	944	13,558	1,775	11,019	764	16,970
Waynesboro	72	2	3	10	57	46	756	86	624	46	319
Williamsburg	18	1	6	4	7	55	651	31	599	21	432
Winchester	74	–	7	20	47	108	1,433	109	1,264	60	1,190
WASHINGTON	21,190	189	2,824	5,852	12,325	21,445	298,447	59,955	195,448	43,044	273,851
Adams	61	–	9	11	41	40	939	265	624	50	624
Asotin	48	1	5	1	41	43	740	129	554	57	852
Benton	389	5	46	60	278	351	5,736	1,226	4,159	351	5,019
Chelan	163	2	46	26	89	144	3,305	570	2,562	173	2,884
Clallam	169	3	47	16	103	114	1,814	398	1,289	127	1,873

See footnotes at end of table.

Table B-8. Counties — **Crime—Number of Offenses**—Con.

[Includes United States, states, and 3,141 counties/county equivalents defined as of February 22, 2005. For more information on these areas, see Appendix C, Geographic Information]

County	Violent crimes[1] 2004						Property crimes[1] 2004				
	Total	Murder and non-negligent man-slaughter	Forcible rape	Robbery	Aggra-vated assault	2000	Total	Burglary	Larceny-theft	Motor vehicle theft	2000
WASHINGTON—Con.											
Clark	984	12	189	212	571	954	15,402	2,698	10,722	1,982	12,382
Columbia	8	–	–	–	8	5	213	29	180	4	181
Cowlitz	357	5	49	61	242	311	5,808	1,306	3,916	586	4,894
Douglas	55	1	12	4	38	48	1,270	238	973	59	1,064
Ferry	7	1	4	–	2	7	39	9	28	2	86
Franklin	161	3	15	38	105	134	2,083	434	1,488	161	1,730
Garfield	9	–	3	–	6	8	65	8	56	1	90
Grant	179	3	31	33	112	236	4,122	930	2,886	306	3,214
Grays Harbor	170	–	34	30	106	123	3,883	818	2,810	255	3,109
Island	47	1	13	4	29	59	695	154	514	27	1,432
Jefferson	45	–	13	2	30	57	967	270	656	41	857
King	7,050	58	672	2,705	3,615	7,429	98,836	18,068	60,914	19,854	91,410
Kitsap	1,058	1	231	125	701	1,002	6,878	1,710	4,543	625	9,029
Kittitas	58	–	15	10	33	61	2,251	522	1,610	119	1,848
Klickitat	34	–	5	–	29	47	538	209	299	30	482
Lewis	217	1	38	32	146	216	3,246	686	2,335	225	3,044
Lincoln	9	–	3	–	6	22	246	79	153	14	151
Mason	182	2	56	19	105	143	2,891	787	1,785	319	2,612
Okanogan	97	3	17	12	65	80	1,152	344	712	96	934
Pacific	45	–	4	4	37	49	922	365	513	44	655
Pend Oreille	17	–	3	–	14	16	485	172	282	31	386
Pierce	4,031	26	385	1,186	2,434	4,540	38,568	8,146	24,042	6,380	41,883
San Juan	7	–	1	1	5	6	234	54	164	16	220
Skagit	281	2	67	62	150	141	7,477	1,288	5,724	465	5,930
Skamania	13	3	7	–	3	9	377	72	276	29	257
Snohomish	1,606	18	274	419	895	1,415	24,534	5,059	14,580	4,895	19,071
Spokane	1,661	15	147	380	1,119	1,749	27,023	5,323	19,020	2,680	23,312
Stevens	40	1	24	3	12	32	1,162	317	768	77	1,026
Thurston	592	8	84	92	408	557	8,266	1,790	5,838	638	7,950
Wahkiakum	9	–	3	–	6	1	73	25	44	4	69
Walla Walla	166	–	44	21	101	219	2,010	351	1,520	139	2,235
Whatcom	437	4	90	96	247	372	9,410	1,785	6,985	640	7,315
Whitman	49	–	16	6	27	58	977	212	706	59	893
Yakima	679	10	122	181	366	647	13,810	3,109	9,218	1,483	12,848
WEST VIRGINIA	4,716	66	319	709	3,622	5,448	42,170	10,138	28,563	3,469	39,134
Barbour	16	1	1	–	14	35	214	86	113	15	139
Berkeley	244	3	7	52	182	308	1,889	404	1,328	157	2,299
Boone	49	–	2	4	43	109	434	115	266	53	327
Braxton	24	–	3	1	20	47	185	44	125	16	170
Brooke	12	–	3	1	8	28	159	38	107	14	166
Cabell	332	6	61	142	123	364	5,065	1,116	3,567	382	4,947
Calhoun	1	–	–	–	1	8	60	18	29	13	55
Clay	24	1	–	–	23	37	117	52	48	17	74
Doddridge	9	–	1	1	7	15	30	11	15	4	21
Fayette	71	1	5	9	56	108	618	200	376	42	869
Gilmer	7	–	1	2	4	18	116	47	60	9	64
Grant	13	–	–	–	13	26	107	65	40	2	115
Greenbrier	44	–	1	4	39	48	297	64	214	19	349
Hampshire	62	2	5	–	55	54	235	82	132	21	258
Hancock	16	–	–	3	13	29	242	26	198	18	234
Hardy	36	–	2	–	34	32	119	43	65	11	132
Harrison	188	5	12	13	158	135	1,799	377	1,302	120	746
Jackson	35	1	1	2	31	69	306	88	184	34	433
Jefferson	34	1	3	6	24	62	486	114	332	40	520
Kanawha	1,209	18	47	219	925	963	9,215	2,330	6,026	859	8,124
Lewis	9	1	2	–	6	32	99	15	73	11	121
Lincoln	41	–	–	4	37	158	522	172	268	82	409
Logan	171	–	3	18	150	53	1,296	264	920	112	370
McDowell	30	1	3	2	24	91	275	81	180	14	350
Marion	91	1	11	15	64	86	895	202	576	117	879
Marshall	50	–	4	3	43	20	385	100	255	30	133
Mason	38	–	1	3	34	76	429	112	262	55	444
Mercer	286	4	17	48	217	338	2,137	623	1,341	173	2,266
Mineral	81	–	4	8	69	76	391	104	267	20	343
Mingo	62	2	–	5	55	97	294	72	174	48	264
Monongalia	252	–	18	39	195	357	2,032	367	1,562	103	2,056
Monroe	17	1	2	–	14	25	85	37	40	8	74
Morgan	14	–	–	2	12	45	174	57	101	16	269
Nicholas	44	–	5	4	35	85	650	126	467	57	597
Ohio	53	6	1	3	43	128	128	30	86	12	1,106

See footnotes at end of table.

[Includes United States, states, and 3,141 counties/county equivalents defined as of February 22, 2005. For more information on these areas, see Appendix C, Geographic Information]

County	Violent crimes[1]						Property crimes[1]				
	2004					2000	2004				2000
	Total	Murder and non-negligent man-slaughter	Forcible rape	Robbery	Aggra-vated assault		Total	Burglary	Larceny-theft	Motor vehicle theft	
WEST VIRGINIA—Con.											
Pendleton.	4	1	1	–	2	8	61	17	37	7	56
Pleasants.	12	–	–	1	11	7	25	9	16	–	28
Pocahontas	23	1	–	–	22	37	117	54	54	9	108
Preston	34	–	1	2	31	33	272	107	141	24	211
Putnam	80	1	11	7	61	158	1,305	255	935	115	1,084
Raleigh	250	2	19	28	201	281	3,321	446	2,656	219	2,299
Randolph	67	–	7	8	52	82	580	136	423	21	544
Ritchie	22	1	2	2	17	16	137	62	69	6	44
Roane	26	2	–	–	24	45	245	53	171	21	294
Summers	25	–	1	1	23	36	115	41	66	8	127
Taylor	7	–	–	–	7	7	54	22	25	7	151
Tucker	16	–	1	–	15	7	108	43	64	1	96
Tyler	5	–	1	1	3	15	59	27	29	3	99
Upshur	22	–	11	–	11	35	276	52	206	18	288
Wayn.	80	1	6	14	59	114	1,044	278	638	128	1,019
Webster	14	1	–	–	13	51	131	41	81	9	145
Wetzel	16	–	3	1	12	11	123	43	71	9	138
Wirt.	7	–	–	–	7	12	95	41	44	10	83
Wood	308	–	28	30	250	262	2,333	578	1,618	137	2,205
Wyoming	33	1	1	1	30	69	284	151	120	13	392
WISCONSIN	11,460	153	1,121	4,062	6,124	12,387	145,068	23,517	110,259	11,292	153,788
Adams.	–	–	–	–	–	10	2	–	2	–	120
Ashland.	37	–	3	–	34	22	430	53	365	12	525
Barron	58	–	10	3	45	62	815	145	630	40	716
Bayfield	40	–	–	–	40	27	297	83	191	23	331
Brown	604	8	78	69	449	370	5,790	1,003	4,463	324	5,864
Buffalo.	5	–	3	–	2	6	86	27	53	6	176
Burnett	72	2	4	1	65	11	407	160	206	41	92
Calumet	39	–	7	6	26	36	744	115	600	29	659
Chippewa.	42	–	8	3	31	47	1,133	159	916	58	1,209
Clark	16	1	7	–	8	23	323	66	239	18	389
Columbia	53	–	6	3	44	47	1,327	195	1,072	60	1,571
Crawford	6	–	2	–	4	2	200	25	166	9	213
Dane.	1,110	3	132	350	625	903	12,024	1,986	9,288	750	11,885
Dodge	54	–	14	6	34	58	1,387	241	1,100	46	1,407
Door	20	–	10	1	9	21	434	67	354	13	526
Douglas.	68	–	13	13	42	70	1,842	370	1,350	122	1,758
Dunn	25	–	6	3	16	23	848	152	636	60	772
Eau Claire	184	1	19	22	142	155	2,843	428	2,322	93	3,107
Florence.	12	1	1	1	9	11	135	64	64	7	58
Fond du Lac.	98	1	20	10	67	65	1,947	223	1,633	91	2,245
Forest	16	1	1	–	14	42	352	125	205	22	344
Grant.	76	–	3	–	73	54	720	119	587	14	843
Green	20	–	14	–	6	24	428	80	331	17	605
Green Lake	14	–	3	–	11	24	312	50	248	14	346
Iowa	18	1	2	1	14	20	340	41	290	9	284
Iron.	6	–	–	–	6	8	141	43	82	16	188
Jackson	25	2	1	11	11	20	398	78	276	44	346
Jefferson	91	1	20	5	65	81	1,431	210	1,160	61	1,727
Juneau	58	–	12	4	42	30	510	159	319	32	417
Kenosha	257	4	29	108	116	621	3,977	811	2,885	281	4,121
Kewaunee	5	–	–	1	4	31	407	30	372	5	211
La Crosse	187	1	16	30	140	125	2,512	320	2,091	101	3,010
Lafayette	11	–	4	–	7	14	143	23	106	14	173
Langlade	48	–	–	–	48	24	749	140	589	20	605
Lincoln.	20	–	2	1	17	45	722	152	538	32	587
Manitowoc	78	1	22	6	49	62	1,853	289	1,489	75	1,818
Marathon	186	1	27	30	128	153	2,448	480	1,860	108	2,516
Marinette	32	–	4	4	24	68	920	239	640	41	737
Marquette.	4	–	1	1	2	22	222	84	115	23	289
Menominee	21	–	1	1	19	73	154	58	71	25	327
Milwaukee	5,242	93	241	2,837	2,071	6,305	43,389	5,992	31,103	6,294	50,619
Monroe	62	–	8	5	49	55	708	138	520	50	992
Oconto	37	1	3	3	30	26	728	265	416	47	643
Oneida	44	2	6	1	35	50	740	135	578	27	800
Outagamie	163	2	43	23	95	127	3,951	430	3,380	141	3,339
Ozaukee	29	–	2	6	21	29	1,004	155	820	29	1,019
Pepin	4	–	–	1	3	2	45	13	27	5	56
Pierce	33	–	3	4	26	34	844	173	635	36	718
Polk	49	2	9	–	38	30	676	210	417	49	565
Portage	99	–	30	2	67	58	1,492	218	1,224	50	1,605

See footnotes at end of table.

Table B-8. Counties — **Crime—Number of Offenses**—Con.

[Includes United States, states, and 3,141 counties/county equivalents defined as of February 22, 2005. For more information on these areas, see Appendix C, Geographic Information]

County	Violent crimes[1] 2004 Total	Murder and non-negligent man-slaughter	Forcible rape	Robbery	Aggra-vated assault	2000	Property crimes[1] 2004 Total	Burglary	Larceny-theft	Motor vehicle theft	2000
WISCONSIN—Con.											
Price	17	–	26	–	17	19	132	47	80	5	228
Racine	396	7	26	247	116	618	6,926	1,337	5,099	490	7,439
Richland	44	1	3	1	39	36	197	46	138	13	220
Rock	350	1	55	91	203	347	5,278	987	4,037	254	5,232
Rusk	49	–	2	5	42	47	364	85	269	10	334
St. Croix	39	–	13	3	23	77	1,481	220	1,195	66	1,121
Sauk	73	1	9	10	53	72	2,128	226	1,840	62	1,622
Sawyer	16	6	4	–	6	8	525	164	314	47	380
Shawano	24	–	8	2	14	13	1,014	165	809	40	905
Sheboygan	122	1	23	15	83	133	2,857	338	2,420	99	3,176
Taylor	14	–	5	–	9	12	346	76	261	9	317
Trempealeau	21	–	5	1	15	21	374	103	260	11	347
Vernon	14	1	4	1	8	14	277	75	189	13	304
Vilas	30	2	2	3	23	23	597	123	426	48	520
Walworth	96	1	18	11	66	99	2,403	328	1,993	82	2,445
Washburn	18	–	1	2	15	20	217	54	150	13	308
Washington	82	–	22	13	47	65	2,288	294	1,899	95	2,518
Waukesha	254	1	30	46	177	237	5,632	805	4,641	186	5,653
Waupaca	40	–	4	2	34	38	1,039	203	767	69	1,077
Waushara	15	–	–	1	14	20	269	79	178	12	409
Winnebago	233	1	27	29	176	205	3,706	618	2,958	130	3,655
Wood	35	1	10	3	21	37	1,688	322	1,312	54	2,105
WYOMING	1,137	11	111	66	949	1,311	16,566	2,685	13,097	784	14,896
Albany	35	1	1	2	31	94	1,239	177	1,013	49	951
Big Horn	4	–	2	–	2	22	48	7	36	5	175
Campbell	54	–	7	2	45	110	1,277	137	1,106	34	1,273
Carbon	60	–	2	3	55	65	564	112	416	36	443
Converse	19	–	3	1	15	13	255	50	195	10	237
Crook	10	–	2	–	8	29	109	22	86	1	84
Fremont	53	3	4	1	45	71	955	157	735	63	1,001
Goshen	46	–	2	–	44	19	270	67	199	4	222
Hot Springs	10	–	–	–	10	19	99	6	86	7	143
Johnson	22	–	–	–	22	13	179	31	142	6	152
Laramie	161	1	32	17	111	177	3,072	428	2,528	116	2,692
Lincoln	40	1	–	–	39	33	204	59	124	21	198
Natrona	132	–	7	16	109	236	3,355	643	2,528	184	2,509
Niobrara	6	–	1	–	5	4	24	10	14	–	24
Park	84	–	15	2	67	45	624	110	503	11	623
Platte	14	–	–	–	14	10	219	31	182	6	193
Sheridan	28	1	6	5	16	68	564	58	479	27	677
Sublette	27	–	2	–	25	15	236	18	203	15	149
Sweetwater	226	2	8	13	203	133	1,721	337	1,261	123	1,669
Teton	49	–	15	3	31	75	574	103	446	25	528
Uinta	22	–	1	–	21	17	727	69	624	34	700
Washakie	28	1	–	1	26	26	73	13	53	7	115
Weston	7	1	1	–	5	17	178	40	138	–	138

– Represents zero.　NA Not available.　X Not applicable.

[1]For individual crime data items, some data are incomplete. The U.S. and state totals are a summation of data for counties. The U.S. and state totals may differ from published Uniform Crime Reports (related Internet site <http://www.fbi.gov/ucr/cius_04/>).

[2]For individual crime data items, some data are not distributed by state.

[3]For individual crime data items, some data are not distributed by county.

[4]Yellowstone National Park County became incorporated with Gallatin and Park Counties, MT; effective November 7, 1997.

[5]Bronx, New York, Queens, and Richmond Counties included with Kings County, NY.

[6]Clifton Forge independent city became incorporated with Alleghany County, VA; effective July 1, 2001.

[7]South Boston independent city became incorporated with Halifax County, VA; effective June 30, 1995.

Survey, Census, or Data Collection Method:　Based on the Uniform Crime Reporting (UCR) Program; for information, see Appendix B, Limitations of the Data and Methodology.

Source:　U.S. Department of Justice, Federal Bureau of Investigation, Uniform Crime Reporting Program, unpublished data, annual (related Internet site <http://www.fbi.gov/>).

Table B-9. Counties — **Personal Income and Earnings by Industries**

[Includes United States, states, and 3,141 counties/county equivalents defined as of February 22, 2005. For more information on these areas, see Appendix C, Geographic Information]

County	Personal income — Total, by place of residence 2005 (mil. dol.)	2004 (mil. dol.)	2000 (mil. dol.)	Percent change 2004–2005	Percent change 2000–2005	Per capita[1] (dol.) 2005	2000	Earnings, by place of work, 2005 Total[2] (mil. dol.)	Construction	Retail trade	Professional and technical services	Health care and social assistance	Government
UNITED STATES	10,220,942	9,716,351	8,422,074	5.2	21.4	34,471	29,845	7,983,652	6.4	6.5	9.4	9.4	16.5
ALABAMA	134,736	126,655	105,807	6.4	27.3	29,623	23,764	98,672	6.4	7.3	7.6	9.4	20.2
Autauga	1,336	1,242	1,011	7.6	32.2	27,567	23,018	529	8.1	12.0	3.2	5.7	18.3
Baldwin	5,029	4,561	3,694	10.3	36.2	30,899	26,119	2,424	12.7	12.7	4.6	9.8	16.5
Barbour	660	626	547	5.4	20.7	23,343	18,820	469	2.5	6.2	(NA)	5.5	17.3
Bibb	466	437	353	6.6	31.9	21,732	17,724	184	18.6	7.1	3.6	(NA)	29.1
Blount	1,306	1,233	1,023	5.9	27.7	23,492	19,967	433	9.8	9.3	3.4	(NA)	19.9
Bullock	212	203	179	4.4	18.6	19,262	15,395	124	(NA)	5.6	3.3	(NA)	26.4
Butler	511	483	404	5.8	26.6	24,749	18,924	296	4.8	9.2	(NA)	(NA)	14.8
Calhoun	3,160	2,967	2,382	6.5	32.6	28,156	21,388	2,314	3.2	6.9	4.8	8.0	34.0
Chambers	833	807	730	3.2	14.1	23,562	19,958	459	4.5	9.2	(NA)	(NA)	13.9
Cherokee	578	545	444	6.1	30.1	23,507	18,472	226	3.4	11.6	1.6	5.2	23.0
Chilton	989	929	782	6.5	26.4	23,754	19,655	375	8.9	11.6	(NA)	(NA)	19.9
Choctaw	359	340	310	5.6	15.8	24,388	19,522	254	3.2	5.0	2.0	(NA)	9.4
Clarke	650	621	563	4.7	15.5	24,006	20,208	384	4.5	11.1	(NA)	(NA)	21.0
Clay	346	327	262	5.8	31.9	24,860	18,391	202	2.7	4.2	(NA)	(NA)	19.4
Cleburne	348	332	260	4.8	34.0	23,997	18,331	161	12.8	8.9	1.0	1.4	21.0
Coffee	1,393	1,312	1,021	6.2	36.4	30,655	23,453	629	4.2	11.0	5.4	11.6	17.5
Colbert	1,385	1,316	1,168	5.2	18.6	25,368	21,216	1,098	7.0	8.7	(NA)	7.2	30.3
Conecuh	311	289	268	7.6	15.9	23,481	19,086	185	2.0	4.4	(NA)	(NA)	19.5
Coosa	257	242	217	6.2	18.5	23,094	18,255	77	(NA)	4.9	(NA)	5.4	22.8
Covington	940	892	732	5.4	28.5	25,419	19,496	567	5.2	9.8	3.8	(NA)	16.5
Crenshaw	386	363	300	6.3	28.7	28,377	21,902	209	4.1	5.1	(NA)	(NA)	12.7
Cullman	2,083	1,983	1,648	5.0	26.4	26,125	21,239	1,272	7.1	8.6	3.6	12.3	13.4
Dale	1,233	1,167	995	5.7	23.9	25,421	20,265	1,382	2.3	2.8	1.8	1.9	52.8
Dallas	1,064	1,015	890	4.8	19.6	24,085	19,247	675	4.5	8.8	1.8	11.5	17.8
DeKalb	1,691	1,646	1,354	2.7	24.9	25,102	20,942	1,132	4.2	7.3	1.9	6.5	11.2
Elmore	2,000	1,860	1,530	7.5	30.7	27,119	23,089	725	10.5	8.6	3.8	8.0	22.3
Escambia	854	798	718	7.0	19.0	22,515	18,687	576	4.4	8.4	(NA)	(NA)	20.2
Etowah	2,744	2,603	2,212	5.4	24.1	26,658	21,410	1,603	5.9	8.6	3.4	18.0	15.3
Fayette	436	405	350	7.7	24.7	23,973	18,928	235	2.8	7.9	(NA)	5.9	22.6
Franklin	742	711	628	4.4	18.1	24,160	20,126	464	2.6	5.3	1.3	(NA)	17.2
Geneva	647	617	520	4.9	24.5	25,232	20,148	265	6.1	7.7	(NA)	4.3	21.9
Greene	218	208	175	4.8	24.7	22,551	17,548	100	2.8	4.2	0.8	(NA)	25.1
Hale	371	351	298	5.7	24.3	20,373	16,291	153	3.5	4.9	1.9	(NA)	26.3
Henry	404	375	324	7.7	24.9	24,394	19,791	208	9.8	4.5	3.0	(NA)	15.2
Houston	2,858	2,685	2,175	6.4	31.4	30,418	24,456	2,212	5.7	10.8	4.7	15.2	15.9
Jackson	1,327	1,267	1,155	4.7	14.9	24,812	21,372	757	3.7	8.4	2.0	4.8	25.5
Jefferson	25,494	24,132	20,130	5.6	26.6	38,861	30,406	24,318	7.2	6.9	9.0	13.3	14.2
Lamar	328	313	296	4.8	10.7	22,085	18,625	183	2.8	5.3	2.1	5.7	14.9
Lauderdale	2,314	2,194	1,946	5.5	18.9	26,462	22,117	1,208	6.5	10.9	4.4	11.2	23.4
Lawrence	859	815	696	5.4	23.5	24,891	19,949	420	4.2	6.3	1.6	(NA)	15.3
Lee	3,054	2,870	2,338	6.4	30.6	24,804	20,254	2,045	6.2	7.7	3.4	6.0	35.8
Limestone	1,881	1,778	1,468	5.8	28.1	26,698	22,258	1,340	5.0	6.8	17.0	(NA)	25.1
Lowndes	283	271	236	4.4	20.1	21,875	17,478	165	9.4	2.8	1.6	(NA)	15.9
Macon	450	432	376	4.2	19.6	19,823	15,620	257	1.9	4.3	2.5	(NA)	47.0
Madison	10,433	9,689	8,009	7.7	30.3	34,987	28,825	10,318	2.7	5.8	22.0	6.2	27.3
Marengo	592	560	481	5.7	23.2	27,140	21,304	375	3.8	6.4	(NA)	4.6	19.1
Marion	730	688	577	6.1	26.5	24,303	18,513	514	2.5	5.3	4.9	8.2	12.8
Marshall	2,346	2,246	1,774	4.5	32.3	27,365	21,547	1,495	4.4	9.6	2.0	4.8	16.6
Mobile	10,237	9,619	8,638	6.4	18.5	25,602	21,590	8,163	8.8	8.3	7.4	11.0	18.4
Monroe	573	545	472	5.1	21.3	24,319	19,457	463	1.9	5.4	(NA)	(NA)	14.4
Montgomery	7,756	7,306	6,089	6.2	27.4	35,130	27,256	7,534	7.9	6.3	8.4	8.9	30.0
Morgan	3,506	3,321	2,766	5.6	26.7	30,814	24,874	2,544	6.8	6.4	2.8	6.8	13.0
Perry	230	224	200	2.7	15.2	20,352	16,894	88	2.7	7.1	(NA)	8.9	28.5
Pickens	476	452	383	5.3	24.3	23,628	18,309	185	5.8	6.5	1.6	(NA)	22.2
Pike	851	811	625	4.9	36.3	28,842	21,010	613	5.7	8.9	1.4	5.7	19.4
Randolph	501	484	403	3.5	24.3	22,189	17,976	245	4.5	8.7	1.6	(NA)	21.6
Russell	1,199	1,121	965	7.0	24.3	24,291	19,412	547	7.4	10.3	2.3	(NA)	20.8
St. Clair	1,940	1,801	1,387	7.7	39.8	26,872	21,305	685	10.4	8.6	3.5	(NA)	18.5
Shelby	6,785	6,274	4,758	8.1	42.6	39,590	32,913	3,437	9.9	6.8	7.5	6.9	9.4
Sumter	282	271	243	4.1	15.8	20,509	16,508	155	4.3	5.5	(NA)	(NA)	35.1
Talladega	2,226	2,038	1,528	9.2	45.7	27,793	19,014	1,579	4.9	5.7	1.7	6.0	15.0
Tallapoosa	1,039	980	886	6.0	17.3	25,519	21,238	541	5.3	7.9	4.6	(NA)	17.2
Tuscaloosa	5,212	4,791	4,044	8.8	28.9	30,951	24,496	4,276	6.8	6.6	3.7	7.0	23.6
Walker	1,830	1,721	1,464	6.3	25.0	26,155	20,711	806	5.5	12.5	5.4	(NA)	17.9
Washington	381	367	330	3.8	15.6	21,494	18,196	271	4.4	2.6	(NA)	(NA)	14.6
Wilcox	243	233	206	4.3	18.0	18,820	15,835	170	5.5	4.9	(NA)	(NA)	21.5
Winston	579	549	475	5.5	22.0	23,630	19,058	374	2.7	5.8	(NA)	(NA)	13.1

See footnotes at end of table.

County and City Data Book: 2007

U.S. Census Bureau

Table B-9. Counties — Personal Income and Earnings by Industries—Con.

[Includes United States, states, and 3,141 counties/county equivalents defined as of February 22, 2005. For more information on these areas, see Appendix C, Geographic Information]

| County | Personal income | | | | | | | Earnings, by place of work, 2005 | | | | | |
| | Total, by place of residence | | | Percent change | | Per capita[1] (dol.) | | | Percent, by selected major industries | | | | |
	2005 (mil. dol.)	2004 (mil. dol.)	2000 (mil. dol.)	2004–2005	2000–2005	2005	2000	Total[2] (mil. dol.)	Con-struc-tion	Retail trade	Profes-sional and tech-nical services	Health care and social assis-tance	Govern-ment
ALASKA	23,588	22,259	18,741	6.0	25.9	35,564	29,867	20,147	8.6	6.5	5.6	9.0	31.9
Aleutians East	75	70	61	7.1	23.1	27,655	22,694	80	0.9	1.4	(NA)	(NA)	15.1
Aleutians West.	151	143	115	5.6	31.8	28,120	21,057	215	1.6	4.2	2.1	2.7	14.2
Anchorage	11,204	10,610	8,778	5.6	27.6	40,670	33,697	10,347	9.7	6.5	8.6	9.7	28.4
Bethel	412	405	312	1.7	32.1	24,054	19,392	289	2.2	4.8	(NA)	(NA)	42.9
Bristol Bay	48	43	43	11.6	12.6	43,966	34,596	74	(NA)	1.6	(NA)	(NA)	21.0
Denali	86	79	70	8.9	22.2	47,551	37,129	105	1.0	0.9	0.2	0.2	27.2
Dillingham.	148	143	130	3.5	13.9	29,775	26,368	120	1.2	4.4	(NA)	20.6	33.3
Fairbanks North Star.	2,939	2,745	2,303	7.1	27.6	33,568	27,842	2,700	9.1	6.3	2.9	7.7	47.3
Haines	90	85	76	5.9	18.2	40,185	31,750	62	(NA)	6.2	2.5	(NA)	15.3
Juneau	1,195	1,134	1,067	5.4	12.0	38,702	34,762	966	6.5	6.7	2.9	7.4	51.0
Kenai Peninsula.	1,594	1,514	1,399	5.3	14.0	30,795	28,156	1,035	8.9	7.9	2.7	7.1	27.2
Ketchikan Gateway.	534	506	481	5.5	11.1	40,291	34,391	413	5.4	9.6	2.1	9.2	35.2
Kodiak Island	430	408	373	5.4	15.2	32,896	26,693	391	3.8	4.4	(NA)	(NA)	37.2
Lake and Peninsula	41	42	38	-2.4	7.6	26,027	21,076	30	(NA)	3.0	(NA)	0.4	45.1
Matanuska-Susitna	2,305	2,124	1,552	8.5	48.6	30,279	25,902	953	15.9	13.2	4.7	12.2	22.6
Nome.	248	238	196	4.2	26.2	26,550	21,436	171	3.5	5.1	0.3	25.8	42.7
North Slope.	287	277	221	3.6	29.9	42,209	29,956	795	(NA)	0.7	1.0	(NA)	12.3
Northwest Arctic.	196	182	160	7.7	22.5	26,339	22,174	166	3.8	2.1	(NA)	(NA)	30.3
Prince of Wales-Outer Ketchikan	132	125	129	5.6	2.6	23,305	20,945	93	2.7	7.2	(NA)	4.9	45.0
Sitka	295	281	257	5.0	14.8	33,115	29,078	245	(NA)	7.7	(NA)	16.2	33.5
Skagway-Hoonah-Angoon	107	100	100	7.0	7.1	34,265	29,104	74	9.9	13.1	(NA)	2.0	36.8
Southeast Fairbanks.	218	179	140	21.8	55.4	33,572	22,756	166	(NA)	4.6	9.3	(NA)	28.2
Valdez-Cordova	343	334	307	2.7	11.6	34,614	30,011	313	9.5	5.2	(NA)	3.0	26.2
Wade Hampton	120	113	99	6.2	21.1	16,012	14,070	64	(NA)	7.5	0.1	(NA)	63.3
Wrangell-Petersburg	208	200	186	4.0	11.6	33,446	27,852	151	3.0	5.8	(NA)	4.0	34.8
Yakutat.	24	23	23	4.3	2.9	33,716	29,237	16	(NA)	5.1	(NA)	0.5	42.4
Yukon-Koyukuk	157	156	126	0.6	25.0	25,674	19,363	112	9.3	4.5	(NA)	13.3	52.3
ARIZONA	178,706	164,122	132,558	8.9	34.8	30,019	25,660	137,109	9.6	8.3	7.6	9.3	16.5
Apache	1,297	1,202	943	7.9	37.6	18,637	13,630	861	3.4	4.2	1.5	6.5	71.0
Cochise	3,392	3,082	2,329	10.1	45.6	26,886	19,734	2,315	5.4	6.3	9.6	6.6	51.9
Coconino	3,473	3,227	2,662	7.6	30.5	28,045	22,815	2,581	6.9	8.4	4.2	13.6	31.9
Gila.	1,245	1,170	973	6.4	27.9	24,165	18,946	605	8.0	8.9	(NA)	11.0	34.6
Graham	630	587	474	7.3	32.9	19,034	14,158	307	5.0	12.1	2.3	11.3	38.6
Greenlee	190	173	173	9.8	10.0	25,319	20,195	212	7.5	1.7	(NA)	(NA)	9.1
La Paz	418	394	308	6.1	35.7	20,683	15,672	241	3.1	12.0	1.9	(NA)	38.8
Maricopa	120,717	110,279	89,772	9.5	34.5	33,178	28,990	99,674	10.3	8.3	8.3	8.7	11.9
Mohave	4,116	3,780	2,908	8.9	41.5	22,055	18,610	2,168	14.8	14.3	4.1	13.1	16.8
Navajo	1,994	1,851	1,421	7.7	40.4	18,380	14,506	1,248	6.5	8.7	2.3	8.7	37.5
Pima	26,704	24,881	20,514	7.3	30.2	28,869	24,175	18,524	7.0	7.4	7.6	12.2	23.9
Pinal	5,001	4,647	3,203	7.6	56.1	20,835	17,669	2,316	4.3	8.0	(NA)	7.6	35.2
Santa Cruz	839	774	651	8.4	28.9	19,967	16,871	621	2.7	11.4	(NA)	3.0	36.3
Yavapai	4,876	4,519	3,574	7.9	36.4	24,521	21,151	2,537	13.7	10.3	4.7	11.8	20.1
Yuma	3,814	3,558	2,654	7.2	43.7	21,005	16,509	2,899	7.6	7.9	2.6	9.6	32.2
ARKANSAS	74,059	70,853	58,726	4.5	26.1	26,681	21,925	54,561	5.6	6.8	5.1	10.5	18.6
Arkansas	536	572	446	-6.3	20.2	26,728	21,575	429	3.3	7.2	1.3	(NA)	13.2
Ashley	557	535	509	4.1	9.4	24,135	21,058	430	6.4	5.0	(NA)	(NA)	12.0
Baxter	1,040	970	847	7.2	22.8	25,738	22,025	588	5.1	10.0	3.7	24.6	12.8
Benton	5,580	5,152	3,873	8.3	44.1	29,779	25,013	4,793	5.8	4.5	8.1	5.1	8.1
Boone	858	808	703	6.2	22.0	23,991	20,650	633	4.4	8.4	1.7	7.7	20.7
Bradley.	278	271	230	2.6	21.0	22,796	18,235	163	5.0	5.1	(NA)	10.6	20.3
Calhoun	127	119	105	6.7	20.7	22,801	18,366	184	2.6	(NA)	(NA)	0.9	11.8
Carroll	572	560	465	2.1	23.0	21,211	18,301	375	4.2	8.4	2.0	(NA)	13.4
Chicot	264	268	242	-1.5	9.2	20,239	17,164	150	9.0	6.7	3.1	(NA)	29.5
Clark	544	524	442	3.8	23.0	23,736	18,814	392	1.7	7.5	2.9	8.6	22.9
Clay.	346	358	319	-3.4	8.6	20,865	18,164	173	5.0	6.9	0.9	8.1	23.7
Cleburne.	644	613	524	5.1	22.8	25,435	21,746	303	7.2	9.2	2.3	(NA)	14.0
Cleveland	227	220	178	3.2	27.8	25,476	20,771	60	3.0	(NA)	(NA)	3.0	27.2
Columbia	678	643	557	5.4	21.8	27,661	21,776	476	3.4	5.2	(NA)	4.7	16.3
Conway	506	495	439	2.2	15.2	24,511	21,610	290	10.3	8.9	(NA)	(NA)	17.9
Craighead.	2,248	2,150	1,793	4.6	25.4	25,944	21,731	1,799	5.5	8.1	3.8	20.0	17.2
Crawford.	1,298	1,209	1,003	7.4	29.4	22,590	18,791	784	10.8	6.5	2.9	6.9	13.5
Crittenden.	1,243	1,213	1,008	2.5	23.3	24,095	19,761	703	5.8	7.6	2.7	10.1	19.0
Cross	366	393	341	-6.9	7.2	19,034	17,515	185	5.3	9.1	1.8	(NA)	26.5
Dallas	201	193	182	4.1	10.2	23,744	19,919	125	3.0	7.8	0.7	(NA)	16.0
Desha	302	302	269	–	12.4	21,205	17,542	217	3.2	7.6	2.0	(NA)	20.0
Drew	438	421	360	4.0	21.7	23,610	19,238	263	3.3	9.4	1.5	(NA)	31.6
Faulkner	2,588	2,407	1,941	7.5	33.3	26,478	22,477	1,640	8.1	8.0	16.8	10.0	18.5
Franklin	436	425	345	2.6	26.4	23,989	19,452	227	4.3	5.6	1.1	6.9	28.1
Fulton	237	226	189	4.9	25.4	20,084	16,204	89	(NA)	5.5	2.0	(NA)	26.6

See footnotes at end of table.

Table B-9. Counties — **Personal Income and Earnings by Industries**—Con.

[Includes United States, states, and 3,141 counties/county equivalents defined as of February 22, 2005. For more information on these areas, see Appendix C, Geographic Information]

County	Personal income — Total, by place of residence 2005 (mil. dol.)	2004 (mil. dol.)	2000 (mil. dol.)	Percent change 2004–2005	2000–2005	Per capita[1] (dol.) 2005	2000	Earnings, by place of work, 2005 Total[2] (mil. dol.)	Construction	Retail trade	Professional and technical services	Health care and social assistance	Government
ARKANSAS—Con.													
Garland	2,601	2,439	2,118	6.6	22.8	27,833	23,963	1,460	7.6	10.1	3.6	21.4	16.1
Grant	454	433	365	4.8	24.3	26,212	22,132	157	9.7	6.4	3.7	(NA)	25.1
Greene	878	849	719	3.4	22.1	22,314	19,166	601	3.3	7.0	(NA)	9.4	13.9
Hempstead	521	511	440	2.0	18.3	22,352	18,681	357	2.3	6.0	(NA)	8.8	20.7
Hot Spring	692	657	557	5.3	24.1	22,058	18,349	331	6.5	7.4	1.2	(NA)	21.8
Howard	349	346	301	0.9	16.1	24,010	21,064	336	2.0	4.9	1.0	(NA)	11.2
Independence	854	830	700	2.9	22.0	24,622	20,409	649	3.0	7.0	(NA)	(NA)	14.0
Izard	276	269	227	2.6	21.7	20,722	17,083	129	4.2	8.6	(NA)	8.5	29.7
Jackson	380	395	348	–3.8	9.2	21,616	18,955	226	4.2	8.3	2.6	17.2	24.3
Jefferson	1,951	1,906	1,654	2.4	18.0	24,053	19,633	1,599	5.8	6.5	3.8	12.4	29.1
Johnson	500	481	407	4.0	23.0	20,756	17,842	331	3.9	7.1	1.5	(NA)	15.7
Lafayette	172	177	151	–2.8	14.2	21,468	17,633	78	(NA)	5.0	(NA)	7.2	22.5
Lawrence	334	346	304	–3.5	10.0	19,469	17,175	164	4.7	9.9	(NA)	6.4	31.5
Lee	208	222	185	–6.3	12.1	18,029	14,795	108	(NA)	5.5	2.8	(NA)	33.6
Lincoln	264	266	214	–0.8	23.2	18,612	14,796	129	2.8	3.0	0.9	(NA)	40.7
Little River	318	312	280	1.9	13.5	24,301	20,567	268	3.4	3.7	(NA)	1.7	13.3
Logan	491	481	409	2.1	20.0	21,523	18,176	255	3.8	6.8	1.2	8.2	22.5
Lonoke	1,520	1,463	1,171	3.9	29.8	25,074	22,026	470	12.6	9.8	3.8	8.6	24.2
Madison	320	321	267	–0.3	20.0	21,361	18,651	167	6.6	6.2	(NA)	(NA)	18.2
Marion	342	325	276	5.2	23.9	20,517	17,070	153	3.2	7.7	1.4	(NA)	18.1
Miller	1,127	1,059	849	6.4	32.7	26,341	20,992	666	7.5	8.7	(NA)	(NA)	14.3
Mississippi	1,136	1,104	953	2.9	19.2	23,778	18,376	921	2.7	5.2	1.0	6.2	13.6
Monroe	188	203	174	–7.4	8.3	20,300	17,062	78	2.8	12.4	(NA)	(NA)	31.5
Montgomery	197	190	167	3.7	17.8	21,294	18,008	91	6.5	4.9	1.3	1.6	25.5
Nevada	229	223	187	2.7	22.2	24,029	18,872	121	(NA)	4.1	1.0	8.4	17.8
Newton	161	155	128	3.9	26.2	19,224	14,766	48	(NA)	5.8	(NA)	(NA)	40.8
Ouachita	646	614	553	5.2	16.8	23,889	19,265	295	3.6	9.3	(NA)	13.4	25.0
Perry	250	246	207	1.6	20.7	23,896	20,214	65	9.0	5.9	(NA)	6.6	27.8
Phillips	505	500	440	1.0	14.7	21,196	16,753	272	2.1	8.2	(NA)	12.8	27.7
Pike	262	255	214	2.7	22.3	23,989	18,919	135	4.6	6.4	0.4	(NA)	22.9
Poinsett	524	531	455	–1.3	15.1	20,740	17,764	257	3.6	6.6	1.7	(NA)	22.8
Polk	431	413	355	4.4	21.3	21,390	17,529	278	3.6	8.5	1.5	10.4	18.1
Pope	1,418	1,313	1,139	8.0	24.5	24,983	20,898	1,140	8.0	6.9	1.9	7.9	15.6
Prairie	185	216	169	–14.4	9.3	20,444	17,791	59	(NA)	8.7	(NA)	8.3	31.2
Pulaski	13,617	13,047	10,859	4.4	25.4	37,279	30,021	14,029	5.0	5.8	7.0	11.5	23.6
Randolph	356	355	305	0.3	16.7	19,341	16,778	180	4.0	8.1	(NA)	(NA)	25.5
St. Francis	554	554	472	–	17.5	19,999	16,101	372	3.2	8.9	2.9	(NA)	35.8
Saline	2,630	2,491	1,955	5.6	34.5	28,832	23,285	825	11.3	15.2	3.2	10.7	23.5
Scott	241	241	202	–	19.2	21,724	18,366	144	3.0	4.6	(NA)	(NA)	15.6
Searcy	148	142	124	4.2	19.0	18,448	15,032	63	8.6	8.3	1.9	10.3	34.5
Sebastian	3,774	3,494	2,923	8.0	29.1	31,820	25,303	3,685	4.1	6.1	7.5	12.3	9.8
Sevier	364	354	291	2.8	25.2	22,274	18,469	254	2.6	5.5	0.5	(NA)	17.2
Sharp	344	329	280	4.6	22.9	19,631	16,285	140	5.4	9.9	2.0	(NA)	23.6
Stone	249	238	198	4.6	26.0	21,152	17,139	120	5.8	13.7	1.1	(NA)	20.9
Union	1,430	1,319	1,157	8.4	23.5	32,467	25,395	1,045	7.6	5.9	2.0	8.9	11.1
Van Buren	347	331	288	4.8	20.4	20,940	17,766	136	6.1	10.9	(NA)	(NA)	23.4
Washington	4,985	4,692	3,463	6.2	44.0	27,486	21,828	4,363	6.6	7.3	4.1	10.6	18.3
White	1,585	1,530	1,268	3.6	25.0	22,210	18,808	994	7.1	9.5	4.0	(NA)	14.9
Woodruff	148	174	149	–14.9	–0.6	18,451	17,124	70	3.8	6.1	(NA)	9.0	32.6
Yell	486	465	398	4.5	22.2	22,729	18,784	278	6.5	4.4	(NA)	(NA)	23.0
CALIFORNIA	1,335,386	1,268,049	1,103,842	5.3	21.0	36,936	32,463	1,065,280	6.9	6.6	11.1	7.8	15.8
Alameda	62,332	59,180	55,791	5.3	11.7	42,956	38,466	52,517	7.1	6.1	12.3	8.7	16.9
Alpine	39	38	32	2.6	22.4	34,093	26,401	34	7.9	(NA)	(NA)	(NA)	29.2
Amador	1,141	1,095	837	4.2	36.3	29,689	23,783	675	8.9	10.2	3.7	(NA)	40.8
Butte	5,811	5,517	4,571	5.3	27.1	27,136	22,428	3,669	9.4	10.1	5.7	16.5	21.2
Calaveras	1,337	1,264	1,008	5.8	32.7	28,572	24,745	527	22.5	9.1	7.0	6.8	23.3
Colusa	534	556	441	–4.0	21.1	25,559	23,401	400	3.3	4.7	1.3	(NA)	23.1
Contra Costa	49,475	47,336	42,418	4.5	16.6	48,618	44,479	28,348	10.7	6.9	10.5	9.8	11.4
Del Norte	617	592	495	4.2	24.6	21,482	18,024	381	4.6	8.1	2.0	13.8	47.3
El Dorado	7,213	6,798	5,596	6.1	28.9	40,906	35,597	3,313	17.4	7.6	14.0	10.1	15.3
Fresno	22,796	21,859	17,628	4.3	29.3	25,961	21,975	17,355	8.3	7.6	5.2	11.2	21.3
Glenn	625	617	511	1.3	22.2	22,561	19,334	384	5.6	6.1	3.2	(NA)	27.9
Humboldt	3,585	3,480	2,936	3.0	22.1	27,932	23,236	2,377	7.9	10.3	5.1	11.3	26.4
Imperial	3,413	3,239	2,530	5.4	34.9	21,899	17,752	2,511	4.8	9.1	2.1	4.2	39.0
Inyo	537	517	435	3.9	23.4	29,793	24,269	349	5.9	10.6	(NA)	(NA)	46.3
Kern	18,924	17,660	13,891	7.2	36.2	24,999	20,927	14,773	8.4	7.1	4.9	7.5	25.4
Kings	3,090	2,959	2,118	4.4	45.9	21,536	16,312	2,427	3.6	5.9	1.7	6.5	48.2
Lake	1,774	1,706	1,388	4.0	27.8	27,225	23,687	761	8.9	9.7	4.1	14.2	27.4
Lassen	743	712	589	4.4	26.1	21,465	17,454	539	5.1	6.4	1.8	7.7	59.5
Los Angeles	342,231	327,363	279,050	4.5	22.6	34,426	29,232	293,031	4.3	6.1	11.4	8.1	13.5
Madera	3,164	2,995	2,265	5.6	39.7	22,198	18,317	2,171	8.6	7.1	(NA)	13.8	23.4

See footnotes at end of table.

[Includes United States, states, and 3,141 counties/county equivalents defined as of February 22, 2005. For more information on these areas, see Appendix C, Geographic Information]

County	Total, by place of residence 2005 (mil. dol.)	2004 (mil. dol.)	2000 (mil. dol.)	Percent change 2004–2005	2000–2005	Per capita[1] (dol.) 2005	2000	Earnings, by place of work, 2005 Total[2] (mil. dol.)	Construction	Retail trade	Professional and technical services	Health care and social assistance	Government
CALIFORNIA—Con.													
Marin	18,751	17,917	16,766	4.7	11.8	75,884	67,692	9,634	8.3	7.6	18.2	10.7	9.4
Mariposa	476	456	379	4.4	25.5	26,366	22,112	242	8.3	4.9	4.0	(NA)	38.9
Mendocino	2,570	2,459	2,151	4.5	19.5	29,117	24,891	1,544	9.3	11.6	4.5	11.8	22.7
Merced	5,538	5,362	4,134	3.3	34.0	22,862	19,531	3,577	7.9	7.7	2.0	8.4	20.5
Modoc	246	238	196	3.4	25.6	25,836	20,796	136	6.4	6.3	1.8	(NA)	45.6
Mono	495	447	330	10.7	50.1	38,975	25,632	392	12.3	6.6	5.3	(NA)	25.8
Monterey	14,752	14,179	12,097	4.0	21.9	35,775	30,005	10,957	5.5	6.7	5.1	6.8	22.2
Napa	5,787	5,405	4,714	7.1	22.8	43,669	37,818	4,212	9.5	6.3	5.9	9.6	13.6
Nevada	3,646	3,441	2,826	6.0	29.0	37,105	30,544	1,906	18.0	9.6	8.6	11.4	15.9
Orange	133,032	125,670	106,004	5.9	25.5	44,453	37,103	110,592	8.6	6.6	10.6	6.7	8.9
Placer	13,070	12,254	9,153	6.7	42.8	41,248	36,419	8,455	16.3	10.6	7.3	9.0	11.5
Plumas	679	659	539	3.0	26.0	31,739	25,936	410	12.9	6.3	3.2	5.1	30.6
Riverside	52,850	49,255	37,015	7.3	42.8	27,167	23,728	32,495	15.6	9.7	5.0	8.3	20.3
Sacramento	46,376	43,742	35,017	6.0	32.4	34,014	28,463	40,701	8.3	6.5	8.0	8.8	31.4
San Benito	1,728	1,699	1,561	1.7	10.7	30,862	28,984	927	11.6	9.6	2.5	4.0	18.6
San Bernardino	51,223	47,996	37,772	6.7	35.6	26,074	21,972	35,423	9.2	8.9	4.2	9.7	21.7
San Diego	119,136	113,062	92,654	5.4	28.6	40,569	32,803	94,878	7.6	6.6	12.1	6.6	22.7
San Francisco	46,398	43,325	43,284	7.1	7.2	62,614	55,729	52,805	3.3	4.6	22.2	5.2	14.8
San Joaquin	17,332	16,603	13,757	4.4	26.0	26,071	24,209	11,811	11.7	8.8	3.6	10.2	19.2
San Luis Obispo	8,766	8,379	6,801	4.6	28.9	34,305	27,455	5,780	12.5	8.9	6.8	10.0	20.1
San Mateo	41,518	39,626	41,730	4.8	-0.5	59,213	58,904	33,467	4.9	6.2	18.2	6.0	6.7
Santa Barbara	16,231	15,389	12,911	5.5	25.7	40,486	32,302	11,617	7.0	7.0	10.2	8.5	19.5
Santa Clara	87,154	82,287	91,386	5.9	-4.6	51,112	54,195	88,794	4.2	4.4	16.9	5.7	7.6
Santa Cruz	10,636	10,258	10,015	3.7	6.2	42,643	39,149	6,041	10.9	9.4	7.6	10.6	17.5
Shasta	5,209	4,991	4,005	4.4	30.1	29,104	24,443	3,455	11.0	10.8	6.1	15.7	20.4
Sierra	88	85	81	3.5	8.7	25,926	22,646	35	10.9	(NA)	(NA)	3.4	56.1
Siskiyou	1,211	1,171	988	3.4	22.6	26,874	22,315	691	6.9	8.3	3.7	11.0	30.1
Solano	13,759	13,048	10,953	5.4	25.6	33,494	27,578	7,885	11.3	9.0	3.2	11.7	27.0
Sonoma	18,890	17,985	16,778	5.0	12.6	40,451	36,438	12,158	10.9	8.1	9.6	10.9	13.6
Stanislaus	13,552	12,886	10,573	5.2	28.2	26,810	23,501	9,386	9.1	9.1	4.3	12.3	16.7
Sutter	2,452	2,371	1,939	3.4	26.4	27,548	24,488	1,414	10.4	12.1	4.2	12.8	15.7
Tehama	1,366	1,307	1,069	4.5	27.8	22,420	19,028	827	6.3	10.5	2.7	9.2	22.6
Trinity	325	318	259	2.2	25.4	23,377	19,918	140	8.8	7.7	3.7	(NA)	44.8
Tulare	9,669	9,190	7,219	5.2	33.9	23,517	19,567	6,803	7.7	7.5	3.1	7.1	22.6
Tuolumne	1,662	1,565	1,269	6.2	31.0	29,218	23,204	934	10.2	9.2	5.7	12.9	31.5
Ventura	32,139	30,534	25,364	5.3	26.7	40,358	33,521	21,506	6.2	6.9	7.6	6.9	15.6
Yolo	5,745	5,513	4,470	4.2	28.5	31,041	26,331	5,542	7.6	5.0	5.8	5.5	37.3
Yuba	1,546	1,494	1,155	3.5	33.9	23,022	19,139	1,167	6.2	4.5	3.5	9.6	55.2
COLORADO	174,919	164,673	144,394	6.2	21.1	37,510	33,371	144,091	8.6	5.9	11.4	7.4	15.6
Adams	11,665	10,968	9,811	6.4	(NA)	29,001	26,732	8,525	14.6	7.5	5.7	5.7	12.8
Alamosa	381	364	308	4.7	23.7	24,985	20,568	315	7.2	10.1	7.5	15.6	28.5
Arapahoe	24,898	23,663	21,053	5.2	18.3	47,039	42,829	22,686	8.0	5.3	13.2	7.3	7.9
Archuleta	270	251	192	7.6	40.4	22,715	19,156	149	19.1	14.3	5.2	(NA)	18.1
Baca	115	109	106	5.5	8.6	28,054	23,527	75	(NA)	5.3	(NA)	1.0	28.4
Bent	114	109	106	4.6	7.3	20,518	17,788	59	0.4	4.1	0.9	2.1	50.0
Boulder	12,815	12,006	11,825	6.7	(NA)	45,849	40,362	11,289	5.1	5.0	20.4	7.7	13.5
Broomfield	1,550	1,480	(X)	4.7	(NA)	35,743	(X)	2,050	4.3	7.2	21.4	2.1	3.1
Chaffee	425	406	353	4.7	20.4	25,166	21,649	249	13.8	11.9	5.3	(NA)	28.6
Cheyenne	67	61	52	9.8	27.8	34,577	23,581	50	(NA)	2.9	5.2	(NA)	24.6
Clear Creek	443	419	321	5.7	38.1	48,150	34,449	200	10.4	4.8	5.7	5.2	14.6
Conejos	159	152	132	4.6	20.8	18,875	15,649	65	8.3	8.1	1.6	8.9	34.0
Costilla	76	72	65	5.6	16.7	22,158	17,755	29	(NA)	2.9	(NA)	(NA)	39.7
Crowley	100	86	85	16.3	17.7	18,661	15,344	71	1.6	3.7	(NA)	(NA)	33.6
Custer	102	102	73	–	38.9	26,309	20,892	41	29.0	9.4	7.3	1.5	20.9
Delta	708	669	583	5.8	21.5	23,612	20,881	348	10.3	9.7	(NA)	7.2	28.0
Denver	26,622	25,127	21,746	5.9	22.4	47,652	39,151	34,688	4.8	3.1	12.2	6.7	13.6
Dolores	48	45	37	6.7	28.6	26,535	20,180	23	8.4	4.9	(NA)	0.7	25.5
Douglas	10,961	9,934	7,844	10.3	39.7	43,919	43,470	4,794	13.9	9.4	12.8	5.1	9.8
Eagle	2,108	1,930	1,584	9.2	33.1	44,200	37,770	1,722	17.8	7.4	7.6	6.4	7.7
Elbert	834	794	626	5.0	33.2	36,692	31,122	198	33.0	4.9	8.8	(NA)	19.3
El Paso	18,966	17,670	15,373	7.3	23.4	33,577	29,603	15,632	7.7	6.4	11.9	7.1	30.6
Fremont	1,012	965	867	4.9	16.7	21,231	18,727	637	9.4	6.7	(NA)	9.9	44.8
Garfield	1,566	1,442	1,241	8.6	26.2	31,460	28,054	1,238	20.7	9.3	6.2	7.7	15.2
Gilpin	182	169	164	7.7	10.8	36,826	34,222	254	4.0	0.3	0.8	(NA)	8.0
Grand	442	422	345	4.7	28.1	33,672	27,639	307	22.6	8.3	4.1	2.4	17.5
Gunnison	425	398	314	6.8	35.2	29,972	22,466	358	14.1	9.0	5.0	2.8	21.0
Hinsdale	22	22	19	–	17.4	28,370	23,871	10	20.9	(NA)	(NA)	(NA)	25.9
Huerfano	156	152	131	2.6	19.1	20,146	16,731	73	11.1	8.7	5.6	(NA)	24.5
Jackson	38	34	31	11.8	20.8	26,603	19,941	20	(NA)	10.0	(NA)	(NA)	34.3

See footnotes at end of table.

[Includes United States, states, and 3,141 counties/county equivalents defined as of February 22, 2005. For more information on these areas, see Appendix C, Geographic Information]

County	Total, by place of residence 2005 (mil. dol.)	2004 (mil. dol.)	2000 (mil. dol.)	Percent change 2004–2005	2000–2005	Per capita[1] (dol.) 2005	2000	Earnings, by place of work, 2005 Total[2] (mil. dol.)	Construction	Retail trade	Professional and technical services	Health care and social assistance	Government
COLORADO—Con.													
Jefferson	22,414	21,374	20,198	4.9	(NA)	42,709	38,231	12,923	7.6	7.3	11.7	8.4	16.5
Kiowa	47	44	56	6.8	−15.8	32,990	34,665	35	(NA)	2.3	(NA)	(NA)	23.8
Kit Carson	223	210	190	6.2	17.1	29,158	23,849	162	4.0	5.6	(NA)	2.4	16.9
Lake	176	167	161	5.4	9.4	22,793	20,596	77	14.8	6.2	2.3	(NA)	39.6
La Plata	1,597	1,484	1,211	7.6	31.9	33,807	27,408	1,198	13.8	8.5	7.8	10.9	20.9
Larimer	9,330	8,816	7,657	5.8	21.8	34,323	30,274	6,995	12.3	7.1	12.3	9.5	18.7
Las Animas	377	361	304	4.4	24.0	24,509	19,878	232	13.4	8.1	2.3	7.7	31.4
Lincoln	111	114	105	−2.6	5.2	19,688	17,378	80	3.2	10.4	1.4	(NA)	51.5
Logan	572	525	502	9.0	14.0	27,634	24,290	420	8.0	8.2	3.4	(NA)	24.2
Mesa	3,744	3,472	2,928	7.8	27.9	28,854	24,921	2,619	12.6	9.5	5.0	14.3	17.1
Mineral	25	25	19	–	35.0	27,066	22,100	17	18.9	5.9	(NA)	(NA)	21.8
Moffat	390	363	295	7.4	32.4	29,133	22,360	266	4.7	8.8	(NA)	(NA)	21.2
Montezuma	657	617	537	6.5	22.3	26,516	22,490	377	12.7	10.8	4.3	8.9	32.3
Montrose	1,029	955	744	7.7	38.3	27,402	22,144	754	15.3	8.8	5.1	8.1	18.2
Morgan	701	670	594	4.6	18.0	25,030	21,787	521	8.2	5.2	1.7	(NA)	17.4
Otero	485	469	448	3.4	8.3	24,882	22,099	271	3.3	8.9	2.6	(NA)	25.3
Ouray	150	143	100	4.9	50.2	35,283	26,424	74	30.4	7.4	7.4	(NA)	17.4
Park	496	472	432	5.1	14.7	29,275	29,420	123	23.2	5.4	11.0	1.9	26.2
Phillips	117	109	110	7.3	6.3	25,492	24,669	75	5.3	4.8	(NA)	(NA)	26.9
Pitkin	1,156	1,076	984	7.4	17.5	77,970	66,627	1,040	14.2	7.2	11.5	2.6	9.6
Prowers	352	339	320	3.8	10.1	25,268	22,106	236	3.8	9.0	2.3	5.1	25.4
Pueblo	3,870	3,745	3,262	3.3	18.7	25,634	22,992	2,426	9.5	9.1	3.0	17.4	23.8
Rio Blanco	198	181	159	9.4	24.3	32,993	26,676	186	12.3	6.7	2.1	(NA)	21.3
Rio Grande	328	317	277	3.5	18.4	26,793	22,272	219	6.9	5.5	(NA)	6.4	18.6
Routt	885	831	649	6.5	36.3	41,558	32,746	759	24.4	8.7	6.0	7.8	9.9
Saguache	127	120	91	5.8	39.1	17,999	15,260	69	10.1	5.5	2.1	2.9	28.2
San Juan	16	15	14	6.7	17.6	28,085	24,475	9	8.4	(NA)	(NA)	(NA)	27.5
San Miguel	292	277	226	5.4	29.0	40,570	34,198	242	18.1	6.2	7.2	2.8	14.5
Sedgwick	70	68	65	2.9	7.7	27,641	23,625	38	(NA)	5.9	1.4	(NA)	28.3
Summit	919	885	819	3.8	12.2	36,796	34,626	774	14.4	10.7	7.5	3.3	12.7
Teller	730	690	617	5.8	18.4	33,379	29,832	299	9.5	6.2	6.9	3.6	17.3
Washington	126	120	109	5.0	15.2	27,260	22,100	67	4.3	6.9	1.5	1.1	26.9
Weld	5,669	5,322	4,586	6.5	(NA)	24,846	25,036	4,150	14.9	6.7	3.8	8.3	13.8
Yuma	272	274	233	−0.7	16.6	27,783	23,742	203	3.9	5.4	1.1	(NA)	17.7
CONNECTICUT	165,890	158,567	141,570	4.6	17.2	47,388	41,489	128,707	5.6	6.0	9.7	9.8	12.2
Fairfield	60,615	57,845	52,190	4.8	16.1	67,269	58,986	46,605	(NA)	5.7	11.2	7.1	6.4
Hartford	37,876	35,954	32,152	5.3	17.8	43,266	37,451	36,994	(NA)	5.3	9.4	10.0	12.5
Litchfield	7,900	7,560	6,949	4.5	13.7	41,722	38,041	3,791	12.9	9.4	8.4	11.9	12.4
Middlesex	6,953	6,695	5,898	3.9	17.9	42,705	37,893	4,751	6.5	6.1	6.8	12.6	13.8
New Haven	33,182	31,856	28,379	4.2	16.9	39,292	34,396	23,832	6.4	6.7	9.5	13.7	12.9
New London	10,379	10,029	8,514	3.5	21.9	39,276	32,810	8,439	5.6	5.9	7.8	9.5	31.7
Tolland	5,408	5,190	4,517	4.2	19.7	36,674	32,997	2,327	9.6	7.6	6.3	11.0	34.4
Windham	3,576	3,437	2,971	4.0	20.4	30,889	27,209	1,968	6.6	8.9	4.3	13.1	18.5
DELAWARE	31,218	29,300	24,277	6.5	28.6	37,088	30,869	26,825	(NA)	6.3	11.6	9.6	14.2
Kent	4,045	3,801	3,021	6.4	33.9	28,196	23,767	3,218	(NA)	8.5	(NA)	9.6	38.9
New Castle	21,895	20,568	17,440	6.5	25.5	41,937	34,750	20,386	6.0	5.2	14.0	9.4	10.6
Sussex	5,278	4,931	3,816	7.0	38.3	29,959	24,234	3,221	11.0	10.8	(NA)	11.5	11.9
DISTRICT OF COLUMBIA	30,739	29,125	23,102	5.5	33.1	52,811	40,456	65,430	(NA)	1.0	22.5	4.9	41.5
District of Columbia	30,739	29,125	23,102	5.5	33.1	52,811	40,456	65,430	(NA)	1.0	22.5	4.9	41.5
FLORIDA	604,131	564,997	457,539	6.9	32.0	34,001	28,509	407,351	8.3	8.1	8.8	10.2	16.0
Alachua	6,809	6,287	5,238	8.3	30.0	30,435	24,010	5,692	5.3	6.5	6.6	16.2	38.3
Baker	574	549	431	4.6	33.1	23,396	19,265	279	10.3	6.5	2.0	(NA)	40.7
Bay	4,888	4,546	3,522	7.5	38.8	30,298	23,756	3,620	8.5	8.0	7.4	9.7	29.9
Bradford	621	586	484	6.0	28.3	22,141	18,552	313	5.5	7.1	4.0	(NA)	39.5
Brevard	16,811	15,780	12,865	6.5	30.7	31,800	26,925	11,467	9.0	7.6	8.8	10.8	16.0
Broward	65,213	60,265	50,138	8.2	30.1	36,595	30,709	42,099	8.0	8.6	9.3	8.8	14.6
Calhoun	251	233	207	7.7	21.0	18,859	15,904	110	9.5	9.5	1.5	(NA)	36.7
Charlotte	4,613	4,334	3,650	6.4	26.4	29,890	25,649	1,928	15.2	12.4	6.5	19.0	15.9
Citrus	3,495	3,233	2,635	8.1	32.6	26,072	22,211	1,409	12.1	11.8	5.5	19.0	14.6
Clay	5,018	4,667	3,730	7.5	34.5	29,410	26,329	1,792	13.5	12.6	5.6	13.7	17.8
Collier	15,237	14,550	10,012	4.7	52.2	49,492	39,402	7,352	15.8	9.3	7.2	10.3	9.7
Columbia	1,414	1,306	1,063	8.3	33.0	22,076	18,734	910	5.7	10.5	3.3	11.8	31.1
DeSoto	635	601	531	5.7	19.5	18,113	16,453	373	5.5	13.5	1.3	(NA)	27.2
Dixie	277	253	211	9.5	31.0	18,945	15,297	122	6.0	8.5	2.0	(NA)	34.9
Duval	27,882	26,515	22,549	5.2	23.7	33,723	28,920	28,096	7.5	7.0	7.8	9.6	18.2

See footnotes at end of table.

Includes United States, states, and 3,141 counties/county equivalents defined as of February 22, 2005. For more information on these areas, see Appendix C, Geographic Information]

County	Total, by place of residence 2005 (mil. dol.)	2004 (mil. dol.)	2000 (mil. dol.)	Percent change 2004–2005	2000–2005	Per capita[1] (dol.) 2005	2000	Earnings, by place of work, 2005 Total[2] (mil. dol.)	Construction	Retail trade	Professional and technical services	Health care and social assistance	Government
FLORIDA—Con.													
Escambia	8,387	7,965	6,852	5.3	22.4	28,371	23,279	6,693	6.4	7.8	6.6	13.8	30.4
Flagler	2,076	1,850	1,194	12.2	73.8	27,297	23,610	820	10.4	9.2	4.5	7.4	17.0
Franklin	266	254	205	4.7	29.6	26,133	20,859	151	10.4	12.6	4.6	(NA)	22.8
Gadsden	1,069	1,029	883	3.9	21.1	23,129	19,588	617	8.4	5.8	1.6	4.3	36.6
Gilchrist	385	361	283	6.6	36.1	23,369	19,448	129	6.0	7.1	2.9	(NA)	37.8
Glades	209	195	163	7.2	28.0	18,513	15,391	68	(NA)	6.9	(NA)	(NA)	26.4
Gulf	333	316	242	5.4	37.3	23,836	16,604	177	10.9	5.7	3.4	7.1	34.5
Hamilton	219	210	194	4.3	12.8	15,721	14,569	189	1.9	3.3	0.7	5.1	31.4
Hardee	530	493	447	7.5	18.5	18,752	16,618	327	6.7	6.5	1.4	10.7	23.3
Hendry	839	784	658	7.0	27.5	21,205	18,089	535	6.0	8.5	1.4	5.7	20.2
Hernando	4,108	3,810	3,087	7.8	33.1	25,975	23,475	1,623	11.6	11.5	3.8	18.4	18.2
Highlands	2,250	2,124	1,771	5.9	27.1	23,511	20,246	1,075	7.6	11.5	3.6	17.2	17.2
Hillsborough	37,379	35,135	28,646	6.4	30.5	33,034	28,556	35,815	6.7	7.1	10.2	8.9	13.5
Holmes	411	389	326	5.7	25.9	21,500	17,611	155	8.0	6.3	2.3	(NA)	36.3
Indian River	5,886	5,643	4,208	4.3	39.9	46,219	37,110	2,326	11.9	11.2	7.7	16.1	12.8
Jackson	1,066	986	842	8.1	26.5	21,837	18,013	619	7.3	9.6	2.0	7.4	43.9
Jefferson	352	340	308	3.5	14.4	24,368	23,815	137	10.6	6.9	4.3	(NA)	27.3
Lafayette	124	118	106	5.1	17.3	15,638	14,979	68	2.6	6.0	(NA)	(NA)	44.0
Lake	8,012	7,307	5,460	9.6	46.7	28,942	25,651	3,591	14.7	10.7	6.3	15.0	15.4
Lee	19,905	18,381	12,875	8.3	54.6	36,577	29,006	11,441	16.7	11.0	6.4	8.8	15.1
Leon	7,861	7,514	6,255	4.6	25.7	32,188	26,068	7,108	5.4	6.4	12.4	10.3	38.4
Levy	838	779	628	7.6	33.4	22,036	18,143	371	9.8	10.5	5.0	6.3	23.6
Liberty	155	149	119	4.0	30.6	20,044	16,975	100	(NA)	2.7	(NA)	6.9	34.1
Madison	378	362	312	4.4	21.1	19,889	16,652	190	3.0	7.2	3.6	12.0	30.0
Manatee	10,766	10,003	8,088	7.6	33.1	35,154	30,439	6,260	8.4	9.2	11.4	9.0	10.7
Marion	8,161	7,495	5,894	8.9	38.5	26,893	22,640	4,277	10.3	11.6	4.7	12.8	16.5
Martin	6,963	6,550	5,347	6.3	30.2	49,992	42,065	3,100	10.9	11.6	9.4	13.3	10.0
Miami-Dade	74,534	70,514	57,922	5.7	28.7	31,347	25,626	61,447	6.1	6.9	9.8	8.9	16.2
Monroe	3,498	3,365	2,941	4.0	18.9	45,946	37,009	1,880	6.0	10.8	5.6	6.1	25.6
Nassau	2,366	2,252	1,747	5.1	35.4	36,583	30,144	914	5.9	8.1	5.3	4.2	25.6
Okaloosa	6,393	5,968	4,611	7.1	38.7	35,275	26,977	5,350	5.4	6.9	8.8	5.7	41.6
Okeechobee	833	783	610	6.4	36.4	20,980	17,002	454	8.0	10.2	(NA)	14.6	21.0
Orange	32,260	29,726	24,437	8.5	32.0	31,569	27,084	35,806	7.4	6.2	10.7	8.0	10.4
Osceola	5,095	4,603	3,503	10.7	45.4	22,008	20,109	2,754	10.1	11.6	(NA)	12.1	19.8
Palm Beach	63,718	59,651	48,955	6.8	30.2	50,371	43,102	33,360	8.7	7.5	10.3	11.0	11.2
Pasco	11,214	10,298	7,844	8.9	43.0	26,076	22,581	3,860	11.7	12.3	5.1	17.6	19.2
Pinellas	35,298	33,449	29,314	5.5	20.4	38,085	31,785	22,721	6.0	8.4	8.6	13.4	11.7
Polk	15,659	14,376	11,517	8.9	36.0	28,896	23,723	9,787	7.6	8.0	6.5	11.0	13.3
Putnam	1,600	1,503	1,282	6.5	24.8	21,814	18,195	797	6.7	9.5	2.1	9.5	26.1
St. Johns	6,946	6,365	4,693	9.1	48.0	43,086	37,704	2,446	8.5	9.7	7.3	10.0	15.1
St. Lucie	6,206	5,745	4,302	8.0	44.2	25,861	22,237	3,000	10.7	10.8	4.9	12.5	20.3
Santa Rosa	3,974	3,665	2,851	8.4	39.4	27,897	24,066	1,542	13.8	8.3	6.0	8.7	27.2
Sarasota	17,148	16,283	12,939	5.3	32.5	46,965	39,565	8,305	12.1	10.0	8.1	14.9	9.7
Seminole	15,585	14,330	11,351	8.8	37.3	38,838	30,924	9,674	12.2	10.5	13.4	7.6	9.2
Sumter	1,398	1,251	826	11.8	69.2	21,878	15,422	672	15.8	8.9	1.8	(NA)	32.8
Suwannee	865	820	666	5.5	29.9	22,415	18,993	419	6.6	11.2	3.0	(NA)	20.2
Taylor	451	419	370	7.6	22.0	22,971	19,239	306	7.6	8.3	2.2	(NA)	21.9
Union	232	219	178	5.9	30.1	15,641	13,249	181	3.5	3.3	(NA)	(NA)	63.1
Volusia	13,830	12,971	10,381	6.6	33.2	28,347	23,327	6,952	9.3	10.9	5.8	15.0	16.7
Wakulla	662	619	512	6.9	29.3	23,451	22,266	223	10.4	5.3	7.7	(NA)	30.5
Walton	1,230	1,139	755	8.0	62.9	24,412	18,504	738	18.2	10.0	4.3	7.2	17.5
Washington	473	437	370	8.2	27.7	21,297	17,627	241	8.3	7.6	1.4	(NA)	39.0
GEORGIA	282,322	264,728	230,356	6.6	22.6	30,914	27,989	229,413	6.1	6.5	8.7	7.9	17.1
Appling	386	371	335	4.0	15.3	21,574	19,214	303	5.2	5.9	1.2	(NA)	18.8
Atkinson	161	154	136	4.5	18.5	20,170	17,856	96	1.1	3.5	(NA)	2.9	17.1
Bacon	214	201	192	6.5	11.6	20,502	18,926	138	1.9	6.4	(NA)	(NA)	16.3
Baker	81	79	82	2.5	-0.8	19,672	20,150	28	(NA)	2.6	(NA)	4.4	23.9
Baldwin	1,125	1,066	952	5.5	18.1	24,816	21,285	776	3.4	7.9	1.9	11.5	38.3
Banks	419	403	315	4.0	33.1	26,006	21,668	175	5.0	6.1	1.9	2.0	14.9
Barrow	1,481	1,375	1,082	7.7	36.8	24,722	23,246	661	13.5	9.0	4.0	6.2	17.7
Bartow	2,393	2,261	1,981	5.8	20.8	26,872	25,820	1,644	9.4	7.5	4.0	6.6	13.4
Ben Hill	426	399	360	6.8	18.2	24,502	20,602	353	2.1	5.9	(NA)	(NA)	16.4
Berrien	399	385	341	3.6	17.1	23,843	20,926	207	5.0	8.7	4.7	(NA)	15.5
Bibb	4,812	4,584	4,161	5.0	15.6	31,171	27,053	4,228	4.6	7.3	5.3	18.6	13.2
Bleckley	299	284	253	5.3	18.0	24,467	21,675	171	6.3	6.6	(NA)	4.1	24.6
Brantley	324	312	260	3.8	24.7	20,947	17,685	94	14.1	5.3	(NA)	3.7	31.6
Brooks	370	347	333	6.6	11.0	22,728	20,236	130	3.7	5.7	1.6	7.8	21.0
Bryan	839	757	567	10.8	48.1	29,363	24,087	259	19.5	6.8	5.1	(NA)	25.1
Bulloch	1,294	1,216	1,100	6.4	17.6	20,866	19,595	861	7.3	9.4	3.2	12.0	30.3
Burke	464	444	388	4.5	19.5	20,030	17,407	320	1.9	4.9	(NA)	(NA)	18.0
Butts	517	495	429	4.4	20.4	22,660	21,774	260	7.5	7.7	1.9	(NA)	22.1
Calhoun	114	109	100	4.6	14.6	18,879	15,735	62	2.5	5.1	(NA)	2.6	42.1
Camden	1,177	1,100	916	7.0	28.5	25,734	20,938	991	2.4	5.3	(NA)	4.0	61.8

See footnotes at end of table.

[Includes United States, states, and 3,141 counties/county equivalents defined as of February 22, 2005. For more information on these areas, see Appendix C, Geographic Information]

County	Total, by place of residence			Percent change		Per capita[1] (dol.)		Earnings, by place of work, 2005					
								Total[2]	Percent, by selected major industries				
	2005 (mil. dol.)	2004 (mil. dol.)	2000 (mil. dol.)	2004– 2005	2000– 2005	2005	2000	(mil. dol.)	Construction	Retail trade	Professional and technical services	Health care and social assistance	Government
GEORGIA—Con.													
Candler	222	211	182	5.2	22.2	21,459	18,960	126	8.8	8.6	2.1	14.1	21.1
Carroll	2,531	2,362	1,902	7.2	33.1	24,244	21,605	1,699	8.4	7.4	2.7	11.3	15.9
Catoosa	1,504	1,421	1,201	5.8	25.3	24,759	22,371	684	7.6	10.9	(NA)	14.4	14.8
Charlton	194	186	160	4.3	21.2	18,064	15,585	93	2.8	6.7	1.2	2.5	28.2
Chatham	8,106	7,566	6,459	7.1	25.5	34,053	27,804	6,755	6.0	7.6	5.2	13.4	19.5
Chattahoochee	318	292	236	8.9	34.8	25,619	15,742	1,131	(NA)	0.1	(NA)	(NA)	95.7
Chattooga	524	503	459	4.2	14.2	19,763	17,998	290	4.2	8.5	2.8	(NA)	21.6
Cherokee	5,965	5,372	4,480	11.0	33.2	32,358	31,148	2,215	17.8	10.4	6.8	7.4	15.9
Clarke	2,586	2,445	2,162	5.8	19.6	23,159	21,253	3,016	3.5	6.5	3.5	14.4	35.3
Clay	77	76	67	1.3	14.8	23,742	19,973	29	22.3	5.6	0.2	7.0	41.6
Clayton	5,961	5,763	5,154	3.4	15.7	22,360	21,609	5,934	(NA)	6.5	4.0	7.5	13.1
Clinch	133	129	117	3.1	14.1	18,982	16,985	92	1.7	3.5	2.7	3.5	23.9
Cobb	26,371	24,752	22,321	6.5	18.1	39,744	36,445	20,565	10.5	7.2	12.4	7.2	8.7
Coffee	884	856	771	3.3	14.7	22,336	20,510	708	6.4	11.0	2.0	(NA)	16.9
Colquitt	958	890	810	7.6	18.3	21,833	19,225	571	4.9	10.3	2.2	(NA)	24.4
Columbia	3,656	3,347	2,672	9.2	36.8	35,324	29,751	1,187	11.4	9.7	(NA)	9.7	15.5
Cook	321	302	285	6.3	12.8	19,663	17,964	169	5.9	6.7	3.0	(NA)	19.7
Coweta	3,109	2,908	2,440	6.9	27.4	28,319	27,066	1,337	8.3	10.4	4.4	10.9	17.1
Crawford	319	300	245	6.3	30.5	24,860	19,630	74	16.0	7.2	1.4	4.4	24.9
Crisp	495	472	432	4.9	14.5	22,614	19,652	332	5.2	10.0	2.3	(NA)	18.8
Dade	374	353	316	5.9	18.3	23,167	20,802	146	(NA)	9.5	2.4	3.5	16.7
Dawson	584	547	433	6.8	35.0	29,478	26,571	261	14.2	14.8	(NA)	3.8	15.7
Decatur	635	598	563	6.2	12.8	22,361	19,931	427	3.8	9.7	1.6	(NA)	24.1
DeKalb	24,977	23,749	21,434	5.2	16.5	34,997	32,068	20,471	4.6	6.2	8.2	8.7	15.2
Dodge	402	382	345	5.2	16.4	20,576	18,049	225	3.2	9.9	1.9	(NA)	37.2
Dooly	248	230	219	7.8	13.1	21,210	19,071	156	1.1	5.0	(NA)	(NA)	21.1
Dougherty	2,477	2,349	2,073	5.4	19.5	26,079	21,608	2,564	4.0	7.2	5.3	13.4	24.1
Douglas	3,058	2,821	2,437	8.4	25.5	27,087	26,272	1,495	11.5	13.9	3.6	8.8	15.8
Early	307	293	258	4.8	19.1	25,465	20,874	259	2.4	(NA)	1.2	(NA)	19.1
Echols	73	70	57	4.3	28.2	17,234	15,039	26	(NA)	1.2	1.1	(NA)	22.4
Effingham	1,238	1,099	854	12.6	45.0	26,426	22,588	410	7.9	6.9	(NA)	2.5	23.4
Elbert	494	476	429	3.8	15.3	23,840	20,898	303	3.5	6.5	2.0	(NA)	21.3
Emanuel	487	468	410	4.1	18.7	21,970	18,752	291	2.5	8.4	3.2	(NA)	29.6
Evans	245	237	203	3.4	20.9	21,589	19,164	177	7.3	7.1	1.3	(NA)	16.1
Fannin	520	494	428	5.3	21.4	23,846	21,470	230	13.1	12.8	3.8	(NA)	16.4
Fayette	4,094	3,880	3,383	5.5	21.0	39,291	36,727	1,959	11.6	8.4	7.0	10.2	14.3
Floyd	2,708	2,550	2,110	6.2	28.3	28,698	23,236	2,048	3.1	6.4	3.2	18.6	14.0
Forsyth	4,720	4,301	3,637	9.7	29.8	33,524	36,173	2,475	15.8	5.8	10.1	5.2	10.5
Franklin	542	526	454	3.0	19.4	25,147	22,321	371	5.4	7.9	1.6	(NA)	11.4
Fulton	46,049	42,720	37,497	7.8	22.8	49,291	45,916	62,399	3.8	3.7	15.0	6.1	11.0
Gilmer	647	605	467	6.9	38.6	23,660	19,632	376	8.2	10.0	2.8	5.7	14.1
Glascock	59	57	50	3.5	17.1	22,191	19,714	23	2.6	(NA)	0.3	(NA)	25.5
Glynn	2,455	2,333	1,959	5.2	25.3	34,272	28,945	1,747	6.7	7.8	3.9	9.0	27.2
Gordon	1,256	1,184	975	6.1	28.8	25,007	21,975	1,001	4.4	7.0	(NA)	6.1	13.7
Grady	542	504	446	7.5	21.6	22,104	18,841	260	6.9	8.8	(NA)	(NA)	21.1
Greene	433	414	338	4.6	28.0	27,818	23,391	216	17.0	7.3	3.7	(NA)	17.6
Gwinnett	22,666	21,088	19,008	7.5	19.2	31,186	31,863	19,011	8.7	9.2	9.2	5.4	8.6
Habersham	999	950	792	5.2	26.1	25,219	21,917	627	5.5	8.2	3.8	(NA)	20.2
Hall	4,405	4,133	3,485	6.6	26.4	26,486	24,733	3,396	7.9	7.1	3.6	12.9	12.9
Hancock	173	168	138	3.0	25.2	17,813	13,747	58	2.2	7.7	(NA)	(NA)	52.3
Haralson	679	641	544	5.9	24.7	23,957	21,080	310	(NA)	9.2	3.4	(NA)	22.2
Harris	1,009	907	727	11.2	38.8	36,416	30,534	206	12.8	4.9	4.8	(NA)	22.0
Hart	538	523	487	2.9	10.5	22,474	21,117	310	6.1	6.1	(NA)	7.9	16.5
Heard	233	230	208	1.3	11.8	20,513	18,766	115	20.5	1.4	0.7	(NA)	19.4
Henry	4,512	4,183	3,285	7.9	37.4	26,826	27,002	1,982	10.5	10.3	4.0	9.0	23.0
Houston	3,580	3,347	2,714	7.0	31.9	28,507	24,390	3,254	2.5	5.1	8.0	4.9	59.7
Irwin	211	198	192	6.6	10.2	20,607	19,206	103	5.0	3.8	2.9	(NA)	28.5
Jackson	1,383	1,277	982	8.3	40.9	26,415	23,421	861	7.9	9.7	(NA)	2.0	14.0
Jasper	318	297	255	7.1	24.7	24,173	22,178	118	6.4	3.8	2.4	(NA)	19.7
Jeff Davis	281	274	256	2.6	9.8	21,479	20,112	185	1.7	9.5	(NA)	3.4	17.5
Jefferson	353	348	311	1.4	13.4	21,035	18,036	222	3.4	7.7	1.6	(NA)	20.4
Jenkins	174	161	153	8.1	13.8	19,920	17,776	104	2.2	4.2	0.6	(NA)	21.4
Johnson	183	174	156	5.2	17.6	19,223	18,171	86	4.2	3.4	0.8	(NA)	27.3
Jones	712	672	552	6.0	28.9	26,613	23,310	141	19.4	6.4	3.7	(NA)	30.1
Lamar	402	387	337	3.9	19.2	24,208	21,096	145	4.5	7.3	1.2	4.4	28.2
Lanier	167	156	134	7.1	24.5	22,187	18,461	44	7.8	8.2	1.1	13.6	34.8
Laurens	1,161	1,116	970	4.0	19.7	24,735	21,569	867	7.5	8.0	2.8	(NA)	26.2
Lee	739	683	566	8.2	30.7	23,724	22,723	197	20.7	8.0	2.2	(NA)	26.9
Liberty	1,408	1,297	1,037	8.6	35.8	23,209	16,911	2,015	1.3	2.4	3.1	1.3	80.6
Lincoln	195	188	162	3.7	20.3	23,593	19,390	62	14.4	7.5	1.3	(NA)	26.8

See footnotes at end of table.

Table B-9. Counties — **Personal Income and Earnings by Industries**—Con.

[Includes United States, states, and 3,141 counties/county equivalents defined as of February 22, 2005. For more information on these areas, see Appendix C, Geographic Information]

County	Personal income — Total, by place of residence 2005 (mil. dol.)	2004 (mil. dol.)	2000 (mil. dol.)	Percent change 2004–2005	Percent change 2000–2005	Per capita[1] (dol.) 2005	Per capita[1] (dol.) 2000	Earnings, by place of work, 2005 Total[2] (mil. dol.)	Percent, by selected major industries Construction	Retail trade	Professional and technical services	Health care and social assistance	Government
GEORGIA—Con.													
Long	209	193	155	8.3	34.7	18,776	15,017	35	6.3	2.9	1.5	2.2	50.1
Lowndes	2,489	2,350	1,960	5.9	27.0	25,729	21,279	2,121	5.6	10.2	3.4	9.4	35.1
Lumpkin	611	574	464	6.4	31.6	24,902	21,938	315	6.9	8.0	2.1	(NA)	31.7
McDuffie	564	545	481	3.5	17.3	26,025	22,591	316	6.8	9.0	2.2	6.6	21.4
McIntosh	240	229	192	4.8	24.8	21,801	17,635	81	7.0	14.8	3.2	1.7	29.4
Macon	295	277	255	6.5	15.6	21,490	18,152	194	6.7	4.8	0.7	(NA)	18.7
Madison	722	686	583	5.2	23.8	26,293	22,547	210	14.2	4.9	3.0	(NA)	22.0
Marion	184	170	138	8.2	33.2	25,479	19,231	75	4.1	5.4	(NA)	(NA)	23.0
Meriwether	504	480	459	5.0	9.7	22,153	20,385	240	10.6	6.4	1.4	(NA)	30.2
Miller	153	144	136	6.3	12.1	24,833	21,371	70	5.0	7.3	3.5	(NA)	37.2
Mitchell	478	445	416	7.4	15.0	20,162	17,342	294	3.4	6.8	(NA)	(NA)	22.8
Monroe	680	640	520	6.3	30.8	28,648	23,792	243	11.7	5.5	(NA)	(NA)	29.3
Montgomery	182	177	146	2.8	24.5	20,339	17,671	71	5.2	12.1	(NA)	0.8	25.5
Morgan	515	496	405	3.8	27.2	29,392	26,104	281	7.0	9.2	4.0	2.4	15.3
Murray	902	860	734	4.9	23.0	22,102	19,931	518	2.3	6.5	(NA)	3.4	12.9
Muscogee	5,840	5,444	4,674	7.3	24.9	31,431	25,070	4,811	4.2	6.3	6.8	11.9	24.5
Newton	1,978	1,816	1,485	8.9	33.2	22,857	23,594	963	9.9	6.4	1.8	8.6	18.5
Oconee	1,030	958	766	7.5	34.4	34,597	29,015	362	10.8	9.5	7.9	7.4	15.9
Oglethorpe	333	318	274	4.7	21.6	24,477	21,533	84	8.4	6.3	2.1	(NA)	23.5
Paulding	2,829	2,601	1,959	8.8	44.4	25,135	23,601	803	19.4	11.3	4.7	6.5	24.0
Peach	607	574	514	5.7	18.1	24,801	21,592	345	4.9	11.1	1.2	(NA)	28.5
Pickens	880	819	619	7.4	42.1	30,927	26,509	336	11.7	9.3	4.1	(NA)	16.8
Pierce	383	365	313	4.9	22.5	22,383	19,904	169	11.1	6.4	1.7	(NA)	18.7
Pike	413	388	310	6.4	33.3	25,669	22,452	118	18.6	3.0	3.7	(NA)	22.9
Polk	880	844	717	4.3	22.8	21,754	18,725	484	7.5	7.7	2.3	4.8	17.5
Pulaski	261	251	221	4.0	18.2	26,785	23,004	128	(NA)	8.3	1.5	(NA)	23.2
Putnam	558	520	435	7.3	28.3	28,313	23,053	299	10.7	13.2	2.0	(NA)	19.6
Quitman	57	56	49	1.8	17.3	23,128	18,644	18	(NA)	(NA)	0.3	(NA)	29.6
Rabun	422	396	345	6.6	22.3	25,943	22,872	243	12.0	10.3	2.4	(NA)	16.1
Randolph	156	151	134	3.3	16.1	21,490	17,314	92	5.7	4.7	1.7	(NA)	32.6
Richmond	5,152	4,955	4,411	4.0	16.8	26,539	22,104	5,718	3.9	5.8	3.6	13.1	40.8
Rockdale	2,327	2,205	1,964	5.5	18.5	29,681	27,824	1,571	11.6	10.0	5.4	9.6	10.8
Schley	87	84	75	3.6	16.1	21,219	19,799	59	(NA)	2.8	0.1	(NA)	17.4
Screven	316	301	277	5.0	14.2	20,698	17,995	151	3.5	6.1	1.4	(NA)	26.6
Seminole	216	207	201	4.3	7.3	23,543	21,468	96	(NA)	8.9	(NA)	17.1	20.4
Spalding	1,570	1,498	1,324	4.8	18.6	25,626	22,637	1,035	7.0	8.7	(NA)	12.0	21.0
Stephens	636	615	563	3.4	12.9	25,409	22,102	411	6.7	9.0	2.6	(NA)	18.6
Stewart	111	106	102	4.7	9.1	22,843	19,389	35	0.6	7.2	(NA)	19.8	33.8
Sumter	794	758	699	4.7	13.5	24,431	21,039	552	3.2	6.1	2.8	12.7	22.2
Talbot	139	135	115	3.0	20.7	20,954	17,626	40	15.0	4.4	(NA)	1.6	29.5
Taliaferro	40	38	34	5.3	19.2	21,646	16,158	9	(NA)	(NA)	0.7	(NA)	53.4
Tattnall	494	465	422	6.2	17.0	21,322	18,911	281	3.1	5.4	1.3	(NA)	31.3
Taylor	183	179	162	2.2	13.2	20,781	18,320	92	3.5	7.7	0.4	7.3	23.0
Telfair	233	223	201	4.5	15.7	17,453	17,062	131	(NA)	7.5	(NA)	(NA)	26.6
Terrell	234	224	205	4.5	14.2	21,891	18,670	102	2.5	6.7	3.0	(NA)	27.6
Thomas	1,282	1,183	993	8.4	29.1	28,718	23,168	988	2.8	7.5	3.1	(NA)	16.2
Tift	1,002	937	841	6.9	19.1	24,589	21,887	851	5.1	8.5	3.9	9.6	23.8
Toombs	627	602	526	4.2	19.2	23,070	20,137	404	5.8	10.5	2.8	16.0	15.1
Towns	278	257	213	8.2	30.8	27,085	22,678	123	11.0	9.4	2.5	(NA)	17.0
Treutlen	126	120	106	5.0	19.3	18,670	15,346	42	(NA)	8.4	(NA)	(NA)	35.7
Troup	1,655	1,583	1,419	4.5	16.7	26,427	24,069	1,422	6.7	11.7	1.9	5.7	16.7
Turner	203	192	168	5.7	21.0	21,504	17,637	101	2.6	8.9	(NA)	4.0	23.7
Twiggs	228	215	184	6.0	24.1	22,172	17,342	71	2.8	2.7	0.5	4.3	22.5
Union	505	466	372	8.4	35.9	25,135	21,328	250	9.8	12.9	4.1	(NA)	22.1
Upson	601	575	556	4.5	8.1	21,744	20,113	315	3.6	8.8	2.5	18.9	21.8
Walker	1,528	1,453	1,335	5.2	14.5	23,942	21,833	617	5.3	7.7	(NA)	(NA)	20.4
Walton	2,038	1,855	1,450	9.9	40.6	26,930	23,525	811	14.4	12.4	4.4	6.4	18.9
Ware	805	772	692	4.3	16.3	22,760	19,514	628	5.2	11.2	(NA)	(NA)	23.0
Warren	129	128	113	0.8	14.6	21,280	17,870	57	2.5	5.7	(NA)	(NA)	18.1
Washington	506	493	426	2.6	18.7	25,324	20,143	373	4.2	6.1	2.9	(NA)	23.3
Wayne	664	624	536	6.4	23.8	23,265	20,152	412	7.2	9.4	(NA)	(NA)	31.6
Webster	58	54	47	7.4	23.5	25,724	19,715	25	(NA)	3.9	0.2	0.2	21.0
Wheeler	109	104	91	4.8	20.0	16,293	14,720	50	5.2	3.4	(NA)	(NA)	26.3
White	575	541	459	6.3	25.3	23,917	22,807	278	14.9	10.8	1.8	(NA)	20.0
Whitfield	2,710	2,556	2,136	6.0	26.9	29,747	25,391	2,999	2.1	6.1	11.1	6.8	8.5
Wilcox	186	181	156	2.8	19.4	21,608	18,184	71	2.4	4.3	(NA)	6.7	32.4
Wilkes	235	226	217	4.0	8.2	22,439	20,333	136	4.3	6.9	2.5	5.8	23.9
Wilkinson	223	215	202	3.7	10.3	22,105	19,759	142	4.1	2.4	0.9	2.8	13.3
Worth	529	500	446	5.8	18.5	24,210	20,319	152	5.3	10.5	1.3	(NA)	24.6

See footnotes at end of table.

Table B-9. Counties — **Personal Income and Earnings by Industries**—Con.

[Includes United States, states, and 3,141 counties/county equivalents defined as of February 22, 2005. For more information on these areas, see Appendix C, Geographic Information]

County	Personal income — Total, by place of residence — 2005 (mil. dol.)	2004 (mil. dol.)	2000 (mil. dol.)	Percent change 2004–2005	Percent change 2000–2005	Per capita[1] (dol.) 2005	Per capita 2000	Earnings, by place of work, 2005 — Total[2] (mil. dol.)	Construction	Retail trade	Professional and technical services	Health care and social assistance	Government
HAWAII	43,913	41,129	34,451	6.8	27.5	34,489	28,422	35,326	7.6	6.6	6.0	8.7	31.3
Hawaii	4,426	4,102	3,195	7.9	38.5	26,591	21,404	3,161	(NA)	8.9	(NA)	9.2	22.2
Honolulu	33,316	31,278	26,605	6.5	25.2	36,828	30,392	27,355	7.0	5.8	6.7	8.8	34.9
Kalawao	–	–	–	–	–	–	–	–	–	–	–	–	–
Kauai	1,815	1,695	1,410	7.1	28.7	29,101	24,090	1,360	(NA)	9.4	(NA)	(NA)	20.1
Maui	4,356	4,053	3,241	7.5	34.4	31,156	25,136	3,450	8.6	9.4	3.6	(NA)	15.6
IDAHO	40,706	38,229	31,290	6.5	30.1	28,478	24,075	30,059	8.4	8.6	9.0	8.9	18.4
Ada	13,576	12,498	10,156	8.6	33.7	39,302	33,510	11,539	8.4	7.9	9.3	10.0	13.8
Adams	94	90	75	4.4	24.7	26,612	21,750	42	(NA)	8.5	6.5	2.3	36.9
Bannock	1,979	1,878	1,577	5.4	25.5	25,436	20,857	1,445	7.1	7.9	5.2	8.8	28.8
Bear Lake	134	131	107	2.3	25.0	21,648	16,689	63	4.0	10.1	2.3	3.9	37.7
Benewah	224	212	186	5.7	20.5	24,394	20,213	161	4.0	6.6	1.0	4.6	32.5
Bingham	944	919	806	2.7	17.2	21,569	19,267	600	8.2	6.1	(NA)	3.6	29.4
Blaine	1,106	1,037	821	6.7	34.6	52,245	42,947	736	21.2	9.0	13.5	4.5	8.7
Boise	185	174	145	6.3	27.3	24,856	21,542	62	11.5	3.6	(NA)	(NA)	40.5
Bonner	1,012	939	754	7.8	34.2	24,844	20,361	628	10.0	17.1	6.8	6.3	16.4
Bonneville	2,718	2,538	1,961	7.1	38.6	29,642	23,652	2,191	7.7	9.6	23.9	12.7	12.1
Boundary	199	199	169	–	17.6	18,885	17,045	134	7.9	8.0	4.8	5.8	31.5
Butte	66	68	60	-2.9	10.5	23,603	20,611	320	0.5	0.5	90.7	(NA)	3.1
Camas	28	26	21	7.7	33.9	26,577	21,314	14	4.5	(NA)	(NA)	(NA)	33.9
Canyon	3,365	3,119	2,624	7.9	28.3	20,397	19,712	2,144	11.8	9.8	4.3	9.8	14.7
Caribou	179	178	151	0.6	18.8	25,257	20,607	173	7.1	4.6	3.2	(NA)	14.8
Cassia	538	525	462	2.5	16.5	25,166	21,575	395	4.3	10.3	2.5	(NA)	16.5
Clark	23	25	24	-8.0	-3.7	24,697	23,254	19	2.9	(NA)	(NA)	(NA)	35.2
Clearwater	213	201	175	6.0	21.4	25,585	19,730	133	7.3	7.3	2.2	11.4	38.9
Custer	95	98	98	-3.1	-3.2	23,301	22,622	71	4.2	5.6	3.6	(NA)	29.9
Elmore	730	707	586	3.3	24.6	25,786	20,142	577	2.8	4.9	(NA)	2.5	70.0
Franklin	279	266	212	4.9	31.7	22,472	18,646	138	9.3	7.3	3.1	(NA)	21.1
Fremont	259	252	213	2.8	21.6	21,192	18,068	122	10.4	6.5	4.9	(NA)	36.5
Gem	363	338	295	7.4	23.1	22,289	19,375	117	11.2	8.4	(NA)	(NA)	30.1
Gooding	445	437	333	1.8	33.5	30,857	23,473	325	4.4	3.6	3.0	(NA)	12.6
Idaho	349	337	294	3.6	18.9	22,292	18,972	189	7.9	8.2	3.7	(NA)	32.8
Jefferson	461	446	360	3.4	27.9	21,315	18,744	220	12.8	6.6	2.6	4.2	20.3
Jerome	536	517	402	3.7	33.4	27,249	21,787	411	3.3	8.6	2.8	(NA)	9.5
Kootenai	3,445	3,205	2,521	7.5	36.7	26,970	23,012	2,220	12.1	11.0	6.4	10.3	18.8
Latah	926	897	741	3.2	25.0	26,458	21,248	589	5.2	9.1	6.4	8.2	46.9
Lemhi	184	182	152	1.1	20.8	23,375	19,673	101	9.4	9.7	(NA)	(NA)	42.3
Lewis	104	102	86	2.0	21.6	27,922	22,829	52	4.3	9.2	1.8	(NA)	28.7
Lincoln	97	97	82	–	18.7	21,318	20,143	66	(NA)	1.8	(NA)	7.7	33.7
Madison	515	488	381	5.5	35.3	16,489	13,878	437	5.8	8.9	7.7	(NA)	15.7
Minidoka	382	379	351	0.8	8.9	20,086	17,446	258	4.9	5.6	3.1	(NA)	19.7
Nez Perce	1,083	1,052	931	2.9	16.3	28,504	24,899	911	4.8	9.3	4.2	15.4	18.9
Oneida	80	76	68	5.3	17.3	19,056	16,521	33	4.0	6.8	(NA)	4.4	39.7
Owyhee	244	243	196	0.4	24.2	22,089	18,376	119	7.5	4.8	(NA)	2.8	21.0
Payette	531	502	387	5.8	37.3	24,025	18,737	267	5.5	6.3	(NA)	6.0	16.0
Power	164	167	155	-1.8	5.8	21,154	20,629	137	2.2	3.4	(NA)	(NA)	18.6
Shoshone	340	321	263	5.9	29.1	26,000	19,151	186	5.9	23.8	3.8	5.9	23.2
Teton	179	167	114	7.2	57.3	23,918	18,628	90	20.9	8.6	8.0	3.2	21.6
Twin Falls	1,822	1,721	1,401	5.9	30.0	26,196	21,778	1,331	6.1	10.8	7.1	9.3	18.5
Valley	284	258	212	10.1	33.8	34,126	27,783	179	14.5	10.2	(NA)	3.5	29.2
Washington	228	220	184	3.6	24.2	22,548	18,407	114	4.3	6.4	3.2	5.8	24.6
ILLINOIS	462,928	442,349	400,373	4.7	15.6	36,264	32,185	367,173	6.0	5.6	11.2	8.6	13.8
Adams	2,007	1,936	1,691	3.7	18.7	29,927	24,797	1,462	5.2	8.7	3.8	15.5	13.4
Alexander	172	169	162	1.8	6.2	19,422	16,887	79	1.9	3.8	0.4	(NA)	37.4
Bond	485	473	413	2.5	17.6	26,932	23,380	219	(NA)	4.7	(NA)	(NA)	25.6
Boone	1,391	1,314	1,178	5.9	18.1	27,589	27,993	789	17.4	5.4	2.0	(NA)	11.1
Brown	142	144	113	-1.4	26.1	21,022	16,185	140	3.6	2.1	(NA)	4.6	18.8
Bureau	1,013	1,010	901	0.3	12.4	28,801	25,379	571	6.3	13.1	1.8	(NA)	17.1
Calhoun	133	131	114	1.5	16.7	25,655	22,381	36	8.6	9.7	(NA)	(NA)	29.2
Carroll	427	426	413	0.2	3.5	26,526	24,829	198	7.2	5.3	2.4	(NA)	18.0
Cass	355	360	319	-1.4	11.3	25,659	23,308	247	3.2	5.0	(NA)	(NA)	14.3
Champaign	5,438	5,293	4,579	2.7	18.7	29,441	25,469	4,616	5.4	5.3	6.0	11.9	37.1
Christian	951	940	840	1.2	13.2	27,042	23,752	455	8.8	9.1	2.6	11.9	19.3
Clark	439	438	373	0.2	17.8	25,833	21,936	220	6.5	5.8	2.6	(NA)	15.3
Clay	369	365	315	1.1	17.0	26,169	21,665	260	2.1	4.8	1.9	(NA)	15.6
Clinton	1,107	1,094	946	1.2	17.0	30,635	26,603	503	11.2	10.5	3.5	10.0	22.3
Coles	1,336	1,300	1,204	2.8	10.9	26,173	22,706	1,041	5.1	6.6	(NA)	13.8	27.3
Cook	209,099	199,275	182,394	4.9	14.6	39,423	33,918	190,453	5.0	4.3	14.9	8.0	11.8
Crawford	520	505	452	3.0	15.0	26,111	22,157	378	6.3	5.6	1.5	(NA)	21.2
Cumberland	281	290	259	-3.1	8.6	25,613	22,972	103	5.7	10.9	1.3	10.5	19.0
DeKalb	2,716	2,582	2,327	5.2	16.7	27,778	26,057	1,704	8.8	7.0	5.8	10.1	31.3
De Witt	447	463	426	-3.5	4.8	26,852	25,391	260	5.6	7.4	(NA)	(NA)	17.4

See footnotes at end of table.

County and City Data Book: 2007

U.S. Census Bureau

[Includes United States, states, and 3,141 counties/county equivalents defined as of February 22, 2005. For more information on these areas, see Appendix C, Geographic Information]

County	Personal income Total, by place of residence 2005 (mil. dol.)	2004 (mil. dol.)	2000 (mil. dol.)	Percent change 2004–2005	2000–2005	Per capita[1] (dol.) 2005	2000	Earnings, by place of work, 2005 Total[2] (mil. dol.)	Construction	Retail trade	Professional and technical services	Health care and social assistance	Government
ILLINOIS—Con.													
Douglas	552	556	486	−0.7	13.5	27,873	24,411	370	6.9	10.1	(NA)	(NA)	9.6
DuPage	45,138	43,275	41,923	4.3	7.7	48,472	46,235	40,546	7.2	6.4	13.1	6.4	7.4
Edgar	461	481	460	−4.2	0.2	24,010	23,412	267	3.9	6.7	3.2	(NA)	20.6
Edwards	177	180	154	−1.7	15.1	26,375	22,067	139	3.3	5.4	1.1	2.2	8.5
Effingham	990	991	859	−0.1	15.3	28,691	25,054	827	6.1	9.3	(NA)	15.8	11.3
Fayette	470	462	408	1.7	15.3	21,660	18,695	255	4.8	9.6	2.8	(NA)	25.6
Ford	422	429	381	−1.6	10.8	29,818	26,774	203	6.8	6.9	2.5	(NA)	16.9
Franklin	927	890	761	4.2	21.8	23,336	19,497	407	4.4	10.9	(NA)	8.5	25.3
Fulton	971	956	844	1.6	15.0	25,924	22,081	337	5.8	9.9	2.6	(NA)	31.8
Gallatin	134	139	133	−3.6	0.8	21,769	20,667	50	4.7	6.5	(NA)	(NA)	22.2
Greene	316	335	278	−5.7	13.6	21,877	18,851	125	4.7	8.6	1.8	(NA)	23.4
Grundy	1,336	1,262	1,090	5.9	22.5	30,542	28,936	945	8.8	6.7	(NA)	7.9	11.6
Hamilton	205	201	169	2.0	21.4	24,656	19,632	80	5.1	5.9	1.9	4.6	28.8
Hancock	503	526	479	−4.4	5.1	26,251	23,826	216	6.7	5.4	4.3	(NA)	20.1
Hardin	103	99	90	4.0	14.9	22,000	18,704	42	(NA)	6.1	(NA)	17.4	23.3
Henderson	194	208	188	−6.7	3.3	24,399	22,840	51	(NA)	4.7	1.9	7.1	31.8
Henry	1,460	1,435	1,303	1.7	12.0	28,910	25,527	592	9.6	9.0	2.8	7.2	22.3
Iroquois	808	818	738	−1.2	9.5	26,317	23,547	336	8.7	8.2	2.7	(NA)	18.5
Jackson	1,537	1,466	1,268	4.8	21.3	26,483	21,294	1,241	5.3	7.6	(NA)	11.6	47.1
Jasper	258	278	227	−7.2	13.7	25,956	22,525	126	3.4	7.6	(NA)	(NA)	22.9
Jefferson	1,053	1,013	866	3.9	21.6	26,061	21,618	894	3.5	6.4	3.1	(NA)	13.9
Jersey	652	626	543	4.2	20.1	29,059	25,045	193	8.3	12.3	5.5	(NA)	28.3
Jo Daviess	768	751	626	2.3	22.7	34,115	28,086	366	10.3	7.6	(NA)	(NA)	15.2
Johnson	263	250	215	5.2	22.1	19,994	16,662	106	5.3	5.9	3.3	(NA)	41.4
Kane	15,711	14,833	12,507	5.9	25.6	32,515	30,677	11,249	10.1	6.9	6.9	9.5	14.8
Kankakee	2,941	2,833	2,571	3.8	14.4	27,275	24,744	1,844	6.5	9.1	(NA)	17.0	17.2
Kendall	2,465	2,233	1,720	10.4	43.3	30,972	31,158	1,037	15.2	7.6	3.0	2.7	15.9
Knox	1,357	1,360	1,288	−0.2	5.3	25,442	23,108	872	3.0	8.9	2.4	19.2	18.6
Lake	34,434	32,879	29,976	4.7	14.9	48,906	46,203	24,713	6.1	7.5	8.5	6.3	14.5
LaSalle	3,200	3,075	2,857	4.1	12.0	28,481	25,618	2,007	5.7	9.7	3.7	9.9	15.4
Lawrence	410	404	380	1.5	7.8	25,666	24,696	202	5.1	5.8	1.8	(NA)	17.4
Lee	947	933	834	1.5	13.5	26,584	23,134	620	4.5	5.8	(NA)	14.5	20.1
Livingston	1,156	1,163	1,007	−0.6	14.8	29,666	25,402	712	4.3	6.8	1.9	9.1	21.5
Logan	738	740	689	−0.3	7.1	24,165	22,122	407	2.7	8.3	2.4	10.3	28.0
McDonough	745	742	683	0.4	9.1	23,279	20,780	528	4.1	6.8	2.5	(NA)	49.7
McHenry	10,745	10,116	8,731	6.2	23.1	35,265	33,365	4,986	13.8	8.0	4.9	8.4	13.2
McLean	5,231	5,074	4,410	3.1	18.6	32,905	29,232	4,728	4.8	5.5	(NA)	8.1	13.6
Macon	3,603	3,437	3,130	4.8	15.1	32,808	27,334	2,962	7.4	5.9	3.5	11.9	9.7
Macoupin	1,368	1,316	1,176	4.0	16.3	27,900	23,996	522	8.1	7.6	3.4	8.4	19.7
Madison	8,176	7,773	6,840	5.2	19.5	30,973	26,400	4,708	8.4	7.9	6.5	10.6	16.5
Marion	1,053	1,007	947	4.6	11.2	26,271	22,699	590	4.4	6.2	(NA)	15.7	18.3
Marshall	395	391	340	1.0	16.1	30,079	25,864	150	5.2	4.3	3.1	7.2	14.1
Mason	403	417	384	−3.4	5.0	25,640	23,968	132	4.4	8.0	1.3	4.9	36.6
Massac	384	372	320	3.2	20.2	25,194	21,125	230	2.8	6.3	1.2	5.3	17.2
Menard	385	386	340	−0.3	13.2	30,560	27,163	94	11.7	6.4	4.5	(NA)	27.8
Mercer	479	485	416	−1.2	15.1	28,443	24,534	134	6.8	6.7	1.6	(NA)	34.8
Monroe	1,065	1,023	855	4.1	24.6	34,042	30,774	355	12.4	11.2	8.7	6.9	16.2
Montgomery	743	721	664	3.1	11.8	24,511	21,677	432	4.2	9.3	3.9	12.8	19.9
Morgan	919	925	835	−0.6	10.0	25,715	22,813	608	4.7	7.5	(NA)	12.9	18.7
Moultrie	394	387	333	1.8	18.5	27,301	23,194	196	8.9	7.0	3.5	(NA)	12.5
Ogle	1,505	1,450	1,329	3.8	13.2	27,833	25,980	868	5.1	5.1	4.8	4.9	14.2
Peoria	6,278	5,868	5,157	7.0	21.7	34,486	28,150	5,531	5.7	5.4	13.4	19.9	11.5
Perry	483	475	411	1.7	17.4	21,191	17,838	262	(NA)	7.6	1.6	8.4	24.8
Piatt	536	538	487	−0.4	10.1	32,313	29,742	149	10.0	7.4	4.7	(NA)	23.3
Pike	416	417	356	−0.2	16.9	24,439	20,522	184	5.8	10.1	3.0	(NA)	22.6
Pope	94	92	81	2.2	15.6	22,455	18,382	33	(NA)	2.2	(NA)	(NA)	41.9
Pulaski	145	139	124	4.3	17.4	21,227	16,867	77	5.2	3.6	(NA)	(NA)	44.1
Putnam	188	185	152	1.6	23.5	31,014	25,003	101	(NA)	3.6	(NA)	(NA)	10.1
Randolph	781	767	673	1.8	16.0	23,596	19,854	534	4.5	10.2	1.9	6.6	28.4
Richland	399	400	371	−0.3	7.4	25,217	23,041	261	2.8	7.9	1.4	(NA)	16.1
Rock Island	4,641	4,426	3,984	4.9	16.5	31,475	26,716	4,476	3.4	5.1	4.3	8.0	22.7
St. Clair	7,785	7,412	6,445	5.0	20.8	30,013	25,157	5,069	5.1	6.8	8.2	11.7	32.7
Saline	661	635	547	4.1	20.9	25,383	20,522	434	4.6	6.5	4.0	(NA)	21.0
Sangamon	6,533	6,278	5,656	4.1	15.5	33,904	29,915	5,577	4.9	5.7	6.5	16.4	33.5
Schuyler	198	201	165	−1.5	19.7	28,132	23,017	107	(NA)	4.8	4.0	4.3	18.6
Scott	125	130	114	−3.8	10.1	22,909	20,454	69	38.5	4.1	1.2	(NA)	19.4
Shelby	548	560	501	−2.1	9.3	24,628	21,952	228	4.9	5.8	5.1	9.8	17.3
Stark	168	176	159	−4.5	5.8	27,262	25,143	54	4.3	15.5	5.5	7.5	22.7
Stephenson	1,429	1,395	1,311	2.4	9.0	29,945	26,800	972	10.3	5.1	3.2	11.7	12.7
Tazewell	4,392	4,044	3,629	8.6	21.0	33,888	28,246	3,530	6.8	5.1	(NA)	4.7	8.8

See footnotes at end of table.

[Includes United States, states, and 3,141 counties/county equivalents defined as of February 22, 2005. For more information on these areas, see Appendix C, Geographic Information]

County	Personal income Total, by place of residence 2005 (mil. dol.)	2004 (mil. dol.)	2000 (mil. dol.)	Percent change 2004–2005	2000–2005	Per capita[1] (dol.) 2005	2000	Earnings, by place of work, 2005 Total[2] (mil. dol.)	Construction	Retail trade	Professional and technical services	Health care and social assistance	Government
ILLINOIS—Con.													
Union	439	419	369	4.8	19.1	24,071	20,195	210	4.7	9.0	2.3	(NA)	36.9
Vermilion	2,060	2,023	1,807	1.8	14.0	25,068	21,561	1,419	3.1	6.5	(NA)	9.2	23.8
Wabash	332	331	288	0.3	15.1	26,486	22,359	165	10.1	7.0	3.5	(NA)	23.1
Warren	419	434	380	-3.5	10.2	23,809	20,343	222	2.1	7.1	2.2	(NA)	15.2
Washington	448	451	386	-0.7	15.9	29,960	25,470	281	4.1	8.8	2.1	(NA)	13.3
Wayne	446	442	382	0.9	16.8	26,573	22,287	221	2.5	7.1	1.0	9.5	16.7
White	420	414	368	1.4	14.3	27,571	23,960	218	3.3	12.0	1.8	(NA)	16.3
Whiteside	1,629	1,571	1,493	3.7	9.1	27,269	24,617	914	6.8	8.1	3.0	9.2	20.1
Will	20,255	18,807	15,224	7.7	33.0	31,520	29,948	9,218	13.4	8.2	4.2	8.6	16.4
Williamson	1,723	1,621	1,368	6.3	26.0	27,169	22,335	1,128	6.8	8.4	3.1	14.2	25.9
Winnebago	8,301	7,939	7,544	4.6	10.0	28,464	27,038	6,704	6.1	7.1	4.4	14.1	11.3
Woodford	1,177	1,154	971	2.0	21.2	31,450	27,347	490	8.6	7.1	2.5	21.5	14.7
INDIANA	195,332	187,533	165,285	4.2	18.2	31,173	27,132	149,311	6.5	6.4	5.0	10.0	14.3
Adams	867	859	773	0.9	12.1	25,696	23,004	653	7.2	6.0	(NA)	(NA)	12.5
Allen	10,911	10,472	9,677	4.2	12.7	31,722	29,084	9,372	6.7	6.0	5.3	14.6	10.5
Bartholomew	2,499	2,402	2,183	4.0	14.5	33,955	30,447	2,340	4.0	4.6	4.0	6.9	11.2
Benton	250	256	230	-2.3	8.6	27,723	24,518	105	6.1	6.2	1.2	3.6	24.3
Blackford	325	316	296	2.8	9.8	23,577	21,128	171	3.1	7.9	1.9	8.2	15.5
Boone	2,230	2,142	1,704	4.1	30.9	42,946	36,726	1,084	13.8	4.9	(NA)	6.0	11.9
Brown	476	459	434	3.7	9.6	31,456	28,946	134	(NA)	8.9	7.3	5.6	23.6
Carroll	568	557	548	2.0	3.6	27,767	27,191	255	7.8	5.5	3.1	(NA)	13.9
Cass	1,092	1,073	1,006	1.8	8.6	27,168	24,547	655	5.3	6.7	1.7	5.7	26.0
Clark	3,056	2,883	2,551	6.0	19.8	30,067	26,353	2,081	8.4	9.2	2.1	8.2	17.3
Clay	664	645	597	2.9	11.3	24,498	22,462	321	7.0	8.8	2.3	5.8	16.2
Clinton	873	853	745	2.3	17.2	25,635	21,930	518	4.2	4.9	2.0	6.9	13.9
Crawford	262	256	213	2.3	22.9	23,481	19,734	103	(NA)	3.5	0.9	4.1	20.3
Daviess	824	791	671	4.2	22.8	27,212	22,487	463	10.9	7.0	(NA)	(NA)	17.4
Dearborn	1,523	1,473	1,273	3.4	19.6	31,122	27,473	740	7.2	8.4	(NA)	(NA)	17.7
Decatur	694	669	621	3.7	11.8	27,758	25,266	547	4.0	6.3	(NA)	4.2	12.0
DeKalb	1,164	1,133	1,028	2.7	13.2	27,950	25,441	1,094	4.3	3.9	1.7	(NA)	8.0
Delaware	3,188	3,083	2,898	3.4	10.0	27,431	24,422	2,305	5.4	6.9	5.0	20.1	22.4
Dubois	1,504	1,459	1,189	3.1	26.5	36,752	29,941	1,346	4.6	7.5	1.8	9.3	7.2
Elkhart	6,195	5,896	4,871	5.1	27.2	31,725	26,538	6,653	4.4	4.3	2.6	6.6	5.8
Fayette	661	650	622	1.7	6.3	26,666	24,335	446	2.3	6.8	1.6	13.2	12.9
Floyd	2,551	2,415	2,139	5.6	19.2	35,413	30,175	1,403	8.6	6.7	5.5	10.4	18.8
Fountain	460	449	416	2.4	10.4	26,399	23,231	244	4.0	6.1	1.7	(NA)	15.0
Franklin	648	614	565	5.5	14.7	27,984	25,423	170	11.0	7.1	2.7	(NA)	24.3
Fulton	549	534	476	2.8	15.2	26,678	23,173	325	8.1	7.1	1.8	(NA)	16.1
Gibson	989	959	768	3.1	28.8	29,649	23,593	1,013	2.3	3.2	(NA)	3.7	5.6
Grant	1,815	1,788	1,641	1.5	10.6	25,756	22,401	1,268	3.7	7.1	2.2	12.9	18.1
Greene	859	831	700	3.4	22.7	25,704	21,076	324	6.6	8.1	12.0	(NA)	25.0
Hamilton	10,677	10,054	8,020	6.2	33.1	44,354	44,655	6,185	8.6	8.9	9.8	7.6	8.2
Hancock	2,296	2,178	1,865	5.4	23.1	36,466	33,514	1,066	11.7	6.6	13.8	5.3	16.7
Harrison	1,019	1,007	878	1.2	16.1	27,744	25,442	464	5.8	8.4	(NA)	(NA)	18.5
Hendricks	4,104	3,896	3,242	5.3	26.6	32,246	30,755	1,994	8.8	10.5	5.9	6.5	18.4
Henry	1,265	1,256	1,211	0.7	4.4	26,787	24,991	619	6.2	9.4	2.2	9.0	24.9
Howard	2,606	2,537	2,435	2.7	7.0	30,713	28,659	2,790	2.3	4.9	2.5	5.4	10.8
Huntington	1,046	1,029	964	1.7	8.5	27,469	25,303	637	4.5	6.7	1.9	(NA)	12.2
Jackson	1,174	1,142	960	2.8	22.3	27,777	23,173	987	3.6	7.6	2.0	(NA)	12.9
Jasper	865	837	759	3.3	13.9	27,250	25,138	504	12.1	7.7	9.4	4.7	16.0
Jay	525	520	449	1.0	17.0	24,338	20,574	332	4.3	4.5	1.1	(NA)	15.6
Jefferson	871	829	681	5.1	27.8	26,896	21,477	622	4.5	7.1	(NA)	(NA)	17.5
Jennings	718	693	604	3.6	18.8	25,231	21,825	352	10.9	5.1	(NA)	(NA)	17.3
Johnson	4,134	3,948	3,453	4.7	19.7	31,845	29,768	1,909	9.8	11.0	5.9	10.0	15.5
Knox	1,081	1,051	895	2.9	20.8	28,238	22,828	704	3.0	7.8	3.5	11.2	31.2
Kosciusko	2,437	2,342	1,948	4.1	25.1	32,054	26,245	1,927	3.7	5.2	1.6	5.9	7.1
LaGrange	840	806	684	4.2	22.9	22,795	19,562	647	4.1	4.8	1.1	(NA)	9.9
Lake	14,327	13,695	12,756	4.6	12.3	29,136	26,318	10,028	9.7	8.0	3.8	13.6	13.5
LaPorte	3,002	2,892	2,683	3.8	11.9	27,222	24,346	2,044	7.4	7.3	2.7	12.3	17.8
Lawrence	1,228	1,189	1,088	3.3	12.9	26,500	23,669	661	4.4	8.6	2.9	9.6	18.3
Madison	3,741	3,631	3,305	3.0	13.2	28,688	24,791	2,173	4.4	6.8	2.7	12.8	16.0
Marion	31,270	29,893	26,403	4.6	18.4	36,286	30,685	36,402	6.6	5.4	8.0	10.1	13.1
Marshall	1,264	1,219	1,085	3.7	16.5	26,905	23,977	785	5.0	6.7	(NA)	7.8	12.9
Martin	265	257	235	3.1	12.6	25,680	22,731	515	(NA)	1.2	3.7	0.6	79.6
Miami	889	869	785	2.3	13.2	25,046	21,697	492	5.2	5.6	1.1	7.1	32.4
Monroe	3,496	3,341	2,796	4.6	25.1	28,781	23,176	2,931	5.9	6.2	4.5	12.6	33.3
Montgomery	1,050	1,018	912	3.1	15.2	27,484	24,235	807	4.4	5.5	1.1	(NA)	11.0
Morgan	2,166	2,072	1,774	4.5	22.1	31,049	26,521	651	11.8	10.3	(NA)	8.4	20.6
Newton	360	357	315	0.8	14.1	24,940	21,674	163	5.6	4.5	1.4	4.5	20.1
Noble	1,237	1,199	1,082	3.2	14.4	25,974	23,290	898	3.6	4.7	1.9	4.6	9.8
Ohio	148	142	134	4.2	10.3	25,419	23,781	69	4.0	2.8	(NA)	3.4	18.5
Orange	465	449	412	3.6	12.8	23,583	21,336	252	16.2	6.7	(NA)	(NA)	16.3
Owen	550	537	460	2.4	19.6	24,077	21,003	206	6.5	5.4	2.5	(NA)	17.7

See footnotes at end of table.

Table B-9. Counties — **Personal Income and Earnings by Industries**—Con.

[Includes United States, states, and 3,141 counties/county equivalents defined as of February 22, 2005. For more information on these areas, see Appendix C, Geographic Information]

County	Personal income — Total, by place of residence — 2005 (mil. dol.)	2004 (mil. dol.)	2000 (mil. dol.)	Percent change 2004–2005	2000–2005	Per capita[1] (dol.) 2005	2000	Earnings, by place of work, 2005 — Total[2] (mil. dol.)	Percent, by selected major industries — Construction	Retail trade	Professional and technical services	Health care and social assistance	Government
INDIANA—Con.													
Parke	412	404	352	2.0	17.0	23,934	20,431	139	5.2	6.6	2.0	(NA)	38.2
Perry	509	491	420	3.7	21.1	26,885	22,261	303	5.5	5.6	1.7	(NA)	23.9
Pike	323	316	272	2.2	18.6	25,287	21,245	157	1.3	3.9	(NA)	4.5	16.7
Porter	5,604	5,295	4,555	5.8	23.0	35,605	30,935	2,840	9.1	6.8	4.9	8.7	14.6
Posey	860	831	746	3.5	15.2	32,045	27,565	568	7.9	4.6	4.4	(NA)	10.3
Pulaski	374	372	309	0.5	21.1	27,137	22,456	244	2.6	5.0	1.5	(NA)	18.8
Putnam	990	960	803	3.1	23.2	26,809	22,243	529	3.7	6.1	(NA)	(NA)	23.7
Randolph	681	675	632	0.9	7.7	25,611	23,087	336	6.2	5.1	(NA)	(NA)	16.1
Ripley	740	721	625	2.6	18.4	26,753	23,447	641	5.4	4.6	1.1	7.9	9.9
Rush	516	511	453	1.0	13.9	29,040	24,868	257	6.8	5.5	2.2	4.5	20.9
St. Joseph	8,607	8,278	7,049	4.0	22.1	32,354	26,515	6,890	5.1	6.7	6.5	12.7	10.4
Scott	584	559	496	4.5	17.8	24,571	21,515	296	2.5	8.6	(NA)	(NA)	19.7
Shelby	1,340	1,299	1,162	3.2	15.3	30,617	26,651	789	7.3	6.0	(NA)	(NA)	15.6
Spencer	589	569	489	3.5	20.5	28,778	23,947	337	4.2	4.1	(NA)	(NA)	12.9
Starke	497	485	440	2.5	12.8	21,667	18,704	164	5.0	9.6	1.8	(NA)	24.4
Steuben	921	895	849	2.9	8.4	27,352	25,495	634	4.5	8.3	(NA)	(NA)	11.5
Sullivan	492	484	423	1.7	16.2	22,699	19,463	237	3.6	6.8	2.2	4.6	39.4
Switzerland	232	215	193	7.9	20.4	23,922	21,192	96	(NA)	2.8	(NA)	4.4	19.9
Tippecanoe	4,411	4,169	3,614	5.8	22.0	28,639	24,232	4,176	4.5	5.7	3.4	11.8	29.3
Tipton	522	516	494	1.2	5.7	31,784	29,830	200	7.7	8.3	3.5	(NA)	26.1
Union	201	197	166	2.0	21.3	27,767	22,537	75	5.2	6.7	2.6	(NA)	26.7
Vanderburgh	5,908	5,642	4,860	4.7	21.6	34,194	28,281	5,494	8.6	6.8	5.5	14.1	9.3
Vermillion	454	442	387	2.7	17.2	27,402	23,078	261	7.1	8.1	(NA)	(NA)	13.0
Vigo	2,818	2,714	2,364	3.8	19.2	27,425	22,363	2,348	5.8	8.7	3.1	15.0	21.0
Wabash	941	920	869	2.3	8.3	27,867	24,840	579	5.7	6.1	2.7	(NA)	14.5
Warren	226	226	192	–	17.4	25,802	22,781	82	3.7	5.1	1.2	11.1	22.2
Warrick	1,895	1,802	1,497	5.2	26.5	33,586	28,480	728	9.1	4.8	3.2	12.8	12.4
Washington	707	683	616	3.5	14.8	25,408	22,590	287	6.7	6.8	2.2	5.0	23.5
Wayne	1,828	1,801	1,705	1.5	7.2	26,422	24,004	1,366	3.6	8.3	(NA)	14.9	16.2
Wells	778	755	716	3.0	8.7	27,738	25,912	482	4.7	6.0	1.9	11.6	12.6
White	628	615	603	2.1	4.2	25,651	23,877	330	4.8	11.8	(NA)	(NA)	20.4
Whitley	931	890	818	4.6	13.8	28,926	26,598	494	4.7	6.7	1.2	6.2	13.4
IOWA	93,919	91,230	77,763	2.9	20.8	31,670	26,554	71,011	6.5	7.0	4.3	9.7	16.4
Adair	228	239	206	−4.6	10.9	29,222	25,040	133	6.4	4.8	2.5	5.7	15.4
Adams	115	125	107	−8.0	7.6	27,297	23,870	61	(NA)	5.6	2.7	16.8	17.1
Allamakee	378	372	323	1.6	17.1	25,579	21,996	242	5.4	7.6	2.0	(NA)	16.4
Appanoose	322	321	280	0.3	15.1	23,705	20,409	196	2.9	8.1	(NA)	11.5	17.8
Audubon	198	206	164	−3.9	20.8	31,100	24,072	112	5.0	4.9	(NA)	5.7	15.6
Benton	772	750	648	2.9	19.1	28,649	25,576	280	9.7	9.3	2.3	5.4	23.8
Black Hawk	3,830	3,702	3,118	3.5	22.8	30,406	24,375	3,378	4.8	7.1	4.4	12.3	16.2
Boone	835	810	713	3.1	17.1	31,499	27,165	435	6.8	6.6	2.9	(NA)	25.7
Bremer	761	739	612	3.0	24.4	32,245	26,263	426	6.4	6.1	2.3	(NA)	15.7
Buchanan	584	568	488	2.8	19.6	27,778	23,172	296	7.1	7.5	1.7	(NA)	23.4
Buena Vista	541	553	482	−2.2	12.2	26,898	23,677	406	3.6	7.1	2.6	(NA)	16.5
Butler	415	417	352	−0.5	17.8	27,578	22,996	167	6.0	5.3	2.3	(NA)	18.0
Calhoun	283	294	253	−3.7	11.7	26,957	22,845	141	3.5	7.6	2.2	(NA)	24.0
Carroll	640	648	554	−1.2	15.6	30,445	25,915	479	5.1	9.2	(NA)	(NA)	11.1
Cass	402	406	355	−1.0	13.2	28,407	24,180	240	9.3	9.5	(NA)	(NA)	25.7
Cedar	562	554	496	1.4	13.2	30,823	27,245	226	7.0	7.3	4.8	(NA)	19.5
Cerro Gordo	1,455	1,409	1,217	3.3	19.6	32,628	26,261	1,149	7.8	8.5	3.3	20.7	12.3
Cherokee	360	370	313	−2.7	15.2	29,430	24,005	242	7.6	6.8	3.0	(NA)	19.4
Chickasaw	354	351	324	0.9	9.4	28,370	24,765	206	7.2	7.2	1.9	(NA)	13.3
Clarke	237	234	200	1.3	18.2	26,007	21,803	175	(NA)	6.4	(NA)	(NA)	16.8
Clay	504	500	444	0.8	13.5	29,950	25,551	393	4.8	12.3	(NA)	9.6	18.9
Clayton	500	506	439	−1.2	13.9	27,415	23,578	282	13.0	6.1	1.9	(NA)	19.8
Clinton	1,407	1,347	1,198	4.5	17.5	28,283	23,913	970	6.5	7.5	2.1	13.9	11.5
Crawford	444	444	368	–	20.7	26,314	21,721	328	6.0	6.1	2.1	7.0	16.5
Dallas	1,824	1,718	1,238	6.2	47.3	35,156	30,162	1,131	10.6	9.5	3.1	4.4	9.6
Davis	200	204	175	−2.0	14.3	23,210	20,457	101	5.0	7.1	(NA)	(NA)	24.7
Decatur	181	177	158	2.3	14.5	20,961	18,211	96	4.3	5.3	(NA)	(NA)	24.8
Delaware	519	503	431	3.2	20.4	28,954	23,424	313	6.1	6.3	(NA)	(NA)	16.4
Des Moines	1,239	1,203	1,100	3.0	12.6	30,231	26,021	1,031	5.0	7.7	3.0	14.0	11.3
Dickinson	569	570	485	−0.2	17.4	33,970	29,430	369	8.9	10.1	(NA)	7.3	13.3
Dubuque	2,808	2,696	2,293	4.2	22.5	30,650	25,690	2,372	5.6	7.8	3.5	13.5	8.5
Emmet	301	302	261	−0.3	15.2	28,590	23,772	197	6.9	7.3	3.2	11.3	17.9
Fayette	540	531	470	1.7	14.9	25,477	21,364	320	3.7	6.3	2.2	(NA)	16.6
Floyd	471	462	375	1.9	25.6	28,638	22,241	274	6.2	6.4	(NA)	(NA)	16.2
Franklin	303	317	268	−4.4	13.2	28,123	25,041	182	6.9	4.8	2.7	4.9	16.8
Fremont	231	237	206	−2.5	12.1	30,066	25,752	164	1.2	5.7	1.5	(NA)	11.8
Greene	278	283	231	−1.8	20.5	27,877	22,300	146	5.3	5.9	4.3	5.2	24.5
Grundy	396	395	326	0.3	21.4	32,152	26,364	196	14.7	5.9	1.9	(NA)	13.5
Guthrie	337	343	273	−1.7	23.5	29,506	24,048	144	9.1	4.4	2.3	6.0	22.3
Hamilton	496	492	426	0.8	16.3	30,552	25,957	382	3.3	3.9	1.7	(NA)	12.9

See footnotes at end of table.

[Includes United States, states, and 3,141 counties/county equivalents defined as of February 22, 2005. For more information on these areas, see Appendix C, Geographic Information]

County	Personal income Total, by place of residence 2005 (mil. dol.)	2004 (mil. dol.)	2000 (mil. dol.)	Percent change 2004–2005	2000–2005	Per capita[1] (dol.) 2005	2000	Earnings, by place of work, 2005 Total[2] (mil. dol.)	Construc-tion	Retail trade	Profes-sional and tech-nical services	Health care and social assis-tance	Govern-ment
IOWA—Con.													
Hancock	368	376	314	−2.1	17.3	31,269	25,926	362	2.2	2.8	1.6	(NA)	7.9
Hardin	503	505	437	−0.4	15.2	28,057	23,195	331	5.5	6.3	2.2	(NA)	21.6
Harrison	431	434	384	−0.7	12.1	27,326	24,478	163	4.0	7.7	(NA)	(NA)	23.4
Henry	562	542	479	3.7	17.3	27,599	23,589	482	3.9	5.2	5.4	(NA)	17.7
Howard	283	274	236	3.3	19.9	29,062	23,812	205	3.8	5.5	1.7	(NA)	14.9
Humboldt	299	305	263	−2.0	13.9	29,932	25,311	183	5.4	6.0	2.3	(NA)	15.9
Ida	214	220	182	−2.7	17.7	29,102	23,288	160	6.4	4.9	1.5	(NA)	11.1
Iowa	531	525	451	1.1	17.8	33,079	28,690	472	3.9	5.6	2.8	(NA)	9.1
Jackson	535	527	452	1.5	18.3	26,412	22,266	239	6.8	9.6	2.6	(NA)	21.7
Jasper	1,074	1,085	968	−1.0	11.0	28,622	25,974	642	4.7	8.2	3.4	5.4	18.2
Jefferson	458	448	434	2.2	5.5	28,649	26,864	343	3.9	14.7	8.7	(NA)	14.5
Johnson	4,050	3,876	3,251	4.5	24.6	34,556	29,216	3,739	5.4	5.9	3.0	6.8	42.9
Jones	494	490	437	0.8	13.1	24,095	21,609	253	6.2	11.1	3.0	8.5	24.2
Keokuk	296	305	263	−3.0	12.4	26,648	23,046	116	6.5	7.1	2.1	7.2	21.1
Kossuth	513	511	421	0.4	21.8	31,732	24,589	340	5.5	6.3	3.4	(NA)	13.6
Lee	1,022	992	888	3.0	15.1	27,997	23,406	787	6.5	7.0	(NA)	9.7	15.2
Linn	7,016	6,690	6,027	4.9	16.4	35,158	31,350	6,267	6.5	7.3	5.0	9.4	10.3
Louisa	339	331	283	2.4	19.6	28,705	23,284	163	3.7	3.4	(NA)	4.2	20.2
Lucas	228	225	204	1.3	11.8	23,671	21,664	142	6.2	7.3	(NA)	6.0	21.7
Lyon	308	307	264	0.3	16.7	26,363	22,458	164	4.7	5.1	6.3	5.8	15.1
Madison	447	440	350	1.6	27.6	29,495	24,904	175	10.5	7.6	3.6	6.1	21.6
Mahaska	637	622	550	2.4	15.8	28,562	24,650	350	6.7	7.8	3.8	5.8	16.8
Marion	951	916	849	3.8	12.0	29,064	26,439	830	3.5	4.7	1.4	7.9	11.7
Marshall	1,208	1,165	1,002	3.7	20.5	30,515	25,485	872	4.4	6.1	2.2	10.3	17.4
Mills	532	512	420	3.9	26.7	34,841	28,822	188	6.5	8.1	3.5	(NA)	42.5
Mitchell	301	302	260	−0.3	15.9	27,672	23,900	181	5.2	4.3	2.3	(NA)	16.2
Monona	243	253	228	−4.0	6.7	25,589	22,767	122	6.9	7.8	2.3	18.1	26.0
Monroe	222	219	197	1.4	12.5	28,527	24,683	117	(NA)	6.4	1.8	6.0	19.5
Montgomery	311	314	290	−1.0	7.3	27,401	24,590	207	6.0	5.8	3.3	(NA)	19.6
Muscatine	1,391	1,342	1,088	3.7	27.9	32,677	26,023	1,184	3.3	4.8	(NA)	5.1	10.8
O'Brien	432	429	368	0.7	17.3	30,007	24,453	250	4.4	6.6	2.8	14.9	16.1
Osceola	174	182	159	−4.4	9.4	26,136	22,781	107	6.4	3.7	(NA)	(NA)	13.1
Page	453	450	392	0.7	15.4	27,780	23,185	276	3.5	8.7	(NA)	(NA)	24.3
Palo Alto	266	266	232	–	14.6	27,471	22,885	168	2.6	7.2	1.5	(NA)	22.3
Plymouth	778	767	654	1.4	19.0	31,261	26,301	526	4.3	5.7	2.3	5.0	11.7
Pocahontas	214	227	200	−5.7	7.2	27,006	23,169	121	2.6	4.7	(NA)	(NA)	19.1
Polk	15,755	15,003	12,299	5.0	28.1	39,215	32,728	15,391	8.5	6.3	6.3	9.6	12.6
Pottawattamie	2,723	2,623	2,249	3.8	21.1	30,366	25,564	1,687	8.9	9.3	3.1	11.6	14.8
Poweshiek	591	584	506	1.2	16.8	31,210	26,847	456	9.3	4.6	3.3	(NA)	8.4
Ringgold	130	134	115	−3.0	13.3	24,739	20,992	73	10.1	6.0	2.0	(NA)	27.2
Sac	314	328	264	−4.3	18.9	29,480	23,010	166	2.9	4.9	1.9	10.0	15.0
Scott	5,644	5,367	4,469	5.2	26.3	35,018	28,157	4,224	6.0	8.6	8.2	12.5	10.0
Shelby	371	369	317	0.5	17.1	29,559	24,212	204	6.0	7.4	3.3	(NA)	19.1
Sioux	948	933	762	1.6	24.5	29,308	24,120	790	6.1	4.6	2.3	5.8	10.8
Story	2,553	2,453	2,067	4.1	23.5	32,002	25,826	2,132	5.3	5.9	4.2	7.3	43.0
Tama	474	486	403	−2.5	17.5	26,414	22,318	234	3.5	4.7	1.4	(NA)	38.9
Taylor	167	172	146	−2.9	14.2	25,539	20,919	89	1.7	3.3	2.4	5.2	19.9
Union	317	310	271	2.3	17.2	26,430	22,033	235	4.0	8.1	(NA)	8.8	23.5
Van Buren	177	181	157	−2.2	12.4	22,854	20,125	84	3.1	4.6	1.5	3.9	28.8
Wapello	971	942	779	3.1	24.6	26,994	21,684	734	4.3	8.1	2.6	14.9	16.4
Warren	1,388	1,320	1,058	5.2	31.2	32,153	25,934	390	11.0	10.9	3.6	10.0	22.7
Washington	651	646	565	0.8	15.3	30,469	27,245	293	12.8	8.4	2.7	(NA)	20.1
Wayne	154	153	136	0.7	13.5	23,580	20,147	76	3.0	5.9	3.1	5.7	29.1
Webster	1,117	1,097	963	1.8	16.0	28,663	23,960	868	5.5	7.6	3.3	14.8	16.7
Winnebago	307	309	258	−0.6	19.2	27,028	21,906	204	7.2	7.1	1.6	(NA)	15.7
Winneshiek	661	653	521	1.2	27.0	31,150	24,439	499	11.4	6.0	2.5	(NA)	16.1
Woodbury	2,955	2,841	2,653	4.0	11.4	28,824	25,544	2,222	6.0	8.5	3.9	16.2	15.9
Worth	192	191	173	0.5	11.1	24,783	21,848	83	(NA)	5.2	2.1	5.3	18.9
Wright	457	458	385	−0.2	18.7	33,635	26,882	271	7.1	4.8	2.2	5.1	18.5
KANSAS	90,320	85,520	74,570	5.6	21.1	32,866	27,694	69,918	5.4	6.2	6.4	9.2	19.8
Allen	347	343	295	1.2	17.8	25,279	20,485	236	4.0	7.0	1.7	(NA)	24.8
Anderson	195	186	168	4.8	16.4	23,893	20,684	86	6.6	9.3	1.9	(NA)	25.3
Atchison	408	392	343	4.1	18.9	24,345	20,466	289	5.9	7.0	3.3	(NA)	15.4
Barber	130	121	106	7.4	22.1	26,371	20,117	79	4.4	6.2	(NA)	3.1	29.0
Barton	867	807	681	7.4	27.3	31,460	24,218	609	6.4	8.3	(NA)	(NA)	15.0
Bourbon	374	364	318	2.7	17.6	25,001	20,662	258	(NA)	6.5	4.0	(NA)	18.0
Brown	290	275	240	5.5	20.9	28,355	22,401	206	2.4	5.0	1.8	12.1	36.4
Butler	1,885	1,787	1,579	5.5	19.4	30,228	26,445	803	8.6	7.8	3.4	10.6	27.8
Chase	103	96	82	7.3	25.4	33,696	27,079	56	(NA)	3.0	4.3	4.9	18.5
Chautauqua	104	102	92	2.0	13.1	25,405	21,131	41	8.7	7.2	1.6	15.4	24.6

See footnotes at end of table.

Table B-9. Counties — **Personal Income and Earnings by Industries**—Con.

[Includes United States, states, and 3,141 counties/county equivalents defined as of February 22, 2005. For more information on these areas, see Appendix C, Geographic Information]

County	Personal income Total, by place of residence 2005 (mil. dol.)	2004 (mil. dol.)	2000 (mil. dol.)	Percent change 2004–2005	Percent change 2000–2005	Per capita[1] (dol.) 2005	Per capita 2000	Earnings, by place of work, 2005 Total[2] (mil. dol.)	Percent, by selected major industries Construction	Retail trade	Professional and technical services	Health care and social assistance	Government
KANSAS—Con.													
Cherokee	541	523	448	3.4	20.7	25,188	19,869	294	9.7	5.4	4.4	(NA)	17.4
Cheyenne	65	49	69	32.7	-5.5	22,232	21,777	35	4.9	6.1	(NA)	13.9	25.7
Clark	64	56	54	14.3	19.4	28,531	22,470	38	(NA)	5.1	6.7	(NA)	41.5
Clay	268	256	217	4.7	23.5	31,163	24,574	141	7.1	15.0	2.8	8.7	23.6
Cloud	244	235	208	3.8	17.1	25,117	20,385	139	(NA)	10.4	2.2	(NA)	22.6
Coffey	287	265	222	8.3	29.3	33,134	25,002	248	2.7	3.7	1.1	1.6	18.9
Comanche	44	38	41	15.8	7.7	22,757	20,884	25	2.9	5.8	(NA)	(NA)	36.3
Cowley	951	921	819	3.3	16.2	27,097	22,567	617	3.6	6.6	(NA)	(NA)	24.9
Crawford	965	928	807	4.0	19.6	25,330	21,115	659	2.7	6.7	1.6	(NA)	31.7
Decatur	83	70	77	18.6	7.5	26,259	22,303	38	(NA)	6.9	(NA)	16.0	25.3
Dickinson	507	487	449	4.1	13.0	26,432	23,155	262	4.3	8.2	(NA)	4.0	23.6
Doniphan	182	177	163	2.8	12.0	23,211	19,704	110	4.9	4.3	1.0	3.7	26.3
Douglas	3,166	3,012	2,423	5.1	30.6	28,394	24,206	2,242	6.5	6.1	5.5	6.5	36.0
Edwards	94	90	86	4.4	8.9	29,036	25,183	60	2.7	4.0	0.8	6.8	15.9
Elk	70	68	64	2.9	10.0	22,359	19,722	26	(NA)	4.7	1.2	2.6	48.2
Ellis	871	835	679	4.3	28.2	32,436	24,773	683	4.4	9.1	3.0	18.2	22.5
Ellsworth	166	159	141	4.4	17.8	26,390	21,579	100	(NA)	4.8	4.1	7.6	37.2
Finney	892	870	836	2.5	6.7	22,827	20,586	743	6.8	9.7	2.9	(NA)	19.5
Ford	842	792	699	6.3	20.5	24,965	21,443	690	3.2	7.2	2.2	(NA)	18.3
Franklin	688	666	573	3.3	20.0	26,281	23,053	391	5.6	10.0	(NA)	(NA)	20.0
Geary	846	805	660	5.1	28.1	34,784	23,807	1,290	1.9	2.8	2.7	1.6	80.2
Gove	82	68	75	20.6	9.0	29,833	24,533	51	4.6	8.0	(NA)	3.3	30.5
Graham	93	73	77	27.4	20.2	34,272	26,480	62	(NA)	6.4	(NA)	7.0	22.4
Grant	215	199	173	8.0	24.5	28,503	21,896	190	8.2	4.1	3.4	(NA)	15.6
Gray	188	166	148	13.3	26.8	31,917	25,086	145	9.2	2.8	2.7	2.6	21.3
Greeley	39	36	36	8.3	8.2	28,805	23,408	28	(NA)	5.2	0.6	(NA)	21.2
Greenwood	182	174	161	4.6	13.2	24,818	20,975	82	3.6	5.6	1.9	(NA)	24.3
Hamilton	83	75	65	10.7	26.9	31,909	24,587	64	(NA)	2.8	1.0	(NA)	21.5
Harper	175	156	148	12.2	18.6	28,962	22,697	105	3.1	8.0	2.0	3.4	28.2
Harvey	1,011	963	830	5.0	21.8	29,977	25,236	709	6.4	7.3	3.2	(NA)	11.4
Haskell	151	141	124	7.1	22.0	35,924	28,754	118	2.2	1.8	1.3	0.7	18.5
Hodgeman	63	54	52	16.7	21.8	30,268	24,819	37	(NA)	2.5	0.4	0.2	28.1
Jackson	386	375	310	2.9	24.6	28,697	24,422	201	(NA)	8.4	2.6	(NA)	26.0
Jefferson	501	483	418	3.7	19.7	26,424	22,659	145	28.7	3.3	1.5	(NA)	31.7
Jewell	94	90	76	4.4	23.3	28,254	20,246	49	(NA)	5.6	1.2	1.2	31.9
Johnson	24,358	23,072	20,079	5.6	21.3	48,123	44,170	19,498	5.6	6.4	13.8	8.1	8.4
Kearny	101	95	91	6.3	11.6	22,449	20,084	63	(NA)	1.3	(NA)	1.6	37.6
Kingman	221	207	190	6.8	16.3	27,137	21,901	109	9.4	5.4	3.0	10.8	19.6
Kiowa	91	87	74	4.6	23.0	30,347	22,734	50	(NA)	5.1	1.2	(NA)	28.2
Labette	588	559	479	5.2	22.8	26,539	21,054	373	(NA)	6.1	(NA)	10.7	31.7
Lane	62	48	54	29.2	14.1	33,116	25,329	40	(NA)	3.9	(NA)	(NA)	22.4
Leavenworth	2,075	1,992	1,695	4.2	22.4	28,521	24,572	1,512	6.8	3.8	7.1	(NA)	55.8
Lincoln	75	71	73	5.6	3.4	21,954	20,282	33	8.6	8.0	1.8	(NA)	43.5
Linn	245	238	202	2.9	21.1	24,654	21,061	99	9.4	5.6	1.2	2.0	28.9
Logan	79	60	59	31.7	34.7	28,523	19,242	51	2.6	5.7	2.3	4.0	29.8
Lyon	877	849	743	3.3	18.0	24,652	20,664	690	3.1	6.3	(NA)	6.3	28.7
McPherson	941	886	760	6.2	23.8	31,890	25,685	742	10.0	4.6	1.9	8.7	10.8
Marion	301	294	261	2.4	15.3	23,336	19,518	143	3.2	6.1	2.7	(NA)	26.1
Marshall	337	332	272	1.5	24.1	32,331	24,834	246	3.2	6.0	(NA)	7.1	11.7
Meade	125	117	112	6.8	11.7	27,240	24,161	75	3.9	3.5	(NA)	(NA)	27.8
Miami	958	898	745	6.7	28.5	31,522	26,151	329	15.2	11.4	3.3	10.7	29.0
Mitchell	182	175	157	4.0	15.9	28,402	22,718	137	3.6	11.8	1.6	(NA)	26.2
Montgomery	915	870	766	5.2	19.5	26,445	21,154	657	3.3	6.3	1.9	12.1	15.8
Morris	155	148	133	4.7	16.6	25,552	21,750	67	6.1	6.4	(NA)	4.8	28.5
Morton	84	70	73	20.0	14.4	26,313	21,099	58	(NA)	5.8	(NA)	1.7	44.6
Nemaha	311	306	259	1.6	20.1	29,984	24,221	191	5.0	5.1	3.1	10.6	15.4
Neosho	414	404	348	2.5	18.9	25,086	20,543	300	4.5	8.7	2.5	8.5	23.4
Ness	106	95	91	11.6	17.0	35,449	26,316	63	4.2	6.4	1.7	1.1	25.9
Norton	144	137	129	5.1	11.3	25,554	21,728	102	3.5	9.6	2.1	9.3	38.1
Osage	424	411	362	3.2	17.0	24,880	21,617	105	7.9	8.5	1.8	7.8	45.0
Osborne	102	96	91	6.3	12.2	25,371	20,507	59	3.5	8.5	5.6	8.0	19.9
Ottawa	149	142	137	4.9	8.6	24,217	22,150	53	5.5	5.0	2.4	13.1	30.5
Pawnee	194	183	163	6.0	18.8	29,027	22,611	151	3.0	3.5	2.0	5.7	58.0
Phillips	165	154	146	7.1	13.4	30,143	24,253	110	2.7	4.6	2.5	5.9	23.4
Pottawatomie	572	538	438	6.3	30.7	30,019	23,927	361	9.7	10.6	(NA)	(NA)	13.6
Pratt	280	264	237	6.1	18.4	29,552	24,562	193	4.8	8.5	3.1	(NA)	23.5
Rawlins	79	62	65	27.4	21.8	29,437	21,920	46	4.2	5.0	(NA)	7.0	26.9
Reno	1,723	1,650	1,549	4.4	11.2	27,109	23,953	1,161	5.4	8.3	3.0	16.0	19.6
Republic	124	122	116	1.6	6.6	24,164	20,042	73	5.8	6.3	3.1	10.4	29.4
Rice	231	223	226	3.6	2.0	22,176	21,095	131	3.0	5.1	2.4	(NA)	27.0

See footnotes at end of table.

Table B-9. Counties — **Personal Income and Earnings by Industries**—Con.

[Includes United States, states, and 3,141 counties/county equivalents defined as of February 22, 2005. For more information on these areas, see Appendix C, Geographic Information]

County	Personal income							Earnings, by place of work, 2005					
	Total, by place of residence					Per capita[1] (dol.)			Percent, by selected major industries				
				Percent change									
	2005 (mil. dol.)	2004 (mil. dol.)	2000 (mil. dol.)	2004–2005	2000–2005	2005	2000	Total[2] (mil. dol.)	Construction	Retail trade	Professional and technical services	Health care and social assistance	Government
KANSAS—Con.													
Riley	1,968	1,851	1,390	6.3	41.6	31,820	22,142	1,259	4.3	6.3	3.0	9.6	52.2
Rooks	140	130	124	7.7	12.5	26,378	21,978	87	2.8	10.2	(NA)	2.6	28.6
Rush	88	77	78	14.3	13.3	25,951	21,933	50	1.4	2.9	3.0	(NA)	25.6
Russell	176	163	173	8.0	1.7	25,822	23,530	95	2.8	6.9	2.1	12.3	24.0
Saline	1,670	1,586	1,489	5.3	12.1	30,930	27,780	1,379	5.7	8.6	5.0	13.6	14.4
Scott	144	131	138	9.9	4.3	30,742	27,062	96	4.1	5.4	(NA)	(NA)	16.0
Sedgwick	16,175	15,103	12,900	7.1	25.4	34,703	28,447	14,257	4.8	5.8	4.3	10.5	13.0
Seward	587	550	498	6.7	17.9	25,224	22,083	541	(NA)	8.0	(NA)	(NA)	18.1
Shawnee	5,588	5,345	4,770	4.5	17.1	32,521	28,048	4,844	5.0	5.8	4.9	13.3	27.0
Sheridan	90	81	67	11.1	34.1	34,465	23,941	60	(NA)	7.5	(NA)	(NA)	17.0
Sherman	162	139	161	16.5	0.5	26,402	23,928	104	3.3	9.7	3.4	6.2	29.6
Smith	110	106	99	3.8	11.3	26,830	21,863	57	4.5	9.9	0.7	(NA)	22.4
Stafford	122	119	112	2.5	8.5	27,097	23,608	66	(NA)	2.5	3.7	5.1	32.8
Stanton	72	66	57	9.1	27.0	31,952	23,618	48	(NA)	2.4	1.1	1.1	23.1
Stevens	160	152	140	5.3	14.6	29,561	25,578	118	4.9	2.6	(NA)	(NA)	23.2
Sumner	691	666	609	3.8	13.4	27,949	23,449	261	3.5	6.8	2.3	(NA)	29.3
Thomas	224	198	190	13.1	18.0	29,522	23,220	170	4.0	8.1	1.6	10.0	24.3
Trego	74	62	64	19.4	16.0	24,280	19,397	42	3.0	9.2	2.3	3.5	33.9
Wabaunsee	193	187	162	3.2	19.2	27,800	23,541	61	9.3	4.4	(NA)	4.2	28.1
Wallace	39	37	37	5.4	5.4	24,956	21,309	22	1.3	5.5	(NA)	(NA)	26.1
Washington	154	148	132	4.1	16.4	25,637	20,438	78	3.1	5.2	1.7	4.7	32.2
Wichita	81	68	73	19.1	11.1	35,014	28,908	64	(NA)	2.3	(NA)	(NA)	17.4
Wilson	262	245	209	6.9	25.3	26,622	20,291	188	7.2	3.5	2.3	4.3	19.6
Woodson	79	76	69	3.9	14.1	22,166	18,386	39	(NA)	5.6	0.6	3.3	24.1
Wyandotte	3,681	3,551	3,121	3.7	17.9	23,640	19,774	4,381	6.9	4.8	1.9	8.6	25.8
KENTUCKY	117,967	111,873	98,845	5.4	19.3	28,272	24,412	90,811	5.7	6.9	5.3	10.6	19.4
Adair	370	346	313	6.9	18.2	21,108	18,111	177	(NA)	6.8	2.0	(NA)	23.2
Allen	436	408	361	6.9	20.6	23,458	20,281	228	4.8	19.9	(NA)	5.5	14.0
Anderson	530	503	464	5.4	14.3	25,979	24,171	194	(NA)	7.8	(NA)	(NA)	19.6
Ballard	260	235	217	10.6	19.8	31,494	26,121	197	(NA)	2.9	(NA)	2.1	8.7
Barren	982	933	850	5.3	15.6	24,479	22,285	745	5.4	9.1	(NA)	13.2	12.3
Bath	234	226	212	3.5	10.4	20,238	19,045	72	(NA)	7.0	(NA)	5.6	32.2
Bell	578	556	498	4.0	16.1	19,531	16,574	356	2.1	11.4	3.1	14.8	23.8
Boone	3,291	3,077	2,588	7.0	27.2	30,963	29,739	3,988	4.4	6.6	3.1	3.8	8.2
Bourbon	601	568	562	5.8	7.0	30,250	28,985	364	5.5	5.2	(NA)	6.6	11.7
Boyd	1,360	1,304	1,201	4.3	13.2	27,555	24,190	1,365	7.8	8.1	5.6	19.3	12.4
Boyle	733	704	665	4.1	10.3	25,808	24,001	657	3.3	8.4	(NA)	17.4	12.6
Bracken	202	192	177	5.2	14.4	23,299	21,294	50	(NA)	6.9	2.1	7.4	32.8
Breathitt	306	292	257	4.8	18.9	19,191	16,015	139	(NA)	10.2	2.1	17.3	34.6
Breckinridge	427	399	366	7.0	16.7	22,224	19,584	143	10.8	9.5	1.9	(NA)	25.3
Bullitt	1,764	1,678	1,474	5.1	19.7	24,693	23,904	584	17.1	7.4	(NA)	4.7	18.1
Butler	273	255	240	7.1	13.9	20,429	18,404	128	6.9	5.4	0.7	(NA)	20.3
Caldwell	334	306	283	9.2	18.0	25,886	21,712	193	3.3	10.9	(NA)	(NA)	18.6
Calloway	909	851	817	6.8	11.3	25,959	23,921	695	5.3	9.2	2.5	5.6	27.5
Campbell	2,713	2,604	2,355	4.2	15.2	31,168	26,561	1,263	(NA)	8.0	5.7	12.1	21.1
Carlisle	137	127	121	7.9	13.5	25,788	22,586	56	7.0	6.6	(NA)	3.6	17.9
Carroll	274	262	222	4.6	23.2	26,177	21,854	342	4.4	5.8	(NA)	(NA)	8.1
Carter	534	504	450	6.0	18.7	19,612	16,745	223	5.9	11.9	(NA)	7.0	25.8
Casey	314	293	270	7.2	16.4	19,330	17,422	144	6.5	7.7	0.8	9.0	20.6
Christian	2,020	1,797	1,526	12.4	32.4	28,960	21,110	3,751	1.1	2.4	(NA)	3.1	71.2
Clark	1,009	963	862	4.8	17.1	28,961	25,917	702	7.1	7.5	4.0	8.5	10.3
Clay	403	385	345	4.7	17.0	16,699	14,067	186	3.4	10.0	2.9	(NA)	46.5
Clinton	210	203	167	3.4	25.7	22,046	17,346	136	4.1	4.4	(NA)	(NA)	17.3
Crittenden	208	187	182	11.2	14.0	23,096	19,399	86	3.9	7.8	(NA)	(NA)	18.2
Cumberland	135	130	122	3.8	11.1	19,101	16,960	55	4.8	8.5	1.8	19.2	28.0
Daviess	2,624	2,492	2,257	5.3	16.3	28,259	24,636	1,881	6.2	8.3	3.3	10.9	19.4
Edmonson	232	216	185	7.4	25.6	19,302	15,827	65	8.8	5.9	1.6	11.5	50.3
Elliott	112	104	93	7.7	20.5	16,126	13,720	31	(NA)	6.0	(NA)	11.3	56.1
Estill	283	272	263	4.0	7.5	18,794	17,190	89	(NA)	10.5	(NA)	(NA)	31.6
Fayette	9,641	9,215	8,135	4.6	18.5	35,982	31,180	9,138	6.2	7.3	10.1	11.7	20.4
Fleming	290	271	259	7.0	12.2	19,868	18,663	139	6.4	10.6	2.2	7.4	31.3
Floyd	921	870	755	5.9	22.0	21,756	17,802	555	5.0	7.7	5.7	15.1	19.7
Franklin	1,491	1,430	1,315	4.3	13.4	30,944	27,490	1,566	(NA)	5.9	(NA)	6.2	55.0
Fulton	189	178	166	6.2	13.6	26,319	21,588	134	1.3	9.1	1.9	8.9	18.1
Gallatin	191	182	161	4.9	18.6	23,430	20,484	114	6.2	4.6	(NA)	(NA)	14.7
Garrard	359	342	302	5.0	19.1	21,722	20,256	110	30.2	8.3	1.7	(NA)	24.5
Grant	563	536	477	5.0	18.0	22,895	21,149	206	(NA)	17.6	2.1	(NA)	23.9
Graves	872	831	789	4.9	10.5	23,156	21,282	486	4.4	9.4	(NA)	(NA)	18.4
Grayson	528	505	448	4.6	17.8	20,940	18,583	309	7.6	8.7	(NA)	6.6	20.5
Green	223	209	199	6.7	11.8	19,235	17,278	73	(NA)	10.1	(NA)	(NA)	37.2
Greenup	965	920	780	4.9	23.7	25,945	21,181	422	5.5	7.0	5.5	20.1	15.7

See footnotes at end of table.

[Includes United States, states, and 3,141 counties/county equivalents defined as of February 22, 2005. For more information on these areas, see Appendix C, Geographic Information]

County	Personal income							Earnings, by place of work, 2005					
	Total, by place of residence			Percent change		Per capita[1] (dol.)		Percent, by selected major industries					
	2005 (mil. dol.)	2004 (mil. dol.)	2000 (mil. dol.)	2004–2005	2000–2005	2005	2000	Total[2] (mil. dol.)	Con-struc-tion	Retail trade	Profes-sional and tech-nical services	Health care and social assis-tance	Govern-ment
KENTUCKY—Con.													
Hancock	199	187	173	6.4	15.1	23,126	20,524	260	(NA)	1.8	0.3	2.4	7.0
Hardin	2,914	2,774	2,304	5.0	26.5	30,097	24,432	2,674	4.5	6.5	3.1	6.2	46.1
Harlan	616	592	527	4.1	16.9	19,462	15,947	356	3.5	7.3	(NA)	(NA)	22.7
Harrison	446	424	397	5.2	12.4	24,232	22,007	219	(NA)	6.7	2.0	14.2	16.9
Hart	339	321	298	5.6	13.8	18,453	16,975	158	(NA)	6.9	1.4	9.2	21.2
Henderson	1,288	1,222	1,075	5.4	19.9	28,259	23,974	1,005	5.5	5.3	1.7	9.9	11.3
Henry	403	389	352	3.6	14.5	25,497	23,318	158	6.4	7.6	2.5	3.8	22.4
Hickman	222	217	158	2.3	40.2	43,723	30,175	152	1.3	3.7	(NA)	2.4	7.0
Hopkins	1,199	1,128	1,014	6.3	18.2	25,706	21,820	801	3.8	8.2	(NA)	16.8	17.4
Jackson	220	211	197	4.3	11.8	16,053	14,557	98	7.0	5.4	1.1	(NA)	28.8
Jefferson	25,950	24,885	21,859	4.3	18.7	37,121	31,504	24,979	5.5	5.7	8.0	12.5	11.0
Jessamine	1,149	1,087	1,013	5.7	13.4	26,471	25,833	681	12.4	14.2	(NA)	3.3	14.0
Johnson	511	486	429	5.1	19.1	21,322	18,380	257	6.0	15.4	6.8	(NA)	24.6
Kenton	5,483	5,115	4,428	7.2	23.8	35,763	29,194	3,410	9.8	5.1	7.8	14.4	18.5
Knott	345	325	282	6.2	22.4	19,600	15,977	222	2.4	3.1	1.4	4.6	16.2
Knox	660	624	519	5.8	27.1	20,475	16,291	395	3.7	10.3	3.7	(NA)	20.4
Larue	366	348	317	5.2	15.6	26,800	23,634	113	11.1	7.1	2.5	(NA)	22.8
Laurel	1,240	1,174	1,055	5.6	17.6	22,013	19,925	947	7.4	9.7	(NA)	11.4	14.4
Lawrence	301	284	239	6.0	26.0	18,633	15,307	134	5.1	9.0	3.5	(NA)	22.1
Lee	142	137	121	3.6	17.5	18,555	15,244	72	3.3	9.3	3.7	9.3	27.1
Leslie	242	228	204	6.1	18.6	20,124	16,476	109	(NA)	5.5	3.9	(NA)	23.3
Letcher	528	494	434	6.9	21.8	21,543	17,177	275	2.2	6.9	2.5	(NA)	18.7
Lewis	232	223	202	4.0	15.0	16,683	14,269	82	11.1	6.5	(NA)	(NA)	30.9
Lincoln	487	464	420	5.0	16.0	19,338	17,887	175	(NA)	9.4	2.8	8.4	25.9
Livingston	259	238	212	8.8	22.4	26,509	21,556	128	10.5	(NA)	1.1	6.5	19.0
Logan	659	614	559	7.3	17.9	24,267	21,013	442	5.0	5.6	(NA)	7.9	11.8
Lyon	187	173	152	8.1	23.2	23,007	18,706	78	12.1	7.5	1.7	(NA)	41.2
McCracken	2,084	1,993	1,817	4.6	14.7	32,217	27,761	1,797	5.3	10.4	5.5	18.0	12.8
McCreary	295	283	233	4.2	26.6	17,110	13,655	134	(NA)	9.3	(NA)	(NA)	48.6
McLean	279	253	268	10.3	3.9	28,048	26,903	131	5.1	6.3	1.5	3.3	15.6
Madison	1,773	1,675	1,437	5.9	23.4	22,806	20,170	1,208	4.1	7.9	2.8	9.5	28.5
Magoffin	253	239	209	5.9	20.8	18,867	15,710	104	(NA)	6.3	(NA)	8.6	26.2
Marion	454	417	364	8.9	24.8	24,107	19,957	297	4.1	4.8	1.7	8.7	12.5
Marshall	839	795	739	5.5	13.6	27,107	24,503	584	(NA)	7.0	(NA)	(NA)	12.3
Martin	248	237	200	4.6	24.2	20,318	15,884	156	(NA)	6.1	1.9	4.6	36.4
Mason	435	424	368	2.6	18.1	25,337	21,918	368	4.7	10.4	1.5	(NA)	13.2
Meade	699	665	567	5.1	23.2	24,729	21,354	182	12.5	9.6	2.3	(NA)	24.0
Menifee	114	109	96	4.6	18.3	16,846	14,590	38	4.7	7.7	1.1	9.3	45.5
Mercer	532	501	479	6.2	11.1	24,583	22,966	355	5.4	5.3	(NA)	(NA)	11.7
Metcalfe	205	192	173	6.8	18.5	20,069	17,275	105	1.6	4.9	(NA)	3.2	20.1
Monroe	250	236	214	5.9	16.7	21,326	18,242	139	3.1	9.1	(NA)	5.2	24.2
Montgomery	565	532	472	6.2	19.7	23,294	20,831	411	(NA)	10.2	(NA)	(NA)	12.3
Morgan	241	230	196	4.8	22.9	16,850	14,046	124	15.3	11.0	(NA)	8.9	36.4
Muhlenberg	704	681	642	3.4	9.6	22,300	20,203	429	6.2	7.8	1.3	9.7	29.5
Nelson	1,120	1,059	938	5.8	19.5	27,266	24,876	649	10.9	7.4	(NA)	9.5	11.9
Nicholas	162	158	145	2.5	11.8	23,117	21,342	33	6.2	8.3	(NA)	21.6	38.0
Ohio	531	490	433	8.4	22.5	22,377	18,900	282	2.8	7.6	(NA)	6.8	19.7
Oldham	1,939	1,824	1,521	6.3	27.5	36,269	32,342	595	11.7	8.8	6.6	9.9	25.2
Owen	220	209	203	5.3	8.6	19,299	19,163	63	8.1	8.5	1.6	13.0	32.7
Owsley	92	90	81	2.2	13.8	19,445	16,638	27	(NA)	7.2	(NA)	20.9	44.0
Pendleton	327	310	302	5.5	8.4	21,538	20,797	104	(NA)	6.1	(NA)	6.2	26.5
Perry	715	672	557	6.4	28.3	24,246	19,006	618	3.4	8.9	3.6	(NA)	17.3
Pike	1,580	1,482	1,347	6.6	17.3	23,673	19,648	1,167	3.5	9.4	4.9	(NA)	14.0
Powell	273	261	230	4.6	18.4	19,899	17,353	115	(NA)	9.4	(NA)	(NA)	26.6
Pulaski	1,443	1,373	1,163	5.1	24.1	24,362	20,651	995	6.0	9.9	2.3	16.7	18.0
Robertson	44	42	41	4.8	6.6	19,540	18,221	8	(NA)	(NA)	(NA)	18.6	75.7
Rockcastle	313	297	262	5.4	19.7	18,661	15,724	121	(NA)	6.8	1.9	20.4	27.5
Rowan	476	459	380	3.7	25.2	21,510	17,227	373	(NA)	8.8	1.4	(NA)	34.6
Russell	354	337	291	5.0	21.5	20,814	17,831	213	(NA)	10.4	1.4	(NA)	20.2
Scott	1,157	1,076	980	7.5	18.0	29,261	29,321	1,486	3.1	3.2	(NA)	(NA)	5.7
Shelby	1,117	1,071	960	4.3	16.4	29,220	28,598	667	4.5	7.0	3.2	7.9	13.0
Simpson	458	430	371	6.5	23.6	26,974	22,559	412	2.6	7.8	(NA)	3.6	8.4
Spencer	357	328	265	8.8	34.8	22,833	22,033	61	16.9	8.6	2.7	12.0	37.6
Taylor	547	515	441	6.2	24.2	23,146	19,230	367	(NA)	11.2	(NA)	(NA)	19.8
Todd	285	261	246	9.2	15.7	23,840	20,604	140	2.2	4.8	1.6	(NA)	16.5
Trigg	418	375	295	11.5	41.9	31,341	23,307	185	5.8	5.8	2.3	(NA)	18.2
Trimble	162	158	129	2.5	25.1	17,906	15,843	38	(NA)	4.3	1.2	9.3	39.7
Union	436	391	344	11.5	26.7	28,002	22,059	297	2.5	6.3	(NA)	(NA)	10.5
Warren	2,868	2,678	2,270	7.1	26.3	28,995	24,463	2,486	6.7	7.6	4.0	11.7	15.1
Washington	265	252	225	5.2	17.8	23,344	20,590	142	11.2	8.1	2.8	(NA)	15.1

See footnotes at end of table.

U.S. Census Bureau

[Includes United States, states, and 3,141 counties/county equivalents defined as of February 22, 2005. For more information on these areas, see Appendix C, Geographic Information]

County	Personal income							Earnings, by place of work, 2005					
	Total, by place of residence					Per capita[1] (dol.)			Percent, by selected major industries				
				Percent change									
	2005 (mil. dol.)	2004 (mil. dol.)	2000 (mil. dol.)	2004–2005	2000–2005	2005	2000	Total[2] (mil. dol.)	Construction	Retail trade	Professional and technical services	Health care and social assistance	Government
KENTUCKY—Con.													
Wayne	407	392	317	3.8	28.3	19,951	15,863	240	2.7	8.6	2.8	6.8	17.7
Webster	433	402	347	7.7	24.7	30,659	24,591	280	5.6	3.1	(NA)	2.3	9.9
Whitley	812	764	656	6.3	23.7	21,431	18,247	484	3.5	11.1	(NA)	(NA)	18.7
Wolfe	128	123	109	4.1	17.1	18,061	15,400	42	(NA)	13.3	1.4	(NA)	41.7
Woodford	941	906	836	3.9	12.6	38,973	35,913	647	4.5	3.7	4.8	3.0	10.2
LOUISIANA	111,167	121,781	103,151	-8.7	7.8	24,664	23,079	88,982	7.2	7.1	6.6	10.2	21.4
Acadia	1,336	1,298	1,089	2.9	22.6	22,544	18,514	663	7.7	7.9	2.9	9.5	17.9
Allen	443	456	394	-2.9	12.5	17,549	15,499	332	2.5	5.1	1.9	(NA)	59.9
Ascension	2,617	2,375	1,840	10.2	42.2	28,939	23,790	1,765	12.3	7.3	5.1	5.9	10.0
Assumption	577	594	448	-2.9	28.7	24,980	19,169	221	4.3	5.3	2.1	4.7	19.6
Avoyelles	869	828	684	5.0	27.1	20,800	16,481	400	6.9	8.7	3.6	(NA)	36.8
Beauregard	701	738	622	-5.0	12.6	20,300	18,833	360	7.3	9.5	(NA)	10.5	19.1
Bienville	337	321	277	5.0	21.6	22,205	17,650	183	5.5	4.7	(NA)	5.6	17.9
Bossier	2,947	2,763	2,235	6.7	31.8	27,988	22,671	2,139	6.0	7.9	(NA)	6.7	40.2
Caddo	7,871	7,626	6,332	3.2	24.3	31,428	25,130	6,486	4.1	6.5	5.3	14.0	18.8
Calcasieu	4,461	4,864	4,134	-8.3	7.9	24,152	22,528	3,977	10.0	6.6	6.3	(NA)	15.5
Caldwell	224	216	181	3.7	23.6	21,050	17,156	97	6.2	13.8	4.1	(NA)	24.3
Cameron	79	183	178	-56.8	-55.7	8,184	17,957	104	9.1	(NA)	(NA)	(NA)	29.8
Catahoula	220	205	183	7.3	20.4	21,018	16,782	100	6.0	7.6	(NA)	(NA)	27.3
Claiborne	388	366	296	6.0	30.9	23,975	17,661	215	4.9	4.6	1.9	(NA)	33.2
Concordia	441	393	325	12.2	35.9	22,844	16,050	215	3.5	9.1	2.3	(NA)	30.4
De Soto	645	610	497	5.7	29.8	24,516	19,463	381	8.4	5.2	(NA)	(NA)	16.4
East Baton Rouge	13,566	12,593	10,993	7.7	23.4	33,104	26,633	11,960	11.5	6.8	8.7	10.8	22.3
East Carroll	164	162	134	1.2	22.6	18,661	14,222	85	0.8	5.3	(NA)	(NA)	35.2
East Feliciana	524	493	417	6.3	25.5	25,325	19,522	232	3.3	3.8	1.6	(NA)	59.0
Evangeline	668	658	561	1.5	19.1	18,830	15,846	285	4.0	9.5	(NA)	23.1	25.1
Franklin	422	406	350	3.9	20.7	20,691	16,437	204	5.7	12.1	1.6	(NA)	27.3
Grant	427	407	331	4.9	29.2	21,960	17,664	150	11.1	2.8	0.9	3.1	51.1
Iberia	1,958	1,804	1,467	8.5	33.5	26,378	20,018	1,587	10.9	6.8	(NA)	6.5	11.2
Iberville	715	749	614	-4.5	16.4	22,234	18,446	905	6.3	3.1	1.9	(NA)	14.8
Jackson	386	371	345	4.0	12.0	25,594	22,404	187	(NA)	6.9	1.3	5.6	21.5
Jefferson	11,381	14,406	12,616	-21.0	-9.8	25,233	27,742	9,479	7.8	9.4	8.5	12.2	12.9
Jefferson Davis	611	638	528	-4.2	15.7	19,594	16,811	294	6.6	11.2	3.1	16.2	23.8
Lafayette	6,467	6,098	5,216	6.1	24.0	32,892	27,389	6,309	5.4	7.2	8.6	12.0	10.6
Lafourche	2,528	2,457	2,028	2.9	24.7	27,509	22,539	1,720	6.6	6.2	3.3	6.2	18.3
La Salle	306	291	236	5.2	29.7	21,876	16,521	164	6.7	8.5	2.5	5.0	28.8
Lincoln	1,011	983	835	2.8	21.1	24,126	19,644	757	5.3	8.5	3.4	(NA)	27.4
Livingston	2,581	2,369	1,960	8.9	31.7	23,685	21,169	826	16.2	9.5	6.6	5.4	24.3
Madison	235	224	192	4.9	22.4	18,823	13,988	125	2.7	9.1	1.4	12.6	39.0
Morehouse	650	631	564	3.0	15.2	21,737	18,214	336	4.4	9.1	1.9	(NA)	18.6
Natchitoches	949	905	704	4.9	34.8	24,771	18,004	658	3.5	6.5	(NA)	4.6	28.5
Orleans	5,804	14,115	12,342	-58.9	-53.0	12,837	25,523	11,293	3.5	4.0	12.2	8.1	29.0
Ouachita	4,047	3,904	3,402	3.7	19.0	27,397	23,107	3,215	4.4	9.0	5.3	14.7	17.2
Plaquemines	309	705	561	-56.2	-44.9	10,691	20,981	843	10.4	(NA)	(NA)	(NA)	22.0
Pointe Coupee	539	522	466	3.3	15.6	24,170	20,484	229	4.9	8.9	(NA)	(NA)	21.8
Rapides	3,863	3,638	2,987	6.2	29.3	30,203	23,627	2,714	7.3	7.9	5.4	17.2	26.4
Red River	199	185	157	7.6	26.4	21,101	16,393	99	(NA)	5.1	(NA)	(NA)	20.1
Richland	439	423	375	3.8	17.1	21,541	17,888	216	6.4	9.4	2.3	(NA)	21.5
Sabine	507	495	413	2.4	22.7	21,372	17,588	243	3.8	9.5	2.3	(NA)	19.7
St. Bernard	335	1,655	1,450	-79.8	-76.9	5,148	21,635	352	16.8	11.9	1.1	21.3	34.4
St. Charles	1,355	1,332	1,167	1.7	16.1	26,811	24,211	1,431	10.9	3.1	2.8	1.9	11.6
St. Helena	251	233	172	7.7	45.7	24,801	16,389	81	(NA)	5.2	(NA)	(NA)	30.4
St. James	481	458	392	5.0	22.6	22,870	18,506	437	2.2	3.4	1.2	(NA)	15.2
St. John the Baptist	1,152	1,080	851	6.7	35.4	24,964	19,721	678	8.2	7.5	2.2	7.0	14.0
St. Landry	1,978	1,872	1,533	5.7	29.0	22,069	17,464	983	6.8	9.4	4.1	12.0	23.0
St. Martin	1,083	1,012	832	7.0	30.1	21,554	17,101	369	10.6	12.0	2.8	6.7	24.8
St. Mary	1,352	1,319	1,123	2.5	20.4	26,404	21,067	1,217	10.4	4.9	2.8	(NA)	16.8
St. Tammany	6,214	6,937	5,618	-10.4	10.6	28,270	29,219	2,860	9.3	11.6	9.2	14.8	22.8
Tangipahoa	2,370	2,370	1,923	–	23.2	22,322	19,072	1,389	5.3	12.7	2.9	9.5	33.7
Tensas	134	126	119	6.3	12.8	21,987	18,042	65	(NA)	3.6	10.5	(NA)	28.7
Terrebonne	2,647	2,610	2,171	1.4	21.9	24,719	20,763	2,240	6.4	7.9	3.1	10.3	11.1
Union	562	546	437	2.9	28.7	24,571	19,170	250	5.6	6.0	2.0	(NA)	17.4
Vermilion	1,062	1,126	1,008	-5.7	5.4	19,210	18,674	547	6.7	9.3	2.8	(NA)	22.7
Vernon	1,449	1,371	1,055	5.7	37.3	29,869	20,100	1,246	2.1	3.0	6.1	3.7	73.1
Washington	840	924	761	-9.1	10.4	18,974	17,336	411	5.8	8.9	(NA)	(NA)	37.3
Webster	1,037	993	833	4.4	24.5	25,195	19,964	561	8.0	8.8	2.1	(NA)	15.9
West Baton Rouge	602	550	499	9.5	20.7	27,844	23,131	475	13.8	4.7	(NA)	(NA)	12.7
West Carroll	233	214	192	8.9	21.2	19,758	15,632	118	(NA)	6.4	(NA)	(NA)	29.3
West Feliciana	291	277	243	5.1	19.7	19,146	16,062	318	1.3	1.9	0.9	2.6	39.4
Winn	324	307	259	5.5	24.9	20,326	15,393	203	3.2	6.1	(NA)	12.6	17.4

See footnotes at end of table.

Table B-9. Counties — **Personal Income and Earnings by Industries**—Con.

[Includes United States, states, and 3,141 counties/county equivalents defined as of February 22, 2005. For more information on these areas, see Appendix C, Geographic Information]

County	Personal income — Total, by place of residence 2005 (mil. dol.)	2004 (mil. dol.)	2000 (mil. dol.)	Percent change 2004–2005	2000–2005	Per capita¹ (dol.) 2005	2000	Earnings, by place of work, 2005 Total² (mil. dol.)	Construction	Retail trade	Professional and technical services	Health care and social assistance	Government
MAINE	40,612	39,236	33,173	3.5	22.4	30,808	25,969	29,134	6.9	8.9	6.2	14.5	19.2
Androscoggin	3,163	3,047	2,532	3.8	24.9	29,542	24,377	2,167	(NA)	8.8	5.7	18.6	11.9
Aroostook.	1,893	1,809	1,540	4.6	22.9	25,923	20,837	1,260	3.3	8.7	2.1	16.8	24.5
Cumberland	10,453	10,157	8,475	2.9	23.3	38,122	31,861	9,437	5.9	8.1	9.5	14.7	14.0
Franklin	762	736	629	3.5	21.2	25,517	21,321	544	8.5	8.8	(NA)	(NA)	16.4
Hancock.	1,631	1,584	1,427	3.0	14.3	30,422	27,503	1,079	10.3	10.4	10.6	12.0	14.5
Kennebec	3,556	3,430	2,981	3.7	19.3	29,442	25,431	2,725	5.8	9.7	5.2	14.8	34.1
Knox	1,299	1,271	1,043	2.2	24.6	31,624	26,264	906	8.7	9.3	(NA)	12.3	15.1
Lincoln	1,087	1,059	904	2.6	20.3	30,891	26,810	504	11.9	10.6	5.8	12.8	14.8
Oxford	1,424	1,359	1,175	4.8	21.2	25,089	21,427	775	6.9	8.9	2.0	12.2	16.7
Penobscot	4,215	4,035	3,422	4.5	23.2	28,711	23,621	3,298	5.7	10.3	5.0	19.4	20.5
Piscataquis	459	438	357	4.8	28.4	26,090	20,700	276	4.1	8.1	2.3	(NA)	20.1
Sagadahoc	1,145	1,116	918	2.6	24.8	31,163	26,045	818	6.9	5.4	4.7	5.4	17.0
Somerset	1,310	1,266	1,090	3.5	20.2	25,369	21,402	861	13.0	7.9	2.5	11.4	15.2
Waldo	1,029	992	802	3.7	28.3	26,717	21,973	530	(NA)	8.7	(NA)	13.0	14.4
Washington	834	805	696	3.6	19.8	25,094	20,536	482	5.9	9.2	1.5	15.9	26.3
York	6,350	6,133	5,184	3.5	22.5	31,426	27,556	3,473	8.2	9.2	4.0	11.3	28.4
MARYLAND.	234,609	220,603	181,957	6.3	28.9	41,972	34,257	163,980	8.0	6.3	13.2	9.6	22.8
Allegany.	1,884	1,783	1,557	5.7	21.0	25,728	20,810	1,297	5.5	7.5	2.5	20.1	24.4
Anne Arundel	23,253	21,949	17,917	5.9	29.8	45,648	36,466	17,383	7.3	6.6	11.7	6.2	30.8
Baltimore	34,764	32,842	27,083	5.9	28.4	44,375	35,824	22,984	8.0	7.7	10.2	12.4	17.7
Calvert	3,270	3,052	2,352	7.1	39.0	37,323	31,284	1,116	13.4	7.7	5.8	12.5	20.5
Caroline	840	794	649	5.8	29.5	26,409	21,734	425	12.2	9.8	(NA)	(NA)	17.0
Carroll	6,209	5,848	4,909	6.2	26.5	36,874	32,374	2,603	16.8	9.0	7.1	11.4	15.7
Cecil	3,238	2,990	2,442	8.3	32.6	33,214	28,240	1,503	6.4	7.7	6.0	8.4	23.4
Charles	5,046	4,715	3,730	7.0	35.3	36,537	30,754	2,141	14.5	13.0	6.8	8.6	28.6
Dorchester	916	866	720	5.8	27.3	29,221	23,526	551	5.7	5.7	2.7	(NA)	20.8
Frederick	8,725	8,144	6,427	7.1	35.8	39,587	32,696	5,148	13.0	7.7	13.4	8.6	19.5
Garrett.	831	781	660	6.4	25.9	27,843	22,126	517	13.6	9.5	4.8	(NA)	15.1
Harford.	9,218	8,618	6,874	7.0	34.1	38,595	31,318	4,691	9.0	7.9	12.1	7.9	31.9
Howard	14,153	13,284	10,893	6.5	29.9	52,580	43,646	9,592	11.8	7.5	22.0	6.0	9.9
Kent	784	725	583	8.1	34.4	39,389	30,261	386	7.0	6.5	7.2	15.0	14.1
Montgomery	55,600	52,215	43,575	6.5	27.6	59,953	49,599	39,063	6.7	4.9	18.5	7.8	21.0
Prince George's.	29,423	27,768	23,195	6.0	26.8	34,912	28,894	20,198	11.3	7.0	10.7	6.4	33.7
Queen Anne's	1,831	1,729	1,390	5.9	31.7	40,262	34,087	666	13.0	11.0	8.6	4.3	17.7
St. Mary's	3,294	3,138	2,511	5.0	31.2	34,004	29,020	2,768	4.3	4.5	23.0	6.2	46.1
Somerset	594	566	455	4.9	30.5	23,125	18,400	337	5.5	3.5	2.4	(NA)	41.9
Talbot.	1,813	1,703	1,287	6.5	40.9	50,872	37,961	929	12.2	10.3	10.7	15.6	10.8
Washington.	4,391	4,084	3,323	7.5	32.2	31,015	25,148	3,083	7.4	10.0	4.7	13.0	13.6
Wicomico	2,716	2,529	2,048	7.4	32.6	30,092	24,120	2,097	8.4	9.2	(NA)	16.9	15.7
Worcester	1,702	1,612	1,299	5.6	31.0	35,016	27,782	947	11.1	12.1	4.7	6.7	19.2
Independent City													
Baltimore city.	20,114	18,867	16,077	6.6	25.1	31,607	24,789	23,556	3.2	2.9	11.9	15.3	20.0
MASSACHUSETTS.	279,860	267,972	240,209	4.4	16.5	43,501	37,756	224,879	5.8	5.7	13.5	11.2	11.5
Barnstable	9,949	9,530	7,980	4.4	24.7	43,992	35,746	5,085	11.3	11.7	8.7	14.7	16.9
Berkshire	4,953	4,651	4,082	6.5	21.3	37,586	30,278	3,290	7.2	8.5	7.6	15.9	11.3
Bristol	18,797	18,006	15,279	4.4	23.0	34,436	28,499	11,352	6.9	9.6	4.9	13.3	13.4
Dukes	729	700	535	4.1	36.3	46,879	35,459	466	17.6	12.9	(NA)	8.8	15.0
Essex	31,252	29,866	27,302	4.6	14.5	42,563	37,627	18,582	6.4	7.4	10.9	12.3	11.9
Franklin	2,472	2,362	2,022	4.7	22.2	34,185	28,276	1,286	7.1	8.5	4.1	10.7	15.9
Hampden	14,988	14,258	12,569	5.1	19.2	32,525	27,527	10,471	5.7	7.5	5.2	16.2	17.5
Hampshire	4,973	4,749	4,174	4.7	19.1	32,427	27,395	3,011	5.1	7.8	5.6	10.5	29.6
Middlesex	75,980	72,801	68,074	4.4	11.6	51,869	46,347	65,570	5.5	4.6	20.3	7.4	8.5
Nantucket	569	540	431	5.4	31.9	56,092	45,100	440	20.6	12.4	(NA)	4.3	11.5
Norfolk.	34,766	33,585	30,494	3.5	14.0	53,278	46,824	22,781	7.7	7.2	10.0	9.7	8.4
Plymouth	19,895	19,076	16,413	4.3	21.2	40,443	34,588	10,563	9.3	8.8	8.8	12.1	17.4
Suffolk	31,723	30,284	26,314	4.8	20.6	45,845	38,139	53,396	3.0	2.2	15.5	13.2	11.1
Worcester	28,806	27,565	24,539	4.5	17.4	36,851	32,602	18,584	6.6	7.5	8.3	13.0	14.2
MICHIGAN.	331,349	320,261	294,227	3.5	12.6	32,804	29,552	257,610	5.7	6.1	9.9	9.6	14.0
Alcona	263	252	236	4.4	11.2	22,501	20,195	82	(NA)	9.8	2.9	13.5	19.7
Alger	213	206	184	3.4	15.8	22,033	18,683	142	4.0	4.2	3.3	5.1	30.6
Allegan.	3,195	3,092	2,801	3.3	14.1	28,259	26,396	1,925	7.9	5.4	3.4	5.4	10.9
Alpena	829	795	730	4.3	13.5	27,304	23,334	564	6.5	9.6	(NA)	10.2	25.7
Antrim	667	649	568	2.8	17.3	27,333	24,431	282	12.4	7.0	3.9	3.1	20.0
Arenac.	401	386	355	3.9	13.0	23,346	20,513	213	5.2	7.0	3.1	(NA)	20.8
Baraga	188	179	165	5.0	13.7	21,581	18,917	135	3.2	4.5	0.5	(NA)	49.8
Barry	1,787	1,712	1,575	4.4	13.5	29,882	27,664	681	8.7	5.8	(NA)	9.9	15.5
Bay	3,047	2,996	2,858	1.7	6.6	27,984	25,949	1,839	4.4	9.8	11.7	13.3	17.5
Benzie	469	450	381	4.2	23.1	26,676	23,648	183	15.9	9.3	3.8	(NA)	17.7

See footnotes at end of table.

Table B-9. Counties — **Personal Income and Earnings by Industries**—Con.

[Includes United States, states, and 3,141 counties/county equivalents defined as of February 22, 2005. For more information on these areas, see Appendix C, Geographic Information]

County	Personal income — Total, by place of residence 2005 (mil. dol.)	2004 (mil. dol.)	2000 (mil. dol.)	Percent change 2004–2005	2000–2005	Per capita[1] (dol.) 2005	2000	Earnings, by place of work, 2005 Total[2] (mil. dol.)	Percent, by selected major industries — Construction	Retail trade	Professional and technical services	Health care and social assistance	Government
MICHIGAN—Con.													
Berrien	4,740	4,607	4,239	2.9	11.8	29,242	26,072	3,322	4.5	6.4	3.8	10.4	11.5
Branch	1,088	1,059	963	2.7	13.0	23,502	20,985	711	5.2	8.8	(NA)	4.9	23.7
Calhoun	3,919	3,807	3,471	2.9	12.9	28,289	25,138	3,226	4.3	5.8	2.2	10.8	19.9
Cass	1,460	1,416	1,265	3.1	15.4	28,322	24,734	516	6.8	5.5	(NA)	(NA)	20.8
Charlevoix	838	827	682	1.3	22.9	31,486	26,070	544	9.2	6.7	4.6	6.8	16.3
Cheboygan	677	651	570	4.0	18.7	24,765	21,468	334	15.1	13.3	3.7	(NA)	18.8
Chippewa	840	809	718	3.8	17.0	21,632	18,620	590	4.4	7.9	1.5	(NA)	56.6
Clare	709	687	599	3.2	18.4	22,497	19,083	342	8.9	11.6	3.9	(NA)	22.1
Clinton	2,128	2,064	1,862	3.1	14.3	30,685	28,657	935	12.3	6.9	(NA)	5.8	17.0
Crawford	319	312	282	2.2	13.0	21,204	19,683	193	8.1	8.2	5.3	17.7	22.8
Delta	1,023	992	892	3.1	14.7	26,799	23,121	692	7.1	8.2	4.6	10.2	16.7
Dickinson	824	797	694	3.4	18.7	29,869	25,257	651	11.2	9.1	3.1	(NA)	22.6
Eaton	3,136	3,091	2,804	1.5	11.8	29,257	26,982	1,631	8.4	8.2	4.4	5.4	19.8
Emmet	1,134	1,098	866	3.3	30.9	33,896	27,459	838	10.5	10.5	(NA)	18.4	15.0
Genesee	12,197	12,110	11,550	0.7	5.6	27,550	26,430	8,506	5.5	7.4	5.8	12.5	15.4
Gladwin	604	594	521	1.7	16.0	22,366	19,933	198	8.7	16.4	1.3	(NA)	22.8
Gogebic	400	392	347	2.0	15.2	23,731	20,033	233	4.3	6.9	3.4	(NA)	34.8
Grand Traverse	2,694	2,610	2,255	3.2	19.5	32,089	28,912	2,430	8.7	10.4	6.6	18.4	12.7
Gratiot	1,005	969	848	3.7	18.5	23,794	20,048	650	3.4	6.4	(NA)	(NA)	20.1
Hillsdale	1,189	1,156	1,062	2.9	12.0	25,208	22,740	740	4.4	6.3	(NA)	(NA)	15.7
Houghton	817	790	699	3.4	16.9	22,976	19,436	534	8.8	7.4	4.1	(NA)	39.5
Huron	997	978	895	1.9	11.4	28,886	24,811	610	5.1	6.7	3.7	(NA)	14.8
Ingham	8,526	8,174	7,401	4.3	15.2	30,656	26,483	8,975	4.2	5.8	6.9	11.5	30.5
Ionia	1,511	1,467	1,291	3.0	17.0	23,442	20,940	778	6.8	7.4	3.4	5.1	27.9
Iosco	612	585	544	4.6	12.5	22,792	19,900	319	7.2	9.1	2.9	(NA)	23.9
Iron	316	306	267	3.3	18.4	25,458	20,344	154	7.5	7.1	4.1	13.6	29.5
Isabella	1,640	1,550	1,301	5.8	26.0	24,978	20,538	1,262	7.0	7.5	3.0	7.8	35.7
Jackson	4,461	4,304	3,966	3.6	12.5	27,299	24,984	3,057	5.0	7.5	3.3	12.4	16.9
Kalamazoo	7,705	7,523	6,643	2.4	16.0	32,089	27,812	6,324	6.0	6.7	4.9	12.8	13.5
Kalkaska	353	344	305	2.6	15.7	20,512	18,350	192	13.3	7.4	1.3	3.4	18.5
Kent	20,041	19,292	16,938	3.9	18.3	33,627	29,392	19,490	5.9	6.6	7.6	10.6	8.1
Keweenaw	56	55	48	1.8	16.0	25,740	20,900	17	(NA)	5.4	(NA)	(NA)	24.2
Lake	252	246	212	2.4	18.9	21,041	18,596	85	9.3	7.0	(NA)	(NA)	28.0
Lapeer	2,674	2,590	2,481	3.2	7.8	28,686	28,089	1,034	7.9	9.3	4.2	4.7	21.2
Leelanau	804	775	595	3.7	35.1	36,502	27,981	282	15.3	6.4	6.8	5.0	29.6
Lenawee	2,963	2,866	2,577	3.4	15.0	29,116	25,998	1,577	5.4	8.5	(NA)	7.4	17.0
Livingston	6,556	6,287	5,675	4.3	15.5	36,140	35,803	2,873	11.8	8.1	7.2	6.2	11.8
Luce	129	136	120	–	7.1	19,115	17,184	79	2.8	7.2	1.1	2.5	58.5
Mackinac	322	315	293	2.2	9.9	28,619	24,558	188	7.2	8.7	3.0	(NA)	33.4
Macomb	28,815	27,774	26,057	3.7	10.6	34,761	32,945	21,424	7.3	6.6	7.3	7.5	11.9
Manistee	625	600	539	4.2	15.9	24,853	21,881	360	4.8	7.0	1.9	(NA)	37.5
Marquette	1,714	1,644	1,442	4.3	18.9	26,506	22,315	1,221	6.2	7.4	4.3	21.4	24.4
Mason	763	740	643	3.1	18.7	26,396	22,678	468	6.5	8.8	2.3	12.3	18.1
Mecosta	914	866	754	5.5	21.2	21,658	18,548	542	4.2	8.9	2.6	7.4	37.6
Menominee	625	605	555	3.3	12.6	25,094	21,945	357	4.2	5.4	1.5	(NA)	26.6
Midland	3,116	3,043	2,622	2.4	18.8	37,099	31,586	2,293	6.6	4.7	(NA)	9.2	8.3
Missaukee	328	323	281	1.5	16.8	21,545	19,296	138	9.0	6.1	1.5	(NA)	16.3
Monroe	4,747	4,592	4,281	3.4	10.9	30,873	29,224	2,501	7.9	6.7	(NA)	7.7	13.0
Montcalm	1,395	1,360	1,164	2.6	19.8	21,868	18,950	871	5.2	8.2	1.3	11.0	19.1
Montmorency	221	215	188	2.8	17.4	21,153	18,142	96	13.6	7.3	2.2	11.2	17.2
Muskegon	4,495	4,363	3,943	3.0	14.0	25,692	23,122	3,077	5.5	10.7	2.7	14.7	15.7
Newaygo	1,180	1,139	1,014	3.6	16.3	23,644	21,123	626	5.4	8.4	(NA)	9.7	22.4
Oakland	63,444	60,925	56,335	4.1	12.6	52,274	47,079	55,206	6.0	5.5	19.2	9.0	6.1
Oceana	667	639	519	4.4	28.6	23,404	19,234	291	10.1	5.9	2.0	4.1	23.5
Ogemaw	475	458	391	3.7	21.4	21,768	18,035	251	5.4	15.8	2.8	(NA)	23.7
Ontonagon	191	184	163	3.8	17.2	26,013	20,887	100	7.7	7.9	0.9	6.5	28.5
Osceola	547	527	452	3.8	21.0	23,093	19,446	372	12.2	5.7	0.6	8.3	14.6
Oscoda	184	177	147	4.0	25.6	19,960	15,552	86	4.9	8.3	1.6	(NA)	21.1
Otsego	666	640	571	4.1	16.7	27,047	24,365	536	7.7	12.7	3.6	(NA)	13.0
Ottawa	7,845	7,539	6,678	4.1	17.5	30,743	27,881	6,056	6.7	5.3	3.5	4.5	11.8
Presque Isle	335	323	289	3.7	15.9	23,547	20,105	133	5.6	9.5	1.2	(NA)	22.1
Roscommon	604	589	505	2.5	19.7	23,141	19,765	256	9.8	15.2	2.0	10.9	28.2
Saginaw	5,665	5,580	5,374	1.5	5.4	27,256	25,596	4,663	4.9	6.9	3.8	14.1	13.6
St. Clair	5,119	4,956	4,585	3.3	11.7	29,922	27,833	2,550	6.8	7.8	3.6	13.7	15.9
St. Joseph	1,639	1,592	1,444	3.0	13.5	26,078	23,097	1,089	3.6	6.5	1.8	4.4	16.5
Sanilac	1,168	1,131	1,040	3.3	12.3	26,189	23,349	530	6.5	11.2	2.0	(NA)	18.8
Schoolcraft	209	204	181	2.5	15.3	23,837	20,337	126	6.2	8.2	(NA)	4.5	36.2
Shiawassee	1,816	1,784	1,660	1.8	9.4	24,916	23,145	742	6.4	10.5	2.8	(NA)	23.7
Tuscola	1,336	1,323	1,252	1.0	6.7	22,932	21,476	568	5.9	9.1	1.4	9.6	29.4

See footnotes at end of table.

Table B-9. Counties — **Personal Income and Earnings by Industries**—Con.

[Includes United States, states, and 3,141 counties/county equivalents defined as of February 22, 2005. For more information on these areas, see Appendix C, Geographic Information]

County	Personal income — Total, by place of residence			Percent change		Per capita[1] (dol.)		Earnings, by place of work, 2005 — Percent, by selected major industries					
	2005 (mil. dol.)	2004 (mil. dol.)	2000 (mil. dol.)	2004–2005	2000–2005	2005	2000	Total[2] (mil. dol.)	Construction	Retail trade	Professional and technical services	Health care and social assistance	Government
MICHIGAN—Con.													
Van Buren	1,991	1,934	1,682	2.9	18.3	25,290	22,032	1,011	4.5	7.7	6.0	5.0	24.8
Washtenaw	13,578	13,087	11,541	3.8	17.6	39,689	35,593	12,503	4.1	4.8	13.3	8.5	27.8
Wayne	61,430	59,299	56,660	3.6	8.4	30,855	27,514	54,864	3.9	4.6	10.7	9.7	14.2
Wexford	782	756	677	3.4	15.5	24,593	22,168	645	3.2	9.2	5.7	12.2	15.9
MINNESOTA	191,175	184,225	157,964	3.8	21.0	37,290	32,017	152,818	6.2	6.0	7.8	10.5	13.8
Aitkin	390	381	327	2.4	19.1	24,196	21,331	174	13.3	9.5	2.1	14.8	22.2
Anoka	11,279	10,820	9,226	4.2	22.3	34,875	30,770	6,422	11.7	7.5	3.9	9.5	12.6
Becker	924	868	727	6.5	27.1	28,968	24,160	576	8.8	9.3	2.7	(NA)	21.9
Beltrami	1,093	1,060	856	3.1	27.6	25,571	21,524	760	8.8	11.0	2.3	13.5	31.6
Benton	1,101	1,060	862	3.9	27.7	28,612	24,991	784	11.6	6.2	(NA)	5.7	9.2
Big Stone	160	156	129	2.6	23.7	29,005	22,328	81	12.9	5.5	1.5	12.3	29.4
Blue Earth	1,819	1,711	1,449	6.3	25.6	31,602	25,910	1,630	8.7	8.3	4.6	16.4	16.6
Brown	814	787	688	3.4	18.3	30,964	25,597	624	6.9	5.8	4.3	10.6	11.8
Carlton	888	863	759	2.9	17.1	26,114	23,911	590	10.3	6.4	1.6	7.8	32.5
Carver	3,749	3,522	2,758	6.4	35.9	44,137	38,913	1,981	8.5	4.9	7.3	8.7	10.9
Cass	844	817	668	3.3	26.4	29,178	24,453	383	7.3	9.4	(NA)	4.1	42.7
Chippewa	388	366	323	6.0	20.2	30,443	24,695	265	9.1	6.4	4.4	(NA)	17.7
Chisago	1,483	1,398	1,157	6.1	28.2	30,047	27,827	648	14.5	7.8	(NA)	20.5	18.8
Clay	1,470	1,412	1,174	4.1	25.2	27,368	22,876	726	9.0	8.7	3.3	(NA)	27.6
Clearwater	190	188	175	1.1	8.8	22,486	20,837	106	11.5	7.0	2.2	4.2	28.7
Cook	171	163	138	4.9	23.5	32,312	26,651	112	12.8	7.3	2.2	2.7	39.7
Cottonwood	365	351	282	4.0	29.4	30,937	23,248	242	4.5	5.0	1.4	9.4	16.2
Crow Wing	1,627	1,582	1,302	2.8	25.0	27,107	23,527	1,137	10.9	12.4	4.8	13.0	19.7
Dakota	15,878	15,250	13,090	4.1	21.3	41,416	36,576	9,769	9.4	7.2	7.9	6.6	11.3
Dodge	631	609	472	3.6	33.8	32,298	26,420	315	11.0	3.6	2.1	(NA)	15.4
Douglas	1,058	1,025	830	3.2	27.5	30,121	25,218	754	11.2	10.1	3.9	8.1	18.6
Faribault	504	448	381	12.5	32.4	32,732	23,573	340	4.3	3.9	(NA)	(NA)	13.9
Fillmore	616	596	499	3.4	23.6	29,020	23,559	316	7.9	7.3	2.0	(NA)	17.0
Freeborn	909	886	780	2.6	16.5	28,626	23,968	549	5.7	9.5	3.1	16.0	13.1
Goodhue	1,530	1,520	1,221	0.7	25.3	33,600	27,649	1,060	4.9	6.9	(NA)	9.6	19.0
Grant	162	163	154	−0.6	5.4	26,640	24,505	83	11.4	5.5	6.5	12.5	19.7
Hennepin	55,452	53,755	48,143	3.2	15.2	49,566	43,075	60,783	4.1	5.0	12.5	8.2	9.6
Houston	611	594	512	2.9	19.2	30,765	25,942	221	8.1	6.5	3.3	9.5	20.8
Hubbard	494	479	390	3.1	26.5	26,208	21,188	245	8.4	8.8	(NA)	15.0	19.7
Isanti	1,108	1,050	830	5.5	33.5	29,489	26,311	509	11.5	10.2	(NA)	19.0	18.1
Itasca	1,172	1,129	977	3.8	19.9	26,359	22,205	704	8.0	8.9	(NA)	12.7	22.7
Jackson	339	319	256	6.3	32.5	30,323	22,761	235	3.9	3.4	1.1	(NA)	14.2
Kanabec	403	394	327	2.3	23.4	24,910	21,673	170	19.1	9.5	3.9	8.2	27.9
Kandiyohi	1,321	1,272	1,102	3.9	19.9	32,085	26,777	960	8.0	8.7	(NA)	13.2	22.3
Kittson	133	133	133	−	−0.3	27,766	25,324	67	3.2	7.1	(NA)	(NA)	29.3
Koochiching	412	413	350	−0.2	17.6	29,830	24,491	282	5.4	6.7	1.6	(NA)	19.6
Lac qui Parle	227	213	190	6.6	19.5	29,829	23,584	131	4.1	6.0	1.4	7.8	21.2
Lake	361	342	269	5.6	34.3	32,655	24,288	209	(NA)	5.9	2.0	(NA)	19.9
Lake of the Woods	108	105	90	2.9	20.3	24,677	19,908	64	3.8	7.6	1.0	(NA)	24.2
Le Sueur	819	793	702	3.3	16.7	29,813	27,533	388	12.2	5.0	2.5	5.8	14.0
Lincoln	178	166	144	7.2	23.7	29,359	22,451	92	8.4	4.9	1.9	17.2	15.7
Lyon	785	740	660	6.1	18.9	31,838	25,956	670	6.3	9.3	(NA)	5.5	19.0
McLeod	1,124	1,076	930	4.5	20.8	30,713	26,676	879	5.2	5.9	(NA)	6.9	13.4
Mahnomen	123	113	103	8.8	19.2	24,305	19,949	82	5.4	4.1	0.3	(NA)	64.6
Marshall	268	258	252	3.9	6.2	26,894	24,922	111	9.3	7.6	1.3	6.3	26.0
Martin	685	667	569	2.7	20.4	32,668	26,117	453	3.4	6.6	(NA)	(NA)	13.0
Meeker	667	642	528	3.9	26.3	28,072	23,274	335	11.1	5.9	6.8	(NA)	16.8
Mille Lacs	615	599	492	2.7	24.9	23,972	21,918	359	7.3	6.0	1.5	11.3	41.2
Morrison	833	805	675	3.5	23.3	25,416	21,241	476	8.9	8.1	5.8	(NA)	21.9
Mower	1,194	1,154	979	3.5	21.9	30,930	25,298	765	4.8	6.5	(NA)	(NA)	15.6
Murray	269	258	217	4.3	24.0	30,404	23,722	145	9.9	4.8	2.5	7.0	17.4
Nicollet	982	938	794	4.7	23.7	31,760	26,544	614	2.5	2.9	3.8	(NA)	20.1
Nobles	608	584	482	4.1	26.0	29,637	23,187	471	4.0	9.2	(NA)	(NA)	16.9
Norman	192	186	179	3.2	7.5	27,414	24,012	92	(NA)	7.5	4.0	13.4	22.1
Olmsted	5,304	5,101	4,064	4.0	30.5	39,204	32,556	5,225	5.2	4.9	3.0	41.8	8.5
Otter Tail	1,598	1,551	1,310	3.0	21.9	27,760	22,928	910	7.9	9.1	3.4	12.6	19.0
Pennington	458	431	357	6.3	28.4	33,671	26,317	382	2.5	5.3	(NA)	(NA)	18.8
Pine	677	663	553	2.1	22.3	23,909	20,757	310	9.4	7.8	1.8	8.2	47.1
Pipestone	298	281	235	6.0	26.8	31,597	23,856	206	5.9	6.3	6.0	7.4	17.4
Polk	855	825	722	3.6	18.4	27,502	23,007	488	5.5	6.2	3.1	15.6	24.5
Pope	339	328	263	3.4	29.0	30,316	23,368	186	6.7	7.3	1.6	(NA)	18.4
Ramsey	20,232	19,641	17,076	3.0	18.5	40,883	33,394	20,675	4.7	4.8	6.6	10.2	16.8
Red Lake	101	95	94	6.3	7.5	23,698	21,941	48	4.9	6.3	1.0	(NA)	26.4
Redwood	464	448	399	3.6	16.2	29,193	23,849	304	6.0	5.9	2.5	(NA)	27.1
Renville	450	444	403	1.4	11.8	27,012	23,486	253	4.2	4.0	(NA)	(NA)	18.7

See footnotes at end of table.

[Includes United States, states, and 3,141 counties/county equivalents defined as of February 22, 2005. For more information on these areas, see Appendix C, Geographic Information]

| County | Personal income | | | | | | | Earnings, by place of work, 2005 | | | | | |
| | Total, by place of residence | | | Percent change | | Per capita[1] (dol.) | | | | Percent, by selected major industries | | | |
	2005 (mil. dol.)	2004 (mil. dol.)	2000 (mil. dol.)	2004–2005	2000–2005	2005	2000	Total[2] (mil. dol.)	Construction	Retail trade	Professional and technical services	Health care and social assistance	Government
MINNESOTA—Con.													
Rice	1,643	1,598	1,363	2.8	20.5	26,906	23,985	1,029	9.8	7.4	(NA)	7.7	18.7
Rock	293	270	239	8.5	22.8	30,721	24,574	175	2.7	5.8	3.4	11.0	16.5
Roseau	517	467	427	10.7	21.1	31,495	26,188	444	1.6	3.9	0.9	(NA)	12.0
St. Louis	6,247	6,067	5,260	3.0	18.8	31,739	26,246	4,645	5.4	7.2	4.0	19.5	19.7
Scott	4,195	3,937	3,072	6.6	36.6	34,955	33,712	2,182	16.6	6.1	8.6	6.1	20.2
Sherburne	2,253	2,154	1,671	4.6	34.8	27,530	25,590	1,117	11.7	8.6	3.0	10.7	17.9
Sibley	419	402	338	4.2	24.1	27,673	21,985	161	12.7	4.0	(NA)	(NA)	24.6
Stearns	4,232	4,086	3,357	3.6	26.0	29,705	25,138	3,610	7.2	8.7	3.6	14.7	16.9
Steele	1,129	1,082	919	4.3	22.9	31,643	27,188	933	5.4	8.1	(NA)	8.6	10.2
Stevens	284	278	248	2.2	14.7	28,985	24,697	218	5.5	6.4	2.8	(NA)	26.8
Swift	272	260	240	4.6	13.1	25,986	20,163	170	5.1	4.1	(NA)	(NA)	24.2
Todd	565	550	479	2.7	17.9	23,073	19,619	274	5.8	6.4	1.4	7.7	23.0
Traverse	104	101	93	3.0	12.3	27,073	22,460	49	4.4	6.6	0.7	7.0	34.4
Wabasha	705	697	567	1.1	24.4	31,817	26,145	315	8.2	7.1	1.1	(NA)	16.2
Wadena	334	324	266	3.1	25.7	24,642	19,375	233	2.4	13.3	1.1	(NA)	23.9
Waseca	544	521	457	4.4	19.0	28,115	23,399	367	4.0	4.6	(NA)	(NA)	19.0
Washington	9,474	9,057	7,383	4.6	28.3	43,030	36,431	3,785	8.6	8.9	5.7	9.4	13.7
Watonwan	333	327	270	1.8	23.2	29,574	22,854	220	4.5	3.6	2.2	7.2	15.3
Wilkin	188	185	161	1.6	16.8	27,846	22,580	94	3.3	8.4	0.6	17.4	19.9
Winona	1,428	1,383	1,214	3.3	17.6	28,943	24,277	1,053	4.2	7.8	(NA)	8.2	16.0
Wright	3,403	3,201	2,509	6.3	35.6	30,778	27,635	1,622	16.0	9.7	3.1	7.7	16.5
Yellow Medicine	309	292	253	5.8	22.3	29,596	22,871	201	12.7	3.9	4.0	(NA)	29.9
MISSISSIPPI	72,862	69,450	59,837	4.9	21.8	25,051	21,005	51,278	5.7	7.6	4.6	9.6	24.1
Adams	792	745	728	6.3	8.8	24,713	21,250	508	12.4	10.3	3.5	(NA)	18.4
Alcorn	806	770	681	4.7	18.3	22,901	19,689	550	4.1	10.6	2.0	7.9	20.7
Amite	287	271	237	5.9	21.3	21,433	17,420	116	3.0	6.5	2.8	(NA)	16.7
Attala	406	388	344	4.6	18.0	20,820	17,502	215	10.3	11.1	1.9	(NA)	23.2
Benton	144	135	125	6.7	15.5	18,463	15,538	55	9.6	6.9	(NA)	7.2	24.3
Bolivar	789	762	690	3.5	14.3	20,570	17,048	488	3.0	10.8	2.7	12.8	24.6
Calhoun	358	345	293	3.8	22.1	24,551	19,479	185	1.2	9.5	0.6	(NA)	17.7
Carroll	233	217	194	7.4	20.0	22,375	18,010	53	11.8	5.6	1.9	(NA)	29.9
Chickasaw	415	402	352	3.2	17.9	21,789	18,148	279	2.2	6.4	2.0	(NA)	13.4
Choctaw	178	166	140	7.2	27.1	18,694	14,352	102	12.5	3.7	1.2	(NA)	19.5
Claiborne	202	193	179	4.7	12.7	17,603	15,143	213	6.4	2.5	1.2	3.1	31.3
Clarke	346	331	313	4.5	10.4	19,705	17,445	135	2.5	6.0	1.2	10.5	23.6
Clay	473	463	426	2.2	11.1	22,388	19,372	309	3.5	7.1	3.8	(NA)	12.7
Coahoma	685	653	602	4.9	13.7	23,892	19,703	414	3.4	7.1	7.4	(NA)	20.7
Copiah	589	568	491	3.7	20.0	20,368	17,059	316	3.8	6.4	2.1	6.4	24.9
Covington	425	403	322	5.5	31.8	21,156	16,571	246	14.2	5.6	1.9	(NA)	19.7
DeSoto	4,049	3,709	2,832	9.2	43.0	29,623	26,070	2,059	16.2	10.6	3.8	8.2	11.4
Forrest	1,863	1,767	1,553	5.4	20.0	24,866	21,337	1,754	4.4	8.6	4.6	15.9	31.8
Franklin	158	150	129	5.3	22.7	19,021	15,215	71	6.3	4.6	1.7	6.1	35.3
George	435	408	360	6.6	20.8	20,550	18,745	177	15.2	11.0	3.6	(NA)	32.1
Greene	226	216	181	4.6	24.6	17,195	13,624	88	(NA)	5.5	(NA)	5.4	45.1
Grenada	539	514	461	4.9	16.9	23,752	19,868	442	2.9	9.3	(NA)	(NA)	19.2
Hancock	1,108	1,106	928	0.2	19.3	23,795	21,451	726	7.4	4.9	11.0	4.5	43.3
Harrison	5,219	5,097	4,632	2.4	12.7	27,014	24,418	4,449	5.7	7.6	4.0	7.8	39.7
Hinds	7,364	7,084	6,210	4.0	18.6	29,680	24,779	7,427	3.9	6.5	8.7	12.7	26.4
Holmes	385	366	299	5.2	28.9	18,395	13,829	163	2.1	8.8	2.8	(NA)	31.3
Humphreys	207	205	199	1.0	4.2	19,863	17,837	114	(NA)	5.6	(NA)	(NA)	20.2
Issaquena	33	35	26	-5.7	28.4	17,464	11,383	16	(NA)	(NA)	(NA)	(NA)	21.7
Itawamba	567	529	444	7.2	27.8	24,348	19,415	239	14.7	6.0	0.6	(NA)	20.5
Jackson	3,475	3,304	2,943	5.2	18.1	25,629	22,315	2,465	4.8	5.6	5.4	6.4	23.8
Jasper	382	362	302	5.5	26.5	21,263	16,657	196	4.0	5.6	7.0	(NA)	19.9
Jefferson	142	134	113	6.0	25.5	15,271	11,639	48	(NA)	(NA)	(NA)	9.6	46.9
Jefferson Davis	264	250	211	5.6	24.8	20,179	15,241	100	16.7	8.1	(NA)	(NA)	29.4
Jones	1,718	1,610	1,370	6.7	25.4	25,990	21,078	1,332	5.4	6.5	2.7	4.9	20.6
Kemper	198	189	174	4.8	13.8	19,381	16,685	77	3.4	6.0	0.7	(NA)	33.5
Lafayette	1,102	1,023	802	7.7	37.5	27,361	20,693	851	4.6	7.2	8.2	13.9	37.5
Lamar	1,155	1,078	823	7.1	40.4	26,007	20,909	525	7.3	16.0	5.5	18.2	14.8
Lauderdale	2,045	1,971	1,754	3.8	16.6	26,578	22,463	1,631	4.6	8.8	3.0	18.9	24.4
Lawrence	327	306	274	6.9	19.3	24,398	20,603	180	2.8	4.0	(NA)	3.5	16.3
Leake	501	477	386	5.0	29.9	22,241	18,416	279	(NA)	6.9	1.1	(NA)	16.7
Lee	2,252	2,196	1,917	2.6	17.5	28,685	25,227	2,331	3.1	7.7	5.0	16.8	10.2
Leflore	799	763	673	4.7	18.8	22,244	17,765	637	5.3	6.9	3.8	(NA)	27.4
Lincoln	798	754	653	5.8	22.2	23,592	19,685	565	8.1	8.4	(NA)	10.3	12.5
Lowndes	1,495	1,426	1,304	4.8	14.7	25,039	21,194	1,220	6.7	9.0	2.7	10.2	26.4
Madison	3,224	3,044	2,380	5.9	35.4	38,307	31,706	2,163	6.1	8.1	9.3	6.9	8.5
Marion	547	518	437	5.6	25.3	21,641	17,067	314	12.0	10.2	3.0	(NA)	19.9
Marshall	766	723	610	5.9	25.5	21,525	17,397	275	8.7	10.3	1.6	(NA)	21.3
Monroe	888	863	737	2.9	20.4	23,644	19,398	534	5.7	6.7	1.3	(NA)	13.6
Montgomery	260	249	214	4.4	21.5	22,149	17,623	123	3.8	12.4	18.1	(NA)	24.0
Neshoba	798	754	587	5.8	36.0	26,704	20,438	645	20.4	6.0	1.3	(NA)	44.4

See footnotes at end of table.

[Includes United States, states, and 3,141 counties/county equivalents defined as of February 22, 2005. For more information on these areas, see Appendix C, Geographic Information]

	Personal income							Earnings, by place of work, 2005					
	Total, by place of residence			Percent change		Per capita[1] (dol.)			Percent, by selected major industries				
County	2005 (mil. dol.)	2004 (mil. dol.)	2000 (mil. dol.)	2004–2005	2000–2005	2005	2000	Total[2] (mil. dol.)	Construction	Retail trade	Professional and technical services	Health care and social assistance	Government
MISSISSIPPI—Con.													
Newton	531	514	421	3.3	26.1	23,890	19,256	304	3.6	6.5	0.9	(NA)	26.4
Noxubee	230	221	202	4.1	13.9	18,950	16,100	128	3.2	6.8	(NA)	(NA)	25.0
Oktibbeha	1,012	954	810	6.1	25.0	24,520	18,857	780	5.9	6.4	(NA)	4.7	51.9
Panola	736	692	591	6.4	24.5	20,908	17,186	461	4.3	10.1	(NA)	(NA)	23.2
Pearl River	1,090	1,022	871	6.7	25.1	20,776	17,855	387	10.8	14.9	3.9	(NA)	29.6
Perry	225	219	180	2.7	25.3	18,661	14,738	122	1.5	4.7	0.8	6.8	18.1
Pike	858	813	713	5.5	20.3	21,886	18,298	576	2.5	11.5	2.6	(NA)	27.4
Pontotoc	661	641	499	3.1	32.5	23,283	18,639	504	1.9	4.0	(NA)	(NA)	9.6
Prentiss	500	487	421	2.7	18.8	19,492	16,444	292	4.9	5.6	3.2	(NA)	22.7
Quitman	190	182	148	4.4	28.4	20,058	14,717	78	1.0	6.4	(NA)	(NA)	23.5
Rankin	3,888	3,651	3,081	6.5	26.2	29,564	26,512	2,556	8.6	8.6	4.7	9.9	15.6
Scott	647	617	515	4.9	25.7	22,608	18,126	505	3.6	5.4	0.9	(NA)	12.6
Sharkey	121	122	101	−0.8	20.2	20,218	15,377	54	(NA)	7.4	1.2	(NA)	33.0
Simpson	699	667	506	4.8	38.1	25,006	18,285	327	4.7	9.3	(NA)	(NA)	20.6
Smith	409	393	319	4.1	28.4	25,721	19,681	241	2.0	2.6	(NA)	2.2	11.1
Stone	356	335	266	6.3	33.8	23,924	19,474	151	3.0	9.6	4.8	9.0	31.6
Sunflower	570	544	537	4.8	6.1	17,879	15,670	373	1.6	5.6	1.3	6.5	38.8
Tallahatchie	293	283	229	3.5	28.0	20,809	15,381	121	3.6	7.2	1.5	(NA)	29.6
Tate	643	611	536	5.2	20.0	24,319	21,049	256	5.8	11.5	2.7	(NA)	27.1
Tippah	473	453	402	4.4	17.6	22,321	19,284	290	3.7	5.7	(NA)	(NA)	15.6
Tishomingo	381	366	347	4.1	9.7	19,953	18,125	212	4.8	7.9	(NA)	(NA)	16.6
Tunica	201	192	160	4.7	25.7	19,656	17,327	554	(NA)	1.7	0.7	(NA)	7.5
Union	607	582	500	4.3	21.4	22,675	19,540	354	3.8	7.9	1.6	11.2	14.4
Walthall	302	286	240	5.6	26.0	19,750	15,864	125	7.9	7.6	1.3	7.1	24.3
Warren	1,443	1,379	1,241	4.6	16.3	29,601	25,029	1,146	3.1	7.4	(NA)	13.1	28.8
Washington	1,248	1,210	1,165	3.1	7.1	21,237	18,568	841	2.1	8.9	4.5	8.5	28.7
Wayne	442	416	355	6.3	24.4	20,951	16,763	268	10.1	8.1	(NA)	(NA)	19.0
Webster	201	188	187	6.9	7.7	20,084	18,117	87	6.8	9.2	1.9	(NA)	21.4
Wilkinson	177	170	147	4.1	20.3	17,424	14,290	73	2.3	6.4	1.2	(NA)	35.4
Winston	419	399	365	5.0	14.9	21,220	18,088	245	5.3	8.9	1.6	(NA)	13.8
Yalobusha	292	280	245	4.3	19.3	21,868	18,640	130	8.2	6.0	(NA)	4.7	25.7
Yazoo	602	572	504	5.2	19.4	21,630	17,898	336	1.3	5.3	1.2	(NA)	29.7
MISSOURI	181,066	173,054	152,722	4.6	18.6	31,231	27,241	140,886	6.9	6.8	7.7	9.9	15.8
Adair	551	524	492	5.2	12.0	22,539	19,746	405	(NA)	9.8	5.8	(NA)	25.3
Andrew	490	476	415	2.9	18.1	29,104	25,099	113	15.0	12.4	(NA)	(NA)	25.1
Atchison	161	170	155	−5.3	3.8	25,874	24,196	77	3.4	6.4	2.6	11.5	19.7
Audrain	610	604	576	1.0	5.9	23,785	22,327	400	4.3	10.6	2.0	(NA)	25.8
Barry	840	803	699	4.6	20.2	23,557	20,527	627	4.3	6.8	(NA)	(NA)	11.6
Barton	288	295	249	−2.4	15.5	22,108	19,869	201	4.8	6.9	2.9	4.1	15.5
Bates	430	425	354	1.2	21.4	25,285	21,190	169	7.9	8.3	4.0	8.6	27.2
Benton	409	392	324	4.3	26.3	21,804	18,773	151	11.9	16.0	2.5	4.4	27.5
Bollinger	259	249	212	4.0	22.3	21,024	17,551	81	10.2	9.2	2.7	7.1	22.3
Boone	4,518	4,261	3,623	6.0	24.7	31,519	26,685	3,751	6.8	7.5	3.8	10.9	36.7
Buchanan	2,342	2,247	2,056	4.2	13.9	27,596	23,885	1,998	7.1	7.7	4.3	14.7	15.3
Butler	1,100	1,065	891	3.3	23.4	26,613	21,833	806	5.7	8.7	2.6	19.3	19.5
Caldwell	237	230	202	3.0	17.3	25,705	22,454	77	18.2	8.6	(NA)	(NA)	28.4
Callaway	999	964	847	3.6	18.0	23,513	20,685	661	10.1	4.9	1.9	(NA)	24.5
Camden	1,105	1,037	919	6.6	20.2	28,084	24,687	689	(NA)	17.8	4.3	12.4	11.2
Cape Girardeau	2,051	1,973	1,738	4.0	18.0	28,844	25,278	1,725	7.1	8.4	3.5	22.1	14.3
Carroll	235	243	214	−3.3	10.0	23,160	20,790	100	7.9	8.3	1.7	(NA)	23.5
Carter	134	128	105	4.7	28.0	22,721	17,603	55	7.5	10.3	1.2	(NA)	33.5
Cass	2,712	2,577	2,199	5.2	23.3	28,932	26,608	1,028	16.9	11.7	3.6	6.8	22.0
Cedar	297	289	242	2.8	22.7	21,060	17,624	131	7.6	10.2	2.2	8.0	25.7
Chariton	200	208	187	−3.8	6.7	24,701	22,262	86	6.5	10.6	(NA)	4.5	20.3
Christian	1,696	1,562	1,253	8.6	35.3	25,195	22,808	633	18.1	11.3	4.2	5.4	16.0
Clark	160	168	150	−4.8	6.5	21,813	20,326	54	3.6	12.1	2.2	4.9	33.0
Clay	6,695	6,375	5,558	5.0	20.5	33,194	30,074	5,133	6.9	11.4	13.1	6.9	12.3
Clinton	578	557	464	3.8	24.5	27,972	24,367	190	10.4	9.6	1.9	(NA)	27.4
Cole	2,449	2,348	1,987	4.3	23.2	33,672	27,805	2,526	(NA)	7.7	5.0	10.4	38.8
Cooper	404	399	343	1.3	17.8	23,351	20,513	230	6.5	7.0	1.8	5.5	22.5
Crawford	605	574	478	5.4	26.6	25,415	20,899	281	7.4	15.5	2.4	3.9	13.3
Dade	179	184	152	−2.7	17.8	22,912	19,191	90	(NA)	4.4	(NA)	1.4	22.1
Dallas	386	366	302	5.5	27.9	23,506	19,241	140	15.1	11.1	2.1	5.5	21.2
Daviess	180	184	167	−2.2	7.7	22,394	20,889	81	9.0	7.2	1.3	4.2	22.6
DeKalb	218	214	182	1.9	19.5	17,740	13,909	105	6.1	7.0	0.9	(NA)	47.7
Dent	336	316	289	6.3	16.4	22,288	19,330	162	(NA)	12.1	1.6	(NA)	22.1
Douglas	273	256	219	6.6	24.5	20,136	16,729	135	7.8	10.4	(NA)	(NA)	16.0
Dunklin	782	754	644	3.7	21.5	24,116	19,443	405	4.0	10.2	(NA)	(NA)	17.5

See footnotes at end of table.

[Includes United States, states, and 3,141 counties/county equivalents defined as of February 22, 2005. For more information on these areas, see Appendix C, Geographic Information]

County	Personal income Total, by place of residence 2005 (mil. dol.)	2004 (mil. dol.)	2000 (mil. dol.)	Percent change 2004–2005	2000–2005	Per capita[1] (dol.) 2005	2000	Earnings, by place of work, 2005 Total[2] (mil. dol.)	Construc-tion	Retail trade	Profes-sional and tech-nical services	Health care and social assis-tance	Govern-ment
MISSOURI—Con.													
Franklin	2,909	2,766	2,421	5.2	20.2	29,392	25,729	1,574	9.8	9.2	3.1	8.9	11.9
Gasconade	399	385	345	3.6	15.5	25,412	22,444	195	(NA)	9.8	(NA)	5.1	20.0
Gentry	161	161	145	–	11.0	24,735	21,145	77	3.3	10.1	(NA)	17.1	22.0
Greene	7,607	7,237	6,192	5.1	22.9	30,371	25,732	7,155	5.1	9.1	6.0	17.0	12.5
Grundy	235	229	215	2.6	9.4	22,877	20,651	133	3.7	10.7	(NA)	(NA)	26.1
Harrison	193	191	174	1.0	11.2	21,664	19,582	94	2.5	18.5	1.3	9.4	27.7
Henry	568	547	482	3.8	17.8	25,180	21,813	312	5.7	9.8	1.9	(NA)	23.0
Hickory	171	166	146	3.0	17.1	18,597	16,321	43	11.5	12.3	(NA)	5.9	35.2
Holt	122	126	118	–3.2	3.0	24,034	22,221	50	5.3	10.4	(NA)	7.3	25.8
Howard	255	256	223	–0.4	14.3	25,691	21,912	82	7.1	7.2	(NA)	(NA)	24.1
Howell	863	821	681	5.1	26.6	22,463	18,301	578	4.1	10.0	3.2	16.7	16.3
Iron	228	216	192	5.6	18.7	22,209	18,056	122	2.1	5.3	0.8	(NA)	17.5
Jackson	22,238	21,339	19,223	4.2	15.7	33,585	29,319	22,831	7.2	5.3	11.2	9.0	16.3
Jasper	2,825	2,706	2,393	4.4	18.0	25,557	22,796	2,417	4.6	9.1	2.8	11.7	11.3
Jefferson	5,927	5,590	4,879	6.0	21.5	27,827	24,539	2,007	14.1	9.6	3.2	10.1	18.6
Johnson	1,244	1,197	970	3.9	28.2	24,573	20,032	945	5.6	5.3	(NA)	4.3	56.6
Knox	91	104	89	–12.5	1.8	21,923	20,490	40	5.5	7.6	2.2	3.5	28.6
Laclede	805	748	633	7.6	27.2	23,393	19,410	552	3.8	10.9	(NA)	7.9	11.3
Lafayette	961	941	814	2.1	18.0	29,023	24,647	354	9.2	10.4	(NA)	(NA)	25.0
Lawrence	800	774	662	3.4	20.9	21,576	18,728	336	7.1	11.2	(NA)	5.3	22.3
Lewis	211	214	189	–1.4	11.6	20,809	17,969	92	5.9	8.4	(NA)	(NA)	26.3
Lincoln	1,202	1,106	884	8.7	36.0	25,119	22,501	481	18.3	8.9	(NA)	4.8	19.7
Linn	316	316	290	–	8.8	24,140	21,153	191	3.1	6.6	3.1	(NA)	17.2
Livingston	373	369	352	1.1	5.9	26,171	24,285	237	6.7	11.2	3.0	(NA)	20.5
McDonald	495	475	377	4.2	31.3	21,717	17,395	261	6.2	12.0	(NA)	2.8	15.2
Macon	378	375	329	0.8	15.0	24,231	20,871	189	5.7	10.3	(NA)	(NA)	36.0
Madison	255	241	204	5.8	25.1	21,081	17,261	116	5.4	11.7	2.6	5.9	27.9
Maries	213	205	174	3.9	22.6	23,665	19,498	67	(NA)	8.9	3.0	7.1	18.1
Marion	718	694	630	3.5	13.9	25,398	22,287	532	8.3	8.8	(NA)	(NA)	15.4
Mercer	88	95	86	–7.4	2.2	24,672	22,859	66	2.4	2.4	(NA)	(NA)	14.1
Miller	538	514	434	4.7	23.9	21,758	18,378	286	14.8	11.5	(NA)	(NA)	16.4
Mississippi	292	293	252	–0.3	15.7	21,389	18,895	140	2.4	8.9	1.2	(NA)	30.7
Moniteau	369	360	307	2.5	20.1	24,376	20,702	159	11.2	7.5	2.3	(NA)	25.0
Monroe	200	209	193	–4.3	3.6	21,363	20,689	92	4.3	5.4	(NA)	(NA)	30.0
Montgomery	306	300	264	2.0	15.8	25,189	21,781	126	12.9	8.2	(NA)	6.2	22.9
Morgan	494	481	368	2.7	34.1	24,165	19,008	180	7.3	12.2	2.6	(NA)	19.8
New Madrid	440	443	396	–0.7	11.2	23,807	20,112	351	1.8	6.9	0.8	(NA)	11.8
Newton	1,439	1,390	1,140	3.5	26.2	25,950	21,617	856	4.9	9.1	1.3	23.9	11.0
Nodaway	482	481	416	0.2	15.9	22,205	19,020	366	4.1	6.7	2.2	(NA)	26.7
Oregon	207	198	159	4.5	29.8	19,964	15,450	97	3.0	11.6	1.5	7.5	20.7
Osage	372	359	304	3.6	22.4	27,741	23,243	145	8.0	10.2	1.0	4.8	18.6
Ozark	186	179	155	3.9	20.2	19,797	16,231	57	5.7	8.0	2.8	5.6	28.7
Pemiscot	446	436	389	2.3	14.7	23,102	19,419	228	2.0	7.6	0.9	(NA)	31.8
Perry	457	443	387	3.2	18.2	24,676	21,299	353	7.9	8.7	(NA)	4.5	12.2
Pettis	1,043	1,008	901	3.5	15.7	26,004	22,848	761	5.6	7.6	2.4	(NA)	17.0
Phelps	1,092	1,047	851	4.3	28.3	26,020	21,349	763	5.3	8.9	3.1	9.7	37.6
Pike	402	402	351	–	14.4	21,568	19,179	224	7.6	9.7	4.2	5.8	29.4
Platte	3,029	2,911	2,460	4.1	23.1	36,899	33,158	1,856	5.9	6.7	4.9	5.2	9.8
Polk	634	591	480	7.3	32.0	21,896	17,742	312	5.4	9.7	2.5	(NA)	28.0
Pulaski	1,329	1,200	950	10.8	39.8	30,161	22,756	1,261	1.3	3.1	(NA)	1.6	81.1
Putnam	107	105	93	1.9	15.4	20,894	17,687	43	3.7	9.9	1.9	2.9	36.6
Halls	232	240	212	6.5	9.2	23,526	21,976	117	5.2	5.7	(NA)	(NA)	13.3
Randolph	611	595	494	2.7	23.8	24,101	20,010	428	2.7	14.4	1.7	10.4	18.5
Ray	675	655	557	3.1	21.2	28,249	23,813	211	10.2	10.1	3.7	(NA)	28.7
Reynolds	151	138	119	9.4	27.2	22,998	17,610	82	4.6	4.7	0.4	5.3	17.6
Ripley	281	269	221	4.5	27.1	20,232	16,383	99	4.5	11.3	1.2	(NA)	28.5
St. Charles	11,052	10,342	8,528	6.9	29.6	33,530	29,794	5,964	13.1	8.0	4.4	9.0	11.4
St. Clair	202	199	168	1.5	20.6	20,949	17,294	74	5.8	10.0	1.9	12.0	36.7
Ste. Genevieve	453	433	396	4.6	14.3	24,963	22,118	229	12.3	6.4	(NA)	(NA)	16.5
St. Francois	1,378	1,314	1,105	4.9	24.7	22,405	19,819	804	6.7	10.1	1.9	15.4	26.7
St. Louis	46,312	44,032	40,644	5.2	13.9	46,207	39,987	39,289	6.9	6.0	10.0	9.9	7.7
Saline	605	613	535	–1.3	13.1	26,297	22,528	365	3.3	6.5	1.7	(NA)	22.9
Schuyler	85	85	75	–	13.4	19,891	17,969	26	9.1	11.3	(NA)	4.7	40.6
Scotland	103	111	98	–7.2	4.8	20,963	19,740	51	3.5	8.3	(NA)	(NA)	44.0
Scott	1,069	1,023	885	4.5	20.8	26,082	21,905	635	5.5	8.4	8.4	12.6	16.3
Shannon	156	150	130	4.0	19.6	18,654	15,675	69	(NA)	6.3	(NA)	3.4	26.6
Shelby	155	167	162	–7.2	–4.1	22,913	23,817	69	3.8	6.2	2.3	3.2	27.7
Stoddard	727	714	594	1.8	22.4	24,443	19,994	440	5.3	9.3	2.2	(NA)	13.6
Stone	799	752	635	6.3	25.8	25,946	22,104	323	13.0	16.1	(NA)	5.5	13.4
Sullivan	170	174	160	–2.3	6.5	24,748	22,116	121	2.0	4.6	0.7	3.6	16.6

See footnotes at end of table.

[Includes United States, states, and 3,141 counties/county equivalents defined as of February 22, 2005. For more information on these areas, see Appendix C, Geographic Information]

County	Personal income — Total, by place of residence — 2005 (mil. dol.)	2004 (mil. dol.)	2000 (mil. dol.)	Percent change 2004–2005	Percent change 2000–2005	Per capita (dol.) 2005	Per capita (dol.) 2000	Earnings, by place of work, 2005 — Total (mil. dol.)	Construction	Retail trade	Professional and technical services	Health care and social assistance	Government
MISSOURI—Con.													
Taney	1,064	1,015	893	4.8	19.1	24,828	22,377	847	8.3	10.9	2.7	9.1	9.9
Texas	469	449	374	4.5	25.2	20,131	16,276	216	3.7	9.7	1.2	3.6	34.2
Vernon	487	488	425	−0.2	14.5	23,853	20,825	285	3.6	8.2	3.2	(NA)	25.5
Warren	790	741	595	6.6	32.7	27,478	24,062	278	13.7	11.0	(NA)	4.7	16.6
Washington	488	461	380	5.9	28.5	20,351	16,206	171	4.8	8.4	1.0	(NA)	36.0
Wayne	273	262	216	4.2	26.2	20,828	16,313	83	3.7	11.0	3.0	5.6	31.0
Webster	732	692	565	5.8	29.6	21,063	18,066	265	10.5	11.1	2.8	3.5	21.3
Worth	47	48	42	−2.1	12.8	21,243	17,522	17	8.5	6.5	(NA)	4.3	40.9
Wright	351	335	301	4.8	16.6	19,151	16,759	154	4.2	12.4	1.1	(NA)	24.6
Independent City													
St. Louis city	9,529	9,189	8,561	3.7	11.3	27,027	24,685	14,892	(NA)	2.2	11.2	9.6	17.0
MONTANA	27,122	25,791	20,716	5.2	30.9	29,015	22,929	19,788	8.3	8.5	6.1	11.7	22.2
Beaverhead	240	232	197	3.4	21.8	27,382	21,418	155	6.6	6.5	3.3	(NA)	31.7
Big Horn	273	251	202	8.8	35.1	20,866	15,940	220	14.5	3.2	(NA)	2.9	44.1
Blaine	139	133	111	4.5	24.8	20,893	15,946	86	2.6	5.3	1.3	(NA)	41.1
Broadwater	110	105	84	4.8	30.2	24,398	19,326	56	4.7	4.9	2.1	5.1	24.8
Carbon	292	282	230	3.5	27.1	29,493	24,050	108	13.5	7.8	5.0	(NA)	23.4
Carter	33	31	25	6.5	30.9	25,209	18,686	18	2.6	3.0	1.3	(NA)	20.4
Cascade	2,436	2,348	1,968	3.7	23.8	30,647	24,527	1,781	6.8	8.2	5.3	16.4	31.0
Chouteau	151	150	120	0.7	26.3	27,610	19,984	73	2.0	5.3	2.2	4.3	24.1
Custer	295	289	254	2.1	16.3	26,240	21,736	194	6.8	9.7	3.3	(NA)	28.3
Daniels	54	55	56	−1.8	−3.8	29,353	27,908	33	3.5	3.8	(NA)	(NA)	21.9
Dawson	213	204	185	4.4	15.0	24,714	20,473	154	3.0	8.5	(NA)	13.8	19.8
Deer Lodge	215	209	188	2.9	14.4	23,945	20,020	111	8.4	7.4	5.7	(NA)	35.8
Fallon	82	71	58	15.5	41.5	30,425	20,605	72	(NA)	5.5	(NA)	6.2	14.1
Fergus	316	307	254	2.9	24.4	27,436	21,348	201	12.4	7.9	5.0	11.2	21.9
Flathead	2,493	2,369	1,794	5.2	39.0	30,008	24,001	1,804	12.5	10.1	5.2	11.6	13.1
Gallatin[3]	2,538	2,337	1,699	8.6	49.4	32,434	24,885	2,040	14.1	10.4	9.5	7.0	19.3
Garfield	36	32	25	12.5	41.5	30,103	20,067	22	1.3	2.7	1.4	(NA)	18.9
Glacier	299	290	216	3.1	38.2	22,091	16,378	215	(NA)	6.1	(NA)	3.7	50.9
Golden Valley	25	23	19	8.7	32.5	21,640	18,444	8	(NA)	(NA)	0.8	(NA)	37.2
Granite	72	69	55	4.3	31.1	24,652	19,317	39	9.8	6.2	(NA)	(NA)	28.1
Hill	478	463	373	3.2	28.3	29,348	22,404	316	3.8	8.3	3.5	(NA)	29.5
Jefferson	328	310	252	5.8	30.2	29,488	24,989	151	8.0	7.1	3.3	6.1	27.4
Judith Basin	53	53	43	–	22.0	24,537	18,601	24	(NA)	1.6	(NA)	1.2	31.9
Lake	614	595	487	3.2	26.0	21,726	18,291	351	9.3	10.0	3.9	10.9	32.6
Lewis and Clark	1,819	1,740	1,424	4.5	27.7	31,151	25,489	1,518	5.9	6.9	8.7	9.9	35.7
Liberty	52	50	43	4.0	20.1	26,471	20,142	34	(NA)	4.1	1.6	(NA)	18.4
Lincoln	418	396	335	5.6	24.8	21,769	17,783	243	6.2	8.9	2.4	(NA)	30.6
McCone	45	43	39	4.7	15.0	25,224	19,905	27	1.9	3.8	(NA)	(NA)	20.9
Madison	197	177	135	11.3	45.5	27,181	19,702	120	14.0	6.0	(NA)	(NA)	18.2
Meagher	49	48	38	2.1	27.5	24,785	19,893	30	(NA)	7.6	(NA)	(NA)	22.3
Mineral	89	84	66	6.0	34.5	22,057	17,036	47	10.4	10.8	1.1	7.2	31.5
Missoula	3,062	2,923	2,343	4.8	30.7	30,608	24,383	2,576	7.1	9.5	7.0	15.5	19.2
Musselshell	95	90	71	5.6	34.7	21,215	15,674	47	8.3	4.7	2.0	9.5	21.2
Park[3]	427	406	332	5.2	28.7	26,745	21,093	231	10.7	9.9	4.8	10.9	15.6
Petroleum	10	10	8	–	32.1	22,058	15,388	6	(NA)	(NA)	1.1	(NA)	33.6
Phillips	100	101	85	−1.0	17.2	24,156	18,726	56	6.5	7.2	(NA)	8.2	30.1
Pondera	154	150	129	2.7	19.1	25,286	20,283	89	17.4	7.2	(NA)	(NA)	20.3
Powder River	39	38	33	2.6	19.1	22,826	17,629	21	(NA)	6.2	3.1	(NA)	34.4
Powell	151	141	127	7.1	19.4	21,624	17,613	105	(NA)	4.3	1.4	(NA)	49.5
Prairie	32	30	25	6.7	26.7	29,269	21,253	17	(NA)	3.2	(NA)	0.3	36.0
Ravalli	986	934	734	5.6	34.4	24,758	20,188	500	13.7	9.8	6.3	7.7	20.9
Richland	267	246	207	8.5	29.1	29,112	21,480	202	10.2	7.7	4.1	(NA)	14.6
Roosevelt	220	223	191	−1.3	15.1	20,755	17,988	145	2.5	7.7	1.0	8.6	51.6
Rosebud	254	245	203	3.7	25.0	27,374	21,654	227	6.9	2.7	1.0	(NA)	32.5
Sanders	222	215	174	3.3	27.8	20,164	16,940	121	7.7	7.0	1.9	(NA)	24.9
Sheridan	103	108	98	−4.6	5.2	29,373	23,991	56	2.4	5.6	3.0	(NA)	29.2
Silver Bow	1,030	964	783	6.8	31.5	31,324	22,690	763	4.1	10.7	8.8	12.8	16.8
Stillwater	259	247	202	4.9	28.2	30,582	24,559	186	(NA)	3.6	2.4	(NA)	10.2
Sweet Grass	94	90	72	4.4	30.5	25,402	19,819	91	7.7	6.2	3.1	0.7	14.5
Teton	171	172	134	−0.6	27.3	27,679	20,864	95	4.2	6.4	3.1	(NA)	20.3
Toole	146	137	112	6.6	30.1	28,161	21,327	119	(NA)	5.0	(NA)	3.3	28.9
Treasure	17	17	15	–	15.7	23,945	17,179	8	(NA)	2.4	(NA)	(NA)	30.0
Valley	224	227	185	−1.3	21.3	31,328	24,166	139	3.8	7.2	2.3	(NA)	24.0
Wheatland	46	44	36	4.5	28.9	22,472	15,842	23	(NA)	3.5	(NA)	(NA)	31.8
Wibaux	24	22	20	9.1	21.0	25,742	18,483	13	(NA)	0.9	1.6	(NA)	29.3
Yellowstone	4,537	4,265	3,421	6.4	32.6	33,215	26,404	3,698	7.2	8.2	7.5	15.5	13.6
Yellowstone National Park[3]	(X)	(X)	(X)	–	(NA)	(X)	(X)	(X)	(NA)	(NA)	(NA)	(NA)	(NA)

See footnotes at end of table.

[Includes United States, states, and 3,141 counties/county equivalents defined as of February 22, 2005. For more information on these areas, see Appendix C, Geographic Information]

County	Personal income							Earnings, by place of work, 2005					
	Total, by place of residence					Per capita[1] (dol.)		Percent, by selected major industries					
				Percent change									
	2005 (mil. dol.)	2004 (mil. dol.)	2000 (mil. dol.)	2004– 2005	2000– 2005	2005	2000	Total[2] (mil. dol.)	Con- struc- tion	Retail trade	Profes- sional and tech- nical services	Health care and social assis- tance	Govern- ment
NEBRASKA	57,885	55,828	47,329	3.7	22.3	32,923	27,625	45,118	6.4	6.5	6.2	10.0	17.8
Adams	858	831	746	3.2	15.0	25,904	23,929	600	5.8	7.8	3.5	(NA)	17.6
Antelope	192	196	172	−2.0	11.8	27,334	23,062	112	4.8	6.8	(NA)	7.2	17.4
Arthur	8	8	4	–	102.5	20,489	8,919	1	47.1	(NA)	(NA)	(NA)	220.1
Banner	20	19	14	5.3	39.8	26,639	17,362	11	(NA)	(NA)	0.7	(NA)	23.1
Blaine	9	10	6	−10.0	60.7	18,141	9,624	3	(NA)	(NA)	(NA)	(NA)	115.8
Boone	157	155	136	1.3	15.2	27,219	21,928	92	2.7	5.6	0.8	5.0	24.3
Box Butte	328	317	305	3.5	7.4	29,023	25,195	280	2.2	4.3	1.7	(NA)	15.2
Boyd	50	48	41	4.2	23.3	22,378	16,711	20	(NA)	6.0	(NA)	8.8	35.6
Brown	89	87	71	2.3	25.6	26,715	20,120	53	4.8	8.2	(NA)	(NA)	30.2
Buffalo	1,258	1,207	977	4.2	28.8	28,817	23,090	1,048	5.3	8.3	(NA)	16.3	16.3
Burt	198	196	179	1.0	10.4	26,799	22,998	78	5.9	5.4	6.2	5.6	28.9
Butler	227	232	203	−2.2	11.8	26,222	22,915	100	5.2	6.2	2.5	(NA)	24.1
Cass	840	815	670	3.1	25.3	32,568	27,465	221	8.5	8.2	3.1	5.8	24.3
Cedar	273	277	225	−1.4	21.2	30,305	23,488	170	5.9	5.7	(NA)	3.1	16.7
Chase	115	115	99	–	16.4	29,733	24,412	72	2.7	8.9	(NA)	2.9	26.0
Cherry	160	156	127	2.6	25.7	26,291	20,722	89	7.5	10.3	5.0	5.6	25.5
Cheyenne	324	316	236	2.5	37.4	32,341	23,993	274	2.5	11.2	(NA)	5.1	11.7
Clay	183	179	174	2.2	5.0	27,489	24,777	114	5.7	3.9	1.6	5.0	31.9
Colfax	277	275	250	0.7	10.8	26,885	23,930	200	(NA)	3.6	1.7	(NA)	12.9
Cuming	300	329	289	−8.8	4.0	30,820	28,366	205	4.5	4.3	1.5	(NA)	12.9
Custer	322	317	270	1.6	19.4	28,283	22,855	206	4.5	5.6	1.7	8.6	16.5
Dakota	477	463	431	3.0	10.6	23,481	21,259	455	5.3	4.4	(NA)	(NA)	11.4
Dawes	194	184	162	5.4	19.9	22,574	17,928	121	5.2	13.6	2.7	10.4	40.3
Dawson	596	572	534	4.2	11.6	24,199	21,884	449	2.5	7.5	1.8	4.0	18.7
Deuel	55	54	44	1.9	25.8	27,489	20,727	21	(NA)	12.8	(NA)	(NA)	33.3
Dixon	176	184	158	−4.3	11.3	28,551	25,039	98	4.8	1.7	(NA)	2.0	15.7
Dodge	1,025	991	904	3.4	13.3	28,433	24,961	644	4.7	11.1	3.4	(NA)	19.6
Douglas	20,068	19,123	16,126	4.9	24.4	41,219	34,714	18,316	7.5	6.0	8.8	10.5	11.7
Dundy	69	69	62	–	11.6	32,301	26,958	33	2.5	(NA)	2.8	5.8	27.7
Fillmore	190	190	174	–	9.4	29,952	26,222	104	12.6	4.5	0.7	4.8	23.4
Franklin	88	89	78	−1.1	13.5	25,822	21,844	36	(NA)	6.9	2.4	4.6	35.2
Frontier	77	75	61	2.7	25.9	27,826	19,807	48	5.8	7.7	(NA)	3.5	24.7
Furnas	126	123	118	2.4	6.4	25,091	22,332	65	5.1	6.5	3.5	(NA)	29.5
Gage	700	704	585	−0.6	19.7	30,083	25,444	414	3.7	7.6	(NA)	10.6	23.8
Garden	56	57	45	−1.8	25.0	27,788	19,649	22	(NA)	16.5	(NA)	(NA)	43.6
Garfield	52	50	45	4.0	16.3	28,717	23,584	27	4.1	9.4	(NA)	8.4	24.0
Gosper	55	53	50	3.8	10.6	27,424	23,211	20	3.9	1.6	(NA)	(NA)	27.5
Grant	10	10	7	–	38.4	15,548	9,669	2	(NA)	25.5	(NA)	(NA)	140.6
Greeley	64	65	56	−1.5	14.6	26,046	20,637	36	3.4	4.5	0.2	2.7	25.2
Hall	1,664	1,580	1,329	5.3	25.2	30,253	24,843	1,382	5.3	10.4	3.3	11.3	16.8
Hamilton	255	250	213	2.0	19.5	26,822	22,728	142	3.1	5.5	(NA)	(NA)	16.9
Harlan	91	89	79	2.2	14.8	26,246	20,998	44	4.3	7.4	1.4	4.8	22.4
Hayes	24	22	18	9.1	33.0	22,374	16,823	15	(NA)	(NA)	(NA)	(NA)	22.2
Hitchcock	68	62	52	9.7	31.5	22,924	16,666	32	3.6	2.2	0.3	(NA)	34.0
Holt	304	310	255	−1.9	19.1	28,140	22,208	206	2.6	7.8	2.1	(NA)	14.6
Hooker	15	17	10	−11.8	45.4	20,171	13,222	6	6.2	5.3	1.1	21.6	50.3
Howard	172	164	141	4.9	22.1	25,821	21,493	73	2.9	6.0	2.4	3.0	30.6
Jefferson	223	225	189	−0.9	17.8	28,068	22,706	131	7.7	8.0	1.5	(NA)	15.3
Johnson	129	132	96	−2.3	34.7	27,452	21,352	79	3.2	4.9	1.0	9.6	41.9
Kearney	206	204	180	1.0	14.3	30,527	26,171	102	4.3	3.5	1.1	10.1	17.9
Keith	212	209	188	1.4	12.6	25,533	21,254	126	5.6	11.8	2.8	(NA)	17.3
Keya Paha	20	20	15	–	32.6	22,528	15,423	10	(NA)	(NA)	(NA)	(NA)	19.1
Kimball	104	101	93	3.0	11.9	27,562	22,878	60	3.1	8.7	2.7	(NA)	26.0
Knox	215	225	188	−4.4	14.2	24,303	20,152	109	3.6	7.4	2.7	5.9	35.9
Lancaster	8,869	8,523	7,341	4.1	20.8	33,506	29,230	7,442	6.3	6.3	7.2	13.5	22.2
Lincoln	997	960	826	3.9	20.8	28,082	23,823	777	4.1	8.5	2.9	14.1	17.7
Logan	19	18	15	5.6	29.6	25,886	19,018	8	3.2	(NA)	(NA)	0.8	25.8
Loup	7	9	5	−22.2	31.6	10,628	7,459	−1	(NA)	(NA)	−9.1	(NA)	−259.5
McPherson	9	9	6	–	45.4	17,938	11,657	3	(NA)	(NA)	(NA)	–	40.2
Madison	1,003	984	832	1.9	20.6	28,238	23,657	892	4.4	8.0	3.1	12.1	17.7
Merrick	209	208	186	0.5	12.5	26,077	22,739	98	9.5	4.4	1.6	(NA)	20.7
Morrill	127	121	103	5.0	23.4	24,543	18,905	67	2.6	8.6	(NA)	4.8	28.8
Nance	103	101	80	2.0	29.0	27,659	19,751	49	(NA)	3.0	(NA)	7.9	26.8
Nemaha	222	240	201	−7.5	10.6	31,216	26,524	198	3.1	3.7	3.3	4.7	51.8
Nuckolls	122	124	106	−1.6	15.5	25,657	21,010	59	3.4	10.1	2.9	17.2	23.6
Otoe	431	424	362	1.7	19.1	27,778	23,458	247	5.9	6.3	(NA)	(NA)	20.7
Pawnee	88	89	73	−1.1	20.3	30,805	23,714	43	(NA)	3.9	(NA)	6.0	24.5
Perkins	85	87	76	−2.3	11.8	27,528	23,935	55	10.7	3.1	(NA)	2.8	22.5
Phelps	301	296	262	1.7	15.0	31,822	26,868	219	(NA)	5.0	(NA)	(NA)	14.5
Pierce	202	205	166	−1.5	21.5	26,412	21,182	94	9.1	5.1	1.9	7.1	20.7

See footnotes at end of table.

[Includes United States, states, and 3,141 counties/county equivalents defined as of February 22, 2005. For more information on these areas, see Appendix C, Geographic Information]

County	Personal income — Total, by place of residence 2005 (mil. dol.)	2004 (mil. dol.)	2000 (mil. dol.)	Percent change 2004–2005	2000–2005	Per capita[1] (dol.) 2005	2000	Earnings, by place of work, 2005 — Total[2] (mil. dol.)	Percent, by selected major industries — Construction	Retail trade	Professional and technical services	Health care and social assistance	Government
NEBRASKA—Con.													
Platte	899	861	775	4.4	16.0	28,455	24,586	758	6.2	6.3	3.3	7.0	15.4
Polk	155	152	135	2.0	15.1	28,687	23,973	74	7.5	4.8	3.0	6.4	23.1
Red Willow	306	296	261	3.4	17.1	27,712	22,819	212	4.0	9.3	4.1	9.9	20.4
Richardson	248	251	218	−1.2	13.7	28,292	22,918	114	4.7	8.0	2.6	10.6	20.1
Rock	36	38	32	−5.3	11.2	22,983	18,420	19	(NA)	(NA)	(NA)	(NA)	34.1
Saline	391	390	305	0.3	28.2	27,457	21,992	311	1.5	3.7	(NA)	(NA)	16.2
Sarpy	4,547	4,266	3,324	6.6	36.8	32,657	26,980	3,194	7.0	4.9	7.6	3.9	32.6
Saunders	637	623	511	2.2	24.5	31,178	25,760	229	15.6	7.0	2.9	(NA)	21.3
Scotts Bluff	1,007	966	880	4.2	14.4	27,471	23,787	749	5.1	8.7	3.4	17.0	17.9
Seward	507	505	434	0.4	16.9	30,315	26,224	269	6.8	5.1	5.6	(NA)	17.6
Sheridan	131	123	120	6.5	9.0	23,248	19,444	58	2.5	10.1	3.4	2.5	39.1
Sherman	74	75	57	−1.3	29.2	23,707	17,381	34	1.9	4.9	(NA)	(NA)	28.2
Sioux	26	29	18	−10.3	43.3	18,087	12,327	4	(NA)	5.9	(NA)	(NA)	64.6
Stanton	174	176	137	−1.1	27.0	26,617	21,326	99	3.5	1.5	(NA)	(NA)	11.4
Thayer	166	169	142	−1.8	16.6	30,545	23,541	108	3.0	4.4	0.9	(NA)	20.7
Thomas	13	14	11	−7.1	15.8	20,536	15,293	6	(NA)	23.2	(NA)	–	48.5
Thurston	164	160	126	2.5	30.0	22,494	17,567	122	4.2	3.6	1.2	9.0	47.1
Valley	114	111	92	2.7	23.5	25,849	19,861	66	3.4	5.7	(NA)	3.9	34.3
Washington	658	629	544	4.6	20.9	33,207	28,956	407	12.8	10.8	1.8	(NA)	25.0
Wayne	255	253	200	0.8	27.3	27,291	20,433	184	2.4	3.8	(NA)	7.0	26.0
Webster	114	111	93	2.7	23.0	30,188	22,849	58	1.8	4.1	(NA)	5.2	19.0
Wheeler	24	27	21	−11.1	14.4	29,202	23,688	19	(NA)	(NA)	0.4	(NA)	11.6
York	476	457	370	4.2	28.5	33,157	25,427	397	2.8	6.7	(NA)	(NA)	12.5
NEVADA	86,224	79,353	61,428	8.7	40.4	35,744	30,437	67,329	12.6	7.3	6.8	6.8	14.2
Churchill	831	786	602	5.7	38.1	33,681	25,051	577	7.0	7.6	(NA)	8.2	33.5
Clark	59,793	54,475	41,239	9.8	45.0	34,980	29,601	48,681	13.4	7.3	6.5	6.4	12.8
Douglas	2,178	2,061	1,640	5.7	32.8	47,303	39,539	1,065	12.0	7.8	6.2	4.7	11.5
Elko	1,373	1,270	1,115	8.1	23.2	30,127	24,611	924	10.9	7.0	2.4	5.5	21.1
Esmeralda	28	28	24	–	18.1	35,345	24,411	12	(NA)	1.4	(NA)	(NA)	29.5
Eureka	42	41	38	2.4	10.3	30,052	23,299	323	(NA)	0.2	0.1	(NA)	2.6
Humboldt	475	444	393	7.0	20.8	27,668	24,702	415	5.3	6.8	(NA)	(NA)	17.9
Lander	163	145	146	12.4	11.8	31,893	25,518	123	(NA)	5.1	1.0	0.9	22.8
Lincoln	100	97	78	3.1	29.0	22,150	18,561	64	(NA)	6.4	(NA)	0.9	45.3
Lyon	1,155	1,055	801	9.5	44.1	24,400	22,965	556	13.2	10.9	3.3	3.8	17.6
Mineral	129	126	122	2.4	6.0	26,363	24,287	85	1.4	4.5	1.3	(NA)	34.9
Nye	1,162	1,051	797	10.6	45.8	28,761	24,201	692	7.9	6.6	32.4	2.8	14.2
Pershing	126	119	113	5.9	11.9	19,764	16,892	93	7.6	5.1	0.6	(NA)	41.4
Storey	129	119	96	8.4	34.5	31,916	28,258	64	8.1	2.8	2.7	0.2	16.4
Washoe	16,130	15,278	12,323	5.6	30.9	41,382	36,100	11,682	11.9	7.6	7.6	9.7	14.6
White Pine	291	261	220	11.5	32.5	32,672	24,293	186	3.7	5.1	(NA)	(NA)	45.1
Independent City													
Carson City	2,118	1,997	1,684	6.1	25.8	37,898	32,043	1,788	(NA)	8.0	5.4	8.4	35.5
NEW HAMPSHIRE	49,356	47,248	41,429	4.5	19.1	37,768	33,396	36,696	7.3	9.6	7.9	10.7	12.1
Belknap	2,149	2,050	1,702	4.8	26.3	34,996	30,080	1,454	(NA)	12.3	6.5	10.4	12.9
Carroll	1,643	1,584	1,336	3.7	23.0	34,911	30,424	938	(NA)	14.1	(NA)	10.7	12.5
Cheshire	2,552	2,424	2,088	5.3	22.2	33,118	28,213	1,764	9.1	10.2	4.6	11.9	12.8
Coos	999	969	837	3.1	19.4	30,121	25,243	635	6.1	10.6	(NA)	14.0	18.3
Grafton	3,287	3,122	2,565	5.3	28.1	38,760	31,348	3,144	3.8	8.3	6.7	19.1	10.2
Hillsborough	15,967	15,385	13,770	3.8	16.0	39,865	36,011	12,878	6.2	8.8	9.0	9.6	9.8
Merrimack	5,112	4,876	4,226	4.8	21.0	34,819	30,907	3,969	7.3	9.1	7.7	12.5	20.2
Rockingham	12,510	11,923	10,726	4.9	16.6	42,519	38,478	8,768	9.0	10.2	9.5	7.8	8.6
Strafford	3,714	3,555	3,058	4.5	21.4	31,210	27,141	2,360	6.7	9.6	5.1	12.3	23.2
Sullivan	1,425	1,360	1,122	4.8	27.0	33,294	27,662	787	6.9	9.9	4.3	7.8	13.4
NEW JERSEY	381,466	363,158	323,554	5.0	17.9	43,831	38,364	278,468	5.4	6.7	11.2	9.5	14.7
Atlantic	9,274	8,720	7,975	6.4	16.3	34,307	31,510	8,118	7.9	7.8	5.7	10.5	17.8
Bergen	51,184	48,583	45,380	5.4	12.8	56,725	51,227	35,241	4.3	6.9	11.0	11.9	8.5
Burlington	18,199	17,333	14,882	5.0	22.3	40,520	35,044	12,948	6.2	8.4	8.5	9.5	17.8
Camden	18,707	17,775	14,968	5.2	25.0	36,297	29,417	12,839	6.2	7.1	9.6	13.7	17.8
Cape May	3,909	3,765	3,239	3.8	20.7	39,563	31,662	2,102	12.2	11.0	4.9	8.9	26.1
Cumberland	4,304	4,058	3,421	6.1	25.8	28,149	23,364	3,223	6.6	8.6	3.0	11.6	26.7
Essex	34,684	33,092	29,355	4.8	18.2	43,951	37,033	28,420	3.4	4.3	11.2	10.5	19.8
Gloucester	9,642	9,066	7,184	6.4	34.2	34,803	28,134	5,633	9.8	9.4	5.9	9.1	17.2
Hudson	20,798	19,763	17,633	5.2	17.9	34,492	28,931	18,863	2.5	5.2	7.0	6.0	15.8
Hunterdon	7,849	7,510	6,479	4.5	21.2	60,357	52,836	4,148	8.7	14.3	15.1	7.6	13.5
Mercer	16,811	15,893	13,872	5.8	21.2	45,923	39,455	15,599	3.3	4.7	16.4	8.5	23.4
Middlesex	32,400	31,076	27,477	4.3	17.9	41,050	36,486	29,114	4.8	5.4	13.6	6.9	12.9
Monmouth	30,794	29,551	26,318	4.2	17.0	48,506	42,636	16,733	8.9	8.1	14.3	12.0	17.3
Morris	30,671	29,363	26,479	4.5	15.8	62,583	56,162	26,232	4.8	5.5	15.0	6.7	8.1
Ocean	19,262	18,331	15,582	5.1	23.6	34,509	30,332	8,073	10.1	11.6	6.4	17.0	20.6

See footnotes at end of table.

Table B-9. Counties — **Personal Income and Earnings by Industries**—Con.

[Includes United States, states, and 3,141 counties/county equivalents defined as of February 22, 2005. For more information on these areas, see Appendix C, Geographic Information]

County	Personal income — Total, by place of residence 2005 (mil. dol.)	2004 (mil. dol.)	2000 (mil. dol.)	Percent change 2004–2005	2000–2005	Per capita¹ (dol.) 2005	2000	Earnings, by place of work, 2005 Total² (mil. dol.)	Construction	Retail trade	Professional and technical services	Health care and social assistance	Government
NEW JERSEY—Con.													
Passaic	17,423	16,306	14,954	6.9	16.5	35,057	30,452	11,267	6.2	8.7	7.0	10.4	16.8
Salem	2,189	2,082	1,777	5.1	23.2	33,146	27,666	1,407	6.7	5.1	(NA)	9.8	17.1
Somerset	19,522	18,680	17,113	4.5	14.1	61,039	57,249	16,121	4.1	5.8	14.3	6.0	7.0
Sussex	6,374	6,034	5,349	5.6	19.2	41,733	36,972	2,380	10.5	9.4	10.0	13.3	19.5
Union	23,376	22,303	20,749	4.8	12.7	44,047	39,649	17,723	6.0	7.3	11.0	8.7	12.4
Warren	4,094	3,872	3,366	5.7	21.6	37,111	32,680	2,288	8.0	8.9	(NA)	10.6	14.6
NEW MEXICO	53,714	50,707	40,318	5.9	33.2	27,889	22,134	39,793	7.1	7.5	9.0	9.5	28.6
Bernalillo	19,657	18,607	15,079	5.6	30.4	32,556	27,078	17,017	7.9	7.4	14.6	10.4	23.4
Catron	63	62	51	1.6	23.0	18,599	14,377	26	(NA)	(NA)	(NA)	3.2	62.9
Chaves	1,539	1,472	1,166	4.6	32.0	24,880	19,007	1,047	4.5	7.3	3.9	11.7	19.8
Cibola	523	497	383	5.2	36.4	18,935	14,935	313	3.5	7.2	(NA)	(NA)	51.0
Colfax	337	330	283	2.1	19.1	24,584	19,881	215	7.8	8.5	4.2	(NA)	31.8
Curry	1,239	1,199	926	3.3	33.8	27,115	20,619	935	4.9	6.5	(NA)	(NA)	42.1
De Baca	46	45	39	2.2	18.0	22,565	17,591	23	(NA)	6.4	(NA)	5.5	31.9
Dona Ana	4,367	4,092	3,120	6.7	40.0	23,070	17,830	2,895	5.8	6.7	6.6	12.2	36.0
Eddy	1,494	1,400	1,060	6.7	41.0	29,132	20,593	1,164	4.7	5.1	3.3	7.6	16.6
Grant	681	635	578	7.2	17.8	22,983	18,702	392	8.5	7.0	1.6	7.0	36.8
Guadalupe	72	70	63	2.9	15.2	16,455	13,351	41	16.1	11.5	0.2	9.3	38.8
Harding	15	15	15	–	1.9	19,885	18,328	8	(NA)	(NA)	(NA)	(NA)	44.5
Hidalgo	105	98	91	7.1	14.8	20,589	15,868	62	(NA)	6.9	1.0	(NA)	39.8
Lea	1,566	1,414	1,103	10.7	41.9	27,636	19,994	1,231	6.6	6.1	1.8	(NA)	11.9
Lincoln	469	454	371	3.3	26.3	22,356	18,999	261	11.9	12.8	7.2	10.0	22.6
Los Alamos	1,021	986	762	3.5	33.9	54,134	41,687	1,568	1.9	1.0	7.0	2.8	72.4
Luna	510	465	365	9.7	39.8	19,165	14,594	314	10.9	11.3	1.7	(NA)	28.9
McKinley	1,324	1,255	1,015	5.5	30.4	18,435	13,547	885	3.1	10.4	1.3	10.2	44.8
Mora	90	89	70	1.1	29.3	17,557	13,378	31	(NA)	5.5	(NA)	(NA)	48.9
Otero	1,354	1,307	1,054	3.6	28.5	21,448	16,929	1,001	6.4	5.9	3.4	7.4	59.0
Quay	207	203	191	2.0	8.5	22,319	18,924	118	4.6	9.2	1.3	10.0	32.1
Rio Arriba	943	902	703	4.5	34.2	23,203	17,035	460	7.0	10.4	1.9	14.9	44.1
Roosevelt	481	478	344	0.6	39.8	26,413	19,132	307	4.1	5.3	0.8	(NA)	29.2
Sandoval	2,909	2,709	2,169	7.4	34.1	27,146	23,754	1,431	9.1	5.9	2.9	3.0	19.9
San Juan	3,052	2,818	2,167	8.3	40.9	24,260	18,968	2,491	7.7	7.2	2.6	8.5	20.0
San Miguel	650	629	496	3.3	31.0	22,074	16,488	325	4.9	7.2	(NA)	14.4	52.3
Santa Fe	5,341	5,019	3,846	6.4	38.9	37,934	29,627	3,553	8.5	10.1	10.5	9.4	25.2
Sierra	266	254	227	4.7	17.0	20,786	17,167	111	7.7	6.8	7.4	(NA)	35.9
Socorro	395	370	279	6.8	41.8	21,694	15,422	249	1.4	5.9	11.9	(NA)	50.6
Taos	816	761	542	7.2	50.7	25,817	18,006	520	9.8	24.1	3.6	11.3	19.0
Torrance	380	370	299	2.7	27.0	21,788	17,627	146	7.9	10.0	(NA)	(NA)	34.0
Union	120	108	99	11.1	20.7	31,345	23,865	83	2.9	3.8	1.1	(NA)	17.8
Valencia	1,685	1,594	1,363	5.7	23.6	24,374	20,511	572	8.8	11.2	2.5	9.6	31.2
NEW YORK	771,990	742,209	663,005	4.0	16.4	39,967	34,897	630,690	4.1	5.0	11.3	10.2	14.5
Albany	11,503	11,186	9,810	2.8	17.3	38,652	33,302	13,594	4.4	5.3	10.3	10.4	30.9
Allegany	1,093	1,051	956	4.0	14.3	21,697	19,159	615	4.6	5.8	2.1	8.0	30.4
Bronx	32,085	31,515	25,817	1.8	24.3	23,513	19,342	12,895	6.6	6.0	3.5	30.9	13.5
Broome	5,723	5,506	5,075	3.9	12.8	29,119	25,343	4,320	5.3	6.9	5.9	14.0	21.9
Cattaraugus	2,164	2,111	1,757	2.5	23.2	26,359	20,936	1,441	3.2	8.7	2.3	14.0	30.8
Cayuga	2,245	2,185	1,860	2.7	20.7	27,594	22,697	1,271	5.5	8.0	3.7	12.5	26.5
Chautauqua	3,391	3,281	2,985	3.4	13.6	24,917	21,384	2,262	4.0	7.5	2.9	13.3	20.8
Chemung	2,444	2,310	2,217	5.8	10.2	27,456	24,349	1,748	5.1	8.5	3.3	15.8	22.1
Chenango	1,319	1,264	1,097	4.4	20.2	25,533	21,334	763	4.2	7.5	2.9	8.3	23.4
Clinton	2,187	2,115	1,801	3.4	21.4	26,639	22,534	1,626	5.1	8.7	(NA)	14.2	28.0
Columbia	2,022	1,975	1,803	2.4	12.2	31,937	28,579	999	6.6	9.5	6.4	16.2	22.4
Cortland	1,213	1,190	1,071	1.9	13.3	25,012	22,042	791	5.4	8.1	6.1	(NA)	24.6
Delaware	1,248	1,193	1,046	4.6	19.3	26,352	21,810	860	7.1	7.5	2.6	(NA)	22.2
Dutchess	10,740	10,147	8,858	5.8	21.3	36,467	31,534	6,847	6.1	6.8	5.5	11.6	19.2
Erie	30,667	29,772	26,426	3.0	16.0	33,039	27,837	23,687	4.3	5.9	7.7	11.2	18.3
Essex	1,031	999	864	3.2	19.4	26,757	22,206	667	8.0	8.4	3.1	10.2	34.4
Franklin	1,139	1,099	962	3.6	18.4	22,366	18,816	793	3.3	7.0	3.1	16.2	50.5
Fulton	1,584	1,526	1,325	3.8	19.5	28,578	24,088	831	5.8	9.0	2.9	16.9	23.6
Genesee	1,646	1,595	1,435	3.2	14.7	27,810	23,791	1,000	5.2	7.4	3.5	9.1	29.0
Greene	1,393	1,329	1,136	4.8	22.6	28,114	23,548	664	7.0	9.1	3.9	6.7	38.6
Hamilton	150	144	126	4.2	19.5	28,904	23,315	67	14.4	9.1	1.3	(NA)	43.1
Herkimer	1,607	1,557	1,377	3.2	16.7	25,261	21,390	721	6.7	8.4	2.2	8.9	27.0
Jefferson	3,482	3,120	2,551	11.6	36.5	30,137	22,888	2,900	3.5	6.1	1.5	9.6	59.0
Kings	71,480	69,738	60,470	2.5	18.2	28,462	24,514	25,285	6.0	7.2	4.7	26.7	10.3
Lewis	633	601	529	5.3	19.6	23,868	19,615	312	6.0	6.2	3.0	(NA)	31.6
Livingston	1,688	1,637	1,475	3.1	14.4	26,300	22,911	900	7.2	9.9	2.8	8.9	39.0
Madison	1,952	1,893	1,748	3.1	11.7	27,881	25,163	955	5.4	7.9	6.6	(NA)	21.2
Monroe	26,399	25,431	22,905	3.8	15.3	36,062	31,134	22,351	4.3	5.2	8.3	11.2	12.4
Montgomery	1,377	1,331	1,193	3.5	15.4	28,096	24,019	778	3.9	9.9	2.2	19.7	18.6
Nassau	73,161	70,643	63,409	3.6	15.4	54,941	47,446	42,056	5.4	8.0	10.0	15.0	14.7

See footnotes at end of table.

County and City Data Book: 2007

U.S. Census Bureau

Table B-9. Counties — **Personal Income and Earnings by Industries**—Con.

[Includes United States, states, and 3,141 counties/county equivalents defined as of February 22, 2005. For more information on these areas, see Appendix C, Geographic Information]

County	Personal income — Total, by place of residence 2005 (mil. dol.)	2004 (mil. dol.)	2000 (mil. dol.)	Percent change 2004–2005	2000–2005	Per capita[1] (dol.) 2005	2000	Earnings, by place of work, 2005 Total[2] (mil. dol.)	Con-struc-tion	Retail trade	Profes-sional and tech-nical services	Health care and social assis-tance	Govern-ment
NEW YORK—Con.													
New York	149,989	141,268	132,138	6.2	13.5	93,377	85,829	279,432	1.3	2.7	16.5	4.6	10.8
Niagara	6,048	5,845	5,380	3.5	12.4	27,923	24,499	3,523	5.0	7.0	3.1	11.6	22.6
Oneida	6,504	6,294	5,669	3.3	14.7	27,798	24,099	4,886	3.5	7.5	5.1	15.0	28.5
Onondaga	15,338	14,771	13,174	3.8	16.4	33,542	28,737	13,431	4.8	6.1	8.4	11.9	16.4
Ontario	3,363	3,207	2,827	4.9	19.0	32,270	28,152	2,270	8.1	10.4	4.8	11.9	17.9
Orange	11,711	11,224	9,521	4.3	23.0	31,419	27,749	6,911	5.7	9.9	6.1	12.4	29.5
Orleans	1,023	986	901	3.8	13.6	23,637	20,387	558	2.7	5.3	(NA)	(NA)	45.9
Oswego	3,001	2,919	2,644	2.8	13.5	24,367	21,578	1,608	4.8	7.7	2.2	11.6	26.3
Otsego	1,641	1,565	1,348	4.9	21.8	26,153	21,857	1,006	3.9	9.6	2.7	22.6	19.8
Putnam	4,422	4,235	3,737	4.4	18.3	43,992	38,840	1,468	12.0	6.6	7.2	16.1	21.3
Queens	72,012	69,807	62,299	3.2	15.6	31,912	27,921	29,077	12.5	5.9	2.9	17.1	9.9
Rensselaer	4,899	4,742	4,171	3.3	17.5	31,686	27,337	2,620	8.2	7.2	6.8	14.1	22.8
Richmond	17,794	17,256	15,230	3.1	16.8	37,459	34,184	4,984	11.0	8.6	6.8	26.9	10.8
Rockland	13,702	13,193	11,828	3.9	15.8	46,505	41,138	7,496	5.8	6.4	12.2	13.8	17.0
St. Lawrence	2,579	2,473	2,225	4.3	15.9	23,180	19,893	1,688	4.5	7.8	2.2	12.8	33.2
Saratoga	7,556	7,210	6,176	4.8	22.4	35,288	30,649	3,790	7.8	9.4	8.1	9.2	18.8
Schenectady	5,336	5,127	4,274	4.1	24.8	35,816	29,184	3,865	5.1	6.4	19.5	12.9	14.7
Schoharie	867	818	738	6.0	17.6	26,973	23,343	400	8.3	9.4	2.9	(NA)	35.8
Schuyler	492	468	418	5.1	17.6	25,438	21,709	219	10.6	10.6	2.9	14.3	27.3
Seneca	903	877	775	3.0	16.6	26,003	23,206	494	5.7	11.4	(NA)	(NA)	25.1
Steuben	3,023	2,815	2,842	7.4	6.4	30,731	28,765	2,369	2.3	4.9	11.7	8.1	16.7
Suffolk	62,377	60,039	52,889	3.9	17.9	42,373	37,136	37,758	7.5	7.7	7.9	11.0	18.5
Sullivan	2,258	2,171	1,901	4.0	18.8	29,645	25,663	1,206	7.2	8.4	3.8	16.3	32.0
Tioga	1,398	1,342	1,239	4.2	12.8	27,229	23,947	784	3.3	5.0	2.1	4.6	15.2
Tompkins	2,849	2,759	2,321	3.3	22.8	28,462	24,037	2,527	2.1	5.3	6.2	(NA)	12.4
Ulster	5,438	5,208	4,546	4.4	19.6	29,811	25,549	2,803	5.9	10.9	4.3	13.8	25.8
Warren	2,033	1,934	1,705	5.1	19.2	31,010	26,920	1,630	6.7	9.9	4.4	17.3	14.6
Washington	1,574	1,508	1,303	4.4	20.8	24,984	21,365	767	5.9	7.1	(NA)	6.0	37.3
Wayne	2,633	2,560	2,348	2.9	12.1	28,263	25,035	1,233	6.3	7.4	3.7	7.2	24.3
Westchester	58,801	56,565	50,992	4.0	15.3	62,045	55,071	34,934	6.8	5.4	10.3	11.6	13.4
Wyoming	1,070	1,021	857	4.8	24.8	25,050	19,758	692	3.7	6.1	(NA)	3.9	33.9
Yates	591	560	502	5.5	17.7	23,772	20,403	260	4.2	6.4	2.4	(NA)	23.9
NORTH CAROLINA	269,203	252,253	218,668	6.7	23.1	31,041	27,068	206,623	6.5	6.9	6.6	8.9	19.4
Alamance	3,863	3,688	3,431	4.7	12.6	27,551	26,098	2,625	7.4	7.9	3.6	11.9	10.8
Alexander	958	926	816	3.5	17.3	26,760	24,241	462	4.8	5.7	3.2	(NA)	15.4
Alleghany	285	269	266	5.9	7.2	26,205	24,835	143	9.4	6.2	2.3	(NA)	19.1
Anson	609	573	531	6.3	14.6	23,713	21,032	349	4.8	4.5	(NA)	(NA)	29.1
Ashe	655	623	567	5.1	15.4	25,899	23,199	355	11.3	9.0	(NA)	(NA)	14.1
Avery	445	420	398	6.0	11.7	25,115	23,164	289	10.7	8.2	(NA)	13.3	17.9
Beaufort	1,181	1,109	1,010	6.5	17.0	25,737	22,439	704	7.2	7.9	(NA)	11.8	17.4
Bertie	461	433	392	6.5	17.7	23,859	19,855	255	10.3	3.2	0.8	(NA)	16.8
Bladen	799	758	680	5.4	17.5	24,304	21,083	535	3.1	3.7	1.7	(NA)	18.6
Brunswick	2,394	2,210	1,653	8.3	44.8	26,866	22,412	1,235	11.7	9.0	4.1	6.5	16.7
Buncombe	6,586	6,181	5,525	6.6	19.2	30,158	26,693	4,974	7.8	8.3	6.4	18.4	16.2
Burke	2,321	2,245	2,049	3.4	13.3	25,945	22,958	1,572	3.8	5.6	3.5	12.6	21.2
Cabarrus	4,803	4,427	3,871	8.5	24.1	32,111	29,273	3,088	8.3	10.2	5.1	6.9	17.3
Caldwell	2,127	2,082	1,855	2.2	14.7	26,814	23,896	1,351	4.3	7.5	(NA)	7.2	12.3
Camden	244	220	176	10.9	38.7	27,167	25,394	88	8.4	9.6	3.7	(NA)	20.6
Carteret	1,946	1,820	1,530	6.9	27.2	30,961	25,756	910	10.2	11.1	4.8	8.0	24.4
Caswell	554	535	510	3.6	8.7	23,564	21,635	121	8.2	5.7	3.7	(NA)	48.6
Catawba	4,328	4,134	3,915	4.7	10.5	28,598	27,479	3,845	4.0	8.1	2.4	9.7	11.3
Chatham	2,232	2,068	1,702	7.9	31.1	38,426	34,232	836	8.1	7.3	8.3	9.0	12.5
Cherokee	561	518	453	8.3	23.8	21,814	18,572	348	11.7	13.9	2.5	(NA)	19.1
Chowan	412	382	327	7.9	26.2	28,456	23,122	241	5.5	6.0	3.3	(NA)	16.2
Clay	227	211	187	7.6	21.7	23,230	21,160	81	22.3	14.1	4.1	8.2	24.7
Cleveland	2,558	2,436	2,211	5.0	15.7	26,104	22,891	1,503	4.8	8.4	2.3	(NA)	15.5
Columbus	1,377	1,294	1,207	6.4	14.1	25,319	22,044	775	4.9	7.7	(NA)	15.0	18.8
Craven	2,889	2,679	2,370	7.8	21.9	30,794	25,857	2,537	4.2	4.9	4.6	6.8	53.1
Cumberland	9,925	9,046	7,238	9.7	37.1	33,192	23,901	9,152	3.3	5.1	2.8	4.6	63.2
Currituck	693	642	468	7.9	48.1	29,982	25,521	217	17.0	15.1	3.9	(NA)	22.7
Dare	1,128	1,074	811	5.0	39.1	33,463	26,852	844	14.4	12.9	(NA)	4.4	16.6
Davidson	4,479	4,252	3,945	5.3	13.5	28,983	26,718	1,982	7.6	7.5	3.4	8.6	14.2
Davie	1,242	1,166	1,026	6.5	21.0	31,836	29,271	463	7.3	12.6	(NA)	6.2	14.2
Duplin	1,237	1,165	1,028	6.2	20.3	23,857	20,900	818	4.5	5.3	(NA)	4.9	18.5
Durham	8,160	7,825	6,888	4.3	18.5	33,669	30,676	12,256	2.7	3.2	13.2	13.5	9.3
Edgecombe	1,370	1,311	1,206	4.5	13.6	25,373	21,804	1,061	8.3	3.8	1.5	(NA)	20.4
Forsyth	11,392	10,770	9,519	5.8	19.7	34,973	31,013	9,884	4.8	7.8	7.5	14.3	8.7
Franklin	1,414	1,337	1,158	5.8	22.1	25,890	24,324	585	11.7	6.2	(NA)	7.7	17.5

See footnotes at end of table.

County and City Data Book: 2007

U.S. Census Bureau

[Includes United States, states, and 3,141 counties/county equivalents defined as of February 22, 2005. For more information on these areas, see Appendix C, Geographic Information]

| County | Personal income | | | | | | | Earnings, by place of work, 2005 | | | | | |
| | Total, by place of residence | | | Percent change | | Per capita[1] (dol.) | | | Percent, by selected major industries | | | | |
	2005 (mil. dol.)	2004 (mil. dol.)	2000 (mil. dol.)	2004–2005	2000–2005	2005	2000	Total[2] (mil. dol.)	Construction	Retail trade	Professional and technical services	Health care and social assistance	Government
NORTH CAROLINA—Con.													
Gaston	5,858	5,578	5,026	5.0	16.5	29,854	26,357	3,432	6.9	8.3	3.3	13.7	12.0
Gates	267	248	205	7.7	30.2	23,920	19,515	83	1.3	3.8	2.6	5.3	30.3
Graham	190	181	157	5.0	21.3	23,763	19,589	107	24.8	4.9	1.9	6.5	19.2
Granville	1,255	1,192	1,090	5.3	15.2	23,490	22,350	900	4.0	4.9	1.6	(NA)	41.1
Greene	470	445	404	5.6	16.4	23,425	21,185	194	11.4	5.0	2.1	8.7	31.1
Guilford	15,348	14,539	13,001	5.6	18.1	34,604	30,783	14,424	5.6	8.5	6.6	10.4	11.3
Halifax	1,297	1,228	1,133	5.6	14.5	23,314	19,775	709	4.0	9.6	3.3	9.5	28.9
Harnett	2,581	2,383	1,980	8.3	30.4	24,869	21,615	1,042	12.5	8.4	4.4	(NA)	20.4
Haywood	1,500	1,426	1,262	5.2	18.9	26,743	23,318	756	9.1	12.1	4.7	9.9	21.6
Henderson	2,974	2,785	2,488	6.8	19.5	30,603	27,755	1,625	8.6	9.5	3.0	11.7	14.4
Hertford	525	499	437	5.2	20.3	22,299	19,022	353	6.1	7.6	(NA)	(NA)	19.4
Hoke	820	747	586	9.8	40.0	20,169	17,272	308	8.1	3.2	1.7	9.2	28.8
Hyde	129	118	110	9.3	17.1	23,692	19,034	83	7.7	4.9	(NA)	3.2	36.2
Iredell	4,168	3,916	3,326	6.4	25.3	29,676	26,910	2,760	6.9	9.6	4.0	10.0	13.3
Jackson	897	834	700	7.6	28.1	25,471	21,048	640	9.7	7.1	(NA)	12.2	36.9
Johnston	4,143	3,833	3,137	8.1	32.1	28,315	25,441	1,926	12.5	8.4	3.5	6.1	17.4
Jones	279	250	210	11.6	32.8	27,093	20,211	108	5.9	4.8	3.6	12.7	20.8
Lee	1,554	1,471	1,243	5.6	25.0	27,884	25,155	1,384	4.9	6.6	2.3	7.3	9.9
Lenoir	1,580	1,508	1,403	4.8	12.6	27,296	23,583	1,158	7.1	8.4	3.8	10.0	24.0
Lincoln	1,868	1,758	1,493	6.3	25.1	26,785	23,313	826	8.9	7.7	2.4	4.6	18.4
McDowell	998	964	889	3.5	12.3	23,113	21,049	674	5.5	7.6	(NA)	(NA)	15.2
Macon	825	775	688	6.5	19.9	25,848	22,966	464	15.9	11.8	6.6	11.9	15.3
Madison	463	449	410	3.1	13.1	22,893	20,786	163	8.8	5.1	(NA)	(NA)	22.8
Martin	608	582	524	4.5	16.0	24,851	20,547	388	4.8	6.9	1.3	(NA)	17.7
Mecklenburg	34,231	31,433	26,104	8.9	31.1	42,984	37,274	37,306	6.5	5.4	8.6	5.5	9.0
Mitchell	357	340	309	5.0	15.5	22,669	19,659	227	4.7	8.9	1.1	12.2	21.5
Montgomery	696	659	586	5.6	18.7	25,452	21,768	453	5.4	5.1	1.8	(NA)	16.7
Moore	2,894	2,689	2,370	7.6	22.1	35,575	31,534	1,498	8.5	8.5	6.6	23.4	12.3
Nash	2,655	2,535	2,216	4.7	19.8	29,116	25,255	1,915	5.6	7.5	3.2	8.2	13.9
New Hanover	5,838	5,339	4,588	9.3	27.2	32,607	28,557	4,601	9.3	9.6	10.0	10.8	19.0
Northampton	574	526	458	9.1	25.2	26,800	20,749	281	4.3	14.4	1.4	(NA)	21.6
Onslow	4,922	4,370	3,437	12.6	43.2	32,705	22,900	4,247	3.2	4.2	1.5	2.8	77.4
Orange	4,668	4,448	3,583	4.9	30.3	39,380	30,912	3,178	3.4	6.5	8.6	5.5	54.4
Pamlico	361	336	300	7.4	20.5	28,214	23,144	109	11.2	10.1	(NA)	(NA)	32.3
Pasquotank	919	856	726	7.4	26.6	24,013	20,815	735	4.5	10.1	4.1	9.8	43.5
Pender	1,125	1,045	877	7.7	28.3	24,218	21,240	425	12.9	8.4	(NA)	6.8	24.4
Perquimans	313	285	232	9.8	34.8	25,996	20,342	108	9.6	4.9	(NA)	(NA)	26.7
Person	951	920	824	3.4	15.5	25,552	23,034	492	5.4	8.5	1.5	8.0	18.0
Pitt	4,012	3,751	3,263	7.0	23.0	28,200	24,331	2,967	5.8	8.0	3.8	11.5	35.4
Polk	696	652	566	6.7	22.9	36,528	30,767	209	16.6	6.3	4.7	21.4	17.0
Randolph	3,514	3,369	3,093	4.3	13.6	25,433	23,592	2,078	8.7	6.3	2.2	7.4	12.6
Richmond	1,070	1,020	942	4.9	13.6	22,900	20,222	634	3.8	8.0	1.8	(NA)	19.7
Robeson	2,610	2,463	2,213	6.0	18.0	20,429	17,931	1,478	6.7	8.5	2.1	16.8	24.5
Rockingham	2,351	2,251	2,044	4.4	15.0	25,418	22,227	1,286	7.2	7.8	(NA)	11.0	15.1
Rowan	3,690	3,515	3,156	5.0	16.9	27,376	24,154	2,345	4.7	6.2	(NA)	9.1	19.3
Rutherford	1,559	1,506	1,342	3.5	16.2	24,496	21,300	944	6.4	8.3	1.9	10.9	14.6
Sampson	1,561	1,461	1,235	6.8	26.4	24,836	20,479	922	4.7	5.7	1.3	5.2	18.8
Scotland	833	798	740	4.4	12.6	22,462	20,540	602	3.9	7.1	1.8	(NA)	16.2
Stanly	1,550	1,447	1,346	7.1	15.2	26,251	23,112	855	8.4	7.8	2.1	11.8	17.6
Stokes	1,199	1,143	1,023	4.9	17.2	26,193	22,809	308	11.8	7.6	3.8	(NA)	24.8
Surry	1,874	1,813	1,674	3.4	11.9	25,875	23,504	1,270	14.2	8.5	2.3	8.0	15.8
Swain	299	282	226	6.0	32.2	22,594	17,369	223	4.3	6.2	1.4	(NA)	44.8
Transylvania	844	791	771	6.7	9.5	28,487	26,234	376	11.8	9.8	3.7	14.8	16.0
Tyrrell	93	86	73	8.1	27.6	22,329	17,567	44	3.4	7.4	(NA)	2.0	39.5
Union	4,744	4,326	3,289	9.7	44.2	29,018	26,170	2,458	19.2	6.1	3.7	3.8	14.9
Vance	1,016	979	905	3.8	12.3	23,331	20,972	588	4.6	12.1	1.9	15.0	21.7
Wake	28,350	26,509	22,767	6.9	24.5	37,756	35,954	23,496	7.5	6.8	13.2	6.9	17.9
Warren	402	391	344	2.8	17.0	20,368	17,232	157	7.5	4.7	(NA)	(NA)	34.4
Washington	317	305	277	3.9	14.5	23,858	20,198	121	3.5	8.6	1.6	(NA)	38.5
Watauga	1,202	1,128	960	6.6	25.2	28,323	22,467	892	7.4	9.7	4.5	16.7	27.8
Wayne	2,976	2,847	2,504	4.5	18.9	26,141	22,089	2,047	5.4	6.8	1.9	12.1	36.3
Wilkes	1,968	1,778	1,555	10.7	26.6	29,314	23,625	1,386	3.8	5.4	(NA)	4.6	13.6
Wilson	2,159	2,024	1,731	6.7	24.8	28,345	23,408	1,820	9.2	5.7	6.1	6.1	15.7
Yadkin	968	925	844	4.6	14.7	25,680	23,110	386	8.6	7.1	(NA)	7.8	16.5
Yancey	386	374	356	3.2	8.4	21,238	19,999	164	13.6	8.3	(NA)	(NA)	21.1
NORTH DAKOTA	19,899	18,509	16,097	7.5	23.6	31,357	25,106	16,282	6.2	7.1	4.3	11.9	22.0
Adams	66	57	57	15.8	15.1	27,719	22,213	42	2.6	10.7	(NA)	30.9	14.7
Barnes	332	307	278	8.1	19.2	30,164	23,763	214	7.5	6.0	3.6	(NA)	18.9
Benson	147	125	117	17.6	25.2	20,897	16,868	100	2.8	2.3	(NA)	0.9	63.0
Billings	27	21	16	28.6	68.9	32,522	18,289	21	0.2	1.7	(NA)	0.4	28.2
Bottineau	217	188	187	15.4	15.9	32,209	26,312	132	5.4	4.8	2.7	(NA)	18.2

See footnotes at end of table.

[Includes United States, states, and 3,141 counties/county equivalents defined as of February 22, 2005. For more information on these areas, see Appendix C, Geographic Information]

	Personal income							Earnings, by place of work, 2005					
	Total, by place of residence			Percent change		Per capita[1] (dol.)			Percent, by selected major industries				
County	2005 (mil. dol.)	2004 (mil. dol.)	2000 (mil. dol.)	2004–2005	2000–2005	2005	2000	Total[2] (mil. dol.)	Construction	Retail trade	Professional and technical services	Health care and social assistance	Government
NORTH DAKOTA—Con.													
Bowman	104	89	76	16.9	36.4	34,420	23,601	74	5.0	5.6	3.7	9.4	12.7
Burke	69	54	59	27.8	16.7	34,141	26,499	47	4.9	(NA)	1.0	(NA)	28.5
Burleigh	2,516	2,381	1,876	5.7	34.1	34,053	26,980	2,182	6.5	7.5	5.8	17.8	21.7
Cass	4,563	4,339	3,647	5.2	25.1	34,978	29,561	4,442	7.5	8.3	7.3	13.4	13.5
Cavalier	135	117	145	15.4	-6.9	31,667	30,155	87	7.4	4.2	1.5	8.3	14.2
Dickey	194	168	144	15.5	34.3	35,486	25,110	143	2.1	5.1	1.1	10.1	8.1
Divide	61	51	55	19.6	10.5	28,453	24,368	37	(NA)	4.9	3.7	(NA)	19.6
Dunn	91	72	74	26.4	22.7	26,648	20,600	56	3.2	3.5	(NA)	5.1	17.2
Eddy	72	60	58	20.0	25.0	27,815	21,026	40	2.6	4.9	(NA)	13.5	19.2
Emmons	106	86	93	23.3	13.7	28,284	21,641	68	6.7	4.5	2.8	8.6	14.6
Foster	102	89	94	14.6	8.4	28,857	25,145	79	4.1	6.9	1.9	13.1	13.8
Golden Valley	41	32	35	28.1	16.6	24,044	18,337	27	(NA)	4.8	2.1	12.2	22.3
Grand Forks	1,940	1,859	1,587	4.4	22.3	29,746	24,091	1,781	6.4	8.9	3.8	13.9	36.4
Grant	67	55	59	21.8	13.3	25,551	20,843	35	(NA)	3.1	(NA)	15.0	19.5
Griggs	77	69	71	11.6	8.2	30,841	26,069	49	(NA)	5.5	2.6	(NA)	15.3
Hettinger	75	66	74	13.6	1.3	29,332	27,499	43	3.6	2.0	(NA)	6.7	17.7
Kidder	74	67	59	10.4	25.2	29,991	21,598	45	(NA)	2.8	(NA)	4.5	16.0
LaMoure	161	147	122	9.5	31.9	36,907	26,074	109	1.3	2.3	(NA)	(NA)	12.5
Logan	71	60	60	18.3	18.3	34,404	26,144	45	3.6	3.2	1.9	(NA)	12.1
McHenry	147	131	118	12.2	24.2	26,803	19,888	67	6.1	2.0	2.6	3.7	24.9
McIntosh	92	85	85	8.2	7.8	30,635	25,266	56	(NA)	5.0	(NA)	19.1	13.2
McKenzie	146	136	124	7.4	18.1	25,938	21,645	115	5.1	2.2	2.6	(NA)	44.4
McLean	272	260	213	4.6	27.8	31,635	22,966	171	8.6	3.1	1.5	7.6	18.9
Mercer	276	266	226	3.8	21.9	33,206	26,310	280	8.7	3.0	1.1	(NA)	8.2
Morton	709	664	559	6.8	26.8	27,815	22,073	404	6.1	8.9	2.1	(NA)	15.9
Mountrail	185	181	154	2.2	19.9	28,350	23,363	111	12.7	4.2	1.1	7.7	26.8
Nelson	90	79	81	13.9	11.5	26,232	21,828	39	4.5	6.8	1.0	13.6	24.1
Oliver	58	54	45	7.4	30.1	31,868	21,688	45	(NA)	(NA)	(NA)	0.9	10.4
Pembina	224	212	250	5.7	-10.4	28,019	29,233	169	8.7	5.3	(NA)	5.2	24.4
Pierce	103	94	102	9.6	0.5	24,165	21,969	70	8.4	7.7	1.5	(NA)	14.2
Ramsey	329	295	280	11.5	17.4	28,996	23,305	234	5.6	11.7	1.8	14.2	25.7
Ransom	181	171	146	5.8	24.3	31,360	24,693	115	4.6	5.5	1.4	9.0	14.3
Renville	82	64	69	28.1	18.3	33,404	26,723	47	(NA)	2.9	(NA)	(NA)	18.8
Richland	498	470	430	6.0	15.8	28,826	23,946	400	5.6	4.1	(NA)	(NA)	20.6
Rolette	296	280	238	5.7	24.6	21,361	17,365	205	4.7	6.3	0.7	(NA)	63.7
Sargent	169	154	131	9.7	29.3	40,663	29,992	191	1.6	1.7	(NA)	0.8	5.5
Sheridan	40	41	32	-2.4	25.9	27,717	18,711	22	(NA)	(NA)	(NA)	(NA)	16.9
Sioux	77	69	55	11.6	40.4	18,280	13,506	75	2.0	1.3	(NA)	(NA)	86.7
Slope	17	15	19	13.3	-11.5	23,961	25,344	10	2.3	(NA)	0.8	0.7	10.5
Stark	676	614	499	10.1	35.5	30,560	22,128	536	6.3	7.5	(NA)	(NA)	16.3
Steele	61	47	59	29.8	2.8	30,056	26,478	36	8.7	4.8	(NA)	0.3	14.2
Stutsman	646	574	518	12.5	24.8	31,129	23,682	510	3.8	6.7	3.3	(NA)	16.3
Towner	81	65	74	24.6	9.1	32,197	25,992	48	3.4	3.3	(NA)	(NA)	14.6
Traill	243	214	213	13.6	14.1	29,246	25,142	150	2.6	3.8	1.8	(NA)	19.0
Walsh	331	309	303	7.1	9.4	28,687	24,483	234	3.7	4.7	1.5	(NA)	20.1
Ward	1,828	1,746	1,469	4.7	24.4	32,815	25,039	1,501	5.8	7.5	(NA)	12.6	38.1
Wells	145	125	115	16.0	26.3	31,761	22,589	91	3.9	6.5	(NA)	11.7	13.1
Williams	589	533	445	10.5	32.4	30,585	22,628	452	6.3	7.4	3.6	(NA)	14.4
OHIO	365,453	352,588	320,538	3.6	14.0	31,860	28,207	282,835	5.5	6.6	7.4	10.9	15.4
Adams	625	594	536	5.2	16.7	21,963	19,595	306	5.5	10.3	1.8	(NA)	22.3
Allen	2,904	2,817	2,633	3.1	10.3	27,382	24,255	2,662	6.2	7.7	3.2	16.0	12.5
Ashland	1,341	1,296	1,175	3.5	14.1	24,743	22,358	844	6.7	6.2	5.7	(NA)	16.0
Ashtabula	2,641	2,536	2,305	4.1	14.6	25,632	22,424	1,415	5.7	7.7	(NA)	12.2	17.4
Athens	1,360	1,320	1,114	3.0	22.1	21,928	17,877	919	3.2	7.9	2.9	12.2	53.8
Auglaize	1,433	1,377	1,306	4.1	9.8	30,380	28,002	898	5.5	5.7	(NA)	7.3	12.2
Belmont	1,753	1,694	1,514	3.5	15.8	25,376	21,592	947	7.7	11.9	(NA)	14.6	19.5
Brown	1,123	1,075	934	4.5	20.2	25,375	21,940	358	(NA)	7.9	(NA)	9.3	32.3
Butler	11,081	10,619	9,547	4.4	16.1	31,662	28,608	7,139	9.5	6.7	4.2	9.1	15.2
Carroll	693	668	635	3.7	9.1	23,701	21,985	288	8.8	8.4	(NA)	(NA)	15.1
Champaign	1,067	1,028	994	3.8	7.4	26,891	25,511	543	5.1	5.9	(NA)	(NA)	17.6
Clark	4,042	3,912	3,735	3.3	8.2	28,485	25,821	2,245	4.8	7.7	(NA)	15.7	16.8
Clermont	6,127	5,891	5,177	4.0	18.3	32,190	29,063	2,913	8.0	8.8	6.7	7.5	13.3
Clinton	1,185	1,129	1,056	5.0	12.3	27,834	25,946	1,205	2.1	4.2	1.3	(NA)	13.8
Columbiana	2,663	2,585	2,459	3.0	8.3	24,072	21,930	1,334	5.5	8.1	2.8	13.3	18.7
Coshocton	909	895	852	1.6	6.7	24,595	23,203	577	4.4	6.1	1.8	11.0	12.7
Crawford	1,146	1,121	1,083	2.2	5.8	25,130	23,091	673	5.1	5.9	3.9	(NA)	14.3
Cuyahoga	49,335	47,818	45,277	3.2	9.0	37,082	32,523	46,407	3.9	4.8	10.9	11.4	13.8
Darke	1,452	1,427	1,363	1.8	6.5	27,419	25,566	804	8.4	7.0	(NA)	8.7	13.0
Defiance	1,105	1,084	1,026	1.9	7.7	28,376	25,996	876	3.7	8.1	1.9	(NA)	11.1

See footnotes at end of table.

[Includes United States, states, and 3,141 counties/county equivalents defined as of February 22, 2005. For more information on these areas, see Appendix C, Geographic Information]

County	Personal income Total, by place of residence 2005 (mil. dol.)	2004 (mil. dol.)	2000 (mil. dol.)	Percent change 2004–2005	2000–2005	Per capita[1] (dol.) 2005	2000	Earnings, by place of work, 2005 Total[2] (mil. dol.)	Construction	Retail trade	Professional and technical services	Health care and social assistance	Government
OHIO—Con.													
Delaware	6,126	5,752	4,686	6.5	30.7	40,703	41,937	3,716	5.6	7.9	19.0	6.5	10.4
Erie	2,620	2,530	2,280	3.6	14.9	33,426	28,645	1,933	4.3	6.6	2.8	10.7	15.0
Fairfield	4,203	4,019	3,467	4.6	21.2	30,371	28,088	1,664	9.1	8.0	4.7	10.0	24.9
Fayette	769	751	637	2.4	20.7	27,267	22,412	450	5.6	10.0	2.0	(NA)	16.6
Franklin	39,813	38,133	33,798	4.4	17.8	36,547	31,540	40,096	5.4	7.5	10.7	9.8	17.1
Fulton	1,287	1,248	1,128	3.1	14.1	29,998	26,775	1,028	7.2	4.9	1.7	(NA)	10.8
Gallia	825	797	687	3.5	20.1	26,407	22,103	553	6.3	7.5	(NA)	(NA)	17.4
Geauga	3,884	3,739	3,397	3.9	14.3	40,863	37,228	1,762	11.0	6.3	4.7	7.8	11.2
Greene	4,977	4,813	4,272	3.4	16.5	32,780	28,834	4,123	3.3	5.5	12.1	5.7	49.7
Guernsey	970	941	809	3.1	19.9	23,664	19,830	620	5.5	8.4	(NA)	14.1	20.6
Hamilton	33,087	31,973	28,330	3.5	16.8	39,937	33,567	33,536	5.3	4.7	10.1	11.7	11.1
Hancock	2,335	2,255	2,027	3.5	15.2	31,771	28,420	2,080	(NA)	8.0	3.1	8.4	8.4
Hardin	730	707	667	3.3	9.5	22,796	20,872	384	3.0	6.5	1.8	(NA)	18.4
Harrison	372	362	336	2.8	10.6	23,428	21,210	155	3.7	4.6	1.8	(NA)	22.2
Henry	827	799	747	3.5	10.7	28,090	25,581	540	7.1	5.9	(NA)	7.0	17.8
Highland	1,032	982	844	5.1	22.2	24,270	20,575	522	5.3	12.3	1.8	7.8	20.9
Hocking	685	661	571	3.6	19.9	23,677	20,230	283	7.8	9.7	1.8	6.9	29.8
Holmes	915	879	707	4.1	29.5	22,087	18,094	830	12.7	7.1	2.0	(NA)	9.3
Huron	1,560	1,516	1,441	2.9	8.3	25,882	24,168	1,143	9.8	5.5	2.6	(NA)	11.7
Jackson	754	726	632	3.9	19.3	22,460	19,362	464	5.5	8.6	(NA)	7.5	16.2
Jefferson	1,869	1,814	1,632	3.0	14.5	26,458	22,145	1,091	6.2	7.7	2.4	15.8	15.2
Knox	1,526	1,452	1,268	5.1	20.4	26,222	23,197	905	7.2	6.6	2.7	9.9	15.2
Lake	7,739	7,461	6,943	3.7	11.5	33,298	30,495	4,913	5.7	8.7	6.4	9.3	13.0
Lawrence	1,449	1,383	1,195	4.8	21.2	23,026	19,191	473	8.6	12.2	2.9	10.9	29.3
Licking	4,719	4,465	3,918	5.7	20.4	30,509	26,820	2,482	8.0	9.9	5.5	9.4	16.8
Logan	1,355	1,301	1,186	4.2	14.2	29,218	25,774	1,057	3.9	5.0	(NA)	6.5	10.8
Lorain	8,735	8,373	7,646	4.3	14.2	29,089	26,808	5,141	6.4	7.3	3.2	10.4	17.6
Lucas	13,890	13,503	12,669	2.9	9.6	31,045	27,853	11,763	6.3	6.8	6.6	15.8	15.1
Madison	1,205	1,155	957	4.3	25.9	29,245	23,788	723	6.6	8.1	5.4	5.5	22.6
Mahoning	7,101	6,909	6,370	2.8	11.5	28,046	24,781	4,726	7.2	10.4	4.8	17.5	16.9
Marion	1,729	1,668	1,490	3.7	16.0	26,257	22,529	1,251	4.4	6.8	2.8	10.4	23.1
Medina	5,585	5,330	4,672	4.8	19.5	33,450	30,761	2,846	9.3	8.3	5.4	8.3	12.9
Meigs	471	455	455	3.5	3.4	20,307	19,765	152	8.5	9.6	2.7	(NA)	29.3
Mercer	1,186	1,151	1,041	3.0	13.9	28,820	25,435	737	7.2	7.2	2.3	4.9	16.7
Miami	3,108	2,989	2,760	4.0	12.6	30,645	27,876	1,888	5.8	8.8	(NA)	9.5	13.5
Monroe	336	334	288	0.6	16.5	22,794	18,995	146	6.7	5.7	1.6	3.2	23.7
Montgomery	17,532	17,046	16,168	2.9	8.4	32,133	28,949	15,301	4.4	5.3	7.7	13.9	15.3
Morgan	301	295	289	2.0	4.1	20,206	19,412	139	8.1	5.8	1.7	6.1	21.8
Morrow	864	833	691	3.7	25.0	25,185	21,727	280	8.8	6.9	3.2	(NA)	26.0
Muskingum	2,199	2,184	1,979	0.7	11.1	25,685	23,350	1,493	5.1	11.7	2.2	17.4	16.6
Noble	251	246	221	2.0	13.6	17,835	15,674	139	3.2	5.4	1.1	8.7	36.3
Ottawa	1,330	1,294	1,193	2.8	11.4	32,095	29,102	689	5.1	7.5	2.4	(NA)	16.6
Paulding	493	482	456	2.3	8.2	25,285	22,512	217	4.3	6.5	3.5	(NA)	25.3
Perry	745	722	628	3.2	18.6	21,211	18,400	282	16.2	5.6	2.2	(NA)	25.9
Pickaway	1,368	1,304	1,152	4.9	18.7	25,896	21,802	699	6.6	7.0	2.1	9.4	30.8
Pike	618	603	547	2.5	12.9	22,024	19,714	470	7.5	5.5	2.3	7.1	16.8
Portage	4,636	4,451	3,999	4.2	15.9	29,878	26,245	2,697	5.5	6.7	3.9	4.6	26.9
Preble	1,128	1,088	1,011	3.7	11.6	26,606	23,867	489	5.3	6.9	(NA)	(NA)	18.2
Putnam	985	953	904	3.4	9.0	28,298	25,997	464	11.5	6.4	2.0	6.0	16.3
Richland	3,432	3,351	3,024	2.4	13.5	26,900	23,478	2,662	5.0	7.5	2.5	11.9	17.1
Ross	1,863	1,800	1,632	3.5	14.2	24,798	22,219	1,333	3.8	7.5	1.6	13.6	28.5
Sandusky	1,669	1,622	1,479	2.9	12.9	27,096	23,923	1,157	5.2	6.9	2.0	(NA)	14.3
Scioto	1,796	1,780	1,559	0.9	15.2	23,473	19,714	988	5.9	8.1	2.5	22.3	28.4
Seneca	1,509	1,465	1,354	3.0	11.5	26,306	23,095	893	7.0	6.8	2.4	10.8	15.2
Shelby	1,472	1,414	1,271	4.1	15.8	30,242	26,479	1,599	5.7	4.3	(NA)	(NA)	8.4
Stark	11,118	10,718	10,114	3.7	9.9	29,236	26,746	7,726	6.7	8.6	4.4	14.8	12.7
Summit	18,789	18,122	16,594	3.7	13.2	34,395	30,527	14,369	4.8	7.3	6.5	12.2	12.5
Trumbull	6,033	5,884	5,619	2.5	7.4	27,590	24,975	4,240	3.7	7.1	2.3	9.8	12.5
Tuscarawas	2,337	2,250	2,043	3.9	14.4	25,461	22,435	1,471	6.0	8.2	3.0	11.2	14.8
Union	1,375	1,311	1,101	4.9	24.9	30,162	26,723	1,852	2.7	2.5	11.1	2.1	8.8
Van Wert	804	776	731	3.6	10.0	27,514	24,661	471	2.9	6.2	(NA)	11.1	13.4
Vinton	260	249	221	4.4	17.9	19,453	17,211	93	4.2	5.4	1.6	6.5	35.9
Warren	6,597	6,239	4,946	5.7	33.4	33,524	30,660	3,575	4.8	8.1	7.1	5.5	12.9
Washington	1,639	1,600	1,437	2.4	14.1	26,370	22,736	1,081	8.0	7.8	4.8	13.9	14.3
Wayne	3,103	2,999	2,676	3.5	16.0	27,340	23,954	2,288	7.4	6.0	2.9	(NA)	14.6
Williams	1,052	1,029	974	2.2	8.1	27,210	24,831	772	4.3	4.6	2.0	9.3	12.7
Wood	3,762	3,633	3,314	3.6	13.5	30,368	27,346	2,926	7.7	5.2	3.0	6.7	20.3
Wyandot	631	629	540	0.3	16.8	27,783	23,582	452	7.2	4.3	(NA)	(NA)	13.3

See footnotes at end of table.

Table B-9. Counties — **Personal Income and Earnings by Industries**—Con.

[Includes United States, states, and 3,141 counties/county equivalents defined as of February 22, 2005. For more information on these areas, see Appendix C, Geographic Information]

	Personal income							Earnings, by place of work, 2005					
County	Total, by place of residence					Per capita[1] (dol.)			Percent, by selected major industries				
				Percent change									
	2005 (mil. dol.)	2004 (mil. dol.)	2000 (mil. dol.)	2004–2005	2000–2005	2005	2000	Total[2] (mil. dol.)	Construction	Retail trade	Professional and technical services	Health care and social assistance	Government
OKLAHOMA.............	106,119	100,027	84,310	6.1	25.9	29,948	24,407	79,336	4.8	6.7	5.6	8.8	20.9
Adair...................	435	411	331	5.8	31.3	19,804	15,720	249	(NA)	6.8	1.5	5.0	22.8
Alfalfa.................	127	122	124	4.1	2.7	22,213	20,299	66	6.2	6.2	(NA)	3.8	27.7
Atoka..................	280	262	217	6.9	29.1	19,499	15,655	162	3.8	10.8	2.8	(NA)	34.2
Beaver.................	137	128	131	7.0	4.6	25,409	22,637	68	8.6	(NA)	2.9	0.9	29.1
Beckham...............	470	432	354	8.8	32.6	25,002	17,942	366	5.3	10.9	(NA)	10.6	12.8
Blaine.................	241	237	215	1.7	12.3	18,722	17,937	152	3.5	5.2	2.9	5.8	21.1
Bryan..................	918	864	695	6.3	32.2	24,336	18,964	573	2.5	6.3	4.2	10.9	37.1
Caddo..................	620	590	533	5.1	16.3	20,593	17,702	335	4.0	8.0	(NA)	(NA)	36.0
Canadian...............	2,845	2,656	2,210	7.1	28.7	28,895	25,054	1,155	9.6	8.5	(NA)	5.0	24.7
Carter.................	1,262	1,196	1,066	5.5	18.4	26,842	23,386	987	5.8	7.0	4.2	12.1	12.9
Cherokee...............	957	909	715	5.3	33.9	21,554	16,751	592	5.6	7.4	1.6	5.7	54.5
Choctaw................	321	300	244	7.0	31.6	20,953	15,891	174	5.2	8.7	2.1	(NA)	29.2
Cimarron...............	64	61	68	4.9	−5.5	22,781	21,499	37	(NA)	8.1	1.8	1.6	31.9
Cleveland..............	6,588	6,247	5,236	5.5	25.8	29,379	25,136	3,023	7.5	9.3	7.1	9.0	31.8
Coal...................	106	100	90	6.0	18.0	18,459	14,947	35	6.3	11.8	2.6	17.4	41.8
Comanche...............	3,127	2,958	2,453	5.7	27.5	28,269	21,397	2,561	2.7	5.6	3.7	5.4	57.4
Cotton.................	175	159	137	10.1	27.5	26,774	20,639	75	(NA)	3.8	1.4	4.3	42.9
Craig..................	359	348	297	3.2	20.9	23,835	19,858	244	3.5	8.5	(NA)	(NA)	32.3
Creek..................	1,665	1,584	1,421	5.1	17.1	24,240	21,036	784	11.5	8.0	(NA)	8.7	16.7
Custer.................	636	595	532	6.9	19.5	25,147	20,424	449	6.1	8.9	4.0	(NA)	25.1
Delaware...............	999	950	765	5.2	30.7	25,466	20,551	362	7.9	11.3	3.4	11.0	23.8
Dewey..................	123	115	98	7.0	25.0	27,137	20,877	56	4.0	9.8	(NA)	1.7	32.0
Ellis..................	104	101	86	3.0	20.2	26,246	21,340	47	2.9	7.2	(NA)	6.6	30.7
Garfield...............	1,731	1,664	1,379	4.0	25.5	30,430	23,904	1,198	4.3	7.0	(NA)	12.6	23.1
Garvin.................	714	678	561	5.3	27.2	26,270	20,578	426	6.3	12.8	2.7	(NA)	22.1
Grady..................	1,152	1,097	928	5.0	24.1	23,331	20,357	566	10.5	8.2	(NA)	7.1	20.1
Grant..................	139	140	118	−0.7	17.5	29,127	23,064	66	2.4	(NA)	2.1	3.0	21.0
Greer..................	143	138	128	3.6	11.3	24,435	21,311	69	(NA)	5.5	(NA)	4.7	49.7
Harmon.................	71	72	60	−1.4	17.9	23,460	18,353	38	(NA)	6.2	1.8	1.1	32.2
Harper.................	114	100	92	14.0	23.3	33,979	26,095	71	(NA)	3.8	1.7	2.7	21.2
Haskell................	281	266	220	5.6	27.9	23,226	18,575	139	7.4	8.5	(NA)	16.6	24.9
Hughes.................	288	274	228	5.1	26.3	20,726	16,131	138	3.8	6.5	1.7	3.9	27.5
Jackson................	729	700	592	4.1	23.1	27,679	20,966	611	1.9	6.0	1.7	4.2	55.7
Jefferson..............	139	134	120	3.7	15.8	21,613	17,698	61	2.2	6.0	(NA)	(NA)	28.3
Johnston...............	224	211	170	6.2	32.0	21,715	16,147	126	1.5	5.1	(NA)	9.6	25.6
Kay....................	1,361	1,292	1,095	5.3	24.3	29,452	22,844	1,005	5.1	6.3	4.5	7.6	13.5
Kingfisher.............	412	393	336	4.8	22.5	28,980	24,200	293	5.7	7.7	2.1	3.4	11.3
Kiowa..................	227	221	199	2.7	13.8	22,968	19,540	103	(NA)	7.6	2.9	(NA)	32.3
Latimer................	249	241	203	3.3	22.9	23,518	18,971	187	(NA)	4.0	0.8	(NA)	24.6
Le Flore...............	1,106	1,045	886	5.8	24.8	22,384	18,404	534	4.4	8.5	2.3	(NA)	28.9
Lincoln................	726	686	611	5.8	18.9	22,447	18,997	295	9.5	6.5	3.5	(NA)	24.1
Logan..................	1,075	1,004	761	7.1	41.2	29,525	22,427	350	7.2	9.2	(NA)	(NA)	23.8
Love...................	222	200	163	11.0	35.9	24,219	18,504	93	3.6	7.6	(NA)	(NA)	54.5
McClain................	833	774	614	7.6	35.6	27,785	22,056	298	14.2	14.4	4.0	(NA)	22.3
McCurtain..............	805	767	638	5.0	26.2	23,754	18,539	566	7.7	5.9	2.6	5.3	18.4
McIntosh...............	432	420	355	2.9	21.6	21,783	18,237	159	4.8	17.6	4.4	12.8	24.8
Major..................	175	172	161	1.7	8.5	23,960	21,386	98	7.5	7.2	2.7	5.0	19.0
Marshall...............	317	301	240	5.3	32.0	22,086	18,226	180	2.3	6.7	1.7	(NA)	17.5
Mayes..................	904	862	767	4.9	17.9	22,942	19,944	468	6.3	11.8	(NA)	5.7	25.0
Murray.................	315	284	231	10.9	36.1	24,565	18,341	177	4.5	8.7	3.1	(NA)	39.4
Muskogee...............	1,683	1,611	1,383	4.5	21.7	23,813	19,910	1,288	5.2	8.8	2.4	9.3	29.9
Noble..................	270	256	252	5.5	7.1	24,112	22,146	187	(NA)	3.9	2.4	4.6	21.9
Nowata.................	216	207	184	4.3	17.1	20,006	17,410	78	9.4	7.3	4.4	8.7	25.5
Okfuskee...............	232	218	178	6.4	30.0	20,330	15,119	115	4.8	6.8	(NA)	9.9	38.5
Oklahoma...............	24,751	23,271	18,731	6.4	32.1	36,176	28,308	25,169	3.8	5.9	6.4	9.9	21.4
Okmulgee...............	884	846	690	4.5	28.2	22,279	17,397	406	2.6	9.0	2.2	(NA)	33.4
Osage..................	1,172	1,102	922	6.4	27.2	25,858	20,683	400	6.8	6.6	(NA)	3.8	24.0
Ottawa.................	798	757	621	5.4	28.5	24,314	18,682	466	2.7	6.9	3.5	(NA)	21.3
Pawnee.................	397	381	332	4.2	19.6	23,634	19,880	152	3.1	9.5	(NA)	15.8	29.3
Payne..................	1,760	1,698	1,434	3.7	22.7	23,966	21,042	1,327	4.9	8.1	4.0	6.8	44.2
Pittsburg..............	1,082	1,028	836	5.3	29.4	24,286	19,015	729	3.4	8.6	(NA)	(NA)	40.7
Pontotoc...............	916	851	728	7.6	25.8	26,037	20,719	657	3.2	7.1	(NA)	11.3	35.7
Pottawatomie...........	1,676	1,587	1,328	5.6	26.2	24,622	20,214	851	5.5	9.4	(NA)	10.2	20.6
Pushmataha.............	246	233	180	5.6	36.9	21,071	15,415	122	11.5	9.3	2.3	17.8	30.8
Roger Mills............	86	83	71	3.6	21.6	25,963	20,663	45	(NA)	8.0	(NA)	(NA)	35.9
Rogers.................	2,159	2,000	1,730	8.0	24.8	26,811	24,246	1,206	9.1	5.5	(NA)	5.4	20.4
Seminole...............	548	515	427	6.4	28.3	22,260	17,165	294	5.1	7.4	1.6	(NA)	25.3
Sequoyah...............	900	857	731	5.0	23.1	22,086	18,712	395	3.4	10.1	9.8	12.4	29.0
Stephens...............	1,150	1,083	943	6.2	22.0	26,787	21,882	723	4.8	8.5	(NA)	8.5	12.6
Texas..................	553	513	570	7.8	−3.0	27,476	28,240	459	(NA)	5.1	3.0	2.9	14.7

See footnotes at end of table.

[Includes United States, states, and 3,141 counties/county equivalents defined as of February 22, 2005. For more information on these areas, see Appendix C, Geographic Information]

| County | Personal income | | | | | | | | Earnings, by place of work, 2005 | | | | |
| | Total, by place of residence | | | Percent change | | Per capita[1] (dol.) | | | Percent, by selected major industries | | | | |
	2005 (mil. dol.)	2004 (mil. dol.)	2000 (mil. dol.)	2004–2005	2000–2005	2005	2000	Total[2] (mil. dol.)	Construction	Retail trade	Professional and technical services	Health care and social assistance	Government
OKLAHOMA—Con.													
Tillman	184	180	154	2.2	19.8	21,611	16,589	103	(NA)	4.6	2.0	3.5	29.8
Tulsa	22,870	21,372	18,669	7.0	22.5	40,079	33,110	21,400	4.8	5.8	7.2	9.3	8.0
Wagoner	1,577	1,479	1,220	6.6	29.2	24,568	21,137	292	11.7	7.9	3.2	(NA)	24.1
Washington	1,615	1,538	1,371	5.0	17.8	32,960	27,985	966	2.9	10.0	4.1	(NA)	9.9
Washita	247	242	195	2.1	26.7	21,606	16,933	113	10.0	5.9	5.9	4.9	27.8
Woods	214	210	185	1.9	15.5	25,217	20,485	118	2.6	10.4	2.6	4.8	36.5
Woodward	490	447	367	9.6	33.7	25,798	19,877	410	8.8	7.7	2.3	(NA)	15.2
OREGON	117,497	111,325	96,402	5.5	21.9	32,289	28,097	91,881	6.5	6.9	6.5	10.1	18.9
Baker	393	376	340	4.5	15.6	24,199	20,317	216	3.9	8.7	3.6	(NA)	33.5
Benton	2,883	2,727	2,259	5.7	27.6	36,685	28,921	2,167	3.3	3.9	6.0	10.7	32.7
Clackamas	14,631	13,847	12,416	5.7	17.8	39,729	36,556	8,473	8.7	7.2	8.0	10.2	12.4
Clatsop	1,063	1,009	862	5.4	23.3	28,854	24,215	788	6.2	9.9	2.2	9.6	20.9
Columbia	1,394	1,318	1,168	5.8	19.3	29,111	26,750	536	6.2	8.0	(NA)	5.5	22.1
Coos	1,740	1,656	1,377	5.1	26.4	26,953	21,959	1,072	4.6	9.0	3.0	9.0	31.7
Crook	524	495	394	5.9	33.1	23,802	20,359	335	6.4	5.1	2.3	6.6	22.1
Curry	603	574	500	5.1	20.7	27,010	23,648	301	11.0	11.6	3.8	(NA)	23.3
Deschutes	4,534	4,164	3,140	8.9	44.4	32,094	26,926	3,280	13.4	10.0	6.9	12.7	14.3
Douglas	2,836	2,708	2,276	4.7	24.6	27,237	22,649	1,847	5.9	7.6	4.3	11.2	25.6
Gilliam	48	46	36	4.3	33.2	26,911	18,851	32	(NA)	3.4	(NA)	4.6	31.4
Grant	205	201	169	2.0	21.5	27,975	21,358	126	6.8	5.7	2.0	(NA)	45.1
Harney	184	174	161	5.7	14.3	26,620	21,140	122	3.6	6.7	(NA)	(NA)	46.7
Hood River	579	546	467	6.0	23.9	30,277	22,818	426	5.3	8.7	5.5	12.4	18.1
Jackson	5,901	5,599	4,531	5.4	30.2	30,239	24,914	4,115	11.6	12.6	4.1	14.3	16.5
Jefferson	470	461	379	2.0	23.9	23,514	19,841	277	2.6	5.9	(NA)	(NA)	47.4
Josephine	2,033	1,930	1,626	5.3	25.0	25,198	21,438	1,137	9.6	11.5	3.3	15.0	18.5
Klamath	1,711	1,631	1,362	4.9	25.6	25,997	21,305	1,130	4.8	8.3	(NA)	11.6	27.4
Lake	193	188	158	2.7	22.1	26,508	21,334	123	4.3	6.0	3.3	(NA)	43.8
Lane	9,981	9,415	8,248	6.0	21.0	29,841	25,500	7,172	6.7	8.2	5.4	12.6	21.4
Lincoln	1,353	1,284	1,084	5.4	24.9	29,445	24,440	829	8.2	12.4	3.9	9.9	26.3
Linn	2,927	2,757	2,328	6.2	25.7	26,870	22,590	2,076	5.9	6.8	1.8	7.7	17.0
Malheur	676	633	600	6.8	12.7	21,609	19,024	560	2.1	9.3	2.2	10.7	33.6
Marion	8,813	8,316	6,981	6.0	26.3	28,826	24,439	6,917	6.3	7.1	3.9	14.0	32.3
Morrow	292	322	226	−9.3	29.1	25,108	20,455	208	1.5	2.4	0.8	1.4	21.1
Multnomah	25,436	24,214	21,384	5.0	18.9	37,798	32,329	27,202	5.1	5.1	10.2	9.8	18.1
Polk	1,978	1,851	1,535	6.9	28.9	28,030	24,498	809	6.1	5.4	2.4	8.2	36.6
Sherman	40	43	37	−7.0	9.0	23,120	19,055	21	(NA)	13.9	(NA)	(NA)	89.7
Tillamook	718	685	576	4.8	24.7	28,449	23,739	421	6.1	7.0	(NA)	8.5	24.9
Umatilla	1,845	1,791	1,514	3.0	21.8	25,322	21,421	1,395	4.0	6.6	(NA)	8.4	31.7
Union	672	661	559	1.7	20.2	27,522	22,771	458	5.2	8.1	2.4	11.2	30.4
Wallowa	197	190	158	3.7	24.6	28,300	21,891	116	6.9	12.2	3.1	5.0	31.5
Wasco	625	608	564	2.8	10.9	26,537	23,663	409	4.6	11.3	3.3	16.4	31.7
Washington	17,338	16,366	14,881	5.9	16.5	34,626	33,178	15,265	6.3	6.3	5.3	6.8	8.3
Wheeler	37	33	30	12.1	24.0	25,923	19,306	14	5.2	5.7	3.2	(NA)	40.6
Yamhill	2,644	2,503	2,078	5.6	27.3	28,713	24,364	1,505	7.0	6.6	3.0	9.8	17.5
PENNSYLVANIA	433,400	413,589	364,838	4.8	18.8	34,937	29,695	323,799	6.1	6.5	9.6	12.4	13.3
Adams	2,925	2,740	2,308	6.8	26.7	29,320	25,192	1,597	9.6	7.7	2.8	(NA)	14.1
Allegheny	51,126	49,155	44,298	4.0	15.4	41,464	34,611	46,111	5.1	5.3	11.3	12.4	9.9
Armstrong	2,007	1,906	1,668	5.3	20.3	28,452	23,070	1,007	5.8	9.8	2.8	11.8	14.4
Beaver	5,166	4,945	4,495	4.5	14.9	29,217	24,812	2,703	6.7	8.0	7.7	13.6	15.0
Bedford	1,189	1,161	1,048	2.4	13.4	23,854	20,949	661	9.4	10.0	2.2	7.7	16.8
Berks	12,543	11,931	10,778	5.1	16.4	31,655	28,776	8,704	7.1	8.7	6.9	11.2	12.6
Blair	3,489	3,368	3,057	3.6	14.1	27,562	23,689	2,632	5.4	9.6	5.5	16.2	16.6
Bradford	1,568	1,512	1,366	3.7	14.8	25,092	21,752	1,040	3.7	7.5	(NA)	19.6	15.3
Bucks	27,856	26,668	22,922	4.5	21.5	44,945	38,236	16,326	11.9	8.7	9.5	10.8	8.9
Butler	6,031	5,736	5,028	5.1	20.0	33,225	28,798	3,722	7.0	9.5	4.6	9.4	14.3
Cambria	3,920	3,742	3,413	4.8	14.8	26,525	22,420	2,470	4.5	8.4	8.1	18.6	20.2
Cameron	148	145	138	2.1	7.3	26,421	23,205	107	2.4	4.1	(NA)	4.6	16.7
Carbon	1,693	1,612	1,424	5.0	18.9	27,368	24,194	732	6.9	9.4	2.5	13.0	18.0
Centre	4,110	3,910	3,266	5.1	25.8	29,295	24,048	3,559	5.5	5.8	7.2	8.2	46.4
Chester	24,059	22,783	20,245	5.6	18.8	50,787	46,453	18,149	5.8	7.1	16.2	7.9	7.6
Clarion	1,131	1,073	917	5.4	23.3	27,996	21,966	748	4.9	7.9	2.3	9.6	23.1
Clearfield	2,108	2,025	1,800	4.1	17.1	25,508	21,583	1,329	4.9	9.5	(NA)	17.8	17.7
Clinton	943	910	791	3.6	19.2	25,321	20,861	590	5.5	8.7	1.6	8.8	23.7
Columbia	1,799	1,721	1,452	4.5	23.9	27,764	22,649	1,256	6.5	8.1	4.5	9.7	18.3
Crawford	2,202	2,108	2,063	4.5	6.8	24,611	22,820	1,353	4.9	8.0	2.8	14.1	16.2
Cumberland	8,116	7,764	6,652	4.5	22.0	36,393	31,090	7,123	4.8	6.6	8.1	11.1	16.9
Dauphin	8,921	8,553	7,422	4.3	20.2	35,269	29,473	9,867	4.6	5.0	6.6	11.2	25.8
Delaware	23,289	22,223	20,328	4.8	14.6	42,008	36,813	13,600	6.6	6.6	9.7	13.8	10.6
Elk	1,003	966	901	3.8	11.4	29,954	25,701	697	3.6	4.9	(NA)	11.6	9.7
Erie	7,754	7,404	6,888	4.7	12.6	27,676	24,538	5,843	4.7	7.7	4.0	15.2	14.8

See footnotes at end of table.

County and City Data Book: 2007

U.S. Census Bureau

Table B-9. Counties — **Personal Income and Earnings by Industries**—Con.

[Includes United States, states, and 3,141 counties/county equivalents defined as of February 22, 2005. For more information on these areas, see Appendix C, Geographic Information]

County	Total, by place of residence 2005 (mil. dol.)	2004 (mil. dol.)	2000 (mil. dol.)	Percent change 2004–2005	2000–2005	Per capita[1] (dol.) 2005	2000	Total[2] (mil. dol.)	Con- struc- tion	Retail trade	Profes- sional and tech- nical services	Health care and social assis- tance	Govern- ment
PENNSYLVANIA—Con.													
Fayette	3,775	3,637	3,265	3.8	15.6	25,821	21,983	1,735	6.3	10.6	4.3	15.0	19.5
Forest	131	117	102	12.0	28.0	20,065	20,710	92	3.4	2.8	(NA)	17.1	49.6
Franklin	4,043	3,788	3,224	6.7	25.4	29,453	24,885	2,550	6.6	7.6	3.9	13.1	17.4
Fulton	430	397	332	8.3	29.4	29,321	23,300	329	7.6	4.0	0.8	(NA)	10.2
Greene	943	896	815	5.2	15.7	23,337	20,027	635	3.6	5.8	(NA)	(NA)	21.1
Huntingdon	1,067	1,018	885	4.8	20.6	23,305	19,402	590	8.8	5.9	1.8	(NA)	25.8
Indiana	2,451	2,310	2,005	6.1	22.2	27,703	22,397	1,745	4.0	8.0	2.4	9.4	21.2
Jefferson	1,165	1,113	1,013	4.7	15.0	25,478	22,056	666	4.4	7.6	2.9	(NA)	14.0
Juniata	650	628	498	3.5	30.5	27,762	21,798	363	8.4	5.5	(NA)	5.3	10.2
Lackawanna	6,559	6,286	5,755	4.3	14.0	31,291	27,029	4,577	5.4	9.0	6.0	17.1	13.5
Lancaster	15,991	15,171	13,570	5.4	17.8	32,638	28,765	11,879	10.9	7.8	5.6	10.9	9.1
Lawrence	2,457	2,357	2,147	4.2	14.5	26,584	22,687	1,463	11.7	7.5	3.7	13.7	16.0
Lebanon	3,957	3,761	3,175	5.2	24.6	31,545	26,365	2,174	5.5	8.2	2.9	12.4	19.0
Lehigh	11,587	10,933	9,708	6.0	19.4	35,093	31,049	9,935	5.7	6.2	5.0	17.0	9.0
Luzerne	9,508	9,131	8,249	4.1	15.3	30,397	25,891	6,693	5.0	7.6	4.4	13.8	15.4
Lycoming	3,311	3,204	2,762	3.3	19.9	28,034	23,026	2,418	5.0	7.1	3.8	13.7	17.2
McKean	1,212	1,165	1,128	4.0	7.4	27,408	24,630	781	4.7	6.5	(NA)	12.1	17.7
Mercer	3,218	3,101	2,816	3.8	14.3	27,019	23,432	2,061	4.1	8.9	2.3	18.2	13.4
Mifflin	1,140	1,090	951	4.6	19.8	24,732	20,460	718	5.9	7.9	(NA)	15.4	12.6
Monroe	4,402	4,156	3,418	5.9	28.8	27,106	24,439	2,739	7.4	9.0	4.0	9.0	25.8
Montgomery	42,059	40,331	34,536	4.3	21.8	54,293	45,991	37,028	7.8	5.6	15.7	11.1	6.3
Montour	600	579	475	3.6	26.2	33,383	26,042	731	4.0	3.4	3.0	(NA)	9.4
Northampton	9,324	8,866	7,722	5.2	20.8	32,451	28,867	5,021	8.2	8.0	5.3	8.9	14.3
Northumberland	2,502	2,404	2,115	4.1	18.3	27,113	22,388	1,346	5.1	6.7	(NA)	9.3	17.3
Perry	1,284	1,236	1,069	3.9	20.1	28,717	24,507	347	13.2	10.3	3.5	6.4	27.2
Philadelphia	45,335	43,155	37,194	5.1	21.9	31,129	24,571	44,156	2.2	3.5	15.1	15.1	17.9
Pike	1,501	1,403	1,120	7.0	34.0	26,719	24,004	504	10.2	10.0	5.1	6.7	25.7
Potter	489	473	438	3.4	11.7	27,582	24,118	351	4.0	6.3	1.5	(NA)	14.0
Schuylkill	3,912	3,729	3,435	4.9	13.9	26,610	22,878	2,170	5.4	8.0	3.3	13.2	17.6
Snyder	1,124	1,079	940	4.2	19.5	29,613	25,041	762	5.2	9.1	(NA)	5.2	15.2
Somerset	1,955	1,884	1,672	3.8	16.9	24,816	20,892	1,137	6.5	9.5	3.0	10.3	19.7
Sullivan	161	157	143	2.5	12.3	25,334	21,839	65	10.0	9.5	2.2	(NA)	23.9
Susquehanna	1,108	1,066	990	3.9	11.9	26,417	23,433	388	8.7	9.7	3.5	10.7	23.8
Tioga	963	931	848	3.4	13.6	23,265	20,492	560	3.1	7.8	(NA)	(NA)	25.4
Union	1,093	1,055	913	3.6	19.7	25,314	21,919	855	6.0	5.3	2.3	(NA)	23.7
Venango	1,527	1,457	1,340	4.8	13.9	27,290	23,317	902	2.9	8.5	2.0	14.9	20.1
Warren	1,146	1,101	1,028	4.1	11.5	27,295	23,473	682	3.2	15.7	5.4	13.2	18.1
Washington	7,026	6,637	5,656	5.9	24.2	34,035	27,859	4,028	9.7	6.5	6.0	12.4	12.2
Wayne	1,355	1,297	1,107	4.5	22.4	26,822	23,094	637	12.9	11.5	3.1	12.1	23.9
Westmoreland	11,872	11,341	9,950	4.7	19.3	32,337	26,906	6,487	6.8	9.4	6.9	11.7	13.1
Wyoming	751	714	639	5.2	17.5	26,688	22,798	476	6.9	5.9	(NA)	(NA)	12.3
York	13,222	12,374	11,019	6.9	20.0	32,393	28,788	9,096	8.1	7.1	4.2	10.4	12.4
RHODE ISLAND	37,923	36,679	30,697	3.4	23.5	35,324	29,214	27,049	5.9	6.4	7.3	13.0	18.1
Bristol	2,265	2,197	1,841	3.1	23.0	43,068	36,287	775	8.4	6.2	4.8	10.8	16.0
Kent	6,485	6,257	5,170	3.6	25.4	37,901	30,862	4,340	6.1	9.2	7.6	11.5	13.1
Newport	3,593	3,481	3,012	3.2	19.3	43,168	35,159	2,561	5.1	6.0	10.7	6.8	36.8
Providence	20,421	19,776	16,611	3.3	22.9	31,978	26,670	16,625	5.8	5.3	7.2	14.9	15.9
Washington	5,159	4,969	4,064	3.8	27.0	40,291	32,767	2,749	5.9	9.4	5.3	10.5	22.6
SOUTH CAROLINA	120,123	113,632	98,270	5.7	22.2	28,285	24,424	89,011	7.2	8.0	6.0	7.9	20.9
Abbeville	576	553	602	4.2	−4.4	22,111	22,967	320	5.9	4.4	(NA)	(NA)	19.5
Aiken	4,264	4,090	3,546	4.3	20.2	28,418	24,831	3,236	11.4	6.8	4.5	5.7	12.3
Allendale	205	194	182	5.7	12.8	18,871	16,244	163	2.1	2.8	(NA)	3.1	29.8
Anderson	4,726	4,511	4,037	4.8	17.1	26,968	24,271	2,836	6.1	9.3	2.9	7.0	19.0
Bamberg	331	319	289	3.8	14.4	20,989	17,395	190	2.8	9.8	2.1	6.9	29.9
Barnwell	475	460	521	3.3	−8.9	20,409	22,216	295	4.6	7.2	5.4	(NA)	21.8
Beaufort	5,426	5,020	3,960	8.1	37.0	39,308	32,452	3,619	11.2	8.3	6.4	5.5	31.4
Berkeley	4,043	3,757	2,884	7.6	40.2	27,040	20,157	2,054	11.2	7.0	(NA)	3.4	20.1
Calhoun	428	403	339	6.2	26.4	28,429	22,219	248	12.2	3.9	1.9	(NA)	13.3
Charleston	11,254	10,535	8,924	6.8	26.1	34,158	28,720	11,076	7.1	8.6	10.4	9.4	27.9
Cherokee	1,215	1,170	1,070	3.8	13.5	22,651	20,313	837	8.5	6.1	2.8	(NA)	13.2
Chester	821	778	681	5.5	20.6	24,814	19,941	531	8.3	4.2	(NA)	(NA)	15.0
Chesterfield	963	935	839	3.0	14.7	22,286	19,558	611	3.1	6.0	1.1	6.8	14.7
Clarendon	704	681	583	3.4	20.8	21,266	17,902	318	6.3	8.9	(NA)	(NA)	29.6
Colleton	898	860	733	4.4	22.6	22,764	19,103	441	6.8	9.7	3.2	9.9	20.4
Darlington	1,734	1,669	1,493	3.9	16.2	25,745	22,115	1,097	4.9	5.8	2.0	(NA)	13.1
Dillon	643	625	552	2.9	16.5	20,850	17,965	366	3.9	11.9	(NA)	(NA)	19.3
Dorchester	2,956	2,725	2,125	8.5	39.1	26,207	21,973	1,248	8.3	9.6	(NA)	5.9	18.1
Edgefield	587	564	465	4.1	26.3	23,157	18,921	251	4.0	4.5	1.0	(NA)	34.4
Fairfield	571	542	472	5.4	21.0	23,926	20,045	317	4.7	5.1	(NA)	(NA)	22.3

See footnotes at end of table.

County and City Data Book: 2007

U.S. Census Bureau

[Includes United States, states, and 3,141 counties/county equivalents defined as of February 22, 2005. For more information on these areas, see Appendix C, Geographic Information]

County	Personal income							Earnings, by place of work, 2005				
	Total, by place of residence					Per capita[1] (dol.)			Percent, by selected major industries				
				Percent change							Profes-sional and tech-nical services	Health care and social assis-tance	
	2005 (mil. dol.)	2004 (mil. dol.)	2000 (mil. dol.)	2004–2005	2000–2005	2005	2000	Total[2] (mil. dol.)	Con-struc-tion	Retail trade			Govern-ment
SOUTH CAROLINA—Con.													
Florence	3,711	3,535	2,994	5.0	24.0	28,486	23,795	2,994	5.2	8.4	4.8	11.6	19.7
Georgetown	1,830	1,694	1,361	8.0	34.5	30,399	24,254	1,105	12.5	8.3	(NA)	10.1	20.2
Greenville	12,931	12,250	11,314	5.6	14.3	31,759	29,689	11,845	7.1	9.0	8.7	7.1	11.8
Greenwood	1,728	1,660	1,532	4.1	12.8	25,471	23,090	1,389	6.3	7.3	4.3	8.3	23.5
Hampton	456	435	396	4.8	15.1	21,566	18,551	258	5.4	6.3	7.4	(NA)	30.8
Horry	6,095	5,654	4,740	7.8	28.6	26,789	23,933	4,475	11.0	12.1	5.2	8.1	14.3
Jasper	507	467	367	8.6	38.3	23,696	17,693	270	16.7	7.9	1.4	(NA)	21.7
Kershaw	1,611	1,522	1,234	5.8	30.5	28,595	23,355	912	8.8	9.4	3.1	5.1	16.7
Lancaster	1,486	1,401	1,264	6.1	17.5	23,560	20,591	857	5.7	7.2	(NA)	8.8	16.7
Laurens	1,689	1,588	1,421	6.4	18.9	24,043	20,391	815	4.8	5.0	(NA)	(NA)	21.2
Lee	418	394	347	6.1	20.5	20,307	17,225	178	2.2	7.3	(NA)	(NA)	30.9
Lexington	7,418	7,038	6,268	5.4	18.3	31,575	28,901	4,355	9.2	9.6	6.8	7.0	17.0
McCormick	206	197	173	4.6	19.1	20,299	17,308	84	2.8	4.2	(NA)	(NA)	44.5
Marion	713	704	637	1.3	12.0	20,485	17,948	391	4.6	10.7	(NA)	(NA)	28.1
Marlboro	572	544	485	5.1	17.9	20,643	16,841	355	2.2	5.4	0.8	(NA)	25.6
Newberry	892	856	743	4.2	20.1	23,901	20,605	547	7.2	6.4	2.5	4.6	19.6
Oconee	1,990	1,908	1,601	4.3	24.3	28,561	24,107	1,264	6.4	6.9	(NA)	5.2	15.7
Orangeburg	2,182	2,105	1,804	3.7	21.0	24,002	19,711	1,411	4.4	9.3	1.8	6.7	25.3
Pickens	2,782	2,659	2,338	4.6	19.0	24,572	21,068	1,601	7.3	8.7	2.3	7.8	29.6
Richland	10,773	10,166	8,713	6.0	23.6	31,518	27,110	11,323	5.0	6.1	8.2	10.1	30.3
Saluda	487	468	403	4.1	20.9	25,667	20,990	184	3.7	5.7	0.7	(NA)	21.0
Spartanburg	7,111	6,831	6,190	4.1	14.9	26,656	24,327	5,977	5.9	6.9	4.8	8.0	14.6
Sumter	2,627	2,515	2,150	4.5	22.2	25,042	20,535	1,987	6.8	6.1	2.4	8.3	35.7
Union	696	667	603	4.3	15.4	24,396	20,178	365	2.8	6.4	(NA)	(NA)	23.2
Williamsburg	706	669	597	5.5	18.2	20,005	16,073	398	4.6	8.9	(NA)	(NA)	25.5
York	5,685	5,316	4,299	6.9	32.2	29,904	25,942	3,617	5.8	7.0	3.9	9.1	13.3
SOUTH DAKOTA	25,201	24,053	19,438	4.8	29.6	32,523	25,720	18,157	6.2	7.6	3.5	12.9	19.3
Aurora	82	93	72	−11.8	14.3	28,465	23,417	34	(NA)	7.0	2.7	6.0	21.7
Beadle	546	527	457	3.6	19.6	34,409	26,892	357	5.8	7.9	2.2	(NA)	18.5
Bennett	84	72	65	16.7	29.0	23,627	18,211	43	7.5	5.3	(NA)	(NA)	35.4
Bon Homme	188	192	159	−2.1	18.2	26,674	21,934	95	(NA)	7.5	1.8	12.7	25.7
Brookings	844	804	673	5.0	25.3	30,409	23,824	680	4.1	5.4	3.0	4.5	28.6
Brown	1,338	1,273	988	5.1	35.4	38,579	27,927	987	6.1	8.3	3.5	15.2	14.5
Brule	142	135	119	5.2	19.0	27,561	22,303	84	5.2	10.7	1.9	14.1	18.1
Buffalo	33	32	24	3.1	36.1	15,784	12,097	28	0.2	(NA)	(NA)	(NA)	74.1
Butte	230	216	177	6.5	30.1	24,594	19,403	115	8.6	12.8	4.5	(NA)	19.7
Campbell	48	45	46	6.7	5.2	30,821	25,625	27	2.4	(NA)	(NA)	1.5	14.8
Charles Mix	260	251	204	3.6	27.7	28,182	21,782	160	4.5	6.0	2.1	(NA)	31.3
Clark	119	117	108	1.7	10.4	31,245	26,126	73	9.2	4.3	2.2	4.0	12.3
Clay	390	392	311	−0.5	25.3	30,100	23,088	263	2.7	7.1	3.3	8.6	40.4
Codington	850	804	677	5.7	25.6	32,641	26,121	630	6.6	10.3	2.5	11.9	13.9
Corson	95	84	70	13.1	36.6	22,038	16,520	53	(NA)	1.7	(NA)	(NA)	46.9
Custer	233	216	161	7.9	44.5	29,824	22,095	113	12.3	7.9	(NA)	8.2	35.4
Davison	659	643	508	2.5	29.8	34,950	27,111	486	7.5	11.1	3.4	(NA)	11.2
Day	166	172	142	−3.5	16.8	28,637	22,759	90	8.9	6.3	2.4	7.9	18.5
Deuel	134	133	113	0.8	18.3	31,102	25,159	83	8.7	5.6	2.8	6.6	11.6
Dewey	133	123	97	8.1	36.5	21,688	16,272	96	(NA)	3.3	(NA)	(NA)	67.8
Douglas	93	92	81	1.1	14.4	28,374	23,627	59	5.0	2.7	(NA)	8.7	11.9
Edmunds	158	158	121	–	30.2	38,589	27,888	88	4.2	6.6	(NA)	3.0	14.2
Fall River	200	190	159	5.3	25.8	27,432	21,438	132	2.2	6.2	1.1	(NA)	44.9
Faulk	80	80	70	–	14.0	33,558	26,662	50	(NA)	2.4	(NA)	5.3	11.2
Grant	235	229	194	2.6	20.8	31,811	24,823	178	4.7	5.8	1.8	(NA)	8.6
Gregory	133	123	105	8.1	26.4	30,929	22,093	71	10.5	10.0	3.0	(NA)	15.8
Haakon	80	64	61	25.0	30.9	41,719	28,118	49	(NA)	6.4	4.2	(NA)	11.4
Hamlin	154	150	122	2.7	25.9	27,404	22,028	76	6.4	5.0	(NA)	4.2	21.9
Hand	128	118	94	8.5	36.7	38,678	25,220	78	3.5	5.1	(NA)	(NA)	11.9
Hanson	93	106	68	−12.3	37.2	24,903	21,479	25	(NA)	3.6	(NA)	(NA)	23.6
Harding	34	29	26	17.2	32.8	28,066	19,059	23	4.7	4.1	(NA)	8.9	20.4
Hughes	569	532	441	7.0	29.0	33,729	26,736	458	4.0	8.9	4.5	11.3	43.4
Hutchinson	229	238	199	−3.8	15.0	30,368	24,655	110	3.8	7.2	(NA)	(NA)	14.9
Hyde	49	45	37	8.9	31.3	30,566	22,366	31	4.9	8.9	(NA)	(NA)	25.4
Jackson	56	46	47	21.7	20.0	19,535	15,879	32	4.1	8.3	(NA)	(NA)	48.5
Jerauld	72	72	63	–	14.7	34,182	27,507	55	7.2	4.9	(NA)	(NA)	9.3
Jones	33	33	30	–	10.7	31,730	25,223	23	(NA)	7.4	1.8	2.5	23.4
Kingsbury	171	175	150	−2.3	14.2	31,102	25,765	98	8.0	4.4	(NA)	7.5	11.6
Lake	328	315	274	4.1	19.8	29,670	24,339	217	6.3	6.9	2.2	8.2	18.4
Lawrence	669	623	482	7.4	38.8	29,725	22,139	438	7.8	9.6	2.8	11.8	17.8
Lincoln	1,131	1,075	697	5.2	62.4	33,872	28,375	461	12.7	7.8	(NA)	13.2	8.7
Lyman	98	93	81	5.4	21.7	24,947	20,603	60	(NA)	11.0	(NA)	(NA)	43.8
McCook	170	181	166	−6.1	2.6	28,706	28,318	74	5.9	8.6	2.6	9.2	17.4
McPherson	71	70	63	1.4	12.7	26,870	21,769	38	1.1	2.1	(NA)	7.2	16.0
Marshall	138	132	110	4.5	25.3	31,260	24,065	89	4.2	4.1	1.7	(NA)	13.8

See footnotes at end of table.

[Includes United States, states, and 3,141 counties/county equivalents defined as of February 22, 2005. For more information on these areas, see Appendix C, Geographic Information]

County	Personal income							Earnings, by place of work, 2005					
	Total, by place of residence					Per capita[1] (dol.)			Percent, by selected major industries				
				Percent change							Professional and technical services	Health care and social assistance	
	2005 (mil. dol.)	2004 (mil. dol.)	2000 (mil. dol.)	2004–2005	2000–2005	2005	2000	Total[2] (mil. dol.)	Construction	Retail trade			Government
SOUTH DAKOTA—Con.													
Meade	832	779	570	6.8	46.0	33,875	23,518	424	8.1	6.8	3.4	(NA)	33.0
Mellette	41	40	32	2.5	27.8	19,654	15,359	18	(NA)	5.6	(NA)	(NA)	42.8
Miner	73	72	68	1.4	8.0	28,456	23,394	41	(NA)	4.5	(NA)	7.9	15.1
Minnehaha	6,023	5,653	4,545	6.5	32.5	37,629	30,503	5,590	6.2	8.0	4.8	17.4	10.0
Moody	215	199	172	8.0	24.9	32,438	26,153	131	9.0	3.2	1.6	5.2	27.0
Pennington	3,070	2,918	2,348	5.2	30.8	32,887	26,450	2,332	7.7	9.2	4.1	16.8	25.6
Perkins	89	81	76	9.9	17.8	29,085	22,624	55	3.5	7.0	1.4	(NA)	18.0
Potter	93	92	81	1.1	14.8	39,401	30,235	43	5.5	6.1	(NA)	9.7	16.5
Roberts	263	259	207	1.5	27.2	26,296	20,674	155	3.5	5.4	1.4	6.8	38.2
Sanborn	103	97	77	6.2	33.7	40,726	28,817	48	3.6	2.5	(NA)	(NA)	12.4
Shannon	221	205	153	7.8	44.4	16,278	12,206	183	(NA)	1.9	(NA)	(NA)	77.5
Spink	239	246	204	-2.8	16.9	34,508	27,509	127	3.1	3.7	(NA)	3.0	30.4
Stanley	106	92	75	15.2	40.7	38,041	27,076	49	35.4	7.0	3.0	(NA)	13.9
Sully	70	75	59	-6.7	18.8	49,119	37,981	46	(NA)	4.0	(NA)	(NA)	9.7
Todd	154	142	119	8.5	29.9	15,611	13,039	120	0.1	2.9	(NA)	3.6	81.1
Tripp	177	166	138	6.6	27.9	29,228	21,670	114	4.5	10.5	2.6	(NA)	15.1
Turner	280	285	241	-1.8	16.2	32,864	27,209	107	7.3	5.7	(NA)	9.7	16.4
Union	578	571	470	1.2	23.0	43,056	37,299	467	4.0	1.6	3.2	(NA)	6.3
Walworth	149	140	132	6.4	12.9	27,248	22,220	84	4.6	11.3	5.1	13.1	18.7
Yankton	629	614	532	2.4	18.2	28,928	24,617	491	4.1	7.3	2.3	(NA)	17.5
Ziebach	46	38	29	21.1	59.8	17,353	11,576	24	(NA)	2.2	(NA)	(NA)	31.7
TENNESSEE	184,443	174,452	148,833	5.7	23.9	30,969	26,097	147,894	5.8	7.6	6.7	11.7	13.9
Anderson	2,104	2,020	1,785	4.2	17.9	29,007	25,035	2,256	3.6	4.7	18.8	8.6	13.0
Bedford	1,132	1,063	878	6.5	29.0	26,780	23,203	803	7.1	5.8	(NA)	3.0	11.7
Benton	359	341	327	5.3	9.7	21,811	19,801	162	5.3	10.6	2.3	10.9	20.0
Bledsoe	277	266	220	4.1	25.8	21,481	17,747	102	6.2	4.6	(NA)	3.5	37.0
Blount	3,161	3,007	2,544	5.1	24.2	27,337	23,947	2,239	11.8	9.8	3.4	6.3	13.4
Bradley	2,617	2,480	2,004	5.5	30.6	28,400	22,727	2,039	4.4	6.6	3.2	(NA)	11.9
Campbell	940	884	711	6.3	32.3	23,179	17,793	471	8.2	8.8	2.3	(NA)	20.2
Cannon	353	334	284	5.7	24.1	26,465	22,026	113	(NA)	8.3	2.8	(NA)	17.9
Carroll	702	657	617	6.8	13.8	24,187	20,938	361	4.9	7.1	(NA)	(NA)	15.9
Carter	1,297	1,244	1,062	4.3	22.1	22,021	18,691	481	11.3	10.6	(NA)	13.1	20.4
Cheatham	1,135	1,069	898	6.2	26.4	29,466	24,870	522	(NA)	5.4	7.0	3.0	11.8
Chester	363	343	309	5.8	17.4	22,849	19,889	167	(NA)	10.6	2.0	(NA)	19.0
Claiborne	721	680	573	6.0	25.8	23,218	19,154	378	4.3	6.2	2.2	(NA)	19.3
Clay	165	163	145	1.2	13.9	20,622	18,141	80	4.2	11.2	1.4	10.3	20.5
Cocke	693	661	604	4.8	14.8	19,870	17,955	317	(NA)	10.1	(NA)	10.6	21.2
Coffee	1,461	1,391	1,113	5.0	31.3	28,716	23,095	1,282	4.1	7.9	24.1	9.1	12.3
Crockett	357	336	330	6.3	8.2	24,599	22,690	183	7.4	5.7	(NA)	(NA)	14.4
Cumberland	1,260	1,174	1,023	7.3	23.2	24,633	21,744	729	8.9	11.0	(NA)	14.2	12.6
Davidson	24,235	22,787	19,029	6.4	27.4	42,192	33,388	28,213	4.6	6.5	9.8	18.1	10.5
Decatur	293	279	236	5.0	24.0	25,330	20,184	165	6.6	6.5	2.4	19.8	15.9
DeKalb	462	432	350	6.9	32.0	25,243	20,040	285	5.3	5.9	(NA)	6.8	11.2
Dickson	1,215	1,141	1,020	6.5	19.1	26,509	23,529	682	9.8	11.7	3.1	11.5	14.7
Dyer	1,024	982	835	4.3	22.6	27,118	22,372	801	6.2	7.0	(NA)	9.0	13.1
Fayette	1,028	935	737	9.9	39.6	29,856	25,292	407	5.3	5.9	3.9	(NA)	15.2
Fentress	390	370	310	5.4	26.0	22,724	18,598	197	9.6	11.3	4.7	(NA)	16.8
Franklin	994	944	827	5.3	20.2	24,312	21,016	456	5.0	9.0	3.4	(NA)	15.5
Gibson	1,234	1,186	1,076	4.0	14.7	25,680	22,333	722	5.3	7.6	2.4	6.4	15.3
Giles	737	700	676	5.3	9.0	25,218	22,940	430	6.7	9.3	(NA)	(NA)	13.0
Grainger	484	458	393	5.7	23.3	21,817	18,946	155	(NA)	5.9	3.5	4.8	20.4
Greene	1,982	1,896	1,434	4.5	38.2	30,371	22,749	1,335	4.5	8.9	2.2	(NA)	12.5
Grundy	313	298	252	5.0	24.2	21,459	17,584	113	6.5	9.3	(NA)	7.5	23.8
Hamblen	1,577	1,524	1,318	3.5	19.7	26,204	22,628	1,621	3.1	7.7	(NA)	9.8	9.4
Hamilton	10,811	10,282	9,186	5.1	17.7	34,799	29,822	10,212	6.1	9.5	6.6	9.3	15.4
Hancock	104	100	94	4.0	10.4	15,526	13,904	30	8.1	11.8	(NA)	11.7	46.9
Hardeman	576	546	468	5.5	23.1	20,500	16,627	343	3.0	5.6	1.8	(NA)	23.3
Hardin	658	622	537	5.8	22.6	25,315	20,972	378	5.2	8.6	2.7	(NA)	17.5
Hawkins	1,318	1,256	1,087	4.9	21.2	23,450	20,248	598	2.7	7.0	(NA)	(NA)	18.0
Haywood	449	426	399	5.4	12.4	23,141	20,148	277	3.5	6.9	(NA)	5.9	16.0
Henderson	635	612	553	3.8	14.9	24,073	21,583	417	4.5	7.3	(NA)	5.3	12.4
Henry	799	759	687	5.3	16.4	25,383	22,045	516	4.1	10.2	(NA)	(NA)	19.6
Hickman	484	455	394	6.4	23.0	20,414	17,540	149	(NA)	6.5	(NA)	7.7	28.7
Houston	190	178	153	6.7	24.2	23,718	19,081	54	(NA)	9.5	1.4	15.2	30.4
Humphreys	465	437	393	6.4	18.4	25,546	21,898	320	(NA)	5.7	3.6	5.7	23.0
Jackson	259	250	204	3.6	27.1	23,406	18,477	111	6.5	7.3	(NA)	7.7	15.6
Jefferson	1,134	1,070	911	6.0	24.5	23,497	20,423	565	9.7	8.3	2.6	(NA)	16.0
Johnson	340	323	266	5.3	27.7	18,813	15,206	170	6.5	9.5	2.1	6.6	20.9
Knox	13,302	12,572	10,931	5.8	21.7	32,815	28,554	11,560	6.5	9.2	8.9	14.1	15.8
Lake	126	119	103	5.9	22.5	16,744	12,955	51	(NA)	7.4	(NA)	(NA)	57.0
Lauderdale	515	487	473	5.7	8.9	19,291	17,486	294	3.1	7.1	(NA)	6.0	25.8
Lawrence	920	906	809	1.5	13.8	22,450	20,232	521	(NA)	9.9	3.3	(NA)	15.5

See footnotes at end of table.

[Includes United States, states, and 3,141 counties/county equivalents defined as of February 22, 2005. For more information on these areas, see Appendix C, Geographic Information]

County	Personal income Total, by place of residence 2005 (mil. dol.)	2004 (mil. dol.)	2000 (mil. dol.)	Percent change 2004–2005	2000–2005	Per capita[1] (dol.) 2005	2000	Earnings, by place of work, 2005 Total[2] (mil. dol.)	Percent, by selected major industries Construction	Retail trade	Professional and technical services	Health care and social assistance	Government
TENNESSEE—Con.													
Lewis	235	226	199	4.0	17.8	20,564	17,536	93	9.1	13.4	2.2	(NA)	24.2
Lincoln	857	799	689	7.3	24.4	26,478	21,938	422	6.2	8.7	3.4	(NA)	20.7
Loudon	1,326	1,248	996	6.3	33.1	30,538	25,399	608	6.3	7.8	(NA)	6.1	14.9
McMinn	1,259	1,189	1,009	5.9	24.8	24,528	20,522	926	4.4	8.0	(NA)	6.1	11.5
McNairy	645	609	524	5.9	23.0	25,488	21,207	375	2.6	6.6	(NA)	7.1	11.7
Macon	508	483	428	5.2	18.7	23,561	20,922	212	6.8	10.4	3.0	(NA)	16.5
Madison	2,789	2,651	2,354	5.2	18.5	29,459	25,587	2,666	8.0	9.2	3.6	12.8	19.8
Marion	705	673	607	4.8	16.2	25,432	21,849	287	(NA)	13.2	(NA)	(NA)	16.6
Marshall	704	681	659	3.4	6.8	24,844	24,530	455	6.4	7.3	(NA)	3.0	14.0
Maury	2,117	2,058	1,847	2.9	14.6	27,775	26,482	1,905	4.4	8.2	2.4	8.9	15.1
Meigs	257	245	201	4.9	27.7	22,206	18,082	100	5.2	6.3	4.4	3.3	17.2
Monroe	974	914	684	6.6	42.4	22,552	17,454	654	3.0	7.1	1.3	5.5	10.5
Montgomery	4,671	4,081	3,245	14.5	44.0	31,812	23,992	1,917	7.9	11.4	3.8	10.7	20.2
Moore	161	151	119	6.6	35.7	26,701	20,562	74	1.1	2.2	(NA)	4.9	34.9
Morgan	390	373	340	4.6	14.6	19,414	17,194	141	8.6	6.2	(NA)	8.2	35.4
Obion	873	832	791	4.9	10.4	27,143	24,339	693	5.4	8.8	3.0	(NA)	10.7
Overton	438	419	371	4.5	18.1	21,385	18,372	208	6.8	8.4	2.9	10.4	20.3
Perry	190	178	166	6.7	14.7	24,841	21,665	104	(NA)	4.1	(NA)	13.5	13.6
Pickett	99	94	86	5.3	14.7	20,405	17,494	36	(NA)	14.5	(NA)	12.5	25.5
Polk	388	367	328	5.7	18.1	24,245	20,396	114	(NA)	12.3	1.5	10.2	30.5
Putnam	1,748	1,678	1,429	4.2	22.3	26,145	22,874	1,435	5.8	9.2	4.3	8.7	21.6
Rhea	680	663	559	2.6	21.7	22,757	19,621	508	3.4	4.8	(NA)	(NA)	29.4
Roane	1,455	1,394	1,161	4.4	25.4	27,584	22,339	1,017	2.2	6.0	40.7	(NA)	18.3
Robertson	1,773	1,656	1,390	7.1	27.6	29,372	25,334	916	7.4	9.1	2.7	3.4	14.5
Rutherford	6,507	6,006	4,885	8.3	33.2	29,784	26,624	5,399	7.0	6.5	2.8	9.8	11.2
Scott	429	413	356	3.9	20.5	19,632	16,804	244	5.1	7.8	1.7	(NA)	19.1
Sequatchie	300	281	219	6.8	37.1	23,604	19,175	109	5.3	7.7	(NA)	6.4	19.7
Sevier	2,224	2,081	1,604	6.9	38.6	28,029	22,374	1,514	11.8	14.9	3.3	4.1	12.7
Shelby	32,750	31,508	27,394	3.9	19.6	36,160	30,496	31,474	4.5	6.6	5.4	9.9	14.3
Smith	470	450	400	4.4	17.4	25,324	22,478	235	7.3	9.7	(NA)	10.3	15.1
Stewart	303	283	240	7.1	26.1	23,341	19,301	138	5.6	5.8	0.6	3.2	56.9
Sullivan	4,435	4,252	3,751	4.3	18.2	29,077	24,528	3,686	7.5	6.9	4.3	15.6	8.7
Sumner	4,493	4,178	3,549	7.5	26.6	31,033	27,061	2,154	14.6	7.3	4.8	10.3	14.0
Tipton	1,454	1,368	1,183	6.3	22.9	25,962	22,946	507	10.9	7.6	2.9	8.5	20.2
Trousdale	178	166	150	7.2	19.0	23,288	20,432	73	2.2	7.5	3.4	9.9	24.5
Unicoi	458	445	382	2.9	20.0	26,044	21,623	262	6.5	2.6	(NA)	(NA)	16.8
Union	375	355	313	5.6	20.0	19,711	17,492	120	(NA)	7.1	(NA)	(NA)	25.4
Van Buren	131	128	103	2.3	27.7	24,051	18,598	57	(NA)	2.7	(NA)	(NA)	22.3
Warren	995	956	821	4.1	21.2	25,119	21,377	777	3.5	6.6	(NA)	(NA)	10.2
Washington	3,161	2,997	2,449	5.5	29.1	28,115	22,786	2,727	5.0	7.8	4.8	15.8	20.0
Wayne	302	297	252	1.7	20.0	17,928	14,943	144	2.5	8.1	0.8	6.0	31.8
Weakley	824	787	716	4.7	15.0	24,524	20,530	496	2.2	6.1	(NA)	9.6	26.6
White	518	499	437	3.8	18.5	21,410	18,900	289	4.2	8.5	4.5	(NA)	15.6
Williamson	7,321	6,692	5,209	9.4	40.5	47,712	40,660	4,890	7.6	7.7	14.5	16.6	7.6
Wilson	3,419	3,204	2,673	6.7	27.9	34,030	29,934	1,906	9.4	10.2	(NA)	8.1	8.7
TEXAS	744,270	690,480	593,139	7.8	25.5	32,460	28,313	618,504	6.5	6.3	8.7	8.2	14.8
Anderson	1,142	1,097	973	4.1	17.3	20,226	17,668	814	3.9	6.8	(NA)	14.8	29.6
Andrews	354	318	265	11.3	33.7	27,727	20,462	254	9.2	4.1	2.9	2.2	18.5
Angelina	2,327	2,216	1,798	5.0	29.4	28,518	22,398	1,775	4.1	10.8	(NA)	14.0	15.0
Aransas	679	633	544	7.3	24.9	27,504	24,116	236	8.6	13.9	7.0	6.7	17.7
Archer	274	262	227	4.6	20.7	29,838	25,317	118	4.2	5.5	(NA)	2.3	17.6
Armstrong	62	61	49	1.6	27.4	28,612	22,446	23	10.2	2.1	9.8	(NA)	20.4
Atascosa	936	876	743	6.8	26.0	21,631	19,086	412	6.8	9.2	3.6	(NA)	21.4
Austin	787	736	630	6.9	25.0	30,259	26,496	476	11.9	9.6	9.5	3.3	13.7
Bailey	160	152	141	5.3	13.8	23,984	21,343	106	3.3	6.5	3.1	2.5	21.7
Bandera	559	528	460	5.9	21.6	27,935	25,771	126	16.1	7.8	9.7	5.7	23.5
Bastrop	1,656	1,564	1,307	5.9	26.7	23,725	22,422	557	9.8	11.7	6.6	6.0	31.6
Baylor	88	88	82	–	7.3	23,006	20,107	41	6.3	7.1	4.2	17.0	24.5
Bee	578	546	483	5.9	19.6	17,564	14,973	350	3.1	8.0	3.0	(NA)	40.8
Bell	7,921	7,143	5,676	10.9	39.5	31,139	23,776	7,745	3.9	4.8	3.6	7.5	59.8
Bexar	46,777	43,888	38,190	6.6	22.5	30,843	27,321	40,788	6.1	6.8	7.5	10.2	22.9
Blanco	282	267	214	5.6	31.7	30,795	25,299	130	15.4	6.2	(NA)	4.2	16.8
Borden	20	18	13	11.1	57.0	31,210	17,792	11	0.5	(NA)	1.8	(NA)	31.9
Bosque	441	419	367	5.3	20.2	24,529	21,276	173	9.3	8.0	(NA)	9.8	24.0
Bowie	2,493	2,350	2,036	6.1	22.5	27,583	22,795	1,905	3.7	8.7	(NA)	18.1	30.7
Brazoria	8,298	7,701	6,574	7.8	26.2	29,869	27,022	4,472	16.1	7.4	5.8	5.2	15.3
Brazos	3,915	3,634	3,006	7.7	30.2	24,994	19,709	3,412	5.9	7.2	6.5	10.3	38.8
Brewster	248	245	192	1.2	29.0	27,422	21,677	180	4.8	9.2	4.2	9.9	33.0
Briscoe	40	36	37	11.1	8.8	24,325	20,669	19	(NA)	5.6	(NA)	2.9	21.7
Brooks	143	135	118	5.9	20.8	18,591	14,878	85	(NA)	8.6	(NA)	(NA)	40.4
Brown	920	861	766	6.9	20.1	23,780	20,305	644	4.1	10.2	2.0	(NA)	18.4

See footnotes at end of table.

[Includes United States, states, and 3,141 counties/county equivalents defined as of February 22, 2005. For more information on these areas, see Appendix C, Geographic Information]

County	Personal income							Earnings, by place of work, 2005					
	Total, by place of residence					Per capita[1] (dol.)			Percent, by selected major industries				
				Percent change									
	2005 (mil. dol.)	2004 (mil. dol.)	2000 (mil. dol.)	2004–2005	2000–2005	2005	2000	Total[2] (mil. dol.)	Construction	Retail trade	Professional and technical services	Health care and social assistance	Government
TEXAS—Con.													
Burleson	425	399	350	6.5	21.5	24,773	21,126	165	14.0	9.1	(NA)	(NA)	21.6
Burnet	1,214	1,119	840	8.5	44.5	29,262	24,336	592	12.7	10.6	(NA)	8.8	15.3
Caldwell	804	754	642	6.6	25.2	21,992	19,778	273	7.8	8.7	(NA)	12.1	24.4
Calhoun	505	476	435	6.1	16.2	24,561	21,048	640	12.3	4.3	3.0	(NA)	9.3
Callahan	317	303	265	4.6	19.4	23,612	20,541	96	14.9	12.3	2.5	3.5	28.7
Cameron	6,597	6,221	5,023	6.0	31.3	17,410	14,913	4,428	4.2	9.1	3.8	18.9	28.1
Camp	347	338	289	2.7	20.2	28,350	24,893	191	(NA)	8.5	2.4	(NA)	11.1
Carson	177	167	175	6.0	1.0	26,841	26,913	370	1.6	1.1	(NA)	0.6	9.8
Cass	746	717	639	4.0	16.8	24,894	20,991	400	4.1	7.6	(NA)	(NA)	20.1
Castro	297	304	241	-2.3	23.2	38,945	29,324	237	1.3	2.3	(NA)	0.7	9.9
Chambers	947	863	723	9.7	31.0	33,249	27,629	494	4.9	5.6	9.3	(NA)	14.2
Cherokee	1,200	1,140	1,035	5.3	16.0	24,879	22,165	725	4.0	6.2	(NA)	8.5	22.9
Childress	140	131	118	6.9	18.5	18,248	15,376	102	2.4	8.8	(NA)	4.6	45.0
Clay	306	289	235	5.9	30.1	27,328	21,173	114	9.6	7.3	(NA)	11.8	18.8
Cochran	103	90	75	14.4	36.5	31,232	20,347	74	(NA)	3.6	0.3	(NA)	18.8
Coke	70	72	71	-2.8	-0.9	19,198	18,319	24	(NA)	7.8	(NA)	1.2	55.0
Coleman	202	193	184	4.7	9.5	23,278	20,062	83	9.9	10.9	4.1	(NA)	33.2
Collin	30,217	26,396	22,708	14.5	33.1	45,720	45,403	18,289	6.7	9.6	7.9	6.9	8.4
Collingsworth	94	87	73	8.0	28.4	31,650	22,905	55	(NA)	4.0	3.2	(NA)	16.6
Colorado	569	529	479	7.6	18.7	27,463	23,548	282	11.2	8.6	2.5	(NA)	15.4
Comal	3,117	2,840	2,296	9.8	35.8	32,522	29,133	1,636	14.2	10.5	4.1	9.2	12.1
Comanche	349	336	288	3.9	21.4	25,377	20,535	191	6.0	8.0	3.2	6.4	19.1
Concho	70	66	57	6.1	21.9	18,644	14,520	40	(NA)	3.6	0.7	4.8	23.1
Cooke	1,157	1,059	881	9.3	31.3	29,771	24,160	733	6.9	7.7	(NA)	3.8	15.6
Coryell	1,908	1,717	1,373	11.1	38.9	25,278	18,267	616	10.4	8.1	6.4	(NA)	41.0
Cottle	47	52	43	-9.6	10.4	27,565	22,579	20	(NA)	9.0	(NA)	5.3	24.8
Crane	90	81	76	11.1	18.6	23,447	19,199	75	(NA)	4.2	(NA)	4.9	18.6
Crockett	68	70	69	-2.9	-1.9	17,318	17,191	38	4.4	9.1	3.1	2.3	39.4
Crosby	212	197	152	7.6	39.1	31,908	21,594	124	0.6	3.0	(NA)	4.7	15.2
Culberson	46	45	41	2.2	12.3	17,727	13,913	30	(NA)	16.5	(NA)	(NA)	52.1
Dallam	183	177	189	3.4	-2.9	29,598	30,285	193	4.5	4.7	3.2	(NA)	14.5
Dallas	93,073	88,337	80,217	5.4	16.0	40,317	36,046	113,920	5.4	5.5	11.8	7.6	8.3
Dawson	302	283	270	6.7	11.8	21,193	18,054	199	3.4	7.5	1.7	3.3	29.5
Deaf Smith	455	400	452	13.8	0.8	24,574	24,385	327	5.4	5.9	1.8	2.4	14.9
Delta	116	113	102	2.7	14.3	21,337	18,994	36	4.6	11.0	10.9	12.6	34.2
Denton	19,004	17,617	14,507	7.9	31.0	34,241	33,060	7,921	8.0	8.4	6.7	9.4	17.5
DeWitt	495	452	409	9.5	21.1	24,281	20,456	309	4.1	6.8	2.6	(NA)	27.4
Dickens	49	47	45	4.3	9.4	18,493	16,407	24	(NA)	6.1	(NA)	1.9	31.0
Dimmit	185	175	135	5.7	36.5	17,837	13,262	105	3.7	7.6	(NA)	(NA)	51.3
Donley	100	92	83	8.7	21.0	25,656	21,549	43	2.4	9.2	(NA)	5.6	35.8
Duval	263	247	202	6.5	30.0	20,925	15,499	131	7.4	2.8	(NA)	4.6	36.9
Eastland	493	456	391	8.1	26.0	26,857	21,368	287	10.6	7.4	2.0	7.3	18.3
Ector	3,206	2,914	2,546	10.0	25.9	25,590	21,093	2,544	8.7	8.5	3.7	8.5	15.6
Edwards	39	40	31	-2.5	24.0	19,544	14,604	16	8.1	14.5	4.9	4.9	51.3
Ellis	3,687	3,491	3,009	5.6	22.5	27,613	26,751	1,682	7.8	8.0	3.5	6.2	15.9
El Paso	16,771	15,727	12,650	6.6	32.6	23,256	18,562	13,500	5.0	7.4	3.6	10.5	28.8
Erath	868	814	734	6.6	18.2	25,627	22,226	584	5.9	8.2	(NA)	9.4	20.7
Falls	369	359	317	2.8	16.2	20,941	17,133	174	3.6	7.9	1.6	(NA)	48.3
Fannin	753	710	625	6.1	20.5	22,755	19,921	351	7.1	9.1	(NA)	(NA)	34.0
Fayette	707	674	561	4.9	26.1	31,456	25,697	383	6.0	10.8	4.1	(NA)	19.4
Fisher	107	98	77	9.2	38.7	26,459	17,798	50	(NA)	2.7	2.0	5.5	25.4
Floyd	209	206	187	1.5	11.6	29,183	24,167	133	1.1	4.3	0.7	3.3	17.9
Foard	35	34	34	2.9	3.7	23,120	20,992	13	(NA)	6.2	(NA)	(NA)	33.9
Fort Bend	16,918	15,285	12,088	10.7	40.0	36,286	33,672	7,609	14.5	6.7	7.0	5.7	12.8
Franklin	286	275	220	4.0	29.9	27,784	23,243	157	7.4	22.3	4.0	17.4	10.4
Freestone	416	393	330	5.9	26.1	22,285	18,417	276	13.5	7.8	2.0	(NA)	18.1
Frio	294	276	241	6.5	21.9	17,997	14,879	160	2.5	6.3	(NA)	(NA)	30.8
Gaines	373	337	271	10.7	37.6	25,307	18,763	281	5.3	5.1	(NA)	1.1	16.2
Galveston	9,192	8,609	7,385	6.8	24.5	33,146	29,449	4,684	6.3	6.5	5.5	6.4	32.1
Garza	118	115	96	2.6	23.0	24,218	19,719	83	8.5	4.4	(NA)	2.9	20.2
Gillespie	756	716	533	5.6	41.9	32,852	25,462	360	13.5	11.6	(NA)	19.2	13.0
Glasscock	38	35	25	8.6	49.6	29,404	18,126	26	1.5	(NA)	(NA)	(NA)	16.9
Goliad	166	158	143	5.1	15.8	23,353	20,555	67	4.7	6.4	3.1	5.4	27.5
Gonzales	519	488	421	6.4	23.3	26,586	22,572	328	1.9	5.9	2.2	5.5	16.0
Gray	651	603	555	8.0	17.2	30,261	24,590	470	2.7	7.4	1.9	(NA)	12.5
Grayson	3,060	2,878	2,559	6.3	19.6	26,207	23,046	1,990	7.5	9.4	3.4	15.6	13.1
Gregg	3,900	3,586	3,028	8.8	28.8	33,768	27,205	3,625	5.8	9.5	4.2	12.7	8.3
Grimes	563	510	422	10.4	33.5	22,279	17,851	357	6.0	3.6	3.3	4.0	23.3
Guadalupe	2,961	2,703	2,077	9.5	42.6	28,720	23,100	1,212	8.4	8.7	(NA)	5.5	18.3
Hale	836	797	757	4.9	10.5	23,120	20,691	639	2.5	6.2	1.9	(NA)	15.9

See footnotes at end of table.

[Includes United States, states, and 3,141 counties/county equivalents defined as of February 22, 2005. For more information on these areas, see Appendix C, Geographic Information]

County	Personal income Total, by place of residence 2005 (mil. dol.)	2004 (mil. dol.)	2000 (mil. dol.)	Percent change 2004–2005	2000–2005	Per capita[1] (dol.) 2005	2000	Earnings, by place of work, 2005 Total[2] (mil. dol.)	Percent, by selected major industries Construction	Retail trade	Professional and technical services	Health care and social assistance	Government
TEXAS—Con.													
Hall	74	69	60	7.2	23.6	20,067	15,901	45	1.6	9.1	3.0	4.3	22.8
Hamilton	210	203	187	3.4	12.2	25,814	22,731	102	12.2	9.8	(NA)	9.6	23.3
Hansford	189	171	180	10.5	5.3	36,283	33,530	153	3.0	3.0	1.9	0.5	13.1
Hardeman	105	101	97	4.0	8.7	24,703	20,494	55	(NA)	7.8	(NA)	5.8	28.4
Hardin	1,416	1,294	1,092	9.4	29.7	27,778	22,683	519	17.7	10.4	4.4	10.8	17.5
Harris	156,921	143,418	121,593	9.4	29.1	41,703	35,606	160,619	6.6	4.3	11.4	5.9	8.6
Harrison	1,714	1,571	1,339	9.1	28.0	27,174	21,560	1,041	6.1	7.6	(NA)	(NA)	12.7
Hartley	153	159	155	−3.8	−1.3	28,655	27,972	81	(NA)	3.6	1.5	(NA)	19.4
Haskell	147	143	115	2.8	27.7	26,519	19,040	86	4.0	9.4	(NA)	5.5	19.9
Hays	3,187	2,944	2,323	8.3	37.2	25,610	23,467	1,793	10.2	11.3	6.0	9.7	23.9
Hemphill	129	125	112	3.2	15.6	37,973	33,584	102	9.7	4.2	1.8	2.2	12.6
Henderson	1,945	1,863	1,677	4.4	16.0	24,401	22,790	678	9.4	12.7	(NA)	13.5	18.8
Hidalgo	11,102	10,229	7,793	8.5	42.5	16,359	13,576	7,832	5.6	10.6	4.1	17.6	26.4
Hill	823	783	652	5.1	26.2	23,309	20,005	370	17.7	13.9	(NA)	(NA)	21.9
Hockley	576	537	464	7.3	24.2	25,274	20,465	366	5.5	5.8	2.0	5.9	20.0
Hood	1,420	1,339	1,150	6.0	23.5	29,734	27,698	435	8.6	15.6	5.1	9.3	18.3
Hopkins	838	796	721	5.3	16.2	25,209	22,531	529	7.9	9.7	4.1	5.3	17.0
Houston	533	548	515	−2.7	3.4	23,121	22,238	327	3.6	6.7	(NA)	7.9	26.1
Howard	776	742	670	4.6	15.9	23,858	20,011	541	6.0	6.5	2.4	13.5	32.6
Hudspeth	49	53	47	−7.5	3.7	14,804	14,137	33	(NA)	3.0	0.3	0.3	75.0
Hunt	2,151	2,007	1,766	7.2	21.8	26,138	22,944	1,287	5.2	8.3	3.2	6.3	21.8
Hutchinson	560	520	556	7.7	0.6	24,969	23,403	413	12.8	4.8	1.7	2.4	16.2
Irion	46	44	41	4.5	12.7	26,392	22,984	16	(NA)	5.5	(NA)	2.0	29.2
Jack	206	187	162	10.2	27.1	22,668	18,488	112	7.7	4.4	(NA)	3.8	19.4
Jackson	340	324	331	4.9	2.8	23,743	22,896	202	16.9	6.2	3.3	2.7	19.0
Jasper	860	788	747	9.1	15.1	24,215	20,970	513	5.5	9.4	3.7	9.0	16.8
Jeff Davis	44	46	38	−4.3	15.6	19,499	17,081	20	(NA)	9.8	(NA)	(NA)	62.1
Jefferson	7,248	6,708	6,124	8.1	18.4	29,324	24,335	6,496	9.3	7.3	11.9	11.2	14.9
Jim Hogg	118	117	92	0.9	28.9	23,480	17,360	57	(NA)	8.9	(NA)	8.0	52.2
Jim Wells	992	916	735	8.3	35.0	24,184	18,653	674	3.0	7.2	3.2	(NA)	14.1
Johnson	3,813	3,600	3,088	5.9	23.5	26,024	24,117	1,689	11.8	10.3	3.8	7.2	15.9
Jones	400	378	336	5.8	18.9	20,239	16,211	205	4.4	8.2	(NA)	(NA)	24.3
Karnes	270	257	233	5.1	16.1	17,677	15,058	150	4.7	6.1	(NA)	6.5	41.1
Kaufman	2,332	2,164	1,819	7.8	28.2	26,228	25,213	1,116	10.6	10.0	(NA)	7.0	20.5
Kendall	1,058	969	736	9.2	43.7	36,868	30,712	451	10.1	16.1	11.4	6.6	16.0
Kenedy	13	14	11	−7.1	22.8	33,108	25,504	17	–	(NA)	(NA)	(NA)	12.7
Kent	18	20	17	−10.0	7.4	23,825	19,759	8	(NA)	(NA)	(NA)	(NA)	68.2
Kerr	1,558	1,456	1,158	7.0	34.6	33,473	26,414	868	10.0	10.9	5.5	15.0	19.3
Kimble	95	91	79	4.4	20.6	20,746	17,519	49	12.5	11.0	(NA)	3.4	31.2
King	8	8	7	–	7.5	25,367	20,664	6	(NA)	0.9	(NA)	0.9	42.8
Kinney	69	67	56	3.0	22.8	20,813	16,614	26	(NA)	3.3	(NA)	2.4	78.5
Kleberg	758	706	567	7.4	33.6	24,761	18,001	522	2.4	11.6	(NA)	(NA)	43.0
Knox	93	91	77	2.2	20.4	24,832	18,195	57	(NA)	4.7	(NA)	4.5	26.3
Lamar	1,240	1,184	1,080	4.7	14.8	24,993	22,201	862	6.3	9.0	(NA)	15.2	14.6
Lamb	349	321	295	8.7	18.3	24,058	20,110	228	(NA)	6.3	1.3	3.4	18.0
Lampasas	599	526	409	13.9	46.4	30,234	22,846	189	17.0	13.1	(NA)	(NA)	20.3
La Salle	106	95	83	11.6	27.0	17,728	14,182	80	0.8	3.0	0.9	2.7	37.1
Lavaca	539	503	430	7.2	25.4	28,507	22,388	262	4.7	8.0	1.8	(NA)	13.1
Lee	427	394	350	8.4	22.1	25,873	22,227	238	14.7	7.7	3.8	(NA)	20.8
Leon	415	400	340	3.8	21.9	25,461	22,049	269	25.4	4.9	1.7	1.3	11.8
Liberty	1,981	1,848	1,490	7.2	33.0	26,332	21,081	883	6.0	9.9	(NA)	9.6	19.9
Limestone	532	509	421	4.5	26.5	23,531	19,060	322	2.6	8.3	1.7	(NA)	32.9
Lipscomb	84	83	76	1.2	9.9	27,394	25,125	61	(NA)	2.8	(NA)	0.3	19.8
Live Oak	245	230	206	6.5	19.0	21,037	16,754	149	(NA)	6.8	2.9	3.0	32.8
Llano	488	464	396	5.2	23.1	26,928	23,146	174	12.1	7.6	3.8	(NA)	26.0
Loving	5	5	5	–	7.3	77,787	71,723	2	(NA)	(NA)	(NA)	(NA)	26.6
Lubbock	7,065	6,635	5,903	6.5	19.7	27,997	24,306	5,418	5.5	9.3	4.3	14.9	22.9
Lynn	186	173	120	7.5	54.4	30,039	18,512	125	0.4	1.0	(NA)	0.9	15.5
McCulloch	212	202	170	5.0	24.6	26,693	20,804	125	4.3	21.2	4.0	5.4	20.9
McLennan	6,026	5,673	4,862	6.2	23.9	26,860	22,715	4,802	5.8	6.8	4.1	10.5	17.2
McMullen	24	24	23	–	6.2	26,712	26,458	11	1.3	3.5	(NA)	(NA)	36.6
Madison	293	274	242	6.9	21.3	22,305	18,608	182	4.0	8.6	3.5	(NA)	25.3
Marion	229	216	184	6.0	24.2	20,871	16,840	94	3.9	10.1	3.3	(NA)	19.0
Martin	113	107	84	5.6	35.1	25,719	17,721	63	(NA)	5.8	1.6	4.9	24.8
Mason	98	92	71	6.5	38.0	25,476	18,952	52	5.6	6.0	(NA)	7.0	18.0
Matagorda	859	830	780	3.5	10.1	22,599	20,548	556	4.3	6.0	2.3	(NA)	18.3
Maverick	752	687	545	9.5	37.9	14,690	11,509	494	2.8	10.2	3.9	(NA)	43.2
Medina	997	939	777	6.2	28.2	23,224	19,693	325	6.7	9.4	3.3	(NA)	34.1
Menard	44	44	37	–	17.9	20,013	15,839	13	(NA)	15.0	(NA)	3.9	54.5
Midland	4,963	4,426	4,092	12.1	21.3	40,855	35,419	3,986	3.6	5.5	6.1	5.2	9.6

See footnotes at end of table.

[Includes United States, states, and 3,141 counties/county equivalents defined as of February 22, 2005. For more information on these areas, see Appendix C, Geographic Information]

County	Personal income							Earnings, by place of work, 2005					
	Total, by place of residence					Per capita[1] (dol.)		Percent, by selected major industries					
				Percent change									
	2005 (mil. dol.)	2004 (mil. dol.)	2000 (mil. dol.)	2004–2005	2000–2005	2005	2000	Total[2] (mil. dol.)	Construction	Retail trade	Professional and technical services	Health care and social assistance	Government
TEXAS—Con.													
Milam	593	552	543	7.4	9.2	23,550	22,379	350	12.4	6.0	3.4	5.5	15.1
Mills	129	122	108	5.7	19.4	24,509	21,023	64	3.6	12.9	(NA)	13.1	24.7
Mitchell	165	158	140	4.4	17.5	17,519	14,568	103	(NA)	5.6	(NA)	2.8	48.1
Montague	527	483	428	9.1	23.2	26,847	22,367	221	8.8	9.3	3.4	(NA)	23.0
Montgomery	13,258	12,041	9,815	10.1	35.1	34,978	32,989	5,955	11.6	9.4	9.9	8.9	11.3
Moore	500	461	432	8.5	15.8	24,624	21,460	413	6.6	7.1	2.1	2.7	14.9
Morris	348	321	288	8.4	21.0	26,879	22,032	282	2.1	2.5	5.6	2.5	9.7
Motley	31	29	24	6.9	31.1	24,255	16,447	16	(NA)	6.7	(NA)	(NA)	24.2
Nacogdoches	1,384	1,312	1,154	5.5	19.9	22,844	19,485	911	6.4	8.8	5.7	14.7	25.6
Navarro	1,127	1,067	944	5.6	19.3	23,136	20,834	643	5.7	8.5	2.8	(NA)	21.3
Newton	281	261	228	7.7	23.0	19,651	15,172	85	1.7	4.4	4.0	6.8	30.1
Nolan	369	346	316	6.6	16.9	24,888	20,036	250	2.9	9.9	4.5	6.2	27.0
Nueces	9,428	8,839	7,499	6.7	25.7	29,541	23,925	7,889	9.3	7.3	7.2	12.9	21.5
Ochiltree	310	289	253	7.3	22.7	32,905	28,097	267	5.8	4.6	(NA)	(NA)	9.9
Oldham	49	48	51	2.1	-3.3	23,260	23,086	36	(NA)	2.9	0.6	(NA)	32.7
Orange	2,275	2,080	1,953	9.4	16.5	26,763	22,985	1,052	6.6	8.1	3.8	6.7	17.5
Palo Pinto	703	657	586	7.0	20.1	25,543	21,616	393	4.9	8.1	2.6	(NA)	19.6
Panola	613	576	487	6.4	25.8	26,904	21,417	374	14.9	5.6	(NA)	5.9	13.7
Parker	3,063	2,853	2,549	7.4	20.2	29,834	28,548	1,029	13.7	12.0	5.9	7.0	20.8
Parmer	257	233	256	10.3	0.5	26,243	25,590	223	(NA)	2.0	1.3	1.6	14.1
Pecos	282	271	233	4.1	20.9	17,704	13,953	197	5.7	7.1	3.7	3.9	36.5
Polk	1,274	1,190	1,010	7.1	26.1	27,432	24,294	445	6.1	11.9	3.7	6.6	26.2
Potter	3,147	2,966	2,711	6.1	16.1	26,219	23,837	3,760	5.4	7.6	7.1	15.6	16.9
Presidio	112	111	99	0.9	13.4	14,583	13,448	62	(NA)	6.9	3.6	(NA)	66.7
Rains	240	224	182	7.1	32.0	21,334	19,720	84	15.1	14.2	5.2	4.9	20.7
Randall	3,341	3,169	2,630	5.4	27.0	30,369	25,126	1,126	8.3	11.9	4.7	8.8	17.7
Reagan	80	68	55	17.6	46.4	26,725	16,599	86	(NA)	2.9	(NA)	0.4	15.1
Real	65	62	56	4.8	16.4	21,472	18,234	19	15.4	6.6	(NA)	14.9	38.3
Red River	293	279	260	5.0	12.7	21,595	18,204	108	5.2	7.5	(NA)	14.8	28.3
Reeves	213	200	207	6.5	3.0	18,439	15,833	134	2.2	9.7	3.3	4.1	45.0
Refugio	223	213	202	4.7	10.5	29,195	25,775	87	(NA)	8.4	1.6	(NA)	29.1
Roberts	24	23	21	4.3	16.6	28,949	23,305	9	4.7	2.0	(NA)	0.6	36.2
Robertson	412	393	317	4.8	29.9	25,514	19,789	182	7.1	4.6	1.7	7.1	21.8
Rockwall	2,286	2,081	1,620	9.9	41.1	36,373	36,943	811	10.7	9.5	(NA)	12.4	13.9
Runnels	240	239	215	0.4	11.5	21,853	18,751	136	4.7	6.5	3.5	4.2	22.6
Rusk	1,186	1,105	997	7.3	19.0	24,767	21,044	662	9.8	7.3	(NA)	6.1	13.6
Sabine	260	242	220	7.4	18.0	24,938	21,098	133	5.7	4.9	(NA)	3.6	17.0
San Augustine	199	190	168	4.7	18.4	22,533	18,797	79	4.0	7.3	(NA)	16.4	21.7
San Jacinto	592	549	448	7.8	32.1	23,898	19,965	101	9.6	6.7	6.7	(NA)	35.1
San Patricio	1,709	1,604	1,306	6.5	30.9	24,674	19,405	944	11.7	5.9	2.6	4.2	39.6
San Saba	137	133	121	3.0	13.6	22,676	19,458	74	3.9	9.2	3.5	4.8	38.0
Schleicher	58	55	51	5.5	14.3	20,854	17,371	31	15.7	2.4	(NA)	3.6	32.1
Scurry	502	445	334	12.8	50.5	31,047	20,532	381	5.5	4.4	1.5	(NA)	15.8
Shackelford	92	90	83	2.2	10.7	28,766	25,235	52	2.0	3.9	4.6	(NA)	17.9
Shelby	624	596	538	4.7	16.0	23,722	21,276	387	4.3	8.9	3.7	4.3	12.9
Sherman	139	149	139	-6.7	0.1	47,084	43,521	109	(NA)	1.6	(NA)	(NA)	9.7
Smith	5,963	5,562	4,922	7.2	21.1	31,301	28,055	4,783	4.6	9.4	5.9	19.4	12.3
Somervell	204	193	167	5.7	21.9	26,781	24,460	237	3.3	2.6	3.1	(NA)	11.5
Starr	738	673	515	9.7	43.4	12,197	9,558	409	2.7	10.1	1.9	13.8	49.7
Stephens	228	210	200	8.6	13.9	23,989	20,751	140	5.4	6.3	(NA)	7.6	21.2
Sterling	24	25	22	-4.0	8.9	18,832	16,026	16	(NA)	13.8	(NA)	(NA)	33.7
Stonewall	44	43	38	2.3	16.8	32,354	22,454	22	21.4	9.5	(NA)	(NA)	31.6
Sutton	117	104	78	12.5	49.3	27,832	19,403	105	12.6	4.0	(NA)	1.4	15.2
Swisher	240	225	207	6.7	16.2	30,725	24,683	165	1.2	2.2	(NA)	(NA)	17.6
Tarrant	55,514	52,317	44,068	6.1	26.0	34,275	30,300	46,245	6.6	7.1	6.3	8.5	11.7
Taylor	3,673	3,480	3,278	5.5	12.0	29,395	25,932	2,862	4.6	7.6	4.0	15.1	29.5
Terrell	20	21	26	-4.8	-24.2	20,039	24,892	8	(NA)	(NA)	4.2	9.7	76.6
Terry	331	313	266	5.8	24.5	26,723	20,907	210	2.3	8.6	(NA)	(NA)	20.5
Throckmorton	52	49	44	6.1	17.4	31,960	24,142	26	(NA)	1.4	(NA)	(NA)	23.2
Titus	732	712	583	2.8	25.5	24,756	20,732	693	2.8	8.7	1.3	(NA)	17.2
Tom Green	2,976	2,846	2,482	4.6	19.9	28,777	23,869	2,134	5.5	7.3	3.4	13.9	27.0
Travis	33,777	31,575	28,865	7.0	17.0	37,972	35,213	35,559	5.5	5.0	12.8	7.5	17.7
Trinity	316	306	259	3.3	22.1	22,076	18,721	93	6.5	7.8	2.5	(NA)	25.2
Tyler	462	427	379	8.2	22.0	22,422	18,152	169	4.3	8.3	(NA)	5.3	40.5
Upshur	927	855	751	8.4	23.5	24,589	21,214	287	10.3	8.3	5.3	7.7	22.7
Upton	83	76	65	9.2	28.4	26,935	19,114	58	(NA)	2.2	(NA)	1.5	27.0
Uvalde	601	568	484	5.8	24.1	22,339	18,669	355	3.7	10.7	3.4	(NA)	32.0
Val Verde	1,055	994	756	6.1	39.5	22,133	16,798	825	2.6	7.7	(NA)	7.1	46.5
Van Zandt	1,434	1,358	1,138	5.6	26.0	27,420	23,525	421	11.4	10.2	3.4	(NA)	20.6
Victoria	2,629	2,447	2,231	7.4	17.8	30,667	26,552	1,834	8.6	11.2	3.8	14.1	14.3

See footnotes at end of table.

[Includes United States, states, and 3,141 counties/county equivalents defined as of February 22, 2005. For more information on these areas, see Appendix C, Geographic Information]

County	Total, by place of residence 2005 (mil. dol.)	2004 (mil. dol.)	2000 (mil. dol.)	Percent change 2004–2005	2000–2005	Per capita[1] (dol.) 2005	2000	Earnings, by place of work, 2005 Total[2] (mil. dol.)	Percent, by selected major industries Construction	Retail trade	Professional and technical services	Health care and social assistance	Government
TEXAS—Con.													
Walker	1,217	1,146	1,048	6.2	16.2	19,223	16,982	919	2.2	7.0	1.9	7.6	60.2
Waller	924	867	652	6.6	41.7	26,543	19,852	585	6.5	16.5	3.0	(NA)	28.0
Ward	244	225	203	8.4	20.1	23,802	18,774	150	4.5	4.8	4.5	3.1	27.9
Washington	1,020	944	847	8.1	20.4	32,399	27,826	602	6.6	9.2	4.3	8.2	19.0
Webb	4,230	3,863	2,934	9.5	44.2	18,809	15,069	3,428	4.1	9.1	3.6	9.5	27.1
Wharton	1,080	1,022	916	5.7	17.9	26,093	22,217	641	4.5	9.6	3.1	(NA)	17.9
Wheeler	185	167	156	10.8	18.3	38,471	29,824	135	2.4	3.4	13.1	(NA)	13.5
Wichita	3,852	3,678	3,250	4.7	18.5	30,639	24,745	3,083	3.5	6.9	3.3	12.3	30.0
Wilbarger	371	342	324	8.5	14.4	26,316	22,176	273	2.1	6.5	1.6	3.9	40.8
Willacy	376	347	272	8.4	38.2	18,417	13,554	149	3.2	8.3	(NA)	9.9	30.9
Williamson	10,678	9,355	8,019	14.1	33.2	31,933	31,449	5,895	9.2	9.0	6.3	7.5	11.9
Wilson	980	899	719	9.0	36.4	26,039	21,964	243	10.9	10.8	3.4	(NA)	34.7
Winkler	165	152	133	8.6	24.4	25,008	18,706	116	(NA)	3.9	2.2	1.5	19.3
Wise	1,411	1,306	1,076	8.0	31.1	24,872	21,768	815	7.7	9.1	(NA)	(NA)	15.2
Wood	948	889	734	6.6	29.2	23,227	19,899	401	6.0	9.7	5.5	(NA)	18.2
Yoakum	220	204	148	7.8	48.7	29,718	20,330	192	5.7	2.9	(NA)	0.6	14.7
Young	536	484	453	10.7	18.3	30,222	25,271	355	4.2	6.3	(NA)	4.7	15.1
Zapata	196	180	149	8.9	31.3	14,592	12,208	146	9.7	4.9	1.1	3.7	27.8
Zavala	173	162	126	6.8	37.1	14,644	10,874	104	(NA)	3.3	0.8	13.0	28.3
UTAH	68,039	63,478	53,561	7.2	27.0	27,321	23,878	57,047	8.1	7.5	8.6	7.7	18.9
Beaver	176	167	128	5.4	37.8	28,362	21,231	140	3.6	3.9	(NA)	2.0	18.0
Box Elder	1,079	1,017	873	6.1	23.6	23,289	20,350	982	5.4	5.2	1.6	3.4	11.3
Cache	2,225	2,126	1,720	4.7	29.4	22,626	18,762	1,705	5.7	7.2	6.2	7.7	25.0
Carbon	520	479	435	8.6	19.5	26,721	21,353	382	4.8	8.0	(NA)	(NA)	23.4
Daggett	18	17	14	5.9	27.5	19,041	15,201	19	12.0	(NA)	(NA)	(NA)	62.1
Davis	7,714	7,225	6,024	6.8	28.1	28,776	25,066	5,290	9.5	6.4	8.2	6.0	36.9
Duchesne	393	353	273	11.3	44.0	25,660	18,981	266	9.4	5.6	1.9	8.3	26.0
Emery	232	218	197	6.4	17.7	21,628	17,992	207	7.4	3.7	1.5	(NA)	15.6
Garfield	104	100	87	4.0	19.5	23,506	18,319	74	5.4	4.8	(NA)	(NA)	34.7
Grand	212	200	170	6.0	25.0	24,079	20,188	156	10.2	10.6	5.7	6.9	26.5
Iron	799	733	557	9.0	43.5	20,789	16,390	592	8.2	9.2	3.4	5.9	27.7
Juab	192	178	149	7.9	28.6	20,957	18,028	128	20.6	6.3	(NA)	(NA)	18.9
Kane	171	158	132	8.2	30.0	27,456	21,637	99	5.7	8.3	1.4	(NA)	30.3
Millard	283	276	216	2.5	31.2	23,066	17,379	216	2.2	6.1	(NA)	4.2	22.0
Morgan	195	183	156	6.6	25.2	24,742	21,746	81	18.1	7.4	(NA)	(NA)	18.6
Piute	31	29	22	6.9	38.9	22,910	15,522	17	6.7	(NA)	(NA)	(NA)	28.2
Rich	52	50	41	4.0	27.0	25,487	20,810	24	14.9	3.9	0.3	(NA)	31.9
Salt Lake	30,720	28,650	24,924	7.2	23.3	31,990	27,674	30,084	7.2	7.4	10.2	7.6	15.3
San Juan	227	215	185	5.6	22.6	16,067	12,881	147	6.2	3.6	(NA)	8.5	49.2
Sanpete	423	405	345	4.4	22.5	17,640	15,142	246	8.2	7.0	2.2	(NA)	38.4
Sevier	401	380	334	5.5	20.1	20,683	17,685	290	5.1	10.8	2.8	(NA)	24.0
Summit	1,775	1,652	1,336	7.4	32.9	50,542	44,548	937	13.0	8.3	8.8	5.1	11.3
Tooele	1,139	1,038	820	9.7	38.9	22,215	19,680	748	4.9	4.9	5.6	(NA)	36.6
Uintah	647	575	428	12.5	51.3	23,851	16,924	563	5.8	6.2	(NA)	4.2	20.4
Utah	9,365	8,703	7,284	7.6	28.6	20,726	19,640	7,544	9.7	7.7	10.0	8.9	14.0
Wasatch	456	421	321	8.3	41.9	23,969	20,817	243	17.8	8.6	6.8	6.1	21.4
Washington	2,689	2,421	1,752	11.1	53.5	22,565	19,203	1,869	17.3	11.8	5.6	12.3	13.9
Wayne	54	53	46	1.9	16.4	22,157	18,292	40	11.2	4.5	(NA)	(NA)	30.5
Weber	5,745	5,455	4,593	5.3	25.1	27,294	23,260	3,959	7.1	8.4	4.5	10.2	25.4
VERMONT	20,362	19,519	16,883	4.3	20.6	32,717	27,680	15,323	7.6	8.5	7.2	12.2	17.9
Addison	1,107	1,066	921	3.8	20.2	29,963	25,549	733	8.4	9.0	5.7	11.2	12.8
Bennington	1,270	1,221	1,080	4.0	17.6	34,469	29,191	893	6.7	13.0	4.5	15.5	11.5
Caledonia	842	798	694	5.5	21.4	27,564	23,306	572	9.5	9.5	5.9	12.4	15.5
Chittenden	5,608	5,420	4,739	3.5	18.3	37,501	32,241	5,398	7.3	7.6	9.9	12.8	16.1
Essex	137	130	121	5.4	12.9	20,620	18,777	81	4.9	4.3	1.9	(NA)	27.0
Franklin	1,419	1,326	1,091	7.0	30.0	29,603	23,930	830	4.8	8.8	2.6	11.3	26.0
Grand Isle	235	230	196	2.2	19.7	30,318	28,279	60	22.6	8.1	6.2	(NA)	24.7
Lamoille	797	757	603	5.3	32.1	32,535	25,843	517	9.9	9.0	6.1	12.9	14.9
Orange	820	780	663	5.1	23.6	27,965	23,437	389	12.1	8.5	6.6	13.0	22.4
Orleans	738	701	579	5.3	27.4	26,764	21,985	473	8.7	9.2	2.9	13.2	20.9
Rutland	2,015	1,928	1,648	4.5	22.3	31,681	25,987	1,363	7.2	9.8	(NA)	13.9	16.3
Washington	2,018	1,926	1,649	4.8	22.4	33,965	28,395	1,670	5.0	8.1	7.2	10.4	26.2
Windham	1,410	1,372	1,234	2.8	14.2	32,058	27,937	1,143	8.3	8.2	(NA)	10.6	11.9
Windsor	1,946	1,864	1,664	4.4	16.9	33,681	28,944	1,202	9.4	7.4	8.8	10.8	23.3
VIRGINIA	283,685	266,751	220,845	6.3	28.5	37,503	31,087	228,461	6.8	5.7	15.0	6.9	23.7
Accomack[4]	879	840	703	4.6	25.0	22,356	18,313	559	5.4	(NA)	6.8	(NA)	29.0
Albemarle[4]	5,083	4,786	4,162	6.2	22.1	38,845	33,392	4,643	6.3	6.7	9.1	9.0	34.5
Alleghany[5]	584	572	526	2.1	11.1	25,585	22,387	448	6.0	7.3	(NA)	(NA)	15.6
Amelia	366	335	265	9.3	38.3	30,010	23,048	148	21.3	4.5	2.5	(NA)	16.6
Amherst	813	772	669	5.3	21.6	25,406	20,957	450	8.9	7.1	(NA)	(NA)	27.0

See footnotes at end of table.

Table B-9. Counties — **Personal Income and Earnings by Industries**—Con.

[Includes United States, states, and 3,141 counties/county equivalents defined as of February 22, 2005. For more information on these areas, see Appendix C, Geographic Information]

County	Total, by place of residence 2005 (mil. dol.)	2004 (mil. dol.)	2000 (mil. dol.)	Percent change 2004–2005	2000–2005	Per capita[1] (dol.) 2005	2000	Earnings, by place of work, 2005 Total[2] (mil. dol.)	Construc-tion	Retail trade	Profes-sional and tech-nical services	Health care and social assis-tance	Govern-ment
VIRGINIA—Con.													
Appomattox	365	347	322	5.2	13.3	26,289	23,502	159	14.1	8.1	2.7	3.8	21.7
Arlington	11,864	11,262	9,378	5.3	26.5	59,389	49,555	16,475	2.2	2.2	21.7	2.5	41.3
Augusta[6]	3,284	3,068	2,628	7.0	25.0	28,806	24,053	2,258	7.4	7.1	3.4	(NA)	16.5
Bath	154	151	130	2.0	18.4	31,520	25,799	92	6.5	2.3	(NA)	(NA)	16.0
Bedford[7]	2,304	2,170	1,868	6.2	23.3	32,333	27,898	882	(NA)	6.9	(NA)	7.1	14.4
Bland	154	144	122	6.9	26.7	22,200	17,721	83	4.7	3.6	(NA)	5.2	29.6
Botetourt	1,043	981	882	6.3	18.3	32,693	28,840	462	11.7	3.8	4.5	4.2	13.3
Brunswick	367	353	319	4.0	14.9	20,540	17,328	190	6.8	4.2	(NA)	(NA)	31.0
Buchanan	578	544	522	6.3	10.7	23,425	19,475	385	6.7	5.0	2.2	(NA)	17.0
Buckingham	322	307	256	4.9	25.6	20,085	16,402	162	9.4	7.0	3.8	(NA)	34.1
Campbell[8]	3,326	3,144	2,768	5.8	20.2	27,979	23,786	3,252	(NA)	7.3	3.7	13.2	10.5
Caroline	720	658	527	9.4	36.6	28,289	23,819	261	13.2	7.4	(NA)	3.0	30.2
Carroll[9]	858	828	723	3.6	18.7	23,853	19,999	533	(NA)	11.9	3.2	(NA)	17.7
Charles City	203	193	162	5.2	25.4	28,578	23,360	80	12.0	4.8	(NA)	1.2	18.5
Charlotte	275	266	243	3.4	13.2	22,131	19,506	124	8.1	6.2	2.3	(NA)	27.5
Chesterfield	10,934	10,098	8,410	8.3	30.0	37,911	32,228	6,356	9.5	8.4	7.3	7.3	15.9
Clarke	487	459	394	6.1	23.7	34,433	30,985	225	13.8	4.0	5.6	(NA)	14.2
Craig	132	125	111	5.6	19.1	25,742	21,737	30	9.4	7.7	(NA)	(NA)	32.0
Culpeper	1,307	1,167	909	12.0	43.7	30,792	26,360	740	10.4	8.5	5.0	(NA)	18.8
Cumberland	219	204	177	7.4	23.9	23,402	19,627	56	12.4	11.9	2.5	2.9	31.5
Dickenson	336	312	282	7.7	19.3	20,651	17,230	146	6.4	8.6	1.4	5.2	25.6
Dinwiddie[10]	2,190	2,097	1,841	4.4	19.0	29,141	24,501	1,455	(NA)	10.8	(NA)	(NA)	26.3
Essex	272	257	223	5.8	21.9	25,965	22,334	142	5.8	14.9	(NA)	(NA)	15.9
Fairfax[11]	62,858	59,226	50,393	6.1	24.7	60,289	50,035	56,205	6.1	4.4	30.6	5.2	14.0
Fauquier	2,929	2,710	2,165	8.1	35.3	45,171	38,947	1,252	20.6	7.3	9.5	8.7	17.5
Floyd	351	327	281	7.3	24.9	23,922	20,144	136	10.6	5.0	4.6	(NA)	18.9
Fluvanna	683	627	470	8.9	45.3	27,640	23,231	184	12.2	4.6	3.4	(NA)	29.9
Franklin	1,384	1,323	1,112	4.6	24.4	27,584	23,438	583	10.6	9.5	(NA)	(NA)	15.5
Frederick[12]	3,000	2,776	2,268	8.1	32.3	31,887	27,238	2,455	(NA)	10.1	4.6	14.6	12.1
Giles	411	385	348	6.8	18.2	23,940	20,813	235	(NA)	8.0	2.2	6.8	14.3
Gloucester	1,105	1,040	853	6.3	29.5	29,271	24,462	377	11.4	14.1	3.5	11.2	28.6
Goochland	1,006	928	687	8.4	46.3	52,212	40,589	972	7.3	2.1	2.5	(NA)	6.9
Grayson	358	341	317	5.0	13.0	21,970	18,769	106	3.8	4.9	1.3	(NA)	25.5
Greene	475	438	340	8.4	39.6	27,389	22,148	140	20.0	12.4	(NA)	(NA)	24.6
Greensville[13]	340	321	299	5.9	13.5	20,505	17,387	315	1.3	6.3	(NA)	14.5	24.3
Halifax[14]	819	787	731	4.1	12.0	22,671	19,592	512	7.5	7.5	1.7	(NA)	17.8
Hanover	3,612	3,410	2,737	5.9	32.0	37,100	31,451	2,023	16.5	8.5	4.7	9.6	12.1
Henrico	11,234	10,577	9,254	6.2	21.4	40,036	35,158	10,404	6.4	6.4	10.4	10.3	7.0
Henry[15]	1,804	1,747	1,581	3.3	14.1	25,312	21,573	1,109	(NA)	10.0	(NA)	(NA)	15.4
Highland	72	68	74	5.9	19.6	28,904	23,765	26	10.3	4.6	2.5	(NA)	21.1
Isle of Wight	1,052	989	811	6.4	29.8	31,495	27,122	649	4.5	4.1	(NA)	(NA)	10.2
James City[16]	2,860	2,681	2,107	6.7	35.7	41,401	34,849	1,854	7.8	7.7	7.6	7.2	22.4
King and Queen	188	176	155	6.8	21.6	27,720	23,359	69	12.7	3.6	3.7	(NA)	37.3
King George	698	638	472	9.4	48.0	33,778	27,879	903	3.5	1.5	23.0	(NA)	56.7
King William	477	444	360	7.4	32.4	32,417	27,282	199	8.9	5.5	(NA)	(NA)	16.0
Lancaster	440	417	352	5.5	25.0	38,304	30,372	208	12.5	9.2	7.3	19.8	10.7
Lee	528	509	409	3.7	29.1	22,283	17,375	237	6.2	8.1	1.9	11.6	36.0
Loudoun	10,563	9,435	7,154	12.0	47.7	41,193	41,123	8,690	10.5	5.5	14.5	4.0	14.0
Louisa	920	852	661	8.0	39.2	30,632	25,657	468	12.4	4.4	(NA)	(NA)	12.6
Lunenburg	269	263	230	2.3	16.9	20,459	17,579	116	9.6	7.0	1.7	6.2	29.4
Madison	373	346	291	7.8	28.1	27,945	23,189	150	12.1	20.0	4.4	(NA)	16.2
Mathews	380	365	281	4.1	35.3	41,630	30,508	91	12.0	7.3	6.9	(NA)	18.8
Mecklenburg	766	738	662	3.8	15.6	23,673	20,468	459	6.4	8.6	2.6	(NA)	21.9
Middlesex	333	316	263	5.4	26.4	31,744	26,422	128	13.3	9.7	(NA)	(NA)	28.2
Montgomery[17]	2,335	2,195	1,887	6.4	23.7	23,637	18,979	2,081	4.9	6.9	5.9	8.3	36.0
Nelson	446	419	361	6.4	23.5	29,572	24,936	144	12.5	5.3	(NA)	5.2	19.9
New Kent	487	457	370	6.6	31.6	30,189	27,341	159	24.7	7.5	(NA)	(NA)	24.0
Northampton	343	328	272	4.6	26.0	25,502	20,840	212	5.2	6.6	5.4	(NA)	20.5
Northumberland	395	373	302	5.9	30.8	30,816	24,596	120	15.9	8.2	5.9	2.5	18.3
Nottoway	382	364	322	4.9	18.6	24,556	20,450	228	4.9	7.5	1.2	(NA)	45.1
Orange	873	813	649	7.4	34.4	28,872	24,960	378	10.6	7.1	5.2	(NA)	20.7
Page	563	520	480	8.3	17.4	23,635	20,667	257	9.1	7.6	(NA)	7.0	21.9
Patrick	390	382	350	2.1	11.5	20,289	18,017	182	5.1	6.1	1.4	10.1	16.9
Pittsylvania[18]	2,788	2,677	2,364	4.1	17.9	25,951	21,487	1,749	(NA)	9.1	2.6	12.6	15.7
Powhatan	851	788	614	8.0	38.5	31,946	27,169	298	26.3	5.9	(NA)	2.3	33.5
Prince Edward	379	363	321	4.4	18.2	18,557	16,275	312	5.0	11.7	1.8	(NA)	29.6
Prince George[19]	1,610	1,508	1,252	6.8	28.6	27,279	22,571	1,548	(NA)	(NA)	(NA)	(NA)	55.5
Prince William[20]	14,618	13,438	10,228	8.8	42.9	36,693	31,038	7,689	16.8	10.4	(NA)	(NA)	25.5
Pulaski	975	916	805	6.4	21.1	27,843	22,921	721	3.0	5.0	(NA)	(NA)	13.1
Rappahannock	247	228	191	8.3	29.1	33,902	27,459	100	18.9	6.0	7.8	(NA)	15.4

See footnotes at end of table.

County and City Data Book: 2007

U.S. Census Bureau

429

Table B-9. Counties — **Personal Income and Earnings by Industries**—Con.

[Includes United States, states, and 3,141 counties/county equivalents defined as of February 22, 2005. For more information on these areas, see Appendix C, Geographic Information]

County	\multicolumn{5}{Personal income}					Earnings, by place of work, 2005					
	Total, by place of residence			Percent change		Per capita[1] (dol.)			Percent, by selected major industries					
	2005 (mil. dol.)	2004 (mil. dol.)	2000 (mil. dol.)	2004–2005	2000–2005	2005	2000	Total[2] (mil. dol.)	Construction	Retail trade	Professional and technical services	Health care and social assistance	Government
VIRGINIA—Con.													
Richmond	195	186	159	4.8	22.7	21,558	18,074	121	6.6	6.1	1.9	(NA)	33.8
Roanoke[21]	3,986	3,853	3,363	3.5	18.5	35,140	30,422	2,978	(NA)	7.7	5.6	(NA)	15.1
Rockbridge[22]	928	891	741	4.2	25.2	26,936	21,778	610	(NA)	7.1	(NA)	(NA)	20.8
Rockingham[23]	2,960	2,782	2,385	6.4	24.1	26,419	22,054	2,572	(NA)	8.1	4.2	9.6	16.2
Russell	629	593	542	6.1	16.0	21,806	18,514	338	8.8	8.2	2.1	(NA)	17.4
Scott	516	491	417	5.1	23.6	22,528	17,857	186	3.8	11.2	2.0	9.1	25.6
Shenandoah	1,102	1,016	839	8.5	31.4	28,229	23,805	655	7.6	7.5	2.4	(NA)	12.9
Smyth	779	734	652	6.1	19.4	24,012	19,722	584	5.7	5.6	(NA)	(NA)	19.5
Southampton[24]	700	660	594	6.1	17.9	26,851	23,046	327	(NA)	8.7	2.9	(NA)	32.5
Spotsylvania[25]	4,577	4,212	3,145	8.7	45.5	33,415	28,360	2,704	12.4	12.3	6.6	14.3	15.8
Stafford	3,955	3,621	2,690	9.2	47.0	33,529	28,747	1,670	13.4	5.6	8.7	3.1	26.8
Surry	175	166	145	5.4	20.4	25,101	21,243	146	5.2	0.8	(NA)	(NA)	13.3
Sussex	274	261	238	5.0	15.3	22,808	19,025	138	2.6	6.5	(NA)	(NA)	44.4
Tazewell	1,121	1,055	904	6.3	24.1	25,180	20,325	653	4.6	11.8	5.0	(NA)	18.9
Warren	1,105	1,012	822	9.2	34.4	31,202	25,925	487	13.5	8.4	4.0	9.6	16.8
Washington[26]	1,880	1,797	1,578	4.6	19.2	27,127	23,044	1,358	3.1	9.4	(NA)	(NA)	16.5
Westmoreland	484	460	386	5.2	25.4	28,253	23,136	145	8.2	8.6	6.0	(NA)	23.0
Wise[27]	1,087	1,034	851	5.1	27.8	23,838	18,469	848	2.8	8.2	3.8	(NA)	22.8
Wythe[28]	686	639	559	7.4	22.7	24,187	20,229	448	3.8	12.9	(NA)	9.6	20.0
York[28]	2,716	2,575	2,025	5.5	34.1	36,964	29,709	1,076	13.8	7.7	7.4	5.5	32.8
Independent Cities													
Alexandria	8,414	7,975	6,212	5.5	35.4	61,147	48,105	7,487	3.8	4.6	26.1	4.5	26.2
Bedford[7]	(NA)	(NA)	(NA)	–	(NA)	(NA)	(NA)	(NA)	(NA)	(NA)	(NA)	(NA)	(NA)
Bristol[26]	(NA)	(NA)	(NA)	–	(NA)	(NA)	(NA)	(NA)	(NA)	(NA)	(NA)	(NA)	(NA)
Buena Vista[22]	(NA)	(NA)	(NA)	–	(NA)	(NA)	(NA)	(NA)	(NA)	(NA)	(NA)	(NA)	(NA)
Charlottesville[4]	(NA)	(NA)	(NA)	–	(NA)	(NA)	(NA)	(NA)	(NA)	(NA)	(NA)	(NA)	(NA)
Chesapeake	7,267	6,872	5,380	5.7	35.1	33,302	26,848	4,402	14.1	9.6	10.0	5.5	18.4
Clifton Forge[5]	(X)	(X)	(X)	–	(NA)	(X)	(NA)	(X)	(NA)	(NA)	(NA)	(NA)	(NA)
Colonial Heights[10]	(NA)	(NA)	(NA)	–	(NA)	(NA)	(NA)	(NA)	(NA)	(NA)	(NA)	(NA)	(NA)
Covington[5]	(NA)	(NA)	(NA)	–	(NA)	(NA)	(NA)	(NA)	(NA)	(NA)	(NA)	(NA)	(NA)
Danville[18]	(NA)	(NA)	(NA)	–	(NA)	(NA)	(NA)	(NA)	(NA)	(NA)	(NA)	(NA)	(NA)
Emporia[13]	(NA)	(NA)	(NA)	–	(NA)	(NA)	(NA)	(NA)	(NA)	(NA)	(NA)	(NA)	(NA)
Fairfax[11]	(NA)	(NA)	(NA)	–	(NA)	(NA)	(NA)	(NA)	(NA)	(NA)	(NA)	(NA)	(NA)
Falls Church[11]	(NA)	(NA)	(NA)	–	(NA)	(NA)	(NA)	(NA)	(NA)	(NA)	(NA)	(NA)	(NA)
Franklin[24]	(NA)	(NA)	(NA)	–	(NA)	(NA)	(NA)	(NA)	(NA)	(NA)	(NA)	(NA)	(NA)
Fredericksburg[25]	(NA)	(NA)	(NA)	–	(NA)	(NA)	(NA)	(NA)	(NA)	(NA)	(NA)	(NA)	(NA)
Galax[9]	(NA)	(NA)	(NA)	–	(NA)	(NA)	(NA)	(NA)	(NA)	(NA)	(NA)	(NA)	(NA)
Hampton	4,411	4,162	3,505	6.0	25.9	30,389	23,945	3,976	(NA)	5.6	10.7	6.4	53.1
Harrisonburg[23]	(NA)	(NA)	(NA)	–	(NA)	(NA)	(NA)	(NA)	(NA)	(NA)	(NA)	(NA)	(NA)
Hopewell[19]	(NA)	(NA)	(NA)	–	(NA)	(NA)	(NA)	(NA)	(NA)	(NA)	(NA)	(NA)	(NA)
Lexington[22]	(NA)	(NA)	(NA)	–	(NA)	(NA)	(NA)	(NA)	(NA)	(NA)	(NA)	(NA)	(NA)
Lynchburg[8]	(NA)	(NA)	(NA)	–	(NA)	(NA)	(NA)	(NA)	(NA)	(NA)	(NA)	(NA)	(NA)
Manassas[20]	(NA)	(NA)	(NA)	–	(NA)	(NA)	(NA)	(NA)	(NA)	(NA)	(NA)	(NA)	(NA)
Manassas Park[20]	(NA)	(NA)	(NA)	–	(NA)	(NA)	(NA)	(NA)	(NA)	(NA)	(NA)	(NA)	(NA)
Martinsville[15]	(NA)	(NA)	(NA)	–	(NA)	(NA)	(NA)	(NA)	(NA)	(NA)	(NA)	(NA)	(NA)
Newport News	5,086	4,854	3,956	4.8	28.6	28,436	21,913	5,386	4.6	5.2	6.9	7.9	27.2
Norfolk[27]	7,045	6,786	5,511	3.8	27.8	30,528	23,546	12,681	(NA)	3.1	5.4	7.4	53.0
Norton[27]	(NA)	(NA)	(NA)	–	(NA)	(NA)	(NA)	(NA)	(NA)	(NA)	(NA)	(NA)	(NA)
Petersburg[10]	(NA)	(NA)	(NA)	–	(NA)	(NA)	(NA)	(NA)	(NA)	(NA)	(NA)	(NA)	(NA)
Poquoson[28]	(NA)	(NA)	(NA)	–	(NA)	(NA)	(NA)	(NA)	(NA)	(NA)	(NA)	(NA)	(NA)
Portsmouth	2,774	2,640	2,149	5.1	29.1	27,799	21,403	2,919	4.6	2.6	2.2	8.4	59.0
Radford[17]	(NA)	(NA)	(NA)	–	(NA)	(NA)	(NA)	(NA)	(NA)	(NA)	(NA)	(NA)	(NA)
Richmond	7,582	7,204	5,894	5.2	28.6	39,245	29,829	10,560	(NA)	2.8	13.4	6.4	27.7
Roanoke	2,986	2,846	2,340	4.9	27.6	32,512	24,698	3,509	(NA)	8.1	8.1	15.9	13.6
Salem[21]	(NA)	(NA)	(NA)	–	(NA)	(NA)	(NA)	(NA)	(NA)	(NA)	(NA)	(NA)	(NA)
South Boston[14]	(X)	(X)	(X)	–	(NA)	(X)	(X)	(X)	(NA)	(NA)	(NA)	(NA)	(NA)
Staunton[6]	(NA)	(NA)	(NA)	–	(NA)	(NA)	(NA)	(NA)	(NA)	(NA)	(NA)	(NA)	(NA)
Suffolk	2,337	2,176	1,626	7.4	43.7	29,661	25,319	1,131	6.6	7.9	5.4	12.1	26.1
Virginia Beach	16,537	15,793	12,842	4.7	28.8	37,839	30,117	10,135	9.2	6.9	10.0	7.0	30.0
Waynesboro[6]	(NA)	(NA)	(NA)	–	(NA)	(NA)	(NA)	(NA)	(NA)	(NA)	(NA)	(NA)	(NA)
Williamsburg[18]	(NA)	(NA)	(NA)	–	(NA)	(NA)	(NA)	(NA)	(NA)	(NA)	(NA)	(NA)	(NA)
Winchester[12]	(NA)	(NA)	(NA)	–	(NA)	(NA)	(NA)	(NA)	(NA)	(NA)	(NA)	(NA)	(NA)
WASHINGTON	223,232	216,921	187,853	2.9	18.8	35,479	31,779	175,684	7.2	7.0	8.2	8.8	19.1
Adams	397	372	337	6.7	17.8	23,575	20,472	275	2.9	6.0	1.3	(NA)	22.2
Asotin	578	559	488	3.4	18.5	27,469	23,716	249	12.7	11.4	3.7	13.9	19.4
Benton	4,964	4,755	3,801	4.4	30.6	31,433	26,559	4,115	7.1	6.2	21.8	7.3	16.3
Chelan	2,074	1,975	1,675	5.0	23.8	29,657	25,101	1,712	7.0	8.7	3.4	16.1	19.7
Clallam	2,034	1,911	1,583	6.4	28.5	29,267	24,617	1,106	9.8	11.5	4.4	9.6	31.2

See footnotes at end of table.

Table B-9. Counties — **Personal Income and Earnings by Industries**—Con.

[Includes United States, states, and 3,141 counties/county equivalents defined as of February 22, 2005. For more information on these areas, see Appendix C, Geographic Information]

County	Personal income — Total, by place of residence 2005 (mil. dol.)	2004 (mil. dol.)	2000 (mil. dol.)	Percent change 2004–2005	2000–2005	Per capita[1] (dol.) 2005	2000	Earnings, by place of work, 2005 Total[2] (mil. dol.)	Construction	Retail trade	Professional and technical services	Health care and social assistance	Government
WASHINGTON—Con.													
Clark	12,566	11,637	10,040	8.0	25.2	31,098	28,890	7,223	11.4	7.2	9.1	11.7	17.2
Columbia	105	107	112	−1.9	−6.6	25,248	27,591	54	(NA)	4.7	2.5	(NA)	41.9
Cowlitz	2,553	2,429	2,202	5.1	15.9	26,268	23,664	1,894	11.2	7.8	2.4	11.2	14.6
Douglas	839	809	703	3.7	19.4	24,047	21,509	368	9.5	9.9	2.9	7.0	29.4
Ferry	151	143	126	5.6	20.0	20,093	17,265	75	(NA)	6.2	(NA)	(NA)	54.9
Franklin	1,296	1,230	955	5.4	35.8	20,573	19,259	1,053	7.0	7.9	3.2	8.9	22.2
Garfield	43	54	58	−20.4	−25.8	18,928	24,225	19	4.7	9.9	(NA)	(NA)	126.5
Grant	1,829	1,761	1,514	3.9	20.8	22,538	20,171	1,307	4.3	7.2	2.1	7.5	27.7
Grays Harbor	1,751	1,668	1,475	5.0	18.7	24,701	21,953	1,158	6.6	8.3	3.5	(NA)	25.0
Island	2,453	2,345	1,910	4.6	28.5	30,665	26,567	1,428	6.4	6.3	3.0	4.0	62.6
Jefferson	1,013	937	752	8.1	34.8	35,319	28,418	426	9.5	7.6	5.7	13.3	24.0
King	86,747	87,418	77,272	−0.8	12.3	48,216	44,437	85,399	6.0	6.1	11.0	7.1	11.5
Kitsap	8,602	8,189	6,853	5.0	25.5	35,616	29,493	5,594	5.7	6.9	6.2	8.6	53.0
Kittitas	932	888	771	5.0	20.9	25,370	23,028	582	12.2	9.0	(NA)	5.3	34.0
Klickitat	511	487	433	4.9	17.9	25,756	22,519	279	8.0	9.7	(NA)	3.2	27.3
Lewis	1,815	1,739	1,527	4.4	18.8	25,070	22,246	1,183	6.3	9.6	2.4	10.6	18.7
Lincoln	265	255	228	3.9	16.3	25,762	22,376	127	5.9	5.9	4.3	(NA)	43.7
Mason	1,443	1,363	1,130	5.9	27.7	26,645	22,793	651	8.5	8.0	(NA)	6.5	33.8
Okanogan	1,028	999	816	2.9	26.0	25,850	20,609	668	4.8	11.4	2.4	7.2	35.7
Pacific	526	500	443	5.2	18.6	24,366	21,175	264	4.1	6.8	(NA)	5.4	35.8
Pend Oreille	289	276	244	4.7	18.6	22,896	20,736	145	3.5	4.4	2.0	1.9	41.7
Pierce	24,440	23,253	19,417	5.1	25.9	32,448	27,580	16,522	9.0	7.0	3.9	11.7	31.9
San Juan	670	637	533	5.2	25.8	44,053	37,620	260	19.1	10.2	(NA)	4.7	16.9
Skagit	3,594	3,333	2,823	7.8	27.3	31,754	27,282	2,487	10.2	12.4	3.8	8.3	19.1
Skamania	274	259	222	5.8	23.3	25,817	22,447	89	4.8	3.6	5.6	(NA)	41.1
Snohomish	22,289	21,143	18,515	5.4	20.4	33,999	30,393	13,619	9.4	7.6	4.7	7.6	17.6
Spokane	12,862	12,202	10,890	5.4	18.1	29,203	26,010	10,023	6.9	9.1	6.0	14.2	20.0
Stevens	918	883	789	4.0	16.4	21,900	19,598	457	6.5	9.1	2.3	12.6	29.6
Thurston	7,724	7,317	6,093	5.6	26.8	33,745	29,250	4,976	6.6	7.5	4.8	10.8	40.2
Wahkiakum	99	94	86	5.3	14.7	25,529	22,493	38	5.0	4.0	1.3	(NA)	30.2
Walla Walla	1,435	1,426	1,252	0.6	14.6	24,982	22,642	1,096	5.2	7.1	(NA)	13.5	24.9
Whatcom	5,420	5,065	4,063	7.0	33.4	29,561	24,240	3,923	12.5	9.2	5.6	10.3	17.9
Whitman	852	855	806	−0.4	5.7	21,219	19,820	691	3.5	4.7	2.2	6.3	60.2
Yakima	5,851	5,647	4,916	3.6	19.0	25,336	22,070	4,148	4.7	7.8	2.8	13.6	19.9
WEST VIRGINIA	47,926	45,819	39,582	4.6	21.1	26,419	21,899	33,284	6.3	7.5	5.5	13.1	22.6
Barbour	324	312	262	3.8	23.5	20,719	16,878	128	8.0	6.6	3.9	(NA)	29.9
Berkeley	2,518	2,324	1,777	8.3	41.7	26,990	23,250	1,570	8.2	7.1	7.0	9.3	30.6
Boone	551	526	493	4.8	11.7	21,503	19,329	539	1.3	4.2	2.5	(NA)	14.2
Braxton	287	275	229	4.4	25.1	19,329	15,586	166	8.8	11.1	2.1	12.8	23.8
Brooke	633	611	568	3.6	11.4	25,883	22,384	418	6.3	6.7	(NA)	(NA)	11.3
Cabell	2,640	2,552	2,285	3.4	15.5	28,088	23,638	2,404	5.6	8.1	5.4	22.2	17.2
Calhoun	135	131	119	3.1	13.7	18,279	15,660	65	(NA)	9.5	(NA)	15.8	23.8
Clay	171	163	142	4.9	20.6	16,560	13,713	98	5.1	4.7	0.2	7.9	25.9
Doddridge	145	138	124	5.1	16.9	19,401	16,724	51	6.5	7.0	(NA)	7.2	40.9
Fayette	1,051	1,005	867	4.6	21.3	22,584	18,237	517	4.8	9.0	4.2	(NA)	28.5
Gilmer	150	143	126	4.9	19.4	21,577	17,531	99	2.1	4.2	(NA)	4.5	49.7
Grant	290	272	236	6.6	22.9	24,781	20,912	199	14.8	5.4	1.2	6.7	22.7
Greenbrier	888	855	721	3.9	23.1	25,502	20,952	579	8.0	10.5	3.8	(NA)	18.5
Hampshire	468	443	381	5.6	22.8	21,268	18,757	183	11.6	8.0	3.5	11.5	32.4
Hancock	818	799	737	2.4	10.9	26,215	22,603	593	(NA)	4.1	3.4	12.6	11.2
Hardy	309	297	243	4.0	27.0	23,216	19,159	259	3.6	7.0	(NA)	(NA)	12.9
Harrison	1,995	1,919	1,649	4.0	21.0	29,135	24,034	1,691	5.1	7.7	6.3	11.6	29.7
Jackson	645	619	561	4.2	15.0	22,802	19,988	410	4.6	9.0	2.3	(NA)	16.6
Jefferson	1,567	1,457	1,130	7.5	38.7	31,877	26,621	653	10.2	9.3	7.2	7.0	27.0
Kanawha	6,646	6,420	5,746	3.5	15.7	34,361	28,775	5,917	5.4	6.6	9.9	15.0	20.1
Lewis	412	389	315	5.9	30.7	24,042	18,675	260	2.6	8.0	(NA)	10.9	25.2
Lincoln	426	401	343	6.2	24.0	18,995	15,520	141	10.3	6.0	3.2	8.3	30.6
Logan	907	857	716	5.8	26.6	25,038	19,059	523	3.1	10.1	4.3	(NA)	18.8
McDowell	436	421	394	3.6	10.8	17,964	14,484	222	2.3	6.3	1.8	6.0	34.0
Marion	1,524	1,450	1,268	5.1	20.2	26,891	22,441	1,001	6.5	7.8	11.3	8.9	20.2
Marshall	898	847	741	6.0	21.1	26,213	20,938	671	4.5	4.4	(NA)	(NA)	14.6
Mason	554	535	487	3.6	13.8	21,503	18,753	304	4.1	5.8	1.7	(NA)	24.9
Mercer	1,564	1,520	1,360	2.9	15.0	25,487	21,604	925	4.9	10.4	4.2	17.7	24.8
Mineral	655	631	543	3.8	20.6	24,330	20,079	316	6.0	9.3	(NA)	(NA)	22.0
Mingo	609	569	543	7.0	12.1	22,416	19,381	438	4.0	4.0	3.1	7.6	14.7
Monongalia	2,516	2,389	1,911	5.3	31.7	29,742	23,340	2,328	5.4	5.9	5.1	18.1	34.0
Monroe	285	276	239	3.3	19.2	21,027	18,093	103	10.9	4.8	2.8	4.7	41.4
Morgan	483	458	354	5.5	36.5	30,229	23,572	167	(NA)	10.3	3.0	(NA)	22.8
Nicholas	607	574	521	5.7	16.6	23,017	19,604	354	4.5	10.9	2.8	(NA)	25.2
Ohio	1,437	1,390	1,284	3.4	11.9	31,959	27,132	1,187	7.1	6.7	7.8	21.6	15.5

See footnotes at end of table.

[Includes United States, states, and 3,141 counties/county equivalents defined as of February 22, 2005. For more information on these areas, see Appendix C, Geographic Information]

County	Personal income Total, by place of residence 2005 (mil. dol.)	2004 (mil. dol.)	2000 (mil. dol.)	Percent change 2004–2005	2000–2005	Per capita[1] (dol.) 2005	2000	Earnings, by place of work, 2005 Total[2] (mil. dol.)	Percent, by selected major industries Construction	Retail trade	Professional and technical services	Health care and social assistance	Government
WEST VIRGINIA—Con.													
Pendleton	193	187	166	3.2	16.3	24,839	20,328	95	2.9	5.2	1.3	8.1	46.0
Pleasants	198	195	160	1.5	24.1	27,029	21,249	180	8.8	3.0	1.2	(NA)	16.0
Pocahontas	219	213	184	2.8	19.3	24,790	20,144	139	5.2	6.3	7.9	5.1	24.7
Preston	701	658	538	6.5	30.2	23,319	18,372	339	9.5	7.0	2.3	(NA)	29.6
Putnam	1,607	1,529	1,299	5.1	23.7	29,540	25,107	1,014	17.7	5.8	4.9	7.0	11.2
Raleigh	2,136	2,016	1,714	6.0	24.6	26,980	21,672	1,506	6.2	9.8	4.6	(NA)	22.0
Randolph	733	701	576	4.6	27.4	25,710	20,396	496	6.4	10.4	(NA)	(NA)	20.7
Ritchie	244	232	194	5.2	25.5	23,147	18,805	149	3.9	5.5	1.2	(NA)	15.4
Roane	311	295	267	5.4	16.3	20,117	17,285	142	7.3	11.5	2.8	15.5	22.2
Summers	260	251	212	3.6	22.7	19,043	14,800	93	4.7	8.6	5.5	(NA)	32.9
Taylor	341	327	276	4.3	23.6	21,068	17,140	127	(NA)	9.3	0.8	7.6	38.7
Tucker	170	163	137	4.3	24.3	24,438	18,735	98	8.4	6.5	(NA)	11.3	25.4
Tyler	194	188	164	3.2	18.2	20,843	17,114	119	4.7	4.2	1.1	5.3	21.0
Upshur	512	489	419	4.7	22.2	21,718	17,899	358	6.3	10.0	3.6	(NA)	17.0
Wayne	922	881	741	4.7	24.4	21,971	17,278	486	5.2	4.9	(NA)	(NA)	39.3
Webster	180	174	137	3.4	31.3	18,501	14,128	110	2.2	4.6	1.0	(NA)	26.5
Wetzel	422	408	368	3.4	14.6	24,880	20,829	173	12.1	16.7	2.4	(NA)	33.8
Wirt	105	103	95	1.9	11.0	17,860	16,084	28	(NA)	7.0	(NA)	9.5	43.2
Wood	2,408	2,355	2,094	2.3	15.0	27,714	23,823	1,886	7.1	9.8	3.1	15.3	20.6
Wyoming	527	487	424	8.2	24.2	21,607	16,572	267	5.4	5.9	0.9	(NA)	21.5
WISCONSIN	183,948	176,482	153,548	4.2	19.8	33,278	28,570	140,151	6.4	6.4	5.5	11.1	14.8
Adams	516	491	408	5.1	26.4	24,768	20,394	230	9.4	6.4	(NA)	6.8	28.0
Ashland	428	409	358	4.6	19.4	25,889	21,270	364	7.7	6.7	(NA)	(NA)	23.8
Barron	1,221	1,180	1,037	3.5	17.7	26,707	23,029	884	6.1	9.3	2.3	10.1	20.5
Bayfield	388	375	322	3.5	20.3	25,613	21,439	155	9.6	8.9	1.6	(NA)	35.0
Brown	8,089	7,814	6,776	3.5	19.4	33,901	29,811	7,565	6.4	6.2	4.8	12.0	11.4
Buffalo	463	441	376	5.0	23.0	33,199	27,225	319	5.1	3.0	1.8	5.9	13.7
Burnett	425	404	334	5.2	27.4	25,758	21,213	212	10.3	7.3	2.5	(NA)	22.5
Calumet	1,556	1,472	1,167	5.7	33.3	35,196	28,660	649	8.8	5.1	(NA)	(NA)	10.1
Chippewa	1,611	1,539	1,385	4.7	16.3	26,990	25,018	993	9.3	10.6	2.5	8.6	16.2
Clark	829	797	688	4.0	20.4	24,316	20,468	468	9.1	6.6	1.7	(NA)	17.9
Columbia	1,863	1,779	1,522	4.7	22.4	33,801	28,933	947	8.5	8.1	2.6	9.4	17.7
Crawford	430	409	357	5.1	20.3	25,265	20,722	304	5.0	17.3	1.6	(NA)	14.9
Dane	18,336	17,428	14,366	5.2	27.6	40,007	33,539	16,637	6.7	5.9	8.6	8.5	24.7
Dodge	2,464	2,367	2,195	4.1	12.3	28,008	25,514	1,652	10.6	5.5	(NA)	9.3	14.7
Door	994	951	816	4.5	21.8	35,212	29,123	547	11.1	9.6	3.6	9.3	14.7
Douglas	1,140	1,103	981	3.4	16.2	25,813	22,612	713	7.2	8.7	2.4	(NA)	20.7
Dunn	1,061	1,011	878	4.9	20.9	25,480	21,964	723	5.7	7.3	3.4	(NA)	24.8
Eau Claire	2,829	2,709	2,419	4.4	17.0	30,073	25,934	2,448	5.7	7.7	5.5	17.8	16.2
Florence	128	126	111	1.6	15.4	25,952	21,750	36	5.1	6.2	(NA)	5.2	32.2
Fond du Lac	3,215	3,088	2,700	4.1	19.1	32,509	27,715	2,327	8.0	6.4	2.7	10.3	12.0
Forest	237	228	189	3.9	25.4	23,985	18,808	140	3.8	5.2	2.4	(NA)	47.7
Grant	1,305	1,257	1,104	3.8	18.2	26,374	22,290	755	7.0	7.3	4.0	(NA)	26.7
Green	1,083	1,048	908	3.3	19.3	30,870	26,909	649	6.0	15.3	(NA)	(NA)	13.5
Green Lake	582	558	492	4.3	18.3	30,400	25,758	326	9.8	7.2	2.1	12.7	14.8
Iowa	739	706	581	4.7	27.3	31,399	25,446	530	7.8	44.7	2.0	(NA)	12.0
Iron	167	163	142	2.5	17.2	25,274	20,772	83	13.0	11.9	(NA)	10.2	19.7
Jackson	535	518	438	3.3	22.2	27,126	22,877	375	18.3	5.9	1.4	(NA)	26.0
Jefferson	2,503	2,373	2,121	5.5	18.0	31,575	27,927	1,697	6.6	7.4	2.6	8.8	11.5
Juneau	626	600	520	4.3	20.4	23,438	21,336	371	5.8	6.9	1.2	(NA)	20.7
Kenosha	4,900	4,666	4,161	5.0	17.8	30,552	27,726	2,782	7.3	6.4	3.0	11.3	16.9
Kewaunee	604	586	506	3.1	19.4	29,097	25,044	356	8.7	4.3	3.6	10.6	15.5
La Crosse	3,361	3,247	2,790	3.5	20.5	30,874	26,015	2,956	5.3	7.2	3.4	19.5	14.7
Lafayette	410	400	335	2.5	22.5	25,153	20,739	170	6.2	6.2	1.1	2.8	25.7
Langlade	543	521	455	4.2	19.3	26,245	21,949	337	8.8	11.0	1.9	(NA)	15.2
Lincoln	825	794	683	3.9	20.8	27,270	22,982	527	6.1	6.5	1.6	6.6	17.0
Manitowoc	2,487	2,405	2,169	3.4	14.7	30,395	26,152	1,683	6.4	5.2	2.1	9.9	12.8
Marathon	4,146	3,946	3,431	5.1	20.9	32,176	27,244	3,393	6.0	7.7	4.4	10.0	11.1
Marinette	1,182	1,139	987	3.8	19.8	27,275	22,705	888	3.9	6.7	1.5	(NA)	12.4
Marquette	374	357	301	4.8	24.4	24,621	20,567	159	7.3	5.8	1.2	4.4	20.6
Menominee	90	86	73	4.7	23.0	19,561	15,959	78	0.6	1.1	0.1	(NA)	92.7
Milwaukee	31,132	30,075	26,521	3.5	17.4	33,888	28,226	29,225	3.2	4.7	8.2	13.7	13.5
Monroe	1,116	1,070	889	4.3	25.6	26,220	21,666	839	4.5	6.2	(NA)	6.5	29.0
Oconto	1,039	999	856	4.0	21.4	27,530	23,900	388	10.8	7.6	2.6	8.0	19.9
Oneida	1,175	1,127	972	4.3	20.9	31,855	26,393	800	14.9	13.8	2.8	16.2	16.4
Outagamie	5,637	5,418	4,705	4.0	19.8	32,980	29,077	5,081	11.0	7.6	4.8	9.5	10.7
Ozaukee	4,513	4,331	3,806	4.2	18.6	52,490	46,092	2,142	6.0	5.9	6.6	9.4	9.5
Pepin	206	198	166	4.0	23.9	27,885	23,109	95	10.4	9.7	2.2	10.1	21.9
Pierce	1,160	1,113	951	4.2	22.0	29,788	25,770	440	8.3	5.6	4.9	7.9	34.2
Polk	1,203	1,157	971	4.0	24.0	27,130	23,404	646	8.1	7.0	(NA)	11.2	17.3
Portage	2,024	1,965	1,670	3.0	21.2	30,080	24,837	1,489	4.9	7.6	3.7	9.0	16.6

See footnotes at end of table.

Table B-9. Counties — **Personal Income and Earnings by Industries**—Con.

[Includes United States, states, and 3,141 counties/county equivalents defined as of February 22, 2005. For more information on these areas, see Appendix C, Geographic Information]

County	Personal income — Total, by place of residence					Per capita¹ (dol.)		Earnings, by place of work, 2005					
	2005 (mil. dol.)	2004 (mil. dol.)	2000 (mil. dol.)	Percent change 2004–2005	Percent change 2000–2005	2005	2000	Total² (mil. dol.)	Construction	Retail trade	Professional and technical services	Health care and social assistance	Government
WISCONSIN—Con.													
Price	417	404	346	3.2	20.5	27,527	21,863	276	4.0	7.2	3.9	7.9	16.1
Racine	6,574	6,304	5,439	4.3	20.9	33,676	28,776	4,179	5.9	5.8	6.0	11.3	12.5
Richland	468	445	377	5.2	24.1	25,467	20,917	262	5.6	9.4	1.6	10.8	16.8
Rock	4,532	4,380	3,993	3.5	13.5	28,804	26,174	3,256	6.1	8.7	2.3	11.9	13.3
Rusk	341	332	297	2.7	14.9	22,481	19,333	227	4.7	7.1	(NA)	(NA)	21.8
St. Croix	2,546	2,415	1,953	5.4	30.4	32,947	30,669	1,233	9.9	8.7	5.3	8.9	14.0
Sauk	1,841	1,756	1,458	4.8	26.2	31,884	26,347	1,539	12.5	9.0	3.8	9.3	14.3
Sawyer	460	437	361	5.3	27.6	27,013	22,200	292	9.5	10.5	4.3	(NA)	26.1
Shawano	1,113	1,070	904	4.0	23.1	26,988	22,165	568	5.8	7.9	2.4	7.7	20.6
Sheboygan	3,937	3,754	3,249	4.9	21.2	34,409	28,814	3,204	5.5	5.0	3.0	10.2	9.8
Taylor	492	476	414	3.4	18.7	24,944	21,013	374	5.7	5.2	(NA)	(NA)	11.3
Trempealeau	783	764	630	2.5	24.2	28,161	23,274	574	3.0	4.0	1.3	(NA)	15.1
Vernon	670	650	540	3.1	24.1	23,108	19,235	338	5.2	7.9	2.0	(NA)	20.6
Vilas	654	627	518	4.3	26.3	29,307	24,497	335	13.7	11.4	2.5	(NA)	26.7
Walworth	2,941	2,822	2,522	4.2	16.6	29,485	27,292	1,800	7.7	7.3	3.4	6.6	18.0
Washburn	414	405	343	2.2	20.6	24,940	21,324	218	4.6	10.5	2.1	(NA)	26.7
Washington	4,740	4,485	3,965	5.7	19.5	37,642	33,604	2,528	7.8	7.2	3.6	8.6	10.8
Waukesha	17,218	16,478	14,860	4.5	15.9	45,454	41,033	13,201	8.9	5.9	7.2	8.3	7.2
Waupaca	1,582	1,517	1,289	4.3	22.8	30,137	24,798	933	4.4	5.9	1.9	(NA)	17.1
Waushara	589	565	483	4.2	21.9	23,798	20,913	238	9.7	9.0	2.2	(NA)	20.8
Winnebago	5,261	5,050	4,431	4.2	18.7	32,978	28,216	4,763	5.1	4.3	5.2	9.3	12.2
Wood	2,480	2,403	2,088	3.2	18.8	33,051	27,622	2,240	4.6	5.7	(NA)	33.6	11.1
WYOMING	18,981	17,723	14,063	7.1	35.0	37,305	28,460	13,689	8.6	6.4	4.7	6.9	23.1
Albany	961	931	743	3.2	29.4	31,165	23,335	647	5.3	6.5	7.6	8.3	48.2
Big Horn	291	270	236	7.8	23.4	25,727	20,640	213	6.7	(NA)	(NA)	2.2	26.4
Campbell	1,396	1,260	930	10.8	50.2	37,318	27,351	1,431	9.4	4.2	3.0	2.9	11.9
Carbon	472	433	369	9.0	27.9	30,961	23,663	312	10.2	6.3	2.7	5.2	28.2
Converse	436	406	306	7.4	42.6	34,176	25,251	286	8.3	3.7	2.3	(NA)	19.7
Crook	221	203	146	8.9	50.9	35,784	24,845	121	9.8	6.3	3.9	2.2	23.2
Fremont	1,065	991	829	7.5	28.5	29,125	23,123	652	8.2	8.3	4.2	(NA)	32.7
Goshen	335	324	283	3.4	18.3	27,624	22,561	188	5.3	11.0	(NA)	12.7	24.1
Hot Springs	145	146	114	-0.7	26.9	31,763	23,496	84	4.4	4.3	4.4	10.7	25.4
Johnson	266	244	175	9.0	51.8	34,192	24,644	157	13.5	5.5	3.3	(NA)	25.5
Laramie	3,124	2,973	2,293	5.1	36.3	36,739	28,052	2,320	6.5	7.0	4.9	7.1	40.5
Lincoln	456	439	338	3.9	35.1	28,632	23,057	298	14.5	5.5	2.8	(NA)	23.2
Natrona	2,888	2,659	2,257	8.6	28.0	41,462	33,905	2,253	6.3	6.7	4.7	11.0	12.1
Niobrara	79	72	59	9.7	34.4	34,274	24,588	42	(NA)	(NA)	2.5	3.4	31.7
Park	917	862	699	6.4	31.1	34,313	27,088	593	11.1	8.5	4.7	8.7	26.0
Platte	262	254	222	3.1	17.8	30,476	25,383	170	7.1	7.0	3.8	(NA)	20.6
Sheridan	1,066	1,017	794	4.8	34.3	38,999	29,829	608	9.4	7.7	7.0	9.7	26.6
Sublette	294	256	165	14.8	78.5	42,181	27,678	217	16.3	5.0	6.1	(NA)	18.0
Sweetwater	1,446	1,283	1,106	12.7	30.7	38,039	29,500	1,347	8.3	5.3	2.5	3.0	13.3
Teton	1,693	1,622	1,153	4.4	46.8	89,028	62,831	973	12.6	7.0	10.1	5.7	12.1
Uinta	648	599	455	8.2	42.4	32,595	23,084	452	13.6	7.1	3.2	7.5	18.8
Washakie	278	256	212	8.6	31.0	35,125	25,678	177	8.7	4.5	2.9	10.9	20.6
Weston	241	221	180	9.0	34.3	36,329	27,021	149	(NA)	5.3	5.8	3.9	20.1

– Represents zero.   NA Not available.   X Not applicable.

¹Based on resident population estimated as of July 1, 2000, and 2005.   ²Includes other industries not shown separately.   ³Yellowstone National Park County became incorporated with Gallatin and Park Counties, MT; effective November 7, 1997.   ⁴Albemarle County, VA, includes Charlottesville city.   ⁵Alleghany County, VA, includes Clifton Forge and Covington cities. Clifton Forge independent city became incorporated with Alleghany County, VA; effective July 1, 2001.   ⁶Augusta County, VA, includes Staunton and Waynesboro cities.   ⁷Bedford County, VA, includes Bedford city.   ⁸Campbell County, VA, includes Lynchburg city.   ⁹Carroll County, VA, includes Galax city.   ¹⁰Dinwiddie County, VA, includes Colonial Heights and Petersburg cities.   ¹¹Fairfax County, VA, includes Fairfax and Falls Church cities.   ¹²Frederick County, VA, includes Winchester city.   ¹³Greensville County, VA, includes Emporia city.   ¹⁴South Boston independent city became incorporated with Halifax County, VA; effective June 30, 1995.   ¹⁵Henry County, VA, includes Martinsville city.   ¹⁶James City County, VA, includes Williamsburg city.   ¹⁷Montgomery County, VA, includes Radford city.   ¹⁸Pittsylvania County, VA, includes Danville city.   ¹⁹Prince George County, VA, includes Hopewell city.   ²⁰Prince William County, VA, includes Manassas and Manassas Park cities.   ²¹Roanoke County, VA, includes Salem city.   ²²Rockbridge County, VA, includes Buena Vista and Lexington cities.   ²³Rockingham County, VA, includes Harrisonburg city.   ²⁴Southampton County, VA, includes Franklin city.   ²⁵Spotsylvania County, VA, includes Fredericksburg city.   ²⁶Washington County, VA, includes Bristol city.   ²⁷Wise County, VA, includes Norton city.   ²⁸York County, VA, includes Poquoson city.

Survey, Census, or Data Collection Method: Based on the Regional Economic Information System; for more information, see <http://www.bea.gov/regional/methods.cfm/>.

Source: U.S. Bureau of Economic Analysis, Regional Economic Information System (REIS), downloaded estimates and software, accessed June 5, 2007 (related Internet site <http://www.bea.gov/regional/docs/reis2005dvd.cfm>).

Table B-10. Counties — **Labor Force and Private Business Establishments and Employment**

[Includes United States, states, and 3,141 counties/county equivalents defined as of February 22, 2005. For more information on these areas, see Appendix C, Geographic Information]

County	Civilian labor force							Private nonfarm businesses					
	Total			Number of unemployed		Unemployment rate[1]		Establishments		Employment[2]		Annual payroll per employee, 2004	
	2006	2000	Net change, 2000–2006	2006	2000	2006	2000	2004	Net change, 2000–2004	2004	Net change, 2000–2004	Amount (dol.)	Percent of U.S. average
UNITED STATES	151,428,000	142,583,000	8,845,000	7,001,000	5,692,000	4.6	4.0	7,387,724	317,676	115,074,924	1,009,948	36,967	100.0
ALABAMA	2,199,562	2,154,545	45,017	78,989	87,398	3.6	4.1	[3]100,802	[3]985	[3]1,629,141	[3]–23,933	[3]30,552	[3]82.6
Autauga	24,538	21,954	2,584	730	784	3.0	3.6	857	88	10,135	1,020	25,328	68.5
Baldwin	80,414	70,300	10,114	2,269	2,291	2.8	3.3	4,370	498	49,300	4,810	25,220	68.2
Barbour	10,877	11,475	–598	555	560	5.1	4.9	560	–17	9,303	–1,629	23,897	64.6
Bibb	9,077	8,643	434	339	406	3.7	4.7	317	–14	3,202	–201	22,898	61.9
Blount	27,102	25,389	1,713	782	783	2.9	3.1	698	–44	6,441	–1,427	26,796	72.5
Bullock	3,758	3,993	–235	301	302	8.0	7.6	130	–6	2,243	–113	22,188	60.0
Butler	9,409	9,212	197	481	636	5.1	6.9	490	–14	6,023	736	23,613	63.9
Calhoun	54,626	53,392	1,234	1,983	2,391	3.6	4.5	2,541	–25	41,664	1,050	26,085	70.6
Chambers	15,943	17,551	–1,608	835	683	5.2	3.9	620	–25	9,303	–2,217	27,783	75.2
Cherokee	12,205	11,419	786	452	454	3.7	4.0	359	3	3,735	321	22,542	61.0
Chilton	20,160	19,677	483	644	747	3.2	3.8	772	–3	7,104	284	23,502	63.6
Choctaw	5,387	6,231	–844	273	361	5.1	5.8	296	–9	3,432	–257	38,762	104.9
Clarke	10,245	11,676	–1,431	578	759	5.6	6.5	691	–44	7,347	–501	24,577	66.5
Clay	6,272	6,618	–346	256	360	4.1	5.4	220	–9	3,908	–648	24,129	65.3
Cleburne	6,813	7,031	–218	209	252	3.1	3.6	184	–11	2,573	318	22,456	60.7
Coffee	20,854	20,072	782	699	1,033	3.4	5.1	949	–6	11,275	–1,957	22,566	61.0
Colbert	25,873	26,178	–305	1,066	1,288	4.1	4.9	1,323	–37	18,504	–883	27,285	73.8
Conecuh	5,223	5,526	–303	260	319	5.0	5.8	235	–24	3,254	–513	25,821	69.8
Coosa	4,890	5,342	–452	244	256	5.0	4.8	112	–16	1,099	–331	25,255	68.3
Covington	17,495	17,441	54	603	1,067	3.4	6.1	871	–46	11,613	693	23,076	62.4
Crenshaw	6,700	6,167	533	239	312	3.6	5.1	247	–9	2,848	–94	20,281	54.9
Cullman	39,955	39,053	902	1,219	1,426	3.1	3.7	1,713	24	22,764	940	25,987	70.3
Dale	20,979	20,979	–	876	971	4.2	4.6	805	–37	12,020	1,862	30,286	81.9
Dallas	16,039	17,926	–1,887	1,189	1,283	7.4	7.2	909	–38	14,180	–941	28,598	77.4
DeKalb	32,124	32,653	–529	1,186	1,163	3.7	3.6	1,224	10	21,029	–	25,919	70.1
Elmore	35,339	31,327	4,012	1,073	1,099	3.0	3.5	1,080	–11	12,280	2,908	24,046	65.0
Escambia	14,567	16,241	–1,674	650	747	4.5	4.6	804	–53	9,531	–2,147	25,256	68.3
Etowah	47,117	48,595	–1,478	1,787	2,512	3.8	5.2	2,137	–18	31,086	–3,259	25,164	68.1
Fayette	8,013	8,345	–332	300	432	3.7	5.2	337	–12	3,919	–1,418	24,721	66.9
Franklin	14,130	14,741	–611	587	855	4.2	5.8	594	–10	9,025	–820	25,081	67.8
Geneva	11,947	12,294	–347	400	553	3.3	4.5	464	8	4,417	7	19,093	51.6
Greene	3,565	3,536	29	176	214	4.9	6.1	130	–4	1,608	291	21,981	59.5
Hale	7,351	7,033	318	344	375	4.7	5.3	197	–33	2,736	–470	22,586	61.1
Henry	7,659	7,708	–49	274	336	3.6	4.4	329	4	3,778	–407	24,852	67.2
Houston	47,253	45,633	1,620	1,440	1,777	3.0	3.9	2,878	98	47,753	1,510	28,528	77.2
Jackson	27,339	28,156	–817	1,097	1,292	4.0	4.6	858	–36	12,655	–2,134	24,506	66.3
Jefferson	324,652	332,550	–7,898	11,527	11,666	3.6	3.5	17,413	–53	349,712	–12,408	37,365	101.1
Lamar	6,178	7,498	–1,320	291	462	4.7	6.2	259	–30	3,597	–1,246	26,711	72.3
Lauderdale	43,549	43,860	–311	1,622	1,935	3.7	4.4	2,002	–2	26,009	–5,266	22,777	61.6
Lawrence	16,141	16,731	–590	686	738	4.3	4.4	396	–19	4,538	–851	34,277	92.7
Lee	65,790	58,646	7,144	1,966	2,072	3.0	3.5	2,205	213	37,540	5,269	23,690	64.1
Limestone	36,039	33,186	2,853	1,165	1,114	3.2	3.4	1,196	105	16,491	–818	28,945	78.3
Lowndes	5,041	5,089	–48	334	312	6.6	6.1	142	–8	2,255	104	43,077	116.5
Macon	8,926	9,157	–231	424	469	4.8	5.1	225	–13	5,353	–994	31,387	84.9
Madison	163,821	150,347	13,474	4,756	4,709	2.9	3.1	7,532	315	135,587	8,816	36,866	99.7
Marengo	8,913	9,095	–182	361	419	4.1	4.6	524	22	6,417	245	27,375	74.1
Marion	13,776	14,309	–533	536	844	3.9	5.9	561	–169	7,602	–2,851	26,233	71.0
Marshall	42,667	40,940	1,727	1,315	1,736	3.1	4.2	1,875	–74	32,740	90	23,914	64.7
Mobile	184,720	186,720	–2,000	6,861	8,147	3.7	4.4	9,140	–91	153,394	–3,047	29,763	80.5
Monroe	9,424	10,352	–928	514	591	5.5	5.7	431	–15	8,265	–102	29,491	79.8
Montgomery	107,668	106,838	830	3,977	3,953	3.7	3.7	6,023	–8	106,382	–8,934	30,383	82.2
Morgan	56,511	56,833	–322	2,028	2,114	3.6	3.7	2,757	22	46,608	–48	29,813	80.6
Perry	3,612	4,120	–508	275	338	7.6	8.2	157	–2	1,845	–292	19,526	52.8
Pickens	8,257	8,653	–396	374	578	4.5	6.7	321	–29	3,131	–120	21,308	57.6
Pike	15,437	14,184	1,253	552	693	3.6	4.9	624	–47	10,077	141	25,128	68.0
Randolph	9,929	10,059	–130	471	434	4.7	4.3	406	19	5,269	164	18,155	49.1
Russell	21,727	22,217	–490	1,137	908	5.2	4.1	834	–71	9,540	–1,625	23,137	62.6
St. Clair	34,556	31,698	2,858	1,095	1,051	3.2	3.3	1,145	23	12,988	478	23,439	63.4
Shelby	97,164	83,285	13,879	2,396	2,009	2.5	2.4	4,373	618	66,058	8,977	34,815	94.2
Sumter	4,869	5,406	–537	296	437	6.1	8.1	235	–11	3,109	229	22,896	61.9
Talladega	40,076	35,923	4,153	1,853	1,647	4.6	4.6	1,358	–23	23,056	2,039	29,964	81.1
Tallapoosa	18,594	19,544	–950	847	847	4.6	4.3	829	6	17,425	–7,945	23,312	63.1
Tuscaloosa	88,366	82,536	5,830	2,584	2,869	2.9	3.5	3,998	43	71,318	1,708	31,324	84.7
Walker	30,614	31,768	–1,154	1,234	1,634	4.0	5.1	1,365	–78	15,557	–271	25,537	69.1
Washington	6,971	7,784	–813	363	472	5.2	6.1	258	–3	2,802	–605	43,620	118.0
Wilcox	3,618	3,959	–341	280	308	7.7	7.8	229	6	2,173	–456	34,258	92.7
Winston	10,722	11,758	–1,036	475	816	4.4	6.9	518	94	8,605	–531	20,855	56.4

See footnotes at end of table.

Table B-10. Counties — **Labor Force and Private Business Establishments and Employment**—Con.

[Includes United States, states, and 3,141 counties/county equivalents defined as of February 22, 2005. For more information on these areas, see Appendix C, Geographic Information]

County	Civilian labor force							Private nonfarm businesses					
	Total			Number of unemployed		Unemployment rate[1]		Establishments		Employment[2]		Annual payroll per employee, 2004	
			Net change, 2000–2006						Net change, 2000–2004		Net change, 2000–2004	Percent of U.S. average	
	2006	2000		2006	2000	2006	2000	2004		2004		Amount (dol.)	Percent of U.S. average
ALASKA	346,769	319,002	27,767	23,238	19,678	6.7	6.2	[3]19,387	[3]886	[3]223,153	[3]18,266	[3]40,890	[3]110.6
Aleutians East.	1,133	938	195	100	79	8.8	8.4	43	−5	1,442	−591	32,444	87.8
Aleutians West	3,180	2,733	447	187	138	5.9	5.0	121	12	3,990	−120	26,775	72.4
Anchorage	150,905	140,456	10,449	8,052	6,909	5.3	4.9	8,250	362	122,801	10,037	44,498	120.4
Bethel	6,980	6,386	594	926	558	13.3	8.7	229	−1	3,972	498	31,644	85.6
Bristol Bay	1,022	922	100	56	57	5.5	6.2	78	12	320	−94	79,891	216.1
Denali	1,706	1,337	369	97	95	5.7	7.1	94	27	505	182	82,463	223.1
Dillingham	2,113	1,958	155	201	140	9.5	7.2	95	−1	1,145	−39	42,225	114.2
Fairbanks North Star	44,914	40,952	3,962	2,611	2,443	5.8	6.0	2,348	173	26,467	4,859	38,040	102.9
Haines.	1,457	1,394	63	119	110	8.2	7.9	121	2	491	−16	33,908	91.7
Juneau	18,446	18,004	442	910	816	4.9	4.5	1,086	−25	10,206	173	34,414	93.1
Kenai Peninsula	25,418	24,539	879	2,101	1,963	8.3	8.0	1,878	71	12,455	1,117	35,547	96.2
Ketchikan Gateway	8,071	8,279	−208	500	505	6.2	6.1	560	−26	4,747	−341	35,327	95.6
Kodiak Island	6,062	6,524	−462	465	526	7.7	8.1	454	1	3,836	−535	33,875	91.6
Lake and Peninsula	1,073	1,034	39	66	53	6.2	5.1	56	5	156	−9	48,359	130.8
Matanuska-Susitna	37,302	28,820	8,482	2,889	2,050	7.7	7.1	1,704	283	11,610	1,967	33,019	89.3
Nome	3,910	3,694	216	475	348	12.1	9.4	171	−15	2,005	204	34,307	92.8
North Slope	4,124	3,396	728	289	278	7.0	8.2	135	3	1,997	39	53,157	143.8
Northwest Arctic	2,967	2,939	28	338	259	11.4	8.8	66	−27	1,621	59	48,463	131.1
Prince of Wales-Outer Ketchikan	2,342	2,655	−313	339	368	14.5	13.9	154	−3	1,173	66	21,716	58.7
Sitka	4,705	4,449	256	256	208	5.4	4.7	408	15	3,125	273	32,225	87.2
Skagway-Hoonah-Angoon	1,872	1,824	48	244	176	13.0	9.6	206	49	687	95	38,661	104.6
Southeast Fairbanks	3,278	2,261	1,017	360	272	11.0	12.0	160	9	969	343	35,082	94.9
Valdez-Cordova.	5,189	5,211	−22	447	386	8.6	7.4	435	−27	2,684	239	50,916	137.7
Wade Hampton	2,554	2,227	327	528	332	20.7	14.9	58	−5	646	−39	16,203	43.8
Wrangell-Petersburg.	2,913	3,068	−155	282	290	9.7	9.5	267	−21	1,544	−102	33,256	90.0
Yakutat	311	370	−59	31	25	10.0	6.8	37	3	179	−107	30,056	81.3
Yukon-Koyukuk	2,825	2,636	189	371	296	13.1	11.2	116	−20	576	4	31,514	85.2
ARIZONA	2,977,094	2,505,306	471,788	122,713	100,390	4.1	4.0	[3]125,693	[3]10,889	[3]2,044,134	[3]124,781	[3]33,834	[3]91.5
Apache	19,988	19,023	965	1,994	1,746	10.0	9.2	518	12	5,902	−612	22,279	60.3
Cochise	56,500	48,549	7,951	2,562	2,196	4.5	4.5	2,304	104	26,659	3,978	25,622	69.3
Coconino	69,015	62,556	6,459	3,006	2,817	4.4	4.5	3,722	264	43,410	4,493	25,063	67.8
Gila	20,783	20,274	509	1,085	1,052	5.2	5.2	1,114	−33	11,021	−1,931	25,367	68.6
Graham	13,296	12,253	1,043	655	676	4.9	5.5	510	−5	5,110	171	20,418	55.2
Greenlee	3,787	3,914	−127	142	167	3.7	4.3	86	−18	2,642	−594	45,124	122.1
La Paz	7,730	7,597	133	446	473	5.8	6.2	352	−10	3,764	−171	20,414	55.2
Maricopa	1,926,869	1,595,203	331,666	67,134	52,507	3.5	3.3	79,345	7,331	1,411,802	57,553	36,256	98.1
Mohave	92,410	68,585	23,825	3,958	2,996	4.3	4.4	3,963	517	42,462	7,617	25,826	69.9
Navajo	37,788	34,227	3,561	2,755	2,511	7.3	7.3	1,845	105	18,286	1,596	27,273	73.8
Pima	449,033	408,961	40,072	18,039	15,245	4.0	3.7	19,735	1,103	306,821	13,439	31,549	85.3
Pinal	90,772	69,574	21,198	4,580	3,211	5.0	4.6	2,373	332	30,127	4,996	26,208	70.9
Santa Cruz.	16,338	14,738	1,600	1,253	1,230	7.7	8.3	1,174	91	10,810	730	23,470	63.5
Yavapai	96,005	75,543	20,462	3,782	2,947	3.9	3.9	5,733	748	52,960	6,897	25,699	69.5
Yuma	76,781	64,311	12,470	11,322	10,616	14.7	16.5	2,740	203	38,171	6,938	24,822	67.1
ARKANSAS.	1,364,646	1,260,256	104,390	71,760	52,904	5.3	4.2	[3]65,291	[3]2,106	[3]1,007,512	[3]16,682	[3]28,457	[3]77.0
Arkansas	11,582	10,159	1,423	905	460	7.8	4.5	580	3	8,583	308	27,101	73.3
Ashley	9,706	10,503	−797	749	612	7.7	5.8	474	−31	7,718	−895	30,427	82.3
Baxter	17,525	16,290	1,235	947	670	5.4	4.1	1,073	34	12,291	398	25,037	67.7
Benton.	102,814	76,889	25,925	3,459	2,125	3.4	2.8	4,565	908	89,174	21,696	34,260	92.7
Boone	17,079	16,245	834	840	674	4.9	4.1	942	−6	12,902	−1,064	27,433	74.2
Bradley	5,610	5,102	508	410	327	7.3	6.4	303	4	3,715	604	21,822	59.0
Calhoun	2,669	2,558	111	188	140	7.0	5.5	86	−7	835	28	26,595	71.9
Carroll	13,902	13,039	863	620	510	4.5	3.9	778	12	8,331	−149	21,558	58.3
Chicot	4,916	5,434	−518	431	395	8.8	7.3	262	−21	3,140	−83	18,542	50.2
Clark	11,061	11,225	−164	624	476	5.6	4.2	575	−11	8,594	322	22,737	61.5
Clay	6,975	8,074	−1,099	594	431	8.5	5.3	321	−32	4,249	−1,031	19,637	53.1
Cleburne	11,631	10,735	896	596	481	5.1	4.5	602	32	5,830	74	22,672	61.3
Cleveland.	4,216	3,902	314	263	192	6.2	4.9	98	−14	822	32	20,327	55.0
Columbia	11,212	11,276	−64	694	573	6.2	5.1	622	−24	8,236	−612	25,901	70.1
Conway	9,897	9,351	546	500	568	5.1	6.1	397	−12	5,199	−496	25,134	68.0
Craighead	45,812	42,782	3,030	2,223	1,680	4.9	3.9	2,343	98	35,891	1,699	26,093	70.6
Crawford	28,033	24,780	3,253	1,278	880	4.6	3.6	991	76	16,877	105	24,774	67.0
Crittenden	22,684	21,963	721	1,545	900	6.8	4.1	967	19	14,878	−908	24,673	66.7
Cross	8,522	8,684	−162	641	404	7.5	4.7	405	25	4,561	−89	22,348	60.5
Dallas	3,958	3,863	95	265	212	6.7	5.5	244	−11	2,968	158	22,271	60.2
Desha	6,200	6,319	−119	590	511	9.5	8.1	392	−2	3,941	−187	25,142	68.0
Drew	8,481	8,743	−262	702	514	8.3	5.9	453	−17	6,169	−1,517	19,520	52.8
Faulkner	52,706	45,478	7,228	2,348	1,634	4.5	3.6	2,043	260	31,258	1,990	27,618	74.7
Franklin	8,690	8,075	615	376	271	4.3	3.4	279	−2	3,473	329	22,468	60.8
Fulton	5,118	4,970	148	269	192	5.3	3.9	175	11	1,348	73	16,045	43.4

See footnotes at end of table.

[Includes United States, states, and 3,141 counties/county equivalents defined as of February 22, 2005. For more information on these areas, see Appendix C, Geographic Information]

County	Civilian labor force							Private nonfarm businesses					
	Total			Number of unemployed		Unemployment rate[1]		Establishments		Employment[2]		Annual payroll per employee, 2004	
	2006	2000	Net change, 2000–2006	2006	2000	2006	2000	2004	Net change, 2000–2004	2004	Net change, 2000–2004	Amount (dol.)	Percent of U.S. average
ARKANSAS—Con.													
Garland	42,497	38,466	4,031	2,243	1,630	5.3	4.2	2,709	138	32,760	1,829	22,923	62.0
Grant	8,782	8,097	685	432	319	4.9	3.9	283	11	2,936	−81	25,302	68.4
Greene	18,938	18,135	803	1,096	858	5.8	4.7	796	7	12,616	−764	24,673	66.7
Hempstead	10,956	11,079	−123	612	504	5.6	4.5	435	13	7,515	−260	23,184	62.7
Hot Spring	15,565	14,293	1,272	819	599	5.3	4.2	525	−49	5,457	−704	25,707	69.5
Howard	6,460	6,633	−173	363	279	5.6	4.2	326	7	6,748	−634	22,144	59.9
Independence	17,683	16,717	966	993	802	5.6	4.8	858	32	14,737	262	25,310	68.5
Izard	5,416	5,224	192	342	242	6.3	4.6	235	−4	2,071	−129	21,448	58.0
Jackson	7,843	7,704	139	626	577	8.0	7.5	387	−43	4,775	−401	24,681	66.8
Jefferson	36,561	35,943	618	2,932	2,059	8.0	5.7	1,637	35	28,007	−553	27,917	75.5
Johnson	11,078	10,202	876	584	425	5.3	4.2	399	1	7,131	−299	21,425	58.0
Lafayette	3,131	3,455	−324	229	204	7.3	5.9	126	−12	1,251	−113	20,353	55.1
Lawrence	7,514	7,868	−354	521	415	6.9	5.3	369	−15	3,477	−856	22,408	60.6
Lee	3,456	3,896	−440	342	288	9.9	7.4	158	−2	1,269	−41	20,477	55.4
Lincoln	5,191	5,039	152	422	306	8.1	6.1	173	13	1,833	156	22,954	62.1
Little River	6,550	6,394	156	303	291	4.6	4.6	211	−18	3,967	18	42,812	115.8
Logan	10,356	9,870	486	515	402	5.0	4.1	402	21	5,360	484	19,338	52.3
Lonoke	31,154	26,436	4,718	1,353	868	4.3	3.3	1,038	95	9,914	1,059	22,087	59.7
Madison	8,021	6,923	1,098	290	214	3.6	3.1	213	15	2,610	666	21,275	57.6
Marion	6,977	6,656	321	370	253	5.3	3.8	247	14	3,259	253	21,589	58.4
Miller	19,744	18,214	1,530	939	808	4.8	4.4	764	25	10,829	−491	29,652	80.2
Mississippi	20,869	22,677	−1,808	1,699	1,743	8.1	7.7	902	−73	14,328	−3,335	32,185	87.1
Monroe	3,782	4,075	−293	289	206	7.6	5.1	217	−16	1,951	−54	17,807	48.2
Montgomery	4,409	4,078	331	211	165	4.8	4.0	142	−35	1,027	−57	21,880	59.2
Nevada	4,420	4,609	−189	252	217	5.7	4.7	149	−12	2,274	308	25,026	67.7
Newton	3,682	3,759	−77	189	160	5.1	4.3	107	−1	726	90	15,709	42.5
Ouachita	12,636	12,401	235	1,029	724	8.1	5.8	604	−17	8,696	702	29,048	78.6
Perry	5,026	4,811	215	252	237	5.0	4.9	111	−10	529	−88	20,335	55.0
Phillips	8,817	9,705	−888	770	594	8.7	6.1	491	−182	5,166	−655	21,441	58.0
Pike	5,344	5,437	−93	280	223	5.2	4.1	240	−12	2,289	−149	19,963	54.0
Poinsett	11,663	11,447	216	778	537	6.7	4.7	421	1	4,461	−374	23,439	63.4
Polk	8,853	8,990	−137	432	364	4.9	4.0	493	3	5,536	118	21,662	58.6
Pope	29,968	26,805	3,163	1,451	1,132	4.8	4.2	1,487	24	20,625	−1,144	26,472	71.6
Prairie	4,405	4,405	–	264	191	6.0	4.3	171	−11	1,298	−32	19,099	51.7
Pulaski	193,080	184,404	8,676	9,293	6,827	4.8	3.7	12,034	−9	224,515	543	33,423	90.4
Randolph	7,902	8,292	−390	574	433	7.3	5.2	336	−4	4,151	−411	20,958	56.7
St. Francis	10,758	10,919	−161	991	753	9.2	6.9	512	−57	6,886	−3,066	22,582	61.1
Saline	48,037	42,739	5,298	2,150	1,387	4.5	3.2	1,596	238	16,894	1,235	24,924	67.4
Scott	4,859	4,935	−76	220	170	4.5	3.4	155	−20	2,190	−644	20,193	54.6
Searcy	3,522	3,309	213	173	162	4.9	4.9	127	1	1,119	−76	16,442	44.5
Sebastian	61,061	56,511	4,550	2,830	1,886	4.6	3.3	3,436	131	67,833	−5,096	29,941	81.0
Sevier	7,704	7,242	462	324	274	4.2	3.8	286	−9	5,583	754	17,595	47.6
Sharp	6,574	6,565	9	446	340	6.8	5.2	353	−22	3,201	22	18,224	49.3
Stone	4,776	4,666	110	268	203	5.6	4.4	227	−13	2,069	−233	19,758	53.4
Union	19,925	20,200	−275	1,350	945	6.8	4.7	1,220	−36	19,503	445	29,236	79.1
Van Buren	7,150	6,628	522	436	350	6.1	5.3	322	5	3,135	208	18,598	50.3
Washington	103,659	82,260	21,399	3,758	2,415	3.6	2.9	4,814	585	78,088	6,802	29,402	79.5
White	32,571	30,991	1,580	1,863	1,462	5.7	4.7	1,471	46	21,453	−303	25,459	68.9
Woodruff	3,514	3,777	−263	304	234	8.7	6.2	154	5	1,335	−306	24,333	65.8
Yell	10,810	9,937	873	499	394	4.6	4.0	329	−46	5,764	−148	22,001	59.5
CALIFORNIA	17,901,874	16,857,578	1,044,296	872,567	833,237	4.9	4.9	[3]841,774	[3]41,911	[3]13,264,918	[3]380,226	[3]41,820	[3]113.1
Alameda	745,890	768,785	−22,895	33,090	27,754	4.4	3.6	36,799	408	626,076	−29,654	47,737	129.1
Alpine	492	555	−63	32	35	6.5	6.3	62	10	1,305	257	12,175	32.9
Amador	17,518	15,252	2,266	937	776	5.3	5.1	890	41	9,133	1,755	28,096	76.0
Butte	101,113	93,083	8,030	6,292	5,709	6.2	6.1	4,838	241	56,846	3,070	26,275	71.1
Calaveras	20,960	18,119	2,841	1,224	990	5.8	5.5	1,026	41	6,517	760	26,048	70.5
Colusa	9,803	9,295	508	1,233	1,068	12.6	11.5	377	18	3,912	482	27,148	73.4
Contra Costa	518,535	500,752	17,783	22,190	17,758	4.3	3.5	22,462	397	326,359	10,592	47,254	127.8
Del Norte	10,914	10,232	682	755	757	6.9	7.4	482	−38	4,068	−327	23,985	64.9
El Dorado	93,570	81,741	11,829	4,292	3,390	4.6	4.1	4,428	472	41,578	3,363	31,559	85.4
Fresno	414,778	388,909	25,869	33,368	40,401	8.0	10.4	15,762	482	235,267	22,317	31,709	85.8
Glenn	11,785	11,298	487	948	949	8.0	8.4	498	−2	4,191	−94	31,967	86.5
Humboldt	60,232	60,104	128	3,354	3,474	5.6	5.8	3,568	30	37,079	−311	25,829	69.9
Imperial	64,182	56,072	8,110	9,828	9,791	15.3	17.5	2,317	44	27,817	2,464	25,362	68.6
Inyo	9,173	8,840	333	422	402	4.6	4.5	620	10	6,128	591	24,824	67.2
Kern	338,348	294,213	44,135	25,589	24,274	7.6	8.3	11,487	594	167,870	17,560	31,785	86.0
Kings	55,583	49,319	6,264	4,709	4,950	8.5	10.0	1,555	16	22,474	3,934	28,156	76.2
Lake	26,520	23,709	2,811	1,892	1,641	7.1	6.9	1,161	51	10,367	853	27,119	73.4
Lassen	12,354	11,360	994	983	819	8.0	7.2	487	−31	4,125	214	23,396	63.3
Los Angeles	4,860,620	4,677,326	183,294	228,994	252,432	4.7	5.4	239,571	13,289	3,883,777	19,906	40,039	108.3
Madera	63,487	55,038	8,449	4,435	4,769	7.0	8.7	1,926	61	24,063	903	29,421	79.6

See footnotes at end of table.

Table B-10. Counties — Labor Force and Private Business Establishments and Employment—Con.

[Includes United States, states, and 3,141 counties/county equivalents defined as of February 22, 2005. For more information on these areas, see Appendix C, Geographic Information]

| County | Civilian labor force | | | | | | | Private nonfarm businesses | | | | | |
| | Total | | | Number of unemployed | | Unemployment rate[1] | | Establishments | | Employment[2] | | Annual payroll per employee, 2004 | |
	2006	2000	Net change, 2000–2006	2006	2000	2006	2000	2004	Net change, 2000–2004	2004	Net change, 2000–2004	Amount (dol.)	Percent of U.S. average
CALIFORNIA—Con.													
Marin	132,235	141,740	−9,505	4,691	4,026	3.5	2.8	10,083	−174	102,053	−4,222	47,493	128.5
Mariposa	9,141	7,969	1,172	516	486	5.6	6.1	356	−6	4,688	1,541	24,034	65.0
Mendocino	43,877	43,586	291	2,302	2,404	5.2	5.5	2,712	−58	24,440	−328	25,986	70.3
Merced	100,211	90,429	9,782	9,366	8,675	9.3	9.6	3,048	89	43,724	4,178	28,685	77.6
Modoc	4,045	3,754	291	313	278	7.7	7.4	190	−9	1,387	−175	23,933	64.7
Mono	8,381	7,399	982	369	348	4.4	4.7	595	44	6,726	613	21,614	58.5
Monterey	204,705	203,714	991	14,350	14,983	7.0	7.4	8,820	245	107,973	2,905	33,884	91.7
Napa	72,560	66,617	5,943	2,820	2,351	3.9	3.5	3,955	208	54,563	5,037	37,837	102.4
Nevada	50,374	45,402	4,972	2,212	1,838	4.4	4.0	3,182	185	27,888	1,874	28,692	77.6
Orange	1,623,569	1,480,917	142,652	55,276	52,233	3.4	3.5	85,368	6,812	1,435,590	56,873	41,974	113.5
Placer	168,934	131,403	37,531	7,072	4,720	4.2	3.6	8,832	1,535	126,077	32,146	39,361	106.5
Plumas	10,309	9,749	560	789	684	7.7	7.0	810	84	5,033	460	30,135	81.5
Riverside	886,407	680,509	205,898	44,367	36,439	5.0	5.4	30,993	4,428	479,752	86,946	30,427	82.3
Sacramento	682,587	605,641	76,946	32,280	26,352	4.7	4.4	27,336	1,614	456,152	32,269	37,797	102.2
San Benito	25,018	27,418	−2,400	1,762	1,649	7.0	6.0	994	29	12,049	1,268	29,858	80.8
San Bernardino	884,106	739,227	144,879	41,768	35,388	4.7	4.8	30,144	3,065	529,498	63,871	31,436	85.0
San Diego	1,518,007	1,375,719	142,288	60,482	53,822	4.0	3.9	74,524	6,602	1,151,140	98,926	39,132	105.9
San Francisco	421,474	472,545	−51,071	17,808	16,055	4.2	3.4	29,529	−1,877	534,015	−21,632	57,924	156.7
San Joaquin	287,754	258,976	28,778	21,360	17,964	7.4	6.9	11,056	869	170,985	16,580	32,090	86.8
San Luis Obispo	133,886	122,421	11,465	5,304	4,876	4.0	4.0	7,657	713	83,672	10,047	30,114	81.5
San Mateo	368,207	397,978	−29,771	13,598	11,376	3.7	2.9	19,544	−863	309,002	−63,906	59,784	161.7
Santa Barbara	214,160	202,453	11,707	8,697	8,792	4.1	4.3	11,161	277	141,120	924	35,474	96.0
Santa Clara	834,317	939,730	−105,413	37,258	29,397	4.5	3.1	44,021	−1,634	849,891	−149,628	69,107	186.9
Santa Cruz	145,893	148,435	−2,542	8,212	7,593	5.6	5.1	6,921	−51	74,477	−4,783	34,726	93.9
Shasta	83,782	74,768	9,014	5,542	4,481	6.6	6.0	4,634	166	50,727	4,611	29,098	78.7
Sierra	1,619	1,798	−179	121	103	7.5	5.7	84	−15	324	−336	29,272	79.2
Siskiyou	18,960	19,128	−168	1,522	1,420	8.0	7.4	1,275	12	9,367	−249	24,709	66.8
Solano	212,415	198,696	13,719	10,294	9,031	4.8	4.5	7,025	520	103,979	9,460	35,505	96.0
Sonoma	258,085	253,182	4,903	10,366	8,435	4.0	3.3	13,670	251	164,735	1,735	37,598	101.7
Stanislaus	227,114	207,888	19,226	18,105	16,149	8.0	7.8	8,768	511	132,987	12,354	32,065	86.7
Sutter	41,028	37,901	3,127	3,652	3,548	8.9	9.4	1,730	80	19,413	2,150	29,698	80.3
Tehama	25,447	23,603	1,844	1,646	1,519	6.5	6.4	1,098	94	13,014	997	29,124	78.8
Trinity	5,109	5,103	6	502	495	9.8	9.7	324	3	1,769	50	23,061	62.4
Tulare	189,425	172,170	17,255	16,143	17,855	8.5	10.4	6,060	134	86,905	9,743	27,310	73.9
Tuolumne	26,237	22,858	3,379	1,554	1,322	5.9	5.8	1,558	62	13,502	1,081	27,640	74.8
Ventura	425,402	392,693	32,714	18,347	17,759	4.3	4.5	18,628	1,422	261,459	23,457	41,697	112.8
Yolo	94,725	85,741	8,984	4,891	4,327	5.2	5.0	3,587	163	60,965	3,575	34,388	93.0
Yuba	26,509	24,320	2,189	2,346	1,928	8.8	7.9	824	−14	9,982	1,009	28,757	77.8
COLORADO	2,651,718	[4]2,364,990	[4]286,728	114,681	[4]64,798	4.3	[4]2.7	[3]147,314	[3]9,786	[3]1,908,508	[3]−4,794	[3]37,505	[3]101.5
Adams	216,237	185,865	(X)	10,707	5,157	5.0	2.8	7,796	(X)	121,273	(X)	34,386	93.0
Alamosa	8,229	7,216	1,013	389	258	4.7	3.6	516	−1	5,141	84	24,497	66.3
Arapahoe	307,801	283,063	24,738	13,309	6,923	4.3	2.4	17,463	1,051	265,146	−27,261	43,860	118.6
Archuleta	6,453	5,027	1,426	266	162	4.1	3.2	504	37	2,723	15	22,952	62.1
Baca	2,449	2,107	342	79	58	3.2	2.8	98	−12	592	15	18,880	51.1
Bent	2,433	2,275	158	139	85	5.7	3.7	77	−	557	−584	22,224	60.1
Boulder	173,079	160,426	(X)	6,436	3,900	3.7	2.4	10,955	(X)	132,973	(X)	43,963	118.9
Broomfield	25,319	(X)	(X)	1,103	(X)	4.4	(X)	1,485	(X)	26,440	(X)	53,364	144.4
Chaffee	8,220	7,362	858	364	243	4.4	3.3	825	81	4,899	128	22,438	60.7
Cheyenne	1,395	1,123	272	37	28	2.7	2.5	59	−1	448	−1	28,725	77.7
Clear Creek	6,020	6,068	−48	244	163	4.1	2.7	341	7	2,350	−413	26,838	72.6
Conejos	3,802	3,340	462	252	163	6.6	4.9	117	−4	678	−184	21,342	57.7
Costilla	1,324	1,261	63	114	87	8.6	6.9	46	−11	244	9	17,869	48.3
Crowley	1,614	1,490	124	111	78	6.9	5.2	44	−5	468	−124	26,985	73.0
Custer	1,944	1,664	280	84	52	4.3	3.1	158	21	727	149	22,028	59.6
Delta	15,886	12,341	3,545	643	434	4.0	3.5	805	55	6,037	463	23,569	63.8
Denver	310,908	306,409	4,499	15,112	9,200	4.9	3.0	21,798	−623	379,953	−31,350	44,030	119.1
Dolores	966	903	63	64	48	6.6	5.3	53	10	200	13	20,730	56.1
Douglas	147,615	106,048	41,567	5,371	2,191	3.6	2.1	5,999	1,921	60,432	22,530	38,356	103.8
Eagle	29,989	25,765	4,224	1,012	642	3.4	2.5	3,128	311	29,810	1,124	30,117	81.5
Elbert	13,314	11,656	1,658	534	264	4.0	2.3	521	68	2,298	−21	28,235	76.4
El Paso	298,840	265,275	33,565	13,744	7,744	4.6	2.9	15,069	1,403	205,184	−4,805	33,882	91.7
Fremont	19,667	17,879	1,788	1,101	688	5.6	3.8	920	42	8,137	90	22,769	61.6
Garfield	33,646	24,849	8,797	975	668	2.9	2.7	2,258	220	16,863	1,170	32,637	88.3
Gilpin	3,440	3,321	119	141	81	4.1	2.4	98	15	4,088	371	31,738	85.9
Grand	8,796	7,652	1,144	291	196	3.3	2.6	854	106	5,234	−1,054	22,359	60.5
Gunnison	9,593	8,213	1,380	304	237	3.2	2.9	952	88	5,973	−1,035	24,632	66.6
Hinsdale	628	652	−24	19	13	3.0	2.0	72	−5	159	−12	23,409	63.3
Huerfano	3,427	3,078	349	206	165	6.0	5.4	176	−27	1,402	−106	22,052	59.7
Jackson	1,115	888	227	34	26	3.0	2.9	62	4	203	−14	23,143	62.6

See footnotes at end of table.

[Includes United States, states, and 3,141 counties/county equivalents defined as of February 22, 2005. For more information on these areas, see Appendix C, Geographic Information]

County	Civilian labor force							Private nonfarm businesses					
	Total			Number of unemployed		Unemployment rate[1]		Establishments		Employment[2]		Annual payroll per employee, 2004	
	2006	2000	Net change, 2000–2006	2006	2000	2006	2000	2004	Net change, 2000–2004	2004	Net change, 2000–2004	Amount (dol.)	Percent of U.S. average
COLORADO—Con.													
Jefferson	313,902	310,044	(X)	13,212	7,413	4.2	2.4	15,980	(X)	181,015	(X)	37,026	100.2
Kiowa	898	783	115	32	24	3.6	3.1	43	-5	265	23	19,415	52.5
Kit Carson	4,555	3,855	700	141	100	3.1	2.6	266	-20	1,799	-199	23,260	62.9
Lake	4,128	4,061	67	171	138	4.1	3.4	209	6	1,259	-91	19,753	53.4
La Plata	30,510	24,521	5,989	1,031	711	3.4	2.9	2,235	234	17,962	134	28,691	77.6
Larimer	171,145	146,678	24,467	6,713	3,679	3.9	2.5	8,888	871	99,726	6,148	33,259	90.0
Las Animas	8,616	6,679	1,937	347	262	4.0	3.9	403	33	4,042	768	20,275	54.8
Lincoln	3,096	2,632	464	114	74	3.7	2.8	150	5	1,328	-19	23,329	63.1
Logan	11,351	10,026	1,325	390	284	3.4	2.8	622	-14	5,444	-261	24,321	65.8
Mesa	74,880	58,945	15,935	2,945	1,886	3.9	3.2	4,331	437	45,814	2,464	28,097	76.0
Mineral	445	422	23	23	17	5.2	4.0	57	-3	158	-2	23,525	63.6
Moffat	8,464	7,015	1,449	315	248	3.7	3.5	426	36	3,698	6	35,026	94.7
Montezuma	13,252	11,806	1,446	584	468	4.4	4.0	788	8	6,641	-101	24,524	66.3
Montrose	20,473	16,252	4,221	819	576	4.0	3.5	1,242	118	10,873	725	26,875	72.7
Morgan	14,448	12,566	1,882	566	369	3.9	2.9	682	20	8,444	153	26,063	70.5
Otero	9,452	8,822	630	577	365	6.1	4.1	520	3	5,132	-12	21,670	58.6
Ouray	3,095	2,220	875	95	58	3.1	2.6	271	23	1,071	280	31,188	84.4
Park	9,933	8,566	1,367	396	218	4.0	2.5	447	49	1,247	-89	26,616	72.0
Phillips	2,426	2,057	369	83	53	3.4	2.6	141	-7	958	-56	22,061	59.7
Pitkin	11,386	10,067	1,319	366	288	3.2	2.9	1,592	60	15,838	347	29,294	79.2
Prowers	7,046	6,943	103	413	198	5.9	2.9	407	-30	4,459	169	22,412	60.6
Pueblo	71,261	63,986	7,275	4,022	2,409	5.6	3.8	3,286	99	44,765	-3,588	27,276	73.8
Rio Blanco	4,826	3,245	1,581	127	95	2.6	2.9	229	8	1,545	-34	33,343	90.2
Rio Grande	6,624	5,826	798	318	255	4.8	4.4	375	-12	2,747	11	22,192	60.0
Routt	15,157	12,550	2,607	485	324	3.2	2.6	1,533	196	15,648	-1,863	32,652	88.3
Saguache	3,234	2,711	523	205	148	6.3	5.5	145	24	823	156	21,691	58.7
San Juan	555	515	40	28	24	5.0	4.7	77	22	258	181	31,814	86.1
San Miguel	5,509	4,751	758	191	147	3.5	3.1	623	89	4,691	441	24,986	67.6
Sedgwick	1,639	1,401	238	53	37	3.2	2.6	91	–	542	24	18,327	49.6
Summit	16,863	16,129	734	534	383	3.2	2.4	1,968	133	21,556	1,935	20,394	55.2
Teller	13,005	11,907	1,098	549	347	4.2	2.9	691	52	5,273	-25	26,488	71.7
Washington	2,925	2,445	480	102	62	3.5	2.5	101	-16	633	-115	24,785	67.0
Weld	115,979	93,722	(X)	5,371	2,521	4.6	2.7	4,643	(X)	60,182	(X)	33,297	90.1
Yuma	6,491	5,045	1,446	176	128	2.7	2.5	342	-8	2,521	335	25,242	68.3
CONNECTICUT	1,844,235	1,736,831	107,404	79,160	39,161	4.3	2.3	[3]93,011	[3]575	[3]1,537,461	[3]-8,789	[3]47,382	[3]128.2
Fairfield	464,411	445,342	19,069	17,597	8,978	3.8	2.0	28,475	-112	450,517	5,587	62,420	168.9
Hartford	449,501	428,466	21,035	21,031	10,625	4.7	2.5	23,196	-2	456,061	-20,579	46,313	125.3
Litchfield	104,829	99,272	5,557	4,140	1,939	3.9	2.0	5,212	20	56,400	-2,518	34,296	92.8
Middlesex	91,681	85,321	6,360	3,338	1,714	3.6	2.0	4,350	114	65,440	4,998	39,392	106.6
New Haven	440,949	413,770	27,179	20,746	10,178	4.7	2.5	20,796	21	335,706	-3,222	38,808	105.0
New London	146,963	131,618	15,345	6,004	2,921	4.1	2.2	6,005	276	111,683	5,913	36,125	97.7
Tolland	83,114	75,553	7,561	3,110	1,371	3.7	1.8	2,529	-2	29,344	(NA)	30,416	82.3
Windham	62,789	57,491	5,298	3,195	1,437	5.1	2.5	2,315	128	29,689	-1,487	31,411	85.0
DELAWARE	440,322	416,503	23,819	15,816	13,726	3.6	3.3	[3]25,391	[3]1,620	[3]391,682	[3]14,405	[3]41,040	[3]111.0
Kent	73,474	63,919	9,555	2,371	2,269	3.2	3.5	3,222	261	48,944	4,544	27,530	74.5
New Castle	274,825	272,540	2,285	10,455	8,710	3.8	3.2	16,881	690	285,654	3,523	45,858	124.1
Sussex	92,024	80,045	11,979	2,991	2,748	3.3	3.4	5,219	600	56,763	6,017	28,365	76.7
DISTRICT OF COLUMBIA	315,874	309,421	6,453	18,917	17,505	6.0	5.7	19,518	-137	436,865	21,882	55,587	150.4
District of Columbia	315,874	309,421	6,453	18,917	17,505	6.0	5.7	19,518	-137	436,865	21,882	55,587	150.4
FLORIDA	8,988,611	7,869,690	1,118,921	295,850	300,284	3.3	3.8	[3]484,938	[3]56,500	[3]6,864,987	[3]647,601	[3]32,017	[3]86.6
Alachua	123,748	116,195	7,553	3,275	3,495	2.6	3.0	5,590	419	83,565	2,156	28,485	77.1
Baker	11,360	10,396	964	325	313	2.9	3.0	363	85	5,130	1,306	25,322	68.5
Bay	84,810	71,998	12,812	2,632	3,340	3.1	4.6	4,532	324	56,873	2,941	27,224	73.6
Bradford	12,022	10,585	1,437	342	397	2.8	3.8	422	38	4,152	38	22,601	61.1
Brevard	261,417	232,007	29,410	8,553	8,420	3.3	3.6	12,938	1,578	174,830	17,132	33,571	90.8
Broward	974,486	855,214	119,272	30,105	31,101	3.1	3.6	56,087	5,759	652,609	33,208	34,287	92.8
Calhoun	5,384	5,154	230	167	243	3.1	4.7	227	6	1,693	-211	19,040	51.5
Charlotte	68,085	55,163	12,922	2,345	2,043	3.4	3.7	3,711	638	35,448	3,763	25,508	69.0
Citrus	54,339	43,743	10,596	2,039	2,044	3.8	4.7	2,701	330	26,042	-2,128	26,328	71.2
Clay	88,534	73,871	14,663	2,662	2,233	3.0	3.0	3,399	583	35,812	4,534	24,381	66.0
Collier	153,365	116,109	37,256	4,652	4,311	3.0	3.7	9,952	1,477	102,376	10,152	32,442	87.8
Columbia	29,520	25,680	3,840	925	1,009	3.1	3.9	1,252	119	16,715	1,543	26,238	71.0
DeSoto	14,412	13,277	1,135	511	589	3.5	4.4	476	53	4,474	-704	23,267	62.9
Dixie	5,774	5,129	645	194	228	3.4	4.4	188	-1	1,526	117	22,033	59.6
Duval	430,322	408,336	21,986	14,945	13,533	3.5	3.3	22,873	1,959	402,356	8,250	36,204	97.9

See footnotes at end of table.

County and City Data Book: 2007

U.S. Census Bureau

Table B-10. Counties — **Labor Force and Private Business Establishments and Employment**—Con.

[Includes United States, states, and 3,141 counties/county equivalents defined as of February 22, 2005. For more information on these areas, see Appendix C, Geographic Information]

County	Civilian labor force							Private nonfarm businesses					
	Total			Number of unemployed		Unemployment rate[1]		Establishments		Employment[2]		Annual payroll per employee, 2004	
	2006	2000	Net change, 2000–2006	2006	2000	2006	2000	2004	Net change, 2000–2004	2004	Net change, 2000–2004	Amount (dol.)	Percent of U.S. average
FLORIDA—Con.													
Escambia	136,211	132,487	3,724	4,329	5,338	3.2	4.0	6,914	331	102,561	–4,033	28,405	76.8
Flagler	31,480	21,008	10,472	1,313	753	4.2	3.6	1,578	533	13,760	3,740	29,102	78.7
Franklin	5,159	4,414	745	150	174	2.9	3.9	360	42	2,329	56	22,320	60.4
Gadsden	20,728	19,954	774	716	799	3.5	4.0	636	61	9,786	403	25,139	68.0
Gilchrist	7,504	6,430	1,074	219	230	2.9	3.6	238	68	1,554	481	21,075	57.0
Glades	4,549	4,086	463	180	192	4.0	4.7	77	–51	729	–820	26,008	70.4
Gulf	6,619	5,247	1,372	194	317	2.9	6.0	296	45	2,356	460	25,272	68.4
Hamilton	4,660	4,581	79	175	244	3.8	5.3	187	15	2,235	104	31,672	85.7
Hardee	12,091	10,754	1,337	466	633	3.9	5.9	414	54	4,012	549	25,669	69.4
Hendry	17,706	16,296	1,410	1,091	1,171	6.2	7.2	557	77	5,869	685	27,118	73.4
Hernando	60,263	49,595	10,668	2,608	2,159	4.3	4.4	2,917	548	28,266	4,658	24,615	66.6
Highlands	41,684	33,174	8,510	1,490	1,587	3.6	4.8	1,978	226	19,520	–22,540	24,108	65.2
Hillsborough	601,719	528,979	72,740	18,935	17,245	3.1	3.3	30,690	3,856	501,501	–1,333	36,387	98.4
Holmes	8,689	7,740	949	261	372	3.0	4.8	285	30	2,046	–186	19,640	53.1
Indian River	59,596	51,057	8,539	2,494	2,604	4.2	5.1	3,873	421	40,234	1,631	27,595	74.6
Jackson	21,502	19,399	2,103	747	890	3.5	4.6	844	70	9,464	98	21,565	58.3
Jefferson	6,906	6,067	839	200	223	2.9	3.7	268	29	1,967	346	22,906	62.0
Lafayette	2,857	2,719	138	78	110	2.7	4.0	87	–19	734	–118	19,617	53.1
Lake	123,126	93,300	29,826	4,090	3,341	3.3	3.6	5,706	1,090	63,295	8,811	26,492	71.7
Lee	283,015	207,750	75,265	8,082	6,703	2.9	3.2	15,126	2,733	177,318	34,264	30,492	82.5
Leon	139,341	134,833	4,508	3,805	4,107	2.7	3.0	7,071	635	94,327	4,202	29,294	79.2
Levy	16,791	14,400	2,391	569	559	3.4	3.9	753	119	5,820	195	21,479	58.1
Liberty	3,561	2,622	939	92	109	2.6	4.2	86	–7	1,364	641	23,720	64.2
Madison	7,431	7,698	–267	370	313	5.0	4.1	337	28	3,912	420	21,214	57.4
Manatee	154,265	123,240	31,025	4,464	3,914	2.9	3.2	7,076	1,474	90,321	8,857	30,186	81.7
Marion	131,653	109,216	22,437	4,453	4,412	3.4	4.0	6,557	1,074	78,223	5,088	26,980	73.0
Martin	65,866	56,357	9,509	2,265	2,344	3.4	4.2	4,814	546	50,768	2,107	29,062	78.6
Miami-Dade	1,158,801	1,103,485	55,316	43,637	56,585	3.8	5.1	72,749	6,240	852,296	–2,093	35,178	95.2
Monroe	44,520	45,192	–672	1,107	1,291	2.5	2.9	3,792	54	32,471	107	23,970	64.8
Nassau	33,424	30,282	3,142	957	999	2.9	3.3	1,473	271	14,410	1,663	28,171	76.2
Okaloosa	98,757	80,410	18,347	2,386	2,959	2.4	3.7	5,432	634	66,074	7,778	27,673	74.9
Okeechobee	17,497	15,662	1,835	711	839	4.1	5.4	734	58	7,061	423	23,287	63.0
Orange	575,990	499,652	76,338	17,678	15,283	3.1	3.1	30,142	3,751	589,727	14,794	32,562	88.1
Osceola	121,189	89,582	31,607	4,084	2,943	3.4	3.3	4,505	1,157	55,113	7,044	24,602	66.5
Palm Beach	631,038	541,759	89,279	22,523	22,812	3.6	4.2	40,988	4,478	470,989	22,338	36,287	98.2
Pasco	187,391	150,276	37,115	6,998	5,540	3.7	3.7	7,504	1,311	72,173	6,932	24,911	67.4
Pinellas	477,891	471,195	6,696	15,149	15,450	3.2	3.3	27,629	1,539	388,767	–52,295	31,788	86.0
Polk	269,119	231,280	37,839	9,364	9,529	3.5	4.1	10,683	1,074	166,646	5,181	29,897	80.9
Putnam	31,508	29,357	2,151	1,168	1,252	3.7	4.3	1,367	148	13,123	424	26,490	71.7
St. Johns	85,415	66,464	18,951	2,323	1,963	2.7	3.0	4,366	958	42,149	4,249	27,764	75.1
St. Lucie	114,980	87,455	27,525	4,840	5,017	4.2	5.7	4,658	851	51,927	10,347	27,366	74.0
Santa Rosa	67,796	54,985	12,811	2,072	2,104	3.1	3.8	2,436	490	21,902	4,098	25,078	67.8
Sarasota	180,823	148,844	31,979	5,360	4,756	3.0	3.2	12,911	1,641	133,183	–27,853	30,831	83.4
Seminole	236,170	212,638	23,532	6,775	6,420	2.9	3.0	12,345	1,771	147,358	10,253	31,821	86.1
Sumter	29,152	16,926	12,226	788	728	2.7	4.3	745	232	11,172	6,185	28,425	76.9
Suwannee	17,013	15,425	1,588	541	552	3.2	3.6	669	41	7,682	292	22,841	61.8
Taylor	8,736	8,279	457	342	407	3.9	4.9	435	54	6,181	1,130	29,164	78.9
Union	5,117	4,530	587	135	197	2.6	4.3	130	17	1,507	62	26,933	72.9
Volusia	248,026	209,694	38,332	8,061	7,071	3.3	3.4	12,310	1,508	137,765	6,505	26,028	70.4
Wakulla	14,596	11,697	2,899	371	375	2.5	3.2	398	52	2,824	332	24,998	67.6
Walton	31,513	19,418	12,095	662	672	2.1	3.5	1,362	463	11,804	2,561	23,798	64.4
Washington	9,604	8,948	656	313	403	3.3	4.5	371	19	4,049	–83	20,466	55.4
GEORGIA	4,741,860	4,242,889	498,971	219,835	147,527	4.6	3.5	[3]214,714	[3]14,272	[3]3,452,451	[3]–31,049	[3]35,147	[3]95.1
Appling	8,869	8,596	273	497	454	5.6	5.3	394	9	5,249	556	33,117	89.6
Atkinson	3,436	3,542	–106	190	204	5.5	5.8	94	8	1,335	67	27,619	74.7
Bacon	4,922	4,684	238	225	209	4.6	4.5	207	6	2,293	–506	23,959	64.8
Baker	1,838	1,750	88	92	73	5.0	4.2	26	5	313	99	21,112	57.1
Baldwin	20,992	19,060	1,932	1,152	913	5.5	4.8	855	4	13,466	–1,805	25,095	67.9
Banks	9,730	7,841	1,889	316	231	3.2	2.9	151	–46	1,202	–1,842	19,338	52.3
Barrow	31,655	25,258	6,397	1,322	750	4.2	3.0	945	134	10,650	1,100	28,961	78.3
Bartow	46,092	40,738	5,354	2,202	1,479	4.8	3.6	1,794	195	28,216	1,666	29,408	79.6
Ben Hill	8,403	8,181	222	484	384	5.8	4.7	373	–3	6,602	–672	25,781	69.7
Berrien	9,039	8,086	953	379	313	4.2	3.9	274	–2	4,032	46	28,463	77.0
Bibb	74,190	70,623	3,567	4,230	2,971	5.7	4.2	4,507	–82	82,506	–1,105	30,331	82.0
Bleckley	5,116	5,190	–74	312	211	6.1	4.1	191	–8	2,733	–461	22,560	61.0
Brantley	7,842	6,814	1,028	360	278	4.6	4.1	186	7	1,398	–64	23,054	62.4
Brooks	8,603	7,591	1,012	353	344	4.1	4.5	186	–22	2,074	–315	24,282	65.7
Bryan	16,044	11,648	4,396	564	355	3.5	3.0	478	80	3,973	821	22,047	59.6
Bulloch	31,674	27,410	4,264	1,333	1,043	4.2	3.8	1,364	144	17,116	635	21,655	58.6
Burke	10,141	9,216	925	676	457	6.7	5.0	341	22	5,061	–320	33,066	89.4
Butts	9,438	9,097	341	510	413	5.4	4.5	387	47	4,951	651	24,072	65.1
Calhoun	2,404	2,367	37	144	151	6.0	6.4	103	1	731	12	20,439	55.3
Camden	20,828	17,940	2,888	875	700	4.2	3.9	803	111	8,078	6	20,409	55.2

See footnotes at end of table.

[Includes United States, states, and 3,141 counties/county equivalents defined as of February 22, 2005. For more information on these areas, see Appendix C, Geographic Information]

County	Civilian labor force							Private nonfarm businesses					
	Total			Number of unemployed		Unemployment rate[1]		Establishments		Employment[2]		Annual payroll per employee, 2004	
	2006	2000	Net change, 2000–2006	2006	2000	2006	2000	2004	Net change, 2000–2004	2004	Net change, 2000–2004	Amount (dol.)	Percent of U.S. average
GEORGIA—Con.													
Candler	4,616	3,998	618	195	178	4.2	4.5	199	−6	2,327	−26	20,819	56.3
Carroll	52,523	45,066	7,457	2,541	1,657	4.8	3.7	1,958	112	26,022	−1,727	30,599	82.8
Catoosa	35,902	29,817	6,085	1,329	785	3.7	2.6	862	105	11,808	992	27,250	73.7
Charlton	4,546	3,967	579	209	161	4.6	4.1	175	−5	1,911	310	23,564	63.7
Chatham	130,632	112,074	18,558	5,247	3,916	4.0	3.5	6,788	166	112,579	5,470	31,235	84.5
Chattahoochee	2,687	2,641	46	254	212	9.5	8.0	71	14	685	−662	25,559	69.1
Chattooga	11,042	11,678	−636	569	426	5.2	3.6	333	–	6,444	−413	20,683	55.9
Cherokee	103,527	83,165	20,362	3,741	2,120	3.6	2.5	4,098	851	37,426	8,143	27,306	73.9
Clarke	61,628	54,489	7,139	2,429	1,848	3.9	3.4	2,901	304	46,120	4,840	27,191	73.6
Clay	1,493	1,346	147	69	71	4.6	5.3	45	−1	528	149	20,538	55.6
Clayton	140,144	126,783	13,361	7,782	4,215	5.6	3.3	4,142	−232	71,746	−16,776	30,260	81.9
Clinch	2,731	2,777	−46	143	146	5.2	5.3	125	−8	1,651	−874	17,530	47.4
Cobb	382,689	362,179	20,510	15,778	10,011	4.1	2.8	19,163	1,212	312,292	−583	41,389	112.0
Coffee	16,915	17,319	−404	921	872	5.4	5.0	832	−5	14,731	−2,139	24,432	66.1
Colquitt	20,921	19,427	1,494	892	873	4.3	4.5	885	9	10,662	−590	23,395	63.3
Columbia	57,433	47,425	10,008	2,358	1,351	4.1	2.8	1,936	132	24,298	1,044	28,048	75.9
Cook	7,056	7,287	−231	388	321	5.5	4.4	332	−13	3,365	−881	21,836	59.1
Coweta	57,810	48,904	8,906	2,366	1,590	4.1	3.3	1,946	281	25,883	2,184	27,709	75.0
Crawford	6,337	5,895	442	325	229	5.1	3.9	90	14	699	52	19,345	52.3
Crisp	10,382	9,797	585	610	474	5.9	4.8	547	−6	7,245	−529	23,913	64.7
Dade	8,686	7,741	945	351	229	4.0	3.0	234	12	3,174	653	22,551	61.0
Dawson	10,679	9,067	1,612	398	241	3.7	2.7	545	50	4,900	679	23,133	62.6
Decatur	12,048	12,346	−298	689	540	5.7	4.4	609	23	8,272	−535	23,698	64.1
DeKalb	380,339	382,767	−2,428	19,327	12,492	5.1	3.3	16,001	−966	272,394	−55,994	37,782	102.2
Dodge	9,583	8,539	1,044	474	395	4.9	4.6	366	−8	4,066	430	21,847	59.1
Dooly	4,895	4,813	82	291	225	5.9	4.7	178	−10	1,642	−1,311	24,391	66.0
Dougherty	42,275	41,670	605	2,555	2,131	6.0	5.1	2,601	17	45,081	−558	29,769	80.5
Douglas	61,650	51,635	10,015	3,038	1,516	4.9	2.9	2,415	310	32,876	3,655	25,647	69.4
Early	5,772	5,373	399	289	259	5.0	4.8	230	−8	3,603	−114	31,638	85.6
Echols	2,403	1,868	535	77	63	3.2	3.4	15	3	64	41	22,266	60.2
Effingham	26,843	19,090	7,753	897	585	3.3	3.1	596	97	6,441	1,088	30,038	81.3
Elbert	10,099	9,745	354	659	496	6.5	5.1	516	−15	5,841	55	24,229	65.5
Emanuel	10,941	9,967	974	561	548	5.1	5.5	423	4	5,827	535	21,902	59.2
Evans	5,056	4,709	347	225	197	4.5	4.2	233	−8	4,159	548	20,876	56.5
Fannin	10,815	9,098	1,717	438	336	4.0	3.7	540	87	4,583	402	21,335	57.7
Fayette	55,088	49,991	5,097	2,132	1,314	3.9	2.6	2,987	576	39,150	9,558	29,387	79.5
Floyd	51,711	44,870	6,841	2,217	1,659	4.3	3.7	2,058	42	35,667	−2,277	28,073	75.9
Forsyth	77,892	57,518	20,374	2,498	1,355	3.2	2.4	3,778	1,410	45,787	16,100	35,855	97.0
Franklin	10,964	9,973	991	565	377	5.2	3.8	492	15	7,694	1,348	26,853	72.6
Fulton	472,795	432,000	40,795	23,155	14,787	4.9	3.4	32,899	1,953	730,700	−37,816	48,364	130.8
Gilmer	14,219	11,345	2,874	513	362	3.6	3.2	513	81	6,583	487	23,985	64.9
Glascock	1,207	1,193	14	62	46	5.1	3.9	25	1	196	11	19,622	53.1
Glynn	40,447	34,936	5,511	1,543	1,192	3.8	3.4	2,485	118	31,436	890	27,280	73.8
Gordon	27,429	24,416	3,013	1,201	805	4.4	3.3	1,047	78	17,962	−1,538	27,982	75.7
Grady	12,330	11,044	1,286	493	476	4.0	4.3	401	26	3,937	−24	22,518	60.9
Greene	6,985	6,392	593	409	272	5.9	4.3	355	32	3,802	−437	25,801	69.8
Gwinnett	412,993	347,889	65,104	16,866	9,393	4.1	2.7	20,150	2,365	294,721	7,255	38,097	103.1
Habersham	19,917	18,436	1,481	808	623	4.1	3.4	901	87	12,810	843	24,928	67.4
Hall	86,559	73,882	12,677	3,296	2,144	3.8	2.9	3,812	450	59,890	2,035	32,851	88.9
Hancock	3,438	3,291	147	291	258	8.5	7.8	84	2	657	−117	16,015	43.3
Haralson	13,286	12,454	832	612	439	4.6	3.5	457	13	5,602	4	26,598	71.9
Harris	15,574	12,962	2,612	584	399	3.7	3.1	452	36	4,021	−275	10,981	54.1
Hart	11,091	11,410	−319	719	436	6.5	3.8	381	−4	5,412	−833	24,533	66.4
Heard	5,105	5,149	−44	248	202	4.9	3.9	115	−4	1,140	−303	25,992	70.3
Henry	91,691	67,821	23,870	4,130	1,780	4.5	2.6	3,073	802	37,973	9,535	26,080	70.5
Houston	66,202	53,848	12,354	2,824	1,802	4.3	3.3	2,153	187	30,678	3,959	25,202	68.2
Irwin	4,761	4,553	208	243	203	5.1	4.5	131	−4	1,890	−106	21,475	58.1
Jackson	26,992	21,448	5,544	1,060	664	3.9	3.1	1,191	207	15,839	1,660	29,320	79.3
Jasper	6,484	5,804	680	309	185	4.8	3.2	176	16	2,001	160	25,837	69.9
Jeff Davis	5,554	5,806	−252	403	261	7.3	4.5	289	−20	4,604	–	22,455	60.7
Jefferson	7,033	6,785	248	454	441	6.5	6.5	359	17	4,496	47	27,616	74.7
Jenkins	3,652	3,739	−87	199	191	5.4	5.1	143	−5	1,858	−456	23,293	63.0
Johnson	3,804	3,420	384	206	209	5.4	6.1	135	−15	1,181	−401	24,871	67.3
Jones	13,962	11,837	2,125	713	445	5.1	3.8	309	70	2,204	94	22,626	61.2
Lamar	8,060	8,084	−24	451	358	5.6	4.4	229	−8	2,662	−465	20,799	56.3
Lanier	3,957	3,348	609	153	162	3.9	4.8	106	−12	738	−244	19,885	53.8
Laurens	22,734	21,528	1,206	1,204	992	5.3	4.6	1,050	−13	16,782	17	26,543	71.8
Lee	16,823	13,203	3,620	626	439	3.7	3.3	295	87	2,808	334	23,997	64.9
Liberty	24,042	19,736	4,306	1,331	1,051	5.5	5.3	758	23	10,614	1,124	23,752	64.3
Lincoln	3,712	3,784	−72	234	211	6.3	5.6	163	2	1,096	−59	19,474	52.7

See footnotes at end of table.

County and City Data Book: 2007

U.S. Census Bureau

[Includes United States, states, and 3,141 counties/county equivalents defined as of February 22, 2005. For more information on these areas, see Appendix C, Geographic Information]

County	Civilian labor force							Private nonfarm businesses					
	Total			Number of unemployed		Unemployment rate[1]		Establishments		Employment[2]		Annual payroll per employee, 2004	
	2006	2000	Net change, 2000–2006	2006	2000	2006	2000	2004	Net change, 2000–2004	2004	Net change, 2000–2004	Amount (dol.)	Percent of U.S. average
GEORGIA—Con.													
Long	6,035	4,343	1,692	224	159	3.7	3.7	54	7	494	274	12,192	33.0
Lowndes	52,383	43,640	8,743	2,053	1,914	3.9	4.4	2,656	248	41,008	4,870	23,317	63.1
Lumpkin	12,820	10,957	1,863	521	318	4.1	2.9	457	75	4,825	779	24,288	65.7
McDuffie	10,722	9,943	779	668	431	6.2	4.3	487	17	12,722	5,297	30,747	83.2
McIntosh	5,407	4,908	499	225	203	4.2	4.1	211	−17	1,655	−371	18,972	51.3
Macon	5,386	5,437	−51	393	352	7.3	6.5	216	7	2,371	−230	28,704	77.6
Madison	16,090	13,867	2,223	579	445	3.6	3.2	402	−109	2,934	−4,007	20,616	55.8
Marion	3,460	3,336	124	153	129	4.4	3.9	85	8	1,510	−661	20,606	55.7
Meriwether	10,160	10,180	−20	655	457	6.4	4.5	326	−16	4,171	−848	25,707	69.5
Miller	3,780	3,263	517	135	128	3.6	3.9	140	−6	1,141	78	20,215	54.7
Mitchell	10,569	9,946	623	521	497	4.9	5.0	446	50	6,711	−22	20,617	55.8
Monroe	12,861	11,398	1,463	585	410	4.5	3.6	406	8	4,060	487	25,488	68.9
Montgomery	4,458	3,938	520	237	226	5.3	5.7	104	−12	1,025	−143	21,654	58.6
Morgan	9,354	8,205	1,149	413	273	4.4	3.3	445	41	4,906	−841	27,309	73.9
Murray	21,771	19,697	2,074	930	651	4.3	3.3	450	−16	9,266	−1,556	25,702	69.5
Muscogee	86,121	83,999	2,122	4,712	3,897	5.5	4.6	4,386	182	81,332	−5,157	28,759	77.8
Newton	43,897	32,438	11,459	2,308	1,041	5.3	3.2	1,413	232	18,133	2,544	31,233	84.5
Oconee	17,878	14,408	3,470	550	363	3.1	2.5	759	180	7,068	1,710	25,371	68.6
Oglethorpe	7,852	6,657	1,195	285	199	3.6	3.0	156	14	901	60	22,008	59.5
Paulding	60,745	46,009	14,736	2,491	1,207	4.1	2.6	1,346	362	11,799	2,618	25,899	70.1
Peach	11,578	10,882	696	683	511	5.9	4.7	492	46	6,332	−273	24,608	66.6
Pickens	14,787	12,541	2,246	546	370	3.7	3.0	587	103	5,537	529	28,826	78.0
Pierce	8,420	7,677	743	354	309	4.2	4.0	309	10	3,368	975	21,059	57.0
Pike	7,952	7,013	939	362	255	4.6	3.6	224	29	1,356	135	21,299	57.6
Polk	21,116	17,655	3,461	916	701	4.3	4.0	626	−4	9,347	910	24,770	67.0
Pulaski	4,631	4,387	244	210	174	4.5	4.0	198	−9	2,326	55	23,912	64.7
Putnam	10,390	9,078	1,312	474	310	4.6	3.4	418	59	5,532	261	22,722	61.5
Quitman	996	1,044	−48	50	65	5.0	6.2	37	2	247	19	21,866	59.2
Rabun	7,842	7,294	548	444	221	5.7	3.0	513	28	5,351	−277	25,424	68.8
Randolph	2,849	3,012	−163	184	173	6.5	5.7	153	−9	1,501	−53	22,302	60.3
Richmond	90,641	87,564	3,077	5,637	3,798	6.2	4.3	4,623	169	84,075	333	31,652	85.6
Rockdale	40,426	37,061	3,365	1,996	1,138	4.9	3.1	2,077	95	31,617	89	30,653	82.9
Schley	1,813	1,727	86	106	73	5.8	4.2	62	2	1,031	78	27,954	75.6
Screven	7,150	6,622	528	359	315	5.0	4.8	240	3	2,792	−106	23,935	64.7
Seminole	4,063	4,021	42	208	192	5.1	4.8	193	−2	1,576	86	19,428	52.6
Spalding	29,057	28,246	811	1,818	1,206	6.3	4.3	1,229	46	20,093	803	26,100	70.6
Stephens	13,588	13,259	329	681	460	5.0	3.5	596	3	8,985	−768	25,599	69.2
Stewart	1,987	2,091	−104	134	108	6.7	5.2	84	−10	592	−350	20,813	56.3
Sumter	14,775	15,418	−643	926	656	6.3	4.3	702	4	10,838	−1,741	23,620	63.9
Talbot	3,060	2,858	202	201	151	6.6	5.3	59	−1	418	−53	30,545	82.6
Taliaferro	761	851	−90	57	42	7.5	4.9	24	–	123	20	15,016	40.6
Tattnall	9,135	8,884	251	488	504	5.3	5.7	291	−10	3,053	24	18,903	51.1
Taylor	3,319	3,419	−100	213	175	6.4	5.1	140	−1	1,270	−51	26,459	71.6
Telfair	5,256	4,435	821	393	335	7.5	7.6	229	−9	3,388	−318	21,286	57.6
Terrell	4,654	4,675	−21	261	242	5.6	5.2	183	−8	1,650	−458	19,779	53.5
Thomas	23,763	19,910	3,853	971	810	4.1	4.1	1,133	74	17,976	−123	27,716	75.0
Tift	20,220	18,985	1,235	1,025	765	5.1	4.0	1,135	7	17,487	−509	26,118	70.7
Toombs	13,389	12,300	1,089	715	806	5.3	6.6	738	7	10,716	416	21,546	58.3
Towns	5,990	4,258	1,732	203	170	3.4	4.0	315	26	2,682	571	21,260	57.5
Treutlen	2,692	2,640	52	163	201	6.1	7.6	91	−1	835	105	14,969	40.5
Troup	30,559	30,196	363	1,823	1,056	6.0	3.5	1,430	13	29,944	−1,944	29,975	81.1
Turner	5,206	4,382	824	300	237	5.8	5.4	171	−8	1,657	−52	19,659	53.2
Twiggs	4,683	4,617	66	273	199	5.8	4.3	79	−14	799	−516	28,860	78.1
Union	10,684	8,122	2,562	397	301	3.7	3.7	566	110	4,864	1,155	23,790	64.4
Upson	11,865	12,842	−977	756	629	6.4	4.9	539	33	6,758	−1,604	26,058	70.5
Walker	33,884	30,561	3,323	1,485	1,065	4.4	3.5	841	−67	13,807	−2,805	27,789	75.2
Walton	39,106	32,650	6,456	1,763	1,001	4.5	3.1	1,526	303	15,530	4,157	27,162	73.5
Ware	14,953	15,294	−341	759	774	5.1	5.1	992	16	13,279	154	22,003	59.5
Warren	2,479	2,650	−171	210	141	8.5	5.3	93	16	1,221	−172	23,906	64.7
Washington	8,347	8,600	−253	490	396	5.9	4.6	415	14	6,638	−333	30,384	82.2
Wayne	11,973	11,398	575	669	552	5.6	4.8	552	11	7,062	−734	26,882	72.7
Webster	1,182	1,073	109	55	39	4.7	3.6	29	5	269	11	30,052	81.3
Wheeler	3,114	2,283	831	175	141	5.6	6.2	82	6	1,009	39	25,728	69.6
White	12,500	10,863	1,637	467	368	3.7	3.4	635	55	5,487	897	20,773	56.2
Whitfield	47,226	43,833	3,393	2,109	1,515	4.5	3.5	2,547	−28	57,040	846	30,547	82.6
Wilcox	3,303	3,265	38	197	150	6.0	4.6	107	1	694	47	19,360	52.4
Wilkes	4,735	5,057	−322	297	227	6.3	4.5	268	2	2,918	−621	23,911	64.7
Wilkinson	4,569	4,528	41	269	188	5.9	4.2	155	2	2,695	−219	35,314	95.5
Worth	10,608	10,321	287	547	442	5.2	4.3	297	9	2,471	38	21,491	58.1

See footnotes at end of table.

Table B-10. Counties — **Labor Force and Private Business Establishments and Employment**—Con.

[Includes United States, states, and 3,141 counties/county equivalents defined as of February 22, 2005. For more information on these areas, see Appendix C, Geographic Information]

County	Civilian labor force							Private nonfarm businesses					
	Total		Net change, 2000–2006	Number of unemployed		Unemployment rate[1]		Establishments	Net change, 2000–2004	Employment[2]	Net change, 2000–2004	Annual payroll per employee, 2004	
	2006	2000		2006	2000	2006	2000	2004		2004		Amount (dol.)	Percent of U.S. average
HAWAII	643,486	609,018	34,468	15,209	24,160	2.4	4.0	[3]31,605	[3]1,752	[3]473,500	[3]41,408	[3]31,837	[3]86.1
Hawaii	83,654	74,216	9,438	2,368	3,488	2.8	4.7	3,929	300	49,749	5,602	28,161	76.2
Honolulu	450,171	433,110	17,061	10,319	16,683	2.3	3.9	21,439	802	333,514	17,652	33,384	90.3
Kalawao	–	–	–	–	–	–	–	–	–	–	–	–	–
Kauai	32,559	30,371	2,188	764	1,372	2.3	4.5	1,897	199	25,185	5,352	26,880	72.7
Maui	77,104	71,321	5,783	1,758	2,617	2.3	3.7	4,295	406	61,020	8,770	28,843	78.0
IDAHO	749,244	662,958	86,286	25,623	30,507	3.4	4.6	[3]41,336	[3]3,907	[3]488,676	[3]37,888	[3]29,074	[3]78.6
Ada	195,589	170,639	24,950	5,287	5,703	2.7	3.3	11,332	1,193	162,352	9,173	34,757	94.0
Adams	2,095	1,910	185	137	189	6.5	9.9	130	21	503	–61	27,068	73.2
Bannock	40,803	38,397	2,406	1,411	1,764	3.5	4.6	1,977	83	25,604	1,497	26,174	70.8
Bear Lake	3,100	2,987	113	95	140	3.1	4.7	128	–3	979	53	17,531	47.4
Benewah	4,353	4,003	350	310	435	7.1	10.9	260	–30	2,560	–4	27,632	74.7
Bingham	20,758	19,849	909	721	859	3.5	4.3	841	65	9,774	756	24,938	67.5
Blaine	14,517	11,890	2,627	365	421	2.5	3.5	1,471	182	11,445	955	31,045	84.0
Boise	3,831	3,431	400	132	166	3.4	4.8	144	20	687	173	19,825	53.6
Bonner	20,843	17,623	3,220	938	1,335	4.5	7.6	1,452	202	11,824	1,399	27,049	73.2
Bonneville	46,988	41,612	5,376	1,314	1,400	2.8	3.4	2,983	380	42,235	4,287	30,305	82.0
Boundary	4,261	4,223	38	302	319	7.1	7.6	355	–3	2,329	–224	24,309	65.8
Butte	1,200	1,462	–262	51	61	4.3	4.2	72	5	1,106	739	45,130	122.1
Camas	636	539	97	17	20	2.7	3.7	30	10	195	48	10,687	28.9
Canyon	82,136	66,038	16,098	2,943	2,907	3.6	4.4	3,431	482	39,762	–434	27,325	73.9
Caribou	3,443	3,287	156	137	163	4.0	5.0	187	3	2,272	–47	39,493	106.8
Cassia	10,482	10,298	184	400	499	3.8	4.8	627	14	5,722	–263	22,593	61.1
Clark	531	539	–8	20	27	3.8	5.0	16	–	240	140	30,763	83.2
Clearwater	3,336	3,674	–338	275	477	8.2	13.0	260	3	1,834	–123	24,749	66.9
Custer	2,577	2,617	–40	105	142	4.1	5.4	150	–3	753	–97	20,853	56.4
Elmore	10,876	10,594	282	447	612	4.1	5.8	429	41	4,015	104	22,740	61.5
Franklin	6,326	5,226	1,100	179	167	2.8	3.2	259	15	1,891	208	22,888	61.9
Fremont	5,994	5,690	304	222	272	3.7	4.8	306	51	1,583	138	24,064	65.1
Gem	7,542	7,040	502	293	357	3.9	5.1	353	40	2,024	–281	19,217	52.0
Gooding	8,616	7,173	1,443	229	263	2.7	3.7	332	–3	2,384	13	22,807	61.7
Idaho	7,167	6,924	243	440	570	6.1	8.2	473	22	2,900	202	23,774	64.3
Jefferson	10,320	9,028	1,292	318	334	3.1	3.7	406	59	3,315	165	20,094	54.4
Jerome	10,330	9,253	1,077	327	388	3.2	4.2	480	62	4,736	379	24,052	65.1
Kootenai	69,381	56,473	12,908	2,638	3,499	3.8	6.2	4,109	446	40,377	3,365	27,955	75.6
Latah	18,593	17,613	980	554	748	3.0	4.2	878	6	8,061	354	20,841	56.4
Lemhi	4,026	3,841	185	222	300	5.5	7.8	317	14	1,676	146	18,940	51.2
Lewis	1,753	1,739	14	53	111	3.0	6.4	122	4	627	–119	22,463	60.8
Lincoln	2,609	2,198	411	102	94	3.9	4.3	79	7	639	46	20,249	54.8
Madison	14,754	12,840	1,914	392	449	2.7	3.5	629	102	10,283	–1,958	19,919	53.9
Minidoka	9,821	10,168	–347	442	573	4.5	5.6	361	–5	4,448	–701	25,561	69.1
Nez Perce	19,254	18,608	646	728	955	3.8	5.1	1,191	–27	16,977	429	29,956	81.0
Oneida	2,233	2,010	223	52	65	2.3	3.2	74	8	515	–59	20,507	55.5
Owyhee	4,951	4,795	156	109	185	2.2	3.9	177	17	1,152	–310	27,739	75.0
Payette	10,402	10,012	390	563	654	5.4	6.5	437	12	4,237	–12	23,300	63.0
Power	3,837	3,611	226	182	206	4.7	5.7	145	–4	1,743	–224	23,093	62.5
Shoshone	5,690	6,119	–429	417	581	7.3	9.5	371	–15	3,184	–631	26,954	72.9
Teton	4,636	3,664	972	104	106	2.2	2.9	346	103	1,455	351	25,368	68.6
Twin Falls	38,563	34,041	4,522	1,227	1,380	3.2	4.1	2,363	207	25,803	1,743	23,445	63.4
Valley	5,024	4,116	908	199	272	4.0	6.6	530	53	2,570	111	22,236	60.2
Washington	5,071	5,168	–97	225	343	4.4	6.6	233	1	2,110	39	20,934	56.6
ILLINOIS	6,613,346	6,467,692	145,654	297,631	290,855	4.5	4.5	[3]315,854	[3]7,787	[3]5,217,160	[3]–283,876	[3]39,846	[3]107.8
Adams	39,222	35,876	3,346	1,368	1,327	3.5	3.7	1,919	5	30,319	–655	29,011	78.5
Alexander	3,495	3,628	–133	275	285	7.9	7.9	143	–19	1,238	–488	23,247	62.9
Bond	8,816	8,326	490	429	390	4.9	4.7	342	–10	3,803	–380	26,010	70.4
Boone	25,630	22,041	3,589	1,453	1,084	5.7	4.9	791	89	11,225	–415	36,814	99.6
Brown	3,421	2,782	639	104	95	3.0	3.4	128	3	2,266	332	30,259	81.9
Bureau	19,544	19,103	441	857	938	4.4	4.9	824	–36	10,509	78	29,593	80.1
Calhoun	2,672	2,541	131	161	141	6.0	5.5	98	–11	561	–136	18,503	50.1
Carroll	8,466	8,613	–147	426	497	5.0	5.8	445	–5	3,445	–573	26,283	71.1
Cass	7,702	7,089	613	324	330	4.2	4.7	299	–2	5,067	505	24,405	66.0
Champaign	104,451	99,093	5,358	3,855	3,540	3.7	3.6	4,195	143	69,707	–968	28,440	76.9
Christian	17,409	17,456	–47	854	930	4.9	5.3	824	3	10,361	654	23,631	63.9
Clark	8,725	8,706	19	441	426	5.1	4.9	374	–16	4,051	–624	25,297	68.4
Clay	6,970	7,168	–198	357	432	5.1	6.0	382	4	5,492	–31	26,195	70.9
Clinton	19,351	18,364	987	859	727	4.4	4.0	875	53	8,985	874	23,305	63.0
Coles	27,094	28,133	–1,039	1,152	1,177	4.3	4.2	1,280	–16	19,965	–2,035	26,021	70.4
Cook	2,630,338	2,728,495	–98,157	123,623	132,124	4.7	4.8	129,113	948	2,342,284	–211,722	44,712	120.9
Crawford	9,525	9,581	–56	508	546	5.3	5.7	447	–10	6,158	–715	31,184	84.4
Cumberland	5,664	5,832	–168	259	282	4.6	4.8	188	1	1,542	–48	20,178	54.6
DeKalb	55,046	51,249	3,797	2,153	1,847	3.9	3.6	2,068	121	25,785	–283	27,880	75.4
De Witt	8,462	9,161	–699	367	505	4.3	5.5	389	–3	4,295	–871	35,997	97.4

See footnotes at end of table.

442

County and City Data Book: 2007

U.S. Census Bureau

Table B-10. Counties — **Labor Force and Private Business Establishments and Employment**—Con.

[Includes United States, states, and 3,141 counties/county equivalents defined as of February 22, 2005. For more information on these areas, see Appendix C, Geographic Information]

County	Civilian labor force							Private nonfarm businesses					
	Total			Number of unemployed		Unemployment rate[1]		Establishments		Employment[2]		Annual payroll per employee, 2004	
	2006	2000	Net change, 2000–2006	2006	2000	2006	2000	2004	Net change, 2000–2004	2004	Net change, 2000–2004	Amount (dol.)	Percent of U.S. average
ILLINOIS—Con.													
Douglas	10,349	10,327	22	430	406	4.2	3.9	687	52	6,687	−903	26,744	72.3
DuPage	531,514	529,697	1,817	17,959	17,684	3.4	3.3	32,908	532	591,755	−28,925	44,392	120.1
Edgar	10,695	9,857	838	512	441	4.8	4.5	412	11	5,569	346	24,973	67.6
Edwards	3,428	3,640	−212	150	189	4.4	5.2	161	−5	2,758	−215	29,826	80.7
Effingham	18,256	18,330	−74	772	817	4.2	4.5	1,154	43	19,021	24	25,528	69.1
Fayette	10,142	10,239	−97	588	642	5.8	6.3	489	−3	5,069	49	22,075	59.7
Ford	7,502	7,319	183	329	280	4.4	3.8	386	−37	4,024	−62	25,478	68.9
Franklin	18,265	17,538	727	1,216	1,207	6.7	6.9	805	−72	7,635	−1,350	20,471	55.4
Fulton	17,935	17,639	296	933	978	5.2	5.5	730	−9	6,727	−667	21,468	58.1
Gallatin	2,621	2,870	−249	151	176	5.8	6.1	125	−12	1,153	−70	41,168	111.4
Greene	7,252	6,940	312	348	370	4.8	5.3	276	−19	2,011	−8	19,810	53.6
Grundy	23,994	21,091	2,903	1,235	1,106	5.1	5.2	1,051	135	12,104	1,176	40,839	110.5
Hamilton	4,258	3,984	274	233	198	5.5	5.0	183	−4	1,265	90	19,524	52.8
Hancock	10,033	10,842	−809	472	487	4.7	4.5	464	−36	4,209	−590	24,027	65.0
Hardin	1,718	1,948	−230	133	129	7.7	6.6	68	−5	774	−57	22,811	61.7
Henderson	4,232	4,285	−53	223	177	5.3	4.1	119	−9	649	−36	17,590	47.6
Henry	28,329	27,308	1,021	1,174	1,343	4.1	4.9	1,121	−42	13,521	−1,308	24,728	66.9
Iroquois	16,692	16,393	299	751	708	4.5	4.3	748	29	6,679	−455	24,299	65.7
Jackson	32,699	30,317	2,382	1,346	1,352	4.1	4.5	1,392	−3	17,959	−401	22,388	60.6
Jasper	5,066	5,328	−262	256	267	5.1	5.0	236	−14	2,205	−243	26,241	71.0
Jefferson	21,085	19,088	1,997	996	1,023	4.7	5.4	1,077	18	16,947	1,119	29,040	78.6
Jersey	11,947	11,147	800	573	514	4.8	4.6	440	23	4,438	−200	22,091	59.8
Jo Daviess	13,565	12,772	793	524	549	3.9	4.3	766	3	6,848	−875	24,983	67.6
Johnson	5,219	4,852	367	281	305	5.4	6.3	195	5	1,409	285	16,236	43.9
Kane	256,553	221,711	34,842	10,911	9,510	4.3	4.3	11,790	1,497	187,957	6,383	34,276	92.7
Kankakee	55,189	52,391	2,798	3,095	2,425	5.6	4.6	2,350	61	36,836	−22,903	30,348	82.1
Kendall	45,957	32,363	13,594	1,828	1,059	4.0	3.3	1,422	272	14,135	1,298	30,367	82.1
Knox	25,702	27,965	−2,263	1,387	1,354	5.4	4.8	1,205	−75	18,535	−2,724	23,377	63.2
Lake	369,959	338,345	31,614	15,655	12,540	4.2	3.7	19,619	1,303	319,539	10,226	48,512	131.2
LaSalle	58,777	56,313	2,464	3,134	3,003	5.3	5.3	2,958	12	37,281	−1,285	29,687	80.3
Lawrence	8,390	8,088	302	413	453	4.9	5.6	331	−35	4,070	18	21,867	59.2
Lee	18,305	17,682	623	835	760	4.6	4.3	788	−16	10,901	−122	29,403	79.5
Livingston	18,866	19,474	−608	808	742	4.3	3.8	890	−20	12,109	−345	31,142	84.2
Logan	13,473	15,024	−1,551	637	592	4.7	3.9	697	−6	8,450	−335	24,206	65.5
McDonough	16,891	16,834	57	718	732	4.3	4.3	754	−37	8,946	−1,086	22,340	60.4
McHenry	172,405	151,357	21,048	6,463	5,419	3.7	3.6	7,679	834	95,200	3,037	34,902	94.4
McLean	90,351	85,473	4,878	3,093	2,913	3.4	3.4	3,649	107	79,984	−2,741	38,392	103.9
Macon	54,604	56,211	−1,607	2,917	2,930	5.3	5.2	2,695	−27	45,874	−11,261	33,561	90.8
Macoupin	25,397	24,404	993	1,306	1,112	5.1	4.6	1,089	18	10,121	−282	26,111	70.6
Madison	140,570	132,802	7,768	6,907	5,856	4.9	4.4	6,053	246	85,327	48	30,674	83.0
Marion	18,604	20,712	−2,108	1,098	1,185	5.9	5.7	1,071	−89	12,302	−3,675	26,040	70.4
Marshall	7,483	6,997	486	288	292	3.8	4.2	271	−26	3,035	137	24,377	65.9
Mason	7,538	7,902	−364	442	459	5.9	5.8	314	−43	2,623	−186	23,842	64.5
Massac	7,621	7,209	412	407	385	5.3	5.3	264	−9	4,499	−7	30,996	83.8
Menard	7,193	7,010	183	284	252	3.9	3.6	253	6	1,537	136	24,306	65.7
Mercer	9,266	8,838	428	491	499	5.3	5.6	305	−45	2,211	−192	20,646	55.9
Monroe	18,014	15,521	2,493	700	514	3.9	3.3	756	97	7,443	1,203	27,684	74.9
Montgomery	13,584	14,140	−556	846	796	6.2	5.6	768	−36	8,265	−833	24,846	67.2
Morgan	17,800	18,810	−1,010	870	790	4.9	4.2	923	−19	14,209	−1,203	23,826	64.5
Moultrie	8,175	7,456	719	295	310	3.6	4.2	298	−4	3,696	180	28,505	77.1
Ogle	27,363	26,983	380	1,377	1,174	5.0	4.4	1,070	73	14,922	−294	32,430	87.7
Peoria	96,663	91,271	5,392	4,089	4,138	4.2	4.5	4,850	8	101,462	−6,840	38,937	105.3
Perry	10,296	10,295	1	703	726	6.8	7.1	437	−19	5,097	−639	25,340	68.5
Piatt	9,430	9,043	387	345	332	3.7	3.7	363	−24	2,648	−214	25,440	68.8
Pike	8,605	8,499	106	387	458	4.5	5.4	375	−16	3,020	−267	22,666	61.3
Pope	1,945	2,033	−88	127	135	6.5	6.6	61	−6	333	−122	16,162	43.7
Pulaski	2,936	3,096	−160	201	220	6.8	7.1	110	−15	736	−437	23,825	64.4
Putnam	3,247	3,141	106	161	157	5.0	5.0	132	3	1,155	−461	42,821	115.8
Randolph	15,587	15,201	386	739	766	4.7	5.0	726	−33	10,252	−728	28,149	76.1
Richland	7,596	7,854	−258	359	484	4.7	6.2	499	−1	5,647	−617	26,821	72.6
Rock Island	80,930	77,604	3,326	3,484	3,574	4.3	4.6	3,570	−75	63,217	−6,242	33,393	90.3
St. Clair	126,310	119,705	6,605	7,286	6,111	5.8	5.1	5,508	73	79,463	4,172	28,254	76.4
Saline	12,424	11,774	650	681	819	5.5	7.0	640	−28	7,495	−420	24,728	66.9
Sangamon	108,444	105,335	3,109	4,549	3,910	4.2	3.7	5,350	−13	81,658	−2,383	30,401	82.2
Schuyler	4,439	3,983	456	184	204	4.1	5.1	159	−1	1,407	46	21,893	59.2
Scott	2,812	2,980	−168	149	144	5.3	4.8	94	−6	615	−373	30,481	82.5
Shelby	11,208	11,706	−498	530	576	4.7	4.9	453	−30	5,273	214	25,813	69.8
Stark	2,969	2,888	81	140	174	4.7	6.0	128	−4	882	−124	23,763	64.3
Stephenson	25,434	25,972	−538	1,244	1,377	4.9	5.3	1,121	−9	17,730	−2,142	31,524	85.3
Tazewell	72,388	67,213	5,175	2,763	2,764	3.8	4.1	2,906	72	42,901	318	29,856	80.8

See footnotes at end of table.

[Includes United States, states, and 3,141 counties/county equivalents defined as of February 22, 2005. For more information on these areas, see Appendix C, Geographic Information]

County	Civilian labor force							Private nonfarm businesses					
	Total			Number of unemployed		Unemployment rate[1]		Establishments		Employment[2]		Annual payroll per employee, 2004	
	2006	2000	Net change, 2000–2006	2006	2000	2006	2000	2004	Net change, 2000–2004	2004	Net change, 2000–2004	Amount (dol.)	Percent of U.S. average
ILLINOIS—Con.													
Union	8,495	8,360	135	508	545	6.0	6.5	357	−7	3,895	−886	22,347	60.4
Vermilion	38,274	38,883	−609	2,174	2,323	5.7	6.0	1,672	−82	27,102	−1,881	28,768	77.8
Wabash	6,577	6,883	−306	315	361	4.8	5.2	296	−23	3,504	−327	24,631	66.6
Warren	9,058	10,044	−986	423	442	4.7	4.4	394	11	5,629	600	22,131	59.9
Washington	8,573	8,349	224	333	332	3.9	4.0	421	8	5,616	397	25,425	68.8
Wayne	8,282	8,397	−115	359	497	4.3	5.9	370	−3	3,609	−252	24,289	65.7
White	7,956	7,481	475	384	374	4.8	5.0	404	−22	3,845	260	24,809	67.1
Whiteside	30,660	30,861	−201	1,606	1,311	5.2	4.2	1,396	−59	18,791	−2,728	26,478	71.6
Will	345,717	278,741	66,976	14,703	11,333	4.3	4.1	12,108	2,053	161,695	18,900	36,090	97.6
Williamson	35,500	29,912	5,588	1,696	1,831	4.8	6.1	1,597	22	24,012	1,221	26,116	70.6
Winnebago	146,715	146,439	276	7,738	6,771	5.3	4.6	6,973	−73	127,956	−7,780	31,975	86.5
Woodford	21,052	18,756	2,296	659	643	3.1	3.4	758	32	8,255	−452	27,724	75.0
INDIANA	3,271,496	3,144,379	127,117	162,690	91,660	5.0	2.9	[3]149,381	[3]3,060	[3]2,586,799	[3]−63,975	[3]32,897	[3]89.0
Adams	16,398	16,652	−254	713	435	4.3	2.6	795	7	13,499	−838	27,490	74.4
Allen	184,398	176,766	7,632	9,121	4,610	4.9	2.6	9,333	384	169,886	−9,097	33,261	90.0
Bartholomew	38,519	37,520	999	1,605	946	4.2	2.5	1,867	−105	36,830	−1,735	37,832	102.3
Benton	4,704	4,859	−155	229	136	4.9	2.8	229	−23	1,880	−226	23,299	63.0
Blackford	6,790	7,063	−273	443	292	6.5	4.1	285	−1	3,391	−856	26,730	72.3
Boone	27,997	24,412	3,585	1,038	493	3.7	2.0	1,330	66	13,317	576	27,725	75.0
Brown	8,203	7,919	284	393	220	4.8	2.8	387	4	2,341	70	19,425	52.5
Carroll	10,736	10,560	176	496	287	4.6	2.7	414	5	4,392	−686	24,748	66.9
Cass	19,082	20,766	−1,684	1,033	607	5.4	2.9	826	−26	14,974	−1,453	25,143	68.0
Clark	55,270	52,760	2,510	2,710	1,810	4.9	3.4	2,571	118	42,809	819	29,336	79.4
Clay	13,383	12,913	470	750	509	5.6	3.9	513	−16	6,133	134	23,340	63.1
Clinton	17,196	16,554	642	859	460	5.0	2.8	676	28	9,706	−578	28,837	78.0
Crawford	5,375	5,135	240	379	237	7.1	4.6	142	−3	1,012	−202	19,364	52.4
Daviess	15,252	14,169	1,083	551	402	3.6	2.8	736	−13	8,863	49	23,517	63.6
Dearborn	26,919	24,603	2,316	1,407	779	5.2	3.2	1,021	48	14,216	894	30,370	82.2
Decatur	12,631	13,509	−878	550	290	4.4	2.1	630	11	11,450	−1,349	30,615	82.8
DeKalb	21,767	21,825	−58	1,311	629	6.0	2.9	1,035	66	21,691	−280	33,689	91.1
Delaware	57,609	58,964	−1,355	3,420	1,958	5.9	3.3	2,638	−60	44,035	−6,428	27,739	75.0
Dubois	22,611	22,285	326	811	472	3.6	2.1	1,296	37	26,910	−1,886	31,875	86.2
Elkhart	105,777	97,347	8,430	4,897	2,462	4.6	2.5	5,149	137	118,921	567	33,727	91.2
Fayette	10,926	12,462	−1,536	872	517	8.0	4.1	533	−5	7,828	−1,828	33,358	90.2
Floyd	38,785	38,248	537	1,859	1,254	4.8	3.3	1,819	98	25,689	−1,070	28,714	77.7
Fountain	8,875	8,700	175	424	258	4.8	3.0	371	−7	4,572	−458	27,185	73.5
Franklin	12,246	11,379	867	698	383	5.7	3.4	381	21	3,744	−244	22,947	62.1
Fulton	10,603	10,815	−212	561	417	5.3	3.9	474	−31	6,514	54	28,143	76.1
Gibson	17,584	16,825	759	782	533	4.4	3.2	732	−17	15,274	3,209	42,307	114.4
Grant	33,382	34,997	−1,615	2,335	1,321	7.0	3.8	1,511	−27	26,758	−4,498	28,355	76.7
Greene	16,938	16,100	838	946	741	5.6	4.6	625	−18	5,446	−518	21,938	59.3
Hamilton	134,885	101,907	32,978	4,383	1,823	3.2	1.8	6,242	922	91,453	11,588	38,343	103.7
Hancock	35,526	30,582	4,944	1,440	665	4.1	2.2	1,390	125	17,376	3,241	32,699	88.5
Harrison	20,174	18,817	1,357	1,067	603	5.3	3.2	709	58	10,816	2,350	25,429	68.8
Hendricks	71,508	57,835	13,673	2,590	1,095	3.6	1.9	2,487	340	34,861	8,350	28,607	77.4
Henry	22,988	23,460	−472	1,334	866	5.8	3.7	929	−33	11,363	−1,287	26,366	71.3
Howard	39,375	41,719	−2,344	2,564	1,272	6.5	3.0	2,008	38	39,312	−5,497	41,331	111.8
Huntington	20,887	20,898	−11	1,094	612	5.2	2.9	936	55	15,279	−505	26,381	71.4
Jackson	22,453	21,823	630	977	557	4.4	2.6	1,076	1	19,193	−24	29,108	78.7
Jasper	15,526	14,780	746	787	483	5.1	3.3	801	19	11,420	1,385	27,469	74.3
Jay	11,876	11,036	840	532	354	4.5	3.2	436	−1	6,027	−880	28,143	76.1
Jefferson	17,667	16,259	1,408	849	513	4.8	3.2	772	42	12,620	561	28,365	76.7
Jennings	13,970	14,132	−162	811	387	5.8	2.7	442	2	6,733	−274	28,302	76.6
Johnson	72,115	63,629	8,486	2,803	1,306	3.9	2.1	2,943	310	43,328	3,589	26,430	71.5
Knox	19,382	19,574	−192	926	687	4.8	3.5	1,014	−14	14,036	−26	26,022	70.4
Kosciusko	42,570	39,480	3,090	2,055	935	4.8	2.4	1,922	26	33,322	566	37,181	100.6
LaGrange	17,799	16,995	804	906	387	5.1	2.3	768	64	11,474	47	31,620	85.5
Lake	230,345	226,616	3,729	13,249	8,221	5.8	3.6	10,207	165	173,109	−6,114	33,410	90.4
LaPorte	53,734	54,111	−377	3,060	1,798	5.7	3.3	2,555	−80	35,318	−4,959	29,382	79.5
Lawrence	23,158	23,031	127	1,594	890	6.9	3.9	950	13	12,400	−1,569	30,617	82.8
Madison	63,189	63,788	−599	3,804	1,913	6.0	3.0	2,661	−112	39,159	−3,187	28,591	77.3
Marion	471,981	457,920	14,061	22,976	12,270	4.9	2.7	24,384	−4	534,364	−30,301	38,848	105.1
Marshall	23,377	23,434	−57	1,236	694	5.3	3.0	1,110	−19	16,807	−1,607	26,211	70.9
Martin	5,369	5,100	269	261	165	4.9	3.2	236	−10	2,552	75	24,149	65.3
Miami	17,327	17,662	−335	1,066	574	6.2	3.2	684	2	8,096	−139	24,731	66.9
Monroe	67,857	64,138	3,719	2,895	1,668	4.3	2.6	3,018	92	50,620	3,273	29,871	80.8
Montgomery	20,015	19,778	237	829	495	4.1	2.5	897	−21	14,455	−1,024	32,159	87.0
Morgan	38,288	35,761	2,527	1,709	845	4.5	2.4	1,371	64	14,297	494	26,826	72.6
Newton	7,236	7,297	−61	357	208	4.9	2.9	293	4	3,144	−64	26,202	70.9
Noble	23,930	24,560	−630	1,450	679	6.1	2.8	950	34	16,999	−2,465	29,656	80.2
Ohio	3,223	3,002	221	167	99	5.2	3.3	87	10	1,517	−278	25,949	70.2
Orange	9,657	9,630	27	693	405	7.2	4.2	402	9	5,216	−1,608	25,683	69.5
Owen	11,916	10,804	1,112	628	319	5.3	3.0	325	10	3,873	346	23,815	64.4

See footnotes at end of table.

Table B-10. Counties — **Labor Force and Private Business Establishments and Employment**—Con.

[Includes United States, states, and 3,141 counties/county equivalents defined as of February 22, 2005. For more information on these areas, see Appendix C, Geographic Information]

County	Civilian labor force							Private nonfarm businesses					
	Total			Number of unemployed		Unemployment rate[1]		Establishments		Employment[2]		Annual payroll per employee, 2004	
	2006	2000	Net change, 2000–2006	2006	2000	2006	2000	2004	Net change, 2000–2004	2004	Net change, 2000–2004	Amount (dol.)	Percent of U.S. average
INDIANA—Con.													
Parke	8,015	8,059	−44	443	271	5.5	3.4	280	−22	2,360	−93	20,278	54.9
Perry	9,873	9,535	338	506	428	5.1	4.5	383	−3	5,404	676	25,966	70.2
Pike	6,248	6,382	−134	283	214	4.5	3.4	193	3	2,669	569	33,456	90.5
Porter	82,916	77,901	5,015	3,630	2,137	4.4	2.7	3,542	255	50,424	247	33,046	89.4
Posey	14,086	13,928	158	611	405	4.3	2.9	521	−10	7,356	−199	41,813	113.1
Pulaski	6,955	6,789	166	316	284	4.5	4.2	358	1	3,552	186	28,783	77.9
Putnam	18,157	17,207	950	965	479	5.3	2.8	673	−10	11,666	681	26,033	70.4
Randolph	13,003	13,596	−593	890	491	6.8	3.6	546	−31	6,639	54	27,758	75.1
Ripley	14,548	13,792	756	696	339	4.8	2.5	748	6	12,509	308	42,412	114.7
Rush	9,620	9,514	106	432	239	4.5	2.5	418	4	4,382	−202	27,313	73.9
St. Joseph	136,217	135,041	1,176	6,988	4,148	5.1	3.1	6,370	−187	119,802	−5,290	32,179	87.0
Scott	11,566	11,340	226	741	362	6.4	3.2	466	13	6,825	−93	24,558	66.4
Shelby	24,335	23,686	649	1,067	604	4.4	2.6	995	35	17,726	2,279	30,470	82.4
Spencer	10,784	11,039	−255	532	375	4.9	3.4	416	1	5,643	−1,486	30,943	83.7
Starke	10,666	10,882	−216	699	502	6.6	4.6	324	−20	3,335	−530	22,933	62.0
Steuben	16,793	18,574	−1,781	1,065	538	6.3	2.9	1,031	13	14,625	−6,645	26,707	72.2
Sullivan	9,331	9,261	70	556	466	6.0	5.0	377	−10	3,591	−280	25,711	69.5
Switzerland	5,730	5,030	700	234	235	4.1	4.7	123	1	1,861	879	26,338	71.2
Tippecanoe	81,016	78,405	2,611	3,429	1,994	4.2	2.5	3,292	100	60,336	−5,073	31,871	86.2
Tipton	8,095	8,726	−631	439	224	5.4	2.6	348	28	3,745	−48	28,921	78.2
Union	3,928	3,812	116	215	113	5.5	3.0	136	−7	806	−163	21,109	57.1
Vanderburgh	92,920	90,188	2,732	4,403	2,775	4.7	3.1	5,147	−105	108,181	−2,961	30,899	83.6
Vermillion	8,216	8,170	46	535	364	6.5	4.5	279	−9	4,662	−209	33,935	91.8
Vigo	50,667	51,023	−356	3,213	1,980	6.3	3.9	2,666	24	48,593	651	26,947	72.9
Wabash	17,934	18,166	−232	990	517	5.5	2.8	842	−3	13,378	−33	25,405	68.7
Warren	4,845	4,508	337	195	115	4.0	2.6	137	29	1,336	294	26,903	72.8
Warrick	31,097	28,566	2,531	1,299	901	4.2	3.2	1,105	68	12,442	761	31,166	84.3
Washington	14,548	14,106	442	886	513	6.1	3.6	481	13	5,610	−244	24,233	65.6
Wayne	34,406	35,681	−1,275	2,021	1,242	5.9	3.5	1,691	−18	29,890	−3,427	29,042	78.6
Wells	15,288	14,964	324	656	352	4.3	2.4	631	23	10,114	−1,305	25,791	69.8
White	12,231	13,661	−1,430	615	389	5.0	2.8	659	−40	6,764	−2,583	25,885	70.0
Whitley	18,214	17,185	1,029	861	422	4.7	2.5	679	−17	10,399	−1,237	27,792	75.2
IOWA	1,664,339	1,601,920	62,419	61,490	44,839	3.7	2.8	[3]81,565	[3]675	[3]1,241,864	[3]−23,200	[3]30,312	[3]82.0
Adair	4,475	4,481	−6	145	123	3.2	2.7	186	−31	2,052	−249	24,312	65.8
Adams	2,084	2,346	−262	95	92	4.6	3.9	123	−2	968	−95	22,483	60.8
Allamakee	8,229	8,005	224	382	286	4.6	3.6	413	1	4,773	−124	23,519	63.6
Appanoose	6,446	6,381	65	346	291	5.4	4.6	348	19	3,839	155	25,696	69.5
Audubon	3,269	3,433	−164	134	103	4.1	3.0	206	−5	1,383	−93	22,380	60.5
Benton	14,775	13,764	1,011	584	337	4.0	2.4	599	−36	4,641	4	25,142	68.0
Black Hawk	72,433	68,937	3,496	2,805	2,029	3.9	2.9	3,167	−2	61,689	1,363	29,167	78.9
Boone	15,617	14,679	938	461	331	3.0	2.3	582	8	6,973	−72	26,167	70.8
Bremer	13,917	12,865	1,052	452	336	3.2	2.6	642	1	7,735	−295	28,908	78.2
Buchanan	11,391	10,732	659	484	319	4.2	3.0	548	10	5,301	−62	26,830	72.6
Buena Vista	10,493	10,320	173	352	254	3.4	2.5	595	−7	9,025	606	22,567	61.0
Butler	8,352	8,037	315	343	269	4.1	3.3	367	−8	2,246	−59	23,145	62.6
Calhoun	5,275	5,371	−96	181	154	3.4	2.9	289	−20	2,201	−94	20,950	56.7
Carroll	12,477	12,013	464	332	281	2.7	2.3	857	20	11,139	957	24,535	66.4
Cass	7,669	7,927	−258	330	295	4.3	3.7	484	−13	4,939	−817	23,613	63.9
Cedar	10,819	10,426	393	352	247	3.3	2.4	486	−8	3,629	−484	21,867	59.2
Cerro Gordo	26,424	25,357	1,067	1,031	775	3.9	3.1	1,460	−27	22,322	−944	28,911	78.2
Cherokee	6,571	6,995	−424	278	170	4.2	2.4	395	5	4,236	−257	25,911	70.1
Chickasaw	6,499	6,927	−428	295	462	4.5	6.7	399	−3	3,296	−1,001	25,380	68.7
Clarke	4,743	4,903	−160	197	162	4.2	3.3	213	−14	3,272	−851	22,964	62.1
Clay	9,921	10,005	−84	329	257	3.3	2.6	620	−23	7,389	−752	26,925	72.8
Clayton	9,694	10,286	−592	494	369	5.1	3.6	532	5	4,870	−974	24,367	65.9
Clinton	27,240	26,264	976	1,077	947	4.0	3.6	1,325	54	18,995	−290	26,630	72.0
Crawford	9,341	8,956	385	293	233	3.1	2.6	468	2	6,034	322	26,521	71.7
Dallas	30,359	23,647	6,712	874	484	2.9	2.0	1,078	261	14,840	5,044	32,351	87.5
Davis	4,146	4,184	−38	197	143	4.8	3.4	183	4	1,520	−83	22,023	59.6
Decatur	4,225	4,293	−68	174	150	4.1	3.5	166	4	2,220	−74	16,368	44.3
Delaware	10,815	10,225	590	402	305	3.7	3.0	496	13	4,666	−247	25,002	67.6
Des Moines	21,131	22,417	−1,286	1,004	820	4.8	3.7	1,193	−28	19,704	−1,393	28,767	77.8
Dickinson	10,188	9,498	690	410	271	4.0	2.9	752	48	7,773	1	26,282	71.1
Dubuque	52,731	48,739	3,992	1,926	1,656	3.7	3.4	2,709	50	47,897	−2,091	29,660	80.2
Emmet	6,093	6,045	48	248	180	4.1	3.0	347	34	3,584	91	24,628	66.6
Fayette	11,113	11,268	−155	511	443	4.6	3.9	620	−37	6,584	−942	21,492	58.1
Floyd	8,863	8,548	315	417	331	4.7	3.9	431	−22	4,355	−242	24,884	67.3
Franklin	5,860	5,724	136	227	163	3.9	2.8	321	−15	2,708	−488	25,745	69.6
Fremont	3,959	4,252	−293	151	104	3.8	2.4	182	−11	1,302	−226	24,366	65.9
Greene	5,074	5,013	61	202	170	4.0	3.4	310	11	2,897	226	20,537	55.6
Grundy	6,949	6,552	397	214	159	3.1	2.4	309	1	3,054	185	29,683	80.3
Guthrie	6,303	6,085	218	228	171	3.6	2.8	322	22	2,301	433	25,621	69.3
Hamilton	8,852	8,990	−138	320	234	3.6	2.6	418	−33	6,429	−508	27,612	74.7

See footnotes at end of table.

[Includes United States, states, and 3,141 counties/county equivalents defined as of February 22, 2005. For more information on these areas, see Appendix C, Geographic Information]

County	Civilian labor force							Private nonfarm businesses					
	Total			Number of unemployed		Unemployment rate[1]		Establishments		Employment[2]		Annual payroll per employee, 2004	
	2006	2000	Net change, 2000–2006	2006	2000	2006	2000	2004	Net change, 2000–2004	2004	Net change, 2000–2004	Amount (dol.)	Percent of U.S. average
IOWA—Con.													
Hancock	6,164	6,349	−185	225	144	3.7	2.3	315	−24	3,195	149	24,831	67.2
Hardin	9,210	9,548	−338	349	303	3.8	3.2	585	−51	5,816	−1,395	24,738	66.9
Harrison	8,247	8,124	123	342	229	4.1	2.8	341	−25	2,696	−546	22,372	60.5
Henry	10,634	10,620	14	561	332	5.3	3.1	570	5	12,179	121	25,427	68.8
Howard	5,288	5,152	136	193	170	3.6	3.3	272	−4	3,598	12	24,595	66.5
Humboldt	5,224	5,297	−73	176	141	3.4	2.7	343	12	3,445	−126	26,421	71.5
Ida	3,987	4,006	−19	140	90	3.5	2.2	266	2	2,816	−508	29,197	79.0
Iowa	8,972	8,884	88	327	195	3.6	2.2	504	4	8,403	−882	27,447	74.2
Jackson	11,353	11,207	146	544	424	4.8	3.8	599	26	5,420	63	20,664	55.9
Jasper	18,433	19,907	−1,474	944	518	5.1	2.6	823	−19	12,826	−931	30,986	83.8
Jefferson	8,269	9,086	−817	353	275	4.3	3.0	677	−22	6,816	−475	27,730	75.0
Johnson	76,074	67,613	8,461	2,005	1,353	2.6	2.0	2,859	193	53,876	2,789	30,670	83.0
Jones	10,661	10,475	186	414	294	3.9	2.8	533	32	4,555	9	24,498	66.3
Keokuk	5,891	5,853	38	238	195	4.0	3.3	265	−6	2,002	156	21,536	58.3
Kossuth	9,083	8,882	201	301	236	3.3	2.7	572	28	5,227	−289	25,159	68.1
Lee	17,534	18,756	−1,222	1,088	881	6.2	4.7	1,007	−37	14,299	−2,235	28,391	76.8
Linn	116,124	111,721	4,403	4,231	2,709	3.6	2.4	5,431	123	104,433	−10,160	35,131	95.0
Louisa	6,479	6,284	195	247	196	3.8	3.1	236	21	2,872	25	25,508	69.0
Lucas	4,977	4,764	213	207	137	4.2	2.9	207	−11	2,699	−8	27,892	75.5
Lyon	6,682	6,391	291	158	132	2.4	2.1	371	2	2,561	92	21,159	57.2
Madison	8,387	7,656	731	332	254	4.0	3.3	365	20	2,666	−108	23,919	64.7
Mahaska	11,907	11,588	319	439	288	3.7	2.5	595	9	6,399	98	25,343	68.6
Marion	18,015	17,701	314	633	414	3.5	2.3	854	44	15,829	−2,327	31,860	86.2
Marshall	20,932	20,704	228	786	591	3.8	2.9	880	−42	15,190	−316	28,947	78.3
Mills	8,374	7,937	437	308	168	3.7	2.1	286	46	2,140	−561	21,245	57.5
Mitchell	5,466	5,482	−16	188	155	3.4	2.8	337	−13	3,017	−90	25,233	68.3
Monona	4,705	5,008	−303	256	160	5.4	3.2	274	−17	2,585	−99	21,149	57.2
Monroe	4,166	3,923	243	171	126	4.1	3.2	177	−30	1,729	−870	20,542	55.6
Montgomery	5,905	6,034	−129	321	202	5.4	3.3	326	−21	3,916	−507	25,433	68.8
Muscatine	24,192	22,391	1,801	781	643	3.2	2.9	972	−26	19,382	−919	37,698	102.0
O'Brien	7,826	7,803	23	239	184	3.1	2.4	540	−22	5,099	−50	22,403	60.6
Osceola	3,441	3,628	−187	120	93	3.5	2.6	206	−4	1,895	89	25,045	67.7
Page	8,402	8,393	9	325	278	3.9	3.3	486	−15	6,356	−469	26,910	72.8
Palo Alto	5,400	5,226	174	177	124	3.3	2.4	315	−1	2,928	230	22,879	61.9
Plymouth	14,419	13,573	846	460	362	3.2	2.7	717	39	9,135	−114	30,054	81.3
Pocahontas	4,102	4,219	−117	130	119	3.2	2.8	243	−34	1,779	−377	22,274	60.3
Polk	234,879	215,941	18,938	8,011	5,383	3.4	2.5	11,805	282	245,103	981	37,679	101.9
Pottawattamie	49,685	48,322	1,363	2,111	1,204	4.2	2.5	1,982	73	30,530	1,461	26,588	71.9
Poweshiek	10,687	10,412	275	411	294	3.8	2.8	589	24	9,159	65	28,645	77.5
Ringgold	2,472	2,599	−127	101	79	4.1	3.0	137	–	974	−146	19,508	52.8
Sac	5,892	5,984	−92	198	161	3.4	2.7	366	−25	2,643	42	19,418	52.5
Scott	88,812	86,140	2,672	3,338	2,922	3.8	3.4	4,508	77	81,549	−223	30,238	81.8
Shelby	7,376	7,115	261	239	174	3.2	2.4	417	−16	4,437	−106	23,194	62.7
Sioux	19,382	17,696	1,686	484	360	2.5	2.0	1,142	49	15,521	512	24,814	67.1
Story	48,122	46,571	1,551	1,280	890	2.7	1.9	1,958	25	27,503	−999	26,511	71.7
Tama	8,987	9,288	−301	383	329	4.3	3.5	393	−19	4,069	−260	25,335	68.5
Taylor	3,432	3,501	−69	133	115	3.9	3.3	146	−22	1,268	−28	22,645	61.3
Union	6,487	6,604	−117	263	232	4.1	3.5	359	4	4,738	−216	24,226	65.5
Van Buren	3,943	4,015	−72	170	133	4.3	3.3	160	−15	1,557	−230	24,441	66.1
Wapello	18,871	17,966	905	851	668	4.5	3.7	836	−28	14,835	1,472	29,262	79.2
Warren	25,379	23,632	1,747	814	539	3.2	2.3	793	14	7,461	−118	22,067	59.7
Washington	12,593	11,375	1,218	377	272	3.0	2.4	664	−45	5,570	−314	22,398	60.6
Wayne	3,199	3,254	−55	130	100	4.1	3.1	176	−6	1,345	−129	21,031	56.9
Webster	19,981	20,011	−30	782	635	3.9	3.2	1,144	−36	15,380	−1,099	29,611	80.1
Winnebago	5,850	6,477	−627	210	135	3.6	2.1	356	−7	8,575	398	29,819	80.7
Winneshiek	12,295	12,229	66	459	328	3.7	2.7	614	−9	9,904	−120	24,098	65.2
Woodbury	54,438	55,718	−1,280	2,323	1,529	4.3	2.7	2,816	−116	44,694	−2,855	27,226	73.6
Worth	4,648	4,384	264	175	135	3.8	3.1	186	6	1,366	−109	25,416	68.8
Wright	7,197	7,624	−427	266	205	3.7	2.7	410	−43	4,408	−680	25,827	69.9
KANSAS	1,466,004	1,405,104	60,900	65,835	53,116	4.5	3.8	[3]75,827	[3]888	[3]1,116,277	[3]−12,455	[3]32,004	[3]86.6
Allen	7,086	7,224	−138	323	333	4.6	4.6	398	−18	4,869	−334	23,856	64.5
Anderson	4,074	4,118	−44	209	171	5.1	4.2	231	−6	1,513	−95	20,322	55.0
Atchison	8,570	8,453	117	427	377	5.0	4.5	403	3	6,737	765	23,449	63.4
Barber	2,621	2,671	−50	88	72	3.4	2.7	211	−2	1,291	−98	23,590	63.8
Barton	14,998	14,545	453	558	487	3.7	3.3	994	−35	10,594	−196	25,805	69.8
Bourbon	8,532	8,110	422	367	316	4.3	3.9	403	−34	5,198	−1,525	24,540	66.4
Brown	5,483	5,355	128	226	270	4.1	5.0	243	−26	3,186	−64	22,943	62.1
Butler	32,123	30,378	1,745	1,506	1,267	4.7	4.2	1,328	47	11,948	−46	25,863	70.0
Chase	1,757	1,625	132	71	48	4.0	3.0	57	−15	312	−160	18,804	50.9
Chautauqua	1,871	1,931	−60	101	81	5.4	4.2	95	5	678	85	17,499	47.3

See footnotes at end of table.

[Includes United States, states, and 3,141 counties/county equivalents defined as of February 22, 2005. For more information on these areas, see Appendix C, Geographic Information]

County	Civilian labor force							Private nonfarm businesses					
	Total			Number of unemployed		Unemployment rate[1]		Establishments		Employment[2]		Annual payroll per employee, 2004	
	2006	2000	Net change, 2000–2006	2006	2000	2006	2000	2004	Net change, 2000–2004	2004	Net change, 2000–2004	Amount (dol.)	Percent of U.S. average
KANSAS—Con.													
Cherokee	10,969	10,892	77	564	531	5.1	4.9	376	−25	5,167	−39	26,144	70.7
Cheyenne	1,463	1,634	−171	53	40	3.6	2.4	105	−9	581	26	19,120	51.7
Clark	1,179	1,234	−55	41	33	3.5	2.7	81	5	423	−25	21,934	59.3
Clay	4,886	4,590	296	175	150	3.6	3.3	297	12	2,440	−155	19,892	53.8
Cloud	5,478	5,227	251	206	191	3.8	3.7	333	−16	2,974	−140	21,463	58.1
Coffey	5,117	4,794	323	266	179	5.2	3.7	255	−6	2,625	−183	40,868	110.6
Comanche	1,081	1,033	48	33	23	3.1	2.2	85	15	397	−26	18,788	50.8
Cowley	17,379	17,600	−221	813	814	4.7	4.6	815	−21	11,705	892	28,891	78.2
Crawford	20,476	19,227	1,249	1,018	854	5.0	4.4	983	−34	14,464	−134	23,559	63.7
Decatur	1,686	1,751	−65	58	42	3.4	2.4	110	−17	657	−139	16,855	45.6
Dickinson	10,594	10,427	167	432	332	4.1	3.2	547	−18	5,463	−439	23,610	63.9
Doniphan	4,472	4,083	389	225	206	5.0	5.0	149	−32	1,256	−791	22,868	61.9
Douglas	61,846	57,774	4,072	2,319	1,717	3.7	3.0	2,742	118	35,792	−1,693	24,437	66.1
Edwards	1,766	1,738	28	56	44	3.2	2.5	99	−8	583	−102	25,528	69.1
Elk	1,421	1,444	−23	74	70	5.2	4.8	74	9	315	31	16,098	43.5
Ellis	16,363	15,596	767	488	417	3.0	2.7	1,063	18	12,131	−162	23,399	63.3
Ellsworth	3,508	3,167	341	124	107	3.5	3.4	181	−10	1,708	−35	24,508	66.3
Finney	18,066	19,858	−1,792	656	557	3.6	2.8	1,012	−8	14,659	−2,096	25,778	69.7
Ford	17,125	16,236	889	562	435	3.3	2.7	824	−12	13,591	261	26,385	71.4
Franklin	13,876	13,086	790	726	507	5.2	3.9	617	34	8,335	623	25,198	68.2
Geary	11,408	11,647	−239	611	575	5.4	4.9	519	−68	6,526	−1,807	21,590	58.4
Gove	1,504	1,599	−95	45	34	3.0	2.1	134	–	833	−1	19,214	52.0
Graham	1,413	1,456	−43	49	40	3.5	2.7	107	−3	644	−45	18,379	49.7
Grant	3,747	3,775	−28	119	113	3.2	3.0	239	−15	2,209	−81	29,940	81.0
Gray	3,144	3,020	124	96	80	3.1	2.6	217	10	1,236	−46	25,892	70.0
Greeley	720	787	−67	25	25	3.5	3.2	52	−8	317	−36	20,710	56.0
Greenwood	3,601	3,766	−165	172	178	4.8	4.7	211	−17	1,205	−175	21,207	57.4
Hamilton	1,296	1,287	9	43	35	3.3	2.7	77	−7	591	−315	22,147	59.9
Harper	3,374	3,201	173	117	115	3.5	3.6	231	2	1,561	123	24,966	67.5
Harvey	18,230	17,452	778	815	645	4.5	3.7	853	35	12,300	584	26,529	71.8
Haskell	2,150	2,104	46	64	51	3.0	2.4	115	1	786	70	24,822	67.1
Hodgeman	958	1,018	−60	36	34	3.8	3.3	50	2	245	−106	19,702	53.3
Jackson	7,016	6,604	412	382	286	5.4	4.3	285	–	3,260	−38	23,928	64.7
Jefferson	9,945	9,687	258	479	388	4.8	4.0	349	−26	2,441	236	24,015	65.0
Jewell	2,059	1,949	110	61	48	3.0	2.5	96	−13	499	−44	19,665	53.2
Johnson	291,371	260,814	30,557	12,227	7,934	4.2	3.0	16,799	905	286,400	3,748	39,501	106.9
Kearny	2,032	2,076	−44	80	58	3.9	2.8	83	−3	532	−58	22,799	61.7
Kingman	4,326	4,285	41	168	153	3.9	3.6	217	−1	1,894	−97	22,746	61.5
Kiowa	1,608	1,664	−56	51	44	3.2	2.6	104	−10	836	−121	22,616	61.2
Labette	10,697	11,566	−869	588	564	5.5	4.9	509	−16	8,210	27	23,309	63.1
Lane	1,057	1,126	−69	39	31	3.7	2.8	73	−13	342	−45	22,944	62.1
Leavenworth	33,106	31,053	2,053	1,873	1,312	5.7	4.2	1,175	52	15,210	166	29,681	80.3
Lincoln	1,812	1,907	−95	68	52	3.8	2.7	108	1	617	21	15,951	43.2
Linn	4,873	4,703	170	307	238	6.3	5.1	188	−5	1,292	−89	32,378	87.6
Logan	1,515	1,637	−122	50	56	3.3	3.4	141	4	856	105	20,856	56.4
Lyon	20,224	19,202	1,022	838	602	4.1	3.1	915	7	15,610	268	24,167	65.4
McPherson	17,850	15,739	2,111	601	456	3.4	2.9	936	−4	13,198	356	28,082	76.0
Marion	6,761	6,747	14	278	201	4.1	3.0	342	−10	2,948	−126	19,109	51.7
Marshall	5,869	5,709	160	211	196	3.6	3.4	383	−5	3,676	264	24,805	67.1
Meade	2,114	2,201	−87	71	59	3.4	2.7	137	−12	759	−133	23,733	64.2
Miami	16,340	15,225	1,115	759	525	4.6	3.4	759	141	6,707	−161	25,259	68.3
Mitchell	3,388	3,536	−148	124	94	3.7	2.7	274	−3	2,579	−35	23,501	63.6
Montgomery	17,178	17,950	−772	836	898	4.9	5.0	976	−47	14,005	−861	25,964	70.2
Morris	2,889	3,190	−301	130	109	4.5	3.4	134	−20	1,073	−149	22,250	60.2
Morton	1,703	1,760	−57	52	50	3.1	2.8	110	−11	704	−173	27,744	75.1
Nemaha	5,324	5,246	78	189	147	3.5	2.8	386	−4	4,200	284	23,810	64.4
Neosho	8,655	8,483	172	378	378	4.4	4.5	544	6	6,403	−380	23,757	64.3
Ness	1,672	1,849	−177	51	43	3.1	2.3	140	−17	823	−190	25,838	69.9
Norton	2,713	2,659	54	93	83	3.4	3.1	197	−20	1,849	−2	24,696	66.8
Osage	8,912	8,773	139	493	407	5.5	4.6	313	−36	2,932	−546	14,859	40.2
Osborne	2,324	2,323	1	81	59	3.5	2.5	160	−6	1,262	−38	16,970	45.9
Ottawa	3,436	3,274	162	121	105	3.5	3.2	138	14	895	63	20,867	56.4
Pawnee	3,834	3,566	268	139	99	3.6	2.8	172	−12	1,756	−225	29,363	79.4
Phillips	3,028	3,121	−93	100	85	3.3	2.7	227	−10	1,807	84	23,614	63.9
Pottawatomie	11,065	9,602	1,463	383	319	3.5	3.3	510	15	6,194	300	27,047	73.2
Pratt	5,386	5,058	328	173	137	3.2	2.7	418	35	3,398	404	24,297	65.7
Rawlins	1,354	1,476	−122	45	41	3.3	2.8	109	10	684	124	19,658	53.2
Reno	33,119	32,572	547	1,519	1,240	4.6	3.8	1,767	44	23,279	−2,918	27,097	73.3
Republic	2,767	3,008	−241	104	83	3.8	2.8	191	−22	1,406	−485	19,248	52.1
Rice	5,424	5,367	57	239	194	4.4	3.6	293	−14	2,677	61	23,172	62.7

See footnotes at end of table.

[Includes United States, states, and 3,141 counties/county equivalents defined as of February 22, 2005. For more information on these areas, see Appendix C, Geographic Information]

County	Civilian labor force							Private nonfarm businesses					
	Total			Number of unemployed		Unemployment rate[1]		Establishments		Employment[2]		Annual payroll per employee, 2004	
	2006	2000	Net change, 2000–2006	2006	2000	2006	2000	2004	Net change, 2000–2004	2004	Net change, 2000–2004	Amount (dol.)	Percent of U.S. average
KANSAS—Con.													
Riley	34,905	31,561	3,344	1,205	950	3.5	3.0	1,542	143	21,634	1,977	20,968	56.7
Rooks	2,624	2,836	−212	105	88	4.0	3.1	199	−9	1,244	−99	23,623	63.9
Rush	1,669	1,784	−115	64	58	3.8	3.3	106	5	871	−62	25,171	68.1
Russell	3,396	3,575	−179	138	141	4.1	3.9	274	−17	1,807	−379	18,379	49.7
Saline	31,100	29,043	2,057	1,180	927	3.8	3.2	1,692	−7	27,332	981	27,027	73.1
Scott	2,804	2,999	−195	81	66	2.9	2.2	192	−22	1,189	−266	24,672	66.7
Sedgwick	245,677	236,415	9,262	11,495	10,088	4.7	4.3	11,963	75	234,214	3,218	35,549	96.2
Seward	10,252	10,255	−3	367	323	3.6	3.1	629	−49	9,058	−776	26,089	70.6
Shawnee	91,240	90,759	481	4,431	3,709	4.9	4.1	4,730	130	74,734	−9,855	30,579	82.7
Sheridan	1,518	1,497	21	45	32	3.0	2.1	104	−3	603	—	22,095	59.8
Sherman	2,932	3,616	−684	113	102	3.9	2.8	263	−20	1,876	−245	20,386	55.1
Smith	2,183	2,227	−44	78	57	3.6	2.6	161	−4	1,115	23	18,183	49.2
Stafford	2,207	2,360	−153	83	72	3.8	3.1	160	7	800	−132	20,966	56.7
Stanton	1,128	1,293	−165	33	32	2.9	2.5	79	6	401	−20	23,307	63.0
Stevens	2,362	2,545	−183	84	72	3.6	2.8	165	−5	1,224	−2	25,641	69.4
Sumner	12,265	12,769	−504	585	611	4.8	4.8	531	−14	4,348	−513	23,387	63.3
Thomas	4,356	4,284	72	136	106	3.1	2.5	357	4	2,650	−30	20,371	55.1
Trego	1,719	1,690	29	56	40	3.3	2.4	136	11	685	−52	19,550	52.9
Wabaunsee	3,687	3,708	−21	142	127	3.9	3.4	121	−7	809	108	19,634	53.1
Wallace	905	938	−33	30	20	3.3	2.1	57	−4	324	−24	17,642	47.7
Washington	3,339	3,464	−125	120	114	3.6	3.3	215	−24	1,599	−11	18,351	49.6
Wichita	1,281	1,257	24	40	37	3.1	2.9	91	1	397	−31	25,476	68.9
Wilson	5,478	5,069	409	211	197	3.9	3.9	254	−6	3,800	265	28,114	76.1
Woodson	1,687	1,741	−54	86	82	5.1	4.7	100	−9	519	−85	17,362	47.0
Wyandotte	73,137	73,804	−667	5,589	4,701	7.6	6.4	2,962	−119	59,658	−1,930	37,489	101.4
KENTUCKY	2,038,971	1,949,013	89,958	116,808	82,665	5.7	4.2	[3]91,797	[3]1,876	[3]1,489,497	[3]−24,225	[3]30,992	[3]83.8
Adair	8,879	8,168	711	507	413	5.7	5.1	314	9	3,508	83	20,571	55.6
Allen	8,458	8,444	14	552	374	6.5	4.4	220	13	3,434	−893	25,880	70.0
Anderson	10,897	10,152	745	570	352	5.2	3.5	295	20	3,182	−324	28,048	75.9
Ballard	4,171	4,203	−32	260	252	6.2	6.0	167	−2	1,851	−118	35,534	96.1
Barren	19,670	19,254	416	1,106	892	5.6	4.6	858	1	14,437	−511	26,840	72.6
Bath	5,196	4,930	266	399	307	7.7	6.2	142	−30	1,550	74	22,403	60.6
Bell	9,698	9,864	−166	761	653	7.8	6.6	585	−48	7,193	−791	24,430	66.1
Boone	60,561	48,904	11,657	2,862	1,465	4.7	3.0	2,678	276	58,611	119	34,096	92.2
Bourbon	9,969	9,950	19	492	337	4.9	3.4	406	10	6,111	679	31,216	84.4
Boyd	23,320	21,387	1,933	1,287	1,251	5.5	5.8	1,491	14	24,089	−1,397	32,885	89.0
Boyle	12,920	13,467	−547	870	541	6.7	4.0	792	15	13,846	−1,559	27,211	73.6
Bracken	4,441	4,173	268	251	149	5.7	3.6	116	—	927	−187	24,393	66.0
Breathitt	5,699	5,380	319	424	367	7.4	6.8	218	3	2,149	−244	20,781	56.2
Breckinridge	9,155	8,628	527	616	415	6.7	4.8	295	−3	2,209	−47	21,530	58.2
Bullitt	36,964	33,363	3,601	2,218	1,095	6.0	3.3	980	56	11,729	1,032	25,867	70.0
Butler	5,885	6,583	−698	459	271	7.8	4.1	200	−9	2,781	−634	22,093	59.8
Caldwell	6,725	6,177	548	350	273	5.2	4.4	292	18	3,131	111	25,039	67.7
Calloway	18,147	17,232	915	1,025	682	5.6	4.0	791	13	11,965	−4	24,236	65.6
Campbell	46,331	46,433	−102	2,342	1,552	5.1	3.3	1,660	45	25,989	2,618	29,133	78.8
Carlisle	2,314	2,398	−84	142	146	6.1	6.1	74	−5	558	−41	17,557	47.5
Carroll	5,751	4,954	797	318	217	5.5	4.4	243	10	5,604	312	42,183	114.1
Carter	13,791	11,704	2,087	1,050	853	7.6	7.3	432	−10	5,999	1,683	18,498	50.0
Casey	7,539	6,839	700	515	315	6.8	4.6	204	3	2,594	207	18,891	51.1
Christian	27,195	26,356	839	1,791	1,277	6.6	4.8	1,354	32	25,140	2,548	27,213	73.6
Clark	17,431	16,950	481	952	642	5.5	3.8	803	39	12,829	360	28,342	76.7
Clay	7,116	7,209	−93	713	487	10.0	6.8	281	−20	2,584	−542	21,385	57.8
Clinton	4,544	4,510	34	273	228	6.0	5.1	199	9	3,228	194	22,882	61.9
Crittenden	4,059	4,334	−275	249	279	6.1	6.4	167	−5	1,840	233	19,053	51.5
Cumberland	3,054	3,172	−118	224	180	7.3	5.7	127	8	1,134	−48	20,011	54.1
Daviess	47,413	46,724	689	2,536	2,039	5.3	4.4	2,356	−53	37,126	−4,129	27,511	74.4
Edmonson	5,550	5,017	533	375	254	6.8	5.1	107	5	831	72	19,426	52.5
Elliott	3,137	2,449	688	258	220	8.2	9.0	52	−7	310	−83	18,003	48.7
Estill	6,133	5,997	136	405	290	6.6	4.8	202	−20	1,713	−353	18,900	51.1
Fayette	149,338	148,870	468	6,474	4,474	4.3	3.0	8,006	116	144,215	−6,968	33,535	90.7
Fleming	6,713	6,460	253	437	305	6.5	4.7	269	−20	2,535	−432	22,748	61.5
Floyd	15,302	13,767	1,535	992	965	6.5	7.0	827	−2	9,525	112	27,748	75.1
Franklin	25,660	25,353	307	1,198	866	4.7	3.4	1,203	33	17,432	512	27,064	73.2
Fulton	2,910	3,134	−224	218	167	7.5	5.3	171	−20	2,419	−434	20,489	55.4
Gallatin	4,053	3,902	151	193	157	4.8	4.0	104	9	1,151	−278	22,845	61.8
Garrard	7,597	7,533	64	446	266	5.9	3.5	210	−20	1,583	−344	22,059	59.7
Grant	12,723	11,534	1,189	679	449	5.3	3.9	426	−21	4,566	−259	22,798	61.7
Graves	15,930	17,066	−1,136	1,140	847	7.2	5.0	730	62	9,234	−1,163	24,848	67.2
Grayson	11,706	11,204	502	973	581	8.3	5.2	466	−1	7,818	209	20,853	56.4
Green	5,624	5,318	306	317	243	5.6	4.6	187	15	1,280	−180	19,808	53.6
Greenup	17,425	15,762	1,663	1,020	928	5.9	5.9	532	20	5,673	779	28,650	77.5

See footnotes at end of table.

— **Labor Force and Private Business Establishments and Employment**—Con.

[Includes United States, states, and 3,141 counties/county equivalents defined as of February 22, 2005. For more information on these areas, see Appendix C, Geographic Information]

County	Civilian labor force							Private nonfarm businesses					
	Total			Number of unemployed		Unemployment rate[1]		Establishments		Employment[2]		Annual payroll per employee, 2004	
	2006	2000	Net change, 2000–2006	2006	2000	2006	2000	2004	Net change, 2000–2004	2004	Net change, 2000–2004	Amount (dol.)	Percent of U.S. average
KENTUCKY—Con.													
Hancock	4,257	4,176	81	252	214	5.9	5.1	148	19	3,600	533	42,788	115.7
Hardin	47,903	42,744	5,159	2,601	1,888	5.4	4.4	2,126	169	33,168	469	27,221	73.6
Harlan	10,232	10,004	228	824	835	8.1	8.3	518	−9	5,850	135	28,112	76.0
Harrison	9,059	9,101	−42	494	325	5.5	3.6	312	9	3,930	−211	30,502	82.5
Hart	7,909	7,601	308	506	361	6.4	4.7	250	−2	3,382	798	22,141	59.9
Henderson	23,325	22,758	567	1,198	807	5.1	3.5	1,071	−14	18,580	−1,420	30,426	82.3
Henry	8,113	7,746	367	460	250	5.7	3.2	215	−34	2,025	−659	24,902	67.4
Hickman	2,071	2,355	−284	140	110	6.8	4.7	85	−11	763	−442	23,232	62.8
Hopkins	23,528	21,167	2,361	1,353	1,145	5.8	5.4	1,046	−22	15,017	41	29,134	78.8
Jackson	4,808	5,025	−217	468	289	9.7	5.8	150	7	2,422	162	21,881	59.2
Jefferson	360,170	361,025	−855	20,338	13,470	5.6	3.7	20,008	176	400,096	−16,294	35,953	97.3
Jessamine	22,374	20,591	1,783	1,060	622	4.7	3.0	986	97	13,849	1,387	25,878	70.0
Johnson	9,665	9,057	608	631	528	6.5	5.8	481	5	4,381	−485	22,004	59.5
Kenton	84,917	82,730	2,187	4,187	2,717	4.9	3.3	3,235	6	63,383	−448	35,519	96.1
Knott	6,580	5,687	893	459	422	7.0	7.4	215	−12	2,803	161	31,970	86.5
Knox	12,251	11,069	1,182	842	639	6.9	5.8	399	−39	4,187	−1,467	23,097	62.5
Larue	7,110	6,376	734	395	287	5.6	4.5	220	−1	2,174	245	18,763	50.8
Laurel	26,007	24,054	1,953	1,515	1,022	5.8	4.2	1,095	57	19,123	1,851	27,574	74.6
Lawrence	5,834	5,476	358	486	384	8.3	7.0	216	7	2,182	−199	27,000	73.0
Lee	2,783	2,480	303	205	146	7.4	5.9	112	5	1,817	102	17,877	48.4
Leslie	3,712	3,918	−206	328	234	8.8	6.0	127	−5	1,050	−166	22,846	61.8
Letcher	9,173	8,770	403	695	694	7.6	7.9	387	−32	5,092	−121	30,870	83.5
Lewis	5,569	5,588	−19	459	484	8.2	8.7	150	13	1,197	216	20,896	56.5
Lincoln	10,849	10,780	69	778	444	7.2	4.1	300	–	2,988	38	23,277	63.0
Livingston	4,873	4,908	−35	300	278	6.2	5.7	152	8	1,526	−333	29,746	80.5
Logan	12,531	13,206	−675	727	487	5.8	3.7	509	−16	7,232	−996	30,630	82.9
Lyon	3,325	3,140	185	221	177	6.6	5.6	169	−2	1,197	−278	17,566	47.5
McCracken	31,200	31,495	−295	1,699	1,458	5.4	4.6	2,154	37	34,891	−2,056	28,440	76.9
McCreary	6,060	6,048	12	613	409	10.1	6.8	173	−1	1,761	−219	18,057	48.8
McLean	4,787	4,753	34	357	249	7.5	5.2	171	−8	1,376	−86	24,088	65.2
Madison	42,815	37,273	5,542	2,046	1,352	4.8	3.6	1,508	71	22,724	314	25,452	68.9
Magoffin	4,356	4,437	−81	449	474	10.3	10.7	191	−3	2,009	40	19,481	52.7
Marion	10,103	8,556	1,547	533	434	5.3	5.1	366	37	6,558	1,046	25,367	68.6
Marshall	14,873	14,690	183	903	751	6.1	5.1	655	4	8,454	−382	34,669	93.8
Martin	3,630	3,439	191	273	255	7.5	7.4	180	5	2,540	560	33,543	90.7
Mason	8,738	8,266	472	459	311	5.3	3.8	490	37	7,504	−918	28,597	77.4
Meade	12,413	11,680	733	782	477	6.3	4.1	314	9	2,792	−230	25,414	68.7
Menifee	2,717	2,592	125	229	164	8.4	6.3	65	−7	484	−88	21,764	58.9
Mercer	10,603	10,649	−46	619	406	5.8	3.8	405	2	6,034	−183	31,581	85.4
Metcalfe	4,528	4,580	−52	246	208	5.4	4.5	118	−13	1,624	−948	24,982	67.6
Monroe	5,093	5,377	−284	319	440	6.3	8.2	215	−6	2,508	−412	21,261	57.5
Montgomery	12,086	11,170	916	728	491	6.0	4.4	548	15	8,465	437	24,363	65.9
Morgan	5,043	4,861	182	443	319	8.8	6.6	179	−21	1,948	−315	25,201	68.2
Muhlenberg	13,016	13,039	−23	1,201	766	9.2	5.9	578	−14	7,000	86	22,260	60.2
Nelson	21,043	19,563	1,480	1,241	827	5.9	4.2	932	54	12,349	−79	28,314	76.6
Nicholas	2,988	3,251	−263	206	230	6.9	7.1	82	−9	629	−106	16,970	45.9
Ohio	11,884	10,529	1,355	720	542	6.1	5.1	370	15	5,171	386	21,795	59.0
Oldham	26,990	23,962	3,028	1,339	719	5.0	3.0	1,136	141	9,781	488	26,564	71.9
Owen	5,220	4,975	245	291	182	5.6	3.7	114	−3	1,096	−45	24,606	66.6
Owsley	1,550	1,518	32	131	87	8.5	5.7	49	4	394	79	16,975	45.9
Pendleton	7,574	7,139	435	422	251	5.6	3.5	187	−17	1,589	−121	24,035	65.0
Perry	11,510	9,958	1,552	795	677	6.9	6.8	679	−32	9,770	214	30,119	81.5
Pike	25,183	24,824	359	1,507	1,541	6.0	6.2	1,419	−100	18,624	−1,601	30,118	81.5
Powell	5,593	5,788	−195	411	288	7.3	5.0	180	−7	1,899	−464	19,235	52.0
Pulaski	27,393	25,580	1,813	1,778	1,121	6.5	4.4	1,501	57	20,991	601	24,323	65.8
Robertson	1,054	1,088	−34	56	48	5.3	4.4	21	−3	131	−13	14,840	40.1
Rockcastle	7,613	7,127	486	522	342	6.9	4.8	228	7	2,722	−119	20,616	55.8
Rowan	12,277	10,745	1,532	704	477	5.7	4.4	475	12	7,073	732	22,442	60.7
Russell	8,173	7,402	771	543	424	6.6	5.7	380	27	4,681	493	20,771	56.2
Scott	21,064	18,263	2,801	1,008	582	4.8	3.2	787	133	20,632	1,171	44,579	120.6
Shelby	20,618	18,260	2,358	1,080	555	5.2	3.0	825	102	12,806	1,029	30,226	81.8
Simpson	9,004	8,437	567	518	292	5.8	3.5	371	3	7,575	−39	28,856	78.1
Spencer	8,478	6,501	1,977	517	196	6.1	3.0	208	37	925	−23	20,694	56.0
Taylor	13,235	11,144	2,091	642	580	4.9	5.2	664	−12	8,573	1,285	23,727	64.2
Todd	5,131	5,728	−597	494	237	9.6	4.1	189	−9	2,167	−206	20,589	55.7
Trigg	6,627	5,926	701	390	267	5.9	4.5	245	−6	3,140	400	23,480	63.5
Trimble	4,490	4,070	420	300	155	6.7	3.8	82	9	657	128	23,758	64.3
Union	7,196	7,385	−189	432	353	6.0	4.8	292	−7	5,216	−1,044	28,678	77.6
Warren	56,832	50,031	6,801	2,717	1,892	4.8	3.8	2,650	150	45,460	1,813	28,895	78.2
Washington	5,374	5,200	174	314	214	5.8	4.1	242	31	2,838	163	25,506	69.0

See footnotes at end of table.

Table B-10. Counties — Labor Force and Private Business Establishments and Employment—Con.

[Includes United States, states, and 3,141 counties/county equivalents defined as of February 22, 2005. For more information on these areas, see Appendix C, Geographic Information]

County	Civilian labor force							Private nonfarm businesses					
	Total			Number of unemployed		Unemployment rate[1]		Establishments		Employment[2]		Annual payroll per employee, 2004	
	2006	2000	Net change, 2000–2006	2006	2000	2006	2000	2004	Net change, 2000–2004	2004	Net change, 2000–2004	Amount (dol.)	Percent of U.S. average
KENTUCKY—Con.													
Wayne	8,767	8,140	627	587	450	6.7	5.5	323	13	4,885	480	20,303	54.9
Webster	6,742	6,748	−6	346	312	5.1	4.6	245	−11	2,884	67	31,962	86.5
Whitley	15,374	14,226	1,148	945	702	6.1	4.9	900	53	13,711	−367	24,275	65.7
Wolfe	2,322	2,510	−188	224	214	9.6	8.5	84	10	703	1	17,757	48.0
Woodford	13,596	13,358	238	573	376	4.2	2.8	530	20	7,311	−989	32,637	88.3
LOUISIANA	1,990,120	2,031,292	−41,172	79,772	100,630	4.0	5.0	[3]103,067	[3]2,051	[3]1,623,680	[3]31,323	[3]30,207	[3]81.7
Acadia	25,712	23,867	1,845	815	1,296	3.2	5.4	1,031	17	10,921	−983	22,643	61.3
Allen	8,610	8,703	−93	399	549	4.6	6.3	346	−6	3,524	84	20,079	54.3
Ascension	46,359	38,356	8,003	1,651	1,895	3.6	4.9	1,651	133	25,983	648	33,651	91.0
Assumption	10,109	9,978	131	490	600	4.8	6.0	260	12	2,271	−202	24,841	67.2
Avoyelles	16,061	15,681	380	705	937	4.4	6.0	712	−3	8,421	−38	18,529	50.1
Beauregard	14,382	13,993	389	562	695	3.9	5.0	601	−7	6,787	232	27,666	74.8
Bienville	6,297	5,921	376	280	372	4.4	6.3	265	−2	3,228	38	24,309	65.8
Bossier	51,853	47,034	4,819	1,707	2,102	3.3	4.5	2,136	168	33,400	2,655	24,196	65.5
Caddo	118,361	114,768	3,593	4,729	5,533	4.0	4.8	6,230	−28	108,211	70	30,086	81.4
Calcasieu	89,090	86,362	2,728	3,067	4,096	3.4	4.7	4,271	31	71,243	2,025	30,311	82.0
Caldwell	4,374	4,340	34	167	276	3.8	6.4	192	−10	1,852	194	19,590	53.0
Cameron	4,426	4,532	−106	133	212	3.0	4.7	173	−3	1,855	−21	33,294	90.1
Catahoula	4,175	4,127	48	208	364	5.0	8.8	187	−12	1,662	−63	17,568	47.5
Claiborne	6,858	6,474	384	291	388	4.2	6.0	248	−28	2,886	118	23,990	64.9
Concordia	7,239	7,737	−498	425	613	5.9	7.9	345	3	3,650	503	22,138	59.9
De Soto	11,439	10,775	664	495	624	4.3	5.8	361	15	5,046	728	33,298	90.1
East Baton Rouge	214,878	206,885	7,993	8,063	8,931	3.8	4.3	11,487	−12	214,405	979	31,209	84.4
East Carroll	2,982	3,093	−111	239	281	8.0	9.1	136	−3	1,043	36	21,663	58.6
East Feliciana	8,319	8,261	58	339	443	4.1	5.4	248	−4	4,894	1,433	25,109	67.9
Evangeline	12,116	12,116	−	492	675	4.1	5.6	542	−18	6,336	330	23,372	63.2
Franklin	7,761	8,185	−424	446	562	5.7	6.9	422	1	4,348	3	17,910	48.4
Grant	8,671	7,890	781	317	465	3.7	5.9	209	7	1,717	263	21,012	56.8
Iberia	34,099	30,433	3,666	1,132	1,650	3.3	5.4	1,651	47	26,666	1,745	32,078	86.8
Iberville	12,650	12,585	65	673	831	5.3	6.6	535	−7	10,950	313	43,530	117.8
Jackson	6,437	6,696	−259	246	357	3.8	5.3	281	−12	2,853	−343	24,283	65.7
Jefferson	181,505	231,695	−50,190	9,151	9,956	5.0	4.3	12,693	−149	203,114	−13,668	30,755	83.2
Jefferson Davis	14,392	12,766	1,626	421	700	2.9	5.5	587	−2	6,346	479	21,096	57.1
Lafayette	107,747	97,296	10,451	2,918	3,720	2.7	3.8	7,098	437	106,532	4,016	31,089	84.1
Lafourche	46,909	41,048	5,861	1,310	1,721	2.8	4.2	1,860	24	27,244	2,979	30,966	83.8
La Salle	6,069	5,885	184	190	321	3.1	5.5	299	−18	2,410	−531	22,585	61.1
Lincoln	18,580	19,049	−469	778	962	4.2	5.1	950	59	13,671	919	24,552	66.4
Livingston	54,262	44,722	9,540	1,886	2,360	3.5	5.3	1,417	189	13,829	1,595	21,615	58.5
Madison	4,649	4,954	−305	256	373	5.5	7.5	202	−8	2,092	−83	18,555	50.2
Morehouse	11,475	12,433	−958	690	891	6.0	7.2	521	−1	6,206	−44	26,169	70.8
Natchitoches	17,758	16,569	1,189	720	912	4.1	5.5	810	31	12,333	2,200	19,763	53.5
Orleans	154,041	210,684	−56,643	7,224	10,744	4.7	5.1	10,500	−119	211,247	2,722	32,972	89.2
Ouachita	71,950	69,776	2,174	2,674	3,092	3.7	4.4	4,271	167	64,215	−1,594	27,026	73.1
Plaquemines	9,246	11,006	−1,760	440	599	4.8	5.4	750	17	10,591	−994	42,165	114.1
Pointe Coupee	9,852	9,732	120	418	575	4.2	5.9	363	13	3,970	194	22,927	62.0
Rapides	60,037	55,629	4,408	2,123	2,818	3.5	5.1	3,141	56	48,112	−174	27,409	74.1
Red River	3,271	3,540	−269	181	230	5.5	6.5	139	−8	2,239	560	22,795	61.7
Richland	8,560	8,653	−93	399	558	4.7	6.4	415	12	4,678	−333	22,466	60.8
Sabine	9,641	9,286	355	329	454	3.4	4.9	470	−	4,704	163	22,131	59.9
St. Bernard	23,991	32,177	−8,186	746	1,642	3.1	5.1	1,183	−8	13,820	−109	28,019	75.8
St. Charles	19,583	23,892	−4,309	1,012	1,246	5.2	5.2	922	40	19,146	1,437	45,510	123.1
St. Helena	4,213	4,052	161	292	219	6.9	5.4	102	12	1,339	593	20,286	54.9
St. James	8,340	8,819	−479	495	710	5.9	8.1	316	3	5,401	−306	42,191	114.1
St. John the Baptist	16,959	19,988	−3,029	1,250	1,271	7.4	6.4	667	41	10,531	−702	33,634	91.0
St. Landry	37,475	32,670	4,805	1,468	1,987	3.9	6.1	1,577	48	20,835	4,218	26,427	71.5
St. Martin	23,421	21,316	2,105	768	1,107	3.3	5.2	766	110	7,787	−659	22,591	61.1
St. Mary	23,057	22,433	624	951	1,550	4.1	6.9	1,367	−63	21,498	−891	32,852	88.9
St. Tammany	86,662	96,404	−9,742	3,925	3,899	4.5	4.0	5,265	630	61,226	9,444	27,447	74.2
Tangipahoa	50,389	45,087	5,302	2,233	2,726	4.4	6.0	2,097	83	30,567	5,559	22,210	60.1
Tensas	2,301	2,473	−172	164	176	7.1	7.1	109	1	757	−32	25,808	69.8
Terrebonne	52,509	45,769	6,740	1,561	1,986	3.0	4.3	2,840	142	41,871	2,609	30,920	83.6
Union	10,394	10,173	221	403	541	3.9	5.3	327	−9	5,203	56	16,150	43.7
Vermilion	23,880	23,278	602	811	1,157	3.4	5.0	988	51	9,514	122	26,834	72.6
Vernon	21,625	18,267	3,358	780	1,050	3.6	5.7	625	−2	8,714	1,321	22,048	59.6
Washington	15,428	16,756	−1,328	802	974	5.2	5.8	695	−21	8,713	398	22,175	60.0
Webster	19,661	18,420	1,241	766	1,053	3.9	5.7	803	−46	10,901	−26	25,247	68.3
West Baton Rouge	10,537	10,152	385	390	502	3.7	4.9	455	25	8,284	−571	32,288	87.3
West Carroll	5,202	4,832	370	304	434	5.8	9.0	180	−21	1,786	−86	21,205	57.4
West Feliciana	4,953	4,798	155	221	302	4.5	6.3	186	14	2,908	214	45,933	124.3
Winn	6,341	6,025	316	253	370	4.0	6.1	327	−8	4,370	347	26,209	70.9

See footnotes at end of table.

[Includes United States, states, and 3,141 counties/county equivalents defined as of February 22, 2005. For more information on these areas, see Appendix C, Geographic Information]

County	Civilian labor force							Private nonfarm businesses				Annual payroll per employee, 2004	
	Total			Number of unemployed		Unemployment rate[1]		Establishments		Employment[2]			
	2006	2000	Net change, 2000–2006	2006	2000	2006	2000	2004	Net change, 2000–2004	2004	Net change, 2000–2004	Amount (dol.)	Percent of U.S. average
MAINE	711,376	672,440	38,936	32,533	22,055	4.6	3.3	[3]41,269	[3]1,803	[3]494,256	[3]2,476	[3]31,237	[3]84.5
Androscoggin	58,435	55,241	3,194	2,712	1,839	4.6	3.3	2,824	38	45,262	−604	29,607	80.1
Aroostook.	36,069	34,627	1,442	2,339	1,426	6.5	4.1	2,181	−134	24,513	−525	25,095	67.9
Cumberland	158,644	148,699	9,945	5,378	3,601	3.4	2.4	11,000	692	155,617	5,520	35,495	96.0
Franklin	14,628	14,365	263	831	708	5.7	4.9	867	22	10,162	−375	26,543	71.8
Hancock	30,320	28,627	1,693	1,596	1,131	5.3	4.0	2,175	35	17,064	−33	32,442	87.8
Kennebec.	63,960	60,826	3,134	2,833	2,085	4.4	3.4	3,350	130	42,941	−296	29,237	79.1
Knox	21,700	20,851	849	920	565	4.2	2.7	1,651	123	14,601	485	28,781	77.9
Lincoln	18,617	17,762	855	795	524	4.3	3.0	1,493	128	8,667	154	28,535	77.2
Oxford	28,583	27,587	996	1,627	1,102	5.7	4.0	1,427	23	14,297	−1,637	26,900	72.8
Penobscot	79,068	74,854	4,214	3,904	2,702	4.9	3.6	4,215	42	56,018	−824	29,114	78.8
Piscataquis	7,698	7,894	−196	510	406	6.6	5.1	481	3	4,542	−639	25,383	68.7
Sagadahoc	18,900	18,795	105	761	490	4.0	2.6	890	106	13,875	−40	34,667	93.8
Somerset	25,437	25,038	399	1,716	1,169	6.7	4.7	1,181	−35	14,809	−1,733	29,833	80.7
Waldo	19,527	18,979	548	1,024	728	5.2	3.8	978	126	9,443	144	30,182	81.6
Washington	15,550	15,668	−118	1,153	914	7.4	5.8	924	8	7,771	−257	25,741	69.6
York	114,242	102,622	11,620	4,436	2,662	3.9	2.6	5,573	437	54,010	2,472	30,438	82.3
MARYLAND.	3,009,143	2,811,657	197,486	116,523	100,275	3.9	3.6	[3]136,062	[3]7,595	[3]2,151,474	[3]93,170	[3]39,204	[3]106.1
Allegany.	35,819	32,993	2,826	2,036	1,958	5.7	5.9	1,793	−54	27,104	1,968	27,473	74.3
Anne Arundel	283,120	268,268	14,852	9,468	8,118	3.3	3.0	13,592	1,417	207,420	22,603	38,375	103.8
Baltimore	431,861	409,441	22,420	17,114	15,191	4.0	3.7	20,291	1,301	325,423	11,024	37,300	100.9
Calvert.	47,336	40,479	6,857	1,499	1,220	3.2	3.0	1,759	269	17,663	2,715	31,897	86.3
Caroline	16,309	15,404	905	708	557	4.3	3.6	681	89	6,872	334	27,590	74.6
Carroll	94,855	84,170	10,685	3,027	2,505	3.2	3.0	4,427	355	48,406	4,881	28,382	76.8
Cecil	50,960	45,904	5,056	2,222	1,621	4.4	3.5	1,759	115	22,619	1,790	35,468	95.9
Charles	74,792	65,300	9,492	2,372	1,930	3.2	3.0	2,800	392	35,173	5,740	27,712	75.0
Dorchester	17,242	15,635	1,607	976	803	5.7	5.1	788	75	10,191	540	27,035	73.1
Frederick	124,318	109,912	14,406	3,913	2,983	3.1	2.7	5,761	823	83,388	11,044	34,097	92.2
Garrett.	16,718	14,560	2,158	830	759	5.0	5.2	973	86	10,148	929	23,201	62.8
Harford	133,094	120,208	12,886	4,849	3,910	3.6	3.3	5,275	442	64,262	5,425	29,824	80.7
Howard	158,974	145,008	13,966	4,570	3,648	2.9	2.5	7,939	597	146,154	11,164	47,123	127.5
Kent	10,880	10,095	785	438	392	4.0	3.9	705	36	7,837	816	25,014	67.7
Montgomery	519,688	489,050	30,638	14,937	12,853	2.9	2.6	26,446	815	412,188	8,038	47,573	128.7
Prince George's.	454,601	430,406	24,195	18,813	15,874	4.1	3.7	14,522	694	258,949	8,255	37,375	101.1
Queen Anne's	25,844	22,763	3,081	876	698	3.4	3.1	1,384	187	10,816	1,241	27,257	73.7
St. Mary's.	50,459	44,467	5,992	1,711	1,445	3.4	3.2	1,797	108	26,807	4,659	35,581	96.3
Somerset	11,702	10,480	1,222	637	655	5.4	6.3	376	−29	3,704	534	30,424	82.3
Talbot	19,128	17,565	1,563	693	588	3.6	3.3	1,587	134	16,944	47	29,972	81.1
Washington	70,138	66,332	3,806	3,094	2,428	4.4	3.7	3,444	116	58,748	144	30,717	83.1
Wicomico	53,135	46,358	6,777	2,150	1,932	4.0	4.2	2,658	124	39,427	2,121	29,625	80.1
Worcester.	28,294	26,077	2,217	1,738	1,609	6.1	6.2	2,238	115	19,227	821	26,286	71.1
Independent City													
Baltimore city	279,877	280,786	−909	17,853	16,599	6.4	5.9	12,919	−721	281,689	−16,689	43,132	116.7
MASSACHUSETTS.	3,404,394	3,365,573	38,821	169,534	92,292	5.0	2.7	[3]175,933	[3]−289	[3]2,979,690	[3]−107,354	[3]45,389	[3]122.8
Barnstable	121,635	113,365	8,270	6,356	3,856	5.2	3.4	8,635	296	76,600	4,413	33,417	90.4
Berkshire	72,947	70,051	2,896	3,332	2,048	4.6	2.9	4,439	56	57,291	−1,644	31,646	85.6
Bristol	289,692	278,203	11,489	18,096	10,432	6.2	3.7	13,400	180	203,088	−59	32,116	86.9
Dukes	10,900	10,068	832	447	280	4.1	2.8	1,001	−5	5,147	131	41,421	112.0
Essex	378,010	372,511	5,499	20,018	10,408	5.3	2.8	18,517	−71	275,148	−7,218	38,785	104.9
Franklin	39,561	39,202	359	1,794	969	4.5	2.5	1,797	−2	22,223	−2,535	30,576	82.7
Hampden	224,928	219,254	5,674	13,775	7,305	6.1	3.3	10,355	−1,245	172,229	−8,978	33,988	91.9
Hampshire	88,038	86,556	1,482	3,684	1,900	4.2	2.2	3,621	33	48,458	2,453	27,873	75.4
Middlesex	814,972	821,779	−6,807	33,593	18,240	4.1	2.2	42,823	−251	787,300	−65,654	51,274	138.7
Nantucket	8,264	7,285	979	204	109	2.5	1.5	840	65	3,827	6	50,523	136.7
Norfolk.	358,885	357,112	1,773	15,482	8,375	4.3	2.3	19,364	−314	328,104	−9,462	43,873	118.7
Plymouth	261,140	251,284	9,856	13,248	6,859	5.1	2.7	12,193	554	153,150	5,391	35,464	95.9
Suffolk.	334,652	351,064	−16,412	18,046	10,764	5.4	3.1	19,739	−850	548,381	−22,736	61,772	167.1
Worcester.	400,768	387,841	12,927	21,458	10,747	5.4	2.8	19,026	1,112	292,652	−726	37,226	100.7
MICHIGAN	5,081,336	5,143,916	−62,580	351,045	190,495	6.9	3.7	[3]237,984	[3]1,072	[3]3,895,914	[3]−176,872	[3]37,917	[3]102.6
Alcona.	4,468	4,465	3	468	298	10.5	6.7	247	1	1,194	−248	24,131	65.3
Alger	4,517	4,374	143	352	232	7.8	5.3	264	−86	2,230	−625	26,140	70.7
Allegan	57,102	57,730	−628	3,441	1,648	6.0	2.9	2,356	189	35,349	−816	32,823	88.8
Alpena	15,166	15,536	−370	1,147	849	7.6	5.5	922	6	11,944	798	28,363	76.7
Antrim	12,207	11,603	604	934	525	7.7	4.5	652	−9	4,440	−1,121	27,460	74.3
Arenac.	7,956	7,648	308	786	437	9.9	5.7	381	−98	3,587	−2,224	22,877	61.9
Baraga	4,312	4,119	193	473	265	11.0	6.4	212	−16	1,852	−404	25,379	68.7
Barry	31,325	30,386	939	1,624	1,011	5.2	3.3	1,036	28	11,422	−307	28,222	76.3
Bay	55,844	56,597	−753	3,880	2,286	6.9	4.0	2,515	−41	33,008	−2,328	31,526	85.3
Benzie	9,336	8,391	945	707	374	7.6	4.5	512	43	3,833	630	24,020	65.0

See footnotes at end of table.

Table B-10. Counties — Labor Force and Private Business Establishments and Employment—Con.

[Includes United States, states, and 3,141 counties/county equivalents defined as of February 22, 2005. For more information on these areas, see Appendix C, Geographic Information]

County	Civilian labor force							Private nonfarm businesses					
	Total			Number of unemployed		Unemployment rate[1]		Establishments		Employment[2]		Annual payroll per employee, 2004	
	2006	2000	Net change, 2000–2006	2006	2000	2006	2000	2004	Net change, 2000–2004	2004	Net change, 2000–2004	Amount (dol.)	Percent of U.S. average
MICHIGAN—Con.													
Berrien..............	79,547	84,375	−4,828	5,545	3,087	7.0	3.7	4,021	30	59,271	−1,228	32,298	87.4
Branch..............	22,846	23,411	−565	1,688	888	7.4	3.8	918	−18	13,120	−230	28,767	77.8
Calhoun.............	72,237	69,600	2,637	4,935	2,905	6.8	4.2	2,922	−107	54,363	−6,356	35,002	94.7
Cass...............	27,965	27,130	835	1,486	853	5.3	3.1	855	35	8,810	−302	27,921	75.5
Charlevoix...........	14,475	13,819	656	1,105	612	7.6	4.4	934	−153	9,200	−1,851	29,695	80.3
Cheboygan...........	13,467	12,943	524	1,273	1,040	9.5	8.0	843	−71	5,736	−592	27,992	75.7
Chippewa............	17,908	17,467	441	1,510	1,108	8.4	6.3	877	−24	8,824	−405	23,282	63.0
Clare..............	13,646	13,028	618	1,392	696	10.2	5.3	579	−65	6,211	−38	23,466	63.5
Clinton.............	37,903	35,658	2,245	1,988	930	5.2	2.6	1,230	61	13,176	−509	29,988	81.1
Crawford............	6,947	6,703	244	521	305	7.5	4.6	344	42	3,596	503	28,328	76.6
Delta..............	20,829	19,809	1,020	1,480	1,034	7.1	5.2	1,174	−33	13,571	64	27,762	75.1
Dickinson...........	14,745	14,000	745	838	569	5.7	4.1	971	−11	12,633	−1,218	31,058	84.0
Eaton..............	59,539	57,957	1,582	3,118	1,631	5.2	2.8	1,931	−56	27,887	−3,386	27,342	74.0
Emmet..............	20,556	18,057	2,499	1,706	980	8.3	5.4	1,649	256	14,944	723	31,358	84.8
Genesee.............	212,853	213,893	−1,040	17,361	9,547	8.2	4.5	8,998	−119	143,474	−8,265	34,460	93.2
Gladwin.............	11,029	10,963	66	1,075	571	9.7	5.2	484	20	4,111	−246	25,454	68.9
Gogebic.............	7,855	7,719	136	585	475	7.4	6.2	482	−18	4,936	175	19,563	52.9
Grand Traverse........	49,534	45,570	3,964	2,944	1,542	5.9	3.4	3,648	80	43,406	−97	30,937	83.7
Gratiot.............	20,666	19,552	1,114	1,751	883	8.5	4.5	821	−48	12,183	−479	26,728	72.3
Hillsdale............	22,509	24,180	−1,671	1,743	885	7.7	3.7	931	−10	13,861	−1,986	27,920	75.5
Houghton............	18,100	17,121	979	1,228	827	6.8	4.8	945	17	9,766	−245	22,316	60.4
Huron..............	17,797	17,600	197	1,410	788	7.9	4.5	1,001	−43	9,913	−1,399	27,655	74.8
Ingham.............	154,682	154,649	33	9,678	4,579	6.3	3.0	7,228	99	129,849	1,998	34,167	92.4
Ionia..............	31,635	29,957	1,678	2,584	1,099	8.2	3.7	1,003	−33	11,455	−501	26,394	71.4
Iosco..............	11,368	11,603	−235	1,020	736	9.0	6.3	761	79	6,817	1,388	26,088	70.6
Iron...............	6,075	5,654	421	430	319	7.1	5.6	421	9	2,948	−163	23,163	62.7
Isabella.............	38,536	34,825	3,711	1,963	1,163	5.1	3.3	1,538	214	21,657	2,323	24,685	66.8
Jackson.............	78,785	79,110	−325	5,625	2,690	7.1	3.4	3,386	−25	50,674	−4,022	32,824	88.8
Kalamazoo...........	134,568	132,817	1,751	6,943	3,960	5.2	3.0	5,801	−103	112,858	2,012	36,203	97.9
Kalkaska............	9,001	8,551	450	690	395	7.7	4.6	379	−16	3,417	−604	31,141	84.2
Kent...............	325,350	318,485	6,865	18,326	9,890	5.6	3.1	16,193	920	321,088	−14,901	35,520	96.1
Keweenaw...........	1,085	1,049	36	108	64	10.0	6.1	62	−5	210	−232	17,157	46.4
Lake...............	4,256	4,456	−200	444	249	10.4	5.6	171	−4	1,311	101	22,458	60.8
Lapeer..............	44,967	45,922	−955	3,529	1,991	7.8	4.3	1,813	−8	19,040	−2,677	27,412	74.2
Leelanau............	11,837	11,325	512	588	342	5.0	3.0	698	9	4,171	−275	25,218	68.2
Lenawee............	50,586	51,729	−1,143	3,689	1,927	7.3	3.7	2,143	12	30,122	−263	28,626	77.4
Livingston...........	94,228	89,658	4,570	5,014	2,362	5.3	2.6	4,192	393	45,889	1,362	32,679	88.4
Luce...............	2,899	2,754	145	218	165	7.5	6.0	189	−7	1,825	242	22,582	61.1
Mackinac............	6,677	6,881	−204	636	513	9.5	7.5	507	−30	2,360	−487	31,808	86.0
Macomb.............	421,446	433,849	−12,403	30,194	15,738	7.2	3.6	19,231	391	308,750	−26,500	39,052	105.6
Manistee	12,369	11,830	539	1,036	622	8.4	5.3	666	54	5,529	−347	28,170	76.2
Marquette	36,301	34,183	2,118	2,176	1,479	6.0	4.3	1,735	99	22,601	1,971	28,217	76.3
Mason	15,177	14,731	446	1,194	703	7.9	4.8	826	−27	8,932	−576	28,016	75.8
Mecosta	20,636	18,923	1,713	1,518	804	7.4	4.2	842	−62	10,005	558	23,484	63.5
Menominee	13,319	13,272	47	838	544	6.3	4.1	483	−39	5,832	−1,170	26,825	72.6
Midland	42,807	42,593	214	2,381	1,380	5.6	3.2	1,850	−97	32,767	−3,777	46,089	124.7
Missaukee	6,888	7,000	−112	521	309	7.6	4.4	269	−72	2,071	−98	23,324	63.1
Monroe	79,051	77,060	1,991	5,115	2,445	6.5	3.2	2,613	127	39,254	−301	32,510	87.9
Montcalm	28,810	29,401	−591	3,643	1,213	12.6	4.1	1,146	35	15,428	−160	29,061	78.6
Montmorency	4,410	4,083	327	519	323	11.8	7.9	264	16	1,842	138	22,336	60.4
Muskegon	91,030	85,500	5,530	6,237	3,489	6.9	4.1	3,672	85	54,342	−3,122	31,384	84.9
Newaygo	23,657	23,002	655	1,692	1,058	7.2	4.6	840	66	9,801	875	29,691	80.3
Oakland............	630,690	675,784	−45,094	36,329	19,446	5.8	2.9	41,828	−71	746,068	−45,022	47,270	127.9
Oceana	14,816	13,217	1,599	1,241	771	8.4	5.8	578	−12	5,004	480	23,516	63.6
Ogemaw	9,990	9,600	390	808	511	8.1	5.3	618	4	6,431	875	22,696	61.4
Ontonagon	3,598	3,648	−50	281	228	7.8	6.3	227	−7	1,820	151	25,319	68.5
Osceola	10,303	11,176	−873	754	502	7.3	4.5	472	54	6,152	−795	33,789	91.4
Oscoda	4,128	3,894	234	431	234	10.4	6.0	212	−44	1,578	−302	22,697	61.4
Otsego	12,810	12,354	456	1,042	508	8.1	4.1	916	7	10,611	110	26,035	70.4
Ottawa.............	138,851	135,248	3,603	7,287	3,618	5.2	2.7	6,080	190	104,319	−3,486	34,222	92.6
Presque Isle	6,364	6,497	−133	751	531	11.8	8.2	392	−49	2,331	−1,051	24,035	65.0
Roscommon	11,179	10,371	808	1,012	554	9.1	5.3	689	−43	4,967	−145	23,377	63.2
Saginaw............	99,133	101,113	−1,980	7,396	4,069	7.5	4.0	4,899	−124	85,375	−7,238	31,724	85.8
St. Clair	84,186	87,056	−2,870	6,767	3,688	8.0	4.2	3,543	12	44,947	−3,536	30,715	83.1
St. Joseph	31,657	32,584	−927	2,063	1,090	6.5	3.3	1,288	−1	19,937	−780	33,188	89.8
Sanilac	23,009	21,933	1,076	1,936	1,001	8.4	4.6	976	−15	9,653	−1,475	25,160	68.1
Schoolcraft..........	4,159	3,925	234	432	315	10.4	8.0	275	−6	2,137	165	26,351	71.3
Shiawassee	37,233	37,396	−163	2,989	1,445	8.0	3.9	1,323	8	15,671	−775	25,555	69.1
Tuscola	29,553	28,771	782	2,491	1,307	8.4	4.5	1,013	−56	10,508	−1,643	26,452	71.6

See footnotes at end of table.

Table B-10. Counties — Labor Force and Private Business Establishments and Employment—Con.

[Includes United States, states, and 3,141 counties/county equivalents defined as of February 22, 2005. For more information on these areas, see Appendix C, Geographic Information]

County	Civilian labor force							Private nonfarm businesses					
	Total			Number of unemployed		Unemployment rate[1]		Establishments		Employment[2]		Annual payroll per employee, 2004	
	2006	2000	Net change, 2000–2006	2006	2000	2006	2000	2004	Net change, 2000–2004	2004	Net change, 2000–2004	Amount (dol.)	Percent of U.S. average
MICHIGAN—Con.													
Van Buren	41,374	39,619	1,755	2,771	1,590	6.7	4.0	1,454	−93	16,348	−689	27,728	75.0
Washtenaw	191,462	185,356	6,106	8,795	4,395	4.6	2.4	8,383	131	153,330	−4,134	42,637	115.3
Wayne	894,058	952,531	−58,473	75,214	41,237	8.4	4.3	35,137	−874	705,771	−51,716	42,669	115.4
Wexford	15,167	15,596	−429	1,215	829	8.0	5.3	898	34	13,728	−326	27,451	74.3
MINNESOTA	2,939,304	2,807,668	131,636	117,007	87,176	4.0	3.1	[3]148,626	[3]9,546	[3]2,393,126	[3]−2,235	[3]38,609	[3]104.4
Aitkin	7,915	7,174	741	465	426	5.9	5.9	433	24	3,277	85	23,814	64.4
Anoka	193,461	179,025	14,436	7,467	4,840	3.9	2.7	7,522	901	106,938	5,698	40,917	110.7
Becker	17,202	15,608	1,594	863	757	5.0	4.9	929	−123	12,778	−3,657	25,012	67.7
Beltrami	21,672	20,310	1,362	1,105	934	5.1	4.6	1,150	126	14,031	1,331	25,160	68.1
Benton	22,738	20,568	2,170	1,003	708	4.4	3.4	942	191	14,153	2,756	30,323	82.0
Big Stone	2,895	2,772	123	123	113	4.2	4.1	205	4	1,542	7	18,623	50.4
Blue Earth	36,759	33,870	2,889	1,192	939	3.2	2.8	1,932	250	32,246	4,699	26,688	72.2
Brown	15,184	15,400	−216	665	565	4.4	3.7	791	90	13,023	512	25,344	68.6
Carlton	17,259	15,864	1,395	906	763	5.2	4.8	783	100	9,751	690	28,618	77.4
Carver	48,969	41,009	7,960	1,616	986	3.3	2.4	2,164	414	30,657	3,110	38,587	104.4
Cass	14,899	13,378	1,521	922	714	6.2	5.3	922	149	6,855	1,554	23,501	63.6
Chippewa	7,389	7,110	279	278	346	3.8	4.9	435	27	4,771	688	23,690	64.1
Chisago	27,595	23,206	4,389	1,330	842	4.8	3.6	1,224	125	12,497	1,828	28,879	78.1
Clay	31,831	28,040	3,791	1,022	902	3.2	3.2	1,192	45	15,034	324	21,456	58.0
Clearwater	3,877	4,193	−316	374	387	9.6	9.2	210	13	1,905	68	29,073	78.6
Cook	3,301	3,130	171	142	124	4.3	4.0	264	5	2,029	−95	23,560	63.7
Cottonwood	6,436	6,258	178	290	290	4.5	4.6	344	−41	3,944	−93	22,954	62.1
Crow Wing	33,074	29,052	4,022	1,594	1,155	4.8	4.0	2,101	181	24,405	2,787	27,363	74.0
Dakota	232,232	216,846	15,386	8,132	5,259	3.5	2.4	9,711	1,108	158,404	4,287	37,696	102.0
Dodge	11,411	10,217	1,194	414	303	3.6	3.0	473	60	4,165	121	31,377	84.9
Douglas	20,425	18,183	2,242	774	587	3.8	3.2	1,399	110	15,214	1,151	28,436	76.9
Faribault	7,982	8,594	−612	356	310	4.5	3.6	505	42	4,867	−11	24,248	65.6
Fillmore	11,444	11,728	−284	470	357	4.1	3.0	661	12	5,210	−669	23,066	62.4
Freeborn	16,715	17,404	−689	732	593	4.4	3.4	891	−122	11,326	−1,973	26,542	71.8
Goodhue	25,217	25,109	108	1,069	756	4.2	3.0	1,407	130	19,027	−577	29,288	79.2
Grant	3,168	3,288	−120	161	157	5.1	4.8	236	36	1,616	206	21,812	59.0
Hennepin	664,469	665,632	−1,163	23,450	17,914	3.5	2.7	40,289	1,152	810,943	−54,425	48,377	130.9
Houston	11,330	10,937	393	485	438	4.3	4.0	464	74	4,633	603	20,913	56.6
Hubbard	9,809	9,139	670	534	441	5.4	4.8	545	−3	4,647	−394	25,155	68.0
Isanti	21,474	17,912	3,562	1,049	606	4.9	3.4	832	82	8,754	1,429	27,093	73.3
Itasca	22,814	21,641	1,173	1,351	1,225	5.9	5.7	1,199	−25	12,929	−976	28,432	76.9
Jackson	6,812	6,140	672	260	184	3.8	3.0	300	−45	3,977	−96	25,400	68.7
Kanabec	7,913	7,913	−	546	373	6.9	4.7	313	24	3,246	−298	26,136	70.7
Kandiyohi	23,673	22,905	768	919	728	3.9	3.2	1,383	84	18,652	−1,782	27,478	74.3
Kittson	2,655	2,575	80	144	138	5.4	5.4	158	−2	1,092	(NA)	20,889	56.5
Koochiching	6,823	7,243	−420	447	371	6.6	5.1	441	−14	4,908	28	27,951	75.6
Lac qui Parle	4,186	4,119	67	157	135	3.8	3.3	224	−54	1,836	−503	24,058	65.1
Lake	6,298	5,915	383	255	243	4.0	4.1	305	22	3,434	391	26,846	72.6
Lake of the Woods	2,402	2,346	56	113	93	4.7	4.0	151	−6	1,284	−18	19,093	51.6
Le Sueur	14,366	14,925	−559	768	564	5.3	3.8	646	−96	6,188	−2,948	27,362	74.0
Lincoln	3,435	3,461	−26	123	121	3.6	3.5	188	15	1,363	(NA)	18,786	50.8
Lyon	14,910	14,650	260	485	417	3.3	2.8	841	75	11,683	−1,559	28,616	77.4
McLeod	21,253	20,257	996	827	655	3.9	3.2	1,000	102	16,516	−77	33,212	89.8
Mahnomen	2,563	2,472	91	141	140	5.5	5.7	112	−22	1,879	(NA)	20,878	56.5
Marshall	5,481	5,193	288	366	403	6.7	7.8	296	−60	1,713	−631	26,946	72.9
Martin	11,220	11,703	−483	482	397	4.3	3.4	683	1	8,216	−262	26,830	72.6
Meeker	12,758	12,310	448	634	518	5.0	4.2	604	−	5,972	100	26,964	72.9
Mille Lacs	12,228	11,853	375	821	520	6.7	4.4	755	129	10,452	983	26,452	71.6
Morrison	17,398	16,676	722	963	761	5.5	4.6	868	31	8,515	−511	23,882	64.6
Mower	20,622	19,941	681	781	557	3.8	2.8	998	86	15,869	2,549	31,689	85.7
Murray	5,724	5,184	540	217	190	3.8	3.7	317	25	2,259	24	22,680	61.4
Nicollet	19,529	18,114	1,415	611	490	3.1	2.7	618	−52	12,328	−1,198	27,091	73.3
Nobles	11,399	11,090	309	356	327	3.1	2.9	647	8	8,641	204	23,067	62.4
Norman	3,673	3,719	−46	183	162	5.0	4.4	212	1	1,533	151	22,550	61.0
Olmsted	80,095	72,625	7,470	2,707	1,921	3.4	2.6	3,362	370	80,397	5,099	38,252	103.5
Otter Tail	30,108	29,296	812	1,433	1,182	4.8	4.0	1,663	94	17,851	−145	24,832	67.2
Pennington	8,545	7,669	876	465	450	5.4	5.9	430	101	7,398	1,538	27,900	75.5
Pine	14,087	13,421	666	893	694	6.3	5.2	621	−22	6,552	1,648	22,384	60.5
Pipestone	5,163	5,406	−243	173	178	3.4	3.3	331	32	3,545	−368	21,383	57.8
Polk	17,291	15,815	1,476	800	754	4.6	4.8	818	−13	9,333	591	23,919	64.7
Pope	6,454	5,861	593	243	169	3.8	2.9	361	54	4,027	817	30,216	81.7
Ramsey	276,503	286,223	−9,720	10,592	8,191	3.8	2.9	14,063	362	301,748	−3,396	42,282	114.4
Red Lake	2,256	2,204	52	153	160	6.8	7.3	109	2	843	−429	22,420	60.6
Redwood	8,263	8,891	−628	334	273	4.0	3.1	564	−66	4,902	−1,041	25,900	70.1
Renville	8,539	9,155	−616	409	354	4.8	3.9	558	−85	5,783	−336	24,257	65.6

See footnotes at end of table.

[Includes United States, states, and 3,141 counties/county equivalents defined as of February 22, 2005. For more information on these areas, see Appendix C, Geographic Information]

County	Civilian labor force							Private nonfarm businesses					
	Total			Number of unemployed		Unemployment rate[1]		Establishments		Employment[2]		Annual payroll per employee, 2004	
	2006	2000	Net change, 2000–2006	2006	2000	2006	2000	2004	Net change, 2000–2004	2004	Net change, 2000–2004	Amount (dol.)	Percent of U.S. average
MINNESOTA—Con.													
Rice	32,481	31,556	925	1,381	969	4.3	3.1	1,503	87	22,894	1,538	26,787	72.5
Rock	5,071	5,236	−165	141	136	2.8	2.6	270	15	2,611	−425	22,186	60.0
Roseau	10,445	9,290	1,155	650	335	6.2	3.6	427	30	8,100	410	28,693	77.6
St. Louis	103,349	103,276	73	5,179	4,444	5.0	4.3	5,639	100	80,028	852	29,520	79.9
Scott	71,171	54,255	16,916	2,495	1,408	3.5	2.6	2,902	690	35,217	4,162	36,031	97.5
Sherburne	47,459	37,835	9,624	2,067	1,136	4.4	3.0	1,763	451	16,920	2,547	29,969	81.1
Sibley	8,982	8,779	203	373	279	4.2	3.2	383	19	2,946	−168	23,996	64.9
Stearns	82,670	78,237	4,433	3,291	2,417	4.0	3.1	4,327	386	72,623	696	29,557	80.0
Steele	20,196	19,474	722	799	556	4.0	2.9	1,047	85	19,272	−1,237	32,894	89.0
Stevens	5,863	5,693	170	195	191	3.3	3.4	349	9	3,794	82	25,525	69.0
Swift	5,463	5,667	−204	245	212	4.5	3.7	316	−4	2,807	−747	23,031	62.3
Todd	12,653	12,364	289	648	471	5.1	3.8	520	−15	4,868	72	23,286	63.0
Traverse	1,976	1,811	165	82	83	4.1	4.6	131	–	855	(NA)	20,235	54.7
Wabasha	12,878	12,298	580	509	355	4.0	2.9	634	−10	6,477	−834	26,054	70.5
Wadena	6,381	6,676	−295	435	335	6.8	5.0	452	139	5,943	1,201	22,120	59.8
Waseca	10,603	10,593	10	434	313	4.1	3.0	509	44	6,465	−543	24,661	66.7
Washington	128,147	117,904	10,243	4,538	2,900	3.5	2.5	5,202	700	64,934	6,925	35,602	96.3
Watonwan	5,736	6,042	−306	251	194	4.4	3.2	338	12	3,981	318	24,100	65.2
Wilkin	3,642	3,691	−49	136	111	3.7	3.0	177	−7	1,744	233	25,068	67.8
Winona	28,794	28,898	−104	1,028	880	3.6	3.0	1,310	3	20,786	−1,953	27,869	75.4
Wright	64,039	52,505	11,534	2,763	1,664	4.3	3.2	2,917	551	28,764	3,097	29,626	80.1
Yellow Medicine	5,737	5,721	16	230	235	4.0	4.1	350	2	3,961	−185	27,823	75.3
MISSISSIPPI	1,307,347	1,314,154	−6,807	88,683	74,295	6.8	5.7	[3]60,534	[3]746	[3]928,313	[3]−28,468	[3]26,734	[3]72.3
Adams	13,204	14,526	−1,322	927	955	7.0	6.6	930	−75	9,851	−1,771	23,583	63.8
Alcorn	15,859	16,683	−824	1,167	851	7.4	5.1	842	−22	12,090	−1,782	25,643	69.4
Amite	5,337	5,547	−210	329	309	6.2	5.6	166	–	1,429	−182	27,726	75.0
Attala	7,528	8,352	−824	600	618	8.0	7.4	386	−15	6,510	498	21,388	57.9
Benton	2,961	3,203	−242	274	217	9.3	6.8	71	8	900	88	25,842	69.9
Bolivar	15,817	16,267	−450	1,347	1,219	8.5	7.5	769	−2	9,317	−1,064	20,913	56.6
Calhoun	6,323	6,937	−614	497	413	7.9	6.0	286	−28	2,834	−448	22,525	60.9
Carroll	4,852	5,033	−181	297	301	6.1	6.0	92	−27	441	−371	16,231	43.9
Chickasaw	7,790	8,790	−1,000	698	492	9.0	5.6	394	−19	6,257	−1,149	22,046	59.6
Choctaw	3,507	4,038	−531	272	315	7.8	7.8	126	−9	1,339	−68	24,861	67.3
Claiborne	3,701	4,289	−588	401	406	10.8	9.5	136	−16	2,067	−331	41,998	113.6
Clarke	7,166	7,632	−466	451	652	6.3	8.5	272	−40	2,307	−1,437	21,251	57.5
Clay	8,274	9,770	−1,496	917	629	11.1	6.4	398	−21	7,336	−649	26,334	71.2
Coahoma	10,694	11,788	−1,094	1,051	945	9.8	8.0	614	−52	8,032	−747	24,962	67.5
Copiah	12,439	12,254	185	870	796	7.0	6.5	440	−18	6,040	33	22,699	61.4
Covington	8,728	8,407	321	508	485	5.8	5.8	323	20	4,499	367	21,210	57.4
DeSoto	71,799	58,900	12,899	2,989	1,478	4.2	2.5	2,127	286	34,590	3,548	26,139	70.7
Forrest	36,968	35,111	1,857	1,943	1,774	5.3	5.1	2,144	11	34,383	713	26,971	73.0
Franklin	3,222	3,447	−225	220	235	6.8	6.8	125	−29	1,202	−196	24,653	66.7
George	8,442	8,405	37	832	665	9.9	7.9	309	5	3,745	798	22,504	60.9
Greene	5,037	4,799	238	385	427	7.6	8.9	130	7	876	8	20,162	54.5
Grenada	9,931	10,549	−618	644	610	6.5	5.8	630	9	9,702	−980	26,068	70.5
Hancock	19,063	19,516	−453	1,941	951	10.2	4.9	810	57	9,978	–	28,785	77.9
Harrison	84,569	90,854	−6,285	9,071	4,384	10.7	4.8	4,537	78	77,751	−2,134	26,359	71.3
Hinds	121,971	122,444	−473	7,015	6,441	5.8	5.3	6,482	−219	117,728	−17,787	31,064	84.0
Holmes	7,275	7,625	−350	774	1,043	10.6	13.7	283	15	2,204	−448	20,249	54.8
Humphreys	4,285	4,253	32	401	413	9.4	9.7	163	−18	1,781	−995	20,318	55.0
Issaquena	742	849	−107	74	90	10.0	10.6	9	−6	33	−65	27,212	73.6
Itawamba	10,556	11,131	−575	669	611	6.3	5.5	355	33	4,381	−51	27,189	73.5
Jackson	59,502	63,505	−4,003	4,837	3,804	8.1	6.0	2,301	−76	40,579	−2,060	31,075	84.1
Jasper	7,700	7,444	256	460	454	6.0	6.1	236	−23	3,163	−617	24,540	66.4
Jefferson	2,751	3,178	−427	359	397	13.0	12.5	62	−16	513	−165	24,244	65.6
Jefferson Davis	5,232	5,447	−215	404	558	7.7	10.2	177	−6	1,425	−196	20,944	56.7
Jones	31,541	29,930	1,611	1,502	1,384	4.8	4.6	1,449	−17	25,534	2,762	26,777	72.4
Kemper	4,226	4,408	−182	354	381	8.4	8.6	129	14	1,142	167	17,956	48.6
Lafayette	22,548	19,749	2,799	1,048	900	4.6	4.6	975	82	11,144	−170	24,684	66.8
Lamar	23,130	20,023	3,107	978	833	4.2	4.2	831	111	9,143	1,436	21,269	57.5
Lauderdale	33,624	34,567	−943	2,162	2,045	6.4	5.9	2,090	−10	31,589	406	25,933	70.2
Lawrence	5,190	5,932	−742	394	475	7.6	8.0	213	−8	2,210	−142	33,831	91.5
Leake	8,407	8,908	−501	573	585	6.8	6.6	314	−27	5,014	−1,013	19,661	53.2
Lee	38,559	39,841	−1,282	2,313	1,834	6.0	4.6	2,386	139	43,148	−6,248	31,008	83.9
Leflore	13,982	14,629	−647	1,233	1,346	8.8	9.2	811	−49	12,825	−222	24,008	64.9
Lincoln	14,527	14,719	−192	880	832	6.1	5.7	779	−18	10,999	245	24,153	65.3
Lowndes	26,288	27,660	−1,372	1,783	1,606	6.8	5.8	1,614	−18	23,049	−1,668	27,400	74.1
Madison	44,140	39,319	4,821	2,075	1,703	4.7	4.3	2,307	350	41,082	13,551	30,451	82.4
Marion	10,376	10,643	−267	679	664	6.5	6.2	582	−10	6,593	−120	21,731	58.8
Marshall	15,284	15,256	28	1,188	663	7.8	4.3	440	5	6,708	−464	20,730	56.1
Monroe	16,804	17,712	−908	1,503	1,301	8.9	7.3	717	−3	10,177	−21	27,927	75.5
Montgomery	4,687	5,337	−650	427	350	9.1	6.6	254	7	2,559	−711	21,851	59.1
Neshoba	14,641	13,355	1,286	731	742	5.0	5.6	562	11	10,178	1,724	31,539	85.3

See footnotes at end of table.

County and City Data Book: 2007

U.S. Census Bureau

[Includes United States, states, and 3,141 counties/county equivalents defined as of February 22, 2005. For more information on these areas, see Appendix C, Geographic Information]

County	Civilian labor force							Private nonfarm businesses					
	Total			Number of unemployed		Unemployment rate[1]		Establishments		Employment[2]		Annual payroll per employee, 2004	
	2006	2000	Net change, 2000–2006	2006	2000	2006	2000	2004	Net change, 2000–2004	2004	Net change, 2000–2004	Amount (dol.)	Percent of U.S. average
MISSISSIPPI—Con.													
Newton	9,612	9,847	−235	564	571	5.9	5.8	398	24	4,736	20	21,917	59.3
Noxubee	4,303	4,729	−426	488	436	11.3	9.2	225	−1	2,854	411	18,911	51.2
Oktibbeha	20,277	20,734	−457	1,154	1,105	5.7	5.3	825	12	11,125	459	19,308	52.2
Panola	15,171	14,738	433	1,181	1,070	7.8	7.3	641	−4	8,886	−324	23,934	64.7
Pearl River	20,328	21,258	−930	1,336	1,119	6.6	5.3	802	42	7,781	−10	19,773	53.5
Perry	5,290	5,193	97	353	333	6.7	6.4	166	15	1,555	−397	32,476	87.9
Pike	15,727	16,088	−361	1,039	1,062	6.6	6.6	992	2	13,671	−242	21,665	58.6
Pontotoc	13,413	13,665	−252	800	648	6.0	4.7	495	22	11,545	1,896	24,316	65.8
Prentiss	11,344	12,279	−935	821	654	7.2	5.3	520	−14	7,479	−465	22,200	60.1
Quitman	3,956	4,033	−77	339	304	8.6	7.5	128	−16	1,104	−32	23,048	62.3
Rankin	71,876	63,330	8,546	2,974	2,364	4.1	3.7	2,973	463	46,465	6,639	29,042	78.6
Scott	13,495	12,737	758	736	624	5.5	4.9	524	18	9,272	−211	23,768	64.3
Sharkey	2,501	2,644	−143	248	270	9.9	10.2	142	16	912	115	20,372	55.1
Simpson	11,989	11,857	132	668	597	5.6	5.0	455	34	6,127	1,360	18,137	49.1
Smith	6,866	7,335	−469	383	363	5.6	4.9	171	−29	2,395	−785	26,286	71.1
Stone	6,308	6,575	−267	550	381	8.7	5.8	277	−15	3,116	749	24,451	66.1
Sunflower	11,464	12,136	−672	1,066	1,123	9.3	9.3	451	−54	5,970	−1,432	22,029	59.6
Tallahatchie	6,238	6,041	197	483	512	7.7	8.5	197	12	1,834	371	22,228	60.1
Tate	11,960	11,708	252	797	443	6.7	3.8	391	−23	4,516	−1,060	22,573	61.1
Tippah	9,597	9,810	−213	659	576	6.9	5.9	387	−10	7,531	407	22,471	60.8
Tishomingo	8,214	8,943	−729	608	654	7.4	7.3	401	−13	4,928	−326	23,974	64.9
Tunica	4,424	4,036	388	362	211	8.2	5.2	225	26	14,534	−4,033	25,125	68.0
Union	11,816	12,522	−706	710	578	6.0	4.6	501	38	7,621	−2,488	24,213	65.5
Walthall	5,825	6,324	−499	392	448	6.7	7.1	231	3	2,405	−241	18,638	50.4
Warren	22,733	24,355	−1,622	1,352	1,279	5.9	5.3	1,154	−35	20,202	−1,668	28,197	76.3
Washington	22,459	26,061	−3,602	2,199	2,087	9.8	8.0	1,400	−108	18,515	−2,498	23,088	62.5
Wayne	8,495	8,826	−331	541	589	6.4	6.7	395	4	5,074	93	25,255	68.3
Webster	3,498	4,694	−1,196	288	241	8.2	5.1	185	−12	1,648	−1,118	21,322	57.7
Wilkinson	3,541	3,530	11	291	312	8.2	8.8	166	−4	1,661	−22	22,357	60.5
Winston	7,963	8,689	−726	559	614	7.0	7.1	379	−18	5,278	−121	25,113	67.9
Yalobusha	5,432	5,745	−313	415	349	7.6	6.1	218	−27	2,616	−128	28,152	76.2
Yazoo	10,060	10,735	−675	884	798	8.8	7.4	424	−15	4,353	−1,209	23,157	62.6
MISSOURI	3,032,434	2,973,092	59,342	146,577	97,756	4.8	3.3	[3]153,985	[3]9,230	[3]2,421,450	[3]22,471	[3]32,690	[3]88.4
Adair	13,363	13,296	67	584	393	4.4	3.0	722	95	8,326	−453	22,687	61.4
Andrew	10,080	8,948	1,132	406	260	4.0	2.9	262	20	1,622	−661	19,872	53.8
Atchison	3,090	3,377	−287	125	84	4.0	2.5	245	38	1,596	104	19,125	51.7
Audrain	11,807	12,780	−973	540	385	4.6	3.0	607	−35	7,204	−1,201	25,027	67.7
Barry	17,244	16,770	474	718	550	4.2	3.3	873	59	14,185	305	28,560	77.3
Barton	5,956	6,575	−619	317	174	5.3	2.6	294	7	4,797	285	21,595	58.4
Bates	8,060	8,257	−197	449	290	5.6	3.5	424	34	3,095	42	19,356	52.4
Benton	8,281	7,499	782	467	382	5.6	5.1	430	11	2,824	404	17,109	46.3
Bollinger	5,990	6,028	−38	320	249	5.3	4.1	222	11	1,370	−3	18,764	50.8
Boone	87,450	79,950	7,500	2,827	1,743	3.2	2.2	4,112	309	63,209	702	28,620	77.4
Buchanan	46,744	42,954	3,790	2,122	1,444	4.5	3.4	2,537	202	38,833	1,752	29,178	78.9
Butler	21,213	19,151	2,062	1,162	889	5.5	4.6	1,352	309	16,431	1,359	23,143	62.6
Caldwell	4,475	4,516	−41	232	144	5.2	3.2	176	−8	975	−29	23,273	63.0
Callaway	22,696	22,077	619	979	605	4.3	2.7	707	28	10,472	−285	29,093	78.7
Camden	21,579	19,139	2,440	1,034	766	4.8	4.0	1,501	−98	12,869	−739	24,071	65.1
Cape Girardeau	39,085	38,876	209	1,586	1,148	4.1	3.0	2,423	102	37,274	680	26,977	73.0
Carroll	5,163	5,083	80	244	160	4.7	3.1	242	−3	1,881	−122	20,781	56.2
Carter	2,895	2,535	360	174	139	6.0	5.5	170	32	1,094	329	18,629	50.4
Cass	49,588	45,465	4,123	2,247	1,204	4.5	2.6	1,959	178	18,246	2,763	23,445	63.4
Cedar	6,185	5,925	260	326	210	5.3	3.5	419	105	2,615	−72	21,296	57.6
Chariton	3,950	4,353	−403	206	155	5.2	3.6	227	25	1,135	−559	21,592	58.4
Christian	38,518	31,026	7,492	1,426	837	3.7	2.7	1,429	224	11,819	653	21,596	58.4
Clark	3,582	3,862	−280	182	134	5.1	3.5	142	−4	915	−35	20,268	54.8
Clay	113,465	108,441	5,024	4,848	2,538	4.3	2.3	4,906	217	86,517	1,924	35,618	96.4
Clinton	10,507	10,093	414	506	288	4.8	2.9	462	40	4,127	694	20,901	56.5
Cole	40,362	40,216	146	1,517	1,008	3.8	2.5	2,362	174	36,671	−578	29,516	79.8
Cooper	8,940	8,175	765	388	258	4.3	3.2	468	43	4,904	1,053	18,935	51.2
Crawford	11,827	11,140	687	691	477	5.8	4.3	596	103	4,813	−339	24,119	65.2
Dade	3,817	3,791	26	182	128	4.8	3.4	163	12	1,387	157	21,803	59.0
Dallas	7,694	7,259	435	385	308	5.0	4.2	264	−9	2,519	−267	15,145	41.0
Daviess	4,013	3,959	54	181	122	4.5	3.1	183	−1	997	−126	22,062	59.7
DeKalb	5,236	5,002	234	279	169	5.3	3.4	209	17	1,141	−351	21,973	59.4
Dent	6,455	6,838	−383	390	320	6.0	4.7	390	49	3,402	−444	25,059	67.8
Douglas	5,853	6,112	−259	322	269	5.5	4.4	206	11	2,025	−20	17,711	47.9
Dunklin	14,067	14,701	−634	1,031	648	7.3	4.4	837	80	8,060	−67	19,653	53.2

See footnotes at end of table.

Table B-10. Counties — **Labor Force and Private Business Establishments and Employment**—Con.

[Includes United States, states, and 3,141 counties/county equivalents defined as of February 22, 2005. For more information on these areas, see Appendix C, Geographic Information]

County	Civilian labor force							Private nonfarm businesses					
	Total			Number of unemployed		Unemployment rate[1]		Establishments		Employment[2]		Annual payroll per employee, 2004	
	2006	2000	Net change, 2000–2006	2006	2000	2006	2000	2004	Net change, 2000–2004	2004	Net change, 2000–2004	Amount (dol.)	Percent of U.S. average
MISSOURI—Con.													
Franklin	53,155	51,752	1,403	2,773	1,765	5.2	3.4	2,716	297	33,054	1,233	27,419	74.2
Gasconade	7,984	7,891	93	441	259	5.5	3.3	497	62	4,396	-302	22,946	62.1
Gentry	3,292	3,341	-49	140	100	4.3	3.0	188	-17	1,613	-174	21,128	57.2
Greene	141,445	133,853	7,592	5,213	3,630	3.7	2.7	8,029	376	143,947	6,818	27,202	73.6
Grundy	4,687	5,214	-527	223	162	4.8	3.1	258	-4	2,485	-1,492	21,645	58.6
Harrison	4,464	4,517	-53	213	134	4.8	3.0	237	-9	2,084	-99	18,855	51.0
Henry	10,548	11,059	-511	557	385	5.3	3.5	686	49	6,936	-431	26,522	71.7
Hickory	3,342	3,347	-5	236	192	7.1	5.7	177	23	745	51	17,188	46.5
Holt	2,650	2,744	-94	109	81	4.1	3.0	132	-	801	-124	24,079	65.1
Howard	5,525	5,437	88	237	159	4.3	2.9	205	-4	1,749	-72	19,482	52.7
Howell	19,346	18,072	1,274	838	668	4.3	3.7	1,098	80	12,966	-473	22,215	60.1
Iron	4,844	4,794	50	274	260	5.7	5.4	677	430	2,315	119	21,416	57.9
Jackson	341,598	351,797	-10,199	19,248	11,930	5.6	3.4	18,292	290	354,979	-21,207	36,603	99.0
Jasper	56,019	54,745	1,274	2,366	1,721	4.2	3.1	3,300	221	51,771	-3,502	28,431	76.9
Jefferson	117,240	111,902	5,338	5,651	3,403	4.8	3.0	3,898	405	37,762	2,083	25,514	69.0
Johnson	25,941	24,327	1,614	1,064	775	4.1	3.2	924	82	9,461	-489	25,876	70.0
Knox	2,289	2,136	153	92	72	4.0	3.4	127	13	742	85	19,449	52.6
Laclede	17,000	16,507	493	822	600	4.8	3.6	873	37	11,690	-405	24,046	65.0
Lafayette	16,972	17,748	-776	798	546	4.7	3.1	843	45	7,225	138	20,369	55.1
Lawrence	18,882	17,956	926	746	561	4.0	3.1	703	60	7,080	401	24,686	66.8
Lewis	5,791	5,740	51	217	178	3.7	3.1	222	-11	2,110	83	18,646	50.4
Lincoln	24,944	20,966	3,978	1,322	660	5.3	3.1	880	120	8,769	1,847	27,938	75.6
Linn	6,430	6,987	-557	431	347	6.7	5.0	427	90	4,472	-63	23,463	63.5
Livingston	6,852	7,311	-459	303	196	4.4	2.7	435	-18	5,009	-193	23,105	62.5
McDonald	12,419	10,957	1,462	467	368	3.8	3.4	348	9	5,168	323	22,154	59.9
Macon	8,045	8,321	-276	395	339	4.9	4.1	414	38	3,513	-411	21,067	57.0
Madison	5,856	5,440	416	322	257	5.5	4.7	270	1	2,699	235	18,675	50.5
Maries	4,773	4,602	171	219	164	4.6	3.6	163	28	1,288	224	21,152	57.2
Marion	14,075	14,585	-510	700	552	5.0	3.8	939	132	12,371	215	23,814	64.4
Mercer	1,799	1,931	-132	79	53	4.4	2.7	83	4	381	-52	22,837	61.8
Miller	13,160	12,457	703	688	530	5.2	4.3	796	224	6,765	936	23,150	62.6
Mississippi	5,758	6,019	-261	385	309	6.7	5.1	295	8	2,560	-180	19,829	53.6
Moniteau	7,593	7,548	45	349	224	4.6	3.0	362	25	3,117	-5	20,897	56.5
Monroe	4,275	4,764	-489	234	175	5.5	3.7	228	10	2,177	-1	21,453	58.0
Montgomery	6,170	6,246	-76	339	206	5.5	3.3	316	-25	2,416	-434	22,016	59.6
Morgan	9,251	9,300	-49	625	371	6.8	4.0	525	12	3,534	104	17,684	47.8
New Madrid	8,481	9,192	-711	567	438	6.7	4.8	349	-4	4,136	-2,224	30,508	82.5
Newton	28,489	27,930	559	1,267	1,015	4.4	3.6	1,090	88	16,565	492	26,635	72.1
Nodaway	12,244	12,030	214	427	278	3.5	2.3	528	22	7,499	527	23,589	63.8
Oregon	4,253	4,338	-85	213	166	5.0	3.8	226	15	1,686	-9	17,576	47.5
Osage	7,552	7,462	90	340	273	4.5	3.7	295	35	2,886	203	23,828	64.5
Ozark	4,353	4,329	24	209	179	4.8	4.1	164	-15	986	-20	16,490	44.6
Pemiscot	7,925	8,210	-285	546	450	6.9	5.5	404	59	4,654	129	20,306	54.9
Perry	10,222	10,012	210	365	255	3.6	2.5	498	15	8,186	-242	26,924	72.8
Pettis	19,994	20,551	-557	1,033	682	5.2	3.3	1,086	41	17,578	-88	25,637	69.4
Phelps	21,849	19,717	2,132	971	666	4.4	3.4	1,193	107	14,668	2,397	23,001	62.2
Pike	8,707	8,600	107	464	300	5.3	3.5	424	17	4,507	697	23,319	63.1
Platte	48,157	45,591	2,566	1,878	989	3.9	2.2	2,142	282	38,275	2,509	32,978	89.2
Polk	14,411	13,261	1,150	626	391	4.3	2.9	665	72	7,517	-155	19,607	53.0
Pulaski	17,947	14,880	3,067	898	735	5.0	4.9	781	117	7,363	1,684	20,729	56.1
Putnam	2,493	2,447	46	126	77	5.1	3.1	107	9	626	-31	18,911	51.2
Ralls	5,399	5,542	-143	269	195	5.0	3.5	177	10	1,779	-700	30,754	83.2
Randolph	12,838	12,010	828	642	449	5.0	3.7	674	95	8,930	1,364	24,078	65.1
Ray	12,021	12,230	-209	608	422	5.1	3.5	395	-11	3,607	-114	20,602	55.7
Reynolds	2,476	2,713	-237	173	191	7.0	7.0	172	13	1,571	-24	22,877	61.9
Ripley	6,430	5,647	783	379	279	5.9	4.9	271	26	2,693	735	15,686	42.4
St. Charles	188,991	168,690	20,301	7,327	4,017	3.9	2.4	7,313	1,059	117,026	21,492	31,770	85.9
St. Clair	4,256	4,351	-95	246	164	5.8	3.8	224	39	1,612	249	17,511	47.4
Ste. Genevieve	9,613	9,407	206	452	295	4.7	3.1	402	24	4,913	-371	27,974	75.7
St. Francois	27,597	25,352	2,245	1,654	1,383	6.0	5.5	1,419	136	19,749	3,172	21,464	58.1
St. Louis	542,763	563,110	-20,347	25,194	15,961	4.6	2.8	29,951	-210	570,526	-16,322	38,848	105.1
Saline	11,608	12,512	-904	548	356	4.7	2.8	579	23	7,048	-600	24,256	65.6
Schuyler	2,261	2,153	108	119	93	5.3	4.3	114	23	413	27	18,063	48.9
Scotland	2,412	2,567	-155	104	72	4.3	2.8	163	28	790	-64	18,732	50.7
Scott	20,079	20,361	-282	1,088	874	5.4	4.3	1,256	164	15,882	2,251	24,196	65.5
Shannon	3,639	3,768	-129	241	200	6.6	5.3	167	28	1,088	-188	17,694	47.9
Shelby	3,143	3,618	-475	165	163	5.2	4.5	200	17	1,262	-141	20,340	55.0
Stoddard	15,461	14,621	840	895	604	5.8	4.1	733	28	9,427	757	21,448	58.0
Stone	15,878	14,428	1,450	1,053	865	6.6	6.0	690	55	5,070	-223	21,580	58.4
Sullivan	3,280	3,661	-381	186	108	5.7	3.0	182	65	2,015	-243	23,979	64.9

See footnotes at end of table.

Labor Force and Private Business Establishments and Employment—Con.

[Includes United States, states, and 3,141 counties/county equivalents defined as of February 22, 2005. For more information on these areas, see Appendix C, Geographic Information]

County	Civilian labor force							Private nonfarm businesses					
	Total			Number of unemployed		Unemployment rate[1]		Establishments		Employment[2]		Annual payroll per employee, 2004	
	2006	2000	Net change, 2000–2006	2006	2000	2006	2000	2004	Net change, 2000–2004	2004	Net change, 2000–2004	Amount (dol.)	Percent of U.S. average
MISSOURI—Con.													
Taney	25,424	23,145	2,279	1,743	1,491	6.9	6.4	1,716	−13	19,201	−867	24,569	66.5
Texas	10,396	10,519	−123	593	518	5.7	4.9	514	29	4,306	−516	21,394	57.9
Vernon	9,845	10,258	−413	449	286	4.6	2.8	621	129	5,420	−424	23,407	63.3
Warren	15,620	13,720	1,900	828	429	5.3	3.1	588	32	6,406	439	24,234	65.6
Washington	10,099	10,041	58	795	562	7.9	5.6	382	63	2,881	−45	19,216	52.0
Wayne	5,557	5,316	241	365	280	6.6	5.3	295	43	1,632	−434	17,934	48.5
Webster	17,239	15,311	1,928	717	505	4.2	3.3	700	78	5,288	−54	23,474	63.5
Worth	1,126	1,179	−53	44	41	3.9	3.5	61	2	240	5	16,213	43.9
Wright	8,001	8,205	−204	418	358	5.2	4.4	430	52	3,734	−36	19,782	53.5
Independent City													
St. Louis city	158,275	163,640	−5,365	10,847	8,501	6.9	5.2	10,407	769	274,157	10,579	40,372	109.2
MONTANA	493,842	468,865	24,977	15,680	22,313	3.2	4.8	[3]34,686	[3]2,837	[3]314,865	[3]18,645	[3]26,288	[3]71.1
Beaverhead	4,946	5,028	−82	140	205	2.8	4.1	373	8	2,277	151	19,973	54.0
Big Horn	5,059	5,446	−387	314	513	6.2	9.4	223	15	2,047	17	28,736	77.7
Blaine	2,819	2,978	−159	89	162	3.2	5.4	149	−17	927	−53	26,283	71.1
Broadwater	2,261	2,236	25	68	99	3.0	4.4	107	−3	657	−137	23,099	62.5
Carbon	5,380	4,994	386	150	220	2.8	4.4	395	89	2,058	102	18,950	51.3
Carter	657	775	−118	21	27	3.2	3.5	32	5	138	12	17,399	47.1
Cascade	38,976	38,331	645	1,222	1,889	3.1	4.9	2,541	−23	28,868	1,110	24,528	66.3
Chouteau	2,533	2,805	−272	66	102	2.6	3.6	168	14	816	66	17,266	46.7
Custer	5,551	5,988	−437	171	267	3.1	4.5	410	19	3,774	−131	23,519	63.6
Daniels	736	974	−238	23	43	3.1	4.4	77	−4	507	−18	25,531	69.1
Dawson	4,119	4,767	−648	113	190	2.7	4.0	300	−14	2,872	395	19,223	52.0
Deer Lodge	3,844	4,246	−402	176	298	4.6	7.0	238	−1	2,179	−155	23,677	64.0
Fallon	1,731	1,547	184	32	56	1.8	3.6	123	5	795	127	26,127	70.7
Fergus	5,662	6,117	−455	219	313	3.9	5.1	424	−24	3,226	167	22,293	60.3
Flathead	43,700	39,331	4,369	1,560	2,064	3.6	5.2	3,774	575	31,219	3,090	26,608	72.0
Gallatin[5]	53,930	41,446	12,484	1,073	1,524	2.0	3.7	4,277	866	33,115	5,080	26,423	71.5
Garfield	636	706	−70	21	29	3.3	4.1	29	4	158	34	14,620	39.5
Glacier	5,801	5,720	81	369	465	6.4	8.1	276	−6	2,037	−24	29,782	80.6
Golden Valley	512	547	−35	18	29	3.5	5.3	17	4	61	−2	16,164	43.7
Granite	1,255	1,355	−100	52	83	4.1	6.1	82	−6	421	−84	20,290	54.9
Hill	7,880	8,008	−128	280	391	3.6	4.9	516	13	4,650	−99	21,041	56.9
Jefferson	5,665	5,377	288	190	254	3.4	4.7	230	36	1,651	270	27,385	74.1
Judith Basin	1,047	1,182	−135	33	53	3.2	4.5	58	7	183	26	16,415	44.4
Lake	11,310	12,321	−1,011	511	671	4.5	5.4	762	76	5,240	−668	23,215	62.8
Lewis and Clark	31,169	31,221	−52	928	1,257	3.0	4.0	2,060	99	22,041	1,059	26,657	72.1
Liberty	809	962	−153	25	39	3.1	4.1	71	−5	420	−114	21,240	57.5
Lincoln	7,585	7,885	−300	484	656	6.4	8.3	606	38	3,799	−82	22,051	59.6
McCone	996	1,103	−107	24	40	2.4	3.6	57	9	347	−9	23,510	63.6
Madison	4,322	3,530	792	115	164	2.7	4.6	346	80	1,343	192	24,231	65.5
Meagher	872	993	−121	37	57	4.2	5.7	69	1	281	−11	19,302	52.2
Mineral	1,971	1,888	83	89	121	4.5	6.4	140	17	947	112	19,328	52.3
Missoula	58,414	54,251	4,163	1,698	2,207	2.9	4.1	4,004	381	46,409	5,092	26,556	71.8
Musselshell	2,039	2,095	−56	75	125	3.7	6.0	136	10	699	115	18,009	48.7
Park[5]	9,310	9,045	265	279	460	3.0	5.1	765	26	4,462	18	22,362	60.5
Petroleum	220	252	−32	9	17	4.1	6.7	12	4	23	8	11,043	29.9
Phillips	2,051	2,323	−272	73	102	3.6	4.4	151	−	807	5	19,473	52.7
Pondera	2,692	2,981	−289	101	140	3.8	4.7	179	−16	1,250	−73	23,386	63.3
Powder River	889	1,002	−113	26	37	2.9	3.7	67	−1	242	52	14,562	39.4
Powell	2,630	2,887	−257	123	167	4.7	5.8	154	6	1,097	−46	20,611	55.8
Prairie	552	616	−64	20	31	3.6	5.0	31	−	117	−58	23,453	63.4
Ravalli	18,443	17,094	1,349	716	896	3.9	5.2	1,374	172	8,037	561	22,551	61.0
Richland	5,023	4,978	45	126	261	2.5	5.2	411	17	3,260	174	25,448	68.8
Roosevelt	3,849	4,263	−414	216	299	5.6	7.0	213	−23	1,615	−200	19,985	54.1
Rosebud	3,859	4,282	−423	197	252	5.1	5.9	188	−2	2,630	−41	34,818	94.2
Sanders	4,676	4,405	271	224	300	4.8	6.8	371	24	2,208	311	20,961	56.7
Sheridan	1,704	2,017	−313	49	89	2.9	4.4	145	−2	889	10	17,756	48.0
Silver Bow	17,132	17,186	−54	596	983	3.5	5.7	1,088	−42	12,466	51	27,598	74.7
Stillwater	4,394	4,423	−29	114	199	2.6	4.5	251	21	2,900	486	42,370	114.6
Sweet Grass	2,801	1,989	812	43	61	1.5	3.1	163	29	701	57	21,174	57.3
Teton	2,973	2,978	−5	87	128	2.9	4.3	195	−1	1,053	−24	23,592	63.8
Toole	2,462	2,528	−66	62	102	2.5	4.0	208	−1	1,588	37	23,743	64.2
Treasure	389	458	−69	12	21	3.1	4.6	25	1	92	−	17,457	47.2
Valley	3,540	3,848	−308	109	167	3.1	4.3	277	20	1,968	195	20,128	54.4
Wheatland	995	1,122	−127	28	52	2.8	4.6	60	2	323	12	16,146	43.7
Wibaux	502	550	−48	13	23	2.6	4.2	28	1	149	−10	20,477	55.4
Yellowstone	78,575	71,492	7,083	2,074	2,917	2.6	4.1	5,166	276	59,966	1,100	29,294	79.2
Yellowstone National Park[5]	(X)	(X)	(NA)	(X)	(X)	(X)	(X)	(X)	(NA)	(X)	(NA)	(NA)	(NA)

See footnotes at end of table.

[Includes United States, states, and 3,141 counties/county equivalents defined as of February 22, 2005. For more information on these areas, see Appendix C, Geographic Information]

County	Civilian labor force							Private nonfarm businesses					
	Total			Number of unemployed		Unemployment rate[1]		Establishments		Employment[2]		Annual payroll per employee, 2004	
	2006	2000	Net change, 2000–2006	2006	2000	2006	2000	2004	Net change, 2000–2004	2004	Net change, 2000–2004	Amount (dol.)	Percent of U.S. average
NEBRASKA............	974,476	949,762	24,714	29,206	26,564	3.0	2.8	[3]50,928	[3]1,305	[3]774,311	[3]23,235	[3]30,584	[3]82.7
Adams..................	16,666	17,332	−666	482	439	2.9	2.5	970	4	13,252	−969	25,832	69.9
Antelope	3,826	3,996	−170	106	107	2.8	2.7	231	−17	1,396	−120	20,777	56.2
Arthur	265	273	−8	9	6	3.4	2.2	10	−6	22	−41	13,227	35.8
Banner	390	429	−39	9	12	2.3	2.8	4	−2	17	(NA)	24,706	66.8
Blaine	268	321	−53	8	11	3.0	3.4	8	−4	21	−20	10,905	29.5
Boone	3,124	3,241	−117	81	77	2.6	2.4	194	−12	1,372	−134	21,278	57.6
Box Butte.............	5,600	6,454	−854	168	251	3.0	3.9	354	−14	3,027	−348	21,604	58.4
Boyd	1,170	1,261	−91	36	36	3.1	2.9	78	−	413	−18	16,029	43.4
Brown	1,894	1,927	−33	54	61	2.9	3.2	142	−4	813	−69	17,843	48.3
Buffalo................	27,430	25,034	2,396	614	576	2.2	2.3	1,415	120	20,781	1,053	26,027	70.4
Burt...................	3,833	4,147	−314	154	149	4.0	3.6	210	−12	1,058	−248	20,528	55.5
Butler	4,702	4,722	−20	128	129	2.7	2.7	198	14	1,932	152	23,040	62.3
Cass	14,108	13,628	480	451	382	3.2	2.8	523	4	3,718	−281	24,015	65.0
Cedar	4,970	5,063	−93	111	120	2.2	2.4	308	27	1,625	−145	20,824	56.3
Chase	2,096	2,126	−30	48	48	2.3	2.3	145	3	1,049	61	23,404	63.3
Cherry.................	3,655	3,539	116	81	89	2.2	2.5	211	−19	1,843	257	17,311	46.8
Cheyenne	5,282	5,682	−400	124	129	2.3	2.3	318	9	4,678	369	33,290	90.1
Clay	3,167	3,659	−492	95	105	3.0	2.9	190	−10	1,156	−123	23,529	63.6
Colfax	5,759	5,709	50	133	119	2.3	2.1	258	−9	3,842	91	23,906	64.7
Cuming	5,257	5,703	−446	149	124	2.8	2.2	357	−1	3,002	−299	23,754	64.3
Custer.................	6,140	6,219	−79	145	152	2.4	2.4	373	4	2,704	120	22,378	60.5
Dakota	10,482	10,916	−434	299	353	2.9	3.2	428	−14	9,543	−1,343	29,653	80.2
Dawes.................	4,648	5,086	−438	130	152	2.8	3.0	296	4	2,362	219	16,915	45.8
Dawson	12,468	12,399	69	388	375	3.1	3.0	688	2	9,836	−214	24,236	65.6
Deuel	1,054	1,180	−126	29	34	2.8	2.9	71	−10	461	−69	20,631	55.8
Dixon..................	3,145	3,360	−215	79	87	2.5	2.6	128	2	1,579	875	27,987	75.7
Dodge	19,717	19,858	−141	670	607	3.4	3.1	1,042	−26	14,822	−467	25,028	67.7
Douglas	267,301	259,962	7,339	9,003	7,890	3.4	3.0	14,427	269	303,032	−2,728	36,306	98.2
Dundy	1,069	1,213	−144	33	25	3.1	2.1	66	−6	431	−22	21,153	57.2
Fillmore	3,334	3,532	−198	89	89	2.7	2.5	221	−6	1,583	−291	23,510	63.6
Franklin	1,841	1,822	19	56	47	3.0	2.6	90	−6	527	9	19,712	53.3
Frontier	1,792	1,751	41	40	42	2.2	2.4	88	7	555	36	20,432	55.3
Furnas	2,469	2,651	−182	74	71	3.0	2.7	185	1	1,215	−100	22,798	61.7
Gage..................	12,803	12,679	124	466	375	3.6	3.0	675	−11	7,781	−407	22,911	62.0
Garden	1,021	1,222	−201	30	31	2.9	2.5	57	−4	415	28	18,280	49.4
Garfield	1,051	1,020	31	27	24	2.6	2.4	92	3	512	−43	16,777	45.4
Gosper	1,079	1,148	−69	30	30	2.8	2.6	56	5	202	8	18,980	51.3
Grant..................	411	441	−30	10	10	2.4	2.3	29	7	85	5	16,059	43.4
Greeley	1,345	1,410	−65	40	40	3.0	2.8	80	−3	408	−13	17,390	47.0
Hall	30,372	29,028	1,344	928	847	3.1	2.9	1,865	41	27,541	−225	26,452	71.6
Hamilton	5,433	5,162	271	121	120	2.2	2.3	280	6	2,466	−129	26,348	71.3
Harlan	1,764	1,931	−167	44	48	2.5	2.5	97	−7	580	−4	17,438	47.2
Hayes	502	589	−87	15	20	3.0	3.4	17	−5	46	−33	27,435	74.2
Hitchcock	1,489	1,547	−58	51	40	3.4	2.6	63	−	370	63	21,043	56.9
Holt...................	6,165	6,289	−124	167	160	2.7	2.5	426	−	3,063	142	20,378	55.1
Hooker................	463	452	11	14	14	3.0	3.1	32	−	162	−11	17,852	48.3
Howard	3,717	3,572	145	104	91	2.8	2.5	147	−8	856	40	19,791	53.5
Jefferson	4,366	4,390	−24	139	135	3.2	3.1	251	8	2,426	−166	23,351	63.2
Johnson...............	3,289	2,516	773	97	153	2.9	6.1	124	−8	1,148	363	22,612	61.2
Kearney...............	3,948	3,761	187	89	78	2.3	2.1	188	1	1,694	136	20,733	56.1
Keith	4,694	4,898	−204	124	131	2.6	2.7	358	−15	2,793	−182	21,980	59.5
Koya Paha	430	501	−71	13	12	3.0	2.4	20	4	58	22	16,948	45.8
Kimball	2,065	2,207	−142	55	52	2.7	2.4	157	−4	1,305	−114	21,027	56.9
Knox...................	4,847	4,834	13	141	177	2.9	3.7	266	−9	1,526	103	16,951	45.9
Lancaster..............	156,396	149,092	7,304	4,321	3,550	2.8	2.4	7,563	436	132,717	6,331	30,244	81.8
Lincoln................	21,138	18,480	2,658	584	583	2.8	3.2	1,016	32	11,609	1,468	21,201	57.4
Logan	450	420	30	10	10	2.2	2.4	20	4	66	11	18,576	50.2
Loup	357	337	20	13	8	3.6	2.4	8	−1	21	(NA)	11,667	31.6
McPherson............	295	275	20	7	5	2.4	1.8	8	1	14	−1	8,357	22.6
Madison...............	19,890	19,368	522	707	626	3.6	3.2	1,362	42	21,435	2,121	27,116	73.4
Merrick	4,349	4,307	42	149	114	3.4	2.6	242	10	1,589	−338	22,861	61.8
Morrill	2,802	2,812	−10	72	96	2.6	3.4	114	−8	799	20	20,740	56.1
Nance	2,038	2,072	−34	56	61	2.7	2.9	99	−8	448	−52	18,482	50.0
Nemaha................	3,607	3,792	−185	137	149	3.8	3.9	208	4	1,823	72	24,631	66.6
Nuckolls...............	2,358	2,589	−231	63	65	2.7	2.5	176	−8	1,222	−42	18,262	49.4
Otoe	8,669	8,361	308	273	256	3.1	3.1	445	5	4,946	190	23,571	63.8
Pawnee	1,623	1,644	−21	49	56	3.0	3.4	74	−6	558	107	20,020	54.2
Perkins	1,590	1,653	−63	36	36	2.3	2.2	112	11	794	59	22,569	61.1
Phelps	5,231	5,392	−161	115	116	2.2	2.2	346	23	3,780	−59	26,054	70.5
Pierce	4,168	4,237	−69	115	109	2.8	2.6	213	−10	1,466	−165	20,405	55.2

See footnotes at end of table.

County and City Data Book: 2007

U.S. Census Bureau

Table B-10. Counties — **Labor Force and Private Business Establishments and Employment**—Con.

[Includes United States, states, and 3,141 counties/county equivalents defined as of February 22, 2005. For more information on these areas, see Appendix C, Geographic Information]

County	Civilian labor force							Private nonfarm businesses					
	Total			Number of unemployed		Unemployment rate[1]		Establishments		Employment[2]		Annual payroll per employee, 2004	
	2006	2000	Net change, 2000–2006	2006	2000	2006	2000	2004	Net change, 2000–2004	2004	Net change, 2000–2004	Amount (dol.)	Percent of U.S. average
NEBRASKA—Con.													
Platte	17,502	17,558	−56	478	485	2.7	2.8	999	6	14,275	−1,434	26,652	72.1
Polk	3,023	3,051	−28	81	66	2.7	2.2	138	−9	1,043	105	21,994	59.5
Red Willow	5,992	6,215	−223	161	158	2.7	2.5	429	−10	3,971	−307	20,500	55.5
Richardson	4,351	4,746	−395	167	234	3.8	4.9	266	−26	1,949	−307	19,130	51.7
Rock	945	1,017	−72	23	27	2.4	2.7	61	1	270	−91	19,974	54.0
Saline	8,170	7,670	500	221	195	2.7	2.5	297	−16	6,094	545	27,438	74.2
Sarpy	73,716	66,308	7,408	2,081	1,526	2.8	2.3	2,672	376	37,109	9,576	31,119	84.2
Saunders	11,219	11,125	94	330	316	2.9	2.8	464	8	3,235	−76	24,656	66.7
Scotts Bluff	19,078	18,862	216	626	748	3.3	4.0	1,219	4	13,799	508	24,856	67.2
Seward	9,297	9,241	56	244	219	2.6	2.4	443	21	5,351	−462	23,442	63.4
Sheridan	3,191	3,306	−115	80	93	2.5	2.8	191	−6	1,216	42	16,609	44.9
Sherman	1,894	1,790	104	53	48	2.8	2.7	80	–	487	54	16,099	43.5
Sioux	742	806	−64	21	15	2.8	1.9	14	−2	42	15	14,405	39.0
Stanton	3,677	3,551	126	109	91	3.0	2.6	99	15	481	−45	19,218	52.0
Thayer	2,848	3,173	−325	74	76	2.6	2.4	216	1	1,899	120	23,294	63.0
Thomas	396	419	−23	12	21	3.0	5.0	32	−7	221	48	25,154	68.0
Thurston	2,998	2,853	145	188	197	6.3	6.9	117	−11	1,261	−252	26,011	70.4
Valley	2,552	2,437	115	64	63	2.5	2.6	169	−2	1,315	161	19,474	52.7
Washington	11,281	10,938	343	309	267	2.7	2.4	530	50	6,240	362	31,136	84.2
Wayne	5,558	5,733	−175	134	147	2.4	2.6	249	5	2,913	−977	21,713	58.7
Webster	1,993	1,970	23	51	51	2.6	2.6	99	2	708	114	18,403	49.8
Wheeler	462	502	−40	11	12	2.4	2.4	19	–	148	62	9,818	26.6
York	8,469	7,880	589	204	191	2.4	2.4	510	8	6,787	170	24,229	65.5
NEVADA	1,295,085	1,062,845	232,240	54,217	47,624	4.2	4.5	[3]55,853	[3]7,675	[3]1,022,011	[3]119,236	[3]34,098	[3]92.2
Churchill	12,930	11,985	945	556	748	4.3	6.2	495	11	5,585	106	27,820	75.3
Clark	924,959	727,521	197,438	38,261	33,588	4.1	4.6	36,181	6,550	739,434	100,279	33,884	91.7
Douglas	22,442	21,712	730	1,083	893	4.8	4.1	1,538	195	19,031	1,435	28,257	76.4
Elko	24,867	24,209	658	880	952	3.5	3.9	990	−23	16,354	−134	36,773	99.5
Esmeralda	473	511	−38	20	44	4.2	8.6	15	5	109	4	36,046	97.5
Eureka	715	793	−78	28	26	3.9	3.3	29	−11	515	−1,876	56,192	152.0
Humboldt	8,110	7,794	316	306	383	3.8	4.9	356	−39	5,150	−472	34,640	93.7
Lander	2,858	2,850	8	112	165	3.9	5.8	82	−8	834	−400	35,263	95.4
Lincoln	1,618	1,655	−37	74	82	4.6	5.0	86	2	586	81	19,384	52.4
Lyon	21,350	17,920	3,430	1,294	1,044	6.1	5.8	628	113	8,966	2,536	28,009	75.8
Mineral	2,066	2,354	−288	147	195	7.1	8.3	73	−15	1,260	16	29,836	80.7
Nye	17,255	14,062	3,193	979	958	5.7	6.8	678	107	7,014	1,017	28,210	76.3
Pershing	2,440	2,553	−113	126	113	5.2	4.4	85	−8	1,253	−25	34,508	93.3
Storey	2,374	1,995	379	104	64	4.4	3.2	79	1	335	−129	18,525	50.1
Washoe	218,296	194,691	23,605	8,739	7,222	4.0	3.7	11,799	662	180,525	11,182	35,074	94.9
White Pine	4,491	3,769	722	171	158	3.8	4.2	199	−18	1,781	−14	29,771	80.5
Independent City													
Carson City	27,842	26,472	1,370	1,337	989	4.8	3.7	2,416	66	25,252	467	32,321	87.4
NEW HAMPSHIRE	736,780	694,254	42,526	25,268	18,713	3.4	2.7	[3]38,843	[3]1,429	[3]551,001	[3]4,601	[3]36,307	[3]98.2
Belknap	32,808	31,236	1,572	1,084	774	3.3	2.5	1,946	62	21,517	−660	31,298	84.7
Carroll	25,393	23,856	1,537	826	646	3.3	2.7	1,976	121	21,152	1,796	22,840	61.8
Cheshire	42,820	40,275	2,545	1,383	1,069	3.2	2.7	2,004	27	30,734	1,796	31,135	84.2
Coos	16,766	17,299	−533	711	642	4.2	3.7	989	–	10,900	(NA)	26,145	70.7
Grafton	47,796	45,266	2,530	1,375	1,081	2.9	2.4	3,046	148	47,015	−1,974	34,687	93.8
Hillsborough	228,202	214,534	13,668	8,092	5,546	3.5	2.6	11,090	186	173,710	−3,238	41,001	110.9
Merrimack	79,995	75,473	4,522	2,492	1,819	3.1	2.4	4,243	189	56,829	1,094	33,667	91.1
Rockingham	172,950	162,039	10,911	6,527	4,889	3.8	3.0	9,780	435	129,151	3,809	38,892	105.2
Strafford	67,657	62,384	5,273	2,118	1,695	3.1	2.7	2,605	142	37,964	2,548	34,886	94.4
Sullivan	22,396	21,892	504	661	550	3.0	2.5	1,081	37	11,549	−1,128	31,229	84.5
NEW JERSEY	4,518,035	4,287,783	230,252	209,014	157,473	4.6	3.7	[3]240,539	[3]6,980	[3]3,609,640	[3]61,211	[3]44,392	[3]120.1
Atlantic	139,723	129,004	10,719	7,983	6,005	5.7	4.7	6,703	326	129,347	8,789	31,939	86.4
Bergen	477,018	469,215	7,803	18,445	14,768	3.9	3.1	33,486	311	470,179	1,004	47,729	129.1
Burlington	245,661	221,419	24,242	10,013	6,868	4.1	3.1	10,733	415	181,100	7,210	37,960	102.7
Camden	271,638	254,319	17,319	13,973	9,855	5.1	3.9	12,596	15	182,252	−1,631	36,880	99.8
Cape May	58,937	55,518	3,419	4,006	3,531	6.8	6.4	4,192	172	26,062	117	33,205	89.8
Cumberland	70,637	65,553	5,084	4,862	3,799	6.9	5.8	3,173	147	47,831	2,007	32,067	86.7
Essex	370,603	366,064	4,539	21,395	16,455	5.8	4.5	20,268	511	317,283	−9,663	46,195	125.0
Gloucester	153,038	134,863	18,175	7,165	4,875	4.7	3.6	5,946	302	85,784	8,008	33,701	91.2
Hudson	294,070	297,756	−3,686	16,117	14,341	5.5	4.8	13,511	247	219,803	1,944	47,965	129.8
Hunterdon	73,056	67,949	5,107	2,417	1,586	3.3	2.3	4,169	267	44,623	2,064	48,958	132.4
Mercer	201,847	180,191	21,656	8,384	5,878	4.2	3.3	9,983	334	185,383	11,266	46,390	125.5
Middlesex	427,703	401,163	26,540	18,460	13,331	4.3	3.3	21,252	654	389,516	−551	46,338	125.3
Monmouth	332,931	318,121	14,810	13,618	10,182	4.1	3.2	19,543	867	226,748	11,452	39,183	106.0
Morris	274,019	261,278	12,741	9,117	6,923	3.3	2.6	17,656	95	295,818	−6,489	56,974	154.1
Ocean	257,236	232,059	25,177	12,763	8,579	5.0	3.7	12,164	1,182	123,524	11,652	30,980	83.8

See footnotes at end of table.

[Includes United States, states, and 3,141 counties/county equivalents defined as of February 22, 2005. For more information on these areas, see Appendix C, Geographic Information]

County	Civilian labor force							Private nonfarm businesses					
	Total			Number of unemployed		Unemployment rate[1]		Establishments		Employment[2]		Annual payroll per employee, 2004	
	2006	2000	Net change, 2000–2006	2006	2000	2006	2000	2004	Net change, 2000–2004	2004	Net change, 2000–2004	Amount (dol.)	Percent of U.S. average
NEW JERSEY—Con.													
Passaic	240,340	236,288	4,052	13,384	10,800	5.6	4.6	12,469	582	169,347	−666	38,150	103.2
Salem	32,137	31,550	587	1,591	1,216	5.0	3.9	1,320	23	19,414	393	41,961	113.5
Somerset	179,911	165,513	14,398	6,224	4,258	3.5	2.6	9,896	115	174,859	−891	58,717	158.8
Sussex	85,256	79,538	5,718	3,490	2,346	4.1	2.9	3,716	173	33,603	3,079	30,221	81.7
Union	271,831	264,749	7,082	13,164	10,260	4.8	3.9	14,725	−34	233,838	492	44,666	120.8
Warren	60,445	55,675	4,770	2,444	1,619	4.0	2.9	2,861	139	31,199	7	41,180	111.4
NEW MEXICO	935,350	852,293	83,057	39,727	42,269	4.2	5.0	[3]44,205	[3]1,423	[3]580,576	[3]31,224	[3]28,957	[3]78.3
Bernalillo	313,412	289,826	23,586	12,233	11,649	3.9	4.0	15,918	248	252,666	2,392	31,618	85.5
Catron	1,523	1,460	63	82	98	5.4	6.7	62	−4	279	23	17,763	48.1
Chaves	26,960	25,826	1,134	1,220	1,448	4.5	5.6	1,477	−31	15,534	360	22,546	61.0
Cibola	11,730	9,967	1,763	565	683	4.8	6.9	366	24	6,809	796	24,361	65.9
Colfax	6,620	7,000	−380	299	351	4.5	5.0	528	27	4,242	68	20,658	55.9
Curry	21,111	18,723	2,388	752	875	3.6	4.7	1,068	9	13,252	2,282	21,181	57.3
De Baca	896	969	−73	37	46	4.1	4.7	59	−2	325	−55	19,572	52.9
Dona Ana	86,216	76,425	9,791	4,092	4,695	4.7	6.1	3,422	211	42,580	5,530	23,710	64.1
Eddy	25,367	23,273	2,094	928	1,322	3.7	5.7	1,164	−61	16,665	1,107	30,967	83.8
Grant	12,455	12,870	−415	551	749	4.4	5.8	705	25	7,366	−363	26,589	71.9
Guadalupe	1,889	1,797	92	102	131	5.4	7.3	98	−8	1,097	82	19,210	52.0
Harding	383	420	−37	17	18	4.4	4.4	16	−1	41	−2	18,317	49.5
Hidalgo	2,768	2,649	119	94	181	3.4	6.8	111	2	945	89	18,578	50.3
Lea	26,803	22,646	4,157	865	1,191	3.2	5.3	1,409	13	16,285	2,301	27,264	73.8
Lincoln	10,605	9,668	937	427	410	4.0	4.2	762	55	5,382	872	20,857	56.4
Los Alamos	11,329	10,512	817	282	323	2.5	3.1	440	10	6,261	−81	36,638	99.1
Luna	12,960	10,820	2,140	1,369	1,679	10.6	15.5	421	13	4,807	1,331	19,287	52.2
McKinley	26,897	24,595	2,302	1,509	1,621	5.6	6.6	1,030	−26	16,304	1,409	23,198	62.8
Mora	2,034	1,971	63	178	208	8.8	10.6	64	9	428	70	20,523	55.5
Otero	26,334	24,383	1,951	1,155	1,300	4.4	5.3	1,047	22	11,961	−520	20,877	56.5
Quay	4,101	4,468	−367	193	221	4.7	4.9	260	−29	1,949	−231	19,212	52.0
Rio Arriba	21,934	19,217	2,717	1,064	1,167	4.9	6.1	692	40	7,223	681	22,900	61.9
Roosevelt	9,424	8,026	1,398	305	355	3.2	4.4	352	5	3,689	1,067	20,494	55.4
Sandoval	51,400	43,281	8,119	2,253	1,842	4.4	4.3	1,404	183	21,953	2,205	37,164	100.5
San Juan	55,944	49,687	6,257	2,438	2,860	4.4	5.8	2,657	170	36,221	1,881	30,664	82.9
San Miguel	13,524	12,600	924	661	733	4.9	5.8	494	−13	6,193	1,247	36,408	98.5
Santa Fe	76,977	70,763	6,214	2,710	2,568	3.5	3.6	5,034	365	47,761	3,066	29,869	80.8
Sierra	5,524	5,275	249	253	234	4.6	4.4	249	−28	2,194	149	17,283	46.8
Socorro	9,401	7,976	1,425	355	403	3.8	5.1	270	−2	2,756	205	25,415	68.7
Taos	17,606	15,384	2,222	976	1,048	5.5	6.8	1,219	79	8,855	367	20,903	56.5
Torrance	7,768	7,585	183	338	380	4.4	5.0	235	12	2,180	334	20,311	54.9
Union	2,053	2,073	−20	62	77	3.0	3.7	113	−8	857	70	19,516	52.8
Valencia	31,407	30,166	1,241	1,364	1,407	4.3	4.7	899	48	11,192	2,234	19,644	53.1
NEW YORK	9,498,563	9,166,972	331,591	425,830	415,531	4.5	4.5	[3]511,440	[3]19,367	[3]7,433,686	[3]80,477	[3]47,521	[3]128.5
Albany	160,451	155,109	5,342	6,075	5,162	3.8	3.3	9,226	350	171,625	3,116	36,209	97.9
Allegany	23,650	22,800	850	1,247	1,108	5.3	4.9	842	−11	12,522	833	21,359	57.8
Bronx	506,221	486,596	19,625	32,863	34,793	6.5	7.2	15,431	1,336	213,672	7,300	36,440	98.6
Broome	97,293	98,223	−930	4,462	3,540	4.6	3.6	4,273	−26	79,338	−3,665	29,277	79.2
Cattaraugus	42,098	41,195	903	2,143	1,853	5.1	4.5	1,859	−1	24,069	−348	26,009	70.4
Cayuga	42,195	40,432	1,763	1,987	1,570	4.7	3.9	1,618	79	18,745	283	27,946	75.6
Chautauqua	66,898	68,217	−1,319	3,001	2,715	4.5	4.0	3,118	−5	44,626	−2,725	26,169	70.8
Chemung	40,837	42,711	−1,874	1,985	1,834	4.9	4.3	1,920	3	32,766	−2,389	29,354	79.4
Chenango	24,704	24,413	291	1,193	972	4.8	4.0	988	−18	12,009	−356	28,645	77.5
Clinton	40,176	38,609	1,567	2,119	1,815	5.3	4.7	1,903	53	26,566	3,016	28,001	75.7
Columbia	32,284	31,627	657	1,200	1,068	3.7	3.4	1,748	89	16,358	600	29,238	79.1
Cortland	23,842	24,187	−345	1,233	1,055	5.2	4.4	1,100	57	15,917	−198	24,043	65.0
Delaware	23,642	22,186	1,456	1,018	908	4.3	4.1	1,212	82	13,073	689	29,164	78.9
Dutchess	148,416	139,432	8,984	5,551	4,486	3.7	3.2	7,496	735	98,683	7,635	38,316	103.6
Erie	472,200	467,713	4,487	23,072	19,508	4.9	4.2	22,834	492	410,777	−1,721	31,666	85.7
Essex	18,782	18,535	247	1,044	879	5.6	4.7	1,189	−7	10,004	64	27,147	73.4
Franklin	22,743	22,072	671	1,247	1,282	5.5	5.8	1,104	14	10,803	309	23,491	63.5
Fulton	27,223	26,435	788	1,449	1,216	5.3	4.6	1,174	91	16,589	3,264	25,969	70.2
Genesee	33,308	32,694	614	1,514	1,285	4.5	3.9	1,370	31	16,704	−160	27,197	73.6
Greene	24,120	22,439	1,681	1,137	1,017	4.7	4.5	1,169	35	10,707	975	23,378	63.2
Hamilton	3,105	2,866	239	169	156	5.4	5.4	201	−10	787	53	25,485	68.9
Herkimer	31,665	31,617	48	1,575	1,336	5.0	4.2	1,180	−3	12,986	−897	25,452	68.9
Jefferson	48,764	45,267	3,497	2,658	2,670	5.5	5.9	2,357	51	26,699	315	26,902	72.8
Kings	1,069,722	1,042,605	27,117	56,296	66,485	5.3	6.4	42,329	4,174	465,242	33,450	32,684	88.4
Lewis	13,210	12,717	493	684	654	5.2	5.1	514	−41	4,408	−381	26,836	72.6
Livingston	32,856	32,938	−82	1,561	1,335	4.8	4.1	1,328	89	12,995	455	25,212	68.2
Madison	36,119	35,077	1,042	1,675	1,346	4.6	3.8	1,473	96	17,680	−2,368	26,743	72.3
Monroe	376,027	376,868	−841	16,127	13,309	4.3	3.5	17,013	174	354,988	−7,785	36,514	98.8
Montgomery	25,000	23,662	1,338	1,382	1,108	5.5	4.7	1,096	−37	14,788	−1,534	27,492	74.4
Nassau	696,597	677,947	18,650	25,837	22,486	3.7	3.3	48,068	867	568,108	5,758	40,811	110.4

See footnotes at end of table.

County and City Data Book: 2007

U.S. Census Bureau

Table B-10. Counties — **Labor Force and Private Business Establishments and Employment**—Con.

[Includes United States, states, and 3,141 counties/county equivalents defined as of February 22, 2005. For more information on these areas, see Appendix C, Geographic Information]

	Civilian labor force							Private nonfarm businesses					
	Total			Number of unemployed		Unemployment rate[1]		Establishments		Employment[2]		Annual payroll per employee, 2004	
County	2006	2000	Net change, 2000–2006	2006	2000	2006	2000	2004	Net change, 2000–2004	2004	Net change, 2000–2004	Amount (dol.)	Percent of U.S. average
NEW YORK—Con.													
New York	903,771	855,263	48,508	38,360	43,413	4.2	5.1	104,728	–3,053	1,988,296	–92,579	80,013	216.4
Niagara	111,811	109,900	1,911	5,980	5,124	5.3	4.7	4,517	23	61,979	–3,174	29,641	80.2
Oneida	110,990	110,667	323	4,748	4,254	4.3	3.8	5,037	71	91,010	3,218	28,498	77.1
Onondaga	234,384	230,882	3,502	9,940	8,112	4.2	3.5	12,051	449	223,649	–5,066	33,629	91.0
Ontario	56,831	54,551	2,280	2,464	1,929	4.3	3.5	2,768	212	41,577	2,044	29,347	79.4
Orange	179,483	162,436	17,047	7,451	5,492	4.2	3.4	8,868	792	103,420	9,459	30,893	83.6
Orleans	19,984	20,295	–311	1,114	945	5.6	4.7	694	10	7,461	93	23,836	64.5
Oswego	60,245	58,778	1,467	3,421	2,803	5.7	4.8	2,065	42	25,011	354	30,409	82.3
Otsego	32,267	29,750	2,517	1,398	1,249	4.3	4.2	1,401	54	18,594	977	28,626	77.4
Putnam	56,546	52,437	4,109	1,953	1,516	3.5	2.9	2,911	287	21,591	2,494	35,807	96.9
Queens	1,090,666	1,064,279	26,387	47,823	56,560	4.4	5.3	40,305	3,996	478,584	2,914	35,988	97.4
Rensselaer	84,392	80,998	3,394	3,380	2,923	4.0	3.6	2,918	188	43,302	1,348	31,615	85.5
Richmond	231,593	217,176	14,417	10,198	11,059	4.4	5.1	7,984	521	87,414	2,741	32,201	87.1
Rockland	152,457	145,323	7,134	5,608	4,752	3.7	3.3	9,068	476	103,241	2,721	36,651	99.1
St. Lawrence	49,747	49,397	350	2,821	2,794	5.7	5.7	2,119	–37	28,174	–66	27,390	74.1
Saratoga	120,805	110,908	9,897	4,192	3,662	3.5	3.3	4,673	536	60,697	6,904	30,990	83.8
Schenectady	75,941	72,745	3,196	3,049	2,519	4.0	3.5	3,048	86	50,696	1,098	34,782	94.1
Schoharie	15,987	15,226	761	800	647	5.0	4.2	594	21	5,820	130	25,975	70.3
Schuyler	9,968	9,405	563	498	418	5.0	4.4	333	–13	3,171	73	23,939	64.8
Seneca	17,423	15,909	1,514	777	677	4.5	4.3	683	25	7,883	170	27,531	74.5
Steuben	44,945	48,074	–3,129	2,319	1,950	5.2	4.1	1,853	81	27,550	–5,222	36,437	98.6
Suffolk	785,622	735,894	49,728	30,527	25,175	3.9	3.4	46,933	3,468	560,912	38,112	39,070	105.7
Sullivan	35,352	33,174	2,178	1,726	1,439	4.9	4.3	2,072	167	18,618	–40	26,805	72.5
Tioga	26,532	26,530	2	1,122	905	4.2	3.4	769	–31	12,397	4,052	41,058	111.1
Tompkins	55,144	50,951	4,193	1,860	1,689	3.4	3.3	2,188	63	46,910	5,110	27,031	73.1
Ulster	92,748	88,709	4,039	3,803	3,154	4.1	3.6	4,796	438	50,302	4,573	26,738	72.3
Warren	35,834	33,258	2,576	1,612	1,380	4.5	4.1	2,369	50	32,942	–2,190	29,456	79.7
Washington	32,363	30,077	2,286	1,319	1,114	4.1	3.7	1,096	22	10,034	–82	28,653	77.5
Wayne	48,908	48,940	–32	2,241	1,860	4.6	3.8	1,825	152	21,323	248	29,232	79.1
Westchester	486,643	465,289	21,354	18,227	15,659	3.7	3.4	32,068	1,298	391,438	–1,301	50,284	136.0
Wyoming	21,990	20,457	1,533	1,054	963	4.8	4.7	825	22	9,444	558	27,124	73.4
Yates	13,045	12,108	937	540	444	4.1	3.7	531	32	5,353	–56	22,086	59.7
NORTH CAROLINA	4,464,875	4,123,812	341,063	214,256	154,577	4.8	3.7	[3]213,057	[3]9,154	[3]3,365,633	[3]–19,859	[3]32,556	[3]88.1
Alamance	69,955	69,342	613	3,866	2,197	5.5	3.2	3,286	–62	57,848	–2,130	29,124	78.8
Alexander	18,499	19,370	–871	902	535	4.9	2.8	575	–2	7,642	–1,103	23,979	64.9
Alleghany	4,999	5,636	–637	252	340	5.0	6.0	295	11	2,750	–564	21,876	59.2
Anson	11,119	11,010	109	817	582	7.3	5.3	451	–8	5,299	–920	26,567	71.9
Ashe	12,858	12,492	366	736	641	5.7	5.1	575	39	6,061	43	22,982	62.2
Avery	8,005	7,937	68	402	320	5.0	4.0	580	28	5,619	–531	20,251	54.8
Beaufort	20,468	20,675	–207	1,204	1,258	5.9	6.1	1,170	6	13,606	–1,839	27,103	73.3
Bertie	8,814	8,376	438	584	594	6.6	7.1	383	–2	5,420	32	19,474	52.7
Bladen	15,390	14,670	720	991	902	6.4	6.1	525	6	10,362	–1,076	23,308	63.0
Brunswick	45,420	35,447	9,973	2,064	1,614	4.5	4.6	2,096	413	20,079	2,403	28,640	77.4
Buncombe	118,930	107,642	11,288	4,525	3,390	3.8	3.1	6,770	389	97,927	–1,098	28,195	76.3
Burke	42,036	46,257	–4,221	2,434	1,643	5.8	3.6	1,561	–6	26,240	–7,403	27,187	73.5
Cabarrus	80,899	71,950	8,949	3,354	2,189	4.1	3.0	3,642	467	53,319	498	31,686	85.7
Caldwell	40,227	42,404	–2,177	3,031	1,240	7.5	2.9	1,512	–56	25,452	–5,626	25,870	70.0
Camden	4,528	3,314	1,214	195	99	4.3	3.0	126	21	608	33	22,808	61.7
Carteret	33,409	29,593	3,816	1,385	1,232	4.1	4.2	2,010	89	18,303	580	22,544	61.0
Caswell	10,803	10,879	–76	778	409	7.2	3.8	249	20	1,690	–60	19,989	54.1
Catawba	77,785	80,222	–2,437	4,210	2,222	5.4	2.8	4,424	9	85,707	–8,955	29,645	80.2
Chatham	32,233	26,810	5,423	1,260	742	3.9	2.8	973	38	12,179	–957	26,571	71.9
Cherokee	10,617	11,466	–849	574	742	5.4	6.5	655	43	7,035	–2,493	22,322	60.4
Chowan	7,082	6,484	598	357	258	5.0	4.0	384	32	4,558	269	23,088	62.5
Clay	4,696	4,032	664	184	165	3.9	4.1	251	24	1,516	39	22,189	60.0
Cleveland	48,052	48,968	–916	3,089	2,432	6.4	5.0	2,154	–21	31,489	–1,805	28,338	76.7
Columbus	23,842	23,509	333	1,353	1,819	5.7	7.7	1,169	–42	14,142	–138	25,065	67.8
Craven	41,865	38,558	3,307	1,844	1,612	4.4	4.2	2,238	63	29,667	1,046	28,677	77.6
Cumberland	130,734	119,209	11,525	7,201	5,339	5.5	4.5	5,470	165	88,406	–722	25,979	70.3
Currituck	12,408	9,213	3,195	429	255	3.5	2.8	607	156	4,505	1,368	24,159	65.4
Dare	22,689	18,771	3,918	1,030	813	4.5	4.3	2,020	324	15,031	2,488	26,137	70.7
Davidson	80,049	79,558	491	4,740	2,601	5.9	3.3	2,834	135	40,999	–3,095	26,172	70.8
Davie	20,494	18,424	2,070	865	778	4.2	4.2	750	58	8,353	–490	25,224	68.2
Duplin	23,560	23,408	152	1,234	1,017	5.2	4.3	890	–62	12,203	294	22,133	59.9
Durham	135,753	122,130	13,623	5,338	3,619	3.9	3.0	6,090	139	159,008	–4,162	48,917	132.3
Edgecombe	24,750	25,057	–307	1,996	1,470	8.1	5.9	953	–1	19,938	2,757	30,452	82.4
Forsyth	173,132	161,676	11,456	7,517	5,213	4.3	3.2	8,614	121	170,822	–3,677	36,791	99.5
Franklin	27,373	24,405	2,968	1,135	796	4.1	3.3	850	94	8,803	653	30,852	83.5

See footnotes at end of table.

Table B-10. Counties — **Labor Force and Private Business Establishments and Employment**—Con.

[Includes United States, states, and 3,141 counties/county equivalents defined as of February 22, 2005. For more information on these areas, see Appendix C, Geographic Information]

County	Civilian labor force — Total 2006	Total 2000	Total Net change, 2000–2006	Number of unemployed 2006	Number of unemployed 2000	Unemployment rate[1] 2006	Unemployment rate[1] 2000	Private nonfarm businesses — Establishments 2004	Establishments Net change, 2000–2004	Employment[2] 2004	Employment[2] Net change, 2000–2004	Annual payroll per employee, 2004 Amount (dol.)	Annual payroll per employee, 2004 Percent of U.S. average
NORTH CAROLINA—Con.													
Gaston	100,564	99,985	579	5,491	5,515	5.5	5.5	4,043	−158	61,467	−9,301	28,368	76.7
Gates	5,001	4,651	350	199	160	4.0	3.4	139	5	992	9	21,661	58.6
Graham	4,173	3,812	361	267	253	6.4	6.6	179	−3	1,848	50	25,540	69.1
Granville	24,395	22,502	1,893	1,284	995	5.3	4.4	811	26	14,480	592	30,014	81.2
Greene	9,301	8,601	700	506	402	5.4	4.7	232	25	1,827	−195	19,666	53.2
Guilford	246,850	232,961	13,889	11,589	7,659	4.7	3.3	13,829	168	254,754	−11,335	34,445	93.2
Halifax	24,100	22,914	1,186	1,586	1,392	6.6	6.1	1,155	23	14,595	−713	23,508	63.6
Harnett	46,958	42,271	4,687	2,321	1,613	4.9	3.8	1,557	85	19,360	−1,434	23,124	62.6
Haywood	28,062	25,868	2,194	1,141	1,013	4.1	3.9	1,460	58	15,629	584	24,329	65.8
Henderson	47,792	42,194	5,598	1,739	1,277	3.6	3.0	2,522	317	32,914	2,919	29,042	78.6
Hertford	9,820	9,509	311	551	496	5.6	5.2	550	−10	7,926	165	24,560	66.4
Hoke	18,857	14,478	4,379	1,048	833	5.6	5.8	331	48	5,477	751	19,651	53.2
Hyde	2,667	2,867	−200	147	165	5.5	5.8	162	−17	775	−269	23,796	64.4
Iredell	76,887	65,911	10,976	3,376	2,318	4.4	3.5	3,757	436	56,888	7,366	29,492	79.8
Jackson	21,573	17,197	4,376	798	680	3.7	4.0	999	98	9,214	914	25,213	68.2
Johnston	74,735	64,032	10,703	2,948	1,865	3.9	2.9	2,878	317	33,467	3,831	26,395	71.4
Jones	5,056	4,668	388	223	213	4.4	4.6	146	−15	1,279	78	23,141	62.6
Lee	26,376	24,612	1,764	1,435	990	5.4	4.0	1,403	21	24,066	−1,289	30,634	82.9
Lenoir	27,576	27,746	−170	1,573	1,466	5.7	5.3	1,484	−31	23,898	−3,313	25,836	69.9
Lincoln	37,967	34,773	3,194	1,915	1,315	5.0	3.8	1,496	135	18,764	−1,812	26,060	70.5
McDowell	21,101	21,414	−313	1,311	927	6.2	4.3	766	−20	14,681	−733	24,858	67.2
Macon	16,243	14,114	2,129	727	552	4.5	3.9	1,192	113	9,908	1,043	25,000	67.6
Madison	10,049	9,373	676	424	352	4.2	3.8	324	9	3,008	−159	21,842	59.1
Martin	11,949	11,802	147	672	822	5.6	7.0	526	−12	5,927	184	22,434	60.7
Mecklenburg	447,144	395,586	51,558	20,019	11,697	4.5	3.0	25,600	1,355	497,949	−745	42,802	115.8
Mitchell	7,612	7,768	−156	483	352	6.3	4.5	390	11	4,801	−270	24,527	66.3
Montgomery	12,318	12,753	−435	832	503	6.8	3.9	541	−14	8,837	−937	26,304	71.2
Moore	36,440	34,607	1,833	1,761	1,261	4.8	3.6	2,164	40	26,729	4	27,401	74.1
Nash	45,100	43,498	1,602	2,506	2,006	5.6	4.6	2,239	−67	36,574	−4,201	28,156	76.2
New Hanover	103,840	87,641	16,199	3,818	3,222	3.7	3.7	6,504	494	83,170	5,731	29,846	80.7
Northampton	9,079	8,694	385	527	475	5.8	5.5	321	−4	4,032	932	22,606	61.2
Onslow	58,957	53,185	5,772	2,726	2,327	4.6	4.4	2,587	−15	30,976	1,799	20,266	54.8
Orange	67,975	64,791	3,184	2,273	1,638	3.3	2.5	3,067	179	39,810	3,785	31,748	85.9
Pamlico	5,859	5,420	439	266	221	4.5	4.1	225	−6	1,832	19	22,000	59.5
Pasquotank	17,854	15,421	2,433	897	587	5.0	3.8	940	12	11,285	754	24,784	67.0
Pender	23,210	19,444	3,766	978	804	4.2	4.1	841	144	6,721	1,148	22,019	59.6
Perquimans	5,336	4,774	562	279	188	5.2	3.9	191	6	1,508	167	19,759	53.5
Person	19,612	18,151	1,461	1,212	795	6.2	4.4	789	42	10,365	−422	28,292	76.5
Pitt	76,671	69,869	6,802	4,043	2,938	5.3	4.2	3,342	123	54,048	1,001	26,826	72.6
Polk	9,455	8,494	961	336	310	3.6	3.6	463	13	3,688	−88	23,995	64.9
Randolph	76,846	72,291	4,555	3,577	2,484	4.7	3.4	2,728	−50	44,577	−2,546	27,267	73.8
Richmond	20,266	20,888	−622	1,555	1,122	7.7	5.4	955	−32	14,072	201	20,303	54.9
Robeson	54,231	53,606	625	3,377	3,626	6.2	6.8	1,942	−48	31,709	−1,753	23,753	64.3
Rockingham	46,747	46,129	618	2,789	2,232	6.0	4.8	1,818	33	25,811	−3,063	27,072	73.2
Rowan	69,799	65,487	4,312	3,518	2,957	5.0	4.5	2,588	106	42,783	−4,819	29,778	80.6
Rutherford	29,804	30,987	−1,183	2,352	1,819	7.9	5.9	1,374	78	18,432	−3,135	24,897	67.3
Sampson	31,450	28,831	2,619	1,447	1,022	4.6	3.5	1,062	−12	13,566	440	24,924	67.4
Scotland	14,939	15,725	−786	1,338	1,010	9.0	6.4	682	−44	13,608	−3,380	25,304	68.4
Stanly	30,314	29,826	488	1,561	1,164	5.1	3.9	1,404	2	17,259	−1,801	25,377	68.6
Stokes	24,584	23,922	662	1,067	841	4.3	3.5	644	36	5,461	−113	23,577	63.8
Surry	35,139	36,968	−1,829	1,828	1,509	5.2	4.1	1,804	−38	32,070	−2,789	27,618	74.7
Swain	7,165	6,197	968	412	554	5.8	8.9	423	20	5,669	126	23,995	64.9
Transylvania	12,597	13,391	−794	544	437	4.3	3.3	785	27	7,665	−1,929	23,617	63.9
Tyrrell	2,107	1,882	225	125	139	5.9	7.4	70	−9	353	6	20,031	54.2
Union	86,298	67,195	19,103	3,450	1,884	4.0	2.8	3,545	639	42,982	3,777	30,059	81.3
Vance	18,934	20,240	−1,306	1,433	1,387	7.6	6.9	919	−15	13,252	−1,456	24,826	67.2
Wake	426,125	366,028	60,097	15,507	8,875	3.6	2.4	22,316	1,856	347,541	14,797	36,480	98.7
Warren	7,903	8,130	−227	512	494	6.5	6.1	246	−19	2,355	104	20,663	55.9
Washington	6,130	5,963	167	415	322	6.8	5.4	267	–	3,632	−39	34,654	93.7
Watauga	23,898	23,232	666	911	678	3.8	2.9	1,598	–	15,610	−321	23,460	63.5
Wayne	52,314	50,900	1,414	2,513	2,043	4.8	4.0	2,303	−37	39,874	2,157	25,223	68.2
Wilkes	31,367	33,989	−2,622	1,739	1,220	5.5	3.6	1,324	−12	22,182	−978	35,369	95.7
Wilson	40,129	37,197	2,932	2,877	2,089	7.2	5.6	1,821	7	33,472	−1,363	30,791	83.3
Yadkin	19,750	19,064	686	853	684	4.3	3.6	639	−28	7,781	−885	23,523	63.6
Yancey	8,055	8,508	−453	453	314	5.6	3.7	344	−2	3,306	−453	22,912	62.0
NORTH DAKOTA	357,960	345,881	12,079	11,601	10,101	3.2	2.9	[3]20,822	[3]683	[3]265,663	[3]10,485	[3]27,531	[3]74.5
Adams	1,299	1,327	−28	39	34	3.0	2.6	94	−18	686	−69	22,891	61.9
Barnes	5,878	6,081	−203	216	188	3.7	3.1	398	34	4,351	401	19,907	53.9
Benson	2,712	2,640	72	163	155	6.0	5.9	111	2	1,187	52	22,314	60.4
Billings	510	492	18	13	13	2.5	2.6	27	−2	148	−38	30,081	81.4
Bottineau	3,408	3,514	−106	129	130	3.8	3.7	262	−3	1,680	30	20,429	55.3

See footnotes at end of table.

Table B-10. Counties — **Labor Force and Private Business Establishments and Employment**—Con.

[Includes United States, states, and 3,141 counties/county equivalents defined as of February 22, 2005. For more information on these areas, see Appendix C, Geographic Information]

County	Civilian labor force							Private nonfarm businesses					
	Total			Number of unemployed		Unemployment rate[1]		Establishments		Employment[2]		Annual payroll per employee, 2004	
	2006	2000	Net change, 2000–2006	2006	2000	2006	2000	2004	Net change, 2000–2004	2004	Net change, 2000–2004	Amount (dol.)	Percent of U.S. average
NORTH DAKOTA—Con.													
Bowman.............	1,760	1,818	−58	40	36	2.3	2.0	152	−14	936	−88	20,684	56.0
Burke..............	1,014	1,062	−48	27	30	2.7	2.8	89	5	320	28	23,325	63.1
Burleigh............	45,219	40,517	4,702	1,194	943	2.6	2.3	2,437	113	36,096	1,009	29,838	80.7
Cass...............	83,463	76,118	7,345	2,134	1,620	2.6	2.1	4,527	354	79,593	6,263	30,879	83.5
Cavalier............	2,118	2,377	−259	73	76	3.4	3.2	173	−10	1,194	−82	23,432	63.4
Dickey.............	3,006	3,091	−85	83	62	2.8	2.0	212	8	1,838	130	20,157	54.5
Divide.............	948	1,075	−127	36	29	3.8	2.7	90	6	539	–	17,616	47.7
Dunn..............	1,727	1,780	−53	57	55	3.3	3.1	77	−4	577	−125	18,629	50.4
Eddy..............	1,309	1,376	−67	68	56	5.2	4.1	78	−3	547	−7	22,724	61.5
Emmons............	1,818	2,097	−279	90	84	5.0	4.0	136	−6	866	−348	20,734	56.1
Foster.............	1,705	1,976	−271	58	54	3.4	2.7	151	−5	1,385	−213	24,359	65.9
Golden Valley........	842	919	−77	28	27	3.3	2.9	75	5	505	50	17,550	47.5
Grand Forks.........	38,194	36,299	1,895	1,163	1,022	3.0	2.8	1,781	42	28,558	903	27,320	73.9
Grant..............	1,233	1,375	−142	46	40	3.7	2.9	71	−11	452	−24	18,781	50.8
Griggs.............	1,302	1,382	−80	42	32	3.2	2.3	100	−11	810	−107	20,804	56.3
Hettinger...........	1,175	1,269	−94	41	37	3.5	2.9	111	12	416	7	20,639	55.8
Kidder.............	1,259	1,315	−56	60	58	4.8	4.4	69	8	443	63	18,354	49.7
LaMoure............	2,267	2,308	−41	72	62	3.2	2.7	146	6	978	96	21,343	57.7
Logan.............	953	1,053	−100	30	27	3.1	2.6	77	11	360	−69	18,531	50.1
McHenry............	2,775	2,840	−65	140	137	5.0	4.8	136	3	655	−2	23,073	62.4
McIntosh...........	1,473	1,573	−100	43	41	2.9	2.6	130	7	1,001	28	19,004	51.4
McKenzie...........	2,789	2,704	85	89	83	3.2	3.1	158	−6	1,026	−110	24,444	66.1
McLean............	4,605	4,600	5	210	211	4.6	4.6	246	7	1,843	−49	32,591	88.2
Mercer.............	4,780	4,539	241	181	194	3.8	4.3	227	−27	3,678	160	42,448	114.8
Morton.............	14,816	13,995	821	483	417	3.3	3.0	703	55	7,809	783	29,930	81.0
Mountrail...........	2,875	3,047	−172	176	139	6.1	4.6	198	4	1,401	−235	21,394	57.9
Nelson.............	1,672	1,837	−165	72	67	4.3	3.6	137	–	753	−42	18,732	50.7
Oliver.............	1,074	1,137	−63	44	46	4.1	4.0	42	8	405	9	55,551	150.3
Pembina............	4,075	4,731	−656	253	242	6.2	5.1	320	−13	2,988	32	23,580	63.8
Pierce.............	1,879	2,213	−334	85	72	4.5	3.3	160	10	1,548	−22	21,225	57.4
Ramsey............	5,866	6,244	−378	242	204	4.1	3.3	427	9	4,572	236	20,532	55.5
Ransom............	3,157	3,127	30	125	70	4.0	2.2	213	8	1,513	18	22,778	61.6
Renville............	1,305	1,318	−13	41	33	3.1	2.5	97	−4	527	−22	24,751	67.0
Richland............	8,991	9,468	−477	317	255	3.5	2.7	519	−31	6,838	−200	26,284	71.1
Rolette.............	5,065	5,281	−216	470	499	9.3	9.4	210	−3	2,661	−298	22,280	60.3
Sargent............	2,509	2,372	137	95	55	3.8	2.3	138	9	1,956	−133	37,859	102.4
Sheridan...........	700	799	−99	38	41	5.4	5.1	50	2	167	−23	23,575	63.8
Sioux..............	1,325	1,276	49	92	72	6.9	5.6	26	−5	932	73	24,988	67.6
Slope.............	517	430	87	12	11	2.3	2.6	10	−2	57	18	30,439	82.3
Stark..............	13,567	12,436	1,131	356	348	2.6	2.8	892	39	9,417	944	24,646	66.7
Steele.............	1,112	1,186	−74	29	23	2.6	1.9	66	−11	337	−70	30,045	81.3
Stutsman...........	11,811	11,956	−145	360	296	3.0	2.5	673	17	8,606	−913	22,913	62.0
Towner............	1,189	1,453	−264	63	40	5.3	2.8	97	3	753	−13	17,928	48.5
Traill..............	4,197	4,307	−110	155	120	3.7	2.8	314	7	2,458	27	23,107	62.5
Walsh.............	5,779	6,516	−737	272	229	4.7	3.5	438	−1	3,645	−426	22,857	61.8
Ward..............	28,274	28,244	30	901	897	3.2	3.2	1,632	6	24,222	2,415	22,785	61.6
Wells.............	2,189	2,371	−182	103	91	4.7	3.8	207	4	1,365	−35	19,540	52.9
Williams...........	12,479	10,628	1,851	256	303	2.1	2.9	828	29	6,806	−26	25,610	69.3
OHIO..............	5,933,957	5,807,036	126,921	324,901	233,882	5.5	4.0	[3]271,733	[3]1,224	[3]4,762,205	[3]−239,775	[3]34,135	[3]92.3
Adams.............	13,238	12,553	685	1,005	888	7.6	7.1	434	−2	4,522	59	23,505	63.6
Allen..............	52,555	51,592	963	3,207	2,248	6.1	4.4	2,765	−74	50,687	−1,152	29,309	79.3
Ashland...........	27,110	27,106	4	1,499	1,067	5.5	3.9	1,092	34	17,026	−1,246	28,568	77.3
Ashtabula..........	50,235	50,529	−294	3,339	2,425	6.6	4.8	2,238	−17	28,283	−2,315	26,104	70.6
Athens............	30,515	27,782	2,733	1,801	1,475	5.9	5.3	1,166	−18	13,110	−468	21,310	57.6
Auglaize...........	26,937	25,155	1,782	1,137	838	4.2	3.3	1,026	−12	18,268	362	29,698	80.3
Belmont...........	32,494	31,019	1,475	1,915	1,874	5.9	6.0	1,635	8	20,091	620	22,758	61.6
Brown.............	22,326	20,648	1,678	1,515	1,055	6.8	5.1	578	−19	5,765	−869	25,932	70.1
Butler.............	189,698	173,564	16,134	10,675	6,204	5.6	3.6	6,892	587	121,556	7,134	34,297	92.8
Carroll............	14,035	14,169	−134	851	612	6.1	4.3	473	−11	4,910	−230	23,483	63.5
Champaign..........	20,746	20,538	208	1,057	732	5.1	3.6	707	3	10,106	522	28,160	76.2
Clark..............	70,432	72,367	−1,935	3,968	3,106	5.6	4.3	2,629	−81	44,858	−6,213	27,841	75.3
Clermont...........	105,638	95,756	9,882	5,359	3,482	5.1	3.6	3,606	329	51,629	3,523	31,880	86.2
Clinton............	24,218	21,917	2,301	1,155	778	4.8	3.5	807	1	21,967	−1,779	34,045	92.1
Columbiana.........	53,454	54,322	−868	3,458	2,593	6.5	4.8	2,364	17	28,182	−1,517	25,306	68.5
Coshocton..........	17,658	18,229	−571	1,227	781	6.9	4.3	725	−20	12,377	−1,249	28,326	76.6
Crawford...........	22,787	23,501	−714	1,472	1,001	6.5	4.3	956	−9	14,652	−1,954	28,263	76.5
Cuyahoga..........	663,367	693,725	−30,358	36,702	28,168	5.5	4.1	37,192	−1,014	689,876	−89,033	39,199	106.0
Darke.............	27,842	27,886	−44	1,586	1,094	5.7	3.9	1,256	−5	16,047	−636	27,371	74.0
Defiance...........	20,677	21,252	−575	1,154	787	5.6	3.7	881	12	15,185	−1,730	35,753	96.7

See footnotes at end of table.

[Includes United States, states, and 3,141 counties/county equivalents defined as of February 22, 2005. For more information on these areas, see Appendix C, Geographic Information]

County	Civilian labor force							Private nonfarm businesses					
	Total			Number of unemployed		Unemployment rate[1]		Establishments		Employment[2]		Annual payroll per employee, 2004	
	2006	2000	Net change, 2000–2006	2006	2000	2006	2000	2004	Net change, 2000–2004	2004	Net change, 2000–2004	Amount (dol.)	Percent of U.S. average
OHIO—Con.													
Delaware	84,846	62,802	22,044	3,334	1,685	3.9	2.7	3,359	840	57,759	14,885	38,656	104.6
Erie	42,663	42,152	511	2,518	1,773	5.9	4.2	2,013	-28	30,655	-2,409	30,726	83.1
Fairfield	74,172	65,660	8,512	3,571	2,168	4.8	3.3	2,632	91	30,739	-373	25,429	68.8
Fayette	16,261	14,946	1,315	807	580	5.0	3.9	681	11	10,549	947	26,732	72.3
Franklin	609,718	594,317	15,401	28,649	18,659	4.7	3.1	28,564	597	597,428	-29,413	37,256	100.8
Fulton	23,387	22,691	696	1,389	908	5.9	4.0	1,106	8	18,608	-1,810	32,755	88.6
Gallia	14,750	13,340	1,410	902	920	6.1	6.9	634	-15	9,572	-308	29,823	80.7
Geauga	51,002	49,120	1,882	2,258	1,532	4.4	3.1	2,733	118	28,869	-302	32,158	87.0
Greene	77,420	76,334	1,086	3,959	2,822	5.1	3.7	2,990	103	46,916	1,754	29,569	80.0
Guernsey	20,011	18,690	1,321	1,292	1,177	6.5	6.3	958	9	13,205	432	26,582	71.9
Hamilton	423,493	428,880	-5,387	21,309	15,805	5.0	3.7	23,581	-1,315	493,298	-63,298	38,345	103.7
Hancock	41,259	39,000	2,259	1,817	1,289	4.4	3.3	1,838	63	38,680	-1,835	34,739	94.0
Hardin	15,931	15,745	186	891	646	5.6	4.1	518	2	7,666	-953	23,983	64.9
Harrison	7,433	7,184	249	446	367	6.0	5.1	299	-29	3,060	-28	29,592	80.0
Henry	16,173	15,268	905	976	650	6.0	4.3	623	1	9,181	-508	30,640	82.9
Highland	21,527	19,582	1,945	1,201	849	5.6	4.3	758	17	10,031	-468	26,759	72.4
Hocking	13,987	13,161	826	872	819	6.2	6.2	543	-18	5,829	-186	21,770	58.9
Holmes	19,433	17,765	1,668	740	508	3.8	2.9	1,049	63	14,843	1,305	26,180	70.8
Huron	30,011	30,708	-697	2,226	1,668	7.4	5.4	1,234	-9	20,642	-2,385	31,472	85.1
Jackson	15,928	14,470	1,458	1,194	843	7.5	5.8	660	-1	11,022	742	24,986	67.6
Jefferson	31,402	31,719	-317	2,196	1,802	7.0	5.7	1,507	-56	24,445	2,119	24,750	67.0
Knox	30,453	27,432	3,021	1,544	1,125	5.1	4.1	1,148	39	18,953	1,721	30,601	82.8
Lake	131,393	129,228	2,165	6,276	4,402	4.8	3.4	6,547	167	91,178	-6,025	32,815	88.8
Lawrence	29,024	26,145	2,879	1,534	1,920	5.3	7.3	859	-60	9,912	-364	21,580	58.4
Licking	82,710	77,542	5,168	4,227	2,860	5.1	3.7	3,008	144	49,222	585	28,606	77.4
Logan	25,065	24,167	898	1,168	864	4.7	3.6	950	-18	18,213	-1,482	34,525	93.4
Lorain	154,436	148,879	5,557	8,910	6,172	5.8	4.1	6,036	213	89,869	-8,929	32,342	87.5
Lucas	226,172	227,291	-1,119	14,289	10,265	6.3	4.5	10,898	-217	212,853	-7,866	33,176	89.7
Madison	20,089	19,368	721	1,049	665	5.2	3.4	793	68	11,871	605	29,743	80.5
Mahoning	119,561	120,236	-675	7,738	6,066	6.5	5.0	6,339	-102	90,470	-9,305	27,616	74.7
Marion	32,435	31,788	647	1,754	1,323	5.4	4.2	1,331	-38	24,217	-208	28,893	78.2
Medina	93,142	84,936	8,206	4,436	2,758	4.8	3.2	4,020	93	51,711	-1,542	31,137	84.2
Meigs	9,095	9,831	-736	772	707	8.5	7.2	339	-12	2,485	-154	19,342	52.3
Mercer	24,110	21,724	2,386	906	868	3.8	4.0	1,013	39	14,256	1,762	25,970	70.3
Miami	55,059	53,949	1,110	3,001	1,892	5.5	3.5	2,258	30	36,361	-2,147	29,810	80.6
Monroe	5,105	6,338	-1,233	575	445	11.3	7.0	286	7	3,607	-54	36,256	98.1
Montgomery	272,811	279,629	-6,818	16,452	11,151	6.0	4.0	12,832	-431	265,330	-24,268	35,145	95.1
Morgan	5,778	6,602	-824	524	437	9.1	6.6	197	-6	1,646	-597	22,414	60.6
Morrow	17,967	16,461	1,506	1,020	624	5.7	3.8	425	16	4,652	-457	24,307	65.8
Muskingum	39,092	42,088	-2,996	2,802	2,177	7.2	5.2	2,016	10	34,969	28	27,549	74.5
Noble	5,883	5,653	230	422	361	7.2	6.4	190	-15	2,036	-516	26,975	73.0
Ottawa	21,944	21,402	542	1,532	1,084	7.0	5.1	1,121	-36	11,220	-1,011	33,517	90.7
Paulding	10,660	10,497	163	520	400	4.9	3.8	323	-20	3,986	-139	25,313	68.5
Perry	16,593	16,145	448	1,222	853	7.4	5.3	510	12	4,672	-571	24,001	64.9
Pickaway	24,206	23,905	301	1,400	969	5.8	4.1	827	13	12,257	131	30,652	82.9
Pike	10,768	11,433	-665	951	784	8.8	6.9	468	-14	8,809	-1,823	31,940	86.4
Portage	90,464	84,756	5,708	4,656	3,290	5.1	3.9	3,215	107	43,563	-3,209	30,548	82.6
Preble	21,933	21,918	15	1,318	839	6.0	3.8	727	6	9,112	-256	30,056	81.3
Putnam	17,817	18,297	-480	846	596	4.7	3.3	734	11	9,210	-1,070	24,775	67.0
Richland	62,535	63,263	-728	3,807	3,189	6.1	5.0	3,013	-5	50,569	-1,218	29,713	80.4
Ross	34,741	33,523	1,218	2,169	1,696	6.2	5.1	1,347	-16	20,817	-1,267	30,182	81.6
Sandusky	33,427	32,810	617	1,919	1,358	5.7	4.1	1,484	27	24,616	-721	29,006	78.5
Scioto	31,314	32,035	-721	2,384	2,316	7.6	7.2	1,457	-7	18,712	548	24,290	65.7
Seneca	31,431	30,949	482	1,662	1,321	5.3	4.3	1,352	9	20,191	-1,229	27,947	75.6
Shelby	28,181	25,560	2,621	1,199	985	4.3	3.9	1,068	11	25,488	-519	39,264	106.2
Stark	188,942	192,885	-3,943	10,998	7,933	5.8	4.1	9,391	-89	152,356	-12,130	30,258	81.9
Summit	294,232	280,304	13,928	15,613	11,613	5.3	4.1	14,535	94	253,928	-1,459	34,795	94.1
Trumbull	105,288	107,499	-2,211	6,669	5,321	6.3	4.9	4,694	-36	78,771	-9,164	33,377	90.3
Tuscarawas	47,992	46,452	1,540	2,439	1,922	5.1	4.1	2,398	50	33,300	411	26,203	70.9
Union	24,853	22,220	2,633	1,132	677	4.6	3.0	909	108	22,657	1,107	49,878	134.9
Van Wert	15,643	15,788	-145	757	652	4.8	4.1	598	-24	10,276	-1,187	27,770	75.1
Vinton	5,713	5,442	271	451	374	7.9	6.9	159	-4	1,733	59	26,691	72.2
Warren	105,550	83,289	22,261	5,196	2,747	4.9	3.3	3,470	532	61,818	2,773	35,593	96.3
Washington	32,996	31,319	1,677	1,740	1,704	5.3	5.4	1,558	-16	21,985	-1,270	28,109	76.0
Wayne	59,994	58,933	1,061	2,789	1,963	4.6	3.3	2,622	31	41,944	-1,923	29,059	78.6
Williams	19,674	21,272	-1,598	1,182	744	6.0	3.5	903	-23	15,830	-1,815	29,747	80.5
Wood	68,447	66,341	2,106	3,590	2,318	5.2	3.5	2,796	162	48,928	820	32,691	88.4
Wyandot	12,475	12,379	96	733	483	5.9	3.9	584	25	9,609	387	28,571	77.3

See footnotes at end of table.

Table B-10. Counties — **Labor Force and Private Business Establishments and Employment**—Con.

[Includes United States, states, and 3,141 counties/county equivalents defined as of February 22, 2005. For more information on these areas, see Appendix C, Geographic Information]

County	Civilian labor force							Private nonfarm businesses					
	Total			Number of unemployed		Unemployment rate[1]		Establishments		Employment[2]		Annual payroll per employee, 2004	
	2006	2000	Net change, 2000–2006	2006	2000	2006	2000	2004	Net change, 2000–2004	2004	Net change, 2000–2004	Amount (dol.)	Percent of U.S. average
OKLAHOMA	1,719,628	1,661,045	58,583	68,751	51,523	4.0	3.1	[3]87,440	[3]2,346	[3]1,195,043	[3]-6,563	[3]29,788	[3]80.6
Adair	10,314	9,219	1,095	454	332	4.4	3.6	229	14	2,811	−591	30,161	81.6
Alfalfa	2,242	2,616	−374	97	78	4.3	3.0	144	−10	802	−137	19,313	52.2
Atoka	5,584	5,194	390	275	189	4.9	3.6	234	2	1,974	−13	19,851	53.7
Beaver	2,890	2,943	−53	80	71	2.8	2.4	171	−2	867	−172	25,231	68.3
Beckham	10,165	8,643	1,522	275	277	2.7	3.2	655	10	6,486	665	22,538	61.0
Blaine	4,764	4,804	−40	202	137	4.2	2.9	286	−12	2,382	−360	22,795	61.7
Bryan	19,834	16,773	3,061	707	500	3.6	3.0	682	103	13,027	3,250	24,828	67.2
Caddo	11,570	12,162	−592	650	459	5.6	3.8	507	−23	4,287	10	24,022	65.0
Canadian	51,536	46,621	4,915	1,736	1,112	3.4	2.4	1,890	188	18,877	−161	24,718	66.9
Carter	24,094	20,924	3,170	916	795	3.8	3.8	1,410	56	17,780	1,374	30,545	82.6
Cherokee	20,894	18,847	2,047	888	606	4.3	3.2	719	50	7,486	107	22,364	60.5
Choctaw	6,536	6,075	461	333	293	5.1	4.8	263	2	3,258	202	17,198	46.5
Cimarron	1,251	1,602	−351	43	36	3.4	2.2	90	−4	434	−65	16,597	44.9
Cleveland	118,983	111,444	7,539	4,048	2,591	3.4	2.3	4,778	508	56,086	8,421	24,880	67.3
Coal	2,303	2,496	−193	139	108	6.0	4.3	67	3	611	−292	18,697	50.6
Comanche	45,594	43,323	2,271	1,918	1,587	4.2	3.7	2,175	−24	29,819	2,226	25,223	68.2
Cotton	3,285	2,867	418	109	93	3.3	3.2	83	−13	852	358	20,379	55.1
Craig	6,675	6,933	−258	285	250	4.3	3.6	354	−25	4,625	−1,101	25,484	68.9
Creek	32,258	31,973	285	1,324	1,042	4.1	3.3	1,295	20	15,491	−342	25,730	69.6
Custer	13,303	13,261	42	410	332	3.1	2.5	847	10	8,360	−35	24,540	66.4
Delaware	17,163	15,997	1,166	772	586	4.5	3.7	640	11	6,007	137	20,665	55.9
Dewey	2,345	2,276	69	75	62	3.2	2.7	127	−14	775	30	28,698	77.6
Ellis	2,161	2,111	50	61	57	2.8	2.7	117	−1	689	28	24,887	67.3
Garfield	28,650	28,113	537	893	797	3.1	2.8	1,651	13	20,793	1,656	28,443	76.9
Garvin	13,308	12,501	807	489	436	3.7	3.5	644	36	6,639	89	26,170	70.8
Grady	23,746	22,002	1,744	1,137	649	4.8	2.9	939	11	10,737	60	22,879	61.9
Grant	2,328	2,569	−241	89	64	3.8	2.5	117	−21	728	−90	29,948	81.0
Greer	2,029	2,269	−240	102	91	5.0	4.0	98	−15	894	54	16,110	43.6
Harmon	1,415	1,436	−21	52	40	3.7	2.8	76	–	479	62	18,656	50.5
Harper	1,784	1,916	−132	56	41	3.1	2.1	108	−10	603	33	21,041	56.9
Haskell	5,289	5,103	186	230	227	4.3	4.4	225	21	2,259	86	20,974	56.7
Hughes	4,958	5,559	−601	310	291	6.3	5.2	232	−14	1,936	38	17,979	48.6
Jackson	12,258	11,909	349	422	362	3.4	3.0	571	17	7,690	181	23,087	62.5
Jefferson	2,310	2,837	−527	105	103	4.5	3.6	121	−4	706	−163	16,972	45.9
Johnston	4,851	4,535	316	211	165	4.3	3.6	160	4	2,123	−205	24,405	66.0
Kay	21,456	22,042	−586	1,062	956	4.9	4.3	1,229	−27	16,140	−2,293	29,732	80.4
Kingfisher	7,846	7,179	667	220	160	2.8	2.2	452	33	4,574	249	28,356	76.7
Kiowa	3,841	4,600	−759	185	130	4.8	2.8	215	−18	2,058	−107	18,872	51.0
Latimer	3,991	4,434	−443	206	212	5.2	4.8	164	3	1,643	−201	25,470	68.9
Le Flore	21,855	20,741	1,114	1,111	893	5.1	4.3	734	11	7,685	−178	21,167	57.3
Lincoln	14,802	14,893	−91	597	442	4.0	3.0	535	29	4,588	−436	22,221	60.1
Logan	18,278	17,008	1,270	664	432	3.6	2.5	607	80	5,924	1,052	18,425	49.8
Love	4,851	4,216	635	169	152	3.5	3.6	142	−1	1,195	−233	23,125	62.6
McClain	14,796	13,850	946	536	357	3.6	2.6	680	107	5,561	509	21,591	58.4
McCurtain	13,700	14,852	−1,152	856	715	6.2	4.8	580	−4	8,274	−307	23,120	62.5
McIntosh	8,122	7,935	187	426	366	5.2	4.6	402	4	3,254	124	18,952	51.3
Major	3,761	4,004	−243	109	95	2.9	2.4	219	6	1,701	−17	21,856	59.1
Marshall	6,160	5,720	440	260	215	4.2	3.8	288	24	3,753	283	23,520	63.6
Mayes	17,033	18,011	−978	735	605	4.3	3.4	753	15	8,656	−1,351	26,438	71.5
Murray	7,528	6,021	1,507	233	213	3.1	3.5	271	4	2,606	159	21,540	58.3
Muskogee	28,682	28,959	−277	1,496	1,131	5.2	3.9	1,573	−3	23,588	−1,448	26,756	72.4
Noble	5,537	5,741	−204	200	134	3.6	2.3	206	−13	3,254	−309	30,659	82.9
Nowata	4,693	4,867	−174	220	169	4.7	3.5	169	−2	1,551	243	20,181	54.6
Okfuskee	4,398	4,539	−141	248	178	5.6	3.9	167	−1	1,700	−108	21,739	58.8
Oklahoma	334,826	326,774	8,052	13,825	9,502	4.1	2.9	21,591	362	335,703	−9,156	31,823	86.1
Okmulgee	17,018	17,116	−98	910	771	5.3	4.5	729	62	7,005	467	23,641	64.0
Osage	21,076	20,844	232	853	668	4.0	3.2	508	−24	3,318	−915	19,950	54.0
Ottawa	16,212	15,611	601	762	717	4.7	4.6	670	−44	7,285	−141	22,662	61.3
Pawnee	7,897	7,929	−32	319	297	4.0	3.7	287	−23	2,279	−432	21,704	58.7
Payne	34,256	36,207	−1,951	1,246	905	3.6	2.5	1,679	106	20,516	754	22,928	62.0
Pittsburg	20,999	17,705	3,294	869	799	4.1	4.5	899	10	10,005	194	22,014	59.5
Pontotoc	19,609	16,710	2,899	718	554	3.7	3.3	914	13	11,641	−640	22,317	60.4
Pottawatomie	31,078	30,208	870	1,418	974	4.6	3.2	1,323	−7	17,142	−1,703	22,747	61.5
Pushmataha	5,353	4,658	695	236	203	4.4	4.4	186	−5	1,945	206	17,122	46.3
Roger Mills	1,741	1,831	−90	48	45	2.8	2.5	86	11	620	137	19,563	52.9
Rogers	40,585	36,138	4,447	1,461	978	3.6	2.7	1,418	111	18,594	3,020	29,288	79.2
Seminole	10,109	10,430	−321	585	452	5.8	4.3	467	−58	4,968	−1,221	22,855	61.8
Sequoyah	18,500	17,206	1,294	1,003	751	5.4	4.4	597	−6	6,834	146	18,668	50.5
Stephens	20,525	19,306	1,219	725	653	3.5	3.4	1,025	−16	12,091	−762	24,366	65.9
Texas	8,963	10,606	−1,643	302	280	3.4	2.6	472	−73	6,057	−1,214	28,102	76.0

See footnotes at end of table.

Table B-10. Counties — **Labor Force and Private Business Establishments and Employment**—Con.

[Includes United States, states, and 3,141 counties/county equivalents defined as of February 22, 2005. For more information on these areas, see Appendix C, Geographic Information]

County	Civilian labor force							Private nonfarm businesses					
	Total			Number of unemployed		Unemployment rate[1]		Establishments		Employment[2]		Annual payroll per employee, 2004	
	2006	2000	Net change, 2000–2006	2006	2000	2006	2000	2004	Net change, 2000–2004	2004	Net change, 2000–2004	Amount (dol.)	Percent of U.S. average
OKLAHOMA—Con.													
Tillman	3,438	3,803	−365	152	124	4.4	3.3	155	−11	1,447	−70	22,297	60.3
Tulsa	298,911	296,841	2,070	11,123	8,419	3.7	2.8	18,816	533	304,046	−20,819	35,201	95.2
Wagoner	32,557	29,477	3,080	1,169	765	3.6	2.6	822	56	6,498	−1,085	23,478	63.5
Washington	25,159	22,860	2,299	882	712	3.5	3.1	1,234	38	15,613	−1,520	35,044	94.8
Washita	5,663	5,561	102	189	149	3.3	2.7	233	−6	1,560	18	19,533	52.8
Woods	4,160	4,570	−410	237	116	5.7	2.5	272	−6	2,278	2	19,959	54.0
Woodward	10,996	9,193	1,803	298	278	2.7	3.0	740	79	7,045	889	24,395	66.0
OREGON	1,898,847	1,810,150	88,697	102,682	93,196	5.4	5.1	[3]105,449	[3]4,804	[3]1,355,542	[3]100	[3]34,191	[3]92.5
Baker	7,203	7,354	−151	473	511	6.6	6.9	548	−3	3,890	−20	24,045	65.0
Benton	42,759	41,180	1,579	2,020	1,618	4.7	3.9	1,992	65	28,090	832	33,092	89.5
Clackamas	196,681	187,388	9,293	9,464	7,691	4.8	4.1	10,333	708	125,202	9,493	36,285	98.2
Clatsop	19,533	17,993	1,540	982	894	5.0	5.0	1,436	72	11,877	495	23,154	62.6
Columbia	23,778	22,443	1,335	1,374	1,248	5.8	5.6	914	68	8,893	−143	32,853	88.9
Coos	28,831	27,351	1,480	1,986	1,996	6.9	7.3	1,749	8	19,435	1,243	25,713	69.6
Crook	9,618	8,649	969	577	627	6.0	7.2	485	56	4,892	−147	32,158	87.0
Curry	9,631	8,688	943	670	596	7.0	6.9	785	96	5,685	797	23,510	63.6
Deschutes	79,505	61,406	18,099	3,683	3,305	4.6	5.4	5,498	1,008	50,488	7,602	28,964	78.3
Douglas	47,712	45,191	2,521	3,609	3,330	7.6	7.4	2,823	126	32,427	2,170	28,006	75.8
Gilliam	1,002	1,149	−147	50	51	5.0	4.4	67	4	618	−25	27,018	73.1
Grant	3,573	3,939	−366	300	369	8.4	9.4	280	−7	1,645	71	25,073	67.8
Harney	3,366	3,789	−423	275	322	8.2	8.5	187	−6	1,539	−252	24,972	67.6
Hood River	12,712	11,623	1,089	705	759	5.5	6.5	846	65	8,381	702	22,205	60.1
Jackson	100,965	91,561	9,404	5,822	5,069	5.8	5.5	6,009	645	67,754	5,500	28,622	77.4
Jefferson	9,206	9,550	−344	527	481	5.7	5.0	362	86	4,176	−60	28,189	76.3
Josephine	35,209	31,334	3,875	2,367	2,159	6.7	6.9	2,122	241	19,941	1,646	25,929	70.1
Klamath	30,583	29,385	1,198	2,073	2,178	6.8	7.4	1,680	94	16,632	−661	30,098	81.4
Lake	3,673	3,389	284	280	279	7.6	8.2	207	4	1,292	−12	24,216	65.5
Lane	178,082	170,410	7,672	9,850	9,184	5.5	5.4	9,789	99	118,928	−597	30,196	81.7
Lincoln	22,141	21,006	1,135	1,357	1,344	6.1	6.4	1,591	−90	13,757	84	24,039	65.0
Linn	52,938	51,847	1,091	3,518	3,393	6.6	6.5	2,544	−18	33,054	−826	30,806	83.3
Malheur	12,687	13,290	−603	827	999	6.5	7.5	743	−15	8,328	−543	23,970	64.8
Marion	151,392	144,000	7,392	8,659	7,980	5.7	5.5	7,675	225	94,543	−72	28,753	77.8
Morrow	5,478	5,435	43	370	420	6.8	7.7	175	22	1,943	283	30,035	81.2
Multnomah	371,888	378,889	−7,001	19,256	17,928	5.2	4.7	23,551	−21	377,679	−27,163	37,726	102.1
Polk	36,493	33,040	3,453	1,845	1,587	5.1	4.8	1,247	104	12,967	174	24,583	66.5
Sherman	884	1,042	−158	55	58	6.2	5.6	45	−2	342	54	13,918	37.6
Tillamook	12,508	11,544	964	706	592	5.6	5.1	709	21	6,392	−25	25,437	68.8
Umatilla	36,279	35,689	590	2,485	2,197	6.8	6.2	1,600	13	21,347	1,385	26,160	70.8
Union	12,034	12,204	−170	725	663	6.0	5.4	763	43	7,170	128	26,517	71.7
Wallowa	3,627	3,595	32	246	262	6.8	7.3	356	25	1,572	−21	23,522	63.6
Wasco	13,275	12,535	740	737	766	5.6	6.1	697	−30	6,210	−1,408	25,325	68.5
Washington	277,520	257,841	19,679	12,404	10,103	4.5	3.9	13,303	855	208,519	−5,913	44,066	119.2
Wheeler	631	728	−97	43	51	6.8	7.0	35	−1	134	9	16,224	43.9
Yamhill	45,457	43,691	1,766	2,366	2,185	5.2	5.0	2,175	136	25,049	955	29,045	78.6
PENNSYLVANIA	6,306,050	6,085,833	220,217	296,192	254,931	4.7	4.2	[3]301,557	[3]6,816	[3]5,107,044	[3]19,807	[3]35,595	[3]96.3
Adams	55,280	49,432	5,848	1,861	1,583	3.4	3.2	1,908	34	27,983	−428	26,339	71.2
Allegheny	631,994	635,816	−3,822	29,044	25,827	4.6	4.1	34,784	−67	679,552	−11,675	37,606	101.7
Armstrong	33,014	33,138	−124	1,794	1,891	5.4	5.7	1,430	−60	15,360	−1,306	24,734	66.9
Beaver	89,605	88,835	770	4,395	3,818	4.9	4.3	3,550	73	49,026	−558	28,639	77.5
Bedford	23,072	24,603	−1,531	1,341	1,362	5.8	5.5	1,094	−12	14,206	−609	24,583	66.5
Berks	201,584	194,612	6,972	9,021	7,679	4.5	3.9	8,488	333	144,424	−4,439	33,722	91.2
Blair	64,616	62,363	2,253	2,998	2,912	4.6	4.7	3,318	29	49,870	−1,981	27,455	74.3
Bradford	30,705	30,234	471	1,440	1,096	4.7	3.6	1,344	8	18,490	−388	28,444	76.9
Bucks	345,674	329,104	16,570	13,799	11,310	4.0	3.4	18,828	1,030	258,373	10,801	34,679	93.8
Butler	95,465	89,074	6,391	4,264	3,649	4.5	4.1	4,514	260	64,741	1,384	30,042	81.3
Cambria	67,954	66,623	1,331	3,753	4,066	5.5	6.1	3,519	−29	49,596	−1,818	25,855	69.9
Cameron	2,594	2,783	−189	167	183	6.4	6.6	148	6	1,922	−173	24,467	66.2
Carbon	30,836	28,993	1,843	1,812	1,498	5.9	5.2	1,157	19	12,644	−1,782	24,357	65.9
Centre	73,094	68,466	4,628	2,819	2,425	3.9	3.5	3,233	106	44,569	−2,185	27,230	73.7
Chester	259,490	235,821	23,669	8,972	7,225	3.5	3.1	13,383	1,206	213,332	23,180	47,856	129.5
Clarion	20,460	19,354	1,106	1,055	989	5.2	5.1	1,016	−22	11,614	−1,046	24,522	66.3
Clearfield	40,886	39,368	1,518	2,284	2,219	5.6	5.6	1,959	52	25,368	−1,264	25,278	68.4
Clinton	18,891	18,201	690	1,079	944	5.7	5.2	758	17	9,662	−824	24,558	66.4
Columbia	34,506	31,954	2,552	1,948	1,681	5.6	5.3	1,523	6	23,814	−1,072	29,123	78.8
Crawford	42,633	42,747	−114	2,259	2,103	5.3	4.9	2,210	51	26,679	−2,042	25,876	70.0
Cumberland	121,795	113,803	7,992	4,212	3,613	3.5	3.2	5,639	69	113,422	−1,998	33,656	91.0
Dauphin	136,296	131,303	4,993	5,559	4,654	4.1	3.5	6,861	281	153,390	17,273	34,863	94.3
Delaware	282,764	277,065	5,699	12,479	10,476	4.4	3.8	13,278	−28	217,136	58	41,504	112.3
Elk	17,611	18,190	−579	848	885	4.8	4.9	974	−27	13,886	−1,291	29,793	80.6
Erie	140,889	140,289	600	7,318	6,380	5.2	4.5	6,759	−204	117,531	−4,869	28,266	76.5

See footnotes at end of table.

County and City Data Book: 2007

U.S. Census Bureau

[Includes United States, states, and 3,141 counties/county equivalents defined as of February 22, 2005. For more information on these areas, see Appendix C, Geographic Information]

County	Civilian labor force							Private nonfarm businesses					
	Total			Number of unemployed		Unemployment rate[1]		Establishments		Employment[2]		Annual payroll per employee, 2004	
	2006	2000	Net change, 2000–2006	2006	2000	2006	2000	2004	Net change, 2000–2004	2004	Net change, 2000–2004	Amount (dol.)	Percent of U.S. average
PENNSYLVANIA—Con.													
Fayette	65,585	64,532	1,053	4,287	3,675	6.5	5.7	2,816	27	36,453	2,423	23,615	63.9
Forest	2,530	2,012	518	171	143	6.8	7.1	128	−17	1,228	82	25,180	68.1
Franklin	78,727	67,502	11,225	2,532	2,535	3.2	3.8	2,940	129	45,549	3,314	28,021	75.8
Fulton	8,299	7,258	1,041	355	281	4.3	3.9	301	12	4,179	−1,455	38,244	103.5
Greene	17,459	16,686	773	1,030	988	5.9	5.9	699	17	8,947	574	28,720	77.7
Huntingdon	22,147	20,810	1,337	1,184	1,271	5.3	6.1	843	11	9,694	−395	23,915	64.7
Indiana	45,626	40,976	4,650	2,402	2,392	5.3	5.8	2,010	6	28,026	2,564	27,606	74.7
Jefferson	22,737	21,486	1,251	1,140	1,137	5.0	5.3	1,170	−20	13,706	39	25,351	68.6
Juniata	12,653	11,485	1,168	551	484	4.4	4.2	495	2	5,915	60	24,901	67.4
Lackawanna	106,211	103,625	2,586	5,352	4,651	5.0	4.5	5,440	18	95,887	2,504	27,926	75.5
Lancaster	267,346	250,562	16,784	9,632	7,103	3.6	2.8	11,811	371	219,344	4,764	32,242	87.2
Lawrence	43,751	44,624	−873	2,402	2,190	5.5	4.9	2,126	−7	28,812	−1,417	27,145	73.4
Lebanon	71,278	64,137	7,141	2,472	2,033	3.5	3.2	2,595	27	42,237	4,607	29,009	78.5
Lehigh	173,908	162,455	11,453	8,097	5,954	4.7	3.7	8,308	129	157,244	−4,185	39,001	105.5
Luzerne	158,721	155,431	3,290	8,778	7,982	5.5	5.1	7,711	50	125,682	−1,646	28,686	77.6
Lycoming	59,002	59,250	−248	3,182	2,573	5.4	4.3	2,810	−69	46,158	−3,289	27,547	74.5
McKean	21,826	21,858	−32	1,170	1,048	5.4	4.8	1,116	−21	14,581	−725	26,931	72.9
Mercer	55,218	56,611	−1,393	3,053	2,810	5.5	5.0	3,033	81	45,865	−541	26,534	71.8
Mifflin	22,564	22,163	401	1,164	951	5.2	4.3	990	64	14,297	−566	26,814	72.5
Monroe	80,003	69,262	10,741	4,153	2,929	5.2	4.2	3,589	307	43,621	2,923	28,961	78.3
Montgomery	427,798	408,793	19,005	15,775	13,002	3.7	3.2	26,164	364	496,707	−507	46,796	126.6
Montour	9,081	8,597	484	377	301	4.2	3.5	398	37	11,880	75	45,858	124.1
Northampton	150,370	138,159	12,211	6,993	5,222	4.7	3.8	6,125	451	88,062	7,703	32,851	88.9
Northumberland	47,187	45,403	1,784	2,557	2,049	5.4	4.5	1,742	−57	22,615	−2,082	27,875	75.4
Perry	24,507	23,299	1,208	971	873	4.0	3.7	817	68	6,369	469	21,673	58.6
Philadelphia	623,622	635,138	−11,516	39,584	35,532	6.3	5.6	26,524	742	578,955	−27,554	40,801	110.4
Pike	26,269	21,183	5,086	1,566	808	6.0	3.8	838	119	6,660	1,215	22,792	61.7
Potter	8,313	8,489	−176	498	382	6.0	4.5	411	−37	5,292	−802	28,383	76.8
Schuylkill	71,480	69,929	1,551	4,005	4,090	5.6	5.8	3,095	−39	41,261	−2,415	28,192	76.3
Snyder	20,028	19,016	1,012	848	694	4.2	3.6	867	45	14,674	1,033	25,524	69.0
Somerset	39,022	38,044	978	2,194	2,004	5.6	5.3	1,878	−38	22,858	782	24,000	64.9
Sullivan	3,027	2,976	51	165	142	5.5	4.8	192	18	1,446	150	21,133	57.2
Susquehanna	21,330	20,359	971	1,015	801	4.8	3.9	859	59	6,421	−21	21,658	58.6
Tioga	20,277	19,993	284	1,116	888	5.5	4.4	856	1	10,078	−401	24,317	65.8
Union	17,858	17,290	568	943	678	5.3	3.9	852	6	16,441	1,553	27,241	73.7
Venango	26,772	26,777	−5	1,427	1,366	5.3	5.1	1,270	−37	16,445	−1,446	26,923	72.8
Warren	21,087	22,126	−1,039	1,086	831	5.2	3.8	942	−28	13,823	−2,046	29,394	79.5
Washington	102,836	98,371	4,465	5,188	4,533	5.0	4.6	5,018	113	75,309	1,039	33,131	89.6
Wayne	25,271	22,629	2,642	1,067	1,025	4.2	4.5	1,571	151	14,040	880	24,673	66.7
Westmoreland	185,702	181,603	4,099	9,507	8,453	5.1	4.7	9,064	48	125,836	−2,583	29,985	81.1
Wyoming	14,437	13,806	631	763	662	5.3	4.8	646	15	8,473	279	32,695	88.4
York	222,476	208,958	13,518	8,916	6,999	4.0	3.3	8,547	349	157,906	4,815	32,616	88.2
RHODE ISLAND	577,338	543,404	33,934	29,720	22,646	5.1	4.2	[3]30,011	[3]1,477	[3]434,706	[3]19,538	[3]34,564	[3]93.5
Bristol	28,870	26,840	2,030	1,303	987	4.5	3.7	1,273	142	13,814	(NA)	26,843	72.6
Kent	98,398	92,827	5,571	4,769	3,655	4.8	3.9	5,188	265	75,465	3,768	32,671	88.4
Newport	45,546	44,980	566	2,138	1,690	4.7	3.8	2,823	121	30,357	1,812	32,916	89.0
Providence	329,951	309,668	20,283	18,324	13,980	5.6	4.5	16,760	479	272,471	8,850	35,798	96.8
Washington	74,571	69,092	5,479	3,185	2,336	4.3	3.4	3,889	393	42,174	6,297	33,331	90.2
SOUTH CAROLINA	2,126,439	1,972,850	153,589	138,061	70,821	6.5	3.6	[3]101,165	[3]4,019	[3]1,560,573	[3]−40,959	[3]29,897	[3]80.9
Abbeville	12,322	12,470	−148	1,085	456	8.8	3.7	351	11	5,531	−1,148	26,442	71.5
Aiken	75,715	69,233	6,482	4,906	2,588	6.5	3.7	2,709	89	51,509	−923	37,630	101.8
Allendale	3,523	3,707	−184	405	188	11.5	5.1	152	−5	1,979	−348	27,942	75.6
Anderson	85,482	83,705	1,777	5,829	2,551	6.8	3.0	3,819	94	56,775	−2,223	26,659	72.1
Bamberg	6,666	6,491	175	658	325	9.9	5.0	285	−18	3,427	−339	23,980	64.9
Barnwell	9,341	10,226	−885	952	501	10.2	4.9	394	3	6,230	−149	38,396	103.9
Beaufort	60,707	51,115	9,592	3,040	1,576	5.0	3.1	4,709	422	50,746	3,575	28,730	77.7
Berkeley	74,571	65,801	8,770	4,200	2,100	5.6	3.2	2,214	409	33,084	6,495	32,228	87.2
Calhoun	7,358	7,096	262	517	263	7.0	3.7	206	4	2,467	379	26,214	70.9
Charleston	172,913	153,058	19,855	8,735	4,902	5.1	3.2	11,242	756	167,036	−2,757	29,602	80.1
Cherokee	25,196	25,539	−343	1,967	1,054	7.8	4.1	1,021	−13	18,665	−1,875	26,662	72.1
Chester	16,369	16,314	55	1,685	819	10.3	5.0	565	−2	9,214	−873	29,175	78.9
Chesterfield	18,667	19,256	−589	1,812	874	9.7	4.5	755	17	12,270	−1,250	27,333	73.9
Clarendon	13,012	13,040	−28	1,223	691	9.4	5.3	501	−27	6,625	−257	23,640	63.9
Colleton	16,602	15,941	661	1,128	596	6.8	3.7	816	−	9,251	535	22,556	61.0
Darlington	31,471	31,495	−24	2,432	1,507	7.7	4.8	1,246	−30	19,551	−2,016	30,914	83.6
Dillon	13,368	13,637	−24	1,273	908	9.5	6.7	507	−34	8,340	−89	20,250	54.8
Dorchester	58,809	47,263	11,546	3,050	1,407	5.2	3.0	1,986	207	22,493	−624	23,841	64.5
Edgefield	11,378	10,373	1,005	878	370	7.7	3.6	308	−32	4,563	−427	25,172	68.1
Fairfield	11,912	11,062	850	1,053	539	8.8	4.9	329	6	4,720	−2,147	35,745	96.7

See footnotes at end of table.

[Includes United States, states, and 3,141 counties/county equivalents defined as of February 22, 2005. For more information on these areas, see Appendix C, Geographic Information]

County	Civilian labor force							Private nonfarm businesses					
	Total			Number of unemployed		Unemployment rate[1]		Establishments		Employment[2]		Annual payroll per employee, 2004	
	2006	2000	Net change, 2000–2006	2006	2000	2006	2000	2004	Net change, 2000–2004	2004	Net change, 2000–2004	Amount (dol.)	Percent of U.S. average
SOUTH CAROLINA—Con.													
Florence	63,153	60,326	2,827	4,610	2,430	7.3	4.0	3,270	9	56,364	14	28,367	76.7
Georgetown	28,758	25,864	2,894	2,144	1,373	7.5	5.3	1,969	175	21,403	476	26,188	70.8
Greenville	216,797	203,590	13,207	11,729	5,294	5.4	2.6	11,744	119	220,568	−21,295	33,687	91.1
Greenwood	31,864	32,603	−739	2,568	1,370	8.1	4.2	1,534	−60	27,171	−2,168	28,950	78.3
Hampton	7,888	8,321	−433	586	352	7.4	4.2	437	−6	4,240	−500	27,317	73.9
Horry	129,708	105,607	24,101	7,057	3,733	5.4	3.5	7,940	753	90,033	3,743	24,593	66.5
Jasper	9,940	9,199	741	503	324	5.1	3.5	475	40	4,480	1,018	25,107	67.9
Kershaw	30,108	27,113	2,995	1,903	996	6.3	3.7	1,222	36	15,643	421	25,732	69.6
Lancaster	30,951	30,112	839	2,807	1,085	9.1	3.6	1,156	−20	14,713	−2,480	28,337	76.7
Laurens	34,412	33,920	492	2,372	1,096	6.9	3.2	890	−25	13,976	−3,175	26,660	72.1
Lee	8,509	8,275	234	822	460	9.7	5.6	233	−13	2,414	−297	20,388	55.2
Lexington	132,510	118,390	14,120	6,177	3,137	4.7	2.6	5,405	437	75,764	7,694	27,987	75.7
McCormick	3,630	3,742	−112	402	233	11.1	6.2	125	−7	1,125	29	21,889	59.2
Marion	13,536	15,470	−1,934	1,648	1,421	12.2	9.2	655	−	8,356	−2,147	23,462	63.5
Marlboro	12,842	12,265	577	1,422	818	11.1	6.7	405	−18	6,468	115	25,305	68.5
Newberry	17,870	17,295	575	1,178	717	6.6	4.1	750	19	11,229	−209	26,672	72.2
Oconee	30,918	32,353	−1,435	2,792	1,116	9.0	3.4	1,552	59	20,054	−2,224	30,558	82.7
Orangeburg	40,358	40,709	−351	3,821	2,327	9.5	5.7	1,886	−52	27,095	−1,531	26,256	71.0
Pickens	59,016	57,617	1,399	3,679	1,721	6.2	3.0	2,228	44	31,005	−778	23,599	63.8
Richland	177,782	161,769	16,013	10,325	5,196	5.8	3.2	9,268	77	174,849	−765	31,881	86.2
Saluda	9,607	9,389	218	598	336	6.2	3.6	224	−21	2,039	−2,156	19,795	53.5
Spartanburg	135,367	129,773	5,594	9,041	4,554	6.7	3.5	6,552	269	116,612	−5,340	34,135	92.3
Sumter	46,248	44,794	1,454	3,667	1,877	7.9	4.2	1,950	86	33,194	−3,826	26,217	70.9
Union	12,584	14,137	−1,553	1,369	713	10.9	5.0	481	−58	6,553	−1,022	24,208	65.5
Williamsburg	15,745	15,124	621	1,565	1,126	9.9	7.4	495	−43	6,533	−991	23,275	63.0
York	100,962	88,274	12,688	6,452	2,801	6.4	3.2	4,077	266	59,762	4,075	31,958	86.5
SOUTH DAKOTA	430,992	408,685	22,307	13,892	11,007	3.2	2.7	[3]24,787	[3]1,004	[3]308,010	[3]1,306	[3]27,380	[3]74.1
Aurora	1,337	1,581	−244	48	37	3.6	2.3	97	−	511	61	15,924	43.1
Beadle	9,129	9,127	2	280	239	3.1	2.6	579	−18	5,723	−596	22,865	61.9
Bennett	1,426	1,342	84	73	52	5.1	3.9	71	5	650	63	18,200	49.2
Bon Homme	3,236	3,332	−96	133	92	4.1	2.8	191	−22	1,550	−166	20,790	56.2
Brookings	18,796	17,566	1,230	474	397	2.5	2.3	809	71	11,790	57	33,880	91.6
Brown	20,864	20,506	358	564	503	2.7	2.5	1,289	−55	16,141	−559	25,949	70.2
Brule	2,895	2,727	168	83	70	2.9	2.6	220	1	1,749	−77	19,646	53.1
Buffalo	540	511	29	80	52	14.8	10.2	8	−	115	61	20,617	55.8
Butte	5,258	4,784	474	150	141	2.9	2.9	298	19	1,811	−150	21,712	58.7
Campbell	871	927	−56	28	53	3.2	5.7	55	2	297	−16	18,168	49.1
Charles Mix	4,072	4,012	60	152	117	3.7	2.9	282	−5	2,578	35	19,659	53.2
Clark	1,838	2,133	−295	76	82	4.1	3.8	113	−5	518	−174	19,736	53.4
Clay	7,504	7,363	141	227	173	3.0	2.3	301	−1	2,816	−200	16,276	44.0
Codington	16,048	15,535	513	488	410	3.0	2.6	1,065	81	12,872	−101	24,831	67.2
Corson	1,375	1,381	−6	89	84	6.5	6.1	50	4	190	−90	16,947	45.8
Custer	4,739	4,167	572	148	132	3.1	3.2	242	21	1,016	−17	25,336	68.5
Davison	10,917	10,358	559	334	251	3.1	2.4	755	12	10,535	−155	24,885	67.3
Day	2,919	3,046	−127	154	131	5.3	4.3	203	−3	1,586	151	18,423	49.8
Deuel	2,666	2,515	151	100	83	3.8	3.3	136	−	1,254	340	29,223	79.1
Dewey	2,597	2,267	330	262	223	10.1	9.8	91	−10	720	−646	23,296	63.0
Douglas	1,731	1,739	−8	49	39	2.8	2.2	117	−4	746	−158	20,672	55.9
Edmunds	2,101	2,141	−40	61	53	2.9	2.5	128	12	638	−83	23,141	62.6
Fall River	3,759	3,533	226	137	141	3.6	4.0	234	26	2,183	−189	38,093	103.0
Faulk	1,173	1,283	−110	37	33	3.2	2.6	76	2	325	−7	19,160	51.8
Grant	4,196	4,152	44	154	136	3.7	3.3	278	17	3,050	82	25,847	69.9
Gregory	2,408	2,435	−27	86	76	3.6	3.1	193	5	1,065	10	16,775	45.4
Haakon	1,182	1,264	−82	33	23	2.8	1.8	81	−9	577	−67	21,844	59.1
Hamlin	2,956	2,790	166	97	76	3.3	2.7	155	6	966	146	23,970	64.8
Hand	1,921	2,043	−122	54	43	2.8	2.1	143	12	944	2	21,600	58.4
Hanson	1,992	1,594	398	59	36	3.0	2.3	55	2	183	−74	18,765	50.8
Harding	771	765	6	23	22	3.0	2.9	33	−2	202	23	19,515	52.8
Hughes	10,109	9,619	490	266	205	2.6	2.1	676	41	6,356	124	23,140	62.6
Hutchinson	3,808	3,984	−176	135	104	3.5	2.6	242	−8	1,955	−340	20,415	55.2
Hyde	768	853	−85	29	23	3.8	2.7	43	−2	567	14	21,437	58.0
Jackson	1,249	1,154	95	74	53	5.9	4.6	54	−1	263	−15	16,418	44.4
Jerauld	1,352	1,232	120	41	30	3.0	2.4	78	8	1,082	606	21,789	58.9
Jones	711	757	−46	18	17	2.5	2.2	49	−7	274	−25	24,033	65.0
Kingsbury	2,985	3,038	−53	101	80	3.4	2.6	198	−6	1,522	153	22,314	60.4
Lake	6,700	6,551	149	212	170	3.2	2.6	359	7	3,650	6	23,561	63.7
Lawrence	12,877	11,548	1,329	377	350	2.9	3.0	899	79	8,919	386	22,078	59.7
Lincoln	19,523	14,502	5,021	494	268	2.5	1.8	786	180	7,387	2,180	31,222	84.5
Lyman	1,989	1,926	63	93	85	4.7	4.4	84	15	674	84	17,369	47.0
McCook	2,999	2,985	14	94	71	3.1	2.4	183	5	1,134	−139	21,489	58.1
McPherson	1,191	1,327	−136	52	38	4.4	2.9	88	−5	359	−110	17,504	47.4
Marshall	2,109	2,223	−114	95	85	4.5	3.8	145	1	1,158	−217	22,383	60.5

See footnotes at end of table.

Table B-10. Counties — **Labor Force and Private Business Establishments and Employment**—Con.

[Includes United States, states, and 3,141 counties/county equivalents defined as of February 22, 2005. For more information on these areas, see Appendix C, Geographic Information]

County	Civilian labor force							Private nonfarm businesses					
	Total			Number of unemployed		Unemployment rate[1]		Establishments		Employment[2]		Annual payroll per employee, 2004	
	2006	2000	Net change, 2000–2006	2006	2000	2006	2000	2004	Net change, 2000–2004	2004	Net change, 2000–2004	Amount (dol.)	Percent of U.S. average
SOUTH DAKOTA—Con.													
Meade	12,698	12,269	429	418	319	3.3	2.6	593	74	5,214	562	26,250	71.0
Mellette	906	853	53	44	35	4.9	4.1	27	−3	184	23	14,402	39.0
Miner	1,181	1,491	−310	47	41	4.0	2.7	68	−5	487	−324	21,193	57.3
Minnehaha	94,654	88,973	5,681	2,678	1,907	2.8	2.1	5,383	247	104,223	5,488	30,271	81.9
Moody	3,987	3,720	267	169	149	4.2	4.0	134	−41	1,422	−92	26,504	71.7
Pennington	52,373	48,840	3,533	1,599	1,230	3.1	2.5	3,431	218	43,249	1,078	26,829	72.6
Perkins	1,709	1,787	−78	54	47	3.2	2.6	121	−11	835	−174	19,193	51.9
Potter	1,339	1,459	−120	43	41	3.2	2.8	116	−18	779	−100	19,669	53.2
Roberts	4,803	4,612	191	217	189	4.5	4.1	251	−	2,179	240	18,709	50.6
Sanborn	1,517	1,482	35	46	38	3.0	2.6	67	8	543	−185	19,245	52.1
Shannon	3,789	2,841	948	337	268	8.9	9.4	71	17	2,001	545	23,771	64.3
Spink	3,451	3,525	−74	116	115	3.4	3.3	168	−13	1,164	−139	20,637	55.8
Stanley	1,931	1,848	83	48	37	2.5	2.0	101	13	706	−118	26,622	72.0
Sully	1,005	910	95	25	22	2.5	2.4	59	3	367	116	18,793	50.8
Todd	3,391	2,955	436	201	147	5.9	5.0	51	−13	1,179	81	25,261	68.3
Tripp	3,051	3,302	−251	102	93	3.3	2.8	223	−	1,715	−50	19,929	53.9
Turner	4,556	4,785	−229	142	117	3.1	2.4	260	−14	1,530	−110	21,007	56.8
Union	7,529	7,296	233	267	195	3.5	2.7	420	20	7,449	−5,513	45,275	122.5
Walworth	2,695	2,888	−193	114	102	4.2	3.5	231	−9	1,809	−158	20,695	56.0
Yankton	11,982	11,482	500	361	275	3.0	2.4	710	21	9,852	−224	25,221	68.2
Ziebach	867	753	114	56	63	6.5	8.4	19	2	160	−24	24,138	65.3
TENNESSEE	2,990,152	2,871,539	118,613	154,622	115,041	5.2	4.0	[3]131,691	[3]815	[3]2,347,335	[3]−42,987	[3]32,770	[3]88.6
Anderson	35,527	34,058	1,469	1,670	1,445	4.7	4.2	1,650	−70	39,280	−284	42,756	115.7
Bedford	22,114	19,755	2,359	1,144	921	5.2	4.7	745	−7	13,145	−447	28,113	76.0
Benton	6,923	7,385	−462	495	557	7.2	7.5	337	−2	3,268	−259	19,595	53.0
Bledsoe	4,798	5,144	−346	313	212	6.5	4.1	125	−11	760	−590	19,876	53.8
Blount	60,841	54,348	6,493	2,630	1,962	4.3	3.6	2,323	149	39,863	1,443	32,195	87.1
Bradley	47,652	45,671	1,981	2,380	1,655	5.0	3.6	1,912	41	37,663	−2,465	29,544	79.9
Campbell	16,737	16,188	549	1,024	996	6.1	6.2	612	−35	6,931	−823	24,120	65.2
Cannon	6,604	6,409	195	330	232	5.0	3.6	163	−5	1,469	117	22,619	61.2
Carroll	13,906	14,349	−443	881	1,145	6.3	8.0	510	−21	6,668	−695	24,442	66.1
Carter	29,290	27,844	1,446	1,473	1,360	5.0	4.9	737	−6	9,719	−272	22,068	59.7
Cheatham	20,930	19,660	1,270	842	555	4.0	2.8	532	8	6,039	−671	28,128	76.1
Chester	7,684	7,679	5	416	319	5.4	4.2	261	17	3,004	−394	20,470	55.4
Claiborne	13,293	12,693	600	721	646	5.4	5.1	454	−15	7,963	−160	23,596	63.8
Clay	3,624	3,729	−105	395	248	10.9	6.7	121	3	1,292	−77	24,978	67.6
Cocke	16,205	15,700	505	1,177	1,024	7.3	6.5	497	−14	6,391	−475	24,283	65.7
Coffee	25,478	23,702	1,776	1,392	964	5.5	4.1	1,229	36	21,260	−272	29,213	79.0
Crockett	6,525	6,878	−353	448	329	6.9	4.8	269	−14	2,749	−415	26,008	70.4
Cumberland	22,839	20,535	2,304	1,417	1,037	6.2	5.0	1,008	39	13,351	1,080	24,214	65.5
Davidson	312,344	311,521	823	12,999	10,014	4.2	3.2	18,235	−365	385,790	−12,757	36,618	99.1
Decatur	5,538	5,719	−181	362	311	6.5	5.4	238	−19	3,009	−345	27,050	73.2
DeKalb	10,152	8,661	1,491	552	416	5.4	4.8	314	6	6,256	1,120	27,351	74.0
Dickson	23,447	22,293	1,154	1,075	816	4.6	3.7	891	5	13,501	97	26,868	72.7
Dyer	17,489	18,145	−656	1,010	952	5.8	5.2	889	−62	14,508	−602	27,898	75.5
Fayette	16,410	14,089	2,321	1,040	647	6.3	4.6	424	−22	4,800	588	28,298	76.5
Fentress	7,569	6,916	653	499	523	6.6	7.6	277	−9	3,053	−55	23,157	62.6
Franklin	20,087	18,866	1,221	1,145	748	5.7	4.0	710	37	10,367	2,159	28,127	76.1
Gibson	21,066	23,404	−2,338	1,617	1,272	7.7	5.4	1,082	3	13,366	−3,062	26,266	71.1
Giles	13,471	15,009	−1,538	958	667	7.1	4.4	551	−23	7,622	−2,017	26,564	71.9
Grainger	10,356	9,760	596	604	450	5.8	4.6	237	−9	2,199	−711	22,695	61.4
Greene	32,822	31,868	954	2,557	1,893	7.8	5.9	1,185	−13	22,674	−363	26,902	72.8
Grundy	5,866	5,706	160	472	288	8.0	5.0	201	13	1,685	178	18,846	51.0
Hamblen	30,324	29,758	566	1,731	1,212	5.7	4.1	1,397	−7	29,405	−2,982	29,732	80.4
Hamilton	161,562	160,657	905	7,171	5,403	4.4	3.4	8,785	−61	172,616	−2,154	31,539	85.3
Hancock	2,470	2,672	−202	174	139	7.0	5.2	56	−8	494	−127	17,854	48.3
Hardeman	11,376	11,118	258	819	582	7.2	5.2	391	−31	6,125	−428	24,664	66.7
Hardin	11,691	11,728	−37	720	640	6.2	5.5	511	−10	6,015	−397	26,152	70.7
Hawkins	26,030	24,690	1,340	1,503	1,058	5.8	4.3	586	−44	11,154	−941	27,337	73.9
Haywood	9,588	9,349	239	736	534	7.7	5.7	342	−39	5,046	507	24,093	65.2
Henderson	12,488	12,931	−443	820	654	6.6	5.1	504	−25	8,428	361	24,059	65.1
Henry	14,095	14,880	−785	1,009	742	7.2	5.0	734	−13	9,088	−1,184	26,082	70.6
Hickman	10,415	9,866	549	555	412	5.3	4.2	305	−2	2,473	135	21,283	57.6
Houston	3,820	3,706	114	287	222	7.5	6.0	118	8	984	−107	21,908	59.3
Humphreys	8,981	8,957	24	568	457	6.3	5.1	346	26	4,468	−207	31,348	84.8
Jackson	5,178	5,106	72	345	327	6.7	6.4	112	3	1,688	85	20,992	56.8
Jefferson	24,207	22,593	1,614	1,368	987	5.7	4.4	669	20	10,637	1	25,244	68.3
Johnson	7,238	6,976	262	482	475	6.7	6.8	241	−4	2,686	28	24,692	66.8
Knox	220,537	202,414	18,123	8,622	6,381	3.9	3.2	11,166	−8	198,854	11,656	31,477	85.1
Lake	2,677	2,568	109	187	163	7.0	6.3	92	−2	636	−46	20,426	55.3
Lauderdale	9,902	11,293	−1,391	796	591	8.0	5.2	338	−51	5,607	−1,049	25,348	68.6
Lawrence	16,899	19,150	−2,251	1,909	1,816	11.3	9.5	755	−45	10,920	−931	23,435	63.4

See footnotes at end of table.

[Includes United States, states, and 3,141 counties/county equivalents defined as of February 22, 2005. For more information on these areas, see Appendix C, Geographic Information]

County	Civilian labor force							Private nonfarm businesses					
	Total			Number of unemployed		Unemployment rate[1]		Establishments		Employment[2]		Annual payroll per employee, 2004	
	2006	2000	Net change, 2000–2006	2006	2000	2006	2000	2004	Net change, 2000–2004	2004	Net change, 2000–2004	Amount (dol.)	Percent of U.S. average
TENNESSEE—Con.													
Lewis	5,244	5,311	−67	375	297	7.2	5.6	192	−23	1,840	−199	20,460	55.3
Lincoln	17,047	15,892	1,155	716	577	4.2	3.6	625	−12	6,542	−740	25,364	68.6
Loudon	22,351	19,614	2,737	987	711	4.4	3.6	826	83	11,256	894	27,229	73.7
McMinn	24,822	23,724	1,098	1,396	1,091	5.6	4.6	909	−30	14,707	−2,482	31,938	86.4
McNairy	12,240	11,825	415	745	534	6.1	4.5	459	6	6,612	−2,597	24,168	65.4
Macon	10,976	10,267	709	741	392	6.8	3.8	333	25	3,493	−582	23,776	64.3
Madison	47,520	47,028	492	2,560	1,769	5.4	3.8	2,586	−35	51,977	−1,276	30,710	83.1
Marion	13,098	13,144	−46	750	601	5.7	4.6	442	8	5,341	−54	24,801	67.1
Marshall	12,649	14,063	−1,414	795	513	6.3	3.6	501	2	8,582	−2,928	25,458	68.9
Maury	36,422	37,051	−629	1,971	1,342	5.4	3.6	1,570	70	28,886	−1,126	37,988	102.8
Meigs	4,841	4,909	−68	331	258	6.8	5.3	95	1	1,367	−69	26,949	72.9
Monroe	19,408	17,528	1,880	1,110	962	5.7	5.5	710	53	11,382	−656	27,085	73.3
Montgomery	67,439	59,818	7,621	3,231	2,298	4.8	3.8	2,349	106	35,815	2,304	25,405	68.7
Moore	3,125	2,934	191	147	93	4.7	3.2	51	−7	798	53	35,754	96.7
Morgan	8,406	8,067	339	553	421	6.6	5.2	159	−9	1,610	−250	25,704	69.5
Obion	15,622	16,392	−770	877	717	5.6	4.4	724	−29	13,303	−1,685	31,468	85.1
Overton	10,036	9,682	354	665	529	6.6	5.5	280	−21	3,475	−102	24,156	65.3
Perry	3,350	3,514	−164	219	187	6.5	5.3	107	−6	1,763	−1,022	31,775	86.0
Pickett	1,868	2,286	−418	159	119	8.5	5.2	97	19	764	−314	23,681	64.1
Polk	7,432	7,540	−108	414	344	5.6	4.6	253	−7	1,762	−272	23,077	62.4
Putnam	34,818	32,015	2,803	1,980	1,433	5.7	4.5	1,715	−1	27,317	−912	25,114	67.9
Rhea	13,403	13,420	−17	824	641	6.1	4.8	518	31	9,111	578	26,429	71.5
Roane	26,627	24,900	1,727	1,431	1,086	5.4	4.4	728	16	9,625	1,236	23,077	62.4
Robertson	32,535	29,796	2,739	1,441	1,076	4.4	3.6	923	−41	13,735	−163	26,360	71.3
Rutherford	122,092	103,339	18,753	4,921	3,225	4.0	3.1	3,905	455	76,992	5,298	36,033	97.5
Scott	8,620	8,696	−76	585	464	6.8	5.3	353	7	5,340	−690	27,263	73.7
Sequatchie	5,921	5,369	552	271	211	4.6	3.9	192	24	2,378	−22	23,513	63.6
Sevier	47,011	39,837	7,174	2,536	2,009	5.4	5.0	2,678	155	30,723	3,084	22,299	60.3
Shelby	440,771	442,438	−1,667	25,150	17,437	5.7	3.9	20,787	−556	441,324	−35,975	37,597	101.7
Smith	9,361	8,969	392	533	395	5.7	4.4	303	−3	4,705	−220	26,698	72.2
Stewart	6,105	5,544	561	474	274	7.8	4.9	167	21	1,840	675	28,370	76.7
Sullivan	73,221	73,338	−117	3,328	2,772	4.5	3.8	3,553	−90	62,132	−2,254	34,072	92.2
Sumner	77,837	70,941	6,896	3,228	2,336	4.1	3.3	2,839	294	39,260	4,183	29,220	79.0
Tipton	27,074	25,307	1,767	1,516	955	5.6	3.8	740	4	8,959	−750	25,727	69.6
Trousdale	3,786	3,577	209	227	125	6.0	3.5	116	−4	1,005	−228	20,144	54.5
Unicoi	8,362	8,351	11	518	581	6.2	7.0	272	13	4,245	512	32,675	88.4
Union	8,948	8,128	820	429	319	4.8	3.9	197	8	1,793	−268	21,807	59.0
Van Buren	2,472	2,679	−207	198	127	8.0	4.7	44	−6	740	85	32,188	87.1
Warren	18,031	19,571	−1,540	1,626	821	9.0	4.2	764	−12	12,094	−1,745	30,463	82.4
Washington	59,070	55,363	3,707	2,675	2,248	4.5	4.1	2,803	55	49,915	−1,734	27,170	73.5
Wayne	6,539	6,757	−218	682	567	10.4	8.4	239	−8	2,784	−105	21,232	57.4
Weakley	15,742	16,934	−1,192	1,063	859	6.8	5.1	604	−43	8,262	−1,671	21,764	58.9
White	10,747	11,017	−270	971	517	9.0	4.7	399	−7	6,076	−753	26,696	72.2
Williamson	83,899	70,444	13,455	2,943	1,795	3.5	2.5	4,956	594	78,154	8,242	40,891	110.6
Wilson	56,210	50,132	6,078	2,494	1,617	4.4	3.2	2,303	260	33,162	6,581	31,967	86.5
TEXAS	11,487,496	10,347,847	1,139,649	565,823	451,845	4.9	4.4	[3]491,092	[3]19,583	[3]8,118,483	[3]92,045	[3]36,161	[3]97.8
Anderson	20,596	19,580	1,016	1,225	1,200	5.9	6.1	937	−13	11,824	1,289	25,882	70.0
Andrews	7,022	5,612	1,410	245	276	3.5	4.9	283	2	2,890	81	29,121	78.8
Angelina	40,735	37,872	2,863	1,914	1,815	4.7	4.8	1,816	11	29,489	−482	26,173	70.8
Aransas	11,178	9,713	1,465	537	578	4.8	6.0	490	13	3,619	27	21,017	56.9
Archer	5,416	4,855	561	187	154	3.5	3.2	147	−4	867	152	28,534	77.2
Armstrong	1,154	1,086	68	41	34	3.6	3.1	37	5	308	(NA)	25,016	67.7
Atascosa	19,693	17,190	2,503	917	710	4.7	4.1	605	60	5,994	78	22,391	60.6
Austin	13,355	11,989	1,366	566	478	4.2	4.0	585	37	7,006	1,207	28,952	78.3
Bailey	3,154	3,184	−30	165	145	5.2	4.6	167	−10	1,502	53	20,469	55.4
Bandera	10,048	8,685	1,363	427	317	4.2	3.6	383	62	1,829	168	20,330	55.0
Bastrop	35,021	29,667	5,354	1,603	1,032	4.6	3.5	895	105	8,385	1,141	23,195	62.7
Baylor	1,921	1,839	82	82	81	4.3	4.4	137	2	1,220	−81	14,609	39.5
Bee	11,580	11,304	276	746	677	6.4	6.0	447	−2	4,075	−317	23,616	63.9
Bell	116,223	101,226	14,997	5,911	4,325	5.1	4.3	4,352	279	79,363	4,086	28,608	77.4
Bexar	741,154	660,867	80,287	34,792	26,902	4.7	4.1	30,690	891	582,905	11,005	31,776	86.0
Blanco	4,680	4,459	221	186	137	4.0	3.1	229	6	1,688	−502	29,911	80.9
Borden	421	421	–	18	27	4.3	6.4	2	−1	[6]10	(NA)	(NA)	(NA)
Bosque	8,270	8,030	240	415	322	5.0	4.0	314	−1	2,717	76	24,974	67.6
Bowie	43,101	40,379	2,722	2,336	1,990	5.4	4.9	2,137	6	31,365	−782	26,272	71.1
Brazoria	138,590	119,857	18,733	6,817	5,998	4.9	5.0	4,141	304	64,800	3,924	34,428	93.1
Brazos	88,190	78,537	9,653	3,563	2,961	4.0	3.8	3,463	247	51,298	3,923	25,042	67.7
Brewster	5,626	4,545	1,081	191	175	3.4	3.9	313	25	2,406	225	18,736	50.7
Briscoe	694	907	−213	35	32	5.0	3.5	36	−17	131	−76	18,092	48.9
Brooks	3,069	2,880	189	194	194	6.3	6.7	144	6	1,766	502	13,994	37.9
Brown	19,407	17,615	1,792	877	774	4.5	4.4	892	−6	12,398	304	25,071	67.8

See footnotes at end of table.

Table B-10. Counties — **Labor Force and Private Business Establishments and Employment**—Con.

[Includes United States, states, and 3,141 counties/county equivalents defined as of February 22, 2005. For more information on these areas, see Appendix C, Geographic Information]

County	Civilian labor force							Private nonfarm businesses					
	Total			Number of unemployed		Unemployment rate[1]		Establishments		Employment[2]		Annual payroll per employee, 2004	
	2006	2000	Net change, 2000–2006	2006	2000	2006	2000	2004	Net change, 2000–2004	2004	Net change, 2000–2004	Amount (dol.)	Percent of U.S. average
TEXAS—Con.													
Burleson	8,773	7,708	1,065	358	314	4.1	4.1	293	14	2,314	23	22,149	59.9
Burnet	21,638	17,126	4,512	890	586	4.1	3.4	930	20	8,144	1,072	25,235	68.3
Caldwell	16,620	15,075	1,545	808	629	4.9	4.2	489	−5	4,519	293	21,734	58.8
Calhoun	9,557	9,326	231	473	436	4.9	4.7	404	−7	6,882	−1,173	43,351	117.3
Callahan	7,169	6,195	974	287	238	4.0	3.8	201	3	1,145	147	21,668	58.6
Cameron	144,709	126,967	17,742	9,594	8,888	6.6	7.0	6,168	372	90,929	4,432	20,497	55.4
Camp	5,556	5,202	354	285	266	5.1	5.1	247	−9	4,333	1,274	28,977	78.4
Carson	3,587	3,345	242	128	109	3.6	3.3	112	−15	3,884	3,046	58,618	158.6
Cass	13,172	13,493	−321	795	781	6.0	5.8	574	3	5,345	104	19,834	53.7
Castro	3,202	3,981	−779	159	146	5.0	3.7	185	−17	1,070	−372	24,689	66.8
Chambers	14,475	13,083	1,392	737	564	5.1	4.3	408	32	4,456	−1,920	35,216	95.3
Cherokee	20,637	20,864	−227	1,118	955	5.4	4.6	764	−58	11,830	−1,239	22,475	60.8
Childress	3,004	2,973	31	174	138	5.8	4.6	163	−5	1,444	212	20,289	54.9
Clay	6,638	5,938	700	256	210	3.9	3.5	139	11	1,103	98	23,586	63.8
Cochran	1,441	1,585	−144	92	92	6.4	5.8	64	−3	435	6	25,384	68.7
Coke	1,369	1,655	−286	78	67	5.7	4.0	65	−12	555	−109	26,580	71.9
Coleman	4,232	4,200	32	187	194	4.4	4.6	205	−6	1,473	29	18,944	51.2
Collin	381,670	299,234	82,436	16,300	8,562	4.3	2.9	14,297	3,216	228,523	45,199	43,034	116.4
Collingsworth	1,599	1,526	73	70	54	4.4	3.5	71	–	595	145	20,030	54.2
Colorado	10,804	9,890	914	476	363	4.4	3.7	533	−22	5,009	−533	25,124	68.0
Comal	50,703	40,308	10,395	2,098	1,420	4.1	3.5	2,352	302	30,386	5,407	27,629	74.7
Comanche	6,430	6,657	−227	296	251	4.6	3.8	299	−11	2,508	−209	21,391	57.9
Concho	1,341	1,433	−92	77	81	5.7	5.7	54	−4	591	19	26,198	70.9
Cooke	20,966	18,609	2,357	814	670	3.9	3.6	839	−7	11,027	−863	25,039	67.7
Coryell	25,895	23,925	1,970	1,682	1,304	6.5	5.5	703	−22	8,372	817	20,620	55.8
Cottle	791	946	−155	43	39	5.4	4.1	42	−5	219	−89	16,406	44.4
Crane	1,739	1,609	130	79	87	4.5	5.4	72	−13	825	−118	31,982	86.5
Crockett	2,056	2,039	17	74	77	3.6	3.8	122	−1	782	−186	23,824	64.4
Crosby	2,992	2,974	18	163	137	5.4	4.6	115	−12	969	45	26,305	71.2
Culberson	1,683	1,489	194	54	85	3.2	5.7	59	−3	526	−61	17,110	46.3
Dallam	2,995	3,277	−282	105	110	3.5	3.4	240	10	1,852	103	22,768	61.6
Dallas	1,184,476	1,184,898	−422	60,317	46,625	5.1	3.9	62,601	−1,206	1,314,123	−163,993	44,686	120.9
Dawson	5,091	5,831	−740	347	306	6.8	5.2	316	−38	2,366	−181	21,587	58.4
Deaf Smith	8,273	8,224	49	362	396	4.4	4.8	419	−28	3,932	−474	25,649	69.4
Delta	2,505	2,564	−59	128	132	5.1	5.1	65	−7	576	105	12,063	32.6
Denton	326,387	267,029	59,358	13,821	7,613	4.2	2.9	9,388	1,366	132,913	22,298	31,938	86.4
DeWitt	9,617	8,951	666	427	374	4.4	4.2	411	46	4,152	464	22,724	61.5
Dickens	1,216	1,132	84	54	58	4.4	5.1	48	−6	348	−33	25,618	69.3
Dimmit	3,843	3,853	−10	300	335	7.8	8.7	167	−15	1,459	18	21,508	58.2
Donley	1,837	1,861	−24	89	74	4.8	4.0	85	−9	381	−23	16,525	44.7
Duval	5,511	5,001	510	298	351	5.4	7.0	136	−15	1,262	151	26,052	70.5
Eastland	8,640	8,555	85	420	396	4.9	4.6	485	26	4,795	−184	23,675	64.0
Ector	66,467	56,487	9,980	2,583	3,058	3.9	5.4	3,129	118	42,590	3,965	29,832	80.7
Edwards	960	952	8	43	41	4.5	4.3	43	6	190	47	18,253	49.4
Ellis	68,919	60,047	8,872	3,460	2,172	5.0	3.6	2,238	190	30,654	2,172	30,292	81.9
El Paso	295,141	274,826	20,315	19,911	18,716	6.7	6.8	12,556	246	199,563	−318	24,863	67.3
Erath	17,777	16,545	1,232	727	598	4.1	3.6	831	−2	10,877	1,298	22,159	59.9
Falls	7,178	7,173	5	455	381	6.3	5.3	261	−16	1,947	−534	20,049	54.2
Fannin	13,710	13,899	−189	833	661	6.1	4.8	503	12	4,937	−827	27,037	73.1
Fayette	12,102	11,387	715	458	370	3.8	3.2	746	9	6,353	224	24,380	66.0
Fisher	1,963	2,148	−185	83	79	4.2	3.7	75	−12	779	81	22,751	61.5
Floyd	3,154	3,466	−312	193	164	6.1	4.7	182	−2	1,192	−87	19,348	52.3
Foard	675	790	−115	30	28	4.4	3.5	33	−7	193	−136	14,767	39.9
Fort Bend	244,666	185,224	59,442	11,532	6,670	4.7	3.6	7,105	1,097	90,649	12,001	36,512	98.8
Franklin	5,451	4,417	1,034	234	182	4.3	4.1	168	−21	5,544	−147	13,102	35.4
Freestone	10,469	7,874	2,595	415	395	4.0	5.0	358	15	3,432	267	29,683	80.3
Frio	6,503	6,156	347	366	379	5.6	6.2	250	−18	2,164	35	20,446	55.3
Gaines	6,135	6,231	−96	287	270	4.7	4.3	307	−6	2,507	122	24,043	65.0
Galveston	143,120	127,783	15,337	7,193	6,318	5.0	4.9	4,940	139	69,101	−57	29,070	78.6
Garza	2,550	2,116	434	106	92	4.2	4.3	121	2	1,011	−11	23,948	64.8
Gillespie	12,920	10,481	2,439	432	381	3.3	3.6	898	87	6,885	652	23,988	64.9
Glasscock	581	726	−145	27	22	4.6	3.0	15	−5	86	−46	28,977	78.4
Goliad	3,480	3,326	154	143	126	4.1	3.8	115	3	853	141	27,783	75.2
Gonzales	9,847	9,082	765	411	308	4.2	3.4	400	5	4,329	327	24,508	66.3
Gray	10,991	9,955	1,036	437	492	4.0	4.9	652	−22	5,884	−307	28,780	77.9
Grayson	57,451	56,210	1,241	2,810	2,240	4.9	4.0	2,645	65	36,644	−2,875	29,284	79.2
Gregg	61,958	55,089	6,869	2,852	2,979	4.6	5.4	3,955	87	62,031	4,557	29,324	79.3
Grimes	10,622	9,939	683	578	531	5.4	5.3	357	12	4,153	−913	31,474	85.1
Guadalupe	53,759	45,260	8,499	2,353	1,545	4.4	3.4	1,627	268	23,903	4,785	27,180	73.5
Hale	16,693	16,909	−216	891	759	5.3	4.5	800	−24	11,792	47	24,339	65.8

See footnotes at end of table.

[Includes United States, states, and 3,141 counties/county equivalents defined as of February 22, 2005. For more information on these areas, see Appendix C, Geographic Information]

County	Civilian labor force							Private nonfarm businesses					
	Total			Number of unemployed		Unemployment rate[1]		Establishments		Employment[2]		Annual payroll per employee, 2004	
	2006	2000	Net change, 2000–2006	2006	2000	2006	2000	2004	Net change, 2000–2004	2004	Net change, 2000–2004	Amount (dol.)	Percent of U.S. average
TEXAS—Con.													
Hall	1,504	1,712	−208	92	88	6.1	5.1	85	−6	453	−326	17,166	46.4
Hamilton	4,065	4,031	34	172	143	4.2	3.5	213	−1	1,760	−62	23,786	64.3
Hansford	2,395	2,818	−423	90	82	3.8	2.9	160	−19	1,025	−117	25,764	69.7
Hardeman	2,396	2,445	−49	99	86	4.1	3.5	91	−11	855	46	23,823	64.4
Hardin	25,294	23,149	2,145	1,371	1,290	5.4	5.6	742	5	8,672	−141	24,560	66.4
Harris	1,895,870	1,722,146	173,724	95,192	75,183	5.0	4.4	86,566	1,774	1,644,612	3,574	43,477	117.6
Harrison	31,651	29,331	2,320	1,648	1,452	5.2	5.0	1,115	−72	16,054	212	24,788	67.1
Hartley	2,216	2,424	−208	92	77	4.2	3.2	67	−17	790	18	19,290	52.2
Haskell	3,070	2,888	182	122	117	4.0	4.1	141	−6	785	−132	18,468	50.0
Hays	69,865	56,579	13,286	2,926	1,852	4.2	3.3	2,574	388	29,840	5,800	25,533	69.1
Hemphill	2,291	1,837	454	65	52	2.8	2.8	144	4	984	57	27,369	74.0
Henderson	34,964	32,766	2,198	1,836	1,342	5.3	4.1	1,241	49	13,062	32	22,431	60.7
Hidalgo	269,586	210,954	58,632	19,837	19,412	7.4	9.2	9,338	1,018	140,725	25,870	21,757	58.9
Hill	15,357	15,182	175	865	676	5.6	4.5	680	−13	6,874	−530	20,961	56.7
Hockley	11,402	10,886	516	493	441	4.3	4.1	475	−14	5,247	173	24,677	66.8
Hood	23,105	20,242	2,863	1,146	781	5.0	3.9	1,025	84	8,784	529	23,430	63.4
Hopkins	17,780	16,341	1,439	754	649	4.2	4.0	730	−4	9,746	697	23,594	63.8
Houston	8,328	9,044	−716	514	455	6.2	5.0	363	−45	3,652	294	25,243	68.3
Howard	13,738	13,566	172	692	690	5.0	5.1	715	−38	9,434	−505	27,076	73.2
Hudspeth	1,362	1,315	47	101	60	7.4	4.6	42	3	201	−20	27,975	75.7
Hunt	40,036	38,815	1,221	2,060	1,665	5.1	4.3	1,351	61	24,623	4,123	33,025	89.3
Hutchinson	10,817	10,987	−170	502	522	4.6	4.8	499	−17	6,258	−296	34,932	94.5
Irion	980	941	39	35	30	3.6	3.2	46	4	249	−5	36,622	99.1
Jack	4,345	3,782	563	188	158	4.3	4.2	181	5	1,817	469	26,026	70.4
Jackson	6,573	6,788	−215	307	247	4.7	3.6	260	−21	3,893	−343	27,186	73.5
Jasper	15,781	15,315	466	1,014	1,096	6.4	7.2	672	−35	8,964	203	25,300	68.4
Jeff Davis	1,202	1,160	42	49	43	4.1	3.7	56	2	401	−31	18,928	51.2
Jefferson	114,074	112,578	1,496	7,050	7,328	6.2	6.5	5,816	−93	101,800	1,398	32,849	88.9
Jim Hogg	2,721	2,177	544	121	130	4.4	6.0	95	−11	979	185	17,053	46.1
Jim Wells	20,567	16,642	3,925	985	993	4.8	6.0	787	−12	10,846	1,157	25,700	69.5
Johnson	74,278	66,317	7,961	3,424	2,533	4.6	3.8	2,304	128	28,088	1,521	25,111	67.9
Jones	8,080	7,664	416	441	392	5.5	5.1	320	2	2,698	−451	22,303	60.3
Karnes	5,452	5,367	85	339	286	6.2	5.3	253	−19	2,098	86	22,321	60.4
Kaufman	44,633	37,543	7,090	2,244	1,540	5.0	4.1	1,566	103	18,273	−2,041	27,894	75.5
Kendall	14,869	12,073	2,796	586	405	3.9	3.4	906	180	7,732	1,533	28,758	77.8
Kenedy	252	206	46	7	7	2.8	3.4	6	3	19	(NA)	20,947	56.7
Kent	394	442	−48	18	16	4.6	3.6	14	−5	[7]175	(NA)	(NA)	(NA)
Kerr	22,893	19,176	3,717	942	682	4.1	3.6	1,400	73	14,905	589	27,072	73.2
Kimble	2,246	2,249	−3	89	75	4.0	3.3	144	5	1,359	206	22,278	60.3
King	160	211	−51	8	7	5.0	3.3	1	–	[6]10	(NA)	(NA)	(NA)
Kinney	1,311	1,203	108	79	87	6.0	7.2	39	7	225	14	19,520	52.8
Kleberg	16,445	13,864	2,581	767	704	4.7	5.1	571	21	6,245	891	22,700	61.4
Knox	1,789	1,851	−62	76	83	4.2	4.5	124	1	853	140	21,232	57.4
Lamar	23,889	22,997	892	1,312	1,117	5.5	4.9	1,223	40	17,376	595	25,517	69.0
Lamb	7,165	6,896	269	342	335	4.8	4.9	296	−18	2,653	−254	27,499	74.4
Lampasas	10,082	8,623	1,459	421	335	4.2	3.9	391	20	4,634	1,062	16,913	45.8
La Salle	2,730	2,198	532	144	156	5.3	7.1	85	−1	912	95	29,781	80.6
Lavaca	10,430	9,566	864	388	282	3.7	2.9	459	−43	6,231	−356	20,050	54.2
Lee	8,887	8,205	682	362	286	4.1	3.5	408	16	3,726	201	27,296	73.8
Leon	7,825	7,004	821	395	349	5.0	5.0	342	22	3,843	209	35,415	95.8
Liberty	32,345	30,195	2,150	1,817	1,800	5.6	6.0	1,049	9	11,445	−223	23,022	62.3
Limestone	10,386	9,545	841	501	445	4.8	4.7	396	−3	4,751	299	23,041	62.3
Lipscomb	1,702	1,480	222	60	49	3.5	3.3	105	7	610	186	26,095	70.6
Live Oak	5,036	4,836	200	241	215	4.8	4.4	246	44	1,790	130	43,078	116.5
Llano	8,291	7,326	965	394	283	4.8	3.9	461	15	3,164	−291	24,302	65.7
Loving	37	49	−12	4	4	10.8	8.2	1	–	[6]10	(NA)	(NA)	(NA)
Lubbock	140,349	127,818	12,531	5,596	4,572	4.0	3.6	6,634	135	99,448	5,931	25,988	70.3
Lynn	2,783	2,985	−202	158	121	5.7	4.1	97	−10	660	−123	27,379	74.1
McCulloch	3,758	3,680	78	172	190	4.6	5.2	220	−2	1,801	−357	21,166	57.3
McLennan	113,340	103,603	9,737	5,484	4,279	4.8	4.1	4,946	106	88,313	−2,350	27,233	73.7
McMullen	336	397	−61	20	15	6.0	3.8	14	–	58	−5	28,845	78.0
Madison	5,003	4,836	167	267	234	5.3	4.8	204	−3	1,741	−134	21,733	58.8
Marion	5,056	4,635	421	275	290	5.4	6.3	180	−8	1,183	34	22,086	59.7
Martin	2,144	2,130	14	92	84	4.3	3.9	90	1	656	99	23,591	63.8
Mason	2,465	2,013	452	76	55	3.1	2.7	136	16	683	148	16,914	45.8
Matagorda	16,079	17,268	−1,189	1,160	1,149	7.2	6.7	786	8	7,441	−446	32,647	88.3
Maverick	19,747	16,484	3,263	2,563	2,484	13.0	15.1	804	−33	8,013	148	19,301	52.2
Medina	20,172	17,929	2,243	926	713	4.6	4.0	608	34	5,252	345	20,666	55.9
Menard	1,069	1,166	−97	46	40	4.3	3.4	47	–	247	−42	15,887	43.0
Midland	70,525	58,115	12,410	2,384	2,441	3.4	4.2	4,026	−12	49,858	3,858	32,841	88.8

See footnotes at end of table.

Table B-10. Counties — **Labor Force and Private Business Establishments and Employment**—Con.

[Includes United States, states, and 3,141 counties/county equivalents defined as of February 22, 2005. For more information on these areas, see Appendix C, Geographic Information]

| County | Civilian labor force | | | | | | | Private nonfarm businesses | | | | | |
| | Total | | | Number of unemployed | | Unemployment rate[1] | | Establishments | | Employment[2] | | Annual payroll per employee, 2004 | |
	2006	2000	Net change, 2000–2006	2006	2000	2006	2000	2004	Net change, 2000–2004	2004	Net change, 2000–2004	Amount (dol.)	Percent of U.S. average
TEXAS—Con.													
Milam	12,129	11,565	564	578	424	4.8	3.7	433	1	4,930	-546	31,939	86.4
Mills	2,472	2,451	21	103	82	4.2	3.3	127	–	967	107	20,456	55.3
Mitchell	3,373	3,423	-50	208	188	6.2	5.5	135	-7	1,088	-175	23,079	62.4
Montague	10,129	9,207	922	421	427	4.2	4.6	452	20	3,213	-82	22,786	61.6
Montgomery	197,136	152,424	44,712	8,577	5,625	4.4	3.7	7,236	1,435	98,965	13,425	38,094	103.0
Moore	10,510	9,676	834	364	319	3.5	3.3	413	-25	6,939	30	30,818	83.4
Morris	6,249	5,929	320	342	373	5.5	6.3	230	-38	4,082	14	34,330	92.9
Motley	637	701	-64	27	23	4.2	3.3	42	-6	203	25	18,493	50.0
Nacogdoches	31,298	29,023	2,275	1,499	1,268	4.8	4.4	1,250	-67	18,212	404	23,342	63.1
Navarro	21,478	21,053	425	1,196	1,038	5.6	4.9	897	-36	13,777	256	23,316	63.1
Newton	5,738	6,094	-356	423	484	7.4	7.9	139	-12	1,159	-465	18,142	49.1
Nolan	7,666	7,321	345	341	349	4.4	4.8	369	-13	4,372	-349	24,917	67.4
Nueces	159,964	147,724	12,240	7,895	7,792	4.9	5.3	7,972	99	116,907	116	29,678	80.3
Ochiltree	5,164	4,762	402	159	148	3.1	3.1	312	5	2,622	130	27,552	74.5
Oldham	1,037	1,151	-114	43	37	4.1	3.2	38	-9	345	-215	19,446	52.6
Orange	41,517	40,581	936	2,478	2,812	6.0	6.9	1,398	-63	18,559	-1,373	30,223	81.8
Palo Pinto	14,837	13,309	1,528	634	542	4.3	4.1	622	4	6,364	-427	24,495	66.3
Panola	12,202	10,371	1,831	538	577	4.4	5.6	467	14	5,063	-432	27,434	74.2
Parker	52,279	46,237	6,042	2,409	1,668	4.6	3.6	1,840	287	17,586	1,928	23,922	64.7
Parmer	4,376	4,484	-108	176	150	4.0	3.3	197	-9	3,395	-42	25,117	67.9
Pecos	6,694	6,985	-291	324	356	4.8	5.1	298	-16	3,192	223	22,775	61.6
Polk	17,049	15,837	1,212	1,063	911	6.2	5.8	676	-19	7,432	128	23,704	64.1
Potter	58,171	52,876	5,295	2,505	2,842	4.3	5.4	3,567	-65	62,194	205	28,219	76.3
Presidio	3,275	3,182	93	349	529	10.7	16.6	120	–	605	-29	16,258	44.0
Rains	5,212	4,348	864	254	166	4.9	3.8	145	6	1,069	165	17,679	47.8
Randall	67,368	60,171	7,197	2,251	1,507	3.3	2.5	2,084	93	22,197	763	25,981	70.3
Reagan	2,337	1,622	715	58	57	2.5	3.5	99	5	687	-111	30,655	82.9
Real	1,301	1,384	-83	67	59	5.1	4.3	63	-5	372	-55	18,672	50.5
Red River	6,346	6,762	-416	356	321	5.6	4.7	211	-13	1,990	-600	20,613	55.8
Reeves	4,149	5,033	-884	267	444	6.4	8.8	189	-25	2,286	-599	18,902	51.1
Refugio	3,827	3,682	145	182	154	4.8	4.2	150	-6	1,279	122	24,499	66.3
Roberts	561	511	50	18	12	3.2	2.3	11	-2	[8]60	(NA)	(NA)	(NA)
Robertson	7,693	6,955	738	374	328	4.9	4.7	238	13	2,070	-33	29,717	80.4
Rockwall	33,691	24,260	9,431	1,514	737	4.5	3.0	1,299	258	13,886	2,952	27,765	75.1
Runnels	4,465	5,266	-801	248	242	5.6	4.6	263	–	3,066	174	22,359	60.5
Rusk	23,205	21,026	2,179	1,100	1,033	4.7	4.9	723	-59	9,014	-503	29,360	79.4
Sabine	3,474	3,754	-280	307	309	8.8	8.2	143	-18	1,792	186	20,748	56.1
San Augustine	3,591	3,733	-142	234	190	6.5	5.1	134	-6	1,198	-16	20,987	56.8
San Jacinto	10,578	9,380	1,198	600	446	5.7	4.8	164	19	1,105	62	18,310	49.5
San Patricio	29,933	27,416	2,517	1,664	1,620	5.6	5.9	1,031	19	12,441	119	25,892	70.0
San Saba	2,559	2,795	-236	132	113	5.2	4.0	158	-8	1,055	-254	16,771	45.4
Schleicher	1,376	1,503	-127	54	55	3.9	3.7	61	-9	622	21	25,561	69.1
Scurry	7,216	7,212	4	347	344	4.8	4.8	389	-21	4,189	-118	27,931	75.6
Shackelford	2,007	1,640	367	63	55	3.1	3.4	110	5	694	152	25,048	67.8
Shelby	12,151	11,323	828	607	581	5.0	5.1	452	-68	5,749	-43	23,423	63.4
Sherman	1,317	1,622	-305	55	43	4.2	2.7	59	-13	278	-332	27,183	73.5
Smith	97,622	86,196	11,426	4,576	3,767	4.7	4.4	5,165	304	80,762	6,864	31,905	86.3
Somervell	3,770	3,452	318	184	140	4.9	4.1	183	33	3,057	-48	43,053	116.5
Starr	21,758	17,725	4,033	2,539	2,983	11.7	16.8	440	43	6,668	1,704	15,018	40.6
Stephens	4,466	4,361	105	187	184	4.2	4.2	267	-1	1,888	-342	24,339	65.8
Sterling	851	726	125	28	23	3.3	3.2	33	2	220	57	23,086	62.5
Stonewall	896	818	78	30	34	3.3	4.2	48	-8	327	-56	25,581	69.2
Sutton	2,852	2,151	701	79	83	2.8	3.9	142	-3	1,264	219	28,732	77.7
Swisher	3,542	3,873	-331	164	153	4.6	4.0	152	-25	1,244	71	20,183	54.6
Tarrant	868,728	792,811	75,917	41,261	28,602	4.7	3.6	35,314	1,946	639,842	-1,085	36,973	100.0
Taylor	66,832	61,244	5,588	2,661	2,487	4.0	4.1	3,363	-138	51,584	2,427	23,855	64.5
Terrell	381	512	-131	23	20	6.0	3.9	19	-2	86	(NA)	23,605	63.9
Terry	5,669	5,593	76	301	272	5.3	4.9	246	6	1,978	-122	23,846	64.5
Throckmorton	941	972	-31	35	32	3.7	3.3	56	–	289	-52	18,758	50.7
Titus	14,674	12,734	1,940	635	558	4.3	4.4	689	13	12,994	851	24,247	65.6
Tom Green	53,011	50,598	2,413	2,241	1,971	4.2	3.9	2,569	-23	36,517	1,745	26,517	71.7
Travis	522,790	490,786	32,004	21,150	15,110	4.0	3.1	25,048	1,500	416,610	-29,479	40,329	109.1
Trinity	5,788	5,738	50	347	295	6.0	5.1	204	-9	1,747	38	19,355	52.4
Tyler	8,300	7,902	398	538	525	6.5	6.6	262	-31	2,300	-1,681	19,062	51.6
Upshur	19,204	16,468	2,736	894	800	4.7	4.9	453	24	4,139	189	22,106	59.8
Upton	1,618	1,506	112	61	72	3.8	4.8	65	-1	588	-153	29,930	81.0
Uvalde	11,762	11,358	404	697	646	5.9	5.7	577	-8	6,388	198	21,854	59.1
Val Verde	20,205	17,307	2,898	1,241	1,091	6.1	6.3	814	9	10,688	1,740	19,539	52.9
Van Zandt	25,690	22,519	3,171	1,183	871	4.6	3.9	787	44	8,680	1,744	22,315	60.4
Victoria	45,103	43,026	2,077	1,859	1,600	4.1	3.7	2,225	18	29,440	-55	27,748	75.1

See footnotes at end of table.

Table B-10. Counties — **Labor Force and Private Business Establishments and Employment**—Con.

[Includes United States, states, and 3,141 counties/county equivalents defined as of February 22, 2005. For more information on these areas, see Appendix C, Geographic Information]

County	Civilian labor force							Private nonfarm businesses					
	Total			Number of unemployed		Unemployment rate[1]		Establishments		Employment[2]		Annual payroll per employee, 2004	
	2006	2000	Net change, 2000–2006	2006	2000	2006	2000	2004	Net change, 2000–2004	2004	Net change, 2000–2004	Amount (dol.)	Percent of U.S. average
TEXAS—Con.													
Walker	26,348	25,095	1,253	1,444	1,195	5.5	4.8	882	34	10,524	−180	20,452	55.3
Waller	16,520	15,298	1,222	857	685	5.2	4.5	960	439	11,970	4,615	30,221	81.8
Ward	4,771	4,442	329	228	277	4.8	6.2	249	12	2,129	48	27,734	75.0
Washington	16,177	15,038	1,139	697	543	4.3	3.6	813	33	11,796	1,003	24,324	65.8
Webb	89,117	70,847	18,270	4,840	4,367	5.4	6.2	4,495	415	61,975	8,759	21,571	58.4
Wharton	20,790	20,141	649	1,015	859	4.9	4.3	962	7	12,372	1,198	23,312	63.1
Wheeler	2,708	2,696	12	96	102	3.5	3.8	161	−12	1,381	206	15,624	42.3
Wichita	63,847	60,830	3,017	2,852	2,820	4.5	4.6	3,279	−53	47,934	983	26,042	70.4
Wilbarger	7,954	7,205	749	284	265	3.6	3.7	326	1	3,820	127	23,782	64.3
Willacy	7,704	7,276	428	711	724	9.2	10.0	217	12	2,174	264	21,017	56.9
Williamson	187,111	144,848	42,263	7,889	4,033	4.2	2.8	5,812	1,008	88,161	19,342	47,383	128.2
Wilson	18,368	15,485	2,883	815	565	4.4	3.6	464	73	3,704	586	20,072	54.3
Winkler	3,221	2,926	295	132	167	4.1	5.7	138	−17	1,079	83	26,338	71.2
Wise	28,434	25,273	3,161	1,248	880	4.4	3.5	1,014	118	11,298	375	30,072	81.3
Wood	18,110	16,212	1,898	928	796	5.1	4.9	834	60	7,493	1,354	21,971	59.4
Yoakum	3,462	3,309	153	148	176	4.3	5.3	172	−10	1,783	72	36,084	97.6
Young	9,768	8,808	960	383	430	3.9	4.9	576	−17	5,027	−136	26,311	71.2
Zapata	4,967	3,972	995	310	318	6.2	8.0	144	−4	1,622	281	21,883	59.2
Zavala	3,793	3,707	86	449	463	11.8	12.5	105	−6	1,539	−465	15,796	42.7
UTAH	1,311,073	1,136,036	175,037	38,272	38,121	2.9	3.4	[3]62,834	[3]7,455	[3]935,126	[3]18,037	[3]30,587	[3]82.7
Beaver	3,095	2,688	407	93	93	3.0	3.5	156	19	1,393	110	16,724	45.2
Box Elder	22,825	19,978	2,847	721	740	3.2	3.7	888	85	16,069	−370	34,112	92.3
Cache	58,027	47,977	10,050	1,357	1,338	2.3	2.8	2,725	368	34,449	3,246	24,387	66.0
Carbon	9,863	9,227	636	342	519	3.5	5.6	551	38	6,660	307	29,867	80.8
Daggett	515	460	55	24	18	4.7	3.9	23	2	97	−38	24,443	66.1
Davis	138,773	119,528	19,245	3,990	3,731	2.9	3.1	5,517	911	68,122	6,131	28,013	75.8
Duchesne	8,270	6,095	2,175	239	301	2.9	4.9	456	78	3,739	775	26,887	72.7
Emery	5,251	4,703	548	183	226	3.5	4.8	171	−13	2,696	−43	38,620	104.5
Garfield	2,668	2,469	199	132	168	4.9	6.8	160	11	1,028	−42	26,980	73.0
Grand	5,065	4,619	446	240	303	4.7	6.6	403	23	2,901	64	22,286	60.3
Iron	20,753	16,809	3,944	583	547	2.8	3.3	1,060	224	10,929	948	21,294	57.6
Juab	4,052	3,731	321	145	132	3.6	3.5	167	19	1,788	40	23,911	64.7
Kane	3,399	3,011	388	119	115	3.5	3.8	224	37	1,649	221	20,070	54.3
Millard	6,179	5,162	1,017	182	178	2.9	3.4	255	18	2,605	67	31,709	85.8
Morgan	3,895	3,400	495	116	117	3.0	3.4	202	53	1,358	297	28,043	75.9
Piute	877	623	254	27	28	3.1	4.5	29	6	152	59	17,829	48.2
Rich	1,377	1,039	338	31	31	2.3	3.0	68	12	226	−96	23,133	62.6
Salt Lake	532,283	483,816	48,467	15,223	15,309	2.9	3.2	27,611	1,676	462,008	−18,867	34,320	92.8
San Juan	4,864	4,699	165	294	375	6.0	8.0	261	23	1,899	138	21,764	58.9
Sanpete	10,652	9,630	1,022	393	424	3.7	4.4	419	50	4,149	369	18,110	49.0
Sevier	9,357	8,293	1,064	297	322	3.2	3.9	507	26	5,580	402	25,469	68.9
Summit	22,068	18,165	3,903	618	632	2.8	3.5	1,767	277	19,660	4,218	22,809	61.7
Tooele	25,888	20,156	5,732	833	742	3.2	3.7	606	140	7,860	1,379	29,400	79.5
Uintah	15,911	11,339	4,572	390	481	2.5	4.2	885	154	7,139	939	28,089	76.0
Utah	212,422	180,176	32,246	5,924	5,297	2.8	2.9	8,797	1,670	138,492	−3,865	27,572	74.6
Wasatch	9,942	7,739	2,203	305	271	3.1	3.5	562	99	3,817	549	26,098	70.6
Washington	61,128	39,148	21,980	1,759	1,377	2.9	3.5	3,380	869	33,878	7,239	24,868	67.3
Wayne	1,381	1,310	71	59	60	4.3	4.6	82	8	614	153	23,010	62.2
Weber	110,296	100,047	10,249	3,652	4,246	3.3	4.2	4,732	454	65,717	−4,601	27,806	75.2
VERMONT	361,044	335,798	25,246	13,018	9,056	3.6	2.7	[3]22,133	[3]569	[3]256,132	[3]2,591	[3]31,049	[3]84.0
Addison	22,500	19,833	2,667	714	503	3.2	2.5	1,160	70	11,836	588	30,427	82.3
Bennington	20,884	19,936	948	746	567	3.6	2.8	1,538	−52	16,841	−153	30,729	83.1
Caledonia	17,176	15,490	1,686	687	503	4.0	3.2	951	−27	9,571	16	27,339	74.0
Chittenden	89,396	85,239	4,157	2,845	1,873	3.2	2.2	5,461	153	83,635	−158	36,032	97.5
Essex	3,332	3,266	66	137	127	4.1	3.9	144	12	1,113	−205	26,288	71.1
Franklin	26,633	24,533	2,100	1,086	703	4.1	2.9	1,104	−18	11,508	−135	29,113	78.8
Grand Isle	4,355	3,786	569	224	143	5.1	3.8	191	7	603	(NA)	26,491	71.7
Lamoille	15,231	13,362	1,869	624	413	4.1	3.1	1,022	69	9,874	375	23,578	63.8
Orange	16,745	15,546	1,199	552	368	3.3	2.4	840	72	6,994	733	27,656	74.8
Orleans	14,603	12,945	1,658	774	552	5.3	4.3	873	28	7,746	463	24,467	66.2
Rutland	36,638	33,601	3,037	1,410	1,021	3.8	3.0	2,360	65	25,968	−1,444	29,222	79.0
Washington	34,806	32,850	1,956	1,309	862	3.8	2.6	2,329	85	25,729	518	30,155	81.6
Windham	25,415	24,392	1,023	926	661	3.6	2.7	1,871	34	22,374	−71	29,182	78.9
Windsor	33,333	31,008	2,325	986	749	3.0	2.4	2,252	35	22,068	2,308	27,181	73.5
VIRGINIA	3,998,569	3,584,037	414,532	119,581	81,513	3.0	2.3	[3]188,989	[3]13,407	[3]3,054,816	[3]151,268	[3]37,610	[3]101.7
Accomack	18,946	18,014	932	778	532	4.1	3.0	854	48	10,047	1,368	23,041	62.3
Albemarle	49,761	43,304	6,457	1,189	742	2.4	1.7	2,069	323	25,386	2,513	35,049	94.8
Alleghany[9]	7,368	7,684	−316	352	231	4.8	3.0	258	109	3,513	1,006	23,376	63.2
Amelia	6,495	5,831	664	191	116	2.9	2.0	302	48	2,066	324	22,716	61.4
Amherst	15,732	15,320	412	493	324	3.1	2.1	625	27	7,127	−92	26,213	70.9

See footnotes at end of table.

Table B-10. Counties — **Labor Force and Private Business Establishments and Employment**—Con.

[Includes United States, states, and 3,141 counties/county equivalents defined as of February 22, 2005. For more information on these areas, see Appendix C, Geographic Information]

County	Civilian labor force							Private nonfarm businesses					
	Total			Number of unemployed		Unemployment rate[1]		Establishments		Employment[2]		Annual payroll per employee, 2004	
	2006	2000	Net change, 2000–2006	2006	2000	2006	2000	2004	Net change, 2000–2004	2004	Net change, 2000–2004	Amount (dol.)	Percent of U.S. average
VIRGINIA—Con.													
Appomattox	6,995	6,727	268	250	166	3.6	2.5	253	−25	2,620	−519	22,093	59.8
Arlington	127,546	118,618	8,928	2,461	1,849	1.9	1.6	5,574	347	121,926	7,186	53,972	146.0
Augusta	37,001	34,388	2,613	951	664	2.6	1.9	1,137	1	17,432	112	31,238	84.5
Bath	2,935	2,721	214	93	72	3.2	2.6	152	12	1,682	931	29,037	78.5
Bedford	35,011	31,926	3,085	1,001	612	2.9	1.9	1,391	449	11,283	2,663	29,432	79.6
Bland	3,211	2,914	297	114	151	3.6	5.2	91	−7	993	−165	30,000	81.2
Botetourt	17,546	16,374	1,172	443	290	2.5	1.8	724	140	7,203	855	29,495	79.8
Brunswick	6,898	6,808	90	299	237	4.3	3.5	316	11	3,771	235	20,787	56.2
Buchanan	8,393	8,680	−287	406	505	4.8	5.8	506	−79	5,875	−634	33,505	90.6
Buckingham	6,840	6,107	733	221	194	3.2	3.2	225	4	1,881	−47	22,557	61.0
Campbell	27,446	26,350	1,096	866	608	3.2	2.3	1,081	113	13,265	−783	28,169	76.2
Caroline	13,230	10,933	2,297	443	237	3.3	2.2	394	30	3,662	687	25,762	69.7
Carroll	14,058	14,727	−669	710	593	5.1	4.0	451	−5	5,004	75	20,930	56.6
Charles City	3,863	3,593	270	149	88	3.9	2.4	190	61	2,153	706	25,243	68.3
Charlotte	5,265	5,485	−220	343	172	6.5	3.1	261	18	2,657	6	21,630	58.5
Chesterfield	163,190	141,459	21,731	4,432	2,521	2.7	1.8	6,197	700	95,883	13,961	32,762	88.6
Clarke	8,019	6,866	1,153	192	108	2.4	1.6	363	62	3,553	276	31,420	85.0
Craig	2,576	2,488	88	86	60	3.3	2.4	67	8	335	−8	22,540	61.0
Culpeper	20,156	16,828	3,328	608	320	3.0	1.9	957	145	11,153	1,008	32,912	89.0
Cumberland	4,573	4,212	361	151	94	3.3	2.2	138	6	859	63	21,236	57.4
Dickenson	5,664	5,330	334	285	307	5.0	5.8	258	−27	2,367	351	28,413	76.9
Dinwiddie	12,879	11,965	914	399	249	3.1	2.1	367	117	5,072	215	31,743	85.9
Essex	5,436	5,120	316	207	136	3.8	2.7	330	−3	3,373	−377	22,018	59.6
Fairfax	587,520	547,422	40,098	12,652	8,877	2.2	1.6	27,213	1,633	526,836	17,695	55,003	148.8
Fauquier	36,663	30,037	6,626	871	462	2.4	1.5	1,781	266	16,731	3,198	32,376	87.6
Floyd	7,041	6,934	107	224	256	3.2	3.7	266	19	1,661	55	22,013	59.5
Fluvanna	13,387	10,166	3,221	311	200	2.3	2.0	387	62	2,898	787	25,784	69.7
Franklin	26,117	24,227	1,890	813	719	3.1	3.0	1,112	158	11,787	575	25,666	69.4
Frederick	40,544	32,723	7,821	1,039	662	2.6	2.0	1,319	134	20,853	2,036	31,001	83.9
Giles	8,406	7,750	656	310	326	3.7	4.2	317	−10	3,737	−882	31,477	85.1
Gloucester	20,189	17,489	2,700	528	336	2.6	1.9	902	94	7,032	747	21,812	59.0
Goochland	10,627	8,863	1,764	256	154	2.4	1.7	534	104	5,201	1,889	35,543	96.1
Grayson	7,323	8,043	−720	386	409	5.3	5.1	180	−5	1,369	−75	19,909	53.9
Greene	10,114	8,350	1,764	229	153	2.3	1.8	310	50	1,973	212	24,348	65.9
Greensville	4,196	3,988	208	166	134	4.0	3.4	108	−9	1,992	72	29,198	79.0
Halifax[10]	15,874	16,101	−227	900	799	5.7	5.0	792	28	10,661	−848	25,086	67.9
Hanover	55,026	47,202	7,824	1,353	776	2.5	1.6	2,958	281	37,891	3,698	30,683	83.0
Henrico	160,768	144,690	16,078	4,499	2,613	2.8	1.8	7,498	286	143,916	−4,490	39,977	108.1
Henry	25,337	28,678	−3,341	1,180	1,389	4.7	4.8	910	27	12,466	−2,089	25,223	68.2
Highland	1,161	1,164	−3	35	33	3.0	2.8	93	−8	403	−14	18,705	50.6
Isle of Wight	17,685	14,819	2,866	543	320	3.1	2.2	584	55	9,834	259	28,467	77.0
James City	29,348	23,153	6,195	775	453	2.6	2.0	1,262	226	17,196	4,847	27,539	74.5
King and Queen	3,350	3,142	208	110	80	3.3	2.5	126	23	830	261	24,329	65.8
King George	9,583	8,356	1,227	297	161	3.1	1.9	424	47	4,370	212	38,708	104.7
King William	8,109	6,987	1,122	217	131	2.7	1.9	347	37	3,903	720	39,317	106.4
Lancaster	5,171	4,815	356	221	276	4.3	5.7	526	30	4,190	470	27,440	74.2
Lee	9,227	8,774	453	393	367	4.3	4.2	345	−12	2,973	−512	23,383	63.3
Loudoun	152,430	99,476	52,954	3,216	1,404	2.1	1.4	6,093	1,584	98,902	30,867	48,488	131.2
Louisa	15,514	12,810	2,704	473	304	3.0	2.4	533	41	4,563	375	36,156	97.8
Lunenburg	5,598	5,341	257	231	184	4.1	3.4	201	12	2,200	411	22,374	60.5
Madison	7,274	6,520	754	187	115	2.6	1.8	299	24	2,371	31	22,380	60.5
Mathews	4,485	4,233	252	116	92	2.6	2.2	230	15	1,214	2	19,748	53.4
Mecklenburg	13,208	14,159	−951	666	473	5.0	3.3	878	37	11,578	−442	21,693	58.7
Middlesex	5,043	4,517	526	155	94	3.1	2.1	390	26	2,382	23	21,480	58.1
Montgomery	43,812	40,573	3,239	1,327	1,019	3.0	2.5	1,903	110	26,626	2,469	27,014	73.1
Nelson	7,786	6,991	795	212	162	2.7	2.3	418	32	3,208	629	23,429	63.4
New Kent	9,037	7,256	1,781	246	132	2.7	1.8	282	18	1,938	−267	25,385	68.7
Northampton	5,946	5,568	378	255	147	4.3	2.6	361	39	3,331	−90	26,437	71.5
Northumberland	5,991	5,404	587	247	242	4.1	4.5	380	43	2,521	390	26,346	71.3
Nottoway	6,445	6,135	310	244	179	3.8	2.9	356	4	3,832	−143	22,074	59.7
Orange	15,082	12,661	2,421	435	259	2.9	2.0	692	78	7,688	587	29,976	81.1
Page	11,356	11,712	−356	512	304	4.5	2.6	482	17	5,330	−424	22,111	59.8
Patrick	8,864	9,450	−586	400	310	4.5	3.3	327	17	3,561	−881	22,063	59.7
Pittsylvania	31,086	31,761	−675	1,674	1,045	5.4	3.3	906	−32	10,189	−1,573	23,049	62.3
Powhatan	13,916	11,183	2,733	354	202	2.5	1.8	571	106	3,561	−1,609	28,996	78.4
Prince Edward	8,791	8,084	707	413	270	4.7	3.3	567	30	7,010	−872	21,770	58.9
Prince George	15,427	13,144	2,283	496	335	3.2	2.5	389	33	6,978	2,578	33,741	91.3
Prince William	196,161	152,695	43,466	4,606	2,686	2.3	1.8	5,994	1,611	80,264	18,305	29,366	79.4
Pulaski	18,253	17,288	965	695	777	3.8	4.5	662	−3	11,205	−2,097	28,246	76.4
Rappahannock	4,349	3,731	618	100	69	2.3	1.8	187	−30	1,027	−406	28,463	77.0

See footnotes at end of table.

[Includes United States, states, and 3,141 counties/county equivalents defined as of February 22, 2005. For more information on these areas, see Appendix C, Geographic Information]

County	Civilian labor force							Private nonfarm businesses					
	Total			Number of unemployed		Unemployment rate[1]		Establishments		Employment[2]		Annual payroll per employee, 2004	
	2006	2000	Net change, 2000–2006	2006	2000	2006	2000	2004	Net change, 2000–2004	2004	Net change, 2000–2004	Amount (dol.)	Percent of U.S. average
VIRGINIA—Con.													
Richmond	3,474	3,404	70	149	146	4.3	4.3	226	3	1,840	29	24,267	65.6
Roanoke	48,130	45,736	2,394	1,239	792	2.6	1.7	2,102	672	33,536	10,095	32,719	88.5
Rockbridge	11,308	10,610	698	304	228	2.7	2.1	311	10	4,123	-349	23,671	64.0
Rockingham	42,332	35,907	6,425	989	604	2.3	1.7	1,253	103	22,146	-1,022	27,233	73.7
Russell	11,796	11,789	7	681	606	5.8	5.1	518	-49	6,818	449	27,556	74.5
Scott	10,059	9,710	349	478	370	4.8	3.8	331	3	3,408	158	24,798	67.1
Shenandoah	20,112	18,401	1,711	577	327	2.9	1.8	931	36	12,563	-203	26,289	71.1
Smyth	15,740	15,764	-24	697	680	4.4	4.3	620	-68	10,827	-1,234	27,286	73.8
Southampton	7,598	7,443	155	271	204	3.6	2.7	257	-18	3,491	-765	41,837	113.2
Spotsylvania	64,038	48,232	15,806	1,520	819	2.4	1.7	1,897	556	25,395	7,237	27,002	73.0
Stafford	63,703	48,134	15,569	1,525	809	2.4	1.7	1,859	414	23,224	5,346	29,660	80.2
Surry	3,672	3,375	297	123	97	3.3	2.9	80	-4	1,421	11	66,160	179.0
Sussex	4,484	4,504	-20	196	165	4.4	3.7	194	-2	2,325	-605	24,825	67.2
Tazewell	19,760	18,877	883	781	959	4.0	5.1	1,219	8	14,454	1,312	23,276	63.0
Warren	19,257	16,483	2,774	528	332	2.7	2.0	816	56	8,658	603	26,555	71.8
Washington	26,702	24,989	1,713	1,071	889	4.0	3.6	1,185	21	14,587	104	26,885	72.7
Westmoreland	8,142	7,637	505	318	269	3.9	3.5	376	-6	2,353	-45	20,592	55.7
Wise	17,269	16,051	1,218	766	673	4.4	4.2	912	-8	10,533	1,071	26,966	72.9
Wythe	15,077	14,074	1,003	598	606	4.0	4.3	711	-11	9,085	-246	24,140	65.3
York	31,175	26,697	4,478	817	517	2.6	1.9	1,349	167	15,080	1,135	24,447	66.1
Independent Cities													
Alexandria	87,612	80,458	7,154	1,895	1,422	2.2	1.8	4,743	102	83,715	2,202	45,752	123.8
Bedford	2,605	2,592	13	96	64	3.7	2.5	339	-146	4,867	-1,098	24,598	66.5
Bristol	7,943	7,468	475	373	237	4.7	3.2	698	6	14,710	-844	26,644	72.1
Buena Vista	3,413	3,207	206	114	73	3.3	2.3	134	9	2,423	326	26,849	72.6
Charlottesville	20,722	19,260	1,462	645	566	3.1	2.9	2,433	140	37,569	-3,904	32,896	89.0
Chesapeake[9]	113,965	97,374	16,591	3,644	2,213	3.2	2.3	5,051	552	88,344	11,894	28,815	77.9
Clifton Forge[9]	(X)	(X)	(NA)	(X)	(X)	(X)	(X)	(X)	(NA)	(X)	(NA)	(NA)	(NA)
Colonial Heights	9,266	8,565	701	289	192	3.1	2.2	676	21	9,630	-555	23,416	63.3
Covington	2,834	2,882	-48	196	113	6.9	3.9	283	6	4,398	-344	37,244	100.7
Danville	20,306	21,255	-949	1,729	926	8.5	4.4	1,551	56	26,613	-601	26,185	70.8
Emporia	2,622	2,352	270	136	73	5.2	3.1	255	-13	4,642	125	22,174	60.0
Fairfax	13,227	12,432	795	314	167	2.4	1.3	2,375	207	36,087	1,863	42,707	115.5
Falls Church	6,634	6,119	515	185	98	2.8	1.6	903	36	17,005	1,624	42,615	115.3
Franklin	3,765	3,548	217	175	112	4.6	3.2	302	61	3,785	638	22,729	61.5
Fredericksburg	11,585	10,262	1,323	450	235	3.9	2.3	1,650	-19	24,394	604	29,597	80.1
Galax	3,082	3,285	-203	181	114	5.9	3.5	366	41	6,716	-1,301	22,533	61.0
Hampton	67,785	63,944	3,841	2,450	1,719	3.6	2.7	2,506	55	45,056	-3,679	28,305	76.6
Harrisonburg	21,976	19,539	2,437	637	444	2.9	2.3	1,722	177	30,068	5,007	25,563	69.1
Hopewell	10,483	9,813	670	473	278	4.5	2.8	464	-13	6,952	-1,156	35,537	96.1
Lexington	2,327	2,230	97	107	79	4.6	3.5	458	12	4,972	323	24,260	65.6
Lynchburg	32,085	30,601	1,484	1,144	740	3.6	2.4	2,379	-160	53,321	-4,218	32,993	89.2
Manassas	21,228	19,160	2,068	531	320	2.5	1.7	1,529	-420	20,841	-3,482	42,541	115.1
Manassas Park	6,752	5,756	996	153	80	2.3	1.4	290	128	3,413	892	39,491	106.8
Martinsville	5,850	6,698	-848	419	523	7.2	7.8	732	-25	13,400	-2,657	24,850	67.2
Newport News	87,490	82,380	5,110	3,048	2,135	3.5	2.6	3,802	108	86,220	1,343	33,529	90.7
Norfolk	97,533	92,428	5,105	4,045	3,015	4.1	3.3	5,760	301	127,492	10,569	35,707	96.6
Norton	1,525	1,479	46	78	61	5.1	4.1	272	-25	4,860	-189	32,256	87.3
Petersburg	14,221	13,832	389	853	470	6.0	3.4	786	-93	12,456	-1,590	30,699	83.0
Poquoson	6,278	5,797	481	146	106	2.3	1.8	203	26	1,539	126	20,391	55.2
Portsmouth	45,435	42,693	2,742	1,975	1,446	4.3	3.4	1,791	112	28,777	3,139	28,499	77.1
Radford	7,323	7,423	-100	272	238	3.7	3.2	363	7	6,305	-808	32,761	88.6
Richmond	97,794	94,849	2,945	4,354	2,498	4.5	2.6	7,772	263	159,105	-3,281	42,829	115.9
Roanoke	46,585	46,423	162	1,685	1,133	3.6	2.4	3,450	-723	63,590	-11,745	31,646	85.6
Salem	13,149	12,897	252	384	247	2.9	1.9	985	25	21,749	-871	34,052	92.1
South Boston[10]	(X)	(X)	(NA)	(X)	(X)	(X)	(X)	(X)	(NA)	(X)	(NA)	(NA)	(NA)
Staunton	11,484	11,574	-90	341	247	3.0	2.1	987	87	12,237	833	23,227	62.8
Suffolk	38,524	29,149	9,375	1,336	728	3.5	2.5	1,239	84	19,451	3,142	29,888	80.8
Virginia Beach	224,325	204,662	19,663	6,424	4,529	2.9	2.2	10,789	532	155,957	10,746	28,115	76.1
Waynesboro	10,002	9,095	907	310	234	3.1	2.6	708	91	9,740	-619	27,707	75.0
Williamsburg	4,816	4,577	239	280	198	5.8	4.3	745	-53	17,202	63	24,403	66.0
Winchester	14,545	12,835	1,710	409	284	2.8	2.2	1,341	96	24,699	1,091	33,485	90.6
WASHINGTON	3,326,524	3,050,021	276,503	166,174	151,344	5.0	5.0	[3]171,529	[3]7,511	[3]2,268,913	[3]1,428	[3]39,735	[3]107.5
Adams	8,040	8,039	1	519	605	6.5	7.5	384	-14	3,917	100	27,944	75.6
Asotin	10,373	9,657	716	498	487	4.8	5.0	437	-6	4,033	-99	27,384	74.1
Benton	84,079	76,077	8,002	4,818	3,753	5.7	4.9	3,617	318	54,917	4,380	38,578	104.4
Chelan	39,784	36,485	3,299	2,055	2,357	5.2	6.5	2,363	78	24,393	173	30,110	81.5
Clallam	29,644	25,823	3,821	1,757	1,773	5.9	6.9	2,216	148	16,753	1,526	26,471	71.6

See footnotes at end of table.

Table B-10. Counties — **Labor Force and Private Business Establishments and Employment**—Con.

[Includes United States, states, and 3,141 counties/county equivalents defined as of February 22, 2005. For more information on these areas, see Appendix C, Geographic Information]

County	Civilian labor force							Private nonfarm businesses					
	Total			Number of unemployed		Unemployment rate[1]		Establishments		Employment[2]		Annual payroll per employee, 2004	
	2006	2000	Net change, 2000–2006	2006	2000	2006	2000	2004	Net change, 2000–2004	2004	Net change, 2000–2004	Amount (dol.)	Percent of U.S. average
WASHINGTON—Con.													
Clark	205,800	179,371	26,429	12,020	8,523	5.8	4.8	8,936	900	102,357	4,438	34,566	93.5
Columbia	1,508	1,778	−270	133	141	8.8	7.9	136	7	875	−145	26,187	70.8
Cowlitz	42,965	43,153	−188	2,816	2,735	6.6	6.3	2,309	−26	31,284	−1,230	34,245	92.6
Douglas	20,198	18,051	2,147	1,010	1,099	5.0	6.1	592	52	5,049	855	25,457	68.9
Ferry	2,918	2,972	−54	276	280	9.5	9.4	144	−5	714	−343	27,941	75.6
Franklin	28,992	22,949	6,043	2,096	1,644	7.2	7.2	1,215	90	15,203	1,257	27,985	75.7
Garfield	1,053	1,035	18	58	48	5.5	4.6	54	−1	371	5	24,383	66.0
Grant	38,821	35,587	3,234	2,579	2,754	6.6	7.7	1,729	47	16,557	151	27,278	73.8
Grays Harbor	31,083	29,227	1,856	2,203	2,134	7.1	7.3	1,913	−3	18,329	377	30,059	81.3
Island	32,521	28,974	3,547	1,677	1,445	5.2	5.0	1,761	150	11,769	616	25,290	68.4
Jefferson	13,577	11,663	1,914	688	628	5.1	5.4	1,095	66	8,436	1,722	24,957	67.5
King	1,044,342	984,531	59,811	43,702	39,864	4.2	4.0	60,825	1,014	984,046	−48,840	49,309	133.4
Kitsap	122,472	105,983	16,489	5,836	5,332	4.8	5.0	5,750	510	54,895	5,006	28,342	76.7
Kittitas	19,606	17,253	2,353	1,032	945	5.3	5.5	1,097	71	9,601	1,881	21,647	58.6
Klickitat	9,505	9,274	231	677	698	7.1	7.5	537	−2	3,109	−524	28,940	78.3
Lewis	31,192	29,745	1,447	2,182	2,175	7.0	7.3	1,955	19	19,692	474	30,074	81.4
Lincoln	4,682	4,612	70	270	218	5.8	4.7	287	−13	1,697	−132	25,265	68.3
Mason	24,537	20,942	3,595	1,449	1,330	5.9	6.4	1,055	42	9,757	958	27,803	75.2
Okanogan	20,803	20,526	277	1,385	1,682	6.7	8.2	1,118	57	7,313	−1,379	23,384	63.3
Pacific	9,141	8,573	568	605	604	6.6	7.0	642	−22	4,268	−103	21,250	57.5
Pend Oreille	5,124	4,604	520	381	350	7.4	7.6	252	33	1,888	332	32,656	88.3
Pierce	373,629	339,966	33,663	19,302	16,970	5.2	5.0	16,460	910	215,580	7,361	34,237	92.6
San Juan	8,186	7,493	693	321	297	3.9	4.0	961	96	4,047	274	28,888	78.1
Skagit	56,528	51,918	4,610	2,950	3,009	5.2	5.8	3,442	185	36,865	1,208	31,095	84.1
Skamania	5,109	4,808	301	362	293	7.1	6.1	182	18	1,291	65	26,705	72.2
Snohomish	357,485	322,902	34,583	16,519	14,552	4.6	4.5	16,346	1,031	206,608	1,895	36,990	100.1
Spokane	227,834	211,201	16,633	11,493	10,922	5.0	5.2	12,156	467	170,031	1,758	31,725	85.8
Stevens	18,144	17,498	646	1,296	1,267	7.1	7.2	964	122	7,496	412	27,149	73.4
Thurston	124,016	108,262	15,754	5,754	4,941	4.6	4.6	5,511	461	59,987	7,018	29,665	80.2
Wahkiakum	1,636	1,655	−19	107	110	6.5	6.6	86	−11	555	5	25,923	70.1
Walla Walla	28,806	27,147	1,659	1,580	1,542	5.5	5.7	1,327	77	17,259	408	26,982	73.0
Whatcom	103,263	88,022	15,241	4,711	4,514	4.6	5.1	5,950	564	64,824	5,187	29,598	80.1
Whitman	20,404	19,271	1,133	831	716	4.1	3.7	857	−1	7,411	282	26,639	72.1
Yakima	118,733	113,000	5,733	8,229	8,612	6.9	7.6	4,707	−52	60,350	86	28,353	76.7
WEST VIRGINIA	806,996	808,861	−1,865	39,862	44,212	4.9	5.5	[3]40,837	[3]−210	[3]568,619	[3]10,448	[3]27,449	[3]74.3
Barbour	6,768	6,662	106	387	525	5.7	7.9	248	−8	2,270	−229	21,211	57.4
Berkeley	44,516	39,607	4,909	1,878	1,427	4.2	3.6	1,625	182	22,512	2,708	29,625	80.1
Boone	9,472	9,809	−337	451	664	4.8	6.8	358	−36	6,243	720	40,249	108.9
Braxton	5,957	5,850	107	331	428	5.6	7.3	315	−6	3,101	16	21,895	59.2
Brooke	11,014	11,801	−787	819	535	7.4	4.5	435	−12	12,586	5,059	32,680	88.4
Cabell	44,765	44,794	−29	2,043	2,137	4.6	4.8	2,721	−71	46,499	1,434	27,081	73.3
Calhoun	2,743	2,932	−189	200	301	7.3	10.3	127	−8	956	−121	22,950	62.1
Clay	3,512	3,643	−131	242	308	6.9	8.5	133	−3	1,312	91	31,923	86.4
Doddridge	2,905	2,909	−4	153	169	5.3	5.8	73	−4	543	−41	19,425	52.5
Fayette	18,110	18,498	−388	1,027	1,312	5.7	7.1	920	−33	8,822	−1,023	24,943	67.5
Gilmer	3,136	2,785	351	147	202	4.7	7.3	125	−1	1,034	77	19,390	52.5
Grant	5,065	5,472	−407	308	290	6.1	5.3	265	−24	2,698	−562	31,838	86.1
Greenbrier	15,716	15,118	598	970	983	6.2	6.5	1,019	2	10,792	717	23,596	63.8
Hampshire	9,860	9,349	511	389	304	3.9	3.3	342	9	2,991	219	20,138	54.5
Hancock	14,604	15,687	−1,083	1,120	705	7.7	4.5	701	27	10,104	−4,067	21,507	58.2
Hardy	7,271	6,684	587	285	255	3.9	3.8	270	10	6,190	1,039	19,688	53.3
Harrison	30,789	31,333	−544	1,453	1,790	4.7	5.7	1,892	25	26,881	1,898	27,242	73.7
Jackson	11,842	12,731	−889	622	751	5.3	5.9	555	13	7,096	−73	29,704	80.4
Jefferson	24,904	23,360	1,544	834	796	3.3	3.4	919	113	11,296	563	23,951	64.8
Kanawha	91,830	97,302	−5,472	4,040	4,802	4.4	4.9	5,850	−141	94,877	−1,845	30,037	81.3
Lewis	7,386	7,462	−76	383	433	5.2	5.8	406	–	4,989	658	22,069	59.7
Lincoln	7,950	8,135	−185	487	595	6.1	7.3	259	27	2,056	275	22,696	61.4
Logan	12,985	13,737	−752	632	1,034	4.9	7.5	762	−52	9,424	104	28,210	76.3
McDowell	6,952	7,089	−137	543	729	7.8	10.3	328	−78	2,986	−753	24,856	67.2
Marion	26,293	25,992	301	1,162	1,490	4.4	5.7	1,299	12	16,831	−42	26,571	71.9
Marshall	15,068	15,884	−816	866	900	5.7	5.7	528	−26	7,557	832	30,445	82.4
Mason	10,539	10,577	−38	736	851	7.0	8.0	345	1	4,569	−519	30,658	82.9
Mercer	23,987	25,643	−1,656	1,208	1,285	5.0	5.0	1,386	−71	18,880	−1,684	24,898	67.4
Mineral	13,381	12,981	400	668	703	5.0	5.4	478	−2	5,571	571	24,702	66.8
Mingo	8,595	9,088	−493	475	718	5.5	7.9	549	−72	5,859	−941	30,684	83.0
Monongalia	46,020	41,267	4,753	1,573	1,808	3.4	4.4	2,074	79	34,091	3,968	28,119	76.1
Monroe	5,962	5,849	113	327	306	5.5	5.2	223	30	1,332	189	22,868	61.9
Morgan	7,166	7,286	−120	336	284	4.7	3.9	278	30	2,467	62	23,495	63.6
Nicholas	10,697	11,071	−374	572	753	5.3	6.8	634	–	6,778	−349	25,543	69.1
Ohio	21,000	22,449	−1,449	1,015	991	4.8	4.4	1,529	−56	28,026	1,023	24,987	67.6

See footnotes at end of table.

Labor Force and Private Business Establishments and Employment—Con.

[Includes United States, states, and 3,141 counties/county equivalents defined as of February 22, 2005. For more information on these areas, see Appendix C, Geographic Information]

| County | Civilian labor force | | | | | | | Private nonfarm businesses | | | | | |
| | Total | | | Number of unemployed | | Unemployment rate[1] | | Establishments | | Employment[2] | | Annual payroll per employee, 2004 | |
	2006	2000	Net change, 2000–2006	2006	2000	2006	2000	2004	Net change, 2000–2004	2004	Net change, 2000–2004	Amount (dol.)	Percent of U.S. average
WEST VIRGINIA—Con.													
Pendleton	3,859	3,964	−105	165	310	4.3	7.8	177	15	1,257	−398	20,549	55.6
Pleasants	3,213	3,325	−112	180	192	5.6	5.8	137	1	1,850	39	37,958	102.7
Pocahontas	3,827	4,034	−207	297	268	7.8	6.6	279	26	3,600	396	18,985	51.4
Preston	14,879	13,400	1,479	676	751	4.5	5.6	606	−19	4,841	−620	21,548	58.3
Putnam	26,821	26,210	611	1,116	1,255	4.2	4.8	1,138	46	15,789	2,857	31,614	85.5
Raleigh	32,937	32,716	221	1,496	2,005	4.5	6.1	1,920	−68	25,518	543	27,008	73.1
Randolph	13,176	12,837	339	671	771	5.1	6.0	765	−5	9,575	367	22,379	60.5
Ritchie	4,768	4,610	158	240	288	5.0	6.2	221	11	2,763	307	28,355	76.7
Roane	5,529	6,205	−676	347	557	6.3	9.0	273	−29	2,482	−373	22,237	60.2
Summers	4,753	4,803	−50	303	331	6.4	6.9	203	7	1,577	33	20,301	54.9
Taylor	7,016	6,973	43	369	379	5.3	5.4	215	1	2,018	−59	22,236	60.2
Tucker	3,077	3,328	−251	191	209	6.2	6.3	203	1	2,270	−142	19,570	52.9
Tyler	3,677	3,840	−163	264	227	7.2	5.9	147	–	1,570	−311	36,953	100.0
Upshur	10,817	10,379	438	517	619	4.8	6.0	554	17	6,953	362	23,317	63.1
Wayne	17,889	17,681	208	966	924	5.4	5.2	599	−29	7,142	−777	31,031	83.9
Webster	3,447	3,259	188	199	237	5.8	7.3	181	−13	2,056	305	26,173	70.8
Wetzel	6,366	7,113	−747	525	566	8.2	8.0	409	−26	4,843	−487	32,627	88.3
Wirt	2,508	2,562	−54	154	179	6.1	7.0	70	−4	392	86	16,161	43.7
Wood	41,329	42,178	−849	2,040	1,918	4.9	4.5	2,282	−39	35,799	−1,397	27,000	73.0
Wyoming	8,349	8,614	−265	467	667	5.6	7.7	392	−11	3,961	−163	25,398	68.7
WISCONSIN	3,062,932	2,996,091	66,841	144,777	101,207	4.7	3.4	[3]144,116	[3]3,701	[3]2,435,143	[3]20,309	[3]34,016	[3]92.0
Adams	9,926	8,904	1,022	660	372	6.6	4.2	325	43	2,511	201	27,304	73.9
Ashland	9,401	8,932	469	563	468	6.0	5.2	601	34	7,148	−190	26,171	70.8
Barron	25,499	25,037	462	1,412	966	5.5	3.9	1,316	30	16,619	−316	27,072	73.2
Bayfield	8,345	7,738	607	530	404	6.4	5.2	461	26	2,262	−39	20,974	56.7
Brown	137,348	131,661	5,687	6,220	3,728	4.5	2.8	6,610	315	136,265	4,389	35,010	94.7
Buffalo	8,810	7,894	916	341	282	3.9	3.6	366	1	4,452	619	35,874	97.0
Burnett	8,544	7,810	734	496	293	5.8	3.8	455	13	3,526	78	25,567	69.2
Calumet	25,411	24,197	1,214	1,037	650	4.1	2.7	818	49	14,220	1,798	31,009	83.9
Chippewa	33,652	30,084	3,568	1,735	1,253	5.2	4.2	1,458	222	18,195	591	29,646	80.2
Clark	18,082	17,586	496	968	739	5.4	4.2	805	5	8,710	80	24,867	67.3
Columbia	31,995	29,944	2,051	1,489	1,074	4.7	3.6	1,569	127	20,516	2,289	26,417	71.5
Crawford	9,938	9,166	772	476	327	4.8	3.6	436	42	6,256	−479	24,905	67.4
Dane	289,005	266,527	22,478	9,378	6,206	3.2	2.3	13,025	645	247,136	25,682	36,235	98.0
Dodge	47,070	47,656	−586	2,353	1,495	5.0	3.1	1,880	46	28,470	−869	32,211	87.1
Door	16,727	16,510	217	901	637	5.4	3.9	1,326	42	10,519	−662	27,037	73.1
Douglas	23,053	22,831	222	1,155	969	5.0	4.2	1,119	10	14,119	105	24,983	67.6
Dunn	24,209	22,574	1,635	1,091	765	4.5	3.4	900	−81	13,007	−381	27,016	73.1
Eau Claire	55,505	53,384	2,121	2,205	1,691	4.0	3.2	2,610	−76	46,952	1,024	28,462	77.0
Florence	2,584	2,628	−44	173	106	6.7	4.0	115	12	687	33	20,001	54.1
Fond du Lac	56,629	55,962	667	2,669	1,669	4.7	3.0	2,517	1	43,859	−1,247	29,663	80.2
Forest	5,036	4,657	379	334	260	6.6	5.6	345	43	2,359	−20	26,004	70.3
Grant	27,496	27,557	−61	1,223	898	4.4	3.3	1,274	10	13,657	−266	23,385	63.3
Green	20,349	20,122	227	887	625	4.4	3.1	962	20	11,969	−1,122	28,344	76.7
Green Lake	10,482	10,768	−286	578	415	5.5	3.9	560	−61	6,181	−667	29,331	79.3
Iowa	14,436	13,702	734	623	388	4.3	2.8	612	17	9,185	−1,198	31,691	85.7
Iron	3,215	3,277	−62	264	219	8.2	6.7	235	10	2,007	−50	20,759	56.2
Jackson	10,007	9,842	165	550	445	5.5	4.5	440	38	5,588	478	30,816	83.4
Jefferson	43,159	43,413	−254	1,948	1,225	4.5	2.8	1,985	48	32,250	−1,114	28,204	76.3
Juneau	13,695	12,855	840	779	627	5.7	4.9	608	−34	6,738	−1,321	26,526	71.8
Kenosha	83,021	81,196	1,825	4,469	3,268	5.4	4.0	3,190	53	50,957	1,661	30,099	81.4
Kewaunee	11,936	11,656	280	529	310	4.4	2.7	483	−9	5,189	−363	29,569	80.0
La Crosse	62,778	61,599	1,179	2,407	1,953	3.8	3.2	3,007	72	58,118	1,101	30,926	83.7
Lafayette	9,158	9,215	−57	378	267	4.1	2.9	357	10	2,368	−437	22,851	61.8
Langlade	10,827	10,830	−3	655	487	6.0	4.5	624	22	6,849	139	25,111	67.9
Lincoln	15,931	16,205	−274	886	661	5.6	4.1	818	40	9,568	75	28,770	77.8
Manitowoc	45,519	47,177	−1,658	2,252	1,503	4.9	3.2	1,888	−55	30,549	−3,840	30,509	82.5
Marathon	75,581	72,349	3,232	3,215	2,354	4.3	3.3	3,363	−74	63,645	8	31,298	84.7
Marinette	22,083	22,555	−472	1,424	969	6.4	4.3	1,209	105	17,759	565	29,497	79.8
Marquette	7,939	7,557	382	469	402	5.9	5.3	378	30	3,460	146	26,476	71.6
Menominee	1,681	1,645	36	186	143	11.1	8.7	20	−75	825	−826	20,942	56.6
Milwaukee	456,542	478,428	−21,886	25,966	20,338	5.7	4.3	21,156	−159	466,863	−13,709	38,583	104.4
Monroe	24,248	21,719	2,529	1,025	790	4.2	3.6	934	63	13,592	−37	27,558	74.5
Oconto	20,544	19,496	1,048	1,252	685	6.1	3.5	829	−22	7,199	−1,508	23,760	64.3
Oneida	20,199	19,802	397	1,177	956	5.8	4.8	1,421	−163	15,685	−694	28,256	76.4
Outagamie	96,174	93,575	2,599	4,440	2,708	4.6	2.9	4,939	226	93,532	−3,458	34,278	92.7
Ozaukee	48,212	47,698	514	1,745	1,181	3.6	2.5	2,815	−67	37,651	293	36,453	98.6
Pepin	4,131	3,931	200	195	135	4.7	3.4	218	17	1,600	−193	28,656	77.5
Pierce	23,809	22,914	895	994	584	4.2	2.5	858	62	7,418	583	25,627	69.3
Polk	24,178	22,800	1,378	1,392	750	5.8	3.3	1,211	149	12,664	919	26,845	72.6
Portage	41,167	38,840	2,327	1,847	1,342	4.5	3.5	1,633	−3	27,199	400	31,577	85.4

See footnotes at end of table.

[Includes United States, states, and 3,141 counties/county equivalents defined as of February 22, 2005. For more information on these areas, see Appendix C, Geographic Information]

County	Civilian labor force							Private nonfarm businesses					
	Total			Number of unemployed		Unemployment rate[1]		Establishments		Employment[2]		Annual payroll per employee, 2004	
	2006	2000	Net change, 2000–2006	2006	2000	2006	2000	2004	Net change, 2000–2004	2004	Net change, 2000–2004	Amount (dol.)	Percent of U.S. average
WISCONSIN—Con.													
Price	8,690	8,403	287	484	416	5.6	5.0	478	10	5,565	−199	26,061	70.5
Racine	98,961	99,866	−905	5,634	3,891	5.7	3.9	4,271	123	71,826	−1,601	35,640	96.4
Richland	10,112	9,650	462	467	326	4.6	3.4	417	57	4,924	220	25,224	68.2
Rock	84,195	82,916	1,279	4,248	3,436	5.0	4.1	3,518	158	60,258	−495	33,964	91.9
Rusk	7,915	7,936	−21	526	404	6.6	5.1	333	−2	4,539	157	26,239	71.0
St. Croix	45,658	38,057	7,601	2,254	911	4.9	2.4	2,009	326	25,887	3,697	36,061	97.5
Sauk	34,983	33,333	1,650	1,569	977	4.5	2.9	1,754	73	29,969	3,994	28,483	77.1
Sawyer	9,388	8,459	929	602	439	6.4	5.2	682	34	4,509	−508	26,671	72.1
Shawano	22,704	22,127	577	1,146	783	5.0	3.5	975	58	10,668	238	24,845	67.2
Sheboygan	65,113	64,605	508	2,594	1,595	4.0	2.5	2,750	146	54,075	−3,153	33,302	90.1
Taylor	11,041	11,020	21	554	406	5.0	3.7	494	22	7,995	279	26,769	72.4
Trempealeau	16,505	15,477	1,028	699	601	4.2	3.9	686	13	12,181	2,405	32,875	88.9
Vernon	14,560	14,407	153	695	523	4.8	3.6	641	5	6,056	−228	23,428	63.4
Vilas	11,928	10,998	930	715	533	6.0	4.8	959	166	6,165	1,775	22,290	60.3
Walworth	56,138	54,199	1,939	2,415	1,580	4.3	2.9	2,658	73	36,369	870	27,822	75.3
Washburn	8,080	8,029	51	533	400	6.6	5.0	643	65	5,891	733	23,478	63.5
Washington	72,883	70,096	2,787	3,052	1,939	4.2	2.8	3,317	213	49,904	2,563	31,562	85.4
Waukesha	214,447	211,346	3,101	8,202	5,667	3.8	2.7	12,746	177	219,724	−5,567	39,067	105.7
Waupaca	28,382	27,906	476	1,427	912	5.0	3.3	1,378	15	18,031	652	27,818	75.3
Waushara	13,134	11,836	1,298	726	483	5.5	4.1	535	13	4,477	64	20,535	55.5
Winnebago	92,491	89,989	2,502	4,147	2,452	4.5	2.7	3,723	5	87,555	5,759	38,581	104.4
Wood	40,360	41,040	−680	2,149	1,557	5.3	3.8	1,919	10	38,533	−881	34,619	93.6
WYOMING	284,690	266,882	17,808	9,073	10,197	3.2	3.8	[3]19,330	[3]1,210	[3]187,360	[3]12,746	[3]30,404	[3]82.2
Albany	18,985	18,300	685	505	612	2.7	3.3	1,063	47	10,170	599	23,383	63.3
Big Horn	5,397	5,317	80	225	267	4.2	5.0	293	−4	2,454	−176	28,050	75.9
Campbell	24,807	19,908	4,899	533	609	2.1	3.1	1,320	135	17,318	2,206	41,768	113.0
Carbon	7,899	8,094	−195	270	337	3.4	4.2	552	−11	4,600	−383	27,346	74.0
Converse	6,955	6,582	373	237	258	3.4	3.9	426	52	3,436	771	32,139	86.9
Crook	3,382	3,173	209	96	116	2.8	3.7	209	26	1,337	−18	27,144	73.4
Fremont	17,846	17,665	181	769	916	4.3	5.2	1,317	22	9,989	−193	24,605	66.6
Goshen	5,913	6,249	−336	231	227	3.9	3.6	378	−5	2,934	−58	21,753	58.8
Hot Springs	2,345	2,643	−298	85	96	3.6	3.6	197	−17	1,592	72	22,138	59.9
Johnson	3,866	3,575	291	120	133	3.1	3.7	355	27	1,976	317	24,588	66.5
Laramie	42,100	40,237	1,863	1,636	1,505	3.9	3.7	2,474	186	29,309	2,408	28,008	75.8
Lincoln	8,017	7,357	660	287	285	3.6	3.9	546	67	4,351	430	29,470	79.7
Natrona	40,620	36,536	4,084	1,208	1,426	3.0	3.9	2,769	144	30,020	2,463	30,965	83.8
Niobrara	1,136	1,236	−100	38	45	3.3	3.6	87	−6	359	−143	18,061	48.9
Park	14,362	14,378	−16	511	579	3.6	4.0	1,267	98	9,378	335	27,889	75.4
Platte	4,011	4,355	−344	178	176	4.4	4.0	276	7	2,148	−10	28,454	77.0
Sheridan	15,540	14,755	785	494	587	3.2	4.0	1,153	67	9,455	860	25,731	69.6
Sublette	5,682	3,560	2,122	100	105	1.8	2.9	401	76	1,960	635	31,670	85.7
Sweetwater	23,198	20,716	2,482	587	819	2.5	4.0	1,185	105	14,109	91	36,623	99.1
Teton	14,204	14,183	21	366	343	2.6	2.4	1,745	73	14,330	−47	27,958	75.6
Uinta	11,048	10,461	587	335	419	3.0	4.0	611	58	6,660	615	28,868	78.1
Washakie	4,264	4,306	−42	156	198	3.7	4.6	362	−18	3,400	230	24,086	65.2
Weston	3,114	3,299	−185	108	140	3.5	4.2	225	17	1,601	41	22,598	61.1

- Represents zero.   NA Not available.   X Not applicable.

[1]Civilian unemployed as percent of total civilian labor force.
[2]For pay period including March 12 of the year shown.
[3]Includes data not distributed by county.
[4]Colorado state total includes Broomfield city.
[5]Yellowstone National Park County became incorporated with Gallatin and Park Counties, MT; effective November 7, 1997.
[6]0 to 19 employees. Figure in table represents midpoint of range.
[7]100 to 249 employees. Figure in table represents midpoint of range.
[8]20 to 99 employees. Figure in table represents midpoint of range.
[9]Clifton Forge independent city became incorporated with Alleghany County, VA; effective July 1, 2001.
[10]South Boston independent city became incorporated with Halifax County, VA; effective June 30, 1995.

Survey, Census, or Data Collection Method: Civilian labor force—Based on the Current Population Survey (CPS), the Current Employment Statistics (CES) survey, and the unemployment insurance (UI) system; for more information, see Appendix B, Limitations of the Data and Methodology, and also <http://www.bls.gov/lau/laumthd.htm>.   Private nonfarm businesses—For data extracted from the Census Bureau's *County Business Patterns,* see Internet site <http://www.census.gov/epcd/cbp/view/cbpmethodology.htm>.

Sources: Civilian labor force—U.S. Bureau of Labor Statistics, *Local Area Unemployment Statistics, Annual Averages,* accessed April 17, 2007 (related Internet site <http://www.bls.gov/lau>). Private nonfarm businesses—U.S. Census Bureau, *County Business Patterns,* accessed July 12, 2006 (related Internet site <http://www.census.gov/epcd/cbp/view/cbpview.html>).

[Includes United States, states, and 3,141 counties/county equivalents defined as of February 22, 2005. For more information on these areas, see Appendix C, Geographic Information]

County	Banking,[1] 2005			Retail trade[2] (NAICS 44–45), 2002				Accommodation and food services[2] (NAICS 72), 2002				
	Offices				Sales					Sales		
	Number	Rate per 10,000 people	Total deposits (mil. dol.)	Estab-lishments	Total ($1,000)	Per capita[3] (dol.)	General merchandise stores,[4] percent of total	Estab-lishments	Total ($1,000)	Per capita[3] (dol.)	Percent change, 1997–2002	Food services,[5] percent of total
UNITED STATES.	91,394	3.1	5,869,879	1,114,637	3,056,421,997	10,615	14.6	565,590	449,498,718	1,561	28.3	71.5
ALABAMA.	1,454	3.2	65,307	19,608	43,784,342	9,771	17.6	7,075	4,692,297	1,047	20.9	85.1
Autauga.	15	3.1	380	176	516,308	11,326	(NA)	67	52,718	1,156	88.6	81.6
Baldwin	72	4.4	3,100	946	1,820,932	12,297	15.6	319	274,788	1,856	22.5	65.2
Barbour	13	4.6	388	123	187,191	6,460	18.0	44	22,470	775	30.2	83.5
Bibb	8	3.7	155	63	79,243	3,763	(NA)	17	5,352	254	(NA)	(NA)
Blount	13	2.3	463	140	247,103	4,656	(NA)	44	16,961	320	23.7	(NA)
Bullock.	2	1.8	143	33	34,140	3,013	(NA)	9	2,629	232	(NA)	(NA)
Butler	11	5.3	251	126	174,487	8,386	15.8	35	22,160	1,065	28.9	84.5
Calhoun	30	2.7	1,377	570	1,160,387	10,413	20.9	188	131,131	1,177	14.7	87.3
Chambers	10	2.8	273	126	241,756	6,686	(NA)	46	26,403	730	44.6	92.8
Cherokee.	7	2.9	233	94	141,575	5,820	13.6	32	9,206	378	34.3	(NA)
Chilton	10	2.4	361	184	286,336	7,069	(NA)	49	23,094	570	25.7	91.6
Choctaw.	5	3.4	195	76	63,054	4,075	7.7	13	5,001	323	–10.6	79.0
Clarke.	17	6.2	425	162	262,080	9,518	(NA)	44	18,477	671	7.7	87.5
Clay	5	3.6	162	46	56,813	3,992	(NA)	16	2,849	200	–11.9	100.0
Cleburne	5	3.5	132	47	56,574	3,888	(NA)	9	4,234	291	(NA)	(NA)
Coffee	14	3.1	591	208	504,964	11,476	(NA)	62	29,391	668	9.4	95.7
Colbert.	21	3.8	613	257	625,300	11,421	17.4	95	51,653	943	11.6	89.3
Conecuh	3	2.3	113	44	40,818	2,969	(NA)	17	7,598	553	25.6	82.0
Coosa	2	1.8	25	27	17,022	1,466	(NA)	4	678	58	(NA)	100.0
Covington.	10	2.7	597	224	327,573	8,855	13.3	61	25,020	676	24.7	90.7
Crenshaw.	5	3.6	177	57	61,301	4,504	6.6	14	4,947	364	31.3	(NA)
Cullman.	35	4.4	1,150	347	683,325	8,765	18.4	107	67,489	866	27.9	91.0
Dale	14	2.9	337	167	249,632	5,066	(NA)	68	29,984	608	11.5	89.0
Dallas	9	2.0	494	224	390,430	8,610	21.9	56	24,802	547	–4.6	77.2
DeKalb	24	3.6	669	261	445,468	6,778	22.2	86	51,191	779	25.3	81.6
Elmore.	19	2.6	580	206	378,429	5,479	(NA)	63	31,707	459	–4.2	95.6
Escambia.	16	4.2	537	181	275,070	7,138	17.3	62	22,248	577	–7.3	89.6
Etowah	28	2.7	1,078	454	912,041	8,858	17.7	171	102,568	996	20.6	91.9
Fayette	7	3.8	236	74	108,752	5,936	34.4	17	7,311	399	(NA)	100.0
Franklin	19	6.2	497	124	158,111	5,129	15.9	43	15,673	508	23.3	(NA)
Geneva	7	2.7	350	117	121,587	4,770	15.1	24	6,522	256	7.5	(NA)
Greene	2	2.1	43	33	33,021	3,323	(NA)	5	1,166	117	–13.4	100.0
Hale	3	1.6	186	52	67,453	3,694	(NA)	8	2,182	120	(NA)	(NA)
Henry	7	4.2	224	65	72,670	4,443	(NA)	12	3,330	204	(NA)	(NA)
Houston.	33	3.5	1,549	613	1,508,753	16,739	(NA)	193	132,240	1,467	8.8	84.8
Jackson.	22	4.1	635	202	353,987	6,564	22.7	68	33,478	621	29.1	92.8
Jefferson.	204	3.1	15,713	2,965	9,086,766	13,781	13.6	1,206	960,838	1,457	20.7	83.8
Lamar	11	7.4	263	55	58,353	3,788	7.0	18	4,497	292	28.9	100.0
Lauderdale	36	4.1	1,363	441	899,201	10,325	24.8	139	85,405	981	27.0	94.4
Lawrence	10	2.9	196	87	151,003	4,349	17.0	39	17,409	501	29.1	(NA)
Lee.	36	2.9	1,407	416	1,013,341	8,617	(NA)	205	139,484	1,186	26.5	84.6
Limestone	15	2.1	630	243	484,420	7,171	(NA)	74	53,530	792	16.7	90.1
Lowndes	5	3.8	128	31	47,486	3,513	(NA)	3	65	5	(NA)	100.0
Macon	3	1.3	106	62	73,901	3,117	(NA)	17	14,012	591	41.3	85.4
Madison	78	2.6	4,221	1,245	3,343,602	11,717	(NA)	541	432,125	1,514	24.9	84.7
Marengo	12	5.5	416	120	164,079	7,325	13.9	32	13,129	586	3.8	79.8
Marion	17	5.6	503	106	147,307	4,845	(NA)	48	16,125	530	(NA)	94.1
Marshall	39	4.6	1,306	481	1,082,162	12,988	15.3	159	82,757	993	17.0	91.4
Mobile	105	2.6	5,235	1,647	4,073,954	10,194	18.9	637	438,793	1,098	18.6	85.9
Monroe	9	3.8	310	105	150,163	6,258	16.2	37	14,132	589	–7.1	93.3
Montgomery	74	3.3	4,172	1,048	2,595,660	11,637	16.0	418	327,952	1,470	17.3	84.3
Morgan	34	3.0	1,405	574	1,204,957	10,782	17.4	183	120,016	1,074	18.7	(NA)
Perry.	3	2.6	124	43	35,999	3,070	(NA)	13	2,969	253	(Z)	(NA)
Pickens	10	5.0	277	84	94,127	4,515	7.6	17	3,441	165	(NA)	(NA)
Pike	11	3.7	534	155	282,587	9,689	(NA)	55	31,731	1,088	23.1	85.4
Randolph	10	4.4	341	85	98,556	4,375	(NA)	28	10,039	446	26.2	93.7
Russell	16	3.2	498	159	324,840	6,591	39.3	73	42,926	871	33.5	92.3
St. Clair	21	2.9	668	203	312,955	4,642	(NA)	76	32,442	481	3.5	93.4
Shelby	46	2.7	1,585	568	1,583,276	10,290	17.8	241	187,297	1,217	55.9	87.1
Sumter.	4	2.9	140	55	61,224	4,292	18.8	20	7,048	494	1.2	80.3
Talladega	18	2.2	761	299	569,635	7,090	(NA)	103	52,349	652	38.0	89.7
Tallapoosa	11	2.7	532	168	271,607	6,622	(NA)	44	23,036	562	7.8	83.1
Tuscaloosa	48	2.8	2,258	766	1,875,902	11,332	18.0	334	236,923	1,431	17.0	(NA)
Walker	26	3.7	879	322	779,732	11,048	22.8	86	54,572	773	25.4	94.7
Washington	5	2.8	146	52	53,985	3,012	(NA)	9	1,756	98	(NA)	(NA)
Wilcox	3	2.3	147	55	58,665	4,492	6.8	19	4,472	342	–0.2	(NA)
Winston	11	4.5	328	119	141,211	5,727	15.4	33	12,376	502	11.1	(NA)

See footnotes at end of table.

Table B-11. Counties — **Banking, Retail Trade, and Accommodation and Food Services**—Con.

[Includes United States, states, and 3,141 counties/county equivalents defined as of February 22, 2005. For more information on these areas, see Appendix C, Geographic Information]

County	Banking,[1] 2005 Offices Number	Rate per 10,000 people	Total deposits (mil. dol.)	Retail trade[2] (NAICS 44–45), 2002 Estab-lishments	Sales Total ($1,000)	Per capita[3] (dol.)	General merchandise stores,[4] percent of total	Accommodation and food services[2] (NAICS 72), 2002 Estab-lishments	Sales Total ($1,000)	Per capita[3] (dol.)	Percent change, 1997–2002	Food services,[5] percent of total
ALASKA	134	2.0	6,435	2,661	7,437,071	11,605	25.2	1,849	1,393,225	2,174	30.8	65.7
Aleutians East	–	–		7	8,166	3,065	(NA)	8	(D)	(NA)	(NA)	(NA)
Aleutians West	1	1.9	21	19	45,584	8,868	(NA)	17	15,541	3,024	103.5	(NA)
Anchorage	38	1.4	3,112	927	3,781,569	14,123	28.0	666	745,408	2,784	29.9	73.4
Bethel	2	1.2	53	55	69,731	4,196	29.6	16	5,491	330	72.1	50.5
Bristol Bay	1	9.0	33	10	6,410	5,584	–	15	4,633	4,036	2.8	(NA)
Denali	–	–	–	11	5,965	3,204	–	31	29,906	16,061	245.0	8.1
Dillingham	2	4.1	30	15	35,158	7,068	(NA)	12	5,395	1,085	–39.7	(NA)
Fairbanks North Star	20	2.3	804	332	1,112,694	13,126	(NA)	195	155,038	1,829	38.3	68.2
Haines	1	4.4	25	20	19,226	8,355	–	16	4,903	2,131	–8.3	51.5
Juneau	13	4.2	578	166	375,342	12,229	33.3	96	61,246	1,996	6.1	61.6
Kenai Peninsula	10	1.9	456	270	482,801	9,461	18.7	249	97,990	1,920	50.2	56.1
Ketchikan Gateway	9	6.8	298	111	219,320	16,155	(NA)	60	30,317	2,233	20.1	53.3
Kodiak Island	4	3.1	133	52	149,058	10,893	(NA)	37	20,917	1,529	13.4	55.6
Lake and Peninsula	–	–	–	8	2,069	1,301	79.9	12	(D)	(NA)	(NA)	(NA)
Matanuska-Susitna	9	1.2	317	210	615,639	9,455	25.3	156	69,571	1,068	58.5	67.9
Nome	1	1.1	63	35	52,004	5,689	(NA)	14	8,654	947	31.8	(NA)
North Slope	1	1.4	37	19	41,109	5,731	16.2	26	29,097	4,056	–10.2	81.1
Northwest Arctic	1	1.3	11	16	25,132	3,435	–	7	(D)	(NA)	(NA)	(NA)
Prince of Wales- Outer Ketchikan	2	3.5	44	33	35,733	6,208	2.8	21	6,839	1,188	–17.0	52.9
Sitka	4	4.5	134	73	86,230	9,735	(NA)	35	24,450	2,760	57.5	45.5
Skagway-Hoonah-Angoon	2	6.4	24	46	34,616	10,550	–	31	12,165	3,708	29.3	32.3
Southeast Fairbanks	3	4.5	36	29	29,531	5,249	(NA)	25	11,977	2,129	80.9	55.4
Valdez-Cordova	5	5.1	107	66	90,599	8,998	(NA)	57	24,004	2,384	21.3	37.4
Wade Hampton	–	–	–	25	31,088	4,340	15.9	2	(D)	(NA)	(NA)	(NA)
Wrangell-Petersburg	4	6.4	112	63	53,418	8,275	–	24	5,469	847	–13.5	59.2
Yakutat	1	13.9	7	4	3,998	5,395	–	8	2,755	3,718	–1.7	(NA)
Yukon-Koyukuk	–	–	–	39	24,881	3,931	6.4	13	3,962	626	–10.4	51.2
ARIZONA	1,140	1.9	72,806	17,238	56,457,863	10,380	(NA)	9,944	8,612,730	1,583	29.8	69.2
Apache	6	0.9	109	124	194,854	2,886	(NA)	62	42,528	630	12.9	41.5
Cochise	23	1.8	905	442	917,299	7,641	20.7	282	123,366	1,028	30.9	74.8
Coconino	27	2.2	882	671	1,340,393	11,174	17.7	455	424,374	3,538	4.1	51.8
Gila	11	2.1	509	180	381,240	7,397	(NA)	135	50,710	984	–9.7	82.6
Graham	4	1.2	192	98	226,262	6,808	(NA)	57	22,063	664	16.3	80.6
Greenlee	2	2.7	38	20	17,310	2,203	(NA)	13	2,714	345	–29.8	100.0
La Paz	5	2.5	164	79	243,687	12,488	(NA)	75	48,013	2,461	107.2	45.3
Maricopa	718	2.0	51,138	9,975	37,448,117	11,370	(NA)	5,615	5,440,107	1,652	29.6	72.9
Mohave	43	2.3	2,172	631	1,757,951	10,604	(NA)	345	199,944	1,206	38.3	73.7
Navajo	20	1.8	533	309	797,334	7,809	(NA)	218	137,652	1,348	16.2	47.3
Pima	164	1.8	10,250	2,818	8,693,151	9,906	16.9	1,599	1,387,756	1,581	33.2	67.0
Pinal	34	1.5	1,081	424	1,052,949	5,401	(NA)	236	198,251	1,017	42.0	53.5
Santa Cruz	8	1.9	753	221	441,798	11,152	25.6	91	48,192	1,217	19.4	76.9
Yavapai	52	2.6	2,857	789	1,608,287	8,978	17.4	490	313,002	1,747	73.5	55.1
Yuma	23	1.3	1,223	457	1,337,231	8,021	22.3	271	174,058	1,044	33.4	72.1
ARKANSAS	1,370	4.9	40,996	12,141	25,611,630	9,459	20.5	4,659	2,766,905	1,022	26.9	82.1
Arkansas	14	7.0	463	130	210,408	10,320	(NA)	47	16,149	792	53.6	85.6
Ashley	15	6.5	246	97	134,632	5,638	18.9	26	12,245	513	23.7	88.4
Baxter	19	4.7	827	229	369,210	9,522	(NA)	102	38,913	1,004	20.4	69.5
Benton	76	4.1	3,215	606	1,487,818	9,000	(NA)	238	163,378	988	65.1	81.6
Boone	17	4.7	687	205	439,059	12,667	(NA)	57	31,565	911	18.4	86.4
Bradley	8	6.6	210	54	55,822	4,477	6.8	16	5,132	412	2.3	(NA)
Calhoun	2	3.6	44	17	13,541	2,390	(NA)	3	(D)	(NA)	(NA)	(NA)
Carroll	20	7.4	470	193	215,470	8,274	(NA)	163	49,211	1,890	19.0	52.9
Chicot	8	6.1	200	60	67,967	5,005	9.1	19	5,872	432	47.7	76.7
Clark	14	6.1	364	100	188,674	8,046	(NA)	48	30,003	1,280	29.0	87.6
Clay	10	6.0	239	62	85,892	5,035	13.0	21	7,378	432	(NA)	(NA)
Cleburne	19	7.5	349	132	163,907	6,708	(NA)	55	20,842	853	–0.8	68.3
Cleveland	5	5.6	47	14	13,806	1,600	(NA)	2	(D)	(NA)	(NA)	(NA)
Columbia	14	5.7	519	123	157,880	6,251	(NA)	45	20,787	823	6.7	82.8
Conway	10	4.8	245	89	172,311	8,419	(NA)	29	12,209	596	17.5	84.7
Craighead	42	4.8	1,659	453	1,047,329	12,506	(NA)	142	107,809	1,287	34.4	93.0
Crawford	28	4.9	574	160	320,181	5,818	(NA)	56	37,087	674	14.3	88.8
Crittenden	18	3.5	464	197	591,704	11,564	(NA)	83	54,218	1,060	6.1	75.6
Cross	10	5.2	284	84	136,517	7,058	(NA)	18	8,680	449	5.0	94.4
Dallas	6	7.0	151	59	69,455	7,860	(NA)	11	2,911	329	(NA)	(NA)
Desha	11	7.7	214	86	132,151	8,923	(NA)	26	7,629	515	–4.2	81.1
Drew	11	5.9	330	102	214,720	11,654	(NA)	35	13,189	716	–13.8	83.6
Faulkner	48	4.9	1,246	350	772,155	8,576	(NA)	127	79,198	880	14.3	90.8
Franklin	9	4.9	271	56	92,884	5,183	(NA)	25	8,970	501	52.6	80.0
Fulton	6	5.0	150	47	28,694	2,472	(NA)	20	4,950	427	47.7	72.1

See footnotes at end of table.

[Includes United States, states, and 3,141 counties/county equivalents defined as of February 22, 2005. For more information on these areas, see Appendix C, Geographic Information]

County	Banking,[1] 2005 Offices			Retail trade[2] (NAICS 44–45), 2002	Sales			Accommodation and food services[2] (NAICS 72), 2002	Sales			
	Number	Rate per 10,000 people	Total deposits (mil. dol.)	Estab-lishments	Total ($1,000)	Per capita[3] (dol.)	General merchan-dise stores,[4] percent of total	Estab-lishments	Total ($1,000)	Per capita[3] (dol.)	Percent change, 1997–2002	Food services,[5] percent of total
ARKANSAS—Con.												
Garland	51	5.5	1,310	533	1,107,218	12,301	(NA)	249	158,113	1,757	31.5	71.0
Grant	5	2.9	158	51	85,290	5,092	20.5	18	6,507	388	(NA)	(NA)
Greene	20	5.1	592	177	287,944	7,569	(NA)	57	28,245	742	35.6	93.6
Hempstead	11	4.7	369	97	153,949	6,562	(NA)	30	16,954	723	13.4	(NA)
Hot Spring	14	4.5	395	96	182,809	5,979	(NA)	30	16,175	529	19.4	95.5
Howard	9	6.2	210	82	110,251	7,707	22.6	16	7,194	503	7.5	(NA)
Independence	19	5.5	553	195	331,482	9,658	(NA)	54	29,338	855	29.5	88.6
Izard	8	6.0	155	49	83,891	6,359	5.0	15	2,881	218	37.3	87.0
Jackson	7	4.0	211	90	118,842	6,698	(NA)	29	8,052	454	−6.2	(NA)
Jefferson	25	3.1	853	354	744,272	8,936	16.4	138	73,779	886	27.5	86.4
Johnson	11	4.6	285	90	170,224	7,334	(NA)	33	13,546	584	−1.4	80.2
Lafayette	4	5.0	130	24	23,154	2,778	11.6	10	1,478	177	−6.0	(NA)
Lawrence	10	5.8	234	81	108,713	6,170	(NA)	21	8,329	473	8.1	(NA)
Lee	3	2.6	73	31	34,431	2,806	12.3	5	2,117	173	(NA)	100.0
Lincoln	6	4.2	100	31	51,817	3,571	(NA)	13	(D)	(NA)	(NA)	(NA)
Little River	8	6.0	134	50	81,155	6,044	(NA)	12	4,726	352	(NA)	(NA)
Logan	13	5.7	302	94	132,477	5,877	(NA)	26	10,985	487	26.8	96.7
Lonoke	29	4.8	660	203	385,232	6,963	(NA)	67	35,767	647	68.0	(NA)
Madison	7	4.7	159	42	63,871	4,457	(NA)	7	1,765	123	−14.9	100.0
Marion	8	4.8	174	46	57,597	3,547	(NA)	31	6,214	383	1.9	64.1
Miller	14	3.2	523	144	309,987	7,500	(NA)	78	95,817	2,318	109.3	91.5
Mississippi	23	4.8	522	216	334,934	6,669	(NA)	83	41,100	818	13.5	74.6
Monroe	6	6.5	182	55	58,175	5,969	18.4	24	9,963	1,022	−16.7	81.3
Montgomery	3	3.2	84	27	23,634	2,584	(NA)	14	11,476	1,255	22.5	(NA)
Nevada	2	2.1	86	34	51,051	5,265	(NA)	8	2,993	309	−20.4	(NA)
Newton	2	2.4	48	20	24,931	2,931	(NA)	16	3,818	449	99.7	46.6
Ouachita	16	5.9	340	134	208,934	7,505	(NA)	34	(D)	(NA)	(NA)	(NA)
Perry	3	2.9	80	20	22,169	2,126	(NA)	3	628	60	−39.4	(NA)
Phillips	12	5.0	262	117	169,099	6,745	(NA)	34	11,654	465	23.9	(NA)
Pike	8	7.2	203	54	56,048	5,007	8.0	18	4,349	388	−10.3	75.1
Poinsett	15	5.9	298	102	139,104	5,474	(NA)	32	12,076	475	27.3	94.8
Polk	11	5.5	274	99	143,779	7,102	(NA)	33	9,881	488	−31.7	78.4
Pope	29	5.1	893	306	685,879	12,420	14.2	105	56,537	1,024	12.0	(NA)
Prairie	4	4.4	84	36	25,378	2,689	12.7	12	3,308	351	−5.0	(NA)
Pulaski	198	5.4	6,901	1,756	5,254,294	14,446	16.7	774	629,128	1,730	23.9	79.6
Randolph	7	3.8	241	72	108,709	5,960	(NA)	28	10,503	576	(NA)	88.9
St. Francis	13	4.7	261	152	262,386	9,163	(NA)	43	26,942	941	11.5	71.5
Saline	31	3.4	755	270	973,769	11,292	(NA)	85	54,322	630	17.4	92.7
Scott	7	6.3	177	30	48,069	4,362	(NA)	14	1,784	162	(NA)	(NA)
Searcy	6	7.5	89	34	33,946	4,193	7.6	9	1,974	244	−5.4	(NA)
Sebastian	54	4.5	1,950	598	1,478,430	12,643	(NA)	241	163,582	1,399	17.8	88.9
Sevier	10	6.1	278	66	113,567	7,210	(NA)	12	6,153	391	(NA)	(NA)
Sharp	14	8.0	356	79	113,924	6,561	(NA)	37	10,960	631	8.1	83.9
Stone	4	3.4	187	64	77,767	6,732	(NA)	30	12,498	1,082	64.7	47.2
Union	26	5.9	1,029	256	430,578	9,523	23.1	75	39,101	865	39.0	76.5
Van Buren	12	7.3	172	77	117,151	7,192	(NA)	21	8,935	549	0.9	90.3
Washington	83	4.6	2,818	772	2,142,085	12,938	(NA)	387	262,849	1,588	43.4	(NA)
White	34	4.8	942	326	568,676	8,228	(NA)	107	76,072	1,101	58.3	94.7
Woodruff	4	4.9	105	35	35,509	4,211	10.8	8	1,275	151	43.6	100.0
Yell	11	5.1	330	69	102,862	4,815	(NA)	19	8,876	415	(NA)	(NA)
CALIFORNIA	6,620	1.8	753,579	108,941	359,120,365	10,264	13.0	66,568	55,559,669	1,588	31.3	74.4
Alameda	286	2.0	28,082	4,420	16,512,174	11,279	10.7	2,937	2,050,993	1,401	30.3	82.6
Alpine	–	–	–	8	1,621	1,333	31.2	15	24,482	20,133	311.3	3.5
Amador	13	3.4	628	167	1,641,687	44,592	(NA)	100	42,480	1,154	41.8	75.1
Butte	49	2.3	2,701	770	2,027,431	9,714	17.6	381	222,714	1,067	42.5	89.5
Calaveras	14	3.0	407	147	208,310	4,828	(NA)	95	28,203	654	31.8	84.1
Colusa	8	3.8	248	64	130,093	6,716	(NA)	39	24,572	1,269	43.8	77.2
Contra Costa	215	2.1	23,538	2,701	10,108,546	10,225	16.1	1,608	1,184,301	1,198	31.1	88.8
Del Norte	5	1.7	220	73	135,822	4,931	(NA)	80	30,621	1,112	27.2	67.4
El Dorado	43	2.4	2,115	571	1,186,870	7,160	(NA)	408	416,729	2,514	99.4	35.7
Fresno	138	1.6	8,417	2,475	7,258,766	8,724	16.5	1,290	823,835	990	30.3	88.5
Glenn	8	2.9	275	81	130,271	4,860	(NA)	51	22,417	836	26.0	83.3
Humboldt	29	2.3	1,306	661	1,321,439	10,370	13.5	360	179,541	1,409	33.8	75.6
Imperial	14	0.9	1,426	481	1,345,422	9,234	23.6	214	126,785	870	42.0	83.0
Inyo	6	3.3	314	123	219,799	12,012	(NA)	94	60,073	3,283	10.5	56.8
Kern	91	1.2	5,064	1,909	5,601,117	8,082	15.0	1,048	642,606	927	30.3	87.4
Kings	19	1.3	915	307	723,565	5,378	19.1	156	86,604	644	33.0	89.8
Lake	15	2.3	733	189	423,825	6,806	(NA)	130	40,757	654	39.8	83.2
Lassen	6	1.7	172	91	191,436	5,690	(NA)	67	32,735	973	27.0	79.9
Los Angeles	1,611	1.6	208,227	28,636	92,100,128	9,433	11.6	17,074	14,211,642	1,456	28.2	80.5
Madera	23	1.6	1,012	334	705,181	5,474	(NA)	170	93,412	725	27.9	68.1

See footnotes at end of table.

[Includes United States, states, and 3,141 counties/county equivalents defined as of February 22, 2005. For more information on these areas, see Appendix C, Geographic Information]

County	Banking,[1] 2005			Retail trade[2] (NAICS 44–45), 2002				Accommodation and food services[2] (NAICS 72), 2002				
	Offices		Total deposits (mil. dol.)	Estab-lishments	Sales			Estab-lishments	Sales			
	Number	Rate per 10,000 people			Total ($1,000)	Per capita[3] (dol.)	General merchan-dise stores,[4] percent of total		Total ($1,000)	Per capita[3] (dol.)	Percent change, 1997–2002	Food services,[5] percent of total
CALIFORNIA—Con.												
Marin	81	3.3	7,913	1,206	3,731,456	15,095	9.9	687	524,076	2,120	25.5	80.6
Mariposa	3	1.7	119	70	70,920	4,095	(NA)	51	114,093	6,588	41.1	(NA)
Mendocino	24	2.7	1,320	495	910,183	10,390	9.8	325	156,739	1,789	25.5	60.3
Merced	30	1.2	1,797	544	1,602,352	7,124	19.3	278	140,824	626	29.5	89.0
Modoc	3	3.1	111	43	43,369	4,634	–	28	6,299	673	27.9	(NA)
Mono	4	3.2	138	93	143,720	11,058	–	139	176,337	13,568	54.3	24.5
Monterey	80	1.9	6,209	1,542	4,063,394	9,873	14.3	958	1,033,917	2,512	23.5	47.7
Napa	44	3.3	2,529	551	1,390,394	10,696	7.6	343	350,932	2,700	22.2	61.8
Nevada	30	3.0	1,664	440	884,272	9,298	(NA)	221	167,704	1,763	41.9	48.5
Orange	615	2.1	63,665	9,559	35,736,615	12,205	12.2	5,911	5,592,425	1,910	31.6	74.8
Placer	98	3.1	5,114	1,123	4,778,965	17,128	12.0	630	547,087	1,961	63.7	76.7
Plumas	9	4.2	304	114	148,285	7,057	(NA)	123	30,685	1,460	30.8	54.3
Riverside	284	1.5	18,931	4,437	16,301,196	9,619	15.3	2,491	2,360,637	1,393	45.7	68.6
Sacramento	206	1.5	18,587	3,739	13,730,077	10,548	14.4	2,206	1,665,556	1,280	39.1	83.6
San Benito	9	1.6	674	137	385,890	6,930	(NA)	85	46,459	834	54.9	92.5
San Bernardino	220	1.1	16,171	4,439	15,969,020	8,828	16.6	2,528	1,841,198	1,018	43.9	86.1
San Diego	566	1.9	46,560	9,486	31,586,056	10,906	14.1	5,761	6,331,146	2,186	49.1	61.2
San Francisco	246	3.3	93,499	3,654	8,883,316	11,658	7.4	3,311	3,546,865	4,655	8.0	58.8
San Joaquin	106	1.6	57,998	1,661	5,473,782	8,936	15.9	938	571,806	933	51.7	88.2
San Luis Obispo	75	2.9	4,436	1,205	2,668,485	10,587	8.9	760	600,487	2,382	56.7	57.4
San Mateo	155	2.2	17,836	2,221	9,017,029	12,858	13.3	1,557	1,471,499	2,098	6.6	72.5
Santa Barbara	98	2.4	8,461	1,633	4,311,187	10,738	14.3	975	840,658	2,094	32.5	67.0
Santa Clara	326	1.9	49,081	5,140	20,035,462	11,964	(NA)	3,690	3,036,675	1,813	17.2	79.4
Santa Cruz	54	2.2	4,112	979	2,618,480	10,335	12.2	606	426,478	1,683	39.0	78.1
Shasta	41	2.3	2,108	705	1,972,157	11,471	18.1	376	231,341	1,346	43.1	75.6
Sierra	2	5.8	18	15	11,757	3,360	–	22	4,895	1,399	-9.2	(NA)
Siskiyou	24	5.3	602	231	311,163	7,035	(NA)	155	64,779	1,465	38.1	60.4
Solano	62	1.5	3,300	1,124	4,155,519	10,148	17.4	669	433,859	1,059	48.6	89.6
Sonoma	123	2.6	8,790	1,870	5,731,948	12,303	12.8	1,068	723,958	1,554	46.9	74.3
Stanislaus	92	1.8	5,740	1,433	4,918,690	10,242	16.2	751	498,507	1,038	58.9	90.7
Sutter	15	1.7	989	282	820,540	9,977	(NA)	117	73,500	894	63.6	91.4
Tehama	12	2.0	560	184	522,436	9,062	(NA)	114	55,140	956	50.3	85.6
Trinity	4	2.9	90	52	59,346	4,477	2.0	50	13,053	985	18.1	52.2
Tulare	63	1.5	3,213	1,059	2,930,759	7,687	18.7	474	258,662	678	11.3	89.1
Tuolumne	21	3.5	982	230	482,649	8,612	19.6	168	69,773	1,245	19.4	73.1
Ventura	163	2.0	11,692	2,429	9,024,777	11,557	12.6	1,287	987,277	1,264	27.3	82.9
Yolo	31	1.7	2,092	466	1,426,316	7,954	(NA)	316	181,556	1,012	29.6	88.4
Yuba	8	1.2	380	142	294,900	4,729	(NA)	82	37,285	598	20.4	80.9
COLORADO	1,464	3.1	70,409	18,851	52,226,983	11,611	14.9	10,799	8,808,846	1,958	31.3	70.2
Adams	73	1.8	2,324	986	3,733,112	10,010	17.0	559	402,132	1,078	39.3	85.1
Alamosa	7	4.6	321	89	233,398	15,433	(NA)	46	23,737	1,570	14.9	73.2
Arapahoe	150	2.8	7,322	2,155	9,263,841	18,158	13.6	1,052	960,284	1,882	40.4	82.8
Archuleta	7	5.9	205	84	87,723	7,922	(NA)	53	25,346	2,289	68.3	46.0
Baca	3	7.4	85	22	20,051	4,568	(NA)	8	1,542	351	21.3	(NA)
Bent	2	3.6	71	15	11,743	2,062	(NA)	8	1,616	284	-27.4	(NA)
Boulder	106	3.8	5,215	1,279	3,463,955	12,448	13.7	720	539,362	1,938	18.8	82.0
Broomfield	17	3.9	497	206	636,212	15,579	12.7	95	93,885	2,299	(NA)	75.6
Chaffee	9	5.3	286	123	192,961	11,467	(NA)	97	38,172	2,268	23.7	56.3
Cheyenne	3	15.4	117	10	9,374	4,356	(NA)	6	869	404	(NA)	100.0
Clear Creek	3	3.3	52	49	47,010	4,924	–	41	20,662	2,164	9.8	77.4
Conejos	2	2.3	45	15	22,493	2,683	–	15	2,648	316	37.8	44.7
Costilla	1	2.9	1	12	5,576	1,542	–	7	831	230	(NA)	70.9
Crowley	1	1.9	34	10	14,747	2,686	–	4	329	60	(NA)	100.0
Custer	2	5.2	47	22	21,705	5,935	–	16	6,008	1,643	42.9	39.9
Delta	14	4.7	445	151	203,745	7,021	2.5	75	18,891	651	24.0	79.5
Denver	170	3.0	20,038	2,313	6,405,054	11,485	9.5	1,641	1,669,129	2,993	25.0	73.8
Dolores	1	5.5	22	8	6,728	3,629	–	6	1,284	693	(NA)	40.3
Douglas	74	3.0	2,004	622	2,011,172	9,501	21.1	286	242,250	1,144	122.1	91.2
Eagle	35	7.4	1,140	443	574,318	12,954	(NA)	242	394,172	8,891	36.8	46.5
Elbert	5	2.2	80	38	52,201	2,369	–	19	4,722	214	97.8	(NA)
El Paso	140	2.5	4,787	1,953	6,079,111	11,220	(NA)	1,082	948,116	1,750	22.7	69.8
Fremont	13	2.7	478	143	271,645	5,714	(NA)	91	32,093	675	7.7	84.5
Garfield	23	4.6	765	319	699,266	14,882	(NA)	153	96,846	2,061	33.5	63.3
Gilpin	–	–	–	5	832	171		9	234,777	48,268	284.0	(NA)
Grand	8	6.1	185	129	131,111	10,163	(NA)	142	70,757	5,485	36.3	40.8
Gunnison	10	7.0	318	137	155,769	11,114	(NA)	120	62,186	4,437	-26.3	45.4
Hinsdale	1	13.1	21	13	5,703	7,312	(NA)	23	3,552	4,554	-3.6	37.2
Huerfano	3	3.9	79	33	39,719	5,024	(NA)	29	7,498	948	28.1	76.0
Jackson	1	6.9	17	13	12,172	7,930	–	8	1,146	747	22.2	(NA)

See footnotes at end of table.

[Includes United States, states, and 3,141 counties/county equivalents defined as of February 22, 2005. For more information on these areas, see Appendix C, Geographic Information]

County	Banking,[1] 2005 Offices Number	Rate per 10,000 people	Total deposits (mil. dol.)	Retail trade[2] (NAICS 44–45), 2002 Establishments	Sales Total ($1,000)	Per capita[3] (dol.)	General merchandise stores,[4] percent of total	Accommodation and food services[2] (NAICS 72), 2002 Establishments	Sales Total ($1,000)	Per capita[3] (dol.)	Percent change, 1997–2002	Food services,[5] percent of total
COLORADO—Con.												
Jefferson	136	2.6	7,248	1,843	5,801,330	10,937	16.1	951	736,562	1,389	25.6	85.4
Kiowa	1	7.0	16	7	6,448	4,322	–	4	287	192	(NA)	(NA)
Kit Carson	7	9.2	198	55	79,791	10,034	(NA)	19	7,657	963	–21.8	49.9
Lake	3	3.9	70	27	35,239	4,513	–	39	9,232	1,182	10.2	71.0
La Plata	17	3.6	874	324	579,110	12,642	(NA)	175	146,406	3,196	2.2	45.1
Larimer	86	3.2	3,713	1,251	3,164,674	11,996	18.5	702	476,556	1,806	38.4	79.4
Las Animas	6	3.9	268	55	125,295	8,107	(NA)	47	18,900	1,223	39.1	72.1
Lincoln	4	7.1	70	28	74,370	12,569	(NA)	21	7,708	1,303	–4.2	62.8
Logan	8	3.9	285	107	221,972	10,562	(NA)	48	21,977	1,046	7.6	77.9
Mesa	45	3.5	1,665	600	1,661,962	13,603	20.1	250	180,411	1,477	44.7	76.2
Mineral	1	10.7	12	14	4,182	4,880	(NA)	17	3,714	4,334	84.1	28.1
Moffat	3	2.2	122	67	123,508	9,204	(NA)	36	19,880	1,481	65.1	73.8
Montezuma	10	4.0	354	130	263,446	10,936	(NA)	83	30,025	1,246	8.1	62.0
Montrose	14	3.7	478	185	409,595	11,592	(NA)	89	35,780	1,013	22.2	74.4
Morgan	12	4.3	414	104	203,973	7,379	8.9	49	23,590	853	20.3	76.8
Otero	13	6.7	306	95	170,666	8,610	(NA)	57	16,191	817	1.8	87.3
Ouray	4	9.4	76	45	18,364	4,633	(NA)	50	15,314	3,863	40.7	46.4
Park	1	0.6	27	39	37,880	2,349	–	39	9,534	591	–3.8	62.1
Phillips	4	8.7	90	24	28,224	6,215	–	7	1,586	349	(NA)	(NA)
Pitkin	11	7.4	816	251	309,870	20,822	0.8	169	221,876	14,909	–3.5	39.5
Prowers	8	5.8	279	74	120,249	8,459	33.2	37	14,093	991	14.3	72.7
Pueblo	41	2.7	1,265	542	1,430,646	9,708	24.3	338	175,891	1,193	23.5	86.0
Rio Blanco	3	5.0	98	36	27,906	4,648	(NA)	27	10,548	1,757	41.2	38.0
Rio Grande	10	8.2	219	66	89,906	7,362	(NA)	40	14,008	1,147	28.7	56.5
Routt	12	5.6	474	212	274,515	13,469	(NA)	129	124,868	6,127	27.3	41.9
Saguache	2	2.8	18	21	29,445	4,551	–	8	1,728	267	(NA)	(NA)
San Juan	1	17.3	6	20	4,699	8,287	–	21	2,926	5,160	47.0	69.0
San Miguel	7	9.7	234	77	60,641	8,471	–	77	66,110	9,235	163.5	45.6
Sedgwick	4	15.8	62	16	26,521	9,783	(NA)	8	996	367	(NA)	(NA)
Summit	15	6.0	511	387	510,968	20,649	(NA)	195	226,339	9,147	–0.1	46.5
Teller	5	2.3	166	80	113,498	5,258	(NA)	65	117,526	5,445	24.0	11.0
Washington	5	10.8	99	21	25,701	5,301	(NA)	5	531	110	(NA)	(NA)
Weld	72	3.1	2,604	582	1,673,132	8,187	(NA)	320	158,337	775	48.3	94.9
Yuma	9	9.2	271	69	106,810	10,935	(NA)	24	6,917	708	46.0	95.1
CONNECTICUT	1,197	3.4	76,936	13,861	41,952,682	12,129	10.0	7,047	6,681,803	1,932	78.3	58.4
Fairfield	340	3.8	22,671	3,876	13,931,143	15,569	7.4	1,874	1,368,615	1,529	22.9	82.7
Hartford	271	3.1	23,998	3,347	10,220,398	11,787	11.2	1,765	1,276,476	1,472	28.2	83.2
Litchfield	90	4.7	3,731	784	2,090,276	11,213	(NA)	384	187,049	1,003	24.2	78.1
Middlesex	69	4.2	2,927	743	1,607,873	10,075	6.5	365	219,011	1,372	27.3	78.0
New Haven	265	3.1	16,485	3,218	9,268,417	11,102	11.9	1,674	1,011,744	1,212	25.7	88.5
New London	87	3.3	3,938	1,119	3,011,905	11,464	15.9	589	2,380,268	9,060	614.9	12.0
Tolland	39	2.6	1,852	387	894,305	6,281	2.7	186	136,584	959	34.7	92.6
Windham	36	3.1	1,335	387	928,365	8,352	(NA)	210	102,056	918	33.9	81.9
DELAWARE	263	3.1	138,758	3,727	10,912,971	13,538	14.0	1,576	1,231,595	1,528	22.1	83.7
Kent	34	2.4	1,404	568	1,719,250	13,061	21.7	211	153,034	1,163	29.3	82.1
New Castle	168	3.2	118,628	2,047	6,936,307	13,594	13.2	905	755,783	1,481	15.2	84.9
Sussex	61	3.5	18,726	1,112	2,257,414	13,745	10.6	460	322,778	1,965	37.7	81.7
DISTRICT OF COLUMBIA	211	3.8	22,630	1,877	3,061,401	5,422	(NA)	1,799	2,943,078	5,212	30.0	55.1
District of Columbia	211	3.8	22,630	1,877	3,061,401	5,422	(NA)	1,799	2,943,078	5,212	30.0	55.1
FLORIDA	5,081	2.9	342,820	69,543	191,805,685	11,498	13.9	30,215	29,366,940	1,760	21.5	65.7
Alachua	59	2.6	2,573	924	2,367,427	10,720	(NA)	438	326,772	1,480	24.2	(NA)
Baker	3	1.2	167	65	129,758	5,584	(NA)	20	14,066	605	43.8	90.1
Bay	52	3.2	2,570	813	1,864,639	12,249	23.0	449	373,164	2,451	11.0	65.9
Bradford	3	1.1	166	84	144,818	5,526	(NA)	32	22,727	867	31.7	94.8
Brevard	128	2.4	6,895	1,913	5,233,118	10,555	17.3	839	604,443	1,219	22.0	78.0
Broward	432	2.4	33,407	7,193	22,012,210	12,917	11.3	3,363	2,799,987	1,643	13.2	76.1
Calhoun	4	3.0	118	49	81,863	6,407	3.0	14	(D)	(NA)	(NA)	(NA)
Charlotte	55	3.5	3,607	558	1,434,629	9,570	26.7	238	138,202	922	11.9	89.5
Citrus	44	3.3	2,023	461	1,176,143	9,505	11.8	184	80,485	650	21.4	85.6
Clay	28	1.6	917	559	1,535,243	10,124	20.5	222	149,730	987	30.7	93.9
Collier	124	4.0	9,655	1,465	4,196,902	15,222	11.3	586	697,888	2,531	30.0	57.0
Columbia	16	2.5	648	250	578,398	9,894	(NA)	104	66,455	1,137	22.8	76.7
DeSoto	7	2.0	329	71	243,399	7,388	(NA)	29	13,552	411	9.2	84.7
Dixie	4	2.7	88	44	42,537	3,044	(NA)	20	5,231	374	47.6	73.8
Duval	177	2.1	21,334	3,157	10,185,744	12,699	14.0	1,474	1,173,952	1,464	28.0	81.0

See footnotes at end of table.

County and City Data Book: 2007

U.S. Census Bureau

[Includes United States, states, and 3,141 counties/county equivalents defined as of February 22, 2005. For more information on these areas, see Appendix C, Geographic Information]

County	Banking,[1] 2005 Offices Number	Offices Rate per 10,000 people	Total deposits (mil. dol.)	Retail trade[2] (NAICS 44–45), 2002 Establishments	Sales Total ($1,000)	Per capita[3] (dol.)	General merchandise stores,[4] percent of total	Accommodation and food services[2] (NAICS 72), 2002 Establishments	Sales Total ($1,000)	Per capita[3] (dol.)	Percent change, 1997–2002	Food services,[5] percent of total
FLORIDA—Con.												
Escambia	79	2.7	4,081	1,253	3,340,536	11,255	(NA)	486	392,107	1,321	11.7	87.6
Flagler	17	2.2	1,323	159	342,357	5,931	(NA)	97	62,587	1,084	47.8	65.4
Franklin	10	9.8	287	75	80,841	8,070	(NA)	40	21,903	2,187	46.6	54.7
Gadsden	6	1.3	200	140	254,369	5,590	(NA)	39	13,882	305	29.4	87.1
Gilchrist	5	3.0	100	29	38,483	2,555	(NA)	15	4,680	311	(NA)	(NA)
Glades	3	2.7	32	9	7,812	715	(NA)	9	2,816	258	−40.1	58.0
Gulf	7	5.0	243	58	58,149	4,410	7.4	22	9,165	695	97.9	(NA)
Hamilton	2	1.4	61	42	53,286	3,873	(NA)	19	4,303	313	16.0	(NA)
Hardee	5	1.8	357	81	150,747	5,474	(NA)	25	9,334	339	27.0	90.0
Hendry	10	2.5	435	136	297,216	8,079	(NA)	48	21,138	575	14.8	86.3
Hernando	37	2.3	2,534	397	1,066,482	7,709	21.1	184	100,504	727	35.7	92.6
Highlands	32	3.4	1,401	366	737,104	8,184	19.4	122	63,160	701	20.7	87.8
Hillsborough	273	2.4	16,878	4,141	13,909,770	13,231	12.4	1,723	1,643,887	1,564	31.7	76.4
Holmes	3	1.6	203	56	50,619	2,703	(NA)	12	4,516	241	−0.3	87.6
Indian River	57	4.4	3,740	667	1,524,526	12,922	17.4	211	139,857	1,185	24.5	91.3
Jackson	16	3.3	424	211	397,784	8,551	19.3	60	30,504	656	17.4	79.2
Jefferson	2	1.4	116	53	65,437	4,751	(NA)	13	3,649	265	8.9	(NA)
Lafayette	2	2.5	53	16	30,563	4,194	8.3	7	(D)	(NA)	(NA)	(NA)
Lake	93	3.4	4,091	827	2,028,795	8,632	(NA)	319	240,784	1,025	55.8	65.6
Lee	188	3.5	10,315	2,181	6,365,752	13,386	14.1	929	839,873	1,766	20.1	65.4
Leon	80	3.3	3,860	1,020	2,685,149	11,198	(NA)	512	393,582	1,641	32.6	79.4
Levy	13	3.4	323	141	269,567	7,517	(NA)	65	25,561	713	31.1	83.5
Liberty	1	1.3	59	16	15,331	2,131	(NA)	2	(D)	(NA)	(NA)	(NA)
Madison	5	2.6	190	70	76,607	4,096	4.7	30	10,946	585	10.1	72.3
Manatee	104	3.4	4,965	994	2,703,995	9,650	16.9	435	297,414	1,061	23.1	82.5
Marion	82	2.7	4,435	1,063	2,860,280	10,496	20.7	378	240,967	884	19.9	88.5
Martin	61	4.4	3,696	726	1,921,445	14,577	(NA)	277	220,032	1,669	31.1	83.6
Miami-Dade	584	2.5	70,222	10,113	24,568,286	10,616	11.5	3,935	4,162,169	1,799	30.1	65.2
Monroe	54	7.1	2,258	762	1,183,949	14,978	6.4	549	638,620	8,079	12.2	42.8
Nassau	18	2.8	698	243	422,949	6,984	(NA)	99	180,124	2,974	25.7	27.2
Okaloosa	81	4.4	3,452	968	2,476,204	14,131	19.1	422	357,413	2,040	36.6	84.3
Okeechobee	11	2.8	504	148	335,976	9,081	(NA)	61	34,759	940	−0.1	88.0
Orange	229	2.2	17,867	4,237	12,403,154	13,128	13.8	1,939	4,688,186	4,962	15.5	38.4
Osceola	51	2.2	2,221	670	1,751,198	9,023	(NA)	437	654,999	3,375	−14.1	46.9
Palm Beach	478	3.8	34,471	5,326	16,480,821	13,879	11.1	2,305	2,266,130	1,908	36.5	69.9
Pasco	109	2.5	5,039	1,156	3,074,472	8,242	19.9	449	275,807	739	12.0	78.5
Pinellas	318	3.4	17,987	3,813	12,038,819	13,018	11.6	1,894	1,567,142	1,695	13.3	69.3
Polk	125	2.3	5,179	1,713	4,522,310	9,041	18.8	649	452,479	905	7.9	85.5
Putnam	16	2.2	553	240	498,261	6,999	(NA)	78	37,432	526	−0.1	86.6
St. Johns	62	3.8	2,148	711	1,340,944	9,834	(NA)	351	330,651	2,425	25.5	52.2
St. Lucie	56	2.3	3,501	613	1,886,487	9,187	(NA)	258	170,144	829	15.2	78.7
Santa Rosa	37	2.6	1,266	334	805,701	6,327	(NA)	150	85,173	669	58.4	94.1
Sarasota	173	4.7	11,012	1,697	4,434,320	13,039	11.6	688	579,129	1,703	20.2	73.0
Seminole	125	3.1	5,514	1,658	5,082,697	13,339	15.1	608	476,453	1,250	12.6	89.4
Sumter	17	2.6	498	120	247,536	4,285	(NA)	49	29,352	508	24.4	81.9
Suwannee	9	2.3	412	140	270,491	7,473	(NA)	35	20,362	563	31.3	85.5
Taylor	4	2.0	133	89	170,746	8,822	(NA)	35	14,647	757	23.3	79.1
Union	2	1.3	56	29	28,928	2,079	(NA)	5	2,291	165	(NA)	100.0
Volusia	152	3.1	7,629	1,888	4,714,294	10,260	16.6	972	734,596	1,599	15.6	72.3
Wakulla	7	2.5	207	59	81,316	3,229	(NA)	24	10,978	436	12.6	(NA)
Walton	30	6.0	960	211	305,302	6,862	(NA)	103	308,779	6,941	188.1	18.5
Washington	4	1.8	131	72	120,694	5,642	(NA)	29	12,754	596	45.4	86.8
GEORGIA	2,643	2.9	149,442	34,050	90,098,578	10,551	15.1	15,463	12,740,423	1,492	31.5	78.6
Appling	5	2.8	212	77	119,636	6,782	3.1	32	17,016	965	61.5	94.1
Atkinson	3	3.7	63	27	27,732	3,601	(NA)	8	1,812	235	5.7	100.0
Bacon	5	4.8	181	44	40,136	4,000	6.4	16	5,488	547	(NA)	(NA)
Baker	1	2.4	16	6	3,735	931	(NA)	−	−	−	−100.0	−
Baldwin	12	2.7	500	207	412,262	9,173	(NA)	74	45,754	1,018	21.0	84.6
Banks	4	2.5	63	37	106,327	7,012	(NA)	6	8,363	552	−50.0	(NA)
Barrow	18	3.0	607	145	525,648	10,260	14.9	59	33,252	649	38.1	97.3
Bartow	25	2.8	1,028	271	810,603	9,814	16.4	138	83,094	1,006	27.3	88.3
Ben Hill	9	5.2	240	93	160,715	9,308	(NA)	31	11,010	638	(NA)	87.3
Berrien	6	3.6	190	71	102,158	6,236	3.4	16	5,189	317	−6.2	(NA)
Bibb	55	3.6	2,466	873	2,254,348	14,592	17.8	356	259,908	1,682	13.1	84.2
Bleckley	3	2.5	144	52	55,526	4,706	5.5	13	5,360	454	−1.2	(NA)
Brantley	3	1.9	63	30	41,415	2,722	(NA)	10	2,983	196	42.5	100.0
Brooks	5	3.1	198	49	72,472	4,440	(NA)	10	2,013	123	(NA)	(NA)
Bryan	5	1.8	237	72	130,961	5,220	(NA)	39	19,255	768	(NA)	(NA)
Bulloch	17	2.8	819	270	569,278	9,964	24.1	101	65,676	1,150	25.1	87.0
Burke	10	4.3	188	73	145,317	6,383	(NA)	24	9,510	418	29.1	87.6
Butts	4	1.9	378	70	170,102	7,948	2.2	34	16,403	766	55.5	(NA)
Calhoun	3	5.0	69	29	21,507	3,404	(NA)	6	(D)	(NA)	(NA)	(NA)
Camden	13	2.8	401	162	447,154	9,831	(NA)	76	55,183	1,213	56.5	73.9

See footnotes at end of table.

[Includes United States, states, and 3,141 counties/county equivalents defined as of February 22, 2005. For more information on these areas, see Appendix C, Geographic Information]

County	Banking,[1] 2005 Offices Number	Banking,[1] 2005 Offices Rate per 10,000 people	Total deposits (mil. dol.)	Retail trade[2] (NAICS 44–45), 2002 Establishments	Retail trade[2] Sales Total ($1,000)	Retail trade[2] Sales Per capita[3] (dol.)	General merchandise stores,[4] percent of total	Accommodation and food services[2] (NAICS 72), 2002 Establishments	Accommodation and food services[2] Sales Total ($1,000)	Accommodation and food services[2] Sales Per capita[3] (dol.)	Percent change, 1997–2002	Food services,[5] percent of total
GEORGIA—Con.												
Candler	7	6.8	143	52	78,966	8,039	(NA)	24	12,606	1,283	63.8	91.1
Carroll	34	3.2	1,567	361	822,550	8,671	20.6	139	78,107	823	23.9	93.0
Catoosa	17	2.8	823	167	513,385	9,074	26.9	62	45,512	804	32.6	87.8
Charlton	2	1.9	78	48	29,034	2,740	9.8	15	5,923	559	55.9	(NA)
Chatham	83	3.5	4,089	1,179	2,887,448	12,276	(NA)	654	566,731	2,409	32.5	69.5
Chattahoochee	1	0.7	31	9	4,792	248	(NA)	2	(D)	(NA)	(NA)	(NA)
Chattooga	6	2.3	260	77	147,453	5,651	15.7	35	10,838	415	7.6	(NA)
Cherokee	59	3.2	2,426	457	1,459,703	9,149	18.1	222	152,327	955	102.6	96.8
Clarke	40	3.8	1,656	546	1,461,556	14,299	(NA)	286	217,937	2,132	73.6	89.0
Clay	2	6.2	19	13	10,210	3,048	(NA)	1	(D)	(NA)	(NA)	(NA)
Clayton	41	1.5	1,489	812	2,787,525	11,000	17.1	372	403,786	1,593	−4.5	82.9
Clinch	2	2.9	70	25	31,013	4,532	9.1	11	5,355	783	(NA)	(NA)
Cobb	182	2.7	8,074	2,330	8,601,411	13,473	13.4	1,213	1,072,870	1,681	26.6	80.0
Coffee	17	4.3	561	200	368,793	9,513	(NA)	59	36,609	944	40.1	93.0
Colquitt	11	2.5	430	183	305,860	7,114	(NA)	57	31,712	738	36.1	90.6
Columbia	26	2.5	1,037	268	1,018,898	10,761	(NA)	105	73,310	774	15.7	93.6
Cook	7	4.3	168	82	110,758	6,934	3.0	38	13,483	844	39.6	80.5
Coweta	36	3.3	1,054	277	879,107	8,981	18.5	131	95,882	980	63.9	91.0
Crawford	2	1.6	44	18	12,576	999	(NA)	2	(D)	(NA)	(NA)	(NA)
Crisp	7	3.2	317	134	244,512	11,046	(NA)	49	24,873	1,124	−5.2	79.7
Dade	4	2.5	115	67	128,428	8,166	3.2	22	11,270	717	7.8	(NA)
Dawson	8	4.1	357	169	240,367	13,637	(NA)	27	19,643	1,114	(NA)	90.7
Decatur	10	3.5	297	145	278,638	9,918	(NA)	36	16,275	579	15.9	80.4
DeKalb	145	2.1	7,495	2,186	6,218,730	9,240	12.4	1,145	839,425	1,247	3.7	78.0
Dodge	7	3.6	265	84	123,527	6,405	17.2	21	8,873	460	5.2	93.8
Dooly	3	2.6	134	35	87,352	7,545	(NA)	12	3,378	292	4.0	61.9
Dougherty	29	3.1	1,328	532	1,210,583	12,648	22.1	208	124,504	1,301	5.5	91.1
Douglas	29	2.6	1,155	407	1,693,487	17,205	19.1	174	146,642	1,490	51.5	94.5
Early	4	3.3	123	61	77,360	6,341	3.5	13	4,924	404	(NA)	(NA)
Echols	–	–	–	3	(D)	(NA)	(NA)	–	–	–	–	–
Effingham	8	1.7	293	87	220,622	5,371	(NA)	40	15,722	383	(NA)	(NA)
Elbert	7	3.4	262	86	137,470	6,652	(NA)	34	12,993	629	12.0	86.5
Emanuel	8	3.6	269	94	152,207	6,987	14.7	31	14,162	650	49.1	94.6
Evans	8	7.0	144	60	118,135	10,641	2.9	18	5,682	512	−11.4	(NA)
Fannin	9	4.1	379	114	219,563	10,499	3.4	45	22,406	1,071	98.1	72.6
Fayette	45	4.3	1,591	384	1,028,463	10,665	18.7	153	133,273	1,382	30.2	86.0
Floyd	28	3.0	1,222	424	960,214	10,366	23.6	185	121,357	1,310	38.3	94.1
Forsyth	44	3.1	1,902	358	1,072,907	9,184	20.3	127	99,321	850	82.1	97.3
Franklin	12	5.6	330	110	276,121	13,207	2.1	38	18,542	887	10.4	89.2
Fulton	293	3.2	48,463	3,652	11,149,163	13,638	10.8	2,608	3,328,579	4,072	40.8	69.1
Gilmer	6	2.2	540	92	217,079	8,594	(NA)	34	14,197	562	27.7	(NA)
Glascock	1	3.7	55	5	3,324	1,281	–	2	(D)	(NA)	(NA)	(NA)
Glynn	37	5.1	1,353	494	974,277	14,036	(NA)	229	336,855	4,853	33.9	43.9
Gordon	11	2.2	644	254	480,065	10,282	19.4	81	49,263	1,055	20.6	92.0
Grady	8	3.3	277	81	153,634	6,413	(NA)	23	9,345	390	14.6	(NA)
Greene	6	3.8	274	58	89,693	5,915	2.6	22	31,551	2,081	400.7	25.3
Gwinnett	193	2.7	9,368	2,513	9,767,435	15,054	12.7	1,170	938,765	1,447	30.3	87.6
Habersham	18	4.5	745	174	350,943	9,280	19.1	68	32,912	870	26.6	90.0
Hall	52	3.1	2,328	551	1,493,130	9,834	17.8	232	198,658	1,308	33.8	74.2
Hancock	2	2.1	122	25	19,623	1,956	(NA)	5	644	64	−46.6	100.0
Haralson	13	4.6	353	98	187,592	6,978	11.7	34	12,828	477	(NA)	(NA)
Harris	4	1.4	87	56	36,467	1,451	(NA)	41	24,968	993	(NA)	(NA)
Hart	7	2.9	279	76	104,522	4,498	(NA)	25	12,856	553	42.2	91.3
Heard	2	1.8	68	27	17,365	1,543	(NA)	9	2,179	194	(NA)	(NA)
Henry	53	3.2	1,607	435	1,266,112	9,035	24.0	235	170,073	1,214	128.4	92.4
Houston	28	2.2	1,068	428	1,218,245	10,460	18.9	201	150,390	1,291	46.8	83.4
Irwin	3	3.0	72	31	22,965	2,285	(NA)	6	2,532	252	25.8	100.0
Jackson	19	3.6	706	259	519,021	11,402	1.1	65	84,363	1,853	29.1	(NA)
Jasper	2	1.5	183	29	27,828	2,275	(NA)	12	3,040	249	35.8	(NA)
Jeff Davis	5	3.8	157	82	208,257	16,189	(NA)	23	8,411	654	(NA)	(NA)
Jefferson	10	5.9	240	83	100,760	5,884	5.1	24	(D)	(NA)	(NA)	(NA)
Jenkins	2	2.3	61	34	41,940	4,840	(NA)	15	3,732	431	(NA)	(NA)
Johnson	2	2.1	82	21	21,279	2,259	(NA)	3	(D)	(NA)	(NA)	(NA)
Jones	5	1.9	323	30	42,124	1,699	(NA)	12	6,661	269	(NA)	(NA)
Lamar	4	2.4	184	43	74,831	4,613	4.3	21	10,294	635	56.6	94.7
Lanier	1	1.3	106	28	(D)	(NA)	(NA)	5	1,457	203	(NA)	(NA)
Laurens	18	3.8	702	268	440,064	9,624	(NA)	78	(D)	(NA)	(NA)	(NA)
Lee	10	3.2	152	43	62,844	2,267	(NA)	15	3,797	137	56.4	(NA)
Liberty	12	2.1	309	177	320,355	5,269	(NA)	77	41,593	684	16.1	(NA)
Lincoln	2	2.4	71	25	28,823	3,405	7.1	9	4,184	494	(NA)	100.0

See footnotes at end of table.

Table B-11. Counties — **Banking, Retail Trade, and Accommodation and Food Services**—Con.

[Includes United States, states, and 3,141 counties/county equivalents defined as of February 22, 2005. For more information on these areas, see Appendix C, Geographic Information]

County	Banking,[1] 2005 Offices Number	Banking,[1] 2005 Offices Rate per 10,000 people	Banking,[1] 2005 Total deposits (mil. dol.)	Retail trade[2] (NAICS 44–45), 2002 Estab- lishments	Retail trade Sales Total ($1,000)	Retail trade Sales Per capita[3] (dol.)	Retail trade Sales General merchan- dise stores,[4] percent of total	Accommodation and food services[2] (NAICS 72), 2002 Estab- lishments	Accommodation Sales Total ($1,000)	Accommodation Sales Per capita[3] (dol.)	Accommodation Sales Percent change, 1997– 2002	Food services,[5] percent of total
GEORGIA—Con.												
Long	2	1.8	13	12	8,099	752	(NA)	7	2,892	269	155.0	(NA)
Lowndes	33	3.4	1,468	575	1,332,541	14,230	20.6	210	184,551	1,971	68.8	86.4
Lumpkin	8	3.3	254	72	169,590	7,507	(NA)	42	24,715	1,094	49.9	83.0
McDuffie	8	3.7	277	115	290,555	13,628	(NA)	35	18,564	871	4.4	82.4
McIntosh	3	2.7	98	89	107,997	9,855	(NA)	23	14,533	1,326	62.4	84.9
Macon	2	1.5	86	47	58,203	4,144	6.4	13	3,820	272	(NA)	(NA)
Madison	10	3.7	166	69	93,822	3,515	(NA)	13	5,121	192	−84.7	100.0
Marion	1	1.4	29	22	36,632	5,112	(NA)	7	(D)	(NA)	(NA)	(NA)
Meriwether	8	3.5	196	90	106,631	4,662	6.1	33	9,173	401	2.0	(NA)
Miller	3	4.8	123	41	41,468	6,484	5.5	10	2,564	401	−6.4	(NA)
Mitchell	9	3.8	244	93	121,284	5,081	13.7	34	12,748	534	9.9	58.4
Monroe	5	2.1	183	67	77,304	3,413	(NA)	39	22,938	1,013	6.2	55.9
Montgomery	4	4.5	164	21	13,395	1,583	(NA)	7	2,334	276	17.0	(NA)
Morgan	7	4.0	252	83	165,618	10,088	(NA)	36	20,233	1,232	20.8	66.3
Murray	7	1.7	241	112	208,731	5,396	3.6	37	18,240	472	−8.7	77.1
Muscogee	47	2.5	3,896	794	2,329,515	12,577	15.8	354	319,761	1,726	(NA)	(NA)
Newton	15	1.7	824	201	459,981	6,405	14.2	86	48,985	682	58.7	90.9
Oconee	12	4.0	461	71	170,140	6,233	(NA)	20	9,021	330	154.4	(NA)
Oglethorpe	3	2.2	84	27	37,932	2,887	(NA)	7	461	35	−66.9	(NA)
Paulding	19	1.7	858	178	624,837	6,613	28.0	72	53,908	571	(NA)	(NA)
Peach	6	2.4	187	123	225,688	9,357	(NA)	55	26,227	1,087	(NA)	79.3
Pickens	9	3.2	724	93	251,144	9,779	1.4	34	16,972	661	50.4	(NA)
Pierce	4	2.3	216	61	88,340	5,523	(NA)	16	7,510	470	33.6	(NA)
Pike	6	3.7	149	23	17,750	1,215	(NA)	9	1,670	114	−21.8	100.0
Polk	10	2.5	353	135	215,323	5,446	(NA)	56	25,706	650	(NA)	95.1
Pulaski	3	3.1	117	46	51,689	5,313	3.3	16	6,166	634	10.6	100.0
Putnam	5	2.5	298	77	170,260	8,784	1.8	25	9,543	492	55.9	86.5
Quitman	1	4.1	4	12	9,684	3,767	(NA)	2	(D)	(NA)	(NA)	(NA)
Rabun	10	6.2	492	93	163,822	10,547	(NA)	52	31,120	2,004	63.7	45.4
Randolph	3	4.1	76	34	28,458	3,757	(NA)	11	3,514	464	35.3	(NA)
Richmond	47	2.4	2,422	868	2,207,714	11,140	(NA)	390	318,891	1,609	24.7	81.1
Rockdale	20	2.5	956	297	1,170,817	16,011	16.2	145	134,408	1,838	55.1	94.1
Schley	1	2.4	127	14	17,329	4,400	(NA)	4	303	77	13.9	100.0
Screven	7	4.5	221	59	76,735	4,971	4.5	18	6,314	409	59.8	89.9
Seminole	5	5.4	129	53	69,499	7,435	4.1	11	3,363	360	14.5	90.2
Spalding	13	2.1	580	246	610,518	10,226	13.9	96	61,213	1,025	31.0	94.6
Stephens	11	4.4	299	118	243,709	9,544	(NA)	43	19,766	774	−7.4	90.7
Stewart	2	4.1	43	21	17,710	3,471	(NA)	9	(D)	(NA)	(NA)	(NA)
Sumter	12	3.6	431	142	279,570	8,410	(NA)	52	27,737	834	18.0	82.9
Talbot	2	3.0	35	15	6,529	989	(NA)	–	–	–	(NA)	–
Taliaferro	1	5.5	15	3	1,501	748	–	2	(D)	(NA)	(NA)	(NA)
Tattnall	7	3.0	247	73	89,711	4,028	(NA)	19	6,106	274	−8.1	(NA)
Taylor	3	3.4	88	28	32,731	3,676	6.4	4	781	88	−40.5	100.0
Telfair	8	6.1	157	61	64,469	5,548	(NA)	19	(D)	(NA)	(NA)	(NA)
Terrell	4	3.7	160	55	60,698	5,610	(NA)	13	4,720	436	(NA)	(NA)
Thomas	15	3.4	1,008	235	450,796	10,449	19.4	69	37,500	869	1.7	87.0
Tift	16	3.9	598	257	538,445	13,779	17.8	83	66,907	1,712	51.1	79.1
Toombs	14	5.1	716	158	297,672	11,333	(NA)	63	32,006	1,218	40.6	87.0
Towns	5	4.8	323	63	61,188	6,318	4.7	32	22,842	2,359	54.6	(NA)
Treutlen	2	3.0	50	22	16,461	2,361	(NA)	8	1,798	258	−20.3	100.0
Troup	21	3.4	874	298	634,188	10,588	12.3	109	63,860	1,066	26.2	89.3
Turner	4	4.2	214	37	56,308	5,853	(NA)	19	6,087	633	1.0	45.1
Twiggs	1	1.0	23	20	16,120	1,534	(NA)	5	(D)	(NA)	(NA)	(NA)
Union	6	3.0	874	102	191,346	10,400	3.0	38	12,866	699	52.4	84.1
Upson	9	3.3	341	121	180,664	6,504	(NA)	39	16,634	599	14.3	93.2
Walker	14	2.2	400	199	350,113	5,638	16.5	60	22,345	360	11.9	(NA)
Walton	16	2.1	826	196	466,805	6,957	5.5	70	39,355	587	(NA)	93.5
Ware	9	2.6	607	238	429,638	12,090	(NA)	64	41,841	1,177	21.6	(NA)
Warren	2	3.3	32	21	16,693	2,667	(NA)	3	(D)	(NA)	(NA)	(NA)
Washington	7	3.5	297	87	137,428	6,579	(NA)	30	17,583	842	(NA)	89.6
Wayne	8	2.8	207	143	214,059	7,895	(NA)	49	22,942	846	46.3	87.8
Webster	1	4.4	7	5	2,930	1,277	–	–	–	–	–	–
Wheeler	2	3.0	54	13	10,151	1,543	(NA)	5	2,181	332	463.6	100.0
White	8	3.3	396	135	194,185	8,789	2.1	78	38,218	1,730	50.9	57.1
Whitfield	33	3.6	1,484	513	1,248,916	14,393	15.2	172	124,757	1,438	35.6	86.5
Wilcox	7	8.0	119	28	19,391	2,238	9.0	4	696	80	(NA)	100.0
Wilkes	5	4.8	244	66	80,207	7,524	4.7	14	10,407	976	(NA)	(NA)
Wilkinson	3	3.0	94	26	28,952	2,820	(NA)	6	1,876	183	(NA)	100.0
Worth	4	1.8	170	64	119,868	5,485	3.1	18	6,723	308	(NA)	93.8

See footnotes at end of table.

[Includes United States, states, and 3,141 counties/county equivalents defined as of February 22, 2005. For more information on these areas, see Appendix C, Geographic Information]

County	Banking,[1] 2005			Retail trade[2] (NAICS 44–45), 2002				Accommodation and food services[2] (NAICS 72), 2002				
	Offices		Total deposits (mil. dol.)	Estab-lishments	Sales			Estab-lishments	Sales			
	Number	Rate per 10,000 people			Total ($1,000)	Per capita[3] (dol.)	General merchan-dise stores,[4] percent of total		Total ($1,000)	Per capita[3] (dol.)	Percent change, 1997–2002	Food services,[5] percent of total
HAWAII................	285	2.2	24,783	4,924	13,008,182	10,537	19.7	3,138	5,551,380	4,497	10.9	42.0
Hawaii...............	34	2.0	2,056	691	1,704,360	11,006	20.7	350	747,901	4,830	36.8	25.2
Honolulu.............	192	2.1	19,617	3,065	8,816,634	9,948	20.0	2,119	2,956,987	3,337	-2.6	55.0
Kalawao.............	–	–	–	–	–	–	–	–	–	–	–	–
Kauai...............	21	3.4	945	352	714,715	11,914	19.1	208	467,176	7,788	59.0	28.8
Maui................	38	2.7	2,165	816	1,772,473	13,297	17.6	461	1,379,316	10,347	22.0	27.8
IDAHO...............	489	3.4	15,125	5,874	13,540,952	10,081	17.1	3,088	1,653,671	1,231	34.1	72.0
Ada.................	125	3.6	4,902	1,352	3,869,329	12,098	20.2	745	497,952	1,557	34.4	82.2
Adams..............	2	5.6	28	19	15,577	4,479	(NA)	18	3,553	1,022	5.2	(NA)
Bannock.............	24	3.1	522	352	806,072	10,633	(NA)	169	91,357	1,205	21.4	79.6
Bear Lake...........	4	6.5	81	35	54,122	8,587	6.4	17	3,357	533	19.9	60.3
Benewah............	5	5.4	89	36	66,165	7,343	–	20	3,833	425	-9.1	(NA)
Bingham.............	9	2.1	219	123	276,113	6,518	(NA)	48	16,708	394	32.9	93.7
Blaine..............	15	7.1	594	194	292,239	14,399	(NA)	107	122,134	6,018	5.9	39.5
Boise...............	–	–	–	21	11,316	1,604	–	25	5,035	714	63.3	82.3
Bonner.............	11	2.7	474	187	301,688	7,892	(NA)	116	46,077	1,205	37.3	59.0
Bonneville...........	26	2.8	886	462	1,224,811	14,363	(NA)	197	115,906	1,359	28.0	81.7
Boundary...........	3	2.8	111	50	68,101	6,821	(NA)	22	(D)	(NA)	(NA)	(NA)
Butte...............	2	7.1	23	15	10,479	3,579	–	8	(D)	(NA)	(NA)	(NA)
Camas..............	1	9.5	7	3	(D)	(NA)	(NA)	5	(D)	(NA)	(NA)	(NA)
Canyon.............	38	2.3	1,098	443	1,263,707	8,683	18.2	204	95,500	656	33.7	93.8
Caribou.............	3	4.2	67	39	55,952	7,728	(NA)	14	2,669	369	-1.1	68.1
Cassia..............	10	4.7	315	115	198,259	9,197	(NA)	43	20,648	958	15.4	(NA)
Clark...............	–	–	–	3	(D)	(NA)	(NA)	2	(D)	(NA)	(NA)	(NA)
Clearwater..........	4	4.8	85	48	43,509	5,139	(NA)	29	4,765	563	1.6	74.6
Custer..............	2	4.9	38	33	23,752	5,701	–	22	6,738	1,617	17.0	26.0
Elmore..............	7	2.4	129	89	184,309	6,306	(NA)	57	22,893	783	69.2	77.6
Franklin.............	4	3.2	87	37	73,250	6,205	(NA)	17	4,115	349	23.7	89.8
Fremont.............	6	4.9	72	42	55,793	4,690	(NA)	36	9,591	806	11.5	52.6
Gem................	4	2.5	134	33	48,866	3,136	(NA)	23	6,429	413	19.9	100.0
Gooding.............	7	4.8	135	50	65,782	4,621	(NA)	24	7,492	526	51.1	72.0
Idaho..............	9	5.7	166	75	71,249	4,591	(NA)	62	11,727	756	20.5	59.9
Jefferson............	5	2.3	122	45	68,504	3,463	(NA)	22	4,036	204	(NA)	91.8
Jerome.............	8	4.1	153	62	191,230	10,229	(NA)	30	9,395	503	35.2	84.2
Kootenai............	40	3.1	1,472	540	1,287,845	11,265	15.7	307	222,209	1,944	61.4	55.0
Latah..............	13	3.7	342	163	279,495	8,025	19.0	97	44,712	1,284	33.4	(NA)
Lemhi..............	3	3.8	86	63	84,814	10,940	5.3	34	7,711	995	18.2	64.7
Lewis...............	3	8.0	38	24	18,358	4,928	–	14	(D)	(NA)	(NA)	(NA)
Lincoln.............	1	2.2	17	11	11,765	2,780	(NA)	7	1,555	367	0.8	100.0
Madison.............	6	1.9	182	97	314,970	10,929	(NA)	37	15,506	538	(NA)	85.9
Minidoka............	5	2.6	145	65	125,774	6,469	(NA)	27	7,126	367	24.8	(NA)
Nez Perce..........	15	4.0	480	222	534,026	14,364	(NA)	101	53,030	1,426	23.3	80.8
Oneida.............	2	4.8	40	15	14,906	3,608	(NA)	6	1,479	358	(NA)	100.0
Owyhee............	3	2.7	35	22	23,481	2,148	(NA)	14	3,500	320	43.7	100.0
Payette.............	7	3.2	188	65	86,165	4,064	(NA)	26	4,386	207	-6.5	100.0
Power..............	4	5.2	52	29	34,521	4,649	(NA)	15	2,148	289	-7.9	86.4
Shoshone...........	10	7.6	142	61	304,971	23,321	(NA)	52	8,833	675	8.7	74.0
Teton...............	4	5.4	83	33	57,279	8,405	(NA)	24	6,228	914	50.3	67.4
Twin Falls...........	30	4.3	996	399	873,941	13,351	(NA)	158	83,347	1,273	33.0	87.8
Valley..............	4	4.8	178	69	83,342	10,950	–	64	18,942	2,489	35.9	66.6
Washington..........	5	5.0	112	33	56,546	5,677	–	23	4,390	441	(NA)	(NA)
ILLINOIS.............	4,645	3.6	303,552	43,022	131,469,518	10,446	14.0	24,245	19,072,168	1,515	28.6	75.4
Adams..............	43	6.4	1,493	367	901,470	13,292	(NA)	141	73,752	1,087	11.9	(NA)
Alexander...........	3	3.4	61	26	25,610	2,708	(NA)	18	3,118	330	-28.2	(NA)
Bond...............	9	5.0	253	65	92,666	5,191	(NA)	33	12,630	708	14.4	(NA)
Boone..............	11	2.2	470	93	281,702	6,288	14.7	54	22,121	494	19.2	97.5
Brown..............	7	10.2	106	24	19,918	2,912	(NA)	11	1,934	283	10.3	100.0
Bureau.............	23	6.5	776	122	265,629	7,531	(NA)	79	23,216	658	12.1	(NA)
Calhoun............	5	9.7	95	18	24,555	4,899	(NA)	19	4,708	939	30.2	100.0
Carroll.............	10	6.2	341	71	88,324	5,392	6.3	49	10,458	638	16.8	81.1
Cass...............	8	5.8	263	48	90,848	6,654	(NA)	34	8,691	637	13.3	93.9
Champaign..........	72	3.9	3,223	675	1,921,255	10,538	22.6	433	287,196	1,575	15.5	82.6
Christian............	22	6.3	536	133	291,014	8,264	(NA)	78	23,195	659	7.5	97.5
Clark...............	11	6.5	290	83	125,530	7,385	(NA)	33	12,701	747	2.3	86.1
Clay................	10	7.1	231	58	85,978	6,015	18.7	34	8,033	562	38.0	87.5
Clinton.............	19	5.3	769	169	332,353	9,284	(NA)	78	24,804	693	(NA)	96.3
Coles...............	25	4.9	770	214	562,399	10,845	29.8	118	63,489	1,224	6.1	(NA)
Cook...............	1,521	2.9	163,070	16,494	50,441,449	9,403	12.7	10,000	9,587,830	1,787	23.4	74.0
Crawford............	14	7.0	327	79	137,091	6,798	(NA)	37	10,867	539	(NA)	(NA)
Cumberland	6	5.5	139	40	31,590	2,846	–	15	3,374	304	(NA)	(NA)
DeKalb.............	33	3.4	1,668	319	860,356	9,352	17.2	179	91,800	998	25.4	89.4
De Witt.............	10	6.0	246	71	159,598	9,583	(NA)	38	12,280	737	10.2	87.4

See footnotes at end of table.

[Includes United States, states, and 3,141 counties/county equivalents defined as of February 22, 2005. For more information on these areas, see Appendix C, Geographic Information]

County	Banking,[1] 2005 Offices Number	Rate per 10,000 people	Total deposits (mil. dol.)	Retail trade[2] (NAICS 44–45), 2002 Estab-lishments	Sales Total ($1,000)	Per capita[3] (dol.)	General merchandise stores,[4] percent of total	Accommodation and food services[2] (NAICS 72), 2002 Estab-lishments	Sales Total ($1,000)	Per capita[3] (dol.)	Percent change, 1997–2002	Food services,[5] percent of total
ILLINOIS—Con.												
Douglas	14	7.0	280	153	195,406	9,794	(NA)	48	17,583	881	1.8	77.1
DuPage	373	4.0	23,724	3,442	15,049,905	16,342	11.2	1,829	1,721,730	1,870	15.1	78.5
Edgar	12	6.3	400	64	137,322	7,073	(NA)	27	8,122	418	34.0	88.5
Edwards	3	4.4	122	23	31,089	4,548	(NA)	6	2,069	303	(NA)	100.0
Effingham	21	6.1	852	204	536,367	15,586	(NA)	102	84,379	2,452	42.5	67.0
Fayette	9	4.1	263	95	162,091	7,514	(NA)	36	13,807	640	10.8	88.4
Ford	12	8.5	361	74	118,709	8,382	(NA)	33	8,796	621	16.8	(NA)
Franklin	16	4.0	479	172	323,514	8,284	(NA)	70	26,176	670	-2.0	93.9
Fulton	21	5.6	599	147	309,997	8,244	15.3	73	21,962	584	7.6	97.2
Gallatin	4	6.5	82	22	14,035	2,260	(NA)	8	1,317	212	-0.2	(NA)
Greene	9	6.2	233	61	71,401	4,857	(NA)	31	6,202	422	(NA)	(NA)
Grundy	25	5.7	775	136	395,171	10,197	(NA)	94	45,404	1,172	38.4	88.0
Hamilton	4	4.8	208	35	39,499	4,691	6.8	8	2,401	285	16.0	100.0
Hancock	17	8.9	350	96	104,581	5,311	0.7	45	12,976	659	65.9	(NA)
Hardin	3	6.4	50	11	10,394	2,197	–	8	1,063	225	(NA)	(NA)
Henderson	6	7.5	173	20	22,613	2,771	–	19	2,666	327	35.7	100.0
Henry	30	5.9	927	205	441,860	8,752	(NA)	98	31,460	623	-4.4	(NA)
Iroquois	25	8.1	657	105	198,433	6,439	(NA)	62	19,038	618	31.6	81.8
Jackson	22	3.8	732	258	618,763	10,641	24.8	140	77,867	1,339	19.1	91.7
Jasper	5	5.0	193	39	73,011	7,246	(NA)	15	2,555	254	11.9	100.0
Jefferson	17	4.2	522	210	501,945	12,458	23.6	76	54,005	1,340	28.9	79.3
Jersey	10	4.5	286	74	190,658	8,670	(NA)	42	18,677	849	16.9	75.9
Jo Daviess	18	8.0	643	146	168,382	7,501	(NA)	86	66,912	2,981	8.3	39.5
Johnson	6	4.6	127	37	52,049	4,054	(NA)	18	5,852	456	60.7	(NA)
Kane	171	3.5	7,563	1,494	4,316,428	9,756	18.5	727	540,613	1,222	47.3	88.2
Kankakee	40	3.7	1,611	396	1,105,228	10,495	20.0	207	111,928	1,063	11.5	91.9
Kendall	28	3.5	1,015	146	528,678	8,556	(NA)	82	39,101	633	38.6	89.6
Knox	19	3.6	731	244	616,204	11,219	17.5	133	57,233	1,042	5.0	86.9
Lake	234	3.3	17,725	2,459	13,098,140	19,407	7.0	1,325	1,042,298	1,544	34.3	82.9
LaSalle	65	5.8	2,362	493	1,406,596	12,586	(NA)	324	125,998	1,127	14.8	83.9
Lawrence	12	7.5	246	50	72,638	4,518	(NA)	25	6,167	384	9.3	(NA)
Lee	18	5.0	573	122	258,829	7,265	(NA)	72	28,021	786	39.2	(NA)
Livingston	27	6.9	835	152	372,567	9,478	12.0	82	28,330	721	6.9	(NA)
Logan	21	6.9	447	117	252,849	8,211	9.2	73	27,552	895	15.0	88.5
McDonough	17	5.3	482	138	255,543	7,777	24.0	87	38,899	1,184	30.7	94.5
McHenry	123	4.0	5,453	827	2,637,228	9,451	16.9	452	252,402	905	43.6	95.0
McLean	61	3.8	9,549	585	1,742,220	11,220	17.0	324	242,713	1,563	21.0	80.2
Macon	44	4.0	1,641	477	1,277,275	11,344	22.9	218	132,570	1,177	7.3	84.4
Macoupin	28	5.7	729	178	303,759	6,196	(NA)	88	23,896	487	-3.2	96.9
Madison	91	3.4	3,726	940	2,523,360	9,649	(NA)	532	286,729	1,096	13.0	88.4
Marion	20	5.0	539	195	298,187	7,258	10.0	86	32,431	789	3.3	89.4
Marshall	9	6.8	285	45	68,703	5,276	(NA)	27	7,691	591	0.4	(NA)
Mason	9	5.7	272	54	89,826	5,618	6.3	34	7,490	468	-9.8	93.9
Massac	4	2.6	224	51	76,335	5,030	(NA)	35	12,297	810	19.7	76.0
Menard	7	5.5	183	34	39,721	3,153	(NA)	18	5,138	408	(NA)	(NA)
Mercer	11	6.5	276	51	72,380	4,255	(NA)	30	5,932	349	6.6	(NA)
Monroe	19	6.1	608	85	351,826	12,106	(NA)	50	21,560	742	(NA)	(NA)
Montgomery	24	7.9	578	147	339,241	11,095	(NA)	63	25,745	842	0.3	89.8
Morgan	23	6.4	656	181	339,212	9,394	(NA)	86	46,194	1,279	35.7	69.1
Moultrie	12	8.3	269	45	79,277	5,517	(NA)	16	4,341	302	-30.3	(NA)
Ogle	24	4.4	855	138	282,955	5,419	(NA)	101	34,025	652	23.3	78.8
Peoria	78	4.3	2,366	774	2,018,864	11,054	17.4	476	274,186	1,501	11.3	(NA)
Perry	7	3.1	258	65	137,650	6,037	(NA)	28	10,607	465	2.2	(NA)
Piatt	11	6.6	322	54	110,651	6,806	(NA)	32	6,862	422	(NA)	(NA)
Pike	15	8.8	514	73	108,265	6,338	(NA)	34	10,801	632	16.0	83.7
Pope	1	2.4	20	9	7,124	1,642	–	5	906	209	-49.7	(NA)
Pulaski	5	7.4	53	19	23,012	3,201	–	8	1,614	225	-1.9	(NA)
Putnam	3	4.9	116	16	17,497	2,864	–	13	1,766	289	(NA)	(NA)
Randolph	22	6.6	609	121	307,000	9,219	(NA)	67	23,169	696	13.8	92.5
Richland	10	6.3	296	78	155,483	9,676	(NA)	29	15,476	963	20.1	92.7
Rock Island	57	3.9	2,125	592	1,447,658	9,751	(NA)	355	181,074	1,220	12.2	86.9
St. Clair	87	3.3	3,448	940	2,601,235	10,104	19.3	495	488,147	1,896	99.2	60.5
Saline	12	4.6	501	134	239,396	9,119	(NA)	50	21,192	807	7.6	93.0
Sangamon	84	4.4	3,879	824	2,386,912	12,462	(NA)	506	327,126	1,708	(NA)	(NA)
Schuyler	4	5.7	118	32	38,336	5,476	(NA)	13	3,610	516	(NA)	100.0
Scott	4	7.4	90	12	25,870	4,699	(NA)	8	1,452	264	17.2	100.0
Shelby	18	8.1	327	73	118,190	5,234	3.1	43	15,113	669	-2.0	(NA)
Stark	4	6.5	149	23	36,595	5,851	–	8	1,042	167	(NA)	100.0
Stephenson	23	4.8	964	196	447,686	9,288	17.5	100	34,763	721	-6.2	94.0
Tazewell	50	3.8	2,018	471	1,471,573	11,460	(NA)	288	303,488	2,364	162.0	(NA)

See footnotes at end of table.

[Includes United States, states, and 3,141 counties/county equivalents defined as of February 22, 2005. For more information on these areas, see Appendix C, Geographic Information]

County	Banking,[1] 2005 Offices Number	Rate per 10,000 people	Total deposits (mil. dol.)	Retail trade[2] (NAICS 44–45), 2002 Estab-lishments	Sales Total ($1,000)	Per capita[3] (dol.)	General merchandise stores,[4] percent of total	Accommodation and food services[2] (NAICS 72), 2002 Estab-lishments	Sales Total ($1,000)	Per capita[3] (dol.)	Percent change, 1997–2002	Food services,[5] percent of total
ILLINOIS—Con.												
Union	9	4.9	244	63	126,983	6,985	(NA)	28	9,349	514	(NA)	(NA)
Vermilion	34	4.1	979	321	717,496	8,618	22.2	168	72,719	873	6.1	89.7
Wabash	6	4.8	219	50	90,295	7,101	4.1	20	8,669	682	10.0	(NA)
Warren	11	6.3	325	71	112,539	6,118	16.6	35	14,403	783	47.3	90.5
Washington	13	8.7	287	75	177,921	11,740	2.6	35	10,506	693	–3.4	84.5
Wayne	6	3.6	275	70	111,282	6,531	(NA)	22	7,080	416	(NA)	(NA)
White	11	7.2	279	72	105,196	6,907	(NA)	21	8,333	547	–22.3	(NA)
Whiteside	28	4.7	1,109	246	611,321	10,130	24.2	115	49,170	815	14.6	89.2
Will	192	3.0	7,556	1,254	4,185,668	7,508	13.8	769	992,006	1,779	240.2	41.4
Williamson	31	4.9	882	307	712,211	11,459	24.4	126	85,965	1,383	26.2	78.5
Winnebago	84	2.9	5,128	1,031	3,208,379	11,375	16.9	534	345,105	1,224	12.7	88.4
Woodford	20	5.3	501	114	299,495	8,320	(NA)	62	19,959	554	6.3	92.7
INDIANA	2,345	3.7	84,543	24,322	67,261,298	10,922	17.4	11,788	9,409,270	1,528	41.6	70.8
Adams	14	4.1	507	170	321,269	9,579	11.1	54	25,429	758	–7.3	92.0
Allen	106	3.1	3,828	1,349	3,957,581	11,723	(NA)	661	471,617	1,397	13.9	89.1
Bartholomew	26	3.5	2,432	323	731,933	10,186	18.0	121	94,786	1,319	–7.4	82.4
Benton	7	7.7	163	49	76,585	8,262	(NA)	11	1,953	211	(NA)	(NA)
Blackford	7	5.1	119	52	100,747	7,264	(NA)	23	(D)	(NA)	(NA)	(NA)
Boone	19	3.6	547	167	358,322	7,393	(NA)	87	40,027	826	6.8	93.0
Brown	4	2.6	90	98	50,217	3,289	(NA)	44	22,373	1,465	21.4	41.5
Carroll	9	4.4	209	60	114,964	5,652	(NA)	27	9,989	491	2.1	92.1
Cass	14	3.5	543	147	334,540	8,257	16.6	79	34,204	844	11.4	92.1
Clark	44	4.3	1,104	465	1,452,504	14,823	16.4	199	(D)	(NA)	(NA)	(NA)
Clay	12	4.4	280	96	231,574	8,719	(NA)	44	15,961	601	16.8	92.5
Clinton	12	3.5	408	112	217,421	6,380	(NA)	54	19,993	587	3.2	(NA)
Crawford	6	5.3	89	33	34,804	3,142	(NA)	15	4,174	377	(NA)	(NA)
Daviess	16	5.3	368	120	297,764	9,986	(NA)	54	19,663	659	–3.5	89.9
Dearborn	22	4.5	828	155	433,395	9,161	(NA)	75	(D)	(NA)	(NA)	(NA)
Decatur	9	3.6	458	126	301,934	12,246	(NA)	48	(D)	(NA)	(NA)	(NA)
DeKalb	16	3.8	440	160	350,016	8,591	(NA)	75	36,724	901	8.0	87.6
Delaware	40	3.4	1,432	525	1,322,539	11,121	21.5	225	146,640	1,233	15.8	92.0
Dubois	27	6.6	1,018	243	643,791	16,083	(NA)	82	47,769	1,193	21.1	(NA)
Elkhart	59	3.0	2,075	727	1,932,227	10,394	21.1	352	224,897	1,210	18.7	88.7
Fayette	11	4.4	295	83	206,173	8,202	18.8	45	20,653	822	–6.2	(NA)
Floyd	42	5.8	1,118	227	567,679	7,945	(NA)	104	67,800	949	23.4	(NA)
Fountain	14	8.0	255	79	180,539	10,130	3.2	38	15,466	868	–5.6	(NA)
Franklin	7	3.0	318	58	94,320	4,183	(NA)	38	15,820	702	25.3	(NA)
Fulton	9	4.4	236	92	182,803	8,855	(NA)	48	16,119	781	13.4	(NA)
Gibson	16	4.8	369	139	329,092	10,072	(NA)	64	30,814	943	47.0	87.3
Grant	28	4.0	700	313	705,178	9,741	17.9	144	83,813	1,158	12.9	94.1
Greene	14	4.2	363	124	193,057	5,824	(NA)	43	16,177	488	(NA)	(NA)
Hamilton	98	4.1	2,380	670	2,279,295	10,925	18.1	355	276,691	1,326	67.1	88.1
Hancock	19	3.0	538	169	468,867	8,046	(NA)	83	46,787	803	12.8	87.2
Harrison	15	4.1	536	142	346,930	9,837	(NA)	51	308,475	8,747	1,340.9	(NA)
Hendricks	51	4.0	1,330	355	1,301,632	11,323	24.8	179	147,048	1,279	103.8	93.7
Henry	21	4.4	639	178	497,982	10,358	8.6	74	36,568	761	20.2	90.1
Howard	33	3.9	914	409	1,123,401	13,259	24.6	178	134,393	1,586	16.8	(NA)
Huntington	17	4.4	470	162	398,882	10,423	11.0	84	31,239	816	–3.4	94.8
Jackson	16	3.8	680	241	478,399	11,515	(NA)	77	46,293	1,114	31.1	82.0
Jasper	13	4.1	461	147	319,515	10,401	(NA)	57	26,057	848	8.2	90.9
Jay	11	5.1	225	77	121,298	5,590	(NA)	39	15,651	721	9.0	93.0
Jefferson	16	4.9	408	171	351,004	10,940	(NA)	74	36,057	1,124	21.8	87.9
Jennings	10	3.5	219	75	148,366	5,258	(NA)	31	13,866	491	38.1	(NA)
Johnson	55	4.3	1,256	533	1,636,663	13,460	26.6	228	164,327	1,351	35.2	94.9
Knox	18	4.7	634	214	410,949	10,539	24.2	74	46,607	1,195	29.2	89.1
Kosciusko	41	5.4	953	331	666,478	8,892	18.3	147	75,491	1,007	28.7	87.1
LaGrange	13	3.5	397	157	234,770	6,578	3.2	61	28,884	809	20.4	77.5
Lake	165	3.3	6,759	1,764	5,456,028	11,224	14.9	912	926,744	1,906	100.1	52.4
LaPorte	36	3.3	1,313	496	1,128,086	10,234	18.4	233	340,958	3,093	221.3	(NA)
Lawrence	14	3.0	418	195	381,436	8,270	19.0	68	39,351	853	3.5	93.3
Madison	53	4.1	1,322	464	1,277,247	9,678	16.4	240	141,946	1,076	1.5	94.7
Marion	283	3.3	17,217	3,328	11,874,187	13,768	14.3	1,920	1,832,567	2,125	20.3	77.0
Marshall	16	3.4	620	205	456,184	9,959	13.9	88	43,002	939	16.0	91.7
Martin	5	4.8	127	41	67,174	6,470	8.8	22	(D)	(NA)	(NA)	(NA)
Miami	11	3.1	328	128	225,099	6,188	(NA)	62	21,723	597	19.1	92.5
Monroe	45	3.7	1,381	484	1,328,285	11,075	(NA)	300	218,600	1,823	23.8	79.9
Montgomery	21	5.5	540	153	311,429	8,214	17.8	82	38,722	1,021	15.0	81.0
Morgan	26	3.7	650	224	584,377	8,596	(NA)	89	54,728	805	21.3	97.4
Newton	10	6.9	192	61	79,361	5,525	(NA)	33	6,977	486	(NA)	68.2
Noble	18	3.8	415	158	265,086	5,647	(NA)	69	32,496	692	9.2	91.1
Ohio	3	5.1	68	11	15,278	2,651	(NA)	11	(D)	(NA)	(NA)	(NA)
Orange	8	4.0	243	81	143,940	7,396	(NA)	28	21,365	1,098	114.2	(NA)
Owen	6	2.6	178	49	97,664	4,343	(NA)	22	10,521	468	(NA)	(NA)

See footnotes at end of table.

Table B-11. Counties — Banking, Retail Trade, and Accommodation and Food Services—Con.

[Includes United States, states, and 3,141 counties/county equivalents defined as of February 22, 2005. For more information on these areas, see Appendix C, Geographic Information]

County	Banking,[1] 2005 Offices Number	Banking Offices Rate per 10,000 people	Total deposits (mil. dol.)	Retail trade[2] (NAICS 44–45), 2002 Estab-lishments	Sales Total ($1,000)	Sales Per capita[3] (dol.)	General merchandise stores,[4] percent of total	Accommodation and food services[2] (NAICS 72), 2002 Estab-lishments	Sales Total ($1,000)	Sales Per capita[3] (dol.)	Percent change, 1997–2002	Food services,[5] percent of total
INDIANA—Con.												
Parke	8	4.6	158	51	70,769	4,102	5.3	29	(D)	(NA)	(NA)	(NA)
Perry	7	3.7	297	77	126,093	6,683	(NA)	40	17,261	915	22.8	90.1
Pike	6	4.7	145	40	46,125	3,560	(NA)	12	2,704	209	(NA)	(NA)
Porter	59	3.7	1,835	533	1,464,858	9,721	19.8	271	157,216	1,043	24.3	88.6
Posey	9	3.4	289	85	164,756	6,093	(NA)	36	12,166	450	(NA)	(NA)
Pulaski	8	5.8	287	69	144,700	10,528	(NA)	24	(D)	(NA)	(NA)	(NA)
Putnam	14	3.8	418	120	251,524	6,909	(NA)	77	31,300	860	12.6	73.0
Randolph	17	6.4	373	99	203,098	7,492	9.1	43	15,496	572	29.8	(NA)
Ripley	16	5.8	493	127	228,168	8,364	2.0	49	20,037	735	1.3	90.1
Rush	7	3.9	203	68	111,395	6,196	(NA)	28	9,580	533	(NA)	(NA)
St. Joseph	71	2.7	3,376	1,017	3,309,503	12,444	20.5	511	347,185	1,305	13.7	86.4
Scott	9	3.8	227	100	207,420	8,866	(NA)	41	24,926	1,065	27.1	(NA)
Shelby	14	3.2	474	139	327,173	7,474	12.1	61	38,122	871	22.4	93.5
Spencer	14	6.8	248	79	146,824	7,237	2.2	26	8,396	414	(NA)	73.9
Starke	8	3.5	218	77	124,055	5,491	12.9	27	9,946	440	(NA)	(NA)
Steuben	15	4.4	392	227	435,989	13,021	24.3	84	41,627	1,243	(Z)	81.5
Sullivan	10	4.6	207	70	134,430	6,152	(NA)	26	8,857	405	(NA)	(NA)
Switzerland	4	4.1	61	23	21,983	2,316	(NA)	12	(D)	(NA)	(NA)	(NA)
Tippecanoe	52	3.4	1,790	571	1,797,913	11,991	(NA)	335	239,626	1,598	23.3	(NA)
Tipton	5	3.1	178	50	135,781	8,195	3.1	29	9,750	588	5.4	(NA)
Union	4	5.5	104	32	35,280	4,801	–	7	1,857	253	(NA)	(NA)
Vanderburgh	57	3.3	3,406	879	2,790,813	16,221	(NA)	414	436,898	2,539	63.5	65.2
Vermillion	8	4.8	164	53	130,342	7,864	(NA)	35	12,605	760	−8.1	(NA)
Vigo	27	2.6	1,562	497	2,320,744	22,182	(NA)	269	170,676	1,631	14.6	86.6
Wabash	13	3.8	321	160	298,731	8,653	13.4	65	26,345	763	(NA)	94.1
Warren	4	4.6	75	15	13,775	1,586	–	10	2,030	234	(NA)	(NA)
Warrick	14	2.5	486	139	240,387	4,483	(NA)	58	25,376	473	(NA)	(NA)
Washington	11	3.9	263	96	167,662	6,058	(NA)	35	(D)	(NA)	(NA)	(NA)
Wayne	38	5.5	1,060	331	875,075	12,422	25.2	145	98,803	1,403	18.0	89.5
Wells	10	3.6	342	104	187,928	6,737	(NA)	34	18,513	664	21.1	(NA)
White	15	6.1	326	117	247,153	9,815	(NA)	76	29,257	1,162	70.5	85.6
Whitley	14	4.3	365	112	302,591	9,628	(NA)	54	23,729	755	1.8	(NA)
IOWA	1,577	5.3	50,984	13,859	31,195,012	10,629	15.8	6,586	3,698,955	1,260	33.9	70.4
Adair	8	10.2	177	39	45,917	5,733	(NA)	16	(D)	(NA)	(NA)	(NA)
Adams	5	11.7	60	29	23,551	5,367	(NA)	9	(D)	(NA)	(NA)	(NA)
Allamakee	9	6.1	389	77	112,879	7,812	4.3	35	6,958	482	13.9	85.3
Appanoose	6	4.4	164	64	100,245	7,448	(NA)	28	7,451	554	1.3	83.2
Audubon	5	7.7	136	26	41,025	6,223	(NA)	12	(D)	(NA)	(NA)	(NA)
Benton	19	7.0	390	106	154,515	5,912	5.5	38	6,057	232	−1.2	91.3
Black Hawk	40	3.2	1,346	567	1,595,272	12,613	(NA)	285	158,805	1,256	16.9	89.5
Boone	10	3.8	396	91	224,273	8,590	(NA)	45	15,276	585	1.0	87.5
Bremer	15	6.3	417	100	176,037	7,560	(NA)	36	13,930	598	2.5	(NA)
Buchanan	11	5.2	294	112	170,182	8,156	(NA)	36	(D)	(NA)	(NA)	(NA)
Buena Vista	18	8.9	488	109	220,039	10,848	(NA)	46	15,736	776	5.0	93.9
Butler	11	7.3	233	77	74,396	4,952	(NA)	23	(D)	(NA)	(NA)	(NA)
Calhoun	10	9.6	191	59	90,236	8,341	(NA)	14	(D)	(NA)	(NA)	(NA)
Carroll	21	10.0	554	150	247,201	11,675	(NA)	48	21,339	1,008	10.7	84.8
Cass	10	7.0	248	96	154,793	10,809	7.6	42	9,547	667	−6.5	87.2
Cedar	13	7.1	276	74	105,003	5,774	12.0	40	9,082	499	12.1	94.8
Cerro Gordo	27	6.0	841	267	680,176	14,998	24.0	141	71,742	1,582	17.7	78.5
Cherokee	11	9.0	282	86	152,785	12,047	7.1	29	8,007	631	−3.3	86.2
Chickasaw	10	8.0	340	59	109,286	8,497	7.5	31	(D)	(NA)	(NA)	(NA)
Clarke	6	6.5	176	43	66,824	7,294	13.9	27	(D)	(NA)	(NA)	(NA)
Clay	12	7.1	453	135	218,197	12,769	(NA)	49	16,797	983	−2.2	78.7
Clayton	16	8.7	427	105	137,449	7,474	(NA)	65	12,841	698	79.3	84.0
Clinton	26	5.2	764	235	510,288	10,234	21.0	119	43,378	870	10.4	83.5
Crawford	14	8.3	322	90	126,789	7,467	(NA)	44	10,831	638	−5.1	90.1
Dallas	24	4.6	632	151	326,369	7,336	(NA)	66	32,993	742	152.6	(NA)
Davis	3	3.5	99	42	44,352	5,145	(NA)	14	2,474	287	−3.0	100.0
Decatur	5	5.8	81	37	31,713	3,674	(NA)	17	4,681	542	108.7	84.3
Delaware	11	6.1	363	83	136,891	7,479	(NA)	29	(D)	(NA)	(NA)	(NA)
Des Moines	23	5.6	709	228	543,819	13,118	28.3	93	46,985	1,133	−1.7	85.7
Dickinson	16	9.6	426	117	207,773	12,650	(NA)	85	38,765	2,360	33.4	60.3
Dubuque	40	4.4	1,710	502	1,094,459	12,232	19.1	240	115,365	1,289	21.8	82.6
Emmet	9	8.5	197	67	79,561	7,344	6.2	26	(D)	(NA)	(NA)	(NA)
Fayette	16	7.5	366	120	154,954	7,188	9.7	46	11,456	531	5.8	92.0
Floyd	7	4.3	330	82	122,898	7,392	14.6	41	10,029	603	13.0	90.3
Franklin	9	8.4	181	50	74,884	7,008	(NA)	19	(D)	(NA)	(NA)	(NA)
Fremont	7	9.0	142	31	27,302	3,481	–	16	(D)	(NA)	(NA)	(NA)
Greene	9	9.0	244	48	74,967	7,362	7.9	20	(D)	(NA)	(NA)	(NA)
Grundy	9	7.3	294	48	57,355	4,643	(NA)	22	4,538	367	(NA)	(NA)
Guthrie	10	8.7	247	47	54,125	4,782	(NA)	32	10,065	889	73.6	(NA)
Hamilton	8	4.9	286	63	110,823	6,795	8.0	27	7,151	438	−15.2	84.3

See footnotes at end of table.

[Includes United States, states, and 3,141 counties/county equivalents defined as of February 22, 2005. For more information on these areas, see Appendix C, Geographic Information]

County	Banking,[1] 2005			Retail trade[2] (NAICS 44–45), 2002				Accommodation and food services[2] (NAICS 72), 2002			
	Offices				Sales					Sales	
	Number	Rate per 10,000 people	Total deposits (mil. dol.)	Estab-lishments	Total ($1,000)	Per capita[3] (dol.)	General merchan-dise stores,[4] percent of total	Estab-lishments	Total ($1,000)	Per capita[3] (dol.)	Percent change, 1997–2002	Food services,[5] percent of total
IOWA—Con.												
Hancock	9	7.6	222	54	89,682	7,577	(NA)	19	(D)	(NA)	(NA)	(NA)
Hardin	16	8.9	430	101	134,990	7,321	17.2	43	11,299	613	20.3	89.8
Harrison	12	7.6	197	62	131,581	8,449	(NA)	32	7,763	498	–9.6	(NA)
Henry	14	6.9	271	81	157,765	7,848	(NA)	47	21,501	1,070	28.4	91.1
Howard	5	5.2	201	57	64,225	6,513	4.1	22	(D)	(NA)	(NA)	(NA)
Humboldt	7	7.0	194	52	81,951	8,086	5.4	25	(D)	(NA)	(NA)	(NA)
Ida	8	10.8	283	43	58,421	7,667	(NA)	18	(D)	(NA)	(NA)	(NA)
Iowa	9	5.6	193	159	183,323	11,581	(NA)	51	27,737	1,752	–8.9	82.7
Jackson	14	6.9	362	99	188,351	9,299	11.6	47	14,819	732	30.1	94.0
Jasper	16	4.2	506	150	262,642	6,984	(NA)	72	26,819	713	3.6	82.5
Jefferson	9	5.6	266	87	429,729	26,920	(NA)	33	10,704	671	–0.4	65.3
Johnson	41	3.5	1,735	503	1,247,292	10,960	(NA)	287	193,807	1,703	34.3	80.4
Jones	14	6.8	290	88	189,857	9,361	9.9	35	8,053	397	4.1	84.2
Keokuk	11	9.9	216	51	106,232	9,305	(NA)	13	1,530	134	–8.9	100.0
Kossuth	18	11.2	400	107	151,277	9,111	12.3	33	9,868	594	6.8	89.1
Lee	26	7.1	626	173	373,302	10,088	(NA)	101	35,679	964	8.2	(NA)
Linn	79	4.0	3,103	799	2,583,158	13,232	17.5	417	272,605	1,396	13.5	84.2
Louisa	7	5.9	141	25	44,920	3,675	–	25	4,253	348	7.4	(NA)
Lucas	6	6.2	127	33	67,126	7,097	(NA)	14	(D)	(NA)	(NA)	(NA)
Lyon	10	8.5	253	60	63,759	5,449	5.1	18	(D)	(NA)	(NA)	(NA)
Madison	8	5.3	209	60	70,830	4,910	(NA)	23	7,125	494	49.2	(NA)
Mahaska	11	4.9	383	111	175,182	7,835	(NA)	40	15,931	713	2.0	88.9
Marion	17	5.2	520	161	293,190	8,999	(NA)	63	22,395	687	9.2	80.3
Marshall	20	5.1	655	175	355,101	9,051	(NA)	88	36,017	918	21.1	88.1
Mills	9	5.9	173	42	67,462	4,579	(NA)	17	4,016	273	–29.6	(NA)
Mitchell	7	6.4	320	79	64,322	5,919	2.8	25	(D)	(NA)	(NA)	(NA)
Monona	11	11.6	190	64	104,129	10,666	5.5	26	(D)	(NA)	(NA)	(NA)
Monroe	5	6.4	150	39	61,762	7,913	(NA)	17	(D)	(NA)	(NA)	(NA)
Montgomery	9	8.0	208	55	80,039	7,043	10.1	25	(D)	(NA)	(NA)	(NA)
Muscatine	17	4.0	633	161	373,785	8,883	(NA)	82	32,201	765	9.8	(NA)
O'Brien	14	9.7	346	108	146,853	9,951	9.1	32	(D)	(NA)	(NA)	(NA)
Osceola	6	9.0	149	31	28,653	4,186	(NA)	12	(D)	(NA)	(NA)	(NA)
Page	12	7.4	309	100	154,382	9,351	16.3	48	12,990	787	29.2	89.8
Palo Alto	9	9.3	195	61	64,150	6,485	(NA)	25	(D)	(NA)	(NA)	(NA)
Plymouth	15	6.0	650	116	200,545	8,129	(NA)	63	(D)	(NA)	(NA)	(NA)
Pocahontas	10	12.6	175	36	45,492	5,421	(NA)	17	(D)	(NA)	(NA)	(NA)
Polk	141	3.5	8,391	1,627	5,443,842	14,151	15.9	928	664,808	1,728	24.4	79.5
Pottawattamie	32	3.6	1,035	350	1,237,642	14,037	(NA)	176	375,619	4,260	101.8	22.3
Poweshiek	11	5.8	314	106	211,035	11,190	(NA)	42	13,848	734	5.0	80.8
Ringgold	5	9.5	66	26	44,580	8,351	(NA)	11	(D)	(NA)	(NA)	(NA)
Sac	16	15.1	285	71	71,814	6,491	(NA)	28	(D)	(NA)	(NA)	(NA)
Scott	56	3.5	2,280	723	2,150,022	13,516	16.0	359	492,950	3,099	110.5	42.5
Shelby	13	10.3	300	78	116,754	9,088	(NA)	33	7,762	604	4.4	91.4
Sioux	24	7.4	829	165	278,465	8,694	8.7	72	21,045	657	6.2	91.7
Story	42	5.3	1,230	339	799,934	9,909	18.7	210	110,943	1,374	24.5	80.1
Tama	13	7.3	291	80	90,363	5,041	3.6	34	8,006	447	2.8	93.5
Taylor	6	9.1	77	33	29,976	4,387	(NA)	11	1,289	189	–8.7	100.0
Union	8	6.7	255	73	126,830	10,435	(NA)	26	(D)	(NA)	(NA)	(NA)
Van Buren	7	9.0	112	26	22,163	2,839	(NA)	13	(D)	(NA)	(NA)	(NA)
Wapello	14	3.9	443	160	374,065	10,408	21.0	80	33,639	936	12.8	82.0
Warren	17	4.0	366	117	289,446	6,984	(NA)	58	20,216	488	10.6	91.5
Washington	12	5.6	420	125	173,094	8,185	(NA)	39	9,497	449	–11.9	90.7
Wayne	6	9.1	86	40	45,556	6,843	(NA)	15	(D)	(NA)	(NA)	(NA)
Webster	18	4.6	596	219	476,575	11,966	27.7	81	46,743	1,174	26.1	85.4
Winnebago	8	7.0	255	72	134,419	11,760	(NA)	26	(D)	(NA)	(NA)	(NA)
Winneshiek	14	6.6	427	133	211,273	9,911	(NA)	54	18,411	864	26.7	80.1
Woodbury	46	4.5	1,596	497	1,177,367	11,384	(NA)	238	147,050	1,422	34.6	89.9
Worth	6	7.7	95	32	27,838	3,570	–	11	1,675	215	(NA)	100.0
Wright	12	8.8	280	72	86,896	6,224	4.7	35	(D)	(NA)	(NA)	(NA)
KANSAS	1,505	5.5	48,304	11,890	26,505,396	9,770	17.9	5,584	3,196,947	1,178	19.0	82.6
Allen	11	8.0	228	79	112,722	7,992	(NA)	36	13,301	943	–2.6	(NA)
Anderson	9	11.0	153	43	56,590	6,933	(NA)	14	3,999	490	–18.3	(NA)
Atchison	11	6.5	302	60	92,425	5,516	28.3	33	13,417	801	63.8	(NA)
Barber	8	16.1	118	38	65,753	12,921	(NA)	16	2,719	534	13.1	76.9
Barton	21	7.5	699	167	274,332	9,922	(NA)	62	28,175	1,019	5.2	91.7
Bourbon	9	6.0	225	61	106,099	6,978	(NA)	34	14,648	963	(NA)	97.1
Brown	11	10.7	280	37	38,284	3,647	(NA)	20	8,029	765	48.2	(NA)
Butler	33	5.3	691	194	431,297	7,129	(NA)	102	45,520	752	21.1	93.3
Chase	3	9.7	39	11	8,082	2,653	(NA)	8	1,677	551	(NA)	(NA)
Chautauqua	3	7.3	47	24	10,609	2,522	(NA)	10	1,039	247	5.3	(NA)

See footnotes at end of table.

[Includes United States, states, and 3,141 counties/county equivalents defined as of February 22, 2005. For more information on these areas, see Appendix C, Geographic Information]

County	Banking,[1] 2005 Offices Number	Rate per 10,000 people	Total deposits (mil. dol.)	Retail trade[2] (NAICS 44–45), 2002 Establishments	Sales Total ($1,000)	Per capita[3] (dol.)	General merchandise stores,[4] percent of total	Accommodation and food services[2] (NAICS 72), 2002 Establishments	Sales Total ($1,000)	Per capita[3] (dol.)	Percent change, 1997–2002	Food services,[5] percent of total
KANSAS—Con.												
Cherokee	12	5.6	231	73	98,072	4,454	13.7	33	8,813	400	20.2	(NA)
Cheyenne	3	10.2	64	25	11,364	3,725	(NA)	8	1,143	375	−2.6	(NA)
Clark	3	13.1	81	16	7,968	3,378	−	6	579	245	(NA)	100.0
Clay	8	9.3	174	46	59,640	6,880	14.1	17	4,696	542	1.8	(NA)
Cloud	10	10.2	183	71	92,569	9,293	(NA)	23	7,199	723	−8.7	85.7
Coffey	10	11.5	192	51	74,986	8,495	(NA)	16	4,805	544	3.8	(NA)
Comanche	3	15.5	60	15	9,110	4,653	(NA)	6	790	403	−19.6	(NA)
Cowley	19	5.4	573	149	255,314	7,018	(NA)	68	27,363	752	6.7	88.0
Crawford	26	6.8	639	182	346,256	9,113	(NA)	93	49,114	1,293	−3.2	90.5
Decatur	5	15.7	74	21	13,903	4,108	(NA)	7	1,258	372	(NA)	(NA)
Dickinson	14	7.3	316	98	132,497	6,928	(NA)	41	14,088	737	11.4	83.8
Doniphan	9	11.5	150	25	19,305	2,360	−	10	1,648	201	25.9	(NA)
Douglas	55	5.3	1,405	422	877,880	8,647	17.6	265	157,035	1,547	30.1	83.4
Edwards	4	12.2	60	16	10,545	3,148	(NA)	7	1,063	317	(NA)	100.0
Elk	4	13.0	30	11	6,748	2,106	−	8	858	268	(NA)	(NA)
Ellis	17	6.4	518	202	399,554	14,628	(NA)	83	43,757	1,602	0.4	77.0
Ellsworth	8	12.6	132	39	33,363	5,222	(NA)	14	2,771	434	−20.1	(NA)
Finney	17	4.4	469	187	426,009	10,820	(NA)	64	44,386	1,127	10.4	72.3
Ford	16	4.7	371	175	366,026	11,279	(NA)	80	34,551	1,065	−2.4	82.5
Franklin	13	5.0	365	97	190,957	7,485	(NA)	40	18,980	744	10.9	90.5
Geary	14	5.7	280	103	214,997	8,121	(NA)	70	29,222	1,104	1.9	84.6
Gove	4	14.5	67	24	26,195	8,838	−	9	2,500	843	(NA)	(NA)
Graham	5	18.4	74	18	19,644	6,835	(NA)	8	1,213	422	−11.7	(NA)
Grant	3	4.0	126	40	50,349	6,367	8.5	22	6,529	826	−7.1	(NA)
Gray	4	6.8	95	31	26,601	4,439	(NA)	10	1,293	216	28.3	100.0
Greeley	1	7.4	33	8	7,907	5,442	−	6	529	364	11.4	(NA)
Greenwood	9	12.3	115	44	39,817	5,207	7.4	21	3,960	518	(NA)	93.3
Hamilton	2	7.7	103	14	17,869	6,682	(NA)	7	972	364	−18.5	(NA)
Harper	6	9.9	132	46	47,819	7,586	(NA)	14	4,914	780	11.4	(NA)
Harvey	22	6.5	470	154	279,305	8,365	(NA)	55	25,600	767	0.3	88.8
Haskell	3	7.1	83	17	12,291	2,903	(NA)	7	1,095	259	−8.8	(NA)
Hodgeman	2	9.5	34	6	4,970	2,305	−	2	(D)	(NA)	(NA)	(NA)
Jackson	9	6.6	218	55	96,274	7,474	(NA)	21	(D)	(NA)	(NA)	(NA)
Jefferson	8	4.2	159	61	50,940	2,723	(NA)	28	(D)	(NA)	(NA)	(NA)
Jewell	7	20.9	67	22	10,849	3,089	−	11	1,272	362	7.1	(NA)
Johnson	218	4.3	11,998	1,938	7,057,213	14,823	16.4	921	835,198	1,754	31.3	83.9
Kearny	3	6.6	81	12	5,582	1,219	(NA)	6	1,364	298	23.6	(NA)
Kingman	4	4.9	137	34	44,972	5,343	8.0	16	4,071	484	−7.5	(NA)
Kiowa	5	16.8	62	24	23,381	7,540	(NA)	11	1,630	526	−9.1	(NA)
Labette	17	7.7	347	115	152,859	6,840	(NA)	42	15,079	675	13.0	89.2
Lane	2	10.6	64	14	7,636	3,833	−	4	362	182	(NA)	100.0
Leavenworth	30	4.1	755	185	427,968	5,997	(NA)	75	35,956	504	−3.9	89.6
Lincoln	5	14.7	82	26	11,900	3,390	(NA)	10	1,049	299	1.7	(NA)
Linn	10	10.1	112	29	38,039	3,913	(NA)	10	1,757	181	−4.3	100.0
Logan	4	14.3	76	23	38,963	13,212	(NA)	17	3,089	1,047	50.6	63.0
Lyon	19	5.3	502	158	337,970	9,460	(NA)	100	45,259	1,267	21.5	(NA)
McPherson	24	8.1	535	161	243,070	8,278	(NA)	61	25,666	874	12.0	86.0
Marion	13	10.0	196	72	99,795	7,504	(NA)	24	5,950	447	11.0	94.6
Marshall	14	13.5	354	78	88,565	8,312	(NA)	29	7,124	669	17.1	63.0
Meade	4	8.6	108	24	18,237	3,900	(NA)	7	1,307	280	−9.3	(NA)
Miami	15	4.9	390	90	184,143	6,362	(NA)	37	15,436	533	37.5	100.0
Mitchell	8	12.5	148	60	68,373	10,206	(NA)	22	5,283	789	3.1	(NA)
Montgomery	21	6.1	523	200	325,412	9,222	(NA)	81	32,818	930	8.4	83.6
Morris	6	9.9	108	42	40,068	6,649	(NA)	12	3,661	608	(NA)	(NA)
Morton	3	9.4	73	17	17,409	5,181	6.2	7	2,277	678	−4.1	(NA)
Nemaha	16	15.3	358	79	93,644	8,918	3.2	24	5,410	515	8.6	91.2
Neosho	17	10.3	287	104	187,047	11,190	(NA)	38	12,343	738	11.7	(NA)
Ness	4	13.3	76	27	20,305	6,191	(NA)	8	916	279	(NA)	(NA)
Norton	6	10.6	132	29	36,606	6,274	(NA)	19	4,542	778	14.0	86.9
Osage	11	6.4	210	64	64,373	3,826	(NA)	22	(D)	(NA)	(NA)	(NA)
Osborne	5	12.3	126	37	38,685	9,026	(NA)	12	1,555	363	14.8	(NA)
Ottawa	5	8.2	153	17	13,379	2,159	(NA)	13	1,727	279	25.1	(NA)
Pawnee	6	8.9	116	34	39,987	5,788	8.7	15	4,729	684	−45.1	(NA)
Phillips	8	14.5	176	37	39,174	6,787	9.9	14	3,333	577	6.5	71.5
Pottawatomie	13	6.8	369	79	156,227	8,471	(NA)	27	5,925	321	−18.8	87.2
Pratt	6	6.3	211	63	108,630	11,323	(NA)	34	13,478	1,405	30.9	78.2
Rawlins	5	18.7	69	19	13,374	4,639	(NA)	8	634	220	(NA)	(NA)
Reno	26	4.1	832	339	682,425	10,660	18.8	132	72,223	1,128	7.0	86.5
Republic	8	15.5	134	40	37,177	6,823	4.0	9	2,612	479	−15.7	(NA)
Rice	11	10.5	182	46	41,905	3,984	(NA)	22	5,433	516	−12.7	(NA)

See footnotes at end of table.

[Includes United States, states, and 3,141 counties/county equivalents defined as of February 22, 2005. For more information on these areas, see Appendix C, Geographic Information]

County	Banking,[1] 2005 Offices Number	Rate per 10,000 people	Total deposits (mil. dol.)	Retail trade[2] (NAICS 44–45), 2002 Estab-lishments	Sales Total ($1,000)	Per capita[3] (dol.)	General merchan-dise stores,[4] percent of total	Accommodation and food services[2] (NAICS 72), 2002 Estab-lishments	Sales Total ($1,000)	Per capita[3] (dol.)	Percent change, 1997–2002	Food services,[5] percent of total
KANSAS—Con.												
Riley	28	4.5	1,043	289	584,993	9,419	(NA)	153	90,589	1,459	21.5	78.4
Rooks	7	13.1	126	37	40,462	7,366	2.3	15	(D)	(NA)	(NA)	(NA)
Rush	5	14.7	81	20	26,181	7,547	(NA)	9	1,243	358	(NA)	(NA)
Russell	7	10.2	163	41	45,660	6,490	(NA)	18	6,147	874	-1.1	(NA)
Saline	25	4.6	1,086	297	767,493	14,226	(NA)	138	83,542	1,548	21.2	(NA)
Scott	3	6.5	146	38	46,845	9,502	6.4	14	3,149	639	-5.9	(NA)
Sedgwick	163	3.5	6,912	1,806	4,960,072	10,774	(NA)	983	653,503	1,419	11.6	85.3
Seward	7	3.0	271	124	263,939	11,472	(NA)	57	28,113	1,222	16.0	76.4
Shawnee	89	5.2	3,547	762	1,968,488	11,542	(NA)	353	(D)	(NA)	(NA)	(NA)
Sheridan	5	19.3	109	24	15,619	5,845	(NA)	4	(D)	(NA)	(NA)	(NA)
Sherman	4	6.5	169	47	92,715	14,421	(NA)	23	8,737	1,359	32.5	59.8
Smith	6	14.6	99	33	22,191	5,158	(NA)	9	1,598	371	-30.1	(NA)
Stafford	6	13.4	120	21	14,997	3,213	(NA)	12	(D)	(NA)	(NA)	(NA)
Stanton	2	8.9	46	9	7,100	2,927	(NA)	5	(D)	(NA)	(NA)	(NA)
Stevens	2	3.7	89	25	27,316	5,129	(NA)	10	(D)	(NA)	(NA)	(NA)
Sumner	15	6.0	380	83	121,811	4,771	(NA)	47	13,299	521	23.9	81.4
Thomas	8	10.5	175	58	92,838	11,496	(NA)	31	16,328	2,022	21.3	68.4
Trego	3	9.8	76	23	24,857	7,909	(NA)	12	2,960	942	(NA)	87.9
Wabaunsee	7	10.1	83	31	18,825	2,779	(NA)	8	664	98	-51.7	100.0
Wallace	1	6.4	21	10	7,089	4,253	–	4	1,263	758	(NA)	(NA)
Washington	9	15.0	132	39	23,315	3,748	(NA)	24	2,955	475	6.3	(NA)
Wichita	2	8.7	57	17	11,363	4,576	(NA)	2	(D)	(NA)	(NA)	(NA)
Wilson	6	6.1	193	47	35,678	3,513	8.1	18	4,148	408	(NA)	100.0
Woodson	4	11.2	40	22	14,138	3,868	(NA)	8	1,320	361	4.4	(NA)
Wyandotte	45	2.9	2,132	393	932,832	5,916	(NA)	223	122,169	775	11.8	93.2
KENTUCKY	1,750	4.2	57,241	16,847	40,062,561	9,795	19.0	6,660	4,908,331	1,200	21.0	84.1
Adair	8	4.6	262	67	106,552	6,124	(NA)	22	7,143	411	-1.7	(NA)
Allen	5	2.7	166	58	81,336	4,481	6.3	19	8,147	449	28.6	(NA)
Anderson	7	3.4	245	48	104,956	5,366	(NA)	20	7,220	369	10.9	(NA)
Ballard	6	7.2	129	38	51,520	6,334	(NA)	13	1,898	233	(NA)	100.0
Barren	17	4.2	535	200	410,128	10,584	(NA)	86	59,720	1,541	33.9	84.6
Bath	7	6.0	140	45	43,180	3,781	(NA)	8	(D)	(NA)	(NA)	(NA)
Bell	12	4.0	405	140	306,840	10,232	35.2	46	30,688	1,023	18.1	96.9
Boone	52	4.9	1,558	468	1,915,938	20,470	22.3	203	214,492	2,292	37.5	(NA)
Bourbon	9	4.5	247	69	133,983	6,870	(NA)	25	15,152	777	53.1	(NA)
Boyd	29	5.8	870	319	835,010	16,800	(NA)	105	74,354	1,496	8.3	(NA)
Boyle	18	6.3	515	160	359,932	12,995	(NA)	58	41,017	1,481	26.2	90.1
Bracken	5	5.8	93	27	25,033	2,961	(NA)	13	(D)	(NA)	(NA)	(NA)
Breathitt	4	2.5	172	50	89,611	5,631	(NA)	12	6,334	398	-36.4	(NA)
Breckinridge	9	4.7	220	56	89,326	4,714	(NA)	18	4,492	237	-4.1	100.0
Bullitt	14	2.0	520	154	328,261	5,149	2.7	73	57,597	903	60.0	78.6
Butler	5	3.7	136	56	63,116	4,799	12.9	13	3,748	285	23.3	(NA)
Caldwell	6	4.6	204	64	115,288	8,952	(NA)	22	7,370	572	2.2	(NA)
Calloway	12	3.4	571	160	394,939	11,542	(NA)	65	36,237	1,059	36.9	90.4
Campbell	37	4.2	1,052	269	715,917	8,105	18.5	167	(D)	(NA)	(NA)	(NA)
Carlisle	5	9.4	110	14	22,179	4,138	(NA)	5	798	149	(NA)	100.0
Carroll	8	7.7	133	55	160,027	15,585	(NA)	27	14,584	1,420	15.1	68.9
Carter	10	3.7	297	120	215,458	7,948	10.9	32	16,187	597	14.3	88.3
Casey	6	3.7	140	55	56,131	3,545	12.7	11	4,556	288	(NA)	(NA)
Christian	21	3.0	721	265	632,646	8,809	(NA)	101	65,812	916	18.5	87.4
Clark	17	4.9	548	164	421,498	12,548	(NA)	53	40,436	1,204	29.8	78.5
Clay	6	2.5	187	74	118,715	4,861	18.7	15	7,864	322	-18.1	(NA)
Clinton	5	3.1	121	54	52,347	5,434	5.1	13	5,876	610	-9.5	65.5
Crittenden	5	5.6	100	38	41,757	4,556	8.8	11	3,650	398	(NA)	100.0
Cumberland	3	4.2	118	38	37,699	5,264	(NA)	11	4,612	644	8.1	(NA)
Daviess	49	5.3	1,487	459	1,046,101	11,384	(NA)	158	132,391	1,441	31.6	(NA)
Edmonson	2	1.7	152	24	26,242	2,218	(NA)	11	(D)	(NA)	(NA)	(NA)
Elliott	2	2.9	40	17	12,243	1,803	(NA)	3	652	96	(NA)	100.0
Estill	5	3.3	122	57	76,728	4,997	8.8	15	7,196	469	(NA)	(NA)
Fayette	107	4.0	4,614	1,155	3,912,042	14,891	19.3	641	599,766	2,283	18.0	78.9
Fleming	9	6.2	245	70	111,140	7,841	2.7	9	5,370	379	48.6	83.1
Floyd	15	3.6	440	191	341,056	8,049	14.6	46	24,660	582	27.6	80.4
Franklin	24	5.0	874	200	567,337	11,788	(NA)	100	68,257	1,418	44.7	(NA)
Fulton	6	8.3	214	57	91,242	12,044	(NA)	15	6,088	804	(NA)	(NA)
Gallatin	2	2.5	34	22	29,427	3,764	(NA)	7	(D)	(NA)	(NA)	(NA)
Garrard	7	4.2	146	39	29,972	1,918	(NA)	12	3,642	233	34.4	100.0
Grant	16	6.5	250	90	231,936	9,835	(NA)	47	(D)	(NA)	(NA)	(NA)
Graves	11	2.9	407	142	274,342	7,389	(NA)	51	17,765	478	13.5	95.1
Grayson	13	5.2	299	96	142,242	5,858	(NA)	30	15,008	618	16.5	90.4
Green	5	4.3	169	38	40,212	3,443	(NA)	10	3,425	293	7.9	100.0
Greenup	17	4.6	350	107	161,465	4,384	(NA)	35	18,964	515	-6.4	(NA)

See footnotes at end of table.

Table B-11. Counties — **Banking, Retail Trade, and Accommodation and Food Services**—Con.

[Includes United States, states, and 3,141 counties/county equivalents defined as of February 22, 2005. For more information on these areas, see Appendix C, Geographic Information]

County	Banking,[1] 2005 Offices — Number	Rate per 10,000 people	Total deposits (mil. dol.)	Retail trade[2] (NAICS 44–45), 2002 Estab-lishments	Sales Total ($1,000)	Per capita[3] (dol.)	General merchandise stores,[4] percent of total	Accommodation and food services[2] (NAICS 72), 2002 Estab-lishments	Sales Total ($1,000)	Per capita[3] (dol.)	Percent change, 1997–2002	Food services,[5] percent of total
KENTUCKY—Con.												
Hancock	5	5.8	133	21	34,842	4,123	(NA)	5	1,427	169	(NA)	(NA)
Hardin	40	4.1	1,146	454	1,111,176	11,658	19.5	154	134,155	1,407	56.6	88.0
Harlan	11	3.5	321	111	159,789	4,910	28.5	30	16,921	520	13.1	90.8
Harrison	10	5.4	249	67	96,503	5,330	(NA)	17	9,365	517	(NA)	100.0
Hart	7	3.8	189	78	81,086	4,582	8.5	17	8,059	455	46.0	74.2
Henderson	17	3.7	492	201	515,959	11,451	(NA)	78	43,252	960	4.7	(NA)
Henry	9	5.7	220	47	79,197	5,166	(NA)	12	3,447	225	10.4	100.0
Hickman	2	3.9	76	13	12,811	2,446	(NA)	6	(D)	(NA)	(NA)	(NA)
Hopkins	21	4.5	534	232	452,002	9,729	(NA)	61	42,698	919	40.3	90.5
Jackson	5	3.7	106	36	33,271	2,439	7.9	11	2,183	160	(NA)	100.0
Jefferson	277	4.0	13,687	2,839	8,456,123	12,148	18.2	1,444	1,277,236	1,835	18.1	82.0
Jessamine	17	3.9	441	158	528,479	12,983	(NA)	48	31,881	783	35.2	90.6
Johnson	10	4.2	295	121	267,789	11,404	(NA)	34	22,012	937	43.7	88.1
Kenton	64	4.2	1,781	406	873,191	5,754	8.5	282	260,171	1,714	9.8	75.7
Knott	3	1.7	127	43	46,573	2,621	(NA)	6	2,453	138	(NA)	100.0
Knox	16	5.0	365	95	224,606	7,092	16.7	21	9,898	313	−37.6	(NA)
Larue	9	6.6	201	37	43,083	3,203	11.8	12	4,350	323	(NA)	100.0
Laurel	24	4.3	601	247	711,993	13,080	(NA)	65	50,389	926	−1.0	79.2
Lawrence	4	2.5	107	57	82,707	5,209	8.0	17	8,778	553	5.9	88.4
Lee	2	2.6	73	25	35,885	4,545	(NA)	6	1,360	172	(NA)	(NA)
Leslie	3	2.5	85	34	38,085	3,104	(NA)	2	(D)	(NA)	(NA)	(NA)
Letcher	9	3.7	256	74	122,531	4,915	(NA)	22	11,971	480	26.0	88.2
Lewis	7	5.0	103	41	40,457	2,925	(NA)	11	1,737	126	(NA)	(NA)
Lincoln	9	3.6	197	62	77,748	3,219	(NA)	15	7,755	321	65.2	100.0
Livingston	5	5.1	99	31	24,214	2,464	(NA)	16	9,826	1,000	13.0	88.4
Logan	11	4.0	356	95	158,388	5,922	(NA)	32	14,732	551	27.1	94.6
Lyon	3	3.7	89	34	42,885	5,267	(NA)	24	9,678	1,189	35.1	70.7
McCracken	25	3.9	971	462	1,208,555	18,649	25.4	173	142,782	2,203	14.1	82.3
McCreary	5	2.9	116	54	74,155	4,329	6.1	13	3,915	229	30.1	(NA)
McLean	7	7.1	124	30	43,894	4,399	(NA)	10	1,854	186	17.5	100.0
Madison	33	4.2	746	305	682,633	9,322	(NA)	139	98,037	1,339	29.8	87.8
Magoffin	5	3.7	101	43	51,515	3,867	8.6	11	4,994	375	3.0	100.0
Marion	9	4.8	247	68	96,689	5,229	(NA)	27	11,698	633	41.7	(NA)
Marshall	12	3.9	464	123	256,130	8,464	(NA)	72	30,707	1,015	28.2	62.9
Martin	3	2.5	96	46	68,629	5,471	(NA)	14	5,237	418	−31.2	(NA)
Mason	11	6.4	261	113	266,727	15,793	(NA)	40	25,311	1,499	25.6	(NA)
Meade	6	2.1	188	69	140,544	5,126	8.1	22	10,455	381	11.4	(NA)
Menifee	1	1.5	28	17	14,836	2,208	(NA)	2	(D)	(NA)	(NA)	(NA)
Mercer	9	4.2	314	79	141,344	6,703	(NA)	34	15,610	740	11.6	77.0
Metcalfe	5	4.9	117	31	37,279	3,722	(NA)	9	2,937	293	47.0	100.0
Monroe	8	6.9	149	54	87,697	7,472	(NA)	16	5,212	444	(NA)	(NA)
Montgomery	13	5.4	413	128	285,852	12,298	(NA)	37	29,442	1,267	43.7	89.0
Morgan	6	4.2	167	51	76,306	5,355	6.4	8	3,271	230	(NA)	(NA)
Muhlenberg	10	3.2	389	122	230,892	7,280	26.2	45	19,140	603	44.8	90.0
Nelson	17	4.1	544	186	313,899	8,057	(NA)	54	31,753	815	16.6	85.3
Nicholas	3	4.3	71	19	18,060	2,607	(NA)	5	766	111	−7.4	100.0
Ohio	14	5.9	257	72	128,486	5,533	(NA)	25	9,682	417	−5.9	100.0
Oldham	13	2.4	399	120	309,208	6,285	(NA)	49	31,378	638	7.6	92.2
Owen	5	4.4	91	21	31,765	2,884	(NA)	8	2,370	215	28.9	100.0
Owsley	1	2.1	35	11	14,193	2,979	(NA)	2	(D)	(NA)	(NA)	(NA)
Pendleton	8	5.3	129	32	38,975	2,627	(NA)	10	4,033	272	(NA)	100.0
Perry	17	5.8	437	163	346,697	11,753	20.2	45	33,113	1,123	−4.2	91.9
Pike	30	4.5	1,057	324	783,587	11,554	26.5	85	57,771	852	28.7	88.2
Powell	4	2.9	112	41	73,629	5,531	4.7	16	9,033	679	(NA)	(NA)
Pulaski	30	5.1	847	338	677,481	11,812	20.7	81	53,253	929	17.3	90.3
Robertson	1	4.4	16	5	1,447	627	(NA)	–	–	–	−100.0	–
Rockcastle	5	3.0	151	59	70,393	4,210	(NA)	21	11,239	672	30.2	84.6
Rowan	8	3.6	215	123	216,225	9,718	(NA)	39	25,501	1,146	6.2	84.0
Russell	9	5.3	238	91	118,321	7,169	15.1	29	11,196	678	14.2	93.3
Scott	20	5.1	411	124	341,593	9,634	(NA)	62	66,901	1,887	54.7	92.3
Shelby	15	3.9	502	127	366,975	10,477	(NA)	53	33,506	957	56.7	89.6
Simpson	10	5.9	271	66	288,715	17,350	(NA)	32	22,221	1,335	−6.1	84.8
Spencer	3	1.9	89	25	28,208	2,075	(NA)	7	2,794	206	(NA)	(NA)
Taylor	12	5.1	312	157	329,342	14,151	(NA)	40	22,671	974	20.5	92.8
Todd	8	6.7	164	39	47,232	3,934	(NA)	10	2,280	190	13.9	(NA)
Trigg	6	4.5	160	49	53,021	4,160	(NA)	19	9,432	740	55.2	78.9
Trimble	3	3.3	118	12	15,335	1,771	(NA)	6	893	103	56.9	100.0
Union	7	4.5	215	75	138,111	8,830	(NA)	22	8,140	520	(NA)	(NA)
Warren	48	4.9	1,299	544	1,243,132	13,197	(NA)	197	(D)	(NA)	(NA)	(NA)
Washington	6	5.3	200	46	76,955	6,902	(NA)	12	5,197	466	26.7	(NA)

See footnotes at end of table.

[Includes United States, states, and 3,141 counties/county equivalents defined as of February 22, 2005. For more information on these areas, see Appendix C, Geographic Information]

County	Banking,[1] 2005			Retail trade[2] (NAICS 44–45), 2002				Accommodation and food services[2] (NAICS 72), 2002				
	Offices				Sales					Sales		
	Number	Rate per 10,000 people	Total deposits (mil. dol.)	Estab-lishments	Total ($1,000)	Per capita[3] (dol.)	General merchan-dise stores,[4] percent of total	Estab-lishments	Total ($1,000)	Per capita[3] (dol.)	Percent change, 1997–2002	Food services,[5] percent of total
KENTUCKY—Con.												
Wayne	7	3.4	246	76	140,966	7,016	(NA)	23	14,997	746	(NA)	63.7
Webster	10	7.1	215	50	57,152	4,055	(NA)	15	3,323	236	6.6	(NA)
Whitley	14	3.7	395	198	434,416	11,802	13.0	78	55,938	1,520	59.4	86.5
Wolfe	3	4.2	52	31	46,942	6,714	5.7	6	(D)	(NA)	(NA)	(NA)
Woodford	9	3.7	423	80	174,000	7,394	(NA)	32	13,579	577	-8.9	(NA)
LOUISIANA	1,547	3.4	57,069	17,613	41,885,192	9,356	18.7	7,535	7,411,702	1,655	40.9	62.6
Acadia	20	3.4	625	206	381,589	6,452	(NA)	55	23,399	396	(NA)	90.8
Allen	10	4.0	150	81	104,295	4,145	19.0	31	12,013	477	10.5	67.8
Ascension	21	2.3	610	333	691,599	8,457	(NA)	113	81,481	996	38.7	85.1
Assumption	7	3.0	119	57	87,762	3,778	(NA)	11	2,787	120	-14.9	100.0
Avoyelles	20	4.8	394	164	224,892	5,413	19.6	43	(D)	(NA)	(NA)	(NA)
Beauregard	12	3.5	290	114	245,233	7,383	(NA)	27	14,819	446	-5.6	(NA)
Bienville	8	5.3	134	60	55,185	3,579	11.3	14	(D)	(NA)	(NA)	(NA)
Bossier	24	2.3	803	399	1,148,002	11,386	17.9	182	687,461	6,818	128.6	15.7
Caddo	74	2.9	2,981	1,018	2,791,765	11,145	16.6	393	644,127	2,571	171.8	39.8
Calcasieu	74	4.0	1,966	800	2,032,091	11,089	(NA)	313	399,830	2,182	30.5	(NA)
Caldwell	4	3.8	142	38	90,620	8,535	3.1	9	(D)	(NA)	(NA)	(NA)
Cameron	6	6.3	100	30	30,960	3,169	(NA)	9	1,602	164	-20.3	(NA)
Catahoula	6	5.7	117	38	41,164	3,826	9.3	9	(D)	(NA)	(NA)	(NA)
Claiborne	8	4.9	171	53	65,476	3,938	(NA)	11	(D)	(NA)	(NA)	(NA)
Concordia	6	3.1	285	80	121,339	6,083	(NA)	26	9,400	471	(NA)	(NA)
De Soto	12	4.5	225	75	138,597	5,375	12.9	17	7,884	306	(NA)	88.4
East Baton Rouge	140	3.4	7,124	1,797	5,031,137	12,262	(NA)	747	594,972	1,450	17.9	87.2
East Carroll	2	2.3	74	26	22,857	2,511	(NA)	7	(D)	(NA)	(NA)	(NA)
East Feliciana	6	2.9	175	43	49,620	2,350	(NA)	12	2,289	108	-33.3	(NA)
Evangeline	12	3.4	431	137	176,751	4,996	11.5	25	(D)	(NA)	(NA)	(NA)
Franklin	9	4.4	233	84	183,502	8,777	(NA)	20	(D)	(NA)	(NA)	(NA)
Grant	7	3.6	72	32	68,456	3,652	(NA)	3	(D)	(NA)	(NA)	(NA)
Iberia	31	4.2	1,027	304	728,376	9,880	(NA)	91	50,250	682	48.3	90.9
Iberville	14	4.3	325	101	210,531	6,365	(NA)	31	14,919	451	14.8	100.0
Jackson	5	3.3	175	50	80,391	5,264	(NA)	16	5,029	329	(NA)	(NA)
Jefferson	132	2.9	6,446	1,961	6,523,229	14,434	17.4	1,018	837,843	1,854	23.0	84.2
Jefferson Davis	16	5.1	388	125	250,115	8,033	(NA)	41	19,083	613	-6.4	(NA)
Lafayette	88	4.5	2,973	1,000	2,666,644	13,828	19.3	421	387,126	2,007	43.3	(NA)
Lafourche	42	4.6	1,291	322	656,241	7,227	(NA)	141	59,326	653	22.0	86.5
La Salle	11	7.8	162	68	84,079	5,901	(NA)	10	(D)	(NA)	(NA)	(NA)
Lincoln	17	4.0	582	177	429,075	10,248	(NA)	68	39,148	935	13.5	(NA)
Livingston	22	2.0	534	236	462,012	4,668	(NA)	86	44,038	445	18.7	95.1
Madison	5	4.0	101	41	69,789	5,287	(NA)	16	7,074	536	(NA)	(NA)
Morehouse	10	3.3	224	107	206,807	6,775	(NA)	29	23,895	783	(NA)	(NA)
Natchitoches	17	4.4	371	149	313,820	8,058	(NA)	66	45,590	1,171	11.6	73.8
Orleans	108	2.4	8,952	1,722	3,158,341	6,684	(NA)	1,228	1,944,816	4,116	41.8	48.9
Ouachita	59	4.0	1,838	728	1,759,682	11,960	23.4	264	199,023	1,353	17.0	(NA)
Plaquemines	7	2.4	277	80	94,776	3,466	(NA)	49	29,626	1,083	-46.6	85.7
Pointe Coupee	10	4.5	292	88	149,597	6,628	(NA)	29	12,988	575	(NA)	90.3
Rapides	50	3.9	1,546	584	1,444,341	11,396	(NA)	194	(D)	(NA)	(NA)	(NA)
Red River	3	3.2	80	31	38,366	4,005	14.7	11	(D)	(NA)	(NA)	(NA)
Richland	10	4.9	226	71	151,889	7,329	12.2	24	10,645	514	22.9	82.2
Sabine	16	6.7	253	80	132,419	5,657	20.6	17	(D)	(NA)	(NA)	(NA)
St. Bernard	19	2.9	909	205	457,970	6,898	21.9	127	48,307	728	12.3	97.0
St. Charles	14	2.8	403	124	251,750	5,125	(NA)	66	27,542	561	45.2	90.8
St. Helena	3	2.9	52	15	37,596	3,605	(NA)	5	889	85	(NA)	(NA)
St. James	8	3.8	262	59	93,681	4,404	3.9	21	(D)	(NA)	(NA)	(NA)
St. John the Baptist	10	2.2	377	109	274,090	6,200	(NA)	49	30,004	679	37.7	83.2
St. Landry	39	4.3	909	326	590,748	6,683	21.5	94	41,844	473	30.1	89.6
St. Martin	17	3.4	441	136	241,243	4,871	12.9	65	31,415	634	(NA)	(NA)
St. Mary	22	4.3	753	237	415,176	7,903	(NA)	89	38,617	735	-6.6	92.6
St. Tammany	76	3.4	2,702	804	2,155,481	10,675	20.8	380	233,040	1,154	36.5	90.1
Tangipahoa	37	3.5	1,065	425	1,057,339	10,324	16.7	179	112,179	1,095	40.8	92.0
Tensas	6	9.8	96	25	21,355	3,326	(NA)	5	369	57	-77.1	100.0
Terrebonne	37	3.4	1,244	495	1,176,348	11,150	(NA)	192	139,598	1,323	31.8	92.6
Union	8	3.5	221	70	113,772	4,985	15.9	18	6,775	297	(NA)	(NA)
Vermilion	27	4.9	682	205	370,330	6,844	(NA)	60	25,905	479	14.5	94.4
Vernon	12	2.5	227	136	242,193	4,728	(NA)	49	28,010	547	21.9	85.0
Washington	16	3.6	460	163	291,967	6,652	(NA)	54	21,782	496	18.9	94.5
Webster	18	4.4	529	180	364,034	8,767	(NA)	55	22,071	532	22.0	86.0
West Baton Rouge	5	2.3	151	71	151,913	7,000	(NA)	50	25,275	1,165	40.0	72.6
West Carroll	6	5.1	108	29	43,774	3,597	(NA)	7	(D)	(NA)	(NA)	(NA)
West Feliciana	2	1.3	69	42	46,949	3,095	(NA)	30	9,511	627	33.6	78.4
Winn	4	2.5	124	67	94,071	5,678	32.8	13	(D)	(NA)	(NA)	(NA)

See footnotes at end of table.

Table B-11. Counties — **Banking, Retail Trade, and Accommodation and Food Services**—Con.

[Includes United States, states, and 3,141 counties/county equivalents defined as of February 22, 2005. For more information on these areas, see Appendix C, Geographic Information]

County	Banking,[1] 2005 Offices — Number	Offices — Rate per 10,000 people	Offices — Total deposits (mil. dol.)	Retail trade[2] (NAICS 44–45), 2002 — Establishments	Sales — Total ($1,000)	Sales — Per capita[3] (dol.)	General merchandise stores,[4] percent of total	Accommodation and food services[2] (NAICS 72), 2002 — Establishments	Sales — Total ($1,000)	Sales — Per capita[3] (dol.)	Percent change, 1997–2002	Food services,[5] percent of total
MAINE	507	3.8	18,105	7,050	16,053,515	12,370	12.2	3,726	2,045,841	1,576	35.5	66.3
Androscoggin	33	3.1	1,125	481	1,468,010	13,951	13.9	195	112,811	1,072	45.7	87.3
Aroostook	34	4.6	782	423	729,225	9,969	16.7	151	54,698	748	9.4	79.6
Cumberland	105	3.8	5,488	1,557	4,386,091	16,252	12.8	837	573,621	2,126	33.3	69.8
Franklin	16	5.4	332	173	295,273	9,932	13.7	93	38,876	1,308	15.7	73.8
Hancock	29	5.4	956	397	665,174	12,733	10.4	318	145,110	2,778	38.2	54.0
Kennebec	44	3.6	1,441	586	1,962,372	16,539	12.9	247	151,669	1,278	39.0	69.2
Knox	23	5.6	926	285	490,405	12,103	11.8	149	82,034	2,025	41.4	57.4
Lincoln	18	5.1	820	254	396,690	11,505	(NA)	166	62,140	1,802	26.6	55.1
Oxford	20	3.5	566	262	403,483	7,225	(NA)	143	105,212	1,884	138.0	27.4
Penobscot	55	3.7	1,682	798	2,087,667	14,212	13.9	302	185,903	1,266	22.9	78.5
Piscataquis	6	3.4	163	113	150,994	8,748	6.9	53	11,123	644	2.6	69.7
Sagadahoc	11	3.0	286	154	253,729	7,049	3.5	65	37,577	1,044	46.6	67.6
Somerset	19	3.7	460	247	430,579	8,436	(NA)	96	39,325	770	51.5	67.6
Waldo	8	2.1	282	172	263,451	6,984	(NA)	87	33,319	883	43.7	77.7
Washington	19	5.7	550	190	265,342	7,942	14.2	97	22,748	681	3.6	77.0
York	67	3.3	2,246	958	1,805,030	9,223	7.8	727	389,675	1,991	32.3	62.2
MARYLAND	1,707	3.0	88,936	19,394	60,039,971	11,034	12.9	9,406	7,832,268	1,439	31.1	79.6
Allegany	23	3.1	617	353	733,824	9,917	(NA)	172	103,998	1,405	37.8	(NA)
Anne Arundel	165	3.2	6,691	2,007	6,445,273	12,837	15.5	895	869,901	1,733	36.5	78.2
Baltimore	303	3.9	13,912	2,963	10,441,440	13,585	13.7	1,345	1,110,178	1,444	31.8	89.7
Calvert	23	2.6	923	202	601,855	7,439	(NA)	95	74,725	924	31.4	85.4
Caroline	17	5.3	357	93	275,151	9,067	(NA)	31	10,399	343	32.2	(NA)
Carroll	60	3.6	2,299	568	1,577,424	9,901	19.7	222	147,037	923	33.3	90.9
Cecil	27	2.8	839	310	816,035	9,030	11.7	146	102,628	1,136	36.5	85.1
Charles	40	2.9	1,531	518	1,939,847	15,130	(NA)	203	172,707	1,347	37.8	91.1
Dorchester	16	5.1	529	119	231,717	7,599	(NA)	49	29,971	983	40.5	(NA)
Frederick	75	3.4	2,938	769	2,346,746	11,223	(NA)	348	264,520	1,265	36.9	87.2
Garrett	14	4.7	608	152	386,684	12,926	(NA)	80	35,320	1,181	32.2	73.3
Harford	82	3.4	2,424	739	2,445,303	10,755	14.9	307	252,487	1,111	35.8	87.3
Howard	72	2.7	3,354	812	3,650,291	14,045	(NA)	394	387,795	1,492	59.9	79.9
Kent	16	8.0	441	123	157,871	8,127	4.2	55	27,777	1,430	38.2	75.4
Montgomery	294	3.2	23,083	2,963	11,390,449	12,572	9.1	1,518	1,338,375	1,477	26.0	79.4
Prince George's	162	1.9	7,154	2,295	7,665,151	9,261	11.9	1,027	881,472	1,065	22.7	83.2
Queen Anne's	18	3.9	648	218	483,728	11,282	(NA)	78	72,781	1,697	32.6	81.8
St. Mary's	21	2.2	775	271	808,441	8,988	(NA)	123	93,129	1,035	48.9	89.0
Somerset	7	2.7	181	67	71,918	2,824	(NA)	32	13,767	541	31.7	82.1
Talbot	23	6.4	857	270	598,946	17,428	(NA)	113	85,386	2,485	22.4	69.6
Washington	50	3.5	1,712	659	1,762,461	13,076	18.3	272	168,252	1,248	31.9	85.7
Wicomico	45	5.0	1,385	457	1,224,086	14,207	(NA)	160	113,246	1,314	30.5	89.7
Worcester	39	8.0	1,143	467	712,235	14,831	(NA)	400	411,522	8,569	32.9	54.5
Independent City												
Baltimore city	115	1.8	14,536	1,999	3,273,095	5,145	(NA)	1,341	1,064,895	1,674	25.3	67.8
MASSACHUSETTS	2,131	3.3	172,205	25,761	73,903,837	11,525	9.7	15,175	11,789,582	1,839	27.0	79.0
Barnstable	122	5.4	5,535	1,663	3,393,996	14,911	4.7	1,141	757,207	3,327	21.3	68.4
Berkshire	57	4.3	2,721	794	1,571,043	11,785	9.9	511	327,334	2,455	32.3	54.3
Bristol	153	2.8	7,412	2,416	7,352,497	13,519	14.3	1,145	727,872	1,338	30.6	93.9
Dukes	18	11.5	590	219	288,858	18,736	1.7	135	87,295	5,662	–0.6	61.0
Essex	254	3.4	14,886	2,722	8,168,806	11,091	8.4	1,624	1,108,870	1,506	27.1	87.5
Franklin	20	2.8	916	306	569,255	7,912	(NA)	141	60,497	841	21.4	88.5
Hampden	143	3.1	7,341	1,757	4,972,531	10,819	13.4	947	538,263	1,171	24.2	88.4
Hampshire	56	3.7	2,570	598	1,268,629	8,312	(NA)	342	188,805	1,237	26.7	89.3
Middlesex	486	3.3	33,919	5,393	16,876,076	11,491	9.3	3,126	2,561,961	1,744	24.5	78.2
Nantucket	5	4.9	436	160	264,487	26,773	–	116	85,791	8,684	24.2	73.7
Norfolk	233	3.6	15,108	2,662	9,539,845	14,593	9.8	1,361	1,069,827	1,637	33.0	85.9
Plymouth	147	3.0	6,253	1,872	5,536,746	11,425	9.4	935	651,742	1,345	34.9	90.0
Suffolk	208	3.2	64,843	2,489	6,007,610	8,768	4.7	2,115	2,684,230	3,918	26.1	67.8
Worcester	229	2.9	9,674	2,710	8,093,458	10,517	11.2	1,536	939,888	1,221	31.2	87.6
MICHIGAN	3,057	3.0	139,351	38,876	109,350,139	10,889	(NA)	19,084	12,248,269	1,220	20.6	84.3
Alcona	3	2.6	41	48	60,811	5,255	–	32	4,683	405	–14.2	(NA)
Alger	8	8.3	108	49	45,193	4,603	4.3	41	13,833	1,409	9.4	55.7
Allegan	33	2.9	717	389	802,530	7,340	17.2	202	92,934	850	41.7	85.2
Alpena	15	4.9	362	175	382,462	12,348	(NA)	67	34,185	1,104	25.6	81.9
Antrim	10	4.1	275	101	146,593	6,143	0.9	64	24,043	1,008	–51.3	95.6
Arenac	6	3.5	134	69	124,508	7,181	6.1	43	15,497	894	5.1	94.2
Baraga	3	3.4	116	34	53,472	6,106	–	16	4,800	548	4.9	77.2
Barry	11	1.8	335	160	289,988	4,983	(NA)	75	28,958	498	3.4	96.0
Bay	35	3.2	1,361	509	1,280,626	11,670	21.3	241	127,043	1,158	19.3	92.8
Benzie	7	4.0	204	87	117,146	6,984	(NA)	57	40,267	2,401	40.4	36.9

See footnotes at end of table.

[Includes United States, states, and 3,141 counties/county equivalents defined as of February 22, 2005. For more information on these areas, see Appendix C, Geographic Information]

County	Banking,[1] 2005 Offices Number	Rate per 10,000 people	Total deposits (mil. dol.)	Retail trade[2] (NAICS 44–45), 2002 Establishments	Sales Total ($1,000)	Per capita[3] (dol.)	General merchandise stores,[4] percent of total	Accommodation and food services[2] (NAICS 72), 2002 Establishments	Sales Total ($1,000)	Per capita[3] (dol.)	Percent change, 1997–2002	Food services,[5] percent of total
MICHIGAN—Con.												
Berrien	62	3.8	1,881	624	1,318,424	8,113	18.3	413	191,020	1,176	16.8	82.8
Branch	23	5.0	542	186	433,764	9,325	28.7	84	39,662	853	32.1	87.1
Calhoun	41	2.9	984	534	1,398,422	10,080	25.5	291	161,061	1,161	9.2	93.0
Cass	13	2.5	297	127	162,693	3,160	4.2	80	21,419	416	7.2	95.1
Charlevoix	13	4.9	299	139	206,286	7,781	7.9	79	51,059	1,926	13.4	60.2
Cheboygan	11	4.0	297	175	266,507	9,774	(NA)	107	41,206	1,511	22.7	67.8
Chippewa	14	3.6	345	176	297,237	7,662	(NA)	133	142,792	3,681	191.4	22.0
Clare	12	3.8	251	125	273,456	8,625	1.6	71	29,883	943	18.5	79.3
Clinton	14	2.0	346	184	472,408	7,072	(NA)	85	40,771	610	25.7	(NA)
Crawford	4	2.7	108	81	177,509	12,099	(NA)	50	22,476	1,532	52.7	63.8
Delta	18	4.7	433	219	405,204	10,541	17.5	126	59,157	1,539	48.0	87.5
Dickinson	16	5.7	410	178	382,431	14,021	18.7	84	27,797	1,019	4.2	81.8
Eaton	34	3.2	936	335	1,088,747	10,320	(NA)	151	121,298	1,150	37.2	(NA)
Emmet	24	7.1	720	326	553,884	17,040	(NA)	163	120,852	3,718	36.5	47.7
Genesee	97	2.2	4,050	1,703	5,026,802	11,401	18.4	717	442,862	1,004	9.7	94.4
Gladwin	7	2.6	166	95	181,818	6,803	9.2	42	18,677	699	60.2	87.9
Gogebic	8	4.7	202	97	128,561	7,351	17.5	69	53,229	3,044	33.2	27.5
Grand Traverse	34	4.0	1,400	656	1,651,746	20,369	21.5	226	204,781	2,525	52.6	60.7
Gratiot	19	4.5	435	160	300,396	7,099	22.2	68	29,891	706	0.3	97.1
Hillsdale	14	3.0	357	157	327,324	6,965	(NA)	77	29,715	632	26.1	84.3
Houghton	21	5.9	493	182	265,268	7,435	20.6	110	35,537	996	17.3	76.9
Huron	29	8.4	691	185	293,080	8,279	(NA)	91	30,630	865	32.0	86.2
Ingham	78	2.8	4,087	1,168	3,523,913	12,583	20.8	618	419,906	1,499	13.8	87.7
Ionia	22	3.4	427	177	353,981	5,602	(NA)	78	28,138	445	8.2	91.4
Iosco	13	4.8	284	168	245,251	9,087	9.7	80	29,200	1,082	13.0	75.6
Iron	7	5.7	156	84	96,848	7,570	7.0	45	12,390	968	7.9	64.0
Isabella	25	3.8	649	250	689,717	10,784	28.4	114	95,146	1,488	38.9	72.2
Jackson	54	3.3	1,621	600	1,548,612	9,606	26.1	282	158,955	986	16.0	90.6
Kalamazoo	70	2.9	2,556	908	2,734,142	11,372	(NA)	458	332,805	1,384	27.7	86.7
Kalkaska	3	1.7	88	57	165,460	9,740	(NA)	33	11,428	673	27.0	89.0
Kent	204	3.4	10,491	2,166	8,203,468	13,985	17.1	1,028	773,516	1,319	25.3	84.1
Keweenaw	1	4.6	10	11	3,015	1,337	–	19	4,183	1,855	(NA)	58.4
Lake	3	2.5	73	34	32,960	2,851	3.8	30	7,791	674	–0.9	82.5
Lapeer	26	2.8	715	304	847,715	9,340	18.1	121	67,089	739	28.8	92.0
Leelanau	9	4.1	169	117	91,071	4,222	–	65	40,330	1,870	24.2	58.7
Lenawee	36	3.5	1,002	375	978,830	9,744	18.2	184	88,090	877	19.9	94.7
Livingston	50	2.8	1,842	528	1,812,089	10,720	18.1	214	142,146	841	22.5	93.8
Luce	2	2.9	59	40	80,416	11,457	(NA)	25	7,757	1,105	5.9	62.9
Mackinac	11	9.7	156	131	128,479	11,085	1.8	129	51,106	4,409	1.4	53.7
Macomb	244	2.9	12,637	2,988	11,008,091	13,624	16.7	1,463	963,452	1,192	21.0	93.6
Manistee	14	5.5	270	127	208,471	8,314	(NA)	84	27,459	1,095	48.4	68.2
Marquette	30	4.6	594	316	620,890	9,594	22.1	169	81,721	1,263	26.4	77.2
Mason	11	3.8	342	163	301,352	10,489	35.4	92	41,457	1,443	40.7	72.5
Mecosta	16	3.8	303	170	398,000	9,600	31.1	75	29,593	714	–28.2	(NA)
Menominee	9	3.6	169	78	127,557	5,075	14.2	50	15,657	623	(NA)	(NA)
Midland	24	2.9	862	338	820,361	9,788	27.2	127	101,237	1,208	29.6	84.2
Missaukee	4	2.6	98	45	92,285	6,155	(NA)	19	6,827	455	47.4	(NA)
Monroe	46	3.0	1,707	441	1,398,052	9,365	15.8	247	131,763	883	34.4	91.5
Montcalm	24	3.8	539	239	469,722	7,509	(NA)	100	33,785	540	21.9	92.5
Montmorency	4	3.8	94	46	61,366	5,853	(NA)	28	8,044	767	13.4	(NA)
Muskegon	40	2.3	1,365	623	1,536,294	8,920	28.0	317	177,047	1,028	15.1	87.5
Newaygo	12	2.4	283	166	314,142	6,421	12.1	71	30,230	618	51.7	83.3
Oakland	397	3.3	33,982	5,368	19,140,544	15,007	13.8	2,559	2,038,414	1,694	22.2	87.1
Oceana	11	3.9	208	106	131,199	4,727	4.7	67	16,610	598	–1.5	65.4
Ogemaw	10	4.6	232	135	316,402	14,524	(NA)	62	30,188	1,386	45.3	88.2
Ontonagon	6	8.1	89	44	60,949	7,918	(NA)	41	7,845	1,019	21.3	62.1
Osceola	8	3.4	163	87	136,178	5,779	1.8	44	18,603	789	75.4	(NA)
Oscoda	3	3.2	61	46	51,805	5,480	(NA)	26	8,635	913	54.4	79.0
Otsego	10	4.1	329	162	488,144	20,226	15.4	67	55,142	2,285	–3.1	64.9
Ottawa	85	3.3	3,348	819	2,142,358	8,693	23.2	348	217,119	881	25.4	93.5
Presque Isle	4	2.8	117	79	99,259	6,923	1.9	46	20,827	1,453	130.1	(NA)
Roscommon	11	4.2	274	145	320,147	12,381	(NA)	91	33,311	1,288	25.9	85.2
Saginaw	66	3.2	1,734	1,052	2,702,863	12,880	18.3	415	339,356	1,617	25.4	82.2
St. Clair	45	2.6	1,917	612	1,512,103	9,031	20.9	277	154,043	920	11.4	87.2
St. Joseph	32	5.1	643	219	448,487	7,183	29.5	119	48,552	778	6.7	86.7
Sanilac	25	5.6	507	187	317,333	7,090	(NA)	72	25,554	571	20.1	86.1
Schoolcraft	7	7.9	149	68	100,042	11,388	8.7	48	10,790	1,228	44.1	71.1
Shiawassee	20	2.7	608	245	654,051	9,055	19.4	107	50,380	697	22.7	95.3
Tuscola	24	4.1	508	188	477,212	8,189	(NA)	77	22,069	379	–23.9	92.6

See footnotes at end of table.

Table B-11. Counties — **Banking, Retail Trade, and Accommodation and Food Services**—Con.

[Includes United States, states, and 3,141 counties/county equivalents defined as of February 22, 2005. For more information on these areas, see Appendix C, Geographic Information]

County	Banking,[1] 2005 Offices Number	Banking,[1] 2005 Offices Rate per 10,000 people	Banking,[1] 2005 Total deposits (mil. dol.)	Retail trade[2] (NAICS 44–45), 2002 Estab-lishments	Retail trade[2] (NAICS 44–45), 2002 Sales Total ($1,000)	Retail trade[2] (NAICS 44–45), 2002 Sales Per capita[3] (dol.)	Retail trade[2] (NAICS 44–45), 2002 Sales General merchan-dise stores,[4] percent of total	Accommodation and food services[2] (NAICS 72), 2002 Estab-lishments	Accommodation and food services[2] (NAICS 72), 2002 Sales Total ($1,000)	Accommodation and food services[2] (NAICS 72), 2002 Sales Per capita[3] (dol.)	Accommodation and food services[2] (NAICS 72), 2002 Sales Percent change, 1997–2002	Accommodation and food services[2] (NAICS 72), 2002 Sales Food services,[5] percent of total
MICHIGAN—Con.												
Van Buren	23	2.9	626	247	483,322	6,239	(NA)	146	67,926	877	31.7	86.8
Washtenaw	101	3.0	4,651	1,160	4,071,538	12,247	14.7	614	511,840	1,540	19.0	83.5
Wayne	402	2.0	25,941	6,593	17,444,033	8,550	15.1	3,254	2,305,993	1,130	14.0	85.3
Wexford	16	5.0	321	191	444,244	14,413	(NA)	84	44,806	1,454	12.7	(NA)
MINNESOTA	1,763	3.4	96,053	21,129	60,015,531	11,943	14.3	10,232	7,959,590	1,584	34.1	72.6
Aitkin	5	3.1	175	65	103,563	6,629	(NA)	54	16,411	1,051	−0.6	73.1
Anoka	61	1.9	2,444	960	3,199,554	10,311	17.7	393	303,999	980	41.1	95.4
Becker	13	4.1	371	157	313,672	10,183	(NA)	81	35,340	1,147	6.1	69.4
Beltrami	20	4.7	584	218	531,725	12,916	24.5	104	56,079	1,362	37.3	75.3
Benton	10	2.6	272	136	409,952	11,181	(NA)	55	32,943	899	22.7	92.4
Big Stone	5	9.1	162	37	41,856	7,317	(NA)	21	3,481	609	5.1	(NA)
Blue Earth	29	5.0	992	358	987,453	17,421	11.4	141	115,843	2,044	59.5	91.4
Brown	15	5.7	548	145	300,583	11,172	11.4	67	25,697	955	9.3	84.1
Carlton	11	3.2	192	145	280,615	8,620	(NA)	70	29,561	908	26.3	87.2
Carver	32	3.8	1,036	210	590,005	7,753	(NA)	119	62,005	815	42.2	(NA)
Cass	16	5.5	378	174	251,019	8,987	(NA)	155	122,942	4,402	358.9	18.2
Chippewa	7	5.5	328	73	106,539	8,247	(NA)	32	9,212	713	21.5	(NA)
Chisago	15	3.0	466	161	346,454	7,705	(NA)	71	33,972	756	83.6	(NA)
Clay	19	3.5	667	186	472,980	9,130	(NA)	93	43,039	831	5.8	(NA)
Clearwater	4	4.7	100	34	37,321	4,422	–	18	3,969	470	(NA)	(NA)
Cook	3	5.6	64	48	50,934	9,782	(NA)	75	41,229	7,918	14.3	18.5
Cottonwood	7	5.9	199	67	161,009	13,403	(NA)	19	6,088	507	1.3	(NA)
Crow Wing	38	6.3	1,037	373	960,272	16,745	(NA)	195	120,776	2,106	−0.4	62.3
Dakota	99	2.6	3,941	1,162	4,852,694	13,153	15.7	555	501,330	1,359	45.3	87.8
Dodge	10	5.1	218	77	81,230	4,365	(NA)	23	10,682	574	(NA)	(NA)
Douglas	16	4.6	686	248	496,029	14,735	27.4	98	52,051	1,546	23.4	71.5
Faribault	15	9.7	381	89	112,752	7,094	(NA)	24	7,584	477	(NA)	(NA)
Fillmore	17	8.0	393	129	159,737	7,491	2.0	64	13,404	629	(NA)	82.8
Freeborn	20	6.3	448	163	350,390	10,908	17.1	82	29,364	914	10.7	81.5
Goodhue	21	4.6	9,942	256	475,275	10,564	(NA)	114	219,107	4,870	455.7	(NA)
Grant	8	13.1	112	46	60,623	9,661	(NA)	11	2,553	407	(NA)	(NA)
Hennepin	263	2.3	29,522	4,542	16,970,984	15,147	12.0	2,301	2,486,397	2,219	19.6	78.6
Houston	9	4.5	230	76	91,423	4,588	(NA)	36	7,051	354	2.9	(NA)
Hubbard	5	2.7	306	111	158,444	8,542	8.7	68	18,485	997	9.5	69.1
Isanti	9	2.4	327	115	348,709	10,284	(NA)	52	24,437	721	69.0	(NA)
Itasca	21	4.7	644	242	452,745	10,271	14.8	109	48,778	1,107	16.5	69.5
Jackson	9	8.0	213	53	72,983	6,474	(NA)	20	6,017	534	(NA)	(NA)
Kanabec	4	2.5	186	62	139,863	9,007	(NA)	30	12,174	784	(NA)	(NA)
Kandiyohi	21	5.1	809	250	491,575	12,030	18.3	87	43,369	1,061	4.5	80.3
Kittson	7	14.6	104	31	35,943	7,126	–	9	(D)	(NA)	(NA)	(NA)
Koochiching	6	4.3	169	90	133,009	9,510	(NA)	48	17,883	1,279	−1.0	55.2
Lac qui Parle	7	9.2	127	48	47,850	6,029	(NA)	14	2,615	330	(NA)	100.0
Lake	5	4.5	110	51	108,224	9,718	4.1	59	25,559	2,295	63.6	50.8
Lake of the Woods	3	6.8	68	32	33,148	7,645	(NA)	36	15,773	3,638	39.3	10.6
Le Sueur	10	3.6	316	106	156,263	5,980	(NA)	45	13,581	520	(NA)	88.0
Lincoln	4	6.6	58	30	29,943	4,795	(NA)	15	2,735	438	19.7	100.0
Lyon	14	5.7	578	141	339,181	13,593	15.6	54	26,399	1,058	19.8	81.2
McLeod	18	4.9	771	183	398,723	11,187	23.2	66	30,819	865	14.4	90.0
Mahnomen	2	3.9	73	28	30,532	5,908	–	13	(D)	(NA)	(NA)	(NA)
Marshall	10	10.0	166	44	71,703	7,202	–	20	(D)	(NA)	(NA)	(NA)
Martin	14	6.7	514	124	255,539	11,981	11.4	51	20,243	949	11.7	(NA)
Meeker	10	4.3	271	108	176,498	7,663	(NA)	40	13,573	589	(NA)	93.4
Mille Lacs	9	3.5	305	128	223,810	9,419	3.2	65	167,749	7,060	(NA)	(NA)
Morrison	14	4.3	407	141	284,944	8,777	(NA)	92	29,246	901	30.5	82.4
Mower	21	5.4	485	187	313,139	8,077	16.3	92	41,195	1,063	30.9	86.2
Murray	8	9.0	197	52	57,704	6,366	(NA)	22	4,337	478	(NA)	(NA)
Nicollet	12	3.9	387	83	166,312	5,461	(NA)	43	22,704	745	−0.9	82.7
Nobles	16	7.8	360	136	268,210	13,019	(NA)	41	17,913	869	1.8	(NA)
Norman	8	11.4	129	34	54,692	7,481	–	12	(D)	(NA)	(NA)	(NA)
Olmsted	41	3.0	1,753	572	1,984,174	15,370	27.1	262	249,779	1,935	22.3	64.1
Otter Tail	27	4.7	815	281	569,006	9,903	17.7	149	48,722	848	28.7	80.1
Pennington	5	3.7	234	91	206,240	15,151	13.1	29	36,719	2,698	66.6	(NA)
Pine	12	4.2	271	115	209,264	7,591	15.9	64	175,607	6,370	534.5	(NA)
Pipestone	8	8.5	211	56	116,020	11,915	(NA)	23	7,830	804	(NA)	90.3
Polk	16	5.1	421	141	241,096	7,796	(NA)	67	31,907	1,032	27.5	90.3
Pope	8	7.1	197	52	91,696	8,164	(NA)	30	8,934	795	(NA)	73.7
Ramsey	102	2.1	12,333	1,824	6,302,759	12,370	14.6	992	823,671	1,617	25.8	90.4
Red Lake	3	6.9	64	25	33,325	7,797	–	10	(D)	(NA)	(NA)	(NA)
Redwood	14	8.7	454	91	131,281	7,999	(NA)	32	9,775	596	−7.1	(NA)
Renville	15	8.9	281	92	113,017	6,659	(NA)	30	(D)	(NA)	(NA)	(NA)

See footnotes at end of table.

Table B-11. Counties — **Banking, Retail Trade, and Accommodation and Food Services**—Con.

[Includes United States, states, and 3,141 counties/county equivalents defined as of February 22, 2005. For more information on these areas, see Appendix C, Geographic Information]

County	Banking,[1] 2005 Offices Number	Rate per 10,000 people	Total deposits (mil. dol.)	Retail trade[2] (NAICS 44–45), 2002 Estab-lishments	Sales Total ($1,000)	Per capita[3] (dol.)	General merchan-dise stores,[4] percent of total	Accommodation and food services[2] (NAICS 72), 2002 Estab-lishments	Sales Total ($1,000)	Per capita[3] (dol.)	Percent change, 1997–2002	Food services,[5] percent of total
MINNESOTA—Con.												
Rice	20	3.3	752	231	511,406	8,717	(NA)	113	71,043	1,211	29.2	90.5
Rock	8	8.4	187	47	90,053	9,300	(NA)	19	6,678	690	(NA)	(NA)
Roseau	7	4.2	275	93	171,778	10,626	7.0	42	13,701	848	-6.1	76.4
St. Louis	80	4.1	2,362	1,027	2,313,080	11,569	(NA)	584	351,099	1,756	21.2	62.3
Scott	29	2.4	1,009	294	736,437	7,091	13.2	161	237,723	2,289	317.2	(NA)
Sherburne	17	2.1	605	185	651,270	9,012	(NA)	78	48,649	673	45.8	(NA)
Sibley	12	7.9	198	63	59,536	3,883	(NA)	21	3,911	255	-6.6	(NA)
Stearns	55	3.9	2,945	714	2,085,612	15,088	(NA)	310	195,165	1,412	29.7	85.2
Steele	16	4.5	466	218	517,241	15,049	(NA)	69	39,261	1,142	48.8	84.6
Stevens	7	7.1	157	58	127,648	12,891	5.1	25	9,882	998	(NA)	(NA)
Swift	10	8.8	178	64	95,882	8,355	(NA)	24	6,495	566	-1.4	(NA)
Todd	11	4.5	275	95	138,159	5,656	2.1	44	12,704	520	(NA)	86.5
Traverse	5	13.1	92	32	30,438	7,739	(NA)	9	(D)	(NA)	(NA)	(NA)
Wabasha	11	5.0	399	107	177,909	8,094	(NA)	46	14,598	664	(NA)	(NA)
Wadena	7	5.1	225	88	133,105	9,692	(NA)	38	9,894	720	(NA)	90.5
Waseca	8	4.1	308	73	122,446	6,262	(NA)	33	9,022	461	(NA)	(NA)
Washington	76	3.4	2,060	691	2,627,480	12,485	(NA)	328	238,940	1,135	44.6	93.6
Watonwan	10	8.9	243	55	61,334	5,224	(NA)	23	5,164	440	(NA)	(NA)
Wilkin	5	7.4	110	28	40,399	5,805	(NA)	17	5,206	748	(NA)	(NA)
Winona	18	3.7	774	200	454,368	9,189	18.9	112	53,049	1,073	16.1	84.0
Wright	35	3.2	1,241	417	1,116,725	11,341	(NA)	151	73,238	744	34.8	88.3
Yellow Medicine	10	9.6	194	64	109,018	10,083	(NA)	23	6,097	564	(NA)	(NA)
MISSISSIPPI	1,136	3.9	35,047	12,561	25,017,531	8,724	20.7	4,329	5,486,105	1,913	79.0	40.0
Adams	12	3.7	485	207	373,577	11,154	(NA)	84	87,863	2,623	133.2	(NA)
Alcorn	14	4.0	452	189	488,150	14,025	19.9	66	32,078	922	19.2	85.2
Amite	3	2.2	71	32	27,972	2,068	(NA)	5	1,405	104	(NA)	100.0
Attala	7	3.6	271	97	167,792	8,519	27.5	26	12,693	644	17.2	89.2
Benton	3	3.8	36	16	18,896	2,401	(NA)	1	(D)	(NA)	(NA)	(NA)
Bolivar	18	4.7	399	182	255,863	6,478	(NA)	51	22,430	568	25.3	94.4
Calhoun	6	4.1	170	75	62,634	4,206	(NA)	12	2,471	166	(NA)	(NA)
Carroll	3	2.9	49	26	16,782	1,583	6.2	8	1,033	97	(NA)	100.0
Chickasaw	7	3.6	198	90	100,472	5,194	(NA)	31	14,088	728	(NA)	88.1
Choctaw	3	3.1	77	32	40,404	4,158	7.2	4	1,338	138	(NA)	100.0
Claiborne	2	1.7	95	32	32,441	2,785	16.7	8	3,590	308	145.9	(NA)
Clarke	8	4.5	161	54	38,766	2,174	(NA)	10	3,139	176	-6.4	(NA)
Clay	10	4.7	210	83	122,527	5,600	15.3	35	14,823	677	29.4	82.6
Coahoma	12	4.1	432	147	251,800	8,411	14.0	41	131,333	4,387	663.9	(NA)
Copiah	12	4.1	223	103	123,445	4,286	(NA)	35	13,320	462	5.6	90.1
Covington	7	3.5	182	66	104,639	5,295	(NA)	16	6,589	333	(NA)	(NA)
DeSoto	53	3.9	1,443	361	1,272,689	10,721	(NA)	168	140,317	1,182	93.1	85.1
Forrest	39	5.2	1,261	454	916,832	12,490	(NA)	165	107,920	1,470	(NA)	88.3
Franklin	6	7.1	116	21	14,651	1,767	(NA)	7	922	111	(NA)	(NA)
George	7	3.3	190	79	131,859	6,577	28.9	23	8,275	413	(NA)	(NA)
Greene	4	3.0	54	30	29,050	2,195	(NA)	5	1,229	93	-31.1	100.0
Grenada	9	3.9	282	140	276,856	12,055	27.9	50	26,796	1,167	9.9	80.6
Hancock	14	3.0	470	156	300,432	6,729	(NA)	84	141,972	3,180	475.3	(NA)
Harrison	66	3.4	2,234	896	2,139,214	11,239	21.4	428	1,435,562	7,542	343.9	(NA)
Hinds	90	3.6	4,396	1,044	3,023,634	12,142	13.7	449	371,086	1,490	15.1	80.6
Holmes	9	4.3	213	85	94,325	4,388	8.4	25	5,434	253	75.7	78.8
Humphreys	4	3.8	153	38	67,803	6,284	6.4	7	2,136	198	(NA)	100.0
Issaquena	1	5.2	3	–	–	–	–	–	–	–	–	–
Itawamba	5	2.1	215	67	128,125	5,576	(NA)	28	9,262	403	33.7	(NA)
Jackson	39	2.9	1,205	470	937,404	7,048	21.7	211	124,255	934	27.6	(NA)
Jasper	7	3.9	159	49	54,775	3,000	4.8	7	3,136	172	(NA)	(NA)
Jefferson	2	2.1	31	15	14,186	1,463	(NA)	5	(D)	(NA)	(NA)	(NA)
Jefferson Davis	3	2.3	118	49	46,357	3,416	9.6	13	5,792	427	(NA)	(NA)
Jones	24	3.6	881	286	559,991	8,600	24.1	94	46,482	714	24.7	(NA)
Kemper	3	2.9	76	34	39,610	3,763	(NA)	4	816	78	28.1	(NA)
Lafayette	22	5.4	630	176	329,029	8,396	(NA)	101	55,249	1,410	27.8	83.5
Lamar	12	2.7	396	181	457,599	11,116	(NA)	50	33,636	817	(NA)	84.6
Lauderdale	37	4.8	940	466	1,028,426	13,241	20.8	151	106,239	1,368	21.6	(NA)
Lawrence	4	3.0	102	49	37,551	2,798	10.9	17	3,043	227	5.3	(NA)
Leake	10	4.5	232	89	120,672	5,555	(NA)	20	9,736	448	(NA)	(NA)
Lee	39	4.9	1,435	529	1,177,537	15,289	(NA)	168	107,477	1,395	26.9	(NA)
Leflore	17	4.7	461	186	304,713	8,287	13.8	48	29,601	805	5.6	82.9
Lincoln	10	2.9	397	158	361,527	10,769	(NA)	54	32,741	975	54.3	90.6
Lowndes	23	3.8	682	352	678,102	11,131	22.0	104	63,496	1,042	6.8	85.0
Madison	42	5.0	1,227	398	901,868	11,581	(NA)	148	114,067	1,465	44.7	86.7
Marion	8	3.2	340	136	175,384	6,949	18.8	32	13,781	546	30.7	93.1
Marshall	12	3.4	259	106	118,521	3,363	(NA)	21	7,432	211	-4.0	78.9
Monroe	20	5.3	497	152	257,216	6,787	21.2	41	12,507	330	-6.9	90.6
Montgomery	7	5.9	212	71	79,177	6,624	20.8	21	6,469	541	19.8	82.1
Neshoba	13	4.3	393	122	245,376	8,526	35.2	46	25,728	894	50.4	81.1

See footnotes at end of table.

500

County and City Data Book: 2007

U.S. Census Bureau

[Includes United States, states, and 3,141 counties/county equivalents defined as of February 22, 2005. For more information on these areas, see Appendix C, Geographic Information]

County	Banking,[1] 2005			Retail trade[2] (NAICS 44–45), 2002				Accommodation and food services[2] (NAICS 72), 2002				
	Offices				Sales					Sales		
	Number	Rate per 10,000 people	Total deposits (mil. dol.)	Estab-lishments	Total ($1,000)	Per capita[3] (dol.)	General merchan-dise stores,[4] percent of total	Estab-lishments	Total ($1,000)	Per capita[3] (dol.)	Percent change, 1997–2002	Food services,[5] percent of total
MISSISSIPPI—Con.												
Newton	10	4.5	230	92	119,152	5,437	14.5	19	8,956	409	(NA)	(NA)
Noxubee	4	3.3	149	49	55,951	4,518	(NA)	11	3,729	301	24.1	(NA)
Oktibbeha	15	3.6	624	179	339,423	8,095	85	53,804	1,283	33.8	81.6
Panola	14	4.0	373	198	272,781	7,811	17.6	43	24,216	693	5.2	85.5
Pearl River	16	3.0	444	160	342,976	6,802	28.7	64	30,379	602	30.7	93.6
Perry	6	4.9	88	36	39,507	3,221	(NA)	4	1,208	98	−18.6	100.0
Pike	19	4.8	538	233	397,956	10,217	(NA)	64	32,791	842	26.3	87.5
Pontotoc	7	2.5	323	95	145,441	5,360	(NA)	23	11,102	409	38.1	(NA)
Prentiss	12	4.7	329	131	157,335	6,150	17.5	30	12,975	507	18.9	(NA)
Quitman	4	4.2	69	31	35,216	3,533	10.2	9	1,790	180	(NA)	(NA)
Rankin	52	3.9	1,375	459	1,392,855	11,448	(NA)	182	135,948	1,117	74.0	91.2
Scott	9	3.1	379	127	159,834	5,649	16.6	34	14,688	519	12.9	86.3
Sharkey	4	6.7	58	25	20,563	3,261	(NA)	4	862	137	(NA)	100.0
Simpson	10	3.6	272	104	182,869	6,595	(NA)	27	16,751	604	(NA)	91.3
Smith	6	3.7	137	41	41,894	2,624	(NA)	8	1,418	89	−9.3	100.0
Stone	6	4.0	190	67	93,222	6,602	(NA)	18	9,474	671	(NA)	(NA)
Sunflower	12	3.7	271	117	189,526	5,597	(NA)	25	10,253	303	4.5	90.3
Tallahatchie	5	3.5	93	44	35,933	2,477	11.0	10	2,465	170	116.8	100.0
Tate	9	3.4	316	87	231,553	9,042	(NA)	26	14,240	556	37.2	89.9
Tippah	10	4.7	314	99	112,526	5,367	21.7	18	7,910	377	(NA)	(NA)
Tishomingo	12	6.2	299	85	89,883	4,708	18.9	29	7,282	381	(NA)	(NA)
Tunica	5	4.8	96	71	99,861	10,296	(NA)	29	1,268,071	130,742	53.3	0.3
Union	7	2.6	392	105	173,739	6,710	(NA)	30	19,088	737	(NA)	95.0
Walthall	4	2.6	137	43	64,677	4,276	(NA)	18	6,455	427	51.2	91.8
Warren	19	3.9	495	275	478,729	9,735	24.4	104	267,816	5,446	66.6	17.7
Washington	23	3.9	647	310	604,920	9,904	20.8	90	81,727	1,338	72.0	53.4
Wayne	12	5.6	277	99	137,440	6,481	30.3	28	9,175	433	(NA)	92.1
Webster	5	5.0	117	49	52,944	5,149	8.2	5	1,964	191	(NA)	100.0
Wilkinson	5	4.9	96	39	41,268	4,007	10.3	6	1,985	193	−8.1	(NA)
Winston	8	4.0	245	92	111,245	5,565	20.6	26	10,725	537	20.2	(NA)
Yalobusha	7	5.2	161	48	57,642	4,331	9.4	7	2,176	163	(NA)	(NA)
Yazoo	11	3.9	298	95	192,019	6,853	(NA)	25	13,136	469	33.0	72.6
MISSOURI	2,225	3.8	92,765	23,837	61,861,163	10,891	16.7	11,280	8,607,025	1,515	26.9	73.5
Adair	9	3.7	499	129	260,371	10,471	(NA)	55	27,483	1,105	−5.1	89.4
Andrew	5	3.0	142	47	76,205	4,565	(NA)	12	3,551	213	1.5	(NA)
Atchison	6	9.6	126	38	50,380	7,996	(NA)	20	3,810	605	(NA)	81.4
Audrain	10	3.9	336	125	378,795	14,660	(NA)	38	12,828	496	−25.0	(NA)
Barry	25	7.0	460	172	309,220	9,001	(NA)	69	26,788	780	49.7	85.4
Barton	9	6.9	204	55	95,352	7,398	(NA)	21	7,473	580	3.5	(NA)
Bates	12	7.0	233	75	87,368	5,149	(NA)	27	9,002	530	26.9	(NA)
Benton	9	4.8	257	81	129,792	7,325	(NA)	55	10,190	575	5.9	81.4
Bollinger	5	4.1	74	32	53,535	4,352	(NA)	9	2,044	166	33.3	(NA)
Boone	57	4.0	2,037	607	1,727,665	12,461	(NA)	335	231,868	1,672	28.7	(NA)
Buchanan	34	4.0	1,279	409	992,745	11,638	(NA)	181	108,243	1,269	12.5	87.6
Butler	20	4.8	633	238	541,264	13,245	(NA)	76	49,600	1,214	36.4	90.4
Caldwell	5	5.4	90	34	24,328	2,680	(NA)	10	2,994	330	199.1	(NA)
Callaway	14	3.3	338	123	211,492	5,006	(NA)	40	28,148	666	24.8	92.4
Camden	22	5.6	788	332	562,590	14,824	(NA)	179	117,485	3,096	13.0	49.6
Cape Girardeau	33	4.6	1,250	467	1,101,797	15,856	24.4	155	110,100	1,584	23.2	(NA)
Carroll	10	9.8	257	45	48,456	4,729	(NA)	15	4,288	418	(NA)	92.7
Carter	5	8.5	78	24	18,552	3,138	(NA)	14	2,836	480	45.4	91.0
Cass	32	3.4	796	258	680,044	7,802	(NA)	111	54,548	626	8.2	93.6
Cedar	8	5.6	253	62	85,585	6,155	6.8	32	6,841	492	6.5	91.7
Chariton	8	9.8	189	43	45,535	5,505	2.5	11	1,470	178	40.0	(NA)
Christian	30	4.5	650	205	425,606	7,181	(NA)	75	40,174	678	97.7	92.3
Clark	6	8.2	123	36	48,781	6,518	(NA)	7	1,102	147	37.1	(NA)
Clay	69	3.4	2,501	732	2,992,473	15,640	(NA)	351	686,477	3,588	30.2	31.5
Clinton	10	4.8	213	80	133,712	6,813	(NA)	24	10,731	547	(NA)	(NA)
Cole	27	3.7	2,142	354	1,270,018	17,663	16.0	158	113,801	1,583	34.6	77.1
Cooper	15	8.7	291	84	123,920	7,263	(NA)	37	12,942	759	27.1	80.1
Crawford	8	3.3	222	81	157,824	6,782	(NA)	49	15,889	683	36.9	68.4
Dade	6	7.7	106	24	27,687	3,497	(NA)	10	1,546	195	(NA)	100.0
Dallas	6	3.7	181	52	91,714	5,758	(NA)	24	7,148	449	6.4	(NA)
Daviess	5	6.2	124	43	42,813	5,368	(NA)	15	2,598	326	20.7	(NA)
DeKalb	13	10.5	191	23	80,022	6,133	(NA)	22	6,815	522	−33.7	(NA)
Dent	7	4.6	193	66	103,805	6,986	(NA)	19	6,936	467	−16.9	76.3
Douglas	5	3.7	132	42	55,040	4,122	(NA)	9	3,740	280	4.5	100.0
Dunklin	15	4.6	415	168	305,180	9,296	(NA)	57	19,344	589	32.2	(NA)

See footnotes at end of table.

[Includes United States, states, and 3,141 counties/county equivalents defined as of February 22, 2005. For more information on these areas, see Appendix C, Geographic Information]

County	Banking,[1] 2005 Offices — Number	Offices — Rate per 10,000 people	Total deposits (mil. dol.)	Retail trade[2] (NAICS 44–45), 2002 Establishments	Sales Total ($1,000)	Per capita[3] (dol.)	General merchandise stores,[4] percent of total	Accommodation and food services[2] (NAICS 72), 2002 Establishments	Sales Total ($1,000)	Per capita[3] (dol.)	Percent change, 1997–2002	Food services,[5] percent of total
MISSOURI—Con.												
Franklin	39	3.9	1,561	433	1,023,983	10,653	(NA)	167	85,487	889	20.5	90.7
Gasconade	9	5.7	274	83	117,751	7,627	(NA)	42	12,465	807	67.9	66.7
Gentry	5	7.6	116	46	45,390	6,811	(NA)	11	1,726	259	36.0	(NA)
Greene	108	4.3	5,032	1,283	3,743,851	15,392	(NA)	622	450,224	1,851	28.5	83.5
Grundy	7	6.8	160	54	71,055	6,964	(NA)	14	5,542	543	10.9	(NA)
Harrison	9	10.1	187	61	145,488	16,561	31.4	19	8,791	1,001	−0.1	83.9
Henry	16	7.1	440	134	228,651	10,275	(NA)	54	18,090	813	11.5	89.1
Hickory	5	5.4	65	41	34,133	3,838	(NA)	21	2,156	242	−39.1	71.4
Holt	7	13.8	80	29	41,857	8,137	(NA)	13	2,903	564	6.5	(NA)
Howard	6	6.0	162	49	57,198	5,694	(NA)	16	2,991	298	2.6	(NA)
Howell	19	4.9	579	241	409,985	10,994	(NA)	68	34,074	914	16.3	84.0
Iron	7	6.8	129	53	45,135	4,306	9.5	16	3,375	322	−11.0	71.5
Jackson	194	2.9	11,341	2,496	7,721,715	11,713	(NA)	1,361	1,187,403	1,801	18.1	75.2
Jasper	60	5.4	1,591	603	1,443,554	13,505	(NA)	224	130,510	1,221	19.1	95.6
Jefferson	44	2.1	1,481	516	1,389,609	6,812	21.0	215	144,365	708	26.8	94.8
Johnson	20	3.9	452	160	310,828	6,255	28.0	88	45,989	926	45.8	(NA)
Knox	2	4.8	70	27	26,587	6,190	(NA)	7	1,491	347	99.3	(NA)
Laclede	13	3.8	525	196	360,695	10,954	(NA)	73	41,448	1,259	48.4	65.9
Lafayette	19	5.7	614	191	257,088	7,787	(NA)	69	25,184	763	(NA)	85.7
Lawrence	13	3.5	339	121	287,262	7,943	8.2	49	18,427	510	4.9	91.2
Lewis	8	7.9	171	40	44,715	4,301	(NA)	14	1,722	166	−18.0	(NA)
Lincoln	14	2.9	529	126	368,395	8,683	(NA)	51	23,325	550	19.9	94.9
Linn	12	9.1	225	64	94,392	6,979	(NA)	28	7,971	589	21.3	89.7
Livingston	10	7.0	442	80	176,280	12,252	(NA)	27	13,488	937	15.1	83.1
McDonald	9	3.9	172	82	94,422	4,346	(NA)	32	7,277	335	1.5	(NA)
Macon	11	7.1	331	83	140,610	9,089	(NA)	27	11,337	733	16.1	86.6
Madison	7	5.8	155	49	77,318	6,506	(NA)	20	6,005	505	5.4	86.7
Maries	6	6.7	142	30	38,029	4,342	5.1	12	1,665	190	(NA)	100.0
Marion	21	7.4	442	162	341,666	12,179	21.5	69	32,831	1,170	13.7	78.4
Mercer	3	8.3	62	18	20,972	5,716	(NA)	8	1,136	310	37.5	(NA)
Miller	14	5.7	261	141	303,630	12,533	(NA)	74	36,353	1,501	−9.0	75.4
Mississippi	7	5.1	207	63	95,318	7,249	(NA)	17	8,164	621	(NA)	87.4
Moniteau	9	6.0	220	63	119,161	7,960	(NA)	21	6,617	442	21.1	(NA)
Monroe	6	6.4	152	41	52,779	5,650	6.0	19	3,978	426	18.2	(NA)
Montgomery	11	9.0	212	56	67,261	5,567	(NA)	18	7,656	634	61.8	(NA)
Morgan	11	5.4	241	102	187,074	9,467	(NA)	42	11,066	560	−2.8	83.3
New Madrid	11	5.9	186	71	172,182	8,935	(NA)	22	5,374	279	−32.3	65.7
Newton	20	3.6	412	185	427,156	8,027	(NA)	88	57,932	1,089	16.0	67.7
Nodaway	11	5.1	433	92	182,353	8,352	(NA)	37	27,695	1,268	50.8	(NA)
Oregon	6	5.8	93	54	80,183	7,814	15.8	17	4,035	393	−3.1	100.0
Osage	9	6.7	203	53	122,103	9,328	(NA)	18	3,166	242	(NA)	(NA)
Ozark	5	5.3	112	38	32,880	3,479	(NA)	16	4,864	515	108.7	19.3
Pemiscot	8	4.1	232	81	134,154	6,751	9.7	27	9,765	491	−7.4	78.5
Perry	9	4.8	340	89	195,843	10,755	(NA)	39	16,830	924	35.0	89.6
Pettis	17	4.2	627	211	432,818	10,973	(NA)	89	48,017	1,217	32.8	90.9
Phelps	17	4.0	647	213	462,951	11,410	(NA)	111	55,610	1,371	23.4	80.4
Pike	9	4.8	291	89	117,784	6,408	12.5	23	7,750	422	−11.4	81.4
Platte	39	4.8	805	218	999,726	12,851	(NA)	179	185,861	2,389	33.5	64.4
Polk	15	5.2	396	117	220,707	7,986	(NA)	49	17,289	626	43.6	94.6
Pulaski	17	3.8	431	142	262,714	5,977	(NA)	79	51,194	1,165	73.4	87.5
Putnam	3	5.8	99	25	26,742	5,154	(NA)	6	985	190	(NA)	100.0
Ralls	3	3.1	98	25	24,896	2,568	—	14	5,693	587	−6.8	35.9
Randolph	12	4.7	319	115	236,254	9,545	(NA)	42	18,359	742	13.9	(NA)
Ray	10	4.1	246	64	136,524	5,752	(NA)	28	10,139	427	42.9	(NA)
Reynolds	6	9.1	67	25	23,361	3,536	(NA)	12	4,033	610	33.5	(NA)
Ripley	6	4.3	131	52	96,309	7,082	(NA)	16	5,106	375	25.4	(NA)
St. Charles	83	2.5	3,178	986	3,372,092	11,110	17.8	498	362,696	1,195	47.9	92.9
St. Clair	7	7.2	119	42	47,086	4,891	(NA)	18	5,658	588	(NA)	(NA)
Ste. Genevieve	8	4.4	273	61	100,784	5,581	(NA)	24	9,042	501	−4.8	85.8
St. Francois	24	3.9	695	236	525,214	9,245	31.3	105	70,270	1,237	55.7	81.9
St. Louis	277	2.8	19,777	4,091	14,370,172	14,159	14.3	1,983	1,965,119	1,936	24.4	73.9
Saline	15	6.5	336	114	173,122	7,529	(NA)	49	13,650	594	−10.9	87.6
Schuyler	3	7.0	41	24	22,203	5,265	—	5	517	123	−35.9	100.0
Scotland	3	6.1	100	31	24,439	4,992	(NA)	11	2,295	469	1.2	(NA)
Scott	18	4.4	591	241	461,739	11,399	(NA)	85	43,255	1,068	23.2	(NA)
Shannon	4	4.8	68	26	19,310	2,313	(NA)	13	3,947	473	84.0	85.6
Shelby	6	8.9	106	37	34,694	5,153	(NA)	16	2,433	361	60.4	(NA)
Stoddard	22	7.4	445	141	287,334	9,616	(NA)	43	17,652	591	21.3	86.8
Stone	19	6.1	297	112	165,871	5,633	(NA)	86	26,860	912	39.6	43.8
Sullivan	5	7.2	93	28	36,328	5,004	(NA)	7	1,312	181	(NA)	100.0

See footnotes at end of table.

Table B-11. Counties — **Banking, Retail Trade, and Accommodation and Food Services**—Con.

[Includes United States, states, and 3,141 counties/county equivalents defined as of February 22, 2005. For more information on these areas, see Appendix C, Geographic Information]

County	Banking,[1] 2005 Offices — Number	Rate per 10,000 people	Total deposits (mil. dol.)	Retail trade[2] (NAICS 44–45), 2002 Sales — Estab-lishments	Total ($1,000)	Per capita[3] (dol.)	General merchan-dise stores,[4] percent of total	Accommodation and food services[2] (NAICS 72), 2002 Sales — Estab-lishments	Total ($1,000)	Per capita[3] (dol.)	Percent change, 1997–2002	Food services,[5] percent of total
MISSOURI—Con.												
Taney	27	6.3	604	414	615,363	15,124	(NA)	293	280,202	6,887	14.2	42.5
Texas	10	4.1	301	98	129,386	5,339	15.6	34	7,237	299	53.5	88.1
Vernon	9	4.4	257	98	152,236	7,505	(NA)	41	17,335	855	25.9	90.6
Warren	7	2.4	290	120	233,766	8,937	(NA)	34	15,610	597	8.8	(NA)
Washington	9	3.7	189	67	87,180	3,685	(NA)	15	6,411	271	(NA)	(NA)
Wayne	7	5.3	106	51	70,269	5,343	(NA)	26	6,041	459	71.0	91.7
Webster	13	3.7	392	118	195,098	5,972	(NA)	31	14,419	441	22.9	(NA)
Worth	2	9.2	29	15	9,808	4,253	(NA)	8	456	198	23.6	100.0
Wright	11	6.0	258	90	194,564	10,709	(NA)	26	7,592	418	−8.5	(NA)
Independent City												
St. Louis city	82	2.4	11,086	1,234	2,821,962	8,127	(NA)	967	1,033,254	2,976	50.5	72.6
MONTANA	370	4.0	12,566	5,145	10,122,625	11,116	16.2	3,260	1,537,986	1,689	28.2	71.9
Beaverhead	4	4.6	131	61	86,233	9,578	(NA)	55	13,981	1,553	26.1	59.4
Big Horn	4	3.0	79	45	56,924	4,436	(NA)	24	13,013	1,014	60.7	73.2
Blaine	3	4.5	56	33	33,864	4,965	–	16	2,124	311	−14.0	67.2
Broadwater	2	4.4	42	13	27,799	6,302	(NA)	14	3,482	789	5.6	(NA)
Carbon	6	6.1	102	64	50,037	5,143	(NA)	45	14,133	1,453	−0.9	60.8
Carter	1	7.6	24	5	4,470	3,289	–	2	(D)	(NA)	(NA)	(NA)
Cascade	25	3.1	931	431	1,011,663	12,683	21.9	257	129,619	1,625	18.2	81.6
Chouteau	4	7.3	84	22	24,741	4,382	–	22	2,590	459	54.4	70.5
Custer	4	3.6	254	61	142,594	12,466	(NA)	43	18,040	1,577	5.1	73.1
Daniels	1	5.4	31	16	20,009	10,335	–	7	833	430	(NA)	(NA)
Dawson	4	4.6	132	55	74,732	8,553	(NA)	29	9,103	1,042	−2.9	68.7
Deer Lodge	4	4.5	93	47	55,308	6,094	(NA)	36	13,046	1,437	6.9	50.8
Fallon	2	7.4	71	18	19,657	7,206	(NA)	14	2,580	946	−11.9	75.9
Fergus	5	4.3	199	79	102,362	8,762	(NA)	45	12,886	1,103	−22.0	73.2
Flathead	29	3.5	1,116	515	1,025,123	13,232	16.6	317	159,629	2,060	20.8	70.9
Gallatin[6]	37	4.7	1,315	538	1,103,191	15,515	15.1	339	222,370	3,127	44.3	53.9
Garfield	1	8.3	23	7	5,718	4,593	–	4	781	627	(NA)	(NA)
Glacier	3	2.2	117	46	80,786	6,116	2.0	51	31,836	2,410	72.1	28.0
Golden Valley	1	8.6	5	1	(D)	(NA)	(NA)	4	(D)	(NA)	(NA)	(NA)
Granite	2	6.7	26	14	12,169	4,242	–	11	1,575	549	−12.1	(NA)
Hill	6	3.7	300	88	157,434	9,618	(NA)	53	23,144	1,414	24.2	89.5
Jefferson	3	2.7	50	19	21,174	2,032	(NA)	18	5,202	499	2.9	75.1
Judith Basin	1	4.5	40	8	4,127	1,829	–	9	1,369	607	(NA)	(NA)
Lake	11	3.9	253	129	194,425	7,199	(NA)	77	26,839	994	30.7	85.9
Lewis and Clark	20	3.4	760	303	649,561	11,502	(NA)	189	89,215	1,580	31.4	78.1
Liberty	2	10.0	26	14	9,348	4,628	–	6	740	366	36.3	100.0
Lincoln	5	2.6	131	99	113,247	6,041	(NA)	57	20,568	1,097	23.3	77.2
McCone	1	5.5	14	11	11,488	6,237	–	4	522	283	(NA)	100.0
Madison	4	5.5	115	42	35,607	5,109	(NA)	61	10,326	1,482	34.5	51.2
Meagher	1	5.0	23	14	13,465	6,951	(NA)	15	1,736	896	−34.2	72.1
Mineral	3	7.5	40	20	24,765	6,490	–	27	8,749	2,293	84.1	78.1
Missoula	35	3.5	1,278	557	1,525,115	15,590	19.8	329	205,956	2,105	41.4	78.1
Musselshell	2	4.4	48	21	16,001	3,586	(NA)	13	1,946	436	(NA)	86.6
Park[6]	8	5.0	248	115	130,975	8,269	(NA)	104	37,670	2,378	10.9	51.2
Petroleum	–	–	–	2	(D)	(NA)	(NA)	3	363	745	(NA)	(NA)
Phillips	3	7.2	100	30	30,522	7,007	(NA)	20	3,358	771	−15.3	62.5
Pondera	4	6.6	87	36	44,623	7,128	–	15	2,882	460	(NA)	(NA)
Powder River	1	5.9	29	15	12,175	6,660	–	6	1,250	684	(NA)	(NA)
Powell	3	4.3	72	15	22,652	3,217	(NA)	27	7,610	1,081	(NA)	73.5
Prairie	1	9.0	30	6	4,024	3,390	–	2	(D)	(NA)	(NA)	(NA)
Ravalli	16	4.0	508	169	235,802	6,246	(NA)	98	28,093	744	33.1	89.1
Richland	5	5.5	173	66	104,540	11,270	(NA)	34	11,631	1,254	12.6	89.9
Roosevelt	5	4.8	121	54	83,386	7,990	–	27	7,563	725	28.9	78.7
Rosebud	4	4.3	88	36	39,216	4,227	(NA)	31	8,400	905	12.4	73.0
Sanders	5	4.5	156	45	45,869	4,395	(NA)	39	8,674	831	78.4	74.6
Sheridan	3	8.5	123	34	26,233	6,891	–	18	3,706	973	(NA)	(NA)
Silver Bow	12	3.6	416	193	432,660	12,934	(NA)	120	58,863	1,760	23.1	74.0
Stillwater	4	4.7	113	43	55,462	6,557	(NA)	23	7,774	919	(NA)	(NA)
Sweet Grass	3	8.2	90	29	37,476	10,344	(NA)	16	6,295	1,738	1.4	30.8
Teton	3	4.8	137	31	37,290	5,899	–	19	2,748	435	−17.9	76.8
Toole	4	8.0	100	27	33,657	6,401	(NA)	26	6,204	1,180	30.0	69.6
Treasure	1	14.5	11	4	4,359	5,610	–	4	342	440	(NA)	(NA)
Valley	5	7.0	150	54	73,562	9,942	6.9	32	8,409	1,137	10.5	64.0
Wheatland	1	4.9	29	9	6,561	3,025	(NA)	12	1,484	684	−18.1	85.2
Wibaux	1	10.5	10	4	2,953	2,953	–	4	448	448	(NA)	(NA)
Yellowstone	42	3.1	1,864	732	1,944,727	14,738	(NA)	387	274,959	2,084	33.9	79.4
Yellowstone National Park[5]	(NA)	(NA)	(NA)	(X)	(X)	(NA)	(NA)	(X)	(X)	(NA)	(NA)	(NA)

See footnotes at end of table.

Table B-11. Counties — **Banking, Retail Trade, and Accommodation and Food Services**—Con.

[Includes United States, states, and 3,141 counties/county equivalents defined as of February 22, 2005. For more information on these areas, see Appendix C, Geographic Information]

County	Banking,[1] 2005 Offices Number	Rate per 10,000 people	Total deposits (mil. dol.)	Retail trade[2] (NAICS 44–45), 2002 Estab-lishments	Sales Total ($1,000)	Per capita[3] (dol.)	General merchandise stores,[4] percent of total	Accommodation and food services[2] (NAICS 72), 2002 Estab-lishments	Sales Total ($1,000)	Per capita[3] (dol.)	Percent change, 1997–2002	Food services,[5] percent of total
NEBRASKA.	1,021	5.8	33,415	8,157	20,249,200	11,729	14.0	3,992	2,088,710	1,210	21.0	84.8
Adams.	18	5.4	635	167	293,103	9,472	19.4	79	34,044	1,100	17.0	88.9
Antelope	7	10.0	137	54	80,452	11,078	(NA)	18	2,714	374	–3.5	(NA)
Arthur	1	26.5	2	4	(D)	(NA)	(NA)	–	–	–	–	–
Banner	1	13.6	24	1	(D)	(NA)	(NA)	–	–	–	–	–
Blaine	1	20.7	16	4	(D)	(NA)	(NA)	1	(D)	(NA)	(NA)	(NA)
Boone	7	12.1	188	52	62,244	10,238	(NA)	15	2,641	434	46.5	(NA)
Box Butte.	6	5.3	157	66	95,272	8,038	13.1	34	9,628	812	–6.1	87.2
Boyd	4	17.7	51	17	(D)	(NA)	(NA)	6	375	159	–22.5	(NA)
Brown	4	12.0	93	30	39,786	11,416	(NA)	8	2,089	599	–9.8	(NA)
Buffalo.	25	5.7	847	248	583,227	13,626	(NA)	120	78,952	1,845	19.9	(NA)
Burt.	6	8.0	123	40	43,032	5,684	(NA)	14	2,875	380	–8.6	100.0
Butler	9	10.3	152	26	48,065	5,399	–	10	1,922	216	(NA)	(NA)
Cass	18	7.0	290	71	149,131	6,005	(NA)	41	11,301	455	9.2	(NA)
Cedar	13	14.3	198	53	61,220	6,564	(NA)	15	2,843	305	(NA)	(NA)
Chase	4	10.3	129	32	75,272	18,818	(NA)	11	2,505	626	41.4	82.8
Cherry.	6	9.8	178	42	67,398	11,085	11.3	27	8,518	1,401	45.1	60.7
Cheyenne	10	10.0	315	64	(D)	(NA)	(NA)	36	15,885	1,598	26.6	71.6
Clay	7	10.4	118	35	42,957	6,231	–	12	3,071	445	(NA)	100.0
Colfax	7	6.7	180	53	74,544	7,097	(NA)	24	4,675	445	(NA)	100.0
Cuming	10	10.3	306	60	121,266	12,123	(NA)	25	6,132	613	–1.7	(NA)
Custer	11	9.6	258	74	79,594	6,882	4.0	24	5,939	513	17.7	79.1
Dakota.	11	5.4	212	75	131,451	6,441	(NA)	40	21,377	1,047	1.1	(NA)
Dawes	5	5.8	124	60	120,282	13,310	(NA)	38	12,416	1,374	32.5	82.0
Dawson	17	6.9	439	132	242,984	9,952	11.1	60	18,869	773	–2.5	(NA)
Deuel	3	15.0	43	17	51,805	25,258	(NA)	5	970	473	–14.0	(NA)
Dixon.	4	6.5	77	19	(D)	(NA)	(NA)	8	1,490	241	8.8	100.0
Dodge	24	6.7	779	179	598,277	16,631	(NA)	91	41,325	1,149	0.1	94.7
Douglas	179	3.7	11,065	1,948	6,453,551	13,691	12.8	1,094	801,979	1,701	29.6	85.4
Dundy	2	9.4	43	13	12,191	5,534	–	6	674	306	(NA)	100.0
Fillmore	9	14.1	192	38	34,536	5,339	4.6	19	(D)	(NA)	(NA)	(NA)
Franklin	5	14.6	63	17	15,511	4,448	–	9	1,033	296	–22.8	100.0
Frontier	3	10.7	90	14	(D)	(NA)	(NA)	4	993	333	(NA)	100.0
Furnas	8	15.9	145	41	70,095	13,359	(NA)	18	1,960	374	(NA)	90.8
Gage	21	9.0	418	145	230,234	9,894	(NA)	52	17,402	748	11.8	91.7
Garden	3	15.0	52	17	(D)	(NA)	(NA)	8	672	305	–37.2	(NA)
Garfield	1	5.5	26	25	17,590	9,282	(NA)	7	894	472	2.8	100.0
Gosper	2	9.9	26	5	1,818	877	–	5	1,535	740	136.9	(NA)
Grant.	2	29.9	10	7	(D)	(NA)	(NA)	3	(D)	(NA)	(NA)	(NA)
Greeley	4	15.9	62	20	25,436	9,595	(NA)	5	596	225	–36.9	100.0
Hall	30	5.4	1,060	337	876,194	16,277	(NA)	152	80,023	1,487	12.0	84.1
Hamilton	10	10.5	206	34	36,307	3,859	(NA)	14	4,352	463	50.6	75.1
Harlan	5	14.4	104	20	23,171	6,336	(NA)	12	2,370	648	(NA)	(NA)
Hayes	1	9.7	14	2	(D)	(NA)	(NA)	2	(D)	(NA)	(NA)	(NA)
Hitchcock	3	10.1	27	12	(D)	(NA)	(NA)	5	505	166	(NA)	100.0
Holt.	8	7.4	243	97	134,570	11,985	5.3	29	7,876	701	8.0	84.8
Hooker.	2	26.9	15	8	(D)	(NA)	(NA)	4	421	570	–18.3	(NA)
Howard	8	11.9	98	30	35,169	5,385	(NA)	12	2,016	309	5.5	(NA)
Jefferson	10	12.6	193	42	58,853	7,151	(NA)	19	4,756	578	(NA)	(NA)
Johnson	7	14.9	99	31	31,178	7,133	(NA)	10	2,003	458	42.4	(NA)
Kearney	4	5.9	149	29	31,063	4,554	(NA)	15	3,601	528	(NA)	(NA)
Keith	6	7.2	209	76	128,119	14,672	6.2	48	21,782	2,495	9.1	56.2
Keya Paha	1	11.1	10	5	(D)	(NA)	(NA)	2	(D)	(NA)	(NA)	(NA)
Kimball	3	7.9	114	33	43,867	11,047	3.5	13	2,427	611	–61.5	71.6
Knox	9	10.1	208	69	68,114	7,483	(NA)	34	3,732	410	8.5	(NA)
Lancaster.	117	4.4	3,943	1,049	2,871,797	11,199	(NA)	553	381,082	1,486	19.7	(NA)
Lincoln.	20	5.6	600	206	446,166	12,929	24.0	88	(D)	(NA)	(NA)	(NA)
Logan	1	13.5	14	3	(D)	(NA)	(NA)	–	–	(NA)	(NA)	–
Loup	1	14.6	21	2	(D)	(NA)	(NA)	2	(D)	(NA)	(NA)	(NA)
McPherson.	–	–	–	2	(D)	(NA)	(NA)	1	(D)	(NA)	(NA)	(NA)
Madison.	26	7.3	818	226	565,879	15,743	21.9	89	45,430	1,264	12.9	86.7
Merrick	6	7.4	112	39	33,882	4,183	(NA)	17	3,767	465	10.3	(NA)
Morrill	4	7.7	73	25	21,576	4,078	10.9	17	3,853	728	65.7	(NA)
Nance	3	8.2	91	19	16,378	4,217	(NA)	5	623	160	59.3	(NA)
Nemaha.	7	10.1	169	46	49,613	6,808	(NA)	22	4,780	656	–1.2	(NA)
Nuckolls.	6	12.7	114	35	41,005	8,437	(NA)	8	2,091	430	(NA)	100.0
Otoe	12	7.7	265	88	99,662	6,446	8.2	42	17,677	1,143	1.6	71.3
Pawnee	7	24.3	52	10	(D)	(NA)	(NA)	6	788	262	–9.9	(NA)
Perkins	5	16.4	67	17	13,835	4,488	–	5	577	187	(NA)	100.0
Phelps	9	9.5	209	53	74,803	7,709	4.9	25	7,533	776	31.5	(NA)
Pierce	4	5.3	118	43	39,528	5,109	–	12	1,808	234	9.6	100.0

See footnotes at end of table.

[Includes United States, states, and 3,141 counties/county equivalents defined as of February 22, 2005. For more information on these areas, see Appendix C, Geographic Information]

County	Banking,[1] 2005 Offices		Total deposits (mil. dol.)	Retail trade[2] (NAICS 44–45), 2002 Estab-lishments	Sales Total ($1,000)	Per capita[3] (dol.)	General merchan-dise stores,[4] percent of total	Accommodation and food services[2] (NAICS 72), 2002 Estab-lishments	Sales Total ($1,000)	Per capita[3] (dol.)	Percent change, 1997–2002	Food services,[5] percent of total
	Number	Rate per 10,000 people										
NEBRASKA—Con.												
Platte	20	6.4	653	165	338,431	10,822	(NA)	79	31,880	1,019	7.3	90.0
Polk	5	9.2	100	23	25,278	4,581	–	11	1,425	258	–6.5	100.0
Red Willow	10	9.0	350	93	171,530	15,177	(NA)	32	15,491	1,371	21.7	83.8
Richardson	9	10.3	202	55	57,184	6,274	(NA)	24	4,385	481	–7.3	88.5
Rock	1	6.4	37	13	(D)	(NA)	(NA)	6	2,065	1,226	213.8	(NA)
Saline	11	7.7	301	55	90,022	6,395	(NA)	41	11,278	801	13.2	(NA)
Sarpy	33	2.4	1,073	324	1,170,215	9,059	(NA)	171	114,436	886	58.5	93.3
Saunders	20	9.8	326	72	100,651	5,061	(NA)	40	8,646	435	(NA)	(NA)
Scotts Bluff	20	5.4	683	225	(D)	(NA)	(NA)	103	43,698	1,189	31.9	81.0
Seward	10	6.0	317	59	97,044	5,833	(NA)	42	12,848	772	1.9	(NA)
Sheridan	5	8.8	164	55	53,608	8,939	(NA)	18	3,277	546	(NA)	88.7
Sherman	4	12.9	61	15	19,601	6,175	(NA)	9	(D)	(NA)	(NA)	(NA)
Sioux	1	6.9	17	6	(D)	(NA)	(NA)	1	(D)	(NA)	(NA)	(NA)
Stanton	3	4.6	58	12	15,272	2,340	–	4	978	150	(NA)	100.0
Thayer	10	18.4	223	48	42,361	7,384	–	13	1,779	310	–25.1	(NA)
Thomas	1	16.1	10	3	(D)	(NA)	(NA)	4	793	1,164	–19.2	(NA)
Thurston	3	4.1	98	25	45,553	6,422	–	8	2,158	304	–28.8	(NA)
Valley	6	13.6	110	40	74,397	16,319	(NA)	14	2,717	596	(NA)	(NA)
Washington	6	3.0	284	62	529,854	27,448	(NA)	43	12,941	670	9.5	73.0
Wayne	9	9.8	190	47	69,238	7,248	7.1	23	7,176	751	–5.6	(NA)
Webster	3	8.0	71	21	19,090	4,905	–	6	1,082	278	–15.5	(NA)
Wheeler	2	24.4	26	4	(D)	(NA)	(NA)	4	(D)	(NA)	(NA)	(NA)
York	16	11.1	383	82	171,844	11,952	13.3	41	24,834	1,727	12.1	79.6
NEVADA	502	2.1	48,231	7,214	26,999,899	12,452	14.2	4,252	19,537,592	9,011	27.5	16.2
Churchill	8	3.3	247	75	205,585	8,477	(NA)	51	37,425	1,543	43.7	47.6
Clark	332	1.9	33,605	4,750	19,302,266	12,734	(NA)	2,787	16,440,741	10,846	32.5	15.3
Douglas	13	2.8	643	150	457,674	10,583	(NA)	95	453,727	10,492	–13.4	14.1
Elko	12	2.6	354	163	423,061	9,485	(NA)	116	325,067	7,288	8.0	(NA)
Esmeralda	–	–	–	–	–	–	–	5	548	612	7.5	100.0
Eureka	1	7.0	33	8	4,222	2,619	–	5	1,483	920	–25.0	(NA)
Humboldt	5	2.9	149	71	197,559	12,254	(NA)	45	44,242	2,744	–4.7	36.4
Lander	1	2.0	19	18	23,082	4,445	–	18	6,921	1,333	19.1	61.2
Lincoln	4	9.1	33	18	23,113	5,456	(NA)	13	3,558	840	41.5	(NA)
Lyon	6	1.3	196	76	190,912	5,020	–	42	18,858	496	19.0	56.4
Mineral	1	2.0	11	16	17,326	3,635	(NA)	13	10,825	2,271	11.4	(NA)
Nye	8	2.0	356	108	206,794	5,974	(NA)	71	61,461	1,776	51.8	23.8
Pershing	2	3.1	32	18	29,509	4,491	(NA)	14	2,764	421	–63.9	(NA)
Storey	1	2.5	10	24	5,818	1,700	–	13	4,695	1,372	96.4	66.8
Washoe	83	2.1	11,200	1,404	4,989,892	13,794	15.8	815	1,999,865	5,529	10.1	20.5
White Pine	3	3.3	102	42	61,888	7,157	(NA)	25	15,293	1,769	–12.0	28.2
Independent City												
Carson City	22	3.9	1,242	273	861,198	15,786	(NA)	124	110,119	2,019	18.3	61.4
NEW HAMPSHIRE	426	3.3	29,654	6,702	20,830,057	16,330	13.9	3,160	2,082,145	1,632	34.8	75.3
Belknap	21	3.4	10,004	391	1,236,784	20,898	9.0	206	114,651	1,937	28.7	72.9
Carroll	24	5.1	945	427	736,155	16,246	7.5	281	193,274	4,265	34.5	45.9
Cheshire	22	2.8	1,396	388	1,218,203	16,195	12.3	156	87,855	1,168	27.4	82.9
Coos	16	4.8	508	221	539,011	16,136	6.3	122	91,904	2,751	63.4	25.0
Grafton	57	6.7	1,596	592	1,442,042	17,388	14.3	342	225,786	2,722	44.5	57.2
Hillsborough	102	2.5	6,435	1,703	6,182,948	15,761	14.5	753	554,370	1,413	34.0	85.6
Merrimack	52	3.5	2,163	657	2,056,720	14,503	13.5	269	172,795	1,218	37.1	86.4
Rockingham	89	3.0	4,714	1,685	5,463,618	18,977	(NA)	751	498,076	1,730	29.7	83.7
Strafford	25	2.1	1,252	440	1,499,781	12,922	(NA)	218	119,516	1,030	41.8	91.7
Sullivan	18	4.2	640	198	454,795	10,968	18.1	62	23,918	577	5.7	80.5
NEW JERSEY	3,222	3.7	222,556	34,741	102,153,833	11,910	10.2	17,537	15,715,595	1,832	17.1	58.7
Atlantic	82	3.0	4,571	1,182	3,310,597	12,768	14.1	749	4,866,281	18,767	–3.0	8.0
Bergen	483	5.4	33,136	4,438	14,090,702	15,746	8.1	1,966	1,474,003	1,647	32.0	80.5
Burlington	148	3.3	8,007	1,555	7,571,497	17,295	8.7	772	529,755	1,210	35.3	78.1
Camden	136	2.6	8,738	1,959	4,797,754	9,370	10.8	893	528,833	1,033	20.1	92.5
Cape May	57	5.7	2,529	772	1,383,058	13,587	(NA)	933	497,530	4,888	35.2	49.7
Cumberland	46	3.0	1,828	553	1,518,709	10,259	11.6	212	104,405	705	32.5	89.5
Essex	262	3.3	14,955	2,909	6,213,743	7,802	8.5	1,460	1,000,271	1,256	17.2	83.5
Gloucester	84	3.0	3,749	965	3,311,510	12,611	16.3	427	287,457	1,095	42.6	94.8
Hudson	179	3.0	33,619	2,301	4,090,693	6,710	8.6	1,146	612,792	1,005	31.4	80.1
Hunterdon	58	4.4	2,660	625	1,636,344	12,908	(NA)	222	118,939	938	16.1	90.7
Mercer	134	3.7	9,302	1,409	4,191,115	11,719	10.8	741	553,731	1,548	40.6	77.9
Middlesex	251	3.2	26,305	2,701	8,893,407	11,549	11.0	1,374	974,839	1,266	26.5	78.2
Monmouth	267	4.2	13,402	2,855	8,785,490	13,980	10.9	1,457	899,102	1,431	30.3	89.2
Morris	226	4.6	11,723	2,112	8,010,002	16,729	9.0	1,123	854,711	1,785	28.4	75.7
Ocean	192	3.4	10,899	1,978	5,774,994	10,746	13.0	981	544,906	1,014	29.7	88.3

See footnotes at end of table.

[Includes United States, states, and 3,141 counties/county equivalents defined as of February 22, 2005. For more information on these areas, see Appendix C, Geographic Information]

County	Banking,[1] 2005 Offices Number	Rate per 10,000 people	Total deposits (mil. dol.)	Retail trade[2] (NAICS 44–45), 2002 Estab-lishments	Sales Total ($1,000)	Per capita[3] (dol.)	General merchandise stores,[4] percent of total	Accommodation and food services[2] (NAICS 72), 2002 Estab-lishments	Sales Total ($1,000)	Per capita[3] (dol.)	Percent change, 1997–2002	Food services,[5] percent of total
NEW JERSEY—Con.												
Passaic	153	3.1	9,080	1,879	5,071,456	10,203	12.8	814	440,449	886	30.0	95.6
Salem	30	4.5	986	216	542,856	8,382	9.5	110	67,138	1,037	48.8	83.5
Somerset	116	3.6	7,728	1,208	4,423,052	14,364	12.1	665	576,442	1,872	61.7	76.5
Sussex	59	3.9	1,987	495	1,345,425	9,037	(NA)	280	129,858	872	22.3	87.3
Union	215	4.0	15,511	2,135	5,877,136	11,099	7.5	995	555,283	1,049	8.2	83.2
Warren	44	4.0	1,840	494	1,314,293	12,226	11.7	217	98,870	920	22.7	89.7
NEW MEXICO	498	2.6	19,667	7,227	18,328,637	9,880	18.3	3,756	2,771,474	1,494	29.1	71.8
Bernalillo	136	2.3	7,555	2,233	7,844,485	13,689	17.0	1,200	1,068,848	1,865	21.5	79.7
Catron	1	2.9	13	12	4,563	1,304	40.4	11	1,913	547	15.9	(NA)
Chaves	21	3.4	645	261	543,649	8,941	16.8	99	60,976	1,003	11.2	80.2
Cibola	6	2.2	124	74	157,325	5,841	(NA)	48	105,820	3,929	395.6	(NA)
Colfax	11	8.0	258	107	113,263	7,970	8.8	72	56,085	3,946	62.2	(NA)
Curry	20	4.4	541	208	429,565	9,598	(NA)	78	47,040	1,051	2.4	85.4
De Baca	1	5.0	22	14	10,690	4,998	–	6	1,148	537	–3.1	(NA)
Dona Ana	41	2.2	1,310	513	1,252,188	7,012	21.1	245	155,290	870	27.6	87.7
Eddy	17	3.3	656	225	398,401	7,762	(NA)	90	51,064	995	–3.5	66.5
Grant	11	3.7	326	124	197,797	6,504	(NA)	76	26,842	883	6.8	76.9
Guadalupe	2	4.6	34	21	52,306	11,275	–	28	11,979	2,582	19.2	(NA)
Harding	1	13.5	8	4	8,309	11,093	–	2	(D)	(NA)	(NA)	(NA)
Hidalgo	3	5.8	49	33	63,787	11,921	(NA)	21	9,521	1,779	20.3	65.0
Lea	17	3.0	510	227	491,816	8,819	21.7	104	48,100	862	14.4	89.8
Lincoln	14	6.7	296	145	208,176	10,543	(NA)	108	41,758	2,115	38.9	71.3
Los Alamos	5	2.7	765	47	92,295	5,060	(NA)	38	21,181	1,161	3.6	(NA)
Luna	6	2.3	223	83	166,907	6,609	(NA)	45	18,734	742	17.0	75.9
McKinley	8	1.1	367	263	744,437	10,101	19.2	136	89,192	1,210	28.7	75.0
Mora	3	5.9	23	14	8,989	1,716	–	2	(D)	(NA)	(NA)	(NA)
Otero	19	3.0	466	199	398,288	6,458	(NA)	97	59,507	965	61.0	56.1
Quay	5	5.4	138	62	93,332	9,616	9.3	44	20,335	2,095	25.7	(NA)
Rio Arriba	9	2.2	342	113	249,811	6,090	(NA)	78	43,675	1,065	28.9	69.0
Roosevelt	7	3.8	157	64	147,174	8,090	(NA)	23	14,682	807	18.1	94.5
Sandoval	13	1.2	542	161	441,646	4,614	(NA)	115	103,457	1,081	125.0	(NA)
San Juan	25	2.0	971	470	1,238,836	10,325	21.8	177	137,499	1,146	37.4	83.6
San Miguel	9	3.0	223	94	178,323	6,014	(NA)	79	31,742	1,070	32.3	74.5
Santa Fe	40	2.8	1,869	910	1,809,469	13,484	(NA)	353	376,204	2,803	23.4	59.8
Sierra	5	3.9	99	51	71,590	5,511	10.2	45	13,563	1,044	4.6	72.1
Socorro	5	2.8	153	46	76,722	4,270	(NA)	39	17,319	964	–7.4	71.3
Taos	13	4.1	348	242	258,622	8,389	(NA)	169	87,148	2,827	36.7	47.5
Torrance	6	3.4	96	44	92,545	5,537	(NA)	32	11,824	707	32.5	(NA)
Union	3	7.8	87	22	20,341	5,130	6.2	18	5,820	1,468	20.3	68.4
Valencia	15	2.2	451	141	462,990	6,794	(NA)	78	32,745	481	15.6	87.3
NEW YORK	4,931	2.6	689,775	76,425	178,067,530	9,298	11.1	39,428	27,835,952	1,453	28.4	75.5
Albany	118	4.0	14,145	1,365	4,499,439	15,201	13.1	847	593,885	2,006	32.2	76.7
Allegany	19	3.8	372	163	233,094	4,625	10.1	89	37,432	743	28.6	94.6
Bronx	129	1.0	9,956	3,319	4,318,169	3,178	8.0	1,164	490,582	361	32.0	94.6
Broome	59	3.0	1,919	796	2,219,433	11,106	17.6	485	263,512	1,319	29.0	85.8
Cattaraugus	27	3.3	749	383	751,114	9,007	15.4	201	89,765	1,076	12.9	72.8
Cayuga	23	2.8	774	258	628,675	7,675	21.1	167	56,926	695	8.4	85.4
Chautauqua	50	3.7	1,293	576	1,198,673	8,660	17.9	363	149,280	1,078	19.5	71.4
Chemung	24	2.7	1,161	401	1,043,436	11,489	20.3	208	104,596	1,152	21.3	89.5
Chenango	15	2.9	698	196	359,928	7,000	(NA)	88	27,290	531	13.8	73.1
Clinton	28	3.4	1,038	388	935,328	11,574	16.4	175	91,738	1,135	41.8	76.2
Columbia	22	3.5	916	270	511,054	8,086	(NA)	152	47,259	748	12.9	81.1
Cortland	17	3.5	540	212	456,035	9,405	14.8	135	53,045	1,094	–0.1	87.5
Delaware	18	3.8	762	228	324,044	6,844	7.4	142	43,780	925	41.0	70.6
Dutchess	88	3.0	3,535	1,091	3,093,409	10,744	15.5	600	323,127	1,122	28.2	79.1
Erie	262	2.8	23,585	3,457	9,838,147	10,448	12.0	2,072	1,213,115	1,288	29.7	86.6
Essex	18	4.7	407	223	355,542	9,095	(NA)	203	106,873	2,734	23.0	36.0
Franklin	18	3.5	426	211	351,363	6,910	8.0	124	38,695	761	26.4	65.7
Fulton	17	3.1	652	217	403,102	7,311	(NA)	110	32,535	590	15.6	87.1
Genesee	17	2.9	792	232	531,542	8,870	(NA)	137	62,551	1,044	21.1	86.7
Greene	22	4.4	703	214	459,733	9,473	(NA)	206	73,256	1,509	17.1	43.2
Hamilton	3	5.7	54	40	28,939	5,484	8.2	55	14,857	2,815	43.1	55.4
Herkimer	20	3.1	531	236	418,527	6,568	(NA)	164	49,609	779	22.0	76.6
Jefferson	38	3.3	1,068	506	1,151,710	10,108	14.9	300	126,958	1,114	23.9	79.2
Kings	275	1.1	31,683	7,687	10,909,140	4,390	8.1	2,553	1,020,122	411	38.9	93.8
Lewis	9	3.4	213	93	124,698	4,681	(NA)	69	13,281	499	21.5	79.7
Livingston	20	3.1	607	220	502,459	7,765	9.9	133	50,538	781	28.7	92.0
Madison	20	2.8	700	232	558,627	8,002	16.9	158	76,653	1,098	27.9	95.8
Monroe	190	2.6	9,362	2,418	7,434,651	10,113	12.2	1,386	869,946	1,183	14.4	86.3
Montgomery	20	4.1	673	207	491,925	9,986	12.2	99	33,314	676	–9.7	94.5
Nassau	447	3.4	46,691	6,684	19,647,827	14,668	10.4	2,889	1,965,422	1,467	27.2	89.7

See footnotes at end of table.

[Includes United States, states, and 3,141 counties/county equivalents defined as of February 22, 2005. For more information on these areas, see Appendix C, Geographic Information]

County	Banking,[1] 2005 Offices			Retail trade[2] (NAICS 44–45), 2002	Sales			Accommodation and food services[2] (NAICS 72), 2002	Sales			
	Number	Rate per 10,000 people	Total deposits (mil. dol.)	Estab-lishments	Total ($1,000)	Per capita[3] (dol.)	General merchandise stores,[4] percent of total	Estab-lishments	Total ($1,000)	Per capita[3] (dol.)	Percent change, 1997–2002	Food services,[5] percent of total
NEW YORK—Con.												
New York	555	3.5	378,494	11,620	25,904,575	16,718	6.4	7,612	10,714,578	6,915	28.8	62.0
Niagara	48	2.2	2,583	798	1,819,454	8,333	13.7	516	211,997	971	2.0	79.5
Oneida	69	2.9	3,802	900	2,325,193	9,931	(NA)	488	228,100	974	26.7	81.3
Onondaga	146	3.2	6,707	1,846	5,329,824	11,619	12.6	1,057	631,909	1,378	23.9	82.5
Ontario	31	3.0	1,263	537	1,455,877	14,287	20.7	288	137,523	1,350	24.3	84.0
Orange	124	3.3	4,991	1,516	4,035,561	11,323	14.0	685	352,408	989	37.4	82.1
Orleans	11	2.5	288	130	215,957	4,921	4.9	62	16,812	383	10.5	96.9
Oswego	32	2.6	990	391	876,299	7,137	11.6	275	114,826	935	31.9	90.0
Otsego	26	4.1	886	302	715,681	11,545	17.7	191	91,390	1,474	45.5	70.9
Putnam	27	2.7	3,627	352	690,307	6,994	5.9	161	60,554	614	32.5	90.5
Queens	370	1.7	36,687	6,395	11,226,779	5,008	9.2	3,149	1,748,340	780	30.0	88.6
Rensselaer	49	3.2	1,926	442	1,105,444	7,247	(NA)	258	115,255	756	25.2	89.5
Richmond	90	1.9	8,558	1,231	3,159,828	6,931	13.1	587	306,863	673	28.1	93.9
Rockland	105	3.6	6,855	1,226	3,142,865	10,786	14.5	603	415,404	1,426	68.5	79.4
St. Lawrence	39	3.5	1,035	444	971,042	8,735	15.4	248	91,981	827	22.9	83.2
Saratoga	80	3.7	2,511	756	2,196,328	10,607	15.9	402	252,207	1,218	27.8	80.0
Schenectady	49	3.3	2,064	499	1,323,289	9,010	14.4	263	112,405	765	5.4	91.2
Schoharie	12	3.7	348	115	238,964	7,548	(NA)	55	19,528	617	35.8	73.7
Schuyler	5	2.6	138	73	109,564	5,641	(NA)	51	13,653	703	19.8	73.9
Seneca	14	4.0	371	188	317,913	9,080	(NA)	68	26,840	767	15.1	(NA)
Steuben	30	3.0	754	372	777,921	7,817	(NA)	202	84,283	847	12.9	77.9
Suffolk	415	2.8	32,984	6,685	18,469,555	12,689	11.5	2,924	1,733,779	1,191	36.8	87.9
Sullivan	35	4.6	994	308	578,761	7,789	15.2	239	127,711	1,719	–13.8	30.7
Tioga	15	2.9	367	153	237,370	4,581	0.9	79	28,649	553	18.2	79.6
Tompkins	33	3.3	1,255	366	804,362	8,181	7.8	317	157,064	1,597	38.8	78.0
Ulster	59	3.2	2,283	827	1,838,068	10,188	14.5	473	272,731	1,512	26.5	56.9
Warren	29	4.4	1,181	459	1,095,627	17,088	12.3	381	212,028	3,307	18.1	(NA)
Washington	19	3.0	554	223	404,190	6,570	4.5	113	23,181	377	16.9	(NA)
Wayne	23	2.5	697	316	701,448	7,478	7.8	150	50,897	543	10.3	96.4
Westchester	336	3.6	27,772	4,174	11,807,085	12,589	11.0	1,924	1,322,936	1,411	29.9	81.2
Wyoming	16	3.7	551	154	287,586	6,658	(NA)	84	27,057	626	64.5	77.1
Yates	6	2.4	254	104	125,050	5,098	(NA)	49	13,121	535	1.1	(NA)
NORTH CAROLINA	2,544	2.9	184,218	35,851	88,821,486	10,686	13.8	15,747	11,237,386	1,352	30.3	78.9
Alamance	47	3.3	2,165	607	1,630,194	12,018	12.0	258	194,801	1,436	34.3	91.2
Alexander	10	2.8	317	95	185,110	5,374	(NA)	39	16,916	491	9.1	97.2
Alleghany	6	5.5	183	46	62,458	5,769	(NA)	23	5,868	542	–4.7	(NA)
Anson	8	3.1	235	83	121,075	4,789	13.3	27	14,854	588	22.5	(NA)
Ashe	13	5.1	453	115	202,870	8,163	(NA)	38	16,368	659	30.5	85.4
Avery	9	5.1	201	95	106,120	5,994	3.4	55	27,333	1,544	23.9	61.7
Beaufort	17	3.7	580	234	435,532	9,619	17.9	71	39,792	879	36.5	87.9
Bertie	7	3.6	147	61	93,036	4,739	(NA)	18	5,487	279	25.9	(NA)
Bladen	8	2.4	201	107	188,003	5,791	10.3	43	16,160	498	–9.6	78.9
Brunswick	39	4.4	1,400	352	648,538	8,218	(NA)	189	92,047	1,166	36.6	82.8
Buncombe	79	3.6	3,177	1,180	2,637,340	12,528	14.8	556	484,765	2,303	45.0	63.8
Burke	18	2.0	670	282	630,333	7,061	(NA)	128	83,106	931	31.6	95.0
Cabarrus	39	2.6	2,049	684	1,854,532	13,261	13.9	203	178,757	1,278	44.5	95.1
Caldwell	20	2.5	767	308	594,571	7,551	12.5	110	46,297	588	13.3	93.4
Camden	3	3.3	20	17	13,287	1,788	(NA)	2	(D)	(NA)	(NA)	(NA)
Carteret	24	3.8	910	402	732,940	12,164	18.8	198	111,182	1,845	4.9	74.7
Caswell	2	0.8	52	37	40,359	1,703	(NA)	12	2,517	106	–7.3	(NA)
Catawba	53	3.5	2,294	771	2,145,348	14,648	14.9	344	226,771	1,548	26.2	90.5
Chatham	16	2.8	463	157	236,573	4,399	(NA)	51	22,167	412	(NA)	96.8
Cherokee	11	4.3	397	135	311,356	12,595	(NA)	56	23,723	960	53.8	88.0
Chowan	8	5.5	192	69	144,884	10,194	(NA)	28	12,180	857	20.8	83.6
Clay	4	4.1	124	50	92,944	10,153	(NA)	10	4,733	517	(NA)	(NA)
Cleveland	32	3.3	1,106	429	802,500	8,210	18.1	147	81,092	830	33.9	90.9
Columbus	16	2.9	568	287	409,325	7,473	14.3	85	30,300	553	13.4	90.2
Craven	20	2.2	982	424	879,490	9,652	15.5	170	116,764	1,281	34.0	(NA)
Cumberland	64	2.1	2,319	1,047	3,006,446	9,873	19.1	492	366,359	1,203	15.1	(NA)
Currituck	5	2.2	124	119	197,238	10,041	0.9	49	21,985	1,119	60.8	78.3
Dare	24	7.1	891	445	697,172	21,699	12.6	289	204,301	6,359	46.0	63.5
Davidson	37	2.4	1,759	525	1,065,470	7,066	11.9	181	106,893	709	22.3	93.5
Davie	10	2.6	429	109	223,104	6,081	(NA)	48	20,752	566	(NA)	81.5
Duplin	16	3.1	402	208	331,012	6,537	11.6	63	28,942	572	1.3	94.6
Durham	67	2.8	3,026	959	2,473,029	10,596	14.3	553	501,332	2,148	32.4	74.2
Edgecombe	11	2.0	279	198	295,860	5,376	15.6	75	35,453	644	60.2	77.6
Forsyth	98	3.0	12,954	1,450	4,589,485	14,599	14.8	629	502,788	1,599	23.2	86.5
Franklin	7	1.3	294	128	274,365	5,422	10.7	42	14,835	293	(NA)	88.3

See footnotes at end of table.

Table B-11. Counties — **Banking, Retail Trade, and Accommodation and Food Services**—Con.

[Includes United States, states, and 3,141 counties/county equivalents defined as of February 22, 2005. For more information on these areas, see Appendix C, Geographic Information]

County	Banking,[1] 2005			Retail trade[2] (NAICS 44–45), 2002				Accommodation and food services[2] (NAICS 72), 2002				
	Offices				Sales					Sales		
	Number	Rate per 10,000 people	Total deposits (mil. dol.)	Estab-lishments	Total ($1,000)	Per capita[3] (dol.)	General merchandise stores,[4] percent of total	Estab-lishments	Total ($1,000)	Per capita[3] (dol.)	Percent change, 1997–2002	Food services,[5] percent of total
NORTH CAROLINA—Con.												
Gaston	56	2.9	1,899	707	1,789,973	9,271	17.3	275	181,829	942	14.6	94.1
Gates	3	2.7	83	29	42,154	3,966	1.1	7	2,002	188	62.6	100.0
Graham	2	2.5	104	35	39,384	4,871	(NA)	15	6,991	865	–9.0	(NA)
Granville	9	1.7	421	161	310,092	5,987	9.7	61	33,211	641	42.5	91.7
Greene	3	1.5	87	38	45,599	2,334	(NA)	13	3,005	154	2.4	100.0
Guilford	134	3.0	6,908	1,975	5,983,875	13,905	11.8	985	800,418	1,860	25.5	78.8
Halifax	20	3.6	550	292	485,164	8,580	(NA)	81	60,330	1,067	16.6	88.6
Harnett	25	2.4	796	285	559,754	5,778	16.8	92	49,451	510	33.4	90.2
Haywood	15	2.7	660	286	635,546	11,540	(NA)	151	80,005	1,453	21.4	63.9
Henderson	27	2.8	1,463	425	1,215,907	13,154	(NA)	183	128,335	1,388	32.0	69.0
Hertford	6	2.5	249	113	188,928	7,935	17.6	32	17,811	748	6.1	89.5
Hoke	4	1.0	104	63	83,144	2,300	4.6	22	7,161	198	32.4	(NA)
Hyde	4	7.4	146	46	28,448	4,957	(NA)	34	12,885	2,245	26.7	57.6
Iredell	44	3.1	1,744	605	1,573,615	12,054	17.3	231	143,189	1,097	21.9	87.8
Jackson	15	4.2	391	198	306,521	9,045	(NA)	92	42,140	1,243	28.1	70.1
Johnston	36	2.5	1,085	504	1,167,881	8,785	10.0	173	106,705	803	17.4	88.3
Jones	3	2.9	57	22	28,831	2,808	(NA)	7	1,680	164	25.6	100.0
Lee	19	3.4	660	269	657,444	13,333	10.7	96	55,106	1,118	36.2	88.9
Lenoir	19	3.3	666	337	699,789	11,893	13.0	91	56,736	964	10.2	90.8
Lincoln	25	3.6	716	239	556,311	8,398	14.1	87	41,572	628	55.2	95.1
McDowell	8	1.9	295	148	347,996	8,136	11.3	64	31,940	747	19.7	90.4
Macon	17	5.3	654	254	388,495	12,589	(NA)	94	40,182	1,302	33.8	76.0
Madison	5	2.5	153	55	81,679	4,096	(NA)	23	7,481	375	23.4	58.8
Martin	8	3.2	294	107	189,455	7,530	15.6	44	20,196	803	15.6	80.8
Mecklenburg	229	2.9	83,121	3,150	10,567,506	14,376	11.5	1,869	1,597,023	2,173	33.7	80.2
Mitchell	7	4.4	198	82	165,732	10,455	(NA)	31	15,141	955	69.5	59.9
Montgomery	14	5.1	285	90	181,242	6,702	(NA)	30	9,964	368	(NA)	(NA)
Moore	37	4.5	1,300	375	773,866	9,930	14.1	171	176,513	2,265	32.7	42.3
Nash	34	3.7	1,228	467	1,059,753	11,918	16.4	172	110,052	1,238	–1.4	89.8
New Hanover	67	3.7	3,217	1,047	2,993,200	18,058	(NA)	511	350,447	2,114	24.6	82.3
Northampton	5	2.3	89	62	79,847	3,651	(NA)	18	4,464	204	(NA)	(NA)
Onslow	24	1.6	807	572	1,441,454	9,622	18.4	250	170,477	1,138	33.3	87.3
Orange	31	2.6	1,646	416	1,109,412	9,475	(NA)	263	181,566	1,551	17.8	77.9
Pamlico	3	2.4	112	46	56,512	4,389	(NA)	21	16,731	1,299	23.3	(NA)
Pasquotank	13	3.4	672	197	526,815	14,795	15.1	67	41,868	1,176	32.0	(NA)
Pender	9	1.9	325	136	172,901	4,033	2.4	58	19,214	448	26.3	86.9
Perquimans	3	2.5	84	35	49,139	4,228	(NA)	12	(D)	(NA)	(NA)	(NA)
Person	8	2.1	397	160	305,362	8,342	(NA)	42	25,319	692	21.9	86.8
Pitt	42	2.9	1,397	656	1,688,455	12,326	(NA)	263	191,984	1,401	25.1	88.8
Polk	10	5.2	326	68	77,584	4,124	(NA)	41	12,109	644	11.1	83.4
Randolph	43	3.1	1,451	452	993,158	7,431	16.4	164	92,207	690	21.5	92.1
Richmond	15	3.2	398	231	420,478	8,972	10.5	77	34,908	745	22.2	85.9
Robeson	32	2.5	823	434	989,527	7,932	12.3	163	103,786	832	21.7	83.7
Rockingham	30	3.2	1,038	371	748,225	8,077	11.8	127	65,426	706	8.7	93.7
Rowan	36	2.7	1,258	440	949,947	7,110	10.4	193	109,771	822	33.2	89.4
Rutherford	21	3.3	664	263	430,951	6,805	25.1	118	48,322	763	29.3	88.0
Sampson	15	2.4	410	224	471,092	7,700	16.0	72	33,961	555	27.9	95.0
Scotland	9	2.4	288	156	299,393	8,362	25.5	42	28,060	784	–2.9	83.6
Stanly	19	3.2	750	243	438,970	7,482	13.2	104	43,718	745	28.1	95.0
Stokes	11	2.4	233	114	160,392	3,564	3.7	49	22,978	511	(NA)	87.6
Surry	29	4.0	1,083	379	886,458	12,303	17.7	131	63,920	887	13.0	93.7
Swain	5	3.8	195	113	93,951	7,213	(NA)	99	379,584	29,143	895.7	(NA)
Transylvania	12	4.1	484	111	222,800	7,548	(NA)	65	44,557	1,509	30.9	47.2
Tyrrell	2	4.8	40	19	21,478	5,167	(NA)	5	494	119	(NA)	(NA)
Union	34	2.1	1,343	421	1,079,392	7,740	15.9	166	89,989	645	23.2	(NA)
Vance	9	2.1	362	214	499,992	11,387	14.8	73	46,474	1,058	20.5	89.4
Wake	210	2.8	11,838	2,881	9,703,181	14,321	12.6	1,375	1,117,422	1,649	24.6	82.4
Warren	4	2.0	100	48	50,855	2,551	(NA)	14	3,189	160	(NA)	100.0
Washington	6	4.5	123	66	95,767	7,104	4.0	22	9,273	688	–3.3	(NA)
Watauga	20	4.7	683	353	631,298	14,703	14.4	162	101,381	2,361	11.1	71.9
Wayne	32	2.8	1,005	519	1,024,042	9,049	23.2	170	103,483	914	22.6	90.1
Wilkes	20	3.0	690	248	511,313	7,653	17.4	90	47,998	718	11.8	88.9
Wilson	23	3.0	813	383	779,219	10,393	15.3	130	90,512	1,207	6.0	87.5
Yadkin	11	2.9	387	136	193,032	5,175	(NA)	60	29,155	782	11.2	80.5
Yancey	5	2.7	236	65	119,911	6,682	6.9	22	8,293	462	12.6	(NA)
NORTH DAKOTA	422	6.6	12,192	3,433	7,723,945	12,187	14.6	1,765	854,656	1,348	24.8	69.9
Adams	3	12.3	54	21	33,213	13,222	(NA)	5	(D)	(NA)	(NA)	(NA)
Barnes	7	6.3	223	63	104,911	9,323	(NA)	39	9,889	879	22.3	81.7
Benson	5	7.1	32	11	10,167	1,482	–	17	2,502	365	(NA)	(NA)
Billings	1	12.3	5	8	1,443	1,651	–	12	7,883	9,019	18.0	(NA)
Bottineau	9	13.4	157	51	57,661	8,369	(NA)	30	5,011	727	4.9	70.7

See footnotes at end of table.

Table B-11. Counties — **Banking, Retail Trade, and Accommodation and Food Services**—Con.

[Includes United States, states, and 3,141 counties/county equivalents defined as of February 22, 2005. For more information on these areas, see Appendix C, Geographic Information]

County	Banking,[1] 2005 Offices Number	Banking,[1] 2005 Offices Rate per 10,000 people	Banking,[1] 2005 Total deposits (mil. dol.)	Retail trade[2] (NAICS 44–45), 2002 Estab-lishments	Retail trade[2] Sales Total ($1,000)	Retail trade[2] Sales Per capita[3] (dol.)	Retail trade[2] Sales General merchandise stores,[4] percent of total	Accommodation and food services[2] (NAICS 72), 2002 Estab-lishments	Accommodation Sales Total ($1,000)	Accommodation Sales Per capita[3] (dol.)	Percent change, 1997–2002	Food services,[5] percent of total
NORTH DAKOTA—Con.												
Bowman	6	19.7	111	23	42,137	13,637	(NA)	19	3,834	1,241	18.9	77.8
Burke	4	19.7	49	12	9,978	4,711	(NA)	12	(D)	(NA)	(NA)	(NA)
Burleigh	30	4.1	1,284	365	997,713	14,061	20.4	149	122,253	1,723	26.4	75.1
Cass	65	5.0	2,745	604	2,035,395	16,254	(NA)	303	224,201	1,790	15.0	(NA)
Cavalier	5	11.5	167	34	59,574	13,002	(NA)	21	2,511	548	(NA)	(NA)
Dickey	4	7.3	91	43	51,334	9,231	(NA)	19	3,511	631	8.8	82.0
Divide	4	18.6	74	14	12,365	5,623	–	8	(D)	(NA)	(NA)	(NA)
Dunn	3	8.7	42	13	27,997	7,909	–	10	(D)	(NA)	(NA)	(NA)
Eddy	1	3.8	20	14	22,186	8,433	–	7	(D)	(NA)	(NA)	(NA)
Emmons	4	10.4	109	26	29,855	7,300	–	18	2,608	638	(NA)	(NA)
Foster	4	11.2	96	36	58,326	16,306	(NA)	11	3,297	922	(NA)	(NA)
Golden Valley	3	17.3	48	16	29,917	16,339	–	6	(D)	(NA)	(NA)	(NA)
Grand Forks	29	4.4	1,001	343	1,080,101	16,649	(NA)	176	102,540	1,581	9.3	81.7
Grant	3	11.5	55	16	12,055	4,485	–	7	1,235	459	19.7	(NA)
Griggs	8	32.0	64	14	6,859	2,637	–	11	1,589	611	-7.4	(NA)
Hettinger	3	12.1	60	15	21,656	8,352	–	9	(D)	(NA)	(NA)	(NA)
Kidder	2	8.1	66	10	14,595	5,629	–	10	(D)	(NA)	(NA)	(NA)
LaMoure	5	11.4	76	24	30,850	6,749	–	16	2,372	519	(NA)	(NA)
Logan	3	14.6	53	10	14,403	6,568	–	9	1,010	461	8.5	100.0
McHenry	6	10.9	75	20	18,229	3,183	(NA)	7	870	152	(NA)	100.0
McIntosh	4	13.3	87	28	48,757	15,090	–	15	2,033	629	38.7	66.9
McKenzie	4	7.2	110	22	20,351	3,587	–	14	1,860	328	-17.7	(NA)
McLean	9	10.5	147	41	33,197	3,682	–	29	4,262	473	1.8	88.8
Mercer	7	8.4	121	41	58,572	6,870	(NA)	31	6,707	787	5.8	74.6
Morton	12	4.7	367	102	272,442	10,798	–	43	19,105	757	21.5	76.4
Mountrail	6	9.2	133	43	49,828	7,665	(NA)	27	5,170	795	26.9	81.1
Nelson	6	17.5	123	28	20,560	5,939	–	12	(D)	(NA)	(NA)	(NA)
Oliver	1	5.5	20	3	5,892	3,018	–	3	(D)	(NA)	(NA)	(NA)
Pembina	11	13.7	249	59	91,280	11,029	(NA)	29	5,347	646	-2.9	81.6
Pierce	3	7.0	92	28	60,711	13,387	(NA)	15	3,476	766	8.8	(NA)
Ramsey	10	8.7	310	90	194,549	16,549	18.8	41	17,316	1,473	13.9	75.9
Ransom	7	12.0	136	41	52,133	8,921	5.6	19	3,778	646	-9.2	(NA)
Renville	4	16.5	35	12	16,801	6,635	–	13	968	382	(NA)	(NA)
Richland	12	6.9	271	83	142,529	8,167	(NA)	47	47,576	2,726	319.6	(NA)
Rolette	5	3.6	117	48	73,198	5,317	(NA)	25	21,223	1,542	482.1	(NA)
Sargent	4	9.6	79	23	17,782	4,149	–	19	1,796	419	(NA)	(NA)
Sheridan	3	21.0	25	11	4,933	3,134	–	6	(D)	(NA)	(NA)	(NA)
Sioux	–	–	–	8	5,554	1,352	–	4	(D)	(NA)	(NA)	(NA)
Slope	–	–	–	–	–	–	–	2	(D)	(NA)	(NA)	(NA)
Stark	15	6.8	431	167	288,585	13,008	19.2	70	30,851	1,391	15.9	(NA)
Steele	3	14.9	58	10	18,210	8,606	–	7	855	404	7.7	100.0
Stutsman	8	3.8	368	123	223,571	10,455	18.2	60	22,038	1,031	-0.4	80.8
Towner	5	19.7	62	18	9,966	3,672	–	9	(D)	(NA)	(NA)	(NA)
Traill	10	12.0	182	49	47,821	5,750	(NA)	33	6,601	794	-4.9	94.5
Walsh	14	12.1	311	80	82,300	6,926	4.9	42	8,070	679	9.3	90.6
Ward	23	4.1	1,014	302	817,500	14,396	(NA)	139	72,768	1,281	0.9	(NA)
Wells	8	17.5	147	38	46,886	9,744	(NA)	22	3,126	650	8.4	87.3
Williams	11	5.7	436	129	237,117	12,155	(NA)	58	22,540	1,155	8.5	74.8
OHIO	3,994	3.5	201,186	42,280	119,778,409	10,497	15.0	22,663	14,875,890	1,304	19.9	87.0
Adams	12	4.2	281	97	172,484	6,213	(NA)	42	17,407	627	25.5	91.0
Allen	37	3.5	1,685	512	1,340,953	12,402	27.1	228	146,943	1,359	15.3	92.1
Ashland	21	3.9	583	178	358,141	6,734	(NA)	105	48,484	912	19.2	84.7
Ashtabula	35	3.4	1,067	436	863,599	8,383	14.1	228	94,684	919	12.9	86.3
Athens	28	4.5	466	220	420,356	6,679	16.7	143	68,438	1,087	19.1	83.6
Auglaize	23	4.9	585	193	388,351	8,316	9.0	91	40,150	860	5.9	91.7
Belmont	40	5.8	1,088	352	888,491	12,744	23.7	145	90,058	1,292	33.2	88.2
Brown	16	3.6	401	110	196,981	4,535	5.7	70	24,068	554	53.9	94.7
Butler	107	3.1	3,411	935	2,951,701	8,690	15.8	560	382,435	1,126	33.6	88.6
Carroll	9	3.1	194	80	126,082	4,303	8.8	45	13,868	473	32.4	92.7
Champaign	15	3.8	641	130	280,506	7,136	(NA)	50	20,704	527	3.4	96.3
Clark	39	2.7	1,464	508	1,327,978	9,233	16.2	251	153,281	1,066	15.4	90.4
Clermont	56	2.9	1,431	595	2,177,528	11,879	23.3	234	184,422	1,006	37.8	89.8
Clinton	16	3.8	505	146	349,319	8,441	(NA)	80	(D)	(NA)	(NA)	(NA)
Columbiana	49	4.4	2,021	423	982,583	8,804	13.8	190	76,229	683	8.8	93.6
Coshocton	12	3.2	397	129	220,782	5,969	(NA)	49	20,209	546	5.5	88.8
Crawford	23	5.0	676	162	299,485	6,457	16.2	93	32,316	697	5.8	91.9
Cuyahoga	464	3.5	53,971	5,143	15,483,267	11,279	9.6	3,005	2,132,004	1,553	15.5	83.1
Darke	27	5.1	867	203	431,859	8,154	(NA)	84	34,933	660	7.9	91.9
Defiance	17	4.3	773	174	472,974	12,045	22.6	80	36,757	936	10.2	93.2

See footnotes at end of table.

[Includes United States, states, and 3,141 counties/county equivalents defined as of February 22, 2005. For more information on these areas, see Appendix C, Geographic Information]

County	Banking,[1] 2005 Offices Number	Rate per 10,000 people	Total deposits (mil. dol.)	Retail trade[2] (NAICS 44–45), 2002 Estab-lishments	Sales Total ($1,000)	Per capita[3] (dol.)	General merchan-dise stores,[4] percent of total	Accommodation and food services[2] (NAICS 72), 2002 Estab-lishments	Sales Total ($1,000)	Per capita[3] (dol.)	Percent change, 1997–2002	Food services,[5] percent of total
OHIO—Con.												
Delaware	54	3.6	1,375	436	1,545,041	12,119	26.9	251	204,957	1,608	158.6	94.3
Erie	26	3.3	863	350	834,234	10,569	21.0	267	181,071	2,294	7.9	58.5
Fairfield	38	2.7	1,365	429	1,109,190	8,578	20.8	185	139,735	1,081	30.8	93.5
Fayette	8	2.8	331	228	466,004	16,532	(NA)	59	33,437	1,186	3.3	93.5
Franklin	315	2.9	22,955	4,017	14,864,623	13,736	14.2	2,419	2,121,534	1,960	27.0	82.3
Fulton	22	5.1	687	172	352,576	8,334	(NA)	77	30,139	712	8.2	87.9
Gallia	11	3.5	487	162	326,463	10,433	(NA)	57	33,852	1,082	9.7	(NA)
Geauga	40	4.2	1,561	294	603,414	6,511	(NA)	142	67,139	724	14.6	93.1
Greene	40	2.6	1,184	564	1,841,722	12,294	24.8	258	204,562	1,365	30.0	87.7
Guernsey	13	3.2	485	167	368,546	8,957	28.9	92	56,796	1,380	15.2	75.4
Hamilton	328	4.1	24,011	3,454	10,618,141	12,788	12.3	1,921	1,521,668	1,833	11.4	86.4
Hancock	28	3.8	828	312	880,998	12,122	25.3	154	108,183	1,489	23.6	86.1
Hardin	13	4.1	347	104	172,508	5,430	12.1	45	19,708	620	14.9	97.6
Harrison	7	4.4	133	51	55,649	3,502	6.1	30	5,594	352	-2.3	82.9
Henry	19	6.5	506	104	224,086	7,617	(NA)	55	14,996	510	(NA)	(NA)
Highland	20	4.7	798	157	303,772	7,267	19.7	60	26,742	640	17.0	95.6
Hocking	9	3.1	272	81	192,818	6,749	(NA)	52	25,675	899	25.7	74.4
Holmes	21	5.1	503	156	350,889	8,689	(NA)	59	34,521	855	32.8	69.8
Huron	28	4.6	698	230	552,087	9,207	11.0	108	54,079	902	24.0	91.4
Jackson	16	4.8	508	136	279,679	8,477	(NA)	67	29,946	908	38.1	(NA)
Jefferson	34	4.8	958	291	615,098	8,518	17.9	154	54,346	753	11.9	(NA)
Knox	19	3.3	582	201	416,930	7,406	13.6	93	45,690	812	23.9	91.0
Lake	85	3.7	3,511	939	3,173,982	13,784	14.0	496	312,372	1,357	21.4	87.4
Lawrence	21	3.3	478	189	462,818	7,453	(NA)	66	34,811	561	8.4	90.7
Licking	42	2.7	1,663	487	1,507,610	10,136	13.0	249	160,157	1,077	28.8	88.3
Logan	21	4.5	613	183	359,294	7,757	17.2	95	40,893	883	10.6	91.6
Lorain	90	3.0	3,216	935	2,759,916	9,578	15.6	517	259,087	899	20.0	94.4
Lucas	128	2.9	5,885	1,746	5,283,306	11,638	17.9	995	695,527	1,532	15.5	89.7
Madison	12	2.9	366	113	466,500	11,546	(NA)	61	46,182	1,143	16.7	84.8
Mahoning	82	3.2	3,490	1,087	2,517,750	9,960	15.8	505	294,133	1,164	15.0	90.7
Marion	29	4.4	732	242	654,812	9,883	23.6	121	64,296	970	11.4	94.5
Medina	60	3.6	2,215	524	1,694,188	10,693	(NA)	252	134,609	850	14.4	93.1
Meigs	10	4.3	232	88	105,843	4,566	4.9	26	10,473	452	3.7	(NA)
Mercer	24	5.8	742	196	349,982	8,549	(NA)	85	35,663	871	29.7	95.0
Miami	40	3.9	1,122	371	1,033,470	10,372	(NA)	174	104,499	1,049	14.3	89.5
Monroe	5	3.4	124	51	56,448	3,766	10.5	19	4,289	286	(NA)	(NA)
Montgomery	162	3.0	7,099	1,916	6,095,475	11,020	15.8	1,090	838,967	1,517	16.9	89.8
Morgan	6	4.0	143	34	48,446	3,265	(NA)	19	4,652	314	10.8	(NA)
Morrow	7	2.0	163	66	150,676	4,570	3.5	34	11,330	344	11.1	90.4
Muskingum	32	3.7	1,257	411	922,196	10,818	15.4	182	107,177	1,257	17.0	90.8
Noble	3	2.1	133	41	79,733	5,695	2.4	17	5,201	372	-15.3	(NA)
Ottawa	23	5.5	613	187	410,654	10,008	(NA)	155	78,951	1,924	26.1	80.2
Paulding	7	3.6	187	60	97,333	4,888	(NA)	29	7,418	373	-26.9	100.0
Perry	12	3.4	274	95	127,575	3,689	3.3	37	12,875	372	55.7	100.0
Pickaway	18	3.4	502	147	310,387	5,819	(NA)	61	32,157	603	1.5	94.5
Pike	10	3.6	203	100	184,960	6,600	(NA)	51	28,166	1,005	33.2	83.4
Portage	47	3.0	1,340	465	1,328,797	8,663	8.2	286	146,703	956	17.8	82.3
Preble	20	4.7	404	107	277,851	6,530	(NA)	67	32,068	754	45.1	85.8
Putnam	16	4.6	589	109	221,170	6,376	(NA)	56	20,611	594	(NA)	(NA)
Richland	47	3.7	1,487	527	1,483,590	11,557	23.6	270	152,542	1,188	8.9	91.7
Ross	21	2.8	673	268	669,423	9,000	22.1	119	77,643	1,044	26.7	90.4
Sandusky	26	4.2	667	224	546,802	8,838	17.2	138	68,180	1,102	36.4	89.9
Scioto	20	2.6	704	309	624,197	7,993	18.1	150	77,808	996	18.9	91.6
Seneca	23	4.0	878	214	450,968	7,776	10.1	115	45,223	780	33.4	87.7
Shelby	26	5.3	681	158	374,881	7,747	(NA)	80	51,519	1,065	5.9	81.6
Stark	118	3.1	4,807	1,511	4,144,570	10,920	15.9	776	450,310	1,186	15.5	94.6
Summit	181	3.3	8,472	2,026	6,144,572	11,251	12.9	1,138	743,132	1,361	21.4	88.6
Trumbull	70	3.2	2,781	835	2,011,435	9,015	17.1	437	231,323	1,037	13.7	93.7
Tuscarawas	38	4.1	1,124	444	937,745	10,234	16.1	220	103,000	1,124	13.6	85.4
Union	11	2.4	373	117	328,701	7,643	13.2	63	36,238	843	57.1	92.9
Van Wert	9	3.1	388	114	230,908	7,868	14.6	56	23,235	792	5.9	92.8
Vinton	3	2.2	160	26	31,128	2,374	7.2	17	(D)	(NA)	(NA)	(NA)
Warren	67	3.4	1,716	476	1,209,967	6,912	15.4	266	211,368	1,208	36.7	83.1
Washington	34	5.5	995	259	557,611	8,916	13.0	114	68,674	1,098	5.0	84.3
Wayne	45	4.0	1,453	408	1,026,225	9,093	13.1	174	97,604	865	23.6	95.5
Williams	26	6.7	674	149	286,090	7,335	17.5	84	32,556	835	7.5	85.7
Wood	47	3.8	1,456	423	1,198,621	9,824	18.4	265	177,652	1,456	32.2	84.9
Wyandot	15	6.6	461	81	131,915	5,791	6.9	58	20,606	905	26.6	(NA)

See footnotes at end of table.

[Includes United States, states, and 3,141 counties/county equivalents defined as of February 22, 2005. For more information on these areas, see Appendix C, Geographic Information]

County	Banking,[1] 2005 Offices		Banking Total deposits (mil. dol.)	Retail trade[2] (NAICS 44–45), 2002 Estab-lishments	Retail Sales Total ($1,000)	Retail Sales Per capita[3] (dol.)	General merchandise stores,[4] percent of total	Accommodation and food services[2] (NAICS 72), 2002 Estab-lishments	Accom. Sales Total ($1,000)	Accom. Sales Per capita[3] (dol.)	Percent change, 1997–2002	Food services,[5] percent of total
	Number	Rate per 10,000 people										
OKLAHOMA	1,280	3.6	48,334	13,922	32,112,960	9,206	19.5	6,506	3,901,754	1,119	23.8	86.7
Adair.	6	2.7	141	60	86,973	4,073	(NA)	16	6,375	299	(NA)	(NA)
Alfalfa	7	12.2	104	25	29,207	4,905	(NA)	6	811	136	(NA)	(NA)
Atoka.	3	2.1	138	45	96,053	6,859	(NA)	20	7,525	537	(NA)	84.5
Beaver.	4	7.4	119	21	13,028	2,342	(NA)	7	1,270	228	(NA)	(NA)
Beckham	12	6.4	497	137	281,861	14,118	16.9	61	25,946	1,300	31.5	68.8
Blaine	8	6.2	182	48	45,833	3,924	(NA)	26	5,017	430	-0.3	92.1
Bryan	11	2.9	561	118	282,440	7,642	(NA)	50	27,441	742	17.0	85.5
Caddo	18	6.0	381	133	171,254	5,707	(NA)	42	10,519	351	30.8	95.4
Canadian	30	3.0	831	224	688,568	7,559	(NA)	131	71,149	781	44.0	91.2
Carter	23	4.9	637	262	442,999	9,608	(NA)	91	57,783	1,253	30.4	(NA)
Cherokee	14	3.1	322	133	282,171	6,500	(NA)	82	32,425	747	22.0	90.0
Choctaw.	4	2.6	171	59	104,257	6,779	(NA)	23	8,671	564	(NA)	92.4
Cimarron	3	10.6	45	20	24,457	8,101	(NA)	9	2,395	793	35.0	(NA)
Cleveland.	51	2.3	1,682	685	1,802,222	8,377	6.2	350	255,236	1,186	35.7	88.8
Coal	1	1.7	46	26	24,936	4,167	(NA)	4	(D)	(NA)	(NA)	(NA)
Comanche	41	3.6	893	422	900,736	8,059	28.0	190	121,504	1,087	25.4	91.0
Cotton	3	4.6	57	18	26,648	4,121	(NA)	7	3,347	518	(NA)	100.0
Craig.	7	4.6	289	65	122,000	8,263	(NA)	31	11,723	794	-16.9	83.5
Creek	22	3.2	629	189	415,591	6,050	(NA)	80	37,309	543	19.5	94.8
Custer	19	7.5	471	163	298,650	11,900	17.5	63	29,167	1,162	5.3	81.1
Delaware	13	3.3	357	140	204,472	5,382	(NA)	64	25,266	665	4.8	79.9
Dewey.	6	13.1	126	37	24,271	5,279	(NA)	5	680	148	(NA)	100.0
Ellis.	3	7.6	59	24	23,520	5,868	(NA)	4	935	233	(NA)	100.0
Garfield	25	4.4	848	291	578,658	10,113	20.0	112	58,915	1,030	13.6	89.8
Garvin	17	6.2	343	116	203,577	7,470	(NA)	37	14,964	549	12.4	92.0
Grady	15	3.0	473	173	295,607	6,312	(NA)	57	34,376	734	40.4	(NA)
Grant.	6	12.6	132	15	26,988	5,362	—	6	(D)	(NA)	(NA)	(NA)
Greer.	6	10.2	96	17	20,749	3,491	(NA)	5	1,168	197	-13.9	100.0
Harmon	3	9.9	72	16	14,407	4,621	(NA)	4	618	198	(NA)	(NA)
Harper	2	6.0	65	20	12,825	3,712	(NA)	6	560	162	-25.2	(NA)
Haskell	3	2.5	98	36	86,148	7,309	18.4	15	3,972	337	(NA)	(NA)
Hughes	4	2.9	117	57	65,608	4,676	(NA)	19	5,846	417	(NA)	95.2
Jackson	13	4.9	322	128	284,704	10,395	(NA)	62	27,399	1,000	13.1	90.9
Jefferson	5	7.7	103	30	23,231	3,555	5.6	8	(D)	(NA)	(NA)	(NA)
Johnston	3	2.9	75	38	33,244	3,185	(NA)	11	2,893	277	2.2	100.0
Kay.	25	5.4	666	242	474,370	9,954	(NA)	99	51,863	1,088	28.6	90.1
Kingfisher.	11	7.7	276	70	121,922	8,751	(NA)	25	8,118	583	(NA)	(NA)
Kiowa	8	8.1	134	42	49,044	4,913	(NA)	19	6,152	616	(NA)	(NA)
Latimer	4	3.8	121	25	28,135	2,664	(NA)	8	(D)	(NA)	(NA)	(NA)
Le Flore	14	2.8	390	164	324,725	6,680	25.1	50	19,044	392	4.6	92.2
Lincoln.	14	4.3	347	95	149,365	4,629	(NA)	40	16,986	526	37.3	(NA)
Logan	12	3.3	233	96	189,242	5,425	(NA)	43	17,513	502	(NA)	(NA)
Love	4	4.4	57	31	30,384	3,422	(NA)	14	5,205	586	-1.3	(NA)
McClain	12	4.0	356	107	262,045	9,338	(NA)	42	21,583	769	(NA)	(NA)
McCurtain.	12	3.5	354	127	186,968	5,475	(NA)	47	17,537	514	17.3	80.0
McIntosh	7	3.5	245	90	184,519	9,356	10.6	46	13,932	706	10.7	82.9
Major.	5	6.8	120	34	83,713	11,103	(NA)	12	2,754	365	(NA)	100.0
Marshall.	5	3.5	138	56	84,293	6,199	(NA)	29	10,391	764	41.6	88.6
Mayes	16	4.1	423	145	319,833	8,251	(NA)	64	25,341	654	28.9	96.8
Murray.	7	5.4	164	58	135,550	10,720	(NA)	26	11,435	904	35.9	70.7
Muskogee	26	3.7	898	316	655,782	9,376	17.8	134	70,746	1,012	20.3	93.0
Noble	4	3.6	211	41	69,792	6,174	(NA)	20	8,192	725	13.2	77.1
Nowata	5	4.6	102	28	22,645	2,125	12.1	12	4,195	394	36.2	96.9
Okfuskee	5	4.4	94	36	47,226	4,056	(NA)	15	(D)	(NA)	(NA)	(NA)
Oklahoma	225	3.3	11,810	2,955	8,291,367	12,346	18.0	1,514	1,153,410	1,718	25.6	84.6
Okmulgee	11	2.8	366	135	253,390	6,378	(NA)	62	26,963	679	30.1	90.3
Osage	12	2.6	274	101	101,809	2,253	17.3	43	13,913	308	46.6	(NA)
Ottawa.	16	4.9	310	126	188,202	5,723	(NA)	70	24,760	753	36.8	85.0
Pawnee	6	3.6	148	52	63,610	3,777	(NA)	26	6,782	403	19.7	(NA)
Payne	22	3.2	1,472	306	589,783	8,542	(NA)	147	92,771	1,344	39.4	87.1
Pittsburg	13	2.9	679	190	430,020	9,741	(NA)	83	46,279	1,048	24.1	80.5
Pontotoc	15	4.2	584	169	312,670	8,968	(NA)	56	31,902	915	8.9	92.1
Pottawatomie	19	2.8	606	262	489,367	7,327	21.1	122	76,668	1,148	0.5	91.8
Pushmataha	4	3.4	95	53	48,422	4,131	(NA)	14	3,591	306	9.5	(NA)
Roger Mills.	2	6.0	83	17	13,963	4,342	(NA)	7	1,072	333	-18.7	(NA)
Rogers.	18	2.2	621	198	550,483	7,315	(NA)	104	47,754	635	25.7	93.7
Seminole	10	4.0	226	86	120,333	4,896	(NA)	33	13,012	529	11.0	(NA)
Sequoyah.	12	2.9	328	135	283,706	7,153	(NA)	67	26,441	667	10.1	78.3
Stephens	22	5.1	720	217	392,744	9,215	21.4	75	30,423	714	-1.5	90.9
Texas	7	3.5	311	85	128,439	6,408	(NA)	44	18,392	918	9.8	82.4

See footnotes at end of table.

[Includes United States, states, and 3,141 counties/county equivalents defined as of February 22, 2005. For more information on these areas, see Appendix C, Geographic Information]

| County | Banking,[1] 2005 Offices | | | Retail trade[2] (NAICS 44–45), 2002 | | | | Accommodation and food services[2] (NAICS 72), 2002 | | | | |
	Number	Rate per 10,000 people	Total deposits (mil. dol.)	Estab-lishments	Sales Total ($1,000)	Per capita[3] (dol.)	General merchan-dise stores,[4] percent of total	Estab-lishments	Sales Total ($1,000)	Per capita[3] (dol.)	Percent change, 1997–2002	Food services,[5] percent of total
OKLAHOMA—Con.												
Tillman	6	7.0	109	37	29,666	3,324	10.1	14	(D)	(NA)	(NA)	(NA)
Tulsa	200	3.5	10,959	2,458	7,298,312	12,806	(NA)	1,337	962,292	1,688	24.8	84.8
Wagoner	11	1.7	278	109	202,504	3,345	(NA)	48	22,360	369	−3.1	(NA)
Washington	17	3.5	648	213	495,022	10,064	27.5	107	53,186	1,081	3.0	95.9
Washita	10	8.7	245	43	58,597	5,155	(NA)	11	(D)	(NA)	(NA)	(NA)
Woods	6	7.0	258	59	80,243	9,143	(NA)	27	7,677	875	21.3	83.3
Woodward	9	4.7	384	122	232,862	12,588	(NA)	46	22,766	1,231	24.3	84.6
OREGON	1,044	2.9	42,285	14,277	37,896,022	10,756	18.5	8,816	5,527,223	1,569	26.0	75.2
Baker	8	4.9	193	90	115,004	6,955	(NA)	61	20,199	1,222	6.0	60.0
Benton	16	2.0	739	269	538,260	6,811	14.6	182	97,057	1,228	12.9	86.8
Clackamas	102	2.8	3,237	1,120	3,774,377	10,710	15.9	625	409,301	1,161	23.6	84.6
Clatsop	13	3.5	384	292	447,325	12,527	(NA)	212	107,415	3,008	19.7	61.9
Columbia	10	2.1	243	115	244,466	5,378	(NA)	87	29,609	651	22.0	89.5
Coos	20	3.1	699	285	547,393	8,739	21.7	173	74,033	1,182	20.6	78.5
Crook	5	2.3	210	56	80,686	3,991	(NA)	39	15,499	767	22.1	84.3
Curry	8	3.6	288	114	194,960	9,081	(NA)	113	37,062	1,726	21.6	64.2
Deschutes	55	3.9	1,990	763	1,863,448	14,836	22.3	373	266,882	2,125	37.2	62.6
Douglas	30	2.9	1,056	457	811,962	8,022	19.1	262	177,082	1,750	28.2	48.2
Gilliam	2	11.1	29	13	8,048	4,325	–	7	2,011	1,081	18.9	(NA)
Grant	4	5.5	63	42	51,262	6,885	(NA)	25	5,834	784	1.4	72.1
Harney	3	4.3	75	30	53,299	7,279	(NA)	24	6,293	859	21.3	54.5
Hood River	6	2.8	243	141	219,415	10,594	(NA)	74	39,637	1,914	9.6	64.9
Jackson	69	3.5	2,362	898	2,580,478	13,803	17.5	552	298,936	1,599	45.6	80.4
Jefferson	5	2.5	111	62	137,456	7,004	(NA)	42	33,254	1,694	179.8	31.0
Josephine	30	3.7	1,138	328	747,296	9,603	17.9	186	81,307	1,045	21.5	79.4
Klamath	18	2.7	826	258	574,594	8,932	23.2	158	65,712	1,022	−10.1	76.1
Lake	3	4.1	79	35	32,884	4,415	(NA)	35	7,206	968	18.3	78.3
Lane	94	2.8	3,349	1,421	3,720,102	11,376	19.2	781	464,782	1,421	19.7	83.1
Lincoln	23	5.0	685	334	449,781	10,101	20.1	253	160,870	3,613	19.3	50.4
Linn	27	2.5	779	407	903,915	8,599	24.7	183	82,890	789	13.3	90.7
Malheur	12	3.8	294	156	333,712	10,620	(NA)	72	34,572	1,100	3.8	76.6
Marion	82	2.7	2,968	1,087	2,985,346	10,124	(NA)	583	(D)	(NA)	(NA)	(NA)
Morrow	5	4.3	82	21	19,308	1,664	–	22	6,250	539	48.7	56.3
Multnomah	176	2.6	12,780	2,894	8,061,820	11,942	16.2	2,070	1,538,580	2,279	16.9	79.1
Polk	13	1.8	373	140	279,105	4,306	(NA)	96	(D)	(NA)	(NA)	(NA)
Sherman	1	5.7	8	15	18,400	10,285	(NA)	7	3,034	1,696	(NA)	(NA)
Tillamook	9	3.6	264	123	176,327	7,197	(NA)	115	37,042	1,512	4.4	69.1
Umatilla	27	3.7	620	258	603,568	8,379	(NA)	161	126,073	1,750	89.1	49.9
Union	11	4.5	262	122	264,721	10,805	17.9	74	26,082	1,065	10.7	82.0
Wallowa	5	7.1	149	54	73,859	10,409	(NA)	39	7,837	1,104	34.8	55.8
Wasco	9	3.8	353	134	268,357	11,386	22.9	64	37,131	1,575	8.1	75.5
Washington	111	2.2	4,560	1,457	6,047,548	12,809	19.7	899	585,218	1,240	18.0	87.8
Wheeler	1	6.9	10	6	9,012	5,890	–	7	461	301	(NA)	100.0
Yamhill	31	3.4	781	280	658,528	7,494	(NA)	160	72,928	830	25.1	90.0
PENNSYLVANIA	4,643	3.7	225,238	48,041	130,713,197	10,603	12.9	24,778	15,305,402	1,241	25.2	79.8
Adams	31	3.1	1,127	370	609,576	6,448	(NA)	192	110,119	1,165	23.3	63.8
Allegheny	458	3.7	40,321	5,006	14,522,461	11,469	13.6	2,944	2,182,494	1,724	27.5	81.1
Armstrong	31	4.4	1,025	264	509,030	7,086	13.9	125	38,279	533	16.7	94.9
Beaver	54	3.0	2,010	617	1,225,841	6,840	18.7	289	137,194	766	26.6	95.9
Bedford	25	5.0	596	232	476,065	9,541	(NA)	109	51,174	1,026	3.4	80.2
Berks	138	3.5	6,327	1,374	3,846,141	10,072	13.1	688	368,743	966	11.6	89.0
Blair	64	5.0	1,811	611	1,695,016	13,277	20.5	270	154,890	1,213	42.3	87.7
Bradford	30	4.8	769	291	626,266	9,981	14.7	104	38,155	608	8.1	83.8
Bucks	243	3.9	10,994	2,514	8,625,586	14,157	10.3	1,080	713,789	1,172	25.4	87.9
Butler	69	3.8	2,583	715	1,950,127	10,943	18.7	327	194,000	1,089	23.9	86.1
Cambria	80	5.4	2,332	613	1,403,524	9,332	19.1	295	129,340	860	16.2	90.3
Cameron	2	3.5	64	24	34,722	5,936	(NA)	15	2,680	458	4.0	100.0
Carbon	27	4.4	848	217	394,557	6,603	(NA)	108	71,071	1,189	70.2	53.4
Centre	65	4.6	1,845	576	1,403,041	10,123	15.9	295	209,187	1,509	35.1	74.4
Chester	192	4.1	7,817	1,530	8,407,068	18,681	5.1	767	556,299	1,236	52.2	84.3
Clarion	21	5.2	641	221	395,993	9,604	23.3	99	41,394	1,004	7.0	79.7
Clearfield	32	3.9	1,186	373	847,821	10,169	20.9	158	73,169	878	30.4	83.8
Clinton	12	3.2	315	152	373,966	9,958	23.1	79	30,701	818	7.5	86.4
Columbia	33	5.1	833	273	587,051	9,099	(NA)	135	63,148	979	6.5	91.7
Crawford	29	3.2	983	367	774,782	8,596	14.9	200	83,664	928	24.2	88.6
Cumberland	102	4.6	3,573	930	3,055,748	14,046	(NA)	451	292,709	1,345	24.4	82.4
Dauphin	99	3.9	4,234	1,038	3,184,837	12,603	(NA)	622	515,073	2,038	30.6	60.3
Delaware	171	3.1	8,288	1,955	5,490,387	9,919	10.5	1,008	606,629	1,096	18.0	88.4
Elk	21	6.3	584	148	244,062	7,067	(NA)	79	21,211	614	14.9	84.3
Erie	87	3.1	3,146	1,159	3,076,390	10,895	15.5	612	320,431	1,135	20.8	85.9

See footnotes at end of table.

County and City Data Book: 2007

U.S. Census Bureau

Table B-11. Counties — **Banking, Retail Trade, and Accommodation and Food Services**—Con.

[Includes United States, states, and 3,141 counties/county equivalents defined as of February 22, 2005. For more information on these areas, see Appendix C, Geographic Information]

County	Banking,[1] 2005 Offices Number	Rate per 10,000 people	Total deposits (mil. dol.)	Retail trade[2] (NAICS 44–45), 2002 Estab-lishments	Sales Total ($1,000)	Per capita[3] (dol.)	General merchandise stores,[4] percent of total	Accom. and food services[2] (NAICS 72), 2002 Estab-lishments	Sales Total ($1,000)	Per capita[3] (dol.)	Percent change, 1997–2002	Food services,[5] percent of total
PENNSYLVANIA—Con.												
Fayette	43	2.9	1,933	566	1,252,517	8,534	14.8	278	208,299	1,419	32.4	50.2
Forest	2	3.5	36	27	18,031	3,619	(NA)	25	8,528	1,712	75.1	47.9
Franklin	56	4.1	1,589	519	1,294,089	9,842	14.3	228	121,356	923	14.7	87.1
Fulton	8	5.5	206	52	95,425	6,654	3.6	25	8,605	600	-14.4	92.4
Greene	12	3.0	533	132	299,191	7,390	3.3	65	22,657	560	17.0	91.1
Huntingdon	22	4.8	468	168	271,911	5,933	4.8	75	26,842	586	17.0	69.6
Indiana	36	4.1	1,809	362	934,000	10,484	17.6	163	87,246	979	34.5	91.6
Jefferson	17	3.7	739	191	350,285	7,646	8.7	93	30,945	675	29.6	87.3
Juniata	12	5.1	355	80	178,584	7,796	2.1	30	8,150	356	-4.1	(NA)
Lackawanna	91	4.3	3,935	997	2,445,058	11,584	(NA)	504	275,502	1,305	25.6	87.9
Lancaster	194	4.0	7,677	2,002	5,379,410	11,240	10.6	857	588,172	1,229	16.1	77.6
Lawrence	34	3.7	1,488	360	869,570	9,268	15.8	201	73,093	779	8.6	91.8
Lebanon	48	3.8	1,510	446	1,282,502	10,544	15.2	206	93,903	772	23.5	89.4
Lehigh	108	3.3	5,081	1,278	3,924,642	12,369	11.9	611	409,479	1,290	-0.8	89.3
Luzerne	133	4.3	5,695	1,332	3,478,413	11,051	14.5	729	386,219	1,227	31.9	83.3
Lycoming	51	4.3	1,464	553	1,276,543	10,744	15.7	254	117,981	993	11.2	87.2
McKean	20	4.5	651	197	363,527	7,992	17.1	110	36,173	795	20.7	83.1
Mercer	50	4.2	1,660	615	1,331,428	11,111	16.3	249	139,405	1,163	23.1	89.1
Mifflin	20	4.3	609	188	461,649	9,925	21.8	78	28,282	608	8.8	(NA)
Monroe	52	3.2	1,921	699	1,621,462	10,867	19.2	364	282,490	1,893	16.9	51.9
Montgomery	358	4.6	17,690	3,509	11,883,312	15,545	12.6	1,642	1,274,038	1,667	39.2	76.8
Montour	6	3.3	192	68	157,486	8,659	(NA)	40	22,588	1,242	42.9	69.2
Northampton	115	4.0	4,084	846	2,464,436	9,005	(NA)	542	258,338	944	32.5	88.0
Northumberland	34	3.7	1,198	339	687,272	7,351	10.3	174	47,354	507	8.4	93.1
Perry	21	4.7	508	136	243,722	5,547	(NA)	70	19,479	443	31.5	86.6
Philadelphia	336	2.3	35,524	4,522	9,093,922	6,117	9.1	3,037	2,135,977	1,437	26.3	73.6
Pike	15	2.7	457	114	239,674	4,785	(NA)	97	84,734	1,692	73.0	32.8
Potter	8	4.5	222	79	105,278	5,795	4.7	44	10,070	554	10.8	70.2
Schuylkill	78	5.3	1,801	618	1,251,409	8,408	12.0	260	98,226	660	15.3	91.8
Snyder	19	5.0	487	206	527,924	13,918	28.8	77	47,494	1,252	28.7	91.4
Somerset	35	4.4	1,042	322	614,428	7,715	8.4	172	64,328	808	18.3	80.6
Sullivan	5	7.8	95	31	36,434	5,579	(NA)	18	4,536	695	15.6	(NA)
Susquehanna	17	4.0	517	160	286,334	6,822	4.8	80	24,106	574	8.8	84.6
Tioga	18	4.3	530	190	358,453	8,613	20.2	91	31,935	767	0.3	79.3
Union	18	4.2	555	144	302,743	7,173	(NA)	79	59,219	1,403	27.9	85.6
Venango	19	3.4	620	244	542,766	9,539	20.6	98	32,203	566	2.3	(NA)
Warren	13	3.1	571	168	680,521	15,754	4.2	94	27,006	625	-3.2	86.7
Washington	74	3.6	3,180	783	1,967,231	9,651	15.3	377	176,806	867	32.9	88.2
Wayne	26	5.2	1,070	269	571,226	11,784	17.2	169	141,993	2,929	33.0	22.4
Westmoreland	139	3.8	5,506	1,426	3,711,256	10,072	15.3	699	359,051	974	11.9	89.9
Wyoming	14	5.0	307	120	250,627	8,950	(NA)	60	17,439	623	-8.4	77.7
York	150	3.7	5,468	1,413	3,848,448	9,873	18.2	662	409,612	1,051	28.5	88.4
RHODE ISLAND	240	2.2	21,826	4,134	10,342,351	9,676	9.4	2,701	1,731,799	1,620	41.9	83.1
Bristol	14	2.7	698	154	264,375	5,070	2.7	116	60,046	1,151	54.2	97.3
Kent	38	2.2	4,338	741	2,727,738	16,040	16.7	445	333,560	1,961	50.7	81.7
Newport	22	2.6	1,186	480	905,153	10,564	6.2	320	275,592	3,216	33.1	62.2
Providence	134	2.1	13,230	2,203	4,984,615	7,860	6.7	1,389	832,499	1,313	43.2	89.7
Washington	32	2.5	2,374	556	1,460,470	11,517	8.4	431	230,102	1,815	33.7	82.5
SOUTH CAROLINA	1,289	3.0	53,844	18,416	40,629,089	9,895	15.4	8,135	6,104,316	1,487	26.2	74.3
Abbeville	10	3.8	217	65	79,390	3,009	(NA)	29	10,235	388	23.6	86.9
Aiken	33	2.2	1,421	527	1,137,091	7,824	18.2	203	121,484	836	22.2	(NA)
Allendale	7	6.4	65	39	31,244	2,820	(NA)	8	1,777	160	3.4	(NA)
Anderson	59	3.4	2,010	734	1,657,795	9,736	17.0	312	175,261	1,029	21.2	92.9
Bamberg	7	4.4	204	71	92,401	5,662	5.0	19	7,004	429	7.9	95.0
Barnwell	6	2.6	229	93	146,337	6,261	(NA)	38	10,655	456	0.1	(NA)
Beaufort	62	4.5	2,782	817	1,814,560	13,972	(NA)	374	469,756	3,617	39.1	54.1
Berkeley	23	1.5	536	352	882,440	6,059	(NA)	164	96,635	664	51.5	88.8
Calhoun	3	2.0	85	33	38,772	2,547	(NA)	9	2,160	142	(NA)	(NA)
Charleston	109	3.3	5,822	1,915	4,638,504	14,639	13.1	914	1,024,476	3,233	44.2	62.9
Cherokee	13	2.4	429	246	472,082	8,815	16.3	95	48,110	898	18.5	90.4
Chester	7	2.1	184	108	174,409	5,114	(NA)	43	20,316	596	5.9	80.4
Chesterfield	13	3.0	365	181	244,637	5,662	13.1	72	25,475	590	9.3	90.8
Clarendon	6	1.8	231	125	208,613	6,335	10.9	50	19,923	605	23.3	70.4
Colleton	11	2.8	339	184	309,122	7,939	14.2	57	31,424	807	19.8	74.9
Darlington	20	3.0	496	280	413,323	6,089	16.7	95	41,766	615	33.1	91.7
Dillon	7	2.3	250	153	260,544	8,381	(NA)	51	25,422	818	-2.2	79.0
Dorchester	29	2.6	801	291	696,055	6,878	(NA)	133	77,147	762	24.9	77.6
Edgefield	7	2.7	141	72	100,897	4,079	3.2	21	6,515	263	8.4	(NA)
Fairfield	7	2.9	167	55	116,561	4,879	(NA)	18	6,161	258	-21.0	(NA)

See footnotes at end of table.

[Includes United States, states, and 3,141 counties/county equivalents defined as of February 22, 2005. For more information on these areas, see Appendix C, Geographic Information]

County	Banking,[1] 2005			Retail trade[2] (NAICS 44–45), 2002				Accommodation and food services[2] (NAICS 72), 2002				
	Offices				Sales					Sales		
	Number	Rate per 10,000 people	Total deposits (mil. dol.)	Estab- lishments	Total ($1,000)	Per capita[3] (dol.)	General merchan- dise stores,[4] percent of total	Estab- lishments	Total ($1,000)	Per capita[3] (dol.)	Percent change, 1997– 2002	Food services,[5] percent of total
SOUTH CAROLINA—Con.												
Florence............	48	3.7	1,847	771	1,773,439	13,937	18.0	248	164,278	1,291	11.7	79.3
Georgetown..........	29	4.8	941	356	559,813	9,638	17.0	160	125,538	2,161	44.4	83.7
Greenville...........	156	3.8	7,734	1,770	4,659,185	11,906	16.8	811	588,727	1,504	16.2	82.4
Greenwood..........	23	3.4	771	317	668,408	9,945	18.2	118	68,258	1,016	5.8	88.1
Hampton............	7	3.3	262	118	141,490	6,643	4.0	34	14,359	674	37.8	73.0
Horry..............	109	4.8	4,752	1,585	3,224,312	15,647	17.3	1,052	1,065,381	5,170	20.8	56.4
Jasper.............	5	2.3	113	92	177,245	8,461	(NA)	51	24,729	1,180	13.7	65.1
Kershaw............	13	2.3	550	209	388,147	7,221	23.0	82	35,951	669	15.9	85.9
Lancaster...........	8	1.3	308	243	417,622	6,711	23.1	77	37,258	599	12.2	93.6
Laurens............	17	2.4	501	188	292,432	4,172	15.0	75	37,433	534	19.5	94.5
Lee...............	4	1.9	101	60	93,303	4,596	(NA)	16	5,979	295	(NA)	(NA)
Lexington...........	57	2.4	2,115	866	2,291,936	10,288	12.0	350	255,838	1,148	25.8	90.9
McCormick..........	3	3.0	76	34	24,689	2,418	(NA)	9	2,393	234	7.9	(NA)
Marion.............	13	3.7	297	170	239,796	6,832	11.6	51	20,186	575	41.7	89.1
Marlboro............	7	2.5	171	112	140,107	4,896	(NA)	31	11,951	418	13.6	88.0
Newberry...........	12	3.2	409	137	256,446	6,974	(NA)	49	20,565	559	23.1	89.7
Oconee............	20	2.9	893	298	590,603	8,691	16.9	118	51,562	759	22.3	91.9
Orangeburg.........	24	2.6	812	444	773,158	8,468	16.0	155	92,752	1,016	28.7	75.1
Pickens............	34	3.0	1,275	344	907,064	8,139	10.8	198	104,757	940	7.0	88.7
Richland............	97	2.9	7,321	1,466	3,823,458	11,663	17.9	716	555,062	1,693	32.6	80.9
Saluda.............	5	2.6	129	51	65,848	3,445	4.6	12	4,499	235	(NA)	100.0
Spartanburg.........	75	2.8	2,824	1,102	2,724,038	10,503	13.7	511	299,561	1,155	22.7	93.1
Sumter............	18	1.7	741	455	853,758	8,114	13.4	132	78,827	749	12.6	89.8
Union..............	9	3.2	321	101	156,402	5,329	(NA)	37	14,044	479	3.8	93.6
Williamsburg.........	12	3.4	235	133	193,052	5,297	4.9	34	9,119	250	–9.3	85.9
York...............	45	2.4	1,567	653	1,678,561	9,648	12.8	303	193,607	1,113	26.7	89.2
SOUTH DAKOTA.......	459	5.9	42,102	4,249	9,601,175	12,626	13.2	2,203	1,226,459	1,613	38.1	64.4
Aurora.............	3	10.3	77	17	25,897	8,881	–	12	1,889	648	41.3	(NA)
Beadle.............	8	5.0	270	104	171,366	10,346	(NA)	53	16,345	987	–4.7	73.7
Bennett............	1	2.8	28	18	18,068	5,108	–	8	1,733	490	30.8	(NA)
Bon Homme.........	5	7.1	102	46	41,843	5,854	–	19	(D)	(NA)	(NA)	(NA)
Brookings..........	14	5.0	715	143	243,443	8,617	(NA)	67	36,430	1,289	35.6	84.3
Brown.............	20	5.8	696	215	539,493	15,460	16.3	90	49,754	1,426	5.0	(NA)
Brule..............	4	7.7	138	45	62,138	11,986	(NA)	24	8,009	1,545	–21.2	61.0
Buffalo.............	–	–	–	2	(D)	(NA)	(NA)	1	(D)	(NA)	(NA)	(NA)
Butte..............	4	4.3	169	50	88,792	9,825	(NA)	27	6,097	675	(NA)	86.2
Campbell...........	2	12.8	39	8	(D)	(NA)	(NA)	10	1,015	592	38.1	(NA)
Charles Mix.........	6	6.5	180	63	63,635	6,907	(NA)	25	20,069	2,178	–48.2	(NA)
Clark..............	5	13.2	82	17	14,752	3,691	(NA)	13	(D)	(NA)	(NA)	(NA)
Clay...............	6	4.6	134	45	(D)	(NA)	(NA)	41	16,784	1,272	8.3	(NA)
Codington..........	20	7.7	540	198	408,268	15,796	(NA)	74	33,376	1,291	0.8	79.5
Corson............	3	6.9	33	9	(D)	(NA)	(NA)	4	290	68	23.4	100.0
Custer.............	2	2.5	63	37	36,979	4,900	(NA)	42	20,329	2,694	37.4	29.2
Davison............	13	6.9	397	148	376,198	20,071	22.4	78	39,077	2,085	17.6	69.0
Day...............	7	12.2	108	36	43,104	7,113	(NA)	18	3,892	642	43.5	74.2
Deuel..............	4	9.3	66	26	22,484	5,061	–	13	(D)	(NA)	(NA)	(NA)
Dewey.............	3	4.9	39	21	16,858	2,787	(NA)	6	(D)	(NA)	(NA)	(NA)
Douglas............	3	9.1	44	19	12,284	3,671	–	8	(D)	(NA)	(NA)	(NA)
Edmunds...........	5	12.2	99	26	38,960	9,141	(NA)	8	1,290	303	–7.2	(NA)
Fall River..........	6	8.2	97	45	36,541	4,987	(NA)	34	9,241	1,261	–25.4	69.4
Faulk..............	2	8.4	38	13	12,723	5,071	–	10	(D)	(NA)	(NA)	(NA)
Grant..............	5	6.8	164	51	78,945	10,321	(NA)	19	6,201	811	8.5	75.2
Gregory............	4	9.3	121	46	33,160	7,340	–	15	2,013	446	–12.6	90.4
Haakon............	2	10.5	94	17	23,707	11,436	(NA)	9	967	466	–23.9	(NA)
Hamlin.............	7	12.3	89	25	35,330	6,315	–	10	824	147	(NA)	100.0
Hand..............	2	6.0	103	26	31,262	8,732	(NA)	13	2,581	721	108.6	(NA)
Hanson............	3	8.0	54	6	5,879	1,743	–	3	633	188	18.1	100.0
Harding............	1	8.2	24	3	(D)	(NA)	(NA)	6	(D)	(NA)	(NA)	(NA)
Hughes............	12	7.1	447	120	231,138	13,909	(NA)	56	28,969	1,743	12.7	(NA)
Hutchinson..........	8	10.6	257	51	56,836	7,256	–	17	3,691	471	(NA)	68.4
Hyde..............	2	12.4	31	9	34,184	21,635	–	4	(D)	(NA)	(NA)	(NA)
Jackson............	1	3.5	22	20	21,525	7,531	–	12	2,294	803	–39.5	51.9
Jerauld............	2	9.4	41	15	34,689	15,556	(NA)	5	(D)	(NA)	(NA)	(NA)
Jones..............	3	29.0	29	12	21,997	19,693	–	11	3,152	2,822	30.2	40.1
Kingsbury..........	7	12.7	128	38	31,245	5,562	–	26	4,054	722	21.5	(NA)
Lake..............	5	4.5	175	58	110,699	9,985	(NA)	31	9,300	839	14.4	93.2
Lawrence...........	11	4.9	335	139	248,009	11,452	(NA)	113	142,070	6,560	139.8	22.3
Lincoln............	13	3.9	213	82	271,790	9,793	(NA)	37	11,384	410	45.4	(NA)
Lyman.............	4	10.2	54	23	38,097	9,699	(NA)	14	10,872	2,768	245.1	(NA)
McCook............	5	8.4	78	30	57,631	9,882	–	18	2,891	496	7.8	(NA)
McPherson.........	2	7.6	45	18	10,869	3,904	–	8	1,736	624	(NA)	(NA)
Marshall...........	5	11.3	87	23	24,720	5,676	–	16	2,895	665	49.9	81.5

See footnotes at end of table.

Table B-11. Counties — **Banking, Retail Trade, and Accommodation and Food Services**—Con.

[Includes United States, states, and 3,141 counties/county equivalents defined as of February 22, 2005. For more information on these areas, see Appendix C, Geographic Information]

County	Banking,[1] 2005 Offices Number	Banking,[1] 2005 Offices Rate per 10,000 people	Banking,[1] 2005 Total deposits (mil. dol.)	Retail trade[2] (NAICS 44–45), 2002 Establishments	Retail trade Sales Total ($1,000)	Retail trade Sales Per capita[3] (dol.)	General merchandise stores,[4] percent of total	Accommodation and food services[2] (NAICS 72), 2002 Establishments	Accommodation Sales Total ($1,000)	Accommodation Sales Per capita[3] (dol.)	Percent change, 1997–2002	Food services,[5] percent of total
SOUTH DAKOTA—Con.												
Meade	6	2.4	242	94	142,232	5,801	(NA)	57	18,499	755	18.1	64.0
Mellette	1	4.8	12	7	(D)	(NA)	(NA)	3	(D)	(NA)	(NA)	(NA)
Miner	3	11.6	36	12	9,757	3,477	–	7	940	335	−6.9	100.0
Minnehaha	95	5.9	31,746	801	2,361,143	15,465	(NA)	400	338,640	2,218	51.6	81.8
Moody	3	4.5	85	19	30,693	4,685	–	15	(D)	(NA)	(NA)	(NA)
Pennington	32	3.4	1,296	596	1,546,123	17,014	(NA)	316	216,169	2,379	32.1	64.2
Perkins	3	9.9	89	21	17,609	5,378	(NA)	9	1,450	443	−6.9	(NA)
Potter	3	12.8	98	26	20,293	8,040	(NA)	13	3,722	1,475	17.7	72.8
Roberts	7	7.0	195	50	65,098	6,573	(NA)	24	4,263	430	−8.2	(NA)
Sanborn	3	11.8	33	11	(D)	(NA)	(NA)	7	569	221	(NA)	100.0
Shannon	–	–	–	13	30,594	2,347	–	7	1,811	139	53.1	(NA)
Spink	9	13.0	141	40	48,070	6,769	(NA)	21	5,138	724	21.5	91.1
Stanley	1	3.5	21	17	23,140	8,445	–	7	1,904	695	30.4	(NA)
Sully	2	14.0	43	15	30,583	20,416	–	6	1,554	1,037	−16.1	35.4
Todd	1	1.0	55	19	25,598	2,722	(NA)	7	(D)	(NA)	(NA)	(NA)
Tripp	5	8.2	138	50	61,848	9,830	(NA)	18	5,226	831	5.9	79.4
Turner	9	10.6	135	48	40,958	4,749	(NA)	18	2,582	299	19.9	(NA)
Union	10	7.4	166	48	(D)	(NA)	(NA)	45	20,485	1,595	30.3	(NA)
Walworth	4	7.3	189	60	68,012	11,942	(NA)	27	6,104	1,072	−4.5	69.2
Yankton	11	5.1	487	135	226,437	10,536	26.2	67	29,276	1,362	24.0	84.9
Ziebach	1	3.8	153	4	(D)	(NA)	(NA)	1	(D)	(NA)	(NA)	(NA)
TENNESSEE	2,113	3.5	95,586	24,029	60,136,403	10,382	17.0	10,070	8,024,900	1,385	18.2	77.9
Anderson	20	2.8	896	295	776,903	10,837	18.5	126	87,033	1,214	21.6	84.8
Bedford	10	2.4	449	148	262,323	6,681	12.5	51	24,790	631	25.2	91.2
Benton	7	4.3	231	82	111,372	6,719	20.6	35	11,847	715	10.9	77.5
Bledsoe	2	1.5	91	34	24,666	1,972	(NA)	9	3,017	241	67.0	(NA)
Blount	43	3.7	1,390	393	1,384,366	12,617	15.3	188	152,486	1,390	56.7	82.2
Bradley	34	3.7	1,246	375	820,497	9,166	19.7	133	98,520	1,101	20.4	(NA)
Campbell	16	3.9	439	148	247,076	6,185	26.3	54	27,840	697	4.7	85.5
Cannon	3	2.2	133	30	37,611	2,869	(NA)	8	3,983	304	39.4	100.0
Carroll	18	6.2	392	117	158,503	5,399	26.5	41	11,803	402	−2.0	94.3
Carter	13	2.2	538	149	327,364	5,752	(NA)	58	30,143	530	37.9	(NA)
Cheatham	13	3.4	314	82	160,786	4,333	(NA)	35	14,233	384	29.8	91.4
Chester	9	5.6	188	62	104,600	6,567	4.8	21	5,353	336	−18.8	83.7
Claiborne	11	3.5	436	98	174,757	5,807	14.4	23	13,922	463	15.5	(NA)
Clay	3	3.8	80	28	34,234	4,294	(NA)	9	3,061	384	−10.6	(NA)
Cocke	10	2.9	387	123	249,535	7,312	(NA)	60	32,740	959	7.4	83.0
Coffee	18	3.5	562	276	620,250	12,609	(NA)	100	67,779	1,378	20.0	(NA)
Crockett	11	7.5	191	59	60,759	4,178	(NA)	11	6,797	467	41.2	47.6
Cumberland	16	3.1	691	232	481,056	9,876	(NA)	77	49,193	1,010	24.3	86.3
Davidson	175	3.0	13,907	2,781	8,361,347	14,690	12.4	1,422	1,706,630	2,998	12.9	61.5
Decatur	7	6.0	204	48	99,164	8,464	(NA)	25	4,588	392	17.1	76.2
DeKalb	9	4.9	288	80	95,861	5,390	7.4	22	10,015	563	50.9	91.8
Dickson	20	4.4	563	192	484,179	10,924	(NA)	77	44,479	1,004	18.1	87.6
Dyer	17	4.5	487	204	382,920	10,304	22.5	81	40,044	1,078	32.8	90.6
Fayette	15	4.4	352	61	59,374	1,903	14.9	23	5,598	179	10.9	88.2
Fentress	6	3.5	220	67	93,960	5,568	20.4	16	6,338	376	6.4	(NA)
Franklin	11	2.7	363	152	283,857	7,073	(NA)	41	19,391	483	14.8	(NA)
Gibson	30	6.2	640	233	370,222	7,689	(NA)	64	23,043	479	4.3	(NA)
Giles	16	5.5	550	127	220,893	7,492	(NA)	39	16,682	566	13.8	91.9
Grainger	6	2.7	125	53	57,413	2,708	(NA)	8	4,269	201	(NA)	(NA)
Greene	25	3.8	923	232	563,413	8,844	(NA)	96	45,930	721	9.2	89.5
Grundy	7	4.8	95	56	70,447	4,919	(NA)	15	9,533	666	395.7	59.4
Hamblen	17	2.8	780	306	828,078	14,169	(NA)	106	71,913	1,230	23.3	89.4
Hamilton	112	3.6	4,895	1,445	3,888,849	12,573	16.0	699	532,613	1,722	17.5	82.3
Hancock	2	3.0	46	20	18,734	2,773	(NA)	1	(D)	(NA)	(NA)	(NA)
Hardeman	14	5.0	300	102	121,545	4,298	21.3	36	12,507	442	52.0	94.9
Hardin	12	4.6	337	119	207,629	8,007	(NA)	47	18,462	712	7.6	87.8
Hawkins	19	3.4	483	129	235,921	4,312	(NA)	43	18,523	339	2.9	(NA)
Haywood	6	3.1	239	79	154,055	7,859	(NA)	27	10,668	544	−6.4	85.4
Henderson	15	5.7	446	113	201,750	7,805	(NA)	33	18,768	726	38.5	95.4
Henry	14	4.4	448	161	280,629	8,950	(NA)	67	25,885	826	17.0	87.5
Hickman	5	2.1	171	66	66,464	2,861	8.6	29	6,162	265	(NA)	(NA)
Houston	3	3.8	83	26	25,970	3,248	(NA)	10	2,141	268	13.0	(NA)
Humphreys	6	3.3	205	83	113,208	6,259	(NA)	32	12,582	696	−5.8	70.8
Jackson	4	3.6	109	30	30,280	2,708	(NA)	10	1,664	149	19.5	(NA)
Jefferson	16	3.3	451	129	294,659	6,429	(NA)	53	35,986	785	46.3	(NA)
Johnson	6	3.3	205	52	75,421	4,232	(NA)	21	6,273	352	19.5	90.4
Knox	137	3.4	6,325	1,856	5,955,939	15,213	15.5	774	720,352	1,840	30.8	85.7
Lake	3	4.0	50	25	21,254	2,694	(NA)	12	6,225	789	58.0	45.1
Lauderdale	15	5.6	303	96	123,525	4,550	(NA)	21	11,035	406	47.6	92.1
Lawrence	17	4.1	509	184	339,164	8,347	(NA)	49	26,536	653	22.6	91.2

See footnotes at end of table.

[Includes United States, states, and 3,141 counties/county equivalents defined as of February 22, 2005. For more information on these areas, see Appendix C, Geographic Information]

County	Banking,[1] 2005 Offices Number	Rate per 10,000 people	Total deposits (mil. dol.)	Retail trade[2] (NAICS 44–45), 2002 Estab-lishments	Sales Total ($1,000)	Per capita[3] (dol.)	General merchandise stores,[4] percent of total	Accommodation and food services[2] (NAICS 72), 2002 Estab-lishments	Sales Total ($1,000)	Per capita[3] (dol.)	Percent change, 1997–2002	Food services,[5] percent of total
TENNESSEE—Con.												
Lewis	5	4.4	82	48	70,280	6,143	(NA)	14	5,979	523	(NA)	(NA)
Lincoln	10	3.1	425	138	249,018	7,852	(NA)	42	18,907	596	(NA)	(NA)
Loudon	21	4.8	611	147	351,118	8,610	(NA)	59	33,829	830	28.5	85.7
McMinn	23	4.5	728	208	422,300	8,422	17.1	75	41,325	824	-0.8	85.1
McNairy	14	5.5	268	103	157,623	6,376	(NA)	28	15,588	631	128.1	94.8
Macon	10	4.6	331	77	124,852	5,985	(NA)	19	7,686	368	23.8	(NA)
Madison	39	4.1	1,277	534	1,364,079	14,600	21.1	183	153,467	1,643	11.4	84.7
Marion	14	5.0	267	115	230,065	8,278	(NA)	37	18,524	666	-9.2	(NA)
Marshall	13	4.6	390	115	186,247	6,789	(NA)	33	16,537	603	28.5	88.9
Maury	28	3.7	1,052	315	661,917	9,257	19.6	111	75,664	1,058	29.7	92.8
Meigs	4	3.4	81	21	26,856	2,374	(NA)	9	2,364	209	23.8	100.0
Monroe	27	6.3	518	160	341,035	8,442	(NA)	71	35,635	882	28.6	87.8
Montgomery	46	3.1	1,338	517	1,356,268	9,910	26.2	241	167,289	1,222	26.4	(NA)
Moore	2	3.3	60	11	9,334	1,564	(NA)	3	561	94	(NA)	100.0
Morgan	3	1.5	117	34	40,832	2,036	(NA)	8	2,758	138	-26.7	(NA)
Obion	19	5.9	567	167	352,834	10,878	(NA)	54	24,084	743	21.3	(NA)
Overton	6	2.9	279	59	90,574	4,472	(NA)	20	9,244	456	21.9	(NA)
Perry	3	4.0	103	21	23,360	3,096	(NA)	5	1,162	154	74.7	100.0
Pickett	2	4.1	97	22	19,684	3,892	(NA)	9	1,756	347	(NA)	(NA)
Polk	10	6.3	188	51	79,236	4,914	7.4	21	8,790	545	82.0	(NA)
Putnam	27	4.1	1,103	372	768,909	12,003	21.7	129	94,461	1,475	14.9	88.2
Rhea	10	3.3	289	91	153,619	5,305	15.4	46	18,402	636	6.3	93.1
Roane	16	3.0	388	162	379,060	7,255	(NA)	55	36,261	694	33.3	88.4
Robertson	16	2.6	562	154	353,488	6,176	(NA)	41	28,918	505	2.0	91.3
Rutherford	61	2.8	2,124	637	1,904,441	9,733	20.6	285	242,448	1,239	26.6	90.0
Scott	8	3.7	260	88	147,004	6,778	(NA)	19	10,570	487	13.3	86.2
Sequatchie	7	5.5	112	38	58,392	4,949	(NA)	14	4,869	413	(NA)	(NA)
Sevier	47	5.9	1,580	732	1,235,138	16,615	10.2	461	487,537	6,558	26.9	53.1
Shelby	252	2.8	23,606	3,342	10,052,067	11,148	15.9	1,578	1,427,456	1,583	4.8	79.2
Smith	10	5.4	367	59	127,191	6,996	(NA)	20	11,257	619	(NA)	(NA)
Stewart	6	4.6	145	34	50,349	3,935	6.6	17	3,331	260	3.2	(NA)
Sullivan	49	3.2	1,753	688	1,697,761	11,112	(NA)	286	196,194	1,284	15.8	86.1
Sumner	45	3.1	1,618	424	948,923	6,954	21.2	182	110,854	812	65.3	87.7
Tipton	19	3.4	410	154	308,495	5,779	11.7	54	21,458	402	18.1	91.8
Trousdale	3	3.9	130	30	27,253	3,684	(NA)	8	2,806	379	29.5	100.0
Unicoi	4	2.3	167	39	71,910	4,072	(NA)	28	7,696	436	8.8	(NA)
Union	6	3.1	114	39	43,927	2,366	(NA)	11	3,331	179	11.7	100.0
Van Buren	1	1.8	29	4	4,503	813	(NA)	2	(D)	(NA)	(NA)	(NA)
Warren	19	4.8	603	184	317,858	8,196	(NA)	49	26,043	672	8.5	95.4
Washington	45	4.0	1,669	536	1,486,860	13,621	16.9	212	164,729	1,509	17.2	89.6
Wayne	10	5.9	295	66	54,622	3,206	(NA)	17	3,372	198	(NA)	(NA)
Weakley	14	4.2	418	132	202,066	5,896	(NA)	55	21,026	613	12.2	(NA)
White	7	2.9	313	76	173,594	7,388	(NA)	26	12,067	514	(NA)	(NA)
Williamson	72	4.7	3,726	672	2,416,245	17,674	16.6	257	238,798	1,747	48.7	81.7
Wilson	36	3.6	1,271	375	832,434	8,906	(NA)	138	89,305	955	30.1	88.5
TEXAS	5,863	2.6	356,111	75,703	228,694,755	10,528	15.6	36,591	29,914,774	1,377	31.8	81.6
Anderson	11	2.0	425	187	353,413	6,472	(NA)	63	35,356	647	19.0	83.3
Andrews	4	3.1	121	44	65,380	5,059	(NA)	22	7,221	559	(NA)	100.0
Angelina	26	3.2	904	344	823,097	10,229	(NA)	119	78,499	976	29.2	88.5
Aransas	7	2.8	244	90	167,419	7,252	(NA)	70	29,163	1,263	17.1	68.0
Archer	4	4.4	62	17	24,668	2,735	(NA)	8	1,565	174	49.6	(NA)
Armstrong	1	4.6	17	5	5,015	2,370	—	6	1,132	535	155.0	(NA)
Atascosa	9	2.1	244	108	257,731	6,265	(NA)	44	18,756	456	39.9	91.0
Austin	13	5.0	562	108	223,009	9,053	(NA)	42	16,424	667	6.6	90.1
Bailey	2	3.0	86	28	42,053	6,448	7.5	12	4,922	755	(NA)	(NA)
Bandera	5	2.5	133	65	55,807	2,943	(NA)	52	14,897	786	49.6	(NA)
Bastrop	16	2.3	444	142	550,737	8,573	(NA)	79	46,505	724	80.8	94.3
Baylor	3	7.8	74	18	18,380	4,696	(NA)	12	2,881	736	52.5	(NA)
Bee	4	1.2	199	85	170,264	5,274	(NA)	47	15,728	487	11.4	92.0
Bell	58	2.3	2,157	854	2,427,637	9,920	(NA)	407	264,265	1,080	30.2	87.3
Bexar	272	1.8	28,633	4,498	15,914,486	11,038	13.9	2,710	2,767,377	1,919	36.5	74.1
Blanco	6	6.6	148	45	35,617	4,042	(NA)	17	4,336	492	-30.3	93.1
Borden	—	—	—	1	(D)	(NA)	(NA)	—	—	—	—	—
Bosque	8	4.4	209	58	68,871	3,915	(NA)	19	11,359	646	304.5	34.9
Bowie	31	3.4	1,016	442	1,151,940	12,859	(NA)	129	93,956	1,049	13.4	93.4
Brazoria	63	2.3	1,825	669	2,143,093	8,341	21.2	311	184,448	718	24.3	90.0
Brazos	40	2.6	1,786	591	1,573,053	10,243	(NA)	312	250,196	1,629	46.6	83.7
Brewster	5	5.5	86	55	82,902	9,134	7.2	46	19,207	2,116	27.0	(NA)
Briscoe	2	12.2	47	5	3,679	2,167	—	3	350	206	(NA)	100.0
Brooks	3	3.9	88	32	53,426	6,875	(NA)	22	9,724	1,251	34.3	69.9
Brown	15	3.9	379	187	405,379	10,662	(NA)	77	37,623	990	18.9	87.1

See footnotes at end of table.

Table B-11. Counties — **Banking, Retail Trade, and Accommodation and Food Services**—Con.

[Includes United States, states, and 3,141 counties/county equivalents defined as of February 22, 2005. For more information on these areas, see Appendix C, Geographic Information]

County	Banking,[1] 2005 Offices Number	Rate per 10,000 people	Total deposits (mil. dol.)	Retail trade[2] (NAICS 44–45), 2002 Estab-lishments	Sales Total ($1,000)	Per capita[3] (dol.)	General merchandise stores,[4] percent of total	Accommodation and food services[2] (NAICS 72), 2002 Estab-lishments	Sales Total ($1,000)	Per capita[3] (dol.)	Percent change, 1997–2002	Food services,[5] percent of total
TEXAS—Con.												
Burleson	7	4.1	251	50	106,964	6,383	(NA)	28	6,477	387	4.2	(NA)
Burnet	14	3.4	522	184	430,820	11,458	(NA)	76	49,890	1,327	47.0	60.8
Caldwell	6	1.6	239	89	169,567	4,862	(NA)	42	19,099	548	35.1	95.2
Calhoun	8	3.9	322	63	139,820	6,844	(NA)	63	19,163	938	26.0	(NA)
Callahan	4	3.0	136	48	79,746	6,168	(NA)	13	4,696	363	62.0	(NA)
Cameron	70	1.9	3,475	1,120	2,756,738	7,808	20.6	570	371,305	1,052	33.5	77.8
Camp	6	4.9	210	52	94,041	8,071	2.7	17	5,729	492	64.6	96.6
Carson	4	6.1	68	27	24,189	3,662	(NA)	12	1,986	301	(NA)	(NA)
Cass	12	4.0	292	122	189,186	6,270	(NA)	42	13,284	440	−9.5	95.4
Castro	5	6.5	77	42	50,426	6,288	(NA)	14	(D)	(NA)	(NA)	(NA)
Chambers	8	2.8	191	79	137,504	5,067	(NA)	39	18,514	682	24.0	84.9
Cherokee	13	2.7	555	142	310,455	6,598	(NA)	51	21,670	461	6.9	92.9
Childress	4	5.2	101	32	48,945	6,455	(NA)	25	10,359	1,366	44.3	61.7
Clay	4	3.5	88	30	72,254	6,411	(NA)	9	1,568	139	7.8	100.0
Cochran	2	6.1	55	13	19,376	5,508	(NA)	6	721	205	54.7	100.0
Coke	2	5.5	48	14	28,750	7,570	−	4	577	152	(NA)	(NA)
Coleman	6	6.9	118	39	44,848	5,053	7.5	23	4,838	545	16.0	(NA)
Collin	204	3.1	6,691	1,953	8,086,129	14,214	17.5	929	896,556	1,576	108.0	89.4
Collingsworth	2	6.7	64	11	19,419	6,238	(NA)	9	1,145	368	15.1	100.0
Colorado	13	6.3	367	104	171,635	8,393	13.4	44	17,458	854	14.0	86.1
Comal	21	2.2	732	347	954,987	11,271	(NA)	181	109,868	1,297	36.6	78.5
Comanche	8	5.8	210	63	85,932	6,343	(NA)	24	(D)	(NA)	(NA)	(NA)
Concho	2	5.4	36	12	14,221	3,721	−	5	2,075	543	−25.1	(NA)
Cooke	11	2.8	471	203	415,944	11,015	(NA)	70	35,322	935	21.9	91.2
Coryell	13	1.7	455	136	334,132	4,477	(NA)	70	40,698	545	33.9	(NA)
Cottle	2	11.5	45	7	12,901	7,280	−	3	657	371	(NA)	100.0
Crane	2	5.2	33	15	13,984	3,573	(NA)	6	(D)	(NA)	(NA)	(NA)
Crockett	3	7.6	84	28	62,729	16,109	(NA)	18	5,812	1,493	−8.5	48.9
Crosby	5	7.5	88	28	40,857	5,953	(NA)	8	712	104	−35.3	(NA)
Culberson	−	−	−	18	56,026	19,811	(NA)	20	7,427	2,626	23.6	32.9
Dallam	5	8.1	148	45	57,152	9,278	(NA)	24	10,535	1,710	21.8	67.6
Dallas	594	2.6	50,057	7,776	26,239,828	11,546	13.1	4,385	4,708,310	2,072	16.4	73.8
Dawson	3	2.1	259	52	87,424	6,016	(NA)	26	8,631	594	−11.9	(NA)
Deaf Smith	5	2.7	178	83	130,105	7,072	(NA)	24	8,166	444	(NA)	(NA)
Delta	4	7.3	45	20	26,162	4,829	(NA)	2	(D)	(NA)	(NA)	(NA)
Denton	135	2.4	3,451	1,327	4,557,662	9,336	16.5	632	495,821	1,016	52.6	93.3
DeWitt	10	4.9	329	79	112,565	5,616	(NA)	31	10,442	521	16.9	95.2
Dickens	1	3.8	27	11	9,686	3,589	(NA)	7	1,288	477	−12.1	100.0
Dimmit	2	1.9	21	36	57,830	5,644	(NA)	14	5,485	535	37.4	(NA)
Donley	3	7.7	80	22	26,904	6,938	(NA)	11	2,046	528	−7.2	(NA)
Duval	4	3.2	76	36	42,778	3,337	4.8	13	2,583	201	−9.3	(NA)
Eastland	8	4.3	234	97	170,924	9,375	(NA)	34	11,717	643	26.7	91.6
Ector	29	2.3	1,240	497	1,357,691	11,091	22.0	219	153,927	1,257	28.4	90.0
Edwards	1	5.0	40	8	9,073	4,394	(NA)	3	282	137	(NA)	(NA)
Ellis	32	2.4	972	348	960,158	7,985	(NA)	140	82,328	685	56.8	94.4
El Paso	78	1.1	4,632	2,138	5,807,166	8,373	25.3	1,090	772,229	1,113	9.8	86.9
Erath	13	3.8	411	149	335,347	10,126	(NA)	61	43,255	1,306	43.0	96.9
Falls	8	4.5	180	61	86,290	4,813	15.2	20	(D)	(NA)	(NA)	(NA)
Fannin	12	3.6	305	90	269,962	8,481	(NA)	39	13,751	432	39.2	(NA)
Fayette	15	6.7	538	137	221,348	9,950	(NA)	56	28,547	1,283	36.3	90.2
Fisher	2	4.9	45	15	11,529	2,726	(NA)	5	687	162	(NA)	100.0
Floyd	4	5.6	109	27	41,012	5,563	(NA)	13	1,314	178	−34.9	100.0
Foard	1	6.6	19	6	4,389	2,810	−	2	(D)	(NA)	(NA)	(NA)
Fort Bend	84	1.8	3,931	1,008	3,384,276	8,486	23.0	446	350,729	879	70.7	92.4
Franklin	6	5.9	111	31	51,065	5,241	(NA)	13	4,112	422	−19.5	(NA)
Freestone	10	5.3	229	77	130,553	7,085	3.6	32	17,085	927	86.4	85.5
Frio	4	2.4	193	43	88,594	5,413	(NA)	20	7,052	431	24.2	91.3
Gaines	3	2.0	171	58	73,359	5,156	21.2	21	4,808	338	(NA)	(NA)
Galveston	80	2.9	2,782	861	2,236,605	8,576	18.5	484	418,713	1,605	38.9	78.7
Garza	2	4.0	57	28	21,420	4,252	(NA)	10	3,506	696	30.3	(NA)
Gillespie	11	4.8	534	175	255,165	11,789	9.6	81	36,498	1,686	41.1	71.4
Glasscock	1	7.5	12	4	(D)	(NA)	(NA)	−	−	(NA)	−	−
Goliad	2	2.8	49	20	24,587	3,479	(NA)	11	3,830	542	44.6	(NA)
Gonzales	6	3.1	224	87	129,048	6,849	(NA)	26	10,802	573	52.5	86.5
Gray	9	4.2	310	120	(D)	(NA)	(NA)	36	17,031	778	−10.2	(NA)
Grayson	41	3.5	1,454	468	1,368,776	12,039	24.0	190	116,108	1,021	10.8	89.1
Gregg	47	4.1	1,926	752	1,903,233	16,820	(NA)	265	173,835	1,536	18.8	90.3
Grimes	7	2.8	254	63	122,786	4,972	(NA)	28	7,387	299	(NA)	82.4
Guadalupe	21	2.0	570	262	755,259	8,007	(NA)	136	82,627	876	(NA)	92.6
Hale	12	3.3	396	141	268,454	7,516	19.7	62	35,838	1,003	38.2	95.1

See footnotes at end of table.

Counties — **Banking, Retail Trade, and Accommodation and Food Services**—Con.

[Includes United States, states, and 3,141 counties/county equivalents defined as of February 22, 2005. For more information on these areas, see Appendix C, Geographic Information]

County	Banking,[1] 2005 Offices Number	Rate per 10,000 people	Total deposits (mil. dol.)	Retail trade[2] (NAICS 44–45), 2002 Estab-lishments	Sales Total ($1,000)	Per capita[3] (dol.)	General merchan-dise stores,[4] percent of total	Accommodation and food services[2] (NAICS 72), 2002 Estab-lishments	Sales Total ($1,000)	Per capita[3] (dol.)	Percent change, 1997–2002	Food services,[5] percent of total
TEXAS—Con.												
Hall	4	10.8	62	16	13,648	3,638	(NA)	5	425	113	(NA)	(NA)
Hamilton	5	6.2	137	47	44,490	5,583	(NA)	13	(D)	(NA)	(NA)	(NA)
Hansford	4	7.6	156	31	40,108	7,640	(NA)	12	2,186	416	(NA)	(NA)
Hardeman	4	9.3	75	19	14,721	3,263	(NA)	10	3,353	743	(NA)	(NA)
Hardin	12	2.4	319	137	402,227	8,175	(NA)	49	23,829	484	45.0	97.6
Harris	896	2.4	86,041	11,810	39,358,036	11,119	13.5	5,881	5,593,840	1,580	27.7	82.4
Harrison	18	2.8	577	214	423,644	6,804	(NA)	79	39,674	637	12.9	85.9
Hartley	1	1.8	27	11	17,240	3,332	(NA)	4	1,109	214	333.2	100.0
Haskell	5	9.0	94	35	59,757	10,231	(NA)	11	(D)	(NA)	(NA)	(NA)
Hays	26	2.1	623	494	1,246,255	11,191	(NA)	209	142,595	1,280	61.2	89.4
Hemphill	3	8.8	96	21	20,575	6,151	(NA)	10	1,910	571	36.2	(NA)
Henderson	26	3.2	666	241	514,217	6,806	(NA)	115	51,184	677	25.8	93.3
Hidalgo	123	1.8	6,791	1,713	5,022,716	8,196	19.0	692	524,508	856	49.0	84.4
Hill	16	4.5	314	218	320,195	9,519	(NA)	75	36,292	1,079	43.4	70.6
Hockley	10	4.4	298	87	155,873	6,864	(NA)	41	12,338	543	-7.2	(NA)
Hood	17	3.5	538	174	485,129	11,037	(NA)	78	37,904	862	34.7	87.4
Hopkins	11	3.3	432	151	358,100	11,072	(NA)	46	24,754	765	-3.1	92.4
Houston	11	4.7	277	68	143,783	6,207	(NA)	30	9,508	410	31.7	74.9
Howard	8	2.5	427	142	281,724	8,494	(NA)	64	25,571	771	5.8	93.4
Hudspeth	1	3.0	10	12	6,824	2,046	–	8	1,630	489	14.3	(NA)
Hunt	18	2.2	641	246	634,937	7,949	(NA)	94	(D)	(NA)	(NA)	(NA)
Hutchinson	5	2.2	150	86	144,197	6,230	(NA)	44	17,906	774	18.6	(NA)
Irion	1	5.7	51	4	1,704	973	–	1	(D)	(NA)	(NA)	(NA)
Jack	4	4.4	168	33	26,627	2,984	(NA)	11	4,386	491	(NA)	(NA)
Jackson	6	4.2	186	57	89,182	6,240	(NA)	17	6,592	461	-5.9	92.0
Jasper	11	3.1	333	171	418,256	11,722	(NA)	46	22,950	643	6.5	90.0
Jeff Davis	1	4.3	19	8	4,836	2,186	–	15	5,585	2,525	25.4	33.6
Jefferson	50	2.0	2,805	1,081	3,104,438	12,466	(NA)	406	316,190	1,270	20.7	88.2
Jim Hogg	4	8.0	103	33	45,474	8,840	(NA)	13	3,265	635	9.7	70.6
Jim Wells	10	2.4	337	152	341,196	8,514	(NA)	56	31,159	777	21.7	(NA)
Johnson	33	2.3	907	384	926,373	6,824	(NA)	154	94,505	696	57.0	95.3
Jones	7	3.5	137	61	150,210	7,424	(NA)	22	6,665	329	78.8	(NA)
Karnes	5	3.3	170	55	78,214	5,103	(NA)	25	6,649	434	30.4	(NA)
Kaufman	23	2.6	757	307	860,887	11,028	(NA)	94	66,798	856	67.5	91.2
Kendall	10	3.5	359	136	443,921	17,532	(NA)	56	35,079	1,385	26.8	66.8
Kenedy	–	–	–	–	(D)	(NA)	(NA)	1	(D)	(NA)	(NA)	(NA)
Kent	1	12.8	19	4	(D)	(NA)	(NA)	2	(D)	(NA)	(NA)	(NA)
Kerr	17	3.7	843	243	528,960	11,801	(NA)	100	66,994	1,495	23.3	56.7
Kimble	2	4.4	62	34	40,268	8,935	(NA)	19	6,764	1,501	0.4	76.0
King	–	–	–	–	–	–	–	–	–	–	(NA)	
Kinney	1	3.0	14	8	5,915	1,733	–	2	(D)	(NA)	(NA)	(NA)
Kleberg	9	2.9	229	107	307,055	9,861	(NA)	70	(D)	(NA)	(NA)	(NA)
Knox	2	5.3	65	23	22,496	5,661	7.0	5	(D)	(NA)	(NA)	(NA)
Lamar	16	3.2	743	249	535,974	10,918	21.7	87	52,029	1,060	13.4	87.6
Lamb	14	9.7	239	53	86,792	5,926	6.0	23	5,041	344	(NA)	(NA)
Lampasas	7	3.6	201	55	183,638	9,754	(NA)	32	11,421	607	(NA)	(NA)
La Salle	1	1.7	28	23	38,967	6,688	4.7	9	2,329	400	-32.5	66.8
Lavaca	9	4.8	467	92	136,625	7,195	11.1	24	6,829	360	-25.5	(NA)
Lee	10	6.1	265	68	130,835	8,017	(NA)	23	6,864	421	-16.1	90.5
Leon	8	4.9	215	74	88,077	5,551	3.4	29	11,584	730	24.7	81.6
Liberty	13	1.7	602	205	632,289	8,588	(NA)	73	40,045	544	21.8	92.5
Limestone	10	4.4	225	89	197,554	8,818	(NA)	32	12,471	557	28.3	92.6
Lipscomb	3	9.7	67	17	11,772	3,871	–	4	(D)	(NA)	(NA)	(NA)
Live Oak	4	3.4	141	41	78,792	6,545	(NA)	28	10,983	912	15.6	84.5
Llano	11	6.0	299	85	104,762	5,858	3.7	40	29,304	1,639	179.1	(NA)
Loving	–	–	–	–	–	–	–	–	–	–	–	–
Lubbock	80	3.2	4,181	1,055	3,274,249	13,240	(NA)	520	414,895	1,678	24.9	(NA)
Lynn	4	6.4	97	16	17,902	2,805	(NA)	4	646	101	-37.2	100.0
McCulloch	3	3.8	136	40	81,241	10,306	(NA)	25	7,753	984	9.3	82.4
McLennan	48	2.1	2,664	818	2,199,055	10,123	19.1	400	292,764	1,348	32.7	86.5
McMullen	1	11.3	13	3	(D)	(NA)	(NA)	1	(D)	(NA)	(NA)	(NA)
Madison	4	3.0	199	40	196,462	15,345	(NA)	22	9,925	775	25.8	87.9
Marion	2	1.8	69	43	53,637	4,863	3.2	26	5,885	534	18.2	64.0
Martin	2	4.6	60	17	27,664	5,954	–	3	(D)	(NA)	(NA)	(NA)
Mason	3	7.7	84	29	16,693	4,444	–	12	3,040	809	133.5	84.6
Matagorda	8	2.1	378	159	266,048	6,994	(NA)	75	30,934	813	16.1	87.8
Maverick	10	2.0	455	186	351,776	7,207	(NA)	54	29,977	614	26.6	80.5
Medina	12	2.8	369	106	289,764	7,115	(NA)	61	21,850	537	68.8	92.7
Menard	2	9.1	40	12	12,332	5,221	(NA)	7	1,156	489	-38.4	(NA)
Midland	41	3.4	2,362	529	1,293,601	11,014	18.4	240	170,001	1,447	37.2	87.9

See footnotes at end of table.

[Includes United States, states, and 3,141 counties/county equivalents defined as of February 22, 2005. For more information on these areas, see Appendix C, Geographic Information]

County	Banking,[1] 2005 Offices			Retail trade[2] (NAICS 44–45), 2002	Sales			Accommodation and food services[2] (NAICS 72), 2002	Sales			
	Number	Rate per 10,000 people	Total deposits (mil. dol.)	Estab-lishments	Total ($1,000)	Per capita[3] (dol.)	General merchandise stores,[4] percent of total	Estab-lishments	Total ($1,000)	Per capita[3] (dol.)	Percent change, 1997–2002	Food services,[5] percent of total
TEXAS—Con.												
Milam	9	3.5	246	77	137,316	5,481	14.5	42	13,380	534	24.5	86.6
Mills	2	3.8	110	31	36,964	7,228	(NA)	8	1,372	268	−2.4	(NA)
Mitchell	3	3.2	81	35	38,159	4,036	9.6	11	3,313	350	−14.9	(NA)
Montague	7	3.6	280	84	120,833	6,284	(NA)	27	7,359	383	−29.2	(NA)
Montgomery	103	2.7	3,488	1,056	3,375,120	10,274	(NA)	414	461,328	1,404	100.4	71.5
Moore	9	4.4	149	73	145,760	7,237	(NA)	42	15,895	789	−21.6	79.2
Morris	9	7.0	156	51	47,317	3,581	(NA)	20	(D)	(NA)	(NA)	(NA)
Motley	1	7.7	11	8	3,962	3,071	−	4	311	241	5.8	100.0
Nacogdoches	21	3.5	783	274	612,898	10,347	(NA)	93	59,475	1,004	4.2	87.5
Navarro	15	3.1	468	181	407,024	8,696	(NA)	57	35,094	750	37.7	91.6
Newton	2	1.4	46	27	32,907	2,208	(NA)	11	2,226	149	−26.9	77.7
Nolan	4	2.7	194	69	115,729	7,630	(NA)	34	14,981	988	27.6	77.0
Nueces	83	2.6	3,177	1,190	3,277,543	10,437	(NA)	736	505,577	1,610	20.8	83.3
Ochiltree	3	3.2	219	45	73,643	8,118	7.6	18	6,639	732	−5.8	83.4
Oldham	1	4.7	11	9	9,202	4,282	−	6	1,656	771	40.9	37.1
Orange	19	2.2	694	289	653,709	7,745	(NA)	110	60,557	717	3.4	92.9
Palo Pinto	16	5.8	362	135	204,446	7,527	(NA)	55	26,398	972	24.2	75.9
Panola	5	2.2	407	89	148,008	6,497	(NA)	26	9,837	432	−9.7	81.1
Parker	18	1.8	832	261	957,274	10,111	(NA)	106	71,055	750	71.3	87.1
Parmer	5	5.1	161	33	38,345	3,894	(NA)	14	1,484	151	(NA)	86.7
Pecos	5	3.2	136	76	113,760	6,973	(NA)	36	14,075	863	10.8	(NA)
Polk	10	2.1	428	146	387,408	8,731	(NA)	48	24,995	563	16.2	89.3
Potter	37	3.1	2,271	583	1,742,876	15,063	(NA)	314	246,736	2,132	29.2	82.7
Presidio	3	3.9	74	34	29,121	3,880	(NA)	16	5,007	667	51.0	38.3
Rains	5	4.4	114	28	36,351	3,501	(NA)	18	5,103	491	77.4	79.5
Randall	25	2.3	854	360	1,072,296	10,080	(NA)	151	87,531	823	22.3	94.3
Reagan	2	6.7	35	14	21,730	6,879	(NA)	7	1,447	458	(NA)	(NA)
Real	2	6.6	42	12	5,561	1,857	−	10	2,416	807	13.3	60.1
Red River	6	4.4	135	52	53,065	3,804	(NA)	12	(D)	(NA)	(NA)	(NA)
Reeves	2	1.7	117	33	73,768	5,885	(NA)	25	11,490	917	37.3	39.5
Refugio	3	3.9	83	31	53,165	6,920	(NA)	21	6,565	854	8.1	92.8
Roberts	1	12.2	10	2	(D)	(NA)	(NA)	−	−	(NA)	−	−
Robertson	5	3.1	205	66	64,627	4,061	(NA)	19	7,779	489	31.3	(NA)
Rockwall	19	3.0	668	179	585,609	11,485	20.3	75	65,307	1,281	144.2	(NA)
Runnels	9	8.2	163	55	81,443	7,342	(NA)	20	3,733	337	15.4	(NA)
Rusk	13	2.7	559	136	245,099	5,163	(NA)	43	17,003	358	11.3	(NA)
Sabine	5	4.8	133	40	38,127	3,667	6.6	11	3,418	329	−20.0	(NA)
San Augustine	5	5.6	99	34	51,530	5,788	4.6	8	1,417	159	−26.2	(NA)
San Jacinto	4	1.6	81	31	38,725	1,665	(NA)	8	3,078	132	−32.4	100.0
San Patricio	21	3.0	394	177	421,325	6,261	(NA)	115	55,346	822	74.3	84.1
San Saba	2	3.3	63	44	64,566	10,660	2.6	15	2,007	331	(NA)	(NA)
Schleicher	1	3.6	35	13	11,568	3,981	(NA)	5	578	199	(NA)	100.0
Scurry	6	3.7	292	61	134,940	8,430	(NA)	30	11,039	690	16.5	89.6
Shackelford	2	6.3	95	16	10,980	3,286	(NA)	4	1,463	438	−17.9	(NA)
Shelby	12	4.6	324	97	168,980	6,625	(NA)	24	9,857	386	16.1	75.3
Sherman	2	6.7	66	11	10,248	3,226	(NA)	3	384	121	−51.8	100.0
Smith	64	3.4	2,853	831	2,332,276	12,902	18.4	297	236,645	1,309	35.1	88.1
Somervell	2	2.6	74	36	35,104	4,919	(NA)	24	9,562	1,340	57.8	66.4
Starr	10	1.6	385	125	299,639	5,330	(NA)	40	17,727	315	63.3	95.4
Stephens	5	5.2	185	50	62,734	6,624	(NA)	18	6,216	656	10.2	92.6
Sterling	1	7.7	25	4	5,929	4,385	−	3	(D)	(NA)	(NA)	(NA)
Stonewall	1	7.3	23	7	4,345	2,897	−	3	(D)	(NA)	(NA)	(NA)
Sutton	2	4.7	89	28	38,071	9,270	(NA)	15	5,094	1,240	8.9	56.2
Swisher	5	6.4	111	25	39,157	4,887	(NA)	17	(D)	(NA)	(NA)	(NA)
Tarrant	396	2.4	47,961	5,306	17,906,814	11,741	15.2	2,619	2,422,367	1,588	33.0	85.6
Taylor	44	3.5	1,470	581	1,565,940	12,537	(NA)	262	183,340	1,468	21.0	89.7
Terrell	2	20.1	31	4	3,141	3,076	(NA)	3	(D)	(NA)	(NA)	(NA)
Terry	3	2.4	162	42	102,096	8,105	12.6	25	8,161	648	3.6	88.8
Throckmorton	3	18.5	32	7	5,124	2,967	−	3	363	210	(NA)	100.0
Titus	11	3.7	450	148	312,856	11,075	(NA)	48	29,708	1,052	41.0	89.3
Tom Green	30	2.9	1,108	468	1,135,305	10,970	18.5	194	(D)	(NA)	(NA)	(NA)
Travis	230	2.6	12,088	3,121	10,544,294	12,469	10.0	1,860	1,953,197	2,310	47.7	75.9
Trinity	3	2.1	79	40	45,554	3,236	11.0	15	8,776	623	17.3	(NA)
Tyler	7	3.4	140	59	85,011	4,102	(NA)	17	5,915	285	(NA)	(NA)
Upshur	11	2.9	395	102	156,055	4,271	(NA)	27	13,388	366	17.9	(NA)
Upton	2	6.5	41	14	30,782	9,405	(NA)	6	1,392	425	(NA)	(NA)
Uvalde	9	3.3	372	105	226,538	8,530	(NA)	51	31,241	1,176	51.8	73.0
Val Verde	9	1.9	311	192	408,931	8,919	22.0	92	48,544	1,059	45.8	77.7
Van Zandt	16	3.0	410	158	348,888	6,951	(NA)	57	22,032	439	13.4	85.2
Victoria	21	2.5	1,340	379	1,007,946	11,843	(NA)	144	89,712	1,054	12.7	88.7

See footnotes at end of table.

[Includes United States, states, and 3,141 counties/county equivalents defined as of February 22, 2005. For more information on these areas, see Appendix C, Geographic Information]

County	Banking,[1] 2005 Offices Number	Banking,[1] 2005 Offices Rate per 10,000 people	Banking,[1] 2005 Total deposits (mil. dol.)	Retail trade[2] (NAICS 44–45), 2002 Estab-lishments	Retail trade Sales Total ($1,000)	Retail trade Sales Per capita[3] (dol.)	General merchan-dise stores,[4] percent of total	Accommodation and food services[2] (NAICS 72), 2002 Estab-lishments	Accom. Sales Total ($1,000)	Accom. Sales Per capita[3] (dol.)	Percent change, 1997–2002	Food services,[5] percent of total
TEXAS—Con.												
Walker	10	1.6	505	166	452,926	7,386	(NA)	88	58,334	951	28.6	85.4
Waller	9	2.6	250	173	771,930	22,631	(NA)	63	49,309	1,446	174.3	92.1
Ward	3	2.9	111	42	61,891	5,919	7.5	15	5,524	528	−4.2	(NA)
Washington	12	3.8	636	136	309,592	10,082	(NA)	74	34,439	1,122	46.9	86.7
Webb	41	1.8	4,509	728	2,035,217	9,845	22.2	288	240,598	1,164	66.2	84.7
Wharton	20	4.8	753	198	338,212	8,219	(NA)	65	33,565	816	35.3	89.1
Wheeler	5	10.4	121	29	35,684	7,134	(NA)	17	7,901	1,580	(NA)	65.9
Wichita	37	2.9	1,594	562	1,449,713	11,266	(NA)	260	181,716	1,412	13.9	(NA)
Wilbarger	7	5.0	266	63	111,965	7,834	29.1	30	12,127	848	12.0	82.6
Willacy	4	2.0	93	38	84,210	4,205	(NA)	22	7,265	363	27.4	(NA)
Williamson	86	2.6	2,354	811	8,513,305	29,304	(NA)	389	312,805	1,077	101.9	88.9
Wilson	9	2.4	209	78	108,472	3,156	(NA)	39	10,038	292	(NA)	(NA)
Winkler	4	6.0	80	25	41,105	5,902	9.8	8	(D)	(NA)	(NA)	(NA)
Wise	18	3.2	547	152	556,181	10,514	(NA)	67	33,812	639	44.6	84.0
Wood	21	5.1	472	158	290,886	7,647	(NA)	57	23,082	607	37.1	91.3
Yoakum	4	5.4	83	32	36,005	4,985	(NA)	17	4,077	564	(NA)	(NA)
Young	8	4.4	383	79	142,131	8,027	(NA)	45	11,367	642	14.2	81.5
Zapata	2	1.5	183	40	36,157	2,841	9.7	21	7,835	616	8.8	76.7
Zavala	3	2.5	48	28	30,806	2,647	(NA)	13	2,980	256	8.6	(NA)
UTAH	594	2.4	118,114	8,135	23,675,432	10,206	16.2	4,106	2,984,632	1,287	29.0	72.6
Beaver	3	4.8	58	31	63,100	10,344	(NA)	29	11,385	1,866	10.6	51.3
Box Elder	10	2.2	273	122	354,644	8,054	(NA)	60	39,778	903	52.8	89.7
Cache	22	2.2	847	354	732,162	7,639	(NA)	132	77,727	811	53.8	89.7
Carbon	9	4.6	205	93	189,204	9,538	(NA)	47	20,526	1,035	21.6	65.1
Daggett	—	—	—	6	1,732	1,924	—	4	(D)	(NA)	(NA)	(NA)
Davis	53	2.0	1,759	688	2,169,665	8,705	16.0	299	188,429	756	23.4	91.4
Duchesne	4	2.6	136	61	102,283	6,884	(NA)	32	9,083	611	6.8	84.6
Emery	4	3.7	52	38	69,661	6,504	—	25	8,523	796	81.8	42.8
Garfield	3	6.7	45	24	16,145	3,502	—	55	30,863	6,695	37.6	10.0
Grand	2	2.3	124	76	88,307	10,221	(NA)	82	43,724	5,061	14.0	50.9
Iron	10	2.6	377	152	361,548	10,228	(NA)	87	44,839	1,268	6.8	68.6
Juab	2	2.2	51	35	69,320	8,023	(NA)	20	7,908	915	16.4	74.0
Kane	3	4.8	93	39	35,812	5,931	(NA)	37	17,839	2,954	27.4	45.1
Millard	4	3.3	124	51	76,998	6,218	(NA)	24	8,402	678	39.0	70.8
Morgan	2	2.5	57	20	46,349	6,244	—	11	2,321	313	24.1	100.0
Piute	1	7.3	12	6	3,300	2,388	—	6	(D)	(NA)	(NA)	(NA)
Rich	1	4.9	19	11	7,485	3,833	—	13	1,873	959	−13.6	61.9
Salt Lake	252	2.7	100,828	3,329	11,441,626	12,472	(NA)	1,710	1,537,310	1,676	27.9	72.2
San Juan	4	2.8	63	35	29,373	2,124	(NA)	32	16,510	1,194	−17.3	(NA)
Sanpete	9	3.7	172	76	127,948	5,476	(NA)	44	8,428	361	18.6	87.3
Sevier	7	3.6	180	107	200,478	10,486	(NA)	48	20,843	1,090	33.0	66.4
Summit	15	4.3	690	257	413,820	12,988	(NA)	139	134,940	4,235	28.5	54.2
Tooele	7	1.4	97	83	295,779	6,429	(NA)	48	25,120	546	57.0	80.4
Uintah	4	1.5	183	119	235,363	8,970	(NA)	54	22,204	846	22.8	75.6
Utah	81	1.8	2,676	1,137	3,279,414	8,375	(NA)	473	326,342	833	42.3	79.7
Wasatch	6	3.2	154	63	110,427	6,528	(NA)	42	22,571	1,334	14.6	66.8
Washington	34	2.9	1,345	459	1,156,928	11,615	21.8	200	155,531	1,561	37.4	60.7
Wayne	1	4.1	18	19	18,106	7,123	(NA)	26	5,791	2,278	44.4	46.1
Weber	41	1.9	7,481	644	1,978,455	9,728	21.1	327	190,685	938	22.9	84.5
VERMONT	276	4.4	9,517	3,946	7,623,872	12,366	7.0	1,950	1,154,048	1,872	26.8	54.5
Addison	15	4.1	446	207	385,616	10,571	2.0	82	39,365	1,079	21.3	57.4
Bennington	19	5.1	684	362	683,926	18,424	6.0	175	93,328	2,514	21.8	49.2
Caledonia	18	5.9	484	173	297,293	9,918	3.1	72	27,927	932	14.6	73.6
Chittenden	53	3.5	2,951	892	2,358,040	15,879	(NA)	403	294,325	1,982	41.7	72.0
Essex	2	3.0	21	19	12,310	1,878	—	14	2,763	422	(NA)	75.9
Franklin	20	4.2	516	243	484,454	10,386	(NA)	105	34,229	734	36.5	79.1
Grand Isle	2	2.6	44	32	26,715	3,652	—	24	6,687	914	(NA)	20.3
Lamoille	11	4.5	344	178	232,610	9,692	3.8	117	158,390	6,599	29.6	22.3
Orange	15	5.1	265	131	249,060	8,632	1.0	56	23,957	830	15.0	65.9
Orleans	11	4.0	390	171	240,256	9,001	5.7	72	29,883	1,120	25.7	50.5
Rutland	26	4.1	851	474	849,938	13,421	8.3	234	120,803	1,908	11.2	60.2
Washington	26	4.4	914	418	732,721	12,432	6.2	163	85,068	1,443	35.0	66.7
Windham	22	5.0	728	312	522,322	11,819	3.0	224	132,938	3,008	25.3	42.8
Windsor	36	6.2	880	334	548,611	9,475	3.3	209	104,385	1,803	12.8	43.3
VIRGINIA	2,438	3.2	155,264	28,914	80,509,062	11,069	15.6	13,305	10,929,429	1,503	32.0	73.4
Accomack	15	3.8	466	189	240,450	6,184	5.1	94	43,911	1,129	33.5	62.7
Albemarle	17	1.9	521	297	1,020,833	11,806	18.9	142	163,531	1,891	42.4	72.7
Alleghany[7]	8	4.8	224	60	128,289	7,556	(NA)	17	8,168	481	18.4	44.9
Amelia	3	2.4	82	30	39,986	3,411	(NA)	8	2,831	242	25.9	(NA)
Amherst	9	2.8	322	111	226,771	7,128	(NA)	42	20,089	631	4.1	90.7

See footnotes at end of table.

Table B-11. Counties — **Banking, Retail Trade, and Accommodation and Food Services**—Con.

[Includes United States, states, and 3,141 counties/county equivalents defined as of February 22, 2005. For more information on these areas, see Appendix C, Geographic Information]

County	Banking,[1] 2005 Offices Number	Rate per 10,000 people	Total deposits (mil. dol.)	Retail trade[2] (NAICS 44–45), 2002 Estab-lishments	Sales Total ($1,000)	Per capita[3] (dol.)	General merchan-dise stores,[4] percent of total	Accommodation and food services[2] (NAICS 72), 2002 Estab-lishments	Sales Total ($1,000)	Per capita[3] (dol.)	Percent change, 1997–2002	Food services,[5] percent of total
VIRGINIA—Con.												
Appomattox	4	2.9	213	56	76,416	5,556	(NA)	16	5,745	418	3.4	(NA)
Arlington	72	3.7	17,265	647	2,107,505	11,169	14.3	494	740,062	3,922	19.8	49.9
Augusta	19	2.7	315	184	394,663	5,903	(NA)	64	34,057	509	3.3	74.4
Bath	4	8.1	71	25	12,440	2,468	(NA)	16	(D)	(NA)	(NA)	(NA)
Bedford	13	2.0	358	171	297,077	4,801	(NA)	47	13,434	217	(NA)	93.1
Bland	1	1.4	37	20	16,651	2,411	–	4	(D)	(NA)	(NA)	(NA)
Botetourt	16	5.0	324	97	151,776	4,870	(NA)	39	21,945	704	–20.4	73.8
Brunswick	5	2.8	122	52	54,899	2,990	3.4	13	6,883	375	19.6	(NA)
Buchanan	11	4.4	440	108	137,290	5,271	8.3	20	11,670	448	19.6	(NA)
Buckingham	3	1.9	69	40	53,969	3,409	10.7	6	(D)	(NA)	(NA)	(NA)
Campbell	18	3.4	576	189	367,924	7,155	(NA)	51	24,229	471	(NA)	(NA)
Caroline	7	2.7	269	72	256,890	11,359	(NA)	30	13,160	582	10.6	(NA)
Carroll	7	2.4	236	117	238,283	8,136	(NA)	42	22,210	758	42.6	67.3
Charles City	1	1.4	18	20	26,182	3,706	–	15	3,558	504	(NA)	78.4
Charlotte	6	4.8	127	45	58,327	4,668	(NA)	8	(D)	(NA)	(NA)	(NA)
Chesterfield	86	3.0	2,766	849	2,865,113	10,581	20.9	350	288,648	1,066	29.7	82.2
Clarke	5	3.5	216	42	52,095	3,940	(NA)	16	4,843	366	(NA)	(NA)
Craig	2	3.9	58	11	7,762	1,529	–	2	(D)	(NA)	(NA)	(NA)
Culpeper	10	2.4	547	152	419,800	11,375	(NA)	60	29,904	810	36.0	84.6
Cumberland	3	3.2	52	36	45,783	5,066	(NA)	5	(D)	(NA)	(NA)	(NA)
Dickenson	7	4.3	162	61	87,495	5,391	4.4	16	(D)	(NA)	(NA)	(NA)
Dinwiddie	5	2.0	156	52	99,873	4,051	(NA)	13	7,889	320	33.4	93.4
Essex	7	6.7	236	67	162,308	16,038	(NA)	23	13,305	1,315	7.1	92.7
Fairfax	291	2.9	38,116	2,907	11,150,720	11,237	11.8	1,717	1,863,695	1,878	36.2	72.7
Fauquier	20	3.1	991	222	606,406	10,194	(NA)	83	65,566	1,102	37.6	70.4
Floyd	3	2.0	171	41	49,117	3,445	(NA)	14	4,051	284	(NA)	(NA)
Fluvanna	3	1.2	85	29	40,310	1,832	(NA)	11	7,192	327	45.0	(NA)
Franklin	14	2.8	642	181	313,940	6,469	(NA)	52	(D)	(NA)	(NA)	(NA)
Frederick	15	2.2	436	182	751,027	11,929	(NA)	63	54,795	870	20.3	74.1
Giles	8	4.7	196	77	137,689	8,137	(NA)	19	8,963	530	47.0	(NA)
Gloucester	12	3.2	368	143	346,121	9,638	(NA)	54	27,874	776	44.6	85.1
Goochland	3	1.5	114	57	112,819	6,376	(NA)	16	5,379	304	38.7	88.8
Grayson	6	3.7	179	37	37,689	2,258	(NA)	15	(D)	(NA)	(NA)	(NA)
Greene	5	2.9	100	41	66,376	4,071	(NA)	14	6,978	428	53.5	(NA)
Greensville	–	–	–	25	48,575	4,195	(NA)	12	5,507	476	–15.9	58.5
Halifax[8]	10	2.8	474	143	269,357	7,304	26.0	59	31,851	864	34.3	89.3
Hanover	37	3.8	1,258	313	1,096,337	11,933	(NA)	134	103,734	1,129	50.3	79.4
Henrico	98	3.5	16,161	1,054	4,025,162	15,016	14.4	480	419,255	1,564	19.6	75.5
Henry	20	3.5	555	201	428,619	7,472	27.2	54	31,555	550	–0.1	90.4
Highland	3	12.1	87	23	9,748	3,951	–	5	(D)	(NA)	(NA)	(NA)
Isle of Wight	7	2.1	320	101	152,201	4,920	(NA)	37	16,603	537	(NA)	94.4
James City	22	3.8	699	212	375,915	7,316	(NA)	78	111,169	2,164	49.0	40.2
King and Queen	1	1.5	18	18	16,248	2,470	–	3	(D)	(NA)	(NA)	(NA)
King George	4	1.9	137	45	109,167	6,127	(NA)	29	10,551	592	(NA)	84.8
King William	7	4.8	219	63	119,487	8,663	(NA)	17	5,395	391	40.1	(NA)
Lancaster	11	9.5	378	96	126,270	10,539	(NA)	31	14,734	1,230	–15.5	86.4
Lee	13	5.5	328	85	116,664	4,944	4.4	14	5,456	231	–3.7	(NA)
Loudoun	73	2.9	2,735	792	2,868,495	14,074	16.4	315	314,609	1,544	103.3	82.4
Louisa	8	2.7	255	65	101,492	3,743	(NA)	21	11,724	432	32.4	85.5
Lunenburg	5	3.8	133	50	46,945	3,561	(NA)	9	1,643	125	64.6	100.0
Madison	2	1.5	97	53	107,837	8,305	(NA)	11	7,305	563	28.3	(NA)
Mathews	2	2.2	118	40	40,696	4,402	(NA)	12	(D)	(NA)	(NA)	(NA)
Mecklenburg	20	6.1	599	188	348,098	10,718	10.6	63	33,868	1,043	16.2	74.6
Middlesex	8	7.6	193	70	88,338	8,751	(NA)	19	6,670	661	–23.8	(NA)
Montgomery	36	4.3	1,108	370	920,896	10,989	(NA)	171	118,141	1,410	23.0	83.1
Nelson	5	3.3	148	58	43,430	2,953	(NA)	24	29,460	2,003	25.0	(NA)
New Kent	2	1.2	116	25	59,422	4,161	–	10	3,170	222	–33.9	(NA)
Northampton	7	5.2	184	80	96,711	7,404	19.2	35	22,641	1,733	45.2	63.1
Northumberland	7	5.4	243	52	61,185	4,857	(NA)	21	5,117	406	62.5	89.3
Nottoway	9	5.8	252	78	135,752	8,657	(NA)	23	10,080	643	3.5	79.2
Orange	11	3.6	346	101	204,941	7,509	4.4	37	16,987	622	16.2	88.9
Page	9	3.8	255	87	139,089	5,953	(NA)	54	50,477	2,160	130.6	28.7
Patrick	9	4.7	226	52	82,365	4,265	(NA)	23	5,225	271	(NA)	93.3
Pittsylvania	11	1.8	272	164	307,166	4,973	38.5	44	12,970	210	–34.2	(NA)
Powhatan	4	1.5	213	56	111,680	4,603	(NA)	13	(D)	(NA)	(NA)	(NA)
Prince Edward	9	4.4	305	111	300,454	14,997	(NA)	44	31,539	1,574	12.9	92.2
Prince George	4	1.1	103	69	117,191	3,448	(NA)	26	18,540	546	–11.3	(NA)
Prince William	67	1.9	2,108	1,013	3,762,787	12,106	16.5	401	347,033	1,116	30.5	91.4
Pulaski	11	3.1	317	125	232,005	6,633	(NA)	65	30,987	886	44.2	83.4
Rappahannock	2	2.8	67	33	36,606	5,119	(NA)	14	11,469	1,604	31.6	94.0

See footnotes at end of table.

[Includes United States, states, and 3,141 counties/county equivalents defined as of February 22, 2005. For more information on these areas, see Appendix C, Geographic Information]

County	Banking,[1] 2005			Retail trade[2] (NAICS 44–45), 2002				Accommodation and food services[2] (NAICS 72), 2002				
	Offices				Sales					Sales		
	Number	Rate per 10,000 people	Total deposits (mil. dol.)	Estab- lishments	Total ($1,000)	Per capita[3] (dol.)	General merchan- dise stores,[4] percent of total	Estab- lishments	Total ($1,000)	Per capita[3] (dol.)	Percent change, 1997– 2002	Food services,[5] percent of total
VIRGINIA—Con.												
Richmond.	5	5.5	158	52	74,280	8,270	7.7	13	4,225	470	(NA)	(NA)
Roanoke	34	3.9	1,031	309	835,274	9,655	(NA)	132	86,200	996	97.7	80.8
Rockbridge.	10	4.7	323	45	171,961	8,246	(NA)	32	22,173	1,063	11.5	33.6
Rockingham	22	3.1	572	213	475,281	6,889	(NA)	60	39,547	573	−27.0	(NA)
Russell	11	3.8	348	97	194,779	6,725	14.0	25	8,333	288	−14.4	(NA)
Scott.	11	4.8	196	95	166,262	7,199	4.1	16	8,904	386	(NA)	(NA)
Shenandoah	18	4.6	642	174	344,941	9,472	(NA)	77	37,807	1,038	23.3	69.1
Smyth	12	3.7	438	152	235,252	7,168	(NA)	50	17,851	544	8.5	86.5
Southampton	7	4.0	85	42	39,500	2,275	(NA)	8	(D)	(NA)	(NA)	(NA)
Spotsylvania	24	2.1	803	267	1,170,499	11,412	16.6	103	81,643	796	31.9	82.7
Stafford	19	1.6	597	221	614,479	5,893	(NA)	138	88,495	849	54.3	77.2
Surry.	2	2.9	27	14	10,242	1,471	–	3	(D)	(NA)	(NA)	(NA)
Sussex	7	5.8	124	46	64,411	5,311	(NA)	17	8,925	736	31.7	(NA)
Tazewell.	31	6.9	727	254	617,088	13,930	32.8	65	35,364	798	9.0	(NA)
Warren	13	3.7	434	133	289,087	8,743	8.8	66	30,292	916	18.2	75.9
Washington	26	5.0	852	232	471,589	9,187	(NA)	93	56,953	1,110	17.4	79.7
Westmoreland.	7	4.1	220	58	89,143	5,327	(NA)	38	11,184	668	15.7	85.2
Wise	17	4.0	414	189	362,695	8,671	10.9	55	26,371	630	28.7	91.7
Wythe	17	6.0	392	188	535,960	19,256	11.6	72	48,064	1,727	25.0	66.2
York	16	2.6	538	257	538,333	9,079	26.1	111	104,215	1,758	33.8	(NA)
Independent Cities												
Alexandria	52	3.8	3,512	551	2,053,604	15,825	12.5	342	395,295	3,046	28.2	75.6
Bedford	6	9.7	354	72	108,730	17,314	(NA)	25	15,597	2,484	(NA)	76.1
Bristol	15	8.7	609	173	382,268	22,359	(NA)	64	41,699	2,439	(NA)	(NA)
Buena Vista	3	4.7	77	26	39,020	6,197	(NA)	13	6,331	1,005	44.7	(NA)
Charlottesville	36	8.9	1,919	382	901,079	23,272	3.8	203	153,514	3,965	26.3	(NA)
Chesapeake	45	2.1	1,829	792	2,587,372	12,589	22.5	322	245,015	1,192	30.8	85.2
Clifton Forge[7]	(NA)	(NA)	(NA)	(X)	(X)	(NA)	(NA)	(X)	(X)	(NA)	(NA)	(NA)
Colonial Heights	12	6.8	402	196	514,751	30,023	45.7	57	50,285	2,933	23.3	(NA)
Covington.	3	4.8	148	67	101,589	16,031	4.3	23	(D)	(NA)	(NA)	(NA)
Danville	32	6.9	1,121	332	672,723	14,219	11.1	123	88,898	1,879	35.2	(NA)
Emporia.	7	12.5	212	90	137,054	24,011	(NA)	24	21,291	3,730	31.4	72.1
Fairfax.	29	13.2	2,347	305	1,727,272	79,313	12.7	151	129,491	5,946	19.9	92.1
Falls Church	13	12.1	790	118	506,846	47,699	(NA)	89	47,044	4,427	(NA)	(NA)
Franklin	6	7.0	160	60	134,521	16,435	(NA)	32	19,981	2,441	97.9	78.7
Fredericksburg	21	10.1	1,238	350	795,191	39,726	14.7	147	131,054	6,547	42.5	83.2
Galax	9	13.5	309	78	142,854	21,475	(NA)	34	14,882	2,237	(NA)	(NA)
Hampton	21	1.4	762	480	1,500,977	10,362	14.2	231	168,280	1,162	12.3	77.6
Harrisonburg.	29	7.2	896	350	891,822	21,764	(NA)	150	108,438	2,646	54.4	(NA)
Hopewell	7	3.1	288	86	111,652	4,975	(NA)	48	43,011	1,916	(NA)	77.0
Lexington	3	4.4	131	76	109,283	15,836	(NA)	76	42,961	6,225	56.9	63.7
Lynchburg	37	5.5	1,495	433	1,420,834	21,875	(NA)	174	130,883	2,015	18.1	87.1
Manassas	16	4.3	901	183	712,711	19,461	(NA)	94	55,896	1,526	(NA)	94.4
Manassas Park	1	0.9	32	25	116,442	10,653	–	10	10,002	915	208.1	(NA)
Martinsville.	9	6.0	577	129	218,572	14,418	11.2	53	27,745	1,830	10.5	91.0
Newport News.	28	1.6	1,162	674	2,078,241	11,565	21.6	306	214,404	1,193	26.1	80.0
Norfolk.	59	2.5	3,933	971	2,231,322	9,362	15.9	530	424,514	1,781	41.8	77.0
Norton.	5	13.6	187	58	194,947	49,643	(NA)	22	11,953	3,044	(NA)	87.9
Petersburg	12	3.7	436	155	346,861	10,469	(NA)	61	31,056	937	−9.3	77.1
Poquoson	1	0.8	46	25	44,676	3,847	(NA)	18	7,208	621	66.2	100.0
Portsmouth.	15	1.5	891	291	522,938	5,263	2.8	157	82,556	831	40.6	76.5
Radford	10	6.9	285	55	97,428	6,355	(NA)	43	21,692	1,415	51.9	(NA)
Richmond.	62	3.2	10,425	1,160	2,526,091	12,868	14.1	601	430,190	2,191	41.4	77.8
Roanoke	40	4.3	2,143	577	1,712,312	18,378	14.8	287	214,221	2,299	5.3	76.5
Salem	16	6.5	596	161	693,001	27,961	(NA)	85	48,165	1,943	6.5	81.2
South Boston[8]	(NA)	(NA)	(NA)	(X)	(X)	(NA)	(NA)	(X)	(X)	(NA)	(NA)	(NA)
Staunton	14	6.0	641	197	447,279	18,796	(NA)	81	47,990	2,017	39.7	80.1
Suffolk.	17	2.2	504	198	576,240	8,253	(NA)	71	43,668	625	33.0	84.8
Virginia Beach.	93	2.1	4,534	1,626	4,168,686	9,674	17.1	959	875,114	2,031	51.9	62.5
Waynesboro	9	4.2	314	124	236,458	11,738	12.7	50	31,551	1,566	20.8	80.8
Williamsburg.	6	5.1	186	146	270,497	23,432	(NA)	140	200,332	17,354	−2.2	47.2
Winchester.	32	12.7	1,280	276	807,467	33,161	(NA)	116	77,560	3,185	33.8	83.1
WASHINGTON.	1,832	2.9	91,469	22,564	65,262,333	10,757	15.9	13,699	8,642,681	1,425	23.4	79.5
Adams.	10	6.0	141	64	109,770	6,669	(NA)	38	15,648	951	28.4	73.9
Asotin	7	3.3	233	49	156,508	7,610	(NA)	37	19,487	948	20.8	77.4
Benton.	41	2.6	1,446	585	1,636,459	10,879	(NA)	289	194,012	1,290	42.5	84.1
Chelan.	25	3.6	1,112	400	737,793	10,981	13.0	235	128,873	1,918	30.5	58.1
Clallam	32	4.6	1,278	307	601,935	9,108	20.1	215	92,332	1,397	21.6	73.5

See footnotes at end of table.

Table B-11. Counties — Banking, Retail Trade, and Accommodation and Food Services—Con.

[Includes United States, states, and 3,141 counties/county equivalents defined as of February 22, 2005. For more information on these areas, see Appendix C, Geographic Information]

County	Banking,[1] 2005 Offices Number	Banking,[1] 2005 Offices Rate per 10,000 people	Banking,[1] 2005 Total deposits (mil. dol.)	Retail trade[2] (NAICS 44-45), 2002 Estab-lishments	Retail trade[2] Sales Total ($1,000)	Retail trade[2] Sales Per capita[3] (dol.)	Retail trade[2] Sales General merchandise stores,[4] percent of total	Accommodation and food services[2] (NAICS 72), 2002 Estab-lishments	Accommodation and food services[2] Sales Total ($1,000)	Accommodation and food services[2] Sales Per capita[3] (dol.)	Accommodation and food services[2] Sales Percent change, 1997-2002	Accommodation and food services[2] Food services,[5] percent of total
WASHINGTON—Con.												
Clark	92	2.3	3,498	920	2,946,201	7,961	18.7	605	359,783	972	32.4	87.2
Columbia	4	9.7	70	27	20,281	4,930	(NA)	11	3,650	887	(NA)	(NA)
Cowlitz	20	2.1	657	392	938,408	9,914	18.6	219	112,475	1,188	15.9	91.4
Douglas	11	3.1	339	95	289,709	8,711	46.2	59	24,096	725	11.5	94.2
Ferry	1	1.3	20	31	34,634	4,749	–	14	3,436	471	-32.0	75.5
Franklin	13	2.1	324	186	608,745	11,492	(NA)	92	39,680	749	14.8	71.1
Garfield	3	12.8	36	15	13,042	5,651	(NA)	6	627	272	(NA)	(NA)
Grant	24	3.0	610	306	590,194	7,608	(NA)	174	69,895	901	18.8	76.6
Grays Harbor	29	4.1	950	313	544,032	7,921	16.3	226	94,763	1,380	27.7	73.3
Island	25	3.2	790	232	413,649	5,472	(NA)	148	58,848	778	31.9	84.4
Jefferson	13	4.5	428	155	168,308	6,172	(NA)	96	31,762	1,165	-10.8	74.1
King	515	2.9	43,563	6,915	24,261,001	13,797	12.7	4,685	3,776,814	2,148	19.4	74.7
Kitsap	70	2.9	2,120	809	2,266,877	9,507	22.2	434	235,184	986	30.4	89.0
Kittitas	13	3.5	455	178	316,207	9,148	14.3	143	58,845	1,702	29.0	78.7
Klickitat	7	3.5	229	62	56,938	2,934	(NA)	52	14,971	771	57.0	85.0
Lewis	28	3.9	796	362	673,931	9,675	14.4	177	71,523	1,027	13.7	87.3
Lincoln	10	9.6	157	55	69,017	6,817	–	28	3,569	353	-15.6	90.2
Mason	12	2.2	378	136	268,476	5,244	(NA)	100	31,526	616	5.4	84.2
Okanogan	14	3.5	331	192	268,864	6,847	(NA)	119	42,423	1,080	(Z)	51.9
Pacific	13	6.0	345	116	93,739	4,520	(NA)	105	27,679	1,335	2.8	74.9
Pend Oreille	3	2.4	78	41	37,931	3,130	(NA)	26	4,947	408	2.5	90.9
Pierce	194	2.6	7,640	2,249	7,089,770	9,694	17.3	1,244	782,231	1,070	29.4	88.9
San Juan	8	5.2	312	123	122,673	8,391	–	94	42,390	2,900	5.7	43.4
Skagit	46	4.1	1,610	618	1,603,785	15,029	18.5	295	186,785	1,750	58.0	68.2
Skamania	3	2.8	50	20	17,157	1,704	–	19	19,973	1,984	353.3	10.5
Snohomish	177	2.7	7,238	2,038	6,643,541	10,511	15.4	1,219	701,420	1,110	25.3	91.5
Spokane	122	2.8	5,515	1,699	4,867,840	11,394	17.7	908	578,623	1,354	27.4	80.8
Stevens	7	1.7	292	153	197,146	4,854	(NA)	88	22,737	560	-3.2	78.6
Thurston	64	2.8	2,313	757	2,236,011	10,299	20.1	399	244,999	1,128	27.0	88.7
Wahkiakum	2	5.2	36	11	7,216	1,893	–	8	1,413	371	-4.6	(NA)
Walla Walla	23	4.0	1,007	207	444,823	7,941	21.5	116	57,201	1,021	33.7	84.6
Whatcom	70	3.8	2,516	819	1,776,574	10,205	16.8	451	245,775	1,412	25.5	81.1
Whitman	24	6.0	592	127	232,749	5,758	(NA)	121	39,673	982	28.3	69.5
Yakima	57	2.5	1,964	800	1,900,399	8,463	20.3	404	202,613	902	13.4	85.2
WEST VIRGINIA	639	3.5	23,340	7,454	16,747,900	9,277	18.9	3,310	1,974,851	1,094	20.9	77.4
Barbour	5	3.2	188	47	74,259	4,778	(NA)	16	4,918	316	(NA)	(NA)
Berkeley	28	3.0	884	281	655,521	8,047	21.4	141	82,880	1,017	22.5	74.6
Boone	6	2.3	226	87	156,269	6,088	(NA)	24	9,623	375	16.4	88.4
Braxton	7	4.7	188	86	123,859	8,364	3.2	33	15,864	1,071	10.6	(NA)
Brooke	7	2.9	353	77	99,118	3,956	(NA)	59	19,648	784	(NA)	(NA)
Cabell	33	3.5	1,608	504	1,246,185	13,058	(NA)	254	172,777	1,810	22.6	(NA)
Calhoun	2	2.7	57	27	25,325	3,435	(NA)	7	1,184	161	-69.4	(NA)
Clay	3	2.9	58	31	36,474	3,508	(NA)	5	1,316	127	169.7	100.0
Doddridge	3	4.0	94	17	14,454	1,940	(NA)	5	816	110	(NA)	100.0
Fayette	16	3.4	434	202	352,540	7,477	24.6	71	32,242	684	15.7	85.6
Gilmer	2	2.9	87	24	26,010	3,707	(NA)	10	2,868	409	12.6	(NA)
Grant	4	3.4	177	47	85,101	7,496	(NA)	21	5,223	460	19.7	73.9
Greenbrier	16	4.6	592	205	376,449	10,877	25.2	74	133,750	3,865	13.0	(NA)
Hampshire	8	3.6	250	58	91,381	4,358	3.9	32	18,667	890	67.4	51.3
Hancock	12	3.8	415	119	234,848	7,323	(NA)	69	27,369	853	(NA)	100.0
Hardy	8	6.0	290	49	88,017	6,854	(NA)	24	10,621	827	41.1	(NA)
Harrison	30	4.4	869	350	956,329	14,063	(NA)	150	84,890	1,248	16.2	(NA)
Jackson	12	4.2	352	109	314,980	11,154	(NA)	41	22,339	791	11.3	85.6
Jefferson	13	2.6	641	139	342,559	7,617	(NA)	93	72,095	1,603	91.9	79.0
Kanawha	66	3.4	3,272	922	2,648,190	13,504	20.3	427	334,019	1,703	19.0	80.8
Lewis	5	2.9	249	80	149,870	8,863	(NA)	31	12,179	720	-1.6	79.1
Lincoln	6	2.7	118	52	61,357	2,748	(NA)	14	3,028	136	(NA)	100.0
Logan	13	3.6	437	165	432,841	11,695	21.9	66	29,221	790	21.5	92.5
McDowell	10	4.1	194	84	106,823	4,099	21.3	14	5,282	203	-5.8	(NA)
Marion	18	3.2	591	221	480,159	8,523	(NA)	114	44,826	796	21.5	86.8
Marshall	11	3.2	312	103	204,034	5,826	13.2	61	18,866	539	-3.8	96.5
Mason	8	3.1	276	77	114,790	4,406	(NA)	28	8,794	338	16.1	(NA)
Mercer	18	2.9	895	305	745,891	11,998	17.8	102	76,943	1,238	19.7	(NA)
Mineral	8	3.0	208	87	182,819	6,742	(NA)	48	16,608	613	26.3	(NA)
Mingo	13	4.8	398	102	124,854	4,502	4.0	36	10,930	394	1.2	(NA)
Monongalia	32	3.8	1,320	368	829,467	10,027	18.8	199	125,094	1,512	30.9	77.1
Monroe	3	2.2	108	36	24,275	1,821	(NA)	19	2,788	209	94.3	(NA)
Morgan	5	3.1	203	53	82,486	5,382	3.1	22	18,003	1,175	52.5	32.2
Nicholas	9	3.4	307	120	267,385	10,136	(NA)	51	25,984	985	39.7	76.3
Ohio	23	5.1	985	222	446,976	9,660	1.1	126	67,880	1,467	12.7	87.2

See footnotes at end of table.

Table B-11. Counties — **Banking, Retail Trade, and Accommodation and Food Services**—Con.

[Includes United States, states, and 3,141 counties/county equivalents defined as of February 22, 2005. For more information on these areas, see Appendix C, Geographic Information]

County	Banking,[1] 2005 Offices Number	Rate per 10,000 people	Total deposits (mil. dol.)	Retail trade[2] (NAICS 44–45), 2002 Establishments	Sales Total ($1,000)	Per capita[3] (dol.)	General merchandise stores,[4] percent of total	Accommodation and food services[2] (NAICS 72), 2002 Establishments	Sales Total ($1,000)	Per capita[3] (dol.)	Percent change, 1997–2002	Food services,[5] percent of total
WEST VIRGINIA—Con.												
Pendleton.	3	3.8	131	29	33,085	4,167	(NA)	12	2,653	334	−1.2	(NA)
Pleasants.	4	5.4	86	24	39,967	5,300	(NA)	9	(D)	(NA)	(NA)	(NA)
Pocahontas.	6	6.8	129	50	55,766	6,225	(NA)	24	45,848	5,118	13.8	(NA)
Preston.	12	4.0	324	102	176,311	5,946	8.1	37	7,887	266	17.7	94.8
Putnam.	18	3.3	728	179	453,027	8,661	7.7	71	40,990	784	27.4	89.4
Raleigh.	23	2.9	1,002	364	918,983	11,596	19.0	136	111,314	1,405	31.9	74.9
Randolph.	11	3.9	376	137	274,397	9,666	20.4	62	24,354	858	3.3	84.4
Ritchie.	8	7.6	103	37	39,704	3,809	(NA)	13	2,247	216	3.2	(NA)
Roane.	6	3.9	217	52	97,915	6,400	(NA)	10	4,749	310	4.9	(NA)
Summers.	3	2.2	120	37	65,555	4,679	9.7	23	8,639	617	17.3	89.4
Taylor.	3	1.8	94	38	80,606	4,995	(NA)	19	5,610	348	54.3	(NA)
Tucker.	5	7.2	100	32	45,097	6,231	(NA)	30	12,535	1,732	6.6	(NA)
Tyler.	4	4.3	84	25	29,350	3,118	−	11	1,804	192	(NA)	(NA)
Upshur.	7	3.0	263	95	240,478	10,276	(NA)	43	16,859	720	22.8	86.0
Wayne.	9	2.1	259	117	216,673	5,106	(NA)	41	14,915	351	20.4	(NA)
Webster.	3	3.1	52	32	31,623	3,244	(NA)	12	1,157	119	(NA)	(NA)
Wetzel.	11	6.4	224	93	196,798	11,399	(NA)	43	17,282	1,001	40.7	94.7
Wirt.	2	3.4	34	12	10,159	1,736	(NA)	6	(D)	(NA)	(NA)	(NA)
Wood.	30	3.4	1,161	440	1,413,387	16,110	(NA)	198	121,481	1,385	9.7	(NA)
Wyoming.	8	3.3	216	103	127,124	5,096	13.5	23	9,674	388	18.6	100.0
WISCONSIN.	2,298	4.2	100,643	21,360	59,978,700	11,025	14.7	13,268	6,885,765	1,266	21.9	80.1
Adams.	6	2.9	183	36	102,774	5,016	5.2	35	17,239	841	18.0	(NA)
Ashland.	9	5.4	241	93	165,438	9,850	(NA)	80	25,605	1,525	23.0	80.4
Barron.	24	5.2	803	253	597,966	13,148	20.8	137	46,953	1,032	18.9	87.6
Bayfield.	11	7.3	188	79	91,446	6,040	(NA)	94	29,335	1,938	32.4	40.5
Brown.	90	3.8	4,951	988	3,051,980	13,155	(NA)	556	332,297	1,432	17.3	83.5
Buffalo.	11	7.9	240	51	58,289	4,217	(NA)	44	(D)	(NA)	(NA)	(NA)
Burnett.	9	5.4	187	80	95,396	5,923	3.2	74	18,084	1,123	(NA)	69.7
Calumet.	15	3.4	399	109	304,950	7,173	(NA)	73	36,673	863	47.3	99.2
Chippewa.	26	4.3	662	234	648,558	11,524	11.0	130	42,883	762	24.9	82.4
Clark.	21	6.2	443	124	233,195	6,892	(NA)	61	16,585	490	(NA)	91.4
Columbia.	30	5.4	864	233	495,075	9,262	(NA)	206	91,833	1,718	47.5	75.9
Crawford.	13	7.6	358	90	180,451	10,600	(NA)	54	19,442	1,142	23.5	77.9
Dane.	172	3.8	9,749	1,775	5,818,321	13,174	(NA)	1,047	718,149	1,626	29.6	82.8
Dodge.	41	4.7	985	262	664,887	7,647	17.5	145	44,505	512	7.1	94.3
Door.	20	7.1	765	288	330,511	11,685	14.0	243	118,861	4,202	23.3	54.1
Douglas.	15	3.4	540	168	443,586	10,149	15.3	178	61,654	1,411	21.2	81.4
Dunn.	27	6.5	354	145	330,214	8,099	21.7	79	35,503	871	6.2	86.2
Eau Claire.	37	3.9	1,201	453	1,275,771	13,557	22.9	247	140,651	1,495	21.3	83.7
Florence.	5	10.1	68	16	20,136	3,927	−	20	3,409	665	(NA)	93.6
Fond du Lac.	34	3.4	1,381	411	1,028,966	10,519	16.1	222	111,884	1,144	20.4	89.8
Forest.	6	6.0	125	50	97,818	9,852	(NA)	39	(D)	(NA)	(NA)	(NA)
Grant.	38	7.7	1,013	224	384,738	7,781	15.6	148	37,336	755	7.7	84.7
Green.	20	5.7	749	155	455,286	13,353	13.2	82	29,125	854	0.1	92.4
Green Lake.	14	7.3	451	100	185,046	9,614	(NA)	61	23,375	1,214	16.6	64.9
Iowa.	14	5.9	331	111	1,609,849	69,588	(NA)	46	13,928	602	(NA)	82.2
Iron.	2	3.0	59	39	58,100	8,548	−	45	14,171	2,085	25.3	51.3
Jackson.	10	5.1	225	82	157,856	8,174	(NA)	52	18,078	936	5.9	81.1
Jefferson.	29	3.7	925	290	684,128	8,890	14.5	192	70,197	912	33.0	90.6
Juneau.	15	5.6	319	104	199,352	7,949	(NA)	69	23,081	920	−32.5	83.1
Kenosha.	41	2.6	1,727	544	1,473,555	9,571	10.6	323	150,679	979	13.0	91.6
Kewaunee.	13	6.2	323	75	137,301	6,692	(NA)	52	12,000	585	3.8	84.2
La Crosse.	41	3.8	1,598	477	1,510,894	13,985	(NA)	294	165,667	1,533	16.8	(NA)
Lafayette.	16	9.8	290	49	73,723	4,520	−	38	(D)	(NA)	(NA)	(NA)
Langlade.	7	3.4	137	112	271,136	13,020	25.3	73	23,003	1,105	22.1	84.2
Lincoln.	13	4.3	363	134	273,235	9,110	(NA)	101	23,350	778	9.6	86.1
Manitowoc.	30	3.7	1,181	300	654,691	7,945	15.8	185	71,868	872	21.1	85.9
Marathon.	53	4.1	2,121	528	1,844,149	14,530	17.9	273	128,050	1,009	21.7	85.9
Marinette.	24	5.5	673	204	425,596	9,805	16.2	145	41,139	948	13.7	(NA)
Marquette.	10	6.6	191	42	58,883	3,998	(NA)	61	15,857	1,077	(NA)	74.5
Menominee.	−	−	−	5	6,505	1,406	−	2	(D)	(NA)	(NA)	(NA)
Milwaukee.	295	3.2	29,010	2,936	8,851,410	9,473	13.6	1,778	1,254,504	1,343	23.7	84.9
Monroe.	20	4.7	548	158	352,910	8,490	(NA)	110	41,402	996	15.6	77.2
Oconto.	16	4.2	303	102	192,670	5,259	(NA)	99	23,652	646	−9.6	87.1
Oneida.	19	5.1	634	273	703,015	19,013	16.2	178	65,190	1,763	5.8	72.4
Outagamie.	65	3.8	2,650	750	2,555,214	15,385	(NA)	383	234,557	1,412	22.1	81.3
Ozaukee.	47	5.5	1,724	342	835,860	9,947	11.7	178	101,492	1,208	35.3	90.7
Pepin.	3	4.1	185	33	103,294	14,073	(NA)	28	(D)	(NA)	(NA)	(NA)
Pierce.	19	4.9	501	103	180,863	4,831	(NA)	104	26,265	702	8.1	95.8
Polk.	22	5.0	628	189	319,124	7,463	12.9	120	31,281	732	18.6	85.4
Portage.	24	3.6	918	268	594,626	8,840	24.5	177	85,453	1,270	−0.9	80.5

See footnotes at end of table.

Table B-11. Counties — **Banking, Retail Trade, and Accommodation and Food Services**—Con.

[Includes United States, states, and 3,141 counties/county equivalents defined as of February 22, 2005. For more information on these areas, see Appendix C, Geographic Information]

County	Banking,[1] 2005 Offices Number	Offices Rate per 10,000 people	Total deposits (mil. dol.)	Retail trade[2] (NAICS 44–45), 2002 Estab-lishments	Sales Total ($1,000)	Per capita[3] (dol.)	General merchandise stores,[4] percent of total	Accommodation and food services[2] (NAICS 72), 2002 Estab-lishments	Sales Total ($1,000)	Per capita[3] (dol.)	Percent change, 1997–2002	Food services,[5] percent of total
WISCONSIN—Con.												
Price	9	5.9	220	83	114,274	7,391	(NA)	48	9,874	639	(NA)	71.3
Racine.	69	3.5	2,629	689	1,895,046	9,924	16.8	349	186,128	975	20.3	87.7
Richland.	9	4.9	240	85	199,696	11,024	(NA)	35	12,756	704	(NA)	93.9
Rock	46	2.9	1,721	558	1,754,016	11,384	18.0	353	183,824	1,193	21.6	90.7
Rusk	9	5.9	179	55	92,887	6,067	5.3	29	(D)	(NA)	(NA)	(NA)
St. Croix.	31	4.0	876	232	775,814	11,331	(NA)	170	83,670	1,222	58.3	81.5
Sauk	35	6.1	1,153	306	849,072	15,178	17.1	235	238,730	4,268	93.2	43.4
Sawyer	11	6.5	377	111	199,945	12,054	(NA)	114	58,527	3,528	140.5	40.0
Shawano	17	4.1	456	159	297,584	7,258	16.1	108	32,336	789	-1.8	86.3
Sheboygan	45	3.9	1,595	423	1,149,300	10,144	18.0	250	138,650	1,224	30.9	61.9
Taylor	9	4.6	358	95	165,315	8,408	(NA)	49	10,247	521	(NA)	100.0
Trempealeau.	19	6.8	503	125	229,557	8,441	(NA)	83	18,908	695	10.7	93.5
Vernon.	16	5.5	354	109	182,901	6,447	(NA)	56	13,571	478	(NA)	90.6
Vilas	14	6.3	384	167	191,135	8,771	2.4	217	65,823	3,021	-5.9	53.4
Walworth	44	4.4	1,396	369	815,244	8,562	13.7	270	185,537	1,949	10.4	58.7
Washburn.	9	5.4	217	113	190,050	11,577	(NA)	89	21,520	1,311	22.0	75.6
Washington	52	4.1	1,852	398	1,295,713	10,706	16.1	223	111,084	918	18.6	91.3
Waukesha	181	4.8	7,586	1,386	5,238,908	14,146	13.6	691	484,504	1,308	30.0	83.7
Waupaca	30	5.7	827	240	473,023	9,029	14.2	141	47,532	907	13.8	85.0
Waushara.	17	6.9	281	87	156,297	6,679	(NA)	62	18,172	776	(NA)	84.4
Winnebago	46	2.9	1,594	553	1,511,094	9,535	12.6	352	167,338	1,056	8.8	88.5
Wood	38	5.1	1,382	350	1,013,092	13,440	17.8	183	75,173	997	15.1	85.9
WYOMING	210	4.1	8,563	2,861	5,783,756	11,586	15.3	1,742	984,684	1,973	21.7	58.2
Albany.	10	3.2	348	167	354,968	11,234	(NA)	101	61,240	1,938	35.8	80.1
Big Horn	6	5.3	189	47	44,506	3,963	–	37	5,470	487	13.1	81.0
Campbell	10	2.7	571	187	445,835	12,327	(NA)	82	53,465	1,478	27.6	80.3
Carbon	8	5.2	218	95	176,255	11,455	3.8	85	30,060	1,954	16.3	48.1
Converse	4	3.1	209	67	88,081	7,127	(NA)	41	14,612	1,182	15.4	67.1
Crook	3	4.9	101	27	32,701	5,543	(NA)	26	9,218	1,562	99.4	(NA)
Fremont.	17	4.7	443	214	385,033	10,682	19.0	139	49,402	1,371	23.9	70.3
Goshen	7	5.7	282	61	72,880	5,929	3.8	35	9,396	764	4.5	86.1
Hot Springs	3	6.6	111	31	23,391	4,949	(NA)	25	8,771	1,856	22.7	57.0
Johnson	4	5.2	224	49	43,394	5,851	(NA)	43	15,313	2,065	57.5	49.7
Laramie.	24	2.8	1,066	366	1,190,629	14,313	14.8	177	138,761	1,668	30.6	77.6
Lincoln.	9	5.6	230	83	116,938	7,824	3.9	63	13,750	920	19.6	64.8
Natrona	19	2.7	1,047	370	876,372	12,979	21.8	177	97,853	1,449	23.9	80.0
Niobrara.	2	8.7	46	14	13,032	5,743	–	13	3,800	1,675	5.4	(NA)
Park	15	5.6	568	198	277,801	10,703	(NA)	133	79,511	3,063	-11.7	(NA)
Platte	7	8.1	168	43	76,914	8,764	(NA)	40	12,242	1,395	34.2	69.5
Sheridan	11	4.0	546	167	319,566	11,853	(NA)	95	48,156	1,786	30.9	59.9
Sublette.	3	4.3	117	45	38,419	6,176	(NA)	41	9,849	1,583	29.8	54.6
Sweetwater.	12	3.2	587	195	496,241	13,303	18.6	100	83,261	2,232	35.9	(NA)
Teton.	17	8.9	993	255	363,169	19,535	(NA)	175	197,559	10,627	18.8	30.5
Uinta	9	4.5	219	90	244,512	12,363	(NA)	52	27,016	1,366	11.4	65.1
Washakie.	7	8.8	156	57	69,038	8,692	(NA)	34	8,640	1,088	3.3	82.2
Weston	3	4.5	124	33	34,081	5,147	(NA)	28	7,339	1,108	76.9	77.6

– Represents zero.   D Data withheld to avoid disclosure.   NA Not available.   X Not applicable.   Z Less than .05 percent.

[1]As of June 30. Covers all FDIC-insured commercial banks and savings institutions.
[2]Includes only establishments with payroll.
[3]Based on resident population estimated as of July 1, 2002.
[4]Represents NAICS code 452.
[5]Represents NAICS code 722. Includes full-service restaurants, limited-service eating places, special food services, and drinking places (alcoholic beverages).
[6]Yellowstone National Park County became incorporated with Gallatin and Park Counties, MT; effective November 7, 1997.
[7]Clifton Forge independent city became incorporated with Alleghany County, VA; effective July 1, 2001.
[8]South Boston independent city became incorporated with Halifax County, VA; effective June 30, 1995.

Survey, Census, or Data Collection Method: Banking—Based on surveys on every FDIC-insured bank and savings association as of June 30 each year conducted by the Federal Deposit Insurance Corporation (FDIC) and the Office of Thrift Supervision (OTS); for information, see Internet site <http://www2.fdic.gov/sod/sodPublications.asp?barItem=5>.   Retail trade and accommodation and food services—Based on the 2002 Economic Census; for more information, see Appendix B, Limitations of the Data and Methodology, and also <http://www.census.gov/econ/census02/>.

Sources: Banking—U.S. Federal Deposit Insurance Corporation (FDIC) and Office of Thrift Supervision (OTS), 2005 Bank and Thrift Branch Office Data Book: Summary of Deposits, accessed August 9, 2006 (related Internet site <http://www2.fdic.gov/sod/index.asp>).   Retail trade—U.S. Census Bureau, 2002 Economic Census, *Retail Trade, Geographic Area Series*, accessed June 21, 2005 (related Internet site <http://www.census.gov/econ/census02/>).   Accommodation and food services—U.S. Census Bureau, 1997 and 2002 Economic Censuses, *Accommodation and Food Services, Geographic Area Series*, accessed June 21, 2005 (related Internet site <http://www.census.gov/econ/census02/>).

Table B-12. Counties — Government Expenditure, Earnings, and Employment

[Includes United States, states, and 3,141 counties/county equivalents defined as of February 22, 2005. For more information on these areas, see Appendix C, Geographic Information]

County	Federal government expenditure 2004 Total (mil. dol.)	Percent change, 2000–2004	Per capita (dol.)	Direct payments to individuals, percent of total	2000 (mil. dol.)	Earnings 2005 Total (mil. dol.)	Percent of total	Percent change, 2000–2005	2000 (mil. dol.)	Employment 2005 Total	Percent of total	Percent change, 2000–2005	2000
UNITED STATES.	[2]2,143,782	[2]31.9	[2]7,300	[2]50.2	[2]1,624,777	1,319,146	16.5	32.5	995,592	23,837,000	13.7	3.9	22,944,000
ALABAMA.	[3]39,047	[3]33.5	[3]8,619	[3]51.9	[3]29,250	19,935	20.2	30.9	15,232	400,711	16.0	3.9	385,840
Autauga.	235	15.8	4,960	74.9	203	97	18.3	36.9	71	2,377	13.1	7.8	2,204
Baldwin.	806	40.2	5,144	82.7	575	401	16.5	38.7	289	9,530	11.6	5.6	9,022
Barbour.	179	27.2	6,270	65.5	141	81	17.3	20.7	67	2,129	14.5	-5.4	2,250
Bibb.	113	30.5	5,300	76.0	87	54	29.1	34.3	40	1,428	22.6	8.3	1,318
Blount.	204	35.9	3,704	77.7	150	86	19.9	38.4	62	2,244	12.5	7.8	2,081
Bullock.	80	24.7	7,085	60.5	64	33	26.4	27.4	26	853	19.0	1.7	839
Butler.	141	24.9	6,794	70.8	113	44	14.8	21.8	36	1,172	12.0	-4.9	1,233
Calhoun.	1,111	20.9	9,884	56.7	919	786	34.0	60.3	490	13,767	21.3	13.5	12,130
Chambers.	226	35.9	6,344	72.6	166	64	13.9	21.2	52	1,689	11.0	-3.5	1,750
Cherokee.	148	30.9	6,050	61.1	113	52	23.0	41.7	37	1,385	16.1	9.7	1,263
Chilton.	195	32.0	4,694	77.1	147	75	19.9	34.4	56	2,003	15.5	6.5	1,881
Choctaw.	161	64.9	10,576	43.3	98	24	9.4	17.9	20	670	11.9	-8.5	732
Clarke.	185	31.6	6,729	66.6	140	80	21.0	19.3	67	2,135	16.6	-0.7	2,149
Clay	89	31.5	6,349	71.2	68	39	19.4	24.0	32	1,147	16.7	-2.4	1,175
Cleburne.	76	29.0	5,279	70.8	59	34	21.0	30.2	26	918	18.6	1.0	909
Coffee.	532	14.6	11,808	45.8	464	110	17.5	31.3	84	2,783	12.8	3.3	2,693
Colbert.	491	26.1	8,953	58.8	389	333	30.3	25.9	264	6,085	21.1	3.4	5,885
Conecuh.	103	12.8	7,655	68.1	91	36	19.5	19.4	30	922	15.4	-4.7	967
Coosa.	63	23.0	5,552	77.1	51	18	22.8	15.8	15	496	19.7	-4.6	520
Covington.	273	30.0	7,395	69.0	210	93	16.5	26.9	74	2,481	13.2	1.6	2,443
Crenshaw.	101	24.7	7,387	64.7	81	27	12.7	28.3	21	739	12.6	2.5	721
Cullman.	423	33.2	5,339	77.3	317	171	13.4	31.4	130	4,637	11.3	6.5	4,353
Dale	552	15.9	11,237	45.1	476	730	52.8	33.5	547	9,509	34.2	-7.9	10,325
Dallas	389	12.5	8,668	59.6	346	120	17.8	14.9	105	3,224	15.3	-7.4	3,481
DeKalb.	333	36.1	4,968	70.3	244	127	11.2	33.0	96	3,332	9.3	3.7	3,214
Elmore.	369	36.7	5,128	76.4	270	162	22.3	28.7	126	4,049	16.9	3.3	3,921
Escambia.	237	23.0	6,187	68.4	193	116	20.2	16.8	99	3,118	18.0	-5.0	3,282
Etowah.	666	28.1	6,455	76.1	520	244	15.3	23.2	198	6,085	12.0	0.7	6,043
Fayette	110	36.9	6,032	68.0	81	53	22.6	27.0	42	1,488	18.2	3.5	1,437
Franklin	209	37.7	6,787	65.9	152	80	17.2	7.5	74	2,096	13.7	-13.1	2,413
Geneva.	227	52.8	8,885	56.4	149	58	21.9	27.6	45	1,718	17.3	2.9	1,670
Greene.	84	18.1	8,606	51.6	71	25	25.1	16.2	21	712	20.9	-11.9	808
Hale	125	35.1	6,819	64.4	92	40	26.3	26.3	32	1,105	19.9	0.5	1,099
Henry	117	20.7	6,990	65.7	97	32	15.2	17.3	27	905	12.9	-1.0	914
Houston.	558	31.4	6,002	66.6	425	352	15.9	33.9	263	8,357	13.5	8.3	7,713
Jackson	555	16.0	10,310	41.0	478	193	25.5	24.0	156	4,377	17.5	3.8	4,216
Jefferson	4,987	23.9	7,574	60.6	4,024	3,444	14.2	27.1	2,710	64,893	13.6	3.3	62,800
Lamar	107	33.5	7,127	66.3	80	27	14.9	19.2	23	733	11.7	-2.9	755
Lauderdale	499	23.8	5,701	77.2	403	282	23.4	14.6	246	6,748	15.6	-8.1	7,346
Lawrence	175	34.9	5,090	61.1	130	64	15.3	19.6	54	1,699	14.0	-3.5	1,761
Lee	504	37.9	4,177	60.5	366	732	35.8	37.8	531	15,917	25.2	7.5	14,808
Limestone	341	44.7	4,917	68.2	236	336	25.1	26.3	266	6,273	17.1	7.8	5,821
Lowndes	96	31.1	7,292	48.4	73	26	15.9	18.6	22	712	13.6	-9.9	790
Macon	250	12.2	10,769	44.9	222	121	47.0	13.1	107	2,250	26.9	-9.6	2,488
Madison.	7,639	59.7	26,067	15.1	4,784	2,818	27.3	36.7	2,061	39,496	18.9	6.3	37,163
Marengo	152	30.5	6,887	63.1	117	72	19.1	26.7	57	1,922	17.6	-0.5	1,932
Marion	192	19.8	6,343	66.1	160	66	12.8	21.9	54	1,752	10.4	-2.0	1,787
Marshall.	524	32.2	6,178	70.4	396	248	16.6	30.8	189	6,155	13.1	5.4	5,841
Mobile	2,458	21.9	6,137	68.2	2,017	1,506	18.4	30.9	1,151	32,180	14.5	4.2	30,870
Monroe	150	26.3	6,316	65.2	119	67	14.4	31.7	51	1,764	14.2	3.2	1,709
Montgomery	3,350	32.0	15,053	32.3	2,538	2,261	30.0	28.7	1,757	38,845	22.3	4.4	37,211
Morgan	674	26.9	5,958	63.7	531	331	13.0	23.5	268	7,891	12.5	0.9	7,817
Perry.	96	23.3	8,362	62.0	78	25	28.5	17.5	21	683	18.7	-5.7	724
Pickens	155	28.9	7,575	66.0	120	41	22.2	19.6	34	1,080	16.6	-5.8	1,147
Pike	325	94.5	11,052	44.5	167	119	19.4	39.5	85	3,012	17.3	12.8	2,671
Randolph	131	24.6	5,798	75.4	105	53	21.6	27.7	41	1,407	16.4	0.5	1,400
Russell	331	32.4	6,714	72.8	250	114	20.8	31.5	86	3,118	18.4	9.2	2,855
St. Clair	335	63.8	4,776	66.6	205	127	18.5	40.5	90	3,118	13.5	11.4	2,800
Shelby	403	38.1	2,434	81.2	292	323	9.4	57.0	206	7,998	10.0	24.4	6,430
Sumter.	119	23.0	8,446	54.1	97	55	35.1	23.7	44	1,508	26.5	-1.7	1,534
Talladega	529	18.3	6,591	68.7	447	237	15.0	24.7	190	5,798	15.0	2.9	5,635
Tallapoosa	288	44.9	7,059	65.1	199	93	17.2	26.9	74	2,361	11.9	1.9	2,317
Tuscaloosa.	1,007	23.6	6,027	61.1	815	1,011	23.6	30.7	773	22,488	21.8	6.5	21,110
Walker	472	26.6	6,742	79.8	373	144	17.9	21.9	118	3,797	11.8	-0.1	3,799
Washington	104	25.8	5,806	69.2	83	40	14.6	27.1	31	1,142	18.2	0.8	1,133
Wilcox	117	23.4	9,016	51.9	95	37	21.5	15.9	32	1,025	22.5	-0.2	1,027
Winston	178	62.3	7,255	64.8	109	49	13.1	26.7	39	1,281	10.6	-1.8	1,305

See footnotes at end of table.

Table B-12. Counties — **Government Expenditure, Earnings, and Employment**—Con.

[Includes United States, states, and 3,141 counties/county equivalents defined as of February 22, 2005. For more information on these areas, see Appendix C, Geographic Information]

County	Federal government expenditure					Federal, state, and local governments[1]							
						Earnings				Employment			
	2004					2005				2005			
	Total (mil. dol.)	Percent change, 2000–2004	Per capita (dol.)	Direct payments to individuals, percent of total	2000 (mil. dol.)	Total (mil. dol.)	Percent of total	Percent change, 2000–2005	2000 (mil. dol.)	Total	Percent of total	Percent change, 2000–2005	2000
ALASKA	[3]8,445	[3]41.6	[3]12,885	[3]19.5	[3]5,963	6,430	31.9	35.0	4,762	101,843	23.3	5.2	96,774
Aleutians East	20	−4.7	7,501	29.0	21	12	15.1	12.9	11	278	8.7	−11.7	315
Aleutians West	77	18.9	14,215	3.4	65	31	14.2	26.1	24	560	11.2	4.5	536
Anchorage	3,003	32.5	11,011	21.0	2,266	2,939	28.4	37.5	2,137	41,290	20.9	7.3	38,496
Bethel	324	52.6	19,109	7.7	212	124	42.9	30.0	95	3,210	36.8	−1.4	3,254
Bristol Bay	39	56.9	35,188	15.1	25	15	21.0	−5.8	16	253	14.3	−33.8	382
Denali	17	−45.3	8,516	16.0	30	29	27.2	7.4	27	449	18.2	−6.5	480
Dillingham	79	58.6	15,962	15.6	50	40	33.3	29.4	31	992	24.9	8.2	917
Fairbanks North Star	1,442	57.4	16,778	12.7	916	1,278	47.3	44.0	887	18,884	32.6	5.2	17,951
Haines	19	−11.2	8,384	38.6	21	9	15.3	12.5	8	209	8.5	1.0	207
Juneau	939	86.3	30,161	9.2	504	492	51.0	25.6	392	7,631	37.2	2.3	7,462
Kenai Peninsula	294	49.7	5,708	44.8	197	281	27.2	33.8	210	5,076	16.5	5.9	4,794
Ketchikan Gateway	129	29.4	9,737	27.5	100	145	35.2	36.7	106	2,315	22.3	6.2	2,179
Kodiak Island	179	29.5	13,487	8.0	138	145	37.2	30.5	111	2,274	24.6	1.7	2,236
Lake and Peninsula	23	97.6	14,742	23.4	12	13	45.1	62.1	8	412	47.4	28.3	321
Matanuska-Susitna	242	36.4	3,347	61.3	177	215	22.6	50.8	142	4,196	14.3	18.0	3,556
Nome	134	71.4	14,315	11.4	78	73	42.7	27.7	57	1,751	37.6	8.5	1,614
North Slope	70	53.8	10,041	13.9	46	98	12.3	−5.9	104	1,623	16.9	−16.6	1,945
Northwest Arctic	85	21.0	11,251	13.2	70	50	30.3	27.1	39	1,264	36.4	10.8	1,141
Prince of Wales-Outer Ketchikan	66	80.5	11,466	14.4	37	42	45.0	29.8	32	866	29.0	−1.9	883
Sitka	128	43.2	14,456	18.1	89	82	33.5	28.9	64	1,443	20.8	2.7	1,405
Skagway-Hoonah-Angoon	31	53.2	10,027	28.2	21	27	36.8	42.4	19	574	22.5	14.3	502
Southeast Fairbanks	205	229.7	34,167	8.0	62	47	28.2	5.6	44	734	20.5	−13.6	850
Valdez-Cordova	156	32.3	15,632	12.6	118	82	26.2	30.2	63	1,498	20.5	4.6	1,432
Wade Hampton	77	38.2	10,265	17.4	56	41	63.3	23.4	33	1,440	52.7	9.9	1,310
Wrangell-Petersburg	59	4.2	9,404	30.2	57	53	34.8	24.8	42	974	21.0	1.7	958
Yakutat	8	203.3	10,610	2.2	2	7	42.4	24.3	5	147	20.6	–	147
Yukon-Koyukuk	164	8.4	25,917	9.9	151	59	52.3	16.1	51	1,500	44.0	−0.1	1,501
ARIZONA	[3]41,979	[3]43.4	[3]7,309	[3]46.7	[3]29,282	22,687	16.5	44.8	15,664	432,718	13.4	11.3	388,894
Apache	1,020	60.7	14,802	23.1	635	612	71.0	41.3	433	12,876	49.1	3.4	12,455
Cochise	1,823	62.7	14,698	33.6	1,120	1,202	51.9	51.7	792	17,649	30.4	5.1	16,800
Coconino	885	39.1	7,206	41.0	636	824	31.9	32.4	622	16,156	20.2	2.7	15,727
Gila	584	83.4	11,359	46.8	319	209	34.6	31.7	159	4,951	22.7	0.6	4,921
Graham	210	43.6	6,361	51.6	146	118	38.6	13.3	105	2,444	23.3	−19.2	3,026
Greenlee	41	12.7	5,494	60.2	37	19	9.1	23.4	16	528	11.3	−7.0	568
La Paz	186	38.3	9,337	33.8	134	94	38.8	40.0	67	2,427	30.0	11.9	2,169
Maricopa	21,300	56.1	6,084	47.8	13,647	11,872	11.9	47.9	8,025	223,748	10.2	17.9	189,739
Mohave	1,045	39.7	5,804	80.8	748	365	16.8	43.2	255	8,141	11.6	9.0	7,471
Navajo	827	57.1	7,768	39.0	527	468	37.5	34.1	349	10,664	27.7	−0.7	10,741
Pima	8,994	40.9	9,915	38.9	6,382	4,420	23.9	39.5	3,168	84,035	17.3	4.9	80,130
Pinal	1,141	39.0	5,324	57.9	821	815	35.2	51.9	537	17,082	28.6	5.7	16,155
Santa Cruz	258	38.2	6,331	40.2	187	225	36.3	52.2	148	3,489	20.1	6.9	3,265
Yavapai	1,091	43.5	5,723	78.4	760	511	20.1	42.7	358	11,131	13.1	11.0	10,024
Yuma	1,072	35.5	6,091	50.1	791	933	32.2	48.0	631	17,397	21.0	10.8	15,703
ARKANSAS	[3]19,489	[3]31.3	[3]7,080	[3]59.5	[3]14,847	10,149	18.6	40.0	7,251	222,969	14.3	8.1	206,332
Arkansas	184	2.2	9,154	49.2	180	57	13.2	21.7	47	1,382	9.9	−11.7	1,565
Ashley	176	34.9	7,438	58.9	131	52	12.0	26.2	41	1,419	12.6	−1.7	1,444
Baxter	291	31.1	7,296	84.5	222	75	12.8	37.2	55	1,877	8.7	3.6	1,812
Benton	630	29.4	3,503	82.2	487	386	8.1	71.6	225	8,794	7.4	24.9	7,040
Boone	269	69.0	7,623	57.9	159	131	20.7	37.5	95	3,241	15.6	11.6	2,903
Bradley	89	13.3	7,225	65.7	79	33	20.3	33.7	25	895	15.4	5.0	852
Calhoun	34	−31.1	6,135	58.7	49	22	11.8	25.1	17	709	15.3	7.8	658
Carroll	143	56.5	5,391	67.9	91	50	13.4	45.3	34	1,283	8.6	10.2	1,164
Chicot	142	14.8	10,718	44.3	124	44	29.5	17.8	37	1,207	22.2	−7.8	1,309
Clark	148	15.7	6,395	65.9	128	90	22.9	30.1	69	2,537	18.9	4.6	2,425
Clay	151	15.0	9,037	55.5	132	41	23.7	42.5	29	1,121	15.1	3.9	1,079
Cleburne	165	33.8	6,576	78.9	123	42	14.0	38.0	31	1,112	8.6	6.6	1,043
Cleveland	47	38.5	5,299	72.5	34	16	27.2	40.4	12	454	21.6	5.3	431
Columbia	188	38.8	7,590	61.3	135	78	16.3	25.8	62	2,086	16.1	0.9	2,068
Conway	143	33.0	6,943	70.7	107	52	17.9	35.6	38	1,495	13.8	8.9	1,373
Craighead	438	23.7	5,087	64.9	355	310	17.2	37.6	225	7,526	13.7	11.0	6,778
Crawford	262	37.1	4,629	75.4	191	106	13.5	45.5	73	2,580	9.8	13.3	2,278
Crittenden	366	42.0	7,117	46.5	258	133	19.0	36.3	98	3,375	15.6	8.8	3,103
Cross	160	28.4	8,388	44.3	125	49	26.5	34.3	37	1,207	14.5	0.5	1,201
Dallas	65	30.9	7,497	67.5	50	20	16.0	29.9	15	572	12.6	−0.9	577
Desha	158	7.8	10,771	40.8	147	43	20.0	18.1	37	1,112	15.2	−13.0	1,278
Drew	156	52.7	8,411	44.6	102	83	31.6	41.4	59	2,173	23.1	16.5	1,866
Faulkner	396	57.8	4,165	67.8	251	303	18.5	49.7	203	7,272	14.7	22.4	5,942
Franklin	114	46.2	6,317	65.0	78	64	28.1	38.3	46	1,286	17.1	2.7	1,252
Fulton	77	36.4	6,442	76.8	56	24	26.6	37.8	17	690	13.5	8.7	635

See footnotes at end of table.

[Includes United States, states, and 3,141 counties/county equivalents defined as of February 22, 2005. For more information on these areas, see Appendix C, Geographic Information]

County	Federal government expenditure					Federal, state, and local governments[1]							
	2004					Earnings				Employment			
						2005				2005			
	Total (mil. dol.)	Percent change, 2000–2004	Per capita (dol.)	Direct payments to individuals, percent of total	2000 (mil. dol.)	Total (mil. dol.)	Percent of total	Percent change, 2000–2005	2000 (mil. dol.)	Total	Percent of total	Percent change, 2000–2005	2000
ARKANSAS—Con.													
Garland	699	30.1	7,589	77.3	538	236	16.1	41.9	166	5,152	10.0	10.5	4,664
Grant	101	89.8	5,870	56.4	53	39	25.1	44.0	27	1,049	17.0	9.6	957
Greene	222	32.8	5,699	62.4	167	84	13.9	45.2	58	2,035	10.3	8.3	1,879
Hempstead	137	31.8	5,840	65.2	104	74	20.7	39.2	53	1,803	15.5	4.2	1,731
Hot Spring	170	57.7	5,537	75.3	108	72	21.8	55.0	46	1,911	16.5	19.4	1,600
Howard	85	30.6	5,847	71.5	65	38	11.2	34.0	28	947	9.3	4.5	906
Independence	210	13.2	6,050	67.3	185	91	14.0	40.5	65	2,401	10.8	13.8	2,110
Izard	95	29.5	7,097	76.9	73	38	29.7	29.7	30	1,113	20.6	12.0	994
Jackson	205	36.7	11,886	47.6	150	55	24.3	55.1	35	1,555	18.0	17.3	1,326
Jefferson	734	11.4	8,884	48.4	659	465	29.1	40.7	331	9,474	21.7	9.4	8,660
Johnson	120	10.3	5,076	72.1	109	52	15.7	46.5	36	1,267	10.6	10.9	1,142
Lafayette	69	28.5	8,392	58.2	54	18	22.5	20.6	15	492	18.6	-10.4	549
Lawrence	154	18.2	8,832	56.5	130	52	31.5	35.9	38	1,433	18.2	4.2	1,375
Lee	128	22.3	10,908	35.7	105	36	33.6	15.3	32	928	24.4	-10.3	1,035
Lincoln	77	4.3	5,357	53.0	74	53	40.7	22.1	43	1,398	31.0	3.3	1,353
Little River	84	29.1	6,332	74.8	65	36	13.3	40.0	26	969	14.9	5.3	920
Logan	137	30.4	5,971	70.8	105	57	22.5	33.3	43	1,503	16.4	2.0	1,474
Lonoke	352	59.6	5,990	58.8	220	114	24.2	60.4	71	2,995	15.1	21.7	2,461
Madison	69	18.1	4,699	70.8	58	30	18.2	58.0	19	798	11.8	18.6	673
Marion	94	31.9	5,709	81.6	71	28	18.1	42.4	19	758	10.8	8.8	697
Miller	243	6.9	5,716	68.4	227	95	14.3	34.3	71	2,352	11.9	5.4	2,232
Mississippi	317	10.4	6,544	62.3	287	125	13.6	21.2	103	3,544	14.5	-3.9	3,687
Monroe	106	19.1	11,254	44.7	89	25	31.5	30.6	19	677	16.3	-0.6	681
Montgomery	55	29.3	5,913	76.0	42	23	25.5	40.1	16	631	16.2	6.1	595
Nevada	66	33.8	6,833	68.2	49	22	17.8	27.8	17	641	16.2	2.6	625
Newton	53	29.3	6,301	61.2	41	19	40.8	20.2	16	564	19.3	-3.6	585
Ouachita	207	7.1	7,552	66.4	193	74	25.0	32.4	56	1,851	18.6	6.0	1,747
Perry	61	30.3	5,829	72.9	47	18	27.8	29.3	14	536	18.1	4.1	515
Phillips	271	28.4	11,161	44.1	211	75	27.7	24.7	60	2,031	21.5	-5.9	2,159
Pike	63	35.4	5,784	71.7	47	31	22.9	41.4	22	819	18.2	4.1	787
Poinsett	216	21.6	8,535	49.1	178	59	22.8	37.5	43	1,651	16.4	9.1	1,513
Polk	128	33.2	6,348	75.5	96	50	18.1	37.7	37	1,398	13.6	8.8	1,285
Pope	289	30.2	5,166	67.2	222	178	15.6	41.3	126	4,288	12.3	12.8	3,801
Prairie	77	8.1	8,422	51.4	72	19	31.2	25.2	15	472	14.7	-9.6	522
Pulaski	3,791	38.2	10,361	41.6	2,744	3,305	23.6	37.7	2,401	57,158	18.6	5.1	54,389
Randolph	115	30.5	6,267	67.3	88	46	25.5	51.9	30	1,326	16.1	20.8	1,098
St. Francis	265	7.1	9,376	42.8	247	133	35.8	56.0	85	2,596	21.9	5.8	2,453
Saline	320	62.8	3,586	66.5	197	194	23.5	40.1	138	4,655	17.2	5.0	4,432
Scott	65	30.1	5,898	72.0	50	23	15.6	41.7	16	549	10.7	3.2	532
Searcy	66	36.8	8,163	60.1	48	22	34.5	32.7	16	595	15.1	4.4	570
Sebastian	597	24.7	5,071	71.5	479	362	9.8	37.1	264	7,678	8.5	11.3	6,897
Sevier	80	33.0	4,954	72.3	60	44	17.2	50.3	29	1,210	15.4	16.9	1,035
Sharp	130	28.8	7,413	78.9	101	33	23.6	30.0	25	996	16.2	1.5	981
Stone	85	14.9	7,234	69.0	74	25	20.9	21.9	21	711	12.8	-5.6	753
Union	299	26.6	6,713	67.7	237	116	11.1	25.3	93	3,084	11.5	3.5	2,981
Van Buren	117	30.6	7,050	75.6	90	32	23.4	45.2	22	875	13.9	6.1	825
Washington	748	37.2	4,298	60.1	545	798	18.3	51.4	527	16,438	14.1	14.1	14,406
White	362	28.9	5,122	74.8	281	148	14.9	44.8	102	4,025	11.5	13.1	3,558
Woodruff	99	22.4	12,116	44.3	81	23	32.6	28.4	18	651	19.1	-1.1	658
Yell	127	21.2	5,965	66.4	105	64	23.0	44.9	44	1,581	15.3	9.2	1,448
CALIFORNIA	[3]232,387	[3]32.1	[3]6,474	[3]48.3	[3]175,967	168,589	15.8	36.5	123,531	2,656,123	12.9	3.7	2,560,477
Alameda	10,766	24.8	7,398	38.7	8,626	8,873	16.9	31.5	6,746	120,047	13.4	-3.0	123,767
Alpine	9	4.7	7,794	68.8	9	10	29.2	74.8	6	207	18.3	17.6	176
Amador	208	40.0	5,508	80.3	149	275	40.8	107.4	133	5,301	27.5	55.0	3,420
Butte	1,267	27.1	5,949	70.5	997	778	21.2	30.1	598	16,104	15.0	-1.5	16,341
Calaveras	245	21.9	5,332	80.2	201	123	23.3	39.0	88	2,475	13.9	3.3	2,397
Colusa	139	4.6	6,858	48.1	133	92	23.1	51.2	61	2,060	18.7	10.7	1,861
Contra Costa	4,803	32.6	4,759	61.2	3,622	3,226	11.4	36.7	2,359	49,880	9.9	3.8	48,047
Del Norte	167	25.3	5,896	66.3	133	180	47.3	41.6	127	3,638	32.1	10.9	3,279
El Dorado	701	11.8	4,052	78.4	627	508	15.3	38.0	368	9,332	10.2	3.5	9,017
Fresno	4,195	23.0	4,840	52.0	3,412	3,697	21.3	36.5	2,708	66,349	15.2	4.8	63,286
Glenn	184	5.2	6,681	49.8	175	107	27.9	31.1	82	2,209	18.2	4.2	2,120
Humboldt	826	21.7	6,424	59.6	678	628	26.4	34.0	468	13,300	18.6	5.4	12,622
Imperial	868	33.9	5,692	47.3	648	980	39.0	50.7	650	16,626	24.7	12.0	14,841
Inyo	256	17.7	14,013	32.8	217	162	46.3	54.7	104	3,170	29.3	18.4	2,678
Kern	4,154	16.6	5,653	50.0	3,563	3,753	25.4	32.3	2,836	60,423	17.3	5.4	57,331
Kings	843	24.5	5,915	36.8	677	1,169	48.2	63.6	714	19,083	33.6	17.9	16,185
Lake	433	25.3	6,722	76.4	346	209	27.4	52.5	137	4,727	19.6	13.2	4,175
Lassen	210	20.8	6,055	50.3	174	321	59.5	43.8	223	5,872	41.0	7.5	5,464
Los Angeles	59,186	26.1	5,956	44.5	46,941	39,546	13.5	31.6	30,049	613,857	10.9	0.9	608,253
Madera	581	32.9	4,179	64.0	437	509	23.4	61.9	315	10,402	17.6	31.4	7,918

See footnotes at end of table.

Table B-12. Counties — **Government Expenditure, Earnings, and Employment**—Con.

[Includes United States, states, and 3,141 counties/county equivalents defined as of February 22, 2005. For more information on these areas, see Appendix C, Geographic Information]

County	Federal government expenditure — 2004 — Total (mil. dol.)	Percent change, 2000–2004	Per capita (dol.)	Direct payments to individuals, percent of total	2000 (mil. dol.)	Federal, state, and local governments[1] — Earnings — 2005 — Total (mil. dol.)	Percent of total	Percent change, 2000–2005	2000 (mil. dol.)	Employment — 2005 — Total	Percent of total	Percent change, 2000–2005	2000
CALIFORNIA—Con.													
Marin	1,270	35.3	5,162	68.0	939	902	9.4	32.7	680	14,415	7.8	−0.4	14,478
Mariposa	125	30.5	6,955	62.6	96	94	38.9	28.5	73	1,815	21.8	9.1	1,663
Mendocino	558	36.4	6,305	61.6	409	350	22.7	33.5	262	7,271	14.2	−0.9	7,336
Merced	975	19.6	4,115	61.3	816	734	20.5	46.3	501	14,534	16.0	3.2	13,681
Modoc	96	47.0	9,957	44.8	65	62	45.6	38.1	45	1,346	28.4	11.5	1,207
Mono	55	35.0	4,287	36.4	41	101	25.8	53.7	66	1,642	15.8	5.9	1,551
Monterey	2,312	30.0	5,577	50.8	1,778	2,429	22.2	40.4	1,730	35,394	15.2	1.1	35,003
Napa	750	33.1	5,666	71.7	563	574	13.6	43.2	401	9,919	11.0	4.1	9,524
Nevada	589	35.6	6,033	65.2	434	304	15.9	49.1	204	5,714	10.0	10.2	5,184
Orange	13,835	44.2	4,631	54.3	9,594	9,805	8.9	36.7	7,171	158,428	7.9	(Z)	158,456
Placer	1,283	36.8	4,181	77.8	938	972	11.5	58.5	613	18,207	9.9	19.7	15,208
Plumas	178	49.7	8,327	56.5	119	125	30.6	39.1	90	2,515	22.1	−0.4	2,526
Riverside	7,515	33.4	4,015	72.5	5,634	6,604	20.3	60.0	4,127	119,170	14.3	23.8	96,227
Sacramento	16,414	39.3	12,136	29.9	11,783	12,797	31.4	33.6	9,581	181,097	22.6	1.2	178,943
San Benito	173	30.7	3,075	60.9	132	172	18.6	39.1	124	2,976	12.6	2.7	2,899
San Bernardino	8,289	30.2	4,315	56.6	6,368	7,686	21.7	42.6	5,389	129,461	15.2	8.6	119,155
San Diego	25,893	36.3	8,832	37.7	18,991	21,549	22.7	38.6	15,544	335,824	17.8	5.9	317,049
San Francisco	7,607	23.5	10,221	36.6	6,159	7,813	14.8	32.7	5,886	97,736	14.0	0.7	97,000
San Joaquin	2,799	25.7	4,307	61.8	2,227	2,267	19.2	40.1	1,617	38,490	13.4	6.7	36,085
San Luis Obispo	1,211	25.2	4,756	72.4	967	1,160	20.1	33.3	870	20,852	13.7	1.2	20,599
San Mateo	3,492	24.2	4,994	60.1	2,812	2,248	6.7	33.4	1,684	31,744	6.9	−0.4	31,877
Santa Barbara	2,964	29.8	7,376	44.1	2,283	2,261	19.5	38.4	1,634	38,081	14.5	4.4	36,492
Santa Clara	11,900	33.6	7,062	33.4	8,905	6,739	7.6	28.9	5,227	95,955	8.6	−3.5	99,399
Santa Cruz	1,082	25.5	4,316	62.5	862	1,056	17.5	40.5	751	18,868	13.0	2.2	18,454
Shasta	1,145	29.6	6,440	69.5	883	706	20.4	34.2	526	14,078	15.2	3.4	13,618
Sierra	27	29.4	7,669	61.8	21	20	56.1	12.3	18	457	34.8	−7.3	493
Siskiyou	347	18.0	7,725	64.9	294	208	30.1	31.8	158	4,466	19.8	1.1	4,417
Solano	2,573	32.0	6,229	50.4	1,949	2,130	27.0	34.5	1,583	32,334	18.2	−2.9	33,312
Sonoma	2,198	27.0	4,691	69.2	1,731	1,649	13.6	30.0	1,269	29,597	10.5	−0.7	29,819
Stanislaus	2,119	28.4	4,253	64.3	1,651	1,566	16.7	40.9	1,111	28,002	12.4	7.9	25,948
Sutter	442	17.3	5,098	67.8	377	223	15.7	24.7	179	4,390	10.2	−1.2	4,442
Tehama	330	21.7	5,487	68.0	271	187	22.6	47.2	127	4,020	16.2	13.0	3,558
Trinity	103	37.6	7,542	64.8	75	63	44.8	22.6	51	1,262	25.1	−10.0	1,403
Tulare	1,694	26.2	4,218	57.6	1,342	1,539	22.6	38.6	1,111	30,731	16.6	5.1	29,239
Tuolumne	332	25.1	5,834	76.6	266	295	31.5	59.5	185	5,927	21.3	26.2	4,698
Ventura	4,147	24.6	5,198	53.5	3,328	3,346	15.6	33.6	2,505	50,460	11.5	1.8	49,544
Yolo	1,158	31.9	6,281	38.8	878	2,069	37.3	67.2	1,237	33,423	28.2	22.0	27,386
Yuba	590	27.5	9,121	41.1	462	644	55.2	51.3	425	10,460	38.8	11.1	9,417
COLORADO	[3]30,060	[3]31.1	[3]6,533	[3]44.4	[3]22,929	22,428	15.6	36.0	16,495	411,010	13.4	6.8	384,788
Adams	1,603	33.9	4,113	52.0	1,198	1,088	12.8	38.5	785	21,843	10.4	11.5	19,591
Alamosa	90	31.6	5,938	46.6	68	90	28.5	31.4	68	2,342	22.3	13.1	2,071
Arapahoe	2,475	23.9	4,735	54.2	1,997	1,797	7.9	38.2	1,300	34,960	8.6	9.6	31,911
Archuleta	48	47.7	4,154	68.5	33	27	18.1	49.9	18	648	8.8	10.6	586
Baca	55	12.9	13,308	37.5	49	21	28.4	22.3	17	733	25.5	−4.4	767
Bent	45	−5.5	8,044	58.2	48	29	50.0	−30.8	43	743	33.0	−24.3	981
Boulder	1,940	29.4	6,956	35.2	1,499	1,526	13.5	27.9	1,193	28,831	12.8	3.4	27,873
Broomfield	23	(NA)	540	(Z)	(X)	63	3.1	(NA)	(X)	1,249	3.4	(NA)	(X)
Chaffee	86	28.1	5,056	75.7	67	71	28.6	19.4	60	1,668	16.1	0.2	1,665
Cheyenne	77	201.6	37,947	11.2	26	12	24.6	42.5	9	332	18.6	3.1	322
Clear Creek	48	139.3	5,211	37.0	20	29	14.6	24.9	23	676	9.6	−0.6	680
Conejos	59	30.3	7,044	48.0	45	22	34.0	23.7	18	630	19.8	−2.8	648
Costilla	35	26.4	9,801	51.9	28	11	39.7	22.3	9	382	27.2	−5.7	405
Crowley	26	31.7	4,686	60.9	20	24	33.6	15.1	21	533	28.7	−2.7	548
Custer	24	54.4	6,268	70.6	16	8	20.9	35.3	6	249	11.1	7.8	231
Delta	173	26.4	5,816	72.5	137	97	28.0	47.5	66	2,397	16.0	15.8	2,070
Denver	6,197	22.8	11,128	33.6	5,045	4,730	13.6	25.9	3,757	73,193	13.7	0.6	72,746
Dolores	13	28.5	7,234	55.0	10	6	25.5	28.3	5	200	20.3	−1.5	203
Douglas	287	34.7	1,206	71.9	213	472	9.8	77.4	266	9,959	9.0	36.1	7,316
Eagle	81	102.7	1,759	44.0	40	132	7.7	39.5	95	2,655	6.4	1.6	2,612
Elbert	54	70.2	2,411	77.3	32	38	19.3	34.5	28	1,039	12.0	7.2	969
El Paso	5,478	38.0	9,878	35.8	3,970	4,779	30.6	52.6	3,132	74,130	20.9	10.5	67,091
Fremont	287	15.9	6,059	59.5	248	285	44.8	17.5	243	5,099	25.8	−3.4	5,277
Garfield	147	30.8	3,038	66.6	113	188	15.2	47.9	127	4,207	12.3	18.3	3,557
Gilpin	17	122.7	3,563	36.7	8	20	8.0	59.3	13	436	7.0	34.2	325
Grand	46	60.7	3,474	60.6	29	54	17.5	40.0	38	1,208	11.2	7.5	1,124
Gunnison	98	14.3	6,934	26.9	86	75	21.0	37.9	55	1,789	14.4	10.9	1,613
Hinsdale	4	54.5	4,928	79.8	3	3	25.9	30.1	2	88	13.3	14.3	77
Huerfano	60	28.2	7,762	66.4	47	18	24.5	28.9	14	493	13.5	2.9	479
Jackson	11	81.3	7,460	41.0	6	7	34.3	22.0	6	184	15.3	−8.5	201

See footnotes at end of table.

Table B-12. Counties — **Government Expenditure, Earnings, and Employment**—Con.

[Includes United States, states, and 3,141 counties/county equivalents defined as of February 22, 2005. For more information on these areas, see Appendix C, Geographic Information]

County	Federal government expenditure 2004 — Total (mil. dol.)	Percent change, 2000–2004	Per capita (dol.)	Direct payments to individuals, percent of total	2000 (mil. dol.)	Earnings 2005 — Total (mil. dol.)	Percent of total	Percent change, 2000–2005	2000 (mil. dol.)	Employment 2005 — Total	Percent of total	Percent change, 2000–2005	2000
COLORADO—Con.													
Jefferson	3,237	22.3	6,150	37.0	2,646	2,133	16.5	28.9	1,655	35,506	13.3	3.4	34,341
Kiowa	40	54.8	27,381	17.7	26	8	23.8	23.6	7	265	20.3	-1.1	268
Kit Carson	95	20.2	12,281	27.7	79	27	16.9	24.2	22	849	16.4	1.2	839
Lake	26	37.3	3,373	57.6	19	30	39.6	36.6	22	824	26.8	12.1	735
La Plata	202	45.3	4,347	58.4	139	250	20.9	51.2	165	5,337	15.0	13.9	4,685
Larimer	1,178	39.5	4,381	54.4	845	1,311	18.7	32.0	993	26,688	14.7	6.1	25,154
Las Animas	119	14.7	7,741	58.6	104	73	31.4	41.0	52	2,108	24.6	15.3	1,828
Lincoln	48	20.2	8,400	39.6	40	41	51.5	23.8	33	948	26.7	-0.4	952
Logan	137	34.1	6,533	51.2	102	102	24.2	22.0	83	2,625	20.3	-2.6	2,695
Mesa	696	28.1	5,472	66.5	544	449	17.1	33.3	337	8,781	11.1	3.6	8,476
Mineral	6	177.9	6,509	47.0	2	4	21.8	29.9	3	104	13.0	2.0	102
Moffat	67	42.6	4,963	50.5	47	56	21.2	23.6	46	1,296	16.8	2.3	1,267
Montezuma	217	93.8	8,768	38.7	112	122	32.3	38.7	88	3,209	22.6	13.2	2,834
Montrose	191	32.3	5,209	67.3	144	137	18.2	36.9	100	3,040	13.1	10.6	2,749
Morgan	133	16.3	4,720	60.0	114	91	17.4	31.5	69	2,532	16.0	6.4	2,380
Otero	164	25.0	8,390	57.9	132	69	25.3	16.8	59	2,027	19.9	-0.9	2,046
Ouray	13	31.9	3,039	81.0	10	13	17.4	46.4	9	329	10.8	9.7	300
Park	41	29.4	2,428	78.7	32	32	26.2	34.9	24	850	14.0	9.4	777
Phillips	44	5.6	9,695	45.1	42	20	26.9	25.2	16	626	21.4	3.5	605
Pitkin	39	50.3	2,643	51.0	26	99	9.6	32.4	75	1,794	7.9	5.0	1,708
Prowers	98	38.4	6,970	44.1	71	60	25.4	23.9	48	1,601	20.7	0.1	1,599
Pueblo	941	21.7	6,265	67.0	773	578	23.8	31.0	441	12,371	17.0	4.9	11,794
Rio Blanco	31	22.3	5,094	60.0	25	40	21.3	16.2	34	1,092	23.2	-4.7	1,146
Rio Grande	78	30.7	6,310	52.0	60	41	18.6	25.1	33	979	12.4	-2.2	1,001
Routt	54	24.7	2,551	58.1	43	75	9.9	32.1	57	1,740	8.3	3.4	1,683
Saguache	36	23.1	5,097	46.8	29	19	28.2	11.4	17	586	20.7	-6.1	624
San Juan	2	1.6	3,595	71.4	2	2	27.5	-1.2	2	70	13.1	-15.7	83
San Miguel	18	50.4	2,487	37.7	12	35	14.5	36.9	26	789	9.6	12.7	700
Sedgwick	28	4.5	10,908	52.8	27	11	28.3	18.8	9	335	19.2	-5.4	354
Summit	41	16.1	1,637	71.4	35	98	12.7	43.1	68	2,177	8.6	12.3	1,939
Teller	75	39.8	3,443	85.6	53	52	17.3	35.9	38	1,242	11.4	7.1	1,160
Washington	53	7.5	11,363	35.0	49	18	26.9	31.7	14	537	17.8	5.9	507
Weld	686	29.9	3,130	62.3	528	571	13.8	40.4	407	13,886	12.6	10.5	12,569
Yuma	74	-7.5	7,521	42.8	80	36	17.7	37.4	26	971	15.2	2.3	949
CONNECTICUT	³30,304	³55.2	³8,649	³44.1	³19,527	15,660	12.2	25.1	12,516	261,041	12.0	1.0	258,498
Fairfield	6,729	50.1	7,450	43.9	4,484	2,996	6.4	24.3	2,410	48,230	8.2	2.7	46,974
Hartford	8,931	66.6	10,200	37.5	5,362	4,632	12.5	22.6	3,778	71,222	11.5	-1.3	72,155
Litchfield	865	26.2	4,570	76.6	685	468	12.4	24.3	377	8,912	9.2	0.8	8,838
Middlesex	799	40.7	4,921	65.5	568	656	13.8	30.8	502	10,378	10.8	3.1	10,064
New Haven	5,458	25.0	6,454	58.9	4,365	3,069	12.9	21.4	2,527	50,849	10.5	-4.6	53,273
New London	5,099	110.5	19,134	19.7	2,422	2,673	31.7	33.8	1,998	48,833	28.2	6.9	45,680
Tolland	528	27.6	3,601	70.2	414	801	34.4	26.9	631	15,442	24.7	7.4	14,383
Windham	557	22.5	4,875	69.4	455	364	18.5	23.9	294	7,175	14.0	0.6	7,131
DELAWARE	³5,253	³32.6	³6,326	³59.8	³3,962	3,805	14.2	38.3	2,752	68,313	12.9	3.1	66,249
Kent	1,235	36.6	8,901	42.5	904	1,252	38.9	44.3	868	21,898	26.3	7.9	20,295
New Castle	2,654	25.6	5,110	61.2	2,114	2,168	10.6	34.6	1,611	38,099	10.9	0.2	38,010
Sussex	1,039	37.3	6,035	76.3	757	385	11.9	41.1	272	8,316	8.8	4.7	7,944
DISTRICT OF COLUMBIA	37,630	37.2	67,982	8.6	27,418	27,185	41.5	40.1	19,410	254,116	31.9	5.5	240,769
District of Columbia	37,630	37.2	67,982	8.6	27,418	27,185	41.5	40.1	19,410	254,116	31.9	5.5	240,769
FLORIDA	³121,934	³31.3	³7,009	³64.6	³92,882	65,282	16.0	34.8	48,439	1,161,853	11.5	6.3	1,093,169
Alachua	1,474	32.3	6,606	49.7	1,114	2,181	38.3	38.0	1,581	40,783	26.6	-2.9	42,018
Baker	103	31.1	4,305	75.9	79	114	40.7	17.2	97	2,610	28.8	-1.4	2,648
Bay	1,599	27.2	10,124	49.5	1,257	1,081	29.9	53.7	704	18,010	18.3	23.4	14,592
Bradford	146	36.9	5,299	65.7	107	123	39.5	26.2	98	2,691	25.3	2.6	2,624
Brevard	5,905	37.0	11,370	46.9	4,312	1,839	16.0	34.1	1,371	31,663	11.3	7.5	29,443
Broward	8,768	28.9	4,996	77.6	6,803	6,148	14.6	41.1	4,356	106,256	10.6	14.6	92,742
Calhoun	78	34.9	5,922	64.3	58	40	36.7	14.1	35	988	22.9	-1.0	998
Charlotte	1,075	31.7	6,840	91.2	816	307	15.9	43.8	213	6,148	9.5	9.3	5,624
Citrus	887	30.5	6,798	93.3	679	205	14.6	35.6	151	4,807	9.7	9.7	4,382
Clay	722	38.2	4,392	88.8	522	318	17.8	41.8	225	6,823	11.4	19.2	5,723
Collier	1,332	33.8	4,491	85.5	996	713	9.7	56.3	456	13,070	7.1	19.1	10,974
Columbia	385	34.3	6,226	65.3	287	283	31.1	27.3	223	5,693	21.7	5.1	5,415
DeSoto	165	28.5	4,741	78.3	129	102	27.2	-2.3	104	2,363	15.5	-18.2	2,887
Dixie	92	40.1	6,457	69.2	66	43	34.9	23.2	35	1,039	22.8	-1.1	1,051
Duval	6,458	25.3	7,862	47.0	5,152	5,120	18.2	36.3	3,755	76,402	12.3	4.4	73,215

See footnotes at end of table.

[Includes United States, states, and 3,141 counties/county equivalents defined as of February 22, 2005. For more information on these areas, see Appendix C, Geographic Information]

County	Federal government expenditure					Federal, state, and local governments[1]							
						Earnings				Employment			
	2004					2005				2005			
	Total (mil. dol.)	Percent change, 2000–2004	Per capita (dol.)	Direct payments to individuals, percent of total	2000 (mil. dol.)	Total (mil. dol.)	Percent of total	Percent change, 2000–2005	2000 (mil. dol.)	Total	Percent of total	Percent change, 2000–2005	2000
FLORIDA—Con.													
Escambia	2,778	25.1	9,294	56.0	2,220	2,036	30.4	14.1	1,785	33,097	18.7	−13.0	38,037
Flagler	386	39.1	5,598	92.3	278	139	17.0	95.3	71	3,282	13.6	47.8	2,220
Franklin	70	22.0	6,963	73.4	58	34	22.8	35.7	25	832	13.7	11.1	749
Gadsden	280	17.0	6,076	59.2	239	226	36.6	20.5	187	5,453	28.2	4.6	5,213
Gilchrist	67	18.7	4,170	82.2	56	49	37.8	23.4	40	1,180	22.4	1.8	1,159
Glades	31	19.2	2,798	82.6	26	18	26.4	36.8	13	451	11.8	8.2	417
Gulf	98	36.3	7,098	78.0	72	61	34.5	25.4	49	1,443	24.6	2.9	1,402
Hamilton	77	27.7	5,462	62.7	61	59	31.4	9.2	54	1,377	28.5	−11.5	1,556
Hardee	132	39.6	4,723	63.8	95	76	23.3	21.7	63	1,780	13.5	0.6	1,770
Hendry	144	13.6	3,768	68.1	127	108	20.2	21.9	89	2,527	12.2	1.2	2,496
Hernando	1,095	28.5	7,281	92.2	852	296	18.2	42.2	208	6,491	11.4	10.7	5,864
Highlands	688	29.7	7,393	85.5	531	185	17.2	28.9	144	4,198	10.5	−0.3	4,209
Hillsborough	7,095	40.7	6,443	54.0	5,044	4,834	13.5	36.1	3,551	81,201	10.1	4.6	77,641
Holmes	140	17.7	7,388	67.5	119	56	36.3	27.3	44	1,421	20.0	1.4	1,402
Indian River	900	32.8	7,252	85.6	677	297	12.8	36.5	218	5,823	8.7	12.6	5,173
Jackson	381	29.8	7,994	54.3	294	271	43.9	20.4	226	6,184	31.4	−2.6	6,346
Jefferson	87	19.3	5,999	58.1	73	37	27.3	7.3	35	924	17.9	−10.7	1,035
Lafayette	26	23.1	3,488	69.2	21	30	44.0	29.0	23	723	29.3	10.2	656
Lake	1,771	43.3	6,789	88.8	1,236	554	15.4	57.0	353	12,397	11.1	25.2	9,905
Lee	2,866	32.2	5,573	84.9	2,167	1,730	15.1	51.9	1,138	32,521	11.1	18.4	27,474
Leon	4,613	57.6	18,915	17.9	2,926	2,731	38.4	14.0	2,395	53,623	29.7	−5.2	56,543
Levy	230	47.7	6,161	70.8	156	87	23.6	29.7	67	2,172	15.3	6.9	2,032
Liberty	36	36.2	4,911	60.7	27	34	34.1	20.4	28	828	28.2	3.6	799
Madison	128	24.6	6,702	61.2	103	57	30.0	4.6	55	1,504	20.1	−5.2	1,586
Manatee	1,557	28.4	5,252	84.5	1,213	671	10.7	35.3	496	12,567	7.2	−0.2	12,596
Marion	1,775	27.3	6,091	85.9	1,394	707	16.5	25.8	562	16,675	12.3	6.2	15,697
Martin	936	35.6	6,782	84.9	690	310	10.0	35.4	229	5,826	6.6	5.9	5,502
Miami-Dade	15,597	34.0	6,599	55.1	11,639	9,979	16.2	34.8	7,403	157,876	11.4	4.5	151,074
Monroe	557	30.8	7,111	56.3	426	482	25.6	35.9	354	7,742	13.8	0.6	7,697
Nassau	366	29.8	5,791	67.3	282	234	25.6	32.2	177	3,836	14.9	10.5	3,473
Okaloosa	2,767	29.1	15,247	38.0	2,144	2,225	41.6	42.7	1,559	30,588	24.1	5.1	29,101
Okeechobee	228	35.2	5,849	80.4	169	95	21.0	31.6	72	2,039	15.0	7.3	1,900
Orange	6,588	26.8	6,655	45.3	5,195	3,718	10.4	31.7	2,823	68,242	8.3	9.4	62,371
Osceola	714	41.6	3,254	85.0	504	546	19.8	63.3	334	11,188	13.2	31.5	8,510
Palm Beach	7,404	7.0	5,955	80.9	6,917	3,751	11.2	35.5	2,768	66,527	8.7	10.5	60,204
Pasco	2,302	33.7	5,645	89.4	1,722	743	19.2	45.8	509	15,498	12.4	12.7	13,747
Pinellas	7,234	23.6	7,791	73.7	5,851	2,653	11.7	28.6	2,063	49,019	8.2	4.3	47,003
Polk	2,770	36.0	5,282	77.4	2,037	1,306	13.3	27.1	1,028	28,380	10.6	−0.5	28,515
Putnam	482	28.2	6,643	72.6	376	208	26.1	17.7	177	4,582	19.9	−5.8	4,863
St. Johns	846	48.8	5,550	68.6	569	370	15.1	52.0	243	7,798	11.5	20.2	6,490
St. Lucie	1,331	31.8	5,868	85.6	1,010	608	20.3	43.2	425	12,042	12.6	14.2	10,549
Santa Rosa	866	50.9	6,263	67.7	574	419	27.2	36.0	308	7,339	15.1	5.4	6,960
Sarasota	2,666	27.3	7,499	90.7	2,095	803	9.7	44.0	558	15,015	6.7	14.5	13,114
Seminole	1,509	27.5	3,855	78.6	1,184	891	9.2	37.4	648	18,093	8.0	10.5	16,375
Sumter	365	22.1	6,019	67.0	299	221	32.8	59.9	138	3,870	19.2	25.5	3,083
Suwannee	234	36.9	6,217	76.6	171	85	20.2	32.4	64	1,877	12.8	4.0	1,805
Taylor	134	14.4	6,924	64.0	117	67	21.9	26.5	53	1,663	18.7	5.3	1,580
Union	50	21.6	3,439	65.0	42	114	63.1	26.2	90	2,479	46.8	3.4	2,397
Volusia	2,974	27.5	6,213	81.3	2,332	1,160	16.7	34.0	866	23,806	11.2	7.2	22,200
Wakulla	91	32.1	3,345	73.2	69	68	30.5	34.6	51	1,634	19.9	8.6	1,505
Walton	604	207.6	12,457	27.5	196	129	17.5	47.2	88	2,866	11.9	13.6	2,522
Washington	155	34.6	7,043	66.3	115	94	39.0	6.8	88	2,008	23.2	−13.3	2,316
GEORGIA	[3]55,153	[3]29.7	[3]6,247	[3]51.0	[3]42,525	39,149	17.1	37.2	28,527	752,395	14.5	8.2	695,234
Appling	105	29.6	5,840	58.9	81	57	18.8	48.4	39	1,604	17.4	29.7	1,237
Atkinson	49	33.8	6,070	54.8	36	17	17.1	32.2	12	516	17.1	14.9	449
Bacon	65	32.4	6,251	63.5	49	23	16.3	24.8	18	635	11.5	0.2	634
Baker	28	8.7	6,575	37.9	26	7	23.9	7.9	6	205	15.6	−15.6	243
Baldwin	219	34.8	4,840	71.3	162	297	38.3	15.2	258	7,815	31.4	−1.9	7,964
Banks	53	−27.0	3,369	68.4	72	26	14.9	52.8	17	776	10.2	25.2	620
Barrow	187	37.5	3,321	72.9	136	117	17.7	49.3	79	2,855	12.5	13.0	2,527
Bartow	326	32.5	3,745	68.4	246	220	13.4	42.4	155	5,349	10.8	16.6	4,589
Ben Hill	112	32.1	6,469	65.0	85	58	16.4	21.2	48	1,688	15.4	3.2	1,635
Berrien	107	38.4	6,427	68.2	77	32	15.5	27.1	25	943	12.1	8.4	870
Bibb	1,218	29.6	7,846	62.2	939	559	13.2	25.2	446	12,123	11.1	4.7	11,574
Bleckley	84	26.4	7,008	73.3	67	42	24.6	32.4	32	1,195	21.8	13.6	1,052
Brantley	71	40.0	4,570	75.2	51	30	31.6	36.6	22	845	21.4	7.2	788
Brooks	107	35.8	6,560	54.8	79	27	21.0	19.9	23	791	15.8	−2.8	814
Bryan	397	−41.6	14,414	20.9	680	65	25.1	70.7	38	1,576	17.5	14.0	1,382
Bulloch	236	25.1	3,908	64.6	188	261	30.3	30.8	200	6,361	21.1	13.3	5,615
Burke	146	24.9	6,315	57.0	117	58	18.0	24.9	46	1,535	17.6	−3.1	1,584
Butts	109	29.7	4,876	68.9	84	57	22.1	25.1	46	1,511	16.7	5.1	1,438
Calhoun	51	21.3	8,375	51.3	42	26	42.1	17.5	22	834	34.8	4.4	799
Camden	523	23.1	11,602	23.6	425	613	61.8	23.9	495	9,529	39.2	−5.8	10,117

See footnotes at end of table.

[Includes United States, states, and 3,141 counties/county equivalents defined as of February 22, 2005. For more information on these areas, see Appendix C, Geographic Information]

	Federal government expenditure					Federal, state, and local governments[1]							
						Earnings				Employment			
County	2004				2000 (mil. dol.)	2005			2000 (mil. dol.)	2005			2000
	Total (mil. dol.)	Percent change, 2000–2004	Per capita (dol.)	Direct payments to individuals, percent of total		Total (mil. dol.)	Percent of total	Percent change, 2000–2005		Total	Percent of total	Percent change, 2000–2005	
GEORGIA—Con.													
Candler	62	32.2	6,077	60.4	47	27	21.1	23.9	21	755	14.8	0.1	754
Carroll	415	31.4	4,089	74.3	316	270	15.9	34.6	200	6,796	14.7	14.9	5,915
Catoosa	173	23.4	2,888	78.5	140	101	14.8	54.2	65	2,532	10.2	17.4	2,157
Charlton	56	32.2	5,241	69.1	42	26	28.2	39.7	19	699	19.9	5.4	663
Chatham	1,997	33.0	8,373	49.0	1,501	1,318	19.5	36.5	966	23,192	13.7	3.6	22,387
Chattahoochee	285	106.9	21,078	4.8	138	1,083	95.7	62.4	667	14,870	88.6	1.5	14,644
Chattooga	137	31.3	5,143	72.7	104	62	21.6	20.9	52	1,702	17.1	-0.7	1,714
Cherokee	391	50.0	2,237	75.6	261	351	15.9	69.9	207	7,409	11.3	26.3	5,867
Clarke	653	31.2	6,283	41.5	498	1,064	35.3	30.5	815	21,155	26.2	13.0	18,716
Clay	44	73.1	13,266	29.7	25	12	41.6	11.6	11	322	28.8	-1.2	326
Clayton	880	38.0	3,323	68.7	638	780	13.1	35.4	576	17,308	12.4	13.9	15,199
Clinch	44	11.6	6,301	65.7	39	22	23.9	25.4	18	623	19.4	-0.8	628
Cobb	2,980	-21.6	4,556	46.6	3,801	1,783	8.7	40.2	1,271	36,159	8.6	11.9	32,316
Coffee	190	25.2	4,837	64.4	152	119	16.9	55.9	77	3,230	13.6	32.2	2,443
Colquitt	266	33.7	6,078	60.3	199	139	24.4	29.0	108	3,654	17.7	2.2	3,577
Columbia	503	-12.9	5,000	47.4	578	184	15.5	58.9	116	4,324	10.5	25.9	3,434
Cook	147	113.4	9,013	39.3	69	33	19.7	25.4	27	1,022	15.6	4.5	978
Coweta	354	28.7	3,358	76.1	275	228	17.1	45.5	157	5,182	11.8	8.4	4,780
Crawford	43	23.8	3,334	68.8	35	18	24.9	24.3	15	522	13.7	-6.8	560
Crisp	156	34.0	7,096	56.0	117	62	18.8	19.9	52	1,591	13.8	-4.2	1,660
Dade	73	4.1	4,588	74.3	70	24	16.7	25.5	20	687	11.3	3.9	661
Dawson	61	46.8	3,213	76.4	42	41	15.7	71.2	24	1,128	11.7	37.6	820
Decatur	177	39.1	6,177	56.6	127	103	24.1	21.6	85	3,008	20.4	4.9	2,867
DeKalb	2,910	34.5	4,306	48.9	2,164	3,118	15.2	42.1	2,194	48,697	11.4	10.1	44,227
Dodge	126	24.9	6,444	61.8	101	84	37.2	31.4	64	2,257	25.5	9.0	2,070
Dooly	87	-0.3	7,522	49.2	88	33	21.1	2.4	32	927	17.6	-13.4	1,070
Dougherty	791	15.8	8,268	52.2	683	617	24.1	26.4	488	11,534	18.3	-4.2	12,035
Douglas	326	47.7	3,040	76.3	221	237	15.8	39.3	170	5,326	10.5	17.2	4,544
Early	95	33.8	7,882	49.3	71	50	19.1	80.9	27	1,292	19.4	42.1	909
Echols	10	57.9	2,522	53.1	7	6	22.4	22.7	5	193	11.7	0.5	192
Effingham	132	50.5	2,957	76.5	88	96	23.4	60.2	60	2,476	19.2	20.4	2,056
Elbert	143	31.5	6,850	62.6	109	65	21.3	24.5	52	1,692	16.7	3.3	1,638
Emanuel	165	31.7	7,482	54.9	126	86	29.6	28.7	67	2,285	20.5	7.6	2,124
Evans	63	32.5	5,640	63.8	48	29	16.1	22.2	23	772	12.0	-0.1	773
Fannin	138	35.9	6,392	76.3	102	38	16.4	30.5	29	990	9.8	2.4	967
Fayette	383	68.7	3,784	75.2	227	281	14.3	64.2	171	5,610	9.5	20.5	4,657
Floyd	474	32.3	5,038	73.2	358	287	14.0	29.3	222	6,809	12.5	6.8	6,373
Forsyth	262	72.1	1,990	67.5	152	261	10.5	94.5	134	5,560	10.2	44.2	3,856
Franklin	128	38.9	5,976	72.5	92	42	11.4	32.2	32	1,191	9.5	7.0	1,113
Fulton	9,504	28.2	11,669	30.3	7,410	6,837	11.0	26.4	5,408	107,935	11.8	2.5	105,313
Gilmer	126	38.9	4,698	75.8	90	53	14.1	54.6	34	1,399	10.7	22.2	1,145
Glascock	20	39.2	7,556	64.8	14	6	25.5	25.3	5	197	20.4	-1.0	199
Glynn	675	39.7	9,456	47.0	483	476	27.2	45.9	326	8,234	16.9	12.0	7,349
Gordon	188	24.1	3,824	74.3	151	137	13.7	71.8	80	3,347	11.8	38.9	2,409
Grady	119	28.4	4,914	64.5	93	55	21.1	32.2	41	1,401	13.5	1.4	1,382
Greene	100	46.3	6,378	66.1	68	38	17.6	30.1	29	993	13.2	4.3	952
Gwinnett	1,560	50.0	2,226	55.4	1,040	1,630	8.6	48.7	1,096	33,674	8.7	27.0	26,517
Habersham	171	37.0	4,376	75.8	125	127	20.2	33.0	95	3,220	15.8	14.1	2,822
Hall	615	42.9	3,822	64.2	430	438	12.9	46.1	300	10,198	11.5	19.8	8,514
Hancock	82	30.4	8,373	63.2	63	30	52.3	5.3	29	910	36.7	-11.8	1,032
Haralson	132	21.8	4,694	74.6	108	69	22.2	53.2	45	1,804	17.4	20.3	1,500
Harris	100	40.2	4,017	75.9	77	45	22.0	36.7	33	1,251	12.5	5.7	1,184
Hart	131	41.9	5,608	61.0	92	51	16.5	38.3	37	1,327	13.0	12.4	1,181
Heard	44	38.6	3,886	70.1	32	22	19.4	36.0	16	653	20.3	6.0	616
Henry	502	45.8	3,146	66.8	344	457	23.0	71.3	267	8,166	13.3	44.5	5,651
Houston	1,989	52.5	16,069	26.1	1,304	1,943	59.7	42.2	1,366	26,626	37.1	11.6	23,855
Irwin	98	109.0	9,863	31.5	47	29	28.5	26.0	23	856	22.3	8.4	790
Jackson	199	14.9	4,007	71.6	173	121	14.0	55.0	78	3,246	13.5	30.6	2,485
Jasper	51	27.3	3,950	69.6	40	23	19.7	27.7	18	655	15.2	-1.5	665
Jeff Davis	72	24.5	5,633	67.6	58	32	17.5	20.9	27	853	12.9	-0.9	861
Jefferson	141	10.3	8,378	53.2	128	45	20.4	28.1	35	1,294	16.9	5.3	1,229
Jenkins	66	28.8	7,553	52.0	51	22	21.4	22.3	18	675	16.8	-3.0	696
Johnson	61	26.2	6,372	60.7	48	23	27.3	-5.5	25	706	22.8	-14.4	825
Jones	86	44.9	3,287	69.1	60	42	30.1	37.6	31	1,127	19.4	9.5	1,029
Lamar	85	36.2	5,162	72.2	62	41	28.2	36.8	30	1,018	18.7	5.2	968
Lanier	40	33.5	5,416	65.2	30	15	34.8	26.7	12	433	20.3	6.7	406
Laurens	340	22.4	7,284	54.3	278	227	26.2	34.2	169	4,590	17.2	4.0	4,413
Lee	73	30.9	2,446	69.0	56	53	26.9	36.2	39	1,468	20.1	14.2	1,286
Liberty	1,016	349.4	16,455	16.2	226	1,623	80.6	61.9	1,002	22,348	61.2	3.1	21,671
Lincoln	50	32.8	5,937	47.2	38	17	26.8	21.9	14	500	17.3	-1.8	509

See footnotes at end of table.

[Includes United States, states, and 3,141 counties/county equivalents defined as of February 22, 2005. For more information on these areas, see Appendix C, Geographic Information]

County	Federal government expenditure 2004 Total (mil. dol.)	Percent change, 2000–2004	Per capita (dol.)	Direct payments to individuals, percent of total	2000 (mil. dol.)	Earnings 2005 Total (mil. dol.)	Percent of total	Percent change, 2000–2005	2000 (mil. dol.)	Employment 2005 Total	Percent of total	Percent change, 2000–2005	2000
GEORGIA—Con.													
Long	33	49.2	2,984	69.3	22	17	50.1	44.8	12	576	33.2	20.8	477
Lowndes	718	31.1	7,500	45.8	548	744	35.1	35.2	551	14,267	22.8	5.8	13,487
Lumpkin	92	44.4	3,864	63.3	64	100	31.7	48.6	67	2,052	20.0	12.3	1,827
McDuffie	126	33.5	5,861	66.4	94	67	21.4	22.3	55	1,738	15.9	-1.5	1,764
McIntosh	66	9.4	5,889	72.6	60	24	29.4	18.6	20	696	17.9	-7.1	749
Macon	94	28.0	6,775	53.3	74	36	18.7	7.1	34	1,044	17.6	-10.6	1,168
Madison	125	41.6	4,575	70.6	88	46	22.0	45.3	32	1,252	15.4	8.9	1,150
Marion	40	43.7	5,582	51.8	28	17	23.0	29.5	13	487	17.5	-4.1	508
Meriwether	130	40.5	5,721	63.1	93	72	30.2	24.6	58	1,970	24.0	-0.5	1,979
Miller	48	22.5	7,753	49.9	39	26	37.2	49.9	17	662	22.9	16.8	567
Mitchell	148	-44.2	6,216	53.2	266	67	22.8	16.8	57	1,860	16.7	-3.3	1,923
Monroe	92	33.2	3,933	69.3	69	71	29.3	30.0	55	1,858	24.3	11.1	1,673
Montgomery	52	36.9	5,823	59.7	38	18	25.5	27.3	14	519	16.7	5.3	493
Morgan	82	41.3	4,798	69.8	58	43	15.3	37.5	31	1,149	11.7	9.5	1,049
Murray	118	40.7	2,914	75.1	84	67	12.9	38.9	48	1,765	11.2	13.9	1,549
Muscogee	2,072	25.6	11,334	41.1	1,649	1,180	24.5	32.2	892	22,562	18.5	-0.5	22,686
Newton	276	44.9	3,383	77.9	190	178	18.5	75.8	102	4,303	16.9	36.1	3,161
Oconee	89	44.6	3,066	74.7	61	58	15.9	46.0	40	1,543	13.0	13.3	1,362
Oglethorpe	47	35.6	3,447	63.0	34	20	23.5	33.1	15	588	18.6	10.1	534
Paulding	187	57.4	1,768	73.9	119	193	24.0	73.0	111	4,636	14.0	41.5	3,276
Peach	188	45.8	7,624	61.4	129	98	28.5	22.7	80	2,285	22.4	2.3	2,233
Pickens	110	13.0	3,951	79.6	97	57	16.8	48.8	38	1,455	13.8	16.7	1,247
Pierce	95	34.8	5,691	70.1	71	32	18.7	31.7	24	884	12.9	-2.1	903
Pike	84	70.7	5,317	55.2	49	27	22.9	43.1	19	765	15.6	15.6	662
Polk	240	15.2	5,950	70.7	208	85	17.5	19.7	71	2,071	12.8	-3.0	2,135
Pulaski	74	29.7	7,475	60.5	57	30	23.2	10.2	27	834	18.5	-7.3	900
Putnam	99	38.5	4,989	75.0	71	59	19.6	57.6	37	1,577	15.8	28.3	1,229
Quitman	21	5.1	8,615	58.1	20	5	29.6	44.3	4	180	23.0	25.0	144
Rabun	104	48.6	6,523	65.5	70	39	16.1	38.3	28	1,006	11.2	4.7	961
Randolph	66	26.2	9,060	50.6	53	30	32.6	27.0	24	916	25.9	2.3	895
Richmond	1,949	55.6	9,931	48.4	1,252	2,332	40.8	36.9	1,703	38,066	27.9	-0.7	38,322
Rockdale	225	33.0	2,929	82.8	169	170	10.8	47.5	116	4,162	9.5	16.0	3,587
Schley	24	48.7	5,864	52.7	16	10	17.4	78.9	6	280	15.3	28.4	218
Screven	98	24.2	6,361	59.1	79	40	26.6	24.6	32	1,113	18.9	2.9	1,082
Seminole	69	30.6	7,397	60.6	53	20	20.4	19.0	17	520	12.9	-9.1	572
Spalding	320	31.5	5,252	67.5	243	217	21.0	50.1	145	5,403	17.3	27.8	4,228
Stephens	161	30.9	6,440	72.6	123	76	18.6	26.3	61	1,975	15.3	5.4	1,873
Stewart	48	38.3	9,540	53.5	34	12	33.8	20.9	10	374	24.0	4.8	357
Sumter	205	26.8	6,236	56.0	162	122	22.2	22.9	100	3,023	17.6	-4.1	3,151
Talbot	46	39.7	6,969	68.1	33	12	29.5	28.2	9	343	21.5	0.3	342
Taliaferro	20	14.9	10,408	50.4	17	5	53.4	38.0	3	151	28.7	16.2	130
Tattnall	131	36.4	5,683	62.6	96	88	31.3	6.4	83	2,448	26.2	-7.1	2,634
Taylor	63	39.2	7,021	63.4	45	21	23.0	19.4	18	591	19.8	-1.8	602
Telfair	105	43.9	8,114	62.3	73	35	26.6	11.4	31	1,004	17.6	-6.5	1,074
Terrell	84	22.0	7,641	50.5	69	28	27.6	29.5	22	729	19.8	6.6	684
Thomas	285	32.3	6,482	64.9	216	160	16.2	24.8	128	4,081	14.4	8.0	3,780
Tift	215	25.1	5,356	62.0	172	203	23.8	29.7	156	4,926	18.8	6.2	4,639
Toombs	169	39.5	6,297	60.7	121	61	15.1	31.0	47	1,683	10.9	4.3	1,614
Towns	70	22.5	6,870	80.3	57	21	17.0	74.2	12	598	10.2	37.8	434
Treutlen	43	31.7	6,048	55.3	32	15	35.7	24.1	12	435	21.4	1.6	428
Troup	342	33.3	5,593	64.4	257	238	16.7	30.4	182	5,772	14.9	7.1	5,389
Turner	68	-34.0	7,232	55.3	103	24	23.7	26.6	19	662	16.3	15.7	572
Twiggs	57	41.4	5,466	64.0	40	16	22.5	10.5	14	479	18.8	-8.1	521
Union	117	33.4	5,950	78.7	87	55	22.1	41.0	39	1,560	15.8	15.0	1,356
Upson	155	27.9	5,502	70.7	121	69	21.8	19.6	57	1,901	17.4	2.7	1,851
Walker	340	28.1	5,358	78.6	265	126	20.4	28.5	98	3,344	16.6	4.6	3,197
Walton	266	53.3	3,692	75.0	173	153	18.9	58.5	97	3,669	15.4	27.0	2,888
Ware	281	31.6	7,880	66.3	213	145	23.0	21.3	119	3,605	17.1	-4.6	3,779
Warren	49	37.4	7,869	57.4	36	10	18.1	14.6	9	322	15.2	-8.0	350
Washington	137	36.9	6,482	59.3	100	87	23.3	16.0	75	2,358	22.2	-4.5	2,468
Wayne	192	38.8	6,798	55.1	138	130	31.6	32.5	98	3,085	24.7	10.4	2,795
Webster	16	27.8	6,736	49.5	12	5	21.0	21.9	4	168	19.3	1.2	166
Wheeler	38	31.8	5,829	54.4	29	13	26.3	31.8	10	391	21.7	5.4	371
White	102	42.5	4,321	77.6	72	56	20.0	58.5	35	1,359	12.5	27.4	1,067
Whitfield	351	22.8	3,928	71.7	286	255	8.5	31.3	194	5,837	8.0	6.9	5,460
Wilcox	63	27.5	7,230	58.0	49	23	32.4	13.7	20	677	25.6	-4.5	709
Wilkes	81	38.7	7,630	65.1	58	33	23.9	16.1	28	903	18.1	-6.3	964
Wilkinson	65	26.5	6,384	69.4	51	19	13.3	15.9	16	603	16.2	1.0	597
Worth	115	23.7	5,226	56.4	93	37	24.6	10.5	34	1,024	16.3	-17.2	1,237

See footnotes at end of table.

[Includes United States, states, and 3,141 counties/county equivalents defined as of February 22, 2005. For more information on these areas, see Appendix C, Geographic Information]

County	Federal government expenditure 2004 — Total (mil. dol.)	Percent change, 2000–2004	Per capita (dol.)	Direct payments to individuals, percent of total	2000 (mil. dol.)	Federal, state, and local governments[1] — Earnings 2005 — Total (mil. dol.)	Percent of total	Percent change, 2000–2005	2000 (mil. dol.)	Employment 2005 — Total	Percent of total	Percent change, 2000–2005	2000
HAWAII	[3]12,187	[3]34.9	[3]9,651	[3]37.8	[3]9,036	11,046	31.3	44.0	7,670	172,708	20.7	3.9	166,273
Hawaii	896	34.7	5,500	60.2	665	701	22.2	50.2	467	12,945	14.0	5.6	12,260
Honolulu	9,732	34.2	10,818	33.8	7,250	9,534	34.9	43.0	6,669	144,886	24.0	3.5	140,028
Kalawao	1	76.0	8,254	81.1	1	–	–	–	–	–	–	–	–
Kauai	367	22.2	5,926	52.5	300	274	20.1	45.6	188	4,884	11.6	1.9	4,793
Maui	611	42.1	4,419	55.8	430	537	15.6	55.0	347	9,993	10.4	8.7	9,192
IDAHO	[3]8,968	[3]27.9	[3]6,437	[3]49.3	[3]7,012	5,532	18.4	32.9	4,164	125,106	14.4	6.2	117,850
Ada	1,859	26.8	5,592	46.8	1,466	1,588	13.8	39.6	1,138	31,917	12.4	10.7	28,839
Adams	30	34.8	8,737	55.2	22	15	36.9	-1.2	16	328	13.9	-18.2	401
Bannock	410	34.2	5,422	59.7	306	416	28.8	36.0	306	10,035	21.4	10.5	9,085
Bear Lake	36	-34.0	5,748	62.4	55	24	37.7	34.4	18	673	22.6	9.6	614
Benewah	73	39.3	8,121	54.8	52	52	32.5	41.8	37	1,278	24.6	11.7	1,144
Bingham	193	21.5	4,467	55.4	159	176	29.4	33.0	133	4,267	20.4	5.7	4,037
Blaine	58	24.4	2,733	64.3	46	64	8.7	28.3	50	1,365	6.5	-0.4	1,370
Boise	52	21.7	7,064	36.5	43	25	40.5	38.8	18	550	20.4	7.0	514
Bonner	187	30.2	4,689	73.3	144	103	16.4	29.7	79	2,490	10.6	5.1	2,369
Bonneville	1,290	5.9	14,394	18.8	1,219	266	12.1	22.2	217	5,686	9.1	0.7	5,645
Boundary	61	20.0	5,873	58.6	51	42	31.5	27.6	33	1,120	21.3	4.1	1,076
Butte	29	0.8	10,143	40.1	29	10	3.1	32.6	7	248	4.9	-3.1	256
Camas	6	18.7	6,379	42.5	5	5	33.9	34.1	4	126	17.7	7.7	117
Canyon	638	47.1	4,034	60.9	433	315	14.7	43.5	220	7,837	10.6	13.7	6,891
Caribou	39	-4.6	5,405	54.6	41	26	14.8	25.3	21	732	15.4	9.9	666
Cassia	108	22.6	5,062	58.2	88	65	16.5	26.5	52	1,712	13.3	0.2	1,709
Clark	8	-45.0	8,464	40.0	14	7	35.2	15.3	6	161	17.9	–	161
Clearwater	71	28.1	8,519	54.5	56	52	38.9	18.5	44	1,180	23.7	-2.3	1,208
Custer	29	49.7	7,102	56.6	20	21	29.9	17.9	18	490	18.1	-0.2	491
Elmore	400	26.4	13,850	22.2	317	404	70.0	33.8	302	6,479	45.6	-1.4	6,570
Franklin	66	80.6	5,403	46.2	36	29	21.1	34.3	22	928	16.9	9.7	846
Fremont	62	8.0	5,024	56.5	57	45	36.5	20.8	37	1,099	21.4	6.1	1,036
Gem	82	33.0	5,153	71.6	62	35	30.1	31.3	27	903	14.7	5.4	857
Gooding	75	29.7	5,261	61.4	58	41	12.6	33.8	30	1,161	13.9	3.1	1,126
Idaho	106	13.4	6,809	57.5	94	62	32.8	9.6	57	1,344	16.2	-5.4	1,421
Jefferson	77	35.0	3,716	63.7	57	45	20.3	28.1	35	1,351	14.2	7.6	1,255
Jerome	80	24.4	4,139	64.0	64	39	9.5	40.9	28	1,032	9.5	5.6	977
Kootenai	678	58.1	5,542	61.0	429	417	18.8	41.8	294	9,557	13.3	10.5	8,645
Latah	240	61.7	6,821	40.0	148	276	46.9	18.0	234	7,024	32.6	-1.4	7,125
Lemhi	64	37.9	8,153	59.7	46	43	42.3	25.8	34	889	18.9	4.8	848
Lewis	51	19.8	13,491	51.5	42	15	28.7	22.1	12	402	18.5	-5.2	424
Lincoln	21	11.8	4,959	52.2	19	22	33.7	53.7	14	523	21.8	8.5	482
Madison	86	39.5	2,789	65.7	62	69	15.7	41.9	48	1,879	11.1	11.6	1,684
Minidoka	96	26.8	5,002	63.6	76	51	19.7	19.2	43	1,455	14.5	-4.7	1,527
Nez Perce	277	28.6	7,333	59.0	216	172	18.9	17.7	146	4,182	15.8	-5.6	4,428
Oneida	24	1.4	5,758	60.6	24	13	39.7	22.7	11	443	21.7	1.6	436
Owyhee	44	31.9	4,036	61.2	34	25	21.0	34.1	19	732	17.1	5.8	692
Payette	99	19.9	4,587	67.2	83	43	16.0	26.9	34	1,171	12.6	4.6	1,119
Power	42	10.9	5,599	42.8	38	25	18.6	26.5	20	718	16.5	-1.8	731
Shoshone	105	16.1	8,148	69.1	90	43	23.2	11.9	39	1,120	18.5	-7.9	1,216
Teton	26	19.0	3,559	48.6	22	19	21.6	52.4	13	500	13.4	12.4	445
Twin Falls	335	26.0	4,929	66.2	266	247	18.5	32.8	186	6,138	13.5	11.2	5,522
Valley	64	29.0	8,030	67.0	50	52	29.2	16.6	45	1,108	16.3	1.9	1,087
Washington	59	23.3	5,872	68.5	48	28	24.6	29.0	22	773	15.6	2.0	758
ILLINOIS	[3]76,828	[3]27.9	[3]6,043	[3]57.6	[3]60,046	50,586	13.8	26.0	40,144	893,899	12.0	-0.1	804,899
Adams	390	19.9	5,836	67.1	326	196	13.4	20.3	163	4,756	10.6	-4.5	4,981
Alexander	88	18.0	9,587	54.6	75	30	37.4	8.4	27	648	22.8	-12.1	737
Bond	107	11.0	5,944	59.1	96	56	25.6	25.8	45	1,044	13.9	1.3	1,031
Boone	138	30.3	2,850	78.8	106	88	11.1	46.0	60	1,922	10.2	18.4	1,623
Brown	32	12.7	4,771	57.5	29	26	18.8	13.1	23	496	12.5	-9.8	550
Bureau	189	2.5	5,370	74.4	184	98	17.1	27.6	77	2,537	13.4	-0.4	2,547
Calhoun	83	131.4	16,087	27.5	36	10	29.2	30.0	8	281	13.4	-3.4	291
Carroll	105	8.1	6,433	73.0	97	36	18.0	17.5	30	945	12.2	-3.2	976
Cass	79	15.6	5,718	67.6	68	35	14.3	29.4	27	994	11.7	5.5	942
Champaign	975	21.3	5,289	45.0	804	1,712	37.1	32.1	1,296	35,246	27.8	7.2	32,884
Christian	224	24.5	6,337	66.9	180	88	19.3	26.8	69	2,104	12.5	-1.7	2,141
Clark	96	8.4	5,685	71.0	89	34	15.3	32.0	26	930	11.4	3.0	903
Clay	90	15.0	6,323	67.3	78	41	15.6	30.1	31	1,007	11.7	2.0	987
Clinton	161	15.4	4,466	79.2	140	112	22.3	28.8	87	2,510	13.4	0.7	2,492
Coles	233	19.2	4,525	74.2	196	285	27.3	30.5	218	6,490	18.5	3.2	6,291
Cook	32,974	22.7	6,189	63.6	26,872	22,568	11.8	22.0	18,503	352,146	10.8	-2.2	360,203
Crawford	105	12.5	5,231	76.5	93	80	21.2	26.8	63	2,025	19.0	(Z)	2,026
Cumberland	55	10.0	4,953	68.2	50	20	19.0	27.8	15	525	11.1	-1.7	534
DeKalb	330	23.8	3,458	71.0	267	533	31.3	36.4	391	12,858	25.2	13.7	11,310
De Witt	86	6.7	5,186	77.0	81	45	17.4	8.5	42	1,178	15.0	-7.5	1,274

See footnotes at end of table.

Table B-12. Counties — Government Expenditure, Earnings, and Employment—Con.

[Includes United States, states, and 3,141 counties/county equivalents defined as of February 22, 2005. For more information on these areas, see Appendix C, Geographic Information]

County	Federal government expenditure — 2004					Federal, state, and local governments[1] — Earnings — 2005				Federal, state, and local governments[1] — Employment — 2005			
	Total (mil. dol.)	Percent change, 2000–2004	Per capita (dol.)	Direct payments to individuals, percent of total	2000 (mil. dol.)	Total (mil. dol.)	Percent of total	Percent change, 2000–2005	2000 (mil. dol.)	Total	Percent of total	Percent change, 2000–2005	2000
ILLINOIS—Con.													
Douglas	82	−4.0	4,088	73.7	85	35	9.6	30.8	27	967	7.8	8.4	892
DuPage	3,325	29.8	3,580	67.9	2,562	2,987	7.4	32.7	2,251	51,876	7.2	5.2	49,330
Edgar	115	7.3	5,985	68.6	108	55	20.6	16.7	47	1,256	13.1	−6.3	1,341
Edwards	37	16.0	5,433	71.2	32	12	8.5	26.8	9	313	6.6	−1.3	317
Effingham	171	21.8	4,946	67.2	140	94	11.3	25.6	74	2,109	8.1	−0.1	2,111
Fayette	114	13.3	5,252	68.4	100	65	25.6	19.3	55	1,432	14.0	−9.7	1,585
Ford	82	3.1	5,715	70.6	79	34	16.9	31.9	26	889	11.1	7.5	827
Franklin	271	11.6	6,867	72.8	243	103	25.3	23.8	83	2,345	15.4	−1.0	2,369
Fulton	223	16.7	5,937	75.1	192	107	31.8	19.7	90	2,644	18.8	−4.6	2,772
Gallatin	64	12.3	10,287	49.9	57	11	22.2	12.7	10	327	14.1	−0.9	330
Greene	93	12.5	6,432	68.5	83	29	23.4	17.9	25	789	13.5	−7.5	853
Grundy	150	11.8	3,655	82.8	134	110	11.6	51.5	73	2,592	12.0	19.8	2,163
Hamilton	61	19.0	7,295	59.8	51	23	28.8	20.3	19	615	18.0	−4.4	643
Hancock	148	35.0	7,651	54.7	110	44	20.1	22.6	36	1,289	13.6	−5.5	1,364
Hardin	36	35.2	7,678	63.5	27	10	23.3	9.1	9	280	14.2	−9.1	308
Henderson	49	10.7	6,093	59.3	44	16	31.8	19.2	14	482	16.9	−3.8	501
Henry	248	10.9	4,907	76.3	224	132	22.3	25.4	105	3,446	14.8	−2.1	3,519
Iroquois	180	5.4	5,856	70.4	170	62	18.5	32.3	47	1,734	11.4	5.1	1,650
Jackson	302	22.6	5,179	63.4	246	585	47.1	24.3	470	13,064	33.8	−1.3	13,240
Jasper	52	−1.0	5,170	65.5	52	29	22.9	24.4	23	763	16.6	−0.8	769
Jefferson	224	24.6	5,542	71.9	180	124	13.9	21.7	102	2,890	11.5	0.4	2,879
Jersey	95	21.0	4,237	77.3	78	54	28.3	33.7	41	1,266	14.9	3.2	1,227
Jo Daviess	115	19.7	5,079	77.2	96	56	15.2	36.9	41	1,381	10.2	1.6	1,359
Johnson	80	31.1	6,127	61.0	61	44	41.4	19.8	37	848	19.0	−8.5	927
Kane	1,782	27.3	3,772	56.0	1,399	1,670	14.8	42.2	1,174	29,762	11.3	12.7	26,417
Kankakee	554	18.1	5,171	72.1	469	316	17.2	25.6	252	6,619	12.4	−0.5	6,654
Kendall	169	48.6	2,324	63.3	113	164	15.9	90.6	86	3,407	12.8	42.7	2,387
Knox	311	14.9	5,780	78.6	271	162	18.6	21.4	134	3,876	14.1	−1.6	3,940
Lake	3,845	34.9	5,550	41.4	2,850	3,593	14.5	21.3	2,962	57,941	13.2	−7.5	62,619
LaSalle	546	17.5	4,865	77.7	465	309	15.4	25.6	246	6,704	11.5	−1.6	6,815
Lawrence	97	7.9	6,059	72.9	90	35	17.4	21.3	29	1,027	15.0	−6.7	1,101
Lee	185	7.1	5,170	71.0	173	125	20.1	20.8	103	2,421	13.0	−6.1	2,578
Livingston	190	11.0	4,879	70.3	172	153	21.5	21.7	126	3,055	14.9	−6.9	3,281
Logan	152	−3.8	4,937	73.6	158	114	28.0	18.5	96	2,228	15.9	−8.9	2,446
McDonough	171	35.4	5,263	61.7	126	263	49.7	26.4	208	5,766	32.1	−10.0	6,409
McHenry	751	40.1	2,532	82.1	536	657	13.2	52.0	432	14,233	11.3	20.3	11,834
McLean	553	26.9	3,498	67.2	436	642	13.6	26.1	509	14,354	13.1	0.2	14,323
Macon	710	34.8	6,394	63.9	527	288	9.7	18.6	243	6,222	9.2	−13.1	7,157
Macoupin	270	21.5	5,513	80.5	223	103	19.7	23.4	84	2,796	14.9	−2.2	2,860
Madison	1,628	41.0	6,160	67.5	1,155	775	16.5	24.0	624	16,817	13.4	−1.0	16,989
Marion	293	23.6	7,219	75.1	237	108	18.3	17.1	92	2,577	14.1	−7.7	2,793
Marshall	67	21.9	5,060	74.9	55	21	14.1	20.1	18	543	9.2	−12.8	623
Mason	99	22.1	6,210	75.7	81	48	36.6	24.5	39	1,210	19.9	−7.5	1,308
Massac	97	23.8	6,378	71.4	79	40	17.2	35.6	29	975	14.8	−1.2	987
Menard	60	23.6	4,720	70.2	49	26	27.8	18.1	22	773	18.2	−4.3	808
Mercer	86	20.9	5,094	70.3	72	47	34.8	24.0	38	1,195	19.4	−9.5	1,321
Monroe	117	31.7	3,821	79.1	88	58	16.2	40.1	41	1,383	10.8	3.8	1,332
Montgomery	179	28.6	5,874	71.4	139	86	19.9	21.1	71	1,921	13.1	−8.7	2,103
Morgan	191	21.0	5,307	72.0	158	114	18.7	22.5	93	2,458	12.4	−5.2	2,594
Moultrie	79	26.1	5,450	77.4	62	25	12.5	20.3	20	624	9.2	−8.8	684
Ogle	216	36.3	4,031	70.9	159	123	14.2	22.5	100	2,905	11.7	−2.5	2,979
Peoria	1,248	18.8	6,843	55.4	1,051	637	11.5	21.8	523	12,009	9.7	−3.3	12,419
Perry	115	18.0	5,062	78.5	98	65	24.8	23.7	52	1,426	15.4	−4.0	1,485
Piatt	81	12.6	4,934	76.0	72	35	23.3	16.7	30	970	15.9	−7.5	1,049
Pike	105	21.8	6,174	69.1	87	41	22.6	21.1	34	1,043	13.6	−5.4	1,103
Pope	33	34.3	7,683	56.7	25	14	41.9	20.3	11	300	22.8	−11.2	338
Pulaski	92	−27.2	13,146	37.8	126	34	44.1	25.9	27	923	31.8	−2.0	942
Putnam	32	33.4	5,198	75.1	24	10	10.1	30.3	8	309	10.6	−4.0	322
Randolph	172	22.4	5,159	75.8	141	152	28.4	23.9	122	2,968	19.6	−6.5	3,175
Richland	98	27.3	6,160	71.2	77	42	16.1	11.4	38	1,071	11.6	−10.2	1,193
Rock Island	1,077	14.9	7,291	55.9	938	1,016	22.7	34.8	753	15,072	15.7	1.0	14,928
St. Clair	2,732	53.9	10,542	42.4	1,775	1,660	32.7	38.5	1,198	24,238	19.1	4.1	23,278
Saline	215	27.4	8,179	59.5	168	91	21.0	20.9	75	2,128	16.0	−4.2	2,221
Sangamon	3,125	33.1	16,274	28.9	2,348	1,871	33.5	20.0	1,558	28,588	21.4	−8.9	31,364
Schuyler	45	33.3	6,387	59.6	34	20	18.6	30.2	15	600	17.3	9.9	546
Scott	35	25.7	6,509	55.6	28	13	19.4	27.3	10	386	15.9	−1.5	392
Shelby	131	27.2	5,851	69.8	103	39	17.3	1.6	39	999	11.0	−25.8	1,347
Stark	41	26.0	6,709	66.5	33	12	22.7	19.0	10	356	14.8	−1.9	363
Stephenson	269	36.0	5,594	68.7	198	124	12.7	26.4	98	3,090	11.0	1.4	3,047
Tazewell	592	30.0	4,581	76.0	455	312	8.8	31.6	237	7,442	10.0	5.5	7,055

See footnotes at end of table.

[Includes United States, states, and 3,141 counties/county equivalents defined as of February 22, 2005. For more information on these areas, see Appendix C, Geographic Information]

County	Federal government expenditure					Federal, state, and local governments[1]							
	2004					Earnings				Employment			
						2005				2005			
	Total (mil. dol.)	Percent change, 2000–2004	Per capita (dol.)	Direct payments to individ-uals, percent of total	2000 (mil. dol.)	Total (mil. dol.)	Percent of total	Percent change, 2000–2005	2000 (mil. dol.)	Total	Percent of total	Percent change, 2000–2005	2000
ILLINOIS—Con.													
Union	114	30.0	6,248	66.6	87	77	36.9	20.8	64	1,777	23.0	−9.0	1,953
Vermilion	548	19.0	6,616	66.4	460	338	23.8	23.1	275	6,209	15.1	−4.3	6,491
Wabash	65	21.8	5,118	75.8	53	38	23.1	26.6	30	1,019	17.4	6.6	956
Warren	102	24.3	5,744	67.7	82	34	15.2	19.5	28	887	10.3	−8.9	974
Washington	85	22.3	5,609	73.7	69	37	13.3	29.2	29	1,020	12.2	−1.4	1,035
Wayne	113	40.0	6,674	63.2	81	37	16.7	22.0	30	1,088	14.0	5.2	1,034
White	128	15.3	8,382	61.3	111	35	16.3	23.2	29	927	12.0	−1.6	942
Whiteside	329	31.7	5,479	80.3	250	184	20.1	28.8	143	4,066	14.0	−0.8	4,099
Will	1,452	36.2	2,366	80.6	1,066	1,516	16.4	54.7	980	31,100	14.1	24.1	25,070
Williamson	535	33.3	8,478	48.4	401	293	25.9	23.7	237	5,316	15.7	−5.6	5,631
Winnebago	1,322	28.0	4,611	66.6	1,034	759	11.3	23.3	616	14,710	8.6	−2.0	15,016
Woodford	141	36.0	3,807	71.6	103	72	14.7	26.9	57	1,831	10.6	2.3	1,790
INDIANA	[3]37,918	[3]31.9	[3]6,079	[3]58.3	[3]28,743	21,423	14.3	29.7	16,517	439,733	11.9	1.9	431,482
Adams	137	22.7	4,062	69.4	112	81	12.5	25.9	65	2,241	9.7	3.7	2,162
Allen	2,104	47.4	6,149	46.6	1,428	982	10.5	28.6	763	19,675	8.6	2.1	19,265
Bartholomew	386	36.7	5,290	60.8	282	262	11.2	28.1	205	6,117	11.6	9.2	5,603
Benton	57	38.0	6,227	61.5	41	25	24.3	13.9	22	696	15.2	−6.7	746
Blackford	70	24.7	5,087	77.4	56	26	15.5	−4.3	28	698	11.5	−20.2	875
Boone	167	25.1	3,291	78.4	134	129	11.9	45.9	88	2,918	9.8	19.4	2,444
Brown	42	37.7	2,749	77.5	30	32	23.6	26.6	25	824	11.5	2.9	801
Carroll	80	24.3	3,956	69.7	65	36	13.9	24.6	29	932	8.6	−0.5	937
Cass	222	15.8	5,489	66.7	192	170	26.0	30.8	130	3,867	18.8	3.1	3,752
Clark	563	−14.7	5,590	66.6	660	360	17.3	−2.3	368	7,698	13.1	−22.8	9,967
Clay	158	29.1	5,810	70.7	122	52	16.2	15.6	45	1,352	10.6	−4.0	1,409
Clinton	153	19.2	4,477	74.2	128	72	13.9	22.2	59	1,743	11.5	2.2	1,705
Crawford	69	21.9	6,223	63.1	57	21	20.3	21.0	17	607	14.1	11.4	545
Daviess	164	31.6	5,438	68.7	125	81	17.4	33.6	60	1,905	11.3	9.6	1,738
Dearborn	185	28.5	3,803	77.5	144	131	17.7	42.9	92	2,864	12.4	16.1	2,466
Decatur	115	25.3	4,609	71.6	92	66	12.0	36.3	48	1,528	9.3	6.8	1,431
DeKalb	144	32.4	3,478	80.0	109	88	8.0	26.2	70	2,065	7.2	3.2	2,001
Delaware	616	25.7	5,228	70.0	490	517	22.4	32.5	390	10,656	16.8	−1.8	10,850
Dubois	207	36.3	5,085	59.2	152	97	7.2	27.5	76	2,188	6.2	4.8	2,088
Elkhart	620	24.7	3,233	77.0	497	387	5.8	27.4	304	8,642	5.6	8.2	7,989
Fayette	146	24.8	5,854	72.5	117	58	12.9	3.6	56	1,392	11.3	−8.4	1,519
Floyd	360	29.9	5,038	72.0	277	263	18.8	35.8	194	5,834	14.5	6.2	5,492
Fountain	105	21.8	5,936	73.3	86	37	15.0	19.6	31	944	11.2	−3.2	975
Franklin	82	22.5	3,575	71.1	67	41	24.3	29.3	32	1,039	14.3	−0.8	1,047
Fulton	91	20.9	4,430	79.9	75	52	16.1	30.0	40	1,267	11.6	8.0	1,173
Gibson	175	24.3	5,251	71.0	141	57	5.6	20.5	47	1,331	6.3	−0.7	1,340
Grant	458	25.3	6,400	67.9	365	230	18.1	21.1	190	4,521	12.7	−1.6	4,596
Greene	238	35.6	7,113	57.5	176	81	25.0	15.6	70	1,943	15.6	−9.3	2,143
Hamilton	469	42.1	2,022	80.3	330	509	8.2	46.1	348	10,906	7.4	21.7	8,960
Hancock	214	34.7	3,505	83.3	159	179	16.7	46.5	122	4,121	11.7	22.6	3,362
Harrison	152	33.5	4,171	77.3	114	86	18.5	30.8	66	2,034	11.9	6.0	1,919
Hendricks	340	40.0	2,757	80.1	243	367	18.4	51.3	243	7,950	12.6	22.0	6,518
Henry	260	20.0	5,434	74.2	216	154	24.9	36.1	113	3,730	18.3	11.6	3,342
Howard	446	27.5	5,272	74.5	350	301	10.8	33.8	225	6,790	12.9	3.6	6,554
Huntington	163	25.5	4,282	78.9	130	78	12.2	9.9	71	1,810	8.7	−7.2	1,951
Jackson	189	7.1	4,500	72.9	176	127	12.9	41.2	90	2,805	10.6	8.3	2,591
Jasper	140	32.4	4,437	74.4	106	81	16.0	36.1	59	2,046	12.2	12.6	1,817
Jay	116	28.7	5,337	71.2	90	52	15.6	23.6	42	1,320	11.7	1.9	1,295
Jefferson	174	11.4	5,409	69.1	156	109	17.5	35.9	80	2,588	13.9	1.8	2,541
Jennings	117	30.0	4,123	71.6	90	61	17.3	−17.5	74	1,387	12.1	−36.6	2,180
Johnson	452	38.1	3,595	76.5	328	297	15.5	37.1	216	6,761	10.6	12.5	6,010
Knox	257	16.5	6,689	67.7	221	219	31.2	23.3	178	5,020	23.2	−10.2	5,593
Kosciusko	261	26.7	3,451	79.2	206	137	7.1	24.9	109	3,376	7.3	6.4	3,173
LaGrange	94	20.5	2,561	79.6	78	64	9.9	24.1	52	1,490	8.1	0.5	1,482
Lake	2,777	20.9	5,658	70.5	2,296	1,354	13.5	17.9	1,148	29,697	12.1	−2.0	30,300
LaPorte	532	27.0	4,850	77.5	419	363	17.8	24.2	292	7,909	13.3	−2.4	8,107
Lawrence	252	24.7	5,425	72.4	202	121	18.3	26.2	96	2,751	13.1	0.5	2,738
Madison	748	22.8	5,724	76.1	609	349	16.0	24.6	280	7,146	12.6	−2.1	7,296
Marion	7,513	28.8	8,699	43.2	5,832	4,755	13.1	31.9	3,605	79,402	11.7	1.4	78,298
Marshall	177	25.1	3,796	75.4	142	101	12.9	24.3	82	2,516	10.1	4.3	2,412
Martin	347	36.7	33,177	13.4	254	410	79.6	29.9	316	4,420	55.9	3.0	4,292
Miami	221	20.0	6,138	61.5	184	159	32.4	16.8	136	3,057	19.8	−5.5	3,234
Monroe	633	20.9	5,233	48.9	524	977	33.3	37.2	712	20,787	25.3	3.2	20,135
Montgomery	179	24.0	4,712	72.3	144	89	11.0	24.7	71	2,185	9.8	4.7	2,087
Morgan	266	30.6	3,833	73.6	204	134	20.6	26.9	105	3,191	14.9	3.9	3,072
Newton	64	29.2	4,418	68.5	49	33	20.1	21.1	27	875	15.7	−0.8	882
Noble	158	30.1	3,350	77.6	122	88	9.8	18.9	74	2,132	8.0	−1.7	2,168
Ohio	24	29.4	4,026	76.0	18	13	18.5	21.4	10	310	11.7	−10.7	347
Orange	108	27.6	5,453	67.9	84	41	16.3	28.3	32	1,036	12.1	8.4	956
Owen	87	28.9	3,753	72.9	67	36	17.7	23.3	29	956	12.8	0.7	949

See footnotes at end of table.

County and City Data Book: 2007

U.S. Census Bureau

[Includes United States, states, and 3,141 counties/county equivalents defined as of February 22, 2005. For more information on these areas, see Appendix C, Geographic Information]

County	Federal government expenditure					Federal, state, and local governments[1]							
						Earnings				Employment			
	2004					2005				2005			
	Total (mil. dol.)	Percent change, 2000–2004	Per capita (dol.)	Direct payments to individuals, percent of total	2000 (mil. dol.)	Total (mil. dol.)	Percent of total	Percent change, 2000–2005	2000 (mil. dol.)	Total	Percent of total	Percent change, 2000–2005	2000
INDIANA—Con.													
Parke	90	33.0	5,229	67.3	68	53	38.2	40.2	38	1,341	23.3	5.8	1,267
Perry	107	35.6	5,625	62.6	79	72	23.9	35.9	53	1,616	18.1	2.5	1,577
Pike	80	37.1	6,153	66.2	58	26	16.7	24.2	21	745	17.3	5.4	707
Porter	603	45.4	3,893	79.5	415	414	14.6	26.4	328	9,531	13.1	5.3	9,049
Posey	122	31.1	4,514	68.6	93	58	10.3	17.7	49	1,345	10.3	−4.1	1,402
Pulaski	71	29.0	5,148	71.4	55	46	18.8	27.7	36	1,172	16.4	10.5	1,061
Putnam	148	36.3	4,022	72.6	109	125	23.7	30.3	96	2,947	17.5	3.7	2,843
Randolph	151	34.5	5,646	72.2	112	54	16.1	6.8	51	1,407	12.8	−10.7	1,575
Ripley	160	45.9	5,814	61.0	110	64	9.9	26.6	50	1,498	8.8	3.5	1,447
Rush	91	17.2	5,057	68.7	78	54	20.9	23.4	43	1,300	15.9	−3.6	1,349
St. Joseph	2,439	71.4	9,153	37.0	1,423	720	10.4	28.9	559	15,498	9.7	2.9	15,054
Scott	130	19.3	5,527	69.5	109	58	19.7	26.4	46	1,429	14.9	3.0	1,387
Shelby	189	23.5	4,316	71.7	153	123	15.6	33.2	93	2,856	12.4	8.5	2,633
Spencer	106	28.0	5,225	65.0	83	43	12.9	24.8	35	1,145	10.9	7.1	1,069
Starke	114	36.1	4,984	73.8	84	40	24.4	14.8	35	1,052	16.6	−5.2	1,110
Steuben	137	29.0	4,070	78.8	106	73	11.5	34.7	54	1,818	9.2	7.8	1,686
Sullivan	120	15.8	5,479	72.1	103	93	39.4	27.7	73	2,165	26.8	−2.9	2,229
Switzerland	45	31.2	4,682	65.4	34	19	19.9	24.6	15	480	12.8	1.1	475
Tippecanoe	682	24.7	4,487	53.4	547	1,224	29.3	53.3	799	21,860	22.3	3.5	21,119
Tipton	77	17.2	4,636	74.9	66	52	26.1	30.7	40	1,299	20.6	1.6	1,278
Union	33	21.2	4,532	73.9	27	20	26.7	46.4	14	513	17.5	10.3	461
Vanderburgh	1,095	17.7	6,322	63.2	930	509	9.3	24.0	411	10,343	8.1	−1.9	10,538
Vermillion	110	23.1	6,639	59.1	89	34	13.0	18.5	29	851	12.8	0.9	843
Vigo	711	28.6	6,886	59.4	553	493	21.0	37.6	358	9,350	14.8	−2.5	9,590
Wabash	166	22.8	4,852	74.8	135	84	14.5	12.6	75	2,040	10.6	−8.9	2,240
Warren	39	25.9	4,477	61.4	31	18	22.2	35.1	13	444	14.9	5.7	420
Warrick	195	17.5	3,514	78.4	166	90	12.4	27.0	71	2,129	10.3	8.5	1,963
Washington	128	29.5	4,579	68.0	99	68	23.5	37.0	49	1,595	15.3	8.1	1,475
Wayne	411	22.4	5,884	69.7	336	222	16.2	28.3	173	5,162	12.7	−1.3	5,232
Wells	107	20.7	3,829	76.1	89	61	12.6	15.3	53	1,507	10.1	−5.0	1,587
White	139	25.4	5,597	73.2	111	67	20.4	22.6	55	1,739	16.5	4.9	1,657
Whitley	163	16.3	5,106	61.1	140	66	13.4	23.0	54	1,565	10.7	2.1	1,533
IOWA	[3]19,218	[3]30.2	[3]6,505	[3]56.3	[3]14,761	11,675	16.4	26.4	9,236	260,403	13.2	1.6	256,251
Adair	52	17.6	6,609	54.8	45	20	15.4	21.0	17	558	9.7	−11.7	632
Adams	33	29.5	7,604	56.7	25	10	17.1	17.7	9	293	11.1	−10.7	328
Allamakee	77	32.8	5,245	61.7	58	40	16.4	27.1	31	1,139	12.1	1.6	1,121
Appanoose	100	27.8	7,313	60.5	78	35	17.8	21.2	29	814	10.4	−8.6	891
Audubon	48	12.7	7,474	58.4	43	17	15.6	21.3	14	501	12.3	−2.7	515
Benton	118	−39.6	4,441	68.1	196	67	23.8	31.8	51	1,675	14.5	1.0	1,658
Black Hawk	670	19.0	5,313	68.2	563	548	16.2	26.6	433	12,399	13.9	0.6	12,326
Boone	136	29.2	5,139	67.8	105	112	25.7	35.5	83	2,731	18.9	12.8	2,421
Bremer	121	29.1	5,150	70.3	94	67	15.7	45.0	46	1,744	12.4	11.2	1,568
Buchanan	108	23.7	5,151	66.1	88	69	23.4	21.0	57	1,742	16.9	−3.7	1,808
Buena Vista	114	16.4	5,671	65.1	98	67	16.5	30.9	51	1,714	12.5	0.8	1,700
Butler	98	30.4	6,478	65.3	75	30	18.0	32.6	23	839	12.0	−3.6	870
Calhoun	78	23.6	7,365	62.8	63	34	24.0	23.1	27	904	15.4	−3.2	934
Carroll	136	37.1	6,527	64.7	99	53	11.1	26.9	42	1,446	8.5	3.4	1,398
Cass	95	22.3	6,674	67.7	78	62	25.7	26.6	49	1,495	15.9	−0.2	1,498
Cedar	88	18.4	4,835	64.5	75	44	19.5	29.3	34	1,167	12.2	1.0	1,155
Cerro Gordo	267	20.2	5,920	68.5	222	141	12.3	26.4	112	3,247	9.3	−0.6	3,268
Cherokee	91	38.2	7,312	68.8	66	47	19.4	23.2	38	1,150	13.9	−2.5	1,179
Chickasaw	77	20.9	6,110	59.9	64	27	13.3	20.1	23	744	10.1	−4.7	781
Clarke	50	37.3	5,426	60.2	36	29	16.8	13.3	26	774	12.0	−4.1	807
Clay	97	2.9	5,770	63.7	95	74	18.9	37.7	54	1,717	13.9	12.7	1,524
Clayton	109	26.2	5,944	62.8	86	56	19.8	22.4	45	1,323	11.8	−4.0	1,378
Clinton	259	18.0	5,199	76.1	220	112	11.5	20.4	93	2,885	9.6	−3.1	2,978
Crawford	116	32.8	6,860	51.1	87	54	16.5	31.5	41	1,287	11.5	2.2	1,259
Dallas	148	19.2	2,994	73.5	125	108	9.6	49.7	72	2,801	9.0	18.0	2,373
Davis	48	30.8	5,547	60.6	37	25	24.7	24.3	20	661	15.1	−0.5	664
Decatur	59	38.9	6,960	54.0	43	24	24.8	13.2	21	674	15.1	−9.4	744
Delaware	84	20.6	4,646	61.3	70	51	16.4	32.7	39	1,309	11.9	5.4	1,242
Des Moines	307	49.6	7,514	57.2	205	117	11.3	19.3	98	2,751	9.8	−3.7	2,858
Dickinson	92	14.8	5,495	74.9	80	49	13.3	36.0	36	1,229	9.1	4.8	1,173
Dubuque	444	24.8	4,874	70.4	355	201	8.5	35.4	148	4,690	7.1	8.2	4,336
Emmet	75	27.2	7,061	63.6	59	35	17.9	21.9	29	914	13.8	−1.9	932
Fayette	135	24.0	6,361	63.8	109	53	16.6	23.2	43	1,412	11.9	−3.2	1,458
Floyd	114	20.3	6,915	62.7	95	44	16.2	25.3	35	1,127	12.7	−3.8	1,172
Franklin	68	28.2	6,327	56.6	53	31	16.8	24.6	24	833	12.4	−3.7	865
Fremont	62	33.0	8,054	57.0	47	19	11.8	25.1	16	566	10.9	−2.1	578
Greene	68	21.5	6,751	61.2	56	36	24.5	22.7	29	976	17.3	−3.5	1,011
Grundy	67	−0.7	5,431	67.7	68	27	13.5	17.2	23	736	11.4	−6.6	788
Guthrie	73	31.2	6,339	63.4	56	32	22.3	29.0	25	903	17.1	−1.4	916
Hamilton	92	16.6	5,680	67.7	79	49	12.9	20.4	41	1,284	11.4	−5.2	1,354

See footnotes at end of table.

Table B-12. Counties — Government Expenditure, Earnings, and Employment—Con.

[Includes United States, states, and 3,141 counties/county equivalents defined as of February 22, 2005. For more information on these areas, see Appendix C, Geographic Information]

County	Federal government expenditure					Federal, state, and local governments[1]							
	2004				2000 (mil. dol.)	Earnings				Employment			
						2005			2000 (mil. dol.)	2005			2000
	Total (mil. dol.)	Percent change, 2000–2004	Per capita (dol.)	Direct payments to individuals, percent of total		Total (mil. dol.)	Percent of total	Percent change, 2000–2005		Total	Percent of total	Percent change, 2000–2005	
IOWA—Con.													
Hancock	66	18.7	5,580	64.7	55	29	7.9	24.2	23	824	7.7	−2.3	843
Hardin	125	20.4	6,872	65.3	104	72	21.6	22.8	58	1,888	17.7	−0.7	1,901
Harrison	102	9.2	6,448	61.9	93	38	23.4	30.6	29	998	14.4	3.0	969
Henry	109	−1.9	5,377	61.8	111	85	17.7	26.1	68	1,955	13.5	−0.2	1,959
Howard	63	36.0	6,380	55.6	46	31	14.9	24.3	25	922	13.1	−1.1	932
Humboldt	66	22.1	6,611	64.5	54	29	15.9	23.9	23	781	11.6	−0.6	786
Ida	52	29.8	7,026	61.1	40	18	11.1	19.8	15	496	9.3	−6.8	532
Iowa	79	28.9	4,951	66.9	62	43	9.1	38.4	31	1,108	8.1	0.3	1,105
Jackson	118	17.3	5,800	65.5	100	52	21.7	24.9	42	1,396	12.9	0.1	1,395
Jasper	186	25.4	4,918	68.0	148	117	18.2	22.1	95	2,695	14.4	−5.8	2,861
Jefferson	80	30.9	4,992	61.4	61	50	14.5	26.9	39	1,183	9.8	−3.4	1,225
Johnson	873	56.6	7,516	26.0	557	1,604	42.9	26.8	1,265	31,968	32.3	11.0	28,801
Jones	100	32.4	4,829	63.3	75	61	24.2	22.9	50	1,493	15.3	−2.1	1,525
Keokuk	80	30.6	7,093	60.3	61	24	21.1	33.0	18	680	13.3	1.0	673
Kossuth	115	25.6	7,043	58.9	92	46	13.6	28.7	36	1,223	11.2	−4.7	1,283
Lee	206	20.4	5,601	71.6	171	120	15.2	30.5	92	2,640	12.1	1.5	2,600
Linn	1,498	24.4	7,594	39.9	1,204	643	10.3	29.7	496	13,576	9.4	3.9	13,066
Louisa	66	41.3	5,473	55.8	47	33	20.2	30.6	25	838	14.5	2.1	821
Lucas	65	35.9	6,724	59.7	48	31	21.7	31.9	23	817	15.1	3.7	788
Lyon	59	20.5	5,024	64.0	49	25	15.1	29.9	19	688	10.5	1.0	681
Madison	69	23.2	4,622	69.6	56	38	21.6	25.2	30	957	14.1	1.1	947
Mahaska	121	23.8	5,451	64.6	98	59	16.8	43.5	41	1,426	11.6	7.7	1,324
Marion	200	26.6	6,110	61.5	158	97	11.7	−4.4	102	2,225	9.4	−9.8	2,468
Marshall	235	29.1	5,954	63.4	182	152	17.4	29.8	117	3,689	15.3	3.7	3,558
Mills	90	38.9	5,989	60.5	65	80	42.5	32.6	60	1,835	29.4	3.2	1,778
Mitchell	69	26.1	6,268	66.6	55	29	16.2	34.0	22	768	12.9	1.7	755
Monona	79	23.4	8,158	62.6	64	32	26.0	18.7	27	949	17.6	−7.1	1,021
Monroe	58	25.1	7,379	61.4	46	23	19.5	35.4	17	550	12.3	−2.8	566
Montgomery	81	32.2	7,114	64.4	61	40	19.6	28.0	32	1,009	13.7	−0.5	1,014
Muscatine	212	25.3	4,976	62.2	169	127	10.8	20.6	106	2,973	10.4	0.2	2,966
O'Brien	95	24.7	6,590	66.2	76	40	16.1	20.8	33	1,161	12.3	−1.9	1,184
Osceola	44	27.8	6,416	63.7	34	14	13.1	20.5	12	394	10.8	−2.5	404
Page	104	18.4	6,399	66.4	88	67	24.3	27.8	53	1,611	16.9	−1.3	1,632
Palo Alto	77	16.5	7,826	57.1	66	37	22.3	14.7	33	1,051	19.4	−6.1	1,119
Plymouth	118	23.7	4,731	65.3	95	62	11.7	34.0	46	1,552	9.7	2.6	1,513
Pocahontas	66	23.9	8,150	61.3	53	23	19.1	18.5	19	627	14.0	−7.4	677
Polk	2,916	41.5	7,416	42.0	2,061	1,938	12.6	27.3	1,522	34,577	10.7	0.8	34,308
Pottawattamie	478	21.4	5,362	68.2	394	249	14.8	23.1	202	5,469	11.1	−2.9	5,634
Poweshiek	100	26.2	5,242	70.5	79	38	8.4	19.6	32	1,026	7.5	−8.9	1,126
Ringgold	40	27.1	7,537	55.7	31	20	27.2	26.1	16	537	18.1	1.3	530
Sac	76	23.2	7,059	62.0	62	25	15.0	10.0	23	710	12.2	−13.4	820
Scott	798	26.4	4,982	71.2	631	422	10.0	22.7	344	9,142	8.3	1.4	9,019
Shelby	91	21.1	7,125	60.7	75	39	19.1	26.1	31	1,048	14.2	−1.7	1,066
Sioux	143	17.7	4,436	64.4	121	85	10.8	40.3	61	2,195	9.0	6.2	2,067
Story	608	67.6	7,556	34.2	363	917	43.0	22.8	746	19,947	35.7	0.4	19,871
Tama	107	28.3	5,962	61.7	83	91	38.9	17.7	77	2,476	29.0	−3.4	2,564
Taylor	51	32.2	7,643	56.4	39	18	19.9	20.4	15	523	15.7	−5.8	555
Union	87	26.4	7,287	62.2	69	55	23.5	29.3	43	1,360	16.5	1.9	1,335
Van Buren	50	23.2	6,483	67.6	41	24	28.8	22.9	20	712	20.1	−3.0	734
Wapello	239	24.8	6,669	67.4	191	120	16.4	23.9	97	2,889	13.3	−3.8	3,004
Warren	150	28.8	3,536	74.0	117	88	22.7	34.5	66	2,220	14.7	3.7	2,141
Washington	115	30.1	5,396	66.1	88	59	20.1	42.4	41	1,530	14.8	6.3	1,440
Wayne	58	31.7	8,803	55.5	44	22	29.1	24.1	18	652	19.3	6.0	615
Webster	278	31.2	7,073	59.4	212	145	16.7	20.2	121	3,241	12.9	−7.0	3,486
Winnebago	71	24.6	6,200	64.1	57	32	15.7	25.8	25	873	12.8	1.7	858
Winneshiek	110	32.3	5,188	61.1	83	80	16.1	33.3	60	2,152	13.4	9.6	1,964
Woodbury	561	18.3	5,441	61.7	474	353	15.9	25.9	280	7,326	11.5	−1.3	7,426
Worth	51	31.7	6,565	61.4	38	16	18.9	23.1	13	414	11.7	−1.9	422
Wright	96	24.4	7,008	65.3	77	50	18.5	46.9	34	1,284	15.8	13.3	1,133
KANSAS	[3]19,131	[3]33.9	[3]6,993	[3]52.5	[3]14,282	13,834	19.8	43.6	9,634	289,010	16.1	3.6	279,003
Allen	89	22.3	6,364	67.9	73	59	24.8	39.9	42	1,755	18.9	5.6	1,662
Anderson	51	16.6	6,190	68.8	43	22	25.3	37.7	16	614	14.3	−2.8	632
Atchison	98	29.1	5,804	69.3	76	45	15.4	30.5	34	1,187	11.2	−7.3	1,281
Barber	38	24.1	7,542	69.8	30	23	29.0	29.1	18	684	19.8	−11.1	769
Barton	162	31.9	5,914	71.3	123	92	15.0	35.2	68	2,697	13.6	1.1	2,668
Bourbon	100	20.7	6,661	69.5	83	47	18.0	36.4	34	1,388	14.0	0.7	1,379
Brown	92	33.3	8,862	50.8	69	75	36.4	34.0	56	2,195	29.7	−2.1	2,243
Butler	237	29.4	3,836	79.1	183	224	27.8	56.4	143	6,067	21.0	15.8	5,239
Chase	27	73.2	8,829	46.1	16	10	18.5	39.6	7	319	10.9	3.9	307
Chautauqua	29	17.2	7,025	73.3	25	10	24.6	29.5	8	316	12.7	−2.2	323

See footnotes at end of table.

Table B-12. Counties — Government Expenditure, Earnings, and Employment—Con.

[Includes United States, states, and 3,141 counties/county equivalents defined as of February 22, 2005. For more information on these areas, see Appendix C, Geographic Information]

| County | Federal government expenditure 2004 | | | | | Federal, state, and local governments[1] | | | | | | | |
| | | | | | | Earnings 2005 | | | | Employment 2005 | | | |
	Total (mil. dol.)	Percent change, 2000–2004	Per capita (dol.)	Direct payments to individuals, percent of total	2000 (mil. dol.)	Total (mil. dol.)	Percent of total	Percent change, 2000–2005	2000 (mil. dol.)	Total	Percent of total	Percent change, 2000–2005	2000
KANSAS—Con.													
Cherokee	132	16.7	6,028	67.6	113	51	17.4	34.8	38	1,485	12.2	3.5	1,435
Cheyenne	43	67.1	14,307	37.6	26	9	25.7	20.9	7	290	15.8	−9.1	319
Clark	19	37.7	8,322	61.9	14	16	41.5	43.9	11	448	26.3	−1.5	455
Clay	63	34.5	7,351	66.5	47	33	23.6	45.9	23	981	14.8	4.8	936
Cloud	79	21.5	8,080	66.5	65	31	22.6	28.0	25	952	15.7	−10.4	1,063
Coffey	57	34.7	6,459	62.7	42	47	18.9	46.6	32	1,296	19.8	5.4	1,230
Comanche	17	35.8	9,075	59.8	13	9	36.3	50.2	6	329	24.8	11.1	296
Cowley	268	48.4	7,495	54.3	181	154	24.9	45.5	106	4,066	19.9	7.9	3,770
Crawford	232	23.3	6,095	67.6	188	209	31.7	53.2	137	5,324	24.3	8.7	4,897
Decatur	43	70.8	13,135	41.8	25	10	25.3	19.3	8	322	15.3	−14.4	376
Dickinson	155	53.0	8,094	58.1	101	62	23.6	40.3	44	1,821	18.4	5.0	1,735
Doniphan	52	24.6	6,505	59.1	42	29	26.3	35.0	21	945	23.9	4.9	901
Douglas	422	35.1	4,110	53.9	313	808	36.0	63.0	496	17,381	25.5	6.5	16,315
Edwards	32	20.3	9,786	50.6	27	10	15.9	28.3	7	266	13.1	−13.4	307
Elk	25	24.4	7,878	69.4	20	12	48.2	19.8	10	421	24.6	−9.5	465
Ellis	139	27.2	5,132	69.0	109	154	22.5	47.3	104	3,795	16.5	2.5	3,703
Ellsworth	42	19.2	6,584	70.5	35	37	37.2	63.7	23	947	23.7	10.9	854
Finney	135	30.9	3,434	59.0	103	145	19.5	37.3	106	3,597	15.7	3.4	3,479
Ford	144	27.5	4,341	56.4	113	126	18.3	53.6	82	3,062	15.1	12.4	2,724
Franklin	143	41.0	5,496	64.4	102	78	20.0	37.8	57	1,949	13.4	0.2	1,946
Geary	702	28.2	27,954	15.3	547	1,034	80.2	50.6	687	14,800	58.1	(Z)	14,807
Gove	40	104.1	14,070	45.3	20	16	30.5	35.5	11	481	21.2	−1.2	487
Graham	38	78.1	13,687	41.5	21	14	22.4	27.5	11	403	14.3	−9.0	443
Grant	35	28.1	4,517	52.3	27	30	15.6	34.4	22	848	16.7	3.5	819
Gray	40	46.3	6,664	39.5	27	31	21.3	44.8	21	1,026	25.2	12.4	913
Greeley	33	155.5	23,616	16.8	13	6	21.2	30.1	5	201	16.8	−5.2	212
Greenwood	58	29.8	7,703	73.1	45	20	24.3	30.5	15	609	19.0	−1.8	620
Hamilton	27	76.2	10,080	40.4	15	14	21.5	42.8	10	435	25.0	10.4	394
Harper	52	27.6	8,273	62.6	40	30	28.2	33.0	22	950	22.0	−1.7	966
Harvey	161	8.3	4,782	82.2	149	81	11.4	37.1	59	2,196	8.9	5.7	2,077
Haskell	30	44.0	7,011	35.3	21	22	18.5	55.1	14	588	25.4	11.8	526
Hodgeman	22	55.6	10,383	41.6	14	10	28.1	27.1	8	346	26.2	−4.2	361
Jackson	73	47.5	5,524	60.1	49	52	26.0	46.2	36	1,369	14.2	10.8	1,236
Jefferson	85	33.2	4,476	75.2	64	46	31.7	32.2	35	1,302	21.3	−3.2	1,345
Jewell	38	32.2	11,147	46.2	29	16	31.9	34.6	12	508	20.9	1.0	503
Johnson	1,882	34.7	3,789	65.1	1,397	1,635	8.4	43.9	1,136	31,640	8.0	11.5	28,386
Kearny	27	38.2	5,918	44.0	19	24	37.6	38.6	17	672	32.6	−0.7	677
Kingman	51	18.0	6,078	71.5	43	21	19.6	24.3	17	662	12.3	−5.8	703
Kiowa	27	29.2	8,904	61.8	21	14	28.2	30.2	11	481	23.2	−0.2	482
Labette	163	35.0	7,330	61.0	121	118	31.7	39.3	85	3,040	21.3	0.5	3,026
Lane	28	71.3	14,401	36.0	16	9	22.4	22.1	7	297	20.5	−11.9	337
Leavenworth	1,177	83.5	16,251	23.7	641	844	55.8	35.0	626	9,960	28.3	−3.9	10,367
Lincoln	27	25.9	7,771	59.2	21	14	43.5	22.1	12	445	20.5	−7.7	482
Linn	91	80.0	9,329	47.1	51	29	28.9	42.7	20	813	19.9	6.7	762
Logan	34	69.7	12,011	40.5	20	15	29.8	36.6	11	457	20.6	−4.0	476
Lyon	149	27.3	4,162	71.9	117	198	28.7	41.9	139	4,929	22.2	1.6	4,851
McPherson	137	17.2	4,672	78.2	117	80	10.8	36.6	59	2,127	9.1	2.1	2,084
Marion	92	46.0	7,070	61.9	63	37	26.1	30.7	29	1,246	20.3	−3.5	1,291
Marshall	93	49.0	8,910	54.6	62	29	11.7	26.7	23	958	12.1	−2.7	985
Meade	32	33.6	6,996	57.1	24	21	27.8	56.1	13	593	22.6	5.3	563
Miami	162	69.8	5,465	53.9	96	95	29.0	47.7	64	2,292	19.6	6.4	2,154
Mitchell	51	27.6	7,766	61.0	40	36	26.2	45.3	25	982	20.0	7.3	915
Montgomery	238	24.3	6,805	71.3	191	104	15.8	29.4	80	2,908	13.8	−4.0	3,030
Morris	43	22.5	7,235	67.6	35	19	28.5	32.7	14	568	23.0	1.4	560
Morton	26	55.7	7,961	49.8	17	26	44.6	42.8	18	708	33.7	8.9	650
Nemaha	75	39.3	7,175	55.0	54	29	15.4	30.5	22	860	12.6	1.2	850
Neosho	98	16.2	5,931	73.5	84	70	23.4	33.2	53	1,738	15.9	−3.4	1,799
Ness	37	49.9	11,894	52.9	24	16	25.9	22.7	13	513	19.3	−11.2	578
Norton	65	104.8	11,260	37.3	32	39	38.1	41.6	27	964	24.9	1.3	952
Osage	88	22.8	5,142	75.5	72	47	45.0	39.8	34	1,408	26.6	2.8	1,369
Osborne	41	31.9	10,098	55.1	31	12	19.9	15.5	10	407	14.0	−11.5	460
Ottawa	36	24.5	5,760	64.1	29	16	30.5	29.1	13	494	17.7	−7.7	535
Pawnee	49	26.5	7,220	57.1	39	87	58.0	61.2	54	2,037	39.2	7.0	1,904
Phillips	53	38.6	9,415	54.7	38	26	23.4	28.3	20	859	19.5	−0.3	862
Pottawatomie	82	22.6	4,348	76.2	67	49	13.6	23.1	40	1,420	9.6	−11.0	1,595
Pratt	63	25.2	6,704	71.5	50	45	23.5	39.6	32	1,235	18.8	−1.4	1,252
Rawlins	46	40.9	16,606	31.6	33	12	26.9	23.7	10	388	13.8	−5.8	412
Reno	340	23.6	5,337	74.9	275	228	19.6	36.9	166	5,821	15.9	1.4	5,743
Republic	45	−0.2	8,675	60.0	45	21	29.4	26.9	17	688	18.8	−9.5	760
Rice	65	27.3	6,206	66.9	51	35	27.0	31.6	27	1,149	23.3	1.3	1,134

See footnotes at end of table.

Table B-12. Counties — Government Expenditure, Earnings, and Employment—Con.

[Includes United States, states, and 3,141 counties/county equivalents defined as of February 22, 2005. For more information on these areas, see Appendix C, Geographic Information]

County	Federal government expenditure					Federal, state, and local governments[1]							
	2004					Earnings				Employment			
						2005				2005			
	Total (mil. dol.)	Percent change, 2000–2004	Per capita (dol.)	Direct payments to individuals, percent of total	2000 (mil. dol.)	Total (mil. dol.)	Percent of total	Percent change, 2000–2005	2000 (mil. dol.)	Total	Percent of total	Percent change, 2000–2005	2000
KANSAS—Con.													
Riley	377	40.3	5,984	42.1	269	657	52.2	71.7	383	12,716	35.7	6.9	11,900
Rooks	47	40.3	8,670	62.0	33	25	28.6	39.5	18	780	24.1	-2.0	796
Rush	35	33.2	10,040	57.5	26	13	25.6	23.7	10	380	16.6	-12.2	433
Russell	57	29.6	8,102	70.7	44	23	24.0	28.0	18	708	18.3	-6.1	754
Saline	302	39.2	5,593	63.9	217	199	14.4	44.5	138	4,748	12.1	7.2	4,429
Scott	35	62.8	7,469	30.8	22	15	16.0	-2.6	16	422	12.7	-25.4	566
Sedgwick	3,214	32.3	6,929	46.1	2,429	1,860	13.0	41.9	1,311	35,733	11.5	6.9	33,425
Seward	80	-51.6	3,450	59.6	166	98	18.1	36.8	72	2,480	16.7	6.9	2,319
Shawnee	1,730	29.5	10,076	42.4	1,336	1,306	27.0	42.6	916	23,553	20.0	2.2	23,035
Sheridan	41	107.0	15,692	25.7	20	10	17.0	23.0	8	336	18.1	-5.4	355
Sherman	71	50.2	11,371	41.7	47	31	29.6	30.7	23	771	18.3	-5.2	813
Smith	43	32.2	10,267	52.8	32	13	22.4	31.1	10	397	14.8	-0.3	398
Stafford	39	28.6	8,558	57.9	30	22	32.8	34.1	16	696	27.6	-8.9	764
Stanton	25	80.5	10,390	28.1	14	11	23.1	36.0	8	352	23.1	7.3	328
Stevens	39	38.8	7,101	44.2	28	27	23.2	29.6	21	796	23.9	-0.3	798
Sumner	153	27.3	6,057	70.7	120	77	29.3	26.9	60	2,074	21.4	-4.9	2,180
Thomas	76	69.8	9,723	39.5	45	41	24.3	37.6	30	1,301	23.4	8.2	1,202
Trego	31	46.1	9,885	52.0	21	14	33.9	35.0	11	458	24.0	-4.0	477
Wabaunsee	91	-5.0	13,136	72.7	96	17	28.1	32.8	13	537	19.2	-3.6	557
Wallace	26	91.8	16,510	29.9	14	6	26.1	31.2	4	196	16.5	-3.9	204
Washington	60	41.4	9,774	51.4	42	25	32.2	29.1	19	844	24.0	-6.6	904
Wichita	79	57.8	33,561	10.2	50	11	17.4	53.5	7	351	20.0	18.2	297
Wilson	72	15.7	7,261	60.0	62	37	19.6	35.9	27	1,027	17.0	-1.6	1,044
Woodson	29	34.0	8,186	70.0	22	9	24.1	37.8	7	298	19.1	2.1	292
Wyandotte	1,120	7.0	7,155	52.6	1,046	1,129	25.8	39.8	808	18,336	20.0	(Z)	18,329
KENTUCKY	31,714[3]	29.6[3]	7,649[3]	52.3[3]	24,472[3]	17,595	19.4	35.8	12,957	356,173	15.0	2.9	346,110
Adair	111	30.2	6,319	63.6	85	41	23.2	35.1	30	1,003	12.2	8.0	929
Allen	104	36.3	5,630	62.3	77	32	14.0	35.2	24	832	10.0	5.3	790
Anderson	83	46.8	4,117	67.6	56	38	19.6	39.8	27	1,006	13.2	11.3	904
Ballard	59	24.4	7,079	76.9	47	17	8.7	19.3	14	473	10.0	-3.9	492
Barren	204	29.2	5,173	64.8	158	91	12.3	25.6	73	2,335	8.8	2.2	2,285
Bath	86	15.0	7,467	48.2	75	23	32.2	27.4	18	605	15.3	-3.7	628
Bell	78	69.0	2,631	196.4	46	85	23.8	27.9	66	2,157	17.8	5.9	2,037
Boone	405	42.4	3,991	57.8	284	328	8.2	65.1	199	6,136	6.7	26.6	4,848
Bourbon	168	98.7	8,546	41.4	84	43	11.7	28.1	33	1,072	10.1	1.5	1,056
Boyd	383	19.5	7,701	68.5	321	169	12.4	20.9	140	3,902	11.4	5.4	3,703
Boyle	147	27.1	5,205	72.8	116	83	12.6	20.7	69	2,037	9.8	0.1	2,034
Bracken	46	24.3	5,228	69.8	37	16	32.8	35.2	12	457	14.1	7.5	425
Breathitt	134	17.4	8,409	53.5	114	48	34.6	17.2	41	1,188	24.3	-3.7	1,234
Breckinridge	110	19.6	5,741	69.7	92	36	25.3	25.9	29	971	13.1	2.4	948
Bullitt	490	116.9	7,355	29.9	226	105	18.1	41.2	75	2,500	10.9	8.3	2,309
Butler	70	26.2	5,240	66.4	55	26	20.3	12.5	23	724	14.6	-7.9	786
Caldwell	80	22.9	6,247	73.4	65	36	18.6	25.0	29	926	14.2	-0.2	928
Calloway	176	29.1	5,051	77.8	136	191	27.5	27.8	150	5,232	23.8	–	5,232
Campbell	443	38.4	5,075	70.7	320	267	21.1	38.9	192	6,037	15.6	1.0	5,978
Carlisle	34	24.2	6,353	73.2	27	10	17.9	24.3	8	269	13.4	2.7	262
Carroll	60	31.2	5,817	61.4	46	28	8.1	18.0	23	742	8.3	-10.0	824
Carter	185	28.1	6,725	59.5	144	57	25.8	32.7	43	1,545	14.7	10.0	1,405
Casey	88	24.8	5,506	63.2	71	30	20.6	39.0	21	811	10.9	15.4	703
Christian	1,748	40.7	24,745	12.5	1,243	2,670	71.2	74.1	1,534	35,815	52.3	12.3	31,897
Clark	190	38.0	5,536	64.5	138	72	10.3	31.5	55	1,723	7.8	4.6	1,647
Clay	231	37.9	9,524	42.5	168	86	46.5	18.9	73	1,792	28.2	-5.0	1,887
Clinton	77	19.0	8,036	58.0	65	23	17.3	25.9	19	648	12.4	1.9	636
Crittenden	59	32.3	6,543	72.0	45	16	18.2	20.0	13	431	11.3	-6.3	460
Cumberland	57	10.2	8,003	59.1	52	16	28.0	21.6	13	408	13.2	-4.4	427
Daviess	476	26.2	5,143	73.4	377	365	19.4	31.5	278	8,678	15.6	6.0	8,189
Edmonson	66	21.3	5,500	57.4	54	33	50.3	34.3	25	803	24.8	8.2	742
Elliott	34	1.3	5,008	57.3	34	17	56.1	81.8	10	489	27.0	45.5	336
Estill	108	18.4	7,140	68.9	91	28	31.6	18.5	24	719	17.2	-9.1	791
Fayette	1,957	13.8	7,348	43.4	1,719	1,866	20.4	28.8	1,449	35,202	16.7	-0.7	35,434
Fleming	93	48.2	6,448	54.9	63	43	31.3	20.0	36	1,115	16.2	15.9	962
Floyd	323	22.9	7,616	67.5	263	109	19.7	27.1	86	2,987	18.8	3.2	2,893
Franklin	1,366	47.4	28,371	21.8	926	861	55.0	17.5	733	16,478	41.0	-1.4	16,709
Fulton	70	24.2	9,466	62.0	56	24	18.1	18.0	21	656	17.0	-2.8	675
Gallatin	76	213.1	9,555	29.9	24	17	14.7	48.9	11	432	13.3	13.1	382
Garrard	69	14.6	4,265	74.8	60	27	24.5	12.9	24	718	12.6	-15.2	847
Grant	97	37.6	4,007	73.4	71	49	23.9	42.6	34	1,215	14.2	10.2	1,103
Graves	230	27.6	6,158	70.9	180	90	18.4	29.9	69	2,122	12.3	2.3	2,075
Grayson	154	31.4	6,173	65.6	117	63	20.5	38.5	46	1,673	13.7	4.0	1,609
Green	63	25.6	5,423	72.2	50	27	37.2	28.7	21	826	17.4	9.1	757
Greenup	212	27.4	5,685	80.1	166	66	15.7	32.5	50	1,760	13.6	5.8	1,663

See footnotes at end of table.

Table B-12. Counties — **Government Expenditure, Earnings, and Employment**—Con.

[Includes United States, states, and 3,141 counties/county equivalents defined as of February 22, 2005. For more information on these areas, see Appendix C, Geographic Information]

County	Federal government expenditure 2004 — Total (mil. dol.)	Percent change, 2000-2004	Per capita (dol.)	Direct payments to individuals, percent of total	2000 (mil. dol.)	Earnings 2005 — Total (mil. dol.)	Percent of total	Percent change, 2000-2005	2000 (mil. dol.)	Employment 2005 — Total	Percent of total	Percent change, 2000-2005	2000
KENTUCKY—Con.													
Hancock	37	25.9	4,384	69.9	29	18	7.0	29.9	14	472	8.5	−0.4	474
Hardin	979	8.0	10,196	43.8	907	1,232	46.1	24.5	989	18,980	30.1	−14.6	22,218
Harlan	398	6.6	12,481	68.8	374	81	22.7	17.8	69	2,082	20.7	−13.4	2,405
Harrison	93	32.9	5,082	68.7	70	37	16.9	22.8	30	946	11.0	−4.6	992
Hart	92	10.4	5,050	65.4	83	34	21.2	24.3	27	887	11.5	5.3	842
Henderson	240	32.1	5,282	71.7	182	114	11.3	25.0	91	2,865	11.8	6.5	2,690
Henry	76	31.8	4,848	68.1	58	35	22.4	43.9	25	849	12.1	11.6	761
Hickman	31	−0.7	5,899	62.4	31	11	7.0	21.5	9	282	15.2	−7.2	304
Hopkins	352	16.0	7,518	56.6	304	140	17.4	32.1	106	3,610	15.4	8.8	3,319
Jackson	131	83.9	9,630	40.1	71	28	28.8	24.8	23	758	14.8	−3.9	789
Jefferson	5,549	55.1	7,927	48.7	3,578	2,748	11.0	33.9	2,052	51,011	9.8	1.4	50,289
Jessamine	145	24.1	3,434	70.5	117	96	14.0	36.6	70	2,417	11.2	8.2	2,233
Johnson	169	25.0	7,064	64.2	135	63	24.6	20.9	52	1,574	18.1	−2.8	1,619
Kenton	834	28.1	5,458	58.6	652	631	18.5	46.8	430	11,535	14.7	8.1	10,670
Knott	119	22.8	6,760	59.3	97	36	16.2	13.4	32	913	17.2	−8.7	1,000
Knox	211	21.5	6,617	56.6	174	81	20.4	23.4	65	2,003	14.2	−4.1	2,089
Larue	74	20.9	5,512	73.3	61	26	22.8	24.8	21	647	11.5	−4.1	675
Laurel	267	−1.6	4,768	65.4	271	136	14.4	27.1	107	3,141	10.2	−0.7	3,163
Lawrence	99	21.5	6,174	64.9	82	30	22.1	27.3	23	764	16.2	−6.9	821
Lee	58	19.8	7,483	62.4	49	19	27.1	29.6	15	529	18.9	−2.0	540
Leslie	97	13.0	8,050	63.7	86	25	23.3	19.2	21	667	22.5	−5.7	707
Letcher	184	19.1	7,458	68.5	155	51	18.7	20.6	43	1,364	17.0	−3.7	1,416
Lewis	80	26.7	5,804	64.1	63	25	30.9	28.9	20	735	15.9	3.8	708
Lincoln	141	28.0	5,679	63.3	110	45	25.9	37.9	33	1,320	16.4	17.9	1,120
Livingston	96	40.0	9,848	48.3	69	24	19.0	35.3	18	588	15.0	−0.2	589
Logan	154	17.7	5,684	69.1	131	52	11.8	26.5	41	1,348	10.0	−3.4	1,396
Lyon	46	23.0	5,562	79.1	37	32	41.2	23.7	26	819	25.4	2.6	798
McCracken	1,391	−12.8	21,504	20.4	1,595	230	12.8	22.2	188	4,762	9.9	−4.1	4,966
McCreary	147	34.9	8,616	51.9	109	65	48.6	103.8	32	1,353	28.3	37.2	986
McLean	59	27.9	5,939	69.6	46	20	15.6	26.9	16	568	17.5	−0.9	573
Madison	415	43.9	5,440	57.5	288	344	28.5	36.4	252	8,404	20.3	21.0	6,948
Magoffin	99	22.1	7,322	57.2	81	27	26.2	28.8	21	769	19.7	−7.3	830
Marion	100	23.8	5,351	61.0	81	37	12.5	28.7	29	957	9.6	−6.6	1,025
Marshall	170	29.4	5,502	82.7	131	72	12.3	29.8	55	1,878	12.1	2.1	1,840
Martin	126	54.6	10,198	53.0	81	57	36.4	151.8	23	1,065	27.2	35.2	788
Mason	93	24.1	5,500	66.7	75	49	13.2	24.5	39	1,288	10.3	10.5	1,166
Meade	99	34.1	3,498	82.2	74	44	24.0	37.0	32	1,148	16.1	10.9	1,035
Menifee	56	43.3	8,239	45.0	39	17	45.5	31.7	13	433	22.2	3.6	418
Mercer	101	29.8	4,683	74.0	78	41	11.7	35.1	31	1,069	9.8	8.7	983
Metcalfe	58	24.1	5,720	64.5	47	21	20.1	32.7	16	590	13.3	−8.1	642
Monroe	92	19.0	7,913	58.9	78	34	24.2	29.4	26	926	16.0	5.1	881
Montgomery	114	16.1	4,830	71.8	98	51	12.3	30.2	39	1,237	8.6	6.5	1,161
Morgan	82	18.9	5,708	58.8	69	45	36.4	20.5	37	1,183	23.0	−2.6	1,214
Muhlenberg	306	9.2	9,629	46.8	280	127	29.5	20.8	105	2,389	18.6	−2.7	2,455
Nelson	165	30.1	4,072	69.5	126	77	11.9	38.5	56	1,908	9.5	7.4	1,776
Nicholas	43	−10.0	6,113	64.2	48	13	38.0	16.9	11	324	12.8	−10.7	363
Ohio	123	21.2	5,238	75.0	102	56	19.7	28.5	43	1,487	14.9	−6.5	1,591
Oldham	98	36.2	1,879	78.7	72	150	25.2	29.7	116	3,471	17.8	6.5	3,258
Owen	42	28.1	3,750	70.3	33	21	32.7	29.9	16	512	13.9	−5.0	539
Owsley	50	20.4	10,534	56.0	42	12	44.0	19.0	10	348	22.3	−9.1	383
Pendleton	57	23.4	3,741	76.1	46	28	26.5	23.5	22	733	16.7	−5.3	774
Perry	242	23.8	8,143	62.3	196	107	17.3	27.1	84	2,990	18.4	4.7	2,857
Pike	520	24.4	7,749	65.2	418	163	14.0	22.8	133	3,901	13.0	0.5	3,880
Powell	62	26.6	4,563	63.4	49	31	26.6	25.5	24	810	17.7	−5.6	858
Pulaski	396	36.7	6,740	62.5	290	179	18.0	37.9	130	4,798	14.2	11.6	4,301
Robertson	12	28.7	5,302	68.2	10	6	75.7	27.1	5	197	21.1	−3.9	205
Rockcastle	96	16.4	5,700	61.6	82	33	27.5	31.4	25	860	15.1	1.1	851
Rowan	141	54.5	6,371	57.5	91	129	34.6	30.9	99	3,248	24.8	2.2	3,177
Russell	116	25.0	6,907	60.8	93	43	20.2	17.6	37	1,148	13.0	−5.5	1,215
Scott	118	20.5	3,112	74.9	98	85	5.7	42.5	60	2,028	7.0	6.7	1,900
Shelby	130	24.3	3,500	67.5	105	87	13.0	61.2	54	2,162	10.6	29.9	1,664
Simpson	77	17.4	4,580	73.1	66	35	8.4	19.8	29	916	8.0	−13.1	1,054
Spencer	42	38.7	2,818	77.1	30	23	37.6	48.2	16	574	15.7	10.8	518
Taylor	150	28.9	6,378	68.9	116	73	19.8	31.7	55	1,819	12.7	9.4	1,662
Todd	67	14.2	5,631	62.7	58	23	16.5	31.8	17	629	12.9	−1.7	640
Trigg	87	22.5	6,576	73.0	71	34	18.2	18.4	28	815	14.1	−4.2	851
Trimble	35	28.0	3,817	76.9	27	15	39.7	50.3	10	401	18.4	31.0	306
Union	306	15.1	19,461	19.7	266	31	10.5	18.3	26	827	10.6	−5.5	875
Warren	461	17.6	4,743	68.7	392	376	15.1	29.1	291	9,268	13.5	7.5	8,618
Washington	71	41.6	6,301	57.2	50	22	15.1	28.7	17	535	9.9	−13.6	619

See footnotes at end of table.

Table B-12. Counties — **Government Expenditure, Earnings, and Employment**—Con.

[Includes United States, states, and 3,141 counties/county equivalents defined as of February 22, 2005. For more information on these areas, see Appendix C, Geographic Information]

County	Federal government expenditure					Federal, state, and local governments[1]						
						Earnings				Employment		
	2004					2005				2005		
	Total (mil. dol.)	Percent change, 2000–2004	Per capita (dol.)	Direct payments to individuals, percent of total	2000 (mil. dol.)	Total (mil. dol.)	Percent of total	Percent change, 2000–2005	2000 (mil. dol.)	Total	Percent of total	Percent change, 2000–2005	2000
KENTUCKY—Con.												
Wayne	139	22.2	6,837	55.7	114	43	17.7	25.1	34	1,156	12.7	3.2	1,120
Webster	84	14.3	5,979	67.8	74	28	9.9	22.9	23	793	14.9	-2.5	813
Whitley	322	33.2	8,571	66.6	242	91	18.7	27.8	71	2,442	15.6	3.9	2,351
Wolfe	60	20.0	8,470	53.6	50	17	41.7	15.6	15	475	20.9	-8.7	520
Woodford	83	26.9	3,452	79.6	65	66	10.2	82.0	36	1,823	11.6	55.5	1,172
LOUISIANA	[3]32,954	[3]26.8	[3]7,298	[3]55.1	[3]25,995	19,035	21.4	34.5	14,158	408,868	16.6	-1.2	413,981
Acadia	372	7.2	6,295	54.9	347	119	17.9	31.4	90	3,483	14.6	-6.5	3,727
Allen	174	7.9	6,868	50.5	162	199	59.9	24.2	160	4,990	40.7	-5.0	5,253
Ascension	278	32.2	3,194	76.7	211	177	10.0	28.1	138	4,273	7.0	5.3	4,059
Assumption	131	38.2	5,622	64.1	95	43	19.6	23.2	35	1,212	18.1	-12.0	1,377
Avoyelles	289	24.3	6,873	57.4	232	147	36.8	15.0	128	4,617	28.1	-10.6	5,167
Beauregard	181	33.6	5,307	73.2	135	69	19.1	25.6	55	1,829	14.1	-6.2	1,949
Bienville	112	26.4	7,276	67.1	88	33	17.9	36.9	24	957	14.5	3.1	928
Bossier	899	32.4	8,641	47.3	679	860	40.2	51.8	567	14,487	25.0	8.2	13,385
Caddo	1,566	26.5	6,226	62.5	1,238	1,219	18.8	30.5	934	24,288	15.4	5.0	23,125
Calcasieu	1,103	55.5	5,966	60.8	710	615	15.5	40.4	438	14,554	13.7	1.7	14,310
Caldwell	72	3.9	6,654	67.1	69	24	24.3	11.9	21	723	18.2	-20.0	904
Cameron	37	-4.5	3,844	60.2	39	31	29.8	19.9	26	819	18.8	-15.3	967
Catahoula	97	5.2	9,136	47.5	92	27	27.3	26.5	22	816	19.1	-5.4	863
Claiborne	105	25.8	6,394	63.3	84	71	33.2	50.1	48	1,854	28.5	5.9	1,751
Concordia	152	11.9	7,720	55.3	136	65	30.4	41.1	46	1,792	22.9	5.5	1,699
De Soto	156	44.8	5,965	63.7	108	62	16.4	36.4	46	1,618	17.3	-3.8	1,682
East Baton Rouge	3,178	33.7	7,702	45.5	2,377	2,673	22.3	42.7	1,874	56,593	19.5	3.5	54,697
East Carroll	91	3.9	10,132	42.8	87	30	35.2	31.1	23	789	25.9	-22.9	1,024
East Feliciana	117	27.5	5,580	64.2	92	137	59.0	45.4	94	3,328	42.2	1.5	3,280
Evangeline	271	26.9	7,643	52.8	213	71	25.1	41.5	51	2,183	19.1	-12.9	2,506
Franklin	174	22.9	8,358	52.3	142	56	27.3	20.0	46	1,543	17.1	-9.2	1,699
Grant	152	45.1	7,951	51.3	105	77	51.1	104.5	37	1,635	30.7	21.7	1,343
Iberia	368	32.2	4,950	66.2	279	178	11.2	23.6	144	4,805	11.7	-1.2	4,862
Iberville	215	29.1	6,630	59.9	167	134	14.8	23.9	108	3,331	19.3	-8.7	3,650
Jackson	108	21.3	7,095	71.7	89	40	21.5	45.6	28	1,020	18.4	-5.2	1,076
Jefferson	2,218	17.9	4,890	73.8	1,882	1,218	12.9	36.2	895	26,063	9.8	0.3	25,986
Jefferson Davis	187	15.6	5,974	60.9	161	70	23.8	40.1	50	1,870	15.5	0.1	1,868
Lafayette	875	33.3	4,469	63.2	656	670	10.6	39.4	481	14,339	9.2	7.5	13,336
Lafourche	509	34.9	5,522	59.6	377	315	18.3	33.8	236	7,818	14.5	-0.7	7,875
La Salle	87	27.2	6,136	70.4	68	47	28.8	38.4	34	1,372	25.3	3.5	1,326
Lincoln	218	32.9	5,154	68.3	164	207	27.4	18.8	174	5,245	23.0	-14.5	6,133
Livingston	344	31.7	3,259	77.2	262	201	24.3	60.0	125	5,696	17.2	23.9	4,599
Madison	134	29.8	10,275	39.1	103	49	39.0	18.4	41	1,293	26.5	-12.5	1,477
Morehouse	254	19.7	8,323	56.1	212	63	18.6	25.2	50	1,697	15.5	-8.4	1,852
Natchitoches	266	29.4	6,870	55.2	206	188	28.5	41.9	132	4,764	24.3	4.3	4,567
Orleans	6,309	14.3	13,648	35.5	5,518	3,271	29.0	24.0	2,638	55,895	19.7	-11.6	63,220
Ouachita	798	25.1	5,379	67.3	638	552	17.2	28.0	431	13,285	14.8	-3.5	13,763
Plaquemines	223	19.7	7,699	40.7	186	185	22.0	27.7	145	3,662	18.7	-3.9	3,811
Pointe Coupee	141	31.1	6,245	55.1	107	50	21.8	18.4	42	1,430	16.6	-8.3	1,560
Rapides	930	30.3	7,266	59.5	714	717	26.4	42.2	505	14,477	19.4	1.7	14,230
Red River	67	13.6	6,998	56.2	59	20	20.1	8.0	18	535	16.4	-27.3	736
Richland	168	23.0	8,205	52.0	137	47	21.5	22.8	38	1,315	16.1	-14.2	1,532
Sabine	158	27.6	6,671	66.2	123	48	19.7	30.7	37	1,460	17.3	3.3	1,413
St. Bernard	372	27.0	5,677	79.7	293	121	34.4	26.4	96	3,101	14.5	-12.7	3,553
St. Charles	211	2.9	4,213	66.0	205	166	11.6	38.5	120	3,814	13.6	9.7	3,477
St. Helena	55	36.6	5,337	53.7	40	25	30.4	31.5	19	734	17.9	-8.3	800
St. James	114	-3.9	5,372	71.7	118	67	15.2	31.4	51	1,725	19.6	0.8	1,712
St. John the Baptist	170	-1.5	3,737	77.4	173	95	14.0	51.9	62	2,127	12.1	-6.6	2,277
St. Landry	604	23.1	6,741	57.9	491	227	23.0	31.4	172	6,014	18.3	-0.3	6,032
St. Martin	235	25.7	4,664	60.0	187	91	24.8	31.3	70	2,537	16.6	-2.3	2,597
St. Mary	320	24.2	6,132	63.9	258	204	16.8	22.9	166	5,290	16.7	-2.3	5,414
St. Tammany	906	48.5	4,241	73.0	610	653	22.8	49.6	437	14,095	14.0	9.6	12,866
Tangipahoa	603	33.4	5,730	67.3	452	468	33.7	36.8	342	11,479	22.8	4.1	11,025
Tensas	72	11.8	11,658	40.0	64	19	28.7	34.8	14	583	23.6	-10.0	648
Terrebonne	507	31.1	4,761	71.7	387	250	11.1	27.0	197	7,164	12.6	-1.3	7,259
Union	139	25.6	6,056	68.3	110	43	17.4	39.1	31	1,239	15.1	-2.5	1,271
Vermilion	284	19.5	5,192	65.6	238	124	22.7	29.4	96	3,256	16.1	-9.1	3,581
Vernon	1,015	56.3	20,492	17.7	650	911	73.1	37.5	663	13,475	49.7	-6.4	14,399
Washington	345	31.8	7,821	69.5	262	153	37.3	49.1	103	3,893	23.4	5.4	3,695
Webster	296	31.3	7,175	67.9	225	89	15.9	30.5	68	2,333	13.2	0.5	2,322
West Baton Rouge	169	23.8	7,739	42.4	137	60	12.7	27.1	48	1,577	13.1	-3.1	1,627
West Carroll	103	31.8	8,637	51.1	78	35	29.3	28.7	27	955	21.8	-5.9	1,015
West Feliciana	42	-9.5	2,752	64.6	46	125	39.4	32.6	94	2,748	39.5	-1.3	2,785
Winn	103	23.7	6,366	64.7	83	35	17.4	18.4	30	974	14.4	-8.0	1,059

See footnotes at end of table.

Table B-12. Counties — **Government Expenditure, Earnings, and Employment**—Con.

[Includes United States, states, and 3,141 counties/county equivalents defined as of February 22, 2005. For more information on these areas, see Appendix C, Geographic Information]

County	Federal government expenditure — 2004: Total (mil. dol.)	Percent change, 2000–2004	Per capita (dol.)	Direct payments to individuals, percent of total	2000 (mil. dol.)	Earnings 2005: Total (mil. dol.)	Percent of total	Percent change, 2000–2005	2000 (mil. dol.)	Employment 2005: Total	Percent of total	Percent change, 2000–2005	2000
MAINE	[3]10,865	[3]38.3	[3]8,248	[3]48.7	[3]7,853	5,591	19.2	34.4	4,159	110,927	13.5	3.0	107,733
Androscoggin	647	27.6	6,044	63.5	507	257	11.9	25.4	205	6,073	9.6	2.4	5,931
Aroostook.	651	30.0	8,877	53.6	501	308	24.5	37.6	224	6,802	16.5	6.2	6,402
Cumberland	1,821	28.9	6,659	51.9	1,413	1,318	14.0	29.5	1,018	24,674	11.0	0.1	24,652
Franklin	162	26.1	5,464	66.7	129	89	16.4	31.6	68	2,198	12.2	4.6	2,102
Hancock	380	29.3	7,086	54.4	294	156	14.5	22.0	128	3,783	9.9	−4.2	3,948
Kennebec.	1,288	35.7	10,679	38.9	949	930	34.1	35.2	688	16,902	21.9	2.0	16,568
Knox	263	37.6	6,410	62.8	191	137	15.1	45.4	94	3,084	10.7	9.4	2,818
Lincoln.	208	35.3	5,897	71.1	154	75	14.8	33.0	56	1,896	9.5	2.0	1,859
Oxford	343	34.6	6,064	65.7	255	130	16.7	27.6	102	3,528	13.7	3.2	3,420
Penobscot	1,020	28.1	6,880	56.6	796	676	20.5	24.9	541	14,511	15.6	−3.6	15,053
Piscataquis.	125	33.2	7,119	69.1	94	55	20.1	46.7	38	1,420	16.1	15.2	1,233
Sagadahoc	1,437	118.6	38,922	9.1	657	139	17.0	39.1	100	2,549	12.0	7.6	2,368
Somerset	323	39.8	6,271	61.5	231	131	15.2	33.5	98	3,156	12.5	1.0	3,126
Waldo	226	11.3	5,891	59.0	203	76	14.4	42.9	53	1,959	10.6	9.5	1,789
Washington	308	29.3	9,192	52.6	239	127	26.3	29.7	98	3,023	16.0	−0.8	3,048
York	1,211	28.2	6,042	57.9	944	987	28.4	52.1	649	15,369	15.7	14.6	13,416
MARYLAND.	[3]64,726	[3]42.7	[3]11,645	[3]32.8	[3]45,365	37,401	22.8	33.9	27,935	530,082	15.9	2.6	516,474
Allegany.	572	15.1	7,745	69.6	497	317	24.4	24.8	254	6,406	16.4	−1.6	6,510
Anne Arundel	4,866	41.4	9,568	40.8	3,442	5,353	30.8	36.6	3,918	77,829	22.6	3.7	75,070
Baltimore	5,231	28.2	6,700	59.1	4,080	4,069	17.7	37.1	2,969	61,405	12.4	6.3	57,790
Calvert	355	46.7	4,105	77.6	242	229	20.5	56.5	146	4,125	12.8	18.7	3,475
Caroline	172	21.6	5,537	66.0	141	72	17.0	33.6	54	1,586	11.4	−0.1	1,588
Carroll	702	33.5	4,223	77.6	525	408	15.7	41.1	289	8,371	10.4	12.1	7,469
Cecil	447	23.6	4,675	67.2	361	351	23.4	49.0	236	5,384	14.1	3.8	5,188
Charles	815	34.5	6,001	57.8	606	613	28.6	41.1	434	9,281	15.9	13.0	8,215
Dorchester	248	16.2	8,038	56.4	214	115	20.8	25.1	92	2,294	13.4	−0.9	2,316
Frederick	1,947	114.9	8,946	31.0	906	1,003	19.5	48.3	676	15,640	12.6	11.0	14,093
Garrett	160	12.9	5,319	69.7	142	78	15.1	27.0	61	1,806	9.0	1.6	1,778
Harford	1,891	28.2	8,027	40.5	1,475	1,494	31.9	32.1	1,131	19,664	17.5	−2.4	20,150
Howard	1,239	38.3	4,646	46.9	896	948	9.9	37.4	690	17,322	9.7	8.8	15,917
Kent	153	27.9	7,795	70.5	119	54	14.1	26.1	43	1,173	9.3	0.9	1,162
Montgomery	15,294	43.8	16,594	19.6	10,636	8,210	21.0	37.0	5,991	89,729	13.9	2.5	87,548
Prince George's.	10,372	41.2	12,305	27.5	7,344	6,807	33.7	35.6	5,021	90,196	21.3	5.5	85,515
Queen Anne's	214	48.1	4,736	62.6	144	118	17.7	45.1	81	2,541	12.1	17.4	2,165
St. Mary's.	2,366	35.2	24,929	14.6	1,751	1,277	46.1	33.9	954	14,104	24.7	1.5	13,896
Somerset	167	28.2	6,464	56.4	130	141	41.9	26.4	112	2,997	26.9	0.3	2,989
Talbot	262	19.4	7,476	68.8	219	100	10.8	34.0	75	1,984	7.2	3.9	1,910
Washington	722	24.0	5,169	68.2	582	419	13.6	26.0	333	8,748	11.1	2.5	8,535
Wicomico	437	13.2	4,923	67.1	386	330	15.7	31.7	250	6,897	12.0	6.6	6,469
Worcester.	1,132	237.2	23,117	21.8	336	182	19.2	43.1	127	3,865	11.4	14.0	3,391
Independent City													
Baltimore city	10,590	28.9	16,644	29.5	8,216	4,712	20.0	17.9	3,997	76,735	18.9	−7.9	83,335
MASSACHUSETTS.	[3]53,120	[3]30.0	[3]8,279	[3]48.5	[3]40,860	25,904	11.5	21.4	21,335	438,013	10.6	−3.7	454,616
Barnstable	1,902	26.6	8,319	68.0	1,503	860	16.9	28.2	671	15,114	10.5	−0.1	15,130
Berkshire	1,174	36.0	8,860	52.4	863	372	11.3	14.7	324	7,797	9.3	−7.2	8,403
Bristol	3,526	26.1	6,432	57.0	2,797	1,526	13.4	24.2	1,229	27,801	9.9	−3.6	28,835
Dukes	76	34.3	4,833	75.5	56	70	15.0	40.0	50	1,416	10.0	9.0	1,299
Essex	4,844	17.1	6,555	55.1	4,135	2,203	11.9	20.0	1,836	40,978	10.3	−1.1	41,431
Franklin	385	26.3	5,331	67.4	305	205	15.9	19.7	171	5,036	12.5	−5.1	5,308
Hampden	3,116	21.7	6,746	58.3	2,560	1,829	17.5	17.2	1,560	34,448	13.9	−4.5	36,067
Hampshire	843	29.3	5,477	55.9	652	891	29.6	37.3	649	17,641	20.5	7.3	16,447
Middlesex	13,924	37.6	9,507	36.0	10,118	5,565	8.5	27.7	4,357	88,171	8.4	0.3	87,886
Nantucket.	44	42.1	4,307	65.1	31	50	11.5	34.7	37	772	7.5	5.9	729
Norfolk.	3,804	28.9	5,820	57.5	2,951	1,915	8.4	23.1	1,556	33,179	7.8	0.1	33,155
Plymouth	2,313	26.0	4,715	69.9	1,836	1,840	17.4	29.0	1,427	31,678	12.5	4.5	30,321
Suffolk	9,891	22.5	14,851	30.2	8,075	5,948	11.1	12.5	5,289	82,687	12.3	−15.8	98,198
Worcester.	4,252	26.5	5,455	63.5	3,361	2,630	14.2	20.7	2,179	51,295	12.3	−0.2	51,407
MICHIGAN	[3]60,489	[3]29.1	[3]5,981	[3]64.0	[3]46,851	36,158	14.0	21.6	29,725	687,129	12.5	−1.6	698,242
Alcona.	96	28.3	8,222	75.2	75	16	19.7	12.8	14	402	10.3	−11.5	454
Alger.	63	21.3	6,477	70.8	52	43	30.6	12.6	38	954	22.4	−2.0	973
Allegan	407	51.6	3,615	65.0	268	210	10.9	23.6	170	4,667	8.3	−2.7	4,795
Alpena	219	19.8	7,111	69.2	182	145	25.7	16.8	124	3,118	17.9	−6.8	3,345
Antrim	126	34.0	5,141	76.7	94	56	20.0	23.3	46	1,464	12.9	1.8	1,438
Arenac.	120	30.9	6,923	70.5	92	44	20.8	16.7	38	944	10.4	−2.6	969
Baraga	65	48.5	7,426	56.6	44	67	49.8	15.2	58	1,766	38.6	−3.3	1,827
Barry	198	25.5	3,327	77.5	157	106	15.5	15.9	91	2,371	9.2	−1.6	2,410
Bay	573	20.2	5,237	76.8	477	322	17.5	12.4	287	6,850	13.4	−4.5	7,173
Benzie	88	32.5	5,035	74.8	66	32	17.7	19.8	27	759	8.8	−1.2	768

See footnotes at end of table.

[Includes United States, states, and 3,141 counties/county equivalents defined as of February 22, 2005. For more information on these areas, see Appendix C, Geographic Information]

County	Federal government expenditure					Federal, state, and local governments[1]							
	2004				2000 (mil. dol.)	Earnings				Employment			
						2005			2000 (mil. dol.)	2005			2000
	Total (mil. dol.)	Percent change, 2000–2004	Per capita (dol.)	Direct payments to individuals, percent of total		Total (mil. dol.)	Percent of total	Percent change, 2000–2005		Total	Percent of total	Percent change, 2000–2005	
MICHIGAN—Con.													
Berrien	903	19.9	5,533	71.8	753	382	11.5	11.8	341	8,369	9.7	−10.9	9,388
Branch	194	17.3	4,174	76.3	165	169	23.7	18.7	142	3,462	15.8	−3.9	3,604
Calhoun	1,026	28.3	7,381	56.3	800	641	19.9	15.0	557	10,808	15.0	−8.7	11,837
Cass	217	23.3	4,185	71.5	176	107	20.8	26.5	85	2,584	14.7	2.4	2,524
Charlevoix	126	31.8	4,730	74.7	96	89	16.3	23.9	72	2,009	13.2	3.5	1,942
Cheboygan	150	33.7	5,496	71.8	112	63	18.8	24.0	51	1,294	9.9	−4.9	1,361
Chippewa	259	23.7	6,687	54.2	210	334	56.6	19.9	279	7,400	39.6	−4.1	7,715
Clare	205	24.5	6,448	78.9	165	75	22.1	26.8	59	1,748	12.6	0.6	1,737
Clinton	206	20.5	2,995	71.5	171	159	17.0	25.4	127	2,848	9.3	1.3	2,811
Crawford	87	24.5	5,881	64.7	70	44	22.8	9.8	40	839	12.4	−10.9	942
Delta	246	29.1	6,419	72.3	191	115	16.7	12.5	103	2,459	11.9	−1.2	2,488
Dickinson	199	37.5	7,259	61.1	144	147	22.6	18.6	124	2,867	15.8	−1.5	2,910
Eaton	431	20.3	4,025	57.4	358	322	19.8	16.9	276	6,293	14.4	−3.1	6,495
Emmet	157	29.2	4,710	72.5	121	126	15.0	43.8	87	2,892	11.9	21.1	2,388
Genesee	2,401	23.7	5,409	72.7	1,942	1,311	15.4	13.0	1,160	26,456	12.9	−2.6	27,149
Gladwin	160	27.1	5,882	82.1	126	45	22.8	18.9	38	1,160	16.5	4.1	1,114
Gogebic	141	21.9	8,298	67.0	116	81	34.8	14.2	71	1,994	24.3	−8.1	2,170
Grand Traverse	423	30.9	5,115	69.4	323	309	12.7	29.3	239	6,694	10.3	9.5	6,115
Gratiot	223	18.8	5,254	65.5	187	131	20.1	19.9	109	2,814	13.4	1.3	2,777
Hillsdale	206	17.4	4,350	73.5	176	116	15.7	17.3	99	2,592	11.9	−7.7	2,809
Houghton	224	18.6	6,285	61.3	188	211	39.5	14.5	184	4,471	24.9	−5.7	4,742
Huron	225	20.6	6,447	70.1	187	90	14.8	13.9	79	2,138	11.1	−6.5	2,287
Ingham	3,749	34.5	13,385	33.7	2,788	2,734	30.5	15.8	2,360	49,857	24.2	−3.2	51,516
Ionia	221	21.4	3,431	73.5	182	217	27.9	18.7	183	4,280	18.5	1.6	4,211
Iosco	194	21.6	7,213	83.9	159	76	23.9	14.5	67	1,853	16.2	−5.7	1,966
Iron	94	13.8	7,440	76.1	82	45	29.5	6.5	43	1,101	19.6	−15.6	1,305
Isabella	228	32.9	3,544	69.0	172	451	35.7	27.5	354	11,134	28.2	4.5	10,658
Jackson	757	22.7	4,647	73.8	617	517	16.9	17.0	442	10,109	13.2	−3.8	10,503
Kalamazoo	1,105	21.4	4,589	65.8	910	854	13.5	14.9	743	15,950	10.6	−17.9	19,439
Kalkaska	67	22.0	3,923	76.5	55	36	18.5	19.8	30	994	17.4	9.6	907
Kent	2,491	21.2	4,195	63.7	2,055	1,582	8.1	19.8	1,321	29,337	7.0	0.8	29,110
Keweenaw	15	25.8	6,774	76.5	12	4	24.2	−36.6	7	140	15.8	−28.6	196
Lake	78	24.0	6,537	74.1	63	24	28.0	17.6	20	555	14.6	−7.8	602
Lapeer	298	31.9	3,221	75.1	226	219	21.2	21.3	181	5,014	14.8	0.8	4,973
Leelanau	95	31.0	4,289	70.7	73	83	29.6	8.5	77	2,034	19.9	−10.8	2,279
Lenawee	471	26.8	4,630	73.4	372	268	17.0	19.0	225	5,909	13.5	−0.3	5,929
Livingston	438	40.7	2,467	75.5	311	340	11.8	31.9	258	6,908	9.2	1.1	6,830
Luce	44	21.0	6,447	67.6	37	46	58.5	21.3	38	983	37.2	−0.7	990
Mackinac	77	31.9	6,779	65.1	59	63	33.4	14.4	55	1,485	21.6	−11.8	1,684
Macomb	5,276	34.4	6,413	55.4	3,925	2,554	11.9	29.3	1,976	41,202	9.9	4.4	39,482
Manistee	149	28.2	5,936	76.2	116	135	37.5	45.0	93	3,031	25.3	16.6	2,599
Marquette	356	23.6	5,487	74.2	288	297	24.4	8.3	275	6,572	18.2	−6.1	6,999
Mason	160	29.1	5,518	74.8	124	85	18.1	13.7	75	2,133	13.6	−1.1	2,157
Mecosta	181	28.1	4,269	79.3	141	204	37.6	19.8	170	4,382	23.4	−5.5	4,638
Menominee	133	29.7	5,277	70.3	102	95	26.6	19.2	80	2,527	21.1	2.1	2,475
Midland	329	26.5	3,892	76.8	260	190	8.3	14.6	166	3,895	8.4	−2.9	4,011
Missaukee	65	27.0	4,266	74.1	51	23	16.3	20.3	19	570	10.2	−7.0	613
Monroe	591	25.4	3,875	80.2	471	325	13.0	21.6	268	6,751	11.4	0.7	6,705
Montcalm	299	28.9	4,695	72.4	232	166	19.1	17.7	141	3,592	14.3	−1.8	3,657
Montmorency	82	23.6	7,779	83.9	66	17	17.2	6.3	16	403	10.6	−15.5	477
Muskegon	924	24.5	5,299	67.3	742	482	15.7	16.7	413	9,683	11.4	−2.4	9,917
Newaygo	197	28.7	3,958	76.9	153	118	22.4	21.0	97	2,784	16.1	−0.6	2,801
Oakland	5,306	28.3	4,373	74.3	4,136	3,355	6.1	22.7	2,735	60,912	6.5	1.8	59,812
Oceana	145	26.3	5,115	70.1	115	69	23.5	30.0	53	1,671	14.9	3.4	1,616
Ogemaw	128	27.3	5,843	80.9	101	60	23.7	26.4	47	1,412	14.4	−2.1	1,443
Ontonagon	63	3.6	8,410	67.2	61	28	28.5	14.6	25	664	19.7	−5.9	706
Osceola	133	26.1	5,590	73.3	106	55	14.6	17.1	47	1,219	14.6	−12.6	1,394
Oscoda	51	29.8	5,432	78.0	39	18	21.1	17.6	15	433	12.2	−6.7	464
Otsego	120	28.2	4,881	70.1	93	70	13.0	14.5	61	1,399	9.0	−1.3	1,417
Ottawa	914	33.5	3,622	65.4	685	715	11.8	27.6	560	15,134	10.7	7.4	14,095
Presque Isle	99	27.7	6,951	75.6	78	29	22.1	16.6	25	707	14.0	−9.5	781
Roscommon	194	30.8	7,414	85.1	148	72	28.2	16.1	62	1,564	16.9	−7.7	1,694
Saginaw	1,192	19.3	5,704	68.1	999	635	13.6	17.1	542	12,942	11.5	1.9	12,702
St. Clair	694	27.1	4,060	71.0	546	404	15.9	25.4	322	7,894	11.6	1.9	7,748
St. Joseph	271	20.9	4,299	76.5	224	180	16.5	24.1	145	4,106	13.9	−0.5	4,126
Sanilac	248	26.6	5,531	69.6	196	100	18.8	18.4	84	2,278	11.8	−4.0	2,374
Schoolcraft	66	1.1	7,408	68.3	65	46	36.2	24.9	36	1,019	26.7	1.8	1,001
Shiawassee	323	22.9	4,421	78.8	263	176	23.7	24.3	141	4,121	16.8	−1.4	4,179
Tuscola	314	37.0	5,351	67.0	229	167	29.4	13.4	147	3,535	18.9	−6.2	3,768

See footnotes at end of table.

Table B-12. Counties — **Government Expenditure, Earnings, and Employment**—Con.

[Includes United States, states, and 3,141 counties/county equivalents defined as of February 22, 2005. For more information on these areas, see Appendix C, Geographic Information]

County	Federal government expenditure — 2004 Total (mil. dol.)	Percent change, 2000–2004	Per capita (dol.)	Direct payments to individuals, percent of total	2000 (mil. dol.)	Earnings 2005 Total (mil. dol.)	Percent of total	Percent change, 2000–2005	2000 (mil. dol.)	Employment 2005 Total	Percent of total	Percent change, 2000–2005	2000
MICHIGAN—Con.													
Van Buren	379	20.3	4,832	69.4	315	251	24.8	31.8	190	5,725	19.8	7.1	5,345
Washtenaw	2,042	31.0	6,021	40.1	1,559	3,477	27.8	31.7	2,639	67,668	27.7	1.1	66,956
Wayne	13,823	20.5	6,856	60.6	11,467	7,791	14.2	22.5	6,362	127,874	13.1	−4.2	133,433
Wexford	294	90.1	9,331	40.7	155	102	15.9	26.9	81	2,198	11.4	4.6	2,102
MINNESOTA	[3]28,791	[3]25.1	[3]5,644	[3]54.2	[3]23,013	21,034	13.8	26.8	16,594	415,134	11.9	2.1	406,659
Aitkin	109	30.0	6,788	71.3	84	39	22.2	25.9	31	921	11.7	−0.4	925
Anoka	661	26.0	2,067	74.1	525	807	12.6	30.2	619	16,173	10.1	5.5	15,329
Becker	203	26.7	6,394	54.2	161	126	21.9	29.7	97	2,782	12.4	4.7	2,656
Beltrami	261	32.7	6,186	50.9	197	240	31.6	25.4	191	5,299	20.0	0.2	5,289
Benton	146	33.4	3,837	73.3	110	72	9.2	38.5	52	1,729	6.5	16.3	1,487
Big Stone	47	10.8	8,369	54.8	42	24	29.4	26.1	19	671	20.1	−0.6	675
Blue Earth	285	25.6	4,959	60.4	227	271	16.6	24.2	218	5,540	11.3	2.8	5,388
Brown	147	15.7	5,488	63.2	127	74	11.8	26.0	58	1,750	8.7	−0.4	1,757
Carlton	196	36.9	5,819	62.2	143	191	32.5	29.1	148	4,658	25.6	6.2	4,387
Carver	182	7.3	2,217	66.8	170	215	10.9	53.3	140	4,534	9.3	17.9	3,845
Cass	222	39.5	7,802	54.0	159	164	42.7	27.2	129	4,062	18.6	3.2	3,937
Chippewa	78	6.1	6,134	54.9	73	47	17.7	32.4	35	1,146	11.8	5.6	1,085
Chisago	163	39.9	3,380	75.1	117	122	18.8	38.7	88	2,795	13.3	13.9	2,453
Clay	246	20.9	4,657	65.1	204	200	27.6	23.1	163	4,493	17.0	−6.6	4,808
Clearwater	60	23.5	7,097	50.1	48	30	28.7	6.2	29	783	16.5	−16.3	936
Cook	34	40.9	6,479	54.6	24	44	39.7	36.9	32	1,044	23.9	10.2	947
Cottonwood	79	−0.2	6,566	61.4	79	39	16.2	27.1	31	986	11.4	1.5	971
Crow Wing	338	36.0	5,687	69.6	248	224	19.7	21.3	185	4,714	13.3	−0.4	4,731
Dakota	1,105	33.1	2,914	58.7	830	1,099	11.3	34.4	818	20,077	8.8	6.9	18,775
Dodge	73	4.4	3,751	64.9	70	48	15.4	41.5	34	1,229	12.2	3.3	1,190
Douglas	184	26.3	5,326	67.9	146	140	18.6	39.8	100	3,178	12.1	10.2	2,883
Faribault	124	27.3	7,936	54.0	98	47	13.9	32.1	36	1,302	14.1	6.5	1,223
Fillmore	126	12.5	5,916	63.1	112	54	17.0	26.6	42	1,449	11.5	0.4	1,443
Freeborn	182	2.2	5,692	69.2	178	72	13.1	23.0	58	1,624	8.7	−6.4	1,735
Goodhue	197	20.6	4,333	69.8	163	202	19.0	19.5	169	4,709	16.0	−0.5	4,735
Grant	53	3.9	8,727	50.9	51	16	19.7	19.3	14	421	11.4	−6.4	450
Hennepin	7,222	18.4	6,443	46.1	6,100	5,865	9.6	24.8	4,699	99,510	9.5	−0.5	100,048
Houston	90	13.9	4,508	69.3	79	46	20.8	30.1	35	1,231	12.9	5.7	1,165
Hubbard	105	24.0	5,590	70.8	85	48	19.7	32.6	36	1,191	14.8	1.9	1,169
Isanti	112	21.2	3,058	69.8	92	92	18.1	29.4	71	2,129	10.1	8.2	1,967
Itasca	263	31.9	5,941	70.6	200	160	22.7	26.7	126	3,658	15.6	9.0	3,356
Jackson	64	−15.7	5,716	55.3	76	33	14.2	19.8	28	962	12.0	−2.4	986
Kanabec	69	35.2	4,275	68.2	51	47	27.9	39.4	34	1,103	15.2	11.5	989
Kandiyohi	223	20.7	5,414	60.2	185	214	22.3	23.7	173	4,588	15.0	1.8	4,509
Kittson	54	−7.1	11,288	40.1	59	20	29.3	33.3	15	412	13.9	−4.0	429
Koochiching	97	32.5	7,010	63.2	73	55	19.6	27.1	43	1,139	15.0	−2.7	1,171
Lac qui Parle	59	3.2	7,578	52.9	57	28	21.2	21.0	23	750	15.0	−4.0	781
Lake	72	19.3	6,446	69.5	61	42	19.9	27.0	33	966	13.7	3.2	936
Lake of the Woods	28	21.9	6,404	59.5	23	15	24.2	25.9	12	328	11.8	−7.6	355
Le Sueur	128	25.4	4,705	64.6	102	54	14.0	24.6	44	1,405	9.5	−5.9	1,493
Lincoln	49	8.3	7,891	54.0	45	14	15.7	19.0	12	405	11.2	−1.7	412
Lyon	129	4.5	5,220	61.5	123	127	19.0	24.6	102	2,996	14.9	0.7	2,974
McLeod	139	25.4	3,833	71.8	111	117	13.4	25.1	94	2,716	11.3	−1.8	2,766
Mahnomen	42	16.5	8,311	45.0	36	53	64.6	40.4	38	1,563	48.4	10.5	1,415
Marshall	94	−7.7	9,417	41.4	102	29	26.0	22.8	23	722	13.1	−4.4	755
Martin	128	5.8	6,077	68.0	121	59	13.0	24.8	47	1,464	10.2	−3.5	1,517
Meeker	108	18.8	4,621	63.5	91	56	16.8	28.6	44	1,439	10.8	3.3	1,393
Mille Lacs	153	41.3	6,095	63.9	108	148	41.2	63.6	90	3,628	28.8	29.0	2,813
Morrison	193	31.0	5,898	55.4	147	104	21.9	24.1	84	2,179	12.1	−0.9	2,199
Mower	237	16.2	6,090	66.8	204	119	15.6	30.5	91	2,729	12.2	5.0	2,598
Murray	62	−0.7	6,880	55.5	62	25	17.4	32.6	19	648	12.1	−3.6	672
Nicollet	95	20.3	3,082	65.0	79	124	20.1	28.3	96	2,753	15.5	7.3	2,565
Nobles	116	7.3	5,653	57.1	108	80	16.9	30.0	61	1,951	13.1	1.3	1,926
Norman	70	12.0	9,934	43.1	63	20	22.1	4.9	19	572	13.9	−10.1	636
Olmsted	739	43.0	5,543	42.8	517	444	8.5	27.7	348	8,474	7.6	3.7	8,173
Otter Tail	340	25.5	5,875	65.7	271	173	19.0	26.4	137	3,963	11.2	−0.8	3,994
Pennington	95	24.2	6,991	49.5	76	72	18.8	29.1	55	1,771	15.0	5.0	1,687
Pine	152	22.1	5,406	62.2	125	146	47.1	22.3	120	3,585	29.9	−0.1	3,587
Pipestone	66	15.1	6,882	55.7	57	36	17.4	27.7	28	923	14.3	−1.8	940
Polk	240	9.0	7,709	48.5	220	120	24.5	19.3	100	2,931	16.1	−2.0	2,992
Pope	75	21.6	6,683	59.2	62	34	18.4	30.8	26	817	12.0	2.8	795
Ramsey	4,514	24.6	9,038	42.2	3,622	3,467	16.8	24.3	2,789	59,543	14.7	2.2	58,266
Red Lake	31	−8.9	7,117	49.2	34	13	26.4	27.4	10	346	18.7	1.5	341
Redwood	111	10.2	6,829	54.7	100	82	27.1	27.0	65	2,378	23.5	1.1	2,353
Renville	113	7.6	6,795	52.3	105	47	18.7	21.5	39	1,205	13.1	−7.5	1,303

See footnotes at end of table.

Table B-12. Counties — **Government Expenditure, Earnings, and Employment**—Con.

[Includes United States, states, and 3,141 counties/county equivalents defined as of February 22, 2005. For more information on these areas, see Appendix C, Geographic Information]

County	Federal government expenditure					Federal, state, and local governments[1]							
	2004				2000 (mil. dol.)	Earnings				Employment			
						2005			2000 (mil. dol.)	2005			2000
	Total (mil. dol.)	Percent change, 2000–2004	Per capita (dol.)	Direct payments to individuals, percent of total		Total (mil. dol.)	Percent of total	Percent change, 2000–2005		Total	Percent of total	Percent change, 2000–2005	
MINNESOTA—Con.													
Rice	238	38.8	3,941	60.4	171	193	18.7	24.0	155	4,106	13.6	-1.0	4,149
Rock	55	-2.8	5,774	63.3	57	29	16.5	18.0	24	776	13.7	-5.3	819
Roseau	88	13.1	5,406	48.1	78	53	12.0	35.9	39	1,285	9.7	6.1	1,211
St. Louis	1,382	27.3	6,975	60.2	1,086	913	19.7	13.5	805	18,832	15.5	-9.4	20,781
Scott	206	43.7	1,794	68.1	143	442	20.2	37.2	322	9,829	18.1	11.2	8,837
Sherburne	161	32.7	2,039	72.7	121	200	17.9	41.1	141	4,036	12.2	14.3	3,530
Sibley	77	16.8	5,073	60.4	66	39	24.6	41.7	28	1,072	16.7	14.9	933
Stearns	609	30.6	4,320	57.3	466	608	16.9	30.1	468	11,739	11.8	2.3	11,478
Steele	137	11.3	3,909	68.4	123	95	10.2	26.5	75	2,141	8.4	7.2	1,997
Stevens	69	3.5	6,979	51.9	67	58	26.8	23.3	47	1,345	20.3	-6.9	1,445
Swift	83	14.6	7,265	57.7	73	41	24.2	30.5	32	1,068	17.5	5.5	1,012
Todd	131	26.2	5,295	59.9	103	63	23.0	33.4	47	1,607	13.7	4.8	1,533
Traverse	38	-12.6	9,874	49.6	44	17	34.4	31.8	13	477	20.7	2.6	465
Wabasha	130	32.5	5,857	56.1	98	51	16.2	32.0	39	1,278	12.2	8.0	1,183
Wadena	91	26.5	6,659	62.7	72	56	23.9	20.0	46	1,448	18.4	-8.4	1,581
Waseca	112	22.9	5,829	47.3	91	70	19.0	24.8	56	1,533	13.6	-0.4	1,539
Washington	437	48.9	2,018	65.6	294	520	13.7	27.8	407	10,641	11.0	7.2	9,922
Watonwan	82	22.6	7,235	50.2	67	34	15.3	31.5	26	883	13.5	6.5	829
Wilkin	51	-5.1	7,487	45.6	54	19	19.9	19.3	16	443	12.2	-8.3	483
Winona	208	25.8	4,251	70.0	166	169	16.0	23.2	137	3,669	11.3	-3.8	3,814
Wright	283	33.5	2,651	71.8	212	268	16.5	48.1	181	6,087	11.8	18.6	5,131
Yellow Medicine	81	3.7	7,675	57.5	78	60	29.9	42.7	42	1,697	27.5	11.6	1,521
MISSISSIPPI	[3]22,338	[3]21.5	[3]7,695	[3]53.3	[3]18,389	12,340	24.1	32.1	9,339	277,407	18.4	1.3	273,722
Adams	239	25.2	7,347	60.6	191	93	18.4	25.4	74	2,380	13.9	-6.0	2,532
Alcorn	207	31.2	5,881	71.4	158	114	20.7	38.8	82	2,847	15.9	4.2	2,733
Amite	81	29.3	6,047	67.3	63	19	16.7	29.4	15	537	10.1	-4.1	560
Attala	132	20.8	6,698	66.2	109	50	23.2	52.5	33	1,371	16.0	15.1	1,191
Benton	57	34.8	7,271	60.6	42	13	24.3	46.0	9	390	16.5	7.4	363
Bolivar	310	14.2	7,962	48.3	271	120	24.6	15.2	104	3,509	20.6	-7.2	3,780
Calhoun	107	33.0	7,217	60.2	81	33	17.7	39.3	23	937	15.5	6.6	879
Carroll	55	25.8	5,222	63.4	44	16	29.9	36.2	12	468	17.5	-0.8	472
Chickasaw	127	32.1	6,561	62.6	96	37	13.4	47.2	25	1,043	11.7	7.3	972
Choctaw	49	30.0	5,148	61.9	38	20	19.5	41.0	14	567	15.3	6.4	533
Claiborne	72	34.2	6,215	56.2	53	67	31.3	17.3	57	1,834	37.4	-5.2	1,935
Clarke	106	35.9	5,994	68.5	78	32	23.6	32.4	24	951	18.8	1.1	941
Clay	123	24.2	5,678	62.6	99	39	12.7	22.4	32	1,088	10.7	-1.4	1,103
Coahoma	256	13.5	8,757	50.0	225	86	20.7	23.6	69	2,337	18.1	-5.6	2,476
Copiah	204	26.9	6,989	66.7	161	79	24.9	34.1	59	2,283	19.8	6.2	2,150
Covington	113	22.9	5,600	65.6	92	48	19.7	44.6	33	1,355	15.8	11.5	1,215
DeSoto	402	44.6	3,080	77.1	278	234	11.4	86.5	125	6,000	10.1	34.1	4,475
Forrest	602	44.9	8,080	55.5	415	558	31.8	28.7	433	12,739	24.6	-0.1	12,754
Franklin	52	12.0	6,161	64.3	46	25	35.3	28.8	19	638	24.6	-0.3	640
George	106	31.2	5,086	78.9	81	57	32.1	51.4	37	1,496	20.2	12.5	1,330
Greene	51	21.8	3,859	70.1	42	40	45.1	21.3	33	1,163	28.7	-5.8	1,235
Grenada	163	33.1	7,191	64.2	123	85	19.2	30.8	65	2,030	14.2	-0.7	2,045
Hancock	535	10.0	11,654	34.4	487	315	43.3	45.8	216	4,440	20.1	5.5	4,208
Harrison	1,903	23.2	9,889	46.6	1,545	1,767	39.7	33.1	1,328	29,122	24.0	-3.7	30,237
Hinds	2,496	28.3	9,985	40.0	1,946	1,959	26.4	27.2	1,540	40,388	23.5	0.4	40,211
Holmes	201	27.1	9,519	52.9	158	51	31.3	31.8	39	1,402	21.8	-0.1	1,404
Humphreys	95	15.1	8,935	50.2	83	23	20.2	17.2	20	598	12.1	-16.9	720
Issaquena	21	-5.9	10,581	20.9	22	3	21.7	16.9	3	119	14.8	-5.6	126
Itawamba	111	40.9	4,778	71.4	79	49	20.5	40.7	35	1,238	14.2	9.9	1,126
Jackson	1,621	15.2	11,969	30.8	1,407	587	23.8	25.1	469	11,870	18.7	-4.7	12,456
Jasper	112	35.0	6,238	63.3	83	39	19.9	39.5	28	1,099	17.7	1.8	1,080
Jefferson	92	(Z)	9,745	44.6	92	22	46.9	24.5	18	675	37.4	-10.9	758
Jefferson Davis	88	32.5	6,741	58.9	67	29	29.4	40.6	21	907	21.9	3.1	880
Jones	388	30.6	5,902	71.3	297	275	20.6	35.2	203	7,410	19.6	4.7	7,074
Kemper	79	48.2	7,613	60.7	53	26	33.5	47.0	18	697	20.9	13.9	612
Lafayette	205	33.6	5,031	48.3	153	319	37.5	42.3	224	7,258	28.9	8.6	6,681
Lamar	124	27.7	2,858	79.7	97	78	14.8	67.0	46	2,154	11.5	16.4	1,851
Lauderdale	588	21.2	7,591	57.4	485	398	24.4	18.0	337	8,246	17.5	-8.8	9,038
Lawrence	97	27.9	7,241	72.2	76	29	16.3	31.1	22	859	18.4	-0.6	864
Leake	140	19.8	6,280	67.1	117	46	16.7	43.5	32	1,355	14.8	11.3	1,217
Lee	396	26.6	5,064	68.8	312	239	10.2	33.2	179	5,713	9.0	-0.3	5,733
Leflore	291	-72.1	8,062	53.1	1,045	175	27.4	26.2	138	4,366	22.0	-4.0	4,546
Lincoln	169	29.7	5,019	72.5	130	70	12.5	33.8	53	1,948	11.4	-0.4	1,955
Lowndes	484	30.3	8,006	44.4	372	322	26.4	30.0	247	6,376	18.7	0.7	6,331
Madison	730	32.7	8,901	30.5	550	183	8.5	39.1	132	4,546	7.9	8.3	4,198
Marion	181	32.9	7,099	63.0	136	62	19.9	29.8	48	1,689	15.0	-1.6	1,716
Marshall	214	17.1	6,023	56.3	183	59	21.3	38.5	42	1,612	16.1	4.6	1,541
Monroe	210	25.9	5,527	70.4	167	73	13.6	20.8	60	1,860	12.0	-12.3	2,120
Montgomery	104	23.4	8,880	56.6	84	30	24.0	34.3	22	864	19.5	-1.6	878
Neshoba	189	58.9	6,401	52.0	119	286	44.4	53.8	186	8,023	42.8	26.3	6,353

See footnotes at end of table.

Table B-12. Counties — **Government Expenditure, Earnings, and Employment**—Con.

[Includes United States, states, and 3,141 counties/county equivalents defined as of February 22, 2005. For more information on these areas, see Appendix C, Geographic Information]

County	Federal government expenditure 2004 — Total (mil. dol.)	Percent change, 2000-2004	Per capita (dol.)	Direct payments to individuals, percent of total	2000 (mil. dol.)	Earnings 2005 — Total (mil. dol.)	Percent of total	Percent change, 2000-2005	2000 (mil. dol.)	Employment 2005 — Total	Percent of total	Percent change, 2000-2005	2000
MISSISSIPPI—Con.													
Newton	163	34.7	7,346	70.6	121	80	26.4	33.6	60	2,200	24.3	5.1	2,093
Noxubee	89	27.3	7,270	52.1	70	32	25.0	32.8	24	857	17.4	−0.3	860
Oktibbeha	264	5.4	6,386	46.6	250	404	51.9	25.5	322	9,710	38.7	4.2	9,323
Panola	216	29.8	6,094	57.4	166	107	23.2	44.9	74	2,764	18.1	9.3	2,528
Pearl River	271	38.0	5,229	78.7	196	115	29.6	50.8	76	3,207	18.7	8.3	2,960
Perry	62	37.2	5,074	67.5	45	22	18.1	11.0	20	683	15.9	−19.9	853
Pike	253	24.2	6,445	70.3	204	158	27.4	35.5	117	3,839	19.4	2.9	3,732
Pontotoc	125	27.7	4,448	68.6	98	48	9.6	34.4	36	1,277	8.0	1.3	1,261
Prentiss	151	36.5	5,885	69.4	111	66	22.7	28.8	52	1,763	17.1	3.0	1,712
Quitman	99	26.8	10,163	45.0	78	18	23.5	37.2	13	522	17.7	−2.8	537
Rankin	532	64.2	4,143	61.0	324	399	15.6	25.1	319	10,324	14.1	−1.1	10,434
Scott	164	33.5	5,715	66.0	123	64	12.6	37.1	46	1,606	10.3	5.9	1,517
Sharkey	54	7.3	8,914	47.4	51	18	33.0	24.2	14	495	19.1	−5.7	525
Simpson	141	26.5	5,079	73.1	112	67	20.6	28.3	53	1,934	17.6	−0.6	1,945
Smith	80	26.2	5,071	65.7	64	27	11.1	27.6	21	776	14.7	−1.4	787
Stone	101	46.5	7,018	78.4	69	48	31.6	37.2	35	1,284	23.8	15.3	1,114
Sunflower	216	13.3	6,455	52.4	190	145	38.8	6.8	135	4,017	28.8	−14.1	4,677
Tallahatchie	133	27.0	9,327	40.6	105	36	29.6	40.5	26	1,066	20.7	5.2	1,013
Tate	138	36.1	5,273	67.9	101	69	27.1	36.2	51	1,915	19.8	9.7	1,746
Tippah	138	31.8	6,563	69.0	104	45	15.6	38.7	33	1,249	12.3	2.2	1,222
Tishomingo	152	16.9	7,961	62.5	130	35	16.6	41.9	25	968	12.9	7.6	900
Tunica	78	26.0	7,723	39.5	62	41	7.5	77.0	23	1,068	6.4	35.7	787
Union	127	32.4	4,787	71.3	96	51	14.4	41.5	36	1,381	11.3	5.5	1,309
Walthall	90	20.3	5,895	62.7	74	30	24.3	32.3	23	899	17.9	3.8	866
Warren	453	13.1	9,218	46.4	400	330	28.8	30.5	252	5,001	16.5	−2.6	5,137
Washington	456	21.4	7,657	51.1	376	241	28.7	39.7	173	5,294	19.3	1.3	5,228
Wayne	104	34.8	4,900	63.9	77	51	19.0	38.2	37	1,352	16.3	0.1	1,350
Webster	69	8.4	6,772	67.9	63	19	21.4	31.3	14	517	14.1	−3.9	538
Wilkinson	63	29.0	6,180	60.2	49	26	35.4	47.1	18	670	22.3	6.2	631
Winston	116	31.7	5,862	66.4	88	34	13.8	26.5	27	940	11.5	−4.6	985
Yalobusha	106	19.5	7,977	67.0	89	33	25.7	37.7	24	917	20.1	3.0	890
Yazoo	223	15.5	7,890	48.5	193	100	29.7	38.3	72	2,115	22.7	4.0	2,034
MISSOURI	[3]45,730	[3]28.0	[3]7,947	[3]49.8	[3]35,730	22,252	15.8	26.0	17,660	475,815	13.3	1.3	469,823
Adair	145	40.5	5,893	55.2	103	102	25.3	12.1	91	2,783	17.1	−8.8	3,051
Andrew	71	10.8	4,200	62.5	64	28	25.1	22.6	23	813	12.7	−3.3	841
Atchison	51	9.7	8,108	55.9	48	15	19.7	12.3	14	452	13.8	−5.2	477
Audrain	157	21.2	6,114	69.1	129	103	25.8	17.1	88	2,859	19.3	−2.1	2,919
Barry	197	30.8	5,577	73.5	151	73	11.6	22.4	60	1,983	8.7	−2.1	2,025
Barton	66	14.9	5,059	68.8	58	31	15.5	24.6	25	945	11.4	−0.1	946
Bates	99	17.0	5,826	69.5	85	46	27.2	32.1	35	1,280	15.5	0.7	1,271
Benton	133	19.4	7,173	80.3	111	41	27.5	30.8	32	1,071	13.7	3.1	1,039
Bollinger	72	31.0	5,842	59.0	55	18	22.3	19.8	15	539	11.0	−2.0	550
Boone	771	26.6	5,453	51.4	609	1,377	36.7	22.8	1,122	30,667	28.2	−2.2	31,356
Buchanan	515	23.8	6,074	69.4	416	306	15.3	20.7	254	7,350	13.1	1.5	7,243
Butler	357	25.6	8,703	55.9	284	157	19.5	31.5	120	3,480	13.1	2.6	3,392
Caldwell	55	3.3	5,977	68.1	53	22	28.4	25.8	17	699	14.4	4.3	670
Callaway	239	54.2	5,673	55.0	155	162	24.5	15.0	141	4,503	21.5	−1.6	4,576
Camden	189	29.4	4,896	85.6	146	77	11.2	31.5	59	2,057	7.3	4.1	1,976
Cape Girardeau	351	28.4	4,961	66.0	273	247	14.3	24.0	199	6,615	12.4	2.6	6,445
Carroll	76	10.4	7,469	60.3	69	24	23.5	22.6	19	711	13.2	−2.2	727
Carter	47	5.1	7,845	65.4	45	18	33.5	15.6	16	486	19.1	−5.8	516
Cass	410	22.1	4,481	67.4	336	226	22.0	44.4	157	5,251	14.1	14.1	4,603
Cedar	93	28.2	6,694	74.7	73	34	25.7	23.2	27	912	13.2	3.9	878
Chariton	66	17.6	8,081	55.5	56	17	20.3	20.5	14	552	10.9	−0.4	554
Christian	211	44.8	3,276	80.0	145	101	16.0	53.8	66	2,579	9.2	18.6	2,174
Clark	45	15.2	6,067	61.4	39	18	33.0	11.0	16	578	16.7	−13.1	665
Clay	601	26.2	3,039	76.3	476	630	12.3	40.9	447	13,742	11.6	9.5	12,553
Clinton	105	34.4	5,089	70.4	78	52	27.4	53.8	34	1,360	17.6	23.0	1,106
Cole	1,617	53.2	22,463	22.2	1,055	980	38.8	19.9	817	22,272	33.7	6.9	20,831
Cooper	93	21.1	5,406	66.2	77	52	22.5	20.2	43	1,416	14.9	−6.3	1,511
Crawford	115	29.2	4,856	77.7	89	37	13.3	31.8	28	1,040	9.4	1.3	1,027
Dade	53	23.6	6,707	67.9	42	20	22.1	19.5	17	645	14.6	−4.7	677
Dallas	86	33.8	5,246	68.7	64	30	21.2	34.8	22	783	10.2	3.8	754
Daviess	56	24.7	6,861	55.2	45	18	22.6	12.4	16	516	12.3	−5.3	545
DeKalb	45	23.2	3,566	65.3	36	50	47.7	1.0	50	1,315	29.7	−18.8	1,620
Dent	121	28.1	8,019	56.3	94	36	22.1	16.8	31	987	14.1	−8.7	1,081
Douglas	77	31.8	5,681	62.1	58	22	16.0	24.4	17	562	7.1	−6.5	601
Dunklin	304	28.3	9,353	51.0	237	71	17.5	22.8	58	1,891	13.0	1.2	1,869

See footnotes at end of table.

Table B-12. Counties — Government Expenditure, Earnings, and Employment—Con.

[Includes United States, states, and 3,141 counties/county equivalents defined as of February 22, 2005. For more information on these areas, see Appendix C, Geographic Information]

County	Federal government expenditure					Federal, state, and local governments[1]							
	2004					Earnings				Employment			
						2005				2005			
	Total (mil. dol.)	Percent change, 2000–2004	Per capita (dol.)	Direct payments to individuals, percent of total	2000 (mil. dol.)	Total (mil. dol.)	Percent of total	Percent change, 2000–2005	2000 (mil. dol.)	Total	Percent of total	Percent change, 2000–2005	2000
MISSOURI—Con.													
Franklin	446	40.2	4,541	73.4	318	187	11.9	28.3	146	4,800	9.5	4.6	4,589
Gasconade	84	28.0	5,385	80.1	66	39	20.0	37.8	28	1,110	12.5	3.9	1,068
Gentry	63	28.0	9,667	57.0	49	17	22.0	14.1	15	509	13.5	-2.5	522
Greene	1,351	30.8	5,451	66.4	1,033	894	12.5	28.2	697	19,737	10.1	5.3	18,737
Grundy	80	23.6	7,827	62.1	65	35	26.1	18.9	29	1,046	18.6	-2.4	1,072
Harrison	73	22.1	8,300	58.4	60	26	27.7	22.6	21	771	15.2	-3.6	800
Henry	148	17.7	6,507	76.0	126	72	23.0	41.1	51	1,749	15.1	2.3	1,709
Hickory	65	23.6	7,110	81.4	53	15	35.2	33.6	11	420	15.1	2.7	409
Holt	55	26.4	10,814	48.2	44	13	25.8	8.6	12	383	14.7	-10.9	430
Howard	64	19.6	6,463	64.4	54	20	24.1	27.9	15	573	12.5	-1.9	584
Howell	247	31.1	6,492	67.0	188	94	16.3	27.0	74	2,576	11.1	1.4	2,540
Iron	78	32.3	7,595	67.2	59	21	17.5	18.0	18	634	14.3	-3.8	659
Jackson	5,942	35.3	9,001	46.5	4,393	3,730	16.3	25.7	2,967	65,668	14.3	1.2	64,906
Jasper	631	-21.1	5,764	69.8	800	274	11.3	26.6	216	7,130	9.4	1.5	7,023
Jefferson	705	30.1	3,352	79.4	542	372	18.6	31.6	283	8,979	12.4	3.7	8,662
Johnson	456	25.7	9,000	33.5	363	534	56.6	38.0	387	10,269	33.9	7.9	9,521
Knox	37	4.2	8,725	57.0	35	11	28.6	2.7	11	388	15.8	-16.7	466
Laclede	184	33.1	5,465	71.7	138	62	11.3	29.9	48	1,662	8.5	1.7	1,634
Lafayette	186	25.6	5,613	72.0	148	88	25.0	21.3	73	2,387	16.1	-1.3	2,419
Lawrence	175	28.2	4,755	72.2	136	75	22.3	31.3	57	2,125	14.8	6.1	2,002
Lewis	71	31.6	6,928	56.7	54	24	26.3	23.6	20	720	15.5	-3.9	749
Lincoln	156	31.0	3,409	76.0	119	95	19.7	49.7	63	2,242	13.0	14.0	1,967
Linn	103	20.8	7,779	68.3	86	33	17.2	12.7	29	925	12.4	-7.0	995
Livingston	110	28.7	7,727	56.3	86	49	20.5	19.1	41	1,270	13.7	-0.5	1,277
McDonald	110	41.3	4,912	61.0	78	40	15.2	47.0	27	991	9.5	10.4	898
Macon	117	39.8	7,500	65.4	83	68	36.0	33.5	51	1,906	22.6	6.2	1,794
Madison	73	13.5	6,147	73.0	65	32	27.9	40.8	23	958	18.2	11.0	863
Maries	43	30.5	4,861	74.6	33	12	18.1	22.3	10	388	7.4	-6.3	414
Marion	176	15.0	6,205	65.7	153	82	15.4	26.3	65	2,132	11.6	0.7	2,117
Mercer	29	21.0	7,952	55.4	24	9	14.1	9.7	8	285	11.2	-5.6	302
Miller	135	32.2	5,470	77.0	102	47	16.4	25.4	38	1,322	11.5	3.6	1,276
Mississippi	124	11.6	9,027	48.1	111	43	30.7	67.2	26	1,215	21.7	35.8	895
Moniteau	68	25.7	4,518	72.8	54	40	25.0	16.3	34	1,114	16.2	-4.7	1,169
Monroe	71	18.7	7,474	59.5	60	28	30.0	20.2	23	810	15.8	-6.0	862
Montgomery	78	16.5	6,473	67.7	67	29	22.9	32.7	22	824	13.3	3.6	795
Morgan	119	23.7	5,857	82.2	96	36	19.8	31.3	27	1,102	15.1	5.2	1,048
New Madrid	197	24.7	10,391	38.9	158	42	11.8	15.4	36	1,135	11.4	-8.1	1,235
Newton	214	30.3	3,899	70.5	164	94	11.0	34.9	70	2,672	10.4	11.4	2,399
Nodaway	112	16.7	5,164	60.5	96	98	26.7	17.9	83	2,872	21.0	-1.3	2,909
Oregon	79	32.2	7,550	62.2	60	20	20.7	30.6	15	595	12.1	3.1	577
Osage	57	28.0	4,268	74.1	44	27	18.6	23.2	22	809	12.2	4.1	777
Ozark	72	30.8	7,625	64.2	55	16	28.7	18.9	14	536	14.8	-2.5	550
Pemiscot	222	20.3	11,354	40.5	185	73	31.8	21.5	60	1,968	23.4	-4.6	2,063
Perry	94	27.8	5,136	67.5	74	43	12.2	31.5	33	1,200	9.5	3.2	1,163
Pettis	237	29.5	5,970	68.8	183	130	17.0	27.5	102	3,354	13.1	4.7	3,204
Phelps	290	28.3	6,953	60.1	226	287	37.6	28.5	223	6,435	26.0	1.7	6,325
Pike	114	30.4	6,204	59.5	88	66	29.4	20.2	55	1,778	20.4	-5.5	1,881
Platte	271	0.2	3,350	65.6	271	181	9.8	37.4	132	3,696	7.6	3.1	3,586
Polk	165	41.9	5,834	69.6	116	88	28.0	69.0	52	2,142	16.5	18.7	1,805
Pulaski	807	24.1	18,139	20.0	650	1,023	81.1	44.7	707	15,398	58.5	-3.9	16,031
Putnam	41	28.5	8,075	59.1	32	16	36.6	31.7	12	507	19.4	10.0	461
Ralls	55	25.4	5,641	59.7	44	16	13.3	16.6	13	426	10.0	-9.7	472
Randolph	158	30.1	6,294	69.1	122	79	18.5	22.3	65	2,157	15.3	–	2,157
Ray	104	3.3	4,327	73.4	100	61	28.7	52.6	40	1,484	15.0	7.7	1,378
Reynolds	51	39.6	7,749	61.2	37	14	17.6	8.5	13	418	15.8	-18.2	511
Ripley	111	30.1	8,033	61.1	85	28	28.5	24.8	23	778	15.5	1.7	765
St. Charles	1,289	65.6	4,018	60.8	778	681	11.4	46.8	464	14,827	9.5	18.0	12,563
St. Clair	70	-8.0	7,380	67.3	77	27	36.7	37.7	20	759	18.8	6.8	711
Ste. Genevieve	76	4.8	4,147	81.1	72	38	16.5	19.0	32	986	12.5	-5.7	1,046
St. Francois	343	28.8	5,643	73.9	266	215	26.7	42.7	151	5,813	19.9	17.9	4,932
St. Louis	5,765	38.5	5,712	67.8	4,162	3,024	7.7	25.4	2,411	61,220	7.8	1.9	60,052
Saline	157	14.4	6,829	62.8	138	84	22.9	11.7	75	2,375	17.7	-7.4	2,566
Schuyler	35	28.5	8,070	63.5	27	11	40.6	17.4	9	356	20.1	-1.7	362
Scotland	36	6.5	7,320	56.2	34	23	44.0	34.2	17	641	25.0	1.4	632
Scott	258	21.9	6,300	64.6	211	103	16.3	19.3	87	2,532	12.3	-3.1	2,613
Shannon	54	31.3	6,456	59.0	41	18	26.6	9.1	17	513	14.0	-8.2	559
Shelby	51	15.2	7,667	61.9	45	19	27.7	19.7	16	660	19.5	-0.5	663
Stoddard	248	25.1	8,318	53.6	198	60	13.6	19.7	50	1,609	10.0	-1.8	1,638
Stone	150	33.1	4,882	85.1	113	43	13.4	32.8	32	1,173	7.9	4.5	1,122
Sullivan	56	22.6	8,046	54.4	46	20	16.6	30.8	15	572	14.6	3.2	554

See footnotes at end of table.

[Includes United States, states, and 3,141 counties/county equivalents defined as of February 22, 2005. For more information on these areas, see Appendix C, Geographic Information]

County	Federal government expenditure					Federal, state, and local governments[1]							
	2004					Earnings				Employment			
						2005				2005			
	Total (mil. dol.)	Percent change, 2000–2004	Per capita (dol.)	Direct payments to individuals, percent of total	2000 (mil. dol.)	Total (mil. dol.)	Percent of total	Percent change, 2000–2005	2000 (mil. dol.)	Total	Percent of total	Percent change, 2000–2005	2000
MISSOURI—Con.													
Taney	229	36.1	5,459	76.0	168	84	9.9	41.5	59	2,116	6.9	12.3	1,885
Texas	151	30.1	6,174	69.6	116	74	34.2	28.1	58	1,992	20.4	4.8	1,901
Vernon	122	19.2	5,984	65.9	102	72	25.5	17.6	62	1,931	17.1	−5.3	2,040
Warren	107	34.1	3,863	80.4	80	46	16.6	48.3	31	1,254	12.0	16.4	1,077
Washington	122	33.5	5,091	65.6	91	62	36.0	19.7	52	1,634	24.8	−4.3	1,707
Wayne	118	30.7	9,006	66.4	90	26	31.0	20.3	21	722	18.3	−4.6	757
Webster	158	35.4	4,627	70.8	117	57	21.3	37.6	41	1,527	13.0	11.9	1,365
Worth	20	20.4	8,517	52.4	16	7	40.9	22.3	6	233	20.3	1.7	229
Wright	133	33.2	7,322	63.6	100	38	24.6	8.3	35	1,068	14.4	−8.6	1,169
Independent City													
St. Louis city	9,095	13.0	26,496	18.5	8,047	2,530	17.0	11.2	2,276	42,128	15.8	−10.7	47,189
MONTANA	3-7,494	3-26.6	3-8,085	3-46.7	3-5,920	4,399	22.2	34.4	3,274	92,756	15.1	4.1	89,095
Beaverhead	70	24.4	7,917	51.0	56	49	31.7	42.5	35	1,117	19.6	10.9	1,007
Big Horn	113	27.2	8,685	28.9	89	97	44.1	18.7	81	2,332	36.0	−6.5	2,493
Blaine	91	20.2	13,607	24.3	75	35	41.1	22.7	29	800	25.9	−1.1	809
Broadwater	30	12.8	6,669	66.5	27	14	24.8	65.4	8	359	15.0	34.5	267
Carbon	52	8.8	5,292	67.5	47	25	23.4	45.0	17	654	11.9	5.8	618
Carter	28	136.4	21,125	15.6	12	4	20.4	21.9	3	112	12.5	−24.8	149
Cascade	807	22.0	10,102	42.9	661	551	31.0	33.9	412	9,458	18.8	1.6	9,305
Chouteau	67	−7.8	11,961	30.2	72	18	24.1	21.0	15	521	16.4	−5.4	551
Custer	87	21.6	7,583	56.2	71	55	28.3	14.5	48	1,100	15.2	−7.3	1,186
Daniels	27	4.2	14,747	34.8	26	7	21.9	19.9	6	189	12.7	−11.3	213
Dawson	58	5.7	6,763	60.4	55	30	19.8	7.3	28	807	14.7	−15.5	955
Deer Lodge	65	12.6	7,099	70.9	57	40	35.8	13.2	35	932	21.3	−8.4	1,017
Fallon	20	15.4	7,319	48.6	18	10	14.1	25.3	8	273	12.9	−5.2	288
Fergus	91	10.3	7,920	56.5	83	44	21.9	20.5	37	1,084	14.1	−4.7	1,137
Flathead	448	31.1	5,512	62.8	341	236	13.1	32.5	178	4,909	8.5	4.7	4,689
Gallatin[4]	347	52.1	4,593	47.6	228	394	19.3	48.0	267	9,151	14.4	7.6	8,507
Garfield	31	93.4	25,606	15.6	16	4	18.9	14.8	4	125	14.3	−13.2	144
Glacier	135	10.0	9,987	29.2	123	109	50.9	43.2	76	2,394	37.7	12.3	2,131
Golden Valley	11	35.6	9,660	40.8	8	3	37.2	28.2	2	93	15.6	−	93
Granite	17	39.0	5,789	66.2	12	11	28.1	28.7	9	290	15.4	1.8	285
Hill	165	14.5	10,056	38.8	144	93	29.5	42.7	65	2,227	22.4	15.3	1,932
Jefferson	64	1.0	5,850	53.6	63	41	27.4	45.6	28	1,010	18.1	8.5	931
Judith Basin	20	−15.0	9,166	41.0	24	8	31.9	22.7	6	215	19.2	−3.2	222
Lake	225	71.0	8,070	42.7	132	115	32.6	30.9	88	2,720	19.3	1.3	2,685
Lewis and Clark	815	40.5	14,051	29.8	580	542	35.7	33.9	405	9,314	22.5	0.4	9,273
Liberty	32	−2.3	15,941	39.7	33	6	18.4	14.8	5	170	13.4	−13.7	197
Lincoln	144	17.8	7,533	60.7	122	74	30.6	24.1	60	1,492	15.9	−0.1	1,494
McCone	20	−19.8	11,166	35.5	25	6	20.9	24.8	5	182	14.2	−0.5	183
Madison	35	20.1	4,963	71.4	29	22	18.2	38.6	16	563	12.0	4.3	540
Meagher	14	−9.4	6,925	55.0	15	7	22.3	31.0	5	176	14.2	−3.8	183
Mineral	26	26.5	6,717	73.5	21	15	31.5	19.7	12	351	16.5	2.9	341
Missoula	554	22.8	5,595	52.5	451	494	19.2	41.6	349	10,544	14.1	15.0	9,165
Musselshell	32	21.5	7,047	60.5	26	10	21.2	32.0	8	290	14.2	3.6	280
Park[4]	96	42.9	6,054	63.0	67	36	15.6	33.9	27	860	8.8	4.5	823
Petroleum	5	−0.9	10,220	31.3	5	2	33.6	25.8	1	61	16.8	−10.3	68
Phillips	47	13.8	11,279	38.8	42	17	30.1	26.7	13	439	16.3	−2.9	452
Pondera	60	9.7	9,752	41.9	55	18	20.3	20.1	15	490	15.1	−5.4	518
Powder River	15	54.3	8,212	34.8	10	7	34.4	22.9	6	221	18.6	−13.0	254
Powell	36	16.0	5,272	65.5	31	52	49.5	30.7	40	1,117	30.8	−3.4	1,156
Prairie	12	−35.1	10,891	48.5	19	6	36.0	59.0	4	177	25.1	−0.6	178
Ravalli	306	82.8	7,776	49.3	167	104	20.9	40.5	74	2,234	11.3	12.9	1,978
Richland	67	1.5	7,358	52.7	66	30	14.6	27.6	23	728	10.6	−6.1	775
Roosevelt	144	43.4	13,529	25.0	101	75	51.6	26.2	59	1,876	35.0	0.7	1,863
Rosebud	83	−3.6	8,992	30.5	86	74	32.5	21.9	61	1,897	31.4	1.4	1,871
Sanders	71	16.5	6,468	70.8	61	30	24.9	24.7	24	759	13.6	2.4	741
Sheridan	52	9.0	14,303	36.7	48	16	29.2	29.8	13	376	14.8	−5.3	397
Silver Bow	271	20.7	8,202	56.6	225	128	16.8	29.0	99	2,745	13.6	6.2	2,585
Stillwater	41	20.3	4,926	67.4	34	19	10.2	33.9	14	512	9.7	7.1	478
Sweet Grass	29	64.5	7,859	40.1	18	13	14.5	56.2	8	387	13.3	16.6	332
Teton	64	20.6	10,122	39.0	53	19	20.3	33.6	14	556	15.5	8.0	515
Toole	51	15.2	9,952	28.8	44	34	28.9	66.8	21	719	20.5	8.3	664
Treasure	5	−54.6	6,541	64.5	11	2	30.0	17.3	2	84	17.3	−2.3	86
Valley	84	10.0	11,555	41.6	76	33	24.0	29.3	26	784	16.3	2.8	763
Wheatland	22	33.6	10,712	49.0	17	7	31.8	24.0	6	213	18.8	0.5	212
Wibaux	15	30.2	15,872	23.4	12	4	29.3	32.9	3	117	17.4	4.5	112
Yellowstone	753	20.8	5,589	59.1	624	502	13.6	35.1	371	9,450	9.6	5.0	9,004
Yellowstone National Park[4]	(X)	(NA)	(X)	(NA)	(X)	(X)	(NA)	(NA)	(X)	(X)	(NA)	(NA)	(X)

See footnotes at end of table.

[Includes United States, states, and 3,141 counties/county equivalents defined as of February 22, 2005. For more information on these areas, see Appendix C, Geographic Information]

County	Federal government expenditure					Federal, state, and local governments[1]							
	2004				2000 (mil. dol.)	Earnings				Employment			
						2005			2000 (mil. dol.)	2005			2000
	Total (mil. dol.)	Percent change, 2000–2004	Per capita (dol.)	Direct payments to individuals, percent of total		Total (mil. dol.)	Percent of total	Percent change, 2000–2005		Total	Percent of total	Percent change, 2000–2005	
NEBRASKA.............	[3]11,795	[3]22.6	[3]6,751	[3]52.6	[3]9,617	8,027	17.8	33.4	6,017	170,891	14.0	5.1	162,618
Adams.................	172	9.2	5,557	63.9	157	106	17.6	21.1	87	2,616	12.6	–5.5	2,768
Antelope	54	–29.6	7,650	48.4	77	19	17.4	18.9	16	581	12.3	–7.3	627
Arthur	2	5.7	5,540	72.8	2	1	220.1	37.0	1	47	13.9	–4.1	49
Banner	8	–11.0	10,492	18.9	9	3	23.1	31.6	2	83	18.1	–	83
Blaine	6	104.8	10,732	32.6	3	3	115.8	22.1	3	92	20.0	–10.7	103
Boone.................	44	–5.5	7,564	52.4	47	22	24.3	28.3	17	637	17.1	–0.3	639
Box Butte.............	69	2.5	6,054	60.4	67	43	15.2	26.0	34	1,151	15.1	2.9	1,119
Boyd	21	27.2	9,356	57.8	17	7	35.6	4.4	7	254	18.6	–15.1	299
Brown	23	7.1	6,779	63.9	22	16	30.2	29.3	12	406	17.5	–8.8	445
Buffalo..............	189	25.4	4,349	62.5	151	170	16.3	37.4	124	4,094	12.1	9.4	3,743
Burt.................	56	2.4	7,521	62.1	55	22	28.9	25.8	18	666	18.8	–2.1	680
Butler................	61	11.1	6,908	48.6	55	24	24.1	38.4	17	666	15.0	2.9	647
Cass.................	127	11.4	4,941	70.1	114	54	24.3	47.4	37	1,376	14.0	8.2	1,272
Cedar	56	4.1	6,211	53.5	54	28	16.7	29.5	22	785	14.1	–0.5	789
Chase	35	–16.0	8,959	47.8	42	19	26.0	33.5	14	571	20.8	–2.9	588
Cherry	35	16.7	5,794	60.1	30	23	25.5	39.0	16	614	14.5	3.2	595
Cheyenne	67	3.8	6,808	56.4	65	32	11.7	28.0	25	891	10.7	1.8	875
Clay	59	–4.6	8,680	46.8	62	36	31.9	18.4	31	858	21.4	–2.6	881
Colfax	59	–2.5	5,639	67.0	61	26	12.9	37.6	19	717	10.5	–0.1	718
Cuming	65	16.7	6,681	52.4	56	27	12.9	31.5	20	755	11.6	–0.3	757
Custer	96	22.5	8,327	48.7	78	34	16.5	25.1	27	952	13.2	–4.6	998
Dakota................	86	–25.2	4,179	61.3	115	52	11.4	56.4	33	1,255	9.4	16.1	1,081
Dawes	68	23.3	7,830	49.2	56	49	40.3	25.3	39	1,250	21.3	7.4	1,164
Dawson................	120	12.3	4,883	57.1	107	84	18.7	36.0	62	2,115	14.0	4.1	2,031
Deuel	28	44.2	13,720	35.6	19	7	33.3	40.3	5	211	18.0	7.7	196
Dixon.................	42	11.7	6,828	49.6	37	15	15.7	27.0	12	460	14.5	–1.9	469
Dodge.................	193	18.9	5,351	72.0	162	126	19.6	34.6	94	2,972	13.5	3.4	2,874
Douglas	2,818	24.9	5,846	56.4	2,257	2,142	11.7	30.8	1,637	41,303	10.6	8.7	37,986
Dundy	25	2.4	11,499	41.4	25	9	27.7	24.5	7	250	18.2	–7.7	271
Fillmore	53	–16.4	8,251	50.6	64	24	23.4	21.4	20	737	18.0	–11.7	835
Franklin	31	–4.1	9,029	52.7	32	13	35.2	59.4	8	412	21.3	23.0	335
Frontier	26	3.2	9,076	39.6	25	12	24.7	14.1	10	367	20.3	–7.6	397
Furnas	58	13.5	11,262	46.6	51	19	29.5	22.3	16	622	21.8	–2.7	639
Gage.................	148	15.3	6,322	60.9	128	99	23.8	36.6	72	2,456	16.5	–1.4	2,490
Garden	33	24.3	15,263	37.9	27	10	43.6	16.7	8	307	19.6	–8.9	337
Garfield	13	15.5	7,338	69.3	12	6	24.0	42.6	4	193	13.5	8.4	178
Gosper	18	–16.4	8,745	51.1	21	6	27.5	20.3	5	188	18.7	–	188
Grant.................	5	73.5	7,024	56.3	3	3	140.6	21.3	2	96	19.2	–5.0	101
Greeley	22	0.9	8,839	47.1	22	9	25.2	28.6	7	301	19.4	–4.4	315
Hall.................	302	13.4	5,498	60.8	266	232	16.8	40.5	165	4,917	12.1	8.7	4,523
Hamilton	56	–19.0	5,895	54.6	69	24	16.9	18.2	20	667	12.1	3.1	647
Harlan	31	–4.8	8,627	52.8	33	10	22.4	27.7	8	310	17.0	–1.3	314
Hayes	14	3.6	12,371	21.0	13	3	22.2	49.1	2	107	15.0	13.8	94
Hitchcock............	35	28.8	11,547	46.8	27	11	34.0	10.5	10	348	21.2	–14.7	408
Holt.................	86	13.0	7,914	50.5	76	30	14.6	27.9	24	903	11.6	–4.7	948
Hooker...............	5	26.3	6,302	78.1	4	3	50.3	20.9	2	101	15.3	–3.8	105
Howard	42	10.9	6,198	59.0	38	22	30.6	34.4	17	635	19.9	–0.9	641
Jefferson	63	2.6	7,768	56.0	61	20	15.3	26.3	16	547	11.4	–2.3	560
Johnson...............	31	3.6	6,739	56.3	30	33	41.9	154.0	13	843	25.9	75.6	480
Kearney	52	3.4	7,598	57.2	51	18	17.9	19.7	15	522	14.4	–8.7	572
Keith	51	–9.6	6,094	62.9	57	22	17.3	10.0	20	586	10.9	–11.9	665
Keya Paha	6	22.3	6,327	49.9	5	2	19.1	12.8	2	79	12.4	–11.2	89
Kimball	31	–4.6	8,251	55.1	33	16	26.0	38.0	11	488	17.7	15.6	422
Knox.................	74	13.6	8,280	52.7	66	39	35.9	35.2	29	1,216	25.6	1.2	1,201
Lancaster............	1,919	49.1	7,339	47.8	1,287	1,652	22.2	36.5	1,210	33,804	16.9	8.0	31,310
Lincoln...............	209	10.6	5,967	66.5	189	138	17.7	30.2	106	2,999	13.4	4.0	2,884
Logan	7	9.1	9,673	49.8	6	2	25.8	18.3	2	73	15.5	–14.1	85
Loup.................	3	15.7	4,824	67.1	3	2	(NA)	42.3	1	64	17.7	10.3	58
McPherson	4	–19.6	7,389	56.4	5	1	40.2	32.4	1	40	13.7	–9.1	44
Madison...............	189	14.9	5,295	60.6	165	158	17.7	39.6	113	3,968	13.5	7.0	3,707
Merrick	53	4.9	6,575	59.6	51	20	20.7	16.4	17	614	15.9	–7.7	665
Morrill	34	4.7	6,412	59.4	32	19	28.8	33.3	14	525	19.3	–3.5	544
Nance	33	10.9	8,875	44.1	30	13	26.8	23.2	11	404	19.8	–8.6	442
Nemaha................	50	10.4	7,027	59.0	45	102	51.8	7.5	95	1,602	30.2	–4.9	1,685
Nuckolls..............	47	13.4	9,760	50.8	42	14	23.6	23.6	11	420	13.7	–7.5	454
Otoe.................	89	15.0	5,740	62.3	77	51	20.7	30.1	39	1,202	12.8	1.9	1,180
Pawnee	29	6.1	10,343	50.4	28	10	24.5	33.1	8	303	18.4	0.3	302
Perkins	35	–9.8	11,469	37.1	39	12	22.5	25.2	10	371	18.0	–9.7	411
Phelps	63	–8.7	6,528	58.8	69	32	14.5	25.5	25	852	12.8	0.2	850
Pierce	47	6.5	6,156	60.5	44	19	20.7	29.3	15	552	15.0	–0.5	555

See footnotes at end of table.

Table B-12. Counties — **Government Expenditure, Earnings, and Employment**—Con.

[Includes United States, states, and 3,141 counties/county equivalents defined as of February 22, 2005. For more information on these areas, see Appendix C, Geographic Information]

County	Federal government expenditure 2004					Federal, state, and local governments[1] Earnings 2005				Employment 2005			
	Total (mil. dol.)	Percent change, 2000–2004	Per capita (dol.)	Direct payments to individuals, percent of total	2000 (mil. dol.)	Total (mil. dol.)	Percent of total	Percent change, 2000–2005	2000 (mil. dol.)	Total	Percent of total	Percent change, 2000–2005	2000
NEBRASKA—Con.													
Platte	128	3.8	4,093	68.3	123	117	15.4	33.2	88	2,652	11.7	8.6	2,442
Polk	39	−4.3	7,215	52.5	41	17	23.1	37.6	12	515	17.1	−1.9	525
Red Willow	79	21.9	7,073	60.8	65	43	20.4	40.2	31	1,156	15.5	4.2	1,109
Richardson	70	8.9	7,881	62.4	64	23	20.1	22.7	19	651	14.0	−6.2	694
Rock	12	0.5	7,407	53.9	12	7	34.1	28.7	5	222	19.2	0.9	220
Saline	89	23.9	6,210	54.1	72	51	16.2	44.4	35	1,410	15.9	10.1	1,281
Sarpy	1,045	41.9	7,686	27.3	736	1,043	32.6	40.7	741	15,205	20.4	5.1	14,463
Saunders	102	8.8	5,037	63.5	94	49	21.3	29.8	38	1,385	17.2	−0.6	1,393
Scotts Bluff	235	24.0	6,413	63.0	190	134	17.9	22.6	109	3,301	14.0	3.5	3,188
Seward	80	5.2	4,786	61.5	76	47	17.6	30.1	36	1,138	12.2	4.9	1,085
Sheridan	43	16.1	7,317	59.7	37	23	39.1	15.9	19	735	21.8	−8.7	805
Sherman	32	9.6	10,055	44.3	29	10	28.2	27.7	7	311	17.8	−1.3	315
Sioux	6	19.7	3,922	41.9	5	3	64.6	33.9	2	104	13.9	−3.7	108
Stanton	23	−3.7	3,552	48.7	24	11	11.4	29.6	9	340	13.4	−5.3	359
Thayer	46	−9.6	8,290	57.8	50	22	20.7	22.2	18	661	17.4	−7.9	718
Thomas	6	15.8	9,782	43.5	5	3	48.5	35.1	2	126	23.6	15.6	109
Thurston	83	4.5	11,593	28.8	79	57	47.1	45.1	40	1,438	41.8	8.7	1,323
Valley	37	3.6	8,122	53.5	35	23	34.3	21.9	19	668	23.9	−5.9	710
Washington	79	12.3	4,044	66.6	71	102	25.0	37.7	74	1,639	15.0	0.2	1,635
Wayne	47	11.4	5,082	56.1	42	48	26.0	29.7	37	1,263	20.2	12.2	1,126
Webster	36	6.0	9,203	53.4	34	11	19.0	29.5	8	345	17.8	–	345
Wheeler	7	−42.2	8,328	39.5	12	2	11.6	23.5	2	71	10.3	−6.6	76
York	86	−2.5	6,046	60.8	88	50	12.5	25.6	40	1,186	10.1	0.3	1,182
NEVADA	[3]12,769	[3]47.9	[3]5,469	[3]57.5	[3]8,633	9,588	14.2	46.2	6,559	155,942	10.2	19.4	130,585
Churchill	276	39.2	11,319	37.7	198	193	33.5	27.3	152	3,137	15.8	−0.7	3,160
Clark	8,002	50.7	4,848	58.0	5,311	6,238	12.8	53.1	4,075	98,404	9.2	24.4	79,105
Douglas	188	51.1	4,134	78.8	124	123	11.5	40.0	88	2,379	7.5	8.8	2,186
Elko	160	42.8	3,600	49.9	112	195	21.1	20.5	162	3,774	15.4	−0.6	3,797
Esmeralda	15	9.0	18,107	80.7	14	3	29.5	13.4	3	97	19.8	−4.9	102
Eureka	9	82.7	6,706	47.1	5	8	2.6	−2.2	9	184	4.3	−19.7	229
Humboldt	71	11.2	4,176	55.5	63	74	17.9	18.5	63	1,388	13.7	−4.5	1,453
Lander	28	23.0	5,545	46.0	23	28	22.8	12.3	25	534	19.4	−6.8	573
Lincoln	30	41.5	6,893	61.4	21	29	45.3	22.7	24	614	30.3	2.0	602
Lyon	196	54.6	4,536	78.5	127	98	17.6	53.8	64	2,121	12.5	25.1	1,696
Mineral	96	36.6	19,591	31.9	70	30	34.9	19.9	25	605	25.0	−4.3	632
Nye	218	46.1	5,789	85.8	149	98	14.2	29.4	76	1,879	11.1	8.3	1,735
Pershing	30	−3.1	4,643	40.8	31	39	41.4	35.1	29	763	30.7	7.6	709
Storey	31	343.3	8,381	18.3	7	10	16.4	46.8	7	201	10.8	4.1	193
Washoe	1,869	39.6	4,908	58.9	1,338	1,703	14.6	38.6	1,229	27,827	10.3	20.8	23,042
White Pine	68	49.8	7,953	47.5	45	84	45.1	30.6	64	1,509	30.7	8.6	1,389
Independent City													
Carson City	671	37.1	11,991	35.8	490	635	35.5	35.8	467	10,526	24.9	5.4	9,982
NEW HAMPSHIRE	[3]7,959	[3]37.1	[3]6,124	[3]53.9	[3]5,805	4,439	12.1	39.8	3,175	92,470	11.1	6.7	86,664
Belknap	332	25.4	5,463	72.9	265	188	12.9	55.5	121	4,309	10.8	19.3	3,613
Carroll	255	33.4	5,451	75.4	191	118	12.5	42.5	83	2,920	9.2	10.7	2,637
Cheshire	377	28.0	4,901	68.4	294	226	12.8	40.0	161	5,746	11.9	8.2	5,312
Coos	243	22.5	7,248	67.1	198	116	18.3	39.7	83	2,993	15.3	7.7	2,778
Grafton	603	32.2	7,166	48.8	456	320	10.2	39.5	229	7,259	10.3	5.2	6,903
Hillsborough	2,482	40.3	6,228	45.6	1,769	1,267	9.8	40.6	901	22,958	8.9	11.4	20,614
Merrimack	1,027	32.7	7,053	43.6	774	800	20.2	34.2	596	16,738	17.6	3.9	16,105
Rockingham	1,401	39.4	4,791	58.9	1,005	752	8.6	42.0	530	15,307	8.0	7.9	14,186
Strafford	615	31.7	5,201	62.5	467	548	23.2	39.6	392	11,570	19.6	−1.8	11,777
Sullivan	255	38.7	6,011	72.8	184	105	13.4	32.9	79	2,670	12.4	−2.5	2,739
NEW JERSEY	[3]55,264	[3]26.6	[3]6,353	[3]59.3	[3]43,654	40,926	14.7	32.5	30,880	655,757	13.1	8.6	604,043
Atlantic	1,783	31.0	6,636	55.2	1,362	1,448	17.8	38.2	1,048	23,403	12.7	14.3	20,473
Bergen	4,562	23.4	5,052	70.5	3,698	3,005	8.5	32.2	2,274	49,132	8.2	9.6	44,827
Burlington	3,733	27.2	8,301	42.7	2,934	2,301	17.8	38.5	1,662	37,346	14.1	9.2	34,210
Camden	2,993	21.0	5,798	64.0	2,473	2,280	17.8	27.7	1,786	37,920	14.1	3.1	36,764
Cape May	730	23.9	7,247	74.1	589	548	26.1	36.5	401	10,961	17.3	8.0	10,148
Cumberland	915	24.0	6,053	61.4	738	861	26.7	33.3	646	15,306	19.9	8.2	14,152
Essex	5,727	18.2	7,189	48.2	4,845	5,631	19.8	34.0	4,201	82,520	17.9	8.7	75,896
Gloucester	1,155	24.6	4,248	73.8	927	972	17.2	43.1	679	18,797	14.5	17.4	16,005
Hudson	3,500	16.0	5,773	48.2	3,016	2,972	15.8	31.7	2,256	45,674	15.2	8.1	42,260
Hunterdon	440	32.0	3,392	77.7	333	560	13.5	44.2	388	9,904	13.0	20.5	8,222
Mercer	4,072	29.1	11,148	36.7	3,154	3,649	23.4	29.4	2,820	53,587	20.2	5.3	50,894
Middlesex	3,635	24.6	4,631	63.3	2,917	3,758	12.9	30.0	2,890	62,028	12.7	9.3	56,749
Monmouth	4,299	21.6	6,756	52.0	3,534	2,901	17.3	27.0	2,284	43,892	12.6	1.8	43,127
Morris	2,112	25.0	4,327	66.8	1,690	2,119	8.1	32.5	1,600	32,061	8.5	8.3	29,617
Ocean	3,375	25.4	6,100	82.6	2,691	1,663	20.6	33.2	1,248	28,748	13.6	9.2	26,329

See footnotes at end of table.

Table B-12. Counties — **Government Expenditure, Earnings, and Employment**—Con.

[Includes United States, states, and 3,141 counties/county equivalents defined as of February 22, 2005. For more information on these areas, see Appendix C, Geographic Information]

County	Federal government expenditure					Federal, state, and local governments[1]							
						Earnings				Employment			
	2004					2005				2005			
	Total (mil. dol.)	Percent change, 2000–2004	Per capita (dol.)	Direct payments to individuals, percent of total	2000 (mil. dol.)	Total (mil. dol.)	Percent of total	Percent change, 2000–2005	2000 (mil. dol.)	Total	Percent of total	Percent change, 2000–2005	2000
NEW JERSEY—Con.													
Passaic	2,704	27.3	5,404	56.3	2,124	1,898	16.8	33.5	1,422	31,583	13.8	11.6	28,301
Salem	361	23.3	5,531	72.9	293	240	17.1	35.3	178	4,775	15.8	10.7	4,315
Somerset	1,139	21.5	3,595	69.5	937	1,121	7.0	34.5	833	17,862	8.2	8.6	16,448
Sussex	519	13.9	3,410	78.1	456	465	19.5	32.4	351	8,239	12.9	10.3	7,468
Union	2,746	25.0	5,162	67.4	2,197	2,200	12.4	32.4	1,662	35,806	12.3	12.0	31,979
Warren	527	32.1	4,790	73.1	399	334	14.6	33.2	251	6,213	12.3	6.0	5,859
NEW MEXICO	[3]19,864	[3]37.1	[3]10,437	[3]34.3	[3]14,484	11,381	28.6	39.7	8,144	219,567	20.6	8.5	202,390
Bernalillo	7,309	42.7	12,310	29.3	5,122	3,983	23.4	39.2	2,862	69,560	16.6	6.6	65,226
Catron	28	20.9	7,999	60.4	23	16	62.9	22.1	13	330	20.5	-7.6	357
Chaves	376	25.5	6,094	58.2	299	208	19.8	25.1	166	4,853	16.7	-1.4	4,922
Cibola	137	23.6	4,986	40.6	111	160	51.0	70.8	93	4,133	39.3	30.1	3,177
Colfax	98	47.6	7,102	61.4	67	68	31.8	31.4	52	1,669	19.8	5.0	1,590
Curry	458	21.4	10,034	36.9	377	394	42.1	37.5	286	6,859	27.7	1.7	6,747
De Baca	19	23.6	9,171	60.4	15	7	31.9	-0.2	7	221	19.8	-10.2	246
Dona Ana	1,389	38.6	7,462	41.1	1,002	1,042	36.0	41.9	734	21,414	24.5	12.2	19,087
Eddy	497	39.6	9,611	39.6	356	194	16.6	40.6	138	3,758	13.9	3.1	3,646
Grant	211	38.9	7,158	65.4	152	144	36.8	27.8	113	3,930	27.5	9.9	3,576
Guadalupe	51	20.9	11,354	31.4	43	16	38.8	22.6	13	446	20.8	8.3	412
Harding	9	68.9	11,163	45.0	5	4	44.5	14.4	3	112	14.4	-3.4	116
Hidalgo	38	20.7	7,385	63.4	32	25	39.8	30.7	19	546	22.1	-1.3	553
Lea	282	27.4	5,015	65.5	221	147	11.9	24.3	118	3,653	11.1	-2.3	3,738
Lincoln	121	47.0	5,846	66.5	82	59	22.6	26.4	47	1,389	12.0	3.6	1,341
Los Alamos	1,990	19.3	105,868	2.2	1,668	1,135	72.4	55.1	732	11,907	54.4	17.6	10,126
Luna	161	30.7	6,164	64.0	123	91	28.9	42.8	64	1,969	18.1	11.1	1,772
McKinley	602	30.7	8,318	29.8	461	397	44.8	36.6	290	7,819	26.7	10.1	7,102
Mora	52	36.1	9,993	38.1	38	15	48.9	26.3	12	388	18.9	-2.8	399
Otero	651	37.5	10,292	37.9	474	591	59.0	32.7	445	11,042	37.6	6.2	10,402
Quay	85	22.4	8,987	54.1	70	38	32.1	9.0	35	1,001	20.7	-13.4	1,156
Rio Arriba	316	49.1	7,773	39.9	212	203	44.1	40.9	144	5,495	29.3	18.0	4,657
Roosevelt	127	29.5	7,012	55.3	98	90	29.2	53.1	59	2,353	24.9	14.2	2,061
Sandoval	428	46.4	4,187	63.0	292	285	19.9	65.3	172	6,889	18.8	31.0	5,258
San Juan	614	31.6	4,949	49.9	467	499	20.0	30.2	383	11,650	18.6	4.8	11,114
San Miguel	273	47.8	9,240	39.8	184	170	52.3	27.6	133	4,427	32.9	0.1	4,421
Santa Fe	1,181	34.2	8,512	35.7	880	896	25.2	38.6	647	19,096	21.5	8.4	17,624
Sierra	118	31.7	9,129	67.9	90	40	35.9	27.0	31	944	19.7	-1.7	960
Socorro	172	68.4	9,473	31.9	102	126	50.6	68.0	75	3,124	36.9	32.7	2,355
Taos	214	51.7	6,789	47.3	141	99	19.0	35.7	73	2,359	12.9	4.8	2,251
Torrance	80	3.0	4,739	58.5	78	50	34.0	21.2	41	1,274	22.0	8.5	1,174
Union	36	-3.8	9,300	50.8	37	15	17.8	23.6	12	390	14.2	-3.7	405
Valencia	324	36.3	4,711	72.1	238	178	31.2	34.4	133	4,567	20.6	3.3	4,419
NEW YORK	[3]143,903	[3]30.3	[3]7,484	[3]51.1	[3]110,459	91,727	14.5	24.8	73,526	1,499,714	13.9	1.1	1,483,872
Albany	5,020	-4.8	16,820	32.1	5,275	4,201	30.9	15.0	3,653	68,901	24.8	-3.1	71,115
Allegany	265	21.6	5,232	67.8	218	187	30.4	22.1	153	4,256	20.1	4.6	4,068
Bronx	(5)	(NA)	(5)	(NA)	(5)	1,737	13.5	7.7	1,613	25,181	7.7	-13.1	28,976
Broome	1,279	21.4	6,472	62.9	1,054	947	21.9	19.6	792	20,634	17.5	5.3	19,595
Cattaraugus	608	45.8	7,307	59.4	417	444	30.8	45.2	306	10,179	24.0	17.3	8,677
Cayuga	433	21.5	5,289	65.0	357	337	26.5	34.5	251	6,234	16.7	3.4	6,029
Chautauqua	845	23.0	6,155	64.9	687	472	20.8	17.3	402	10,217	14.1	-4.1	10,658
Chemung	556	20.3	6,180	65.5	462	385	22.1	22.7	314	7,073	14.5	-9.1	7,784
Chenango	276	26.4	5,324	65.9	218	178	23.4	24.7	143	4,326	18.1	3.9	4,163
Clinton	468	34.8	5,722	58.8	348	456	28.0	20.5	378	8,145	18.4	-1.9	8,299
Columbia	377	23.5	5,922	63.4	305	224	22.4	21.4	184	4,911	15.0	5.0	4,679
Cortland	231	25.6	4,724	64.3	184	195	24.6	16.2	168	3,890	15.4	0.5	3,870
Delaware	336	(Z)	7,094	56.1	336	191	22.2	11.8	171	4,829	17.0	3.9	4,648
Dutchess	1,391	28.2	4,740	66.7	1,085	1,316	19.2	33.1	989	23,254	15.1	2.7	22,633
Erie	6,464	20.2	6,903	59.6	5,376	4,329	18.3	22.4	3,538	77,833	13.9	1.2	76,890
Essex	276	28.0	7,106	57.4	216	230	34.4	27.7	180	4,760	21.6	5.4	4,517
Franklin	303	31.4	5,940	56.8	231	400	50.5	34.9	297	8,308	35.2	12.5	7,385
Fulton	283	27.0	5,110	69.1	223	196	23.6	17.2	167	4,197	15.3	-6.3	4,477
Genesee	352	29.8	5,903	63.7	272	290	29.0	37.4	211	6,046	19.5	9.0	5,546
Greene	271	31.9	5,517	68.7	206	257	38.6	46.1	176	4,243	21.4	1.7	4,174
Hamilton	33	12.4	6,231	79.8	29	29	43.1	30.8	22	759	25.8	11.6	680
Herkimer	347	20.7	5,434	71.4	288	195	27.0	21.6	160	4,775	18.6	-5.4	5,045
Jefferson	1,405	50.0	12,603	25.7	936	1,710	59.0	68.7	1,014	25,808	38.3	14.3	22,583
Kings	[5]63,703	[5]34.9	[5]25,735	[5]43.2	[5]47,237	2,614	10.3	16.3	2,247	39,385	5.7	-0.2	39,462
Lewis	139	34.2	5,247	60.9	104	99	31.6	22.8	80	2,426	21.8	4.7	2,317
Livingston	281	26.7	4,340	70.9	222	351	39.0	20.4	291	7,427	24.8	4.3	7,120
Madison	323	32.5	4,594	68.4	244	202	21.2	20.7	167	4,634	14.8	4.4	4,438
Monroe	4,444	27.2	6,045	58.4	3,495	2,780	12.4	46.2	1,902	52,168	19.8	7.3	48,626
Montgomery	320	20.7	6,484	72.4	265	145	18.6	31.1	110	3,359	14.2	2.5	3,276
Nassau	8,049	21.4	6,008	68.3	6,631	6,186	14.7	32.7	4,661	86,755	10.9	2.9	84,307

See footnotes at end of table.

Table B-12. Counties — **Government Expenditure, Earnings, and Employment**—Con.

[Includes United States, states, and 3,141 counties/county equivalents defined as of February 22, 2005. For more information on these areas, see Appendix C, Geographic Information]

County	Federal government expenditure 2004 Total (mil. dol.)	Percent change, 2000-2004	Per capita (dol.)	Direct payments to individuals, percent of total	2000 (mil. dol.)	Federal, state, and local governments[1] Earnings 2005 Total (mil. dol.)	Percent of total	Percent change, 2000-2005	2000 (mil. dol.)	Employment 2005 Total	Percent of total	Percent change, 2000-2005	2000
NEW YORK—Con.													
New York	(5)	(NA)	(5)	(NA)	(5)	30,247	10.8	20.7	25,061	456,422	16.9	-2.2	466,460
Niagara	1,300	18.6	5,963	68.5	1,097	794	22.6	30.5	609	15,478	16.7	13.2	13,677
Oneida	1,689	20.1	7,189	60.3	1,407	1,395	28.5	37.5	1,014	27,250	20.1	16.8	23,338
Onondaga	3,141	24.7	6,831	52.5	2,520	2,197	16.4	33.7	1,643	40,976	13.4	0.3	40,836
Ontario	580	33.7	5,602	63.4	434	407	17.9	12.6	361	8,295	12.5	-2.3	8,493
Orange	1,913	17.1	5,166	55.7	1,634	2,042	29.5	42.4	1,433	33,832	19.2	5.2	32,163
Orleans	218	35.0	4,929	63.8	161	256	45.9	39.8	183	4,396	28.0	-3.0	4,532
Oswego	590	25.8	4,769	68.0	469	423	26.3	-0.7	426	9,760	21.4	-1.0	9,855
Otsego	348	27.7	5,562	65.1	272	199	19.8	11.0	179	4,987	16.0	-1.6	5,069
Putnam	344	30.5	3,417	78.0	263	313	21.3	71.7	182	4,693	12.1	10.0	4,267
Queens	(5)	(NA)	(5)	(NA)	(5)	2,869	9.9	34.0	2,141	39,741	5.7	4.2	38,137
Rensselaer	2,425	158.0	15,741	23.2	940	597	22.8	19.6	499	11,575	16.9	3.4	11,196
Richmond	(5)	(NA)	(5)	(NA)	(5)	539	10.8	24.3	434	7,979	6.1	0.6	7,932
Rockland	1,526	30.3	5,196	63.9	1,171	1,271	17.0	21.8	1,043	21,336	14.3	5.2	20,287
St. Lawrence	659	25.9	5,923	60.8	524	561	33.2	13.5	494	10,999	21.9	-2.1	11,233
Saratoga	844	28.7	3,969	72.8	656	711	18.8	22.5	581	14,118	13.3	3.9	13,592
Schenectady	2,353	48.3	15,892	26.6	1,586	567	14.7	30.9	434	11,234	14.8	8.1	10,388
Schoharie	177	33.6	5,522	63.0	132	143	35.8	13.8	126	2,935	22.8	2.6	2,862
Schuyler	101	27.7	5,191	64.4	79	60	27.3	36.3	44	1,198	13.1	4.0	1,152
Seneca	180	24.8	5,132	68.1	144	124	25.1	28.3	97	2,706	17.0	5.0	2,576
Steuben	644	34.7	6,515	61.2	478	395	16.7	21.5	325	8,469	17.3	3.1	8,214
Suffolk	8,649	27.8	5,862	57.6	6,767	6,997	18.5	23.7	5,655	106,129	13.4	2.5	103,572
Sullivan	520	26.5	6,830	59.2	411	386	32.0	44.3	267	6,407	17.9	0.4	6,383
Tioga	716	16.4	13,900	21.7	615	119	15.2	20.0	99	2,826	14.9	–	2,826
Tompkins	665	29.5	6,637	37.5	513	314	12.4	23.6	254	6,616	9.8	0.6	6,577
Ulster	918	30.1	5,048	65.2	705	723	25.8	17.4	616	14,815	17.1	2.7	14,427
Warren	356	25.8	5,469	69.4	283	238	14.6	34.4	177	4,981	10.8	2.7	4,851
Washington	310	29.5	4,935	67.7	239	286	37.3	28.7	222	5,503	25.1	2.1	5,390
Wayne	548	48.6	5,836	58.1	369	299	24.3	6.8	280	6,841	18.6	-8.1	7,440
Westchester	5,331	21.1	5,657	65.8	4,404	4,677	13.4	27.1	3,679	66,371	11.8	3.1	64,401
Wyoming	229	53.0	5,328	56.9	150	235	33.9	27.4	184	4,597	25.1	2.8	4,471
Yates	131	22.0	5,324	72.9	108	62	23.9	42.2	44	1,336	14.4	7.9	1,238
NORTH CAROLINA	[3]55,233	[3]33.4	[3]6,467	[3]55.3	[3]41,414	40,012	19.4	35.9	29,436	803,802	15.7	8.6	740,400
Alamance	639	32.9	4,618	73.3	481	284	10.8	27.1	223	7,232	9.1	7.1	6,754
Alexander	127	38.4	3,652	78.3	92	71	15.4	54.2	46	1,903	12.1	27.8	1,489
Alleghany	74	28.5	6,821	64.4	58	27	19.1	34.9	20	748	12.3	15.6	647
Anson	162	23.7	6,467	62.5	131	102	29.1	33.7	76	2,798	25.4	14.3	2,448
Ashe	170	39.9	6,735	59.0	121	50	14.1	31.6	38	1,377	9.7	11.8	1,232
Avery	105	30.8	5,902	71.4	80	52	17.9	34.3	38	1,470	11.8	16.8	1,259
Beaufort	305	20.5	6,657	66.0	253	123	17.4	16.0	106	3,218	13.6	0.9	3,189
Bertie	255	82.9	13,074	35.2	140	43	16.8	1.6	42	1,120	11.9	-13.6	1,297
Bladen	218	22.4	6,609	60.9	178	100	18.6	22.2	82	2,559	14.2	1.3	2,526
Brunswick	520	35.9	6,145	73.3	382	207	16.7	38.8	149	4,809	11.9	11.3	4,319
Buncombe	1,357	31.9	6,294	63.2	1,029	808	16.2	25.2	645	16,430	11.1	3.8	15,830
Burke	437	40.8	4,889	66.0	311	334	21.2	14.9	290	8,561	16.6	1.8	8,407
Cabarrus	606	34.6	4,149	76.3	450	533	17.3	42.9	373	11,960	14.2	16.0	10,308
Caldwell	343	31.8	4,344	77.0	260	166	12.3	22.0	136	4,642	11.8	5.5	4,402
Camden	53	28.4	6,288	68.7	41	18	20.6	32.9	14	471	14.7	11.6	422
Carteret	443	34.7	7,144	69.0	329	222	24.4	26.6	175	5,155	14.5	6.7	4,832
Caswell	124	39.1	5,245	62.1	89	59	48.6	12.7	52	1,528	25.5	-4.7	1,603
Catawba	609	34.5	4,072	74.9	452	434	11.3	24.2	350	10,040	9.8	3.3	9,721
Chatham	204	23.2	3,586	75.4	166	104	12.5	36.3	77	2,541	6.8	10.6	2,297
Cherokee	177	29.5	6,995	68.2	137	66	19.1	28.1	52	1,630	12.1	8.5	1,502
Chowan	105	32.6	7,253	64.8	79	39	16.2	14.9	34	963	11.9	-4.8	1,012
Clay	63	35.4	6,699	72.9	47	20	24.7	36.6	15	525	14.5	7.8	487
Cleveland	517	27.6	5,265	70.4	405	233	15.5	26.0	185	6,257	14.0	10.1	5,684
Columbus	415	29.9	7,590	61.7	320	145	18.8	18.6	123	3,840	15.2	1.2	3,796
Craven	1,273	34.3	13,901	35.4	948	1,347	53.1	29.2	1,042	22,035	35.9	-2.0	22,479
Cumberland	4,489	34.0	14,551	27.4	3,350	5,785	63.2	57.2	3,680	80,769	41.6	6.4	75,936
Currituck	135	80.6	6,116	60.5	75	49	22.7	36.6	36	1,202	13.9	14.9	1,046
Dare	220	51.0	6,552	55.8	145	140	16.6	40.9	100	3,036	10.2	9.9	2,763
Davidson	567	27.2	3,686	76.1	446	281	14.2	17.1	240	7,110	9.8	0.8	7,057
Davie	160	36.9	4,220	76.9	117	66	14.2	22.5	54	1,541	9.4	-0.8	1,554
Duplin	293	29.8	5,665	61.5	226	152	18.5	40.3	108	3,986	15.0	12.8	3,535
Durham	2,279	37.8	9,506	29.3	1,654	1,138	9.3	31.6	864	18,745	8.9	3.9	18,045
Edgecombe	362	5.3	6,616	55.0	344	216	20.4	15.6	187	5,056	17.8	-1.1	5,110
Forsyth	1,691	36.8	5,270	65.1	1,236	857	8.7	23.6	694	19,389	8.6	5.2	18,432
Franklin	223	36.8	4,163	66.0	163	103	17.5	28.2	80	2,507	12.5	5.1	2,386

See footnotes at end of table.

[Includes United States, states, and 3,141 counties/county equivalents defined as of February 22, 2005. For more information on these areas, see Appendix C, Geographic Information]

	Federal government expenditure					Federal, state, and local governments[1]							
	2004					Earnings				Employment			
						2005				2005			
County	Total (mil. dol.)	Percent change, 2000–2004	Per capita (dol.)	Direct payments to individuals, percent of total	2000 (mil. dol.)	Total (mil. dol.)	Percent of total	Percent change, 2000–2005	2000 (mil. dol.)	Total	Percent of total	Percent change, 2000–2005	2000
NORTH CAROLINA—Con.													
Gaston	876	27.1	4,504	76.6	689	413	12.0	14.8	360	9,526	9.9	−5.9	10,127
Gates	67	28.7	6,136	65.8	52	25	30.3	9.3	23	665	25.4	−2.6	683
Graham	56	42.3	6,973	62.1	40	20	19.2	10.3	19	520	12.9	−14.2	606
Granville	308	38.6	5,826	48.9	222	370	41.1	26.8	292	7,668	31.4	4.0	7,376
Greene	92	30.6	4,562	59.0	71	60	31.1	26.2	48	1,558	17.2	9.6	1,422
Guilford	2,378	25.6	5,420	59.2	1,894	1,633	11.3	28.2	1,273	32,827	9.8	3.5	31,717
Halifax	446	26.9	7,959	60.2	351	205	28.9	14.0	180	5,176	22.2	−3.9	5,388
Harnett	470	51.8	4,629	58.8	310	213	20.4	23.7	172	5,122	13.1	1.9	5,026
Haywood	393	44.3	6,985	65.1	272	163	21.6	25.4	130	4,125	15.7	6.6	3,869
Henderson	563	29.6	5,906	81.2	435	235	14.4	28.6	182	5,571	11.5	5.5	5,283
Hertford	163	30.0	6,907	62.3	125	86	19.4	16.5	59	1,837	15.2	−1.4	1,863
Hoke	143	43.4	3,638	63.0	100	89	28.8	20.4	74	2,379	19.0	4.6	2,275
Hyde	54	11.9	9,771	41.6	48	30	36.2	17.1	26	793	24.4	−3.3	820
Iredell	532	35.8	3,889	78.8	392	366	13.3	36.2	269	8,811	11.3	17.9	7,476
Jackson	168	33.3	4,804	70.0	126	236	36.9	34.3	176	6,193	28.3	10.6	5,600
Johnston	553	30.6	3,904	65.5	423	335	17.4	43.5	234	8,222	12.8	23.0	6,684
Jones	78	24.8	7,451	62.5	62	22	20.8	22.7	18	619	19.2	7.3	577
Lee	287	34.8	5,834	74.6	213	137	9.9	25.9	109	3,447	9.8	9.8	3,140
Lenoir	454	22.9	7,771	62.1	369	278	24.0	15.6	240	6,843	19.2	−1.6	6,956
Lincoln	249	29.2	3,659	78.8	192	152	18.4	33.1	114	3,763	14.9	11.3	3,380
McDowell	207	31.1	4,771	73.0	158	102	15.2	22.4	84	2,916	13.9	7.3	2,717
Macon	212	32.5	6,763	71.8	160	71	15.3	24.0	57	1,730	9.9	2.5	1,688
Madison	135	5.6	6,772	56.3	128	37	22.8	18.6	31	1,045	12.9	2.2	1,023
Martin	180	22.6	7,270	62.6	147	69	17.7	15.1	60	1,956	15.6	1.8	1,921
Mecklenburg	3,227	25.6	4,183	54.0	2,570	3,345	9.0	39.6	2,396	62,321	9.7	14.2	54,595
Mitchell	119	42.8	7,488	57.5	83	49	21.5	30.5	37	1,465	18.2	10.6	1,325
Montgomery	171	53.3	6,229	55.0	112	76	16.7	25.6	60	1,916	13.8	5.4	1,817
Moore	529	36.5	6,610	80.2	388	184	12.3	25.2	147	4,690	10.9	3.2	4,543
Nash	486	28.4	5,355	68.7	378	266	13.9	22.2	217	6,592	13.1	7.7	6,118
New Hanover	1,055	40.3	6,081	61.7	752	876	19.0	38.8	631	18,489	14.9	16.9	15,820
Northampton	185	31.9	8,547	55.4	140	61	21.6	18.4	51	1,585	19.1	−0.7	1,596
Onslow	2,395	50.4	15,520	21.6	1,593	3,289	77.4	57.8	2,084	55,741	56.7	14.4	48,744
Orange	834	38.7	7,096	36.0	601	1,730	54.4	35.6	1,276	33,231	43.8	16.1	28,629
Pamlico	98	41.7	7,673	62.7	69	35	32.3	29.8	27	959	20.9	6.3	902
Pasquotank	358	54.7	9,718	45.4	231	320	43.5	34.2	238	6,690	30.0	7.8	6,204
Pender	216	21.1	4,779	74.2	178	104	24.4	27.3	82	2,600	16.9	5.4	2,467
Perquimans	88	30.2	7,497	70.2	68	29	26.7	28.5	22	765	19.2	7.0	715
Person	177	31.9	4,803	63.8	134	88	18.0	21.7	73	2,398	15.6	5.4	2,275
Pitt	689	28.8	4,904	61.7	535	1,051	35.4	37.3	766	21,424	25.3	16.3	18,420
Polk	114	30.0	5,985	80.6	88	35	17.0	27.0	28	899	11.7	4.7	859
Randolph	469	33.4	3,441	76.7	351	262	12.6	27.7	205	6,882	10.9	8.0	6,370
Richmond	300	27.2	6,423	69.8	236	125	19.7	17.1	107	3,437	17.7	1.5	3,385
Robeson	764	31.6	6,041	58.8	580	361	24.5	27.9	283	9,119	18.0	6.9	8,529
Rockingham	507	30.1	5,481	71.4	390	195	15.1	18.5	164	4,936	11.9	0.7	4,900
Rowan	683	30.7	5,088	67.2	523	452	19.3	35.7	333	8,719	15.1	9.1	7,989
Rutherford	335	32.9	5,273	70.8	252	138	14.6	18.9	116	3,707	12.4	−0.4	3,723
Sampson	348	33.5	5,580	57.9	261	174	18.8	31.1	133	4,326	17.9	5.9	4,084
Scotland	224	33.1	6,191	58.8	169	97	16.2	34.2	73	2,523	13.1	17.0	2,157
Stanly	278	32.6	4,724	75.6	210	150	17.6	28.1	117	3,791	14.2	8.3	3,501
Stokes	170	39.1	3,750	75.0	122	76	24.8	17.7	65	2,059	15.2	6.6	1,932
Surry	385	24.7	5,324	73.1	309	201	15.8	24.4	161	5,289	12.4	7.2	4,934
Swain	120	32.6	9,092	48.9	90	100	44.8	57.8	63	2,395	32.2	31.3	1,824
Transylvania	193	36.3	6,530	78.8	141	60	16.0	17.3	51	1,460	10.4	−2.7	1,500
Tyrrell	30	14.9	7,246	51.3	26	17	39.5	29.6	13	467	27.1	9.4	427
Union	393	37.7	2,559	72.2	286	366	14.9	59.7	229	8,985	13.1	33.8	6,713
Vance	278	34.4	6,361	60.8	207	128	21.7	11.3	115	3,342	17.1	−8.7	3,661
Wake	4,628	18.5	6,432	36.3	3,906	4,206	17.9	35.9	3,096	83,202	16.4	15.7	71,941
Warren	126	20.7	6,321	59.1	104	54	34.4	16.3	47	1,472	25.5	−0.5	1,480
Washington	95	22.4	7,117	62.8	78	47	38.5	16.5	40	1,223	24.0	−5.6	1,296
Watauga	164	15.1	3,860	71.8	142	248	27.8	28.9	192	5,812	19.1	8.8	5,342
Wayne	1,026	34.5	8,983	45.1	763	742	36.3	26.1	589	14,254	24.2	−1.2	14,434
Wilkes	334	36.5	4,984	67.4	245	189	13.6	25.4	150	4,889	14.1	3.3	4,731
Wilson	436	24.4	5,723	63.4	350	286	15.7	29.7	220	6,622	14.4	3.5	6,399
Yadkin	171	33.2	4,584	72.1	128	64	16.5	17.2	54	1,676	11.2	−4.1	1,748
Yancey	112	35.7	6,162	64.3	82	35	21.1	16.6	30	985	13.7	3.9	948
NORTH DAKOTA	[3]6,035	[3]15.0	[3]9,513	[3]38.1	[3]5,246	3,583	22.0	37.6	2,605	80,693	17.1	5.1	76,779
Adams	30	13.9	12,223	39.6	26	6	14.7	22.8	5	187	10.2	−8.3	204
Barnes	109	−12.7	9,754	43.7	124	40	18.9	26.2	32	1,111	14.1	−5.8	1,179
Benson	126	42.7	18,025	19.9	88	63	63.0	41.1	45	1,742	47.2	13.6	1,534
Billings	7	14.6	7,902	23.0	6	6	28.2	56.4	4	140	17.0	8.5	129
Bottineau	78	−3.2	11,463	40.8	81	24	18.2	33.5	18	619	13.3	−4.2	646

See footnotes at end of table.

[Includes United States, states, and 3,141 counties/county equivalents defined as of February 22, 2005. For more information on these areas, see Appendix C, Geographic Information]

County	Federal government expenditure 2004 — Total (mil. dol.)	Percent change, 2000–2004	Per capita (dol.)	Direct payments to individuals, percent of total	2000 (mil. dol.)	Federal, state, and local governments[1] — Earnings 2005 — Total (mil. dol.)	Percent of total	Percent change, 2000–2005	2000 (mil. dol.)	Employment 2005 — Total	Percent of total	Percent change, 2000–2005	2000
NORTH DAKOTA—Con.													
Bowman	27	−18.8	8,658	52.5	33	9	12.7	31.1	7	274	11.1	−5.8	291
Burke	45	42.7	21,792	26.6	32	13	28.5	67.8	8	268	15.8	6.3	252
Burleigh	694	20.9	9,560	35.4	574	474	21.7	37.9	344	10,441	16.9	10.5	9,446
Cass	734	28.9	5,711	42.6	570	599	13.5	44.2	416	12,598	11.1	9.1	11,544
Cavalier	71	−19.8	16,155	29.3	88	12	14.2	22.1	10	332	10.0	−14.4	388
Dickey	57	−5.7	10,374	41.9	60	12	8.1	25.0	9	362	9.3	−5.5	383
Divide	50	57.1	22,821	22.1	32	7	19.6	37.0	5	182	10.4	0.6	181
Dunn	27	6.5	7,821	38.7	25	10	17.2	27.4	8	283	14.4	−5.4	299
Eddy	25	−5.6	9,750	52.1	27	8	19.2	31.9	6	228	14.9	1.3	225
Emmons	50	20.5	12,701	36.3	41	10	14.6	16.2	9	262	10.2	−14.9	308
Foster	49	2.1	14,078	31.7	48	11	13.8	30.8	8	283	11.1	−4.1	295
Golden Valley	17	−8.8	9,486	51.9	18	6	22.3	26.5	5	199	15.7	2.1	195
Grand Forks	608	25.4	9,364	27.2	485	648	36.4	40.1	463	13,347	25.9	7.8	12,385
Grant	34	16.5	12,917	39.2	29	7	19.5	24.2	5	201	10.9	−11.5	227
Griggs	29	−20.2	11,347	44.0	36	7	15.3	28.1	6	234	11.7	14.7	204
Hettinger	41	−2.0	16,120	33.7	42	8	17.7	15.9	7	209	11.9	−14.0	243
Kidder	30	12.6	11,839	38.2	27	7	16.0	26.2	6	217	11.9	−0.9	219
LaMoure	59	−0.5	13,051	35.6	59	14	12.5	36.3	10	372	13.7	−0.8	375
Logan	28	19.8	13,140	36.2	23	5	12.1	21.4	4	161	10.5	−10.6	180
McHenry	57	−6.2	10,111	49.7	61	17	24.9	32.2	13	485	16.8	−6.2	517
McIntosh	38	6.0	12,292	51.8	36	7	13.2	25.4	6	227	10.8	−8.1	247
McKenzie	44	22.7	7,917	37.4	35	51	44.4	31.9	39	1,392	33.1	8.6	1,282
McLean	106	4.9	11,991	40.3	101	32	18.9	29.7	25	808	15.2	−6.2	861
Mercer	42	11.3	4,982	65.4	38	23	8.2	21.8	19	670	10.6	−8.2	730
Morton	172	49.0	6,800	50.7	116	64	15.9	34.7	48	1,716	14.6	1.2	1,695
Mountrail	91	31.7	13,876	31.3	69	30	26.8	28.5	23	744	19.6	−3.6	772
Nelson	49	−9.9	14,264	43.6	55	9	24.1	14.2	8	272	13.2	−10.2	303
Oliver	10	−13.5	5,572	48.3	12	5	10.4	26.9	4	151	12.4	−0.7	152
Pembina	115	41.4	14,100	30.1	82	41	24.4	55.9	27	838	14.2	10.7	757
Pierce	39	−14.2	8,871	49.9	45	10	14.2	23.3	8	266	8.6	−9.8	295
Ramsey	116	−8.6	10,157	44.5	127	60	25.7	31.0	46	1,537	18.4	1.0	1,522
Ransom	53	2.6	9,112	43.5	52	16	14.3	28.5	13	514	14.3	−3.4	532
Renville	39	−1.5	15,943	31.9	40	9	18.8	37.0	6	246	15.0	5.6	233
Richland	115	−1.8	6,530	48.9	117	83	20.6	36.5	61	2,238	20.2	4.4	2,144
Rolette	157	2.4	11,324	29.4	153	131	63.7	45.2	90	2,927	44.7	15.0	2,546
Sargent	46	1.6	11,160	33.7	45	11	5.5	38.4	8	308	8.3	−4.6	323
Sheridan	21	−11.3	14,299	37.7	24	4	16.9	19.3	3	123	12.3	−14.0	143
Sioux	76	68.2	18,389	15.3	45	65	86.7	38.7	47	1,514	70.9	7.1	1,413
Slope	9	−7.6	12,756	18.6	10	1	10.5	39.5	1	47	9.5	−13.0	54
Stark	130	8.2	5,887	62.4	120	87	16.3	39.3	62	2,402	14.3	12.8	2,130
Steele	26	−22.6	12,841	35.0	34	5	14.2	18.5	4	155	12.0	−9.9	172
Stutsman	177	1.3	8,456	44.8	175	83	16.3	24.8	66	1,977	13.8	−1.9	2,016
Towner	45	−21.8	17,514	28.3	58	7	14.6	24.6	6	199	10.6	−2.9	205
Traill	68	−7.0	8,075	50.3	73	28	19.0	36.7	21	815	17.3	5.2	775
Walsh	107	−1.1	9,200	47.9	108	47	20.1	17.5	40	1,466	19.0	−6.0	1,560
Ward	630	30.6	11,210	32.5	483	572	38.1	38.6	412	10,225	24.9	3.3	9,900
Wells	55	−12.2	11,751	45.0	62	12	13.1	19.8	10	343	10.3	−11.6	388
Williams	129	15.0	6,683	61.5	112	65	14.4	28.5	51	1,836	13.0	3.1	1,780
OHIO	[3]73,195	[3]27.5	[3]6,388	[3]58.7	[3]57,387	43,647	15.4	29.0	33,839	843,041	12.4	2.5	822,856
Adams	212	31.8	7,466	51.6	161	68	22.3	33.4	51	1,731	13.5	3.7	1,669
Allen	745	24.8	6,972	72.1	597	333	12.5	8.1	308	7,181	10.2	−10.2	7,998
Ashland	205	23.2	3,797	75.7	167	135	16.0	23.8	109	2,997	11.1	−2.8	3,083
Ashtabula	541	19.1	5,246	76.4	454	246	17.4	25.9	195	5,643	11.6	−1.2	5,714
Athens	331	23.7	5,240	58.0	268	494	53.8	30.8	378	10,418	35.6	3.1	10,108
Auglaize	200	29.0	4,260	73.6	155	109	12.2	9.0	100	2,540	9.9	−16.3	3,034
Belmont	420	17.3	6,057	77.9	358	185	19.5	25.3	147	4,579	14.0	1.9	4,493
Brown	192	24.1	4,344	66.9	155	115	32.3	49.6	77	2,850	16.3	24.2	2,294
Butler	1,851	75.7	5,342	51.3	1,054	1,085	15.2	42.6	761	22,564	12.6	7.1	21,070
Carroll	108	33.1	3,636	71.5	81	44	15.1	28.3	34	1,118	9.7	3.9	1,076
Champaign	200	23.0	5,042	60.3	162	95	17.6	34.4	71	2,222	12.9	6.7	2,083
Clark	887	25.1	6,220	68.7	709	378	16.8	19.2	317	8,090	12.0	−4.1	8,437
Clermont	555	29.3	2,941	71.4	429	388	13.3	40.9	275	8,382	10.1	14.0	7,353
Clinton	211	21.7	4,994	66.3	174	167	13.8	39.4	120	3,722	12.2	13.1	3,290
Columbiana	610	27.5	5,473	73.3	479	250	18.7	25.5	199	5,693	12.3	0.2	5,679
Coshocton	179	25.2	4,824	69.0	143	73	12.7	22.6	60	1,824	9.2	−2.9	1,878
Crawford	244	18.3	5,310	75.1	206	96	14.3	21.9	79	2,252	10.1	−4.0	2,347
Cuyahoga	10,166	22.9	7,525	58.0	8,270	6,426	13.8	24.7	5,153	105,728	11.5	−2.5	108,492
Darke	241	18.5	4,528	71.1	203	104	13.0	30.4	80	2,430	8.6	−0.4	2,439
Defiance	176	19.3	4,509	72.2	148	97	11.1	30.8	74	2,236	9.6	0.6	2,223

See footnotes at end of table.

Table B-12. Counties — Government Expenditure, Earnings, and Employment—Con.

[Includes United States, states, and 3,141 counties/county equivalents defined as of February 22, 2005. For more information on these areas, see Appendix C, Geographic Information]

County	Federal government expenditure 2004					Federal, state, and local governments[1] Earnings 2005				Employment 2005			
	Total (mil. dol.)	Percent change, 2000-2004	Per capita (dol.)	Direct payments to individuals, percent of total	2000 (mil. dol.)	Total (mil. dol.)	Percent of total	Percent change, 2000-2005	2000 (mil. dol.)	Total	Percent of total	Percent change, 2000-2005	2000
OHIO—Con.													
Delaware	385	−8.3	2,702	57.3	420	387	10.4	90.4	203	7,708	7.9	49.5	5,157
Erie	454	29.2	5,745	68.8	351	289	15.0	36.4	212	6,033	11.9	5.9	5,695
Fairfield	473	31.6	3,475	76.9	359	414	24.9	45.5	284	8,961	15.5	15.4	7,766
Fayette	142	14.5	5,064	64.6	124	75	16.6	31.0	57	1,735	10.9	3.6	1,674
Franklin	8,603	38.0	7,901	37.4	6,234	6,847	17.1	30.9	5,232	128,262	15.2	4.3	123,000
Fulton	177	21.3	4,134	78.6	146	111	10.8	33.2	83	2,576	9.1	6.1	2,429
Gallia	204	30.2	6,511	63.5	156	96	17.4	25.7	77	2,142	12.4	−0.6	2,155
Geauga	257	40.0	2,714	82.3	183	197	11.2	37.5	143	4,382	8.4	8.8	4,028
Greene	2,334	15.5	15,330	19.2	2,021	2,050	49.7	34.8	1,521	26,593	27.8	5.8	25,129
Guernsey	238	29.0	5,772	66.0	185	128	20.6	22.5	104	2,760	12.7	−4.7	2,897
Hamilton	7,030	16.1	8,630	45.3	6,053	3,730	11.1	24.7	2,992	65,052	10.1	−0.8	65,547
Hancock	257	16.2	3,496	72.3	222	174	8.4	34.7	129	3,857	7.2	9.6	3,518
Hardin	133	14.7	4,135	61.4	116	71	18.4	30.2	54	1,885	13.7	2.9	1,831
Harrison	100	18.9	6,245	71.6	84	34	22.2	31.3	26	980	17.9	−0.8	988
Henry	148	31.5	5,035	63.6	112	96	17.8	27.4	75	2,302	14.2	1.2	2,274
Highland	223	21.4	5,236	65.4	184	109	20.9	40.7	78	2,557	14.8	10.4	2,316
Hocking	128	24.3	4,436	72.4	103	84	29.8	37.5	61	1,875	18.4	6.6	1,759
Holmes	89	39.8	2,158	62.3	64	77	9.3	48.7	52	1,862	6.9	13.2	1,645
Huron	291	27.1	4,811	75.3	229	134	11.7	26.3	106	3,114	9.5	1.0	3,084
Jackson	200	22.8	5,980	59.1	163	75	16.2	38.8	54	1,826	11.3	15.2	1,585
Jefferson	545	23.3	7,637	76.1	442	166	15.2	17.5	141	4,146	13.1	−3.2	4,284
Knox	258	29.8	4,462	71.3	199	137	15.2	31.2	104	3,173	11.0	6.7	2,975
Lake	987	30.3	4,253	80.6	757	641	13.0	28.3	500	13,292	10.6	4.9	12,676
Lawrence	418	28.7	6,665	66.4	325	139	29.3	10.6	126	3,612	18.9	−11.1	4,061
Licking	747	18.4	4,888	61.2	631	417	16.8	39.3	300	8,833	11.9	12.7	7,839
Logan	223	15.2	4,780	70.7	193	114	10.8	38.3	83	2,630	10.2	5.5	2,494
Lorain	1,377	28.0	4,680	70.2	1,076	903	17.6	31.7	685	16,564	12.7	4.6	15,831
Lucas	2,714	23.9	6,024	62.7	2,192	1,775	15.1	26.5	1,403	34,070	12.1	0.5	33,906
Madison	198	39.4	4,821	61.4	142	164	22.6	26.7	129	3,364	16.8	4.7	3,213
Mahoning	1,729	25.3	6,923	69.1	1,380	798	16.9	26.2	632	17,110	12.4	−1.8	17,420
Marion	343	23.7	5,180	69.3	278	289	23.1	20.8	239	6,335	17.6	(Z)	6,334
Medina	520	26.4	3,149	80.6	411	366	12.9	41.3	259	7,781	9.4	11.8	6,957
Meigs	142	30.2	6,088	63.6	109	45	29.3	26.0	35	1,198	18.7	−7.6	1,296
Mercer	112	25.1	2,721	60.5	89	123	16.7	37.8	89	2,967	12.9	4.5	2,840
Miami	474	8.2	4,701	70.8	438	255	13.5	31.9	194	5,431	10.1	5.8	5,133
Monroe	90	21.5	5,977	65.9	74	35	23.7	21.7	28	981	16.4	−1.1	992
Montgomery	4,211	23.2	7,655	56.6	3,418	2,345	15.3	20.5	1,946	39,588	11.6	−1.5	40,193
Morgan	78	22.9	5,220	64.6	63	30	21.8	23.1	25	776	14.1	−3.6	805
Morrow	101	20.4	2,937	72.7	84	73	26.0	44.9	50	1,812	16.1	13.5	1,596
Muskingum	466	22.9	5,437	68.0	379	248	16.6	35.0	183	5,960	12.6	11.3	5,356
Noble	55	27.1	3,955	62.1	44	50	36.3	20.3	42	1,160	23.0	−3.0	1,196
Ottawa	221	21.4	5,333	79.0	182	114	16.6	24.7	92	2,516	12.3	4.1	2,416
Paulding	84	25.6	4,288	57.7	67	55	25.3	34.3	41	1,340	17.0	2.2	1,311
Perry	174	24.5	4,968	70.1	140	73	25.9	35.4	54	2,013	20.9	6.7	1,886
Pickaway	214	21.4	3,996	66.7	177	215	30.8	17.0	184	4,421	21.8	−3.8	4,594
Pike	246	−18.7	8,692	38.9	302	79	16.8	32.9	59	1,914	14.4	3.0	1,859
Portage	649	34.2	4,190	68.5	483	725	26.9	39.5	520	15,795	20.8	8.3	14,578
Preble	181	12.4	4,242	74.9	161	89	18.2	29.4	69	2,249	13.9	2.8	2,188
Putnam	112	24.1	3,223	64.2	90	75	16.3	25.0	60	1,914	12.2	−6.9	2,056
Richland	654	22.5	5,102	71.0	534	454	17.1	26.0	361	9,491	13.3	−0.6	9,552
Ross	444	22.6	5,965	57.5	362	380	28.5	25.9	302	6,772	19.2	0.1	6,762
Sandusky	273	24.6	4,411	72.8	219	165	14.3	28.3	129	3,770	11.4	1.4	3,717
Scioto	577	22.6	7,495	62.3	471	280	28.4	31.1	214	6,407	19.7	4.7	6,120
Seneca	288	18.6	4,987	77.5	243	136	15.2	16.1	117	3,165	11.0	−7.6	3,424
Shelby	171	18.7	3,527	74.4	144	135	8.4	35.6	100	3,006	8.3	5.4	2,852
Stark	2,017	26.4	5,291	73.3	1,596	985	12.7	28.9	764	21,136	9.8	2.9	20,543
Summit	3,365	35.3	6,148	59.3	2,487	1,800	12.5	27.5	1,412	35,012	10.4	1.7	34,435
Trumbull	1,207	24.5	5,473	78.3	970	529	12.5	23.0	430	11,393	10.7	−4.7	11,954
Tuscarawas	416	28.3	4,515	74.1	325	218	14.8	27.6	171	5,105	11.1	−2.2	5,219
Union	126	17.8	2,832	68.9	107	163	8.8	43.8	113	3,481	10.8	12.8	3,086
Van Wert	111	15.4	3,808	71.0	97	63	13.4	28.7	49	1,558	10.3	0.1	1,556
Vinton	65	28.7	4,895	61.2	51	33	35.9	38.3	24	853	25.2	−3.4	883
Warren	510	39.5	2,695	74.2	366	463	12.9	51.8	305	9,468	10.3	22.5	7,729
Washington	349	26.7	5,583	70.8	276	155	14.3	24.3	125	3,607	10.9	0.7	3,583
Wayne	451	29.3	3,975	72.2	349	333	14.6	23.9	269	7,853	12.6	3.5	7,587
Williams	166	21.2	4,264	76.8	137	98	12.7	29.4	76	2,398	10.8	2.2	2,347
Wood	445	23.2	3,610	74.3	361	593	20.3	37.4	431	13,432	17.9	6.8	12,581
Wyandot	115	21.7	5,023	65.8	94	60	13.3	39.8	43	1,527	11.8	8.8	1,404

See footnotes at end of table.

County and City Data Book: 2007

U.S. Census Bureau

[Includes United States, states, and 3,141 counties/county equivalents defined as of February 22, 2005. For more information on these areas, see Appendix C, Geographic Information]

County	Federal government expenditure					Federal, state, and local governments[1]							
						Earnings				Employment			
	2004					2005				2005			
	Total (mil. dol.)	Percent change, 2000–2004	Per capita (dol.)	Direct payments to individuals, percent of total	2000 (mil. dol.)	Total (mil. dol.)	Percent of total	Percent change, 2000–2005	2000 (mil. dol.)	Total	Percent of total	Percent change, 2000–2005	2000
OKLAHOMA	[3]26,644	[3]28.4	[3]7,562	[3]53.7	[3]20,758	16,603	20.9	30.5	12,727	347,025	16.7	5.0	330,563
Adair	169	29.2	7,792	45.6	131	57	22.8	25.5	45	1,536	16.9	4.1	1,476
Alfalfa	47	8.5	8,043	59.5	43	18	27.7	11.9	16	517	16.2	−7.3	558
Atoka	83	−5.8	5,840	61.5	88	56	34.2	28.6	43	1,406	20.2	6.1	1,325
Beaver	36	7.1	6,664	49.5	34	20	29.1	20.8	16	555	16.1	−1.6	564
Beckham	114	16.1	5,894	62.0	98	47	12.8	30.5	36	1,224	9.9	5.2	1,164
Blaine	76	17.2	6,764	61.4	65	32	21.1	12.6	29	974	15.3	−3.0	1,004
Bryan	314	37.4	8,316	52.0	229	212	37.1	71.7	124	5,630	25.6	38.6	4,062
Caddo	279	38.1	9,252	46.8	202	120	36.0	31.3	92	2,925	23.0	2.7	2,847
Canadian	401	16.1	4,201	65.6	346	285	24.7	37.5	207	6,151	15.8	10.7	5,554
Carter	272	23.8	5,783	72.5	220	127	12.9	33.1	96	3,354	11.1	7.6	3,117
Cherokee	341	46.2	7,720	47.5	233	323	54.5	47.1	219	7,826	35.6	15.7	6,763
Choctaw	197	58.1	12,747	40.7	125	51	29.2	41.8	36	1,492	20.1	21.5	1,228
Cimarron	31	−2.4	10,536	38.5	31	12	31.9	8.7	11	351	16.0	−12.7	402
Cleveland	922	29.5	4,153	74.8	712	963	31.8	32.4	727	23,614	22.4	11.4	21,199
Coal	49	29.5	8,245	57.0	38	15	41.8	15.7	13	422	17.2	−3.2	436
Comanche	1,430	22.6	12,938	34.9	1,166	1,469	57.4	33.0	1,105	23,668	37.5	−7.7	25,641
Cotton	49	6.4	7,458	63.4	46	32	42.9	138.8	13	914	30.0	91.2	478
Craig	101	26.1	6,798	69.0	80	79	32.3	18.8	66	1,968	21.2	1.7	1,936
Creek	317	35.2	4,621	73.4	235	131	16.7	24.2	106	3,367	11.6	1.8	3,306
Custer	125	20.7	4,938	64.9	103	113	25.1	18.0	95	3,120	18.8	−0.4	3,132
Delaware	200	32.5	5,126	74.3	151	86	23.8	54.6	56	2,274	15.1	25.0	1,819
Dewey	38	13.7	8,094	63.2	33	18	32.0	10.3	16	552	17.9	−4.7	579
Ellis	29	7.4	7,448	68.1	27	15	30.7	8.0	13	412	16.4	−5.9	438
Garfield	477	17.7	8,330	51.3	405	277	23.1	21.3	228	4,951	14.0	−8.2	5,395
Garvin	253	18.5	9,303	56.2	214	94	22.1	29.5	73	2,492	16.3	3.7	2,402
Grady	221	14.1	4,583	71.5	193	114	20.1	23.6	92	2,905	13.1	−0.3	2,913
Grant	45	−12.5	9,368	55.6	52	14	21.0	13.1	12	400	13.5	−5.2	422
Greer	56	14.0	9,544	61.7	49	34	49.7	11.1	31	856	32.6	−11.0	962
Harmon	35	−7.4	11,631	48.3	38	12	32.2	10.9	11	377	23.1	−5.0	397
Harper	26	−3.6	7,612	63.4	27	15	21.2	10.5	14	429	21.0	−6.5	459
Haskell	99	29.6	8,217	62.2	77	35	24.9	23.2	28	941	14.3	−6.3	1,004
Hughes	112	25.9	8,006	62.3	89	38	27.5	17.4	32	1,098	18.8	−4.0	1,144
Jackson	351	18.4	12,928	37.6	297	340	55.7	21.9	279	5,899	35.7	−2.8	6,070
Jefferson	56	23.4	8,681	62.3	45	17	28.3	3.1	17	461	18.1	−20.8	582
Johnston	79	16.6	7,540	61.3	67	32	25.6	20.8	27	950	19.3	3.0	922
Kay	379	6.5	8,104	53.6	356	136	13.5	22.1	111	3,754	13.7	2.3	3,669
Kingfisher	106	58.7	7,492	48.0	67	33	11.3	18.2	28	941	9.8	1.5	927
Kiowa	95	9.5	9,610	58.8	87	33	32.3	10.2	30	929	19.1	−15.7	1,102
Latimer	68	25.5	6,376	72.1	54	46	24.6	−6.9	50	1,358	21.7	−23.9	1,785
Le Flore	329	30.7	6,692	66.7	252	154	28.9	42.2	109	4,330	22.1	21.8	3,554
Lincoln	191	42.0	5,905	66.2	135	71	24.1	30.5	54	1,967	13.4	10.0	1,788
Logan	187	33.9	5,151	58.6	140	83	23.8	25.5	66	2,134	11.9	−1.0	2,155
Love	51	31.2	5,602	70.7	39	51	54.5	269.8	14	1,802	38.6	286.7	466
McClain	126	32.2	4,325	79.3	95	66	22.3	31.4	50	1,719	15.3	8.9	1,578
McCurtain	281	30.3	8,253	54.4	216	104	18.4	26.0	83	2,843	17.1	6.0	2,681
McIntosh	159	28.1	7,986	72.4	124	39	24.8	14.5	34	1,078	13.6	−7.8	1,169
Major	48	16.1	6,475	64.9	41	19	19.0	22.6	15	497	10.1	−4.6	521
Marshall	88	29.0	6,335	76.0	68	31	17.5	23.9	25	876	13.4	4.5	838
Mayes	194	28.3	4,937	76.4	151	117	25.0	32.8	88	2,598	16.0	4.5	2,485
Murray	92	27.5	7,270	63.7	72	70	39.4	71.0	41	2,076	30.1	58.6	1,309
Muskogee	605	34.6	8,570	55.7	450	385	29.9	31.2	293	7,839	19.7	5.9	7,402
Noble	81	39.7	7,187	53.8	58	41	21.9	30.7	31	1,152	17.4	7.6	1,071
Nowata	63	27.5	5,923	70.5	50	20	25.5	15.9	17	554	13.0	−1.6	563
Okfuskee	96	1.6	8,278	61.1	95	44	38.5	48.6	30	1,196	25.7	28.1	934
Oklahoma	7,099	25.4	10,428	37.0	5,663	5,391	21.4	28.1	4,209	86,419	16.6	1.6	85,056
Okmulgee	284	29.8	7,130	62.3	219	136	33.4	32.7	102	3,398	21.9	7.3	3,168
Osage	203	45.0	4,487	51.0	140	96	24.0	27.5	75	2,441	13.3	0.2	2,437
Ottawa	288	41.2	8,795	59.0	204	99	21.3	32.9	75	2,735	17.3	3.7	2,638
Pawnee	101	30.6	6,012	66.6	78	45	29.3	29.7	34	1,011	16.4	−0.2	1,013
Payne	395	31.0	5,665	55.3	301	587	44.2	26.7	464	15,952	35.1	4.1	15,318
Pittsburg	380	29.2	8,657	55.5	295	297	40.7	47.7	201	5,685	24.8	15.8	4,909
Pontotoc	325	55.1	9,285	51.3	210	234	35.7	61.0	145	6,011	25.7	35.2	4,447
Pottawatomie	462	53.0	6,891	58.8	302	176	20.6	46.3	120	4,629	15.2	25.2	3,697
Pushmataha	102	25.8	8,668	60.5	81	37	30.8	21.1	31	1,029	18.2	−2.6	1,057
Roger Mills	25	9.5	7,647	59.0	23	16	35.9	27.5	13	406	18.9	−4.9	427
Rogers	296	34.7	3,743	72.7	220	246	20.4	76.9	139	5,936	15.0	39.0	4,269
Seminole	194	25.1	7,869	64.3	155	75	25.3	26.8	59	2,127	19.0	0.9	2,109
Sequoyah	249	22.5	6,137	64.4	203	115	29.0	45.1	79	2,914	20.4	12.3	2,595
Stephens	308	31.6	7,183	66.6	234	91	12.6	16.9	78	2,419	10.5	−0.5	2,432
Texas	96	6.8	4,713	54.9	90	68	14.7	22.3	55	1,892	14.5	1.0	1,874

See footnotes at end of table.

[Includes United States, states, and 3,141 counties/county equivalents defined as of February 22, 2005. For more information on these areas, see Appendix C, Geographic Information]

County	Federal government expenditure 2004 Total (mil. dol.)	Percent change, 2000–2004	Per capita (dol.)	Direct payments to individuals, percent of total	2000 (mil. dol.)	Earnings 2005 Total (mil. dol.)	Percent of total	Percent change, 2000–2005	2000 (mil. dol.)	Employment 2005 Total	Percent of total	Percent change, 2000–2005	2000
OKLAHOMA—Con.													
Tillman	82	3.5	9,308	52.7	79	31	29.8	29.6	24	858	20.8	13.8	754
Tulsa	3,013	24.0	5,294	67.2	2,430	1,717	8.0	25.0	1,374	37,382	8.8	2.6	36,428
Wagoner	187	30.7	2,968	72.2	143	70	24.1	34.0	52	1,838	14.8	6.3	1,729
Washington	256	25.0	5,231	82.1	205	96	9.9	18.2	81	2,484	9.6	1.9	2,438
Washita	88	15.2	7,604	59.4	76	31	27.8	22.0	26	866	17.2	−1.5	879
Woods	70	15.3	8,208	57.8	61	43	36.5	22.3	35	1,379	24.5	3.9	1,327
Woodward	89	21.1	4,737	75.1	73	62	15.2	−0.3	63	1,560	12.2	−16.4	1,865
OREGON	3 21,871	3 32.0	3 6,084	3 59.7	3 16,568	17,329	18.9	47.4	11,753	284,292	12.7	2.3	277,838
Baker	122	19.0	7,412	62.2	103	72	33.5	29.1	56	1,244	13.8	−9.8	1,379
Benton	450	40.5	5,665	46.5	320	709	32.7	71.4	413	14,319	26.1	28.7	11,122
Clackamas	1,487	33.8	4,094	68.1	1,112	1,052	12.4	40.4	749	17,616	8.2	–	17,616
Clatsop	248	20.7	6,816	61.6	205	165	20.9	34.4	122	2,994	12.8	−5.6	3,171
Columbia	187	27.5	3,972	78.5	146	119	22.1	39.3	85	2,055	12.5	−4.8	2,158
Coos	465	32.8	7,294	68.7	350	340	31.7	41.4	240	6,117	18.1	−1.2	6,194
Crook	114	31.0	5,330	69.9	87	74	22.1	35.8	55	1,271	12.2	−2.0	1,297
Curry	171	31.2	7,717	82.6	130	70	23.3	40.9	50	1,315	11.2	−2.4	1,348
Deschutes	581	41.0	4,322	75.4	412	469	14.3	47.6	318	7,787	8.4	0.5	7,747
Douglas	743	34.5	7,203	66.0	552	472	25.6	36.4	346	8,302	14.9	−4.1	8,657
Gilliam	23	42.4	12,455	37.3	16	10	31.4	30.9	8	212	15.3	−11.7	240
Grant	63	13.4	8,493	54.4	55	57	45.1	32.9	43	1,057	23.3	−2.2	1,081
Harney	56	18.6	7,904	50.5	48	57	46.7	37.8	41	1,052	23.5	−4.0	1,096
Hood River	111	38.6	5,267	53.8	80	77	18.1	41.3	54	1,410	9.3	−4.5	1,477
Jackson	1,071	25.8	5,550	69.3	852	677	16.5	41.3	479	11,754	10.0	−2.5	12,051
Jefferson	101	25.0	5,064	63.8	80	132	47.4	43.1	92	2,532	28.3	−1.8	2,578
Josephine	515	31.3	6,443	77.3	392	211	18.5	39.0	152	3,738	9.6	−7.8	4,053
Klamath	442	38.4	6,784	63.6	319	309	27.4	43.4	215	5,530	16.1	1.6	5,444
Lake	61	25.2	8,218	58.3	48	54	43.8	41.5	38	967	21.7	1.8	950
Lane	1,840	31.1	5,550	64.6	1,404	1,537	21.4	48.3	1,036	28,479	14.2	4.8	27,174
Lincoln	303	22.9	6,688	73.6	246	218	26.3	20.4	181	4,051	15.1	−12.8	4,648
Linn	552	28.4	5,141	74.1	430	353	17.0	44.3	245	6,885	12.7	−0.9	6,946
Malheur	164	25.0	5,209	61.6	131	188	33.6	41.4	133	3,377	18.2	−4.8	3,549
Marion	2,098	36.4	6,952	50.1	1,538	2,234	32.3	47.5	1,515	33,510	19.3	0.1	33,486
Morrow	83	6.4	7,136	36.6	78	44	21.1	45.3	30	839	15.1	1.5	827
Multnomah	4,985	24.7	7,416	46.8	3,999	4,930	18.1	47.2	3,349	69,676	12.5	1.6	68,584
Polk	408	54.8	6,036	38.7	263	296	36.6	68.5	176	6,096	23.2	12.4	5,425
Sherman	25	−7.3	14,706	36.6	27	18	89.7	46.5	13	275	21.5	0.4	274
Tillamook	162	27.2	6,511	74.6	128	105	24.9	43.0	73	1,855	13.9	−3.9	1,930
Umatilla	543	43.6	7,392	43.3	378	442	31.7	53.0	289	7,353	18.5	4.0	7,067
Union	158	30.9	6,471	65.4	121	139	30.4	45.6	96	2,842	18.5	3.0	2,759
Wallowa	55	29.9	7,914	60.5	42	36	31.5	29.6	28	692	14.6	−12.1	787
Wasco	168	30.9	7,091	58.4	128	129	31.7	30.8	99	2,196	17.1	−9.6	2,429
Washington	1,240	29.0	2,540	70.3	961	1,266	8.3	69.0	749	20,281	7.1	14.2	17,752
Wheeler	11	30.9	7,125	73.6	8	6	40.6	12.6	5	132	16.0	−27.5	182
Yamhill	384	17.3	4,238	68.9	328	263	17.5	47.2	179	4,481	10.4	2.8	4,360
PENNSYLVANIA	3 94,900	3 28.7	3 7,649	3 60.0	3 73,745	43,137	13.3	26.8	34,025	813,076	11.4	3.5	785,266
Adams	465	37.6	4,727	67.7	338	225	14.1	28.0	176	4,561	8.9	−7.6	4,938
Allegheny	11,850	18.7	9,474	54.1	9,987	4,546	9.9	18.0	3,851	78,260	9.1	−3.6	81,204
Armstrong	486	18.8	6,810	76.1	409	145	14.4	13.8	127	3,209	10.3	−7.8	3,481
Beaver	1,157	26.7	6,476	77.2	913	404	15.0	22.6	330	9,139	12.3	−2.9	9,409
Bedford	293	19.7	5,838	70.3	245	111	16.8	25.2	89	2,624	11.1	2.3	2,566
Berks	1,840	30.9	4,698	73.5	1,406	1,101	12.6	35.7	811	23,876	11.0	13.1	21,116
Blair	867	20.7	6,804	69.9	719	438	16.6	24.1	353	9,830	13.1	5.9	9,284
Bradford	344	14.7	5,504	68.9	300	159	15.3	30.3	122	3,670	11.3	5.1	3,493
Bucks	2,693	28.7	4,360	77.4	2,092	1,459	8.9	32.0	1,105	25,790	7.2	9.6	23,527
Butler	1,231	45.0	6,813	56.9	849	531	14.3	35.8	391	10,853	10.9	12.2	9,674
Cambria	1,323	24.6	8,906	63.0	1,062	499	20.2	22.8	407	10,600	14.0	−0.2	10,620
Cameron	40	10.2	7,045	68.3	36	18	16.7	16.5	15	439	13.3	−3.1	453
Carbon	398	41.7	6,506	74.6	281	132	18.0	29.8	101	3,188	13.1	6.4	2,995
Centre	941	22.6	6,696	42.8	768	1,652	46.4	47.1	1,124	43,088	40.6	18.5	36,357
Chester	1,928	15.8	4,138	69.5	1,665	1,377	7.6	50.3	916	25,314	8.1	19.1	21,248
Clarion	251	25.6	6,103	74.0	200	173	23.1	25.3	138	4,088	18.5	4.1	3,926
Clearfield	516	29.9	6,223	69.8	397	235	17.7	21.9	193	5,393	12.8	2.9	5,241
Clinton	209	17.1	5,576	73.1	178	140	23.7	32.6	105	3,250	17.4	9.1	2,978
Columbia	341	23.0	5,251	76.6	277	230	18.3	38.0	167	5,460	15.3	13.1	4,828
Crawford	496	22.7	5,514	75.8	404	219	16.2	20.4	182	4,853	10.8	−1.8	4,944
Cumberland	1,483	21.9	6,696	61.0	1,216	1,200	16.9	19.8	1,002	18,858	11.8	−1.6	19,162
Dauphin	4,968	50.8	19,616	28.0	3,295	2,547	25.8	28.6	1,980	46,899	21.6	6.1	44,190
Delaware	4,218	58.0	7,600	56.5	2,670	1,446	10.6	30.3	1,110	26,761	9.5	2.9	26,000
Elk	182	21.0	5,337	81.8	150	67	9.7	22.7	55	1,557	7.8	0.1	1,555
Erie	1,553	22.4	5,499	69.0	1,268	864	14.8	24.9	692	18,088	11.0	3.4	17,494

See footnotes at end of table.

Table B-12. Counties — **Government Expenditure, Earnings, and Employment**—Con.

[Includes United States, states, and 3,141 counties/county equivalents defined as of February 22, 2005. For more information on these areas, see Appendix C, Geographic Information]

County	Federal government expenditure 2004 — Total (mil. dol.)	Percent change, 2000–2004	Per capita (dol.)	Direct payments to individuals, percent of total	2000 (mil. dol.)	Federal, state, and local governments[1] — Earnings 2005 — Total (mil. dol.)	Percent of total	Percent change, 2000–2005	2000 (mil. dol.)	Employment 2005 — Total	Percent of total	Percent change, 2000–2005	2000
PENNSYLVANIA—Con.													
Fayette	1,178	21.0	8,089	70.4	974	339	19.5	39.5	243	7,253	12.4	13.2	6,405
Forest	44	32.7	8,876	76.1	33	46	49.6	181.0	16	911	31.4	105.6	443
Franklin	822	30.2	6,095	66.3	631	443	17.4	33.1	333	8,564	11.7	7.4	7,972
Fulton	87	36.0	5,934	63.0	64	34	10.2	20.6	28	841	10.4	2.1	824
Greene	327	21.5	8,141	59.6	269	134	21.1	14.7	117	2,817	16.7	−4.8	2,959
Huntingdon	248	24.4	5,402	69.9	200	152	25.8	18.9	128	3,279	17.2	2.1	3,210
Indiana	556	26.6	6,247	68.9	439	370	21.2	28.4	288	8,120	17.6	4.4	7,777
Jefferson	292	25.5	6,357	74.0	233	93	14.0	26.6	74	2,174	9.8	0.5	2,163
Juniata	110	36.0	4,708	74.4	81	37	10.2	36.1	27	864	7.1	8.1	799
Lackawanna	1,801	35.2	8,580	59.7	1,333	616	13.5	23.6	499	12,667	10.0	5.3	12,026
Lancaster	2,060	22.8	4,228	73.3	1,677	1,081	9.1	30.8	826	22,784	7.5	10.3	20,660
Lawrence	658	18.8	7,045	76.5	554	233	16.0	19.4	196	4,889	11.6	−1.8	4,980
Lebanon	779	35.4	6,262	61.4	576	413	19.0	35.6	304	7,923	13.4	8.5	7,299
Lehigh	1,594	26.5	4,888	71.9	1,260	895	9.0	31.5	680	18,544	8.6	8.2	17,134
Luzerne	2,311	18.0	7,374	69.9	1,958	1,027	15.4	23.4	832	19,633	11.2	−0.9	19,810
Lycoming	713	25.7	6,014	67.2	567	416	17.2	46.1	285	9,650	14.2	42.2	6,788
McKean	288	15.4	6,443	68.1	250	138	17.7	15.1	120	2,871	12.3	−6.3	3,063
Mercer	760	18.2	6,342	77.4	643	276	13.4	23.4	223	6,194	9.8	(Z)	6,197
Mifflin	279	7.8	6,048	70.3	259	90	12.6	27.9	71	2,030	9.0	4.4	1,944
Monroe	804	39.0	5,059	63.3	578	706	25.8	52.7	462	12,748	16.8	18.3	10,775
Montgomery	4,488	29.9	5,799	67.0	3,456	2,318	6.3	28.0	1,811	39,844	6.6	3.8	38,388
Montour	102	26.9	5,624	77.5	80	69	9.4	20.3	57	1,518	8.5	4.1	1,458
Northampton	1,566	29.7	5,544	78.2	1,208	719	14.3	32.0	544	14,772	11.8	7.4	13,757
Northumberland	578	19.1	6,226	75.2	486	232	17.3	37.2	169	5,357	13.4	8.2	4,949
Perry	205	37.9	4,581	77.0	148	94	27.2	31.9	72	2,348	17.7	10.1	2,132
Philadelphia	16,055	19.5	10,921	45.8	13,431	7,907	17.9	18.1	6,696	116,176	15.4	−6.8	124,649
Pike	186	40.9	3,437	82.4	132	130	25.7	53.7	84	2,706	15.3	21.4	2,229
Potter	109	28.4	6,056	66.5	85	49	14.0	26.0	39	1,228	12.4	4.5	1,175
Schuylkill	948	15.8	6,417	77.5	818	382	17.6	25.0	306	8,165	12.8	1.1	8,077
Snyder	169	34.6	4,445	74.1	126	116	15.2	7.9	108	2,591	11.4	−6.4	2,767
Somerset	538	32.8	6,770	66.8	405	224	19.7	30.5	172	4,825	13.0	1.2	4,770
Sullivan	42	17.9	6,519	73.5	35	16	23.9	14.2	14	394	13.5	−1.0	398
Susquehanna	211	24.5	5,021	76.8	170	92	23.8	30.9	71	2,173	13.4	3.6	2,098
Tioga	276	29.3	6,592	61.5	213	142	25.4	25.7	113	3,494	18.0	5.5	3,313
Union	289	17.1	6,759	45.3	247	203	23.7	8.5	187	3,134	14.0	−16.1	3,734
Venango	356	24.0	6,332	73.8	287	182	20.1	17.3	155	3,789	14.1	−7.6	4,099
Warren	252	23.6	5,920	73.0	204	123	18.1	16.9	105	2,533	12.4	−11.5	2,862
Washington	1,352	21.1	6,571	78.0	1,116	490	12.2	19.5	410	10,705	10.6	0.4	10,658
Wayne	314	30.5	6,338	78.2	241	152	23.9	42.7	107	2,965	14.3	12.2	2,643
Westmoreland	2,320	23.9	6,292	77.3	1,873	852	13.1	22.7	695	17,391	9.6	−0.3	17,444
Wyoming	137	25.5	4,861	77.8	109	59	12.3	30.0	45	1,353	11.3	6.0	1,277
York	2,296	33.8	5,718	55.7	1,716	1,128	12.4	46.4	770	21,211	9.6	14.8	18,478
RHODE ISLAND	[3]8,245	[3]19.9	[3]7,630	[3]53.3	[3]6,879	4,894	18.1	28.6	3,806	75,375	12.4	−1.4	76,410
Bristol	283	32.3	5,347	70.4	214	124	16.0	34.8	92	2,251	10.0	3.8	2,168
Kent	964	22.2	5,599	73.5	789	568	13.1	35.3	420	9,579	9.2	−0.7	9,647
Newport	1,240	8.3	14,591	30.3	1,145	943	36.8	18.1	798	10,408	19.1	−9.3	11,473
Providence	4,568	19.0	7,116	51.5	3,837	2,639	15.9	29.2	2,042	40,321	11.4	−2.1	41,173
Washington	709	19.2	5,513	62.5	595	621	22.6	36.7	455	12,816	17.6	7.3	11,949
SOUTH CAROLINA	[3]30,051	[3]34.6	[3]7,158	[3]53.7	[3]22,323	18,562	20.9	28.3	14,469	383,221	16.2	(Z)	383,222
Abbeville	130	36.0	4,928	64.1	95	63	19.5	24.1	50	1,619	14.2	−2.1	1,653
Aiken	2,532	26.8	16,999	21.8	1,996	397	12.3	18.6	335	8,666	10.9	6.2	8,160
Allendale	88	28.1	7,952	48.3	69	49	29.8	−2.0	50	1,331	30.1	−13.8	1,544
Anderson	801	26.8	4,616	76.2	632	540	19.0	27.2	424	12,330	14.9	0.7	12,248
Bamberg	131	23.5	8,193	53.8	106	57	29.9	25.6	45	1,518	20.5	4.4	1,454
Barnwell	149	31.6	6,385	58.6	114	64	21.8	17.3	55	1,766	18.3	−9.8	1,957
Beaufort	1,153	42.9	8,492	48.0	807	1,135	31.4	35.5	837	20,260	22.0	−0.2	20,302
Berkeley	619	29.6	4,138	70.5	478	413	20.1	37.1	301	8,468	14.4	7.9	7,850
Calhoun	70	22.6	4,574	58.8	57	33	13.3	14.9	29	989	12.0	−7.8	1,073
Charleston	4,020	44.4	12,303	34.0	2,783	3,088	27.9	34.4	2,298	53,503	19.8	2.4	52,261
Cherokee	240	28.0	4,465	71.6	188	110	13.2	31.6	84	2,652	10.8	2.9	2,577
Chester	185	22.3	5,504	70.6	151	80	15.0	−12.0	91	1,978	13.4	−31.1	2,871
Chesterfield	241	25.3	5,571	60.9	192	90	14.7	22.6	73	2,324	12.6	−2.5	2,383
Clarendon	225	34.3	6,799	57.7	168	94	29.6	18.5	80	2,337	20.1	−12.5	2,672
Colleton	257	27.8	6,479	65.6	201	90	20.4	20.4	75	2,386	15.1	−6.2	2,543
Darlington	368	27.0	5,439	64.2	289	144	13.1	29.4	111	3,656	12.8	2.7	3,559
Dillon	204	23.6	6,535	57.1	165	71	19.3	25.8	56	1,808	14.3	−1.1	1,828
Dorchester	505	39.5	4,716	74.9	362	225	18.1	31.9	171	5,630	15.2	4.1	5,409
Edgefield	137	33.5	5,512	45.3	102	86	34.4	15.9	75	1,757	21.6	−0.1	1,758
Fairfield	140	32.8	5,790	63.3	105	71	22.3	28.0	55	1,728	20.4	1.8	1,698

See footnotes at end of table.

Table B-12. Counties — **Government Expenditure, Earnings, and Employment**—Con.

[Includes United States, states, and 3,141 counties/county equivalents defined as of February 22, 2005. For more information on these areas, see Appendix C, Geographic Information]

County	Federal government expenditure					Federal, state, and local governments[1]							
						Earnings				Employment			
	2004					2005				2005			
	Total (mil. dol.)	Percent change, 2000–2004	Per capita (dol.)	Direct payments to individuals, percent of total	2000 (mil. dol.)	Total (mil. dol.)	Percent of total	Percent change, 2000–2005	2000 (mil. dol.)	Total	Percent of total	Percent change, 2000–2005	2000
SOUTH CAROLINA—Con.													
Florence	810	34.7	6,246	61.6	601	589	19.7	21.8	484	13,108	16.2	−2.8	13,489
Georgetown	404	31.8	6,753	79.4	306	223	20.2	44.5	154	4,909	14.2	12.3	4,373
Greenville	2,055	37.1	5,123	61.4	1,499	1,396	11.8	34.7	1,036	28,317	9.7	5.4	26,862
Greenwood	358	32.0	5,303	71.2	271	327	23.5	33.4	245	7,797	20.3	8.6	7,182
Hampton	173	23.4	8,140	50.0	140	79	30.8	20.7	66	1,720	22.3	−4.0	1,792
Horry	1,078	27.0	4,955	73.7	849	638	14.3	45.8	438	13,969	9.9	16.7	11,969
Jasper	110	44.3	5,173	52.8	76	59	21.7	23.9	47	1,483	16.9	−4.1	1,547
Kershaw	274	32.1	4,935	73.9	207	152	16.7	38.3	110	3,618	13.9	4.1	3,476
Lancaster	299	34.8	4,730	73.1	222	143	16.7	14.9	124	3,636	14.8	−9.1	4,000
Laurens	328	37.5	4,665	67.9	238	173	21.2	17.5	147	4,481	17.4	−5.7	4,751
Lee	123	24.0	6,012	56.1	99	55	30.9	10.8	50	1,430	22.8	−8.8	1,568
Lexington	1,010	43.8	4,372	66.9	703	742	17.0	48.4	500	16,664	13.1	15.0	14,492
McCormick	77	37.6	7,643	59.9	56	37	44.5	7.3	35	925	31.7	−13.4	1,068
Marion	319	27.8	9,090	47.1	250	110	28.1	21.4	90	2,832	19.3	−3.0	2,920
Marlboro	202	27.6	7,186	56.9	159	91	25.6	42.8	64	2,062	20.2	4.4	1,975
Newberry	226	36.3	6,078	64.4	166	107	19.6	38.2	77	2,676	15.6	10.2	2,428
Oconee	351	30.8	5,078	79.7	268	198	15.7	37.4	144	4,700	15.1	12.3	4,187
Orangeburg	607	25.0	6,685	61.3	486	357	25.3	23.2	290	7,874	18.4	−6.3	8,406
Pickens	514	30.2	4,574	70.6	395	475	29.6	34.4	353	9,722	20.3	7.1	9,074
Richland	3,450	22.7	10,312	37.1	2,811	3,426	30.3	16.0	2,953	66,045	25.1	−11.1	74,324
Saluda	86	28.6	4,549	60.2	67	39	21.0	21.8	32	1,025	16.2	−1.4	1,040
Spartanburg	1,202	31.7	4,548	74.1	912	871	14.6	27.8	681	19,067	13.1	7.1	17,795
Sumter	947	33.8	8,943	45.1	708	709	35.7	31.8	538	12,653	23.2	−1.5	12,843
Union	167	26.6	5,786	74.7	132	85	23.2	2.9	82	2,174	19.9	−16.9	2,616
Williamsburg	256	32.3	7,238	52.9	194	102	25.5	35.2	75	2,470	18.8	1.1	2,443
York	671	37.0	3,652	76.7	490	482	13.3	34.6	358	11,158	12.6	3.3	10,802
SOUTH DAKOTA	[3]6,602	[3]28.4	[3]8,564	[3]45.7	[3]5,141	3,495	19.3	33.0	2,628	80,055	14.9	2.7	77,984
Aurora	24	14.0	8,194	47.5	21	7	21.7	−28.6	10	221	12.7	−40.1	369
Beadle	165	22.8	10,264	42.5	134	66	18.5	12.2	59	1,353	12.8	−12.3	1,543
Bennett	33	25.0	9,243	32.3	26	15	35.4	66.3	9	411	26.1	33.9	307
Bon Homme	46	−3.9	6,446	63.5	47	24	25.7	42.6	17	671	17.3	2.9	652
Brookings	145	25.8	5,137	58.3	115	194	28.6	26.8	153	5,026	23.5	−2.9	5,175
Brown	334	30.7	9,605	48.1	256	143	14.5	29.2	111	3,261	12.0	1.3	3,218
Brule	41	1.4	7,823	50.5	40	15	18.1	29.9	12	408	11.6	−5.8	433
Buffalo	30	70.3	14,214	13.9	17	21	74.1	29.7	16	477	61.5	0.2	476
Butte	55	31.3	5,984	60.3	42	23	19.7	31.6	17	669	13.6	5.0	637
Campbell	26	22.6	15,935	42.5	21	4	14.8	24.5	3	139	12.9	−6.1	148
Charles Mix	97	21.8	10,663	36.2	80	50	31.3	19.6	42	1,370	23.1	−4.9	1,441
Clark	41	−3.6	10,407	39.2	43	9	21.3	23.4	7	297	12.9	−0.3	298
Clay	87	14.2	6,679	44.7	76	106	40.4	16.9	91	2,852	25.3	−4.4	2,983
Codington	145	27.2	5,614	55.5	114	88	13.9	30.6	67	2,106	10.3	2.1	2,062
Corson	47	13.9	10,750	41.2	41	25	46.9	47.5	17	686	40.0	12.6	609
Custer	68	42.3	8,911	47.7	48	40	35.4	35.6	29	833	15.5	3.2	807
Davison	112	4.0	5,901	64.2	108	55	11.2	33.5	41	1,402	9.1	2.4	1,369
Day	67	8.7	11,477	42.5	62	17	18.5	20.4	14	487	12.9	−11.0	547
Deuel	33	1.8	7,697	50.5	32	10	11.6	29.7	7	329	10.6	−0.9	332
Dewey	82	30.4	13,410	22.4	63	65	67.8	38.9	47	1,559	52.7	7.9	1,445
Douglas	26	11.8	7,736	54.4	23	7	11.9	30.5	5	213	11.2	−1.8	217
Edmunds	37	−1.8	9,064	45.1	38	13	14.2	31.6	10	423	17.3	−1.9	431
Fall River	89	12.5	12,173	52.6	80	59	44.9	33.8	44	1,117	30.7	0.8	1,108
Faulk	27	5.4	11,201	41.2	26	6	11.2	15.9	5	180	13.6	−13.0	207
Grant	59	25.4	7,720	52.9	47	15	8.6	20.9	13	438	8.0	−9.5	484
Gregory	39	−11.8	8,893	57.4	44	11	15.8	25.3	9	361	11.9	−3.7	375
Haakon	26	24.5	13,228	31.6	21	6	11.4	14.4	5	162	9.9	−12.0	184
Hamlin	31	−6.1	5,536	56.6	33	17	21.9	27.6	13	530	22.0	−3.3	548
Hand	59	30.9	17,446	21.8	45	9	11.9	16.4	8	259	10.8	−15.1	305
Hanson	26	50.8	6,989	48.1	18	6	23.6	39.7	4	199	15.5	12.4	177
Harding	17	76.0	13,800	22.3	10	5	20.4	20.2	4	132	12.3	−18.0	161
Hughes	335	51.4	19,996	18.8	221	199	43.4	29.8	153	3,931	29.3	2.9	3,821
Hutchinson	57	0.3	7,411	57.8	57	16	14.9	21.5	14	515	11.4	−9.5	569
Hyde	18	19.1	11,299	34.0	15	8	25.4	65.8	5	221	19.9	20.1	184
Jackson	29	96.0	9,992	24.2	15	16	48.5	35.0	12	377	26.4	5.0	359
Jerauld	19	3.2	9,262	54.8	19	5	9.3	6.1	5	168	8.4	−21.1	213
Jones	32	125.5	29,117	13.1	14	6	23.4	59.6	3	169	17.4	24.3	136
Kingsbury	48	−3.1	8,722	56.9	49	11	11.6	26.3	9	343	10.9	−2.8	353
Lake	77	22.7	7,055	55.6	63	40	18.4	28.4	31	1,092	15.5	0.5	1,087
Lawrence	128	25.8	5,738	68.0	102	78	17.8	29.2	60	1,942	12.4	−0.4	1,950
Lincoln	69	−33.8	2,200	62.0	104	40	8.7	63.8	25	1,156	6.4	19.2	970
Lyman	40	−28.2	9,950	30.8	55	26	43.8	40.5	19	725	30.0	8.7	667
McCook	38	−0.6	6,454	56.2	38	13	17.4	35.3	10	390	12.6	4.0	375
McPherson	25	19.6	9,233	35.9	21	6	16.0	23.1	5	198	14.5	−7.5	214
Marshall	43	4.1	9,866	43.4	41	12	13.8	27.8	10	375	15.2	−6.3	400

See footnotes at end of table.

Table B-12. Counties — **Government Expenditure, Earnings, and Employment**—Con.

[Includes United States, states, and 3,141 counties/county equivalents defined as of February 22, 2005. For more information on these areas, see Appendix C, Geographic Information]

County	Federal government expenditure 2004					Federal, state, and local governments[1]								
						Earnings 2005				Employment 2005			
	Total (mil. dol.)	Percent change, 2000–2004	Per capita (dol.)	Direct payments to individuals, percent of total	2000 (mil. dol.)	Total (mil. dol.)	Percent of total	Percent change, 2000–2005	2000 (mil. dol.)	Total	Percent of total	Percent change, 2000–2005	2000
SOUTH DAKOTA—Con.													
Meade	216	41.9	8,677	37.6	152	140	33.0	29.2	108	2,796	16.0	3.3	2,706
Mellette	17	45.9	8,332	33.9	12	8	42.8	67.3	5	245	29.6	26.3	194
Miner	27	12.3	10,390	45.5	24	6	15.1	16.8	5	193	12.6	–11.9	219
Minnehaha	1,089	65.5	6,920	62.6	658	559	10.0	40.0	399	10,748	7.9	7.3	10,014
Moody	45	-0.2	6,869	45.4	45	35	27.0	26.1	28	945	26.6	-2.0	964
Pennington	758	25.0	8,186	46.2	607	596	25.6	36.3	437	10,720	17.2	3.1	10,402
Perkins	41	51.2	13,138	37.3	27	10	18.0	26.3	8	309	13.0	-9.1	340
Potter	37	10.4	14,864	36.3	33	7	16.5	13.7	6	201	12.6	-12.6	230
Roberts	98	18.5	9,735	35.5	83	59	38.2	50.7	39	1,609	29.6	16.9	1,376
Sanborn	22	6.4	8,423	49.5	21	6	12.4	24.1	5	196	13.2	-6.7	210
Shannon	198	41.7	14,803	18.8	139	142	77.5	40.5	101	3,399	68.8	20.5	2,821
Spink	77	3.2	11,068	42.5	75	39	30.4	28.4	30	1,129	29.1	4.7	1,078
Stanley	21	38.5	7,566	38.4	15	7	13.9	35.3	5	189	10.2	-1.0	191
Sully	28	6.0	19,389	16.5	26	4	9.7	25.0	4	133	11.6	-7.6	144
Todd	111	38.8	11,420	21.3	80	97	81.1	40.4	69	2,526	68.3	6.9	2,362
Tripp	51	25.4	8,438	45.6	41	17	15.1	36.2	13	497	12.4	2.7	484
Turner	59	12.8	6,852	67.0	52	18	16.4	31.8	13	547	13.1	–	547
Union	178	51.1	13,290	24.2	118	29	6.3	39.0	21	806	8.0	3.6	778
Walworth	39	14.9	7,069	45.6	34	16	18.7	23.0	13	463	12.4	-6.3	494
Yankton	116	11.7	5,394	62.1	104	86	17.5	35.7	63	2,020	13.9	7.6	1,878
Ziebach	18	48.3	6,937	25.7	12	8	31.7	36.9	6	211	25.7	2.4	206
TENNESSEE	[3]45,441	[3]35.3	[3]7,701	[3]51.3	[3]33,588	20,546	13.9	30.3	15,765	438,664	12.1	4.3	420,670
Anderson	3,574	55.9	49,465	9.3	2,292	292	13.0	20.5	243	5,240	9.9	-2.1	5,354
Bedford	172	31.2	4,175	72.3	131	94	11.7	41.1	66	2,604	10.1	7.4	2,425
Benton	119	32.8	7,191	74.9	89	32	20.0	20.1	27	906	12.8	-1.2	917
Bledsoe	63	30.7	4,957	62.3	49	38	37.0	38.8	27	1,116	27.9	7.5	1,038
Blount	555	26.2	4,879	75.1	440	301	13.4	43.6	209	7,338	12.6	15.8	6,335
Bradley	409	33.8	4,486	76.2	306	243	11.9	32.5	183	5,857	11.6	7.6	5,441
Campbell	312	21.7	7,706	64.2	256	95	20.2	34.3	71	2,598	16.8	13.2	2,296
Cannon	76	35.6	5,694	73.7	56	20	17.9	45.4	14	603	10.8	17.3	514
Carroll	310	70.8	10,557	47.8	181	57	15.9	29.9	44	1,622	12.0	0.4	1,615
Carter	303	26.3	5,173	70.4	240	98	20.4	27.6	77	2,502	12.4	0.8	2,482
Cheatham	127	34.1	3,334	74.9	95	61	11.8	25.3	49	1,628	10.1	-4.6	1,706
Chester	87	33.7	5,496	58.1	65	32	19.0	36.6	23	961	13.7	3.0	933
Claiborne	229	34.7	7,460	63.4	170	73	19.3	41.2	52	2,282	15.3	11.3	2,050
Clay	58	37.8	7,289	53.3	42	16	20.5	35.9	12	463	11.0	2.2	453
Cocke	234	33.9	6,756	61.6	175	67	21.2	30.5	52	1,880	14.6	5.2	1,787
Coffee	667	23.0	13,296	31.9	542	158	12.3	24.4	127	3,611	10.6	1.3	3,565
Crockett	101	24.5	6,929	58.9	81	26	14.4	33.7	20	746	11.3	5.8	705
Cumberland	236	51.9	4,716	105.0	155	92	12.6	34.4	68	2,378	9.4	11.0	2,142
Davidson	5,230	34.4	9,137	39.8	3,893	2,951	10.5	34.7	2,191	52,916	9.7	7.1	49,395
Decatur	81	31.4	6,947	71.4	62	26	15.9	28.3	20	767	12.1	-4.5	803
DeKalb	118	26.7	6,504	63.5	93	32	11.2	40.2	23	872	9.3	6.6	818
Dickson	209	27.4	4,617	74.2	164	100	14.7	23.6	81	2,574	10.8	-4.2	2,686
Dyer	247	28.0	6,561	62.2	193	104	13.1	25.1	84	2,692	11.2	-1.4	2,731
Fayette	169	26.0	5,029	53.0	134	62	15.2	42.4	43	1,870	9.4	14.3	1,636
Fentress	135	36.5	7,946	65.5	99	33	16.8	37.1	24	911	11.5	-1.9	929
Franklin	264	48.8	6,488	66.4	177	71	15.5	35.5	52	1,970	12.1	5.5	1,868
Gibson	334	21.8	6,950	67.1	275	110	15.3	26.3	87	2,886	12.6	2.5	2,815
Giles	176	30.2	6,023	69.3	135	56	13.0	28.3	44	1,523	10.0	-1.0	1,539
Grainger	138	44.1	6,282	63.1	96	32	20.4	28.8	25	898	12.2	8.5	828
Greene	419	26.3	6,472	61.5	332	167	12.5	33.4	125	4,299	10.9	5.1	4,089
Grundy	95	27.9	6,543	70.1	74	27	23.8	42.6	19	806	15.6	7.6	749
Hamblen	330	32.2	5,555	68.4	250	152	9.4	26.5	121	3,803	8.6	1.7	3,741
Hamilton	2,847	19.6	9,173	47.9	2,380	1,576	15.4	24.0	1,271	28,295	11.6	2.5	27,602
Hancock	60	32.5	8,974	49.3	45	14	46.9	40.5	10	470	20.2	2.2	460
Hardeman	211	30.0	7,504	53.6	163	80	23.3	35.8	59	2,176	20.0	7.6	2,022
Hardin	200	40.7	7,697	56.2	142	66	17.5	34.6	49	1,753	13.7	7.1	1,637
Hawkins	320	42.0	5,722	64.9	225	108	18.0	37.2	79	2,624	13.0	5.1	2,496
Haywood	165	36.2	8,426	44.4	121	44	16.0	28.8	34	1,213	14.4	3.7	1,170
Henderson	169	16.8	6,432	63.9	145	52	12.4	34.4	38	1,362	9.7	12.2	1,214
Henry	212	20.2	6,738	71.8	177	101	19.6	39.1	73	2,618	15.1	10.8	2,362
Hickman	106	32.5	4,472	72.5	80	43	28.7	46.1	29	1,238	17.7	8.4	1,142
Houston	56	32.6	6,991	68.2	42	16	30.4	45.1	11	536	17.8	7.0	501
Humphreys	363	8.4	20,030	21.1	335	74	23.0	27.3	58	1,428	16.5	8.0	1,322
Jackson	69	37.4	6,221	61.8	50	17	15.6	42.3	12	544	7.7	19.0	457
Jefferson	288	51.9	6,042	69.3	189	90	16.0	41.0	64	2,427	12.9	6.7	2,274
Johnson	122	35.7	6,747	66.8	90	35	20.9	37.2	26	1,094	15.8	6.7	1,025
Knox	2,834	26.3	7,083	54.4	2,244	1,822	15.8	26.0	1,445	39,051	13.3	4.1	37,521
Lake	61	24.0	7,929	53.0	49	29	57.0	35.9	22	843	42.5	8.4	778
Lauderdale	188	30.3	7,024	55.4	145	76	25.8	31.1	58	2,063	22.3	3.5	1,993
Lawrence	270	46.4	6,608	64.8	185	81	15.5	26.8	64	2,106	11.1	-1.5	2,139

See footnotes at end of table.

[Includes United States, states, and 3,141 counties/county equivalents defined as of February 22, 2005. For more information on these areas, see Appendix C, Geographic Information]

County	Federal government expenditure					Federal, state, and local governments[1]							
	2004					Earnings				Employment			
						2005				2005			
	Total (mil. dol.)	Percent change, 2000–2004	Per capita (dol.)	Direct payments to individ-uals, percent of total	2000 (mil. dol.)	Total (mil. dol.)	Percent of total	Percent change, 2000–2005	2000 (mil. dol.)	Total	Percent of total	Percent change, 2000–2005	2000
TENNESSEE—Con.													
Lewis.	67	41.4	5,891	63.9	48	23	24.2	38.7	16	692	15.6	6.6	649
Lincoln.	202	46.2	6,299	61.3	138	88	20.7	34.0	65	2,684	17.4	2.7	2,614
Loudon.	264	26.7	6,239	78.8	208	90	14.9	35.0	67	2,166	11.6	11.5	1,943
McMinn	292	28.4	5,722	68.9	227	107	11.5	27.7	83	2,741	10.3	4.1	2,633
McNairy.	199	36.9	7,904	62.8	145	44	11.7	32.7	33	1,327	11.9	4.7	1,267
Macon	106	28.2	4,957	64.6	83	35	16.5	31.1	27	1,045	10.5	2.0	1,025
Madison.	567	36.0	6,002	60.6	417	527	19.8	32.4	398	11,654	17.1	5.8	11,012
Marion	179	39.7	6,485	67.7	128	48	16.6	29.7	37	1,318	12.7	2.6	1,285
Marshall	135	34.9	4,818	70.7	100	64	14.0	28.2	50	1,621	11.0	1.7	1,594
Maury	348	33.6	4,658	72.4	260	287	15.1	31.7	218	6,590	15.0	4.6	6,300
Meigs	74	23.1	6,393	61.1	60	17	17.2	41.1	12	471	8.2	1.9	462
Monroe	224	41.0	5,319	70.7	159	69	10.5	45.7	47	1,900	10.1	21.4	1,565
Montgomery	760	41.4	5,346	67.5	538	387	20.2	33.4	290	9,014	14.7	0.5	8,970
Moore	19	22.6	3,187	80.4	16	26	34.9	24.2	21	736	27.2	-3.3	761
Morgan	104	35.7	5,152	66.4	76	50	35.4	40.8	35	1,654	26.0	16.9	1,415
Obion	208	13.6	6,412	69.0	183	74	10.7	21.2	61	1,894	10.1	-3.2	1,956
Overton	138	37.3	6,737	65.4	100	42	20.3	37.5	31	1,238	14.3	7.4	1,153
Perry	55	37.0	7,186	68.1	40	14	13.6	37.4	10	413	10.3	12.5	367
Pickett	36	33.5	7,348	59.8	27	9	25.5	35.6	7	303	15.7	17.4	258
Polk	119	29.6	7,396	68.4	92	35	30.5	45.0	24	920	20.9	10.6	832
Putnam	434	43.5	6,580	61.5	302	310	21.6	36.2	227	7,697	17.9	7.5	7,163
Rhea	250	15.3	8,403	49.9	217	149	29.4	15.2	130	2,463	16.6	0.5	2,450
Roane	417	28.3	7,873	61.5	325	186	18.3	28.6	145	4,248	19.8	-2.6	4,363
Robertson	236	24.3	3,985	76.4	190	133	14.5	37.4	97	3,384	11.9	8.7	3,112
Rutherford	1,194	117.7	5,687	38.7	549	603	11.2	19.8	503	13,704	10.7	3.6	13,229
Scott	260	46.7	11,927	36.1	178	47	19.1	30.7	36	1,353	14.6	4.4	1,296
Sequatchie	77	18.5	6,270	52.6	65	21	19.7	44.2	15	618	14.3	7.5	575
Sevier	333	38.1	4,312	76.6	241	192	12.7	38.8	139	4,613	9.2	4.2	4,425
Shelby	7,072	28.4	7,787	43.0	5,509	4,499	14.3	28.0	3,515	79,470	12.6	-0.2	79,646
Smith	102	24.1	5,565	70.8	83	35	15.1	39.4	25	947	11.0	8.4	874
Stewart	140	41.7	10,976	45.5	99	79	56.9	40.4	56	1,210	28.9	10.3	1,097
Sullivan	1,014	41.1	6,652	68.8	719	320	8.7	21.5	263	7,793	8.5	-1.8	7,933
Sumner	635	29.9	4,481	65.3	488	302	14.0	38.9	217	7,228	13.5	10.5	6,542
Tipton	283	36.8	5,175	64.8	207	103	20.2	36.3	75	2,681	16.4	8.4	2,474
Trousdale	41	29.2	5,539	69.8	32	18	24.5	32.6	13	455	8.6	-0.2	456
Unicoi	239	46.6	13,524	38.9	163	44	16.8	32.8	33	1,171	16.6	5.7	1,108
Union	79	39.6	4,159	66.5	56	30	25.4	44.4	21	859	18.0	14.8	748
Van Buren	26	30.7	4,842	64.1	20	13	22.3	36.1	9	365	15.3	9.3	334
Warren	233	30.5	5,885	72.6	178	79	10.2	31.1	60	2,069	9.6	3.1	2,006
Washington	743	24.1	6,690	64.0	599	544	20.0	27.9	426	11,824	15.3	2.1	11,583
Wayne	94	33.3	5,567	62.5	70	46	31.8	39.1	33	1,412	23.0	6.5	1,326
Weakley.	197	29.1	5,838	66.0	153	132	26.6	27.7	103	3,871	22.4	7.4	3,605
White.	145	36.4	6,083	69.8	106	45	15.6	42.1	32	1,416	12.3	12.4	1,260
Williamson	395	44.2	2,690	78.2	274	371	7.6	54.9	240	8,327	8.3	22.2	6,813
Wilson	382	40.7	3,899	75.1	271	166	8.7	45.6	114	4,142	8.5	12.2	3,691
TEXAS	[3]141,858	[3]33.0	[3]6,308	[3]48.7	[3]106,671	91,458	14.8	34.9	67,784	1,828,003	14.0	6.3	1,720,427
Anderson	280	25.3	4,996	72.4	224	241	29.6	16.3	207	5,898	22.7	-0.4	5,920
Andrews	58	26.8	4,547	72.7	46	47	18.5	22.1	38	1,153	17.3	0.3	1,149
Angelina	435	29.8	5,337	72.8	335	265	15.0	27.8	208	6,893	14.6	4.4	6,601
Aransas	125	29.0	5,198	83.7	97	42	17.7	21.2	35	1,080	10.1	-1.0	1,091
Archer	61	17.7	6,614	62.6	52	21	17.6	32.9	16	556	13.1	4.3	533
Armstrong	16	8.6	7,217	53.1	14	5	20.4	6.9	4	139	12.5	-14.2	162
Atascosa	182	25.6	4,272	67.5	145	88	21.4	26.1	70	2,444	14.5	6.6	2,292
Austin	504	-6.0	19,523	18.6	536	65	13.7	33.9	49	1,629	10.0	7.7	1,513
Bailey	54	13.5	8,113	44.2	48	23	21.7	25.1	18	666	16.9	3.7	642
Bandera	95	41.7	4,796	83.5	67	30	23.5	26.8	23	854	11.6	7.4	795
Bastrop	266	33.3	3,880	68.3	200	176	31.6	35.2	130	3,937	16.8	5.5	3,730
Baylor	37	-0.8	9,374	65.5	37	10	24.5	8.3	9	279	12.6	-7.3	301
Bee	162	31.8	4,913	64.7	123	143	40.8	12.2	127	3,600	30.1	-8.0	3,914
Bell	3,736	34.1	14,924	24.7	2,785	4,633	59.8	57.6	2,940	67,873	40.4	5.2	64,492
Bexar	12,575	30.2	8,417	46.1	9,655	9,328	22.9	28.2	7,276	157,290	17.2	0.2	157,017
Blanco	68	7.5	7,498	88.8	63	22	16.8	29.6	17	546	8.2	4.8	521
Borden	4	-3.7	6,583	27.9	5	4	31.9	16.2	3	93	16.3	-2.1	95
Bosque	104	25.0	5,792	79.6	83	42	24.0	42.8	29	1,177	14.2	15.6	1,018
Bowie	812	42.8	8,996	51.7	569	585	30.7	48.7	394	10,619	20.8	14.9	9,241
Brazoria	820	27.2	3,025	77.5	645	685	15.3	34.8	508	16,732	14.4	7.3	15,600
Brazos	928	60.8	5,938	34.0	577	1,323	38.8	36.1	972	31,562	31.5	10.1	28,661
Brewster	63	45.1	6,816	57.0	43	59	33.0	30.0	46	1,444	22.2	4.3	1,385
Briscoe	26	34.3	15,354	35.2	20	4	21.7	6.0	4	124	12.1	-13.9	144
Brooks	74	25.8	9,542	42.2	59	34	40.4	34.1	26	727	20.6	-3.2	751
Brown	238	23.7	6,220	73.3	192	118	18.4	24.0	96	3,019	13.4	-0.1	3,021

See footnotes at end of table.

Table B-12. Counties — **Government Expenditure, Earnings, and Employment**—Con.

[Includes United States, states, and 3,141 counties/county equivalents defined as of February 22, 2005. For more information on these areas, see Appendix C, Geographic Information]

County	Federal government expenditure					Federal, state, and local governments[1]							
	2004				2000 (mil. dol.)	Earnings				Employment			
						2005			2000 (mil. dol.)	2005			2000
	Total (mil. dol.)	Percent change, 2000–2004	Per capita (dol.)	Direct payments to individuals, percent of total		Total (mil. dol.)	Percent of total	Percent change, 2000–2005		Total	Percent of total	Percent change, 2000–2005	
TEXAS—Con.													
Burleson	99	21.2	5,823	66.1	82	36	21.6	26.9	28	1,017	13.5	8.4	938
Burnet	188	30.4	4,659	82.6	144	91	15.3	35.0	67	2,275	9.5	9.1	2,085
Caldwell	159	28.4	4,347	68.4	124	67	24.4	30.0	51	1,753	14.5	3.5	1,694
Calhoun	112	37.6	5,422	60.5	81	59	9.3	16.2	51	1,527	11.9	-2.2	1,561
Callahan	74	20.9	5,540	75.1	61	27	28.7	23.0	22	765	13.9	5.2	727
Cameron	1,793	32.4	4,823	50.8	1,354	1,245	28.1	35.4	919	27,884	17.9	6.6	26,150
Camp	84	37.5	6,995	69.0	61	21	11.1	25.4	17	614	11.0	8.1	568
Carson	43	0.6	6,569	56.4	42	36	9.8	6.5	34	620	10.0	-2.8	638
Cass	215	24.1	7,177	71.6	174	80	20.1	20.8	66	2,193	16.6	2.0	2,150
Castro	64	0.1	8,379	35.6	64	24	9.9	5.4	22	720	16.4	-10.4	804
Chambers	154	95.1	5,458	41.6	79	70	14.2	31.0	54	1,766	15.4	11.3	1,587
Cherokee	242	30.9	5,026	70.5	185	166	22.9	21.3	137	4,312	18.2	2.4	4,211
Childress	45	-7.3	5,904	59.4	48	46	45.0	20.9	38	1,149	29.4	1.6	1,131
Clay	49	10.5	4,325	76.0	44	21	18.8	26.4	17	604	10.6	2.9	587
Cochran	43	3.3	12,775	31.4	41	14	18.8	7.4	13	399	21.1	-1.5	405
Coke	20	17.0	5,417	78.4	17	13	55.0	17.3	11	424	21.8	-6.6	454
Coleman	80	21.7	9,206	69.2	66	27	33.2	15.7	24	780	15.6	-5.8	828
Collin	1,675	53.8	2,667	49.1	1,089	1,532	8.4	73.3	884	33,111	9.2	39.7	23,708
Collingsworth	41	3.2	13,533	37.5	40	9	16.6	-8.2	10	261	11.0	-24.8	347
Colorado	138	21.7	6,642	60.3	113	43	15.4	23.0	35	1,177	9.6	-0.5	1,183
Comal	433	32.9	4,716	77.8	326	198	12.1	39.1	142	4,676	9.7	8.5	4,310
Comanche	95	24.3	6,946	70.1	76	37	19.1	28.3	28	1,066	12.1	6.5	1,001
Concho	28	-6.2	7,360	47.1	29	9	23.1	22.8	7	280	13.0	1.1	277
Cooke	169	22.6	4,379	79.5	138	114	15.6	32.5	86	2,956	11.9	11.9	2,641
Coryell	287	31.8	3,820	78.0	218	252	41.0	21.3	208	6,281	28.5	2.3	6,140
Cottle	21	12.9	12,197	45.9	19	5	24.8	-6.8	5	155	14.8	-14.4	181
Crane	15	24.4	3,885	86.8	12	14	18.6	12.8	12	369	18.6	-1.6	375
Crockett	24	41.4	6,180	45.4	17	15	39.4	26.5	12	459	20.6	10.6	415
Crosby	70	26.1	10,464	46.7	55	19	15.2	13.8	17	558	16.7	-1.9	569
Culberson	15	9.6	5,586	55.7	14	16	52.1	22.7	13	373	23.0	-3.9	388
Dallam	62	8.4	10,115	45.3	58	28	14.5	18.0	24	687	12.5	-3.2	710
Dallas	12,174	30.4	5,305	45.3	9,338	9,407	8.3	33.1	7,067	165,935	9.1	7.0	155,138
Dawson	129	11.8	8,986	47.1	116	59	29.5	16.2	51	1,556	21.5	-3.6	1,614
Deaf Smith	118	20.8	6,390	45.2	98	49	14.9	16.8	42	1,321	13.5	-6.2	1,408
Delta	40	25.0	7,345	62.8	32	12	34.2	18.8	10	340	15.3	-3.1	351
Denton	1,058	52.1	1,994	65.6	695	1,383	17.5	56.7	883	30,823	15.1	19.7	25,755
DeWitt	117	18.2	5,739	66.5	99	85	27.4	20.3	70	2,343	18.9	3.2	2,271
Dickens	26	19.5	9,728	61.9	22	8	31.0	34.1	6	229	15.2	12.3	204
Dimmit	88	42.0	8,568	38.0	62	54	51.3	37.2	39	1,164	28.4	0.3	1,161
Donley	28	22.5	7,233	68.4	23	15	35.8	22.3	13	498	22.0	2.5	486
Duval	115	31.7	9,107	49.8	88	48	36.9	27.5	38	1,298	23.5	–	1,298
Eastland	136	16.1	7,388	74.6	117	52	18.3	22.1	43	1,487	13.2	-0.6	1,496
Ector	508	25.3	4,083	77.8	406	396	15.6	19.0	333	9,416	13.7	-3.0	9,707
Edwards	19	40.3	9,244	75.6	13	8	51.3	37.5	6	221	15.1	9.4	202
Ellis	468	47.2	3,639	70.6	318	268	15.9	51.8	176	6,712	12.6	21.3	5,532
El Paso	4,446	32.0	6,235	47.9	3,368	3,888	28.8	41.3	2,751	71,901	20.6	5.9	67,870
Erath	158	30.6	4,688	78.1	121	121	20.7	27.0	95	3,500	16.2	3.5	3,382
Falls	128	16.9	7,218	56.4	110	84	48.3	18.6	71	2,120	25.9	-0.1	2,123
Fannin	475	169.7	14,554	28.7	176	119	34.0	23.1	97	2,443	17.6	-1.0	2,467
Fayette	148	29.4	6,561	72.0	114	74	19.4	30.9	57	1,631	10.2	5.2	1,550
Fisher	40	-0.7	9,661	52.3	40	13	25.4	12.2	11	358	15.5	-10.1	398
Floyd	79	17.3	10,730	36.9	67	24	17.9	20.4	20	673	17.8	5.3	639
Foard	19	-11.8	12,150	46.2	21	4	33.9	9.6	4	129	14.4	-7.2	139
Fort Bend	883	74.7	1,994	60.6	505	976	12.8	45.3	672	21,837	11.5	16.8	18,699
Franklin	54	56.1	5,337	69.6	34	16	10.4	31.2	12	433	6.6	5.1	412
Freestone	92	27.0	4,930	70.8	72	50	18.1	26.0	40	1,313	12.1	2.6	1,280
Frio	87	13.0	5,302	50.9	77	49	30.8	19.2	41	1,342	21.5	2.1	1,315
Gaines	124	19.8	8,525	31.7	104	46	16.2	26.8	36	1,277	15.6	2.3	1,248
Galveston	1,471	25.4	5,415	59.3	1,174	1,503	32.1	30.4	1,153	29,755	23.9	0.6	29,574
Garza	38	49.0	7,520	51.7	26	17	20.2	45.0	12	472	14.6	26.2	374
Gillespie	130	29.8	5,799	88.2	101	47	13.0	31.5	36	1,163	7.4	8.9	1,068
Glasscock	19	-15.9	14,021	15.8	22	4	16.9	-0.2	4	128	13.5	-19.5	159
Goliad	40	26.9	5,597	68.6	31	18	27.5	26.4	15	508	15.5	5.4	482
Gonzales	145	42.7	7,535	53.6	102	53	16.0	29.5	41	1,474	13.6	7.3	1,374
Gray	133	15.2	6,194	80.7	115	59	12.5	12.3	52	1,509	12.2	-5.6	1,599
Grayson	583	16.6	5,032	77.7	500	261	13.1	27.9	204	6,308	10.9	3.3	6,109
Gregg	630	25.2	5,480	76.2	504	299	8.3	19.4	251	7,783	8.6	1.3	7,684
Grimes	117	33.4	4,637	65.5	88	83	23.3	19.8	69	1,996	18.1	1.7	1,962
Guadalupe	472	46.8	4,738	80.0	322	221	18.3	43.7	154	5,563	14.8	13.3	4,912
Hale	229	18.7	6,344	55.4	193	102	15.9	16.6	87	2,669	13.6	-1.9	2,722

See footnotes at end of table.

[Includes United States, states, and 3,141 counties/county equivalents defined as of February 22, 2005. For more information on these areas, see Appendix C, Geographic Information]

County	Federal government expenditure					Federal, state, and local governments[1]							
	2004				2000 (mil. dol.)	Earnings				Employment			
						2005			2000 (mil. dol.)	2005			2000
	Total (mil. dol.)	Percent change, 2000–2004	Per capita (dol.)	Direct payments to individuals, percent of total		Total (mil. dol.)	Percent of total	Percent change, 2000–2005		Total	Percent of total	Percent change, 2000–2005	
TEXAS—Con.													
Hall	42	12.7	11,132	45.8	37	10	22.8	5.0	10	333	15.4	−11.7	377
Hamilton	52	18.7	6,427	78.0	44	24	23.3	25.5	19	653	14.0	7.4	608
Hansford	40	−1.1	7,603	43.0	40	20	13.1	19.1	17	575	16.9	−1.2	582
Hardeman	42	25.2	9,541	55.3	33	16	28.4	19.1	13	440	18.7	−3.9	458
Hardin	228	33.0	4,529	80.9	171	91	17.5	24.2	73	2,566	14.1	1.9	2,518
Harris	15,799	1.8	4,335	51.0	15,521	13,868	8.6	37.1	10,115	256,430	10.6	7.9	237,752
Harrison	331	24.5	5,279	62.9	266	132	12.7	32.2	100	3,504	11.4	1.5	3,452
Hartley	23	−20.4	4,212	17.0	29	16	19.4	19.8	13	510	29.5	3.0	495
Haskell	61	10.7	10,856	52.0	55	17	19.9	11.9	15	493	13.1	−12.4	563
Hays	435	57.3	3,647	60.6	277	429	23.9	48.3	289	11,230	17.9	14.2	9,836
Hemphill	14	11.5	4,069	80.7	12	13	12.6	12.9	11	361	12.9	1.1	357
Henderson	339	35.6	4,282	75.1	250	128	18.8	34.5	95	3,433	11.5	8.4	3,166
Hidalgo	2,684	38.3	4,077	51.7	1,940	2,069	26.4	43.8	1,438	48,656	18.2	14.5	42,480
Hill	211	18.9	6,004	72.0	178	81	21.9	29.4	62	2,248	14.5	3.3	2,176
Hockley	153	32.8	6,716	55.2	115	73	20.0	26.8	58	2,056	16.8	10.1	1,868
Hood	230	36.8	4,948	89.2	168	80	18.3	41.6	56	2,035	12.9	12.4	1,811
Hopkins	168	23.1	5,064	72.4	137	90	17.0	31.5	68	2,354	12.3	7.0	2,199
Houston	171	26.3	7,348	61.9	136	85	26.1	17.4	73	2,274	20.8	(Z)	2,275
Howard	301	20.4	9,157	48.6	250	176	32.6	23.1	143	3,666	23.3	−2.8	3,772
Hudspeth	36	−5.7	10,897	25.2	38	25	75.0	56.3	16	456	30.2	15.2	396
Hunt	885	−3.2	10,816	33.0	913	280	21.8	29.5	216	7,476	18.5	10.5	6,766
Hutchinson	114	19.4	5,059	79.2	96	67	16.2	18.5	56	1,835	17.0	−0.9	1,851
Irion	8	23.7	4,551	76.4	6	5	29.2	25.0	4	134	13.2	3.1	130
Jack	40	28.1	4,490	72.1	31	22	19.4	28.4	17	548	12.5	0.2	547
Jackson	97	6.9	6,739	55.5	91	39	19.0	17.4	33	1,127	14.4	−1.6	1,145
Jasper	217	11.3	6,096	70.4	195	86	16.8	18.3	73	2,319	13.0	1.7	2,281
Jeff Davis	17	37.4	7,598	49.0	12	12	62.1	33.8	9	281	20.8	–	281
Jefferson	2,430	61.9	9,788	43.3	1,500	965	14.9	21.6	794	19,794	13.4	−3.2	20,440
Jim Hogg	45	25.6	8,902	46.6	36	30	52.2	69.7	17	554	21.5	1.5	546
Jim Wells	254	29.3	6,218	59.8	196	95	14.1	24.6	76	2,447	11.2	1.5	2,412
Johnson	503	35.7	3,510	82.2	371	268	15.9	44.2	186	6,740	11.3	11.8	6,031
Jones	117	13.1	5,831	62.6	104	50	24.3	−44.1	89	1,492	17.0	−46.4	2,783
Karnes	102	30.7	6,580	55.4	78	61	41.1	14.5	54	1,658	23.0	−2.9	1,708
Kaufman	410	31.5	4,802	79.5	312	229	20.5	44.5	158	5,777	16.0	12.8	5,120
Kendall	168	55.9	6,156	79.5	107	72	16.0	55.5	46	1,737	12.4	27.2	1,366
Kenedy	2	−63.6	3,762	59.5	4	2	12.7	22.7	2	78	14.2	−6.0	83
Kent	9	4.8	11,821	50.2	8	6	68.2	21.4	5	207	28.7	0.5	206
Kerr	344	33.3	7,530	78.2	258	168	19.3	29.1	130	3,422	11.9	0.5	3,404
Kimble	24	19.0	5,331	78.7	20	15	31.2	39.2	11	410	12.9	13.9	360
King	3	18.8	9,201	30.4	3	3	42.8	20.4	2	78	24.2	5.4	74
Kinney	30	32.0	9,051	60.8	23	20	78.5	48.7	14	361	26.9	4.0	347
Kleberg	286	−9.0	9,125	39.2	314	224	43.0	22.8	183	5,064	31.0	(Z)	5,065
Knox	42	−0.1	10,909	49.0	43	15	26.3	9.1	14	441	18.8	−6.4	471
Lamar	313	25.2	6,299	64.8	250	126	14.6	19.6	105	3,213	11.2	0.6	3,193
Lamb	121	14.1	8,345	49.0	106	41	18.0	21.2	34	1,128	14.6	1.5	1,111
Lampasas	121	34.1	5,861	86.2	91	38	20.3	26.7	30	953	11.6	−4.8	1,001
La Salle	61	47.3	10,187	33.2	41	30	37.1	38.2	21	620	22.7	10.9	559
Lavaca	147	23.6	7,769	70.2	119	34	13.1	22.0	28	982	8.2	1.1	971
Lee	67	38.8	4,060	69.6	48	49	20.8	22.5	40	1,273	13.2	−0.1	1,274
Leon	128	38.1	7,936	67.2	93	32	11.8	30.2	24	890	9.3	9.7	811
Liberty	357	24.3	4,768	74.6	287	176	19.9	29.2	136	4,601	16.7	5.3	4,369
Limestone	138	27.4	6,053	66.4	108	106	32.9	23.0	86	2,987	25.1	1.1	2,955
Lipscomb	17	7.2	5,622	63.6	16	12	19.8	28.3	9	400	18.9	12.0	357
Live Oak	74	−29.4	6,362	46.7	105	49	32.8	16.5	42	919	17.4	−5.5	972
Llano	116	26.1	6,376	89.3	92	45	26.0	35.7	33	1,132	15.6	8.1	1,047
Loving	1	23.2	11,442	55.8	(Z)	–	26.6	22.9	–	16	20.3	−15.8	19
Lubbock	1,269	0.6	5,055	66.6	1,261	1,239	22.9	29.5	956	25,220	15.8	6.2	23,754
Lynn	62	−1.4	10,080	40.6	63	19	15.5	24.6	16	581	20.1	1.2	574
McCulloch	61	16.8	7,493	67.9	52	26	20.9	24.4	21	767	15.4	4.2	736
McLennan	1,367	26.5	6,146	59.6	1,080	827	17.2	33.1	621	17,579	13.4	9.2	16,093
McMullen	4	−36.0	4,204	68.7	6	4	36.6	21.7	3	117	16.2	−0.8	118
Madison	54	24.9	4,117	71.2	44	46	25.3	14.4	40	1,239	20.1	−0.3	1,243
Marion	79	16.4	7,116	57.7	68	18	19.0	21.2	15	478	12.1	−4.2	499
Martin	46	−2.6	10,412	32.2	48	16	24.8	19.6	13	388	15.0	−5.8	412
Mason	25	26.4	6,467	73.6	20	9	18.0	22.4	8	272	9.7	−6.2	290
Matagorda	217	19.6	5,695	58.0	181	102	18.3	22.5	83	2,698	16.5	−5.3	2,850
Maverick	259	29.7	5,127	49.9	199	214	43.2	48.7	144	4,963	26.9	19.3	4,161
Medina	179	27.0	4,241	74.5	141	111	34.1	25.3	88	3,030	20.3	5.1	2,884
Menard	18	38.6	7,955	66.1	13	7	54.5	12.7	6	223	15.3	0.5	222
Midland	459	29.9	3,816	74.8	353	384	9.6	24.1	309	8,463	9.8	−2.1	8,641

See footnotes at end of table.

Table B-12. Counties — **Government Expenditure, Earnings, and Employment**—Con.

[Includes United States, states, and 3,141 counties/county equivalents defined as of February 22, 2005. For more information on these areas, see Appendix C, Geographic Information]

County	Federal government expenditure 2004 — Total (mil. dol.)	Percent change, 2000–2004	Per capita (dol.)	Direct payments to individuals, percent of total	2000 (mil. dol.)	Earnings 2005 — Total (mil. dol.)	Percent of total	Percent change, 2000–2005	2000 (mil. dol.)	Employment 2005 — Total	Percent of total	Percent change, 2000–2005	2000
TEXAS—Con.													
Milam	149	17.5	5,904	64.4	127	53	15.1	29.8	41	1,422	11.5	1.7	1,398
Mills	34	29.8	6,619	74.3	26	16	24.7	32.5	12	458	13.6	10.9	413
Mitchell	53	-2.5	5,680	62.5	55	49	48.1	18.8	42	1,315	33.1	0.7	1,306
Montague	123	26.2	6,285	80.5	97	51	23.0	24.6	41	1,429	14.1	5.0	1,361
Montgomery	1,034	37.3	2,853	80.6	753	676	11.3	53.7	439	15,604	10.3	21.3	12,869
Moore	74	8.1	3,640	62.2	68	61	14.9	30.8	47	1,590	13.8	4.7	1,518
Morris	92	27.5	7,062	75.2	72	27	9.7	12.3	24	733	11.6	-2.4	751
Motley	15	13.7	11,323	51.0	13	4	24.2	21.7	3	123	11.3	-1.6	125
Nacogdoches	330	28.2	5,480	64.6	258	233	25.6	28.7	181	5,265	17.3	6.5	4,942
Navarro	270	27.6	5,593	67.4	212	137	21.3	36.3	100	3,796	15.4	16.8	3,251
Newton	79	34.5	5,540	67.3	59	26	30.1	17.0	22	777	23.3	0.6	772
Nolan	100	20.8	6,594	72.0	83	68	27.0	21.4	56	1,857	21.0	-0.9	1,874
Nueces	2,408	33.2	7,584	47.0	1,808	1,693	21.5	33.0	1,273	30,642	15.7	2.0	30,034
Ochiltree	39	-12.8	4,303	57.5	45	26	9.9	19.5	22	736	11.9	0.5	732
Oldham	14	-35.0	6,539	56.9	22	12	32.7	17.8	10	293	23.5	1.4	289
Orange	463	27.1	5,454	76.2	364	184	17.5	19.3	154	4,748	15.2	-1.0	4,795
Palo Pinto	156	33.3	5,695	71.1	117	77	19.6	28.2	60	1,938	14.5	3.4	1,875
Panola	126	28.1	5,506	72.5	98	51	13.7	10.2	46	1,262	10.5	-15.5	1,493
Parker	358	45.9	3,565	78.3	245	214	20.8	45.7	147	5,267	12.3	14.1	4,618
Parmer	77	5.7	7,757	35.3	73	31	14.1	25.6	25	940	14.1	5.9	888
Pecos	59	21.9	3,714	63.9	49	72	36.5	14.7	63	1,882	27.7	-4.0	1,961
Polk	372	34.1	8,020	84.5	278	116	26.2	25.6	93	3,155	19.2	3.8	3,040
Potter	2,082	22.8	17,580	27.3	1,695	634	16.9	26.2	503	13,600	13.2	6.2	12,809
Presidio	56	30.4	7,306	42.3	43	41	66.7	28.7	32	834	30.6	7.5	776
Rains	47	28.0	4,242	80.2	37	17	20.7	47.2	12	480	11.1	16.2	413
Randall	205	79.3	1,878	75.1	114	199	17.7	26.7	157	5,238	14.1	8.7	4,819
Reagan	17	-5.1	5,661	48.2	18	13	15.1	15.8	11	361	14.7	-12.2	411
Real	25	38.0	8,317	69.4	18	7	38.3	37.3	5	239	16.6	-6.6	256
Red River	124	23.7	9,064	55.9	100	30	28.3	22.4	25	900	16.4	3.9	866
Reeves	86	47.6	7,232	46.4	58	60	45.0	43.5	42	1,631	31.2	11.0	1,470
Refugio	56	18.2	7,290	62.7	47	25	29.1	23.8	20	711	21.0	0.7	706
Roberts	5	-57.0	5,404	59.5	11	3	36.2	25.2	3	105	19.2	6.1	99
Robertson	118	24.3	7,284	55.1	95	40	21.8	29.1	31	1,063	14.5	0.9	1,053
Rockwall	207	60.2	3,547	54.3	129	113	13.9	76.4	64	2,759	10.8	38.8	1,988
Runnels	80	12.5	7,307	62.8	71	31	22.6	15.0	27	886	15.0	-6.3	946
Rusk	221	24.5	4,603	71.5	177	90	13.6	19.1	76	2,389	12.1	3.6	2,306
Sabine	99	31.0	9,472	77.4	75	22	17.0	22.2	18	604	16.3	3.6	583
San Augustine	69	28.3	7,786	64.9	54	17	21.7	14.3	15	457	15.1	-11.1	514
San Jacinto	106	34.9	4,294	72.0	79	36	35.1	37.0	26	1,085	20.1	22.0	889
San Patricio	482	18.0	7,064	49.4	408	374	39.6	18.4	316	7,015	27.3	-7.8	7,609
San Saba	51	29.5	8,404	50.9	40	28	38.0	17.0	24	715	17.9	-10.1	795
Schleicher	15	0.7	5,566	66.8	15	10	32.1	18.5	8	287	17.3	-4.7	301
Scurry	91	12.2	5,639	67.0	81	60	15.8	11.3	54	1,560	17.2	-7.9	1,693
Shackelford	21	25.1	6,355	73.5	16	9	17.9	34.0	7	254	11.5	11.9	227
Shelby	182	26.7	6,947	61.1	143	50	12.9	21.2	41	1,357	11.3	-0.7	1,366
Sherman	28	-25.1	8,966	31.6	37	11	9.7	22.2	9	315	17.6	2.9	306
Smith	973	28.2	5,219	71.2	759	590	12.3	26.3	467	13,061	10.8	3.5	12,622
Somervell	28	31.4	3,786	79.4	21	27	11.5	31.2	21	685	13.4	12.5	609
Starr	260	33.0	4,352	46.7	196	203	49.7	56.5	130	5,316	26.1	17.5	4,523
Stephens	52	25.1	5,489	77.7	42	30	21.2	17.7	25	780	14.8	-2.5	800
Sterling	6	49.0	4,713	58.0	4	5	33.7	23.3	4	173	17.4	3.0	168
Stonewall	14	5.0	10,004	57.5	13	7	31.6	28.3	6	219	16.7	9.0	201
Sutton	15	16.9	3,664	72.4	13	16	15.2	26.2	13	424	12.8	-6.2	452
Swisher	72	16.4	9,133	43.5	62	29	17.6	18.6	25	806	19.9	-0.5	810
Tarrant	15,410	78.2	9,704	24.9	8,646	5,425	11.7	37.8	3,937	102,349	10.8	9.6	93,374
Taylor	984	26.6	7,869	49.7	778	843	29.5	38.7	608	15,740	19.3	5.0	14,994
Terrell	13	91.8	13,350	37.9	7	6	76.6	-28.6	8	144	20.4	-42.4	250
Terry	109	30.0	8,704	46.1	84	43	20.5	40.4	36	1,184	18.8	1.5	1,167
Throckmorton	15	8.1	8,904	60.8	13	6	23.2	14.2	5	188	15.8	-7.4	203
Titus	137	24.7	4,696	71.0	110	119	17.2	33.6	89	3,005	14.1	5.1	2,860
Tom Green	722	28.3	6,954	54.1	563	577	27.0	26.7	455	12,027	18.6	-1.8	12,250
Travis	7,850	47.6	9,024	26.3	5,317	6,301	17.7	33.9	4,706	116,855	16.7	5.0	111,314
Trinity	106	11.4	7,367	76.4	95	23	25.2	14.1	21	713	15.2	-3.3	737
Tyler	119	-9.2	5,740	79.0	131	68	40.5	20.5	57	1,859	28.4	1.3	1,835
Upshur	195	12.5	5,210	79.1	173	65	22.7	25.9	52	1,781	15.1	5.1	1,694
Upton	18	11.7	5,797	69.9	16	16	27.0	15.6	14	436	22.8	-4.6	457
Uvalde	154	27.0	5,788	58.7	121	113	32.0	28.9	88	2,729	19.9	-0.2	2,734
Val Verde	412	29.8	8,697	32.4	318	384	46.5	37.3	280	5,958	25.4	1.3	5,880
Van Zandt	241	26.3	4,639	82.8	191	87	20.6	32.6	65	2,363	12.7	4.1	2,271
Victoria	400	22.9	4,663	71.3	326	263	14.3	17.0	225	6,592	13.0	-3.3	6,818

See footnotes at end of table.

Table B-12. Counties — **Government Expenditure, Earnings, and Employment**—Con.

[Includes United States, states, and 3,141 counties/county equivalents defined as of February 22, 2005. For more information on these areas, see Appendix C, Geographic Information]

County	Federal government expenditure 2004 — Total (mil. dol.)	Percent change, 2000–2004	Per capita (dol.)	Direct payments to individuals, percent of total	2000 (mil. dol.)	Earnings 2005 — Total (mil. dol.)	Percent of total	Percent change, 2000–2005	2000 (mil. dol.)	Employment 2005 — Total	Percent of total	Percent change, 2000–2005	2000
TEXAS—Con.													
Walker	229	38.0	3,684	69.0	166	553	60.2	16.5	474	12,568	44.0	-2.2	12,847
Waller	149	34.4	4,276	62.2	111	164	28.0	54.6	106	4,605	27.4	37.1	3,359
Ward	61	38.2	5,860	65.8	44	42	27.9	17.6	36	1,110	24.6	-4.6	1,164
Washington	177	34.5	5,654	67.1	131	115	19.0	26.5	91	3,103	14.4	5.0	2,956
Webb	961	33.1	4,379	45.0	722	929	27.1	51.5	614	19,586	19.0	20.9	16,194
Wharton	272	15.6	6,540	56.5	235	115	17.9	20.8	95	3,108	14.3	-3.1	3,209
Wheeler	39	-14.7	8,136	73.1	46	18	13.5	16.6	16	571	17.2	2.1	559
Wichita	1,210	20.4	9,507	45.4	1,006	924	30.0	11.6	828	17,919	22.7	-16.7	21,521
Wilbarger	94	12.6	6,660	67.8	84	111	40.8	23.3	90	2,854	30.5	1.4	2,815
Willacy	126	26.0	6,244	47.3	100	46	30.9	9.8	42	1,288	22.6	-11.5	1,455
Williamson	1,406	72.6	4,422	39.6	815	699	11.9	55.5	449	16,767	12.3	26.4	13,266
Wilson	139	32.2	3,792	75.8	105	84	34.7	49.2	56	2,372	19.8	26.2	1,879
Winkler	35	21.4	5,172	80.6	29	22	19.3	16.8	19	593	18.8	-10.2	660
Wise	177	41.7	3,179	75.2	125	124	15.2	52.6	81	3,241	12.1	21.4	2,670
Wood	239	35.8	5,931	81.0	176	73	18.2	33.2	55	1,976	13.4	2.2	1,934
Yoakum	48	19.6	6,567	46.3	40	28	14.7	24.6	23	799	17.2	10.4	724
Young	109	20.8	6,068	76.2	90	53	15.1	24.4	43	1,478	12.3	-2.4	1,514
Zapata	62	38.3	4,679	60.9	44	41	27.8	46.3	28	1,158	23.0	12.0	1,034
Zavala	76	29.1	6,455	47.1	58	29	28.3	19.0	25	885	18.9	-6.6	948
UTAH	[3]13,684	[3]36.3	[3]5,728	[3]43.8	[3]10,043	10,783	18.9	36.5	7,901	220,758	14.6	8.4	203,739
Beaver	38	45.0	6,265	54.0	26	25	18.0	26.8	20	691	21.8	0.3	689
Box Elder	297	-44.3	6,637	41.5	534	111	11.3	24.0	90	2,703	10.3	5.5	2,561
Cache	377	41.7	3,869	49.7	266	426	25.0	38.8	307	10,155	16.8	8.1	9,390
Carbon	110	32.8	5,570	75.7	83	89	23.4	22.4	73	2,266	19.3	-5.2	2,390
Daggett	10	17.0	10,900	34.4	9	12	62.1	39.0	8	245	37.1	20.1	204
Davis	2,646	58.3	10,130	23.4	1,671	1,949	36.9	41.4	1,379	30,091	21.4	12.2	26,826
Duchesne	79	41.7	5,271	59.7	50	60	26.0	44.2	48	1,693	18.6	6.1	1,596
Emery	50	37.8	4,672	62.0	36	32	15.6	6.5	30	882	15.5	-3.7	916
Garfield	41	18.7	9,366	39.4	35	26	34.7	23.1	21	581	17.6	-1.0	587
Grand	56	50.1	6,407	45.0	37	41	26.5	39.8	30	870	14.1	3.0	845
Iron	183	66.7	5,049	51.2	110	164	27.7	34.2	122	4,059	18.5	4.8	3,872
Juab	46	90.7	5,075	49.8	24	24	18.9	39.2	17	630	13.6	7.7	585
Kane	38	20.7	6,177	64.6	32	30	30.3	30.3	23	746	18.1	5.5	707
Millard	52	19.2	4,207	65.9	43	48	22.0	26.7	38	1,130	17.5	5.1	1,075
Morgan	21	10.0	2,777	101.6	19	15	18.6	28.7	12	400	11.5	6.1	377
Piute	11	37.5	8,156	55.9	8	5	28.2	20.5	4	137	19.8	5.4	130
Rich	10	52.2	4,714	59.2	6	8	31.9	31.6	6	200	15.8	4.7	191
Salt Lake	4,793	30.5	5,125	43.0	3,672	4,593	15.3	34.5	3,414	92,376	13.3	6.1	87,056
San Juan	112	35.0	8,019	27.0	83	72	49.2	28.2	56	1,838	32.5	1.9	1,803
Sanpete	93	14.8	3,947	66.2	81	94	38.4	37.3	69	2,593	24.1	8.2	2,397
Sevier	99	28.0	5,092	65.0	77	70	24.0	24.7	56	1,696	15.7	-0.9	1,711
Summit	74	-18.2	2,200	58.8	91	106	11.3	37.9	77	2,438	8.3	10.6	2,204
Tooele	428	52.0	8,613	28.8	281	274	36.6	51.8	180	4,296	22.3	16.1	3,699
Uintah	130	36.1	4,884	49.9	96	115	20.4	29.3	89	2,686	16.6	0.7	2,668
Utah	1,122	38.9	2,783	62.0	808	1,055	14.0	40.9	748	26,422	11.7	15.9	22,796
Wasatch	47	32.9	2,591	65.9	35	52	21.4	39.0	37	1,191	12.7	13.0	1,054
Washington	477	51.6	4,336	72.9	314	259	13.9	49.6	173	6,323	9.9	24.5	5,080
Wayne	15	30.5	6,183	49.3	12	12	30.5	24.2	10	278	16.5	-3.1	287
Weber	1,317	25.1	6,313	54.6	1,052	1,007	25.4	31.7	765	21,142	18.6	5.5	20,043
VERMONT	[3]4,633	[3]37.7	[3]7,456	[3]47.1	[3]3,364	2,746	17.9	42.2	1,931	55,527	13.1	5.3	52,752
Addison	175	19.0	4,742	54.4	147	93	12.8	35.5	69	2,302	9.4	1.7	2,264
Bennington	217	32.5	5,864	66.3	164	103	11.5	23.2	83	2,306	8.7	-7.6	2,497
Caledonia	167	27.2	5,469	63.7	131	89	15.5	35.2	66	2,176	11.7	-1.8	2,215
Chittenden	1,215	35.3	8,137	34.8	898	869	16.1	41.8	613	15,787	12.8	7.9	14,636
Essex	44	26.3	6,574	64.0	35	22	27.0	83.3	12	468	18.4	14.7	408
Franklin	285	35.4	5,992	45.8	211	216	26.0	68.3	128	3,981	16.9	19.4	3,335
Grand Isle	40	51.9	5,269	56.5	27	15	24.7	47.5	10	386	14.5	14.2	338
Lamoille	111	28.4	4,538	63.5	86	77	14.9	40.5	55	1,814	11.1	3.0	1,762
Orange	147	36.5	5,048	63.0	108	87	22.4	36.7	64	2,120	14.7	-3.9	2,206
Orleans	283	118.9	10,353	35.2	129	99	20.9	55.3	64	2,240	14.2	9.4	2,048
Rutland	398	29.7	6,255	62.0	307	223	16.3	38.3	161	4,922	12.3	2.9	4,782
Washington	615	35.2	10,415	34.6	455	438	26.2	44.5	303	8,544	18.9	5.9	8,068
Windham	240	30.6	5,420	66.5	184	136	11.9	45.2	94	3,246	9.5	9.0	2,977
Windsor	416	27.8	7,167	53.9	325	280	23.3	33.0	210	5,235	14.7	0.4	5,216
VIRGINIA	[3]90,638	[3]44.3	[3]12,150	[3]32.2	[3]62,808	54,200	23.7	36.4	39,726	847,623	17.9	4.9	807,976
Accomack	364	32.8	9,237	43.9	274	162	29.0	31.3	123	3,081	16.8	8.2	2,847
Albemarle	264	32.3	2,975	83.2	199	[6]1,600	[6]34.5	[6]40.4	[6]1,139	[6]28,817	[6]26.3	[6]10.9	[6]25,983
Alleghany	75	206.4	4,507	70.6	25	[8]70	[8]15.6	[8]25.2	[8]956	[8]1,836	[8]15.2	[8]1.7	[9]1,805
Amelia	52	35.2	4,400	74.5	39	25	16.6	25.6	20	626	12.4	4.5	599
Amherst	145	32.5	4,521	74.2	109	122	27.0	24.1	98	3,159	22.6	5.1	3,005

See footnotes at end of table.

Table B-12. Counties — **Government Expenditure, Earnings, and Employment**—Con.

[Includes United States, states, and 3,141 counties/county equivalents defined as of February 22, 2005. For more information on these areas, see Appendix C, Geographic Information]

County	Federal government expenditure					Federal, state, and local governments[1]							
						Earnings				Employment			
	2004					2005				2005			
	Total (mil. dol.)	Percent change, 2000–2004	Per capita (dol.)	Direct payments to individuals, percent of total	2000 (mil. dol.)	Total (mil. dol.)	Percent of total	Percent change, 2000–2005	2000 (mil. dol.)	Total	Percent of total	Percent change, 2000–2005	2000
VIRGINIA—Con.													
Appomattox	61	26.0	4,411	73.5	49	35	21.7	21.0	29	908	15.5	0.2	906
Arlington	9,725	49.9	52,254	6.9	6,486	6,801	41.3	36.5	4,983	57,470	28.7	0.7	57,087
Augusta	215	33.3	3,126	77.6	161	[10]374	[10]16.5	[10]17.2	[10]319	[10]9,197	[10]14.2	[10]-2.0	[10]9,388
Bath	35	36.4	7,017	74.2	26	15	16.0	11.1	13	430	14.2	-0.7	433
Bedford	268	36.7	4,204	84.4	196	[11]127	[11]14.4	[11]39.8	[11]191	[11]3,287	[11]9.9	[11]13.3	[11]2,901
Bland	40	37.3	5,696	73.5	29	25	29.6	16.3	21	635	21.8	2.8	618
Botetourt	129	29.7	4,055	82.1	99	61	13.3	31.2	47	1,385	9.3	4.2	1,329
Brunswick	103	24.3	5,686	73.9	83	59	31.0	23.9	48	1,600	23.5	1.5	1,577
Buchanan	206	19.6	8,172	76.5	172	65	17.0	12.6	58	1,771	17.4	-12.2	2,018
Buckingham	71	30.2	4,479	65.2	55	55	34.1	42.7	39	1,391	21.9	18.5	1,174
Campbell	189	27.9	3,649	77.2	147	[12]341	[12]10.5	[12]24.0	[12]275	[12]7,974	[12]9.7	[12]-0.6	[12]8,023
Caroline	135	36.9	5,622	64.0	99	79	30.2	46.8	54	1,653	17.8	11.2	1,487
Carroll	131	28.9	4,452	72.1	102	[13]94	[13]17.7	[13]26.1	[13]75	[13]2,641	[13]12.7	[13]2.5	[13]2,577
Charles City	34	22.2	4,762	74.0	28	15	18.5	24.2	12	363	14.1	-5.0	382
Charlotte	88	13.1	7,073	72.3	78	34	27.5	38.8	25	979	18.2	7.7	909
Chesterfield	710	57.1	2,510	72.5	452	1,008	15.9	31.7	765	19,910	12.7	6.5	18,701
Clarke	59	31.6	4,282	77.4	45	32	14.2	35.6	24	777	11.4	2.0	762
Craig	47	58.9	9,129	36.6	30	10	32.0	20.8	8	258	16.0	-3.7	268
Culpeper	179	38.4	4,449	73.4	129	139	18.8	27.2	109	3,224	15.9	3.1	3,128
Cumberland	41	23.0	4,465	62.0	33	18	31.5	44.3	12	463	21.4	9.7	422
Dickenson	117	19.1	7,210	79.6	98	37	25.6	25.7	30	1,081	22.3	3.5	1,044
Dinwiddie	110	33.3	4,355	73.5	82	[14]382	[14]26.3	[14]4.6	[14]366	[14]8,978	[14]21.1	[14]-14.8	[14]10,533
Essex	102	110.7	9,848	47.6	48	23	15.9	23.1	18	526	9.7	3.5	508
Fairfax	17,383	66.9	17,329	15.7	10,412	[15]7,878	[15]14.0	[15]44.7	[15]5,446	[15]103,615	[15]12.6	[15]11.1	[15]93,243
Fauquier	317	66.0	5,011	63.5	191	219	17.5	97.4	111	3,996	11.8	27.1	3,145
Floyd	63	31.5	4,329	79.7	48	26	18.9	38.3	19	674	11.0	10.1	612
Fluvanna	95	35.8	4,034	84.2	70	55	29.9	42.8	39	1,289	19.5	14.0	1,131
Franklin	204	34.3	4,086	77.9	152	90	15.5	38.2	65	2,209	10.5	11.7	1,977
Frederick	189	16.4	2,844	85.0	163	[16]297	[16]12.1	[16]57.4	[16]189	[16]6,258	[16]9.7	[16]20.7	[16]5,186
Giles	101	25.0	5,935	78.7	81	34	14.3	27.4	26	974	13.9	-2.0	994
Gloucester	206	54.1	5,518	73.6	133	108	28.6	30.1	83	2,571	17.6	-1.8	2,617
Goochland	69	49.0	3,691	76.5	46	67	6.9	45.7	46	1,587	9.5	17.8	1,347
Grayson	88	28.6	5,317	68.7	68	27	25.5	20.0	22	785	16.0	6.8	735
Greene	53	40.6	3,135	77.4	38	34	24.6	31.6	26	848	17.8	-1.2	858
Greensville	30	16.7	2,630	59.0	26	[17]77	[17]24.3	[17]12.5	[17]68	[17]1,885	[17]18.7	[17]-5.4	[17]1,992
Halifax[18]	229	14.6	6,311	68.8	200	91	17.8	24.5	73	2,335	13.0	-1.8	2,377
Hanover	342	35.7	3,562	85.3	252	246	12.1	46.0	168	5,522	10.0	15.5	4,783
Henrico	739	47.1	2,673	68.8	502	733	7.0	30.4	562	15,667	7.6	10.7	14,158
Henry	233	28.3	4,096	81.1	182	[19]171	[19]15.4	[19]17.7	[19]145	[19]4,254	[19]11.6	[19]-0.8	[19]4,290
Highland	18	38.9	7,192	71.1	13	5	21.1	23.7	4	172	11.8	-3.4	178
Isle of Wight	162	38.6	4,956	79.3	117	66	10.2	39.1	48	1,488	8.7	-0.1	1,490
James City	145	49.9	2,617	81.2	97	[20]415	[20]22.4	[20]27.9	[20]325	[20]8,958	[20]16.3	[20]4.2	[20]8,598
King and Queen	35	29.3	5,192	76.3	27	26	37.3	39.3	18	472	19.6	-3.1	487
King George	678	23.8	35,043	10.7	548	513	56.7	21.7	421	5,175	33.9	-5.0	5,447
King William	65	19.2	4,509	70.6	54	32	16.0	38.8	23	810	15.2	9.3	741
Lancaster	107	28.6	8,888	85.4	83	22	10.7	27.3	17	565	8.0	-0.2	566
Lee	404	12.6	16,931	30.8	359	85	36.0	96.1	44	1,811	19.6	26.9	1,427
Loudoun	2,296	129.8	9,599	17.9	999	1,220	14.0	57.6	774	19,122	12.4	38.6	13,798
Louisa	130	38.2	4,508	81.4	94	59	12.6	43.5	41	1,486	10.1	10.8	1,341
Lunenburg	63	23.2	4,790	74.1	51	34	29.4	13.2	30	876	18.8	-5.2	924
Madison	64	24.0	4,889	69.8	52	24	16.2	27.9	19	613	9.3	0.8	608
Mathews	85	60.4	9,187	72.4	53	17	18.8	30.5	13	461	11.6	4.3	442
Mecklenburg	208	12.8	6,416	72.7	185	100	21.9	24.9	80	2,556	14.9	0.7	2,537
Middlesex	75	35.4	7,117	80.5	55	36	28.2	31.9	27	981	18.8	4.0	943
Montgomery	428	33.9	5,093	48.7	319	[21]749	[21]36.0	[21]26.5	[21]592	[21]15,959	[21]27.4	[21]-0.5	[21]16,041
Nelson	109	42.8	7,339	67.2	77	29	19.9	36.7	21	698	12.7	5.1	664
New Kent	65	35.7	4,197	80.4	48	38	24.0	76.5	22	878	16.8	39.4	630
Northampton	187	39.7	14,045	33.8	134	43	20.5	11.3	39	1,149	16.6	-19.7	1,431
Northumberland	93	30.9	7,221	84.0	71	22	18.3	32.0	17	544	11.2	-0.7	548
Nottoway	198	105.7	12,649	37.6	96	103	45.1	22.5	84	2,501	32.4	3.8	2,410
Orange	182	39.4	6,279	84.9	130	78	20.7	45.9	54	2,126	18.0	17.6	1,808
Page	119	-3.0	5,016	78.7	123	56	21.9	36.1	41	1,279	13.6	6.7	1,199
Patrick	98	29.1	5,076	75.1	76	31	16.9	24.6	25	902	12.0	3.2	874
Pittsylvania	285	34.3	4,612	60.9	212	[22]275	[22]15.7	[22]23.4	[22]222	[22]6,935	[22]12.8	[22]5.2	[22]6,591
Powhatan	76	51.9	2,942	81.3	50	100	33.5	16.9	85	2,303	24.5	-1.4	2,336
Prince Edward	108	21.4	5,328	75.0	89	92	29.6	35.5	68	2,295	20.0	11.3	2,062
Prince George	559	29.7	16,299	15.9	431	[23]859	[23]55.5	[23]39.4	[23]616	[23]11,913	[23]39.8	[23]-1.1	[23]12,045
Prince William	1,915	53.1	5,689	40.2	1,250	[24]1,963	[24]25.5	[24]55.0	[24]1,267	[24]31,996	[24]17.8	[24]17.8	[24]27,157
Pulaski	187	27.0	5,328	80.3	147	94	13.1	23.7	76	2,384	12.8	1.0	2,360
Rappahannock	48	38.5	6,664	80.0	35	15	15.4	34.8	11	379	9.9	3.0	368

See footnotes at end of table.

Table B-12. Counties — Government Expenditure, Earnings, and Employment—Con.

[Includes United States, states, and 3,141 counties/county equivalents defined as of February 22, 2005. For more information on these areas, see Appendix C, Geographic Information]

County	Federal government expenditure, 2004 — Total (mil. dol.)	Percent change, 2000–2004	Per capita (dol.)	Direct payments to individuals, percent of total	2000 (mil. dol.)	Federal, state, and local governments[1] — Earnings, 2005 Total (mil. dol.)	2005 Percent of total	2005 Percent change, 2000–2005	2000 (mil. dol.)	Employment, 2005 Total	2005 Percent of total	2005 Percent change, 2000–2005	2000
VIRGINIA—Con.													
Richmond	57	−54.1	6,348	71.5	124	41	33.8	18.1	35	944	24.3	−0.4	948
Roanoke	195	24.5	2,228	83.7	157	[25]450	[25]15.1	[25]23.0	[25]366	[25]8,594	[25]11.1	[25]−1.3	[25]8,708
Rockbridge	185	209.1	8,752	29.8	60	[26]127	[26]20.8	[26]26.1	[26]101	[26]2,975	[26]14.9	[26]4.1	[26]2,858
Rockingham	244	22.0	3,473	77.3	200	[27]418	[27]16.2	[27]33.9	[27]312	[27]9,962	[27]13.3	[27]8.6	[27]9,175
Russell	194	19.7	6,721	70.3	162	59	17.4	−6.2	63	1,439	11.8	−22.5	1,856
Scott	168	34.2	7,326	66.7	126	48	25.6	29.4	37	1,227	15.3	4.8	1,171
Shenandoah	188	31.1	4,945	83.9	143	85	12.9	38.0	61	2,109	10.3	10.9	1,901
Smyth	209	17.8	6,410	68.3	177	114	19.5	23.2	93	2,984	15.8	−1.6	3,031
Southampton	93	16.2	5,276	62.8	80	[28]106	[28]32.5	[28]20.3	[28]88	[28]2,650	[28]21.8	[28]1.8	[28]2,604
Spotsylvania	303	93.5	2,707	68.7	156	[29]427	[29]15.8	[29]45.2	[29]294	[29]9,102	[29]12.5	[29]15.1	[29]7,906
Stafford	362	56.6	3,154	73.5	231	448	26.8	58.5	283	7,512	18.6	20.7	6,224
Surry	39	33.5	5,564	68.8	29	19	13.3	23.0	16	501	18.0	0.4	499
Sussex	78	22.6	6,510	68.2	63	61	44.4	12.3	55	1,370	31.5	−7.2	1,476
Tazewell	320	18.9	7,148	80.7	269	124	18.9	17.7	105	3,400	15.8	−1.7	3,460
Warren	145	33.6	4,214	77.7	108	82	16.8	39.1	59	1,812	11.7	9.3	1,658
Washington	254	28.6	4,887	73.9	198	[30]225	[30]16.5	[30]25.5	[30]179	[30]5,291	[30]12.4	[30]5.9	[30]4,994
Westmoreland	130	33.4	7,620	81.7	97	33	23.0	33.4	25	878	15.0	2.1	860
Wise	363	14.8	8,684	61.6	316	[31]194	[31]22.8	[31]34.0	[31]145	[31]4,852	[31]13.3	[31]13.3	[31]4,284
Wythe	163	25.6	5,823	77.9	130	90	20.0	23.0	73	2,492	16.2	5.7	2,357
York	695	102.9	11,409	42.6	342	[32]353	[32]32.8	[32]32.9	[32]266	[32]6,445	[32]18.9	[32]4.6	[32]6,161
Independent Cities													
Alexandria	4,105	63.6	32,018	19.7	2,510	1,965	26.2	38.8	1,416	21,576	18.6	2.2	21,110
Bedford	70	20.5	11,190	88.5	58	[11]	(NA)	(NA)	[11]	[11]	(NA)	(NA)	[11]
Bristol	163	18.2	9,405	70.9	138	[30]	(NA)	(NA)	[30]	[30]	(NA)	(NA)	[30]
Buena Vista	42	36.4	6,680	76.3	31	[26]	(NA)	(NA)	[26]	[26]	(NA)	(NA)	[26]
Charlottesville	641	30.5	17,503	29.0	491	[6]	(NA)	(NA)	[6]	[6]	(NA)	(NA)	[6]
Chesapeake	1,145	32.9	5,302	66.7	862	808	18.4	29.0	627	17,083	14.3	3.0	16,591
Clifton Forge[7]	(X)	(NA)	(X)	(NA)	33	[14]	(NA)	(NA)	[14]	[14]	(NA)	(NA)	[14]
Colonial Heights	270	17.6	15,400	40.6	229	[8]	(NA)	(NA)	[8]	[8]	(NA)	(NA)	[8]
Covington	77	22.5	12,379	84.2	63	[9]	(NA)	(NA)	[9]	[9]	(NA)	(NA)	[9]
Danville	348	20.0	7,498	74.9	290	[22]	(NA)	(NA)	[22]	[22]	(NA)	(NA)	[22]
Emporia	59	29.3	10,369	76.9	46	[17]	(NA)	(NA)	[17]	[17]	(NA)	(NA)	[17]
Fairfax	3,046	22.1	138,060	13.7	2,495	[15]	(NA)	(NA)	[15]	[15]	(NA)	(NA)	[15]
Falls Church	1,565	−20.0	145,164	8.9	1,956	[15]	(NA)	(NA)	[15]	[15]	(NA)	(NA)	[15]
Franklin	76	13.3	9,012	71.4	67	[28]	(NA)	(NA)	[28]	[28]	(NA)	(NA)	[28]
Fredericksburg	326	48.3	15,935	79.7	220	[29]	(NA)	(NA)	[29]	[29]	(NA)	(NA)	[29]
Galax	75	19.8	11,260	81.7	63	[13]	(NA)	(NA)	[13]	[13]	(NA)	(NA)	[13]
Hampton	2,769	50.1	18,974	24.3	1,844	2,110	53.1	39.2	1,515	27,375	33.4	3.2	26,533
Harrisonburg	145	33.8	3,533	68.8	108	[27]	(NA)	(NA)	[27]	[27]	(NA)	(NA)	[27]
Hopewell	296	37.4	13,215	39.9	215	[23]	(NA)	(NA)	[23]	[23]	(NA)	(NA)	[23]
Lexington	71	33.9	10,337	76.2	53	[26]	(NA)	(NA)	[26]	[26]	(NA)	(NA)	[26]
Lynchburg	1,076	46.9	16,571	29.3	733	[12]	(NA)	(NA)	[12]	[12]	(NA)	(NA)	[12]
Manassas	1,064	52.5	28,281	18.5	697	[24]	(NA)	(NA)	[24]	[24]	(NA)	(NA)	[24]
Manassas Park	21	90.4	1,837	18.8	11	[24]	(NA)	(NA)	[24]	[24]	(NA)	(NA)	[24]
Martinsville	155	19.1	10,316	81.2	130	[19]	(NA)	(NA)	[19]	[19]	(NA)	(NA)	[19]
Newport News	2,382	9.3	13,092	30.2	2,178	1,465	27.2	26.2	1,161	24,135	20.4	−6.5	25,801
Norfolk	6,224	26.4	26,167	15.3	4,922	6,727	53.0	38.1	4,871	94,815	41.7	0.9	93,995
Norton	55	28.9	14,644	57.0	43	[31]	(NA)	(NA)	[31]	[31]	(NA)	(NA)	[31]
Petersburg	342	9.9	10,437	68.8	311	[14]	(NA)	(NA)	[14]	[14]	(NA)	(NA)	[14]
Poquoson	35	37.6	2,996	80.3	25	[32]	(NA)	(NA)	[32]	[32]	(NA)	(NA)	[32]
Portsmouth	1,835	35.7	18,484	28.2	1,352	1,722	59.0	39.2	1,237	22,389	39.6	6.6	21,002
Radford	146	84.7	9,909	38.5	79	[21]	(NA)	(NA)	[21]	[21]	(NA)	(NA)	[21]
Richmond	4,161	37.8	21,615	36.3	3,020	2,922	27.7	22.8	2,380	50,819	27.8	0.7	50,482
Roanoke	1,040	36.1	11,264	54.3	764	478	13.6	25.9	380	9,412	11.4	7.5	8,755
Salem	266	20.3	10,915	55.5	221	[25]	(NA)	(NA)	[25]	[25]	(NA)	(NA)	[25]
South Boston[18]	(X)	(NA)	(X)	(NA)	(X)	(X)	(NA)	(NA)	(X)	(X)	(NA)	(NA)	(X)
Staunton	177	31.1	7,408	79.3	135	[10]	(NA)	(NA)	[10]	[10]	(NA)	(NA)	[10]
Suffolk	585	53.8	7,633	48.9	380	295	26.1	62.7	181	5,491	18.0	15.5	4,755
Virginia Beach	3,873	44.9	8,801	43.8	2,674	3,044	30.0	36.2	2,235	49,313	19.7	0.8	48,911
Waynesboro	130	33.3	6,245	87.2	97	[10]	(NA)	(NA)	[10]	[10]	(NA)	(NA)	[10]
Williamsburg	284	44.2	24,766	73.8	197	[20]	(NA)	(NA)	[20]	[20]	(NA)	(NA)	[20]
Winchester	196	42.9	7,895	65.6	137	[16]	(NA)	(NA)	[16]	[16]	(NA)	(NA)	[16]
WASHINGTON	[3]44,841	[3]32.2	[3]7,228	[3]48.5	[3]33,923	33,585	19.1	33.3	25,204	598,542	16.0	6.2	563,358
Adams	106	−1.3	6,411	36.0	108	61	22.2	29.6	47	1,583	17.4	6.5	1,486
Asotin	169	71.1	8,128	53.9	99	48	19.4	30.6	37	1,259	15.1	15.2	1,093
Benton	3,065	49.5	19,651	13.6	2,050	673	16.3	34.2	501	11,793	13.4	12.2	10,509
Chelan	363	28.5	5,267	64.1	283	337	19.7	26.7	266	6,653	12.7	1.9	6,527
Clallam	541	41.4	7,970	71.2	382	346	31.2	26.2	274	7,186	20.0	1.6	7,074

See footnotes at end of table.

[Includes United States, states, and 3,141 counties/county equivalents defined as of February 22, 2005. For more information on these areas, see Appendix C, Geographic Information]

County	Federal government expenditure					Federal, state, and local governments[1]							
	2004					Earnings				Employment			
						2005				2005			
	Total (mil. dol.)	Percent change, 2000–2004	Per capita (dol.)	Direct payments to individuals, percent of total	2000 (mil. dol.)	Total (mil. dol.)	Percent of total	Percent change, 2000–2005	2000 (mil. dol.)	Total	Percent of total	Percent change, 2000–2005	2000
WASHINGTON—Con.													
Clark	1,576	35.1	4,017	65.4	1,167	1,245	17.2	39.3	894	23,796	13.4	16.6	20,416
Columbia	41	9.9	9,753	46.4	37	23	41.9	26.3	18	522	24.5	4.4	500
Cowlitz	502	19.2	5,215	72.0	421	276	14.6	24.9	221	6,097	12.9	4.8	5,820
Douglas	153	16.0	4,458	66.5	132	108	29.4	34.1	81	2,208	17.2	9.3	2,020
Ferry	46	52.0	6,105	60.8	30	41	54.9	37.6	30	975	34.4	4.3	935
Franklin	254	26.7	4,266	49.2	200	234	22.2	35.1	173	4,949	16.9	12.9	4,383
Garfield	28	-2.1	12,132	41.6	29	25	126.5	35.2	18	499	37.0	2.9	485
Grant	400	21.9	4,997	55.9	328	363	27.7	34.3	270	7,424	18.2	3.7	7,159
Grays Harbor	456	18.3	6,476	68.4	385	289	25.0	27.4	227	6,659	19.7	8.2	6,152
Island	798	26.9	10,060	40.1	629	894	62.6	42.5	627	13,151	36.1	4.8	12,552
Jefferson	211	43.3	7,498	72.4	147	102	24.0	31.5	78	2,230	14.8	8.2	2,061
King	11,786	28.8	6,632	42.5	9,151	9,796	11.5	27.4	7,688	167,743	11.6	3.2	162,547
Kitsap	2,917	23.3	12,200	34.1	2,367	2,963	53.0	35.3	2,191	40,913	32.4	4.4	39,194
Kittitas	161	32.5	4,495	70.3	121	198	34.0	27.7	155	4,432	23.5	4.9	4,224
Klickitat	120	21.1	6,038	63.7	99	76	27.3	25.8	61	1,755	18.6	2.3	1,715
Lewis	423	27.9	5,909	72.6	331	222	18.7	18.6	187	5,206	14.6	-0.8	5,246
Lincoln	85	0.5	8,130	60.0	84	55	43.7	37.8	40	1,451	28.7	10.4	1,314
Mason	314	30.9	5,859	82.0	240	220	33.8	33.6	165	5,006	24.7	12.8	4,438
Okanogan	260	15.6	6,604	58.4	225	239	35.7	25.9	190	5,529	23.2	1.4	5,453
Pacific	167	29.4	7,861	71.9	129	95	35.8	33.0	71	2,059	20.7	4.7	1,967
Pend Oreille	72	22.7	5,739	70.9	58	61	41.7	59.9	38	1,330	32.7	26.5	1,051
Pierce	5,376	32.5	7,211	47.6	4,057	5,268	31.9	52.8	3,448	83,603	22.8	12.1	74,611
San Juan	82	48.6	5,394	71.9	55	44	16.9	24.4	35	1,046	9.8	2.8	1,018
Skagit	582	28.7	5,237	71.8	452	476	19.1	31.2	363	10,644	16.6	8.0	9,857
Skamania	46	19.9	4,391	53.5	39	36	41.1	6.3	34	799	26.7	-8.2	870
Snohomish	2,555	29.0	3,966	61.7	1,980	2,398	17.6	30.8	1,833	44,368	14.7	7.0	41,449
Spokane	2,679	25.6	6,149	60.7	2,133	2,008	20.0	28.6	1,561	38,018	14.5	5.4	36,058
Stevens	216	28.3	5,228	68.9	168	135	29.6	25.1	108	3,138	19.5	-1.1	3,173
Thurston	2,459	49.5	10,946	37.2	1,645	2,002	40.2	25.6	1,594	36,638	29.4	3.0	35,556
Wahkiakum	23	29.5	6,049	81.9	18	11	30.2	34.1	8	283	17.3	8.0	262
Walla Walla	352	21.5	6,130	59.4	289	273	24.9	28.7	212	5,313	15.9	6.3	4,997
Whatcom	1,167	43.8	6,479	45.7	812	704	17.9	58.2	445	15,119	14.0	15.9	13,048
Whitman	282	14.2	7,026	39.3	247	416	60.2	12.6	370	9,367	41.1	-2.4	9,593
Yakima	1,188	19.5	5,184	55.3	994	823	19.9	27.5	646	17,798	14.7	7.6	16,545
WEST VIRGINIA	[3]15,183	[3]29.2	[3]8,364	[3]58.5	[3]11,751	7,510	22.6	26.3	5,947	151,623	16.7	(Z)	151,638
Barbour	115	35.6	7,438	61.4	85	38	29.9	27.9	30	906	16.2	-1.6	921
Berkeley	688	36.2	7,696	43.3	505	481	30.6	32.7	362	6,998	17.6	4.0	6,729
Boone	161	16.0	6,259	75.6	139	76	14.2	31.6	58	1,780	16.4	8.3	1,644
Braxton	99	22.3	6,638	59.3	81	40	23.8	28.4	31	977	16.5	2.4	954
Brooke	153	41.7	6,162	83.3	108	47	11.3	19.4	40	1,143	10.4	-3.6	1,186
Cabell	783	29.8	8,261	63.1	603	414	17.2	21.4	341	7,732	11.8	-3.4	8,002
Calhoun	60	26.6	8,082	59.8	47	16	23.8	11.8	14	387	14.4	-5.4	409
Clay	73	24.2	7,000	62.5	59	25	25.9	16.8	22	627	21.3	-5.6	664
Doddridge	38	31.1	5,110	64.8	29	21	40.9	70.6	12	516	19.2	33.3	387
Fayette	371	24.2	7,885	71.0	299	147	28.5	19.6	123	3,402	20.2	-2.0	3,473
Gilmer	69	26.4	9,929	46.5	55	49	49.7	102.0	24	862	27.2	11.4	774
Grant	80	52.6	6,908	63.7	52	45	22.7	26.8	36	1,032	17.4	1.9	1,013
Greenbrier	261	32.5	7,489	66.8	197	107	18.5	21.6	88	2,408	12.7	-2.7	2,476
Hampshire	107	2.8	4,950	72.6	104	59	32.4	36.0	44	1,475	19.6	9.3	1,350
Hancock	246	39.0	7,810	84.2	177	66	11.2	18.3	56	1,478	9.3	-8.1	1,609
Hardy	119	-34.0	9,020	39.1	181	33	12.9	39.2	24	810	9.3	14.9	705
Harrison	603	39.5	8,833	55.8	432	503	29.7	27.2	395	7,897	18.2	-1.6	8,027
Jackson	162	26.4	5,691	72.6	128	68	16.6	26.4	54	1,579	12.8	0.8	1,566
Jefferson	341	68.5	7,158	47.9	202	176	27.0	41.2	125	3,575	17.9	7.4	3,329
Kanawha	2,354	44.5	12,058	44.2	1,629	1,192	20.1	28.3	930	23,429	17.5	2.4	22,878
Lewis	129	30.2	7,540	65.6	99	65	25.2	17.7	56	1,575	19.6	-5.3	1,664
Lincoln	158	26.1	6,988	62.8	125	43	30.6	18.0	37	996	20.9	-6.0	1,060
Logan	332	19.4	9,099	71.1	278	98	18.8	19.3	82	2,218	16.0	-3.9	2,309
McDowell	278	-0.9	11,235	64.1	280	76	34.0	11.0	68	1,897	30.9	-11.6	2,147
Marion	596	67.0	10,555	47.4	357	202	20.2	25.5	161	4,511	16.3	-0.6	4,538
Marshall	182	29.5	5,253	75.2	141	98	14.6	25.7	78	2,208	11.9	-2.1	2,256
Mason	168	33.0	6,465	67.0	126	76	24.9	31.0	58	1,758	19.0	8.7	1,618
Mercer	485	24.7	7,814	73.6	389	230	24.8	14.1	201	4,947	17.3	-3.7	5,135
Mineral	206	22.3	7,583	60.0	168	69	22.0	18.9	58	1,634	16.3	-3.5	1,694
Mingo	269	22.0	9,833	60.5	221	64	14.7	5.0	61	1,447	15.1	-14.4	1,690
Monongalia	563	19.3	6,713	45.8	472	793	34.0	20.3	659	16,396	28.0	0.5	16,314
Monroe	106	16.4	7,811	63.1	91	43	41.4	24.3	34	813	18.8	-3.2	840
Morgan	91	43.5	5,739	74.3	63	38	22.8	37.9	28	975	20.0	8.3	900
Nicholas	190	34.4	7,248	66.7	142	89	25.2	27.4	70	2,030	17.9	-0.8	2,046
Ohio	393	27.4	8,646	62.2	308	184	15.5	17.1	157	4,119	12.6	-5.8	4,373

See footnotes at end of table.

[Includes United States, states, and 3,141 counties/county equivalents defined as of February 22, 2005. For more information on these areas, see Appendix C, Geographic Information]

County	Federal government expenditure 2004 — Total (mil. dol.)	Percent change, 2000–2004	Per capita (dol.)	Direct payments to individuals, percent of total	2000 (mil. dol.)	Federal, state, and local governments[1] — Earnings 2005 — Total (mil. dol.)	Percent of total	Percent change, 2000–2005	2000 (mil. dol.)	Employment 2005 — Total	Percent of total	Percent change, 2000–2005	2000
WEST VIRGINIA—Con.													
Pendleton	72	35.5	9,097	48.3	53	44	46.0	36.0	32	811	21.9	4.1	779
Pleasants	40	13.5	5,370	77.9	35	29	16.0	30.8	22	709	16.5	11.5	636
Pocahontas	62	−34.9	6,890	68.2	95	34	24.7	31.1	26	894	16.9	3.2	866
Preston	186	−36.0	6,236	67.6	291	100	29.6	67.9	60	2,148	18.8	18.2	1,817
Putnam	225	39.3	4,188	71.3	162	113	11.2	18.9	95	2,577	10.5	−1.5	2,617
Raleigh	642	24.4	8,114	63.2	516	332	22.0	29.3	256	5,844	14.2	−0.7	5,888
Randolph	206	27.7	7,217	63.9	161	103	20.7	21.7	84	2,294	13.9	−0.7	2,311
Ritchie	64	22.9	6,148	68.4	52	23	15.4	17.6	19	582	11.1	−4.1	607
Roane	97	27.5	6,321	66.3	76	32	22.2	22.2	26	761	13.1	0.3	759
Summers	112	27.0	8,077	60.3	88	31	32.9	26.1	24	850	21.2	−2.9	875
Taylor	107	45.8	6,591	59.1	73	49	38.7	24.4	40	1,224	25.9	−1.7	1,245
Tucker	62	32.5	8,825	50.3	47	25	25.4	26.0	20	672	17.3	−11.7	761
Tyler	48	15.0	5,128	74.6	42	25	21.0	33.7	19	602	18.0	4.9	574
Upshur	140	33.9	5,851	67.8	105	61	17.0	23.3	49	1,443	12.4	−0.6	1,451
Wayne	293	16.6	6,892	51.0	251	191	39.3	37.8	139	3,276	27.0	−5.1	3,453
Webster	79	18.9	8,061	63.4	67	29	26.5	25.2	23	710	21.5	−0.7	715
Wetzel	125	28.8	7,333	70.6	97	59	33.8	30.7	45	1,331	20.5	4.8	1,270
Wirt	36	3.3	6,237	65.3	35	12	43.2	16.3	10	307	20.5	−1.6	312
Wood	684	25.2	7,856	58.3	546	388	20.6	33.8	290	6,704	13.0	1.7	6,595
Wyoming	194	17.2	7,854	72.6	166	57	21.5	15.0	50	1,347	18.9	−5.6	1,427
WISCONSIN	[3]31,554	[3]29.8	[3]5,728	[3]58.8	[3]24,308	20,698	14.8	26.0	16,425	426,577	12.1	2.1	417,767
Adams	112	18.8	5,492	58.3	95	64	28.0	25.5	51	1,255	13.8	5.4	1,191
Ashland	125	27.1	7,485	56.1	98	87	23.8	27.6	68	2,207	18.1	5.7	2,087
Barron	234	23.1	5,129	67.1	190	182	20.5	27.5	142	4,711	15.1	1.4	4,644
Bayfield	95	23.3	6,280	60.3	77	54	35.0	28.2	42	1,433	18.7	4.8	1,367
Brown	936	26.0	3,946	63.3	743	863	11.4	27.6	677	18,100	10.0	5.5	17,156
Buffalo	78	10.4	5,670	61.6	71	44	13.7	24.0	35	970	9.1	−5.4	1,025
Burnett	98	29.4	5,946	66.4	76	48	22.5	25.7	38	1,299	15.0	4.4	1,244
Calumet	113	32.3	2,583	68.2	85	65	10.1	27.8	51	1,557	6.7	0.5	1,549
Chippewa	296	33.4	5,029	62.2	222	160	16.2	20.1	134	3,584	11.3	−4.6	3,756
Clark	168	24.6	4,922	67.0	135	84	17.9	22.5	68	2,098	11.4	−5.1	2,210
Columbia	288	14.5	5,261	68.0	252	167	17.7	27.5	131	3,895	12.9	4.7	3,719
Crawford	98	18.2	5,765	58.9	83	45	14.9	23.5	37	1,092	8.7	−1.7	1,111
Dane	3,729	42.3	8,222	31.2	2,621	4,106	24.7	31.5	3,123	77,399	20.3	6.9	72,393
Dodge	267	14.8	3,030	74.1	232	243	14.7	34.1	181	5,279	10.8	7.0	4,932
Door	157	20.4	5,544	77.5	130	81	14.7	27.5	63	1,887	9.0	0.5	1,877
Douglas	259	17.4	5,873	68.9	220	147	20.7	20.0	123	3,318	15.4	−5.6	3,514
Dunn	171	28.0	4,127	60.8	134	180	24.8	27.5	141	4,426	18.6	4.3	4,245
Eau Claire	449	34.2	4,760	63.3	334	396	16.2	21.8	325	8,431	11.9	0.2	8,410
Florence	26	6.7	5,195	71.1	24	11	32.2	13.4	10	302	18.3	−7.6	327
Fond du Lac	443	24.4	4,494	72.0	357	278	12.0	25.8	221	6,136	10.2	−0.1	6,145
Forest	75	30.6	7,499	55.2	57	67	47.7	46.2	46	1,728	32.8	15.8	1,492
Grant	279	34.0	5,624	62.6	208	201	26.7	22.6	164	5,140	18.1	−0.1	5,144
Green	146	21.3	4,216	74.0	120	88	13.5	26.9	69	2,145	9.6	2.5	2,092
Green Lake	120	38.3	6,232	63.4	87	48	14.8	25.7	38	1,222	10.7	−1.0	1,234
Iowa	94	18.4	4,040	58.8	80	63	12.0	23.3	51	1,515	9.2	−0.1	1,517
Iron	48	34.3	7,238	65.0	36	16	19.7	18.4	14	387	10.1	−2.8	398
Jackson	101	24.3	5,150	62.5	81	98	26.0	−13.8	113	2,602	21.3	−30.0	3,715
Jefferson	405	45.6	5,157	61.9	278	195	11.5	24.2	157	4,425	8.9	2.5	4,319
Juneau	180	33.0	7,068	57.7	136	77	20.7	25.6	61	1,808	14.7	−1.0	1,826
Kenosha	626	18.9	3,954	74.2	527	470	16.9	35.7	346	10,044	13.1	10.9	9,053
Kewaunee	89	−29.6	4,307	73.1	127	55	15.5	31.0	42	1,240	11.7	4.9	1,182
La Crosse	538	34.0	4,944	60.6	401	435	14.7	23.5	352	9,850	11.9	1.1	9,747
Lafayette	85	19.6	5,197	57.9	71	44	25.7	15.9	38	1,150	16.2	−5.1	1,212
Langlade	119	24.0	5,668	70.5	96	51	15.2	17.6	44	1,249	11.0	−4.4	1,307
Lincoln	160	24.1	5,276	73.3	129	90	17.0	27.2	71	2,070	12.7	–	2,070
Manitowoc	379	20.6	4,628	75.6	314	215	12.8	25.5	171	4,749	10.6	0.7	4,717
Marathon	535	25.5	4,192	66.0	427	375	11.1	30.1	289	8,166	9.0	5.4	7,744
Marinette	258	−1.3	5,954	69.0	262	110	12.4	22.9	89	2,509	9.6	2.4	2,450
Marquette	109	42.3	7,268	69.1	76	33	20.6	31.9	25	855	14.1	−0.5	859
Menominee	51	31.0	11,252	26.6	39	72	92.7	19.2	61	2,021	87.7	(Z)	2,020
Milwaukee	5,904	17.3	6,362	57.2	5,033	3,941	13.5	21.0	3,257	67,789	11.3	−1.9	69,097
Monroe	373	39.0	8,807	42.7	269	243	29.0	17.7	206	4,468	17.0	−6.2	4,761
Oconto	162	28.7	4,305	69.2	126	77	19.9	27.1	61	1,960	13.2	3.3	1,897
Oneida	226	24.9	6,072	75.9	181	131	16.4	21.1	108	2,675	10.0	−5.6	2,835
Outagamie	639	37.0	3,774	66.8	467	544	10.7	35.9	400	10,800	8.7	5.8	10,204
Ozaukee	423	61.1	4,920	60.5	263	203	9.5	23.3	164	4,152	8.0	0.1	4,146
Pepin	40	12.3	5,357	68.4	35	21	21.9	18.2	18	563	16.1	−2.8	579
Pierce	149	29.0	3,878	66.3	115	151	34.2	27.9	118	3,766	21.8	7.3	3,509
Polk	198	33.6	4,522	68.5	149	112	17.3	30.6	85	2,721	11.9	4.2	2,611
Portage	260	27.7	3,854	70.4	203	247	16.6	21.7	203	5,773	13.5	0.2	5,760

See footnotes at end of table.

Table B-12. Counties — **Government Expenditure, Earnings, and Employment**—Con.

[Includes United States, states, and 3,141 counties/county equivalents defined as of February 22, 2005. For more information on these areas, see Appendix C, Geographic Information]

County	Federal government expenditure					Federal, state, and local governments[1]							
	2004					Earnings				Employment			
						2005				2005			
	Total (mil. dol.)	Percent change, 2000–2004	Per capita (dol.)	Direct payments to individuals, percent of total	2000 (mil. dol.)	Total (mil. dol.)	Percent of total	Percent change, 2000–2005	2000 (mil. dol.)	Total	Percent of total	Percent change, 2000–2005	2000
WISCONSIN—Con.													
Price	95	25.9	6,165	69.8	76	44	16.1	21.4	37	1,100	12.1	−1.3	1,115
Racine	853	25.0	4,393	72.0	683	524	12.5	23.3	425	10,223	10.9	(Z)	10,219
Richland	87	17.8	4,724	64.8	74	44	16.8	23.5	36	1,194	12.0	−0.4	1,199
Rock	796	36.7	5,085	60.7	582	433	13.3	20.7	359	9,270	10.8	−0.6	9,330
Rusk	88	18.4	5,744	63.6	74	50	21.8	21.1	41	1,298	14.5	−3.7	1,348
St. Croix	199	28.6	2,670	71.8	154	172	14.0	38.8	124	3,992	10.3	8.6	3,675
Sauk	260	17.9	4,547	69.4	220	219	14.3	41.4	155	5,335	11.5	11.9	4,768
Sawyer	179	101.6	10,565	39.0	89	76	26.1	27.8	60	2,081	19.3	4.0	2,001
Shawano	199	17.8	4,818	68.0	168	117	20.6	25.8	93	3,123	15.4	2.9	3,035
Sheboygan	475	20.6	4,166	72.0	394	315	9.8	25.4	251	6,573	8.4	1.2	6,497
Taylor	87	24.7	4,419	66.4	70	42	11.3	16.2	36	1,067	8.4	−3.9	1,110
Trempealeau	153	19.3	5,580	62.2	129	87	15.1	25.2	69	2,205	12.8	2.7	2,148
Vernon	147	20.2	5,108	63.6	122	70	20.6	22.6	57	1,877	13.1	−3.5	1,946
Vilas	143	19.8	6,446	73.9	120	89	26.7	24.3	72	2,314	21.6	1.6	2,278
Walworth	355	27.1	3,613	77.6	280	325	18.0	27.9	254	7,307	13.2	6.2	6,882
Washburn	130	30.1	7,823	66.1	100	58	26.7	19.6	49	1,376	18.0	0.7	1,366
Washington	397	30.7	3,186	79.8	303	273	10.8	27.9	213	5,741	8.6	1.7	5,646
Waukesha	1,384	16.9	3,669	77.3	1,184	945	7.2	26.8	746	18,570	6.6	1.7	18,262
Waupaca	275	17.4	5,206	75.4	234	160	17.1	26.4	126	3,945	14.7	5.6	3,737
Waushara	124	29.9	5,188	71.8	95	50	20.8	31.2	38	1,230	13.7	2.8	1,197
Winnebago	1,644	70.1	10,337	28.9	966	582	12.2	25.2	465	12,550	11.8	2.2	12,281
Wood	396	21.9	5,268	73.0	325	248	11.1	25.0	198	5,285	10.2	−0.8	5,328
WYOMING	[3]4,393	[3]36.4	[3]8,673	[3]39.4	[3]3,221	3,163	23.1	41.3	2,239	68,507	19.0	5.5	64,946
Albany	196	39.3	6,242	46.1	141	312	48.2	42.3	219	7,787	36.6	10.5	7,045
Big Horn	75	30.8	6,565	60.8	57	56	26.4	37.2	41	1,525	22.2	5.5	1,445
Campbell	93	7.1	2,541	57.6	87	170	11.9	57.9	108	3,911	14.1	14.4	3,420
Carbon	247	2.5	16,153	21.0	241	88	28.2	32.3	67	2,074	20.7	1.7	2,039
Converse	58	43.4	4,614	61.1	40	56	19.7	45.8	39	1,368	18.4	4.1	1,314
Crook	38	44.9	6,330	52.2	26	28	23.2	36.7	21	737	18.6	4.7	704
Fremont	254	33.2	7,009	52.2	191	213	32.7	43.8	148	5,307	23.3	9.8	4,835
Goshen	87	15.7	7,055	58.2	75	45	24.1	30.5	35	1,248	17.9	−2.9	1,285
Hot Springs	38	7.9	8,326	64.2	35	21	25.4	27.8	17	566	18.1	−3.9	589
Johnson	54	69.4	6,989	52.3	32	40	25.5	58.4	25	942	16.9	13.1	833
Laramie	1,085	40.2	12,726	31.7	774	939	40.5	45.2	647	16,580	28.2	5.4	15,730
Lincoln	72	25.4	4,616	61.3	58	69	23.2	50.4	46	1,703	18.3	12.4	1,515
Natrona	356	12.2	5,158	62.0	317	273	12.1	33.2	205	5,797	11.6	0.3	5,782
Niobrara	18	21.0	8,105	59.0	15	13	31.7	35.6	10	351	20.4	2.3	343
Park	215	48.7	8,090	46.4	144	154	26.0	32.1	117	3,436	17.7	1.3	3,391
Platte	62	28.9	7,149	61.8	48	35	20.6	41.2	25	900	15.6	6.3	847
Sheridan	194	26.4	7,153	55.9	154	162	26.6	41.7	114	3,085	16.6	2.2	3,020
Sublette	29	23.0	4,302	60.2	23	39	18.0	78.4	22	840	14.7	23.7	679
Sweetwater	142	17.4	3,768	64.4	121	180	13.3	29.2	139	4,242	15.4	−1.1	4,288
Teton	77	18.2	4,043	42.5	65	118	12.1	44.2	82	2,264	9.2	8.2	2,093
Uinta	73	53.7	3,690	56.8	47	85	18.8	31.9	64	2,167	17.4	0.2	2,163
Washakie	68	51.5	8,508	49.0	45	36	20.6	26.3	29	885	15.7	6.0	835
Weston	72	46.4	10,777	35.8	49	30	20.1	39.0	22	792	15.9	5.5	751

— Represents zero.   NA Not available.   X Not applicable.   Z Less than .05 percent.

[1]Government includes federal civilian and military and state and local.   [2]Includes data not distributed by state.   [3]Includes data not distributed by county.   [4]Yellowstone National Park County became incorporated with Gallatin and Park Counties, MT; effective November 7, 1997.   [5]Bronx, New York, Queens, and Richmond Counties included with Kings County, NY.   [6]Albemarle County, VA, includes Charlottesville city.   [7]Clifton Forge independent city became incorporated with Alleghany County, VA; effective July 1, 2001.   [8]Alleghany County, VA, includes Covington city.   [9]Alleghany County, VA, includes Clifton Forge and Covington cities.   [10]Augusta County, VA, includes Staunton and Waynesboro cities.   [11]Bedford County, VA, includes Bedford city.   [12]Campbell County, VA, includes Lynchburg city.   [13]Carroll County, VA, includes Galax city.   [14]Dinwiddie County, VA, includes Colonial Heights and Petersburg cities.   [15]Fairfax County, VA, includes Fairfax and Falls Church cities.   [16]Frederick County, VA, includes Winchester city.   [17]Greensville County, VA, includes Emporia city.   [18]South Boston indepentent city became incorporated with Halifax County, VA; effective June 30, 1995.   [19]Henry County, VA, includes Martinsville city.   [20]James City County, VA, includes Williamsburg city.   [21]Montgomery County, VA, includes Radford city.   [22]Pittsylvania County, VA, includes Danville city.   [23]Prince George County, VA, includes Hopewell city.   [24]Prince William County, VA, includes Manassas and Manassas Park cities.   [25]Roanoke County, VA, includes Salem city.   [26]Rockbridge County, VA, includes Buena Vista and Lexington cities.   [27]Rockingham County, VA, includes Harrisonburg city.   [28]Southampton County, VA, includes Franklin city.   [29]Spotsylvania County, VA, includes Fredericksburg city.   [30]Washington County, VA, includes Bristol city.   [31]Wise County, VA, includes Norton city.   [32]York County, VA, includes Poquoson city.

Survey, Census, or Data Collection Method: Federal government expenditure—Based on information systems in various federal government agencies; for information, see <http://ftp2.census.gov/govs/cffr/generictech.pdf>.   Government earnings and employment—Based on the Regional Economic Information System; for more information, see Appendix B, Limitations of the Data and Methodology, and also <http://www.bea.gov/regional/methods.cfm>.

Sources: Federal government expenditure—U.S. Census Bureau, *Consolidated Federal Funds Report*, accessed February 28, 2006 (related Internet site <http://www.census.gov/govs/www /cffr.html>).   Government earnings and employment—U.S. Bureau of Economic Analysis, Regional Economic Information System (REIS), downloaded estimates and software, accessed June 5, 2007 (related Internet site <http://www.bea.gov/regional/docs/reis2005dvd.cfm>).

Table B-13. Counties — **Local Government Finances and Elections**

[Includes United States, states, and 3,141 counties/county equivalents defined as of February 22, 2005. For more information on these areas, see Appendix C, Geographic Information]

County	Local government employment, March 2002		Local government finances, 2002						Elections, 2004[1]			
			General revenue				Total debt outstanding		Votes cast for President			
					Taxes							
	Total employ-ment	Total payroll ($1,000)	Total ($1,000)	Per capita (dol.)	Total ($1,000)	Prop-erty, percent of total (taxes)	Amount ($1,000)	Per capita (dol.)	Total	Percent change, 2000–2004	Repub-lican cand-idate, percent of total	Demo-cratic cand-idate, percent of total
UNITED STATES.	13,277,647	37,483,436	995,855,965	3,458	369,730,209	72.9	1,043,904,090	3,625	122,295,345	16.0	48.3	50.7
ALABAMA.	196,725	461,639	12,485,697	2,787	3,209,062	39.8	12,651,831	2,824	1,883,449	13.0	62.5	36.8
Autauga.	1,570	3,157	87,739	1,926	18,750	26.4	105,041	2,305	20,081	16.7	75.7	23.7
Baldwin.	6,482	15,073	396,390	2,678	113,956	41.4	342,319	2,313	69,320	22.7	76.4	22.5
Barbour.	1,408	2,716	65,252	2,253	13,691	34.7	35,409	1,223	10,777	161.8	54.7	44.8
Bibb	987	1,919	44,798	2,128	3,993	38.8	15,106	718	7,600	7.0	72.0	27.5
Blount	1,770	2,690	73,794	1,391	15,940	58.9	52,229	984	21,504	19.6	80.9	18.3
Bullock.	473	880	22,963	2,027	3,627	47.9	19,503	1,722	4,717	–3.8	31.7	68.1
Butler	990	1,994	47,440	2,281	10,193	39.0	30,769	1,479	8,416	7.9	59.2	40.6
Calhoun	5,307	12,594	361,935	3,249	73,889	33.1	165,240	1,483	45,249	16.3	65.9	33.3
Chambers	1,342	2,658	55,640	1,540	16,382	36.9	61,928	1,714	13,032	10.1	58.5	41.0
Cherokee	1,048	2,032	38,934	1,601	9,404	51.2	12,239	503	9,049	15.7	65.5	33.6
Chilton	1,399	2,729	63,895	1,578	14,737	48.7	25,812	637	16,693	10.6	76.9	22.6
Choctaw.	637	1,187	27,865	1,801	5,703	67.5	25,946	1,677	7,227	–2.0	53.9	45.7
Clarke	1,122	2,137	59,459	2,160	16,201	33.6	77,934	2,831	11,394	6.0	59.1	40.6
Clay	884	1,732	36,972	2,599	4,378	51.3	11,271	792	6,576	11.8	70.3	28.8
Cleburne	557	1,112	26,292	1,808	4,335	61.1	8,321	572	5,798	13.9	75.4	24.0
Coffee	2,021	4,098	79,060	1,797	23,256	30.2	13,992	318	17,616	14.1	73.9	25.4
Colbert.	3,220	7,400	173,873	3,177	27,813	36.6	114,601	2,094	23,935	11.2	55.1	44.3
Conecuh	550	1,254	26,389	1,920	4,810	54.1	20,292	1,477	6,021	8.5	54.3	45.2
Coosa	404	694	16,297	1,404	3,174	48.3	3,434	296	5,001	9.5	58.1	41.1
Covington.	1,609	3,346	72,108	1,950	15,801	40.4	89,288	2,415	14,627	7.4	76.0	23.4
Crenshaw.	533	1,050	24,704	1,816	3,520	67.3	10,685	785	5,500	14.7	68.7	30.9
Cullman	3,424	7,176	182,620	2,343	35,622	35.7	134,458	1,725	35,191	19.2	76.2	22.9
Dale	1,928	4,168	99,416	2,018	17,087	49.0	55,653	1,130	18,231	15.3	74.7	24.6
Dallas	1,925	4,059	102,567	2,263	29,651	46.8	52,928	1,168	18,573	0.6	39.5	60.2
DeKalb	2,111	4,719	112,890	1,718	27,304	37.6	96,819	1,474	24,169	19.1	69.9	29.3
Elmore.	2,214	4,356	114,406	1,657	19,097	33.1	57,671	835	20,000	20.5	76.9	22.6
Escambia	1,615	3,284	117,316	3,045	16,578	31.3	35,493	921	12,395	6.3	68.7	30.8
Etowah	3,697	8,439	201,181	1,955	69,493	29.6	105,871	1,029	42,680	8.5	63.3	35.9
Fayette	540	1,173	28,933	1,580	3,925	39.5	24,578	1,342	8,002	2.5	69.2	30.1
Franklin	1,164	2,512	57,454	1,864	10,660	50.9	46,983	1,524	12,269	10.5	62.7	36.8
Geneva	1,277	2,338	70,401	2,762	6,763	49.4	24,909	977	10,520	10.1	79.3	20.1
Greene	579	1,069	20,180	2,032	3,965	59.4	9,121	918	4,748	8.0	20.2	79.3
Hale	814	1,558	33,411	1,830	3,466	49.2	9,990	547	7,945	2.8	41.3	58.3
Henry	832	1,510	35,143	2,149	4,938	45.3	12,643	773	7,361	6.2	66.3	33.3
Houston.	5,772	13,461	385,884	4,283	66,373	32.7	380,017	4,218	36,201	12.9	74.2	25.3
Jackson	2,402	5,386	96,622	1,792	20,278	31.8	77,792	1,443	20,321	13.5	56.8	42.5
Jefferson	29,944	82,710	2,126,716	3,225	906,526	40.5	4,395,836	6,667	292,967	7.0	54.2	45.2
Lamar	574	1,144	31,569	2,050	4,886	27.1	20,013	1,300	6,885	–5.0	71.1	28.4
Lauderdale	5,305	13,394	370,972	4,261	78,335	66.0	296,436	3,405	37,107	15.5	59.7	39.4
Lawrence	1,278	2,534	65,832	1,897	7,844	60.8	201,182	5,797	14,001	14.9	55.2	44.0
Lee	5,789	12,802	395,852	3,367	80,053	43.8	428,736	3,647	44,610	16.6	62.7	36.4
Limestone	2,686	6,436	133,078	1,971	20,150	36.8	125,242	1,855	29,073	23.0	67.8	31.4
Lowndes	642	1,280	29,186	2,160	4,014	47.7	5,196	385	6,021	–3.6	29.7	70.3
Macon	1,067	2,180	37,048	1,563	7,541	52.5	33,188	1,400	9,407	6.5	16.7	82.9
Madison.	14,918	41,187	1,785,050	6,248	223,651	39.9	1,446,323	5,062	131,062	15.7	58.9	40.2
Marengo	1,370	2,935	75,998	3,394	12,592	51.1	36,016	1,608	10,322	7.4	50.9	48.8
Marion	1,163	2,415	55,348	1,821	12,534	35.0	37,886	1,247	12,875	9.5	69.8	29.6
Marshall.	3,780	8,724	261,173	3,136	48,063	37.8	196,560	2,360	31,491	12.5	72.4	26.8
Mobile	15,407	33,834	984,641	2,465	373,294	33.8	1,005,317	2,516	156,771	12.2	58.7	40.7
Monroe	1,206	3,214	65,705	2,739	6,989	52.6	14,988	625	9,534	6.5	61.2	38.5
Montgomery	8,421	21,247	460,384	2,065	178,016	24.9	264,689	1,187	89,650	11.6	49.2	50.4
Morgan	5,622	13,856	360,624	3,228	74,700	56.6	380,667	3,407	47,007	10.1	69.1	30.1
Perry.	700	1,242	30,987	2,643	4,254	41.5	11,508	982	5,523	–4.6	31.5	68.2
Pickens	830	1,622	40,738	1,955	6,523	42.9	64,946	3,116	9,132	6.9	56.6	42.9
Pike	1,166	2,402	51,423	1,764	11,950	36.9	44,044	1,510	11,883	12.7	63.0	36.5
Randolph	943	1,893	39,727	1,764	10,178	70.1	17,116	760	9,001	13.7	68.1	31.3
Russell	1,789	4,450	95,378	1,936	28,740	42.2	122,762	2,492	16,809	13.8	49.6	49.8
St. Clair	2,007	4,719	106,168	1,575	30,442	41.1	78,583	1,166	29,161	21.1	80.6	18.7
Shelby	4,409	9,853	269,602	1,753	108,310	53.8	253,425	1,648	78,906	27.0	80.4	18.8
Sumter.	707	1,385	31,048	2,177	7,433	34.3	17,170	1,204	6,433	5.7	29.2	70.4
Talladega	3,019	6,570	145,278	1,809	36,401	39.6	113,897	1,418	29,898	17.5	61.3	38.0
Tallapoosa	2,045	4,339	90,999	2,220	18,221	43.4	62,071	1,514	17,952	10.5	69.0	30.4
Tuscaloosa	10,014	24,964	649,032	3,922	121,402	35.7	426,034	2,575	69,830	16.2	61.4	37.9
Walker	2,487	5,178	103,440	1,466	25,396	31.0	66,867	948	28,367	10.6	67.6	31.8
Washington	870	1,669	42,123	2,351	9,162	83.8	19,415	1,083	8,247	8.6	61.4	38.1
Wilcox	694	1,309	32,509	2,490	3,440	47.7	74,248	5,687	5,682	10.8	32.3	67.6
Winston	1,266	2,492	57,846	2,346	9,269	38.0	25,185	1,021	10,423	11.9	78.0	21.5

See footnotes at end of table.

[Includes United States, states, and 3,141 counties/county equivalents defined as of February 22, 2005. For more information on these areas, see Appendix C, Geographic Information]

County	Local government employment, March 2002		Local government finances, 2002							Elections, 2004[1]			
			General revenue				Total debt outstanding			Votes cast for President			
					Taxes							Repub- lican cand- idate, percent of total	Demo- cratic cand- idate, percent of total
	Total employ- ment	Total payroll ($1,000)	Total ($1,000)	Per capita (dol.)	Total ($1,000)	Prop- erty, percent of total (taxes)	Amount ($1,000)	Per capita (dol.)		Total	Percent change, 2000– 2004		
ALASKA	31,883	96,526	2,678,056	4,180	980,404	79.6	3,337,621	5,209		312,598	9.5	61.1	35.5
Aleutians East.	290	578	20,501	7,696	4,921	19.7	9,115	3,422		(NA)	(NA)	(NA)	(NA)
Aleutians West	293	1,005	45,215	8,800	12,989	30.6	11,498	2,238		(NA)	(NA)	(NA)	(NA)
Anchorage	10,518	37,471	894,634	3,342	321,827	89.5	1,371,204	5,123		(NA)	(NA)	(NA)	(NA)
Bethel	492	911	35,730	2,151	5,387	0.6	76,276	4,592		(NA)	(NA)	(NA)	(NA)
Bristol Bay	114	268	9,846	8,592	4,183	66.5	–	–		(NA)	(NA)	(NA)	(NA)
Denali	118	241	5,958	3,202	1,833	10.7	–	–		(NA)	(NA)	(NA)	(NA)
Dillingham	298	812	23,235	4,675	3,775	31.6	168	34		(NA)	(NA)	(NA)	(NA)
Fairbanks North Star	3,425	9,945	241,366	2,848	81,532	90.3	143,400	1,692		(NA)	(NA)	(NA)	(NA)
Haines	171	399	10,462	4,549	4,359	54.0	3,775	1,641		(NA)	(NA)	(NA)	(NA)
Juneau	2,351	7,172	179,623	5,837	64,134	41.7	60,669	1,972		(NA)	(NA)	(NA)	(NA)
Kenai Peninsula	2,366	6,725	179,784	3,524	74,378	58.5	50,393	988		(NA)	(NA)	(NA)	(NA)
Ketchikan Gateway	960	2,896	79,962	5,892	24,421	47.9	76,287	5,621		(NA)	(NA)	(NA)	(NA)
Kodiak Island	794	2,160	66,508	4,861	16,314	49.4	18,987	1,388		(NA)	(NA)	(NA)	(NA)
Lake and Peninsula	264	604	17,376	10,935	2,077	50.8	9,840	6,193		(NA)	(NA)	(NA)	(NA)
Matanuska-Susitna	2,614	5,839	191,340	2,940	64,102	79.1	137,345	2,110		(NA)	(NA)	(NA)	(NA)
Nome	632	1,294	29,139	3,189	5,389	43.1	6,219	681		(NA)	(NA)	(NA)	(NA)
North Slope	2,129	7,485	323,271	45,080	225,982	99.6	821,920	114,617		(NA)	(NA)	(NA)	(NA)
Northwest Arctic	750	1,925	67,012	9,161	6,467	59.8	26,258	3,590		(NA)	(NA)	(NA)	(NA)
Prince of Wales- Outer Ketchikan	318	770	19,830	3,446	2,301	17.5	19,936	3,465		(NA)	(NA)	(NA)	(NA)
Sitka	550	1,811	40,697	4,597	11,405	35.5	61,263	6,920		(NA)	(NA)	(NA)	(NA)
Skagway-Hoonah-Angoon	211	513	14,986	4,569	5,390	28.1	2,496	761		(NA)	(NA)	(NA)	(NA)
Southeast Fairbanks	16	22	632	112	10	–	–	–		(NA)	(NA)	(NA)	(NA)
Valdez-Cordova	561	1,795	89,787	8,920	25,071	88.5	414,099	41,138		(NA)	(NA)	(NA)	(NA)
Wade Hampton	332	506	8,794	1,228	881	24.1	131	18		(NA)	(NA)	(NA)	(NA)
Wrangell-Petersburg	627	1,899	41,174	6,381	9,212	53.2	10,123	1,569		(NA)	(NA)	(NA)	(NA)
Yakutat	64	185	5,453	7,359	1,448	52.3	1,313	1,772		(NA)	(NA)	(NA)	(NA)
Yukon-Koyukuk	625	1,294	35,741	5,650	616	31.3	4,906	776		(NA)	(NA)	(NA)	(NA)
ARIZONA	223,850	607,207	16,455,137	3,026	5,943,001	66.0	22,258,843	4,093		2,012,585	31.4	54.9	44.4
Apache	3,309	7,950	232,764	3,444	26,784	87.7	454,003	6,718		24,198	24.5	34.7	64.7
Cochise	6,123	13,147	319,319	2,661	88,572	76.6	160,847	1,340		44,483	34.0	59.7	39.4
Coconino	5,609	13,137	381,020	3,177	132,602	63.8	428,783	3,576		52,267	27.8	43.1	56.0
Gila	2,548	5,607	147,794	2,869	44,970	62.6	102,944	1,998		20,843	17.5	59.2	39.9
Graham	1,808	3,586	96,373	2,901	16,546	60.6	29,787	897		10,720	10.9	69.7	29.7
Greenlee	523	1,139	29,329	3,735	9,908	82.4	68,644	8,741		3,067	3.6	61.9	37.4
La Paz	954	2,099	54,642	2,801	13,313	71.1	24,167	1,239		5,055	12.8	62.5	36.6
Maricopa	127,552	376,466	10,405,706	3,160	3,912,867	63.8	16,575,181	5,033		1,192,751	32.6	57.0	42.3
Mohave	6,270	14,108	396,461	2,392	149,838	72.5	329,786	1,990		57,807	31.0	63.7	35.5
Navajo	5,088	10,723	315,218	3,088	71,150	68.7	205,061	2,009		32,343	28.6	53.4	45.8
Pima	39,126	102,547	2,528,690	2,883	942,245	73.6	2,753,368	3,139		366,907	27.6	46.6	52.6
Pinal	8,150	18,975	503,381	2,586	169,288	71.5	399,351	2,051		64,622	56.5	57.3	42.2
Santa Cruz	2,072	5,301	114,876	2,901	32,914	71.8	34,417	869		11,668	31.2	40.0	59.2
Yavapai	7,196	15,939	487,969	2,725	207,176	64.3	376,617	2,103		87,389	28.4	61.2	37.9
Yuma	7,522	16,483	441,595	2,649	124,828	54.6	315,887	1,895		38,465	34.2	57.7	41.7
ARKANSAS	112,313	221,070	5,689,968	2,102	1,234,805	41.9	5,751,659	2,125		1,054,945	14.4	54.3	44.6
Arkansas	1,361	2,151	54,241	2,662	11,767	35.8	23,912	1,174		6,946	9.0	54.6	44.8
Ashley	1,044	1,908	57,722	2,418	10,719	47.2	179,993	7,541		8,512	2.9	53.7	45.6
Baxter	1,265	2,279	62,226	1,605	14,593	45.1	118,459	3,056		18,530	10.9	60.1	38.5
Benton	5,907	12,894	311,711	1,886	75,102	40.6	234,754	1,420		68,121	27.0	68.4	30.5
Boone	1,280	2,567	59,173	1,708	10,906	39.6	23,147	668		14,777	8.4	66.3	31.4
Bradley	523	849	23,762	1,907	3,974	49.5	10,434	837		4,249	6.8	47.3	51.9
Calhoun	277	410	16,119	2,846	2,054	57.3	89,332	15,772		2,299	5.2	58.3	40.8
Carroll	965	1,673	43,985	1,689	11,088	44.0	32,256	1,239		10,481	9.3	59.0	39.7
Chicot	1,046	1,670	42,883	3,159	5,527	59.1	13,555	998		4,757	6.9	36.3	62.9
Clark	875	1,623	48,364	2,063	8,861	39.7	118,844	5,070		9,211	6.8	45.0	54.2
Clay	983	1,567	33,183	1,946	5,232	48.9	13,600	798		6,096	3.3	45.3	53.5
Cleburne	816	1,542	33,273	1,362	7,534	52.3	10,385	425		11,761	15.2	60.4	38.4
Cleveland	388	559	14,888	1,726	3,582	85.3	5,611	651		3,496	9.9	57.5	41.5
Columbia	932	1,737	78,765	3,120	9,296	30.7	59,555	2,359		9,909	6.5	57.8	41.5
Conway	910	1,635	34,701	1,696	6,483	38.5	29,233	1,429		8,084	11.8	49.6	49.3
Craighead	3,199	6,356	195,372	2,334	45,958	46.7	412,464	4,927		29,801	18.5	53.1	45.9
Crawford	2,043	4,096	98,718	1,795	18,405	44.3	77,553	1,410		20,401	15.8	65.6	33.2
Crittenden	2,608	5,254	121,587	2,377	28,314	30.1	91,011	1,779		15,300	15.6	45.3	54.1
Cross	935	1,731	38,302	1,981	6,506	53.0	12,449	644		7,074	13.8	54.6	44.3
Dallas	506	741	16,749	1,896	3,231	48.2	10,714	1,213		3,388	1.9	50.2	49.3
Desha	911	1,664	45,683	3,086	8,549	69.5	24,631	1,664		4,647	3.4	37.2	61.4
Drew	1,054	1,830	47,953	2,604	8,797	33.2	17,119	929		6,249	5.5	52.2	47.2
Faulkner	2,712	5,820	165,972	1,844	35,904	45.0	182,537	2,028		36,686	25.6	58.6	39.6
Franklin	751	1,299	31,629	1,766	5,222	51.2	24,861	1,388		7,289	18.7	57.4	41.3
Fulton	501	824	17,687	1,525	2,187	46.4	5,119	441		4,955	20.6	50.9	47.8

See footnotes at end of table.

[Includes United States, states, and 3,141 counties/county equivalents defined as of February 22, 2005. For more information on these areas, see Appendix C, Geographic Information]

County	Local government employment, March 2002		Local government finances, 2002							Elections, 2004[1]			
			General revenue				Total debt outstanding			Votes cast for President			
					Taxes							Republican candidate, percent of total	Democratic candidate, percent of total
	Total employment	Total payroll ($1,000)	Total ($1,000)	Per capita (dol.)	Total ($1,000)	Property, percent of total (taxes)	Amount ($1,000)	Per capita (dol.)		Total	Percent change, 2000–2004		
ARKANSAS—Con.													
Garland	2,867	6,628	181,564	2,018	45,992	32.8	145,844	1,621		40,154	11.7	54.1	44.9
Grant	835	1,674	35,153	2,099	4,510	64.9	17,909	1,070		6,770	12.6	62.1	37.3
Greene	1,539	2,930	71,978	1,893	12,336	31.4	89,229	2,346		13,955	11.8	51.9	47.0
Hempstead	1,111	1,924	46,828	1,997	8,990	25.7	23,559	1,005		7,452	2.2	48.0	51.2
Hot Spring	1,275	2,348	52,305	1,711	8,999	53.8	74,949	2,452		12,065	9.9	49.4	48.9
Howard	809	1,325	32,576	2,278	5,568	41.8	19,934	1,394		4,943	10.9	55.4	43.8
Independence	1,617	2,809	77,100	2,247	12,628	52.5	106,834	3,113		13,011	12.2	57.1	41.8
Izard	528	756	20,055	1,521	4,067	45.6	13,930	1,056		5,493	9.2	51.6	47.1
Jackson	825	1,307	31,378	1,769	6,348	44.5	11,194	631		6,219	2.4	42.2	56.5
Jefferson	3,053	6,470	165,837	1,992	36,913	42.1	107,402	1,290		30,493	12.1	33.5	64.5
Johnson	925	1,572	37,184	1,602	6,463	49.4	33,596	1,448		8,044	12.3	53.6	45.0
Lafayette	416	663	16,203	1,945	3,201	65.4	5,466	656		3,191	-5.7	50.3	49.1
Lawrence	1,109	1,838	42,339	2,404	5,652	44.4	21,964	1,247		6,615	9.5	44.6	53.6
Lee	503	924	22,005	1,794	2,715	39.1	2,302	188		4,080	-1.0	36.6	62.5
Lincoln	488	857	19,631	1,353	2,566	56.5	6,164	425		4,109	15.9	46.8	52.3
Little River	733	1,207	39,081	2,912	6,652	40.9	95,614	7,124		5,294	0.6	48.6	50.6
Logan	821	1,468	33,616	1,492	5,140	52.3	17,069	758		8,551	5.6	59.4	39.3
Lonoke	2,140	3,888	97,436	1,762	18,259	36.1	48,865	884		22,030	22.8	65.4	33.8
Madison	474	1,008	22,531	1,573	3,106	60.1	15,008	1,048		6,384	13.4	60.7	37.9
Marion	590	918	22,958	1,414	4,134	53.0	12,446	767		6,867	14.2	60.1	37.9
Miller	1,699	3,231	88,392	2,139	17,953	43.1	111,336	2,694		14,678	6.8	57.6	41.8
Mississippi	2,500	4,363	159,219	3,171	20,140	32.5	764,201	15,221		14,153	12.5	43.3	53.7
Monroe	547	913	21,754	2,233	3,474	53.0	3,477	357		3,667	11.4	43.3	55.9
Montgomery	346	548	13,674	1,495	2,233	50.8	9,231	1,010		3,958	5.9	59.8	38.5
Nevada	587	772	21,997	2,269	2,203	60.3	20,300	2,094		3,477	-7.0	50.4	48.7
Newton	336	565	13,874	1,632	1,125	64.4	5,230	615		4,378	11.5	63.5	34.4
Ouachita	2,083	3,213	55,548	1,996	9,482	45.7	29,443	1,058		10,650	2.5	50.2	48.7
Perry	413	690	15,495	1,486	1,746	61.5	6,017	577		4,431	10.6	55.0	43.4
Phillips	1,326	2,387	56,042	2,236	9,461	39.2	25,388	1,013		8,868	-4.8	35.7	63.6
Pike	508	768	24,773	2,213	3,129	50.7	11,897	1,063		3,367	-15.2	59.8	38.9
Poinsett	1,280	2,031	47,978	1,889	7,743	42.6	15,938	627		7,723	6.7	46.0	52.7
Polk	858	1,409	36,290	1,793	5,291	36.1	18,177	898		7,799	8.4	66.6	31.7
Pope	2,259	4,244	105,225	1,906	23,037	43.2	145,737	2,640		20,902	13.5	65.1	34.0
Prairie	437	647	15,896	1,686	2,796	65.5	6,258	664		3,624	3.3	56.0	43.1
Pulaski	16,600	40,464	1,029,563	2,832	275,444	46.6	980,988	2,698		153,620	20.8	44.2	55.0
Randolph	617	1,184	26,678	1,463	4,544	38.5	7,587	416		6,667	13.4	47.4	51.2
St. Francis	1,387	2,128	61,594	2,152	11,971	28.7	19,392	677		9,588	12.9	39.8	59.3
Saline	2,280	5,038	117,678	1,365	23,552	55.4	59,121	686		39,376	21.6	63.2	35.9
Scott	463	618	19,946	1,811	2,096	49.3	5,785	525		4,038	1.4	62.3	36.5
Searcy	356	559	13,707	1,694	1,438	58.4	5,097	630		3,992	-1.6	64.3	34.3
Sebastian	4,305	9,923	263,926	2,258	84,430	36.1	257,251	2,200		44,211	10.1	61.8	37.3
Sevier	678	1,159	25,660	1,628	3,842	47.8	5,814	369		4,601	7.2	54.7	44.2
Sharp	761	1,174	27,993	1,613	3,926	44.7	5,835	336		7,470	4.8	54.9	43.7
Stone	443	700	16,846	1,459	2,995	39.5	2,981	258		5,549	14.2	57.5	40.6
Union	1,972	3,753	92,265	2,041	21,170	36.3	82,056	1,816		17,832	14.2	58.9	39.7
Van Buren	675	983	22,283	1,368	3,841	53.6	24,058	1,477		7,374	5.6	54.1	44.9
Washington	6,178	13,329	359,509	2,172	106,267	26.8	277,085	1,674		64,103	24.6	55.7	43.1
White	2,561	4,475	114,477	1,657	18,289	36.6	126,005	1,824		26,425	19.3	64.3	34.6
Woodruff	487	715	20,723	2,459	2,448	49.0	9,509	1,129		3,026	14.1	33.7	65.2
Yell	921	1,897	38,567	1,806	4,709	73.3	19,659	920		6,659	2.8	55.2	43.8
CALIFORNIA	1,689,444	5,799,895	159,819,813	4,568	42,668,690	66.3	138,036,602	3,945		12,421,852	13.3	44.4	54.3
Alameda	68,868	271,061	8,019,359	5,478	2,436,473	60.6	10,734,915	7,333		562,090	13.7	23.3	75.2
Alpine	200	443	16,914	13,898	5,431	78.9	577	474		701	19.6	44.4	53.2
Amador	1,409	4,034	98,213	2,668	33,347	81.8	17,086	464		17,891	15.7	62.1	36.6
Butte	9,702	26,648	787,517	3,774	150,304	72.5	229,468	1,100		96,157	14.9	53.7	44.1
Calaveras	1,633	5,078	129,645	3,006	42,911	85.7	79,838	1,851		22,343	18.4	60.9	37.1
Colusa	1,342	3,554	102,533	5,294	19,806	82.8	18,457	953		6,166	10.3	67.2	31.6
Contra Costa	42,409	147,775	4,170,449	4,219	1,240,348	75.7	3,334,957	3,374		413,028	8.3	36.5	62.3
Del Norte	1,911	4,874	100,920	3,665	15,682	75.3	15,752	572		9,421	13.6	56.9	41.3
El Dorado	7,911	23,991	659,735	3,981	189,635	79.7	359,677	2,171		86,364	19.7	61.2	37.3
Fresno	45,197	133,700	3,668,620	4,410	634,781	72.2	2,388,762	2,872		247,463	12.1	57.4	41.7
Glenn	1,806	4,855	142,696	5,323	20,505	78.0	27,499	1,026		9,454	8.5	66.7	31.7
Humboldt	8,224	19,561	518,737	4,073	100,708	74.7	133,128	1,045		65,886	17.7	39.0	57.7
Imperial	11,848	33,744	844,055	5,794	103,891	73.4	508,644	3,491		34,274	18.4	46.4	52.4
Inyo	1,931	5,273	129,880	7,100	39,888	69.9	17,863	976		8,616	10.2	59.1	38.9
Kern	37,587	120,432	3,749,310	5,411	579,604	78.9	1,562,629	2,255		211,174	15.8	66.5	32.5
Kings	5,873	17,434	443,448	3,297	67,544	73.2	173,699	1,291		32,110	13.3	65.4	33.7
Lake	3,078	8,319	208,103	3,343	46,065	80.9	50,662	814		24,719	18.2	44.9	53.2
Lassen	2,079	4,504	124,758	3,716	20,428	81.0	60,812	1,812		11,450	8.2	63.0	34.7
Los Angeles	487,133	1,702,684	47,020,998	4,816	11,982,815	58.3	42,997,440	4,404		3,023,280	12.2	35.6	63.1
Madera	4,603	14,004	406,568	3,157	80,968	76.0	100,278	779		38,850	16.3	64.0	34.7

See footnotes at end of table.

[Includes United States, states, and 3,141 counties/county equivalents defined as of February 22, 2005. For more information on these areas, see Appendix C, Geographic Information]

County	Local government employment, March 2002		Local government finances, 2002							Elections, 2004[1]			
			General revenue				Total debt outstanding			Votes cast for President			
					Taxes								
	Total employment	Total payroll ($1,000)	Total ($1,000)	Per capita (dol.)	Total ($1,000)	Property, percent of total (taxes)	Amount ($1,000)	Per capita (dol.)		Total	Percent change, 2000–2004	Republican candidate, percent of total	Democratic candidate, percent of total
CALIFORNIA—Con.													
Marin	10,635	37,687	946,618	3,830	435,199	77.8	567,986	2,298		135,325	9.9	25.4	73.2
Mariposa	1,048	2,528	71,285	4,118	21,202	56.8	13,046	754		8,658	7.2	60.2	37.6
Mendocino	5,282	15,093	514,014	5,869	93,642	77.0	182,573	2,085		38,429	11.7	33.7	63.5
Merced	12,825	35,389	990,655	4,405	139,474	77.2	342,155	1,521		57,960	15.0	56.5	42.3
Modoc	899	2,123	74,882	8,004	8,571	88.8	1,038	111		4,467	8.8	72.4	25.7
Mono	1,189	3,691	102,791	7,911	40,542	69.0	55,040	4,236		5,338	22.1	49.1	49.2
Monterey	20,770	74,064	2,112,076	5,132	478,091	68.8	704,530	1,712		124,653	6.1	38.4	60.4
Napa	6,200	19,446	548,903	4,222	208,328	74.9	163,303	1,256		56,599	9.4	39.0	59.5
Nevada	4,566	14,632	354,321	3,727	101,637	80.6	185,878	1,955		53,920	13.6	53.4	44.9
Orange	121,275	418,917	10,600,707	3,621	3,738,288	67.9	12,043,216	4,113		1,075,399	10.8	59.7	39.0
Placer	14,359	41,645	1,271,381	4,558	444,179	67.6	1,135,600	4,072		153,278	30.1	62.6	36.3
Plumas	1,735	4,128	142,125	6,766	27,509	83.7	19,804	943		11,190	7.6	61.7	36.9
Riverside	73,932	262,245	6,923,325	4,087	1,600,679	73.8	5,645,130	3,332		557,579	23.6	57.8	41.0
Sacramento	68,874	234,686	6,143,694	4,721	1,230,645	63.1	8,848,840	6,800		477,866	10.7	49.3	49.5
San Benito	2,984	8,731	241,266	4,333	57,634	83.4	143,779	2,582		18,725	11.3	46.5	52.6
San Bernardino	83,607	272,584	7,937,288	4,387	1,360,683	68.1	6,021,366	3,328		523,276	15.0	55.3	43.5
San Diego	134,801	430,772	11,595,637	4,000	3,296,242	72.5	8,707,341	3,003		1,136,344	18.5	52.5	46.3
San Francisco	46,147	220,022	5,979,900	7,848	2,012,483	50.5	8,638,384	11,337		357,465	11.8	15.2	83.0
San Joaquin	29,684	94,464	2,641,655	4,314	511,323	68.7	1,510,966	2,467		189,864	13.5	53.2	45.8
San Luis Obispo	11,559	35,806	966,513	3,836	369,132	77.9	295,684	1,173		129,050	18.5	52.7	45.5
San Mateo	26,933	104,552	2,968,002	4,233	1,260,932	76.8	1,988,851	2,836		284,857	9.8	29.3	69.5
Santa Barbara	22,039	72,454	1,883,150	4,689	507,823	74.1	833,580	2,076		169,861	9.6	45.2	53.2
Santa Clara	73,702	313,273	8,708,892	5,200	3,498,984	70.7	7,589,708	4,532		603,816	10.2	34.6	63.9
Santa Cruz	13,881	41,918	1,096,838	4,330	328,520	71.6	558,854	2,206		122,084	12.7	24.9	73.0
Shasta	10,402	26,091	741,231	4,313	144,493	75.9	441,268	2,568		77,731	16.8	67.2	31.3
Sierra	481	1,183	29,731	8,502	5,540	89.3	4,232	1,210		1,948	5.5	64.1	33.2
Siskiyou	3,301	7,601	221,816	5,017	36,323	78.4	11,362	257		20,899	5.4	60.6	37.7
Solano	16,877	57,295	1,734,925	4,239	408,996	64.7	1,450,886	3,545		148,837	13.0	41.9	57.2
Sonoma	20,115	69,092	1,933,326	4,151	574,320	76.1	1,544,089	3,315		220,690	12.0	30.9	67.2
Stanislaus	22,697	73,313	2,047,743	4,265	405,894	65.8	2,408,357	5,016		145,624	13.5	58.7	40.4
Sutter	3,592	11,686	329,473	4,006	65,766	73.8	62,582	761		30,145	13.5	67.2	31.9
Tehama	3,144	8,042	211,721	3,674	37,337	76.6	8,597	149		23,444	12.4	66.4	32.0
Trinity	1,631	3,962	83,844	6,327	8,432	85.8	20,938	1,580		6,513	12.4	54.7	42.7
Tulare	24,566	68,678	2,104,047	5,520	222,408	70.1	638,295	1,674		98,860	10.1	66.2	32.9
Tuolumne	2,723	7,557	206,597	3,688	46,590	81.3	74,328	1,327		26,235	10.6	60.0	38.5
Ventura	35,596	118,636	3,092,451	3,962	905,163	75.8	1,705,700	2,185		313,193	10.8	51.2	47.5
Yolo	6,537	22,152	654,174	3,648	192,734	64.8	568,771	3,172		72,269	17.6	38.8	59.3
Yuba	4,112	11,366	270,358	4,336	31,818	79.7	88,402	1,418		18,024	11.8	67.0	31.6
COLORADO	201,382	559,644	16,153,765	3,591	6,976,853	59.7	21,299,122	4,735		2,130,330	22.3	51.7	47.0
Adams	14,052	35,850	1,210,580	3,256	501,100	54.5	1,336,861	3,596		136,677	(NA)	48.2	50.6
Alamosa	940	1,853	47,986	3,174	17,069	58.3	17,455	1,154		6,279	11.0	50.6	48.1
Arapahoe	20,829	62,056	1,766,539	3,464	856,539	67.6	2,759,987	5,412		232,365	22.3	51.4	47.5
Archuleta	524	1,395	46,232	4,177	25,076	77.7	22,135	2,000		5,839	22.7	61.7	36.7
Baca	652	1,048	25,902	5,904	7,497	66.1	11,055	2,520		2,186	-4.0	76.9	22.1
Bent	400	781	32,423	5,695	4,677	95.6	16,903	2,969		2,155	9.8	62.1	36.4
Boulder	11,922	32,690	915,485	3,286	519,928	60.0	1,045,298	3,752		159,259	(NA)	32.4	66.3
Broomfield	723	2,409	104,281	2,582	81,050	12.6	701,295	17,364		23,235	(NA)	51.7	47.1
Chaffee	1,188	2,492	56,228	3,343	17,204	64.5	25,118	1,493		8,770	15.2	55.6	42.9
Cheyenne	260	362	17,720	8,238	6,032	93.2	16,173	7,519		1,134	-6.4	81.4	17.5
Clear Creek	532	1,190	33,261	3,486	18,974	80.9	46,822	4,907		5,613	14.0	44.9	53.3
Conejos	699	1,246	28,173	3,361	4,347	86.4	8,821	1,052		3,803	3.6	49.0	49.8
Costilla	338	540	9,028	2,497	3,325	92.1	6,601	1,825		1,760	6.8	32.2	66.5
Crowley	202	322	8,491	1,547	2,417	74.1	2,774	506		1,493	3.3	67.4	32.0
Custer	220	398	9,642	2,637	4,910	78.0	5,228	1,430		2,428	15.0	68.3	30.4
Delta	1,686	3,232	89,969	3,101	21,817	66.1	24,077	830		14,159	11.6	68.7	29.8
Denver	28,473	100,507	3,479,538	6,240	1,327,905	37.0	6,570,284	11,782		238,826	20.4	29.3	69.6
Dolores	157	264	7,510	4,051	2,668	92.8	4,874	2,629		1,146	1.1	68.5	29.1
Douglas	6,017	18,758	674,184	3,186	342,967	74.1	1,096,114	5,180		121,201	40.6	66.5	32.7
Eagle	2,206	5,930	224,253	5,059	142,233	65.2	289,593	6,533		18,511	21.9	46.1	52.6
Elbert	875	1,812	48,384	2,197	20,562	88.8	26,987	1,226		11,364	26.8	73.8	24.9
El Paso	22,564	68,755	1,648,824	3,033	547,879	59.8	1,981,571	3,645		241,788	20.4	66.7	32.1
Fremont	1,462	3,188	83,012	1,747	29,707	56.6	29,076	612		18,526	15.4	66.5	32.0
Garfield	2,331	5,795	157,306	3,348	77,748	66.1	170,306	3,625		20,647	20.7	53.9	44.7
Gilpin	338	848	48,386	9,952	26,414	25.4	65,144	13,399		3,196	29.7	41.6	56.5
Grand	908	2,086	76,969	5,968	38,529	68.5	70,536	5,470		7,609	19.8	56.0	42.6
Gunnison	890	1,948	58,629	4,184	27,456	63.4	38,929	2,778		8,420	16.4	41.3	56.8
Hinsdale	79	120	3,078	3,977	1,939	69.3	1,475	1,906		602	6.4	59.0	39.2
Huerfano	701	1,283	24,004	3,037	8,943	82.4	6,733	852		3,402	7.2	50.0	48.9
Jackson	160	249	6,858	4,471	2,182	78.4	4,345	2,832		934	1.0	76.0	22.5

See footnotes at end of table.

U.S. Census Bureau

[Includes United States, states, and 3,141 counties/county equivalents defined as of February 22, 2005. For more information on these areas, see Appendix C, Geographic Information]

County	Local government employment, March 2002		Local government finances, 2002						Elections, 2004[1]			
			General revenue				Total debt outstanding		Votes cast for President			
					Taxes							
	Total employment	Total payroll ($1,000)	Total ($1,000)	Per capita (dol.)	Total ($1,000)	Property, percent of total (taxes)	Amount ($1,000)	Per capita (dol.)	Total	Percent change, 2000–2004	Republican candidate, percent of total	Democratic candidate, percent of total
COLORADO—Con.												
Jefferson	20,253	57,660	1,392,744	2,624	683,074	74.1	1,279,280	2,410	271,568	(NA)	51.8	46.6
Kiowa	264	382	14,576	9,769	4,600	92.4	3,090	2,071	892	−7.9	79.8	19.3
Kit Carson	789	1,524	34,720	4,368	10,094	89.9	11,435	1,439	3,502	1.3	77.7	20.8
Lake	1,902	3,252	84,481	10,817	35,640	92.2	8,007	1,025	2,949	12.2	42.8	55.0
La Plata	1,974	4,911	130,803	2,857	71,795	64.3	74,336	1,623	25,513	24.5	45.9	52.6
Larimer	11,852	33,185	838,323	3,179	397,020	63.5	1,077,233	4,085	146,436	23.5	51.8	46.6
Las Animas	805	1,806	46,015	2,979	15,712	62.9	27,282	1,766	6,592	8.2	48.5	50.1
Lincoln	497	933	25,971	4,391	6,863	68.2	8,769	1,483	2,337	6.3	77.8	21.5
Logan	1,558	2,998	72,878	3,469	20,856	65.8	37,703	1,795	8,766	8.3	70.4	28.4
Mesa	4,685	13,912	323,952	2,653	132,443	55.9	240,059	1,966	61,885	21.2	67.1	31.6
Mineral	84	161	4,451	5,200	1,785	72.4	108	126	619	27.4	61.9	36.7
Moffat	780	1,692	84,379	6,290	28,587	81.9	243,385	18,143	5,725	7.3	74.2	23.7
Montezuma	1,251	2,563	70,862	2,943	24,224	68.4	35,749	1,485	11,015	17.4	63.4	35.1
Montrose	2,257	5,420	137,456	3,891	35,873	58.3	56,314	1,594	16,219	14.1	69.2	29.5
Morgan	1,662	3,186	81,864	2,963	33,940	83.2	85,766	3,104	9,936	10.4	68.3	30.6
Otero	1,253	2,487	64,908	3,277	15,381	55.3	18,492	934	8,180	11.9	60.5	38.7
Ouray	255	484	13,094	3,308	6,685	74.2	13,420	3,391	2,721	21.9	51.5	47.0
Park	755	1,416	40,620	2,521	18,663	90.6	27,353	1,698	8,357	25.4	57.2	41.2
Phillips	462	930	23,338	5,135	6,191	84.5	7,090	1,560	2,325	4.6	73.9	25.0
Pitkin	1,521	4,482	182,962	12,305	78,219	53.4	195,680	13,160	9,256	18.7	30.1	68.4
Prowers	1,072	2,420	62,999	4,432	14,083	59.0	14,250	1,003	4,745	4.9	71.5	27.6
Pueblo	6,016	15,351	379,032	2,573	150,642	60.8	425,331	2,887	67,187	24.5	46.3	52.6
Rio Blanco	1,038	1,955	48,352	8,107	12,403	89.4	10,231	1,715	3,003	5.2	80.0	18.9
Rio Grande	769	1,660	39,289	3,218	11,648	73.7	13,241	1,085	5,526	8.9	62.4	36.3
Routt	1,243	2,832	90,221	4,428	57,120	56.8	67,332	3,305	11,762	22.0	44.2	54.3
Saguache	475	842	18,536	2,866	6,446	93.3	5,710	883	2,803	10.8	41.5	56.9
San Juan	78	149	3,660	6,444	2,318	51.9	–	–	486	11.5	44.4	52.1
San Miguel	638	1,701	54,007	7,548	31,673	63.2	87,878	12,282	4,019	23.5	26.9	71.6
Sedgwick	414	651	14,697	5,421	3,811	83.9	1,722	635	1,360	4.4	71.4	27.5
Summit	1,832	5,313	139,829	5,651	90,808	67.8	154,332	6,238	13,735	24.1	39.1	59.3
Teller	1,070	2,467	70,987	3,290	31,469	58.1	42,946	1,990	11,842	20.3	68.4	30.0
Washington	351	680	18,819	3,883	6,682	94.2	1,707	352	2,530	3.5	81.0	18.0
Weld	8,498	19,375	551,108	2,694	226,825	75.9	612,124	2,993	88,653	(NA)	62.7	36.0
Yuma	701	1,453	50,957	5,218	14,196	87.3	9,197	942	4,559	4.6	75.8	23.3
CONNECTICUT	128,740	427,008	10,679,196	3,088	6,092,141	98.4	6,983,652	2,019	1,578,769	8.2	44.0	54.3
Fairfield	33,654	124,874	3,021,980	3,377	1,983,555	98.2	2,549,423	2,849	400,967	8.3	47.3	51.4
Hartford	30,242	102,791	2,529,743	2,918	1,486,654	98.7	1,046,340	1,207	391,808	6.6	39.5	58.7
Litchfield	6,491	18,834	515,327	2,764	323,292	98.8	249,230	1,337	96,668	10.7	51.9	46.2
Middlesex	5,699	18,128	429,276	2,691	279,784	98.4	210,188	1,317	83,984	8.5	42.0	56.3
New Haven	31,876	103,182	2,724,143	3,264	1,325,985	98.3	2,085,544	2,499	366,392	7.4	43.8	54.3
New London	10,806	32,223	796,917	3,035	396,854	98.5	573,336	2,183	118,360	8.4	42.2	55.8
Tolland	5,456	15,146	364,378	2,560	182,611	98.1	168,470	1,183	71,729	14.4	43.6	54.6
Windham	4,516	11,829	297,432	2,676	113,406	98.6	101,121	910	48,861	11.1	45.7	52.1
DELAWARE	24,381	72,238	1,888,857	2,344	513,498	77.9	1,494,267	1,854	375,190	14.5	45.8	53.4
Kent	4,166	11,902	313,349	2,381	51,104	91.5	160,712	1,221	55,980	16.0	56.4	42.7
New Castle	14,263	46,495	1,185,678	2,325	365,958	77.2	1,083,360	2,124	241,461	13.3	38.6	60.5
Sussex	5,952	13,842	389,830	2,375	96,436	73.4	250,195	1,524	77,749	17.3	60.5	38.7
DISTRICT OF COLUMBIA	46,408	190,598	6,922,336	12,260	3,227,909	24.9	5,436,087	9,628	227,586	12.7	9.3	89.2
District of Columbia	46,408	190,598	6,922,336	12,260	3,227,909	24.9	5,436,087	9,628	227,586	12.7	9.3	89.2
FLORIDA	685,418	1,851,207	54,956,082	3,295	19,488,212	78.6	70,010,245	4,198	7,609,810	27.6	52.1	47.1
Alachua	10,579	25,077	576,013	2,613	187,424	86.8	830,482	3,767	111,328	29.9	42.9	56.1
Baker	840	1,705	68,088	2,932	11,669	66.0	27,620	1,189	9,955	22.1	77.7	21.9
Bay	8,664	18,276	581,560	3,821	145,727	65.7	461,797	3,034	75,024	27.6	71.2	28.1
Bradford	956	1,911	48,014	1,833	14,551	72.9	19,319	738	10,855	25.2	69.6	29.9
Brevard	19,681	47,520	1,320,335	2,664	408,487	78.9	1,287,022	2,597	265,462	21.6	57.7	41.6
Broward	75,309	232,096	6,696,119	3,930	2,278,716	79.5	6,304,701	3,700	706,872	22.9	34.6	64.2
Calhoun	547	1,068	27,533	2,156	5,700	63.1	1,969	154	5,963	15.2	63.4	35.5
Charlotte	4,405	10,857	373,888	2,495	176,806	69.2	271,283	1,810	79,786	19.3	55.7	42.9
Citrus	4,318	7,909	255,308	2,064	101,266	91.2	391,883	3,168	69,467	21.4	56.9	42.2
Clay	5,185	12,448	327,635	2,161	114,793	69.7	354,851	2,341	81,495	42.1	76.2	23.3
Collier	9,216	25,770	779,569	2,828	427,572	88.8	757,269	2,747	128,683	39.6	65.0	34.1
Columbia	2,570	5,332	142,534	2,439	38,397	63.7	68,538	1,173	24,991	35.0	67.1	32.1
DeSoto	1,087	2,269	64,054	1,944	20,868	72.5	15,210	462	9,510	21.8	58.1	41.2
Dixie	556	845	30,017	2,150	7,323	77.9	3,533	253	6,442	38.1	68.8	30.4
Duval	27,227	77,695	2,272,762	2,835	878,395	72.8	7,217,635	9,002	381,061	44.0	57.8	41.6

See footnotes at end of table.

County and City Data Book: 2007

U.S. Census Bureau

Table B-13. Counties — **Local Government Finances and Elections**—Con.

[Includes United States, states, and 3,141 counties/county equivalents defined as of February 22, 2005. For more information on these areas, see Appendix C, Geographic Information]

County	Local government employment, March 2002		Local government finances, 2002							Elections, 2004[1]			
			General revenue				Total debt outstanding			Votes cast for President			
					Taxes								
	Total employment	Total payroll ($1,000)	Total ($1,000)	Per capita (dol.)	Total ($1,000)	Property, percent of total (taxes)	Amount ($1,000)	Per capita (dol.)		Total	Percent change, 2000–2004	Republican candidate, percent of total	Democratic candidate, percent of total
FLORIDA—Con.													
Escambia	12,143	27,399	839,170	2,820	233,829	67.7	1,623,077	5,455		143,278	22.8	65.3	33.7
Flagler	2,155	3,402	119,998	2,079	58,973	82.6	94,549	1,638		38,480	41.9	51.0	48.3
Franklin	421	753	31,952	3,191	13,160	91.0	12,555	1,254		5,931	27.7	58.5	40.5
Gadsden	1,843	4,063	107,894	2,372	22,542	68.6	35,217	774		20,984	42.5	29.8	69.7
Gilchrist	652	1,213	29,872	1,984	7,606	80.9	8,163	542		7,015	30.0	70.4	28.8
Glades	373	772	21,711	1,986	10,511	69.5	–	–		4,188	24.5	58.3	41.0
Gulf	651	1,381	38,689	2,935	15,218	92.3	19,508	1,480		7,277	18.4	66.0	33.1
Hamilton	629	1,492	82,294	5,984	32,828	37.6	13,794	1,003		5,079	28.1	55.0	44.5
Hardee	1,305	2,739	63,491	2,306	19,965	80.0	17,492	635		7,249	16.3	69.7	29.7
Hendry	1,606	3,558	120,541	3,277	37,418	82.3	57,220	1,555		9,775	20.1	58.9	40.5
Hernando	4,947	11,498	426,269	3,083	203,533	95.8	394,578	2,853		80,547	23.5	52.9	46.2
Highlands	3,250	7,325	200,648	2,228	67,060	77.6	161,758	1,796		41,496	18.1	62.4	37.0
Hillsborough	43,982	113,277	3,477,890	3,309	1,197,892	76.9	5,465,728	5,201		463,222	28.6	53.0	46.2
Holmes	815	1,531	47,639	2,545	6,299	72.9	15,383	822		8,300	12.2	77.3	21.8
Indian River	4,134	10,656	334,989	2,840	175,520	81.0	325,331	2,758		61,414	23.8	60.2	39.0
Jackson	3,097	5,937	158,517	3,409	23,671	55.2	26,851	577		19,807	21.5	61.2	38.1
Jefferson	533	935	28,759	2,089	8,427	73.7	2,017	147		7,478	32.5	44.1	55.3
Lafayette	292	549	12,278	1,685	3,124	83.0	4,961	681		3,325	32.7	74.0	25.4
Lake	7,717	16,615	523,918	2,230	197,956	69.5	349,295	1,487		123,950	39.9	60.0	38.9
Lee	21,569	55,456	2,118,291	4,456	618,286	86.4	2,731,968	5,747		240,667	30.5	59.9	39.0
Leon	11,131	27,895	771,221	3,217	239,681	69.0	2,142,708	8,939		136,379	32.2	37.9	61.5
Levy	1,444	2,874	78,786	2,198	24,673	73.2	18,592	519		16,652	30.9	62.5	36.5
Liberty	288	522	14,766	2,053	2,572	89.1	5,751	800		3,021	25.4	63.8	35.4
Madison	1,088	1,970	53,140	2,842	13,784	49.6	5,124	274		8,304	34.8	50.5	48.8
Manatee	10,948	25,851	806,285	2,878	281,262	85.6	613,427	2,190		143,621	30.3	56.6	42.7
Marion	9,385	21,260	600,969	2,206	174,664	84.7	482,019	1,769		139,677	35.7	58.2	41.0
Martin	4,117	10,994	400,340	3,038	216,850	94.7	317,208	2,407		72,453	16.8	57.1	41.7
Miami-Dade	104,944	342,067	9,594,847	4,145	2,965,203	74.7	11,299,610	4,882		774,726	23.9	46.6	52.9
Monroe	3,988	11,321	393,967	4,986	170,851	78.9	267,429	3,384		39,535	16.7	49.2	49.7
Nassau	2,244	5,048	143,660	2,373	68,252	80.7	129,713	2,143		32,743	37.7	72.6	26.2
Okaloosa	6,886	15,922	428,406	2,445	142,393	83.3	150,444	859		89,756	27.0	77.7	21.6
Okeechobee	1,625	3,557	84,362	2,281	28,124	71.3	63,438	1,715		12,190	23.7	57.2	42.3
Orange	44,248	124,231	3,873,716	4,101	1,322,452	75.4	8,920,507	9,444		388,044	38.5	49.6	49.8
Osceola	8,034	19,881	561,847	2,894	212,055	70.3	992,295	5,112		82,204	47.7	52.5	47.0
Palm Beach	44,623	132,315	4,338,507	3,654	2,096,464	83.8	4,696,437	3,956		544,622	25.7	39.1	60.4
Pasco	11,952	26,651	717,113	1,923	225,680	89.3	512,383	1,374		190,916	33.8	54.1	44.4
Pinellas	36,256	95,464	2,723,255	2,946	1,113,813	75.4	3,180,324	3,440		455,357	14.3	49.6	49.5
Polk	21,160	48,532	1,170,924	2,342	363,337	81.4	1,703,848	3,408		210,830	25.0	58.6	40.8
Putnam	4,063	9,830	324,038	4,553	119,951	95.5	255,491	3,590		30,973	18.1	59.1	40.1
St. Johns	4,161	10,674	372,192	2,730	157,428	89.9	477,870	3,505		86,290	42.1	68.6	30.6
St. Lucie	9,377	23,054	598,268	2,914	215,934	85.3	1,201,531	5,853		100,063	28.3	47.6	51.8
Santa Rosa	3,900	8,803	233,567	1,835	75,166	86.4	117,594	924		67,307	33.8	77.4	21.8
Sarasota	14,713	42,453	1,369,792	4,030	461,310	76.1	1,135,481	3,340		195,652	21.6	53.5	45.2
Seminole	13,829	33,693	973,095	2,555	382,377	73.7	508,446	1,335		186,195	35.3	58.1	41.3
Sumter	1,591	2,999	87,115	1,508	34,941	71.3	36,494	632		31,842	43.0	62.2	36.4
Suwannee	1,331	2,849	69,714	1,926	14,191	79.1	29,541	816		15,802	26.9	70.6	28.6
Taylor	938	1,892	57,985	2,997	19,078	77.2	34,181	1,767		8,581	26.0	63.7	35.5
Union	504	796	24,533	1,764	3,972	73.4	4,283	308		4,675	22.2	72.6	26.8
Volusia	19,406	47,856	1,475,641	3,213	469,851	81.2	1,254,774	2,732		228,939	24.7	48.9	50.5
Wakulla	802	1,595	66,555	2,643	13,284	75.8	17,390	691		11,763	37.0	57.6	41.6
Walton	1,781	4,231	119,793	2,694	76,658	79.3	45,257	1,018		23,976	30.9	73.2	25.9
Washington	1,407	2,796	79,414	3,713	10,449	73.4	18,098	846		10,366	29.2	71.1	28.1
GEORGIA	390,042	975,155	26,907,860	3,135	10,286,233	64.0	26,057,766	3,036		3,301,875	27.2	58.0	41.4
Appling	1,246	2,567	92,302	5,234	23,336	64.0	37,670	2,136		6,370	4.4	70.6	29.0
Atkinson	382	673	19,784	2,570	5,467	61.3	4,157	540		2,470	19.3	67.5	32.4
Bacon	508	1,026	46,560	4,604	8,424	55.6	7,755	767		3,792	26.6	75.2	24.5
Baker	169	296	8,909	2,221	3,603	81.5	44	11		1,764	16.1	46.5	53.1
Baldwin	1,851	4,148	160,361	3,569	32,281	54.1	86,568	1,927		14,560	20.1	53.0	46.5
Banks	516	1,045	30,232	1,994	16,294	49.3	29,494	1,946		5,592	23.4	78.9	20.6
Barrow	2,137	5,012	111,226	2,172	48,648	57.9	58,440	1,141		17,744	46.6	76.2	23.1
Bartow	3,522	7,853	233,838	2,832	99,940	54.6	226,308	2,741		30,277	32.9	73.7	25.6
Ben Hill	1,237	2,604	65,484	3,793	15,704	59.7	12,957	751		5,540	18.9	60.1	39.4
Berrien	770	1,363	33,635	2,054	12,045	54.8	14,857	907		5,599	27.0	70.0	29.3
Bibb	7,067	16,579	860,519	5,575	201,649	60.9	486,916	3,155		57,754	16.0	48.7	50.8
Bleckley	629	1,362	32,417	2,748	8,103	59.4	4,735	401		4,468	19.2	70.9	28.7
Brantley	666	1,307	28,236	1,856	8,015	70.5	6,050	398		5,621	23.1	77.1	22.4
Brooks	658	1,367	33,073	2,027	9,175	71.4	7,443	456		5,116	12.4	56.9	42.9
Bryan	1,062	2,316	55,734	2,222	23,558	63.8	10,039	400		9,983	41.4	73.8	25.9
Bulloch	2,360	5,987	131,535	2,303	44,528	53.9	34,092	597		19,195	29.9	63.8	35.6
Burke	1,390	2,801	132,861	5,838	40,811	86.1	902,909	39,673		8,482	18.9	49.9	49.7
Butts	815	1,649	45,093	2,104	22,164	61.8	26,400	1,232		7,735	37.3	66.2	33.3
Calhoun	463	772	20,487	3,243	4,938	70.1	2,851	451		2,019	7.0	44.1	55.4
Camden	2,141	6,467	122,056	2,699	49,265	55.5	44,863	992		14,175	40.1	66.9	32.7

See footnotes at end of table.

U.S. Census Bureau

Table B-13. Counties — **Local Government Finances and Elections**—Con.

[Includes United States, states, and 3,141 counties/county equivalents defined as of February 22, 2005. For more information on these areas, see Appendix C, Geographic Information]

County	Local government employment, March 2002		Local government finances, 2002						Elections, 2004[1]			
			General revenue				Total debt outstanding		Votes cast for President			
					Taxes							
	Total employ-ment	Total payroll ($1,000)	Total ($1,000)	Per capita (dol.)	Total ($1,000)	Prop-erty, percent of total (taxes)	Amount ($1,000)	Per capita (dol.)	Total	Percent change, 2000–2004	Repub-lican cand-idate, percent of total	Demo-cratic cand-idate, percent of total

GEORGIA—Con.

County												
Candler	681	1,373	37,774	3,837	9,137	57.7	19,969	2,029	3,151	15.8	65.0	34.8
Carroll	3,932	8,964	201,308	2,122	81,568	48.9	202,903	2,139	35,317	37.2	70.3	29.0
Catoosa	3,150	7,535	203,333	3,595	41,733	47.2	56,761	1,003	22,328	26.0	73.5	26.0
Charlton	532	1,089	33,696	3,181	9,076	71.1	13,151	1,241	3,387	20.3	68.2	31.4
Chatham	10,804	24,761	784,946	3,338	361,718	63.6	829,682	3,528	91,607	19.8	49.7	49.8
Chattahoochee	166	342	7,469	487	2,067	42.3	1,765	115	1,689	39.9	53.6	45.8
Chattooga	1,100	2,450	54,134	2,075	16,871	53.9	21,719	833	7,853	21.2	63.6	35.8
Cherokee	5,002	13,239	341,524	2,141	167,814	68.1	291,785	1,829	73,686	40.8	79.0	20.1
Clarke	4,666	11,128	467,042	4,570	101,729	66.4	254,624	2,491	37,388	29.4	40.3	58.1
Clay	172	303	8,341	2,488	2,974	66.3	1,544	461	1,309	2.5	38.9	61.0
Clayton	11,126	28,177	653,079	2,578	273,915	55.3	399,871	1,578	79,600	29.6	29.0	70.5
Clinch	457	985	25,901	3,787	6,214	74.3	2,208	323	2,266	17.5	66.2	33.1
Cobb	20,874	65,828	1,520,952	2,383	751,398	74.1	1,488,467	2,332	279,866	19.1	62.0	37.1
Coffee	1,802	4,095	84,765	2,187	27,276	60.0	13,144	339	12,332	30.8	67.4	32.3
Colquitt	2,527	6,171	149,786	3,486	31,762	53.9	51,130	1,190	11,745	17.8	70.6	28.8
Columbia	4,287	8,212	205,456	2,171	90,153	59.6	158,593	1,676	47,170	31.0	75.4	24.3
Cook	1,026	1,623	41,772	2,615	12,842	52.1	20,394	1,277	4,820	22.2	63.6	36.0
Coweta	3,431	9,243	224,921	2,299	107,767	57.1	199,134	2,035	42,545	36.2	74.5	25.0
Crawford	409	794	24,366	1,936	7,568	79.7	1,319	105	4,406	23.5	64.2	35.2
Crisp	1,778	3,802	67,705	3,059	24,570	52.9	54,479	2,462	6,251	11.4	61.8	37.7
Dade	561	1,267	29,670	1,887	12,130	45.9	1,878	119	6,247	23.7	69.9	29.2
Dawson	660	1,305	44,969	2,552	26,634	55.6	37,548	2,131	8,117	37.6	81.9	17.3
Decatur	1,982	3,871	106,849	3,789	28,249	49.9	20,986	744	8,951	17.0	59.8	40.0
DeKalb	29,938	90,580	2,045,252	3,038	772,456	69.5	1,213,568	1,803	276,509	25.7	26.6	72.6
Dodge	1,118	2,479	84,082	4,361	11,089	55.6	7,439	386	6,995	19.0	65.5	34.1
Dooly	621	1,134	29,313	2,533	11,681	68.3	12,599	1,089	3,844	9.2	48.2	51.3
Dougherty	5,138	11,920	368,225	3,848	129,096	56.0	226,780	2,370	33,662	15.8	40.7	58.8
Douglas	3,933	10,570	252,405	2,564	115,741	59.8	153,946	1,564	42,104	36.0	61.4	38.0
Early	614	1,374	33,140	2,718	11,009	56.7	6,785	556	4,213	17.5	59.2	40.4
Echols	189	366	7,598	1,971	2,552	86.3	427	111	991	10.4	76.4	23.3
Effingham	1,872	4,151	105,760	2,576	32,802	61.2	47,767	1,163	16,167	51.8	77.3	22.4
Elbert	1,206	2,667	66,522	3,220	18,718	60.3	38,127	1,846	7,659	30.9	60.4	39.0
Emanuel	1,582	3,444	61,756	2,835	18,541	57.2	18,882	867	7,470	19.3	62.5	37.1
Evans	477	1,001	30,016	2,704	7,829	43.4	1,531	138	3,514	14.1	65.2	34.5
Fannin	740	1,772	42,877	2,051	19,222	54.6	6,871	329	9,666	15.2	71.0	28.2
Fayette	4,335	11,624	260,451	2,702	134,160	80.0	270,227	2,803	52,587	23.9	71.0	28.3
Floyd	5,984	16,447	422,987	4,569	90,582	59.4	198,049	2,139	31,625	17.9	67.7	31.7
Forsyth	2,633	7,748	265,703	2,275	154,099	54.5	336,162	2,878	56,904	59.1	83.1	16.2
Franklin	1,034	2,050	52,327	2,504	21,417	50.5	27,214	1,302	7,502	30.2	69.6	29.9
Fulton	45,331	134,860	4,499,652	5,205	1,923,581	67.6	10,755,463	12,441	336,407	27.8	39.9	59.3
Gilmer	1,037	2,035	49,787	1,972	22,622	57.2	16,370	648	10,014	35.9	74.0	25.1
Glascock	195	294	6,803	2,623	2,382	75.6	932	359	1,269	24.4	80.1	19.7
Glynn	4,121	11,162	335,360	4,833	112,262	63.3	112,441	1,621	27,696	23.7	67.2	32.4
Gordon	2,121	4,585	112,132	2,402	42,962	40.5	43,739	937	15,792	29.4	73.9	25.5
Grady	1,058	2,250	49,999	2,088	17,560	62.6	14,245	595	8,194	22.2	61.9	37.7
Greene	833	1,816	49,589	3,271	22,451	65.0	15,065	994	6,874	32.3	59.2	40.4
Gwinnett	24,574	65,896	1,831,949	2,824	951,860	67.7	1,349,033	2,079	244,179	27.8	65.7	33.5
Habersham	1,867	3,890	111,969	2,961	34,334	58.0	47,840	1,265	13,269	36.9	78.6	20.7
Hall	6,254	15,992	652,077	4,293	182,373	56.2	434,446	2,860	49,744	30.4	78.2	21.1
Hancock	896	1,303	32,227	3,214	10,210	85.3	15,649	1,561	3,550	15.0	23.2	76.5
Haralson	1,265	2,854	63,245	2,354	23,387	59.4	28,914	1,076	10,193	24.8	75.6	23.9
Harris	986	2,072	50,513	2,010	22,961	69.0	22,107	880	12,350	44.2	71.9	27.5
Hart	830	1,756	53,483	2,303	22,652	63.2	17,804	767	9,029	19.8	60.9	38.5
Heard	508	1,189	32,900	2,925	14,511	47.6	26,043	2,315	3,956	23.7	70.5	29.0
Henry	4,382	11,917	370,500	2,645	176,871	68.8	647,063	4,619	64,153	65.1	66.7	32.9
Houston	6,453	15,646	385,523	3,311	108,290	55.1	133,670	1,148	45,198	22.2	66.1	33.3
Irwin	655	1,314	22,728	2,268	7,240	72.0	2,460	246	3,414	19.7	68.8	30.8
Jackson	2,216	5,015	123,877	2,716	44,783	54.8	105,085	2,304	16,173	39.0	78.0	21.4
Jasper	596	1,263	30,317	2,480	12,177	72.5	17,547	1,435	4,742	20.3	66.6	32.9
Jeff Davis	740	1,644	39,102	3,040	10,262	52.7	16,701	1,298	4,845	14.8	73.3	26.4
Jefferson	1,133	2,195	52,019	3,039	14,815	65.1	21,183	1,238	6,537	17.4	46.9	52.7
Jenkins	480	974	22,620	2,612	5,886	57.4	4,917	568	3,404	31.3	55.8	43.9
Johnson	346	718	16,015	1,701	3,794	61.4	1,764	187	3,553	23.2	64.1	35.6
Jones	959	1,918	45,787	1,848	16,590	59.4	20,027	808	10,853	34.5	63.9	35.5
Lamar	596	1,190	33,293	2,052	11,775	67.7	22,427	1,382	6,498	24.2	62.0	37.4
Lanier	354	662	14,386	2,003	4,113	60.6	2,210	308	2,587	35.9	63.4	36.0
Laurens	2,732	5,814	134,815	2,942	34,083	49.1	34,409	751	17,237	22.8	63.1	36.4
Lee	1,117	2,770	59,322	2,140	23,546	64.2	43,066	1,553	10,421	32.2	78.7	20.9
Liberty	2,570	5,581	155,380	2,556	44,292	55.1	43,849	721	12,805	28.4	47.9	51.7
Lincoln	540	872	20,378	2,408	7,594	76.3	7,118	841	3,657	17.9	63.1	36.6

See footnotes at end of table.

Table B-13. Counties — **Local Government Finances and Elections**—Con.

[Includes United States, states, and 3,141 counties/county equivalents defined as of February 22, 2005. For more information on these areas, see Appendix C, Geographic Information]

County	Local government employment, March 2002		Local government finances, 2002					Total debt outstanding		Elections, 2004[1]			
			General revenue							Votes cast for President			
					Taxes							Republican candidate, percent of total	Democratic candidate, percent of total
	Total employ-ment	Total payroll ($1,000)	Total ($1,000)	Per capita (dol.)	Total ($1,000)	Property, percent of total (taxes)	Amount ($1,000)	Per capita (dol.)	Total	Percent change, 2000–2004		
GEORGIA—Con.													
Long	426	701	17,675	1,643	5,427	74.6	9,111	847	3,039	31.3	65.6	34.0
Lowndes	6,360	14,987	412,487	4,405	99,656	47.4	60,537	646	31,654	24.5	60.0	39.5
Lumpkin	856	1,730	51,772	2,291	25,785	58.5	66,804	2,956	8,886	31.6	75.3	23.5
McDuffie	1,298	2,392	76,172	3,574	21,136	51.7	8,715	409	7,773	18.7	62.3	37.3
McIntosh	484	995	24,353	2,223	10,813	54.6	2,856	261	5,379	40.2	52.7	46.9
Macon	796	1,489	34,841	2,482	10,843	68.2	25,549	1,820	4,777	9.7	38.8	60.8
Madison	960	2,206	50,090	1,878	19,356	68.2	7,778	292	9,843	23.1	73.7	25.7
Marion	451	923	18,220	2,544	4,709	67.2	7,181	1,003	2,955	35.3	56.5	43.2
Meriwether	1,049	2,452	54,546	2,386	17,546	70.6	34,551	1,511	8,155	21.6	54.0	45.5
Miller	554	1,126	15,327	2,397	5,186	72.6	2,451	383	2,442	13.6	69.4	30.1
Mitchell	1,141	2,374	61,603	2,581	19,530	62.0	34,758	1,456	7,267	25.3	53.5	46.2
Monroe	1,137	2,624	75,630	3,340	29,139	64.7	228,575	10,095	9,789	29.8	66.6	32.9
Montgomery	334	637	13,812	1,633	4,006	61.2	1,848	218	3,169	26.3	67.8	31.8
Morgan	911	2,027	47,402	2,888	21,137	70.1	6,296	384	7,243	22.7	67.7	31.8
Murray	1,401	3,267	68,606	1,775	23,070	63.7	35,631	922	10,689	27.7	72.5	27.1
Muscogee	10,146	22,978	520,523	2,808	176,993	68.5	349,972	1,888	64,006	22.7	48.2	51.4
Newton	3,284	7,655	219,624	3,059	74,444	62.7	138,934	1,935	29,179	58.8	62.0	37.5
Oconee	1,135	2,520	66,891	2,451	32,651	65.0	32,274	1,183	14,182	27.0	72.5	26.7
Oglethorpe	523	1,076	22,934	1,746	7,515	68.6	4,829	368	5,631	28.4	65.5	33.7
Paulding	3,160	7,622	191,028	2,025	84,045	58.5	109,615	1,162	40,496	66.9	76.2	23.3
Peach	1,247	2,342	76,632	3,178	25,760	46.7	24,752	1,026	8,549	19.8	53.3	46.3
Pickens	1,025	2,177	54,703	2,131	26,332	71.3	18,456	719	10,630	29.6	76.3	23.0
Pierce	844	1,468	33,151	2,073	11,586	56.2	5,125	321	5,924	26.6	79.0	20.8
Pike	505	1,032	24,651	1,688	9,167	64.5	12,889	882	6,745	38.1	77.0	22.3
Polk	1,581	3,743	83,406	2,110	31,323	59.9	40,847	1,033	12,414	22.7	68.2	31.2
Pulaski	554	1,126	20,703	2,129	7,075	60.7	3,974	409	3,516	5.1	62.6	36.8
Putnam	910	1,860	57,453	2,965	25,233	56.8	37,177	1,918	8,111	28.8	64.0	35.5
Quitman	104	186	5,891	2,292	1,937	76.5	4,693	1,826	965	6.7	42.4	56.3
Rabun	894	1,775	51,694	3,328	23,690	64.4	13,967	899	6,638	24.3	70.1	28.9
Randolph	737	1,344	32,465	4,288	6,062	66.6	1,871	247	3,047	18.6	46.5	52.9
Richmond	8,904	20,639	524,247	2,646	170,038	61.4	524,402	2,647	69,349	20.5	42.9	56.6
Rockdale	3,477	8,391	192,583	2,636	100,276	63.6	216,395	2,962	31,181	27.3	60.5	38.9
Schley	195	480	9,813	2,494	2,722	73.1	7,936	2,017	1,530	30.1	69.5	30.3
Screven	938	1,799	42,530	2,756	10,538	63.0	5,041	327	5,923	25.5	56.7	42.8
Seminole	393	870	21,925	2,346	8,821	61.5	717	77	3,275	13.8	60.4	39.0
Spalding	3,081	7,355	172,312	2,886	65,591	59.3	105,950	1,774	21,026	36.6	64.0	35.5
Stephens	1,275	2,877	91,200	3,564	25,065	59.0	69,802	2,728	9,670	15.4	71.4	28.1
Stewart	320	607	12,434	2,435	3,893	70.0	1,171	229	2,031	3.9	39.2	60.1
Sumter	1,904	3,586	149,891	4,487	28,481	65.4	48,519	1,453	11,291	16.4	50.4	49.3
Talbot	328	497	13,188	1,999	5,545	69.6	3,695	560	2,945	16.4	37.5	62.1
Taliaferro	106	186	6,726	3,355	1,624	77.0	295	147	951	14.3	35.2	64.4
Tattnall	877	1,602	41,271	1,854	13,164	64.3	17,941	806	6,463	15.2	72.1	27.7
Taylor	395	848	18,900	2,123	6,031	56.9	8,209	922	3,381	21.6	56.6	43.1
Telfair	537	1,019	24,712	2,127	8,620	52.5	5,273	454	3,775	8.1	57.5	42.1
Terrell	543	1,106	24,691	2,283	8,060	56.8	2,522	233	3,824	22.8	48.6	51.0
Thomas	2,364	5,444	124,893	2,896	26,434	58.2	30,511	708	15,707	30.3	61.5	38.2
Tift	2,735	5,822	187,832	4,810	39,363	51.1	69,307	1,775	12,529	21.3	68.8	30.8
Toombs	1,359	2,640	61,712	2,350	17,667	39.2	12,518	477	8,814	22.2	70.3	29.1
Towns	340	671	18,632	1,924	8,443	47.4	12,661	1,308	5,280	17.4	72.4	27.1
Treutlen	334	590	13,931	1,999	2,977	66.8	1,409	202	2,758	40.5	61.3	38.1
Troup	3,417	8,008	190,271	3,178	68,067	58.7	113,923	1,903	21,927	23.2	64.7	34.8
Turner	610	1,182	26,037	2,707	8,657	59.6	7,270	756	2,964	20.7	61.2	38.3
Twiggs	423	864	20,340	1,936	8,235	78.7	331	32	4,365	20.7	48.4	50.9
Union	1,061	2,027	63,720	3,465	15,419	53.4	16,841	916	9,228	32.7	74.2	25.2
Upson	1,083	2,341	57,997	2,089	22,297	63.9	30,469	1,097	10,091	21.8	65.7	33.9
Walker	2,547	5,466	117,707	1,896	34,345	57.9	28,494	459	21,453	13.5	71.5	27.9
Walton	3,135	7,317	204,981	3,056	83,077	58.6	104,052	1,551	27,624	44.8	78.2	21.3
Ware	2,064	4,659	116,751	3,287	38,756	51.9	56,030	1,577	11,281	17.2	69.1	30.6
Warren	273	515	14,479	2,314	5,172	67.3	5,201	831	2,489	16.0	45.0	54.6
Washington	923	2,015	70,958	3,398	21,800	65.4	21,689	1,039	7,847	17.3	52.0	47.6
Wayne	1,609	2,573	86,776	3,202	22,465	67.5	16,655	614	9,555	19.4	71.4	28.1
Webster	140	235	6,991	3,057	1,971	78.9	6,649	2,907	1,008	10.9	48.1	51.1
Wheeler	267	606	12,497	1,900	3,176	68.3	911	139	2,049	30.1	58.2	41.3
White	817	1,837	47,366	2,145	23,888	57.7	24,241	1,098	9,498	34.9	77.9	21.2
Whitfield	4,090	10,168	337,210	3,886	113,701	56.8	394,060	4,541	26,378	13.2	73.2	26.3
Wilcox	370	743	16,898	1,954	5,320	69.4	1,118	129	2,619	10.7	65.1	34.4
Wilkes	713	1,419	35,864	3,365	9,806	70.4	7,604	713	4,544	12.9	54.8	44.6
Wilkinson	512	964	25,695	2,503	13,788	57.0	4,755	463	4,514	20.7	50.1	49.5
Worth	903	1,827	47,367	2,165	15,457	64.1	3,620	165	7,353	21.3	69.4	30.2

See footnotes at end of table.

County and City Data Book: 2007

U.S. Census Bureau

Table B-13. Counties — **Local Government Finances and Elections**—Con.

[Includes United States, states, and 3,141 counties/county equivalents defined as of February 22, 2005. For more information on these areas, see Appendix C, Geographic Information]

County	Local government employment, March 2002		Local government finances, 2002						Elections, 2004[1]			
			General revenue				Total debt outstanding		Votes cast for President			
					Taxes						Republican candidate, percent of total	Democratic candidate, percent of total
	Total employment	Total payroll ($1,000)	Total ($1,000)	Per capita (dol.)	Total ($1,000)	Property, percent of total (taxes)	Amount ($1,000)	Per capita (dol.)	Total	Percent change, 2000–2004		
HAWAII	15,495	49,576	1,542,547	1,250	818,886	75.1	2,791,939	2,262	[2]429,013	[2]16.6	[2]45.3	[2]54.0
Hawaii	2,260	7,046	214,724	1,387	118,015	83.7	155,939	1,007	57,702	13.5	38.2	60.9
Honolulu	10,072	32,359	1,021,205	1,152	534,404	71.6	2,297,001	2,592	298,547	16.6	48.3	51.1
Kalawao	-	-	-	-	-	-	-	-	-	-	-	-
Kauai	1,092	3,543	101,467	1,692	48,542	78.4	83,104	1,386	24,876	14.3	39.2	60.0
Maui	2,071	6,627	205,151	1,539	117,925	81.1	255,895	1,920	47,430	20.8	38.3	60.7
IDAHO	67,536	140,405	3,698,592	2,752	1,020,020	94.0	1,440,447	1,072	598,447	19.3	68.4	30.3
Ada	12,726	28,495	779,235	2,437	301,304	92.9	453,933	1,420	155,030	25.5	61.1	37.8
Adams	256	443	12,754	3,670	2,910	88.1	4,819	1,387	2,063	8.1	71.2	26.9
Bannock	4,167	9,792	242,518	3,154	51,047	95.9	76,341	993	34,844	12.9	61.6	37.0
Bear Lake	369	624	23,955	3,802	3,819	95.4	2,800	444	3,040	4.9	82.4	16.3
Benewah	618	1,129	29,476	3,273	5,921	96.0	6,353	705	4,050	9.8	69.7	28.4
Bingham	2,496	5,023	106,724	2,520	19,573	97.2	29,106	687	16,565	14.5	76.9	21.8
Blaine	1,027	2,516	70,878	3,493	42,976	88.1	28,993	1,429	10,147	27.8	39.8	59.1
Boise	357	603	14,619	2,072	4,480	95.6	5,046	715	3,527	15.5	70.9	27.5
Bonner	1,450	2,832	72,111	1,887	29,430	97.3	13,181	345	17,684	21.6	60.5	37.6
Bonneville	3,959	8,919	199,359	2,339	54,098	96.6	78,771	924	38,871	15.8	77.3	21.5
Boundary	683	1,205	28,336	2,839	6,675	96.6	5,938	595	4,379	12.7	68.8	29.0
Butte	261	481	13,094	4,477	2,317	96.1	5,691	1,946	1,406	-3.7	76.6	22.8
Camas	85	128	3,617	3,485	893	96.9	837	806	595	17.4	75.6	23.4
Canyon	5,045	11,048	311,860	2,143	93,598	93.0	190,154	1,307	55,698	29.5	74.7	24.1
Caribou	586	1,164	30,761	4,249	7,886	98.9	9,103	1,257	3,281	3.3	83.9	15.0
Cassia	1,197	2,278	56,041	2,600	13,741	90.0	23,916	1,110	7,821	7.4	83.9	14.7
Clark	105	143	4,507	4,710	1,090	95.7	3,946	4,123	353	-7.6	85.6	13.0
Clearwater	576	856	25,254	2,984	7,013	96.3	766	91	4,034	3.5	70.4	27.7
Custer	300	570	14,761	3,544	5,735	98.2	570	137	2,358	1.2	74.7	23.7
Elmore	1,353	2,572	55,537	1,901	12,651	95.0	13,062	447	8,061	15.7	74.6	24.3
Franklin	810	1,351	30,048	2,546	5,133	90.0	2,063	175	5,054	10.1	89.6	9.0
Fremont	625	1,121	31,547	2,653	11,370	93.4	12,098	1,017	5,769	13.4	86.1	12.8
Gem	720	1,376	32,090	2,060	6,861	94.1	14,984	962	7,134	19.2	75.9	22.8
Gooding	904	1,474	38,814	2,727	7,703	98.9	24,469	1,719	5,325	5.9	74.6	24.0
Idaho	849	1,429	38,172	2,460	6,267	96.6	8,738	563	7,970	7.0	75.5	21.2
Jefferson	1,140	2,246	43,233	2,186	8,336	95.7	17,750	898	8,906	13.7	86.5	12.2
Jerome	814	1,493	39,846	2,132	10,114	96.8	7,988	427	6,580	9.5	78.7	20.4
Kootenai	6,880	14,864	479,498	4,196	89,314	94.1	105,246	921	54,603	24.6	66.3	32.2
Latah	1,411	3,014	78,105	2,243	25,794	93.5	25,917	744	17,553	14.6	49.5	48.0
Lemhi	526	908	22,842	2,947	3,988	96.0	3,603	465	4,055	11.4	75.9	22.6
Lewis	349	601	19,456	5,224	4,715	98.4	3,243	871	1,820	7.8	74.7	24.2
Lincoln	253	446	11,993	2,835	2,820	93.2	5,478	1,295	1,876	19.2	74.0	24.8
Madison	1,286	2,346	71,904	2,495	10,889	91.5	23,363	811	11,637	29.7	91.9	7.1
Minidoka	1,329	2,429	57,837	2,976	9,103	94.2	19,670	1,012	7,201	10.5	80.5	18.5
Nez Perce	1,678	4,297	99,123	2,667	37,512	95.6	37,050	997	17,700	10.5	62.2	36.6
Oneida	293	443	13,646	3,303	2,716	87.0	4,357	1,055	2,133	18.6	83.9	14.3
Owyhee	566	1,185	28,763	2,632	6,883	96.5	10,564	967	3,590	12.6	79.6	19.1
Payette	988	1,830	42,958	2,027	11,882	86.2	12,843	606	8,181	19.3	76.5	22.6
Power	692	1,240	31,009	4,116	11,477	99.3	21,728	2,884	2,958	9.2	71.2	28.0
Shoshone	914	1,611	49,858	3,814	10,786	97.4	13,974	1,069	5,337	-0.9	54.8	43.7
Teton	411	800	17,287	2,538	3,703	94.0	9,199	1,350	3,690	38.2	60.6	38.4
Twin Falls	5,156	10,636	248,445	3,796	42,486	94.7	68,259	1,043	26,435	17.3	74.4	24.4
Valley	657	1,270	42,981	5,649	13,971	94.8	26,305	3,458	4,774	20.0	60.0	38.6
Washington	669	1,174	33,740	3,387	9,040	96.8	8,232	826	4,359	7.1	75.1	23.7
ILLINOIS	605,373	1,714,128	42,483,591	3,375	19,094,806	82.8	46,175,609	3,669	5,274,322	11.2	44.5	54.8
Adams	3,546	6,990	150,220	2,216	47,528	90.3	75,406	1,112	31,477	4.5	66.2	33.4
Alexander	455	826	25,829	2,733	3,695	86.5	4,042	428	3,873	-3.7	47.3	52.1
Bond	767	1,271	32,369	1,814	8,707	97.3	17,287	969	7,369	4.8	55.2	43.8
Boone	1,662	3,806	115,797	2,586	57,994	93.5	81,441	1,819	19,541	25.9	57.0	42.4
Brown	368	508	13,820	2,021	3,725	96.2	5,328	779	2,585	-2.8	65.0	34.6
Bureau	2,549	4,460	106,335	3,016	33,280	96.3	29,026	823	17,902	6.4	54.9	44.5
Calhoun	331	392	10,818	2,159	2,849	99.2	3,538	706	2,706	4.0	48.7	50.5
Carroll	1,134	1,536	37,650	2,299	17,772	94.3	25,038	1,529	8,135	13.3	55.7	43.5
Cass	909	1,402	34,125	2,500	9,883	91.4	10,130	742	5,700	-3.4	55.5	43.7
Champaign	9,163	20,419	494,205	2,711	200,168	84.1	216,582	1,188	82,434	11.0	48.4	50.4
Christian	1,933	3,306	72,003	2,045	26,072	97.1	23,264	661	15,267	3.4	59.2	40.0
Clark	812	1,309	35,698	2,101	10,136	96.5	10,143	597	8,007	6.6	63.5	35.9
Clay	947	1,722	46,594	3,260	7,613	96.3	19,935	1,395	6,554	6.8	67.4	32.1
Clinton	1,441	2,697	65,705	1,836	22,124	98.3	37,799	1,056	17,131	11.0	59.7	39.7
Coles	2,819	5,838	156,852	3,026	52,421	92.3	63,277	1,221	22,780	13.4	57.1	42.0
Cook	255,810	877,622	21,454,899	3,999	10,019,873	75.1	30,870,796	5,754	2,049,434	9.8	29.2	70.3
Crawford	1,201	2,363	58,331	2,894	14,613	96.1	18,017	894	9,332	9.8	65.2	34.2
Cumberland	583	982	23,547	2,122	6,490	98.5	14,397	1,297	5,416	8.9	64.6	34.4
DeKalb	4,376	9,245	242,910	2,641	119,054	91.2	166,621	1,812	40,768	22.7	51.7	47.3
De Witt	1,336	2,463	58,371	3,506	24,657	98.5	17,094	1,027	7,798	10.6	63.1	36.4

See footnotes at end of table.

Table B-13. Counties — **Local Government Finances and Elections**—Con.

[Includes United States, states, and 3,141 counties/county equivalents defined as of February 22, 2005. For more information on these areas, see Appendix C, Geographic Information]

County	Local government employment, March 2002		Local government finances, 2002						Elections, 2004[1]			
			General revenue				Total debt outstanding		Votes cast for President			
					Taxes							
	Total employment	Total payroll ($1,000)	Total ($1,000)	Per capita (dol.)	Total ($1,000)	Property, percent of total (taxes)	Amount ($1,000)	Per capita (dol.)	Total	Percent change, 2000–2004	Republican candidate, percent of total	Democratic candidate, percent of total
ILLINOIS—Con.												
Douglas	876	1,485	43,330	2,172	17,389	97.4	27,535	1,381	8,540	4.8	66.8	32.4
DuPage	39,717	124,345	3,062,079	3,325	1,772,951	89.3	2,661,483	2,890	402,446	10.5	54.4	44.8
Edgar	1,122	1,838	45,066	2,322	16,026	92.7	12,447	641	8,429	2.4	62.4	36.7
Edwards	356	467	11,874	1,737	3,511	99.7	5,298	775	3,364	3.2	71.7	27.7
Effingham	1,673	3,116	78,942	2,295	25,982	94.2	36,970	1,075	16,278	12.4	72.3	27.0
Fayette	992	1,634	45,422	2,106	11,020	97.0	15,175	704	9,549	2.3	61.6	37.4
Ford	938	1,519	42,081	2,972	18,413	98.3	15,920	1,124	6,479	5.3	69.6	29.5
Franklin	1,955	3,811	87,483	2,241	17,627	93.2	37,687	965	19,352	0.7	53.7	45.6
Fulton	2,633	4,336	104,881	2,791	33,499	97.1	41,468	1,103	17,035	4.7	45.9	53.3
Gallatin	443	551	14,130	2,276	4,977	66.2	3,853	621	3,225	-9.4	50.2	48.8
Greene	893	1,159	30,193	2,055	8,609	95.9	6,503	443	6,068	5.2	58.7	40.5
Grundy	2,144	4,780	123,495	3,188	74,152	97.6	88,859	2,294	19,831	19.6	56.5	42.7
Hamilton	716	896	24,974	2,967	4,194	99.7	8,675	1,031	4,514	-1.6	58.8	40.2
Hancock	1,530	1,888	50,221	2,551	15,527	97.7	10,395	528	9,899	2.1	59.0	40.2
Hardin	297	497	11,186	2,365	847	98.9	570	121	2,437	-7.6	61.6	37.9
Henderson	545	691	17,123	2,098	5,730	98.5	4,660	571	4,153	7.4	44.7	54.6
Henry	3,235	5,919	139,115	2,757	42,163	96.1	49,880	988	25,241	7.5	52.3	47.1
Iroquois	2,010	2,604	71,545	2,322	28,221	96.4	20,774	674	13,835	3.1	71.7	27.7
Jackson	2,655	5,666	143,765	2,473	42,044	75.8	95,740	1,647	25,826	11.8	43.3	55.4
Jasper	622	1,133	24,135	2,396	9,550	98.8	3,283	326	5,336	6.3	66.1	33.4
Jefferson	2,448	4,617	108,529	2,695	25,646	84.7	20,181	501	16,948	10.3	60.0	39.6
Jersey	1,128	2,463	55,526	2,526	9,869	95.5	5,554	253	10,137	7.7	53.6	45.4
Jo Daviess	1,327	2,359	69,434	3,094	33,355	93.8	24,202	1,078	11,584	12.2	53.3	45.9
Johnson	408	821	19,346	1,508	4,417	97.5	13,459	1,049	5,865	9.4	68.2	30.9
Kane	23,089	66,010	1,607,027	3,632	808,809	90.9	2,021,206	4,568	167,297	18.3	55.0	44.1
Kankakee	4,808	11,251	284,394	2,702	98,102	94.1	143,886	1,367	45,036	12.1	54.9	44.4
Kendall	2,313	5,560	160,249	2,595	83,238	95.1	144,635	2,342	32,527	42.9	60.8	38.4
Knox	3,358	7,100	156,018	2,841	49,149	91.1	66,629	1,213	24,708	6.6	45.0	54.3
Lake	29,035	89,560	2,414,502	3,577	1,344,705	89.3	2,240,240	3,319	275,295	13.7	50.5	48.8
LaSalle	5,595	11,530	307,398	2,751	132,156	91.2	178,285	1,596	50,729	10.3	51.5	47.8
Lawrence	930	1,569	30,249	1,882	6,455	98.7	9,156	570	6,729	2.3	61.9	37.4
Lee	2,539	3,483	94,844	2,663	37,861	92.3	21,357	600	15,876	8.6	58.6	40.4
Livingston	2,464	4,488	113,656	2,892	46,666	98.4	31,903	812	16,039	4.0	64.3	35.1
Logan	1,290	2,412	56,487	1,835	24,523	98.9	9,592	312	13,467	3.1	67.7	31.7
McDonough	2,101	4,227	109,981	3,348	25,061	97.8	22,370	681	14,929	14.7	51.3	47.7
McHenry	10,732	26,903	738,537	2,647	391,810	94.0	686,917	2,462	127,948	20.5	59.7	39.3
McLean	7,039	15,665	410,364	2,644	208,375	84.5	298,113	1,920	71,620	17.6	57.6	41.7
Macon	5,237	12,717	327,512	2,914	106,332	87.8	175,285	1,560	51,746	4.5	54.3	45.1
Macoupin	2,633	4,421	106,569	2,174	29,061	96.9	39,796	812	22,785	6.5	50.1	49.1
Madison	11,053	26,710	667,141	2,557	213,069	91.6	438,112	1,679	123,678	11.3	48.0	51.3
Marion	2,822	5,377	146,559	3,569	29,284	92.8	36,052	878	17,224	3.4	54.7	44.7
Marshall	667	966	28,635	2,200	13,394	95.9	10,901	837	6,584	11.5	56.7	42.6
Mason	1,216	2,448	51,272	3,208	16,884	97.2	11,710	733	7,183	6.1	54.4	44.8
Massac	893	1,682	58,100	3,830	9,457	95.2	12,823	845	7,424	10.1	61.7	37.8
Menard	787	1,285	33,693	2,676	12,062	99.3	18,644	1,481	6,574	6.0	67.1	32.5
Mercer	1,313	2,631	49,066	2,885	13,409	99.1	16,856	991	8,974	7.9	49.1	50.3
Monroe	1,193	2,545	60,767	2,092	23,704	92.9	51,707	1,780	16,370	18.7	57.8	41.5
Montgomery	1,790	2,935	67,071	2,194	21,161	96.9	31,391	1,027	12,930	-1.2	53.0	46.2
Morgan	1,586	3,136	69,311	1,920	27,389	93.8	14,875	412	15,180	5.9	61.9	37.2
Moultrie	762	1,244	33,129	2,306	14,520	99.2	15,481	1,078	6,466	12.9	62.3	36.9
Ogle	3,442	7,573	170,044	3,258	83,398	96.1	127,473	2,442	24,091	16.9	61.9	37.4
Peoria	8,590	22,625	502,202	2,750	164,812	81.7	293,840	1,609	82,771	7.8	49.6	49.7
Perry	1,047	2,159	54,065	2,372	9,761	90.1	24,142	1,059	10,425	4.9	53.6	45.8
Piatt	964	1,764	52,232	3,214	18,690	97.6	26,212	1,613	8,586	2.4	62.8	36.4
Pike	1,190	1,709	37,422	2,191	10,930	99.1	16,112	944	7,980	-1.6	63.1	35.7
Pope	192	309	9,922	2,287	1,969	94.3	1,226	283	2,436	4.5	61.6	37.7
Pulaski	612	1,427	19,054	2,652	2,311	81.4	4,162	579	3,108	3.1	55.3	44.1
Putnam	331	516	11,472	1,879	4,516	98.8	519	85	3,352	5.4	48.4	50.8
Randolph	2,020	3,877	96,677	2,904	18,101	95.0	37,748	1,134	14,956	4.7	54.0	45.3
Richland	1,406	3,190	65,131	4,054	12,531	94.6	21,657	1,348	7,749	4.3	66.5	32.6
Rock Island	7,625	18,762	447,978	3,019	152,190	89.6	245,297	1,653	69,972	7.5	42.4	57.0
St. Clair	11,837	28,736	789,344	3,066	194,391	90.4	479,991	1,864	113,189	12.7	44.4	55.1
Saline	1,827	3,110	77,621	2,958	15,722	97.6	38,350	1,461	11,814	1.4	59.7	39.8
Sangamon	9,927	27,408	522,994	2,731	212,546	90.5	587,159	3,066	95,375	4.3	58.6	40.5
Schuyler	648	926	28,168	4,025	4,920	99.8	8,951	1,279	4,031	6.9	59.6	39.5
Scott	377	600	13,239	2,406	3,401	93.0	622	113	2,636	6.8	64.3	35.2
Shelby	1,083	1,577	40,777	1,807	15,048	98.2	8,861	393	10,577	4.1	63.9	35.4
Stark	428	1,144	16,881	2,700	9,108	99.5	3,297	527	3,061	2.4	60.1	38.8
Stephenson	2,727	5,799	133,505	2,771	52,503	93.1	67,254	1,396	21,320	10.0	57.3	41.8
Tazewell	7,046	13,683	360,082	2,805	132,718	88.4	122,452	954	62,338	6.8	57.8	41.4

See footnotes at end of table.

County and City Data Book: 2007

U.S. Census Bureau

[Includes United States, states, and 3,141 counties/county equivalents defined as of February 22, 2005. For more information on these areas, see Appendix C, Geographic Information]

County	Local government employment, March 2002		Local government finances, 2002					Total debt outstanding		Elections, 2004[1]			
			General revenue							Votes cast for President			
					Taxes							Republican candidate, percent of total	Democratic candidate, percent of total
	Total employ-ment	Total payroll ($1,000)	Total ($1,000)	Per capita (dol.)	Total ($1,000)	Property, percent of total (taxes)		Amount ($1,000)	Per capita (dol.)	Total	Percent change, 2000–2004		
ILLINOIS—Con.													
Union	1,533	2,947	63,483	3,494	10,736	98.7		13,079	720	9,119	5.3	58.5	41.0
Vermilion	4,142	8,589	228,210	2,742	64,318	88.0		72,476	871	33,714	5.0	55.6	43.7
Wabash	745	1,540	37,340	2,938	6,614	94.8		16,935	1,332	6,006	9.0	70.1	29.2
Warren	1,082	1,564	39,302	2,137	14,297	94.3		18,751	1,020	8,457	10.8	52.9	46.6
Washington	1,038	1,535	39,585	2,613	10,329	98.8		13,915	918	8,104	13.5	62.6	36.9
Wayne	1,036	1,526	33,948	1,993	8,526	94.5		3,257	191	8,287	7.7	73.6	25.8
White	798	1,014	32,989	2,167	8,454	90.1		6,959	457	8,301	8.7	62.4	37.0
Whiteside	3,746	7,980	211,939	3,513	50,289	96.9		51,163	848	26,873	8.2	48.2	51.1
Will	19,596	51,897	1,453,892	2,599	680,576	90.2		1,463,299	2,616	249,609	30.2	52.4	46.9
Williamson	2,861	5,993	154,861	2,493	43,756	90.0		79,725	1,283	29,960	11.2	60.4	39.0
Winnebago	13,396	33,197	815,175	2,891	337,626	95.5		609,936	2,163	121,425	11.1	50.1	49.2
Woodford	2,031	3,848	81,573	2,266	38,710	94.1		43,135	1,198	18,802	12.0	67.5	31.9
INDIANA	276,500	674,315	18,538,509	3,012	6,786,047	88.0		14,614,998	2,375	2,468,002	12.2	59.9	39.3
Adams	2,067	3,833	99,089	2,955	29,182	92.6		37,236	1,111	13,340	6.0	73.0	26.3
Allen	12,854	34,469	815,381	2,416	371,943	89.1		554,842	1,644	129,609	13.4	63.3	36.0
Bartholomew	4,574	11,310	298,914	4,161	75,732	83.0		152,434	2,122	28,515	10.7	67.0	32.2
Benton	667	1,275	28,774	3,105	12,378	90.9		11,934	1,288	3,992	3.0	70.1	28.4
Blackford	781	1,668	42,290	3,046	12,853	87.3		31,817	2,291	5,380	10.0	64.1	35.4
Boone	2,312	5,496	174,816	3,608	59,556	80.8		230,700	4,762	22,898	24.5	74.5	24.6
Brown	620	1,303	39,219	2,571	14,049	79.6		8,823	578	7,330	7.5	61.6	37.2
Carroll	839	1,789	44,901	2,208	19,508	85.9		28,648	1,409	8,638	4.5	67.9	31.1
Cass	2,585	5,631	136,196	3,363	39,639	88.8		48,794	1,205	13,931	−7.8	68.1	31.0
Clark	4,735	12,474	311,749	3,183	85,830	97.4		128,161	1,308	42,337	13.4	57.9	41.7
Clay	1,082	2,148	67,782	2,553	18,378	85.2		37,026	1,395	10,783	6.2	68.3	30.9
Clinton	1,755	4,173	86,331	2,534	31,550	86.8		30,609	898	11,877	8.1	71.3	28.1
Crawford	490	972	24,712	2,232	6,706	90.0		17,887	1,616	4,574	8.7	57.0	42.2
Daviess	1,544	3,454	90,242	3,027	23,412	85.7		66,799	2,241	10,599	8.6	74.9	24.3
Dearborn	2,659	6,188	211,299	4,468	51,387	90.7		87,063	1,841	20,969	18.8	67.9	31.5
Decatur	1,264	3,036	85,194	3,457	23,986	84.9		49,171	1,995	10,199	11.2	73.5	25.7
DeKalb	1,788	3,967	134,236	3,297	41,550	83.6		79,492	1,952	15,403	11.7	68.0	31.2
Delaware	4,610	10,174	283,927	2,388	110,735	90.2		98,323	827	47,939	8.6	56.5	42.6
Dubois	1,685	3,873	105,432	2,634	42,831	87.8		85,654	2,140	17,066	10.1	68.7	30.5
Elkhart	7,788	19,092	466,609	2,511	204,255	84.7		396,604	2,134	61,380	12.7	70.0	29.3
Fayette	1,480	3,473	65,198	2,595	25,726	83.9		20,789	827	9,468	9.5	60.9	38.3
Floyd	3,893	9,331	288,041	4,033	67,512	97.0		97,200	1,361	33,890	12.9	58.7	40.9
Fountain	860	1,729	39,309	2,207	14,838	77.3		23,810	1,337	7,804	7.2	67.4	31.7
Franklin	679	1,310	36,789	1,632	13,825	81.9		12,160	540	9,992	19.8	69.8	29.3
Fulton	1,120	2,218	63,988	3,100	18,628	87.4		39,481	1,913	8,703	4.5	69.3	30.0
Gibson	1,178	2,528	81,171	2,485	33,414	97.1		209,637	6,419	14,614	6.1	62.5	36.8
Grant	3,079	6,860	160,629	2,220	65,902	83.6		60,087	830	27,460	4.1	68.4	31.0
Greene	1,666	3,582	106,333	3,209	28,443	85.6		28,372	856	13,352	5.8	64.5	34.5
Hamilton	8,759	23,215	604,828	2,920	284,501	80.5		593,528	2,866	104,906	38.2	74.4	25.2
Hancock	2,998	7,274	254,278	4,365	59,266	80.3		192,483	3,304	27,867	21.4	74.5	24.8
Harrison	1,493	3,619	116,542	3,306	27,697	87.8		51,126	1,450	17,310	16.2	63.6	35.7
Hendricks	5,258	12,829	335,032	2,916	129,212	83.7		423,415	3,685	52,302	30.0	73.5	25.9
Henry	3,182	6,990	172,449	3,589	43,663	80.9		67,593	1,407	20,504	12.0	64.1	35.0
Howard	5,109	13,172	293,508	3,466	115,015	89.2		172,807	2,040	37,021	8.6	64.1	35.1
Huntington	1,416	3,408	91,276	2,386	36,327	86.0		50,818	1,328	15,627	6.9	74.3	24.8
Jackson	2,087	5,013	142,800	3,438	30,141	82.0		72,476	1,745	16,309	11.7	68.0	31.2
Jasper	1,710	3,543	97,783	3,184	31,290	88.1		180,157	5,867	11,844	6.1	68.0	31.1
Jay	1,225	2,420	72,628	3,349	18,507	93.5		17,664	814	8,232	2.5	65.9	33.3
Jefferson	1,177	2,506	79,588	2,482	32,714	97.8		44,569	1,390	12,971	8.7	59.9	39.5
Jennings	960	2,229	58,447	2,072	20,819	70.6		48,861	1,732	10,517	10.8	65.3	33.6
Johnson	5,103	11,329	362,144	2,979	118,937	83.4		274,251	2,256	51,255	21.2	73.7	25.6
Knox	3,223	7,286	194,487	4,990	29,960	95.9		93,181	2,391	15,746	4.6	63.4	35.9
Kosciusko	3,169	7,220	178,108	2,377	78,102	89.5		85,926	1,147	28,360	12.2	78.1	21.1
LaGrange	1,313	2,990	74,898	2,099	31,731	82.6		66,176	1,855	9,003	8.0	71.4	28.0
Lake	23,452	58,686	1,815,179	3,736	671,764	94.9		1,033,177	2,126	188,022	6.8	38.2	61.0
LaPorte	4,999	11,507	337,965	3,067	134,825	92.6		168,464	1,529	42,606	7.2	49.1	49.6
Lawrence	2,144	5,122	126,351	2,741	36,705	88.8		66,878	1,451	17,698	9.6	69.0	30.2
Madison	5,867	13,756	320,386	2,429	113,040	88.7		148,185	1,123	54,855	5.1	59.3	39.9
Marion	36,659	111,272	3,122,736	3,622	1,243,372	88.1		4,369,654	5,068	320,838	14.6	48.7	50.6
Marshall	1,879	4,079	100,523	2,195	41,657	93.9		72,246	1,578	17,814	10.3	67.8	31.4
Martin	507	871	22,674	2,184	9,052	65.2		10,051	968	4,996	8.4	68.3	30.5
Miami	2,226	4,884	131,431	3,615	25,239	88.4		33,831	930	13,628	5.4	70.4	28.5
Monroe	4,144	9,233	299,175	2,495	105,711	80.6		219,294	1,829	50,467	25.5	45.3	53.4
Montgomery	1,819	3,777	106,136	2,800	44,513	88.0		90,069	2,376	14,548	11.0	74.9	24.3
Morgan	2,802	6,210	159,743	2,351	52,954	79.9		52,131	767	26,029	18.1	73.8	25.6
Newton	908	1,580	41,900	2,918	16,363	89.6		22,686	1,580	5,848	6.1	64.2	34.8
Noble	1,744	3,880	103,073	2,196	40,163	86.8		75,474	1,608	15,679	10.3	69.3	30.0
Ohio	292	593	28,499	4,946	14,982	20.4		4,616	801	2,958	18.7	60.7	38.5
Orange	1,000	2,122	52,529	2,700	13,469	83.4		40,470	2,080	8,652	16.0	65.7	33.3
Owen	788	1,618	42,796	1,904	13,638	82.3		31,237	1,390	7,604	16.9	65.8	33.4

See footnotes at end of table.

[Includes United States, states, and 3,141 counties/county equivalents defined as of February 22, 2005. For more information on these areas, see Appendix C, Geographic Information]

County	Local government employment, March 2002		Local government finances, 2002						Elections, 2004[1]			
			General revenue				Total debt outstanding		Votes cast for President			
					Taxes							
	Total employment	Total payroll ($1,000)	Total ($1,000)	Per capita (dol.)	Total ($1,000)	Property, percent of total (taxes)	Amount ($1,000)	Per capita (dol.)	Total	Percent change, 2000–2004	Republican candidate, percent of total	Democratic candidate, percent of total
INDIANA—Con.												
Parke	770	1,264	34,061	1,975	12,127	84.1	14,148	820	6,971	8.1	65.3	33.9
Perry	1,076	2,126	61,740	3,273	18,962	68.2	70,043	3,713	8,315	12.6	49.8	49.7
Pike	668	1,095	33,097	2,556	12,746	88.4	25,320	1,955	6,212	−1.4	60.3	38.9
Porter	7,515	17,898	469,913	3,119	132,679	93.5	378,652	2,514	64,873	9.3	53.6	45.3
Posey	1,132	2,977	65,935	2,439	36,214	99.5	50,067	1,852	11,986	7.9	65.4	34.1
Pulaski	921	1,812	54,428	3,961	14,360	86.5	33,338	2,426	5,614	1.7	67.6	31.2
Putnam	2,111	4,222	110,955	3,049	35,579	88.0	109,381	3,006	13,136	10.7	67.8	31.2
Randolph	1,335	2,710	76,698	2,830	23,161	84.6	13,614	502	11,092	9.5	64.7	34.4
Ripley	1,263	2,493	63,390	2,324	24,657	84.2	23,963	879	11,834	10.9	69.5	29.7
Rush	970	2,065	53,347	2,968	16,412	89.3	18,422	1,025	7,421	1.9	72.3	27.0
St. Joseph	10,487	26,508	795,203	2,991	312,553	93.5	712,617	2,680	108,619	11.4	50.9	48.5
Scott	1,124	2,442	74,698	3,194	17,328	83.4	55,210	2,361	8,677	10.6	55.2	44.1
Shelby	2,347	5,480	148,432	3,391	40,461	85.1	155,383	3,550	16,027	4.7	71.1	28.2
Spencer	940	1,872	51,120	2,521	25,803	91.6	41,222	2,033	9,924	10.4	59.8	39.5
Starke	1,051	1,994	69,417	3,073	18,408	94.2	73,407	3,250	8,937	2.7	54.2	44.6
Steuben	1,386	2,976	76,048	2,272	33,588	85.6	64,106	1,915	12,905	14.4	65.4	33.7
Sullivan	1,157	2,240	74,658	3,418	19,955	98.4	218,392	9,999	8,394	1.6	59.6	39.8
Switzerland	395	753	34,971	3,686	6,846	85.8	7,465	787	3,671	13.3	58.9	40.3
Tippecanoe	4,623	12,291	346,041	2,308	156,440	85.5	183,944	1,227	52,360	13.1	59.0	39.8
Tipton	1,417	2,720	61,800	3,731	18,321	80.3	34,041	2,055	7,892	7.9	71.3	27.9
Union	393	767	20,245	2,756	7,685	87.9	18,147	2,470	3,344	18.2	67.8	31.3
Vanderburgh	5,857	14,920	443,608	2,579	190,859	79.9	194,013	1,128	70,654	6.7	58.7	40.7
Vermillion	755	1,524	36,273	2,189	17,654	98.1	34,188	2,063	7,017	5.8	50.4	48.8
Vigo	4,136	9,563	216,111	2,066	95,583	98.3	92,931	889	39,744	9.7	52.8	46.4
Wabash	2,095	4,387	105,596	3,060	31,540	87.3	51,863	1,503	13,602	5.6	70.6	28.8
Warren	415	808	20,340	2,343	7,204	85.5	5,803	668	3,960	5.1	64.8	34.2
Warrick	1,690	4,252	120,653	2,251	56,662	90.6	112,449	2,098	26,025	16.7	65.1	34.5
Washington	1,260	2,814	78,666	2,843	19,953	88.0	26,009	940	10,880	11.0	63.6	35.7
Wayne	3,213	7,272	181,732	2,581	73,682	81.6	57,485	816	27,657	10.0	60.0	39.0
Wells	1,143	2,528	61,031	2,189	22,938	84.6	64,659	2,319	12,354	9.5	74.2	25.2
White	1,607	3,324	85,058	3,379	32,660	89.3	83,796	3,329	10,366	4.7	67.3	31.6
Whitley	1,182	2,624	84,801	2,699	43,950	77.3	43,868	1,396	13,481	8.4	70.6	28.8
IOWA	154,390	331,304	9,117,686	3,107	3,324,163	86.6	5,781,408	1,970	1,506,908	14.5	49.9	49.2
Adair	396	693	18,671	2,332	7,252	95.7	11,952	1,493	4,278	3.8	56.2	43.1
Adams	254	423	10,966	2,499	4,067	98.1	7,498	1,709	2,325	8.4	56.7	42.0
Allamakee	732	1,209	42,190	2,920	13,925	94.3	11,462	793	7,062	9.3	50.0	48.8
Appanoose	782	1,295	33,813	2,513	10,400	95.8	10,512	781	6,450	13.1	51.8	47.5
Audubon	447	795	16,893	2,563	6,638	96.6	3,051	463	3,592	−5.1	54.5	44.8
Benton	1,164	2,310	56,558	2,162	20,146	97.1	42,870	1,639	13,501	14.7	49.3	50.0
Black Hawk	5,414	12,560	379,440	3,001	141,185	77.8	239,172	1,892	63,907	16.0	43.9	55.4
Boone	1,338	2,815	76,240	2,921	24,761	86.8	86,946	3,331	14,009	14.4	49.0	50.2
Bremer	1,238	2,497	74,573	3,204	22,646	92.6	41,250	1,772	12,779	14.4	52.2	47.2
Buchanan	1,064	1,896	54,524	2,614	16,639	90.7	16,598	796	10,475	11.3	45.8	53.5
Buena Vista	1,395	2,631	67,778	3,341	19,196	90.3	25,489	1,257	8,490	6.4	57.6	41.5
Butler	707	1,094	33,366	2,222	13,210	94.4	14,527	967	7,475	11.2	59.1	40.2
Calhoun	717	1,271	33,545	3,101	13,856	98.1	6,150	569	5,542	9.9	58.7	40.5
Carroll	1,004	1,882	57,766	2,729	22,233	97.8	34,277	1,620	10,524	10.0	54.8	44.6
Cass	1,058	2,319	56,213	3,927	15,387	92.7	27,051	1,890	7,543	9.6	63.6	35.5
Cedar	967	1,876	45,851	2,522	19,322	91.8	19,358	1,065	9,694	16.2	50.2	49.0
Cerro Gordo	2,600	5,058	139,506	3,077	52,663	84.7	44,807	988	24,516	10.6	44.7	54.5
Cherokee	674	1,270	30,883	2,436	12,193	92.7	21,099	1,664	6,796	3.1	55.3	44.0
Chickasaw	627	1,207	32,842	2,554	13,665	91.7	9,903	770	6,806	3.4	44.7	54.5
Clarke	612	1,215	33,540	3,662	10,564	89.8	24,353	2,659	4,566	9.3	48.2	50.9
Clay	1,351	3,074	84,075	4,922	17,170	85.4	45,461	2,661	8,588	13.3	57.0	41.3
Clayton	993	1,837	49,946	2,717	20,241	84.6	10,233	557	9,168	7.0	47.0	51.7
Clinton	3,630	6,795	132,118	2,651	54,069	81.0	90,466	1,815	24,684	11.3	43.2	56.0
Crawford	946	1,993	52,917	3,115	15,820	88.4	7,496	441	7,242	10.5	54.6	44.5
Dallas	2,250	4,704	115,790	2,607	48,159	94.2	111,984	2,521	26,293	36.0	57.8	41.5
Davis	534	876	32,076	3,719	10,370	98.5	11,125	1,290	3,918	4.3	54.8	44.2
Decatur	690	1,102	28,907	3,349	7,230	91.1	8,052	933	4,011	8.1	52.1	46.4
Delaware	1,018	2,101	57,815	3,160	17,894	90.7	16,207	886	9,200	10.2	53.4	46.0
Des Moines	1,922	3,797	136,146	3,285	49,822	74.8	71,249	1,719	20,874	7.8	39.4	59.7
Dickinson	1,078	2,273	64,538	3,931	29,270	79.8	49,212	2,997	9,553	17.6	55.9	43.3
Dubuque	3,529	8,383	234,763	2,625	85,902	82.5	66,918	748	47,043	16.7	42.7	56.5
Emmet	632	1,162	56,163	5,186	14,556	88.6	10,202	942	5,156	11.4	52.3	46.6
Fayette	1,138	2,175	54,944	2,549	19,604	88.1	15,629	725	10,392	8.0	49.4	49.9
Floyd	979	1,987	56,350	3,390	17,556	88.6	17,999	1,083	8,167	12.8	45.9	53.3
Franklin	844	1,456	37,335	3,496	12,469	87.9	9,393	879	5,521	11.8	56.7	42.4
Fremont	472	830	22,983	2,932	9,583	87.9	7,856	1,002	3,911	8.2	60.4	38.6
Greene	891	1,637	42,071	4,132	12,601	96.5	9,079	892	5,113	8.3	51.2	48.1
Grundy	771	1,337	36,334	2,942	13,119	91.6	15,847	1,283	6,849	12.1	64.7	34.8
Guthrie	822	1,412	39,377	3,481	12,338	95.8	15,323	1,355	5,994	9.6	55.5	43.6
Hamilton	1,210	2,308	60,400	3,705	20,234	96.2	36,469	2,237	8,335	10.0	52.4	46.7

See footnotes at end of table.

[Includes United States, states, and 3,141 counties/county equivalents defined as of February 22, 2005. For more information on these areas, see Appendix C, Geographic Information]

County	Local government employment, March 2002		Local government finances, 2002							Elections, 2004[1]			
			General revenue				Total debt outstanding		Votes cast for President				
					Taxes								
	Total employ- ment	Total payroll ($1,000)	Total ($1,000)	Per capita (dol.)	Total ($1,000)	Prop- erty, percent of total (taxes)	Amount ($1,000)	Per capita (dol.)		Total	Percent change, 2000– 2004	Repub- lican cand- idate, percent of total	Demo- cratic cand- idate, percent of total
IOWA—Con.													
Hancock	696	1,298	35,458	2,997	13,075	92.8	10,900	921		5,905	8.6	57.0	42.1
Hardin	1,069	1,833	64,812	3,516	22,254	88.3	24,702	1,340		8,949	6.1	54.5	44.9
Harrison	878	1,669	41,077	2,639	16,817	92.9	22,693	1,458		7,680	17.4	60.9	37.8
Henry	1,302	2,684	67,168	3,343	20,381	89.8	51,797	2,578		9,457	9.1	55.2	43.6
Howard	847	1,476	33,538	3,402	11,079	88.6	9,491	963		4,697	4.6	43.2	55.7
Humboldt	717	1,315	32,199	3,178	11,415	97.3	11,590	1,144		5,350	8.3	59.1	40.1
Ida	395	706	18,675	2,452	7,664	96.5	7,154	939		3,774	8.1	62.1	37.5
Iowa	743	1,447	45,746	2,891	17,785	81.4	14,989	947		8,454	14.0	53.8	45.4
Jackson	1,155	2,390	57,173	2,824	16,292	85.9	10,940	540		10,011	10.8	42.4	56.5
Jasper	2,084	4,166	131,028	3,486	41,501	92.2	49,070	1,305		20,062	12.5	47.2	52.0
Jefferson	867	1,711	43,598	2,732	14,081	88.8	10,131	635		8,281	9.7	44.1	54.2
Johnson	3,741	8,514	259,366	2,279	111,744	91.1	386,780	3,398		65,373	23.9	34.8	64.0
Jones	936	1,735	47,590	2,347	17,965	91.4	28,312	1,396		9,978	9.1	48.5	50.7
Keokuk	714	1,229	33,484	2,934	12,587	94.7	15,223	1,334		5,480	10.8	56.9	41.9
Kossuth	994	1,923	55,411	3,339	21,443	89.2	11,516	694		9,258	4.3	54.5	44.6
Lee	1,688	3,529	95,223	2,574	40,048	76.2	55,505	1,501		17,858	7.8	41.8	56.9
Linn	10,715	23,315	624,570	3,200	230,701	92.2	476,897	2,444		110,740	20.3	44.7	54.6
Louisa	724	1,401	44,256	3,622	14,013	96.0	113,798	9,312		4,916	6.0	52.3	46.7
Lucas	599	1,172	33,268	3,519	8,630	89.7	10,533	1,114		4,571	6.2	55.6	43.5
Lyon	602	1,095	29,457	2,519	12,266	88.9	11,272	964		6,101	14.2	77.9	21.4
Madison	890	1,854	59,267	4,109	14,286	96.7	99,997	6,934		8,004	14.9	56.7	42.2
Mahaska	1,060	2,339	65,239	2,919	22,790	86.0	34,297	1,535		10,728	12.4	63.9	35.3
Marion	1,489	2,974	77,919	2,392	29,720	91.2	67,186	2,063		16,696	15.9	59.8	39.4
Marshall	2,170	5,111	118,947	3,032	41,254	85.5	48,238	1,230		19,164	8.7	49.9	49.3
Mills	802	1,512	35,567	2,415	14,043	96.2	10,678	725		6,940	17.3	65.7	33.3
Mitchell	672	1,337	33,569	3,090	10,639	91.4	12,058	1,110		5,480	6.2	48.3	50.8
Monona	562	1,017	27,910	2,860	12,524	86.8	4,261	437		5,018	10.0	51.3	47.8
Monroe	457	745	25,406	3,256	7,703	97.5	6,276	804		3,963	8.7	52.2	46.8
Montgomery	835	1,761	50,388	4,435	14,450	82.6	23,744	2,090		5,556	3.0	64.8	34.2
Muscatine	2,146	5,497	120,703	2,869	47,304	80.6	162,338	3,859		18,717	16.4	48.2	51.0
O'Brien	1,014	1,866	47,775	3,237	17,706	92.4	21,153	1,433		7,731	9.8	68.9	30.1
Osceola	326	578	14,402	2,105	6,003	96.1	7,658	1,119		3,266	6.6	70.3	28.6
Page	969	1,778	49,886	3,023	16,024	84.4	26,757	1,621		7,513	6.4	69.8	29.4
Palo Alto	834	1,433	38,560	3,899	11,888	91.1	10,554	1,067		5,191	7.6	51.5	47.8
Plymouth	1,270	2,506	71,742	2,909	23,418	90.9	27,938	1,133		12,222	20.8	63.9	35.0
Pocahontas	541	972	23,829	2,840	8,458	94.0	8,119	968		4,313	4.2	56.6	42.2
Polk	18,224	49,868	1,353,633	3,516	556,135	85.7	1,193,105	3,099		202,618	16.3	47.3	51.9
Pottawattamie	3,857	9,965	273,243	3,100	110,244	77.7	151,381	1,718		41,820	21.3	58.7	40.4
Poweshiek	861	1,814	45,501	2,413	18,746	90.2	23,840	1,265		10,091	12.4	49.2	50.0
Ringgold	445	960	21,334	3,998	5,586	98.6	1,862	349		2,778	3.2	52.8	46.3
Sac	682	1,137	27,877	2,521	11,378	98.0	6,152	556		5,374	6.8	58.2	41.2
Scott	7,292	17,838	502,121	3,156	213,147	78.1	409,059	2,571		82,722	17.2	48.3	50.9
Shelby	910	1,747	54,741	4,245	16,965	90.8	28,809	2,234		6,670	11.0	63.8	35.3
Sioux	1,532	3,105	90,781	2,841	27,394	88.0	69,895	2,187		16,570	12.8	85.9	13.6
Story	3,433	7,704	289,066	3,581	82,753	88.7	131,082	1,624		44,652	26.3	46.6	52.2
Tama	1,172	1,977	49,863	2,785	19,147	91.1	9,934	555		9,001	8.3	49.5	49.9
Taylor	546	748	19,503	2,856	5,739	91.9	9,142	1,339		3,190	3.0	59.8	39.3
Union	1,005	2,117	62,656	5,157	12,425	98.8	21,671	1,784		5,978	4.1	52.9	46.0
Van Buren	565	1,013	27,145	3,479	6,137	94.4	11,397	1,461		3,836	7.7	57.6	40.9
Wapello	2,137	3,883	129,652	3,609	39,182	79.5	50,640	1,410		16,707	10.4	44.3	54.6
Warren	1,734	3,577	94,005	2,269	35,080	96.2	68,456	1,652		23,053	17.3	52.8	46.5
Washington	1,182	2,840	61,713	2,919	19,839	94.2	43,247	2,046		10,688	17.5	55.9	43.0
Wayne	489	904	22,808	3,428	6,055	96.7	4,663	701		3,133	3.7	55.3	44.0
Webster	2,182	4,157	126,244	3,171	42,867	86.1	54,739	1,375		18,631	9.3	48.1	51.3
Winnebago	725	1,389	36,506	3,195	14,455	90.7	14,586	1,276		5,952	7.7	53.3	45.5
Winneshiek	1,434	2,887	84,426	3,962	23,398	82.8	20,010	939		10,784	14.5	49.4	49.7
Woodbury	6,118	13,210	334,329	3,233	123,982	78.0	203,278	1,966		44,195	16.6	50.8	48.6
Worth	367	758	18,758	2,406	7,700	92.5	10,368	1,330		4,123	3.0	43.5	55.5
Wright	1,105	2,260	47,369	3,394	17,903	89.4	15,022	1,076		6,603	4.2	55.0	44.4
KANSAS	164,726	347,345	8,469,363	3,122	3,166,614	78.0	10,024,660	3,696		1,187,756	10.8	62.0	36.6
Allen	1,264	1,935	43,797	3,106	12,173	74.3	17,680	1,254		5,873	1.9	65.8	32.7
Anderson	511	855	20,002	2,452	7,642	87.4	28,303	3,469		3,863	11.1	64.7	33.5
Atchison	931	1,750	41,489	2,477	14,918	74.8	36,325	2,168		7,118	3.2	54.5	43.8
Barber	533	795	25,477	5,009	8,304	84.1	6,049	1,189		2,403	−3.8	74.2	24.5
Barton	2,272	3,985	93,160	3,317	31,352	81.1	74,833	2,665		11,706	6.9	74.0	24.6
Bourbon	1,078	1,920	41,334	2,720	12,707	78.8	29,163	1,919		6,686	6.0	65.4	33.1
Brown	621	995	25,093	2,391	8,877	82.8	20,779	1,980		4,418	−5.8	70.0	28.7
Butler	4,492	8,364	194,617	3,218	56,304	88.0	259,785	4,296		26,280	25.1	70.2	28.5
Chase	311	386	9,477	3,112	3,845	97.2	3,972	1,304		1,501	14.0	70.3	27.9
Chautauqua	298	398	10,180	2,421	2,933	86.7	3,307	786		1,960	4.3	78.0	20.6

See footnotes at end of table.

Table B-13. Counties — **Local Government Finances and Elections**—Con.

[Includes United States, states, and 3,141 counties/county equivalents defined as of February 22, 2005. For more information on these areas, see Appendix C, Geographic Information]

County	Local government employment, March 2002		Local government finances, 2002							Elections, 2004[1]			
			General revenue				Total debt outstanding			Votes cast for President			
					Taxes								
	Total employ-ment	Total payroll ($1,000)	Total ($1,000)	Per capita (dol.)	Total ($1,000)	Prop-erty, percent of total (taxes)	Amount ($1,000)	Per capita (dol.)		Total	Percent change, 2000–2004	Repub-lican cand-idate, percent of total	Demo-cratic cand-idate, percent of total
KANSAS—Con.													
Cherokee	1,188	2,005	45,042	2,047	12,651	78.8	10,411	473		9,913	8.6	61.4	37.6
Cheyenne	285	403	8,980	2,944	3,777	82.4	83	27		1,692	-2.0	80.0	18.9
Clark	366	686	18,935	8,027	5,140	98.6	1,694	718		1,291	2.4	78.5	19.9
Clay	860	1,469	31,735	3,662	8,225	87.5	15,112	1,744		4,010	-1.9	79.2	19.8
Cloud	840	1,378	36,448	3,660	11,329	82.9	13,308	1,336		4,503	–	71.5	26.9
Coffey	1,031	2,043	51,539	5,840	28,704	99.3	15,576	1,765		4,408	9.1	73.9	24.8
Comanche	283	335	9,563	4,887	4,142	94.5	1,521	777		981	-2.5	78.5	20.4
Cowley	2,825	6,055	130,550	3,590	30,297	85.8	68,051	1,871		14,447	1.7	65.1	33.4
Crawford	2,568	4,497	92,614	2,438	31,214	64.3	57,810	1,522		16,527	9.9	52.2	46.1
Decatur	393	465	10,350	3,058	3,980	92.4	1,817	537		1,740	-1.1	77.9	20.4
Dickinson	1,522	2,595	55,708	2,914	15,849	84.6	24,449	1,279		8,791	8.6	71.6	26.9
Doniphan	879	1,281	31,854	3,896	6,055	83.9	9,127	1,116		3,603	-1.3	69.1	29.6
Douglas	4,659	12,055	308,304	3,038	106,797	71.2	258,613	2,548		50,111	25.8	41.0	57.1
Edwards	289	409	10,032	2,996	5,232	93.8	1,410	421		1,496	-4.3	72.5	25.8
Elk	459	593	13,336	4,164	2,805	91.7	2,668	833		1,515	-2.3	73.9	24.4
Ellis	1,497	2,780	63,522	2,326	26,035	81.8	30,596	1,121		12,187	9.2	64.8	33.1
Ellsworth	513	744	19,679	3,081	9,354	89.3	21,933	3,434		3,102	9.3	72.8	25.8
Finney	2,799	5,550	142,573	3,621	52,878	81.6	110,575	2,809		9,933	8.6	75.3	23.7
Ford	2,193	4,213	106,819	3,291	39,375	76.4	89,906	2,770		9,016	1.1	73.6	25.4
Franklin	1,671	3,190	87,877	3,434	25,062	72.1	45,793	1,790		11,476	18.8	64.4	34.2
Geary	1,996	4,174	112,410	4,247	22,661	64.7	48,940	1,849		7,328	6.7	64.2	34.5
Gove	464	732	17,884	6,034	3,856	88.6	3,635	1,226		1,467	-1.9	81.5	16.8
Graham	417	592	13,868	4,827	4,018	93.8	1,871	651		1,440	-2.3	75.1	23.2
Grant	619	1,120	29,186	3,691	20,905	96.1	16,848	2,131		2,758	-3.4	78.6	20.3
Gray	428	774	18,362	3,064	7,896	91.1	10,899	1,819		2,245	3.9	80.9	18.2
Greeley	164	220	6,623	4,561	4,014	95.6	5,010	3,450		735	-8.5	79.5	18.8
Greenwood	569	795	18,578	2,431	7,669	91.3	14,111	1,846		3,244	-8.9	70.4	28.1
Hamilton	214	358	11,444	4,277	6,921	94.5	8,826	3,298		1,130	-5.2	78.6	20.3
Harper	795	1,309	30,389	4,823	8,666	89.7	11,992	1,903		2,930	-4.1	73.5	24.8
Harvey	1,775	3,590	84,518	2,532	29,839	75.3	113,955	3,414		15,110	10.4	63.1	35.3
Haskell	405	761	20,754	4,902	11,643	96.2	11,170	2,638		1,599	-1.1	84.8	14.2
Hodgeman	180	270	11,914	5,531	3,581	91.8	–	–		1,183	8.7	80.6	18.9
Jackson	1,051	1,477	31,428	2,441	8,604	82.4	19,595	1,522		5,888	12.2	63.4	35.1
Jefferson	1,197	2,057	49,116	2,627	15,551	91.1	24,882	1,331		8,793	11.6	61.5	37.0
Jewell	433	574	15,360	4,375	4,918	87.7	1,329	379		1,915	2.0	78.1	20.1
Johnson	22,699	60,964	1,544,096	3,244	782,728	72.7	2,327,527	4,890		258,687	18.9	61.1	37.8
Kearny	587	1,135	26,222	5,732	14,625	97.6	13,528	2,957		1,455	1.3	80.9	18.7
Kingman	550	838	22,736	2,702	8,221	98.3	22,819	2,712		3,764	-1.2	74.4	24.0
Kiowa	360	441	11,168	3,603	5,431	94.0	3,226	1,041		1,565	-2.7	81.5	16.4
Labette	1,933	3,708	89,473	4,006	18,486	75.5	29,101	1,303		9,139	7.0	59.1	39.6
Lane	276	393	10,341	5,191	3,741	95.7	2,941	1,476		1,014	-10.5	81.2	17.9
Leavenworth	3,058	7,006	161,515	2,269	56,595	79.4	123,922	1,741		27,331	17.4	58.4	40.4
Lincoln	407	625	14,535	4,143	4,450	92.8	3,316	945		1,800	-4.8	76.0	21.7
Linn	768	1,160	32,647	3,360	14,596	97.5	31,026	3,194		4,741	11.3	64.3	34.4
Logan	435	586	13,516	4,585	4,383	91.1	1,328	450		1,523	9.0	82.4	16.3
Lyon	2,706	5,630	144,230	4,038	28,202	79.6	121,813	3,410		13,440	7.9	59.2	38.9
McPherson	1,922	3,563	79,610	2,712	32,123	84.6	112,807	3,843		13,367	7.3	71.8	26.9
Marion	1,083	1,407	35,674	2,683	12,531	87.2	28,363	2,133		6,159	4.3	73.3	24.9
Marshall	824	1,223	32,080	3,012	11,204	90.1	15,120	1,420		5,108	-0.1	63.8	35.0
Meade	502	754	22,586	4,829	8,234	91.6	9,830	2,102		2,121	3.3	82.4	16.8
Miami	1,543	3,038	66,634	2,303	29,049	83.0	90,108	3,114		14,016	20.8	64.3	34.5
Mitchell	728	1,152	23,387	3,492	8,843	80.4	3,268	488		3,349	2.5	77.9	20.7
Montgomery	2,566	5,329	143,335	4,063	34,020	69.3	93,218	2,642		14,116	2.7	68.0	30.7
Morris	395	569	11,929	1,980	3,725	81.5	4,690	779		2,936	11.2	66.8	31.7
Morton	463	954	29,786	8,870	10,835	96.3	6,699	1,995		1,576	1.2	81.7	17.5
Nemaha	678	1,065	26,690	2,543	8,875	86.9	14,715	1,402		5,463	3.3	73.7	24.8
Neosho	1,499	2,847	64,983	3,889	13,038	65.0	83,243	4,981		7,231	5.0	65.1	33.5
Ness	471	578	16,117	4,915	5,152	96.9	2,426	740		1,818	-3.1	77.4	21.0
Norton	609	934	23,486	4,026	7,639	94.9	2,481	425		2,599	6.0	80.5	18.2
Osage	985	1,671	37,815	2,248	10,736	89.4	29,333	1,744		7,463	12.9	64.3	34.0
Osborne	392	393	9,677	2,258	4,422	91.4	3,626	846		2,075	2.2	76.5	21.9
Ottawa	537	762	18,915	3,053	6,459	87.9	6,688	1,080		2,971	6.4	78.5	20.0
Pawnee	631	900	23,854	3,454	8,587	88.6	5,797	839		2,988	1.6	72.7	25.9
Phillips	458	670	23,895	4,141	9,130	95.5	9,031	1,565		2,847	2.0	79.2	19.6
Pottawatomie	1,492	2,419	66,116	3,586	25,427	96.0	54,721	2,968		8,823	14.1	71.7	24.7
Pratt	863	1,506	32,634	3,403	12,771	88.6	26,990	2,814		4,384	-0.7	71.2	27.4
Rawlins	288	357	8,857	3,073	4,086	92.1	1,066	370		1,720	-1.1	82.2	16.8
Reno	3,829	7,979	181,289	2,833	71,563	76.1	118,748	1,856		27,324	7.4	65.0	33.4
Republic	581	829	18,135	3,329	7,935	92.8	10,135	1,860		2,889	-3.2	77.5	21.0
Rice	1,100	1,587	33,407	3,176	12,142	88.9	15,787	1,501		4,376	-3.2	72.7	25.8

See footnotes at end of table.

Table B-13. Counties — **Local Government Finances and Elections**—Con.

[Includes United States, states, and 3,141 counties/county equivalents defined as of February 22, 2005. For more information on these areas, see Appendix C, Geographic Information]

County	Local government employment, March 2002 Total employ-ment	Total payroll ($1,000)	General revenue Total ($1,000)	Per capita (dol.)	Taxes Total ($1,000)	Property, percent of total (taxes)	Total debt outstanding Amount ($1,000)	Per capita (dol.)	Votes cast for President Total	Percent change, 2000–2004	Repub-lican cand-idate, percent of total	Demo-cratic cand-idate, percent of total
KANSAS—Con.												
Riley	2,754	4,700	104,898	1,686	45,486	72.6	113,290	1,821	20,911	14.6	60.6	37.8
Rooks	692	885	23,257	4,235	6,977	93.5	6,663	1,213	2,710	-2.3	78.3	19.7
Rush	410	569	14,545	4,194	5,502	97.0	2,734	788	1,789	-3.5	68.5	28.9
Russell	660	1,140	30,993	4,407	9,638	86.9	12,179	1,732	3,525	1.2	75.8	23.0
Saline	2,409	6,071	153,041	2,838	63,607	66.4	181,140	3,359	23,041	7.0	65.6	32.7
Scott	346	579	16,090	3,266	7,264	91.2	21,233	4,310	2,299	-0.2	83.7	15.1
Sedgwick	19,347	48,126	1,218,225	2,647	426,483	73.2	1,891,826	4,111	177,679	8.7	62.1	36.5
Seward	2,317	4,345	113,296	4,924	30,642	70.1	74,320	3,230	5,439	6.7	78.5	20.6
Shawnee	9,922	23,882	562,367	3,299	222,590	76.6	972,541	5,704	81,577	9.7	54.2	44.5
Sheridan	321	464	12,276	4,596	4,154	93.2	964	361	1,406	-5.6	81.4	17.0
Sherman	605	1,049	28,017	4,360	8,840	76.6	5,286	823	2,762	3.0	75.6	22.9
Smith	447	559	12,886	2,997	5,045	96.3	2,113	491	2,370	8.5	76.1	22.8
Stafford	583	777	20,410	4,373	8,113	92.1	4,271	915	2,186	-0.6	75.4	23.2
Stanton	261	498	14,151	5,838	8,634	97.4	2,140	883	966	-6.1	82.4	17.1
Stevens	602	1,150	28,575	5,366	17,607	97.0	6,663	1,251	2,265	7.3	85.5	13.7
Sumner	1,648	3,170	77,071	3,020	20,554	90.1	86,284	3,381	10,488	2.5	67.6	30.7
Thomas	946	1,416	31,732	3,931	10,019	84.5	9,074	1,124	3,870	2.4	77.7	21.1
Trego	426	614	14,724	4,686	4,294	96.9	7,892	2,512	1,686	-8.2	72.7	25.7
Wabaunsee	477	756	16,452	2,430	6,237	88.8	15,310	2,261	3,604	5.4	70.2	27.8
Wallace	183	255	6,388	3,834	2,592	98.4	2,720	1,633	876	1.7	84.7	12.8
Washington	682	904	27,192	4,373	7,492	92.2	6,061	975	3,190	-2.4	78.3	20.2
Wichita	265	414	11,746	4,732	4,496	88.9	1,373	553	1,062	-2.6	81.8	17.2
Wilson	874	1,400	29,341	2,889	8,187	86.0	12,311	1,212	4,398	7.4	74.2	24.1
Woodson	223	312	8,435	2,308	3,458	97.1	1,052	288	1,763	10.5	68.3	30.1
Wyandotte	8,970	25,412	539,965	3,425	180,021	78.9	1,602,071	10,162	53,401	10.6	33.6	65.4
KENTUCKY	168,339	365,852	8,731,629	2,136	2,806,067	54.9	19,954,998	4,881	1,795,882	16.3	59.6	39.7
Adair	999	2,167	22,741	1,307	4,803	62.9	28,206	1,622	7,447	1.6	75.6	23.7
Allen	719	1,256	28,502	1,571	7,657	60.4	37,662	2,076	7,163	11.4	72.6	26.9
Anderson	766	1,475	31,805	1,627	10,229	74.5	33,569	1,717	9,591	20.4	66.3	32.8
Ballard	401	771	24,988	3,073	4,392	62.9	134,204	16,505	4,177	10.8	57.2	42.1
Barren	1,648	3,322	81,965	2,116	23,355	59.6	130,486	3,369	16,140	16.6	67.1	32.3
Bath	458	877	16,254	1,424	2,996	74.4	9,532	835	4,919	10.0	46.1	53.0
Bell	1,463	2,897	54,584	1,821	11,417	50.0	25,866	863	11,002	3.7	61.1	38.3
Boone	3,021	7,407	205,100	2,192	105,151	59.2	562,416	6,011	45,082	41.0	71.7	27.5
Bourbon	825	1,698	39,040	2,003	12,784	53.4	36,013	1,847	8,217	15.7	60.3	38.9
Boyd	2,259	4,794	104,672	2,107	31,801	67.0	262,056	5,274	21,780	13.5	52.8	46.5
Boyle	1,234	2,645	58,932	2,129	21,004	56.7	71,685	2,589	12,490	21.0	62.2	37.2
Bracken	376	831	13,885	1,643	3,302	75.7	8,853	1,047	3,610	19.6	65.5	33.6
Breathitt	678	1,343	30,604	1,924	5,138	49.0	23,843	1,499	5,944	17.2	42.8	56.0
Breckinridge	751	1,325	30,507	1,611	6,153	76.5	33,197	1,753	8,520	14.3	65.5	33.9
Bullitt	1,986	4,776	87,279	1,369	29,399	75.7	45,222	710	28,627	26.1	67.9	31.6
Butler	543	1,096	29,502	2,244	6,171	37.5	42,993	3,270	5,578	11.3	73.7	25.7
Caldwell	553	1,130	20,626	1,602	5,850	46.9	46,106	3,582	6,349	15.8	64.0	35.4
Calloway	2,171	4,828	120,329	3,518	15,893	70.8	46,138	1,349	15,145	10.8	61.4	37.8
Campbell	2,856	7,262	143,751	1,628	69,505	60.2	327,615	3,710	40,178	18.8	63.6	35.5
Carlisle	208	317	7,481	1,396	1,382	72.4	6,592	1,230	2,845	9.7	61.0	38.7
Carroll	503	907	115,676	11,271	8,632	56.8	1,600,461	155,945	3,897	11.4	55.8	43.3
Carter	1,288	2,421	40,924	1,510	6,739	62.1	35,218	1,300	11,117	24.1	48.8	50.2
Casey	600	1,122	21,815	1,378	4,360	71.8	9,205	581	6,321	15.6	80.8	18.6
Christian	2,259	4,662	110,084	1,533	30,525	48.7	155,403	2,165	21,015	18.2	66.3	33.2
Clark	1,423	3,156	67,740	2,018	22,622	55.2	126,137	3,757	15,317	22.8	62.3	37.0
Clay	1,073	2,105	36,502	1,495	4,939	55.5	23,435	960	7,687	14.4	74.5	24.7
Clinton	434	765	17,114	1,778	3,064	51.2	9,797	1,018	4,352	1.1	77.4	21.9
Crittenden	356	664	12,296	1,342	2,666	67.4	16,788	1,833	4,190	0.9	65.1	34.3
Cumberland	433	679	12,559	1,754	2,367	46.3	4,073	569	3,239	7.8	72.7	26.2
Daviess	4,209	9,764	230,306	2,507	60,371	61.5	1,014,936	11,049	41,483	14.5	61.2	38.1
Edmonson	473	893	17,623	1,490	3,122	76.4	21,539	1,821	5,481	9.7	65.6	33.9
Elliott	284	548	11,543	1,700	1,106	79.1	7,845	1,156	2,957	24.2	29.5	69.8
Estill	594	1,132	23,446	1,527	4,108	64.9	18,925	1,233	5,575	18.4	65.2	34.2
Fayette	9,585	26,044	545,184	2,076	326,186	39.7	695,221	2,647	125,584	19.1	52.9	46.2
Fleming	695	1,338	35,719	2,521	4,570	72.1	21,901	1,546	6,203	19.8	60.4	38.8
Floyd	1,682	3,147	80,861	1,909	17,480	77.4	71,095	1,678	17,885	16.2	37.0	62.2
Franklin	1,890	4,572	103,898	2,160	46,950	46.3	115,025	2,391	24,134	11.5	50.9	48.2
Fulton	523	919	21,186	2,798	3,986	57.4	30,493	4,027	2,890	3.7	52.8	46.4
Gallatin	347	644	24,852	3,180	4,035	71.6	208,867	26,726	3,073	25.0	60.8	38.7
Garrard	711	1,204	29,010	1,857	7,013	73.1	12,088	774	6,658	14.3	71.9	27.7
Grant	849	1,724	38,195	1,620	9,699	73.5	31,910	1,354	8,824	24.2	67.4	31.9
Graves	1,312	2,588	57,224	1,542	15,589	54.2	198,230	5,341	16,231	14.0	61.0	38.2
Grayson	1,027	2,011	43,145	1,777	9,717	51.2	77,686	3,201	10,143	18.6	70.7	28.6
Green	611	970	25,620	2,195	3,134	63.2	13,696	1,173	5,206	9.5	74.3	25.2
Greenup	1,333	2,693	59,636	1,620	15,570	85.8	32,681	888	16,435	12.1	52.9	46.4

See footnotes at end of table.

Table B-13. Counties — **Local Government Finances and Elections**—Con.

[Includes United States, states, and 3,141 counties/county equivalents defined as of February 22, 2005. For more information on these areas, see Appendix C, Geographic Information]

County	Local government employment, March 2002 — Total employment	Total payroll ($1,000)	Local government finances, 2002 — General revenue — Total ($1,000)	Per capita (dol.)	Taxes — Total ($1,000)	Property, percent of total (taxes)	Total debt outstanding — Amount ($1,000)	Per capita (dol.)	Elections, 2004[1] — Votes cast for President — Total	Percent change, 2000–2004	Republican candidate, percent of total	Democratic candidate, percent of total
KENTUCKY—Con.												
Hancock	442	811	68,290	8,085	6,933	41.2	679,602	80,455	4,029	11.6	56.7	42.4
Hardin	4,926	11,258	254,275	2,669	45,743	58.5	206,688	2,169	36,441	18.7	67.6	31.6
Harlan	1,279	2,583	65,198	2,004	9,798	74.2	24,510	754	11,070	5.1	60.2	39.1
Harrison	742	1,433	30,026	1,659	9,064	46.5	37,807	2,089	7,731	16.9	62.8	36.3
Hart	574	1,152	23,440	1,325	5,461	60.6	26,322	1,488	6,784	12.7	62.9	36.4
Henderson	2,045	4,319	113,045	2,510	24,645	58.5	489,508	10,867	18,701	16.6	56.0	43.3
Henry	574	1,155	24,094	1,572	6,271	75.2	21,551	1,406	6,499	18.7	63.0	36.4
Hickman	229	410	7,896	1,508	1,658	73.3	6,813	1,301	2,342	10.3	59.6	39.5
Hopkins	2,033	4,274	85,938	1,850	26,183	55.6	85,740	1,846	18,843	14.3	65.4	34.1
Jackson	680	1,280	19,395	1,422	2,608	72.5	9,145	671	5,178	6.7	84.4	14.9
Jefferson	27,746	70,007	1,802,234	2,590	767,609	51.2	4,774,527	6,862	337,351	11.6	48.8	50.4
Jessamine	1,727	3,316	66,930	1,645	25,926	62.9	71,617	1,760	18,580	23.4	69.8	29.5
Johnson	1,035	2,050	49,477	2,108	12,225	52.8	37,350	1,591	9,304	13.7	63.8	35.3
Kenton	6,182	15,379	425,281	2,803	148,261	56.3	1,381,364	9,105	67,124	19.3	65.1	34.0
Knott	694	1,395	34,243	1,928	4,842	76.5	13,283	748	7,394	14.5	35.8	63.4
Knox	1,629	2,678	63,091	1,993	9,909	59.7	30,753	971	12,028	21.4	67.4	31.8
Larue	564	1,037	21,426	1,594	4,010	75.5	21,982	1,635	5,968	15.2	68.9	30.6
Laurel	1,858	3,697	92,520	1,700	22,532	53.3	79,221	1,456	22,264	22.9	75.5	23.8
Lawrence	620	1,226	42,755	2,694	3,902	71.2	374,438	23,593	6,513	22.7	57.7	41.5
Lee	421	683	15,259	1,933	2,263	68.2	15,210	1,927	2,920	5.6	69.1	30.1
Leslie	513	1,095	24,164	1,970	3,353	78.7	7,712	629	4,964	12.0	73.8	25.5
Letcher	1,017	1,896	41,262	1,656	7,803	70.6	18,693	750	9,065	0.9	53.0	46.2
Lewis	558	1,014	22,286	1,612	3,554	70.3	105,529	7,632	5,484	20.1	68.9	30.4
Lincoln	1,109	1,774	37,650	1,559	7,044	59.8	33,662	1,394	8,863	16.7	67.7	31.6
Livingston	407	682	13,530	1,377	3,934	65.2	6,315	643	4,706	11.3	56.8	42.7
Logan	1,049	1,852	42,385	1,585	11,935	56.6	38,085	1,425	10,644	14.1	64.0	35.4
Lyon	295	526	15,577	1,913	4,076	73.2	17,153	2,107	3,925	14.8	54.3	45.1
McCracken	2,650	6,341	144,994	2,238	54,269	50.9	124,657	1,924	29,797	11.6	61.1	38.1
McCreary	828	1,531	29,071	1,697	3,336	81.5	16,238	948	5,693	18.6	72.4	26.9
McLean	448	736	21,114	2,117	4,054	63.5	34,350	3,444	4,435	10.3	58.3	41.1
Madison	2,018	4,634	124,514	1,701	44,437	49.2	212,197	2,899	30,707	29.8	61.6	37.5
Magoffin	1,020	1,265	24,151	1,814	3,467	68.8	18,002	1,352	5,718	4.9	49.6	49.7
Marion	668	1,294	33,267	1,800	9,543	52.0	57,921	3,134	7,354	19.1	53.1	46.2
Marshall	1,309	2,606	90,167	2,980	22,676	56.8	441,045	14,579	15,521	12.8	58.3	41.1
Martin	689	1,350	24,946	1,990	3,544	77.3	13,438	1,072	4,539	1.9	66.0	33.1
Mason	732	1,616	57,042	3,379	13,673	49.8	339,330	20,104	7,079	20.5	61.9	37.4
Meade	894	1,841	36,946	1,348	8,583	79.1	34,484	1,258	10,951	20.7	65.3	34.0
Menifee	248	488	9,192	1,369	1,688	73.3	10,280	1,531	2,528	12.4	48.1	50.8
Mercer	862	1,764	34,804	1,651	12,175	55.7	49,244	2,336	10,028	16.2	67.3	32.2
Metcalfe	421	708	14,757	1,474	3,682	49.2	12,509	1,249	4,157	8.0	63.6	35.4
Monroe	566	932	20,515	1,749	4,382	62.6	10,490	894	5,843	4.9	79.7	19.8
Montgomery	1,037	2,163	56,634	2,437	14,246	54.6	139,322	5,996	10,230	20.1	55.2	44.1
Morgan	550	1,015	26,687	1,874	3,818	66.0	7,218	507	5,272	24.3	50.9	48.0
Muhlenberg	1,202	2,835	47,168	1,488	9,482	84.6	72,650	2,292	13,479	12.7	50.1	49.2
Nelson	1,477	3,026	71,289	1,830	18,335	78.9	180,646	4,638	16,844	24.9	60.3	38.7
Nicholas	287	487	11,374	1,642	2,617	63.6	9,527	1,376	3,059	14.4	55.6	43.5
Ohio	1,236	2,321	50,068	2,157	8,431	60.1	246,631	10,624	10,028	12.9	62.9	36.2
Oldham	1,834	4,046	73,759	1,500	33,416	81.4	231,993	4,717	27,132	33.9	69.3	29.8
Owen	295	559	16,534	1,502	3,840	71.5	11,893	1,080	4,741	16.5	65.1	34.1
Owsley	303	488	9,652	2,026	961	66.3	5,479	1,150	1,999	9.5	77.9	21.5
Pendleton	563	1,250	28,797	1,942	5,291	74.9	12,938	872	6,025	25.4	67.1	32.2
Perry	1,712	3,224	81,951	2,779	14,024	66.7	226,005	7,664	11,655	6.0	53.1	46.3
Pike	2,889	6,133	119,020	1,756	30,390	70.0	64,253	948	26,770	7.4	47.1	52.3
Powell	595	1,158	21,828	1,640	3,746	51.5	14,372	1,080	4,960	13.7	54.2	45.3
Pulaski	2,371	4,819	100,694	1,756	31,163	58.7	99,324	1,732	25,516	18.5	76.6	22.8
Robertson	112	179	3,528	1,531	612	71.7	1,295	562	1,090	9.2	61.5	37.9
Rockcastle	1,062	2,165	45,577	2,727	4,904	70.9	22,955	1,373	6,166	17.5	77.9	21.4
Rowan	789	1,501	35,443	1,593	11,976	39.0	26,207	1,178	8,706	20.5	46.7	52.3
Russell	590	1,203	27,568	1,671	6,128	60.9	22,655	1,373	7,821	10.6	76.8	22.7
Scott	1,873	3,075	123,378	3,481	40,360	28.7	690,895	19,493	17,051	23.7	62.2	37.1
Shelby	1,547	3,011	60,241	1,720	26,531	67.6	65,371	1,867	16,314	28.1	66.9	32.4
Simpson	729	1,315	36,929	2,220	9,759	59.0	36,923	2,219	7,043	20.9	60.7	38.8
Spencer	395	727	21,564	1,587	8,141	87.4	13,792	1,015	6,822	43.0	70.6	28.9
Taylor	1,435	2,978	76,499	3,288	11,665	51.6	28,801	1,238	10,295	13.7	70.4	28.9
Todd	463	813	19,672	1,639	3,637	57.7	93,096	7,757	4,754	13.5	68.2	31.4
Trigg	492	909	18,339	1,439	5,373	68.7	11,633	913	6,111	14.4	65.8	33.5
Trimble	344	569	38,688	4,470	3,967	60.7	405,908	46,893	3,790	23.0	61.5	37.7
Union	695	1,349	25,158	1,609	6,366	74.0	17,223	1,102	5,977	11.3	59.1	40.1
Warren	3,693	8,274	186,423	1,980	69,465	50.9	567,859	6,030	39,712	20.4	63.2	36.1
Washington	452	818	18,932	1,699	5,236	48.0	39,364	3,532	5,236	14.1	66.4	32.9

See footnotes at end of table.

[Includes United States, states, and 3,141 counties/county equivalents defined as of February 22, 2005. For more information on these areas, see Appendix C, Geographic Information]

County	Local government employment, March 2002		Local government finances, 2002						Elections, 2004[1]			
			General revenue				Total debt outstanding		Votes cast for President			
					Taxes							
	Total employment	Total payroll ($1,000)	Total ($1,000)	Per capita (dol.)	Total ($1,000)	Property, percent of total (taxes)	Amount ($1,000)	Per capita (dol.)	Total	Percent change, 2000–2004	Republican candidate, percent of total	Democratic candidate, percent of total
KENTUCKY—Con.												
Wayne.	882	1,630	28,766	1,432	5,269	64.6	21,223	1,057	7,685	18.7	65.4	34.0
Webster.	636	1,113	28,865	2,048	5,560	74.8	31,361	2,225	5,547	9.4	57.8	41.5
Whitley.	1,758	3,244	67,765	1,842	12,166	52.8	41,997	1,141	13,629	15.8	70.1	29.2
Wolfe.	415	642	11,859	1,697	1,547	52.7	3,866	553	3,155	30.1	43.9	55.3
Woodford.	916	1,834	39,128	1,663	19,662	51.6	36,649	1,558	11,502	13.5	60.3	39.0
LOUISIANA.	206,183	458,667	12,648,133	2,826	4,825,129	39.5	11,752,840	2,626	1,943,106	10.1	56.7	42.2
Acadia.	2,393	4,514	116,565	1,972	41,322	28.2	51,175	866	25,230	8.6	63.8	35.4
Allen.	1,358	1,725	55,176	2,195	17,457	41.2	17,860	711	9,124	10.0	56.3	41.6
Ascension.	3,441	7,589	215,685	2,639	116,287	33.9	163,172	1,997	39,100	26.8	63.1	35.7
Assumption.	1,061	2,025	49,176	2,119	16,065	38.2	9,857	425	10,735	6.8	46.3	52.0
Avoyelles.	1,622	3,162	83,643	2,015	17,424	23.9	16,715	403	15,525	6.0	53.5	44.9
Beauregard	1,975	3,151	87,742	2,644	28,267	44.4	36,709	1,106	13,281	8.8	71.3	27.6
Bienville.	788	1,191	39,676	2,579	15,560	55.6	15,751	1,024	7,157	2.2	50.5	47.5
Bossier.	4,578	8,880	241,626	2,400	114,607	33.0	124,204	1,234	42,705	18.9	70.3	28.8
Caddo.	11,978	28,641	716,083	2,860	343,840	49.7	757,081	3,023	106,595	11.5	50.9	48.5
Calcasieu.	8,748	19,156	587,938	3,210	270,198	35.8	774,064	4,226	79,698	8.2	57.8	41.2
Caldwell.	413	690	24,934	2,353	5,643	45.1	4,310	407	4,752	9.8	69.6	29.1
Cameron.	671	1,152	46,698	4,794	18,571	97.1	13,767	1,413	4,640	10.9	68.8	29.5
Catahoula.	587	915	22,521	2,103	6,040	44.1	8,035	750	4,954	4.0	65.0	33.8
Claiborne.	1,222	2,240	48,228	2,902	10,887	52.5	23,779	1,431	6,630	5.6	55.9	43.1
Concordia.	1,075	2,025	70,771	3,549	15,411	54.3	20,628	1,035	8,980	5.7	60.4	38.4
De Soto.	1,283	2,613	77,249	2,997	26,999	58.5	170,479	6,614	11,336	7.0	54.8	44.3
East Baton Rouge.	15,983	39,763	1,074,004	2,619	549,219	34.5	1,073,177	2,617	183,642	8.7	54.4	44.8
East Carroll.	501	922	30,569	3,360	4,595	47.6	2,639	290	3,395	4.6	40.0	58.3
East Feliciana.	771	1,214	27,652	1,310	8,812	41.8	13,263	628	9,201	13.6	54.6	44.5
Evangeline.	1,578	2,872	62,977	1,781	18,292	40.2	20,755	587	13,979	2.7	56.9	41.2
Franklin.	937	1,828	59,596	2,851	12,789	28.6	7,761	371	9,103	8.9	67.5	31.1
Grant.	783	1,351	30,036	1,603	4,644	51.5	6,900	368	7,991	13.3	74.0	24.7
Iberia.	4,216	7,524	200,270	2,718	60,602	33.0	86,896	1,179	32,273	7.5	60.2	38.5
Iberville.	1,532	3,124	84,775	2,564	43,510	39.7	70,922	2,145	14,827	2.2	42.7	55.7
Jackson.	964	1,911	33,904	2,221	12,461	30.9	114,591	7,506	7,647	7.6	65.9	33.0
Jefferson.	20,397	51,500	1,442,583	3,193	524,478	35.4	1,356,440	3,003	191,663	7.0	61.5	37.6
Jefferson Davis.	1,545	2,657	66,148	2,125	24,140	43.9	36,859	1,184	13,007	3.7	61.9	36.5
Lafayette.	7,620	16,650	400,582	2,079	191,516	31.9	713,584	3,704	89,923	14.9	64.2	34.7
Lafourche.	4,781	10,915	325,873	3,590	83,509	43.9	147,525	1,625	37,864	9.9	60.0	38.1
La Salle.	962	1,758	51,487	3,615	9,968	61.8	6,526	458	6,238	2.1	80.4	18.5
Lincoln.	1,649	3,020	82,695	1,976	36,592	42.4	28,411	679	18,218	10.1	59.2	39.8
Livingston.	3,835	7,162	164,970	1,667	54,323	27.6	43,089	435	44,253	20.0	76.8	22.4
Madison.	605	999	30,111	2,282	7,627	46.8	18,193	1,379	4,673	-1.5	49.0	50.0
Morehouse.	1,850	3,354	106,509	3,490	22,228	41.3	163,175	5,348	12,971	5.3	57.6	41.1
Natchitoches.	2,378	4,462	139,114	3,574	28,579	40.2	66,470	1,707	16,966	14.2	54.6	43.6
Orleans.	21,590	58,900	1,536,705	3,253	641,603	39.8	2,046,386	4,332	197,103	8.8	21.7	77.4
Ouachita.	6,819	13,842	423,953	2,883	196,224	35.0	343,421	2,335	64,444	10.7	64.8	34.2
Plaquemines.	1,576	3,431	112,741	4,123	46,178	63.2	81,268	2,972	12,153	11.2	64.7	34.4
Pointe Coupee.	1,147	2,325	68,441	3,034	21,281	45.0	63,277	2,805	11,271	4.1	48.2	50.7
Rapides.	6,061	14,362	309,061	2,439	117,781	44.2	249,780	1,972	54,069	10.3	63.8	35.0
Red River.	563	1,005	24,173	2,524	6,715	52.1	10,839	1,132	4,717	4.3	53.2	45.4
Richland.	1,343	2,608	72,627	3,506	13,507	31.6	16,938	818	8,665	2.1	63.1	35.6
Sabine.	1,060	1,784	47,824	2,044	14,943	42.9	31,650	1,353	9,576	8.1	70.1	28.6
St. Bernard.	2,395	4,868	131,589	1,983	60,534	32.8	131,671	1,984	29,838	4.3	65.7	33.4
St. Charles.	3,132	7,982	222,411	4,529	115,603	61.3	517,324	10,535	23,007	10.8	61.9	37.2
St. Helena.	524	948	20,858	2,001	4,137	46.5	5,122	491	5,508	4.8	40.6	57.6
St. James.	1,408	2,784	87,624	4,121	44,893	62.1	138,912	6,533	11,108	3.8	40.9	57.7
St. John the Baptist.	1,808	3,102	110,800	2,507	45,259	43.7	186,685	4,224	19,617	10.7	46.1	52.5
St. Landry.	4,083	8,619	231,524	2,620	50,141	32.5	53,664	607	36,760	7.6	49.8	49.4
St. Martin.	2,076	3,676	91,787	1,854	26,174	57.4	41,822	845	22,824	9.8	53.0	45.2
St. Mary.	3,343	7,550	209,149	3,983	54,759	46.7	79,298	1,510	22,694	4.1	56.7	42.1
St. Tammany.	7,658	18,219	626,846	3,106	226,060	39.9	510,195	2,528	100,592	20.1	74.7	24.5
Tangipahoa.	5,145	12,826	342,070	3,341	72,310	27.1	139,891	1,367	42,135	13.4	62.1	36.4
Tensas.	374	560	19,842	3,091	4,727	58.3	18,552	2,890	2,963	-1.6	49.0	49.6
Terrebonne.	5,322	12,307	402,477	3,816	100,776	28.3	165,636	1,571	40,574	10.6	65.0	33.7
Union.	913	1,422	43,402	1,903	11,063	29.6	7,606	333	10,718	14.7	69.6	28.8
Vermilion.	2,499	5,191	130,036	2,398	38,607	44.3	29,959	552	24,552	10.4	61.4	37.0
Vernon.	2,541	4,401	100,654	1,965	25,770	33.5	23,895	467	15,229	10.1	72.4	26.5
Washington.	2,117	4,094	103,444	2,358	29,355	37.4	20,667	471	17,841	5.6	61.7	36.7
Webster.	1,491	2,884	88,437	2,131	30,265	35.4	47,163	1,136	18,449	8.0	60.0	37.0
West Baton Rouge.	1,004	2,215	65,233	3,007	26,058	46.2	112,093	5,167	10,835	6.5	53.7	45.5
West Carroll.	583	1,121	21,591	1,775	6,042	35.5	3,830	315	5,033	7.7	74.3	24.5
West Feliciana.	769	1,857	74,958	4,943	22,669	72.0	475,414	31,349	5,218	7.4	56.2	42.4
Winn.	759	1,133	30,310	1,830	9,233	44.5	15,120	913	6,507	2.3	67.1	31.6

See footnotes at end of table.

[Includes United States, states, and 3,141 counties/county equivalents defined as of February 22, 2005. For more information on these areas, see Appendix C, Geographic Information]

County	Local government employment, March 2002 — Total employment	Local government employment, March 2002 — Total payroll ($1,000)	Local government finances, 2002 — General revenue — Total ($1,000)	General revenue — Per capita (dol.)	General revenue — Taxes — Total ($1,000)	Taxes — Property, percent of total (taxes)	Total debt outstanding — Amount ($1,000)	Total debt outstanding — Per capita (dol.)	Elections, 2004[1] — Votes cast for President — Total	Percent change, 2000–2004	Republican candidate, percent of total	Democratic candidate, percent of total
MAINE	65,421	133,870	3,531,360	2,723	1,914,316	97.4	2,024,883	1,561	740,752	13.6	44.6	53.6
Androscoggin	4,802	10,658	275,995	2,624	134,313	97.9	178,314	1,695	56,067	13.9	43.7	54.4
Aroostook	4,405	8,364	250,325	3,423	103,620	97.1	69,550	951	37,733	7.4	46.6	51.9
Cumberland	12,926	31,600	807,337	2,993	468,666	97.8	629,331	2,333	162,962	14.3	40.1	58.2
Franklin	1,802	3,325	96,567	3,234	53,894	97.6	87,750	2,939	17,257	11.7	42.8	54.9
Hancock	2,880	4,716	133,042	2,548	87,331	97.3	63,063	1,208	33,122	15.9	43.5	54.5
Kennebec	6,134	11,958	292,550	2,465	141,558	97.6	194,498	1,639	66,772	13.4	44.6	53.3
Knox	1,668	3,068	95,902	2,368	69,840	98.7	51,754	1,278	23,247	13.4	43.5	54.6
Lincoln	2,323	3,915	105,450	3,060	70,290	97.8	25,807	749	22,142	12.6	46.8	51.3
Oxford	2,873	5,467	146,982	2,633	82,445	98.3	62,276	1,116	31,546	14.7	45.0	52.7
Penobscot	6,926	13,837	376,203	2,573	174,743	95.0	206,342	1,411	82,112	12.2	49.1	49.2
Piscataquis	1,273	2,334	63,756	3,696	20,194	95.2	18,648	1,081	9,940	7.4	53.3	44.4
Sagadahoc	1,981	4,092	100,442	2,792	57,386	98.4	57,035	1,585	21,079	14.5	45.1	52.7
Somerset	3,101	6,183	141,536	2,774	72,182	98.6	56,245	1,102	27,108	13.2	47.8	50.0
Waldo	1,807	3,141	87,401	2,318	51,428	96.1	36,861	978	22,322	16.6	46.2	51.8
Washington	2,192	3,101	82,940	2,482	41,680	96.4	24,522	734	17,310	10.2	49.8	48.5
York	8,328	18,113	474,932	2,426	284,749	97.1	262,887	1,343	110,033	16.4	45.0	53.4
MARYLAND	222,233	707,198	17,656,587	3,244	9,053,005	56.8	13,354,398	2,454	2,386,678	18.1	42.9	55.9
Allegany	3,089	8,770	215,530	2,910	64,677	63.6	131,445	1,775	29,855	13.2	63.6	35.4
Anne Arundel	16,545	59,294	1,444,277	2,876	854,489	53.4	1,532,389	3,052	239,667	19.4	55.6	43.1
Baltimore	24,886	79,746	2,130,628	2,770	1,216,101	54.6	1,244,487	1,618	353,479	16.2	47.0	51.6
Calvert	3,000	9,521	238,025	2,943	120,537	61.6	136,509	1,688	39,351	32.0	58.5	40.6
Caroline	1,255	3,209	78,037	2,572	23,475	56.6	40,091	1,321	11,356	26.9	65.1	33.6
Carroll	5,706	15,632	415,140	2,604	217,245	59.7	310,146	1,946	79,349	23.9	69.7	29.0
Cecil	3,410	9,541	230,967	2,557	109,458	61.4	99,726	1,104	37,674	30.5	59.9	39.0
Charles	6,009	15,912	388,812	3,033	185,573	61.3	172,572	1,346	58,241	30.6	48.8	50.4
Dorchester	1,329	3,409	90,129	2,954	31,848	64.5	35,751	1,172	13,339	17.1	58.5	40.6
Frederick	10,370	26,603	699,317	3,344	378,508	61.8	485,602	2,322	100,594	27.9	59.6	39.3
Garrett	1,611	3,408	84,854	2,837	32,349	58.1	27,683	926	12,484	17.2	72.8	26.4
Harford	9,685	26,028	600,821	2,643	319,587	57.4	315,106	1,386	112,728	23.3	63.5	35.2
Howard	11,050	35,111	891,534	3,431	544,628	58.5	701,697	2,700	133,810	18.6	44.6	54.0
Kent	877	1,982	51,071	2,607	26,008	60.6	13,951	712	9,285	14.8	52.8	46.1
Montgomery	41,119	153,389	3,785,618	4,174	2,429,156	55.5	3,341,773	3,685	415,225	11.7	32.8	66.0
Prince George's	32,759	100,128	2,453,955	2,969	1,053,549	53.0	1,915,315	2,317	318,474	19.3	17.4	81.8
Queen Anne's	1,942	5,277	142,047	3,315	75,254	58.2	71,211	1,662	21,794	30.0	66.5	32.4
St. Mary's	3,153	9,387	248,037	2,758	125,308	56.4	221,600	2,464	37,916	28.5	62.6	36.3
Somerset	847	2,084	59,596	2,342	15,691	63.4	17,363	682	8,994	18.3	54.3	44.9
Talbot	1,390	3,603	104,577	3,044	62,310	59.6	66,112	1,924	18,864	23.8	59.8	39.1
Washington	5,511	15,041	331,306	2,459	147,291	60.4	201,643	1,497	57,904	22.0	63.8	35.2
Wicomico	3,537	8,314	221,330	2,574	94,439	60.5	142,175	1,653	37,503	18.0	58.7	40.4
Worcester	2,486	6,971	184,868	3,851	115,706	65.6	170,161	3,545	25,229	21.6	60.8	38.2
Independent City												
Baltimore city	30,667	104,843	2,566,111	4,030	809,818	61.6	1,959,890	3,078	213,563	11.0	17.0	82.0
MASSACHUSETTS	264,423	838,996	20,912,683	3,262	9,072,844	96.1	20,106,252	3,136	2,912,388	7.7	36.8	61.9
Barnstable	9,046	28,430	725,611	3,189	427,570	93.6	635,119	2,791	132,148	9.1	44.3	54.6
Berkshire	6,345	16,818	377,724	2,834	160,508	96.4	295,948	2,221	65,291	9.9	25.7	73.1
Bristol	21,981	64,967	1,438,763	2,646	521,439	96.2	1,045,753	1,923	232,878	10.2	35.4	63.5
Dukes	1,291	2,938	94,183	6,111	54,522	95.3	93,786	6,086	9,997	12.9	26.0	72.7
Essex	28,558	89,013	2,119,863	2,879	952,925	97.4	1,967,125	2,672	333,234	7.4	40.6	58.2
Franklin	3,916	8,099	218,135	3,033	90,038	97.5	164,004	2,280	37,381	12.0	29.6	68.4
Hampden	21,281	63,128	1,445,558	3,147	468,405	98.0	1,915,849	4,170	186,639	8.5	38.0	60.9
Hampshire	6,147	15,739	343,448	2,251	152,172	97.5	278,714	1,827	74,422	8.4	28.6	69.4
Middlesex	58,454	188,434	4,607,749	3,138	2,390,965	97.1	2,965,526	2,019	688,960	4.9	34.5	64.0
Nantucket	767	2,198	56,349	5,706	39,769	92.7	49,104	4,973	5,724	16.2	35.6	63.0
Norfolk	24,053	78,419	1,782,196	2,724	1,061,444	97.2	1,165,414	1,781	331,137	4.4	38.6	60.2
Plymouth	19,687	59,680	1,354,793	2,797	648,137	95.7	930,738	1,921	233,297	10.6	45.3	53.7
Suffolk	32,567	128,834	3,923,337	5,727	1,137,815	93.4	5,909,632	8,626	240,645	10.9	22.8	75.9
Worcester	30,330	92,300	2,424,974	3,152	967,135	94.6	2,689,540	3,496	340,636	9.8	42.3	56.4
MICHIGAN	455,318	1,251,509	34,134,413	3,400	8,780,132	90.0	32,247,783	3,212	4,839,252	14.3	47.8	51.2
Alcona	559	759	28,220	2,439	9,142	97.0	22,323	1,930	6,531	8.9	55.0	44.0
Alger	552	1,013	27,238	2,775	6,351	97.9	18,248	1,859	4,765	9.1	48.7	50.3
Allegan	4,674	10,486	261,216	2,390	66,696	97.8	244,998	2,242	53,907	20.1	63.1	35.9
Alpena	3,199	7,478	211,388	6,827	22,021	98.4	49,503	1,599	15,211	7.6	50.4	48.7
Antrim	1,321	2,578	79,082	3,316	28,106	97.9	38,422	1,611	13,619	18.4	61.5	37.2
Arenac	759	1,475	41,678	2,405	10,599	98.8	36,862	2,127	8,216	13.1	49.6	49.6
Baraga	656	1,363	40,064	4,576	6,062	99.4	21,354	2,439	3,684	8.6	53.7	45.1
Barry	2,258	5,050	121,781	2,094	25,948	98.5	80,168	1,378	30,272	15.3	61.6	37.4
Bay	6,151	15,030	427,668	3,899	91,363	98.0	135,556	1,236	57,059	10.5	44.6	54.4
Benzie	848	1,584	54,756	3,266	16,373	98.6	26,175	1,561	9,778	21.1	54.0	44.8

See footnotes at end of table.

[Includes United States, states, and 3,141 counties/county equivalents defined as of February 22, 2005. For more information on these areas, see Appendix C, Geographic Information]

County	Local government employment, March 2002		Local government finances, 2002						Elections, 2004[1]			
			General revenue				Total debt outstanding		Votes cast for President			
					Taxes							
	Total employment	Total payroll ($1,000)	Total ($1,000)	Per capita (dol.)	Total ($1,000)	Property, percent of total (taxes)	Amount ($1,000)	Per capita (dol.)	Total	Percent change, 2000–2004	Republican candidate, percent of total	Democratic candidate, percent of total
MICHIGAN—Con.												
Berrien	7,766	18,546	472,351	2,908	114,186	97.2	224,806	1,384	74,671	14.5	55.0	44.0
Branch	2,600	6,243	178,139	3,831	23,054	95.9	83,135	1,788	17,967	13.8	60.0	39.0
Calhoun	6,884	17,704	455,131	3,282	100,186	83.3	311,678	2,247	62,667	13.8	51.2	47.7
Cass	2,248	4,654	125,747	2,443	24,845	97.0	88,304	1,716	22,697	14.5	57.1	42.0
Charlevoix	1,684	4,076	100,803	3,804	32,819	99.6	73,803	2,785	14,139	13.2	58.1	40.5
Cheboygan	1,154	2,438	62,827	2,305	20,213	98.3	38,590	1,416	13,887	10.1	56.2	42.8
Chippewa	1,834	3,919	111,732	2,881	21,574	99.6	113,546	2,928	16,488	14.9	55.3	43.7
Clare	1,793	3,633	96,957	3,059	18,655	98.0	41,472	1,309	14,226	12.8	49.8	49.1
Clinton	2,320	5,605	142,910	2,140	30,652	96.6	183,391	2,746	37,807	17.4	58.2	41.0
Crawford	638	1,150	37,270	2,541	11,763	94.0	26,278	1,792	7,235	13.7	55.5	43.2
Delta	2,110	4,971	117,284	3,052	26,050	99.9	86,709	2,257	19,238	11.1	50.3	48.8
Dickinson	2,071	5,581	119,744	4,392	23,186	99.2	67,494	2,476	13,549	5.6	57.1	41.7
Eaton	3,908	9,887	239,675	2,272	59,109	95.4	275,431	2,611	55,755	13.2	53.4	45.6
Emmet	1,828	4,097	151,257	4,655	50,768	98.0	183,290	5,641	17,372	18.1	59.5	39.4
Genesee	21,813	63,486	1,332,517	3,024	232,397	96.9	603,301	1,369	213,775	12.0	39.2	60.0
Gladwin	1,162	2,120	53,979	2,020	14,707	98.0	21,590	808	13,227	13.7	51.2	48.0
Gogebic	988	2,210	73,321	4,194	11,306	99.4	30,305	1,733	8,452	1.4	46.6	52.3
Grand Traverse	4,745	10,736	313,883	3,872	74,373	96.8	441,346	5,444	46,191	20.8	59.4	39.5
Gratiot	2,089	4,405	102,058	2,413	16,551	98.2	61,252	1,448	17,379	14.5	56.6	42.5
Hillsdale	1,904	4,098	121,315	2,582	20,124	98.8	153,577	3,269	20,216	15.7	63.3	35.2
Houghton	1,918	3,970	132,841	3,725	15,748	98.8	94,084	2,638	15,851	11.5	56.1	42.5
Huron	1,925	3,841	113,005	3,193	29,832	97.9	88,468	2,500	17,466	8.5	55.4	43.7
Ingham	16,124	46,877	1,129,916	4,036	285,869	85.9	1,325,454	4,734	133,053	10.3	41.1	57.8
Ionia	2,782	6,311	158,537	2,510	25,651	99.1	207,300	3,282	27,618	15.2	60.2	38.6
Iosco	1,919	3,578	97,795	3,625	22,654	98.1	80,663	2,990	14,006	5.9	52.1	46.8
Iron	669	1,436	46,562	3,638	10,338	99.2	20,596	1,609	6,511	5.2	49.5	49.4
Isabella	1,860	4,222	203,608	3,185	25,965	94.0	118,784	1,858	24,390	15.8	48.2	50.6
Jackson	6,708	16,185	465,941	2,891	75,241	87.8	312,349	1,938	71,795	15.9	55.8	43.2
Kalamazoo	10,459	26,289	664,562	2,765	187,527	97.5	883,814	3,677	119,783	19.0	47.7	51.3
Kalkaska	1,063	1,918	48,623	2,863	12,325	97.5	19,049	1,122	8,380	22.4	60.7	38.1
Kent	25,182	73,480	1,965,612	3,352	483,056	86.9	2,642,236	4,506	290,891	16.2	58.9	40.2
Keweenaw	135	147	6,417	2,847	1,400	96.9	648	287	1,439	7.1	54.3	43.8
Lake	463	768	28,764	2,489	8,910	99.8	12,094	1,047	5,246	11.8	47.7	51.0
Lapeer	3,572	7,792	217,176	2,394	41,937	92.1	118,228	1,303	44,147	18.6	57.9	41.0
Leelanau	916	1,786	51,107	2,370	22,205	97.3	40,521	1,879	13,917	15.9	55.6	43.5
Lenawee	4,913	10,540	258,591	2,575	52,542	96.4	155,740	1,551	47,012	17.3	54.6	44.2
Livingston	6,069	15,017	400,996	2,373	102,372	97.8	681,635	4,034	93,742	24.2	62.8	36.3
Luce	787	1,705	44,089	6,284	4,024	98.1	4,836	689	2,829	11.6	61.8	36.9
Mackinac	999	1,674	52,047	4,493	15,897	97.2	38,541	3,327	6,599	10.5	56.2	42.7
Macomb	29,712	92,578	2,422,304	2,998	696,207	97.0	1,970,739	2,439	402,410	16.5	50.2	48.8
Manistee	1,603	3,347	103,579	4,133	20,211	98.6	72,401	2,889	12,740	11.5	49.4	49.2
Marquette	3,899	8,304	222,745	3,443	45,200	97.5	145,794	2,254	32,488	11.3	45.2	53.6
Mason	1,999	4,022	119,116	4,147	28,970	99.0	22,552	785	14,611	12.3	55.6	43.3
Mecosta	2,143	4,768	119,537	2,884	24,145	91.2	91,402	2,205	17,581	19.2	55.2	44.0
Menominee	1,111	2,306	58,366	2,323	12,601	98.3	30,979	1,233	11,419	9.4	52.0	46.6
Midland	3,571	9,889	277,931	3,317	91,657	98.9	297,461	3,550	43,275	11.3	56.3	42.4
Missaukee	668	1,122	40,875	2,727	8,458	89.3	13,844	924	7,421	14.2	68.1	31.3
Monroe	6,006	15,764	438,184	2,936	119,570	96.4	559,216	3,747	74,132	20.0	50.5	48.7
Montcalm	3,464	7,394	175,166	2,801	35,466	96.7	163,138	2,609	26,734	16.7	56.0	42.9
Montmorency	505	817	23,311	2,224	7,426	97.1	17,204	1,641	5,563	11.1	59.3	39.5
Muskegon	8,552	22,254	619,866	3,600	112,756	80.9	463,159	2,690	80,313	15.9	44.0	55.1
Newaygo	2,930	6,081	148,002	3,026	25,372	97.6	97,583	1,995	22,873	17.0	59.5	39.6
Oakland	48,465	151,066	4,135,103	3,437	1,548,424	95.9	3,605,955	2,998	641,977	12.6	49.3	49.8
Oceana	1,292	2,477	66,146	2,384	18,245	91.5	38,151	1,374	12,297	14.2	54.3	44.3
Ogemaw	1,398	2,862	74,762	3,433	13,587	96.2	42,646	1,958	10,796	9.5	50.5	48.3
Ontonagon	719	1,462	23,731	3,084	5,818	99.5	15,985	2,077	4,192	1.0	54.0	44.4
Osceola	1,346	2,752	73,046	3,101	14,104	99.4	31,275	1,328	11,188	12.7	59.0	39.9
Oscoda	485	785	19,504	2,064	6,173	98.5	5,692	602	4,409	10.4	58.3	40.6
Otsego	1,148	2,725	70,088	2,905	27,462	99.6	61,438	2,547	12,307	17.2	60.7	38.0
Ottawa	9,017	23,922	628,119	2,550	174,092	97.4	849,934	3,450	128,643	16.3	71.6	27.6
Presque Isle	665	1,205	31,861	2,223	8,931	100.0	8,452	590	7,516	6.2	53.0	45.7
Roscommon	1,439	2,883	77,160	2,985	29,399	98.7	22,452	869	14,359	11.1	51.3	47.4
Saginaw	9,318	23,788	617,320	2,943	118,548	83.0	427,045	2,036	102,852	9.7	45.9	53.4
St. Clair	6,849	17,874	493,068	2,946	129,182	92.7	338,948	2,025	79,743	16.4	53.6	45.4
St. Joseph	3,769	8,243	237,603	3,807	39,897	98.8	150,156	2,406	25,239	14.6	60.8	38.2
Sanilac	2,375	4,384	127,951	2,860	27,434	98.4	98,995	2,213	20,763	11.8	60.8	38.0
Schoolcraft	579	1,215	32,074	3,652	6,127	99.3	11,309	1,288	4,441	5.8	51.1	48.1
Shiawassee	3,735	8,303	194,808	2,698	32,506	96.4	103,433	1,433	36,651	13.8	53.0	46.1
Tuscola	3,222	6,780	154,694	2,656	28,533	97.4	78,395	1,346	28,338	15.0	54.3	44.6

See footnotes at end of table.

Table B-13. Counties — **Local Government Finances and Elections**—Con.

[Includes United States, states, and 3,141 counties/county equivalents defined as of February 22, 2005. For more information on these areas, see Appendix C, Geographic Information]

County	Local government employment, March 2002		Local government finances, 2002						Elections, 2004[1]			
			General revenue				Total debt outstanding		Votes cast for President			
					Taxes							
	Total employment	Total payroll ($1,000)	Total ($1,000)	Per capita (dol.)	Total ($1,000)	Property, percent of total (taxes)	Amount ($1,000)	Per capita (dol.)	Total	Percent change, 2000–2004	Republican candidate, percent of total	Democratic candidate, percent of total
MICHIGAN—Con.												
Van Buren	4,676	10,704	296,405	3,827	53,276	96.7	286,891	3,704	34,174	15.9	51.6	47.3
Washtenaw	14,267	42,097	1,016,955	3,059	369,952	97.5	1,110,507	3,341	173,264	19.5	35.5	63.5
Wayne	91,752	299,758	9,102,137	4,463	2,249,970	75.7	10,316,228	5,058	864,728	12.5	29.8	69.4
Wexford	1,660	3,669	104,716	3,399	17,761	99.7	70,497	2,288	15,160	16.8	59.1	39.8
MINNESOTA	260,581	668,341	19,723,791	3,926	5,232,373	93.8	25,601,836	5,096	2,828,387	16.0	47.6	51.1
Aitkin	1,017	1,721	52,089	3,335	15,027	98.6	34,720	2,223	9,452	14.4	50.4	48.0
Anoka	12,966	29,133	999,312	3,222	274,053	95.2	1,037,598	3,345	174,066	19.5	52.8	46.1
Becker	1,630	3,123	91,701	2,978	23,452	98.1	51,923	1,686	16,801	17.2	58.3	40.2
Beltrami	2,634	5,381	145,707	3,541	26,178	97.5	140,392	3,411	21,131	22.7	48.5	50.1
Benton	1,336	3,184	90,782	2,476	25,487	96.2	150,012	4,091	18,384	23.3	54.6	43.8
Big Stone	580	941	37,883	6,628	4,536	98.5	255,734	44,740	3,067	2.9	48.4	50.1
Blue Earth	2,883	6,465	195,656	3,453	54,504	90.3	186,958	3,300	33,119	20.9	47.5	50.9
Brown	1,610	3,465	85,191	3,167	19,317	93.8	108,316	4,027	13,778	7.4	60.9	37.4
Carlton	2,467	4,786	137,425	4,223	25,399	98.2	178,287	5,479	18,334	21.6	36.2	62.5
Carver	4,035	10,650	264,730	3,480	98,979	93.0	409,760	5,386	45,411	29.7	62.8	36.2
Cass	1,861	3,567	103,280	3,699	31,468	99.0	76,726	2,748	15,910	17.0	55.8	43.0
Chippewa	966	1,940	51,675	4,001	10,705	98.6	43,970	3,405	6,606	4.0	46.8	51.8
Chisago	1,894	4,599	133,536	2,971	34,010	93.5	157,521	3,505	28,260	28.5	55.6	43.2
Clay	2,791	5,982	176,972	3,417	29,715	96.6	274,682	5,304	27,737	18.7	51.8	46.8
Clearwater	846	1,426	29,639	3,513	8,264	99.8	26,421	3,132	4,361	14.0	55.9	42.9
Cook	602	1,336	40,188	7,718	8,210	82.5	29,239	5,615	3,303	17.1	45.1	52.5
Cottonwood	1,032	1,794	50,055	4,168	11,151	99.5	42,834	3,567	6,369	3.0	55.9	42.8
Crow Wing	3,336	7,021	191,484	3,340	54,248	97.1	167,998	2,931	33,545	19.3	57.0	41.8
Dakota	15,803	44,167	1,197,931	3,249	374,789	95.4	1,501,003	4,071	215,846	18.4	50.5	48.5
Dodge	1,115	2,256	63,517	3,415	14,272	98.2	58,216	3,130	9,868	22.6	56.7	41.7
Douglas	1,649	3,463	156,072	4,638	26,232	97.1	68,013	2,021	20,309	18.0	58.1	40.5
Faribault	1,225	2,050	63,921	4,023	12,219	97.8	48,238	3,036	8,681	3.1	55.2	43.4
Fillmore	1,208	2,275	62,569	2,936	13,115	98.4	41,598	1,952	11,698	14.4	48.7	49.8
Freeborn	1,507	3,062	92,116	2,869	23,418	91.4	61,608	1,919	17,666	9.5	43.5	55.1
Goodhue	2,533	5,534	179,515	3,991	58,972	98.0	270,673	6,018	25,608	15.1	51.3	47.3
Grant	527	824	25,163	4,011	6,217	97.8	23,989	3,824	3,819	5.4	49.6	48.6
Hennepin	55,710	181,629	5,060,479	4,517	1,614,460	92.6	6,308,934	5,632	646,981	12.7	39.4	59.3
Houston	1,098	1,912	57,557	2,890	12,048	98.6	47,926	2,406	11,082	9.0	50.8	47.6
Hubbard	1,049	1,779	58,156	3,137	16,509	98.0	75,200	4,057	11,340	18.0	56.8	41.8
Isanti	1,480	3,528	92,281	2,722	25,304	95.0	86,734	2,559	19,313	29.4	57.9	40.8
Itasca	3,019	6,237	183,935	4,175	45,127	99.3	184,894	4,197	24,367	12.2	43.9	54.5
Jackson	882	1,418	40,652	3,607	9,678	99.5	38,910	3,453	5,779	6.3	52.3	45.9
Kanabec	1,048	2,239	60,162	3,876	8,543	98.2	47,983	3,091	8,248	21.1	54.9	43.6
Kandiyohi	3,038	7,175	195,330	4,781	34,726	92.5	176,494	4,320	21,349	10.7	54.8	43.7
Kittson	501	758	23,230	4,605	6,562	99.9	8,752	1,735	2,682	1.7	48.7	49.7
Koochiching	1,040	2,077	52,432	3,749	7,893	97.8	49,047	3,507	7,309	6.3	48.4	50.1
Lac qui Parle	887	1,613	38,805	4,892	7,115	99.5	16,749	2,111	4,541	2.0	46.1	52.6
Lake	703	1,436	50,994	4,580	9,948	96.8	56,376	5,064	7,071	7.7	39.2	59.6
Lake of the Woods	308	683	19,770	4,562	3,021	98.0	332,740	76,774	2,400	9.7	59.5	38.4
Le Sueur	1,403	2,433	75,590	2,894	18,206	98.1	56,767	2,173	14,424	17.0	53.7	44.8
Lincoln	433	583	19,339	3,098	5,193	99.6	11,800	1,890	3,342	1.8	51.9	46.6
Lyon	2,154	4,257	112,476	4,509	20,767	96.6	108,400	4,346	12,673	10.3	56.8	41.8
McLeod	2,300	5,339	168,245	4,722	26,725	97.1	115,655	3,246	18,412	19.6	62.0	36.5
Mahnomen	641	994	29,371	5,685	4,001	99.6	5,120	991	2,508	12.8	45.1	53.4
Marshall	836	1,154	39,478	3,966	8,410	99.6	11,453	1,151	5,562	7.0	57.3	41.5
Martin	1,354	2,810	65,754	3,084	17,805	98.4	41,532	1,948	11,047	6.5	57.1	41.6
Meeker	1,759	3,415	97,255	4,224	17,031	98.2	88,498	3,844	12,334	15.6	55.6	42.9
Mille Lacs	1,446	3,173	84,405	3,553	19,530	97.8	77,763	3,273	13,065	27.4	55.1	43.5
Morrison	1,846	3,503	90,431	2,787	19,181	98.3	63,926	1,970	16,758	14.2	57.9	40.5
Mower	1,896	4,704	132,197	3,411	21,324	98.0	1,186,503	30,612	20,222	9.4	37.5	61.0
Murray	713	1,069	34,923	3,855	7,008	99.4	15,374	1,697	4,998	5.2	54.4	44.4
Nicollet	1,258	2,464	87,469	2,873	18,070	97.1	62,032	2,038	17,741	15.7	49.0	49.6
Nobles	1,686	3,503	87,268	4,236	14,884	98.6	61,890	3,004	9,204	3.7	56.1	42.4
Norman	775	1,201	38,212	5,230	8,618	98.7	18,037	2,468	3,810	4.6	47.1	51.3
Olmsted	5,195	14,894	459,942	3,564	112,070	86.3	1,421,961	11,019	71,575	20.5	52.2	46.5
Otter Tail	3,161	5,825	178,558	3,109	39,637	98.2	154,191	2,685	32,178	12.9	61.3	37.4
Pennington	1,087	1,866	50,605	3,717	10,943	98.1	29,776	2,187	7,017	11.0	53.7	44.4
Pine	1,577	2,753	78,515	2,849	17,356	97.7	64,385	2,337	14,518	11.1	48.4	49.8
Pipestone	740	1,202	47,003	4,829	9,338	98.0	36,088	3,707	5,032	2.8	60.9	37.8
Polk	2,057	3,690	159,331	5,154	25,063	96.3	112,847	3,650	15,668	10.8	55.7	43.0
Pope	844	1,614	46,711	4,160	9,863	79.1	20,338	1,811	6,700	11.9	49.3	49.3
Ramsey	24,198	84,399	2,884,232	5,662	682,503	92.1	4,454,880	8,746	272,577	11.6	35.6	63.0
Red Lake	365	497	16,423	3,844	3,289	99.5	10,218	2,392	2,177	4.2	53.5	44.2
Redwood	1,376	2,149	71,115	4,334	14,047	98.3	61,816	3,767	8,139	5.0	60.2	38.1
Renville	1,026	2,278	66,861	3,941	15,266	98.5	55,897	3,295	8,349	2.8	53.1	45.4

See footnotes at end of table.

[Includes United States, states, and 3,141 counties/county equivalents defined as of February 22, 2005. For more information on these areas, see Appendix C, Geographic Information]

County	Local government employment, March 2002		Local government finances, 2002						Elections, 2004[1]			
			General revenue				Total debt outstanding		Votes cast for President			
					Taxes						Republican candidate, percent of total	Democratic candidate, percent of total
	Total employment	Total payroll ($1,000)	Total ($1,000)	Per capita (dol.)	Total ($1,000)	Property, percent of total (taxes)	Amount ($1,000)	Per capita (dol.)	Total	Percent change, 2000–2004		
MINNESOTA—Con.												
Rice	2,765	6,652	205,733	3,508	36,901	94.8	244,365	4,167	30,745	18.2	45.2	53.4
Rock	669	1,196	35,821	3,701	7,424	94.9	40,135	4,147	5,191	3.6	59.9	38.5
Roseau	1,148	2,189	71,229	4,408	9,643	98.6	57,025	3,529	7,911	10.4	67.7	30.9
St. Louis	11,563	30,934	862,785	4,317	173,424	89.1	608,906	3,047	119,565	11.3	33.6	65.2
Scott	3,424	8,933	264,602	2,549	89,375	91.5	416,399	4,011	60,639	38.5	59.5	39.5
Sherburne	2,891	8,040	227,141	3,143	80,776	96.9	438,877	6,073	41,454	34.4	60.8	38.2
Sibley	941	1,762	54,809	3,576	11,772	98.7	38,954	2,541	7,949	8.4	58.7	39.1
Stearns	8,004	16,558	467,383	3,380	117,634	92.2	715,672	5,176	75,577	21.0	55.2	43.2
Steele	2,087	4,424	101,228	2,944	24,316	97.3	87,358	2,540	18,695	16.4	55.6	42.8
Stevens	657	1,218	31,349	3,167	7,093	99.4	18,442	1,863	5,949	3.4	50.9	47.4
Swift	928	1,608	52,835	4,606	5,790	98.8	25,601	2,232	5,735	5.5	43.3	55.2
Todd	1,305	2,516	77,679	3,181	15,010	96.0	38,383	1,572	12,214	10.1	56.9	41.2
Traverse	494	738	26,019	6,616	4,298	87.7	9,110	2,316	2,141	1.7	50.3	47.9
Wabasha	1,225	2,133	67,563	3,075	14,613	97.3	52,185	2,375	11,835	12.4	51.7	46.9
Wadena	1,306	2,544	52,476	3,822	8,759	98.5	40,935	2,982	7,093	11.1	59.4	39.4
Waseca	1,251	2,951	67,594	3,459	16,134	96.0	50,625	2,590	9,800	10.6	55.7	42.6
Washington	7,868	20,640	609,961	2,899	213,957	94.8	750,897	3,569	128,449	20.0	51.2	47.8
Watonwan	822	1,472	40,846	3,481	9,169	98.9	28,418	2,422	5,583	8.7	53.2	45.0
Wilkin	525	888	29,291	4,211	5,755	99.1	24,217	3,481	3,527	6.7	65.3	33.1
Winona	1,992	4,109	124,769	2,524	30,575	94.2	108,546	2,196	27,422	14.7	46.3	51.9
Wright	4,920	11,176	323,897	3,291	88,895	95.1	548,552	5,573	59,534	37.3	60.8	38.0
Yellow Medicine	854	1,256	55,180	5,106	10,061	98.9	33,919	3,139	5,758	4.4	50.0	48.6
MISSISSIPPI	142,895	280,353	7,394,493	2,580	1,794,817	91.7	5,773,746	2,014	1,152,145	15.9	59.5	39.8
Adams	1,881	3,725	107,080	3,198	25,429	85.4	150,134	4,484	15,470	4.0	45.2	54.5
Alcorn	2,131	4,721	145,059	4,170	17,000	93.1	74,636	2,145	14,239	12.7	60.6	38.3
Amite	503	602	16,577	1,226	4,034	91.4	2,456	182	7,197	12.3	57.6	41.9
Attala	999	1,766	51,087	2,595	10,020	92.9	13,002	660	8,207	14.4	61.1	38.3
Benton	404	521	13,722	1,744	2,896	99.7	2,573	327	4,247	22.0	46.4	52.9
Bolivar	2,179	3,988	81,828	2,072	22,404	92.6	44,801	1,135	15,307	13.1	36.2	62.9
Calhoun	778	1,362	27,614	1,855	6,686	92.3	11,458	770	6,389	11.0	64.7	35.0
Carroll	474	720	13,247	1,250	4,508	98.9	11,367	1,073	5,592	13.6	65.5	34.0
Chickasaw	1,006	1,649	35,450	1,833	8,219	91.7	12,241	633	8,343	16.3	50.3	48.9
Choctaw	428	592	17,553	1,807	3,911	93.5	7,906	814	4,082	9.8	66.0	33.5
Claiborne	656	1,194	37,163	3,191	3,859	88.9	149,098	12,803	5,355	16.0	17.7	81.5
Clarke	789	1,223	29,830	1,673	7,921	89.3	11,002	617	7,505	8.5	67.5	32.0
Clay	908	1,675	38,386	1,755	12,365	94.8	33,479	1,531	9,139	11.9	47.5	52.0
Coahoma	1,661	3,121	83,347	2,785	23,155	82.6	102,363	3,421	10,608	11.0	34.7	64.2
Copiah	1,747	3,113	83,934	2,915	14,893	93.7	36,908	1,282	11,388	7.6	56.0	43.6
Covington	1,094	2,022	45,136	2,285	7,716	93.2	6,875	348	8,252	19.9	61.1	38.3
DeSoto	3,769	7,571	192,740	1,624	68,602	93.9	170,698	1,438	50,200	43.7	72.3	27.1
Forrest	6,577	14,626	405,488	5,526	56,615	87.8	204,312	2,784	26,733	20.1	61.0	38.2
Franklin	394	731	17,372	2,096	3,908	98.1	1,755	212	4,491	13.6	64.4	35.1
George	1,042	2,009	49,772	2,484	8,533	92.5	28,175	1,406	8,001	9.8	77.8	21.6
Greene	495	825	18,512	1,404	5,109	95.8	2,473	187	5,299	19.5	72.7	26.8
Grenada	1,384	3,137	82,726	3,604	14,415	92.8	45,992	2,004	10,105	16.9	58.1	41.4
Hancock	1,759	3,812	122,682	2,749	33,965	89.4	83,800	1,878	17,869	22.8	70.4	28.6
Harrison	9,179	21,943	718,254	3,778	172,899	83.4	399,907	2,104	63,267	20.2	62.8	36.5
Hinds	13,458	26,225	652,066	2,620	220,028	93.0	738,257	2,966	92,500	5.4	40.0	59.3
Holmes	1,440	2,463	56,459	2,627	9,991	94.7	22,480	1,046	8,383	12.9	23.4	75.9
Humphreys	617	847	25,046	2,322	6,360	92.4	11,497	1,066	4,899	24.2	34.3	64.7
Issaquena	25	29	5,520	2,593	1,156	96.5	4,994	2,346	970	3.1	45.3	53.2
Itawamba	1,120	2,346	66,155	2,880	12,969	98.3	32,428	1,412	9,710	13.4	70.4	28.9
Jackson	7,908	17,623	429,465	3,230	117,624	91.2	515,381	3,877	51,049	13.2	68.8	30.5
Jasper	921	1,431	36,544	2,002	9,895	90.7	13,804	756	8,009	24.2	48.1	51.4
Jefferson	603	952	21,539	2,222	4,413	90.2	14,290	1,474	3,466	1.7	18.2	81.4
Jefferson Davis	795	1,460	28,238	2,081	4,794	97.7	8,612	635	5,765	8.4	46.3	51.3
Jones	4,560	8,748	206,206	3,169	36,142	92.6	180,503	2,774	26,666	9.6	71.7	27.7
Kemper	861	1,574	51,359	4,882	6,694	95.9	8,953	851	4,603	8.0	45.8	53.6
Lafayette	1,160	2,182	65,185	1,664	22,435	90.4	81,383	2,077	15,388	21.4	58.5	40.4
Lamar	1,417	2,580	64,555	1,569	22,715	95.0	53,328	1,296	20,465	23.3	80.2	19.2
Lauderdale	3,386	6,972	178,279	2,296	50,252	92.6	113,835	1,466	30,166	16.2	65.4	34.1
Lawrence	609	898	27,524	2,051	7,773	97.3	6,320	471	6,306	–4.3	62.7	36.6
Leake	699	1,205	30,850	1,421	7,310	93.5	19,523	899	8,212	18.1	60.4	39.1
Lee	3,291	6,677	177,291	2,303	54,709	94.6	198,190	2,574	30,621	22.0	66.1	33.1
Leflore	2,857	6,075	138,162	3,759	21,268	95.1	45,331	1,233	12,463	10.5	37.2	60.7
Lincoln	1,370	2,409	58,803	1,752	16,778	92.3	48,655	1,450	14,491	11.5	69.1	30.5
Lowndes	2,288	4,998	135,824	2,230	38,170	92.1	172,455	2,832	24,268	26.2	56.4	42.9
Madison	2,754	5,512	164,882	2,118	59,626	92.7	218,625	2,808	37,724	26.3	64.3	35.2
Marion	1,251	2,247	61,763	2,448	11,519	93.5	36,442	1,444	11,947	8.6	67.0	32.5
Marshall	1,284	2,258	45,764	1,299	16,033	93.6	32,790	931	14,649	16.3	40.8	58.7
Monroe	1,558	2,744	61,424	1,621	17,619	92.7	29,933	790	15,632	17.0	59.5	39.9
Montgomery	676	1,231	23,631	1,978	5,504	90.1	5,671	475	5,496	13.3	54.6	45.0
Neshoba	872	1,611	40,961	1,424	10,136	90.9	22,906	796	10,418	14.9	74.7	25.0

See footnotes at end of table.

[Includes United States, states, and 3,141 counties/county equivalents defined as of February 22, 2005. For more information on these areas, see Appendix C, Geographic Information]

County	Local government employment, March 2002		Local government finances, 2002						Elections, 2004[1]			
			General revenue				Total debt outstanding		Votes cast for President			
					Taxes							
	Total employment	Total payroll ($1,000)	Total ($1,000)	Per capita (dol.)	Total ($1,000)	Property, percent of total (taxes)	Amount ($1,000)	Per capita (dol.)	Total	Percent change, 2000–2004	Republican candidate, percent of total	Democratic candidate, percent of total
MISSISSIPPI—Con.												
Newton	1,265	2,105	50,818	2,320	9,175	91.4	12,430	567	8,487	9.7	72.6	26.9
Noxubee	693	1,249	31,267	2,525	6,261	92.7	14,273	1,153	6,097	23.1	28.3	71.3
Oktibbeha	1,875	3,927	95,705	2,283	19,958	98.2	44,067	1,051	16,279	10.0	55.7	43.1
Panola	1,609	2,899	69,551	1,992	17,116	88.7	35,708	1,023	13,440	18.0	50.4	49.2
Pearl River	2,627	4,534	109,541	2,173	26,138	93.6	24,720	490	19,487	18.3	76.4	23.0
Perry	640	1,006	69,614	5,679	6,378	93.7	578,265	47,171	5,030	15.4	74.5	25.1
Pike	2,713	6,258	157,185	4,037	20,459	96.8	33,583	863	16,632	17.4	52.1	47.4
Pontotoc	989	1,869	52,324	1,929	11,632	90.8	21,173	781	11,240	18.2	75.4	23.7
Prentiss	1,339	2,866	69,734	2,727	11,928	97.4	37,408	1,463	9,932	17.1	65.8	33.5
Quitman	688	960	16,223	1,628	5,002	90.8	7,466	749	3,416	0.1	39.8	59.5
Rankin	3,533	7,202	189,019	1,554	66,774	94.4	209,213	1,720	54,717	32.1	78.7	20.1
Scott	1,077	1,872	47,794	1,690	12,177	89.7	28,473	1,007	10,228	11.1	62.5	37.2
Sharkey	360	581	14,310	2,270	3,808	93.2	4,091	649	3,093	6.5	36.2	50.4
Simpson	1,305	1,788	43,461	1,568	9,512	91.7	11,011	397	10,474	9.4	68.2	31.2
Smith	594	1,101	26,187	1,641	6,537	90.9	4,061	254	7,120	9.1	78.3	21.0
Stone	1,479	3,129	81,017	5,739	18,427	96.7	15,380	1,090	5,735	3.8	72.3	26.6
Sunflower	2,245	3,853	88,322	2,609	16,446	93.4	30,740	908	10,015	19.0	35.3	63.5
Tallahatchie	836	1,315	35,212	2,428	6,639	93.9	7,173	495	6,217	12.6	44.0	55.0
Tate	1,550	3,332	82,067	3,206	17,674	95.4	43,229	1,689	11,167	28.5	60.5	38.9
Tippah	941	1,639	46,921	2,238	8,705	86.5	3,499	167	9,275	10.4	66.6	32.5
Tishomingo	746	1,210	27,372	1,434	7,286	90.1	5,007	262	8,326	19.1	64.6	34.2
Tunica	659	1,397	71,739	7,399	9,635	91.7	32,298	3,331	3,129	32.2	30.4	68.4
Union	1,154	1,895	43,022	1,663	12,007	94.5	37,029	1,431	10,819	16.2	73.1	26.2
Walthall	774	1,348	30,889	2,043	5,585	91.6	3,141	208	6,352	7.8	61.2	38.3
Warren	2,486	4,388	116,874	2,378	38,685	94.7	80,802	1,644	19,679	5.7	57.7	41.8
Washington	3,788	8,342	229,986	3,767	44,230	90.0	95,689	1,567	19,597	6.9	39.5	59.0
Wayne	1,108	2,022	58,320	2,751	8,765	91.5	18,650	880	8,794	14.1	63.3	36.3
Webster	531	791	17,086	1,662	4,606	93.1	10,936	1,064	5,065	11.4	73.2	26.5
Wilkinson	475	748	18,984	1,844	4,091	94.8	5,315	516	4,385	7.0	35.6	63.7
Winston	779	1,346	34,213	1,712	7,665	88.2	17,454	873	9,409	12.4	57.2	42.3
Yalobusha	744	1,274	32,952	2,477	5,714	93.0	18,591	1,397	5,971	14.2	54.9	44.5
Yazoo	1,276	2,170	48,670	1,738	14,818	94.7	38,874	1,388	10,987	4.5	51.6	45.6
MISSOURI	259,747	601,701	15,182,868	2,673	6,394,500	60.4	11,551,697	2,033	[2]2,731,364	[2]15.7	[2]53.3	[2]46.1
Adair	1,062	1,908	57,874	2,328	23,766	65.5	20,296	817	11,404	8.1	55.8	43.3
Andrew	657	1,135	25,587	1,533	7,262	85.7	3,277	196	8,266	13.6	62.1	37.1
Atchison	456	715	18,515	2,939	7,617	69.9	1,488	236	3,156	9.9	67.7	31.8
Audrain	1,207	2,125	49,345	1,911	19,291	61.1	24,720	957	10,683	7.0	58.9	40.4
Barry	1,704	3,068	78,602	2,289	26,801	64.1	20,486	597	13,927	12.6	68.9	30.3
Barton	948	1,358	31,075	2,412	8,488	70.7	12,386	961	5,991	11.6	76.3	22.9
Bates	924	1,406	32,780	1,933	11,221	65.6	31,860	1,878	8,466	8.6	59.1	40.1
Benton	741	1,318	28,099	1,586	9,416	68.2	9,007	508	9,009	19.6	61.9	37.5
Bollinger	436	696	16,956	1,379	5,348	76.8	420	34	5,895	11.4	69.6	29.8
Boone	6,040	12,402	345,391	2,492	144,698	59.7	344,264	2,484	76,046	27.6	49.7	49.5
Buchanan	3,373	7,749	201,884	2,367	86,756	54.4	261,896	3,071	37,950	9.2	52.2	46.9
Butler	2,085	3,641	79,974	1,958	27,744	53.1	22,830	559	16,441	14.2	71.1	28.4
Caldwell	719	948	31,360	3,456	8,631	81.6	6,886	759	4,268	10.9	60.8	38.5
Callaway	1,239	2,726	65,768	1,557	26,212	77.1	52,018	1,232	17,773	16.1	62.5	36.9
Camden	1,327	2,389	77,255	2,036	38,528	59.7	79,482	2,095	19,519	14.2	67.2	32.3
Cape Girardeau	3,054	5,548	169,746	2,444	88,766	63.6	113,433	1,633	34,565	15.8	68.9	30.6
Carroll	689	929	20,674	2,018	7,473	78.0	5,971	583	4,741	3.5	66.6	33.1
Carter	267	503	10,971	1,856	2,466	82.0	3,605	610	2,779	−1.0	64.7	34.7
Cass	3,857	8,448	223,253	2,562	83,267	75.7	242,006	2,777	44,217	23.3	61.6	37.7
Cedar	713	1,282	30,086	2,164	8,006	83.7	4,852	349	6,203	9.5	68.3	30.8
Chariton	529	663	15,270	1,847	5,467	83.6	3,123	378	4,340	4.5	55.8	43.6
Christian	1,927	3,596	95,649	1,615	37,227	67.9	82,119	1,386	31,348	35.0	70.5	28.9
Clark	523	814	17,765	2,374	4,735	77.7	6,603	883	3,736	−1.7	50.8	48.0
Clay	11,596	26,885	695,078	3,634	223,294	68.4	391,753	2,048	96,460	20.3	53.1	46.3
Clinton	772	1,687	37,598	1,917	14,087	71.3	27,589	1,407	9,540	11.8	55.4	43.7
Cole	2,241	5,410	128,010	1,781	65,502	61.7	101,013	1,405	36,701	12.0	67.4	32.0
Cooper	1,013	1,569	43,048	2,524	11,820	64.1	24,641	1,445	7,508	10.6	67.4	32.0
Crawford	912	1,551	28,926	1,243	9,672	76.1	9,704	417	9,381	13.0	60.6	38.7
Dade	535	667	17,887	2,260	3,701	88.7	3,508	443	4,089	9.0	72.5	27.0
Dallas	404	855	21,247	1,334	5,212	65.7	3,575	225	7,259	16.7	66.0	33.2
Daviess	454	706	17,015	2,134	5,392	85.2	5,175	649	3,794	8.6	62.0	37.0
DeKalb	339	563	13,274	1,024	4,154	83.0	1,830	141	4,686	15.7	62.8	36.4
Dent	789	1,399	44,856	3,021	11,205	80.9	5,577	376	6,304	5.3	69.3	29.6
Douglas	488	835	17,201	1,289	4,141	79.5	1,634	122	6,327	19.8	71.1	27.5
Dunklin	1,535	2,916	60,921	1,856	19,092	70.0	24,044	733	11,677	10.9	57.6	42.0

See footnotes at end of table.

[Includes United States, states, and 3,141 counties/county equivalents defined as of February 22, 2005. For more information on these areas, see Appendix C, Geographic Information]

County	Local government employment, March 2002		Local government finances, 2002							Elections, 2004[1]			
			General revenue				Total debt outstanding			Votes cast for President			
					Taxes								
	Total employ- ment	Total payroll ($1,000)	Total ($1,000)	Per capita (dol.)	Total ($1,000)	Prop- erty, percent of total (taxes)	Amount ($1,000)	Per capita (dol.)		Total	Percent change, 2000– 2004	Repub- lican cand- idate, percent of total	Demo- cratic cand- idate, percent of total
MISSOURI—Con.													
Franklin	3,720	7,882	177,455	1,847	82,389	68.8	132,967	1,384		45,318	15.6	58.3	41.0
Gasconade	812	1,540	36,961	2,395	13,340	73.9	19,696	1,276		7,171	8.2	66.3	32.8
Gentry	467	735	15,703	2,357	5,020	80.4	4,457	669		3,312	6.7	63.0	36.3
Greene	10,371	26,218	535,185	2,201	242,681	50.6	597,107	2,456		125,266	21.7	62.2	37.3
Grundy	974	1,507	31,096	3,049	6,907	69.9	29,121	2,855		4,808	2.1	66.0	32.5
Harrison	725	1,135	24,371	2,775	6,032	78.1	5,027	572		4,048	1.4	67.4	31.6
Henry	1,493	2,711	84,131	3,782	20,250	53.2	29,979	1,348		10,877	11.2	58.5	41.0
Hickory	377	740	15,362	1,728	4,777	80.1	7,549	849		4,866	14.8	57.4	42.0
Holt	268	438	13,531	2,631	5,577	73.4	2,442	475		2,691	1.1	69.3	30.1
Howard	461	780	16,544	1,648	5,194	78.7	7,191	716		4,921	9.1	59.2	40.1
Howell	1,930	3,351	68,926	1,849	21,825	64.7	25,700	689		16,379	16.4	67.8	31.3
Iron	571	1,000	21,706	2,072	8,193	83.5	3,338	319		4,679	6.0	52.9	46.1
Jackson	32,534	92,678	2,453,866	3,713	1,166,605	48.1	2,077,909	3,144		174,570	−35.8	54.1	45.3
Jasper	4,679	8,613	232,852	2,179	97,197	56.4	84,674	792		45,085	20.3	70.6	28.8
Jefferson	7,473	16,658	351,755	1,725	144,693	68.9	229,277	1,124		93,264	20.8	50.0	49.4
Johnson	2,643	5,214	115,412	2,327	31,113	63.9	57,789	1,165		20,236	20.5	60.6	38.5
Knox	341	450	10,183	2,371	3,055	78.6	3,564	830		1,978	−3.7	61.0	38.5
Laclede	1,436	2,820	55,703	1,692	20,618	58.5	29,839	907		14,869	14.0	71.1	28.3
Lafayette	1,439	2,612	59,059	1,790	19,748	72.9	49,430	1,498		16,182	11.4	59.7	39.6
Lawrence	1,640	2,726	65,281	1,806	16,071	74.7	21,322	590		15,806	22.5	70.8	28.5
Lewis	579	867	20,370	1,960	5,754	70.9	4,556	438		4,644	3.6	61.6	37.8
Lincoln	1,908	4,172	86,566	2,041	27,142	63.4	55,927	1,319		19,839	24.7	57.0	42.2
Linn	858	1,432	29,851	2,208	8,065	78.2	13,751	1,017		5,898	−1.9	58.0	41.4
Livingston	899	1,606	36,536	2,540	11,257	61.4	3,798	264		6,346	1.1	63.5	35.9
McDonald	745	1,220	29,073	1,338	6,621	80.3	1,303	60		7,725	18.3	70.5	28.7
Macon	1,364	2,120	46,589	3,012	9,951	65.4	10,801	698		7,570	5.5	61.7	37.7
Madison	701	1,444	27,177	2,288	4,863	83.1	1,657	139		4,918	12.5	59.1	40.1
Maries	366	560	11,936	1,363	5,043	69.9	250	29		4,424	14.8	63.9	35.3
Marion	1,530	3,052	102,550	3,657	34,538	67.7	100,414	3,581		12,453	6.3	62.8	36.7
Mercer	278	384	9,293	2,533	3,181	88.4	2,732	745		1,817	−1.4	66.4	32.0
Miller	1,280	2,342	49,651	2,050	21,332	73.2	26,660	1,101		10,831	15.8	72.0	27.3
Mississippi	737	1,281	27,961	2,127	8,235	68.1	10,535	801		5,298	1.6	54.8	44.8
Moniteau	617	1,031	21,224	1,418	7,215	82.1	12,503	836		6,691	10.3	70.9	28.6
Monroe	631	1,058	24,340	2,606	7,135	73.1	33,955	3,636		4,307	5.2	61.1	38.2
Montgomery	491	904	18,431	1,526	6,667	76.3	4,461	369		5,760	8.6	61.9	37.3
Morgan	650	1,109	23,966	1,213	10,299	73.2	3,408	173		8,771	11.3	64.5	34.8
New Madrid	1,254	2,108	39,789	2,066	14,918	79.6	9,830	510		7,907	8.8	52.5	47.0
Newton	1,910	3,976	90,391	1,699	27,128	71.0	17,168	323		23,889	12.9	72.0	27.5
Nodaway	1,155	1,804	43,431	1,990	18,332	65.4	27,669	1,268		10,119	11.8	61.5	37.9
Oregon	515	789	16,849	1,642	4,480	67.0	1,982	193		4,673	10.4	59.3	39.0
Osage	503	767	15,861	1,212	5,569	78.4	7,272	556		6,671	8.0	74.6	25.1
Ozark	521	790	18,866	1,997	4,942	78.6	5,324	564		4,707	9.7	65.5	33.2
Pemiscot	1,228	2,244	48,570	2,445	10,745	76.6	8,615	434		6,806	12.3	49.9	49.7
Perry	664	1,214	40,659	2,234	13,733	59.2	27,516	1,512		8,247	19.5	67.7	31.8
Pettis	2,774	5,725	141,003	3,575	30,925	54.4	69,784	1,770		17,496	11.1	66.3	33.2
Phelps	2,836	6,011	172,817	4,261	36,651	57.7	64,492	1,590		18,700	15.8	63.5	35.7
Pike	1,007	1,800	38,000	2,068	9,853	66.0	7,413	403		8,040	9.4	53.7	45.7
Platte	2,935	6,455	161,059	2,071	82,544	72.2	158,526	2,039		41,970	23.2	55.5	43.9
Polk	1,701	3,436	85,286	3,087	15,861	62.4	18,483	669		12,453	21.0	69.0	30.3
Pulaski	1,879	3,373	84,050	1,913	17,957	76.9	8,413	191		12,221	16.0	70.5	29.1
Putnam	421	591	12,208	2,353	4,690	80.5	6,935	1,337		2,445	4.8	67.9	31.6
Ralls	269	417	9,715	1,003	4,108	74.9	9,459	976		5,034	10.8	59.3	40.4
Randolph	1,586	2,717	66,948	2,706	22,541	62.7	24,550	992		10,198	11.0	64.2	35.2
Ray	1,282	2,411	59,214	2,496	14,162	73.1	27,799	1,172		10,788	10.7	52.6	46.7
Reynolds	433	662	12,507	1,894	4,062	90.4	1,586	240		3,364	7.4	56.4	43.1
Ripley	626	1,351	19,150	1,409	5,069	75.0	1,220	90		5,653	11.6	65.3	33.7
St. Charles	10,653	27,490	708,296	2,335	370,627	70.3	1,019,437	3,360		163,488	27.0	58.6	40.9
St. Clair	650	1,083	30,824	3,202	4,412	84.9	5,484	570		4,965	4.8	62.4	37.1
Ste. Genevieve	482	968	42,360	2,347	9,476	83.2	14,591	808		8,146	11.4	46.5	52.6
St. Francois	3,003	5,956	119,064	2,097	35,442	64.0	68,223	1,201		22,933	21.7	52.7	46.9
St. Louis	36,128	105,159	2,667,459	2,629	1,538,226	69.1	1,793,898	1,768		542,983	11.5	45.1	54.4
Saline	1,190	2,297	65,255	2,839	15,880	65.3	18,897	822		9,939	6.2	54.2	45.1
Schuyler	275	401	10,269	2,436	2,582	81.6	5,250	1,245		2,031	1.2	55.3	44.0
Scotland	491	883	20,312	4,150	3,105	83.3	2,252	460		2,197	0.8	61.5	37.7
Scott	1,870	3,993	80,438	1,987	27,796	68.2	240,806	5,947		17,448	11.1	64.9	34.7
Shannon	302	566	11,884	1,424	2,797	63.8	3,210	385		4,167	10.2	60.3	38.8
Shelby	584	757	16,174	2,403	5,023	76.6	3,704	550		3,502	7.5	65.1	34.3
Stoddard	1,314	2,298	54,032	1,809	18,636	71.2	13,308	446		13,252	6.4	69.7	29.8
Stone	1,024	1,807	49,912	1,696	24,349	84.3	37,274	1,266		15,189	25.0	69.4	30.1
Sullivan	444	652	17,004	2,343	4,858	80.0	3,057	421		3,089	0.8	60.9	38.1

See footnotes at end of table.

[Includes United States, states, and 3,141 counties/county equivalents defined as of February 22, 2005. For more information on these areas, see Appendix C, Geographic Information]

County	Local government employment, March 2002		Local government finances, 2002				Total debt outstanding		Elections, 2004[1]			
			General revenue						Votes cast for President			
					Taxes							
	Total employ-ment	Total payroll ($1,000)	Total ($1,000)	Per capita (dol.)	Total ($1,000)	Prop-erty, percent of total (taxes)	Amount ($1,000)	Per capita (dol.)	Total	Percent change, 2000–2004	Repub-lican cand-idate, percent of total	Demo-cratic cand-idate, percent of total
MISSOURI—Con.												
Taney	1,726	3,246	103,601	2,547	55,095	39.5	136,223	3,349	19,280	27.6	70.4	29.1
Texas	1,381	2,583	50,172	2,071	9,610	79.2	8,577	354	11,018	10.9	65.7	33.3
Vernon	1,383	2,625	45,084	2,223	18,680	43.6	38,561	1,902	8,992	6.9	63.8	35.7
Warren	826	1,660	39,707	1,519	19,733	61.5	26,780	1,024	13,432	25.1	58.7	40.7
Washington	1,041	1,947	48,182	2,037	8,730	75.1	12,680	536	9,178	11.0	50.6	48.6
Wayne	541	831	19,765	1,503	5,812	66.9	3,614	275	6,204	6.1	63.2	36.3
Webster	1,069	1,977	45,812	1,403	12,505	63.5	21,295	652	14,944	25.8	68.2	31.2
Worth	197	258	5,882	2,552	1,229	91.3	3,800	1,649	1,132	-2.2	61.0	38.5
Wright	979	1,721	50,801	2,797	19,509	29.4	6,500	358	8,346	6.4	73.0	26.2
Independent City												
St. Louis city	23,152	67,097	1,904,670	5,462	667,077	38.9	1,902,080	5,454	144,638	15.9	19.2	80.3
MONTANA	43,133	86,449	2,219,274	2,438	692,451	96.9	1,210,984	1,330	450,445	9.6	59.1	38.6
Beaverhead	549	1,090	29,137	3,237	7,087	99.5	6,267	696	4,242	1.1	72.3	26.0
Big Horn	786	2,116	36,454	2,842	10,061	99.7	555	43	4,311	3.6	47.0	51.4
Blaine	563	994	27,613	4,051	4,735	99.2	3,046	447	2,768	0.3	51.5	47.0
Broadwater	204	343	14,391	3,263	3,291	99.0	5,756	1,305	2,356	13.6	75.5	22.6
Carbon	492	787	21,629	2,224	8,481	93.3	10,243	1,053	5,321	11.1	62.8	34.7
Carter	93	161	4,446	3,272	2,234	99.9	283	208	709	9.9	87.9	10.7
Cascade	3,455	7,003	167,842	2,105	54,478	97.8	59,568	747	33,459	0.4	56.9	41.0
Chouteau	432	655	19,574	3,468	6,905	99.8	3,747	664	2,921	1.2	65.5	32.4
Custer	621	1,179	29,190	2,553	8,033	97.6	2,607	228	5,048	2.9	65.3	32.3
Daniels	220	372	10,283	5,317	2,315	99.9	2,924	1,512	1,119	0.8	68.3	29.1
Dawson	675	1,190	28,319	3,242	8,605	99.4	8,037	920	4,484	5.0	64.3	33.3
Deer Lodge	427	802	17,196	1,896	4,547	96.7	12,326	1,359	4,543	0.2	38.0	59.4
Fallon	220	419	24,335	8,924	2,280	99.9	2,287	839	1,491	8.9	79.0	19.4
Fergus	669	1,116	27,764	2,378	9,210	98.7	6,184	530	6,127	2.2	72.2	25.8
Flathead	3,333	7,005	173,875	2,245	61,168	90.5	66,350	857	38,678	14.3	67.3	30.0
Gallatin[3]	2,556	5,088	139,278	1,960	51,341	93.5	78,968	1,111	39,842	24.4	56.2	41.2
Garfield	128	146	3,860	3,103	1,568	99.8	45	36	655	-12.0	90.1	7.9
Glacier	834	1,639	41,684	3,157	8,401	99.4	4,163	315	4,562	10.6	40.1	57.9
Golden Valley	73	99	3,137	2,943	1,388	99.9	1,215	1,140	522	-1.7	75.9	22.8
Granite	222	315	8,800	3,067	2,865	99.9	4,611	1,607	1,605	0.9	71.3	25.2
Hill	994	1,821	45,688	2,793	10,748	99.1	15,690	959	6,657	1.5	52.7	45.0
Jefferson	387	760	20,585	1,976	6,711	99.6	11,178	1,073	5,868	13.7	65.5	32.1
Judith Basin	165	236	7,085	3,141	3,238	99.8	2,125	942	1,286	-7.7	73.4	25.0
Lake	1,167	2,166	55,749	2,065	16,221	98.7	16,177	599	12,576	9.9	57.6	39.4
Lewis and Clark	2,372	5,635	139,067	2,463	45,170	98.0	74,805	1,325	29,843	9.4	55.3	42.6
Liberty	154	253	6,359	3,150	2,669	99.5	2,371	1,174	1,033	-1.1	71.1	27.2
Lincoln	1,016	1,896	41,232	2,200	9,091	99.3	6,380	340	8,449	7.7	69.7	27.5
McCone	141	202	5,093	2,765	2,042	99.4	843	458	1,137	-0.4	69.6	28.1
Madison	516	836	24,463	3,511	8,576	98.5	6,898	990	3,933	7.6	72.9	25.0
Meagher	151	204	4,778	2,468	2,244	99.6	257	133	973	4.1	71.7	25.4
Mineral	265	428	11,553	3,028	3,662	99.8	4,377	1,147	1,837	12.1	67.6	29.5
Missoula	3,708	8,387	192,606	1,970	79,440	97.3	119,606	1,223	52,454	12.6	45.7	51.4
Musselshell	205	441	9,384	2,104	2,855	99.8	1,191	267	2,247	1.8	74.0	23.9
Park[3]	594	1,166	32,278	2,039	10,147	97.9	8,848	559	8,218	11.0	58.1	38.9
Petroleum	49	90	1,981	4,068	590	99.8	183	376	292	-4.6	78.1	18.8
Phillips	345	522	17,342	3,984	4,719	99.0	5,505	1,265	2,170	-2.6	77.3	21.0
Pondera	422	663	18,340	2,931	5,408	99.1	3,259	521	2,860	-1.2	64.8	33.4
Powder River	196	280	6,629	3,628	1,963	99.9	32	18	1,029	2.1	83.2	15.0
Powell	289	511	13,918	1,977	4,507	97.5	235	133	2,830	-0.1	70.4	26.9
Prairie	194	180	5,313	4,476	1,412	99.1	1,866	1,572	736	-1.3	74.2	24.6
Ravalli	1,378	2,414	61,555	1,631	19,220	98.4	24,151	640	19,867	15.3	66.8	30.9
Richland	536	1,091	26,322	2,839	7,039	99.7	9,001	971	4,308	6.8	72.2	26.0
Roosevelt	1,054	1,753	42,571	4,081	8,944	99.5	3,603	345	4,028	5.6	43.7	54.5
Rosebud	713	1,378	63,735	6,873	11,958	99.8	422,544	45,567	3,585	4.7	55.3	42.4
Sanders	509	895	24,495	2,348	8,466	99.3	2,081	199	5,153	9.2	67.2	29.2
Sheridan	278	481	15,984	4,200	4,559	99.8	1,770	465	2,038	3.7	56.9	41.5
Silver Bow	1,239	2,785	74,827	2,238	25,615	97.6	69,599	2,081	16,084	-3.7	39.7	57.9
Stillwater	376	626	20,585	2,435	8,085	99.7	7,506	888	4,213	7.5	73.3	24.3
Sweet Grass	266	432	13,421	3,704	3,418	99.9	294	81	1,983	7.4	76.1	22.4
Teton	549	854	23,859	3,776	5,374	98.3	6,532	1,034	3,359	1.4	66.5	31.2
Toole	549	879	23,201	4,360	4,176	98.8	13,132	2,468	2,311	-2.8	68.5	29.9
Treasure	78	112	3,526	4,544	2,152	99.9	723	932	482	0.6	72.2	25.1
Valley	498	782	24,402	3,299	7,167	99.3	8,808	1,191	4,018	1.4	61.6	35.6
Wheatland	251	250	5,861	2,703	2,233	99.7	35	16	979	-2.0	72.1	25.5
Wibaux	95	140	4,764	4,759	1,119	99.2	379	379	560	8.1	72.7	25.7
Yellowstone	4,882	12,380	301,916	2,289	92,520	95.1	79,818	605	66,286	15.3	61.7	36.4
Yellowstone National Park[3]	(X)	(X)	(X)	(NA)	(X)	(NA)	(X)	(NA)	(X)	(NA)	(X)	(X)

See footnotes at end of table.

[Includes United States, states, and 3,141 counties/county equivalents defined as of February 22, 2005. For more information on these areas, see Appendix C, Geographic Information]

County	Local government employment, March 2002		Local government finances, 2002						Elections, 2004[1]			
			General revenue				Total debt outstanding		Votes cast for President			
					Taxes							
	Total employment	Total payroll ($1,000)	Total ($1,000)	Per capita (dol.)	Total ($1,000)	Property, percent of total (taxes)	Amount ($1,000)	Per capita (dol.)	Total	Percent change, 2000–2004	Republican candidate, percent of total	Democratic candidate, percent of total
NEBRASKA.	100,486	228,892	5,392,362	3,123	2,323,819	75.0	5,690,799	3,296	778,186	11.6	65.9	32.7
Adams.	2,524	5,045	122,704	3,853	47,665	84.6	82,822	2,601	13,286	6.8	69.5	28.5
Antelope	702	1,016	22,069	3,040	10,128	88.1	4,575	630	3,424	1.7	80.6	17.9
Arthur	57	89	1,944	4,860	1,136	96.1	–	–	266	–2.2	90.2	9.0
Banner	70	112	3,009	3,944	1,779	93.4	–	–	437	–5.4	86.7	12.8
Blaine	65	74	2,323	4,216	1,563	95.5	–	–	339	–2.9	88.8	11.2
Boone	628	1,075	25,751	4,236	8,451	85.5	4,361	717	2,895	1.2	79.8	18.9
Box Butte.	763	1,843	47,101	3,975	14,971	70.9	8,241	696	5,152	1.2	65.9	32.2
Boyd.	263	417	13,038	5,539	5,603	86.0	885	376	1,148	–7.6	79.4	19.9
Brown	359	599	16,512	4,739	4,623	78.7	14,269	4,096	1,733	2.9	82.3	15.5
Buffalo.	1,864	3,854	107,012	2,501	45,825	73.9	35,759	836	18,608	13.0	76.4	22.0
Burt.	579	1,035	25,353	3,350	11,781	82.6	5,815	768	3,668	8.1	64.0	34.7
Butler	622	1,037	29,855	3,355	14,836	77.7	13,047	1,466	4,168	8.9	72.4	25.6
Cass	1,054	1,945	56,795	2,288	26,059	84.9	60,137	2,423	11,529	12.1	67.3	31.4
Cedar	624	1,023	25,617	2,748	12,088	80.4	8,073	866	4,536	6.3	74.7	23.9
Chase	732	732	17,186	4,299	6,926	91.2	5,541	1,386	1,973	5.2	83.7	15.3
Cherry	437	823	28,859	4,748	12,004	79.4	1,513	249	3,042	6.8	82.5	15.9
Cheyenne	739	1,410	35,714	3,595	17,143	66.7	20,688	2,083	4,746	13.4	79.9	18.8
Clay.	738	1,240	29,829	4,328	12,855	76.9	3,667	532	3,337	3.8	76.2	22.3
Colfax	601	943	23,571	2,244	11,844	88.2	12,345	1,175	3,633	9.6	71.3	27.3
Cuming	576	981	26,449	2,646	14,057	79.9	10,234	1,024	4,349	3.2	76.6	22.2
Custer	865	1,615	33,940	2,935	15,215	82.3	17,960	1,553	5,612	3.7	80.5	18.5
Dakota.	933	1,781	43,303	2,122	16,557	77.9	23,724	1,162	6,615	9.1	53.3	45.8
Dawes	462	923	23,827	2,638	8,696	71.4	7,766	860	3,994	10.3	70.3	28.0
Dawson	1,654	3,613	89,965	3,685	28,904	79.6	55,274	2,264	7,956	6.0	77.3	21.7
Deuel	189	327	8,541	4,164	4,739	74.0	2,163	1,055	1,053	1.9	77.9	21.1
Dixon.	495	769	21,832	3,530	8,424	79.3	1,449	234	3,009	7.8	67.4	31.2
Dodge	2,730	6,720	155,753	4,331	47,880	64.1	61,727	1,716	16,172	11.7	66.3	32.5
Douglas.	23,609	66,945	1,506,818	3,198	725,238	71.2	2,061,712	4,376	207,071	13.1	58.3	40.2
Dundy	219	445	10,381	4,714	3,394	95.0	366	166	1,053	4.2	81.5	17.7
Fillmore	618	976	28,464	4,401	11,663	82.7	5,866	907	3,193	6.5	72.5	25.9
Franklin	285	448	14,056	4,031	5,293	76.7	651	187	1,714	2.8	74.5	24.0
Frontier	301	551	16,127	5,404	6,071	90.7	310	104	1,467	5.3	79.1	18.8
Furnas	483	804	22,325	4,256	9,462	76.9	18,966	3,616	2,467	1.5	79.0	19.9
Gage.	1,167	2,317	62,803	2,699	24,238	78.2	50,041	2,151	10,384	9.2	63.3	35.2
Garden	301	548	13,899	6,301	6,030	92.7	392	178	1,183	–3.0	82.0	17.0
Garfield	145	225	6,658	3,515	2,188	79.3	915	483	1,017	5.6	79.3	19.3
Gosper	116	165	9,605	4,631	3,795	77.6	1,573	758	1,119	10.4	79.5	19.8
Grant.	78	108	2,547	3,523	1,952	95.6	750	1,037	396	2.9	88.9	10.4
Greeley	238	368	11,427	4,312	4,126	90.4	2,107	795	1,248	–4.7	69.3	28.9
Hall.	2,498	6,274	148,940	2,768	62,966	74.0	137,820	2,561	21,154	14.1	69.0	29.4
Hamilton	424	821	27,090	2,880	12,729	84.4	2,204	234	4,866	8.4	77.8	20.8
Harlan	249	360	11,079	3,029	3,941	76.1	956	261	1,897	2.4	77.3	21.0
Hayes	95	130	3,616	3,266	1,709	92.9	959	866	598	4.7	87.6	11.0
Hitchcock	358	575	10,305	3,383	3,650	82.1	5,063	1,662	1,486	0.4	78.8	19.9
Holt.	830	1,257	32,362	2,883	16,014	76.9	10,400	927	5,174	4.3	81.5	17.3
Hooker.	129	173	4,304	5,832	2,142	91.9	100	136	461	12.7	85.0	14.1
Howard.	562	989	28,501	4,366	7,999	84.4	5,707	874	2,979	5.4	67.8	30.2
Jefferson	509	981	24,219	2,943	11,956	81.8	5,485	667	4,011	4.3	64.8	33.7
Johnson.	371	649	19,263	4,409	8,023	83.9	13,826	3,165	2,394	13.4	61.4	37.0
Kearney.	537	953	24,859	3,646	11,701	83.5	7,485	1,098	3,379	8.2	77.6	20.9
Keith	493	960	26,969	3,009	12,579	74.6	3,638	417	4,137	7.5	81.1	18.0
Keya Paha	61	58	2,473	2,614	1,633	94.9	321	339	549	7.0	80.5	17.9
Kimball	311	716	22,029	5,549	6,693	68.3	4,365	1,099	1,877	3.1	79.4	19.5
Knox	656	894	25,018	2,750	10,050	81.5	8,481	932	4,213	5.9	72.7	25.8
Lancaster	14,193	32,582	764,905	2,984	336,269	75.5	889,501	3,470	124,509	16.2	56.0	42.4
Lincoln.	1,877	4,189	120,021	3,479	54,542	59.8	59,679	1,730	16,199	7.2	68.3	30.3
Logan	82	106	2,782	3,704	1,392	85.1	99	132	429	4.1	83.2	15.6
Loup	65	104	1,820	2,423	1,069	94.4	104	138	386	2.1	81.4	17.6
McPherson	38	55	1,662	3,033	1,113	97.0	418	763	312	3.7	83.0	15.7
Madison.	2,269	4,438	122,063	3,397	51,180	72.5	45,867	1,277	14,089	9.6	77.9	20.8
Merrick	562	988	31,858	3,935	10,540	78.1	16,840	2,080	3,657	9.5	75.8	22.8
Morrill	434	700	21,674	4,099	7,071	74.8	9,196	1,739	2,293	7.2	76.5	21.6
Nance	298	453	15,338	3,952	6,040	89.8	2,749	708	1,731	4.0	71.5	26.5
Nemaha	564	1,176	32,629	4,480	7,558	85.1	1,703	234	3,715	10.3	69.9	28.7
Nuckolls	162	260	6,795	1,399	2,776	68.0	703	145	2,471	1.1	76.2	21.9
Otoe	940	1,855	42,125	2,726	18,983	80.5	18,893	1,222	7,386	10.9	67.9	30.8
Pawnee	232	428	11,711	3,893	3,509	89.2	2,369	788	1,483	–2.4	66.5	32.4
Perkins	516	881	16,414	5,324	5,430	86.1	1,839	596	1,558	7.3	82.5	16.8
Phelps.	645	1,180	29,417	3,033	15,086	72.1	7,295	752	4,743	2.5	81.6	17.5
Pierce	531	935	27,769	3,591	10,566	71.9	10,228	1,322	3,398	5.9	83.1	16.1

See footnotes at end of table.

Table B-13. Counties — **Local Government Finances and Elections**—Con.

[Includes United States, states, and 3,141 counties/county equivalents defined as of February 22, 2005. For more information on these areas, see Appendix C, Geographic Information]

County	Local government employment, March 2002		Local government finances, 2002						Elections, 2004[1]			
			General revenue				Total debt outstanding		Votes cast for President			
					Taxes						Repub-lican cand-idate, percent of total	Demo-cratic cand-idate, percent of total
	Total employ-ment	Total payroll ($1,000)	Total ($1,000)	Per capita (dol.)	Total ($1,000)	Prop-erty, percent of total (taxes)	Amount ($1,000)	Per capita (dol.)	Total	Percent change, 2000–2004		
NEBRASKA—Con.												
Platte	3,875	14,665	93,442	2,989	33,218	76.4	1,350,923	43,212	13,987	8.8	79.6	19.0
Polk	449	752	21,148	3,834	11,153	87.0	2,911	528	2,727	4.4	78.7	20.1
Red Willow	675	1,222	34,355	3,041	12,836	74.0	9,966	882	5,258	4.6	78.5	20.1
Richardson	585	1,052	23,118	2,537	9,919	85.3	7,163	786	4,278	3.1	68.4	30.3
Rock	191	295	5,896	3,497	3,317	79.7	685	406	883	−1.2	83.8	14.7
Saline	788	1,393	51,058	3,627	17,639	76.6	15,646	1,112	5,566	8.2	55.2	43.5
Sarpy	4,014	9,886	281,303	2,178	116,003	75.8	241,837	1,873	58,334	28.8	68.9	29.9
Saunders	1,239	2,276	52,062	2,619	23,300	84.2	22,491	1,131	9,489	6.4	67.9	30.4
Scotts Bluff	2,404	4,793	124,148	3,380	44,508	64.1	14,466	394	14,390	4.0	72.1	26.7
Seward	754	1,611	44,349	2,666	22,665	83.5	22,325	1,342	7,565	7.8	70.8	27.9
Sheridan	707	1,357	27,640	4,611	8,080	76.5	6,100	1,018	2,599	0.9	82.2	16.5
Sherman	213	326	8,434	2,658	3,879	89.3	5,732	1,806	1,643	−3.6	65.3	32.9
Sioux	95	115	4,099	2,817	2,962	94.1	292	201	809	7.6	83.7	15.2
Stanton	186	328	10,496	1,609	4,242	93.0	22,972	3,521	2,745	10.4	78.7	20.4
Thayer	374	603	26,481	4,617	10,664	84.5	3,728	650	2,878	−4.3	72.1	26.6
Thomas	78	93	2,784	4,088	1,626	94.5	232	341	444	12.4	85.1	13.5
Thurston	561	1,133	26,918	3,797	4,557	84.1	22,053	3,110	2,387	14.6	48.4	50.8
Valley	605	1,237	23,622	5,181	5,857	83.9	4,901	1,075	2,391	5.7	75.3	23.6
Washington	770	1,640	45,532	2,360	23,950	81.1	20,768	1,076	9,950	15.3	71.2	27.7
Wayne	460	1,110	26,884	2,815	12,318	70.8	9,304	974	4,085	3.7	72.7	25.9
Webster	283	434	15,108	3,884	5,467	74.4	3,273	841	2,002	2.9	70.1	27.8
Wheeler	62	89	2,612	3,106	1,798	92.5	23	27	453	–	80.8	17.9
York	742	1,417	37,901	2,636	21,750	69.5	23,031	1,602	6,797	5.2	79.3	19.2
NEVADA	78,394	261,047	7,998,424	3,690	2,487,235	63.9	12,105,157	5,584	829,587	36.2	50.5	47.9
Churchill	1,158	3,302	91,763	3,784	12,744	84.9	29,474	1,216	10,237	16.0	71.7	26.4
Clark	52,961	184,192	5,571,314	3,676	1,770,409	62.4	9,579,519	6,321	545,397	42.7	46.8	51.7
Douglas	1,842	5,364	145,332	3,362	48,660	68.7	49,622	1,148	23,898	33.0	63.6	34.6
Elko	1,874	5,218	143,395	3,216	27,496	64.3	35,057	786	15,309	8.0	78.0	19.9
Esmeralda	119	217	5,368	5,998	1,782	96.5	–	–	481	−2.0	76.3	20.6
Eureka	200	528	14,492	9,001	7,233	97.6	1,238	769	738	−11.8	77.4	19.5
Humboldt	971	2,689	73,592	4,559	16,177	76.5	104,941	6,501	5,367	6.7	72.6	25.4
Lander	408	1,134	29,101	5,605	11,678	81.8	11,535	2,222	2,053	−3.1	78.0	20.2
Lincoln	397	972	22,525	5,320	4,157	93.5	6,090	1,438	2,047	4.7	77.1	20.4
Lyon	1,435	3,685	91,424	2,405	24,230	82.4	55,180	1,451	17,151	43.0	64.9	32.9
Mineral	387	914	25,627	5,377	3,505	79.7	5,220	1,095	2,327	1.5	57.4	40.0
Nye	1,151	3,841	112,472	3,250	26,899	88.0	57,698	1,667	14,510	19.1	58.5	38.7
Pershing	440	1,184	29,517	4,495	5,635	83.6	10,688	1,628	1,917	6.4	70.0	28.1
Storey	179	457	11,601	3,391	4,686	76.9	2,874	840	2,168	20.6	57.8	40.2
Washoe	11,631	38,368	1,377,957	3,810	478,518	63.5	2,023,287	5,595	159,079	30.1	51.3	47.1
White Pine	459	1,192	28,888	3,342	5,182	80.1	16,258	1,881	3,802	7.3	68.5	28.5
Independent City												
Carson City	2,782	7,790	224,056	4,108	38,244	64.8	116,476	2,135	23,106	18.8	57.0	40.9
NEW HAMPSHIRE	55,489	131,378	3,440,977	2,700	1,701,841	98.0	1,824,741	1,432	677,738	19.1	48.9	50.2
Belknap	2,819	6,852	196,310	3,318	101,665	98.8	61,186	1,034	32,298	20.5	55.5	43.6
Carroll	2,507	4,879	137,949	3,046	73,199	98.9	29,805	658	28,222	18.2	51.8	47.2
Cheshire	4,139	8,947	205,502	2,736	102,427	98.9	63,160	841	41,347	23.8	39.8	59.1
Coos	2,093	3,718	103,783	3,108	45,074	99.4	52,975	1,587	16,925	15.9	48.1	50.7
Grafton	4,497	9,687	259,045	3,134	135,419	98.8	82,999	1,004	46,971	21.3	43.2	55.7
Hillsborough	14,488	39,195	1,031,564	2,632	467,338	96.9	822,797	2,099	195,427	17.9	51.0	48.2
Merrimack	6,487	14,941	363,254	2,562	181,727	98.6	220,874	1,558	76,647	20.4	47.1	52.2
Rockingham	11,545	28,503	750,022	2,607	403,716	98.6	259,124	901	158,816	18.4	51.7	47.5
Strafford	4,818	10,894	285,155	2,456	137,533	96.1	192,473	1,658	59,281	20.0	43.6	55.6
Sullivan	2,096	3,763	108,393	2,615	53,743	98.5	39,348	949	21,804	16.8	46.5	52.4
NEW JERSEY	391,066	1,373,633	31,721,374	3,699	16,299,990	98.4	25,497,303	2,973	3,611,691	13.3	46.6	52.9
Atlantic	15,042	48,164	1,129,011	4,355	549,731	98.0	965,013	3,723	106,097	16.5	47.4	52.5
Bergen	37,578	143,052	3,273,361	3,659	2,069,794	99.2	1,563,790	1,748	400,244	9.1	46.1	51.9
Burlington	20,671	65,062	1,598,088	3,652	850,268	98.2	1,192,235	2,725	207,956	17.1	36.9	53.1
Camden	27,379	95,665	2,375,784	4,642	796,824	98.9	3,173,286	6,200	220,933	12.2	56.8	62.4
Cape May	6,604	20,502	518,294	5,094	278,755	97.2	515,325	5,064	50,762	6.7	45.8	42.3
Cumberland	8,907	27,238	601,207	4,062	134,598	98.0	275,045	1,858	53,185	9.2	28.8	52.4
Essex	33,855	135,247	2,956,511	3,712	1,333,432	95.8	2,201,633	2,765	289,348	11.5	46.9	70.4
Gloucester	13,360	41,394	905,631	3,444	415,017	99.0	804,887	3,061	127,964	19.3	32.0	52.2
Hudson	20,817	73,173	1,973,439	3,237	755,763	97.6	1,545,893	2,535	189,446	13.2	59.8	67.3
Hunterdon	5,709	19,416	631,664	4,984	476,924	99.2	391,811	3,092	66,680	18.1	37.9	39.1
Mercer	18,903	67,903	1,637,723	4,581	796,622	98.8	1,564,859	4,377	149,510	10.3	42.8	61.3
Middlesex	34,537	117,729	2,481,128	3,222	1,396,310	98.2	2,413,013	3,134	295,805	14.3	54.6	56.3
Monmouth	30,700	109,653	2,453,662	3,906	1,335,183	98.6	2,068,461	3,293	299,939	14.4	57.5	44.6
Morris	21,826	80,881	1,755,068	3,667	1,171,667	99.1	1,255,435	2,623	235,154	13.9	60.2	41.7
Ocean	22,057	70,800	1,629,819	3,033	904,471	98.6	1,469,184	2,734	256,306	18.4	43.9	39.0

See footnotes at end of table.

[Includes United States, states, and 3,141 counties/county equivalents defined as of February 22, 2005. For more information on these areas, see Appendix C, Geographic Information]

County	Local government employment, March 2002		Local government finances, 2002							Elections, 2004[1]			
			General revenue				Total debt outstanding		Votes cast for President				
					Taxes								
	Total employ- ment	Total payroll ($1,000)	Total ($1,000)	Per capita (dol.)	Total ($1,000)	Prop- erty, percent of total (taxes)	Amount ($1,000)	Per capita (dol.)	Total	Percent change, 2000– 2004	Repub- lican cand- idate, percent of total	Demo- cratic cand- idate, percent of total
NEW JERSEY—Con.												
Passaic	18,304	66,748	1,452,126	2,922	753,651	99.3	897,776	1,806	171,311	9.4	52.8	55.4
Salem	3,967	12,155	282,425	4,362	99,447	98.5	521,705	8,058	29,781	10.4	51.7	46.2
Somerset	12,369	45,628	1,100,553	3,575	706,433	98.7	849,706	2,760	140,279	16.5	64.1	47.4
Sussex	7,144	23,389	531,168	3,569	297,782	99.1	342,196	2,299	69,396	20.7	40.6	34.6
Union	25,465	90,951	2,035,232	3,844	985,458	98.8	1,242,378	2,346	203,387	9.1	61.3	58.7
Warren	5,872	18,885	399,480	3,717	191,860	99.0	243,672	2,267	48,208	18.2	46.2	37.4
NEW MEXICO	81,800	193,774	5,162,757	2,783	1,249,559	56.3	4,109,904	2,215	756,304	26.3	49.8	49.1
Bernalillo	22,723	59,188	1,601,041	2,798	477,412	60.2	1,405,484	2,456	256,811	25.7	47.3	51.5
Catron	158	276	9,438	2,699	841	95.8	2,000	572	1,993	16.5	71.6	27.7
Chaves	2,691	6,084	161,827	2,662	33,337	47.6	94,492	1,554	21,705	19.6	68.1	31.0
Cibola	807	1,738	50,531	1,877	9,554	44.2	21,440	796	7,487	5.6	46.4	52.3
Colfax	814	1,807	54,741	3,853	10,031	56.2	13,609	958	5,968	9.3	51.6	47.3
Curry	2,367	4,785	121,090	2,706	20,322	42.9	34,391	769	14,286	19.4	74.5	24.8
De Baca	129	255	7,606	3,559	817	71.0	3,673	1,719	993	1.1	71.1	28.3
Dona Ana	8,040	19,190	459,499	2,573	110,697	49.2	268,618	1,504	61,960	32.8	47.7	51.3
Eddy	2,538	6,396	157,070	3,061	36,908	49.3	54,968	1,071	20,270	14.0	65.5	33.9
Grant	1,837	4,774	106,167	3,492	13,265	50.0	32,282	1,062	13,392	19.1	45.8	53.0
Guadalupe	311	575	23,712	5,111	4,150	63.3	5,964	1,286	2,267	37.3	40.3	59.1
Harding	93	155	5,081	6,784	481	83.4	1,157	1,545	644	8.6	59.0	40.2
Hidalgo	370	734	20,215	3,779	4,313	79.2	6,972	1,303	1,964	7.1	55.0	43.8
Lea	3,432	7,195	178,771	3,207	40,832	38.1	36,208	650	18,181	27.5	79.4	20.1
Lincoln	997	2,293	67,433	3,417	16,390	71.3	30,799	1,560	9,014	33.1	67.3	31.3
Los Alamos	1,441	4,025	128,618	7,053	18,671	48.0	113,843	6,243	11,197	9.6	51.9	46.5
Luna	1,223	2,700	63,804	2,527	8,589	54.9	13,500	535	7,593	14.8	54.8	44.0
McKinley	3,365	12,226	201,119	2,727	28,072	52.4	78,990	1,071	20,623	29.9	35.6	63.3
Mora	288	536	15,735	3,005	1,515	74.1	2,855	545	2,826	29.0	32.8	66.4
Otero	1,978	4,172	109,293	1,772	23,021	54.4	16,573	755	20,764	28.1	67.7	31.0
Quay	772	1,527	37,042	3,818	6,937	41.1	9,244	953	4,117	7.1	64.6	34.5
Rio Arriba	1,669	2,840	98,050	2,391	23,877	75.7	47,188	1,151	14,999	24.0	34.3	65.0
Roosevelt	868	1,623	43,113	2,371	6,637	48.5	17,038	937	7,144	26.4	70.0	29.1
Sandoval	3,211	7,431	210,337	2,182	50,995	59.9	102,269	1,061	44,541	40.3	50.8	48.1
San Juan	6,041	14,536	414,147	3,453	85,402	55.0	1,050,005	8,754	45,006	29.9	65.6	33.0
San Miguel	1,615	3,325	90,183	3,042	15,396	58.9	27,439	926	12,116	32.3	27.3	71.7
Santa Fe	5,119	9,518	355,093	2,633	129,015	54.6	435,636	3,231	66,200	33.8	27.9	71.1
Sierra	627	1,189	27,364	2,106	5,934	55.6	12,963	998	5,157	12.5	61.3	37.4
Socorro	722	1,651	42,934	2,390	10,161	69.4	6,176	344	7,851	15.0	47.1	51.3
Taos	1,353	2,968	79,374	2,576	16,684	52.7	29,524	958	14,835	36.2	24.7	74.1
Torrance	1,126	2,209	57,280	3,428	8,216	76.5	24,947	1,493	6,507	31.2	61.9	36.7
Union	313	558	17,211	4,344	2,609	61.6	745	188	1,881	7.2	77.3	21.9
Valencia	2,762	5,295	147,838	2,170	27,678	59.3	78,912	1,158	26,012	21.7	55.6	43.3
NEW YORK	1,052,354	3,970,678	105,031,843	5,480	45,615,975	58.8	107,338,897	5,601	7,391,036	8.3	40.1	58.4
Albany	15,185	47,320	1,195,839	4,041	596,096	63.3	945,289	3,194	147,199	3.7	37.3	60.7
Allegany	3,154	6,908	203,600	4,042	62,107	75.7	216,710	4,302	19,270	3.1	63.9	34.1
Bronx	(4)	(4)	(4)	(4)	(4)	(4)	(4)	(4)	342,929	11.3	16.5	82.8
Broome	12,507	33,846	813,418	4,072	306,998	68.5	540,239	2,704	91,890	5.5	47.4	50.4
Cattaraugus	5,821	14,489	401,721	4,819	123,655	64.2	286,656	3,439	34,262	1.6	58.5	39.4
Cayuga	4,618	11,399	304,732	3,740	104,136	69.3	202,863	2,490	36,052	6.1	49.2	48.6
Chautauqua	9,488	25,020	605,953	4,379	183,021	76.6	457,360	3,305	60,942	3.8	53.2	44.7
Chemung	4,397	11,006	333,862	3,683	109,681	65.8	230,561	2,543	39,075	3.6	54.6	43.7
Chenango	3,476	7,965	209,246	4,067	62,880	82.5	153,793	2,989	21,341	5.4	54.3	43.5
Clinton	4,679	12,470	316,661	3,920	103,376	69.2	193,825	2,399	33,736	10.4	45.4	52.2
Columbia	3,836	9,546	248,245	3,929	114,339	76.1	129,129	2,044	31,103	8.4	46.5	51.2
Cortland	2,840	7,076	184,752	3,811	62,162	68.6	153,837	3,174	22,760	9.8	51.0	46.9
Delaware	3,631	8,072	229,004	4,839	81,374	87.4	136,495	2,884	21,166	4.9	56.5	41.2
Dutchess	14,189	42,480	1,052,457	3,655	535,766	75.7	770,304	2,675	123,881	10.8	51.2	47.0
Erie	48,072	159,351	3,816,536	4,052	1,402,166	69.9	2,390,503	2,538	445,138	4.8	41.4	56.4
Essex	2,432	5,647	184,685	4,744	86,702	79.4	120,794	3,103	19,082	6.4	51.7	46.0
Franklin	3,348	7,618	222,811	4,389	61,825	80.3	194,222	3,826	18,316	5.0	45.8	52.1
Fulton	3,408	7,917	234,038	4,253	75,640	76.2	209,914	3,814	22,215	2.5	56.6	41.4
Genesee	4,321	11,130	273,944	4,573	91,646	68.0	184,418	3,078	27,580	5.8	60.6	37.5
Greene	2,695	6,757	182,789	3,769	93,502	78.7	98,378	2,028	22,398	6.2	58.0	39.9
Hamilton	611	1,180	39,251	7,440	27,108	90.6	14,609	2,769	3,692	0.3	67.0	31.0
Herkimer	4,611	10,213	259,851	4,079	84,698	74.8	200,356	3,145	28,310	2.2	56.6	41.2
Jefferson	6,264	16,011	430,854	3,782	127,637	71.2	354,935	3,115	38,800	6.5	54.7	43.5
Kings	4462,697	42,068,619	455,539,943	422,401	422,235,234	440.0	472,168,531	429,108	687,780	11.5	24.3	74.9
Lewis	2,290	5,079	135,652	5,094	32,044	80.5	101,662	3,818	11,397	4.3	58.1	39.9
Livingston	3,608	9,582	242,173	3,753	77,797	79.4	213,213	3,304	29,948	10.0	59.2	38.4
Madison	3,757	9,704	243,434	3,488	86,108	84.0	168,245	2,411	30,287	6.8	54.6	43.3
Monroe	40,344	125,965	3,103,377	4,215	1,241,353	75.2	2,216,510	3,010	342,981	7.9	47.7	50.6
Montgomery	3,138	7,634	214,610	4,358	68,594	75.1	180,554	3,667	21,221	2.0	53.4	44.5
Nassau	68,663	283,533	7,189,199	5,368	4,614,173	80.3	6,410,328	4,786	618,343	4.9	46.6	52.3

See footnotes at end of table.

Table B-13. Counties — **Local Government Finances and Elections**—Con.

[Includes United States, states, and 3,141 counties/county equivalents defined as of February 22, 2005. For more information on these areas, see Appendix C, Geographic Information]

County	Local government employment, March 2002		Local government finances, 2002						Elections, 2004[1]			
			General revenue				Total debt outstanding		Votes cast for President			
					Taxes							
	Total employment	Total payroll ($1,000)	Total ($1,000)	Per capita (dol.)	Total ($1,000)	Property, percent of total (taxes)	Amount ($1,000)	Per capita (dol.)	Total	Percent change, 2000–2004	Republican candidate, percent of total	Democratic candidate, percent of total
NEW YORK—Con.												
New York	(4)	(4)	(4)	(4)	(4)	(4)	(4)	(4)	641,747	13.9	16.7	82.1
Niagara	11,803	35,985	915,033	4,192	325,045	74.9	1,023,978	4,691	96,580	3.6	48.8	49.3
Oneida	12,633	33,790	889,819	3,802	306,235	66.9	745,156	3,184	95,369	-0.7	54.9	42.8
Onondaga	25,475	79,510	1,831,634	3,996	668,789	68.4	1,437,333	3,136	214,589	5.4	43.8	54.2
Ontario	6,603	17,812	442,903	4,348	184,389	69.5	301,681	2,961	50,102	9.0	55.9	42.3
Orange	18,499	58,990	1,471,311	4,130	679,560	76.5	947,962	2,661	144,673	14.3	54.7	43.8
Orleans	2,224	6,030	161,393	3,700	51,758	75.9	125,906	2,887	16,573	4.6	62.3	36.0
Oswego	7,591	20,463	524,906	4,277	180,671	79.9	298,752	2,434	51,607	6.5	51.0	46.8
Otsego	3,533	8,081	223,612	3,609	82,357	74.0	139,340	2,249	26,652	5.1	50.1	47.7
Putnam	4,139	16,017	383,814	3,887	240,629	85.5	217,699	2,204	46,563	9.4	56.6	42.0
Queens	(4)	(4)	(4)	(4)	(4)	(4)	(4)	(4)	605,062	8.8	27.4	71.7
Rensselaer	8,609	24,648	630,274	4,133	221,992	75.8	501,988	3,292	72,514	6.0	47.9	49.8
Richmond	(4)	(4)	(4)	(4)	(4)	(4)	(4)	(4)	160,126	12.7	56.4	42.8
Rockland	15,292	56,706	1,386,545	4,758	805,831	83.3	615,662	2,113	131,231	7.1	49.6	48.9
St. Lawrence	6,239	15,441	458,319	4,122	132,151	71.2	302,278	2,718	41,755	5.0	43.2	54.7
Saratoga	9,161	23,986	690,387	3,335	323,088	72.9	428,261	2,069	106,873	12.4	52.6	45.6
Schenectady	7,284	22,050	596,579	4,064	251,931	72.7	387,488	2,640	69,469	3.8	46.2	51.8
Schoharie	2,051	5,006	132,730	4,194	48,694	80.8	92,204	2,913	14,557	7.4	59.0	38.7
Schuyler	971	2,020	65,157	3,356	21,620	74.6	60,202	3,100	8,590	5.4	57.7	40.1
Seneca	1,946	4,369	123,646	3,537	43,137	72.2	90,205	2,580	15,325	6.9	52.1	45.5
Steuben	6,905	18,293	456,484	4,589	144,449	73.0	274,901	2,764	42,284	4.2	63.8	34.4
Suffolk	67,120	261,421	6,963,192	4,786	3,968,847	76.6	4,734,154	3,254	638,712	11.3	48.5	49.5
Sullivan	4,850	13,957	384,744	5,191	173,508	85.8	186,102	2,511	30,966	8.6	49.5	48.6
Tioga	2,791	6,691	169,615	3,275	54,568	75.2	91,123	1,759	23,902	6.4	57.6	40.6
Tompkins	5,097	13,896	348,351	3,543	151,290	71.2	250,721	2,550	42,402	5.8	33.0	64.2
Ulster	9,411	26,939	735,554	4,081	370,473	77.3	358,069	1,987	87,712	12.1	43.1	54.3
Warren	4,006	10,336	280,235	4,372	138,845	72.0	126,659	1,976	31,059	8.5	54.6	43.2
Washington	4,147	9,757	247,037	4,019	81,311	81.8	149,686	2,435	25,103	6.6	55.1	42.3
Wayne	6,222	15,572	393,828	4,200	129,311	83.5	243,590	2,598	41,200	7.5	60.0	38.1
Westchester	45,672	180,272	5,455,002	5,817	2,899,895	81.6	3,371,013	3,594	395,770	6.5	40.3	58.1
Wyoming	2,678	6,224	176,936	4,109	47,209	72.6	119,384	2,772	18,164	3.0	64.7	33.8
Yates	1,322	2,878	80,166	3,269	36,574	82.4	73,167	2,984	10,711	6.6	58.9	39.3
NORTH CAROLINA	391,764	967,993	24,592,246	2,958	7,039,053	77.0	22,332,254	2,687	3,501,007	20.3	56.0	43.6
Alamance	5,169	12,953	289,627	2,136	83,262	76.4	133,046	981	54,175	15.0	61.5	38.2
Alexander	1,205	2,568	56,000	1,626	15,355	66.2	16,256	472	15,600	15.6	70.1	29.6
Alleghany	470	1,043	22,976	2,122	7,330	76.0	4,881	451	4,827	11.9	59.7	39.8
Anson	1,510	3,138	70,543	2,791	14,037	75.5	16,646	659	9,225	15.5	41.2	58.7
Ashe	910	1,954	46,870	1,886	15,318	72.2	17,075	687	11,823	14.6	61.7	37.9
Avery	771	1,573	39,770	2,247	14,367	75.3	15,429	872	7,524	12.4	75.5	24.0
Beaufort	2,502	5,581	151,108	3,338	30,721	75.0	100,204	2,214	19,522	12.8	63.7	36.0
Bertie	944	1,925	47,492	2,420	10,032	78.4	33,320	1,698	8,032	11.9	38.1	61.5
Bladen	1,991	4,233	122,784	3,783	22,112	78.8	40,248	1,240	12,313	12.9	50.1	49.6
Brunswick	3,240	7,421	244,996	3,106	101,788	79.7	114,696	1,454	37,977	31.7	60.4	39.2
Buncombe	9,674	22,216	538,641	2,560	185,498	73.4	363,705	1,728	105,013	22.9	50.0	49.4
Burke	4,168	9,036	208,298	2,334	50,823	87.5	58,453	655	30,762	0.3	61.5	38.1
Cabarrus	5,127	13,215	337,674	2,415	129,388	80.6	348,750	2,495	60,824	23.2	67.1	32.6
Caldwell	3,387	7,990	173,211	2,200	43,048	74.6	36,366	462	31,348	20.0	67.6	31.9
Camden	290	694	19,483	2,622	5,322	76.7	11,088	1,492	3,830	35.3	64.8	35.0
Carteret	2,747	6,163	220,234	3,656	62,831	73.5	99,258	1,648	25,575	-3.3	69.3	30.2
Caswell	881	1,965	45,242	1,909	10,182	67.8	14,979	632	9,437	12.1	51.6	48.1
Catawba	7,824	19,771	585,567	3,999	118,071	76.5	224,675	1,534	58,688	15.4	67.5	32.1
Chatham	1,611	3,934	104,087	1,935	43,788	78.1	42,148	784	25,922	23.8	49.7	49.8
Cherokee	1,182	2,612	61,831	2,502	14,568	65.0	13,557	549	11,199	15.8	67.1	32.5
Chowan	685	1,647	35,092	2,470	9,241	73.1	21,357	1,503	5,386	10.1	55.1	44.7
Clay	353	749	19,179	2,095	4,977	66.2	2,445	267	4,866	26.3	66.0	33.5
Cleveland	5,593	13,875	418,769	4,286	62,980	79.1	168,947	1,729	37,079	13.2	61.4	38.3
Columbus	3,014	6,255	152,125	2,778	29,851	76.9	90,802	1,658	21,191	15.0	50.8	48.8
Craven	4,619	10,620	377,075	4,136	53,480	71.3	141,986	1,558	37,756	18.0	62.4	37.1
Cumberland	18,668	49,116	1,036,550	3,405	210,017	77.0	657,754	2,161	95,226	23.4	51.6	48.1
Currituck	839	1,933	62,480	3,185	30,473	69.2	17,211	877	8,976	33.2	67.0	32.4
Dare	1,600	4,365	127,350	3,965	70,221	68.2	65,266	2,032	15,548	19.6	60.1	39.5
Davidson	5,925	14,140	297,469	1,973	90,387	75.7	79,882	530	59,496	14.3	70.7	28.9
Davie	1,488	3,300	71,925	1,961	23,700	78.1	17,697	482	16,680	19.2	74.2	25.4
Duplin	2,890	5,826	131,318	2,594	29,416	77.5	48,970	967	16,583	15.2	58.0	41.8
Durham	10,419	28,442	684,919	2,933	272,889	80.9	614,117	2,630	109,651	29.6	31.6	68.0
Edgecombe	2,684	5,696	156,691	2,856	32,640	79.9	23,926	436	21,079	15.8	38.7	61.1
Forsyth	13,376	35,111	793,033	2,523	296,899	79.7	666,683	2,121	139,125	15.0	54.1	45.5
Franklin	1,740	4,011	102,196	2,020	32,382	76.9	55,900	1,105	20,918	30.3	55.2	44.4

See footnotes at end of table.

Table B-13. Counties — **Local Government Finances and Elections**—Con.

[Includes United States, states, and 3,141 counties/county equivalents defined as of February 22, 2005. For more information on these areas, see Appendix C, Geographic Information]

County	Local government employment, March 2002		Local government finances, 2002				Total debt outstanding		Elections, 2004[1]			
			General revenue		Taxes				Votes cast for President			
	Total employ-ment	Total payroll ($1,000)	Total ($1,000)	Per capita (dol.)	Total ($1,000)	Prop-erty, percent of total (taxes)	Amount ($1,000)	Per capita (dol.)	Total	Percent change, 2000–2004	Repub-lican cand-idate, percent of total	Demo-cratic cand-idate, percent of total
NORTH CAROLINA—Con.												
Gaston	9,124	22,490	489,610	2,536	148,692	81.6	306,417	1,587	63,755	7.7	67.8	31.8
Gates	492	1,114	21,970	2,068	5,292	74.8	47,908	4,509	4,053	17.6	47.5	52.3
Graham	412	858	21,479	2,658	4,364	70.1	4,438	549	3,987	18.6	67.5	31.9
Granville	1,644	3,927	110,878	2,141	26,126	72.2	48,112	929	18,601	22.4	51.0	48.7
Greene	750	1,604	43,602	2,232	9,129	74.5	5,994	307	6,472	10.3	58.7	41.2
Guilford	18,420	48,357	1,200,559	2,791	441,932	81.1	848,848	1,973	199,314	19.9	49.3	50.2
Halifax	3,387	7,071	166,617	2,948	36,825	77.4	89,136	1,577	19,647	15.8	41.2	58.7
Harnett	3,473	8,487	191,986	1,982	48,122	71.6	122,674	1,267	32,571	34.8	64.2	35.5
Haywood	3,580	7,762	153,803	2,794	40,616	74.9	112,449	2,042	25,932	16.4	56.1	43.3
Henderson	4,839	11,293	296,070	3,203	65,939	73.5	92,257	998	43,234	12.0	64.8	34.7
Hertford	1,589	3,192	83,151	3,493	15,454	76.0	89,856	3,775	8,132	3.0	36.2	63.2
Hoke	1,221	2,824	59,926	1,659	13,418	76.3	16,937	469	11,088	29.2	47.4	52.3
Hyde	326	719	22,173	3,864	5,583	74.1	3,787	660	2,293	2.5	53.9	45.7
Iredell	5,111	12,286	270,891	2,076	95,448	74.4	122,781	941	56,973	25.0	67.9	31.7
Jackson	1,506	2,955	72,723	2,146	25,545	69.5	24,225	715	14,174	16.9	51.9	47.5
Johnston	6,515	15,168	361,351	2,719	92,162	73.6	238,934	1,798	54,357	32.1	67.9	31.8
Jones	437	973	30,054	2,928	5,153	76.9	1,105	108	4,513	13.8	57.8	42.0
Lee	2,879	6,441	138,272	2,656	40,551	80.8	70,328	1,351	19,543	20.0	60.6	39.2
Lenoir	4,061	9,489	218,185	3,709	41,584	77.6	55,111	937	23,179	9.5	55.8	44.0
Lincoln	2,224	5,460	137,638	2,078	45,266	74.7	130,500	1,970	29,579	20.6	67.8	31.9
McDowell	1,854	3,966	81,410	1,904	21,171	67.6	27,929	653	16,002	14.2	66.2	33.3
Macon	1,251	2,876	66,767	2,164	27,406	74.7	28,284	917	15,024	13.5	62.9	36.5
Madison	907	1,683	48,103	2,413	9,946	76.4	6,748	339	9,463	13.7	54.7	44.7
Martin	1,587	3,303	99,886	3,971	18,572	78.6	368,051	14,632	10,452	11.6	51.0	48.8
Mecklenburg	39,015	114,686	3,753,092	5,107	1,088,967	76.9	4,197,083	5,711	323,102	22.8	48.0	51.6
Mitchell	917	1,854	42,578	2,687	9,243	69.3	4,516	285	7,798	18.2	72.9	26.7
Montgomery	1,260	2,885	66,982	2,478	15,265	76.9	36,322	1,344	10,080	12.3	57.0	42.8
Moore	3,898	9,116	178,021	2,285	58,329	77.2	77,287	992	38,382	22.6	64.4	35.3
Nash	7,188	18,202	438,072	4,928	65,171	78.4	48,957	551	37,673	23.5	58.1	41.7
New Hanover	11,239	32,740	935,371	5,645	209,769	78.9	705,002	4,255	81,247	22.5	55.8	43.8
Northampton	1,007	2,132	58,334	2,669	13,606	82.3	19,394	887	8,770	7.0	36.2	63.7
Onslow	6,014	12,760	370,159	2,472	72,782	69.8	105,922	707	37,277	23.4	69.5	30.2
Orange	5,213	13,747	332,227	2,838	145,734	83.4	241,556	2,063	64,153	30.0	32.4	66.9
Pamlico	690	1,470	35,751	2,777	8,647	78.2	11,618	903	6,038	15.2	60.9	38.7
Pasquotank	3,930	8,831	204,902	5,757	23,951	72.9	63,259	1,777	13,648	25.2	48.4	51.2
Pender	1,659	3,551	97,792	2,282	29,815	76.6	39,744	927	17,085	20.7	58.8	41.0
Perquimans	501	1,070	29,814	2,566	6,712	78.2	8,337	718	4,958	15.1	59.8	39.8
Person	1,749	3,956	99,021	2,706	29,620	79.4	133,959	3,661	15,214	28.6	59.0	40.7
Pitt	6,568	16,171	359,997	2,629	87,512	73.3	226,244	1,652	53,643	24.5	53.3	46.5
Polk	576	1,459	34,718	1,846	13,654	80.1	8,513	453	9,021	8.6	57.0	42.0
Randolph	4,976	11,500	258,014	1,931	78,798	76.1	136,802	1,024	50,910	19.2	74.2	25.5
Richmond	2,471	5,494	127,336	2,718	25,921	73.5	20,976	448	16,145	13.1	47.8	51.9
Robeson	6,017	13,750	292,114	2,342	62,997	71.8	87,784	704	33,871	13.9	47.0	52.8
Rockingham	4,314	9,793	221,606	2,393	61,912	80.0	95,606	1,032	37,388	14.9	61.1	38.6
Rowan	5,287	12,738	276,183	2,068	85,604	78.6	138,666	1,038	51,867	17.5	67.3	32.3
Rutherford	3,120	6,946	153,320	2,422	36,657	72.6	60,598	957	24,658	13.5	66.3	33.2
Sampson	2,743	6,120	143,666	2,349	31,543	73.8	92,495	1,512	22,288	15.8	56.5	43.3
Scotland	2,004	4,650	95,979	2,682	26,608	78.2	34,694	969	11,547	22.8	44.5	55.3
Stanly	2,774	6,287	135,372	2,308	40,161	78.1	56,255	959	25,553	12.0	69.7	29.9
Stokes	1,610	3,670	79,807	1,774	24,631	74.4	30,818	685	19,414	13.0	70.0	29.7
Surry	4,328	10,256	180,175	2,501	47,648	73.1	94,678	1,314	25,992	11.3	67.7	32.0
Swain	559	1,245	26,371	2,026	5,526	59.7	7,151	549	5,044	15.4	51.4	48.0
Transylvania	1,095	2,606	63,130	2,139	25,576	76.6	29,358	995	15,588	9.6	60.2	39.1
Tyrrell	244	549	14,893	3,584	2,915	79.1	825	199	1,590	1.5	53.8	46.0
Union	4,823	12,305	278,006	1,994	90,412	74.5	248,553	1,783	61,001	29.3	70.2	29.5
Vance	3,153	6,408	137,754	3,138	28,697	72.6	65,503	1,492	15,677	23.4	43.9	55.9
Wake	25,101	69,334	1,895,927	2,797	728,444	77.3	7,620,418	11,244	348,844	30.1	50.8	48.7
Warren	998	2,110	48,526	2,435	13,300	80.4	21,948	1,101	8,027	18.1	35.4	64.4
Washington	829	1,818	41,222	3,059	8,049	77.7	16,898	1,254	5,471	11.9	45.4	54.3
Watauga	1,717	3,699	93,290	2,173	32,898	70.0	39,285	915	24,050	28.5	52.6	46.7
Wayne	5,591	11,633	285,591	2,524	57,346	71.1	94,996	840	40,046	18.2	62.1	37.7
Wilkes	3,205	6,825	149,129	2,233	42,602	72.6	52,176	781	27,154	11.6	70.7	29.0
Wilson	4,019	9,251	211,804	2,826	57,293	79.0	107,996	1,441	30,535	23.0	53.3	46.5
Yadkin	1,369	3,047	67,212	1,802	22,628	75.6	7,335	197	15,313	11.9	77.2	22.5
Yancey	908	1,963	39,279	2,189	10,420	71.1	2,195	122	9,431	7.6	52.4	47.0
NORTH DAKOTA	35,800	62,049	1,682,914	2,656	611,456	86.8	1,231,883	1,944	312,833	8.5	62.9	35.5
Adams	218	211	5,943	2,367	2,409	95.0	311	124	1,291	11.3	70.9	27.3
Barnes	792	913	29,647	2,635	9,428	95.3	17,399	1,547	5,813	1.1	60.9	37.6
Benson	535	703	19,984	2,913	3,909	99.5	162	24	2,246	4.3	44.6	53.3
Billings	66	147	5,020	5,750	876	61.2	—	—	564	7.4	79.6	17.6
Bottineau	635	637	15,114	2,194	5,506	98.5	2,408	350	3,674	-0.4	67.2	31.8

See footnotes at end of table.

Table B-13. Counties — **Local Government Finances and Elections**—Con.

[Includes United States, states, and 3,141 counties/county equivalents defined as of February 22, 2005. For more information on these areas, see Appendix C, Geographic Information]

County	Local government employment, March 2002		Local government finances, 2002						Elections, 2004[1]			
			General revenue				Total debt outstanding		Votes cast for President			
					Taxes						Republican candidate, percent of total	Democratic candidate, percent of total
	Total employment	Total payroll ($1,000)	Total ($1,000)	Per capita (dol.)	Total ($1,000)	Property, percent of total (taxes)	Amount ($1,000)	Per capita (dol.)	Total	Percent change, 2000–2004		
NORTH DAKOTA—Con.												
Bowman	298	381	9,518	3,081	2,714	97.1	44	14	1,716	16.7	74.6	23.1
Burke	332	243	5,851	2,764	2,167	97.8	404	191	1,165	12.1	69.4	28.8
Burleigh	2,800	6,332	173,231	2,443	65,535	83.2	109,286	1,541	38,814	12.6	68.5	29.9
Cass	4,494	11,211	358,010	2,860	150,067	83.1	409,686	3,273	66,711	13.1	59.4	39.0
Cavalier	478	455	12,268	2,678	5,630	95.0	2,069	452	2,444	3.1	62.3	36.3
Dickey	389	421	12,404	2,231	4,992	94.4	2,488	448	2,821	1.3	67.0	31.3
Divide	265	203	7,975	3,627	2,893	90.9	1,001	455	1,268	59.7	59.2	38.4
Dunn	231	379	10,022	2,836	3,149	97.7	–	–	1,774	2.7	66.4	32.2
Eddy	288	241	8,523	3,239	4,303	98.2	2,126	808	1,213	–4.3	54.0	44.0
Emmons	258	396	10,393	2,541	4,695	99.1	1,414	346	2,113	6.1	68.6	28.9
Foster	252	296	9,846	2,752	3,904	84.2	1,457	407	1,766	1.3	69.0	29.3
Golden Valley	208	253	6,596	3,604	2,059	96.0	616	337	927	14.2	77.6	21.0
Grand Forks	2,882	7,060	203,045	3,131	66,018	76.9	255,007	3,932	30,470	7.3	56.8	41.5
Grant	238	257	8,226	3,060	3,149	97.1	1,302	484	1,242	–13.0	76.7	21.3
Griggs	267	309	9,777	3,759	3,952	99.6	2,403	924	1,439	–2.0	63.0	35.1
Hettinger	334	348	7,765	2,995	2,961	99.0	1,807	697	1,494	–1.6	69.9	27.1
Kidder	360	274	8,209	3,167	2,795	99.4	1,372	529	1,369	7.3	65.9	31.6
LaMoure	487	566	24,027	5,258	6,293	97.0	1,507	330	2,335	–5.4	68.2	30.5
Logan	148	202	5,205	2,373	2,139	96.0	1,105	504	1,130	–1.3	74.7	23.5
McHenry	627	561	12,950	2,262	4,939	95.4	1,796	314	2,820	3.0	61.8	36.5
McIntosh	234	292	6,940	2,149	3,046	96.1	323	100	1,722	5.9	72.8	25.3
McKenzie	449	810	19,013	3,352	4,715	97.3	293	52	2,762	16.8	68.7	30.7
McLean	720	1,038	20,014	2,221	5,311	98.5	6,843	759	4,750	2.2	63.5	35.0
Mercer	489	909	32,721	3,839	6,146	94.4	96,393	11,308	4,617	6.1	71.2	27.0
Morton	1,190	2,411	60,834	2,412	22,022	92.4	42,606	1,689	12,633	12.6	65.9	32.2
Mountrail	720	867	24,030	3,699	5,337	95.7	2,521	388	3,030	4.6	50.4	48.4
Nelson	371	377	10,641	3,075	4,975	99.5	6,276	1,813	1,922	4.5	57.6	40.5
Oliver	127	181	10,353	5,304	1,235	94.7	77,323	39,612	1,119	6.5	70.6	27.7
Pembina	593	961	21,506	2,601	10,649	95.9	5,289	640	3,856	2.0	64.0	34.3
Pierce	308	407	9,580	2,113	4,236	91.4	1,122	247	2,195	11.4	67.2	31.3
Ramsey	751	1,176	29,170	2,482	11,215	82.1	11,565	984	4,900	–1.5	60.1	38.5
Ransom	441	513	17,988	3,080	6,081	95.5	5,076	869	2,602	–4.3	52.0	46.1
Renville	352	372	9,606	3,792	3,673	98.7	976	385	1,469	10.3	64.9	33.8
Richland	1,050	1,401	38,500	2,207	16,953	97.6	16,799	963	8,215	2.5	64.1	34.3
Rolette	821	2,065	32,333	2,350	3,815	91.6	5,517	401	4,044	–8.0	34.4	63.4
Sargent	334	381	10,391	2,424	4,357	99.1	5,198	1,213	2,200	0.7	52.1	46.4
Sheridan	194	140	3,738	2,376	1,553	97.6	15	10	944	1.7	77.0	21.2
Sioux	273	501	11,135	2,709	792	99.6	21	5	1,140	9.5	28.0	70.5
Slope	150	62	1,871	2,515	555	99.3	15	20	432	–2.3	77.6	20.6
Stark	974	2,063	47,466	2,140	16,545	82.8	7,253	327	10,400	6.4	69.4	29.0
Steele	247	211	5,950	2,813	2,938	99.2	130	61	1,213	0.2	48.3	50.8
Stutsman	1,312	1,953	48,606	2,274	19,653	85.4	50,387	2,357	10,122	11.0	64.4	34.0
Towner	314	287	7,408	2,731	3,142	98.0	2,548	939	1,391	17.0	54.2	43.6
Traill	501	764	20,698	2,491	9,728	97.9	4,549	547	4,248	3.3	59.9	38.9
Walsh	767	1,044	25,788	2,171	10,437	93.8	6,895	581	5,186	0.1	61.6	36.7
Ward	2,576	5,408	119,532	2,105	43,640	77.2	52,660	928	25,612	13.9	66.4	32.2
Wells	540	582	12,808	2,662	5,085	96.3	18	4	2,561	6.3	64.6	33.5
Williams	1,120	1,871	44,745	2,294	17,160	89.0	6,102	313	8,929	14.4	70.3	28.1
OHIO	548,000	1,478,129	40,285,092	3,532	16,034,775	66.3	31,335,000	2,748	5,627,908	19.7	50.8	48.7
Adams	1,540	2,908	88,842	3,202	22,710	95.8	48,206	1,737	12,000	17.2	63.8	35.7
Allen	5,244	13,130	333,973	3,090	111,265	67.5	113,876	1,054	49,256	12.5	66.1	33.4
Ashland	2,136	4,722	131,211	2,468	50,118	67.5	28,514	536	24,979	17.5	64.9	34.3
Ashtabula	5,112	11,721	311,731	3,027	103,893	80.2	74,267	721	45,407	15.0	46.3	53.0
Athens	2,939	6,664	183,749	2,921	51,813	69.4	90,355	1,436	30,045	18.1	36.1	63.2
Auglaize	2,130	4,652	129,964	2,784	50,999	61.4	63,560	1,362	23,034	15.8	73.9	25.6
Belmont	3,142	6,290	181,463	2,597	52,564	71.3	89,110	1,275	33,322	10.6	46.8	52.8
Brown	2,213	4,864	135,601	3,123	25,522	80.5	30,513	703	19,892	21.1	63.6	35.9
Butler	13,487	36,807	1,017,589	2,997	388,558	76.1	1,275,931	3,758	166,819	22.0	65.9	33.7
Carroll	1,025	2,037	52,087	1,778	14,506	81.9	7,828	267	14,112	15.1	54.5	44.6
Champaign	1,928	4,220	125,946	3,205	39,218	67.3	25,700	654	18,776	19.7	62.4	37.1
Clark	6,723	17,315	414,517	2,883	144,867	68.5	160,028	1,113	68,807	19.5	50.8	48.7
Clermont	6,110	16,568	501,185	2,743	170,026	82.0	442,544	2,422	89,079	27.5	70.7	29.1
Clinton	2,822	6,755	224,273	5,421	38,990	77.3	394,915	9,545	18,414	22.2	70.3	29.4
Columbiana	4,394	9,810	262,942	2,357	73,527	74.0	92,825	832	49,465	11.3	52.1	47.4
Coshocton	1,751	3,709	102,770	2,780	33,753	75.1	67,178	1,817	17,303	21.3	56.9	42.6
Crawford	2,150	4,991	118,136	2,548	43,999	67.5	39,903	861	21,801	13.7	63.7	35.7
Cuyahoga	84,044	261,101	6,728,549	4,903	2,953,401	58.9	7,385,258	5,382	673,777	17.9	32.9	66.6
Darke	2,559	5,362	136,767	2,583	46,767	67.7	26,460	500	26,313	13.1	69.6	29.8
Defiance	1,941	4,499	115,602	2,945	38,997	63.5	38,208	973	18,516	14.0	61.6	37.7

See footnotes at end of table.

[Includes United States, states, and 3,141 counties/county equivalents defined as of February 22, 2005. For more information on these areas, see Appendix C, Geographic Information]

County	Local government employment, March 2002		Local government finances, 2002						Elections, 2004[1]			
			General revenue		Taxes		Total debt outstanding		Votes cast for President			
	Total employment	Total payroll ($1,000)	Total ($1,000)	Per capita (dol.)	Total ($1,000)	Property, percent of total (taxes)	Amount ($1,000)	Per capita (dol.)	Total	Percent change, 2000–2004	Republican candidate, percent of total	Democratic candidate, percent of total
OHIO—Con.												
Delaware	4,346	10,815	307,107	2,409	162,965	71.6	356,013	2,793	80,456	45.2	66.1	33.6
Erie	4,348	11,478	287,490	3,644	118,773	75.2	135,295	1,715	40,085	14.5	46.4	53.4
Fairfield	4,788	12,697	322,779	2,497	128,307	66.7	319,703	2,473	67,882	25.5	62.9	36.5
Fayette	1,733	3,884	104,224	3,699	28,729	69.4	27,785	986	11,757	26.7	62.7	36.9
Franklin	48,661	160,578	4,631,651	4,281	2,150,860	61.4	5,013,480	4,634	525,827	27.0	45.1	54.4
Fulton	2,192	4,680	119,970	2,837	56,948	66.2	94,070	2,224	21,954	16.2	62.1	37.5
Gallia	1,547	3,487	97,716	3,124	24,149	74.7	9,140	292	13,993	9.5	61.3	38.4
Geauga	3,718	9,006	236,390	2,552	123,211	88.6	84,707	914	50,442	18.4	60.2	39.4
Greene	6,263	16,908	427,353	2,854	182,668	75.0	322,736	2,155	79,282	21.6	61.0	38.5
Guernsey	1,798	3,803	129,235	3,142	31,213	71.0	44,814	1,090	17,840	15.6	55.8	43.5
Hamilton	39,863	118,051	3,405,381	4,103	1,585,551	65.9	3,321,191	4,001	424,025	12.2	52.5	47.1
Hancock	3,293	7,482	198,340	2,730	80,683	69.1	105,421	1,451	35,619	16.3	70.5	29.1
Hardin	1,785	3,213	101,943	3,210	26,601	57.2	25,791	812	13,392	11.0	63.0	36.5
Harrison	1,028	1,584	41,666	2,624	10,600	84.8	9,411	593	8,109	13.2	52.7	46.6
Henry	1,746	3,632	97,904	3,329	36,643	74.2	44,393	1,510	15,105	14.0	65.6	33.8
Highland	2,268	4,818	137,616	3,293	26,768	64.0	53,111	1,271	18,481	19.6	66.1	33.5
Hocking	1,202	2,356	86,816	3,039	18,351	78.1	38,801	1,358	13,199	22.7	52.6	46.8
Holmes	1,376	2,888	92,980	2,304	27,144	81.9	36,999	917	11,220	22.7	75.5	24.0
Huron	3,038	6,422	180,377	3,009	64,484	59.3	70,115	1,170	25,558	19.7	58.0	41.4
Jackson	1,488	3,360	97,121	2,945	17,865	74.4	75,189	2,280	14,334	14.8	59.9	39.8
Jefferson	3,564	7,440	182,892	2,533	62,666	78.4	70,690	979	36,372	5.0	47.3	52.3
Knox	2,289	5,081	152,361	2,707	54,281	73.3	71,897	1,278	27,045	27.2	63.1	36.3
Lake	11,707	32,813	781,628	3,394	402,361	71.6	267,719	1,163	121,823	18.8	51.1	48.5
Lawrence	2,460	5,539	204,292	3,291	28,489	65.4	31,334	505	27,710	13.3	55.8	43.7
Licking	5,785	14,130	377,732	2,540	169,673	63.3	221,057	1,487	79,420	27.1	61.7	37.8
Logan	2,211	4,629	149,782	3,235	55,351	83.1	77,384	1,671	21,398	15.9	67.6	31.9
Lorain	13,970	36,998	922,579	3,203	331,358	71.1	784,986	2,725	140,742	25.5	43.5	56.1
Lucas	19,759	62,323	1,722,918	3,797	714,464	59.9	1,506,209	3,320	220,430	17.7	39.5	60.2
Madison	1,815	4,173	104,581	2,589	41,021	78.1	39,625	981	17,398	18.6	63.9	35.7
Mahoning	10,737	27,419	797,538	3,156	264,454	73.5	373,940	1,480	132,904	16.5	36.7	62.6
Marion	3,081	7,476	248,555	3,757	68,214	72.0	271,864	4,110	29,258	17.9	58.7	40.8
Medina	6,808	17,527	474,162	2,994	194,121	84.7	330,355	2,086	84,878	26.9	56.8	42.7
Meigs	1,247	2,274	79,714	3,440	11,628	80.4	36,670	1,583	10,771	10.0	58.2	41.2
Mercer	2,382	5,439	150,554	3,679	38,350	66.5	57,940	1,416	20,890	14.2	74.9	24.5
Miami	4,733	11,654	298,852	3,001	120,315	70.4	188,398	1,892	51,760	20.8	65.7	34.0
Monroe	934	1,669	49,022	3,272	14,199	78.6	5,540	370	7,729	8.6	44.3	54.9
Montgomery	29,326	82,033	2,230,440	4,034	869,153	60.7	1,612,727	2,917	282,584	22.3	49.0	50.6
Morgan	747	1,493	56,013	3,776	19,833	75.0	9,228	622	6,703	11.8	56.1	42.9
Morrow	1,777	3,464	93,346	2,833	22,080	71.2	83,378	2,530	16,328	27.2	64.2	35.4
Muskingum	4,450	10,470	274,642	3,223	81,842	66.7	130,745	1,534	38,866	19.1	57.3	42.3
Noble	684	1,198	32,740	2,340	7,199	85.0	3,732	267	6,540	9.2	58.7	40.6
Ottawa	1,874	4,390	133,924	3,264	59,381	82.4	69,056	1,683	23,259	16.5	51.9	47.8
Paulding	1,259	2,399	79,234	3,981	15,926	70.2	37,059	1,862	9,879	10.4	62.8	36.5
Perry	1,664	3,261	119,112	3,445	16,174	81.5	40,863	1,182	15,189	18.4	51.7	47.8
Pickaway	2,531	6,482	180,303	3,489	45,496	73.3	50,834	984	22,852	28.8	62.0	37.5
Pike	1,662	3,290	105,164	3,754	19,213	90.7	18,061	645	12,576	19.1	51.8	47.6
Portage	7,560	19,195	528,181	3,437	166,264	75.3	287,894	1,874	76,647	21.9	46.4	53.1
Preble	2,187	4,117	107,290	2,522	38,979	62.0	57,576	1,354	21,127	16.3	65.0	34.4
Putnam	2,130	3,763	110,895	3,198	28,636	65.3	53,062	1,530	18,849	8.7	76.2	23.3
Richland	6,827	15,367	426,929	3,327	146,467	67.8	176,813	1,378	61,840	17.2	59.6	39.8
Ross	3,359	7,608	251,621	3,392	68,335	61.4	119,106	1,606	31,671	21.7	54.4	44.1
Sandusky	3,058	7,197	183,011	2,959	62,801	66.6	72,007	1,164	29,014	12.7	55.9	43.7
Scioto	3,946	7,916	256,341	3,284	43,198	65.8	161,825	2,073	35,203	17.6	51.9	47.8
Seneca	2,500	5,516	150,188	2,591	54,362	65.2	47,597	821	26,991	10.8	58.9	40.6
Shelby	1,917	4,484	140,849	2,912	61,802	61.0	96,161	1,988	22,855	16.2	70.9	28.6
Stark	17,275	42,827	1,099,149	2,897	394,125	74.7	417,135	1,100	188,459	17.9	48.9	50.6
Summit	25,324	75,186	1,880,484	3,443	868,888	64.9	1,273,313	2,331	276,320	22.9	42.9	56.7
Trumbull	9,575	23,921	624,542	2,800	216,868	74.7	229,573	1,029	108,145	12.4	37.9	61.7
Tuscarawas	4,255	9,405	243,028	2,653	86,733	74.6	97,289	1,062	42,906	15.6	55.5	43.9
Union	2,284	5,755	161,561	3,761	56,458	64.0	131,724	3,067	22,631	32.9	70.1	29.5
Van Wert	1,309	2,903	82,150	2,800	28,596	64.9	44,765	1,526	14,827	12.2	72.0	27.6
Vinton	722	1,376	43,402	3,311	5,882	75.9	9,717	741	5,928	19.9	54.8	44.7
Warren	6,506	16,399	443,186	2,530	210,439	71.0	548,386	3,131	94,422	36.7	72.1	27.6
Washington	2,590	5,407	188,545	3,016	63,498	71.5	86,742	1,388	30,216	14.0	58.0	41.5
Wayne	6,026	14,103	397,769	3,526	115,562	74.7	114,861	1,018	51,848	22.2	61.5	38.2
Williams	2,282	4,650	101,922	2,614	38,851	68.5	32,858	843	18,639	17.1	64.6	34.8
Wood	5,753	13,913	385,995	3,165	173,814	69.7	194,513	1,595	63,346	21.4	53.0	46.4
Wyandot	1,288	2,790	75,039	3,295	18,969	61.6	7,448	327	11,043	12.4	65.7	33.6

See footnotes at end of table.

[Includes United States, states, and 3,141 counties/county equivalents defined as of February 22, 2005. For more information on these areas, see Appendix C, Geographic Information]

County	Local government employment, March 2002		Local government finances, 2002				Total debt outstanding		Elections, 2004[1]			
			General revenue						Votes cast for President			
					Taxes						Repub-lican cand-idate,	Demo-cratic cand-idate,
	Total employ-ment	Total payroll ($1,000)	Total ($1,000)	Per capita (dol.)	Total ($1,000)	Prop-erty, percent of total (taxes)	Amount ($1,000)	Per capita (dol.)	Total	Percent change, 2000–2004	percent of total	percent of total
OKLAHOMA	158,385	338,337	8,455,104	2,425	2,729,209	54.3	6,031,032	1,730	1,463,758	18.6	65.6	34.4
Adair.	1,215	2,404	47,002	2,202	6,827	49.9	15,127	709	7,533	26.0	66.0	34.0
Alfalfa	339	465	9,451	1,588	3,257	70.9	2,059	346	2,671	6.5	82.4	17.6
Atoka	650	1,297	29,846	2,132	4,979	66.0	4,471	319	5,088	17.7	61.8	38.3
Beaver.	418	772	22,950	4,127	9,882	87.7	2,746	494	2,569	4.6	88.4	11.6
Beckham	790	1,821	53,012	2,656	22,341	60.5	7,848	393	7,385	13.1	73.9	26.2
Blaine	928	1,375	32,221	2,759	5,337	74.0	4,071	349	4,421	8.0	72.4	27.6
Bryan	1,640	3,026	68,537	1,855	16,791	57.0	23,444	635	14,360	22.3	60.0	40.0
Caddo	1,869	3,417	75,590	2,520	14,379	61.6	9,038	301	10,407	13.0	62.4	37.6
Canadian	4,026	8,081	183,066	2,010	59,626	67.8	120,086	1,319	43,009	37.1	77.4	22.6
Carter	2,243	4,104	103,279	2,241	34,490	55.7	25,168	546	18,644	13.3	65.3	34.7
Cherokee	2,103	4,051	96,700	2,228	14,340	43.4	20,020	461	18,192	25.7	52.6	47.4
Choctaw.	1,013	1,715	28,359	1,845	5,806	38.4	6,001	390	5,807	9.3	54.6	45.5
Cimarron	303	487	9,846	3,262	2,545	83.7	943	312	1,426	–3.9	87.1	12.9
Cleveland.	8,769	21,268	508,566	2,365	141,815	58.1	205,809	957	99,727	30.9	65.9	34.1
Coal	416	683	15,311	2,559	2,838	72.1	3,378	565	2,599	10.0	53.7	46.3
Comanche	6,789	15,336	321,846	2,881	61,155	49.4	119,547	1,070	33,192	13.2	63.8	36.2
Cotton	338	564	12,939	2,002	2,093	65.1	3,193	494	2,640	6.4	66.0	34.0
Craig.	885	1,838	35,278	2,390	12,827	79.0	8,815	597	6,398	16.7	60.9	39.1
Creek	3,163	6,100	130,060	1,894	37,349	60.0	75,678	1,102	28,777	21.2	65.5	34.5
Custer	1,423	2,674	70,600	2,814	19,971	48.6	38,333	1,528	10,640	9.2	73.7	26.3
Delaware	1,313	2,897	57,864	1,524	17,387	67.4	22,108	582	15,608	16.9	64.2	35.8
Dewey.	507	838	18,154	3,950	3,876	78.1	4,161	905	2,251	1.4	81.9	18.1
Ellis.	260	424	11,057	2,760	3,262	76.6	1,689	422	2,080	3.3	81.0	19.0
Garfield	2,439	5,692	118,410	2,070	46,288	51.7	57,425	1,004	23,271	7.3	76.0	24.0
Garvin	1,239	2,260	69,599	2,555	20,248	66.4	18,779	689	11,317	15.0	67.2	32.8
Grady	2,121	4,705	107,714	2,301	21,932	57.2	26,186	559	20,106	23.5	70.3	29.7
Grant.	488	662	14,830	2,948	4,923	87.1	2,988	594	2,521	0.7	77.4	22.7
Greer.	451	781	16,343	2,750	2,112	70.6	2,306	388	2,248	4.5	68.0	32.0
Harmon	237	431	6,998	2,245	1,385	70.0	988	317	1,192	–1.1	70.3	29.7
Harper	341	649	8,975	2,598	2,911	80.8	14	4	1,665	–1.1	83.9	16.1
Haskell	921	1,488	23,612	2,004	4,878	50.6	1,269	108	5,324	15.0	55.3	44.7
Hughes	1,053	1,784	35,122	2,504	6,792	65.1	17,338	1,236	5,349	16.7	57.3	42.7
Jackson	2,217	4,793	112,438	4,107	13,206	52.4	39,905	1,457	9,256	13.4	75.9	24.1
Jefferson	472	796	17,124	2,622	2,595	57.7	42,086	6,444	2,603	0.4	59.4	40.6
Johnston	517	846	16,780	1,608	3,448	76.8	4,741	454	4,348	10.6	60.6	39.4
Kay.	2,560	4,519	102,227	2,146	32,108	65.9	64,587	1,356	20,078	10.5	70.3	29.7
Kingfisher	931	1,620	35,454	2,546	12,152	69.6	9,683	695	6,652	9.8	84.6	15.4
Kiowa	1,012	1,565	25,319	2,537	7,132	76.1	4,735	474	4,023	7.3	64.9	35.1
Latimer	1,118	1,795	38,584	3,654	14,032	84.3	3,882	368	4,480	22.1	56.6	43.4
Le Flore	2,185	3,958	96,893	1,994	17,060	55.2	19,192	395	17,424	16.3	61.3	38.7
Lincoln.	1,141	2,175	51,601	1,600	14,022	54.7	20,411	633	14,190	21.3	71.5	28.5
Logan	1,021	1,932	53,350	1,530	10,605	61.5	21,542	618	16,343	27.0	70.2	29.8
Love	437	789	14,354	1,617	3,336	60.0	3,760	424	3,833	13.7	59.9	40.1
McClain	1,531	3,138	63,513	2,264	25,964	73.2	26,151	932	13,783	30.8	72.9	27.2
McCurtain	2,241	4,152	71,731	2,101	13,515	62.4	18,271	535	11,156	6.4	67.0	33.0
McIntosh	747	1,418	41,805	2,120	8,476	42.1	13,113	665	9,180	18.0	51.1	48.9
Major.	528	878	20,089	2,666	4,644	80.9	3,780	502	3,659	9.2	85.3	14.7
Marshall	575	1,065	28,230	2,077	5,844	53.8	5,541	408	5,451	11.2	61.7	38.3
Mayes	1,682	3,150	65,055	1,679	19,252	49.0	15,671	404	16,879	20.6	58.9	41.1
Murray.	645	1,366	23,520	1,861	5,610	49.1	6,407	507	5,795	17.7	63.2	36.8
Muskogee	3,428	6,805	246,738	3,529	63,614	54.6	178,521	2,554	27,709	12.2	54.6	45.4
Noble	775	1,362	34,219	3,028	9,058	80.8	17,827	1,578	5,328	13.4	74.9	25.1
Nowata	503	848	18,292	1,717	3,564	66.9	6,582	618	4,465	16.0	62.8	37.2
Okfuskee	593	958	28,225	2,425	4,566	63.6	9,017	775	4,285	13.1	59.3	40.7
Oklahoma	24,398	59,070	1,758,427	2,619	696,427	44.4	1,838,841	2,739	272,039	21.9	64.2	35.8
Okmulgee	1,693	3,423	83,648	2,106	16,742	44.9	18,462	465	15,730	19.4	53.2	46.8
Osage	1,169	2,036	51,785	1,146	10,959	62.1	12,389	274	19,535	22.8	58.7	41.3
Ottawa	1,717	3,065	77,646	2,362	21,699	73.2	13,416	408	12,529	9.8	59.4	40.6
Pawnee	675	1,296	29,133	1,731	5,896	56.4	14,313	850	6,976	17.7	63.3	36.8
Payne	3,835	8,282	152,371	2,208	50,577	51.8	90,706	1,314	29,661	18.9	66.0	34.1
Pittsburg	2,826	5,580	126,938	2,877	33,439	32.7	89,877	2,037	18,586	13.6	59.9	40.1
Pontotoc	1,643	3,408	71,697	2,057	22,603	40.4	31,739	911	14,812	15.4	65.1	34.9
Pottawatomie	2,652	5,804	155,420	2,328	42,584	44.6	45,233	678	25,853	15.8	66.6	33.4
Pushmataha	821	1,430	24,391	2,082	3,427	51.3	1,651	141	4,797	10.3	59.7	40.3
Roger Mills	201	457	14,102	4,388	3,240	54.0	1,110	345	1,770	4.9	78.4	21.6
Rogers.	2,671	5,268	122,584	1,630	39,882	69.6	54,027	718	36,894	27.4	67.7	32.3
Seminole	1,105	2,206	61,667	2,511	12,862	58.9	21,821	888	9,272	17.9	60.7	39.3
Sequoyah	1,995	3,766	71,915	1,814	12,141	50.4	27,358	690	14,775	20.6	60.0	40.0
Stephens	1,936	3,744	80,859	1,898	26,306	56.6	41,927	984	19,161	9.6	71.2	28.8
Texas	1,331	2,519	67,774	3,381	15,376	66.6	8,281	413	6,466	6.2	84.3	15.7

See footnotes at end of table.

[Includes United States, states, and 3,141 counties/county equivalents defined as of February 22, 2005. For more information on these areas, see Appendix C, Geographic Information]

County	Local government employment, March 2002 Total employment	Local government employment, March 2002 Total payroll ($1,000)	Local government finances, 2002 General revenue Total ($1,000)	Local government finances, 2002 General revenue Per capita (dol.)	Local government finances, 2002 General revenue Taxes Total ($1,000)	Local government finances, 2002 General revenue Taxes Property, percent of total (taxes)	Total debt outstanding Amount ($1,000)	Total debt outstanding Per capita (dol.)	Elections, 2004[1] Votes cast for President Total	Elections, 2004[1] Votes cast for President Percent change, 2000–2004	Elections, 2004[1] Votes cast for President Republican candidate, percent of total	Elections, 2004[1] Votes cast for President Democratic candidate, percent of total
OKLAHOMA—Con.												
Tillman	703	1,254	25,893	2,902	3,458	63.3	10,757	1,206	3,448	3.0	65.9	34.1
Tulsa	23,461	60,113	1,667,233	2,926	709,714	56.8	2,196,498	3,855	253,672	16.0	64.4	35.6
Wagoner	1,206	2,679	58,247	963	19,106	50.6	46,860	774	28,238	31.2	67.6	32.4
Washington	2,133	4,330	100,147	2,037	39,150	53.8	45,428	924	23,413	12.9	70.7	29.3
Washita	739	1,201	31,825	2,801	8,626	81.0	6,138	540	5,045	12.9	73.4	26.6
Woods	849	1,439	25,152	2,867	10,018	72.0	9,305	1,061	4,098	1.3	77.3	22.7
Woodward	1,077	1,947	47,572	2,573	16,532	49.3	18,464	999	7,651	7.8	80.9	19.1
OREGON	161,419	422,669	12,118,367	3,440	3,839,550	81.1	11,159,367	3,168	1,836,782	19.7	47.2	51.4
Baker	759	1,521	45,205	2,735	11,180	92.2	7,775	470	9,034	9.4	69.2	29.0
Benton	2,859	7,235	202,644	2,565	68,548	89.7	125,330	1,586	45,735	19.6	40.4	58.0
Clackamas	13,669	35,811	1,010,480	2,869	370,542	89.5	848,008	2,407	195,000	20.2	50.1	48.8
Clatsop	2,111	4,509	143,041	4,007	49,730	85.3	82,101	2,300	19,309	17.2	44.0	54.2
Columbia	1,949	5,103	126,730	2,789	39,826	91.2	159,107	3,501	24,917	17.6	47.6	50.4
Coos	4,228	10,132	292,790	4,676	49,469	84.4	86,300	1,378	33,362	13.6	54.8	43.1
Crook	819	1,820	74,028	3,663	22,221	85.4	26,888	1,330	10,051	21.4	68.0	30.1
Curry	1,116	2,486	63,133	2,941	21,061	88.1	48,878	2,277	12,799	11.2	57.3	40.8
Deschutes	5,792	13,760	391,227	3,116	152,250	83.1	341,649	2,721	74,048	27.9	56.4	42.1
Douglas	5,143	11,425	335,734	3,318	61,367	92.6	93,475	924	54,984	16.4	65.4	32.9
Gilliam	185	455	15,188	8,166	3,213	93.8	1,107	595	1,138	4.4	66.3	32.5
Grant	740	1,480	42,903	5,763	4,652	95.3	12,343	1,658	4,061	5.6	78.9	19.2
Harney	648	1,274	35,501	4,851	4,664	97.9	3,124	427	3,702	-0.9	76.0	22.7
Hood River	888	2,125	73,178	3,534	14,737	85.5	31,948	1,543	9,859	15.3	41.8	56.7
Jackson	6,941	18,288	506,938	2,709	166,206	82.0	303,422	1,621	102,189	20.5	55.3	43.4
Jefferson	1,181	2,817	74,528	3,799	15,669	85.7	73,124	3,727	8,115	17.7	58.7	40.0
Josephine	3,530	8,543	241,593	3,107	47,487	82.5	94,590	1,216	42,275	15.1	62.1	36.0
Klamath	2,697	6,676	198,183	3,082	35,841	92.5	386,562	6,011	31,515	13.2	72.1	26.2
Lake	578	1,193	37,427	5,026	5,833	92.3	7,873	1,057	3,905	4.7	77.8	20.5
Lane	15,091	39,424	1,081,627	3,309	301,547	85.9	844,021	2,582	185,872	22.1	40.4	58.0
Lincoln	2,014	5,620	188,097	4,226	72,618	88.3	116,075	2,608	24,325	15.2	41.8	56.5
Linn	5,736	12,616	332,052	3,160	92,349	87.1	175,062	1,666	52,041	17.2	60.1	38.3
Malheur	2,068	4,111	115,717	3,683	20,261	85.8	86,180	2,743	10,846	4.2	74.9	23.8
Marion	13,069	35,303	980,859	3,327	257,493	88.7	684,825	2,323	129,619	14.4	53.9	44.5
Morrow	754	1,657	49,485	4,266	14,972	90.5	38,312	3,303	4,149	15.0	65.9	32.8
Multnomah	38,144	114,464	3,309,788	4,904	1,211,241	67.4	4,597,000	6,812	362,694	22.2	27.1	71.6
Polk	1,681	3,863	115,036	1,775	27,846	84.4	80,105	1,236	35,489	24.7	55.0	43.6
Sherman	174	306	10,414	5,824	3,721	95.8	693	388	1,104	4.0	62.9	35.3
Tillamook	1,458	3,330	84,818	3,462	26,961	90.3	49,067	2,003	13,951	12.7	50.2	48.4
Umatilla	3,261	7,627	224,281	3,114	54,123	90.9	153,104	2,126	26,322	14.1	64.8	33.8
Union	1,035	2,132	80,790	3,298	15,600	90.1	18,662	762	13,519	11.9	65.7	32.8
Wallowa	574	1,048	30,060	4,237	5,800	93.8	22,051	3,108	4,521	5.3	69.3	28.1
Wasco	1,326	2,901	99,415	4,219	23,107	95.1	101,041	4,288	12,002	12.5	51.0	47.4
Washington	15,570	42,698	1,258,575	2,667	500,953	87.5	1,285,797	2,724	231,308	24.4	46.4	52.4
Wheeler	135	219	7,250	4,735	1,032	98.8	353	231	880	4.6	69.6	27.8
Yamhill	3,496	8,696	239,652	2,728	65,430	86.6	173,415	1,974	42,142	18.6	56.6	41.7
PENNSYLVANIA	459,188	1,332,171	38,501,369	3,124	15,491,083	70.1	62,826,518	5,098	[5]5,769,590	[5]17.4	[5]48.4	[5]50.9
Adams	3,143	6,191	196,310	2,077	100,120	72.2	259,139	2,742	42,228	26.3	66.9	32.6
Allegheny	52,861	161,787	5,308,629	4,194	2,023,506	72.3	11,163,920	8,820	645,469	10.8	42.1	57.2
Armstrong	2,566	6,312	184,316	2,567	64,659	85.1	151,971	2,117	31,097	13.4	60.9	38.7
Beaver	8,342	20,055	593,684	3,314	173,522	80.7	1,453,106	8,111	82,543	12.2	48.4	51.1
Bedford	1,639	3,588	104,167	2,089	31,824	77.8	77,957	1,563	22,679	16.7	73.2	26.5
Berks	15,248	39,471	1,128,614	2,957	493,716	79.2	1,879,786	4,925	164,487	21.7	53.0	46.4
Blair	5,118	11,720	297,984	2,335	96,232	71.4	310,943	2,437	54,178	20.0	66.0	33.4
Bradford	2,985	6,812	197,262	3,145	49,991	75.6	645,246	10,288	25,652	10.0	66.1	33.5
Bucks	20,264	67,711	1,732,488	2,844	946,566	80.3	2,022,356	3,320	319,816	21.4	48.3	51.1
Butler	6,020	15,421	446,869	2,509	164,395	76.0	750,083	4,211	85,425	20.6	64.3	35.2
Cambria	7,361	16,399	415,783	2,765	105,684	77.6	608,929	4,050	66,983	11.1	50.8	48.7
Cameron	259	517	14,954	2,558	5,268	83.5	15,370	2,629	2,406	7.1	66.5	33.0
Carbon	2,324	5,257	152,610	2,555	64,455	78.5	193,197	3,234	25,043	17.7	50.0	48.8
Centre	4,469	10,413	280,176	2,022	125,451	70.8	312,354	2,254	64,253	29.7	51.6	47.8
Chester	13,129	42,713	1,265,177	2,812	712,902	82.3	1,979,029	4,399	230,823	23.1	52.0	47.5
Clarion	1,806	3,852	95,988	2,329	29,281	77.8	78,426	1,903	17,184	8.5	64.4	35.2
Clearfield	3,160	7,348	185,047	2,220	63,160	80.0	178,126	2,137	34,233	11.8	60.0	39.5
Clinton	1,717	3,514	88,242	2,351	30,871	76.3	78,381	2,088	13,967	16.4	57.5	41.7
Columbia	2,561	5,382	138,806	2,152	58,783	72.6	143,480	2,225	26,869	22.7	59.7	39.7
Crawford	2,785	7,383	202,746	2,250	67,014	82.1	187,889	2,086	38,322	15.0	57.3	41.8
Cumberland	7,733	21,096	508,103	2,336	264,589	68.3	721,734	3,319	106,082	20.5	63.8	35.8
Dauphin	11,863	32,087	971,521	3,846	339,941	70.8	2,183,500	8,643	121,208	20.4	53.9	45.6
Delaware	19,258	56,587	1,720,021	3,108	760,680	90.5	3,678,676	6,648	284,538	14.7	42.3	57.2
Elk	1,136	2,636	79,576	2,305	30,212	75.3	78,454	2,273	14,550	7.2	54.1	45.4
Erie	9,174	25,716	763,666	2,704	250,391	80.2	1,188,518	4,208	125,898	12.1	45.6	54.0

See footnotes at end of table.

County and City Data Book: 2007

U.S. Census Bureau

Table B-13. Counties — **Local Government Finances and Elections**—Con.

[Includes United States, states, and 3,141 counties/county equivalents defined as of February 22, 2005. For more information on these areas, see Appendix C, Geographic Information]

County	Local government employment, March 2002		Local government finances, 2002						Elections, 2004[1]			
			General revenue				Total debt outstanding		Votes cast for President			
					Taxes						Republican candidate, percent of total	Democratic candidate, percent of total
	Total employment	Total payroll ($1,000)	Total ($1,000)	Per capita (dol.)	Total ($1,000)	Property, percent of total (taxes)	Amount ($1,000)	Per capita (dol.)	Total	Percent change, 2000-2004		
PENNSYLVANIA—Con.												
Fayette	3,911	10,369	284,543	1,939	70,616	74.8	237,537	1,619	54,707	10.4	45.8	53.2
Forest	269	493	14,436	2,899	6,434	86.4	10,785	2,166	2,573	12.7	61.1	38.4
Franklin	4,101	10,692	259,457	1,973	98,136	76.1	176,132	1,339	58,569	19.6	71.4	28.3
Fulton	519	1,111	33,103	2,309	11,036	81.5	34,286	2,392	6,271	18.7	76.1	23.5
Greene	1,430	3,533	103,861	2,566	40,490	85.8	134,802	3,331	15,565	14.2	50.0	49.3
Huntingdon	1,536	2,717	79,247	1,730	24,351	76.1	98,119	2,142	18,058	13.2	67.2	32.6
Indiana	2,746	6,929	192,374	2,160	65,163	77.6	182,570	2,050	36,248	15.4	55.9	43.7
Jefferson	1,686	3,523	94,712	2,068	29,900	76.1	87,465	1,910	19,560	11.3	68.4	31.1
Juniata	758	1,384	28,562	1,247	11,029	68.6	2,013	88	10,006	15.4	71.4	28.0
Lackawanna	6,598	18,118	533,715	2,530	229,006	71.2	724,080	3,432	105,819	9.8	42.3	56.3
Lancaster	13,414	39,561	1,089,300	2,277	504,565	78.8	1,962,321	4,102	221,278	26.2	65.8	33.6
Lawrence	2,948	7,488	219,135	2,336	69,783	76.5	173,527	1,850	43,442	9.6	50.5	49.2
Lebanon	4,534	11,398	294,846	2,425	112,362	76.1	349,946	2,878	55,665	21.3	66.6	32.5
Lehigh	12,116	34,110	1,003,019	3,162	409,620	78.3	2,324,607	7,328	145,091	24.8	48.4	51.0
Luzerne	10,758	28,377	718,670	2,284	308,558	72.3	939,701	2,987	136,028	13.7	47.8	51.2
Lycoming	4,304	11,372	307,172	2,586	107,953	69.8	457,123	3,849	50,049	15.9	67.9	31.3
McKean	2,042	4,437	123,084	2,707	34,295	77.4	132,904	2,923	17,426	10.3	62.8	36.1
Mercer	4,186	9,943	275,853	2,303	92,846	74.3	363,050	3,031	51,564	5.8	51.0	48.2
Mifflin	1,387	3,444	86,269	1,855	31,153	75.9	93,531	2,012	16,802	15.0	69.8	29.1
Monroe	5,160	14,094	371,940	2,494	227,921	87.8	566,154	3,796	56,342	20.2	49.7	49.6
Montgomery	24,514	79,959	2,302,000	3,013	1,312,718	81.9	3,368,097	4,408	399,591	20.2	44.0	55.6
Montour	631	1,404	52,180	2,870	17,514	68.5	243,008	13,365	7,624	17.4	64.3	35.0
Northampton	11,377	30,511	844,768	3,087	371,698	78.7	1,396,886	5,104	126,740	21.1	49.0	50.1
Northumberland	3,723	8,168	219,154	2,345	58,251	63.0	198,835	2,128	37,134	11.7	60.0	39.3
Perry	1,572	3,553	89,074	2,028	38,204	65.9	99,947	2,276	19,427	20.9	71.7	27.9
Philadelphia	72,370	272,911	7,925,192	5,331	2,643,494	31.3	13,085,155	8,802	674,069	20.1	19.3	80.4
Pike	1,094	2,750	81,328	1,624	46,331	95.0	67,556	1,349	21,299	22.7	58.4	40.6
Potter	790	1,576	46,342	2,552	16,791	82.1	51,251	2,822	7,962	12.3	70.8	28.5
Schuylkill	4,918	11,058	350,748	2,358	111,120	72.8	332,074	2,232	65,269	12.0	54.6	44.8
Snyder	1,309	2,902	70,796	1,867	30,864	65.8	55,165	1,455	14,983	16.7	70.5	29.0
Somerset	2,464	5,531	155,495	1,953	53,026	77.6	172,361	2,165	36,778	11.5	64.7	34.9
Sullivan	306	553	15,519	2,378	7,387	87.8	4,236	649	3,285	5.8	62.6	36.9
Susquehanna	1,663	3,782	98,869	2,356	37,549	90.5	60,475	1,441	19,040	10.2	60.8	38.6
Tioga	2,236	4,386	101,019	2,428	31,675	78.5	112,471	2,704	17,571	18.9	68.4	30.9
Union	1,084	2,253	72,475	1,718	28,818	66.1	115,437	2,736	16,123	22.4	64.1	35.4
Venango	2,378	5,671	164,909	2,899	45,377	77.3	231,724	4,074	23,659	15.3	61.2	38.1
Warren	1,356	3,366	86,738	2,009	38,934	79.3	51,949	1,203	19,273	9.9	57.1	41.7
Washington	6,678	17,086	526,505	2,584	190,182	78.9	731,893	3,592	96,177	13.9	49.6	50.1
Wayne	1,995	4,966	132,650	2,738	69,108	95.4	165,805	3,422	21,967	16.1	62.4	36.7
Westmoreland	12,372	31,287	916,342	2,488	358,568	80.0	1,364,877	3,706	178,696	14.0	56.0	43.5
Wyoming	1,101	2,486	69,033	2,466	28,675	82.5	70,316	2,155	12,832	9.7	60.7	38.8
York	11,933	32,952	994,196	2,552	416,369	77.0	1,465,777	3,762	179,269	24.3	63.7	35.5
RHODE ISLAND	35,864	122,676	2,706,973	2,533	1,494,635	97.7	1,489,112	1,394	[5]437,134	[5]6.9	[5]38.7	[5]59.4
Bristol	1,581	4,990	122,121	2,342	72,563	99.1	85,218	1,635	24,677	6.1	39.9	58.6
Kent	5,549	18,341	422,786	2,487	266,140	96.6	255,167	1,501	77,842	6.0	43.3	55.0
Newport	3,006	9,215	245,433	2,865	149,517	95.2	93,480	1,091	40,337	6.7	41.2	57.0
Providence	21,087	75,743	1,582,139	2,495	789,456	98.4	834,253	1,316	230,947	5.9	35.7	62.7
Washington	4,641	14,387	334,494	2,639	216,959	98.1	220,994	1,743	62,486	11.3	42.5	55.5
SOUTH CAROLINA	177,000	432,517	10,910,956	2,660	3,663,909	84.2	12,756,903	3,109	1,617,730	17.0	58.0	40.9
Abbeville	910	1,894	48,850	1,853	17,455	88.7	20,906	793	9,925	18.5	54.8	44.2
Aiken	5,794	12,188	280,777	1,933	92,861	86.2	124,218	855	59,492	17.2	65.7	33.3
Allendale	995	1,666	35,136	3,173	9,783	84.9	8,802	795	3,591	7.5	27.4	71.4
Anderson	5,311	12,917	332,310	1,952	126,006	86.1	193,748	1,138	64,722	14.2	67.0	32.0
Bamberg	1,106	2,190	33,107	2,030	9,539	95.1	12,825	786	6,036	8.7	35.4	63.6
Barnwell	1,300	3,309	68,283	2,923	14,263	81.6	31,141	1,333	8,685	4.9	53.0	45.9
Beaufort	5,568	13,066	419,621	3,277	175,008	88.3	594,286	4,641	55,235	25.1	60.3	38.9
Berkeley	5,166	13,619	264,061	1,820	75,712	80.2	462,104	3,186	52,937	22.2	60.7	38.1
Calhoun	559	1,089	25,378	1,668	10,330	95.7	4,784	314	6,919	8.6	49.8	49.0
Charleston	12,283	31,084	1,009,419	3,186	439,995	75.2	1,422,312	4,489	136,316	22.3	51.6	46.8
Cherokee	2,069	4,884	125,461	2,344	37,798	82.7	1,364,777	25,494	18,714	14.6	64.6	34.6
Chester	1,915	4,644	109,174	3,203	28,113	88.8	65,668	1,926	11,729	12.4	49.4	49.4
Chesterfield	1,484	3,419	82,534	1,911	24,271	72.3	49,708	1,151	14,049	12.2	51.6	47.9
Clarendon	1,589	3,458	86,819	2,638	17,407	82.4	49,255	1,496	13,200	16.9	45.9	53.7
Colleton	1,760	3,593	81,670	2,098	29,762	82.1	20,562	528	14,106	5.3	51.5	47.5
Darlington	2,573	5,310	130,194	1,918	47,053	85.3	70,537	1,039	25,454	16.4	52.7	46.5
Dillon	1,362	2,789	61,186	1,969	11,592	62.0	13,040	420	9,235	2.7	46.6	52.3
Dorchester	4,116	8,789	194,346	1,922	64,044	88.9	103,167	1,020	41,317	22.8	62.9	35.7
Edgefield	849	1,950	45,586	1,844	14,374	90.8	16,474	666	9,746	10.3	57.6	41.6
Fairfield	1,074	2,546	56,664	2,372	33,573	97.2	26,185	1,096	9,435	12.3	37.4	61.1

See footnotes at end of table.

[Includes United States, states, and 3,141 counties/county equivalents defined as of February 22, 2005. For more information on these areas, see Appendix C, Geographic Information]

County	Local government employment, March 2002		Local government finances, 2002						Elections, 2004[1]			
			General revenue				Total debt outstanding		Votes cast for President			
					Taxes							
	Total employ-ment	Total payroll ($1,000)	Total ($1,000)	Per capita (dol.)	Total ($1,000)	Prop-erty, percent of total (taxes)	Amount ($1,000)	Per capita (dol.)	Total	Percent change, 2000–2004	Repub-lican cand-idate, percent of total	Demo-cratic cand-idate, percent of total
SOUTH CAROLINA—Con.												
Florence	6,316	11,322	269,960	2,122	91,010	74.3	298,901	2,350	49,545	19.6	55.9	43.3
Georgetown	2,981	6,860	181,550	3,127	73,256	87.4	266,314	4,587	23,593	15.9	53.4	44.9
Greenville	19,905	56,423	1,573,224	4,022	379,227	87.3	1,763,400	4,508	168,833	20.3	66.0	32.8
Greenwood	2,651	6,711	293,631	4,370	46,558	90.9	188,390	2,804	23,442	12.4	60.9	38.2
Hampton	1,241	2,418	45,687	2,146	14,072	89.3	8,893	418	8,016	3.3	38.6	60.3
Horry	8,347	21,981	655,922	3,184	271,343	72.7	575,647	2,795	81,347	14.1	62.0	36.3
Jasper	635	1,186	37,796	1,805	14,440	78.5	14,042	671	6,846	5.8	42.8	56.1
Kershaw	2,641	6,447	143,648	2,673	35,064	86.4	92,949	1,730	22,915	16.5	61.8	37.2
Lancaster	2,334	5,282	119,994	1,929	36,097	88.3	129,605	2,083	20,814	0.5	62.1	36.7
Laurens	2,752	5,740	154,922	2,211	33,690	86.7	90,073	1,286	23,829	16.8	60.7	38.6
Lee	738	1,528	35,358	1,742	11,629	86.4	17,620	868	7,898	18.9	36.7	62.8
Lexington	12,732	31,256	760,326	3,414	220,152	94.0	493,090	2,214	93,432	12.5	71.9	27.2
McCormick	385	704	25,288	2,478	5,735	91.1	27,571	2,701	5,122	39.9	46.8	51.7
Marion	1,516	3,246	122,756	3,499	17,130	80.1	62,346	1,777	13,507	11.2	41.4	57.5
Marlboro	1,227	3,069	54,781	1,915	12,556	87.2	29,615	1,035	8,560	8.6	40.0	58.2
Newberry	1,789	3,944	79,482	2,164	27,799	90.4	31,900	869	12,409	0.3	61.7	36.1
Oconee	2,510	5,977	130,266	1,918	65,492	94.4	125,274	1,844	27,532	16.8	68.3	30.5
Orangeburg	4,937	12,384	289,042	3,159	81,644	80.0	122,946	1,344	37,564	14.8	33.8	65.8
Pickens	3,472	8,049	171,178	1,536	68,991	70.0	96,584	867	40,510	17.1	73.5	25.4
Richland	12,490	33,449	765,075	2,334	326,123	88.7	797,039	2,431	133,801	15.9	42.0	57.0
Saluda	629	1,198	26,627	1,394	7,703	91.6	22,415	1,173	7,578	10.0	59.9	39.6
Spartanburg	13,672	38,293	703,215	2,711	242,089	89.1	2,168,876	8,361	96,758	15.8	64.1	34.8
Sumter	3,953	8,213	214,582	2,041	67,175	77.6	117,376	1,116	37,003	20.6	48.8	50.5
Union	1,645	3,891	96,283	3,282	19,824	93.2	42,837	1,460	11,934	12.7	55.2	43.9
Williamsburg	1,860	4,004	71,120	1,952	17,511	85.2	25,090	689	13,918	22.8	34.5	65.0
York	5,859	14,538	398,667	2,292	198,660	85.4	493,611	2,838	70,181	29.1	64.5	34.5
SOUTH DAKOTA	40,812	70,985	1,811,740	2,383	864,852	77.2	1,143,217	1,504	388,215	22.7	59.9	38.4
Aurora	276	288	7,372	2,529	3,814	81.8	2,375	815	1,649	16.7	61.2	37.6
Beadle	948	1,347	34,608	2,090	17,084	85.3	21,802	1,317	8,480	9.6	58.0	40.6
Bennett	294	559	13,197	3,734	2,715	77.5	50	14	1,630	46.1	51.1	46.6
Bon Homme	438	596	18,264	2,556	7,230	83.8	20,853	2,918	3,408	8.6	60.5	37.9
Brookings	1,826	3,419	92,341	3,269	27,721	74.5	39,824	1,410	13,375	21.8	57.3	40.7
Brown	1,622	2,593	73,389	2,104	42,747	70.1	31,363	899	18,599	12.3	55.8	42.7
Brule	381	537	13,627	2,630	6,906	76.0	5,410	1,044	2,629	21.3	58.7	39.6
Buffalo	18	18	555	277	392	81.4	–	–	841	106.1	26.5	71.7
Butte	501	805	19,964	2,210	7,627	79.6	15,653	1,733	4,271	15.8	74.1	23.6
Campbell	139	157	4,180	2,436	2,391	85.5	239	139	959	4.6	73.8	24.9
Charles Mix	680	953	27,123	2,945	8,619	83.9	10,292	1,117	4,798	34.1	53.3	44.9
Clark	372	319	9,406	2,354	5,276	89.2	4,319	1,081	2,327	10.4	61.7	37.6
Clay	580	941	21,842	1,648	11,108	83.7	16,753	1,264	6,136	20.2	43.9	54.0
Codington	1,482	3,031	65,767	2,546	27,687	64.2	21,187	820	12,751	14.5	61.0	37.7
Corson	342	451	12,790	3,004	1,915	75.6	101	24	1,724	38.7	41.8	56.4
Custer	331	402	13,991	1,855	8,936	77.0	7,210	956	4,304	20.5	67.9	29.6
Davison	1,107	1,988	50,975	2,721	21,455	65.8	30,796	1,644	8,952	18.9	62.1	36.5
Day	497	503	14,656	2,423	7,041	75.3	2,184	361	3,540	10.7	47.2	51.3
Deuel	312	293	7,923	1,784	4,384	85.7	828	186	2,412	8.5	58.3	39.8
Dewey	331	350	9,525	1,575	2,176	79.4	769	127	2,564	52.5	35.9	62.6
Douglas	262	232	6,628	1,981	3,669	78.6	1,558	466	2,012	17.7	79.3	19.5
Edmunds	625	670	12,372	2,905	5,046	91.4	2,571	604	2,234	12.5	64.2	34.2
Fall River	411	614	15,895	2,170	7,957	81.5	4,099	560	3,845	12.1	62.8	34.5
Faulk	328	336	7,616	3,037	3,063	92.3	35	14	1,369	3.0	69.0	30.5
Grant	481	616	18,453	2,412	10,138	80.6	33,851	4,426	4,090	6.8	58.5	39.9
Gregory	392	455	11,655	2,580	5,151	77.0	2,975	659	2,546	12.8	66.2	31.9
Haakon	163	256	8,213	3,966	3,081	74.8	962	465	1,240	9.8	81.2	17.7
Hamlin	436	614	15,504	2,772	6,997	87.3	10,096	1,805	3,011	10.6	64.6	33.7
Hand	327	325	7,904	2,208	4,687	82.8	5,530	1,545	2,187	7.7	67.8	30.5
Hanson	247	271	6,181	1,832	2,726	90.0	2,154	639	2,150	51.3	64.1	34.7
Harding	97	170	4,502	3,476	2,425	80.1	–	–	815	11.5	86.4	11.5
Hughes	693	1,530	38,477	2,316	18,456	74.1	40,480	2,437	8,835	17.3	68.1	30.5
Hutchinson	575	716	19,406	2,479	9,779	86.4	9,729	1,243	4,147	14.4	69.9	28.4
Hyde	84	131	3,542	2,242	2,268	86.0	1,850	1,171	900	7.8	70.1	28.8
Jackson	170	185	4,719	1,651	1,672	84.8	1,084	379	1,271	22.2	57.1	40.0
Jerauld	278	260	5,699	2,558	2,770	84.0	213	96	1,236	10.2	59.6	39.0
Jones	140	145	2,602	2,329	1,554	85.0	31	28	717	8.0	78.8	18.7
Kingsbury	478	519	13,437	2,393	6,562	88.3	4,717	840	3,014	10.5	59.9	38.6
Lake	653	1,038	25,070	2,252	11,584	80.6	64,071	5,757	6,007	16.6	55.9	41.8
Lawrence	791	1,632	57,928	2,676	28,442	76.7	84,035	3,882	11,619	23.5	64.5	33.2
Lincoln	841	1,309	41,869	1,509	25,819	83.1	26,818	967	17,066	61.7	65.4	33.4
Lyman	248	220	6,054	1,542	3,374	79.5	636	162	1,940	40.0	53.0	45.0
McCook	369	558	13,137	2,253	7,835	86.8	10,491	1,799	3,271	24.3	61.7	36.7
McPherson	203	242	5,690	2,045	3,182	88.4	546	196	1,579	11.4	74.7	23.4
Marshall	381	394	10,301	2,366	5,378	80.8	2,486	571	2,364	13.7	52.5	46.5

See footnotes at end of table.

[Includes United States, states, and 3,141 counties/county equivalents defined as of February 22, 2005. For more information on these areas, see Appendix C, Geographic Information]

County	Local government employment, March 2002		Local government finances, 2002						Elections, 2004[1]			
			General revenue				Total debt outstanding		Votes cast for President			
					Taxes						Repub-lican cand-idate,	Demo-cratic cand-idate,
	Total employ-ment	Total payroll ($1,000)	Total ($1,000)	Per capita (dol.)	Total ($1,000)	Prop-erty, percent of total (taxes)	Amount ($1,000)	Per capita (dol.)	Total	Percent change, 2000–2004	percent of total	percent of total
SOUTH DAKOTA—Con.												
Meade	770	1,531	43,169	1,762	17,036	82.9	16,108	658	11,504	22.8	72.6	25.6
Mellette	235	269	7,993	3,895	1,534	83.1	425	207	931	27.0	59.4	38.8
Miner	317	369	7,206	2,569	3,972	86.1	362	129	1,470	16.1	55.1	43.6
Minnehaha	5,834	14,488	387,507	2,539	216,218	78.8	326,511	2,139	77,632	26.5	56.9	41.6
Moody	399	585	13,575	2,073	5,748	87.9	13,795	2,107	3,451	26.2	51.9	46.6
Pennington	4,599	10,773	231,147	2,544	114,976	68.4	114,966	1,266	44,968	23.0	66.7	31.6
Perkins	394	334	8,724	2,662	3,806	85.9	1,600	488	1,813	12.3	73.3	23.1
Potter	155	218	6,329	2,509	4,146	86.2	1,012	401	1,618	8.3	70.6	28.6
Roberts	711	919	19,937	2,015	7,474	82.9	3,048	308	4,982	22.3	48.1	50.7
Sanborn	226	246	5,067	1,967	2,063	89.2	14	5	1,426	12.5	57.3	40.7
Shannon	410	915	17,345	1,331	718	48.9	–	–	4,214	115.8	12.5	84.6
Spink	732	929	22,072	3,107	9,313	81.7	3,800	535	3,774	14.9	59.9	39.2
Stanley	133	264	7,262	2,651	3,664	77.3	1,404	513	1,623	17.5	69.6	28.6
Sully	150	233	4,208	2,813	2,681	87.3	200	134	917	5.3	76.6	21.9
Todd	555	1,148	24,060	2,559	1,949	67.1	–	–	3,524	135.9	25.2	72.2
Tripp	524	573	14,087	2,241	7,125	72.6	10,010	1,592	3,245	17.4	68.7	30.0
Turner	527	796	17,503	2,031	8,811	80.4	13,838	1,605	4,834	20.7	63.8	34.1
Union	671	1,127	34,038	2,651	20,331	82.9	36,758	2,863	7,048	22.1	56.6	42.6
Walworth	287	527	12,109	2,127	5,706	75.1	2,586	454	2,880	12.8	68.3	30.5
Yankton	915	1,617	49,975	2,319	25,749	75.4	53,754	2,494	10,431	19.3	57.6	40.6
Ziebach	118	137	4,078	1,579	993	77.8	–	–	1,116	54.8	40.1	57.4
TENNESSEE	245,521	599,913	14,333,478	2,475	5,176,087	66.7	17,500,115	3,022	2,437,319	17.4	56.8	42.5
Anderson	3,271	7,404	170,025	2,373	69,264	71.8	192,533	2,687	31,682	10.1	58.4	40.7
Bedford	2,034	3,919	96,242	2,452	24,136	66.2	47,124	1,200	13,706	12.3	60.9	38.4
Benton	646	1,315	22,953	1,385	5,567	59.2	17,327	1,046	7,090	12.3	44.6	54.6
Bledsoe	563	956	19,839	1,587	3,350	74.9	17,524	1,402	4,809	14.6	59.2	40.1
Blount	5,887	13,306	314,894	2,871	71,604	76.8	308,034	2,809	48,712	19.8	68.2	30.9
Bradley	4,142	9,640	211,181	2,360	48,923	71.7	160,730	1,796	35,637	21.0	72.8	26.5
Campbell	1,771	3,252	61,294	1,535	16,704	65.2	54,376	1,362	14,118	13.7	55.7	43.7
Cannon	485	885	19,320	1,474	4,377	68.3	15,866	1,211	5,481	16.7	53.5	45.9
Carroll	1,207	2,230	47,635	1,623	8,173	49.6	35,904	1,223	11,757	8.6	56.2	43.1
Carter	1,869	3,550	74,045	1,301	18,092	69.8	37,316	656	22,313	16.8	70.7	28.7
Cheatham	1,454	2,710	64,823	1,748	23,855	62.1	56,095	1,512	15,697	24.4	61.6	37.7
Chester	543	971	22,579	1,418	6,629	52.2	13,425	843	6,357	11.0	64.3	35.3
Claiborne	1,630	3,029	65,124	2,165	10,885	67.5	31,921	1,061	10,540	17.1	61.2	38.3
Clay	284	534	14,033	1,760	3,764	70.3	2,129	267	3,357	-2.5	49.2	49.9
Cocke	1,318	2,498	57,286	1,679	16,037	67.1	26,957	790	12,311	20.2	67.4	32.0
Coffee	2,302	4,657	90,572	1,842	34,652	59.1	63,093	1,283	20,167	13.4	58.5	40.9
Crockett	720	1,111	26,204	1,803	6,558	67.9	29,170	2,007	5,722	5.2	56.7	43.0
Cumberland	1,497	3,127	67,419	1,385	23,134	56.4	59,565	1,223	23,637	24.3	64.1	35.2
Davidson	21,628	69,974	1,664,290	2,925	686,106	86.0	3,992,283	7,016	242,302	16.2	44.5	54.8
Decatur	736	1,365	17,779	1,518	3,941	56.2	20,467	1,748	4,879	11.6	52.6	46.5
DeKalb	848	1,437	27,293	1,535	5,964	70.9	37,098	2,087	7,173	14.5	51.4	48.0
Dickson	1,568	3,473	93,328	2,106	37,879	57.8	148,442	3,350	19,298	24.1	54.8	44.6
Dyer	1,810	3,714	68,663	1,848	17,525	72.3	90,358	2,432	13,809	16.6	61.2	38.3
Fayette	1,119	2,001	41,384	1,327	14,229	63.7	17,662	566	14,737	27.8	60.8	38.7
Fentress	599	987	24,861	1,474	6,236	48.1	17,815	1,056	6,700	11.1	64.1	35.4
Franklin	1,461	2,509	61,471	1,532	21,467	64.9	48,766	1,216	17,077	16.2	53.5	45.7
Gibson	2,459	4,415	101,112	2,101	28,489	63.3	65,893	1,369	19,221	12.2	55.1	44.3
Giles	940	1,949	53,224	1,806	19,230	67.3	35,671	1,210	11,537	14.6	53.4	45.7
Grainger	669	1,154	27,336	1,290	5,770	64.4	17,046	804	7,527	21.5	65.2	34.1
Greene	2,204	4,685	97,794	1,536	30,074	66.5	82,293	1,292	24,194	16.2	67.7	31.6
Grundy	617	1,017	24,059	1,680	5,006	78.4	14,060	982	4,929	7.2	42.8	56.6
Hamblen	1,935	4,355	99,614	1,705	45,329	51.9	79,066	1,353	22,318	13.3	66.1	33.3
Hamilton	15,525	39,130	1,197,675	3,873	337,390	72.9	1,197,603	3,873	136,936	13.8	57.4	41.9
Hancock	361	533	15,473	2,292	1,589	73.4	14,539	2,153	2,551	22.9	68.8	30.5
Hardeman	1,189	1,945	43,995	1,556	11,262	58.3	21,310	754	10,466	18.9	45.0	54.3
Hardin	1,259	2,225	54,517	2,103	13,114	58.0	18,051	696	9,954	13.3	61.2	38.5
Hawkins	2,085	3,730	76,893	1,406	26,630	65.6	44,076	806	20,233	18.3	66.5	33.0
Haywood	1,080	2,110	38,920	1,986	11,069	69.0	1,280	65	7,548	16.5	41.6	57.8
Henderson	1,022	2,249	42,526	1,646	13,088	45.5	46,360	1,794	10,096	20.2	65.2	34.2
Henry	1,681	3,337	100,574	3,209	18,402	49.4	42,008	1,340	13,177	7.1	55.7	43.5
Hickman	809	1,165	34,423	1,483	8,325	65.8	16,723	720	8,673	19.4	50.3	49.2
Houston	374	588	14,702	1,841	3,361	70.5	14,590	1,827	3,598	15.1	40.0	59.1
Humphreys	883	1,924	35,089	1,941	9,488	68.3	82,383	4,557	7,793	16.6	41.9	57.6
Jackson	435	732	17,210	1,540	3,612	74.4	6,647	595	5,056	6.4	40.1	59.3
Jefferson	1,270	2,548	64,691	1,412	19,750	67.5	43,619	952	17,215	22.2	67.5	31.8
Johnson	530	965	25,791	1,448	6,444	69.4	17,958	1,008	6,480	14.5	71.5	28.0
Knox	13,680	33,332	902,467	2,306	480,615	59.3	1,172,752	2,996	178,419	18.5	62.1	37.0
Lake	360	588	11,728	1,487	2,955	59.6	7,098	900	4,740	113.1	43.8	55.6
Lauderdale	1,107	2,033	45,310	1,669	12,682	61.8	26,592	980	8,682	14.0	48.0	51.5
Lawrence	1,867	4,215	69,822	1,719	24,367	56.4	63,758	1,570	16,658	15.1	59.8	39.6

See footnotes at end of table.

[Includes United States, states, and 3,141 counties/county equivalents defined as of February 22, 2005. For more information on these areas, see Appendix C, Geographic Information]

County	Local government employment, March 2002		Local government finances, 2002						Elections, 2004[1]			
			General revenue				Total debt outstanding		Votes cast for President			
					Taxes						Repub-lican cand-idate, percent of total	Demo-cratic cand-idate, percent of total
	Total employ-ment	Total payroll ($1,000)	Total ($1,000)	Per capita (dol.)	Total ($1,000)	Prop-erty, percent of total (taxes)	Amount ($1,000)	Per capita (dol.)	Total	Percent change, 2000–2004		
TENNESSEE—Con.												
Lewis	409	819	19,015	1,663	4,729	54.8	10,949	957	5,054	14.3	55.8	43.4
Lincoln	2,000	3,586	95,300	3,006	15,062	53.8	82,026	2,587	12,457	16.9	62.9	36.5
Loudon	1,487	3,509	77,728	1,907	25,158	58.5	132,109	3,241	19,864	21.1	70.7	28.7
McMinn	2,373	4,697	105,381	2,103	28,716	64.6	56,857	1,135	18,003	8.5	66.5	32.7
McNairy	960	1,538	37,375	1,512	8,612	68.1	44,377	1,796	9,924	10.4	58.3	41.3
Macon	830	1,495	31,211	1,496	8,699	67.4	26,806	1,285	7,433	14.5	62.8	36.8
Madison	7,708	17,994	590,367	6,321	109,102	50.1	358,577	3,839	38,675	14.0	56.1	43.5
Marion	1,011	2,030	45,443	1,636	13,699	49.9	37,878	1,363	11,492	12.1	51.0	48.3
Marshall	1,134	2,455	53,065	1,935	22,719	69.1	77,961	2,843	10,615	13.4	54.9	44.5
Maury	4,631	12,574	296,221	4,144	53,681	56.6	200,807	2,809	30,043	28.4	58.3	41.2
Meigs	422	744	16,557	1,464	3,374	73.4	8,918	789	4,132	21.9	60.5	38.6
Monroe	1,389	2,752	59,691	1,478	18,626	53.5	29,991	742	15,568	19.7	65.0	34.4
Montgomery	5,265	11,517	265,643	1,942	111,523	60.4	408,699	2,987	48,998	25.5	58.4	41.0
Moore	220	416	11,120	1,864	2,663	92.1	2,395	402	2,774	20.6	60.1	39.1
Morgan	622	1,092	28,133	1,403	6,765	81.3	10,505	524	7,360	19.4	59.8	39.7
Obion	1,299	2,664	56,409	1,740	20,439	55.4	18,023	556	13,535	8.8	58.1	41.0
Overton	843	1,418	30,027	1,483	7,345	58.1	33,271	1,643	8,510	13.5	46.3	53.1
Perry	340	580	15,936	2,113	3,850	74.2	8,728	1,157	3,150	9.9	48.3	50.1
Pickett	249	464	10,655	2,107	2,497	56.9	7,886	1,560	2,645	18.1	60.5	39.1
Polk	477	912	24,009	1,489	6,534	65.7	13,078	811	6,700	19.8	58.6	40.7
Putnam	3,638	8,966	218,068	3,406	42,817	60.4	153,750	2,401	26,442	17.8	59.1	40.0
Rhea	1,325	2,254	59,536	2,057	12,476	63.8	33,047	1,142	11,054	13.1	66.1	33.2
Roane	2,384	5,030	105,604	2,022	31,524	61.6	81,583	1,562	23,338	9.4	62.0	37.3
Robertson	1,865	4,493	97,766	1,709	39,319	60.3	100,446	1,756	25,323	25.6	60.5	39.0
Rutherford	6,357	16,364	363,328	1,858	146,741	66.5	515,650	2,636	84,409	35.7	61.8	37.5
Scott	1,082	1,992	40,036	1,847	6,683	71.0	45,222	2,086	7,628	15.3	59.1	40.5
Sequatchie	499	796	17,971	1,523	5,684	70.1	18,089	1,533	4,983	28.2	59.2	39.9
Sevier	3,370	7,178	191,793	2,581	95,134	29.7	271,825	3,658	30,970	22.1	71.5	27.8
Shelby	42,654	134,185	2,976,010	3,302	1,309,312	66.6	4,241,992	4,706	377,282	12.0	41.9	57.5
Smith	718	1,071	30,705	1,690	9,410	54.9	27,850	1,532	7,828	6.5	47.8	51.7
Stewart	526	812	23,416	1,831	5,042	71.8	22,698	1,774	5,583	16.8	47.9	51.2
Sullivan	5,752	13,451	289,829	1,898	125,721	68.9	268,565	1,758	62,639	12.4	67.9	31.4
Sumner	4,750	11,094	254,624	1,867	101,661	65.9	180,345	1,322	61,968	22.8	64.8	34.6
Tipton	2,075	4,464	92,961	1,742	26,017	69.7	60,981	1,143	21,677	31.0	65.4	34.0
Trousdale	288	549	12,397	1,676	3,256	91.5	5,211	705	3,191	8.4	41.2	58.0
Unicoi	799	1,629	48,169	2,729	8,226	69.3	27,958	1,584	7,463	16.1	67.4	31.8
Union	560	1,177	26,806	1,444	4,582	68.1	14,984	807	6,710	15.3	61.8	37.6
Van Buren	252	385	8,822	1,594	2,020	63.7	4,071	736	2,347	10.1	47.7	51.5
Warren	1,464	3,029	67,113	1,731	23,144	64.5	47,592	1,228	14,400	9.7	52.1	47.3
Washington	4,096	9,434	206,370	1,891	88,002	61.0	359,393	3,293	45,006	18.6	66.1	33.2
Wayne	775	1,164	29,607	1,738	6,576	62.5	21,828	1,282	5,984	12.8	66.8	32.6
Weakley	1,478	2,524	57,159	1,668	18,745	56.7	42,740	1,247	13,496	13.9	57.9	41.4
White	875	1,869	34,730	1,479	9,862	61.9	26,979	1,149	9,495	22.1	55.5	43.7
Williamson	5,598	14,915	407,048	2,978	181,217	62.5	517,808	3,789	79,650	36.3	72.1	27.3
Wilson	2,939	6,353	164,842	1,764	72,031	61.8	166,311	1,780	44,452	23.8	65.1	34.4
TEXAS	1,074,656	2,697,240	64,879,272	2,987	30,318,113	80.9	98,801,444	4,548	7,410,765	15.7	61.1	38.2
Anderson	1,939	4,071	85,965	1,575	40,668	80.0	22,883	419	16,301	8.1	70.7	28.7
Andrews	1,075	2,459	63,147	4,888	36,979	94.9	33,632	2,603	4,536	12.7	84.6	14.9
Angelina	5,061	10,210	223,314	2,775	72,604	73.9	161,795	2,011	28,364	5.2	66.8	32.8
Aransas	816	1,832	44,013	1,907	27,806	85.0	23,539	1,020	9,268	12.4	70.9	28.5
Archer	469	925	21,605	2,306	8,940	83.7	17,810	1,975	4,451	11.4	79.9	19.7
Armstrong	136	240	4,346	2,057	1,508	86.3	–	–	1,004	7.0	82.7	16.9
Atascosa	2,108	4,369	84,520	2,055	26,059	83.1	36,165	879	12,116	12.7	63.0	36.5
Austin	1,092	2,378	53,757	2,182	26,579	84.2	47,493	1,928	10,702	16.0	75.4	24.1
Bailey	564	1,085	23,934	3,672	5,890	83.6	4,878	748	2,412	15.4	78.0	21.8
Bandera	764	1,465	32,077	1,692	16,643	87.7	8,018	423	8,741	20.2	79.3	19.9
Bastrop	2,644	6,258	140,750	2,191	54,547	88.0	149,810	2,332	23,441	28.0	56.7	41.8
Baylor	321	607	10,670	2,728	3,499	85.9	2,230	570	1,640	-17.3	71.3	28.5
Bee	1,807	3,505	77,686	2,407	19,051	76.1	23,489	728	9,518	14.3	57.0	42.5
Bell	13,705	32,800	709,061	2,897	206,221	75.6	817,946	3,342	79,724	26.0	65.4	34.1
Bexar	79,530	208,010	4,489,594	3,114	1,652,912	82.0	8,836,407	6,130	475,314	15.2	54.9	44.4
Blanco	403	818	18,236	2,070	10,647	88.6	12,664	1,438	4,584	21.7	71.5	27.6
Borden	79	187	6,464	9,395	5,660	99.1	–	–	359	1.7	84.4	15.3
Bosque	846	1,760	38,523	2,191	15,404	86.8	23,360	1,328	7,586	12.1	75.6	23.9
Bowie	4,256	9,237	219,785	2,455	73,194	74.8	126,062	1,408	33,760	11.3	64.6	35.2
Brazoria	12,089	27,488	649,145	2,527	372,353	86.7	858,179	3,341	93,248	16.5	68.3	31.0
Brazos	6,709	15,197	332,394	2,165	174,441	76.9	388,676	2,532	54,309	15.7	69.2	29.7
Brewster	651	1,416	35,840	3,950	8,778	71.3	11,294	1,245	3,760	5.0	52.7	46.0
Briscoe	102	180	3,913	2,306	1,761	88.7	8,867	5,225	811	5.1	76.5	23.6
Brooks	515	1,111	25,334	3,261	10,675	92.3	4,407	567	2,674	10.0	31.6	68.2
Brown	1,896	3,994	92,767	2,442	33,706	77.6	52,699	1,387	14,253	10.3	81.7	17.7

See footnotes at end of table.

[Includes United States, states, and 3,141 counties/county equivalents defined as of February 22, 2005. For more information on these areas, see Appendix C, Geographic Information]

County	Local government employment, March 2002		Local government finances, 2002						Elections, 2004[1]			
			General revenue				Total debt outstanding		Votes cast for President			
					Taxes						Repub-lican cand-idate, percent of total	Demo-cratic cand-idate, percent of total
	Total employ-ment	Total payroll ($1,000)	Total ($1,000)	Per capita (dol.)	Total ($1,000)	Prop-erty, percent of total (taxes)	Amount ($1,000)	Per capita (dol.)	Total	Percent change, 2000–2004		
TEXAS—Con.												
Burleson	822	1,604	37,397	2,233	17,181	86.9	16,115	962	6,721	14.6	65.5	33.9
Burnet	1,583	3,966	83,030	2,210	50,344	86.7	68,404	1,821	15,742	19.0	72.8	26.3
Caldwell	1,446	3,060	68,186	1,956	20,158	84.4	39,781	1,141	11,587	22.9	55.6	43.6
Calhoun	1,452	2,763	103,012	5,043	62,498	93.2	62,870	3,078	6,929	5.6	62.8	37.0
Callahan	674	1,305	28,415	2,198	9,962	73.5	18,493	1,431	5,654	15.5	80.3	19.0
Cameron	19,980	44,325	995,855	2,821	247,649	74.9	1,007,177	2,854	69,156	11.4	50.3	49.2
Camp	490	988	22,529	1,932	8,853	83.2	21,961	1,884	4,439	17.3	59.4	40.1
Carson	379	825	18,303	2,772	13,002	94.5	786	119	2,944	7.4	83.2	16.5
Cass	1,825	3,982	88,452	2,931	24,523	87.9	24,632	816	12,049	9.3	61.3	38.4
Castro	704	1,037	29,626	3,695	8,105	88.5	3,688	460	2,430	3.2	73.8	26.0
Chambers	1,415	3,450	102,612	3,780	70,847	92.7	116,618	4,296	11,649	18.8	74.0	25.4
Cherokee	2,099	4,116	90,077	1,915	27,402	83.5	42,611	906	15,839	9.0	71.5	28.0
Childress	554	1,144	24,225	3,197	4,315	75.2	4,520	597	2,144	0.8	76.0	23.8
Clay	610	1,235	40,243	3,572	8,694	94.1	189,592	16,830	5,288	14.0	75.1	24.6
Cochran	359	763	16,882	4,800	9,090	93.7	459	131	1,110	−5.2	77.1	22.4
Coke	369	715	15,492	4,080	4,817	92.7	913	240	1,610	6.3	83.1	16.5
Coleman	690	1,475	30,875	3,480	5,737	80.7	10,500	1,183	3,826	6.9	79.3	20.3
Collin	20,638	55,242	1,561,979	2,746	1,071,179	87.0	2,917,320	5,129	245,154	39.8	71.2	28.1
Collingsworth	286	527	11,804	3,793	2,817	86.7	432	139	1,398	−1.2	75.2	24.8
Colorado	997	2,184	48,888	2,389	22,487	86.9	23,131	1,130	7,690	6.1	71.4	28.1
Comal	3,754	7,418	239,929	2,833	161,830	86.4	289,775	3,421	41,043	25.3	76.9	22.3
Comanche	920	1,683	43,499	3,211	8,755	86.8	10,373	766	5,268	4.9	72.4	27.2
Concho	232	379	12,718	3,329	4,250	92.1	2,198	575	1,193	8.2	76.4	22.6
Cooke	2,505	5,355	122,892	3,256	38,176	78.8	64,494	1,709	15,107	12.2	78.8	20.8
Coryell	2,847	6,148	122,650	1,643	31,301	77.8	96,987	1,300	17,625	16.8	70.5	29.1
Cottle	97	212	5,195	2,933	2,427	88.9	757	427	768	1.5	71.5	27.9
Crane	259	615	23,993	6,135	19,315	96.6	4,150	1,061	1,574	−4.8	83.5	16.1
Crockett	236	500	25,448	6,530	22,370	98.3	2,090	536	1,728	23.6	72.2	27.4
Crosby	481	1,011	21,283	3,103	6,108	87.3	314	46	2,275	13.6	72.4	27.3
Culberson	268	598	9,283	3,284	5,263	88.7	5,795	2,050	788	−22.1	51.7	47.6
Dallam	446	898	18,113	2,941	9,108	79.0	5,754	934	1,782	2.2	82.7	17.1
Dallas	108,172	327,284	8,243,853	3,627	4,567,623	75.4	11,419,316	5,023	687,709	12.2	50.4	49.0
Dawson	962	2,294	48,636	3,348	18,517	86.3	70,586	4,859	4,545	−6.1	75.2	24.5
Deaf Smith	1,132	2,352	54,031	2,938	16,590	87.5	23,895	1,299	5,291	6.2	78.2	21.4
Delta	308	578	13,533	2,495	3,989	85.7	13,001	2,397	2,082	9.6	69.5	30.1
Denton	15,588	43,274	979,001	2,006	632,996	87.0	2,167,929	4,442	201,410	37.2	70.0	29.5
DeWitt	1,628	3,274	77,903	3,890	15,395	86.6	22,213	1,109	6,732	8.9	75.8	23.9
Dickens	192	435	6,853	2,539	3,063	78.5	1,400	519	1,063	20.7	76.7	23.1
Dimmit	769	1,820	35,468	3,462	7,892	76.4	14,751	1,440	3,566	−5.0	33.3	66.3
Donley	375	746	15,752	4,063	3,375	80.1	17,692	4,563	1,784	3.8	80.1	19.6
Duval	1,135	2,797	46,104	3,598	15,667	87.8	22,216	1,734	4,091	−18.7	28.4	71.3
Eastland	1,473	2,672	59,698	3,278	12,861	81.1	23,028	1,265	6,857	6.9	76.6	23.1
Ector	8,362	20,117	487,270	3,982	136,112	79.4	261,047	2,133	36,310	10.4	75.7	23.6
Edwards	244	402	9,869	4,779	5,415	96.9	899	435	963	2.8	77.4	22.5
Ellis	5,028	11,768	264,695	2,202	133,718	83.3	390,375	3,248	46,444	24.5	74.5	25.1
El Paso	37,115	89,950	2,086,811	3,008	639,753	78.6	1,755,375	2,531	169,573	16.9	43.2	56.1
Erath	1,375	3,010	65,666	1,979	29,943	79.6	57,529	1,734	12,281	10.5	77.4	22.1
Falls	858	1,668	33,403	1,864	9,865	72.7	16,275	908	5,902	3.3	58.5	41.1
Fannin	1,255	2,594	60,065	1,888	20,542	85.8	45,747	1,438	11,960	15.7	66.0	33.5
Fayette	1,128	2,129	47,803	2,147	28,518	88.7	10,983	493	10,397	10.8	72.4	27.0
Fisher	341	657	19,536	4,623	6,194	93.3	12,615	2,985	1,923	2.7	60.4	39.4
Floyd	691	1,384	22,683	3,078	5,881	88.9	335	45	2,584	6.8	78.6	21.1
Foard	122	229	4,869	3,117	2,040	91.9	1,028	658	587	5.6	59.1	40.0
Fort Bend	13,888	37,857	914,920	2,294	545,295	88.3	1,606,448	4,028	163,169	32.1	57.4	42.1
Franklin	324	779	17,764	1,821	11,521	91.0	14,882	1,526	4,217	21.5	75.5	24.0
Freestone	772	1,504	47,505	2,579	30,466	93.5	21,835	1,186	7,161	7.8	70.6	28.9
Frio	855	1,824	45,872	2,804	9,568	81.7	233,692	14,285	3,930	−4.8	50.7	49.1
Gaines	1,064	2,137	69,035	4,851	38,303	96.7	2,174	153	4,164	20.4	85.0	14.6
Galveston	14,731	36,689	917,054	3,516	531,451	88.0	1,220,792	4,681	105,981	14.0	57.8	41.4
Garza	357	666	19,146	3,801	9,128	90.2	207	41	1,812	2.4	81.7	18.0
Gillespie	807	1,673	44,207	2,041	27,314	81.6	33,433	1,543	11,553	16.5	80.5	18.2
Glasscock	101	213	9,202	6,816	7,933	97.6	–	–	533	−6.7	91.6	8.3
Goliad	454	897	19,772	2,799	11,475	94.0	3,744	530	3,501	3.2	64.8	34.8
Gonzales	1,235	2,468	60,094	3,190	14,981	82.5	19,692	1,045	6,022	−0.8	71.3	28.4
Gray	1,005	2,133	46,813	2,138	25,975	86.6	23,979	1,095	8,572	4.7	84.7	15.0
Grayson	5,466	12,495	278,248	2,448	114,375	79.8	297,713	2,620	44,423	11.2	69.3	30.3
Gregg	6,397	15,473	349,866	3,093	157,669	75.0	359,988	3,182	42,398	10.3	70.6	29.0
Grimes	927	2,033	44,332	1,795	22,831	88.1	24,217	981	8,030	18.1	65.5	33.8
Guadalupe	4,525	10,377	166,642	1,766	81,611	84.4	200,908	2,130	38,752	26.8	72.8	26.6
Hale	1,934	4,004	85,222	2,387	28,573	72.6	18,824	527	10,154	11.5	79.0	20.5

See footnotes at end of table.

[Includes United States, states, and 3,141 counties/county equivalents defined as of February 22, 2005. For more information on these areas, see Appendix C, Geographic Information]

County	Local government employment, March 2002		Local government finances, 2002						Elections, 2004[1]			
			General revenue				Total debt outstanding		Votes cast for President			
					Taxes						Repub-lican cand-idate, percent of total	Demo-cratic cand-idate, percent of total
	Total employ-ment	Total payroll ($1,000)	Total ($1,000)	Per capita (dol.)	Total ($1,000)	Prop-erty, percent of total (taxes)	Amount ($1,000)	Per capita (dol.)	Total	Percent change, 2000–2004		
TEXAS—Con.												
Hall	325	531	16,264	4,341	4,172	83.2	700	187	1,277	–11.7	67.4	32.3
Hamilton	605	1,060	25,574	3,208	7,405	82.5	13,446	1,687	3,730	10.5	76.6	22.7
Hansford	512	989	28,999	5,524	15,034	94.7	24,750	4,714	2,147	2.8	88.6	11.2
Hardeman	486	957	18,284	4,053	7,911	90.0	687	152	1,702	9.3	71.3	28.2
Hardin	2,495	4,995	97,820	1,989	38,213	88.9	80,002	1,627	20,710	16.1	72.6	27.1
Harris	171,537	473,328	11,939,625	3,373	6,124,731	80.1	24,414,922	6,896	1,067,968	9.6	54.8	44.6
Harrison	2,794	5,894	122,627	1,970	69,597	87.1	114,433	1,838	26,223	14.2	62.8	36.8
Hartley	288	585	4,618	893	3,184	87.9	644	124	2,059	1.4	84.3	15.3
Haskell	434	885	18,838	3,225	5,869	87.7	2,667	457	2,416	–17.5	63.7	35.9
Hays	4,176	10,181	283,363	2,549	127,817	76.2	520,286	4,680	47,823	39.4	56.5	42.1
Hemphill	304	667	19,749	5,906	14,828	94.5	4,844	1,449	1,643	11.5	84.0	15.6
Henderson	3,009	6,206	140,655	1,862	63,350	81.6	98,492	1,304	28,849	12.6	70.1	29.5
Hidalgo	34,632	75,767	1,786,259	2,915	426,001	78.7	1,396,922	2,280	113,683	12.5	44.8	54.9
Hill	1,922	3,781	82,065	2,439	28,912	77.9	72,056	2,141	13,053	21.6	70.7	28.7
Hockley	2,233	4,250	106,034	4,670	37,281	93.4	131,019	5,771	7,577	12.3	81.3	18.3
Hood	1,699	3,252	76,502	1,741	47,200	85.5	127,525	2,902	21,293	21.6	76.5	22.9
Hopkins	1,804	4,528	98,514	3,047	29,359	79.5	48,038	1,486	12,062	10.6	71.2	28.5
Houston	1,020	2,441	39,563	1,709	15,408	82.9	17,157	741	8,806	6.9	66.4	33.2
Howard	2,521	4,864	148,814	4,488	34,234	80.5	193,610	5,839	10,201	6.8	73.3	26.1
Hudspeth	218	459	15,924	4,773	5,212	94.8	5,157	1,546	886	–3.9	65.1	34.1
Hunt	4,270	9,404	210,412	2,634	65,254	79.2	242,367	3,034	28,194	15.2	71.2	28.3
Hutchinson	1,722	3,564	94,784	4,094	34,996	85.2	25,504	1,101	9,369	0.2	83.7	16.0
Irion	98	196	5,800	3,311	4,767	96.3	50	29	828	4.4	82.6	17.0
Jack	502	979	22,866	2,563	9,239	85.6	10,645	1,193	3,126	5.1	79.0	20.6
Jackson	1,028	2,149	50,102	3,509	20,708	89.3	58,078	4,068	5,077	4.6	74.2	25.5
Jasper	1,686	3,700	77,921	2,184	32,330	87.0	77,609	2,176	12,873	9.6	64.8	34.7
Jeff Davis	138	297	7,396	3,344	3,005	90.0	1,078	487	1,167	10.1	65.5	32.4
Jefferson	11,851	29,274	720,077	2,928	388,764	81.5	1,239,043	4,977	91,866	5.7	48.4	51.2
Jim Hogg	399	710	16,307	3,168	8,185	93.9	5,305	1,031	2,065	–4.3	34.5	65.1
Jim Wells	2,021	3,922	97,342	2,430	33,752	68.6	131,260	3,277	12,691	5.6	45.8	53.8
Johnson	5,352	12,016	271,835	2,003	115,188	86.2	374,233	2,758	47,422	22.5	73.4	26.0
Jones	1,315	2,377	46,542	2,301	12,686	76.5	10,729	530	5,931	–1.9	71.7	28.0
Karnes	856	1,560	35,621	2,325	9,994	83.7	9,745	636	4,673	8.5	66.6	33.0
Kaufman	3,699	8,371	177,139	2,269	72,108	86.2	206,827	2,649	30,366	31.7	70.2	29.5
Kendall	1,206	3,001	72,945	2,881	51,829	92.7	73,458	2,901	14,072	27.1	81.3	18.0
Kenedy	83	152	4,604	11,284	4,404	99.4	–	–	169	–25.9	48.5	50.3
Kent	119	220	4,867	6,016	4,283	99.4	2,343	2,896	522	–2.6	73.2	26.4
Kerr	1,819	4,033	90,477	2,019	50,125	83.8	66,340	1,481	21,246	10.5	77.8	21.5
Kimble	301	603	17,167	3,808	4,776	82.2	1,663	369	1,816	9.0	81.6	17.8
King	37	89	3,767	12,074	3,441	97.4	508	1,628	156	13.9	87.8	11.5
Kinney	239	422	10,012	2,935	2,873	86.0	1,954	573	1,600	10.8	65.7	33.9
Kleberg	1,910	3,582	83,652	2,688	31,019	82.7	14,960	481	9,973	8.5	53.8	45.6
Knox	388	726	17,426	4,386	4,714	81.7	2,358	594	1,552	–1.5	69.7	29.9
Lamar	2,264	5,207	124,852	2,544	51,614	77.9	102,555	2,090	17,470	13.2	69.0	30.6
Lamb	906	1,811	56,895	3,884	19,126	91.5	20,193	1,378	4,271	–7.1	79.8	20.1
Lampasas	851	1,829	33,507	1,781	11,901	84.3	13,742	730	7,025	13.1	77.2	22.7
La Salle	436	904	21,004	3,606	5,591	86.0	5,020	862	2,230	10.7	44.4	55.1
Lavaca	864	1,790	39,196	2,064	18,173	86.4	13,817	728	8,177	8.4	73.1	26.3
Lee	716	1,542	33,231	2,037	15,752	85.2	20,880	1,280	6,088	10.0	68.3	31.2
Leon	689	1,350	34,301	2,163	18,446	88.8	13,271	837	6,799	7.5	73.9	25.8
Liberty	2,930	6,470	142,629	1,938	60,667	89.1	95,137	1,293	21,691	8.0	68.3	31.3
Limestone	1,167	2,439	58,619	2,617	27,419	88.8	18,457	824	7,818	10.5	64.3	35.2
Lipscomb	268	529	12,568	4,131	7,825	92.9	28	9	1,337	3.3	85.8	13.8
Live Oak	605	1,132	24,429	2,030	16,149	92.1	4,462	371	4,201	4.9	74.9	24.7
Llano	577	1,147	33,467	1,876	25,414	95.4	25,396	1,424	9,563	10.8	75.7	23.6
Loving	30	41	1,176	17,818	1,052	98.9	–	–	80	–48.7	81.3	15.0
Lubbock	11,358	29,093	751,293	3,038	230,526	75.8	484,951	1,961	93,151	22.6	75.3	24.1
Lynn	484	845	22,954	3,592	6,397	90.2	4,472	700	2,271	9.0	78.2	21.6
McCulloch	624	1,191	27,852	3,535	6,812	76.5	9,066	1,151	3,220	10.3	76.6	23.1
McLennan	10,417	24,391	739,117	3,403	216,969	73.5	3,092,518	14,240	79,254	15.2	65.7	33.8
McMullen	81	191	6,273	7,311	5,673	97.3	3,621	4,220	564	28.5	82.8	16.8
Madison	554	1,054	25,733	2,011	8,949	79.4	22,378	1,749	4,101	13.2	69.2	30.1
Marion	421	768	16,205	1,466	9,100	87.1	723	65	4,348	10.6	56.1	43.3
Martin	347	797	18,410	3,964	8,582	95.2	423	91	1,807	–7.3	83.8	15.9
Mason	238	390	8,376	2,231	3,397	87.7	1,777	473	2,077	15.3	77.0	22.1
Matagorda	2,475	5,552	134,593	3,539	64,845	90.0	91,073	2,395	12,521	0.5	64.8	34.8
Maverick	2,874	5,729	150,530	3,085	22,010	71.0	85,526	1,753	10,034	8.7	40.1	59.3
Medina	2,083	4,604	84,366	2,072	26,730	79.0	55,814	1,371	14,826	15.2	70.1	29.2
Menard	222	434	7,702	3,262	2,338	89.9	1,534	650	1,103	11.4	69.0	30.0
Midland	7,256	17,584	449,912	3,832	161,323	79.0	243,934	2,078	44,834	12.8	81.6	17.9

See footnotes at end of table.

[Includes United States, states, and 3,141 counties/county equivalents defined as of February 22, 2005. For more information on these areas, see Appendix C, Geographic Information]

County	Local government employment, March 2002		Local government finances, 2002						Elections, 2004[1]			
			General revenue				Total debt outstanding		Votes cast for President			
					Taxes						Republican candidate, percent of total	Democratic candidate, percent of total
	Total employment	Total payroll ($1,000)	Total ($1,000)	Per capita (dol.)	Total ($1,000)	Property, percent of total (taxes)	Amount ($1,000)	Per capita (dol.)	Total	Percent change, 2000–2004		
TEXAS—Con.												
Milam	1,203	2,643	57,410	2,293	23,938	84.6	24,319	971	8,783	6.2	60.2	39.2
Mills	300	655	12,769	2,497	3,534	85.5	2,504	490	2,231	–3.6	80.4	18.7
Mitchell	666	1,377	30,933	3,273	11,196	88.0	13,819	1,462	2,558	–0.6	74.8	25.0
Montague	1,307	2,559	63,880	3,320	15,394	85.1	33,135	1,722	7,897	7.7	74.8	24.6
Montgomery	12,481	29,534	713,334	2,171	386,594	89.1	1,370,682	4,171	133,988	26.2	78.1	21.4
Moore	1,363	2,918	67,369	3,344	30,445	92.0	18,380	912	5,628	6.4	81.8	17.9
Morris	630	1,336	26,034	1,970	16,094	88.9	11,162	845	5,278	8.0	53.4	46.2
Motley	79	172	3,071	2,382	1,463	88.7	279	216	684	6.5	82.5	16.5
Nacogdoches	3,130	7,337	190,236	3,212	45,389	81.5	135,719	2,291	21,466	8.4	66.0	33.3
Navarro	2,846	5,741	132,689	2,835	42,379	76.1	101,560	2,170	16,034	15.4	66.8	32.8
Newton	666	1,352	25,745	1,728	9,101	92.6	23,746	1,594	5,700	14.2	55.4	44.1
Nolan	1,157	2,571	55,608	3,667	18,143	84.0	26,829	1,769	5,289	–0.4	70.4	29.1
Nueces	16,628	41,594	928,835	2,958	402,777	79.5	950,194	3,026	104,560	7.4	56.8	42.5
Ochiltree	628	1,248	31,313	3,450	14,391	82.3	9,561	1,053	3,177	7.3	92.0	7.9
Oldham	271	711	13,592	6,322	3,297	84.1	412	192	843	8.9	87.0	12.8
Orange	3,703	8,297	238,207	2,823	96,422	83.0	615,040	7,288	31,908	7.6	63.6	36.0
Palo Pinto	1,659	3,686	90,674	3,340	30,399	83.1	68,037	2,506	10,014	9.8	71.3	28.1
Panola	1,101	2,584	73,781	3,238	49,891	94.2	27,297	1,198	10,007	10.3	70.2	29.6
Parker	4,257	10,155	236,505	2,499	86,357	85.5	279,038	2,948	40,957	23.3	77.6	21.9
Parmer	692	1,293	25,423	2,578	8,938	83.6	3,266	331	2,773	1.1	85.7	14.0
Pecos	1,007	2,261	71,927	4,411	44,690	93.6	40,370	2,476	4,428	2.9	71.5	28.1
Polk	1,581	3,372	81,929	1,847	36,841	85.1	264,340	5,959	20,846	9.8	66.1	33.4
Potter	9,295	21,572	516,322	4,464	203,394	69.9	340,630	2,945	29,056	14.5	73.7	25.8
Presidio	461	991	24,176	3,221	5,001	79.6	19,279	2,568	1,890	7.6	37.8	61.3
Rains	377	639	16,620	1,601	7,265	84.9	7,707	742	4,229	26.9	70.9	28.7
Randall	1,654	3,350	68,763	647	39,655	93.0	47,233	444	48,587	16.3	83.4	16.2
Reagan	329	716	16,607	5,259	10,763	95.6	5,749	1,820	1,143	–8.9	83.6	16.1
Real	118	185	9,895	3,305	4,760	93.4	10,524	3,515	1,645	10.4	79.9	19.8
Red River	739	1,550	32,254	2,313	8,884	84.0	15,106	1,083	5,490	5.5	61.6	38.2
Reeves	1,145	2,241	74,457	5,941	14,395	85.8	105,961	8,455	3,395	6.9	52.3	47.1
Refugio	606	1,169	29,885	3,890	15,463	92.4	11,936	1,554	3,455	18.3	64.0	35.7
Roberts	89	157	5,715	6,638	5,068	97.7	738	857	507	–7.7	90.9	9.1
Robertson	1,032	2,221	49,223	3,093	25,668	92.0	9,226	580	6,795	6.7	55.8	43.8
Rockwall	2,096	4,980	118,293	2,320	79,300	85.9	204,275	4,006	25,581	44.9	78.7	20.8
Runnels	805	1,555	36,391	3,282	9,661	86.1	14,054	1,267	4,049	0.1	80.0	19.6
Rusk	1,808	5,288	98,660	2,079	52,702	90.8	67,197	1,416	18,344	10.3	73.0	26.7
Sabine	486	967	22,210	2,137	6,571	79.8	2,375	228	4,639	1.0	67.6	31.8
San Augustine	401	837	14,982	1,681	4,366	78.8	9,079	1,019	3,757	–1.3	59.5	40.1
San Jacinto	782	1,432	34,137	1,468	14,763	92.8	18,440	793	8,125	5.3	66.4	33.1
San Patricio	3,898	8,277	182,480	2,709	73,344	89.5	139,809	2,075	21,320	14.0	63.2	36.4
San Saba	334	719	14,496	2,394	4,416	80.9	3,336	551	2,431	4.2	77.9	21.8
Schleicher	261	539	11,910	4,100	5,396	91.1	847	292	1,329	13.3	76.2	23.5
Scurry	1,302	2,611	47,950	2,996	21,472	82.1	12,412	776	5,572	4.6	82.1	17.6
Shackelford	216	383	11,022	3,300	3,918	89.4	2,530	757	1,527	13.4	84.6	15.0
Shelby	1,168	2,474	49,912	1,958	15,298	83.3	28,886	1,133	9,279	3.0	67.8	31.8
Sherman	273	508	12,622	3,972	7,782	94.8	4,733	1,489	1,066	–8.3	88.4	11.6
Smith	8,698	19,320	405,069	2,241	175,841	76.6	305,617	1,691	73,664	21.5	72.5	27.1
Somervell	557	1,293	42,510	5,959	36,585	97.7	1,400	196	3,551	21.7	76.1	23.4
Starr	3,762	7,287	164,268	2,922	27,828	88.0	76,494	1,361	9,781	15.6	26.1	73.6
Stephens	552	1,203	26,635	2,813	10,399	83.1	6,683	706	3,519	6.9	79.7	20.0
Sterling	107	246	6,342	4,694	5,505	97.3	–	–	615	–6.7	88.5	11.5
Stonewall	183	353	7,555	5,043	3,548	92.9	408	272	752	–5.9	66.4	33.2
Sutton	275	571	15,287	3,723	10,565	89.2	64	16	1,453	–5.6	80.7	19.3
Swisher	612	1,207	27,455	3,428	7,113	85.0	2,970	371	2,120	–15.2	70.1	29.5
Tarrant	68,657	192,366	4,536,420	2,974	2,450,247	79.2	8,248,660	5,408	560,141	18.6	62.4	37.0
Taylor	5,722	13,436	296,387	2,373	128,178	76.1	157,792	1,263	48,099	11.8	77.3	22.1
Terrell	96	201	6,723	6,585	5,546	95.9	168	165	469	–1.7	65.3	33.9
Terry	922	1,874	47,547	3,777	15,767	89.0	16,509	1,311	3,970	–2.1	79.8	20.0
Throckmorton	164	298	6,171	3,559	3,097	94.9	198	114	863	2.5	76.0	23.4
Titus	2,556	5,454	140,623	4,974	34,910	80.4	122,836	4,344	8,907	9.9	64.1	35.6
Tom Green	4,618	9,411	219,603	2,122	93,627	73.6	211,449	2,043	37,417	8.1	75.3	24.1
Travis	40,960	114,975	2,858,815	3,381	1,722,777	78.9	8,574,163	10,140	352,113	16.9	42.0	56.0
Trinity	610	1,134	25,577	1,818	9,378	87.9	4,180	297	6,213	17.3	64.1	35.5
Tyler	1,065	2,081	50,110	2,418	16,614	92.2	23,173	1,118	7,745	8.8	65.1	34.3
Upshur	1,543	3,335	66,982	1,833	27,366	89.4	17,702	484	14,526	13.4	70.4	29.1
Upton	418	947	28,185	8,614	22,086	98.0	824	252	1,197	–6.0	84.3	15.5
Uvalde	2,554	5,009	109,043	4,108	18,453	68.7	55,515	2,091	8,483	0.7	60.7	38.9
Val Verde	2,316	5,316	112,371	2,452	26,659	69.8	88,217	1,925	11,795	2.8	59.1	40.3
Van Zandt	1,963	4,219	90,426	1,802	32,416	85.5	46,305	923	19,856	11.0	75.4	24.3
Victoria	6,022	14,104	321,839	3,781	107,275	79.3	270,267	3,175	29,602	8.0	70.5	28.9

See footnotes at end of table.

[Includes United States, states, and 3,141 counties/county equivalents defined as of February 22, 2005. For more information on these areas, see Appendix C, Geographic Information]

County	Local government employment, March 2002		Local government finances, 2002							Elections, 2004[1]			
			General revenue				Total debt outstanding			Votes cast for President			
					Taxes								
	Total employ-ment	Total payroll ($1,000)	Total ($1,000)	Per capita (dol.)	Total ($1,000)	Prop-erty, percent of total (taxes)	Amount ($1,000)	Per capita (dol.)	Total	Percent change, 2000–2004	Repub-lican cand-idate, percent of total	Demo-cratic cand-idate, percent of total
TEXAS—Con.												
Walker	2,024	5,015	197,955	3,229	41,966	76.3	845,320	13,788	17,822	24.0	65.7	33.5
Waller	1,597	3,583	78,407	2,305	37,817	90.1	83,448	2,453	13,881	27.8	55.3	44.3
Ward	677	1,407	38,524	3,687	20,470	93.4	726	69	3,768	-2.7	75.8	23.9
Washington	2,355	5,115	117,159	3,815	38,517	83.3	74,371	2,422	13,063	10.6	73.5	25.9
Webb	13,187	29,585	693,656	3,355	196,715	75.3	827,908	4,004	41,556	31.6	42.7	56.9
Wharton	2,863	6,427	132,753	3,225	47,683	85.1	44,128	1,072	14,039	4.6	66.2	33.5
Wheeler	446	935	26,446	5,289	13,743	95.1	7,865	1,573	2,394	0.2	81.9	17.5
Wichita	6,427	14,599	293,300	2,280	135,368	74.1	281,278	2,187	45,545	6.6	71.3	28.2
Wilbarger	1,253	2,498	60,469	4,235	21,272	87.2	15,394	1,078	4,990	9.0	73.9	25.7
Willacy	1,250	2,378	55,811	2,788	15,231	82.8	34,455	1,721	4,962	-2.0	44.5	55.1
Williamson	13,340	30,542	822,765	2,833	517,045	87.2	1,629,295	5,609	128,198	33.6	65.0	33.6
Wilson	1,670	3,656	69,727	2,029	22,548	90.9	57,389	1,670	14,885	27.2	69.9	29.6
Winkler	636	1,337	31,003	4,454	17,707	91.4	5,623	808	2,002	-2.0	80.1	19.5
Wise	2,047	4,089	100,719	1,905	51,009	89.7	76,680	1,450	20,047	22.5	75.7	23.9
Wood	1,447	2,800	65,617	1,726	33,500	87.0	28,750	756	16,929	21.9	75.8	23.8
Yoakum	762	1,635	47,059	6,519	33,501	97.0	3,968	550	2,613	6.0	85.3	14.4
Young	1,203	2,384	49,094	2,772	15,043	79.2	13,855	782	7,409	6.5	79.3	20.4
Zapata	881	1,933	40,736	3,197	29,135	100.0	11,718	920	2,898	10.8	42.4	57.4
Zavala	750	1,367	29,820	2,564	4,641	90.2	15,996	1,375	3,118	-8.1	24.9	74.8
UTAH	97,911	214,192	6,017,440	2,575	2,100,760	67.6	8,520,440	3,646	927,844	20.4	71.5	26.0
Beaver	438	899	24,031	3,940	5,947	77.0	34,166	5,602	2,544	13.0	79.5	19.4
Box Elder	2,183	3,995	104,237	2,336	31,505	74.8	71,969	1,613	18,368	18.6	85.8	12.2
Cache	3,792	6,752	189,796	1,983	49,395	61.5	159,772	1,669	39,731	19.9	81.8	16.1
Carbon	1,409	2,291	60,085	3,030	20,102	72.9	83,531	4,212	8,508	15.2	58.2	40.1
Daggett	150	232	7,041	7,832	1,529	81.7	7,044	7,835	499	14.7	76.2	21.6
Davis	10,608	21,566	587,750	2,359	181,902	68.6	302,691	1,215	109,268	24.4	78.9	19.1
Duchesne	997	1,686	67,858	4,569	11,929	73.9	30,907	2,081	5,556	22.2	85.4	13.3
Emery	684	1,294	60,502	5,652	19,216	90.8	291,350	27,216	4,678	6.4	80.8	17.8
Garfield	313	424	22,720	4,932	4,625	65.0	21,767	4,725	2,162	9.9	85.5	12.2
Grand	480	968	28,623	3,317	11,385	57.3	23,185	2,687	4,165	15.2	51.1	44.6
Iron	1,620	2,944	90,605	2,564	28,021	69.2	110,956	3,140	15,446	22.6	83.0	14.7
Juab	499	993	25,898	2,999	6,486	75.0	25,806	2,988	3,417	22.7	78.5	17.7
Kane	581	963	28,883	4,785	7,423	74.2	16,802	2,784	3,051	8.9	79.1	18.9
Millard	955	1,754	48,120	3,887	21,699	91.4	11,416	922	4,877	2.1	83.7	12.8
Morgan	357	654	17,180	2,315	5,439	77.8	5,235	705	3,841	21.1	85.9	12.3
Piute	108	132	5,322	3,854	832	73.2	2,001	1,449	773	-1.0	83.6	15.9
Rich	166	252	8,303	4,254	2,775	84.7	3,006	1,540	1,037	14.8	88.9	10.5
Salt Lake	36,927	92,495	2,477,472	2,700	970,788	66.1	5,091,373	5,549	362,138	17.9	59.6	37.5
San Juan	1,175	2,256	52,895	3,826	10,077	76.5	25,502	1,845	4,950	4.3	60.0	38.5
Sanpete	1,343	2,298	62,370	2,670	11,828	64.0	42,568	1,822	8,507	14.5	82.3	14.0
Sevier	970	1,658	53,225	2,785	14,134	68.2	51,550	2,698	7,641	8.0	86.3	12.0
Summit	1,748	3,965	141,985	4,457	86,703	73.5	115,059	3,612	15,312	26.3	51.8	45.6
Tooele	1,906	4,110	116,825	2,540	27,944	74.1	153,571	3,339	16,664	33.5	73.1	24.8
Uintah	1,465	2,194	89,111	3,397	25,973	59.9	121,129	4,618	9,957	18.6	85.6	12.7
Utah	15,133	30,832	872,462	2,138	277,508	65.6	1,025,693	2,513	149,173	24.0	86.0	11.6
Wasatch	832	1,714	65,299	3,860	17,933	70.5	84,721	5,008	7,512	32.4	73.3	24.7
Washington	3,521	7,427	226,897	2,279	83,567	63.8	331,676	3,331	44,018	35.6	81.0	17.1
Wayne	200	269	7,610	2,996	1,740	66.3	4,031	1,587	1,360	11.0	78.1	20.5
Weber	7,351	17,178	474,335	2,333	162,355	69.0	271,963	1,338	72,691	15.9	70.4	27.3
VERMONT	29,346	61,704	1,510,640	2,451	446,653	96.9	743,968	1,207	312,309	6.1	38.8	58.9
Addison	1,848	3,298	88,608	2,430	28,205	98.9	33,872	929	18,579	6.6	38.1	60.0
Bennington	1,462	2,983	85,934	2,316	26,348	96.2	15,897	428	19,065	7.9	40.0	58.1
Caledonia	1,229	2,325	68,161	2,274	18,230	95.4	30,186	1,007	14,211	4.2	47.6	50.0
Chittenden	6,940	16,511	373,182	2,514	111,009	93.1	305,249	2,056	77,696	7.9	34.0	63.5
Essex	391	549	14,598	2,228	3,789	96.4	3,256	497	2,937	1.6	54.2	43.5
Franklin	1,885	4,109	100,337	2,152	22,850	97.1	66,235	1,421	19,920	3.8	44.9	53.2
Grand Isle	199	356	15,557	2,127	5,304	99.0	5,822	796	4,077	12.1	43.0	55.1
Lamoille	1,230	2,328	58,568	2,442	17,553	98.7	35,054	1,462	12,181	8.3	35.0	62.7
Orange	1,558	2,953	74,967	2,599	21,735	99.7	30,031	1,041	14,895	1.4	43.1	54.8
Orleans	1,393	2,513	57,181	2,143	13,534	99.3	22,179	831	12,242	0.9	46.3	51.7
Rutland	3,128	6,488	162,719	2,570	45,511	97.0	53,576	846	30,975	5.5	46.6	51.3
Washington	2,856	6,111	140,726	2,389	40,592	99.5	89,959	1,527	31,448	5.7	36.4	61.0
Windham	2,394	5,039	117,609	2,662	42,893	99.0	18,228	413	23,316	8.5	31.2	66.4
Windsor	2,833	6,140	152,493	2,635	49,100	98.6	34,424	595	30,767	5.6	37.4	60.3
VIRGINIA	335,348	863,011	21,734,543	2,983	9,350,097	71.6	21,637,063	2,970	3,198,367	16.8	53.7	45.5
Accomack	1,361	3,008	74,107	1,906	26,010	72.6	35,544	914	13,356	12.0	57.9	41.3
Albemarle	3,314	7,808	201,595	2,332	104,023	67.5	198,089	2,291	43,726	18.7	48.5	50.5
Alleghany[6]	846	1,714	45,615	2,690	14,391	84.1	47,660	2,810	7,195	40.4	55.1	44.5
Amelia	428	856	18,950	1,617	5,533	72.8	15,649	1,336	5,397	12.7	64.8	34.5
Amherst	1,036	2,265	55,414	1,742	18,050	66.7	30,937	973	12,695	8.4	61.1	38.3

See footnotes at end of table.

Table B-13. Counties — **Local Government Finances and Elections**—Con.

[Includes United States, states, and 3,141 counties/county equivalents defined as of February 22, 2005. For more information on these areas, see Appendix C, Geographic Information]

County	Local government employment, March 2002		Local government finances, 2002						Elections, 2004[1]			
			General revenue		Taxes		Total debt outstanding		Votes cast for President			
	Total employment	Total payroll ($1,000)	Total ($1,000)	Per capita (dol.)	Total ($1,000)	Property, percent of total (taxes)	Amount ($1,000)	Per capita (dol.)	Total	Percent change, 2000–2004	Republican candidate, percent of total	Democratic candidate, percent of total
VIRGINIA—Con.												
Appomattox	569	1,069	26,634	1,937	8,161	75.0	17,969	1,307	6,655	12.3	65.6	32.9
Arlington	9,541	35,276	1,250,283	6,402	471,177	71.9	2,311,314	11,835	94,650	13.3	31.3	67.6
Augusta	2,648	5,101	139,577	2,088	44,060	66.3	87,548	1,310	29,704	17.5	74.4	23.6
Bath	267	553	15,500	3,077	10,994	91.8	8,452	1,678	2,282	3.3	62.8	36.3
Bedford	2,681	5,097	137,960	2,230	43,466	83.2	106,223	1,717	31,404	20.1	69.8	29.0
Bland	260	434	15,241	2,208	2,725	74.9	3,978	576	2,865	6.6	68.5	29.5
Botetourt	1,299	2,488	53,581	1,720	24,323	77.0	43,503	1,396	15,797	14.1	68.8	30.4
Brunswick	799	1,375	32,324	1,761	7,735	74.7	4,410	240	6,926	15.5	41.2	58.7
Buchanan	1,148	2,013	63,663	2,445	22,555	51.1	30,718	1,180	9,829	-0.3	45.9	53.7
Buckingham	573	1,171	28,127	1,777	7,244	76.6	12,075	763	6,027	10.5	52.9	46.3
Campbell	2,116	4,386	94,440	1,836	31,536	75.5	78,670	1,530	22,997	13.1	69.1	29.8
Caroline	924	1,900	44,225	1,956	16,855	76.8	18,964	839	9,954	19.2	50.2	49.0
Carroll	1,026	2,237	47,625	1,627	14,456	73.0	44,694	1,526	12,128	10.2	67.4	32.1
Charles City	302	655	17,818	2,523	5,275	85.4	23,806	3,371	3,439	12.2	36.5	62.7
Charlotte	593	1,121	25,088	2,009	6,033	79.3	4,063	325	5,438	8.9	58.2	40.9
Chesterfield	11,523	30,276	658,496	2,433	300,877	73.9	552,759	2,042	133,814	20.6	62.6	36.9
Clarke	502	1,068	26,203	1,983	14,260	85.9	8,170	618	6,505	23.1	57.5	41.5
Craig	196	368	9,788	1,928	2,667	80.6	4,524	891	2,621	5.1	65.1	34.4
Culpeper	1,543	3,505	82,922	2,248	34,700	70.3	47,588	1,290	15,605	27.5	64.3	35.1
Cumberland	349	720	17,552	1,943	6,076	82.6	14,365	1,590	4,126	17.7	57.6	41.7
Dickenson	874	1,502	47,070	2,901	12,781	53.5	12,399	764	7,406	2.5	48.5	50.8
Dinwiddie	930	1,948	51,467	2,089	19,221	80.2	36,935	1,499	10,839	18.6	57.1	42.2
Essex	387	820	21,557	2,131	9,002	68.5	15,048	1,488	4,344	13.4	53.0	46.2
Fairfax	41,567	144,207	3,362,069	3,388	1,963,828	78.3	3,258,797	3,284	461,379	11.5	45.9	53.3
Fauquier	2,455	5,996	161,354	2,714	83,503	78.9	70,979	1,194	29,915	27.4	63.6	35.8
Floyd	592	1,168	22,343	1,568	7,547	73.3	9,750	684	6,734	17.3	61.8	37.0
Fluvanna	601	1,388	31,053	1,394	12,205	84.7	6,672	300	10,957	25.9	58.9	40.3
Franklin	1,704	3,945	81,876	1,688	31,058	69.9	39,104	806	22,223	18.0	63.2	36.0
Frederick	2,350	5,623	146,549	2,329	69,012	81.1	87,973	1,398	28,540	27.5	67.9	31.0
Giles	822	1,519	33,664	1,990	11,724	76.9	26,752	1,582	7,498	9.9	57.6	40.6
Gloucester	1,528	3,220	70,264	1,957	29,609	74.1	61,236	1,706	16,333	19.2	67.9	31.3
Goochland	725	1,385	44,488	2,515	28,048	85.7	30,204	1,710	10,338	17.8	64.5	34.7
Grayson	632	1,176	26,417	1,583	7,008	77.5	1,787	107	7,137	4.2	65.2	34.1
Greene	692	1,322	35,452	2,175	11,031	76.3	15,830	971	6,939	28.2	65.9	32.3
Greensville	716	1,524	33,335	2,880	5,706	75.3	27,271	2,356	4,258	9.0	40.7	59.0
Halifax[7]	1,961	3,399	72,887	1,977	21,828	65.2	26,346	715	14,656	4.2	57.1	42.4
Hanover	3,999	9,688	217,891	2,372	99,962	74.8	154,919	1,687	49,611	19.3	71.4	28.1
Henrico	10,847	28,168	718,761	2,683	331,218	68.3	689,260	2,573	133,418	16.8	53.8	45.6
Henry	2,036	4,242	98,022	1,708	33,410	58.9	22,719	396	23,458	9.3	56.9	42.0
Highland	133	214	5,987	2,428	2,009	85.7	2,053	833	1,520	5.8	64.6	34.3
Isle of Wight	1,107	2,474	65,246	2,110	35,343	79.1	7,092	229	15,871	22.6	62.6	37.0
James City	1,127	3,033	133,249	2,594	80,897	75.1	167,274	3,256	31,090	26.9	61.0	38.4
King and Queen	280	547	19,357	2,944	4,510	83.1	11,801	1,795	3,286	14.9	52.9	45.8
King George	646	1,544	45,398	2,549	13,838	77.6	48,643	2,732	7,921	35.4	64.7	34.6
King William	646	1,329	36,542	2,650	16,737	86.0	21,439	1,555	6,872	19.1	64.0	35.5
Lancaster	446	849	20,171	1,754	10,219	85.2	29,704	2,583	6,230	14.2	59.8	39.8
Lee	1,043	2,031	48,433	2,053	9,608	70.8	9,477	402	9,770	11.7	58.0	41.0
Loudoun	10,508	27,730	695,793	3,415	414,195	78.5	712,598	3,497	108,430	43.3	55.7	43.6
Louisa	1,010	2,088	53,560	1,976	29,101	89.6	81,732	3,015	12,035	19.2	58.9	40.3
Lunenburg	599	1,240	20,789	1,578	6,521	78.2	11,970	908	5,245	14.2	54.5	45.0
Madison	439	980	21,516	1,658	9,506	74.9	9,341	720	5,772	14.8	61.6	37.7
Mathews	393	762	16,284	1,758	7,974	86.0	21,560	2,327	5,129	11.3	68.2	31.0
Mecklenburg	1,479	2,619	63,914	1,969	24,171	72.6	15,235	469	12,780	9.7	57.3	41.4
Middlesex	457	695	18,431	1,827	9,429	80.3	25,984	2,575	5,377	14.7	62.0	35.6
Montgomery	3,643	6,516	156,076	1,863	58,556	66.6	143,967	1,718	31,515	16.0	54.2	44.8
Nelson	519	1,067	29,207	1,986	13,361	75.9	37,156	2,527	7,139	16.2	49.6	49.6
New Kent	540	1,263	29,196	2,045	12,163	81.8	5,399	378	7,946	30.0	68.1	30.8
Northampton	985	2,151	75,570	5,788	9,572	74.0	243,850	18,676	5,499	12.4	48.5	50.5
Northumberland	396	845	22,296	1,771	10,562	86.5	3,612	287	6,409	14.3	59.8	39.8
Nottoway	771	1,348	30,304	1,933	7,869	64.1	16,287	1,039	6,030	9.8	54.8	43.7
Orange	1,003	2,053	48,005	1,760	22,719	79.5	15,713	576	12,928	23.3	59.9	38.8
Page	961	1,739	44,085	1,888	12,719	72.7	11,110	476	9,603	20.1	64.8	34.6
Patrick	682	1,236	29,348	1,520	8,372	74.7	5,178	268	8,215	11.2	67.0	31.3
Pittsylvania	2,010	4,115	102,756	1,664	27,577	74.3	68,900	1,116	27,417	13.0	64.5	33.8
Powhatan	704	1,408	34,782	1,434	17,711	68.6	56,655	2,336	12,163	25.2	73.6	25.6
Prince Edward	696	1,362	36,987	1,847	12,631	55.6	26,847	1,341	7,316	15.0	48.8	49.6
Prince George	1,449	3,365	77,242	2,198	22,509	82.5	87,480	2,489	13,254	21.6	61.4	38.2
Prince William	13,707	41,601	1,053,069	3,389	414,648	72.9	1,029,097	3,312	132,063	31.4	52.8	46.4
Pulaski	1,595	3,050	80,411	2,300	23,696	69.5	50,410	1,442	14,251	12.2	61.5	37.3
Rappahannock	347	616	13,351	1,868	7,446	87.0	–	–	4,050	15.3	53.6	45.4

See footnotes at end of table.

[Includes United States, states, and 3,141 counties/county equivalents defined as of February 22, 2005. For more information on these areas, see Appendix C, Geographic Information]

County	Local government employment, March 2002		Local government finances, 2002						Elections, 2004[1]			
			General revenue				Total debt outstanding		Votes cast for President			
					Taxes							
	Total employ-ment	Total payroll ($1,000)	Total ($1,000)	Per capita (dol.)	Total ($1,000)	Property, percent of total (taxes)	Amount ($1,000)	Per capita (dol.)	Total	Percent change, 2000–2004	Republican candidate, percent of total	Democratic candidate, percent of total
VIRGINIA—Con.												
Richmond	359	859	22,093	2,461	6,924	74.1	13,796	1,537	3,361	14.0	62.0	37.0
Roanoke	3,886	9,959	222,197	2,569	96,740	71.8	251,446	2,908	46,973	9.7	65.1	34.2
Rockbridge	899	1,621	45,493	2,182	16,215	69.3	33,958	1,629	9,181	17.3	59.0	39.5
Rockingham	2,960	6,040	135,059	1,957	48,465	80.2	71,503	1,036	29,216	21.8	74.4	24.9
Russell	944	2,325	58,918	2,035	14,876	67.1	87,552	3,024	11,423	5.8	53.2	45.2
Scott	889	1,761	52,465	2,273	12,049	64.2	14,648	634	9,967	6.8	65.0	33.4
Shenandoah	1,478	3,014	74,186	2,038	31,386	71.6	68,273	1,875	17,146	18.6	68.9	30.3
Smyth	1,651	3,007	65,346	1,992	17,090	67.3	36,076	1,100	12,319	4.9	64.2	33.6
Southampton	842	1,536	37,836	2,180	12,855	84.2	24,384	1,405	7,492	11.6	53.6	45.8
Spotsylvania	3,965	9,396	232,339	2,266	108,570	72.8	268,130	2,615	45,445	29.8	62.8	36.6
Stafford	4,252	10,552	252,663	2,424	104,412	79.7	223,168	2,141	45,986	34.3	62.0	37.4
Surry	369	894	22,486	3,231	15,501	97.1	5,483	788	3,522	9.0	43.8	55.5
Sussex	444	1,069	26,401	2,178	7,209	82.3	28,498	2,351	4,345	11.2	43.5	55.7
Tazewell	1,769	3,014	99,287	2,242	26,122	65.7	40,892	923	17,480	7.0	57.4	41.1
Warren	1,100	2,213	58,957	1,784	26,322	73.6	25,547	773	14,068	26.0	61.1	37.3
Washington	2,011	4,120	88,507	1,725	33,565	67.3	46,906	914	22,514	11.3	65.5	32.6
Westmoreland	608	1,192	31,570	1,887	11,856	82.4	18,310	1,095	6,848	13.6	50.1	49.2
Wise	2,203	4,333	99,695	2,385	26,440	60.1	30,916	740	14,312	7.5	58.2	40.5
Wythe	1,300	2,465	66,520	2,391	20,695	59.1	79,695	2,864	11,554	13.0	68.5	31.0
York	2,451	4,668	154,076	2,600	71,612	74.9	114,290	1,929	29,880	21.5	64.9	34.4
Independent Cities												
Alexandria	4,787	17,981	470,970	3,502	293,326	69.9	286,765	2,132	61,515	11.4	32.3	66.8
Bedford	1,951	4,022	13,828	2,203	5,628	62.0	34,208	5,449	2,542	4.1	57.9	41.0
Bristol	931	2,409	53,435	3,127	18,482	53.5	67,007	3,921	6,724	7.1	63.6	35.7
Buena Vista	310	547	16,507	2,623	4,789	68.6	5,976	949	2,389	21.0	59.3	39.2
Charlottesville	2,376	4,921	127,176	3,105	59,225	56.3	59,805	1,460	15,450	16.8	27.0	71.8
Chesapeake	11,107	30,690	758,893	3,695	264,098	67.2	828,856	4,030	91,541	22.7	57.1	42.3
Clifton Forge[6]	(X)	(X)	(X)	(NA)	(X)	(NA)	(X)	(NA)	(X)	(NA)	(X)	(X)
Colonial Heights	726	1,931	45,051	2,628	28,836	55.5	20,124	1,174	8,231	5.8	74.5	25.0
Covington	330	772	20,350	3,213	9,298	68.0	16,339	2,580	2,301	3.9	48.0	51.2
Danville	2,936	6,531	141,761	2,997	40,020	56.2	192,901	4,078	19,112	4.4	49.2	49.4
Emporia	119	345	8,034	1,408	4,715	70.0	9,831	1,723	2,221	6.8	43.7	56.2
Fairfax	372	1,875	75,448	3,465	56,236	56.8	31,315	1,438	10,546	10.4	47.8	51.2
Falls Church	726	2,250	45,399	4,272	30,880	68.6	27,180	2,557	6,098	9.0	34.0	64.7
Franklin	691	1,594	35,632	4,355	9,595	55.3	21,312	2,605	3,536	10.8	45.6	54.0
Fredericksburg	1,491	3,566	101,933	5,094	39,718	48.6	202,599	10,125	7,542	12.9	45.0	54.2
Galax	376	804	20,562	3,092	7,186	50.2	6,907	1,038	2,335	5.5	57.2	42.3
Hampton	8,346	17,264	374,456	2,586	158,411	66.5	218,708	1,510	55,741	16.4	42.0	57.4
Harrisonburg	1,340	3,223	88,632	2,163	40,412	44.4	310,834	7,586	11,030	10.8	55.9	42.9
Hopewell	1,331	3,033	76,291	3,401	25,206	74.1	74,738	3,331	7,936	13.7	53.6	45.0
Lexington	334	621	17,882	2,592	5,653	54.0	26,651	3,863	2,349	9.8	41.8	57.1
Lynchburg	3,215	7,350	206,748	3,186	80,699	60.8	274,325	4,227	26,340	12.1	54.7	44.5
Manassas	1,472	4,665	114,993	3,141	57,107	75.9	75,164	2,053	12,903	4.0	56.2	43.1
Manassas Park	472	1,286	29,095	2,662	13,289	71.6	21,563	1,973	3,332	29.1	54.2	45.0
Martinsville	987	2,556	44,663	2,956	12,905	49.4	23,848	1,579	5,603	–1.6	45.3	54.2
Newport News	9,551	23,653	580,154	3,230	216,931	67.1	753,167	4,193	67,952	17.5	47.4	52.0
Norfolk	16,761	43,426	1,149,319	4,824	288,216	55.8	1,479,666	6,210	70,570	13.9	37.4	61.7
Norton	256	505	13,044	3,312	4,993	33.9	4,947	1,256	1,504	–1.7	51.1	48.2
Petersburg	3,466	8,037	217,794	6,574	32,742	66.8	58,974	1,780	11,949	8.0	18.7	81.0
Poquoson	567	1,211	28,906	2,490	12,265	79.4	28,543	2,459	6,480	10.6	77.2	22.0
Portsmouth	5,593	13,589	327,738	3,299	94,060	63.6	282,943	2,848	39,534	11.5	38.5	61.0
Radford	486	1,107	25,766	1,681	8,607	59.6	6,451	421	4,845	8.9	52.9	46.3
Richmond	9,481	29,870	924,073	4,705	332,288	68.8	1,170,956	5,962	74,325	12.7	29.1	70.2
Roanoke	5,086	13,196	356,599	3,829	130,974	54.3	433,937	4,659	36,000	7.6	46.3	52.4
Salem	1,299	3,125	73,809	2,978	40,628	65.6	46,747	1,886	11,484	6.6	62.0	37.0
South Boston[7]	(X)	(X)	(X)	(NA)	(X)	(NA)	(X)	(NA)	(X)	(NA)	(X)	(X)
Staunton	1,081	2,124	54,122	2,275	22,713	55.8	36,734	1,544	9,629	13.1	60.3	39.0
Suffolk	3,104	7,282	181,337	2,598	77,140	70.1	259,443	3,717	32,189	30.5	52.1	47.3
Virginia Beach	21,705	50,952	1,213,375	2,817	582,688	67.4	1,114,256	2,587	175,687	17.3	59.1	40.2
Waynesboro	915	2,001	55,420	2,752	23,908	67.0	15,122	751	7,963	12.1	64.0	35.1
Williamsburg	1,794	4,840	118,182	10,238	82,453	79.8	132,300	11,461	4,320	16.0	47.8	51.3
Winchester	1,514	3,240	94,470	3,880	37,821	44.9	169,197	6,949	9,343	18.5	56.6	42.5
WASHINGTON	247,940	794,763	21,261,782	3,505	6,884,936	62.9	32,008,374	5,276	2,859,084	14.9	45.6	52.8
Adams	1,183	2,882	83,112	5,051	15,276	74.2	36,238	2,202	5,127	3.1	73.2	25.7
Asotin	740	1,905	49,948	2,430	11,387	76.6	31,304	1,523	8,786	10.0	60.6	37.8
Benton	7,911	27,293	723,952	4,814	132,820	61.6	6,775,428	45,055	66,886	11.9	66.3	32.2
Chelan	3,721	11,451	238,682	3,553	67,860	68.8	1,057,169	15,738	29,396	10.9	62.9	35.6
Clallam	3,726	10,470	249,923	3,783	55,100	64.5	98,257	1,487	36,766	14.1	51.3	46.4

See footnotes at end of table.

[Includes United States, states, and 3,141 counties/county equivalents defined as of February 22, 2005. For more information on these areas, see Appendix C, Geographic Information]

County	Local government employment, March 2002		Local government finances, 2002						Elections, 2004[1]		
			General revenue				Total debt outstanding		Votes cast for President		
					Taxes					Republican candidate, percent of total	Democratic candidate, percent of total
	Total employment	Total payroll ($1,000)	Total ($1,000)	Per capita (dol.)	Total ($1,000)	Property, percent of total (taxes)	Amount ($1,000)	Per capita (dol.)	Total	Percent change, 2000–2004		
WASHINGTON—Con.												
Clark	11,891	38,573	1,015,988	2,746	329,121	74.4	1,688,823	4,565	170,439	25.7	52.0	46.7
Columbia	382	738	20,025	4,869	3,299	81.7	7,900	1,921	2,107	–	69.8	28.7
Cowlitz	4,018	12,002	303,704	3,209	86,753	69.3	335,562	3,546	42,473	14.9	47.6	50.8
Douglas	1,464	4,249	103,887	3,124	27,086	81.8	269,297	8,098	13,372	4.0	66.6	32.2
Ferry	550	1,076	31,680	4,346	3,067	77.5	5,700	782	3,341	10.0	60.4	36.0
Franklin	2,305	6,496	170,168	3,218	41,791	62.4	209,162	3,955	16,159	18.7	66.6	32.1
Garfield	265	541	13,134	5,693	2,049	76.2	4,171	1,808	1,320	-0.7	70.8	27.7
Grant	5,255	15,196	325,878	4,201	62,293	72.8	691,739	8,917	25,995	9.2	68.5	29.9
Grays Harbor	3,265	9,196	236,888	3,450	63,560	60.4	196,190	2,858	27,953	7.6	46.1	52.2
Island	2,541	7,238	178,698	2,362	48,139	71.7	115,262	1,523	38,559	16.8	51.2	47.2
Jefferson	1,501	3,855	99,851	3,663	31,516	70.6	56,868	2,086	18,616	17.6	35.7	62.4
King	75,823	268,629	7,865,593	4,472	2,992,681	54.9	11,910,514	6,772	893,534	12.5	33.7	65.0
Kitsap	7,808	24,194	622,143	2,608	202,064	72.7	475,886	1,995	118,453	15.5	47.0	51.3
Kittitas	1,728	4,108	107,032	3,098	28,151	61.9	97,302	2,816	16,084	14.2	56.3	41.9
Klickitat	1,294	3,312	89,751	4,626	14,627	65.7	75,371	3,885	9,237	13.2	54.3	43.7
Lewis	3,117	8,744	197,889	2,842	55,687	61.9	239,056	3,433	32,428	8.1	64.9	33.1
Lincoln	1,289	2,394	61,239	6,052	10,534	86.3	20,137	1,990	5,811	11.8	69.1	29.4
Mason	2,380	6,570	169,238	3,306	40,984	77.9	111,310	2,175	25,394	13.0	47.2	50.8
Okanogan	2,424	6,179	140,239	3,572	24,559	70.5	61,031	1,555	16,342	10.4	59.0	38.6
Pacific	1,251	3,415	87,732	4,231	22,168	70.2	50,212	2,422	10,431	9.6	44.4	53.4
Pend Oreille	955	2,542	44,830	3,701	8,758	81.8	30,541	2,522	6,198	14.0	59.6	37.3
Pierce	26,198	91,424	2,159,813	2,954	724,035	70.7	2,275,065	3,112	313,331	16.7	48.1	50.5
San Juan	731	1,857	46,889	3,208	20,152	71.1	26,257	1,797	10,088	20.0	32.6	65.3
Skagit	5,642	15,396	486,808	4,563	114,585	68.0	335,487	3,145	52,230	15.5	50.1	48.1
Skamania	535	1,234	33,984	3,376	5,133	71.8	3,521	350	5,159	21.4	52.2	46.0
Snohomish	22,041	72,115	1,979,097	3,132	638,718	66.6	2,525,677	3,997	294,997	17.5	45.5	53.0
Spokane	15,164	47,312	1,212,184	2,839	361,812	68.2	804,481	1,884	202,587	17.7	55.1	43.2
Stevens	1,638	3,875	92,946	2,289	22,413	73.9	41,932	1,033	20,340	13.0	64.0	33.5
Thurston	7,864	24,101	622,703	2,869	218,028	70.0	432,658	1,994	112,789	15.8	42.6	55.6
Wahkiakum	210	523	15,356	4,028	2,478	66.3	4,376	1,148	2,235	13.3	52.4	45.7
Walla Walla	2,134	5,697	153,364	2,739	47,108	72.8	158,401	2,829	22,925	7.3	62.5	36.0
Whatcom	6,033	17,478	451,245	2,593	166,986	65.0	374,686	2,153	90,394	22.6	44.6	53.4
Whitman	2,141	4,807	122,906	3,041	32,334	72.4	44,354	1,097	18,012	10.9	52.2	46.0
Yakima	8,822	25,696	653,283	2,910	149,824	66.7	331,049	1,475	72,790	8.2	59.6	39.1
WEST VIRGINIA	65,544	156,675	3,782,611	2,096	1,089,593	82.3	3,547,252	1,966	755,887	16.6	56.1	43.2
Barbour	621	1,259	30,798	1,983	4,609	91.5	39,480	2,542	6,655	10.0	60.2	39.2
Berkeley	2,591	6,241	148,716	1,826	40,374	93.9	170,397	2,093	33,785	46.8	63.0	36.2
Boone	1,164	2,949	77,835	3,034	24,145	97.2	4,884	190	10,198	11.6	41.3	58.2
Braxton	590	1,200	28,222	1,906	4,619	92.1	86,428	5,838	6,051	13.6	49.4	50.2
Brooke	856	1,750	43,478	1,736	17,029	88.5	30,044	1,200	10,773	14.5	48.2	51.0
Cabell	3,236	8,393	210,482	2,206	77,524	74.2	79,442	833	37,950	17.8	55.4	43.7
Calhoun	294	562	13,143	1,784	2,127	97.2	3,151	428	2,889	10.5	55.0	43.8
Clay	433	1,947	18,448	1,775	2,995	94.0	1,041	100	4,072	13.7	54.0	45.1
Doddridge	255	568	13,345	1,791	3,472	99.2	–	–	3,179	12.9	74.3	25.2
Fayette	1,510	3,780	81,558	1,730	23,027	85.3	92,177	1,956	16,967	16.1	46.5	52.9
Gilmer	284	510	18,039	2,572	3,694	96.6	1,939	276	2,852	4.1	58.4	40.6
Grant	820	1,795	54,785	4,828	7,547	98.1	131,208	11,562	5,047	11.3	80.5	19.1
Greenbrier	1,212	5,085	66,848	1,932	14,685	91.0	74,817	2,163	14,553	13.6	57.4	41.8
Hampshire	690	1,449	30,979	1,478	8,590	96.8	13,132	626	7,996	31.1	68.7	30.7
Hancock	1,107	2,642	66,728	2,082	23,412	83.6	111,660	3,483	14,321	6.3	51.0	48.2
Hardy	425	836	26,131	2,036	5,814	91.2	7,732	602	5,276	16.9	68.9	30.7
Harrison	2,693	6,453	147,752	2,174	55,780	75.2	142,771	2,100	30,588	15.1	55.9	43.3
Jackson	1,068	2,415	55,801	1,977	18,174	90.9	27,831	986	13,158	14.2	58.4	40.9
Jefferson	1,358	3,041	69,069	1,536	28,545	90.8	39,699	883	19,993	39.1	52.7	46.5
Kanawha	7,006	16,487	473,135	2,413	181,917	70.5	452,485	2,308	87,928	14.7	50.5	48.9
Lewis	603	1,410	27,265	1,613	7,915	89.2	3,549	210	6,999	14.1	63.5	35.4
Lincoln	635	1,855	36,340	1,628	7,348	89.1	3,885	174	8,312	11.4	49.4	48.7
Logan	1,162	2,751	114,161	3,086	26,919	96.0	28,559	772	14,987	3.8	47.0	52.6
McDowell	1,156	2,457	50,646	1,944	10,822	88.9	2,922	112	7,299	-0.1	37.8	61.7
Marion	1,619	3,854	128,346	2,279	26,048	89.1	421,485	7,485	25,194	10.1	48.2	50.7
Marshall	1,307	2,865	83,822	2,394	25,566	82.7	258,836	7,393	15,072	11.7	56.5	42.7
Mason	1,043	2,260	49,007	1,882	14,415	92.7	64,347	2,471	11,990	6.8	54.1	45.1
Mercer	2,925	7,149	197,562	3,179	28,891	80.6	138,130	2,223	22,379	18.6	58.3	41.0
Mineral	925	2,079	45,285	1,671	11,254	90.9	13,026	481	11,461	17.2	68.5	30.7
Mingo	918	2,370	62,702	2,262	18,637	82.3	3,091	111	10,655	6.1	43.3	56.2
Monongalia	2,290	6,354	139,504	1,687	54,310	78.3	183,136	2,215	34,306	25.4	51.5	47.6
Monroe	434	1,627	20,603	1,546	2,966	92.8	7,170	538	5,951	15.8	60.3	38.8
Morgan	640	1,419	37,605	2,454	7,697	94.7	7,657	500	6,847	18.6	65.9	33.2
Nicholas	1,499	3,433	77,122	2,925	14,535	83.0	16,515	626	10,351	20.7	53.0	46.3
Ohio	2,326	4,690	94,287	2,039	34,484	65.4	97,543	2,109	20,392	13.5	57.4	41.9

See footnotes at end of table.

Table B-13. Counties — **Local Government Finances and Elections**—Con.

[Includes United States, states, and 3,141 counties/county equivalents defined as of February 22, 2005. For more information on these areas, see Appendix C, Geographic Information]

County	Local government employment, March 2002 — Total employment	Local government employment, March 2002 — Total payroll ($1,000)	General revenue — Total ($1,000)	General revenue — Per capita (dol.)	Taxes — Total ($1,000)	Taxes — Property, percent of total (taxes)	Total debt outstanding — Amount ($1,000)	Total debt outstanding — Per capita (dol.)	Votes cast for President — Total	Votes cast for President — Percent change, 2000–2004	Votes cast for President — Republican candidate, percent of total	Votes cast for President — Democratic candidate, percent of total
WEST VIRGINIA—Con.												
Pendleton	267	613	12,105	1,525	2,344	89.6	962	121	3,544	10.0	60.6	39.0
Pleasants	349	829	33,429	4,435	9,166	95.4	216,423	28,715	3,435	7.1	60.0	39.3
Pocahontas	424	861	24,137	2,695	4,766	77.9	4,605	514	3,918	13.0	58.6	40.2
Preston	1,254	2,307	44,411	1,498	7,904	94.6	23,956	808	11,929	14.3	65.9	33.2
Putnam	1,452	3,385	96,568	1,847	30,013	94.8	208,498	3,987	25,151	23.1	62.5	37.0
Raleigh	2,422	5,928	157,439	1,987	49,106	81.6	84,895	1,072	30,525	26.9	60.7	38.7
Randolph	1,050	2,405	69,978	2,466	15,412	37.8	30,757	1,084	11,490	20.4	56.7	42.6
Ritchie	375	753	16,443	1,578	4,222	98.9	3,322	319	4,196	10.1	73.6	25.5
Roane	610	1,316	24,579	1,607	4,090	86.4	12,341	807	6,100	8.4	56.4	42.8
Summers	365	755	17,442	1,246	3,934	71.2	2,922	209	5,524	17.2	53.9	45.3
Taylor	519	1,312	24,232	1,502	5,826	85.7	6,643	412	6,551	14.7	59.4	40.0
Tucker	326	596	16,795	2,321	3,796	84.0	1,861	257	3,600	7.6	60.5	38.9
Tyler	474	1,421	26,022	2,765	5,726	97.4	16,467	1,750	4,245	8.1	65.9	33.0
Upshur	726	1,836	40,388	1,726	9,570	90.8	13,755	588	9,293	14.4	66.6	32.7
Wayne	1,558	3,662	66,454	1,566	18,198	93.6	12,056	284	18,609	14.6	54.1	45.2
Webster	437	850	15,975	1,639	3,056	87.3	1,648	169	3,714	12.3	46.4	52.9
Wetzel	1,024	2,287	60,235	3,490	11,009	80.1	32,009	1,855	7,038	11.9	52.0	47.3
Wirt	228	453	9,340	1,597	1,776	97.2	310	53	2,654	11.4	65.1	33.8
Wood	3,073	7,302	136,415	1,555	46,267	90.9	93,764	1,069	39,227	15.9	63.6	35.8
Wyoming	916	1,867	50,675	2,032	13,526	89.3	19,889	798	8,718	10.7	57.2	42.4
WISCONSIN	273,406	716,314	19,507,188	3,586	6,796,085	93.8	15,457,196	2,842	2,997,007	15.3	49.3	49.7
Adams	903	1,804	55,141	2,692	21,818	92.3	42,141	2,057	10,456	14.7	46.8	52.1
Ashland	1,062	2,213	66,630	3,969	15,906	91.1	42,404	2,526	9,199	16.6	36.0	63.1
Barron	2,394	5,218	153,484	3,376	46,230	91.3	113,295	2,492	23,937	20.3	50.3	48.9
Bayfield	1,135	1,853	59,427	3,926	22,631	93.3	32,068	2,119	9,699	17.4	38.7	60.3
Brown	11,122	32,033	940,686	4,056	289,543	97.9	881,001	3,799	123,294	14.4	54.5	44.6
Buffalo	928	1,571	46,164	3,341	12,062	94.0	26,404	1,911	7,591	14.3	46.1	52.7
Burnett	769	1,462	54,151	3,365	19,519	94.2	48,645	3,023	9,321	14.4	50.9	48.3
Calumet	1,370	2,680	84,931	1,998	27,438	97.2	87,813	2,066	25,276	26.7	58.2	40.7
Chippewa	2,798	5,927	167,979	2,986	48,836	91.1	120,645	2,145	30,524	16.6	50.6	48.3
Clark	2,279	4,157	117,763	3,481	25,053	98.2	59,322	1,754	15,125	6.9	52.7	46.1
Columbia	3,201	6,755	192,442	3,602	70,380	92.3	155,285	2,906	29,555	15.5	50.6	48.4
Crawford	1,069	1,851	55,776	3,277	15,008	90.1	47,783	2,808	8,459	14.4	43.5	55.0
Dane	21,212	57,680	1,645,616	3,728	699,740	91.5	1,466,466	3,322	274,249	17.8	33.0	66.0
Dodge	3,387	7,769	225,224	2,592	76,068	92.3	174,683	2,011	44,336	17.6	61.4	37.6
Door	1,589	3,543	101,998	3,607	53,711	92.7	69,283	2,450	17,491	14.9	50.9	47.8
Douglas	2,646	6,264	197,646	4,524	63,210	92.4	165,748	3,794	25,187	16.0	33.5	65.7
Dunn	1,683	4,062	134,701	3,305	37,639	91.9	107,356	2,634	23,172	19.9	47.0	52.0
Eau Claire	4,345	13,064	327,887	3,486	112,914	96.4	218,357	2,322	55,437	15.8	44.5	54.2
Florence	332	597	17,940	3,500	6,320	98.4	13,652	2,664	2,724	13.3	62.5	36.5
Fond du Lac	5,193	13,228	338,751	3,463	113,124	97.5	308,272	3,152	53,036	13.8	62.8	36.2
Forest	687	1,681	35,414	3,568	13,046	96.6	19,398	1,954	5,153	9.3	50.6	48.7
Grant	2,997	6,437	177,987	3,601	43,787	98.8	99,156	2,006	25,264	15.1	48.3	50.9
Green	2,057	4,504	113,996	3,343	35,704	97.1	87,938	2,579	18,248	19.5	46.6	52.5
Green Lake	1,134	2,326	67,698	3,516	27,854	97.9	51,302	2,664	10,178	11.8	63.6	35.4
Iowa	1,370	2,659	73,525	3,180	26,353	93.5	58,670	2,538	12,542	19.0	42.6	56.8
Iron	449	931	27,731	4,081	9,072	92.7	16,279	2,396	3,879	10.6	48.6	50.4
Jackson	1,325	2,532	72,734	3,773	16,815	92.7	32,522	1,687	9,726	15.6	45.1	54.0
Jefferson	3,803	8,810	250,357	3,255	89,410	92.1	178,535	2,321	42,115	16.7	56.5	42.6
Juneau	1,329	2,683	84,258	3,361	23,671	92.7	116,527	4,648	12,379	21.1	52.3	46.3
Kenosha	7,849	22,504	587,365	3,814	219,580	93.6	552,718	3,589	70,420	20.0	46.6	52.5
Kewaunee	1,124	2,306	66,075	3,222	18,646	98.3	41,960	2,046	11,273	11.8	53.0	45.9
La Crosse	6,329	15,748	423,199	3,919	134,752	91.2	301,687	2,794	62,136	11.8	45.5	53.4
Lafayette	1,221	2,491	70,680	4,335	16,590	98.8	48,802	2,993	8,388	15.5	46.8	52.5
Langlade	1,212	2,514	69,810	3,352	22,606	92.6	45,882	2,203	11,074	13.9	56.3	42.9
Lincoln	1,697	3,797	103,798	3,462	33,126	93.6	71,104	2,371	15,700	10.3	51.1	47.7
Manitowoc	3,939	9,604	242,946	2,950	70,799	96.9	221,936	2,695	44,160	13.7	52.1	46.8
Marathon	7,400	16,805	469,782	3,703	153,281	91.8	299,690	2,362	68,059	16.6	53.5	45.4
Marinette	2,247	4,924	140,351	3,234	44,359	96.9	118,798	2,737	22,270	11.8	53.3	45.8
Marquette	843	1,471	41,761	2,835	17,477	93.8	22,499	1,528	8,477	17.8	54.3	44.7
Menominee	468	951	24,485	5,291	2,880	99.2	9,761	2,109	1,710	38.7	16.8	82.6
Milwaukee	45,994	156,779	4,051,227	4,338	1,218,097	91.8	2,740,295	2,934	482,236	11.2	37.4	61.7
Monroe	2,143	4,519	132,258	3,183	33,403	90.1	121,087	2,914	19,554	19.7	53.1	45.9
Oconto	1,727	3,294	99,415	2,715	32,473	93.3	101,956	2,784	19,794	19.3	55.8	43.1
Oneida	2,140	5,090	144,035	3,897	80,555	94.0	91,884	2,486	22,039	16.7	51.5	47.5
Outagamie	8,825	23,539	629,457	3,791	215,636	97.3	604,480	3,641	90,050	18.9	54.3	44.6
Ozaukee	3,284	9,161	251,344	2,992	128,552	92.5	223,231	2,657	53,032	11.1	65.8	33.4
Pepin	365	760	29,258	3,987	8,357	94.3	14,386	1,960	4,066	11.0	45.6	53.6
Pierce	2,342	4,776	125,631	3,357	41,772	94.1	113,184	3,025	21,876	21.8	47.7	51.1
Polk	2,389	4,768	147,839	3,459	45,499	93.4	142,625	3,337	23,503	18.9	51.5	47.5
Portage	2,860	6,982	206,117	3,065	66,213	91.0	108,645	1,616	38,961	15.4	42.5	56.1

See footnotes at end of table.

[Includes United States, states, and 3,141 counties/county equivalents defined as of February 22, 2005. For more information on these areas, see Appendix C, Geographic Information]

County	Local government employment, March 2002		Local government finances, 2002						Elections, 2004[1]			
			General revenue				Total debt outstanding		Votes cast for President			
					Taxes						Repub-lican cand-idate, percent of total	Demo-cratic cand-idate, percent of total
	Total employ-ment	Total payroll ($1,000)	Total ($1,000)	Per capita (dol.)	Total ($1,000)	Prop-erty, percent of total (taxes)	Amount ($1,000)	Per capita (dol.)	Total	Percent change, 2000–2004		
WISCONSIN—Con.												
Price	1,041	2,094	52,435	3,393	16,517	93.0	27,779	1,798	8,763	10.5	49.2	49.6
Racine	7,540	23,788	602,103	3,154	190,850	97.1	438,226	2,296	101,569	14.3	51.7	47.5
Richland	1,173	1,883	60,204	3,325	14,571	92.1	37,644	2,079	9,420	13.6	51.3	47.8
Rock	8,227	21,845	555,145	3,606	165,863	97.7	344,154	2,235	80,479	14.3	41.2	57.9
Rusk	1,497	2,593	73,664	4,813	13,720	92.8	40,383	2,639	7,927	7.6	50.3	48.2
St. Croix	3,061	6,783	201,432	2,944	71,972	87.3	198,829	2,906	41,835	39.7	54.2	44.9
Sauk	3,147	7,031	195,294	3,492	73,741	83.2	160,942	2,878	30,417	18.6	47.4	51.6
Sawyer	909	1,952	51,483	3,105	24,423	92.1	25,855	1,559	9,453	21.7	52.4	46.7
Shawano	2,224	4,201	119,732	2,922	33,537	92.1	85,617	2,089	20,999	19.3	57.9	41.2
Sheboygan	6,578	16,727	408,382	3,606	144,068	96.9	298,547	2,636	62,625	13.4	55.0	44.1
Taylor	1,164	2,182	64,951	3,305	17,185	93.2	47,324	2,408	9,543	6.1	58.5	40.1
Trempealeau	1,939	4,094	120,359	4,428	30,667	95.2	87,779	3,229	14,062	15.6	41.8	57.4
Vernon	1,541	2,833	93,122	3,284	22,821	93.7	61,952	2,185	14,845	13.8	45.6	53.4
Vilas	884	2,077	67,291	3,089	39,547	92.0	56,774	2,606	14,002	13.6	58.2	40.8
Walworth	4,677	11,623	327,493	3,441	147,714	91.7	367,789	3,864	48,446	19.7	59.4	39.6
Washburn	1,051	2,145	59,303	3,614	25,755	95.4	26,550	1,618	9,567	18.9	49.8	49.2
Washington	4,924	13,093	361,948	2,992	156,747	92.1	380,251	3,143	72,467	18.0	69.9	29.3
Waukesha	16,038	43,978	1,171,879	3,166	610,744	96.8	1,106,946	2,990	230,363	13.1	67.3	32.0
Waupaca	3,186	7,055	174,879	3,340	55,411	93.5	202,949	3,876	26,974	18.3	59.1	40.0
Waushara	1,167	2,480	62,052	2,547	24,226	94.3	40,456	1,661	12,246	19.5	56.3	42.9
Winnebago	6,276	16,509	459,490	2,901	159,666	96.9	438,936	2,771	88,596	16.5	52.5	46.2
Wood	4,196	10,270	279,677	3,712	88,825	97.4	143,954	1,910	40,071	12.1	51.4	47.3
WYOMING	37,275	80,496	2,394,227	4,798	723,966	75.7	1,089,978	2,184	243,428	11.5	68.9	29.1
Albany	1,780	3,919	133,980	4,241	22,369	54.5	45,305	1,434	16,624	17.5	54.2	42.8
Big Horn	1,181	2,071	56,009	4,989	11,979	85.3	24,660	2,196	5,283	7.4	80.1	18.2
Campbell	2,968	7,419	241,075	6,668	114,393	77.2	49,901	1,380	15,099	20.4	82.2	16.3
Carbon	1,144	2,177	80,218	5,215	34,541	82.0	10,517	684	7,077	1.6	67.2	30.5
Converse	1,044	2,108	53,895	4,362	20,468	84.8	25,268	2,045	5,725	10.6	77.7	20.7
Crook	524	1,035	28,765	4,877	6,731	88.7	2,195	372	3,396	24.0	83.5	14.8
Fremont	2,742	5,268	157,704	4,377	31,918	92.4	28,429	789	17,096	10.7	66.9	31.2
Goshen	906	1,789	44,349	3,609	8,899	64.1	11,638	947	5,779	4.7	71.2	27.1
Hot Springs	421	825	26,419	5,594	8,450	77.5	5,638	1,194	2,480	5.4	73.1	25.1
Johnson	634	1,283	33,753	4,553	7,965	75.3	11,869	1,601	3,991	12.4	81.0	16.9
Laramie	5,695	13,086	330,955	3,980	68,510	51.2	119,836	1,441	39,879	12.9	65.1	33.0
Lincoln	1,125	2,372	68,542	4,588	24,520	85.1	93,951	6,289	7,914	15.6	81.2	17.2
Natrona	4,170	8,876	231,859	3,434	56,617	67.5	68,413	1,013	32,068	13.0	67.1	30.8
Niobrara	262	403	10,241	4,515	3,090	76.3	18,522	8,167	1,314	16.6	81.0	17.5
Park	2,287	4,293	138,808	5,349	28,241	91.7	51,124	1,970	14,231	10.9	76.7	21.1
Platte	611	1,179	40,089	4,570	10,223	80.1	78,368	8,934	4,574	4.6	68.9	29.0
Sheridan	2,073	4,818	132,170	4,904	21,828	51.6	25,891	961	14,029	14.7	69.1	29.0
Sublette	490	939	52,697	8,475	35,607	98.8	22,204	3,571	3,651	13.5	78.0	20.0
Sweetwater	3,282	7,998	229,216	6,146	99,525	83.3	195,182	5,234	16,272	3.7	65.5	32.0
Teton	1,446	3,960	127,072	6,838	44,681	58.6	45,125	2,428	11,359	8.9	45.1	52.6
Uinta	1,558	2,933	103,225	5,222	50,653	81.4	140,253	7,095	8,081	8.9	75.3	22.5
Washakie	509	971	25,001	3,149	6,335	92.2	9,677	1,219	4,114	1.6	77.8	20.8
Weston	423	775	48,185	7,280	6,423	78.4	6,012	908	3,392	10.8	80.8	17.1

- Represents zero.   NA Not available.   X Not applicable.

[1] Data subject to copyright; see source citation.
[2] State total includes overseas ballots.
[3] Yellowstone National Park County became incorporated with Gallatin and Park Counties, MT; effective November 7, 1997.
[4] Bronx, New York, Queens, and Richmond Counties included with Kings County, NY.
[5] State total includes write-in votes.
[6] Clifton Forge independent city became incorporated with Alleghany County, VA; effective July 1, 2001.
[7] South Boston independent city became incorporated with Halifax County, VA; effective June 30, 1995.

Survey, Census, or Data Collection Method: Local government employment and finances—For information about these data collections and surveys, see Appendix B, Limitations of the Data and Methodology, and Internet site <http://www.census.gov/govs/www/apesloc02.html>.   Elections—For information, see CQ Press, 2005, *America Votes 2003–2004*, Washington, DC, and Internet site <http://www.cqpress.com>.

Sources: Local government employment and finances—U.S. Census Bureau, 2002 Census of Governments, Compendium of Government Employment, accessed November 20, 2006; Finances, accessed August 6, 2006 (related Internet site <http://www.census.gov/govs/www/cog2002.html>).   Elections, 2004—CQ Press, 2005, *America Votes 2003–2004*, Washington, DC, (copyrighted and printed with permission of CQ Press) (related Internet site <http://www.cqpress.com>).

Table B-14. Counties — Farm Earnings, Agriculture, and Water Use

[Includes United States, states, and 3,141 counties/county equivalents defined as of February 22, 2005. For more information on these areas, see Appendix C, Geographic Information]

County	Farm earnings, 2005		Agriculture (NAICS 111–112), 2002									Water use, 2000[4]			
			Farms			Land in farms		Value of farm products sold						By selected major use (mil. gal. per day)	
				Percent						Percent from					
	Total ($1,000)	Per-cent of total[1]	Number	Less than 50 acres	500 acres or more	Total acres (1,000)	Aver-age size of farm (acres)	Total (mil. dol.)	Average per farm (dol.)	Crops[2]	Live-stock and poultry[3]	Total (mil. gal. per day)	Ground water, percent of total	Irri-gation	Public supply
UNITED STATES	50,903,000	0.6	2,128,982	34.9	15.9	938,279	441	200,646	94,245	47.4	52.6	405,042	20.8	136,905	42,781
ALABAMA	1,324,547	1.3	45,126	37.1	8.3	8,904	197	3,265	72,352	18.1	81.9	9,990	4.4	43	834
Autauga	7,902	1.5	373	26.8	12.9	118	318	19	49,871	43.7	56.3	37	28.6	(Z)	6
Baldwin	17,173	0.7	1,062	48.2	8.1	181	171	86	80,697	82.9	17.1	35	78.1	6	20
Barbour	49,846	10.6	531	17.7	18.5	191	359	61	114,056	24.7	75.3	7	85.7	1	5
Bibb	1,535	0.8	187	26.7	15.0	45	240	2	8,909	25.0	75.0	4	100.0	–	4
Blount	34,349	7.9	1,248	40.1	2.9	143	115	114	91,532	6.3	93.7	32	9.1	(Z)	32
Bullock	14,323	11.5	273	17.6	33.3	146	536	29	105,293	70.0	30.0	3	82.5	1	3
Butler	36,194	12.2	425	25.9	5.6	83	196	58	135,529	2.9	97.1	4	100.0	(Z)	3
Calhoun	9,467	0.4	673	45.8	2.4	75	111	43	63,975	18.2	81.8	25	84.9	1	22
Chambers	1,875	0.4	306	23.9	17.3	93	303	6	18,294	22.3	77.7	12	2.3	(Z)	6
Cherokee	13,899	6.1	546	32.1	9.0	121	222	34	62,125	42.4	57.6	6	22.3	2	3
Chilton	12,365	3.3	667	35.8	4.3	98	147	13	19,651	68.8	31.2	5	72.6	(Z)	4
Choctaw	4,718	1.9	244	27.5	12.3	55	226	6	24,873	6.4	93.6	52	3.3	–	1
Clarke	740	0.2	284	25.4	8.8	57	201	2	6,468	25.9	74.1	23	11.1	–	3
Clay	10,027	5.0	427	21.1	6.6	84	198	23	53,400	2.2	97.8	2	34.1	–	1
Cleburne	27,633	17.2	326	31.0	3.1	44	136	52	159,448	2.6	97.4	2	71.6	–	1
Coffee	54,246	8.6	854	28.7	10.5	197	231	134	156,919	9.1	90.9	13	86.2	2	7
Colbert	21,401	1.9	584	32.9	8.9	132	226	35	59,250	32.2	67.8	1,346	0.3	1	8
Conecuh	4,751	2.6	369	25.5	10.3	82	222	5	14,070	26.6	73.4	2	100.0	–	2
Coosa	1,923	2.5	228	26.8	6.1	39	173	1	6,465	(NA)	(NA)	1	47.7	–	(Z)
Covington	31,418	5.5	1,013	24.8	8.2	202	199	68	66,644	18.8	81.2	29	25.6	1	7
Crenshaw	67,185	32.1	570	22.6	10.9	130	229	74	130,084	2.1	97.9	2	84.4	(Z)	2
Cullman	98,278	7.7	2,301	48.5	2.7	231	101	337	146,658	2.9	97.1	41	1.4	(Z)	40
Dale	24,863	1.8	459	23.5	14.8	139	304	45	97,089	18.8	81.2	9	92.3	1	7
Dallas	12,843	1.9	490	23.3	24.7	236	481	26	52,622	33.7	66.3	54	24.9	1	10
DeKalb	108,345	9.6	2,177	46.6	3.2	237	109	268	123,254	3.8	96.2	18	13.2	(Z)	17
Elmore	3,491	0.5	633	38.7	6.8	104	165	12	18,956	57.0	43.0	6	63.4	(Z)	5
Escambia	6,544	1.1	444	47.1	10.4	94	213	9	21,020	62.3	37.7	43	19.5	1	6
Etowah	34,106	2.1	974	52.1	2.3	90	93	48	49,003	5.5	94.5	271	1.9	1	23
Fayette	2,531	1.1	365	17.5	8.5	75	206	12	33,249	12.5	87.5	3	27.4	–	2
Franklin	54,813	11.8	929	30.7	5.3	146	157	107	115,601	1.8	98.2	5	37.4	(Z)	4
Geneva	43,136	16.3	998	28.6	10.1	227	228	103	103,092	17.4	82.6	4	74.8	1	2
Greene	10,691	10.7	349	24.6	23.5	128	367	20	56,473	1.8	98.2	361	1.0	1	1
Hale	17,626	11.5	433	19.6	18.9	161	371	44	102,464	3.6	96.4	6	100.0	(Z)	2
Henry	7,893	3.8	346	20.2	22.3	151	436	26	75,618	53.6	46.4	5	60.7	2	2
Houston	10,337	0.5	700	34.3	13.9	188	269	40	56,553	61.4	38.6	130	18.3	4	19
Jackson	25,926	3.4	1,375	40.4	7.1	229	167	70	51,141	14.6	85.4	1,563	0.1	(Z)	7
Jefferson	1,138	(Z)	463	58.3	2.4	42	91	14	31,181	12.2	87.8	103	19.1	–	59
Lamar	−1,456	(X)	463	33.0	6.9	87	187	5	11,073	20.2	79.8	2	87.2	(Z)	2
Lauderdale	6,981	0.6	1,485	45.8	4.7	208	140	28	18,943	40.6	59.4	15	19.1	(Z)	13
Lawrence	38,736	9.2	1,597	44.1	4.6	234	147	90	56,053	18.7	81.3	60	1.9	1	2
Lee	14,212	0.7	336	34.8	10.7	74	220	29	86,131	(NA)	(NA)	17	12.2	1	13
Limestone	25,558	1.9	1,235	44.5	7.0	226	183	52	42,338	57.6	42.4	2,121	0.2	2	11
Lowndes	10,736	6.5	420	28.6	23.3	197	468	42	98,862	15.0	85.0	2	77.4	1	1
Macon	4,961	1.9	368	25.8	19.3	129	351	9	25,573	73.2	26.8	5	18.4	1	3
Madison	5,690	0.1	1,117	46.6	6.2	198	178	38	33,693	70.4	29.6	54	58.1	2	50
Marengo	4,967	1.3	508	21.9	18.9	189	372	15	28,724	11.6	88.4	23	22.1	(Z)	2
Marion	28,527	5.6	756	28.3	4.4	119	158	45	59,085	3.3	96.7	6	11.0	–	5
Marshall	63,088	4.2	1,686	53.4	2.5	161	95	186	110,464	2.2	97.8	19	18.3	(Z)	18
Mobile	19,572	0.2	740	56.8	6.8	101	136	75	101,446	87.1	12.9	1,295	3.1	1	136
Monroe	5,986	1.3	443	31.4	14.0	120	271	10	22,878	39.8	60.2	81	26.6	(Z)	5
Montgomery	15,452	0.2	703	33.3	16.2	213	303	36	51,004	25.5	74.5	47	49.1	(Z)	44
Morgan	29,038	1.1	1,308	47.6	2.6	149	114	79	60,717	6.1	93.9	162	2.7	(Z)	33
Perry	5,122	5.8	376	21.8	18.1	165	439	18	47,532	9.4	90.6	4	100.0	–	3
Pickens	10,415	5.6	493	26.2	9.9	143	289	74	149,923	2.6	97.4	3	89.3	(Z)	3
Pike	54,659	8.9	612	21.9	17.6	187	306	66	107,100	8.9	91.1	7	77.3	2	4
Randolph	24,920	10.2	610	25.9	6.6	110	180	52	85,770	1.9	98.1	2	39.3	–	1
Russell	4,422	0.8	245	32.7	19.2	105	430	8	34,171	82.1	17.9	32	3.9	1	8
St. Clair	7,064	1.0	667	42.7	3.7	83	124	47	70,144	14.9	85.1	8	93.7	(Z)	6
Shelby	4,177	0.1	486	46.7	4.7	64	132	13	26,936	70.5	29.5	780	1.8	1	13
Sumter	3,729	2.4	443	26.0	21.9	177	399	13	29,451	6.1	93.9	2	100.0	–	1
Talladega	8,170	0.5	584	34.4	9.1	109	187	27	45,719	20.1	79.9	93	11.9	(Z)	15
Tallapoosa	−487	(X)	377	26.5	6.1	78	207	5	13,748	27.3	72.7	11	2.9	(Z)	11
Tuscaloosa	4,236	0.1	547	36.4	8.4	103	188	21	37,501	30.4	69.6	35	26.5	1	27
Walker	3,101	0.4	543	47.3	5.2	75	138	51	93,742	2.3	97.7	693	0.2	(Z)	58
Washington	10,196	3.8	396	28.8	5.6	74	187	22	54,513	3.5	96.5	124	9.0	(Z)	1
Wilcox	3,067	1.8	306	20.6	25.8	160	523	5	16,480	20.8	79.2	24	4.9	(Z)	1
Winston	24,177	6.5	650	39.1	2.2	66	102	61	93,729	0.5	99.5	1	100.0	–	(Z)

See footnotes at end of table.

Table B-14. Counties — **Farm Earnings, Agriculture, and Water Use**—Con.

[Includes United States, states, and 3,141 counties/county equivalents defined as of February 22, 2005. For more information on these areas, see Appendix C, Geographic Information]

County	Farm earnings, 2005 Total ($1,000)	Farm earnings, 2005 Percent of total[1]	Farms Number	Farms Percent Less than 50 acres	Farms Percent 500 acres or more	Land in farms Total acres (1,000)	Land in farms Average size of farm (acres)	Value of farm products sold Total (mil. dol.)	Value of farm products sold Average per farm (dol.)	Value Percent from Crops[2]	Value Percent from Livestock and poultry[3]	Water use Total (mil. gal. per day)	Water use Ground water, percent of total	By selected major use Irrigation	By selected major use Public supply
ALASKA	13,263	0.1	609	42.0	16.1	901	1,479	46	75,768	44.5	55.5	305	46.2	1	80
Aleutians East	–											3	0.9	–	1
Aleutians West	437	0.2	36	19.4	50.0	707	19,639	(Z)	9,139	(NA)	(NA)	5	7.2	–	2
Anchorage	–	–	251	48.6	10.4	47	187	28	109,610	51.6	48.4	42	31.8	(Z)	37
Bethel	–	–	–	–	–	–	–	–	–	–	–	(Z)	91.7	–	(Z)
Bristol Bay	–	–				–	–					(Z)	100.0	–	(Z)
Denali	–	–	–	–	–	–	–	–	–	–	–	14	1.1	(Z)	(Z)
Dillingham	–	–										(Z)	100.0	–	(Z)
Fairbanks North Star	1,049	(Z)	187	24.1	24.1	110	588	5	28,262	82.3	17.7	43	34.4	(Z)	8
Haines	–	–				–	–					1	5.3	–	(Z)
Juneau	168	(Z)	37	94.6	–	1	15	11	296,270	5.4	94.6	4	68.9	–	4
Kenai Peninsula	[5]25	(NA)	98	48.0	9.2	36	370	2	20,980	(NA)	(NA)	9	90.0	(Z)	4
Ketchikan Gateway	–	–	–	–	–	–	–	–	–	–	–	7	–	–	5
Kodiak Island	–	–	–	–	–	–	–	–	–	–	–	6	4.3	–	5
Lake and Peninsula	–	–	–	–	–	–	–	–	–	–	–	(Z)	27.7	–	(Z)
Matanuska-Susitna	11,641	1.2	–	–	–	–	–	–	–	–	–	4	98.6	(Z)	1
Nome	–	–	–	–	–	–	–	–	–	–	–	1	63.8	–	1
North Slope	–	–	–	–	–	–	–	–	–	–	–	140	64.1	–	(Z)
Northwest Arctic	–	–	–	–	–	–	–	–	–	–	–	7	0.7	–	1
Prince of Wales-Outer Ketchikan	–	–	–	–	–	–	–	–	–	–	–	3	0.4	–	3
Sitka	–	–	–	–	–	–	–	–	–	–	–	1	–	–	1
Skagway-Hoonah-Angoon	–	–	–	–	–	–	–	–	–	–	–	1	47.7	–	1
Southeast Fairbanks	–	–	–	–	–	–	–	–	–	–	–	3	21.5	(Z)	(Z)
Valdez-Cordova	–	–	–	–	–	–	–	–	–	–	–	4	67.2	–	4
Wade Hampton	–	–	–	–	–	–	–	–	–	–	–	(Z)	79.1	–	(Z)
Wrangell-Petersburg	–	–	–	–	–	–	–	–	–	–	–	1	3.4	–	1
Yakutat	–	–	–	–	–	–	–	–	–	–	–	(Z)	100.0	–	(Z)
Yukon-Koyukuk	–	–	–	–	–	–	–	–	–	–	–	3	7.6	–	(Z)
ARIZONA	836,378	0.6	7,294	58.0	17.6	26,587	3,645	2,395	328,413	66.3	33.7	6,730	51.0	5,400	1,080
Apache	−11,330	(X)	363	41.0	19.6	(D)	(D)	8	22,722	2.9	97.1	48	57.1	24	5
Cochise	76,402	3.3	950	33.8	26.8	969	1,020	78	82,428	71.2	28.8	233	99.2	214	11
Coconino	−8,388	(X)	213	49.8	22.5	(D)	(D)	11	52,183	7.0	93.0	53	42.8	6	19
Gila	−3,675	(X)	164	59.1	10.4	(D)	(D)	3	16,220	10.1	89.9	15	89.8	6	6
Graham	31,122	10.2	277	54.9	21.7	(D)	(D)	82	295,668	95.1	4.9	172	74.5	167	5
Greenlee	125	0.1	124	44.4	8.1	27	221	4	33,177	22.0	78.0	33	75.5	14	1
La Paz	26,045	10.8	101	24.8	39.6	(D)	(D)	87	857,653	99.3	0.7	879	32.9	875	3
Maricopa	300,362	0.3	2,110	76.7	7.7	627	297	740	350,798	52.8	47.2	2,151	56.7	1,357	739
Mohave	2,509	0.1	239	49.8	28.0	793	3,318	16	68,356	65.9	34.1	154	76.9	132	20
Navajo	416	(Z)	291	49.5	22.7	4,595	15,791	27	92,003	2.5	97.5	70	98.1	29	10
Pima	29,925	0.2	517	72.7	11.6	(D)	(D)	69	133,228	81.8	18.2	300	94.5	89	170
Pinal	227,225	9.8	687	51.5	29.8	1,162	1,691	425	618,281	41.8	58.2	1,052	51.8	1,010	34
Santa Cruz	−349	(X)	152	21.7	27.0	133	874	6	38,355	4.5	95.5	23	96.1	13	9
Yavapai	−1,866	(X)	575	66.1	15.0	720	1,253	37	64,960	(NA)	(NA)	82	86.0	37	23
Yuma	167,855	5.8	531	56.9	18.3	231	435	802	1,511,051	(NA)	(NA)	1,463	24.9	1,432	29
ARKANSAS	1,005,559	1.8	47,483	27.3	14.5	14,503	305	4,950	104,256	32.7	67.3	10,900	63.5	7,910	421
Arkansas	−24,163	(X)	502	10.0	51.8	390	777	96	190,833	99.1	0.9	1,138	55.4	1,125	5
Ashley	−6,256	(X)	336	31.8	23.2	167	497	52	155,604	75.8	24.2	152	71.8	107	2
Baxter	9,803	1.7	572	32.0	8.0	103	181	12	21,143	3.7	96.3	6	30.3	–	5
Benton	95,374	2.0	2,376	44.7	4.3	313	132	361	151,907	1.3	98.7	374	0.4	(Z)	18
Boone	24,195	3.8	1,305	24.1	9.5	284	218	79	60,822	1.5	98.5	4	40.3	–	3
Bradley	9,102	5.6	222	35.6	3.2	29	132	21	96,752	31.6	68.4	3	61.1	–	2
Calhoun	−59	(X)	116	22.4	5.2	19	165	2	19,276	8.2	91.8	1	100.0	–	(Z)
Carroll	49,499	13.2	1,089	24.2	10.8	269	247	158	144,702	0.8	99.2	5	26.5	–	5
Chicot	11,196	7.5	357	11.8	39.5	269	753	70	195,650	66.9	33.1	222	78.4	174	2
Clark	3,730	1.0	374	24.1	13.9	98	261	13	33,885	13.4	86.6	4	11.2	1	3
Clay	5,685	3.3	702	22.9	28.6	343	488	66	93,523	95.9	4.1	270	98.1	268	2
Cleburne	13,912	4.6	807	29.2	4.6	125	155	58	71,887	1.8	98.2	7	1.0	(Z)	7
Cleveland	16,498	27.7	220	30.9	5.0	36	162	58	261,850	0.5	99.5	1	100.0	–	1
Columbia	21,202	4.5	339	28.3	6.2	55	162	37	108,696	(NA)	(NA)	4	65.8	–	2
Conway	23,675	8.2	779	22.0	8.2	173	223	101	129,030	6.5	93.5	16	11.3	6	2
Craighead	13,514	0.8	730	29.3	29.7	350	480	89	121,360	96.3	3.7	392	90.0	376	14
Crawford	23,320	3.0	916	38.0	6.7	151	165	57	62,225	27.6	72.4	19	0.7	1	17
Crittenden	11,463	1.6	238	14.3	52.9	306	1,284	64	268,975	99.4	0.6	133	98.0	122	10
Cross	−25,330	(X)	346	19.4	49.4	326	942	67	193,396	99.0	1.0	438	93.7	436	2
Dallas	1,300	1.0	125	24.0	13.6	26	207	2	14,232	(NA)	(NA)	1	100.0	–	1
Desha	11,228	5.2	264	14.0	55.3	285	1,078	72	271,326	92.9	7.1	415	79.3	384	2
Drew	2,109	0.8	296	19.9	19.9	116	393	27	91,605	71.9	28.1	64	86.7	60	3
Faulkner	−1,420	(X)	1,317	35.7	7.1	225	171	20	15,226	28.6	71.4	13	10.7	4	9
Franklin	31,087	13.7	832	25.8	9.4	176	211	96	115,163	2.3	97.7	3	0.7	(Z)	3
Fulton	8,988	10.1	820	14.5	16.3	250	304	16	19,115	4.2	95.8	2	41.0	(Z)	1

See footnotes at end of table.

[Includes United States, states, and 3,141 counties/county equivalents defined as of February 22, 2005. For more information on these areas, see Appendix C, Geographic Information]

County	Farm earnings, 2005		Agriculture (NAICS 111–112), 2002								Water use, 2000[4]			
			Farms			Land in farms		Value of farm products sold					By selected major use (mil. gal. per day)	
				Percent						Percent from				
	Total ($1,000)	Percent of total[1]	Number	Less than 50 acres	500 acres or more	Total acres (1,000)	Average size of farm (acres)	Total (mil. dol.)	Average per farm (dol.)	Crops[2]	Live-stock and poultry[3]	Total (mil. gal. per day)	Ground water, percent of total	Irrigation	Public supply
ARKANSAS—Con.														
Garland	15,185	1.0	386	42.0	3.6	46	120	10	24,938	22.9	77.1	17	5.8	1	14
Grant	1,603	1.0	251	39.8	4.8	37	147	6	24,179	18.0	82.0	2	100.0	–	1
Greene	4,607	0.8	827	27.2	17.8	262	317	50	60,696	84.2	15.8	165	96.6	157	4
Hempstead	40,994	11.5	783	25.3	14.0	204	260	144	183,434	1.6	98.4	6	82.2	–	5
Hot Spring	2,889	0.9	486	28.4	4.1	74	153	11	22,638	10.4	89.6	415	0.1	3	2
Howard	48,849	14.6	642	30.5	5.8	110	171	135	209,858	0.6	99.4	7	5.2	–	5
Independence	8,312	1.3	1,117	24.1	12.8	288	258	90	80,259	12.7	87.3	79	44.8	42	6
Izard	7,640	5.9	741	15.7	15.4	215	290	26	34,428	2.4	97.6	2	100.0	–	2
Jackson	–15,346	(X)	398	19.1	35.9	332	835	60	151,887	95.3	4.7	386	94.4	382	2
Jefferson	–16,156	(X)	378	28.0	30.4	276	729	69	181,648	90.0	10.0	569	82.9	494	16
Johnson	24,753	7.5	694	23.5	6.3	118	170	98	141,866	2.3	97.7	6	16.8	1	5
Lafayette	16,267	20.8	284	22.9	15.8	104	366	78	273,271	8.6	91.4	12	90.5	10	1
Lawrence	–4,625	(X)	614	18.4	27.2	296	482	60	98,316	69.9	30.1	325	91.1	323	2
Lee	15,095	14.0	257	9.7	45.9	278	1,082	68	263,420	97.5	2.5	242	97.3	240	1
Lincoln	16,256	12.6	315	19.4	27.3	199	632	97	306,476	40.4	59.6	190	89.2	188	2
Little River	12,249	4.6	424	27.8	13.2	147	347	40	94,075	14.2	85.8	4	34.0	1	1
Logan	33,667	13.2	962	22.9	7.1	200	208	114	118,569	2.6	97.4	4	22.7	(Z)	3
Lonoke	–13,306	(X)	777	26.4	23.4	361	465	98	126,069	71.0	29.0	485	81.7	422	4
Madison	35,165	21.1	1,270	19.8	10.6	295	232	108	85,291	1.5	98.5	2	50.5	(Z)	1
Marion	9,120	6.0	526	20.9	14.6	143	272	21	39,644	1.2	98.8	3	1.0	–	3
Miller	7,602	1.1	516	29.8	14.5	158	307	38	72,756	22.4	77.6	90	7.4	86	4
Mississippi	27,595	3.0	388	13.9	54.9	469	1,207	136	349,302	99.8	0.2	193	97.5	183	7
Monroe	–9,194	(X)	250	14.0	53.2	232	928	50	200,884	91.3	8.7	256	92.2	254	2
Montgomery	19,298	21.3	413	24.9	9.0	78	189	43	103,024	1.5	98.5	1	64.9	(Z)	1
Nevada	16,841	13.9	393	21.1	9.9	82	208	31	79,115	1.2	98.8	1	43.7	–	1
Newton	2,211	4.6	613	18.8	9.3	131	214	7	10,848	4.6	95.4	1	94.7	(Z)	(Z)
Ouachita	2,837	1.0	195	39.0	7.7	33	169	6	29,559	4.3	95.7	68	3.6	–	4
Perry	11,843	18.2	380	28.4	8.9	68	178	32	85,297	13.8	86.2	6	9.6	5	1
Phillips	17,469	6.4	301	15.9	49.5	329	1,093	83	276,947	99.2	0.8	469	43.9	199	4
Pike	26,507	19.7	393	28.0	8.4	68	173	46	117,690	1.1	98.9	2	21.1	(Z)	2
Poinsett	1,231	0.5	448	12.9	57.1	382	852	92	205,600	98.3	1.7	666	87.9	661	3
Polk	45,811	16.5	845	31.5	7.1	146	173	82	96,568	0.5	99.5	3	25.5	(Z)	2
Pope	39,613	3.5	1,044	30.2	6.0	169	161	106	101,357	2.6	97.4	999	0.2	1	12
Prairie	–2,864	(X)	431	15.8	41.5	308	714	64	148,418	87.3	12.7	355	76.2	309	1
Pulaski	195	(Z)	575	49.0	10.3	118	206	20	35,530	77.8	22.2	107	24.8	33	73
Randolph	1,581	0.9	710	14.1	19.4	246	347	36	50,958	49.3	50.7	116	74.0	114	1
St. Francis	–4,448	(X)	347	16.7	35.2	279	805	54	155,343	96.2	3.8	264	95.8	257	4
Saline	482	0.1	432	50.2	5.1	56	130	4	8,891	34.4	65.6	14	23.7	1	11
Scott	42,431	29.4	697	24.4	6.5	124	177	93	132,849	0.4	99.6	2	25.3	–	2
Searcy	–580	(X)	615	15.9	13.5	183	298	9	15,145	4.1	95.9	1	62.1	–	1
Sebastian	11,523	0.3	812	37.4	5.3	122	150	50	61,599	6.0	94.0	30	0.3	(Z)	30
Sevier	30,463	12.0	590	29.3	7.8	124	210	114	193,617	0.6	99.4	5	41.8	(Z)	4
Sharp	14,423	10.3	680	19.6	14.0	178	262	40	58,454	1.4	98.6	2	65.0	(Z)	2
Stone	17,702	14.8	681	19.5	11.9	164	241	39	57,050	2.4	97.6	1	42.9	–	1
Union	11,267	1.1	342	44.4	3.8	40	118	59	173,015	0.5	99.5	18	100.0	–	8
Van Buren	–1,162	(X)	603	16.1	8.6	132	218	15	24,816	7.4	92.6	2	0.5	–	2
Washington	94,270	2.2	2,800	41.0	4.6	368	131	314	112,012	1.4	98.6	28	4.7	(Z)	25
White	–6,927	(X)	1,823	31.4	10.2	394	216	50	27,446	42.8	57.2	129	38.1	116	10
Woodruff	–11,130	(X)	225	9.3	59.6	275	1,221	53	233,969	(NA)	(NA)	433	81.6	366	1
Yell	25,807	9.3	829	28.6	9.2	181	219	113	136,516	3.5	96.5	4	16.6	1	3
CALIFORNIA	9,315,861	0.9	79,631	61.7	10.5	27,589	346	25,737	323,205	74.4	25.6	51,200	30.1	30,500	6,120
Alameda	13,021	(Z)	424	52.4	15.1	218	514	43	101,962	83.8	16.2	258	19.2	20	220
Alpine	–	–	14	21.4	28.6	(D)	(D)	1	43,929	(NA)	(NA)	15	23.3	15	(Z)
Amador	13,933	2.1	451	43.2	10.9	194	430	21	47,078	57.8	42.2	32	58.7	25	6
Butte	102,816	2.8	2,128	58.9	7.4	382	179	252	118,407	96.0	4.0	1,078	31.3	973	45
Calaveras	–5,978	(X)	576	50.2	16.5	261	453	13	22,307	32.4	67.6	17	22.2	7	7
Colusa	62,637	15.7	821	23.5	26.7	485	591	241	293,966	97.6	2.4	914	31.4	909	3
Contra Costa	786	(Z)	592	67.9	9.3	126	213	90	152,383	86.7	13.3	1,242	3.2	96	160
Del Norte	14,490	3.8	89	67.4	5.6	13	150	21	239,854	50.5	49.5	22	49.8	17	4
El Dorado	4,090	0.1	1,116	78.0	2.7	117	105	16	14,071	85.7	14.3	55	22.0	18	36
Fresno	692,773	4.0	6,281	58.1	11.5	1,929	307	2,759	439,328	77.9	22.1	3,745	49.6	3,490	196
Glenn	51,837	13.5	1,283	44.9	14.5	506	395	230	179,392	74.7	25.3	684	34.2	675	4
Humboldt	46,954	2.0	993	49.7	15.1	634	638	97	97,603	45.6	54.4	153	38.7	71	34
Imperial	191,015	7.6	537	22.0	43.9	514	957	1,043	1,942,791	62.2	37.8	2,887	3.6	2,835	31
Inyo	–4,309	(X)	85	47.1	31.8	227	2,668	14	163,165	59.9	40.1	121	70.9	67	3
Kern	943,837	6.4	2,147	36.4	26.8	2,731	1,272	2,059	958,875	86.6	13.4	2,885	56.4	2,583	181
Kings	171,738	7.1	1,154	48.7	18.7	646	559	793	687,228	49.8	50.2	1,536	53.5	1,486	22
Lake	18,818	2.5	880	62.5	6.3	144	164	65	74,143	94.9	5.1	52	77.2	44	6
Lassen	6,816	1.3	419	42.5	28.6	482	1,150	28	66,888	56.9	43.1	485	39.8	477	6
Los Angeles	230,224	0.1	1,543	86.8	3.5	111	72	281	182,309	96.9	3.1	5,365	16.1	65	1,575
Madera	271,611	12.5	1,780	45.2	13.3	682	383	710	399,120	71.1	28.9	993	32.1	954	19

See footnotes at end of table.

[Includes United States, states, and 3,141 counties/county equivalents defined as of February 22, 2005. For more information on these areas, see Appendix C, Geographic Information]

County	Farm earnings, 2005		Agriculture (NAICS 111–112), 2002									Water use, 2000[4]			
			Farms			Land in farms		Value of farm products sold						By selected major use (mil. gal. per day)	
				Percent						Percent from					
	Total ($1,000)	Percent of total[1]	Number	Less than 50 acres	500 acres or more	Total acres (1,000)	Average size of farm (acres)	Total (mil. dol.)	Average per farm (dol.)	Crops[2]	Livestock and poultry[3]	Total (mil. gal. per day)	Ground water, percent of total	Irrigation	Public supply
CALIFORNIA—Con.															
Marin	7,774	0.1	254	39.4	33.9	151	593	43	169,398	15.6	84.4	44	39.9	4	38
Mariposa	−4,697	(X)	284	38.0	20.8	219	772	6	22,130	7.5	92.5	6	49.9	4	1
Mendocino	12,703	0.8	1,184	48.9	17.2	707	598	95	80,276	90.5	9.5	57	44.6	42	10
Merced	509,056	14.2	2,964	50.0	11.9	1,006	339	1,409	475,457	42.4	57.6	1,880	34.0	1,744	48
Modoc	15,057	11.1	428	18.0	37.9	609	1,423	53	122,745	62.7	37.3	241	33.9	237	1
Mono	−1,836	(X)	63	30.2	39.7	54	863	9	141,810	64.8	35.2	193	40.4	180	3
Monterey	1,071,659	9.8	1,216	42.5	21.8	1,261	1,037	2,190	1,801,086	98.7	1.3	1,782	44.9	835	43
Napa	195,838	4.6	1,456	70.5	7.2	238	163	429	294,650	99.1	0.9	81	25.8	53	19
Nevada	−1,578	(X)	599	78.1	4.2	82	137	7	11,903	75.1	24.9	48	23.7	32	15
Orange	127,615	0.1	348	79.3	2.3	68	195	279	800,592	99.6	0.4	723	43.2	48	496
Placer	−6,585	(X)	1,438	78.2	3.3	131	91	37	25,847	76.2	23.8	189	19.9	126	59
Plumas	14,436	3.5	142	40.8	20.4	171	1,201	7	51,669	17.6	82.4	55	22.4	49	4
Riverside	241,965	0.7	3,186	81.1	4.5	572	180	1,008	316,470	66.2	33.8	1,688	26.6	1,231	410
Sacramento	77,036	0.2	1,513	70.0	8.9	314	208	239	158,140	68.1	31.9	783	38.7	410	303
San Benito	101,972	11.0	677	52.7	21.3	578	854	198	292,310	80.6	19.4	93	89.0	83	6
San Bernardino	89,796	0.3	1,386	77.9	3.7	514	371	618	445,776	19.5	80.5	653	63.8	183	372
San Diego	373,524	0.4	5,255	89.1	1.9	408	78	951	180,925	92.8	7.2	4,394	1.4	329	438
San Francisco	–	–	8	100.0	–	(D)	(D)	1	126,500	(NA)	(NA)	253	0.9	1	81
San Joaquin	339,448	2.9	4,026	62.6	8.2	813	202	1,222	303,640	74.3	25.7	1,746	44.4	1,597	99
San Luis Obispo	134,155	2.3	2,322	54.2	16.0	1,318	568	396	170,712	92.4	7.6	3,111	6.0	179	34
San Mateo	64,309	0.2	306	61.1	6.2	42	136	173	566,516	99.3	0.7	103	12.9	8	94
Santa Barbara	416,887	3.6	1,444	60.9	14.2	757	524	717	496,715	95.9	4.1	427	76.0	347	63
Santa Clara	129,870	0.1	1,026	75.6	7.7	321	313	208	203,214	90.2	9.8	342	44.3	38	287
Santa Cruz	234,039	3.9	754	74.1	2.1	67	89	362	479,975	97.5	2.5	78	77.5	44	27
Shasta	18,259	0.5	1,126	64.1	10.6	334	296	22	19,496	38.0	62.0	434	40.9	295	37
Sierra	−2,414	(X)	52	13.5	28.8	59	1,128	2	43,635	(NA)	(NA)	44	14.9	43	1
Siskiyou	21,998	3.2	796	36.1	23.1	610	767	109	137,391	78.0	22.0	562	24.8	510	8
Solano	29,790	0.4	915	60.3	12.3	351	384	191	208,567	83.1	16.9	518	23.1	445	70
Sonoma	144,581	1.2	3,447	70.7	5.9	627	182	572	165,857	75.6	24.4	159	55.3	74	56
Stanislaus	488,025	5.2	4,267	66.4	6.1	790	185	1,229	287,932	46.2	53.8	1,615	39.3	1,401	116
Sutter	57,739	4.1	1,391	44.9	12.4	372	267	251	180,173	97.7	2.3	922	28.0	905	16
Tehama	42,950	5.2	1,573	57.0	11.0	862	548	110	70,018	66.5	33.5	412	48.8	347	7
Trinity	136	0.1	135	37.0	11.9	105	781	2	13,104	37.2	62.8	45	28.4	22	1
Tulare	879,873	12.9	5,738	61.2	8.4	1,393	243	2,339	407,560	51.1	48.9	2,409	54.1	2,248	82
Tuolumne	425	(Z)	358	57.5	15.1	150	418	24	65,835	4.8	95.2	33	13.9	5	7
Ventura	578,799	2.7	2,318	73.6	4.4	332	143	1,019	439,544	98.7	1.3	1,111	17.3	230	157
Yolo	70,972	1.3	1,060	47.1	18.9	550	519	315	297,606	96.0	4.0	1,028	31.8	982	40
Yuba	15,176	1.3	863	50.5	10.3	234	271	115	133,422	78.1	21.9	372	26.6	358	11
COLORADO	721,421	0.5	31,369	32.8	29.0	31,093	991	4,525	144,257	26.9	73.1	12,600	18.4	11,400	899
Adams	13,912	0.2	728	40.2	28.2	701	964	99	135,536	87.7	12.3	134	20.2	45	75
Alamosa	19,676	6.2	318	14.2	34.0	205	644	94	297,016	93.7	6.3	225	55.7	223	2
Arapahoe	300	(Z)	448	46.9	20.3	333	742	20	44,587	76.2	23.8	112	14.1	3	95
Archuleta	−6,031	(X)	258	28.3	18.2	103	400	5	17,977	7.1	92.9	67	1.2	64	2
Baca	32,033	42.9	608	5.3	65.5	1,080	1,777	61	100,495	28.5	71.5	112	100.0	111	(Z)
Bent	8,464	14.4	265	14.7	48.3	736	2,777	82	310,008	5.8	94.2	325	2.3	324	1
Boulder	9,943	0.1	736	63.6	6.8	108	146	33	44,617	66.4	33.6	182	3.2	105	71
Broomfield	927	(Z)	(NA)	(NA)	(NA)	(NA)	(NA)	(NA)	(NA)	(NA)	(NA)	(X)	(NA)	(X)	(X)
Chaffee	−3,814	(X)	212	35.8	13.7	71	336	9	40,264	25.7	74.3	72	1.3	69	3
Cheyenne	7,662	15.3	283	2.5	71.0	740	2,617	23	81,929	50.5	49.5	33	90.2	32	(Z)
Clear Creek	–	–	9	–	55.6	(D)	(D)	(Z)	889	(NA)	(NA)	2	32.6	–	2
Conejos	6,002	9.2	494	18.4	29.4	268	542	23	46,259	52.5	47.5	254	13.7	253	1
Costilla	5,175	18.0	205	26.3	24.4	354	1,727	26	128,024	86.1	13.9	100	50.5	100	(Z)
Crowley	26,194	36.9	217	12.0	44.7	375	1,730	53	246,009	3.0	97.0	98	1.0	97	1
Custer	−3,107	(X)	158	18.4	26.6	122	771	3	17,348	10.0	90.0	49	0.9	49	(Z)
Delta	2,455	0.7	1,063	54.1	7.8	262	247	39	36,761	36.9	63.1	679	0.7	672	5
Denver	850	(Z)	10	100.0	–	(Z)	4	1	128,900	(NA)	(NA)	159	4.3	–	141
Dolores	2,188	9.4	216	17.6	37.5	159	734	4	17,468	47.8	52.2	55	3.3	54	(Z)
Douglas	−7,538	(X)	903	50.8	9.5	199	221	12	12,829	56.7	43.3	43	36.3	11	27
Eagle	−5,546	(X)	114	30.7	23.7	116	1,018	4	32,886	8.1	91.9	141	1.7	129	10
Elbert	−7,952	(X)	1,153	30.1	24.0	1,068	927	28	24,174	18.3	81.7	18	61.2	16	1
El Paso	−7,342	(X)	1,175	35.7	23.1	812	691	32	27,203	43.7	56.3	138	12.2	15	114
Fremont	1,735	0.3	700	61.9	14.7	265	378	15	20,911	31.8	68.2	160	0.5	107	11
Garfield	−514	(X)	499	46.9	19.6	404	810	23	45,633	31.1	68.9	421	1.1	410	9
Gilpin	–	–	26	23.1	3.8	6	233	(Z)	8,192	(NA)	(NA)	1	82.5	–	(Z)
Grand	−2,549	(X)	173	27.7	35.8	220	1,269	7	42,156	14.7	85.3	110	1.0	108	2
Gunnison	−3,963	(X)	186	24.2	31.7	165	890	9	49,134	10.7	89.3	242	1.4	239	2
Hinsdale	−334	(X)	19	–	21.1	9	457	(Z)	16,579	(NA)	(NA)	10	1.2	10	(Z)
Huerfano	−6,517	(X)	292	13.4	45.5	608	2,082	8	26,068	3.7	96.3	68	2.8	67	1
Jackson	−1,494	(X)	89	10.1	74.2	438	4,917	16	178,461	5.5	94.5	323	(Z)	323	(Z)

See footnotes at end of table.

[Includes United States, states, and 3,141 counties/county equivalents defined as of February 22, 2005. For more information on these areas, see Appendix C, Geographic Information]

County	Farm earnings, 2005 Total ($1,000)	Per-cent of total[1]	Agriculture (NAICS 111–112), 2002 Farms Number	Percent Less than 50 acres	500 acres or more	Land in farms Total acres (1,000)	Aver-age size of farm (acres)	Value of farm products sold Total (mil. dol.)	Average per farm (dol.)	Percent from Crops[2]	Live-stock and poultry[3]	Water use, 2000[4] Total (mil. gal. per day)	Ground water, percent of total	By selected major use (mil. gal. per day) Irri-gation	Public supply
COLORADO—Con.															
Jefferson	7,649	0.1	457	65.9	8.3	90	198	20	44,853	90.3	9.7	144	11.6	22	99
Kiowa	20,075	57.9	357	1.1	67.8	897	2,512	19	53,176	(NA)	(NA)	29	92.6	29	(Z)
Kit Carson	55,672	34.4	678	8.0	61.5	1,247	1,840	206	303,177	19.6	80.4	186	100.0	185	1
Lake	–	–	34	17.6	44.1	17	507	(Z)	10,735	(NA)	(NA)	41	1.6	40	1
La Plata	–3,941	(X)	923	38.7	14.1	563	610	16	17,294	24.4	75.6	221	1.8	211	7
Larimer	23,447	0.3	1,564	61.5	9.8	522	334	101	64,639	32.6	67.4	272	9.9	212	57
Las Animas	–6,282	(X)	567	7.9	60.5	2,305	4,065	21	36,838	3.6	96.4	122	2.4	118	3
Lincoln	–5,391	(X)	455	7.0	69.9	1,428	3,139	36	78,262	33.7	66.3	20	99.1	19	1
Logan	50,638	12.0	930	13.1	47.8	1,111	1,195	350	376,401	10.8	89.2	309	18.1	306	2
Mesa	12,941	0.5	1,599	66.4	7.6	385	241	59	37,038	49.9	50.1	1,202	0.6	1,122	32
Mineral	–59	(X)	14	14.3	7.1	4	317	(Z)	11,857	(NA)	(NA)	(Z)	100.0	–	(Z)
Moffat	–831	(X)	443	20.5	37.0	1,018	2,297	20	45,551	5.5	94.5	209	0.6	193	4
Montezuma	3,601	1.0	829	39.2	14.7	819	988	15	17,516	44.5	55.5	429	0.3	421	7
Montrose	16,301	2.2	915	46.8	12.6	335	366	58	63,378	36.3	63.7	598	1.0	589	6
Morgan	56,999	10.9	761	15.2	37.8	758	996	448	588,650	14.0	86.0	288	38.8	278	5
Otero	18,360	6.8	488	31.8	24.8	546	1,120	106	217,195	11.0	89.0	282	3.6	278	3
Ouray	–3,249	(X)	96	39.6	30.2	108	1,126	3	33,688	12.2	87.8	82	0.4	81	1
Park	–1,841	(X)	217	20.7	28.1	298	1,375	4	19,346	5.5	94.5	28	6.1	26	(Z)
Phillips	19,484	25.8	334	9.6	60.2	471	1,410	89	267,311	48.4	51.6	130	98.7	129	1
Pitkin	–2,482	(X)	84	45.2	8.3	24	284	1	8,976	28.9	71.1	43	1.1	39	4
Prowers	40,873	17.3	531	13.4	50.8	862	1,623	183	343,832	15.1	84.9	429	22.5	420	2
Pueblo	–6,663	(X)	801	38.2	27.3	774	967	42	52,000	26.6	73.4	246	4.3	130	35
Rio Blanco	–1,045	(X)	245	27.3	33.9	377	1,537	13	52,739	8.6	91.4	217	0.8	215	1
Rio Grande	21,937	10.0	344	17.4	29.9	171	497	74	216,520	92.4	7.6	285	60.1	284	1
Routt	–14,893	(X)	593	31.5	25.3	450	759	25	42,430	8.5	91.5	271	1.1	264	4
Saguache	12,768	18.6	252	9.1	54.8	477	1,893	82	324,810	86.8	13.2	647	55.3	646	1
San Juan	–	–	1	–	100.0	(D)	(D)	–	–	–	–	(Z)	11.8	–	(Z)
San Miguel	–1,030	(X)	112	28.6	37.5	151	1,349	4	32,250	0.1	90.9	10	3.3	9	1
Sedgwick	10,827	28.6	188	5.9	60.6	274	1,459	58	306,920	30.6	69.4	112	55.7	112	(Z)
Summit	–1,284	(X)	36	22.2	25.0	28	773	(Z)	12,917	8.2	91.8	5	51.8	–	3
Teller	–1,163	(X)	118	44.1	17.8	74	624	2	13,195	26.1	73.9	7	20.5	3	3
Washington	16,200	24.3	861	5.9	58.0	1,409	1,636	72	83,870	46.4	53.6	64	91.2	64	(Z)
Weld	229,559	5.5	3,121	31.5	21.3	1,812	581	1,128	361,376	18.2	81.8	1,064	13.4	1,020	37
Yuma	73,429	36.2	864	9.4	59.7	1,354	1,567	543	628,108	19.9	80.1	321	98.1	320	1
CONNECTICUT	166,000	0.1	4,191	62.3	2.8	357	85	471	112,297	69.6	30.4	4,150	3.4	30	424
Fairfield	4,968	(Z)	287	76.0	0.3	13	45	30	105,477	72.1	27.9	(6)	(NA)	5	158
Hartford	43,406	0.1	724	68.5	1.9	50	69	127	175,119	78.7	21.3	(6)	(NA)	14	45
Litchfield	5,814	0.2	789	55.8	5.2	94	119	30	38,141	52.3	47.7	(6)	(NA)	2	80
Middlesex	15,393	0.3	326	71.8	0.9	18	55	44	135,589	95.9	4.1	(6)	(NA)	1	6
New Haven	25,550	0.1	486	71.4	1.2	26	53	57	117,650	91.9	8.1	(6)	(NA)	5	80
New London	53,280	0.6	677	56.0	2.4	59	87	123	181,516	58.9	41.1	(6)	(NA)	1	47
Tolland	11,259	0.5	398	59.0	3.3	37	92	28	70,746	53.2	46.8	(6)	(NA)	2	6
Windham	6,330	0.3	504	51.6	4.8	61	121	31	61,631	25.5	74.5	(6)	(NA)	1	3
DELAWARE	283,786	1.1	2,391	52.3	11.0	540	226	619	258,826	24.3	75.7	1,320	8.7	44	95
Kent	55,301	1.7	721	44.5	11.7	185	257	129	178,467	42.3	57.7	30	92.4	12	10
New Castle	15,646	0.1	358	59.5	10.6	71	199	27	76,385	84.5	15.5	820	4.1	3	72
Sussex	212,839	6.6	1,312	54.6	10.7	284	216	463	352,768	15.7	84.3	473	11.4	29	13
DISTRICT OF COLUMBIA	–	–	(X)	(NA)	(NA)	(X)	(X)	(X)	(NA)	(NA)	(NA)	10	–	(Z)	–
District of Columbia	–	–	(X)	(NA)	(NA)	(X)	(X)	(X)	(NA)	(NA)	(NA)	10	–	(Z)	–
FLORIDA	1,604,522	0.4	44,081	64.9	6.8	10,415	236	6,242	141,609	80.8	19.2	20,100	25.0	4,290	2,440
Alachua	18,668	0.3	1,493	64.8	4.9	223	149	59	39,293	64.1	35.9	58	99.0	22	28
Baker	3,980	1.4	204	62.3	3.9	18	89	25	124,632	37.4	62.6	8	76.9	5	1
Bay	2,376	0.1	116	73.3	2.6	11	94	2	18,595	87.2	12.8	323	3.8	4	51
Bradford	1,495	0.5	378	64.0	3.4	45	119	18	47,389	9.3	90.7	1	98.7	1	1
Brevard	6,270	0.1	555	73.5	7.6	188	338	42	75,962	83.7	16.3	1,261	11.3	152	28
Broward	16,924	(Z)	494	90.3	2.6	24	48	50	100,455	89.9	10.1	1,814	15.0	41	258
Calhoun	6,176	5.6	151	31.1	15.9	49	325	14	95,298	91.4	8.6	6	70.8	4	1
Charlotte	13,658	0.7	284	60.9	13.4	192	674	48	170,077	88.3	11.7	64	56.1	51	7
Citrus	2,303	0.2	432	70.6	3.0	47	109	7	15,292	71.2	28.8	425	7.1	7	14
Clay	2,816	0.2	340	73.8	3.8	79	231	37	108,976	10.2	89.8	34	98.5	8	15
Collier	97,089	1.3	273	56.8	21.6	181	662	268	980,352	98.6	1.4	230	88.0	169	52
Columbia	–2,352	(X)	688	56.4	4.8	90	131	47	67,975	17.0	83.0	14	98.5	6	4
DeSoto	23,292	6.2	1,153	65.9	9.5	388	337	180	156,198	83.5	16.5	133	92.9	118	11
Dixie	1,374	1.1	215	56.3	6.0	31	145	7	30,428	(NA)	(NA)	3	99.1	2	1
Duval	11,234	(Z)	382	69.9	2.9	31	82	22	58,775	31.2	68.8	814	18.6	12	119

See footnotes at end of table.

[Includes United States, states, and 3,141 counties/county equivalents defined as of February 22, 2005. For more information on these areas, see Appendix C, Geographic Information]

County	Farm earnings, 2005 Total ($1,000)	Per-cent of total[1]	Farms Number	Farms Percent Less than 50 acres	Farms Percent 500 acres or more	Land in farms Total acres (1,000)	Land in farms Average size of farm (acres)	Value of farm products sold Total (mil. dol.)	Value of farm products sold Average per farm (dol.)	Percent from Crops[2]	Percent from Live-stock and poultry[3]	Water use, 2000[4] Total (mil. gal. per day)	Ground water, percent of total	By selected major use (mil. gal. per day) Irri-gation	By selected major use (mil. gal. per day) Public supply
FLORIDA—Con.															
Escambia	4,007	0.1	674	63.4	4.0	65	96	16	23,258	66.2	33.8	314	28.2	8	45
Flagler	12,695	1.5	100	35.0	22.0	68	684	24	237,890	93.8	6.2	28	87.3	21	6
Franklin	–	–	20	85.0	5.0	(D)	(D)	(Z)	19,250	–	(NA)	2	100.0	(Z)	2
Gadsden	48,602	7.9	343	44.6	6.1	68	199	91	266,405	98.8	1.2	16	52.6	9	4
Gilchrist	5,163	4.0	408	48.8	9.3	81	200	45	109,211	13.9	86.1	16	98.0	12	(Z)
Glades	4,967	7.3	231	34.6	23.4	408	1,766	72	311,965	72.8	27.2	75	28.1	69	1
Gulf	–	–	30	46.7	3.3	5	151	(Z)	16,300	(NA)	(NA)	4	62.8	(Z)	1
Hamilton	-1,876	(X)	239	38.1	9.6	52	218	12	50,916	52.9	47.1	42	99.7	6	1
Hardee	27,551	8.4	1,142	50.6	11.6	346	303	166	145,537	78.0	22.0	91	99.3	80	2
Hendry	45,609	8.5	456	49.1	20.6	552	1,211	376	824,149	95.0	5.0	512	38.5	504	5
Hernando	6,978	0.4	617	70.5	4.5	65	106	22	35,183	37.7	62.3	50	98.0	8	20
Highlands	42,940	4.0	1,035	57.5	12.8	577	557	236	228,024	86.8	13.2	174	90.1	161	9
Hillsborough	196,884	0.5	2,969	79.3	3.2	285	96	392	132,176	85.0	15.0	3,479	5.7	95	166
Holmes	6,622	4.3	672	31.5	3.9	91	135	30	44,975	9.7	90.3	4	92.2	1	1
Indian River	19,336	0.8	480	64.4	12.3	191	399	117	243,569	94.3	5.7	287	30.4	233	14
Jackson	10,180	1.6	920	33.5	11.5	227	247	36	39,641	68.1	31.9	112	18.3	16	2
Jefferson	9,754	7.1	418	54.1	10.0	133	318	21	50,608	44.0	56.0	8	98.0	7	1
Lafayette	10,578	15.7	195	34.4	14.4	92	472	48	246,749	7.0	93.0	7	97.6	4	(Z)
Lake	51,209	1.4	1,798	75.0	3.6	180	100	178	99,041	93.4	6.6	100	90.2	45	40
Lee	36,449	0.3	643	75.3	7.5	126	197	113	176,370	96.2	3.8	652	18.4	83	52
Leon	2,359	(Z)	281	67.6	5.7	74	263	7	23,698	66.5	33.5	46	99.3	3	36
Levy	24,294	6.6	897	59.2	6.2	180	201	83	92,783	31.2	68.8	31	91.5	22	2
Liberty	[5]25	(NA)	67	52.2	4.5	10	148	1	22,343	(NA)	(NA)	2	100.0	(Z)	(Z)
Madison	4,344	2.3	529	29.7	12.1	157	297	25	46,588	40.9	59.1	9	98.1	6	2
Manatee	92,123	1.5	852	52.9	14.0	301	354	268	315,117	92.0	8.0	187	65.4	110	50
Marion	33,743	0.8	2,930	75.4	3.1	271	92	88	29,874	20.9	79.1	69	96.9	23	28
Martin	15,524	0.5	418	64.8	17.2	206	493	128	305,395	78.0	22.0	199	21.8	148	18
Miami-Dade	149,710	0.2	2,244	89.6	1.5	90	40	578	257,576	99.2	0.8	598	89.7	124	394
Monroe	–	–	18	100.0	–	(Z)	6	3	140,722	26.5	73.5	2	68.4	2	–
Nassau	1,465	0.2	315	61.9	4.4	(D)	(D)	27	87,292	7.8	92.2	48	96.6	4	7
Okaloosa	813	(Z)	465	49.7	3.4	55	119	7	14,065	54.7	45.3	28	98.4	4	23
Okeechobee	32,396	7.1	638	46.2	22.4	392	615	144	226,295	25.4	74.6	71	83.2	63	2
Orange	75,769	0.2	901	76.6	3.0	147	163	243	269,354	98.7	1.3	275	93.9	52	212
Osceola	12,210	0.4	519	63.0	14.6	653	1,258	65	125,127	67.7	32.3	143	81.8	108	30
Palm Beach	160,183	0.5	1,110	83.3	6.9	536	483	760	684,565	99.1	0.9	1,712	16.0	1,020	230
Pasco	19,740	0.5	1,222	75.1	4.3	169	138	84	68,903	41.1	58.9	2,098	6.6	28	103
Pinellas	4,949	(Z)	111	93.7	–	2	14	8	71,712	95.8	4.2	466	9.3	6	40
Polk	66,794	0.7	3,114	65.1	6.0	627	201	285	91,454	87.5	12.5	363	90.7	175	75
Putnam	13,062	1.6	466	66.5	7.9	93	199	47	100,150	87.8	12.2	89	45.1	16	3
St. Johns	13,715	0.6	204	62.3	14.2	38	185	60	292,554	95.4	4.6	56	94.3	37	16
St. Lucie	16,642	0.6	477	53.7	13.6	222	464	128	268,149	87.8	12.2	1,758	4.6	245	18
Santa Rosa	5,100	0.3	505	60.2	8.7	84	166	21	41,578	91.2	8.8	31	98.9	11	13
Sarasota	8,285	0.1	371	68.7	10.2	121	327	18	47,981	75.0	25.0	46	86.8	16	29
Seminole	10,649	0.1	376	85.4	1.1	28	74	19	51,093	93.4	6.6	90	98.0	21	67
Sumter	12,678	1.9	902	61.3	4.9	187	208	31	33,973	45.8	54.2	44	60.1	16	4
Suwannee	20,228	4.8	1,054	45.2	5.7	170	161	136	128,994	23.9	76.1	128	20.6	19	1
Taylor	472	0.2	101	37.6	16.8	54	532	13	132,218	5.4	94.6	50	93.9	2	2
Union	425	0.2	275	54.2	5.8	60	217	11	38,949	39.9	60.1	3	99.2	1	(Z)
Volusia	58,893	0.8	1,114	80.8	3.2	94	84	106	95,419	92.6	7.4	235	41.3	45	55
Wakulla	463	0.2	126	66.7	3.2	11	87	2	12,571	40.5	59.5	33	14.4	(Z)	2
Walton	3,051	0.4	540	41.3	5.2	80	148	20	37,139	22.6	77.4	12	85.2	4	7
Washington	1,475	0.6	391	37.9	4.9	53	136	6	14,082	41.6	58.4	4	100.0	1	1
GEORGIA	1,839,814	0.8	49,311	39.2	9.9	10,744	218	4,912	99,608	32.2	67.8	6,500	22.3	1,140	1,250
Appling	12,936	4.3	557	37.0	10.8	119	213	56	100,047	36.3	63.7	64	7.3	4	1
Atkinson	29,244	30.3	194	21.6	22.2	71	365	42	214,588	22.2	77.8	7	48.5	6	(Z)
Bacon	10,155	7.3	331	34.4	11.8	67	202	40	119,462	32.5	67.5	6	77.9	5	(Z)
Baker	6,901	24.6	147	27.9	33.3	126	860	28	189,762	61.4	38.6	42	92.7	41	(Z)
Baldwin	717	0.1	194	32.5	7.2	36	184	7	35,948	5.0	95.0	9	7.4	(Z)	7
Banks	43,672	24.9	614	47.2	2.3	58	94	103	168,526	0.8	99.2	2	41.4	(Z)	1
Barrow	19,523	3.0	452	56.9	1.3	36	80	52	114,091	1.2	98.8	8	26.7	1	5
Bartow	9,983	0.6	586	50.3	5.1	82	139	49	83,635	15.1	84.9	66	9.7	2	17
Ben Hill	14,756	4.2	174	30.5	14.4	57	330	14	77,810	65.4	34.6	11	75.1	6	4
Berrien	9,144	4.4	481	29.1	15.6	126	262	27	55,518	76.6	23.4	15	55.8	14	1
Bibb	1,427	(Z)	168	41.1	8.9	30	181	6	35,077	20.7	79.3	155	3.7	2	33
Bleckley	3,006	1.8	265	25.3	10.6	55	209	6	22,053	83.7	16.3	16	51.6	15	1
Brantley	5,912	6.3	270	43.0	5.2	32	120	12	46,096	21.1	78.9	2	86.9	(Z)	(Z)
Brooks	24,468	18.9	446	24.9	20.0	203	455	55	124,011	73.3	26.7	6	78.2	4	2
Bryan	-887	(X)	65	58.5	10.8	17	264	1	18,985	80.3	19.7	3	99.6	1	2
Bulloch	24,029	2.8	641	33.4	17.6	206	322	43	66,629	77.9	22.1	15	81.3	10	3
Burke	12,405	3.9	494	24.5	23.9	219	443	26	53,130	59.1	40.9	98	27.8	29	4
Butts	1,582	0.6	173	36.4	9.2	37	212	2	14,312	32.4	67.6	4	12.6	(Z)	3
Calhoun	9,388	15.1	119	20.2	44.5	118	992	26	217,193	75.7	24.3	35	66.0	33	1
Camden	747	0.1	47	36.2	17.0	12	264	1	21,170	83.2	16.8	49	84.8	1	4

See footnotes at end of table.

[Includes United States, states, and 3,141 counties/county equivalents defined as of February 22, 2005. For more information on these areas, see Appendix C, Geographic Information]

County	Farm earnings, 2005 Total ($1,000)	Percent of total[1]	Farms Number	Farms Percent Less than 50 acres	Farms Percent 500 acres or more	Land in farms Total acres (1,000)	Land in farms Average size of farm (acres)	Value of farm products sold Total (mil. dol.)	Value of farm products sold Average per farm (dol.)	Percent from Crops[2]	Percent from Livestock and poultry[3]	Water use, 2000[4] Total (mil. gal. per day)	Ground water, percent of total	By selected major use (mil. gal. per day) Irrigation	By selected major use (mil. gal. per day) Public supply
GEORGIA—Con.															
Candler	6,452	5.1	272	26.1	12.9	63	231	12	43,423	65.4	34.6	6	54.0	5	1
Carroll	35,700	2.1	975	45.4	1.9	94	97	106	109,085	4.6	95.4	12	26.4	(Z)	9
Catoosa	11,240	1.6	296	50.3	2.4	27	92	24	81,807	3.0	97.0	11	84.6	1	8
Charlton	816	0.9	101	41.6	6.9	15	147	4	41,238	14.5	85.5	1	93.2	(Z)	1
Chatham	2,170	(Z)	58	46.6	10.3	9	157	2	36,138	90.5	9.5	214	33.2	9	33
Chattahoochee	[5]25	(NA)	16	37.5	12.5	4	272	(D)	(NA)	(NA)	(NA)	10	5.2	(Z)	10
Chattooga	1,365	0.5	329	28.9	5.8	55	167	6	17,073	13.7	86.3	12	55.6	(Z)	4
Cherokee	20,321	0.9	606	71.1	1.8	36	60	51	84,134	10.7	89.3	20	12.0	1	15
Clarke	3,949	0.1	104	42.3	5.8	14	136	35	338,106	13.9	86.1	19	2.1	1	19
Clay	3,709	12.6	49	10.2	36.7	42	866	7	135,102	91.5	8.5	6	25.5	5	(Z)
Clayton	[5]25	(NA)	62	71.0	–	3	52	(Z)	7,726	68.1	31.9	27	0.1	1	26
Clinch	2,883	3.1	118	46.6	19.5	31	260	6	49,508	61.8	38.2	2	80.6	1	1
Cobb	2,036	(Z)	191	74.9	2.1	11	57	5	28,152	94.4	5.6	467	0.3	2	97
Coffee	33,271	4.7	692	28.8	13.2	189	273	124	179,171	31.5	68.5	21	60.0	14	5
Colquitt	53,995	9.5	588	31.3	20.4	228	388	129	220,179	80.5	19.5	46	39.5	39	4
Columbia	3,683	0.3	196	54.6	4.1	23	119	5	24,806	27.5	72.5	17	14.4	4	13
Cook	16,273	9.6	254	37.0	13.4	68	266	39	152,969	96.6	3.4	12	66.4	9	2
Coweta	2,984	0.2	480	51.0	5.2	61	127	7	14,790	57.5	42.5	560	1.0	2	10
Crawford	8,236	11.1	179	31.8	6.7	38	213	19	107,866	63.4	36.6	6	75.1	3	(Z)
Crisp	18,698	5.6	223	32.3	25.1	104	466	28	127,112	89.7	10.3	17	87.0	16	1
Dade	2,902	2.0	253	49.0	3.2	28	110	11	42,874	3.1	96.9	3	18.2	1	2
Dawson	11,500	4.4	222	56.8	6.3	20	91	40	177,968	2.5	97.5	2	27.0	(Z)	1
Decatur	37,988	8.9	396	25.0	18.4	160	405	101	253,811	86.3	13.7	63	88.0	58	3
DeKalb	827	(Z)	37	81.1	–	1	29	1	23,162	99.4	0.6	92	3.4	2	87
Dodge	4,905	2.2	491	24.6	12.8	139	282	13	25,998	83.1	16.9	16	25.9	14	1
Dooly	25,323	16.3	326	22.4	25.8	171	524	55	167,457	62.5	37.5	26	94.1	24	2
Dougherty	8,443	0.3	162	46.3	20.4	98	603	22	138,778	94.2	5.8	222	24.9	23	19
Douglas	−753	(X)	153	64.1	0.7	8	52	2	12,908	41.6	58.4	12	6.6	2	10
Early	20,713	8.0	347	25.6	23.3	160	462	26	75,648	90.8	9.2	157	24.7	47	(Z)
Echols	4,675	18.2	78	23.1	17.9	29	376	24	305,397	98.2	1.8	7	92.0	6	(Z)
Effingham	1,509	0.4	206	35.0	13.1	53	258	4	18,131	72.1	27.9	149	3.5	1	33
Elbert	4,186	1.4	438	29.9	4.6	63	145	23	52,822	12.9	87.1	3	27.1	1	2
Emanuel	6,578	2.3	554	20.6	14.6	160	288	12	21,439	67.5	32.5	6	83.1	3	2
Evans	5,049	2.8	242	30.2	11.6	48	199	23	92,983	40.0	60.0	4	73.9	2	1
Fannin	4,772	2.1	208	54.8	1.0	15	74	11	51,115	9.1	90.9	2	34.9	(Z)	1
Fayette	3,193	0.2	235	55.3	0.9	18	77	4	17,855	78.5	21.5	17	16.4	2	14
Floyd	8,416	0.4	663	41.2	4.7	91	138	29	43,163	7.9	92.1	586	0.6	7	14
Forsyth	30,261	1.2	528	65.5	1.5	34	64	56	105,773	10.2	89.8	19	12.7	(Z)	16
Franklin	55,197	14.9	825	41.1	2.1	86	104	181	219,072	0.8	99.2	4	34.2	(Z)	2
Fulton	1,890	(Z)	328	69.5	4.9	28	85	6	18,220	61.7	38.3	171	0.7	4	165
Gilmer	29,436	7.8	303	50.5	1.3	25	82	99	326,264	1.4	98.6	7	27.1	(Z)	5
Glascock	−902	(X)	100	13.0	11.0	21	210	2	18,710	16.4	83.6	(Z)	75.0	(Z)	(Z)
Glynn	155	(Z)	59	45.8	5.1	8	129	(Z)	3,068	43.1	56.9	146	42.3	2	12
Gordon	25,400	2.5	804	51.6	2.2	76	95	100	124,724	3.5	96.5	16	14.6	1	13
Grady	28,699	11.0	501	35.9	11.2	127	254	74	146,794	78.3	21.7	20	46.9	17	2
Greene	10,976	5.1	255	29.0	11.8	52	205	25	97,882	(NA)	(NA)	13	5.2	10	2
Gwinnett	3,527	(Z)	312	75.0	1.3	18	56	21	68,907	87.4	12.6	94	0.4	3	90
Habersham	43,489	6.9	517	60.3	1.2	39	75	120	231,333	0.8	99.2	8	23.5	(Z)	6
Hall	43,326	1.3	834	61.0	1.4	62	74	170	204,137	0.8	99.2	25	22.7	1	19
Hancock	2,961	5.1	144	12.5	16.0	42	293	2	10,764	16.6	83.4	1	33.0	(Z)	1
Haralson	5,391	1.7	332	36.7	3.0	40	120	19	57,108	3.4	96.6	4	12.3	1	2
Harris	1,854	0.9	298	33.6	10.4	67	225	3	8,993	53.5	46.5	7	16.9	1	2
Hart	17,482	5.6	567	40.7	3.4	65	115	82	145,451	2.4	97.6	4	29.7	1	2
Heard	7,980	6.9	209	34.9	8.1	42	201	22	105,344	1.3	98.7	74	0.9	(Z)	2
Henry	2,215	0.1	439	63.8	4.1	58	132	6	13,431	58.2	41.8	14	5.4	(Z)	13
Houston	5,129	0.2	360	48.6	10.3	75	210	24	65,567	34.0	66.0	28	96.1	6	21
Irwin	12,943	12.6	349	21.5	20.9	138	396	29	84,158	80.8	19.2	13	59.8	11	1
Jackson	103,358	12.0	915	50.8	3.8	100	109	154	168,691	1.7	98.3	7	36.2	1	3
Jasper	5,441	4.6	210	27.1	9.0	51	243	26	122,543	8.4	91.6	3	46.6	1	1
Jeff Davis	3,198	1.7	254	34.3	11.4	56	221	11	41,563	61.6	38.4	7	68.7	5	1
Jefferson	5,293	2.4	388	15.5	18.3	137	354	38	98,778	76.4	23.6	27	49.0	18	2
Jenkins	5,649	5.5	240	20.4	24.6	95	394	14	58,567	52.5	47.5	7	70.7	6	1
Johnson	5,417	6.3	286	21.7	12.2	76	266	4	15,524	57.7	42.3	3	76.4	2	(Z)
Jones	2,258	1.6	194	31.4	8.8	35	181	8	41,392	6.5	93.5	3	88.4	(Z)	1
Lamar	5,660	3.9	243	37.0	7.0	42	172	23	94,728	17.4	82.6	7	22.5	1	4
Lanier	900	2.1	134	35.1	14.9	52	386	10	75,022	94.8	5.2	3	83.9	2	1
Laurens	8,385	1.0	709	30.3	9.7	194	273	13	18,216	71.0	29.0	32	33.3	10	4
Lee	11,621	5.9	171	30.4	35.7	147	858	24	137,550	68.3	31.7	35	95.3	33	1
Liberty	−238	(X)	68	33.8	13.2	16	234	(Z)	4,603	63.6	36.4	15	99.3	(Z)	6
Lincoln	1,697	2.7	207	36.2	5.3	31	149	3	12,135	8.6	91.4	1	52.1	(Z)	1

See footnotes at end of table.

Table B-14. Counties — **Farm Earnings, Agriculture, and Water Use**—Con.

[Includes United States, states, and 3,141 counties/county equivalents defined as of February 22, 2005. For more information on these areas, see Appendix C, Geographic Information]

County	Farm earnings, 2005 Total ($1,000)	Percent of total[1]	Farms Number	Farms Percent Less than 50 acres	Farms Percent 500 acres or more	Land in farms Total acres (1,000)	Land in farms Average size of farm (acres)	Value of farm products sold Total (mil. dol.)	Value of farm products sold Average per farm (dol.)	Percent from Crops[2]	Percent from Livestock and poultry[3]	Water use Total (mil. gal. per day)	Ground water, percent of total	By selected major use Irrigation	By selected major use Public supply
GEORGIA—Con.															
Long	2,328	6.7	76	21.1	21.1	24	311	8	104,605	19.2	80.8	1	86.6	(Z)	(Z)
Lowndes	8,406	0.4	462	48.1	7.1	74	160	24	51,794	93.5	6.5	33	90.7	11	9
Lumpkin	16,696	5.3	250	59.2	1.6	21	85	44	176,496	7.6	92.4	4	37.7	(Z)	1
McDuffie	11,383	3.6	296	48.3	9.5	47	158	30	102,963	(NA)	(NA)	5	22.5	2	3
McIntosh	157	0.2	39	25.6	12.8	11	290	(D)	(NA)	(NA)	(NA)	1	87.3	(Z)	1
Macon	33,416	17.2	360	28.6	15.3	114	318	123	342,700	15.5	84.5	32	51.5	19	1
Madison	39,832	18.9	763	48.6	1.4	76	100	123	161,275	1.2	98.8	3	68.2	1	(Z)
Marion	7,200	9.6	181	24.3	14.4	52	286	13	71,122	20.8	79.2	4	70.5	1	2
Meriwether	3,666	1.5	339	27.4	10.0	84	248	7	20,646	46.0	54.0	6	44.2	1	2
Miller	10,591	15.2	207	16.9	29.0	95	460	29	138,425	81.1	18.9	34	91.1	33	(Z)
Mitchell	20,274	6.9	496	31.5	21.0	185	373	128	257,486	37.9	62.1	78	79.2	74	3
Monroe	6,520	2.7	236	31.4	14.0	62	261	45	190,695	3.3	96.7	126	2.7	(Z)	2
Montgomery	2,791	3.9	252	23.4	15.1	74	294	9	35,587	61.5	38.5	3	68.3	2	(Z)
Morgan	13,955	5.0	525	36.8	7.2	89	170	48	91,179	7.2	92.8	3	33.2	(Z)	2
Murray	9,922	1.9	306	44.8	4.6	42	137	27	88,516	5.8	94.2	5	43.6	1	2
Muscogee	−651	(X)	96	47.9	9.4	15	161	1	11,823	83.9	16.1	46	0.2	3	41
Newton	405	(Z)	355	54.4	5.4	45	126	8	22,110	6.9	93.1	13	11.2	(Z)	12
Oconee	15,864	4.4	411	45.3	5.6	54	132	51	123,611	15.7	84.3	3	83.1	(Z)	2
Oglethorpe	24,683	29.4	362	36.2	5.0	56	155	80	219,713	2.1	97.9	2	50.8	(Z)	(Z)
Paulding	[5]25	(NA)	265	58.1	–	17	63	14	53,664	20.5	79.5	4	34.0	(Z)	3
Peach	13,209	3.8	217	41.9	6.9	39	179	20	90,286	81.9	18.1	13	93.1	10	2
Pickens	19,971	5.9	243	57.6	0.8	17	71	48	196,687	1.2	98.8	3	39.1	(Z)	2
Pierce	7,617	4.5	434	40.6	11.8	99	227	29	67,166	65.1	34.9	8	90.9	7	1
Pike	7,794	6.6	327	38.8	4.6	44	134	10	30,618	28.8	71.2	2	57.9	(Z)	1
Polk	6,296	1.3	428	48.6	3.5	52	122	19	45,145	5.6	94.4	9	47.9	1	6
Pulaski	7,360	5.8	187	33.7	19.8	67	360	13	70,128	75.9	24.1	17	82.0	15	1
Putnam	3,513	1.2	225	35.1	9.8	41	181	27	118,218	2.7	97.3	988	0.1	2	1
Quitman	−95	(X)	23	13.0	34.8	14	623	(D)	(NA)	(NA)	(NA)	(Z)	62.9	(Z)	(Z)
Rabun	3,412	1.4	146	63.7	2.1	10	68	11	72,164	22.2	77.8	4	16.5	1	1
Randolph	6,290	6.8	136	12.5	30.9	79	583	13	98,257	86.7	13.3	9	55.2	8	1
Richmond	1,219	(Z)	140	58.6	1.4	12	89	3	22,314	54.0	46.0	126	19.3	8	44
Rockdale	−626	(X)	140	70.7	1.4	9	63	1	6,086	45.2	54.8	2	16.4	(Z)	2
Schley	4,047	6.8	115	13.0	20.9	35	308	10	83,983	15.3	84.7	1	60.5	(Z)	(Z)
Screven	9,667	6.4	347	15.6	23.9	184	531	19	54,161	85.7	14.3	25	76.3	22	1
Seminole	10,578	11.0	206	22.8	21.8	93	451	24	116,684	82.0	18.0	71	90.4	69	1
Spalding	−857	(X)	249	47.0	3.2	26	103	4	17,779	15.0	85.0	11	8.2	1	9
Stephens	15,265	3.7	238	52.1	1.3	20	82	44	186,647	0.5	99.5	4	10.6	(Z)	3
Stewart	1,477	4.2	85	12.9	31.8	34	398	4	47,294	51.5	48.5	3	27.8	2	1
Sumter	48,318	8.8	381	27.0	21.3	167	437	49	128,331	64.8	35.2	42	57.6	38	4
Talbot	292	0.7	160	23.1	16.9	45	283	2	10,150	20.0	80.0	3	55.3	–	(Z)
Taliaferro	542	6.2	73	11.0	19.2	19	254	3	42,014	2.7	97.3	(Z)	78.3	–	(Z)
Tattnall	81,378	28.9	644	35.2	7.5	143	223	139	216,203	29.9	70.1	8	66.5	6	1
Taylor	14,702	16.0	227	13.2	18.1	75	328	24	107,683	42.2	57.8	9	62.8	8	1
Telfair	4,446	3.4	304	18.1	12.5	73	240	8	24,888	83.9	16.1	6	79.3	4	2
Terrell	10,329	10.1	239	18.4	29.7	123	516	19	81,008	97.0	3.0	22	50.6	20	1
Thomas	12,327	1.2	510	33.7	16.7	198	389	26	51,733	71.4	28.6	21	84.4	12	7
Tift	32,667	3.8	398	41.7	11.3	98	246	45	113,405	94.4	5.6	28	62.1	20	7
Toombs	18,797	4.7	382	20.4	12.3	93	243	33	86,751	82.3	17.7	14	50.6	11	3
Towns	−149	(X)	148	56.1	0.7	11	74	2	13,527	33.3	66.7	1	16.0	(Z)	1
Treutlen	2,377	5.6	182	31.9	12.6	35	191	4	19,802	84.8	15.2	2	78.1	1	(Z)
Troup	−914	(X)	294	29.9	10.5	61	208	3	10,381	22.8	77.2	13	5.1	2	11
Turner	12,692	12.5	282	22.3	18.1	98	348	35	124,830	68.5	31.5	17	42.1	16	1
Twiggs	5,637	7.9	119	40.3	16.8	40	338	2	19,319	76.9	23.1	20	98.4	1	(Z)
Union	10,376	4.2	330	57.3	1.5	25	75	16	48,194	26.4	73.6	2	56.0	(Z)	1
Upson	2,583	0.8	291	40.2	7.2	47	160	14	46,447	10.3	89.7	10	25.3	1	3
Walker	8,021	1.3	642	38.6	4.2	82	127	34	53,653	3.4	96.6	15	62.0	1	11
Walton	14,006	1.7	679	51.3	2.2	66	97	32	47,330	24.5	75.5	9	31.6	2	5
Ware	5,150	0.8	323	42.4	10.8	65	202	23	69,820	41.2	58.8	10	83.4	5	4
Warren	2,179	3.8	165	26.1	16.4	48	291	4	27,261	8.3	91.7	3	39.2	(Z)	1
Washington	−501	(X)	411	29.4	16.5	124	302	16	37,871	76.7	23.3	26	94.2	7	4
Wayne	4,075	1.0	341	39.3	7.0	64	189	16	47,974	55.2	44.8	65	99.3	2	2
Webster	5,424	21.4	98	4.1	30.6	66	676	9	89,276	79.8	20.2	4	13.1	4	(Z)
Wheeler	6,273	12.6	156	12.8	26.9	60	383	10	63,827	95.2	4.8	5	25.5	4	(Z)
White	26,124	9.4	376	58.0	2.1	30	81	73	195,319	1.6	98.4	4	37.6	(Z)	2
Whitfield	15,001	0.5	418	45.2	2.4	43	104	74	177,383	1.3	98.7	66	0.3	1	64
Wilcox	23,090	32.5	311	28.9	16.1	102	329	48	154,309	41.9	58.1	23	79.3	22	1
Wilkes	8,019	5.9	349	22.1	12.9	99	284	21	60,716	8.2	91.8	3	13.3	(Z)	2
Wilkinson	208	0.1	127	32.3	10.2	31	241	1	9,118	68.1	31.9	28	96.9	(Z)	1
Worth	19,704	13.0	487	35.1	20.5	179	368	38	79,035	80.8	19.2	42	65.6	38	1

See footnotes at end of table.

Table B-14. Counties — **Farm Earnings, Agriculture, and Water Use**—Con.

[Includes United States, states, and 3,141 counties/county equivalents defined as of February 22, 2005. For more information on these areas, see Appendix C, Geographic Information]

County	Farm earnings, 2005 Total ($1,000)	Farm earnings, 2005 Percent of total[1]	Agriculture (NAICS 111–112), 2002 Farms Number	Farms Percent Less than 50 acres	Farms Percent 500 acres or more	Land in farms Total acres (1,000)	Land in farms Average size of farm (acres)	Value of farm products sold Total (mil. dol.)	Value of farm products sold Average per farm (dol.)	Percent from Crops[2]	Percent from Live-stock and poultry[3]	Water use, 2000[4] Total (mil. gal. per day)	Ground water, percent of total	By selected major use (mil. gal. per day) Irrigation	By selected major use (mil. gal. per day) Public supply
HAWAII	217,252	0.6	5,398	88.0	3.1	1,300	241	533	98,819	83.5	16.5	641	67.7	364	250
Hawaii	70,702	2.2	3,216	87.9	2.9	821	255	188	58,376	76.7	23.3	(6)	(NA)	20	34
Honolulu	63,802	0.2	794	91.4	2.4	71	89	179	225,845	83.1	16.9	(6)	(NA)	39	165
Kalawao	–	–	–	–	–	–	–	–	–	–	–	(6)	(NA)	–	(Z)
Kauai	12,519	0.9	565	84.8	4.8	152	269	42	74,080	85.4	14.6	(6)	(NA)	30	15
Maui	70,229	2.0	823	87.1	3.6	257	312	125	151,289	93.7	6.3	(6)	(NA)	275	37
IDAHO	969,612	3.2	25,017	49.2	18.0	11,767	470	3,908	156,224	45.7	54.3	19,500	21.2	17,100	244
Ada	37,373	0.3	1,420	76.4	4.9	223	157	127	89,246	33.9	66.1	1,193	10.2	1,116	58
Adams	-2,404	(X)	316	42.4	25.0	196	622	8	25,190	10.1	89.9	85	3.8	84	1
Bannock	3,775	0.3	1,030	58.9	15.3	357	347	32	31,259	74.5	25.5	403	12.8	353	21
Bear Lake	6,561	10.5	424	30.7	22.9	212	499	13	30,545	25.4	74.6	108	4.1	105	2
Benewah	2,454	1.5	241	32.4	24.5	138	572	14	59,805	95.6	4.4	3	51.7	1	1
Bingham	47,881	8.0	1,273	56.2	19.6	821	645	269	211,224	73.6	26.4	1,378	33.8	1,335	6
Blaine	3,371	0.5	224	48.2	24.6	226	1,009	19	85,817	43.6	56.4	304	22.9	288	3
Boise	-238	(X)	89	47.2	15.7	50	563	3	28,708	72.7	27.3	10	14.3	8	(Z)
Bonner	1,328	0.2	743	59.6	3.6	91	122	7	9,623	61.7	38.3	22	47.6	8	4
Bonneville	17,199	0.8	963	55.9	17.7	478	496	119	123,717	75.1	24.9	836	16.3	808	22
Boundary	7,051	5.3	432	54.9	9.0	77	177	23	52,829	87.5	12.5	4	40.5	2	1
Butte	1,963	0.6	197	28.4	29.4	121	616	49	246,584	21.7	78.3	213	49.3	194	4
Camas	1,449	10.0	106	17.0	41.5	134	1,266	6	60,038	84.8	15.2	28	60.4	28	(Z)
Canyon	79,493	3.7	2,233	70.1	6.2	272	122	269	120,443	49.7	50.3	710	40.6	648	25
Caribou	10,588	6.1	490	23.9	36.7	427	871	42	85,192	(NA)	(NA)	282	16.6	249	2
Cassia	95,008	24.0	692	37.6	34.2	744	1,076	383	552,789	37.5	62.5	792	63.2	779	4
Clark	756	4.0	85	21.2	54.1	178	2,092	28	330,129	88.2	11.8	161	36.2	160	(Z)
Clearwater	-156	(X)	193	32.6	21.2	71	366	6	29,249	67.5	32.5	2	42.2	1	1
Custer	-1,586	(X)	285	38.6	20.4	132	462	13	44,667	23.6	76.4	232	9.0	205	(Z)
Elmore	33,593	5.8	364	49.7	23.6	346	951	293	804,544	(NA)	(NA)	299	26.8	291	4
Franklin	32,731	23.7	792	43.2	17.6	244	308	49	62,385	15.5	84.5	225	9.8	220	3
Fremont	11,118	9.1	518	36.3	24.1	287	555	72	139,054	88.8	11.2	391	13.1	382	2
Gem	1,959	1.7	802	66.1	8.5	221	276	27	34,248	32.2	67.8	727	1.8	723	1
Gooding	150,688	46.4	663	50.8	12.8	195	294	353	531,928	9.9	90.1	1,414	8.1	417	2
Idaho	-4,582	(X)	663	19.6	35.7	639	963	35	53,163	66.6	33.4	19	15.6	8	1
Jefferson	20,782	9.4	784	51.0	16.7	305	389	159	202,423	62.7	37.3	1,959	22.8	1,953	2
Jerome	141,392	34.4	635	52.1	15.4	186	293	289	454,753	26.1	73.9	1,681	4.8	1,530	2
Kootenai	-964	(X)	828	58.0	7.7	154	186	14	17,077	85.2	14.8	57	68.5	27	24
Latah	3,642	0.6	890	32.2	19.7	340	382	40	44,789	93.2	6.8	8	94.4	1	5
Lemhi	-3,769	(X)	303	45.9	28.1	174	573	17	55,914	7.6	92.4	285	2.6	273	1
Lewis	3,834	7.4	177	12.4	50.3	217	1,224	28	156,791	94.1	5.9	2	44.4	1	1
Lincoln	13,806	21.0	280	28.6	24.6	128	457	54	192,514	28.4	71.6	389	27.9	385	1
Madison	11,393	2.6	479	48.4	19.4	190	397	93	193,470	93.6	6.4	802	13.2	792	5
Minidoka	31,184	12.1	694	51.2	14.1	228	329	191	274,994	76.1	23.9	752	49.5	744	3
Nez Perce	1,879	0.2	441	41.0	32.9	343	779	40	91,615	87.4	12.6	188	1.8	3	6
Oneida	1,425	4.3	428	23.1	34.6	363	848	16	38,164	56.3	43.7	141	44.4	140	(Z)
Owyhee	42,311	35.6	571	34.9	23.6	571	1,000	127	222,019	29.3	70.7	425	22.3	414	1
Payette	28,796	10.8	639	61.2	5.8	155	242	107	167,003	23.7	76.3	246	11.9	241	2
Power	20,805	15.2	334	18.6	49.4	425	1,273	112	333,967	71.3	28.7	341	62.4	326	2
Shoshone	-262	(X)	46	58.7	–	4	94	(Z)	1,935	14.6	85.4	5	34.3	(Z)	2
Teton	2,509	2.8	302	36.4	22.5	125	413	24	79,887	82.9	17.1	168	24.9	166	1
Twin Falls	106,327	8.0	1,297	47.3	14.7	441	340	292	225,022	36.8	63.2	1,877	15.7	1,380	17
Valley	-2,043	(X)	156	56.4	19.2	66	420	3	22,397	27.6	72.4	127	2.1	115	1
Washington	9,192	8.0	495	36.4	26.5	472	954	45	91,000	44.1	55.9	165	20.9	163	1
ILLINOIS	826,217	0.2	73,027	26.9	24.0	27,311	374	7,676	105,115	76.5	23.5	13,700	5.9	154	1,760
Adams	25,344	1.7	1,347	23.8	21.8	444	330	124	92,258	60.8	39.2	22	66.8	1	9
Alexander	1,382	1.7	149	14.1	24.2	78	526	10	68,678	96.3	3.7	3	67.3	2	1
Bond	15,480	7.1	668	33.8	19.8	193	288	41	61,847	71.2	28.8	1	93.1	–	(Z)
Boone	9,475	1.2	476	40.8	17.0	147	309	48	100,504	78.5	21.5	6	100.0	(Z)	4
Brown	11,730	8.4	417	23.3	19.4	144	346	24	57,357	74.5	25.5	(Z)	100.0	(Z)	(Z)
Bureau	19,331	3.4	1,091	18.2	31.8	491	450	204	186,914	84.9	15.1	8	99.1	3	3
Calhoun	3,045	8.5	480	24.2	7.3	90	188	13	26,398	78.8	21.2	1	100.0	–	(Z)
Carroll	13,003	6.6	656	25.3	22.1	248	377	111	169,162	56.2	43.8	7	100.0	2	1
Cass	16,391	6.6	427	24.4	28.6	199	465	64	149,717	66.8	33.2	9	96.5	5	2
Champaign	-1,476	(X)	1,285	21.4	32.1	577	449	168	130,928	95.0	5.0	29	100.0	5	23
Christian	5,918	1.3	796	25.8	34.4	411	516	111	138,961	93.3	6.7	754	0.4	(Z)	3
Clark	10,630	4.8	581	28.6	28.1	275	474	60	102,620	84.8	15.2	3	100.0	1	1
Clay	10,789	4.1	703	31.3	23.5	243	346	37	53,060	74.8	25.2	2	57.0	(Z)	1
Clinton	39,381	7.8	915	29.2	16.4	255	278	141	153,809	29.8	70.2	5	62.1	–	2
Coles	525	(NA)	684	29.5	26.6	261	382	61	89,165	92.4	7.6	5	23.3	(Z)	2
Cook	6,062	(Z)	211	60.7	4.7	24	113	21	100,867	98.6	1.4	1,738	1.0	2	1,043
Crawford	5,515	1.5	567	33.9	23.3	214	377	46	80,489	82.3	17.7	86	7.0	1	2
Cumberland	16,132	15.7	583	30.4	18.5	173	297	51	87,098	61.8	38.2	1	88.5	(Z)	(Z)
DeKalb	10,767	0.6	816	23.8	32.6	359	440	175	213,897	53.3	46.7	11	97.6	(Z)	8
De Witt	-2,330	(X)	459	27.7	32.0	203	442	56	122,582	88.9	11.1	631	0.4	1	1

See footnotes at end of table.

Table B-14. Counties — **Farm Earnings, Agriculture, and Water Use**—Con.

[Includes United States, states, and 3,141 counties/county equivalents defined as of February 22, 2005. For more information on these areas, see Appendix C, Geographic Information]

County	Farm earnings, 2005 Total ($1,000)	Farm earnings, 2005 Percent of total[1]	Farms Number	Farms Percent Less than 50 acres	Farms Percent 500 acres or more	Land in farms Total acres (1,000)	Land in farms Average size of farm (acres)	Value of farm products sold Total (mil. dol.)	Value of farm products sold Average per farm (dol.)	Value of farm products sold Percent from Crops[2]	Value of farm products sold Percent from Live-stock and poultry[3]	Water use, 2000[4] Total (mil. gal. per day)	Water use, 2000[4] Ground water, percent of total	Water use, 2000[4] By selected major use (mil. gal. per day) Irrigation	Water use, 2000[4] By selected major use (mil. gal. per day) Public supply
ILLINOIS—Con.															
Douglas	782	0.2	576	28.0	28.3	233	404	63	108,701	90.7	9.3	1	100.0	(Z)	(Z)
DuPage	5,483	(Z)	79	64.6	5.1	8	97	9	115,468	98.1	1.9	13	100.0	(Z)	10
Edgar	3,336	1.3	667	20.5	37.0	355	532	140	209,367	(NA)	(NA)	3	52.4	(Z)	2
Edwards	4,374	3.1	379	32.5	23.5	123	325	22	58,063	68.6	31.4	1	76.0	–	(Z)
Effingham	18,318	2.2	1,134	29.4	13.5	278	245	72	63,751	52.6	47.4	5	47.9	–	3
Fayette	10,287	4.0	1,248	32.1	18.2	366	293	66	53,278	84.2	15.8	3	62.2	(Z)	1
Ford	-2,743	(X)	530	16.2	40.0	286	540	82	155,426	87.7	12.3	3	100.0	(Z)	2
Franklin	7,173	1.8	727	40.0	12.7	180	247	27	36,993	61.1	38.9	15	2.3	(Z)	14
Fulton	11,937	3.5	1,055	21.4	24.0	413	392	90	85,392	74.8	25.2	237	0.7	(Z)	2
Gallatin	-1,712	(X)	187	23.0	35.3	154	826	29	155,642	93.4	6.6	13	94.3	9	3
Greene	13,482	10.8	678	22.1	27.7	315	464	88	129,162	61.9	38.1	2	100.0	1	1
Grundy	-3,241	(X)	407	19.2	34.6	213	524	53	129,644	94.1	5.9	979	1.2	(Z)	3
Hamilton	8,090	10.1	694	31.4	15.4	234	338	30	42,537	89.1	10.9	1	100.0	(Z)	–
Hancock	19,676	9.1	1,095	18.4	25.6	432	394	117	106,723	69.6	30.4	4	68.9	1	1
Hardin	3,816	9.1	179	12.8	9.5	40	222	3	16,246	(NA)	(NA)	(Z)	100.0	(Z)	(Z)
Henderson	3,749	7.3	392	17.1	36.2	201	513	59	151,048	72.6	27.4	13	99.6	6	6
Henry	14,133	2.4	1,284	22.7	26.7	481	375	180	140,566	63.6	36.4	9	100.0	3	4
Iroquois	6,791	2.0	1,386	18.8	34.3	679	490	229	164,907	81.4	18.6	5	100.0	2	2
Jackson	10,574	0.9	740	28.9	13.2	200	270	29	38,972	73.6	26.4	117	0.5	–	6
Jasper	17,738	14.1	791	26.2	25.2	271	343	69	87,102	63.9	36.1	529	0.4	(Z)	1
Jefferson	13,898	1.6	1,168	33.4	11.9	259	222	32	27,451	73.9	26.1	2	100.0	(Z)	–
Jersey	4,217	2.2	520	26.7	21.0	173	333	41	78,963	79.5	20.5	2	100.0	(Z)	1
Jo Daviess	31,145	8.5	989	24.4	13.7	264	267	70	70,943	42.5	57.5	7	100.0	(Z)	2
Johnson	11,061	10.4	636	26.6	7.4	121	190	11	17,046	52.3	47.7	2	50.5	(Z)	1
Kane	12,861	0.1	619	42.6	20.5	198	320	116	187,488	87.2	12.8	55	61.8	1	53
Kankakee	14,085	0.8	722	22.6	32.3	347	481	120	166,150	92.0	8.0	23	44.2	6	14
Kendall	[5]25	(NA)	412	24.5	29.6	168	408	58	141,095	89.0	11.0	6	100.0	(Z)	2
Knox	16,856	1.9	921	23.9	26.0	394	428	130	140,776	67.0	33.0	2	100.0	(Z)	(Z)
Lake	11,011	(Z)	337	69.7	6.2	39	115	28	83,855	86.2	13.8	752	2.2	1	66
LaSalle	-6,436	(X)	1,478	19.1	27.8	579	392	162	109,407	90.5	9.5	78	22.2	1	11
Lawrence	12,767	6.3	355	25.6	32.1	192	541	56	158,992	59.7	40.3	2	100.0	2	–
Lee	1,682	0.3	842	21.4	30.8	389	462	129	153,754	83.5	16.5	10	86.2	4	4
Livingston	18,873	2.7	1,330	17.1	35.3	636	479	183	137,794	82.4	17.6	7	47.9	(Z)	5
Logan	-3,139	(X)	692	21.5	37.7	359	518	110	159,285	85.6	14.4	5	100.0	1	3
McDonough	7,400	1.4	752	19.8	28.9	325	432	82	109,677	86.8	13.2	4	38.7	(Z)	3
McHenry	1,834	(Z)	870	49.0	14.5	233	268	92	105,306	75.3	24.7	35	99.9	2	21
McLean	-4,423	(X)	1,442	21.3	35.0	688	477	207	143,669	86.8	13.2	13	67.5	1	10
Macon	-2,761	(X)	646	28.3	36.1	321	496	91	140,646	93.5	6.5	42	9.6	(Z)	39
Macoupin	15,507	3.0	1,214	26.6	21.7	427	352	129	106,409	71.8	28.2	6	46.7	(Z)	3
Madison	2,909	0.1	1,152	37.2	14.6	296	257	78	67,878	83.4	16.6	647	7.2	–	54
Marion	11,610	2.0	1,095	34.6	14.0	262	239	39	35,526	73.5	26.5	6	7.4	(Z)	5
Marshall	-3,908	(X)	454	17.4	27.5	191	421	53	115,643	88.8	11.2	6	97.9	3	2
Mason	-9,530	(X)	443	19.2	42.9	285	644	72	163,594	93.2	6.8	123	32.3	37	(Z)
Massac	5,724	2.5	434	29.3	14.5	125	287	17	38,947	67.8	32.2	565	1.8	2	1
Menard	7,421	7.9	329	25.2	31.3	155	471	42	126,985	82.7	17.3	1	100.0	1	(Z)
Mercer	12,105	9.0	746	26.3	25.6	293	392	90	120,823	75.5	24.5	4	100.0	2	1
Monroe	16,649	4.7	531	32.8	20.7	177	334	39	72,589	66.3	33.7	3	100.0	(Z)	(Z)
Montgomery	12,911	3.0	1,001	26.7	24.0	362	362	93	92,755	82.3	17.7	442	0.3	–	1
Morgan	2,488	0.4	682	22.6	30.1	293	429	84	123,177	79.9	20.1	202	4.2	1	(Z)
Moultrie	6,612	3.4	441	29.9	30.2	186	423	49	110,789	89.0	11.0	2	100.0	(Z)	1
Ogle	2,079	0.2	1,129	30.9	21.1	372	330	131	116,434	65.0	35.0	59	15.3	(Z)	5
Peoria	5,858	0.1	892	29.1	18.0	266	299	78	87,015	81.2	18.8	379	9.1	3	26
Perry	10,143	3.9	549	25.7	20.8	194	353	24	43,843	79.4	20.6	2	53.6	(Z)	1
Piatt	-2,705	(X)	442	20.1	42.1	258	583	72	162,002	96.1	3.9	4	100.0	(Z)	2
Pike	22,916	12.5	1,041	21.0	23.8	426	409	100	95,924	68.8	31.2	4	83.7	(Z)	2
Pope	2,647	8.0	341	21.1	10.9	77	226	4	12,630	67.5	32.5	(Z)	100.0	(Z)	–
Pulaski	1,745	2.3	253	26.5	19.4	86	341	15	58,040	86.9	13.1	1	100.0	(Z)	(Z)
Putnam	9,725	9.6	175	20.0	25.1	71	407	43	242,874	93.7	6.3	180	0.4	(Z)	(Z)
Randolph	19,497	3.7	823	24.5	17.9	254	308	39	47,644	71.3	28.7	37	6.1	(Z)	3
Richland	12,110	4.6	506	29.6	26.1	209	414	53	104,783	56.7	43.3	2	32.2	–	1
Rock Island	6,036	0.1	659	34.1	16.8	170	257	46	69,178	76.7	23.3	1,130	0.5	2	16
St. Clair	5,373	0.1	811	28.9	21.5	270	333	70	86,773	86.1	13.9	73	26.6	(Z)	54
Saline	5,032	1.2	446	38.3	17.3	130	291	20	45,471	65.6	34.4	(Z)	100.0	(Z)	–
Sangamon	1,915	(Z)	970	33.5	27.8	468	483	146	150,422	90.0	10.0	355	1.7	(Z)	36
Schuyler	15,707	14.7	538	20.8	21.0	207	386	42	77,796	68.0	32.0	2	100.0	(Z)	1
Scott	2,373	3.4	291	26.5	26.1	116	398	27	93,667	81.3	18.7	6	100.0	1	5
Shelby	14,868	6.5	1,228	27.0	22.9	420	342	95	77,328	77.1	22.9	4	74.0	(Z)	2
Stark	349	0.6	335	21.2	37.0	174	520	57	169,328	85.1	14.9	1	100.0	1	(Z)
Stephenson	30,075	3.1	1,075	29.0	16.7	324	302	125	116,223	47.8	52.2	9	100.0	(Z)	4
Tazewell	4,780	0.1	918	28.8	24.9	327	356	107	116,228	83.8	16.2	855	5.9	19	15

See footnotes at end of table.

Table B-14. Counties — Farm Earnings, Agriculture, and Water Use—Con.

[Includes United States, states, and 3,141 counties/county equivalents defined as of February 22, 2005. For more information on these areas, see Appendix C, Geographic Information]

County	Farm earnings, 2005 Total ($1,000)	Percent of total[1]	Agriculture (NAICS 111–112), 2002 Farms Number	Percent Less than 50 acres	500 acres or more	Land in farms Total acres (1,000)	Average size of farm (acres)	Value of farm products sold Total (mil. dol.)	Average per farm (dol.)	Percent from Crops[2]	Live-stock and poultry[3]	Water use, 2000[4] Total (mil. gal. per day)	Ground water, percent of total	By selected major use (mil. gal. per day) Irrigation	Public supply
ILLINOIS—Con.															
Union	1,180	0.6	666	28.5	11.6	152	229	23	33,788	80.5	19.5	2	97.2	(Z)	(Z)
Vermilion	−7,784	(X)	909	26.7	35.4	450	495	125	137,201	93.6	6.4	16	33.0	(Z)	10
Wabash	−247	(X)	199	24.6	36.2	111	556	23	113,191	87.7	12.3	2	100.0	(Z)	2
Warren	3,329	1.5	633	14.1	38.1	327	516	106	167,773	77.9	22.1	4	100.0	(Z)	3
Washington	20,386	7.3	756	18.8	28.7	332	440	80	105,380	58.5	41.5	3	75.4	(Z)	1
Wayne	23,138	10.5	1,092	29.4	17.1	356	326	57	51,886	69.3	30.7	3	47.0	(Z)	2
White	8,425	3.9	482	26.8	27.0	281	583	44	91,052	88.3	11.7	4	96.5	2	1
Whiteside	10,752	1.2	1,001	24.5	23.7	379	379	144	143,962	66.7	33.3	25	99.0	11	5
Will	−2,363	(X)	830	38.2	20.8	265	320	82	99,061	93.0	7.0	2,095	2.8	1	42
Williamson	9,881	0.9	631	35.8	7.3	105	167	10	15,491	59.9	40.1	109	2.0	(Z)	2
Winnebago	1,312	(Z)	695	39.9	16.5	191	275	62	89,468	73.0	27.0	40	100.0	(Z)	33
Woodford	−2,400	(X)	919	25.0	22.4	310	337	104	112,976	75.2	24.8	13	35.1	(Z)	10
INDIANA	700,191	0.5	60,296	39.9	13.8	15,059	250	4,783	79,328	62.6	37.4	10,100	6.5	101	670
Adams	9,920	1.5	1,296	48.4	9.4	229	177	99	76,090	39.3	60.7	7	72.8	–	3
Allen	8,309	0.1	1,550	46.5	9.1	284	183	75	48,166	75.0	25.0	54	17.7	(Z)	41
Bartholomew	5,990	0.3	608	42.3	15.1	161	264	42	69,689	83.0	17.0	19	86.2	1	12
Benton	3,169	3.0	394	16.8	42.9	248	629	70	176,604	96.5	3.5	1	88.6	(Z)	(Z)
Blackford	1,484	0.9	279	34.8	21.1	97	348	26	92,839	78.1	21.9	3	88.3	(Z)	1
Boone	8,881	0.8	672	48.7	20.2	226	336	75	111,259	85.6	14.4	5	84.4	(Z)	2
Brown	125	0.1	222	53.2	2.3	20	92	2	8,775	65.2	34.8	(Z)	90.3	–	–
Carroll	13,582	5.3	529	31.0	23.6	202	381	95	179,992	54.0	46.0	7	60.5	(Z)	1
Cass	12,266	1.9	717	36.8	18.7	208	291	72	100,876	68.5	31.5	33	16.9	(Z)	6
Clark	2,573	0.1	638	41.2	7.8	101	158	22	34,481	73.8	26.2	25	86.3	–	21
Clay	7,525	2.3	555	40.5	16.2	152	273	32	58,422	82.3	17.7	1	90.8	–	(Z)
Clinton	8,840	1.7	604	36.9	27.8	245	405	105	174,402	64.6	35.4	6	99.4	(Z)	5
Crawford	1,739	1.7	427	26.7	2.8	55	129	4	8,422	36.8	63.2	6	36.5	–	2
Daviess	17,617	3.8	1,138	45.8	7.7	207	182	104	91,185	31.2	68.8	7	93.8	(Z)	2
Dearborn	603	0.1	676	32.4	2.7	74	110	7	10,194	64.0	36.0	860	1.1	–	4
Decatur	8,951	1.6	676	29.3	18.3	207	306	87	128,632	54.7	45.3	4	60.5	–	2
DeKalb	9,719	0.9	1,000	41.0	8.8	179	179	42	42,338	58.2	41.8	12	90.8	(Z)	4
Delaware	8,864	0.4	687	48.5	13.5	190	276	50	73,048	86.9	13.1	18	31.6	(Z)	12
Dubois	17,195	1.3	758	24.9	12.9	189	249	105	138,863	19.2	80.8	7	19.7	–	5
Elkhart	21,276	0.3	1,516	52.8	5.9	201	133	136	89,718	30.6	69.4	35	91.1	7	14
Fayette	827	0.2	424	36.1	14.9	107	252	20	46,573	76.1	23.9	4	96.3	–	3
Floyd	867	0.1	299	56.5	2.7	24	80	4	11,716	69.2	30.8	337	0.6	–	2
Fountain	5,383	2.2	487	27.7	24.4	205	422	52	107,464	89.8	10.2	4	96.7	(Z)	1
Franklin	4,236	2.5	817	31.6	7.1	139	171	25	30,464	56.9	43.1	4	90.9	(Z)	2
Fulton	13,505	4.2	616	36.0	18.7	193	313	53	85,396	73.6	26.4	7	91.6	4	1
Gibson	11,500	1.1	557	32.1	22.6	211	379	54	97,826	81.3	18.7	47	8.3	(Z)	2
Grant	6,709	0.5	598	36.3	22.6	198	332	54	90,005	81.5	18.5	14	63.9	–	7
Greene	12,961	4.0	822	34.5	8.4	171	207	41	50,027	41.6	58.4	5	78.8	(Z)	3
Hamilton	9,626	0.2	726	57.4	10.2	140	193	56	76,616	91.8	8.2	129	18.6	(Z)	33
Hancock	4,680	0.4	616	51.6	14.6	162	262	44	71,690	82.1	17.9	6	95.3	(Z)	3
Harrison	4,409	0.9	1,176	37.8	4.6	160	136	42	36,080	31.1	68.9	3	89.2	–	2
Hendricks	−188	(X)	703	54.9	12.9	182	259	52	74,329	86.4	13.6	10	91.7	–	4
Henry	6,873	1.1	745	46.6	13.7	173	232	47	63,601	74.1	25.9	8	71.0	(Z)	4
Howard	9,725	0.3	536	39.2	18.7	156	291	57	105,959	68.7	31.3	21	36.4	–	12
Huntington	11,320	1.8	675	38.8	19.0	200	296	63	93,604	66.7	33.3	6	80.4	–	3
Jackson	19,226	1.9	806	36.7	16.6	207	257	80	99,783	39.4	60.6	9	46.9	1	5
Jasper	16,774	3.3	641	35.4	30.9	280	437	133	207,340	54.2	45.8	45	11.7	15	1
Jay	14,895	4.5	857	39.8	11.8	195	228	94	109,740	29.1	70.9	4	82.5	(Z)	2
Jefferson	184	(Z)	778	42.4	5.0	109	140	16	20,226	75.8	24.2	1,310	0.2	–	6
Jennings	7,727	2.2	669	45.3	10.0	143	213	41	61,019	50.3	49.7	3	19.3	–	1
Johnson	5,475	0.3	598	53.3	14.0	135	226	49	82,672	69.3	30.7	13	98.7	(Z)	11
Knox	12,980	1.8	508	25.0	31.3	300	591	86	169,764	84.1	15.9	93	10.8	3	5
Kosciusko	21,018	1.1	1,203	42.3	11.6	262	218	122	101,633	39.8	60.2	20	83.5	6	4
LaGrange	23,795	3.7	1,551	41.6	4.4	189	122	107	69,090	38.3	61.7	13	76.9	8	1
Lake	4,524	(Z)	482	51.7	15.8	128	265	39	80,797	92.6	7.4	2,317	0.4	14	81
LaPorte	11,612	0.6	817	41.2	17.6	243	298	79	97,140	70.2	29.8	40	34.2	11	10
Lawrence	3,231	0.5	825	35.2	7.4	147	179	15	17,613	43.3	56.7	9	18.0	–	6
Madison	7,372	0.3	807	45.2	19.1	244	302	75	93,311	90.1	9.9	21	86.1	(Z)	14
Marion	10,521	(Z)	303	74.6	3.3	24	78	33	110,347	(NA)	(NA)	296	17.6	(Z)	125
Marshall	11,434	1.5	842	35.7	13.4	204	243	63	74,791	63.3	36.7	7	86.9	1	3
Martin	4,576	0.9	350	32.0	6.6	64	181	28	79,017	16.5	83.5	2	78.9	–	1
Miami	7,406	1.5	685	36.4	16.9	191	279	59	85,699	60.9	39.1	9	39.6	(Z)	2
Monroe	2,047	0.1	547	41.7	3.5	61	111	7	12,590	49.9	50.1	15	3.3	–	14
Montgomery	5,184	0.6	644	37.6	24.8	273	425	94	146,592	74.0	26.0	5	87.0	(Z)	2
Morgan	2,152	0.3	690	57.1	7.5	112	162	25	36,680	77.9	22.1	277	2.9	–	6
Newton	6,592	4.0	344	28.2	36.3	182	528	119	346,619	39.9	60.1	5	71.8	2	1
Noble	8,427	0.9	1,029	39.7	8.6	173	168	51	49,214	48.6	51.4	9	87.5	2	3
Ohio	−859	(X)	213	41.8	2.3	24	112	2	11,042	82.2	17.8	1	95.0	(Z)	1
Orange	3,918	1.6	535	26.4	7.9	106	198	18	34,402	44.2	55.8	2	50.0	–	1
Owen	1,303	0.6	588	34.0	6.1	99	168	13	22,131	72.7	27.3	2	93.3	–	1

See footnotes at end of table.

Table B-14. Counties — **Farm Earnings, Agriculture, and Water Use**—Con.

[Includes United States, states, and 3,141 counties/county equivalents defined as of February 22, 2005. For more information on these areas, see Appendix C, Geographic Information]

County	Farm earnings, 2005 Total ($1,000)	Farm earnings, 2005 Percent of total[1]	Farms Number	Farms Percent Less than 50 acres	Farms Percent 500 acres or more	Land in farms Total acres (1,000)	Land in farms Average size of farm (acres)	Value of farm products sold Total (mil. dol.)	Value of farm products sold Average per farm (dol.)	Percent from Crops[2]	Percent from Livestock and poultry[3]	Water use Total (mil. gal. per day)	Water use Ground water, percent of total	By selected major use (mil. gal. per day) Irrigation	By selected major use (mil. gal. per day) Public supply
INDIANA—Con.															
Parke	4,594	3.3	470	33.2	17.7	165	351	33	70,468	80.3	19.7	2	94.0	(Z)	1
Perry	3,875	1.3	470	24.3	6.0	76	162	9	18,581	30.4	69.6	1	80.6	–	(Z)
Pike	6,030	3.8	288	30.2	14.2	76	263	15	53,302	70.5	29.5	501	0.3	–	1
Porter	5,283	0.2	606	49.5	16.0	146	241	37	61,579	83.7	16.3	722	1.7	2	15
Posey	5,627	1.0	396	29.3	29.3	192	485	50	127,374	84.5	15.5	20	11.0	(Z)	2
Pulaski	12,889	5.3	524	33.4	24.2	223	425	81	155,351	61.9	38.1	10	43.1	3	(Z)
Putnam	3,743	0.7	853	44.3	10.8	181	212	45	52,183	74.9	25.1	8	86.0	(Z)	4
Randolph	11,269	3.4	786	34.9	21.2	258	328	70	89,452	68.3	31.7	4	71.9	–	2
Ripley	6,231	1.0	904	36.4	9.2	173	191	44	48,770	71.0	29.0	3	27.1	–	2
Rush	10,496	4.1	606	26.7	25.9	224	369	67	111,101	66.5	33.5	3	76.0	(Z)	1
St. Joseph	10,116	0.1	855	52.2	9.8	165	193	50	58,936	74.7	25.3	55	92.7	5	31
Scott	1,842	0.6	387	44.2	7.5	69	179	13	32,344	83.4	16.6	4	3.8	–	2
Shelby	10,245	1.3	651	41.3	20.1	200	307	59	90,702	86.1	13.9	7	91.7	(Z)	4
Spencer	9,376	2.8	593	30.7	14.5	155	261	35	58,610	59.6	40.4	32	9.2	(Z)	2
Starke	862	0.5	518	47.7	13.7	134	259	28	54,792	93.2	6.8	6	63.9	4	1
Steuben	8,452	1.3	674	38.1	6.5	113	167	21	30,533	61.1	38.9	5	81.4	1	1
Sullivan	9,163	3.9	437	29.1	21.5	179	409	38	87,915	87.7	12.3	464	0.7	1	2
Switzerland	–1,740	(X)	464	35.8	2.6	60	130	6	13,940	72.8	27.2	2	95.0	–	1
Tippecanoe	10,526	0.3	705	49.6	17.2	221	313	78	110,790	78.2	21.8	35	96.5	(Z)	14
Tipton	8,114	4.1	360	28.3	26.9	152	421	56	154,769	78.6	21.4	2	98.6	–	1
Union	3,183	4.2	262	22.1	25.2	85	325	22	82,603	68.1	31.9	1	92.2	–	(Z)
Vanderburgh	1,784	(Z)	306	44.4	16.7	82	268	20	66,552	90.3	9.7	22	4.3	(Z)	21
Vermillion	–1,141	(X)	221	29.4	26.2	110	497	28	128,412	78.5	21.5	608	1.8	(Z)	1
Vigo	5,366	0.2	476	46.8	16.6	123	258	28	59,658	91.2	8.8	535	3.4	1	10
Wabash	11,031	1.9	799	35.2	14.8	215	269	103	129,191	37.0	63.0	8	92.9	(Z)	4
Warren	7,412	9.0	346	33.5	26.0	167	482	52	151,592	(NA)	(NA)	2	96.5	(Z)	1
Warrick	6,125	0.8	401	45.9	13.7	94	236	17	42,499	83.6	16.4	786	0.7	–	2
Washington	10,245	3.6	977	34.8	7.1	181	185	40	41,121	36.6	63.4	4	33.0	–	2
Wayne	6,740	0.5	850	38.5	11.8	171	201	45	52,660	72.8	27.2	11	48.1	(Z)	7
Wells	9,594	2.0	631	29.5	24.7	226	359	62	98,960	71.4	28.6	5	71.9	–	2
White	10,963	3.3	589	33.6	29.5	284	482	116	197,774	60.8	39.2	5	75.1	1	1
Whitley	9,321	1.9	840	41.0	10.5	172	205	46	54,907	59.6	40.4	4	94.8	(Z)	2
IOWA	2,237,042	3.2	90,655	23.3	22.7	31,729	350	12,274	135,388	49.5	50.5	3,360	20.2	22	383
Adair	16,154	12.2	843	16.7	27.2	373	443	93	110,654	57.6	42.4	1	79.7	–	(Z)
Adams	13,568	22.1	567	16.4	28.4	238	419	51	89,832	55.6	44.4	2	34.1	–	(Z)
Allamakee	26,898	11.1	1,083	19.5	17.4	326	301	91	84,049	31.3	68.7	239	1.3	–	1
Appanoose	6,464	3.3	816	20.0	17.3	236	289	25	30,984	51.3	48.7	6	21.9	–	5
Audubon	26,409	23.6	638	22.4	26.2	261	409	113	176,658	41.5	58.5	2	81.1	–	(Z)
Benton	13,311	4.8	1,186	24.1	23.1	401	338	148	124,750	64.4	35.6	3	91.9	(Z)	1
Black Hawk	22,620	0.7	939	30.6	18.8	275	293	114	121,814	60.9	39.1	35	85.4	(Z)	19
Boone	12,003	2.8	827	29.9	25.8	313	378	106	128,093	71.4	28.6	3	91.8	–	2
Bremer	32,984	7.7	956	27.5	15.3	255	267	108	113,041	58.0	42.0	3	91.5	(Z)	2
Buchanan	27,701	9.3	1,067	24.7	20.5	340	319	142	132,720	59.3	40.7	4	90.2	(Z)	1
Buena Vista	38,114	9.4	825	20.8	32.2	342	414	213	257,862	37.3	62.7	6	93.5	(Z)	4
Butler	34,724	20.8	1,076	30.4	19.6	328	305	135	125,040	55.4	44.6	2	89.0	(Z)	1
Calhoun	27,124	19.3	762	24.5	33.3	341	447	141	184,459	58.7	41.3	3	72.4	–	1
Carroll	34,306	7.2	1,045	22.3	22.4	364	348	264	252,648	28.6	71.4	5	88.2	(Z)	3
Cass	13,912	5.8	764	19.8	30.6	337	441	117	153,288	44.7	55.3	3	79.1	(Z)	2
Cedar	13,740	6.1	971	24.5	23.3	338	349	123	126,674	66.9	33.1	3	90.8	(Z)	1
Cerro Gordo	32,122	2.8	795	31.2	28.4	323	407	112	141,204	74.6	25.4	10	68.9	(Z)	6
Cherokee	31,284	12.9	837	19.6	27.7	335	401	155	184,780	42.9	57.1	4	90.3	(Z)	3
Chickasaw	35,703	17.3	951	26.5	18.1	271	285	120	126,074	46.9	53.1	2	84.3	(Z)	1
Clarke	16,202	9.3	726	16.9	15.8	216	298	44	60,132	26.3	73.7	2	90.8	–	1
Clay	18,911	4.8	691	20.4	33.1	312	451	157	227,305	40.6	59.4	4	94.2	(Z)	2
Clayton	37,597	13.3	1,601	17.3	15.2	433	270	160	99,905	33.6	66.4	4	86.0	(Z)	1
Clinton	17,524	1.8	1,219	25.5	20.9	388	318	138	113,456	63.9	36.1	277	47.3	(Z)	5
Crawford	22,402	6.8	927	24.2	29.4	446	481	157	169,540	57.2	42.8	5	92.7	–	2
Dallas	30,675	2.7	938	37.4	20.9	309	330	92	98,611	69.9	30.1	6	90.4	(Z)	3
Davis	9,547	9.4	1,007	17.5	14.4	291	289	50	49,293	41.4	58.6	2	62.0	–	(Z)
Decatur	15,179	15.9	788	17.8	18.3	278	353	42	53,274	34.3	65.7	2	68.8	–	1
Delaware	48,737	15.6	1,253	18.8	14.9	345	276	190	151,863	33.1	66.9	5	82.6	–	1
Des Moines	4,267	0.4	674	28.8	16.3	181	269	47	70,473	78.4	21.6	114	7.4	(Z)	7
Dickinson	3,429	0.9	492	21.5	30.9	203	413	76	155,303	56.2	43.8	3	31.7	(Z)	2
Dubuque	35,654	1.5	1,481	19.9	8.5	316	213	152	102,612	22.7	77.3	95	28.5	(Z)	8
Emmet	22,631	11.5	510	20.0	36.9	235	462	107	209,445	49.4	50.6	3	72.7	(Z)	1
Fayette	51,303	16.0	1,344	26.4	19.6	415	309	181	134,548	44.2	55.8	4	87.9	(Z)	1
Floyd	20,872	7.6	895	26.6	22.2	291	325	116	129,964	61.1	38.9	3	90.6	(Z)	2
Franklin	25,276	13.9	825	22.9	29.5	337	409	160	193,896	51.7	48.3	3	56.6	(Z)	1
Fremont	15,623	9.5	547	15.2	36.0	318	582	62	114,207	79.6	20.4	2	92.1	(Z)	1
Greene	14,934	10.2	727	22.4	34.1	347	477	120	165,154	65.4	34.6	2	85.1	(Z)	1
Grundy	27,757	14.2	724	25.8	28.9	324	448	140	193,844	65.9	34.1	2	82.8	(Z)	1
Guthrie	21,488	14.9	885	22.5	21.0	324	366	111	125,631	46.6	53.4	2	78.0	(Z)	1
Hamilton	45,161	11.8	797	28.1	30.4	348	437	235	294,730	37.3	62.7	4	85.3	(Z)	2

See footnotes at end of table.

[Includes United States, states, and 3,141 counties/county equivalents defined as of February 22, 2005. For more information on these areas, see Appendix C, Geographic Information]

County	Farm earnings, 2005 Total ($1,000)	Percent of total[1]	Farms Number	Farms Percent Less than 50 acres	Farms Percent 500 acres or more	Land in farms Total acres (1,000)	Average size of farm (acres)	Value Total (mil. dol.)	Average per farm (dol.)	Percent from Crops[2]	Percent from Live-stock and poultry[3]	Water Total (mil. gal. per day)	Ground water, percent of total	Irrigation	Public supply
IOWA—Con.															
Hancock	31,859	8.8	827	23.9	27.8	322	390	142	171,209	56.6	43.4	4	57.5	(Z)	1
Hardin	42,932	13.0	829	27.3	28.7	328	395	252	303,945	32.2	67.8	6	62.6	(Z)	2
Harrison	10,705	6.6	828	20.7	32.0	428	517	111	134,289	76.3	23.7	5	85.6	2	1
Henry	8,741	1.8	857	27.0	16.6	251	293	79	91,718	50.5	49.5	3	90.5	–	2
Howard	24,822	12.1	891	25.5	17.7	269	302	105	118,110	52.0	48.0	2	80.1	(Z)	1
Humboldt	21,583	11.8	606	19.3	30.2	271	447	97	159,467	68.1	31.9	3	57.8	–	1
Ida	12,499	7.8	618	26.5	27.3	266	430	111	180,228	52.9	47.1	2	87.4	–	1
Iowa	15,659	3.3	1,024	21.3	18.0	340	332	133	129,877	67.0	33.0	2	88.8	(Z)	1
Jackson	10,265	4.3	1,336	20.6	14.4	349	261	107	80,011	31.1	68.9	3	88.3	–	1
Jasper	28,674	4.5	1,212	27.7	24.1	410	339	149	122,889	59.5	40.5	7	94.0	(Z)	5
Jefferson	12,845	3.7	808	20.8	18.1	233	289	49	60,097	54.6	45.4	3	94.5	–	2
Johnson	9,134	0.2	1,261	27.0	13.3	301	239	105	82,971	54.2	45.8	42	12.5	(Z)	9
Jones	11,456	4.5	1,024	21.3	20.1	312	304	119	116,670	48.3	51.7	3	88.6	–	1
Keokuk	14,505	12.6	1,093	23.0	21.0	344	315	99	90,431	51.1	48.9	2	67.4	–	(Z)
Kossuth	42,552	12.5	1,340	18.8	32.8	592	442	261	194,789	55.7	44.3	4	88.5	(Z)	1
Lee	8,886	1.1	945	24.1	18.1	270	286	66	69,398	58.1	41.9	30	68.9	(Z)	11
Linn	12,751	0.2	1,445	32.5	13.3	349	241	105	72,910	69.6	30.4	265	20.3	(Z)	39
Louisa	13,784	8.5	601	21.5	21.8	201	334	70	117,008	60.9	39.1	11	98.7	2	1
Lucas	6,208	4.4	747	19.3	16.1	222	298	27	35,930	41.4	58.6	1	40.7	–	1
Lyon	34,153	20.8	1,045	20.8	21.9	342	327	248	237,221	27.1	72.9	5	87.4	(Z)	2
Madison	9,041	5.2	990	23.3	17.5	304	307	71	71,214	47.3	52.7	2	85.2	–	1
Mahaska	24,161	6.9	1,043	19.8	20.5	329	315	133	127,275	42.0	58.0	4	89.9	–	2
Marion	9,965	1.2	1,051	27.8	15.4	277	263	68	65,140	67.4	32.6	5	91.2	(Z)	4
Marshall	19,726	2.3	848	30.0	27.1	335	395	132	155,772	64.8	35.2	12	77.3	–	6
Mills	10,501	5.6	462	19.3	39.2	247	535	48	104,152	88.6	11.4	2	96.2	–	1
Mitchell	37,102	20.5	828	22.8	25.6	289	349	155	186,700	40.4	59.6	3	83.2	(Z)	1
Monona	8,715	7.1	625	13.1	39.2	392	628	105	168,136	67.4	32.6	8	97.8	6	1
Monroe	8,807	7.6	714	16.2	20.3	253	354	41	57,329	36.7	63.3	2	84.3	–	(Z)
Montgomery	13,785	6.7	583	19.9	29.3	243	416	83	141,559	59.7	40.3	2	93.9	–	1
Muscatine	5,833	0.5	816	27.9	19.0	230	282	72	88,417	70.8	29.2	326	17.4	2	27
O'Brien	37,977	15.2	993	18.6	26.4	362	365	204	205,752	40.4	59.6	4	89.7	(Z)	2
Osceola	23,562	22.0	636	20.3	30.7	257	404	163	255,830	35.1	64.9	4	87.7	(Z)	2
Page	21,302	7.7	873	17.6	29.0	339	388	69	79,211	61.8	38.2	3	51.7	–	2
Palo Alto	37,590	22.4	783	23.9	30.5	327	417	191	244,070	39.3	60.7	3	90.2	1	1
Plymouth	48,862	9.3	1,339	17.2	27.4	531	397	278	207,911	38.2	61.8	7	89.7	1	3
Pocahontas	29,722	24.5	730	17.7	37.9	354	485	142	194,684	61.2	38.8	2	92.0	(Z)	1
Polk	9,328	0.1	764	41.4	17.8	227	297	69	89,682	86.3	13.7	53	47.4	1	51
Pottawattamie	22,029	1.3	1,255	25.7	31.4	540	431	163	130,093	65.5	34.5	455	3.6	(Z)	14
Poweshiek	26,362	5.8	925	21.6	26.2	345	373	111	120,066	60.1	39.9	3	81.9	–	1
Ringgold	17,739	24.3	758	14.5	22.2	299	395	52	67,967	35.2	64.8	2	60.4	(Z)	(Z)
Sac	40,796	24.6	791	21.4	31.4	339	429	183	231,794	44.3	55.7	4	84.4	(Z)	1
Scott	6,083	0.1	750	27.5	19.5	229	305	96	127,620	66.5	33.5	122	4.3	(Z)	20
Shelby	24,040	11.8	868	15.9	30.3	348	401	124	142,762	59.9	40.1	2	88.2	(Z)	1
Sioux	124,576	15.8	1,673	25.5	18.5	505	302	617	368,711	17.6	82.4	15	89.1	2	7
Story	16,939	0.8	977	30.9	24.5	360	368	119	121,525	77.9	22.1	13	88.1	(Z)	9
Tama	28,316	12.1	1,159	19.4	23.3	418	361	128	110,464	75.5	24.5	5	95.4	(Z)	2
Taylor	23,641	26.7	794	14.9	22.5	308	388	60	75,831	51.2	48.8	1	54.0	–	(Z)
Union	10,581	4.5	698	20.3	19.9	238	341	63	90,100	36.8	63.2	4	14.1	–	3
Van Buren	7,418	8.8	870	18.0	16.0	253	291	48	55,025	42.5	57.5	1	58.3	–	(Z)
Wapello	6,485	0.9	845	25.9	14.1	206	244	38	44,764	66.2	33.8	22	2.2	–	7
Warren	9,595	2.5	1,330	34.6	11.7	299	224	53	39,941	65.1	34.9	2	91.3	(Z)	1
Washington	24,747	8.4	1,200	26.4	18.4	335	279	175	145,683	34.7	65.3	4	80.8	–	2
Wayne	13,394	17.5	788	12.6	23.0	305	387	41	52,348	58.5	41.5	1	61.2	–	(Z)
Webster	18,513	2.1	932	22.4	30.3	417	447	154	165,206	69.4	30.6	10	87.0	–	5
Winnebago	13,572	6.6	631	30.3	25.4	240	381	98	155,036	56.1	43.9	2	96.7	(Z)	2
Winneshiek	36,579	7.3	1,501	23.3	13.9	380	253	148	98,886	33.2	66.8	5	79.9	(Z)	2
Woodbury	18,792	0.8	1,148	24.0	24.2	442	385	142	123,994	57.8	42.2	959	3.2	1	17
Worth	11,297	13.6	588	28.2	30.3	224	381	68	115,371	78.0	22.0	3	29.9	(Z)	(Z)
Wright	41,246	15.2	752	24.9	33.5	345	459	226	300,195	38.9	61.1	4	86.3	(Z)	1
KANSAS	1,066,237	1.5	64,414	17.4	34.6	47,228	733	8,746	135,782	27.7	72.3	6,610	57.3	3,710	416
Allen	-5,659	(X)	619	17.1	27.5	280	453	25	40,068	49.6	50.4	4	2.4	(Z)	1
Anderson	4,406	5.1	654	16.8	30.6	379	579	44	67,844	46.7	53.3	3	3.0	1	1
Atchison	5,972	2.1	619	19.1	20.7	227	366	32	51,929	49.4	50.6	5	7.9	(Z)	4
Barber	-3,770	(X)	471	8.3	52.7	697	1,480	50	105,815	29.6	70.4	6	100.0	4	1
Barton	14,490	2.4	772	13.3	41.8	650	842	171	221,707	26.3	73.7	41	100.0	34	3
Bourbon	1,050	0.4	838	14.7	22.6	339	405	29	35,044	23.9	76.1	3	0.3	(Z)	2
Brown	6,725	3.3	591	16.4	31.0	324	548	53	89,091	59.3	40.7	2	57.6	(Z)	1
Butler	9,875	1.2	1,309	27.7	21.5	701	536	116	88,939	20.9	79.1	15	11.7	1	10
Chase	13,024	23.4	260	14.2	45.0	362	1,391	44	167,592	11.2	88.8	4	28.0	2	(Z)
Chautauqua	-1,860	(X)	371	7.0	39.4	390	1,052	30	81,951	23.8	76.2	2	31.3	(Z)	(Z)

See footnotes at end of table.

County and City Data Book: 2007

U.S. Census Bureau

Table B-14. Counties — **Farm Earnings, Agriculture, and Water Use**—Con.

[Includes United States, states, and 3,141 counties/county equivalents defined as of February 22, 2005. For more information on these areas, see Appendix C, Geographic Information]

County	Farm earnings, 2005 Total ($1,000)	Farm earnings, 2005 Percent of total[1]	Farms Number	Farms Percent Less than 50 acres	Farms Percent 500 acres or more	Land in farms Total acres (1,000)	Land in farms Average size of farm (acres)	Value of farm products sold Total (mil. dol.)	Value of farm products sold Average per farm (dol.)	Value of farm products sold Percent from Crops[2]	Value of farm products sold Percent from Livestock and poultry[3]	Water use, 2000[4] Total (mil. gal. per day)	Water use, 2000[4] Ground water, percent of total	By selected major use (mil. gal. per day) Irrigation	By selected major use (mil. gal. per day) Public supply
KANSAS—Con.															
Cherokee	7,145	2.4	746	26.9	20.5	291	389	50	66,469	58.1	41.9	95	3.3	(Z)	3
Cheyenne	4,329	12.5	441	7.7	54.0	576	1,307	54	123,401	36.3	63.7	60	100.0	58	1
Clark	6,760	17.7	302	7.0	46.7	492	1,628	98	324,079	5.1	94.9	6	100.0	4	(Z)
Clay	8,325	5.9	571	14.4	42.6	393	689	49	85,278	53.9	46.1	18	99.4	15	1
Cloud	5,570	4.0	520	10.2	47.7	431	829	38	72,723	64.1	35.9	22	97.3	19	1
Coffey	4,225	1.7	607	15.2	29.7	336	553	38	63,194	44.3	55.7	677	(Z)	(Z)	1
Comanche	−866	(X)	274	7.7	57.3	447	1,631	26	93,996	(NA)	(NA)	8	100.0	7	(Z)
Cowley	6,128	1.0	1,004	18.3	28.6	690	687	62	62,156	36.6	63.4	8	49.4	1	5
Crawford	6,540	1.0	825	22.1	21.6	341	413	42	50,888	51.7	48.3	7	71.8	1	5
Decatur	6,106	15.9	350	14.3	55.7	469	1,340	108	308,263	14.2	85.8	17	100.0	15	1
Dickinson	9,590	3.7	976	17.3	34.4	551	564	97	98,950	30.9	69.1	8	85.1	3	2
Doniphan	4,991	4.5	469	18.1	26.0	206	439	32	68,446	78.2	21.8	1	96.1	(Z)	(Z)
Douglas	2,294	0.1	874	35.8	11.3	201	230	24	27,446	53.3	46.7	25	21.7	1	16
Edwards	19,721	32.7	353	4.8	47.3	420	1,190	131	372,249	28.6	71.4	114	100.0	112	(Z)
Elk	−852	(X)	407	11.1	38.1	370	910	26	63,307	15.6	84.4	1	2.0	–	(Z)
Ellis	12,704	1.9	758	12.5	39.4	578	762	52	68,960	26.9	73.1	5	95.8	2	2
Ellsworth	3,218	3.2	478	17.2	40.2	413	864	25	51,659	54.2	45.8	3	72.9	(Z)	1
Finney	37,216	5.0	485	8.5	59.2	802	1,653	488	1,005,610	16.0	84.0	310	100.0	288	7
Ford	46,496	6.7	701	14.4	46.6	649	926	215	306,217	17.4	82.6	109	99.8	94	5
Franklin	830	0.2	977	26.0	17.6	339	347	41	41,512	37.1	62.9	4	9.0	(Z)	2
Geary	−1,877	(X)	245	18.8	40.8	180	733	17	68,188	38.1	61.9	10	93.2	3	6
Gove	11,133	21.8	395	10.4	58.7	592	1,498	110	278,339	17.5	82.5	22	99.8	20	(Z)
Graham	9,118	14.8	431	10.0	42.5	517	1,200	32	75,299	40.4	59.6	14	99.9	13	1
Grant	28,956	15.2	304	10.2	48.0	302	993	317	1,041,151	9.8	90.2	155	100.0	149	2
Gray	54,418	37.5	470	8.1	51.9	501	1,066	354	752,206	16.1	83.9	238	99.4	234	1
Greeley	10,054	35.5	303	5.0	51.8	456	1,506	52	171,706	17.6	82.4	30	100.0	29	(Z)
Greenwood	5,813	7.1	575	11.5	38.6	594	1,034	51	88,670	12.5	87.5	3	0.4	(Z)	1
Hamilton	30,960	48.3	393	7.4	51.4	536	1,363	176	447,654	7.2	92.8	46	86.7	43	1
Harper	5,021	4.8	523	9.9	45.1	470	898	63	120,436	44.3	55.7	4	93.3	2	1
Harvey	11,739	1.7	832	26.0	26.7	352	423	60	72,475	57.6	42.4	45	98.8	27	16
Haskell	58,591	49.5	227	5.3	70.0	406	1,788	482	2,124,119	12.5	87.5	251	99.9	246	1
Hodgeman	19,425	52.6	381	5.5	59.3	471	1,235	98	257,619	13.7	86.3	32	99.2	31	(Z)
Jackson	−5,112	(X)	1,099	22.7	17.1	337	307	28	25,279	35.6	64.4	2	73.1	(Z)	1
Jefferson	2,568	1.8	1,041	23.4	11.8	280	269	35	33,463	37.3	62.7	4	90.9	2	2
Jewell	10,429	21.4	572	11.0	45.8	496	867	50	87,448	53.1	46.9	92	3.5	91	1
Johnson	9,676	(Z)	659	45.5	11.1	149	226	27	40,616	65.1	34.9	25	55.2	2	14
Kearny	16,557	26.2	347	9.5	45.2	558	1,607	181	520,735	20.6	79.4	249	58.8	246	1
Kingman	−3,395	(X)	837	14.6	36.0	556	664	52	61,879	52.8	47.2	20	96.3	15	1
Kiowa	3,520	7.0	379	8.4	47.2	435	1,147	36	96,282	56.1	43.9	59	100.0	58	(Z)
Labette	3,430	0.9	889	18.9	22.8	361	406	62	70,228	27.9	72.1	5	1.7	(Z)	3
Lane	13,704	34.2	312	6.1	59.9	460	1,476	124	397,628	11.7	88.3	19	100.0	17	(Z)
Leavenworth	5,477	0.4	1,094	34.8	7.0	197	180	22	20,181	48.0	52.0	9	53.7	(Z)	7
Lincoln	2,578	7.8	458	10.9	48.9	446	974	35	76,832	49.0	51.0	2	60.1	1	(Z)
Linn	1,705	1.7	903	16.9	17.9	311	344	23	25,540	45.0	55.0	1,153	(Z)	(Z)	1
Logan	7,917	15.5	318	7.5	62.6	610	1,918	40	126,409	32.3	67.7	10	100.0	8	1
Lyon	6,574	1.0	898	19.3	29.4	494	550	76	84,523	24.3	75.7	7	3.1	(Z)	5
McPherson	21,068	2.8	1,161	17.5	31.0	575	495	99	85,640	49.7	50.3	35	93.9	26	5
Marion	8,002	5.6	996	19.4	34.6	588	591	81	81,617	38.8	61.2	4	47.6	1	1
Marshall	30,416	12.4	954	12.5	42.6	581	609	64	67,453	49.3	50.7	3	69.0	1	1
Meade	25,302	33.8	454	6.4	52.6	611	1,345	106	233,672	40.4	59.6	163	100.0	161	1
Miami	−6,200	(X)	1,424	37.6	10.1	320	225	44	30,963	36.2	63.8	5	–	(Z)	4
Mitchell	11,163	8.2	473	11.6	49.7	449	949	74	156,218	37.0	63.0	16	12.9	14	2
Montgomery	4,522	0.7	983	23.3	16.5	346	352	40	40,192	41.8	58.2	11	0.5	(Z)	5
Morris	3,645	5.5	466	16.5	41.0	386	828	54	114,818	20.8	79.2	5	10.8	(Z)	4
Morton	2,960	5.1	309	7.1	46.0	353	1,141	41	133,731	31.3	68.7	52	100.0	49	1
Nemaha	30,275	15.9	1,020	12.0	27.5	417	408	79	77,841	23.3	76.7	3	99.3	(Z)	1
Neosho	−1,364	(X)	769	18.1	25.1	341	444	39	50,553	42.8	57.2	4	0.3	(Z)	2
Ness	3,502	5.5	547	9.7	55.8	655	1,198	31	57,026	50.3	49.7	5	92.9	4	(Z)
Norton	5,972	5.9	482	16.6	43.6	517	1,074	54	112,324	27.5	72.5	15	67.5	13	1
Osage	−2,883	(X)	925	20.5	21.4	367	397	33	35,489	47.6	52.4	2	1.6	(Z)	2
Osborne	4,785	8.1	449	8.7	52.1	499	1,111	34	76,800	51.8	48.2	6	56.1	4	1
Ottawa	2,867	5.4	512	11.1	41.4	416	812	49	95,961	41.5	58.5	5	91.6	3	1
Pawnee	15,052	10.0	430	13.5	45.1	520	1,210	139	324,381	22.4	77.6	79	99.6	76	1
Phillips	10,521	9.6	531	16.2	47.8	587	1,106	48	90,348	27.9	72.1	29	25.0	27	1
Pottawatomie	6,804	1.9	842	18.8	29.3	465	553	54	63,899	24.0	76.0	40	39.9	6	7
Pratt	12,082	6.3	591	10.3	39.6	501	848	131	221,095	30.0	70.0	85	100.0	81	2
Rawlins	6,277	13.6	405	8.6	65.4	651	1,607	35	85,247	51.4	48.6	23	99.9	21	1
Reno	20,883	1.8	1,570	21.7	26.4	735	468	112	71,127	49.5	50.5	70	100.0	44	8
Republic	7,742	10.6	642	9.7	42.8	424	660	83	129,276	46.7	53.3	35	84.9	32	1
Rice	9,679	7.4	500	18.4	41.2	416	832	106	211,574	31.7	68.3	25	100.0	21	2

See footnotes at end of table.

[Includes United States, states, and 3,141 counties/county equivalents defined as of February 22, 2005. For more information on these areas, see Appendix C, Geographic Information]

County	Farm earnings, 2005 Total ($1,000)	Per-cent of total[1]	Agriculture (NAICS 111–112), 2002 — Farms Number	Percent Less than 50 acres	Percent 500 acres or more	Land in farms Total acres (1,000)	Aver-age size of farm (acres)	Value of farm products sold Total (mil. dol.)	Average per farm (dol.)	Percent from Crops[2]	Percent from Live-stock and poultry[3]	Water use, 2000[4] Total (mil. gal. per day)	Ground water, percent of total	By selected major use (mil. gal. per day) Irri-gation	Public supply
KANSAS—Con.															
Riley	3,503	0.3	493	23.5	29.0	222	451	24	47,992	39.0	61.0	8	90.6	3	3
Rooks	5,160	5.9	485	12.8	46.2	560	1,155	40	82,790	34.3	65.7	18	20.6	17	1
Rush	3,031	6.1	504	11.1	41.5	418	829	29	57,724	58.5	41.5	10	99.4	9	1
Russell	2,751	2.9	617	13.6	37.1	484	784	28	45,629	47.4	52.6	1	12.7	–	1
Saline	585	(Z)	758	19.7	29.8	437	576	41	54,429	53.7	46.3	12	75.2	3	7
Scott	26,696	27.8	327	14.1	56.0	495	1,515	335	1,025,688	8.0	92.0	64	99.7	58	1
Sedgwick	4,488	(Z)	1,355	32.3	21.1	534	394	75	55,663	63.8	36.2	103	62.8	34	54
Seward	28,950	5.4	350	10.0	39.4	363	1,036	276	788,894	11.2	88.8	155	100.0	144	5
Shawnee	2,617	0.1	903	35.8	13.1	217	240	22	24,336	69.7	30.3	46	28.3	8	30
Sheridan	19,103	31.9	404	5.9	63.1	511	1,266	142	352,634	22.3	77.7	89	99.9	87	1
Sherman	11,446	11.0	443	5.6	57.6	607	1,369	68	153,736	52.3	47.7	130	100.0	127	2
Smith	7,266	12.8	546	11.9	53.7	518	949	46	83,650	48.8	51.2	5	85.0	4	1
Stafford	13,023	19.8	534	9.9	44.2	473	885	111	207,401	37.7	62.3	86	100.0	84	(Z)
Stanton	21,732	45.1	313	4.5	52.7	438	1,399	105	337,019	34.4	65.6	151	100.0	149	1
Stevens	34,810	29.5	401	9.7	46.4	491	1,223	152	378,731	37.6	62.4	216	100.0	212	1
Sumner	10,335	4.0	1,072	15.8	39.1	732	683	78	72,633	74.3	25.7	9	88.8	6	3
Thomas	27,681	16.3	476	7.8	59.7	690	1,450	93	195,252	48.0	52.0	123	100.0	120	2
Trego	1,300	3.1	423	11.6	54.4	455	1,075	40	93,563	29.5	70.5	6	96.1	5	(Z)
Wabaunsee	1,915	3.1	631	16.0	30.7	464	736	35	55,189	21.0	79.0	5	68.5	3	(Z)
Wallace	4,981	22.5	290	7.6	61.0	415	1,431	24	82,410	52.2	47.8	73	100.0	73	(Z)
Washington	16,359	21.0	796	16.5	35.9	497	624	82	102,698	30.9	69.1	8	72.6	5	1
Wichita	28,814	44.8	326	9.2	58.9	471	1,444	314	964,598	(NA)	(NA)	81	100.0	77	(Z)
Wilson	-2,440	(X)	556	13.1	35.3	337	607	32	57,002	64.8	35.2	3	1.1	1	1
Woodson	5,305	13.7	308	13.0	41.9	255	828	28	91,104	30.5	69.5	2	–	–	(Z)
Wyandotte	52	(Z)	161	68.3	3.1	14	86	3	18,062	79.2	20.8	398	0.8	(Z)	96
KENTUCKY	1,456,122	1.6	86,541	34.8	5.6	13,844	160	3,080	35,591	36.0	64.0	4,160	4.5	29	525
Adair	8,836	5.0	1,395	31.5	2.9	170	122	31	22,429	19.3	80.7	(6)	(NA)	(Z)	1
Allen	3,072	1.4	1,191	30.4	2.9	168	141	41	34,665	15.1	84.9	(6)	(NA)	(Z)	1
Anderson	-5,249	(X)	748	37.3	1.7	84	112	9	11,964	31.6	68.4	(6)	(NA)	(Z)	2
Ballard	33,614	17.1	486	33.7	11.3	113	233	34	70,646	44.7	55.3	(6)	(NA)	(Z)	1
Barren	21,255	2.9	2,021	37.4	3.8	240	119	63	31,071	25.5	74.5	(6)	(NA)	(Z)	6
Bath	-4,171	(X)	692	28.3	6.1	108	155	13	18,428	48.4	51.6	(6)	(NA)	(Z)	(Z)
Bell	-170	(X)	63	33.3	3.2	7	110	(Z)	3,429	27.9	72.1	(6)	(NA)	–	3
Boone	3,430	0.1	743	50.1	2.4	75	101	18	24,425	62.3	37.7	(6)	(NA)	(Z)	(Z)
Bourbon	54,965	15.1	913	38.2	11.0	185	202	98	107,129	18.0	82.0	(6)	(NA)	1	1
Boyd	-444	(X)	274	36.5	2.6	34	122	1	4,591	35.0	65.0	(6)	(NA)	(Z)	8
Boyle	-3,865	(X)	715	41.1	5.0	99	138	22	31,466	19.7	80.3	(6)	(NA)	(Z)	4
Bracken	-6,502	(X)	639	27.4	3.8	94	148	10	16,208	58.0	42.0	(6)	(NA)	(Z)	1
Breathitt	-1,669	(X)	209	29.7	13.9	51	245	1	6,426	72.0	28.0	(6)	(NA)	(Z)	1
Breckinridge	11,755	8.2	1,443	25.6	7.6	276	192	29	19,899	44.0	56.0	(6)	(NA)	(Z)	1
Bullitt	-2,717	(X)	616	50.3	2.9	61	100	7	11,735	48.4	51.6	(6)	(NA)	(Z)	–
Butler	11,776	9.2	729	19.1	9.2	162	222	19	26,196	37.0	63.0	(6)	(NA)	(Z)	1
Caldwell	23,148	12.0	673	25.0	9.2	147	219	18	26,664	68.1	31.9	(6)	(NA)	(Z)	1
Calloway	60,653	8.7	819	42.5	9.8	169	207	54	65,902	51.7	48.3	(6)	(NA)	(Z)	3
Campbell	-2,725	(X)	581	43.4	0.9	50	87	6	10,074	51.2	48.8	(6)	(NA)	(Z)	33
Carlisle	24,858	44.6	380	33.4	10.3	107	283	31	82,824	49.1	50.9	(6)	(NA)	1	(Z)
Carroll	-1,052	(X)	339	27.4	5.6	61	180	8	23,619	76.8	23.2	(6)	(NA)	(Z)	4
Carter	-3,554	(X)	925	28.6	3.0	120	130	7	7,603	50.5	49.5	(6)	(NA)	(Z)	3
Casey	4,594	3.2	1,353	29.7	3.9	191	141	22	16,052	38.0	62.0	(6)	(NA)	(Z)	1
Christian	50,640	1.3	1,267	27.8	12.0	342	270	77	60,798	69.7	30.3	(6)	(NA)	1	8
Clark	-1,708	(X)	861	41.0	7.4	143	166	25	29,367	28.3	71.7	(6)	(NA)	(Z)	6
Clay	-3,121	(X)	386	28.2	4.1	55	143	4	9,619	80.8	19.2	(6)	(NA)	(Z)	3
Clinton	12,682	9.3	629	39.1	3.2	72	114	21	32,769	14.0	86.0	(6)	(NA)	–	2
Crittenden	17,489	20.3	698	20.1	8.5	157	224	12	17,576	36.8	63.2	(6)	(NA)	(Z)	1
Cumberland	951	1.7	473	24.9	6.8	89	189	7	15,698	33.0	67.0	(6)	(NA)	(Z)	1
Daviess	37,575	2.0	1,062	43.6	11.1	254	239	63	59,070	73.4	26.6	(6)	(NA)	1	14
Edmonson	711	1.1	670	30.3	3.9	94	140	10	14,858	33.5	66.5	(6)	(NA)	–	1
Elliott	-999	(X)	427	26.5	3.5	56	131	3	6,602	64.7	35.3	(6)	(NA)	(Z)	(Z)
Estill	-1,725	(X)	457	25.6	3.7	64	140	4	8,444	41.8	58.2	(6)	(NA)	(Z)	1
Fayette	113,701	1.2	738	47.0	8.0	119	161	179	242,401	8.1	91.9	(6)	(NA)	(Z)	44
Fleming	-907	(X)	1,071	24.7	6.8	184	171	34	31,698	26.2	73.8	(6)	(NA)	(Z)	(Z)
Floyd	140	(Z)	68	45.6	1.5	7	99	1	7,500	87.1	12.9	(6)	(NA)	(Z)	4
Franklin	-3,252	(X)	689	35.8	2.9	82	119	12	17,624	60.6	39.4	(6)	(NA)	1	8
Fulton	32,930	24.6	193	31.1	28.5	112	581	30	156,342	65.7	34.3	(6)	(NA)	1	1
Gallatin	-2,069	(X)	247	28.7	5.3	38	152	4	15,348	64.6	35.4	(6)	(NA)	(Z)	1
Garrard	-7,492	(X)	873	31.0	3.9	120	137	21	24,281	29.4	70.6	(6)	(NA)	(Z)	1
Grant	-4,992	(X)	1,020	32.4	1.7	116	114	13	12,940	41.8	58.2	(6)	(NA)	(Z)	2
Graves	50,329	10.4	1,712	39.7	7.0	300	175	150	87,741	26.9	73.1	(6)	(NA)	(Z)	3
Grayson	15,986	5.2	1,650	30.1	4.3	233	141	32	19,177	23.9	76.1	(6)	(NA)	(Z)	3
Green	1,713	2.4	1,134	35.3	3.2	135	119	21	18,635	35.6	64.4	(6)	(NA)	(Z)	1
Greenup	3,502	0.8	728	29.4	3.6	103	142	5	7,471	56.5	43.5	(6)	(NA)	(Z)	3

See footnotes at end of table.

County and City Data Book: 2007

U.S. Census Bureau

Table B-14. Counties — **Farm Earnings, Agriculture, and Water Use**—Con.

[Includes United States, states, and 3,141 counties/county equivalents defined as of February 22, 2005. For more information on these areas, see Appendix C, Geographic Information]

County	Farm earnings, 2005 Total ($1,000)	Farm earnings, 2005 Percent of total[1]	Farms Number	Farms Percent Less than 50 acres	Farms Percent 500 acres or more	Land in farms Total acres (1,000)	Land in farms Average size of farm (acres)	Value of farm products sold Total (mil. dol.)	Value of farm products sold Average per farm (dol.)	Percent from Crops[2]	Percent from Live-stock and poultry[3]	Water use Total (mil. gal. per day)	Ground water, percent of total	Irrigation	Public supply
KENTUCKY—Con.															
Hancock	4,162	1.6	418	25.8	5.3	69	165	9	22,679	54.3	45.7	(6)	(NA)	(Z)	1
Hardin	16,468	0.6	1,732	44.5	5.7	240	138	36	20,726	51.2	48.8	(6)	(NA)	(Z)	9
Harlan	−167	(X)	23	47.8	–	2	81	(Z)	5,391	75.0	25.0	(6)	(NA)	(Z)	3
Harrison	−7,103	(X)	1,085	30.7	5.2	159	147	21	19,393	51.1	48.9	(6)	(NA)	1	2
Hart	3,230	2.0	1,392	27.1	3.4	195	140	30	21,392	35.3	64.7	(6)	(NA)	(Z)	3
Henderson	38,912	3.9	525	44.0	18.9	192	366	52	98,850	55.8	44.2	(6)	(NA)	1	8
Henry	−2,095	(X)	883	27.5	4.8	142	160	26	29,034	56.8	43.2	(6)	(NA)	1	2
Hickman	111,605	73.4	347	32.6	14.1	125	361	66	189,061	31.2	68.8	(6)	(NA)	1	(Z)
Hopkins	28,224	3.5	678	29.9	9.7	164	242	38	56,618	34.9	65.1	(6)	(NA)	(Z)	9
Jackson	−3,001	(X)	727	35.2	1.8	82	113	8	10,865	56.1	43.9	(6)	(NA)	–	1
Jefferson	5,359	(Z)	526	63.9	2.5	41	78	13	25,338	74.6	25.4	(6)	(NA)	1	140
Jessamine	9,423	1.4	770	50.5	3.8	82	107	50	64,594	15.9	84.1	(6)	(NA)	(Z)	4
Johnson	−1,101	(X)	195	35.4	2.6	24	122	1	6,313	81.2	18.8	(6)	(NA)	(Z)	2
Kenton	−3,743	(X)	495	38.4	1.8	46	94	5	10,729	53.2	46.8	(6)	(NA)	–	5
Knott	−238	(X)	22	22.7	9.1	4	204	(Z)	2,864	6.3	93.7	(6)	(NA)	–	(Z)
Knox	−370	(X)	347	37.8	4.3	41	119	2	7,199	65.9	34.1	(6)	(NA)	(Z)	(Z)
Larue	7,336	6.5	888	36.1	4.3	134	151	21	23,713	50.5	49.5	(6)	(NA)	(Z)	1
Laurel	−4,819	(X)	1,137	48.7	1.7	108	95	16	13,822	43.7	56.3	(6)	(NA)	(Z)	11
Lawrence	−1,576	(X)	318	20.8	6.3	57	179	2	5,635	58.0	42.0	(6)	(NA)	(Z)	1
Lee	160	0.2	173	32.9	4.0	23	136	1	6,647	54.1	45.9	(6)	(NA)	(Z)	1
Leslie	25[5]	(NA)	20	50.0	5.0	3	174	(Z)	1,700	82.4	17.6	(6)	(NA)	–	1
Letcher	25[5]	(NA)	46	54.3	–	3	62	(Z)	3,935	66.9	33.1	(6)	(NA)	(Z)	1
Lewis	304	0.4	733	22.5	7.9	144	196	9	12,951	59.4	40.6	(6)	(NA)	(Z)	1
Lincoln	4,785	2.7	1,275	38.5	4.9	171	134	35	27,511	32.7	67.3	(6)	(NA)	(Z)	2
Livingston	18,649	14.5	518	18.7	13.3	146	282	11	21,834	33.7	66.3	(6)	(NA)	(Z)	1
Logan	38,752	8.8	1,212	29.8	9.2	276	228	56	45,901	68.9	31.1	(6)	(NA)	(Z)	3
Lyon	3,478	4.5	304	23.4	6.3	56	186	5	15,474	63.1	36.9	(6)	(NA)	(Z)	2
McCracken	18,106	1.0	531	50.3	6.0	85	161	16	29,778	73.7	26.3	(6)	(NA)	(Z)	8
McCreary	−907	(X)	154	42.9	0.6	15	97	1	3,675	22.3	77.7	(6)	(NA)	–	1
McLean	63,980	48.8	413	33.2	17.2	129	312	65	156,816	32.0	68.0	(6)	(NA)	(Z)	1
Madison	−5,259	(X)	1,396	38.8	6.2	218	156	36	25,530	34.1	65.9	(6)	(NA)	(Z)	12
Magoffin	−958	(X)	345	38.3	3.8	46	132	2	4,806	71.2	28.8	(6)	(NA)	(Z)	1
Marion	20,095	6.8	1,054	33.2	5.6	171	162	29	27,281	30.1	69.9	(6)	(NA)	(Z)	4
Marshall	25,383	4.3	902	40.7	4.4	121	134	27	29,947	32.3	67.7	(6)	(NA)	(Z)	4
Martin	25[5]	(NA)	13	–	23.1	5	365	(Z)	9,154	7.6	92.4	(6)	(NA)	(Z)	3
Mason	−3,023	(X)	726	31.3	8.0	128	176	22	30,791	42.7	57.3	(6)	(NA)	(Z)	3
Meade	5,954	3.3	955	43.1	4.5	135	141	16	16,933	42.5	57.5	(6)	(NA)	(Z)	1
Menifee	−517	(X)	334	33.2	2.1	37	111	3	7,760	66.6	33.4	(6)	(NA)	(Z)	–
Mercer	−2,308	(X)	1,086	41.0	3.0	134	123	29	26,611	31.0	69.0	(6)	(NA)	(Z)	3
Metcalfe	16,495	15.7	950	33.2	3.9	132	139	30	31,349	19.8	80.2	(6)	(NA)	(Z)	–
Monroe	17,277	12.4	980	31.5	7.0	162	166	33	33,615	15.4	84.6	(6)	(NA)	(Z)	1
Montgomery	−2,243	(X)	676	37.9	4.7	91	135	16	23,146	32.8	67.2	(6)	(NA)	(Z)	2
Morgan	−4,876	(X)	804	25.5	4.4	116	144	8	9,505	54.9	45.1	(6)	(NA)	–	1
Muhlenberg	39,995	9.3	667	28.3	8.1	138	207	42	62,678	22.0	78.0	(6)	(NA)	(Z)	4
Nelson	2,677	0.4	1,407	39.2	4.1	189	134	33	23,626	33.2	66.8	(6)	(NA)	(Z)	4
Nicholas	−2,484	(X)	582	27.8	6.5	106	181	12	20,404	51.4	48.6	(6)	(NA)	(Z)	2
Ohio	24,415	8.6	1,006	29.7	5.1	167	166	61	61,087	18.5	81.5	(6)	(NA)	(Z)	2
Oldham	7,383	1.2	481	53.2	5.4	63	130	21	44,214	42.1	57.9	(6)	(NA)	2	4
Owen	−6,140	(X)	788	18.5	7.7	155	196	17	21,381	47.4	52.6	(6)	(NA)	1	2
Owsley	−1,267	(X)	227	24.7	4.4	33	145	2	7,533	83.1	16.9	(6)	(NA)	–	(Z)
Pendleton	−5,428	(X)	964	25.1	2.5	132	137	9	9,130	61.8	38.2	(6)	(NA)	(Z)	1
Perry	145	(Z)	44	38.6	15.9	7	161	1	13,045	40.8	59.2	(6)	(NA)	(Z)	4
Pike	25[5]	(NA)	45	35.6	4.4	7	160	(Z)	3,311	53.0	47.0	(6)	(NA)	(Z)	4
Powell	2,573	2.2	239	28.9	4.6	38	157	2	10,393	59.2	40.8	(6)	(NA)	–	1
Pulaski	11,577	1.2	1,977	36.3	2.5	232	117	35	17,713	35.4	64.6	(6)	(NA)	(Z)	7
Robertson	−2,994	(X)	247	20.2	5.7	43	174	2	10,065	63.3	36.7	(6)	(NA)	(Z)	–
Rockcastle	−3,589	(X)	803	36.5	2.9	94	117	9	11,481	41.2	58.8	(6)	(NA)	(Z)	2
Rowan	800	0.2	436	40.1	4.1	51	117	6	12,933	43.4	56.6	(6)	(NA)	–	5
Russell	701	0.3	930	44.3	2.7	97	105	23	24,263	21.2	78.8	(6)	(NA)	(Z)	3
Scott	14,717	1.0	848	37.6	6.5	137	162	49	57,236	27.1	72.9	(6)	(NA)	1	2
Shelby	67	(Z)	1,557	44.4	4.1	202	130	46	29,311	57.3	42.7	(6)	(NA)	1	3
Simpson	19,060	4.6	550	38.4	10.4	128	233	42	75,687	51.3	48.7	(6)	(NA)	(Z)	1
Spencer	−3,078	(X)	623	41.3	2.4	78	124	11	18,268	61.2	38.8	(6)	(NA)	(Z)	–
Taylor	1,987	0.5	957	39.1	3.7	112	117	20	20,972	39.9	60.1	(6)	(NA)	(Z)	3
Todd	37,888	27.1	676	25.0	12.9	184	272	62	92,414	51.7	48.3	(6)	(NA)	(Z)	1
Trigg	11,845	6.4	425	28.0	11.5	123	289	20	47,047	71.6	28.4	(6)	(NA)	(Z)	2
Trimble	−4,030	(X)	562	40.0	3.0	65	115	6	11,512	70.2	29.8	(6)	(NA)	(Z)	1
Union	43,448	14.6	328	30.2	25.0	209	637	43	132,155	87.7	12.3	(6)	(NA)	1	2
Warren	27,502	1.1	1,881	44.3	4.1	255	136	61	32,684	38.7	61.3	(6)	(NA)	(Z)	17
Washington	6,502	4.6	1,119	27.8	2.7	150	134	27	24,182	44.9	55.1	(6)	(NA)	(Z)	1

See footnotes at end of table.

Table B-14. Counties — **Farm Earnings, Agriculture, and Water Use**—Con.

[Includes United States, states, and 3,141 counties/county equivalents defined as of February 22, 2005. For more information on these areas, see Appendix C, Geographic Information]

County	Farm earnings, 2005 Total ($1,000)	Percent of total[1]	Farms Number	Farms Percent Less than 50 acres	Farms Percent 500 acres or more	Land in farms Total acres (1,000)	Land in farms Average size of farm (acres)	Value of farm products sold Total (mil. dol.)	Value Average per farm (dol.)	Percent from Crops[2]	Percent from Livestock and poultry[3]	Water use Total (mil. gal. per day)	Ground water, percent of total	By selected major use Irrigation	By selected major use Public supply
KENTUCKY—Con.															
Wayne	24,895	10.4	860	35.3	7.0	139	162	44	50,917	13.0	87.0	(6)	(NA)	(Z)	2
Webster	106,071	37.9	595	26.4	10.9	159	268	77	129,993	22.1	77.9	(6)	(NA)	(Z)	6
Whitley	−110	(X)	530	34.5	2.8	64	121	5	9,138	24.8	75.2	(6)	(NA)	–	1
Wolfe	−402	(X)	371	26.7	6.5	60	161	3	6,749	78.6	21.4	(6)	(NA)	(Z)	(Z)
Woodford	145,652	22.5	708	43.1	9.7	123	174	172	242,821	5.6	94.4	(6)	(NA)	1	3
LOUISIANA	461,215	0.5	27,413	41.2	13.9	7,831	286	1,816	66,239	58.7	41.3	10,400	15.7	1,020	753
Acadia	−5,369	(X)	751	42.9	20.0	257	342	33	44,150	89.8	10.2	186	78.5	162	5
Allen	−1,051	(X)	360	40.3	15.6	103	286	8	23,456	61.0	39.0	39	95.1	34	3
Ascension	2,548	0.1	329	61.4	6.7	50	151	19	57,325	88.1	11.9	217	6.1	(Z)	5
Assumption	6,384	2.9	105	38.1	43.8	66	628	36	343,229	93.9	6.1	30	46.7	–	5
Avoyelles	17,726	4.4	890	39.3	16.2	272	305	52	58,940	90.9	9.1	23	80.8	17	4
Beauregard	1,043	0.3	793	36.7	7.3	143	180	11	14,352	21.5	78.5	30	99.8	4	4
Bienville	5,006	2.7	222	37.8	5.4	44	198	24	108,225	1.5	98.5	13	99.3	–	2
Bossier	−1,495	(X)	456	46.7	12.1	107	235	9	19,939	35.6	64.4	14	30.9	(Z)	12
Caddo	3,579	0.1	555	39.1	16.6	172	309	24	44,036	64.2	35.8	146	3.9	3	48
Calcasieu	−3,704	(X)	870	49.3	11.5	303	349	16	18,121	50.5	49.5	367	35.4	32	25
Caldwell	2,031	2.1	285	38.6	11.6	61	213	5	17,418	79.1	20.9	2	73.5	1	2
Cameron	−303	(X)	409	30.3	27.1	249	608	6	15,352	(NA)	(NA)	30	28.5	24	2
Catahoula	15,883	15.8	435	21.4	26.9	232	534	29	65,706	83.7	16.3	31	99.4	26	1
Claiborne	19,764	9.2	275	26.2	10.2	56	202	52	189,051	1.5	98.5	3	99.2	–	2
Concordia	15,759	7.3	336	19.0	34.5	212	630	29	87,143	89.8	10.2	48	53.2	30	4
De Soto	4,467	1.2	628	35.7	9.7	137	218	18	28,317	8.0	92.0	22	11.0	(Z)	3
East Baton Rouge	−1,651	(X)	489	56.9	5.1	61	126	11	23,100	51.1	48.9	154	88.0	(Z)	64
East Carroll	13,745	16.2	234	11.5	41.0	217	925	45	192,137	97.1	2.9	42	85.1	40	1
East Feliciana	3,241	1.4	460	41.3	13.5	123	268	7	16,220	16.0	84.0	4	94.8	(Z)	3
Evangeline	6,502	2.3	648	38.9	15.3	184	284	22	34,573	81.6	18.4	182	30.7	50	6
Franklin	24,616	12.1	856	28.6	16.7	258	302	60	69,565	74.4	25.6	50	93.3	23	2
Grant	614	0.4	196	41.8	9.7	36	182	3	16,964	56.1	43.9	6	32.9	–	4
Iberia	5,401	0.3	340	60.9	17.6	111	327	53	155,065	98.0	2.0	30	65.2	2	9
Iberville	5,298	0.6	183	36.1	28.4	97	528	44	243,153	95.6	4.4	1,159	2.4	–	3
Jackson	14,432	7.7	235	47.7	1.7	21	89	32	136,464	2.7	97.3	2	100.0	–	2
Jefferson	2,436	(Z)	52	40.4	7.7	8	147	2	32,346	90.3	9.7	1,147	0.3	(Z)	85
Jefferson Davis	−1,077	(X)	641	37.4	30.9	323	504	32	50,415	86.6	13.4	170	84.7	157	4
Lafayette	568	(Z)	715	71.2	5.0	75	105	20	28,354	88.3	11.7	42	92.6	11	21
Lafourche	4,797	0.3	405	38.5	11.9	151	373	27	66,067	83.5	16.5	47	3.5	–	23
La Salle	−143	(X)	161	41.0	1.9	17	105	1	6,348	18.3	81.7	3	88.7	(Z)	3
Lincoln	18,418	2.4	392	35.7	6.4	66	168	70	179,240	3.3	96.7	9	99.7	(Z)	8
Livingston	3,415	0.4	451	65.6	2.4	34	76	7	15,683	18.3	81.7	12	99.6	(Z)	10
Madison	10,692	8.5	274	18.2	43.8	237	865	45	164,825	98.7	1.3	18	93.7	15	2
Morehouse	25,961	7.7	412	21.6	34.2	245	595	51	123,910	97.3	2.7	75	52.2	46	4
Natchitoches	23,687	3.6	565	28.7	14.7	193	341	57	101,315	16.2	83.8	33	11.8	10	6
Orleans	–	–	8	100.0	–	(D)	(D)	(Z)	5,125	(NA)	(NA)	743	0.7	(Z)	155
Ouachita	6,534	0.2	493	44.0	10.3	95	192	20	40,164	50.3	49.7	236	10.7	13	23
Plaquemines	818	0.1	192	75.0	6.3	35	181	7	34,391	67.9	32.1	104	0.1	(Z)	8
Pointe Coupee	6,410	2.8	465	35.3	21.7	199	429	52	111,133	89.9	10.1	294	6.5	3	4
Rapides	14,918	0.5	996	47.3	9.7	201	202	67	66,976	82.4	17.6	452	8.1	10	29
Red River	2,762	2.8	236	30.5	20.8	138	587	11	44,822	53.6	46.4	2	81.7	1	1
Richland	9,875	4.6	536	22.8	24.1	216	403	28	51,396	86.9	13.1	41	83.4	36	3
Sabine	27,413	11.3	403	34.7	6.5	63	155	67	165,501	0.7	99.3	5	45.8	(Z)	2
St. Bernard	[5]25	(NA)	24	58.3	8.3	(D)	(D)	(Z)	15,667	67.8	32.2	281	(Z)	–	10
St. Charles	1,093	0.1	62	38.7	4.8	9	141	5	85,548	(NA)	(NA)	2,701	0.1	–	10
St. Helena	17,517	21.6	326	31.3	6.1	51	156	20	62,822	2.7	97.3	1	99.1	–	(Z)
St. James	5,926	1.4	69	26.1	42.0	53	765	27	386,217	99.5	0.5	245	2.1	–	3
St. John the Baptist	982	0.1	34	29.4	32.4	22	647	6	170,353	99.5	0.5	94	11.0	–	7
St. Landry	8,937	0.9	1,228	52.4	12.0	290	236	52	42,331	83.8	16.2	63	82.9	28	9
St. Martin	6,189	1.7	328	52.7	16.2	81	246	28	86,329	92.5	7.5	59	21.7	7	6
St. Mary	1,902	0.2	99	23.2	47.5	73	742	36	358,869	98.2	1.8	200	1.5	–	11
St. Tammany	2,289	0.1	603	71.5	3.2	51	85	13	20,748	52.5	47.5	26	97.5	1	18
Tangipahoa	16,625	1.2	1,065	49.8	3.3	118	111	57	53,275	15.1	84.9	18	96.7	1	13
Tensas	12,258	18.8	228	11.4	45.2	226	992	49	213,974	99.7	0.3	17	90.6	16	1
Terrebonne	2,131	0.1	156	45.5	19.2	53	340	15	98,231	62.1	37.9	7	1.8	–	6
Union	47,711	19.1	504	38.7	4.4	73	144	121	239,567	0.7	99.3	6	96.9	–	5
Vermilion	−4,571	(X)	1,116	43.0	16.9	359	322	53	47,047	86.4	13.6	226	78.4	190	5
Vernon	4,047	0.3	460	45.4	3.0	50	108	9	18,809	4.7	95.3	8	98.0	–	6
Washington	2,974	0.7	836	42.0	2.2	102	122	35	42,197	21.2	78.8	36	66.5	–	10
Webster	1,987	0.4	426	39.2	4.2	57	133	8	17,688	7.9	92.1	7	97.0	–	6
West Baton Rouge	11,267	2.4	108	57.4	10.2	22	199	29	265,869	(NA)	(NA)	20	79.7	–	6
West Carroll	9,318	7.9	709	24.1	15.1	184	259	31	44,017	91.7	8.3	32	90.9	30	1
West Feliciana	−310	(X)	165	30.3	23.0	68	413	5	30,945	64.5	35.5	50	12.2	–	5
Winn	1,022	0.5	130	26.9	4.6	21	159	5	38,623	10.4	89.6	4	97.1	–	2

See footnotes at end of table.

[Includes United States, states, and 3,141 counties/county equivalents defined as of February 22, 2005. For more information on these areas, see Appendix C, Geographic Information]

County	Farm earnings, 2005 Total ($1,000)	Farm earnings, 2005 Percent of total[1]	Farms Number	Farms Percent Less than 50 acres	Farms Percent 500 acres or more	Land in farms Total acres (1,000)	Land in farms Average size of farm (acres)	Value of farm products sold Total (mil. dol.)	Value of farm products sold Average per farm (dol.)	Percent from Crops[2]	Percent from Livestock and poultry[3]	Water use, 2000[4] Total (mil. gal. per day)	Water use Ground water, percent of total	By selected major use (mil. gal. per day) Irrigation	By selected major use (mil. gal. per day) Public supply
MAINE	117,376	0.4	7,196	38.6	8.0	1,370	190	464	64,425	48.0	52.0	799	10.1	6	102
Androscoggin	13,535	0.6	334	40.7	7.5	56	167	97	289,368	7.4	92.6	(6)	(NA)	(Z)	10
Aroostook	32,810	2.6	1,084	15.9	17.8	392	361	121	111,769	96.8	3.2	(6)	(NA)	2	6
Cumberland	7,728	0.1	596	60.7	3.2	54	91	18	29,520	66.9	33.1	(6)	(NA)	1	28
Franklin	761	0.1	317	32.2	6.3	50	157	6	18,874	24.2	75.8	(6)	(NA)	(Z)	3
Hancock	5,640	0.5	317	46.1	7.6	50	156	29	90,467	(NA)	(NA)	(6)	(NA)	(Z)	4
Kennebec	8,492	0.3	575	36.5	6.6	86	150	30	52,572	22.8	77.2	(6)	(NA)	(Z)	8
Knox	877	0.1	275	50.9	2.2	29	104	5	18,349	69.7	30.3	(6)	(NA)	(Z)	3
Lincoln	2,059	0.4	292	45.9	2.7	31	105	8	25,829	47.0	53.0	(6)	(NA)	(Z)	1
Oxford	4,295	0.6	469	48.0	6.8	67	144	15	31,239	76.6	23.4	(6)	(NA)	1	3
Penobscot	6,997	0.2	575	35.8	9.4	107	186	29	50,357	34.9	65.1	(6)	(NA)	1	10
Piscataquis	1,855	0.7	201	32.3	10.0	39	196	4	19,075	(NA)	(NA)	(6)	(NA)	(Z)	1
Sagadahoc	1,203	0.1	158	37.3	4.4	20	128	4	27,032	(NA)	(NA)	(6)	(NA)	(Z)	2
Somerset	6,186	0.7	504	25.6	10.9	110	219	24	48,200	26.3	73.7	(6)	(NA)	(Z)	3
Waldo	3,603	0.7	415	35.7	6.7	69	167	15	35,318	20.0	80.0	(6)	(NA)	(Z)	1
Washington	15,696	3.3	399	40.9	8.0	152	382	41	103,544	43.8	56.2	(6)	(NA)	1	1
York	5,639	0.2	685	55.8	2.3	57	84	19	27,372	76.8	23.2	(6)	(NA)	(Z)	16
MARYLAND	352,785	0.2	12,198	47.8	7.8	2,078	170	1,293	106,026	34.8	65.2	7,910	2.8	42	824
Allegany	−325	(X)	278	30.2	5.8	39	142	2	7,680	45.2	54.8	49	2.8	(Z)	1
Anne Arundel	5,638	(Z)	432	65.0	3.0	35	82	11	25,412	90.3	9.7	824	5.2	1	31
Baltimore	36,095	0.2	784[7]	62.8[7]	3.1[7]	71[7]	91[7]	62[7]	79,286[7]	74.3[7]	25.7[7]	901	1.0	1	271
Calvert	−659	(X)	321	51.7	1.9	30	94	3	10,106	87.5	12.5	3,277	0.2	(Z)	2
Caroline	13,676	3.2	506	39.9	14.2	115	227	104	206,241	27.6	72.4	21	72.9	15	1
Carroll	17,325	0.7	1,058	52.6	5.0	147	139	69	65,176	45.2	54.8	15	66.2	(Z)	7
Cecil	23,146	1.5	468	51.5	7.9	77	165	69	146,607	44.1	55.9	9	72.3	1	4
Charles	−1,207	(X)	418	49.5	4.1	52	125	6	15,273	74.4	25.6	1,205	1.0	(Z)	7
Dorchester	12,921	2.3	351	38.5	22.5	125	357	84	238,934	30.6	69.4	14	89.5	9	2
Frederick	30,624	0.6	1,273	44.1	5.8	196	154	97	76,004	21.4	78.6	39	35.2	1	15
Garrett	10,971	2.1	634	24.6	4.9	101	160	21	32,897	18.0	82.0	9	35.2	(Z)	3
Harford	24,385	0.5	683	58.9	4.8	81	119	26	38,205	49.6	50.4	18	71.0	(Z)	9
Howard	15,457	0.2	346	64.2	5.5	38	109	22	62,604	75.8	24.2	3	87.9	1	–
Kent	22,812	5.9	318	25.8	19.5	117	369	67	210,176	56.8	43.2	4	91.3	2	1
Montgomery	17,709	(Z)	577	60.3	5.7	75	130	42	72,156	87.0	13.0	708	0.6	1	380
Prince George's	15,475	0.1	452	58.8	3.8	45	101	12	27,009	86.2	13.8	625	0.9	1	52
Queen Anne's	12,373	1.9	443	35.9	21.7	156	351	66	149,038	68.9	31.1	8	83.1	4	2
St. Mary's	3,404	0.1	577	46.3	3.6	68	118	12	21,137	73.7	26.3	9	96.6	(Z)	4
Somerset	9,480	2.8	301	43.9	10.0	57	188	127	422,847	7.0	93.0	4	99.5	(Z)	2
Talbot	8,142	0.9	288	36.1	20.5	106	367	33	116,149	42.8	57.2	6	92.2	1	2
Washington	7,901	0.3	775	40.1	5.4	125	161	60	76,874	18.6	81.4	81	12.6	(Z)	14
Wicomico	42,426	2.0	512	54.9	9.8	88	173	175	341,004	15.0	85.0	16	96.3	4	6
Worcester	25,016	2.6	403	43.7	16.1	131	326	123	306,328	13.1	86.9	13	97.0	1	8
Independent City															
Baltimore city	–	–	(7)	(NA)	(NA)	(7)	(7)	(7)	(NA)	(NA)	(NA)	55	0.2	–	–
MASSACHUSETTS	118,981	0.1	6,075	60.0	2.7	519	85	384	63,262	72.1	27.9	4,660	5.8	126	739
Barnstable	3,546	0.1	285	89.1	–	6	21	14	48,516	62.2	37.8	400	6.7	12	26
Berkshire	3,884	0.1	401	43.9	10.2	69	171	22	54,177	44.7	55.3	33	24.2	1	19
Bristol	18,965	0.2	624	66.8	1.1	36	58	29	47,053	76.0	24.0	1,215	1.5	8	58
Dukes	1,281	0.3	83	86.7	2.4	8	94	1	17,518	61.6	38.4	3	89.5	(Z)	2
Essex	11,197	0.1	400	71.5	3.0	28	70	24	61,173	82.0	18.0	685	1.0	2	74
Franklin	11,487	0.9	586	36.5	4.3	74	127	43	73,200	63.4	36.6	9	61.3	1	5
Hampden	7,751	0.1	458	54.4	1.7	38	82	24	51,716	85.3	14.7	176	11.2	1	54
Hampshire	8,755	0.3	542	50.6	2.4	51	94	35	64,721	68.7	31.3	17	61.3	1	12
Middlesex	32,121	(Z)	579	68.0	0.9	33	57	66	113,843	83.7	16.3	834	6.7	4	67
Nantucket	–	–	13	84.6	–	(D)	(D)	3	205,923	100.0	–	4	47.6	3	1
Norfolk	4,545	(Z)	208	81.3	2.4	13	61	11	54,356	93.1	6.9	48	71.5	2	45
Plymouth	3,506	(Z)	794	70.7	2.3	59	75	43	54,142	94.1	5.9	576	7.1	87	40
Suffolk	–	–	8	87.5	–	(D)	(D)	(Z)	44,250	80.2	19.8	303	0.6	(Z)	–
Worcester	11,943	0.1	1,094	51.4	2.4	104	95	69	62,682	50.8	49.2	359	10.2	3	337
MICHIGAN	820,687	0.3	53,315	41.1	9.0	10,143	190	3,772	70,757	62.6	37.4	10,000	7.3	201	1,140
Alcona	1,500	1.8	244	27.9	9.4	41	168	6	22,816	49.6	50.4	1	96.0	(Z)	(Z)
Alger	429	0.3	67	23.9	11.9	15	223	2	22,552	33.2	66.8	7	20.9	(Z)	1
Allegan	58,783	3.1	1,489	49.4	7.0	243	163	230	154,646	48.9	51.1	26	76.7	7	5
Alpena	−1,020	(X)	460	28.7	6.3	74	160	13	27,289	33.4	66.6	129	1.5	(Z)	3
Antrim	4,104	1.5	382	33.8	6.0	63	166	16	41,503	69.8	30.2	4	97.6	2	1
Arenac	5,933	2.8	381	32.5	12.1	84	220	23	59,136	72.6	27.4	38	3.5	(Z)	36
Baraga	79	0.1	63	27.0	12.7	15	241	1	17,778	57.8	42.2	2	19.8	(Z)	1
Barry	7,465	1.1	1,063	40.9	7.4	182	171	48	45,007	39.9	60.1	7	92.3	1	2
Bay	7,319	0.4	787	38.8	13.6	186	236	59	75,442	91.9	8.1	678	0.3	2	10
Benzie	2,985	1.6	181	35.4	3.3	23	127	4	23,326	79.2	20.8	3	99.6	1	1

See footnotes at end of table.

Table B-14. Counties — **Farm Earnings, Agriculture, and Water Use**—Con.

[Includes United States, states, and 3,141 counties/county equivalents defined as of February 22, 2005. For more information on these areas, see Appendix C, Geographic Information]

County	Farm earnings, 2005 Total ($1,000)	Farm earnings, 2005 Per-cent of total[1]	Agriculture (NAICS 111–112), 2002 Farms Number	Farms Percent Less than 50 acres	Farms Percent 500 acres or more	Land in farms Total acres (1,000)	Land in farms Aver-age size of farm (acres)	Value of farm products sold Total (mil. dol.)	Value of farm products sold Average per farm (dol.)	Percent from Crops[2]	Percent from Live-stock and poultry[3]	Water use, 2000[4] Total (mil. gal. per day)	Ground water, percent of total	By selected major use (mil. gal. per day) Irri-gation	By selected major use (mil. gal. per day) Public supply
MICHIGAN—Con.															
Berrien	29,049	0.9	1,093	53.4	7.6	174	159	97	88,487	87.4	12.6	1,141	1.4	7	17
Branch	16,030	2.3	1,123	36.7	11.1	254	226	65	57,795	60.5	39.5	18	71.1	11	3
Calhoun	13,004	0.4	1,147	32.8	10.1	240	209	64	56,184	56.1	43.9	34	85.5	5	15
Cass	15,572	3.0	808	41.6	11.9	189	234	64	79,545	59.4	40.6	15	88.5	9	2
Charlevoix	885	0.2	299	42.1	4.3	39	130	4	13,348	46.1	53.9	45	28.4	1	2
Cheboygan	1,118	0.3	268	35.1	7.5	50	187	7	24,612	43.2	56.8	4	92.1	(Z)	2
Chippewa	1,306	0.2	372	16.7	12.4	94	252	6	15,565	45.1	54.9	5	45.0	(Z)	3
Clare	3,210	0.9	414	30.9	6.0	64	155	12	27,923	18.0	82.0	4	84.1	1	1
Clinton	21,715	2.3	1,179	39.5	10.1	256	217	99	83,681	42.0	58.0	9	96.0	1	3
Crawford	–	–	47	46.8	10.6	6	134	(Z)	3,170	(NA)	(NA)	2	96.7	(Z)	1
Delta	2,237	0.3	273	19.0	15.4	74	272	10	37,432	47.2	52.8	65	3.7	1	2
Dickinson	165	(Z)	146	32.2	7.5	29	196	4	25,801	43.8	56.2	22	18.1	(Z)	3
Eaton	5,434	0.3	1,221	41.0	9.0	238	195	53	43,435	76.2	23.8	10	85.2	1	3
Emmet	647	0.1	274	33.9	6.2	44	159	6	21,412	48.6	51.4	6	100.0	1	3
Genesee	3,460	(Z)	1,051	59.1	6.6	143	136	29	28,004	73.6	26.4	22	94.8	2	7
Gladwin	2,949	1.5	534	29.4	4.9	72	135	8	15,571	58.6	41.4	2	98.8	(Z)	1
Gogebic	–270	(X)	49	32.7	–	4	82	(Z)	4,102	78.5	21.5	3	100.0	–	2
Grand Traverse	3,811	0.2	489	49.9	5.1	62	127	11	23,243	66.5	33.5	12	56.4	1	6
Gratiot	17,344	2.7	1,018	35.6	15.3	289	284	115	112,697	56.2	43.8	6	80.5	1	3
Hillsdale	20,591	2.8	1,509	40.1	8.1	275	182	79	52,296	51.8	48.2	8	85.1	2	2
Houghton	[5]25	(NA)	158	29.1	5.1	26	164	3	17,854	48.4	51.6	5	99.4	(Z)	4
Huron	23,958	3.9	1,189	29.4	21.6	432	363	211	177,056	51.6	48.4	82	5.2	1	3
Ingham	12,922	0.1	1,018	54.9	8.4	185	182	51	50,438	67.3	32.7	249	15.8	2	34
Ionia	18,378	2.4	1,146	41.4	10.6	230	201	113	98,668	32.0	68.0	10	95.3	1	5
Iosco	3,156	1.0	285	37.2	7.4	45	156	13	45,568	20.2	79.8	3	53.3	1	1
Iron	–289	(X)	106	25.5	10.4	31	296	3	30,321	84.6	15.4	3	92.7	(Z)	2
Isabella	13,403	1.1	953	31.1	9.0	195	205	50	52,598	48.4	51.6	7	95.3	1	4
Jackson	6,252	0.2	1,265	46.2	6.0	193	153	43	34,068	49.2	50.8	21	95.4	2	13
Kalamazoo	32,248	0.5	808	53.7	9.5	148	183	155	191,312	70.5	29.5	84	79.1	6	26
Kalkaska	–197	(X)	175	38.3	4.0	24	138	6	32,206	87.2	12.8	4	93.4	2	1
Kent	46,459	0.2	1,212	51.5	5.5	173	143	150	123,490	75.5	24.5	76	38.3	4	51
Keweenaw	–	–	11	54.5	–	1	65	(D)	(NA)	(NA)	(NA)	(Z)	90.9	(Z)	(Z)
Lake	327	0.4	173	31.2	5.2	23	135	2	12,237	46.6	53.4	1	97.4	(Z)	(Z)
Lapeer	7,505	0.7	1,187	47.7	8.6	189	159	51	42,641	65.8	34.2	8	85.2	1	(Z)
Leelanau	7,995	2.8	429	35.2	4.9	62	145	16	37,268	78.4	21.6	3	96.8	1	(Z)
Lenawee	12,909	0.8	1,446	37.6	13.7	353	244	103	71,478	62.2	37.8	12	68.9	1	6
Livingston	3,559	0.1	877	60.2	4.6	96	110	25	29,032	64.6	35.4	18	97.9	2	6
Luce	894	1.1	30	33.3	23.3	10	342	3	87,833	85.1	14.9	1	100.0	(Z)	1
Mackinac	146	0.1	76	17.1	13.2	20	269	3	37,066	17.4	82.6	10	8.3	(Z)	2
Macomb	17,479	0.1	512	58.2	5.9	68	133	44	85,531	91.2	8.8	13	53.3	2	5
Manistee	2,653	0.7	315	31.4	5.1	46	147	8	25,495	85.9	14.1	43	10.9	1	2
Marquette	–198	(X)	160	39.4	8.1	30	188	4	23,106	48.9	51.1	294	1.6	(Z)	6
Mason	9,190	2.0	478	32.8	7.3	80	167	25	52,207	66.3	33.7	23	11.7	1	2
Mecosta	7,388	1.4	794	27.3	5.4	120	151	31	38,544	43.8	56.2	7	74.2	3	1
Menominee	8,404	2.4	372	17.2	13.7	99	265	21	56,962	14.4	85.6	5	30.4	(Z)	1
Midland	1,155	0.1	510	43.5	8.2	85	166	22	42,627	66.3	33.7	9	33.0	(Z)	(Z)
Missaukee	12,631	9.1	412	23.5	12.4	98	237	40	95,983	27.1	72.9	2	95.2	1	(Z)
Monroe	19,698	0.8	1,183	51.2	10.1	217	184	92	77,974	93.4	6.6	1,734	1.2	3	13
Montcalm	17,415	2.0	1,139	35.2	9.3	255	224	106	93,338	68.3	31.7	27	87.7	19	4
Montmorency	792	0.8	139	23.0	4.3	21	152	3	23,986	34.6	65.4	1	84.7	(Z)	(Z)
Muskegon	10,713	0.3	545	55.2	5.1	74	136	46	84,956	63.8	36.2	323	4.1	4	18
Newaygo	13,451	2.6	902	37.7	6.3	135	150	61	67,481	34.1	65.9	8	91.7	2	3
Oakland	15,591	(Z)	643	71.4	1.9	41	64	45	70,698	91.3	8.7	50	96.6	4	23
Oceana	20,693	7.1	648	33.0	9.0	127	197	58	90,096	68.1	31.9	6	87.7	1	1
Ogemaw	5,273	2.1	256	23.8	14.8	68	265	23	88,828	18.2	81.8	3	94.8	(Z)	(Z)
Ontonagon	476	0.5	108	9.3	18.5	34	312	2	22,343	20.3	79.7	20	2.0	(Z)	(Z)
Osceola	4,269	1.1	591	25.7	8.3	116	196	19	32,462	24.0	76.0	5	96.6	1	3
Oscoda	591	0.7	123	33.3	3.3	17	138	3	27,976	9.8	90.2	1	81.8	(Z)	(Z)
Otsego	–788	(X)	170	32.9	12.9	35	203	5	27,859	72.6	27.4	4	98.7	1	1
Ottawa	87,851	1.5	1,291	54.3	5.0	165	128	278	214,952	59.4	40.6	734	2.0	8	41
Presque Isle	2,699	2.0	303	19.8	9.2	68	225	11	37,307	65.2	34.8	8	35.3	2	1
Roscommon	[5]25	(NA)	46	39.1	8.7	7	161	(D)	(NA)	(NA)	(NA)	3	99.6	(Z)	(Z)
Saginaw	9,037	0.2	1,359	38.8	12.1	325	239	91	67,132	88.2	11.8	18	19.6	2	12
St. Clair	5,237	0.2	1,260	48.7	5.2	182	145	40	31,910	78.0	22.0	1,717	0.3	(Z)	172
St. Joseph	10,915	1.0	907	40.2	12.7	231	254	94	103,264	81.2	18.8	58	73.5	44	4
Sanilac	29,700	5.6	1,595	29.8	15.4	435	273	137	85,826	56.2	43.8	8	91.9	3	2
Schoolcraft	–240	(X)	51	33.3	15.7	14	266	2	29,804	54.9	45.1	12	4.8	(Z)	1
Shiawassee	8,246	1.1	1,037	38.2	12.2	235	226	44	42,906	72.5	27.5	8	93.3	1	3
Tuscola	12,657	2.2	1,292	35.9	13.5	336	260	94	72,598	77.6	22.4	9	80.2	3	2

See footnotes at end of table.

Table B-14. Counties — **Farm Earnings, Agriculture, and Water Use**—Con.

[Includes United States, states, and 3,141 counties/county equivalents defined as of February 22, 2005. For more information on these areas, see Appendix C, Geographic Information]

County	Farm earnings, 2005 Total ($1,000)	Farm earnings, 2005 Percent of total[1]	Farms Number	Farms Percent Less than 50 acres	Farms Percent 500 acres or more	Land in farms Total acres (1,000)	Land in farms Average size of farm (acres)	Value of farm products sold Total (mil. dol.)	Value of farm products sold Average per farm (dol.)	Value Percent from Crops[2]	Value Percent from Live-stock and poultry[3]	Water use Total (mil. gal. per day)	Water use Ground water, percent of total	Water use Irrigation	Water use Public supply
MICHIGAN—Con.															
Van Buren	31,892	3.2	1,160	45.3	4.6	176	152	97	83,383	87.7	12.3	152	10.3	8	4
Washtenaw	8,303	0.1	1,325	51.4	6.5	175	132	55	41,221	68.6	31.4	34	47.4	3	21
Wayne	9,273	(Z)	319	74.0	2.5	21	67	28	86,392	97.8	2.2	1,727	(Z)	2	493
Wexford	2,776	0.4	395	40.5	3.0	46	116	10	24,101	66.9	33.1	8	98.6	(Z)	3
MINNESOTA	1,818,993	1.2	80,839	24.9	19.0	27,512	340	8,576	106,083	53.2	46.8	3,870	18.6	227	500
Aitkin	−1,338	(X)	674	16.9	11.9	174	259	12	18,082	56.3	43.7	4	37.5	2	(Z)
Anoka	6,407	0.1	552	55.8	4.9	60	109	50	90,112	86.5	13.5	132	19.8	3	124
Becker	27,547	4.8	1,254	15.3	14.2	417	332	98	78,441	47.2	52.8	9	99.4	5	2
Beltrami	2,935	0.4	746	14.3	17.0	233	312	17	23,209	26.5	73.5	7	55.6	3	2
Benton	13,671	1.7	965	27.4	8.3	196	203	88	91,518	21.9	78.1	22	54.5	8	3
Big Stone	10,435	12.9	446	14.1	40.8	274	614	58	129,305	77.9	22.1	1	97.1	1	1
Blue Earth	67,540	4.1	1,125	27.3	25.0	406	361	210	186,960	46.4	53.6	33	36.1	(Z)	5
Brown	49,346	7.9	1,047	19.0	22.4	348	333	165	157,983	44.0	56.0	5	96.3	1	2
Carlton	−1,416	(X)	607	15.7	5.6	114	188	8	13,338	34.8	65.2	11	27.1	(Z)	2
Carver	11,704	0.6	820	35.6	8.9	172	210	62	76,067	48.3	51.7	10	97.9	1	7
Cass	1,922	0.5	646	11.8	13.8	197	305	14	22,176	27.6	72.4	4	98.5	1	(Z)
Chippewa	15,721	5.9	694	21.6	32.0	340	489	103	148,244	85.3	14.7	2	81.9	(Z)	1
Chisago	4,683	0.7	943	46.1	3.5	117	124	29	30,487	70.1	29.9	5	86.0	1	2
Clay	13,818	1.9	877	20.2	33.1	601	685	135	153,847	83.5	16.5	7	41.4	1	5
Clearwater	2,608	2.5	627	10.2	17.9	226	361	20	31,941	45.0	55.0	12	8.7	11	(Z)
Cook	−	−	20	25.0	5.0	3	163	(Z)	17,400	81.0	19.0	296	0.1	(Z)	(Z)
Cottonwood	50,318	20.8	832	21.8	33.5	375	450	147	176,512	51.9	48.1	4	86.2	1	1
Crow Wing	−418	(X)	755	24.2	7.4	145	192	14	18,181	36.5	63.5	11	68.1	2	3
Dakota	15,864	0.2	997	44.1	11.7	236	236	112	112,337	66.5	33.5	243	25.2	15	32
Dodge	27,402	8.7	697	34.4	20.1	233	335	109	156,151	52.4	47.6	2	93.0	(Z)	1
Douglas	8,068	1.1	1,177	22.8	10.9	273	232	53	45,200	47.2	52.8	6	98.6	2	2
Faribault	33,573	9.9	909	22.9	33.3	432	475	167	183,323	68.3	31.7	3	100.0	(Z)	1
Fillmore	42,988	13.6	1,600	25.8	16.5	441	276	143	89,221	45.2	54.8	4	99.5	(Z)	2
Freeborn	42,816	7.8	1,172	31.7	23.8	394	337	167	142,314	60.3	39.7	6	99.1	(Z)	4
Goodhue	35,316	3.3	1,679	35.4	12.0	384	229	157	93,515	41.1	58.9	631	1.4	1	4
Grant	8,233	9.9	606	24.6	27.4	317	524	69	114,444	89.8	10.2	2	100.0	1	(Z)
Hennepin	14,894	(Z)	626	60.7	4.3	65	105	58	92,086	88.8	11.2	298	31.9	3	83
Houston	9,575	4.3	1,031	19.0	11.1	254	246	67	64,558	28.8	71.2	3	99.2	(Z)	1
Hubbard	3,956	1.6	535	17.2	10.5	140	262	23	42,912	75.4	24.6	14	99.4	10	1
Isanti	−4,711	(X)	952	46.7	6.5	139	146	26	26,888	63.5	36.5	4	99.7	1	1
Itasca	−1,711	(X)	494	23.7	10.9	120	243	6	13,036	52.7	47.3	201	2.4	(Z)	2
Jackson	50,509	21.5	989	21.9	28.4	398	402	159	161,140	51.9	48.1	2	97.8	(Z)	1
Kanabec	−4,147	(X)	796	26.4	7.9	159	199	19	23,862	33.1	66.9	2	98.2	(Z)	(Z)
Kandiyohi	41,807	4.4	1,286	28.3	17.5	408	317	231	179,546	36.0	64.0	10	97.7	4	4
Kittson	7,271	10.9	659	6.4	42.2	556	843	70	106,168	86.5	13.5	1	80.9	1	(Z)
Koochiching	−184	(X)	258	8.1	16.7	74	288	4	14,795	36.1	63.9	53	1.0	(Z)	1
Lac qui Parle	39,099	29.9	910	15.9	34.8	435	478	113	124,343	69.1	30.9	4	97.1	1	1
Lake	−160	(X)	46	32.6	2.2	5	105	(Z)	7,630	80.6	19.4	136	0.3	(Z)	1
Lake of the Woods	−2,391	(X)	266	12.4	27.4	152	573	6	21,056	79.1	20.9	1	33.6	1	(Z)
Le Sueur	15,521	4.0	974	29.8	12.6	238	244	88	90,561	51.5	48.5	19	50.1	5	2
Lincoln	27,590	30.1	761	22.9	23.0	271	357	73	96,372	50.6	49.4	2	98.4	(Z)	1
Lyon	43,863	6.5	949	22.2	32.2	404	426	157	165,526	47.9	52.1	7	94.5	(Z)	3
McLeod	14,515	1.7	987	29.7	15.4	263	266	81	82,160	63.8	36.2	7	97.7	(Z)	3
Mahnomen	3,540	4.3	363	16.0	31.1	195	537	24	66,047	72.3	27.7	1	100.0	(Z)	(Z)
Marshall	9,244	8.3	1,409	8.3	36.1	935	664	107	76,267	91.4	8.6	1	76.3	(Z)	(Z)
Martin	67,071	14.8	954	22.2	31.2	423	443	249	260,785	41.3	58.7	21	14.1	(Z)	2
Meeker	20,828	6.2	1,141	28.7	16.2	341	298	129	113,120	45.9	54.1	6	99.3	3	1
Mille Lacs	2,742	0.8	847	29.5	5.8	132	156	23	26,581	36.6	63.4	3	97.6	1	1
Morrison	29,598	6.2	1,924	16.6	9.5	452	235	166	86,119	18.2	81.8	14	98.9	9	2
Mower	52,075	6.8	1,088	33.6	23.2	412	379	179	164,229	59.0	41.0	9	92.1	(Z)	4
Murray	38,001	26.3	911	21.1	32.6	407	447	139	152,366	54.4	45.6	2	94.6	(Z)	1
Nicollet	40,565	6.6	730	21.0	22.6	257	352	148	203,199	38.9	61.1	6	98.1	(Z)	4
Nobles	51,684	11.0	1,043	22.0	24.9	404	388	188	179,825	40.0	60.0	5	97.5	(Z)	3
Norman	13,501	14.7	660	13.2	42.6	527	799	91	137,458	82.9	17.1	1	100.0	(Z)	(Z)
Olmsted	31,485	0.6	1,395	36.3	11.9	313	224	104	74,668	55.2	44.8	42	47.2	(Z)	14
Otter Tail	34,937	3.8	3,013	16.2	15.3	881	292	220	73,118	40.8	59.2	105	30.4	25	4
Pennington	6,500	1.7	610	11.3	29.3	332	544	24	40,048	89.2	10.8	3	20.0	1	1
Pine	5,096	1.6	1,199	19.7	8.3	255	213	34	28,683	36.9	63.1	3	98.0	(Z)	1
Pipestone	43,939	21.3	703	23.9	24.6	249	355	106	150,532	35.0	65.0	4	95.8	1	2
Polk	26,812	5.5	1,518	11.9	39.4	1,111	732	197	129,900	93.0	7.0	15	14.8	6	8
Pope	16,668	9.0	924	19.6	20.6	350	379	91	98,037	57.5	42.5	18	98.6	16	1
Ramsey	3,093	(Z)	36	77.8	−	1	29	4	122,361	79.6	20.4	161	14.7	1	23
Red Lake	5,696	11.9	378	9.8	34.7	227	600	23	61,156	76.4	23.6	4	36.5	2	1
Redwood	42,886	14.1	1,198	19.2	34.4	545	455	220	184,048	55.3	44.7	3	94.2	(Z)	1
Renville	36,238	14.3	1,164	19.5	35.8	664	570	317	272,348	64.3	35.7	3	91.4	(Z)	1

See footnotes at end of table.

Table B-14. Counties — **Farm Earnings, Agriculture, and Water Use**—Con.

[Includes United States, states, and 3,141 counties/county equivalents defined as of February 22, 2005. For more information on these areas, see Appendix C, Geographic Information]

County	Farm earnings, 2005 Total ($1,000)	Farm earnings, 2005 Percent of total[1]	Farms Number	Farms Percent Less than 50 acres	Farms Percent 500 acres or more	Land in farms Total acres (1,000)	Land in farms Average size of farm (acres)	Value of farm products sold Total (mil. dol.)	Value of farm products sold Average per farm (dol.)	Value Percent from Crops[2]	Value Percent from Livestock and poultry[3]	Water use Total (mil. gal. per day)	Water use Ground water, percent of total	By selected major use Irrigation	By selected major use Public supply
MINNESOTA—Con.															
Rice	16,854	1.6	1,296	37.9	9.6	249	192	99	76,640	45.7	54.3	9	91.2	(Z)	5
Rock	48,662	27.8	721	26.4	25.0	299	415	152	211,395	35.9	64.1	2	93.4	(Z)	1
Roseau	7,648	1.7	1,238	10.3	29.1	703	568	45	35,981	59.4	40.6	2	100.0	–	1
St. Louis	2,335	0.1	978	25.9	6.6	175	179	11	11,409	52.6	47.4	324	2.0	(Z)	39
Scott	4,172	0.2	1,004	56.4	5.0	131	130	54	53,297	52.1	47.9	14	93.7	1	8
Sherburne	9,970	0.9	677	50.2	9.0	126	186	49	71,696	77.9	22.1	91	33.5	23	3
Sibley	23,335	14.5	963	22.2	18.7	339	352	169	175,079	49.4	50.6	3	100.0	(Z)	2
Stearns	71,167	2.0	3,152	23.7	8.1	681	216	344	109,029	20.2	79.8	38	78.3	17	13
Steele	25,999	2.8	899	36.3	15.5	282	314	128	142,327	62.7	37.3	9	66.8	(Z)	5
Stevens	19,259	8.8	556	26.4	37.2	313	563	120	216,203	54.2	45.8	5	96.7	3	1
Swift	17,907	10.5	807	18.8	32.6	416	515	158	195,437	55.4	44.6	10	99.2	8	1
Todd	17,555	6.4	1,825	18.1	7.8	370	203	96	52,644	26.8	73.2	10	94.5	6	2
Traverse	4,148	8.5	452	22.1	45.8	344	761	80	177,511	90.9	9.1	1	96.7	(Z)	(Z)
Wabasha	19,184	6.1	999	22.3	14.0	267	267	96	95,795	39.5	60.5	5	100.0	(Z)	2
Wadena	8,499	3.7	734	17.3	8.0	166	226	39	53,556	33.5	66.5	11	86.3	9	1
Waseca	35,205	9.6	759	28.5	20.2	231	305	111	145,943	51.0	49.0	3	97.4	(Z)	2
Washington	23,450	0.6	810	56.2	5.9	96	119	62	76,227	89.8	10.2	321	8.3	2	16
Watonwan	48,338	22.0	601	22.8	28.8	272	452	127	211,436	51.6	48.4	4	98.9	1	2
Wilkin	10,755	11.5	414	14.0	51.9	425	1,025	106	256,604	92.3	7.7	1	86.6	(Z)	(Z)
Winona	35,227	3.3	1,125	20.1	14.4	311	276	125	111,132	25.3	74.7	8	100.0	(Z)	3
Wright	9,485	0.6	1,646	40.7	7.5	266	161	94	57,214	53.0	47.0	334	3.4	2	5
Yellow Medicine	32,601	16.3	989	23.9	32.8	448	453	139	140,393	62.4	37.6	3	93.0	(Z)	2
MISSISSIPPI	1,231,711	2.4	42,186	30.0	9.9	11,098	263	3,116	73,870	32.9	67.1	2,960	73.6	1,410	359
Adams	717	0.1	269	32.0	11.5	91	340	6	21,673	70.0	30.0	49	100.0	(Z)	5
Alcorn	2,184	0.4	564	35.3	5.5	93	166	8	14,191	80.3	19.7	6	93.4	(Z)	5
Amite	16,163	14.0	626	27.8	7.5	157	250	30	48,522	2.3	97.7	2	91.9	(Z)	1
Attala	2,494	1.2	526	21.7	8.4	126	240	9	16,975	48.6	51.4	3	93.3	(Z)	2
Benton	1,463	2.7	302	24.2	10.3	100	333	9	28,570	89.5	10.5	1	89.2	(Z)	(Z)
Bolivar	21,773	4.5	435	20.0	40.9	440	1,011	107	246,124	98.3	1.7	286	95.0	269	3
Calhoun	28,252	15.3	634	20.8	10.4	170	268	32	50,823	79.7	20.3	5	83.3	1	3
Carroll	2,509	4.7	556	18.3	14.7	168	302	14	25,583	62.4	37.6	5	97.3	2	1
Chickasaw	17,346	6.2	655	25.0	10.7	172	263	24	35,963	28.3	71.7	4	46.7	1	1
Choctaw	2,958	2.9	284	22.9	8.8	64	225	10	36,606	8.1	91.9	2	72.8	(Z)	1
Claiborne	1,912	0.9	298	20.1	16.1	101	339	6	19,973	57.4	42.6	34	98.8	1	1
Clarke	5,394	4.0	362	33.1	5.8	56	155	8	21,936	8.3	91.7	3	91.5	(Z)	2
Clay	1,285	0.4	497	23.1	10.3	129	260	12	23,304	23.5	76.5	9	92.9	–	6
Coahoma	32,256	7.8	255	20.0	43.1	272	1,068	80	312,553	93.0	7.0	161	95.5	145	12
Copiah	19,471	6.2	690	28.7	8.8	158	228	41	58,812	6.7	93.3	5	99.4	(Z)	3
Covington	25,478	10.4	565	26.5	6.5	103	183	62	110,572	3.6	96.4	6	79.9	(Z)	2
DeSoto	4,011	0.2	639	53.2	7.7	143	224	21	33,484	86.5	13.5	32	97.1	19	11
Forrest	8,622	0.5	440	45.0	2.5	45	103	14	31,018	14.4	85.6	53	25.2	1	10
Franklin	279	0.4	208	23.1	9.6	44	214	4	17,832	11.8	88.2	1	96.0	(Z)	1
George	3,405	1.9	537	56.1	2.8	63	117	13	24,302	76.3	23.7	2	80.3	1	1
Greene	8,821	10.0	393	29.5	3.8	59	151	18	45,122	6.9	93.1	7	31.2	(Z)	1
Grenada	10,653	2.4	339	20.9	10.6	91	268	6	17,106	75.5	24.5	16	69.5	6	3
Hancock	−1,695	(X)	298	41.6	3.0	38	127	3	8,487	27.0	73.0	5	99.2	(Z)	2
Harrison	−983	(X)	418	66.7	1.0	25	60	3	7,981	54.6	45.4	341	11.2	(Z)	24
Hinds	18,108	0.2	1,247	37.3	8.4	279	223	51	40,987	19.3	80.7	47	32.1	(Z)	40
Holmes	8,383	5.1	516	18.2	18.0	219	425	32	62,647	87.3	12.7	48	95.9	39	2
Humphroye	21,085	18.5	289	18.7	30.8	182	628	75	258,983	51.9	48.1	136	98.0	53	1
Issaquena	5,361	33.4	91	14.3	44.0	117	1,281	22	242,099	(NA)	(NA)	14	97.0	8	(Z)
Itawamba	8,930	3.7	514	25.3	5.8	96	187	22	42,457	15.5	84.5	3	95.8	(Z)	2
Jackson	−775	(X)	568	63.2	1.6	43	76	6	11,252	48.9	51.1	71	30.1	(Z)	11
Jasper	21,612	11.0	475	27.4	6.5	80	168	40	83,800	2.0	98.0	2	88.9	(Z)	1
Jefferson	3,685	7.8	315	14.9	12.4	91	289	13	40,832	26.8	73.2	1	100.0	–	(Z)
Jefferson Davis	12,322	12.3	442	26.9	4.1	64	145	22	50,762	5.8	94.2	2	92.0	(Z)	2
Jones	68,046	5.1	1,080	40.7	2.3	132	122	130	120,242	1.7	98.3	19	98.9	(Z)	12
Kemper	8,776	11.4	503	20.7	9.3	123	245	10	19,511	8.1	91.9	1	75.9	(Z)	(Z)
Lafayette	−480	(X)	572	22.6	8.6	135	236	6	9,645	58.4	41.6	6	99.0	(Z)	4
Lamar	11,395	2.2	565	40.5	4.2	75	133	28	49,430	7.1	92.9	17	99.5	(Z)	5
Lauderdale	2,309	0.1	505	37.2	6.5	93	183	7	14,095	33.8	66.2	12	99.4	(Z)	9
Lawrence	20,693	11.5	424	28.1	5.2	66	156	33	77,483	5.4	94.6	36	6.9	(Z)	1
Leake	71,182	25.5	742	25.6	5.1	110	148	121	162,481	0.8	99.2	3	82.6	–	1
Lee	2,211	0.1	613	40.3	9.8	144	235	18	29,352	53.8	46.2	17	44.8	(Z)	12
Leflore	22,365	3.5	287	10.8	42.9	283	986	104	361,362	61.0	39.0	207	96.4	150	4
Lincoln	16,710	3.0	643	27.8	4.4	112	174	28	43,395	4.2	95.8	5	99.1	(Z)	3
Lowndes	16,409	1.3	492	30.5	17.1	150	304	39	79,313	20.0	80.0	42	34.2	(Z)	9
Madison	4,007	0.2	719	30.2	11.4	192	268	16	22,740	74.9	25.1	13	93.2	1	11
Marion	20,228	6.4	581	29.1	4.6	99	170	37	63,775	2.2	97.8	4	86.9	(Z)	3
Marshall	1,039	0.4	670	28.8	12.7	193	287	14	20,648	57.6	42.4	4	95.6	(Z)	2
Monroe	3,056	0.6	713	27.3	7.9	183	257	32	44,252	38.8	61.2	20	93.4	(Z)	4
Montgomery	1,388	1.1	352	16.8	11.9	86	244	7	18,918	45.2	54.8	4	99.8	(Z)	2
Neshoba	19,502	3.0	692	23.6	5.3	146	211	125	181,312	0.6	99.4	4	96.1	(Z)	3

See footnotes at end of table.

Table B-14. Counties — **Farm Earnings, Agriculture, and Water Use**—Con.

[Includes United States, states, and 3,141 counties/county equivalents defined as of February 22, 2005. For more information on these areas, see Appendix C, Geographic Information]

County	Farm earnings, 2005		Agriculture (NAICS 111–112), 2002									Water use, 2000[4]			
			Farms			Land in farms		Value of farm products sold						By selected major use (mil. gal. per day)	
				Percent						Percent from					
	Total ($1,000)	Percent of total[1]	Number	Less than 50 acres	500 acres or more	Total acres (1,000)	Average size of farm (acres)	Total (mil. dol.)	Average per farm (dol.)	Crops[2]	Livestock and poultry[3]	Total (mil. gal. per day)	Ground water, percent of total	Irrigation	Public supply
MISSISSIPPI—Con.															
Newton	62,235	20.5	745	34.9	4.7	119	160	95	127,274	1.1	98.9	2	89.5	(Z)	1
Noxubee	11,012	8.6	571	22.1	18.0	210	368	50	87,739	29.0	71.0	31	5.9	2	1
Oktibbeha	486	0.1	502	34.9	9.6	94	186	10	18,940	22.5	77.5	6	94.1	(Z)	4
Panola	5,135	1.1	725	16.3	15.4	272	375	30	41,557	86.3	13.7	17	96.3	13	3
Pearl River	−696	(X)	881	49.0	4.4	120	136	12	13,304	28.4	71.6	8	98.3	(Z)	5
Perry	8,109	6.6	331	40.8	2.1	35	106	12	36,586	3.3	96.7	18	9.5	(Z)	1
Pike	21,613	3.8	563	33.2	3.6	80	142	50	87,943	3.2	96.8	12	97.8	(Z)	9
Pontotoc	3,233	0.6	864	30.1	6.4	140	162	11	12,681	41.8	58.2	2	88.9	(Z)	2
Prentiss	−454	(X)	572	29.2	5.9	102	179	7	11,404	67.5	32.5	4	99.7	(Z)	4
Quitman	12,765	16.3	243	15.6	32.1	182	751	32	133,576	97.3	2.7	81	95.3	77	(Z)
Rankin	34,920	1.4	804	41.4	4.7	131	163	62	77,153	8.8	91.2	13	95.3	(Z)	11
Scott	100,685	19.9	771	35.9	4.4	114	148	205	265,711	1.0	99.0	9	99.2	(Z)	9
Sharkey	8,205	15.2	101	6.9	64.4	165	1,632	48	477,020	84.2	15.8	37	94.9	28	1
Simpson	77,271	23.7	684	26.9	4.1	104	152	127	185,896	1.7	98.3	2	96.4	(Z)	2
Smith	96,161	39.8	727	29.0	4.3	104	143	154	212,281	2.2	97.8	4	97.7	(Z)	4
Stone	−461	(X)	330	36.7	5.8	57	174	7	21,088	45.6	54.4	2	73.2	(Z)	(Z)
Sunflower	23,806	6.4	343	9.6	41.7	336	981	119	347,230	58.2	41.8	264	96.6	180	2
Tallahatchie	13,133	10.8	417	15.8	26.9	293	703	45	108,254	95.0	5.0	114	95.5	102	1
Tate	3,757	1.5	662	32.9	10.1	155	234	24	36,918	46.2	53.8	18	95.8	15	2
Tippah	1,410	0.5	733	28.2	4.1	121	165	13	17,147	49.7	50.3	3	97.3	(Z)	3
Tishomingo	369	0.2	358	28.5	3.9	53	147	3	9,128	32.1	67.9	3	100.0	–	2
Tunica	16,085	2.9	98	5.1	62.2	201	2,053	53	545,347	87.3	12.7	94	95.7	81	2
Union	3,370	1.0	819	30.3	4.4	139	170	10	12,195	47.8	52.2	3	96.4	(Z)	2
Walthall	23,167	18.5	662	24.8	4.7	107	162	51	77,640	1.5	98.5	2	92.3	–	1
Warren	1,393	0.1	281	33.5	20.6	115	408	10	37,014	87.3	12.7	72	20.8	(Z)	13
Washington	26,122	3.1	333	19.8	39.9	321	963	94	283,568	86.0	14.0	292	73.9	184	12
Wayne	43,628	16.3	547	33.3	5.3	84	154	101	183,969	2.0	98.0	2	93.2	(Z)	2
Webster	2,220	2.5	351	19.1	10.8	77	220	14	39,382	45.3	54.7	1	95.7	(Z)	1
Wilkinson	712	1.0	298	21.1	18.8	105	353	3	9,628	(NA)	(NA)	4	47.1	3	1
Winston	4,401	1.8	530	26.2	8.1	101	190	13	24,930	9.3	90.7	3	96.2	(Z)	2
Yalobusha	−190	(X)	374	21.1	12.6	100	268	8	20,364	78.4	21.6	3	65.9	–	2
Yazoo	25,794	7.7	566	17.1	25.6	360	636	67	118,606	79.8	20.2	60	69.2	25	4
MISSOURI	640,223	0.5	106,797	23.1	14.0	29,946	280	4,983	46,661	40.0	60.0	8,230	21.6	1,430	872
Adair	−1,825	(X)	915	17.9	17.0	269	294	20	22,150	51.7	48.3	4	10.6	(Z)	3
Andrew	2,889	2.5	847	23.8	15.5	223	264	31	36,406	69.9	30.1	1	52.9	(Z)	1
Atchison	7,642	9.9	465	12.3	43.4	318	683	48	104,030	88.5	11.5	7	97.4	6	1
Audrain	3,925	1.0	1,089	20.6	21.7	415	381	90	82,299	58.4	41.6	14	33.5	10	2
Barry	37,211	5.9	1,669	28.6	7.4	321	193	201	120,670	1.9	98.1	21	36.1	(Z)	5
Barton	6,760	3.4	960	20.1	21.8	337	351	66	69,142	41.0	59.0	11	75.7	8	2
Bates	9,737	5.8	1,293	19.0	17.8	468	362	57	44,336	46.1	53.9	3	10.3	(Z)	2
Benton	2,364	1.6	839	16.3	15.4	259	309	31	37,197	19.0	81.0	3	85.7	(Z)	1
Bollinger	1,315	1.6	913	14.9	11.7	228	250	20	21,451	(NA)	(NA)	14	97.4	12	(Z)
Boone	−1,427	(X)	1,388	34.1	8.5	270	194	36	25,793	55.0	45.0	23	95.4	1	19
Buchanan	1,056	0.1	848	29.8	12.6	200	236	28	32,996	76.0	24.0	68	2.1	(Z)	16
Butler	13,985	1.7	673	23.5	20.5	248	368	43	64,248	92.1	7.9	350	98.1	344	4
Caldwell	2,317	3.0	959	23.4	11.5	230	240	25	25,688	36.7	63.3	2	66.5	1	(Z)
Callaway	2,613	0.4	1,494	24.6	11.6	358	239	51	34,159	42.7	57.3	33	22.5	5	4
Camden	2,686	0.4	623	12.4	14.8	178	287	16	26,276	5.4	94.6	5	85.6	(Z)	3
Cape Girardeau	−1,602	(X)	1,204	22.8	9.6	261	217	44	36,809	53.7	46.3	28	69.6	10	9
Carroll	3,983	4.0	1,081	16.3	20.0	417	386	62	57,191	76.2	23.8	3	88.4	1	1
Carter	550	1.0	228	18.0	16.2	93	406	3	12,114	8.3	91.7	1	92.5	–	1
Cass	7,670	0.7	1,635	37.7	7.7	314	192	48	29,612	59.7	40.3	4	4.9	2	1
Cedar	3,010	2.3	952	19.4	10.3	228	240	24	24,765	13.6	86.4	2	74.4	(Z)	1
Chariton	−253	(X)	1,095	14.0	20.6	379	346	66	60,223	58.6	41.4	1	50.7	(Z)	(Z)
Christian	2,818	0.4	1,294	35.3	6.1	213	165	27	20,841	11.1	88.9	9	93.4	2	4
Clark	−1,868	(X)	685	13.4	23.6	254	370	29	41,945	68.7	31.3	2	85.9	1	1
Clay	3,366	0.1	683	43.3	9.4	128	188	25	35,873	36.5	63.5	173	20.0	(Z)	166
Clinton	2,245	1.2	889	30.1	10.7	226	255	31	35,322	50.7	49.3	3	4.7	–	2
Cole	3,567	0.1	1,098	25.1	4.4	186	169	25	22,457	24.5	75.5	12	57.7	(Z)	11
Cooper	2,318	1.0	923	16.7	17.9	294	318	47	51,243	43.3	56.7	3	29.7	–	2
Crawford	2,112	0.8	751	17.7	16.0	218	290	9	12,483	20.3	79.7	2	89.6	–	1
Dade	5,378	6.0	893	20.3	16.2	296	332	41	46,022	32.3	67.7	4	76.7	3	1
Dallas	4,766	3.4	1,243	26.0	7.8	235	189	37	29,501	6.2	93.8	2	71.2	–	1
Daviess	11,902	14.8	1,029	16.8	15.8	330	321	45	43,404	40.1	59.9	2	59.8	(Z)	1
DeKalb	4,294	4.1	833	19.8	15.0	225	271	28	33,062	39.1	60.9	1	52.6	(Z)	(Z)
Dent	1,003	0.6	693	15.0	17.3	210	303	10	14,742	9.9	90.1	28	5.5	(Z)	1
Douglas	5,218	3.9	1,160	17.1	12.1	312	269	26	22,718	3.9	96.1	2	67.1	(Z)	1
Dunklin	14,150	3.5	429	18.4	42.4	297	692	82	191,821	98.4	1.6	79	98.0	74	4

See footnotes at end of table.

[Includes United States, states, and 3,141 counties/county equivalents defined as of February 22, 2005. For more information on these areas, see Appendix C, Geographic Information]

County	Farm earnings, 2005 Total ($1,000)	Farm earnings, 2005 Percent of total[1]	Farms Number	Farms Percent Less than 50 acres	Farms Percent 500 acres or more	Land in farms Total acres (1,000)	Land in farms Average size of farm (acres)	Value of farm products sold Total (mil. dol.)	Value of farm products sold Average per farm (dol.)	Percent from Crops[2]	Percent from Livestock and poultry[3]	Water use Total (mil. gal. per day)	Water use Ground water, percent of total	By selected major use (mil. gal. per day) Irrigation	By selected major use (mil. gal. per day) Public supply
MISSOURI—Con.															
Franklin	940	0.1	1,833	30.7	5.9	300	164	40	21,588	38.8	61.2	1,016	1.0	(Z)	7
Gasconade	683	0.3	877	14.1	10.9	222	253	19	21,233	30.5	69.5	2	78.5	(Z)	1
Gentry	9,700	12.5	821	18.3	19.9	292	355	54	66,308	26.1	73.9	2	37.5	(Z)	1
Greene	−129	(X)	2,122	44.3	4.8	275	130	39	18,434	16.5	83.5	255	5.9	(Z)	47
Grundy	2,308	1.7	735	18.6	14.3	212	288	27	37,201	58.2	41.8	3	26.1	1	2
Harrison	5,494	5.8	1,101	18.6	17.6	388	353	48	43,156	40.9	59.1	1	22.7	(Z)	(Z)
Henry	3,213	1.0	1,010	21.7	18.1	338	335	45	44,484	31.2	68.8	399	0.2	1	3
Hickory	1,071	2.5	534	13.9	15.5	156	292	16	30,105	10.0	90.0	1	75.4	(Z)	(Z)
Holt	3,190	6.4	486	14.0	27.2	252	519	48	98,348	84.6	15.4	19	99.3	19	1
Howard	[5]25	(NA)	806	17.1	16.6	270	335	29	36,325	67.2	32.8	3	70.8	2	1
Howell	5,389	0.9	1,743	25.0	9.5	414	237	44	25,111	8.2	91.8	7	84.2	(Z)	4
Iron	1,723	1.4	299	10.7	13.4	71	236	4	12,174	12.4	87.6	1	76.2	−	(Z)
Jackson	1,137	(Z)	807	53.3	6.6	145	180	21	26,447	74.3	25.7	388	9.3	(Z)	34
Jasper	20,773	0.9	1,390	32.9	9.2	289	208	66	47,717	33.5	66.5	32	45.9	8	18
Jefferson	−1,285	(X)	764	33.1	5.2	125	163	11	13,857	41.6	58.4	813	1.7	−	10
Johnson	5,594	0.6	1,811	28.3	10.8	413	228	56	30,864	34.5	65.5	6	79.7	(Z)	5
Knox	903	2.3	643	8.9	23.5	249	387	27	42,012	56.8	43.2	1	46.7	(Z)	(Z)
Laclede	3,196	0.6	1,394	22.7	11.8	319	229	31	22,518	8.2	91.8	26	19.1	(Z)	4
Lafayette	9,774	2.8	1,286	27.4	14.9	363	282	76	59,010	64.5	35.5	4	14.3	1	3
Lawrence	19,881	5.9	1,852	34.5	7.3	316	171	110	59,338	10.5	89.5	7	63.0	1	3
Lewis	1,695	1.8	838	19.9	16.7	284	339	49	58,647	47.1	52.9	1	61.4	(Z)	1
Lincoln	−277	(X)	1,102	31.3	12.2	252	228	49	44,582	50.7	49.3	6	93.1	2	2
Linn	5,556	2.9	969	17.6	20.8	340	351	38	39,160	40.2	59.8	2	15.5	(Z)	1
Livingston	1,619	0.7	903	19.2	15.5	300	332	39	43,004	68.6	31.4	4	94.5	1	2
McDonald	28,881	11.0	1,113	23.9	8.3	216	194	120	107,717	1.1	98.9	7	83.5	(Z)	3
Macon	−538	(X)	1,351	16.1	14.5	406	301	41	30,454	46.4	53.6	3	5.2	−	2
Madison	1,329	1.2	463	18.1	12.3	123	265	9	19,369	7.2	92.8	1	49.6	−	1
Maries	1,543	2.3	883	12.6	12.9	234	265	20	22,275	11.9	88.1	2	66.9	−	(Z)
Marion	−73	(X)	744	19.8	16.7	230	309	40	53,716	57.9	42.1	8	32.5	2	4
Mercer	38,268	58.0	569	12.7	20.6	212	373	83	146,538	(NA)	(NA)	12	88.9	10	(Z)
Miller	16,275	5.7	1,111	16.7	11.2	268	241	72	64,756	3.9	96.1	4	76.8	1	1
Mississippi	4,161	3.0	247	15.4	56.7	272	1,100	66	267,243	97.3	2.7	78	100.0	76	2
Moniteau	14,345	9.0	1,139	19.8	10.3	258	227	84	74,010	13.4	86.6	3	81.2	−	2
Monroe	−401	(X)	960	19.0	16.5	316	329	49	51,415	51.0	49.0	5	3.9	(Z)	3
Montgomery	−2,278	(X)	761	19.1	19.2	259	340	36	47,466	68.8	31.2	1	59.9	(Z)	1
Morgan	27,888	15.5	930	18.7	9.4	222	239	81	87,627	7.5	92.5	2	72.6	−	1
New Madrid	21,579	6.1	364	9.1	62.4	395	1,085	99	270,766	98.9	1.1	1,092	23.8	257	2
Newton	35,344	4.1	1,752	35.1	5.1	269	153	138	78,566	4.9	95.1	8	64.8	−	4
Nodaway	7,746	2.1	1,396	15.1	22.3	506	362	69	49,688	60.7	39.3	4	31.3	(Z)	2
Oregon	2,093	2.2	843	16.1	15.4	266	316	23	27,856	8.0	92.0	3	80.4	−	2
Osage	7,775	5.4	1,219	12.6	12.5	315	258	53	43,308	9.1	90.9	64	2.1	(Z)	1
Ozark	3,822	6.8	820	12.1	17.1	282	343	26	31,978	4.0	96.0	2	58.5	(Z)	(Z)
Pemiscot	14,064	6.2	258	15.5	55.4	296	1,149	70	269,814	99.6	0.4	50	100.0	47	3
Perry	−204	(X)	914	19.1	10.6	222	243	31	33,573	47.4	52.6	2	45.7	−	1
Pettis	13,318	1.8	1,278	20.3	16.2	402	315	102	79,714	23.9	76.1	7	66.9	(Z)	3
Phelps	−76	(X)	824	24.2	11.0	201	244	10	12,535	13.3	86.7	12	40.3	(Z)	4
Pike	−545	(X)	1,061	19.1	17.2	344	325	55	51,759	51.2	48.8	10	12.1	1	3
Platte	3,568	0.2	736	34.6	11.5	185	251	28	37,416	77.5	22.5	337	0.9	1	3
Polk	7,713	2.5	1,768	28.2	9.2	369	209	60	33,917	7.4	92.6	5	67.5	1	2
Pulaski	290	(Z)	573	18.5	14.3	142	247	11	19,276	12.3	87.7	8	35.1	(Z)	7
Putnam	2,015	4.7	723	15.9	20.9	293	406	57	78,530	12.0	88.0	2	25.3	(Z)	(Z)
Ralls	731	0.6	674	18.7	17.8	253	376	36	52,786	65.8	34.2	1	7.5	(Z)	2
Randolph	1,016	0.2	971	23.5	11.2	246	253	33	33,775	34.0	66.0	812	0.1	1	2
Ray	2,331	1.1	1,231	26.3	10.6	292	237	35	28,500	60.6	39.4	5	91.4	2	4
Reynolds	818	1.0	379	15.6	14.0	118	311	4	10,739	12.1	87.9	4	97.2	−	(Z)
Ripley	1,816	1.8	478	17.6	16.1	140	293	10	20,186	47.7	52.3	36	81.6	35	1
St. Charles	−515	(X)	739	34.2	13.8	185	250	34	45,518	80.0	20.0	502	4.4	(Z)	20
St. Clair	1,768	2.4	766	15.4	20.5	268	350	23	29,790	40.5	59.5	2	70.5	(Z)	(Z)
Ste. Genevieve	1,462	0.6	677	19.4	11.7	184	272	18	26,312	44.5	55.5	3	90.2	−	1
St. Francois	2,958	0.4	735	28.8	5.6	129	175	15	20,792	46.4	53.6	8	77.8	−	4
St. Louis	6,412	(Z)	[8]328	[8]57.6	[8]6.1	[8]39	[8]120	[8]21	[8]64,896	[8]92.5	[8]7.5	499	1.2	(Z)	179
Saline	7,206	2.0	945	19.0	26.2	413	437	92	97,019	63.9	36.1	7	90.9	2	4
Schuyler	380	1.5	480	14.8	16.7	146	305	12	25,917	29.6	70.4	1	17.0	−	(Z)
Scotland	2,513	4.9	654	14.4	21.4	234	358	32	48,222	52.4	47.6	1	36.9	(Z)	(Z)
Scott	6,849	1.1	514	28.8	23.0	224	435	71	138,321	62.3	37.7	100	99.9	90	5
Shannon	−144	(X)	516	21.3	15.1	135	262	6	11,607	7.1	92.9	1	79.4	−	(Z)
Shelby	4,571	6.6	676	13.2	27.8	299	442	59	87,281	50.1	49.9	3	72.6	2	(Z)
Stoddard	22,906	5.2	960	29.7	20.9	415	432	127	132,758	69.6	30.4	372	99.4	368	4
Stone	1,452	0.4	645	25.1	6.8	114	176	12	19,192	8.6	91.4	3	89.9	(Z)	4
Sullivan	30,818	25.4	850	12.8	26.5	365	429	74	86,864	(NA)	(NA)	9	66.5	6	1

See footnotes at end of table.

640

Table B-14. Counties — **Farm Earnings, Agriculture, and Water Use**—Con.

[Includes United States, states, and 3,141 counties/county equivalents defined as of February 22, 2005. For more information on these areas, see Appendix C, Geographic Information]

County	Farm earnings, 2005 Total ($1,000)	Farm earnings, 2005 Percent of total[1]	Farms Number	Farms Percent Less than 50 acres	Farms Percent 500 acres or more	Land in farms Total acres (1,000)	Land in farms Average size of farm (acres)	Value of farm products sold Total (mil. dol.)	Value of farm products sold Average per farm (dol.)	Value of farm products sold Percent from Crops[2]	Value of farm products sold Percent from Livestock and poultry[3]	Water use, 2000[4] Total (mil. gal. per day)	Water use Ground water, percent of total	By selected major use (mil. gal. per day) Irrigation	By selected major use (mil. gal. per day) Public supply
MISSOURI—Con.															
Taney	123	(Z)	512	18.9	12.7	154	301	10	19,887	6.0	94.0	27	18.6	(Z)	10
Texas	5,398	2.5	1,600	18.6	13.4	472	295	40	24,981	10.2	89.8	4	76.2	(Z)	2
Vernon	6,341	2.2	1,399	23.8	14.9	426	305	80	57,415	27.9	72.1	10	36.6	5	3
Warren	−1,662	(X)	670	33.7	10.1	142	211	19	28,490	62.8	37.2	3	92.4	(Z)	2
Washington	4,249	2.5	576	19.6	8.5	133	230	8	13,269	14.9	85.1	5	83.5	1	1
Wayne	381	0.5	445	13.3	11.9	114	256	5	10,461	20.0	80.0	2	68.1	–	1
Webster	5,293	2.0	1,962	33.6	6.4	320	163	62	31,470	5.4	94.6	4	69.0	(Z)	1
Worth	1,917	11.2	368	12.8	22.6	140	381	11	29,731	47.5	52.5	(Z)	31.3	–	(Z)
Wright	6,926	4.5	1,348	18.9	11.9	318	236	44	32,716	6.1	93.9	3	71.1	–	1
Independent City															
St. Louis city	–	–	(8)	(NA)	(NA)	(8)	(8)	(8)	(NA)	(NA)	(NA)	147	(NA)	–	147
MONTANA	463,802	2.3	27,870	23.3	46.4	59,612	2,139	1,882	67,532	39.0	61.0	8,290	2.3	7,950	149
Beaverhead	14,527	9.4	421	24.5	46.3	1,279	3,038	63	150,276	14.9	85.1	506	0.3	504	2
Big Horn	11,410	5.2	584	16.3	55.3	2,811	4,814	66	113,418	26.9	73.1	152	2.2	151	1
Blaine	11,339	13.2	588	8.2	66.2	2,261	3,846	53	90,638	45.4	54.6	286	2.1	286	1
Broadwater	4,463	8.0	279	19.7	41.2	470	1,684	19	68,165	60.4	39.6	198	1.1	197	1
Carbon	5,866	5.4	703	20.6	35.1	754	1,072	47	66,220	28.8	71.2	422	0.4	420	2
Carter	7,342	41.6	289	5.2	85.5	1,667	5,768	30	105,301	3.7	96.3	5	9.0	5	(Z)
Cascade	16,872	0.9	1,037	26.8	37.0	1,389	1,339	51	49,160	36.8	63.2	169	0.9	153	15
Chouteau	27,326	37.3	787	4.3	76.5	2,301	2,924	56	70,704	75.3	24.7	43	3.1	41	1
Custer	4,192	2.2	425	20.0	48.7	1,904	4,480	41	95,734	14.8	85.2	77	1.2	75	2
Daniels	6,645	19.9	364	3.3	74.5	815	2,240	27	74,734	77.7	22.3	3	46.8	3	(Z)
Dawson	8,116	5.3	522	8.4	66.9	1,411	2,703	36	69,247	53.8	46.2	75	0.9	72	2
Deer Lodge	435	0.4	109	24.8	45.9	135	1,239	4	39,404	15.0	85.0	48	8.0	44	4
Fallon	9,572	13.2	327	8.9	67.0	932	2,851	22	68,621	9.7	90.3	3	29.4	3	(Z)
Fergus	16,050	8.0	830	14.1	62.4	2,282	2,749	61	73,743	30.8	69.2	63	5.1	61	2
Flathead	5,957	0.3	1,075	53.0	9.1	235	218	31	28,384	63.5	36.5	71	26.1	57	6
Gallatin[9]	17,501	0.9	1,074	38.5	23.2	709	660	76	70,852	53.3	46.7	409	2.3	399	9
Garfield	9,745	43.6	268	6.3	86.2	2,182	8,141	32	119,399	20.0	80.0	7	8.4	7	(Z)
Glacier	19,137	8.9	472	8.7	65.0	1,645	3,486	39	83,180	52.1	47.9	103	2.0	101	2
Golden Valley	1,126	14.1	140	7.1	68.6	661	4,720	8	57,143	12.0	88.0	52	0.1	52	(Z)
Granite	3,510	9.0	140	9.3	61.4	283	2,021	11	79,136	10.8	89.2	99	0.6	99	(Z)
Hill	21,423	6.8	836	6.1	66.3	1,809	2,164	43	51,981	77.2	22.8	12	16.2	10	2
Jefferson	1,812	1.2	372	29.8	26.1	387	1,041	10	26,086	12.7	87.3	89	3.5	87	2
Judith Basin	8,913	37.9	316	11.7	71.8	830	2,626	32	102,032	26.2	73.8	69	0.9	69	(Z)
Lake	4,860	1.4	1,185	47.8	11.9	602	508	39	33,215	46.2	53.8	342	1.0	339	2
Lewis and Clark	4,770	0.3	635	47.9	20.9	842	1,326	23	35,628	30.8	69.2	176	5.5	166	8
Liberty	11,033	32.8	297	3.4	82.5	905	3,048	26	87,209	66.8	33.2	20	0.4	20	(Z)
Lincoln	1,890	0.8	310	45.8	8.1	54	175	3	8,116	31.1	68.9	29	5.8	13	1
McCone	6,926	25.5	496	7.1	73.2	1,346	2,714	30	59,788	58.9	41.1	15	1.3	15	(Z)
Madison	3,947	3.3	513	23.4	39.8	1,029	2,005	37	72,279	18.5	81.5	484	0.2	483	(Z)
Meagher	7,126	24.0	136	16.2	66.2	857	6,303	20	144,956	11.3	88.7	324	0.1	324	(Z)
Mineral	430	0.9	85	34.1	12.9	16	191	1	8,635	24.4	75.6	8	42.0	4	(Z)
Missoula	−2,629	(X)	641	55.5	11.4	258	403	8	13,044	33.3	66.7	103	36.3	51	28
Musselshell	5,786	12.3	319	12.9	53.0	1,034	3,240	16	49,379	13.8	86.2	80	1.3	79	1
Park[9]	8,118	3.5	527	27.1	38.5	847	1,607	21	39,787	20.1	79.9	263	1.8	260	3
Petroleum	2,006	35.9	89	2.2	73.0	538	6,045	9	101,876	11.3	88.7	43	0.9	43	(Z)
Phillips	3,297	5.9	525	6.9	66.7	1,897	3,613	38	72,015	32.1	67.9	250	1.5	249	(Z)
Pondera	13,743	15.5	520	11.9	63.7	900	1,731	48	92,656	64.4	35.6	231	1.4	230	1
Powder River	4,151	19.6	301	9.0	80.4	1,522	5,055	30	98,010	3.8	96.2	15	2.8	15	(Z)
Powell	6,294	6.0	274	23.0	44.2	619	2,258	19	69,792	14.2	85.8	178	0.9	176	1
Prairie	6,289	36.1	162	6.2	75.9	620	3,825	19	114,500	29.3	70.7	50	3.1	50	–
Ravalli	7,876	1.6	1,441	64.5	6.6	245	170	29	19,876	36.0	64.0	175	3.1	169	4
Richland	8,109	4.0	587	13.1	60.6	1,201	2,047	68	115,695	44.3	55.7	373	0.7	339	1
Roosevelt	13,423	9.3	683	6.3	64.1	1,441	2,111	51	74,366	77.3	22.7	71	2.6	70	1
Rosebud	8,022	3.5	412	11.7	58.7	2,541	6,167	42	102,583	18.4	81.6	189	1.2	161	1
Sanders	−457	(X)	464	32.5	20.7	346	745	14	30,343	47.3	52.7	109	3.3	107	1
Sheridan	10,041	17.8	626	3.7	70.6	1,047	1,672	43	68,832	78.1	21.9	11	85.2	11	(Z)
Silver Bow	766	0.1	155	32.3	22.6	74	476	3	18,439	8.4	91.6	44	4.4	30	12
Stillwater	4,197	2.3	552	21.7	47.1	890	1,613	29	52,788	12.8	87.2	133	4.0	132	1
Sweet Grass	2,757	3.0	357	16.2	53.8	867	2,429	17	46,717	10.1	89.9	193	0.3	193	(Z)
Teton	13,666	14.3	700	13.0	53.7	1,231	1,758	73	103,579	47.3	52.7	556	0.3	555	1
Toole	11,620	9.8	405	4.4	75.8	1,088	2,686	34	84,978	74.3	25.7	11	3.7	10	(Z)
Treasure	2,195	26.4	115	12.2	62.6	607	5,277	20	170,104	24.7	75.3	101	1.1	100	(Z)
Valley	23,848	17.1	743	6.6	63.9	2,052	2,761	67	90,763	48.0	52.0	157	2.9	156	1
Wheatland	4,078	17.4	163	8.0	71.8	842	5,163	18	110,000	14.6	85.4	91	1.3	91	(Z)
Wibaux	3,842	29.8	215	6.0	65.1	536	2,492	12	57,493	38.6	61.4	2	4.8	2	(Z)
Yellowstone	28,503	0.8	1,279	37.1	25.6	1,569	1,226	118	92,107	20.6	79.4	502	1.3	414	24
Yellowstone National Park[9]	(X)	(NA)	(X)	(NA)	(NA)	(X)	(X)	(X)	(NA)	(NA)	(NA)	(X)	(NA)	(X)	(X)

See footnotes at end of table.

[Includes United States, states, and 3,141 counties/county equivalents defined as of February 22, 2005. For more information on these areas, see Appendix C, Geographic Information]

County	Farm earnings, 2005 Total ($1,000)	Percent of total[1]	Farms Number	Farms Percent Less than 50 acres	Farms Percent 500 acres or more	Land in farms Total acres (1,000)	Land in farms Average size of farm (acres)	Value of farm products sold Total (mil. dol.)	Value of farm products sold Average per farm (dol.)	Percent from Crops[2]	Percent from Livestock and poultry[3]	Water use 2000[4] Total (mil. gal. per day)	Ground water, percent of total	Irrigation	Public supply
NEBRASKA	1,500,483	3.3	49,355	14.8	41.6	45,903	930	9,704	196,609	34.9	65.1	12,300	63.9	8,790	330
Adams	14,768	2.5	561	11.4	47.6	344	614	157	278,979	46.0	54.0	218	98.3	204	9
Antelope	28,703	25.6	792	8.8	44.9	527	665	196	247,958	38.9	61.1	224	97.8	219	1
Arthur	-2,670	(X)	76	10.5	81.6	436	5,740	14	183,513	7.7	92.3	16	99.6	16	–
Banner	6,366	57.6	226	1.8	65.9	411	1,819	56	247,916	14.9	85.1	38	88.1	37	(Z)
Blaine	-2,182	(X)	106	4.7	67.0	441	4,162	22	204,500	2.9	97.1	12	94.1	11	(Z)
Boone	29,973	32.6	692	7.5	42.5	431	622	197	284,796	27.3	72.7	133	96.3	130	1
Box Butte	24,502	8.7	476	6.9	54.4	675	1,418	130	273,233	44.1	55.9	234	96.4	230	3
Boyd	615	3.0	314	6.1	58.3	308	981	30	96,831	14.7	85.3	6	63.8	5	(Z)
Brown	11,604	21.9	311	8.0	56.9	686	2,207	93	300,055	14.4	85.6	68	35.1	66	1
Buffalo	21,923	2.1	989	16.2	41.2	601	608	179	180,995	43.8	56.2	251	94.5	233	9
Burt	11,641	15.0	621	15.6	32.9	310	499	95	153,385	54.6	45.4	56	96.4	53	2
Butler	11,836	11.9	840	15.1	32.3	375	446	95	112,513	56.2	43.8	107	96.1	104	1
Cass	10,831	4.9	679	26.5	30.2	320	472	46	68,159	81.7	18.3	40	73.3	3	26
Cedar	64,515	38.0	949	15.0	33.7	460	485	168	176,997	32.3	67.7	70	95.4	65	1
Chase	14,221	19.7	326	9.5	63.5	540	1,655	142	436,282	47.6	52.4	268	99.2	265	1
Cherry	13,150	14.8	557	6.1	79.2	3,777	6,781	119	214,158	9.3	90.7	47	94.8	42	1
Cheyenne	1,786	0.7	616	5.4	62.2	803	1,304	88	143,042	34.5	65.5	94	95.2	88	2
Clay	14,742	12.9	503	15.7	50.3	374	744	160	317,380	47.0	53.0	228	95.7	222	2
Colfax	25,721	12.9	589	21.2	31.1	244	415	170	287,946	22.8	77.2	68	93.7	59	3
Cuming	73,782	36.0	904	18.1	27.1	366	405	581	642,698	9.6	90.4	54	81.5	39	2
Custer	64,968	31.6	1,149	11.1	57.0	1,502	1,307	282	245,368	21.8	78.2	256	88.4	246	3
Dakota	8,514	1.9	296	20.3	28.7	152	512	30	102,084	81.8	18.2	27	98.7	19	3
Dawes	-8,021	(X)	406	9.6	60.3	786	1,937	26	64,626	14.3	85.7	35	63.9	28	2
Dawson	32,157	7.2	718	15.2	44.2	623	867	371	517,175	20.1	79.9	354	70.0	339	9
Deuel	1,974	9.3	252	6.3	61.1	294	1,167	30	117,484	48.5	51.5	39	80.7	36	(Z)
Dixon	31,274	32.1	660	16.2	27.6	277	419	102	154,224	33.7	66.3	21	83.4	17	1
Dodge	17,285	2.7	734	21.3	32.0	339	462	132	179,195	50.1	49.9	100	94.5	87	6
Douglas	-2,224	(X)	361	47.4	10.6	95	262	36	98,440	61.8	38.2	535	6.9	16	68
Dundy	10,431	31.7	262	3.4	61.8	567	2,164	92	350,527	43.0	57.0	131	96.2	129	(Z)
Fillmore	22,057	21.2	499	7.6	55.5	364	729	128	256,519	61.9	38.1	213	96.4	210	1
Franklin	7,267	19.9	378	9.3	47.4	331	876	54	143,257	62.5	37.5	111	83.0	107	1
Frontier	14,258	30.0	318	7.2	65.7	487	1,530	65	204,035	36.0	64.0	86	96.0	85	1
Furnas	8,432	13.0	412	10.4	54.1	441	1,070	84	203,871	36.8	63.2	83	75.9	80	1
Gage	38,876	9.4	1,272	19.8	31.4	552	434	102	80,089	51.1	48.9	63	60.4	53	6
Garden	845	3.8	253	7.9	64.4	1,072	4,237	53	210,992	23.6	76.4	64	75.3	62	(Z)
Garfield	4,290	16.1	190	10.0	56.3	293	1,543	34	177,342	8.3	91.7	17	65.0	16	(Z)
Gosper	4,978	24.8	242	5.0	59.5	262	1,084	48	197,062	59.6	40.4	101	81.2	100	1
Grant	-4,031	(X)	73	17.8	67.1	490	6,711	14	197,726	(NA)	(NA)	3	97.3	2	(Z)
Greeley	14,299	39.4	361	7.2	47.1	293	812	61	168,307	25.6	74.4	54	96.3	53	(Z)
Hall	14,351	1.0	595	19.0	36.8	316	531	132	222,452	48.7	51.3	219	96.6	195	12
Hamilton	16,659	11.7	603	13.3	45.8	348	577	158	261,745	60.3	39.7	244	99.2	239	2
Harlan	6,477	14.7	346	12.1	47.1	309	893	59	171,673	46.3	53.7	129	96.1	126	1
Hayes	9,439	65.0	260	3.5	60.0	408	1,570	71	271,219	24.5	75.5	61	97.0	60	(Z)
Hitchcock	3,282	10.1	299	5.4	67.2	434	1,450	32	108,645	54.3	45.7	63	64.7	59	1
Holt	36,127	17.5	1,166	8.8	54.9	1,481	1,270	206	176,888	37.1	62.9	238	95.3	230	2
Hooker	-3,897	(X)	81	3.7	79.0	424	5,233	11	141,444	4.8	95.2	6	93.9	6	(Z)
Howard	23,667	32.6	600	17.2	32.3	294	489	99	164,627	30.3	69.7	122	63.8	119	1
Jefferson	19,092	14.5	631	13.0	40.1	364	576	79	125,342	48.8	51.2	72	81.1	67	2
Johnson	2,848	3.6	571	13.7	24.9	205	360	23	39,898	42.6	57.4	12	72.4	9	2
Kearney	29,846	29.2	412	7.0	60.2	331	804	205	497,791	40.6	59.4	189	78.4	185	1
Keith	6,524	5.2	363	11.3	49.9	628	1,730	96	263,245	39.3	60.7	136	84.4	132	2
Keya Paha	5,178	52.1	185	4.3	70.8	463	2,504	29	157,805	11.2	88.8	15	65.3	14	(Z)
Kimball	63	0.1	362	5.2	57.7	550	1,518	22	60,423	64.2	35.8	64	93.2	61	2
Knox	22,692	20.8	1,016	9.3	41.6	599	590	160	157,906	17.6	82.4	47	72.8	39	2
Lancaster	14,145	0.2	1,607	39.2	17.1	449	279	71	44,354	68.6	31.4	19	91.9	14	1
Lincoln	22,186	2.9	959	15.3	51.0	1,529	1,594	289	301,231	24.6	75.4	1,009	28.2	315	8
Logan	2,862	34.8	119	6.7	62.2	359	3,017	17	145,874	34.7	65.3	22	97.7	22	(Z)
Loup	-3,427	(X)	120	2.5	65.8	338	2,813	18	152,233	5.8	94.2	12	62.4	11	–
McPherson	1,093	37.7	128	4.7	73.4	529	4,130	19	145,563	6.9	93.1	10	97.9	9	–
Madison	33,847	3.8	766	18.8	31.1	342	447	140	182,879	35.8	64.2	103	90.6	86	7
Merrick	20,410	20.9	513	16.2	39.6	283	552	113	219,468	48.7	51.3	187	98.7	183	1
Morrill	13,712	20.5	443	9.9	49.2	872	1,969	163	366,989	18.3	81.7	196	27.3	191	1
Nance	18,507	37.8	392	13.8	40.1	229	584	55	140,957	38.4	61.6	64	64.4	63	(Z)
Nemaha	14,492	7.3	483	11.2	34.2	255	529	38	78,207	54.9	45.1	730	0.4	2	2
Nuckolls	8,187	13.9	476	9.7	49.4	351	736	49	103,851	68.3	31.7	77	76.0	75	1
Otoe	8,147	3.3	797	21.7	29.2	343	430	44	54,627	54.0	46.0	424	1.4	3	2
Pawnee	14,805	34.8	531	11.1	31.8	257	484	22	41,629	48.4	51.6	3	28.5	2	(Z)
Perkins	14,230	25.9	438	4.3	57.5	548	1,252	83	190,148	68.2	31.8	210	99.8	208	1
Phelps	46,376	21.2	470	8.5	53.6	366	779	341	726,128	25.6	74.4	325	64.0	318	2
Pierce	22,729	24.2	697	16.5	32.3	333	477	122	174,549	37.2	62.8	124	97.0	121	1

See footnotes at end of table.

Table B-14. Counties — **Farm Earnings, Agriculture, and Water Use**—Con.

[Includes United States, states, and 3,141 counties/county equivalents defined as of February 22, 2005. For more information on these areas, see Appendix C, Geographic Information]

County	Farm earnings, 2005 Total ($1,000)	Percent of total[1]	Farms Number	Farms Percent Less than 50 acres	Farms Percent 500 acres or more	Land in farms Total acres (1,000)	Land in farms Average size of farm (acres)	Value of farm products sold Total (mil. dol.)	Average per farm (dol.)	Percent from Crops[2]	Percent from Livestock and poultry[3]	Water use Total (mil. gal. per day)	Ground water, percent of total	By selected major use Irrigation	By selected major use Public supply
NEBRASKA—Con.															
Platte	49,331	6.5	1,000	19.0	30.7	435	435	199	199,414	36.3	63.7	132	93.7	109	8
Polk	21,996	29.7	527	12.0	37.0	264	502	149	281,899	33.3	66.7	136	99.1	133	1
Red Willow	15,653	7.4	380	17.4	55.0	429	1,129	96	251,374	24.7	75.3	79	65.4	70	4
Richardson	24,819	21.9	732	10.9	29.5	321	438	53	72,335	54.3	45.7	3	83.2	1	1
Rock	4,444	23.2	271	8.1	64.2	629	2,320	55	203,483	16.3	83.7	46	96.0	45	(Z)
Saline	25,412	8.2	728	13.5	34.6	345	474	66	90,268	71.6	28.4	101	87.2	96	2
Sarpy	2,487	0.1	355	41.4	20.8	105	296	47	131,777	34.2	65.8	41	87.0	9	22
Saunders	43,460	19.0	1,157	22.7	26.8	458	396	151	130,786	50.7	49.3	133	90.7	86	36
Scotts Bluff	18,143	2.4	780	17.9	26.2	427	548	191	245,060	23.7	76.3	316	19.9	296	10
Seward	32,458	12.1	862	22.2	30.0	364	422	117	135,455	50.9	49.1	93	83.0	89	2
Sheridan	3,029	5.3	613	7.7	57.3	1,486	2,424	70	114,830	25.7	74.3	100	79.8	97	1
Sherman	10,513	31.1	448	10.5	41.7	316	706	43	97,074	42.3	57.7	76	77.3	74	1
Sioux	−978	(X)	318	3.8	65.4	1,103	3,469	67	211,223	12.5	87.5	72	17.5	70	(Z)
Stanton	20,867	21.1	655	13.4	26.7	243	371	82	125,869	32.0	68.0	25	89.3	21	1
Thayer	18,400	17.1	558	9.9	45.7	380	682	101	181,475	59.3	40.7	169	93.1	161	1
Thomas	−2,850	(X)	79	6.3	77.2	349	4,415	11	133,709	(NA)	(NA)	8	64.1	5	(Z)
Thurston	15,524	12.7	438	18.5	31.5	214	489	93	211,550	38.6	61.4	12	88.9	9	2
Valley	13,310	20.0	419	11.7	47.5	315	751	71	168,542	30.2	69.8	78	52.2	76	1
Washington	7,143	1.8	760	31.1	22.5	242	319	86	112,808	46.1	53.9	574	2.2	16	7
Wayne	35,438	19.2	623	17.3	30.5	281	452	117	187,022	33.8	66.2	35	95.1	32	2
Webster	18,494	32.1	449	11.8	43.9	318	709	84	187,641	27.0	73.0	62	77.9	59	1
Wheeler	13,691	73.2	194	10.8	58.8	338	1,743	146	753,371	7.7	92.3	53	99.2	52	(Z)
York	21,594	5.4	617	13.9	45.4	354	573	161	260,669	56.3	43.7	253	98.7	246	3
NEVADA	109,563	0.2	2,989	46.7	24.2	6,331	2,118	447	149,545	35.3	64.7	2,810	26.9	2,110	629
Churchill	14,261	2.5	498	53.6	9.6	149	300	51	101,637	22.2	77.8	158	8.6	152	3
Clark	6,234	(Z)	253	79.8	3.2	69	272	17	67,206	39.0	61.0	529	16.2	25	463
Douglas	227	(Z)	178	59.0	16.9	211	1,185	9	51,303	46.3	53.7	150	11.1	138	11
Elko	13,400	1.4	397	31.5	41.8	2,472	6,227	45	114,134	3.7	96.3	526	8.0	511	13
Esmeralda	450	3.9	18	27.8	61.1	(D)	(D)	(D)	(NA)	(NA)	(NA)	27	88.8	27	(Z)
Eureka	2,889	0.9	73	5.5	58.9	266	3,650	13	173,411	70.7	29.3	109	64.4	109	(Z)
Humboldt	15,690	3.8	233	28.8	47.2	761	3,267	55	235,833	68.4	31.6	396	46.7	391	4
Lander	7,489	6.1	116	37.9	33.6	620	5,347	21	177,716	49.8	50.2	98	55.1	96	2
Lincoln	1,959	3.1	109	34.9	20.2	(D)	(D)	11	105,055	62.0	38.0	58	66.6	56	2
Lyon	16,105	2.9	330	47.6	18.8	226	686	74	225,670	49.3	50.7	224	31.3	210	9
Mineral	−1,452	(X)	17	41.2	29.4	(D)	(D)	3	180,882	(NA)	(NA)	14	52.7	12	2
Nye	15,093	2.2	172	55.2	22.1	98	567	22	130,349	19.5	80.5	53	73.2	45	6
Pershing	3,978	4.3	115	17.4	41.7	131	1,140	26	223,548	33.5	66.5	109	22.2	108	2
Storey	–	–	6	100.0	–	(Z)	15	(D)	(NA)	(NA)	(NA)	8	40.9	2	1
Washoe	9,177	0.1	332	64.2	14.2	802	2,416	18	53,554	55.7	44.3	209	25.3	108	93
White Pine	4,435	2.4	121	24.8	34.7	203	1,679	76	628,306	5.2	94.8	112	16.9	110	3
Independent City															
Carson City	−372	(X)	21	52.4	19.0	4	209	1	44,190	21.8	78.2	25	48.4	7	17
NEW HAMPSHIRE	46,175	0.1	3,363	45.9	5.2	445	132	145	43,067	57.4	42.6	1,210	7.0	5	97
Belknap	1,360	0.1	231	48.1	3.5	23	101	5	21,139	65.2	34.8	6	52.5	(Z)	3
Carroll	2,011	0.2	229	43.7	4.8	30	130	4	18,035	68.4	31.6	7	67.6	(Z)	4
Cheshire	8,559	0.5	323	43.0	5.6	41	128	12	38,108	27.3	72.7	8	67.7	(Z)	4
Coos	3,532	0.6	208	30.3	9.1	44	212	9	43,351	18.8	81.2	44	3.9	(Z)	4
Grafton	3,450	0.1	421	28.7	10.5	86	204	20	47,033	17.3	82.7	18	38.8	(Z)	8
Hillsborough	5,062	(Z)	481	59.9	1.7	40	83	15	30,701	76.0	24.0	56	39.4	1	37
Merrimack	11,000	0.3	502	45.0	7.2	79	158	41	81,996	82.7	17.3	253	3.9	1	9
Rockingham	5,302	0.1	445	60.0	1.1	32	71	17	38,101	78.2	21.8	790	2.7	1	13
Strafford	2,751	0.1	281	47.0	3.2	34	120	10	35,135	62.9	37.1	21	37.2	(Z)	12
Sullivan	3,148	0.4	242	39.3	6.6	36	149	12	49,326	32.8	67.2	5	47.4	(Z)	3
NEW JERSEY	264,521	0.1	9,924	70.5	3.5	806	81	750	75,561	87.7	12.3	5,560	10.5	140	1,050
Atlantic	28,342	0.3	456	70.8	1.8	30	67	79	172,167	99.0	1.0	44	93.1	8	29
Bergen	12,879	(Z)	91	93.4	–	1	14	8	83,121	96.4	3.6	132	22.3	(Z)	112
Burlington	26,550	0.2	906	69.2	6.8	111	123	83	91,891	87.5	12.5	173	25.4	105	50
Camden	5,421	(Z)	216	79.2	1.4	10	47	14	63,139	99.0	1.0	51	96.9	1	46
Cape May	5,046	0.2	197	77.2	1.0	10	51	11	57,112	95.6	4.4	183	9.7	1	12
Cumberland	43,169	1.3	616	62.8	5.4	71	115	123	199,143	97.8	2.2	111	41.1	6	18
Essex	1,103	(Z)	15	100.0	–	(Z)	10	1	49,133	98.8	1.2	33	79.0	(Z)	32
Gloucester	31,095	0.6	692	69.4	3.2	51	73	66	95,389	93.9	6.1	59	58.4	5	21
Hudson	–	–	–	–	–	–	–	–	–	–	–	518	(Z)	–	–
Hunterdon	10,443	0.3	1,514	70.2	2.4	109	72	42	27,917	82.1	17.9	100	15.7	1	86
Mercer	3,459	(Z)	304	72.4	4.6	25	82	12	40,286	89.0	11.0	693	2.0	(Z)	41
Middlesex	9,144	(Z)	275	77.5	4.0	22	79	23	82,556	93.8	6.2	213	20.8	2	31
Monmouth	33,077	0.2	892	80.5	2.7	47	53	82	91,425	89.1	10.9	65	36.3	3	56
Morris	17,576	0.1	407	77.1	0.7	17	42	42	102,897	97.5	2.5	124	49.9	1	103
Ocean	7,724	0.1	217	79.7	2.3	12	56	11	49,433	83.6	16.4	667	8.3	1	50

See footnotes at end of table.

County and City Data Book: 2007

U.S. Census Bureau

Table B-14. Counties — **Farm Earnings, Agriculture, and Water Use**—Con.

[Includes United States, states, and 3,141 counties/county equivalents defined as of February 22, 2005. For more information on these areas, see Appendix C, Geographic Information]

County	Farm earnings, 2005 Total ($1,000)	Farm earnings, 2005 Percent of total[1]	Farms Number	Farms Percent Less than 50 acres	Farms Percent 500 acres or more	Land in farms Total acres (1,000)	Land in farms Average size of farm (acres)	Value of farm products sold Total (mil. dol.)	Value of farm products sold Average per farm (dol.)	Value of farm products sold Percent from Crops[2]	Value of farm products sold Percent from Live-stock and poultry[3]	Water use, 2000[4] Total (mil. gal. per day)	Water use, 2000[4] Ground water, percent of total	Water use, 2000[4] By selected major use (mil. gal. per day) Irri-gation	Water use, 2000[4] By selected major use (mil. gal. per day) Public supply
NEW JERSEY—Con.															
Passaic	2,801	(Z)	70	94.3	–	2	22	6	86,771	98.5	1.5	201	4.3	(Z)	184
Salem	18,488	1.3	753	58.6	6.4	96	128	73	96,311	76.9	23.1	1,970	0.6	4	4
Somerset	2,554	(Z)	442	73.8	4.1	36	82	15	34,081	54.9	45.1	148	9.3	1	142
Sussex	452	(Z)	1,029	66.2	1.7	75	73	15	14,340	54.7	45.3	22	59.5	(Z)	6
Union	2,785	(Z)	18	100.0	–	(Z)	10	7	375,000	99.7	0.3	32	49.9	(Z)	18
Warren	2,413	0.1	814	63.8	4.4	78	96	40	48,773	46.4	53.6	24	86.0	(Z)	7
NEW MEXICO	659,356	1.7	15,170	44.7	28.8	44,810	2,954	1,700	112,065	23.4	76.6	3,260	47.2	2,860	296
Bernalillo	777	(Z)	618	83.2	3.9	(D)	(D)	20	32,403	27.6	72.4	170	67.4	58	106
Catron	-2,005	(X)	206	15.0	49.5	1,645	7,985	8	40,568	3.8	96.2	18	3.6	18	(Z)
Chaves	123,012	11.8	604	40.1	36.6	2,516	4,165	284	470,114	10.6	89.4	319	93.2	301	16
Cibola	-951	(X)	155	29.0	54.2	1,691	10,909	4	26,477	(NA)	(NA)	8	51.8	4	3
Colfax	-2,517	(X)	284	10.9	45.8	2,216	7,804	21	72,303	4.3	95.7	47	3.4	44	3
Curry	90,625	9.7	677	13.9	49.8	916	1,354	233	343,576	11.4	88.6	183	100.0	175	8
De Baca	3,453	15.1	188	32.4	52.1	1,409	7,497	15	81,069	23.6	76.4	45	20.6	44	(Z)
Dona Ana	159,891	5.5	1,691	81.1	5.6	581	343	252	148,934	48.9	51.1	494	25.2	456	34
Eddy	27,895	2.4	510	44.7	31.6	1,183	2,320	82	161,198	30.2	69.8	219	57.2	203	14
Grant	-2,867	(X)	272	26.5	46.7	1,218	4,478	8	27,732	1.9	98.1	31	26.3	27	4
Guadalupe	-3,970	(X)	208	20.2	61.1	1,462	7,028	10	50,409	3.3	96.7	13	14.2	12	1
Harding	-317	(X)	129	4.7	76.0	992	7,689	11	88,434	(NA)	(NA)	3	100.0	3	(Z)
Hidalgo	5,770	9.3	144	17.4	54.2	1,128	7,830	17	115,611	68.3	31.7	38	79.7	37	1
Lea	33,413	2.7	554	28.5	38.8	2,258	4,076	98	177,433	23.0	77.0	137	100.0	116	13
Lincoln	-4,915	(X)	343	36.2	40.2	1,606	4,681	11	32,408	2.1	97.9	25	33.0	21	4
Los Alamos	–	–	6	83.3	–	(D)	(D)	(Z)	2,667	(NA)	(NA)	4	100.0	–	4
Luna	17,602	5.6	171	25.1	43.9	710	4,149	47	277,421	70.0	30.0	90	96.2	85	4
McKinley	-3,833	(X)	150	16.7	48.0	3,170	21,132	6	42,673	(NA)	(NA)	14	84.1	2	5
Mora	-3,986	(X)	410	19.0	33.7	955	2,328	15	35,683	6.6	93.4	30	2.1	29	(Z)
Otero	4,469	0.4	622	60.5	15.4	1,208	1,941	11	16,952	53.1	46.9	42	64.8	30	11
Quay	8,444	7.2	594	14.5	51.7	1,652	2,780	23	38,951	11.8	88.2	104	7.6	102	2
Rio Arriba	-4,352	(X)	988	55.8	16.4	1,431	1,449	11	10,679	16.6	83.4	104	4.3	100	2
Roosevelt	95,648	31.2	804	14.6	42.7	1,501	1,867	190	236,422	13.0	87.0	137	100.0	133	4
Sandoval	-2,368	(X)	347	55.6	18.7	763	2,199	6	16,256	47.3	52.7	72	24.0	56	11
San Juan	56,733	2.3	808	71.2	5.3	1,757	2,174	37	45,829	72.9	27.1	263	0.6	197	17
San Miguel	-5,751	(X)	565	21.6	38.4	2,092	3,702	12	21,731	10.0	90.0	46	2.6	43	3
Santa Fe	-2,752	(X)	460	65.2	13.3	684	1,486	12	25,615	74.1	25.9	46	60.4	30	14
Sierra	4,817	4.4	223	41.3	28.7	1,363	6,112	19	86,933	29.8	70.2	33	35.9	31	2
Socorro	14,635	5.9	388	48.2	25.5	1,523	3,926	36	92,206	12.3	87.7	161	20.3	158	2
Taos	-360	(X)	453	59.2	12.6	466	1,029	3	7,558	17.7	82.3	92	5.4	89	2
Torrance	12,320	8.4	461	20.4	46.2	1,697	3,681	36	78,920	26.1	73.9	32	100.0	30	1
Union	37,777	45.3	419	2.1	70.2	2,243	5,354	143	342,360	10.1	89.9	75	92.4	75	1
Valencia	3,019	0.5	718	85.7	3.6	369	514	18	24,673	20.9	79.1	159	9.2	151	5
NEW YORK	992,222	0.2	37,255	30.4	9.4	7,661	206	3,118	83,689	36.4	63.6	12,100	7.4	36	2,570
Albany	6,819	0.1	484	38.2	3.3	69	143	19	39,990	48.4	51.6	103	10.8	(Z)	48
Allegany	22,994	3.7	867	14.9	8.9	180	208	46	52,552	21.7	78.3	8	71.5	2	3
Bronx	–	–	–	–	–	–	–	–	–	–	–	3	100.0	–	–
Broome	13,364	0.3	588	23.6	5.4	98	167	29	48,966	20.0	80.0	115	27.6	–	31
Cattaraugus	17,544	1.2	1,157	22.3	5.8	202	175	58	50,434	26.9	73.1	14	89.0	–	9
Cayuga	50,433	4.0	881	26.2	13.1	238	270	128	145,335	26.6	73.4	13	27.0	–	13
Chautauqua	44,433	2.0	1,734	36.3	4.5	256	148	99	57,232	36.0	64.0	481	2.2	–	10
Chemung	4,261	0.2	427	26.9	6.8	69	162	12	28,253	32.6	67.4	17	65.3	(Z)	13
Chenango	14,086	1.8	960	24.9	8.3	190	198	52	54,460	10.0	90.0	85	7.8	–	3
Clinton	25,894	1.6	604	21.4	13.9	169	279	78	129,863	21.7	78.3	14	27.2	1	7
Columbia	23,594	2.4	498	32.9	13.7	120	240	52	104,807	34.1	65.9	7	69.6	(Z)	4
Cortland	11,975	1.5	569	21.6	9.5	127	223	40	69,786	8.8	91.2	8	100.0	–	5
Delaware	20,416	2.4	788	18.4	11.0	192	243	51	64,112	14.4	85.6	456	1.2	–	453
Dutchess	8,897	0.1	667	45.6	8.7	112	168	32	47,544	66.7	33.3	35	57.0	1	25
Erie	32,511	0.1	1,289	45.3	4.0	162	125	92	71,654	45.9	54.1	875	0.8	1	178
Essex	3,578	0.5	236	26.7	13.1	55	233	9	36,576	43.2	56.8	8	21.4	–	6
Franklin	14,813	1.9	532	18.6	14.5	138	260	48	90,231	13.0	87.0	9	40.5	1	6
Fulton	3,384	0.4	246	31.3	6.1	38	153	8	34,240	15.6	84.4	8	27.3	–	5
Genesee	21,718	2.2	580	39.0	12.6	177	306	125	215,410	38.2	61.8	9	53.1	(Z)	5
Greene	6,525	1.0	342	38.6	8.5	58	169	14	42,032	40.1	59.9	5	47.8	–	3
Hamilton	–	–	24	54.2	–	1	59	(Z)	8,583	(NA)	(NA)	1	63.3	–	1
Herkimer	15,597	2.2	690	17.2	9.1	159	231	50	72,213	13.5	86.5	10	41.0	–	7
Jefferson	31,508	1.1	1,028	14.7	18.0	331	322	100	96,831	10.4	89.6	17	23.0	–	10
Kings	–	–	1	100.0	–	(D)	(D)	(D)	(NA)	(NA)	(NA)	14	100.0	1	–
Lewis	19,773	6.3	721	16.1	13.5	197	273	72	100,108	9.8	90.2	5	58.0	–	2
Livingston	20,148	2.2	801	32.5	12.9	209	262	84	104,943	34.3	65.7	8	42.4	(Z)	5
Madison	16,035	1.7	734	25.2	11.7	168	229	62	83,929	12.1	87.9	6	72.9	–	2
Monroe	12,777	0.1	631	59.6	9.5	107	169	54	85,477	84.6	15.4	236	3.5	(Z)	77
Montgomery	12,297	1.6	624	22.8	12.5	152	244	52	83,010	19.5	80.5	11	26.0	–	8
Nassau	2,369	(Z)	65	87.7	–	1	17	8	126,938	(NA)	(NA)	499	39.9	5	183

See footnotes at end of table.

County and City Data Book: 2007

U.S. Census Bureau

Table B-14. Counties — **Farm Earnings, Agriculture, and Water Use**—Con.

[Includes United States, states, and 3,141 counties/county equivalents defined as of February 22, 2005. For more information on these areas, see Appendix C, Geographic Information]

County	Farm earnings, 2005 Total ($1,000)	Farm earnings, 2005 Percent of total[1]	Farms Number	Farms Percent Less than 50 acres	Farms Percent 500 acres or more	Land in farms Total acres (1,000)	Land in farms Average size of farm (acres)	Value of farm products sold Total (mil. dol.)	Value of farm products sold Average per farm (dol.)	Percent from Crops[2]	Percent from Live-stock and poultry[3]	Water use Total (mil. gal. per day)	Water use Ground water, percent of total	By selected major use Irrigation	By selected major use Public supply
NEW YORK—Con.															
New York	–	–	4	100.0	–	(Z)	1	(Z)	97,500	100.0	–	259	8.5	–	–
Niagara	22,676	0.6	801	43.2	7.7	148	185	60	74,789	66.4	33.6	284	0.6	–	46
Oneida	24,835	0.5	1,087	25.9	9.6	220	203	78	72,098	28.9	71.1	34	18.9	–	27
Onondaga	24,525	0.2	725	39.3	10.6	156	216	82	113,330	29.9	70.1	95	11.2	(Z)	73
Ontario	26,852	1.2	896	41.5	11.7	195	217	87	97,183	43.2	56.8	11	25.3	–	6
Orange	23,963	0.3	706	40.2	6.9	108	153	66	93,803	61.7	38.3	644	3.5	2	27
Orleans	22,038	3.9	504	33.9	10.7	133	264	69	136,740	88.7	11.3	4	24.3	(Z)	2
Oswego	8,671	0.5	682	30.5	4.8	103	151	32	46,226	56.3	43.7	975	1.1	(Z)	14
Otsego	11,715	1.2	1,028	19.0	8.5	206	201	51	49,322	13.0	87.0	6	73.2	–	3
Putnam	2,332	0.2	52	61.5	5.8	7	129	2	46,654	96.5	3.5	124	5.8	(Z)	118
Queens	–	–	2	100.0	–	(D)	(D)	(D)	(NA)	(NA)	(NA)	1,754	3.5	1	48
Rensselaer	4,756	0.2	549	37.9	7.3	92	168	28	51,224	42.7	57.3	27	23.3	(Z)	18
Richmond	–	–	16	100.0	–	(Z)	3	2	107,500	(NA)	(NA)	324	0.5	–	–
Rockland	1,546	(Z)	29	62.1	–	(D)	(D)	3	108,931	95.2	4.8	592	4.5	–	25
St. Lawrence	31,074	1.8	1,451	11.8	14.8	403	278	100	68,722	8.9	91.1	14	42.7	–	8
Saratoga	15,123	0.4	592	48.8	5.2	75	127	33	56,128	30.0	70.0	20	72.6	1	12
Schenectady	197	(Z)	200	45.0	2.0	22	109	4	20,040	60.0	40.0	28	99.8	(Z)	25
Schoharie	8,544	2.1	579	24.0	7.1	113	195	27	46,596	27.7	72.3	117	2.0	(Z)	115
Schuyler	4,654	2.1	405	29.4	6.2	74	182	18	44,225	25.4	74.6	2	70.6	(Z)	1
Seneca	15,077	3.1	466	29.4	14.6	127	273	45	97,090	40.8	59.2	4	28.4	–	2
Steuben	22,334	0.9	1,501	17.6	11.9	373	249	85	56,498	31.6	68.4	75	17.4	3	8
Suffolk	53,139	0.1	651	76.3	1.5	34	52	201	309,035	88.3	11.7	985	17.9	13	125
Sullivan	10,591	0.9	381	35.2	7.1	64	167	38	99,089	7.1	92.9	141	6.0	(Z)	138
Tioga	12,783	1.6	604	22.8	9.3	128	212	30	49,568	20.4	79.6	7	95.0	–	4
Tompkins	12,718	0.5	563	38.9	8.9	101	179	42	74,437	21.1	78.9	250	0.6	–	10
Ulster	12,919	0.5	532	44.7	6.6	83	157	34	64,692	83.5	16.5	449	2.5	2	440
Warren	921	0.1	72	59.7	1.4	6	89	3	34,944	90.3	9.7	12	16.8	(Z)	8
Washington	25,947	3.4	887	24.2	13.9	206	232	82	92,413	14.5	85.5	8	59.1	1	4
Wayne	32,099	2.6	904	37.8	8.4	165	183	104	114,885	69.7	30.3	437	0.8	–	6
Westchester	3,069	(Z)	129	68.2	3.9	10	77	9	68,636	95.4	4.6	1,234	1.5	–	126
Wyoming	61,998	9.0	767	28.4	12.4	215	281	178	232,078	17.0	83.0	6	49.0	(Z)	4
Yates	17,383	6.7	722	22.6	5.3	115	159	50	69,769	41.8	58.2	83	1.3	(Z)	1
NORTH CAROLINA	2,464,936	1.2	53,930	45.6	7.2	9,079	168	6,962	129,087	28.9	71.1	11,400	5.1	287	945
Alamance	3,182	0.1	831	43.2	3.7	98	118	29	34,552	36.5	63.5	27	18.5	4	18
Alexander	24,614	5.3	661	54.8	2.3	58	88	67	101,171	5.0	95.0	5	40.5	(Z)	1
Alleghany	14,423	10.1	544	47.4	5.0	73	134	24	43,820	44.8	55.2	3	35.1	2	(Z)
Anson	24,939	7.1	539	33.4	8.2	100	186	107	199,416	2.9	97.1	10	23.0	1	6
Ashe	32,861	9.2	1,152	49.6	2.3	108	94	29	25,331	79.9	20.1	3	60.4	1	1
Avery	25,471	8.8	495	62.8	1.4	31	62	28	56,317	98.8	1.2	6	27.4	3	1
Beaufort	11,860	1.7	395	30.4	26.1	170	430	74	187,051	66.0	34.0	48	98.6	3	3
Bertie	20,807	8.2	330	28.5	21.5	143	432	85	257,652	34.6	65.4	12	53.6	6	1
Bladen	64,281	12.0	551	35.9	12.5	145	264	255	462,158	15.5	84.5	51	20.2	2	31
Brunswick	5,900	0.5	271	48.3	6.6	41	152	35	128,620	48.9	51.1	1,640	0.3	11	1
Buncombe	16,978	0.3	1,192	63.8	1.9	95	80	22	18,314	60.6	39.4	42	20.6	3	25
Burke	27,312	1.7	439	62.9	1.4	32	73	31	70,403	55.5	44.5	24	12.8	2	19
Cabarrus	12,287	0.4	658	43.9	3.0	73	111	31	46,464	19.1	80.9	26	12.6	2	21
Caldwell	24,143	1.8	411	54.0	2.4	35	85	16	38,550	59.4	40.6	12	18.5	2	8
Camden	3,141	3.6	70	24.3	45.7	(D)	(D)	20	281,614	(NA)	(NA)	(Z)	94.7	(Z)	(Z)
Carteret	3,004	0.3	128	60.2	5.5	60	467	16	123,992	97.5	2.5	8	95.2	1	4
Caswell	–3,799	(X)	517	22.8	9.1	117	226	24	46,547	54.2	45.8	3	92.6	1	(Z)
Catawba	13,626	0.4	715	47.3	3.9	79	110	21	29,997	35.3	64.7	1,188	0.5	3	18
Chatham	39,237	4.7	1,128	48.0	2.4	119	105	122	108,045	4.7	95.3	365	1.4	1	5
Cherokee	12,056	3.5	262	55.0	1.9	22	85	11	42,309	10.6	89.4	4	41.1	(Z)	2
Chowan	26,587	11.0	173	31.2	24.3	60	346	38	220,549	73.0	27.0	6	40.3	3	2
Clay	–1,184	(X)	168	54.8	1.8	13	80	1	7,940	34.6	65.4	1	55.2	1	(Z)
Cleveland	36,105	2.4	1,131	40.5	2.7	117	104	41	36,073	26.3	73.7	192	1.3	3	14
Columbus	65,099	8.4	828	40.5	10.4	160	193	106	128,320	39.0	61.0	50	13.9	2	3
Craven	12,561	0.5	275	33.1	16.7	79	287	49	178,804	51.2	48.8	32	50.0	3	12
Cumberland	13,254	0.1	478	46.4	10.9	90	189	58	120,513	25.0	75.0	48	19.6	5	40
Currituck	3,774	1.7	82	50.0	23.2	35	424	9	112,293	96.8	3.2	3	75.8	2	1
Dare	–	–	8	50.0	37.5	(D)	(D)	1	114,500	100.0	–	7	93.7	1	6
Davidson	6,692	0.3	1,138	46.7	2.7	105	92	26	22,871	30.4	69.6	21	7.9	2	18
Davie	3,034	0.7	705	46.7	2.8	76	108	14	19,908	30.9	69.1	6	26.7	2	3
Duplin	150,399	18.4	1,190	43.4	10.2	235	197	715	601,057	8.3	91.7	31	82.3	7	5
Durham	1,844	(Z)	238	58.4	3.8	26	110	7	27,987	82.3	17.7	38	12.8	3	30
Edgecombe	42,285	4.0	281	30.6	27.4	164	582	98	348,345	41.5	58.5	13	38.8	5	4
Forsyth	1,200	(Z)	783	61.2	1.1	52	66	14	18,064	80.4	19.6	58	10.9	6	47
Franklin	9,497	1.6	574	36.9	9.2	128	224	40	70,199	65.5	34.5	9	35.7	3	2

See footnotes at end of table.

Table B-14. Counties — Farm Earnings, Agriculture, and Water Use—Con.

[Includes United States, states, and 3,141 counties/county equivalents defined as of February 22, 2005. For more information on these areas, see Appendix C, Geographic Information]

County	Farm earnings, 2005 Total ($1,000)	Farm earnings, 2005 Percent of total[1]	Agriculture — Farms Number	Farms Percent Less than 50 acres	Farms Percent 500 acres or more	Land in farms Total acres (1,000)	Land in farms Average size of farm (acres)	Value of farm products sold Total (mil. dol.)	Value Average per farm (dol.)	Percent from Crops[2]	Percent from Live-stock and poultry[3]	Water use, 2000[4] Total (mil. gal. per day)	Ground water, percent of total	By selected major use (mil. gal. per day) Irrigation	Public supply
NORTH CAROLINA—Con.															
Gaston	7,203	0.2	450	47.3	1.6	42	93	12	26,540	23.8	76.2	972	0.8	3	29
Gates	22,600	27.3	129	30.2	24.8	64	496	32	249,000	45.9	54.1	2	92.4	(Z)	1
Graham	2,131	2.0	143	60.1	1.4	8	56	2	12,343	27.3	72.7	1	42.4	–	1
Granville	-7,550	(X)	674	30.4	10.5	147	217	22	32,829	86.3	13.7	8	34.3	2	3
Greene	34,074	17.6	271	29.5	24.4	98	361	159	586,395	18.5	81.5	6	82.5	1	2
Guilford	26,597	0.2	1,095	54.0	3.9	111	102	45	41,509	67.8	32.2	79	16.1	10	57
Halifax	35,140	5.0	380	31.1	23.9	195	512	64	169,658	45.5	54.5	38	7.5	3	7
Harnett	30,759	3.0	730	47.1	7.8	114	157	105	143,881	28.5	71.5	18	20.9	4	10
Haywood	8,860	1.2	795	58.9	2.1	65	81	12	15,420	45.9	54.1	35	5.1	2	6
Henderson	56,608	3.5	525	58.3	3.2	49	93	61	115,745	88.2	11.8	17	21.6	5	8
Hertford	7,002	2.0	136	30.1	30.1	80	587	96	708,926	22.0	78.0	9	74.5	4	2
Hoke	12,557	4.1	201	48.8	13.9	63	315	45	221,438	23.7	76.3	4	76.2	1	2
Hyde	11,484	13.8	144	41.0	39.6	103	716	33	228,250	97.8	2.2	2	40.6	1	1
Iredell	43,455	1.6	1,262	43.3	3.5	147	116	146	115,370	5.2	94.8	19	42.7	3	10
Jackson	5,807	0.9	248	67.3	1.6	16	66	8	32,875	95.3	4.7	4	42.3	1	1
Johnston	51,809	2.7	1,144	45.2	7.7	194	170	146	127,197	45.8	54.2	19	52.0	4	7
Jones	31,689	29.3	154	20.8	27.3	76	494	90	582,643	21.5	78.5	2	84.7	(Z)	1
Lee	10,100	0.7	304	48.7	6.3	46	152	22	72,586	43.9	56.1	11	22.7	2	7
Lenoir	32,100	2.8	428	32.7	18.7	122	284	141	330,315	29.5	70.5	15	87.6	2	9
Lincoln	11,182	1.4	618	50.6	2.9	58	93	18	28,929	22.0	78.0	10	38.0	1	5
McDowell	30,352	4.5	282	48.9	2.5	24	87	23	80,681	68.1	31.9	8	51.8	1	3
Macon	4,161	0.9	347	57.3	0.3	22	65	5	13,248	52.9	47.1	6	25.3	2	2
Madison	-2,876	(X)	973	47.9	1.5	84	86	10	10,690	81.8	18.2	2	70.8	(Z)	1
Martin	12,596	3.2	305	25.9	23.3	111	363	40	130,790	63.1	36.9	89	8.8	1	2
Mecklenburg	51,426	0.1	300	60.0	2.0	25	85	72	238,380	93.3	6.7	2,767	0.3	11	107
Mitchell	5,449	2.4	358	61.7	1.7	26	73	4	10,818	87.3	12.7	3	30.7	(Z)	1
Montgomery	27,953	6.2	292	38.0	7.5	42	143	68	233,849	4.0	96.0	7	24.4	1	3
Moore	53,991	3.6	820	47.8	3.4	101	123	91	111,017	18.0	82.0	27	39.9	14	7
Nash	34,164	1.8	478	41.4	16.9	160	335	108	226,851	50.6	49.4	32	14.7	14	16
New Hanover	5,857	0.1	77	70.1	–	(D)	(D)	3	43,442	96.4	3.6	36	47.0	4	8
Northampton	62,679	22.3	328	33.5	25.3	151	459	61	187,088	29.0	71.0	4	79.6	1	1
Onslow	22,985	0.5	404	44.3	5.7	64	158	90	222,911	19.4	80.6	25	97.6	3	17
Orange	6,490	0.2	627	43.2	4.3	71	113	22	35,270	50.9	49.1	17	18.7	2	13
Pamlico	3,745	3.4	68	35.3	35.3	52	770	16	242,338	93.0	7.0	2	100.0	(Z)	1
Pasquotank	11,376	1.5	157	27.4	35.0	99	633	35	220,624	98.1	1.9	8	89.5	2	5
Pender	33,762	7.9	296	43.2	11.1	63	212	102	343,453	22.0	78.0	8	69.4	3	1
Perquimans	23,410	21.7	193	16.6	34.7	94	489	38	199,192	61.1	38.9	3	91.7	1	1
Person	-14,143	(X)	374	34.8	11.2	95	254	18	48,455	82.2	17.8	1,059	0.2	1	4
Pitt	14,458	0.5	448	30.1	25.4	186	415	120	268,087	47.8	52.2	14	90.2	4	6
Polk	3,277	1.6	260	55.0	1.5	27	104	5	17,465	61.3	38.7	3	45.6	1	1
Randolph	95,341	4.6	1,583	45.5	2.6	157	99	148	93,478	9.5	90.5	22	42.9	4	8
Richmond	54,423	8.6	257	33.9	6.6	49	192	66	256,942	7.8	92.2	12	23.0	1	7
Robeson	45,232	3.1	873	43.6	17.2	287	328	191	218,371	31.3	68.7	38	52.2	3	20
Rockingham	-598	(X)	871	36.6	6.0	136	156	29	32,784	78.5	21.5	241	1.6	4	18
Rowan	28,506	1.2	951	43.3	4.8	115	121	36	38,120	59.4	40.6	312	1.7	3	13
Rutherford	1,957	0.2	653	39.5	2.6	68	104	9	14,096	19.9	80.1	16	17.8	2	12
Sampson	244,802	26.6	1,178	37.1	12.1	298	253	676	573,592	11.6	88.4	25	74.1	8	3
Scotland	10,957	1.8	159	37.7	20.1	58	367	47	293,101	11.4	88.6	12	56.0	2	4
Stanly	28,362	3.3	719	44.9	6.3	108	150	57	78,777	14.5	85.5	13	31.6	1	8
Stokes	4,288	1.4	934	39.3	3.3	107	115	23	24,506	70.1	29.9	968	0.2	1	2
Surry	54,397	4.3	1,268	47.5	2.8	129	102	89	70,274	24.1	75.9	19	25.7	3	8
Swain	66	(Z)	83	49.4	4.8	7	86	1	13,771	(NA)	(NA)	2	47.4	(Z)	1
Transylvania	11,285	3.0	256	64.1	1.2	18	71	17	64,910	75.4	24.6	24	7.9	2	2
Tyrrell	7,887	18.0	91	19.8	39.6	74	809	29	323,110	72.6	27.4	1	60.2	(Z)	(Z)
Union	112,979	4.6	1,224	52.9	6.1	191	156	261	213,482	10.8	89.2	24	45.8	3	8
Vance	-3,002	(X)	228	24.6	18.9	75	329	14	60,715	96.3	3.7	9	18.7	2	5
Wake	1,834	(Z)	846	55.7	4.3	93	110	56	66,520	74.7	25.3	128	11.6	14	73
Warren	13,596	8.6	297	24.9	12.8	75	254	27	90,902	32.6	67.4	3	45.9	2	(Z)
Washington	6,215	5.1	193	32.1	33.7	114	593	46	239,114	73.7	26.3	4	88.2	2	1
Watauga	11,927	1.3	731	54.9	1.0	52	71	12	15,889	56.7	43.3	6	25.4	1	3
Wayne	31,619	1.5	722	42.5	13.3	171	237	318	440,064	13.7	86.3	42	25.5	4	12
Wilkes	101,710	7.3	1,273	50.6	2.5	124	98	208	163,005	2.5	97.5	22	30.4	1	7
Wilson	-7,589	(X)	315	38.1	21.9	115	364	79	250,689	76.5	23.5	16	25.7	5	9
Yadkin	26,328	6.8	1,044	50.1	3.7	117	112	65	62,283	23.6	76.4	6	70.2	2	2
Yancey	10,225	6.2	622	66.9	0.8	39	62	6	8,997	77.0	23.0	3	56.4	1	1
NORTH DAKOTA	1,082,886	6.7	30,619	6.7	56.8	39,295	1,283	3,233	105,600	76.1	23.9	1,140	10.8	145	64
Adams	6,866	16.4	394	6.1	61.4	605	1,535	24	61,396	27.3	72.7	(Z)	61.5	(Z)	–
Barnes	28,189	13.2	838	9.2	46.3	857	1,023	94	112,428	91.7	8.3	2	55.6	(Z)	1
Benson	10,142	10.1	567	5.1	62.1	733	1,293	55	97,390	77.1	22.9	3	99.3	1	1
Billings	8,073	37.9	238	3.4	68.5	811	3,407	13	53,017	19.4	80.6	1	57.1	(Z)	(Z)
Bottineau	30,682	23.3	879	5.0	51.1	948	1,079	72	82,198	89.8	10.2	2	85.8	(Z)	1

See footnotes at end of table.

Table B-14. Counties — **Farm Earnings, Agriculture, and Water Use**—Con.

[Includes United States, states, and 3,141 counties/county equivalents defined as of February 22, 2005. For more information on these areas, see Appendix C, Geographic Information]

County	Farm earnings, 2005 Total ($1,000)	Percent of total[1]	Farms Number	Farms Percent Less than 50 acres	Farms Percent 500 acres or more	Land in farms Total acres (1,000)	Land in farms Average size of farm (acres)	Value of farm products sold Total (mil. dol.)	Value of farm products sold Average per farm (dol.)	Percent from Crops[2]	Percent from Live-stock and poultry[3]	Water use Total (mil. gal. per day)	Ground water, percent of total	By selected major use Irri-gation	By selected major use Public supply
NORTH DAKOTA—Con.															
Bowman	18,726	25.4	360	3.1	63.1	759	2,109	26	72,831	32.4	67.6	1	39.8	1	(Z)
Burke	13,973	29.7	455	2.0	64.0	600	1,319	32	70,070	87.4	12.6	1	47.8	(Z)	(Z)
Burleigh	26,324	1.2	946	14.3	41.1	866	915	45	47,632	44.4	55.6	13	16.8	3	10
Cass	75,590	1.7	961	14.5	54.8	1,127	1,173	209	217,437	93.6	6.4	16	34.1	2	13
Cavalier	9,729	11.2	607	3.1	65.2	819	1,349	91	149,142	98.3	1.7	1	21.1	–	1
Dickey	56,297	39.4	533	8.8	51.6	599	1,125	72	135,066	70.1	29.9	4	93.7	3	1
Divide	10,015	27.3	532	3.9	68.0	761	1,430	41	77,053	85.1	14.9	2	98.0	2	(Z)
Dunn	21,698	38.6	582	4.6	68.2	1,106	1,900	47	79,986	33.2	66.8	1	31.8	1	(Z)
Eddy	12,495	31.2	325	4.3	60.0	349	1,073	21	65,197	69.6	30.4	1	86.0	(Z)	(Z)
Emmons	24,630	36.2	699	2.9	61.1	838	1,199	47	67,631	33.4	66.6	9	30.2	9	(Z)
Foster	12,250	15.4	309	7.1	58.6	383	1,239	40	128,531	65.9	34.1	1	95.6	1	(Z)
Golden Valley	5,188	19.5	231	3.9	63.2	580	2,513	19	84,113	43.1	56.9	1	25.3	1	(Z)
Grand Forks	10,906	0.6	863	11.7	42.3	756	876	145	167,833	89.1	10.9	11	86.2	9	2
Grant	10,824	31.2	548	5.7	70.1	1,057	1,928	42	76,712	22.7	77.3	11	2.0	11	(Z)
Griggs	11,605	23.8	423	5.7	45.6	379	896	30	70,296	83.5	16.5	2	100.0	1	(Z)
Hettinger	15,019	35.1	489	6.3	57.7	681	1,392	35	72,493	79.2	20.8	(Z)	69.2	(Z)	–
Kidder	17,453	38.4	584	4.8	63.7	794	1,360	44	76,074	44.1	55.9	12	97.5	12	(Z)
LaMoure	55,298	50.9	621	5.3	50.6	677	1,090	80	128,105	78.2	21.8	4	97.5	4	(Z)
Logan	23,462	52.0	445	3.6	63.1	578	1,298	36	79,973	26.0	74.0	2	99.4	1	(Z)
McHenry	18,925	28.4	901	5.0	59.6	1,126	1,250	67	74,880	54.0	46.0	19	34.4	18	(Z)
McIntosh	21,116	37.8	526	5.9	54.9	569	1,081	39	74,791	43.9	56.1	(Z)	100.0	(Z)	(Z)
McKenzie	10,754	9.4	632	5.2	66.5	1,193	1,888	56	88,408	58.9	41.1	13	12.2	12	(Z)
McLean	23,168	13.6	918	6.0	58.0	1,095	1,193	84	91,798	82.2	17.8	14	11.3	2	1
Mercer	6,159	2.2	456	6.1	50.9	536	1,176	22	48,798	45.0	55.0	422	0.4	1	4
Morton	17,525	4.3	855	6.9	63.0	1,276	1,493	69	81,035	28.5	71.5	47	1.7	1	3
Mountrail	16,438	14.8	682	2.3	66.9	1,068	1,566	53	78,302	74.6	25.4	1	63.6	(Z)	(Z)
Nelson	3,159	8.2	598	5.4	41.0	532	889	41	68,893	83.1	16.9	1	100.0	(Z)	(Z)
Oliver	6,190	13.7	307	6.8	60.3	404	1,315	23	73,547	38.4	61.6	442	0.1	3	(Z)
Pembina	6,030	3.6	524	5.9	52.3	614	1,171	142	271,214	96.3	3.7	2	70.0	(Z)	1
Pierce	2,959	4.2	487	6.4	61.4	531	1,090	36	74,528	71.0	29.0	1	97.6	(Z)	1
Ramsey	15,412	6.6	554	8.8	52.3	636	1,148	55	99,570	95.3	4.7	(Z)	76.1	(Z)	(Z)
Ransom	31,353	27.3	528	5.9	42.4	501	948	60	113,313	70.6	29.4	12	88.6	10	1
Renville	16,725	35.4	353	3.4	70.8	527	1,493	44	125,031	91.9	8.1	(Z)	100.0	–	(Z)
Richland	73,246	18.3	813	10.7	56.3	891	1,096	201	247,663	87.2	12.8	6	72.2	2	2
Rolette	3,272	1.6	523	3.1	51.8	508	971	32	61,279	68.0	32.0	2	100.0	(Z)	1
Sargent	42,125	22.0	469	7.5	52.9	505	1,077	78	166,719	81.7	18.3	4	98.7	4	(Z)
Sheridan	8,615	38.9	393	1.8	62.8	469	1,193	25	62,791	72.3	27.7	(Z)	100.0	(Z)	(Z)
Sioux	4,365	5.8	179	7.3	80.4	702	3,925	13	73,670	13.3	86.7	(Z)	82.8	(Z)	(Z)
Slope	6,910	67.2	259	2.3	68.0	763	2,944	20	78,274	41.2	58.8	1	12.1	1	(Z)
Stark	14,999	2.8	774	11.5	49.5	777	1,004	48	61,721	45.3	54.7	2	77.7	(Z)	(Z)
Steele	12,849	35.3	318	6.6	59.1	401	1,261	52	164,148	96.6	3.4	1	100.0	1	–
Stutsman	58,542	11.5	988	7.1	56.7	1,215	1,230	97	97,865	74.9	25.1	9	96.7	3	4
Towner	15,613	32.4	418	6.2	63.2	549	1,313	45	107,227	92.1	7.9	(Z)	93.3	(Z)	(Z)
Traill	34,115	22.7	427	6.3	66.7	530	1,240	101	236,445	98.3	1.7	1	64.9	(Z)	1
Walsh	34,042	14.6	905	7.1	42.3	759	839	150	165,655	97.3	2.7	2	49.5	(Z)	1
Ward	29,659	2.0	966	11.1	58.7	1,109	1,148	91	94,127	83.0	17.0	8	93.5	1	7
Wells	26,224	28.7	579	3.8	57.9	668	1,154	61	105,829	82.9	17.1	1	100.0	(Z)	(Z)
Williams	6,962	1.5	858	6.6	60.4	1,181	1,376	66	76,873	83.7	16.3	26	31.8	23	2
OHIO	708,005	0.3	77,797	39.5	9.0	14,583	187	4,264	54,804	54.1	45.9	11,100	7.9	32	1,470
Adams	[5]25	(NA)	1,320	33.9	5.8	198	150	20	15,501	50.8	49.2	648	0.4	(Z)	2
Allen	–561	(X)	968	36.9	11.3	188	194	41	42,628	73.3	26.7	40	26.8	(Z)	30
Ashland	3,953	0.5	1,089	34.3	5.9	161	148	50	46,127	30.9	69.1	7	90.4	(Z)	4
Ashtabula	5,214	0.4	1,283	37.9	4.1	170	133	40	31,125	49.8	50.2	285	0.9	(Z)	9
Athens	2,081	0.2	673	26.7	4.8	105	156	8	11,886	44.0	56.0	8	80.4	–	7
Auglaize	10,696	1.2	1,020	31.3	11.0	218	214	70	69,044	43.4	56.6	16	58.5	(Z)	5
Belmont	2,615	0.3	753	26.4	6.6	142	188	15	19,623	29.7	70.3	257	2.5	(Z)	8
Brown	–738	(X)	1,400	38.7	7.0	221	158	31	22,270	82.4	17.6	5	73.2	(Z)	4
Butler	464	(Z)	1,060	53.7	5.1	138	130	35	33,258	68.4	31.6	147	47.6	1	45
Carroll	34,587	12.0	749	28.4	4.5	124	165	23	31,085	52.1	47.9	3	87.4	(Z)	1
Champaign	11,616	2.1	937	45.9	11.8	208	222	50	53,839	74.1	25.9	9	92.8	2	3
Clark	19,818	0.9	756	52.1	12.8	165	219	71	93,796	78.3	21.7	24	94.6	2	19
Clermont	–3,942	(X)	973	59.0	5.1	116	119	18	18,662	87.5	12.5	652	2.8	(Z)	19
Clinton	3,534	0.3	811	37.4	18.4	239	294	53	65,184	89.0	11.0	2	71.9	–	1
Columbiana	11,216	0.8	1,184	45.1	3.3	136	115	44	36,790	30.1	69.9	16	41.9	(Z)	11
Coshocton	12,421	2.2	1,043	28.0	7.2	180	172	35	33,132	35.3	64.7	330	5.9	(Z)	8
Crawford	6,444	1.0	693	29.1	18.0	234	338	69	99,358	56.2	43.8	5	30.7	(Z)	3
Cuyahoga	6,194	(Z)	159	86.2	–	4	26	19	117,113	96.5	3.5	518	0.1	(Z)	261
Darke	13,270	1.7	1,764	41.8	10.2	339	192	304	172,452	17.3	82.7	8	66.9	(Z)	3
Defiance	7,704	0.9	982	37.7	11.8	209	213	43	43,995	75.3	24.7	6	26.0	(Z)	5

See footnotes at end of table.

[Includes United States, states, and 3,141 counties/county equivalents defined as of February 22, 2005. For more information on these areas, see Appendix C, Geographic Information]

County	Farm earnings, 2005 Total ($1,000)	Percent of total[1]	Farms Number	Percent Less than 50 acres	500 acres or more	Land in farms Total acres (1,000)	Average size of farm (acres)	Value of farm products sold Total (mil. dol.)	Average per farm (dol.)	Percent from Crops[2]	Live-stock and poultry[3]	Water use Total (mil. gal. per day)	Ground water, percent of total	By selected major use (mil. gal. per day) Irrigation	Public supply
OHIO—Con.															
Delaware	7,121	0.2	785	54.9	14.0	163	207	50	64,270	77.8	22.2	19	33.5	1	11
Erie	4,830	0.2	392	41.6	16.3	95	242	33	83,181	90.0	10.0	24	2.8	2	11
Fairfield	3,232	0.2	1,173	50.3	8.6	196	167	41	35,020	70.6	29.4	13	97.5	(Z)	9
Fayette	1,818	0.4	480	33.8	28.1	203	423	46	96,523	87.8	12.2	4	47.6	(Z)	2
Franklin	6,053	(Z)	561	62.4	7.8	82	145	32	56,153	91.1	8.9	201	16.1	2	184
Fulton	18,733	1.8	783	39.8	14.4	197	252	70	89,539	62.1	37.9	6	27.5	(Z)	4
Gallia	−845	(X)	936	32.5	2.8	118	126	14	15,271	37.1	62.9	1,193	0.4	–	4
Geauga	1,997	0.1	975	56.7	1.4	66	68	23	23,318	58.6	41.4	7	95.4	(Z)	1
Greene	4,786	0.1	819	53.7	10.5	169	206	51	61,731	83.1	16.9	14	89.0	1	9
Guernsey	1,529	0.2	910	28.8	3.7	137	151	13	14,126	26.8	73.2	5	34.8	(Z)	4
Hamilton	5,907	(Z)	399	67.9	2.8	30	74	24	59,236	81.6	18.4	423	13.9	1	159
Hancock	7,090	0.3	976	35.0	16.0	262	269	46	47,319	77.5	22.5	21	29.7	(Z)	15
Hardin	8,375	2.2	842	29.6	16.6	246	293	96	113,479	35.9	64.1	4	93.4	(Z)	2
Harrison	1,963	1.3	450	18.4	12.4	138	308	17	37,400	12.8	87.2	1	65.6	–	1
Henry	7,273	1.3	844	29.3	14.9	236	280	59	69,808	90.5	9.5	9	14.6	(Z)	2
Highland	−1,246	(X)	1,381	35.8	9.8	273	198	44	31,560	72.7	27.3	5	42.5	–	2
Hocking	−1,739	(X)	434	32.5	1.8	50	115	4	8,189	58.5	41.5	5	98.9	–	3
Holmes	15,868	1.9	1,809	31.1	2.2	207	114	97	53,645	10.6	89.4	7	82.6	–	3
Huron	13,179	1.2	865	34.0	13.4	228	264	66	76,760	80.3	19.7	10	17.6	1	7
Jackson	4,649	1.0	458	27.9	6.1	74	161	6	13,893	37.8	62.2	2	39.5	–	2
Jefferson	2,418	0.2	461	29.1	5.4	67	146	7	14,675	39.2	60.8	2,047	0.4	(Z)	9
Knox	14,348	1.6	1,258	39.3	7.2	209	166	55	43,576	44.0	56.0	9	70.9	(Z)	4
Lake	39,091	0.8	333	70.6	1.5	20	59	72	217,694	98.9	1.1	870	0.1	5	27
Lawrence	−1,404	(X)	644	34.8	1.2	65	101	4	5,793	47.8	52.2	7	70.4	–	5
Licking	23,181	0.9	1,482	47.4	5.9	237	160	106	71,338	37.3	62.7	20	52.3	(Z)	14
Logan	10,284	1.0	1,055	41.5	11.5	225	213	49	46,417	56.7	43.3	7	95.3	–	3
Lorain	28,312	0.6	975	52.5	8.6	162	166	98	100,294	86.8	13.2	426	0.2	(Z)	39
Lucas	15,339	0.1	405	62.5	12.1	78	192	41	102,351	92.9	7.1	728	1.3	1	90
Madison	17,427	2.4	730	37.8	22.5	246	337	61	83,248	76.8	23.2	3	94.3	(Z)	2
Mahoning	5,379	0.1	652	45.1	2.6	77	117	28	42,179	45.8	54.2	7	16.0	(Z)	6
Marion	4,598	0.4	520	29.8	23.3	206	395	48	91,544	74.3	25.7	11	62.3	(Z)	7
Medina	5,093	0.2	1,188	59.6	4.3	123	103	40	34,069	59.0	41.0	16	59.4	1	7
Meigs	16,511	10.8	552	24.8	5.6	90	164	19	34,661	75.6	24.4	6	73.4	–	2
Mercer	31,119	4.2	1,268	33.0	10.6	269	212	277	218,748	12.7	87.3	9	74.2	(Z)	3
Miami	3,445	0.2	1,071	53.1	10.0	184	172	40	37,170	78.4	21.6	16	81.0	1	11
Monroe	−3,839	(X)	654	17.6	4.1	107	164	7	10,898	19.8	80.2	10	36.9	(Z)	1
Montgomery	3,120	(Z)	832	63.5	5.8	102	122	33	39,591	87.5	12.5	257	47.5	1	96
Morgan	3,132	2.3	508	16.3	6.5	100	197	9	18,293	26.3	73.7	5	65.4	(Z)	1
Morrow	7,145	2.5	863	41.4	9.7	179	207	36	41,422	65.4	34.6	3	91.9	(Z)	1
Muskingum	668	(Z)	1,222	30.9	6.6	193	158	26	20,961	38.6	61.4	21	55.2	(Z)	10
Noble	−502	(X)	602	22.4	4.8	107	178	5	8,754	40.1	59.9	1	26.2	–	1
Ottawa	3,735	0.5	517	39.1	11.4	114	221	24	46,242	92.0	8.0	52	16.1	(Z)	(Z)
Paulding	9,955	4.6	651	32.4	22.6	238	366	67	102,416	52.0	48.0	4	50.3	–	2
Perry	4,238	1.5	639	36.0	3.9	92	144	14	22,277	60.1	39.9	3	30.2	–	1
Pickaway	8,377	1.2	791	42.5	20.0	275	348	59	74,062	82.1	17.9	79	19.3	2	4
Pike	−2,558	(X)	505	28.1	4.4	84	166	8	16,414	55.6	44.4	5	65.6	(Z)	2
Portage	7,500	0.3	962	56.2	2.9	97	101	25	25,670	66.5	33.5	18	73.3	(Z)	9
Preble	2,653	0.5	1,065	45.2	10.0	198	186	58	54,610	55.7	44.3	5	93.4	–	3
Putnam	22,959	5.0	1,348	25.5	12.9	332	246	88	65,524	61.4	38.6	5	60.9	(Z)	3
Richland	3,210	0.1	1,086	37.0	4.9	159	146	46	42,683	42.6	57.4	19	49.7	(Z)	16
Ross	2,200	0.2	952	31.7	12.1	247	259	37	39,357	77.4	22.6	41	82.5	(Z)	8
Sandusky	9,228	0.8	802	38.8	15.1	196	245	51	63,647	88.9	11.1	16	17.7	(Z)	6
Scioto	−2,319	(X)	709	36.7	4.2	96	136	15	20,969	40.3	59.7	18	23.8	(Z)	12
Seneca	3,944	0.4	1,185	29.4	14.0	280	237	56	46,919	78.5	21.5	6	52.8	(Z)	3
Shelby	10,744	0.7	1,022	31.2	10.2	207	203	65	63,848	41.5	58.5	7	58.2	(Z)	4
Stark	14,066	0.2	1,337	53.9	4.2	145	109	69	51,642	41.1	58.9	52	89.0	1	33
Summit	2,234	(Z)	377	73.7	1.9	21	56	11	29,294	90.6	9.4	73	27.7	1	52
Trumbull	2,604	0.1	1,016	40.4	4.2	126	124	31	30,087	50.7	49.3	212	2.2	(Z)	16
Tuscarawas	14,871	1.0	1,076	32.4	5.5	160	148	52	48,394	19.3	80.7	30	91.6	(Z)	18
Union	10,566	0.6	1,021	45.2	14.5	256	251	89	86,944	46.3	53.7	7	82.2	(Z)	2
Van Wert	762	0.2	681	28.6	25.0	250	367	59	86,721	81.7	18.3	6	52.9	(Z)	4
Vinton	−957	(X)	237	25.3	5.9	44	184	4	16,004	78.9	21.1	1	95.6	–	(Z)
Warren	2,343	0.1	1,036	63.3	5.9	126	122	30	28,590	88.3	11.7	20	91.3	1	17
Washington	4,439	0.4	952	22.7	4.2	141	149	18	19,380	42.0	58.0	998	0.9	(Z)	8
Wayne	34,694	1.5	1,894	40.5	5.9	267	141	159	83,758	20.3	79.7	15	90.9	(Z)	7
Williams	11,896	1.5	1,099	37.9	9.8	213	194	45	40,588	58.6	41.4	5	94.0	(Z)	3
Wood	19,422	0.7	1,066	37.5	19.0	306	287	81	76,151	76.2	23.8	11	47.2	(Z)	6
Wyandot	25,168	5.6	607	31.6	21.3	201	331	72	118,853	35.7	64.3	6	79.3	(Z)	1

See footnotes at end of table.

[Includes United States, states, and 3,141 counties/county equivalents defined as of February 22, 2005. For more information on these areas, see Appendix C, Geographic Information]

County	Farm earnings, 2005 Total ($1,000)	Percent of total[1]	Farms Number	Farms Percent Less than 50 acres	Farms Percent 500 acres or more	Land in farms Total acres (1,000)	Land in farms Average size of farm (acres)	Value of farm products sold Total (mil. dol.)	Value Average per farm (dol.)	Percent from Crops[2]	Percent from Livestock and poultry[3]	Water use Total (mil. gal. per day)	Ground water, percent of total	Irrigation	Public supply
OKLAHOMA	796,487	1.0	83,300	24.2	18.0	33,662	404	4,456	53,498	18.4	81.6	2,020	51.0	718	675
Adair	27,149	10.9	1,130	27.9	8.1	238	211	80	71,183	1.7	98.3	9	10.0	1	6
Alfalfa	11,867	18.0	666	8.1	37.8	461	693	71	107,324	21.2	78.8	8	64.1	1	2
Atoka	8,926	5.5	1,206	18.3	14.5	492	408	22	18,517	7.9	92.1	76	0.4	(Z)	74
Beaver	4,519	6.7	960	5.7	42.3	1,019	1,061	120	124,834	6.4	93.6	44	99.5	37	1
Beckham	494	0.1	1,012	15.4	25.4	533	527	35	34,762	24.5	75.5	10	87.9	4	4
Blaine	15,925	10.5	825	9.6	36.0	537	651	77	93,594	24.3	75.7	9	66.6	3	2
Bryan	−3,142	(X)	1,673	24.0	12.9	458	274	55	32,581	21.8	78.2	18	15.5	4	5
Caddo	28,311	8.5	1,504	13.0	27.7	711	473	89	59,106	37.4	62.6	63	71.6	41	9
Canadian	−5,272	(X)	1,360	29.3	21.2	501	368	85	62,352	26.6	73.4	13	77.7	3	4
Carter	1,363	0.1	1,353	24.3	13.5	431	318	24	17,625	7.3	92.7	180	83.5	1	28
Cherokee	44,362	7.5	1,221	29.1	7.4	221	181	94	77,043	70.2	29.8	11	9.7	3	6
Choctaw	8,620	5.0	1,095	18.9	15.5	337	308	29	26,501	10.3	89.7	15	8.3	(Z)	8
Cimarron	8,805	24.0	545	4.0	56.3	1,122	2,058	182	334,022	9.2	90.8	81	98.9	78	(Z)
Cleveland	−3,239	(X)	1,294	50.5	5.3	165	128	13	10,218	31.7	68.3	27	39.2	(Z)	25
Coal	−2,277	(X)	617	13.8	19.4	263	426	14	22,569	6.4	93.6	6	6.4	(Z)	4
Comanche	9,303	0.4	1,188	23.7	16.8	425	358	33	27,687	25.2	74.8	20	14.0	2	16
Cotton	18,003	24.0	488	6.8	34.0	334	685	38	77,641	21.7	78.3	3	36.7	1	1
Craig	−5,112	(X)	1,289	24.0	12.9	436	338	58	44,717	12.6	87.4	3	18.9	−	(Z)
Creek	−3,242	(X)	1,838	36.0	6.9	366	199	17	9,419	19.6	80.4	23	67.4	(Z)	8
Custer	5,589	1.2	802	16.5	34.7	545	679	44	55,433	33.1	66.9	10	66.7	4	4
Delaware	51,335	14.2	1,393	26.7	8.5	282	203	132	94,478	2.9	97.1	6	46.8	−	2
Dewey	4,302	7.7	774	7.6	35.7	584	755	26	33,769	25.9	74.1	7	83.9	2	(Z)
Ellis	3,557	7.5	727	5.6	37.7	673	925	43	58,550	9.7	90.3	46	99.5	43	1
Garfield	10,421	0.9	1,083	17.9	30.8	632	584	75	68,985	43.7	56.3	6	69.8	(Z)	3
Garvin	2,880	0.7	1,637	25.0	13.9	469	286	38	23,395	22.8	77.2	14	73.7	1	5
Grady	13,164	2.3	1,804	25.2	17.0	602	333	96	53,011	14.0	86.0	23	55.8	13	2
Grant	6,965	10.5	744	10.2	42.7	595	799	58	78,022	54.8	45.2	4	77.5	(Z)	1
Greer	11,153	16.3	515	8.3	31.7	325	631	18	34,839	41.3	58.7	7	76.5	4	2
Harmon	11,515	30.4	397	5.8	41.6	296	747	27	69,038	39.0	61.0	21	97.5	19	1
Harper	28,014	39.6	517	5.2	44.5	601	1,163	142	274,752	2.3	97.7	15	53.3	11	1
Haskell	13,270	9.5	901	20.1	15.4	275	305	67	73,991	2.5	97.5	5	11.4	(Z)	1
Hughes	32,025	23.2	955	14.3	18.3	374	392	55	57,241	4.1	95.9	9	26.9	4	2
Jackson	23,324	3.8	732	17.1	33.3	454	620	68	92,667	54.1	45.9	105	9.2	97	5
Jefferson	14,200	23.2	483	11.8	34.6	407	843	50	103,685	7.6	92.4	9	16.2	(Z)	6
Johnston	7,178	5.7	682	20.7	16.0	326	478	26	38,428	7.2	92.8	11	13.4	4	1
Kay	−5,998	(X)	1,003	21.7	26.1	480	478	47	47,302	58.6	41.4	29	47.5	1	22
Kingfisher	19,051	6.5	1,063	12.8	29.4	553	520	88	82,965	22.7	77.3	16	64.1	4	7
Kiowa	7,199	7.0	662	11.9	43.4	580	877	50	75,495	42.3	57.7	13	24.5	2	9
Latimer		(X)	738	24.8	10.8	206	279	14	19,064	3.0	97.0	2	8.3	(Z)	1
Le Flore	53,681	10.1	1,927	31.8	8.8	411	213	169	87,790	5.1	94.9	18	10.4	3	11
Lincoln	1,746	0.6	2,218	23.3	9.3	472	213	25	11,385	14.0	86.0	12	77.6	3	1
Logan	1,485	0.4	1,205	24.9	14.4	366	303	41	34,407	24.0	76.0	10	53.3	1	2
Love	−1,594	(X)	725	23.4	17.0	244	337	17	22,883	16.6	83.4	3	59.7	1	1
McClain	5,472	1.8	1,273	36.1	12.5	307	241	35	27,379	26.8	73.2	6	63.4	2	2
McCurtain	65,665	11.6	1,855	30.8	7.5	358	193	149	80,410	3.0	97.0	11	11.0	1	5
McIntosh	−1,139	(X)	944	21.1	11.7	266	282	18	18,601	12.1	87.9	5	6.6	−	4
Major	−90	(X)	879	13.7	31.7	509	579	72	82,397	14.1	85.9	17	99.8	8	5
Marshall	−2,802	(X)	477	26.2	11.9	164	344	12	24,631	33.7	66.3	4	25.7	2	2
Mayes	6,906	1.5	1,552	31.8	8.2	302	195	45	29,227	9.4	90.6	97	0.6	−	83
Murray	2,369	1.3	525	22.3	17.7	202	385	20	38,884	4.4	95.6	19	22.0	2	13
Muskogee	8,525	0.7	1,740	32.6	7.7	352	202	36	20,794	30.9	69.1	110	2.6	7	16
Noble	−10,587	(X)	776	13.3	26.9	395	509	35	44,526	38.5	61.5	5	45.7	(Z)	2
Nowata	−3,346	(X)	887	21.2	16.0	311	351	29	32,893	6.5	93.5	6	44.9	(Z)	1
Okfuskee	7,172	6.2	901	18.5	15.3	290	322	24	26,335	6.8	93.2	4	36.0	(Z)	2
Oklahoma	1,193	(Z)	1,268	52.1	5.3	172	136	21	16,859	57.7	42.3	90	26.2	3	74
Okmulgee	−3,179	(X)	1,268	26.3	9.0	289	228	15	11,520	19.4	80.6	12	7.8	(Z)	9
Osage	19,305	4.8	1,420	26.1	23.6	1,186	835	63	44,049	6.9	93.1	19	8.1	(Z)	14
Ottawa	29,644	6.4	1,137	32.9	7.4	226	199	71	62,727	40.3	59.7	6	78.5	−	3
Pawnee	−4,089	(X)	826	23.2	7.5	281	340	25	29,806	9.4	90.6	16	14.0	(Z)	3
Payne	−5,686	(X)	1,445	30.4	10.9	341	236	29	19,907	11.5	88.5	8	33.6	(Z)	4
Pittsburg	6,370	0.9	1,687	26.3	13.8	505	299	30	17,724	15.4	84.6	11	3.7	(Z)	7
Pontotoc	4,382	0.7	1,368	25.4	11.6	368	269	26	19,014	8.1	91.9	19	74.5	1	4
Pottawatomie	13,859	1.6	1,663	28.0	7.5	343	206	22	13,134	21.5	78.5	16	52.8	1	6
Pushmataha	−1,342	(X)	780	19.5	15.9	310	397	10	12,226	9.5	90.5	3	9.8	(Z)	1
Roger Mills	2,247	5.0	677	7.2	47.6	739	1,091	27	40,316	8.5	91.5	8	69.9	6	1
Rogers	−1,001	(X)	1,803	45.7	6.3	310	172	26	14,397	17.6	82.4	79	1.2	1	64
Seminole	2,400	0.8	1,167	23.5	10.9	279	239	18	15,838	13.4	86.6	24	44.2	(Z)	3
Sequoyah	4,855	1.2	1,259	32.4	7.5	222	177	25	20,026	19.0	81.0	16	4.5	2	11
Stephens	1,969	0.3	1,359	23.5	14.8	420	309	34	25,007	9.7	90.3	14	84.4	1	1
Texas	109,891	23.9	1,002	7.5	44.7	1,181	1,179	663	661,186	8.1	91.9	279	99.9	254	6

See footnotes at end of table.

Table B-14. Counties — **Farm Earnings, Agriculture, and Water Use**—Con.

[Includes United States, states, and 3,141 counties/county equivalents defined as of February 22, 2005. For more information on these areas, see Appendix C, Geographic Information]

County	Farm earnings, 2005 Total ($1,000)	Farm earnings, 2005 Percent of total[1]	Farms Number	Farms Percent Less than 50 acres	Farms Percent 500 acres or more	Land in farms Total acres (1,000)	Land in farms Average size of farm (acres)	Value of farm products sold Total (mil. dol.)	Value of farm products sold Average per farm (dol.)	Value of farm products sold Percent from Crops[2]	Value of farm products sold Percent from Live-stock and poultry[3]	Water use, 2000[4] Total (mil. gal. per day)	Water use, 2000[4] Ground water, percent of total	By selected major use (mil. gal. per day) Irrigation	By selected major use (mil. gal. per day) Public supply
OKLAHOMA—Con.															
Tillman.	22,153	21.4	592	9.1	38.7	485	818	53	90,319	43.0	57.0	10	73.6	7	1
Tulsa.	7,077	(Z)	1,146	54.5	5.4	151	132	23	20,447	73.4	26.6	23	38.1	8	7
Wagoner.	683	0.2	1,217	40.7	8.2	260	214	35	29,105	64.4	35.6	20	0.8	(Z)	18
Washington.	2,553	0.3	847	39.2	10.2	223	263	20	23,289	20.8	79.2	3	35.3	(Z)	1
Washita.	6,522	5.8	1,006	13.3	34.3	568	565	69	68,997	29.3	70.7	12	62.8	7	3
Woods.	3,838	3.2	761	9.6	41.5	816	1,073	56	72,997	16.1	83.9	6	99.2	2	2
Woodward.	16,899	4.1	842	13.2	34.6	726	863	67	79,885	5.5	94.5	17	95.8	5	6
OREGON	1,172,970	1.3	40,033	62.5	10.2	17,080	427	3,195	79,822	68.7	31.3	6,930	14.3	6,080	566
Baker.	−2,878	(X)	703	34.7	27.0	870	1,237	47	67,454	23.9	76.1	(6)	(NA)	468	3
Benton.	19,098	0.9	912	71.2	5.5	130	143	85	92,747	87.7	12.3	(6)	(NA)	32	6
Clackamas.	187,625	2.2	4,676	82.2	1.3	215	46	332	71,002	82.3	17.7	(6)	(NA)	118	174
Clatsop.	1,516	0.2	248	55.2	2.4	22	90	7	29,746	18.3	81.7	(6)	(NA)	3	9
Columbia.	12,716	2.4	878	72.2	1.6	62	71	29	32,756	82.5	17.5	(6)	(NA)	11	6
Coos.	17,452	1.6	748	47.7	6.4	144	193	22	29,357	38.0	62.0	(6)	(NA)	35	8
Crook.	−8,037	(X)	685	56.1	19.9	938	1,369	33	47,990	30.8	69.2	(6)	(NA)	224	1
Curry.	330	0.1	207	43.5	18.4	70	340	12	56,681	66.2	33.8	(6)	(NA)	10	3
Deschutes.	−10,215	(X)	1,632	78.6	2.8	138	85	21	12,857	42.7	57.3	(6)	(NA)	107	22
Douglas.	10,115	0.5	2,110	53.7	7.5	390	185	37	17,615	36.5	63.5	(6)	(NA)	112	6
Gilliam.	−1,386	(X)	156	5.8	73.1	643	4,122	17	111,346	70.2	29.8	(6)	(NA)	9	(Z)
Grant.	3,623	2.9	394	26.1	39.1	892	2,265	17	43,335	17.9	82.1	(6)	(NA)	185	3
Harney.	11,586	9.5	524	22.3	43.7	1,575	3,006	36	67,845	20.6	79.4	(6)	(NA)	464	3
Hood River.	38,562	9.1	562	70.5	0.5	29	52	60	106,048	97.4	2.6	(6)	(NA)	49	3
Jackson.	24,630	0.6	1,953	70.3	3.6	252	129	54	27,748	69.8	30.2	(6)	(NA)	202	39
Jefferson.	−12,405	(X)	428	34.1	24.3	701	1,639	41	95,292	84.4	15.6	(6)	(NA)	137	3
Josephine.	7,586	0.7	728	78.4	1.0	32	44	13	17,867	49.2	50.8	(6)	(NA)	52	5
Klamath.	23,082	2.0	1,228	42.8	19.5	703	572	105	85,568	56.9	43.1	(6)	(NA)	708	10
Lake.	2,116	1.7	462	19.0	40.0	748	1,619	57	123,351	47.3	52.7	(6)	(NA)	662	2
Lane.	31,522	0.4	2,577	71.8	3.6	235	91	88	34,080	66.7	33.3	(6)	(NA)	80	58
Lincoln.	791	0.1	374	64.2	3.5	33	88	6	16,874	53.5	46.5	(6)	(NA)	1	5
Linn.	61,204	2.9	2,346	63.8	7.7	386	164	152	64,713	72.7	27.3	(6)	(NA)	78	12
Malheur.	61,183	10.9	1,272	34.7	21.1	1,175	924	232	182,134	47.9	52.1	(6)	(NA)	1,019	6
Marion.	199,715	2.9	3,203	72.0	4.3	341	106	431	134,457	84.6	15.4	(6)	(NA)	133	86
Morrow.	50,140	24.1	375	21.9	54.7	1,125	2,999	237	632,816	43.9	56.1	(6)	(NA)	218	5
Multnomah.	35,187	0.1	710	83.2	1.5	34	48	68	95,144	97.8	2.2	(6)	(NA)	29	11
Polk.	45,376	5.6	1,324	64.4	5.2	169	128	90	67,663	74.9	25.1	(6)	(NA)	41	5
Sherman.	−10,148	(X)	210	10.5	65.2	508	2,418	15	71,357	88.9	11.1	(6)	(NA)	9	(Z)
Tillamook.	34,074	8.1	333	37.8	3.3	40	119	89	267,111	1.1	98.9	(6)	(NA)	3	4
Umatilla.	57,635	4.1	1,648	53.9	23.1	1,331	808	206	124,803	76.2	23.8	(6)	(NA)	306	25
Union.	5,368	1.2	993	49.3	19.4	478	482	48	48,352	63.7	36.3	(6)	(NA)	194	4
Wallowa.	3,509	3.0	503	37.8	32.4	518	1,030	21	41,302	34.1	65.9	(6)	(NA)	152	1
Wasco.	9,313	2.3	538	34.0	30.5	1,087	2,020	43	80,340	77.9	22.1	(6)	(NA)	65	2
Washington.	128,167	0.8	1,900	74.4	2.6	131	69	232	122,011	93.4	6.6	(6)	(NA)	69	26
Wheeler.	2,337	16.8	164	17.7	47.6	738	4,501	6	38,152	9.9	90.1	(6)	(NA)	32	(Z)
Yamhill.	132,481	8.8	2,329	73.8	4.2	196	84	209	89,548	82.4	17.6	(6)	(NA)	59	11
PENNSYLVANIA	1,268,303	0.4	58,105	37.8	4.2	7,745	133	4,257	73,263	31.0	69.0	9,950	6.7	14	1,460
Adams.	32,933	2.1	1,261	49.2	6.5	181	144	140	110,871	38.2	61.8	(6)	(NA)	2	10
Allegheny.	1,453	(Z)	464	61.6	1.3	34	73	9	20,239	87.3	12.7	(6)	(NA)	(Z)	219
Armstrong.	22,366	2.2	739	21.5	6.6	131	177	46	62,687	76.1	23.9	(6)	(NA)	(Z)	5
Beaver.	1,478	0.1	645	39.1	1.6	63	97	11	16,788	36.2	63.8	(6)	(NA)	(Z)	21
Bedford.	13,524	2.0	1,093	22.3	5.9	193	176	57	52,595	15.3	84.7	(6)	(NA)	(Z)	8
Berks.	79,360	0.9	1,791	48.4	4.5	216	120	287	160,233	41.8	58.2	(6)	(NA)	1	32
Blair.	20,728	0.8	504	31.0	6.7	86	170	63	125,698	9.4	90.6	(6)	(NA)	(Z)	15
Bradford.	20,745	2.0	1,495	22.3	8.4	302	202	100	66,753	7.2	92.8	(6)	(NA)	(Z)	4
Bucks.	21,801	0.1	917	70.1	3.4	77	84	62	67,219	80.7	19.3	(6)	(NA)	(Z)	55
Butler.	7,131	0.2	1,174	33.8	3.5	144	123	32	27,647	51.1	48.9	(6)	(NA)	(Z)	9
Cambria.	7,616	0.3	634	34.4	5.8	88	139	18	28,773	43.1	56.9	(6)	(NA)	(Z)	15
Cameron.	−116	(X)	35	17.1	−	4	122	(Z)	9,571	54.9	45.1	(6)	(NA)	−	(Z)
Carbon.	2,389	0.3	206	49.5	2.4	19	93	8	39,549	87.0	13.0	(6)	(NA)	(Z)	24
Centre.	19,192	0.5	1,213	37.6	4.2	165	136	53	44,011	27.8	72.2	(6)	(NA)	(Z)	23
Chester.	150,264	0.8	1,918	59.6	2.9	168	88	377	196,440	76.5	23.5	(6)	(NA)	(Z)	42
Clarion.	5,926	0.8	591	18.3	6.9	109	184	18	29,843	27.7	72.3	(6)	(NA)	(Z)	2
Clearfield.	2,396	0.2	468	33.5	3.2	61	130	11	23,910	45.5	54.5	(6)	(NA)	(Z)	6
Clinton.	10,797	1.8	420	36.0	4.5	53	127	27	63,595	22.7	77.3	(6)	(NA)	(Z)	5
Columbia.	13,803	1.1	884	32.6	4.6	124	140	35	39,732	55.0	45.0	(6)	(NA)	(Z)	6
Crawford.	10,450	0.8	1,416	29.1	4.8	222	157	58	41,025	21.4	78.6	(6)	(NA)	(Z)	5
Cumberland.	29,787	0.4	1,116	38.0	4.6	143	128	90	80,351	19.2	80.8	(6)	(NA)	(Z)	24
Dauphin.	14,846	0.2	852	47.2	2.9	95	111	46	54,562	21.2	78.8	(6)	(NA)	(Z)	31
Delaware.	3,336	(Z)	76	82.9	−	(D)	(D)	7	94,132	98.7	1.3	(6)	(NA)	(Z)	28
Elk.	−1,967	(X)	226	38.9	0.4	22	98	3	12,757	36.3	63.7	(6)	(NA)	−	6
Erie.	16,147	0.3	1,283	37.7	3.9	166	129	64	50,187	65.2	34.8	(6)	(NA)	(Z)	43

See footnotes at end of table.

[Includes United States, states, and 3,141 counties/county equivalents defined as of February 22, 2005. For more information on these areas, see Appendix C, Geographic Information]

County	Farm earnings, 2005 Total ($1,000)	Farm earnings, 2005 Percent of total[1]	Farms Number	Farms Percent Less than 50 acres	Farms Percent 500 acres or more	Land in farms Total acres (1,000)	Land in farms Average size of farm (acres)	Value of farm products sold Total (mil. dol.)	Value of farm products sold Average per farm (dol.)	Value of farm products sold Percent from Crops[2]	Value of farm products sold Percent from Live-stock and poultry[3]	Water use, 2000[4] Total (mil. gal. per day)	Ground water, percent of total	By selected major use (mil. gal. per day) Irrigation	By selected major use (mil. gal. per day) Public supply
PENNSYLVANIA—Con.															
Fayette	5,336	0.3	978	36.2	3.7	125	128	21	21,824	41.2	58.8	(6)	(NA)	(Z)	40
Forest	–113	(X)	59	40.7	1.7	6	96	1	11,288	32.9	67.1	(6)	(NA)	–	(Z)
Franklin	59,735	2.3	1,418	31.1	6.1	245	173	218	153,986	10.6	89.4	(6)	(NA)	1	8
Fulton	11,229	3.4	561	18.0	6.2	101	179	26	45,770	10.4	89.6	(6)	(NA)	(Z)	(Z)
Greene	1,113	0.2	881	19.4	3.5	142	161	7	8,169	30.9	69.1	(6)	(NA)	(Z)	1
Huntingdon	15,983	2.7	848	28.4	6.1	143	169	43	51,238	14.4	85.6	(6)	(NA)	(Z)	3
Indiana	22,576	1.3	903	25.2	5.4	157	174	56	62,004	65.3	34.7	(6)	(NA)	(Z)	4
Jefferson	3,754	0.6	548	22.4	4.0	87	159	12	22,036	31.5	68.5	(6)	(NA)	(Z)	2
Juniata	27,098	7.5	644	34.9	3.1	86	134	68	104,998	6.8	93.2	(6)	(NA)	(Z)	1
Lackawanna	1,873	(Z)	289	33.2	1.4	33	114	14	46,820	65.7	34.3	(6)	(NA)	(Z)	36
Lancaster	217,248	1.8	5,293	44.5	1.2	412	78	798	150,831	11.1	88.9	(6)	(NA)	2	71
Lawrence	3,515	0.2	703	35.3	3.8	87	124	22	31,808	24.5	75.5	(6)	(NA)	(Z)	10
Lebanon	60,558	2.8	1,104	46.4	1.5	125	113	191	173,101	9.0	91.0	(6)	(NA)	(Z)	2
Lehigh	7,974	0.1	618	62.1	5.5	91	148	50	80,694	73.0	27.0	(6)	(NA)	(Z)	29
Luzerne	5,219	0.1	548	40.5	3.5	73	134	22	40,887	81.0	19.0	(6)	(NA)	(Z)	21
Lycoming	20,475	0.8	1,323	30.7	3.3	177	134	49	37,187	32.9	67.1	(6)	(NA)	1	11
McKean	2,588	0.3	265	30.6	4.9	42	157	5	18,083	21.8	78.2	(6)	(NA)	(Z)	7
Mercer	17,592	0.9	1,239	28.1	3.2	164	133	44	35,300	31.9	68.1	(6)	(NA)	(Z)	13
Mifflin	18,581	2.6	752	29.8	2.8	90	120	55	73,787	8.6	91.4	(6)	(NA)	(Z)	4
Monroe	1,625	0.1	324	52.8	2.5	33	102	7	20,306	71.2	28.8	(6)	(NA)	(Z)	7
Montgomery	6,624	(Z)	729	67.6	1.6	48	66	35	48,608	71.5	28.5	(6)	(NA)	(Z)	65
Montour	9,544	1.3	304	29.6	4.6	40	131	27	90,178	71.2	28.8	(6)	(NA)	(Z)	2
Northampton	7,104	0.1	487	56.3	9.9	78	159	22	44,871	63.2	36.8	(6)	(NA)	(Z)	15
Northumberland	15,781	1.2	719	39.9	6.0	119	166	99	138,008	26.8	73.2	(6)	(NA)	(Z)	11
Perry	25,936	7.5	752	27.0	5.3	129	172	70	92,783	13.3	86.7	(6)	(NA)	(Z)	1
Philadelphia	150	(Z)	9	88.9	–	(D)	(D)	(Z)	40,333	100.0	–	(6)	(NA)	–	294
Pike	693	0.1	51	37.3	11.8	10	198	2	35,216	70.3	29.7	(6)	(NA)	(Z)	3
Potter	18,113	5.2	343	16.3	10.5	94	275	26	77,090	35.4	64.6	(6)	(NA)	–	1
Schuylkill	12,536	0.6	838	43.2	5.4	111	132	70	83,878	45.0	55.0	(6)	(NA)	(Z)	26
Snyder	35,242	4.6	784	35.6	3.8	100	128	81	102,807	9.6	90.4	(6)	(NA)	(Z)	2
Somerset	28,654	2.5	1,194	22.0	7.3	223	187	66	55,112	13.5	86.5	(6)	(NA)	(Z)	32
Sullivan	448	0.7	170	18.8	7.1	31	183	7	41,529	10.2	89.8	(6)	(NA)	(Z)	3
Susquehanna	5,644	1.5	1,116	28.9	5.6	189	170	43	38,659	6.5	93.5	(6)	(NA)	(Z)	1
Tioga	9,966	1.8	973	13.9	7.9	200	206	49	49,959	13.1	86.9	(6)	(NA)	1	2
Union	22,034	2.6	521	27.4	4.0	69	133	55	105,597	10.2	89.8	(6)	(NA)	(Z)	4
Venango	1,876	0.2	473	30.9	4.0	65	136	8	16,463	33.2	66.8	(6)	(NA)	–	7
Warren	4,005	0.6	499	27.5	4.2	78	156	15	30,347	14.1	85.9	(6)	(NA)	–	5
Washington	3,497	0.1	2,506	41.1	2.0	261	104	30	12,038	45.7	54.3	(6)	(NA)	(Z)	7
Wayne	3,943	0.6	661	20.3	5.0	113	171	21	32,487	14.3	85.7	(6)	(NA)	(Z)	2
Westmoreland	6,588	0.1	1,353	36.7	2.4	151	112	35	26,211	44.1	55.9	(6)	(NA)	(Z)	40
Wyoming	5,165	1.1	358	21.5	5.3	62	173	12	34,651	21.7	78.3	(6)	(NA)	(Z)	1
York	34,416	0.4	2,546	61.5	3.9	285	112	148	57,985	38.1	61.9	(6)	(NA)	(Z)	27
RHODE ISLAND	18,978	0.1	858	59.8	1.3	61	71	56	64,739	84.9	15.1	429	6.7	3	119
Bristol	449	0.1	37	73.0	–	1	34	4	100,135	99.1	0.9	3	29.2	(Z)	3
Kent	533	(Z)	100	63.0	1.0	8	78	4	37,550	90.1	9.9	3	79.4	(Z)	1
Newport	5,386	0.2	166	63.3	1.2	11	65	15	90,916	87.3	12.7	10	13.7	(Z)	9
Providence	4,126	(Z)	290	59.3	0.7	17	58	12	40,848	70.6	29.4	395	2.4	(Z)	96
Washington	8,484	0.3	265	55.1	2.3	25	93	21	79,804	87.7	12.3	17	81.3	3	11
SOUTH CAROLINA	488,366	0.5	24,541	41.7	8.3	4,846	197	1,490	60,705	39.8	60.2	7,170	4.6	267	566
Abbeville	5,442	1.7	538	35.1	8.7	95	177	11	20,734	25.5	74.5	5	13.8	(Z)	3
Aiken	17,941	0.6	929	43.5	4.6	144	155	50	54,306	15.8	84.2	258	4.9	4	19
Allendale	6,106	3.7	156	20.5	24.4	108	690	10	66,532	80.2	19.8	18	53.2	14	1
Anderson	12,419	0.4	1,644	49.9	3.5	177	108	37	22,534	40.3	59.7	123	0.3	2	20
Bamberg	7,936	4.2	340	17.9	16.8	105	310	15	44,297	67.8	32.2	13	47.5	12	1
Barnwell	4,768	1.6	370	33.2	10.8	85	230	7	19,103	66.4	33.6	17	44.9	12	3
Beaufort	2,094	0.1	116	61.2	12.1	44	383	10	85,181	96.0	4.0	30	88.6	14	14
Berkeley	11,996	0.6	398	56.3	5.3	57	143	26	65,241	95.8	4.2	649	1.2	1	65
Calhoun	10,938	4.4	281	27.0	19.9	95	337	12	41,214	68.8	31.2	108	1.8	16	1
Charleston	7,935	0.1	417	64.5	5.3	48	114	18	43,329	88.5	11.5	14	79.7	4	6
Cherokee	2,988	0.4	430	39.3	4.2	64	149	24	55,791	7.9	92.1	16	2.8	2	12
Chester	5,054	1.0	430	30.2	8.4	97	226	18	40,877	8.6	91.4	6	28.1	1	4
Chesterfield	39,995	6.5	595	27.6	10.3	129	216	62	104,903	12.4	87.6	10	14.5	2	6
Clarendon	11,681	3.7	390	31.5	20.3	148	379	62	158,000	45.6	54.4	13	61.0	10	2
Colleton	3,307	0.7	495	36.8	10.3	137	278	13	26,661	78.2	21.8	8	55.8	1	2
Darlington	13,813	1.3	361	33.0	18.8	161	447	40	109,637	47.7	52.3	829	1.4	4	6
Dillon	9,355	2.6	197	15.7	27.9	112	570	69	351,508	32.9	67.1	6	87.3	1	5
Dorchester	11,052	0.9	365	51.0	5.8	58	158	13	34,685	20.8	79.2	58	8.1	1	13
Edgefield	6,868	2.7	325	35.1	11.4	74	229	49	149,397	91.8	8.2	14	0.8	10	4
Fairfield	3,940	1.2	237	33.3	13.5	56	238	16	68,806	4.6	95.4	674	0.1	(Z)	2

See footnotes at end of table.

[Includes United States, states, and 3,141 counties/county equivalents defined as of February 22, 2005. For more information on these areas, see Appendix C, Geographic Information]

County	Farm earnings, 2005 Total ($1,000)	Per-cent of total[1]	Agriculture (NAICS 111–112), 2002 Farms Number	Farms Percent Less than 50 acres	Farms Percent 500 acres or more	Land in farms Total acres (1,000)	Land in farms Aver-age size of farm (acres)	Value of farm products sold Total (mil. dol.)	Value of farm products sold Average per farm (dol.)	Percent from Crops[2]	Percent from Live-stock and poultry[3]	Water use, 2000[4] Total (mil. gal. per day)	Ground water, percent of total	By selected major use (mil. gal. per day) Irri-gation	By selected major use Public supply
SOUTH CAROLINA—Con.															
Florence	1,012	(Z)	612	37.3	13.7	171	280	35	57,279	84.9	15.1	58	35.8	2	15
Georgetown	4,121	0.4	226	44.7	13.3	55	242	24	105,938	91.8	8.2	55	16.3	6	7
Greenville	7,732	0.1	909	56.9	3.2	87	96	18	19,971	81.9	18.1	56	5.4	4	48
Greenwood	7,540	0.5	501	43.3	5.2	81	161	6	11,415	21.2	78.8	16	9.3	1	13
Hampton	4,997	1.9	248	19.4	23.0	128	516	6	24,907	89.3	10.7	19	44.3	6	12
Horry	−1,721	(X)	988	40.9	8.9	188	191	54	55,112	70.8	29.2	157	11.6	19	30
Jasper	1,573	0.6	163	37.4	12.9	79	485	9	52,423	96.5	3.5	4	100.0	3	1
Kershaw	8,949	1.0	479	47.0	5.6	70	146	84	176,357	2.5	97.5	22	25.8	1	7
Lancaster	14,590	1.7	637	43.5	4.6	81	128	46	71,758	3.6	96.4	27	2.9	(Z)	12
Laurens	13,023	1.6	931	38.8	6.6	143	153	16	16,808	13.2	86.8	8	12.1	2	5
Lee	16,358	9.2	324	25.3	18.2	123	378	34	103,935	30.9	69.1	9	55.7	4	2
Lexington	23,741	0.5	1,086	56.4	2.8	103	95	96	88,133	36.2	63.8	268	5.6	12	44
McCormick	7,970	9.5	97	34.0	14.4	23	240	2	15,773	8.6	91.4	3	2.6	1	2
Marion	5,371	1.4	213	38.0	16.9	93	438	24	113,413	67.7	32.3	15	52.9	7	5
Marlboro	4,252	1.2	222	23.4	26.1	115	518	23	101,432	48.2	51.8	16	25.5	2	3
Newberry	16,925	3.1	633	34.0	6.6	104	164	57	89,866	(NA)	(NA)	8	14.6	1	6
Oconee	22,773	1.8	878	54.0	2.5	78	89	56	64,235	(NA)	(NA)	2,576	(Z)	1	10
Orangeburg	35,496	2.5	968	28.2	13.4	274	283	69	71,413	46.8	53.2	73	61.6	49	10
Pickens	6,271	0.4	622	61.3	1.3	47	75	7	10,732	78.2	21.8	34	5.6	1	29
Richland	5,069	(Z)	429	48.3	5.4	63	148	7	15,632	(NA)	(NA)	540	1.1	5	32
Saluda	26,822	14.6	574	28.2	8.7	107	186	64	111,564	8.6	91.4	8	14.1	7	(Z)
Spartanburg	9,442	0.2	1,412	55.7	2.3	126	90	25	17,894	64.5	35.5	61	6.6	6	48
Sumter	16,480	0.8	537	42.8	12.5	136	253	55	102,693	27.7	72.3	32	79.2	11	16
Union	1,684	0.5	299	31.8	6.0	51	170	2	5,763	(NA)	(NA)	8	3.0	(Z)	4
Williamsburg	13,175	3.3	681	27.0	15.9	206	302	28	40,593	80.9	19.1	9	95.8	(Z)	2
York	19,093	0.5	858	42.8	5.0	119	139	83	96,589	(NA)	(NA)	217	3.9	3	15
SOUTH DAKOTA	1,254,104	6.9	31,736	13.6	49.0	43,785	1,380	3,835	120,829	41.1	58.9	528	42.0	373	93
Aurora	9,158	27.1	401	9.5	49.1	351	875	52	129,314	22.7	77.3	1	51.7	(Z)	(Z)
Beadle	47,406	13.3	728	15.5	51.4	810	1,112	97	133,773	36.6	63.4	12	78.8	9	2
Bennett	11,350	26.6	231	2.6	71.4	727	3,148	23	100,619	27.5	72.5	9	96.6	8	(Z)
Bon Homme	10,085	10.7	665	11.0	39.8	345	518	67	100,095	36.0	64.0	6	33.6	5	(Z)
Brookings	30,110	4.4	962	22.6	28.3	418	435	98	101,449	43.8	56.2	15	95.9	9	5
Brown	47,355	4.8	1,155	18.1	46.4	1,155	1,000	169	146,469	66.0	34.0	5	26.8	1	3
Brule	12,738	15.2	365	9.6	60.0	447	1,225	51	139,627	24.2	75.8	3	10.1	1	1
Buffalo	4,465	15.7	73	4.1	74.0	285	3,903	13	181,068	15.3	84.7	4	15.9	4	–
Butte	6,672	5.8	639	12.2	46.9	1,262	1,976	57	88,856	21.9	78.1	131	2.4	129	1
Campbell	12,147	44.9	293	6.8	60.8	391	1,335	25	86,519	41.7	58.3	4	38.3	3	(Z)
Charles Mix	33,397	20.8	755	10.6	52.3	736	975	97	128,001	37.9	62.1	14	25.3	11	3
Clark	36,333	49.8	588	11.1	47.4	526	894	102	174,250	31.1	68.9	5	87.4	4	1
Clay	6,908	2.6	536	15.1	52.4	373	695	75	140,047	87.6	12.4	7	93.9	5	2
Codington	29,875	4.7	694	25.8	32.4	387	557	74	106,069	46.4	53.6	8	90.8	3	4
Corson	19,654	37.4	344	4.1	80.5	1,389	4,038	38	109,331	10.6	89.4	2	34.2	1	(Z)
Custer	−1,801	(X)	303	15.5	42.6	589	1,944	12	41,155	7.5	92.5	5	20.5	4	(Z)
Davison	8,004	1.6	481	26.0	31.6	279	579	43	88,861	43.7	56.3	4	15.8	1	3
Day	18,206	20.2	704	9.7	39.2	531	754	57	80,614	62.8	37.2	1	77.1	1	(Z)
Deuel	16,285	19.7	583	13.0	34.8	328	562	66	112,751	34.0	66.0	2	80.5	1	(Z)
Dewey	6,412	6.7	358	3.6	72.9	1,368	3,821	29	80,810	4.4	95.6	2	23.3	(Z)	1
Douglas	19,573	32.9	394	14.5	44.4	237	601	62	157,792	22.8	77.2	2	82.6	1	–
Edmunds	39,706	44.9	386	7.3	62.2	585	1,516	75	194,440	41.6	58.4	1	47.1	–	–
Fall River	7,257	5.5	278	9.4	68.0	982	3,533	51	184,540	4.5	95.5	38	3.5	36	1
Faulk	27,756	55.9	265	3.8	77.0	535	2,018	64	240,177	52.7	47.3	1	40.3	(Z)	(Z)
Grant	30,559	17.1	548	13.0	38.1	350	639	82	149,956	47.8	52.2	9	44.9	4	1
Gregory	15,322	21.6	587	8.9	58.4	651	1,109	44	74,365	22.9	77.1	2	46.6	1	1
Haakon	18,758	38.3	268	3.0	77.6	1,222	4,558	39	145,041	15.8	84.2	3	54.3	1	1
Hamlin	17,058	22.5	451	17.3	41.2	307	681	58	128,818	62.3	37.7	4	94.3	4	(Z)
Hand	34,446	44.3	480	7.1	67.1	868	1,809	77	160,294	34.2	65.8	2	66.3	1	(Z)
Hanson	5,921	23.5	319	17.6	48.6	249	780	49	152,241	48.8	51.2	1	31.2	(Z)	–
Harding	4,878	20.8	223	4.0	87.4	1,674	7,507	31	137,507	(NA)	(NA)	1	33.6	(Z)	(Z)
Hughes	11,443	2.5	258	14.3	53.1	368	1,425	21	82,992	49.0	51.0	23	20.7	18	4
Hutchinson	22,486	20.4	768	12.4	48.4	506	658	99	128,954	44.7	55.3	3	71.0	2	(Z)
Hyde	9,974	31.7	187	4.8	70.6	469	2,507	23	122,032	21.2	78.8	1	54.0	(Z)	–
Jackson	5,414	16.7	308	2.9	76.9	1,191	3,866	23	76,156	8.7	91.3	1	45.1	(Z)	(Z)
Jerauld	9,480	17.2	272	8.1	47.1	336	1,237	34	125,283	28.7	71.3	2	72.5	1	(Z)
Jones	5,958	25.8	163	3.7	74.8	516	3,169	19	113,798	25.9	74.1	1	22.7	(Z)	(Z)
Kingsbury	30,958	31.7	599	14.9	48.1	519	866	86	143,913	45.1	54.9	3	89.0	1	2
Lake	25,793	11.9	513	18.7	42.3	325	634	67	129,663	54.4	45.6	2	84.2	1	3
Lawrence	2,877	0.7	239	18.4	28.5	141	589	10	41,803	9.9	90.1	8	53.5	2	3
Lincoln	27,158	5.9	841	27.2	25.3	310	368	88	104,599	62.8	37.2	3	85.8	1	2
Lyman	11,416	19.1	420	7.6	64.3	885	2,108	42	100,431	33.5	66.5	3	22.0	1	1
McCook	18,002	24.4	539	17.8	44.2	345	640	73	134,933	57.6	42.4	1	71.0	(Z)	(Z)
McPherson	18,302	48.4	413	5.3	62.2	537	1,300	60	146,208	10.8	89.2	2	58.4	1	(Z)
Marshall	35,047	39.3	529	10.4	52.7	525	992	101	191,830	35.9	64.1	1	61.2	(Z)	(Z)

See footnotes at end of table.

Table B-14. Counties — **Farm Earnings, Agriculture, and Water Use**—Con.

[Includes United States, states, and 3,141 counties/county equivalents defined as of February 22, 2005. For more information on these areas, see Appendix C, Geographic Information]

County	Farm earnings, 2005 Total ($1,000)	Per-cent of total[1]	Farms Number	Farms Percent Less than 50 acres	Farms Percent 500 acres or more	Land in farms Total acres (1,000)	Land in farms Average size of farm (acres)	Value of farm products sold Total (mil. dol.)	Value of farm products sold Average per farm (dol.)	Percent from Crops[2]	Percent from Live-stock and poultry[3]	Water use, 2000[4] Total (mil. gal. per day)	Ground water, percent of total	By selected major use (mil. gal. per day) Irrigation	By selected major use (mil. gal. per day) Public supply
SOUTH DAKOTA—Con.															
Meade	17,902	4.2	895	12.4	58.3	2,229	2,490	66	74,160	9.5	90.5	6	41.3	3	1
Mellette	5,825	32.4	200	4.5	78.5	660	3,302	31	153,055	(NA)	(NA)	1	35.2	(Z)	(Z)
Miner	15,629	38.0	370	7.6	44.9	291	787	41	111,143	48.3	51.7	1	43.1	–	(Z)
Minnehaha	24,217	0.4	1,209	32.1	24.2	422	349	120	99,184	56.0	44.0	21	36.7	2	16
Moody	37,492	28.7	580	21.6	30.5	283	488	78	134,267	49.6	50.4	4	69.5	2	1
Pennington	13,546	0.6	696	18.8	41.8	1,210	1,738	43	61,981	24.5	75.5	20	83.5	3	13
Perkins	13,664	24.8	452	2.9	81.6	1,782	3,942	46	100,781	6.3	93.7	1	47.9	(Z)	(Z)
Potter	12,368	29.0	256	9.4	57.4	453	1,769	29	113,719	57.4	42.6	3	42.6	2	(Z)
Roberts	31,544	20.4	936	12.7	39.9	593	633	88	94,020	64.1	35.9	3	85.5	2	(Z)
Sanborn	18,143	38.1	394	8.1	46.7	380	965	43	108,350	37.5	62.5	1	53.1	(Z)	(Z)
Shannon	11,236	6.2	200	6.0	60.0	1,267	6,333	13	64,900	6.6	93.4	1	83.6	–	(Z)
Spink	44,899	35.2	682	8.1	61.9	911	1,336	134	196,792	61.3	38.7	17	88.8	16	(Z)
Stanley	7,397	15.1	166	8.4	72.9	866	5,219	18	107,000	33.6	66.4	1	53.0	(Z)	(Z)
Sully	29,136	63.6	228	5.3	68.4	573	2,515	36	157,123	72.0	28.0	12	7.0	11	(Z)
Todd	4,370	3.6	249	2.8	73.5	917	3,681	27	107,410	14.7	85.3	9	89.8	8	(Z)
Tripp	33,464	29.3	666	8.7	63.4	1,054	1,582	91	136,932	15.8	84.2	6	56.7	3	2
Turner	29,437	27.6	713	16.0	35.5	348	487	99	139,344	45.7	54.3	19	97.3	17	1
Union	46,634	10.0	522	18.0	37.7	277	530	80	153,056	61.1	38.9	22	98.1	20	1
Walworth	8,020	9.5	299	12.0	54.8	427	1,429	31	102,415	45.9	54.1	7	9.5	1	5
Yankton	17,863	3.6	690	17.8	35.5	342	496	78	113,458	58.3	41.7	13	42.1	6	6
Ziebach	11,017	46.2	227	4.8	79.7	1,173	5,167	21	93,709	5.7	94.3	1	38.6	(Z)	–
TENNESSEE	337,443	0.2	87,595	43.6	4.3	11,682	133	2,200	25,113	48.8	51.2	10,800	3.9	22	890
Anderson	–1,124	(X)	596	53.2	1.3	48	80	4	6,656	34.3	65.7	(6)	(NA)	(Z)	22
Bedford	15,673	2.0	1,667	42.7	5.0	219	132	86	51,366	6.6	93.4	(6)	(NA)	(Z)	7
Benton	–212	(X)	595	37.5	3.5	78	131	5	8,718	30.5	69.5	(6)	(NA)	–	2
Bledsoe	22,076	21.7	560	27.1	6.3	93	166	26	45,796	25.7	74.3	(6)	(NA)	(Z)	1
Blount	–4,047	(X)	1,302	54.6	1.5	105	81	24	18,806	61.8	38.2	(6)	(NA)	1	12
Bradley	12,008	0.6	921	48.0	3.3	95	103	59	64,244	7.3	92.7	(6)	(NA)	(Z)	12
Campbell	–289	(X)	419	45.1	1.7	34	82	3	8,136	33.9	66.1	(6)	(NA)	(Z)	4
Cannon	–3,426	(X)	974	38.9	3.3	122	125	14	14,348	42.0	58.0	(6)	(NA)	(Z)	1
Carroll	10,332	2.9	973	33.6	5.7	183	188	25	25,350	82.4	17.6	(6)	(NA)	(Z)	3
Carter	–1,302	(X)	573	63.2	1.6	37	65	7	12,908	35.2	64.8	(6)	(NA)	(Z)	18
Cheatham	–1,884	(X)	669	38.4	2.4	72	108	8	11,299	76.8	23.2	(6)	(NA)	(Z)	3
Chester	–611	(X)	512	28.1	4.9	79	154	5	9,402	66.8	33.2	(6)	(NA)	(Z)	1
Claiborne	2,722	0.7	1,388	47.6	2.2	135	97	17	12,483	32.7	67.3	(6)	(NA)	–	3
Clay	–150	(X)	514	37.7	5.3	70	137	21	40,362	10.5	89.5	(6)	(NA)	(Z)	1
Cocke	1,184	0.4	880	43.4	1.1	73	83	15	16,527	44.1	55.9	(6)	(NA)	1	4
Coffee	7,322	0.6	1,069	48.0	5.8	145	136	30	28,210	41.6	58.4	(6)	(NA)	(Z)	5
Crockett	7,129	3.9	420	37.4	16.2	145	345	35	83,595	95.6	4.4	(6)	(NA)	1	2
Cumberland	19,711	2.7	854	41.7	4.7	110	129	36	41,779	15.6	84.4	(6)	(NA)	2	4
Davidson	–325	(X)	560	53.6	2.5	51	90	11	19,579	79.8	20.2	(6)	(NA)	1	120
Decatur	–2,267	(X)	438	19.4	6.4	88	202	4	9,932	35.2	64.8	(6)	(NA)	(Z)	1
DeKalb	8,833	3.1	887	44.6	3.2	100	113	37	41,879	85.2	14.8	(6)	(NA)	(Z)	1
Dickson	–2,952	(X)	1,448	40.0	2.0	158	109	12	8,347	36.9	63.1	(6)	(NA)	–	4
Dyer	13,372	1.7	534	36.0	18.5	213	398	45	84,434	92.2	7.8	(6)	(NA)	(Z)	6
Fayette	7,657	1.9	894	34.7	11.2	274	306	38	42,544	77.1	22.9	(6)	(NA)	(Z)	2
Fentress	9,329	4.7	573	41.2	5.4	80	139	33	57,222	(NA)	(NA)	(6)	(NA)	(Z)	1
Franklin	23,194	5.1	1,135	48.5	5.8	153	135	59	52,110	42.0	58.0	(6)	(NA)	(Z)	4
Gibson	17,438	2.4	1,092	42.4	11.5	311	285	64	58,984	85.5	14.5	(6)	(NA)	(Z)	7
Giles	–1,613	(X)	1,922	30.1	3.9	271	141	29	14,925	17.6	82.4	(6)	(NA)	(Z)	4
Grainger	–749	(X)	1,216	46.3	1.2	103	85	16	13,308	56.0	44.0	(6)	(NA)	(Z)	(Z)
Greene	6,377	0.5	3,367	56.9	1.2	247	73	55	16,285	21.8	78.2	(6)	(NA)	(Z)	8
Grundy	9,691	8.6	409	49.1	2.4	42	103	42	103,090	20.5	79.5	(6)	(NA)	(Z)	2
Hamblen	–1,126	(X)	736	55.6	1.8	58	79	20	27,785	45.4	54.6	(6)	(NA)	(Z)	9
Hamilton	–903	(X)	700	54.1	2.7	63	91	11	16,009	20.3	79.7	(6)	(NA)	1	61
Hancock	–2,192	(X)	568	38.4	2.5	64	113	6	11,118	38.6	61.4	(6)	(NA)	–	(Z)
Hardeman	2,712	0.8	602	23.3	10.8	154	255	13	21,249	77.0	23.0	(6)	(NA)	(Z)	3
Hardin	1,062	0.3	634	31.9	6.9	112	177	9	13,844	71.8	28.2	(6)	(NA)	(Z)	3
Hawkins	–2,167	(X)	2,014	49.4	1.3	168	83	22	10,879	48.0	52.0	(6)	(NA)	(Z)	4
Haywood	20,479	7.4	408	23.0	22.8	211	517	45	109,135	97.5	2.5	(6)	(NA)	(Z)	2
Henderson	–950	(X)	1,084	27.1	6.8	173	160	18	16,749	31.7	68.3	(6)	(NA)	(Z)	4
Henry	11,249	2.2	965	33.5	7.5	194	201	46	47,888	51.6	48.4	(6)	(NA)	(Z)	3
Hickman	–1,327	(X)	756	29.4	5.7	129	170	9	11,291	28.1	71.9	(6)	(NA)	(Z)	2
Houston	–1,624	(X)	336	26.5	4.8	49	145	5	13,485	14.4	85.6	(6)	(NA)	(Z)	1
Humphreys	–4,014	(X)	718	29.7	8.1	135	188	10	13,710	37.1	62.9	(6)	(NA)	(Z)	2
Jackson	–1,903	(X)	609	37.3	4.8	79	130	4	7,186	46.3	53.7	(6)	(NA)	–	(Z)
Jefferson	–1,666	(X)	1,311	52.6	1.3	108	82	23	17,573	16.6	83.4	(6)	(NA)	(Z)	3
Johnson	–1,844	(X)	666	55.1	1.1	49	74	7	10,505	44.4	55.6	(6)	(NA)	(Z)	2
Knox	–2,853	(X)	1,410	60.3	1.1	94	66	20	14,352	67.5	32.5	(6)	(NA)	1	62
Lake	2,437	4.7	64	15.6	54.7	90	1,409	18	276,281	99.9	0.1	(6)	(NA)	(Z)	1
Lauderdale	14,914	5.1	624	38.0	15.9	215	345	38	61,125	94.7	5.3	(6)	(NA)	1	4
Lawrence	–125	(X)	1,869	38.7	3.4	236	126	30	15,858	31.1	68.9	(6)	(NA)	(Z)	4

See footnotes at end of table.

[Includes United States, states, and 3,141 counties/county equivalents defined as of February 22, 2005. For more information on these areas, see Appendix C, Geographic Information]

County	Farm earnings, 2005 Total ($1,000)	Percent of total[1]	Agriculture (NAICS 111–112), 2002 Farms Number	Percent Less than 50 acres	500 acres or more	Land in farms Total acres (1,000)	Average size of farm (acres)	Value of farm products sold Total (mil. dol.)	Average per farm (dol.)	Percent from Crops[2]	Livestock and poultry[3]	Water use, 2000[4] Total (mil. gal. per day)	Ground water, percent of total	By selected major use (mil. gal. per day) Irrigation	Public supply
TENNESSEE—Con.															
Lewis	−2,122	(X)	251	26.3	6.8	37	147	3	10,183	59.0	41.0	(6)	(NA)	(Z)	2
Lincoln	19,473	4.6	1,926	35.5	5.7	284	148	46	24,065	37.8	62.2	(6)	(NA)	(Z)	4
Loudon	24,167	4.0	954	56.4	2.3	83	87	51	53,069	(NA)	(NA)	(6)	(NA)	(Z)	10
McMinn	3,324	0.4	1,204	46.3	3.1	128	106	33	27,452	9.4	90.6	(6)	(NA)	–	5
McNairy	−1,053	(X)	822	23.7	5.1	134	163	9	10,807	68.9	31.1	(6)	(NA)	(Z)	3
Macon	9,922	4.7	1,317	40.7	3.0	145	110	26	19,371	68.1	31.9	(6)	(NA)	–	3
Madison	9,855	0.4	740	38.6	9.7	162	219	27	36,657	80.2	19.8	(6)	(NA)	(Z)	15
Marion	1,682	0.6	298	35.2	8.4	51	171	14	48,510	11.1	88.9	(6)	(NA)	–	4
Marshall	−2,583	(X)	1,312	36.5	4.2	175	133	22	16,752	11.0	89.0	(6)	(NA)	(Z)	3
Maury	−360	(X)	1,754	38.4	4.7	241	137	21	11,819	25.2	74.8	(6)	(NA)	(Z)	12
Meigs	−688	(X)	340	30.9	4.4	49	144	6	16,594	14.9	85.1	(6)	(NA)	(Z)	1
Monroe	−2,539	(X)	955	45.2	2.6	99	104	22	22,712	11.7	88.3	(6)	(NA)	(Z)	6
Montgomery	1,955	0.1	1,090	39.8	6.6	167	153	28	25,623	69.3	30.7	(6)	(NA)	(Z)	21
Moore	1,806	2.5	387	27.9	7.2	63	162	10	24,907	6.5	93.5	(6)	(NA)	–	1
Morgan	−363	(X)	403	33.0	3.0	57	140	10	25,194	9.2	90.8	(6)	(NA)	–	1
Obion	11,657	1.7	701	33.2	15.4	264	376	63	89,678	68.0	32.0	(6)	(NA)	(Z)	6
Overton	175	0.1	1,106	44.1	2.9	124	112	16	14,817	14.6	85.4	(6)	(NA)	(Z)	3
Perry	−1,625	(X)	266	27.4	7.9	50	187	3	9,583	35.6	64.4	(6)	(NA)	(Z)	1
Pickett	−551	(X)	401	45.9	2.2	42	104	11	26,309	22.9	77.1	(6)	(NA)	–	1
Polk	6,055	5.3	274	50.7	4.7	32	115	22	78,639	8.8	91.2	(6)	(NA)	(Z)	1
Putnam	−2,251	(X)	1,302	49.2	2.4	119	91	11	8,779	31.3	68.7	(6)	(NA)	(Z)	12
Rhea	2,479	0.5	455	42.0	4.4	61	134	18	39,141	44.4	55.6	(6)	(NA)	(Z)	4
Roane	−4,073	(X)	722	47.9	1.2	63	88	6	7,839	31.5	68.5	(6)	(NA)	–	6
Robertson	6,431	0.7	1,621	47.8	5.6	233	144	65	40,025	76.5	23.5	(6)	(NA)	(Z)	5
Rutherford	−1,486	(X)	2,088	49.8	2.9	211	101	19	9,299	23.7	76.3	(6)	(NA)	1	27
Scott	839	0.3	296	39.9	3.4	35	117	6	19,760	4.5	95.5	(6)	(NA)	(Z)	2
Sequatchie	−63	(X)	208	38.5	6.3	28	136	5	23,067	14.8	85.2	(6)	(NA)	(Z)	1
Sevier	−7,779	(X)	907	49.6	1.2	75	83	10	10,878	24.2	75.8	(6)	(NA)	(Z)	6
Shelby	3,810	(Z)	716	59.2	6.6	116	162	24	33,144	92.3	7.7	(6)	(NA)	(Z)	188
Smith	2,140	0.9	1,126	33.0	3.3	141	126	11	9,879	39.7	60.3	(6)	(NA)	(Z)	2
Stewart	−2,482	(X)	367	28.9	5.2	55	151	5	13,455	65.3	34.7	(6)	(NA)	(Z)	1
Sullivan	−1,863	(X)	1,453	61.3	1.3	101	69	23	15,557	25.5	74.5	(6)	(NA)	(Z)	25
Sumner	−1,399	(X)	1,957	50.2	2.5	193	99	26	13,371	54.1	45.9	(6)	(NA)	(Z)	25
Tipton	9,961	2.0	627	46.4	9.7	169	269	32	50,429	93.1	6.9	(6)	(NA)	1	6
Trousdale	−142	(X)	360	33.9	3.3	47	129	7	18,489	67.2	32.8	(6)	(NA)	–	1
Unicoi	−262	(X)	166	60.8	1.8	9	56	4	24,837	(NA)	(NA)	(6)	(NA)	(Z)	2
Union	−1,859	(X)	585	43.9	1.2	48	82	3	5,014	39.2	60.8	(6)	(NA)	–	1
Van Buren	−154	(X)	230	35.7	4.3	32	137	3	11,965	15.2	84.8	(6)	(NA)	(Z)	1
Warren	32,198	4.1	1,594	49.6	3.9	173	108	94	58,901	86.6	13.4	(6)	(NA)	1	12
Washington	15,790	0.6	1,913	63.1	2.0	134	70	38	20,018	33.2	66.8	(6)	(NA)	1	6
Wayne	−743	(X)	713	25.5	7.2	125	175	10	13,739	13.6	86.4	(6)	(NA)	(Z)	1
Weakley	15,122	3.0	1,231	42.2	7.9	240	195	59	47,722	57.2	42.8	(6)	(NA)	(Z)	3
White	−4,302	(X)	1,168	41.6	2.9	137	118	19	16,506	13.3	86.7	(6)	(NA)	–	3
Williamson	−1,356	(X)	1,712	46.7	3.2	202	118	26	15,144	41.6	58.4	(6)	(NA)	1	2
Wilson	−2,556	(X)	2,142	44.3	2.7	235	110	19	8,684	21.8	78.2	(6)	(NA)	(Z)	12
TEXAS	3,220,629	0.5	228,926	32.6	18.0	129,878	567	14,135	61,744	26.4	73.6	29,600	30.3	8,630	4,230
Anderson	−3,064	(X)	1,735	33.0	8.3	365	210	23	13,293	28.6	71.4	(6)	(NA)	1	12
Andrews	2,788	1.1	169	30.8	39.6	804	4,757	9	51,308	25.8	74.2	(6)	(NA)	11	3
Angelina	1,795	0.1	931	47.0	4.2	117	125	18	19,801	4.1	95.9	(6)	(NA)	(Z)	13
Aransas	−833	(X)	62	51.6	11.3	50	807	(D)	(NA)	(NA)	(NA)	(6)	(NA)	–	(Z)
Archer	13,221	11.2	495	13.9	42.8	536	1,083	58	117,147	2.6	97.4	(6)	(NA)	–	9
Armstrong	5,093	22.3	269	5.9	53.5	506	1,882	27	98,978	15.7	84.3	(6)	(NA)	11	(Z)
Atascosa	11,142	2.7	1,539	24.6	19.9	670	435	52	33,663	33.3	66.7	(6)	(NA)	33	5
Austin	−295	(X)	2,086	35.0	8.1	367	176	24	11,524	23.6	76.4	(6)	(NA)	8	2
Bailey	11,528	10.9	436	9.4	45.2	394	905	128	293,197	18.2	81.8	(6)	(NA)	114	1
Bandera	−1,759	(X)	780	29.4	20.8	367	470	7	8,924	12.6	87.4	(6)	(NA)	(Z)	1
Bastrop	5,517	1.0	2,187	40.8	8.0	423	193	28	12,722	15.4	84.6	(6)	(NA)	(Z)	8
Baylor	−145	(X)	253	13.8	46.6	328	1,295	43	168,209	7.4	92.6	(6)	(NA)	1	3
Bee	5,608	1.6	866	24.4	22.6	510	588	19	22,484	38.2	61.8	(6)	(NA)	2	1
Bell	8,072	0.1	2,080	44.1	8.6	451	217	41	19,631	42.7	57.3	(6)	(NA)	3	83
Bexar	50,877	0.1	2,385	51.4	6.1	441	185	81	33,844	73.5	26.5	(6)	(NA)	31	231
Blanco	4,159	3.2	784	21.0	25.3	389	497	12	15,370	53.9	46.1	(6)	(NA)	(Z)	1
Borden	4,376	39.4	132	1.5	70.5	480	3,636	8	59,371	49.5	50.5	(6)	(NA)	2	–
Bosque	10,747	6.2	1,285	22.5	18.0	563	438	38	29,533	31.0	69.0	(6)	(NA)	2	2
Bowie	20,300	1.1	1,337	33.5	8.2	308	230	37	27,930	18.5	81.5	(6)	(NA)	5	52
Brazoria	6,472	0.1	2,455	51.1	11.5	614	250	47	19,316	52.3	47.7	(6)	(NA)	66	28
Brazos	13,099	0.4	1,350	40.3	10.5	309	229	47	34,859	18.8	81.2	(6)	(NA)	4	28
Brewster	−8,302	(X)	136	16.2	63.2	1,676	12,320	5	38,294	9.6	90.4	(6)	(NA)	(Z)	2
Briscoe	2,779	14.5	264	8.3	48.1	426	1,612	15	55,223	54.0	46.0	(6)	(NA)	21	1
Brooks	857	1.0	351	15.7	21.7	440	1,253	3	21,575	3.6	96.4	(6)	(NA)	(Z)	1
Brown	2,834	0.4	1,347	23.8	19.3	482	358	26	19,101	13.5	86.5	(6)	(NA)	14	6

See footnotes at end of table.

[Includes United States, states, and 3,141 counties/county equivalents defined as of February 22, 2005. For more information on these areas, see Appendix C, Geographic Information]

County	Farm earnings, 2005		Agriculture (NAICS 111–112), 2002									Water use, 2000[4]			
			Farms			Land in farms		Value of farm products sold						By selected major use (mil. gal. per day)	
				Percent						Percent from					
	Total ($1,000)	Per-cent of total[1]	Number	Less than 50 acres	500 acres or more	Total acres (1,000)	Average size of farm (acres)	Total (mil. dol.)	Average per farm (dol.)	Crops[2]	Live-stock and poultry[3]	Total (mil. gal. per day)	Ground water, percent of total	Irri-gation	Public supply
TEXAS—Con.															
Burleson	7,034	4.3	1,550	27.6	11.6	389	251	36	23,386	28.8	71.2	(6)	(NA)	1	2
Burnet	−3,555	(X)	1,370	30.1	17.4	565	413	10	7,487	7.9	92.1	(6)	(NA)	(Z)	3
Caldwell	11,076	4.1	1,402	37.5	9.9	305	217	35	25,029	11.9	88.1	(6)	(NA)	1	3
Calhoun	6,145	1.0	328	26.5	29.6	248	756	19	57,601	48.6	51.4	(6)	(NA)	32	2
Callahan	−686	(X)	893	25.0	20.8	515	577	17	18,906	12.0	88.0	(6)	(NA)	1	(Z)
Cameron	52,641	1.2	1,120	59.0	14.9	350	313	75	66,640	83.5	16.5	(6)	(NA)	188	51
Camp	48,709	25.5	399	36.6	4.0	69	174	82	204,692	1.1	98.9	(6)	(NA)	(Z)	2
Carson	5,025	1.4	363	12.4	57.6	452	1,244	44	121,361	32.2	67.8	(6)	(NA)	65	1
Cass	25,671	6.4	956	28.9	9.0	193	202	32	33,753	9.8	90.2	(6)	(NA)	(Z)	1
Castro	161,830	68.3	535	7.1	55.1	564	1,053	593	1,107,742	12.7	87.3	(6)	(NA)	356	3
Chambers	3,631	0.7	610	41.1	21.3	275	451	13	21,925	41.0	59.0	(6)	(NA)	109	3
Cherokee	122,376	16.9	1,508	32.7	7.0	286	190	123	81,684	70.1	29.9	(6)	(NA)	(Z)	8
Childress	13,652	13.4	300	8.3	40.3	369	1,229	14	45,307	53.4	46.6	(6)	(NA)	3	–
Clay	8,112	7.1	892	17.7	28.8	654	734	39	43,906	10.0	90.0	(6)	(NA)	1	24
Cochran	30,675	41.5	292	3.4	58.2	439	1,504	40	135,397	94.2	5.8	(6)	(NA)	88	1
Coke	−5,789	(X)	335	6.6	44.8	485	1,449	13	38,042	4.5	95.5	(6)	(NA)	(Z)	11
Coleman	−4,180	(X)	829	6.8	38.0	642	775	16	18,983	21.8	78.2	(6)	(NA)	1	57
Collin	7,014	(Z)	2,135	58.5	5.4	310	145	38	17,855	67.2	32.8	(6)	(NA)	(Z)	202
Collingsworth	18,906	34.3	449	12.9	35.2	507	1,129	34	76,223	72.9	27.1	(6)	(NA)	38	1
Colorado	6,931	2.5	1,770	26.8	14.6	539	304	42	23,495	44.8	55.2	(6)	(NA)	194	2
Comal	−4,150	(X)	852	35.9	11.6	203	239	6	6,609	26.5	73.5	(6)	(NA)	(Z)	17
Comanche	30,416	15.9	1,352	19.2	19.0	543	402	103	75,823	14.3	85.7	(6)	(NA)	25	3
Concho	4,551	11.5	411	8.8	51.8	544	1,324	14	34,815	48.0	52.0	(6)	(NA)	5	1
Cooke	−2,899	(X)	1,765	38.4	12.0	459	260	46	26,215	16.0	84.0	(6)	(NA)	(Z)	4
Coryell	3,923	0.6	1,221	22.7	21.8	493	404	35	28,412	14.8	85.2	(6)	(NA)	(Z)	(Z)
Cottle	2,346	11.6	233	2.6	46.4	574	2,464	13	55,918	31.2	68.8	(6)	(NA)	7	(Z)
Crane	−4,025	(X)	44	31.8	59.1	(D)	(D)	1	29,614	0.2	99.8	(6)	(NA)	(Z)	1
Crockett	−9,000	(X)	198	3.5	71.7	1,735	8,765	10	51,707	(NA)	(NA)	(6)	(NA)	1	1
Crosby	50,181	40.5	373	5.9	54.7	490	1,313	40	105,997	91.0	9.0	(6)	(NA)	134	2
Culberson	−2,959	(X)	74	4.1	68.9	1,695	22,899	7	100,959	46.7	53.3	(6)	(NA)	10	1
Dallam	46,676	24.2	412	3.4	62.9	884	2,146	370	897,376	22.5	77.5	(6)	(NA)	395	2
Dallas	19,394	(Z)	730	61.2	4.9	89	122	19	26,008	88.4	11.6	(6)	(NA)	1	235
Dawson	35,294	17.7	581	7.7	55.4	572	985	55	95,332	94.7	5.3	(6)	(NA)	94	1
Deaf Smith	93,019	28.5	703	13.1	54.1	964	1,372	842	1,197,464	4.6	95.4	(6)	(NA)	72	4
Delta	415	1.2	507	32.0	11.8	142	280	11	21,055	44.8	55.2	(6)	(NA)	–	1
Denton	−1,492	(X)	2,358	62.4	5.3	349	148	49	20,824	24.0	76.0	(6)	(NA)	(Z)	370
DeWitt	5,676	1.8	1,786	21.7	16.3	577	323	30	16,530	7.7	92.3	(6)	(NA)	(Z)	3
Dickens	1,934	8.0	396	4.0	37.9	567	1,432	12	29,740	41.8	58.2	(6)	(NA)	7	(Z)
Dimmit	327	0.3	268	22.4	38.8	571	2,129	27	102,567	9.2	90.8	(6)	(NA)	9	2
Donley	7,266	16.8	440	5.9	34.5	584	1,328	74	167,305	12.1	87.9	(6)	(NA)	9	4
Duval	−7,735	(X)	1,228	8.2	25.8	850	692	13	10,546	14.0	86.0	(6)	(NA)	3	2
Eastland	4,137	1.4	1,166	15.7	20.5	498	427	30	26,035	30.0	70.0	(6)	(NA)	2	3
Ector	−10,322	(X)	287	65.9	16.4	504	1,755	2	6,526	14.9	85.1	(6)	(NA)	4	2
Edwards	−4,444	(X)	349	6.9	53.9	974	2,789	7	21,413	2.3	97.7	(6)	(NA)	(Z)	(Z)
Ellis	408	(Z)	2,089	45.0	9.0	464	222	43	20,793	62.0	38.0	(6)	(NA)	(Z)	18
El Paso	18,024	0.1	600	74.2	7.7	114	190	68	113,140	42.8	57.2	(6)	(NA)	216	129
Erath	76,116	13.0	1,977	25.1	14.2	581	294	208	105,065	4.8	95.2	(6)	(NA)	10	3
Falls	7,057	4.1	1,199	24.9	17.2	409	341	68	56,709	25.7	74.3	(6)	(NA)	2	3
Fannin	5,680	1.6	1,976	31.2	11.8	483	245	57	29,030	34.3	65.7	(6)	(NA)	3	4
Fayette	9,953	2.6	2,973	27.9	7.6	552	186	52	17,388	10.2	89.8	(6)	(NA)	1	2
Fisher	11,967	24.1	595	10.3	37.0	479	805	19	31,790	52.1	47.9	(6)	(NA)	3	–
Floyd	64,183	48.4	551	5.1	47.9	574	1,041	159	288,132	(NA)	(NA)	(6)	(NA)	213	(Z)
Foard	1,519	12.0	203	6.4	45.8	286	1,411	9	46,631	43.9	56.1	(6)	(NA)	5	–
Fort Bend	45,247	0.6	1,560	48.2	11.4	415	266	50	31,956	73.3	26.7	(6)	(NA)	36	69
Franklin	21,605	13.8	549	29.7	12.0	132	241	64	116,364	2.0	98.0	(6)	(NA)	(Z)	2
Freestone	−2,313	(X)	1,468	27.3	12.9	429	292	33	22,176	6.4	93.6	(6)	(NA)	(Z)	2
Frio	20,568	12.9	537	13.8	38.4	603	1,123	71	132,153	45.1	54.9	(6)	(NA)	72	2
Gaines	81,197	28.9	724	8.1	49.4	759	1,048	145	199,743	73.0	27.0	(6)	(NA)	421	2
Galveston	−1,455	(X)	664	60.1	8.3	127	192	6	8,509	40.8	59.2	(6)	(NA)	8	5
Garza	473	0.6	246	13.0	48.8	500	2,031	10	39,585	64.6	35.4	(6)	(NA)	7	–
Gillespie	1,370	0.4	1,812	26.5	19.9	645	356	24	13,223	20.6	79.4	(6)	(NA)	1	3
Glasscock	8,485	32.9	199	5.5	72.9	493	2,477	14	68,528	83.7	16.3	(6)	(NA)	22	–
Goliad	4,673	7.0	984	19.2	18.1	506	514	17	17,208	10.2	89.8	(6)	(NA)	(Z)	(Z)
Gonzales	108,429	33.1	1,816	20.3	19.3	696	383	278	152,849	7.8	92.2	(6)	(NA)	1	5
Gray	24,218	5.1	351	12.5	43.3	453	1,290	95	270,276	7.9	92.1	(6)	(NA)	21	1
Grayson	1,367	0.1	2,597	46.9	6.6	441	170	42	16,121	47.8	52.2	(6)	(NA)	4	27
Gregg	−2,760	(X)	444	52.5	3.4	47	105	2	5,441	22.8	77.2	(6)	(NA)	(Z)	28
Grimes	5,130	1.4	1,704	34.6	10.0	415	243	32	18,660	14.2	85.8	(6)	(NA)	(Z)	2
Guadalupe	8,694	0.7	2,442	43.8	6.3	385	158	37	15,235	44.0	56.0	(6)	(NA)	(Z)	7
Hale	102,490	16.0	915	10.1	44.0	605	661	225	246,170	45.7	54.3	(6)	(NA)	329	3

See footnotes at end of table.

[Includes United States, states, and 3,141 counties/county equivalents defined as of February 22, 2005. For more information on these areas, see Appendix C, Geographic Information]

County	Farm earnings, 2005 Total ($1,000)	Percent of total[1]	Agriculture (NAICS 111–112), 2002 — Farms Number	Percent Less than 50 acres	Percent 500 acres or more	Land in farms Total acres (1,000)	Average size of farm (acres)	Value of farm products sold Total (mil. dol.)	Average per farm (dol.)	Percent from Crops[2]	Percent from Livestock and poultry[3]	Water use, 2000[4] Total (mil. gal. per day)	Ground water, percent of total	By selected major use (mil. gal. per day) Irrigation	Public supply
TEXAS—Con.															
Hall	6,748	14.8	311	5.1	45.7	432	1,388	21	66,363	78.3	21.7	(6)	(NA)	17	(Z)
Hamilton	9,318	9.1	996	11.1	23.6	450	451	42	41,770	6.3	93.7	(6)	(NA)	1	(Z)
Hansford	79,210	51.7	290	9.0	65.5	593	2,045	367	1,265,145	6.5	93.5	(6)	(NA)	187	1
Hardeman	2,093	3.8	344	5.8	41.6	346	1,006	17	48,980	40.6	59.4	(6)	(NA)	5	(Z)
Hardin	−1,007	(X)	517	64.0	3.7	69	133	(D)	(NA)	(NA)	(NA)	(6)	(NA)	3	13
Harris	22,280	(Z)	2,452	61.7	4.7	305	124	53	21,565	66.2	33.8	(6)	(NA)	10	332
Harrison	7,150	0.7	1,116	37.8	10.8	229	205	12	11,037	13.8	86.2	(6)	(NA)	(Z)	9
Hartley	43,461	53.7	253	7.1	63.6	789	3,120	447	1,767,885	15.3	84.7	(6)	(NA)	332	(Z)
Haskell	20,899	24.4	579	9.2	41.1	492	850	41	70,459	65.0	35.0	(6)	(NA)	36	9
Hays	−6,602	(X)	1,106	43.0	11.3	278	252	15	13,213	27.3	72.7	(6)	(NA)	(Z)	14
Hemphill	17,195	16.8	239	7.9	53.6	546	2,286	92	386,987	0.5	99.5	(6)	(NA)	3	(Z)
Henderson	1,693	0.2	1,798	38.7	7.1	341	190	43	24,037	31.5	68.5	(6)	(NA)	(Z)	211
Hidalgo	60,770	0.8	2,104	59.8	12.1	593	282	202	96,042	90.3	9.7	(6)	(NA)	310	78
Hill	5,776	1.6	2,014	32.4	11.0	504	250	54	26,822	55.2	44.8	(6)	(NA)	(Z)	8
Hockley	20,663	5.6	767	15.0	40.4	491	641	90	117,623	(NA)	(NA)	(6)	(NA)	171	1
Hood	6,859	1.6	935	48.8	8.8	202	216	22	23,240	19.0	81.0	(6)	(NA)	4	8
Hopkins	50,094	9.5	1,923	28.5	10.0	431	224	134	69,797	3.0	97.0	(6)	(NA)	3	7
Houston	10,082	3.1	1,514	22.5	13.8	465	307	34	22,776	18.4	81.6	(6)	(NA)	1	4
Howard	8,555	1.6	466	18.7	39.9	518	1,112	15	32,416	77.9	22.1	(6)	(NA)	4	(Z)
Hudspeth	−2,166	(X)	131	7.6	62.6	2,122	16,196	27	207,458	79.7	20.3	(6)	(NA)	267	(Z)
Hunt	−2,621	(X)	2,784	47.1	5.6	400	144	28	10,081	41.7	58.3	(6)	(NA)	1	147
Hutchinson	722	0.2	262	23.7	42.0	553	2,111	29	111,882	20.0	80.0	(6)	(NA)	49	76
Irion	−6,353	(X)	151	23.8	51.7	536	3,552	3	23,099	3.3	96.7	(6)	(NA)	1	(Z)
Jack	−3,072	(X)	884	13.2	24.2	596	674	16	17,593	5.1	94.9	(6)	(NA)	–	1
Jackson	−1,507	(X)	917	23.1	26.0	471	513	42	45,649	73.1	26.9	(6)	(NA)	45	1
Jasper	−611	(X)	763	59.9	2.9	96	126	5	6,308	31.2	68.8	(6)	(NA)	(Z)	4
Jeff Davis	−7,785	(X)	79	12.7	74.7	1,489	18,845	6	80,570	2.3	97.7	(6)	(NA)	(Z)	(Z)
Jefferson	−1,261	(X)	775	47.5	17.0	388	501	17	21,772	45.2	54.8	(6)	(NA)	167	22
Jim Hogg	−3,107	(X)	234	4.3	50.0	604	2,579	7	29,658	2.1	97.9	(6)	(NA)	(Z)	1
Jim Wells	7,465	1.1	912	23.1	20.6	498	546	47	51,912	28.1	71.9	(6)	(NA)	1	6
Johnson	4,799	0.3	2,579	56.1	4.7	362	140	44	16,906	15.5	84.5	(6)	(NA)	–	13
Jones	9,573	4.7	918	16.9	28.0	517	563	39	42,728	49.3	50.7	(6)	(NA)	3	1
Karnes	−2,662	(X)	1,157	13.8	19.6	475	410	18	15,768	14.7	85.3	(6)	(NA)	1	3
Kaufman	3,530	0.3	2,438	51.9	5.7	420	172	30	12,321	21.7	78.3	(6)	(NA)	(Z)	5
Kendall	−7,809	(X)	967	34.1	17.3	327	338	7	7,263	13.8	86.2	(6)	(NA)	1	2
Kenedy	921	5.4	28	10.7	75.0	474	16,931	9	320,786	–	100.0	(6)	(NA)	–	(Z)
Kent	−1,682	(X)	182	5.5	51.6	561	3,081	5	29,016	12.9	87.1	(6)	(NA)	–	(Z)
Kerr	−5,870	(X)	977	27.2	19.2	564	578	12	12,276	9.4	90.6	(6)	(NA)	1	6
Kimble	−7,341	(X)	528	16.5	43.0	616	1,166	7	13,932	8.9	91.1	(6)	(NA)	1	1
King	2,064	35.2	41	4.9	56.1	547	13,334	12	286,732	11.0	89.0	(6)	(NA)	(Z)	(Z)
Kinney	−4,723	(X)	148	5.4	72.3	614	4,146	5	32,088	14.3	85.7	(6)	(NA)	4	1
Kleberg	8,693	1.7	348	46.6	14.7	(D)	(D)	58	166,055	17.0	83.0	(6)	(NA)	(Z)	5
Knox	6,170	10.7	271	12.9	48.7	564	2,082	46	170,406	31.8	68.2	(6)	(NA)	30	(Z)
Lamar	−2,593	(X)	1,725	28.5	12.8	470	273	39	22,600	30.2	69.8	(6)	(NA)	3	15
Lamb	50,682	22.2	931	6.0	41.8	629	675	260	279,504	36.7	63.3	(6)	(NA)	304	2
Lampasas	−4,535	(X)	861	25.1	21.5	412	479	13	15,534	10.1	89.9	(6)	(NA)	(Z)	(Z)
La Salle	3,793	4.8	315	6.7	54.9	559	1,773	23	73,565	12.1	87.9	(6)	(NA)	3	1
Lavaca	5,073	1.9	2,861	29.1	8.5	602	210	46	15,959	7.7	92.3	(6)	(NA)	8	1
Lee	9,499	4.0	1,848	29.9	8.7	366	198	23	12,417	18.6	81.4	(6)	(NA)	1	2
Leon	−852	(X)	1,908	25.5	13.7	563	295	51	26,883	5.8	94.2	(6)	(NA)	–	2
Liberty	−2,084	(X)	1,596	50.3	7.1	305	191	21	13,119	53.8	46.2	(6)	(NA)	76	494
Limestone	7,985	2.5	1,430	20.3	18.5	530	371	33	22,922	12.6	87.4	(6)	(NA)	–	4
Lipscomb	7,305	11.9	307	3.9	55.7	578	1,883	42	137,909	8.0	92.0	(6)	(NA)	26	1
Live Oak	−6,705	(X)	845	14.7	29.1	525	622	14	16,560	13.1	86.9	(6)	(NA)	1	5
Llano	−5,041	(X)	692	18.8	34.8	533	771	12	16,964	4.8	95.2	(6)	(NA)	1	3
Loving	−103	(X)	14	–	100.0	515	36,799	1	37,357	–	100.0	(6)	(NA)	1	–
Lubbock	79,508	1.5	1,142	32.0	29.4	557	488	144	125,783	45.7	54.3	(6)	(NA)	191	9
Lynn	68,495	54.6	478	9.6	56.7	530	1,110	49	102,180	96.6	3.4	(6)	(NA)	59	(Z)
McCulloch	1,163	0.9	621	10.0	32.2	546	880	13	20,879	22.5	77.5	(6)	(NA)	2	3
McLennan	17,012	0.4	2,571	46.7	8.8	538	209	61	23,746	35.6	64.4	(6)	(NA)	2	22
McMullen	326	2.9	223	4.5	71.3	597	2,677	6	28,691	2.8	97.2	(6)	(NA)	–	1
Madison	45,193	24.8	890	24.6	12.2	245	275	61	68,064	(NA)	(NA)	(6)	(NA)	(Z)	2
Marion	305	0.3	252	28.2	9.9	60	237	4	16,218	18.2	81.8	(6)	(NA)	(Z)	2
Martin	6,459	10.2	379	10.6	54.1	526	1,388	14	37,135	91.7	8.3	(6)	(NA)	17	4
Mason	2,336	4.5	633	10.4	43.4	556	878	45	70,771	5.3	94.7	(6)	(NA)	8	1
Matagorda	24,253	4.4	991	26.2	24.9	619	625	116	116,781	75.5	24.5	(6)	(NA)	219	4
Maverick	3,785	0.8	214	34.6	26.2	476	2,225	35	162,243	12.0	88.0	(6)	(NA)	99	6
Medina	10,007	3.1	1,951	27.8	18.7	805	413	61	31,134	38.1	61.9	(6)	(NA)	55	6
Menard	−5,077	(X)	336	10.7	44.3	549	1,633	7	22,098	10.5	89.5	(6)	(NA)	4	(Z)
Midland	−2,140	(X)	477	48.6	16.6	362	758	7	15,516	54.0	46.0	(6)	(NA)	37	1

See footnotes at end of table.

Table B-14. Counties — **Farm Earnings, Agriculture, and Water Use**—Con.

[Includes United States, states, and 3,141 counties/county equivalents defined as of February 22, 2005. For more information on these areas, see Appendix C, Geographic Information]

County	Farm earnings, 2005 Total ($1,000)	Per-cent of total[1]	Farms Number	Farms Percent Less than 50 acres	Farms Percent 500 acres or more	Land in farms Total acres (1,000)	Land in farms Aver-age size of farm (acres)	Value of farm products sold Total (mil. dol.)	Value of farm products sold Average per farm (dol.)	Percent from Crops[2]	Percent from Live-stock and poultry[3]	Water use Total (mil. gal. per day)	Ground water, percent of total	Irri-gation	Public supply
TEXAS—Con.															
Milam	11,239	3.2	1,991	26.2	12.5	577	290	72	36,339	24.4	75.6	(6)	(NA)	1	3
Mills	5,274	8.2	768	16.1	25.9	427	556	22	28,629	8.0	92.0	(6)	(NA)	2	1
Mitchell	4,171	4.1	451	12.0	33.0	488	1,082	12	27,370	57.2	42.8	(6)	(NA)	2	(Z)
Montague	525	(NA)	1,399	19.4	17.1	504	360	32	22,782	11.8	88.2	(6)	(NA)	(Z)	2
Montgomery	8,210	0.1	1,701	61.8	4.8	198	116	20	11,798	57.5	42.5	(6)	(NA)	–	49
Moore	20,280	4.9	276	10.9	63.4	550	1,991	303	1,098,815	14.0	86.0	(6)	(NA)	247	6
Morris	11,326	4.0	403	33.3	10.9	100	247	20	49,965	2.0	98.0	(6)	(NA)	(Z)	(Z)
Motley	2,376	14.4	201	2.5	57.2	487	2,423	10	49,224	32.4	67.6	(6)	(NA)	8	(Z)
Nacogdoches	9,725	1.1	1,290	32.2	6.3	274	212	198	153,467	1.2	98.8	(6)	(NA)	1	7
Navarro	5,211	0.8	1,864	29.9	11.9	537	288	37	19,598	32.4	67.6	(6)	(NA)	–	12
Newton	-938	(X)	385	56.6	2.1	69	180	1	3,416	28.7	71.3	(6)	(NA)	1	1
Nolan	5,577	2.2	516	14.0	34.3	481	933	13	25,955	53.1	46.9	(6)	(NA)	2	1
Nueces	38,250	0.5	649	36.7	29.4	524	807	63	96,502	94.9	5.1	(6)	(NA)	–	47
Ochiltree	52,993	19.8	367	11.2	61.3	559	1,524	242	658,997	(NA)	(NA)	(6)	(NA)	64	2
Oldham	7,636	21.5	136	5.9	65.4	936	6,885	66	484,919	3.5	96.5	(6)	(NA)	2	(Z)
Orange	-1,563	(X)	496	70.2	6.0	73	148	4	7,639	27.6	72.4	(6)	(NA)	3	13
Palo Pinto	-2,190	(X)	965	31.2	19.8	485	503	15	15,890	15.5	84.5	(6)	(NA)	(Z)	6
Panola	23,095	6.2	948	27.6	13.0	223	235	46	48,756	3.0	97.0	(6)	(NA)	–	4
Parker	2,314	0.2	3,215	59.3	5.0	487	151	48	14,806	26.9	73.1	(6)	(NA)	(Z)	6
Parmer	53,236	23.9	660	8.6	52.9	576	873	604	915,015	11.9	88.1	(6)	(NA)	314	1
Pecos	7,191	3.6	270	10.7	68.9	2,916	10,800	38	141,548	61.8	38.2	(6)	(NA)	75	4
Polk	605	0.1	689	38.9	7.4	130	189	6	8,388	20.6	79.4	(6)	(NA)	(Z)	8
Potter	-1,245	(X)	305	34.1	24.3	522	1,711	19	63,902	6.7	93.3	(6)	(NA)	5	(Z)
Presidio	-3,669	(X)	123	9.8	67.5	1,504	12,225	51	415,870	(NA)	(NA)	(6)	(NA)	20	1
Rains	6,673	7.9	584	42.8	7.7	94	160	12	20,188	19.4	80.6	(6)	(NA)	(Z)	1
Randall	39,681	3.5	748	29.4	29.7	512	685	261	349,112	4.2	95.8	(6)	(NA)	30	2
Reagan	1,216	1.4	123	1.6	70.7	538	4,376	7	53,398	67.0	33.0	(6)	(NA)	18	1
Real	-3,356	(X)	301	16.6	45.8	400	1,329	3	8,967	10.0	90.0	(6)	(NA)	(Z)	1
Red River	3,515	3.3	1,217	21.9	16.1	423	347	31	25,353	14.1	85.9	(6)	(NA)	5	2
Reeves	2,546	1.9	166	10.8	48.2	1,010	6,084	19	111,825	39.5	60.5	(6)	(NA)	110	2
Refugio	5,177	6.0	274	24.1	29.9	506	1,847	21	78,172	58.6	41.4	(6)	(NA)	–	1
Roberts	1,317	14.4	94	2.1	74.5	495	5,262	13	140,766	16.8	83.2	(6)	(NA)	7	(Z)
Robertson	6,534	3.6	1,555	23.9	14.5	515	331	75	48,059	15.4	84.6	(6)	(NA)	15	3
Rockwall	-201	(X)	385	60.5	4.2	46	121	3	7,790	35.1	64.9	(6)	(NA)	–	–
Runnels	8,965	6.6	897	13.2	32.6	585	652	27	30,541	54.1	45.9	(6)	(NA)	3	1
Rusk	23,699	3.6	1,391	29.3	8.4	272	196	39	28,288	35.5	64.5	(6)	(NA)	(Z)	5
Sabine	6,526	4.9	219	36.5	5.5	31	141	7	31,292	5.5	94.5	(6)	(NA)	–	2
San Augustine	12,822	16.3	308	27.6	6.5	59	191	25	81,104	4.0	96.0	(6)	(NA)	(Z)	1
San Jacinto	3,119	3.1	598	49.8	5.0	93	156	6	9,227	26.0	74.0	(6)	(NA)	–	2
San Patricio	16,739	1.8	575	38.8	28.3	345	601	69	119,762	77.0	23.0	(6)	(NA)	1	9
San Saba	1,144	1.5	706	10.9	39.0	709	1,005	23	32,490	17.0	83.0	(6)	(NA)	2	1
Schleicher	-2,378	(X)	307	5.9	64.2	778	2,535	9	30,023	9.9	90.1	(6)	(NA)	3	(Z)
Scurry	7,028	1.8	674	16.2	30.9	565	838	23	34,163	39.5	60.5	(6)	(NA)	3	12
Shackelford	-3,699	(X)	252	13.5	45.6	557	2,211	15	59,726	8.4	91.6	(6)	(NA)	(Z)	–
Shelby	77,176	20.0	1,100	26.4	6.8	192	175	241	218,763	0.8	99.2	(6)	(NA)	(Z)	5
Sherman	81,547	75.1	322	7.8	64.9	546	1,696	295	916,366	16.1	83.9	(6)	(NA)	292	1
Smith	34,131	0.7	2,264	47.8	4.5	287	127	64	28,051	75.0	25.0	(6)	(NA)	1	41
Somervell	-1,237	(X)	339	35.7	13.3	84	249	2	5,973	25.6	74.4	(6)	(NA)	(Z)	(Z)
Starr	13,678	3.3	870	6.3	30.6	570	656	67	76,717	16.1	83.9	(6)	(NA)	29	9
Stephens	-6,038	(X)	435	7.4	37.9	428	984	9	20,133	5.7	94.3	(6)	(NA)	(Z)	11
Sterling	-5,912	(X)	66	12.1	65.2	633	9,591	6	87,697	1.0	99.0	(6)	(NA)	1	(Z)
Stonewall	396	1.8	316	5.4	50.6	524	1,659	9	28,573	33.8	66.2	(6)	(NA)	2	–
Sutton	-8,385	(X)	191	5.2	75.4	880	4,606	6	33,592	3.7	96.3	(6)	(NA)	2	1
Swisher	90,762	54.9	578	6.9	47.9	566	980	296	512,611	10.4	89.6	(6)	(NA)	162	1
Tarrant	6,511	(Z)	1,227	65.9	6.1	173	141	29	23,701	74.7	25.3	(6)	(NA)	(Z)	178
Taylor	2,284	0.1	1,183	30.3	20.2	534	451	55	46,840	11.8	88.2	(6)	(NA)	4	10
Terrell	-5,867	(X)	76	6.6	89.5	1,413	18,593	4	51,250	(NA)	(NA)	(6)	(NA)	(Z)	(Z)
Terry	51,901	24.7	620	12.9	46.5	445	718	63	102,179	93.8	6.2	(6)	(NA)	148	(Z)
Throckmorton	4,799	18.5	257	5.1	48.6	561	2,184	16	63,887	14.8	85.2	(6)	(NA)	–	(Z)
Titus	2,885	0.4	776	32.7	8.5	178	230	56	72,666	1.5	98.5	(6)	(NA)	–	8
Tom Green	19,203	0.9	1,024	43.1	28.4	845	825	97	94,944	19.4	80.6	(6)	(NA)	33	22
Travis	1,401	(Z)	1,306	46.4	9.9	298	229	17	13,106	58.5	41.5	(6)	(NA)	1	122
Trinity	7,034	7.6	555	29.5	8.1	105	189	9	16,132	3.9	96.1	(6)	(NA)	–	4
Tyler	-1,481	(X)	615	54.5	4.9	80	129	5	7,646	33.9	66.1	(6)	(NA)	(Z)	2
Upshur	8,309	2.9	1,236	40.9	6.2	196	159	41	33,024	5.3	94.7	(6)	(NA)	(Z)	5
Upton	-2,218	(X)	83	6.0	71.1	723	8,716	5	58,000	57.8	42.2	(6)	(NA)	6	1
Uvalde	8,728	2.5	686	20.6	38.0	969	1,412	69	100,633	39.6	60.4	(6)	(NA)	68	6
Val Verde	-9,420	(X)	285	31.9	47.0	1,661	5,829	11	38,263	6.3	93.7	(6)	(NA)	1	13
Van Zandt	17,606	4.2	2,842	46.0	6.0	422	149	73	25,696	45.5	54.5	(6)	(NA)	1	6
Victoria	-538	(X)	1,286	34.8	16.2	514	400	29	22,600	48.0	52.0	(6)	(NA)	7	10

See footnotes at end of table.

Table B-14. Counties — Farm Earnings, Agriculture, and Water Use—Con.

[Includes United States, states, and 3,141 counties/county equivalents defined as of February 22, 2005. For more information on these areas, see Appendix C, Geographic Information]

County	Farm earnings, 2005 Total ($1,000)	Percent of total[1]	Farms Number	Farms Percent Less than 50 acres	Farms Percent 500 acres or more	Land in farms Total acres (1,000)	Land in farms Average size of farm (acres)	Value of farm products sold Total (mil. dol.)	Value of farm products sold Average per farm (dol.)	Percent from Crops[2]	Percent from Live-stock and poultry[3]	Water use, 2000[4] Total (mil. gal. per day)	Ground water, percent of total	By selected major use (mil. gal. per day) Irrigation	By selected major use (mil. gal. per day) Public supply
TEXAS—Con.															
Walker	−603	(X)	1,043	43.3	8.6	206	198	25	24,326	54.5	45.5	(6)	(NA)	(Z)	5
Waller	−4,359	(X)	1,453	49.1	8.6	277	191	38	26,073	57.9	42.1	(6)	(NA)	18	3
Ward	−5,838	(X)	86	23.3	36.0	466	5,414	2	19,547	(NA)	(NA)	(6)	(NA)	8	8
Washington	6,023	1.0	2,303	38.1	5.3	355	154	37	15,927	18.2	81.8	(6)	(NA)	(Z)	3
Webb	−4,842	(X)	568	7.9	49.1	2,043	3,596	24	41,618	5.4	94.6	(6)	(NA)	6	41
Wharton	41,908	6.5	1,538	31.7	22.1	638	415	146	95,169	67.8	32.2	(6)	(NA)	307	4
Wheeler	56,197	41.6	565	9.9	38.8	534	944	94	166,411	3.5	96.5	(6)	(NA)	3	1
Wichita	2,319	0.1	606	38.0	17.7	302	498	16	26,120	51.4	48.6	(6)	(NA)	40	2
Wilbarger	10,607	3.9	502	18.7	34.7	872	1,738	32	63,892	57.8	42.2	(6)	(NA)	30	4
Willacy	17,178	11.6	334	27.8	33.5	370	1,107	19	56,608	77.5	22.5	(6)	(NA)	–	–
Williamson	3,404	0.1	2,510	45.0	11.2	583	232	46	18,484	65.9	34.1	(6)	(NA)	–	30
Wilson	7,690	3.2	2,157	32.4	8.8	446	207	43	19,799	17.8	82.2	(6)	(NA)	12	4
Winkler	−3,330	(X)	44	13.6	45.5	492	11,175	2	43,773	(NA)	(NA)	(6)	(NA)	–	2
Wise	−2,033	(X)	2,696	49.9	6.8	493	183	33	12,352	22.7	77.3	(6)	(NA)	1	4
Wood	43,723	10.9	1,495	41.0	5.9	228	153	58	38,662	6.4	93.6	(6)	(NA)	(Z)	5
Yoakum	22,933	11.9	298	9.4	53.0	455	1,527	50	167,426	83.7	16.3	(6)	(NA)	99	1
Young	−116	(X)	755	13.8	29.4	510	675	24	31,690	7.2	92.8	(6)	(NA)	–	3
Zapata	−1,128	(X)	388	4.6	49.5	398	1,025	10	25,369	(NA)	(NA)	(6)	(NA)	4	2
Zavala	19,892	19.2	257	4.7	59.9	707	2,752	49	189,471	22.2	77.8	(6)	(NA)	60	2
UTAH	244,518	0.4	15,282	54.8	14.0	11,731	768	1,116	73,020	23.1	76.9	4,970	21.1	3,860	638
Beaver	64,116	45.8	256	30.9	23.8	139	544	161	630,254	6.5	93.5	(6)	(NA)	120	2
Box Elder	23,062	2.3	1,113	47.4	21.7	1,401	1,259	114	102,286	25.9	74.1	(6)	(NA)	421	23
Cache	12,867	0.8	1,194	51.1	9.4	247	207	97	80,925	15.2	84.8	(6)	(NA)	259	34
Carbon	−2,662	(X)	243	66.3	15.2	199	821	3	13,708	17.5	82.5	(6)	(NA)	36	6
Daggett	−311	(X)	28	10.7	39.3	(D)	(D)	2	60,107	(NA)	(NA)	(6)	(NA)	23	1
Davis	−7,727	(X)	682	80.4	2.4	66	113	30	52,211	87.1	12.9	(6)	(NA)	92	44
Duchesne	−1,269	(X)	932	42.9	16.1	1,305	1,400	46	49,407	10.6	89.4	(6)	(NA)	218	4
Emery	3,657	1.8	459	39.2	14.8	(D)	(D)	11	24,950	13.1	86.9	(6)	(NA)	162	2
Garfield	−1,877	(X)	225	37.3	17.8	80	355	6	26,831	8.1	91.9	(6)	(NA)	70	2
Grand	−1,259	(X)	94	59.6	11.7	53	561	2	23,149	34.0	66.0	(6)	(NA)	10	3
Iron	43,021	7.3	438	40.6	28.8	479	1,094	77	176,717	48.2	51.8	(6)	(NA)	200	9
Juab	5,764	4.5	236	32.2	33.5	270	1,146	12	51,750	33.4	66.6	(6)	(NA)	80	6
Kane	−65	(X)	131	29.0	37.4	156	1,190	3	25,840	(NA)	(NA)	(6)	(NA)	12	2
Millard	40,764	18.9	646	29.9	31.1	445	689	113	175,169	25.5	74.5	(6)	(NA)	381	5
Morgan	−243	(X)	255	61.2	12.5	(D)	(D)	7	29,341	10.2	89.8	(6)	(NA)	39	1
Piute	5,941	35.3	108	32.4	20.4	(D)	(D)	9	83,593	8.4	91.6	(6)	(NA)	74	1
Rich	3,184	13.2	135	21.5	51.9	509	3,772	13	97,415	2.4	97.6	(6)	(NA)	222	1
Salt Lake	−11,486	(X)	712	82.3	3.1	82	116	19	27,232	71.2	28.8	(6)	(NA)	60	258
San Juan	−3,404	(X)	231	23.4	44.2	1,559	6,747	8	32,537	21.2	78.8	(6)	(NA)	20	3
Sanpete	11,522	4.7	759	42.7	18.3	357	471	94	123,412	5.1	94.9	(6)	(NA)	143	4
Sevier	11,159	3.8	568	52.1	11.4	165	290	52	92,120	26.2	73.8	(6)	(NA)	171	6
Summit	4,520	0.5	557	53.5	15.8	376	674	20	35,023	5.8	94.2	(6)	(NA)	91	10
Tooele	9,294	1.2	380	48.7	18.4	415	1,092	18	47,734	14.2	85.8	(6)	(NA)	68	8
Uintah	−7,790	(X)	908	56.8	11.1	(D)	(D)	30	32,522	11.2	88.8	(6)	(NA)	194	8
Utah	50,721	0.7	2,046	73.6	5.2	343	168	117	57,187	37.5	62.5	(6)	(NA)	399	103
Wasatch	−1,429	(X)	380	69.7	3.7	70	183	6	14,966	16.1	83.9	(6)	(NA)	46	3
Washington	−2,243	(X)	481	53.2	14.3	217	451	7	15,085	41.6	58.4	(6)	(NA)	59	35
Wayne	3,970	10.0	173	30.6	8.7	42	245	11	60,827	7.1	92.9	(6)	(NA)	45	1
Weber	−7,279	(X)	1,012	74.7	2.8	87	86	27	26,292	25.4	74.6	(6)	(NA)	148	52
VERMONT	199,593	1.3	6,571	33.7	8.4	1,245	189	473	71,993	15.1	84.9	447	9.7	4	60
Addison	40,394	5.5	676	31.8	16.4	193	286	106	156,691	10.7	89.3	4	72.5	(Z)	2
Bennington	3,329	0.4	228	44.7	8.8	41	180	8	34,289	30.6	69.4	6	50.3	(Z)	4
Caledonia	13,238	2.3	505	30.7	7.5	84	167	24	47,071	17.0	83.0	4	62.0	(Z)	2
Chittenden	12,577	0.2	473	40.2	7.6	77	162	28	59,427	36.9	63.1	28	15.6	1	24
Essex	2,747	3.4	98	31.6	12.2	20	202	7	69,286	14.3	85.7	2	25.9	(Z)	(Z)
Franklin	44,066	5.3	770	25.2	11.8	190	247	115	149,916	6.0	94.0	6	54.1	(Z)	3
Grand Isle	4,693	7.8	99	35.4	6.1	16	165	9	93,293	15.9	84.1	1	24.1	(Z)	(Z)
Lamoille	7,649	1.5	317	29.7	6.0	54	170	14	43,319	27.5	72.5	3	89.1	(Z)	1
Orange	12,243	3.1	680	30.6	4.9	110	162	32	47,071	19.0	81.0	3	81.4	(Z)	1
Orleans	27,709	5.9	583	23.8	10.8	132	227	57	98,353	5.7	94.3	3	78.7	(Z)	2
Rutland	8,601	0.6	623	33.7	9.8	121	195	24	38,502	17.2	82.8	9	53.2	(Z)	6
Washington	6,981	0.4	425	37.9	2.6	54	127	15	34,680	26.3	73.7	9	50.0	(Z)	6
Windham	9,605	0.8	397	45.8	8.6	62	155	18	46,149	41.8	58.2	362	1.1	(Z)	3
Windsor	5,761	0.5	697	42.9	2.7	90	129	16	22,723	34.1	65.9	8	81.2	(Z)	5
VIRGINIA	548,236	0.2	47,606	35.9	7.5	8,625	181	2,361	49,593	30.4	69.6	8,830	3.6	26	720
Accomack	13,165	2.4	318	46.9	14.5	91	286	109	343,186	43.5	56.5	9	70.6	4	1
Albemarle	[10]8,522	[10]0.2	[10]919	[10]34.5	[10]9.4	[10]177	[10]193	[10]19	[10]20,857	[10]35.3	[10]64.7	15	22.9	1	12
Alleghany[11]	[12]1,328	[12]0.3	[12]202	[12]28.7	[12]4.5	[12]33	[12]163	[12]2	[12]9,837	[12]14.4	[12]85.7	64	5.1	–	1
Amelia	14,555	9.8	456	29.2	9.9	91	200	52	113,164	6.5	93.5	2	95.0	(Z)	–
Amherst	2,088	0.5	460	19.8	8.7	100	217	6	13,843	15.9	84.1	20	4.5	–	13

See footnotes at end of table.

Table B-14. Counties — **Farm Earnings, Agriculture, and Water Use**—Con.

[Includes United States, states, and 3,141 counties/county equivalents defined as of February 22, 2005. For more information on these areas, see Appendix C, Geographic Information]

County	Farm earnings, 2005 — Total ($1,000)	Farm earnings, 2005 — Percent of total[1]	Farms — Number	Farms — Percent Less than 50 acres	Farms — Percent 500 acres or more	Land in farms — Total acres (1,000)	Land in farms — Average size of farm (acres)	Value of farm products sold — Total (mil. dol.)	Value — Average per farm (dol.)	Percent from Crops[2]	Percent from Live-stock and poultry[3]	Water use — Total (mil. gal. per day)	Water use — Ground water, percent of total	By selected major use — Irrigation	By selected major use — Public supply
VIRGINIA—Con.															
Appomattox	1,849	1.2	389	19.3	8.0	85	218	7	17,177	21.7	78.3	1	96.0	(Z)	(Z)
Arlington	–	–	2	100.0	–	(D)	(D)	(D)	(NA)	(NA)	(NA)	(Z)	81.8	(Z)	–
Augusta	[13]27,815	[13]1.2	[13]1,691	[13]39.9	[13]8.3	[13]306	[13]181	[13]144	[13]85,106	[13]9.9	[13]90.1	14	83.4	(Z)	8
Bath	661	0.7	124	15.3	21.8	52	422	3	20,323	4.0	96.0	(Z)	53.1	(Z)	(Z)
Bedford	[14]3,794	[14]0.4	[14]1,289	[14]30.2	[14]4.7	[14]199	[14]155	[14]19	[14]15,031	[14]18.4	[14]81.6	6	64.8	(Z)	1
Bland	1,030	1.2	417	23.3	10.8	94	226	9	20,537	5.6	94.4	(Z)	100.0	–	(Z)
Botetourt	4,180	0.9	610	34.9	7.4	97	159	10	16,364	18.5	81.5	16	16.0	(Z)	15
Brunswick	-1,316	(X)	333	27.9	10.5	79	237	13	37,934	58.2	41.8	21	4.5	(Z)	19
Buchanan	420	0.1	94	37.2	–	9	97	(D)	(NA)	(NA)	(NA)	2	72.2	–	–
Buckingham	5,953	3.7	389	27.8	9.3	81	209	20	52,067	9.4	90.6	1	67.2	–	(Z)
Campbell	[15]1,025	(Z)	[15]664	[15]19.3	[15]9.8	[15]139	[15]209	[15]16	[15]23,476	[15]28.5	[15]71.5	9	33.0	(Z)	4
Caroline	5,624	2.2	237	37.1	12.7	59	250	12	48,599	83.3	16.7	4	31.3	1	(Z)
Carroll	[16]10,866	[16]2.0	953	30.8	3.3	122	128	26	27,190	25.3	74.7	2	82.0	(Z)	1
Charles City	1,789	2.2	88	45.5	18.2	29	326	6	71,341	78.4	21.6	1	72.2	(Z)	(Z)
Charlotte	2,699	2.2	535	18.7	9.2	134	250	16	29,542	41.7	58.3	1	69.3	(Z)	(Z)
Chesterfield	4,643	0.1	[17]214	[17]52.8	[17]4.7	[17]23	[17]109	[17]9	[17]40,556	[17]59.0	[17]41.0	997	0.3	(Z)	33
Clarke	2,426	1.1	472	43.9	6.4	74	157	16	33,085	33.8	66.2	1	64.2	–	(Z)
Craig	1,223	4.1	228	25.4	9.2	48	212	4	15,829	14.1	85.9	(Z)	100.0	–	(Z)
Culpeper	8,292	1.1	669	39.3	8.1	125	187	37	54,877	51.3	48.7	3	53.1	–	2
Cumberland	5,608	10.1	283	21.2	10.6	63	221	28	100,014	9.0	91.0	1	97.3	(Z)	(Z)
Dickenson	726	0.5	117	32.5	2.6	12	101	1	6,291	28.0	72.0	4	13.4	–	3
Dinwiddie	[18]1,494	[18]0.1	[19]361	[19]28.0	[19]10.5	[19]92	[19]256	[19]15	[19]40,706	[19]64.3	[19]35.7	2	72.4	1	–
Essex	2,863	2.0	127	22.8	26.0	58	459	8	63,756	95.2	4.8	1	77.3	(Z)	(Z)
Fairfax	[20]2,690	(Z)	[21]151	[21]66.9	[21]0.7	[21]10	[21]66	[21]5	[21]35,550	[21]82.1	[21]17.9	79	4.8	(Z)	75
Fauquier	9,813	0.8	1,344	43.4	6.2	238	177	45	33,810	21.0	79.0	5	66.5	1	2
Floyd	12,880	9.5	829	25.2	5.5	135	163	33	39,567	31.7	68.3	1	96.9	(Z)	(Z)
Fluvanna	2,860	1.6	328	26.8	6.4	60	184	4	12,607	21.7	78.3	137	0.7	–	1
Franklin	8,229	1.4	1,012	24.2	6.4	173	170	37	36,068	17.3	82.7	4	91.2	(Z)	1
Frederick	[22]8,582	[22]0.3	[22]720	[22]39.2	[22]5.6	[22]113	[22]156	[22]22	[22]30,058	[22]67.0	[22]33.0	5	55.6	(Z)	2
Giles	2,136	0.9	407	27.5	6.4	68	168	5	13,123	22.0	78.0	329	1.4	–	(Z)
Gloucester	2,023	0.9	153	57.5	9.2	26	168	5	30,059	82.1	17.9	3	61.6	(Z)	1
Goochland	2,698	0.3	315	42.9	6.7	52	166	6	18,254	25.8	74.2	1	88.1	(Z)	(Z)
Grayson	6,653	6.3	[23]399	[23]36.0	[23]6.4	[23]151	[23]160	[23]28	[23]29,636	[23]24.5	[23]75.5	1	93.2	(Z)	(Z)
Greene	922	0.7	214	28.5	3.7	33	152	6	27,173	14.3	85.7	1	87.1	(Z)	–
Greensville	[24]1,234	[24]0.4	[24]113	[24]20.4	[24]18.6	[24]42	[24]376	[24]6	[24]49,221	[24]90.3	[24]9.7	2	41.3	(Z)	–
Halifax[25]	-3,147	(X)	905	19.7	11.7	222	245	28	30,634	65.2	34.8	17	16.0	1	2
Hanover	11,021	0.5	682	48.2	6.2	101	147	32	46,626	78.4	21.6	7	48.1	1	4
Henrico	9,319	0.1	[26]185	[26]50.8	[26]4.9	[26]28	[26]152	[26]8	[26]41,135	[26]88.6	[26]11.4	5	94.1	(Z)	(Z)
Henry	[27]4,767	[27]0.4	[27]305	[27]27.2	[27]4.6	[27]53	[27]174	[27]4		[27]32.7	[27]67.3	20	25.6	(Z)	5
Highland	4,586	17.6	293	10.6	17.4	96	328	13	43,478	2.9	97.1	5	100.0	–	(Z)
Isle of Wight	7,139	1.1	204	35.8	24.5	87	424	32	157,147	42.0	58.0	39	92.7	(Z)	2
James City	[28]721	(Z)	[28]64	[28]54.7	[28]4.7	[28]9	[28]140	[28]2	[28]36,578	[28]86.8	[28]13.2	12	92.3	(Z)	10
King and Queen	3,092	4.5	154	21.4	14.3	59	382	7	45,792	76.0	24.0	1	76.2	(Z)	(Z)
King George	1,435	0.2	169	29.0	5.3	32	189	3	17,574	78.7	21.3	3	35.5	(Z)	1
King William	4,997	2.5	135	28.1	21.5	61	455	14	106,630	88.2	11.8	21	97.1	1	1
Lancaster	1,218	0.6	61	44.3	11.5	12	204	2	37,131	96.9	3.1	1	94.3	(Z)	(Z)
Lee	[5]25	(NA)	1,103	37.4	2.6	128	116	12	10,985	45.0	55.0	1	100.0	–	1
Loudoun	7,742	0.1	1,516	64.4	4.5	165	109	39	25,515	49.4	50.6	23	33.8	(Z)	16
Louisa	1,160	0.2	474	29.7	8.0	87	184	10	21,335	23.5	76.5	2,129	0.1	(Z)	(Z)
Lunenburg	-971	(X)	375	18.9	12.0	92	244	14	37,131	56.8	43.2	1	70.1	(Z)	(Z)
Madison	2,001	1.3	531	36.3	8.1	103	194	18	33,955	18.4	81.6	1	98.8	(Z)	(Z)
Mathews	3,185	3.5	47	55.3	8.5	(D)	(D)	4	92,468	92.6	7.4	1	100.0	(Z)	–
Mecklenburg	5,687	1.2	581	20.8	15.1	168	289	27	45,850	69.1	30.9	10	19.7	1	2
Middlesex	1,375	1.1	100	53.5	8.9	21	210	5	51,554	89.2	10.8	1	83.5	(Z)	(Z)
Montgomery	[29]4,286	[29]0.2	[29]650	[29]40.2	[29]6.6	[29]100	[29]153	[29]18	[29]27,560	[29]32.4	[29]67.6	22	11.1	(Z)	7
Nelson	3,160	2.2	456	28.5	7.0	85	186	8	16,590	64.3	35.7	1	97.8	(Z)	(Z)
New Kent	1,357	0.9	100	29.0	7.0	19	193	3	30,860	90.7	9.3	29	3.1	(Z)	28
Northampton	21,021	9.9	187	43.3	19.3	52	281	44	236,321	74.6	25.4	3	47.1	2	(Z)
Northumberland	3,178	2.7	128	38.3	18.0	40	314	7	57,875	95.3	4.7	1	100.0	–	(Z)
Nottoway	5,048	2.2	408	25.7	6.4	71	175	27	67,343	9.1	90.9	1	46.9	(Z)	1
Orange	11,536	3.1	486	31.1	8.8	105	216	37	75,693	52.3	47.7	1	66.7	(Z)	(Z)
Page	19,821	7.7	549	46.4	4.0	64	117	109	198,033	1.2	98.8	3	90.9	(Z)	2
Patrick	3,885	2.1	629	34.8	3.5	91	144	15	24,208	44.3	55.7	2	80.6	(Z)	–
Pittsylvania	[30]8,715	[30]0.5	[30]1,304	[30]22.1	[30]9.7	[30]289	[30]221	[30]55	[30]41,866	[30]56.2	[30]43.8	10	36.6	1	1
Powhatan	2,059	0.7	229	35.8	10.0	55	239	8	35,376	19.3	80.7	2	96.9	(Z)	(Z)
Prince Edward	3,282	1.1	395	20.3	7.6	79	200	12	29,914	22.4	77.6	2	44.8	(Z)	1
Prince George	[31]1,516	[31]0.1	[31]218	[31]32.6	[31]9.6	[31]55	[31]253	[31]4	[31]19,683	[31]88.6	[31]11.4	18	6.6	(Z)	(Z)
Prince William	[32]2,872	(Z)	[32]350	[32]59.1	[32]2.0	[32]33	[32]93	[32]10	[32]27,203	[32]39.9	[32]60.1	310	1.9	(Z)	65
Pulaski	2,366	0.3	448	36.8	8.3	81	181	14	32,203	6.1	93.9	5	13.3	(Z)	4
Rappahannock	864	0.9	443	40.2	6.8	78	177	7	16,002	29.5	70.5	1	94.9	(Z)	(Z)

See footnotes at end of table.

Table B-14. Counties — **Farm Earnings, Agriculture, and Water Use**—Con.

[Includes United States, states, and 3,141 counties/county equivalents defined as of February 22, 2005. For more information on these areas, see Appendix C, Geographic Information]

County	Farm earnings, 2005 Total ($1,000)	Percent of total[1]	Farms Number	Farms Percent Less than 50 acres	Farms Percent 500 acres or more	Land in farms Total acres (1,000)	Land in farms Average size of farm (acres)	Value of farm products sold Total (mil. dol.)	Value of farm products sold Average per farm (dol.)	Percent from Crops[2]	Percent from Livestock and poultry[3]	Water use Total (mil. gal. per day)	Ground water, percent of total	Irrigation	Public supply
VIRGINIA—Con.															
Richmond	6,976	5.8	141	20.6	19.9	45	318	7	47,199	87.5	12.5	(Z)	97.8	(Z)	(Z)
Roanoke	[32]2,167	[33]0.1	[34]342	[34]51.5	[34]1.5	[34]31	[34]90	[34]4	[34]11,202	[34]50.6	[34]49.4	14	26.4	(Z)	12
Rockbridge	[35]5,714	[35]0.9	[35]789	[35]31.9	[35]8.9	[35]157	[35]199	[35]19	[35]23,504	[35]13.6	[35]86.4	6	75.1	(Z)	3
Rockingham	[36]61,854	[36]2.4	[36]2,043	[36]40.7	[36]3.9	[36]249	[36]122	[36]447	[36]218,631	[36]3.0	[36]97.0	31	69.6	1	13
Russell	3,848	1.1	1,128	36.6	5.5	169	150	21	18,615	16.1	83.9	18	10.0	(Z)	1
Scott	4,442	2.4	1,490	38.3	2.1	158	106	13	8,519	53.7	46.3	2	42.8	(Z)	1
Shenandoah	19,197	2.9	989	41.3	4.6	133	135	70	70,433	9.2	90.8	6	72.6	(Z)	2
Smyth	3,983	0.7	877	48.6	6.3	125	142	22	24,941	13.4	86.6	7	87.4	(Z)	6
Southampton	[37]9,732	[37]3.0	[37]275	[37]17.8	[37]33.1	[37]169	[37]613	[37]35	[37]127,280	[37]62.6	[37]37.4	8	78.7	1	1
Spotsylvania	[38]1,156	(Z)	[38]369	[38]46.1	[38]7.0	[38]56	[38]153	[38]6	[38]16,089	[38]29.3	[38]70.7	5	12.7	(Z)	3
Stafford	909	0.1	236	50.8	3.8	26	111	2	10,530	46.4	53.6	8	12.5	(Z)	7
Surry	4,150	2.8	121	24.0	24.0	48	394	19	156,008	(NA)	(NA)	1,967	0.1	(Z)	(Z)
Sussex	5,750	4.2	130	16.9	30.8	74	571	25	192,877	(NA)	(NA)	1	54.8	1	1
Tazewell	2,924	0.4	551	31.6	13.6	139	252	18	32,183	6.5	93.5	2	19.2	(Z)	2
Warren	1,846	0.4	361	44.0	5.0	49	136	6	15,377	18.8	81.2	11	13.6	(Z)	9
Washington	[39]6,331	[39]0.5	[39]1,821	[39]49.8	[39]3.5	[39]197	[39]108	[39]51	[39]27,785	[39]19.7	[39]80.3	10	31.1	–	10
Westmoreland	8,226	5.7	165	25.5	27.3	68	410	20	121,879	95.0	5.0	2	80.6	(Z)	1
Wise	[40]570	[40]0.1	[40]140	[40]44.3	[40]6.4	[40]19	[40]136	[40]1	[40]6,729	[40]32.0	[40]68.0	6	12.6	–	5
Wythe	4,372	1.0	876	31.5	6.4	151	172	31	34,849	7.6	92.4	4	47.1	(Z)	3
York	[41]1,626	[41]0.2	[42]44	[42]88.6	–	[42]1	[42]17	[42]3	[42]66,409	[42]89.2	[42]10.8	938	0.4	–	30
Independent Cities															
Alexandria	–	–	[21]	(NA)	(NA)	[21]	[21]	[21]	(NA)	(NA)	(NA)	360	0.3	(Z)	–
Bedford	[14]	(NA)	[14]	(NA)	(NA)	[14]	[14]	[14]	(NA)	(NA)	(NA)	–	–	–	–
Bristol	[39]	(NA)	[39]	(NA)	(NA)	[39]	[39]	[39]	(NA)	(NA)	(NA)	–	–	–	–
Buena Vista	[35]	(NA)	[35]	(NA)	(NA)	[35]	[35]	[35]	(NA)	(NA)	(NA)	–	–	–	–
Charlottesville	[10]	(NA)	[10]	(NA)	(NA)	[10]	[10]	[10]	(NA)	(NA)	(NA)	–	–	–	–
Chesapeake	20,023	0.5	[43]268	[43]64.2	[43]10.4	[43]61	[43]228	[43]36	[43]133,951	[43]92.1	[43]7.9	539	1.3	(Z)	12
Clifton Forge[11]	(X)	(NA)	(X)	(NA)	(NA)	(X)	(X)	(X)	(NA)	(NA)	(NA)	–	–	–	–
Colonial Heights	[18]	(NA)	[17]	(NA)	(NA)	[17]	[17]	[17]	(NA)	(NA)	(NA)	(Z)	100.0	–	–
Covington	[12]	(NA)	[12]	(NA)	(NA)	[12]	[12]	[12]	(NA)	(NA)	(NA)	2	–	–	2
Danville	[30]	(NA)	[30]	(NA)	(NA)	[30]	[30]	[30]	(NA)	(NA)	(NA)	15	–	(Z)	7
Emporia	[24]	(NA)	[24]	(NA)	(NA)	[24]	[24]	[24]	(NA)	(NA)	(NA)	1	–	–	1
Fairfax	[20]	(NA)	[21]	(NA)	(NA)	[21]	[21]	[21]	(NA)	(NA)	(NA)	–	–	–	–
Falls Church	[20]	(NA)	[21]	(NA)	(NA)	[21]	[21]	[21]	(NA)	(NA)	(NA)	–	–	–	–
Franklin	[37]	(NA)	[37]	(NA)	(NA)	[37]	[37]	[37]	(NA)	(NA)	(NA)	1	100.0	–	1
Fredericksburg	[38]	(NA)	[38]	(NA)	(NA)	[38]	[38]	[38]	(NA)	(NA)	(NA)	1	–	–	1
Galax	[16]	(NA)	[23]	(NA)	(NA)	[23]	[23]	[23]	(NA)	(NA)	(NA)	2	13.9	–	2
Hampton	–		[42]	(NA)	(NA)	[42]	[42]	[42]	(NA)	(NA)	(NA)	1	2.6	(Z)	1
Harrisonburg	[36]	(NA)	[36]	(NA)	(NA)	[36]	[36]	[36]	(NA)	(NA)	(NA)	(Z)	100.0	–	–
Hopewell	[31]	(NA)	[31]	(NA)	(NA)	[31]	[31]	[31]	(NA)	(NA)	(NA)	154	–	–	21
Lexington	[35]	(NA)	[35]	(NA)	(NA)	[35]	[35]	[35]	(NA)	(NA)	(NA)	–	–	–	–
Lynchburg	[15]	(NA)	[15]	(NA)	(NA)	[15]	[15]	[15]	(NA)	(NA)	(NA)	(Z)	–	–	(Z)
Manassas	[32]	(NA)	[32]	(NA)	(NA)	[32]	[32]	[32]	(NA)	(NA)	(NA)	3	100.0	–	–
Manassas Park	[32]	(NA)	[32]	(NA)	(NA)	[32]	[32]	[32]	(NA)	(NA)	(NA)	(Z)	100.0	–	(Z)
Martinsville	[27]	(NA)	[42]	(NA)	(NA)	[42]	[42]	[42]	(NA)	(NA)	(NA)	–	–	–	–
Newport News	–		[42]	(NA)	(NA)	[42]	[42]	[42]	(NA)	(NA)	(NA)	40	5.9	(Z)	29
Norfolk	–		[43]	(NA)	(NA)	[43]	[43]	[43]	(NA)	(NA)	(NA)	3	9.5	(Z)	2
Norton	[40]	(NA)	[40]	(NA)	(NA)	[40]	[40]	[40]	(NA)	(NA)	(NA)	1	–	–	1
Petersburg	[18]	(NA)	[19]	(NA)	(NA)	[19]	[19]	[19]	(NA)	(NA)	(NA)	–	–	–	–
Poquoson	[41]	(NA)	[42]	(NA)	(NA)	[42]	[42]	[42]	(NA)	(NA)	(NA)	–	–	–	–
Portsmouth	–		[43]	(NA)	(NA)	[43]	[43]	[43]	(NA)	(NA)	(NA)	2	98.2	(Z)	–
Radford	[29]	(NA)	[29]	(NA)	(NA)	[29]	[29]	[29]	(NA)	(NA)	(NA)	3	–	–	3
Richmond	–		[26]	(NA)	(NA)	[26]	[26]	[26]	(NA)	(NA)	(NA)	89	0.1	(Z)	89
Roanoke	–		[34]	(NA)	(NA)	[34]	[34]	[34]	(NA)	(NA)	(NA)	(Z)	100.0	(Z)	–
Salem	[33]	(NA)	[34]	(NA)	(NA)	[34]	[34]	[34]	(NA)	(NA)	(NA)	3	–	–	3
South Boston[25]	(X)	(NA)	(X)	(NA)	(NA)	(X)	(X)	(X)	(NA)	(NA)	(NA)	(X)	(NA)	(X)	(X)
Staunton	[13]	(NA)	[13]	(NA)	(NA)	[13]	[13]	[13]	(NA)	(NA)	(NA)	–	–	(Z)	–
Suffolk	14,797	1.3	247	52.2	15.4	71	286	41	165,745	87.3	12.7	81	8.2	(Z)	79
Virginia Beach	3,298	(Z)	172	58.1	5.2	28	165	10	56,169	79.9	20.1	4	89.7	(Z)	(Z)
Waynesboro	[13]	(NA)	[13]	(NA)	(NA)	[13]	[13]	[13]	(NA)	(NA)	(NA)	8	99.5	(Z)	3
Williamsburg	[28]	(NA)	[28]	(NA)	(NA)	[28]	[28]	[28]	(NA)	(NA)	(NA)	(Z)	12.5	(Z)	–
Winchester	[22]	(NA)	[22]	(NA)	(NA)	[22]	[22]	[22]	(NA)	(NA)	(NA)	(Z)	100.0	–	–
WASHINGTON	1,596,733	0.9	35,939	57.5	12.8	15,318	426	5,331	148,327	67.2	32.8	5,310	27.7	3,040	1,020
Adams	38,988	14.2	717	15.9	50.2	1,067	1,488	203	282,921	77.3	22.7	197	59.4	187	7
Asotin	−2,630	(X)	180	30.0	51.1	280	1,558	9	50,478	64.0	36.0	5	93.9	(Z)	5
Benton	86,515	2.1	1,313	73.4	7.8	608	463	401	305,081	91.5	8.5	780	5.6	239	19
Chelan	120,092	7.0	1,193	69.1	2.6	112	94	169	142,000	97.1	2.9	80	19.2	51	12
Clallam	1,688	0.2	455	74.3	0.7	22	49	18	39,051	(NA)	(NA)	16	60.0	6	8

See footnotes at end of table.

Table B-14. Counties — **Farm Earnings, Agriculture, and Water Use**—Con.

[Includes United States, states, and 3,141 counties/county equivalents defined as of February 22, 2005. For more information on these areas, see Appendix C, Geographic Information]

County	Farm earnings, 2005 Total ($1,000)	Farm earnings, 2005 Percent of total[1]	Agriculture — Farms Number	Farms Percent Less than 50 acres	Farms Percent 500 acres or more	Land in farms Total acres (1,000)	Land in farms Average size of farm (acres)	Value of farm products sold Total (mil. dol.)	Value of farm products sold Average per farm (dol.)	Percent from Crops[2]	Percent from Livestock and poultry[3]	Water use Total (mil. gal. per day)	Ground water, percent of total	By selected major use — Irrigation	By selected major use — Public supply
WASHINGTON—Con.															
Clark	17,962	0.2	1,596	79.2	1.1	71	44	54	34,091	52.3	47.7	183	64.8	6	40
Columbia	−2,985	(X)	255	24.7	42.4	295	1,156	27	103,984	85.6	14.4	5	23.2	4	1
Cowlitz	8,934	0.5	532	66.0	1.7	40	74	31	57,444	35.5	64.5	170	3.3	4	12
Douglas	27,155	7.4	947	49.9	24.9	879	928	124	131,307	95.0	5.0	33	33.9	25	4
Ferry	355	0.5	207	21.7	22.7	799	3,862	4	20,995	21.2	78.8	6	37.0	5	1
Franklin	111,040	10.5	943	36.3	29.0	665	705	350	371,668	84.9	15.1	457	27.6	438	15
Garfield	−16,746	(X)	198	18.2	61.1	312	1,578	20	99,889	79.3	20.7	1	50.0	1	(Z)
Grant	192,007	14.7	1,801	32.4	27.0	1,074	596	882	489,592	71.1	28.9	963	29.9	933	22
Grays Harbor	12,482	1.1	510	55.9	3.5	54	105	30	58,853	46.4	53.6	26	42.8	3	12
Island	4,789	0.3	348	77.3	0.6	15	43	10	28,164	22.1	77.9	9	71.9	1	7
Jefferson	3,517	0.8	207	71.5	0.5	12	59	7	32,232	14.6	85.4	12	25.8	1	3
King	43,643	0.1	1,548	88.2	0.3	42	27	120	77,555	60.5	39.5	360	28.1	7	331
Kitsap	8,926	0.2	587	89.6	0.5	16	27	31	52,322	43.4	56.6	30	76.4	2	23
Kittitas	22,898	3.9	931	51.2	9.2	231	248	56	60,541	68.2	31.8	209	4.0	200	7
Klickitat	17,043	6.1	702	36.2	25.4	607	864	52	74,681	76.7	23.3	34	58.3	27	4
Lewis	23,467	2.0	1,402	57.9	2.3	131	93	89	63,802	24.0	76.0	25	54.9	7	7
Lincoln	10,859	8.5	747	12.6	61.2	1,233	1,651	94	125,241	91.1	8.9	39	78.8	36	2
Mason	14,164	2.2	320	78.8	2.2	22	68	52	162,525	9.7	90.3	17	38.9	1	4
Okanogan	89,302	13.4	1,486	49.4	14.9	1,241	835	137	92,475	84.8	15.2	88	38.5	73	7
Pacific	12,045	4.6	341	56.6	5.0	52	152	31	89,933	14.1	85.9	9	35.8	3	4
Pend Oreille	[5]25	(NA)	263	38.4	9.5	61	233	3	12,798	46.9	53.1	3	51.0	1	1
Pierce	38,763	0.2	1,474	80.7	0.7	57	39	94	63,887	37.1	62.9	227	33.2	8	120
San Juan	1,441	0.6	225	67.1	1.8	17	76	3	13,840	36.8	63.2	2	64.3	(Z)	1
Skagit	94,185	3.8	872	59.7	4.9	114	131	217	249,294	70.1	29.9	44	27.7	9	25
Skamania	[5]25	(NA)	99	60.6	–	6	58	12	116,444	13.9	86.1	13	5.8	1	1
Snohomish	35,767	0.3	1,574	80.8	1.3	69	44	127	80,652	45.7	54.3	144	15.3	5	71
Spokane	−8,044	(X)	2,225	52.2	12.1	643	289	94	42,181	82.3	17.7	176	78.7	11	110
Stevens	1,592	0.3	1,269	34.5	12.6	528	416	28	22,258	40.9	59.1	25	35.5	10	5
Thurston	31,815	0.6	1,155	76.0	2.1	74	64	115	99,286	43.0	57.0	45	65.2	7	25
Wahkiakum	−152	(X)	125	43.2	2.4	12	99	3	23,832	2.8	97.2	1	43.1	(Z)	(Z)
Walla Walla	31,830	2.9	890	47.4	28.2	701	787	339	381,003	(NA)	(NA)	154	30.3	125	12
Whatcom	97,092	2.5	1,485	62.2	2.4	148	100	288	193,845	26.4	73.6	88	31.1	25	50
Whitman	−44,698	(X)	1,087	14.4	58.3	1,328	1,222	163	149,615	95.5	4.5	9	75.0	3	5
Yakima	471,669	11.4	3,730	66.5	5.7	1,679	450	844	226,239	60.2	39.8	627	15.7	571	36
WEST VIRGINIA	−29,891	(X)	20,812	27.3	6.3	3,585	172	483	23,199	14.4	85.6	5,150	1.8	(Z)	190
Barbour	−1,046	(X)	445	24.5	7.9	79	176	4	8,715	16.9	83.1	([6])	(NA)	–	1
Berkeley	−936	(X)	676	51.8	3.0	76	113	18	27,263	66.4	33.6	([6])	(NA)	–	9
Boone	−68	(X)	24	16.7	–	3	134	(Z)	2,458	66.1	33.9	([6])	(NA)	–	1
Braxton	−1,255	(X)	314	13.1	9.2	66	212	2	5,417	15.1	84.9	([6])	(NA)	–	1
Brooke	−425	(X)	98	32.7	5.1	14	141	1	7,429	25.5	74.5	([6])	(NA)	–	5
Cabell	−1,448	(X)	438	31.5	1.6	42	97	3	6,781	78.9	21.1	([6])	(NA)	–	16
Calhoun	−524	(X)	244	14.3	7.4	50	206	1	4,988	10.8	89.2	([6])	(NA)	–	(Z)
Clay	[5]25	(NA)	117	7.7	3.4	19	160	(Z)	3,094	14.1	85.9	([6])	(NA)	–	(Z)
Doddridge	−1,711	(X)	455	20.0	7.0	95	208	1	3,240	24.8	75.2	([6])	(NA)	–	(Z)
Fayette	−430	(X)	240	38.3	2.1	24	101	2	6,479	41.5	58.5	([6])	(NA)	–	5
Gilmer	−1,514	(X)	249	9.6	16.1	66	265	3	10,237	5.6	94.4	([6])	(NA)	–	(Z)
Grant	3,335	1.7	357	23.8	17.6	108	302	39	109,947	1.0	99.0	([6])	(NA)	–	1
Greenbrier	−68	(X)	783	25.0	11.0	193	246	35	44,667	3.0	97.0	([6])	(NA)	–	4
Hampshire	1,094	0.6	635	29.6	9.9	139	218	20	30,932	14.6	85.4	([6])	(NA)	–	1
Hancock	−192	(X)	85	48.2	1.2	7	83	1	7,012	77.2	22.8	([6])	(NA)	–	2
Hardy	8,470	3.3	468	29.7	13.7	128	274	124	264,160	0.8	99.2	([6])	(NA)	–	3
Harrison	−3,617	(X)	798	28.2	4.5	120	150	5	6,419	19.2	80.8	([6])	(NA)	–	9
Jackson	−3,295	(X)	842	20.7	3.8	129	153	5	5,576	23.5	76.5	([6])	(NA)	–	2
Jefferson	1,133	0.2	474	58.6	7.2	72	152	17	36,584	41.0	59.0	([6])	(NA)	(Z)	2
Kanawha	[5]25	(NA)	210	44.3	–	20	95	1	3,100	33.5	66.5	([6])	(NA)	–	33
Lewis	−485	(X)	372	15.1	9.1	79	212	3	7,175	13.5	86.5	([6])	(NA)	–	1
Lincoln	345	0.2	242	30.6	3.3	35	144	1	4,000	75.8	24.2	([6])	(NA)	–	1
Logan	[5]25	(NA)	21	42.9	–	2	112	(Z)	13,667	(NA)	(NA)	([6])	(NA)	–	4
McDowell	–	–	7	28.6	–	1	122	(Z)	6,571	(NA)	(NA)	([6])	(NA)	–	4
Marion	−1,333	(X)	464	32.8	1.9	50	108	2	3,634	40.9	59.1	([6])	(NA)	–	7
Marshall	−1,919	(X)	706	21.0	1.4	91	128	3	4,171	32.9	67.1	([6])	(NA)	–	3
Mason	−3,262	(X)	939	28.0	4.8	142	151	17	17,972	59.9	40.1	([6])	(NA)	–	2
Mercer	−1,484	(X)	393	28.5	3.8	56	142	3	7,023	24.9	75.1	([6])	(NA)	–	5
Mineral	1,162	0.4	465	30.5	7.3	81	174	14	30,527	6.7	93.3	([6])	(NA)	–	2
Mingo	–	–	35	88.6	5.7	2	45	(Z)	800	(NA)	(NA)	([6])	(NA)	–	3
Monongalia	−3,864	(X)	478	28.2	2.7	60	126	2	5,136	16.9	83.1	([6])	(NA)	–	10
Monroe	−1,821	(X)	682	20.7	10.1	145	213	17	25,273	5.9	94.1	([6])	(NA)	–	(Z)
Morgan	−968	(X)	178	27.5	3.9	23	129	1	7,152	53.6	46.4	([6])	(NA)	–	1
Nicholas	−294	(X)	332	28.9	3.9	44	132	2	7,479	11.2	88.8	([6])	(NA)	–	3
Ohio	−680	(X)	166	22.3	2.4	22	134	2	10,506	23.3	76.7	([6])	(NA)	–	7

See footnotes at end of table.

[Includes United States, states, and 3,141 counties/county equivalents defined as of February 22, 2005. For more information on these areas, see Appendix C, Geographic Information]

County	Farm earnings, 2005 Total ($1,000)	Farm earnings, 2005 Percent of total[1]	Farms Number	Farms Percent Less than 50 acres	Farms Percent 500 acres or more	Land in farms Total acres (1,000)	Land in farms Average size of farm (acres)	Value of farm products sold Total (mil. dol.)	Value of farm products sold Average per farm (dol.)	Value Percent from Crops[2]	Value Percent from Livestock and poultry[3]	Water use Total (mil. gal. per day)	Water use Ground water, percent of total	By major use Irrigation	By major use Public supply
WEST VIRGINIA—Con.															
Pendleton	3,637	3.8	546	19.0	17.6	171	313	74	135,553	1.1	98.9	(6)	(NA)	(Z)	(Z)
Pleasants	-193	(X)	203	29.6	1.0	23	113	1	2,744	45.7	54.3	(6)	(NA)	-	1
Pocahontas	-845	(X)	376	17.6	18.4	123	327	5	12,556	7.6	92.4	(6)	(NA)	-	1
Preston	-1,570	(X)	917	22.9	4.5	142	155	10	11,161	16.8	83.2	(6)	(NA)	-	1
Putnam	-1,123	(X)	505	34.9	1.8	57	112	6	12,634	81.7	18.3	(6)	(NA)	-	3
Raleigh	-614	(X)	230	39.6	4.8	33	142	2	8,600	22.0	78.0	(6)	(NA)	-	9
Randolph	573	0.1	446	28.3	11.9	101	227	6	13,832	10.3	89.7	(6)	(NA)	-	3
Ritchie	-3,105	(X)	363	16.8	7.2	81	223	3	7,377	19.0	81.0	(6)	(NA)	-	1
Roane	-1,989	(X)	538	15.6	6.1	99	184	3	5,928	14.0	86.0	(6)	(NA)	-	1
Summers	-3,085	(X)	313	18.8	7.0	55	175	5	16,419	43.7	56.3	(6)	(NA)	-	3
Taylor	1,263	1.0	348	39.9	3.7	43	125	4	11,555	47.2	52.8	(6)	(NA)	-	2
Tucker	-426	(X)	198	25.8	8.6	35	178	1	5,970	15.1	84.9	(6)	(NA)	-	1
Tyler	374	0.3	300	21.7	4.7	53	177	1	4,840	21.6	78.4	(6)	(NA)	-	(Z)
Upshur	-2,347	(X)	480	33.3	4.6	69	145	3	5,794	18.2	81.8	(6)	(NA)	-	2
Wayne	-845	(X)	217	17.1	5.5	36	166	1	6,410	59.2	40.8	(6)	(NA)	-	3
Webster	-71	(X)	110	45.5	0.9	11	102	(Z)	1,355	33.6	66.4	(6)	(NA)	-	(Z)
Wetzel	-806	(X)	336	22.6	2.4	49	146	1	2,137	26.0	74.0	(6)	(NA)	-	1
Wirt	-264	(X)	223	21.1	6.3	40	181	4	18,036	55.5	44.5	(6)	(NA)	-	(Z)
Wood	-1,290	(X)	696	29.5	1.4	77	111	3	4,885	31.3	68.7	(6)	(NA)	-	9
Wyoming	5/25	(NA)	35	40.0	2.9	4	104	(Z)	4,714	79.4	20.6	(6)	(NA)	-	2
WISCONSIN	1,164,589	0.8	77,131	27.6	8.2	15,742	204	5,623	72,906	30.1	69.9	7,590	10.7	196	623
Adams	11,845	5.1	414	25.8	11.8	124	298	53	127,309	85.5	14.5	42	100.0	40	(Z)
Ashland	-559	(X)	227	12.3	11.5	59	259	6	27,454	14.7	85.3	47	2.3	(Z)	1
Barron	30,049	3.4	1,647	22.8	9.4	352	214	150	91,025	20.8	79.2	16	92.4	6	4
Bayfield	1,483	1.0	468	16.9	11.1	112	239	12	25,075	31.4	68.6	9	34.6	(Z)	(Z)
Brown	42,294	0.6	1,117	44.0	6.4	197	176	150	134,070	11.1	88.9	522	3.4	1	31
Buffalo	12,622	4.0	1,128	16.6	14.6	316	280	96	84,997	13.7	86.3	234	4.4	5	1
Burnett	3,356	1.6	451	16.9	9.8	98	218	16	34,625	28.2	71.8	3	87.0	1	(Z)
Calumet	16,765	2.6	733	33.8	8.6	150	205	82	111,674	18.2	81.8	8	98.2	(Z)	5
Chippewa	22,174	2.2	1,621	18.6	9.1	374	231	106	65,589	18.5	81.5	11	98.2	2	5
Clark	34,488	7.4	2,200	14.6	6.3	461	210	174	79,289	8.8	91.2	5	95.9	(Z)	2
Columbia	13,445	1.4	1,526	29.0	11.3	348	228	105	68,881	44.3	55.7	10	85.4	(Z)	4
Crawford	6,382	2.1	1,278	19.1	7.3	255	199	42	32,649	31.6	68.4	3	98.3	(Z)	2
Dane	61,370	0.4	2,887	40.4	7.6	515	179	288	99,632	29.7	70.3	125	49.2	1	48
Dodge	37,266	2.3	1,968	29.4	8.3	404	205	179	90,888	30.0	70.0	14	97.9	(Z)	7
Door	10,982	2.0	877	35.0	5.6	135	154	40	45,701	37.9	62.1	7	73.1	1	2
Douglas	948	0.1	391	15.9	8.4	85	217	5	12,010	33.7	66.3	9	13.3	(Z)	4
Dunn	18,478	2.6	1,683	21.7	9.8	399	237	104	61,544	32.9	67.1	14	99.1	8	2
Eau Claire	14,376	0.6	1,174	26.6	5.1	204	174	50	42,456	35.4	64.6	31	50.8	1	10
Florence	-1,096	(X)	121	21.5	4.1	21	177	1	11,901	31.3	68.7	1	100.0	(Z)	(Z)
Fond du Lac	28,992	1.2	1,634	27.2	8.8	344	211	166	101,700	25.0	75.0	41	45.6	(Z)	13
Forest	476	0.3	164	23.8	11.0	34	205	4	21,500	20.8	79.2	2	70.8	(Z)	(Z)
Grant	28,060	3.7	2,490	20.2	10.1	606	243	187	74,958	20.8	79.2	275	3.1	(Z)	3
Green	15,958	2.5	1,490	30.5	8.4	307	206	117	78,668	23.1	76.9	6	96.6	1	3
Green Lake	12,185	3.7	670	23.0	9.6	148	221	46	68,294	43.5	56.5	4	95.9	1	2
Iowa	14,623	2.8	1,686	23.1	9.9	367	218	116	69,051	25.3	74.7	4	96.6	(Z)	1
Iron	-276	(X)	62	12.9	11.3	13	206	(D)	(NA)	(NA)	(NA)	1	100.0	(Z)	1
Jackson	23,779	6.3	914	19.7	12.6	258	282	70	76,328	45.7	54.3	3	96.7	(Z)	1
Jefferson	33,391	2.0	1,421	37.1	6.4	248	174	139	97,621	46.2	53.8	52	52.1	2	10
Juneau	11,328	3.1	805	26.8	8.9	180	224	51	63,280	52.7	47.3	7	99.6	5	1
Kenosha	5,613	0.2	466	51.9	8.6	89	190	34	73,043	66.4	33.6	34	7.9	(Z)	16
Kewaunee	20,221	5.7	915	27.2	7.0	174	190	105	114,552	23.3	76.7	702	0.4	(Z)	1
La Crosse	10,993	0.4	868	24.0	9.2	174	201	42	47,986	23.3	76.7	67	42.3	(Z)	18
Lafayette	18,089	10.6	1,205	24.1	13.3	343	284	131	109,057	29.1	70.9	3	95.4	(Z)	1
Langlade	13,959	4.1	542	22.1	11.4	141	260	56	103,972	66.5	33.5	14	81.3	4	1
Lincoln	8,423	1.6	593	27.0	5.1	98	166	24	40,091	40.0	60.0	10	42.5	(Z)	3
Manitowoc	37,402	2.2	1,469	35.1	6.7	257	175	147	100,271	14.0	86.0	1,324	0.4	(Z)	11
Marathon	41,627	1.2	2,898	25.8	5.9	531	183	205	70,890	17.1	82.9	178	14.2	2	16
Marinette	11,520	1.3	729	25.8	8.5	149	204	41	56,036	23.0	77.0	41	29.1	2	4
Marquette	5,853	3.7	624	25.8	10.6	146	233	38	60,188	47.2	52.8	5	91.0	(Z)	1
Menominee	-	-	4	75.0	-	(Z)	89	(D)	(NA)	(NA)	(NA)	1	63.1	(Z)	(Z)
Milwaukee	3,394	(Z)	78	62.8	1.3	6	72	9	115,308	96.6	3.4	2,057	0.3	1	174
Monroe	27,426	3.3	1,938	22.5	6.6	352	182	103	52,927	27.3	72.7	6	98.2	(Z)	3
Oconto	15,085	3.9	1,132	22.3	6.7	219	193	74	65,360	20.7	79.3	6	72.4	1	1
Oneida	4,469	0.6	183	24.6	14.8	51	279	13	69,410	81.4	18.6	32	13.8	(Z)	3
Outagamie	37,474	0.7	1,430	36.7	8.1	263	184	146	102,431	21.7	78.3	72	28.1	(Z)	15
Ozaukee	6,819	0.3	533	41.8	4.3	75	142	38	71,901	37.8	62.2	128	6.1	1	6
Pepin	8,303	8.8	501	23.0	9.0	111	222	35	69,431	20.8	79.2	1	97.9	(Z)	(Z)
Pierce	10,766	2.4	1,510	30.6	6.2	267	177	72	47,900	33.1	66.9	5	97.4	(Z)	2
Polk	14,293	2.2	1,659	28.7	7.7	293	177	72	43,696	26.8	73.2	10	98.9	(Z)	3
Portage	29,894	2.0	1,197	27.6	9.2	292	244	139	116,081	71.3	28.7	84	92.5	61	9

See footnotes at end of table.

Table B-14. Counties — **Farm Earnings, Agriculture, and Water Use**—Con.

[Includes United States, states, and 3,141 counties/county equivalents defined as of February 22, 2005. For more information on these areas, see Appendix C, Geographic Information]

County	Farm earnings, 2005 Total ($1,000)	Farm earnings, 2005 Percent of total[1]	Farms Number	Farms Percent Less than 50 acres	Farms Percent 500 acres or more	Land in farms Total acres (1,000)	Land in farms Average size of farm (acres)	Value of farm products sold Total (mil. dol.)	Value of farm products sold Average per farm (dol.)	Value of farm products sold Percent from Crops[2]	Value of farm products sold Percent from Livestock and poultry[3]	Water use, 2000[4] Total (mil. gal. per day)	Water use, 2000[4] Ground water, percent of total	By selected major use (mil. gal. per day) Irrigation	By selected major use (mil. gal. per day) Public supply
WISCONSIN—Con.															
Price	3,905	1.4	477	15.9	9.2	104	218	15	31,314	29.2	70.8	9	21.9	(Z)	1
Racine	16,917	0.4	631	53.2	8.9	124	197	73	115,949	50.9	49.1	40	34.2	2	27
Richland	13,409	5.1	1,358	19.5	6.0	258	190	52	38,529	18.3	81.7	3	97.5	(Z)	1
Rock	17,269	0.5	1,529	45.4	10.2	344	225	118	77,242	53.8	46.2	163	17.7	3	20
Rusk	8,789	3.9	715	13.8	9.4	173	242	30	42,326	10.0	90.0	3	77.7	1	1
St. Croix	15,162	1.2	1,864	35.7	6.4	310	166	98	52,502	29.2	70.8	8	98.9	(Z)	4
Sauk	19,667	1.3	1,673	22.6	9.4	353	211	116	69,375	21.5	78.5	14	99.1	1	6
Sawyer	3,137	1.1	230	15.7	10.0	54	235	13	54,370	47.4	52.6	3	86.6	(Z)	1
Shawano	45,352	8.0	1,465	23.6	6.7	271	185	130	88,816	10.1	89.9	6	96.3	(Z)	2
Sheboygan	20,796	0.6	1,116	40.9	8.3	195	175	104	93,154	20.6	79.4	513	1.8	(Z)	20
Taylor	11,446	3.1	1,056	17.2	8.6	257	244	56	52,948	11.0	89.0	2	97.0	(Z)	1
Trempealeau	21,621	3.8	1,744	17.6	8.2	368	211	120	68,660	18.0	82.0	6	96.6	(Z)	3
Vernon	12,835	3.8	2,230	22.9	5.5	382	171	90	40,453	19.4	80.6	206	2.9	(Z)	1
Vilas	2,942	0.9	71	52.1	7.0	10	137	5	71,014	96.9	3.1	8	25.6	(Z)	(Z)
Walworth	15,205	0.8	988	41.1	11.2	220	222	88	88,563	43.0	57.0	15	99.5	1	9
Washburn	4,112	1.9	471	16.1	9.1	105	224	17	36,363	32.7	67.3	4	73.5	1	1
Washington	10,401	0.4	844	39.7	6.2	130	154	73	86,342	38.2	61.8	16	81.8	(Z)	10
Waukesha	8,407	0.1	762	58.3	5.5	98	129	36	47,088	65.2	34.8	38	99.1	3	27
Waupaca	18,337	2.0	1,398	28.5	7.2	247	177	86	61,675	20.9	79.1	12	98.9	2	6
Waushara	19,445	8.2	717	28.7	10.9	193	269	86	119,775	77.8	22.2	32	99.9	27	1
Winnebago	11,622	0.2	963	32.6	8.1	170	177	58	60,541	33.4	66.6	73	18.1	(Z)	22
Wood	26,956	1.2	1,108	26.1	8.5	228	206	80	72,528	40.1	59.9	133	15.4	3	7
WYOMING	184,198	1.3	9,422	21.4	44.5	34,403	3,651	864	91,688	15.9	84.1	5,170	14.8	4,500	107
Albany	2,443	0.4	320	9.4	61.9	2,384	7,451	28	88,644	6.8	93.2	344	1.4	336	7
Big Horn	11,572	5.4	501	25.5	27.9	412	822	37	74,295	41.9	58.1	411	6.2	387	3
Campbell	11,800	0.8	532	16.2	61.8	2,986	5,613	33	62,252	1.3	98.7	115	52.5	42	2
Carbon	11,829	3.8	290	17.6	56.6	2,330	8,033	43	148,766	2.4	97.6	320	1.9	313	3
Converse	6,662	2.3	339	13.9	58.4	2,518	7,427	31	92,891	5.5	94.5	398	5.8	188	2
Crook	10,318	8.5	440	6.1	69.1	1,523	3,462	37	84,441	1.2	98.8	78	19.8	66	7
Fremont	10,831	1.7	1,019	29.3	25.8	2,504	2,457	60	58,738	25.0	75.0	433	4.1	411	7
Goshen	24,172	12.9	665	9.9	48.1	1,258	1,892	120	179,710	16.0	84.0	400	24.7	397	3
Hot Springs	2,370	2.8	147	27.9	41.5	877	5,963	8	55,367	12.7	87.3	105	27.7	77	1
Johnson	3,466	2.2	272	11.8	68.8	2,155	7,924	26	97,276	2.3	97.7	124	2.8	119	1
Laramie	18,014	0.8	755	18.9	46.9	1,755	2,324	66	86,784	26.9	73.1	217	69.1	198	15
Lincoln	5,640	1.9	495	30.9	24.2	365	737	24	48,873	15.3	84.7	196	5.8	177	8
Natrona	6,110	0.3	380	21.8	42.6	2,871	7,555	29	75,050	10.1	89.9	227	21.6	174	12
Niobrara	7,292	17.2	243	2.1	86.8	1,600	6,583	35	143,527	10.0	90.0	62	90.8	61	(Z)
Park	11,000	1.9	711	40.5	21.5	810	1,140	53	74,335	47.1	52.9	390	12.6	338	3
Platte	12,670	7.4	462	13.6	49.1	1,344	2,910	80	172,957	9.3	90.7	275	16.9	255	2
Sheridan	5,067	0.8	561	26.4	40.6	1,638	2,920	42	74,349	9.2	90.8	227	0.4	220	6
Sublette	7,493	3.5	270	29.6	45.6	586	2,169	27	100,511	11.4	88.6	242	11.0	238	3
Sweetwater	171	(Z)	170	24.7	32.4	1,480	8,707	7	41,753	9.7	90.3	171	29.9	93	9
Teton	−85	(X)	110	33.6	23.6	57	519	7	67,336	16.8	83.2	46	14.5	39	6
Uinta	2,648	0.6	335	29.9	35.8	918	2,740	19	58,024	4.3	95.7	189	10.7	183	5
Washakie	5,204	2.9	184	25.5	47.3	427	2,318	25	137,342	42.5	57.5	170	4.1	168	(Z)
Weston	7,511	5.0	221	7.7	75.1	1,606	7,265	26	115,416	2.1	97.9	25	13.8	22	1

– Represents zero. D Data withheld to avoid disclosure. NA Not available. X Not applicable. Z Less than .05 percent or .5 of the unit presented.

[1]For total earnings, see Table B-9. [2]Includes nursery and greenhouse crops. [3]Includes related products. [4]Withdrawals. [5]Represents $0 to $50,000. Figure in table represents midpoint of range. [6]Data not collected. [7]Baltimore County, MD, includes Baltimore city. [8]St. Louis County, MO, includes St. Louis city. [9]Yellowstone National Park County became incorporated with Gallatin and Park Counties, MT; effective November 7, 1997. [10]Albemarle County, VA, includes Charlottesville city. [11]Clifton Forge independent city became incorporated with Alleghany County, VA; effective July 1, 2001. [12]Alleghany County, VA, includes Covington city. [13]Augusta County, VA, includes Staunton and Waynesboro cities. [14]Bedford County, VA, includes Bedford city. [15]Campbell County, VA, includes Lynchburg city. [16]Carroll County, VA, includes Galax city. [17]Chesterfield County, VA, includes Colonial Heights city. [18]Dinwiddie County, VA, includes Colonial Heights and Petersburg cities. [19]Dinwiddie County, VA, includes Petersburg city. [20]Fairfax County, VA, includes Fairfax and Falls Church cities. [21]Fairfax County, VA, includes Alexandria, Fairfax, and Falls Church cities. [22]Frederick County, VA, includes Winchester city. [23]Grayson County, VA, includes Galax city. [24]Greenville County, VA, includes Emporia city. [25]South Boston independent city became incorporated with Halifax County, VA; effective June 30, 1995. [26]Henrico County, VA, includes Richmond city. [27]Henry County, VA, includes Martinsville city. [28]James City County, VA, includes Williamsburg city. [29]Montgomery County, VA, includes Radford city. [30]Pittsylvania County, VA, includes Danville city. [31]Prince George County, VA, includes Hopewell city. [32]Prince William County, VA, includes Manassas and Manassas Park cities. [33]Roanoke County, VA, includes Salem city. [34]Roanoke County, VA, includes Roanoke and Salem cities. [35]Rockbridge County, VA, includes Buena Vista and Lexington cities. [36]Rockingham County, VA, includes Harrisonburg city. [37]Southampton County, VA, includes Franklin city. [38]Spotsylvania County, VA, includes Fredericksburg city. [39]Washington County, VA, includes Bristol city. [40]Wise County, VA, includes Norton city. [41]York County, VA, includes Poquoson city. [42]York County, VA, includes Hampton, Newport News, and Poquoson cities. [43]Chesapeake city, VA, includes Norfolk and Portsmouth cities.

Survey, Census, or Data Collection Method: Farm earnings—Based on the Regional Economic Information System (REIS); for more information, see <http://www.bea.gov/regional/methods.cfm>. Agriculture—Based on the 2002 Census of Agriculture; for information, see Appendix B, Limitations of the Data and Methodology, and <http://www.agcensus.usda.gov/>. Water use—For information, see <http://pubs.usgs.gov/chapter11/>.

Sources: Farm earnings—U.S. Bureau of Economic Analysis, Regional Economic Information System (REIS), downloaded estimates and software, accessed June 5, 2007 (related Internet site <http://www.bea.gov/regional/docs/reis2005dvd.cfm>). Agriculture—U.S. Department of Agriculture, National Agricultural Statistics Service, 2002 Census of Agriculture, *Volume 1, Geographic Area Series*, accessed April 9, 2007 (related Internet site <http://www.agcensus.usda.gov/>). Water use—U.S. Geological Survey (USGS), *Water Use in the United States*, individual state/county and United States by state, accessed May 19, 2006 (related Internet site <http://water.usgs.gov/watuse>).

Table B-15. Counties — **Manufacturing**

[Includes United States, states, and 3,141 counties/county equivalents defined as of February 22, 2005. For more information on these areas, see Appendix C, Geographic Information]

County	Establishments, 2002[1] Total	Percent change, 1997–2002	Employment, 2005[2] Total	Percent of all employees	Percent change, 2001–2005	Earnings, 2005[2] Total ($1,000)	Percent of all earnings	Value added by manufactures, 2002[1] Total ($1,000)	Percent change, 1997–2002	Capital expenditures, 2002[1] Total ($1,000)	Percent change, 1997–2002
UNITED STATES........	350,828	−3.6	14,860,900	8.5	−12.5	1,015,266,000	12.7	1,887,792,650	3.4	125,536,189	−16.8
ALABAMA..............	5,119	−6.0	307,616	12.2	−8.0	17,326,159	17.6	28,641,670	−2.0	3,070,882	0.4
Autauga...............	29	−23.7	1,827	10.1	−13.8	116,715	22.1	(D)	(NA)	(D)	(NA)
Baldwin...............	145	5.1	5,602	6.8	−0.1	241,577	10.0	525,997	43.6	28,564	24.7
Barbour...............	40	−2.4	4,404	30.1	−9.1	151,005	32.2	311,384	12.7	10,350	−46.3
Bibb..................	(NA)	(NA)	389	6.2	−38.7	19,898	10.8	(NA)	(NA)	(NA)	(NA)
Blount................	49	−18.3	(D)	(NA)	(NA)	(D)	(NA)	71,297	−73.8	5,208	−21.3
Bullock...............	5	−16.7	(D)	(NA)	(NA)	(D)	(NA)	(D)	(NA)	(D)	(NA)
Butler................	26	−3.7	1,481	15.2	2.5	57,612	19.5	85,964	−39.7	4,855	−37.8
Calhoun...............	150	0.7	8,103	12.6	−15.3	403,931	17.5	995,122	38.6	47,943	−11.6
Chambers..............	37	−7.5	4,033	26.2	−23.8	171,665	37.4	334,859	25.7	12,789	−73.6
Cherokee..............	26	23.8	1,362	15.9	20.3	49,026	21.7	81,427	98.0	14,019	647.3
Chilton...............	51	−5.6	1,700	13.2	22.5	71,066	18.9	110,116	66.7	18,083	353.5
Choctaw...............	6	−50.0	1,521	27.1	−16.3	146,287	57.7	(D)	(NA)	(D)	(NA)
Clarke................	30	−6.3	1,922	15.0	−22.5	103,476	27.0	224,625	13.2	21,045	(NA)
Clay..................	12	−20.0	2,302	33.5	−13.2	97,061	48.1	161,746	67.9	(D)	(NA)
Cleburne..............	12	20.0	915	18.5	−23.4	37,185	23.1	60,310	25.5	(D)	(NA)
Coffee................	40	2.6	3,053	14.1	0.4	107,055	17.0	157,892	−43.4	6,041	−26.7
Colbert...............	110	−6.8	3,992	13.8	−6.4	216,432	19.7	456,999	134.3	36,412	−41.1
Conecuh...............	15	−28.6	499	8.3	−38.8	15,774	8.5	53,539	35.3	2,640	−38.1
Coosa.................	10	−9.1	636	25.2	−35.7	34,097	44.1	31,399	−41.9	1,670	(NA)
Covington.............	31	3.3	2,622	13.9	−11.8	111,548	19.7	231,834	42.9	12,183	18.3
Crenshaw..............	9	−40.0	741	12.7	101.9	28,128	13.4	32,303	91.9	(D)	(NA)
Cullman...............	109	−11.4	5,307	12.9	−15.0	230,324	18.1	336,224	−0.6	22,045	−18.1
Dale..................	32	23.1	5,504	19.8	−4.4	309,705	22.4	51,726	61.6	2,359	−4.9
Dallas................	57	7.5	4,430	21.1	−12.5	205,327	30.4	490,879	7.3	57,001	42.6
DeKalb................	191	−11.6	10,171	28.4	−22.9	430,482	38.0	705,619	31.2	36,292	−19.4
Elmore................	66	29.4	2,910	12.1	−2.2	162,954	22.5	311,681	137.3	20,794	78.0
Escambia..............	47	−11.3	2,831	16.4	−16.5	178,858	31.1	311,179	−14.1	15,072	−75.1
Etowah................	138	1.5	6,392	12.6	−8.7	314,259	19.6	440,326	−35.2	15,700	−73.6
Fayette...............	25	−24.2	1,555	19.0	−14.0	56,649	24.1	77,533	−38.8	3,588	−69.9
Franklin..............	51	−20.3	4,682	30.7	7.4	162,661	35.1	414,326	137.1	10,261	31.1
Geneva................	23	−11.5	(D)	(NA)	(NA)	(D)	(NA)	47,252	−40.4	1,882	−20.2
Greene................	(NA)	(NA)	395	11.6	26.2	17,785	17.9	(NA)	(NA)	(NA)	(NA)
Hale..................	17	6.3	1,053	18.9	−12.6	36,360	23.8	(D)	(NA)	(D)	(NA)
Henry.................	20	11.1	1,418	20.2	−8.8	62,988	30.2	106,061	−25.6	3,415	−58.6
Houston...............	118	−5.6	5,637	9.1	−10.4	255,879	11.6	626,169	−6.2	39,764	−30.6
Jackson...............	79	−4.8	6,578	26.3	−2.2	269,644	35.6	509,862	6.2	78,383	−57.5
Jefferson.............	727	−11.0	30,324	6.3	−15.2	2,181,385	9.0	3,076,948	−3.7	246,122	19.5
Lamar.................	21	−4.5	1,462	23.3	−29.5	77,559	42.3	141,797	−0.2	8,034	−37.5
Lauderdale............	103	−10.4	3,683	8.5	−39.4	159,140	13.2	273,965	−33.6	20,640	−16.5
Lawrence..............	23	−20.7	2,012	16.5	6.5	182,603	43.5	(D)	(NA)	(D)	(NA)
Lee...................	100	13.6	7,112	11.2	17.1	343,344	16.8	890,988	33.9	48,225	−27.1
Limestone.............	72	4.3	5,467	14.9	−14.6	362,280	27.0	755,417	−12.0	40,031	(NA)
Lowndes...............	12	20.0	1,205	23.1	34.6	66,046	40.0	(D)	(NA)	(D)	(NA)
Macon.................	(NA)	(NA)	160	1.9	26.0	5,087	2.0	(NA)	(NA)	(NA)	(NA)
Madison...............	337	0.6	25,654	12.3	−6.2	1,803,908	17.5	2,391,726	−15.0	226,112	(NA)
Marengo...............	25	38.9	2,607	23.8	−5.8	123,500	32.9	220,760	9.6	17,882	−36.9
Marion................	45	−15.1	5,130	30.5	5.9	217,717	42.4	333,015	−27.4	12,471	−42.2
Marshall..............	134	−11.8	12,175	25.9	−1.5	501,646	33.6	816,576	−18.5	43,212	−7.2
Mobile................	403	−9.4	15,069	6.8	−21.4	914,182	11.2	2,345,352	−8.0	228,061	−33.1
Monroe................	20	−28.6	3,600	29.0	8.2	210,889	45.6	354,898	−31.1	36,983	0.6
Montgomery............	215	0.5	14,046	8.1	18.0	740,464	9.8	1,256,940	20.7	48,907	−3.1
Morgan................	211	−1.4	12,268	19.4	−10.7	1,013,304	39.8	(D)	(NA)	(D)	(NA)
Perry.................	9	12.5	528	14.5	(NA)	19,179	21.7	27,767	−39.8	2,047	−46.1
Pickens...............	20	−4.8	888	13.7	−4.8	44,672	24.2	39,569	−14.1	(D)	(NA)
Pike..................	29	−9.4	2,539	14.6	11.9	99,804	16.3	121,732	−3.7	5,179	−73.6
Randolph..............	25	−10.7	1,751	20.4	−13.8	65,961	27.0	74,644	−23.4	4,273	66.5
Russell...............	35	−28.6	2,683	15.9	−27.2	172,529	31.5	140,830	−74.0	5,701	−93.6
St. Clair.............	70	−17.6	2,612	11.3	2.4	166,499	24.3	340,579	78.5	14,750	−34.1
Shelby................	160	1.3	6,356	7.9	−21.3	425,498	12.4	593,995	36.0	243,459	441.5
Sumter................	(NA)	(NA)	485	8.5	−31.8	20,595	13.2	(NA)	(NA)	(NA)	(NA)
Talladega.............	101	1.0	11,090	28.7	32.0	754,604	47.8	473,209	−18.7	359,214	401.0
Tallapoosa............	46	−13.2	4,387	22.2	−24.4	111,216	20.6	246,417	−28.3	12,926	−41.5
Tuscaloosa............	162	1.3	13,459	13.0	7.7	1,103,304	25.8	1,359,420	46.7	(D)	(NA)
Walker................	60	−16.7	2,223	6.9	16.3	72,404	9.0	70,389	−44.5	7,335	5.8
Washington............	12	–	1,436	22.9	−12.8	132,102	48.7	(D)	(NA)	(D)	(NA)
Wilcox................	12	–	847	18.6	−8.9	70,068	41.1	(D)	(NA)	(D)	(NA)
Winston...............	79	−9.2	4,468	37.0	1.6	159,233	42.6	288,316	−4.3	18,754	38.7

See footnotes at end of table.

Table B-15. Counties — **Manufacturing**—Con.

[Includes United States, states, and 3,141 counties/county equivalents defined as of February 22, 2005. For more information on these areas, see Appendix C, Geographic Information]

County	Establishments, 2002[1] Total	Percent change, 1997–2002	Employment, 2005[2] Total	Percent of all employees	Percent change, 2001–2005	Earnings, 2005[2] Total ($1,000)	Percent of all earnings	Value added by manufactures, 2002[1] Total ($1,000)	Percent change, 1997–2002	Capital expenditures, 2002[1] Total ($1,000)	Percent change, 1997–2002
ALASKA	514	5.3	14,779	3.4	3.3	737,183	3.7	1,283,586	10.7	79,278	–39.1
Aleutians East	4	100.0	(D)	(NA)	(NA)	(D)	(NA)	(D)	(NA)	(D)	(NA)
Aleutians West	6	–25.0	2,255	45.0	42.8	102,229	47.5	132,132	(NA)	8,554	–18.0
Anchorage	203	8.6	2,624	1.3	–0.4	158,799	1.5	209,364	32.7	14,345	25.7
Bethel	(NA)	(NA)	(D)	(NA)	(NA)	(D)	(NA)	(NA)	(NA)	(NA)	(NA)
Bristol Bay	(NA)	(NA)	(D)	(NA)	(NA)	(D)	(NA)	(NA)	(NA)	(NA)	(NA)
Denali	(NA)	(NA)	(D)	(NA)	(NA)	(D)	(NA)	(NA)	(NA)	(NA)	(NA)
Dillingham	(NA)	(NA)	(D)	(NA)	(NA)	(D)	(NA)	(NA)	(NA)	(NA)	(NA)
Fairbanks North Star	(NA)	(NA)	911	1.6	79.0	38,897	1.4	(NA)	(NA)	(NA)	(NA)
Haines	(NA)	(NA)	205	8.3	(NA)	10,761	17.5	(NA)	(NA)	(NA)	(NA)
Juneau	(NA)	(NA)	317	1.5	9.7	15,118	1.6	(NA)	(NA)	(NA)	(NA)
Kenai Peninsula	62	10.7	1,250	4.1	1.4	85,396	8.2	139,540	–50.7	16,454	–67.0
Ketchikan Gateway	17	–5.6	545	5.3	–24.1	22,766	5.5	(D)	(NA)	658	–70.4
Kodiak Island	17	–32.0	1,456	15.8	–31.9	87,932	22.5	90,002	9.0	5,058	–35.4
Lake and Peninsula	(NA)	(NA)	65	7.5	(NA)	2,943	10.0	(NA)	(NA)	(NA)	(NA)
Matanuska-Susitna	(NA)	(NA)	606	2.1	29.2	27,187	2.9	(NA)	(NA)	(NA)	(NA)
Nome	(NA)	(NA)	(D)	(NA)	(NA)	(D)	(NA)	(NA)	(NA)	(NA)	(NA)
North Slope	(NA)	(NA)	(D)	(NA)	(NA)	(D)	(NA)	(NA)	(NA)	(NA)	(NA)
Northwest Arctic	(NA)	(NA)	(D)	(NA)	(NA)	(D)	(NA)	(NA)	(NA)	(NA)	(NA)
Prince of Wales-Outer Ketchikan	(NA)	(NA)	203	6.8	130.7	4,251	4.6	(NA)	(NA)	(NA)	(NA)
Sitka	(NA)	(NA)	(D)	(NA)	(NA)	(D)	(NA)	(NA)	(NA)	(NA)	(NA)
Skagway-Hoonah-Angoon	(NA)	(NA)	(D)	(NA)	(NA)	(D)	(NA)	(NA)	(NA)	(NA)	(NA)
Southeast Fairbanks	(NA)	(NA)	(D)	(NA)	(NA)	(D)	(NA)	(NA)	(NA)	(NA)	(NA)
Valdez-Cordova	(NA)	(NA)	520	7.1	20.9	24,729	7.9	(NA)	(NA)	(NA)	(NA)
Wade Hampton	(NA)	(NA)	(D)	(NA)	(NA)	(D)	(NA)	(NA)	(NA)	(NA)	(NA)
Wrangell-Petersburg	(NA)	(NA)	494	10.7	3.6	27,453	18.2	(NA)	(NA)	(NA)	(NA)
Yakutat	(NA)	(NA)	(D)	(NA)	(NA)	(D)	(NA)	(NA)	(NA)	(NA)	(NA)
Yukon-Koyukuk	(NA)	(NA)	(D)	(NA)	(NA)	(D)	(NA)	(NA)	(NA)	(NA)	(NA)
ARIZONA	4,935	0.4	193,962	6.0	–8.3	13,652,988	10.0	25,976,992	–3.4	977,257	–61.0
Apache	(NA)	(NA)	(D)	(NA)	(NA)	(D)	(NA)	(NA)	(NA)	(NA)	(NA)
Cochise	(NA)	(NA)	1,108	1.9	17.5	34,284	1.5	(NA)	(NA)	(NA)	(NA)
Coconino	100	5.3	3,666	4.6	12.6	199,081	7.7	597,513	(NA)	18,351	(NA)
Gila	21	–38.2	830	3.8	–20.6	51,513	8.5	(D)	(NA)	(D)	(NA)
Graham	(NA)	(NA)	290	2.8	–1.7	9,054	3.0	(NA)	(NA)	(NA)	(NA)
Greenlee	(NA)	(NA)	(D)	(NA)	(NA)	(D)	(NA)	(NA)	(NA)	(NA)	(NA)
La Paz	(NA)	(NA)	335	4.1	15.5	13,249	5.5	(NA)	(NA)	(NA)	(NA)
Maricopa	3,353	–0.3	140,507	6.4	–10.3	10,298,360	10.3	19,303,904	–13.7	668,329	–68.5
Mohave	164	5.1	4,417	6.3	32.7	191,075	8.8	353,329	2.7	31,671	84.3
Navajo	47	4.4	1,128	2.9	15.8	60,974	4.9	(D)	(NA)	11,475	(NA)
Pima	748	–2.1	30,388	6.3	–13.0	2,305,983	12.4	3,937,005	67.5	162,644	5.4
Pinal	93	25.7	3,597	6.0	18.5	172,270	7.4	893,841	23.5	24,388	–79.6
Santa Cruz	41	17.1	619	3.6	–37.2	22,748	3.7	(D)	(NA)	(D)	(NA)
Yavapai	200	5.8	3,844	4.5	16.1	163,334	6.4	246,821	–5.9	13,765	–13.1
Yuma	80	21.2	3,016	3.6	31.6	127,478	4.4	206,649	30.8	16,369	59.3
ARKANSAS	3,185	–4.0	207,441	13.3	–10.9	9,472,372	17.4	21,965,415	13.5	1,209,902	–19.0
Arkansas	29	3.6	3,742	26.7	16.2	173,742	40.5	223,007	58.2	17,180	–2.7
Ashley	27	12.5	3,066	27.2	–9.8	222,643	51.7	(D)	(NA)	38,921	(NA)
Baxter	53	–5.4	2,745	12.7	–20.5	113,303	19.3	295,157	41.0	20,813	682.7
Benton	164	–15.5	14,080	11.9	–11.5	609,785	12.7	1,467,484	24.4	66,102	25.7
Boone	62	–7.5	2,288	11.0	–17.6	95,806	15.1	177,463	–19.8	(D)	(NA)
Bradley	8	–11.1	1,133	19.5	4.0	43,552	26.6	42,649	12.1	(D)	(NA)
Calhoun	(NA)	(NA)	2,656	57.2	27.5	130,111	70.8	(NA)	(NA)	(NA)	(NA)
Carroll	32	–22.0	3,309	22.2	–9.6	99,018	26.4	(D)	(NA)	8,241	76.3
Chicot	11	–	434	8.0	–51.1	19,762	13.2	65,434	208.2	(D)	(NA)
Clark	30	–3.2	2,460	18.3	–19.1	109,640	28.0	135,037	–12.2	11,467	–36.6
Clay	23	–	1,304	17.6	–47.2	40,702	23.5	87,237	–10.8	5,095	28.5
Cleburne	43	26.5	1,929	15.0	1.4	75,003	24.8	102,545	–57.7	3,542	–47.6
Cleveland	(NA)	(NA)	103	4.9	43.1	2,576	4.3	(NA)	(NA)	(NA)	(NA)
Columbia	35	–10.3	2,800	21.5	–5.1	166,028	34.9	352,111	20.9	21,116	–54.9
Conway	27	17.4	1,149	10.6	–0.4	59,467	20.5	152,459	–7.2	(D)	(NA)
Craighead	123	0.8	7,155	13.0	–14.1	321,685	17.9	638,672	25.8	(D)	(NA)
Crawford	58	–6.5	3,658	13.9	–9.4	127,012	16.2	301,493	(NA)	9,549	–63.3
Crittenden	50	11.1	1,539	7.1	–16.5	91,105	13.0	149,883	–33.2	19,890	–7.1
Cross	17	–	865	10.4	–29.9	39,176	21.2	84,869	8.0	7,396	33.8
Dallas	14	–6.7	884	19.5	–9.3	35,012	28.0	42,148	–18.2	1,335	–37.0
Desha	18	12.5	1,304	17.8	14.7	66,026	30.4	147,675	14.7	3,007	
Drew	30	–9.1	1,018	10.8	–31.4	32,864	12.5	75,342	–26.4	2,811	–60.1
Faulkner	92	–1.1	5,305	10.8	–24.9	282,049	17.2	743,340	27.6	35,599	19.6
Franklin	21	31.3	1,054	14.0	–13.4	38,514	17.0	68,620	–35.2	8,566	94.4
Fulton	(NA)	(NA)	198	3.9	(NA)	4,126	4.6	(NA)	(NA)	(NA)	(NA)

See footnotes at end of table.

Table B-15. Counties — **Manufacturing**—Con.

[Includes United States, states, and 3,141 counties/county equivalents defined as of February 22, 2005. For more information on these areas, see Appendix C, Geographic Information]

County	Manufacturing (NAICS 31–33)										
	Establishments, 2002[1]		Employment, 2005[2]			Earnings, 2005[2]		Value added by manufactures, 2002[1]		Capital expenditures, 2002[1]	
	Total	Percent change, 1997–2002	Total	Percent of all employ-ees	Percent change, 2001–2005	Total ($1,000)	Percent of all earnings	Total ($1,000)	Percent change, 1997–2002	Total ($1,000)	Percent change, 1997–2002
ARKANSAS—Con.											
Garland	124	14.8	3,623	7.0	−12.7	145,796	10.0	302,916	17.4	25,667	−3.1
Grant	18	−28.0	893	14.5	−13.8	33,942	21.6	(D)	(NA)	(D)	(NA)
Greene	53	12.8	5,536	27.9	1.4	254,947	42.4	400,837	−14.3	17,852	39.0
Hempstead	32	–	2,862	24.6	−25.9	111,068	31.1	(D)	(NA)	(D)	(NA)
Hot Spring	40	−14.9	1,698	14.6	−23.4	83,181	25.1	153,116	12.5	9,042	−59.2
Howard	27	3.8	4,252	42.0	−9.6	154,839	46.1	399,817	−11.7	40,879	23.4
Independence	53	−1.9	5,138	23.2	−9.9	207,775	32.0	454,001	−3.0	32,441	−33.7
Izard	(NA)	(NA)	405	7.5	−35.0	26,877	20.8	(NA)	(NA)	(NA)	(NA)
Jackson	24	4.3	1,058	12.2	1.5	57,383	25.4	103,020	36.9	11,461	107.6
Jefferson	75	−10.7	6,474	14.8	−17.7	336,748	21.1	(D)	(NA)	(D)	(NA)
Johnson	33	−15.4	3,238	27.1	−2.4	108,360	32.7	255,007	7.3	8,755	−18.2
Lafayette	(NA)	(NA)	(D)	(NA)	(NA)	(D)	(NA)	(NA)	(NA)	(NA)	(NA)
Lawrence	25	−32.4	704	9.0	−42.0	25,437	15.5	64,224	−49.5	1,481	−75.7
Lee	(NA)	(NA)	(D)	(NA)	(NA)	(D)	(NA)	(NA)	(NA)	(NA)	(NA)
Lincoln	(NA)	(NA)	466	10.3	−27.1	17,197	13.3	(NA)	(NA)	(NA)	(NA)
Little River	11	−31.3	1,541	23.7	4.3	128,364	47.8	(D)	(NA)	28,601	(NA)
Logan	25	−30.6	1,866	20.3	−9.4	70,902	27.8	144,798	−10.8	16,994	62.9
Lonoke	41	5.1	1,486	7.5	−4.4	63,031	13.4	159,648	11.5	(D)	(NA)
Madison	24	26.3	1,185	17.6	16.7	39,858	23.9	30,504	−21.4	5,292	212.6
Marion	21	−8.7	1,759	25.1	−9.9	56,472	36.9	80,590	17.5	2,561	−22.3
Miller	25	–	2,867	14.5	0.8	175,151	26.3	372,848	41.5	9,338	−62.9
Mississippi	47	−24.2	5,157	21.1	−10.9	403,135	43.8	999,131	−11.1	51,516	−49.2
Monroe	(NA)	(NA)	168	4.0	−40.2	4,734	6.1	(NA)	(NA)	(NA)	(NA)
Montgomery	(NA)	(NA)	293	7.5	0.7	8,151	9.0	(NA)	(NA)	(NA)	(NA)
Nevada	5	−37.5	(D)	(NA)	(NA)	(D)	(NA)	(D)	(NA)	(D)	(NA)
Newton	(NA)	(NA)	135	4.6	−14.6	4,057	8.5	(NA)	(NA)	(NA)	(NA)
Ouachita	40	21.2	826	8.3	−17.9	36,721	12.4	(D)	(NA)	(D)	(NA)
Perry	(NA)	(NA)	95	3.2	37.7	2,378	3.6	(NA)	(NA)	(NA)	(NA)
Phillips	14	−26.3	451	4.8	−44.7	17,463	6.4	81,238	−14.9	2,135	−82.5
Pike	(NA)	(NA)	518	11.5	−11.9	15,628	11.6	(NA)	(NA)	(NA)	(NA)
Poinsett	24	−11.1	1,524	15.2	−14.5	61,024	23.7	113,002	−9.9	(D)	(NA)
Polk	40	37.9	1,468	14.3	−35.6	53,579	19.3	171,997	23.9	4,861	−4.5
Pope	74	−9.8	5,050	14.5	6.6	199,207	17.5	567,991	11.8	32,236	9.7
Prairie	(NA)	(NA)	(D)	(NA)	(NA)	(D)	(NA)	(NA)	(NA)	(NA)	(NA)
Pulaski	391	−9.3	16,633	5.4	−14.2	934,267	6.7	1,897,490	−3.7	122,175	−22.0
Randolph	38	18.8	1,153	14.0	−31.9	37,713	21.0	123,921	32.8	4,538	−37.3
St. Francis	23	−14.8	1,367	11.5	−31.6	50,834	13.7	(D)	(NA)	9,006	−11.9
Saline	73	1.4	1,970	7.3	−11.7	98,478	11.9	200,769	43.2	14,155	−31.8
Scott	16	−15.8	1,237	24.2	−14.3	33,925	23.5	(D)	(NA)	843	−66.7
Searcy	(NA)	(NA)	350	8.9	27.3	8,458	13.4	(NA)	(NA)	(NA)	(NA)
Sebastian	217	−6.9	21,815	24.3	−2.9	1,017,302	27.6	2,588,712	31.1	116,460	−3.0
Sevier	14	−6.7	2,420	30.7	−2.5	72,051	28.4	116,360	−8.9	5,051	101.7
Sharp	(NA)	(NA)	(D)	(NA)	(NA)	(D)	(NA)	(NA)	(NA)	(NA)	(NA)
Stone	26	–	541	9.8	−27.5	14,184	11.9	21,420	18.7	758	−36.8
Union	62	−1.6	5,265	19.7	−13.1	286,049	27.4	803,923	−7.5	41,208	−45.5
Van Buren	11	−26.7	641	10.2	−2.7	18,887	13.9	29,670	21.2	2,887	198.6
Washington	214	10.9	16,065	13.8	−3.2	645,300	14.8	1,608,089	50.1	59,306	−26.9
White	80	6.7	3,972	11.4	−18.4	178,594	18.0	386,652	28.7	17,372	−9.3
Woodruff	(NA)	(NA)	499	14.7	3.3	17,527	25.2	(NA)	(NA)	(NA)	(NA)
Yell	24	9.1	3,038	29.3	0.9	91,874	33.1	235,027	135.4	7,471	−24.7
CALIFORNIA	48,478	−1.9	1,605,418	7.8	−14.7	127,108,414	11.9	197,574,490	0.9	16,279,856	−0.9
Alameda	2,355	−6.1	80,263	9.0	−15.6	7,119,453	13.6	14,628,752	41.2	716,220	−40.4
Alpine	(NA)	(NA)	10	0.9	(NA)	[3]25	(NA)	(NA)	(NA)	(NA)	(NA)
Amador	52	2.0	880	4.6	−9.6	32,611	4.8	47,394	−30.1	4,141	−21.4
Butte	235	1.3	4,890	4.6	0.6	190,178	5.2	425,336	12.7	90,281	118.5
Calaveras	(NA)	(NA)	696	3.9	7.9	20,908	4.0	(NA)	(NA)	(NA)	(NA)
Colusa	28	40.0	983	8.9	12.9	84,579	21.1	87,646	16.2	5,776	(NA)
Contra Costa	677	−6.4	22,416	4.5	−11.4	2,757,260	9.7	3,971,347	3.6	445,998	7.6
Del Norte	(NA)	(NA)	244	2.2	−33.0	9,486	2.5	(NA)	(NA)	(NA)	(NA)
El Dorado	181	25.7	2,153	2.4	−9.8	122,153	3.7	627,790	368.6	(D)	(NA)
Fresno	701	0.7	28,896	6.6	−2.0	1,676,090	9.7	2,530,737	7.8	166,468	3.6
Glenn	30	3.4	645	5.3	−8.9	34,605	9.0	114,752	68.8	(D)	(NA)
Humboldt	166	−6.7	4,379	6.1	−9.0	200,564	8.4	266,054	−41.5	22,983	−30.1
Imperial	60	−1.6	2,510	3.7	40.5	103,074	4.1	219,088	131.3	17,643	50.7
Inyo	(NA)	(NA)	259	2.4	−1.1	8,795	2.5	(NA)	(NA)	(NA)	(NA)
Kern	398	2.1	13,693	3.9	20.5	756,076	5.1	1,656,177	3.0	165,680	14.1
Kings	79	21.5	4,066	7.2	13.2	249,795	10.3	689,495	176.2	27,258	17.5
Lake	(NA)	(NA)	311	1.3	−51.0	15,551	2.0	(NA)	(NA)	(NA)	(NA)
Lassen	(NA)	(NA)	119	0.8	−62.6	2,309	0.4	(NA)	(NA)	(NA)	(NA)
Los Angeles	17,205	−4.0	504,531	8.9	−18.3	33,043,837	11.3	55,525,812	3.4	5,619,927	58.3
Madera	103	9.6	3,546	6.0	10.0	182,881	8.4	589,761	30.9	39,857	7.6

See footnotes at end of table.

County and City Data Book: 2007

U.S. Census Bureau

[Includes United States, states, and 3,141 counties/county equivalents defined as of February 22, 2005. For more information on these areas, see Appendix C, Geographic Information]

County	Establishments, 2002[1] Total	Percent change, 1997–2002	Employment, 2005[2] Total	Percent of all employees	Percent change, 2001–2005	Earnings, 2005[2] Total ($1,000)	Percent of all earnings	Value added by manufactures, 2002[1] Total ($1,000)	Percent change, 1997–2002	Capital expenditures, 2002[1] Total ($1,000)	Percent change, 1997–2002
CALIFORNIA—Con.											
Marin	290	−15.0	3,483	1.9	−24.7	165,750	1.7	328,477	−1.4	13,106	−27.8
Mariposa	(NA)	(NA)	156	1.9	23.8	5,705	2.4	(NA)	(NA)	(NA)	(NA)
Mendocino	152	−5.0	3,645	7.1	−23.9	144,192	9.3	311,764	−16.8	21,609	7.2
Merced	127	3.3	11,307	12.5	9.8	489,982	13.7	941,111	41.5	49,293	−33.2
Modoc	(NA)	(NA)	52	1.1	18.2	377	0.3	(NA)	(NA)	(NA)	(NA)
Mono	(NA)	(NA)	116	1.1	(NA)	4,422	1.1	(NA)	(NA)	(NA)	(NA)
Monterey	307	1.7	7,528	3.2	−29.2	645,836	5.9	1,037,074	48.5	51,514	−20.2
Napa	381	37.5	11,750	13.1	7.7	869,671	20.6	1,994,584	66.4	159,612	−4.7
Nevada	168	−3.4	2,308	4.0	8.4	123,678	6.5	255,772	21.1	13,077	17.2
Orange	5,621	−2.5	195,331	9.7	−12.7	14,501,185	13.1	21,686,041	2.5	1,559,583	−28.2
Placer	299	15.0	10,204	5.5	−13.1	811,730	9.6	1,497,416	−10.4	(D)	(NA)
Plumas	31	34.8	738	6.5	−13.2	40,279	9.8	40,194	−25.9	(D)	(NA)
Riverside	1,627	14.6	59,833	7.2	7.5	3,281,402	10.1	5,989,543	50.6	357,218	38.8
Sacramento	975	7.1	33,549	4.2	−1.9	2,722,773	6.7	3,443,846	−34.2	196,388	3.2
San Benito	77	2.7	3,000	12.7	12.1	155,736	16.8	248,787	52.8	10,917	18.1
San Bernardino	2,177	9.3	70,404	8.2	−2.0	3,791,116	10.7	7,234,767	31.1	567,475	−4.3
San Diego	3,473	1.9	114,176	6.1	−12.7	9,165,437	9.7	14,187,111	29.0	1,116,270	21.4
San Francisco	932	−25.3	14,249	2.0	−30.5	962,923	1.8	1,818,070	−9.0	38,402	−42.8
San Joaquin	609	10.1	22,045	7.7	−5.1	1,138,387	9.6	3,515,538	21.2	220,366	5.6
San Luis Obispo	383	18.6	6,324	4.2	−16.5	357,448	6.2	614,992	−0.8	59,166	13.6
San Mateo	858	−15.8	30,976	6.7	−16.8	4,904,802	14.7	5,814,332	33.2	392,478	−2.1
Santa Barbara	532	6.0	15,300	5.8	−10.2	1,141,011	9.8	1,773,463	21.1	121,593	38.0
Santa Clara	2,981	−13.9	175,411	15.7	−29.7	25,120,905	28.3	26,640,059	−39.5	2,549,187	−40.0
Santa Cruz	377	−2.6	8,251	5.7	−10.1	509,550	8.4	617,269	−45.9	31,289	−62.2
Shasta	178	0.6	2,950	3.2	−19.4	156,708	4.5	262,551	0.3	(D)	(NA)
Sierra	(NA)	(NA)	57	4.3	(NA)	3,039	8.6	(NA)	(NA)	(NA)	(NA)
Siskiyou	40	−2.4	973	4.3	9.8	39,902	5.8	80,566	3.1	7,809	48.7
Solano	303	9.4	9,481	5.3	−8.7	779,611	9.9	1,779,527	45.4	164,579	60.0
Sonoma	874	10.2	26,537	9.5	−15.2	1,769,453	14.6	3,437,229	19.2	190,348	−20.7
Stanislaus	488	12.2	22,958	10.2	−0.9	1,356,442	14.5	3,284,159	6.6	153,161	−10.1
Sutter	76	8.6	1,855	4.3	−23.3	92,341	6.5	394,495	144.8	21,694	101.2
Tehama	56	16.7	2,495	10.1	−3.2	125,058	15.1	180,467	−0.1	7,118	−20.7
Trinity	(NA)	(NA)	287	5.7	2.5	11,721	8.4	(NA)	(NA)	(NA)	(NA)
Tulare	293	3.9	11,791	6.4	1.0	576,361	8.5	1,262,113	13.7	74,981	−21.1
Tuolumne	81	24.6	1,182	4.2	−0.2	57,668	6.2	105,025	38.9	5,397	−25.0
Ventura	1,051	4.3	41,160	9.4	−4.7	4,005,294	18.6	4,525,268	35.0	259,332	11.7
Yolo	176	0.6	6,958	5.9	9.8	425,389	7.7	627,400	−0.7	28,453	−45.3
Yuba	46	4.5	1,108	4.1	−8.2	44,878	3.8	126,753	62.6	3,179	−56.2
COLORADO	5,349	−2.4	162,694	5.3	−15.5	11,329,982	7.9	17,798,062	−13.9	1,975,737	19.1
Adams	442	(NA)	15,159	7.2	−3.4	923,371	10.8	1,144,260	(NA)	81,374.0	(NA)
Alamosa	(NA)	(NA)	160	1.5	30.1	4,274	1.4	(NA)	(NA)	(NA)	(NA)
Arapahoe	511	−6.9	10,752	2.6	−13.9	720,503	3.2	1,019,898	−65.9	40,367	−66.4
Archuleta	(NA)	(NA)	106	1.4	23.3	1,745	1.2	(NA)	(NA)	(NA)	(NA)
Baca	(NA)	(NA)	(D)	(NA)	(NA)	(D)	(NA)	(NA)	(NA)	(NA)	(NA)
Bent	(NA)	(NA)	15	0.7	−28.6	180	0.3	(NA)	(NA)	(NA)	(NA)
Boulder	581	(NA)	20,330	9.0	−32.7	2,065,391	18.3	2,191,400	(NA)	199,511	(NA)
Broomfield	77	(NA)	4,615	12.6	(NA)	360,439	17.6	1,079,909	(NA)	147,052	(NA)
Chaffee	(NA)	(NA)	132	1.3	−59.1	3,982	1.6	(NA)	(NA)	(NA)	(NA)
Cheyenne	(NA)	(NA)	(D)	(NA)	(NA)	(D)	(NA)	(NA)	(NA)	(NA)	(NA)
Clear Creek	(NA)	(NA)	(D)	(NA)	(NA)	(D)	(NA)	(NA)	(NA)	(NA)	(NA)
Conejos	(NA)	(NA)	65	2.0	−21.7	802	1.2	(NA)	(NA)	(NA)	(NA)
Costilla	(NA)	(NA)	(D)	(NA)	(NA)	(D)	(NA)	(NA)	(NA)	(NA)	(NA)
Crowley	(NA)	(NA)	(D)	(NA)	(NA)	(D)	(NA)	(NA)	(NA)	(NA)	(NA)
Custer	(NA)	(NA)	(D)	(NA)	(NA)	(D)	(NA)	(NA)	(NA)	(NA)	(NA)
Delta	(NA)	(NA)	716	4.8	5.0	24,248	7.0	(NA)	(NA)	(NA)	(NA)
Denver	895	−8.3	25,013	4.7	−15.5	1,530,387	4.4	2,304,647	−8.7	130,872	−20.7
Dolores	(NA)	(NA)	13	1.3	−27.8	574	2.5	(NA)	(NA)	(NA)	(NA)
Douglas	102	−14.3	2,393	2.2	0.7	160,541	3.3	149,623	−12.4	18,248	12.4
Eagle	(NA)	(NA)	498	1.2	−11.2	49,852	2.9	(NA)	(NA)	(NA)	(NA)
Elbert	(NA)	(NA)	173	2.0	68.0	6,771	3.4	(NA)	(NA)	(NA)	(NA)
El Paso	507	1.6	19,663	5.5	−26.0	1,241,183	7.9	2,606,368	−12.1	451,243	18.7
Fremont	48	2.1	880	4.5	−12.1	38,925	6.1	67,345	−31.4	(D)	(NA)
Garfield	(NA)	(NA)	492	1.4	29.5	27,080	2.2	(NA)	(NA)	(NA)	(NA)
Gilpin	(NA)	(NA)	(D)	(NA)	(NA)	(D)	(NA)	(NA)	(NA)	(NA)	(NA)
Grand	(NA)	(NA)	135	1.2	8.0	4,367	1.4	(NA)	(NA)	(NA)	(NA)
Gunnison	(NA)	(NA)	121	1.0	−17.7	3,394	0.9	(NA)	(NA)	(NA)	(NA)
Hinsdale	(NA)	(NA)	(D)	(NA)	(NA)	(D)	(NA)	(NA)	(NA)	(NA)	(NA)
Huerfano	(NA)	(NA)	113	3.1	−13.7	3,392	4.6	(NA)	(NA)	(NA)	(NA)
Jackson	(NA)	(NA)	(D)	(NA)	(NA)	(D)	(NA)	(NA)	(NA)	(NA)	(NA)

See footnotes at end of table.

Table B-15. Counties — **Manufacturing**—Con.

[Includes United States, states, and 3,141 counties/county equivalents defined as of February 22, 2005. For more information on these areas, see Appendix C, Geographic Information]

County	Establishments, 2002[1]		Employment, 2005[2]			Earnings, 2005[2]		Value added by manufactures, 2002[1]		Capital expenditures, 2002[1]	
	Total	Percent change, 1997–2002	Total	Percent of all employees	Percent change, 2001–2005	Total ($1,000)	Percent of all earnings	Total ($1,000)	Percent change, 1997–2002	Total ($1,000)	Percent change, 1997–2002
COLORADO—Con.											
Jefferson	504	(NA)	19,462	7.3	−14.6	1,865,586	14.4	2,876,528	(NA)	230,076	(NA)
Kiowa	(NA)	(NA)	(D)	(NA)	(NA)	(D)	(NA)	(NA)	(NA)	(NA)	(NA)
Kit Carson	(NA)	(NA)	140	2.7	−2.1	4,463	2.8	(NA)	(NA)	(NA)	(NA)
Lake	(NA)	(NA)	(D)	(NA)	(NA)	(D)	(NA)	(NA)	(NA)	(NA)	(NA)
La Plata	73	10.6	817	2.3	−3.3	22,266	1.9	49,001	66.5	(D)	(NA)
Larimer	390	1.6	13,455	7.4	−26.0	1,015,701	14.5	1,559,876	−21.8	272,344	7.9
Las Animas	(NA)	(NA)	195	2.3	27.5	5,646	2.4	(NA)	(NA)	(NA)	(NA)
Lincoln	(NA)	(NA)	(D)	(NA)	(NA)	(D)	(NA)	(NA)	(NA)	(NA)	(NA)
Logan	(NA)	(NA)	385	3.0	−17.4	13,788	3.3	(NA)	(NA)	(NA)	(NA)
Mesa	161	−3.6	3,893	4.9	2.3	161,636	6.2	225,575	−14.1	18,393	−27.4
Mineral	(NA)	(NA)	(D)	(NA)	(NA)	(D)	(NA)	(NA)	(NA)	(NA)	(NA)
Moffat	(NA)	(NA)	100	1.3	2.0	3,176	1.2	(NA)	(NA)	(NA)	(NA)
Montezuma	(NA)	(NA)	521	3.7	14.0	14,632	3.9	(NA)	(NA)	(NA)	(NA)
Montrose	64	–	1,686	7.2	7.4	52,046	6.9	100,927	10.9	(D)	(NA)
Morgan	27	8.0	2,579	16.3	−7.3	97,761	18.8	(D)	(NA)	(D)	(NA)
Otero	(NA)	(NA)	594	5.8	−2.0	22,606	8.3	(NA)	(NA)	(NA)	(NA)
Ouray	(NA)	(NA)	71	2.3	−22.8	2,323	3.1	(NA)	(NA)	(NA)	(NA)
Park	(NA)	(NA)	78	1.3	−44.7	2,548	2.1	(NA)	(NA)	(NA)	(NA)
Phillips	(NA)	(NA)	41	1.4	−12.8	613	0.8	(NA)	(NA)	(NA)	(NA)
Pitkin	(NA)	(NA)	151	0.7	−32.3	7,645	0.7	(NA)	(NA)	(NA)	(NA)
Prowers	17	−15.0	856	11.0	−11.6	32,735	13.9	37,051	(NA)	870	(NA)
Pueblo	122	14.0	4,201	5.8	−14.0	248,380	10.2	540,720	8.1	26,231	−27.9
Rio Blanco	(NA)	(NA)	103	2.2	60.9	5,156	2.8	(NA)	(NA)	(NA)	(NA)
Rio Grande	(NA)	(NA)	186	2.4	8.8	5,070	2.3	(NA)	(NA)	(NA)	(NA)
Routt	(NA)	(NA)	141	0.7	−37.1	5,253	0.7	(NA)	(NA)	(NA)	(NA)
Saguache	(NA)	(NA)	71	2.5	(NA)	1,397	2.0	(NA)	(NA)	(NA)	(NA)
San Juan	(NA)	(NA)	(D)	(NA)	(NA)	(D)	(NA)	(NA)	(NA)	(NA)	(NA)
San Miguel	(NA)	(NA)	148	1.8	5.0	5,872	2.4	(NA)	(NA)	(NA)	(NA)
Sedgwick	(NA)	(NA)	(D)	(NA)	(NA)	(D)	(NA)	(NA)	(NA)	(NA)	(NA)
Summit	(NA)	(NA)	(D)	(NA)	(NA)	(D)	(NA)	(NA)	(NA)	(NA)	(NA)
Teller	(NA)	(NA)	(D)	(NA)	(NA)	(D)	(NA)	(NA)	(NA)	(NA)	(NA)
Washington	(NA)	(NA)	(D)	(NA)	(NA)	(D)	(NA)	(NA)	(NA)	(NA)	(NA)
Weld	231	(NA)	10,234	9.3	−12.7	533,367	12.9	1,289,514	(NA)	65,789	(NA)
Yuma	(NA)	(NA)	74	1.2	−38.8	1,613	0.8	(NA)	(NA)	(NA)	(NA)
CONNECTICUT	5,384	−7.9	203,271	9.3	−13.1	18,409,179	14.3	27,673,466	1.4	1,448,543	−22.3
Fairfield	1,164	−11.6	44,529	7.6	−15.9	5,638,206	12.1	9,458,645	31.0	420,323	−13.1
Hartford	1,485	−6.7	61,870	10.0	−11.4	5,341,495	14.4	6,460,588	−0.3	419,975	−6.0
Litchfield	422	−5.8	11,576	12.0	−21.3	675,348	17.8	1,567,864	−18.5	79,131	−18.4
Middlesex	297	−3.9	11,318	11.8	−11.0	889,442	18.7	1,313,457	−11.2	66,459	−13.4
New Haven	1,455	−8.6	44,936	9.3	−15.3	3,549,293	14.9	5,367,899	−24.2	306,034	−33.0
New London	209	−11.8	17,957	10.4	−0.6	1,660,835	19.7	2,226,256	21.3	98,412	−55.2
Tolland	155	2.0	3,838	6.1	−1.6	211,952	9.1	409,318	−10.3	26,366	−16.8
Windham	197	−0.5	7,247	14.2	−15.5	442,608	22.5	869,439	6.2	31,843	−38.7
DELAWARE	705	4.4	34,273	6.5	−14.8	2,765,603	10.3	5,063,899	−6.0	481,872	−5.5
Kent	76	−7.3	4,008	4.8	−31.6	221,379	6.9	1,262,907	16.3	76,375	91.0
New Castle	462	0.9	17,859	5.1	−20.0	2,023,792	9.9	2,851,516	−6.4	344,844	−16.1
Sussex	167	23.7	12,406	13.2	2.8	520,432	16.2	949,476	−24.4	60,653	3.5
DISTRICT OF COLUMBIA	146	−27.0	2,510	0.3	−35.4	223,184	0.3	163,118	−4.5	13,331	35.6
District of Columbia	146	−27.0	2,510	0.3	−35.4	223,184	0.3	163,118	−4.5	13,331	35.6
FLORIDA	15,202	−4.9	423,934	4.2	−6.5	25,241,963	6.2	41,912,600	4.2	2,465,056	−17.3
Alachua	154	2.0	4,267	2.8	−11.1	210,551	3.7	393,735	−14.1	24,600	−66.4
Baker	(NA)	(NA)	285	3.1	(NA)	13,350	4.8	(NA)	(NA)	(NA)	(NA)
Bay	133	−2.2	3,401	3.4	13.1	182,571	5.0	404,555	22.4	30,348	−21.2
Bradford	(NA)	(NA)	505	4.7	−28.1	20,548	6.6	(NA)	(NA)	(NA)	(NA)
Brevard	459	−7.1	24,452	8.7	2.2	1,802,737	15.7	2,580,956	39.1	131,769	24.8
Broward	1,836	−6.7	34,096	3.4	−11.8	2,266,085	5.4	3,751,169	14.1	153,167	−5.9
Calhoun	(NA)	(NA)	96	2.2	−19.3	1,912	1.7	(NA)	(NA)	(NA)	(NA)
Charlotte	86	16.2	1,129	1.7	3.9	41,300	2.1	64,113	64.6	1,906	3.6
Citrus	62	6.9	910	1.8	−16.1	25,312	1.8	26,709	−39.1	1,537	−36.5
Clay	71	−4.1	1,964	3.3	19.7	91,157	5.1	(D)	(NA)	11,765	23.3
Collier	252	22.9	3,661	2.0	11.4	205,064	2.8	235,764	66.4	10,058	−18.5
Columbia	39	11.4	2,530	9.7	46.3	125,723	13.8	60,758	−43.0	2,451	−40.1
DeSoto	(NA)	(NA)	399	2.6	9.6	18,496	5.0	(NA)	(NA)	(NA)	(NA)
Dixie	(NA)	(NA)	522	11.4	9.9	25,493	20.9	(NA)	(NA)	(NA)	(NA)
Duval	690	−8.5	28,954	4.7	−6.7	1,671,790	6.0	3,975,300	2.1	221,828	−12.9

See footnotes at end of table.

Table B-15. Counties — **Manufacturing**—Con.

[Includes United States, states, and 3,141 counties/county equivalents defined as of February 22, 2005. For more information on these areas, see Appendix C, Geographic Information]

County	Establishments, 2002[1] Total	Percent change, 1997-2002	Employment, 2005[2] Total	Percent of all employees	Percent change, 2001-2005	Earnings, 2005[2] Total ($1,000)	Percent of all earnings	Value added by manufactures, 2002[1] Total ($1,000)	Percent change, 1997-2002	Capital expenditures, 2002[1] Total ($1,000)	Percent change, 1997-2002
FLORIDA—Con.											
Escambia	223	-5.5	6,469	3.7	-9.6	372,622	5.6	812,864	-16.9	49,417	(NA)
Flagler	50	19.0	1,294	5.3	-8.7	51,674	6.3	165,543	50.9	7,469	25.3
Franklin	(NA)	(NA)	(D)	(NA)	(NA)	(D)	(NA)	(NA)	(NA)	(NA)	(NA)
Gadsden	33	3.1	1,570	8.1	-1.9	62,350	10.1	77,692	-1.4	(D)	(NA)
Gilchrist	(NA)	(NA)	157	3.0	-8.2	7,634	5.9	(NA)	(NA)	(NA)	(NA)
Glades	(NA)	(NA)	(D)	(NA)	(NA)	(D)	(NA)	(NA)	(NA)	(NA)	(NA)
Gulf	(NA)	(NA)	246	4.2	251.4	8,481	4.8	(NA)	(NA)	(NA)	(NA)
Hamilton	3	-25.0	(D)	(NA)	(NA)	(D)	(NA)	(D)	(NA)	(D)	(NA)
Hardee	(NA)	(NA)	284	2.2	25.7	10,367	3.2	(NA)	(NA)	(NA)	(NA)
Hendry	15	-31.8	1,232	6.0	10.8	79,247	14.8	(D)	(NA)	(D)	(NA)
Hernando	75	4.2	1,249	2.2	-19.1	56,074	3.5	118,485	-21.3	9,325	-32.9
Highlands	49	-9.3	1,094	2.7	-4.1	53,887	5.0	96,027	34.5	3,011	-86.8
Hillsborough	930	-3.1	33,667	4.2	-1.4	2,283,580	6.4	3,157,296	16.6	200,814	-7.3
Holmes	(NA)	(NA)	203	2.9	-17.1	6,556	4.2	(NA)	(NA)	(NA)	(NA)
Indian River	100	-13.8	2,324	3.5	-29.3	98,797	4.2	184,361	77.7	7,107	-21.9
Jackson	18	-30.8	774	3.9	14.5	48,248	7.8	70,419	14.8	2,303	-59.9
Jefferson	(NA)	(NA)	91	1.8	-15.0	2,805	2.1	(NA)	(NA)	(NA)	(NA)
Lafayette	(NA)	(NA)	147	6.0	54.7	3,494	5.2	(NA)	(NA)	(NA)	(NA)
Lake	165	0.6	4,685	4.2	5.1	202,882	5.7	333,511	42.2	19,592	9.6
Lee	403	12.9	7,607	2.6	8.1	373,768	3.3	582,985	49.9	29,088	31.0
Leon	103	-18.9	2,260	1.3	-3.6	113,128	1.6	149,246	-41.0	10,153	16.3
Levy	(NA)	(NA)	839	5.9	171.5	29,938	8.1	(NA)	(NA)	(NA)	(NA)
Liberty	(NA)	(NA)	307	10.4	(NA)	14,494	14.5	(NA)	(NA)	(NA)	(NA)
Madison	10	-9.1	815	10.9	-17.1	32,776	17.2	(D)	(NA)	(D)	(NA)
Manatee	268	-5.6	10,406	5.9	-13.2	565,713	9.0	1,009,947	47.3	129,526	6.0
Marion	245	14.0	10,080	7.5	2.0	486,880	11.4	724,731	13.2	31,763	-15.3
Martin	152	-11.6	3,415	3.9	11.2	172,744	5.6	214,640	-27.4	10,804	-41.3
Miami-Dade	2,608	-14.0	53,213	3.9	-18.8	2,867,698	4.7	5,021,323	3.4	225,097	-1.4
Monroe	(NA)	(NA)	411	0.7	-24.3	12,817	0.7	(NA)	(NA)	(NA)	(NA)
Nassau	36	5.9	1,217	4.7	-12.6	119,737	13.1	300,417	0.6	11,548	-64.9
Okaloosa	125	-6.0	4,644	3.7	43.5	261,948	4.9	203,117	21.1	8,951	-23.8
Okeechobee	(NA)	(NA)	264	1.9	15.8	40,418	8.9	(NA)	(NA)	(NA)	(NA)
Orange	827	-7.0	31,954	3.9	-2.4	2,184,886	6.1	4,072,426	19.7	245,387	-42.6
Osceola	83	7.8	1,712	2.0	6.9	95,789	3.5	124,227	-34.9	15,441	8.7
Palm Beach	1,078	2.6	21,394	2.8	-20.0	1,650,634	4.9	1,718,538	-58.2	104,618	-34.6
Pasco	208	-2.3	3,718	3.0	18.4	180,226	4.7	229,564	-13.2	29,106	80.4
Pinellas	1,240	-7.1	40,536	6.8	-9.6	2,392,853	10.5	3,923,790	22.8	188,674	-30.2
Polk	452	-5.8	19,066	7.1	4.3	1,216,476	12.4	2,229,138	-13.8	207,531	8.9
Putnam	38	-20.8	2,669	11.6	-14.8	171,993	21.6	363,832	28.4	34,813	-0.8
St. Johns	92	4.5	3,340	4.9	-5.3	188,198	7.7	172,392	5.3	(D)	(NA)
St. Lucie	146	17.7	3,208	3.3	5.8	136,837	4.6	322,990	41.4	42,186	-2.1
Santa Rosa	62	5.1	1,193	2.5	-0.5	54,076	3.5	108,545	-52.6	12,251	(NA)
Sarasota	386	1.8	9,448	4.2	7.9	506,842	6.1	631,906	33.4	36,485	-3.2
Seminole	431	-0.7	8,518	3.8	-25.7	421,974	4.4	1,316,175	54.5	49,880	-26.5
Sumter	25	-16.7	1,126	5.6	24.4	50,502	7.5	62,949	21.5	3,310	36.8
Suwannee	21	10.5	2,007	13.7	(NA)	65,398	15.6	32,970	(NA)	(D)	(NA)
Taylor	24	20.0	1,670	18.8	0.1	92,436	30.2	227,781	-15.9	13,588	-59.7
Union	(NA)	(NA)	223	4.2	38.5	7,830	4.3	(NA)	(NA)	(NA)	(NA)
Volusia	383	-2.3	10,705	5.0	1.4	501,171	7.2	687,362	0.6	63,634	34.4
Wakulla	(NA)	(NA)	543	6.6	-5.2	32,305	14.5	(NA)	(NA)	(NA)	(NA)
Walton	31	-11.4	625	2.6	-23.7	25,055	3.4	71,348	50.4	1,744	56.6
Washington	9	-35.7	912	10.5	6.4	30,652	12.7	(D)	(NA)	(D)	(NA)
GEORGIA	8,805	-3.1	465,899	9.0	-9.7	26,678,517	11.6	59,651,286	7.4	3,212,978	-22.9
Appling	25	–	788	8.6	-27.8	30,868	10.2	104,612	1.4	2,157	-71.9
Atkinson	14	7.7	809	26.8	-1.5	31,419	32.6	73,648	64.3	739	(NA)
Bacon	12	-14.3	1,035	18.8	-2.6	33,090	23.9	38,312	-40.6	(D)	(NA)
Baker	(NA)	(NA)	(D)	(NA)	(NA)	(D)	(NA)	(NA)	(NA)	(NA)	(NA)
Baldwin	20	–	3,628	14.6	18.1	165,073	21.3	(D)	(NA)	(D)	(NA)
Banks	(NA)	(NA)	1,217	16.0	6.8	40,251	22.9	(NA)	(NA)	(NA)	(NA)
Barrow	58	-9.4	2,361	10.3	1.3	114,756	17.4	173,816	-6.3	29,652	35.2
Bartow	119	-5.6	8,435	17.1	-9.5	490,437	29.8	1,421,853	2.5	64,398	-44.6
Ben Hill	30	-11.8	3,180	29.1	-12.7	157,511	44.7	204,828	-21.3	(D)	(NA)
Berrien	19	11.8	2,012	25.9	20.9	79,475	38.4	79,060	-15.1	4,875	107.9
Bibb	156	-12.8	7,912	7.2	-30.0	572,659	13.5	(D)	(NA)	89,830	-62.3
Bleckley	7	16.7	(D)	(NA)	(NA)	(D)	(NA)	(D)	(NA)	(D)	(NA)
Brantley	(NA)	(NA)	157	4.0	-25.9	5,456	5.8	(NA)	(NA)	(NA)	(NA)
Brooks	13	8.3	513	10.3	-28.8	20,515	15.8	(D)	(NA)	(D)	(NA)
Bryan	(NA)	(NA)	352	3.9	53.7	14,898	5.8	(NA)	(NA)	(NA)	(NA)
Bulloch	51	24.4	2,228	7.4	-10.8	83,553	9.7	182,838	-33.9	18,499	-10.0
Burke	15	-6.3	810	9.3	-45.8	32,945	10.3	80,759	64.0	(D)	(NA)
Butts	15	-16.7	1,067	11.8	10.3	43,604	16.8	160,834	52.9	942	-70.1
Calhoun	(NA)	(NA)	264	11.0	(NA)	6,653	10.7	(NA)	(NA)	(NA)	(NA)
Camden	18	-14.3	728	3.0	-52.2	43,861	4.4	192,728	-18.8	(D)	(NA)

See footnotes at end of table.

[Includes United States, states, and 3,141 counties/county equivalents defined as of February 22, 2005. For more information on these areas, see Appendix C, Geographic Information]

County	Manufacturing (NAICS 31–33)										
	Establishments, 2002[1]		Employment, 2005[2]			Earnings, 2005[2]		Value added by manufactures, 2002[1]		Capital expenditures, 2002[1]	
	Total	Percent change, 1997–2002	Total	Percent of all employ-ees	Percent change, 2001–2005	Total ($1,000)	Percent of all earnings	Total ($1,000)	Percent change, 1997–2002	Total ($1,000)	Percent change, 1997–2002
GEORGIA—Con.											
Candler	(NA)	(NA)	242	4.8	−11.0	10,143	8.1	(NA)	(NA)	(NA)	(NA)
Carroll	123	1.7	7,616	16.4	−4.1	518,749	30.5	738,564	11.3	40,241	−35.9
Catoosa	53	−17.2	2,350	9.5	−9.5	102,800	15.0	203,406	11.6	19,396	−22.1
Charlton	(NA)	(NA)	462	13.2	13.2	17,749	19.1	(NA)	(NA)	(NA)	(NA)
Chatham	189	−8.7	11,979	7.1	−13.6	866,638	12.8	1,863,091	(NA)	(D)	(NA)
Chattahoochee	(NA)	(NA)	[4]5	(NA)	(NA)	52	(Z)	(NA)	(NA)	(NA)	(NA)
Chattooga	22	−4.3	3,541	35.5	−13.1	135,303	46.7	320,027	−31.1	21,552	−37.4
Cherokee	167	9.9	4,846	7.4	19.5	199,411	9.0	267,277	8.1	19,114	4.9
Clarke	98	8.9	8,203	10.1	−14.5	474,475	15.7	603,968	4.6	46,615	−50.8
Clay	(NA)	(NA)	–	–	(NA)	–	–	(NA)	(NA)	(NA)	(NA)
Clayton	148	−11.4	5,862	4.2	−21.3	335,546	5.7	876,343	11.0	34,297	−9.7
Clinch	10	−9.1	843	26.3	12.7	33,266	36.2	101,858	104.8	(D)	(NA)
Cobb	597	−1.2	23,067	5.5	35.3	1,719,686	8.4	3,057,777	42.4	181,907	64.3
Coffee	43	−4.4	4,189	17.6	−22.9	151,149	21.4	282,776	−4.1	27,011	20.8
Colquitt	56	1.8	3,156	15.3	−6.1	96,567	16.9	103,889	−31.2	6,930	−59.2
Columbia	56	−27.3	3,142	7.6	2.4	164,776	13.9	716,558	4.9	13,146	−67.2
Cook	30	−14.3	1,096	16.8	−9.0	42,583	25.2	71,623	−28.6	16,217	32.5
Coweta	84	10.5	4,609	10.5	−12.0	234,481	17.5	530,239	36.0	76,145	64.3
Crawford	(NA)	(NA)	83	2.2	−60.7	1,439	1.9	(NA)	(NA)	(NA)	(NA)
Crisp	26	−3.7	1,356	11.7	−10.4	54,242	16.4	145,019	−21.9	9,553	−5.9
Dade	24	9.1	1,052	17.2	−0.8	42,054	28.8	78,538	66.5	5,313	16.2
Dawson	21	(NA)	687	7.1	49.7	39,212	15.0	55,509	(NA)	10,240	(NA)
Decatur	24	−31.4	1,531	10.4	−46.5	66,846	15.6	220,956	−24.4	11,200	−56.0
DeKalb	588	−15.6	20,181	4.7	−19.0	1,480,731	7.2	4,006,557	47.4	103,697	−35.1
Dodge	(NA)	(NA)	550	6.2	−2.0	22,098	9.8	(NA)	(NA)	(NA)	(NA)
Dooly	9	−25.0	1,344	25.5	−0.9	42,891	27.5	(D)	(NA)	3,595	−33.7
Dougherty	80	−11.1	6,709	10.6	−15.6	462,865	18.1	2,554,112	34.1	211,579	(NA)
Douglas	112	17.9	3,650	7.2	1.1	163,711	11.0	302,349	82.7	17,667	51.3
Early	13	8.3	981	14.7	−30.2	87,631	33.8	356,744	114.9	8,644	(NA)
Echols	(NA)	(NA)	(D)	(NA)	(NA)	(D)	(NA)	(NA)	(NA)	(NA)	(NA)
Effingham	16	45.5	1,840	14.3	1.1	134,594	32.8	474,394	(NA)	(D)	(NA)
Elbert	119	6.3	2,617	25.9	−11.1	100,344	33.1	274,256	32.8	12,444	−40.3
Emanuel	34	−5.6	2,459	22.0	18.7	81,498	28.1	153,492	22.2	9,087	43.1
Evans	14	–	1,894	29.5	−9.2	64,806	36.6	172,159	184.3	4,391	−33.7
Fannin	27	−3.6	(D)	(NA)	(NA)	(D)	(NA)	46,019	−32.2	1,574	−42.4
Fayette	104	22.4	4,196	7.1	−12.8	245,143	12.5	476,570	−22.8	25,469	−37.6
Floyd	119	−0.8	9,484	17.5	3.1	585,524	28.6	735,657	−3.9	64,931	−30.3
Forsyth	169	31.0	8,087	14.9	18.0	464,419	18.8	815,225	147.6	20,920	9.1
Franklin	47	2.2	2,251	17.9	20.2	91,902	24.8	320,078	137.8	9,512	3.6
Fulton	794	−11.5	35,448	3.9	−13.2	3,388,450	5.4	6,126,659	−11.8	234,530	−22.3
Gilmer	31	−8.8	2,892	22.1	−9.7	106,838	28.4	129,857	30.7	2,874	−62.4
Glascock	(NA)	(NA)	10	1.0	(NA)	52	0.2	(NA)	(NA)	(NA)	(NA)
Glynn	68	−4.2	3,128	6.4	−11.4	209,268	12.0	412,139	7.7	36,686	6.7
Gordon	109	6.9	8,994	31.8	−4.9	464,194	46.4	932,129	16.3	38,612	−35.7
Grady	16	−15.8	977	9.4	13.1	35,214	13.6	68,725	−12.7	9,837	26.9
Greene	15	−21.1	522	6.9	−60.3	21,525	10.0	81,177	−17.6	7,237	−50.9
Gwinnett	762	3.4	27,045	7.0	−20.7	1,986,058	10.4	2,350,716	−30.9	144,695	−56.0
Habersham	67	−2.9	4,069	20.0	−7.5	161,637	25.8	270,093	−32.8	13,673	−17.1
Hall	240	6.2	16,637	18.8	−13.7	870,389	25.6	1,777,531	−3.2	170,921	28.0
Hancock	(NA)	(NA)	10	0.4	(NA)	52	0.1	(NA)	(NA)	(NA)	(NA)
Haralson	33	−5.7	1,939	18.7	7.1	88,086	28.4	145,833	−0.9	7,566	15.8
Harris	21	10.5	1,042	10.4	−27.3	26,640	12.9	(D)	(NA)	(D)	(NA)
Hart	29	−19.4	1,982	19.5	−29.1	102,248	33.0	101,444	−62.7	4,273	−82.3
Heard	(NA)	(NA)	(D)	(NA)	(NA)	(D)	(NA)	(NA)	(NA)	(NA)	(NA)
Henry	81	19.1	3,629	5.9	−8.3	184,812	9.3	561,182	39.8	20,956	−25.8
Houston	58	−12.1	4,696	6.5	8.3	211,772	6.5	619,016	(NA)	20,515	(NA)
Irwin	(NA)	(NA)	554	14.4	−4.8	19,646	19.1	(NA)	(NA)	(NA)	(NA)
Jackson	67	3.1	4,280	17.8	−7.9	199,243	23.1	403,792	−2.7	19,788	−59.3
Jasper	25	31.6	1,016	23.5	9.2	43,016	36.5	73,703	46.2	4,458	−30.2
Jeff Davis	25	8.7	1,500	22.6	−19.8	54,007	29.2	173,352	12.2	12,560	15.5
Jefferson	26	−7.1	1,493	19.5	−15.2	59,750	26.9	134,464	114.2	3,669	−54.1
Jenkins	8	100.0	1,228	30.6	1.6	43,536	42.0	53,429	−38.2	(D)	(NA)
Johnson	(NA)	(NA)	402	13.0	−13.9	10,903	12.7	(NA)	(NA)	(NA)	(NA)
Jones	(NA)	(NA)	81	1.4	−6.9	2,334	1.7	(NA)	(NA)	(NA)	(NA)
Lamar	13	–	845	15.5	−32.0	35,242	24.2	38,748	−46.3	2,953	−70.4
Lanier	(NA)	(NA)	90	4.2	(NA)	2,483	5.7	(NA)	(NA)	(NA)	(NA)
Laurens	44	2.3	3,774	14.1	−24.7	185,798	21.4	496,500	29.5	(D)	(NA)
Lee	(NA)	(NA)	233	3.2	194.9	9,186	4.7	(NA)	(NA)	(NA)	(NA)
Liberty	16	14.3	1,118	3.1	−3.3	61,140	3.0	(D)	(NA)	15,352	(NA)
Lincoln	(NA)	(NA)	106	3.7	−7.0	2,402	3.9	(NA)	(NA)	(NA)	(NA)

See footnotes at end of table.

Table B-15. Counties — **Manufacturing**—Con.

[Includes United States, states, and 3,141 counties/county equivalents defined as of February 22, 2005. For more information on these areas, see Appendix C, Geographic Information]

County	Manufacturing (NAICS 31–33)										
	Establishments, 2002[1]		Employment, 2005[2]			Earnings, 2005[2]		Value added by manufactures, 2002[1]		Capital expenditures, 2002[1]	
	Total	Percent change, 1997–2002	Total	Percent of all employees	Percent change, 2001–2005	Total ($1,000)	Percent of all earnings	Total ($1,000)	Percent change, 1997–2002	Total ($1,000)	Percent change, 1997–2002
GEORGIA—Con.											
Long	(NA)	(NA)	32	1.8	(NA)	1,069	3.1	(NA)	(NA)	(NA)	(NA)
Lowndes	104	6.1	5,839	9.3	8.0	247,991	11.7	532,212	15.5	(D)	(NA)
Lumpkin	16	–5.9	1,164	11.3	–5.1	47,672	15.2	49,712	19.2	1,818	–73.5
McDuffie	30	15.4	1,739	16.0	–7.3	76,443	24.2	93,137	11.4	(D)	(NA)
McIntosh	(NA)	(NA)	64	1.6	–3.0	1,362	1.7	(NA)	(NA)	(NA)	(NA)
Macon	15	7.1	1,187	20.0	4.8	60,879	31.3	134,916	30.3	(D)	(NA)
Madison	23	–25.8	701	8.6	36.6	25,121	11.9	43,726	36.2	1,693	–32.3
Marion	5	–	686	24.7	(NA)	20,844	27.8	(D)	(NA)	(D)	(NA)
Meriwether	16	–27.3	912	11.1	–41.0	49,170	20.5	161,538	26.9	10,712	29.1
Miller	(NA)	(NA)	(D)	(NA)	(NA)	(D)	(NA)	(NA)	(NA)	(NA)	(NA)
Mitchell	20	17.6	3,207	28.8	7.3	89,540	30.5	94,751	212.5	2,261	29.4
Monroe	(NA)	(NA)	328	4.3	26.2	10,478	4.3	(NA)	(NA)	(NA)	(NA)
Montgomery	(NA)	(NA)	245	7.9	41.6	7,808	11.0	(NA)	(NA)	(NA)	(NA)
Morgan	26	30.0	1,334	13.6	–8.3	62,090	22.1	113,093	0.3	14,694	32.6
Murray	94	–6.0	6,327	40.1	–10.5	254,046	49.1	300,660	–10.7	12,109	–25.8
Muscogee	141	–10.8	10,346	8.5	–21.0	530,817	11.0	1,213,141	(NA)	(D)	(NA)
Newton	85	37.1	4,900	19.2	5.0	294,195	30.6	1,363,200	80.1	69,533	65.0
Oconee	31	3.3	757	6.4	5.3	35,694	9.9	82,678	5.5	2,945	–19.6
Oglethorpe	(NA)	(NA)	182	5.8	34.8	4,546	5.4	(NA)	(NA)	(NA)	(NA)
Paulding	48	26.3	1,186	3.6	25.2	50,778	6.3	93,799	24.7	2,814	–10.5
Peach	28	–12.5	1,741	17.1	55.4	99,103	28.8	110,407	(NA)	7,765	(NA)
Pickens	35	–	814	7.7	–10.0	38,836	11.6	69,577	–6.2	5,048	–32.3
Pierce	(NA)	(NA)	420	6.1	–4.3	14,840	8.8	(NA)	(NA)	(NA)	(NA)
Pike	(NA)	(NA)	524	10.7	28.7	20,185	17.1	(NA)	(NA)	(NA)	(NA)
Polk	37	5.7	3,292	20.3	11.7	144,540	29.9	258,971	18.7	13,464	31.5
Pulaski	(NA)	(NA)	(D)	(NA)	(NA)	(D)	(NA)	(NA)	(NA)	(NA)	(NA)
Putnam	26	8.3	1,340	13.5	–24.1	52,451	17.6	111,455	–23.0	2,654	–36.1
Quitman	(NA)	(NA)	(D)	(NA)	(NA)	(D)	(NA)	(NA)	(NA)	(NA)	(NA)
Rabun	29	7.4	1,597	17.7	–5.1	59,168	24.4	147,702	9.2	5,741	–61.4
Randolph	(NA)	(NA)	244	6.9	–43.4	9,156	9.9	(NA)	(NA)	(NA)	(NA)
Richmond	144	7.5	10,220	7.5	–16.8	629,840	11.0	2,106,998	–7.0	169,309	44.1
Rockdale	97	–16.4	5,584	12.7	–12.9	314,875	20.0	740,767	–0.4	39,434	–0.6
Schley	9	–	735	40.0	8.1	29,764	50.1	83,912	69.9	(D)	(NA)
Screven	17	30.8	1,001	17.0	5.8	38,290	25.3	59,825	–21.6	8,039	189.2
Seminole	(NA)	(NA)	(D)	(NA)	(NA)	(D)	(NA)	(NA)	(NA)	(NA)	(NA)
Spalding	64	–8.6	4,457	14.2	–7.1	219,804	21.2	653,759	27.6	26,850	–27.6
Stephens	57	–10.9	2,426	18.8	–31.7	106,008	25.8	238,648	–9.2	14,916	12.2
Stewart	(NA)	(NA)	79	5.1	(NA)	1,721	4.9	(NA)	(NA)	(NA)	(NA)
Sumter	34	–10.5	2,422	14.1	–19.6	102,938	18.7	311,183	68.2	(D)	(NA)
Talbot	(NA)	(NA)	10	0.6	(NA)	52	0.1	(NA)	(NA)	(NA)	(NA)
Taliaferro	(NA)	(NA)	31	5.9	(NA)	716	8.2	(NA)	(NA)	(NA)	(NA)
Tattnall	(NA)	(NA)	127	1.4	21.0	3,087	1.1	(NA)	(NA)	(NA)	(NA)
Taylor	(NA)	(NA)	153	5.1	–0.6	5,000	5.4	(NA)	(NA)	(NA)	(NA)
Telfair	11	–21.4	(D)	(NA)	(NA)	(D)	(NA)	(D)	(NA)	(D)	(NA)
Terrell	(NA)	(NA)	486	13.2	–20.8	15,292	15.0	(NA)	(NA)	(NA)	(NA)
Thomas	59	–18.1	3,840	13.5	–7.0	208,564	21.1	239,922	–43.0	18,191	–20.1
Tift	57	11.8	3,036	11.6	–16.1	125,383	14.7	271,607	33.1	7,134	–47.9
Toombs	34	–10.5	1,984	12.9	11.0	58,572	14.5	74,710	–6.5	4,530	–18.9
Towns	(NA)	(NA)	235	4.0	128.2	4,698	3.8	(NA)	(NA)	(NA)	(NA)
Treutlen	(NA)	(NA)	(D)	(NA)	(NA)	(D)	(NA)	(NA)	(NA)	(NA)	(NA)
Troup	100	–1.0	7,315	18.9	–30.9	392,048	27.6	899,387	26.3	80,323	5.1
Turner	(NA)	(NA)	385	9.5	–1.3	11,079	10.9	(NA)	(NA)	(NA)	(NA)
Twiggs	(NA)	(NA)	44	1.7	22.2	1,281	1.8	(NA)	(NA)	(NA)	(NA)
Union	(NA)	(NA)	305	3.1	–29.1	10,663	4.3	(NA)	(NA)	(NA)	(NA)
Upson	23	–11.5	1,846	16.9	–34.3	80,906	25.7	222,421	–11.5	11,204	–22.8
Walker	71	–7.8	5,343	26.6	–9.4	235,639	38.2	538,472	–6.5	35,253	–48.9
Walton	49	–10.9	2,573	10.8	5.0	129,649	16.0	218,962	15.2	15,920	0.3
Ware	35	–16.7	1,764	8.4	2.7	59,395	9.5	89,830	–29.0	(D)	(NA)
Warren	5	–16.7	578	27.4	–27.3	22,267	39.2	28,237	–54.6	(D)	(NA)
Washington	(NA)	(NA)	544	5.1	5.8	26,852	7.2	(NA)	(NA)	(NA)	(NA)
Wayne	25	8.7	1,781	14.3	–8.8	116,437	28.3	278,291	16.5	(D)	(NA)
Webster	(NA)	(NA)	(D)	(NA)	(NA)	(D)	(NA)	(NA)	(NA)	(NA)	(NA)
Wheeler	(NA)	(NA)	–	–	(NA)	–	–	(NA)	(NA)	(NA)	(NA)
White	31	10.7	900	8.3	–9.1	37,253	13.4	58,134	–34.1	3,520	–40.9
Whitfield	354	–6.6	25,558	34.9	0.3	1,277,433	42.6	2,563,777	4.9	73,507	–15.4
Wilcox	(NA)	(NA)	47	1.8	–54.4	808	1.1	(NA)	(NA)	(NA)	(NA)
Wilkes	21	–8.7	892	17.9	–20.1	30,665	22.5	78,526	–40.1	4,622	–54.2
Wilkinson	13	–7.1	243	6.5	1.7	10,824	7.6	275,823	–1.3	(D)	(NA)
Worth	(NA)	(NA)	383	6.1	23.5	13,001	8.6	(NA)	(NA)	(NA)	(NA)

See footnotes at end of table.

[Includes United States, states, and 3,141 counties/county equivalents defined as of February 22, 2005. For more information on these areas, see Appendix C, Geographic Information]

County	Establishments, 2002[1]		Employment, 2005[2]			Earnings, 2005[2]		Value added by manufactures, 2002[1]		Capital expenditures, 2002[1]	
	Total	Percent change, 1997–2002	Total	Percent of all employees	Percent change, 2001–2005	Total ($1,000)	Percent of all earnings	Total ($1,000)	Percent change, 1997–2002	Total ($1,000)	Percent change, 1997–2002
HAWAII	929	0.9	18,941	2.3	−3.2	904,754	2.6	1,217,728	−3.5	82,960	−17.6
Hawaii	114	7.5	(D)	(NA)	(NA)	(D)	(NA)	97,719	20.3	6,371	−55.2
Honolulu	683	−0.3	13,966	2.3	−2.6	629,366	2.3	948,546	−9.0	59,572	−23.3
Kalawao	(NA)	(NA)	−	−	−	−	−	(NA)	(NA)	(NA)	(NA)
Kauai	(NA)	(NA)	(D)	(NA)	(NA)	(D)	(NA)	(NA)	(NA)	(NA)	(NA)
Maui	93	−7.0	2,212	2.3	−18.4	173,870	5.0	157,060	27.3	16,574	312.3
IDAHO	1,814	10.1	68,151	7.8	−6.5	3,912,923	13.0	7,440,111	16.4	1,243,409	49.0
Ada	405	2.5	22,762	8.8	−7.7	1,933,512	16.8	3,437,063	53.3	(D)	(NA)
Adams	(NA)	(NA)	(D)	(NA)	(NA)	(D)	(NA)	(NA)	(NA)	(NA)	(NA)
Bannock	72	16.1	2,502	5.3	−10.0	151,638	10.5	(D)	(NA)	(D)	(NA)
Bear Lake	(NA)	(NA)	93	3.1	−7.0	1,937	3.1	(NA)	(NA)	(NA)	(NA)
Benewah	9	12.5	666	12.8	0.6	32,148	20.0	40,682	−6.9	(D)	(NA)
Bingham	48	9.1	2,227	10.7	−8.6	100,260	16.7	228,967	22.0	36,673	−9.3
Blaine	(NA)	(NA)	625	3.0	21.8	33,691	4.6	(NA)	(NA)	(NA)	(NA)
Boise	(NA)	(NA)	80	3.0	48.1	2,253	3.6	(NA)	(NA)	(NA)	(NA)
Bonner	89	3.5	2,486	10.6	45.1	92,878	14.8	135,838	7.2	9,250	−16.1
Bonneville	120	4.3	2,796	4.5	9.0	101,350	4.6	246,476	81.2	(D)	(NA)
Boundary	(NA)	(NA)	468	8.9	−5.3	17,021	12.7	(NA)	(NA)	(NA)	(NA)
Butte	(NA)	(NA)	41	0.8	(NA)	626	0.2	(NA)	(NA)	(NA)	(NA)
Camas	(NA)	(NA)	14	2.0	(NA)	150	1.0	(NA)	(NA)	(NA)	(NA)
Canyon	201	14.2	8,858	11.9	−17.4	375,485	17.5	751,995	−34.3	(D)	(NA)
Caribou	10	42.9	709	14.9	−13.7	68,593	39.6	(D)	(NA)	(D)	(NA)
Cassia	30	25.0	935	7.3	−20.6	41,329	10.5	(D)	(NA)	(D)	(NA)
Clark	(NA)	(NA)	(D)	(NA)	(NA)	(D)	(NA)	(NA)	(NA)	(NA)	(NA)
Clearwater	(NA)	(NA)	332	6.7	9.6	9,645	7.3	(NA)	(NA)	(NA)	(NA)
Custer	(NA)	(NA)	48	1.8	(NA)	596	0.8	(NA)	(NA)	(NA)	(NA)
Elmore	(NA)	(NA)	313	2.2	−33.7	6,987	1.2	(NA)	(NA)	(NA)	(NA)
Franklin	(NA)	(NA)	251	4.6	−7.7	12,773	9.2	(NA)	(NA)	(NA)	(NA)
Fremont	(NA)	(NA)	123	2.4	7.9	1,603	1.3	(NA)	(NA)	(NA)	(NA)
Gem	(NA)	(NA)	174	2.8	−47.7	4,285	3.7	(NA)	(NA)	(NA)	(NA)
Gooding	(NA)	(NA)	766	9.2	11.0	31,839	9.8	(NA)	(NA)	(NA)	(NA)
Idaho	31	(NA)	585	7.1	−2.3	26,267	13.9	38,992	(NA)	1,588	(NA)
Jefferson	31	82.4	983	10.3	34.3	36,927	16.8	52,587	−7.9	(D)	(NA)
Jerome	28	47.4	1,155	10.6	7.4	39,768	9.7	162,376	114.2	21,937	(NA)
Kootenai	218	11.8	4,665	6.5	8.2	207,212	9.3	274,972	−0.2	13,362	−24.7
Latah	(NA)	(NA)	531	2.5	13.0	21,936	3.7	(NA)	(NA)	(NA)	(NA)
Lemhi	(NA)	(NA)	205	4.4	−1.0	6,109	6.1	(NA)	(NA)	(NA)	(NA)
Lewis	(NA)	(NA)	136	6.3	8.8	4,679	9.0	(NA)	(NA)	(NA)	(NA)
Lincoln	(NA)	(NA)	(D)	(NA)	(NA)	(D)	(NA)	(NA)	(NA)	(NA)	(NA)
Madison	27	28.6	1,089	6.5	−7.2	37,051	8.5	198,219	132.0	7,777	55.8
Minidoka	26	44.4	1,113	11.1	−41.4	51,949	20.2	(D)	(NA)	(D)	(NA)
Nez Perce	45	−18.2	2,559	9.7	−11.1	145,051	15.9	(D)	(NA)	(D)	(NA)
Oneida	(NA)	(NA)	32	1.6	(NA)	793	2.4	(NA)	(NA)	(NA)	(NA)
Owyhee	(NA)	(NA)	185	4.3	19.4	6,198	5.2	(NA)	(NA)	(NA)	(NA)
Payette	23	−4.2	1,400	15.1	−2.4	65,359	24.5	(D)	(NA)	(D)	(NA)
Power	7	−12.5	1,013	23.2	−35.3	53,507	39.1	(D)	(NA)	(D)	(NA)
Shoshone	(NA)	(NA)	298	4.9	10.4	9,257	5.0	(NA)	(NA)	(NA)	(NA)
Teton	(NA)	(NA)	164	4.4	(NA)	5,202	5.8	(NA)	(NA)	(NA)	(NA)
Twin Falls	102	7.4	3,503	7.7	−4.2	137,309	10.3	307,077	7.2	13,086	−21.2
Valley	(NA)	(NA)	141	2.1	−32.9	2,509	1.4	(NA)	(NA)	(NA)	(NA)
Washington	(NA)	(NA)	676	13.6	19.9	21,157	18.5	(NA)	(NA)	(NA)	(NA)
ILLINOIS	16,860	−6.1	710,010	9.6	−14.9	50,284,578	13.7	91,825,126	−3.6	5,960,080	−19.2
Adams	91	7.1	5,568	12.4	−4.7	319,160	21.8	(D)	(NA)	(D)	(NA)
Alexander	(NA)	(NA)	169	5.9	−27.2	7,046	8.9	(NA)	(NA)	(NA)	(NA)
Bond	11	−31.3	760	10.1	−4.2	34,986	16.0	65,564	−17.0	(D)	(NA)
Boone	65	3.2	3,757	19.9	−21.7	336,047	42.6	631,473	26.2	(D)	(NA)
Brown	(NA)	(NA)	(D)	(NA)	(NA)	(D)	(NA)	(NA)	(NA)	(NA)	(NA)
Bureau	48	17.1	1,763	9.3	−26.6	100,329	17.6	262,369	9.4	(D)	(NA)
Calhoun	(NA)	(NA)	(D)	(NA)	(NA)	(D)	(NA)	(NA)	(NA)	(NA)	(NA)
Carroll	27	−18.2	923	11.9	−15.7	47,041	23.7	144,565	7.4	8,080	28.6
Cass	11	−15.4	2,437	28.6	10.7	91,846	37.2	(D)	(NA)	(D)	(NA)
Champaign	151	−0.7	9,760	7.7	−7.5	480,649	10.4	1,495,778	28.3	95,625	29.0
Christian	24	−20.0	1,849	11.0	20.3	79,490	17.5	192,861	35.0	6,771	−74.0
Clark	20	−16.7	1,756	21.5	−7.7	76,530	34.8	155,051	−17.9	11,770	−8.6
Clay	20	−13.0	2,145	24.9	−7.7	107,439	41.3	182,167	−17.4	16,317	−17.5
Clinton	44	12.8	1,304	7.0	−7.1	46,723	9.3	120,730	11.7	5,233	169.9
Coles	48	−15.8	3,290	9.4	−3.8	166,189	16.0	(D)	(NA)	(D)	(NA)
Cook	6,937	−12.9	262,095	8.0	−20.2	19,514,454	10.2	33,292,244	−12.7	1,947,998	−27.3
Crawford	19	−5.0	2,284	21.5	−5.1	158,365	41.9	520,591	51.6	(D)	(NA)
Cumberland	(NA)	(NA)	377	7.9	29.1	12,464	12.1	(NA)	(NA)	(NA)	(NA)
DeKalb	139	1.5	4,547	8.9	−22.7	244,807	14.4	596,251	−31.9	32,745	−12.7
De Witt	12	−20.0	593	7.6	−36.0	32,785	12.6	79,009	−43.2	1,799	−64.9

See footnotes at end of table.

Table B-15. Counties — **Manufacturing**—Con.

[Includes United States, states, and 3,141 counties/county equivalents defined as of February 22, 2005. For more information on these areas, see Appendix C, Geographic Information]

County	Establishments, 2002[1]		Employment, 2005[2]			Earnings, 2005[2]		Value added by manufactures, 2002[1]		Capital expenditures, 2002[1]	
	Total	Percent change, 1997–2002	Total	Percent of all employees	Percent change, 2001–2005	Total ($1,000)	Percent of all earnings	Total ($1,000)	Percent change, 1997–2002	Total ($1,000)	Percent change, 1997–2002
ILLINOIS—Con.											
Douglas	89	36.9	3,350	27.2	−8.5	162,505	44.0	252,208	4.7	16,995	−0.5
DuPage	1,985	−2.4	60,917	8.5	−17.2	4,731,836	11.7	7,707,637	16.2	438,876	1.6
Edgar	27	−	1,931	20.1	11.4	83,413	31.3	137,197	36.4	16,607	73.1
Edwards	6	−25.0	(D)	(NA)	(NA)	(D)	(NA)	(D)	(NA)	(D)	(NA)
Effingham	68	15.3	3,950	15.2	−5.1	182,590	22.1	564,109	48.7	54,214	57.3
Fayette	19	−13.6	965	9.4	−15.1	40,056	15.7	84,286	−43.1	13,565	36.4
Ford	20	−9.1	856	10.7	1.9	35,458	17.5	(D)	(NA)	2,544	−49.1
Franklin	37	−14.0	1,400	9.2	−13.5	72,756	17.9	120,579	40.8	6,048	24.6
Fulton	(NA)	(NA)	279	2.0	3.3	9,104	2.7	(NA)	(NA)	(NA)	(NA)
Gallatin	(NA)	(NA)	15	0.6	−79.5	139	0.3	(NA)	(NA)	(NA)	(NA)
Greene	(NA)	(NA)	276	4.7	−3.2	11,605	9.3	(NA)	(NA)	(NA)	(NA)
Grundy	45	36.4	1,706	7.9	5.0	130,987	13.9	566,152	47.2	12,499	−43.0
Hamilton	(NA)	(NA)	106	3.1	19.1	2,817	3.5	(NA)	(NA)	5,440	−36.0
Hancock	26	−7.1	1,300	13.7	−29.3	52,370	24.2	100,266	−16.7	(NA)	(NA)
Hardin	(NA)	(NA)	(D)	(NA)	(NA)	(D)	(NA)	(NA)	(NA)	(NA)	(NA)
Henderson	(NA)	(NA)	(D)	(NA)	(NA)	(D)	(NA)	(NA)	(NA)	(NA)	(NA)
Henry	52	−1.9	1,794	7.7	−8.4	72,569	12.3	330,740	57.5	6,694	4.0
Iroquois	28	−6.7	1,042	6.9	−22.4	29,901	8.9	70,369	−34.9	(D)	(NA)
Jackson	35	−	1,047	2.7	−13.8	40,707	3.3	75,255	22.2	2,979	−21.1
Jasper	(NA)	(NA)	284	6.2	−25.7	8,287	6.6	(NA)	(NA)	(NA)	(NA)
Jefferson	42	−4.5	3,002	12.0	5.0	188,829	21.1	(D)	(NA)	(D)	(NA)
Jersey	(NA)	(NA)	122	1.4	−29.1	4,508	2.3	(NA)	(NA)	(NA)	(NA)
Jo Daviess	43	30.3	1,334	9.8	−35.2	61,067	16.7	156,389	−1.4	6,707	−64.3
Johnson	(NA)	(NA)	80	1.8	(NA)	1,520	1.4	(NA)	(NA)	(NA)	(NA)
Kane	908	3.5	36,185	13.8	−6.1	2,271,030	20.2	4,240,714	−2.7	240,052	−20.1
Kankakee	116	−	4,884	9.1	−24.2	327,488	17.8	967,841	5.8	(D)	(NA)
Kendall	73	10.6	4,045	15.2	−11.4	317,458	30.6	300,841	31.4	18,002	59.3
Knox	44	−21.4	1,381	5.0	−71.8	76,754	8.8	338,378	−8.7	14,964	−35.1
Lake	928	−4.2	52,712	12.0	−6.2	5,328,439	21.6	8,552,279	16.2	691,713	−27.7
LaSalle	150	−1.3	6,982	12.0	6.8	394,145	19.6	837,138	6.0	90,118	4.6
Lawrence	15	(NA)	797	11.6	14.3	37,490	18.6	(D)	(NA)	23,022	26.7
Lee	37	5.7	3,159	17.0	−4.4	170,187	27.4	425,582	5.1	54,761	11.3
Livingston	55	7.8	2,839	13.9	−16.9	193,562	27.2	613,722	14.3	8,947	−28.5
Logan	24	−	1,659	11.9	1.8	82,278	20.2	198,922	16.6	5,426	−60.4
McDonough	30	−	1,266	7.0	−22.3	56,376	10.7	102,313	−27.0		
McHenry	592	1.5	19,731	15.7	−8.9	1,131,347	22.7	2,092,055	6.4	131,922	−16.5
McLean	113	0.9	6,630	6.1	−8.2	431,940	9.1	1,039,530	6.6	(D)	(NA)
Macon	126	−6.0	11,300	16.8	−12.2	930,244	31.4	1,760,168	−19.4	144,881	−25.1
Macoupin	44	25.7	944	5.0	−18.0	61,493	11.8	67,240	2.8	5,760	93.0
Madison	212	−5.4	14,575	11.6	−27.2	1,044,271	22.2	2,215,881	−20.9	145,606	−33.2
Marion	57	−12.3	2,857	15.7	−28.1	135,278	22.9	443,355	0.8	15,115	−50.0
Marshall	18	−	1,290	22.0	16.8	64,120	42.9	106,808	11.9	5,237	−23.9
Mason	(NA)	(NA)	193	3.2	−65.4	7,691	5.8	(NA)	(NA)	(NA)	(NA)
Massac	9	−25.0	570	8.6	−13.1	43,755	19.0	104,930	−21.1	14,280	92.9
Menard	(NA)	(NA)	42	1.0	23.5	796	0.8	(NA)	(NA)	(NA)	(NA)
Mercer	(NA)	(NA)	442	7.2	14.5	15,941	11.9	(NA)	(NA)	(NA)	(NA)
Monroe	(NA)	(NA)	521	4.1	38.9	22,666	6.4	(NA)	(NA)	(NA)	(NA)
Montgomery	37	−	1,293	8.8	−4.1	57,954	13.4	122,283	3.9	3,646	−68.5
Morgan	27	−25.0	2,810	14.2	−22.4	141,759	23.3	(D)	(NA)	(D)	(NA)
Moultrie	21	5.0	1,188	17.6	10.1	63,653	32.5	167,236	105.4	8,911	39.0
Ogle	71	1.4	4,672	18.9	−10.4	227,845	26.2	399,771	−5.8	41,943	91.2
Peoria	170	−4.0	11,361	9.2	−12.0	898,777	16.2	1,549,477	−24.0	110,069	−26.5
Perry	27	22.7	1,451	15.7	−13.6	70,399	26.9	132,812	10.8	(D)	(NA)
Piatt	(NA)	(NA)	386	6.3	−33.1	18,519	12.4	(NA)	(NA)	(NA)	(NA)
Pike	(NA)	(NA)	144	1.9	−32.1	4,365	2.4	(NA)	(NA)	(NA)	(NA)
Pope	(NA)	(NA)	52	4.0	(NA)	1,421	4.3	(NA)	(NA)	(NA)	(NA)
Pulaski	(NA)	(NA)	163	5.6	17.3	6,831	8.8	(NA)	(NA)	(NA)	(NA)
Putnam	(NA)	(NA)	628	21.6	−28.1	42,085	41.5	(NA)	(NA)	(NA)	(NA)
Randolph	31	−3.1	3,340	22.1	−1.9	133,232	24.9	203,894	23.4	(D)	(NA)
Richland	39	14.7	810	8.8	−2.4	31,513	12.1	89,912	−11.0	2,534	−46.0
Rock Island	169	−14.2	11,098	11.5	−8.2	690,315	15.4	1,325,275	−30.7	48,010	−59.4
St. Clair	204	3.0	6,643	5.2	−5.6	378,816	7.5	795,578	32.0	60,335	35.6
Saline	(NA)	(NA)	579	4.4	37.2	18,845	4.3	(NA)	(NA)	(NA)	(NA)
Sangamon	130	−3.0	3,511	2.6	−11.5	179,488	3.2	(D)	(NA)	(D)	(NA)
Schuyler	(NA)	(NA)	121	3.5	−9.0	3,322	3.1	(NA)	(NA)	(NA)	(NA)
Scott	(NA)	(NA)	(D)	(NA)	(NA)	(D)	(NA)	(NA)	(NA)	(NA)	(NA)
Shelby	15	7.1	1,194	13.1	−16.2	46,675	20.5	128,565	24.1	5,935	(NA)
Stark	(NA)	(NA)	158	6.6	7.5	7,297	13.5	(NA)	(NA)	(NA)	(NA)
Stephenson	65	4.8	5,046	18.0	−18.1	302,083	31.1	515,051	−20.4	15,692	−67.1
Tazewell	124	5.1	15,550	20.9	0.5	1,641,898	46.5	856,974	−26.2	83,739	43.3

See footnotes at end of table.

[Includes United States, states, and 3,141 counties/county equivalents defined as of February 22, 2005. For more information on these areas, see Appendix C, Geographic Information]

County	Establishments, 2002[1] Total	Percent change, 1997–2002	Employment, 2005[2] Total	Percent of all employees	Percent change, 2001–2005	Earnings, 2005[2] Total ($1,000)	Percent of all earnings	Value added by manufactures, 2002[1] Total ($1,000)	Percent change, 1997–2002	Capital expenditures, 2002[1] Total ($1,000)	Percent change, 1997–2002
ILLINOIS—Con.											
Union	(NA)	(NA)	606	7.8	2.9	28,569	13.6	(NA)	(NA)	(NA)	(NA)
Vermilion	108	3.8	6,214	15.1	-3.0	332,677	23.4	587,220	-10.7	38,464	-43.3
Wabash	16	6.7	264	4.5	-59.5	15,500	9.4	47,393	16.7	2,837	23.6
Warren	26	36.8	1,649	19.1	-0.5	70,957	31.9	47,303	(NA)	2,695	41.2
Washington	16	–	1,495	17.8	-9.4	94,669	33.7	223,633	114.5	9,861	-38.2
Wayne	16	-20.0	1,027	13.2	-9.0	47,957	21.7	(D)	(NA)	(D)	(NA)
White	(NA)	(NA)	290	3.7	-9.1	10,565	4.9	(NA)	(NA)	(NA)	(NA)
Whiteside	100	-2.0	4,597	15.9	-25.8	262,096	28.7	415,400	-24.1	28,083	-26.8
Will	593	12.5	19,450	8.8	2.9	1,347,271	14.6	3,774,946	17.6	308,712	0.1
Williamson	50	-2.0	3,011	8.9	1.9	151,458	13.4	206,176	27.5	35,291	366.1
Winnebago	720	-7.6	28,870	16.8	-17.6	1,850,310	27.6	3,864,987	1.9	(D)	(NA)
Woodford	47	-14.5	2,295	13.2	-19.4	96,348	19.7	386,249	-4.9	6,864	-70.7
INDIANA	9,223	-0.9	585,556	15.9	-6.7	39,292,654	26.3	78,023,817	16.1	5,617,894	1.2
Adams	68	1.5	6,547	28.2	8.1	313,358	48.0	742,573	53.0	33,106	4.4
Allen	551	-4.3	30,950	13.6	-7.7	1,971,599	21.0	5,174,437	37.5	152,019	-34.2
Bartholomew	136	-6.2	15,067	28.7	-6.2	1,102,342	47.1	1,522,537	15.2	76,056	-38.3
Benton	16	–	573	12.5	-11.8	21,460	20.5	29,213	-2.0	1,071	-2.6
Blackford	28	–	1,698	27.9	-9.9	76,324	44.6	146,170	2.1	6,353	-43.6
Boone	85	16.4	2,498	8.4	14.4	124,296	11.5	197,119	82.4	11,201	141.3
Brown	(NA)	(NA)	348	4.9	10.8	10,815	8.1	(NA)	(NA)	(NA)	(NA)
Carroll	32	-3.0	2,079	19.2	-13.8	84,522	33.1	140,515	16.7	2,146	-27.1
Cass	47	-21.7	5,050	24.5	-18.8	214,724	32.8	444,426	22.7	17,050	-41.7
Clark	173	6.1	7,808	13.3	0.3	408,915	19.7	(D)	(NA)	55,787	4.1
Clay	31	-8.8	2,615	20.6	46.4	112,896	35.1	128,523	(NA)	6,894	(NA)
Clinton	50	2.0	4,567	30.1	-2.1	235,894	45.5	1,052,397	56.5	35,309	-16.5
Crawford	(NA)	(NA)	522	12.1	(NA)	20,008	19.4	(NA)	(NA)	(NA)	(NA)
Daviess	58	13.7	2,408	14.2	6.1	89,709	19.4	142,280	19.9	13,080	76.1
Dearborn	40	2.6	2,054	8.9	-6.0	136,114	18.4	(D)	(NA)	(D)	(NA)
Decatur	54	3.8	5,136	31.2	-12.0	260,395	47.6	709,465	58.1	(D)	(NA)
DeKalb	115	-3.4	10,015	34.7	-8.4	591,044	54.0	1,415,209	44.0	59,935	-11.6
Delaware	162	-8.0	6,451	10.2	-25.1	412,824	17.9	777,890	-11.9	42,521	-37.5
Dubois	113	-0.9	12,246	35.0	-8.2	570,196	42.4	1,084,555	33.0	(D)	(NA)
Elkhart	906	1.3	65,527	42.2	14.6	3,717,423	55.9	4,607,324	19.3	200,169	-6.9
Fayette	32	-11.1	3,023	24.5	-23.0	215,487	48.3	55,957	-91.9	26,733	(NA)
Floyd	119	-11.9	6,536	16.3	-9.5	360,751	25.7	764,387	14.4	38,058	-31.7
Fountain	23	4.5	2,527	30.0	1.0	119,019	48.8	205,719	32.1	4,808	-84.8
Franklin	19	–	422	5.8	-7.0	20,789	12.2	(D)	(NA)	(D)	(NA)
Fulton	55	5.8	2,563	23.5	-0.1	124,641	38.4	232,770	21.8	8,128	-33.4
Gibson	45	7.1	6,679	31.8	51.5	583,725	57.6	(D)	(NA)	(D)	(NA)
Grant	79	-1.3	5,526	15.5	-32.2	403,520	31.8	736,785	(Z)	52,242	-47.9
Greene	26	–	385	3.1	-35.0	10,805	3.3	(D)	(NA)	620	-73.5
Hamilton	200	4.7	6,642	4.5	5.8	426,607	6.9	568,049	15.6	28,591	0.3
Hancock	70	6.1	2,917	8.3	6.3	179,619	16.9	359,070	31.3	36,565	-30.6
Harrison	47	23.7	1,991	11.6	-33.2	84,124	18.1	(D)	(NA)	26,964	187.2
Hendricks	91	13.8	2,485	4.0	28.0	186,324	9.3	240,756	122.3	41,745	210.7
Henry	45	-21.1	2,666	13.1	-23.7	166,064	26.8	323,514	8.8	(D)	(NA)
Howard	79	-1.3	14,986	28.5	-12.7	1,696,678	60.8	(D)	(NA)	(D)	(NA)
Huntington	72	-7.7	4,765	23.0	-11.3	231,177	36.3	618,226	-5.3	22,741	-42.8
Jackson	83	-7.8	6,940	26.3	-5.5	411,045	41.7	914,514	68.0	57,100	23.3
Jasper	41	24.2	1,546	9.2	–	77,582	15.4	162,061	20.6	23,797	44.1
Jay	37	-5.1	3,013	26.8	-9.0	138,959	41.8	261,594	10.7	12,713	-61.7
Jefferson	54	5.9	3,826	20.5	7.2	217,974	35.0	344,682	33.9	24,560	-19.1
Jennings	44	4.8	2,328	20.3	-0.8	94,916	26.9	166,445	14.5	(D)	(NA)
Johnson	138	9.5	5,576	8.7	-20.4	287,984	15.1	547,476	3.1	68,925	-15.3
Knox	40	-9.1	1,848	8.5	20.7	79,675	11.3	158,514	29.4	9,060	-44.5
Kosciusko	193	3.8	16,106	34.8	4.7	1,096,312	56.9	3,123,359	82.0	166,046	54.7
LaGrange	111	44.2	6,600	35.9	11.0	384,816	59.5	529,728	42.5	17,110	-10.7
Lake	412	-2.6	26,831	11.0	-16.8	2,190,837	21.8	4,524,870	-24.3	204,612	-67.6
LaPorte	195	3.2	9,624	16.2	-9.9	511,572	25.0	924,395	-13.3	33,428	-57.2
Lawrence	68	-9.3	3,828	18.3	-16.6	232,772	35.2	435,850	-2.9	37,763	-3.8
Madison	130	-2.3	6,699	11.9	-31.9	671,388	30.9	874,696	-5.5	41,334	-48.1
Marion	1,074	-10.1	72,587	10.7	-7.9	6,957,494	19.1	13,631,065	13.9	610,660	1.7
Marshall	126	-11.9	6,897	27.6	-9.1	306,375	39.0	550,777	-23.3	27,835	-45.5
Martin	14	55.6	546	6.9	-5.7	26,785	5.2	71,221	23.0	(D)	(NA)
Miami	57	14.0	2,994	19.4	-5.7	128,586	26.1	276,874	21.2	9,159	35.6
Monroe	123	0.8	7,505	9.1	-7.9	398,345	13.6	647,366	-40.8	104,911	136.2
Montgomery	62	-7.5	6,168	27.8	-8.2	388,833	48.2	960,177	7.8	177,286	110.6
Morgan	73	12.3	2,402	11.2	-2.2	131,641	20.2	265,189	5.2	13,267	-6.0
Newton	26	-10.3	1,321	23.7	-1.8	50,771	31.1	83,694	-5.8	4,469	-36.0
Noble	145	1.4	10,274	38.5	-9.3	526,760	58.7	935,096	7.0	67,111	-1.0
Ohio	(NA)	(NA)	(D)	(NA)	(NA)	(D)	(NA)	(NA)	(NA)	(NA)	(NA)
Orange	27	-20.6	1,475	17.2	-24.1	61,577	24.5	103,891	-24.6	5,526	-34.0
Owen	29	20.8	1,771	23.7	17.8	81,942	39.9	(D)	(NA)	2,689	-61.4

See footnotes at end of table.

Table B-15. Counties — **Manufacturing**—Con.

[Includes United States, states, and 3,141 counties/county equivalents defined as of February 22, 2005. For more information on these areas, see Appendix C, Geographic Information]

County	Establishments, 2002[1]		Employment, 2005[2]			Earnings, 2005[2]		Value added by manufactures, 2002[1]		Capital expenditures, 2002[1]	
	Total	Percent change, 1997–2002	Total	Percent of all employees	Percent change, 2001–2005	Total ($1,000)	Percent of all earnings	Total ($1,000)	Percent change, 1997–2002	Total ($1,000)	Percent change, 1997–2002
INDIANA—Con.											
Parke	18	5.9	497	8.6	-25.7	17,223	12.4	43,815	5.1	3,688	-15.4
Perry	28	3.7	1,957	22.0	17.6	121,045	39.9	182,346	135.2	10,364	176.2
Pike	(NA)	(NA)	138	3.2	-27.0	6,117	3.9	(NA)	(NA)	(NA)	(NA)
Porter	152	4.1	9,182	12.6	-16.8	788,405	27.8	1,657,586	-3.3	90,423	-67.3
Posey	32	3.2	2,982	22.9	-3.7	286,584	50.5	1,266,749	(NA)	(D)	(NA)
Pulaski	19	-5.0	1,426	20.0	12.3	102,466	42.1	136,942	73.5	(D)	(NA)
Putnam	28	12.0	2,595	15.4	-13.9	144,953	27.4	237,753	26.9	55,943	140.7
Randolph	62	14.8	2,236	20.3	-26.7	109,240	32.5	302,701	55.4	13,500	61.6
Ripley	40	14.3	3,113	18.2	-16.3	170,741	26.6	744,221	31.1	13,268	(NA)
Rush	31	-3.1	1,414	17.3	-20.2	77,837	30.3	176,884	-6.4	(D)	(NA)
St. Joseph	452	-1.1	18,845	11.8	-4.7	1,745,952	25.3	2,671,007	33.6	363,068	147.2
Scott	36	5.9	2,630	27.4	-3.9	122,235	41.3	424,077	(NA)	29,215	2.1
Shelby	93	8.1	5,490	23.8	-15.2	290,416	36.8	654,386	28.4	49,491	-50.1
Spencer	25	31.6	1,504	14.3	-22.4	87,472	26.0	1,017,061	1,292.6	(D)	(NA)
Starke	21	10.5	999	15.8	-14.3	42,933	26.1	63,876	-11.7	3,502	-37.8
Steuben	101	-8.2	5,508	28.0	-17.4	278,624	43.9	505,865	-2.3	23,307	-39.4
Sullivan	(NA)	(NA)	561	7.0	2.7	22,183	9.4	(NA)	(NA)	(NA)	(NA)
Switzerland	(NA)	(NA)	(D)	(NA)	(NA)	(D)	(NA)	(NA)	(NA)	(NA)	(NA)
Tippecanoe	127	12.4	14,981	15.3	-12.6	1,094,697	26.2	1,887,822	-27.0	192,730	-50.4
Tipton	22	–	1,026	16.3	-8.9	53,039	26.6	(D)	(NA)	(D)	(NA)
Union	(NA)	(NA)	287	9.8	36.7	13,291	17.7	(NA)	(NA)	(NA)	(NA)
Vanderburgh	275	1.5	15,376	12.0	-9.7	975,793	17.8	1,972,320	-14.9	(D)	(NA)
Vermillion	13	30.0	878	13.2	-20.0	83,652	32.1	(D)	(NA)	(D)	(NA)
Vigo	132	-3.6	8,242	13.0	-0.4	485,903	20.7	1,424,267	44.0	136,030	(NA)
Wabash	76	-1.3	4,233	22.0	-23.1	217,416	37.5	427,423	20.7	22,870	-9.4
Warren	(NA)	(NA)	538	18.1	35.5	18,888	23.0	(NA)	(NA)	(NA)	(NA)
Warrick	54	1.9	2,951	14.2	-9.5	229,803	31.5	(D)	(NA)	(D)	(NA)
Washington	39	-2.5	2,139	20.5	-15.3	95,876	33.4	(D)	(NA)	5,328	-42.7
Wayne	129	-2.3	7,785	19.2	-7.6	395,425	28.9	934,318	30.6	50,254	-33.7
Wells	51	4.1	2,698	18.0	-20.3	168,468	34.9	(D)	(NA)	20,664	-58.9
White	48	-14.3	1,923	18.3	-36.4	82,764	25.1	224,680	-2.0	5,988	-71.8
Whitley	74	12.1	4,296	29.3	1.1	219,791	44.5	(D)	(NA)	19,471	3.0
IOWA	3,804	1.5	236,301	12.0	-4.4	13,644,409	19.2	31,394,257	9.5	1,705,013	-13.8
Adair	6	-25.0	740	12.9	11.1	31,889	24.0	(D)	(NA)	(D)	(NA)
Adams	(NA)	(NA)	184	7.0	-24.0	7,385	12.0	(NA)	(NA)	(NA)	(NA)
Allamakee	28	7.7	1,549	16.5	-14.4	59,000	24.3	121,556	47.4	6,480	163.0
Appanoose	18	20.0	1,184	15.1	-16.9	48,790	24.9	101,587	20.8	(D)	(NA)
Audubon	(NA)	(NA)	339	8.3	21.1	10,557	9.4	(NA)	(NA)	(NA)	(NA)
Benton	31	(NA)	914	7.9	-5.5	41,693	14.9	83,516	(NA)	4,629	(NA)
Black Hawk	157	-4.8	14,263	16.0	-4.7	966,115	28.6	2,058,977	-8.8	95,932	45.7
Boone	35	34.6	917	6.3	-8.8	41,694	9.6	(D)	(NA)	8,604	184.6
Bremer	37	-5.1	1,821	13.0	3.2	90,228	21.2	116,611	-8.0	(D)	(NA)
Buchanan	34	-2.9	1,569	15.2	21.8	72,277	24.4	107,784	38.1	7,423	-17.7
Buena Vista	29	3.6	2,889	21.0	-0.4	108,019	26.6	157,743	40.4	(D)	(NA)
Butler	(NA)	(NA)	630	9.0	24.3	26,218	15.7	(NA)	(NA)	(NA)	(NA)
Calhoun	(NA)	(NA)	153	2.6	-11.6	5,186	3.7	(NA)	(NA)	(NA)	(NA)
Carroll	35	-10.3	1,497	8.8	10.6	62,143	13.0	141,510	-31.3	15,205	-5.5
Cass	23	-8.0	668	7.1	-23.1	29,770	12.4	61,942	-13.0	2,566	-56.0
Cedar	30	20.0	673	7.0	-30.5	29,137	12.9	53,867	0.8	914	-66.0
Cerro Gordo	55	-9.8	4,037	11.6	-9.2	200,769	17.5	396,710	43.9	(D)	(NA)
Cherokee	17	13.3	1,003	12.1	-17.8	45,579	18.9	52,584	23.7	1,339	-68.9
Chickasaw	33	32.0	970	13.2	-12.3	45,638	22.1	110,052	-30.3	7,030	-49.0
Clarke	14	-26.3	1,047	16.3	-23.3	51,696	29.6	92,841	3.6	4,943	(NA)
Clay	29	3.6	1,434	11.6	-5.6	75,513	19.2	118,943	21.5	5,582	-29.8
Clayton	32	3.2	1,001	8.9	-25.9	37,934	13.5	49,493	-32.9	9,762	171.5
Clinton	57	-3.4	4,949	16.4	-4.6	302,172	31.1	1,355,105	23.5	40,343	-58.9
Crawford	24	9.1	2,440	21.8	16.3	112,912	34.4	119,145	-9.4	19,162	297.8
Dallas	39	-4.9	2,353	7.6	6.4	102,705	9.1	144,083	8.5	11,211	12.5
Davis	(NA)	(NA)	387	8.8	-18.9	18,380	18.2	(NA)	(NA)	(NA)	(NA)
Decatur	(NA)	(NA)	210	4.7	-9.1	6,343	6.6	(NA)	(NA)	(NA)	(NA)
Delaware	38	11.8	1,411	12.8	-2.4	74,255	23.7	62,109	-63.7	3,671	-45.6
Des Moines	65	-1.5	5,055	18.0	-19.2	344,876	33.5	(D)	(NA)	(D)	(NA)
Dickinson	31	–	2,469	18.3	5.0	104,780	28.4	357,127	205.2	7,292	31.5
Dubuque	144	8.3	9,768	14.9	-3.2	601,610	25.4	1,222,906	-12.1	56,868	4.4
Emmet	18	20.0	802	12.1	-9.0	42,927	21.8	97,596	146.6	7,049	99.3
Fayette	35	45.8	1,081	9.1	-7.1	44,544	13.9	111,571	18.6	2,211	-68.3
Floyd	17	–	1,467	16.5	22.5	94,630	34.5	74,793	145.1	23,639	150.0
Franklin	21	-4.5	819	12.2	-11.0	35,372	19.4	44,715	10.9	(D)	(NA)
Fremont	(NA)	(NA)	1,466	28.4	8.0	82,818	50.4	(NA)	(NA)	(NA)	(NA)
Greene	14	-17.6	626	11.1	22.0	28,746	19.7	33,182	-8.5	1,305	-23.8
Grundy	(NA)	(NA)	533	8.3	-11.6	21,483	11.0	(NA)	(NA)	(NA)	(NA)
Guthrie	(NA)	(NA)	226	4.3	17.1	9,883	6.9	(NA)	(NA)	(NA)	(NA)
Hamilton	30	–	3,166	28.2	4.7	152,283	39.9	155,480	-3.6	4,697	-60.5

See footnotes at end of table.

[Includes United States, states, and 3,141 counties/county equivalents defined as of February 22, 2005. For more information on these areas, see Appendix C, Geographic Information]

County	Manufacturing (NAICS 31–33)										
	Establishments, 2002[1]		Employment, 2005[2]			Earnings, 2005[2]		Value added by manufactures, 2002[1]		Capital expenditures, 2002[1]	
	Total	Percent change, 1997–2002	Total	Percent of all employees	Percent change, 2001–2005	Total ($1,000)	Percent of all earnings	Total ($1,000)	Percent change, 1997–2002	Total ($1,000)	Percent change, 1997–2002
IOWA—Con.											
Hancock	31	14.8	4,118	38.7	0.5	201,350	55.7	82,413	50.0	3,421	−23.3
Hardin	40	2.6	1,016	9.5	−16.7	40,553	12.2	147,400	62.0	4,911	−61.5
Harrison	(NA)	(NA)	302	4.4	−1.0	11,248	6.9	(NA)	(NA)	(NA)	(NA)
Henry	31	−8.8	2,884	20.0	3.5	150,756	31.3	205,736	−42.4	8,224	−43.9
Howard	23	15.0	1,834	26.0	7.9	86,063	41.9	114,504	25.1	1,939	−49.6
Humboldt	26	−7.1	1,158	17.2	5.9	47,954	26.3	76,126	−5.6	6,350	33.5
Ida	11	22.2	1,125	21.0	−1.2	52,654	33.0	89,777	18.6	4,984	−0.9
Iowa	30	−3.2	4,481	32.6	5.4	256,399	54.4	545,542	92.3	40,803	41.6
Jackson	43	26.5	1,026	9.5	−24.1	37,413	15.7	74,432	−7.7	4,730	27.0
Jasper	49	6.5	2,980	15.9	−34.5	222,324	34.6	474,860	−4.1	(D)	(NA)
Jefferson	43	16.2	1,447	12.0	−12.2	66,635	19.4	108,398	−27.7	6,649	−18.4
Johnson	75	−15.7	5,382	5.4	−4.7	312,869	8.4	3,032,308	63.2	74,642	35.4
Jones	29	26.1	1,157	11.8	−3.6	49,054	19.4	77,878	−1.4	2,843	−58.3
Keokuk	(NA)	(NA)	346	6.8	−25.8	10,984	9.5	(NA)	(NA)	(NA)	(NA)
Kossuth	24	−20.0	1,110	10.2	16.7	86,790	25.5	93,951	1.1	6,056	54.9
Lee	66	−5.7	4,367	20.0	−14.1	272,869	34.7	(D)	(NA)	(D)	(NA)
Linn	234	−2.1	18,799	13.1	−7.7	1,550,573	24.7	2,938,626	−18.8	179,402	−15.7
Louisa	11	–	1,469	25.4	−0.2	55,099	33.9	(D)	(NA)	(D)	(NA)
Lucas	(NA)	(NA)	217	4.0	−26.2	8,004	5.6	(NA)	(NA)	(NA)	(NA)
Lyon	22	(NA)	611	9.3	−17.4	25,170	15.3	37,511	(NA)	3,143	(NA)
Madison	(NA)	(NA)	404	6.0	−22.5	37,917	21.7	(NA)	(NA)	(NA)	(NA)
Mahaska	28	7.7	1,451	11.8	1.4	78,998	22.6	100,621	−10.2	6,075	2.7
Marion	47	6.8	7,659	32.3	−3.4	439,114	52.9	876,110	26.9	40,956	16.1
Marshall	47	6.8	5,350	22.2	−5.4	317,661	36.4	1,058,620	104.9	17,315	−0.5
Mills	(NA)	(NA)	203	3.3	−4.2	9,017	4.8	(NA)	(NA)	(NA)	(NA)
Mitchell	20	25.0	934	15.7	−5.2	43,763	24.2	109,853	5.2	4,016	−32.1
Monona	(NA)	(NA)	146	2.7	–	4,819	4.0	(NA)	(NA)	(NA)	(NA)
Monroe	(NA)	(NA)	560	12.5	−46.5	21,561	18.5	(NA)	(NA)	(NA)	(NA)
Montgomery	12	9.1	965	13.1	11.0	47,602	23.0	64,180	−30.8	6,167	101.8
Muscatine	73	4.3	7,873	27.7	−8.1	556,428	47.0	(D)	(NA)	(D)	(NA)
O'Brien	28	(NA)	673	6.1	−29.2	23,540	9.4	66,736	(NA)	12,584	(NA)
Osceola	14	(NA)	585	16.0	−10.3	27,309	25.5	54,210	(NA)	2,107	(NA)
Page	25	−7.4	1,081	11.3	−4.6	52,894	19.1	275,987	−6.9	9,679	−20.3
Palo Alto	21	(NA)	667	12.3	28.0	27,384	16.3	51,556	(NA)	2,075	(NA)
Plymouth	30	15.4	2,674	16.7	21.2	173,625	33.0	(D)	(NA)	(D)	(NA)
Pocahontas	18	−5.3	567	12.7	−21.8	22,615	18.7	38,806	−27.9	677	−80.1
Polk	399	−2.7	16,808	5.2	−6.6	996,646	6.5	2,286,551	8.5	111,405	−20.4
Pottawattamie	65	10.2	5,097	10.4	5.7	280,191	16.6	498,198	16.0	(D)	(NA)
Poweshiek	32	–	1,715	12.5	−6.7	83,536	18.3	142,152	30.5	4,652	−30.2
Ringgold	(NA)	(NA)	115	3.9	−21.2	2,682	3.7	(NA)	(NA)	(NA)	(NA)
Sac	(NA)	(NA)	402	6.9	28.0	15,181	9.2	(NA)	(NA)	(NA)	(NA)
Scott	201	−4.3	12,894	11.7	−1.9	787,202	18.6	2,086,645	−4.7	137,498	2.1
Shelby	(NA)	(NA)	299	4.0	−7.1	15,424	7.6	(NA)	(NA)	(NA)	(NA)
Sioux	86	28.4	5,521	22.6	12.6	237,645	30.1	254,410	−16.8	20,792	80.0
Story	69	−8.0	4,303	7.7	15.0	320,786	15.0	590,384	−9.5	39,508	21.8
Tama	(NA)	(NA)	488	5.7	−24.7	25,882	11.0	(NA)	(NA)	(NA)	(NA)
Taylor	(NA)	(NA)	499	15.0	6.6	17,626	19.9	(NA)	(NA)	(NA)	(NA)
Union	15	−21.1	1,329	16.1	−12.9	53,834	22.9	85,702	61.3	4,155	−78.1
Van Buren	(NA)	(NA)	653	18.4	3.5	26,562	31.6	(NA)	(NA)	(NA)	(NA)
Wapello	32	45.5	4,373	20.1	31.0	235,779	32.1	710,036	144.2	51,712	39.9
Warren	(NA)	(NA)	576	3.8	16.8	30,293	7.8	(NA)	(NA)	(NA)	(NA)
Washington	40	25.0	1,081	10.5	−16.3	47,478	16.2	111,584	15.3	4,137	−30.3
Wayne	(NA)	(NA)	378	11.2	−12.1	13,702	17.9	(NA)	(NA)	(NA)	(NA)
Webster	52	−13.3	2,518	10.0	−8.6	171,143	19.7	613,126	−18.1	40,811	−69.9
Winnebago	18	38.5	1,260	18.5	9.4	67,023	32.8	415,690	58.2	12,824	31.4
Winneshiek	28	−3.4	1,702	10.6	−21.3	115,386	23.1	111,894	12.3	5,392	−15.7
Woodbury	108	−4.4	6,319	9.9	−11.9	318,339	14.3	(D)	(NA)	38,566	−61.2
Worth	(NA)	(NA)	590	16.7	36.9	21,379	25.8	(NA)	(NA)	(NA)	(NA)
Wright	30	20.0	1,150	14.2	−12.7	63,733	23.5	205,079	56.5	6,245	−33.3
KANSAS	3,218	−2.8	186,457	10.4	−6.7	11,661,073	16.7	21,347,336	20.9	1,281,375	−12.2
Allen	25	−10.7	1,938	20.8	5.3	85,981	36.4	141,298	−14.4	9,239	51.5
Anderson	(NA)	(NA)	255	5.9	−4.1	8,978	10.5	(NA)	(NA)	(NA)	(NA)
Atchison	22	−8.3	1,801	17.0	2.5	88,179	30.5	147,311	23.5	17,160	33.8
Barber	(NA)	(NA)	185	5.4	7.6	9,530	12.1	(NA)	(NA)	(NA)	(NA)
Barton	49	8.9	1,304	6.6	−15.4	51,222	8.4	98,700	−12.2	10,922	110.3
Bourbon	29	–	1,366	13.7	−12.0	49,714	19.3	74,726	−6.8	2,385	−28.4
Brown	(NA)	(NA)	718	9.7	35.5	34,991	17.0	(NA)	(NA)	(NA)	(NA)
Butler	53	1.9	1,737	6.0	−24.4	109,861	13.7	210,067	−13.8	7,733	−66.0
Chase	(NA)	(NA)	(D)	(NA)	(NA)	(D)	(NA)	(NA)	(NA)	(NA)	(NA)
Chautauqua	(NA)	(NA)	71	2.9	26.8	1,808	4.4	(NA)	(NA)	(NA)	(NA)

See footnotes at end of table.

Table B-15. Counties — **Manufacturing**—Con.

[Includes United States, states, and 3,141 counties/county equivalents defined as of February 22, 2005. For more information on these areas, see Appendix C, Geographic Information]

County	Establishments, 2002[1] Total	Percent change, 1997–2002	Employment, 2005[2] Total	Percent of all employees	Percent change, 2001–2005	Earnings, 2005[2] Total ($1,000)	Percent of all earnings	Value added by manufactures, 2002[1] Total ($1,000)	Percent change, 1997–2002	Capital expenditures, 2002[1] Total ($1,000)	Percent change, 1997–2002
KANSAS—Con.											
Cherokee	37	−15.9	1,785	14.7	−14.3	81,144	27.6	142,969	18.2	17,163	−3.6
Cheyenne	(NA)	(NA)	41	2.2	(NA)	690	2.0	(NA)	(NA)	(NA)	(NA)
Clark	(NA)	(NA)	(D)	(NA)	(NA)	(D)	(NA)	(NA)	(NA)	(NA)	(NA)
Clay	(NA)	(NA)	422	6.4	−16.6	14,444	10.2	(NA)	(NA)	(NA)	(NA)
Cloud	(NA)	(NA)	420	6.9	132.0	17,917	12.9	(NA)	(NA)	(NA)	(NA)
Coffey	(NA)	(NA)	219	3.4	8.4	15,017	6.1	(NA)	(NA)	(NA)	(NA)
Comanche	(NA)	(NA)	80	6.0	6.7	2,708	10.7	(NA)	(NA)	(NA)	(NA)
Cowley	52	10.6	3,404	16.7	1.1	181,299	29.4	288,169	−21.5	54,613	124.6
Crawford	73	−1.4	3,104	14.2	−25.2	122,539	18.6	282,258	18.2	16,130	22.8
Decatur	(NA)	(NA)	(D)	(NA)	(NA)	(D)	(NA)	(NA)	(NA)	(NA)	(NA)
Dickinson	21	−16.0	1,428	14.4	6.6	52,238	19.9	100,635	15.0	2,235	−87.0
Doniphan	(NA)	(NA)	578	14.6	−24.3	28,832	26.2	(NA)	(NA)	(NA)	(NA)
Douglas	86	13.2	4,456	6.5	15.0	252,634	11.3	524,692	33.4	33,299	−22.1
Edwards	(NA)	(NA)	259	12.8	13.6	9,035	15.0	(NA)	(NA)	(NA)	(NA)
Elk	(NA)	(NA)	(D)	(NA)	(NA)	(D)	(NA)	(NA)	(NA)	(NA)	(NA)
Ellis	33	17.9	930	4.0	−11.8	31,208	4.6	(D)	(NA)	(D)	(NA)
Ellsworth	(NA)	(NA)	341	8.5	−18.2	14,943	14.9	(NA)	(NA)	(NA)	(NA)
Finney	32	−15.8	3,614	15.8	−12.1	131,982	17.8	269,342	−1.2	8,032	−66.9
Ford	30	3.4	5,756	28.3	13.4	212,048	30.7	452,993	(NA)	33,736	43.0
Franklin	29	16.0	975	6.7	−5.9	46,529	11.9	139,534	131.7	2,930	−43.3
Geary	11	(NA)	708	2.8	−6.8	28,209	2.2	70,769	(NA)	(D)	(NA)
Gove	(NA)	(NA)	88	3.9	−26.7	2,237	4.4	(NA)	(NA)	(NA)	(NA)
Graham	(NA)	(NA)	(D)	(NA)	(NA)	(D)	(NA)	(NA)	(NA)	(NA)	(NA)
Grant	(NA)	(NA)	171	3.4	3.0	8,969	4.7	(NA)	(NA)	(NA)	(NA)
Gray	(NA)	(NA)	46	1.1	(NA)	1,579	1.1	(NA)	(NA)	(NA)	(NA)
Greeley	(NA)	(NA)	10	0.8	(NA)	56	0.2	(NA)	(NA)	(NA)	(NA)
Greenwood	(NA)	(NA)	97	3.0	−50.5	3,113	3.8	(NA)	(NA)	(NA)	(NA)
Hamilton	(NA)	(NA)	10	0.6	(NA)	130	0.2	(NA)	(NA)	(NA)	(NA)
Harper	(NA)	(NA)	338	7.8	17.4	14,185	13.6	(NA)	(NA)	(NA)	(NA)
Harvey	61	10.9	4,014	16.3	14.1	184,797	26.1	271,421	38.8	15,074	8.4
Haskell	(NA)	(NA)	(D)	(NA)	(NA)	(D)	(NA)	(NA)	(NA)	(NA)	(NA)
Hodgeman	(NA)	(NA)	(D)	(NA)	(NA)	(D)	(NA)	(NA)	(NA)	(NA)	(NA)
Jackson	(NA)	(NA)	405	4.2	−9.6	13,869	6.9	(NA)	(NA)	(NA)	(NA)
Jefferson	(NA)	(NA)	123	2.0	−38.8	5,084	3.5	(NA)	(NA)	(NA)	(NA)
Jewell	(NA)	(NA)	(D)	(NA)	(NA)	(D)	(NA)	(NA)	(NA)	(NA)	(NA)
Johnson	523	−5.1	22,533	5.7	7.7	1,666,692	8.5	2,314,954	27.7	147,256	1.8
Kearny	(NA)	(NA)	10	0.5	(NA)	152	0.2	(NA)	(NA)	(NA)	(NA)
Kingman	(NA)	(NA)	369	6.9	12.5	16,847	15.5	(NA)	(NA)	(NA)	(NA)
Kiowa	(NA)	(NA)	(D)	(NA)	(NA)	(D)	(NA)	(NA)	(NA)	(NA)	(NA)
Labette	35	−12.5	2,000	14.0	−18.0	84,710	22.7	146,474	3.0	5,474	−31.3
Lane	(NA)	(NA)	(D)	(NA)	(NA)	(D)	(NA)	(NA)	(NA)	(NA)	(NA)
Leavenworth	34	−5.6	1,388	3.9	41.8	75,724	5.0	38,519	8.7	4,173	106.8
Lincoln	(NA)	(NA)	(D)	(NA)	(NA)	(D)	(NA)	(NA)	(NA)	(NA)	(NA)
Linn	(NA)	(NA)	85	2.1	−23.4	3,005	3.0	(NA)	(NA)	(NA)	(NA)
Logan	(NA)	(NA)	50	2.3	(NA)	2,620	5.1	(NA)	(NA)	(NA)	(NA)
Lyon	39	−2.5	4,860	21.9	−3.4	207,100	30.0	(D)	(NA)	(D)	(NA)
McPherson	67	−1.5	3,402	14.5	1.1	188,170	25.4	525,522	−16.9	35,253	−66.2
Marion	(NA)	(NA)	360	5.9	−8.9	13,165	9.2	(NA)	(NA)	(NA)	(NA)
Marshall	21	—	1,132	14.3	18.3	50,268	20.4	71,247	52.9	3,101	51.5
Meade	(NA)	(NA)	20	0.8	−16.7	656	0.9	(NA)	(NA)	(NA)	(NA)
Miami	29	−6.5	636	5.4	4.3	28,431	8.6	39,962	11.1	1,627	5.6
Mitchell	(NA)	(NA)	472	9.6	11.8	22,573	16.5	(NA)	(NA)	(NA)	(NA)
Montgomery	53	−13.1	3,902	18.5	−8.2	204,814	31.2	426,254	−2.0	29,721	−16.8
Morris	(NA)	(NA)	174	7.0	−30.4	7,203	10.8	(NA)	(NA)	(NA)	(NA)
Morton	(NA)	(NA)	(D)	(NA)	(NA)	(D)	(NA)	(NA)	(NA)	(NA)	(NA)
Nemaha	26	36.8	942	13.8	8.3	37,482	19.6	95,652	40.4	5,112	69.0
Neosho	35	−12.5	1,996	18.3	3.5	83,101	27.7	157,092	14.6	9,572	68.8
Ness	(NA)	(NA)	39	1.5	21.9	1,106	1.7	(NA)	(NA)	(NA)	(NA)
Norton	(NA)	(NA)	227	5.9	26.1	8,106	7.9	(NA)	(NA)	(NA)	(NA)
Osage	(NA)	(NA)	233	4.4	−9.3	7,121	6.8	(NA)	(NA)	(NA)	(NA)
Osborne	(NA)	(NA)	204	7.0	−12.4	5,542	9.4	(NA)	(NA)	(NA)	(NA)
Ottawa	(NA)	(NA)	241	8.6	65.1	6,669	12.5	(NA)	(NA)	(NA)	(NA)
Pawnee	(NA)	(NA)	68	1.3	−8.1	2,007	1.3	(NA)	(NA)	(NA)	(NA)
Phillips	(NA)	(NA)	339	7.7	−9.4	19,667	17.9	(NA)	(NA)	(NA)	(NA)
Pottawatomie	25	13.6	1,364	9.2	27.8	62,539	17.3	88,750	19.5	5,874	30.2
Pratt	(NA)	(NA)	139	2.1	15.8	5,160	2.7	(NA)	(NA)	(NA)	(NA)
Rawlins	(NA)	(NA)	44	1.6	4.8	1,709	3.7	(NA)	(NA)	(NA)	(NA)
Reno	93	−4.1	4,099	11.2	−13.0	189,562	16.3	337,958	−22.9	17,188	−72.1
Republic	(NA)	(NA)	180	4.9	−42.5	5,872	8.1	(NA)	(NA)	(NA)	(NA)
Rice	(NA)	(NA)	469	9.5	20.6	19,480	14.9	(NA)	(NA)	(NA)	(NA)

See footnotes at end of table.

[Includes United States, states, and 3,141 counties/county equivalents defined as of February 22, 2005. For more information on these areas, see Appendix C, Geographic Information]

County	Manufacturing (NAICS 31–33)										
	Establishments, 2002[1]		Employment, 2005[2]			Earnings, 2005[2]		Value added by manufactures, 2002[1]		Capital expenditures, 2002[1]	
	Total	Percent change, 1997–2002	Total	Percent of all employees	Percent change, 2001–2005	Total ($1,000)	Percent of all earnings	Total ($1,000)	Percent change, 1997–2002	Total ($1,000)	Percent change, 1997–2002
KANSAS—Con.											
Riley	(NA)	(NA)	1,056	3.0	88.2	45,265	3.6	(NA)	(NA)	(NA)	(NA)
Rooks	(NA)	(NA)	281	8.7	-7.3	11,429	13.1	(NA)	(NA)	(NA)	(NA)
Rush	(NA)	(NA)	266	11.6	-0.4	12,775	25.8	(NA)	(NA)	(NA)	(NA)
Russell	(NA)	(NA)	267	6.9	-9.5	11,382	12.0	(NA)	(NA)	(NA)	(NA)
Saline	85	-2.3	6,153	15.7	-9.6	310,701	22.5	(D)	(NA)	(D)	(NA)
Scott	(NA)	(NA)	31	0.9	19.2	752	0.8	(NA)	(NA)	(NA)	(NA)
Sedgwick	583	-2.0	55,476	17.9	-17.8	4,622,829	32.4	7,341,431	39.0	383,969	-15.9
Seward	10	—	(D)	(NA)	(NA)	(D)	(NA)	(D)	(NA)	(D)	(NA)
Shawnee	122	-12.9	7,873	6.7	2.4	488,785	10.1	964,510	1.6	50,428	14.0
Sheridan	(NA)	(NA)	(D)	(NA)	(NA)	(D)	(NA)	(NA)	(NA)	(NA)	(NA)
Sherman	(NA)	(NA)	78	1.8	-9.3	2,580	2.5	(NA)	(NA)	(NA)	(NA)
Smith	(NA)	(NA)	222	8.3	13.8	7,567	13.3	(NA)	(NA)	(NA)	(NA)
Stafford	(NA)	(NA)	(D)	(NA)	(NA)	(D)	(NA)	(NA)	(NA)	(NA)	(NA)
Stanton	(NA)	(NA)	(D)	(NA)	(NA)	(D)	(NA)	(NA)	(NA)	(NA)	(NA)
Stevens	(NA)	(NA)	80	2.4	105.1	2,761	2.3	(NA)	(NA)	(NA)	(NA)
Sumner	46	4.5	1,020	10.5	-6.1	45,434	17.4	74,558	-22.0	5,146	(NA)
Thomas	(NA)	(NA)	70	1.3	-53.6	3,197	1.9	(NA)	(NA)	(NA)	(NA)
Trego	(NA)	(NA)	26	1.4	(NA)	551	1.3	(NA)	(NA)	(NA)	(NA)
Wabaunsee	(NA)	(NA)	156	5.6	26.8	12,589	20.5	(NA)	(NA)	(NA)	(NA)
Wallace	(NA)	(NA)	(D)	(NA)	(NA)	(D)	(NA)	(NA)	(NA)	(NA)	(NA)
Washington	(NA)	(NA)	166	4.7	13.7	4,310	5.5	(NA)	(NA)	(NA)	(NA)
Wichita	(NA)	(NA)	(D)	(NA)	(NA)	(D)	(NA)	(NA)	(NA)	(NA)	(NA)
Wilson	26	-10.3	1,665	27.6	25.3	74,802	39.7	84,294	2.8	10,408	60.6
Woodson	(NA)	(NA)	26	1.7	-75.7	996	2.6	(NA)	(NA)	(NA)	(NA)
Wyandotte	246	-6.1	12,639	13.8	-10.3	917,372	20.9	3,217,849	12.0	207,078	4.3
KENTUCKY	4,283	1.5	270,289	11.4	-9.7	16,368,826	18.0	34,075,367	-11.1	2,562,414	-23.9
Adair	(NA)	(NA)	557	6.8	7.7	15,491	8.8	(NA)	(NA)	(NA)	(NA)
Allen	15	25.0	1,044	12.5	-44.7	55,451	24.4	96,453	-12.8	14,333	(NA)
Anderson	21	5.0	1,234	16.2	-12.2	71,550	37.0	165,452	(NA)	(D)	(NA)
Ballard	12	—	712	15.0	-10.7	61,849	31.4	(D)	(NA)	(D)	(NA)
Barren	57	3.6	5,329	20.1	-12.0	252,712	33.9	513,521	57.7	(D)	(NA)
Bath	(NA)	(NA)	452	11.4	-15.7	15,428	21.4	(NA)	(NA)	(NA)	(NA)
Bell	22	—	892	7.4	10.0	32,550	9.1	71,442	41.3	(D)	(NA)
Boone	164	22.4	11,591	12.7	-0.6	674,969	16.9	1,261,086	43.2	68,619	-24.1
Bourbon	18	-5.3	1,900	18.0	26.8	111,283	30.6	(D)	(NA)	11,939	(NA)
Boyd	37	-11.9	2,599	7.6	-26.2	221,235	16.2	844,367	26.4	(D)	(NA)
Boyle	30	-9.1	3,373	16.2	-29.8	179,451	27.3	(D)	(NA)	(D)	(NA)
Bracken	(NA)	(NA)	254	7.8	-6.3	12,634	25.5	(NA)	(NA)	(NA)	(NA)
Breathitt	(NA)	(NA)	97	2.0	-45.8	1,779	1.3	(NA)	(NA)	(NA)	(NA)
Breckinridge	(NA)	(NA)	300	4.0	26.1	9,624	6.7	(NA)	(NA)	(NA)	(NA)
Bullitt	47	-4.1	2,794	12.2	-6.8	137,653	23.6	176,547	2.6	11,219	(NA)
Butler	15	—	808	16.3	-52.4	35,939	28.2	73,865	-67.7	(D)	(NA)
Caldwell	14	-26.3	1,047	16.1	13.4	47,325	24.5	89,196	80.4	(D)	(NA)
Calloway	31	10.7	3,244	14.7	3.0	134,566	19.4	167,143	-67.8	7,176	-57.3
Campbell	75	-9.6	2,531	6.5	-25.2	160,915	12.7	199,247	-50.2	24,603	107.5
Carlisle	(NA)	(NA)	99	4.9	-26.1	1,959	3.5	(NA)	(NA)	(NA)	(NA)
Carroll	15	-16.7	2,502	28.1	1.8	188,886	55.2	581,676	-8.4	(D)	(NA)
Carter	(NA)	(NA)	956	9.1	-4.5	27,070	12.2	(NA)	(NA)	(NA)	(NA)
Casey	(NA)	(NA)	1,006	13.5	-11.8	26,516	18.5	(NA)	(NA)	(NA)	(NA)
Christian	70	25.0	6,830	10.0	4.2	354,149	9.4	465,251	40.1	68,416	195.0
Clark	49	6.5	4,280	19.5	-3.6	216,612	30.9	448,428	77.7	40,369	(NA)
Clay	(NA)	(NA)	162	2.6	-60.7	4,366	2.3	(NA)	(NA)	(NA)	(NA)
Clinton	18	20.0	1,609	30.8	-8.3	49,267	36.3	275,023	1,035.7	2,315	347.8
Crittenden	(NA)	(NA)	345	9.1	-20.3	10,580	12.3	(NA)	(NA)	(NA)	(NA)
Cumberland	(NA)	(NA)	319	10.4	-15.6	8,424	15.2	(NA)	(NA)	(NA)	(NA)
Daviess	111	-2.6	6,514	11.7	-0.5	350,016	18.6	1,260,110	13.9	(D)	(NA)
Edmonson	(NA)	(NA)	(D)	(NA)	(NA)	(D)	(NA)	(NA)	(NA)	(NA)	(NA)
Elliott	(NA)	(NA)	11	0.6	(NA)	[3]25	(NA)	(NA)	(NA)	(NA)	(NA)
Estill	(NA)	(NA)	342	8.2	-16.8	9,662	10.8	(NA)	(NA)	(NA)	(NA)
Fayette	265	-6.4	14,885	7.1	-8.5	1,111,435	12.2	2,964,854	38.0	103,171	4.4
Fleming	21	10.5	696	10.1	-11.6	26,603	19.2	37,757	69.3	6,779	165.6
Floyd	(NA)	(NA)	347	2.2	26.2	12,164	2.2	(NA)	(NA)	(NA)	(NA)
Franklin	47	17.5	3,281	8.2	-2.5	180,906	11.6	293,791	-2.7	(D)	(NA)
Fulton	11	-21.4	608	15.7	-40.7	22,262	16.6	81,879	1.7	(D)	(NA)
Gallatin	(NA)	(NA)	(D)	(NA)	(NA)	(D)	(NA)	(NA)	(NA)	(NA)	(NA)
Garrard	(NA)	(NA)	(D)	(NA)	(NA)	(D)	(NA)	(NA)	(NA)	(NA)	(NA)
Grant	21	31.3	710	8.3	-25.9	36,250	17.6	(D)	(NA)	(D)	(NA)
Graves	54	8.0	2,395	13.9	-31.4	96,665	19.9	256,844	23.0	23,937	138.3
Grayson	35	12.9	2,398	19.6	-10.8	94,048	30.5	117,458	8.9	9,252	28.7
Green	(NA)	(NA)	188	4.0	-47.6	4,917	6.8	(NA)	(NA)	(NA)	(NA)
Greenup	(NA)	(NA)	819	6.3	-6.9	66,903	15.8	(NA)	(NA)	(NA)	(NA)

See footnotes at end of table.

[Includes United States, states, and 3,141 counties/county equivalents defined as of February 22, 2005. For more information on these areas, see Appendix C, Geographic Information]

County	Manufacturing (NAICS 31–33)										
	Establishments, 2002[1]		Employment, 2005[2]			Earnings, 2005[2]		Value added by manufactures, 2002[1]		Capital expenditures, 2002[1]	
	Total	Percent change, 1997–2002	Total	Percent of all employees	Percent change, 2001–2005	Total ($1,000)	Percent of all earnings	Total ($1,000)	Percent change, 1997–2002	Total ($1,000)	Percent change, 1997–2002
KENTUCKY—Con.											
Hancock	20	53.8	2,734	49.1	−19.5	199,710	76.8	(D)	(NA)	(D)	(NA)
Hardin	89	30.9	6,271	10.0	−8.6	380,819	14.2	(D)	(NA)	130,478	81.0
Harlan	(NA)	(NA)	210	2.1	−18.9	6,074	1.7	(NA)	(NA)	(NA)	(NA)
Harrison	20	5.3	1,374	16.0	−10.1	82,472	37.7	282,684	44.0	37,810	(NA)
Hart	15	50.0	1,658	21.5	−3.2	56,922	36.0	116,105	(NA)	16,388	3,848.9
Henderson	85	9.0	6,330	26.0	−15.3	337,706	33.6	770,205	−15.6	71,300	−5.3
Henry	10	25.0	744	10.6	−14.2	40,053	25.4	(D)	(NA)	(D)	(NA)
Hickman	(NA)	(NA)	(D)	(NA)	(NA)	(D)	(NA)	(NA)	(NA)	(NA)	(NA)
Hopkins	50	−9.1	3,062	13.0	17.9	157,027	19.6	323,843	32.1	59,753	243.0
Jackson	16	23.1	1,033	20.2	6.4	26,990	27.5	53,180	889.9	1,450	−76.5
Jefferson	864	−1.0	48,406	9.3	−15.9	3,992,355	16.0	5,643,059	−63.1	308,091	(NA)
Jessamine	66	−1.5	2,935	13.5	8.2	146,585	21.5	330,114	1.0	27,612	(NA)
Johnson	(NA)	(NA)	147	1.7	−60.6	4,117	1.6	(NA)	(NA)	(NA)	(NA)
Kenton	153	−5.0	4,988	6.4	0.5	325,894	9.6	572,218	−33.5	89,758	87.5
Knott	(NA)	(NA)	39	0.7	8.3	498	0.2	(NA)	(NA)	(NA)	(NA)
Knox	16	−5.9	1,356	9.6	10.4	60,004	15.2	(D)	(NA)	(D)	(NA)
Larue	17	41.7	760	13.5	3.3	22,938	20.4	(D)	(NA)	2,518	566.1
Laurel	50	13.6	3,507	11.4	−25.6	146,905	15.5	316,278	142.2	8,385	−32.3
Lawrence	(NA)	(NA)	(D)	(NA)	(NA)	(D)	(NA)	(NA)	(NA)	(NA)	(NA)
Lee	(NA)	(NA)	167	6.0	(NA)	4,370	6.1	(NA)	(NA)	(NA)	(NA)
Leslie	(NA)	(NA)	(D)	(NA)	(NA)	(D)	(NA)	(NA)	(NA)	(NA)	(NA)
Letcher	(NA)	(NA)	186	2.3	24.0	12,097	4.4	(NA)	(NA)	(NA)	(NA)
Lewis	(NA)	(NA)	518	11.2	80.5	13,609	16.6	(NA)	(NA)	(NA)	(NA)
Lincoln	14	−22.2	900	11.2	6.5	43,490	24.8	(D)	(NA)	(D)	(NA)
Livingston	(NA)	(NA)	(D)	(NA)	(NA)	(D)	(NA)	(NA)	(NA)	(NA)	(NA)
Logan	48	17.1	3,313	24.7	−19.6	184,049	41.6	1,146,273	190.6	21,058	148.3
Lyon	(NA)	(NA)	(D)	(NA)	(NA)	(D)	(NA)	(NA)	(NA)	(NA)	(NA)
McCracken	55	−5.2	3,376	7.0	−13.1	222,152	12.4	(D)	(NA)	(D)	(NA)
McCreary	(NA)	(NA)	424	8.9	−51.2	19,980	14.9	(NA)	(NA)	(NA)	(NA)
McLean	(NA)	(NA)	230	7.1	11.1	8,393	6.4	(NA)	(NA)	(NA)	(NA)
Madison	69	1.5	5,494	13.3	−5.9	309,503	25.6	651,257	19.8	30,540	(NA)
Magoffin	(NA)	(NA)	(D)	(NA)	(NA)	(D)	(NA)	(NA)	(NA)	(NA)	(NA)
Marion	30	36.4	2,826	28.3	22.9	140,393	47.3	202,559	132.4	30,982	155.0
Marshall	40	14.3	2,848	18.4	−3.9	246,187	42.1	882,089	18.1	(D)	(NA)
Martin	(NA)	(NA)	(D)	(NA)	(NA)	(D)	(NA)	(NA)	(NA)	(NA)	(NA)
Mason	19	—	2,144	17.1	−30.5	104,032	28.2	(D)	(NA)	(D)	(NA)
Meade	(NA)	(NA)	317	4.4	−26.5	24,903	13.7	(NA)	(NA)	(NA)	(NA)
Menifee	(NA)	(NA)	153	7.8	−6.7	4,528	12.0	(NA)	(NA)	(NA)	(NA)
Mercer	16	—	2,488	22.7	−8.7	168,319	47.4	170,594	−37.4	29,975	−34.9
Metcalfe	12	−7.7	951	21.5	−7.8	38,446	36.5	47,833	−55.7	(D)	(NA)
Monroe	20	−37.5	960	16.6	−8.1	35,962	25.8	61,075	−24.2	2,321	−18.0
Montgomery	36	12.5	3,773	26.3	8.7	169,129	41.2	(D)	(NA)	(D)	(NA)
Morgan	(NA)	(NA)	270	5.2	−27.6	8,756	7.1	(NA)	(NA)	(NA)	(NA)
Muhlenberg	32	−11.1	986	7.7	−20.2	36,619	8.5	90,992	15.9	(D)	(NA)
Nelson	57	1.8	4,004	19.9	−0.5	212,033	32.7	334,775	−36.7	34,254	−13.6
Nicholas	(NA)	(NA)	74	2.9	(NA)	2,012	6.1	(NA)	(NA)	(NA)	(NA)
Ohio	27	—	2,320	23.2	33.8	90,274	32.0	152,172	41.8	6,497	28.5
Oldham	43	4.9	928	4.7	−18.6	45,797	7.7	149,212	47.2	(D)	(NA)
Owen	(NA)	(NA)	(D)	(NA)	(NA)	(D)	(NA)	(NA)	(NA)	(NA)	(NA)
Owsley	(NA)	(NA)	(D)	(NA)	(NA)	(D)	(NA)	(NA)	(NA)	(NA)	(NA)
Pendleton	12	—	439	10.0	−5.2	16,309	15.7	44,839	(NA)	(D)	(NA)
Perry	13	44.4	797	4.9	79.1	28,911	4.7	63,950	47.6	(D)	(NA)
Pike	27	3.8	562	1.9	−22.1	23,769	2.0	49,535	77.5	(D)	(NA)
Powell	12	−25.0	544	11.9	−49.1	17,873	15.5	19,589	−85.8	1,402	−47.0
Pulaski	92	9.5	4,113	12.1	−8.5	161,786	16.3	404,159	25.3	16,542	−60.0
Robertson	(NA)	(NA)	11	1.2	(NA)	[3]25	(NA)	(NA)	(NA)	(NA)	(NA)
Rockcastle	10	−9.1	478	8.4	−29.1	17,796	14.7	28,878	(NA)	1,989	(NA)
Rowan	19	46.2	1,254	9.6	−8.3	46,493	12.5	152,773	77.2	6,129	(NA)
Russell	28	16.7	1,927	21.8	−2.4	67,514	31.7	68,183	−69.0	12,429	438.3
Scott	41	−8.9	9,151	31.5	−17.0	928,496	62.5	(D)	(NA)	103,600	(NA)
Shelby	42	—	4,706	23.1	−10.0	276,284	41.4	508,897	29.7	33,801	−14.3
Simpson	36	5.9	3,666	32.0	3.8	200,914	48.8	436,456	85.2	37,168	51.4
Spencer	(NA)	(NA)	56	1.5	(NA)	1,792	2.9	(NA)	(NA)	(NA)	(NA)
Taylor	43	13.2	2,294	16.0	14.4	81,779	22.3	109,353	−62.7	(D)	(NA)
Todd	21	10.5	854	17.5	−28.7	31,189	22.3	51,730	−0.1	1,138	−45.3
Trigg	20	5.3	1,344	23.3	8.6	78,185	42.2	115,985	58.8	8,070	(NA)
Trimble	(NA)	(NA)	59	2.7	(NA)	2,197	5.9	(NA)	(NA)	(NA)	(NA)
Union	16	−11.1	1,014	13.0	2.3	42,310	14.2	92,176	−10.2	2,092	−65.7
Warren	107	2.9	9,797	14.3	10.9	597,751	24.0	(D)	(NA)	(D)	(NA)
Washington	12	−7.7	884	16.3	−3.8	49,921	35.1	80,481	42.8	17,319	138.9

See footnotes at end of table.

[Includes United States, states, and 3,141 counties/county equivalents defined as of February 22, 2005. For more information on these areas, see Appendix C, Geographic Information]

County	Establishments, 2002[1]		Employment, 2005[2]			Earnings, 2005[2]		Value added by manufactures, 2002[1]		Capital expenditures, 2002[1]	
	Total	Percent change, 1997–2002	Total	Percent of all employ-ees	Percent change, 2001–2005	Total ($1,000)	Percent of all earnings	Total ($1,000)	Percent change, 1997–2002	Total ($1,000)	Percent change, 1997–2002
KENTUCKY—Con.											
Wayne	34	3.0	2,340	25.7	10.2	75,597	31.5	122,142	56.1	14,588	259.5
Webster	21	10.5	636	11.9	–17.3	20,787	7.4	70,978	47.8	1,637	–9.9
Whitley	35	6.1	1,470	9.4	–9.2	66,297	13.7	114,630	8.1	8,051	3.5
Wolfe	(NA)	(NA)	57	2.5	(NA)	998	2.4	(NA)	(NA)	(NA)	(NA)
Woodford	23	4.5	2,669	17.0	–23.9	167,507	25.9	(D)	(NA)	34,027	–31.7
LOUISIANA	3,524	–0.6	158,696	6.4	–10.8	10,418,563	11.7	28,404,879	–2.3	3,488,400	1.6
Acadia	52	10.6	1,440	6.0	–27.5	51,118	7.7	114,248	24.7	4,615	(NA)
Allen	(NA)	(NA)	496	4.0	9.0	22,110	6.7	(NA)	(NA)	(NA)	(NA)
Ascension	94	9.3	5,121	8.4	–15.7	490,106	27.8	2,489,897	–39.2	(D)	(NA)
Assumption	(NA)	(NA)	1,056	15.8	–49.4	85,968	38.9	(NA)	(NA)	(NA)	(NA)
Avoyelles	19	–5.0	526	3.2	–32.2	22,219	5.6	41,885	–8.3	(D)	(NA)
Beauregard	20	–23.1	1,041	8.0	–20.5	83,522	23.2	257,975	2.9	32,161	7.7
Bienville	12	–14.3	1,077	16.3	1.0	38,500	21.1	107,073	59.0	(D)	(NA)
Bossier	80	5.3	2,098	3.6	–26.5	108,000	5.0	(D)	(NA)	(D)	(NA)
Caddo	218	0.9	11,675	7.4	–4.5	787,386	12.1	(D)	(NA)	150,037	–0.6
Calcasieu	137	2.2	8,928	8.4	–15.5	849,240	21.4	2,892,830	–4.2	(D)	(NA)
Caldwell	(NA)	(NA)	108	2.7	10.2	2,304	2.4	(NA)	(NA)	(NA)	(NA)
Cameron	(NA)	(NA)	244	5.6	–20.3	15,179	14.6	(NA)	(NA)	(NA)	(NA)
Catahoula	(NA)	(NA)	(D)	(NA)	(NA)	(D)	(NA)	(NA)	(NA)	(NA)	(NA)
Claiborne	(NA)	(NA)	402	6.2	–19.1	19,624	9.1	(NA)	(NA)	(NA)	(NA)
Concordia	(NA)	(NA)	105	1.3	(NA)	5,394	2.5	(NA)	(NA)	(NA)	(NA)
De Soto	15	–6.3	1,144	12.2	–8.0	72,586	19.1	(D)	(NA)	(D)	(NA)
East Baton Rouge	346	–2.3	12,436	4.3	–13.3	1,004,113	8.4	3,819,231	41.1	508,189	216.5
East Carroll	(NA)	(NA)	144	4.7	0.7	4,381	5.1	(NA)	(NA)	(NA)	(NA)
East Feliciana	(NA)	(NA)	433	5.5	38.3	17,911	7.7	(NA)	(NA)	(NA)	(NA)
Evangeline	17	–5.6	689	6.0	–27.1	39,538	13.9	(D)	(NA)	13,464	(NA)
Franklin	(NA)	(NA)	533	5.9	–23.1	9,556	4.7	(NA)	(NA)	(NA)	(NA)
Grant	(NA)	(NA)	380	7.1	–29.1	15,105	10.1	(NA)	(NA)	(NA)	(NA)
Iberia	97	–3.0	4,299	10.4	–7.4	221,311	13.9	413,576	–28.1	27,854	8.5
Iberville	33	–15.4	3,707	21.5	–5.8	443,297	49.0	1,023,866	14.9	(D)	(NA)
Jackson	(NA)	(NA)	(D)	(NA)	(NA)	(D)	(NA)	(NA)	(NA)	(NA)	(NA)
Jefferson	399	–10.1	16,986	6.4	–3.4	869,902	9.2	1,069,557	–20.6	69,391	–38.9
Jefferson Davis	(NA)	(NA)	466	3.9	–8.6	22,272	7.6	(NA)	(NA)	(NA)	(NA)
Lafayette	251	16.7	7,621	4.9	–0.4	358,515	5.7	555,167	27.0	34,941	(NA)
Lafourche	57	–13.6	3,271	6.1	–12.8	150,683	8.8	206,449	40.2	10,324	(NA)
La Salle	(NA)	(NA)	93	1.7	–79.5	2,600	1.6	(NA)	(NA)	(NA)	(NA)
Lincoln	34	–2.9	1,698	7.5	–25.1	84,832	11.2	(D)	(NA)	(D)	(NA)
Livingston	59	9.3	2,016	6.1	6.9	97,188	11.8	129,572	22.2	4,957	–50.5
Madison	(NA)	(NA)	238	4.9	–49.6	9,130	7.3	(NA)	(NA)	(NA)	(NA)
Morehouse	14	–4.0	981	9.0	–22.1	75,920	22.6	189,688	(NA)	(D)	(NA)
Natchitoches	22	22.2	2,252	11.5	–7.7	168,235	25.6	373,916	81.7	31,764	188.4
Orleans	225	–13.8	8,345	2.9	–26.5	510,800	4.5	1,221,934	14.8	53,149	23.8
Ouachita	149	–2.0	7,471	8.3	–10.2	433,329	13.5	819,734	–4.8	(D)	(NA)
Plaquemines	42	–4.5	1,946	9.9	–12.4	160,447	19.0	469,399	4.0	25,470	–50.7
Pointe Coupee	(NA)	(NA)	529	6.1	–1.3	19,647	8.6	(NA)	(NA)	(NA)	(NA)
Rapides	70	–4.1	3,639	4.9	–1.3	297,459	11.0	824,894	14.2	(D)	(NA)
Red River	(NA)	(NA)	(D)	(NA)	(NA)	(D)	(NA)	(NA)	(NA)	(NA)	(NA)
Richland	17	21.4	595	7.3	–13.8	20,506	9.5	(D)	(NA)	1,338	–53.8
Sabine	18	–5.3	1,055	12.5	–6.6	47,045	19.4	80,734	22.9	(D)	(NA)
St. Bernard	58	7.4	1,607	7.5	6.8	136,182	38.7	394,835	21.4	70,313	53.6
St. Charles	38	2.7	4,563	16.3	–13.1	546,603	38.2	3,175,388	–15.0	218,003	–16.0
St. Helena	(NA)	(NA)	201	4.9	–26.1	7,277	9.0	(NA)	(NA)	(NA)	(NA)
St. James	26	–	2,732	31.0	10.8	264,695	60.6	697,207	–6.5	231,867	167.0
St. John the Baptist	24	–17.2	2,212	12.5	–3.2	207,029	30.5	1,006,079	59.5	71,624	14.3
St. Landry	48	–15.8	1,916	5.8	–2.3	99,352	10.1	211,720	37.0	32,599	(NA)
St. Martin	47	6.8	1,298	8.5	–30.6	36,370	9.9	67,359	–91.7	5,688	(NA)
St. Mary	90	34.3	3,747	11.8	5.0	203,111	16.7	464,225	–7.2	38,580	–38.2
St. Tammany	127	–	2,389	2.4	–11.1	91,008	3.2	195,878	27.1	8,480	–36.4
Tangipahoa	81	9.5	3,270	6.5	20.2	120,545	8.7	264,994	43.3	15,707	39.4
Tensas	(NA)	(NA)	(D)	(NA)	(NA)	(D)	(NA)	(NA)	(NA)	(NA)	(NA)
Terrebonne	125	5.0	5,594	9.9	20.5	346,802	15.5	357,385	23.4	28,759	(NA)
Union	13	(NA)	(D)	(NA)	(NA)	(D)	(NA)	64,785	(NA)	(D)	(NA)
Vermilion	39	44.4	1,143	5.7	–34.1	47,615	8.7	164,798	90.6	5,156	(NA)
Vernon	(NA)	(NA)	463	1.7	–31.0	13,900	1.1	(NA)	(NA)	(NA)	(NA)
Washington	36	28.6	1,261	7.6	–28.1	80,398	19.5	250,639	46.4	9,925	–27.9
Webster	39	–13.3	2,776	15.7	3.2	134,873	24.1	151,385	–24.9	19,736	1.5
West Baton Rouge	39	–	1,337	11.1	–45.2	98,135	20.7	474,395	9.6	27,046	–12.9
West Carroll	(NA)	(NA)	(D)	(NA)	(NA)	(D)	(NA)	(NA)	(NA)	(NA)	(NA)
West Feliciana	6	–	906	13.0	–3.1	66,272	20.8	(D)	(NA)	(D)	(NA)
Winn	17	–29.2	973	14.3	–4.0	49,499	24.4	52,577	–29.3	6,931	–42.9

See footnotes at end of table.

[Includes United States, states, and 3,141 counties/county equivalents defined as of February 22, 2005. For more information on these areas, see Appendix C, Geographic Information]

County	Establishments, 2002[1] Total	Percent change, 1997–2002	Employment, 2005[2] Total	Percent of all employees	Percent change, 2001–2005	Earnings, 2005[2] Total ($1,000)	Percent of all earnings	Value added by manufactures, 2002[1] Total ($1,000)	Percent change, 1997–2002	Capital expenditures, 2002[1] Total ($1,000)	Percent change, 1997–2002
MAINE	1,880	3.8	66,627	8.1	−16.0	3,829,547	13.1	7,122,274	9.1	543,895	−8.5
Androscoggin	169	−7.7	6,789	10.7	−9.5	370,803	17.1	864,123	22.5	142,447	187.9
Aroostook	102	14.6	3,818	9.2	−13.0	186,851	14.8	512,782	44.2	27,361	−58.2
Cumberland	415	8.6	11,862	5.3	−15.3	729,286	7.7	1,178,933	0.4	86,008	8.7
Franklin	46	−13.2	2,210	12.3	−12.3	144,098	26.5	318,752	−9.9	24,749	−17.5
Hancock	104	10.6	2,921	7.7	−10.0	148,363	13.8	313,966	16.8	12,092	−28.5
Kennebec	127	−1.6	2,999	3.9	−36.0	132,688	4.9	271,535	−21.5	18,503	−41.5
Knox	88	−4.3	1,961	6.8	−1.2	126,107	13.9	139,024	−4.9	5,501	−56.2
Lincoln	79	16.2	1,164	5.8	−3.3	45,303	9.0	51,663	(NA)	3,381	−52.3
Oxford	90	7.1	(D)	(NA)	(NA)	(D)	(NA)	559,970	46.2	22,544	−42.7
Penobscot	173	11.6	5,262	5.7	−29.0	334,723	10.1	416,544	−52.2	57,042	−40.4
Piscataquis	28	7.7	1,458	16.5	−16.2	97,815	35.5	89,694	25.3	5,884	−0.3
Sagadahoc	35	20.7	(D)	(NA)	(NA)	(D)	(NA)	(D)	(NA)	10,356	84.6
Somerset	77	1.3	3,980	15.7	−13.4	253,323	29.4	549,200	5.1	55,177	15.9
Waldo	46	−13.2	1,531	8.3	−7.0	103,560	19.5	86,562	49.4	4,789	23.2
Washington	44	7.3	1,642	8.7	−11.9	74,768	15.5	182,247	77.3	11,998	−43.0
York	257	−0.4	9,314	9.5	−17.9	505,143	14.5	(D)	(NA)	56,063	−32.4
MARYLAND	3,999	0.1	147,812	4.4	−15.6	10,887,094	6.6	19,265,920	2.9	1,594,941	8.6
Allegany	59	−11.9	3,435	8.8	−10.1	176,706	13.6	432,450	9.1	(D)	(NA)
Anne Arundel	342	0.9	14,910	4.3	−9.9	1,651,899	9.5	1,919,110	16.9	209,272	112.1
Baltimore	556	−3.3	27,568	5.5	−17.6	2,104,864	9.2	4,154,684	6.0	186,198	−28.7
Calvert	46	(NA)	857	2.7	−16.8	36,030	3.2	73,020	(NA)	1,944	(NA)
Caroline	35	12.9	1,526	11.0	−18.8	68,297	16.1	152,977	87.3	8,997	80.9
Carroll	153	6.3	5,091	6.3	−4.3	271,890	10.4	475,107	40.8	(D)	(NA)
Cecil	59	7.3	4,527	11.8	15.9	315,773	21.0	438,953	13.9	101,087	90.9
Charles	63	8.6	1,435	2.5	−0.1	69,308	3.2	78,129	5.5	7,134	(NA)
Dorchester	55	14.6	2,966	17.4	−8.9	133,975	24.3	278,869	−13.7	10,670	−30.9
Frederick	201	24.1	6,593	5.3	−13.2	402,526	7.8	1,764,746	112.1	56,563	−25.0
Garrett	62	26.5	1,043	5.2	7.1	35,407	6.9	57,026	22.5	1,923	(NA)
Harford	164	7.9	5,460	4.9	9.8	296,426	6.3	787,936	17.2	42,494	−0.8
Howard	249	1.6	6,876	3.9	−19.5	487,443	5.1	884,629	57.4	(D)	(NA)
Kent	34	25.9	908	7.2	−12.7	36,871	9.5	139,627	124.8	2,501	−48.4
Montgomery	506	−4.0	16,027	2.5	−20.9	1,616,772	4.1	1,469,808	−21.1	113,474	−33.0
Prince George's	382	2.7	11,893	2.8	−8.3	799,342	4.0	1,124,263	11.3	70,044	−38.8
Queen Anne's	48	41.2	925	4.4	−15.7	77,260	11.6	66,639	37.8	1,898	−6.5
St. Mary's	(NA)	(NA)	637	1.1	−10.9	37,001	1.3	(NA)	(NA)	(NA)	(NA)
Somerset	(NA)	(NA)	375	3.4	−6.7	15,020	4.5	(NA)	(NA)	(NA)	(NA)
Talbot	51	−5.6	1,634	5.9	−39.6	73,018	7.9	469,498	8.7	14,064	−29.3
Washington	149	1.4	9,151	11.6	−8.1	543,040	17.6	1,139,530	21.1	49,280	−38.0
Wicomico	94	−1.1	4,535	7.9	−18.7	232,536	11.1	(D)	(NA)	36,432	32.3
Worcester	45	18.4	1,078	3.2	−48.0	43,544	4.6	116,971	19.7	(D)	(NA)
Independent City											
Baltimore city	591	−14.1	18,362	4.5	−28.0	1,362,146	5.8	2,807,410	−37.0	277,457	24.5
MASSACHUSETTS	8,859	−7.3	318,080	7.7	−20.7	26,013,264	11.6	44,508,791	0.4	2,349,095	−32.6
Barnstable	221	−2.2	2,231	1.6	−28.4	137,959	2.7	262,445	14.3	16,219	(NA)
Berkshire	203	−1.9	6,856	8.2	−24.9	449,756	13.7	694,785	−12.6	44,844	−28.3
Bristol	883	−3.5	34,803	12.4	−20.0	2,081,687	18.3	3,994,700	2.7	221,333	−21.1
Dukes	(NA)	(NA)	(D)	(NA)	(NA)	(D)	(NA)	(NA)	(NA)	(NA)	(NA)
Essex	1,134	−5.5	46,041	11.6	−21.8	3,930,946	21.2	8,128,805	7.8	468,030	−33.2
Franklin	120	0.8	4,872	12.1	−26.1	246,167	19.1	619,289	49.4	87,046	84.4
Hampden	748	−6.7	24,892	10.0	−16.0	1,469,950	14.0	2,902,052	−9.7	140,426	−32.1
Hampshire	188	4.4	4,681	5.4	−14.2	265,141	8.8	436,199	−11.6	33,581	21.5
Middlesex	2,189	−10.2	92,447	8.8	−25.1	9,481,094	14.5	13,764,714	−0.9	626,091	−39.2
Nantucket	(NA)	(NA)	(D)	(NA)	(NA)	(D)	(NA)	(NA)	(NA)	(NA)	(NA)
Norfolk	813	−5.8	28,587	6.8	−15.0	2,290,104	10.1	4,177,358	14.1	182,709	−30.0
Plymouth	620	1.1	13,253	5.2	−9.4	827,860	7.8	1,280,522	2.7	51,978	−32.4
Suffolk	468	−25.0	15,683	2.3	−23.3	1,767,660	3.3	2,361,083	−9.4	134,154	−52.7
Worcester	1,243	−7.0	43,268	10.4	−17.3	3,055,003	16.4	5,870,004	−7.5	342,131	−30.3
MICHIGAN	15,193	−5.3	700,904	12.7	−16.9	56,530,416	21.9	97,575,395	4.0	5,699,658	−38.3
Alcona	(NA)	(NA)	314	8.0	−11.0	10,817	13.1	(NA)	(NA)	(NA)	(NA)
Alger	9	−30.8	665	15.6	−10.1	42,490	30.0	75,441	−8.4	5,848	20.3
Allegan	208	2.5	12,732	22.5	−23.1	768,074	39.9	2,101,598	20.6	92,857	−10.7
Alpena	52	−10.3	2,063	11.8	−1.6	119,596	21.2	224,722	−12.8	9,086	−64.4
Antrim	55	−1.8	1,154	10.1	−8.0	57,334	20.3	103,212	14.7	5,261	−33.6
Arenac	32	−13.5	718	7.9	−11.9	24,895	11.7	43,358	−9.3	3,043	35.4
Baraga	(NA)	(NA)	685	15.0	32.0	30,125	22.4	(NA)	(NA)	(NA)	(NA)
Barry	75	5.6	2,834	11.0	−13.3	167,564	24.6	363,253	32.2	15,295	−6.4
Bay	138	−9.2	4,371	8.6	−24.4	328,394	17.9	512,860	−51.9	43,237	(NA)
Benzie	(NA)	(NA)	662	7.7	3.6	21,557	11.8	(NA)	(NA)	(NA)	(NA)

See footnotes at end of table.

[Includes United States, states, and 3,141 counties/county equivalents defined as of February 22, 2005. For more information on these areas, see Appendix C, Geographic Information]

County	Manufacturing (NAICS 31–33)										
	Establishments, 2002[1]		Employment, 2005[2]			Earnings, 2005[2]		Value added by manufactures, 2002[1]		Capital expenditures, 2002[1]	
	Total	Percent change, 1997–2002	Total	Percent of all employees	Percent change, 2001–2005	Total ($1,000)	Percent of all earnings	Total ($1,000)	Percent change, 1997–2002	Total ($1,000)	Percent change, 1997–2002
MICHIGAN—Con.											
Berrien	370	−6.8	15,738	18.3	−10.3	1,111,740	33.5	1,257,131	−0.7	78,786	−25.9
Branch	94	4.4	3,302	15.0	−12.8	156,470	22.0	347,710	29.0	45,051	7.7
Calhoun	202	−9.0	14,195	19.7	−9.5	1,041,245	32.3	2,202,344	−7.3	212,284	1.7
Cass	87	–	3,229	18.4	4.2	153,015	29.7	269,418	31.8	10,488	−27.9
Charlevoix	58	−15.9	2,699	17.8	−4.2	165,681	30.5	343,927	−12.4	22,597	−27.4
Cheboygan	32	−13.5	635	4.8	−28.5	25,313	7.6	40,376	−17.0	17,293	261.9
Chippewa	25	−19.4	678	3.6	−6.0	26,362	4.5	(D)	(NA)	5,887	39.6
Clare	27	−3.6	1,123	8.1	0.5	54,386	15.9	51,963	−1.9	2,536	−36.9
Clinton	65	4.8	3,306	10.8	16.4	216,219	23.1	(D)	(NA)	15,060	(NA)
Crawford	18	5.9	583	8.6	−27.9	33,019	17.1	61,047	86.3	5,918	35.2
Delta	63	6.8	2,805	13.6	−14.8	186,884	27.0	409,537	15.2	35,172	−12.1
Dickinson	51	2.0	2,700	14.9	0.2	166,760	25.6	(D)	(NA)	(D)	(NA)
Eaton	82	−12.8	3,195	7.3	−6.0	185,086	11.3	(D)	(NA)	19,493	(NA)
Emmet	66	15.8	1,653	6.8	−15.3	77,865	9.3	168,677	106.7	6,262	23.1
Genesee	347	−2.3	22,553	11.0	−21.3	2,117,760	24.9	2,677,385	−25.5	140,474	−22.2
Gladwin	42	−8.7	686	9.8	−27.2	37,536	19.0	80,577	−29.3	9,861	12.2
Gogebic	26	−3.7	773	9.4	3.8	29,493	12.6	36,421	30.1	1,694	−34.2
Grand Traverse	206	8.4	5,482	8.4	−13.3	285,057	11.7	544,825	11.7	29,948	(NA)
Gratiot	60	17.6	2,227	10.6	−22.8	104,070	16.0	211,775	49.2	14,422	0.1
Hillsdale	102	−1.9	4,244	19.5	−30.5	255,001	34.5	525,585	6.5	49,777	−13.9
Houghton	46	7.0	812	4.5	−10.3	27,730	5.2	(D)	(NA)	(D)	(NA)
Huron	78	16.4	3,001	15.5	−19.6	155,361	25.5	363,617	11.5	29,704	−5.4
Ingham	265	−2.6	15,126	7.3	−24.3	1,199,632	13.4	(D)	(NA)	149,184	(NA)
Ionia	76	−5.0	3,858	16.7	0.1	218,238	28.0	344,720	−8.2	19,015	−17.0
Iosco	37	8.8	1,132	9.9	−3.7	46,344	14.5	116,257	39.9	7,633	26.9
Iron	(NA)	(NA)	407	7.2	24.1	14,457	9.4	(NA)	(NA)	(NA)	(NA)
Isabella	57	−1.7	2,362	6.0	−0.8	122,822	9.7	204,160	23.6	14,059	72.9
Jackson	317	−9.7	10,301	13.4	−7.5	647,417	21.2	1,177,854	8.8	117,403	30.6
Kalamazoo	385	−3.5	20,913	13.9	−13.5	1,699,001	26.9	4,273,710	145.0	163,956	−31.1
Kalkaska	17	−10.5	530	9.3	−20.3	21,517	11.2	49,276	−40.8	8,733	−49.0
Kent	1,183	−1.8	67,545	16.0	−15.2	4,981,393	25.6	7,278,648	−12.7	454,988	−38.8
Keweenaw	(NA)	(NA)	(D)	(NA)	(NA)	(D)	(NA)	(NA)	(NA)	(NA)	(NA)
Lake	(NA)	(NA)	117	3.1	0.9	3,266	3.8	(NA)	(NA)	(NA)	(NA)
Lapeer	133	−4.3	5,111	15.1	−7.9	254,501	24.6	516,432	31.7	45,948	−18.8
Leelanau	(NA)	(NA)	248	2.4	−17.1	6,655	2.4	(NA)	(NA)	(NA)	(NA)
Lenawee	170	4.3	7,707	17.6	−16.2	526,985	33.4	980,385	26.6	62,371	−23.0
Livingston	272	3.0	9,067	12.1	0.4	618,978	21.5	1,364,089	26.9	89,636	35.4
Luce	(NA)	(NA)	(D)	(NA)	(NA)	(D)	(NA)	(NA)	(NA)	(NA)	(NA)
Mackinac	(NA)	(NA)	160	2.3	(NA)	4,827	2.6	(NA)	(NA)	(NA)	(NA)
Macomb	1,959	−7.4	83,569	20.1	−11.7	7,464,272	34.8	9,707,782	6.1	617,353	−39.6
Manistee	30	−3.2	1,108	9.3	−26.9	67,623	18.8	158,315	12.6	14,610	−53.7
Marquette	47	20.5	938	2.6	1.2	37,805	3.1	60,897	56.3	(D)	(NA)
Mason	42	5.0	2,485	15.8	−6.5	115,649	24.7	236,102	−18.4	10,270	−72.8
Mecosta	34	−17.1	1,635	8.7	−11.9	82,986	15.3	195,274	9.2	11,652	−56.0
Menominee	62	10.7	2,521	21.0	−17.6	117,508	32.9	246,803	5.9	13,284	13.9
Midland	69	−2.8	6,541	14.1	57.5	764,235	33.3	651,105	−16.9	(D)	(NA)
Missaukee	(NA)	(NA)	664	11.8	11.4	26,247	19.0	(NA)	(NA)	(NA)	(NA)
Monroe	151	9.4	8,419	14.2	−14.9	730,082	29.2	1,142,085	−12.8	136,842	−32.2
Montcalm	80	3.9	5,608	22.4	−23.2	311,525	35.8	433,588	−6.6	28,915	60.7
Montmorency	(NA)	(NA)	366	9.6	−5.7	13,207	13.7	(NA)	(NA)	(NA)	(NA)
Muskegon	332	−0.9	13,897	16.4	−4.8	864,649	28.1	1,554,642	2.2	96,486	−26.2
Newaygo	39	−15.2	1,924	11.2	−22.0	130,355	24.8	136,857	−50.7	12,116	6.4
Oakland	2,160	−8.7	81,511	8.7	−22.8	8,680,858	15.7	12,578,604	−1.1	423,028	−56.1
Oceana	42	−17.6	1,634	14.6	18.5	53,993	18.5	124,170	19.5	6,545	0.1
Ogemaw	34	17.2	655	6.7	−28.0	24,478	9.7	61,517	17.0	4,155	22.5
Ontonagon	(NA)	(NA)	384	11.4	−3.3	26,562	26.7	(NA)	(NA)	(NA)	(NA)
Osceola	49	36.1	2,158	25.9	−32.0	147,042	39.5	335,341	−4.3	33,269	91.2
Oscoda	(NA)	(NA)	434	12.3	1.6	16,248	18.9	(NA)	(NA)	(NA)	(NA)
Otsego	44	12.8	1,655	10.7	−1.0	77,189	14.4	87,754	−30.2	5,458	−47.2
Ottawa	616	4.2	38,663	27.2	−10.1	2,492,732	41.2	4,672,629	28.2	224,845	−42.2
Presque Isle	(NA)	(NA)	277	5.5	13.5	8,084	6.1	(NA)	(NA)	(NA)	(NA)
Roscommon	(NA)	(NA)	564	6.1	(NA)	22,776	8.9	(NA)	(NA)	(NA)	(NA)
Saginaw	241	0.8	14,181	12.6	−26.0	1,313,831	28.2	2,768,531	12.7	186,038	2.6
St. Clair	282	−4.1	9,490	13.9	−6.0	528,731	20.7	1,059,083	−4.7	46,638	−59.6
St. Joseph	157	−3.7	8,908	30.0	−10.4	524,528	48.1	1,294,691	−6.9	100,110	16.2
Sanilac	83	−5.7	2,840	14.7	−14.9	134,846	25.4	260,862	−27.4	20,856	−17.0
Schoolcraft	(NA)	(NA)	246	6.5	−1.2	15,439	12.3	(NA)	(NA)	(NA)	(NA)
Shiawassee	82	−4.7	2,671	10.9	−11.0	123,478	16.6	275,895	33.0	10,290	−30.5
Tuscola	56	−13.8	2,321	12.4	−9.5	115,515	20.4	173,806	−11.8	11,215	−36.3

See footnotes at end of table.

[Includes United States, states, and 3,141 counties/county equivalents defined as of February 22, 2005. For more information on these areas, see Appendix C, Geographic Information]

| County | Manufacturing (NAICS 31–33) | | | | | | | | | | |
| | Establishments, 2002[1] | | Employment, 2005[2] | | | Earnings, 2005[2] | | Value added by manufactures, 2002[1] | | Capital expenditures, 2002[1] | |
	Total	Percent change, 1997–2002	Total	Percent of all employees	Percent change, 2001–2005	Total ($1,000)	Percent of all earnings	Total ($1,000)	Percent change, 1997–2002	Total ($1,000)	Percent change, 1997–2002
MICHIGAN—Con.											
Van Buren	104	-18.1	3,819	13.2	-17.8	204,407	20.2	762,247	35.3	48,210	-19.5
Washtenaw	393	-4.6	21,973	9.0	-18.8	2,158,558	17.3	3,333,991	5.3	117,071	-68.6
Wayne	2,059	-13.8	106,488	10.9	-27.7	10,398,420	19.0	18,890,667	-12.1	1,275,878	-40.7
Wexford	62	8.8	3,863	20.1	-7.0	185,458	28.8	(D)	(NA)	(D)	(NA)
MINNESOTA	8,139	0.6	362,545	10.4	-7.5	23,518,176	15.4	39,610,449	8.1	2,815,001	-11.3
Aitkin	(NA)	(NA)	550	7.0	12.7	14,758	8.5	(NA)	(NA)	(NA)	(NA)
Anoka	655	6.7	23,699	14.7	-6.4	1,837,836	28.6	2,506,784	14.7	106,719	-24.4
Becker	41	-2.4	2,257	10.1	19.8	100,494	17.5	142,990	48.8	22,736	112.9
Beltrami	47	9.3	1,623	6.1	-2.3	76,151	10.0	98,631	45.5	(D)	(NA)
Benton	70	32.1	5,184	19.4	22.6	278,884	35.6	333,636	81.3	12,634	51.1
Big Stone	(NA)	(NA)	67	2.0	3.1	1,487	1.8	(NA)	(NA)	(NA)	(NA)
Blue Earth	86	10.3	3,846	7.8	1.2	195,478	12.0	657,410	87.4	32,653	-10.2
Brown	41	–	3,693	18.4	-9.7	187,686	30.1	589,630	-30.6	34,223	8.9
Carlton	37	23.3	1,866	10.3	-21.2	113,234	19.2	(D)	(NA)	(NA)	(NA)
Carver	157	9.8	9,758	20.0	-2.2	654,501	33.0	1,297,151	33.4	86,943	6.8
Cass	(NA)	(NA)	695	3.2	-2.1	14,993	3.9	(NA)	(NA)	(NA)	(NA)
Chippewa	24	–	1,338	13.8	3.6	59,828	22.5	56,213	-14.4	2,090	-67.1
Chisago	98	-3.0	2,270	10.8	2.0	109,326	16.9	126,746	-8.3	10,192	-28.6
Clay	40	5.3	967	3.6	-9.0	37,689	5.2	91,746	59.4	5,831	-46.8
Clearwater	17	(NA)	477	10.0	-10.2	18,819	17.8	43,977	(NA)	2,043	(NA)
Cook	(NA)	(NA)	(D)	(NA)	(NA)	(D)	(NA)	(NA)	(NA)	(NA)	(NA)
Cottonwood	22	37.5	1,438	16.6	44.4	48,868	20.2	110,992	-37.2	11,767	16.7
Crow Wing	111	16.8	3,049	8.6	-8.3	136,076	12.0	212,507	-14.4	(D)	(NA)
Dakota	486	10.7	20,340	8.9	-3.4	1,294,255	13.2	2,290,263	0.3	151,999	8.6
Dodge	27	-6.9	1,595	15.8	34.0	90,443	28.7	41,806	-64.9	(D)	(NA)
Douglas	89	23.6	2,938	11.2	8.8	133,662	17.7	316,927	14.7	19,541	51.3
Faribault	33	17.9	1,406	15.2	-16.5	61,373	18.1	153,127	74.3	10,333	39.2
Fillmore	37	-11.9	1,120	8.9	-14.3	63,894	20.2	49,532	-60.1	3,978	-21.0
Freeborn	62	-6.1	2,582	13.8	-19.9	113,258	20.6	250,333	13.2	12,552	-21.6
Goodhue	90	11.1	3,974	13.5	-19.7	234,195	22.1	412,114	2.1	11,928	-56.9
Grant	(NA)	(NA)	105	2.8	-45.9	2,321	2.8	(NA)	(NA)	(NA)	(NA)
Hennepin	2,107	-12.4	89,969	8.6	-11.1	7,218,722	11.9	9,475,432	-2.9	591,937	-42.9
Houston	27	(NA)	953	10.0	31.1	32,450	14.7	(D)	(NA)	(D)	(NA)
Hubbard	34	6.3	1,319	16.4	-5.9	52,819	21.6	97,050	31.7	5,805	-21.2
Isanti	72	22.0	1,650	7.9	-5.8	68,984	13.5	116,957	43.8	5,104	-44.2
Itasca	54	-6.9	1,618	6.9	-6.4	86,460	12.3	228,093	-8.5	20,505	-52.5
Jackson	12	-33.3	1,351	16.9	43.4	63,889	27.2	(D)	(NA)	(D)	(NA)
Kanabec	17	–	573	7.9	-19.7	21,606	12.7	38,041	-23.7	(D)	(NA)
Kandiyohi	64	-3.0	3,190	10.5	-2.7	143,759	15.0	232,399	-4.6	5,564	-84.6
Kittson	(NA)	(NA)	83	2.8	53.7	2,630	3.9	(NA)	(NA)	(NA)	(NA)
Koochiching	20	81.8	1,159	15.3	-14.3	78,270	27.8	(D)	(NA)	(D)	(NA)
Lac qui Parle	(NA)	(NA)	382	7.7	8.8	13,496	10.3	(NA)	(NA)	(NA)	(NA)
Lake	(NA)	(NA)	667	9.5	13.1	35,926	17.2	(NA)	(NA)	(NA)	(NA)
Lake of the Woods	(NA)	(NA)	(D)	(NA)	(NA)	(D)	(NA)	(NA)	(NA)	(NA)	(NA)
Le Sueur	48	-5.9	2,772	18.7	-9.6	121,213	31.2	557,357	45.6	10,096	-34.5
Lincoln	(NA)	(NA)	33	0.9	13.8	740	0.8	(NA)	(NA)	(NA)	(NA)
Lyon	33	17.9	2,341	11.6	-44.2	101,612	15.2	219,795	64.9	40,894	164.6
McLeod	73	9.0	6,552	27.2	-5.0	408,704	46.5	(D)	(NA)	141,874	50.6
Mahnomen	(NA)	(NA)	(D)	(NA)	(NA)	(D)	(NA)	(NA)	(NA)	(NA)	(NA)
Marshall	(NA)	(NA)	373	6.8	-4.6	14,123	12.7	(NA)	(NA)	(NA)	(NA)
Martin	45	2.3	1,754	12.3	-6.1	81,336	18.0	146,564	-12.7	(D)	(NA)
Meeker	53	-8.6	1,634	12.3	-5.5	72,063	21.5	145,121	21.3	12,901	-48.3
Mille Lacs	56	47.4	933	7.4	-40.3	36,387	10.1	118,371	93.4	5,145	104.1
Morrison	54	22.7	2,150	11.9	1.6	84,984	17.9	163,680	57.2	11,978	78.4
Mower	36	-2.7	4,522	20.2	2.6	262,751	34.4	733,771	(NA)	10,877	-56.9
Murray	(NA)	(NA)	299	5.6	-23.9	9,901	6.8	(NA)	(NA)	(NA)	(NA)
Nicollet	40	17.6	4,845	27.2	-9.1	191,897	31.3	299,474	12.9	8,055	-53.9
Nobles	27	12.5	2,858	19.2	14.2	124,724	26.5	185,374	-21.6	6,288	-35.8
Norman	(NA)	(NA)	10	0.2	-50.0	[3]25	(NA)	(NA)	(NA)	(NA)	(NA)
Olmsted	98	27.3	10,031	9.1	-20.4	807,620	15.5	1,340,537	28.8	(D)	(NA)
Otter Tail	86	-5.5	3,630	10.2	-1.3	140,729	15.5	312,419	19.8	27,851	197.5
Pennington	24	50.0	1,578	13.4	-7.6	74,922	19.6	172,100	-36.3	27,755	124.1
Pine	(NA)	(NA)	306	2.6	-17.7	10,221	3.3	(NA)	(NA)	(NA)	(NA)
Pipestone	13	-13.3	727	11.3	-8.8	28,040	13.6	79,542	76.4	8,808	855.3
Polk	37	-7.5	1,735	9.5	-2.9	73,701	15.1	235,776	81.3	8,246	93.9
Pope	30	3.4	615	9.0	3.4	34,721	18.6	28,211	-19.1	3,125	61.1
Ramsey	700	-8.5	33,207	8.2	-12.6	2,856,977	13.8	4,900,623	-2.2	179,904	-46.5
Red Lake	(NA)	(NA)	(D)	(NA)	(NA)	(D)	(NA)	(NA)	(NA)	(NA)	(NA)
Redwood	25	19.0	862	8.5	-14.6	39,455	13.0	60,253	-19.8	3,667	-25.6
Renville	33	-2.9	1,025	11.2	-12.0	50,292	19.8	172,907	168.6	11,470	39.9

See footnotes at end of table.

Table B-15. Counties — **Manufacturing**—Con.

[Includes United States, states, and 3,141 counties/county equivalents defined as of February 22, 2005. For more information on these areas, see Appendix C, Geographic Information]

County	Establishments, 2002[1]		Employment, 2005[2]			Earnings, 2005[2]		Value added by manufactures, 2002[1]		Capital expenditures, 2002[1]	
	Total	Percent change, 1997–2002	Total	Percent of all employees	Percent change, 2001–2005	Total ($1,000)	Percent of all earnings	Total ($1,000)	Percent change, 1997–2002	Total ($1,000)	Percent change, 1997–2002
MINNESOTA—Con.											
Rice	85	−1.2	4,250	14.0	−18.4	220,013	21.4	566,649	25.9	30,648	−34.2
Rock	(NA)	(NA)	384	6.8	−14.7	15,360	8.8	(NA)	(NA)	(NA)	(NA)
Roseau	21	16.7	5,286	40.1	8.1	286,475	64.6	(D)	(NA)	9,788	2.9
St. Louis	231	1.3	6,154	5.1	0.3	283,438	6.1	484,921	4.9	(D)	(NA)
Scott	160	8.1	4,496	8.3	−21.9	310,256	14.2	504,749	14.0	47,662	36.5
Sherburne	125	30.2	3,439	10.4	10.7	187,804	16.8	221,299	−18.7	16,796	−14.3
Sibley	25	–	547	8.5	3.8	22,059	13.7	133,198	3.1	3,434	22.2
Stearns	255	16.4	12,682	12.7	−7.7	596,405	16.5	1,181,105	28.5	91,932	27.2
Steele	75	11.9	5,942	23.2	−9.1	323,626	34.7	561,382	8.5	30,147	−20.9
Stevens	(NA)	(NA)	581	8.8	9.2	30,716	14.1	(NA)	(NA)	(NA)	(NA)
Swift	(NA)	(NA)	765	12.5	−10.7	33,827	19.9	(NA)	(NA)	(NA)	(NA)
Todd	44	−6.4	2,007	17.1	2.6	83,029	30.3	140,734	34.7	8,187	−23.6
Traverse	(NA)	(NA)	69	3.0	−5.5	1,943	4.0	(NA)	(NA)	(D)	(NA)
Wabasha	34	−12.8	2,153	20.5	0.9	109,120	34.6	199,028	23.6	(D)	(NA)
Wadena	20	−4.8	807	10.3	−27.4	28,187	12.1	49,482	15.0	2,270	32.6
Waseca	28	−3.4	2,496	22.1	67.5	127,172	34.7	307,642	15.7	34,213	76.3
Washington	229	9.0	11,682	12.1	−2.9	857,635	22.7	1,424,628	34.1	125,894	21.4
Watonwan	18	−14.3	1,492	22.9	−12.5	58,506	26.6	64,510	3.7	4,295	−3.0
Wilkin	(NA)	(NA)	29	0.8	−38.3	393	0.4	(NA)	(NA)	(NA)	(NA)
Winona	114	−1.7	6,217	19.2	−8.5	310,139	29.5	484,631	−1.0	26,242	−18.6
Wright	199	11.2	5,698	11.1	11.1	268,089	16.5	420,858	39.8	28,682	42.7
Yellow Medicine	(NA)	(NA)	337	5.5	−35.9	13,261	6.6	(NA)	(NA)	(NA)	(NA)
MISSISSIPPI	2,796	−7.0	183,616	12.2	−10.6	8,526,643	16.6	16,126,629	−5.6	1,111,609	−21.5
Adams	26	−31.6	619	3.6	−64.9	22,810	4.5	(D)	(NA)	(D)	(NA)
Alcorn	52	−10.3	3,982	22.3	−19.0	180,143	32.7	281,516	−24.2	80,673	360.4
Amite	11	10.0	531	10.0	−40.3	18,762	16.2	52,762	59.9	(D)	(NA)
Attala	21	−4.5	1,132	13.2	−16.7	36,394	16.9	47,121	0.6	1,971	−27.5
Benton	(NA)	(NA)	283	12.0	−39.9	9,045	16.4	(NA)	(NA)	(NA)	(NA)
Bolivar	24	9.1	1,572	9.2	−39.3	72,851	14.9	152,207	−35.8	8,201	(NA)
Calhoun	28	−17.6	1,309	21.7	−17.7	59,963	32.5	127,070	43.5	4,644	−40.8
Carroll	(NA)	(NA)	204	7.6	(NA)	6,727	12.6	(NA)	(NA)	(NA)	(NA)
Chickasaw	74	−7.5	3,277	36.7	−7.8	139,449	50.0	160,137	−1.4	4,110	−34.4
Choctaw	(NA)	(NA)	348	9.4	−4.1	13,135	12.9	(NA)	(NA)	(NA)	(NA)
Claiborne	(NA)	(NA)	255	5.2	−48.4	10,072	4.7	(NA)	(NA)	(NA)	(NA)
Clarke	20	11.1	620	12.3	−61.7	31,375	23.3	51,285	−65.3	2,650	−71.7
Clay	26	4.0	2,988	29.3	−24.1	122,216	39.6	215,980	−46.8	20,295	40.9
Coahoma	21	−25.0	841	6.5	−28.8	37,765	9.1	(D)	(NA)	(D)	(NA)
Copiah	32	–	2,298	19.9	−2.0	85,220	27.0	182,117	28.3	13,832	14.1
Covington	12	−29.4	1,734	20.2	1.2	50,599	20.6	77,344	14.0	(D)	(NA)
DeSoto	124	−5.3	6,163	10.4	−6.1	296,355	14.4	638,080	12.9	72,306	66.8
Forrest	81	−3.6	2,672	5.2	−12.9	122,685	7.0	453,733	8.0	38,967	−7.1
Franklin	(NA)	(NA)	144	5.6	27.4	5,531	7.8	(NA)	(NA)	(NA)	(NA)
George	(NA)	(NA)	299	4.0	−22.9	11,593	6.6	(NA)	(NA)	(NA)	(NA)
Greene	(NA)	(NA)	(D)	(NA)	(NA)	(D)	(NA)	(NA)	(NA)	(NA)	(NA)
Grenada	26	8.3	3,511	24.6	−4.8	159,568	36.1	147,201	−37.0	10,919	−64.1
Hancock	29	(NA)	1,102	5.0	−22.0	83,819	11.5	(D)	(NA)	(D)	(NA)
Harrison	135	−2.9	4,059	3.3	−23.4	208,642	4.7	(NA)	(NA)	(D)	(NA)
Hinds	183	−12.0	6,105	3.5	−30.7	348,129	4.7	634,634	−36.6	44,740	−25.9
Holmes	9	−35.7	766	11.9	72.5	31,110	19.1	23,972	−70.8	(D)	(NA)
Humphreys	4	–	(D)	(NA)	(NA)	(D)	(NA)	(D)	(NA)	(D)	(NA)
Issaquena	(NA)	(NA)	12	1.5	(NA)	90	0.6	(NA)	(NA)	(NA)	(NA)
Itawamba	35	−12.5	1,645	18.8	19.5	64,365	27.0	149,450	15.5	6,015	102.6
Jackson	86	−12.2	15,708	24.8	1.0	1,021,485	41.4	(D)	(NA)	(D)	(NA)
Jasper	13	−13.3	1,439	23.2	−13.8	52,997	27.1	(D)	(NA)	4,011	32.6
Jefferson	(NA)	(NA)	45	(NA)	(NA)	–	–	(NA)	(NA)	(NA)	(NA)
Jefferson Davis	(NA)	(NA)	(D)	(NA)	(NA)	(D)	(NA)	(NA)	(NA)	(NA)	(NA)
Jones	76	11.8	7,902	20.9	7.4	326,397	24.5	(D)	(NA)	26,616	−34.1
Kemper	(NA)	(NA)	485	14.6	52.0	12,917	16.7	(NA)	(NA)	(NA)	(NA)
Lafayette	23	−20.7	1,703	6.8	−12.3	76,046	8.9	151,596	29.6	8,872	−9.9
Lamar	20	−9.1	1,120	6.0	−8.6	45,277	8.6	43,526	19.4	(D)	(NA)
Lauderdale	74	−10.8	3,951	8.4	−19.2	172,578	10.6	295,891	−37.2	25,241	−31.6
Lawrence	9	–	825	17.7	1.2	81,898	45.4	(D)	(NA)	(D)	(NA)
Leake	13	−27.8	(D)	(NA)	(NA)	(D)	(NA)	262,621	46.5	(D)	(NA)
Lee	159	−16.8	14,869	23.4	−16.0	711,894	30.5	1,169,302	−1.9	52,803	−36.6
Leflore	39	−2.5	2,922	14.7	−16.4	98,458	15.5	(D)	(NA)	(D)	(NA)
Lincoln	27	−3.6	1,252	7.3	−5.1	104,012	18.4	130,685	0.8	6,917	32.8
Lowndes	72	1.4	3,949	11.6	−30.2	219,786	18.0	501,549	−18.8	20,532	−48.3
Madison	72	26.3	9,302	16.1	208.5	519,476	24.0	240,959	38.1	12,625	−66.3
Marion	26	–	1,153	10.3	−16.3	29,277	9.3	60,249	14.8	2,658	100.0
Marshall	32	10.3	949	9.5	−31.6	49,094	17.8	73,047	−28.8	4,009	−51.2
Monroe	59	−16.9	3,970	25.6	3.0	227,314	42.5	580,270	34.9	36,204	−49.9
Montgomery	21	–	380	8.6	−9.1	10,636	8.6	49,227	23.4	1,054	(NA)
Neshoba	24	−25.0	984	5.2	−47.2	55,890	8.7	122,846	−7.2	17,231	−24.6

See footnotes at end of table.

Table B-15. Counties — **Manufacturing**—Con.

[Includes United States, states, and 3,141 counties/county equivalents defined as of February 22, 2005. For more information on these areas, see Appendix C, Geographic Information]

County	Manufacturing (NAICS 31–33)												
	Establishments, 2002[1]		Employment, 2005[2]			Earnings, 2005[2]		Value added by manufactures, 2002[1]		Capital expenditures, 2002[1]			
	Total	Percent change, 1997–2002	Total	Percent of all employees	Percent change, 2001–2005	Total ($1,000)	Percent of all earnings	Total ($1,000)	Percent change, 1997–2002	Total ($1,000)	Percent change, 1997–2002		
MISSISSIPPI—Con.													
Newton	23	15.0	1,641	18.1	−6.7	67,625	22.3	100,116	11.8	2,276	−12.0		
Noxubee	22	10.0	1,297	26.4	−14.7	41,687	32.6	66,862	−1.9	8,930	37.9		
Oktibbeha	28	−20.0	1,650	6.6	−15.4	80,218	10.3	116,053	−29.5	8,122	40.7		
Panola	40	−9.1	2,282	14.9	−19.4	92,027	20.0	278,914	−3.7	5,936	−26.9		
Pearl River	47	–	815	4.8	0.4	41,020	10.6	92,136	1.3	6,497	6.1		
Perry	8	14.3	811	18.8	−17.0	56,544	46.2	134,680	(NA)	(D)	(NA)		
Pike	34	−5.6	3,197	16.2	−13.0	95,000	16.5	148,761	−24.0	(D)	(NA)		
Pontotoc	83	−9.8	7,276	45.3	17.3	300,205	59.6	493,640	34.6	14,712	0.1		
Prentiss	52	13.0	2,895	28.1	−17.9	111,968	38.3	418,230	12.6	20,383	83.7		
Quitman	(NA)	(NA)	265	9.0	−8.3	8,028	10.2	(NA)	(NA)	(NA)	(NA)		
Rankin	121	−4.7	4,989	6.8	−15.6	227,699	8.9	821,462	47.0	31,024	−25.9		
Scott	32	14.3	6,128	39.2	4.3	190,155	37.7	721,372	219.5	24,012	13.0		
Sharkey	(NA)	(NA)	(D)	(NA)	(NA)	(D)	(NA)	(NA)	(NA)	(NA)	(NA)		
Simpson	(NA)	(NA)	315	2.9	−37.9	6,545	2.0	(NA)	(NA)	(NA)	(NA)		
Smith	15	−11.8	1,484	28.1	−17.0	65,181	27.0	93,644	−32.5	2,776	−36.3		
Stone	11	−26.7	647	12.0	−5.7	28,552	19.0	(D)	(NA)	(D)	(NA)		
Sunflower	23	4.5	1,377	9.9	−27.9	34,585	9.3	212,686	3.8	30,970	349.8		
Tallahatchie	(NA)	(NA)	129	2.5	−51.9	3,459	2.9	(NA)	(NA)	(NA)	(NA)		
Tate	14	−12.5	884	9.1	−26.0	32,384	12.7	92,838	−5.3	(D)	(NA)		
Tippah	33	−21.4	2,991	29.5	−0.6	126,455	43.5	197,558	22.8	11,938	86.2		
Tishomingo	34	−26.1	2,178	28.9	−15.3	80,235	37.9	148,096	16.8	3,110	−18.4		
Tunica	8	(NA)	(D)	(NA)	(NA)	(D)	(NA)	18,179	(NA)	(D)	(NA)		
Union	36	−7.7	2,884	23.6	−10.6	117,381	33.1	153,597	−32.9	4,450	−37.1		
Walthall	21	−12.5	693	13.8	−11.0	19,548	15.6	31,065	−17.8	1,181	−41.8		
Warren	50	16.3	4,689	15.5	−6.6	216,134	18.9	473,124	35.3	28,774	−54.1		
Washington	55	−15.4	2,351	8.6	−35.7	108,351	12.9	343,992	−30.1	18,724	−40.1		
Wayne	20	25.0	919	11.1	−19.9	36,270	13.5	111,466	11.0	1,450	−66.7		
Webster	15	−11.8	560	15.2	−54.4	17,964	20.6	49,268	−46.5	1,384	−38.2		
Wilkinson	(NA)	(NA)	152	5.1	−33.6	4,905	6.7	(NA)	(NA)	(NA)	(NA)		
Winston	20	−23.1	1,707	20.8	13.8	83,984	34.2	81,880	−38.8	6,774	−55.0		
Yalobusha	12	−29.4	778	17.0	−38.4	45,278	34.9	129,726	18.8	5,840	45.9		
Yazoo	25	19.0	863	9.3	−39.4	55,059	16.4	104,249	2.8	5,390	(NA)		
MISSOURI	7,210	−3.8	321,452	9.0	−8.8	19,457,633	13.8	41,528,244	−3.8	2,280,359	−14.1		
Adair	13	30.0	1,273	7.8	−2.2	51,096	12.6	(D)	(NA)	(D)	(NA)		
Andrew	(NA)	(NA)	105	1.6	22.1	2,444	2.2	(NA)	(NA)	(NA)	(NA)		
Atchison	(NA)	(NA)	25	0.8	−21.9	451	0.6	(NA)	(NA)	(NA)	(NA)		
Audrain	32	−15.8	2,236	15.1	−17.1	96,581	24.1	190,196	−8.7	9,060	−52.7		
Barry	55	−9.8	6,002	26.2	−10.7	222,137	35.4	423,255	−13.0	22,057	94.0		
Barton	18	−5.3	1,807	21.7	−19.2	78,025	38.8	170,486	31.7	4,130	−2.5		
Bates	(NA)	(NA)	418	5.1	6.6	17,901	10.6	(NA)	(NA)	(NA)	(NA)		
Benton	(NA)	(NA)	457	5.8	56.0	13,764	9.1	(NA)	(NA)	(NA)	(NA)		
Bollinger	(NA)	(NA)	293	6.0	−21.4	6,763	8.3	(NA)	(NA)	(NA)	(NA)		
Boone	95	9.2	5,179	4.8	−9.1	262,526	7.0	732,218	−14.4	(D)	(NA)		
Buchanan	85	−11.5	6,361	11.3	−15.7	363,390	18.2	(D)	(NA)	58,923	(NA)		
Butler	56	5.7	4,157	15.6	19.3	148,151	18.4	226,340	−15.0	5,545	−45.6		
Caldwell	(NA)	(NA)	55	1.1	−21.4	851	1.1	(NA)	(NA)	(NA)	(NA)		
Callaway	35	−5.4	1,662	7.9	−12.2	87,215	13.2	57,738	−60.4	2,965	−59.2		
Camden	59	11.3	1,615	5.7	17.5	53,846	7.8	75,912	9.4	4,048	75.8		
Cape Girardeau	105	12.9	5,058	9.5	−14.7	263,072	15.3	(D)	(NA)	(D)	(NA)		
Carroll	(NA)	(NA)	387	7.2	−18.2	12,786	12.7	(NA)	(NA)	(NA)	(NA)		
Carter	(NA)	(NA)	251	9.9	−3.1	6,461	11.8	(NA)	(NA)	(NA)	(NA)		
Cass	87	22.5	1,461	3.9	4.4	54,002	5.3	143,823	201.7	7,124	−31.5		
Cedar	(NA)	(NA)	517	7.5	−5.7	17,001	13.0	(NA)	(NA)	(NA)	(NA)		
Chariton	(NA)	(NA)	283	5.6	−18.0	13,310	15.5	(NA)	(NA)	(NA)	(NA)		
Christian	113	11.9	1,552	5.5	−33.3	50,087	7.9	134,512	(NA)	7,142	−14.5		
Clark	(NA)	(NA)	189	5.5	−2.6	5,550	10.3	(NA)	(NA)	(NA)	(NA)		
Clay	230	7.5	12,905	10.9	−7.6	1,003,926	19.6	3,364,943	−23.8	95,826	−45.6		
Clinton	(NA)	(NA)	240	3.1	20.0	7,568	4.0	(NA)	(NA)	(NA)	(NA)		
Cole	61	15.1	2,769	4.2	−12.8	148,678	5.9	830,935	(NA)	37,122	(NA)		
Cooper	(NA)	(NA)	952	10.0	0.5	39,301	17.1	(NA)	(NA)	(NA)	(NA)		
Crawford	43	−17.3	2,054	18.7	2.6	71,500	25.4	117,453	57.2	5,327	−44.3		
Dade	(NA)	(NA)	234	5.3	0.4	6,770	7.5	(NA)	(NA)	(NA)	(NA)		
Dallas	(NA)	(NA)	673	8.7	160.9	15,918	11.3	(NA)	(NA)	(NA)	(NA)		
Daviess	(NA)	(NA)	427	10.2	22.3	15,499	19.2	(NA)	(NA)	(NA)	(NA)		
DeKalb	(NA)	(NA)	75	1.7	(NA)	2,019	1.9	(NA)	(NA)	(NA)	(NA)		
Dent	27	–	568	8.1	−6.9	17,430	10.7	58,591	157.9	(D)	(NA)		
Douglas	12	(NA)	489	6.2	−29.8	32,472	24.0	44,850	(NA)	(D)	(NA)		
Dunklin	29	11.5	1,245	8.6	−13.5	81,027	20.0	114,995	−15.2	3,317	−13.0		

See footnotes at end of table.

[Includes United States, states, and 3,141 counties/county equivalents defined as of February 22, 2005. For more information on these areas, see Appendix C, Geographic Information]

County	Manufacturing (NAICS 31–33)										
	Establishments, 2002[1]		Employment, 2005[2]			Earnings, 2005[2]		Value added by manufactures, 2002[1]		Capital expenditures, 2002[1]	
	Total	Percent change, 1997–2002	Total	Percent of all employees	Percent change, 2001–2005	Total ($1,000)	Percent of all earnings	Total ($1,000)	Percent change, 1997–2002	Total ($1,000)	Percent change, 1997–2002
MISSOURI—Con.											
Franklin	217	3.3	10,065	19.9	−6.5	491,768	31.2	1,078,963	13.2	54,406	15.2
Gasconade	39	2.6	1,614	18.1	−8.1	56,023	28.7	105,941	40.1	15,614	7.1
Gentry	(NA)	(NA)	337	9.0	3.1	12,468	16.1	(NA)	(NA)	(NA)	(NA)
Greene	345	−7.0	14,328	7.3	−16.9	887,189	12.4	1,604,662	−6.8	106,407	25.9
Grundy	13	18.2	627	11.1	−14.0	28,452	21.4	48,848	−71.9	12,609	143.1
Harrison	(NA)	(NA)	72	1.4	−16.3	1,267	1.3	(NA)	(NA)	(NA)	(NA)
Henry	39	21.9	1,503	13.0	−16.7	66,721	21.4	137,660	32.6	12,510	98.9
Hickory	(NA)	(NA)	86	3.1	−26.5	1,837	4.3	(NA)	(NA)	(NA)	(NA)
Holt	(NA)	(NA)	174	6.7	11.5	6,142	12.3	(NA)	(NA)	(NA)	(NA)
Howard	(NA)	(NA)	256	5.6	−34.4	10,752	13.2	(NA)	(NA)	(NA)	(NA)
Howell	90	28.6	3,686	15.8	−2.6	129,697	22.4	279,818	17.5	13,718	41.1
Iron	(NA)	(NA)	386	8.7	−40.3	18,292	14.9	(NA)	(NA)	(NA)	(NA)
Jackson	824	−9.2	28,956	6.3	−8.3	1,792,288	7.9	5,831,043	8.1	195,080	−14.9
Jasper	199	0.5	12,185	16.1	−1.7	589,946	24.4	1,085,831	20.2	60,093	−37.7
Jefferson	185	1.6	5,061	7.0	1.9	256,113	12.8	515,128	−7.7	26,204	−59.6
Johnson	29	−6.5	2,221	7.3	16.1	94,829	10.0	107,704	2.5	3,661	−69.2
Knox	(NA)	(NA)	113	4.6	11.9	3,158	8.0	(NA)	(NA)	(NA)	(NA)
Laclede	62	8.8	5,236	26.8	−4.5	236,198	42.8	398,252	12.9	14,475	−68.6
Lafayette	38	−9.5	1,267	8.6	5.8	42,828	12.1	105,855	137.3	2,955	−32.3
Lawrence	51	−5.6	1,631	11.4	−3.6	62,386	18.6	148,010	31.9	14,124	19.3
Lewis	(NA)	(NA)	156	3.4	(NA)	5,338	5.8	(NA)	(NA)	(NA)	(NA)
Lincoln	43	–	1,623	9.4	17.3	84,870	17.6	219,843	119.4	13,799	33.4
Linn	21	−12.5	1,033	13.8	−15.2	40,441	21.1	122,602	32.5	5,971	40.3
Livingston	24	−14.3	693	7.5	−34.3	30,287	12.8	71,856	1.3	4,764	47.9
McDonald	31	−8.8	2,595	24.9	−3.8	83,478	31.9	215,928	18.3	14,848	−28.2
Macon	10	−33.3	643	7.6	5.2	27,396	14.5	20,296	(NA)	(D)	(NA)
Madison	(NA)	(NA)	470	8.9	−21.1	13,172	11.4	(NA)	(NA)	(NA)	(NA)
Maries	(NA)	(NA)	269	5.1	−7.9	11,174	16.6	(NA)	(NA)	(NA)	(NA)
Marion	46	–	2,105	11.5	−27.8	119,613	22.5	(D)	(NA)	(D)	(NA)
Mercer	(NA)	(NA)	(D)	(NA)	(NA)	(D)	(NA)	(NA)	(NA)	(NA)	(NA)
Miller	24	−17.2	1,180	10.2	−4.1	40,343	14.1	68,517	3.3	(D)	(NA)
Mississippi	(NA)	(NA)	293	5.2	−5.2	13,727	9.8	(NA)	(NA)	(NA)	(NA)
Moniteau	24	9.1	845	12.3	−30.0	28,866	18.2	46,271	−59.7	3,098	−19.1
Monroe	8	14.3	821	16.0	−7.1	22,348	24.3	60,820	33.7	(D)	(NA)
Montgomery	29	−9.4	648	10.5	−17.5	23,374	18.5	45,030	21.1	2,048	52.2
Morgan	29	–	714	9.8	−4.2	24,195	13.5	35,343	−45.9	1,616	−14.1
New Madrid	17	–	2,728	27.5	−20.2	141,769	40.4	168,929	−36.8	(D)	(NA)
Newton	72	14.3	4,501	17.6	−11.3	205,489	24.0	338,415	17.1	10,472	−67.4
Nodaway	22	−4.3	2,149	15.7	7.2	109,522	29.9	391,251	6.7	28,807	32.9
Oregon	(NA)	(NA)	329	6.7	−28.8	7,863	8.1	(NA)	(NA)	(NA)	(NA)
Osage	28	16.7	1,072	16.2	1.6	39,061	27.0	120,048	106.0	2,110	−2.6
Ozark	(NA)	(NA)	253	7.0	8.1	5,067	9.0	(NA)	(NA)	(NA)	(NA)
Pemiscot	14	16.7	771	9.2	−18.2	30,559	13.4	49,385	2.8	843	−45.2
Perry	36	16.1	3,206	25.5	2.8	130,235	36.9	276,789	−4.0	32,415	168.0
Pettis	64	−7.2	4,842	18.9	−12.9	234,623	30.8	479,456	9.4	23,615	−47.2
Phelps	53	−3.6	1,940	7.8	22.8	77,363	10.1	114,929	7.9	7,289	−70.2
Pike	28	3.7	660	7.6	−12.4	36,369	16.2	103,082	−19.2	3,053	−66.3
Platte	51	8.5	2,917	6.0	11.5	168,566	9.1	203,600	94.2	11,566	97.2
Polk	34	–	828	6.4	15.0	31,508	10.1	74,560	56.4	(D)	(NA)
Pulaski	(NA)	(NA)	200	0.8	13.6	5,288	0.4	(NA)	(NA)	(NA)	(NA)
Putnam	(NA)	(NA)	165	6.3	135.7	3,203	7.5	(NA)	(NA)	(NA)	(NA)
Ralls	(NA)	(NA)	1,288	30.2	27.5	55,221	47.1	(NA)	(NA)	(NA)	(NA)
Randolph	28	−24.3	1,570	11.2	12.6	66,684	15.6	95,348	15.6	4,542	−39.9
Ray	18	−14.3	647	6.5	−4.1	26,327	12.5	52,771	34.7	(D)	(NA)
Reynolds	(NA)	(NA)	331	12.5	−24.8	9,791	12.0	(NA)	(NA)	(NA)	(NA)
Ripley	39	−7.1	692	13.8	21.2	17,971	18.1	20,908	−13.4	996	−51.4
St. Charles	273	−2.2	12,916	8.3	−1.6	933,412	15.6	2,494,300	19.1	75,818	−46.0
St. Clair	(NA)	(NA)	79	2.0	(NA)	2,074	2.8	(NA)	(NA)	(NA)	(NA)
Ste. Genevieve	35	9.4	1,583	20.0	−9.3	68,124	29.7	130,874	0.5	22,096	31.2
St. Francois	57	−13.6	2,539	8.7	4.9	90,071	11.2	168,060	−25.2	37,173	179.7
St. Louis	1,141	−10.3	63,209	8.0	−12.9	5,744,712	14.6	7,123,344	−17.0	448,795	−15.2
Saline	24	–	2,055	15.3	−9.1	85,292	23.3	216,040	−3.2	(D)	(NA)
Schuyler	(NA)	(NA)	23	1.3	(NA)	472	1.8	(NA)	(NA)	(NA)	(NA)
Scotland	(NA)	(NA)	147	5.7	4.3	5,953	11.6	(NA)	(NA)	(NA)	(NA)
Scott	76	−1.3	1,780	8.6	−4.2	68,012	10.7	288,150	22.8	15,355	27.7
Shannon	(NA)	(NA)	806	22.1	−0.9	19,783	28.7	(NA)	(NA)	(NA)	(NA)
Shelby	(NA)	(NA)	304	9.0	−30.6	13,354	19.2	(NA)	(NA)	(NA)	(NA)
Stoddard	43	7.5	3,142	19.4	14.1	120,288	27.4	453,102	204.0	10,701	217.3
Stone	(NA)	(NA)	(D)	(NA)	(NA)	(D)	(NA)	(NA)	(NA)	(NA)	(NA)
Sullivan	4	−20.0	(D)	(NA)	(NA)	(D)	(NA)	(D)	(NA)	(D)	(NA)

See footnotes at end of table.

County and City Data Book: 2007

U.S. Census Bureau

Table B-15. Counties — **Manufacturing**—Con.

[Includes United States, states, and 3,141 counties/county equivalents defined as of February 22, 2005. For more information on these areas, see Appendix C, Geographic Information]

County	Establishments, 2002[1]		Employment, 2005[2]			Earnings, 2005[2]		Value added by manufactures, 2002[1]		Capital expenditures, 2002[1]	
	Total	Percent change, 1997-2002	Total	Percent of all employ-ees	Percent change, 2001-2005	Total ($1,000)	Percent of all earnings	Total ($1,000)	Percent change, 1997-2002	Total ($1,000)	Percent change, 1997-2002
MISSOURI—Con.											
Taney	56	−5.1	712	2.3	−5.4	21,754	2.6	39,005	−20.9	(D)	(NA)
Texas	46	−13.2	1,061	10.9	−12.8	37,694	17.5	54,787	−30.6	1,720	−66.3
Vernon	21	−	1,161	10.3	−18.0	60,822	21.4	268,399	−4.2	6,643	(NA)
Warren	36	−2.7	1,468	14.0	−20.3	73,535	26.5	133,211	13.8	5,315	−13.2
Washington	23	(NA)	695	10.5	−13.7	33,861	19.8	34,422	(NA)	8,078	(NA)
Wayne	(NA)	(NA)	468	11.9	−1.3	12,634	15.2	(NA)	(NA)	(NA)	(NA)
Webster	57	29.5	1,389	11.8	4.0	54,535	20.5	95,760	(NA)	3,753	−14.8
Worth	(NA)	(NA)	(D)	(NA)	(NA)	(D)	(NA)	(NA)	(NA)	(NA)	(NA)
Wright	22	22.2	732	9.8	−1.7	27,779	18.0	32,799	−44.9	1,187	4.1
Independent City											
St. Louis city	685	−14.6	24,706	9.3	−14.1	1,906,803	12.8	4,870,268	−4.3	233,313	−36.2
MONTANA	1,234	6.4	23,244	3.8	−5.4	1,125,661	5.7	1,673,980	−3.4	220,108	45.8
Beaverhead	(NA)	(NA)	100	1.8	−18.7	2,408	1.6	(NA)	(NA)	(NA)	(NA)
Big Horn	(NA)	(NA)	29	0.4	(NA)	757	0.3	(NA)	(NA)	(NA)	(NA)
Blaine	(NA)	(NA)	28	0.9	(NA)	370	0.4	(NA)	(NA)	(NA)	(NA)
Broadwater	(NA)	(NA)	381	15.9	12.7	13,013	23.2	(NA)	(NA)	(NA)	(NA)
Carbon	(NA)	(NA)	159	2.9	−17.2	3,473	3.2	(NA)	(NA)	(NA)	(NA)
Carter	(NA)	(NA)	10	1.1	−	125	0.7	(NA)	(NA)	(NA)	(NA)
Cascade	76	−5.0	947	1.9	−13.3	46,699	2.6	84,296	45.1	6,159	−52.6
Chouteau	(NA)	(NA)	78	2.5	36.8	1,235	1.7	(NA)	(NA)	(NA)	(NA)
Custer	(NA)	(NA)	104	1.4	−34.2	2,795	1.4	(NA)	(NA)	(NA)	(NA)
Daniels	(NA)	(NA)	(D)	(NA)	(NA)	(D)	(NA)	(NA)	(NA)	(NA)	(NA)
Dawson	(NA)	(NA)	47	0.9	−13.0	1,356	0.9	(NA)	(NA)	(NA)	(NA)
Deer Lodge	(NA)	(NA)	109	2.5	(NA)	3,809	3.4	(NA)	(NA)	(NA)	(NA)
Fallon	(NA)	(NA)	(D)	(NA)	(NA)	(D)	(NA)	(NA)	(NA)	(NA)	(NA)
Fergus	(NA)	(NA)	375	4.9	−14.0	20,032	9.9	(NA)	(NA)	(NA)	(NA)
Flathead	153	23.4	3,657	6.4	−3.5	167,037	9.3	267,563	−24.2	23,873	−26.1
Gallatin[5]	165	11.5	2,645	4.2	−14.9	147,016	7.2	183,790	37.7	11,845	35.4
Garfield	(NA)	(NA)	(D)	(NA)	(NA)	(D)	(NA)	(NA)	(NA)	(NA)	(NA)
Glacier	(NA)	(NA)	(D)	(NA)	(NA)	(D)	(NA)	(NA)	(NA)	(NA)	(NA)
Golden Valley	(NA)	(NA)	(D)	(NA)	(NA)	(D)	(NA)	(NA)	(NA)	(NA)	(NA)
Granite	(NA)	(NA)	91	4.8	−9.9	2,245	5.7	(NA)	(NA)	(NA)	(NA)
Hill	(NA)	(NA)	80	0.8	−21.6	3,848	1.2	(NA)	(NA)	(NA)	(NA)
Jefferson	(NA)	(NA)	207	3.7	(NA)	11,118	7.4	(NA)	(NA)	(NA)	(NA)
Judith Basin	(NA)	(NA)	(D)	(NA)	(NA)	(D)	(NA)	(NA)	(NA)	(NA)	(NA)
Lake	42	40.0	955	6.8	−11.7	29,925	8.5	68,398	20.5	4,684	33.0
Lewis and Clark	(NA)	(NA)	902	2.2	−12.2	50,843	3.3	(NA)	(NA)	(NA)	(NA)
Liberty	(NA)	(NA)	(D)	(NA)	(NA)	(D)	(NA)	(NA)	(NA)	(NA)	(NA)
Lincoln	27	−18.2	459	4.9	−46.5	15,499	6.4	34,796	−27.8	755	−89.7
McCone	(NA)	(NA)	(D)	(NA)	(NA)	(D)	(NA)	(NA)	(NA)	(NA)	(NA)
Madison	(NA)	(NA)	147	3.1	−6.4	4,649	3.9	(NA)	(NA)	(NA)	(NA)
Meagher	(NA)	(NA)	(D)	(NA)	(NA)	(D)	(NA)	(NA)	(NA)	(NA)	(NA)
Mineral	(NA)	(NA)	208	9.8	16.2	6,470	13.8	(NA)	(NA)	(NA)	(NA)
Missoula	116	−14.7	3,124	4.2	5.1	151,065	5.9	245,709	12.4	9,426	−29.7
Musselshell	(NA)	(NA)	47	2.3	−2.1	1,116	2.4	(NA)	(NA)	(NA)	(NA)
Park[5]	(NA)	(NA)	481	4.9	16.7	17,317	7.5	(NA)	(NA)	(NA)	(NA)
Petroleum	(NA)	(NA)	10	2.7	(NA)	−	−	(NA)	(NA)	(NA)	(NA)
Phillips	(NA)	(NA)	42	1.6	−17.6	867	1.5	(NA)	(NA)	(NA)	(NA)
Pondera	(NA)	(NA)	65	2.0	−16.7	1,651	1.9	(NA)	(NA)	(NA)	(NA)
Powder River	(NA)	(NA)	(D)	(NA)	(NA)	(D)	(NA)	(NA)	(NA)	(NA)	(NA)
Powell	(NA)	(NA)	(D)	(NA)	(NA)	(D)	(NA)	(NA)	(NA)	(NA)	(NA)
Prairie	(NA)	(NA)	(D)	(NA)	(NA)	(D)	(NA)	(NA)	(NA)	(NA)	(NA)
Ravalli	91	37.9	1,327	6.7	−9.3	47,651	9.5	64,174	52.5	3,585	26.1
Richland	(NA)	(NA)	359	5.2	−3.2	14,413	7.1	(NA)	(NA)	(NA)	(NA)
Roosevelt	(NA)	(NA)	98	1.8	−1.0	2,828	2.0	(NA)	(NA)	(NA)	(NA)
Rosebud	(NA)	(NA)	23	0.4	(NA)	407	0.2	(NA)	(NA)	(NA)	(NA)
Sanders	(NA)	(NA)	287	5.1	−25.6	8,355	6.9	(NA)	(NA)	(NA)	(NA)
Sheridan	(NA)	(NA)	20	0.8	−37.5	410	0.7	(NA)	(NA)	(NA)	(NA)
Silver Bow	(NA)	(NA)	601	3.0	14.0	35,496	4.6	(NA)	(NA)	(NA)	(NA)
Stillwater	(NA)	(NA)	400	7.6	2.3	13,714	7.4	(NA)	(NA)	(NA)	(NA)
Sweet Grass	(NA)	(NA)	100	3.4	6.4	3,518	3.8	(NA)	(NA)	(NA)	(NA)
Teton	(NA)	(NA)	40	1.1	−20.0	1,144	1.2	(NA)	(NA)	(NA)	(NA)
Toole	(NA)	(NA)	(D)	(NA)	(NA)	(D)	(NA)	(NA)	(NA)	(NA)	(NA)
Treasure	(NA)	(NA)	10	2.1	(NA)	114	1.4	(NA)	(NA)	(NA)	(NA)
Valley	(NA)	(NA)	78	1.6	−15.2	2,323	1.7	(NA)	(NA)	(NA)	(NA)
Wheatland	(NA)	(NA)	26	2.3	(NA)	402	1.7	(NA)	(NA)	(NA)	(NA)
Wibaux	(NA)	(NA)	10	1.5	−	127	1.0	(NA)	(NA)	(NA)	(NA)
Yellowstone	179	−1.6	3,847	3.9	3.9	272,651	7.4	420,070	−25.1	45,906	39.5
Yellowstone National Park[5]	(X)	(NA)	(X)	(NA)	(NA)	(X)	(NA)	(X)	(NA)	(X)	(NA)

See footnotes at end of table.

Table B-15. Counties — **Manufacturing**—Con.

[Includes United States, states, and 3,141 counties/county equivalents defined as of February 22, 2005. For more information on these areas, see Appendix C, Geographic Information]

County	Establishments, 2002[1]		Employment, 2005[2]			Earnings, 2005[2]		Value added by manufactures, 2002[1]		Capital expenditures, 2002[1]	
	Total	Percent change, 1997–2002	Total	Percent of all employees	Percent change, 2001–2005	Total ($1,000)	Percent of all earnings	Total ($1,000)	Percent change, 1997–2002	Total ($1,000)	Percent change, 1997–2002
NEBRASKA	1,976	0.8	104,711	8.6	-7.6	5,193,739	11.5	11,469,004	6.0	799,333	-2.8
Adams	61	-3.2	2,874	13.8	-8.7	120,163	20.0	(D)	(NA)	19,368	25.7
Antelope	(NA)	(NA)	137	2.9	6.2	4,861	4.3	(NA)	(NA)	(NA)	(NA)
Arthur	(NA)	(NA)	(D)	(NA)	(NA)	(D)	(NA)	(NA)	(NA)	(NA)	(NA)
Banner	(NA)	(NA)	[4]5	(NA)	(NA)	302	2.7	(NA)	(NA)	(NA)	(NA)
Blaine	(NA)	(NA)	[4]5	(NA)	(NA)	152	5.3	(NA)	(NA)	(NA)	(NA)
Boone	(NA)	(NA)	94	2.5	-19.0	3,595	3.9	(NA)	(NA)	(NA)	(NA)
Box Butte	(NA)	(NA)	366	4.8	-14.5	15,280	5.5	(NA)	(NA)	(NA)	(NA)
Boyd	(NA)	(NA)	30	2.2	-6.3	821	4.1	(NA)	(NA)	(NA)	(NA)
Brown	(NA)	(NA)	54	2.3	-6.9	1,739	3.3	(NA)	(NA)	(NA)	(NA)
Buffalo	56	19.1	4,215	12.5	7.7	217,879	20.8	(D)	(NA)	(D)	(NA)
Burt	(NA)	(NA)	116	3.3	-16.5	4,017	5.2	(NA)	(NA)	(NA)	(NA)
Butler	(NA)	(NA)	573	12.9	20.1	21,842	22.0	(NA)	(NA)	(NA)	(NA)
Cass	(NA)	(NA)	468	4.8	-5.8	26,431	11.9	(NA)	(NA)	(NA)	(NA)
Cedar	(NA)	(NA)	210	3.8	-38.8	9,861	5.8	(NA)	(NA)	(NA)	(NA)
Chase	(NA)	(NA)	64	2.3	1.6	3,832	5.3	(NA)	(NA)	(NA)	(NA)
Cherry	(NA)	(NA)	77	1.8	-2.5	2,925	3.3	(NA)	(NA)	(NA)	(NA)
Cheyenne	(NA)	(NA)	427	5.1	-25.6	40,338	14.7	(NA)	(NA)	(NA)	(NA)
Clay	(NA)	(NA)	373	9.3	-20.5	14,270	12.5	(NA)	(NA)	(NA)	(NA)
Colfax	6	50.0	(D)	(NA)	(NA)	(D)	(NA)	(D)	(NA)	(D)	(NA)
Cuming	19	-36.7	739	11.4	-15.2	26,913	13.1	(D)	(NA)	6,402	107.1
Custer	(NA)	(NA)	542	7.5	4.8	27,182	13.2	(NA)	(NA)	(NA)	(NA)
Dakota	37	60.9	4,439	33.2	-33.3	182,381	40.1	(D)	(NA)	(D)	(NA)
Dawes	(NA)	(NA)	65	1.1	14.0	2,453	2.0	(NA)	(NA)	(NA)	(NA)
Dawson	28	7.7	3,747	24.7	-9.8	160,222	35.6	(D)	(NA)	(D)	(NA)
Deuel	(NA)	(NA)	(D)	(NA)	(NA)	(D)	(NA)	(NA)	(NA)	(NA)	(NA)
Dixon	2	(NA)	(D)	(NA)	(NA)	(D)	(NA)	(D)	(NA)	(D)	(NA)
Dodge	70	4.5	3,307	15.0	-10.9	139,469	21.7	382,457	20.5	8,430	-31.6
Douglas	520	-6.3	23,664	6.1	-13.1	1,211,999	6.6	3,151,364	-3.8	257,395	15.3
Dundy	(NA)	(NA)	16	1.2	(NA)	498	1.5	(NA)	(NA)	(NA)	(NA)
Fillmore	(NA)	(NA)	200	4.9	27.4	6,864	6.6	(NA)	(NA)	(NA)	(NA)
Franklin	(NA)	(NA)	(D)	(NA)	(NA)	(D)	(NA)	(NA)	(NA)	(NA)	(NA)
Frontier	(NA)	(NA)	29	1.6	(NA)	893	1.9	(NA)	(NA)	(NA)	(NA)
Furnas	(NA)	(NA)	45	1.6	-6.3	1,436	2.2	(NA)	(NA)	(NA)	(NA)
Gage	41	20.6	2,173	14.6	-1.7	105,845	25.6	177,462	31.6	6,578	-49.6
Garden	(NA)	(NA)	(D)	(NA)	(NA)	(D)	(NA)	(NA)	(NA)	(NA)	(NA)
Garfield	(NA)	(NA)	102	7.1	12.1	3,068	11.5	(NA)	(NA)	(NA)	(NA)
Gosper	(NA)	(NA)	23	2.3	(NA)	1,600	8.0	(NA)	(NA)	(NA)	(NA)
Grant	(NA)	(NA)	–	–	–	–	–	(NA)	(NA)	(NA)	(NA)
Greeley	(NA)	(NA)	46	3.0	-14.8	1,142	3.1	(NA)	(NA)	(NA)	(NA)
Hall	86	6.2	6,402	15.8	-7.7	342,733	24.8	(D)	(NA)	(D)	(NA)
Hamilton	20	-4.8	627	11.4	45.1	31,382	22.0	154,701	-3.7	6,291	-75.4
Harlan	(NA)	(NA)	32	1.8	-13.5	3,879	8.8	(NA)	(NA)	(NA)	(NA)
Hayes	(NA)	(NA)	(D)	(NA)	(NA)	(D)	(NA)	(NA)	(NA)	(NA)	(NA)
Hitchcock	(NA)	(NA)	123	7.5	215.4	5,658	17.5	(NA)	(NA)	(NA)	(NA)
Holt	(NA)	(NA)	219	2.8	23.7	25,264	12.2	(NA)	(NA)	(NA)	(NA)
Hooker	(NA)	(NA)	(D)	(NA)	(NA)	(D)	(NA)	(NA)	(NA)	(NA)	(NA)
Howard	(NA)	(NA)	21	0.7	-27.6	545	0.8	(NA)	(NA)	(NA)	(NA)
Jefferson	(NA)	(NA)	524	10.9	10.3	22,815	17.4	(NA)	(NA)	(NA)	(NA)
Johnson	(NA)	(NA)	(D)	(NA)	(NA)	(D)	(NA)	(NA)	(NA)	(NA)	(NA)
Kearney	(NA)	(NA)	260	7.2	51.2	12,039	11.8	(NA)	(NA)	(NA)	(NA)
Keith	(NA)	(NA)	358	6.6	-14.8	15,497	12.3	(NA)	(NA)	(NA)	(NA)
Keya Paha	(NA)	(NA)	(D)	(NA)	(NA)	(D)	(NA)	(NA)	(NA)	(NA)	(NA)
Kimball	(NA)	(NA)	354	12.8	4.4	9,237	15.3	(NA)	(NA)	(NA)	(NA)
Knox	(NA)	(NA)	197	4.1	10.1	4,805	4.4	(NA)	(NA)	(NA)	(NA)
Lancaster	271	1.5	14,793	7.4	-16.0	881,729	11.8	2,048,203	4.3	(D)	(NA)
Lincoln	(NA)	(NA)	412	1.8	-5.1	13,869	1.8	(NA)	(NA)	(NA)	(NA)
Logan	(NA)	(NA)	[4]5	(NA)	(NA)	267	3.2	(NA)	(NA)	(NA)	(NA)
Loup	(NA)	(NA)	[4]5	(NA)	(NA)	–	–	(NA)	(NA)	(NA)	(NA)
McPherson	(NA)	(NA)	–	–	–	–	–	(NA)	(NA)	(NA)	(NA)
Madison	62	19.2	4,746	16.2	26.6	203,981	22.9	453,867	-6.7	(D)	(NA)
Merrick	(NA)	(NA)	222	5.7	-41.1	8,199	8.4	(NA)	(NA)	(NA)	(NA)
Morrill	(NA)	(NA)	63	2.3	96.9	3,452	5.2	(NA)	(NA)	(NA)	(NA)
Nance	(NA)	(NA)	(D)	(NA)	(NA)	(D)	(NA)	(NA)	(NA)	(NA)	(NA)
Nemaha	(NA)	(NA)	593	11.2	14.5	29,710	15.0	(NA)	(NA)	(NA)	(NA)
Nuckolls	(NA)	(NA)	14	0.5	-6.7	383	0.6	(NA)	(NA)	(NA)	(NA)
Otoe	13	-23.5	1,487	15.8	12.9	68,172	27.6	119,164	22.4	13,249	157.5
Pawnee	(NA)	(NA)	140	8.5	-3.4	4,933	11.6	(NA)	(NA)	(NA)	(NA)
Perkins	(NA)	(NA)	24	1.2	-22.6	945	1.7	(NA)	(NA)	(NA)	(NA)
Phelps	7	-12.5	(D)	(NA)	(NA)	(D)	(NA)	(D)	(NA)	(D)	(NA)
Pierce	(NA)	(NA)	101	2.7	106.1	4,220	4.5	(NA)	(NA)	(NA)	(NA)

See footnotes at end of table.

[Includes United States, states, and 3,141 counties/county equivalents defined as of February 22, 2005. For more information on these areas, see Appendix C, Geographic Information]

County	Manufacturing (NAICS 31–33) Establishments, 2002[1] Total	Establishments, 2002[1] Percent change, 1997–2002	Employment, 2005[2] Total	Employment Percent of all employees	Employment Percent change, 2001–2005	Earnings, 2005[2] Total ($1,000)	Earnings Percent of all earnings	Value added by manufactures, 2002[1] Total ($1,000)	Value added Percent change, 1997–2002	Capital expenditures, 2002[1] Total ($1,000)	Capital expenditures Percent change, 1997–2002
NEBRASKA—Con.											
Platte	74	–	5,295	23.3	–13.6	254,175	33.5	756,911	37.4	56,202	73.7
Polk	(NA)	(NA)	26	0.9	13.0	619	0.8	(NA)	(NA)	(NA)	(NA)
Red Willow	(NA)	(NA)	571	7.7	–12.8	21,785	10.3	(NA)	(NA)	(NA)	(NA)
Richardson	(NA)	(NA)	244	5.3	–33.7	7,151	6.3	(NA)	(NA)	(NA)	(NA)
Rock	(NA)		(D)	(NA)	(NA)	(D)	(NA)	(NA)	(NA)	(NA)	(NA)
Saline	20	5.3	2,912	32.9	7.8	153,037	49.1	182,816	–23.3	7,051	–32.0
Sarpy	70	27.3	2,692	3.6	30.0	151,817	4.8	287,877	(NA)	(D)	(NA)
Saunders	(NA)	(NA)	486	6.0	–19.0	18,675	8.2	(NA)	(NA)	(NA)	(NA)
Scotts Bluff	43	–20.4	1,350	5.7	–1.1	45,492	6.1	57,196	–57.6	1,756	–93.0
Seward	14	–22.2	972	10.4	–2.1	52,195	19.4	65,753	143.4	(D)	(NA)
Sheridan	(NA)	(NA)	72	2.1	111.8	2,097	3.6	(NA)	(NA)	(NA)	(NA)
Sherman	(NA)	(NA)	24	1.4	–7.7	618	1.8	(NA)	(NA)	(NA)	(NA)
Sioux	(NA)	(NA)	[4]5	(NA)	(NA)	303	6.8	(NA)	(NA)	(NA)	(NA)
Stanton	(NA)	(NA)	(D)	(NA)	(NA)	(D)	(NA)	(NA)	(NA)	(NA)	(NA)
Thayer	(NA)	(NA)	610	16.1	9.7	31,480	29.3	(NA)	(NA)	(NA)	(NA)
Thomas	(NA)	(NA)	(D)	(NA)	(NA)	(D)	(NA)	(NA)	(NA)	(NA)	(NA)
Thurston	(NA)	(NA)	221	6.4	–14.7	9,160	7.5	(NA)	(NA)	(NA)	(NA)
Valley	(NA)	(NA)	32	1.1	23.1	1,030	1.5	(NA)	(NA)	(NA)	(NA)
Washington	24	14.3	1,212	11.1	20.8	77,150	18.9	(NA)	(NA)	29,836	(NA)
Wayne	14	–6.7	1,057	16.9	69.1	38,795	21.1	50,825	–38.8	1,003	–91.4
Webster	(NA)	(NA)	22	1.1	–42.1	521	0.9	(NA)	(NA)	(NA)	(NA)
Wheeler	(NA)	(NA)	(D)	(NA)	(NA)	(D)	(NA)	(NA)	(NA)	(NA)	(NA)
York	25	–24.2	1,101	9.4	–3.3	59,228	14.9	87,072	11.3	6,640	–37.2
NEVADA	1,764	9.2	51,662	3.4	11.0	2,984,083	4.4	4,654,748	41.1	340,170	7.6
Churchill	(NA)	(NA)	671	3.4	–8.3	26,649	4.6	(NA)	(NA)	(NA)	(NA)
Clark	926	13.8	27,019	2.5	21.0	1,588,542	3.3	2,214,524	(NA)	191,290	68.3
Douglas	63	–3.1	1,925	6.1	6.2	113,083	10.6	221,833	55.1	9,240	(NA)
Elko	(NA)	(NA)	246	1.0	8.8	7,363	0.8	(NA)	(NA)	(NA)	(NA)
Esmeralda	(NA)	(NA)	(D)	(NA)	(NA)	(D)	(NA)	(NA)	(NA)	(NA)	(NA)
Eureka	(NA)	(NA)	(D)	(NA)	(NA)	(D)	(NA)	(NA)	(NA)	(NA)	(NA)
Humboldt	(NA)	(NA)	351	3.5	6.0	17,607	4.2	(NA)	(NA)	(NA)	(NA)
Lander	(NA)	(NA)	(D)	(NA)	(NA)	(D)	(NA)	(NA)	(NA)	(NA)	(NA)
Lincoln	(NA)	(NA)	(D)	(NA)	(NA)	(D)	(NA)	(NA)	(NA)	(NA)	(NA)
Lyon	66	32.0	2,626	15.5	25.8	127,009	22.8	195,717	44.4	15,066	(NA)
Mineral	(NA)	(NA)	21	0.9	(NA)	1,338	1.6	(NA)	(NA)	(NA)	(NA)
Nye	(NA)	(NA)	282	1.7	28.8	9,927	1.4	(NA)	(NA)	(NA)	(NA)
Pershing	(NA)	(NA)	89	3.6	(NA)	2,901	3.1	(NA)	(NA)	(NA)	(NA)
Storey	(NA)	(NA)	277	14.9	66.9	15,415	24.3	(NA)	(NA)	(NA)	(NA)
Washoe	449	7.4	14,849	5.5	1.7	895,785	7.7	(D)	(NA)	(D)	(NA)
White Pine	(NA)	(NA)	55	1.1	37.5	1,315	0.7	(NA)	(NA)	(NA)	(NA)
Independent City											
Carson City	163	–12.4	3,149	7.4	–18.3	172,893	9.7	360,680	21.3	19,593	(NA)
NEW HAMPSHIRE	2,213	–4.9	84,617	10.1	–16.8	5,820,192	15.9	8,527,926	–24.7	539,919	–23.4
Belknap	121	–9.0	4,098	10.2	–22.5	290,225	20.0	267,679	–12.6	17,014	–7.9
Carroll	85	–8.6	1,481	4.6	–4.3	48,618	5.2	65,028	–30.3	3,441	–49.3
Cheshire	170	1.2	6,044	12.6	–5.2	340,829	19.3	555,335	15.6	32,839	–6.7
Coos	39	–22.0	1,955	10.0	–13.3	120,793	19.0	105,826	–58.5	10,173	–58.9
Grafton	138	–6.8	5,999	8.5	–14.7	503,712	16.0	457,035	–10.2	21,251	–58.2
Hillsborough	678	–8.0	32,077	12.4	–19.3	2,483,469	19.3	3,418,772	–3.1	252,764	–27.5
Merrimack	220	–1.8	7,758	8.1	–9.5	426,607	10.7	644,114	–4.9	48,010	18.1
Rockingham	493	–1.4	16002	8.3	–12.6	1,031,090	11.8	2,128,331	–42.9	87,712	–1.7
Strafford	155	–2.5	5,646	9.6	–28.5	318,398	13.5	497,778	–61.9	23,884	–67.3
Sullivan	114	–1.7	3,557	16.5	–24.6	256,451	32.6	388,028	–10.7	42,831	147.1
NEW JERSEY	10,656	–9.8	341,916	6.8	–17.0	30,488,889	10.9	51,602,288	3.0	3,021,021	–3.0
Atlantic	155	–3.1	4,746	2.6	–8.7	249,221	3.1	381,713	12.8	13,696	–10.3
Bergen	1,581	–12.5	45,910	7.7	–18.1	4,212,167	12.0	7,352,552	33.0	326,263	–9.6
Burlington	468	0.9	19,807	7.5	–9.6	1,451,558	11.2	2,623,652	26.0	116,262	6.3
Camden	590	–12.9	18,257	6.8	–8.7	1,440,270	11.2	2,382,791	24.3	132,361	17.3
Cape May	86	4.9	998	1.6	–16.5	37,373	1.8	66,403	26.3	2,011	–23.5
Cumberland	200	–4.8	10,188	13.2	–13.1	575,881	17.9	1,282,657	31.0	76,113	–15.1
Essex	1,090	–9.6	26,406	5.7	–22.0	2,831,629	10.0	5,185,679	3.4	239,141	–26.6
Gloucester	283	–2.4	10,476	8.1	–9.8	1,006,706	17.9	2,664,772	21.8	245,694	91.2
Hudson	687	–29.8	13,562	4.5	–34.4	794,085	4.2	1,601,479	–22.4	61,488	–34.6
Hunterdon	177	1.1	3,565	4.7	–15.6	240,267	5.8	460,947	–18.1	29,211	–18.1
Mercer	315	–10.5	8,864	3.3	–26.3	648,817	4.2	1,457,405	10.8	57,202	–27.4
Middlesex	908	–7.1	44,377	9.1	–21.8	4,377,141	15.0	5,306,723	–15.6	336,922	–37.5
Monmouth	525	–10.6	10,872	3.1	–8.5	715,849	4.3	1,091,568	–4.0	61,469	–7.3
Morris	685	–8.5	28,265	7.5	–4.5	3,297,220	12.6	3,567,401	–25.4	164,058	–19.3
Ocean	346	12.0	6,607	3.1	–0.1	361,643	4.5	724,543	41.8	25,017	–21.5

See footnotes at end of table.

Table B-15. Counties — **Manufacturing**—Con.

[Includes United States, states, and 3,141 counties/county equivalents defined as of February 22, 2005. For more information on these areas, see Appendix C, Geographic Information]

County	Establishments, 2002[1] Total	Percent change, 1997–2002	Employment, 2005[2] Total	Percent of all employees	Percent change, 2001–2005	Earnings, 2005[2] Total ($1,000)	Percent of all earnings	Value added by manufactures, 2002[1] Total ($1,000)	Percent change, 1997–2002	Capital expenditures, 2002[1] Total ($1,000)	Percent change, 1997–2002
NEW JERSEY—Con.											
Passaic	981	-7.4	23,120	10.1	-22.8	1,590,067	14.1	3,491,981	-7.2	152,310	-24.7
Salem	44	-8.3	3,238	10.7	-11.5	279,240	19.8	654,486	8.3	60,233	19.9
Somerset	363	-3.5	19,135	8.8	-8.1	2,222,125	13.8	2,882,195	-8.2	387,421	51.8
Sussex	139	-4.8	2,363	3.7	-5.9	144,052	6.1	233,860	20.1	11,866	-29.3
Union	884	-11.2	34,865	12.0	-21.3	3,480,262	19.6	7,039,805	9.3	479,311	60.7
Warren	149	-9.1	6,295	12.5	-13.2	533,316	23.3	1,149,676	-4.3	42,972	-55.8
NEW MEXICO	1,587	-0.4	41,896	3.9	-9.1	2,317,315	5.8	5,990,566	-55.4	307,101	-46.4
Bernalillo	668	-5.0	17,441	4.2	-17.5	953,132	5.6	(D)	(NA)	(D)	(NA)
Catron	(NA)	(NA)	(D)	(NA)	(NA)	(D)	(NA)	(NA)	(NA)	(NA)	(NA)
Chaves	51	—	1,235	4.2	-43.3	77,595	7.4	194,636		22,842	37.6
Cibola	(NA)	(NA)	441	4.2	1.8	15,502	5.0	(NA)	(NA)	(NA)	(NA)
Colfax	(NA)	(NA)	293	3.5	6.9	7,806	3.6	(NA)	(NA)	(NA)	(NA)
Curry	(NA)	(NA)	509	2.1	30.5	21,459	2.3	(NA)	(NA)	(NA)	(NA)
De Baca	(NA)	(NA)	(D)	(NA)	(NA)	(D)	(NA)	(NA)	(NA)	(NA)	(NA)
Dona Ana	137	23.4	3,599	4.1	5.3	149,583	5.2	330,183	115.1	10,434	-27.9
Eddy	34	-17.1	755	2.8	-17.8	51,200	4.4	554,927	61.9	12,827	(NA)
Grant	(NA)	(NA)	476	3.3	(NA)	24,361	6.2	(NA)	(NA)	(NA)	(NA)
Guadalupe	(NA)	(NA)	(D)	(NA)	(NA)	(D)	(NA)	(NA)	(NA)	(NA)	(NA)
Harding	(NA)	(NA)	45	(NA)	(NA)	102	1.3	(NA)	(NA)	(NA)	(NA)
Hidalgo	(NA)	(NA)	(D)	(NA)	(NA)	(D)	(NA)	(NA)	(NA)	(NA)	(NA)
Lea	37	-17.8	357	1.1	-11.0	15,267	1.2	80,533	-18.2	5,690	213.8
Lincoln	(NA)	(NA)	167	1.4	22.8	4,081	1.6	(NA)	(NA)	(NA)	(NA)
Los Alamos	(NA)	(NA)	(D)	(NA)	(NA)	(D)	(NA)	(NA)	(NA)	(NA)	(NA)
Luna	(NA)	(NA)	1,229	11.3	16.8	33,088	10.5	(NA)	(NA)	(NA)	(NA)
McKinley	36	(NA)	1,616	5.5	83.8	32,897	3.7	70,981	(NA)	6,528	(NA)
Mora	(NA)	(NA)	(D)	(NA)	(NA)	(D)	(NA)	(NA)	(NA)	(NA)	(NA)
Otero	(NA)	(NA)	270	0.9	-52.2	7,283	0.7	(NA)	(NA)	(NA)	(NA)
Quay	(NA)	(NA)	(D)	(NA)	(NA)	(D)	(NA)	(NA)	(NA)	(NA)	(NA)
Rio Arriba	(NA)	(NA)	449	2.4	-31.2	14,008	3.0	(NA)	(NA)	(NA)	(NA)
Roosevelt	(NA)	(NA)	363	3.8	29.6	12,974	4.2	(NA)	(NA)	(NA)	(NA)
Sandoval	72	26.3	6,627	18.0	-5.5	559,272	39.1	(D)	(NA)	(D)	(NA)
San Juan	76	7.0	1,903	3.0	18.6	81,841	3.3	92,681	2.6	3,268	-70.0
San Miguel	(NA)	(NA)	194	1.4	12.8	3,883	1.2	(NA)	(NA)	(NA)	(NA)
Santa Fe	166	2.5	1,857	2.1	-8.3	182,568	5.1	71,056	-2.4	3,088	-32.4
Sierra	(NA)	(NA)	129	2.7	(NA)	3,936	3.6	(NA)	(NA)	(NA)	(NA)
Socorro	(NA)	(NA)	203	2.4	9.1	7,319	2.9	(NA)	(NA)	(NA)	(NA)
Taos	(NA)	(NA)	398	2.2	-5.7	10,345	2.0	(NA)	(NA)	(NA)	(NA)
Torrance	(NA)	(NA)	129	2.2	5.7	3,375	2.3	(NA)	(NA)	(NA)	(NA)
Union	(NA)	(NA)	16	0.6	-23.8	320	0.4	(NA)	(NA)	(NA)	(NA)
Valencia	29	-27.5	941	4.2	-4.5	38,066	6.7	(D)	(NA)	4,437	-27.9
NEW YORK	21,066	-11.9	613,482	5.7	-15.7	44,911,729	7.1	83,874,558	8.9	4,172,544	-27.1
Albany	260	-4.4	8,847	3.2	-6.9	579,309	4.3	1,521,615	40.1	107,950	8.4
Allegany	54	-5.3	2,581	12.2	-4.8	131,171	21.3	309,633	27.6	7,053	-48.1
Bronx	465	-11.8	10,391	3.2	-6.4	445,530	3.5	790,349	8.9	30,784	-23.5
Broome	225	-7.0	12,862	10.9	-23.4	789,801	18.3	1,547,469	-5.2	(D)	(NA)
Cattaraugus	98	3.2	4,896	11.5	-17.4	254,843	17.7	504,348	-4.8	33,129	8.9
Cayuga	100	—	3,885	10.4	-7.1	210,509	16.6	318,755	2.2	17,117	-15.4
Chautauqua	226	1.8	11,687	16.2	-12.6	597,949	26.4	1,504,507	3.1	80,949	-26.5
Chemung	94	—	6,003	12.3	-22.5	342,503	19.6	601,441	-21.4	51,092	-21.3
Chenango	79	-8.1	3,510	14.7	-14.7	198,091	25.9	667,444	34.0	19,031	-61.9
Clinton	103	25.6	5,271	11.9	-7.8	299,379	18.4	405,144	12.7	41,778	-21.4
Columbia	80	-7.0	2,276	7.0	-12.4	111,601	11.2	165,210	5.8	4,848	60.7
Cortland	73	4.3	2,388	9.4	-30.7	143,229	18.1	309,161	-22.8	20,758	-71.9
Delaware	55	-8.3	4,720	16.6	5.7	257,440	29.9	611,073	46.2	27,136	-1.5
Dutchess	209	-0.5	15,427	10.0	35.8	1,623,833	23.7	3,197,716	241.1	(D)	(NA)
Erie	1,146	-8.4	54,047	9.7	-15.9	4,296,037	18.1	6,925,165	-2.0	598,739	11.1
Essex	33	-17.5	1,269	5.8	10.8	75,973	11.4	185,874	42.9	(D)	(NA)
Franklin	28	7.7	658	2.8	-24.5	22,373	2.8	44,181	-38.3	1,907	(NA)
Fulton	102	-12.1	2,624	9.5	-21.1	118,905	14.3	272,901	23.7	7,131	-57.6
Genesee	98	-8.4	3,165	10.2	-13.9	165,716	16.6	300,051	-10.5	16,813	-48.1
Greene	39	5.4	963	4.9	10.8	52,212	7.9	90,063	55.8	2,703	-49.0
Hamilton	(NA)	(NA)	55	1.9	-6.8	662	1.0	(NA)	(NA)	(NA)	(NA)
Herkimer	68	-4.2	3,336	13.0	-14.6	143,005	19.8	455,219	10.5	16,277	-28.3
Jefferson	89	6.0	2,622	3.9	-16.7	124,668	4.3	263,750	-26.3	21,209	-35.0
Kings	2,327	-12.9	31,865	4.6	-23.1	1,479,974	5.9	3,881,178	28.7	113,369	-18.4
Lewis	28	16.7	1,478	13.3	5.1	77,179	24.7	182,003	39.7	5,367	-66.8
Livingston	60	25.0	2,301	7.7	-9.4	104,908	11.7	245,503	-24.9	23,645	19.6
Madison	71	2.9	3,025	9.6	1.0	133,377	14.0	312,640	95.5	18,217	-4.1
Monroe	973	-3.4	62,821	13.1	-20.8	5,289,286	23.7	9,107,331	-26.3	434,129	-48.7
Montgomery	70	-16.7	4,386	18.6	2.5	173,631	22.3	364,140	5.4	16,166	-28.7
Nassau	1,446	-12.5	29,204	3.7	-21.4	2,069,945	4.9	5,914,795	44.5	288,506	24.2

See footnotes at end of table.

Table B-15. Counties — **Manufacturing**—Con.

[Includes United States, states, and 3,141 counties/county equivalents defined as of February 22, 2005. For more information on these areas, see Appendix C, Geographic Information]

County	Establishments, 2002[1]		Employment, 2005[2]			Earnings, 2005[2]		Value added by manufactures, 2002[1]		Capital expenditures, 2002[1]	
	Total	Percent change, 1997–2002	Total	Percent of all employees	Percent change, 2001–2005	Total ($1,000)	Percent of all earnings	Total ($1,000)	Percent change, 1997–2002	Total ($1,000)	Percent change, 1997–2002
NEW YORK—Con.											
New York	3,523	−31.8	46,677	1.7	−27.8	5,508,470	2.0	5,122,003	−20.2	165,845	−29.8
Niagara	291	−6.1	12,535	13.6	−22.3	927,378	26.3	1,628,410	−35.7	71,599	−68.2
Oneida	271	−3.2	11,054	8.1	−16.3	532,798	10.9	1,078,748	−7.8	58,376	−18.6
Onondaga	513	0.6	27,832	9.1	−16.5	1,994,367	14.8	3,197,380	−11.6	188,115	−29.5
Ontario	162	0.6	7,331	11.1	−6.5	468,745	20.7	796,323	41.7	61,867	−42.3
Orange	341	−1.4	8,406	4.8	−16.7	423,612	6.1	880,801	(NA)	(D)	(NA)
Orleans	45	−6.3	2,041	13.0	12.5	93,805	16.8	182,897	−20.7	8,147	−27.2
Oswego	96	−11.1	3,824	8.4	−24.1	229,194	14.2	559,004	4.6	25,329	−58.9
Otsego	72	5.9	1,424	4.6	−8.1	65,718	6.5	135,786	3.6	6,343	−37.3
Putnam	87	17.6	1,576	4.1	−1.9	98,866	6.7	230,409	41.3	12,816	0.7
Queens	1,755	−14.1	34,942	5.0	−24.1	2,152,924	7.4	3,376,319	−5.3	118,424	−76.1
Rensselaer	113	2.7	(D)	(NA)	(NA)	(D)	(NA)	328,996	9.0	29,117	−26.7
Richmond	158	−2.5	(D)	(NA)	(NA)	(D)	(NA)	188,312	26.5	6,406	−88.8
Rockland	292	−5.5	11,969	8.0	−1.5	1,104,726	14.7	5,450,809	106.3	125,616	−37.6
St. Lawrence	79	−7.1	3,825	7.6	−20.8	256,829	15.2	814,427	34.3	65,635	−42.1
Saratoga	128	−7.9	5,964	5.6	−10.9	402,214	10.6	736,522	2.2	61,915	−38.4
Schenectady	115	−3.4	6,108	8.0	−12.9	658,774	17.0	1,918,864	153.7	72,292	54.3
Schoharie	(NA)	(NA)	374	2.9	−52.2	11,520	2.9	(NA)	(NA)	(NA)	(NA)
Schuyler	(NA)	(NA)	671	7.4	−14.3	28,945	13.2	(NA)	(NA)	(NA)	(NA)
Seneca	36	16.1	2,070	13.0	(NA)	116,914	23.7	189,137	−14.4	6,433	−74.6
Steuben	84	13.5	6,872	14.1	−17.8	678,641	28.6	722,527	−10.1	41,039	−22.8
Suffolk	2,527	−0.3	61,489	7.8	−5.7	4,076,408	10.8	10,072,735	42.1	351,829	−15.8
Sullivan	51	−5.6	1,260	3.5	18.1	42,216	3.5	50,961	(NA)	12,073	326.6
Tioga	41	−14.6	5,175	27.3	3.9	427,121	54.4	175,171	−85.4	(D)	(NA)
Tompkins	91	−3.2	4,145	6.1	−8.3	243,730	9.6	452,053	49.1	20,913	−36.3
Ulster	211	−1.9	5,026	5.8	−26.8	252,408	9.0	450,597	(Z)	18,328	−30.0
Warren	92	9.5	4,343	9.4	13.0	232,886	14.3	467,837	10.4	29,857	−14.8
Washington	105	6.1	2,948	13.4	−18.9	162,140	21.1	394,717	13.7	27,231	−31.4
Wayne	150	3.4	6,301	17.1	−13.9	321,372	26.1	897,275	19.2	36,896	−40.4
Westchester	793	−8.7	20,260	3.6	−13.9	2,661,261	7.6	2,056,105	43.6	116,430	9.7
Wyoming	57	3.6	2,434	13.3	−3.7	122,067	17.6	167,572	−14.4	10,877	−36.7
Yates	31	14.8	1,203	13.0	11.5	51,200	19.7	71,403	−21.7	3,325	−38.9
NORTH CAROLINA	10,762	−4.8	590,341	11.5	−18.1	34,269,266	16.6	87,355,207	11.1	4,428,770	−17.8
Alamance	254	−9.9	13,464	17.0	−22.1	610,764	23.3	1,717,939	21.4	96,796	−27.8
Alexander	91	−8.1	4,929	31.4	−13.1	201,468	43.6	298,373	1.0	7,449	−52.7
Alleghany	20	−9.1	647	10.6	−51.2	19,904	13.9	112,051	40.0	1,542	−23.3
Anson	32	−13.5	1,950	17.7	−16.1	74,657	21.4	122,924	−29.4	8,212	−58.9
Ashe	32	−13.5	2,102	14.8	−18.5	83,705	23.6	103,142	4.0	14,565	69.7
Avery	(NA)	(NA)	392	3.1	−61.6	11,429	4.0	(NA)	(NA)	(NA)	(NA)
Beaufort	62	−4.6	3,345	14.1	−20.0	187,285	26.6	356,424	8.7	58,749	76.7
Bertie	18	12.5	(D)	(NA)	(NA)	(D)	(NA)	172,147	(NA)	3,344	−36.4
Bladen	35	−2.8	5,912	32.8	−10.2	190,887	35.7	341,603	−277.4	10,930	−81.6
Brunswick	68	19.3	1,928	4.8	−24.1	86,651	7.0	263,125	−42.6	20,589	(NA)
Buncombe	329	−0.9	12,776	8.7	−18.0	681,901	13.7	1,385,763	(NA)	85,072	−19.3
Burke	160	−6.4	11,325	21.9	−9.5	509,110	32.4	1,142,298	11.3	91,226	24.1
Cabarrus	166	–	8,252	9.8	−31.9	577,277	18.7	9,915,722	62.6	66,083	−77.1
Caldwell	155	−7.2	10,756	27.3	−29.3	469,152	34.7	884,591	6.3	28,911	−17.7
Camden	(NA)	(NA)	121	3.8	8.0	4,987	5.7	(NA)	(NA)	(NA)	(NA)
Carteret	77	11.6	1,740	4.9	−2.7	50,829	5.6	100,839	39.0	5,924	19.1
Caswell	(NA)	(NA)	426	7.1	−46.5	13,245	10.9	(NA)	(NA)	(NA)	(NA)
Catawba	530	−7.8	29,294	28.7	−27.8	1,388,672	36.1	2,752,999	8.9	109,276	−48.5
Chatham	81	6.6	6,180	16.5	−2.6	219,941	26.3	388,053	−10.1	15,791	−65.0
Cherokee	27	–	1,635	12.2	−31.2	59,977	17.3	111,118	−18.6	5,635	−7.1
Chowan	18	–	1,185	14.7	−0.7	45,326	18.8	75,293	40.8	3,146	7.7
Clay	(NA)	(NA)	202	5.6	30.3	6,469	8.0	(NA)	(NA)	(NA)	(NA)
Cleveland	175	1.2	7,877	17.6	−28.1	468,579	31.2	1,084,034	−17.9	71,497	−40.3
Columbus	43	−6.5	2,916	11.6	−7.4	170,442	22.0	398,770	5.1	22,000	−81.2
Craven	76	−11.6	4,915	8.0	4.2	261,781	10.3	544,454	129.2	60,121	15.5
Cumberland	117	−3.3	8,991	4.6	−24.2	534,409	5.8	(D)	(NA)	82,266	−11.8
Currituck	(NA)	(NA)	150	1.7	−11.8	4,593	2.1	(NA)	(NA)	(NA)	(NA)
Dare	41	(NA)	923	3.1	19.7	38,475	4.6	45,773	(NA)	2,012	(NA)
Davidson	319	−2.1	14,279	19.6	−19.5	604,110	30.5	(D)	(NA)	123,685	6.4
Davie	52	15.6	2,826	17.3	−25.0	115,599	24.9	249,837	40.2	9,640	(NA)
Duplin	40	−16.7	5,605	21.1	−11.8	198,619	24.3	257,534	35.3	7,807	−56.1
Durham	181	–	32,435	15.3	−18.1	3,850,547	31.4	2,442,681	−17.5	315,064	73.6
Edgecombe	57	14.0	4,841	17.0	−19.6	239,239	22.5	1,633,173	203.0	65,272	−22.4
Forsyth	383	−4.0	25,835	11.5	−14.3	1,940,790	19.6	7,970,784	38.2	134,659	−38.5
Franklin	63	14.5	2,740	13.7	10.9	178,342	30.5	300,323	15.9	11,517	−19.5

See footnotes at end of table.

[Includes United States, states, and 3,141 counties/county equivalents defined as of February 22, 2005. For more information on these areas, see Appendix C, Geographic Information]

County	Manufacturing (NAICS 31–33)										
	Establishments, 2002[1]		Employment, 2005[2]			Earnings, 2005[2]		Value added by manufactures, 2002[1]		Capital expenditures, 2002[1]	
	Total	Percent change, 1997–2002	Total	Percent of all employ-ees	Percent change, 2001–2005	Total ($1,000)	Percent of all earnings	Total ($1,000)	Percent change, 1997–2002	Total ($1,000)	Percent change, 1997–2002
NORTH CAROLINA—Con.											
Gaston	392	−20.3	17,315	18.0	−22.8	1,105,673	32.2	1,528,182	−44.6	134,987	−32.0
Gates	(NA)	(NA)	194	7.4	3.2	7,668	9.3	(NA)	(NA)	(NA)	(NA)
Graham	6	100.0	(D)	(NA)	(NA)	(D)	(NA)	(D)	(NA)	287	−80.4
Granville	50	−12.3	5,566	22.8	−8.6	305,371	33.9	1,480,454	56.7	52,477	6.1
Greene	(NA)	(NA)	333	3.7	−46.5	12,437	6.4	(NA)	(NA)	(NA)	(NA)
Guilford	805	−6.6	40,678	12.1	−14.6	2,462,084	17.1	6,720,318	9.5	403,935	23.6
Halifax	45	−23.7	2,276	9.8	−23.2	120,377	17.0	340,882	61.2	30,118	−45.8
Harnett	64	−22.0	2,982	7.7	−3.8	124,278	11.9	155,330	−49.7	8,171	−55.7
Haywood	52	6.1	2,454	9.3	−2.7	129,811	17.2	279,261	56.2	(D)	(NA)
Henderson	128	−3.0	6,657	13.8	−14.7	381,773	23.5	781,141	−7.9	63,408	−1.8
Hertford	25	−16.7	1,235	10.3	−7.0	75,446	21.4	149,008	40.9	11,866	36.6
Hoke	12	9.1	2,496	19.9	−11.3	83,057	26.9	(D)	(NA)	20,071	51.7
Hyde	(NA)	(NA)	191	5.9	38.4	2,634	3.2	(NA)	(NA)	(NA)	(NA)
Iredell	275	4.6	12,591	16.2	−14.5	625,359	22.7	1,758,357	36.4	87,339	−26.5
Jackson	25	−30.6	589	2.7	−20.1	26,029	4.1	56,378	55.1	2,902	26.1
Johnston	117	2.6	7,411	11.5	−5.4	476,311	24.7	859,371	25.9	68,558	−7.5
Jones	(NA)	(NA)	67	2.1	−66.8	2,666	2.5	(NA)	(NA)	(NA)	(NA)
Lee	98	−9.3	11,018	31.4	−2.1	652,725	47.2	1,081,237	−8.4	164,317	26.5
Lenoir	65	−20.7	5,121	14.4	−6.5	235,047	20.3	470,116	−27.8	33,629	67.3
Lincoln	112	–	6,472	25.6	−2.1	288,497	34.9	487,944	3.6	60,852	149.7
McDowell	60	−4.8	7,133	34.1	−11.2	293,821	43.6	531,220	38.9	20,364	−49.7
Macon	37	8.8	1,068	6.1	−8.0	39,764	8.6	75,781	−22.7	4,114	−58.6
Madison	19	(NA)	566	7.0	(NA)	24,252	14.8	51,805	(NA)	(D)	(NA)
Martin	20	−9.1	2,322	18.5	−19.0	151,187	38.9	132,612	37.6	31,726	1,362.7
Mecklenburg	939	−6.2	36,727	5.7	−22.2	3,039,807	8.1	4,226,071	−3.6	277,079	−7.2
Mitchell	33	3.1	1,071	13.3	−12.6	39,834	17.5	75,170	16.6	4,860	−23.0
Montgomery	72	−7.7	4,958	35.6	−16.6	187,783	41.5	310,041	2.2	20,882	−28.1
Moore	89	−15.2	2,464	5.7	−40.4	127,972	8.5	251,045	−31.6	8,623	−50.0
Nash	94	−9.6	7,721	15.3	−17.8	526,755	27.5	226,021	−73.7	8,444	−84.7
New Hanover	213	4.9	6,232	5.0	−29.6	456,595	9.9	1,034,150	−36.0	37,113	(NA)
Northampton	(NA)	(NA)	519	6.2	−25.9	25,311	9.0	(NA)	(NA)	(NA)	(NA)
Onslow	41	10.8	1,144	1.2	−26.8	39,335	0.9	46,289	−72.7	3,313	−34.3
Orange	66	−15.4	1,595	2.1	−33.2	99,987	3.1	54,252	−22.2	3,486	−39.4
Pamlico	(NA)	(NA)	195	4.3	−1.5	4,850	4.5	(NA)	(NA)	(NA)	(NA)
Pasquotank	30	−3.2	775	3.5	−3.0	29,867	4.1	(D)	(NA)	3,223	−53.3
Pender	32	−17.9	857	5.6	−18.8	35,072	8.3	50,221	21.7	2,074	−24.1
Perquimans	(NA)	(NA)	130	3.3	3.2	3,224	3.0	(NA)	(NA)	(NA)	(NA)
Person	40	2.6	2,540	16.5	−29.0	139,477	28.4	548,522	16.3	42,127	4.9
Pitt	106	−10.9	6,999	8.3	−18.3	379,982	12.8	(D)	(NA)	(D)	(NA)
Polk	24	−4.0	735	9.6	−7.2	25,377	12.2	32,875	−54.5	1,893	−72.7
Randolph	356	−13.4	19,019	30.1	1.3	773,832	37.2	1,654,711	−10.7	107,168	−4.7
Richmond	54	−6.9	4,136	21.3	−11.0	144,272	22.8	336,256	−12.5	16,125	6.2
Robeson	89	−7.3	7,028	13.9	−15.2	272,391	18.4	1,473,999	12.9	47,752	17.0
Rockingham	125	0.8	8,928	21.6	−25.2	439,687	34.2	1,623,446	38.9	62,385	−45.3
Rowan	191	−5.0	11,974	20.8	−1.7	688,658	29.4	1,009,776	−33.0	121,991	29.2
Rutherford	87	−10.3	5,231	17.5	−44.1	289,988	30.7	568,596	8.5	45,591	−18.3
Sampson	56	−8.2	3,477	14.4	−13.3	151,435	16.4	300,466	44.7	(D)	(NA)
Scotland	42	−28.8	5,039	26.2	−29.2	205,948	34.2	643,208	−10.2	28,538	−46.3
Stanly	121	−2.4	5,124	19.1	−14.8	255,144	29.8	414,579	−24.2	22,329	−58.0
Stokes	38	15.2	1,175	8.6	−6.0	43,812	14.2	75,411	0.4	3,042	(NA)
Surry	134	−10.1	7,907	18.6	−30.2	286,756	22.6	572,000	−25.0	30,681	−47.3
Swain	(NA)	(NA)	472	6.3	74.8	17,293	7.7	(NA)	(NA)	(NA)	(NA)
Transylvania	31	10.7	586	4.2	−75.6	24,140	6.4	118,141	−72.9	7,622	−72.2
Tyrrell	(NA)	(NA)	106	6.2	−20.3	1,354	3.1	(NA)	(NA)	(NA)	(NA)
Union	245	7.5	11,865	17.4	−7.9	584,305	23.8	979,246	−22.1	65,225	−30.7
Vance	47	−11.3	2,361	12.1	−47.7	96,184	16.4	297,955	−35.9	19,416	−19.1
Wake	687	7.5	22,716	4.5	−19.6	1,718,118	7.3	7,300,439	20.2	330,480	90.1
Warren	11	−15.4	783	13.6	9.5	27,289	17.3	30,167	−17.5	666	−89.2
Washington	15	–	198	3.9	−23.8	7,417	6.1	(D)	(NA)	13,734	(NA)
Watauga	56	–	1,099	3.6	−27.0	55,129	6.2	75,787	39.0	2,687	−11.4
Wayne	93	−7.9	6,528	11.1	−5.3	294,471	14.4	877,472	35.7	57,645	21.0
Wilkes	98	−9.3	5,438	15.7	−26.4	191,966	13.9	749,974	85.8	26,175	56.7
Wilson	95	−1.0	8,703	19.0	−8.9	599,640	32.9	4,710,766	80.8	104,761	1.1
Yadkin	42	−2.3	2,480	16.6	−20.9	93,742	24.3	112,655	−51.4	8,628	(NA)
Yancey	19	−9.5	705	9.8	−34.8	24,765	15.1	50,597	−45.2	3,084	−35.4
NORTH DAKOTA	724	2.8	27,314	5.8	8.1	1,410,799	8.7	2,679,559	48.7	201,839	2.9
Adams	(NA)	(NA)	64	3.5	156.0	2,045	4.9	(NA)	(NA)	(NA)	(NA)
Barnes	(NA)	(NA)	553	7.0	15.7	32,165	15.0	(NA)	(NA)	(NA)	(NA)
Benson	(NA)	(NA)	(D)	(NA)	(NA)	(D)	(NA)	(NA)	(NA)	(NA)	(NA)
Billings	(NA)	(NA)	–	–	–	–	–	(NA)	(NA)	(NA)	(NA)
Bottineau	(NA)	(NA)	86	1.8	−7.5	9,371	7.1	(NA)	(NA)	(NA)	(NA)

See footnotes at end of table.

Table B-15. Counties — **Manufacturing**—Con.

[Includes United States, states, and 3,141 counties/county equivalents defined as of February 22, 2005. For more information on these areas, see Appendix C, Geographic Information]

County	Establishments, 2002[1]		Employment, 2005[2]			Earnings, 2005[2]		Value added by manufactures, 2002[1]		Capital expenditures, 2002[1]	
	Total	Percent change, 1997–2002	Total	Percent of all employees	Percent change, 2001–2005	Total ($1,000)	Percent of all earnings	Total ($1,000)	Percent change, 1997–2002	Total ($1,000)	Percent change, 1997–2002
NORTH DAKOTA—Con.											
Bowman	(NA)	(NA)	23	0.9	−34.3	1,106	1.5	(NA)	(NA)	(NA)	(NA)
Burke	(NA)	(NA)	11	0.7	–	764	1.6	(NA)	(NA)	(NA)	(NA)
Burleigh	64	18.5	2,254	3.6	12.0	154,922	7.1	176,724	(NA)	7,920	(NA)
Cass	186	1.6	8,393	7.4	15.5	402,192	9.1	617,756	−1.3	38,212	−17.2
Cavalier	(NA)	(NA)	53	1.6	3.9	17,598	20.2	(NA)	(NA)	(NA)	(NA)
Dickey	(NA)	(NA)	339	8.7	20.2	19,940	14.0	(NA)	(NA)	(NA)	(NA)
Divide	(NA)	(NA)	(D)	(NA)	(NA)	(D)	(NA)	(NA)	(NA)	(NA)	(NA)
Dunn	(NA)	(NA)	(D)	(NA)	(NA)	(D)	(NA)	(NA)	(NA)	(NA)	(NA)
Eddy	(NA)	(NA)	(D)	(NA)	(NA)	(D)	(NA)	(NA)	(NA)	(NA)	(NA)
Emmons	(NA)	(NA)	26	1.0	(NA)	1,029	1.5	(NA)	(NA)	(NA)	(NA)
Foster	(NA)	(NA)	315	12.4	−2.2	14,177	17.8	(NA)	(NA)	(NA)	(NA)
Golden Valley	(NA)	(NA)	(D)	(NA)	(NA)	(D)	(NA)	(NA)	(NA)	(NA)	(NA)
Grand Forks	56	7.7	2,441	4.7	22.0	106,733	6.0	157,672	8.5	14,065	5.7
Grant	(NA)	(NA)	42	2.3	−23.6	1,735	5.0	(NA)	(NA)	(NA)	(NA)
Griggs	(NA)	(NA)	156	7.8	34.5	5,967	12.2	(NA)	(NA)	(NA)	(NA)
Hettinger	(NA)	(NA)	(D)	(NA)	(NA)	(D)	(NA)	(NA)	(NA)	(NA)	(NA)
Kidder	(NA)	(NA)	(D)	(NA)	(NA)	(D)	(NA)	(NA)	(NA)	(NA)	(NA)
LaMoure	(NA)	(NA)	108	4.0	16.1	3,493	3.2	(NA)	(NA)	(NA)	(NA)
Logan	(NA)	(NA)	(D)	(NA)	(NA)	(D)	(NA)	(NA)	(NA)	(NA)	(NA)
McHenry	(NA)	(NA)	(D)	(NA)	(NA)	(D)	(NA)	(NA)	(NA)	(NA)	(NA)
McIntosh	(NA)	(NA)	124	5.9	44.2	4,004	7.2	(NA)	(NA)	(NA)	(NA)
McKenzie	(NA)	(NA)	37	0.9	−37.3	1,444	1.3	(NA)	(NA)	(NA)	(NA)
McLean	(NA)	(NA)	(D)	(NA)	(NA)	(D)	(NA)	(NA)	(NA)	(NA)	(NA)
Mercer	(NA)	(NA)	59	0.9	63.9	2,117	0.8	(NA)	(NA)	(NA)	(NA)
Morton	35	29.6	950	8.1	−12.4	65,782	16.3	223,507	103.5	22,001	(NA)
Mountrail	(NA)	(NA)	(D)	(NA)	(NA)	(D)	(NA)	(NA)	(NA)	(NA)	(NA)
Nelson	(NA)	(NA)	75	3.6	10.3	2,512	6.5	(NA)	(NA)	(NA)	(NA)
Oliver	(NA)	(NA)	30	2.5	30.4	1,251	2.8	(NA)	(NA)	(NA)	(NA)
Pembina	13	−18.8	700	11.9	−37.1	37,725	22.3	183,919	(NA)	12,455	(NA)
Pierce	(NA)	(NA)	149	4.8	(NA)	8,737	12.5	(NA)	(NA)	(NA)	(NA)
Ramsey	(NA)	(NA)	239	2.9	7.7	9,513	4.1	(NA)	(NA)	(NA)	(NA)
Ransom	(NA)	(NA)	310	8.7	8.8	12,885	11.2	(NA)	(NA)	(NA)	(NA)
Renville	(NA)	(NA)	(D)	(NA)	(NA)	(D)	(NA)	(NA)	(NA)	(NA)	(NA)
Richland	33	−2.9	2,061	18.6	−1.1	104,306	26.1	351,285	191.4	(D)	(NA)
Rolette	(NA)	(NA)	(D)	(NA)	(NA)	(D)	(NA)	(NA)	(NA)	(NA)	(NA)
Sargent	7	40.0	1,724	46.4	(NA)	113,651	59.4	(D)	(NA)	(D)	(NA)
Sheridan	(NA)	(NA)	(D)	(NA)	(NA)	(D)	(NA)	(NA)	(NA)	(NA)	(NA)
Sioux	(NA)	(NA)	–	–	–	–	–	(NA)	(NA)	(NA)	(NA)
Slope	(NA)	(NA)	–	–	–	–	–	(NA)	(NA)	(NA)	(NA)
Stark	35	16.7	1,016	6.0	3.5	42,624	8.0	55,950	53.1	5,578	81.5
Steele	(NA)	(NA)	149	11.5	65.6	4,884	13.4	(NA)	(NA)	(NA)	(NA)
Stutsman	24	−14.3	1,427	9.9	4.5	75,324	14.8	72,541	−34.1	(D)	(NA)
Towner	(NA)	(NA)	106	5.7	−43.0	3,456	7.2	(NA)	(NA)	(NA)	(NA)
Traill	(NA)	(NA)	382	8.1	10.1	19,562	13.0	(NA)	(NA)	(NA)	(NA)
Walsh	9	(NA)	669	8.7	4.0	37,997	16.3	40,937	(NA)	2,026	(NA)
Ward	44	−24.1	789	1.9	14.2	26,327	1.8	(D)	(NA)	(D)	(NA)
Wells	(NA)	(NA)	46	1.4	−6.1	1,510	1.7	(NA)	(NA)	(NA)	(NA)
Williams	(NA)	(NA)	299	2.1	41.7	13,839	3.1	(NA)	(NA)	(NA)	(NA)
OHIO	17,494	−2.7	837,501	12.3	−14.1	55,005,108	19.4	113,243,351	0.7	7,427,634	−17.4
Adams	35	12.9	910	7.1	1.3	57,648	18.8	40,368	(NA)	1,307	(NA)
Allen	142	7.6	11,126	15.7	−7.3	807,402	30.3	3,720,876	35.1	87,949	−65.0
Ashland	96	−2.0	4,312	16.0	−25.7	205,822	24.4	611,651	5.4	22,351	−47.5
Ashtabula	193	10.3	8,911	18.2	−8.9	460,355	32.5	768,197	−16.6	48,901	−33.7
Athens	37	−14.0	940	3.2	−17.7	34,176	3.7	(D)	(NA)	(D)	(NA)
Auglaize	97	4.3	7,131	27.9	0.8	421,640	47.0	734,140	−11.5	64,436	8.9
Belmont	57	3.6	1,390	4.2	−11.3	71,623	7.6	159,744	43.3	1,431	−92.8
Brown	23	−8.0	916	5.2	−1.8	39,336	11.0	24,621	−71.3	1,465	−80.3
Butler	439	10.9	19,889	11.1	−5.0	1,390,588	19.5	2,471,499	−42.9	201,034	2.5
Carroll	41	2.5	1,290	11.2	−34.0	61,101	21.2	125,550	−9.5	7,373	−47.6
Champaign	49	−10.9	3,629	21.0	−3.0	228,494	42.1	579,165	17.4	70,255	−8.5
Clark	204	−11.3	8,532	12.7	−28.8	483,100	21.5	1,195,373	−24.1	70,425	−15.0
Clermont	176	5.4	7,361	8.9	−15.1	584,667	20.1	877,308	−1.1	34,255	−59.3
Clinton	47	−6.0	4,579	15.0	−0.2	255,784	21.2	367,804	4.4	36,481	12.4
Columbiana	210	0.5	6,974	15.1	−18.2	292,822	21.9	520,557	−10.7	47,648	31.4
Coshocton	54	−1.8	3,680	18.6	−10.3	180,974	31.4	400,451	−22.0	17,440	−61.0
Crawford	90	–	5,379	24.2	−13.6	261,215	38.8	655,104	−2.9	26,743	−30.3
Cuyahoga	2,477	−8.7	89,295	9.7	−19.4	6,973,062	15.0	10,396,627	−10.0	686,506	−44.7
Darke	81	−12.0	4,609	16.3	−1.5	228,129	28.4	551,743	1.2	30,092	−27.5
Defiance	54	12.5	5,497	23.7	−9.6	397,734	45.4	615,677	−4.7	154,996	423.1

See footnotes at end of table.

[Includes United States, states, and 3,141 counties/county equivalents defined as of February 22, 2005. For more information on these areas, see Appendix C, Geographic Information]

County	Establishments, 2002[1]		Employment, 2005[2]			Earnings, 2005[2]		Value added by manufactures, 2002[1]		Capital expenditures, 2002[1]	
	Total	Percent change, 1997–2002	Total	Percent of all employees	Percent change, 2001–2005	Total ($1,000)	Percent of all earnings	Total ($1,000)	Percent change, 1997–2002	Total ($1,000)	Percent change, 1997–2002
OHIO—Con.											
Delaware	144	23.1	6,027	6.2	19.2	399,910	10.8	536,360	−26.0	(D)	(NA)
Erie	126	7.7	7,419	14.7	−20.1	570,740	29.5	1,198,890	19.1	69,334	−35.9
Fairfield	128	−16.9	5,306	9.2	−11.3	254,788	15.3	424,825	−8.5	31,007	−5.1
Fayette	40	−11.1	2,513	15.7	−19.1	131,163	29.1	295,045	22.4	34,184	72.3
Franklin	1,039	−2.1	45,047	5.4	−22.0	3,208,687	8.0	6,996,698	11.8	326,307	−30.7
Fulton	111	0.9	9,361	33.2	−2.1	492,592	47.9	1,157,011	43.2	74,275	−29.7
Gallia	21	16.7	876	5.1	−18.3	41,595	7.5	(D)	(NA)	(D)	(NA)
Geauga	223	−4.3	10,394	20.0	2.3	543,056	30.8	956,420	38.1	44,288	−7.3
Greene	119	−15.6	4,367	4.6	−16.5	260,612	6.3	504,130	17.1	31,843	−22.4
Guernsey	63	6.8	2,802	12.9	7.9	141,046	22.7	417,436	4.4	28,525	6.4
Hamilton	1,308	−9.8	61,931	9.6	−16.0	4,871,637	14.5	10,288,806	0.1	984,429	15.4
Hancock	99	2.1	12,028	22.3	−2.8	699,338	33.6	1,439,857	8.2	113,635	−8.8
Hardin	41	7.9	2,480	18.1	5.3	124,529	32.4	229,819	7.9	95,202	523.0
Harrison	20	−16.7	709	12.9	1.0	28,802	18.6	47,854	17.7	4,648	(NA)
Henry	50	−7.4	4,047	25.0	10.3	216,622	40.1	1,140,575	−0.4	52,834	−16.0
Highland	44	7.3	3,121	18.1	0.4	137,657	26.4	323,711	15.3	25,868	−20.0
Hocking	31	19.2	1,205	11.9	−20.4	58,898	20.8	133,794	−23.3	8,625	8.9
Holmes	206	25.6	7,530	28.0	−1.5	294,479	35.5	474,041	44.1	26,706	17.9
Huron	106	−3.6	8,640	26.5	−15.1	417,584	36.5	1,028,262	4.0	30,482	−41.4
Jackson	37	–	4,406	27.2	20.1	174,446	37.6	621,778	47.1	(D)	(NA)
Jefferson	42	−6.7	2,874	9.1	−15.2	207,696	19.0	437,634	133.3	9,946	−44.8
Knox	75	4.2	4,828	16.7	1.5	287,741	31.8	423,306	6.0	48,094	72.1
Lake	735	−4.4	22,055	17.6	−16.3	1,363,934	27.8	2,390,248	−13.0	144,851	−22.3
Lawrence	39	−11.4	683	3.6	2.7	29,570	6.2	64,486	−87.9	8,959	−73.3
Licking	158	5.3	8,366	11.3	−8.4	472,884	19.0	1,122,231	−14.7	62,041	32.5
Logan	55	−5.2	5,864	22.7	−11.4	505,552	47.8	1,760,650	31.9	64,048	−18.9
Lorain	432	−1.1	21,854	16.7	−18.2	1,684,854	32.8	2,884,019	−37.0	190,229	−47.3
Lucas	615	−5.7	27,290	9.7	−15.0	2,105,723	17.9	3,724,116	−0.5	189,999	−28.6
Madison	49	−3.9	3,026	15.1	−8.9	210,336	29.1	(D)	(NA)	78,416	10.2
Mahoning	398	−1.7	10,702	7.8	−10.5	507,244	10.7	942,642	−1.2	52,216	1.4
Marion	87	1.2	7,092	19.7	0.9	369,916	29.6	1,082,747	29.3	54,399	−10.7
Medina	294	−3.9	10,360	12.5	−5.5	543,948	19.1	793,574	−10.8	66,903	−27.5
Meigs	(NA)	(NA)	156	2.4	−11.9	5,118	3.4	(NA)	(NA)	(NA)	(NA)
Mercer	69	11.3	4,833	21.0	20.6	228,191	31.0	337,868	−18.2	31,970	−31.1
Miami	256	−3.4	10,598	19.6	−21.1	632,291	33.5	1,358,190	1.5	101,593	−18.3
Monroe	15	−28.6	307	5.1	−85.5	27,908	19.1	(D)	(NA)	(D)	(NA)
Montgomery	900	−2.9	41,250	12.1	−21.3	2,926,153	19.1	8,410,079	17.7	301,412	−25.1
Morgan	(NA)	(NA)	420	7.7	−35.3	18,956	13.6	(NA)	(NA)	(NA)	(NA)
Morrow	30	11.1	1,461	13.0	−7.4	69,962	25.0	(D)	(NA)	(D)	(NA)
Muskingum	109	−3.5	6,087	12.9	−37.4	261,267	17.5	768,691	0.4	50,533	−32.5
Noble	15	25.0	542	10.7	−21.4	29,389	21.1	65,157	(NA)	1,604	(NA)
Ottawa	56	–	2,580	12.6	−9.3	142,165	20.6	232,483	−27.2	12,912	−70.0
Paulding	40	2.6	1,568	19.9	−6.3	65,412	30.2	137,518	26.2	10,197	16.4
Perry	30	−14.3	1,171	12.1	−25.3	48,851	17.3	144,521	−2.7	4,885	−44.3
Pickaway	44	–	2,619	12.9	−42.0	175,095	25.0	420,631	−31.0	103,113	58.6
Pike	35	25.0	3,643	27.4	−35.3	218,679	46.6	641,176	−15.9	12,532	−48.3
Portage	287	−3.7	12,624	16.6	−10.3	743,125	27.6	1,137,665	2.6	81,264	−14.6
Preble	61	–	3,525	21.8	−3.1	202,277	41.4	330,929	−6.1	38,133	−24.5
Putnam	50	19.0	2,901	18.5	−29.9	160,045	34.5	357,607	3.5	25,114	−80.2
Richland	207	−5.9	13,896	19.4	−12.2	896,041	33.7	1,385,581	15.5	104,894	−17.4
Ross	45	−6.3	4,406	12.5	−5.3	327,682	24.6	699,705	(NA)	40,705	−29.4
Sandusky	119	−4.0	8,870	26.7	−12.6	484,879	41.9	1,495,771	20.3	51,277	−34.8
Scioto	61	−3.2	2,407	7.4	−3.7	106,049	10.7	164,463	46.2	14,727	50.1
Seneca	93	−7.9	5,199	18.2	−14.9	276,763	31.0	599,210	−9.5	26,372	−47.3
Shelby	149	9.6	14,154	39.1	3.4	917,571	57.4	1,261,874	−13.8	(D)	(NA)
Stark	604	−4.0	30,918	14.4	−23.4	1,810,860	23.4	4,123,786	1.5	256,051	−14.2
Summit	1,043	−4.4	38,331	11.3	−5.1	2,585,262	18.0	4,510,125	25.4	342,722	−11.1
Trumbull	269	−4.6	21,833	20.4	−19.4	1,829,371	43.1	3,484,792	−4.9	114,305	−37.6
Tuscarawas	232	2.7	8,343	18.1	−9.3	402,880	27.4	850,881	−5.0	64,978	29.7
Union	40	–	10,209	31.8	−4.6	1,065,383	57.5	(D)	(NA)	(D)	(NA)
Van Wert	46	−8.0	3,784	24.9	−10.9	186,233	39.6	323,026	−23.2	16,152	−38.2
Vinton	(NA)	(NA)	537	15.8	5.5	23,007	24.8	(NA)	(NA)	(NA)	(NA)
Warren	216	9.1	13,311	14.5	1.1	811,656	22.7	1,093,335	24.9	108,716	−25.5
Washington	110	5.8	4,254	12.9	−17.1	264,163	24.4	756,303	−18.9	45,478	−57.1
Wayne	280	11.1	14,513	23.3	−8.4	828,433	36.2	1,609,486	0.1	106,738	−13.0
Williams	141	7.6	7,363	33.2	−17.8	377,013	48.8	796,555	−6.3	88,690	136.3
Wood	226	17.7	13,123	17.5	−14.7	856,287	29.3	1,612,246	36.3	132,728	32.0
Wyandot	45	−15.1	4,212	32.5	−10.3	207,440	45.9	344,137	22.2	22,321	−6.8

See footnotes at end of table.

Table B-15. Counties — **Manufacturing**—Con.

[Includes United States, states, and 3,141 counties/county equivalents defined as of February 22, 2005. For more information on these areas, see Appendix C, Geographic Information]

County	Establishments, 2002[1]		Employment, 2005[2]			Earnings, 2005[2]		Value added by manufactures, 2002[1]		Capital expenditures, 2002[1]	
	Total	Percent change, 1997–2002	Total	Percent of all employees	Percent change, 2001–2005	Total ($1,000)	Percent of all earnings	Total ($1,000)	Percent change, 1997–2002	Total ($1,000)	Percent change, 1997–2002
OKLAHOMA	4,027	-1.5	152,296	7.4	-13.8	12,178,517	15.4	17,005,404	-1.3	1,046,987	-6.0
Adair	15	7.1	1,972	21.7	9.3	88,535	35.6	113,434	10.6	15,789	103.5
Alfalfa	(NA)	(NA)	70	2.2	(NA)	2,447	3.7	(NA)	(NA)	(NA)	(NA)
Atoka	(NA)	(NA)	412	5.9	9.9	27,384	16.9	(NA)	(NA)	(NA)	(NA)
Beaver	(NA)	(NA)	73	2.1	(NA)	3,221	4.8	(NA)	(NA)	(NA)	(NA)
Beckham	(NA)	(NA)	324	2.6	87.3	18,157	5.0	(NA)	(NA)	(NA)	(NA)
Blaine	(NA)	(NA)	494	7.7	8.6	26,754	17.6	(NA)	(NA)	(NA)	(NA)
Bryan	43	38.7	1,540	7.0	6.6	77,164	13.5	89,847	123.5	8,073	91.0
Caddo	(NA)	(NA)	93	0.7	-28.5	5,536	1.7	(NA)	(NA)	(NA)	(NA)
Canadian	73	14.1	3,250	8.3	-27.7	174,769	15.1	519,573	-14.9	9,498	-41.5
Carter	42	-6.7	3,218	10.6	13.0	232,960	23.6	(D)	(NA)	(D)	(NA)
Cherokee	(NA)	(NA)	305	1.4	51.0	6,635	1.1	(NA)	(NA)	(NA)	(NA)
Choctaw	(NA)	(NA)	150	2.0	35.1	12,237	7.0	(NA)	(NA)	(NA)	(NA)
Cimarron	(NA)	(NA)	(D)	(NA)	(NA)	(D)	(NA)	(NA)	(NA)	(NA)	(NA)
Cleveland	144	-4.6	3,699	3.5	1.8	190,003	6.3	441,555	3.5	13,934	-27.6
Coal	(NA)	(NA)	(D)	(NA)	(NA)	(D)	(NA)	(NA)	(NA)	(NA)	(NA)
Comanche	53	3.9	3,994	6.3	5.9	253,472	9.9	379,997	-25.4	13,406	-69.6
Cotton	(NA)	(NA)	29	1.0	-17.1	679	0.9	(NA)	(NA)	(NA)	(NA)
Craig	18	–	774	8.3	-25.4	36,950	15.2	73,734	0.1	3,667	-34.0
Creek	105	9.4	3,616	12.5	-21.1	176,630	22.5	475,643	2.1	22,705	-26.9
Custer	31	34.8	1,290	7.8	-6.2	68,893	15.3	157,287	(NA)	10,298	-17.3
Delaware	23	-23.3	574	3.8	-37.3	25,108	6.9	24,163	44.4	2,103	(NA)
Dewey	(NA)	(NA)	61	2.0	38.6	3,161	5.6	(NA)	(NA)	(NA)	(NA)
Ellis	(NA)	(NA)	31	1.2	14.8	1,152	2.4	(NA)	(NA)	(NA)	(NA)
Garfield	63	-4.5	2,729	7.7	6.1	141,634	11.8	140,901	-39.4	12,155	66.3
Garvin	25	-3.8	1,049	6.9	4.7	53,663	12.6	(D)	(NA)	8,908	-11.0
Grady	65	1.6	2,584	11.7	-15.9	113,440	20.0	285,434	-30.8	7,069	-37.5
Grant	(NA)	(NA)	36	1.2	50.0	833	1.3	(D)	(NA)	(NA)	(NA)
Greer	(NA)	(NA)	(D)	(NA)	(NA)	(D)	(NA)	(NA)	(NA)	(NA)	(NA)
Harmon	(NA)	(NA)	(D)	(NA)	(NA)	(D)	(NA)	(NA)	(NA)	(NA)	(NA)
Harper	(NA)	(NA)	(D)	(NA)	(NA)	(D)	(NA)	(NA)	(NA)	(NA)	(NA)
Haskell	(NA)	(NA)	93	1.4	-56.1	5,820	4.2	(NA)	(NA)	(NA)	(NA)
Hughes	(NA)	(NA)	86	1.5	-37.7	3,918	2.8	(NA)	(NA)	(NA)	(NA)
Jackson	16	33.3	869	5.3	-8.6	38,130	6.2	83,062	-0.1	(D)	(NA)
Jefferson	(NA)	(NA)	88	3.5	-60.4	3,140	5.1	(NA)	(NA)	(NA)	(NA)
Johnston	14	40.0	716	14.5	4.2	27,848	22.1	59,100	81.9	638	(NA)
Kay	78	5.4	2,742	10.0	-27.5	114,062	11.3	218,623	-57.8	122,140	105.3
Kingfisher	(NA)	(NA)	1,103	11.4	157.1	55,817	19.0	(NA)	(NA)	(NA)	(NA)
Kiowa	(NA)	(NA)	(D)	(NA)	(NA)	(D)	(NA)	(NA)	(NA)	(NA)	(NA)
Latimer	(NA)	(NA)	(D)	(NA)	(NA)	(D)	(NA)	(NA)	(NA)	(NA)	(NA)
Le Flore	27	-15.6	2,308	11.8	8.3	75,109	14.1	(D)	(NA)	(D)	(NA)
Lincoln	(NA)	(NA)	546	3.7	-23.0	17,792	6.0	(NA)	(NA)	(NA)	(NA)
Logan	(NA)	(NA)	427	2.4	27.1	12,851	3.7	(NA)	(NA)	(NA)	(NA)
Love	9	(NA)	131	2.8	(NA)	4,740	5.1	(D)	(NA)	(D)	(NA)
McClain	(NA)	(NA)	256	2.3	-33.5	30,653	10.3	(NA)	(NA)	(NA)	(NA)
McCurtain	24	-4.0	2,129	12.8	-39.7	144,411	25.5	526,850	75.8	40,257	(NA)
McIntosh	(NA)	(NA)	301	3.8	-0.7	15,347	9.7	(NA)	(NA)	(NA)	(NA)
Major	(NA)	(NA)	126	2.6	-35.1	7,488	7.6	(NA)	(NA)	(NA)	(NA)
Marshall	19	-5.0	1,274	19.5	2.7	64,631	36.0	50,410	-10.8	2,830	28.6
Mayes	68	–	2,503	15.4	-24.6	125,665	26.8	395,234	9.3	20,718	-43.5
Murray	(NA)	(NA)	227	3.3	11.8	15,397	8.7	(NA)	(NA)	(NA)	(NA)
Muskogee	78	-10.3	4,980	12.5	-4.9	264,149	20.5	615,986	6.0	37,690	35.6
Noble	12	-7.7	(D)	(NA)	(NA)	(D)	(NA)	(D)	(NA)	2,195	-67.6
Nowata	(NA)	(NA)	328	7.7	-10.9	16,567	21.3	(NA)	(NA)	(NA)	(NA)
Okfuskee	(NA)	(NA)	84	1.8	-79.3	11,946	10.4	(NA)	(NA)	(NA)	(NA)
Oklahoma	793	-6.8	29,659	5.7	-22.3	3,700,163	14.7	4,367,792	-5.7	227,710	11.0
Okmulgee	40	14.3	1,534	9.9	3.7	94,041	23.2	225,402	11.4	17,545	48.1
Osage	(NA)	(NA)	670	3.7	74.5	52,850	13.2	(NA)	(NA)	(NA)	(NA)
Ottawa	55	-17.9	1,838	11.6	12.2	117,215	25.2	109,540	5.6	6,977	32.4
Pawnee	(NA)	(NA)	192	3.1	20.0	10,584	7.0	(NA)	(NA)	(NA)	(NA)
Payne	63	5.0	2,790	6.1	13.9	164,215	12.4	234,565	-48.6	20,104	-21.2
Pittsburg	26	-3.7	1,764	7.7	-15.2	84,085	11.5	37,159	-63.7	2,672	-26.8
Pontotoc	55	17.0	1,752	7.5	-22.1	68,260	10.4	178,117	119.5	5,186	24.4
Pottawatomie	63	-12.5	3,080	10.1	-1.4	168,310	19.8	286,873	-12.7	54,899	204.6
Pushmataha	(NA)	(NA)	186	3.3	-10.1	11,574	9.5	(NA)	(NA)	(NA)	(NA)
Roger Mills	(NA)	(NA)	(D)	(NA)	(NA)	(D)	(NA)	(NA)	(NA)	(NA)	(NA)
Rogers	136	11.5	5,706	14.5	-1.4	338,017	28.0	497,670	16.2	25,966	15.0
Seminole	23	-23.3	970	8.7	-40.2	37,133	12.6	462,096	450.1	3,394	-38.5
Sequoyah	(NA)	(NA)	725	5.1	-18.0	55,288	14.0	(NA)	(NA)	(NA)	(NA)
Stephens	53	-8.6	2,337	10.2	-15.5	110,548	15.3	121,065	-60.5	7,939	-41.3
Texas	9	-30.8	(D)	(NA)	(NA)	(D)	(NA)	(D)	(NA)	(D)	(NA)

See footnotes at end of table.

[Includes United States, states, and 3,141 counties/county equivalents defined as of February 22, 2005. For more information on these areas, see Appendix C, Geographic Information]

County	Manufacturing (NAICS 31–33)										
	Establishments, 2002[1]		Employment, 2005[2]			Earnings, 2005[2]		Value added by manufactures, 2002[1]		Capital expenditures, 2002[1]	
	Total	Percent change, 1997–2002	Total	Percent of all employ-ees	Percent change, 2001–2005	Total ($1,000)	Percent of all earnings	Total ($1,000)	Percent change, 1997–2002	Total ($1,000)	Percent change, 1997–2002
OKLAHOMA—Con.											
Tillman.	(NA)	(NA)	(D)	(NA)	(NA)	(D)	(NA)	(NA)	(NA)	(NA)	(NA)
Tulsa.	1,103	−2.9	37,052	8.7	−15.6	3,970,137	18.6	4,147,984	15.6	236,574	−19.3
Wagoner.	81	22.7	1,219	9.8	−11.8	60,989	20.9	148,711	−44.1	6,512	(NA)
Washington.	48	–	835	3.2	−49.7	34,369	3.6	50,022	−52.9	3,485	−67.6
Washita.	(NA)	(NA)	99	2.0	−31.3	5,977	5.3	(NA)	(NA)	(NA)	(NA)
Woods.	(NA)	(NA)	189	3.4	34.0	10,293	8.7	(NA)	(NA)	(NA)	(NA)
Woodward.	(NA)	(NA)	488	3.8	17.9	25,751	6.3	(NA)	(NA)	(NA)	(NA)
OREGON	5,597	−3.0	217,267	9.7	−4.6	13,705,426	14.9	26,440,699	5.4	1,265,365	−53.4
Baker.	22	(NA)	771	8.5	8.4	27,600	12.8	44,437	(NA)	2,439	(NA)
Benton.	103	−2.8	5,816	10.6	−17.2	508,422	23.5	270,924	−63.2	20,731	−83.1
Clackamas.	588	−0.2	20,070	9.3	−0.4	1,233,388	14.6	2,036,297	18.1	142,596	−3.4
Clatsop.	48	−2.0	2,390	10.3	3.2	157,470	20.0	62,620	23.0	1,833	−33.7
Columbia	51	−10.5	2,066	12.6	−4.0	124,029	23.1	510,945	−2.4	25,007	−53.2
Coos.	76	−26.9	1,698	5.0	−4.4	73,128	6.8	116,405	2.0	5,090	−49.9
Crook.	26	23.8	1,481	14.3	1.4	53,520	16.0	84,028	10.5	3,388	−47.8
Curry.	29	−9.4	750	6.4	−9.0	34,681	11.5	42,566	6.6	(D)	(NA)
Deschutes.	245	21.3	6,823	7.4	6.8	313,586	9.6	365,085	11.1	14,745	−18.5
Douglas.	139	−11.5	6,921	12.4	5.9	336,611	18.2	417,251	−21.8	30,297	−39.9
Gilliam.	(NA)	(NA)	12	0.9	(NA)	77	0.2	(NA)	(NA)	(NA)	(NA)
Grant.	(NA)	(NA)	300	6.6	4.2	10,874	8.6	(NA)	(NA)	(NA)	(NA)
Harney.	(NA)	(NA)	(D)	(NA)	(NA)	(D)	(NA)	(NA)	(NA)	(NA)	(NA)
Hood River.	54	−6.9	1,403	9.3	20.1	51,583	12.1	(D)	(NA)	1,586	−53.4
Jackson.	310	3.0	7,997	6.8	−2.8	319,720	7.8	811,621	58.4	30,955	−54.9
Jefferson.	22	4.8	1,758	19.7	7.7	72,177	26.0	60,392	−21.8	4,280	−50.4
Josephine	133	13.7	3,923	10.0	8.6	138,324	12.2	199,907	4.1	22,362	275.0
Klamath.	71	−1.4	2,879	8.4	4.8	134,580	11.9	293,640	34.5	18,758	60.3
Lake.	(NA)	(NA)	330	7.4	2.5	13,852	11.3	(NA)	(NA)	(NA)	(NA)
Lane.	612	−1.9	20,532	10.3	2.8	1,089,459	15.2	2,393,189	42.9	163,328	−78.5
Lincoln.	56	−5.1	1,289	4.8	−1.5	74,849	9.0	194,619	166.7	5,309	−57.4
Linn.	182	−1.1	8,868	16.3	−3.7	611,536	29.5	953,390	2.1	76,268	41.9
Malheur.	28	–	1,196	6.5	−18.4	41,700	7.4	(D)	(NA)	(D)	(NA)
Marion.	378	−6.0	12,431	7.2	−1.8	530,690	7.7	1,173,708	24.5	61,568	(NA)
Morrow.	8	−20.0	898	16.1	7.9	36,605	17.6	(D)	(NA)	(D)	(NA)
Multnomah.	1,220	−6.8	39,427	7.1	−14.7	2,643,991	9.7	4,015,118	−4.3	245,340	−24.1
Polk.	60	−4.8	2,790	10.6	−1.6	115,622	14.3	137,642	−6.3	9,480	(NA)
Sherman.	(NA)	(NA)	(D)	(NA)	(NA)	(D)	(NA)	(NA)	(NA)	(NA)	(NA)
Tillamook.	22	−29.0	1,608	12.0	10.7	73,581	17.5	151,736	51.4	4,623	−43.6
Umatilla.	76	1.3	3,791	9.6	−6.6	151,626	10.9	(D)	(NA)	(D)	(NA)
Union.	31	10.7	1,635	10.6	20.1	78,479	17.1	97,439	13.0	6,203	−8.5
Wallowa.	(NA)	(NA)	285	6.0	11.3	14,816	12.8	(NA)	(NA)	(NA)	(NA)
Wasco.	(NA)	(NA)	724	5.6	−22.1	34,478	8.4	(NA)	(NA)	(NA)	(NA)
Washington.	763	−7.9	47,833	16.8	−7.1	4,248,943	27.8	10,436,863	1.5	261,813	−65.5
Wheeler.	(NA)	(NA)	12	1.5	(NA)	76	0.5	(NA)	(NA)	(NA)	(NA)
Yamhill.	177	11.3	6,237	14.4	2.8	342,281	22.7	578,773	7.1	56,822	−46.1
PENNSYLVANIA.	16,665	−2.7	708,692	9.9	−16.6	47,879,355	14.8	92,319,195	7.1	4,922,598	−28.7
Adams.	127	–	8,115	15.8	−3.2	404,456	25.3	844,564	16.1	62,050	67.1
Allegheny.	1,355	−9.7	45,865	5.3	−21.7	6,356,716	13.8	5,847,341	14.5	206,200	−42.0
Armstrong.	96	4.3	3,167	10.1	−0.4	149,620	14.9	202,084	−11.4	15,778	−0.4
Beaver.	215	−2.7	8,236	11.1	−20.5	482,051	17.8	1,058,000	−25.2	59,614	−49.7
Bedford.	72	18.0	2,372	10.0	−44.8	108,184	16.4	221,545	8.9	16,857	62.8
Berks.	579	−1.4	31,481	14.5	−19.8	1,928,489	22.2	3,504,867	−9.3	228,181	−33.8
Blair.	153	−2.5	8,543	11.4	−12.1	418,202	15.9	816,174	−5.7	37,458	−36.6
Bradford.	78	6.8	6,041	18.6	−8.6	296,913	28.5	633,762	0.7	26,508	−42.8
Bucks.	1,187	−4.0	34,576	9.6	−14.8	2,529,521	15.5	5,733,332	67.9	193,685	−53.9
Butler.	302	9.4	13,260	13.3	−8.8	821,964	22.1	1,341,354	−1.2	88,618	−14.9
Cambria.	151	−1.3	5,151	6.8	−15.0	225,314	9.1	355,646	−30.9	24,398	−16.0
Cameron.	20	–	(D)	(NA)	(NA)	(D)	(NA)	66,693	−24.1	4,174	−75.2
Carbon.	58	−7.9	2,271	9.4	−24.8	98,472	13.5	170,190	−4.1	6,039	−50.4
Centre.	159	–	5,168	4.9	−33.2	243,213	6.8	584,717	−26.0	42,096	−66.9
Chester.	627	−0.3	25,139	8.1	−18.6	2,114,065	11.6	2,592,519	10.6	147,133	12.7
Clarion.	51	4.1	3,038	13.7	2.2	201,601	26.9	240,583	10.6	12,904	45.0
Clearfield.	110	2.8	3,877	9.2	−13.1	154,160	11.6	223,518	−26.2	10,251	−59.6
Clinton.	45	−16.7	3,341	17.9	−10.5	159,049	27.0	304,970	−7.7	26,640	−7.8
Columbia	101	1.0	6,700	18.8	−9.9	418,428	33.3	(D)	(NA)	(D)	(NA)
Crawford.	323	7.3	8,023	17.8	−8.8	402,132	29.7	735,735	−3.2	68,310	4.1
Cumberland .	207	−6.3	10,784	6.8	−13.5	561,562	7.9	1,084,088	−31.1	54,055	−55.1
Dauphin.	222	–	15,275	7.0	−8.8	933,785	9.5	1,662,779	−0.5	58,575	−17.7
Delaware.	466	−10.7	18,019	6.4	−17.5	1,907,279	14.0	2,529,833	−18.9	129,875	−78.2
Elk.	142	9.2	6,911	34.5	−7.7	361,375	51.9	716,145	7.1	47,484	−39.5
Erie.	584	2.5	25,006	15.3	−19.6	1,463,652	25.1	2,873,649	−8.1	139,403	−31.1

See footnotes at end of table.

[Includes United States, states, and 3,141 counties/county equivalents defined as of February 22, 2005. For more information on these areas, see Appendix C, Geographic Information]

	Manufacturing (NAICS 31–33)										
County	Establishments, 2002[1]		Employment, 2005[2]			Earnings, 2005[2]		Value added by manufactures, 2002[1]		Capital expenditures, 2002[1]	
	Total	Percent change, 1997–2002	Total	Percent of all employ-ees	Percent change, 2001–2005	Total ($1,000)	Percent of all earnings	Total ($1,000)	Percent change, 1997–2002	Total ($1,000)	Percent change, 1997–2002
PENNSYLVANIA—Con.											
Fayette	135	5.5	4,419	7.5	−15.1	212,278	12.2	263,593	−17.3	38,901	62.9
Forest	(NA)	(NA)	(D)	(NA)	(NA)	(D)	(NA)	(NA)	(NA)	(NA)	(NA)
Franklin	207	8.4	10,736	14.7	(Z)	534,645	21.0	947,304	−2.9	44,505	−40.0
Fulton	19	−13.6	2,451	30.3	15.6	176,429	53.7	(D)	(NA)	(D)	(NA)
Greene	24	−11.1	578	3.4	−23.7	20,577	3.2	55,124	38.0	1,851	−25.7
Huntingdon	45	2.3	2,618	13.8	1.6	121,475	20.6	228,274	−26.0	30,930	241.5
Indiana	105	19.3	3,352	7.3	−7.0	195,363	11.2	276,921	81.2	9,887	−0.6
Jefferson	91	3.4	4,455	20.1	0.3	198,288	29.8	335,906	−8.9	53,875	112.2
Juniata	51	−10.5	3,095	25.5	26.9	141,389	38.9	157,014	−23.4	3,510	−54.4
Lackawanna	293	−4.2	13,674	10.8	−20.4	688,062	15.0	(D)	(NA)	(D)	(NA)
Lancaster	988	7.6	49,308	16.3	−10.8	2,564,337	21.6	6,541,146	15.6	327,261	−26.2
Lawrence	176	4.1	4,483	10.6	−11.6	223,688	15.3	689,104	51.3	37,798	−26.1
Lebanon	219	10.1	10,002	16.9	−4.2	514,098	23.7	817,772	20.0	83,062	82.4
Lehigh	458	−9.1	19,287	9.0	−37.1	1,277,457	12.9	3,293,223	−36.8	193,821	−37.2
Luzerne	372	−8.8	19,351	11.0	−17.5	975,389	14.6	2,278,627	−3.0	146,118	−46.3
Lycoming	206	−1.0	11,859	17.5	−13.7	703,710	29.1	1,306,732	9.9	62,703	4.4
McKean	71	6.0	4,433	19.0	−11.3	225,753	28.9	472,514	3.6	26,545	−34.6
Mercer	202	2.0	9,151	14.5	−16.0	488,704	23.7	935,301	−5.6	51,649	−31.7
Mifflin	83	15.3	4,403	19.6	−23.6	214,423	29.9	412,785	−15.9	15,728	−62.5
Monroe	122	8.0	5,373	7.1	−3.0	397,860	14.5	948,369	73.1	(D)	(NA)
Montgomery	1,280	−8.4	57,044	9.5	−23.7	5,468,364	14.8	14,647,572	26.7	562,647	−21.5
Montour	23	4.5	659	3.7	−21.8	27,902	3.8	(D)	(NA)	(D)	(NA)
Northampton	363	2.8	15,092	12.0	−12.2	921,393	18.4	1,986,946	32.8	130,702	7.5
Northumberland	111	−3.5	6,890	17.2	−20.7	342,478	25.4	463,991	−43.9	59,093	67.1
Perry	42	31.3	534	4.0	−50.7	19,955	5.7	64,851	62.5	2,376	−10.5
Philadelphia	1,142	−14.9	32,389	4.3	−22.2	2,084,387	4.7	4,738,528	18.5	213,094	−32.8
Pike	(NA)	(NA)	484	2.7	−8.3	25,202	5.0	(NA)	(NA)	(NA)	(NA)
Potter	26	−10.3	918	9.3	−14.8	33,806	9.6	73,088	17.3	4,224	−26.0
Schuylkill	202	−10.6	11,477	17.9	−13.6	536,915	24.7	1,409,129	5.1	60,665	−30.2
Snyder	75	15.4	5,789	25.4	−7.1	274,506	36.0	333,861	83.8	11,935	−3.6
Somerset	128	8.5	4,488	12.1	−18.0	191,238	16.8	333,241	10.5	18,055	−4.6
Sullivan	(NA)	(NA)	202	6.9	−26.5	6,267	9.6	(NA)	(NA)	(NA)	(NA)
Susquehanna	59	15.7	1,072	6.6	−13.5	25,816	6.6	76,272	40.6	12,010	230.9
Tioga	42	−8.7	2,971	15.3	−20.3	133,835	23.9	245,697	13.6	19,163	−8.3
Union	33	−8.3	2,854	12.7	−14.4	142,102	16.6	274,442	20.1	12,495	−15.4
Venango	90	1.1	4,199	15.6	−6.8	236,310	26.2	342,508	−10.7	22,919	−41.3
Warren	78	−3.7	3,055	14.9	−23.1	146,497	21.5	395,007	−0.2	16,555	−41.5
Washington	268	−3.6	10,726	10.7	−10.6	610,669	15.2	1,109,413	−2.5	50,253	−52.3
Wayne	74	8.8	699	3.4	−17.5	30,535	4.8	57,099	−19.6	2,141	−40.7
Westmoreland	596	−0.2	20,328	11.2	−19.8	1,165,965	18.0	2,035,002	13.9	130,474	−32.7
Wyoming	36	2.9	2,643	22.1	−20.6	196,460	41.3	(D)	(NA)	(D)	(NA)
York	657	−0.6	39,038	17.7	−11.3	2,569,349	28.2	4,593,119	−0.8	378,054	26.0
RHODE ISLAND	2,131	−15.9	57,232	9.4	−18.5	3,310,118	12.2	6,148,634	12.1	306,180	−23.1
Bristol	104	4.0	2,626	11.6	−10.8	126,877	16.4	201,122	28.1	13,238	62.8
Kent	322	−21.7	9,859	9.5	−16.8	691,057	15.9	1,400,994	32.1	90,773	18.3
Newport	97	−1.0	3,259	6.0	−7.9	240,580	9.4	454,732	160.0	13,489	69.6
Providence	1,436	−19.1	33,661	9.5	−24.2	1,781,477	10.7	3,204,400	−6.1	155,376	−27.0
Washington	172	13.2	7,827	10.7	5.1	470,127	17.1	887,386	31.0	33,304	−64.1
SOUTH CAROLINA	4,457	0.2	270,969	11.5	−15.4	15,766,873	17.7	38,611,266	14.7	2,911,246	−14.7
Abbeville	35	−2.8	2,769	24.2	−34.3	117,957	36.8	217,780	−8.2	15,331	−58.6
Aiken	106	7.1	8,153	10.3	−10.2	451,005	13.9	2,329,321	−31.6	150,730	−48.9
Allendale	10	−28.6	1,097	24.8	−21.2	50,572	31.0	128,367	−5.0	21,125	149.2
Anderson	253	5.4	14,768	17.8	−18.2	951,684	33.6	1,666,236	−4.2	154,149	−19.8
Bamberg	23	−4.2	913	12.4	−21.5	34,059	18.0	82,870	−17.5	6,001	(NA)
Barnwell	24	9.1	2,748	28.5	−18.2	117,506	39.9	230,671	13.2	16,277	−43.5
Beaufort	96	2.1	1,192	1.3	5.1	70,891	2.0	92,967	22.6	(D)	(NA)
Berkeley	90	20.0	6,370	10.9	−16.9	489,512	23.8	1,150,795	−6.6	65,702	(NA)
Calhoun	14	−22.2	1,507	18.3	−1.8	92,545	37.4	64,756	215.5	(D)	(NA)
Charleston	270	3.4	9,903	3.7	0.4	626,533	5.7	1,529,048	4.3	69,351	(NA)
Cherokee	64	−15.8	6,486	26.4	−19.2	320,867	38.3	1,220,585	33.9	42,360	−21.2
Chester	53	−1.9	4,303	29.1	−15.5	231,336	43.6	561,359	27.2	26,204	−14.7
Chesterfield	60	3.4	5,247	28.4	−23.0	245,358	40.2	655,144	6.7	43,223	0.1
Clarendon	18	−25.0	1,259	10.8	−3.5	50,973	16.0	85,459	14.7	9,727	73.6
Colleton	33	26.9	1,740	11.0	4.4	82,400	18.7	103,723	19.4	(D)	(NA)
Darlington	65	3.2	5,968	21.0	−12.2	429,322	39.1	687,324	−8.3	38,199	−56.9
Dillon	27	8.0	2,674	21.1	−8.7	99,039	27.1	129,151	−16.9	8,154	−65.8
Dorchester	91	15.2	5,513	14.9	5.7	342,871	27.5	357,009	−8.0	44,166	(NA)
Edgefield	19	−32.1	1,287	15.8	−14.6	57,683	23.0	129,574	5.3	8,507	20.2
Fairfield	17	−15.0	991	11.7	−50.5	44,806	14.1	203,605	−55.1	(D)	(NA)

See footnotes at end of table.

[Includes United States, states, and 3,141 counties/county equivalents defined as of February 22, 2005. For more information on these areas, see Appendix C, Geographic Information]

County	Establishments, 2002[1]		Employment, 2005[2]			Earnings, 2005[2]		Value added by manufactures, 2002[1]		Capital expenditures, 2002[1]	
	Total	Percent change, 1997–2002	Total	Percent of all employ-ees	Percent change, 2001–2005	Total ($1,000)	Percent of all earnings	Total ($1,000)	Percent change, 1997–2002	Total ($1,000)	Percent change, 1997–2002
SOUTH CAROLINA—Con.											
Florence.	128	-7.9	9,097	11.3	-19.3	587,442	19.6	1,414,368	45.4	103,636	-20.2
Georgetown	64	-17.9	2,380	6.9	-22.1	174,010	15.8	406,107	-5.9	33,115	-26.7
Greenville.	607	-9.7	35,973	12.4	-17.7	2,121,832	17.9	9,462,724	105.9	515,871	23.7
Greenwood.	85	-8.6	7,998	20.8	-24.6	434,495	31.3	998,856	5.7	133,570	113.6
Hampton	20	–	956	12.4	-12.9	46,521	18.0	65,251	-33.1	3,100	-79.8
Horry.	166	3.8	4,249	3.0	-25.4	201,512	4.5	276,715	-51.0	24,755	-47.3
Jasper.	(NA)	(NA)	552	6.3	40.8	21,390	7.9	(NA)	(NA)	(NA)	(NA)
Kershaw.	66	6.5	4,219	16.2	-13.0	297,881	32.7	601,454	-38.6	57,064	-0.8
Lancaster.	64	18.5	4,544	18.5	-25.3	261,347	30.5	659,063	29.1	19,481	-71.5
Laurens.	69	-4.2	4,623	17.9	-23.0	229,497	28.2	378,920	-6.5	25,048	-23.6
Lee.	(NA)	(NA)	477	7.6	-10.0	25,423	14.3	(NA)	(NA)	(NA)	(NA)
Lexington.	234	4.0	12,100	9.5	-5.6	608,605	14.0	1,043,163	0.8	65,026	-1.0
McCormick.	(NA)	(NA)	274	9.4	-26.1	11,169	13.3	(NA)	(NA)	(NA)	(NA)
Marion.	29	-9.4	2,365	16.1	-33.5	96,827	24.8	201,333	-48.2	7,163	-57.5
Marlboro.	31	40.9	3,127	30.6	-3.5	146,496	41.3	421,550	32.2	33,815	228.0
Newberry.	46	-6.1	4,384	25.5	-4.6	186,337	34.1	262,757	-13.6	15,408	-22.1
Oconee.	92	15.0	6,910	22.1	-25.0	458,665	36.3	699,502	9.7	29,088	-56.6
Orangeburg.	89	-1.1	7,496	17.5	-5.5	384,487	27.2	781,738	21.4	218,681	189.2
Pickens.	131	-2.2	6,413	13.4	-21.4	361,428	22.6	585,352	-5.1	39,335	-48.4
Richland.	248	5.5	11,558	4.4	-5.2	712,414	6.3	2,408,782	64.5	253,512	114.1
Saluda.	8	-42.9	1,735	27.5	-9.2	58,025	31.6	49,272	-66.0	(D)	(NA)
Spartanburg.	521	8.3	29,739	20.4	-15.6	1,903,612	31.8	3,581,177	12.9	412,031	17.7
Sumter.	77	-8.3	9,422	17.3	-19.0	404,294	20.3	989,934	1.3	52,331	-16.5
Union	35	-18.6	2,590	23.7	-25.8	142,008	38.9	232,066	-32.1	16,964	-51.1
Williamsburg.	25	-26.5	2,250	17.2	-15.5	91,022	22.9	224,551	-8.9	14,959	-45.0
York	230	3.6	10,650	12.0	-3.2	893,215	24.7	1,163,203	(Z)	81,341	4.8
SOUTH DAKOTA	926	4.3	41,748	7.8	-2.1	1,982,618	10.9	5,176,605	33.4	193,948	-26.6
Aurora.	(NA)	(NA)	(D)	(NA)	(NA)	(D)	(NA)	(NA)	(NA)	(NA)	(NA)
Beadle.	28	33.3	813	7.7	-8.5	39,255	11.0	(D)	(NA)	2,636	-17.5
Bennett.	(NA)	(NA)	(D)	(NA)	(NA)	(D)	(NA)	(NA)	(NA)	(NA)	(NA)
Bon Homme.	(NA)	(NA)	290	7.5	-3.3	12,724	13.5	(NA)	(NA)	(NA)	(NA)
Brookings.	33	6.5	4,759	22.2	9.9	212,507	31.2	724,224	54.2	39,964	26.5
Brown.	32	-15.8	2,136	7.8	-4.0	171,852	17.4	(D)	(NA)	(D)	(NA)
Brule.	(NA)	(NA)	42	1.2	68.0	954	1.1	(NA)	(NA)	(NA)	(NA)
Buffalo.	(NA)	(NA)	10	1.3	(NA)	220	0.8	(NA)	(NA)	(NA)	(NA)
Butte.	(NA)	(NA)	160	3.3	60.0	7,752	6.7	(NA)	(NA)	(NA)	(NA)
Campbell	(NA)	(NA)	(D)	(NA)	(NA)	(D)	(NA)	(NA)	(NA)	(NA)	(NA)
Charles Mix	(NA)	(NA)	115	1.9	12.7	7,476	4.7	(NA)	(NA)	(NA)	(NA)
Clark.	(NA)	(NA)	72	3.1	(NA)	2,021	2.8	(NA)	(NA)	(NA)	(NA)
Clay.	(NA)	(NA)	116	1.0	12.6	16,610	6.3	(NA)	(NA)	(NA)	(NA)
Codington.	71	12.7	3,135	15.4	-13.5	135,847	21.5	(D)	(NA)	(D)	(NA)
Corson.	(NA)	(NA)	10	0.6	(NA)	221	0.4	(NA)	(NA)	(NA)	(NA)
Custer.	(NA)	(NA)	110	2.0	57.1	4,803	4.3	(NA)	(NA)	(NA)	(NA)
Davison.	35	-2.8	1,829	11.9	3.0	103,199	21.2	(D)	(NA)	(D)	(NA)
Day.	(NA)	(NA)	333	8.8	18.1	11,055	12.3	(NA)	(NA)	(NA)	(NA)
Deuel.	(NA)	(NA)	380	12.2	13.1	14,359	17.4	(NA)	(NA)	(NA)	(NA)
Dewey.	(NA)	(NA)	(D)	(NA)	(NA)	(D)	(NA)	(NA)	(NA)	(NA)	(NA)
Douglas.	(NA)	(NA)	123	6.5	10.8	4,144	7.0	(NA)	(NA)	(NA)	(NA)
Edmunds.	(NA)	(NA)	39	1.6	(NA)	5,054	5.7	(NA)	(NA)	(NA)	(NA)
Fall River.	(NA)	(NA)	39	1.1	–	2,897	2.2	(NA)	(NA)	(NA)	(NA)
Faulk.	(NA)	(NA)	(D)	(NA)	(NA)	(D)	(NA)	(NA)	(NA)	(NA)	(NA)
Grant.	(NA)	(NA)	555	10.2	24.2	27,110	15.2	(NA)	(NA)	(NA)	(NA)
Gregory.	(NA)	(NA)	16	0.5	(NA)	308	0.4	(NA)	(NA)	(NA)	(NA)
Haakon.	(NA)	(NA)	(D)	(NA)	(NA)	(D)	(NA)	(NA)	(NA)	(NA)	(NA)
Hamlin.	(NA)	(NA)	(D)	(NA)	(NA)	(NA)	(NA)	(NA)	(NA)	(NA)	(NA)
Hand.	(NA)	(NA)	47	2.0	-7.8	1,551	2.0	(NA)	(NA)	(NA)	(NA)
Hanson	(NA)	(NA)	58	4.5	7.4	1,649	6.6	(NA)	(NA)	(NA)	(NA)
Harding.	(NA)	(NA)	10	0.9	(NA)	450	1.9	(NA)	(NA)	(NA)	(NA)
Hughes.	(NA)	(NA)	134	1.0	54.0	3,943	0.9	(NA)	(NA)	(NA)	(NA)
Hutchinson.	(NA)	(NA)	241	5.3	-14.8	9,068	8.2	(NA)	(NA)	(NA)	(NA)
Hyde.	(NA)	(NA)	10	0.9	(NA)	221	0.7	(NA)	(NA)	(NA)	(NA)
Jackson.	(NA)	(NA)	(D)	(NA)	(NA)	(D)	(NA)	(NA)	(NA)	(NA)	(NA)
Jerauld	(NA)	(NA)	(D)	(NA)	(NA)	(D)	(NA)	(NA)	(NA)	(NA)	(NA)
Jones	(NA)	(NA)	–	–	–	–	–	(NA)	(NA)	(NA)	(NA)
Kingsbury.	(NA)	(NA)	330	10.5	-2.1	11,645	11.9	(NA)	(NA)	(NA)	(NA)
Lake	27	17.4	1,142	16.2	2.0	46,424	21.4	85,695	15.2	2,268	-64.7
Lawrence	34	13.3	665	4.2	12.3	39,970	9.1	(D)	(NA)	2,358	-13.3
Lincoln.	37	23.3	1,482	8.2	63.6	60,127	13.0	89,731	(NA)	5,532	36.7
Lyman.	(NA)	(NA)	10	0.4	(NA)	221	0.4	(NA)	(NA)	(NA)	(NA)
McCook.	(NA)	(NA)	160	5.2	-3.0	6,162	8.3	(NA)	(NA)	(NA)	(NA)
McPherson.	(NA)	(NA)	64	4.7	18.5	1,781	4.7	(NA)	(NA)	(NA)	(NA)
Marshall.	(NA)	(NA)	283	11.5	21.5	13,903	15.6	(NA)	(NA)	(NA)	(NA)

See footnotes at end of table.

Table B-15. Counties — **Manufacturing**—Con.

[Includes United States, states, and 3,141 counties/county equivalents defined as of February 22, 2005. For more information on these areas, see Appendix C, Geographic Information]

County	Manufacturing (NAICS 31–33)										
	Establishments, 2002[1]		Employment, 2005[2]			Earnings, 2005[2]		Value added by manufactures, 2002[1]		Capital expenditures, 2002[1]	
	Total	Percent change, 1997–2002	Total	Percent of all employees	Percent change, 2001–2005	Total ($1,000)	Percent of all earnings	Total ($1,000)	Percent change, 1997–2002	Total ($1,000)	Percent change, 1997–2002
SOUTH DAKOTA—Con.											
Meade	(NA)	(NA)	457	2.6	0.9	15,161	3.6	(NA)	(NA)	(NA)	(NA)
Mellette	(NA)	(NA)	10	1.2	(NA)	221	1.2	(NA)	(NA)	(NA)	(NA)
Miner	(NA)	(NA)	53	3.5	(NA)	1,682	4.1	(NA)	(NA)	(NA)	(NA)
Minnehaha	173	3.0	11,171	8.2	–3.7	532,968	9.5	902,086	(NA)	54,643	–27.5
Moody	(NA)	(NA)	235	6.6	21.1	11,882	9.1	(NA)	(NA)	(NA)	(NA)
Pennington	122	–9.0	3,575	5.7	–18.7	162,069	7.0	257,903	–19.0	10,930	–56.9
Perkins	(NA)	(NA)	(D)	(NA)	(NA)	(D)	(NA)	(NA)	(NA)	(NA)	(NA)
Potter	(NA)	(NA)	72	4.5	7.5	2,396	5.6	(NA)	(NA)	(NA)	(NA)
Roberts	(NA)	(NA)	261	4.8	68.4	11,202	7.2	(NA)	(NA)	(NA)	(NA)
Sanborn	(NA)	(NA)	(D)	(NA)	(NA)	(D)	(NA)	(NA)	(NA)	(NA)	(NA)
Shannon	(NA)	(NA)	10	0.2	(NA)	195	0.1	(NA)	(NA)	(NA)	(NA)
Spink	(NA)	(NA)	43	1.1	26.5	853	0.7	(NA)	(NA)	(NA)	(NA)
Stanley	(NA)	(NA)	10	0.5	(NA)	221	0.5	(NA)	(NA)	(NA)	(NA)
Sully	(NA)	(NA)	10	0.9	(NA)	221	0.5	(NA)	(NA)	(NA)	(NA)
Todd	(NA)	(NA)	10	0.3	(NA)	221	0.2	(NA)	(NA)	(NA)	(NA)
Tripp	(NA)	(NA)	79	2.0	3.9	2,281	2.0	(NA)	(NA)	(NA)	(NA)
Turner	(NA)	(NA)	157	3.8	–7.6	5,680	5.3	(NA)	(NA)	(NA)	(NA)
Union	24	–7.7	1,648	16.4	–38.0	79,584	17.1	(D)	(NA)	12,973	–46.2
Walworth	(NA)	(NA)	(D)	(NA)	(NA)	(D)	(NA)	(NA)	(NA)	(NA)	(NA)
Yankton	31	3.3	2,619	18.0	1.2	125,456	25.6	202,926	21.6	7,691	–44.5
Ziebach	(NA)	(NA)	(D)	(NA)	(NA)	(D)	(NA)	(NA)	(NA)	(NA)	(NA)
TENNESSEE	6,948	–6.2	424,041	11.7	–9.2	25,713,333	17.4	49,811,004	12.3	4,526,574	16.9
Anderson	118	10.3	10,245	19.4	3.1	684,655	30.4	1,181,542	18.8	(D)	(NA)
Bedford	57	–10.9	6,754	26.2	–0.2	308,914	38.5	386,773	–25.3	26,684	–50.3
Benton	19	11.8	753	10.6	–22.4	28,860	17.8	64,154	24.0	3,894	6.2
Bledsoe	13	(NA)	174	4.4	–69.5	6,108	6.0	(D)	(NA)	(D)	(NA)
Blount	117	–7.1	8,022	13.8	–3.0	520,561	23.3	1,391,478	6.5	156,524	157.9
Bradley	128	–9.9	10,275	20.3	–16.3	589,122	28.9	2,154,458	33.3	(D)	(NA)
Campbell	46	–13.2	2,455	15.9	32.1	125,435	26.6	112,290	0.2	(D)	(NA)
Cannon	(NA)	(NA)	452	8.1	19.3	26,591	23.5	(NA)	(NA)	(NA)	(NA)
Carroll	44	–12.0	2,077	15.4	8.6	100,505	27.8	144,570	–20.1	16,682	26.0
Carter	43	–10.4	1,613	8.0	–9.8	67,214	14.0	160,607	15.7	4,793	(NA)
Cheatham	39	–7.1	3,130	19.3	44.6	228,041	43.7	62,729	–79.1	(D)	(NA)
Chester	20	–16.7	616	8.8	–14.2	24,235	14.5	34,997	20.6	945	–80.7
Claiborne	38	11.8	2,989	20.1	80.7	104,258	27.6	222,821	38.9	3,658	–24.6
Clay	(NA)	(NA)	393	9.3	–42.6	18,146	22.8	(NA)	(NA)	(NA)	(NA)
Cocke	35	–12.5	2,091	16.3	–8.4	90,243	28.4	262,813	62.5	15,782	–3.8
Coffee	67	–	5,526	16.2	–0.8	291,622	22.7	(D)	(NA)	(D)	(NA)
Crockett	21	31.3	1,163	17.7	–28.1	58,507	31.9	142,578	133.1	7,552	63.5
Cumberland	55	17.0	2,577	10.2	–3.8	100,470	13.8	211,788	–7.3	15,373	84.4
Davidson	666	–11.4	29,393	5.4	–14.4	2,456,420	8.7	3,617,798	5.8	150,656	–29.6
Decatur	33	–5.7	715	11.3	–31.2	28,569	17.3	69,495	4.1	4,901	142.6
DeKalb	25	–10.7	2,127	22.6	40.3	100,812	35.4	227,020	62.1	24,103	(NA)
Dickson	54	5.9	3,734	15.6	–6.5	175,031	25.7	393,029	12.6	72,517	114.2
Dyer	42	–	5,964	24.8	2.6	292,237	36.5	615,351	24.4	75,426	41.9
Fayette	37	–5.1	2,006	10.1	18.2	107,226	26.3	179,384	7.8	5,185	–1.9
Fentress	(NA)	(NA)	622	7.8	12.7	23,240	11.8	(NA)	(NA)	(NA)	(NA)
Franklin	47	9.3	2,166	13.3	–8.2	98,170	21.6	(D)	(NA)	(D)	(NA)
Gibson	77	–14.4	4,601	20.1	–23.2	250,707	34.7	522,127	–1.5	20,067	–22.9
Giles	43	–10.4	3,172	20.8	–27.8	167,147	38.9	362,564	–2.1	9,940	–34.2
Grainger	36	2.9	1,342	18.2	–15.1	54,148	35.0	70,046	–1.6	(D)	(NA)
Greene	107	–	8,628	21.8	–6.5	505,003	37.8	562,812	20.9	62,609	64.7
Grundy	(NA)	(NA)	494	9.6	60.9	17,977	16.0	(NA)	(NA)	(NA)	(NA)
Hamblen	123	–4.7	12,498	28.4	–15.8	638,512	39.4	1,331,027	39.2	89,832	–11.3
Hamilton	498	–3.3	25,870	10.6	–14.9	1,403,187	13.7	3,175,258	27.1	222,649	–1.1
Hancock	(NA)	(NA)	162	7.0	–48.6	4,460	14.8	(NA)	(NA)	(NA)	(NA)
Hardeman	38	2.7	2,094	19.2	5.5	109,536	31.9	225,551	128.6	42,520	945.7
Hardin	51	–1.9	2,252	17.6	–6.3	126,857	33.6	278,785	38.2	34,987	0.4
Hawkins	48	–4.0	4,396	21.8	–16.3	253,742	42.4	(D)	(NA)	(D)	(NA)
Haywood	22	–4.3	1,975	23.4	7.6	89,806	32.4	108,920	–31.7	8,840	–16.5
Henderson	42	–10.6	4,006	28.6	–9.2	188,768	45.3	242,960	–4.2	12,814	–50.5
Henry	52	–21.2	3,228	18.6	–24.9	141,985	27.5	163,403	–19.2	6,255	–57.0
Hickman	32	3.2	724	10.4	–14.4	26,814	18.0	29,589	–60.0	(D)	(NA)
Houston	(NA)	(NA)	260	8.6	6.1	9,427	17.4	(NA)	(NA)	(NA)	(NA)
Humphreys	30	3.4	1,428	16.5	–14.0	116,635	36.4	363,487	–27.3	34,860	–35.0
Jackson	8	–	746	10.6	1.5	23,329	21.0	80,065	17.2	(D)	(NA)
Jefferson	59	5.4	2,792	14.9	3.1	161,158	28.5	361,967	76.4	(D)	(NA)
Johnson	19	–	653	9.4	–5.5	30,892	18.2	61,277	–35.6	2,507	–52.7
Knox	458	–7.1	18,309	6.2	–8.0	985,852	8.5	1,851,301	24.5	114,667	13.4
Lake	(NA)	(NA)	(D)	(NA)	(NA)	(D)	(NA)	(NA)	(NA)	(NA)	(NA)
Lauderdale	16	–27.3	1,998	21.6	–35.4	90,056	30.7	219,123	12.6	10,006	–23.2
Lawrence	65	16.1	3,309	17.5	–23.2	168,816	32.4	314,037	–22.5	13,617	–34.5

See footnotes at end of table.

Table B-15. Counties — **Manufacturing**—Con.

[Includes United States, states, and 3,141 counties/county equivalents defined as of February 22, 2005. For more information on these areas, see Appendix C, Geographic Information]

County	Establishments, 2002[1] Total	Percent change, 1997–2002	Employment, 2005[2] Total	Percent of all employees	Percent change, 2001–2005	Earnings, 2005[2] Total ($1,000)	Percent of all earnings	Value added by manufactures, 2002[1] Total ($1,000)	Percent change, 1997–2002	Capital expenditures, 2002[1] Total ($1,000)	Percent change, 1997–2002
TENNESSEE—Con.											
Lewis	(NA)	(NA)	364	8.2	−32.6	12,363	13.3	(NA)	(NA)	(NA)	(NA)
Lincoln	48	11.6	2,987	19.4	12.3	138,773	32.9	401,844	100.3	14,019	59.7
Loudon	53	17.8	3,153	16.8	5.5	154,983	25.5	819,664	78.8	(D)	(NA)
McMinn	65	−12.2	6,706	25.1	7.6	419,074	45.3	777,056	1.8	76,232	8.3
McNairy	43	−10.4	3,053	27.3	−12.5	188,658	50.3	185,946	−5.0	10,024	18.8
Macon	38	–	958	9.6	−16.1	28,854	13.6	34,936	14.2	1,812	−62.1
Madison	127	−8.0	10,280	15.1	−14.8	573,433	21.5	1,954,410	29.2	125,782	−31.6
Marion	27	−6.9	1,433	13.9	−20.5	71,060	24.8	142,684	55.0	(D)	(NA)
Marshall	48	6.7	4,272	29.0	−35.2	206,766	45.5	327,109	−48.3	20,193	−59.1
Maury	77	2.7	7,710	17.6	−25.2	673,041	35.3	1,659,273	−16.8	(D)	(NA)
Meigs	11	−15.4	741	12.9	−7.5	34,973	35.1	48,155	51.7	1,348	(NA)
Monroe	73	−13.1	5,827	31.1	22.2	334,721	51.2	380,772	1.9	31,540	−10.8
Montgomery	75	−9.6	6,231	10.1	−16.9	355,228	18.5	931,154	30.1	46,996	−25.4
Moore	(NA)	(NA)	(D)	(NA)	(NA)	(D)	(NA)	(NA)	(NA)	(NA)	(NA)
Morgan	(NA)	(NA)	330	5.2	−67.2	14,646	10.4	(NA)	(NA)	(NA)	(NA)
Obion	40	−13.0	4,761	25.4	−20.5	296,889	42.9	611,612	−8.1	(D)	(NA)
Overton	27	−6.9	1,236	14.3	−21.5	55,482	26.7	101,824	109.3	(D)	(NA)
Perry	11	−26.7	1,403	34.9	−12.8	53,437	51.5	84,130	44.1	2,574	−84.1
Pickett	(NA)	(NA)	156	8.1	−25.4	4,109	11.4	(NA)	(NA)	(NA)	(NA)
Polk	(NA)	(NA)	318	7.2	−36.3	13,508	11.9	(NA)	(NA)	(NA)	(NA)
Putnam	122	−13.5	7,721	17.9	−7.7	346,843	24.1	689,023	−6.4	19,311	−48.0
Rhea	38	−5.0	4,711	31.7	−2.9	205,651	40.5	342,464	46.5	17,142	211.8
Roane	32	−23.8	1,601	7.5	−31.1	63,431	6.2	(D)	(NA)	5,083	−60.9
Robertson	71	−4.1	6,461	22.8	13.6	347,032	37.9	431,926	45.8	23,506	(NA)
Rutherford	190	−0.5	23,005	18.0	13.8	1,634,815	30.3	1,273,914	−48.7	(D)	(NA)
Scott	46	15.0	2,253	24.3	−2.1	79,337	32.5	145,492	1.7	8,645	−12.9
Sequatchie	11	–	831	19.2	−8.8	26,117	24.0	85,002	9.2	(D)	(NA)
Sevier	82	−20.4	1,493	3.0	−28.4	77,720	5.1	117,345	−17.1	5,998	−42.9
Shelby	800	−11.3	41,172	6.5	−6.0	3,215,092	10.2	5,264,544	9.7	450,208	10.1
Smith	24	4.3	1,355	15.7	−22.4	67,535	28.7	220,929	48.0	(D)	(NA)
Stewart	13	(NA)	449	10.7	−18.5	18,053	13.1	63,607	(NA)	1,117	(NA)
Sullivan	167	−8.2	14,381	15.8	−14.5	1,187,302	32.2	2,044,917	−13.5	724,169	133.5
Sumner	216	5.4	7,789	14.5	−14.9	507,162	23.6	772,203	−3.9	65,065	0.7
Tipton	39	–	2,567	15.7	−24.0	119,889	23.6	247,166	−24.2	14,571	−45.2
Trousdale	(NA)	(NA)	338	6.4	−35.5	12,741	17.5	(NA)	(NA)	(NA)	(NA)
Unicoi	26	18.2	1,867	26.4	6.9	102,987	39.3	85,291	−34.2	9,009	(NA)
Union	19	−5.0	825	17.3	−19.7	41,992	35.1	83,854	98.8	(D)	(NA)
Van Buren	(NA)	(NA)	(D)	(NA)	(NA)	(D)	(NA)	(NA)	(NA)	(NA)	(NA)
Warren	65	−11.0	6,282	29.1	−2.2	382,636	49.2	418,815	−20.0	21,016	−54.3
Washington	143	−5.3	8,010	10.4	−15.2	456,981	16.8	592,217	8.4	28,991	(NA)
Wayne	25	−10.7	829	13.5	−22.9	30,280	21.0	50,704	(Z)	1,262	−71.7
Weakley	42	−6.7	1,909	11.1	−31.0	73,344	14.8	306,531	43.4	4,705	−52.7
White	50	2.0	2,419	21.0	−22.4	102,560	35.5	260,546	2.4	17,468	−0.7
Williamson	121	5.2	3,429	3.4	−11.3	166,187	3.4	289,867	−22.4	18,205	−41.4
Wilson	110	−3.5	6,870	14.1	−6.1	562,026	29.5	3,194,966	786.0	41,914	26.3
TEXAS	21,450	−1.6	951,778	7.3	−11.2	78,687,109	12.7	124,462,554	−3.8	9,916,978	−20.7
Anderson	(NA)	(NA)	535	2.1	−12.2	22,534	2.8	(NA)	(NA)	(NA)	(NA)
Andrews	(NA)	(NA)	344	5.2	−6.3	14,189	5.6	(NA)	(NA)	(NA)	(NA)
Angelina	79	−10.2	6,616	14.0	−3.6	485,514	27.4	420,874	−17.7	39,533	−34.0
Aransas	(NA)	(NA)	137	1.3	−25.9	4,950	2.1	(NA)	(NA)	(NA)	(NA)
Archer	(NA)	(NA)	121	2.9	317.2	3,397	2.9	(NA)	(NA)	(NA)	(NA)
Armstrong	(NA)	(NA)	(D)	(NA)	(NA)	(D)	(NA)	(NA)	(NA)	(NA)	(NA)
Atascosa	(NA)	(NA)	305	1.8	−30.4	7,838	1.9	(NA)	(NA)	(NA)	(NA)
Austin	39	21.9	2,090	12.9	7.0	125,374	26.3	(D)	(NA)	18,433	444.9
Bailey	(NA)	(NA)	158	4.0	−12.7	5,932	5.6	(NA)	(NA)	(NA)	(NA)
Bandera	(NA)	(NA)	139	1.9	93.1	1,395	1.1	(NA)	(NA)	(NA)	(NA)
Bastrop	55	5.8	1,183	5.0	28.2	41,983	7.5	96,422	150.0	(D)	(NA)
Baylor	(NA)	(NA)	87	3.9	(NA)	2,281	5.5	(NA)	(NA)	(NA)	(NA)
Bee	(NA)	(NA)	305	2.5	−2.9	12,376	3.5	(NA)	(NA)	(NA)	(NA)
Bell	140	3.7	7,780	4.6	−8.5	362,169	4.7	931,638	33.7	56,692	14.4
Bexar	1,019	−7.4	38,550	4.2	−14.8	2,876,250	7.1	3,035,203	11.7	183,902	−22.7
Blanco	(NA)	(NA)	69	1.0	−37.3	1,753	1.3	(NA)	(NA)	(NA)	(NA)
Borden	(NA)	(NA)	10	1.8	(NA)	–	–	(NA)	(NA)	(NA)	(NA)
Bosque	(NA)	(NA)	773	9.3	22.3	26,776	15.5	(NA)	(NA)	(NA)	(NA)
Bowie	70	−6.7	2,840	5.6	−0.1	144,675	7.6	465,661	29.7	25,805	−19.5
Brazoria	227	14.1	12,093	10.4	−11.9	1,244,469	27.8	4,596,289	78.2	912,227	14.9
Brazos	112	10.9	5,752	5.7	1.0	261,603	7.7	339,367	93.3	14,573	18.0
Brewster	(NA)	(NA)	94	1.4	2.2	3,028	1.7	(NA)	(NA)	(NA)	(NA)
Briscoe	(NA)	(NA)	(D)	(NA)	(NA)	(D)	(NA)	(NA)	(NA)	(NA)	(NA)
Brooks	(NA)	(NA)	(D)	(NA)	(NA)	(D)	(NA)	(NA)	(NA)	(NA)	(NA)
Brown	38	−2.6	3,481	15.5	−1.4	188,869	29.3	497,755	1.7	11,245	−63.2

See footnotes at end of table.

Table B-15. Counties — **Manufacturing**—Con.

[Includes United States, states, and 3,141 counties/county equivalents defined as of February 22, 2005. For more information on these areas, see Appendix C, Geographic Information]

County	Establishments, 2002[1]		Employment, 2005[2]			Earnings, 2005[2]		Value added by manufactures, 2002[1]		Capital expenditures, 2002[1]	
	Total	Percent change, 1997–2002	Total	Percent of all employees	Percent change, 2001–2005	Total ($1,000)	Percent of all earnings	Total ($1,000)	Percent change, 1997–2002	Total ($1,000)	Percent change, 1997–2002
TEXAS—Con.											
Burleson	(NA)	(NA)	272	3.6	−19.3	9,965	6.0	(NA)	(NA)	(NA)	(NA)
Burnet	48	14.3	1,198	5.0	28.1	51,270	8.7	58,114	39.1	(D)	(NA)
Caldwell	(NA)	(NA)	269	2.2	−29.8	9,891	3.6	(NA)	(NA)	(D)	(NA)
Calhoun	22	10.0	3,215	25.1	−22.0	357,470	55.9	(D)	(NA)	(D)	(NA)
Callahan	(NA)	(NA)	171	3.1	25.7	6,680	7.0	(NA)	(NA)	(NA)	(NA)
Cameron	242	3.0	7,808	5.0	−35.8	293,766	6.6	758,186	−2.2	117,015	263.0
Camp	(NA)	(NA)	203	3.6	−70.3	5,822	3.1	(NA)	(NA)	(NA)	(NA)
Carson	(NA)	(NA)	(D)	(NA)	(NA)	(D)	(NA)	(NA)	(NA)	(NA)	(NA)
Cass	24	−7.7	1,774	13.4	−1.0	107,535	26.9	27,691	−21.1	(D)	(NA)
Castro	(NA)	(NA)	81	1.8	−46.4	4,070	1.7	(NA)	(NA)	(NA)	(NA)
Chambers	15	–	1,320	11.5	−22.0	130,712	26.5	(D)	(NA)	(D)	(NA)
Cherokee	82	−9.9	3,605	15.2	1.1	125,191	17.3	198,626	18.9	16,379	−5.9
Childress	(NA)	(NA)	(D)	(NA)	(NA)	(D)	(NA)	(NA)	(NA)	(NA)	(NA)
Clay	(NA)	(NA)	344	6.0	7.5	8,797	7.7	(NA)	(NA)	(NA)	(NA)
Cochran	(NA)	(NA)	(D)	(NA)	(NA)	(D)	(NA)	(NA)	(NA)	(NA)	(NA)
Coke	(NA)	(NA)	(D)	(NA)	(NA)	(D)	(NA)	(NA)	(NA)	(NA)	(NA)
Coleman	(NA)	(NA)	183	3.7	131.6	3,917	4.7	(NA)	(NA)	(NA)	(NA)
Collin	404	27.0	22,516	6.3	−1.7	2,195,143	12.0	2,001,275	−42.0	168,177	−48.1
Collingsworth	(NA)	(NA)	(D)	(NA)	(NA)	(D)	(NA)	(NA)	(NA)	(NA)	(NA)
Colorado	32	10.3	991	8.1	3.0	36,609	13.0	43,033	3.9	3,127	39.3
Comal	101	20.2	3,373	7.0	−34.9	255,918	15.6	336,585	−2.3	35,052	65.3
Comanche	(NA)	(NA)	219	2.5	5.3	6,475	3.4	(NA)	(NA)	(NA)	(NA)
Concho	(NA)	(NA)	(D)	(NA)	(NA)	(D)	(NA)	(NA)	(NA)	(NA)	(NA)
Cooke	67	−1.5	2,871	11.6	−3.9	154,756	21.1	265,807	26.8	23,604	−10.0
Coryell	(NA)	(NA)	663	3.0	16.7	27,336	4.4	(NA)	(NA)	(NA)	(NA)
Cottle	(NA)	(NA)	(D)	(NA)	(NA)	(D)	(NA)	(NA)	(NA)	(NA)	(NA)
Crane	(NA)	(NA)	(D)	(NA)	(NA)	(D)	(NA)	(NA)	(NA)	(NA)	(NA)
Crockett	(NA)	(NA)	10	0.4	(NA)	79	0.2	(NA)	(NA)	(NA)	(NA)
Crosby	(NA)	(NA)	54	1.6	−26.0	1,506	1.2	(NA)	(NA)	(NA)	(NA)
Culberson	(NA)	(NA)	(D)	(NA)	(NA)	(D)	(NA)	(NA)	(NA)	(NA)	(NA)
Dallam	(NA)	(NA)	150	2.7	−2.0	7,039	3.7	(NA)	(NA)	(NA)	(NA)
Dallas	2,982	−11.9	153,378	8.4	−15.5	14,197,697	12.5	16,691,677	−4.9	1,181,795	−27.0
Dawson	(NA)	(NA)	157	2.2	−15.6	5,191	2.6	(NA)	(NA)	(NA)	(NA)
Deaf Smith	26	−18.8	874	8.9	8.4	30,987	9.5	105,696	−15.5	3,564	−44.7
Delta	(NA)	(NA)	19	0.9	(NA)	336	0.9	(NA)	(NA)	(NA)	(NA)
Denton	351	15.1	13,427	6.6	−0.9	1,201,737	15.2	1,165,937	−16.4	46,266	−49.9
DeWitt	27	12.5	1,258	10.1	−6.5	52,820	17.1	71,082	81.8	1,524	14.1
Dickens	(NA)	(NA)	10	0.7	(NA)	79	0.3	(NA)	(NA)	(NA)	(NA)
Dimmit	(NA)	(NA)	25	0.6	(NA)	346	0.3	(NA)	(NA)	(NA)	(NA)
Donley	(NA)	(NA)	33	1.5	3.1	765	1.8	(NA)	(NA)	(NA)	(NA)
Duval	(NA)	(NA)	33	0.6	(NA)	413	0.3	(NA)	(NA)	(NA)	(NA)
Eastland	31	24.0	878	7.8	−36.1	34,222	11.9	52,172	24.9	(D)	(NA)
Ector	224	10.3	4,024	5.8	−15.5	216,459	8.5	554,909	13.4	20,637	−52.3
Edwards	(NA)	(NA)	10	0.7	(NA)	79	0.5	(NA)	(NA)	(NA)	(NA)
Ellis	170	−2.3	9,502	17.9	−9.3	523,583	31.1	1,216,685	9.6	135,369	10.2
El Paso	643	−1.4	24,799	7.1	−32.0	1,587,100	11.8	3,165,254	−4.1	204,631	−12.6
Erath	41	10.8	1,530	7.1	−25.1	65,622	11.2	194,646	63.6	15,570	79.3
Falls	(NA)	(NA)	265	3.2	−28.6	9,069	5.2	(NA)	(NA)	(NA)	(NA)
Fannin	35	−12.5	881	6.3	−37.6	34,634	9.9	85,474	−38.7	4,910	−33.5
Fayette	49	25.6	1,148	7.2	−2.3	45,309	11.8	65,901	14.4	4,181	−10.3
Fisher	(NA)	(NA)	(D)	(NA)	(NA)	(D)	(NA)	(NA)	(NA)	(NA)	(NA)
Floyd	(NA)	(NA)	79	2.1	−9.2	2,874	2.2	(NA)	(NA)	(NA)	(NA)
Foard	(NA)	(NA)	(D)	(NA)	(NA)	(D)	(NA)	(NA)	(NA)	(NA)	(NA)
Fort Bend	307	13.7	13,782	7.3	9.4	1,244,082	16.3	1,249,654	−16.3	133,292	−10.4
Franklin	(NA)	(NA)	(D)	(NA)	(NA)	(D)	(NA)	(NA)	(NA)	(NA)	(NA)
Freestone	(NA)	(NA)	410	3.8	50.7	23,740	8.6	(NA)	(NA)	(NA)	(NA)
Frio	(NA)	(NA)	67	1.1	−32.3	1,973	1.2	(NA)	(NA)	(NA)	(NA)
Gaines	(NA)	(NA)	119	1.5	−28.7	3,310	1.2	(NA)	(NA)	(NA)	(NA)
Galveston	176	10.0	6,140	4.9	−20.6	713,633	15.2	1,010,084	−42.7	458,730	149.8
Garza	(NA)	(NA)	45	1.4	25.0	1,331	1.6	(NA)	(NA)	(NA)	(NA)
Gillespie	(NA)	(NA)	848	5.4	21.0	32,880	9.1	(NA)	(NA)	(NA)	(NA)
Glasscock	(NA)	(NA)	–	–	–	–	–	(NA)	(NA)	(NA)	(NA)
Goliad	(NA)	(NA)	85	2.6	(NA)	3,632	5.4	(NA)	(NA)	(NA)	(NA)
Gonzales	20	5.3	944	8.7	19.0	33,877	10.3	53,755	20.7	3,468	18.4
Gray	21	5.0	1,047	8.5	−11.6	99,891	21.2	189,828	−0.1	(D)	(NA)
Grayson	132	−5.7	6,569	11.3	−25.5	480,502	24.2	1,614,367	−26.2	89,969	−57.7
Gregg	208	1.5	11,738	12.9	26.1	662,996	18.3	1,308,911	−6.0	80,959	−51.0
Grimes	24	14.3	1,496	13.6	−19.4	126,945	35.6	188,015	−7.5	12,199	2.9
Guadalupe	100	11.1	5,553	14.7	1.7	352,721	29.1	685,248	11.1	45,522	8.5
Hale	28	−12.5	2,660	13.5	−0.3	99,323	15.5	(D)	(NA)	12,828	−23.5

See footnotes at end of table.

[Includes United States, states, and 3,141 counties/county equivalents defined as of February 22, 2005. For more information on these areas, see Appendix C, Geographic Information]

County	Establishments, 2002[1] Total	Percent change, 1997–2002	Employment, 2005[2] Total	Percent of all employees	Percent change, 2001–2005	Earnings, 2005[2] Total ($1,000)	Percent of all earnings	Value added by manufactures, 2002[1] Total ($1,000)	Percent change, 1997–2002	Capital expenditures, 2002[1] Total ($1,000)	Percent change, 1997–2002
TEXAS—Con.											
Hall	(NA)	(NA)	92	4.3	22.7	2,301	5.1	(NA)	(NA)	(NA)	(NA)
Hamilton	(NA)	(NA)	211	4.5	-11.3	10,777	10.6	(NA)	(NA)	(NA)	(NA)
Hansford	(NA)	(NA)	63	1.9	28.6	2,437	1.6	(NA)	(NA)	(NA)	(NA)
Hardeman	(NA)	(NA)	(D)	(NA)	(NA)	(D)	(NA)	(NA)	(NA)	(NA)	(NA)
Hardin	30	-18.9	1,023	5.6	-9.1	49,416	9.5	76,811	22.5	2,617	-60.8
Harris	4,224	-3.4	176,215	7.3	-9.3	20,198,605	12.6	25,231,576	-15.3	2,415,591	-20.2
Harrison	75	-16.7	4,646	15.1	-25.8	233,450	22.4	280,812	-6.8	39,750	12.1
Hartley	(NA)	(NA)	(D)	(NA)	(NA)	(NA)	(NA)	(NA)	(NA)	(NA)	(NA)
Haskell	(NA)	(NA)	40	1.1	-2.4	564	0.7	(NA)	(NA)	(NA)	(NA)
Hays	125	15.7	3,755	6.0	6.3	209,386	11.7	323,715	29.5	(D)	(NA)
Hemphill	(NA)	(NA)	30	1.1	30.4	522	0.5	(NA)	(NA)	(NA)	(NA)
Henderson	60	22.4	1,644	5.5	-25.1	61,071	9.0	184,241	44.8	6,528	53.0
Hidalgo	283	8.4	9,355	3.5	-21.6	303,758	3.9	746,312	11.1	48,438	19.2
Hill	41	10.8	720	4.6	-47.0	36,869	10.0	57,723	-26.5	1,784	-48.0
Hockley	(NA)	(NA)	304	2.5	48.3	9,297	2.5	(NA)	(NA)	(NA)	(NA)
Hood	42	(NA)	498	3.2	8.7	28,528	6.6	(D)	(NA)	2,620	(NA)
Hopkins	43	—	1,375	7.2	-9.3	63,996	12.1	349,591	52.4	13,776	-25.9
Houston	22	-8.3	632	5.8	-29.1	50,535	15.4	66,229	30.1	3,886	15.9
Howard	26	-3.7	844	5.4	-33.4	54,413	10.1	144,446	-8.5	24,487	132.6
Hudspeth	(NA)	(NA)	(D)	(NA)	(NA)	(D)	(NA)	(NA)	(NA)	(NA)	(NA)
Hunt	64	10.3	6,977	17.2	19.7	452,228	35.1	(D)	(NA)	(D)	(NA)
Hutchinson	19	-36.7	1,051	9.7	-39.7	95,597	23.2	413,605	10.7	72,620	(NA)
Irion	(NA)	(NA)	(D)	(NA)	(NA)	(D)	(NA)	(NA)	(NA)	(NA)	(NA)
Jack	(NA)	(NA)	54	1.2	-10.0	2,378	2.1	(D)	(NA)	(NA)	(NA)
Jackson	8	-27.3	(D)	(NA)	(NA)	(D)	(NA)	(D)	(NA)	(D)	(NA)
Jasper	25	-13.8	1,896	10.6	-4.2	154,107	30.0	368,353	57.2	48,329	295.1
Jeff Davis	(NA)	(NA)	(D)	(NA)	(NA)	(D)	(NA)	(NA)	(NA)	(NA)	(NA)
Jefferson	231	0.4	14,071	9.5	-9.8	1,329,166	20.5	4,458,875	1.4	478,977	-29.0
Jim Hogg	(NA)	(NA)	(D)	(NA)	(NA)	(D)	(NA)	(NA)	(NA)	(NA)	(NA)
Jim Wells	(NA)	(NA)	342	1.6	62.9	13,784	2.0	(NA)	(NA)	(NA)	(NA)
Johnson	166	-2.4	6,270	10.6	-13.6	332,885	19.7	453,484	-13.4	20,541	-53.8
Jones	(NA)	(NA)	737	8.4	224.7	31,984	15.6	(NA)	(NA)	(NA)	(NA)
Karnes	(NA)	(NA)	174	2.4	-31.8	4,963	3.3	(NA)	(NA)	(NA)	(NA)
Kaufman	117	7.3	4,130	11.4	-15.6	197,858	17.7	317,773	18.9	25,623	100.5
Kendall	41	(NA)	834	5.9	-8.0	38,159	8.5	105,352	(NA)	4,731	(NA)
Kenedy	(NA)	(NA)	—	—	—	—	—	(NA)	(NA)	(NA)	(NA)
Kent	(NA)	(NA)	—	—	—	—	—	(NA)	(NA)	(NA)	(NA)
Kerr	51	4.1	1,357	4.7	30.7	56,051	6.5	57,865	8.1	2,939	10.7
Kimble	(NA)	(NA)	285	9.0	-19.9	10,242	21.0	(NA)	(NA)	(NA)	(NA)
King	(NA)	(NA)	[4]5	(NA)	(NA)	69	1.2	(NA)	(NA)	(NA)	(NA)
Kinney	(NA)	(NA)	(D)	(NA)	(NA)	(D)	(NA)	(NA)	(NA)	(NA)	(NA)
Kleberg	(NA)	(NA)	215	1.3	-16.0	10,417	2.0	(NA)	(NA)	(NA)	(NA)
Knox	(NA)	(NA)	(D)	(NA)	(NA)	(D)	(NA)	(NA)	(NA)	(NA)	(NA)
Lamar	54	-10.0	4,575	15.9	-7.1	252,288	29.3	1,567,092	17.2	54,133	-2.3
Lamb	13	-7.1	(D)	(NA)	(NA)	(D)	(NA)	46,152	-13.9	2,538	(NA)
Lampasas	(NA)	(NA)	707	8.6	15.9	24,880	13.2	(NA)	(NA)	(NA)	(NA)
La Salle	(NA)	(NA)	10	0.4	(NA)	78	0.1	(NA)	(NA)	(NA)	(NA)
Lavaca	45	-2.2	2,196	18.2	8.9	96,449	36.8	138,443	49.2	15,215	221.4
Lee	(NA)	(NA)	412	4.3	-8.6	18,732	7.9	(NA)	(NA)	(NA)	(NA)
Leon	(NA)	(NA)	416	4.3	-20.9	38,896	14.5	(NA)	(NA)	(NA)	(NA)
Liberty	35	-14.6	2,292	8.3	20.6	219,464	24.9	(D)	(NA)	(D)	(NA)
Limestone	22	29.4	934	7.9	22.3	42,471	13.2	72,129	77.7	3,456	-17.9
Lipscomb	(NA)	(NA)	(D)	(NA)	(NA)	(D)	(NA)	(NA)	(NA)	(NA)	(NA)
Live Oak	(NA)	(NA)	(D)	(NA)	(NA)	(D)	(NA)	(NA)	(NA)	(NA)	(NA)
Llano	(NA)	(NA)	149	2.1	-16.8	4,701	2.7	(NA)	(NA)	(NA)	(NA)
Loving	(NA)	(NA)	(D)	(NA)	(NA)	(D)	(NA)	(NA)	(NA)	(NA)	(NA)
Lubbock	261	1.2	5,449	3.4	-20.4	286,350	5.3	546,929	-37.9	(D)	(NA)
Lynn	(NA)	(NA)	68	2.4	54.5	1,855	1.5	(NA)	(NA)	(NA)	(NA)
McCulloch	(NA)	(NA)	268	5.4	7.6	15,743	12.6	(NA)	(NA)	(NA)	(NA)
McLennan	247	-5.4	16,099	12.2	9.2	998,146	20.8	2,603,132	23.9	73,397	4.7
McMullen	(NA)	(NA)	—	—	—	—	—	(NA)	(NA)	(NA)	(NA)
Madison	(NA)	(NA)	91	1.5	31.9	1,950	1.1	(NA)	(NA)	(NA)	(NA)
Marion	(NA)	(NA)	467	11.8	53.1	22,752	24.2	(NA)	(NA)	(NA)	(NA)
Martin	(NA)	(NA)	(D)	(NA)	(NA)	(D)	(NA)	(NA)	(NA)	(NA)	(NA)
Mason	(NA)	(NA)	104	3.7	89.1	11,020	21.4	(NA)	(NA)	(NA)	(NA)
Matagorda	(NA)	(NA)	516	3.2	-31.9	40,261	7.2	(NA)	(NA)	(NA)	(NA)
Maverick	(NA)	(NA)	439	2.4	-31.3	16,082	3.3	(NA)	(NA)	(NA)	(NA)
Medina	21	-8.7	592	4.0	10.4	19,351	6.0	30,654	-7.6	1,135	-20.0
Menard	(NA)	(NA)	(D)	(NA)	(NA)	(D)	(NA)	(NA)	(NA)	(NA)	(NA)
Midland	119	-11.9	2,660	3.1	10.8	172,405	4.3	115,757	-31.2	13,220	55.1

See footnotes at end of table.

[Includes United States, states, and 3,141 counties/county equivalents defined as of February 22, 2005. For more information on these areas, see Appendix C, Geographic Information]

County	Manufacturing (NAICS 31–33)										
	Establishments, 2002[1]		Employment, 2005[2]			Earnings, 2005[2]		Value added by manufactures, 2002[1]		Capital expenditures, 2002[1]	
	Total	Percent change, 1997–2002	Total	Percent of all employees	Percent change, 2001–2005	Total ($1,000)	Percent of all earnings	Total ($1,000)	Percent change, 1997–2002	Total ($1,000)	Percent change, 1997–2002
TEXAS—Con.											
Milam	14	55.6	1,607	13.0	−12.8	106,215	30.4	294,456	126.9	11,057	−23.0
Mills	(NA)	(NA)	110	3.3	−8.3	3,173	5.0	(NA)	(NA)	(NA)	(NA)
Mitchell	(NA)	(NA)	(D)	(NA)	(NA)	(D)	(NA)	(NA)	(NA)	(NA)	(NA)
Montague	(NA)	(NA)	443	4.4	5.2	14,941	6.8	(NA)	(NA)	(NA)	(NA)
Montgomery	334	17.2	8,725	5.8	22.0	509,545	8.6	791,983	9.6	53,153	−8.8
Moore	17	−10.5	3,465	30.1	4.3	166,189	40.2	(D)	(NA)	(D)	(NA)
Morris	17	6.3	2,030	32.1	0.2	155,377	55.2	288,793	16.7	17,536	(NA)
Motley	(NA)	(NA)	(D)	(NA)	(NA)	(D)	(NA)	(NA)	(NA)	(NA)	(NA)
Nacogdoches	69	15.0	3,963	13.0	−10.0	159,573	17.5	470,574	77.0	22,024	12.2
Navarro	55	12.2	3,172	12.9	−5.9	131,004	20.4	283,768	54.3	26,552	238.6
Newton	(NA)	(NA)	159	4.8	−63.9	12,331	14.4	(NA)	(NA)	(NA)	(NA)
Nolan	13	−23.5	918	10.4	9.0	42,208	16.9	116,951	−7.1	4,981	−58.3
Nueces	217	−2.7	9,116	4.7	−12.1	731,236	9.3	(D)	(NA)	(D)	(NA)
Ochiltree	(NA)	(NA)	32	0.5	−53.6	703	0.3	(NA)	(NA)	(NA)	(NA)
Oldham	(NA)	(NA)	(D)	(NA)	(NA)	(D)	(NA)	(NA)	(NA)	(NA)	(NA)
Orange	92	12.2	4,679	14.9	−16.1	366,014	34.8	854,578	−28.2	75,419	−48.4
Palo Pinto	39	5.4	1,720	12.8	7.8	116,300	29.6	80,064	4.8	(D)	(NA)
Panola	15	25.0	1,035	8.6	−18.4	37,396	10.0	135,919	37.6	3,601	−55.9
Parker	118	16.8	2,615	6.1	17.7	96,636	9.4	157,742	−3.8	11,108	9.8
Parmer	6	–	(D)	(NA)	(NA)	(D)	(NA)	(D)	(NA)	(D)	(NA)
Pecos	(NA)	(NA)	79	1.2	−21.8	3,661	1.9	(NA)	(NA)	(NA)	(NA)
Polk	27	8.0	1,468	8.9	0.6	68,880	15.5	(D)	(NA)	8,903	7.7
Potter	139	−4.1	7,110	6.9	−0.3	298,476	7.9	431,595	(NA)	(D)	(NA)
Presidio	(NA)	(NA)	(D)	(NA)	(NA)	(D)	(NA)	(NA)	(NA)	(NA)	(NA)
Rains	(NA)	(NA)	221	5.1	36.4	7,658	9.1	(NA)	(NA)	(NA)	(NA)
Randall	59	1.7	2,100	5.6	18.6	93,003	8.3	(D)	(NA)	(D)	(NA)
Reagan	(NA)	(NA)	(D)	(NA)	(NA)	(D)	(NA)	(NA)	(NA)	(NA)	(NA)
Real	(NA)	(NA)	(D)	(NA)	(NA)	(D)	(NA)	(NA)	(NA)	(NA)	(NA)
Red River	16	−11.1	693	12.6	−23.2	24,477	22.7	36,754	−38.5	(D)	(NA)
Reeves	(NA)	(NA)	183	3.5	3.0	4,024	3.0	(NA)	(NA)	(NA)	(NA)
Refugio	(NA)	(NA)	(D)	(NA)	(NA)	(D)	(NA)	(NA)	(NA)	(NA)	(NA)
Roberts	(NA)	(NA)	10	1.8	(NA)	–	–	(NA)	(NA)	(NA)	(NA)
Robertson	(NA)	(NA)	582	7.9	16.6	25,434	14.0	(NA)	(NA)	(NA)	(NA)
Rockwall	59	5.4	1,401	5.5	−4.2	62,322	7.7	(D)	(NA)	(D)	(NA)
Runnels	12	−20.0	710	12.0	−40.3	33,764	24.8	113,421	39.8	3,436	19.8
Rusk	33	−35.3	1,607	8.2	−20.0	59,999	9.1	82,601	−3.7	3,991	2.4
Sabine	(NA)	(NA)	710	19.2	2.5	53,967	40.7	(NA)	(NA)	(NA)	(NA)
San Augustine	(NA)	(NA)	(D)	(NA)	(NA)	(D)	(NA)	(NA)	(NA)	(NA)	(NA)
San Jacinto	(NA)	(NA)	97	1.8	−50.3	2,122	2.1	(NA)	(NA)	(NA)	(NA)
San Patricio	49	8.9	1,845	7.2	−36.9	134,340	14.2	(D)	(NA)	(D)	(NA)
San Saba	(NA)	(NA)	47	1.2	−23.0	1,574	2.1	(NA)	(NA)	(NA)	(NA)
Schleicher	(NA)	(NA)	(D)	(NA)	(NA)	(D)	(NA)	(NA)	(NA)	(NA)	(NA)
Scurry	(NA)	(NA)	226	2.5	−25.7	10,526	2.8	(NA)	(NA)	(NA)	(NA)
Shackelford	(NA)	(NA)	28	1.3	27.3	688	1.3	(NA)	(NA)	(NA)	(NA)
Shelby	29	–	2,260	18.9	−8.4	89,081	23.0	131,325	−34.1	9,740	247.7
Sherman	(NA)	(NA)	(D)	(NA)	(NA)	(D)	(NA)	(NA)	(NA)	(NA)	(NA)
Smith	218	2.3	9,496	7.8	−13.4	587,015	12.3	1,170,235	5.1	86,046	73.5
Somervell	(NA)	(NA)	279	5.5	−4.8	7,494	3.2	(NA)	(NA)	(NA)	(NA)
Starr	(NA)	(NA)	211	1.0	−2.8	4,386	1.1	(NA)	(NA)	(NA)	(NA)
Stephens	(NA)	(NA)	432	8.2	−25.5	17,023	12.2	(NA)	(NA)	(NA)	(NA)
Sterling	(NA)	(NA)	–	–	(NA)	–	–	(NA)	(NA)	(NA)	(NA)
Stonewall	(NA)	(NA)	(D)	(NA)	(NA)	(D)	(NA)	(NA)	(NA)	(NA)	(NA)
Sutton	(NA)	(NA)	25	0.8	66.7	1,047	1.0	(NA)	(NA)	(NA)	(NA)
Swisher	(NA)	(NA)	138	3.4	−1.4	3,733	2.3	(NA)	(NA)	(NA)	(NA)
Tarrant	1,869	−7.0	90,493	9.6	−8.9	7,848,854	17.0	14,599,482	55.4	558,990	−9.4
Taylor	120	1.7	2,571	3.2	−19.5	97,429	3.4	263,702	−50.4	(D)	(NA)
Terrell	(NA)	(NA)	(D)	(NA)	(NA)	(D)	(NA)	(NA)	(NA)	(NA)	(NA)
Terry	(NA)	(NA)	136	2.2	100.0	5,348	2.5	(NA)	(NA)	(NA)	(NA)
Throckmorton	(NA)	(NA)	(D)	(NA)	(NA)	(D)	(NA)	(NA)	(NA)	(NA)	(NA)
Titus	37	−11.9	7,686	36.1	13.2	288,420	41.6	925,417	390.3	6,166	−2.5
Tom Green	102	2.0	3,689	5.7	−14.5	197,394	9.3	(D)	(NA)	(D)	(NA)
Travis	747	−3.5	47,501	6.8	−27.4	5,587,728	15.7	10,910,293	−4.3	(D)	(NA)
Trinity	(NA)	(NA)	243	5.2	6.6	6,427	6.9	(NA)	(NA)	(NA)	(NA)
Tyler	(NA)	(NA)	159	2.4	−7.6	9,278	5.5	(NA)	(NA)	(NA)	(NA)
Upshur	(NA)	(NA)	493	4.2	−21.2	24,991	8.7	(NA)	(NA)	(NA)	(NA)
Upton	(NA)	(NA)	(D)	(NA)	(NA)	(D)	(NA)	(NA)	(NA)	(NA)	(NA)
Uvalde	(NA)	(NA)	512	3.7	−28.3	16,012	4.5	(NA)	(NA)	(NA)	(NA)
Val Verde	(NA)	(NA)	2,208	9.4	254.4	102,159	12.4	(NA)	(NA)	(NA)	(NA)
Van Zandt	42	10.5	625	3.4	42.7	23,203	5.5	50,193	30.7	2,678	−38.6
Victoria	75	5.6	2,682	5.3	−14.3	178,341	9.7	(D)	(NA)	(D)	(NA)

See footnotes at end of table.

[Includes United States, states, and 3,141 counties/county equivalents defined as of February 22, 2005. For more information on these areas, see Appendix C, Geographic Information]

County	Establishments, 2002[1] Total	Percent change, 1997–2002	Employment, 2005[2] Total	Percent of all employ- ees	Percent change, 2001– 2005	Earnings, 2005[2] Total ($1,000)	Percent of all earnings	Value added by manufactures, 2002[1] Total ($1,000)	Percent change, 1997– 2002	Capital expenditures, 2002[1] Total ($1,000)	Percent change, 1997– 2002
TEXAS—Con.											
Walker	35	–7.9	879	3.1	–34.5	50,781	5.5	71,779	77.2	2,840	26.6
Waller	56	30.2	2,428	14.5	6.6	131,246	22.4	226,906	77.4	(D)	(NA)
Ward	(NA)	(NA)	178	3.9	161.8	4,559	3.0	(NA)	(NA)	(NA)	(NA)
Washington	56	36.6	2,735	12.7	–11.3	135,784	22.6	354,485	26.3	13,592	–30.0
Webb	95	9.2	1,712	1.7	10.2	47,206	1.4	180,648	32.1	14,187	–23.3
Wharton	52	13.0	1,664	7.7	–20.5	75,578	11.8	169,787	6.0	4,706	–36.7
Wheeler	(NA)	(NA)	27	0.8	(NA)	273	0.2	(NA)	(NA)	(NA)	(NA)
Wichita	147	–3.9	7,621	9.6	–10.1	460,814	14.9	881,250	14.5	42,098	(NA)
Wilbarger	9	–	1,084	11.6	17.7	46,719	17.1	113,709	13.8	4,935	329.1
Willacy	(NA)	(NA)	(D)	(NA)	(NA)	(D)	(NA)	(NA)	(NA)	(NA)	(NA)
Williamson	247	2.9	7,533	5.5	–10.5	490,828	8.3	1,097,204	–70.1	115,336	29.8
Wilson	(NA)	(NA)	395	3.3	18.3	15,098	6.2	(D)	(NA)	(NA)	(NA)
Winkler	(NA)	(NA)	(D)	(NA)	(NA)	(D)	(NA)	(NA)	(NA)	(NA)	(NA)
Wise	64	18.5	1,798	6.7	1.7	88,516	10.9	102,534	–4.2	3,159	–61.3
Wood	50	11.1	902	6.1	–3.0	35,717	8.9	66,160	77.6	3,153	89.9
Yoakum	(NA)	(NA)	98	2.1	50.8	4,971	2.6	(NA)	(NA)	(NA)	(NA)
Young	32	14.3	1,011	8.4	0.8	51,040	14.4	80,278	–43.6	3,156	–62.3
Zapata	(NA)	(NA)	43	0.9	–2.3	614	0.4	(NA)	(NA)	(NA)	(NA)
Zavala	(NA)	(NA)	(D)	(NA)	(NA)	(D)	(NA)	(NA)	(NA)	(NA)	(NA)
UTAH	3,061	7.0	126,202	8.4	–1.0	6,860,384	12.0	12,158,925	7.2	786,006	–16.6
Beaver	(NA)	(NA)	86	2.7	–17.3	4,251	3.0	(NA)	(NA)	(NA)	(NA)
Box Elder	60	17.6	7,737	29.6	6.7	528,979	53.9	974,430	47.3	39,498	281.8
Cache	182	22.1	10,742	17.8	26.1	436,910	25.6	654,784	22.6	32,017	–20.0
Carbon	(NA)	(NA)	462	3.9	10.8	20,762	5.4	(NA)	(NA)	(NA)	(NA)
Daggett	(NA)	(NA)	(D)	(NA)	(NA)	(D)	(NA)	(NA)	(NA)	(NA)	(NA)
Davis	276	21.6	11,533	8.2	7.3	558,269	10.6	939,417	48.0	(D)	(NA)
Duchesne	(NA)	(NA)	154	1.7	–7.2	5,602	2.1	(NA)	(NA)	(NA)	(NA)
Emery	(NA)	(NA)	70	1.2	9.4	1,121	0.5	(NA)	(NA)	(NA)	(NA)
Garfield	(NA)	(NA)	113	3.4	(NA)	2,244	3.0	(NA)	(NA)	(NA)	(NA)
Grand	(NA)	(NA)	100	1.6	5.3	1,834	1.2	(NA)	(NA)	(NA)	(NA)
Iron	50	–	1,833	8.3	14.8	69,585	11.8	199,853	93.0	19,212	5.0
Juab	(NA)	(NA)	475	10.3	16.4	19,220	15.0	(NA)	(NA)	(NA)	(NA)
Kane	(NA)	(NA)	214	5.2	(NA)	6,755	6.8	(NA)	(NA)	(NA)	(NA)
Millard	(NA)	(NA)	214	3.3	12.6	7,601	3.5	(NA)	(NA)	(NA)	(NA)
Morgan	(NA)	(NA)	257	7.4	–8.9	12,132	15.0	(NA)	(NA)	(NA)	(NA)
Piute	(NA)	(NA)	(D)	(NA)	(NA)	(D)	(NA)	(NA)	(NA)	(NA)	(NA)
Rich	(NA)	(NA)	(D)	(NA)	(NA)	(D)	(NA)	(NA)	(NA)	(NA)	(NA)
Salt Lake	1,434	–0.5	53,623	7.7	–3.6	3,317,317	11.0	5,550,134	11.7	343,315	–7.2
San Juan	(NA)	(NA)	246	4.4	25.5	6,516	4.4	(NA)	(NA)	(NA)	(NA)
Sanpete	21	16.7	1,011	9.4	–0.3	26,142	10.6	43,089	–19.0	(D)	(NA)
Sevier	(NA)	(NA)	540	5.0	–19.0	17,497	6.0	(NA)	(NA)	(NA)	(NA)
Summit	40	3.7	608	2.1	5.7	33,626	3.6	48,695	25.0	2,377	(NA)
Tooele	28	3.7	1,585	8.2	0.4	80,141	10.7	132,848	–21.6	7,874	–52.7
Uintah	(NA)	(NA)	262	1.6	0.4	5,848	1.0	(NA)	(NA)	(NA)	(NA)
Utah	445	14.1	18,779	8.3	–9.6	901,821	12.0	1,490,084	25.0	132,834	–16.0
Wasatch	(NA)	(NA)	363	3.9	20.6	19,317	8.0	(NA)	(NA)	(NA)	(NA)
Washington	122	32.6	3,269	5.1	35.9	119,464	6.4	145,283	8.6	5,927	–43.3
Wayne	(NA)	(NA)	15	0.9	–68.1	159	0.4	(NA)	(NA)	(NA)	(NA)
Weber	231	10.0	11,860	10.4	–14.8	656,746	16.6	1,777,081	–31.8	111,493	–28.4
VERMONT	1,176	–4.1	40,153	9.5	–16.9	2,378,975	15.5	5,163,905	27.7	450,230	–38.6
Addison	61	–	2,270	9.3	–3.6	118,911	16.2	220,047	19.2	7,513	(NA)
Bennington	82	–6.8	2,962	11.2	–19.7	191,220	21.4	233,551	–6.6	10,545	(NA)
Caledonia	58	5.5	2,103	11.3	–9.0	103,782	18.2	139,399	20.6	6,346	–65.1
Chittenden	221	–5.6	12,520	10.1	–26.4	975,356	18.1	2,608,551	26.8	(D)	(NA)
Essex	16	45.5	686	26.9	–29.4	32,722	40.4	40,768	27.5	2,705	(NA)
Franklin	56	–17.6	3,152	13.4	–2.2	163,575	19.7	237,238	13.5	(D)	(NA)
Grand Isle	(NA)	(NA)	(D)	(NA)	(NA)	(D)	(NA)	(NA)	(NA)	(NA)	(NA)
Lamoille	60	17.6	(D)	(NA)	(NA)	(D)	(NA)	60,466	28.8	1,633	(NA)
Orange	57	–1.7	1,006	7.0	–6.7	36,252	9.3	162,289	152.2	8,144	(NA)
Orleans	45	–	1,817	11.5	–13.6	73,261	15.5	153,797	95.8	9,741	98.8
Rutland	117	–4.9	4,183	10.4	–5.1	226,520	16.6	299,899	–3.6	17,731	–27.5
Washington	149	–2.0	3,200	7.1	–22.6	144,662	8.7	571,364	161.6	17,607	(NA)
Windham	105	–12.5	2,552	7.4	–11.2	134,255	11.7	243,415	1.4	15,850	–50.9
Windsor	143	–7.7	2,684	7.5	–15.0	113,872	9.5	191,263	–18.8	13,440	–33.8
VIRGINIA	5,909	–1.3	306,221	6.5	–13.0	17,918,413	7.8	48,261,833	10.8	2,384,729	–30.4
Accomack	36	12.5	3,399	18.5	–3.0	112,818	20.2	426,183	304.0	10,896	37.9
Albemarle	46	–14.8	[6]3,761	[6]3.4	(NA)	[6]240,320	[6]5.2	106,304	37.3	(D)	(NA)
Alleghany[7]	13	(NA)	(D)	(NA)	(NA)	(D)	(NA)	63,158	(NA)	5,422	(NA)
Amelia	(NA)	(NA)	270	5.4	–26.8	15,159	10.2	(NA)	(NA)	(NA)	(NA)
Amherst	41	–6.8	1,680	12.0	–8.9	123,920	27.5	272,244	29.9	8,079	–60.3

See footnotes at end of table.

Table B-15. Counties — **Manufacturing**—Con.

[Includes United States, states, and 3,141 counties/county equivalents defined as of February 22, 2005. For more information on these areas, see Appendix C, Geographic Information]

County	Manufacturing (NAICS 31–33)										
	Establishments, 2002[1]		Employment, 2005[2]			Earnings, 2005[2]		Value added by manufactures, 2002[1]		Capital expenditures, 2002[1]	
	Total	Percent change, 1997–2002	Total	Percent of all employees	Percent change, 2001–2005	Total ($1,000)	Percent of all earnings	Total ($1,000)	Percent change, 1997–2002	Total ($1,000)	Percent change, 1997–2002
VIRGINIA—Con.											
Appomattox	18	–	729	12.4	-14.4	29,381	18.5	39,374	-39.9	919	-68.7
Arlington	54	-5.3	(D)	(NA)	(NA)	(D)	(NA)	35,868	-1.1	1,044	-26.2
Augusta	52	-21.2	(D)	(NA)	(NA)	(D)	(NA)	765,880	7.9	22,717	-74.8
Bath	(NA)	(NA)	93	3.1	-21.2	2,922	3.2	(NA)	(NA)	(NA)	(NA)
Bedford	68	51.1	[8]3,024	[8]9.1	[8]-4.9	[8]173,613	[8]19.7	275,241	186.9	23,773	-28.9
Bland	(NA)	(NA)	436	15.0	-5.4	24,229	29.1	(NA)	(NA)	(NA)	(NA)
Botetourt	28	21.7	1,955	13.2	6.0	122,659	26.5	143,746	29.8	15,951	48.8
Brunswick	19	–	484	7.1	-27.3	21,158	11.1	39,913	-10.3	3,427	-29.5
Buchanan	(NA)	(NA)	357	3.5	-1.1	22,365	5.8	(NA)	(NA)	(NA)	(NA)
Buckingham	(NA)	(NA)	240	3.8	-8.4	7,046	4.3	(NA)	(NA)	(NA)	(NA)
Campbell	57	-8.1	[9]14,125	[9]17.3	[9]-18.5	[9]994,718	[9]30.6	578,642	-35.0	52,415	27.2
Caroline	(NA)	(NA)	389	4.2	-12.8	17,382	6.7	(NA)	(NA)	(NA)	(NA)
Carroll	27	-22.9	[10]4,168	[10]20.0	[10]-22.0	[10]134,810	[10]25.3	110,008	-2.5	8,146	-71.9
Charles City	(NA)	(NA)	270	10.5	-3.9	11,813	14.8	(NA)	(NA)	(NA)	(NA)
Charlotte	15	–	712	13.2	-42.5	24,525	19.7	51,920	11.9	2,900	-74.8
Chesterfield	176	7.3	10,467	6.7	-16.9	907,680	14.3	1,484,825	9.1	113,108	-15.8
Clarke	16	23.1	1,212	17.7	-1.9	57,170	25.4	158,250	22.4	(D)	(NA)
Craig	(NA)	(NA)	19	1.2	(NA)	197	0.7	(NA)	(NA)	(NA)	(NA)
Culpeper	33	17.9	1,432	7.0	1.6	81,163	11.0	176,829	38.6	11,462	-9.1
Cumberland	(NA)	(NA)	70	3.2	(NA)	2,747	4.9	(NA)	(NA)	(NA)	(NA)
Dickenson	(NA)	(NA)	(D)	(NA)	(NA)	(D)	(NA)	(NA)	(NA)	(NA)	(NA)
Dinwiddie	10	(NA)	[11]3,541	[11]8.3	[11]-3.5	[11]216,155	[11]14.9	(D)	(NA)	3,803	(NA)
Essex	15	-16.7	494	9.1	-38.9	15,945	11.3	26,086	-42.9	1,091	-85.2
Fairfax	437	-8.6	(D)	(NA)	(NA)	(D)	(NA)	1,017,563	-29.2	46,223	-66.2
Fauquier	47	30.6	1,083	3.2	1.2	51,913	4.1	56,358	10.7	2,424	-37.1
Floyd	(NA)	(NA)	449	7.3	10.6	16,824	12.4	(NA)	(NA)	(NA)	(NA)
Fluvanna	(NA)	(NA)	376	5.7		13,819	7.5	(NA)	(NA)	(NA)	(NA)
Franklin	55	-16.7	3,479	16.6	-6.2	139,459	23.9	198,894	-22.0	9,069	-42.1
Frederick	76	10.1	[12]9,652	[12]15.0	[12]-13.1	[12]557,007	[12]22.7	(D)	(NA)	(D)	(NA)
Giles	13	-13.3	1,279	18.3	-15.8	82,305	35.0	228,391	-24.9	15,015	-44.4
Gloucester	(NA)	(NA)	367	2.5	3.7	12,765	3.4	(NA)	(NA)	(NA)	(NA)
Goochland	(NA)	(NA)	339	2.0	24.6	19,104	2.0	(NA)	(NA)	(NA)	(NA)
Grayson	17	-5.6	662	13.5	21.7	30,691	29.1	135,184	81.8	16,203	724.6
Greene	10	(NA)	199	4.2	(NA)	8,247	5.9	(D)	(NA)	(D)	(NA)
Greensville	7	40.0	[13]2,252	[13]22.4	[13]5.0	[13]90,364	[13]28.7	173,251	376.1	7,172	(NA)
Halifax[14]	42	–	2,610	14.5	-35.5	119,445	23.3	320,981	27.5	26,944	14.2
Hanover	143	-4.7	3,864	7.0	-6.9	186,120	9.2	353,736	37.4	14,710	(NA)
Henrico	209	-3.2	10,427	5.1	-20.4	665,473	6.4	1,713,776	14.1	103,770	-72.7
Henry	72	2.9	[15]9,068	[15]24.6	[15]-21.3	[15]375,727	[15]33.9	474,391	5.9	25,463	12.6
Highland	(NA)	(NA)	44	3.0	-18.5	1,247	4.8	(NA)	(NA)	(NA)	(NA)
Isle of Wight	21	23.5	6,060	35.6	-2.3	306,046	47.2	(D)	(NA)	(D)	(NA)
James City	37	42.3	[16]1,909	[16]3.5	(NA)	[16]155,173	[16]8.4	996,692	(NA)	56,173	549.3
King and Queen	(NA)	(NA)	232	9.6	-26.8	7,649	11.2	(NA)	(NA)	(NA)	(NA)
King George	(NA)	(NA)	184	1.2	-12.0	12,321	1.4	(NA)	(NA)	(NA)	(NA)
King William	16	23.1	843	15.8	2.4	74,042	37.3	313,596	90.9	3,745	(NA)
Lancaster	(NA)	(NA)	205	2.9	-17.7	4,955	2.4	(NA)	(NA)	(NA)	(NA)
Lee	(NA)	(NA)	428	4.6	-35.1	11,997	5.1	(NA)	(NA)	(NA)	(NA)
Loudoun	161	25.8	5,301	3.4	19.5	382,229	4.4	524,480	97.4	33,721	25.6
Louisa	23	-20.7	1,560	10.6	12.3	77,343	16.5	51,918	1.6	2,942	-61.2
Lunenburg	8	-50.0	711	15.3	11.6	22,189	19.2	(D)	(NA)	(D)	(NA)
Madison	(NA)	(NA)	287	4.4	-54.0	15,376	10.2	(NA)	(NA)	(NA)	(NA)
Mathews	(NA)	(NA)	152	3.8	-12.1	4,485	4.9	(NA)	(NA)	(NA)	(NA)
Mecklenburg	38	-7.3	1,737	10.1	-48.7	58,446	12.7	135,812	-60.1	7,885	-69.5
Middlesex	(NA)	(NA)	254	4.9	2.8	8,591	6.7	(NA)	(NA)	(NA)	(NA)
Montgomery	65	-4.4	[17]7,112	[17]12.2	[17]1.5	[17]420,428	[17]20.2	369,607	-23.3	47,109	127.3
Nelson	(NA)	(NA)	264	4.8	35.4	9,490	6.6	(NA)	(NA)	(NA)	(NA)
New Kent	(NA)	(NA)	220	4.2	20.2	7,142	4.5	(NA)	(NA)	(NA)	(NA)
Northampton	(NA)	(NA)	438	6.3	-22.5	16,552	7.8	(NA)	(NA)	(NA)	(NA)
Northumberland	(NA)	(NA)	586	12.1	0.5	22,271	18.6	(NA)	(NA)	(NA)	(NA)
Nottoway	20	11.1	588	7.6	-27.5	20,648	9.0	67,586	67.4	(D)	(NA)
Orange	24	-31.4	1,219	10.3	–	58,147	15.4	332,653	62.3	23,710	-23.2
Page	22	37.5	1,658	17.7	-34.0	57,774	22.5	459,182	132.0	3,190	-71.4
Patrick	30	-21.1	1,840	24.5	-34.5	61,669	33.8	71,843	-34.3	4,295	-82.9
Pittsylvania	57	-3.4	[18]10,182	[18]18.8	[18]-27.3	[18]528,747	[18]30.2	254,315	(NA)	13,098	-56.6
Powhatan	(NA)	(NA)	204	2.2	14.0	6,538	2.2	(NA)	(NA)	(NA)	(NA)
Prince Edward	22	22.2	596	5.2	-0.5	20,147	6.5	41,606	(NA)	3,114	0.8
Prince George	23	(NA)	[19]3,024	[19]10.1	[19]-2.6	[19]242,055	[19]15.6	216,015	(NA)	34,512	(NA)
Prince William	98	-10.1	(D)	(NA)	(NA)	(D)	(NA)	181,760	-2.9	10,257	-11.1
Pulaski	49	19.5	6,087	32.8	5.0	361,924	50.2	489,190	40.1	42,336	41.1
Rappahannock	(NA)	(NA)	124	3.3	53.1	5,328	5.3	(NA)	(NA)	(NA)	(NA)

See footnotes at end of table.

[Includes United States, states, and 3,141 counties/county equivalents defined as of February 22, 2005. For more information on these areas, see Appendix C, Geographic Information]

County	Manufacturing (NAICS 31–33)										
	Establishments, 2002[1]		Employment, 2005[2]			Earnings, 2005[2]		Value added by manufactures, 2002[1]		Capital expenditures, 2002[1]	
	Total	Percent change, 1997–2002	Total	Percent of all employees	Percent change, 2001–2005	Total ($1,000)	Percent of all earnings	Total ($1,000)	Percent change, 1997–2002	Total ($1,000)	Percent change, 1997–2002
VIRGINIA—Con.											
Richmond	(NA)	(NA)	225	5.8	61.9	7,540	6.2	(NA)	(NA)	(NA)	(NA)
Roanoke	62	−3.1	[20]10,020	[20]13.0	[20]−5.7	[20]671,250	[20]22.5	287,453	(Z)	8,207	(NA)
Rockbridge	23	−4.2	(D)	(NA)	(NA)	(D)	(NA)	123,908	13.9	9,450	−17.6
Rockingham	78	5.4	[21]12,236	[21]16.4	[21]−18.2	[21]609,969	[21]23.7	2,641,962	30.7	184,993	46.0
Russell	20	−23.1	1,457	11.9	−19.1	56,462	16.7	90,809	40.1	3,264	−37.3
Scott	9	(NA)	797	10.0	46.0	37,280	20.1	(D)	(NA)	(D)	(NA)
Shenandoah	40	−14.9	4,620	22.7	−5.5	239,189	36.5	316,633	−4.0	26,983	62.2
Smyth	48	−9.4	5,023	26.6	−1.6	244,871	41.9	267,171	−20.4	15,641	34.6
Southampton	18	12.5	[22]851	[22]7.0	[22]0.7	[22]32,671	[22]10.0	551,472	40.0	51,238	(NA)
Spotsylvania	42	5.0	(D)	(NA)	(NA)	(D)	(NA)	163,292	28.4	9,536	(NA)
Stafford	40	−14.9	566	1.4	−27.0	26,637	1.6	58,615	20.2	7,539	100.1
Surry	(NA)	(NA)	(D)	(NA)	(NA)	(D)	(NA)	(NA)	(NA)	(NA)	(NA)
Sussex	(NA)	(NA)	118	2.7	−63.8	3,887	2.8	(NA)	(NA)	(NA)	(NA)
Tazewell	62	6.9	1,813	8.4	−3.6	78,694	12.1	105,766	83.6	(D)	(NA)
Warren	27	–	(D)	(NA)	(NA)	(D)	(NA)	368,078	61.9	4,767	(NA)
Washington	62	−4.6	[23]6,685	[23]15.7	[23]−18.6	[23]318,991	[23]23.5	212,007	20.4	9,802	(NA)
Westmoreland	(NA)	(NA)	658	11.2	14.8	24,873	17.1	(NA)	(NA)	(NA)	(NA)
Wise	(NA)	(NA)	[24]549	[24]2.5	[24]−8.8	[24]21,038	[24]2.5	(NA)	(NA)	(NA)	(NA)
Wythe	41	−8.9	2,139	13.9	24.9	89,565	20.0	156,068	−2.4	6,950	−27.8
York	39	39.3	(D)	(NA)	(NA)	(D)	(NA)	(D)	(NA)	(D)	(NA)
Independent Cities											
Alexandria	98	−14.0	[8]	(NA)	(NA)	[8]	(NA)	161,756	−16.9	6,150	−35.5
Bedford	21	−30.0	[8]	(NA)	(NA)	[8]	(NA)	65,193	−46.8	4,692	−51.8
Bristol	40	−2.4	[23]	(NA)	(NA)	[23]	(NA)	257,487	−45.8	8,066	−76.0
Buena Vista	15	50.0	[25]	(NA)	(NA)	[25]	(NA)	153,027	(NA)	2,800	−69.5
Charlottesville	68	1.5	[6]	(NA)	(NA)	[6]	(NA)	377,564	(NA)	11,952	−31.3
Chesapeake[7]	145	9.8	5,072	4.2	3.7	289,448	6.6	460,428	36.8	23,771	−49.6
Clifton Forge[7]	(X)	(NA)	(X)	(NA)	(NA)	(X)	(NA)	(X)	(NA)	(X)	(NA)
Colonial Heights	11	−21.4	[11]	(NA)	(NA)	[11]	(NA)	145,606	−0.6	5,782	30.6
Covington	9	−18.2	[26]	(NA)	(NA)	[26]	(NA)	(D)	(NA)	(D)	(NA)
Danville	46	−2.1	[18]	(NA)	(NA)	[18]	(NA)	640,066	(NA)	39,823	−34.3
Emporia	13	–	[13]	(NA)	(NA)	[13]	(NA)	87,130	20.4	2,619	(NA)
Fairfax	(NA)	(NA)	[27]	(NA)	(NA)	[27]	(NA)	(NA)	(NA)	(NA)	(NA)
Falls Church	(NA)	(NA)	[27]	(NA)	(NA)	[27]	(NA)	(NA)	(NA)	(NA)	(NA)
Franklin	(NA)	(NA)	[22]	(NA)	(NA)	[22]	(NA)	(NA)	(NA)	(NA)	(NA)
Fredericksburg	46	12.2	[28]	(NA)	(NA)	[28]	(NA)	73,302	−17.2	2,717	−87.3
Galax	21	−12.5	[10]	(NA)	(NA)	[10]	(NA)	143,523	−16.9	6,328	−9.2
Hampton	85	6.3	2,813	3.4	−56.5	159,940	4.0	581,677	37.6	26,796	−1.3
Harrisonburg	59	55.3	[21]	(NA)	(NA)	[21]	(NA)	406,886	60.0	29,978	50.1
Hopewell	17	−10.5	[19]	(NA)	(NA)	[19]	(NA)	569,553	−23.4	36,156	−55.0
Lexington	(NA)	(NA)	[25]	(NA)	(NA)	[25]	(NA)	(NA)	(NA)	(NA)	(NA)
Lynchburg	118	0.9	[9]	(NA)	(NA)	[9]	(NA)	1,186,198	−26.0	49,087	−70.9
Manassas	43	26.5	[29]	(NA)	(NA)	[29]	(NA)	558,690	−6.0	19,557	(NA)
Manassas Park	(NA)	(NA)	[29]	(NA)	(NA)	[29]	(NA)	(NA)	(NA)	(NA)	(NA)
Martinsville	33	−15.4	[15]	(NA)	(NA)	[15]	(NA)	167,523	−51.5	8,306	−52.6
Newport News	121	−7.6	23,852	20.2	5.5	1,506,882	28.0	2,730,794	65.1	109,990	17.9
Norfolk	194	−2.5	9,483	4.2	−5.5	628,413	5.0	1,564,248	−43.9	92,479	1.4
Norton	(NA)	(NA)	[24]	(NA)	(NA)	[24]	(NA)	(NA)	(NA)	(NA)	(NA)
Petersburg	41	−4.7	[11]	(NA)	(NA)	[11]	(NA)	328,090	125.7	42,986	(NA)
Poquoson	(NA)	(NA)	[30]	(NA)	(NA)	[30]	(NA)	(NA)	(NA)	(NA)	(NA)
Portsmouth	66	−7.0	(D)	(NA)	(NA)	(D)	(NA)	263,282	83.3	(D)	(NA)
Radford	21	–	[17]	(NA)	(NA)	[17]	(NA)	189,258	2.1	6,158	−54.2
Richmond	297	−8.6	10,914	6.0	−25.1	869,081	8.2	11,347,830	37.9	138,524	−67.7
Roanoke	126	−17.1	4,938	6.0	−19.1	264,882	7.5	556,855	−54.1	16,983	(NA)
Salem	76	4.1	[20]	(NA)	(NA)	[20]	(NA)	769,741	38.7	29,463	−16.6
South Boston[14]	(X)	(NA)	(X)	(NA)	(NA)	(X)	(NA)	(X)	(NA)	(X)	(NA)
Staunton	(NA)	(NA)	[31]	(NA)	(NA)	[31]	(NA)	(NA)	(NA)	(NA)	(NA)
Suffolk	55	5.8	2,377	7.8	−6.8	143,632	12.7	573,164	6.2	27,169	46.7
Virginia Beach	225	−4.7	6,385	2.5	4.9	264,583	2.6	605,058	59.1	34,609	28.2
Waynesboro	39	25.8	[31]	(NA)	(NA)	[31]	(NA)	451,836	−0.1	23,733	−52.6
Williamsburg	(NA)	(NA)	[16]	(NA)	(NA)	[16]	(NA)	(NA)	(NA)	(NA)	(NA)
Winchester	45	4.7	[12]	(NA)	(NA)	[12]	(NA)	(D)	(NA)	46,593	−1.0
WASHINGTON	7,535	−3.4	288,975	7.7	−13.0	21,147,231	12.0	35,398,551	16.3	1,769,708	−33.0
Adams	14	7.7	1,080	11.9	19.1	45,491	16.5	(D)	(NA)	9,126	(NA)
Asotin	(NA)	(NA)	582	7.0	28.2	23,613	9.5	(NA)	(NA)	(NA)	(NA)
Benton	116	−4.1	4,155	4.7	−2.7	243,685	5.9	442,756	4.1	25,145	−49.1
Chelan	77	−12.5	2,315	4.4	−15.5	111,043	6.5	168,667	−13.5	13,209	−48.4
Clallam	76	1.3	1,792	5.0	8.3	81,625	7.4	126,291	−16.3	11,848	27.9

See footnotes at end of table.

Table B-15. Counties — **Manufacturing**—Con.

[Includes United States, states, and 3,141 counties/county equivalents defined as of February 22, 2005. For more information on these areas, see Appendix C, Geographic Information]

County	Establishments, 2002[1] Total	Establishments, 2002[1] Percent change, 1997–2002	Employment, 2005[2] Total	Employment, 2005[2] Percent of all employees	Employment, 2005[2] Percent change, 2001–2005	Earnings, 2005[2] Total ($1,000)	Earnings, 2005[2] Percent of all earnings	Value added by manufactures, 2002[1] Total ($1,000)	Value added by manufactures, 2002[1] Percent change, 1997–2002	Capital expenditures, 2002[1] Total ($1,000)	Capital expenditures, 2002[1] Percent change, 1997–2002
WASHINGTON—Con.											
Clark	444	5.5	13,712	7.7	−22.6	848,086	11.7	1,670,288	−15.9	120,964	−76.5
Columbia	(NA)	(NA)	(D)	(NA)	(NA)	(D)	(NA)	(NA)	(NA)	(NA)	(NA)
Cowlitz	132	5.6	7,668	16.2	−8.9	509,963	26.9	721,675	−31.4	103,885	−42.4
Douglas	(NA)	(NA)	251	2.0	30.1	12,253	3.3	(NA)	(NA)	(NA)	(NA)
Ferry	(NA)	(NA)	(D)	(NA)	(NA)	(D)	(NA)	(NA)	(NA)	(NA)	(NA)
Franklin	51	8.5	2,170	7.4	19.4	92,993	8.8	257,546	16.3	16,039	1.2
Garfield	(NA)	(NA)	13	1.0	(NA)	59	0.3	(NA)	(NA)	(NA)	(NA)
Grant	64	14.3	3,748	9.2	−23.9	183,710	14.1	330,155	−24.7	32,329	−27.1
Grays Harbor	94	−3.1	4,508	13.4	30.2	243,937	21.1	326,410	−3.4	15,706	−29.9
Island	50	2.0	1,082	3.0	32.4	33,815	2.4	(D)	(NA)	2,400	22.4
Jefferson	75	33.9	789	5.2	−15.3	40,960	9.6	85,633	(NA)	(D)	(NA)
King	2,583	−13.7	115,055	7.9	−18.5	10,222,042	12.0	14,265,827	36.4	507,944	−30.0
Kitsap	171	19.6	1,843	1.5	0.8	86,218	1.5	168,239	106.8	6,885	79.2
Kittitas	31	−3.1	763	4.1	12.2	28,328	4.9	51,881	−13.1	2,275	38.6
Klickitat	25	–	552	5.9	−48.5	17,422	6.2	103,679	(NA)	3,449	−52.4
Lewis	119	3.5	3,640	10.2	17.1	177,555	15.0	288,770	10.2	33,321	38.1
Lincoln	(NA)	(NA)	114	2.3	(NA)	3,186	2.5	(NA)	(NA)	(NA)	(NA)
Mason	50	−3.8	1,923	9.5	0.7	94,491	14.5	118,047	−7.8	33,649	116.5
Okanogan	(NA)	(NA)	461	1.9	55.2	6,616	1.0	(NA)	(NA)	(NA)	(NA)
Pacific	37	2.8	1,010	10.1	18.3	33,813	12.8	44,825	−3.4	(D)	(NA)
Pend Oreille	(NA)	(NA)	415	10.2	−20.0	44,556	30.7	(NA)	(NA)	(NA)	(NA)
Pierce	664	−2.4	19,977	5.4	−8.9	1,259,659	7.6	1,777,490	−5.6	108,461	−44.3
San Juan	(NA)	(NA)	452	4.2	16.5	11,552	4.4	(NA)	(NA)	(NA)	(NA)
Skagit	191	3.2	5,831	9.1	−4.5	437,264	17.6	764,942	10.6	120,904	121.6
Skamania	(NA)	(NA)	230	7.7	8.5	11,785	13.3	(NA)	(NA)	(NA)	(NA)
Snohomish	838	0.1	46,643	15.5	−11.5	3,759,339	27.6	8,467,858	14.7	211,202	−27.5
Spokane	583	1.9	17,723	6.7	−11.9	1,006,945	10.0	1,505,042	−16.9	87,794	−43.6
Stevens	48	20.0	1,490	9.3	−26.7	73,295	16.0	102,762	−18.8	7,164	−30.8
Thurston	174	11.5	3,252	2.6	−5.5	177,917	3.6	300,144	−1.4	26,409	−9.6
Wahkiakum	(NA)	(NA)	65	4.0	8.3	2,280	6.1	(NA)	(NA)	(NA)	(NA)
Walla Walla	88	33.3	3,738	11.2	−8.6	188,281	17.2	236,007	−3.9	26,418	20.6
Whatcom	314	–	8,911	8.2	3.2	509,716	13.0	1,751,804	108.1	164,696	90.6
Whitman	26	(NA)	1,151	5.0	64.0	77,352	11.2	101,259	(NA)	(D)	(NA)
Yakima	244	2.1	9,511	7.9	−17.1	434,718	10.5	726,948	−4.6	49,251	−45.2
WEST VIRGINIA	1,480	−1.7	65,081	7.2	−13.0	3,932,819	11.8	7,983,845	−14.3	675,453	−26.2
Barbour	(NA)	(NA)	240	4.3	17.6	9,841	7.7	(NA)	(NA)	(NA)	(NA)
Berkeley	40	5.3	2,779	7.0	−8.0	159,163	10.1	(D)	(NA)	104,740	39.7
Boone	(NA)	(NA)	79	0.7	−34.2	2,713	0.5	(NA)	(NA)	(NA)	(NA)
Braxton	(NA)	(NA)	465	7.9	0.6	22,690	13.7	(NA)	(NA)	(NA)	(NA)
Brooke	27	22.7	2,168	19.6	−16.0	191,015	45.7	688,372	397.2	42,158	(NA)
Cabell	113	0.9	5,159	7.9	−4.7	305,552	12.7	559,834	−18.9	(D)	(NA)
Calhoun	(NA)	(NA)	(D)	(NA)	(NA)	(D)	(NA)	(NA)	(NA)	(NA)	(NA)
Clay	(NA)	(NA)	(D)	(NA)	(NA)	(D)	(NA)	(NA)	(NA)	(NA)	(NA)
Doddridge	(NA)	(NA)	(D)	(NA)	(NA)	(D)	(NA)	(NA)	(NA)	(NA)	(NA)
Fayette	36	5.9	713	4.2	−22.8	41,281	8.0	92,905	22.0	11,313	(NA)
Gilmer	(NA)	(NA)	261	8.2	8.3	7,687	7.8	(NA)	(NA)	(NA)	(NA)
Grant	13	−27.8	445	7.5	−51.9	20,408	10.3	54,083	44.2	3,750	163.5
Greenbrier	32	−15.8	941	4.9	−12.0	39,804	6.9	62,284	30.1	1,579	−47.1
Hampshire	(NA)	(NA)	251	3.3	−20.8	10,159	5.6	(NA)	(NA)	(NA)	(NA)
Hancock	30	−18.9	4,316	27.2	−26.8	243,084	41.0	299,172	−66.5	30,146	(NA)
Hardy	16	−20.0	(D)	(NA)	(NA)	(D)	(NA)	164,894	15.5	6,100	11.0
Harrison	63	−7.4	2,570	5.9	16.6	144,835	8.6	153,416	−17.2	(D)	(NA)
Jackson	19	18.8	2,180	17.7	−18.3	153,571	37.5	279,363	(NA)	27,779	68.1
Jefferson	24	−7.7	1,111	5.6	−28.8	52,682	8.1	150,121	−22.8	9,695	−57.8
Kanawha	144	2.1	4,875	3.6	−33.0	411,797	7.0	892,878	−54.1	84,028	7.7
Lewis	(NA)	(NA)	523	6.5	−24.5	21,096	8.1	(NA)	(NA)	(NA)	(NA)
Lincoln	(NA)	(NA)	62	1.3	264.7	2,249	1.6	(NA)	(NA)	(NA)	(NA)
Logan	37	−5.1	671	4.9	−23.1	30,995	5.9	37,544	−10.9	4,903	46.5
McDowell	(NA)	(NA)	72	1.2	−15.3	2,413	1.1	(NA)	(NA)	(NA)	(NA)
Marion	56	−9.7	1,389	5.0	−19.1	65,213	6.5	139,414	−8.1	(D)	(NA)
Marshall	(NA)	(NA)	1,885	10.2	−18.9	196,478	29.3	(NA)	(NA)	(NA)	(NA)
Mason	16	–	596	6.4	−14.7	36,420	12.0	(D)	(NA)	(D)	(NA)
Mercer	61	8.9	1,539	5.4	−9.4	68,418	7.4	126,570	−14.4	(D)	(NA)
Mineral	17	6.3	1,426	14.2	10.1	90,368	28.6	158,377	55.6	(D)	(NA)
Mingo	(NA)	(NA)	442	4.6	13.0	14,090	3.2	(NA)	(NA)	(NA)	(NA)
Monongalia	55	−5.2	2,995	5.1	22.5	224,337	9.6	275,426	−4.2	20,673	−48.6
Monroe	(NA)	(NA)	(D)	(NA)	(NA)	(D)	(NA)	(NA)	(NA)	(NA)	(NA)
Morgan	(NA)	(NA)	252	5.2	−24.6	42,757	25.6	(NA)	(NA)	(NA)	(NA)
Nicholas	30	11.1	1,114	9.8	0.8	50,680	14.3	73,247	8.6	1,282	−74.2
Ohio	53	−8.6	1,569	4.8	9.0	65,532	5.5	144,975	(NA)	(D)	(NA)

See footnotes at end of table.

Table B-15. Counties — **Manufacturing**—Con.

[Includes United States, states, and 3,141 counties/county equivalents defined as of February 22, 2005. For more information on these areas, see Appendix C, Geographic Information]

County	Manufacturing (NAICS 31–33)										
	Establishments, 2002[1]		Employment, 2005[2]			Earnings, 2005[2]		Value added by manufactures, 2002[1]		Capital expenditures, 2002[1]	
	Total	Percent change, 1997–2002	Total	Percent of all employees	Percent change, 2001–2005	Total ($1,000)	Percent of all earnings	Total ($1,000)	Percent change, 1997–2002	Total ($1,000)	Percent change, 1997–2002
WEST VIRGINIA—Con.											
Pendleton	(NA)	(NA)	113	3.1	9.7	3,816	4.0	(NA)	(NA)	(NA)	(NA)
Pleasants	6	—	(D)	(NA)	(NA)	(D)	(NA)	(D)	(NA)	(D)	(NA)
Pocahontas	(NA)	(NA)	424	8.0	-10.5	16,068	11.6	(NA)	(NA)	(NA)	(NA)
Preston	27	-3.6	1,015	8.9	-14.4	59,517	17.6	52,361	62.8	2,115	-27.6
Putnam	41	17.1	1,923	7.8	-16.1	161,539	15.9	423,398	342.1	44,049	157.0
Raleigh	58	3.6	1,225	3.0	30.7	56,189	3.7	66,027	15.3	8,968	92.3
Randolph	34	17.2	2,082	12.6	14.2	81,641	16.5	129,111	112.3	8,499	86.4
Ritchie	22	4.8	1,346	25.6	-4.7	57,270	38.6	122,035	82.1	6,152	(NA)
Roane	(NA)	(NA)	385	6.6	-35.6	13,299	9.4	(NA)	(NA)	(NA)	(NA)
Summers	(NA)	(NA)	193	4.8	201.6	3,944	4.2	(NA)	(NA)	(NA)	(NA)
Taylor	(NA)	(NA)	335	7.1	-42.7	15,465	12.1	(NA)	(NA)	(NA)	(NA)
Tucker	(NA)	(NA)	326	8.4	-13.8	18,117	18.5	(NA)	(NA)	(NA)	(NA)
Tyler	12	—	728	21.8	-16.6	59,346	49.8	(D)	(NA)	(D)	(NA)
Upshur	26	—	1,100	9.4	-6.2	57,092	16.0	113,784	55.6	6,398	-6.6
Wayne	36	9.1	776	6.4	-22.3	44,043	9.1	117,585	-22.9	(D)	(NA)
Webster	(NA)	(NA)	243	7.4	-14.1	8,973	8.2	(NA)	(NA)	(NA)	(NA)
Wetzel	18	—	156	2.4	20.0	4,507	2.6	284,358	(NA)	(D)	(NA)
Wirt	(NA)	(NA)	(D)	(NA)	(NA)	(D)	(NA)	(NA)	(NA)	(NA)	(NA)
Wood	75	-3.8	4,482	8.7	-31.8	323,025	17.1	(D)	(NA)	(D)	(NA)
Wyoming	(NA)	(NA)	203	2.9	22.3	8,358	3.1	(NA)	(NA)	(NA)	(NA)
WISCONSIN	9,915	-0.2	524,975	14.8	-8.7	31,463,590	22.4	61,501,462	11.9	3,279,381	-19.9
Adams	(NA)	(NA)	508	5.6	-0.4	23,445	10.2	(NA)	(NA)	(NA)	(NA)
Ashland	31	10.7	1,445	11.8	-11.7	57,882	15.9	66,933	-9.1	4,895	-33.6
Barron	95	-1.0	5,982	19.2	-12.5	245,685	27.8	474,578	17.6	19,687	-29.9
Bayfield	(NA)	(NA)	276	3.6	2.6	6,826	4.4	(NA)	(NA)	(NA)	(NA)
Brown	442	11.6	26,615	14.7	-6.0	1,543,366	20.4	4,066,544	57.1	207,197	-7.9
Buffalo	(NA)	(NA)	401	3.8	0.8	16,138	5.1	(NA)	(NA)	(NA)	(NA)
Burnett	29	-9.4	1,058	12.2	-1.9	46,098	21.7	97,697	-2.5	13,815	40.6
Calumet	63	-1.6	4,478	19.4	-10.5	220,166	33.9	551,620	13.1	24,877	-24.1
Chippewa	131	17.0	5,617	17.6	-18.9	297,506	30.0	565,428	28.4	21,918	-41.4
Clark	88	1.1	3,222	17.5	9.1	128,114	27.4	291,863	46.1	20,295	48.2
Columbia	104	-3.7	4,822	15.9	-7.4	255,699	27.0	671,139	31.9	34,148	8.9
Crawford	28	40.0	1,975	15.8	11.3	76,848	25.3	381,701	4.0	9,975	29.3
Dane	584	3.5	28,565	7.5	-5.9	1,795,632	10.8	2,997,689	20.6	159,409	20.5
Dodge	171	4.3	11,059	22.6	-10.5	546,891	33.1	1,346,930	21.2	56,433	-53.3
Door	65	3.2	2,228	10.7	5.6	114,300	20.9	160,615	18.0	3,771	-62.6
Douglas	61	8.9	1,302	6.0	0.1	65,533	9.2	(D)	(NA)	(D)	(NA)
Dunn	49	-18.3	2,525	10.6	6.3	137,286	19.0	672,145	29.7	27,952	-23.5
Eau Claire	106	-0.9	6,095	8.6	16.3	287,993	11.8	672,494	81.8	63,712	-5.7
Florence	(NA)	(NA)	248	15.0	-6.1	7,371	20.7	(NA)	(NA)	(NA)	(NA)
Fond du Lac	166	5.1	10,886	18.1	-19.5	808,544	34.7	1,097,909	-3.3	42,464	-38.2
Forest	(NA)	(NA)	419	7.9	-6.3	14,503	10.4	(NA)	(NA)	(NA)	(NA)
Grant	67	17.5	2,980	10.5	-7.9	127,718	16.9	375,903	-7.4	16,687	-0.1
Green	78	1.3	3,363	15.0	6.3	158,130	24.4	224,695	-40.9	(D)	(NA)
Green Lake	52	-14.8	1,833	16.0	4.7	77,630	23.8	154,475	0.9	5,055	-30.4
Iowa	37	8.8	732	4.4	-6.6	42,480	8.0	45,895	-14.4	2,756	9.4
Iron	(NA)	(NA)	369	9.6	-21.0	12,328	14.9	(NA)	(NA)	(NA)	(NA)
Jackson	22	10.0	907	7.4	7.2	37,085	9.9	59,511	-17.9	3,647	-36.9
Jefferson	160	-3.0	10,646	21.4	-8.7	599,806	35.3	1,280,233	40.3	71,871	2.0
Juneau	48	2.1	2,291	18.6	-13.6	112,214	30.2	168,884	-31.9	6,928	-55.9
Kenosha	205	0.5	10,887	14.2	-9.6	707,954	25.4	1,041,892	18.2	86,318	-41.2
Kewaunee	46	2.2	2,018	19.0	-6.1	89,145	25.0	108,669	-26.8	17,251	45.6
La Crosse	173	7.5	9,002	10.8	-9.9	490,892	16.6	(D)	(NA)	(D)	(NA)
Lafayette	(NA)	(NA)	565	7.9	-10.3	27,790	16.3	(NA)	(NA)	(NA)	(NA)
Langlade	48	23.1	1,848	16.3	7.8	74,133	22.0	125,356	40.0	11,857	91.7
Lincoln	59	-6.3	3,609	22.1	-9.0	184,341	35.0	346,066	32.1	47,756	243.2
Manitowoc	193	7.2	11,247	25.1	-12.0	616,451	36.6	1,238,392	11.5	61,851	-12.7
Marathon	233	0.4	19,321	21.2	2.1	969,944	28.6	1,569,985	21.2	100,574	-17.5
Marinette	97	18.3	6,446	24.7	0.7	362,351	40.8	711,960	45.4	43,278	-41.7
Marquette	25	4.2	1,313	21.7	2.7	56,630	35.7	102,713	48.0	10,837	26.1
Menominee	(NA)	(NA)	[4]5	(NA)	(NA)	—	(NA)	(NA)	(NA)	(NA)	(NA)
Milwaukee	1,293	-11.6	64,798	10.8	-16.3	4,859,382	16.6	7,983,283	-4.8	455,580	-25.2
Monroe	62	6.9	4,323	16.5	20.7	164,254	19.6	289,584	-0.8	16,993	104.1
Oconto	68	11.5	2,632	17.7	-12.8	99,502	25.6	189,241	39.7	7,555	-72.3
Oneida	60	-11.8	1,590	6.0	-17.1	79,615	10.0	173,048	-5.3	7,098	-55.8
Outagamie	327	7.9	19,662	15.8	-3.3	1,220,209	24.0	1,930,172	-16.8	141,868	-17.6
Ozaukee	230	-5.0	10,310	19.8	-12.9	675,792	31.5	1,190,133	-18.7	87,569	0.2
Pepin	(NA)	(NA)	169	4.8	-19.5	6,428	6.8	(NA)	(NA)	(NA)	(NA)
Pierce	52	30.0	1,081	6.3	11.7	47,165	10.7	97,196	5.1	6,147	-40.2
Polk	109	14.7	4,138	18.2	-4.3	192,558	29.8	248,323	-8.2	19,477	-16.9
Portage	81	-2.4	4,834	11.3	-20.7	241,388	16.2	542,866	-20.6	33,787	-64.7

See footnotes at end of table.

County and City Data Book: 2007

U.S. Census Bureau

Table B-15. Counties — **Manufacturing**—Con.

[Includes United States, states, and 3,141 counties/county equivalents defined as of February 22, 2005. For more information on these areas, see Appendix C, Geographic Information]

County	Manufacturing (NAICS 31–33)										
	Establishments, 2002[1]		Employment, 2005[2]			Earnings, 2005[2]		Value added by manufactures, 2002[1]		Capital expenditures, 2002[1]	
	Total	Percent change, 1997–2002	Total	Percent of all employees	Percent change, 2001–2005	Total ($1,000)	Percent of all earnings	Total ($1,000)	Percent change, 1997–2002	Total ($1,000)	Percent change, 1997–2002
WISCONSIN—Con.											
Price	47	2.2	2,688	29.5	5.7	122,857	44.5	290,583	24.8	9,538	−28.0
Racine	341	−10.0	19,225	20.4	−12.6	1,528,683	36.6	3,836,814	18.5	144,953	−24.7
Richland	29	11.5	1,765	17.8	0.9	87,485	33.4	134,607	−3.9	5,494	−22.7
Rock	238	1.7	14,641	17.0	−13.8	990,205	30.4	5,753,424	47.3	67,629	−67.8
Rusk	29	−3.3	2,139	24.0	−4.3	84,168	37.0	150,570	78.8	3,186	−67.2
St. Croix	155	3.3	5,791	15.0	−14.2	295,078	23.9	487,562	22.0	24,238	−30.7
Sauk	107	−6.1	7,030	15.2	1.0	332,345	21.6	628,214	22.9	36,430	−37.8
Sawyer	47	20.5	618	5.7	−5.1	23,297	8.0	39,980	−34.2	1,515	−80.8
Shawano	74	10.4	2,538	12.5	4.6	111,514	19.6	162,836	24.2	7,760	−39.0
Sheboygan	242	1.3	23,828	30.5	−8.5	1,487,226	46.4	2,212,591	8.7	103,418	−29.2
Taylor	36	−16.3	2,952	23.4	−1.2	121,664	32.5	198,811	11.5	19,718	172.4
Trempealeau	58	−6.5	5,440	31.5	5.0	266,782	46.5	400,227	54.9	14,487	−36.1
Vernon	32	−13.5	1,045	7.3	11.8	33,614	9.9	81,548	−6.0	5,391	−19.7
Vilas	(NA)	(NA)	396	3.7	−28.6	14,183	4.2	(NA)	(NA)	(NA)	(NA)
Walworth	219	0.5	9,342	16.9	0.7	486,994	27.1	1,303,832	69.1	62,976	9.2
Washburn	37	5.7	1,113	14.6	−5.1	43,979	20.2	126,773	219.3	4,827	133.0
Washington	337	5.0	14,400	21.6	−7.9	794,413	31.4	1,359,694	10.2	96,523	1.9
Waukesha	1,107	−3.6	50,029	17.8	−4.7	3,181,139	24.1	4,509,751	−8.8	296,805	−2.7
Waupaca	106	1.0	5,166	19.2	−4.2	313,824	33.6	589,488	0.5	51,747	77.7
Waushara	34	6.3	1,022	11.4	26.5	44,629	18.7	41,921	8.0	2,536	−57.8
Winnebago	310	−1.9	24,347	22.9	−20.3	1,645,257	34.5	2,929,411	1.9	203,748	−13.2
Wood	138	17.9	6,811	13.1	−24.0	425,113	19.0	1,021,921	2.5	64,938	−29.1
WYOMING	560	11.3	11,352	3.1	−0.9	618,361	4.5	1,430,036	38.7	102,325	32.9
Albany	28	−15.2	631	3.0	−11.7	23,193	3.6	58,551	25.7	1,937	−29.8
Big Horn	(NA)	(NA)	235	3.4	−4.5	9,833	4.6	(NA)	(NA)	(NA)	(NA)
Campbell	33	(NA)	632	2.3	29.2	42,892	3.0	50,445	(NA)	8,835	(NA)
Carbon	(NA)	(NA)	(D)	(NA)	(NA)	(D)	(NA)	(NA)	(NA)	(NA)	(NA)
Converse	(NA)	(NA)	143	1.9	10.0	4,787	1.7	(NA)	(NA)	(NA)	(NA)
Crook	(NA)	(NA)	168	4.2	12.8	7,745	6.4	(NA)	(NA)	(NA)	(NA)
Fremont	(NA)	(NA)	618	2.7	14.0	14,693	2.3	(NA)	(NA)	(NA)	(NA)
Goshen	(NA)	(NA)	282	4.0	2.2	10,022	5.3	(NA)	(NA)	(NA)	(NA)
Hot Springs	(NA)	(NA)	57	1.8	–	2,303	2.7	(NA)	(NA)	(NA)	(NA)
Johnson	(NA)	(NA)	124	2.2	30.5	3,423	2.2	(NA)	(NA)	(NA)	(NA)
Laramie	53	10.4	1,761	3.0	1.1	131,964	5.7	189,548	9.1	32,260	104.0
Lincoln	(NA)	(NA)	351	3.8	−14.6	10,466	3.5	(NA)	(NA)	(NA)	(NA)
Natrona	95	4.4	1,979	3.9	9.8	100,023	4.4	149,240	61.9	6,531	32.7
Niobrara	(NA)	(NA)	(D)	(NA)	(NA)	(D)	(NA)	(NA)	(NA)	(NA)	(NA)
Park	(NA)	(NA)	750	3.9	9.8	23,680	4.0	(NA)	(NA)	(NA)	(NA)
Platte	(NA)	(NA)	140	2.4	4.5	4,636	2.7	(NA)	(NA)	(NA)	(NA)
Sheridan	(NA)	(NA)	480	2.6	9.8	14,896	2.4	(NA)	(NA)	(NA)	(NA)
Sublette	(NA)	(NA)	92	1.6	(NA)	2,712	1.3	(NA)	(NA)	(NA)	(NA)
Sweetwater	31	6.9	1,236	4.5	−12.1	114,005	8.5	535,642	84.5	(D)	(NA)
Teton	(NA)	(NA)	264	1.1	−21.0	8,717	0.9	(NA)	(NA)	(NA)	(NA)
Uinta	(NA)	(NA)	388	3.1	−12.4	26,425	5.8	(NA)	(NA)	(NA)	(NA)
Washakie	(NA)	(NA)	428	7.6	−21.5	22,414	12.7	(NA)	(NA)	(NA)	(NA)
Weston	(NA)	(NA)	(D)	(NA)	(NA)	(D)	(NA)	(NA)	(NA)	(NA)	(NA)

– Represents zero.   D Data withheld to avoid disclosure.   NA Not available.   X Not applicable.   Z Less than .05 percent.

[1]Census Bureau, 2002 Economic Census.   [2]Bureau of Economic Analysis.   [3]Represents less than $50,000; data are included in totals. Figure in table represents midpoint of range.
[4]Represents less than 10. Figure in table represents midpoint of range.   [5]Yellowstone National Park County became incorporated with Gallatin and Park Counties, MT; effective November 7, 1997.
[6]Albemarle County, VA, includes Charlottesville city.   [7]Clifton Forge independent city became incorporated with Alleghany County, VA; effective July 1, 2001.   [8]Bedford County, VA, includes
Bedford city.   [9]Campbell County, VA, includes Lynchburg city.   [10]Carroll County, VA, includes Galax city.   [11]Dinwiddie County, VA, includes Colonial Heights and Petersburg cities.   [12]Frederick
County, VA, includes Winchester city.   [13]Greensville County, VA, includes Emporia city.   [14]South Boston independent city became incorporated with Halifax County, VA; effective June 30, 1995.
[15]Henry County, VA, includes Martinsville city.   [16]James City County, VA, includes Williamsburg city.   [17]Montgomery County, VA, includes Radford city.   [18]Pittsylvania County, VA, includes
Danville city.   [19]Prince George County, VA, includes Hopewell city.   [20]Roanoke County, VA, includes Salem city.   [21]Rockingham County, VA, includes Harrisonburg city.   [22]Southampton
County, VA, includes Franklin city.   [23]Washington County, VA, includes Bristol city.   [24]Wise County, VA, includes Norton city.   [25]Rockbridge County, VA, includes Buena Vista and Lexington cities.
[26]Alleghany County, VA, includes Covington city.   [27]Fairfax County, VA, includes Fairfax and Falls Church cities.   [28]Spotsylvania County, VA, includes Fredericksburg city.   [29]Prince William
County, VA, includes Manassas and Manassas Park cities.   [30]York County, VA, includes Poquoson city.   [31]Augusta County, VA, includes Staunton and Waynesboro cities.

Survey, Census, or Data Collection Method: Manufacturing, general (U.S. Census Bureau)—Based on the 2002 Economic Census; for information, see Appendix B, Limitations of the Data and Methodology, and <http://www.census.gov/prod/ec02/ec0231sg1.pdf>.   Establishments—Based on the 2002 Economic Census; for information, see <http://www.census.gov/econ/census02/>. Employment and earnings—Based on the Regional Economic Information System; for information, see Appendix B, Limitations of the Data and Methodology, and <http://www.bea.gov/regional /methods.cfm/>.   Value added and capital expenditures—Based on the Annual Survey of Manufactures and the 2002 Economic Census; for information, see Appendix B, Limitations of the Data and Methodology, and <http://www.census.gov/econ/census02/>.

Sources: Establishments—U.S. Census Bureau, 2002 Economic Census (related Internet site <http://www.census.gov/econ/census02/>).   Employment and earnings—U.S. Bureau of Economic Analysis, Regional Economic Information System (REIS), downloaded estimates and software, accessed June 5, 2007 (related Internet site <http://www.bea.gov/regional/docs/reis2005dvd.cfm/>). Value added and capital expenditures—U.S. Census Bureau, 2002 Economic Census, *Manufacturing, Geographic Area Series*, accessed December 2005 (related Internet site <http://www.census.gov /econ/census02/>).

Figure 3.
Top 40 Cities in the United States by Population: 2005

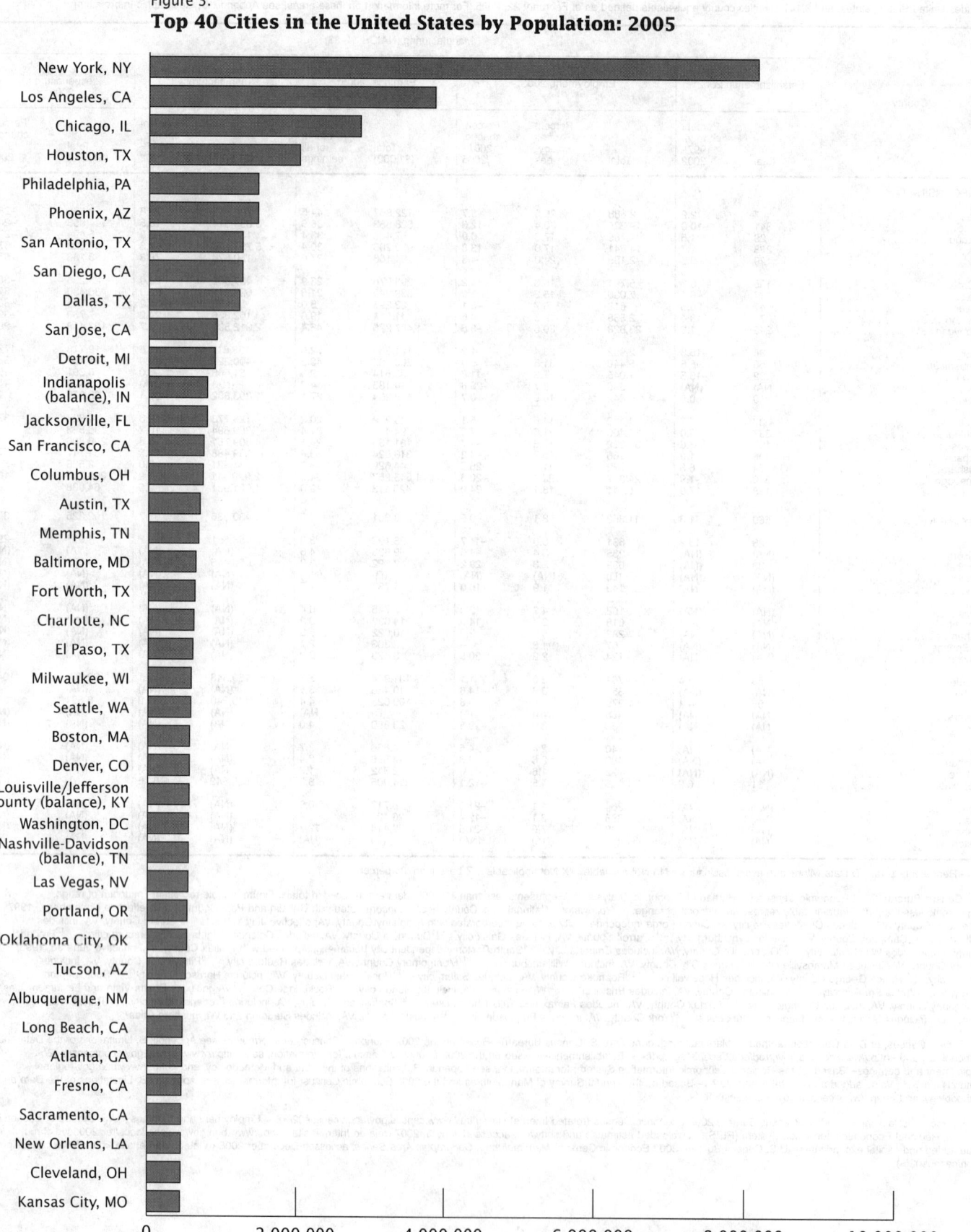

County and City Data Book: 2007

U.S. Census Bureau

Cities

Table C

You may visit us on the Web at
http://www.census.gov/compendia/ccdb

Cities

Table C

Table C-1. Cities — **Area and Population**

[Includes states and 1,265 incorporated places of 25,000 or more population as of April 1, 2000, in all states except Hawaii, which has no incorporated places recognized by the U.S. Census Bureau. Two census designated places (CDPs) are also included (Honolulu CDP in Hawaii and Arlington CDP in Virginia). For more information on these areas, see Appendix C, Geographic Information]

FIPS state and place code[1]	City	County[2]	Land area, 2000 (square miles) Total	Rank[3]	Population 2005 Number	Per square mile[4]	2000[5]	1990[6]	Rank 2005[7]	2000[7]	1990[8]	Percent change 2000–2005	1990–2000
01 00000	ALABAMA		50,744.0	(X)	4,557,808	89.8	4,447,351	4,040,389	(X)	(X)	(X)	2.5	10.1
01 03076	Auburn city	Lee	39.1	281	49,928	1,276.0	43,308	34,465	667	726	787	15.3	25.7
01 05980	Bessemer city	Jefferson, Shelby	40.7	264	28,641	703.7	29,874	33,305	1,146	1,063	825	−4.1	−10.3
01 07000	Birmingham city	Jefferson, Shelby	149.9	41	231,483	1,544.0	242,764	265,674	79	71	59	−4.6	−8.6
01 20104	Decatur city	Limestone, Morgan .	53.4	183	54,909	1,028.1	53,983	50,042	596	561	522	1.7	7.9
01 21184	Dothan city	Dale, Henry, Houston	86.6	85	62,713	724.0	58,059	55,315	487	502	448	8.0	5.0
01 26896	Florence city	Lauderdale	24.9	512	36,480	1,463.3	36,287	36,518	920	875	740	0.5	−0.6
01 28696	Gadsden city	Etowah . .	36.0	312	37,405	1,039.9	39,003	42,842	892	818	619	−4.1	−9.0
01 35800	Homewood city	Jefferson	8.3	1,073	23,963	2,883.6	25,117	23,269	1,266	1,264	1,123	−4.6	7.9
01 35896	Hoover city	Jefferson, Shelby	43.1	240	67,469	1,564.3	63,038	41,222	449	451	649	7.0	52.9
01 37000	Huntsville city	Limestone, Madison	174.1	36	166,313	955.5	159,586	160,616	134	127	108	4.2	−0.6
01 45784	Madison city	Limestone, Madison	23.2	557	35,893	1,549.8	29,326	16,018	936	1,080	1,207	22.4	83.1
01 50000	Mobile city	Mobile	117.9	54	191,544	1,624.6	199,191	198,106	112	90	78	−3.8	0.5
01 51000	Montgomery city	Montgomery	155.4	37	200,127	1,288.0	201,716	190,563	97	87	84	−0.8	5.9
01 59472	Phenix City city	Lee, Russell	24.6	518	29,460	1,197.6	28,447	25,935	1,121	1,108	1,055	3.6	9.7
01 62328	Prattville city	Autauga, Elmore . .	23.2	556	30,043	1,296.6	25,685	20,280	1,097	1,240	1,168	17.0	26.7
01 62496	Prichard city	Mobile . .	25.4	504	27,963	1,101.3	28,641	34,180	1,168	1,098	799	−2.4	−16.2
01 77256	Tuscaloosa city	Tuscaloosa . .	56.2	162	81,358	1,446.6	77,834	79,128	354	350	277	4.5	−1.6
01 78552	Vestavia Hills city	Jefferson, Shelby	14.6	820	31,022	2,120.4	30,534	20,523	1,067	1,037	1,164	1.6	48.8
02 00000	ALASKA		571,951.3	(X)	663,661	1.2	626,931	550,043	(X)	(X)	(X)	5.9	14.0
02 03000	Anchorage municipality	Anchorage	1,697.2	2	275,043	162.1	260,283	226,338	68	66	68	5.7	15.0
02 24230	Fairbanks city	Fairbanks North Star	31.9	377	31,324	983.2	30,224	30,941	1,059	1,046	894	3.6	−2.3
02 36400	Juneau city and borough	Juneau	2,716.7	1	30,987	11.4	30,711	26,752	1,070	1,031	1,023	0.9	14.8
04 00000	ARIZONA		113,634.6	(X)	5,939,292	52.3	5,130,632	3,665,339	(X)	(X)	(X)	15.8	40.0
04 02830	Apache Junction city	Maricopa, Pinal	34.2	340	32,297	943.5	31,630	18,545	1,028	1,002	1,191	2.1	70.6
04 04720	Avondale city	Maricopa	41.3	257	66,706	1,616.7	35,906	17,936	456	887	1,196	85.8	100.2
04 08220	Bullhead City city	Mohave	45.2	221	39,101	864.5	33,769	21,999	848	945	1,149	15.8	53.5
04 10530	Casa Grande city	Pinal	48.2	207	32,855	682.1	25,768	19,201	1,010	1,235	1,181	27.5	34.2
04 12000	Chandler city	Maricopa	57.9	156	234,939	4,058.4	176,997	90,769	75	116	228	32.7	95.0
04 23620	Flagstaff city	Coconino	63.6	137	57,391	902.7	52,960	45,909	564	575	572	8.4	15.4
04 27400	Gilbert town	Maricopa	43.0	243	173,989	4,050.0	110,061	30,124	127	207	921	58.1	265.4
04 27820	Glendale city	Maricopa	55.7	169	239,435	4,300.2	218,802	151,011	73	81	117	9.4	44.9
04 39370	Lake Havasu City city	Mohave	43.0	242	55,338	1,285.7	41,938	24,390	594	749	1,098	32.0	71.9
04 46000	Mesa city	Maricopa	125.0	52	442,780	3,542.5	397,770	290,811	41	43	53	11.3	36.8
04 51600	Oro Valley town	Pima	31.8	379	38,438	1,207.6	31,938	9,235	870	992	1,224	20.4	245.8
04 54050	Peoria city	Maricopa, Yavapai	138.2	45	138,200	999.9	108,939	51,101	169	211	508	26.9	113.2
04 55000	Phoenix city	Maricopa	474.9	7	1,461,575	3,077.9	1,321,627	989,058	6	6	10	10.6	33.6
04 57380	Prescott city	Yavapai	37.1	301	40,360	1,088.8	34,054	27,290	818	933	1,004	18.5	24.8
04 65000	Scottsdale city	Maricopa	184.2	30	226,013	1,227.0	202,625	129,944	80	86	140	11.5	55.9
04 66820	Sierra Vista city	Cochise	153.5	39	41,908	273.1	37,781	33,436	791	845	820	10.9	13.0
04 71510	Surprise city	Maricopa	69.5	122	74,411	1,070.8	30,904	7,286	395	1,028	1,227	140.8	324.2
04 73000	Tempe city	Maricopa	40.1	272	161,143	4,022.5	158,625	142,130	139	128	125	1.6	11.6
04 77000	Tucson city	Pima	194.7	28	515,526	2,648.2	487,337	417,724	32	31	34	5.8	16.7
04 85540	Yuma city	Yuma	106.7	65	84,688	794.1	77,645	62,544	331	353	382	9.1	24.1
05 00000	ARKANSAS		52,068.2	(X)	2,779,154	53.4	2,673,398	2,350,624	(X)	(X)	(X)	4.0	13.7
05 15190	Conway city	Faulkner	35.1	330	51,999	1,483.6	43,447	28,898	640	723	949	19.7	50.3
05 23290	Fayetteville city	Washington	43.4	237	66,655	1,534.8	58,072	42,753	457	501	622	14.8	35.8
05 24550	Fort Smith city	Sebastian	50.4	194	82,481	1,638.2	80,295	73,068	346	335	308	2.7	9.9
05 33400	Hot Springs city	Garland	32.9	364	37,847	1,150.7	35,863	33,165	881	889	831	5.5	8.1
05 34750	Jacksonville city	Pulaski	26.4	484	30,367	1,151.1	29,961	29,109	1,089	1,058	945	1.4	2.9
05 35710	Jonesboro city	Craighead	79.6	97	59,358	745.3	55,513	46,716	536	541	561	6.9	18.8
05 41000	Little Rock city	Pulaski	116.2	56	184,564	1,588.3	183,170	177,208	116	111	97	0.8	3.4
05 50450	North Little Rock city	Pulaski	44.8	226	58,803	1,312.3	60,471	62,284	542	473	386	−2.8	−2.9
05 55310	Pine Bluff city	Jefferson	45.6	220	52,693	1,155.3	55,147	57,575	627	546	425	−4.4	−4.2
05 60410	Rogers city	Benton	33.5	352	48,353	1,442.1	39,596	25,471	690	801	1,067	22.1	55.5
05 66080	Springdale city	Benton, Washington	31.3	388	60,096	1,920.0	46,672	30,152	523	670	919	28.8	54.8
05 68810	Texarkana city	Miller	31.9	378	30,006	942.1	27,837	25,666	1,099	1,132	1,059	7.8	8.5
05 74540	West Memphis city	Crittenden	26.5	479	28,181	1,063.8	27,674	28,635	1,159	1,142	962	1.8	−3.4
06 00000	CALIFORNIA		155,959.3	(X)	36,132,147	231.7	33,871,653	29,811,427	(X)	(X)	(X)	6.7	13.6
06 00562	Alameda city	Alameda	10.8	973	70,576	6,534.8	72,259	73,986	419	381	303	−2.3	−2.3
06 00884	Alhambra city	Los Angeles	7.6	1,097	87,410	11,471.1	85,806	82,129	313	298	266	1.9	4.5
06 00947	Aliso Viejo city	Orange	(X)	(X)	41,541	(NA)	40,018	(X)	799	791	(X)	3.8	(NA)
06 02000	Anaheim city	Orange	48.9	203	331,804	6,779.8	328,005	266,229	55	56	58	1.2	23.2
06 02252	Antioch city	Contra Costa	27.0	463	100,631	3,734.0	90,529	62,125	250	276	387	11.2	45.7
06 02364	Apple Valley town	San Bernardino	73.3	115	65,156	888.5	54,254	46,146	466	555	568	20.1	17.6
06 02462	Arcadia city	Los Angeles	11.0	962	56,153	5,114.1	53,054	48,741	580	573	539	5.8	8.8
06 03064	Atascadero city	San Luis Obispo	26.7	470	27,130	1,014.6	26,411	23,910	1,197	1,195	1,113	2.7	10.5
06 03386	Azusa city	Los Angeles	8.9	1,050	47,120	5,294.4	44,712	40,819	719	706	655	5.4	9.5
06 03526	Bakersfield city	Kern	113.1	61	295,536	2,613.1	243,213	187,662	61	70	88	21.5	29.6

See footnotes at end of table.

County and City Data Book: 2007

U.S. Census Bureau

Table C-1. Cities — **Area and Population**—Con.

[Includes states and 1,265 incorporated places of 25,000 or more population as of April 1, 2000, in all states except Hawaii, which has no incorporated places recognized by the U.S. Census Bureau. Two census designated places (CDPs) are also included (Honolulu CDP in Hawaii and Arlington CDP in Virginia). For more information on these areas, see Appendix C, Geographic Information]

FIPS state and place code[1]	City	County[2]	Land area, 2000 (square miles) Total	Rank[3]	Population 2005 Number	Per square mile[4]	2000[5]	1990[6]	Rank 2005[7]	2000[7]	1990[8]	Percent change 2000–2005	1990–2000
	CALIFORNIA—Con.												
06 03666	Baldwin Park city	Los Angeles	6.7	1,132	78,861	11,841.0	75,837	69,344	371	364	334	4.0	9.4
06 04870	Bell city	Los Angeles	2.5	1,245	37,521	15,129.4	36,664	34,266	889	865	792	2.3	7.0
06 04982	Bellflower city	Los Angeles	6.1	1,154	74,570	12,285.0	72,878	61,848	392	377	391	2.3	17.8
06 04996	Bell Gardens city	Los Angeles	2.5	1,244	45,135	18,126.5	44,054	42,319	749	714	629	2.5	4.1
06 05108	Belmont city	San Mateo	4.5	1,207	24,522	5,413.2	25,099	24,049	1,261	1,265	1,109	-2.3	4.4
06 05290	Benicia city	Solano	12.9	888	26,489	2,053.4	26,865	24,464	1,219	1,178	1,095	-1.4	9.8
06 06000	Berkeley city	Alameda	10.5	988	100,744	9,631.4	102,743	102,734	249	231	194	-1.9	(Z)
06 06308	Beverly Hills city	Los Angeles	5.7	1,167	35,078	6,186.6	33,784	32,038	958	944	862	3.8	5.4
06 08100	Brea city	Orange	10.5	985	38,465	3,649.4	35,450	33,193	868	901	828	8.5	6.8
06 08786	Buena Park city	Orange	10.6	982	79,174	7,490.4	77,962	68,594	369	349	338	1.6	13.7
06 08954	Burbank city	Los Angeles	17.4	729	104,108	6,000.5	100,316	93,632	239	242	219	3.8	7.1
06 09066	Burlingame city	San Mateo	4.3	1,209	27,380	6,323.3	28,135	26,651	1,186	1,116	1,031	-2.7	5.6
06 09710	Calexico city	Imperial	6.2	1,151	36,005	5,779.3	27,112	19,123	932	1,168	1,183	32.8	41.8
06 10046	Camarillo city	Ventura	18.9	690	61,576	3,252.8	57,128	52,618	504	512	487	7.8	8.6
06 10345	Campbell city	Santa Clara	5.6	1,171	37,042	6,602.9	38,138	36,366	905	837	742	-2.9	4.9
06 11194	Carlsbad city	San Diego	37.4	296	90,773	2,424.5	78,306	63,011	296	347	378	15.9	24.3
06 11530	Carson city	Los Angeles	18.8	694	93,955	4,987.0	89,730	84,067	280	279	263	4.7	6.7
06 12048	Cathedral City city	Riverside	19.2	675	51,713	2,696.2	42,859	30,202	644	734	916	20.7	41.9
06 12524	Ceres city	Stanislaus	6.9	1,123	40,571	5,846.0	34,675	26,843	811	922	1,020	17.0	29.2
06 12552	Cerritos city	Los Angeles	8.6	1,060	52,561	6,097.6	51,488	53,345	628	596	476	2.1	-3.5
06 13014	Chico city	Butte	27.7	448	71,427	2,574.9	65,305	48,068	413	432	546	9.4	35.9
06 13210	Chino city	San Bernardino	21.1	622	77,578	3,685.4	69,749	59,967	378	399	405	11.2	16.3
06 13214	Chino Hills city	San Bernardino	44.8	226	75,722	1,689.8	66,787	(X)	384	421	(X)	13.4	(NA)
06 13392	Chula Vista city	San Diego	48.9	204	210,497	4,306.4	173,555	135,065	90	121	133	21.3	28.5
06 13588	Citrus Heights city	Sacramento	14.4	829	86,272	6,012.0	85,071	(X)	321	306	(X)	1.4	(NA)
06 13756	Claremont city	Los Angeles	13.1	879	35,182	2,677.5	33,998	33,191	953	934	829	3.5	2.4
06 14218	Clovis city	Fresno	17.1	734	86,527	5,054.1	69,046	51,086	318	404	510	25.3	35.2
06 14890	Colton city	San Bernardino	15.1	804	51,300	3,398.4	47,662	39,850	649	654	675	7.7	19.6
06 15044	Compton city	Los Angeles	10.1	1,003	95,659	9,443.1	93,493	90,002	271	263	230	2.3	3.9
06 16000	Concord city	Contra Costa	30.1	409	123,252	4,089.3	121,875	111,230	191	180	168	1.1	9.6
06 16350	Corona city	Riverside	35.2	328	149,387	4,250.0	127,768	76,396	151	169	292	16.9	67.2
06 16532	Costa Mesa city	Orange	15.6	790	109,830	7,026.9	109,490	96,354	218	209	212	0.3	13.6
06 16742	Covina city	Los Angeles	7.0	1,121	47,850	6,865.1	46,837	43,275	697	667	612	2.2	8.2
06 17568	Culver City city	Los Angeles	5.1	1,188	39,603	7,750.1	38,816	38,858	840	821	695	2.0	-0.1
06 17610	Cupertino city	Santa Clara	10.9	964	52,171	4,768.8	52,520	44,162	636	582	601	-0.7	18.9
06 17750	Cypress city	Orange	6.6	1,136	47,383	7,168.4	46,604	42,634	709	673	625	1.7	9.3
06 17918	Daly City city	San Mateo	7.6	1,100	100,339	13,272.4	103,625	91,968	251	226	225	-3.2	12.7
06 17946	Dana Point city	Orange	6.6	1,134	35,867	5,401.7	35,110	31,781	937	912	867	2.2	10.5
06 17988	Danville town	Contra Costa	18.1	709	41,852	2,313.5	41,711	31,331	792	753	880	0.3	33.1
06 18100	Davis city	Yolo	10.5	989	60,709	5,809.5	58,656	46,372	516	494	565	3.5	26.5
06 18394	Delano city	Kern	10.1	1,006	45,531	4,508.0	39,522	23,215	743	803	1,124	15.2	70.2
06 19192	Diamond Bar city	Los Angeles	14.8	815	57,975	3,927.8	56,287	53,762	551	524	471	3.0	4.7
06 19766	Downey city	Los Angeles	12.4	903	109,718	8,834.0	107,323	91,488	219	214	227	2.2	17.3
06 20018	Dublin city	Alameda	12.6	898	39,328	3,123.7	30,037	23,294	844	1,054	1,121	30.9	28.9
06 20956	East Palo Alto city	San Mateo	2.6	1,242	32,242	12,643.9	29,506	23,490	1,030	1,074	1,120	9.3	25.6
06 21712	El Cajon city	San Diego	14.6	824	92,487	6,347.8	94,926	89,119	287	255	235	-2.6	6.5
06 21782	El Centro city	Imperial	9.6	1,029	39,636	4,137.4	38,023	32,882	839	840	841	4.2	15.6
06 22020	Elk Grove city	Sacramento	(X)	(X)	112,338	(NA)	81,100	(X)	213	329	(X)	38.5	(NA)
06 22230	El Monte city	Los Angeles	9.6	1,031	122,513	12,828.6	115,965	105,890	193	193	186	5.6	9.5
06 22678	Encinitas city	San Diego	19.1	680	59,525	3,114.9	57,955	55,768	534	504	443	2.7	3.9
06 22804	Escondido city	San Diego	36.3	309	134,085	3,695.8	133,808	109,019	175	161	176	0.2	22.7
06 23042	Eureka city	Humboldt	9.5	1,032	25,579	2,706.8	26,127	25,804	1,243	1,216	1,057	-2.1	1.3
06 23182	Fairfield city	Solano	37.7	293	104,476	2,774.9	96,184	78,683	236	253	280	8.6	22.2
06 24638	Folsom city	Sacramento	21.7	590	65,611	3,018.0	51,884	29,798	465	590	928	26.5	74.1
06 24680	Fontana city	San Bernardino	36.1	311	163,860	4,536.5	129,147	87,810	138	166	238	26.9	47.1
06 25338	Foster City city	San Mateo	3.8	1,226	28,756	7,647.9	28,803	28,160	1,144	1,092	975	-0.2	2.3
06 25380	Fountain Valley city	Orange	8.9	1,049	55,942	6,278.6	54,978	54,204	584	547	464	1.8	1.4
06 26000	Fremont city	Alameda	76.7	106	200,468	2,614.0	203,413	173,338	96	85	99	-1.4	17.4
06 27000	Fresno city	Fresno	104.4	71	461,116	4,418.5	428,945	354,834	36	38	48	7.5	20.9
06 28000	Fullerton city	Orange	22.2	582	132,787	5,981.4	126,280	114,235	177	172	161	5.2	10.5
06 28168	Gardena city	Los Angeles	5.8	1,166	59,891	10,290.5	58,015	52,996	526	503	482	3.2	9.5
06 29000	Garden Grove city	Orange	18.0	715	166,075	9,216.1	165,215	144,216	136	125	121	0.5	14.6
06 29504	Gilroy city	Santa Clara	15.9	785	45,718	2,884.4	41,474	31,530	739	757	874	10.2	31.5
06 30000	Glendale city	Los Angeles	30.7	399	200,065	6,527.4	194,973	180,040	98	98	94	2.6	8.3
06 30014	Glendora city	Los Angeles	19.1	677	50,540	2,640.5	49,394	47,864	658	625	548	2.3	3.2
06 30378	Goleta city	Santa Barbara	(X)	(X)	29,367	(NA)	28,630	(X)	1,125	1,099	(X)	2.6	(NA)
06 31960	Hanford city	Kings	13.1	884	47,485	3,627.6	41,796	30,760	705	751	899	13.6	35.9
06 32548	Hawthorne city	Los Angeles	6.1	1,155	85,697	14,141.4	84,113	70,828	328	310	327	1.9	18.8
06 33000	Hayward city	Alameda	44.3	232	140,293	3,164.7	140,031	114,663	165	152	159	0.2	22.1
06 33182	Hemet city	Riverside	25.6	498	68,063	2,654.6	58,894	49,191	444	492	535	15.6	19.7

See footnotes at end of table.

Table C-1. Cities — **Area and Population**—Con.

[Includes states and 1,265 incorporated places of 25,000 or more population as of April 1, 2000, in all states except Hawaii, which has no incorporated places recognized by the U.S. Census Bureau. Two census designated places (CDPs) are also included (Honolulu CDP in Hawaii and Arlington CDP in Virginia). For more information on these areas, see Appendix C, Geographic Information]

FIPS state and place code[1]	City	County[2]	Land area, 2000 (square miles) Total	Rank[3]	Population 2005 Number	Per square mile[4]	2000[5]	1990[6]	Rank 2005[7]	Rank 2000[7]	Rank 1990[8]	Percent change 2000–2005	Percent change 1990–2000
	CALIFORNIA—Con.												
06 33434	Hesperia city	San Bernardino	67.4	128	77,984	1,157.9	62,711	50,679	376	453	517	24.4	23.7
06 33588	Highland city	San Bernardino	13.6	858	50,892	3,733.8	44,681	34,528	654	707	784	13.9	29.4
06 34120	Hollister city	San Benito	6.6	1,138	35,941	5,470.5	34,411	20,250	934	925	1,170	4.4	69.9
06 36000	Huntington Beach city	Orange	26.4	482	194,457	7,368.6	189,627	181,379	105	102	92	2.5	4.5
06 36056	Huntington Park city	Los Angeles	3.0	1,237	62,491	20,624.1	61,348	56,027	492	464	438	1.9	9.5
06 36294	Imperial Beach city	San Diego	4.3	1,210	26,374	6,176.6	26,992	26,495	1,224	1,173	1,038	-2.3	1.9
06 36448	Indio city	Riverside	26.7	474	70,542	2,643.0	49,121	37,598	421	632	725	43.6	30.6
06 36546	Inglewood city	Los Angeles	9.1	1,039	114,467	12,523.7	112,572	110,973	207	201	170	1.7	1.4
06 36770	Irvine city	Orange	46.2	214	186,852	4,046.2	143,159	110,734	114	146	171	30.5	29.3
06 39220	Laguna Hills city	Orange	6.4	1,142	32,198	5,070.6	32,010	(X)	1,033	990	(X)	0.6	(NA)
06 39248	Laguna Niguel city	Orange	14.7	819	64,664	4,410.9	62,749	45,049	472	452	583	3.1	39.3
06 39290	La Habra city	Orange	7.3	1,109	59,326	8,093.6	58,974	51,312	538	489	503	0.6	14.9
06 39486	Lake Elsinore city	Riverside	33.8	347	39,258	1,161.5	28,930	19,662	845	1,089	1,176	35.7	47.1
06 39496	Lake Forest city	Orange	12.5	902	76,412	6,117.9	75,987	(X)	381	363	(X)	0.6	(NA)
06 39892	Lakewood city	Los Angeles	9.4	1,033	80,467	8,533.1	79,333	73,512	359	343	305	1.4	7.9
06 40004	La Mesa city	San Diego	9.3	1,036	53,081	5,732.3	54,751	52,976	621	550	484	-3.1	3.4
06 40032	La Mirada city	Los Angeles	7.9	1,088	49,640	6,323.6	46,783	40,455	673	669	664	6.1	15.6
06 40130	Lancaster city	Los Angeles	94.0	81	134,032	1,425.9	118,718	97,427	176	186	208	12.9	21.9
06 40340	La Puente city	Los Angeles	3.5	1,231	41,762	11,966.2	41,063	36,833	794	767	735	1.7	11.5
06 40830	La Verne city	Los Angeles	8.3	1,073	33,185	3,993.4	31,626	30,800	1,000	1,003	897	4.9	2.7
06 40886	Lawndale city	Los Angeles	2.0	1,251	32,193	16,259.1	31,711	27,315	1,034	1,000	1,002	1.5	16.1
06 41992	Livermore city	Alameda	23.9	536	78,409	3,278.0	73,412	57,304	373	374	428	6.8	28.1
06 42202	Lodi city	San Joaquin	12.2	913	62,133	5,076.2	57,063	51,980	497	513	497	8.9	9.8
06 42524	Lompoc city	Santa Barbara	11.6	934	39,985	3,435.1	41,103	37,689	826	766	722	-2.7	9.1
06 43000	Long Beach city	Los Angeles	50.4	193	474,014	9,397.6	461,522	429,789	34	35	32	2.7	7.4
06 43280	Los Altos city	Santa Clara	6.4	1,142	27,096	4,267.1	27,696	26,605	1,199	1,139	1,034	-2.2	4.1
06 44000	Los Angeles city	Los Angeles	469.1	9	3,844,829	8,196.7	3,694,484	3,485,567	2	2	2	4.1	6.0
06 44028	Los Banos city	Merced	8.0	1,084	33,506	4,167.4	25,891	14,749	991	1,231	1,214	29.4	75.5
06 44112	Los Gatos town	Santa Clara	10.7	974	28,029	2,617.1	28,647	27,576	1,166	1,097	996	-2.2	3.9
06 44574	Lynwood city	Los Angeles	4.9	1,196	71,208	14,682.1	69,845	61,855	416	397	389	2.0	12.9
06 45022	Madera city	Madera	12.3	909	52,147	4,243.0	43,248	29,477	637	727	935	20.6	46.7
06 45400	Manhattan Beach city	Los Angeles	3.9	1,221	36,481	9,282.7	33,852	31,991	919	941	865	7.8	5.8
06 45484	Manteca city	San Joaquin	15.9	778	62,651	3,937.8	49,297	41,760	488	629	640	27.1	18.0
06 46114	Martinez city	Contra Costa	12.3	912	35,916	2,931.9	35,866	33,556	935	888	815	0.1	6.9
06 46492	Maywood city	Los Angeles	1.2	1,256	28,600	24,237.3	28,083	27,907	1,149	1,118	987	1.8	0.6
06 46870	Menlo Park city	San Mateo	10.1	1,003	29,661	2,928.0	30,785	28,696	1,114	1,029	961	-3.7	7.3
06 46898	Merced city	Merced	19.9	655	73,767	3,714.4	64,115	57,102	396	437	431	15.1	12.3
06 47766	Milpitas city	Santa Clara	13.6	862	63,383	4,674.3	62,698	50,753	481	454	516	1.1	23.5
06 48256	Mission Viejo city	Orange	18.7	697	94,982	5,090.1	92,602	79,494	275	266	275	2.6	16.5
06 48354	Modesto city	Stanislaus	35.8	314	207,011	5,784.0	188,920	165,809	93	104	106	9.6	13.9
06 48648	Monrovia city	Los Angeles	13.8	853	37,954	2,760.3	36,929	35,423	880	860	761	2.8	4.3
06 48788	Montclair city	San Bernardino	5.1	1,189	35,474	6,955.7	33,172	28,458	949	959	965	6.9	16.6
06 48816	Montebello city	Los Angeles	8.3	1,077	63,290	7,671.5	62,150	59,552	483	457	410	1.8	4.4
06 48872	Monterey city	Monterey	8.4	1,066	29,211	3,461.7	29,712	32,157	1,128	1,068	860	-1.7	-7.6
06 48914	Monterey Park city	Los Angeles	7.6	1,096	62,065	8,134.3	60,051	60,704	499	479	399	3.4	-1.1
06 49138	Moorpark city	Ventura	19.0	685	35,844	1,884.5	31,411	25,521	940	1,012	1,065	14.1	23.1
06 49270	Moreno Valley city	Riverside	51.2	190	178,367	3,481.7	142,379	118,717	121	149	153	25.3	19.9
06 49278	Morgan Hill city	Santa Clara	11.7	932	34,852	2,986.5	32,956	24,323	964	964	1,101	5.8	35.5
06 49670	Mountain View city	Santa Clara	12.1	919	69,276	5,744.3	70,705	66,044	433	392	356	-2.0	7.1
06 50076	Murrieta city	Riverside	28.4	435	82,778	2,915.7	50,866	(X)	343	605	(X)	62.7	(NA)
06 50258	Napa city	Napa	17.7	720	74,782	4,225.0	72,750	62,486	390	378	384	2.8	16.4
06 50398	National City city	San Diego	7.4	1,106	61,419	8,311.1	54,224	54,288	507	556	462	13.3	-0.1
06 50916	Newark city	Alameda	14.0	843	41,956	3,003.3	42,471	37,862	789	742	717	-1.2	12.2
06 51182	Newport Beach city	Orange	14.8	814	79,834	5,401.5	77,143	66,501	365	359	351	3.5	16.0
06 52526	Norwalk city	Los Angeles	9.7	1,026	105,834	10,933.3	104,323	94,232	231	223	217	1.4	10.7
06 52582	Novato city	Marin	27.7	449	50,335	1,817.1	47,668	47,636	660	653	553	5.6	0.1
06 53000	Oakland city	Alameda	56.1	163	395,274	7,050.9	399,484	372,248	44	42	41	-1.1	7.3
06 53070	Oakley city	Contra Costa	12.4	903	27,177	2,188.2	25,619	(X)	1,195	1,243	(X)	6.1	(NA)
06 53322	Oceanside city	San Diego	40.6	267	166,108	4,092.3	161,039	128,215	135	126	141	3.1	25.6
06 53896	Ontario city	San Bernardino	49.8	197	172,679	3,468.8	158,011	135,001	128	129	134	9.3	17.0
06 53980	Orange city	Orange	23.4	551	134,950	5,769.6	129,567	111,399	173	165	167	4.2	16.3
06 54652	Oxnard city	Ventura	25.3	505	183,628	7,255.2	170,642	142,454	117	123	123	7.6	19.8
06 54806	Pacifica city	San Mateo	12.6	894	37,092	2,936.8	38,392	37,612	902	830	724	-3.4	2.1
06 55156	Palmdale city	Los Angeles	105.0	68	134,570	1,282.1	116,848	78,023	174	190	284	15.2	49.8
06 55184	Palm Desert city	Riverside	24.4	524	47,058	1,931.0	41,158	30,168	722	764	917	14.3	36.4
06 55254	Palm Springs city	Riverside	94.3	80	47,082	499.5	42,751	40,355	721	737	666	10.1	5.9
06 55282	Palo Alto city	Santa Clara	23.7	546	56,982	2,407.4	58,596	55,850	568	496	441	-2.8	4.9
06 55520	Paradise town	Butte	18.3	702	26,517	1,453.0	26,408	25,510	1,217	1,197	1,066	0.4	3.5
06 55618	Paramount city	Los Angeles	4.7	1,199	56,540	11,953.5	55,230	47,591	576	545	554	2.4	16.1
06 56000	Pasadena city	Los Angeles	23.1	558	143,731	6,222.1	134,019	131,969	160	160	138	7.2	1.6

See footnotes at end of table.

Table C-1. Cities — **Area and Population**—Con.

[Includes states and 1,265 incorporated places of 25,000 or more population as of April 1, 2000, in all states except Hawaii, which has no incorporated places recognized by the U.S. Census Bureau. Two census designated places (CDPs) are also included (Honolulu CDP in Hawaii and Arlington CDP in Virginia). For more information on these areas, see Appendix C, Geographic Information]

FIPS state and place code[1]	City	County[2]	Land area, 2000 (square miles) Total	Rank[3]	Population 2005 Number	Per square mile[4]	2000[5]	1990[6]	Rank 2005[7]	2000[7]	1990[8]	Percent change 2000–2005	1990–2000
	CALIFORNIA—Con.												
06 56700	Perris city	Riverside	31.4	387	45,671	1,455.9	36,189	21,625	741	879	1,154	26.2	67.3
06 56784	Petaluma city	Sonoma	13.8	851	54,846	3,974.3	54,666	43,860	598	551	604	0.3	24.6
06 56924	Pico Rivera city	Los Angeles	8.3	1,075	64,679	7,792.7	63,428	59,188	470	444	413	2.0	7.2
06 57456	Pittsburg city	Contra Costa	15.6	791	62,547	4,009.4	56,769	47,741	491	516	550	10.2	18.9
06 57526	Placentia city	Orange	6.6	1,137	49,795	7,556.1	46,545	41,050	670	675	651	7.0	13.4
06 57764	Pleasant Hill city	Contra Costa	7.1	1,117	33,153	4,676.0	32,837	31,689	1,003	970	872	1.0	3.6
06 57792	Pleasanton city	Alameda	21.7	595	65,950	3,043.4	63,846	50,984	462	439	512	3.3	25.2
06 58072	Pomona city	Los Angeles	22.8	564	153,787	6,733.2	147,906	132,216	144	140	137	4.0	11.9
06 58240	Porterville city	Tulare	14.0	840	44,959	3,209.1	39,747	29,895	752	799	925	13.1	33.0
06 58520	Poway city	San Diego	39.2	279	48,476	1,236.0	48,028	43,434	688	646	610	0.9	10.6
06 59444	Rancho Cordova city	Sacramento	(X)	(X)	57,164	(NA)	53,605	(X)	567	563	(X)	6.6	(NA)
06 59451	Rancho Cucamonga city	San Bernardino	37.5	295	169,353	4,522.1	127,743	101,482	129	170	197	32.6	25.9
06 59514	Rancho Palos Verdes city	Los Angeles	13.7	856	41,949	3,070.9	41,026	41,771	790	768	639	2.2	−1.8
06 59587	Rancho Santa Margarita city	Orange	12.3	910	50,682	4,130.6	47,784	(X)	656	652	(X)	6.1	(NA)
06 59920	Redding city	Shasta	58.4	154	89,641	1,533.9	81,127	67,814	305	328	344	10.5	19.6
06 59962	Redlands city	San Bernardino	35.5	322	69,995	1,973.4	63,603	62,679	425	442	379	10.0	1.5
06 60018	Redondo Beach city	Los Angeles	6.3	1,148	66,824	10,640.8	63,261	60,542	455	448	402	5.6	4.5
06 60102	Redwood City city	San Mateo	19.5	665	73,114	3,753.3	75,399	66,015	401	366	357	−3.0	14.2
06 60466	Rialto city	San Bernardino	21.9	587	99,513	4,550.2	92,326	72,706	256	268	310	7.8	27.0
06 60620	Richmond city	Contra Costa	30.0	411	102,186	3,408.5	99,216	85,976	246	245	250	3.0	15.4
06 62000	Riverside city	Riverside	78.1	102	290,086	3,714.3	255,193	226,602	62	67	67	13.7	12.6
06 62364	Rocklin city	Placer	16.2	769	49,626	3,069.0	36,470	18,736	674	868	1,188	36.1	94.7
06 62546	Rohnert Park city	Sonoma	6.4	1,140	41,101	6,392.1	41,322	36,211	802	759	747	−0.5	14.1
06 62896	Rosemead city	Los Angeles	5.2	1,185	55,119	10,702.7	53,505	51,551	595	564	502	3.0	3.8
06 62938	Roseville city	Placer	30.5	402	105,940	3,475.7	79,920	44,710	230	339	590	32.6	78.8
06 64000	Sacramento city	Sacramento	97.2	73	456,441	4,697.8	407,018	369,900	37	41	43	12.1	10.0
06 64224	Salinas city	Monterey	19.0	686	146,431	7,702.8	142,943	108,851	153	148	178	2.4	31.3
06 65000	San Bernardino city	San Bernardino	58.8	150	198,550	3,376.1	185,975	171,246	100	108	101	6.8	8.6
06 65028	San Bruno city	San Mateo	5.5	1,175	39,752	7,280.6	40,165	38,907	835	785	693	−1.0	3.2
06 65042	San Buenaventura (Ventura) city	Ventura	21.1	621	104,017	4,936.7	100,938	93,568	240	238	220	3.1	7.9
06 65070	San Carlos city	San Mateo	5.9	1,158	26,821	4,530.6	27,715	26,369	1,206	1,138	1,041	−3.2	5.1
06 65084	San Clemente city	Orange	17.6	723	60,235	3,418.6	49,936	41,166	521	616	650	20.6	21.3
06 66000	San Diego city	San Diego	324.3	15	1,255,540	3,871.1	1,223,413	1,110,910	8	7	6	2.6	10.1
06 66070	San Dimas city	Los Angeles	15.5	794	35,850	2,311.4	34,980	32,795	939	916	844	2.5	6.7
06 67000	San Francisco city	San Francisco	46.7	210	739,426	15,836.9	776,733	723,959	14	13	14	−4.8	7.3
06 67042	San Gabriel city	Los Angeles	4.1	1,214	41,056	9,940.9	39,815	37,249	805	798	729	3.1	6.9
06 68000	San Jose city	Santa Clara	174.9	35	912,332	5,217.5	895,279	783,233	10	11	11	1.9	14.3
06 68028	San Juan Capistrano city	Orange	14.2	835	34,673	2,440.0	33,826	26,187	970	943	1,049	2.5	29.2
06 68084	San Leandro city	Alameda	13.1	881	78,178	5,954.2	79,452	68,211	375	341	342	−1.6	16.5
06 68154	San Luis Obispo city	San Luis Obispo	10.7	979	43,509	4,081.5	44,193	42,084	770	711	633	−1.5	5.0
06 68196	San Marcos city	San Diego	23.8	543	73,487	3,092.9	54,974	39,141	399	548	683	33.7	40.5
06 68252	San Mateo city	San Mateo	12.2	914	91,081	7,453.4	92,472	85,832	295	267	252	−1.5	7.7
06 68294	San Pablo city	Contra Costa	2.6	1,241	31,004	12,017.1	30,256	25,051	1,068	1,045	1,077	2.5	20.8
06 68364	San Rafael city	Marin	16.6	753	55,716	3,358.4	56,063	48,298	588	529	544	−0.6	16.1
06 68378	San Ramon city	Contra Costa	11.6	937	49,999	4,317.7	44,752	35,277	666	705	765	11.7	26.9
06 69000	Santa Ana city	Orange	27.1	457	340,368	12,541.2	337,977	294,214	54	52	52	0.7	14.9
06 69070	Santa Barbara city	Santa Barbara	19.0	688	85,899	4,525.8	89,634	85,518	325	281	254	−4.2	4.8
06 69084	Santa Clara city	Santa Clara	18.4	701	105,402	5,731.5	102,361	93,823	232	232	218	3.0	9.1
06 69088	Santa Clarita city	Los Angeles	47.8	208	168,253	3,517.7	151,170	122,690	130	135	148	11.3	23.2
06 69112	Santa Cruz city	Santa Cruz	12.5	901	54,760	4,370.3	55,856	49,726	599	533	529	−2.0	12.3
06 69196	Santa Maria city	Santa Barbara	19.3	670	84,346	4,363.5	77,454	62,001	336	355	388	8.9	24.9
06 70000	Santa Monica city	Los Angeles	8.3	1,076	87,800	10,629.5	84,084	86,599	311	312	244	4.4	−2.9
06 70042	Santa Paula city	Ventura	4.6	1,203	28,478	6,190.9	28,605	25,109	1,154	1,100	1,076	−0.4	13.9
06 70098	Santa Rosa city	Sonoma	40.1	271	153,158	3,816.5	148,116	120,644	145	139	151	3.4	22.8
06 70224	Santee city	San Diego	16.1	773	52,306	3,256.9	52,968	52,783	631	574	486	−1.2	0.4
06 70280	Saratoga city	Santa Clara	12.1	917	29,663	2,449.5	29,866	28,103	1,113	1,064	976	−0.7	6.3
06 70742	Seaside city	Monterey	8.8	1,055	34,214	3,874.7	33,097	38,850	980	961	696	3.4	−14.8
06 72016	Simi Valley city	Ventura	39.2	280	118,687	3,029.3	111,372	100,325	198	206	200	6.6	11.0
06 73080	South Gate city	Los Angeles	7.4	1,107	98,897	13,418.9	96,375	86,308	260	251	247	2.6	11.7
06 73262	South San Francisco city	San Mateo	9.0	1,042	60,735	6,733.4	60,552	54,427	515	471	459	0.3	11.3
06 73962	Stanton city	Orange	3.1	1,234	37,661	12,070.8	37,423	30,353	885	854	915	0.6	23.3
06 75000	Stockton city	San Joaquin	54.7	178	286,926	5,244.5	244,011	211,970	63	69	74	17.6	15.1
06 75630	Suisun City city	Solano	4.0	1,218	26,762	6,673.8	26,118	22,783	1,208	1,217	1,138	2.5	14.6
06 77000	Sunnyvale city	Santa Clara	21.9	585	128,902	5,875.2	131,844	117,481	181	164	155	−2.2	12.2
06 78120	Temecula city	Riverside	26.3	486	85,799	3,267.3	63,298	27,138	326	447	1,012	35.5	133.2
06 78148	Temple City city	Los Angeles	4.0	1,218	37,363	9,317.5	33,377	31,136	893	955	885	11.9	7.2
06 78582	Thousand Oaks city	Ventura	54.9	175	124,359	2,266.8	117,005	104,187	189	189	190	6.3	12.3
06 80000	Torrance city	Los Angeles	20.5	638	142,384	6,932.0	137,733	133,507	161	157	136	3.4	3.2
06 80238	Tracy city	San Joaquin	21.0	627	79,964	3,807.8	56,897	34,647	363	515	782	40.5	64.2
06 80644	Tulare city	Tulare	16.6	751	50,127	3,017.9	44,023	34,189	664	715	798	13.9	28.8

See footnotes at end of table.

Table C-1. Cities — **Area and Population**—Con.

[Includes states and 1,265 incorporated places of 25,000 or more population as of April 1, 2000, in all states except Hawaii, which has no incorporated places recognized by the U.S. Census Bureau. Two census designated places (CDPs) are also included (Honolulu CDP in Hawaii and Arlington CDP in Virginia). For more information on these areas, see Appendix C, Geographic Information]

FIPS state and place code[1]	City	County[2]	Land area, 2000 (square miles) Total	Rank[3]	Population 2005 Number	Per square mile[4]	2000[5]	1990[6]	Rank 2005[7]	2000[7]	1990[8]	Percent change 2000–2005	1990–2000
	CALIFORNIA—Con.												
06 80812	Turlock city	Stanislaus	13.3	872	67,669	5,087.9	56,000	43,098	447	530	616	20.8	29.9
06 80854	Tustin city	Orange	11.4	942	69,096	6,061.1	67,630	51,567	436	415	501	2.2	31.1
06 80994	Twentynine Palms city	San Bernardino	54.8	176	28,409	518.2	28,590	11,784	1,155	1,101	1,219	−0.6	142.6
06 81204	Union City city	Alameda	19.3	672	69,176	3,593.6	66,869	53,774	435	420	470	3.5	24.4
06 81344	Upland city	San Bernardino	15.1	803	73,589	4,867.0	68,552	63,351	398	408	375	7.3	8.2
06 81554	Vacaville city	Solano	27.1	460	92,985	3,433.7	88,656	71,507	284	285	322	4.9	24.0
06 81666	Vallejo city	Solano	30.2	407	117,483	3,891.5	116,760	109,323	200	191	175	0.6	6.8
06 82590	Victorville city	San Bernardino	72.8	117	91,264	1,254.0	64,058	50,379	294	438	520	42.5	27.2
06 82954	Visalia city	Tulare	28.6	430	108,669	3,802.3	91,964	77,052	222	269	290	18.2	19.4
06 82996	Vista city	San Diego	18.7	696	90,402	4,839.5	90,032	73,193	299	278	307	0.4	23.0
06 83332	Walnut city	Los Angeles	9.0	1,044	31,424	3,499.3	30,004	29,149	1,054	1,056	944	4.7	2.9
06 83346	Walnut Creek city	Contra Costa	19.9	653	64,196	3,224.3	64,506	61,098	476	435	395	−0.5	5.6
06 83668	Watsonville city	Santa Cruz	6.4	1,142	47,927	7,547.6	46,449	34,218	695	677	796	3.2	35.7
06 84200	West Covina city	Los Angeles	16.1	770	108,185	6,715.4	105,080	96,015	223	222	213	3.0	9.4
06 84410	West Hollywood city	Los Angeles	1.9	1,253	36,732	19,538.3	35,794	36,021	911	893	750	2.6	−0.6
06 84550	Westminster city	Orange	10.1	1,005	89,523	8,854.9	88,188	78,603	306	287	282	1.5	12.2
06 84816	West Sacramento city	Yolo	20.9	629	41,744	1,993.5	31,615	28,900	797	1,005	948	32.0	9.4
06 85292	Whittier city	Los Angeles	14.6	820	84,473	5,774.0	83,627	77,663	334	314	287	1.0	7.7
06 86328	Woodland city	Yolo	10.3	997	51,020	4,948.6	49,572	40,580	653	620	660	2.9	22.2
06 86832	Yorba Linda city	Orange	19.4	667	64,476	3,328.7	58,922	52,797	473	491	485	9.4	11.6
06 86972	Yuba City city	Sutter	9.4	1,035	58,628	6,257.0	50,544	29,218	545	611	941	16.0	73.0
06 87042	Yucaipa city	San Bernardino	27.8	446	49,100	1,767.5	41,207	33,060	680	763	834	19.2	24.6
08 00000	COLORADO		103,717.5	(X)	4,665,177	45.0	4,302,015	3,294,473	(X)	(X)	(X)	8.4	30.6
08 03455	Arvada city	Adams, Jefferson	32.7	368	103,966	3,183.3	102,239	89,823	241	234	231	1.7	13.8
08 04000	Aurora city	Adams, Arapahoe, Douglas	142.5	43	297,235	2,085.9	275,921	221,713	60	63	72	7.7	24.4
08 07850	Boulder city	Boulder	24.4	524	91,685	3,762.2	94,578	85,975	291	259	251	−3.1	10.0
08 09280	Broomfield city	Broomfield	27.1	459	43,478	1,603.8	39,198	24,746	771	809	1,089	10.9	58.4
08 12815	Centennial city	Arapahoe	(X)	(X)	98,243	(NA)	102,767	(X)	265	229	(X)	−4.4	(NA)
08 16000	Colorado Springs city	El Paso	185.7	29	369,815	1,991.0	361,022	282,355	49	49	54	2.4	27.9
08 20000	Denver city	Denver	153.4	40	557,917	3,638.2	553,693	467,549	25	25	28	0.8	18.4
08 24785	Englewood city	Arapahoe	6.6	1,139	32,350	4,938.9	31,727	29,918	1,023	998	924	2.0	6.0
08 27425	Fort Collins city	Larimer	46.5	213	128,026	2,750.9	119,020	88,831	185	185	236	7.6	34.0
08 31660	Grand Junction city	Mesa	30.8	397	45,299	1,470.3	43,898	35,448	745	716	760	3.2	23.8
08 32155	Greeley city	Weld	29.9	414	87,596	2,929.6	77,737	60,759	312	352	398	12.7	27.9
08 43000	Lakewood city	Jefferson	41.6	255	140,671	3,382.3	144,363	125,968	164	144	145	−2.6	14.6
08 45255	Littleton city	Arapahoe, Douglas, Jefferson	13.5	863	40,396	2,987.9	40,340	33,746	816	783	810	0.1	19.5
08 45970	Longmont city	Boulder, Weld	21.8	589	81,818	3,754.8	71,113	52,203	348	391	493	15.1	36.2
08 46465	Loveland city	Larimer	24.6	520	59,563	2,424.2	51,194	37,778	531	600	720	16.3	35.5
08 54330	Northglenn city	Adams, Weld	7.4	1,103	32,906	4,434.8	31,575	27,259	1,009	1,009	1,007	4.2	15.8
08 62000	Pueblo city	Pueblo	45.1	224	103,495	2,295.8	102,129	98,723	242	235	205	1.3	3.5
08 77290	Thornton city	Adams, Weld	26.9	467	105,182	3,915.9	82,890	55,307	234	319	449	26.9	49.9
08 83835	Westminster city	Adams, Jefferson	31.5	384	105,084	3,334.9	101,020	74,166	235	237	302	4.0	36.2
08 84440	Wheat Ridge city	Jefferson	9.1	1,041	31,242	3,437.0	32,913	29,387	1,063	965	937	−5.1	12.0
09 00000	CONNECTICUT		4,844.8	(X)	3,510,297	724.5	3,405,602	3,287,116	(X)	(X)	(X)	3.1	3.6
09 08000	Bridgeport city	Fairfield	16.0	774	139,008	8,688.0	139,529	141,719	168	153	127	−0.4	−1.5
09 08420	Bristol city	Hartford	26.5	478	61,353	2,314.3	60,187	60,645	508	477	401	1.9	−0.8
09 18430	Danbury city	Fairfield	42.1	250	78,736	1,869.8	74,848	65,627	372	368	360	5.2	14.1
09 37000	Hartford city	Hartford	17.3	732	124,397	7,186.4	124,121	137,382	188	177	132	0.2	−9.7
09 46450	Meriden city	New Haven	23.8	545	59,653	2,511.7	58,244	59,451	528	500	411	2.4	−2.0
09 47290	Middletown city	Middlesex	40.9	260	47,438	1,159.9	45,563	42,776	708	688	621	4.1	6.5
09 47515	Milford city (balance)	New Haven	22.3	581	53,045	2,380.8	50,594	48,149	622	610	545	4.8	5.1
09 49880	Naugatuck borough	New Haven	16.4	761	31,864	1,944.1	30,989	30,556	1,045	1,024	909	2.8	1.4
09 50370	New Britain city	Hartford	13.3	871	71,254	5,341.4	71,538	75,484	415	387	296	−0.4	−5.2
09 52000	New Haven city	New Haven	18.9	692	124,791	6,620.2	123,777	130,159	187	178	139	0.8	−4.9
09 52280	New London city	New London	5.5	1,173	26,174	4,724.5	26,185	28,556	1,230	1,214	963	(Z)	−8.3
09 55990	Norwalk city	Fairfield	22.8	567	84,437	3,701.8	82,951	78,412	335	317	283	1.8	5.8
09 56200	Norwich city	New London	28.3	437	36,598	1,291.8	36,117	37,470	916	882	726	1.3	−3.6
09 68100	Shelton city	Fairfield	30.6	400	39,477	1,291.4	38,101	35,414	841	838	762	3.6	7.6
09 73000	Stamford city	Fairfield	37.8	292	120,045	3,180.0	117,072	108,089	196	188	181	2.5	8.3
09 76500	Torrington city	Litchfield	39.8	274	35,995	904.6	35,202	33,704	933	909	811	2.3	4.4
09 80000	Waterbury city	New Haven	28.6	431	107,902	3,776.8	107,271	108,226	225	215	180	0.6	−0.9
09 82800	West Haven city	New Haven	10.8	969	52,923	4,882.2	52,360	54,283	623	586	463	1.1	−3.5
10 00000	DELAWARE		1,953.6	(X)	843,524	431.8	783,600	666,168	(X)	(X)	(X)	7.6	17.6
10 21200	Dover city	Kent	22.4	578	34,288	1,531.4	32,083	27,913	979	989	986	6.9	14.9
10 50670	Newark city	New Castle	8.9	1,048	30,060	3,370.0	28,853	26,702	1,096	1,091	1,029	4.2	8.1
10 77580	Wilmington city	New Castle	10.9	967	72,786	6,708.4	72,644	71,493	405	380	323	0.2	1.6

See footnotes at end of table.

Table C-1. Cities — **Area and Population**—Con.

[Includes states and 1,265 incorporated places of 25,000 or more population as of April 1, 2000, in all states except Hawaii, which has no incorporated places recognized by the U.S. Census Bureau. Two census designated places (CDPs) are also included (Honolulu CDP in Hawaii and Arlington CDP in Virginia). For more information on these areas, see Appendix C, Geographic Information]

FIPS state and place code[1]	City	County[2]	Land area, 2000 (square miles) Total	Rank[3]	Population 2005 Number	Per square mile[4]	2000[5]	1990[6]	Rank 2005[7]	2000[7]	1990[8]	Percent change 2000–2005	1990–2000
11 00000	DISTRICT OF COLUMBIA ..		61.4	(X)	550,521	8,966.1	572,059	606,900	(X)	(X)	(X)	–3.8	–5.7
11 50000	Washington city	District of Columbia	61.4	144	550,521	8,966.1	572,059	606,900	27	21	19	–3.8	–5.7
12 00000	FLORIDA		53,926.8	(X)	17,789,864	329.9	15,982,824	12,938,071	(X)	(X)	(X)	11.3	23.5
12 00950	Altamonte Springs city	Seminole	8.9	1,050	41,057	4,613.1	41,381	35,030	804	758	770	–0.8	18.1
12 01700	Apopka city	Orange	24.0	532	34,728	1,444.6	27,443	15,169	967	1,151	1,212	26.5	80.9
12 02681	Aventura city	Miami-Dade	2.7	1,240	29,391	10,885.6	25,267	(X)	1,123	1,255	(X)	16.3	(NA)
12 07300	Boca Raton city	Palm Beach	27.2	456	86,632	3,186.2	83,015	61,250	317	316	394	4.4	35.5
12 07525	Bonita Springs city	Lee	35.3	327	37,992	1,076.6	32,808	(X)	876	971	(X)	15.8	(NA)
12 07875	Boynton Beach city	Palm Beach	15.9	782	66,885	4,211.9	60,441	47,004	454	474	559	10.7	28.6
12 07950	Bradenton city	Manatee	12.1	917	53,917	4,452.3	49,516	43,018	608	622	617	8.9	15.1
12 10275	Cape Coral city	Lee	105.2	66	140,010	1,331.0	102,275	74,940	166	233	299	36.9	36.5
12 12875	Clearwater city	Pinellas	25.3	506	108,687	4,297.6	109,452	99,380	221	210	203	–0.7	10.1
12 13275	Coconut Creek city	Broward	11.6	938	49,017	4,243.9	43,592	27,414	682	722	999	12.4	59.0
12 14125	Cooper City city	Broward	6.4	1,142	30,022	4,727.9	28,267	20,253	1,098	1,113	1,169	6.2	39.6
12 14250	Coral Gables city	Miami-Dade	13.1	881	42,871	3,265.1	42,805	41,528	780	735	646	0.2	3.1
12 14400	Coral Springs city	Broward	23.9	538	128,804	5,387.0	117,549	79,259	182	187	276	9.6	48.3
12 16335	Dania Beach city	Broward	6.1	1,153	28,782	4,726.1	27,293	17,736	1,141	1,160	1,198	5.5	53.9
12 16475	Davie town	Broward	33.4	353	84,204	2,518.8	75,720	54,868	337	365	455	11.2	38.0
12 16525	Daytona Beach city	Volusia	58.7	152	64,421	1,097.8	63,777	62,609	474	440	381	1.0	1.9
12 16725	Deerfield Beach city	Broward	13.4	868	76,348	5,684.9	74,306	55,037	382	369	452	2.7	35.0
12 17100	Delray Beach city	Palm Beach	15.4	796	64,757	4,213.2	60,037	47,789	469	480	549	7.9	25.6
12 17200	Deltona city	Volusia	35.8	315	82,788	2,313.8	69,567	(X)	342	400	(X)	19.0	(NA)
12 18575	Dunedin city	Pinellas	10.4	993	36,690	3,534.7	35,977	34,234	913	884	795	2.0	5.1
12 24000	Fort Lauderdale city	Broward	31.7	381	167,380	5,275.1	154,198	149,868	133	131	118	8.5	2.9
12 24125	Fort Myers city	Lee	31.8	379	58,428	1,835.6	52,274	44,487	546	587	592	11.8	17.5
12 24300	Fort Pierce city	St. Lucie	14.7	817	38,552	2,615.5	37,738	38,319	864	847	706	2.2	–1.5
12 25175	Gainesville city	Alachua	48.2	206	108,184	2,245.4	111,405	90,250	224	205	229	–2.9	23.4
12 27322	Greenacres city	Palm Beach	4.7	1,202	32,525	6,979.6	27,833	19,358	1,016	1,133	1,178	16.9	43.8
12 28452	Hallandale Beach city	Broward	4.2	1,212	37,083	8,808.3	34,282	30,948	903	927	893	8.2	10.8
12 30000	Hialeah city	Miami-Dade	19.2	673	220,485	11,459.7	226,434	188,008	84	75	87	–2.6	20.4
12 32000	Hollywood city	Broward	27.3	452	145,629	5,326.6	139,443	122,111	154	154	149	4.4	14.2
12 32275	Homestead city	Miami-Dade	14.3	832	44,494	3,115.8	31,909	28,287	759	994	971	39.4	12.8
12 35000	Jacksonville city	Duval	757.7	3	782,623	1,032.9	735,606	635,078	13	14	17	6.4	15.8
12 35875	Jupiter town	Palm Beach	20.0	650	47,909	2,395.5	39,422	29,802	696	805	927	21.5	32.3
12 36550	Key West city	Monroe	6.0	1,157	23,935	4,022.7	25,478	24,853	1,267	1,250	1,082	–6.1	2.5
12 36950	Kissimmee city	Osceola	16.7	749	59,364	3,559.0	48,016	30,578	535	647	907	23.6	57.0
12 38250	Lakeland city	Polk	45.8	218	88,711	1,935.3	84,448	72,642	308	308	311	5.1	16.3
12 39075	Lake Worth city	Palm Beach	5.6	1,169	36,342	6,443.6	35,663	28,803	923	896	954	1.9	23.8
12 39425	Largo city	Pinellas	15.7	788	74,473	4,755.6	74,076	68,448	394	371	339	0.5	8.2
12 39525	Lauderdale Lakes city	Broward	3.6	1,229	31,826	8,865.2	31,229	27,902	1,046	1,018	988	1.9	11.9
12 39550	Lauderhill city	Broward	7.3	1,111	59,621	8,167.3	57,585	48,810	529	509	538	3.5	18.0
12 43125	Margate city	Broward	8.8	1,057	56,002	6,356.6	53,909	42,837	583	562	620	3.9	25.8
12 43975	Melbourne city	Brevard	30.2	406	76,646	2,537.9	71,856	60,773	380	385	397	6.7	18.2
12 45000	Miami city	Miami-Dade	35.7	317	386,417	10,833.1	362,436	358,894	45	48	47	6.6	1.0
12 45025	Miami Beach city	Miami-Dade	7.0	1,118	87,925	12,507.1	87,933	92,639	310	289	224	(Z)	–5.1
12 45060	Miami Gardens city	Miami-Dade	(X)	(X)	99,438	(NA)	100,515	(X)	257	241	(X)	–1.1	(NA)
12 45975	Miramar city	Broward	29.5	420	106,623	3,614.3	72,739	41,596	228	379	643	46.6	74.9
12 49425	North Lauderdale city	Broward	3.9	1,224	42,262	10,892.3	38,523	27,031	786	828	1,015	9.7	42.5
12 49450	North Miami city	Miami-Dade	8.5	1,065	57,654	6,814.9	59,880	50,590	558	481	518	–3.7	18.4
12 49475	North Miami Beach city	Miami-Dade	5.0	1,194	39,442	7,952.0	40,786	34,911	842	771	773	–3.3	16.8
12 50575	Oakland Park city	Broward	6.3	1,147	31,713	5,033.8	30,966	25,635	1,047	1,025	1,060	2.4	20.8
12 50750	Ocala city	Marion	38.6	284	49,745	1,287.7	45,909	42,742	672	682	623	8.4	7.4
12 53000	Orlando city	Orange	93.5	82	213,223	2,280.5	192,432	165,851	87	100	105	10.8	16.0
12 53150	Ormond Beach city	Volusia	25.8	496	38,613	1,499.5	36,405	31,430	861	870	879	6.1	15.8
12 53575	Oviedo city	Seminole	15.1	802	29,848	1,972.8	26,326	11,258	1,105	1,201	1,221	13.4	133.8
12 54000	Palm Bay city	Brevard	63.7	136	92,833	1,458.5	79,426	62,652	285	342	380	16.9	26.8
12 54075	Palm Beach Gardens city	Palm Beach	55.7	169	48,989	879.8	36,266	24,287	683	876	1,102	35.1	49.3
12 54200	Palm Coast city	Flagler	50.7	192	60,952	1,201.7	32,737	(X)	514	973	(X)	86.2	(NA)
12 54700	Panama City city	Bay	20.5	639	37,188	1,812.3	36,585	34,855	898	867	778	1.6	5.0
12 55775	Pembroke Pines city	Broward	33.1	360	150,380	4,550.1	137,415	65,437	148	158	362	9.4	110.0
12 55925	Pensacola city	Escambia	22.7	570	54,055	2,381.3	56,255	59,181	606	526	414	–3.9	–4.9
12 56975	Pinellas Park city	Pinellas	14.8	816	47,352	3,210.3	46,852	44,667	711	666	591	1.1	4.9
12 57425	Plantation city	Broward	21.7	590	85,989	3,955.3	82,934	66,665	323	318	349	3.7	24.4
12 57550	Plant City city	Hillsborough	22.6	573	31,450	1,389.7	29,916	23,022	1,052	1,060	1,132	5.1	29.9
12 58050	Pompano Beach city	Broward	20.6	636	104,179	5,069.5	100,205	72,344	237	244	313	4.0	38.5
12 58575	Port Orange city	Volusia	24.7	515	53,746	2,175.1	46,252	36,969	610	679	733	16.2	25.1
12 58715	Port St. Lucie city	St. Lucie	75.5	108	131,692	1,743.3	88,878	55,771	178	284	442	48.2	59.4
12 60975	Riviera Beach city	Palm Beach	8.3	1,071	33,772	4,049.4	29,888	27,290	988	1,062	1,004	13.0	9.5

See footnotes at end of table.

Table C-1. Cities — **Area and Population**—Con.

[Includes states and 1,265 incorporated places of 25,000 or more population as of April 1, 2000, in all states except Hawaii, which has no incorporated places recognized by the U.S. Census Bureau. Two census designated places (CDPs) are also included (Honolulu CDP in Hawaii and Arlington CDP in Virginia). For more information on these areas, see Appendix C, Geographic Information]

FIPS state and place code[1]	City	County[2]	Land area, 2000 (square miles) Total	Rank[3]	Population 2005 Number	Per square mile[4]	2000[5]	1990[6]	Rank 2005[7]	2000[7]	1990[8]	Percent change 2000–2005	1990–2000
	FLORIDA—Con.												
12 63000	St. Petersburg city	Pinellas	59.6	148	249,079	4,177.1	248,896	240,443	71	68	64	0.1	3.5
12 63650	Sanford city	Seminole	19.1	680	47,257	2,472.9	38,696	32,845	714	823	842	22.1	17.8
12 64175	Sarasota city	Sarasota	14.9	811	53,711	3,607.2	52,725	51,007	611	579	511	1.9	3.4
12 69700	Sunrise city	Broward	18.2	706	90,589	4,977.4	85,787	66,201	298	299	353	5.6	29.6
12 70600	Tallahassee city	Leon	95.7	77	158,500	1,656.0	152,307	125,845	141	132	146	4.1	21.0
12 70675	Tamarac city	Broward	11.4	943	59,923	5,261.0	55,588	44,437	525	540	593	7.8	25.1
12 71000	Tampa city	Hillsborough	112.1	62	325,989	2,908.8	303,475	280,306	56	58	55	7.4	8.3
12 71900	Titusville city	Brevard	21.3	611	43,767	2,058.7	40,691	39,706	767	773	679	7.6	2.5
12 75812	Wellington village	Palm Beach	31.1	391	53,583	1,725.7	38,826	(X)	613	820	(X)	38.0	(NA)
12 76582	Weston city	Broward	23.8	543	65,679	2,764.3	49,286	(X)	464	630	(X)	33.3	(NA)
12 76600	West Palm Beach city	Palm Beach	55.1	173	97,498	1,768.2	82,379	67,995	267	321	343	18.4	21.2
12 78275	Winter Haven city	Polk	17.7	722	29,501	1,668.6	27,100	25,924	1,120	1,170	1,056	8.9	4.5
12 78300	Winter Park city	Orange	7.3	1,108	28,179	3,839.1	27,774	24,602	1,160	1,135	1,093	1.5	12.9
12 78325	Winter Springs city	Seminole	14.4	829	32,583	2,270.6	31,046	22,184	1,014	1,021	1,148	5.0	39.9
13 00000	**GEORGIA**		57,906.1	(X)	9,072,576	156.7	8,186,816	6,478,149	(X)	(X)	(X)	10.8	26.4
13 01052	Albany city	Dougherty	55.5	172	75,394	1,357.7	76,925	78,610	386	360	281	-2.0	-2.1
13 01696	Alpharetta city	Fulton	21.4	606	40,128	1,878.7	37,983	14,188	821	842	1,216	5.6	167.7
13 03440	Athens-Clarke County (balance)	Clarke	117.8	55	103,238	876.8	100,269	86,553	243	243	245	3.0	15.8
13 04000	Atlanta city	DeKalb, Fulton	131.8	50	470,688	3,572.6	416,425	393,962	35	40	36	13.0	5.7
13 04204	Augusta-Richmond County (balance)	Richmond	302.1	18	190,782	631.5	195,182	186,108	113	97	90	-2.3	4.9
13 19000	Columbus city	Muscogee	(X)	(X)	185,271	(NA)	186,291	(X)	115	107	(X)	-0.5	(NA)
13 21380	Dalton city	Whitfield	19.8	657	32,140	1,621.6	27,921	22,535	1,036	1,124	1,142	15.1	23.9
13 25720	East Point city	Fulton	13.8	853	40,680	2,958.5	40,033	34,590	810	790	783	1.6	15.7
13 31908	Gainesville city	Hall	27.1	460	32,444	1,198.1	25,891	17,974	1,021	1,231	1,195	25.3	44.0
13 38964	Hinesville city	Liberty	16.2	766	28,615	1,764.2	30,446	22,591	1,148	1,040	1,141	-6.0	34.8
13 44340	LaGrange city	Troup	29.0	423	27,362	944.8	26,212	25,603	1,187	1,209	1,061	4.4	2.4
13 49000	Macon city	Bibb, Jones	55.8	167	94,316	1,690.3	97,255	106,779	278	249	184	-3.0	-8.9
13 49756	Marietta city	Cobb	21.9	586	61,261	2,798.6	59,324	44,290	510	487	599	3.3	33.9
13 59724	Peachtree City city	Fayette	23.3	553	34,524	1,483.6	31,580	18,951	972	1,008	1,186	9.3	66.6
13 66668	Rome city	Floyd	29.4	419	35,816	1,219.1	35,471	32,163	941	899	858	1.0	10.3
13 67284	Roswell city	Fulton	38.0	289	85,920	2,259.9	80,076	57,039	324	337	432	7.3	40.4
13 69000	Savannah city	Chatham	74.7	111	128,453	1,718.7	133,412	137,776	183	162	131	-3.7	-3.2
13 71492	Smyrna city	Cobb	13.9	848	47,643	3,427.6	44,094	34,250	701	713	793	8.0	28.7
13 78800	Valdosta city	Lowndes	29.9	412	45,205	1,509.9	44,280	41,305	747	710	648	2.1	7.2
13 80508	Warner Robins city	Houston, Peach	22.8	568	57,907	2,544.2	49,117	44,718	553	633	589	17.9	9.8
15 00000	**HAWAII**		6,422.6	(X)	1,275,194	198.5	1,211,537	1,108,229	(X)	(X)	(X)	5.3	9.3
15 17000	Honolulu CDP	Honolulu	85.7	86	377,379	4,403.5	371,657	376,386	47	47	39	1.5	-1.3
16 00000	**IDAHO**		82,747.2	(X)	1,429,096	17.3	1,293,956	1,006,734	(X)	(X)	(X)	10.4	28.5
16 08830	Boise City city	Ada	63.8	135	193,161	3,028.6	188,905	141,825	111	105	126	2.3	33.2
16 12250	Caldwell city	Canyon	11.3	948	34,433	3,036.4	26,941	19,055	974	1,175	1,185	27.8	41.4
16 16750	Coeur d'Alene city	Kootenai	13.1	881	40,059	3,051.0	34,616	24,848	822	924	1,083	15.7	39.3
16 39700	Idaho Falls city	Bonneville	17.1	737	52,338	3,066.1	50,846	44,323	620	607	597	2.9	14.7
16 46540	Lewiston city	Nez Perce	16.5	756	31,081	1,883.7	30,906	28,290	1,065	1,027	970	0.6	9.2
16 52120	Meridian city	Ada	11.8	928	52,240	4,430.9	35,853	10,333	635	890	1,222	45.7	247.0
16 56260	Nampa city	Canyon	19.9	656	71,713	3,612.7	52,814	30,655	411	578	905	35.8	72.3
16 64090	Pocatello city	Bannock, Power	28.2	439	53,372	1,889.9	51,536	46,102	615	594	569	3.6	11.8
16 82810	Twin Falls city	Twin Falls	12.0	921	38,630	3,216.5	34,746	28,072	860	919	978	11.2	23.8
17 00000	**ILLINOIS**		55,583.6	(X)	12,763,371	229.6	12,419,647	11,430,602	(X)	(X)	(X)	2.8	8.7
17 00243	Addison village	DuPage	9.4	1,033	36,811	3,903.6	36,160	33,100	908	881	832	1.8	9.2
17 01114	Alton city	Madison	15.6	789	29,433	1,881.9	30,504	33,170	1,122	1,039	830	-3.5	-8.0
17 02154	Arlington Heights village	Cook, Lake	16.4	759	74,620	4,547.2	76,429	75,205	391	361	297	-2.4	1.6
17 03012	Aurora city	DuPage, Kane, Kendall, Will	38.5	286	168,181	4,364.9	143,108	100,341	131	147	199	17.5	42.6
17 04013	Bartlett village	Cook, DuPage, Kane	14.8	813	38,479	2,598.2	36,736	19,714	867	864	1,174	4.7	86.3
17 04845	Belleville city	St. Clair	18.9	692	41,143	2,182.7	42,133	43,120	801	745	615	-2.3	-2.3
17 05573	Berwyn city	Cook	3.9	1,223	51,409	13,215.7	54,016	45,538	648	559	577	-4.8	18.6
17 06613	Bloomington city	McLean	22.5	574	69,749	3,100.0	65,353	52,288	429	431	492	6.7	25.0
17 07133	Bolingbrook village	DuPage, Will	20.5	640	68,365	3,333.3	56,381	41,041	441	520	653	21.3	37.4
17 09447	Buffalo Grove village	Cook, Lake	9.2	1,038	43,115	4,691.5	43,195	36,465	777	729	741	-0.2	18.5
17 09642	Burbank city	Cook	4.2	1,213	27,634	6,626.9	27,902	27,588	1,177	1,127	994	-1.0	1.1
17 10487	Calumet City city	Cook	7.3	1,113	37,795	5,205.9	39,074	37,783	883	814	718	-3.3	3.4
17 11163	Carbondale city	Jackson	11.9	925	24,806	2,086.3	25,751	27,577	1,258	1,236	995	-3.7	-6.6
17 11332	Carol Stream village	DuPage	8.9	1,050	40,040	4,498.9	40,481	31,726	824	779	870	-1.1	27.6
17 11358	Carpentersville village	Kane	7.5	1,101	37,204	4,993.8	30,594	23,109	897	1,033	1,130	21.6	32.4

See footnotes at end of table.

Table C-1. Cities — **Area and Population**—Con.

[Includes states and 1,265 incorporated places of 25,000 or more population as of April 1, 2000, in all states except Hawaii, which has no incorporated places recognized by the U.S. Census Bureau. Two census designated places (CDPs) are also included (Honolulu CDP in Hawaii and Arlington CDP in Virginia). For more information on these areas, see Appendix C, Geographic Information]

FIPS state and place code[1]	City	County[2]	Land area, 2000 (square miles) Total	Rank[3]	Population 2005 Number	Per square mile[4]	2000[5]	1990[6]	Rank 2005[7]	2000[7]	1990[8]	Percent change 2000–2005	1990–2000
	ILLINOIS—Con.												
17 12385	Champaign city	Champaign	17.0	740	71,568	4,212.4	69,263	64,664	412	403	366	3.3	7.1
17 14000	Chicago city	Cook, DuPage	227.1	26	2,842,518	12,514.9	2,896,021	2,783,485	3	3	3	-1.8	4.0
17 14026	Chicago Heights city	Cook	9.6	1,030	31,373	3,278.3	32,799	32,970	1,057	972	837	-4.3	-0.5
17 14351	Cicero town	Cook	5.9	1,163	82,741	14,143.8	85,616	67,441	344	301	346	-3.4	26.9
17 17887	Crystal Lake city	McHenry	16.2	765	40,922	2,519.8	38,161	25,457	808	836	1,068	7.2	49.9
17 18563	Danville city	Vermilion	17.0	739	32,920	1,936.5	33,917	35,502	1,008	935	759	-2.9	-4.5
17 18823	Decatur city	Macon	41.6	256	77,836	1,872.9	82,060	85,464	377	323	256	-5.1	-4.0
17 19161	DeKalb city	DeKalb	12.6	895	42,085	3,337.4	39,074	35,887	788	814	752	7.7	8.9
17 19642	Des Plaines city	Cook	14.4	827	56,551	3,921.7	56,975	54,410	575	514	460	-0.7	4.7
17 20292	Dolton village	Cook	4.6	1,205	24,504	5,385.5	25,614	24,023	1,262	1,245	1,110	-4.3	6.6
17 20591	Downers Grove village	DuPage	14.3	834	49,094	3,445.2	49,416	47,726	681	624	551	-0.7	3.5
17 22255	East St. Louis city	St. Clair	14.1	836	29,843	2,122.5	31,622	40,871	1,106	1,004	654	-5.6	-22.6
17 23074	Elgin city	Cook, Kane	25.0	510	98,645	3,945.8	94,628	77,323	264	257	289	4.2	22.4
17 23256	Elk Grove Village village	Cook, DuPage	11.0	960	34,025	3,082.0	34,725	33,488	985	921	818	-2.0	3.7
17 23620	Elmhurst city	Cook, DuPage	10.3	998	44,976	4,383.6	42,775	42,084	751	736	633	5.1	1.6
17 23724	Elmwood Park village	Cook	1.9	1,252	24,499	12,826.7	25,405	23,206	1,263	1,252	1,126	-3.6	9.5
17 24582	Evanston city	Cook	7.8	1,091	75,236	9,707.9	74,239	73,224	387	370	306	1.3	1.4
17 27884	Freeport city	Stephenson	11.4	941	25,612	2,244.7	26,460	26,246	1,242	1,194	1,046	-3.2	0.8
17 28326	Galesburg city	Knox	16.9	742	32,017	1,894.5	33,714	33,749	1,043	947	809	-5.0	-0.1
17 29730	Glendale Heights village	DuPage	5.4	1,177	32,465	6,012.0	31,851	27,787	1,020	997	990	1.9	14.6
17 29756	Glen Ellyn village	DuPage	6.6	1,135	27,193	4,107.7	27,147	25,978	1,193	1,166	1,054	0.2	4.5
17 29938	Glenview village	Cook	13.5	865	45,989	3,419.3	43,077	38,997	734	733	689	6.8	10.5
17 30926	Granite City city	Madison	16.7	749	30,796	1,846.3	31,934	34,159	1,078	993	800	-3.6	-6.5
17 32018	Gurnee village	Lake	13.4	870	30,772	2,296.4	29,011	14,379	1,080	1,086	1,215	6.1	101.8
17 32746	Hanover Park village	Cook, DuPage	6.8	1,128	37,229	5,482.9	38,278	32,906	896	832	840	-2.7	16.3
17 33383	Harvey city	Cook	6.2	1,152	28,771	4,640.5	30,000	30,060	1,142	1,057	922	-4.1	-0.2
17 34722	Highland Park city	Lake	12.4	908	31,380	2,538.8	30,257	31,012	1,056	1,044	888	3.7	-2.4
17 35411	Hoffman Estates village	Cook, Kane	19.7	661	52,046	2,640.6	49,682	46,250	638	619	566	4.8	7.4
17 38570	Joliet city	Kendall, Will	38.1	287	136,208	3,578.8	106,870	79,046	170	217	279	27.5	35.2
17 38934	Kankakee city	Kankakee	12.3	910	26,642	2,171.3	27,648	27,916	1,210	1,145	985	-3.6	-1.0
17 42028	Lansing village	Cook	6.8	1,129	27,324	4,042.0	28,343	28,222	1,188	1,110	973	-3.6	0.4
17 44407	Lombard village	DuPage	9.7	1,025	42,816	4,418.6	42,597	39,865	781	740	673	0.5	6.9
17 47774	Maywood village	Cook	2.7	1,239	25,777	9,511.8	26,987	27,139	1,239	1,174	1,011	-4.5	-0.6
17 49867	Moline city	Rock Island	15.6	791	42,892	2,749.5	43,811	43,510	779	718	608	-2.1	0.7
17 51089	Mount Prospect village	Cook	10.2	1,000	54,482	5,336.1	56,268	53,091	603	525	478	-3.2	6.0
17 51349	Mundelein village	Lake	8.6	1,060	32,774	3,802.1	31,037	21,497	1,011	1,022	1,157	5.6	44.4
17 51622	Naperville city	DuPage, Will	35.4	325	141,579	4,001.7	128,682	87,320	163	167	241	10.0	47.4
17 53000	Niles village	Cook	5.9	1,160	29,330	4,988.1	30,068	28,716	1,126	1,052	960	-2.5	4.7
17 53234	Normal town	McLean	13.6	859	49,927	3,665.7	45,453	40,148	668	692	670	9.8	13.2
17 53481	Northbrook village	Cook	12.9	887	34,190	2,646.3	33,470	32,626	981	953	849	2.2	2.6
17 53559	North Chicago city	Lake	7.8	1,089	33,376	4,262.6	35,919	35,785	995	886	755	-7.1	0.4
17 54638	Oak Forest city	Cook	5.7	1,168	28,116	4,976.3	28,077	27,310	1,163	1,119	1,003	0.1	2.8
17 54820	Oak Lawn village	Cook	8.6	1,062	53,991	6,278.0	55,245	56,256	607	544	437	-2.3	-1.8
17 54885	Oak Park village	Cook	4.7	1,200	50,757	10,799.4	52,524	53,696	655	581	472	-3.4	-2.2
17 56640	Orland Park village	Cook, Will	19.1	677	55,461	2,897.6	51,122	37,685	591	601	723	8.5	35.7
17 57225	Palatine village	Cook	13.0	886	67,232	5,183.7	66,136	57,527	451	425	426	1.7	15.0
17 57875	Park Ridge city	Cook	7.0	1,118	36,983	5,260.7	37,775	37,106	906	846	731	-2.1	1.8
17 58447	Pekin city	Peoria, Tazewell	13.2	878	33,331	2,534.7	33,901	32,168	998	936	857	-1.7	5.4
17 59000	Peoria city	Peoria	44.4	231	112,685	2,538.0	112,980	113,642	212	200	164	-0.3	-0.6
17 62367	Quincy city	Adams	14.6	823	39,841	2,725.1	40,709	40,719	833	772	657	-2.1	(Z)
17 65000	Rockford city	Winnebago	56.0	164	152,916	2,730.2	150,742	144,061	146	136	122	1.4	4.6
17 65078	Rock Island city	Rock Island	15.9	776	38,702	2,431.0	39,728	40,683	858	800	658	-2.6	-2.3
17 66040	Round Lake Beach village	Lake	5.0	1,193	28,253	5,650.6	25,882	16,753	1,157	1,234	1,202	9.2	54.5
17 66703	St. Charles city	DuPage, Kane	14.0	842	32,332	2,311.1	27,953	23,207	1,024	1,122	1,125	15.7	20.5
17 68003	Schaumburg village	Cook, DuPage	19.0	687	72,865	3,831.8	75,397	68,731	404	367	336	-3.4	9.7
17 70122	Skokie village	Cook	10.0	1,010	64,678	6,442.0	63,348	59,431	471	446	412	2.1	6.6
17 72000	Springfield city	Sangamon	54.0	181	115,668	2,142.0	111,644	107,460	204	204	182	3.6	3.9
17 73157	Streamwood village	Cook	7.3	1,111	37,312	5,111.2	36,430	31,464	894	869	877	2.4	15.8
17 75484	Tinley Park village	Cook, Will	15.0	809	57,477	3,844.6	48,823	38,311	561	635	707	17.7	27.4
17 77005	Urbana city	Champaign	10.5	986	38,463	3,666.6	37,725	37,200	869	848	730	2.0	1.4
17 79293	Waukegan city	Lake	23.0	559	91,396	3,972.0	87,917	69,290	293	290	335	4.0	26.9
17 81048	Wheaton city	DuPage	11.2	953	54,700	4,875.2	55,368	51,889	601	543	499	-1.2	6.7
17 81087	Wheeling village	Cook, Lake	8.4	1,068	36,641	4,362.0	36,196	30,045	915	878	923	1.2	20.5
17 82075	Wilmette village	Cook	5.4	1,178	26,922	5,004.1	27,637	26,751	1,203	1,146	1,025	-2.6	3.3
17 83245	Woodridge village	Cook, DuPage, Will	8.3	1,072	34,058	4,093.5	31,030	26,743	984	1,023	1,026	9.8	16.0

See footnotes at end of table.

Table C-1. Cities — **Area and Population**—Con.

[Includes states and 1,265 incorporated places of 25,000 or more population as of April 1, 2000, in all states except Hawaii, which has no incorporated places recognized by the U.S. Census Bureau. Two census designated places (CDPs) are also included (Honolulu CDP in Hawaii and Arlington CDP in Virginia). For more information on these areas, see Appendix C, Geographic Information]

FIPS state and place code[1]	City	County[2]	Land area, 2000 (square miles) Total	Rank[3]	Population 2005 Number	Per square mile[4]	2000[5]	1990[6]	Rank 2005[7]	Rank 2000[7]	Rank 1990[8]	Percent change 2000–2005	Percent change 1990–2000
18 00000	INDIANA		35,866.9	(X)	6,271,973	174.9	6,080,517	5,544,156	(X)	(X)	(X)	3.1	9.7
18 01468	Anderson city	Madison	40.1	273	57,500	1,435.7	59,735	59,570	560	483	409	−3.7	0.3
18 05860	Bloomington city.	Monroe	19.7	660	69,017	3,498.1	71,617	64,134	437	386	373	−3.6	11.7
18 10342	Carmel city	Hamilton	17.8	717	59,243	3,326.4	51,484	26,311	539	597	1,042	15.1	95.7
18 14734	Columbus city	Bartholomew	26.0	493	39,380	1,517.5	39,065	34,319	843	816	790	0.8	13.8
18 19486	East Chicago city	Lake	12.0	924	30,946	2,583.1	32,414	33,858	1,071	979	805	−4.5	−4.3
18 20728	Elkhart city	Elkhart	21.4	606	52,270	2,447.1	52,474	45,983	633	583	571	−0.4	14.1
18 22000	Evansville city	Vanderburgh	40.7	264	115,918	2,848.1	121,582	126,376	203	181	144	−4.7	−3.8
18 23278	Fishers town	Hamilton	21.7	594	57,220	2,638.1	37,946	10,254	566	843	1,223	50.8	270.1
18 25000	Fort Wayne city	Allen	79.0	98	223,341	2,828.9	224,978	205,947	81	77	75	−0.7	9.2
18 27000	Gary city.	Lake	50.2	195	98,715	1,965.3	102,746	116,456	263	230	157	−3.9	−11.8
18 28386	Goshen city.	Elkhart	13.2	877	31,269	2,370.7	29,589	24,268	1,061	1,072	1,104	5.7	21.9
18 29898	Greenwood city	Johnson	14.3	833	42,236	2,959.8	36,372	27,226	787	871	1,009	16.1	33.6
18 31000	Hammond city	Lake	22.9	561	79,217	3,462.3	83,048	84,258	368	315	261	−4.6	−1.4
18 34114	Hobart city	Lake	26.2	488	27,768	1,059.4	25,363	24,269	1,173	1,253	1,103	9.5	4.5
18 36003	Indianapolis city (balance)	Marion	361.5	12	784,118	2,169.2	781,864	731,706	12	12	13	0.3	6.9
18 38358	Jeffersonville city	Clark	13.6	861	28,621	2,107.6	27,839	24,614	1,147	1,131	1,092	2.8	13.1
18 40392	Kokomo city	Howard	16.2	767	46,178	2,850.5	46,578	45,055	731	674	582	−0.9	3.4
18 40788	Lafayette city	Tippecanoe	20.1	648	60,459	3,009.4	61,213	49,836	519	467	526	−1.2	22.8
18 42426	Lawrence city	Marion	20.1	649	40,959	2,039.8	38,915	26,416	807	819	1,039	5.3	47.3
18 46908	Marion city	Grant	13.3	872	30,644	2,304.1	32,088	32,693	1,084	988	847	−4.5	−1.9
18 48528	Merrillville town	Lake	33.3	356	31,525	947.3	30,560	27,948	1,050	1,036	981	3.2	9.3
18 48798	Michigan City city	LaPorte	19.6	662	32,205	1,643.1	32,900	33,819	1,032	967	806	−2.1	−2.7
18 49932	Mishawaka city	St. Joseph	15.7	787	48,497	3,087.0	46,627	43,207	687	671	613	4.0	7.9
18 51876	Muncie city	Delaware	24.2	528	66,164	2,736.3	68,015	71,724	461	412	320	−2.7	−5.2
18 52326	New Albany city	Floyd	14.6	820	36,772	2,513.5	37,882	38,150	910	844	713	−2.9	−0.7
18 54180	Noblesville city.	Hamilton	17.9	716	38,825	2,166.6	28,885	18,605	853	1,090	1,189	34.4	55.3
18 61092	Portage city.	Porter.	25.5	503	35,687	1,401.7	33,496	29,239	946	952	940	6.5	14.6
18 64260	Richmond city	Wayne	23.2	555	37,560	1,618.3	39,178	39,743	888	810	678	−4.1	−1.4
18 71000	South Bend city	St. Joseph	38.7	283	105,262	2,721.4	108,369	105,960	233	213	185	−2.9	2.3
18 75428	Terre Haute city	Vigo.	31.2	389	56,893	1,821.2	59,626	61,085	569	486	396	−4.6	−2.4
18 78326	Valparaiso city	Porter.	10.9	965	29,102	2,669.9	27,655	24,658	1,130	1,144	1,090	5.2	12.2
18 82862	West Lafayette city.	Tippecanoe	5.5	1,174	28,599	5,190.4	28,786	26,230	1,150	1,093	1,048	−0.6	9.7
19 00000	IOWA		55,869.4	(X)	2,966,334	53.1	2,926,382	2,776,831	(X)	(X)	(X)	1.4	5.4
19 01855	Ames city	Story	21.6	599	52,263	2,422.9	50,883	47,483	634	603	555	2.7	7.2
19 02305	Ankeny city	Polk.	16.8	746	36,681	2,187.3	27,264	18,604	914	1,161	1,190	34.5	46.5
19 06355	Bettendorf city	Scott	21.2	613	31,890	1,501.4	31,258	27,940	1,044	1,017	983	2.0	11.9
19 09550	Burlington city	Des Moines.	14.1	837	25,436	1,810.4	26,846	27,433	1,247	1,180	997	−5.3	−2.1
19 11755	Cedar Falls city	Black Hawk.	28.3	438	36,471	1,288.7	36,161	34,017	921	880	801	0.9	6.3
19 12000	Cedar Rapids city	Linn.	63.1	138	123,119	1,949.9	121,367	109,709	192	182	174	1.4	10.6
19 14430	Clinton city	Clinton	35.6	318	27,086	761.5	27,772	29,254	1,200	1,136	938	−2.5	−5.1
19 16860	Council Bluffs city.	Pottawattamie	37.4	297	59,568	1,593.6	58,288	54,825	530	498	457	2.2	6.3
19 19000	Davenport city	Scott	62.8	139	98,845	1,574.2	98,359	95,718	261	246	216	0.5	2.8
19 21000	Des Moines city	Polk, Warren	75.8	107	194,163	2,561.5	198,733	193,459	106	92	80	−2.3	2.7
19 22395	Dubuque city.	Dubuque	26.5	480	57,798	2,182.7	57,711	57,860	555	508	422	0.2	−0.3
19 28515	Fort Dodge city	Webster	14.6	825	25,493	1,750.9	26,309	26,238	1,246	1,203	1,047	−3.1	0.3
19 38595	Iowa City city	Johnson	24.2	529	62,887	2,602.9	62,406	59,745	485	456	407	0.8	4.5
19 49485	Marion city	Linn.	12.0	922	30,233	2,519.4	26,400	20,405	1,092	1,198	1,165	14.5	29.4
19 49755	Marshalltown city	Marshall	18.0	714	25,977	1,440.8	26,012	25,162	1,237	1,221	1,075	−0.1	3.4
19 50160	Mason City city	Cerro Gordo	25.8	495	27,909	1,082.2	29,172	29,174	1,170	1,081	942	−4.3	(Z)
19 73335	Sioux City city	Plymouth, Woodbury.	54.8	177	83,148	1,517.3	85,056	80,566	339	307	271	−2.2	5.6
19 79950	Urbandale city	Dallas, Polk.	20.7	635	34,696	1,676.9	29,074	23,733	969	1,084	1,118	19.3	22.5
19 82425	Waterloo city	Black Hawk.	60.7	145	66,483	1,094.6	68,749	66,486	459	406	352	−3.3	3.4
19 83910	West Des Moines city	Dallas, Polk.	26.8	468	52,768	1,970.4	47,070	32,336	626	663	854	12.1	45.6
20 00000	KANSAS		81,814.9	(X)	2,744,687	33.5	2,688,824	2,477,588	(X)	(X)	(X)	2.1	8.5
20 18250	Dodge City city	Ford.	12.6	895	26,104	2,070.1	25,179	21,179	1,231	1,261	1,159	3.7	18.9
20 21275	Emporia city	Lyon	9.9	1,016	26,456	2,672.3	26,801	25,571	1,222	1,181	1,062	−1.3	4.8
20 25325	Garden City city	Finney	8.5	1,064	27,098	3,176.8	28,494	24,203	1,198	1,104	1,107	−4.9	17.7
20 33625	Hutchinson city	Reno	21.1	617	40,961	1,940.4	41,904	39,300	806	750	682	−2.3	6.6
20 36000	Kansas City city	Wyandotte	124.3	53	144,210	1,160.6	146,866	151,304	158	141	116	−1.8	−2.9
20 38900	Lawrence city	Douglas	28.1	440	81,816	2,910.6	80,192	65,958	349	336	358	2.0	21.6
20 39000	Leavenworth city	Leavenworth	23.5	549	35,213	1,497.8	35,450	38,716	952	901	700	−0.7	−8.4
20 39075	Leawood city	Johnson	15.1	805	30,145	1,999.0	27,656	19,705	1,094	1,143	1,175	9.0	40.4
20 39350	Lenexa city	Johnson	34.3	339	43,434	1,267.0	40,238	34,519	772	784	785	7.9	16.6
20 44250	Manhattan city	Pottawatomie, Riley	15.0	806	48,668	3,240.2	45,643	43,332	686	687	611	6.6	5.3
20 52575	Olathe city	Johnson	54.2	180	111,334	2,055.6	93,049	64,157	216	264	372	19.7	45.0
20 53775	Overland Park city	Johnson	56.8	160	164,811	2,904.2	149,434	111,606	137	137	166	10.3	33.9
20 62700	Salina city.	Saline	22.7	569	45,956	2,021.8	45,751	42,572	735	685	626	0.4	7.5
20 64500	Shawnee city.	Johnson	41.7	254	57,628	1,380.6	47,996	37,863	559	648	716	20.1	26.8
20 71000	Topeka city	Shawnee	56.0	164	121,946	2,177.2	122,920	121,223	194	179	150	−0.8	1.4
20 79000	Wichita city	Sedgwick	135.8	46	354,865	2,614.1	351,241	311,106	51	50	51	1.0	12.9

See footnotes at end of table.

Table C-1. Cities — **Area and Population**—Con.

[Includes states and 1,265 incorporated places of 25,000 or more population as of April 1, 2000, in all states except Hawaii, which has no incorporated places recognized by the U.S. Census Bureau. Two census designated places (CDPs) are also included (Honolulu CDP in Hawaii and Arlington CDP in Virginia). For more information on these areas, see Appendix C, Geographic Information]

FIPS state and place code[1]	City	County[2]	Land area, 2000 (square miles) Total	Rank[3]	Population 2005 Number	Per square mile[4]	2000[5]	1990[6]	Rank 2005[7]	2000[7]	1990[8]	Percent change 2000–2005	1990–2000
21 00000	KENTUCKY		39,728.2	(X)	4,173,405	105.0	4,042,285	3,686,892	(X)	(X)	(X)	3.2	9.6
21 08902	Bowling Green city	Warren	35.4	323	52,272	1,476.2	49,363	42,287	632	628	630	5.9	16.7
21 17848	Covington city	Kenton	13.1	879	42,811	3,258.1	43,370	43,869	782	725	603	−1.3	−1.1
21 28900	Frankfort city	Franklin	14.7	818	27,210	1,847.3	27,722	26,586	1,192	1,137	1,036	−1.8	4.3
21 35866	Henderson city	Henderson	15.0	808	27,666	1,848.1	27,413	26,110	1,176	1,154	1,051	0.9	5.0
21 37918	Hopkinsville city	Christian	24.0	533	28,821	1,199.4	30,131	30,138	1,140	1,049	920	−4.3	(Z)
21 40222	Jeffersontown city	Jefferson	10.0	1,013	26,100	2,623.1	26,528	23,127	1,232	1,188	1,129	−1.6	14.7
21 46027	Lexington-Fayette	Fayette	284.5	20	268,080	942.2	260,512	225,366	69	65	69	2.9	15.6
21 48006	Louisville/Jefferson County (balance)	Jefferson	(X)	(X)	556,429	(NA)	551,183	(X)	26	26	(X)	1.0	(NA)
21 58620	Owensboro city	Daviess	17.4	728	55,459	3,183.6	54,217	53,998	592	557	465	2.3	0.4
21 58836	Paducah city	McCracken	19.5	665	25,575	1,312.9	26,312	27,416	1,244	1,202	998	−2.8	−4.0
21 65226	Richmond city	Madison	19.1	679	30,893	1,615.7	27,530	21,792	1,074	1,148	1,152	12.2	26.3
22 00000	LOUISIANA		43,561.9	(X)	4,523,628	103.8	4,468,958	4,221,826	(X)	(X)	(X)	1.2	5.9
22 00975	Alexandria city	Rapides	26.4	481	45,693	1,730.1	46,188	49,343	740	680	533	−1.1	−6.4
22 05000	Baton Rouge city	East Baton Rouge	76.8	105	222,064	2,890.0	228,037	222,928	82	74	71	−2.6	2.3
22 08920	Bossier City city	Bossier	40.8	262	60,505	1,481.5	56,467	53,024	518	519	480	7.2	6.5
22 36255	Houma city	Terrebonne	14.0	839	32,105	2,288.3	32,393	(9)	1,037	981	(X)	−0.9	(NA)
22 39475	Kenner city	Jefferson	15.1	801	69,911	4,617.6	70,517	71,953	428	394	318	−0.9	−2.0
22 40735	Lafayette city	Lafayette	47.6	209	112,030	2,354.1	111,861	103,711	214	203	192	0.2	7.9
22 41155	Lake Charles city	Calcasieu	40.2	270	70,555	1,756.4	72,081	72,024	420	383	316	−2.1	0.1
22 51410	Monroe city	Ouachita	28.7	426	51,914	1,810.1	53,157	55,587	641	570	445	−2.3	−4.4
22 54035	New Iberia city	Iberia	10.6	983	32,495	3,077.2	32,663	32,196	1,019	975	856	−0.5	1.5
22 55000	New Orleans city	Orleans	180.6	33	454,863	2,519.2	484,674	496,938	38	32	25	−6.2	−2.5
22 70000	Shreveport city	Bossier, Caddo . . .	103.1	72	198,874	1,928.2	200,696	198,972	99	88	77	−0.9	0.9
22 70805	Slidell city	St. Tammany	11.8	928	26,840	2,276.5	25,243	25,177	1,205	1,256	1,074	6.3	0.3
23 00000	MAINE		30,861.6	(X)	1,321,505	42.8	1,274,923	1,227,928	(X)	(X)	(X)	3.7	3.8
23 02795	Bangor city	Penobscot	34.5	337	31,074	902.0	31,473	35,892	1,066	1,010	751	−1.3	−12.3
23 38740	Lewiston city	Androscoggin	34.1	342	36,050	1,057.5	35,690	39,816	930	895	676	1.0	−10.4
23 60545	Portland city	Cumberland	21.2	614	63,889	3,012.2	64,249	63,125	477	436	377	−0.6	1.8
24 00000	MARYLAND		9,773.8	(X)	5,600,388	573.0	5,296,506	4,780,753	(X)	(X)	(X)	5.7	10.8
24 01600	Annapolis city	Anne Arundel	6.7	1,130	36,300	5,393.8	35,852	33,323	924	891	824	1.2	7.6
24 04000	Baltimore city	Baltimore IC	80.8	93	635,815	7,869.0	651,154	736,014	18	18	12	−2.4	−11.5
24 08775	Bowie city	Prince George's . .	16.1	771	53,878	3,346.5	51,369	38,179	609	599	701	4.9	34.5
24 30325	Frederick city	Frederick	20.4	642	57,907	2,835.8	52,816	40,569	553	577	661	9.6	30.2
24 31175	Gaithersburg city	Montgomery	10.1	1,008	57,698	5,718.3	52,455	39,997	556	585	671	10.0	31.1
24 36075	Hagerstown city	Washington	10.7	979	38,326	3,595.3	36,796	35,815	872	863	754	4.2	2.7
24 67675	Rockville city	Montgomery	13.5	865	57,402	4,267.8	47,388	45,226	563	656	580	21.1	4.8
25 00000	MASSACHUSETTS		7,840.0	(X)	6,398,743	816.2	6,349,105	6,016,425	(X)	(X)	(X)	0.8	5.5
25 00765	Agawam city	Hampden	23.2	554	28,599	1,230.6	28,143	(X)	1,150	1,115	(X)	1.6	(NA)
25 02690	Attleboro city	Bristol	27.5	451	43,382	1,577.0	42,068	38,366	773	747	705	3.1	9.6
25 03690	Barnstable Town city	Barnstable	60.0	147	47,826	796.6	47,821	(X)	698	651	(Z)	(Z)	(NA)
25 05595	Beverly city	Essex	16.6	752	39,876	2,402.2	39,862	38,153	831	794	712	(Z)	4.5
25 07000	Boston city	Suffolk	48.4	205	559,034	11,543.1	589,141	574,759	24	20	20	−5.1	2.5
25 09000	Brockton city	Plymouth	21.5	601	94,632	4,407.6	94,304	92,783	277	260	223	0.3	1.6
25 11000	Cambridge city	Middlesex	6.4	1,140	100,135	15,573.1	101,355	95,849	254	236	214	−1.2	5.7
25 13205	Chelsea city	Suffolk	2.2	1,247	32,518	14,848.4	35,080	28,352	1,017	914	969	−7.3	23.7
25 13660	Chicopee city	Hampden	22.9	563	54,680	2,390.9	54,653	56,662	602	552	435	(Z)	−3.5
25 21990	Everett city	Middlesex	3.4	1,233	36,837	10,898.5	38,037	35,744	907	839	756	−3.2	6.4
25 23000	Fall River city	Bristol	31.0	393	91,802	2,959.4	91,938	92,992	290	270	221	−0.1	−1.1
25 23875	Fitchburg city	Worcester	27.8	447	40,045	1,442.5	39,102	41,573	823	812	644	2.4	−5.9
25 25100	Franklin city	Norfolk	26.7	470	30,893	1,155.3	29,560	(X)	1,074	1,073	(X)	4.5	(NA)
25 26150	Gloucester city	Essex	26.0	492	30,713	1,183.1	30,273	28,719	1,082	1,043	959	1.5	5.4
25 29405	Haverhill city	Essex	33.3	354	60,242	1,807.4	58,969	51,165	520	490	507	2.2	15.3
25 30840	Holyoke city	Hampden	21.3	608	39,958	1,876.8	39,838	43,705	827	796	607	0.3	−8.8
25 34550	Lawrence city	Essex	7.0	1,122	71,314	10,246.3	72,043	69,867	414	384	332	−1.0	3.1
25 35075	Leominster city	Worcester	28.9	425	41,804	1,447.5	41,303	37,927	793	760	715	1.2	8.9
25 37000	Lowell city	Middlesex	13.8	852	103,111	7,488.1	105,167	103,423	244	221	193	−2.0	1.7
25 37490	Lynn city	Essex	10.8	970	88,792	8,206.3	89,050	81,414	307	282	269	−0.3	9.4
25 37875	Malden city	Middlesex	5.1	1,191	55,871	11,019.9	56,340	53,674	585	522	473	−0.8	5.0
25 38715	Marlborough city	Middlesex	21.1	620	37,444	1,775.4	36,255	31,821	891	877	866	3.3	13.9
25 39835	Medford city	Middlesex	8.1	1,078	53,523	6,575.3	55,638	57,281	614	536	429	−3.8	−2.9
25 40115	Melrose city	Middlesex	4.7	1,201	26,365	5,621.5	27,134	28,285	1,225	1,167	972	−2.8	−4.1
25 40710	Methuen city	Essex	22.4	577	44,609	1,991.5	43,789	(X)	756	719	(X)	1.9	(NA)
25 45000	New Bedford city	Bristol	20.1	647	93,102	4,627.3	93,768	98,475	283	262	206	−0.7	−4.8
25 45560	Newton city	Middlesex	18.1	712	83,158	4,607.1	83,829	83,132	338	313	264	−0.8	0.8
25 46330	Northampton city	Hampshire	34.5	336	28,715	833.3	28,978	29,250	1,145	1,087	939	−0.9	−0.9
25 52490	Peabody city	Essex	16.4	760	51,239	3,124.3	48,129	47,241	650	643	558	6.5	1.9
25 53960	Pittsfield city	Berkshire	40.7	263	43,860	1,076.8	45,787	48,703	766	683	540	−4.2	−6.0

See footnotes at end of table.

Table C-1. Cities — **Area and Population**—Con.

[Includes states and 1,265 incorporated places of 25,000 or more population as of April 1, 2000, in all states except Hawaii, which has no incorporated places recognized by the U.S. Census Bureau. Two census designated places (CDPs) are also included (Honolulu CDP in Hawaii and Arlington CDP in Virginia). For more information on these areas, see Appendix C, Geographic Information]

FIPS state and place code[1]	City	County[2]	Land area, 2000 (square miles) Total	Rank[3]	Population 2005 Number	Per square mile[4]	2000[5]	1990[6]	Rank 2005[7]	Rank 2000[7]	Rank 1990[8]	Percent change 2000–2005	Percent change 1990–2000
	MASSACHUSETTS—Con.												
25 55745	Quincy city	Norfolk	16.8	745	90,250	5,378.4	88,025	85,005	301	288	257	2.5	3.6
25 56585	Revere city	Suffolk	5.9	1,159	45,807	7,750.8	47,283	42,733	737	660	624	-3.1	10.6
25 59105	Salem city	Essex	8.1	1,082	41,756	5,155.1	40,407	38,231	796	781	709	3.3	5.7
25 62535	Somerville city	Middlesex	4.1	1,216	74,963	18,239.2	77,605	75,842	388	354	294	-3.4	2.3
25 67000	Springfield city	Hampden	32.1	375	151,732	4,726.9	152,080	156,944	147	133	112	-0.2	-3.1
25 69170	Taunton city	Bristol	46.6	211	56,251	1,206.8	55,976	49,903	578	532	525	0.5	12.2
25 72600	Waltham city	Middlesex	12.7	890	59,556	4,689.4	59,226	58,168	532	488	420	0.6	1.8
25 73440	Watertown city	Middlesex	4.1	1,216	32,303	7,859.6	32,986	(X)	1,027	963	(X)	-2.1	(NA)
25 76030	Westfield city	Hampden	46.6	212	40,525	870.0	40,072	38,474	812	788	704	1.1	4.2
25 77850	West Springfield city	Hampden	(X)	(X)	27,989	(NA)	27,900	(X)	1,167	1,128	(X)	0.3	(NA)
25 81035	Woburn city	Middlesex	12.7	893	37,147	2,931.9	37,257	36,085	901	858	749	-0.3	3.2
25 82000	Worcester city	Worcester	37.6	294	175,898	4,683.1	172,648	169,689	126	122	103	1.9	1.7
26 00000	**MICHIGAN**		56,803.8	(X)	10,120,860	178.2	9,938,480	9,295,287	(X)	(X)	(X)	1.8	6.9
26 01380	Allen Park city	Wayne	7.0	1,120	28,083	4,006.1	29,376	31,087	1,164	1,078	887	-4.4	-5.5
26 03000	Ann Arbor city	Washtenaw	27.0	462	113,271	4,193.7	114,344	110,324	210	197	172	-0.9	3.6
26 05920	Battle Creek city	Calhoun	42.8	245	53,202	1,242.2	53,364	53,453	618	566	475	-0.3	-0.2
26 06020	Bay City city	Bay	10.4	991	34,879	3,350.5	36,817	38,670	962	862	702	-5.3	-4.8
26 12060	Burton city	Genesee	23.5	550	30,916	1,317.3	30,308	27,244	1,072	1,042	1,008	2.0	11.2
26 21000	Dearborn city	Wayne	24.4	526	94,090	3,862.5	97,775	89,171	279	247	234	-3.8	9.6
26 21020	Dearborn Heights city	Wayne	11.7	930	56,176	4,793.2	58,264	60,649	579	499	400	-3.6	-3.9
26 22000	Detroit city	Wayne	138.8	44	886,671	6,389.5	951,270	1,028,067	11	10	7	-6.8	-7.5
26 24120	East Lansing city	Clinton, Ingham	11.3	951	46,419	4,126.1	46,607	51,090	729	672	509	-0.4	-8.8
26 24290	Eastpointe city	Macomb	5.1	1,189	33,180	6,505.9	34,077	35,300	1,002	932	763	-2.6	-3.5
26 27440	Farmington Hills city	Oakland	33.3	355	80,223	2,409.8	82,111	74,614	361	322	300	-2.3	10.0
26 29000	Flint city	Genesee	33.6	350	118,551	3,525.2	124,943	142,141	199	173	124	-5.1	-12.1
26 31420	Garden City city	Wayne	5.9	1,162	28,960	4,942.0	30,047	32,018	1,135	1,053	863	-3.6	-6.2
26 34000	Grand Rapids city	Kent	44.6	228	193,780	4,340.9	197,800	189,093	107	94	85	-2.0	4.6
26 38640	Holland city	Allegan, Ottawa	16.6	754	34,429	2,077.8	35,048	30,956	975	915	892	-1.8	13.2
26 40680	Inkster city	Wayne	6.3	1,150	28,870	4,611.8	30,115	30,960	1,139	1,050	891	-4.1	-2.7
26 41420	Jackson city	Jackson	11.1	958	34,879	3,145.1	36,316	37,416	962	873	727	-4.0	-2.9
26 42160	Kalamazoo city	Kalamazoo	24.7	516	72,700	2,945.7	77,145	80,336	406	358	272	-5.8	-4.0
26 42820	Kentwood city	Kent	21.0	623	46,491	2,209.6	45,255	37,779	728	697	719	2.7	19.8
26 46000	Lansing city	Eaton, Ingham	35.1	330	115,518	3,295.8	119,373	127,330	205	184	143	-3.2	-6.2
26 47800	Lincoln Park city	Wayne	5.9	1,163	38,237	6,536.2	40,009	41,854	873	792	638	-4.4	-4.4
26 49000	Livonia city	Wayne	35.7	316	97,977	2,742.9	100,545	100,850	266	240	198	-2.6	-0.3
26 50560	Madison Heights city	Oakland	7.2	1,116	30,251	4,225.0	31,101	32,345	1,091	1,020	853	-2.7	-3.8
26 53780	Midland city	Bay, Midland	33.2	358	41,760	1,257.1	41,748	38,972	795	752	690	(Z)	7.1
26 56020	Mount Pleasant city	Isabella	7.8	1,090	26,253	3,365.8	25,947	23,187	1,227	1,224	1,127	1.2	11.9
26 56320	Muskegon city	Muskegon	14.4	829	39,919	2,781.8	40,105	40,270	829	786	668	-0.5	-0.4
26 59440	Novi city	Oakland	30.5	403	53,115	1,743.2	47,386	32,995	619	657	836	12.1	43.6
26 59920	Oak Park city	Oakland	5.0	1,192	31,194	6,213.9	32,399	30,573	1,064	980	908	-3.7	6.0
26 65440	Pontiac city	Oakland	20.0	651	67,331	3,368.2	67,561	71,136	450	416	325	-0.3	-5.0
26 65560	Portage city	Kalamazoo	32.2	374	45,277	1,406.1	44,897	41,042	746	702	652	0.8	9.4
26 65820	Port Huron city	St. Clair	8.1	1,083	31,501	3,898.6	32,338	33,685	1,051	982	813	-2.6	-4.0
26 69035	Rochester Hills city	Oakland	32.9	367	69,995	2,130.7	68,853	61,855	425	405	389	1.7	11.3
26 69800	Roseville city	Macomb	9.8	1,020	47,708	4,863.2	48,129	51,275	699	643	505	-0.9	-6.1
26 70040	Royal Oak city	Oakland	11.8	926	58,299	4,932.2	60,062	64,710	548	478	365	-2.9	-7.2
26 70520	Saginaw city	Saginaw	17.4	727	58,361	3,346.4	61,792	69,562	547	462	333	-5.6	-11.2
26 70760	St. Clair Shores city	Macomb	11.5	940	61,561	5,339.2	63,096	68,297	505	450	340	-2.4	-7.6
26 74900	Southfield city	Oakland	26.2	487	76,818	2,928.6	78,296	75,700	379	348	295	-1.9	3.4
26 74960	Southgate city	Wayne	6.9	1,126	29,572	4,310.8	30,151	30,773	1,117	1,048	898	-1.9	-2.0
26 76460	Sterling Heights city	Macomb	36.6	306	128,034	3,494.4	124,471	117,810	184	176	154	2.9	5.7
26 79000	Taylor city	Wayne	23.6	548	64,962	2,751.5	65,868	70,811	468	428	328	-1.4	-7.0
26 80700	Troy city	Oakland	33.5	351	81,168	2,420.0	80,957	72,884	356	330	309	0.3	11.1
26 84000	Warren city	Macomb	34.3	338	135,311	3,946.1	138,247	145,101	172	156	120	-2.1	-4.7
26 86000	Westland city	Wayne	20.5	641	85,623	4,186.9	86,602	84,493	329	294	259	-1.1	2.5
26 88900	Wyandotte city	Wayne	5.3	1,179	26,940	5,073.4	27,990	30,913	1,202	1,121	896	-3.8	-9.5
26 88940	Wyoming city	Kent	24.4	523	70,122	2,871.5	69,374	63,986	424	402	374	1.1	8.4
27 00000	**MINNESOTA**		79,610.1	(X)	5,132,799	64.5	4,919,492	4,375,665	(X)	(X)	(X)	4.3	12.4
27 01486	Andover city	Anoka	34.1	341	29,745	872.0	26,588	15,197	1,111	1,186	1,210	11.9	75.0
27 01900	Apple Valley city	Dakota	17.3	730	49,856	2,875.2	45,527	34,651	669	689	781	9.5	31.4
27 06382	Blaine city	Anoka, Ramsey	33.9	346	54,084	1,597.8	45,014	38,859	605	700	694	20.1	15.8
27 06616	Bloomington city	Hennepin	35.5	321	81,164	2,287.6	85,172	86,306	357	304	248	-4.7	-1.3
27 07948	Brooklyn Center city	Hennepin	7.9	1,086	27,551	3,469.9	29,153	28,877	1,180	1,082	951	-5.5	1.0
27 07966	Brooklyn Park city	Hennepin	26.1	491	68,550	2,630.5	67,388	56,367	439	417	436	1.7	19.6
27 08794	Burnsville city	Dakota	24.9	513	59,159	2,378.7	60,220	51,284	540	476	504	-1.8	17.4
27 13114	Coon Rapids city	Anoka	22.7	571	62,417	2,753.3	61,607	52,977	493	463	483	1.3	16.3
27 13456	Cottage Grove city	Washington	34.0	344	32,553	958.0	30,582	22,951	1,015	1,035	1,135	6.4	33.2
27 17000	Duluth city	St. Louis	68.0	127	84,896	1,248.3	86,319	85,478	330	295	255	-1.6	1.0

See footnotes at end of table.

722

Table C-1. Cities — **Area and Population**—Con.

[Includes states and 1,265 incorporated places of 25,000 or more population as of April 1, 2000, in all states except Hawaii, which has no incorporated places recognized by the U.S. Census Bureau. Two census designated places (CDPs) are also included (Honolulu CDP in Hawaii and Arlington CDP in Virginia). For more information on these areas, see Appendix C, Geographic Information]

FIPS state and place code[1]	City	County[2]	Land area, 2000 (square miles) Total	Rank[3]	Population 2005 Number	Per square mile[4]	2000[5]	1990[6]	Rank 2005[7]	2000[7]	1990[8]	Percent change 2000–2005	1990–2000
	MINNESOTA—Con.												
27 17288	Eagan city	Dakota	32.3	372	63,665	1,971.1	63,557	47,368	478	443	557	0.2	34.2
27 18116	Eden Prairie city	Hennepin	32.4	371	60,649	1,872.5	54,901	39,308	517	549	681	10.5	39.7
27 18188	Edina city	Hennepin	15.8	786	45,567	2,893.1	47,425	46,041	742	655	570	-3.9	3.0
27 22814	Fridley city	Anoka	10.2	1,001	26,515	2,609.7	27,449	28,355	1,218	1,150	968	-3.4	-3.2
27 31076	Inver Grove Heights city	Dakota	28.6	427	33,182	1,158.6	29,745	22,448	1,001	1,066	1,143	11.6	32.5
27 35180	Lakeville city	Dakota	36.2	310	51,484	1,423.4	43,128	24,839	646	730	1,084	19.4	73.6
27 39878	Mankato city	Blue Earth, Le Sueur, Nicollet	15.2	798	34,976	2,299.5	32,534	31,729	960	978	869	7.5	2.5
27 40166	Maple Grove city	Hennepin	32.9	366	59,756	1,817.9	50,365	38,800	527	612	698	18.6	29.8
27 40382	Maplewood city	Ramsey	17.3	731	35,085	2,025.7	35,258	30,580	957	908	906	-0.5	15.3
27 43000	Minneapolis city	Hennepin	54.9	174	372,811	6,792.0	382,747	368,397	48	46	44	-2.6	3.9
27 43252	Minnetonka city	Hennepin	27.1	457	50,045	1,844.0	51,102	48,383	665	602	543	-2.1	5.6
27 43864	Moorhead city	Clay	13.4	867	34,081	2,535.8	32,234	32,472	983	983	852	5.7	-0.7
27 47680	Oakdale city	Washington	11.1	959	27,389	2,474.2	26,657	18,501	1,183	1,184	1,192	2.7	44.1
27 51730	Plymouth city	Hennepin	32.9	363	69,701	2,117.9	65,894	50,898	430	427	515	5.8	29.5
27 54214	Richfield city	Hennepin	6.9	1,124	33,497	4,854.6	34,310	35,702	993	926	758	-2.4	-3.9
27 54880	Rochester city	Olmsted	39.6	276	94,950	2,397.1	87,243	72,269	276	291	315	8.8	20.7
27 55852	Roseville city	Ramsey	13.2	875	32,079	2,422.9	33,690	33,485	1,040	949	819	-4.8	0.6
27 56896	St. Cloud city	Benton, Sherburne, Stearns	30.2	408	65,792	2,181.4	59,686	55,977	463	484	439	10.2	6.6
27 57220	St. Louis Park city	Hennepin	10.7	976	43,296	4,046.4	44,102	43,839	774	712	605	-1.8	0.6
27 58000	St. Paul city	Ramsey	52.8	185	275,150	5,214.1	286,788	272,065	67	60	57	-4.1	5.4
27 59998	Shoreview city	Ramsey	11.2	954	26,865	2,399.9	25,924	24,642	1,204	1,227	1,091	3.6	5.2
27 71032	Winona city	Winona	18.2	703	26,587	1,458.4	27,069	26,617	1,213	1,171	1,033	-1.8	1.7
27 71428	Woodbury city	Washington	35.0	332	52,479	1,499.4	46,463	20,075	629	676	1,172	12.9	131.4
28 00000	**MISSISSIPPI**		46,907.0	(X)	2,921,088	62.3	2,844,656	2,575,475	(X)	(X)	(X)	2.7	10.5
28 06220	Biloxi city	Harrison	38.0	288	50,209	1,320.2	50,848	49,787	662	606	528	-1.3	2.1
28 14420	Clinton city	Hinds	23.8	539	26,017	1,091.3	25,032	21,471	1,236	1,266	1,158	3.9	16.6
28 15380	Columbus city	Lowndes	21.4	603	24,425	1,140.3	25,969	27,693	1,264	1,223	993	-5.9	-6.2
28 29180	Greenville city	Washington	26.9	466	38,724	1,440.6	41,633	45,463	855	754	578	-7.0	-8.4
28 29700	Gulfport city	Harrison	56.9	159	72,464	1,273.3	71,127	64,726	408	389	364	1.9	9.9
28 31020	Hattiesburg city	Forrest, Lamar	49.3	201	47,176	957.7	44,837	45,681	716	703	575	5.2	-1.8
28 36000	Jackson city	Hinds, Madison, Rankin	104.9	69	177,977	1,696.6	184,256	196,817	123	110	79	-3.4	-6.4
28 46640	Meridian city	Lauderdale	45.1	223	38,605	855.6	39,968	41,987	863	793	636	-3.4	-4.8
28 55360	Pascagoula city	Jackson	15.2	799	25,173	1,658.3	26,200	26,008	1,253	1,212	1,052	-3.9	0.7
28 69280	Southaven city	DeSoto	33.8	348	38,840	1,149.8	28,949	21,166	852	1,088	1,160	34.2	36.8
28 74840	Tupelo city	Lee	51.1	191	35,673	698.0	34,211	30,983	947	928	890	4.3	10.4
28 76720	Vicksburg city	Warren	32.9	365	25,752	783.2	26,410	26,737	1,240	1,196	1,027	-2.5	-1.2
29 00000	**MISSOURI**		68,885.9	(X)	5,800,310	84.2	5,596,683	5,116,901	(X)	(X)	(X)	3.6	9.4
29 03160	Ballwin city	St. Louis	9.0	1,047	30,481	3,405.7	31,283	28,753	1,086	1,015	958	-2.6	8.8
29 06652	Blue Springs city	Jackson	18.2	707	53,099	2,919.1	48,167	40,525	620	642	662	10.2	18.9
29 11242	Cape Girardeau city	Cape Girardeau, Scott	24.3	527	36,204	1,491.7	35,370	34,892	927	904	775	2.4	1.4
29 13600	Chesterfield city	St. Louis	31.5	384	47,020	1,492.2	46,828	42,341	724	668	628	0.4	10.6
29 15670	Columbia city	Boone	53.1	184	91,814	1,730.1	85,101	70,164	289	305	330	7.9	21.3
29 24778	Florissant city	St. Louis	11.4	944	51,812	4,556.9	54,009	53,871	642	560	467	-4.1	0.3
29 27190	Gladstone city	Clay	8.0	1,085	27,306	3,413.3	26,371	26,296	1,189	1,200	1,044	3.5	0.3
29 31276	Hazelwood city	St. Louis	15.9	782	25,535	1,608.0	26,206	26,836	1,245	1,210	1,022	-2.6	-2.3
29 35000	Independence city	Clay, Jackson	78.3	101	110,208	1,407.0	113,288	112,373	217	199	165	-2.7	0.8
29 37000	Jefferson City city	Callaway, Cole	27.3	454	39,062	1,433.5	40,071	35,861	849	789	753	-2.5	11.7
29 37592	Joplin city	Jasper, Newton	31.4	386	47,183	1,501.7	45,497	41,569	715	690	645	3.7	9.4
29 38000	Kansas City city	Cass, Clay, Jackson, Platte	313.5	16	444,965	1,419.2	441,564	434,953	40	37	31	0.8	1.5
29 39044	Kirkwood city	St. Louis	9.2	1,037	27,038	2,929.4	27,324	28,211	1,201	1,159	974	-1.0	-3.1
29 41348	Lee's Summit city	Cass, Jackson	59.5	149	80,338	1,350.0	70,702	46,423	360	393	563	13.6	52.3
29 42032	Liberty city	Clay	27.0	463	29,042	1,077.6	26,232	20,546	1,131	1,208	1,163	10.7	27.7
29 46586	Maryland Heights city	St. Louis	21.4	604	26,544	1,241.0	27,203	25,536	1,215	1,163	1,064	-2.4	6.5
29 54074	O'Fallon city	St. Charles	22.5	575	69,694	3,101.6	48,816	19,104	431	636	1,184	42.8	155.5
29 60788	Raytown city	Jackson	9.9	1,015	28,923	2,918.6	30,388	30,680	1,137	1,041	903	-4.8	-1.0
29 64082	St. Charles city	St. Charles	20.4	643	62,304	3,060.1	60,595	52,330	495	470	491	2.8	15.8
29 64550	St. Joseph city	Buchanan	43.8	236	72,661	1,657.4	73,990	71,969	407	372	317	-1.8	2.8
29 65000	St. Louis city	St. Louis IC	61.9	142	344,362	5,561.4	348,189	396,685	52	51	35	-1.1	-12.2
29 65126	St. Peters city	St. Charles	21.2	615	54,209	2,559.4	51,438	41,606	604	598	642	5.4	23.6
29 70000	Springfield city	Christian, Greene	73.2	116	150,298	2,054.4	152,034	141,486	149	134	128	-1.1	7.5
29 75220	University City city	St. Louis	5.9	1,160	37,170	6,321.4	37,644	39,889	900	851	672	-1.3	-5.6
29 79820	Wildwood city	St. Louis	66.0	131	34,831	527.5	32,890	(X)	965	968	(X)	5.9	(NA)
30 00000	**MONTANA**		145,552.4	(X)	935,670	6.4	902,195	799,065	(X)	(X)	(X)	3.7	12.9
30 06550	Billings city	Yellowstone	33.7	349	98,721	2,928.5	91,683	81,530	262	272	268	7.7	12.5
30 08950	Bozeman city	Gallatin	12.6	897	33,535	2,661.5	27,686	22,733	989	1,140	1,140	21.1	21.8
30 11397	Butte-Silver Bow (balance)	Silver Bow	716.1	4	32,282	45.1	33,892	33,249	1,029	937	827	-4.8	1.9
30 32800	Great Falls city	Cascade	19.5	664	56,338	2,890.6	56,701	55,269	577	517	450	-0.6	2.6
30 35600	Helena city	Lewis and Clark	14.0	840	27,383	1,954.5	25,883	24,572	1,185	1,233	1,094	5.8	5.3
30 50200	Missoula city	Missoula	23.8	541	62,923	2,643.8	57,275	49,594	484	510	530	9.9	15.5

See footnotes at end of table.

Table C-1. Cities — **Area and Population**—Con.

[Includes states and 1,265 incorporated places of 25,000 or more population as of April 1, 2000, in all states except Hawaii, which has no incorporated places recognized by the U.S. Census Bureau. Two census designated places (CDPs) are also included (Honolulu CDP in Hawaii and Arlington CDP in Virginia). For more information on these areas, see Appendix C, Geographic Information]

FIPS state and place code[1]	City	County[2]	Land area, 2000 (square miles) Total	Rank[3]	Population 2005 Number	Per square mile[4]	2000[5]	1990[6]	Rank 2005[7]	2000[7]	1990[8]	Percent change 2000–2005	1990–2000
31 00000	NEBRASKA		76,872.4	(X)	1,758,787	22.9	1,711,265	1,578,417	(X)	(X)	(X)	2.8	8.4
31 03950	Bellevue city	Sarpy	13.3	874	47,334	3,569.7	44,382	44,173	712	709	600	6.7	0.5
31 17670	Fremont city	Dodge	7.4	1,103	25,314	3,411.6	25,212	23,803	1,250	1,260	1,115	0.4	5.9
31 19595	Grand Island city	Hall	21.5	601	44,546	2,074.8	43,095	38,932	758	732	692	3.4	10.7
31 25055	Kearney city	Buffalo	11.0	962	28,958	2,637.3	27,435	24,780	1,136	1,152	1,087	5.6	10.7
31 28000	Lincoln city	Lancaster	74.6	112	239,213	3,204.9	226,310	192,949	74	76	81	5.7	17.3
31 37000	Omaha city	Douglas	115.7	57	414,521	3,582.7	391,405	373,081	43	45	40	5.9	4.9
32 00000	NEVADA		109,826.0	(X)	2,414,807	22.0	1,998,257	1,201,675	(X)	(X)	(X)	20.8	66.3
32 09700	Carson City	Carson City IC	143.4	42	56,062	391.1	52,457	40,443	581	584	665	6.9	29.7
32 31900	Henderson city	Clark	79.7	96	232,146	2,913.1	175,405	64,978	76	117	363	32.3	169.9
32 40000	Las Vegas city	Clark	113.3	60	545,147	4,811.1	480,044	259,212	29	33	62	13.6	85.2
32 51800	North Las Vegas city . . .	Clark	78.5	99	176,635	2,249.8	115,488	48,018	125	195	547	52.9	140.5
32 60600	Reno city	Washoe	69.1	123	203,550	2,945.3	180,900	138,978	95	113	130	12.5	30.2
32 68400	Sparks city	Washoe	23.9	536	82,051	3,430.2	66,294	53,797	347	424	468	23.8	23.2
33 00000	NEW HAMPSHIRE		8,968.1	(X)	1,309,940	146.1	1,235,786	1,109,252	(X)	(X)	(X)	6.0	11.4
33 14200	Concord city	Merrimack	64.3	134	42,336	658.5	40,687	36,526	784	774	739	4.1	11.4
33 18820	Dover city	Strafford	26.7	472	28,486	1,066.1	26,884	25,326	1,153	1,177	1,070	6.0	6.2
33 45140	Manchester city	Hillsborough	33.0	361	109,691	3,323.0	107,006	99,123	220	216	204	2.5	8.0
33 50260	Nashua city	Hillsborough	30.9	396	87,321	2,826.8	86,605	79,765	314	293	274	0.8	8.6
33 65140	Rochester city	Strafford	45.2	222	30,004	664.5	28,462	26,752	1,100	1,106	1,023	5.4	6.4
34 00000	NEW JERSEY		7,417.3	(X)	8,717,925	1,175.3	8,414,347	7,747,750	(X)	(X)	(X)	3.6	8.6
34 02080	Atlantic City city	Atlantic	11.4	945	40,368	3,556.7	40,517	37,962	817	776	714	−0.4	6.7
34 03580	Bayonne city	Hudson	5.6	1,170	59,987	10,654.9	61,842	61,464	524	460	393	−3.0	0.6
34 05170	Bergenfield borough	Bergen	2.9	1,238	26,056	8,984.8	26,247	24,461	1,234	1,206	1,096	−0.7	7.3
34 10000	Camden city	Camden	8.8	1,056	80,010	9,071.4	79,904	87,471	362	340	240	0.1	−8.7
34 13690	Clifton city	Passaic	11.3	949	79,922	7,072.7	79,062	72,271	364	345	314	1.1	9.4
34 19390	East Orange city	Essex	3.9	1,221	68,190	17,351.1	69,824	73,603	443	398	304	−2.3	−5.1
34 21000	Elizabeth city	Union	12.2	914	125,809	10,295.3	120,568	110,105	186	183	173	4.3	9.5
34 21480	Englewood city	Bergen	4.9	1,195	26,207	5,326.6	26,203	24,820	1,228	1,211	1,085	(Z)	5.6
34 22470	Fair Lawn borough	Bergen	5.2	1,184	31,408	6,075.0	31,637	30,496	1,055	1,001	912	−0.7	3.7
34 24420	Fort Lee borough	Bergen	2.5	1,243	37,175	14,693.7	35,404	31,997	899	903	864	5.0	10.6
34 25770	Garfield city	Bergen	2.1	1,249	29,772	13,977.5	29,786	26,727	1,109	1,065	1,028	(Z)	11.4
34 28680	Hackensack city	Bergen	4.1	1,215	43,735	10,615.3	42,677	36,923	768	739	734	2.5	15.6
34 32250	Hoboken city	Hudson	1.3	1,254	39,900	31,171.9	38,577	33,392	830	827	822	3.4	15.5
34 36000	Jersey City city	Hudson	14.9	810	239,614	16,059.9	240,055	228,564	72	72	66	−0.2	5.0
34 36510	Kearny town	Hudson	9.1	1,039	38,771	4,241.9	40,513	34,882	854	777	776	−4.3	16.1
34 40350	Linden city	Union	10.8	972	40,014	3,701.6	39,394	36,742	825	806	737	1.6	7.2
34 41310	Long Branch city	Monmouth	5.2	1,181	32,091	6,147.7	31,340	28,760	1,038	1,014	956	2.4	9.0
34 46680	Millville city	Cumberland	42.4	248	27,886	658.5	26,847	26,169	1,171	1,179	1,050	3.9	2.6
34 51000	Newark city	Essex	23.8	541	280,666	11,792.7	272,528	275,225	65	64	56	3.0	−1.0
34 51210	New Brunswick city	Middlesex	5.2	1,180	50,156	9,590.1	48,238	41,498	663	641	647	4.0	16.2
34 55950	Paramus borough	Bergen	10.5	987	26,545	2,535.3	25,737	24,934	1,214	1,237	1,080	3.1	3.2
34 56550	Passaic city	Passaic	3.1	1,235	68,338	21,973.6	67,861	58,195	442	413	419	0.7	16.6
34 57000	Paterson city	Passaic	8.4	1,066	149,843	17,753.9	149,222	140,737	150	138	129	0.4	6.0
34 58200	Perth Amboy city	Middlesex	4.8	1,198	48,797	10,208.6	47,303	41,900	685	659	637	3.2	12.9
34 59190	Plainfield city	Union	6.0	1,156	47,642	7,887.7	47,829	46,578	702	650	562	−0.4	2.7
34 61530	Rahway city	Union	4.0	1,220	27,563	6,908.0	26,500	25,312	1,178	1,191	1,071	4.0	4.7
34 65790	Sayreville borough	Middlesex	15.9	779	43,017	2,705.5	40,377	36,572	778	782	738	6.5	10.4
34 74000	Trenton city	Mercer	7.7	1,094	84,639	11,049.5	85,397	88,578	332	302	237	−0.9	−3.6
34 74630	Union City city	Hudson	1.3	1,255	65,128	51,281.9	67,088	57,968	467	419	421	−2.9	15.7
34 76070	Vineland city	Cumberland	68.7	124	58,164	846.8	55,825	54,739	549	534	458	4.2	2.0
34 79040	Westfield town	Union	6.7	1,130	29,918	4,445.5	29,644	28,878	1,103	1,070	950	0.9	2.7
34 79610	West New York town	Hudson	1.0	1,257	46,667	45,752.0	45,768	38,712	726	684	701	2.0	18.2
35 00000	NEW MEXICO		121,355.5	(X)	1,928,384	15.9	1,819,046	1,515,069	(X)	(X)	(X)	6.0	20.1
35 01780	Alamogordo city	Otero	19.4	669	36,245	1,873.1	35,597	27,758	926	897	991	1.8	28.2
35 02000	Albuquerque city	Bernalillo	180.6	32	494,236	2,736.0	448,354	387,035	33	36	38	10.2	15.8
35 12150	Carlsbad city	Eddy	28.4	436	25,300	891.8	25,642	25,266	1,251	1,241	1,072	−1.3	1.5
35 16420	Clovis city	Curry	22.4	578	33,357	1,489.8	32,667	31,215	997	974	882	2.1	4.7
35 25800	Farmington city	San Juan	26.6	477	43,161	1,624.4	38,345	34,333	776	831	788	12.6	11.7
35 32520	Hobbs city	Lea	18.9	690	29,006	1,532.3	28,659	29,150	1,133	1,095	943	1.2	−1.7
35 39380	Las Cruces city	Dona Ana	52.1	186	82,671	1,587.1	73,512	62,531	345	373	383	12.5	17.6
35 63460	Rio Rancho city	Bernalillo, Sandoval . .	73.4	114	66,599	907.1	51,765	32,542	458	591	850	28.7	59.1
35 64930	Roswell city	Chaves	28.9	424	45,199	1,561.8	45,297	44,370	748	696	595	−0.2	2.1
35 70500	Santa Fe city	Santa Fe	37.3	300	70,631	1,892.1	62,543	57,267	418	455	430	12.9	9.2

See footnotes at end of table.

County and City Data Book: 2007

U.S. Census Bureau

Table C-1. Cities — **Area and Population**—Con.

[Includes states and 1,265 incorporated places of 25,000 or more population as of April 1, 2000, in all states except Hawaii, which has no incorporated places recognized by the U.S. Census Bureau. Two census designated places (CDPs) are also included (Honolulu CDP in Hawaii and Arlington CDP in Virginia). For more information on these areas, see Appendix C, Geographic Information]

FIPS state and place code[1]	City	County[2]	Land area, 2000 (square miles)		Population				Rank			Percent change	
					2005								
			Total	Rank[3]	Number	Per square mile[4]	2000[5]	1990[6]	2005[7]	2000[7]	1990[8]	2000–2005	1990–2000
36 00000	NEW YORK		47,213.8	(X)	19,254,630	407.8	18,976,821	17,990,778	(X)	(X)	(X)	1.5	5.5
36 01000	Albany city	Albany	21.4	605	93,523	4,374.3	94,301	100,022	282	261	201	−0.8	−5.7
36 03078	Auburn city	Cayuga	8.4	1,069	27,941	3,330.3	28,574	31,484	1,169	1,102	876	−2.2	−9.2
36 06607	Binghamton city	Broome	10.4	990	45,492	4,357.5	47,380	53,784	744	658	469	−4.0	−11.9
36 11000	Buffalo city	Erie	40.6	266	279,745	6,888.6	292,648	328,233	66	59	50	−4.4	−10.8
36 24229	Elmira city	Chemung	7.3	1,110	29,928	4,088.5	30,940	33,786	1,102	1,026	807	−3.3	−8.4
36 27485	Freeport village	Nassau	4.6	1,204	43,519	9,481.3	43,783	39,814	769	720	677	−0.6	10.0
36 29113	Glen Cove city	Nassau	6.7	1,133	26,633	4,005.0	26,622	24,195	1,211	1,185	1,108	(Z)	10.0
36 33139	Hempstead village	Nassau	3.7	1,228	52,829	14,355.7	53,127	45,900	625	571	574	−0.6	15.7
36 38077	Ithaca city	Tompkins	5.5	1,175	29,766	5,451.6	28,775	29,550	1,110	1,094	932	3.4	−2.6
36 38264	Jamestown city	Chautauqua	9.0	1,044	30,381	3,383.2	31,984	35,058	1,088	991	769	−5.0	−8.8
36 42554	Lindenhurst village	Suffolk	3.8	1,227	28,248	7,532.8	27,820	26,851	1,158	1,134	1,019	1.5	3.6
36 43335	Long Beach city	Nassau	2.1	1,248	35,336	16,512.1	35,462	33,518	950	900	816	−0.4	5.8
36 47042	Middletown city	Orange	5.1	1,186	26,067	5,071.4	25,325	24,343	1,233	1,254	1,099	2.9	4.0
36 49121	Mount Vernon city	Westchester	4.4	1,208	67,924	15,578.9	68,381	67,034	445	409	348	−0.7	2.0
36 50034	Newburgh city	Orange	3.8	1,225	28,548	7,473.3	28,259	26,383	1,152	1,114	1,040	1.0	7.1
36 50617	New Rochelle city	Westchester	10.4	995	72,967	7,050.0	72,182	67,323	402	382	347	1.1	7.2
36 51000	New York city	Bronx, Kings, New York, Queens, Richmond	303.3	17	8,143,197	26,847.8	8,008,654	7,322,564	1	1	1	1.7	9.4
36 51055	Niagara Falls city	Niagara	14.1	837	52,866	3,762.7	55,593	62,463	624	539	385	−4.9	−11.0
36 53682	North Tonawanda city	Niagara	10.1	1,006	32,072	3,175.4	33,262	34,987	1,041	956	772	−3.6	−4.9
36 59223	Port Chester village	Westchester	2.4	1,246	27,886	11,816.1	27,867	25,002	1,171	1,129	1,079	0.1	11.5
36 59641	Poughkeepsie city	Dutchess	5.1	1,186	30,355	5,905.6	29,893	28,875	1,090	1,061	952	1.5	3.5
36 63000	Rochester city	Monroe	35.8	313	211,091	5,891.5	219,774	230,463	88	80	65	−4.0	−4.6
36 63418	Rome city	Oneida	74.9	110	34,344	458.3	34,950	44,342	978	917	596	−1.7	−21.2
36 65255	Saratoga Springs city	Saratoga	28.4	434	28,036	986.1	26,186	25,225	1,165	1,213	1,073	7.1	3.8
36 65508	Schenectady city	Schenectady	10.9	967	61,280	5,647.9	61,821	65,557	509	461	361	−0.9	−5.7
36 70420	Spring Valley village	Rockland	2.1	1,250	25,355	12,073.8	25,565	21,526	1,248	1,248	1,156	−0.8	18.8
36 73000	Syracuse city	Onondaga	25.1	509	141,683	5,647.0	146,464	163,897	162	142	107	−3.3	−10.6
36 75484	Troy city	Rensselaer	10.4	991	48,310	4,640.7	49,170	55,018	691	631	454	−1.7	−10.6
36 76540	Utica city	Oneida	16.4	762	59,336	3,629.1	60,523	68,699	537	472	337	−2.0	−11.9
36 76705	Valley Stream village	Nassau	3.4	1,232	35,799	10,406.7	36,320	34,002	942	872	802	−1.4	6.8
36 78608	Watertown city	Jefferson	9.0	1,046	27,220	3,037.9	26,705	29,857	1,191	1,182	926	1.9	−10.6
36 81677	White Plains city	Westchester	9.8	1,021	56,733	5,789.1	53,077	48,684	571	572	541	6.9	9.0
36 84000	Yonkers city	Westchester	18.1	710	196,425	10,864.2	196,019	188,440	102	95	86	0.2	4.0
37 00000	NORTH CAROLINA		48,710.9	(X)	8,683,242	178.3	8,046,491	6,632,448	(X)	(X)	(X)	7.9	21.3
37 02140	Asheville city	Buncombe	40.9	259	72,231	1,765.2	71,120	65,950	410	390	359	1.6	7.8
37 09060	Burlington city	Alamance, Guilford	21.3	610	47,592	2,236.5	45,656	40,620	703	686	659	4.2	12.4
37 10740	Cary town	Chatham, Wake	42.1	251	106,439	2,528.8	96,255	45,647	229	252	576	10.6	110.9
37 11800	Chapel Hill town	Durham, Orange	19.8	659	49,543	2,508.5	47,830	38,823	677	649	697	3.6	23.2
37 12000	Charlotte city	Mecklenburg	242.3	25	610,949	2,521.8	561,973	427,990	20	24	33	8.7	31.3
37 14100	Concord city	Cabarrus	51.6	188	61,092	1,184.4	56,334	37,742	512	523	721	8.4	49.3
37 19000	Durham city	Durham, Orange, Wake	94.6	79	204,845	2,164.7	187,725	148,505	94	106	119	9.1	26.4
37 22920	Fayetteville city	Cumberland	58.8	151	129,928	2,210.8	132,367	116,822	179	163	156	−1.8	13.3
37 25580	Gastonia city	Gaston	46.1	216	68,964	1,497.3	67,648	60,015	438	414	404	1.9	12.7
37 26880	Goldsboro city	Wayne	24.8	514	38,670	1,559.9	39,272	45,025	859	808	584	−1.5	−12.8
37 28000	Greensboro city	Guilford	104.7	70	231,962	2,215.3	224,465	191,920	77	78	82	3.3	17.0
37 28080	Greenville city	Pitt	25.6	501	69,517	2,717.6	62,000	49,277	432	458	534	12.1	25.8
37 31060	Hickory city	Burke, Caldwell, Catawba	28.1	442	40,232	1,433.3	37,452	32,913	819	853	839	7.4	13.8
37 31400	High Point city	Davidson, Forsyth, Guilford, Randolph	49.1	202	95,086	1,938.6	86,061	69,977	274	296	331	10.5	23.0
37 33120	Huntersville town	Mecklenburg	31.2	390	36,377	1,167.8	25,470	8,663	922	1,251	1,226	42.8	194.0
37 34200	Jacksonville city	Onslow	44.5	230	62,628	1,408.0	66,719	79,126	489	422	278	−6.1	−15.7
37 35200	Kannapolis city	Cabarrus, Rowan	29.9	415	39,041	1,307.9	36,948	33,701	850	859	812	5.7	9.6
37 43920	Monroe city	Union	24.6	520	29,987	1,220.5	27,109	19,162	1,101	1,169	1,182	10.6	41.5
37 55000	Raleigh city	Durham, Wake	114.6	59	341,530	2,980.2	284,800	221,331	53	61	73	19.9	28.7
37 57500	Rocky Mount city	Edgecombe, Nash	35.6	318	56,626	1,592.0	55,997	54,392	574	531	461	1.1	3.0
37 58860	Salisbury city	Rowan	17.8	718	27,563	1,550.2	27,601	23,959	1,178	1,147	1,112	−0.1	15.2
37 74440	Wilmington city	New Hanover	41.0	258	95,476	2,328.7	89,692	64,557	272	280	367	6.4	38.9
37 74540	Wilson city	Wilson	23.3	552	46,967	2,016.6	44,789	39,022	725	704	687	4.9	14.8
37 75000	Winston-Salem city	Forsyth	108.9	64	193,755	1,780.0	185,854	167,570	109	109	104	4.3	10.9
38 00000	NORTH DAKOTA		68,975.9	(X)	636,677	9.2	642,204	638,800	(X)	(X)	(X)	−0.9	0.5
38 07200	Bismarck city	Burleigh	26.9	465	57,377	2,133.8	55,614	49,979	565	538	524	3.2	11.3
38 25700	Fargo city	Cass	37.9	290	90,672	2,389.9	90,640	74,265	297	275	301	(Z)	22.0
38 32060	Grand Forks city	Grand Forks	19.2	673	49,792	2,587.9	49,366	49,586	671	627	531	0.9	−0.4
38 53380	Minot city	Ward	14.6	826	34,984	2,404.4	36,625	34,862	959	866	777	−4.5	5.1

See footnotes at end of table.

Table C-1. Cities — **Area and Population**—Con.

[Includes states and 1,265 incorporated places of 25,000 or more population as of April 1, 2000, in all states except Hawaii, which has no incorporated places recognized by the U.S. Census Bureau. Two census designated places (CDPs) are also included (Honolulu CDP in Hawaii and Arlington CDP in Virginia). For more information on these areas, see Appendix C, Geographic Information]

FIPS state and place code[1]	City	County[2]	Land area, 2000 (square miles) Total	Rank[3]	Population 2005 Number	Per square mile[4]	2000[5]	1990[6]	Rank 2005[7]	2000[7]	1990[8]	Percent change 2000–2005	1990–2000
39 00000	OHIO		40,948.4	(X)	11,464,042	280.0	11,353,145	10,847,115	(X)	(X)	(X)	1.0	4.7
39 01000	Akron city	Summit	62.1	141	210,795	3,396.1	217,070	223,142	89	82	70	-2.9	-2.7
39 03828	Barberton city	Summit	9.0	1,043	27,192	3,018.0	27,933	27,880	1,194	1,123	989	-2.7	0.2
39 04720	Beavercreek city	Greene	26.4	482	39,655	1,502.7	37,984	33,604	838	841	814	4.4	13.0
39 07972	Bowling Green city	Wood	10.2	1,002	29,793	2,935.3	29,668	28,873	1,108	1,069	953	0.4	2.8
39 09680	Brunswick city	Medina	12.5	900	35,159	2,803.7	33,436	28,506	954	954	964	5.2	17.3
39 12000	Canton city	Stark	20.6	636	79,478	3,867.5	80,927	84,147	366	331	262	-1.8	-3.8
39 15000	Cincinnati city	Hamilton	78.0	103	308,728	3,959.6	331,283	364,831	58	55	46	-6.8	-9.2
39 16000	Cleveland city	Cuyahoga . . .	77.6	104	452,208	5,828.9	477,472	505,629	39	34	23	-5.3	-5.6
39 16014	Cleveland Heights city . .	Cuyahoga . . .	8.1	1,080	48,029	5,922.2	50,769	53,947	693	608	466	-5.4	-5.9
39 18000	Columbus city	Delaware, Fairfield, Franklin . . .	210.3	27	730,657	3,474.9	712,016	639,215	15	15	16	2.6	11.4
39 19778	Cuyahoga Falls city	Summit	25.5	502	50,494	1,977.1	49,377	48,862	659	626	536	2.3	1.1
39 21000	Dayton city	Montgomery . . .	55.8	168	158,873	2,848.2	166,197	182,422	140	124	91	-4.4	-8.9
39 21434	Delaware city	Delaware	15.0	807	31,322	2,088.1	25,615	20,356	1,060	1,244	1,166	22.3	25.8
39 22694	Dublin city	Delaware, Franklin, Union . .	21.1	616	34,964	1,655.5	31,585	17,079	961	1,007	1,200	10.7	84.9
39 23380	East Cleveland city	Cuyahoga . . .	3.1	1,235	25,708	8,266.2	27,217	33,086	1,241	1,162	833	-5.5	-17.7
39 25256	Elyria city	Lorain	19.9	654	56,061	2,818.6	56,068	56,877	582	528	434	(Z)	-1.4
39 25704	Euclid city	Cuyahoga . . .	10.7	974	49,619	4,633.0	52,715	54,863	675	580	456	-5.9	-3.9
39 25914	Fairborn city	Greene	13.1	885	31,650	2,423.4	31,590	31,152	1,048	1,006	884	0.2	1.4
39 25970	Fairfield city	Butler, Hamilton . .	21.0	628	42,294	2,015.0	42,097	39,673	785	746	680	0.5	6.1
39 27048	Findlay city	Hancock	17.2	733	39,118	2,275.6	39,159	36,187	847	811	748	-0.1	8.2
39 29106	Gahanna city	Franklin	12.4	905	33,077	2,667.5	32,639	24,232	1,006	977	1,106	1.3	34.7
39 29428	Garfield Heights city . . .	Cuyahoga . . .	7.2	1,114	29,042	4,016.9	30,734	31,724	1,131	1,030	871	-5.5	-3.1
39 32592	Grove City city	Franklin	14.0	844	30,892	2,214.5	27,352	19,766	1,076	1,157	1,173	12.9	38.4
39 33012	Hamilton city	Butler	21.6	596	61,943	2,866.4	60,839	61,492	501	468	392	1.8	-1.1
39 36610	Huber Heights city	Miami, Montgomery .	21.0	624	38,089	1,811.2	38,241	38,737	875	833	699	-0.4	-1.3
39 39872	Kent city	Portage	8.7	1,059	28,135	3,237.6	28,128	29,782	1,162	1,117	930	(Z)	-5.6
39 40040	Kettering city	Greene, Montgomery . .	18.7	695	55,481	2,968.5	57,759	60,387	590	506	403	-3.9	-4.4
39 41664	Lakewood city	Cuyahoga . . .	5.6	1,172	53,244	9,593.5	56,646	59,652	617	518	408	-6.0	-5.0
39 41720	Lancaster city	Fairfield	18.1	711	36,063	1,995.7	35,319	34,774	929	906	779	2.1	1.6
39 43554	Lima city	Allen	12.8	889	38,608	3,021.0	41,581	45,241	862	755	579	-7.1	-8.1
39 44856	Lorain city	Lorain	24.0	534	67,820	2,823.5	68,652	71,255	446	407	324	-1.2	-3.7
39 47138	Mansfield city	Richland	29.9	413	50,615	1,692.2	51,745	50,900	657	592	514	-2.2	1.7
39 47306	Maple Heights city	Cuyahoga . . .	5.2	1,183	24,739	4,766.7	26,156	27,102	1,260	1,215	1,014	-5.4	-3.5
39 47754	Marion city	Marion	11.4	945	36,494	3,215.3	37,406	36,269	918	855	744	-2.4	3.1
39 48244	Massillon city	Stark	16.8	747	32,150	1,919.4	31,432	31,235	1,035	1,011	881	2.3	0.6
39 48790	Medina city	Medina	11.1	956	26,461	2,377.4	25,136	19,295	1,221	1,263	1,179	5.3	30.3
39 49056	Mentor city	Lake	26.8	469	51,485	1,923.2	50,284	47,460	645	613	556	2.4	6.0
39 49840	Middletown city	Butler, Warren . .	25.7	497	51,472	2,005.9	51,596	51,788	647	593	500	-0.2	-0.4
39 54040	Newark city	Licking	19.6	663	47,301	2,419.5	46,360	44,877	713	678	588	2.0	3.3
39 56882	North Olmsted city	Cuyahoga . . .	11.6	935	32,653	2,807.7	34,113	34,202	1,012	930	797	-4.3	-0.3
39 57008	North Royalton city	Cuyahoga . . .	21.3	608	29,538	1,387.4	28,648	23,180	1,119	1,096	1,128	3.1	23.6
39 61000	Parma city	Cuyahoga . . .	20.0	652	81,469	4,081.6	85,655	87,724	352	300	239	-4.9	-2.4
39 66390	Reynoldsburg city	Fairfield, Franklin, Licking	10.6	981	33,059	3,124.7	32,122	26,264	1,007	986	1,045	2.9	22.3
39 70380	Sandusky city	Erie	10.1	1,009	26,666	2,653.3	27,844	29,519	1,209	1,130	934	-4.2	-5.7
39 71682	Shaker Heights city	Cuyahoga . . .	6.3	1,148	27,723	4,414.5	29,405	30,941	1,175	1,077	894	-5.7	-5.0
39 74118	Springfield city	Clark	22.5	575	63,302	2,817.2	65,958	71,006	482	426	326	-4.0	-7.1
39 74944	Stow city	Summit	17.1	735	34,404	2,010.8	32,139	27,966	976	985	980	7.0	14.9
39 75098	Strongsville city	Cuyahoga . . .	24.6	517	43,949	1,783.6	43,858	35,297	765	717	764	0.2	24.3
39 77000	Toledo city	Lucas	80.6	94	301,285	3,737.1	313,782	332,983	59	57	49	-4.0	-5.8
39 77504	Trotwood city	Montgomery . . .	30.5	401	26,608	871.5	27,432	29,411	1,212	1,153	936	-3.0	-6.7
39 79002	Upper Arlington city	Franklin	9.8	1,024	31,550	3,232.6	33,686	34,248	1,049	950	794	-6.3	-1.6
39 80892	Warren city	Trumbull	16.1	772	45,796	2,848.0	48,244	50,979	738	640	513	-5.1	-5.4
39 83342	Westerville city	Delaware, Franklin .	12.4	906	34,722	2,802.4	35,331	30,693	968	905	902	-1.7	15.1
39 83622	Westlake city	Cuyahoga . . .	15.9	779	31,331	1,970.5	31,719	27,018	1,058	999	1,016	-1.2	17.4
39 88000	Youngstown city	Mahoning, Trumbull . .	33.9	345	82,837	2,443.6	82,026	95,728	341	324	215	1.0	-14.3
39 88084	Zanesville city	Muskingum . . .	11.2	952	25,253	2,246.7	25,595	27,276	1,252	1,246	1,006	-1.3	-6.2
40 00000	OKLAHOMA		68,667.1	(X)	3,547,884	51.7	3,450,652	3,145,576	(X)	(X)	(X)	2.8	9.7
40 04450	Bartlesville city	Osage, Washington .	21.1	617	34,734	1,645.4	34,744	34,320	966	920	789	(Z)	1.2
40 09050	Broken Arrow city	Tulsa, Wagoner . .	45.0	225	86,228	1,916.6	80,419	59,101	322	333	415	7.2	36.1
40 23200	Edmond city	Oklahoma	85.1	88	74,881	879.5	68,315	52,343	389	410	490	9.6	30.5
40 23950	Enid city	Garfield	74.0	113	46,416	627.5	47,045	45,226	730	664	580	-1.3	4.0
40 41850	Lawton city	Comanche . . .	75.1	109	90,234	1,200.9	92,779	92,955	302	265	222	-2.7	-0.2
40 48350	Midwest City city	Oklahoma	24.6	519	54,890	2,232.2	54,088	52,605	597	558	488	1.5	2.8
40 49200	Moore city	Cleveland	21.7	592	47,697	2,195.0	41,138	40,205	700	765	669	15.9	2.3
40 50050	Muskogee city	Muskogee . . .	37.3	299	39,766	1,065.0	39,277	38,249	834	807	708	1.2	2.7
40 52500	Norman city	Cleveland	177.0	34	101,719	574.7	96,780	80,057	247	250	273	5.1	20.9
40 55000	Oklahoma City city	Canadian, Cleveland, Oklahoma, Pottawatomie . . .	607.0	5	531,324	875.3	506,129	444,566	31	30	30	5.0	13.8
40 59850	Ponca City city	Kay, Osage . . .	18.1	708	25,070	1,384.3	25,945	26,604	1,255	1,225	1,035	-3.4	-2.5
40 66800	Shawnee city	Pottawatomie . . .	42.3	249	29,824	705.7	29,107	26,505	1,107	1,083	1,037	2.5	9.8
40 70300	Stillwater city	Payne	27.9	444	40,906	1,468.8	39,080	36,760	809	813	736	4.7	6.3
40 75000	Tulsa city	Osage, Rogers, Tulsa, Wagoner	182.7	31	382,457	2,093.9	393,120	367,077	46	44	45	-2.7	7.1

See footnotes at end of table.

Table C-1. Cities — **Area and Population**—Con.

[Includes states and 1,265 incorporated places of 25,000 or more population as of April 1, 2000, in all states except Hawaii, which has no incorporated places recognized by the U.S. Census Bureau. Two census designated places (CDPs) are also included (Honolulu CDP in Hawaii and Arlington CDP in Virginia). For more information on these areas, see Appendix C, Geographic Information]

FIPS state and place code[1]	City	County[2]	Land area, 2000 (square miles) Total	Rank[3]	Population 2005 Number	Per square mile[4]	2000[5]	1990[6]	Rank 2005[7]	2000[7]	1990[8]	Percent change 2000–2005	1990–2000
41 00000	OREGON		95,996.8	(X)	3,641,056	37.9	3,421,436	2,842,337	(X)	(X)	(X)	6.4	20.4
41 01000	Albany city	Benton, Linn	15.9	782	44,797	2,821.0	40,866	33,296	754	770	826	9.6	22.7
41 05350	Beaverton city	Washington	16.3	763	85,775	5,255.8	77,208	55,859	327	357	440	11.1	38.2
41 05800	Bend city	Deschutes	32.0	376	67,152	2,097.2	52,029	33,947	452	588	804	29.1	53.3
41 15800	Corvallis city	Benton	13.6	860	49,553	3,643.6	49,434	45,005	676	623	585	0.2	9.8
41 23850	Eugene city	Lane	40.5	268	144,515	3,566.5	138,509	114,069	156	155	163	4.3	21.4
41 30550	Grants Pass city	Josephine	7.6	1,099	28,882	3,810.3	25,732	18,822	1,138	1,238	1,187	12.2	36.7
41 31250	Gresham city	Multnomah	22.2	583	96,072	4,337.3	90,205	68,216	270	277	341	6.5	32.2
41 34100	Hillsboro city	Washington	21.6	599	84,533	3,919.0	70,214	38,999	333	396	688	20.4	80.0
41 38500	Keizer city	Marion	7.2	1,114	34,644	4,791.7	32,190	21,881	971	984	1,150	7.6	47.1
41 40550	Lake Oswego city	Clackamas, Multnomah, Washington	10.4	995	36,502	3,526.8	35,287	31,511	917	907	875	3.4	12.0
41 45000	McMinnville city	Yamhill	9.9	1,016	29,646	2,994.5	26,523	18,081	1,115	1,190	1,194	11.8	46.7
41 47000	Medford city	Jackson	21.7	593	70,147	3,232.6	65,428	48,847	423	430	537	7.2	33.9
41 55200	Oregon City city	Clackamas	8.1	1,078	30,221	3,712.7	26,485	17,902	1,093	1,192	1,197	14.1	47.9
41 59000	Portland city	Clackamas, Multnomah, Washington	134.3	49	533,427	3,971.3	529,191	485,995	30	29	27	0.8	8.9
41 64900	Salem city	Marion, Polk	45.7	219	148,751	3,252.8	137,026	108,951	152	159	177	8.6	25.8
41 69600	Springfield city	Lane	14.4	828	55,641	3,864.0	53,256	44,988	589	568	586	4.5	18.4
41 73650	Tigard city	Washington	10.9	966	47,968	4,416.9	42,373	30,360	694	743	914	13.2	39.6
42 00000	PENNSYLVANIA		44,816.6	(X)	12,429,616	277.3	12,281,054	11,882,842	(X)	(X)	(X)	1.2	3.4
42 02000	Allentown city	Lehigh	17.7	719	106,992	6,031.1	106,632	105,719	226	218	187	0.3	0.9
42 02184	Altoona city	Blair	9.8	1,023	47,176	4,828.7	49,523	52,406	716	621	489	–4.7	–5.5
42 06064	Bethel Park borough	Allegheny	11.7	931	32,313	2,764.2	33,556	33,783	1,025	951	808	–3.7	–0.7
42 06088	Bethlehem city	Lehigh, Northampton	19.3	671	72,895	3,784.8	71,329	71,804	403	388	319	2.2	–0.7
42 13208	Chester city	Delaware	4.9	1,196	37,058	7,640.8	36,854	42,072	904	861	635	0.6	–12.4
42 21648	Easton city	Northampton	4.3	1,211	26,267	6,166.0	26,258	26,301	1,226	1,205	1,043	(Z)	–0.2
42 24000	Erie city	Erie	22.0	584	102,612	4,672.7	103,688	108,749	245	225	179	–1.0	–4.7
42 32800	Harrisburg city	Dauphin	8.1	1,080	47,472	5,853.6	48,950	51,995	706	634	495	–3.0	–5.9
42 41216	Lancaster city	Lancaster	7.4	1,105	54,757	7,399.6	56,356	55,750	600	521	444	–2.8	1.1
42 52330	Municipality of Monroeville borough	Allegheny	19.8	658	28,175	1,423.7	29,344	29,044	1,161	1,079	946	–4.0	1.0
42 53368	New Castle city	Lawrence	8.5	1,063	25,030	2,930.9	26,309	28,400	1,256	1,203	967	–4.9	–7.4
42 54656	Norristown borough	Montgomery	3.5	1,230	30,689	8,693.8	31,282	30,505	1,083	1,016	911	–1.9	2.5
42 60000	Philadelphia city	Philadelphia	135.1	48	1,463,281	10,831.9	1,517,550	1,585,577	5	5	5	–3.6	–4.3
42 61000	Pittsburgh city	Allegheny	55.6	171	316,718	5,698.4	334,563	369,962	57	53	42	–5.3	–9.6
42 61536	Plum borough	Allegheny	28.6	428	26,452	923.9	26,940	25,707	1,223	1,176	1,058	–1.8	4.8
42 63624	Reading city	Berks	9.8	1,019	80,855	8,233.7	81,207	77,843	358	326	286	–0.4	4.3
42 69000	Scranton city	Lackawanna	25.2	507	73,120	2,898.1	76,081	81,879	400	362	267	–3.9	–7.1
42 73808	State College borough	Centre	4.5	1,206	38,720	8,528.6	38,420	39,025	856	829	686	0.8	–1.6
42 85152	Wilkes-Barre city	Luzerne	6.9	1,127	41,337	6,034.6	43,123	47,672	800	731	552	–4.1	–9.5
42 85312	Williamsport city	Lycoming	8.9	1,054	30,112	3,391.0	30,706	32,159	1,095	1,032	859	–1.9	–4.5
42 87048	York city	York	5.2	1,182	40,418	7,772.7	41,301	42,250	815	762	631	–2.1	–2.2
44 00000	RHODE ISLAND		1,044.9	(X)	1,076,189	1,029.9	1,048,319	1,003,464	(X)	(X)	(X)	2.7	4.5
44 19180	Cranston city	Providence	28.6	431	81,614	2,856.6	79,272	76,256	351	344	293	3.0	4.0
44 22960	East Providence city	Providence	13.4	869	49,515	3,692.4	48,688	50,460	678	637	519	1.7	–3.5
44 49960	Newport city	Newport	7.9	1,086	25,340	3,191.4	26,475	28,447	1,249	1,193	966	–4.3	–6.9
44 54640	Pawtucket city	Providence	8.7	1,058	73,742	8,437.3	72,958	72,531	397	376	312	1.1	0.6
44 59000	Providence city	Providence	18.5	698	176,862	9,575.6	173,621	160,591	124	119	109	1.9	8.1
44 74300	Warwick city	Kent	35.5	320	87,233	2,457.3	85,808	85,540	315	297	253	1.7	0.3
44 80780	Woonsocket city	Providence	7.7	1,093	44,328	5,749.4	43,224	44,305	760	728	598	2.6	–2.4
45 00000	SOUTH CAROLINA		30,109.5	(X)	4,255,083	141.3	4,011,816	3,486,310	(X)	(X)	(X)	6.1	15.1
45 00550	Aiken city	Aiken	16.2	768	27,490	1,699.0	25,152	20,946	1,181	1,262	1,161	9.3	20.1
45 01360	Anderson city	Anderson	13.8	849	25,899	1,871.3	25,633	26,661	1,238	1,242	1,030	1.0	–3.9
45 13330	Charleston city	Berkeley, Charleston	97.0	74	106,712	1,100.2	97,514	91,686	227	248	226	9.4	6.4
45 16000	Columbia city	Lexington, Richland	125.2	51	117,088	935.1	115,984	116,452	202	192	158	1.0	–0.4
45 25810	Florence city	Florence	17.7	720	31,269	1,766.6	30,588	30,722	1,061	1,034	900	2.2	–0.4
45 29815	Goose Creek city	Berkeley, Charleston	31.7	382	32,516	1,026.1	30,163	26,626	1,018	1,047	1,032	7.8	13.3
45 30850	Greenville city	Greenville	26.1	490	56,676	2,174.0	56,078	58,286	573	527	418	1.1	–3.8
45 34045	Hilton Head Island town	Beaufort	42.1	252	34,497	820.2	33,858	23,692	973	940	1,119	1.9	42.9
45 48535	Mount Pleasant town	Charleston	41.9	253	57,932	1,383.0	48,105	31,536	552	645	873	20.4	52.5
45 50875	North Charleston city	Berkeley, Charleston, Dorchester	58.5	153	86,313	1,474.4	81,203	86,483	320	327	246	6.3	–6.1
45 61405	Rock Hill city	York	31.0	392	59,554	1,919.2	49,960	43,002	533	615	618	19.2	16.2
45 68290	Spartanburg city	Spartanburg	19.2	676	38,379	2,004.1	39,860	44,155	871	795	602	–3.7	–9.7
45 70270	Summerville town	Berkeley, Charleston, Dorchester	15.4	797	37,714	2,455.3	27,918	23,289	884	1,125	1,122	35.1	19.9
45 70405	Sumter city	Sumter	26.6	476	39,679	1,492.3	40,499	43,500	836	778	609	–2.0	–6.9
46 00000	SOUTH DAKOTA		75,884.6	(X)	775,933	10.2	754,840	696,004	(X)	(X)	(X)	2.8	8.5
46 52980	Rapid City city	Pennington	44.6	229	62,167	1,394.2	59,648	55,553	496	485	446	4.2	7.4
46 59020	Sioux Falls city	Lincoln, Minnehaha	56.3	161	139,517	2,477.2	124,650	101,720	167	174	195	11.9	22.5

See footnotes at end of table.

Table C-1. Cities — **Area and Population**—Con.

[Includes states and 1,265 incorporated places of 25,000 or more population as of April 1, 2000, in all states except Hawaii, which has no incorporated places recognized by the U.S. Census Bureau. Two census designated places (CDPs) are also included (Honolulu CDP in Hawaii and Arlington CDP in Virginia). For more information on these areas, see Appendix C, Geographic Information]

FIPS state and place code[1]	City	County[2]	Land area, 2000 (square miles) Total	Rank[3]	Population 2005 Number	Per square mile[4]	2000[5]	1990[6]	Rank 2005[7]	2000[7]	1990[8]	Percent change 2000–2005	1990–2000
47 00000	TENNESSEE		41,217.1	(X)	5,962,959	144.7	5,689,262	4,877,203	(X)	(X)	(X)	4.8	16.7
47 03440	Bartlett city	Shelby	19.1	683	43,263	2,267.5	40,624	28,042	775	775	979	6.5	44.9
47 08280	Brentwood city	Williamson	34.7	334	32,426	935.8	26,104	16,926	1,022	1,218	1,201	24.2	54.2
47 08540	Bristol city	Sullivan	29.4	420	24,994	851.6	25,229	24,755	1,257	1,258	1,088	-0.9	1.9
47 14000	Chattanooga city	Hamilton, Marion	135.2	47	154,762	1,144.6	156,057	152,926	143	130	114	-0.8	2.0
47 15160	Clarksville city	Montgomery	94.9	78	112,878	1,189.9	103,473	77,659	211	227	288	9.1	33.2
47 15400	Cleveland city	Bradley	25.0	511	38,186	1,530.5	37,357	32,522	874	856	851	2.2	14.9
47 16420	Collierville town	Shelby	24.6	522	37,564	1,530.1	32,866	14,991	887	969	1,213	14.3	119.2
47 16540	Columbia city	Maury	29.6	417	33,777	1,141.1	33,202	28,773	987	958	955	1.7	15.4
47 16920	Cookeville city	Putnam	21.9	588	27,743	1,269.1	25,913	22,220	1,174	1,228	1,145	7.1	16.6
47 27740	Franklin city	Williamson	30.0	410	53,311	1,775.3	44,905	20,629	616	701	1,162	18.7	117.7
47 28960	Germantown city	Shelby	17.6	724	37,480	2,132.0	37,667	33,019	890	849	835	-0.5	14.1
47 33280	Hendersonville city	Sumner	27.3	453	44,876	1,642.0	40,923	32,665	753	769	848	9.7	25.3
47 37640	Jackson city	Madison	49.5	198	62,099	1,254.8	59,814	51,232	498	482	506	3.8	16.8
47 38320	Johnson City city	Carter, Sullivan, Washington	39.3	278	58,718	1,495.2	55,485	51,989	544	542	496	5.8	6.7
47 39560	Kingsport city	Hawkins, Sullivan	44.1	234	44,130	1,001.4	45,052	42,357	763	699	627	-2.0	6.4
47 40000	Knoxville city	Knox	92.7	83	180,130	1,944.0	175,368	173,820	119	118	98	2.7	0.9
47 48000	Memphis city	Shelby	279.3	21	672,277	2,406.8	682,953	663,575	17	16	15	-1.6	2.9
47 50280	Morristown city	Hamblen, Jefferson	20.9	630	26,187	1,253.0	25,720	23,012	1,229	1,239	1,133	1.8	11.8
47 51560	Murfreesboro city	Rutherford	39.0	282	86,793	2,226.0	69,443	46,390	316	401	564	25.0	49.7
47 52006	Nashville-Davidson (balance)	Davidson	473.3	8	549,110	1,160.1	545,537	488,224	28	27	26	0.7	11.7
47 55120	Oak Ridge city	Anderson, Roane	85.6	87	27,297	319.1	27,387	27,322	1,190	1,155	1,001	-0.3	0.2
47 69420	Smyrna town	Rutherford	22.8	565	33,497	1,467.2	27,191	16,279	993	1,164	1,204	23.2	67.0
48 00000	TEXAS		261,797.1	(X)	22,859,968	87.3	20,851,792	16,986,335	(X)	(X)	(X)	9.6	22.8
48 01000	Abilene city	Jones, Taylor	105.1	67	114,757	1,091.6	115,930	106,785	206	194	183	-1.0	8.6
48 01924	Allen city	Collin	26.3	485	69,222	2,628.0	43,619	19,433	434	721	1,177	58.7	124.5
48 03000	Amarillo city	Potter, Randall	89.9	84	183,021	2,036.7	173,608	157,680	118	120	111	5.4	10.1
48 04000	Arlington city	Tarrant	95.8	76	362,805	3,786.3	333,202	261,973	50	54	60	8.9	27.2
48 05000	Austin city	Hays, Travis, Williamson	251.5	22	690,252	2,744.3	659,829	497,091	16	17	24	4.6	32.7
48 06128	Baytown city	Chambers, Harris	32.7	369	68,371	2,094.1	66,477	64,207	440	423	371	2.8	3.5
48 07000	Beaumont city	Jefferson	85.0	89	111,799	1,315.1	113,698	114,233	215	198	162	-1.7	-0.5
48 07132	Bedford city	Tarrant	10.0	1,011	48,390	4,839.0	47,152	43,768	689	662	606	2.6	7.7
48 08236	Big Spring city	Howard	19.1	680	24,253	1,269.1	25,233	23,106	1,265	1,257	1,131	-3.9	9.2
48 10768	Brownsville city	Cameron	80.4	95	167,493	2,083.2	142,120	114,487	132	150	160	17.9	24.1
48 10912	Bryan city	Brazos	43.3	239	66,306	1,529.9	65,668	55,545	460	429	447	1.0	18.2
48 13024	Carrollton city	Collin, Dallas, Denton	36.5	308	118,870	3,259.4	109,572	82,211	197	208	265	8.5	33.3
48 13492	Cedar Hill city	Dallas, Ellis	35.2	328	41,582	1,183.0	32,110	20,231	798	987	1,171	29.5	58.7
48 13552	Cedar Park city	Travis, Williamson	17.0	741	48,139	2,836.7	26,075	8,976	692	1,219	1,225	84.6	190.5
48 15364	Cleburne city	Johnson	27.8	445	29,184	1,050.2	26,061	22,775	1,129	1,220	1,139	12.0	14.4
48 15976	College Station city	Brazos	40.3	269	72,388	1,798.0	68,238	53,013	409	411	481	6.1	28.7
48 16432	Conroe city	Montgomery	37.8	291	47,042	1,244.8	38,632	29,792	723	825	929	21.8	29.7
48 16612	Coppell city	Dallas, Denton	14.9	812	38,704	2,602.8	35,958	17,095	857	885	1,199	7.6	110.3
48 16624	Copperas Cove city	Bell, Coryell, Lampasas	13.9	845	30,643	2,199.8	29,592	24,324	1,085	1,071	1,100	3.6	21.7
48 17000	Corpus Christi city	Aransas, Kleberg, Nueces, San Patricio	154.6	38	283,474	1,833.1	277,499	258,340	64	62	63	2.2	7.4
48 19000	Dallas city	Collin, Dallas, Denton, Kaufman, Rockwall	342.5	13	1,213,825	3,543.6	1,188,623	1,006,964	9	8	8	2.1	18.0
48 19624	Deer Park city	Harris	10.4	994	28,993	2,798.6	28,520	27,393	1,134	1,103	1,000	1.7	4.1
48 19792	Del Rio city	Val Verde	15.4	795	36,020	2,332.9	33,871	30,988	931	938	889	6.3	9.3
48 19972	Denton city	Denton	61.5	143	104,153	1,693.8	82,451	66,572	238	320	350	26.3	23.9
48 20092	DeSoto city	Dallas	21.6	598	44,653	2,069.2	37,647	30,538	755	850	910	18.6	23.3
48 21628	Duncanville city	Dallas	11.3	950	35,150	3,113.4	36,071	35,024	955	883	771	-2.6	3.0
48 22660	Edinburg city	Hidalgo	37.4	298	62,735	1,678.8	48,472	36,358	486	638	743	29.4	33.3
48 24000	El Paso city	El Paso	249.1	23	598,590	2,403.2	563,657	515,632	21	22	22	6.2	9.3
48 24768	Euless city	Tarrant	16.3	764	51,226	3,148.5	45,976	38,225	651	681	710	11.4	20.3
48 25452	Farmers Branch city	Dallas	12.0	922	26,487	2,207.3	27,508	24,868	1,220	1,149	1,081	-3.7	10.6
48 26232	Flower Mound town	Dallas, Denton, Tarrant	40.9	261	63,526	1,554.3	50,696	15,808	479	609	1,208	25.3	220.7
48 27000	Fort Worth city	Denton, Parker, Tarrant, Wise	292.5	19	624,067	2,133.3	541,339	448,560	19	28	29	15.3	20.7
48 27648	Friendswood city	Galveston, Harris	21.0	626	33,094	1,574.4	29,037	22,951	1,005	1,085	1,135	14.0	26.5
48 27684	Frisco city	Collin, Denton	69.9	121	70,793	1,013.1	33,708	7,026	417	948	1,229	110.0	379.8
48 28068	Galveston city	Galveston	46.2	215	57,466	1,245.2	57,247	59,063	562	511	416	0.4	-3.1
48 29000	Garland city	Collin, Dallas, Rockwall	57.1	158	216,346	3,788.2	215,794	180,886	86	83	93	0.3	19.3
48 29336	Georgetown city	Williamson	22.8	565	39,015	1,708.9	28,466	16,167	851	1,105	1,205	37.1	76.1
48 30464	Grand Prairie city	Dallas, Ellis, Tarrant	71.4	119	144,337	2,021.5	127,166	99,661	157	171	202	13.5	27.6
48 30644	Grapevine city	Dallas, Denton, Tarrant	32.3	373	47,460	1,470.3	42,059	29,543	707	748	933	12.8	42.4
48 31928	Haltom City city	Tarrant	12.4	906	39,875	3,218.3	39,018	32,775	832	817	845	2.2	19.0
48 32372	Harlingen city	Cameron	34.1	343	62,318	1,829.1	57,937	49,980	494	505	523	7.6	15.9
48 35000	Houston city	Fort Bend, Harris, Montgomery	579.4	6	2,016,582	3,480.3	1,957,018	1,697,154	4	4	4	3.0	15.3
48 35528	Huntsville city	Walker	30.9	394	36,699	1,187.7	35,115	30,674	912	911	904	4.5	14.5
48 35576	Hurst city	Tarrant	9.9	1,016	37,967	3,835.1	36,290	33,435	879	874	821	4.6	8.5
48 37000	Irving city	Dallas	67.2	129	193,649	2,880.4	191,641	155,023	110	101	113	1.0	23.6

See footnotes at end of table.

Table C-1. Cities — **Area and Population**—Con.

[Includes states and 1,265 incorporated places of 25,000 or more population as of April 1, 2000, in all states except Hawaii, which has no incorporated places recognized by the U.S. Census Bureau. Two census designated places (CDPs) are also included (Honolulu CDP in Hawaii and Arlington CDP in Virginia). For more information on these areas, see Appendix C, Geographic Information]

FIPS state and place code[1]	City	County[2]	Land area, 2000 (square miles)		Population					Rank			Percent change	
					2005									
			Total	Rank[3]	Number	Per square mile[4]	2000[5]	1990[6]		2005[7]	2000[7]	1990[8]	2000–2005	1990–2000
	TEXAS—Con.													
48 38632	Keller city	Tarrant	18.4	699	35,706	1,936.3	27,345	13,673		945	1,158	1,217	30.6	100.0
48 39148	Killeen city	Bell	35.4	326	100,233	2,835.4	86,862	64,499		252	292	368	15.4	34.7
48 39352	Kingsville city	Kleberg	13.8	850	24,740	1,788.9	25,575	25,387		1,259	1,247	1,069	-3.3	0.7
48 40588	Lake Jackson city	Brazoria	19.0	684	27,386	1,438.3	26,386	22,849		1,184	1,199	1,137	3.8	15.5
48 41212	Lancaster city	Dallas	29.3	421	32,233	1,100.5	25,894	22,211		1,031	1,230	1,146	24.5	16.6
48 41440	La Porte city	Harris	18.9	689	33,136	1,749.5	31,880	27,943		1,004	996	982	3.9	14.1
48 41464	Laredo city	Webb	78.5	100	208,754	2,660.6	177,611	125,787		92	115	147	17.5	41.2
48 41980	League City city	Galveston, Harris	51.2	189	61,490	1,200.0	45,447	30,167		506	693	918	35.3	50.7
48 42508	Lewisville city	Dallas, Denton	36.8	305	90,348	2,455.8	77,742	46,242		300	351	567	16.2	68.1
48 43888	Longview city	Gregg, Harrison	54.7	179	75,609	1,383.3	73,342	70,372		385	375	329	3.1	4.2
48 45000	Lubbock city	Lubbock	114.8	58	209,737	1,826.8	199,575	187,361		91	89	89	5.1	6.5
48 45072	Lufkin city	Angelina	26.7	473	33,522	1,255.5	32,904	30,486		990	966	913	1.9	7.9
48 45384	McAllen city	Hidalgo	46.0	217	123,622	2,689.2	106,451	86,157		190	219	249	16.1	23.6
48 45744	McKinney city	Collin	58.0	155	96,581	1,664.3	54,403	21,683		269	554	1,153	77.5	150.9
48 46452	Mansfield city	Ellis, Johnson, Tarrant	36.5	307	37,976	1,041.0	28,031	15,435		877	1,120	1,209	35.5	81.6
48 47892	Mesquite city	Dallas, Kaufman	43.4	238	129,902	2,991.8	124,533	101,621		180	175	196	4.3	22.5
48 48072	Midland city	Martin, Midland	66.6	130	99,227	1,489.7	95,238	89,392		258	254	233	4.2	6.5
48 48768	Mission city	Hidalgo	24.1	530	60,146	2,492.6	45,480	31,100		522	691	886	32.2	46.2
48 48804	Missouri City city	Fort Bend, Harris	29.7	416	69,941	2,354.9	52,903	36,265		427	576	746	32.2	45.9
48 50256	Nacogdoches city	Nacogdoches	25.2	507	30,806	1,221.0	30,009	31,206		1,077	1,055	883	2.7	-3.8
48 50820	New Braunfels city	Comal, Guadalupe	29.3	422	47,168	1,612.6	38,217	28,093		718	834	977	23.4	36.0
48 52356	North Richland Hills city	Tarrant	18.2	704	61,115	3,356.1	55,634	45,902		511	537	573	9.9	21.2
48 53388	Odessa city	Ector, Midland	36.8	304	93,546	2,542.0	90,943	89,737		281	273	232	2.9	1.3
48 55080	Paris city	Lamar	42.8	247	26,539	620.8	25,897	25,992		1,216	1,229	1,053	2.5	-0.4
48 56000	Pasadena city	Harris	44.2	233	143,852	3,257.5	141,674	119,622		159	151	152	1.5	18.4
48 56348	Pearland city	Brazoria, Fort Bend, Harris	39.3	277	56,790	1,443.9	37,472	23,776		570	852	1,116	51.6	57.6
48 57200	Pharr city	Hidalgo	20.8	633	58,986	2,831.8	46,976	34,686		541	665	780	25.6	35.4
48 58016	Plano city	Collin, Denton	71.6	118	250,096	3,494.4	222,000	128,096		70	79	142	12.7	73.3
48 58820	Port Arthur city	Jefferson, Orange	82.9	92	56,684	683.6	57,755	58,612		572	507	417	-1.9	-1.5
48 61796	Richardson city	Collin, Dallas	28.6	433	99,187	3,472.9	91,776	74,966		259	271	298	8.1	22.4
48 63500	Round Rock city	Travis, Williamson	26.1	489	86,316	3,302.1	61,317	31,745		319	465	868	40.8	93.2
48 63572	Rowlett city	Dallas, Rockwall	20.2	644	53,664	2,652.7	44,503	23,744		612	708	1,117	20.6	87.4
48 64472	San Angelo city	Tom Green	55.9	166	88,014	1,574.5	88,450	84,934		309	286	258	-0.5	4.1
48 65000	San Antonio city	Bexar, Comal	407.6	10	1,256,509	3,083.0	1,151,447	998,043		7	9	9	9.1	15.4
48 65516	San Juan city	Hidalgo	11.0	961	30,773	2,795.0	26,525	16,497		1,079	1,189	1,203	16.0	60.8
48 65600	San Marcos city	Caldwell, Guadalupe, Hays	18.2	704	46,111	2,532.2	35,720	28,956		733	894	947	29.1	23.4
48 67496	Sherman city	Grayson	38.6	285	36,790	954.3	35,095	32,221		909	913	855	4.8	8.9
48 68636	Socorro city	El Paso	17.5	726	29,685	1,695.3	27,680	23,005		1,112	1,141	1,134	7.2	20.3
48 70808	Sugar Land city	Fort Bend	24.1	531	75,754	3,144.6	63,252	44,892		383	449	587	19.8	40.9
48 72176	Temple city	Bell	65.4	132	55,447	848.5	54,475	48,666		593	553	542	1.8	11.9
48 72368	Texarkana city	Bowie	25.6	500	35,746	1,394.7	34,792	35,153		944	918	768	2.7	-1.0
48 72392	Texas City city	Chambers, Galveston	62.4	140	44,274	709.9	41,550	40,786		762	756	656	6.6	1.9
48 72530	The Colony city	Denton	13.7	856	37,972	2,779.8	26,549	22,201		878	1,187	1,147	43.0	19.6
48 74144	Tyler city	Smith	49.3	200	91,936	1,864.8	84,336	78,022		288	309	285	9.0	8.1
48 75428	Victoria city	Victoria	33.0	362	61,790	1,874.1	60,615	55,265		502	469	451	1.9	9.7
48 76000	Waco city	McLennan	84.2	90	120,465	1,430.7	114,419	104,884		195	196	188	5.3	9.1
48 77272	Weslaco city	Hidalgo	12.7	891	31,442	2,477.7	27,915	24,404		1,053	1,126	1,097	12.6	14.4
48 79000	Wichita Falls city	Archer, Wichita	70.7	120	99,846	1,412.4	104,197	96,807		255	224	210	-4.2	7.6
49 00000	**UTAH**		82,143.7	(X)	2,469,585	30.1	2,233,198	1,722,850		(X)	(X)	(X)	10.6	29.6
49 07690	Bountiful city	Davis	13.5	864	41,085	3,050.1	41,303	39,080		803	760	685	-0.5	5.7
49 13850	Clearfield city	Davis	7.8	1,091	27,413	3,537.2	25,974	21,601		1,182	1,222	1,155	5.5	20.2
49 20120	Draper city	Salt Lake, Utah	30.3	404	35,119	1,157.5	25,216	7,120		956	1,259	1,228	39.3	254.2
49 43660	Layton city	Davis	20.7	634	61,782	2,983.2	58,634	42,183		503	495	632	5.4	39.0
49 45860	Logan city	Cache	16.5	755	47,357	2,866.6	42,696	32,757		710	738	846	10.9	30.3
49 49710	Midvale city	Salt Lake	5.8	1,165	27,170	4,652.4	27,018	24,254		1,196	1,172	1,105	0.6	11.4
49 53230	Murray city	Salt Lake	9.6	1,027	44,555	4,636.3	45,338	31,458		757	695	878	-1.7	44.1
49 55980	Ogden city	Weber	26.6	475	78,309	2,939.5	77,291	64,222		374	356	370	1.3	20.3
49 57300	Orem city	Utah	18.4	699	89,713	4,865.1	84,110	67,580		303	311	345	6.7	24.5
49 62470	Provo city	Utah	39.6	275	113,459	2,862.2	105,509	86,993		208	220	243	7.5	21.3
49 64340	Riverton city	Salt Lake	12.6	899	32,089	2,552.8	25,011	11,596		1,039	1,267	1,220	28.3	115.7
49 65110	Roy city	Weber	7.6	1,098	35,229	4,635.4	33,021	25,005		951	962	1,078	6.7	32.1
49 65330	St. George city	Washington	64.4	133	64,201	996.9	49,728	28,760		475	618	956	29.1	72.9
49 67000	Salt Lake City city	Salt Lake	109.1	63	178,097	1,632.7	181,764	159,962		122	112	110	-2.0	13.6
49 67440	Sandy city	Salt Lake	22.3	580	89,664	4,015.4	89,018	76,472		304	283	291	0.7	16.4
49 70850	South Jordan city	Salt Lake	20.9	632	40,209	1,926.6	29,437	12,216		820	1,076	1,218	36.6	141.0
49 75360	Taylorsville city	Salt Lake	10.7	977	58,009	5,431.6	58,757	(X)		550	493	(X)	-1.3	(NA)
49 82950	West Jordan city	Salt Lake	30.9	394	91,444	2,959.4	78,729	43,172		292	346	614	16.2	82.4
49 83470	West Valley City city	Salt Lake	35.4	324	113,300	3,200.6	108,896	87,114		209	212	242	4.0	25.0

See footnotes at end of table.

Table C-1. Cities — **Area and Population**—Con.

[Includes states and 1,265 incorporated places of 25,000 or more population as of April 1, 2000, in all states except Hawaii, which has no incorporated places recognized by the U.S. Census Bureau. Two census designated places (CDPs) are also included (Honolulu CDP in Hawaii and Arlington CDP in Virginia). For more information on these areas, see Appendix C, Geographic Information]

FIPS state and place code[1]	City	County[2]	Land area, 2000 (square miles) Total	Rank[3]	Population 2005 Number	Per square mile[4]	Population 2000[5]	Population 1990[6]	Rank 2005[7]	Rank 2000[7]	Rank 1990[8]	Percent change 2000–2005	Percent change 1990–2000
50 00000	VERMONT............		9,249.6	(X)	623,050	67.4	608,827	562,758	(X)	(X)	(X)	2.3	8.2
50 10675	Burlington city...........	Chittenden	10.6	983	38,531	3,648.8	39,819	39,104	866	797	684	–3.2	1.8
51 00000	VIRGINIA...........		39,594.1	(X)	7,567,465	191.1	7,079,030	6,189,197	(X)	(X)	(X)	6.9	14.4
51 01000	Alexandria city........	Alexandria IC.......	15.2	799	135,337	8,915.5	128,283	111,183	171	168	169	5.5	15.4
51 03000	Arlington CDP.........	Arlington........	25.9	494	195,965	7,575.0	189,453	170,895	103	103	102	3.4	10.9
51 07784	Blacksburg town........	Montgomery	19.4	668	39,130	2,021.2	39,588	35,179	846	802	767	–1.2	12.5
51 14968	Charlottesville city	Charlottesville IC	10.3	998	40,437	3,941.2	40,088	40,470	814	787	663	0.9	–0.9
51 16000	Chesapeake city	Chesapeake IC	340.7	14	218,968	642.7	199,184	151,982	85	91	115	9.9	31.1
51 21344	Danville city........	Danville IC........	43.1	241	46,143	1,071.6	48,411	53,056	732	639	479	–4.7	–8.8
51 35000	Hampton city........	Hampton IC........	51.8	187	145,579	2,811.5	146,437	133,773	155	143	135	–0.6	9.5
51 35624	Harrisonburg city	Harrisonburg IC........	17.6	725	40,438	2,302.8	40,453	30,707	813	780	901	(Z)	31.7
51 44984	Leesburg town........	Loudoun........	11.6	936	36,269	3,126.6	28,311	16,152	925	1,111	1,206	28.1	75.3
51 47672	Lynchburg city	Lynchburg IC........	49.4	199	66,973	1,356.0	65,228	66,120	453	433	355	2.7	–1.3
51 48952	Manassas city	Manassas IC........	9.9	1,014	37,569	3,783.4	35,135	27,757	886	910	992	6.9	26.6
51 56000	Newport News city	Newport News IC......	68.3	126	179,899	2,634.3	180,697	171,477	120	114	100	–0.4	5.4
51 57000	Norfolk city	Norfolk IC........	53.7	182	231,954	4,317.0	234,403	261,250	78	73	61	–1.0	–10.3
51 61832	Petersburg city........	Petersburg IC.......	22.9	561	32,604	1,425.0	33,756	37,071	1,013	946	732	–3.4	–8.9
51 64000	Portsmouth city	Portsmouth IC......	33.2	359	100,169	3,020.8	100,565	103,910	253	239	191	–0.4	–3.2
51 67000	Richmond city	Richmond IC.......	60.1	146	193,777	3,225.9	197,952	202,713	108	93	76	–2.1	–2.3
51 68000	Roanoke city	Roanoke IC........	42.9	244	92,631	2,160.2	94,911	96,487	286	256	211	–2.4	–1.6
51 76432	Suffolk city	Suffolk IC........	400.0	11	78,994	197.5	63,677	52,143	370	441	494	24.1	22.1
51 82000	Virginia Beach city	Virginia Beach IC.........	248.3	24	438,415	1,765.7	425,257	393,089	42	39	37	3.1	8.2
53 00000	WASHINGTON.........		66,544.1	(X)	6,287,759	94.5	5,894,140	4,866,669	(X)	(X)	(X)	6.7	21.1
53 03180	Auburn city	King, Pierce	21.3	611	47,086	2,214.8	43,394	34,281	720	724	791	8.5	26.6
53 05210	Bellevue city	King.........	30.8	398	117,137	3,809.3	112,469	98,438	201	202	207	4.2	14.3
53 05280	Bellingham city	Whatcom	25.6	498	74,547	2,907.4	67,312	53,458	393	418	474	10.7	25.9
53 07380	Bothell city	King, Snohomish	12.1	920	30,916	2,565.6	30,103	23,851	1,072	1,051	1,114	2.7	26.2
53 07695	Bremerton city	Kitsap.........	22.7	572	37,828	1,669.4	37,260	39,854	882	857	674	1.5	–6.5
53 08850	Burien city	King.........	7.4	1,102	30,737	4,131.3	31,881	(X)	1,081	995	(X)	–3.6	(NA)
53 17635	Des Moines city	King.........	6.3	1,146	28,767	4,537.4	29,736	26,987	1,143	1,067	1,017	–3.3	10.2
53 20750	Edmonds city........	Snohomish	8.9	1,050	39,937	4,487.3	39,450	38,961	828	804	691	1.2	1.3
53 22640	Everett city	Snohomish	32.5	370	96,604	2,972.4	94,580	71,655	268	258	321	2.1	32.0
53 23515	Federal Way city	King.........	21.0	624	83,088	3,950.9	85,251	(X)	340	303	(X)	–2.5	(NA)
53 35275	Kennewick city	Benton	22.9	560	60,997	2,660.1	55,696	44,423	513	535	594	9.5	25.4
53 35415	Kent city	King.........	28.0	443	81,800	2,918.3	80,417	59,917	350	334	406	1.7	34.2
53 35940	Kirkland city	King.........	10.7	977	45,814	4,289.7	45,054	40,314	736	698	667	1.7	11.8
53 36745	Lacey city	Thurston.......	16.0	775	33,368	2,092.0	31,111	20,296	996	1,019	1,167	7.3	53.3
53 38038	Lakewood city	Pierce	17.1	735	57,671	3,370.6	58,296	(X)	557	497	(X)	–1.1	(NA)
53 40245	Longview city........	Cowlitz........	13.7	855	36,137	2,637.7	34,665	32,101	928	923	861	4.2	8.0
53 40840	Lynnwood city	Snohomish	7.6	1,095	33,504	4,385.3	33,859	29,669	992	939	931	–1.0	14.1
53 43955	Marysville city	Snohomish	9.6	1,028	29,889	3,116.7	25,937	15,182	1,104	1,226	1,211	15.2	70.8
53 47560	Mount Vernon city	Skagit	11.1	957	29,271	2,634.7	26,237	18,310	1,127	1,207	1,193	11.6	43.3
53 51300	Olympia city	Thurston.......	16.7	748	44,114	2,640.0	42,505	33,957	764	741	803	3.8	25.2
53 53545	Pasco city.........	Franklin	28.1	441	46,494	1,655.8	33,840	24,012	727	942	1,111	37.4	40.9
53 56695	Puyallup city	Pierce	12.1	916	35,861	2,954.0	33,242	25,561	938	957	1,063	7.9	30.0
53 57535	Redmond city	King.........	15.9	781	47,579	2,994.3	45,436	36,266	704	694	745	4.7	25.3
53 57745	Renton city	King.........	17.0	738	55,817	3,277.6	50,249	41,695	586	614	641	11.1	20.5
53 58235	Richland city	Benton	34.8	333	44,317	1,272.7	38,734	32,938	761	822	838	14.4	17.6
53 61115	Sammamish city	King.........	18.1	712	34,364	1,903.8	34,104	(X)	977	931	(X)	0.8	(NA)
53 62288	SeaTac city	King.........	10.0	1,012	25,081	2,518.2	25,496	(X)	1,254	1,249	(X)	–1.6	(NA)
53 63000	Seattle city	King.........	83.9	91	573,911	6,842.9	563,375	516,262	23	23	21	1.9	9.1
53 63960	Shoreline city.......	King.........	11.7	933	52,024	4,461.7	53,293	(X)	639	567	(X)	–2.4	(NA)
53 67000	Spokane city	Spokane.......	57.8	157	196,818	3,407.5	195,629	178,096	101	96	95	0.6	9.8
53 67167	Spokane Valley city	Spokane.......	(X)	(X)	81,380	(NA)	80,902	(X)	353	332	(X)	0.6	(NA)
53 70000	Tacoma city........	Pierce	50.1	196	195,898	3,911.7	193,571	177,245	104	99	96	1.2	9.2
53 73465	University Place city	Pierce	8.4	1,069	30,425	3,626.3	29,933	(X)	1,087	1,059	(X)	1.6	(NA)
53 74060	Vancouver city.......	Clark	42.8	246	157,493	3,680.6	143,645	104,265	142	145	189	9.6	37.8
53 75775	Walla Walla city	Walla Walla	10.8	970	30,989	2,864.0	30,513	27,158	1,069	1,038	1,010	1.6	12.4
53 77105	Wenatchee city	Chelan........	6.9	1,125	29,374	4,269.5	28,393	22,402	1,124	1,109	1,144	3.5	26.7
53 80010	Yakima city	Yakima........	20.1	646	81,214	4,034.5	80,059	64,232	355	338	369	1.4	24.6
54 00000	WEST VIRGINIA.........		24,077.7	(X)	1,816,856	75.5	1,808,350	1,793,477	(X)	(X)	(X)	0.5	0.8
54 14600	Charleston city........	Kanawha	31.6	383	51,176	1,619.5	53,405	57,689	652	565	424	–4.2	–7.4
54 39460	Huntington city.......	Cabell, Wayne	15.9	776	49,198	3,090.3	51,511	55,019	679	595	453	–4.5	–6.4
54 55756	Morgantown city.......	Monongalia	9.8	1,021	28,292	2,886.9	26,675	27,923	1,156	1,183	984	6.1	–4.5
54 62140	Parkersburg city........	Wood........	11.8	926	32,020	2,709.0	33,154	34,479	1,042	960	786	–3.4	–3.8
54 86452	Wheeling city.........	Marshall, Ohio	13.9	846	29,639	2,130.8	31,397	34,893	1,116	1,013	774	–5.6	–10.0

See footnotes at end of table.

Table C-1. Cities — **Area and Population**—Con.

[Includes states and 1,265 incorporated places of 25,000 or more population as of April 1, 2000, in all states except Hawaii, which has no incorporated places recognized by the U.S. Census Bureau. Two census designated places (CDPs) are also included (Honolulu CDP in Hawaii and Arlington CDP in Virginia). For more information on these areas, see Appendix C, Geographic Information]

FIPS state and place code[1]	City	County[2]	Land area, 2000 (square miles)		Population					Rank			Percent change	
					2005									
			Total	Rank[3]	Number	Per square mile[4]	2000[5]	1990[6]		2005[7]	2000[7]	1990[8]	2000–2005	1990–2000
55 00000	WISCONSIN		54,310.1	(X)	5,536,201	101.9	5,363,715	4,891,954		(X)	(X)	(X)	3.2	9.6
55 02375	Appleton city	Calumet, Outagamie, Winnebago	20.9	631	70,217	3,362.9	70,234	66,134		422	395	354	(Z)	6.2
55 06500	Beloit city	Rock	16.4	758	35,621	2,166.7	35,827	35,738		948	892	757	−0.6	0.2
55 10025	Brookfield city	Waukesha.	27.2	455	39,656	1,457.9	38,649	35,189		837	824	766	2.6	9.8
55 22300	Eau Claire city	Chippewa, Eau Claire	30.3	405	62,570	2,066.4	61,934	57,819		490	459	423	1.0	7.1
55 26275	Fond du Lac city	Fond du Lac	16.9	743	42,435	2,515.4	42,242	38,539		783	744	703	0.5	9.6
55 27300	Franklin city.	Milwaukee.	34.6	335	33,263	960.5	29,494	21,855		999	1,075	1,151	12.8	35.0
55 31000	Green Bay city.	Brown	43.9	235	101,203	2,306.9	102,809	96,831		248	228	209	−1.6	6.2
55 31175	Greenfield city	Milwaukee.	11.6	938	35,753	3,095.5	35,476	33,343		943	898	823	0.8	6.4
55 37825	Janesville city	Rock	27.5	450	61,962	2,249.9	60,242	53,277		500	475	477	2.9	13.1
55 39225	Kenosha city	Kenosha.	23.8	540	95,240	4,000.0	90,832	81,080		273	274	270	4.9	12.0
55 40775	La Crosse city	La Crosse.	20.1	645	50,287	2,496.9	51,965	51,899		661	589	498	−3.2	0.1
55 48000	Madison city	Dane	68.7	125	221,551	3,226.3	209,187	190,867		83	84	83	5.9	9.6
55 48500	Manitowoc city	Manitowoc	16.9	743	33,917	2,010.5	34,152	32,817		986	929	843	−0.7	4.1
55 51000	Menomonee Falls village	Waukesha.	33.3	356	34,125	1,025.4	32,647	26,840		982	976	1,021	4.5	21.6
55 53000	Milwaukee city	Milwaukee, Washington, Waukesha	96.1	75	578,887	6,026.3	596,988	628,568		22	19	18	−3.0	−5.0
55 56375	New Berlin city	Waukesha.	36.8	303	38,547	1,046.3	38,217	33,504		865	834	817	0.9	14.1
55 58800	Oak Creek city	Milwaukee.	28.6	429	32,312	1,129.0	28,456	19,206		1,026	1,107	1,180	13.6	48.2
55 60500	Oshkosh city	Winnebago	23.6	547	63,485	2,686.6	63,364	57,012		480	445	433	0.2	11.1
55 66000	Racine city	Racine	15.5	793	79,392	5,108.9	81,855	84,398		367	325	260	−3.0	−3.0
55 72975	Sheboygan city	Sheboygan	13.9	846	48,872	3,513.4	50,868	49,795		684	604	527	−3.9	2.2
55 78650	Superior city	Douglas	36.9	302	26,779	724.9	27,368	27,135		1,207	1,156	1,013	−2.2	0.9
55 84250	Waukesha city	Waukesha.	21.6	597	67,658	3,132.3	65,050	57,491		448	434	427	4.0	13.1
55 84475	Wausau city	Marathon	16.5	757	37,292	2,261.5	38,614	37,405		895	826	728	−3.4	3.2
55 84675	Wauwatosa city	Milwaukee.	13.2	875	45,014	3,399.8	47,282	49,359		750	661	532	−4.8	−4.2
55 85300	West Allis city	Milwaukee.	11.4	945	58,798	5,180.4	61,254	63,198		543	466	376	−4.0	−3.1
55 85350	West Bend city	Washington	12.7	891	29,549	2,328.5	28,299	24,818		1,118	1,112	1,086	4.4	14.0
56 00000	WYOMING.		97,100.4	(X)	509,294	5.2	493,782	453,589		(X)	(X)	(X)	3.1	8.9
56 13150	Casper city	Natrona	24.0	535	51,738	2,160.3	49,737	46,734		643	617	560	4.0	6.4
56 13900	Cheyenne city	Laramie	21.1	617	55,731	2,640.0	53,192	50,215		587	569	521	4.8	5.9
56 45050	Laramie city	Albany	11.1	955	26,050	2,338.4	27,171	26,880		1,235	1,165	1,018	−4.1	1.1

NA Not available.   X Not applicable.   Z Less than .05 percent.

[1]Federal Information Processing Standards (FIPS) codes for states and places defined as of January 2000.

[2]County refers to the county (or counties) in which the city is located. IC = independent city, a county equivalent. If a city is located in more than one county, counties are listed in alphabetical order.

[3]Based on 1,257 places (1,255 incorporated places, 1 CDP in Hawaii, and 1 CDP in Virginia). When places share the same rank, the next lower rank is omitted.

[4]Persons per square mile were calculated on the basis of land area data from the 2000 census.

[5]The April 1, 2000, Population Estimates Base reflects modifications to the Census 2000 population as documented in the Count Question Resolution program, updates from the Boundary and Annexation Survey, and geographic program revisions.

[6]The April 1, 1990, Population Estimates Base reflects governmental unit boundaries legally effective as of January 1, 2000, including any post-1990 corrections and other changes due to annexations, new incorporations, or mergers.

[7]Based on 1,267 places (1,265 incorporated places, 1 CDP in Hawaii, and 1 CDP in Virginia). When places share the same rank, the next lower rank is omitted.

[8]Based on 1,229 places (1,227 incorporated places, 1 CDP in Hawaii, and 1 CDP in Virginia). When places share the same rank, the next lower rank is omitted.

[9]Houma city, LA, was left out of the evaluation estimates universe for 1990 because its government merged with Terrebonne Parish.

Survey, Census, or Data Collection Method: Based on the Census of Population and Housing; for information, see Appendix B, Limitations of the Data and Methodology, and also <http://www.census.gov/main/www/cen2000.html> and <http://www.census.gov/popest/topics/methodology/>.

Sources: Land area—U.S. Census Bureau, 2000 Census of Population and Housing, Summary Population and Housing Characteristics, Series PHC-1, using American FactFinder, accessed August 21, 2006 (related Internet site <http://factfinder.census.gov>).   Population, 2005 and 2000—U.S. Census Bureau, "Subcounty Population Estimates, April 1, 2000 to July 1, 2005 (SUB-EST2005)," released June 21, 2006 (related Internet site <http://www.census.gov/popest/cities/>).   Population, 1990—U.S. Census Bureau, "Population Estimates for States, Counties, Places and Minor Civil Divisions: Annual Time Series, April 1, 1990 Census to July 1, 2000 Estimate (SU-2000-10)," released November 1, 2005 (related Internet site <http://www.census.gov/popest/eval-estimates/subcounty/subcounty-2000c4.html>).

Table C-2. Cities — Crime

[Includes states and 1,265 incorporated places of 25,000 or more population as of April 1, 2000, in all states except Hawaii, which has no incorporated places recognized by the U.S. Census Bureau. Two census designated places (CDPs) are also included (Honolulu CDP in Hawaii and Arlington CDP in Virginia). For more information on these areas, see Appendix C, Geographic Information]

City	Number											Rate per 100,000 population[1]			
	Violent						Property					Violent		Property	
	2005						2005								
	Total	Murder and non-negligent man-slaughter	Forcible rape	Robbery	Aggra-vated assault	2000	Total	Burglary	Larceny-theft	Motor vehicle theft	2000	2005	2000	2005	2000
ALABAMA	19,678	374	1,564	6,447	11,293	21,620	177,393	43,473	120,780	13,140	180,539	432	486	3,892	4,060
Auburn city	154	1	18	52	83	125	2,172	464	1,639	69	1,924	317	288	4,465	4,438
Bessemer city	555	3	24	234	294	447	3,531	903	2,336	292	3,483	1,920	1,433	12,217	11,168
Birmingham city	3,449	104	241	1,429	1,675	2,947	18,923	4,933	11,962	2,028	17,802	1,470	1,161	8,067	7,012
Decatur city	200	1	12	62	125	(NA)	3,994	742	3,035	217	(NA)	365	(NA)	7,280	(NA)
Dothan city	333	8	57	156	112	310	3,532	760	2,617	155	2,834	540	522	5,728	4,770
Florence city	223	5	23	63	132	137	1,763	410	1,297	56	1,674	611	345	4,833	4,215
Gadsden city	315	6	46	146	117	(NA)	3,120	663	2,243	214	(NA)	832	(NA)	8,239	(NA)
Homewood city	(NA)	(NA)	(NA)	(NA)	(NA)	104	(NA)	(NA)	(NA)	(NA)	1,703	(NA)	462	(NA)	7,570
Hoover city	(NA)	(NA)	(NA)	(NA)	(NA)	111	(NA)	(NA)	(NA)	(NA)	1,906	(NA)	178	(NA)	3,050
Huntsville city	1,220	22	88	500	610	1,244	11,513	2,446	7,979	1,088	10,995	739	687	6,971	6,073
Madison city	(NA)	(NA)	(NA)	(NA)	(NA)	59	(NA)	(NA)	(NA)	(NA)	812	(NA)	214	(NA)	2,943
Mobile city	1,165	35	74	597	459	1,496	14,349	3,832	9,396	1,121	16,118	466	613	5,744	6,606
Montgomery city	1,641	29	109	847	656	1,563	12,997	3,528	8,449	1,020	14,698	812	785	6,428	7,380
Phenix City city	(NA)	(NA)	(NA)	(NA)	(NA)	140	(NA)	(NA)	(NA)	(NA)	1,013	(NA)	499	(NA)	3,613
Prattville city	87	–	9	22	56	158	1,276	226	978	72	1,356	314	574	4,612	4,928
Prichard city	103	8	7	37	51	503	737	193	407	137	2,934	371	1,550	2,652	9,043
Tuscaloosa city	504	7	39	200	258	903	5,033	1,191	3,582	260	10,307	625	1,042	6,239	11,891
Vestavia Hills city	31	–	4	11	16	14	267	93	151	23	338	99	62	856	1,496
ALASKA	4,194	32	538	537	3,087	3,554	23,975	4,131	17,249	2,595	23,087	632	567	3,613	3,683
Anchorage municipality	2,031	16	224	384	1,407	1,524	11,365	1,783	8,248	1,334	11,342	736	584	4,116	4,347
Fairbanks city	306	2	47	65	192	206	1,587	227	1,155	205	1,474	993	621	5,150	4,445
Juneau city and borough	135	–	30	14	91	(NA)	1,296	125	1,124	47	(NA)	428	(NA)	4,113	(NA)
ARIZONA	30,478	445	2,006	8,579	19,448	27,281	287,345	56,328	176,112	54,905	271,811	513	532	4,838	5,298
Apache Junction city	114	1	14	6	93	81	1,605	385	986	234	1,347	330	334	4,639	5,560
Avondale city	(NA)	(NA)	(NA)	(NA)	(NA)	154	(NA)	(NA)	(NA)	(NA)	1,902	(NA)	467	(NA)	5,769
Bullhead City city	172	–	4	30	138	199	2,211	498	1,454	259	1,535	443	641	5,692	4,945
Casa Grande city	266	3	4	53	206	190	3,337	1,208	1,761	368	2,467	825	740	10,346	9,610
Chandler city	826	8	54	200	564	445	8,323	1,439	5,684	1,200	7,856	357	245	3,593	4,328
Flagstaff city	529	1	48	62	418	320	4,277	511	3,560	206	4,524	897	522	7,252	7,382
Gilbert town	215	–	27	35	153	123	4,455	975	3,057	423	3,643	133	117	2,746	3,477
Glendale city	1,409	19	84	393	913	1,308	12,413	3,332	5,980	3,101	13,213	578	605	5,095	6,108
Lake Havasu City city	142	3	17	11	111	67	1,842	315	1,345	182	1,308	258	149	3,348	2,904
Mesa city	2,280	29	194	460	1,597	2,393	24,071	3,560	16,263	4,248	23,132	504	604	5,321	5,841
Oro Valley town	24	–	3	4	17	15	847	134	644	69	458	62	61	2,175	1,867
Peoria city	289	1	38	69	181	265	5,984	1,127	3,710	1,147	4,685	211	262	4,368	4,633
Phoenix city	10,691	220	533	4,237	5,701	9,754	93,328	16,255	52,537	24,536	87,744	729	750	6,365	6,745
Prescott city	143	–	12	22	109	(NA)	1,878	386	1,365	127	(NA)	355	(NA)	4,665	(NA)
Scottsdale city	465	4	51	125	285	571	7,733	1,869	4,703	1,161	8,732	203	266	3,372	4,067
Sierra Vista city	123	4	11	33	75	96	1,482	240	1,116	126	1,556	291	232	3,511	3,767
Surprise city	84	1	12	15	56	90	1,863	290	1,332	241	803	134	464	2,969	4,139
Tempe city	1,060	4	72	326	658	978	12,400	1,835	8,260	2,305	14,230	638	543	7,463	7,901
Tucson city	5,048	55	378	1,685	2,930	4,542	31,299	5,130	19,642	6,527	39,983	953	907	5,912	7,981
Yuma city	565	10	30	76	449	(NA)	3,863	749	2,523	591	(NA)	656	(NA)	4,484	(NA)
ARKANSAS	14,659	186	1,193	2,531	10,749	11,904	112,775	30,143	75,348	7,284	98,115	527	445	4,058	3,670
Conway city	135	–	25	41	69	80	2,748	425	2,154	169	2,142	266	180	5,405	4,820
Fayetteville city	313	2	51	33	227	201	2,945	458	2,338	149	2,692	483	330	4,544	4,417
Fort Smith city	865	5	95	117	648	601	5,459	971	4,146	342	6,573	1,047	765	6,606	8,370
Hot Springs city	496	4	26	87	379	361	4,528	894	3,348	286	3,707	1,319	888	12,041	9,123
Jacksonville city	223	1	8	58	156	174	1,961	431	1,427	103	1,383	722	579	6,347	4,602
Jonesboro city	481	2	27	101	351	192	3,719	1,397	2,154	168	2,930	810	349	6,265	5,320
Little Rock city	3,293	41	116	860	2,276	1,887	16,322	3,803	11,409	1,110	15,664	1,772	1,022	8,782	8,487
North Little Rock city	794	4	60	205	525	442	5,638	1,121	3,979	538	5,213	1,322	708	9,389	8,355
Pine Bluff city	725	16	41	209	459	1,162	4,820	1,681	2,727	412	5,139	1,344	2,122	8,937	9,387
Rogers city	95	1	36	24	34	79	2,633	257	2,278	98	1,371	210	193	5,810	3,344
Springdale city	198	–	57	15	126	106	2,398	267	1,984	147	1,518	350	239	4,243	3,422
Texarkana city	455	1	6	45	403	216	1,732	357	1,264	111	1,747	1,528	858	5,816	6,943
West Memphis city	523	11	32	131	349	322	2,251	1,043	1,038	170	1,263	1,842	1,143	7,929	4,482
CALIFORNIA	190,178	2,503	9,392	63,622	114,661	210,531	1,200,531	250,521	692,467	257,543	1,056,183	526	622	3,323	3,118
Alameda city	232	–	11	88	133	302	1,959	367	1,285	307	2,533	324	391	2,736	3,281
Alhambra city	321	1	12	154	154	253	2,607	575	1,472	560	1,867	362	292	2,943	2,152
Aliso Viejo city	32	2	3	8	19	(NA)	553	115	394	44	(NA)	77	(NA)	1,325	(NA)
Anaheim city	1,616	10	81	554	971	1,413	9,512	1,929	5,537	2,046	8,496	481	460	2,831	2,765
Antioch city	553	10	28	232	283	526	2,920	733	1,269	918	2,280	544	612	2,874	2,655
Apple Valley town	253	4	20	43	186	186	2,224	603	1,227	394	1,725	401	313	3,527	2,907
Arcadia city	136	2	7	61	66	139	1,849	433	1,254	162	1,361	241	266	3,280	2,600
Atascadero city	113	–	12	10	91	134	607	118	431	58	637	413	528	2,220	2,510
Azusa city	198	–	15	47	136	145	1,297	269	738	290	1,068	415	333	2,719	2,452
Bakersfield city	1,706	32	45	530	1,099	716	16,438	3,746	10,034	2,658	9,563	597	315	5,751	4,209

See footnotes at end of table.

Table C-2. Cities — **Crime**—Con.

[Includes states and 1,265 incorporated places of 25,000 or more population as of April 1, 2000, in all states except Hawaii, which has no incorporated places recognized by the U.S. Census Bureau. Two census designated places (CDPs) are also included (Honolulu CDP in Hawaii and Arlington CDP in Virginia). For more information on these areas, see Appendix C, Geographic Information]

	Number											Rate per 100,000 population[1]			
	Violent						Property					Violent		Property	
	2005						2005								
City	Total	Murder and non-negligent man-slaughter	Forcible rape	Robbery	Aggra-vated assault	2000	Total	Burglary	Larceny-theft	Motor vehicle theft	2000	2005	2000	2005	2000
CALIFORNIA—Con.															
Baldwin Park city	353	5	14	100	234	302	2,103	439	1,036	628	1,423	445	406	2,648	1,913
Bell city	166	5	7	65	89	259	458	132	133	193	632	436	717	1,204	1,750
Bellflower city	537	9	14	247	267	436	2,500	477	1,170	853	2,046	712	664	3,313	3,117
Bell Gardens city	284	5	25	73	181	377	944	251	316	377	838	622	825	2,067	1,834
Belmont city	10	–	1	9	–	81	636	94	478	64	399	41	305	2,584	1,504
Benicia city	53	–	3	14	36	51	550	160	303	87	487	196	183	2,037	1,750
Berkeley city	570	3	18	354	195	754	7,976	1,229	5,503	1,244	6,934	558	681	7,805	6,264
Beverly Hills city	134	1	10	58	65	123	1,052	314	700	38	1,407	379	369	2,978	4,216
Brea city	87	1	2	40	44	156	1,622	277	1,179	166	1,298	224	423	4,183	3,521
Buena Park city	306	2	14	124	166	286	1,926	449	1,042	435	1,742	383	376	2,411	2,291
Burbank city	246	3	13	67	163	297	2,771	586	1,690	495	2,875	235	293	2,644	2,841
Burlingame city	68	–	3	28	37	64	939	145	697	97	850	246	223	3,402	2,966
Calexico city	138	–	4	25	109	65	1,313	396	504	413	1,109	399	228	3,800	3,884
Camarillo city	94	1	15	30	48	84	1,046	259	710	77	1,081	153	135	1,707	1,736
Campbell city	71	–	5	13	53	96	1,217	225	872	120	928	191	246	3,266	2,376
Carlsbad city	256	2	11	79	164	179	2,411	517	1,648	246	1,876	286	227	2,690	2,378
Carson city	646	7	19	221	399	834	2,402	543	1,270	589	2,564	685	916	2,546	2,816
Cathedral City city	252	3	10	44	195	266	2,079	559	1,023	497	1,524	493	665	4,069	3,807
Ceres city	170	2	8	38	122	179	2,229	280	1,294	655	2,086	438	525	5,745	6,120
Cerritos city	175	1	5	97	72	203	2,020	453	1,287	280	2,151	329	366	3,793	3,874
Chico city	253	3	32	79	139	192	2,671	719	1,462	490	1,878	358	362	3,780	3,540
Chino city	210	2	9	75	124	259	2,539	521	1,576	442	1,784	274	383	3,317	2,640
Chino Hills city	100	3	8	18	71	79	1,092	259	705	128	937	131	131	1,435	1,552
Chula Vista city	927	5	66	338	518	846	7,489	1,235	3,758	2,496	6,202	449	502	3,631	3,680
Citrus Heights city	(NA)	(NA)	(NA)	(NA)	(NA)	(NA)	(NA)	(NA)	(NA)	(NA)	(NA)	(NA)	(NA)	(NA)	(NA)
Claremont city	60	3	2	30	25	64	1,116	310	731	75	963	170	180	3,159	2,712
Clovis city	151	4	21	47	79	96	3,286	642	2,222	422	2,891	182	143	3,963	4,303
Colton city	267	5	17	105	140	207	1,941	472	983	486	1,660	516	456	3,753	3,657
Compton city	1,731	65	40	474	1,152	1,525	2,615	638	971	1,006	3,413	1,787	1,607	2,699	3,596
Concord city	508	1	14	197	296	472	6,248	1,114	3,972	1,162	4,477	406	392	4,992	3,716
Corona city	321	4	33	140	144	326	4,448	926	2,587	935	3,286	219	267	3,039	2,689
Costa Mesa city	306	3	30	119	154	275	3,843	596	2,692	555	3,187	275	259	3,458	3,003
Covina city	213	–	9	85	119	270	2,136	468	1,359	309	1,918	440	590	4,412	4,189
Culver City city	183	1	9	130	43	164	1,282	246	898	138	1,420	456	400	3,192	3,462
Cupertino city	56	–	–	10	46	104	933	250	632	51	1,060	108	222	1,803	2,263
Cypress city	67	1	5	28	33	108	1,003	174	707	122	904	140	219	2,093	1,830
Daly City city	286	2	20	122	142	328	2,158	251	1,439	468	1,800	282	324	2,131	1,775
Dana Point city	61	–	7	9	45	69	529	120	371	38	638	168	195	1,459	1,805
Danville town	41	–	1	9	31	46	621	119	477	25	529	97	109	1,462	1,259
Davis city	232	–	26	45	161	254	1,909	483	1,239	187	1,554	362	441	2,976	2,699
Delano city	209	5	5	48	151	95	2,121	669	845	607	1,520	472	265	4,790	4,239
Diamond Bar city	107	2	3	38	64	118	899	282	463	154	775	182	210	1,531	1,379
Downey city	448	7	30	250	161	340	3,532	579	1,851	1,102	2,739	403	352	3,181	2,837
Dublin city	79	–	1	15	63	93	807	170	499	138	548	212	294	2,167	1,734
East Palo Alto city	429	15	21	108	285	287	1,125	387	432	306	1,002	1,330	1,128	3,488	3,937
El Cajon city	518	2	40	171	305	626	4,045	769	2,140	1,136	3,191	548	648	4,275	3,302
El Centro city	348	–	18	43	287	358	2,115	758	1,097	260	1,737	901	888	5,479	4,308
Elk Grove city	(NA)	(NA)	(NA)	(NA)	(NA)	(NA)	(NA)	(NA)	(NA)	(NA)	(NA)	(NA)	(NA)	(NA)	(NA)
El Monte city	711	4	21	241	445	1,070	3,487	702	1,650	1,135	2,598	578	928	2,836	2,252
Encinitas city	171	3	11	45	112	174	1,234	324	724	186	1,192	283	278	2,041	1,904
Escondido city	692	2	31	186	473	669	4,911	801	3,031	1,079	4,430	507	534	3,601	3,537
Eureka city	170	1	25	63	81	146	1,851	503	1,000	348	2,016	655	569	7,126	7,864
Fairfield city	585	9	38	218	320	541	4,460	748	2,876	836	3,746	559	574	4,262	3,973
Folsom city	89	–	11	18	60	64	1,716	305	1,238	173	1,147	138	131	2,665	2,341
Fontana city	734	10	50	232	442	899	3,681	782	1,496	1,403	3,168	459	766	2,304	2,698
Foster City city	29	–	–	7	22	26	421	80	308	33	464	100	84	1,450	1,495
Fountain Valley city	72	1	6	30	35	146	1,383	303	884	196	1,500	127	249	2,438	2,563
Fremont city	521	1	40	188	292	387	4,803	1,009	3,035	759	4,922	256	182	2,358	2,309
Fresno city	3,897	49	149	1,275	2,424	3,843	25,546	4,170	16,088	5,288	29,025	846	931	5,544	7,028
Fullerton city	390	–	37	149	204	312	4,584	805	3,152	627	3,786	290	248	3,413	3,006
Gardena city	496	3	16	295	182	661	1,594	453	715	426	2,014	825	1,168	2,651	3,559
Garden Grove city	745	6	22	229	488	726	4,505	803	2,591	1,111	4,414	442	463	2,674	2,813
Gilroy city	203	–	13	67	123	304	1,735	246	1,309	180	1,372	455	773	3,886	3,490
Glendale city	350	19	14	136	181	726	3,790	723	2,453	614	4,183	173	380	1,870	2,190
Glendora city	56	–	5	24	27	86	1,265	183	954	128	907	109	167	2,469	1,762
Goleta city	43	–	7	12	24	(NA)	486	141	325	20	(NA)	152	(NA)	1,713	(NA)
Hanford city	185	–	17	51	117	152	1,855	224	1,407	224	1,639	393	393	3,936	4,241
Hawthorne city	520	10	18	225	267	1,272	2,196	785	841	570	2,467	599	1,678	2,528	3,254
Hayward city	641	9	37	301	294	774	5,473	1,147	2,338	1,988	4,893	452	578	3,862	3,654
Hemet city	381	3	19	141	218	324	3,419	910	1,943	566	2,444	569	522	5,103	3,940

See footnotes at end of table.

Table C-2. Cities — **Crime**—Con.

[Includes states and 1,265 incorporated places of 25,000 or more population as of April 1, 2000, in all states except Hawaii, which has no incorporated places recognized by the U.S. Census Bureau. Two census designated places (CDPs) are also included (Honolulu CDP in Hawaii and Arlington CDP in Virginia). For more information on these areas, see Appendix C, Geographic Information]

City	Number											Rate per 100,000 population[1]			
	Violent						Property					Violent		Property	
	2005						2005								
	Total	Murder and non-negligent man-slaughter	Forcible rape	Robbery	Aggra-vated assault	2000	Total	Burglary	Larceny-theft	Motor vehicle theft	2000	2005	2000	2005	2000
CALIFORNIA—Con.															
Hesperia city	223	4	14	81	124	163	2,032	484	945	603	1,690	302	249	2,751	2,585
Highland city	204	7	10	77	110	200	1,403	316	705	382	1,311	403	453	2,774	2,968
Hollister city	155	–	8	29	118	296	1,033	214	659	160	712	424	923	2,825	2,221
Huntington Beach city	466	1	32	92	341	378	4,103	789	2,783	531	4,148	237	185	2,087	2,033
Huntington Park city	577	2	18	357	200	614	2,671	287	1,336	1,048	2,395	910	1,018	4,213	3,972
Imperial Beach city	132	–	3	41	88	156	790	188	335	267	720	491	529	2,938	2,440
Indio city	299	6	28	96	169	349	2,924	802	1,479	643	1,885	469	730	4,587	3,944
Inglewood city	1,057	26	42	555	434	1,376	3,091	822	1,347	922	3,292	911	1,185	2,663	2,836
Irvine city	151	2	17	42	90	221	3,225	709	2,211	305	2,987	84	152	1,797	2,048
Laguna Hills city	53	–	4	16	33	65	703	160	486	57	762	163	178	2,157	2,091
Laguna Niguel city	62	2	2	15	43	75	780	143	600	37	811	95	134	1,193	1,454
La Habra city	190	4	6	77	103	137	1,614	284	1,014	316	1,338	316	244	2,681	2,383
Lake Elsinore city	172	4	11	32	125	274	1,511	319	883	309	1,086	462	926	4,056	3,672
Lake Forest city	121	2	8	33	78	130	971	198	675	98	1,066	156	220	1,253	1,804
Lakewood city	371	–	13	193	165	366	2,788	418	1,880	490	2,435	455	465	3,416	3,091
La Mesa city	201	2	10	107	82	218	2,229	328	1,345	556	1,868	371	380	4,112	3,255
La Mirada city	125	1	3	41	80	158	1,258	307	741	210	869	250	338	2,518	1,862
Lancaster city	1,186	16	54	347	769	1,176	4,707	1,260	2,436	1,011	3,147	914	928	3,627	2,484
La Puente city	237	4	8	57	168	308	827	165	404	258	819	560	771	1,953	2,049
La Verne city	67	–	7	23	37	94	889	159	658	72	647	201	280	2,664	1,927
Lawndale city	208	1	12	80	115	315	622	154	316	152	683	637	1,046	1,905	2,267
Livermore city	141	1	27	27	86	132	1,659	422	1,006	231	1,606	180	171	2,113	2,081
Lodi city	260	1	17	74	168	449	2,974	538	1,900	536	2,387	417	771	4,768	4,098
Lompoc city	228	1	14	40	173	143	1,191	155	948	88	1,231	554	339	2,892	2,917
Long Beach city	3,399	42	104	1,403	1,850	3,216	13,506	2,955	6,808	3,743	14,451	709	723	2,815	3,251
Los Altos city	10	–	2	4	4	23	325	130	181	14	306	37	81	1,196	1,079
Los Angeles city	31,767	489	1,105	13,797	16,376	50,241	117,285	22,592	65,972	28,721	130,297	821	1,353	3,030	3,509
Los Banos city	227	–	13	23	191	85	1,092	268	699	125	551	708	384	3,408	2,492
Los Gatos town	37	–	5	15	17	55	580	145	393	42	630	132	185	2,063	2,123
Lynwood city	676	21	23	258	374	923	1,910	295	578	1,037	1,759	937	1,413	2,649	2,692
Madera city	399	4	22	88	285	607	1,808	367	1,085	356	1,837	792	1,589	3,589	4,809
Manhattan Beach city	73	1	5	32	35	70	818	216	535	67	1,135	200	196	2,237	3,184
Manteca city	283	2	15	71	195	204	3,362	553	2,147	662	1,745	458	402	5,439	3,440
Martinez city	115	–	9	28	78	49	1,424	235	979	210	982	315	131	3,896	2,634
Maywood city	158	4	5	70	79	124	447	77	138	232	502	545	423	1,541	1,712
Menlo Park city	88	–	9	43	36	63	747	159	497	91	726	294	201	2,494	2,315
Merced city	572	10	24	167	371	418	4,189	697	2,957	535	3,672	784	676	5,741	5,934
Milpitas city	195	2	17	36	140	248	2,168	315	1,575	278	1,799	309	395	3,435	2,867
Mission Viejo city	110	2	3	36	69	134	1,259	225	953	81	1,299	114	134	1,299	1,296
Modesto city	1,316	8	65	388	855	967	13,046	1,742	8,290	3,014	9,696	632	503	6,268	5,040
Monrovia city	118	–	11	54	53	146	1,167	149	851	167	1,028	307	377	3,037	2,656
Montclair city	222	5	12	89	116	211	2,047	253	1,339	455	1,668	626	673	5,770	5,322
Montebello city	282	5	18	125	134	333	2,143	300	1,094	749	1,871	440	534	3,342	3,002
Monterey city	172	–	16	31	125	195	1,295	245	977	73	1,124	576	600	4,336	3,458
Monterey Park city	149	2	4	89	54	181	1,395	274	707	414	1,157	237	281	2,221	1,795
Moorpark city	45	2	2	9	32	53	357	91	238	28	276	125	170	988	887
Moreno Valley city	757	11	57	344	345	1,132	6,260	1,522	3,274	1,464	5,170	452	744	3,740	3,398
Morgan Hill city	60	1	11	16	32	57	1,058	244	728	86	1,002	171	175	3,013	3,073
Mountain View city	302	1	5	63	233	361	2,176	253	1,660	263	1,954	435	494	3,132	2,675
Murrieta city	122	1	9	36	76	69	1,815	489	1,058	268	748	163	213	2,420	2,307
Napa city	384	–	19	34	331	207	2,080	359	1,553	168	1,535	505	299	2,738	2,215
National City city	456	4	16	182	254	432	2,726	376	1,409	941	2,236	830	765	4,962	3,958
Newark city	175	2	17	71	85	130	1,977	331	1,321	325	1,620	409	292	4,620	3,634
Newport Beach city	122	3	12	26	81	104	2,496	589	1,715	192	2,245	152	137	3,101	2,968
Norwalk city	473	11	17	189	256	651	2,831	558	1,399	874	2,439	440	648	2,636	2,427
Novato city	88	1	13	22	52	155	1,233	334	754	145	1,186	178	310	2,488	2,370
Oakland city	5,692	93	306	2,672	2,621	5,038	23,027	5,783	8,227	9,017	20,022	1,421	1,350	5,748	5,365
Oakley city	72	–	3	17	52	(NA)	686	117	441	128	(NA)	267	(NA)	2,541	(NA)
Oceanside city	983	7	78	264	634	851	5,657	1,065	3,846	746	5,002	583	532	3,356	3,127
Ontario city	866	12	56	294	504	1,126	6,744	991	3,714	2,039	6,527	506	741	3,940	4,296
Orange city	225	2	2	100	121	334	3,419	537	2,301	581	3,015	167	260	2,538	2,347
Oxnard city	830	19	47	386	378	864	4,384	941	2,681	762	4,797	449	541	2,372	3,002
Pacifica city	67	–	7	12	48	109	794	122	567	105	591	179	262	2,121	1,420
Palmdale city	1,042	15	48	318	661	981	4,115	967	2,384	764	3,411	789	863	3,117	3,000
Palm Desert city	145	2	6	38	99	166	2,662	714	1,691	257	1,671	309	435	5,673	4,378
Palm Springs city	347	4	23	112	208	458	3,102	872	1,659	571	2,780	742	1,013	6,636	6,152
Palo Alto city	91	1	5	46	39	93	2,043	371	1,548	124	1,812	159	155	3,569	3,013
Paradise town	33	–	6	7	20	109	796	249	463	84	872	123	413	2,965	3,306
Paramount city	452	10	4	221	217	492	2,082	358	956	768	2,100	789	929	3,635	3,965
Pasadena city	803	6	23	285	489	732	4,389	788	3,041	560	4,905	554	528	3,026	3,537

See footnotes at end of table.

Table C-2. Cities — **Crime**—Con.

[Includes states and 1,265 incorporated places of 25,000 or more population as of April 1, 2000, in all states except Hawaii, which has no incorporated places recognized by the U.S. Census Bureau. Two census designated places (CDPs) are also included (Honolulu CDP in Hawaii and Arlington CDP in Virginia). For more information on these areas, see Appendix C, Geographic Information]

City	Number — Violent 2005 Total	Murder and non-negligent man-slaughter	Forcible rape	Robbery	Aggra-vated assault	Violent 2000	Property 2005 Total	Burglary	Larceny-theft	Motor vehicle theft	Property 2000	Rate Violent 2005	Rate Violent 2000	Rate Property 2005	Rate Property 2000
CALIFORNIA—Con.															
Perris city	229	4	12	80	133	391	2,104	368	1,137	599	1,561	497	1,128	4,564	4,503
Petaluma city	215	–	34	24	157	83	1,300	128	1,036	136	1,343	386	154	2,333	2,489
Pico Rivera city	373	15	17	117	224	405	1,535	264	773	498	1,158	568	644	2,339	1,843
Pittsburg city	248	5	7	114	122	256	2,604	458	1,516	630	2,023	394	465	4,132	3,676
Placentia city	124	3	8	30	83	131	1,043	231	668	144	794	247	267	2,074	1,619
Pleasant Hill city	127	1	10	47	69	140	1,874	334	1,304	236	1,306	376	407	5,552	3,793
Pleasanton city	96	–	10	24	62	83	1,555	260	1,152	143	1,426	145	122	2,342	2,099
Pomona city	1,235	21	44	385	785	1,375	5,308	997	2,775	1,536	4,487	789	978	3,392	3,190
Porterville city	257	2	18	48	189	174	2,287	506	1,351	430	1,587	580	468	5,162	4,264
Poway city	95	1	11	20	63	101	815	172	551	92	743	193	197	1,653	1,452
Rancho Cordova city	(NA)	(NA)	(NA)	(NA)	(NA)	(NA)	(NA)	(NA)	(NA)	(NA)	(NA)	(NA)	(NA)	(NA)	(NA)
Rancho Cucamonga city	372	2	35	134	201	257	4,393	768	2,921	704	3,252	232	203	2,739	2,572
Rancho Palos Verdes city	45	2	3	4	36	75	387	116	247	24	413	106	169	909	932
Rancho Santa Margarita city	32	–	–	7	25	(NA)	453	80	342	31	(NA)	64	(NA)	900	(NA)
Redding city	550	2	80	75	393	380	4,102	943	2,665	494	2,660	617	466	4,601	3,264
Redlands city	310	1	19	92	198	344	2,799	553	1,799	447	1,946	442	493	3,990	2,787
Redondo Beach city	178	–	9	68	101	206	1,599	319	1,080	200	1,865	265	311	2,382	2,816
Redwood City city	388	3	22	103	260	197	2,553	354	1,831	368	1,896	526	259	3,458	2,495
Rialto city	804	11	33	214	546	654	3,490	715	1,602	1,173	2,812	801	749	3,479	3,221
Richmond city	1,174	40	35	526	573	1,200	5,808	1,062	2,350	2,396	(NA)	1,140	1,248	5,639	(NA)
Riverside city	1,954	10	113	675	1,156	2,006	13,425	2,498	8,157	2,770	10,222	673	739	4,625	3,764
Rocklin city	70	–	6	15	49	33	1,304	254	900	150	679	143	94	2,663	1,942
Rohnert Park city	277	–	12	21	244	74	1,045	156	811	78	1,357	656	176	2,474	3,232
Rosemead city	195	3	8	75	109	374	1,540	403	662	475	1,230	350	680	2,767	2,236
Roseville city	363	–	28	87	248	234	4,750	852	3,188	710	2,848	348	297	4,554	3,617
Sacramento city	5,265	52	170	2,018	3,025	3,117	26,083	5,841	13,320	6,922	24,221	1,151	750	5,703	5,825
Salinas city	1,030	7	43	335	645	1,262	6,778	935	4,339	1,504	5,195	691	999	4,544	4,113
San Bernardino city	2,510	58	72	912	1,468	2,104	11,226	2,525	5,527	3,174	9,766	1,257	1,090	5,621	5,058
San Bruno city	141	1	8	33	99	81	947	127	654	166	903	353	197	2,372	2,191
San Buenaventura (Ventura) city	297	1	19	107	170	(NA)	3,911	815	2,695	401	(NA)	284	(NA)	3,733	(NA)
San Carlos city	31	–	3	10	18	43	580	105	419	56	490	114	151	2,141	1,721
San Clemente city	80	1	5	15	59	102	853	200	579	74	723	133	210	1,423	1,488
San Diego city	6,603	51	376	1,862	4,314	7,160	46,213	7,462	24,613	14,138	39,199	519	566	3,633	3,096
San Dimas city	74	1	3	23	47	135	880	202	552	126	607	204	376	2,424	1,691
San Francisco city	5,985	96	172	3,078	2,639	6,499	34,269	6,208	19,887	8,174	35,675	799	852	4,574	4,675
San Gabriel city	202	4	9	99	90	180	1,089	327	584	178	757	486	466	2,622	1,961
San Jose city	3,492	26	263	884	2,319	4,928	22,930	4,049	13,374	5,507	17,880	384	555	2,518	2,012
San Juan Capistrano city	59	–	2	21	36	54	465	105	303	57	513	168	166	1,324	1,581
San Leandro city	465	4	23	237	201	500	4,069	701	2,328	1,040	3,448	583	652	5,105	4,494
San Luis Obispo city	170	2	23	35	110	134	1,793	361	1,335	97	1,948	384	306	4,045	4,444
San Marcos city	237	–	15	57	165	206	1,630	359	989	282	1,240	344	389	2,369	2,344
San Mateo city	403	4	22	117	260	343	2,780	355	2,205	220	2,151	439	366	3,026	2,293
San Pablo city	269	3	5	160	101	466	1,831	316	874	641	1,775	861	1,691	5,860	6,442
San Rafael city	172	2	22	65	83	252	2,052	427	1,247	378	1,583	308	483	3,669	3,035
San Ramon city	66	1	5	14	46	87	972	146	733	93	911	144	185	2,117	1,941
Santa Ana city	1,845	17	74	644	1,110	1,829	10,292	1,194	5,515	3,583	8,623	535	579	2,983	2,728
Santa Barbara city	560	–	31	76	453	456	2,944	680	2,060	204	2,535	637	517	3,347	2,875
Santa Clara city	190	5	18	49	118	292	3,420	553	2,470	397	2,829	181	286	3,267	2,767
Santa Clarita city	336	3	17	106	210	335	3,552	838	2,200	514	2,346	203	245	2,141	1,715
Santa Cruz city	503	2	49	96	356	544	3,137	573	2,316	248	2,420	922	995	5,748	4,425
Santa Maria city	601	3	36	92	470	310	2,354	383	1,342	629	2,186	713	440	2,792	3,100
Santa Monica city	551	4	21	241	285	642	3,496	788	2,286	422	4,046	623	690	3,954	4,347
Santa Paula city	100	–	8	29	63	105	641	140	407	94	639	346	383	2,216	2,329
Santa Rosa city	1,021	2	61	168	790	546	4,900	803	3,508	589	4,743	660	390	3,168	3,390
Santee city	163	1	16	30	116	168	1,316	281	800	235	1,146	308	284	2,486	1,936
Saratoga city	21	1	3	2	15	42	377	115	249	13	298	70	138	1,264	979
Seaside city	171	–	10	42	119	255	738	129	545	64	650	498	878	2,148	2,239
Simi Valley city	172	–	17	47	108	134	2,315	583	1,515	217	1,549	144	115	1,934	1,327
South Gate city	527	6	19	305	197	787	2,897	444	1,164	1,289	2,368	525	866	2,889	2,605
South San Francisco city	175	3	8	46	118	152	1,541	609	640	292	1,563	290	252	2,556	2,590
Stanton city	149	3	6	63	77	147	937	201	526	210	873	390	434	2,454	2,575
Stockton city	4,202	41	109	1,357	2,695	2,972	18,861	3,434	11,487	3,940	13,877	1,491	1,187	6,694	5,542
Suisun City city	127	–	13	39	75	67	576	124	304	148	518	468	241	2,124	1,865
Sunnyvale city	232	3	27	73	129	191	2,661	495	1,794	372	2,447	180	147	2,065	1,881
Temecula city	269	4	16	73	176	206	2,808	684	1,725	399	1,708	326	430	3,398	3,561
Temple City city	76	–	3	31	42	95	557	181	296	80	459	205	288	1,499	1,390
Thousand Oaks city	174	2	13	56	103	183	1,784	379	1,289	116	1,757	138	150	1,417	1,442
Torrance city	320	1	20	211	88	465	3,290	641	2,144	505	3,881	223	327	2,288	2,732
Tracy city	149	–	7	60	82	122	3,301	473	2,366	462	1,832	192	230	4,264	3,450
Tulare city	497	8	17	85	387	381	3,187	904	1,809	474	2,044	1,014	889	6,501	4,769

See footnotes at end of table.

Table C-2. Cities — **Crime**—Con.

[Includes states and 1,265 incorporated places of 25,000 or more population as of April 1, 2000, in all states except Hawaii, which has no incorporated places recognized by the U.S. Census Bureau. Two census designated places (CDPs) are also included (Honolulu CDP in Hawaii and Arlington CDP in Virginia). For more information on these areas, see Appendix C, Geographic Information]

City	Number Violent 2005						Number Property 2005					Rate per 100,000 population[1]			
												Violent		Property	
	Total	Murder and non-negligent man-slaughter	Forcible rape	Robbery	Aggra-vated assault	2000	Total	Burglary	Larceny-theft	Motor vehicle theft	2000	2005	2000	2005	2000
CALIFORNIA—Con.															
Turlock city	411	2	18	97	294	297	3,705	637	2,014	1,054	2,848	623	554	5,621	5,316
Tustin city	228	2	10	60	156	228	1,926	438	1,146	342	1,901	330	348	2,789	2,897
Twentynine Palms city	105	–	11	5	89	64	530	194	270	66	416	347	438	1,750	2,850
Union City city	416	3	15	167	231	342	2,507	603	1,325	579	2,026	599	507	3,613	3,003
Upland city	282	4	21	104	153	306	3,025	466	2,107	452	2,487	381	440	4,087	3,577
Vacaville city	262	2	23	69	168	347	2,518	353	1,899	266	1,909	276	392	2,653	2,157
Vallejo city	(NA)	(NA)	(NA)	(NA)	(NA)	1,297	(NA)	(NA)	(NA)	(NA)	5,773	(NA)	1,111	(NA)	4,947
Victorville city	435	12	30	153	240	331	4,229	865	2,536	828	3,079	522	460	5,074	4,281
Visalia city	1,055	10	39	192	814	777	6,765	1,216	4,347	1,202	4,239	1,001	829	6,421	4,520
Vista city	530	4	21	190	315	352	2,971	771	1,621	579	2,309	575	420	3,223	2,752
Walnut city	45	–	1	21	23	69	492	178	236	78	456	141	214	1,546	1,415
Walnut Creek city	130	1	8	38	83	129	2,919	507	2,142	270	2,117	199	193	4,473	3,168
Watsonville city	237	2	17	81	137	303	2,043	284	1,481	278	1,588	499	806	4,304	4,225
West Covina city	350	6	19	150	175	387	4,050	744	2,398	908	3,951	320	378	3,702	3,862
West Hollywood city	342	2	19	167	154	364	1,647	312	1,073	262	1,608	920	981	4,430	4,335
Westminster city	351	3	14	96	238	329	2,866	561	1,769	536	2,735	388	374	3,169	3,110
West Sacramento city	361	2	23	60	276	401	1,433	563	480	390	1,271	911	1,296	3,618	4,108
Whittier city	307	5	15	125	162	248	2,592	429	1,655	508	2,142	357	303	3,011	2,619
Woodland city	142	1	14	34	93	259	1,794	307	1,182	305	1,049	273	574	3,448	2,326
Yorba Linda city	49	–	2	5	42	136	797	169	553	75	814	76	215	1,244	1,285
Yuba City city	188	3	17	48	120	182	2,304	453	1,604	247	1,862	358	504	4,391	5,159
Yucaipa city	71	3	3	12	53	69	855	208	468	179	796	147	181	1,775	2,087
COLORADO	18,498	173	2,026	3,948	12,351	14,367	188,449	34,746	127,602	26,101	156,937	397	334	4,039	3,649
Arvada city	196	2	23	52	119	115	3,877	524	2,772	581	3,286	188	109	3,728	3,116
Aurora city	1,836	28	223	644	941	1,539	14,718	2,474	9,502	2,742	13,987	621	574	4,974	5,214
Boulder city	216	–	42	34	140	218	3,624	551	2,821	252	3,353	231	225	3,877	3,466
Broomfield city	42	–	9	11	22	55	1,697	124	1,403	170	1,207	97	136	3,902	2,980
Centennial city	217	3	33	38	143	(NA)	2,022	422	1,400	200	(NA)	218	(NA)	2,030	(NA)
Colorado Springs city	1,792	12	251	439	1,090	1,716	19,619	3,676	14,164	1,779	16,968	479	462	5,239	4,569
Denver city	4,492	59	328	1,432	2,673	2,885	33,902	7,360	18,518	8,024	23,417	796	544	6,005	4,418
Englewood city	185	–	27	35	123	(NA)	2,229	431	1,382	416	(NA)	563	(NA)	6,779	(NA)
Fort Collins city	442	2	118	57	265	367	4,434	764	3,239	431	4,509	343	305	3,444	3,749
Grand Junction city	299	–	23	32	244	151	3,360	542	2,583	235	2,877	660	348	7,415	6,637
Greeley city	556	2	48	60	446	270	5,475	1,149	3,878	448	3,892	647	350	6,367	5,043
Lakewood city	671	5	93	187	386	433	8,331	1,259	5,650	1,422	7,025	468	296	5,815	4,803
Littleton city	66	–	6	33	27	(NA)	1,796	306	1,184	306	(NA)	161	(NA)	4,379	(NA)
Longmont city	(NA)	(NA)	(NA)	(NA)	(NA)	(NA)	(NA)	(NA)	(NA)	(NA)	(NA)	(NA)	(NA)	(NA)	(NA)
Loveland city	108	2	21	17	68	106	1,790	271	1,418	101	1,640	184	207	3,055	3,196
Northglenn city	138	–	2	28	108	103	1,959	258	1,390	311	1,558	410	311	5,814	4,702
Pueblo city	686	13	22	162	489	982	6,981	1,525	4,978	478	4,212	653	892	6,645	3,825
Thornton city	368	1	69	61	237	417	4,825	672	3,402	751	4,055	356	507	4,662	4,928
Westminster city	318	2	25	72	219	(NA)	5,109	701	3,453	955	(NA)	299	(NA)	4,810	(NA)
Wheat Ridge city	162	1	17	27	117	140	2,076	308	1,462	306	1,783	509	439	6,519	5,596
CONNECTICUT	9,635	102	702	3,966	4,865	11,058	89,794	15,343	64,033	10,418	99,033	274	325	2,558	2,908
Bridgeport city	1,508	19	65	648	776	1,984	7,118	1,383	4,452	1,283	6,916	1,076	1,395	5,078	4,864
Bristol city	133	2	14	52	65	237	1,588	425	1,059	104	1,494	218	386	2,598	2,434
Danbury city	128	1	22	58	47	133	1,579	223	1,220	136	1,950	163	191	2,014	2,806
Hartford city	1,442	25	46	692	679	1,490	9,513	1,398	6,255	1,860	9,730	1,153	1,119	7,605	7,305
Meriden city	186	1	14	93	78	94	2,298	504	1,617	177	2,070	314	161	3,879	3,539
Middletown city	59	2	1	25	31	48	1,588	195	1,245	148	1,437	125	105	3,361	3,147
Milford city (balance)	57	–	6	20	31	50	1,628	144	1,331	153	1,864	104	96	2,982	3,592
Naugatuck borough	21	–	3	11	7	51	584	73	448	63	629	66	163	1,833	2,011
New Britain city	359	2	10	189	158	364	3,330	782	2,171	377	3,609	500	501	4,636	4,968
New Haven city	(NA)	(NA)	(NA)	(NA)	(NA)	1,696	(NA)	(NA)	(NA)	(NA)	8,030	(NA)	1,338	(NA)	6,333
New London city	178	1	27	63	87	213	936	195	627	114	1,029	675	792	3,550	3,828
Norwalk city	308	7	9	92	200	(NA)	2,578	365	1,889	324	(NA)	364	(NA)	3,049	(NA)
Norwich city	185	–	27	51	107	149	1,048	224	748	76	1,076	504	412	2,854	2,975
Shelton city	15	–	1	7	7	34	448	97	277	74	593	38	86	1,137	1,494
Stamford city	355	1	18	157	179	287	2,390	427	1,740	223	2,778	295	250	1,984	2,416
Torrington city	114	–	3	13	98	122	1,042	213	776	53	914	317	340	2,895	2,547
Waterbury city	434	6	32	214	182	(NA)	6,027	1,198	4,212	617	(NA)	399	(NA)	5,548	(NA)
West Haven city	152	–	4	67	81	74	1,661	251	1,209	201	1,854	286	138	3,123	3,461
DELAWARE	5,332	37	377	1,306	3,612	5,363	26,245	5,811	18,085	2,349	29,727	632	684	3,111	3,794
Dover city	207	2	13	40	152	(2)	1,642	93	1,434	115	2,088	606	(NA)	4,808	6,255
Newark city	160	1	18	48	93	(2)	1,088	197	806	85	1,233	528	(NA)	3,591	4,187
Wilmington city	1,049	12	27	433	577	(2)	3,434	817	2,104	513	5,459	1,419	(NA)	4,644	7,343

See footnotes at end of table.

Table C-2. Cities — **Crime**—Con.

[Includes states and 1,265 incorporated places of 25,000 or more population as of April 1, 2000, in all states except Hawaii, which has no incorporated places recognized by the U.S. Census Bureau. Two census designated places (CDPs) are also included (Honolulu CDP in Hawaii and Arlington CDP in Virginia). For more information on these areas, see Appendix C, Geographic Information]

City	Number Violent 2005 Total	Murder and non-negligent man-slaughter	Forcible rape	Robbery	Aggra-vated assault	Violent 2000	Number Property 2005 Total	Burglary	Larceny-theft	Motor vehicle theft	Property 2000	Rate Violent 2005	Rate Violent 2000	Rate Property 2005	Rate Property 2000
DISTRICT OF COLUMBIA ...	8,032	195	166	3,700	3,971	8,626	26,133	3,577	14,836	7,720	33,000	1,459	1,508	4,747	5,769
Washington city.............	8,032	195	166	3,700	3,971	8,626	26,133	3,577	14,836	7,720	33,000	1,459	1,508	4,747	5,769
FLORIDA	125,957	883	6,592	30,141	88,341	129,777	712,998	164,783	472,912	75,303	780,377	708	812	4,008	4,883
Altamonte Springs city	199	1	14	51	133	141	1,808	283	1,319	206	1,800	477	338	4,335	4,311
Apopka city	369	2	19	105	243	278	1,695	389	1,196	110	1,706	1,125	1,191	5,170	7,306
Aventura city..............	35	–	1	26	8	107	1,611	139	1,416	56	3,050	126	503	5,784	14,332
Boca Raton city.............	241	–	15	53	173	210	2,844	591	2,071	182	3,102	302	272	3,563	4,020
Bonita Springs city..........	(NA)	(NA)	(NA)	(NA)	(NA)	(NA)	(NA)	(NA)	(NA)	(NA)	(NA)	(NA)	(NA)	(NA)	(NA)
Boynton Beach city	497	1	4	139	353	501	3,408	720	2,381	307	4,490	750	861	5,145	7,718
Bradenton city.............	318	3	18	111	186	461	2,832	597	1,944	291	2,937	585	925	5,212	5,891
Cape Coral city.............	361	5	45	74	237	213	3,900	1,026	2,567	307	3,417	276	215	2,980	3,455
Clearwater city	993	9	48	210	726	865	5,077	949	3,695	433	4,929	894	818	4,571	4,663
Coconut Creek city..........	119	–	17	28	74	91	1,151	201	831	119	1,012	238	220	2,302	2,443
Cooper City city............	101	–	2	17	82	48	598	107	467	24	519	335	157	1,986	1,703
Coral Gables city	152	–	4	40	108	233	2,208	471	1,613	124	2,711	350	519	5,086	6,039
Coral Springs city	224	–	9	58	157	306	2,642	424	1,975	243	3,679	171	249	2,013	2,995
Dania Beach city	(NA)	(NA)	(NA)	(NA)	(NA)	(NA)	(NA)	(NA)	(NA)	(NA)	(NA)	(NA)	(NA)	(NA)	(NA)
Davie town................	298	2	19	71	206	288	3,160	556	2,293	311	3,353	353	391	3,742	4,556
Daytona Beach city	1,079	8	65	342	664	1,130	4,827	1,399	2,698	730	5,646	1,638	1,651	7,327	8,250
Deerfield Beach city	593	2	35	144	412	298	2,517	485	1,767	265	1,863	876	550	3,719	3,437
Delray Beach city...........	658	6	26	132	494	593	3,207	595	2,293	319	4,273	1,003	1,036	4,889	7,465
Deltona city	(NA)	(NA)	(NA)	(NA)	(NA)	87	(NA)	(NA)	(NA)	(NA)	(NA)	(NA)	(NA)	(NA)	(NA)
Dunedin city	135	–	15	16	104	87	1,069	222	788	59	1,182	360	231	2,854	3,132
Fort Lauderdale city	1,503	15	67	741	680	1,762	11,216	2,555	7,564	1,097	11,020	893	1,082	6,665	6,765
Fort Myers city	964	13	32	309	610	1,127	3,059	592	1,848	619	4,923	1,782	2,304	5,655	10,063
Fort Pierce city	736	10	36	195	495	797	2,877	872	1,629	376	3,332	1,896	2,032	7,412	8,497
Gainesville city	973	5	99	168	701	983	4,870	1,178	3,262	430	5,788	874	1,007	4,375	5,930
Greenacres city............	256	1	14	41	200	136	1,136	242	811	83	1,435	782	500	3,470	5,277
Hallandale Beach city........	367	1	9	99	258	419	1,472	349	963	160	1,851	987	1,301	3,960	5,747
Hialeah city...............	1,348	8	38	387	915	1,669	8,772	1,542	5,698	1,532	12,277	587	742	3,821	5,461
Hollywood city.............	773	6	60	330	377	1,081	6,498	1,314	4,366	818	8,535	523	775	4,397	6,121
Homestead city	818	5	8	328	477	709	3,055	782	1,980	293	3,186	2,107	2,163	7,871	9,721
Jacksonville city...........	6,600	91	189	2,253	4,067	8,206	43,517	8,998	29,583	4,936	42,866	830	1,115	5,472	5,824
Jupiter town	162	1	8	59	94	167	1,352	316	963	73	1,363	339	482	2,828	3,936
Key West city	153	1	27	48	77	254	1,454	250	1,044	160	2,218	604	970	5,741	8,472
Kissimmee city	541	1	30	131	379	488	2,652	716	1,732	204	3,152	942	1,166	4,619	7,532
Lakeland city	437	6	26	140	265	447	5,045	912	3,755	378	5,555	484	562	5,584	6,986
Lake Worth city	540	4	14	276	246	397	3,083	919	1,843	321	2,626	1,488	1,293	8,496	8,550
Largo city................	349	4	26	77	242	328	2,556	468	1,860	228	2,478	476	464	3,486	3,506
Lauderdale Lakes city.......	415	4	17	113	281	261	1,388	399	773	216	1,113	1,283	856	4,290	3,648
Lauderhill city	561	3	30	157	371	387	2,027	608	1,072	347	1,822	921	718	3,329	3,381
Margate city	192	–	4	39	149	195	1,115	209	799	107	1,563	340	357	1,977	2,864
Melbourne city.............	684	1	30	124	529	(NA)	3,657	884	2,557	216	(NA)	888	(NA)	4,745	(NA)
Miami city................	6,134	54	62	2,019	3,999	7,877	23,321	5,377	13,930	4,014	31,879	1,580	2,017	6,006	8,163
Miami Beach city	1,173	3	62	515	593	1,323	8,121	1,463	5,681	977	11,070	1,287	1,278	8,913	10,696
Miami Gardens city	1,913	11	57	540	1,305	(NA)	6,598	1,395	4,235	968	(NA)	1,854	(NA)	6,396	(NA)
Miramar city	486	3	35	152	296	356	3,212	939	1,831	442	2,484	468	548	3,095	3,824
North Lauderdale city	321	–	17	68	236	203	1,110	226	758	126	1,024	912	635	3,155	3,201
North Miami city	687	6	25	339	317	880	4,091	1,025	2,538	528	4,715	1,144	1,645	6,810	8,813
North Miami Beach city	493	1	26	201	265	323	2,328	593	1,412	323	2,228	1,208	872	5,703	6,015
Oakland Park city	476	3	23	139	311	314	2,047	451	1,357	239	2,030	1,477	1,052	6,353	6,800
Ocala city................	587	4	43	157	383	724	3,416	804	2,408	204	4,520	1,174	1,428	6,831	8,917
Orlando city	3,801	22	165	1,204	2,410	3,926	18,226	3,882	12,175	2,169	18,443	1,808	2,059	8,667	9,671
Ormond Beach city	88	–	4	17	67	117	1,065	181	834	50	1,189	227	313	2,746	3,183
Oviedo city...............	104	–	8	9	87	85	567	94	445	28	607	353	337	1,925	2,407
Palm Bay city	482	2	42	79	359	698	3,269	1,032	1,999	238	3,268	531	839	3,602	3,929
Palm Beach Gardens city	113	1	10	37	65	93	1,879	377	1,319	183	1,932	249	252	4,147	5,227
Palm Coast city............	(NA)	(NA)	(NA)	(NA)	(NA)	(NA)	(NA)	(NA)	(NA)	(NA)	(NA)	(NA)	(NA)	(NA)	(NA)
Panama City city	336	2	19	76	239	307	2,074	363	1,607	104	2,126	886	728	5,470	5,042
Pembroke Pines city.........	353	6	25	95	227	402	4,471	743	3,295	433	3,451	230	313	2,913	2,690
Pensacola city.............	448	1	37	89	321	(NA)	2,424	423	1,824	177	(NA)	800	(NA)	4,331	(NA)
Pinellas Park city...........	296	1	26	46	223	251	2,784	483	2,153	148	2,520	614	535	5,772	5,368
Plantation city	226	4	15	114	93	245	3,508	587	2,586	335	4,076	259	282	4,012	4,692
Plant City city	262	3	13	96	150	382	1,540	231	1,118	191	2,462	829	1,316	4,873	8,479
Pompano Beach city	1,382	5	57	420	900	878	5,248	958	3,676	614	4,298	1,521	1,087	5,775	5,323
Port Orange city	35	4	2	9	20	33	1,084	181	849	54	998	65	69	2,008	2,076
Port St. Lucie city	287	1	17	27	242	217	2,697	770	1,783	144	2,205	237	251	2,228	2,547
Riviera Beach city	655	12	11	240	392	581	2,902	891	1,435	576	4,229	1,970	1,852	8,726	13,483

See footnotes at end of table.

Table C-2. Cities — **Crime**—Con.

[Includes states and 1,265 incorporated places of 25,000 or more population as of April 1, 2000, in all states except Hawaii, which has no incorporated places recognized by the U.S. Census Bureau. Two census designated places (CDPs) are also included (Honolulu CDP in Hawaii and Arlington CDP in Virginia). For more information on these areas, see Appendix C, Geographic Information]

City	Number											Rate per 100,000 population[1]			
	Violent						Property					Violent		Property	
	2005					2000	2005				2000	2005	2000	2005	2000
	Total	Murder and non-negligent man-slaughter	Forcible rape	Robbery	Aggra-vated assault		Total	Burglary	Larceny-theft	Motor vehicle theft					
FLORIDA—Con.															
St. Petersburg city	3,937	30	101	959	2,847	4,029	16,323	3,534	10,395	2,394	16,375	1,546	1,623	6,408	6,598
Sanford city	316	5	25	130	156	582	3,601	759	2,393	449	3,506	680	1,482	7,746	8,925
Sarasota city	522	5	37	154	326	607	3,562	769	2,535	258	3,671	957	1,131	6,529	6,838
Sunrise city	381	1	22	128	230	365	3,148	554	2,288	306	4,405	413	420	3,412	5,068
Tallahassee city	1,646	9	132	386	1,119	1,824	8,519	2,614	5,191	714	10,746	1,028	1,269	5,319	7,474
Tamarac city	194	1	4	65	124	164	1,229	268	818	143	1,157	320	290	2,028	2,045
Tampa city	4,707	20	210	1,160	3,317	6,381	20,271	4,914	12,564	2,793	27,285	1,431	2,073	6,161	8,866
Titusville city	346	4	21	79	242	349	1,512	417	909	186	1,472	794	793	3,470	3,347
Wellington village	148	2	24	18	104	105	1,472	326	1,019	127	1,100	290	355	2,880	3,716
Weston city	131	–	4	18	109	80	773	141	599	33	595	202	640	1,190	4,757
West Palm Beach city	1,221	22	71	528	600	1,210	7,182	1,605	4,610	967	10,186	1,252	1,486	7,366	12,512
Winter Haven city	222	2	21	54	145	200	2,057	392	1,514	151	1,814	779	691	7,222	6,267
Winter Park city	47	–	6	20	21	77	841	194	545	102	984	173	308	3,091	3,936
Winter Springs city	58	–	5	4	49	63	639	139	472	28	597	177	203	1,954	1,924
GEORGIA	40,725	564	2,143	14,041	23,977	41,319	378,534	84,463	249,594	44,477	347,630	449	505	4,172	4,246
Albany city	516	8	40	216	252	542	4,991	1,704	2,958	329	5,112	659	679	6,370	6,405
Alpharetta city	84	1	4	19	60	102	1,469	182	1,198	89	2,327	239	355	4,175	8,109
Athens-Clarke County (balance)	357	5	41	135	176	420	5,593	1,047	4,185	361	6,377	338	446	5,290	6,767
Atlanta city	7,213	90	223	2,861	4,039	11,583	31,397	6,648	18,993	5,756	43,885	1,675	2,743	7,290	10,393
Augusta-Richmond County (balance)	(NA)	(NA)	(NA)	(NA)	(NA)	(NA)	(NA)	(NA)	(NA)	(NA)	(NA)	(NA)	(NA)	(NA)	(NA)
Columbus city	992	22	24	446	500	(NA)	13,125	2,681	8,763	1,681	(NA)	528	(NA)	6,986	(NA)
Dalton city	(NA)	(NA)	(NA)	(NA)	(NA)	159	(NA)	(NA)	(NA)	(NA)	1,883	(NA)	629	(NA)	7,449
East Point city	346	4	15	159	168	(NA)	2,393	682	1,364	347	(NA)	950	(NA)	6,568	(NA)
Gainesville city	149	1	15	31	102	222	2,191	235	1,790	166	2,355	466	1,032	6,855	10,945
Hinesville city	172	–	14	55	103	206	1,899	414	1,425	60	1,892	548	728	6,046	6,683
LaGrange city	184	2	9	83	90	122	2,233	379	1,685	169	1,852	664	465	8,062	7,055
Macon city	816	20	58	332	406	841	9,217	2,028	6,124	1,065	10,541	836	706	9,443	8,848
Marietta city	331	6	11	194	120	322	2,371	426	1,548	397	2,942	532	600	3,811	5,482
Peachtree City city	11	–	3	3	5	11	335	26	258	51	270	32	32	964	795
Rome city	269	2	17	76	174	633	2,652	597	1,908	147	2,899	736	1,843	7,260	8,440
Roswell city	146	–	7	71	68	(NA)	2,340	442	1,724	174	(NA)	167	(NA)	2,678	(NA)
Savannah city	[3]1,390	[3]30	[3]83	[3]704	[3]573	1,415	[3]11,671	[3]2,530	[3]7,603	[3]1,538	9,678	[3]651	1,039	[3]5,464	7,107
Smyrna city	227	6	14	127	80	172	2,144	461	1,387	296	2,376	483	434	4,560	5,998
Valdosta city	312	7	29	106	170	(NA)	3,461	666	2,602	193	(NA)	669	(NA)	7,423	(NA)
Warner Robins city	253	1	12	94	146	269	3,106	834	2,104	168	3,096	437	518	5,369	5,963
HAWAII	3,253	24	343	1,001	1,885	2,954	61,115	9,792	42,188	9,135	60,033	255	244	4,793	4,955
Honolulu CDP	2,570	15	234	841	1,480	2,302	42,383	6,209	29,376	6,798	44,357	283	261	4,665	5,020
IDAHO	3,670	35	577	266	2,792	3,267	38,556	8,066	27,606	2,884	37,961	257	252	2,698	2,934
Boise City city	748	5	120	86	537	653	7,484	1,358	5,627	499	7,682	384	375	3,838	4,414
Caldwell city	170	3	14	9	144	135	1,907	462	1,259	186	1,403	507	559	5,683	5,807
Coeur d'Alene city	215	1	32	18	164	214	2,133	365	1,587	181	2,185	546	615	5,417	6,280
Idaho Falls city	156	–	27	9	120	132	1,923	339	1,454	130	2,165	292	263	3,595	4,307
Lewiston city	38	–	9	4	25	55	1,394	251	1,072	71	1,244	119	174	4,380	3,933
Meridian city	87	1	12	7	67	28	1,253	254	931	68	1,260	189	98	2,717	4,402
Nampa city	(NA)	(NA)	(NA)	(NA)	(NA)	202	(NA)	(NA)	(NA)	(NA)	2,577	(NA)	424	(NA)	5,405
Pocatello city	159	1	35	7	116	123	1,763	283	1,416	64	1,722	306	225	3,389	3,156
Twin Falls city	138	4	20	22	92	162	1,968	368	1,448	152	2,038	358	457	5,100	5,745
ILLINOIS[4]	70,392	766	4,297	23,187	42,142	81,567	393,148	77,462	276,301	39,385	450,748	552	657	3,080	3,629
Addison village	(NA)	(NA)	(NA)	(NA)	(NA)	(NA)	(NA)	(NA)	(NA)	(NA)	(NA)	(NA)	(NA)	(NA)	(NA)
Alton city	(NA)	(NA)	(NA)	(NA)	(NA)	(NA)	(NA)	(NA)	(NA)	(NA)	(NA)	(NA)	(NA)	(NA)	(NA)
Arlington Heights village	(NA)	(NA)	(NA)	(NA)	(NA)	(NA)	(NA)	(NA)	(NA)	(NA)	(NA)	(NA)	(NA)	(NA)	(NA)
Aurora city	(NA)	14	(NA)	176	480	[2]	4,832	883	3,642	307	5,156	(NA)	(NA)	2,889	3,892
Bartlett village	(NA)	(NA)	(NA)	(NA)	(NA)	(NA)	(NA)	(NA)	(NA)	(NA)	(NA)	(NA)	(NA)	(NA)	(NA)
Belleville city	(NA)	(NA)	(NA)	(NA)	(NA)	(NA)	(NA)	(NA)	(NA)	(NA)	(NA)	(NA)	(NA)	(NA)	(NA)
Berwyn city	(NA)	(NA)	(NA)	(NA)	(NA)	(NA)	(NA)	(NA)	(NA)	(NA)	(NA)	(NA)	(NA)	(NA)	(NA)
Bloomington city	(NA)	(NA)	(NA)	(NA)	(NA)	(NA)	(NA)	(NA)	(NA)	(NA)	(NA)	(NA)	(NA)	(NA)	(NA)
Bolingbrook village	(NA)	(NA)	(NA)	(NA)	(NA)	(NA)	(NA)	(NA)	(NA)	(NA)	(NA)	(NA)	(NA)	(NA)	(NA)
Buffalo Grove village	(NA)	(NA)	(NA)	(NA)	(NA)	(NA)	(NA)	(NA)	(NA)	(NA)	(NA)	(NA)	(NA)	(NA)	(NA)
Burbank city	(NA)	(NA)	(NA)	(NA)	(NA)	(NA)	(NA)	(NA)	(NA)	(NA)	(NA)	(NA)	(NA)	(NA)	(NA)
Calumet City city	(NA)	(NA)	(NA)	(NA)	(NA)	(NA)	(NA)	(NA)	(NA)	(NA)	(NA)	(NA)	(NA)	(NA)	(NA)
Carbondale city	(NA)	(NA)	(NA)	(NA)	(NA)	(NA)	(NA)	(NA)	(NA)	(NA)	(NA)	(NA)	(NA)	(NA)	(NA)
Carol Stream village	(NA)	(NA)	(NA)	(NA)	(NA)	(NA)	(NA)	(NA)	(NA)	(NA)	(NA)	(NA)	(NA)	(NA)	(NA)
Carpentersville village	(NA)	(NA)	(NA)	(NA)	(NA)	(NA)	(NA)	(NA)	(NA)	(NA)	(NA)	(NA)	(NA)	(NA)	(NA)

See footnotes at end of table.

Table C-2. Cities — **Crime**—Con.

[Includes states and 1,265 incorporated places of 25,000 or more population as of April 1, 2000, in all states except Hawaii, which has no incorporated places recognized by the U.S. Census Bureau. Two census designated places (CDPs) are also included (Honolulu CDP in Hawaii and Arlington CDP in Virginia). For more information on these areas, see Appendix C, Geographic Information]

City	Number											Rate per 100,000 population[1]			
	Violent						Property					Violent		Property	
	2005					2000	2005				2000	2005	2000	2005	2000
	Total	Murder and non-negligent manslaughter	Forcible rape	Robbery	Aggravated assault		Total	Burglary	Larceny-theft	Motor vehicle theft					
ILLINOIS—Con.															
Champaign city	(NA)	(NA)	(NA)	(NA)	(NA)	(NA)	(NA)	(NA)	(NA)	(NA)	(NA)	(NA)	(NA)	(NA)	(NA)
Chicago city	(NA)	448	(NA)	15,964	17,943	(²)	131,183	25,314	83,373	22,496	169,699	(NA)	(NA)	4,565	5,921
Chicago Heights city.	(NA)	(NA)	(NA)	(NA)	(NA)	(NA)	(NA)	(NA)	(NA)	(NA)	(NA)	(NA)	(NA)	(NA)	(NA)
Cicero town	(NA)	(NA)	(NA)	(NA)	(NA)	(NA)	(NA)	(NA)	(NA)	(NA)	(NA)	(NA)	(NA)	(NA)	(NA)
Crystal Lake city	(NA)	(NA)	(NA)	(NA)	(NA)	(NA)	(NA)	(NA)	(NA)	(NA)	(NA)	(NA)	(NA)	(NA)	(NA)
Danville city	(NA)	(NA)	(NA)	(NA)	(NA)	(NA)	(NA)	(NA)	(NA)	(NA)	(NA)	(NA)	(NA)	(NA)	(NA)
Decatur city	(NA)	(NA)	(NA)	(NA)	(NA)	(NA)	(NA)	(NA)	(NA)	(NA)	(NA)	(NA)	(NA)	(NA)	(NA)
DeKalb city.	(NA)	(NA)	(NA)	(NA)	(NA)	(NA)	(NA)	(NA)	(NA)	(NA)	(NA)	(NA)	(NA)	(NA)	(NA)
Des Plaines city.	(NA)	(NA)	(NA)	(NA)	(NA)	(NA)	(NA)	(NA)	(NA)	(NA)	(NA)	(NA)	(NA)	(NA)	(NA)
Dolton village	(NA)	(NA)	(NA)	(NA)	(NA)	(NA)	(NA)	(NA)	(NA)	(NA)	(NA)	(NA)	(NA)	(NA)	(NA)
Downers Grove village	(NA)	(NA)	(NA)	(NA)	(NA)	(NA)	(NA)	(NA)	(NA)	(NA)	(NA)	(NA)	(NA)	(NA)	(NA)
East St. Louis city	(NA)	(NA)	(NA)	(NA)	(NA)	(NA)	(NA)	(NA)	(NA)	(NA)	(NA)	(NA)	(NA)	(NA)	(NA)
Elgin city	(NA)	(NA)	(NA)	(NA)	(NA)	(NA)	(NA)	(NA)	(NA)	(NA)	(NA)	(NA)	(NA)	(NA)	(NA)
Elk Grove Village village	(NA)	(NA)	(NA)	(NA)	(NA)	(NA)	(NA)	(NA)	(NA)	(NA)	(NA)	(NA)	(NA)	(NA)	(NA)
Elmhurst city	(NA)	(NA)	(NA)	(NA)	(NA)	(NA)	(NA)	(NA)	(NA)	(NA)	(NA)	(NA)	(NA)	(NA)	(NA)
Elmwood Park village	(NA)	(NA)	(NA)	(NA)	(NA)	(NA)	(NA)	(NA)	(NA)	(NA)	(NA)	(NA)	(NA)	(NA)	(NA)
Evanston city	(NA)	(NA)	(NA)	(NA)	(NA)	(NA)	(NA)	(NA)	(NA)	(NA)	(NA)	(NA)	(NA)	(NA)	(NA)
Freeport city	(NA)	(NA)	(NA)	(NA)	(NA)	(NA)	(NA)	(NA)	(NA)	(NA)	(NA)	(NA)	(NA)	(NA)	(NA)
Galesburg city	(NA)	(NA)	(NA)	(NA)	(NA)	(NA)	(NA)	(NA)	(NA)	(NA)	(NA)	(NA)	(NA)	(NA)	(NA)
Glendale Heights village	(NA)	(NA)	(NA)	(NA)	(NA)	(NA)	(NA)	(NA)	(NA)	(NA)	(NA)	(NA)	(NA)	(NA)	(NA)
Glen Ellyn village.	(NA)	(NA)	(NA)	(NA)	(NA)	(NA)	(NA)	(NA)	(NA)	(NA)	(NA)	(NA)	(NA)	(NA)	(NA)
Glenview village	(NA)	(NA)	(NA)	(NA)	(NA)	(NA)	(NA)	(NA)	(NA)	(NA)	(NA)	(NA)	(NA)	(NA)	(NA)
Granite City city	(NA)	(NA)	(NA)	(NA)	(NA)	(NA)	(NA)	(NA)	(NA)	(NA)	(NA)	(NA)	(NA)	(NA)	(NA)
Gurnee village.	(NA)	(NA)	(NA)	(NA)	(NA)	(NA)	(NA)	(NA)	(NA)	(NA)	(NA)	(NA)	(NA)	(NA)	(NA)
Hanover Park village	(NA)	(NA)	(NA)	(NA)	(NA)	(NA)	(NA)	(NA)	(NA)	(NA)	(NA)	(NA)	(NA)	(NA)	(NA)
Harvey city	(NA)	(NA)	(NA)	(NA)	(NA)	(NA)	(NA)	(NA)	(NA)	(NA)	(NA)	(NA)	(NA)	(NA)	(NA)
Highland Park city	(NA)	(NA)	(NA)	(NA)	(NA)	(NA)	(NA)	(NA)	(NA)	(NA)	(NA)	(NA)	(NA)	(NA)	(NA)
Hoffman Estates village	(NA)	(NA)	(NA)	(NA)	(NA)	(NA)	(NA)	(NA)	(NA)	(NA)	(NA)	(NA)	(NA)	(NA)	(NA)
Joliet city	(NA)	11	(NA)	145	309	(NA)	4,228	745	3,312	171	(NA)	(NA)	(NA)	3,252	(NA)
Kankakee city	(NA)	(NA)	(NA)	(NA)	(NA)	(NA)	(NA)	(NA)	(NA)	(NA)	(NA)	(NA)	(NA)	(NA)	(NA)
Lansing village	(NA)	(NA)	(NA)	(NA)	(NA)	(NA)	(NA)	(NA)	(NA)	(NA)	(NA)	(NA)	(NA)	(NA)	(NA)
Lombard village	(NA)	(NA)	(NA)	(NA)	(NA)	(NA)	(NA)	(NA)	(NA)	(NA)	(NA)	(NA)	(NA)	(NA)	(NA)
Maywood village	(NA)	(NA)	(NA)	(NA)	(NA)	(NA)	(NA)	(NA)	(NA)	(NA)	(NA)	(NA)	(NA)	(NA)	(NA)
Moline city	(NA)	(NA)	(NA)	(NA)	(NA)	(NA)	(NA)	(NA)	(NA)	(NA)	(NA)	(NA)	(NA)	(NA)	(NA)
Mount Prospect village	(NA)	(NA)	(NA)	(NA)	(NA)	(NA)	(NA)	(NA)	(NA)	(NA)	(NA)	(NA)	(NA)	(NA)	(NA)
Mundelein village.	(NA)	(NA)	(NA)	(NA)	(NA)	(NA)	(NA)	(NA)	(NA)	(NA)	(NA)	(NA)	(NA)	(NA)	(NA)
Naperville city	(NA)	3	(NA)	25	45	(²)	2,472	290	2,108	74	2,199	(NA)	(NA)	1,758	1,746
Niles village	(NA)	(NA)	(NA)	(NA)	(NA)	(NA)	(NA)	(NA)	(NA)	(NA)	(NA)	(NA)	(NA)	(NA)	(NA)
Normal town	(NA)	(NA)	(NA)	(NA)	(NA)	(NA)	(NA)	(NA)	(NA)	(NA)	(NA)	(NA)	(NA)	(NA)	(NA)
Northbrook village	(NA)	(NA)	(NA)	(NA)	(NA)	(NA)	(NA)	(NA)	(NA)	(NA)	(NA)	(NA)	(NA)	(NA)	(NA)
North Chicago city	(NA)	(NA)	(NA)	(NA)	(NA)	(NA)	(NA)	(NA)	(NA)	(NA)	(NA)	(NA)	(NA)	(NA)	(NA)
Oak Forest city	(NA)	(NA)	(NA)	(NA)	(NA)	(NA)	(NA)	(NA)	(NA)	(NA)	(NA)	(NA)	(NA)	(NA)	(NA)
Oak Lawn village.	(NA)	(NA)	(NA)	(NA)	(NA)	(NA)	(NA)	(NA)	(NA)	(NA)	(NA)	(NA)	(NA)	(NA)	(NA)
Oak Park village	(NA)	(NA)	(NA)	(NA)	(NA)	(NA)	(NA)	(NA)	(NA)	(NA)	(NA)	(NA)	(NA)	(NA)	(NA)
Orland Park village.	(NA)	(NA)	(NA)	(NA)	(NA)	(NA)	(NA)	(NA)	(NA)	(NA)	(NA)	(NA)	(NA)	(NA)	(NA)
Palatine village	(NA)	(NA)	(NA)	(NA)	(NA)	(NA)	(NA)	(NA)	(NA)	(NA)	(NA)	(NA)	(NA)	(NA)	(NA)
Park Ridge city	(NA)	(NA)	(NA)	(NA)	(NA)	(NA)	(NA)	(NA)	(NA)	(NA)	(NA)	(NA)	(NA)	(NA)	(NA)
Pekin city	(NA)	(NA)	(NA)	(NA)	(NA)	(NA)	(NA)	(NA)	(NA)	(NA)	(NA)	(NA)	(NA)	(NA)	(NA)
Peoria city	(NA)	14	(NA)	380	528	(²)	7,470	1,839	4,848	783	9,334	(NA)	(NA)	6,601	8,203
Quincy city	(NA)	(NA)	(NA)	(NA)	(NA)	(NA)	(NA)	(NA)	(NA)	(NA)	(NA)	(NA)	(NA)	(NA)	(NA)
Rockford city.	(NA)	19	(NA)	537	764	(²)	10,106	2,371	6,758	977	11,206	(NA)	(NA)	6,603	7,609
Rock Island city.	(NA)	(NA)	(NA)	(NA)	(NA)	(NA)	(NA)	(NA)	(NA)	(NA)	(NA)	(NA)	(NA)	(NA)	(NA)
Round Lake Beach village.	(NA)	(NA)	(NA)	(NA)	(NA)	(NA)	(NA)	(NA)	(NA)	(NA)	(NA)	(NA)	(NA)	(NA)	(NA)
St. Charles city	(NA)	(NA)	(NA)	(NA)	(NA)	(NA)	(NA)	(NA)	(NA)	(NA)	(NA)	(NA)	(NA)	(NA)	(NA)
Schaumburg village	(NA)	(NA)	(NA)	(NA)	(NA)	(NA)	(NA)	(NA)	(NA)	(NA)	(NA)	(NA)	(NA)	(NA)	(NA)
Skokie village	(NA)	(NA)	(NA)	(NA)	(NA)	(NA)	(NA)	(NA)	(NA)	(NA)	(NA)	(NA)	(NA)	(NA)	(NA)
Springfield city.	(NA)	5	(NA)	258	1,306	(²)	7,345	1,719	5,288	338	7,272	(NA)	(NA)	6,377	6,025
Streamwood village	(NA)	(NA)	(NA)	(NA)	(NA)	(NA)	(NA)	(NA)	(NA)	(NA)	(NA)	(NA)	(NA)	(NA)	(NA)
Tinley Park village	(NA)	(NA)	(NA)	(NA)	(NA)	(NA)	(NA)	(NA)	(NA)	(NA)	(NA)	(NA)	(NA)	(NA)	(NA)
Urbana city.	(NA)	(NA)	(NA)	(NA)	(NA)	(NA)	(NA)	(NA)	(NA)	(NA)	(NA)	(NA)	(NA)	(NA)	(NA)
Waukegan city	(NA)	(NA)	(NA)	(NA)	(NA)	(NA)	(NA)	(NA)	(NA)	(NA)	(NA)	(NA)	(NA)	(NA)	(NA)
Wheaton city.	(NA)	(NA)	(NA)	(NA)	(NA)	(NA)	(NA)	(NA)	(NA)	(NA)	(NA)	(NA)	(NA)	(NA)	(NA)
Wheeling village	(NA)	(NA)	(NA)	(NA)	(NA)	(NA)	(NA)	(NA)	(NA)	(NA)	(NA)	(NA)	(NA)	(NA)	(NA)
Wilmette village	(NA)	(NA)	(NA)	(NA)	(NA)	(NA)	(NA)	(NA)	(NA)	(NA)	(NA)	(NA)	(NA)	(NA)	(NA)
Woodridge village	(NA)	(NA)	(NA)	(NA)	(NA)	(NA)	(NA)	(NA)	(NA)	(NA)	(NA)	(NA)	(NA)	(NA)	(NA)

See footnotes at end of table.

Table C-2. Cities — **Crime**—Con.

[Includes states and 1,265 incorporated places of 25,000 or more population as of April 1, 2000, in all states except Hawaii, which has no incorporated places recognized by the U.S. Census Bureau. Two census designated places (CDPs) are also included (Honolulu CDP in Hawaii and Arlington CDP in Virginia). For more information on these areas, see Appendix C, Geographic Information]

City	Number Violent 2005 Total	Murder and non-negligent manslaughter	Forcible rape	Robbery	Aggravated assault	Violent 2000	Number Property 2005 Total	Burglary	Larceny-theft	Motor vehicle theft	Property 2000	Rate Violent 2005	Rate Violent 2000	Rate Property 2005	Rate Property 2000
INDIANA	20,302	356	1,856	6,809	11,281	21,230	216,778	43,756	151,278	21,744	206,905	324	349	3,456	3,403
Anderson city	150	2	19	63	66	(NA)	2,688	611	1,886	191	(NA)	257	(NA)	4,614	(NA)
Bloomington city	171	–	25	54	92	122	2,683	566	1,969	148	2,606	247	179	3,880	3,816
Carmel city	24	–	8	6	10	11	989	134	814	41	743	41	23	1,690	1,569
Columbus city	81	–	7	18	56	72	2,488	247	2,115	126	2,419	205	189	6,304	6,356
East Chicago city	714	12	12	125	565	(NA)	1,860	397	1,124	339	(NA)	2,273	(NA)	5,922	(NA)
Elkhart city	200	5	39	146	10	285	3,761	775	2,724	262	4,784	383	643	7,210	10,790
Evansville city	478	8	59	176	235	623	6,008	1,255	4,469	284	5,592	406	500	5,100	4,485
Fishers town	30	–	7	9	14	38	599	61	511	27	626	55	122	1,096	2,017
Fort Wayne city	732	25	84	375	248	820	10,732	2,233	7,841	658	11,295	332	407	4,866	5,612
Gary city	718	58	70	306	284	1,063	5,310	1,593	2,556	1,161	5,238	718	942	5,307	4,643
Goshen city	73	1	–	7	65	283	1,366	142	1,188	36	1,430	238	1,048	4,446	5,295
Greenwood city	144	1	1	15	127	179	2,049	207	1,753	89	1,696	351	501	4,993	4,743
Hammond city	712	9	30	279	394	900	4,554	1,047	2,728	779	5,311	885	1,137	5,662	6,710
Hobart city	186	3	11	13	159	(NA)	1,484	165	1,199	120	(NA)	672	(NA)	5,365	(NA)
Indianapolis city (balance)	7,948	108	527	3,274	4,039	6,843	50,081	11,548	29,541	8,992	30,546	993	891	6,258	3,977
Jeffersonville city	95	2	5	32	56	143	1,086	234	709	143	1,398	330	517	3,771	5,050
Kokomo city	196	11	24	71	90	237	2,990	666	2,181	143	2,499	423	512	6,455	5,401
Lafayette city	258	4	35	70	149	164	3,267	649	2,394	224	2,797	429	326	5,437	5,567
Lawrence city	145	1	13	76	55	94	1,119	305	616	198	855	353	263	2,722	2,394
Marion city	113	1	18	50	44	(NA)	1,786	302	1,388	96	(NA)	365	(NA)	5,761	(NA)
Merrillville town	89	–	4	18	67	71	990	82	754	154	1,035	283	222	3,150	3,233
Michigan City city	136	4	14	70	48	155	1,883	213	1,515	155	2,535	420	463	5,820	7,565
Mishawaka city	189	1	24	52	112	267	3,317	346	2,804	167	4,015	388	566	6,818	8,513
Muncie city	314	1	74	65	174	(NA)	2,783	552	2,059	172	(NA)	465	(NA)	4,121	(NA)
New Albany city	166	–	11	62	93	237	2,331	486	1,678	167	2,685	448	575	6,286	6,516
Noblesville city	36	2	6	4	24	13	760	152	567	41	612	101	44	2,133	2,091
Portage city	57	–	7	7	43	42	1,279	204	970	105	1,266	161	123	3,606	3,696
Richmond city	154	–	6	77	71	191	1,879	366	1,355	158	2,374	404	488	4,925	6,061
South Bend city	794	12	69	348	365	797	6,612	1,678	4,366	568	7,699	749	787	6,233	7,605
Terre Haute city	152	1	31	63	57	137	5,155	934	3,718	503	5,004	264	254	8,959	9,287
Valparaiso city	73	1	4	2	66	26	886	86	758	42	782	253	94	3,065	2,826
West Lafayette city	49	–	8	7	34	39	539	93	425	21	597	170	125	1,874	1,919
IOWA	8,642	38	827	1,154	6,623	7,796	84,056	17,987	60,594	5,475	86,834	291	266	2,834	2,967
Ames city	98	–	14	14	70	70	1,537	465	1,028	44	1,522	187	141	2,926	3,060
Ankeny city	36	–	1	3	32	44	872	157	670	45	856	104	165	2,522	3,214
Bettendorf city	95	–	7	11	77	62	692	96	566	30	746	299	193	2,180	2,318
Burlington city	137	1	10	18	108	155	1,086	312	723	51	1,328	533	572	4,229	4,898
Cedar Falls city	70	–	12	4	54	120	662	88	540	34	870	192	341	1,814	2,470
Cedar Rapids city	417	–	45	121	250	350	6,391	1,067	5,022	302	5,895	340	296	5,209	4,993
Clinton city	147	3	6	18	120	(NA)	1,439	275	1,093	71	(NA)	536	(NA)	5,246	(NA)
Council Bluffs city	725	–	61	79	585	491	5,145	1,034	3,435	676	5,296	1,217	839	8,635	9,053
Davenport city	1,323	7	54	272	990	1,599	7,080	1,451	5,213	416	6,367	1,340	1,596	7,170	6,354
Des Moines city	1,228	5	110	294	819	715	13,799	2,630	10,045	1,124	12,937	629	367	7,073	6,643
Dubuque city	315	1	16	10	288	121	1,770	398	1,306	66	1,856	546	209	3,066	3,207
Fort Dodge city	151	2	17	15	117	163	1,718	375	1,221	122	1,826	585	624	6,652	6,996
Iowa City city	184	–	32	37	115	321	1,480	326	1,082	72	1,717	291	513	2,339	2,747
Marion city	24	–	10	2	12	(NA)	430	115	288	27	(NA)	80	(NA)	1,436	(NA)
Marshalltown city	182	1	5	4	172	228	1,097	177	847	73	1,084	696	862	4,193	4,097
Mason City city	72	–	12	12	48	52	1,594	306	1,227	61	2,032	255	178	5,634	6,945
Sioux City city	400	2	54	52	292	474	3,590	797	2,562	231	5,075	476	561	4,273	6,007
Urbandale city	39	–	7	7	25	24	582	130	417	35	782	116	84	1,737	2,729
Waterloo city	360	1	36	80	243	321	3,251	825	2,242	184	3,605	537	501	4,850	5,629
West Des Moines city	88	–	14	11	63	66	1,807	279	1,459	69	1,694	171	145	3,504	3,721
KANSAS	10,634	102	1,055	1,793	7,684	[4]10,470	103,941	18,917	75,702	9,322	[4]108,057	387	[4]389	3,787	[4]4,019
Dodge City city	(NA)	(NA)	(NA)	(NA)	(NA)	(NA)	(NA)	(NA)	(NA)	(NA)	(NA)	(NA)	(NA)	(NA)	(NA)
Emporia city	64	1	14	9	40	(NA)	1,478	189	1,248	41	(NA)	239	(NA)	5,530	(NA)
Garden City city	137	1	22	8	106	(NA)	1,189	160	980	49	(NA)	500	(NA)	4,339	(NA)
Hutchinson city	158	1	21	16	120	(NA)	2,539	426	2,025	88	(NA)	384	(NA)	6,165	(NA)
Kansas City city	1,166	37	100	416	613	(NA)	10,678	1,842	5,924	2,912	(NA)	801	(NA)	7,339	(NA)
Lawrence city	276	2	30	41	203	(NA)	3,493	545	2,797	151	(NA)	336	(NA)	4,252	(NA)
Leavenworth city	294	–	23	51	220	(NA)	1,410	300	1,024	86	(NA)	830	(NA)	3,982	(NA)
Leawood city	17	–	5	3	9	(NA)	463	85	360	18	(NA)	57	(NA)	1,564	(NA)
Lenexa city	96	4	10	23	59	(NA)	2,044	536	1,417	91	(NA)	225	(NA)	4,780	(NA)
Manhattan city	(NA)	(NA)	(NA)	(NA)	(NA)	(NA)	(NA)	(NA)	(NA)	(NA)	(NA)	(NA)	(NA)	(NA)	(NA)
Olathe city	336	1	45	29	261	(NA)	3,328	249	2,818	261	(NA)	309	(NA)	3,060	(NA)
Overland Park city	494	2	30	63	399	(NA)	4,559	488	3,661	410	(NA)	303	(NA)	2,792	(NA)
Salina city	(NA)	(NA)	(NA)	(NA)	(NA)	(NA)	(NA)	(NA)	(NA)	(NA)	(NA)	(NA)	(NA)	(NA)	(NA)
Shawnee city	87	–	10	30	47	(NA)	1,233	156	964	113	(NA)	154	(NA)	2,187	(NA)
Topeka city	682	7	50	275	350	1,278	9,662	1,719	7,244	699	11,778	558	1,013	7,906	9,337
Wichita city	(NA)	(NA)	(NA)	(NA)	(NA)	2,081	(NA)	(NA)	(NA)	(NA)	19,588	(NA)	612	(NA)	5,763

See footnotes at end of table.

County and City Data Book: 2007

U.S. Census Bureau

Table C-2. Cities — **Crime**—Con.

[Includes states and 1,265 incorporated places of 25,000 or more population as of April 1, 2000, in all states except Hawaii, which has no incorporated places recognized by the U.S. Census Bureau. Two census designated places (CDPs) are also included (Honolulu CDP in Hawaii and Arlington CDP in Virginia). For more information on these areas, see Appendix C, Geographic Information]

	Number											Rate per 100,000 population[1]			
	Violent						Property					Violent		Property	
	2005						2005								
City	Total	Murder and non-negligent man-slaughter	Forcible rape	Robbery	Aggra-vated assault	2000	Total	Burglary	Larceny-theft	Motor vehicle theft	2000	2005	2000	2005	2000
KENTUCKY	11,134	190	1,421	3,690	5,833	[4]11,903	105,608	26,458	70,354	8,796	[4]107,723	267	[4]294	2,530	[4]2,665
Bowling Green city	328	3	47	88	190	279	3,020	584	2,282	154	2,682	635	600	5,849	5,770
Covington city	(NA)	(NA)	(NA)	(NA)	(NA)	(NA)	(NA)	(NA)	(NA)	(NA)	(NA)	(NA)	(NA)	(NA)	(NA)
Frankfort city	81	–	13	25	43	(NA)	1,190	255	844	91	(NA)	295	(NA)	4,333	(NA)
Henderson city	(NA)	(NA)	(NA)	(NA)	(NA)	(NA)	(NA)	(NA)	(NA)	(NA)	(NA)	(NA)	(NA)	(NA)	(NA)
Hopkinsville city	146	1	26	52	67	(NA)	1,732	409	1,253	70	(NA)	501	(NA)	5,943	(NA)
Jeffersontown city	49	–	3	28	18	(NA)	603	111	422	70	(NA)	186	(NA)	2,284	(NA)
Lexington-Fayette[5]	1,476	15	147	575	739	1,888	10,308	2,172	7,391	745	11,769	550	759	3,844	4,731
Louisville/Jefferson County (balance)	[6]3,896	[6]55	[6]209	[6]1,822	[6]1,810	(NA)	[6]27,446	[6]7,146	[6]17,150	[6]3,150	(NA)	[6]625	(NA)	[6]4,400	(NA)
Owensboro city	148	4	16	50	78	115	2,072	438	1,564	70	2,690	268	209	3,749	4,881
Paducah city	200	–	21	44	135	170	1,782	253	1,386	143	1,793	778	646	6,930	6,816
Richmond city	106	–	8	22	76	(NA)	1,124	203	862	59	(NA)	351	(NA)	3,721	(NA)
LOUISIANA	26,889	450	1,421	5,337	19,681	30,440	166,611	39,382	112,840	14,389	211,904	594	681	3,683	4,742
Alexandria city	1,022	9	21	147	845	540	3,787	948	2,629	210	5,072	2,219	1,149	8,223	10,797
Baton Rouge city	2,698	49	83	993	1,573	(NA)	14,378	3,940	8,949	1,489	(NA)	1,202	(NA)	6,405	(NA)
Bossier City city	1,247	–	32	89	1,126	487	3,131	627	2,241	263	3,685	2,088	845	5,243	6,390
Houma city	319	6	14	67	232	435	1,725	290	1,379	56	1,881	994	1,308	5,378	5,655
Kenner city	253	4	19	68	162	401	2,799	716	1,734	349	3,482	360	548	3,977	4,760
Lafayette city	991	8	91	141	751	856	6,342	1,233	4,691	418	7,403	884	717	5,654	6,200
Lake Charles city	562	6	44	153	359	629	3,638	1,720	1,678	240	3,849	792	853	5,128	5,217
Monroe city	607	3	33	61	510	949	4,685	988	3,575	122	5,759	1,162	1,781	8,970	10,811
New Iberia city	(NA)	(NA)	(NA)	(NA)	(NA)	78	(NA)	(NA)	(NA)	(NA)	882	(NA)	229	(NA)	2,590
New Orleans city	(NA)	(NA)	(NA)	(NA)	(NA)	5,330	(NA)	(NA)	(NA)	(NA)	28,671	(NA)	1,131	(NA)	6,086
Shreveport city	2,249	39	151	628	1,431	1,875	12,878	2,969	8,893	1,016	15,184	1,130	979	6,471	7,927
Slidell city	143	1	8	28	106	170	1,923	352	1,422	149	2,102	532	613	7,151	7,578
MAINE	1,483	19	326	323	815	1,397	31,889	6,323	24,218	1,348	32,003	112	110	2,413	2,510
Bangor city	65	–	6	26	33	55	1,568	219	1,304	45	1,820	205	166	4,947	5,477
Lewiston city	91	2	22	35	32	56	1,250	241	967	42	1,663	254	152	3,483	4,516
Portland city	267	3	39	100	125	210	2,970	536	2,261	173	2,659	416	333	4,633	4,220
MARYLAND.	39,369	552	1,266	14,378	23,173	41,663	198,483	35,922	128,491	34,070	213,422	703	787	3,544	4,030
Annapolis city	445	4	11	186	244	530	1,652	314	1,188	150	1,888	1,219	1,562	4,527	5,565
Baltimore city	11,248	269	162	3,910	6,907	16,003	33,241	7,338	19,691	6,212	49,883	1,754	2,470	5,185	7,699
Bowie city	(NA)	(NA)	(NA)	(NA)	(NA)	(NA)	(NA)	(NA)	(NA)	(NA)	(NA)	(NA)	(NA)	(NA)	(NA)
Frederick city	490	–	11	118	361	622	1,575	256	1,244	75	1,922	853	1,247	2,742	3,853
Gaithersburg city	(NA)	(NA)	(NA)	(NA)	(NA)	(NA)	(NA)	(NA)	(NA)	(NA)	(NA)	(NA)	(NA)	(NA)	(NA)
Hagerstown city	279	2	4	84	189	217	1,487	328	1,024	135	1,523	738	612	3,932	4,297
Rockville city	(NA)	(NA)	(NA)	(NA)	(NA)	(NA)	(NA)	(NA)	(NA)	(NA)	(NA)	(NA)	(NA)	(NA)	(NA)
MASSACHUSETTS.	29,237	175	1,732	7,615	19,715	30,230	151,241	34,624	97,737	18,880	161,901	457	476	2,364	2,550
Agawam city	43	–	5	4	34	202	521	206	239	76	510	151	736	1,826	1,859
Attleboro city	114	–	9	12	93	110	919	176	654	89	932	263	268	2,118	2,272
Barnstable Town city	346	2	34	25	285	([7])	1,238	429	724	85	1,296	715	(NA)	2,558	2,736
Beverly city	93	–	8	17	68	(NA)	635	145	445	45	(NA)	232	(NA)	1,585	(NA)
Boston city	7,479	73	268	2,649	4,489	7,322	25,205	4,531	15,957	4,717	28,548	1,318	1,283	4,441	5,001
Brockton city	([7])	10	47	211	([7])	996	3,707	687	2,282	738	3,877	(NA)	1,034	3,913	4,026
Cambridge city	494	3	18	239	234	520	3,309	623	2,396	290	3,870	492	544	3,293	4,050
Chelsea city	([7])	4	21	151	([7])	467	1,195	286	627	282	1,080	(NA)	1,656	3,606	3,830
Chicopee city	343	2	27	46	268	([7])	1,750	479	1,048	223	1,565	627	(NA)	3,200	2,832
Everett city	116	–	6	40	70	324	1,186	292	709	185	895	313	906	3,197	2,503
Fall River city	(NA)	(NA)	(NA)	(NA)	(NA)	548	(NA)	(NA)	(NA)	(NA)	3,079	(NA)	589	(NA)	3,307
Fitchburg city	([7])	1	25	47	([7])	431	1,080	340	658	82	1,692	(NA)	1,037	2,714	4,073
Franklin city	7	–	2	–	5	37	130	43	72	15	87	23	125	432	293
Gloucester city	47	–	6	8	33	34	591	100	456	35	453	153	111	1,923	1,481
Haverhill city	296	–	13	52	231	245	1,417	593	708	116	1,777	491	429	2,349	3,113
Holyoke city	([7])	3	30	92	([7])	460	2,213	356	1,560	297	2,312	(NA)	1,100	5,540	5,528
Lawrence city	584	–	17	159	408	649	1,711	601	577	533	3,431	815	904	2,388	4,781
Leominster city	(NA)	(NA)	(NA)	(NA)	(NA)	86	(NA)	(NA)	(NA)	(NA)	1,367	(NA)	207	(NA)	3,294
Lowell city	1,009	2	41	213	753	737	3,295	664	1,942	689	3,262	976	709	3,188	3,138
Lynn city	1,070	5	12	270	783	([7])	2,925	816	1,527	582	3,756	1,199	(NA)	3,278	4,511
Malden city	213	2	9	78	124	(NA)	1,293	366	782	145	(NA)	386	(NA)	2,343	(NA)
Marlborough city	38	–	8	11	19	61	616	126	442	48	608	101	178	1,639	1,770
Medford city	71	1	8	47	15	127	1,460	327	944	189	1,275	131	222	2,701	2,232
Melrose city	50	–	4	14	32	11	352	89	229	34	364	189	39	1,330	1,300
Methuen city	83	1	3	27	52	78	1,000	205	709	86	1,073	186	179	2,236	2,463
New Bedford city	1,024	8	52	257	707	789	3,116	877	1,924	315	2,377	1,093	810	3,325	2,439
Newton city	114	1	6	15	92	62	1,098	269	783	46	1,028	136	75	1,314	1,248
Northampton city	114	–	9	9	96	47	805	122	626	57	565	395	161	2,790	1,934
Peabody city	165	1	8	24	132	148	1,142	199	829	114	1,112	328	293	2,273	2,198
Pittsfield city	352	2	32	36	282	139	1,041	309	668	64	1,208	797	298	2,357	2,594

See footnotes at end of table.

Table C-2. Cities — **Crime**—Con.

[Includes states and 1,265 incorporated places of 25,000 or more population as of April 1, 2000, in all states except Hawaii, which has no incorporated places recognized by the U.S. Census Bureau. Two census designated places (CDPs) are also included (Honolulu CDP in Hawaii and Arlington CDP in Virginia). For more information on these areas, see Appendix C, Geographic Information]

City	Number											Rate per 100,000 population[1]			
	Violent						Property					Violent		Property	
	2005					2000	2005				2000	2005	2000	2005	2000
	Total	Murder and non-negligent man-slaughter	Forcible rape	Robbery	Aggra-vated assault		Total	Burglary	Larceny-theft	Motor vehicle theft					
MASSACHUSETTS—Con.															
Quincy city	339	2	26	92	219	235	1,422	387	883	152	2,065	378	266	1,586	2,341
Revere city	302	1	16	72	213	(7)	1,806	347	1,139	320	1,290	656	(NA)	3,923	3,005
Salem city	98	–	2	27	69	97	973	171	735	67	1,190	234	246	2,328	3,019
Somerville city	262	1	7	139	115	165	1,673	521	833	319	1,883	347	217	2,218	2,479
Springfield city	2,691	18	109	771	1,793	2,762	8,703	2,141	4,974	1,588	9,616	1,774	1,825	5,738	6,353
Taunton city	(NA)	(NA)	(NA)	(NA)	(NA)	256	(NA)	(NA)	(NA)	(NA)	1,410	(NA)	469	(NA)	2,582
Waltham city	77	–	7	15	55	31	661	85	498	78	988	130	51	1,119	1,639
Watertown city	62	–	1	15	46	70	669	116	518	35	673	191	211	2,058	2,028
Westfield city	(7)	2	16	13	(7)	(7)	646	243	333	70	794	(NA)	(NA)	1,597	2,053
West Springfield city	125	2	4	32	87	(NA)	1,259	195	934	130	(NA)	447	(NA)	4,501	(NA)
Woburn city	64	1	3	16	44	68	842	116	622	104	834	171	177	2,255	2,168
Worcester city	1,390	6	143	389	852	1,488	6,078	1,248	3,673	1,157	7,339	792	866	3,464	4,271
MICHIGAN	55,877	616	5,193	13,342	36,726	55,159	312,843	70,519	194,101	48,223	353,297	552	555	3,091	3,555
Allen Park city	66	–	12	15	39	60	666	112	428	126	684	232	190	2,337	2,162
Ann Arbor city	358	–	37	102	219	303	3,379	859	2,282	238	3,676	315	274	2,973	3,324
Battle Creek city	755	6	61	109	579	853	3,472	691	2,594	187	4,194	1,197	1,577	5,506	7,751
Bay City city	168	–	30	31	107	190	1,155	292	789	74	1,536	475	542	3,268	4,381
Burton city	163	2	22	35	104	120	1,473	334	970	169	1,763	527	436	4,759	6,403
Dearborn city	571	3	30	223	315	770	4,924	651	3,191	1,082	5,065	598	866	5,153	5,699
Dearborn Heights city	206	–	25	82	99	143	1,808	424	967	417	1,744	362	246	3,179	2,997
Detroit city	21,240	354	589	6,820	13,477	22,112	53,972	15,304	17,383	21,285	73,649	2,358	2,274	5,991	7,574
East Lansing city	175	–	20	40	115	145	1,129	202	874	53	1,513	375	309	2,417	3,225
Eastpointe city	198	2	22	74	100	191	1,361	238	736	387	1,341	593	562	4,074	3,949
Farmington Hills city	178	3	23	38	114	161	1,642	403	1,086	153	1,790	220	201	2,031	2,229
Flint city	2,708	48	105	566	1,989	1,828	7,709	2,634	3,492	1,583	9,175	2,260	1,386	6,434	6,959
Garden City city	100	–	8	22	70	34	760	174	475	111	639	341	105	2,591	1,970
Grand Rapids city	1,962	8	66	674	1,214	2,114	9,766	2,038	7,050	678	10,831	1,005	1,134	5,001	5,810
Holland city	139	–	46	8	85	113	1,177	204	934	39	1,365	401	333	3,398	4,026
Inkster city	259	13	22	75	149	401	1,047	320	461	266	1,214	885	1,289	3,578	3,903
Jackson city	297	3	47	66	181	364	2,272	413	1,706	153	2,803	845	997	6,462	7,680
Kalamazoo city	596	3	55	178	360	813	4,541	1,106	3,116	319	5,169	805	1,066	6,135	6,781
Kentwood city	166	–	36	40	90	125	1,759	368	1,303	88	1,507	356	289	3,777	3,487
Lansing city	1,407	8	115	254	1,030	1,219	4,745	1,129	3,204	412	5,664	1,202	947	4,054	4,402
Lincoln Park city	146	4	8	47	87	204	1,919	361	1,155	403	1,872	377	483	4,949	4,434
Livonia city	170	3	13	62	92	190	2,301	444	1,574	283	2,852	172	188	2,324	2,826
Madison Heights city	80	–	13	36	31	79	1,300	175	822	303	1,356	262	248	4,257	4,263
Midland city	50	–	13	1	36	76	1,045	199	814	32	921	119	185	2,478	2,242
Mount Pleasant city	63	1	12	7	43	47	637	92	528	17	674	245	197	2,481	2,830
Muskegon city	464	3	57	99	305	381	2,817	523	2,056	238	3,140	1,160	960	7,045	7,910
Novi city	61	–	2	11	48	70	1,259	197	993	69	1,330	117	153	2,422	2,903
Oak Park city	173	–	18	71	84	(NA)	1,257	300	655	302	(NA)	595	(NA)	4,320	(NA)
Pontiac city	1,255	9	82	253	911	1,260	2,799	1,117	1,194	488	3,374	1,855	1,835	4,138	4,914
Portage city	127	1	15	28	83	94	1,955	287	1,604	64	2,048	281	212	4,321	4,620
Port Huron city	199	2	24	34	139	142	1,344	275	976	93	1,243	627	436	4,235	3,815
Rochester Hills city	(NA)	(NA)	(NA)	(NA)	(NA)	(NA)	(NA)	(NA)	(NA)	(NA)	(NA)	(NA)	(NA)	(NA)	(NA)
Roseville city	153	3	21	35	94	168	2,302	237	1,722	343	2,222	319	328	4,796	4,337
Royal Oak city	127	1	20	34	72	138	1,421	278	954	189	1,720	217	215	2,424	2,680
Saginaw city	1,606	17	44	212	1,333	1,188	2,610	1,286	948	376	3,217	2,718	1,889	4,417	5,115
St. Clair Shores city	161	–	11	35	115	152	1,455	266	942	247	1,459	260	231	2,350	2,216
Southfield city	939	4	22	159	754	736	3,747	748	2,149	850	4,696	1,211	978	4,831	6,237
Southgate city	104	–	8	27	69	108	1,388	161	1,000	227	1,163	347	330	4,635	3,554
Sterling Heights city	282	–	19	46	217	256	2,840	314	2,287	239	3,361	221	204	2,226	2,678
Taylor city	233	1	26	67	139	376	3,043	455	2,117	471	3,449	356	518	4,650	4,752
Troy city	72	1	8	19	44	105	1,991	277	1,578	136	2,319	88	132	2,443	2,911
Warren city	862	5	67	223	567	(NA)	(8)	812	2,251	(8)	(NA)	633	(NA)	(NA)	(NA)
Westland city	303	–	54	72	177	247	2,619	533	1,621	465	2,634	351	284	3,032	3,027
Wyandotte city	46	–	9	8	29	50	786	107	592	87	815	169	157	2,882	2,556
Wyoming city	295	–	32	72	191	258	1,997	568	1,218	211	2,365	419	370	2,838	3,388
MINNESOTA	15,243	115	2,258	4,724	8,146	13,813	158,301	29,716	114,304	14,281	157,798	297	281	3,084	3,208
Andover city	43	–	12	5	26	35	758	117	606	35	690	145	136	2,558	2,675
Apple Valley city	57	–	16	11	30	52	1,582	255	1,290	37	1,317	114	108	3,169	2,726
Blaine city	94	–	5	17	72	(NA)	2,387	242	2,042	103	(NA)	179	(NA)	4,550	(NA)
Bloomington city	(NA)	(NA)	(NA)	(NA)	(NA)	241	(NA)	(NA)	(NA)	(NA)	4,483	(NA)	271	(NA)	5,047
Brooklyn Center city	168	–	21	59	88	136	1,927	180	1,512	235	2,147	599	476	6,876	7,513
Brooklyn Park city	309	1	47	81	180	311	2,932	594	2,036	302	3,126	452	474	4,290	4,759
Burnsville city	114	3	18	32	61	62	1,693	249	1,355	89	1,896	191	100	2,833	3,052
Coon Rapids city	108	1	26	24	57	120	3,071	227	2,709	135	2,363	171	184	4,866	3,614
Cottage Grove city	43	–	15	5	23	35	864	148	670	46	767	133	106	2,671	2,333
Duluth city	(NA)	(NA)	(NA)	(NA)	(NA)	314	(NA)	(NA)	(NA)	(NA)	3,487	(NA)	376	(NA)	4,180

See footnotes at end of table.

Table C-2. Cities — **Crime**—Con.

[Includes states and 1,265 incorporated places of 25,000 or more population as of April 1, 2000, in all states except Hawaii, which has no incorporated places recognized by the U.S. Census Bureau. Two census designated places (CDPs) are also included (Honolulu CDP in Hawaii and Arlington CDP in Virginia). For more information on these areas, see Appendix C, Geographic Information]

City	Number											Rate per 100,000 population[1]			
	Violent						Property					Violent		Property	
	2005						2005								
	Total	Murder and non-negligent man-slaughter	Forcible rape	Robbery	Aggra-vated assault	2000	Total	Burglary	Larceny-theft	Motor vehicle theft	2000	2005	2000	2005	2000
MINNESOTA—Con.															
Eagan city	45	–	8	13	24	76	1,595	266	1,270	59	1,819	70	123	2,473	2,944
Eden Prairie city	57	–	13	21	23	61	1,177	182	955	40	1,518	94	122	1,936	3,037
Edina city	25	–	4	12	9	31	1,046	172	843	31	1,366	54	66	2,256	2,901
Fridley city	121	–	10	43	68	(NA)	1,523	124	1,259	140	(NA)	446	(NA)	5,618	(NA)
Inver Grove Heights city	56	–	13	10	33	62	1,080	144	859	77	948	172	199	3,319	3,041
Lakeville city	38	–	9	7	22	21	984	177	784	23	933	76	49	1,978	2,197
Mankato city	118	–	41	15	62	76	1,730	256	1,403	71	1,802	340	236	4,989	5,588
Maple Grove city	63	–	20	16	27	64	1,384	190	1,144	50	1,187	107	127	2,346	2,358
Maplewood city	90	–	4	32	54	(NA)	2,496	312	1,934	250	(NA)	252	(NA)	6,982	(NA)
Minneapolis city	5,472	47	402	2,584	2,439	4,404	22,417	5,535	12,988	3,894	23,085	1,454	1,210	5,958	6,341
Minnetonka city	44	–	12	13	19	38	1,123	219	848	56	1,435	87	71	2,229	2,689
Moorhead city	59	1	16	5	37	68	839	94	694	51	834	176	198	2,497	2,424
Oakdale city	63	–	12	21	30	51	1,124	148	875	101	978	227	182	4,051	3,482
Plymouth city	65	–	14	17	34	91	1,629	336	1,230	63	1,470	93	142	2,319	2,296
Richfield city	143	–	23	63	57	105	1,430	266	1,047	117	1,242	419	302	4,191	3,578
Rochester city	261	–	51	71	139	259	2,465	421	1,917	127	2,345	278	311	2,626	2,818
Roseville city	44	2	6	16	20	58	1,523	164	1,210	149	1,663	134	164	4,629	4,694
St. Cloud city	251	2	59	34	156	111	2,780	398	2,245	137	1,194	388	185	4,294	1,995
St. Louis Park city	88	–	13	35	40	74	1,506	299	1,106	101	1,473	201	169	3,432	3,368
St. Paul city	2,443	24	220	778	1,421	2,393	13,693	3,484	7,761	2,448	16,326	877	907	4,913	6,186
Shoreview city	8	–	2	1	5	(NA)	389	47	321	21	(NA)	29	(NA)	1,432	(NA)
Winona city	29	–	3	4	22	56	677	124	535	18	1,017	109	218	2,544	3,954
Woodbury city	33	2	7	5	19	39	1,237	157	1,022	58	999	66	85	2,458	2,181
MISSISSIPPI	8,131	214	1,147	2,405	4,365	10,267	95,231	26,866	60,873	7,492	103,644	278	361	3,260	3,643
Biloxi city	(NA)	(NA)	(NA)	(NA)	(NA)	316	(NA)	(NA)	(NA)	(NA)	4,844	(NA)	644	(NA)	9,871
Clinton city	(NA)	(NA)	(NA)	(NA)	(NA)	(NA)	(NA)	(NA)	(NA)	(NA)	(NA)	(NA)	(NA)	(NA)	(NA)
Columbus city	79	1	4	33	41	66	1,295	195	1,045	55	1,714	317	249	5,191	6,477
Greenville city	245	6	45	90	104	391	2,859	925	1,793	141	4,729	625	912	7,289	11,029
Gulfport city	227	6	34	110	77	265	4,597	1,164	3,108	325	5,675	314	399	6,358	8,540
Hattiesburg city	175	5	21	75	74	157	2,818	747	1,889	182	3,294	374	310	6,030	6,512
Jackson city	1,225	38	158	612	417	(NA)	12,008	3,139	6,960	1,909	(NA)	679	(NA)	6,656	(NA)
Meridian city	198	6	29	79	84	196	2,030	744	1,181	105	1,898	507	462	5,195	4,477
Pascagoula city	139	3	38	54	44	163	2,019	703	1,133	183	2,197	534	580	7,755	7,820
Southaven city	(NA)	(NA)	(NA)	(NA)	(NA)	72	(NA)	(NA)	(NA)	(NA)	1,905	(NA)	255	(NA)	6,753
Tupelo city	126	1	33	38	54	109	1,809	342	1,338	129	2,058	354	288	5,076	5,440
Vicksburg city	261	6	53	39	163	274	1,937	376	1,439	122	1,626	1,006	981	7,468	5,821
MISSOURI	30,477	402	1,625	7,196	21,254	27,419	227,809	42,822	159,288	25,699	225,739	525	490	3,928	4,035
Ballwin city	38	–	1	3	34	11	291	53	227	11	307	122	53	938	1,490
Blue Springs city	76	–	13	22	41	(NA)	2,022	293	1,589	140	(NA)	152	(NA)	4,055	(NA)
Cape Girardeau city	187	–	13	32	142	110	2,125	324	1,750	51	2,382	515	293	5,857	6,346
Chesterfield city	40	1	1	6	32	34	755	92	649	14	968	84	75	1,590	2,140
Columbia city	477	7	19	114	337	374	3,065	506	2,386	173	3,233	528	454	3,394	3,925
Florissant city	98	–	4	60	34	51	1,147	182	871	94	1,240	188	100	2,206	2,421
Gladstone city	58	–	1	17	40	40	884	129	646	109	839	212	138	3,227	2,891
Hazelwood city	119	–	5	25	89	(NA)	1,060	144	819	97	(NA)	460	(NA)	4,100	(NA)
Independence city	796	6	45	123	622	618	8,190	1,304	5,956	930	7,365	711	514	7,319	6,124
Jefferson City city	312	8	25	34	245	220	1,733	310	1,344	79	1,446	800	607	4,446	3,991
Joplin city	323	2	34	87	200	205	4,206	656	3,146	404	4,038	684	445	8,911	8,767
Kansas City city	6,536	126	295	2,000	4,115	7,181	34,822	7,429	21,603	5,790	39,944	1,459	1,603	7,774	8,918
Kirkwood city	70	1	1	8	60	29	758	54	677	27	610	256	105	2,769	2,199
Lee's Summit city	134	1	12	32	89	52	2,237	350	1,770	117	1,864	169	74	2,822	2,642
Liberty city	58	–	11	6	41	43	788	103	623	62	768	202	158	2,740	2,828
Maryland Heights city	29	–	–	13	16	54	1,005	107	800	98	1,272	113	222	3,924	5,232
O'Fallon city	59	1	6	9	43	49	1,827	187	1,587	53	1,638	87	121	2,705	4,054
Raytown city	77	1	2	41	33	82	1,321	243	952	126	1,017	260	277	4,466	3,438
St. Charles city	146	1	10	21	114	75	1,996	267	1,593	136	1,767	236	124	3,225	2,913
St. Joseph city	216	2	22	60	132	224	4,204	763	3,079	362	3,703	295	315	5,743	5,202
St. Louis city	8,323	131	276	2,965	4,951	7,936	38,245	7,213	22,886	8,146	42,717	2,405	2,322	11,053	12,501
St. Peters city	92	–	11	11	70	106	1,264	108	1,116	40	1,648	169	198	2,326	3,073
Springfield city	892	5	85	203	599	842	12,723	1,759	10,060	904	12,509	587	577	8,376	8,569
University City city	180	–	10	66	104	152	1,850	330	1,360	160	2,305	476	403	4,895	6,109
Wildwood city	(NA)	(NA)	(NA)	(NA)	(NA)	(NA)	(NA)	(NA)	(NA)	(NA)	(NA)	(NA)	(NA)	(NA)	(NA)
MONTANA	2,634	18	301	177	2,138	[4]2,171	29,407	3,642	23,794	1,971	[4]29,707	282	[4]241	3,143	[4]3,293
Billings city	201	5	34	50	112	(NA)	5,520	598	4,563	359	(NA)	205	(NA)	5,639	(NA)
Bozeman city	71	–	17	10	44	(NA)	1,577	207	1,249	121	(NA)	217	(NA)	4,819	(NA)
Butte-Silver Bow (balance)	(NA)	(NA)	(NA)	(NA)	(NA)	(NA)	(NA)	(NA)	(NA)	(NA)	(NA)	(NA)	(NA)	(NA)	(NA)
Great Falls city	171	2	20	25	124	316	3,394	297	2,959	138	3,842	300	549	5,950	6,673
Helena city	99	2	14	10	73	(NA)	1,046	119	862	65	(NA)	361	(NA)	3,810	(NA)
Missoula city	254	1	40	40	173	(NA)	3,629	395	3,046	188	(NA)	407	(NA)	5,818	(NA)

See footnotes at end of table.

Table C-2. Cities — **Crime**—Con.

[Includes states and 1,265 incorporated places of 25,000 or more population as of April 1, 2000, in all states except Hawaii, which has no incorporated places recognized by the U.S. Census Bureau. Two census designated places (CDPs) are also included (Honolulu CDP in Hawaii and Arlington CDP in Virginia). For more information on these areas, see Appendix C, Geographic Information]

	Number											Rate per 100,000 population[1]			
	Violent						Property					Violent		Property	
	2005						2005								
City	Total	Murder and non-negligent man-slaughter	Forcible rape	Robbery	Aggra-vated assault	2000	Total	Burglary	Larceny-theft	Motor vehicle theft	2000	2005	2000	2005	2000
NEBRASKA	5,048	44	579	1,040	3,385	5,606	60,207	9,363	45,277	5,567	64,479	287	328	3,423	3,768
Bellevue city	57	1	10	10	36	38	1,481	152	1,188	141	1,456	120	83	3,107	3,169
Fremont city	34	–	12	2	20	22	832	122	676	34	863	134	87	3,271	3,417
Grand Island city	99	1	17	13	68	157	2,545	384	2,057	104	2,838	222	364	5,709	6,586
Kearney city	57	–	13	4	40	76	876	127	722	27	1,391	198	261	3,039	4,772
Lincoln city	1,364	4	112	225	1,023	1,201	12,703	1,893	10,388	422	12,960	574	542	5,344	5,843
Omaha city	2,327	31	199	682	1,415	3,164	22,056	3,164	15,079	3,813	23,655	565	796	5,352	5,955
NEVADA	14,654	206	1,016	4,702	8,730	10,474	102,424	23,481	52,012	26,931	74,823	607	524	4,241	3,744
Carson City	(NA)	(NA)	(NA)	(NA)	(NA)	(NA)	(NA)	(NA)	(NA)	(NA)	(NA)	(NA)	(NA)	(NA)	(NA)
Henderson city	432	9	40	133	250	465	6,654	1,556	3,645	1,453	5,122	186	253	2,861	2,787
Las Vegas city[9]	9,530	145	616	3,494	5,275	6,349	62,013	14,368	27,695	19,950	41,059	744	622	4,838	4,025
North Las Vegas city	1,356	20	56	408	872	1,197	7,581	1,866	3,249	2,466	5,667	826	1,064	4,617	5,038
Reno city	1,518	8	110	421	979	896	10,989	1,916	7,547	1,526	9,069	741	487	5,367	4,927
Sparks city	359	5	56	96	202	281	3,235	740	2,045	450	3,084	428	395	3,861	4,340
NEW HAMPSHIRE	1,729	18	405	359	947	2,167	23,532	4,153	18,042	1,337	27,901	132	175	1,796	2,258
Concord city	69	–	18	16	35	(NA)	949	160	747	42	(NA)	162	(NA)	2,223	(NA)
Dover city	29	1	8	5	15	(NA)	492	44	432	16	(NA)	101	(NA)	1,713	(NA)
Manchester city	308	4	73	140	91	242	3,518	693	2,570	255	3,693	280	229	3,193	3,491
Nashua city	164	2	20	28	114	(NA)	2,061	308	1,622	131	(NA)	186	(NA)	2,339	(NA)
Rochester city	75	–	43	10	22	81	916	96	789	31	844	250	279	3,054	2,905
NEW JERSEY	30,919	417	1,208	13,215	16,079	32,298	203,391	38,980	136,728	27,683	233,637	355	384	2,333	2,777
Atlantic City city	753	9	44	374	326	530	4,514	522	3,838	154	6,533	1,852	1,360	11,099	16,767
Bayonne city	220	2	7	79	132	171	933	191	602	140	1,185	361	275	1,532	1,905
Bergenfield borough	20	–	–	12	8	22	192	22	153	17	258	76	87	731	1,016
Camden city	1,680	33	47	702	898	1,667	4,307	1,020	2,332	955	4,837	2,097	1,958	5,375	5,681
Clifton city	169	2	9	85	73	220	1,889	305	1,285	299	2,064	211	281	2,358	2,640
East Orange city	1,061	14	31	551	465	1,225	3,503	876	1,637	990	3,825	1,536	1,698	5,071	5,303
Elizabeth city	823	17	18	541	247	867	4,996	647	2,903	1,446	6,195	658	759	3,997	5,422
Englewood city	74	1	5	26	42	57	577	141	368	68	662	280	219	2,185	2,541
Fair Lawn borough	35	–	2	19	14	46	363	48	290	25	477	110	143	1,146	1,484
Fort Lee borough	25	–	1	12	12	26	373	67	273	33	620	67	74	998	1,772
Garfield city	73	1	–	40	32	57	592	140	381	71	620	244	203	1,980	2,203
Hackensack city	134	–	5	39	90	157	1,060	59	874	127	1,228	306	404	2,421	3,156
Hoboken city	114	1	2	54	57	141	1,370	390	815	165	1,294	283	408	3,403	3,748
Jersey City city	3,136	38	43	1,642	1,413	2,856	8,729	2,216	4,658	1,855	9,581	1,309	1,199	3,643	4,024
Kearny town	113	–	6	39	68	83	1,068	151	653	264	1,244	285	230	2,698	3,440
Linden city	104	–	2	60	42	150	1,465	172	924	369	1,555	259	392	3,654	4,063
Long Branch city	138	–	1	51	86	149	816	186	591	39	945	437	492	2,583	3,121
Millville city	241	1	18	80	142	191	1,494	315	1,108	71	1,229	871	695	5,399	4,475
Newark city	2,821	97	83	1,250	1,391	4,092	12,720	2,056	4,974	5,690	15,571	1,004	1,505	4,526	5,728
New Brunswick city	343	3	17	204	119	331	1,825	519	1,106	200	2,666	684	770	3,641	6,206
Paramus borough	66	1	1	28	36	136	1,491	68	1,349	74	2,337	247	509	5,588	8,740
Passaic city	684	4	6	331	343	834	1,619	363	977	279	2,270	994	1,319	2,353	3,591
Paterson city	1,444	20	32	588	804	1,204	4,433	1,413	2,107	913	5,239	955	784	2,932	3,411
Perth Amboy city	168	2	3	59	104	214	1,200	270	778	152	1,392	343	490	2,452	3,187
Plainfield city	517	15	16	244	242	676	1,577	371	853	353	2,098	1,075	1,415	3,279	4,392
Rahway city	87	–	2	44	41	69	551	95	376	80	813	315	265	1,994	3,121
Sayreville borough	57	1	7	18	31	94	688	103	519	66	803	133	236	1,609	2,012
Trenton city	1,515	31	21	805	658	1,374	3,574	962	1,940	672	4,995	1,771	1,576	4,177	5,728
Union City city	325	3	10	178	134	321	1,499	396	836	267	2,099	490	546	2,261	3,567
Vineland city	721	2	15	198	506	406	2,845	591	2,084	170	2,661	1,240	710	4,894	4,652
Westfield town	17	–	1	5	11	13	328	53	266	9	367	56	43	1,089	1,214
West New York town	168	3	8	89	68	162	861	227	508	126	1,198	363	398	1,858	2,942
NEW MEXICO	13,541	143	1,044	1,904	10,450	13,786	79,995	21,095	50,907	7,993	86,605	702	758	4,148	4,761
Alamogordo city	111	–	25	9	77	93	1,019	121	860	38	1,196	303	313	2,777	4,026
Albuquerque city	4,670	53	285	1,150	3,182	5,136	30,243	5,744	20,703	3,796	34,311	952	1,168	6,164	7,803
Carlsbad city	(NA)	(NA)	(NA)	(NA)	(NA)	134	(NA)	(NA)	(NA)	(NA)	1,594	(NA)	488	(NA)	5,805
Clovis city	240	2	21	34	183	450	2,031	624	1,285	122	1,989	716	1,366	6,063	6,039
Farmington city	(8)	3	66	27	(8)	384	1,523	412	918	193	1,704	(NA)	905	3,544	4,014
Hobbs city	333	4	22	20	287	274	2,478	324	2,088	66	1,256	1,145	974	8,519	4,466
Las Cruces city	465	5	96	101	263	460	3,949	750	2,954	245	6,305	577	581	4,901	7,957
Rio Rancho city	204	3	9	15	177	201	1,395	404	870	121	1,369	325	370	2,222	2,517
Roswell city	438	10	30	24	374	500	3,192	745	2,317	130	3,017	959	1,004	6,990	6,057
Santa Fe city	379	5	44	70	260	404	4,022	1,837	1,978	207	4,511	550	558	5,834	6,226

See footnotes at end of table.

Table C-2. Cities — **Crime**—Con.

[Includes states and 1,265 incorporated places of 25,000 or more population as of April 1, 2000, in all states except Hawaii, which has no incorporated places recognized by the U.S. Census Bureau. Two census designated places (CDPs) are also included (Honolulu CDP in Hawaii and Arlington CDP in Virginia). For more information on these areas, see Appendix C, Geographic Information]

City	Number Violent 2005 Total	Murder and non-negligent man-slaughter	Forcible rape	Robbery	Aggra-vated assault	Violent 2000	Property 2005 Total	Burglary	Larceny-theft	Motor vehicle theft	Property 2000	Rate Violent 2005	Rate Violent 2000	Rate Property 2005	Rate Property 2000
NEW YORK	85,839	874	3,636	35,179	46,150	105,111	405,990	68,034	302,220	35,736	483,078	446	554	2,109	2,546
Albany city	1,275	8	68	439	760	1,114	4,883	1,328	3,186	369	5,978	1,351	1,136	5,175	6,099
Auburn city	(NA)	(NA)	(NA)	(NA)	(NA)	74	(NA)	(NA)	(NA)	(NA)	1,056	(NA)	244	(NA)	3,485
Binghamton city	177	3	19	61	94	178	1,902	236	1,646	20	2,186	385	366	4,141	4,491
Buffalo city	3,938	56	184	1,667	2,031	3,657	16,730	4,240	10,089	2,401	16,591	1,390	1,186	5,906	5,382
Elmira city	121	2	14	39	66	(NA)	1,621	282	1,295	44	(NA)	402	(NA)	5,383	(NA)
Freeport village	157	2	8	66	81	(NA)	885	142	603	140	(NA)	359	(NA)	2,021	(NA)
Glen Cove city	(NA)	(NA)	(NA)	(NA)	(NA)	(NA)	(NA)	(NA)	(NA)	(NA)	(NA)	(NA)	(NA)	(NA)	(NA)
Hempstead village	395	4	16	210	165	354	1,085	204	565	316	1,039	742	726	2,039	2,130
Ithaca city	(NA)	(NA)	(NA)	(NA)	(NA)	(NA)	(NA)	(NA)	(NA)	(NA)	(NA)	(NA)	(NA)	(NA)	(NA)
Jamestown city	213	1	23	46	143	125	1,132	364	728	40	1,171	693	372	3,683	3,484
Lindenhurst village	(NA)	(NA)	(NA)	(NA)	(NA)	(NA)	(NA)	(NA)	(NA)	(NA)	(NA)	(NA)	(NA)	(NA)	(NA)
Long Beach city	94	–	1	30	63	81	355	30	281	44	511	264	226	997	1,426
Middletown city	122	2	12	58	50	85	810	114	657	39	691	466	336	3,097	2,729
Mount Vernon city	631	5	9	334	283	376	1,677	344	1,084	249	1,937	922	539	2,451	2,776
Newburgh city	432	3	12	174	243	438	1,077	294	707	76	1,292	1,511	1,606	3,767	4,737
New Rochelle city	260	3	4	146	107	212	1,428	177	1,147	104	1,649	356	301	1,954	2,341
New York city	54,623	539	1,412	24,722	27,950	75,745	162,509	23,210	120,918	18,381	212,623	673	978	2,002	2,745
Niagara Falls city	685	4	24	242	415	486	2,687	703	1,728	256	2,700	1,274	833	4,996	4,629
North Tonawanda city	47	1	3	12	31	41	568	126	415	27	639	146	121	1,762	1,889
Port Chester village	84	–	4	63	17	(NA)	851	92	724	35	(NA)	301	(NA)	3,046	(NA)
Poughkeepsie city	371	2	16	149	204	191	1,108	234	787	87	1,155	1,221	660	3,646	3,991
Rochester city	1,974	53	100	1,026	795	1,632	13,828	2,758	8,826	2,244	15,618	928	730	6,499	6,983
Rome city	49	–	8	10	31	47	627	164	428	35	678	142	114	1,812	1,638
Saratoga Springs city	34	–	3	4	27	28	577	98	457	22	731	123	104	2,081	2,720
Schenectady city	609	8	41	252	308	462	3,049	795	1,975	279	2,715	995	729	4,981	4,283
Spring Valley village	180	4	7	49	120	259	462	84	335	43	713	704	1,124	1,806	3,095
Syracuse city	1,570	19	73	554	924	1,565	6,486	1,867	3,639	980	7,565	1,096	997	4,526	4,818
Troy city	309	4	18	78	209	296	2,053	517	1,333	203	1,957	641	554	4,257	3,665
Utica city	268	8	18	133	109	287	2,672	619	1,967	86	2,509	448	468	4,471	4,095
Valley Stream village	(NA)	(NA)	(NA)	(NA)	(NA)	(NA)	(NA)	(NA)	(NA)	(NA)	(NA)	(NA)	(NA)	(NA)	(NA)
Watertown city	129	3	14	28	84	78	1,441	227	1,143	71	852	491	273	5,484	2,977
White Plains city	177	1	7	46	123	193	1,267	69	1,142	56	2,187	313	368	2,239	4,174
Yonkers city	970	9	21	518	422	981	3,406	641	2,277	488	4,699	491	491	1,725	2,353
NORTH CAROLINA	40,650	585	2,302	12,635	25,128	40,051	353,855	104,298	221,091	28,466	355,921	468	498	4,075	4,422
Asheville city	434	2	16	229	187	488	5,266	991	3,642	633	4,684	606	703	7,358	6,748
Burlington city	420	4	13	91	312	266	3,207	719	2,352	136	2,940	886	600	6,763	6,627
Cary town	133	–	13	50	70	78	1,963	432	1,428	103	2,217	129	81	1,907	2,310
Chapel Hill town	219	2	13	59	145	219	2,080	425	1,571	84	2,347	436	480	4,144	5,148
Charlotte city[10]	7,933	85	323	3,649	3,876	7,515	46,589	12,783	26,708	7,098	41,948	1,172	1,202	6,880	6,708
Concord city	221	5	15	74	127	(NA)	2,995	505	2,245	245	(NA)	363	(NA)	4,913	(NA)
Durham city	1,477	35	89	627	726	1,846	12,037	3,157	7,944	936	14,551	720	979	5,869	7,717
Fayetteville city	1,152	14	47	429	662	743	10,551	2,531	7,234	786	8,454	905	660	8,287	7,512
Gastonia city	670	5	36	257	372	901	6,190	1,268	4,389	533	5,745	965	1,379	8,916	8,792
Goldsboro city	325	7	3	109	206	442	2,694	594	1,956	144	3,126	824	942	6,834	6,665
Greensboro city	1,941	30	85	787	1,039	1,892	14,360	3,954	9,198	1,208	13,081	825	901	6,100	6,230
Greenville city	509	6	12	177	314	527	4,321	1,505	2,617	199	5,704	729	863	6,188	9,342
Hickory city	368	2	28	112	226	229	3,435	773	2,381	281	2,905	902	652	8,423	8,275
High Point city	616	8	27	217	364	739	5,957	1,970	3,509	478	5,882	653	913	6,310	7,265
Huntersville town	72	1	4	20	47	47	1,204	258	871	75	666	206	324	3,450	4,584
Jacksonville city	105	–	21	23	61	255	799	128	635	36	2,751	143	354	1,087	3,814
Kannapolis city	(NA)	(NA)	(NA)	(NA)	(NA)	103	(NA)	(NA)	(NA)	(NA)	815	(NA)	277	(NA)	2,193
Monroe city	218	5	13	54	146	238	2,005	401	1,482	122	2,112	754	1,013	6,939	8,987
Raleigh city	2,051	20	88	762	1,181	2,049	12,528	3,040	8,480	1,008	17,375	618	746	3,773	6,323
Rocky Mount city	497	8	22	197	270	602	4,876	1,380	3,264	232	5,143	868	985	8,511	8,416
Salisbury city	251	5	12	83	151	191	2,025	406	1,500	119	1,914	931	691	7,511	6,929
Wilmington city	794	8	57	292	437	753	6,558	1,855	4,000	703	7,214	837	1,097	6,915	10,508
Wilson city	233	4	8	55	166	350	1,927	561	1,271	95	2,704	493	806	4,076	6,229
Winston-Salem city	1,639	16	118	608	897	2,406	12,118	4,016	7,146	956	14,348	842	1,361	6,224	8,114
NORTH DAKOTA	625	7	154	47	417	523	12,595	1,986	9,552	1,057	14,171	98	81	1,978	2,207
Bismarck city	51	–	8	8	35	31	1,488	197	1,164	127	1,868	90	56	2,619	3,345
Fargo city	104	2	42	11	49	108	2,348	438	1,697	213	2,771	114	121	2,569	3,103
Grand Forks city	65	1	9	6	49	85	2,074	271	1,628	175	2,075	132	182	4,219	4,454
Minot city	81	1	28	4	48	40	1,041	108	855	78	1,163	230	111	2,951	3,217

See footnotes at end of table.

See footnotes at end of table.

Table C-2. Cities — **Crime**—Con.

[Includes states and 1,265 incorporated places of 25,000 or more population as of April 1, 2000, in all states except Hawaii, which has no incorporated places recognized by the U.S. Census Bureau. Two census designated places (CDPs) are also included (Honolulu CDP in Hawaii and Arlington CDP in Virginia). For more information on these areas, see Appendix C, Geographic Information]

City	Number Violent 2005 Total	Murder and non-negligent man-slaughter	Forcible rape	Robbery	Aggra-vated assault	Violent 2000	Property 2005 Total	Burglary	Larceny-theft	Motor vehicle theft	Property 2000	Rate Violent 2005	Rate Violent 2000	Rate Property 2005	Rate Property 2000
OHIO	40,273	585	4,557	18,696	16,435	37,935	419,899	100,063	278,457	41,379	420,939	351	334	3,663	3,708
Akron city	1,265	27	183	625	430	(NA)	12,040	3,409	7,253	1,378	(NA)	596	(NA)	5,672	(NA)
Barberton city	62	–	22	21	19	101	1,295	225	1,002	68	1,397	226	366	4,731	5,063
Beavercreek city	45	–	4	11	30	35	1,181	106	1,013	62	1,603	114	85	2,995	3,890
Bowling Green city	34	–	7	13	14	36	930	95	813	22	1,141	115	122	3,156	3,879
Brunswick city	(NA)	(NA)	(NA)	(NA)	(NA)	(NA)	(NA)	(NA)	(NA)	(NA)	(NA)	(NA)	(NA)	(NA)	(NA)
Canton city	668	4	57	381	226	1,154	6,051	1,566	3,939	546	5,268	836	1,456	7,569	6,647
Cincinnati city	3,723	79	315	2,319	1,010	2,671	22,411	5,430	14,029	2,952	18,975	1,185	800	7,131	5,685
Cleveland city	6,416	109	478	3,743	2,086	6,041	28,543	8,598	13,145	6,800	26,543	1,398	1,194	6,220	5,246
Cleveland Heights city	21	–	–	21	–	18	618	78	453	87	824	43	33	1,270	1,533
Columbus city	6,111	102	518	3,777	1,714	5,998	54,141	14,604	31,724	7,813	57,096	837	886	7,413	8,437
Cuyahoga Falls city	67	–	19	18	30	86	1,879	194	1,553	132	1,616	133	152	3,718	2,857
Dayton city	1,533	32	140	851	510	2,044	11,471	3,229	6,031	2,211	14,337	956	1,197	7,153	8,395
Delaware city	84	1	41	19	23	40	1,115	243	830	42	889	280	159	3,714	3,535
Dublin city	9	–	2	7	–	16	574	141	402	31	768	26	58	1,673	2,783
East Cleveland city	(NA)	(NA)	(NA)	(NA)	(NA)	(NA)	(NA)	(NA)	(NA)	(NA)	(NA)	(NA)	(NA)	(NA)	(NA)
Elyria city	(NA)	(NA)	(NA)	(NA)	(NA)	(NA)	(NA)	(NA)	(NA)	(NA)	(NA)	(NA)	(NA)	(NA)	(NA)
Euclid city	176	3	14	104	55	135	1,612	342	1,075	195	2,174	349	270	3,197	4,355
Fairborn city	163	1	39	46	77	79	1,425	312	1,033	80	1,467	503	232	4,395	4,306
Fairfield city	164	–	19	33	112	146	1,658	250	1,292	116	2,151	387	343	3,911	5,049
Findlay city	98	–	23	24	51	(NA)	1,871	375	1,457	39	(NA)	244	(NA)	4,655	(NA)
Gahanna city	43	–	5	27	11	45	887	179	647	61	911	131	148	2,704	3,006
Garfield Heights city	136	2	20	34	80	(NA)	918	234	620	64	(NA)	462	(NA)	3,116	(NA)
Grove City city	(NA)	(NA)	(NA)	(NA)	(NA)	50	(NA)	(NA)	(NA)	(NA)	1,133	(NA)	178	(NA)	4,033
Hamilton city	500	3	84	220	193	558	4,449	1,013	2,966	470	4,101	819	908	7,291	6,677
Huber Heights city	(NA)	(NA)	(NA)	(NA)	(NA)	87	(NA)	(NA)	(NA)	(NA)	1,719	(NA)	202	(NA)	4,000
Kent city	74	–	11	19	44	63	834	201	571	62	843	268	242	3,020	3,242
Kettering city	73	3	30	32	8	69	1,910	347	1,428	135	2,037	131	120	3,415	3,534
Lakewood city	114	2	5	37	70	157	1,334	237	961	136	1,413	211	287	2,471	2,584
Lancaster city	102	–	24	32	46	(NA)	1,952	339	1,509	104	(NA)	284	(NA)	5,430	(NA)
Lima city	453	5	92	126	230	360	2,678	839	1,687	152	2,944	1,151	837	6,806	6,847
Lorain city	341	6	14	119	202	279	2,321	661	1,499	161	2,211	502	411	3,416	3,254
Mansfield city	161	–	31	94	36	195	3,343	906	2,217	220	3,296	318	377	6,609	6,367
Maple Heights city	(NA)	(NA)	(NA)	(NA)	(NA)	(NA)	(NA)	(NA)	(NA)	(NA)	(NA)	(NA)	(NA)	(NA)	(NA)
Marion city	83	1	24	26	32	(NA)	1,493	345	1,115	33	(NA)	223	(NA)	4,019	(NA)
Massillon city	(NA)	(NA)	(NA)	(NA)	(NA)	(NA)	(NA)	(NA)	(NA)	(NA)	(NA)	(NA)	(NA)	(NA)	(NA)
Medina city	–	–	–	–	–	(NA)	128	20	100	8	(NA)	–	(NA)	1,524	(NA)
Mentor city	57	–	12	29	16	74	1,385	159	1,133	93	1,455	111	142	2,697	2,791
Middletown city	237	2	44	110	81	120	3,540	721	2,657	162	3,118	457	225	6,830	5,842
Newark city	114	–	29	56	29	106	2,495	570	1,801	124	2,092	244	221	5,335	4,357
North Olmsted city	45	1	8	16	20	(NA)	543	85	396	62	(NA)	136	(NA)	1,639	(NA)
North Royalton city	(NA)	(NA)	(NA)	(NA)	(NA)	(NA)	(NA)	(NA)	(NA)	(NA)	(NA)	(NA)	(NA)	(NA)	(NA)
Parma city	146	–	12	63	71	(NA)	1,966	573	1,216	177	(NA)	177	(NA)	2,377	(NA)
Reynoldsburg city	84	–	13	44	27	67	1,158	204	862	92	1,306	255	219	3,514	4,276
Sandusky city	189	1	7	49	132	200	1,831	385	1,379	67	1,871	700	710	6,784	6,642
Shaker Heights city	(NA)	(NA)	(NA)	(NA)	(NA)	59	(NA)	(NA)	(NA)	(NA)	718	(NA)	207	(NA)	2,516
Springfield city	548	7	70	280	191	842	6,321	1,832	4,027	462	5,207	861	1,281	9,933	7,924
Stow city	27	–	12	7	8	27	659	83	555	21	744	78	83	1,915	2,294
Strongsville city	38	–	5	13	20	31	805	116	659	30	781	86	77	1,816	1,930
Toledo city	3,725	28	179	1,356	2,162	2,380	23,630	7,101	13,331	3,198	21,643	1,221	766	7,745	6,968
Trotwood city	(NA)	(NA)	(NA)	(NA)	(NA)	210	(NA)	(NA)	(NA)	(NA)	1,748	(NA)	740	(NA)	6,162
Upper Arlington city	22	–	3	11	8	32	421	85	327	9	670	69	101	1,321	2,105
Warren city	65	–	1	5	59	(NA)	306	80	200	26	(NA)	1,031	(NA)	4,854	(NA)
Westerville city	32	–	2	17	13	23	958	151	784	23	972	92	66	2,748	2,810
Westlake city	(NA)	(NA)	(NA)	(NA)	(NA)	24	(NA)	(NA)	(NA)	(NA)	442	(NA)	80	(NA)	1,482
Youngstown city	917	34	60	347	476	967	4,698	1,718	2,216	764	5,329	1,179	1,159	6,043	6,385
Zanesville city	(NA)	(NA)	(NA)	(NA)	(NA)	(NA)	(NA)	(NA)	(NA)	(NA)	(NA)	(NA)	(NA)	(NA)	(NA)
OKLAHOMA	18,044	187	1,481	3,230	13,146	17,177	143,406	35,692	93,814	13,900	140,125	509	498	4,042	4,061
Bartlesville city	123	2	16	10	95	155	1,339	303	965	71	1,357	353	448	3,839	3,919
Broken Arrow city	188	–	11	22	155	130	2,070	415	1,484	171	2,094	221	168	2,436	2,705
Edmond city	111	1	26	18	66	51	1,922	389	1,453	80	1,530	151	74	2,612	2,230
Enid city	199	–	25	32	142	216	2,706	785	1,820	101	2,479	424	465	5,764	5,338
Lawton city	669	6	41	135	487	542	4,653	1,362	3,078	213	4,548	753	660	5,239	5,537
Midwest City city	147	–	19	37	91	165	2,428	553	1,616	259	2,092	266	296	4,398	3,758
Moore city	123	–	21	23	79	118	1,635	353	1,149	133	1,550	264	253	3,514	3,320
Muskogee city	272	3	30	52	187	308	2,052	720	1,210	122	2,361	695	780	5,246	5,978
Norman city	229	–	34	40	155	209	3,213	654	2,299	260	3,390	225	216	3,162	3,502
Oklahoma City city	4,538	54	358	1,193	2,933	3,951	42,145	8,925	28,635	4,585	43,894	854	809	7,927	8,987
Ponca City city	156	1	23	13	119	121	1,306	264	968	74	1,270	614	452	5,142	4,744
Shawnee city	167	–	15	30	122	84	1,702	454	1,063	185	1,638	558	292	5,683	5,697
Stillwater city	123	–	30	10	83	110	1,519	317	1,147	55	1,177	300	278	3,704	2,979
Tulsa city	4,995	58	303	1,096	3,538	4,411	25,169	6,592	14,847	3,730	22,442	1,293	1,125	6,513	5,724

See footnotes at end of table.

Table C-2. Cities — **Crime**—Con.

[Includes states and 1,265 incorporated places of 25,000 or more population as of April 1, 2000, in all states except Hawaii, which has no incorporated places recognized by the U.S. Census Bureau. Two census designated places (CDPs) are also included (Honolulu CDP in Hawaii and Arlington CDP in Virginia). For more information on these areas, see Appendix C, Geographic Information]

City	Number — Violent — 2005 Total	Murder and non-negligent man-slaughter	Forcible rape	Robbery	Aggra-vated assault	2000	Number — Property — 2005 Total	Burglary	Larceny-theft	Motor vehicle theft	2000	Rate per 100,000 population[1] Violent 2005	2000	Property 2005	2000
OREGON	10,444	80	1,266	2,478	6,620	12,000	160,199	27,621	113,316	19,262	153,780	287	351	4,400	4,495
Albany city	63	–	8	22	33	88	3,114	337	2,446	331	2,690	142	220	7,005	6,724
Beaverton city	189	1	32	43	113	163	2,957	340	2,301	316	2,749	225	245	3,521	4,127
Bend city	133	2	21	19	91	133	3,159	509	2,401	249	2,738	209	356	4,955	7,329
Corvallis city	69	1	11	18	39	75	1,994	247	1,656	91	2,192	135	143	3,907	4,184
Eugene city	328	5	54	119	150	620	9,902	1,603	6,639	1,660	9,282	227	460	6,851	6,894
Grants Pass city	37	2	10	14	11	53	1,742	140	1,459	143	1,864	134	226	6,324	7,953
Gresham city	500	3	69	148	280	386	5,347	882	3,216	1,249	5,239	518	430	5,535	5,830
Hillsboro city	163	2	30	63	68	(NA)	3,647	473	2,807	367	(NA)	197	(NA)	4,399	(NA)
Keizer city	86	1	9	12	64	30	999	164	717	118	1,285	247	98	2,866	4,176
Lake Oswego city	8	–	1	1	6	28	551	124	397	30	754	22	78	1,496	2,091
McMinnville city	46	1	8	16	21	29	985	125	800	60	1,203	157	115	3,356	4,771
Medford city	325	1	28	53	243	208	4,290	556	3,455	279	3,787	471	336	6,219	6,124
Oregon City city	29	–	7	12	10	51	1,329	186	1,024	119	1,194	96	202	4,408	4,740
Portland city	3,858	20	325	1,137	2,376	5,698	37,645	6,121	25,794	5,730	35,245	714	1,097	6,966	6,783
Salem city	706	3	53	134	516	337	9,004	1,170	6,752	1,082	9,646	477	252	6,083	7,211
Springfield city	195	–	10	36	149	92	4,859	814	3,207	838	4,323	350	176	8,714	8,257
Tigard city	103	–	16	29	58	93	2,289	307	1,824	158	2,303	217	236	4,822	5,841
PENNSYLVANIA	52,761	756	3,586	19,214	29,205	51,584	300,444	56,134	214,916	29,394	316,274	424	420	2,417	2,575
Allentown city	863	21	45	512	285	688	5,771	1,393	3,905	473	4,828	807	671	5,397	4,708
Altoona city	186	5	26	69	86	192	1,653	463	1,117	73	1,684	388	380	3,449	3,332
Bethel Park borough	18	–	–	4	14	(NA)	316	46	261	9	(NA)	55	(NA)	965	(NA)
Bethlehem city	268	2	17	114	135	222	2,301	409	1,700	192	2,226	369	312	3,170	3,128
Chester city	934	15	34	229	656	1,113	1,480	480	710	290	1,723	2,525	2,707	4,001	4,191
Easton city	176	3	16	47	110	177	1,078	189	745	144	1,033	669	683	4,096	3,989
Erie city	472	6	75	200	191	467	2,867	632	2,129	106	3,370	453	449	2,754	3,243
Harrisburg city	805	12	52	480	261	(NA)	2,336	600	1,583	153	(NA)	1,687	(NA)	4,895	(NA)
Lancaster city	420	1	32	189	198	609	3,025	549	2,271	205	3,232	760	1,128	5,472	5,988
Municipality of Monroeville borough	93	2	5	29	57	103	837	114	636	87	886	326	364	2,933	3,128
New Castle city	(NA)	(NA)	(NA)	(NA)	(NA)	179	(NA)	(NA)	(NA)	(NA)	881	(NA)	677	(NA)	3,330
Norristown borough	(NA)	(NA)	(NA)	(NA)	(NA)	358	(NA)	(NA)	(NA)	(NA)	1,543	(NA)	1,194	(NA)	5,147
Philadelphia city	21,609	377	1,024	10,069	10,139	22,812	60,419	10,960	38,039	11,420	75,188	1,467	1,572	4,102	5,180
Pittsburgh city	3,385	63	117	1,617	1,588	3,267	15,628	3,018	10,337	2,273	16,189	1,023	929	4,725	4,602
Plum borough	5	–	4	1	–	(NA)	232	52	165	15	(NA)	19	(NA)	868	(NA)
Reading city	936	22	51	372	491	897	5,093	1,512	2,520	1,061	4,996	1,157	1,187	6,297	6,613
Scranton city	452	1	47	89	315	(NA)	2,371	630	1,569	172	(NA)	610	(NA)	3,201	(NA)
State College borough	32	–	4	6	22	52	884	138	726	20	1,385	61	98	1,673	2,603
Wilkes-Barre city	207	3	30	112	62	(NA)	1,602	338	1,143	121	(NA)	497	(NA)	3,848	(NA)
Williamsport city	134	3	16	64	51	(NA)	1,202	219	917	66	(NA)	443	(NA)	3,976	(NA)
York city	413	13	39	242	119	(NA)	2,314	400	1,703	211	(NA)	1,029	(NA)	5,768	(NA)
RHODE ISLAND	2,703	34	321	776	1,572	3,121	29,260	5,318	19,544	4,398	33,323	251	298	2,719	3,179
Cranston city	137	–	12	48	77	142	2,073	322	1,480	271	2,076	168	179	2,539	2,616
East Providence city	64	–	10	18	36	112	761	149	530	82	898	129	221	1,536	1,774
Newport city	110	–	16	13	81	152	1,157	241	861	55	1,431	427	593	4,489	5,582
Pawtucket city	261	3	24	106	128	375	2,763	512	1,815	436	2,568	353	524	3,736	3,587
Providence city	1,207	20	106	424	657	1,170	9,124	1,835	5,025	2,264	11,670	680	738	5,143	7,359
Warwick city	122	4	18	24	76	169	2,614	277	2,021	316	2,618	140	190	2,994	2,946
Woonsocket city	(NA)	(NA)	(NA)	(NA)	(NA)	154	(NA)	(NA)	(NA)	(NA)	1,064	(NA)	352	(NA)	2,429
SOUTH CAROLINA	32,384	315	1,809	5,622	24,638	32,293	184,646	42,589	125,699	16,358	177,189	761	805	4,339	4,416
Aiken city	105	1	6	23	75	(NA)	1,356	192	1,102	62	(NA)	379	(NA)	4,901	(NA)
Anderson city	166	2	10	32	122	(NA)	1,614	334	1,145	135	(NA)	637	(NA)	6,192	(NA)
Charleston city	1,003	10	49	290	654	(NA)	4,756	810	3,464	482	(NA)	943	(NA)	4,474	(NA)
Columbia city	1,311	15	56	381	859	1,500	7,682	1,332	5,513	837	8,467	1,112	1,333	6,515	7,524
Florence city	555	4	18	201	332	605	3,387	592	2,582	213	3,626	1,773	1,950	10,820	11,685
Goose Creek city	77	1	5	19	52	(NA)	762	125	579	58	(NA)	236	(NA)	2,331	(NA)
Greenville city	656	5	32	161	458	845	3,794	776	2,710	308	4,674	1,150	1,439	6,650	7,960
Hilton Head Island town	(NA)	(NA)	(NA)	(NA)	(NA)	(NA)	(NA)	(NA)	(NA)	(NA)	(NA)	(NA)	(NA)	(NA)	(NA)
Mount Pleasant town	194	–	12	36	146	(NA)	1,295	181	1,006	108	(NA)	340	(NA)	2,267	(NA)
North Charleston city	1,473	11	82	519	861	(NA)	7,328	1,365	5,033	930	(NA)	1,725	(NA)	8,579	(NA)
Rock Hill city	709	4	41	85	579	(NA)	2,770	464	2,111	195	(NA)	1,208	(NA)	4,720	(NA)
Spartanburg city	692	11	28	149	504	964	4,097	939	2,866	292	4,010	1,769	2,294	10,472	9,541
Summerville town	133	1	10	34	88	(NA)	1,342	185	1,059	98	(NA)	383	(NA)	3,867	(NA)
Sumter city	602	3	8	117	474	(NA)	2,324	616	1,580	128	(NA)	1,497	(NA)	5,780	(NA)
SOUTH DAKOTA	1,363	18	362	144	839	1,259	13,784	2,517	10,426	841	16,252	176	167	1,776	2,153
Rapid City city	257	1	58	38	160	219	2,551	459	1,980	112	2,608	415	365	4,124	4,347
Sioux Falls city	473	4	145	71	253	401	4,264	682	3,253	329	3,886	344	334	3,099	3,234

See footnotes at end of table.

Table C-2. Cities — **Crime**—Con.

[Includes states and 1,265 incorporated places of 25,000 or more population as of April 1, 2000, in all states except Hawaii, which has no incorporated places recognized by the U.S. Census Bureau. Two census designated places (CDPs) are also included (Honolulu CDP in Hawaii and Arlington CDP in Virginia). For more information on these areas, see Appendix C, Geographic Information]

City	Number Violent 2005 Total	Murder and non-negligent man-slaughter	Forcible rape	Robbery	Aggra-vated assault	Violent 2000	Property 2005 Total	Burglary	Larceny-theft	Motor vehicle theft	Property 2000	Rate Violent 2005	Rate Violent 2000	Rate Property 2005	Rate Property 2000
TENNESSEE	44,891	432	2,171	9,974	32,314	40,233	254,948	61,233	168,637	25,078	237,985	753	707	4,276	4,183
Bartlett city	60	–	7	21	32	65	1,069	161	844	64	934	139	169	2,468	2,425
Brentwood city	21	–	1	7	13	11	550	73	461	16	646	68	44	1,780	2,577
Bristol city	139	–	9	12	118	126	1,394	234	1,088	72	932	552	494	5,533	3,657
Chattanooga city	1,754	23	116	442	1,173	2,734	12,606	2,190	9,365	1,051	15,250	1,121	1,791	8,056	9,991
Clarksville city	881	5	52	138	686	598	4,129	1,071	2,802	256	4,370	800	582	3,750	4,252
Cleveland city	(NA)	(NA)	(NA)	(NA)	(NA)	196	(NA)	(NA)	(NA)	(NA)	1,736	(NA)	523	(NA)	4,630
Collierville town	64	3	2	11	48	45	614	98	460	56	456	173	169	1,662	1,715
Columbia city	433	3	22	72	336	411	1,796	347	1,341	108	1,932	1,275	1,226	5,290	5,764
Cookeville city	(NA)	(NA)	(NA)	(NA)	(NA)	134	(NA)	(NA)	(NA)	(NA)	1,288	(NA)	495	(NA)	4,762
Franklin city	115	2	7	14	92	(NA)	906	97	751	58	(NA)	236	(NA)	1,860	(NA)
Germantown city	37	–	3	13	21	57	690	120	533	37	1,013	97	145	1,818	2,584
Hendersonville city	143	1	7	14	121	109	950	162	714	74	1,005	323	264	2,143	2,438
Jackson city	836	5	49	177	605	863	4,885	1,269	3,141	475	3,834	1,339	1,539	7,826	6,839
Johnson City city	375	5	20	73	277	361	3,697	692	2,797	208	3,407	642	588	6,328	5,551
Kingsport city	403	3	32	71	297	325	3,253	521	2,553	179	2,144	905	732	7,305	4,832
Knoxville city	1,728	25	99	545	1,059	1,849	11,062	2,471	7,370	1,221	8,887	960	1,019	6,146	4,899
Memphis city	12,629	137	400	4,464	7,628	9,610	56,780	15,844	32,632	8,304	49,951	1,860	1,528	8,362	7,943
Morristown city	248	2	11	37	198	199	1,788	204	1,441	143	1,581	964	823	6,949	6,540
Murfreesboro city [11]	641	2	35	113	491	432	4,021	790	2,994	237	3,408	778	681	4,882	5,369
Nashville-Davidson (balance) [11]	8,974	95	336	2,440	6,103	8,901	35,796	6,448	25,900	3,448	39,689	1,611	1,668	6,426	7,440
Oak Ridge city	169	1	11	51	106	116	1,880	383	1,350	147	1,469	613	417	6,815	5,286
Smyrna town	190	–	8	17	165	107	1,112	192	861	59	1,238	589	410	3,447	4,742
TEXAS	121,091	1,407	8,511	35,790	75,383	113,653	990,293	219,828	644,042	93,423	919,658	530	545	4,332	4,410
Abilene city	576	5	78	146	347	404	5,504	1,521	3,685	298	4,393	494	356	4,717	3,874
Allen city	53	–	9	14	30	63	1,528	286	1,188	54	1,076	79	144	2,266	2,458
Amarillo city	1,537	10	88	347	1,092	1,434	11,850	2,549	8,245	1,056	12,294	836	802	6,448	6,872
Arlington city	2,369	24	178	768	1,399	2,157	20,403	3,984	14,609	1,810	19,323	648	665	5,584	5,954
Austin city	3,393	26	312	1,182	1,873	3,063	41,668	7,285	31,835	2,548	35,611	490	501	6,013	5,823
Baytown city	291	4	32	112	143	239	3,042	705	2,100	237	3,016	425	330	4,446	4,166
Beaumont city	1,130	11	97	337	685	1,073	8,320	2,057	5,735	528	7,170	990	940	7,289	6,283
Bedford city	240	2	14	35	189	115	1,825	342	1,344	139	1,490	488	219	3,708	2,839
Big Spring city	87	1	18	13	55	95	872	346	483	43	1,092	349	415	3,498	4,773
Brownsville city	903	4	53	128	718	912	8,313	1,236	6,647	430	10,508	551	594	5,073	6,839
Bryan city	617	6	45	93	473	440	4,216	1,207	2,784	225	4,044	915	718	6,255	6,598
Carrollton city	300	5	12	95	188	208	4,090	916	2,675	499	3,501	250	194	3,415	3,258
Cedar Hill city	123	–	9	37	77	96	1,427	311	972	144	994	301	312	3,491	3,234
Cedar Park city	85	1	14	10	60	24	686	157	499	30	517	184	85	1,488	1,833
Cleburne city	151	1	22	16	112	91	1,529	278	1,142	109	1,713	516	334	5,223	6,285
College Station city	206	2	38	38	128	134	2,929	555	2,292	82	2,532	281	211	3,992	3,982
Conroe city	340	2	24	101	213	307	2,638	569	1,897	172	2,279	771	766	5,980	5,688
Coppell city	22	1	2	3	16	10	930	206	666	58	165	56	31	2,350	518
Copperas Cove city	107	1	22	24	60	146	1,037	245	769	23	1,023	351	452	3,401	3,168
Corpus Christi city	2,048	8	217	481	1,342	2,104	20,133	3,357	15,870	906	17,905	717	718	7,044	6,108
Dallas city	15,429	202	562	6,882	7,783	16,042	88,955	22,363	52,315	14,277	89,008	1,254	1,433	7,230	7,950
Deer Park city	43	1	9	9	24	25	629	126	456	47	549	148	78	2,160	1,713
Del Rio city	58	1	1	10	46	145	1,245	211	973	61	1,377	159	390	3,420	3,705
Denton city	378	5	72	76	225	270	4,110	684	3,180	246	2,963	378	328	4,114	3,596
DeSoto city	141	1	6	35	99	190	1,762	552	1,072	138	1,389	322	505	4,027	3,695
Duncanville city	169	1	7	53	108	168	1,422	346	905	171	1,344	470	449	3,958	3,958
Edinburg city	442	1	31	67	343	327	4,945	712	3,887	346	4,365	744	692	8,324	9,231
El Paso city	2,614	14	295	448	1,857	4,396	19,675	2,151	14,925	2,599	30,276	434	690	3,269	4,749
Euless city	162	3	7	49	103	102	1,892	371	1,379	142	1,415	315	214	3,680	2,963
Farmers Branch city	57	3	5	22	27	82	1,249	244	795	210	1,338	210	299	4,601	4,876
Flower Mound town	31	1	1	5	24	38	673	104	524	45	666	49	74	1,064	1,302
Fort Worth city	3,920	60	311	1,379	2,170	3,816	37,210	8,684	24,811	3,715	34,327	639	730	6,068	6,568
Friendswood city	42	–	6	5	31	67	433	103	308	22	399	126	219	1,302	1,304
Frisco city	74	1	15	10	48	42	2,542	608	1,850	84	782	117	126	4,010	2,342
Galveston city	530	8	87	172	263	(NA)	3,580	687	2,530	363	(NA)	909	(NA)	6,141	(NA)
Garland city	655	7	41	239	368	471	8,206	2,011	5,445	750	8,202	297	234	3,717	4,079
Georgetown city	44	–	10	5	29	17	695	105	546	44	571	119	50	1,875	1,696
Grand Prairie city	449	9	56	170	214	446	7,468	1,439	4,979	1,050	6,075	315	373	5,236	5,082
Grapevine city	91	2	9	25	55	44	1,457	238	1,095	124	1,721	189	100	3,033	3,929
Haltom City city	164	1	17	36	110	127	2,272	511	1,453	308	1,220	402	325	5,570	3,127
Harlingen city	330	–	24	63	243	303	4,959	1,128	3,598	233	3,806	527	510	7,921	6,403
Houston city	23,987	334	872	11,128	11,653	21,491	120,425	27,541	72,476	20,408	110,220	1,173	1,119	5,887	5,740
Huntsville city	135	–	7	29	99	154	1,404	269	1,058	77	1,245	371	460	3,854	3,723
Hurst city	169	–	16	27	126	134	2,080	268	1,686	126	2,040	439	346	5,400	5,266
Irving city	910	2	66	270	572	784	9,548	1,730	6,658	1,160	8,241	460	420	4,828	4,413

See footnotes at end of table.

Table C-2. Cities — **Crime**—Con.

[Includes states and 1,265 incorporated places of 25,000 or more population as of April 1, 2000, in all states except Hawaii, which has no incorporated places recognized by the U.S. Census Bureau. Two census designated places (CDPs) are also included (Honolulu CDP in Hawaii and Arlington CDP in Virginia). For more information on these areas, see Appendix C, Geographic Information]

City	Number Violent 2005 Total	Murder and non-negligent man-slaughter	Forcible rape	Robbery	Aggra-vated assault	Violent 2000	Number Property 2005 Total	Burglary	Larceny-theft	Motor vehicle theft	Property 2000	Rate Violent 2005	Rate Violent 2000	Rate Property 2005	Rate Property 2000
TEXAS—Con.															
Keller city	35	1	8	5	21	76	601	95	483	23	437	99	291	1,693	1,672
Killeen city	806	8	85	224	489	575	5,862	2,071	3,644	147	4,628	818	679	5,949	5,465
Kingsville city	182	1	9	16	156	115	1,593	477	1,080	36	1,118	709	445	6,205	4,330
Lake Jackson city	34	–	3	12	19	26	809	111	670	28	898	124	92	2,945	3,162
Lancaster city	158	3	6	24	125	197	1,691	520	974	197	1,338	513	770	5,490	5,227
La Porte city	32	–	6	4	22	76	574	138	365	71	612	95	218	1,698	1,759
Laredo city	1,054	18	64	246	726	972	12,462	1,552	9,953	957	12,412	510	510	6,033	6,514
League City city	42	1	11	9	21	49	1,537	365	1,088	84	1,018	71	105	2,608	2,176
Lewisville city	199	2	23	55	119	168	3,772	510	2,913	349	3,148	220	209	4,163	3,912
Longview city	846	8	67	127	644	474	4,926	1,087	3,272	567	4,673	1,105	603	6,435	5,947
Lubbock city	2,222	11	105	309	1,797	2,508	12,786	2,697	9,312	777	11,985	1,052	1,269	6,052	6,064
Lufkin city	188	2	22	39	125	209	1,165	341	744	80	2,019	552	600	3,421	5,797
McAllen city	421	8	34	129	250	389	8,187	734	6,877	576	8,351	343	339	6,671	7,278
McKinney city	228	1	44	41	142	(NA)	2,059	451	1,469	139	(NA)	254	(NA)	2,291	(NA)
Mansfield city	108	–	7	19	82	56	1,124	261	776	87	708	306	217	3,184	2,739
Mesquite city	530	7	15	169	339	427	5,510	837	3,964	709	5,632	402	353	4,179	4,660
Midland city	408	1	80	50	277	395	3,765	779	2,808	178	2,906	409	386	3,777	2,842
Mission city	72	4	5	20	43	55	3,437	619	2,497	321	2,788	123	120	5,849	6,098
Missouri City city	167	2	13	73	79	96	1,288	345	826	117	1,174	247	139	1,903	1,701
Nacogdoches city	111	–	13	33	65	223	1,173	221	914	38	1,306	356	696	3,766	4,076
New Braunfels city	122	–	8	19	95	194	2,028	295	1,643	90	2,502	267	487	4,441	6,283
North Richland Hills city	158	–	21	37	100	188	2,144	416	1,599	129	2,257	257	322	3,487	3,864
Odessa city	590	3	12	72	503	500	3,720	756	2,785	179	4,323	625	538	3,942	4,654
Paris city	250	1	55	41	153	(NA)	2,555	432	2,036	87	2,415	925	(NA)	9,458	8,856
Pasadena city	632	5	51	146	430	543	4,914	1,063	3,397	454	5,799	431	391	3,353	4,171
Pearland city	86	1	34	22	29	64	1,373	364	921	88	1,074	161	176	2,578	2,955
Pharr city	198	4	17	52	125	266	2,912	573	2,183	156	3,010	343	558	5,040	6,311
Plano city	721	2	54	119	546	623	8,677	1,365	6,723	589	7,247	289	257	3,478	2,991
Port Arthur city	370	11	26	118	215	431	2,809	938	1,632	239	2,442	642	732	4,872	4,149
Richardson city	261	2	12	98	149	280	3,478	764	2,437	277	3,596	259	308	3,447	3,950
Round Rock city	121	–	21	24	76	116	2,205	281	1,873	51	1,373	145	166	2,644	1,965
Rowlett city	69	–	3	17	49	58	1,011	185	747	79	938	129	139	1,885	2,242
San Angelo city	373	3	55	40	275	342	5,358	1,137	3,941	280	4,454	416	373	5,983	4,852
San Antonio city	8,007	86	593	2,154	5,174	7,908	80,987	14,365	60,649	5,973	78,424	637	663	6,445	6,571
San Juan city	149	1	6	14	128	(NA)	1,893	385	1,399	109	(NA)	493	(NA)	6,262	(NA)
San Marcos city	157	3	24	25	105	181	1,406	208	1,071	127	1,400	346	429	3,100	3,320
Sherman city	159	3	6	19	131	198	1,932	439	1,405	88	1,980	428	558	5,196	5,581
Socorro city	82	–	8	8	66	38	505	77	371	57	525	288	133	1,773	1,833
Sugar Land city	117	1	4	62	50	95	1,829	285	1,434	110	1,703	156	133	2,441	2,392
Temple city	175	3	5	57	110	177	2,546	502	1,893	151	2,558	316	326	4,596	4,715
Texarkana city	500	3	31	69	397	316	2,646	556	1,926	164	2,232	1,386	941	7,335	6,646
Texas City city	191	2	19	87	83	434	2,812	859	1,735	218	3,166	432	977	6,355	7,127
The Colony city	29	–	4	7	18	34	862	165	631	66	1,084	79	126	2,335	4,020
Tyler city	574	6	52	172	344	638	4,728	1,119	3,412	197	5,624	631	732	5,194	6,452
Victoria city	300	2	34	58	206	442	3,654	829	2,670	155	3,261	479	689	5,828	5,081
Waco city	895	12	60	257	566	938	8,845	2,413	5,740	692	8,396	746	831	7,369	7,437
Weslaco city	144	1	8	36	99	121	2,447	468	1,811	168	2,151	456	370	7,746	6,584
Wichita Falls city	733	6	43	239	445	586	7,641	1,703	5,386	552	5,685	715	569	7,448	5,525
UTAH	5,612	56	920	1,095	3,541	5,711	95,546	14,971	72,082	8,493	94,247	227	256	3,869	4,220
Bountiful city	69	1	19	11	38	104	1,045	175	798	72	955	162	241	2,455	2,212
Clearfield city	37	–	14	6	17	44	891	120	714	57	856	131	155	3,166	3,015
Draper city	33	1	8	4	20	(NA)	1,144	182	897	65	(NA)	97	(NA)	3,349	(NA)
Layton city	95	2	32	17	44	105	1,897	289	1,500	108	2,193	150	177	2,998	3,704
Logan city	38	1	16	5	16	(NA)	1,044	162	842	40	(NA)	81	(NA)	2,219	(NA)
Midvale city	111	–	28	17	66	96	1,605	178	1,232	195	1,632	397	306	5,747	5,207
Murray city	164	–	22	40	102	131	3,903	472	3,069	362	3,018	366	385	8,714	8,870
Ogden city	383	5	40	121	217	443	4,931	797	3,723	411	5,083	472	619	6,075	7,107
Orem city	65	–	16	13	36	54	3,483	392	2,909	182	3,421	71	62	3,802	3,933
Provo city	182	3	55	17	107	128	3,298	673	2,417	208	3,789	177	110	3,202	3,265
Riverton city	(NA)	(NA)	(NA)	(NA)	(NA)	(NA)	(NA)	(NA)	(NA)	(NA)	(NA)	(NA)	(NA)	(NA)	(NA)
Roy city	53	–	17	7	29	87	764	113	603	48	853	145	259	2,093	2,541
St. George city	224	1	13	12	198	(NA)	1,865	385	1,249	231	(NA)	362	(NA)	3,018	(NA)
Salt Lake City city	1,283	10	72	417	784	1,301	15,859	2,172	11,608	2,079	15,530	695	725	8,590	8,654
Sandy city	161	1	14	27	119	126	3,240	474	2,530	236	2,950	173	118	3,483	2,762
South Jordan city	30	–	6	3	21	32	889	116	724	49	625	79	109	2,338	2,128
Taylorsville city	(NA)	(NA)	(NA)	(NA)	(NA)	(NA)	(NA)	(NA)	(NA)	(NA)	(NA)	(NA)	(NA)	(NA)	(NA)
West Jordan city	(NA)	(NA)	(NA)	(NA)	(NA)	124	(NA)	(NA)	(NA)	(NA)	2,588	(NA)	182	(NA)	3,789
West Valley City city	519	10	89	93	327	492	7,086	1,039	5,233	814	6,644	446	457	6,084	6,169

See footnotes at end of table.

Table C-2. Cities — **Crime**—Con.

[Includes states and 1,265 incorporated places of 25,000 or more population as of April 1, 2000, in all states except Hawaii, which has no incorporated places recognized by the U.S. Census Bureau. Two census designated places (CDPs) are also included (Honolulu CDP in Hawaii and Arlington CDP in Virginia). For more information on these areas, see Appendix C, Geographic Information]

City	Number											Rate per 100,000 population[1]			
	Violent					Property						Violent		Property	
	2005					2005									
	Total	Murder and non-negligent man-slaughter	Forcible rape	Robbery	Aggra-vated assault	2000	Total	Burglary	Larceny-theft	Motor vehicle theft	2000	2005	2000	2005	2000
VERMONT	746	8	145	73	520	691	14,210	3,064	10,505	641	17,494	120	113	2,281	2,873
Burlington city	(NA)	(NA)	(NA)	(NA)	(NA)	178	(NA)	(NA)	(NA)	(NA)	2,845	(NA)	453	(NA)	7,238
VIRGINIA	21,400	461	1,721	7,507	11,711	19,943	199,644	29,672	154,000	15,972	194,405	283	282	2,638	2,746
Alexandria city.	462	3	22	199	238	(NA)	3,331	294	2,570	467	(NA)	355	(NA)	2,561	(NA)
Arlington CDP	(NA)	(NA)	(NA)	(NA)	(NA)	(NA)	(NA)	(NA)	(NA)	(NA)	(NA)	(NA)	(NA)	(NA)	(NA)
Blacksburg town	55	–	8	13	34	59	562	105	435	22	655	138	166	1,413	1,846
Charlottesville city	307	2	35	72	198	399	1,875	264	1,442	169	1,924	827	1,052	5,049	5,074
Chesapeake city	1,117	14	51	298	754	(NA)	7,870	1,426	5,905	539	(NA)	513	(NA)	3,613	(NA)
Danville city	248	8	12	88	140	(NA)	2,178	322	1,745	111	(NA)	527	(NA)	4,630	(NA)
Hampton city	595	11	47	276	261	(NA)	5,388	887	3,941	560	(NA)	402	(NA)	3,639	(NA)
Harrisonburg city	98	2	14	35	47	137	1,164	205	883	76	1,391	235	390	2,794	3,957
Leesburg town	84	–	8	22	54	74	720	40	631	49	557	238	268	2,038	2,017
Lynchburg city.	257	6	23	73	155	292	2,390	412	1,805	173	2,460	390	444	3,628	3,736
Manassas city	188	–	21	64	103	135	1,196	137	937	122	1,286	493	391	3,134	3,728
Newport News city	1,439	20	103	542	774	1,340	8,216	1,470	5,887	859	8,617	780	726	4,452	4,671
Norfolk city	1,841	59	92	886	804	1,663	13,061	1,769	10,153	1,139	14,250	763	715	5,414	6,126
Petersburg city	364	9	25	149	181	373	2,625	803	1,534	288	2,386	1,095	1,053	7,899	6,735
Portsmouth city	901	22	41	366	472	(NA)	5,164	1,049	3,708	407	(NA)	895	(NA)	5,127	(NA)
Richmond city	2,385	84	80	1,196	1,025	2,344	12,898	2,529	8,168	2,201	14,366	1,221	1,200	6,605	7,353
Roanoke city	895	16	55	228	596	(NA)	6,369	1,011	4,912	446	(NA)	955	(NA)	6,798	(NA)
Suffolk city	466	9	34	119	304	345	2,743	434	2,192	117	2,550	600	517	3,531	3,821
Virginia Beach city	1,140	20	96	622	402	936	13,342	2,213	10,376	753	16,746	255	210	2,988	3,751
WASHINGTON.	21,745	205	2,811	5,788	12,941	21,788	307,661	60,343	198,031	49,287	279,144	346	370	4,893	4,736
Auburn city	268	1	14	85	168	(NA)	4,001	623	2,509	869	(NA)	588	(NA)	8,776	(NA)
Bellevue city	172	2	29	49	92	139	4,665	595	3,503	567	4,372	145	129	3,937	4,046
Bellingham city	174	3	28	53	90	134	5,573	709	4,555	309	4,015	235	208	7,533	6,222
Bothell city.	47	–	11	13	23	46	838	180	503	155	769	151	148	2,696	2,476
Bremerton city.	402	2	80	73	247	387	1,890	425	1,267	198	2,551	1,103	931	5,185	6,135
Burien city	160	2	24	52	82	205	2,037	340	1,090	607	2,477	511	747	6,507	9,026
Des Moines city	116	1	18	45	52	96	1,403	244	741	418	978	397	353	4,799	3,592
Edmonds city	55	–	5	29	21	30	1,384	235	903	246	985	137	72	3,448	2,361
Everett city	537	3	48	173	313	567	7,600	1,272	4,243	2,085	5,661	551	634	7,803	6,329
Federal Way city	315	6	55	153	101	335	6,159	800	3,786	1,573	4,454	382	440	7,469	5,847
Kennewick city	215	4	26	35	150	192	3,150	523	2,410	217	2,816	353	370	5,170	5,422
Kent city	479	3	57	165	254	295	6,153	1,187	3,492	1,474	5,156	579	435	7,437	7,603
Kirkland city	74	–	21	20	33	60	1,757	297	1,215	245	1,431	160	128	3,805	3,062
Lacey city	91	1	6	33	51	88	1,756	235	1,405	116	1,363	272	276	5,253	4,270
Lakewood city	491	3	61	124	303	618	3,918	872	2,488	558	4,389	834	912	6,657	6,479
Longview city	147	3	24	32	88	162	3,136	748	2,076	312	2,734	404	462	8,608	7,795
Lynnwood city	93	1	7	45	40	128	2,856	308	2,028	520	2,736	275	367	8,432	7,851
Marysville city	57	1	16	16	24	49	1,283	244	725	314	1,042	195	221	4,395	4,704
Mount Vernon city	76	–	23	17	36	44	2,618	330	2,107	181	2,159	260	180	8,962	8,824
Olympia city	115	–	24	26	65	148	2,549	467	1,849	233	2,730	258	362	5,718	6,682
Pasco city	98	–	19	29	50	121	2,015	413	1,389	213	1,489	229	425	4,701	5,235
Puyallup city	128	–	17	39	72	90	3,188	362	2,288	538	3,183	356	279	8,861	9,857
Redmond city	86	–	21	16	49	95	1,788	203	1,393	192	1,584	181	208	3,756	3,460
Renton city	223	2	24	95	102	233	5,311	680	3,670	961	3,564	401	479	9,561	7,322
Richland city	120	–	17	11	92	63	1,467	240	1,140	87	1,237	273	164	3,333	3,217
Sammamish city	16	–	8	1	7	14	537	96	404	37	511	46	45	1,546	1,659
SoaTac city	130	1	22	42	65	(NA)	2,206	346	1,172	688	(NA)	510	(NA)	8,653	(NA)
Seattle city	4,109	25	138	1,607	2,339	4,333	43,471	6,761	27,147	9,563	40,967	709	788	7,505	7,448
Shoreline city	124	–	21	42	61	128	2,354	468	1,358	528	1,582	236	240	4,471	2,968
Spokane city	1,120	13	78	286	743	1,234	12,170	2,436	7,932	1,802	15,083	562	654	6,104	7,992
Spokane Valley city	331	1	33	55	242	(NA)	3,900	629	2,708	563	(NA)	402	(NA)	4,739	(NA)
Tacoma city	2,014	13	120	690	1,191	2,397	16,802	3,255	9,989	3,558	16,208	1,013	1,300	8,454	8,793
University Place city	97	–	12	26	59	149	1,128	235	737	156	1,133	315	552	3,661	4,198
Vancouver city	626	8	111	161	346	593	7,943	1,218	5,573	1,152	7,128	398	488	5,054	5,863
Walla Walla city	175	–	64	13	98	175	1,370	237	1,064	69	1,700	570	592	4,465	5,752
Wenatchee city	105	1	19	16	69	110	1,751	287	1,348	116	1,831	357	434	5,953	7,230
Yakima city	452	10	62	149	231	376	7,532	1,451	5,021	1,060	6,261	551	507	9,187	8,436
WEST VIRGINIA	4,957	80	321	811	3,745	5,723	47,696	11,286	32,594	3,816	41,344	273	316	2,625	2,286
Charleston city	555	7	16	128	404	(NA)	3,836	818	2,712	306	(NA)	1,073	(NA)	7,416	(NA)
Huntington city	325	11	36	164	114	336	3,677	1,071	2,296	310	3,440	651	642	7,364	6,576
Morgantown city	109	–	21	30	58	(NA)	1,030	251	758	21	(NA)	387	(NA)	3,655	(NA)
Parkersburg city	140	3	12	30	95	(NA)	1,645	347	1,191	107	(NA)	435	(NA)	5,111	(NA)
Wheeling city	138	–	20	32	86	(NA)	961	227	645	89	(NA)	461	(NA)	3,212	(NA)

See footnotes at end of table.

Table C-2. Cities — **Crime**—Con.

[Includes states and 1,265 incorporated places of 25,000 or more population as of April 1, 2000, in all states except Hawaii, which has no incorporated places recognized by the U.S. Census Bureau. Two census designated places (CDPs) are also included (Honolulu CDP in Hawaii and Arlington CDP in Virginia). For more information on these areas, see Appendix C, Geographic Information]

City	Number											Rate per 100,000 population[1]			
	Violent					Property						Violent		Property	
	2005					2005									
	Total	Murder and non-negligent man-slaughter	Forcible rape	Robbery	Aggra-vated assault	2000	Total	Burglary	Larceny-theft	Motor vehicle theft	2000	2005	2000	2005	2000
WISCONSIN	13,371	194	1,142	4,550	7,485	12,700	147,275	24,406	110,323	12,546	159,424	242	237	2,660	2,972
Appleton city	173	–	27	16	130	97	2,083	403	1,635	45	1,637	245	141	2,949	2,385
Beloit city	150	4	13	48	85	108	1,859	306	1,444	109	1,536	417	296	5,167	4,208
Brookfield city	6	–	–	5	1	31	193	20	161	12	1,098	94	79	3,030	2,807
Eau Claire city	116	–	7	24	85	137	1,929	329	1,522	78	2,438	184	223	3,068	3,963
Fond du Lac city	75	–	3	11	61	52	1,195	138	1,015	42	1,548	176	124	2,804	3,697
Franklin city	24	–	3	5	16	32	589	99	464	26	610	74	111	1,809	2,125
Green Bay city	495	5	58	72	360	312	2,931	605	2,099	227	3,166	487	311	2,885	3,151
Greenfield city	34	–	3	21	10	41	1,120	159	893	68	1,259	94	114	3,107	3,497
Janesville city	170	–	34	64	72	165	2,968	515	2,317	136	3,020	275	268	4,794	4,906
Kenosha city	249	3	35	124	87	516	2,899	575	2,130	194	2,636	264	565	3,076	2,885
La Crosse city	99	1	16	20	62	98	1,627	213	1,348	66	1,970	194	194	3,194	3,903
Madison city	839	2	80	329	428	688	7,737	1,449	5,682	606	7,304	379	320	3,494	3,394
Manitowoc city	(NA)	(NA)	(NA)	(NA)	(NA)	33	(NA)	(NA)	(NA)	(NA)	1,143	(NA)	96	(NA)	3,341
Menomonee Falls village	17	–	6	7	4	15	487	60	399	28	506	50	46	1,431	1,552
Milwaukee city	6,010	121	158	2,927	2,804	5,711	32,812	4,570	21,611	6,631	38,381	1,025	977	5,595	6,564
New Berlin city	16	–	–	5	11	32	547	90	437	20	497	41	82	1,406	1,268
Oak Creek city	30	1	10	9	10	20	1,018	127	855	36	778	93	69	3,150	2,701
Oshkosh city	183	–	12	17	154	142	1,853	297	1,496	60	1,887	287	230	2,903	3,062
Racine city	391	16	31	242	102	536	4,557	982	3,235	340	5,075	486	649	5,661	6,141
Sheboygan city	68	–	25	10	33	87	2,098	266	1,746	86	2,244	138	172	4,259	4,432
Superior city	64	–	16	12	36	56	1,565	299	1,177	89	1,430	236	201	5,779	5,120
Waukesha city	95	–	27	19	49	66	1,322	266	959	97	1,333	141	102	1,956	2,063
Wausau city	117	–	23	21	73	103	1,125	251	826	48	1,431	313	275	3,012	3,814
Wauwatosa city	101	–	15	57	29	140	2,152	275	1,722	155	2,367	220	302	4,696	5,103
West Allis city	190	4	18	81	87	160	2,659	476	1,960	223	2,471	318	264	4,446	4,077
West Bend city	24	–	2	8	14	10	713	57	637	19	865	82	34	2,421	2,910
WYOMING	1,172	14	122	78	958	1,316	16,070	2,426	12,905	739	14,969	230	267	3,155	3,031
Casper city	135	2	7	14	112	173	2,699	525	2,077	97	2,009	262	348	5,239	4,046
Cheyenne city	97	4	12	17	64	103	2,585	272	2,222	91	2,079	174	186	4,644	3,745
Laramie city	26	2	–	1	23	75	824	91	700	33	747	98	293	3,099	2,913

– Represents zero.   NA Not available.

[1]Per 100,000 resident population provided by the Federal Bureau of Investigation (FBI).

[2]The data collection methodology for the offense of forcible rape used by these agencies does not comply with national Uniform Crime Reporting (UCR) Program guidelines. Consequently, their figures for forcible rape and violent crime are not included.

[3]Data are for Savannah-Chatham Metropolitan, GA, a city-county government that includes the Savannah and Chatham County police departments; data for Savannah city not available.

[4]Limited data were available.

[5]Data are for Lexington city, KY; data not available for Lexington-Fayette.

[6]Data are for Louisville Metro, KY; data for Louisville/Jefferson County (balance) not available.

[7]The data collection methodology for the offense of aggravated assault used by these agencies does not comply with national UCR guidelines. Consequently, their figures for aggravated assault and violent crime are not included.

[8]After examining the data and making inquiries, the FBI determined that the agency's offense count was inflated. Consequently, this figure is not included.

[9]Data are for area covered by Las Vegas Metropolitan Police Department.

[10]Data are for Charlotte-Mecklenburg, NC; data for Charlotte city not available.

[11]Data are for Nashville city, TN; data for Nashville-Davidson (balance) not available.

Survey, Census, or Data Collection Method: Based on the Uniform Crime Reporting Program; for information, see Appendix B, Limitations of the Data and Methodology.

Source: U.S. Department of Justice, Federal Bureau of Investigation, *Crime in the United States*, annual, accessed September 18, 2006 (related Internet site <http://www.fbi.gov/ucr/ucr.htm>).

Table C-3. Cities — Civilian Labor Force

[Includes states and 1,265 incorporated places of 25,000 or more population as of April 1, 2000, in all states except Hawaii, which has no incorporated places recognized by the U.S. Census Bureau. Two census designated places (CDPs) are also included (Honolulu CDP in Hawaii and Arlington CDP in Virginia). For more information on these areas, see Appendix C, Geographic Information]

City	Total			Percent change		Employed			Unemployed			Unemployment rate[3]		
	2005[1]	2000[1]	1990[2]	2000–2005	1990–2000	2005[1]	2000[1]	1990[2]	2005[1]	2000[1]	1990[2]	2005[1]	2000[1]	1990[2]
ALABAMA	2,154,897	2,154,545	1,903,248	(Z)	13.2	2,069,173	2,067,147	1,782,700	85,724	87,398	120,548	4.0	4.1	6.3
Auburn city	24,624	20,683	15,544	19.1	33.1	23,963	19,830	14,639	661	853	905	2.7	4.1	5.8
Bessemer city	10,998	11,955	13,178	-8.0	-9.3	10,309	11,066	12,157	689	889	1,021	6.3	7.4	7.7
Birmingham city	104,127	112,633	120,641	-7.6	-6.6	98,895	106,383	112,512	5,232	6,250	8,129	5.0	5.5	6.7
Decatur city	26,730	27,363	24,915	-2.3	9.8	25,615	26,299	23,305	1,115	1,064	1,610	4.2	3.9	6.5
Dothan city	29,753	29,183	26,826	2.0	8.8	28,799	27,934	25,696	954	1,249	1,130	3.2	4.3	4.2
Florence city	16,537	17,460	17,495	-5.3	-0.2	15,785	16,398	15,927	752	1,062	1,568	4.5	6.1	9.0
Gadsden city	15,073	16,154	19,219	-6.7	-15.9	14,277	15,041	16,198	796	1,113	3,021	5.3	6.9	15.7
Homewood city	14,471	14,439	(NA)	0.2	(NA)	14,075	14,226	(NA)	396	213	(NA)	2.7	1.5	(NA)
Hoover city	38,174	37,376	22,964	2.1	62.8	37,265	36,717	22,550	909	659	414	2.4	1.8	1.8
Huntsville city	87,685	84,345	87,593	4.0	-3.7	84,788	81,184	83,506	2,897	3,161	4,087	3.3	3.7	4.7
Madison city	21,099	17,785	(NA)	18.6	(NA)	20,646	17,452	(NA)	453	333	(NA)	2.1	1.9	(NA)
Mobile city	86,328	92,507	90,391	-6.7	2.3	82,332	88,015	84,376	3,996	4,492	6,015	4.6	4.9	6.7
Montgomery city	96,000	96,832	90,489	-0.9	7.0	92,092	93,225	85,044	3,908	3,607	5,445	4.1	3.7	6.0
Phenix City city	12,905	12,668	11,624	1.9	9.0	12,368	12,138	10,729	537	530	895	4.2	4.2	7.7
Prattville city	13,831	12,362	(NA)	11.9	(NA)	13,448	12,039	(NA)	383	323	(NA)	2.8	2.6	(NA)
Prichard city	9,492	10,081	11,777	-5.8	-14.4	8,846	9,496	10,758	646	585	1,019	6.8	5.8	8.7
Tuscaloosa city	39,757	38,262	35,087	3.9	9.0	38,408	36,675	33,332	1,349	1,587	1,755	3.4	4.1	5.0
Vestavia Hills city	15,433	12,598	(NA)	22.5	(NA)	15,114	12,399	(NA)	319	199	(NA)	2.1	1.6	(NA)
ALASKA	339,305	319,002	270,040	6.4	18.1	316,289	299,324	251,026	23,016	19,678	19,014	6.8	6.2	7.0
Anchorage municipality	147,838	140,456	122,869	5.3	14.3	139,888	133,547	116,623	7,950	6,909	6,246	5.4	4.9	5.1
Fairbanks city	14,397	13,225	13,193	8.9	0.2	13,345	12,233	11,929	1,052	992	1,264	7.3	7.5	9.6
Juneau city and borough	18,083	18,004	15,186	0.4	18.6	17,121	17,188	14,412	962	816	774	5.3	4.5	5.1
ARIZONA	2,843,997	2,505,306	1,788,243	13.5	40.1	2,710,087	2,404,916	1,694,080	133,910	100,390	94,163	4.7	4.0	5.3
Apache Junction city	16,925	14,133	(NA)	19.8	(NA)	16,286	13,680	(NA)	639	453	(NA)	3.8	3.2	(NA)
Avondale city	20,165	17,558	(NA)	14.8	(NA)	19,372	16,998	(NA)	793	560	(NA)	3.9	3.2	(NA)
Bullhead City city	20,595	16,182	11,800	27.3	37.1	19,814	15,511	11,163	781	671	637	3.8	4.1	5.4
Casa Grande city	13,855	11,544	(NA)	20.0	(NA)	13,150	11,044	(NA)	705	500	(NA)	5.1	4.3	(NA)
Chandler city	118,100	102,998	51,903	14.7	98.4	114,427	100,401	50,222	3,673	2,597	1,681	3.1	2.5	3.2
Flagstaff city	33,929	31,617	25,843	7.3	22.3	32,693	30,635	24,317	1,236	982	1,526	3.6	3.1	5.9
Gilbert town	71,625	62,567	16,027	14.5	290.4	69,984	61,406	15,541	1,641	1,161	486	2.3	1.9	3.0
Glendale city	133,344	116,044	81,714	14.9	42.0	127,729	112,073	78,188	5,615	3,971	3,526	4.2	3.4	4.3
Lake Havasu City city	23,604	18,531	12,375	27.4	49.7	22,902	17,928	12,056	702	603	319	3.0	3.3	2.6
Mesa city	237,671	207,034	149,426	14.8	38.6	228,830	200,781	143,959	8,841	6,253	5,467	3.7	3.0	3.7
Oro Valley town	14,591	13,741	(NA)	6.2	(NA)	14,129	13,388	(NA)	462	353	(NA)	3.2	2.6	(NA)
Peoria city	63,286	55,219	23,962	14.6	130.4	61,466	53,932	23,165	1,820	1,287	797	2.9	2.3	3.3
Phoenix city	790,976	687,574	536,292	15.0	28.2	753,099	660,788	510,853	37,877	26,786	25,439	4.8	3.9	4.7
Prescott city	17,315	14,552	11,351	19.0	28.2	16,693	14,049	10,778	622	503	573	3.6	3.5	5.0
Scottsdale city	133,049	116,063	77,048	14.6	50.6	129,064	113,245	74,651	3,985	2,818	2,397	3.0	2.4	3.1
Sierra Vista city	17,548	15,334	12,989	14.4	18.1	17,032	14,920	12,345	516	414	644	2.9	2.7	5.0
Surprise city	13,549	11,771	(NA)	15.1	(NA)	12,857	11,281	(NA)	692	490	(NA)	5.1	4.2	(NA)
Tempe city	113,650	99,035	88,229	14.8	12.2	109,631	96,193	84,977	4,019	2,842	3,252	3.5	2.9	3.7
Tucson city	253,519	237,870	195,879	6.6	21.4	240,699	228,073	186,048	12,820	9,797	9,831	5.1	4.1	5.0
Yuma city	41,098	34,973	25,343	17.5	38.0	36,061	30,547	21,755	5,037	4,426	3,588	12.3	12.7	14.2
ARKANSAS	1,361,844	1,260,256	1,125,962	8.1	11.9	1,295,341	1,207,352	1,049,819	66,503	52,904	76,143	4.9	4.2	6.8
Conway city	25,838	22,533	14,443	14.7	56.0	24,954	21,843	13,388	884	690	1,055	3.4	3.1	7.3
Fayetteville city	38,532	31,090	23,279	23.9	33.6	37,360	30,170	22,382	1,172	920	897	3.0	3.0	3.9
Fort Smith city	42,088	39,203	38,610	7.4	1.5	40,173	37,730	35,839	1,915	1,473	2,771	4.5	3.8	7.2
Hot Springs city	16,889	15,320	13,746	10.2	11.5	15,824	14,514	12,643	1,065	806	1,103	6.3	5.3	8.0
Jacksonville city	13,677	12,880	12,281	6.2	4.9	12,900	12,288	11,271	777	592	1,010	5.7	4.6	8.2
Jonesboro city	31,214	29,342	25,823	6.4	13.6	29,711	28,092	24,354	1,503	1,250	1,469	4.8	4.3	5.7
Little Rock city	100,322	94,642	97,726	6.0	-3.2	95,531	90,994	92,519	4,791	3,648	5,207	4.8	3.9	5.3
North Little Rock city	32,118	30,321	31,075	5.9	-2.4	30,704	29,245	29,363	1,414	1,076	1,712	4.4	3.5	5.5
Pine Bluff city	22,985	21,954	25,107	4.7	-12.6	21,045	20,482	22,609	1,940	1,472	2,498	8.4	6.7	9.9
Rogers city	25,690	19,611	13,135	31.0	49.3	25,019	19,094	12,688	671	517	447	2.6	2.6	3.4
Springdale city	28,589	23,000	16,317	24.3	41.0	27,605	22,228	15,780	984	772	537	3.4	3.4	3.3
Texarkana city	13,200	12,119	10,032	8.9	20.8	12,531	11,504	9,473	669	615	559	5.1	5.1	5.6
West Memphis city	11,967	11,498	13,542	4.1	-15.1	11,088	10,942	12,664	879	556	878	7.3	4.8	6.5
CALIFORNIA	17,695,567	16,857,578	15,168,531	5.0	11.1	16,746,860	16,024,341	14,294,115	948,707	833,237	874,416	5.4	4.9	5.8
Alameda city	39,754	41,092	37,414	-3.3	9.8	38,356	40,095	36,321	1,398	997	1,093	3.5	2.4	2.9
Alhambra city	45,134	43,783	41,184	3.1	6.3	43,081	41,762	39,217	2,053	2,021	1,967	4.5	4.6	4.8
Aliso Viejo city	28,319	(X)	(X)	(NA)	(NA)	27,767	(X)	(X)	552	(X)	(X)	1.9	(X)	(X)
Anaheim city	173,328	160,079	149,547	8.3	7.0	164,830	152,734	143,464	8,498	7,345	6,083	4.9	4.6	4.1
Antioch city	47,648	46,522	32,194	2.4	44.5	45,038	44,639	30,464	2,610	1,883	1,730	5.5	4.0	5.4
Apple Valley town	26,025	22,277	19,619	16.8	13.5	24,585	21,101	18,438	1,440	1,176	1,181	5.5	5.3	6.0
Arcadia city	28,035	27,189	24,575	3.1	10.6	27,206	26,373	23,874	829	816	701	3.0	3.0	2.9
Atascadero city	14,817	13,752	(NA)	7.7	(NA)	14,325	13,307	(NA)	492	445	(NA)	3.3	3.2	(NA)
Azusa city	20,949	20,326	21,185	3.1	-4.1	19,733	19,129	19,792	1,216	1,197	1,393	5.8	5.9	6.6
Bakersfield city	140,258	125,499	89,989	11.8	39.5	132,276	118,386	82,759	7,982	7,113	7,230	5.7	5.7	8.0

See footnotes at end of table.

Table C-3. Cities — **Civilian Labor Force**—Con.

[Includes states and 1,265 incorporated places of 25,000 or more population as of April 1, 2000, in all states except Hawaii, which has no incorporated places recognized by the U.S. Census Bureau. Two census designated places (CDPs) are also included (Honolulu CDP in Hawaii and Arlington CDP in Virginia). For more information on these areas, see Appendix C, Geographic Information]

City	Total			Percent change		Employed			Unemployed			Unemployment rate[3]		
	2005[1]	2000[1]	1990[2]	2000–2005	1990–2000	2005[1]	2000[1]	1990[2]	2005[1]	2000[1]	1990[2]	2005[1]	2000[1]	1990[2]
CALIFORNIA—Con.														
Baldwin Park city	32,548	31,584	31,035	3.1	1.8	30,356	29,426	28,953	2,192	2,158	2,082	6.7	6.8	6.7
Bell city	15,426	14,970	14,528	3.0	3.0	14,318	13,879	13,090	1,108	1,091	1,438	7.2	7.3	9.9
Bellflower city	36,008	34,933	32,263	3.1	8.3	34,063	33,019	30,761	1,945	1,914	1,502	5.4	5.5	4.7
Bell Gardens city	16,622	16,136	17,178	3.0	−6.1	15,166	14,702	15,334	1,456	1,434	1,844	8.8	8.9	10.7
Belmont city	14,074	15,432	15,531	−8.8	−0.6	13,557	15,057	15,200	517	375	331	3.7	2.4	2.1
Benicia city	16,894	16,023	13,908	5.4	15.2	16,333	15,579	13,464	561	444	444	3.3	2.8	3.2
Berkeley city	57,916	59,593	59,484	−2.8	0.2	55,058	57,554	57,248	2,858	2,039	2,236	4.9	3.4	3.8
Beverly Hills city	19,187	18,610	17,558	3.1	6.0	18,490	17,924	17,034	697	686	524	3.6	3.7	3.0
Brea city	21,635	20,013	19,650	8.1	1.8	21,083	19,536	19,178	552	477	472	2.6	2.4	2.4
Buena Park city	41,868	38,671	37,223	8.3	3.9	39,872	36,946	35,673	1,996	1,725	1,550	4.8	4.5	4.2
Burbank city	59,909	58,112	52,948	3.1	9.8	57,352	55,596	50,811	2,557	2,516	2,137	4.3	4.3	4.0
Burlingame city	15,317	16,828	15,672	−9.0	7.4	14,841	16,483	15,399	476	345	273	3.1	2.1	1.7
Calexico city	12,134	11,084	(NA)	9.5	(NA)	9,966	8,905	(NA)	2,168	2,179	(NA)	17.9	19.7	(NA)
Camarillo city	31,515	29,396	26,847	7.2	9.5	30,464	28,461	25,618	1,051	935	1,229	3.3	3.2	4.6
Campbell city	21,215	24,291	22,795	−12.7	6.6	20,225	23,644	22,139	990	647	656	4.7	2.7	2.9
Carlsbad city	46,572	42,624	34,696	9.3	22.8	45,267	41,539	33,404	1,305	1,085	1,292	2.8	2.5	3.7
Carson city	45,328	43,976	44,126	3.1	−0.3	42,895	41,582	41,613	2,433	2,394	2,513	5.4	5.4	5.7
Cathedral City city	24,373	19,541	15,207	24.7	28.5	23,169	18,519	14,231	1,204	1,022	976	4.9	5.2	6.4
Ceres city	17,735	16,022	12,628	10.7	26.9	15,882	14,445	11,120	1,853	1,577	1,508	10.4	9.8	11.9
Cerritos city	29,131	28,251	29,253	3.1	−3.4	28,310	27,443	28,406	821	808	847	2.8	2.9	2.9
Chico city	32,545	30,531	20,358	6.6	50.0	30,573	28,796	18,697	1,972	1,735	1,661	6.1	5.7	8.2
Chino city	35,096	30,057	26,614	16.8	12.9	33,535	28,782	25,531	1,561	1,275	1,083	4.4	4.2	4.1
Chino Hills city	41,228	35,343	(X)	16.7	(NA)	40,220	34,520	(X)	1,008	823	(X)	2.4	2.3	(X)
Chula Vista city	87,645	80,044	63,719	9.5	25.6	83,207	76,354	60,597	4,438	3,690	3,122	5.1	4.6	4.9
Citrus Heights city	50,908	45,883	(X)	11.0	(NA)	49,222	44,512	(X)	1,686	1,371	(X)	3.3	3.0	(X)
Claremont city	16,603	16,101	17,448	3.1	−7.7	16,154	15,659	16,869	449	442	579	2.7	2.7	3.3
Clovis city	41,247	38,780	28,620	6.4	35.5	39,317	36,660	26,568	1,930	2,120	2,052	4.7	5.5	7.2
Colton city	24,858	21,279	18,876	16.8	12.7	23,502	20,171	17,502	1,356	1,108	1,374	5.5	5.2	7.3
Compton city	34,702	33,687	34,870	3.0	−3.4	31,425	30,462	30,852	3,277	3,225	4,018	9.4	9.6	11.5
Concord city	68,049	66,490	64,430	2.3	3.2	64,498	63,927	62,029	3,551	2,563	2,401	5.2	3.9	3.7
Corona city	79,790	63,918	40,592	24.8	57.5	76,878	61,447	38,180	2,912	2,471	2,412	3.6	3.9	5.9
Costa Mesa city	66,767	61,728	61,360	8.2	0.6	64,523	59,788	59,499	2,244	1,940	1,861	3.4	3.1	3.0
Covina city	25,846	25,069	23,458	3.1	6.9	24,893	24,131	22,468	953	938	990	3.7	3.7	4.2
Culver City city	24,443	23,709	23,028	3.1	3.0	23,568	22,847	22,280	875	862	748	3.6	3.6	3.2
Cupertino city	23,065	26,550	24,381	−13.1	8.9	22,261	26,025	23,816	804	525	565	3.5	2.0	2.3
Cypress city	27,161	25,100	24,674	8.2	1.7	26,076	24,162	23,866	1,085	938	808	4.0	3.7	3.3
Daly City city	51,869	56,529	51,514	−8.2	9.7	49,072	54,501	49,749	2,797	2,028	1,765	5.4	3.6	3.4
Dana Point city	22,489	20,801	18,962	8.1	9.7	21,882	20,276	18,435	607	525	527	2.7	2.5	2.8
Danville town	23,161	22,802	18,068	1.6	26.2	22,589	22,389	17,718	572	413	350	2.5	1.8	1.9
Davis city	37,689	34,417	27,198	9.5	26.5	36,410	33,329	25,774	1,279	1,088	1,424	3.4	3.2	5.2
Delano city	15,629	13,974	11,065	11.8	26.3	12,115	10,843	8,147	3,514	3,131	2,918	22.5	22.4	26.4
Diamond Bar city	32,331	31,358	30,701	3.1	2.1	31,122	30,169	29,844	1,209	1,189	857	3.7	3.8	2.8
Downey city	53,501	51,897	47,450	3.1	9.4	51,239	49,670	45,415	2,262	2,227	2,035	4.2	4.3	4.3
Dublin city	15,386	15,926	11,450	−3.4	39.1	14,910	15,586	11,181	476	340	269	3.1	2.1	2.3
East Palo Alto city	12,261	13,115	11,013	−6.5	19.1	10,960	12,172	10,261	1,301	943	752	10.6	7.2	6.8
El Cajon city	50,053	45,673	42,618	9.6	7.2	47,067	43,191	40,218	2,986	2,482	2,400	6.0	5.4	5.6
El Centro city	17,986	16,371	14,369	9.9	13.9	15,307	13,678	10,813	2,679	2,693	3,556	14.9	16.4	24.7
Elk Grove city	35,309	(X)	(X)	(NA)	(NA)	33,948	(X)	(X)	1,361	(X)	(X)	3.9	(X)	(X)
El Monte city	50,475	48,980	47,048	3.1	4.1	47,113	45,671	43,528	3,362	3,309	3,520	6.7	6.8	7.5
Encinitas city	37,839	34,625	33,058	9.3	4.7	36,700	33,678	32,020	1,139	947	1,038	3.0	2.7	3.1
Escondido city	70,057	64,014	55,174	9.4	16.0	66,914	61,402	52,530	3,143	2,612	2,644	4.5	4.1	4.8
Eureka city	11,717	11,668	12,435	0.4	−6.2	10,958	10,947	11,439	759	721	996	6.5	6.2	8.0
Fairfield city	48,176	45,483	36,160	5.9	25.8	45,297	43,207	34,255	2,879	2,276	1,905	6.0	5.0	5.3
Folsom city	27,827	25,111	12,445	10.8	101.8	27,241	24,634	12,066	586	477	379	2.1	1.9	3.0
Fontana city	62,307	53,341	39,589	16.8	34.7	59,041	50,673	37,426	3,266	2,668	2,163	5.2	5.0	5.5
Foster City city	16,002	17,578	18,389	−9.0	−4.4	15,498	17,213	17,999	504	365	390	3.1	2.1	2.1
Fountain Valley city	33,014	30,527	31,519	8.1	−3.1	31,984	29,637	30,612	1,030	890	907	3.1	2.9	2.9
Fremont city	109,088	112,693	101,258	−3.2	11.3	105,050	109,812	98,424	4,038	2,881	2,834	3.7	2.6	2.8
Fresno city	216,475	204,860	167,869	5.7	22.0	198,343	184,941	150,319	18,132	19,919	17,550	8.4	9.7	10.5
Fullerton city	70,853	65,465	65,131	8.2	0.5	67,837	62,858	62,924	3,016	2,607	2,207	4.3	4.0	3.4
Gardena city	29,178	28,306	27,216	3.1	4.0	27,729	26,880	25,950	1,449	1,426	1,266	5.0	5.0	4.7
Garden Grove city	84,137	77,713	75,882	8.3	2.4	80,127	74,247	72,428	4,010	3,466	3,454	4.8	4.5	4.6
Gilroy city	19,438	21,889	15,983	−11.2	37.0	17,816	20,829	14,923	1,622	1,060	1,060	8.3	4.8	6.6
Glendale city	103,523	100,425	93,410	3.1	7.5	98,759	95,736	88,271	4,764	4,689	5,139	4.6	4.7	5.5
Glendora city	28,244	27,390	25,366	3.1	8.0	27,485	26,643	24,508	759	747	858	2.7	2.7	3.4
Goleta city	17,303	(X)	(X)	(NA)	(NA)	16,943	(X)	(X)	360	(X)	(X)	2.1	(X)	(X)
Hanford city	21,611	19,577	13,889	10.4	41.0	19,844	17,869	12,522	1,767	1,708	1,367	8.2	8.7	9.8
Hawthorne city	41,008	39,795	39,637	3.0	0.4	38,118	36,951	37,466	2,890	2,844	2,171	7.0	7.1	5.5
Hayward city	68,775	70,563	59,163	−2.5	19.3	64,768	67,704	56,727	4,007	2,859	2,436	5.8	4.1	4.1
Hemet city	24,263	19,471	11,127	24.6	75.0	22,686	18,133	10,006	1,577	1,338	1,121	6.5	6.9	10.1

See footnotes at end of table.

Table C-3. Cities — **Civilian Labor Force**—Con.

[Includes states and 1,265 incorporated places of 25,000 or more population as of April 1, 2000, in all states except Hawaii, which has no incorporated places recognized by the U.S. Census Bureau. Two census designated places (CDPs) are also included (Honolulu CDP in Hawaii and Arlington CDP in Virginia). For more information on these areas, see Appendix C, Geographic Information]

City	Total			Percent change		Employed			Unemployed			Unemployment rate[3]		
	2005[1]	2000[1]	1990[2]	2000–2005	1990–2000	2005[1]	2000[1]	1990[2]	2005[1]	2000[1]	1990[2]	2005[1]	2000[1]	1990[2]
CALIFORNIA—Con.														
Hesperia city	29,999	25,665	20,167	16.9	27.3	28,021	24,049	18,779	1,978	1,616	1,388	6.6	6.3	6.9
Highland city	22,650	19,379	15,698	16.9	23.4	21,187	18,184	14,654	1,463	1,195	1,044	6.5	6.2	6.7
Hollister city	16,271	17,782	(NA)	−8.5	(NA)	14,813	16,573	(NA)	1,458	1,209	(NA)	9.0	6.8	(NA)
Huntington Beach city	122,871	113,621	112,546	8.1	1.0	119,119	110,378	109,578	3,752	3,243	2,968	3.1	2.9	2.6
Huntington Park city	25,691	24,936	25,571	3.0	−2.5	23,592	22,869	22,950	2,099	2,067	2,621	8.2	8.3	10.2
Imperial Beach city	13,060	11,904	11,048	9.7	7.7	12,132	11,133	10,178	928	771	870	7.1	6.5	7.9
Indio city	25,217	20,225	17,126	24.7	18.1	23,827	19,045	15,396	1,390	1,180	1,730	5.5	5.8	10.1
Inglewood city	52,634	51,075	55,128	3.1	−7.4	49,078	47,575	50,725	3,556	3,500	4,403	6.8	6.9	8.0
Irvine city	84,321	77,986	63,937	8.1	22.0	81,957	75,943	62,380	2,364	2,043	1,557	2.8	2.6	2.4
Laguna Hills city	17,969	16,615	(X)	8.1	(NA)	17,399	16,122	(X)	570	493	(X)	3.2	3.0	(X)
Laguna Niguel city	37,872	35,024	26,499	8.1	32.2	36,768	34,070	25,951	1,104	954	548	2.9	2.7	2.1
La Habra city	31,517	29,120	28,249	8.2	3.1	30,165	27,951	27,112	1,352	1,169	1,137	4.3	4.0	4.0
Lake Elsinore city	16,020	12,843	(NA)	24.7	(NA)	15,236	12,178	(NA)	784	665	(NA)	4.9	5.2	(NA)
Lake Forest city	37,133	34,349	(X)	8.1	(NA)	36,177	33,522	(X)	956	827	(X)	2.6	2.4	(X)
Lakewood city	44,871	43,519	39,162	3.1	11.1	43,360	42,032	37,823	1,511	1,487	1,339	3.4	3.4	3.4
La Mesa city	32,979	30,162	28,452	9.3	6.0	31,803	29,184	27,368	1,176	978	1,084	3.6	3.2	3.8
La Mirada city	24,495	23,755	21,622	3.1	9.9	23,720	22,993	20,843	775	762	779	3.2	3.2	3.6
Lancaster city	54,071	52,476	45,906	3.0	14.3	49,926	48,397	43,359	4,145	4,079	2,547	7.7	7.8	5.5
La Puente city	18,644	18,091	17,223	3.1	5.0	17,467	16,932	15,959	1,177	1,159	1,264	6.3	6.4	7.3
La Verne city	18,435	17,879	16,254	3.1	10.0	17,885	17,338	15,750	550	541	504	3.0	3.0	3.1
Lawndale city	16,158	15,676	15,000	3.1	4.5	15,306	14,837	14,104	852	839	896	5.3	5.4	6.0
Livermore city	41,031	42,437	32,892	−3.3	29.0	39,664	41,462	31,973	1,367	975	919	3.3	2.3	2.8
Lodi city	31,063	28,196	26,636	10.2	5.9	29,296	26,743	24,678	1,767	1,453	1,958	5.7	5.2	7.4
Lompoc city	19,281	18,081	17,343	6.6	4.3	17,775	16,655	16,170	1,506	1,426	1,173	7.8	7.9	6.8
Long Beach city	232,328	225,418	211,198	3.1	6.7	218,647	211,952	199,740	13,681	13,466	11,458	5.9	6.0	5.4
Los Altos city	12,130	14,011	14,248	−13.4	−1.7	11,800	13,795	13,904	330	216	344	2.7	1.5	2.4
Los Angeles city	1,875,671	1,819,887	1,812,933	3.1	0.4	1,764,781	1,710,743	1,692,706	110,890	109,144	120,227	5.9	6.0	6.6
Los Banos city	12,523	11,270	(NA)	11.1	(NA)	11,229	10,129	(NA)	1,294	1,141	(NA)	10.3	10.1	(NA)
Los Gatos town	14,586	16,786	16,673	−13.1	0.7	14,069	16,448	16,263	517	338	410	3.5	2.0	2.5
Lynwood city	26,628	25,848	24,820	3.0	4.1	24,312	23,568	22,342	2,316	2,280	2,478	8.7	8.8	10.0
Madera city	21,848	19,283	13,581	13.3	42.0	19,432	16,880	10,969	2,416	2,403	2,612	11.1	12.5	19.2
Manhattan Beach city	22,759	22,068	21,065	3.1	4.8	22,348	21,664	20,674	411	404	391	1.8	1.8	1.9
Manteca city	26,655	24,174	20,331	10.3	18.9	24,898	22,729	18,714	1,757	1,445	1,617	6.6	6.0	8.0
Martinez city	21,570	21,158	18,528	1.9	14.2	20,748	20,565	17,921	822	593	607	3.8	2.8	3.3
Maywood city	11,792	11,444	12,681	3.0	−9.8	10,855	10,522	11,441	937	922	1,240	7.9	8.1	9.8
Menlo Park city	15,392	16,890	15,086	−8.9	12.0	14,861	16,505	14,782	531	385	304	3.4	2.3	2.0
Merced city	29,759	26,785	23,375	11.1	14.6	26,875	24,242	20,393	2,884	2,543	2,982	9.7	9.5	12.8
Milpitas city	29,789	33,961	27,609	−12.3	23.0	28,110	32,863	26,473	1,679	1,098	1,136	5.6	3.2	4.1
Mission Viejo city	55,539	51,370	40,653	8.1	26.4	54,040	50,074	39,795	1,499	1,296	858	2.7	2.5	2.1
Modesto city	99,818	90,371	82,113	10.5	10.1	92,770	84,374	73,397	7,048	5,997	8,716	7.1	6.6	10.6
Monrovia city	20,489	19,876	19,218	3.1	3.4	19,536	18,938	18,275	953	938	943	4.7	4.7	4.9
Montclair city	16,279	13,939	14,077	16.8	−1.0	15,498	13,301	13,288	781	638	789	4.8	4.6	5.6
Montebello city	28,244	27,404	28,181	3.1	−2.8	26,555	25,742	26,679	1,689	1,662	1,502	6.0	6.1	5.3
Monterey city	17,315	16,828	15,508	2.9	8.5	16,757	16,284	14,966	558	544	542	3.2	3.2	3.5
Monterey Park city	29,333	28,452	28,757	3.1	−1.1	28,171	27,308	27,360	1,162	1,144	1,397	4.0	4.0	4.9
Moorpark city	18,298	17,060	14,401	7.3	18.5	17,493	16,343	13,773	805	717	628	4.4	4.2	4.4
Moreno Valley city	80,399	64,496	57,141	24.7	12.9	75,630	60,449	52,738	4,769	4,047	4,403	5.9	6.3	7.7
Morgan Hill city	16,310	18,469	12,895	−11.7	43.2	15,148	17,709	12,493	1,162	760	402	7.1	4.1	3.1
Mountain View city	39,783	45,689	43,564	−12.9	4.9	38,190	44,647	42,373	1,593	1,042	1,191	4.0	2.3	2.7
Murrieta city	26,139	20,935	(X)	24.9	(NA)	25,290	20,214	(X)	849	721	(X)	3.2	3.4	(X)
Napa city	43,034	39,676	32,027	8.5	23.9	41,135	38,210	30,486	1,899	1,466	1,541	4.4	3.7	4.8
National City city	22,484	20,463	19,724	9.9	3.7	20,536	18,844	18,053	1,948	1,619	1,671	8.7	7.9	8.5
Newark city	22,114	22,762	21,776	−2.8	4.5	21,047	22,001	21,003	1,067	761	773	4.8	3.3	3.5
Newport Beach city	45,196	41,813	41,044	8.1	1.9	44,147	40,907	40,149	1,049	906	895	2.3	2.2	2.2
Norwalk city	48,240	46,804	45,303	3.1	3.3	45,521	44,128	42,921	2,719	2,676	2,382	5.6	5.7	5.3
Novato city	25,432	27,701	26,308	−8.2	5.3	24,252	26,760	25,708	1,180	941	600	4.6	3.4	2.3
Oakland city	194,257	197,864	177,556	−1.8	11.4	178,591	186,687	166,137	15,666	11,177	11,419	8.1	5.6	6.4
Oakley city	13,590	13,344	(X)	1.8	(NA)	13,125	13,009	(X)	465	335	(X)	3.4	2.5	(X)
Oceanside city	82,754	75,647	58,532	9.4	29.2	79,373	72,836	55,243	3,381	2,811	3,289	4.1	3.7	5.6
Ontario city	81,865	70,080	65,075	16.8	7.7	77,477	66,496	61,551	4,388	3,584	3,524	5.4	5.1	5.4
Orange city	73,224	67,693	63,265	8.2	7.0	70,686	65,499	61,156	2,538	2,194	2,109	3.5	3.2	3.3
Oxnard city	86,726	80,773	74,861	7.4	7.9	81,053	75,723	68,668	5,673	5,050	6,193	6.5	6.3	8.3
Pacifica city	21,645	23,624	22,358	−8.4	5.7	20,568	22,843	21,889	1,077	781	469	5.0	3.3	2.1
Palmdale city	54,133	52,528	33,152	3.1	58.4	50,507	48,960	31,336	3,626	3,568	1,816	6.7	6.8	5.5
Palm Desert city	24,031	19,242	12,390	24.9	55.3	23,331	18,648	11,862	700	594	528	2.9	3.1	4.3
Palm Springs city	24,869	19,925	20,139	24.8	−1.1	23,908	19,109	19,019	961	816	1,120	3.9	4.1	5.6
Palo Alto city	30,003	34,633	33,403	−13.4	3.7	29,142	34,070	32,729	861	563	674	2.9	1.6	2.0
Paradise town	11,635	10,923	9,248	6.5	18.1	11,053	10,411	8,636	582	512	612	5.0	4.7	6.6
Paramount city	23,793	23,093	21,581	3.0	7.0	21,895	21,225	19,881	1,898	1,868	1,700	8.0	8.1	7.9
Pasadena city	75,915	73,636	70,028	3.1	5.2	72,878	70,647	66,538	3,037	2,989	3,490	4.0	4.1	5.0

See footnotes at end of table.

Table C-3. Cities — **Civilian Labor Force**—Con.

[Includes states and 1,265 incorporated places of 25,000 or more population as of April 1, 2000, in all states except Hawaii, which has no incorporated places recognized by the U.S. Census Bureau. Two census designated places (CDPs) are also included (Honolulu CDP in Hawaii and Arlington CDP in Virginia). For more information on these areas, see Appendix C, Geographic Information]

City	Total			Percent change		Employed			Unemployed			Unemployment rate[3]		
	2005[1]	2000[1]	1990[2]	2000–2005	1990–2000	2005[1]	2000[1]	1990[2]	2005[1]	2000[1]	1990[2]	2005[1]	2000[1]	1990[2]
CALIFORNIA—Con.														
Perris city	17,443	14,012	8,875	24.5	57.9	16,015	12,800	7,959	1,428	1,212	916	8.2	8.6	10.3
Petaluma city	31,526	31,189	24,030	1.1	29.8	30,259	30,247	23,271	1,267	942	759	4.0	3.0	3.2
Pico Rivera city	28,705	27,847	27,209	3.1	2.3	27,287	26,452	25,385	1,418	1,395	1,824	4.9	5.0	6.7
Pittsburg city	28,914	28,048	23,829	3.1	17.7	26,650	26,414	22,470	2,264	1,634	1,359	7.8	5.8	5.7
Placentia city	28,103	25,982	23,988	8.2	8.3	27,165	25,171	23,236	938	811	752	3.3	3.1	3.1
Pleasant Hill city	20,017	19,632	19,123	2.0	2.7	19,243	19,073	18,630	774	559	493	3.9	2.8	2.6
Pleasanton city	35,509	36,816	31,270	-3.6	17.7	34,598	36,166	30,634	911	650	636	2.6	1.8	2.0
Pomona city	65,184	63,246	60,698	3.1	4.2	61,303	59,426	56,310	3,881	3,820	4,388	6.0	6.0	7.2
Porterville city	19,308	17,901	13,245	7.9	35.2	17,658	16,204	11,289	1,650	1,697	1,956	8.5	9.5	14.8
Poway city	27,560	25,231	23,127	9.2	9.1	26,871	24,658	22,440	689	573	687	2.5	2.3	3.0
Rancho Cordova city	30,268	(X)	(X)	(NA)	(NA)	28,582	(X)	(X)	1,686	(X)	(X)	5.6	(X)	(X)
Rancho Cucamonga city	79,299	67,955	53,585	16.7	26.8	76,768	65,887	51,670	2,531	2,068	1,915	3.2	3.0	3.6
Rancho Palos Verdes city	21,740	21,080	22,062	3.1	-4.5	21,360	20,706	21,657	380	374	405	1.7	1.8	1.8
Rancho Santa Margarita city	29,439	27,235	(X)	8.1	(NA)	28,740	26,631	(X)	699	604	(X)	2.4	2.2	(X)
Redding city	41,592	37,845	32,160	9.9	17.7	39,054	35,885	29,381	2,538	1,960	2,779	6.1	5.2	8.6
Redlands city	37,717	32,315	29,484	16.7	9.6	36,361	31,207	28,423	1,356	1,108	1,061	3.6	3.4	3.6
Redondo Beach city	45,490	44,116	41,654	3.1	5.9	44,243	42,888	40,538	1,247	1,228	1,116	2.7	2.8	2.7
Redwood City city	40,320	44,111	38,202	-8.6	15.5	38,586	42,854	37,287	1,734	1,257	915	4.3	2.8	2.4
Rialto city	43,097	36,871	32,489	16.9	13.5	40,270	34,562	30,524	2,827	2,309	1,965	6.6	6.3	6.0
Richmond city	50,268	48,738	43,243	3.1	12.7	46,240	45,831	39,915	4,028	2,907	3,328	8.0	6.0	7.7
Riverside city	149,169	119,604	114,147	24.7	4.8	141,554	113,141	106,002	7,615	6,463	8,145	5.1	5.4	7.1
Rocklin city	25,015	20,301	10,432	23.2	94.6	24,313	19,787	10,017	702	514	415	2.8	2.5	4.0
Rohnert Park city	24,985	24,698	20,638	1.2	19.7	23,903	23,893	19,737	1,082	805	901	4.3	3.3	4.4
Rosemead city	24,669	23,931	22,989	3.1	4.1	23,522	22,802	21,455	1,147	1,129	1,534	4.6	4.7	6.7
Roseville city	50,966	41,313	23,569	23.4	75.3	48,929	39,820	22,516	2,037	1,493	1,053	4.0	3.6	4.5
Sacramento city	211,064	189,768	176,219	11.2	7.7	199,019	179,972	166,289	12,045	9,796	9,930	5.7	5.2	5.6
Salinas city	71,594	69,600	56,993	2.9	22.1	64,098	62,285	49,785	7,496	7,315	7,208	10.5	10.5	12.6
San Bernardino city	82,693	70,736	67,732	16.9	4.4	76,979	66,069	62,189	5,714	4,667	5,543	6.9	6.6	8.2
San Bruno city	21,413	23,475	22,231	-8.8	5.6	20,616	22,897	21,655	797	578	576	3.7	2.5	2.6
San Buenaventura (Ventura) city	60,066	56,004	51,368	7.3	9.0	57,509	53,728	49,038	2,557	2,276	2,330	4.3	4.1	4.5
San Carlos city	15,015	16,508	15,641	-9.0	5.5	14,581	16,194	15,404	434	314	237	2.9	1.9	1.5
San Clemente city	29,447	27,230	22,977	8.1	18.5	28,555	26,459	22,356	892	771	621	3.0	2.8	2.7
San Diego city	671,973	614,135	557,587	9.4	10.1	643,083	590,119	531,258	28,890	24,016	26,329	4.3	3.9	4.7
San Dimas city	20,171	19,562	18,127	3.1	7.9	19,559	18,960	17,640	612	602	487	3.0	3.1	2.7
San Francisco city	420,565	472,545	409,538	-11.0	15.4	399,047	456,490	394,065	21,518	16,055	15,473	5.1	3.4	3.8
San Gabriel city	20,454	19,840	18,371	3.1	8.0	19,571	18,971	17,478	883	869	893	4.3	4.4	4.9
San Jose city	430,431	489,677	434,202	-12.1	12.8	404,169	472,506	413,900	26,262	17,171	20,302	6.1	3.5	4.7
San Juan Capistrano city	17,745	16,406	13,817	8.2	18.7	17,156	15,897	13,449	589	509	368	3.3	3.1	2.7
San Leandro city	40,973	42,133	35,934	-2.8	17.3	38,871	40,633	34,654	2,102	1,500	1,280	5.1	3.6	3.6
San Luis Obispo city	26,482	24,569	21,677	7.8	13.3	25,285	23,487	20,583	1,197	1,082	1,094	4.5	4.4	5.0
San Marcos city	29,910	27,335	18,805	9.4	45.4	28,624	26,266	17,968	1,286	1,069	837	4.3	3.9	4.5
San Mateo city	48,121	52,813	50,482	-8.9	4.6	46,484	51,627	49,134	1,637	1,186	1,348	3.4	2.2	2.7
San Pablo city	13,017	12,549	11,325	3.7	10.8	11,706	11,603	10,387	1,311	946	938	10.1	7.5	8.3
San Rafael city	29,475	32,104	28,151	-8.2	14.0	28,103	31,010	27,148	1,372	1,094	1,003	4.7	3.4	3.6
San Ramon city	28,433	28,034	22,149	1.4	26.6	27,885	27,638	21,656	548	396	493	1.9	1.4	2.2
Santa Ana city	156,863	144,752	151,850	8.4	-4.7	147,234	136,429	142,316	9,629	8,323	9,534	6.1	5.7	6.3
Santa Barbara city	55,014	51,566	49,596	6.7	4.0	53,370	50,008	47,536	1,644	1,558	2,060	3.0	3.0	4.2
Santa Clara city	53,231	60,863	57,533	-12.5	5.8	50,576	59,127	55,381	2,655	1,736	2,152	5.0	2.9	3.7
Santa Clarita city	89,865	87,156	63,688	3.1	36.8	86,999	84,335	61,932	2,866	2,821	1,756	3.2	3.2	2.8
Santa Cruz city	31,684	32,611	30,199	-2.8	8.0	30,025	31,236	28,294	1,659	1,375	1,905	5.2	4.2	6.3
Santa Maria city	38,267	35,884	29,361	6.6	22.2	35,642	33,397	27,287	2,625	2,487	2,074	6.9	6.9	7.1
Santa Monica city	56,929	55,223	53,056	3.1	4.1	54,458	52,791	51,045	2,471	2,432	2,011	4.3	4.4	3.8
Santa Paula city	14,069	13,094	12,645	7.4	3.6	12,937	12,086	11,476	1,132	1,008	1,169	8.0	7.7	9.2
Santa Rosa city	81,376	80,425	59,043	1.2	36.2	77,785	77,753	56,813	3,591	2,672	2,230	4.4	3.3	3.8
Santee city	31,867	29,144	27,534	9.3	5.8	30,728	28,197	26,455	1,139	947	1,079	3.6	3.2	3.9
Saratoga city	12,748	14,727	15,011	-13.4	-1.9	12,404	14,502	14,651	344	225	360	2.7	1.5	2.4
Seaside city	16,136	15,682	15,020	2.9	4.4	15,454	15,017	13,787	682	665	1,233	4.2	4.2	8.2
Simi Valley city	68,540	63,917	60,741	7.2	5.2	65,890	61,558	57,699	2,650	2,359	3,042	3.9	3.7	5.0
South Gate city	40,194	39,005	38,360	3.0	1.7	37,421	36,275	35,048	2,773	2,730	3,312	6.9	7.0	8.6
South San Francisco city	30,359	33,092	29,673	-8.3	11.5	28,737	31,916	28,688	1,622	1,176	985	5.3	3.6	3.3
Stanton city	18,102	16,703	16,362	8.4	2.1	16,971	15,725	15,345	1,131	978	1,017	6.2	5.9	6.2
Stockton city	118,415	107,089	93,786	10.6	14.2	107,310	97,960	82,821	11,105	9,129	10,965	9.4	8.5	11.7
Suisun City city	14,632	13,823	10,726	5.9	28.9	13,811	13,174	10,106	821	649	620	5.6	4.7	5.8
Sunnyvale city	70,884	81,168	72,829	-12.7	11.5	67,583	79,010	70,369	3,301	2,158	2,460	4.7	2.7	3.4
Temecula city	34,977	28,014	14,047	24.9	99.4	33,801	27,016	13,412	1,176	998	635	3.4	3.6	4.5
Temple City city	18,161	17,613	16,031	3.1	9.9	17,549	17,011	15,450	612	602	581	3.4	3.4	3.6
Thousand Oaks city	70,174	65,447	61,840	7.2	5.8	67,629	63,182	58,865	2,545	2,265	2,975	3.6	3.5	4.8
Torrance city	80,537	78,102	76,331	3.1	2.3	78,468	76,066	73,952	2,069	2,036	2,379	2.6	2.6	3.1
Tracy city	32,385	29,427	18,084	10.1	62.7	30,883	28,192	16,584	1,502	1,235	1,500	4.6	4.2	8.3
Tulare city	21,650	20,056	15,268	7.9	31.4	19,935	18,293	13,649	1,715	1,763	1,619	7.9	8.8	10.6

See footnotes at end of table.

Table C-3. Cities — **Civilian Labor Force**—Con.

[Includes states and 1,265 incorporated places of 25,000 or more population as of April 1, 2000, in all states except Hawaii, which has no incorporated places recognized by the U.S. Census Bureau. Two census designated places (CDPs) are also included (Honolulu CDP in Hawaii and Arlington CDP in Virginia). For more information on these areas, see Appendix C, Geographic Information]

City	Total			Percent change		Employed			Unemployed			Unemployment rate[3]		
	2005[1]	2000[1]	1990[2]	2000–2005	1990–2000	2005[1]	2000[1]	1990[2]	2005[1]	2000[1]	1990[2]	2005[1]	2000[1]	1990[2]
CALIFORNIA—Con.														
Turlock city	28,463	25,785	20,976	10.4	22.9	26,708	24,291	18,784	1,755	1,494	2,192	6.2	5.8	10.5
Tustin city	41,867	38,697	28,583	8.2	35.4	40,313	37,354	27,563	1,554	1,343	1,020	3.7	3.5	3.6
Twentynine Palms city	6,060	5,185	(NA)	16.9	(NA)	5,689	4,882	(NA)	371	303	(NA)	6.1	5.8	(NA)
Union City city	33,845	34,834	29,248	−2.8	19.1	32,199	33,659	28,370	1,646	1,175	878	4.9	3.4	3.0
Upland city	41,208	35,310	34,185	16.7	3.3	39,821	34,177	32,881	1,387	1,133	1,304	3.4	3.2	3.8
Vacaville city	45,301	42,916	33,457	5.6	28.3	43,493	41,486	32,156	1,808	1,430	1,301	4.0	3.3	3.9
Vallejo city	63,459	59,830	51,987	6.1	15.1	59,167	56,436	49,217	4,292	3,394	2,770	6.8	5.7	5.3
Victorville city	29,616	25,343	16,292	16.9	55.6	27,797	23,857	15,028	1,819	1,486	1,264	6.1	5.9	7.8
Visalia city	51,060	47,176	37,056	8.2	27.3	48,157	44,191	34,102	2,903	2,985	2,954	5.7	6.3	8.0
Vista city	46,771	42,724	34,268	9.5	24.7	44,520	40,853	32,457	2,251	1,871	1,811	4.8	4.4	5.3
Walnut city	16,700	16,195	15,618	3.1	3.7	16,282	15,783	15,091	418	412	527	2.5	2.5	3.4
Walnut Creek city	33,961	33,369	32,800	1.8	1.7	32,877	32,586	31,937	1,084	783	863	3.2	2.3	2.6
Watsonville city	21,329	21,557	16,498	−1.1	30.7	18,338	19,078	14,026	2,991	2,479	2,472	14.0	11.5	15.0
West Covina city	54,753	53,114	50,331	3.1	5.5	52,204	50,605	48,362	2,549	2,509	1,969	4.7	4.7	3.9
West Hollywood city	26,784	25,981	23,662	3.1	9.8	25,591	24,807	22,343	1,193	1,174	1,319	4.5	4.5	5.6
Westminster city	45,948	42,455	42,015	8.2	1.0	44,008	40,778	40,254	1,940	1,677	1,761	4.2	4.0	4.2
West Sacramento city	15,352	13,968	13,128	9.9	6.4	14,030	12,843	11,954	1,322	1,125	1,174	8.6	8.1	8.9
Whittier city	43,557	42,247	39,101	3.1	8.0	41,930	40,646	37,608	1,627	1,601	1,493	3.7	3.8	3.8
Woodland city	27,316	24,891	21,169	9.7	17.6	25,557	23,394	19,569	1,759	1,497	1,600	6.4	6.0	7.6
Yorba Linda city	35,786	33,105	30,004	8.1	10.3	34,903	32,342	29,412	883	763	592	2.5	2.3	2.0
Yuba City city	18,990	17,568	14,193	8.1	23.8	16,994	15,724	11,883	1,996	1,844	2,310	10.5	10.5	16.3
Yucaipa city	22,335	19,132	13,503	16.7	41.7	21,448	18,408	12,984	887	724	519	4.0	3.8	3.8
COLORADO	2,547,895	2,364,990	1,768,954	7.7	33.7	2,419,241	2,300,192	1,678,229	128,654	64,798	90,725	5.0	2.7	5.1
Arvada city	58,479	58,403	52,079	0.1	12.1	55,126	56,791	49,766	3,353	1,612	2,313	5.7	2.8	4.4
Aurora city	164,242	154,569	127,986	6.3	20.8	154,028	149,907	122,511	10,214	4,662	5,475	6.2	3.0	4.3
Boulder city	55,624	53,089	51,634	4.8	2.8	52,796	51,615	48,989	2,828	1,474	2,645	5.1	2.8	5.1
Broomfield city	24,002	22,587	14,276	6.3	58.2	22,872	22,050	13,758	1,130	537	518	4.7	2.4	3.6
Centennial city	61,964	(X)	(X)	(NA)	(NA)	59,650	(X)	(X)	2,314	(X)	(X)	3.7	(X)	(X)
Colorado Springs city	206,238	190,764	142,253	8.1	34.1	195,491	185,344	132,139	10,747	5,420	10,114	5.2	2.8	7.1
Denver city	305,104	306,409	252,894	−0.4	21.2	286,897	297,209	238,837	18,207	9,200	14,057	6.0	3.0	5.6
Englewood city	19,812	18,744	16,595	5.7	12.9	18,646	18,207	15,874	1,166	537	721	5.9	2.9	4.3
Fort Collins city	78,644	69,750	50,207	12.8	38.9	74,706	67,732	47,594	3,938	2,018	2,613	5.0	2.9	5.2
Grand Junction city	25,167	21,088	13,476	19.3	56.5	23,977	20,410	12,499	1,190	678	977	4.7	3.2	7.2
Greeley city	45,423	38,550	30,993	17.8	24.4	42,691	37,314	29,212	2,732	1,236	1,781	6.0	3.2	5.7
Lakewood city	84,021	84,273	75,966	−0.3	10.9	79,523	82,108	72,855	4,498	2,165	3,111	5.4	2.6	4.1
Littleton city	24,547	23,402	19,010	4.9	23.1	23,452	22,898	18,241	1,095	504	769	4.5	2.2	4.0
Longmont city	39,078	37,389	28,783	4.5	29.9	37,292	36,458	27,035	1,786	931	1,748	4.6	2.5	6.1
Loveland city	31,753	28,316	19,764	12.1	43.3	30,556	27,703	18,845	1,197	613	919	3.8	2.2	4.6
Northglenn city	18,534	16,992	15,843	9.1	7.3	17,418	16,503	15,103	1,116	489	740	6.0	2.9	4.7
Pueblo city	47,703	44,232	41,436	7.8	6.7	44,085	42,357	38,333	3,618	1,875	3,103	7.6	4.2	7.5
Thornton city	48,720	44,987	30,923	8.3	45.5	46,406	43,973	29,441	2,314	1,014	1,482	4.7	2.3	4.8
Westminster city	62,537	60,009	44,779	4.2	34.0	59,570	58,653	43,149	2,967	1,356	1,630	4.7	2.3	3.6
Wheat Ridge city	17,724	17,717	15,995	(Z)	10.8	16,666	17,208	15,308	1,058	509	687	6.0	2.9	4.3
CONNECTICUT	1,817,025	1,736,831	1,814,924	4.6	−4.3	1,727,927	1,697,670	1,725,381	89,098	39,161	89,543	4.9	2.3	4.9
Bridgeport city	61,970	60,350	69,675	2.7	−13.4	57,190	58,173	63,506	4,780	2,177	6,169	7.7	3.6	8.9
Bristol city	33,450	32,560	35,485	2.7	−8.2	31,608	31,807	33,475	1,842	753	2,010	5.5	2.3	5.7
Danbury city	43,333	41,649	38,318	4.0	8.7	41,629	40,911	36,463	1,704	738	1,855	3.9	1.8	4.8
Hartford city	48,074	46,165	62,592	4.1	−26.2	43,404	43,988	57,085	4,670	2,177	5,507	9.7	4.7	8.8
Meriden city	30,768	29,381	32,600	4.7	−9.9	28,938	28,538	30,822	1,830	843	1,778	5.9	2.9	5.5
Middletown city	25,766	24,794	25,294	3.9	−2.0	24,566	24,246	24,224	1,200	548	1,070	4.7	2.2	4.2
Milford city (balance)[4]	30,737	29,355	28,682	4.7	2.3	29,391	28,803	27,266	1,346	552	1,416	4.4	1.9	4.9
Naugatuck borough	16,944	16,363	17,656	3.6	−7.3	16,034	15,924	16,609	910	439	1,047	5.4	2.7	5.9
New Britain city	34,290	33,442	39,867	2.5	−16.1	31,719	32,255	36,946	2,571	1,187	2,921	7.5	3.5	7.3
New Haven city	54,449	51,884	62,896	4.9	−17.5	50,546	50,151	58,947	3,903	1,733	3,949	7.2	3.3	6.3
New London city	13,595	12,395	13,698	9.7	−9.5	12,784	12,017	12,703	811	378	995	6.0	3.0	7.3
Norwalk city	47,568	46,616	48,465	2.0	−3.8	45,608	45,741	46,553	1,960	875	1,912	4.1	1.9	3.9
Norwich city	20,501	18,559	19,145	10.5	−3.1	19,388	18,063	17,868	1,113	496	1,277	5.4	2.7	6.7
Shelton city	22,013	21,299	20,625	3.4	3.3	21,068	20,858	19,543	945	441	1,082	4.3	2.1	5.2
Stamford city	65,491	63,667	64,030	2.9	−0.6	62,714	62,454	61,452	2,777	1,213	2,578	4.2	1.9	4.0
Torrington city	19,320	18,273	19,741	5.7	−7.4	18,232	17,842	18,677	1,088	431	1,064	5.6	2.4	5.4
Waterbury city	50,006	48,084	57,207	4.0	−15.9	46,066	46,417	52,789	3,940	1,667	4,418	7.9	3.5	7.7
West Haven city	29,079	27,813	30,705	4.6	−9.4	27,481	27,133	29,030	1,598	680	1,675	5.5	2.4	5.5
DELAWARE	438,003	416,503	362,098	5.2	15.0	419,531	402,777	347,038	18,472	13,726	15,060	4.2	3.3	4.2
Dover city	16,946	15,226	14,537	11.3	4.7	16,405	14,638	13,949	541	588	588	3.2	3.9	4.0
Newark city	15,638	15,672	13,775	−0.2	13.8	15,155	15,259	12,935	483	413	840	3.1	2.6	6.1
Wilmington city	32,829	33,567	34,859	−2.2	−3.7	30,771	32,096	33,009	2,058	1,471	1,850	6.3	4.4	5.3

See footnotes at end of table.

Table C-3. Cities — **Civilian Labor Force**—Con.

[Includes states and 1,265 incorporated places of 25,000 or more population as of April 1, 2000, in all states except Hawaii, which has no incorporated places recognized by the U.S. Census Bureau. Two census designated places (CDPs) are also included (Honolulu CDP in Hawaii and Arlington CDP in Virginia). For more information on these areas, see Appendix C, Geographic Information]

City	Total			Percent change		Employed			Unemployed			Unemployment rate[3]		
	2005[1]	2000[1]	1990[2]	2000–2005	1990–2000	2005[1]	2000[1]	1990[2]	2005[1]	2000[1]	1990[2]	2005[1]	2000[1]	1990[2]
DISTRICT OF COLUMBIA . . .	296,131	309,421	331,700	−4.3	−6.7	276,972	291,916	311,838	19,159	17,505	19,862	6.5	5.7	6.0
Washington city	296,131	309,421	331,700	−4.3	−6.7	276,972	291,916	311,838	19,159	17,505	19,862	6.5	5.7	6.0
FLORIDA	8,653,670	7,869,690	6,465,579	10.0	21.7	8,328,661	7,569,406	6,060,994	325,009	300,284	404,585	3.8	3.8	6.3
Altamonte Springs city	26,926	27,114	23,723	−0.7	14.3	26,010	26,249	22,480	916	865	1,243	3.4	3.2	5.2
Apopka city	17,643	14,724	(NA)	19.8	(NA)	17,102	14,315	(NA)	541	409	(NA)	3.1	2.8	(NA)
Aventura city	12,825	12,250	(X)	4.7	(NA)	12,370	11,878	(X)	455	372	(X)	3.5	3.0	(X)
Boca Raton city	41,675	38,019	33,077	9.6	14.9	40,350	37,135	31,508	1,325	884	1,569	3.2	2.3	4.7
Bonita Springs city	18,088	14,869	(X)	21.6	(NA)	17,592	14,558	(X)	496	311	(X)	2.7	2.1	(X)
Boynton Beach city	32,662	29,796	21,965	9.6	35.7	31,516	28,643	20,314	1,146	1,153	1,651	3.5	3.9	7.5
Bradenton city	26,564	23,374	19,826	13.6	17.9	25,769	22,386	18,901	795	988	925	3.0	4.2	4.7
Cape Coral city	72,826	53,218	35,397	36.8	50.3	70,845	51,467	34,027	1,981	1,751	1,370	2.7	3.3	3.9
Clearwater city	57,257	55,917	50,041	2.4	11.7	55,300	54,030	47,525	1,957	1,887	2,516	3.4	3.4	5.0
Coconut Creek city	26,395	22,543	12,996	17.1	73.5	25,475	22,051	12,105	920	492	891	3.5	2.2	6.9
Cooper City city	17,643	16,125	12,240	9.4	31.7	17,147	15,810	11,848	496	315	392	2.8	2.0	3.2
Coral Gables city	23,669	22,572	21,878	4.9	3.2	22,980	22,112	20,976	689	460	902	2.9	2.0	4.1
Coral Springs city	75,054	66,822	45,593	12.3	46.6	72,633	64,586	43,655	2,421	2,236	1,938	3.2	3.3	4.3
Dania Beach city	16,245	11,204	(NA)	45.0	(NA)	15,795	10,797	(NA)	450	407	(NA)	2.8	3.6	(NA)
Davie town	48,336	43,046	28,649	12.3	50.3	46,825	41,709	27,176	1,511	1,337	1,473	3.1	3.1	5.1
Daytona Beach city	32,566	30,022	29,567	8.5	1.5	31,312	28,646	27,504	1,254	1,376	2,063	3.9	4.6	7.0
Deerfield Beach city	33,617	31,606	21,755	6.4	45.3	32,318	30,630	20,607	1,299	976	1,148	3.9	3.1	5.3
Delray Beach city	31,422	29,023	22,604	8.3	28.4	30,228	27,483	20,303	1,194	1,540	2,301	3.8	5.3	10.2
Deltona city	42,350	35,214	(X)	20.3	(NA)	40,791	33,891	(X)	1,559	1,323	(X)	3.7	3.8	(X)
Dunedin city	18,269	17,744	15,986	3.0	11.0	17,616	17,248	15,334	653	496	652	3.6	2.8	4.1
Fort Lauderdale city	90,780	81,590	82,247	11.3	−0.8	87,563	78,232	76,207	3,217	3,358	6,040	3.5	4.1	7.3
Fort Myers city	27,477	23,354	22,506	17.7	3.8	26,706	22,080	21,259	771	1,274	1,247	2.8	5.5	5.5
Fort Pierce city	17,091	16,693	17,608	2.4	−5.2	16,009	15,083	13,852	1,082	1,610	3,756	6.3	9.6	21.3
Gainesville city	56,144	47,570	42,765	18.0	11.2	54,627	45,984	40,901	1,517	1,586	1,864	2.7	3.3	4.4
Greenacres city	15,569	13,108	10,430	18.8	25.7	15,064	12,651	9,716	505	457	714	3.2	3.5	6.8
Hallandale Beach city	16,557	15,177	11,401	9.1	33.1	15,818	14,439	10,486	739	738	915	4.5	4.9	8.0
Hialeah city	95,198	99,788	98,633	−4.6	1.2	89,870	93,618	90,559	5,328	6,170	8,074	5.6	6.2	8.2
Hollywood city	78,830	73,702	63,363	7.0	16.3	75,832	70,882	59,137	2,998	2,820	4,226	3.8	3.8	6.7
Homestead city	17,040	15,217	12,268	12.0	24.0	16,423	14,251	11,357	617	966	911	3.6	6.3	7.4
Jacksonville city	393,852	382,029	330,982	3.1	15.4	377,905	369,176	312,710	15,947	12,853	18,272	4.0	3.4	5.5
Jupiter town	25,741	21,239	14,304	21.2	48.5	25,081	20,583	13,562	660	656	742	2.6	3.1	5.2
Key West city	14,735	15,009	13,194	−1.8	13.8	14,344	14,634	12,836	391	375	358	2.7	2.5	2.7
Kissimmee city	30,760	26,327	18,780	16.8	40.2	29,733	25,404	17,684	1,027	923	1,096	3.3	3.5	5.8
Lakeland city	42,584	36,527	35,108	16.6	4.0	41,156	35,009	31,778	1,428	1,518	3,330	3.4	4.2	9.5
Lake Worth city	18,831	18,697	14,722	0.7	27.0	18,127	17,465	13,540	704	1,232	1,182	3.7	6.6	8.0
Largo city	35,198	33,858	31,626	4.0	7.1	33,866	32,910	30,331	1,332	948	1,295	3.8	2.8	4.1
Lauderdale Lakes city	14,322	14,232	12,477	0.6	14.1	13,650	13,287	11,450	672	945	1,027	4.7	6.6	8.2
Lauderhill city	30,063	28,377	25,750	5.9	10.2	28,807	27,063	24,176	1,256	1,314	1,574	4.2	4.6	6.1
Margate city	29,389	27,681	21,258	6.2	30.2	28,242	26,813	20,019	1,147	868	1,239	3.9	3.1	5.8
Melbourne city	38,270	36,041	31,213	6.2	15.5	36,918	34,798	29,236	1,352	1,243	1,977	3.5	3.4	6.3
Miami city	157,380	158,769	172,198	−0.9	−7.8	150,038	147,929	152,798	7,342	10,840	19,400	4.7	6.8	11.3
Miami Beach city	47,225	48,544	42,039	−2.7	15.5	45,492	46,381	38,205	1,733	2,163	3,834	3.7	4.5	9.1
Miami Gardens city	(NA)	(X)	(X)	(NA)	(NA)	(NA)	(X)	(X)	(NA)	(X)	(X)	(NA)	(X)	(X)
Miramar city	54,505	38,550	23,634	41.4	63.1	52,678	36,675	22,384	1,827	1,875	1,250	3.4	4.9	5.3
North Lauderdale city	19,188	17,587	16,276	9.1	8.1	18,506	16,864	15,374	682	723	902	3.6	4.1	5.5
North Miami city	26,717	28,653	27,157	−6.8	5.5	25,468	26,653	24,869	1,249	2,000	2,288	4.7	7.0	8.4
North Miami Beach city	18,189	19,550	17,674	−7.0	10.6	17,308	18,313	16,535	881	1,237	1,139	4.8	6.3	6.4
Oakland Park city	19,841	18,867	16,878	5.2	11.8	19,178	18,191	16,022	663	676	856	3.3	3.6	5.1
Ocala city	22,284	20,871	19,346	6.8	7.9	21,553	20,012	18,088	731	859	1,258	3.3	4.1	6.5
Orlando city	119,499	107,779	92,438	10.9	16.6	115,440	104,524	86,861	4,059	3,255	5,577	3.4	3.0	6.0
Ormond Beach city	19,126	17,290	13,664	10.6	26.5	18,549	16,913	13,159	577	377	505	3.0	2.2	3.7
Oviedo city	17,130	15,579	(NA)	10.0	(NA)	16,664	15,222	(NA)	466	357	(NA)	2.7	2.3	(NA)
Palm Bay city	44,780	40,411	33,492	10.8	20.7	43,160	38,819	31,572	1,620	1,592	1,920	3.6	3.9	5.7
Palm Beach Gardens city	24,071	18,680	13,252	28.9	41.0	23,511	18,143	12,759	560	537	493	2.3	2.9	3.7
Palm Coast city	19,274	13,813	(X)	39.5	(NA)	18,548	13,389	(X)	726	424	(X)	3.8	3.1	(X)
Panama City city	17,337	16,407	16,622	5.7	−1.3	16,675	15,557	14,788	662	850	1,834	3.8	5.2	11.0
Pembroke Pines city	82,471	72,873	35,227	13.2	106.9	79,754	70,936	33,860	2,717	1,937	1,367	3.3	2.7	3.9
Pensacola city	25,908	27,359	27,174	−5.3	0.7	24,935	26,126	25,419	973	1,233	1,755	3.8	4.5	6.5
Pinellas Park city	24,480	23,614	22,121	3.7	6.7	23,552	22,932	21,152	928	682	969	3.8	2.9	4.4
Plantation city	52,139	48,935	39,740	6.5	23.1	50,478	47,559	38,027	1,661	1,376	1,713	3.2	2.8	4.3
Plant City city	14,558	14,357	(NA)	1.4	(NA)	14,192	13,800	(NA)	366	557	(NA)	2.5	3.9	(NA)
Pompano Beach city	43,742	37,567	35,921	16.4	4.6	42,113	35,892	33,419	1,629	1,675	2,502	3.7	4.5	7.0
Port Orange city	27,908	22,969	17,213	21.5	33.4	27,169	22,461	16,525	739	508	688	2.6	2.2	4.0
Port St. Lucie city	60,341	43,947	28,591	37.3	53.7	58,284	41,866	25,642	2,057	2,081	2,949	3.4	4.7	10.3
Riviera Beach city	14,605	13,504	14,035	8.2	−3.8	13,984	12,500	12,249	621	1,004	1,786	4.3	7.4	12.7

See footnotes at end of table.

Table C-3. Cities — **Civilian Labor Force**—Con.

[Includes states and 1,265 incorporated places of 25,000 or more population as of April 1, 2000, in all states except Hawaii, which has no incorporated places recognized by the U.S. Census Bureau. Two census designated places (CDPs) are also included (Honolulu CDP in Hawaii and Arlington CDP in Virginia). For more information on these areas, see Appendix C, Geographic Information]

City	Total					Employed			Unemployed			Unemployment rate[3]		
				Percent change										
	2005[1]	2000[1]	1990[2]	2000–2005	1990–2000	2005[1]	2000[1]	1990[2]	2005[1]	2000[1]	1990[2]	2005[1]	2000[1]	1990[2]
FLORIDA—Con.														
St. Petersburg city	131,663	131,188	121,957	0.4	7.6	126,837	126,236	115,287	4,826	4,952	6,670	3.7	3.8	5.5
Sanford city	22,535	19,035	16,867	18.4	12.9	21,730	18,152	15,720	805	883	1,147	3.6	4.6	6.8
Sarasota city	27,864	25,700	25,838	8.4	−0.5	27,048	24,663	24,617	816	1,037	1,221	2.9	4.0	4.7
Sunrise city	48,990	45,297	33,076	8.2	36.9	47,178	43,568	31,302	1,812	1,729	1,774	3.7	3.8	5.4
Tallahassee city	85,078	83,161	72,402	2.3	14.9	82,264	80,144	69,439	2,814	3,017	2,963	3.3	3.6	4.1
Tamarac city	28,204	25,494	18,282	10.6	39.4	26,996	24,595	17,112	1,208	899	1,170	4.3	3.5	6.4
Tampa city	160,863	152,818	145,256	5.3	5.2	154,968	146,608	136,350	5,895	6,210	8,906	3.7	4.1	6.1
Titusville city	19,982	19,284	20,400	3.6	−5.5	19,237	18,399	19,285	745	885	1,115	3.7	4.6	5.5
Wellington village	27,535	20,528	(X)	34.1	(NA)	26,792	19,991	(X)	743	537	(X)	2.7	2.6	(X)
Weston city	33,623	25,343	(X)	32.7	(NA)	32,755	24,682	(X)	868	661	(X)	2.6	2.6	(X)
West Palm Beach city	50,059	41,892	38,255	19.5	9.5	48,374	40,004	34,721	1,685	1,888	3,534	3.4	4.5	9.2
Winter Haven city	12,164	11,384	(NA)	6.9	(NA)	11,679	10,824	(NA)	485	560	(NA)	4.0	4.9	(NA)
Winter Park city	13,468	12,039	(NA)	11.9	(NA)	13,067	11,849	(NA)	401	190	(NA)	3.0	1.6	(NA)
Winter Springs city	18,282	18,065	12,969	1.2	39.3	17,681	17,503	12,367	601	562	602	3.3	3.1	4.6
GEORGIA	4,588,023	4,242,889	3,300,136	8.1	28.6	4,346,289	4,095,362	3,129,389	241,734	147,527	170,747	5.3	3.5	5.2
Albany city	32,217	32,440	33,862	−0.7	−4.2	30,189	30,559	31,156	2,028	1,881	2,706	6.3	5.8	8.0
Alpharetta city	19,915	20,752	(NA)	−4.0	(NA)	19,094	20,375	(NA)	821	377	(NA)	4.1	1.8	(NA)
Athens-Clarke County (balance)[5]	59,063	54,489	43,495	8.4	25.3	56,547	52,641	41,082	2,516	1,848	2,413	4.3	3.4	5.5
Atlanta city	200,950	203,158	190,292	−1.1	6.8	187,783	193,100	176,677	13,167	10,058	13,615	6.6	5.0	7.2
Augusta-Richmond County (balance)[6]	91,237	87,564	85,639	4.2	2.2	84,793	83,766	81,197	6,444	3,798	4,442	7.1	4.3	5.2
Columbus city[7]	85,130	(X)	(X)	(NA)	(NA)	79,937	(X)	(X)	5,193	(X)	(X)	6.1	(X)	(X)
Dalton city	14,916	13,729	(NA)	8.6	(NA)	14,260	13,153	(NA)	656	576	(NA)	4.4	4.2	(NA)
East Point city	17,089	19,307	17,852	−11.5	8.2	15,796	18,385	16,661	1,293	922	1,191	7.6	4.8	6.7
Gainesville city	14,283	12,074	(NA)	18.3	(NA)	13,710	11,619	(NA)	573	455	(NA)	4.0	3.8	(NA)
Hinesville city	13,260	11,271	7,105	17.6	58.6	12,511	10,657	6,657	749	614	448	5.6	5.4	6.3
LaGrange city	13,022	12,683	11,829	2.7	7.2	12,101	12,256	10,889	921	427	940	7.1	3.4	7.9
Macon city	41,174	41,259	47,287	−0.2	−12.7	38,438	38,994	44,523	2,736	2,265	2,764	6.6	5.5	5.8
Marietta city	35,470	35,463	25,898	(Z)	36.9	33,833	34,140	24,586	1,637	1,323	1,312	4.6	3.7	5.1
Peachtree City city	17,651	17,088	9,325	3.3	83.2	17,012	16,686	8,938	639	402	387	3.6	2.4	4.2
Rome city	17,550	16,231	14,625	8.1	11.0	16,623	15,511	13,231	927	720	1,394	5.3	4.4	9.5
Roswell city	50,684	48,447	28,690	4.6	68.9	48,763	47,675	28,110	1,921	772	580	3.8	1.6	2.0
Savannah city	63,685	59,475	60,405	7.1	−1.5	60,405	56,581	57,240	3,280	2,894	3,165	5.2	4.9	5.2
Smyrna city	28,045	26,085	20,911	7.5	24.7	26,760	25,141	20,136	1,285	944	775	4.6	3.6	3.7
Valdosta city	24,460	21,031	17,755	16.3	18.5	23,441	19,942	16,792	1,019	1,089	963	4.2	5.2	5.4
Warner Robins city	27,520	23,234	20,880	18.4	11.3	26,235	22,260	20,021	1,285	974	859	4.7	4.2	4.1
HAWAII	634,613	609,018	551,028	4.2	10.5	616,869	584,858	537,620	17,744	24,160	13,408	2.8	4.0	2.4
Honolulu CDP[8]	445,126	433,110	409,270	2.8	5.8	432,929	416,427	401,256	12,197	16,683	8,014	2.7	3.9	2.0
IDAHO	738,739	662,958	494,121	11.4	34.2	710,556	632,451	467,102	28,183	30,507	27,019	3.8	4.6	5.5
Boise City city	120,203	108,544	70,325	10.7	54.3	116,163	104,635	67,763	4,040	3,909	2,562	3.4	3.6	3.6
Caldwell city	15,009	12,539	(NA)	19.7	(NA)	14,315	11,914	(NA)	694	625	(NA)	4.6	5.0	(NA)
Coeur d'Alene city	21,783	18,199	(NA)	19.7	(NA)	20,853	17,044	(NA)	930	1,155	(NA)	4.3	6.3	(NA)
Idaho Falls city	30,397	25,644	23,904	18.5	7.3	29,420	24,688	23,005	977	956	899	3.2	3.7	3.8
Lewiston city	16,061	15,647	16,672	2.6	−6.1	15,398	14,872	16,112	663	775	560	4.1	5.0	3.4
Meridian city	21,090	19,030	(NA)	10.8	(NA)	20,615	18,570	(NA)	475	460	(NA)	2.3	2.4	(NA)
Nampa city	30,961	25,864	13,082	19.7	97.7	29,582	24,622	12,193	1,379	1,242	889	4.5	4.8	6.8
Pocatello city	28,710	26,859	22,417	6.9	19.8	27,756	25,782	20,919	954	1,077	1,498	3.3	4.0	6.7
Twin Falls city	19,854	17,953	13,319	10.6	34.8	19,153	17,217	12,696	701	736	623	3.5	4.1	4.7
ILLINOIS	6,469,338	6,467,692	5,931,619	(Z)	9.0	6,100,807	6,176,837	5,560,548	368,531	290,855	371,071	5.7	4.5	6.3
Addison village	19,636	19,992	19,125	−1.8	4.5	18,344	19,019	17,834	1,292	973	1,291	6.6	4.9	6.8
Alton city	14,098	14,199	14,879	−0.7	−4.6	13,109	13,395	13,777	989	804	1,102	7.0	5.7	7.4
Arlington Heights village	41,757	44,443	43,738	−6.0	1.6	39,876	42,994	42,189	1,881	1,449	1,549	4.5	3.3	3.5
Aurora city	86,502	77,713	53,673	11.3	44.8	81,071	74,262	49,625	5,431	3,451	4,048	6.3	4.4	7.5
Bartlett village	21,336	21,672	11,205	−1.6	93.4	20,318	20,982	10,719	1,018	690	486	4.8	3.2	4.3
Belleville city	22,166	21,991	22,405	0.8	−1.8	20,341	20,648	20,091	1,825	1,343	2,314	8.2	6.1	10.3
Berwyn city	25,783	27,785	23,532	−7.2	18.1	24,144	26,542	22,128	1,639	1,243	1,404	6.4	4.5	6.0
Bloomington city	40,079	38,324	30,716	4.6	24.8	38,388	36,978	29,752	1,691	1,346	964	4.2	3.5	3.1
Bolingbrook village	36,741	33,067	23,155	11.1	42.8	34,810	31,768	21,990	1,931	1,299	1,165	5.3	3.9	5.0
Buffalo Grove village	24,439	24,974	22,765	−2.1	9.7	23,513	24,240	22,096	926	734	669	3.8	2.9	2.9
Burbank city	14,267	14,917	14,736	−4.4	1.2	13,404	14,288	13,692	863	629	1,044	6.0	4.2	7.1
Calumet City city	18,301	19,309	19,158	−5.2	0.8	16,791	18,189	17,699	1,510	1,120	1,459	8.3	5.8	7.6
Carbondale city	13,923	13,069	12,168	6.5	7.4	13,398	12,586	11,727	525	483	441	3.8	3.7	3.6
Carol Stream village	22,898	23,919	18,780	−4.3	27.4	21,722	23,113	17,927	1,176	806	853	5.1	3.4	4.5
Carpentersville village	17,463	15,653	12,208	11.6	28.2	16,108	14,705	11,164	1,355	948	1,044	7.8	6.1	8.6

See footnotes at end of table.

Table C-3. Cities — **Civilian Labor Force**—Con.

[Includes states and 1,265 incorporated places of 25,000 or more population as of April 1, 2000, in all states except Hawaii, which has no incorporated places recognized by the U.S. Census Bureau. Two census designated places (CDPs) are also included (Honolulu CDP in Hawaii and Arlington CDP in Virginia). For more information on these areas, see Appendix C, Geographic Information]

City	Total			Percent change		Employed			Unemployed			Unemployment rate[3]		
	2005[1]	2000[1]	1990[2]	2000–2005	1990–2000	2005[1]	2000[1]	1990[2]	2005[1]	2000[1]	1990[2]	2005[1]	2000[1]	1990[2]
ILLINOIS—Con.														
Champaign city	39,009	37,843	34,985	3.1	8.2	37,472	36,472	34,401	1,537	1,371	584	3.9	3.6	1.7
Chicago city	1,312,540	1,383,553	1,327,862	−5.1	4.2	1,220,265	1,307,933	1,208,686	92,275	75,620	119,176	7.0	5.5	9.0
Chicago Heights city	13,442	14,314	14,395	−6.1	−0.6	12,153	13,306	13,676	1,289	1,008	719	9.6	7.0	5.0
Cicero town	32,754	34,996	31,918	−6.4	9.6	30,005	32,697	29,111	2,749	2,299	2,807	8.4	6.6	8.8
Crystal Lake city	21,484	21,036	13,788	2.1	52.6	20,233	20,212	13,085	1,251	824	703	5.8	3.9	5.1
Danville city	13,960	14,260	15,842	−2.1	−10.0	12,793	13,150	14,141	1,167	1,110	1,701	8.4	7.8	10.7
Decatur city	36,660	38,652	41,778	−5.2	−7.5	34,036	36,325	38,594	2,624	2,327	3,184	7.2	6.0	7.6
DeKalb city	22,074	21,757	19,083	1.5	14.0	20,997	20,991	18,317	1,077	766	766	4.9	3.5	4.0
Des Plaines city	29,893	31,323	31,166	−4.6	0.5	27,755	29,800	29,317	2,138	1,523	1,849	7.2	4.9	5.9
Dolton village	12,403	13,213	12,590	−6.1	4.9	11,316	12,386	11,623	1,087	827	967	8.8	6.3	7.7
Downers Grove village	27,201	28,477	26,719	−4.5	6.6	25,898	27,526	25,511	1,303	951	1,208	4.8	3.3	4.5
East St. Louis city	10,202	10,506	13,188	−2.9	−20.3	9,177	9,561	11,457	1,025	945	1,731	10.0	9.0	13.1
Elgin city	52,196	52,382	42,425	−0.4	23.5	48,365	49,659	39,583	3,831	2,723	2,842	7.3	5.2	6.7
Elk Grove Village village	20,315	21,584	19,977	−5.9	8.0	19,341	20,872	19,235	974	712	742	4.8	3.3	3.7
Elmhurst city	23,846	24,122	23,505	−1.1	2.6	22,805	23,345	22,559	1,041	777	946	4.4	3.2	4.0
Elmwood Park village	13,207	14,163	(NA)	−6.7	(NA)	12,502	13,633	(NA)	705	530	(NA)	5.3	3.7	(NA)
Evanston city	41,034	42,573	42,405	−3.6	0.4	38,980	40,922	40,441	2,054	1,651	1,964	5.0	3.9	4.6
Freeport city	12,980	13,438	13,640	−3.4	−1.5	12,110	12,547	12,560	870	891	1,080	6.7	6.6	7.9
Galesburg city	15,113	16,117	16,495	−6.2	−2.3	13,942	15,307	15,445	1,171	810	1,050	7.7	5.0	6.4
Glendale Heights village	19,051	19,403	17,239	−1.8	12.6	18,020	18,641	16,441	1,031	762	798	5.4	3.9	4.6
Glen Ellyn village	14,552	15,113	14,112	−3.7	7.1	13,818	14,564	13,510	734	549	602	5.0	3.6	4.3
Glenview village	23,132	22,817	19,643	1.4	16.2	22,149	22,056	18,864	983	761	779	4.2	3.3	4.0
Granite City city	15,536	15,593	16,280	−0.4	−4.2	14,398	14,698	14,834	1,138	895	1,446	7.3	5.7	8.9
Gurnee village	17,165	16,447	8,755	4.4	87.9	16,459	15,942	8,550	706	505	205	4.1	3.1	2.3
Hanover Park village	20,820	22,002	19,374	−5.4	13.6	19,456	21,075	18,373	1,364	927	1,001	6.6	4.2	5.2
Harvey city	11,147	11,931	13,074	−6.6	−8.7	9,995	10,928	11,234	1,152	1,003	1,840	10.3	8.4	14.1
Highland Park city	16,463	16,272	17,531	1.2	−7.2	15,959	15,820	17,100	504	452	431	3.1	2.8	2.5
Hoffman Estates village	28,520	29,693	27,799	−4.0	6.8	27,229	28,738	26,870	1,291	955	929	4.5	3.2	3.3
Joliet city	62,215	54,136	37,004	14.9	46.3	57,886	51,152	32,907	4,329	2,984	4,097	7.0	5.5	11.1
Kankakee city	11,775	12,073	12,212	−2.5	−1.1	10,581	11,260	11,175	1,194	813	1,037	10.1	6.7	8.5
Lansing village	14,451	15,335	15,386	−5.8	−0.3	13,506	14,689	14,571	945	646	815	6.5	4.2	5.3
Lombard village	24,249	25,007	23,218	−3.0	7.7	22,941	24,067	22,027	1,308	940	1,191	5.4	3.8	5.1
Maywood village	11,787	12,579	13,598	−6.3	−7.5	10,687	11,704	12,010	1,100	875	1,588	9.3	7.0	11.7
Moline city	23,617	23,319	22,265	1.3	4.7	22,547	22,294	21,162	1,070	1,025	1,103	4.5	4.4	5.0
Mount Prospect village	30,754	32,816	31,881	−6.3	2.9	29,316	31,723	30,726	1,438	1,093	1,155	4.7	3.3	3.6
Mundelein village	17,619	16,964	13,338	3.9	27.2	16,739	16,260	12,795	880	704	543	5.0	4.1	4.1
Naperville city	74,624	72,248	47,463	3.3	52.2	71,291	69,959	46,104	3,333	2,289	1,359	4.5	3.2	2.9
Niles village	14,481	15,338	14,952	−5.6	2.6	13,690	14,707	14,333	791	631	619	5.5	4.1	4.1
Normal town	26,817	25,186	22,964	6.5	9.7	25,877	24,378	22,450	940	808	514	3.5	3.2	2.2
Northbrook village	17,247	17,687	17,349	−2.5	1.9	16,503	17,113	16,728	744	574	621	4.3	3.2	3.6
North Chicago city	9,376	10,093	9,249	−7.1	9.1	8,466	9,337	8,536	910	756	713	9.7	7.5	7.7
Oak Forest city	15,764	16,394	15,215	−3.8	7.7	14,875	15,767	14,368	889	627	847	5.6	3.8	5.6
Oak Lawn village	26,518	28,030	29,367	−5.4	−4.6	24,894	26,845	27,753	1,624	1,185	1,614	6.1	4.2	5.5
Oak Park village	30,799	33,188	32,453	−7.2	2.3	29,461	32,097	31,092	1,338	1,091	1,361	4.3	3.3	4.2
Orland Park village	28,334	27,767	19,587	2.0	41.8	26,895	26,750	18,642	1,439	1,017	945	5.1	3.7	4.8
Palatine village	39,821	41,337	30,507	−3.7	35.5	37,884	39,889	29,165	1,937	1,448	1,342	4.9	3.5	4.4
Park Ridge city	19,147	20,350	19,447	−5.9	4.6	18,308	19,697	18,828	839	653	619	4.4	3.2	3.2
Pekin city	17,000	16,763	15,968	1.4	5.0	15,997	15,893	14,966	1,003	870	1,002	5.9	5.2	6.3
Peoria city	55,119	53,672	55,879	2.7	−3.9	52,181	51,035	52,608	2,938	2,637	3,271	5.3	4.9	5.9
Quincy city	21,566	20,752	19,728	3.9	5.2	20,601	19,858	18,671	965	894	1,057	4.5	4.3	5.4
Rockford city	72,052	74,485	75,545	−3.3	−1.4	66,226	70,286	70,016	5,826	4,199	5,529	8.1	5.6	7.3
Rock Island city	19,987	19,792	19,167	1.0	3.3	19,065	18,908	18,221	922	884	946	4.6	4.5	4.9
Round Lake Beach village	14,735	13,752	(NA)	7.1	(NA)	13,873	13,111	(NA)	862	641	(NA)	5.9	4.7	(NA)
St. Charles city	18,602	16,965	12,742	9.6	33.1	17,540	16,317	12,324	1,062	648	418	5.7	3.8	3.3
Schaumburg village	45,427	48,674	43,935	−6.7	10.8	43,315	47,122	42,464	2,112	1,552	1,471	4.6	3.2	3.3
Skokie village	32,311	33,433	32,128	−3.4	4.1	30,736	32,247	30,815	1,575	1,186	1,313	4.9	3.5	4.1
Springfield city	63,037	61,685	60,678	2.2	1.7	59,819	59,056	58,138	3,218	2,629	2,540	5.1	4.3	4.2
Streamwood village	21,721	22,235	19,006	−2.3	17.0	20,436	21,359	17,979	1,285	876	1,027	5.9	3.9	5.4
Tinley Park village	30,825	28,218	19,616	9.2	43.9	29,421	27,246	18,714	1,404	972	902	4.6	3.4	4.6
Urbana city	20,790	20,050	19,828	3.7	1.1	19,934	19,253	19,170	856	797	658	4.1	4.0	3.3
Waukegan city	43,818	42,756	38,075	2.5	12.3	41,028	40,360	35,760	2,790	2,396	2,315	6.4	5.6	6.1
Wheaton city	29,435	31,008	28,816	−5.1	7.6	28,173	30,101	27,827	1,262	907	989	4.3	2.9	3.4
Wheeling village	21,899	22,556	18,993	−2.9	18.8	20,848	21,788	18,297	1,051	768	696	4.8	3.4	3.7
Wilmette village	12,925	13,822	13,657	−6.5	1.2	12,442	13,430	13,280	483	392	377	3.7	2.8	2.8
Woodridge village	19,721	18,985	16,492	3.9	15.1	18,816	18,332	15,839	905	653	653	4.6	3.4	4.0

See footnotes at end of table.

Table C-3. Cities — **Civilian Labor Force**—Con.

[Includes states and 1,265 incorporated places of 25,000 or more population as of April 1, 2000, in all states except Hawaii, which has no incorporated places recognized by the U.S. Census Bureau. Two census designated places (CDPs) are also included (Honolulu CDP in Hawaii and Arlington CDP in Virginia). For more information on these areas, see Appendix C, Geographic Information]

City	Total			Percent change		Employed			Unemployed			Unemployment rate[3]		
	2005[1]	2000[1]	1990[2]	2000–2005	1990–2000	2005[1]	2000[1]	1990[2]	2005[1]	2000[1]	1990[2]	2005[1]	2000[1]	1990[2]
INDIANA	3,208,969	3,144,379	2,830,551	2.1	11.1	3,035,204	3,052,719	2,688,858	173,765	91,660	141,693	5.4	2.9	5.0
Anderson city	27,670	27,745	29,181	−0.3	−4.9	25,623	26,648	27,094	2,047	1,097	2,087	7.4	4.0	7.2
Bloomington city	36,648	33,800	28,747	8.4	17.6	34,936	32,802	27,679	1,712	998	1,068	4.7	3.0	3.7
Carmel city.	30,309	20,220	14,245	49.9	41.9	29,607	19,881	13,980	702	339	265	2.3	1.7	1.9
Columbus city	19,551	19,881	16,735	−1.7	18.8	18,532	19,377	15,898	1,019	504	837	5.2	2.5	5.0
East Chicago city	10,851	11,609	13,203	−6.5	−12.1	9,805	10,702	11,837	1,046	907	1,366	9.6	7.8	10.3
Elkhart city	26,363	26,508	23,717	−0.5	11.8	24,707	25,381	22,066	1,656	1,127	1,651	6.3	4.3	7.0
Evansville city	60,310	62,562	64,031	−3.6	−2.3	56,681	60,219	60,247	3,629	2,343	3,784	6.0	3.7	5.9
Fishers town	32,752	23,341	(NA)	40.3	(NA)	31,909	23,020	(NA)	843	321	(NA)	2.6	1.4	(NA)
Fort Wayne city	112,283	107,009	92,354	4.9	15.9	105,916	103,374	86,778	6,367	3,635	5,576	5.7	3.4	6.0
Gary city	37,161	39,817	46,481	−6.7	−14.3	33,949	36,808	40,812	3,212	3,009	5,669	8.6	7.6	12.2
Goshen city	15,840	15,032	12,997	5.4	15.7	15,103	14,629	12,372	737	403	625	4.7	2.7	4.8
Greenwood city	23,247	20,646	15,285	12.6	35.1	22,227	20,244	14,972	1,020	402	313	4.4	1.9	2.0
Hammond city	35,077	37,139	39,353	−5.6	−5.6	32,531	35,562	36,842	2,546	1,577	2,511	7.3	4.2	6.4
Hobart city	13,804	12,903	(NA)	7.0	(NA)	13,011	12,585	(NA)	793	318	(NA)	5.7	2.5	(NA)
Indianapolis city (balance)[9]	422,423	415,566	391,419	1.7	6.2	398,800	404,124	377,387	23,623	11,442	14,032	5.6	2.8	3.6
Jeffersonville city	15,002	14,912	(NA)	0.6	(NA)	14,209	14,276	(NA)	793	636	(NA)	5.3	4.3	(NA)
Kokomo city	21,233	22,425	21,759	−5.3	3.1	19,576	21,575	19,950	1,657	850	1,809	7.8	3.8	8.3
Lafayette city	32,851	33,023	23,496	−0.5	40.5	31,111	32,103	22,903	1,740	920	593	5.3	2.8	2.5
Lawrence city	22,932	21,846	14,527	5.0	50.4	21,880	21,312	14,065	1,052	534	462	4.6	2.4	3.2
Marion city	13,264	13,474	15,256	−1.6	−11.7	11,972	12,760	13,684	1,292	714	1,572	9.7	5.3	10.3
Merrillville town	16,170	15,974	14,177	1.2	12.7	15,270	15,651	13,762	900	323	415	5.6	2.0	2.9
Michigan City city	14,744	15,269	16,176	−3.4	−5.6	13,687	14,577	15,034	1,057	692	1,142	7.2	4.5	7.1
Mishawaka city	26,449	25,772	23,027	2.6	11.9	25,074	25,127	21,807	1,375	645	1,220	5.2	2.5	5.3
Muncie city	30,964	31,670	33,958	−2.2	−6.7	28,716	30,284	31,676	2,248	1,386	2,282	7.3	4.4	6.7
New Albany city	18,479	19,419	18,060	−4.8	7.5	17,351	18,641	17,029	1,128	778	1,031	6.1	4.0	5.7
Noblesville city	19,471	15,947	(NA)	22.1	(NA)	18,671	15,591	(NA)	800	356	(NA)	4.1	2.2	(NA)
Portage city	17,592	17,369	14,268	1.3	21.7	16,646	16,766	13,581	946	603	687	5.4	3.5	4.8
Richmond city	17,253	18,787	18,814	−8.2	−0.1	15,955	17,923	16,996	1,298	864	1,818	7.5	4.6	9.7
South Bend city	49,047	52,210	52,337	−6.1	−0.2	45,922	49,725	48,364	3,125	2,485	3,973	6.4	4.8	7.6
Terre Haute city	26,512	26,349	25,124	0.6	4.9	24,511	25,231	23,676	2,001	1,118	1,448	7.5	4.2	5.8
Valparaiso city	15,006	13,760	12,723	9.1	8.2	14,282	13,417	12,352	724	343	371	4.8	2.5	2.9
West Lafayette city	14,001	13,413	12,394	4.4	8.2	13,458	13,092	11,981	543	321	413	3.9	2.4	3.3
IOWA	1,659,800	1,601,920	1,458,858	3.6	9.8	1,584,059	1,557,081	1,393,302	75,741	44,839	65,556	4.6	2.8	4.5
Ames city	31,481	28,767	27,134	9.4	6.0	30,610	28,151	25,986	871	616	1,148	2.8	2.1	4.2
Ankeny city	21,584	16,937	(NA)	27.4	(NA)	21,112	16,712	(NA)	472	225	(NA)	2.2	1.3	(NA)
Bettendorf city	17,922	17,419	15,721	2.9	10.8	17,332	16,997	15,222	590	422	499	3.3	2.4	3.2
Burlington city	12,876	13,830	13,742	−6.9	0.6	12,104	13,239	12,872	772	591	870	6.0	4.3	6.3
Cedar Falls city	23,149	19,912	18,697	16.3	6.5	22,408	19,495	17,761	741	417	936	3.2	2.1	5.0
Cedar Rapids city	70,391	69,926	62,638	0.7	11.6	67,348	68,053	58,789	3,043	1,873	3,849	4.3	2.7	6.1
Clinton city	14,097	13,789	14,450	2.2	−4.6	13,401	13,186	13,397	696	603	1,053	4.9	4.4	7.3
Council Bluffs city	31,788	31,270	28,383	1.7	10.2	30,646	30,384	27,038	1,142	886	1,345	3.6	2.8	4.7
Davenport city	53,116	51,745	48,549	2.6	6.6	50,842	49,689	45,972	2,274	2,056	2,577	4.3	4.0	5.3
Des Moines city.	109,074	109,026	108,889	(Z)	0.1	103,738	105,189	104,225	5,336	3,837	4,664	4.9	3.5	4.3
Dubuque city	31,515	30,410	30,728	3.6	−1.0	30,140	29,306	28,612	1,375	1,104	2,116	4.4	3.6	6.9
Fort Dodge city	13,345	12,668	12,606	5.3	0.5	12,793	12,227	11,886	552	441	720	4.1	3.5	5.7
Iowa City city	41,215	37,569	35,570	9.7	5.6	40,039	36,705	34,350	1,176	864	1,220	2.9	2.3	3.4
Marion city	18,205	16,220	(NA)	12.2	(NA)	17,586	15,895	(NA)	619	325	(NA)	3.4	2.0	(NA)
Marshalltown city	13,162	13,194	13,085	−0.2	0.8	12,496	12,749	12,604	666	445	481	5.1	3.4	3.7
Mason City city	16,374	15,602	15,506	4.9	0.6	15,619	15,057	14,743	755	545	763	4.6	3.5	4.9
Sioux City city	43,385	45,125	41,646	−3.9	8.4	41,490	43,820	39,569	1,895	1,305	2,077	4.4	2.9	5.0
Urbandale city	20,663	17,826	(NA)	15.9	(NA)	20,062	17,568	(NA)	601	258	(NA)	2.9	1.4	(NA)
Waterloo city	36,142	36,005	31,958	0.4	12.7	34,234	34,652	29,684	1,908	1,353	2,274	5.3	3.8	7.1
West Des Moines city	32,674	29,182	19,616	12.0	48.8	31,808	28,882	19,137	866	300	479	2.7	1.0	2.4
KANSAS	1,475,791	1,405,104	1,270,352	5.0	10.6	1,400,838	1,351,988	1,215,102	74,953	53,116	55,250	5.1	3.8	4.3
Dodge City city	13,331	12,494	(NA)	6.7	(NA)	12,782	12,113	(NA)	549	381	(NA)	4.1	3.0	(NA)
Emporia city	14,915	13,921	13,256	7.1	5.0	14,118	13,397	12,544	797	524	712	5.3	3.8	5.4
Garden City city	13,016	13,895	(NA)	−6.3	(NA)	12,378	13,471	(NA)	638	424	(NA)	4.9	3.1	(NA)
Hutchinson city	19,472	19,691	19,593	−1.1	0.5	18,242	18,770	18,602	1,230	921	991	6.3	4.7	5.1
Kansas City city	69,579	68,371	73,142	1.8	−6.5	63,269	63,876	66,715	6,310	4,495	6,427	9.1	6.6	8.8
Lawrence city	50,764	46,572	35,887	9.0	29.8	48,597	45,094	34,010	2,167	1,478	1,877	4.3	3.2	5.2
Leavenworth city	15,037	13,952	12,828	7.8	8.8	13,827	13,176	12,069	1,210	776	759	8.0	5.6	5.9
Leawood city	15,379	13,937	(NA)	10.3	(NA)	14,886	13,637	(NA)	493	300	(NA)	3.2	2.2	(NA)
Lenexa city.	27,419	24,693	21,101	11.0	17.0	26,034	23,849	20,503	1,385	844	598	5.1	3.4	2.8
Manhattan city	27,727	24,532	19,419	13.0	26.3	26,746	23,816	18,681	981	716	738	3.5	2.9	3.8
Olathe city	60,290	54,373	37,020	10.9	46.9	57,496	52,672	35,758	2,794	1,701	1,262	4.6	3.1	3.4
Overland Park city	94,792	85,496	68,221	10.9	25.3	90,425	82,837	66,393	4,367	2,659	1,828	4.6	3.1	2.7
Salina city	26,468	24,549	22,943	7.8	7.0	25,255	23,728	22,020	1,213	821	923	4.6	3.3	4.0
Shawnee city	31,641	28,618	23,410	10.6	22.2	30,444	27,889	22,594	1,197	729	816	3.8	2.5	3.5
Topeka city	66,095	63,759	63,566	3.7	0.3	61,746	60,673	59,997	4,349	3,086	3,569	6.6	4.8	5.6
Wichita city	186,031	179,616	163,538	3.6	9.8	174,692	171,316	155,980	11,339	8,300	7,558	6.1	4.6	4.6

See footnotes at end of table.

County and City Data Book: 2007

Table C-3. Cities — **Civilian Labor Force**—Con.

[Includes states and 1,265 incorporated places of 25,000 or more population as of April 1, 2000, in all states except Hawaii, which has no incorporated places recognized by the U.S. Census Bureau. Two census designated places (CDPs) are also included (Honolulu CDP in Hawaii and Arlington CDP in Virginia). For more information on these areas, see Appendix C, Geographic Information]

City	Total			Percent change		Employed			Unemployed			Unemployment rate[3]		
	2005[1]	2000[1]	1990[2]	2000–2005	1990–2000	2005[1]	2000[1]	1990[2]	2005[1]	2000[1]	1990[2]	2005[1]	2000[1]	1990[2]
KENTUCKY	1,999,658	1,949,013	1,747,605	2.6	11.5	1,878,341	1,866,348	1,640,875	121,317	82,665	106,730	6.1	4.2	6.1
Bowling Green city	28,207	25,570	21,737	10.3	17.6	26,874	24,863	20,835	1,333	707	902	4.7	2.8	4.1
Covington city	21,273	21,109	20,519	0.8	2.9	20,041	20,411	19,648	1,232	698	871	5.8	3.3	4.2
Frankfort city	13,934	13,976	14,378	-0.3	-2.8	13,186	13,450	13,863	748	526	515	5.4	3.8	3.6
Henderson city	13,763	13,496	13,249	2.0	1.9	12,921	12,967	12,386	842	529	863	6.1	3.9	6.5
Hopkinsville city	13,576	13,258	13,347	2.4	-0.7	12,649	12,666	12,387	927	592	960	6.8	4.5	7.2
Jeffersontown city	14,765	15,201	(NA)	-2.9	(NA)	14,260	14,890	(NA)	505	311	(NA)	3.4	2.0	(NA)
Lexington-Fayette	147,298	148,870	127,381	-1.1	16.9	140,498	144,396	122,655	6,800	4,474	4,726	4.6	3.0	3.7
Louisville/Jefferson County (balance)[10]	354,767	(X)	(X)	(NA)	(NA)	332,856	(X)	(X)	21,911	(X)	(X)	6.2	(X)	(X)
Owensboro city	26,617	26,803	26,546	-0.7	1.0	24,989	25,531	24,815	1,628	1,272	1,731	6.1	4.7	6.5
Paducah city	10,860	10,927	11,620	-0.6	-6.0	10,096	10,517	11,029	764	410	591	7.0	3.8	5.1
Richmond city	15,112	13,641	10,852	10.8	25.7	14,279	13,071	9,846	833	570	1,006	5.5	4.2	9.3
LOUISIANA	2,071,486	2,031,292	1,877,388	2.0	8.2	1,923,440	1,930,662	1,767,306	148,046	100,630	110,082	7.1	5.0	5.9
Alexandria city	19,946	19,174	20,840	4.0	-8.0	18,552	17,912	19,280	1,394	1,262	1,560	7.0	6.6	7.5
Baton Rouge city	112,311	108,277	109,839	3.7	-1.4	103,969	102,369	103,970	8,342	5,908	5,869	7.4	5.5	5.3
Bossier City city	28,260	25,945	24,265	8.9	6.9	26,753	24,764	22,902	1,507	1,181	1,363	5.3	4.6	5.6
Houma city	15,153	14,072	12,524	7.7	12.4	14,135	13,341	11,995	1,018	731	529	6.7	5.2	4.2
Kenner city	(NA)	36,677	38,579	(NA)	-4.9	(NA)	34,999	36,516	(NA)	1,678	2,063	(NA)	4.6	5.3
Lafayette city	60,082	56,142	47,977	7.0	17.0	56,853	53,926	45,858	3,229	2,216	2,119	5.4	3.9	4.4
Lake Charles city	34,356	32,856	32,652	4.6	0.6	31,732	30,970	30,493	2,624	1,886	2,159	7.6	5.7	6.6
Monroe city	22,827	22,054	22,410	3.5	-1.6	21,184	20,695	20,772	1,643	1,359	1,638	7.2	6.2	7.3
New Iberia city	13,480	12,895	13,136	4.5	-1.8	12,502	12,007	12,434	978	888	702	7.3	6.9	5.3
New Orleans city	(NA)	210,684	207,466	(NA)	1.6	(NA)	199,940	193,596	(NA)	10,744	13,870	(NA)	5.1	6.7
Shreveport city	93,448	90,768	91,316	3.0	-0.6	87,746	86,020	85,637	5,702	4,748	5,679	6.1	5.2	6.2
Slidell city	(NA)	12,508	11,743	(NA)	6.5	(NA)	11,904	11,195	(NA)	604	548	(NA)	4.8	4.7
MAINE	711,885	672,440	631,147	5.9	6.5	677,429	650,385	597,902	34,456	22,055	33,245	4.8	3.3	5.3
Bangor city	17,370	16,659	17,554	4.3	-5.1	16,578	16,090	16,528	792	569	1,026	4.6	3.4	5.8
Lewiston city	18,171	17,757	20,978	2.3	-15.4	17,191	17,157	19,468	980	600	1,510	5.4	3.4	7.2
Portland city	39,505	37,716	36,276	4.7	4.0	37,938	36,753	34,701	1,567	963	1,575	4.0	2.6	4.3
MARYLAND	2,935,064	2,811,657	2,582,827	4.4	8.9	2,813,781	2,711,382	2,465,249	121,283	100,275	117,578	4.1	3.6	4.6
Annapolis city	21,085	20,631	19,181	2.2	7.6	20,004	19,898	18,042	1,081	733	1,139	5.1	3.6	5.9
Baltimore city	275,558	280,786	336,970	-1.9	-16.7	256,000	264,187	310,511	19,558	16,599	26,459	7.1	5.9	7.9
Bowie city	30,771	28,921	22,884	6.4	26.4	29,532	28,481	22,436	1,239	440	448	4.0	1.5	2.0
Frederick city	31,801	29,700	22,382	7.1	32.7	30,335	28,416	21,293	1,466	1,284	1,089	4.6	4.3	4.9
Gaithersburg city	33,313	30,616	24,123	8.8	26.9	32,052	29,686	23,391	1,261	930	732	3.8	3.0	3.0
Hagerstown city	19,169	18,856	18,012	1.7	4.7	17,826	17,947	16,718	1,343	909	1,294	7.0	4.8	7.2
Rockville city	30,558	25,674	25,345	19.0	1.3	29,510	24,997	24,614	1,048	677	731	3.4	2.6	2.9
MASSACHUSETTS	3,364,496	3,365,573	3,226,368	(Z)	4.3	3,202,985	3,273,281	3,022,393	161,511	92,292	203,975	4.8	2.7	6.3
Agawam city	15,933	15,714	(X)	1.4	(NA)	15,208	15,299	(X)	725	415	(X)	4.6	2.6	(X)
Attleboro city	24,678	23,629	21,575	4.4	9.5	23,366	22,857	19,919	1,312	772	1,656	5.3	3.3	7.7
Barnstable Town city	26,783	25,365	(X)	5.6	(NA)	25,617	24,616	(X)	1,166	749	(X)	4.4	3.0	(X)
Beverly city	21,546	21,786	21,280	-1.1	2.4	20,628	21,308	20,193	918	478	1,087	4.3	2.2	5.1
Boston city	289,512	304,205	304,507	-4.8	-0.1	274,327	294,967	286,374	15,185	9,238	18,133	5.2	3.0	6.0
Brockton city	44,442	45,329	46,338	-2.0	-2.2	41,732	43,783	41,953	2,710	1,546	4,385	6.1	3.4	9.5
Cambridge city	57,475	59,301	56,009	-3.1	5.9	55,545	58,152	53,753	1,930	1,149	2,256	3.4	1.9	4.0
Chelsea city	13,339	14,104	13,017	-5.4	8.4	12,394	13,588	11,886	945	516	1,131	7.1	3.7	8.7
Chicopee city	27,630	27,424	29,065	0.8	-5.6	26,042	26,527	27,039	1,588	897	2,026	5.7	3.3	7.0
Everett city	18,712	19,406	19,034	-3.6	2.0	17,708	18,811	17,695	1,004	595	1,339	5.4	3.1	7.0
Fall River city	44,481	43,249	46,036	2.8	-6.1	40,888	41,024	40,138	3,593	2,225	5,898	8.1	5.1	12.8
Fitchburg city	18,276	18,539	19,481	-1.4	-4.8	16,996	17,882	17,663	1,280	657	1,818	7.0	3.5	9.3
Franklin city	15,838	15,854	(X)	-0.1	(NA)	15,227	15,519	(X)	611	335	(X)	3.9	2.1	(X)
Gloucester city	16,457	16,444	16,151	0.1	1.8	15,485	15,842	14,409	972	602	1,742	5.9	3.7	10.8
Haverhill city	30,574	31,484	26,570	-2.9	18.5	28,936	30,642	24,679	1,638	842	1,891	5.4	2.7	7.1
Holyoke city	16,227	15,920	17,703	1.9	-10.1	15,017	15,269	16,161	1,210	651	1,542	7.5	4.1	8.7
Lawrence city	28,979	28,396	27,934	2.1	1.7	26,042	26,816	24,601	2,937	1,580	3,333	10.1	5.6	11.9
Leominster city	20,706	21,270	20,921	-2.7	1.7	19,485	20,620	19,340	1,221	650	1,581	5.9	3.1	7.6
Lowell city	50,104	51,148	52,174	-2.0	-2.0	46,839	49,530	47,682	3,265	1,618	4,492	6.5	3.2	8.6
Lynn city	41,736	41,876	38,901	-0.3	7.6	39,179	40,525	35,836	2,557	1,351	3,065	6.1	3.2	7.9
Malden city	30,634	31,674	30,453	-3.3	4.0	29,176	30,864	28,567	1,458	810	1,886	4.8	2.6	6.2
Marlborough city	22,129	21,712	19,100	1.9	13.7	21,240	21,220	18,008	889	492	1,092	4.0	2.3	5.7
Medford city	29,313	30,686	32,030	-4.5	-4.2	28,020	29,947	30,306	1,293	739	1,724	4.4	2.4	5.4
Melrose city	14,860	15,499	15,509	-4.1	-0.1	14,278	15,168	14,789	582	331	720	3.9	2.1	4.6
Methuen city	22,992	22,428	(X)	2.5	(NA)	21,591	21,690	(X)	1,401	738	(X)	6.1	3.3	(X)
New Bedford city	42,123	42,056	45,332	0.2	-7.2	38,705	39,758	39,663	3,418	2,298	5,669	8.1	5.5	12.5
Newton city	46,239	47,341	47,892	-2.3	-1.2	44,704	46,481	46,233	1,535	860	1,659	3.3	1.8	3.5
Northampton city	16,955	17,090	16,405	-0.8	4.2	16,359	16,738	15,580	596	352	825	3.5	2.1	5.0
Peabody city	26,560	25,831	26,502	2.8	-2.5	25,309	25,199	24,859	1,251	632	1,643	4.7	2.4	6.2
Pittsfield city	22,993	22,867	23,807	0.6	-3.9	21,943	22,133	22,141	1,050	734	1,666	4.6	3.2	7.0

See footnotes at end of table.

Table C-3. Cities — **Civilian Labor Force**—Con.

[Includes states and 1,265 incorporated places of 25,000 or more population as of April 1, 2000, in all states except Hawaii, which has no incorporated places recognized by the U.S. Census Bureau. Two census designated places (CDPs) are also included (Honolulu CDP in Hawaii and Arlington CDP in Virginia). For more information on these areas, see Appendix C, Geographic Information]

City	Total			Percent change		Employed			Unemployed			Unemployment rate[3]		
	2005[1]	2000[1]	1990[2]	2000–2005	1990–2000	2005[1]	2000[1]	1990[2]	2005[1]	2000[1]	1990[2]	2005[1]	2000[1]	1990[2]
MASSACHUSETTS—Con.														
Quincy city	50,967	50,924	49,242	0.1	3.4	48,610	49,545	46,343	2,357	1,379	2,899	4.6	2.7	5.9
Revere city	21,878	22,621	21,980	–3.3	2.9	20,547	21,870	20,331	1,331	751	1,649	6.1	3.3	7.5
Salem city	23,466	23,031	21,172	1.9	8.8	22,346	22,445	19,877	1,120	586	1,295	4.8	2.5	6.1
Somerville city.	46,195	48,376	45,394	–4.5	6.6	44,566	47,423	43,162	1,629	953	2,232	3.5	2.0	4.9
Springfield city.	65,773	65,025	69,961	1.2	–7.1	61,008	62,331	64,373	4,765	2,694	5,588	7.2	4.1	8.0
Taunton city	30,649	30,170	26,782	1.6	12.7	29,077	29,279	24,546	1,572	891	2,236	5.1	3.0	8.3
Waltham city.	34,508	35,184	34,067	–1.9	3.3	33,071	34,363	32,209	1,437	821	1,858	4.2	2.3	5.5
Watertown city	19,666	20,350	(X)	–3.4	(NA)	18,968	19,935	(X)	698	415	(X)	3.5	2.0	(X)
Westfield city	21,170	20,986	19,756	0.9	6.2	20,201	20,414	18,690	969	572	1,066	4.6	2.7	5.4
West Springfield city[11]	14,588	(X)	(X)	(NA)	(NA)	13,817	(X)	(X)	771	(X)	(X)	5.3	(X)	(X)
Woburn city	21,177	21,461	21,700	–1.3	–1.1	20,254	20,971	20,409	923	490	1,291	4.4	2.3	5.9
Worcester city	82,762	82,201	80,966	0.7	1.5	78,042	79,639	74,802	4,720	2,562	6,164	5.7	3.1	7.6
MICHIGAN	5,097,457	5,143,916	4,619,988	–0.9	11.3	4,753,822	4,953,421	4,262,409	343,635	190,495	357,579	6.7	3.7	7.7
Allen Park city.	13,709	14,775	14,684	–7.2	0.6	13,202	14,510	14,084	507	265	600	3.7	1.8	4.1
Ann Arbor city	66,015	63,699	62,004	3.6	2.7	63,059	62,083	59,470	2,956	1,616	2,534	4.5	2.5	4.1
Battle Creek city	27,309	25,935	24,548	5.3	5.7	25,261	24,666	22,488	2,048	1,269	2,060	7.5	4.9	8.4
Bay City city	18,353	18,367	17,809	–0.1	3.1	16,999	17,567	15,943	1,354	800	1,866	7.4	4.4	10.5
Burton city	15,015	15,076	12,761	–0.4	18.1	14,119	14,557	11,411	896	519	1,350	6.0	3.4	10.6
Dearborn city	40,061	42,762	41,508	–6.3	3.0	37,867	41,618	39,571	2,194	1,144	1,937	5.5	2.7	4.7
Dearborn Heights city . . .	26,713	28,584	30,141	–6.5	–5.2	25,368	27,882	28,815	1,345	702	1,326	5.0	2.5	4.4
Detroit city	375,076	381,590	401,936	–1.7	–5.1	321,996	353,900	340,569	53,080	27,690	61,367	14.2	7.3	15.3
East Lansing city.	20,819	20,723	28,654	0.5	–27.7	19,358	20,023	26,671	1,461	700	1,983	7.0	3.4	6.9
Eastpointe city	17,961	18,395	17,511	–2.4	5.0	16,712	17,711	16,296	1,249	684	1,215	7.0	3.7	6.9
Farmington Hills city	43,512	46,169	43,311	–5.8	6.6	41,455	45,065	41,492	2,057	1,104	1,819	4.7	2.4	4.2
Flint city	54,425	52,746	56,734	3.2	–7.0	46,984	48,441	47,593	7,441	4,305	9,141	13.7	8.2	16.1
Garden City city.	15,022	16,081	16,800	–6.6	–4.3	14,277	15,692	16,060	745	389	740	5.0	2.4	4.4
Grand Rapids city	104,504	101,291	95,931	3.2	5.6	96,193	96,841	88,406	8,311	4,450	7,525	8.0	4.4	7.8
Holland city.	18,263	18,147	16,352	0.6	11.0	17,046	17,504	15,307	1,217	643	1,045	6.7	3.5	6.4
Inkster city	12,853	13,391	13,623	–4.0	–1.7	11,580	12,727	12,188	1,273	664	1,435	9.9	5.0	10.5
Jackson city	17,958	17,511	17,072	2.6	2.6	16,250	16,628	15,316	1,708	883	1,756	9.5	5.0	10.3
Kalamazoo city	39,940	39,481	40,332	1.2	–2.1	37,098	37,826	37,195	2,842	1,655	3,137	7.1	4.2	7.8
Kentwood city	27,509	27,030	22,514	1.8	20.1	26,099	26,275	21,689	1,410	755	825	5.1	2.8	3.7
Lansing city	67,024	66,154	65,950	1.3	0.3	61,414	63,455	60,839	5,610	2,699	5,111	8.4	4.1	7.7
Lincoln Park city	19,399	20,597	20,266	–5.8	1.6	18,147	19,944	19,082	1,252	653	1,184	6.5	3.2	5.8
Livonia city	50,104	54,124	53,946	–7.4	0.3	48,469	53,271	52,138	1,635	853	1,808	3.3	1.6	3.4
Madison Heights city	16,483	17,344	18,204	–5.0	–4.7	15,438	16,783	16,766	1,045	561	1,438	6.3	3.2	7.9
Midland city	20,898	21,350	19,540	–2.1	9.3	19,978	20,826	18,744	920	524	796	4.4	2.5	4.1
Mount Pleasant city	14,229	12,926	(NA)	10.1	(NA)	13,538	12,466	(NA)	691	460	(NA)	4.9	3.6	(NA)
Muskegon city.	18,356	17,037	16,157	7.7	5.4	16,740	16,120	14,363	1,616	917	1,794	8.8	5.4	11.1
Novi city.	26,520	28,308	19,390	–6.3	46.0	25,573	27,800	18,508	947	508	882	3.6	1.8	4.5
Oak Park city	14,556	15,132	15,656	–3.8	–3.3	13,299	14,457	14,533	1,257	675	1,123	8.6	4.5	7.2
Pontiac city.	30,686	30,816	32,183	–0.4	–4.2	26,066	28,336	26,868	4,620	2,480	5,315	15.1	8.0	16.5
Portage city.	26,185	26,251	23,590	–0.3	11.3	25,160	25,654	22,799	1,025	597	791	3.9	2.3	3.4
Port Huron city	16,445	16,520	15,500	–0.5	6.6	14,599	15,509	13,566	1,846	1,011	1,934	11.2	6.1	12.5
Rochester Hills city	36,515	39,039	34,556	–6.5	13.0	35,323	38,399	32,913	1,192	640	1,643	3.3	1.6	4.8
Roseville city.	25,929	26,200	27,890	–1.0	–6.1	23,431	24,832	25,179	2,498	1,368	2,711	9.6	5.2	9.7
Royal Oak city	36,195	38,656	37,617	–6.4	2.8	34,938	37,981	35,706	1,257	675	1,911	3.5	1.7	5.1
Saginaw city	26,474	25,871	27,034	2.3	–4.3	22,983	24,025	23,432	3,491	1,846	3,602	13.2	7.1	13.3
St. Clair Shores city	32,508	33,256	36,259	–2.2	–8.3	30,170	31,975	33,600	2,338	1,281	2,659	7.2	3.9	7.3
Southfield city	41,994	43,971	43,405	–4.5	1.3	38,941	42,332	40,495	3,053	1,639	2,910	7.3	3.7	6.7
Southgate city	15,024	16,069	16,051	–6.5	0.1	14,258	15,670	15,321	766	399	730	5.1	2.5	4.5
Sterling Heights city	68,540	70,820	68,109	–3.2	4.0	64,989	68,875	63,638	3,551	1,945	4,471	5.2	2.7	6.6
Taylor city.	30,886	32,758	34,726	–5.7	–5.7	28,827	31,684	32,403	2,059	1,074	2,323	6.7	3.3	6.7
Troy city.	43,553	46,170	41,602	–5.7	11.0	41,415	45,022	40,053	2,138	1,148	1,549	4.9	2.5	3.7
Warren city.	70,410	71,751	77,615	–1.9	–7.6	64,807	68,682	70,427	5,603	3,069	7,188	8.0	4.3	9.3
Westland city.	44,864	48,089	46,718	–6.7	2.9	42,753	46,988	44,533	2,111	1,101	2,185	4.7	2.3	4.7
Wyandotte city	14,237	15,146	14,364	–6.0	5.4	13,368	14,693	13,493	869	453	871	6.1	3.0	6.1
Wyoming city	41,561	40,671	36,578	2.2	11.2	39,079	39,342	34,570	2,482	1,329	2,008	6.0	3.3	5.5
MINNESOTA	2,947,198	2,807,668	2,390,010	5.0	17.5	2,828,547	2,720,492	2,275,853	118,651	87,176	114,157	4.0	3.1	4.8
Andover city	17,422	15,740	(NA)	10.7	(NA)	16,839	15,372	(NA)	583	368	(NA)	3.3	2.3	(NA)
Apple Valley city	31,362	28,709	20,600	9.2	39.4	30,349	28,061	19,928	1,013	648	672	3.2	2.3	3.3
Blaine city	32,616	28,221	23,755	15.6	18.8	31,520	27,502	22,729	1,096	719	1,026	3.4	2.5	4.3
Bloomington city	50,091	51,457	55,610	–2.7	–7.5	48,163	50,107	53,447	1,928	1,350	2,163	3.8	2.6	3.9
Brooklyn Center city	15,724	16,157	16,414	–2.7	–1.6	14,971	15,666	15,740	753	491	674	4.8	3.0	4.1
Brooklyn Park city	41,932	41,103	35,177	2.0	16.8	40,191	39,988	33,808	1,741	1,115	1,369	4.2	2.7	3.9
Burnsville city	38,410	38,408	33,243	(Z)	15.5	36,987	37,496	32,043	1,423	912	1,200	3.7	2.4	3.6
Coon Rapids city	38,497	37,406	32,044	2.9	16.7	37,005	36,436	30,710	1,492	970	1,334	3.9	2.6	4.2
Cottage Grove city	19,210	18,154	12,880	5.8	40.9	18,562	17,720	12,439	648	434	441	3.4	2.4	3.4
Duluth city	46,246	45,496	41,183	1.6	10.5	44,038	43,606	38,916	2,208	1,890	2,267	4.8	4.2	5.5

See footnotes at end of table.

Table C-3. Cities — **Civilian Labor Force**—Con.

[Includes states and 1,265 incorporated places of 25,000 or more population as of April 1, 2000, in all states except Hawaii, which has no incorporated places recognized by the U.S. Census Bureau. Two census designated places (CDPs) are also included (Honolulu CDP in Hawaii and Arlington CDP in Virginia). For more information on these areas, see Appendix C, Geographic Information]

City	Total			Percent change		Employed			Unemployed			Unemployment rate[3]		
	2005[1]	2000[1]	1990[2]	2000–2005	1990–2000	2005[1]	2000[1]	1990[2]	2005[1]	2000[1]	1990[2]	2005[1]	2000[1]	1990[2]
MINNESOTA—Con.														
Eagan city	40,838	40,150	31,079	1.7	29.2	39,562	39,270	30,117	1,276	880	962	3.1	2.2	3.1
Eden Prairie city	36,742	33,407	30,971	10.0	7.9	35,654	32,610	30,118	1,088	797	853	3.0	2.4	2.8
Edina city	24,132	24,607	24,960	−1.9	−1.4	23,326	24,005	24,239	806	602	721	3.3	2.4	2.9
Fridley city	16,711	16,803	17,810	−0.5	−5.7	16,002	16,323	17,053	709	480	757	4.2	2.9	4.3
Inver Grove Heights city	20,330	18,536	(NA)	9.7	(NA)	19,611	18,087	(NA)	719	449	(NA)	3.5	2.4	(NA)
Lakeville city	28,865	25,213	14,860	14.5	69.7	28,075	24,717	14,394	790	496	466	2.7	2.0	3.1
Mankato city	22,088	20,139	18,094	9.7	11.3	21,361	19,575	17,368	727	564	726	3.3	2.8	4.0
Maple Grove city	37,652	32,836	24,143	14.7	36.0	36,643	32,126	23,308	1,009	710	835	2.7	2.2	3.5
Maplewood city	20,308	19,986	17,245	1.6	15.9	19,552	19,451	16,750	756	535	495	3.7	2.7	2.9
Minneapolis city	222,097	224,636	207,023	−1.1	8.5	212,872	217,867	198,037	9,225	6,769	8,986	4.2	3.0	4.3
Minnetonka city	30,997	31,414	29,957	−1.3	4.9	30,061	30,700	29,004	936	714	953	3.0	2.3	3.2
Moorhead city	20,358	17,956	17,973	13.4	−0.1	19,787	17,464	17,156	571	492	817	2.8	2.7	4.5
Oakdale city	16,510	15,860	(NA)	4.1	(NA)	15,940	15,471	(NA)	570	389	(NA)	3.5	2.5	(NA)
Plymouth city	42,740	40,129	32,162	6.5	24.8	41,422	39,206	31,058	1,318	923	1,104	3.1	2.3	3.4
Richfield city	20,868	20,918	21,737	−0.2	−3.8	20,065	20,378	20,877	803	540	860	3.8	2.6	4.0
Rochester city	55,121	50,153	41,229	9.9	21.6	53,169	48,775	40,000	1,952	1,378	1,229	3.5	2.7	3.0
Roseville city	19,028	19,419	19,630	−2.0	−1.1	18,380	18,954	19,058	648	465	572	3.4	2.4	2.9
St. Cloud city	38,715	36,006	28,208	7.5	27.6	37,088	34,959	26,569	1,627	1,047	1,639	4.2	2.9	5.8
St. Louis Park city	28,569	28,613	28,152	−0.2	1.6	27,603	27,972	27,228	966	641	924	3.4	2.2	3.3
St. Paul city	149,832	153,292	144,052	−2.3	6.4	143,172	148,335	137,443	6,660	4,957	6,609	4.4	3.2	4.6
Shoreview city	16,828	16,138	15,435	4.3	4.6	16,311	15,759	14,973	517	379	462	3.1	2.3	3.0
Winona city	15,442	15,314	13,923	0.8	10.0	14,836	14,782	13,108	606	532	815	3.9	3.5	5.9
Woodbury city	29,843	27,769	12,111	7.5	129.3	28,974	27,206	11,763	869	563	348	2.9	2.0	2.9
MISSISSIPPI	1,343,287	1,314,154	1,175,744	2.2	11.8	1,237,269	1,239,859	1,085,419	106,018	74,295	90,325	7.9	5.7	7.7
Biloxi city	23,416	22,556	16,991	3.8	32.8	20,527	21,392	15,692	2,889	1,164	1,299	12.3	5.2	7.6
Clinton city	(NA)	(NA)	(NA)	(NA)	(NA)	(NA)	(NA)	(NA)	(NA)	(NA)	(NA)	(NA)	(NA)	(NA)
Columbus city	10,733	11,491	11,400	−6.6	0.8	9,520	10,604	10,279	1,213	887	1,121	11.3	7.7	9.8
Greenville city	15,400	16,988	19,592	−9.3	−13.3	13,492	15,674	17,597	1,908	1,314	1,995	12.4	7.7	10.2
Gulfport city	34,838	33,669	18,484	3.5	82.2	31,005	31,897	16,696	3,833	1,772	1,788	11.0	5.3	9.7
Hattiesburg city	23,169	21,926	20,783	5.7	5.5	21,444	20,675	19,246	1,725	1,251	1,537	7.4	5.7	7.4
Jackson city	91,428	87,851	98,043	4.1	−10.4	84,136	82,509	91,867	7,292	5,342	6,176	8.0	6.1	6.3
Meridian city	16,042	16,485	17,856	−2.7	−7.7	14,613	15,359	16,559	1,429	1,126	1,297	8.9	6.8	7.3
Pascagoula city	10,980	11,597	12,910	−5.3	−10.2	9,838	10,699	11,634	1,142	898	1,276	10.4	7.7	9.9
Southaven city	20,125	16,544	(NA)	21.6	(NA)	19,379	16,104	(NA)	746	440	(NA)	3.7	2.7	(NA)
Tupelo city	17,938	17,992	16,647	−0.3	8.1	16,833	17,214	15,740	1,105	778	907	6.2	4.3	5.4
Vicksburg city	11,598	12,116	11,491	−4.3	5.4	10,519	11,348	10,564	1,079	768	927	9.3	6.3	8.1
MISSOURI	3,024,478	2,973,092	2,607,584	1.7	14.0	2,862,153	2,875,336	2,456,998	162,325	97,756	150,586	5.4	3.3	5.8
Ballwin city	17,373	17,947	(NA)	−3.2	(NA)	16,901	17,682	(NA)	472	265	(NA)	2.7	1.5	(NA)
Blue Springs city	28,040	28,985	22,069	−3.3	31.3	26,952	28,391	21,412	1,088	594	657	3.9	2.0	3.0
Cape Girardeau city	18,979	19,277	18,237	−1.5	5.7	17,940	18,573	17,105	1,039	704	1,132	5.5	3.7	6.2
Chesterfield city	25,331	26,099	20,289	−2.9	28.6	24,499	25,632	19,845	832	467	444	3.3	1.8	2.2
Columbia city	53,203	48,919	40,580	8.8	20.5	51,018	47,655	38,951	2,185	1,264	1,629	4.1	2.6	4.0
Florissant city	27,167	27,743	28,394	−2.1	−2.3	25,766	26,957	27,433	1,401	786	961	5.2	2.8	3.4
Gladstone city	16,111	15,683	15,626	2.7	0.4	15,498	15,374	15,144	613	309	482	3.8	2.0	3.1
Hazelwood city	15,656	15,977	(NA)	−2.0	(NA)	14,824	15,510	(NA)	832	467	(NA)	5.3	2.9	(NA)
Independence city	60,311	61,715	60,552	−2.3	1.9	56,734	59,763	57,937	3,577	1,952	2,615	5.9	3.2	4.3
Jefferson City city	21,490	21,131	18,705	1.7	13.0	20,493	20,530	17,947	997	601	758	4.6	2.8	4.1
Joplin city	24,008	23,617	20,458	1.7	15.4	22,801	22,821	19,250	1,207	796	1,208	5.0	3.4	5.9
Kansas City city	237,680	236,879	232,421	0.3	1.9	220,994	227,919	218,631	16,686	8,960	13,790	7.0	3.8	5.9
Kirkwood city	15,248	15,697	14,621	−2.9	7.4	14,721	15,401	14,180	527	296	441	3.5	1.9	3.0
Lee's Summit city	39,575	40,982	25,547	−3.4	60.4	38,317	40,297	24,830	1,258	685	717	3.2	1.7	2.8
Liberty city	15,048	14,614	(NA)	3.0	(NA)	14,405	14,290	(NA)	643	324	(NA)	4.3	2.2	(NA)
Maryland Heights city	16,245	16,719	17,064	−2.8	−2.0	15,676	16,400	16,625	569	319	439	3.5	1.9	2.6
O'Fallon city	29,125	26,556	(NA)	9.7	(NA)	27,977	25,936	(NA)	1,148	620	(NA)	3.9	2.3	(NA)
Raytown city	15,913	16,426	16,733	−3.1	−1.8	15,250	16,064	16,218	663	362	515	4.2	2.2	3.1
St. Charles city	39,115	35,540	32,609	10.1	9.0	37,248	34,531	31,099	1,867	1,009	1,510	4.8	2.8	4.6
St. Joseph city	38,870	36,235	34,710	7.3	4.4	36,459	34,944	32,234	2,411	1,291	2,476	6.2	3.6	7.1
St. Louis city	160,920	163,640	180,645	−1.7	−9.4	147,825	155,139	165,620	13,095	8,501	15,025	8.1	5.2	8.3
St. Peters city	34,507	31,579	26,287	9.3	20.1	33,445	31,005	25,214	1,062	574	1,073	3.1	1.8	4.1
Springfield city	85,774	81,919	72,867	4.7	12.4	81,717	79,362	68,947	4,057	2,557	3,920	4.7	3.1	5.4
University City city	21,093	21,531	22,502	−2.0	−4.3	19,984	20,908	21,097	1,109	623	1,405	5.3	2.9	6.2
Wildwood city	17,774	18,334	(X)	−3.1	(NA)	17,233	18,030	(X)	541	304	(X)	3.0	1.7	(X)
MONTANA	493,407	468,865	408,301	5.2	14.8	473,636	446,552	383,706	19,771	22,313	24,595	4.0	4.8	6.0
Billings city	55,102	49,381	45,356	11.6	8.9	53,518	47,587	43,111	1,584	1,794	2,245	2.9	3.6	4.9
Bozeman city [12]	19,300	17,011	13,257	13.5	28.3	18,746	16,375	12,537	554	636	720	2.9	3.7	5.4
Butte-Silver Bow (balance)[12]	17,547	17,186	16,304	2.1	5.4	16,799	16,203	15,165	748	983	1,139	4.3	5.7	7.0
Great Falls city	28,447	27,563	26,832	3.2	2.7	27,195	26,089	25,310	1,252	1,474	1,522	4.4	5.3	5.7
Helena city	14,514	14,387	13,663	0.9	5.3	13,946	13,769	13,081	568	618	582	3.9	4.3	4.3
Missoula city	35,122	32,480	23,962	8.1	35.5	33,697	31,017	22,390	1,425	1,463	1,572	4.1	4.5	6.6

See footnotes at end of table.

Table C-3. Cities — **Civilian Labor Force**—Con.

[Includes states and 1,265 incorporated places of 25,000 or more population as of April 1, 2000, in all states except Hawaii, which has no incorporated places recognized by the U.S. Census Bureau. Two census designated places (CDPs) are also included (Honolulu CDP in Hawaii and Arlington CDP in Virginia). For more information on these areas, see Appendix C, Geographic Information]

City	Total			Percent change		Employed			Unemployed			Unemployment rate[3]		
	2005[1]	2000[1]	1990[2]	2000–2005	1990–2000	2005[1]	2000[1]	1990[2]	2005[1]	2000[1]	1990[2]	2005[1]	2000[1]	1990[2]
NEBRASKA.............	986,296	949,762	816,703	3.8	16.3	949,070	923,198	797,799	37,226	26,564	18,904	3.8	2.8	2.3
Bellevue city.............	26,053	24,550	15,259	6.1	60.9	24,960	23,847	14,896	1,093	703	363	4.2	2.9	2.4
Fremont city.............	14,113	13,780	(NA)	2.4	(NA)	13,433	13,340	(NA)	680	440	(NA)	4.8	3.2	(NA)
Grand Island city.........	24,155	22,944	21,619	5.3	6.1	23,143	22,239	21,129	1,012	705	490	4.2	3.1	2.3
Kearney city.............	18,576	16,456	14,077	12.9	16.9	18,051	16,060	13,676	525	396	401	2.8	2.4	2.8
Lincoln city.............	143,159	134,612	111,312	6.3	20.9	138,018	131,250	108,809	5,141	3,362	2,503	3.6	2.5	2.2
Omaha city.............	227,836	216,392	178,555	5.3	21.2	216,540	209,254	173,301	11,296	7,138	5,254	5.0	3.3	2.9
NEVADA.............	1,215,957	1,062,845	655,896	14.4	62.0	1,166,624	1,015,221	622,516	49,333	47,624	33,380	4.1	4.5	5.1
Carson City	27,178	26,472	20,488	2.7	29.2	25,914	25,483	19,203	1,264	989	1,285	4.7	3.7	6.3
Henderson city...........	127,653	100,682	35,283	26.8	185.4	123,858	97,259	33,883	3,795	3,423	1,400	3.0	3.4	4.0
Las Vegas city	270,534	245,183	144,056	10.3	70.2	259,497	233,195	137,116	11,037	11,988	6,940	4.1	4.9	4.8
North Las Vegas city	70,874	52,966	22,293	33.8	137.6	68,103	49,907	20,421	2,771	3,059	1,872	3.9	5.8	8.4
Reno city..............	106,921	102,493	78,186	4.3	31.1	102,687	98,237	73,739	4,234	4,256	4,447	4.0	4.2	5.7
Sparks city	44,673	38,614	31,208	15.7	23.7	43,057	37,399	29,712	1,616	1,215	1,496	3.6	3.1	4.8
NEW HAMPSHIRE........	732,036	694,254	620,037	5.4	12.0	705,562	675,541	585,032	26,474	18,713	35,005	3.6	2.7	5.6
Concord city............	21,907	21,640	17,158	1.2	26.1	21,190	21,122	16,236	717	518	922	3.3	2.4	5.4
Dover city..............	17,400	15,963	14,442	9.0	10.5	16,861	15,558	13,728	539	405	714	3.1	2.5	4.9
Manchester city..........	62,035	58,978	57,227	5.2	3.1	59,603	57,452	53,493	2,432	1,526	3,734	3.9	2.6	6.5
Nashua city.............	50,258	48,589	48,381	3.4	0.4	48,138	47,242	45,749	2,120	1,347	2,632	4.2	2.8	5.4
Rochester city...........	16,624	15,414	14,242	7.9	8.2	15,985	14,947	13,158	639	467	1,084	3.8	3.0	7.6
NEW JERSEY..........	4,430,373	4,287,783	4,072,494	3.3	5.3	4,235,937	4,130,310	3,864,958	194,436	157,473	207,536	4.4	3.7	5.1
Atlantic City city..........	17,676	17,642	19,057	0.2	−7.4	16,254	16,274	17,001	1,422	1,368	2,056	8.0	7.8	10.8
Bayonne city............	29,003	29,946	30,654	−3.1	−2.3	27,472	28,820	29,148	1,531	1,126	1,506	5.3	3.8	4.9
Bergenfield borough.......	13,921	14,276	13,668	−2.5	4.4	13,434	13,874	13,062	487	402	606	3.5	2.8	4.4
Camden city............	27,051	26,465	32,771	2.2	−19.2	24,310	23,585	27,344	2,741	2,880	5,427	10.1	10.9	16.6
Clifton city	40,302	40,636	38,604	−0.8	5.3	38,444	39,382	36,978	1,858	1,254	1,626	4.6	3.1	4.2
East Orange city	29,971	30,801	37,687	−2.7	−18.3	27,765	28,760	34,489	2,206	2,041	3,198	7.4	6.6	8.5
Elizabeth city	54,199	53,170	56,994	1.9	−6.7	50,553	49,708	51,959	3,646	3,462	5,035	6.7	6.5	8.8
Englewood city	13,380	13,737	(NA)	−2.6	(NA)	12,768	13,067	(NA)	612	670	(NA)	4.6	4.9	(NA)
Fair Lawn borough........	16,566	16,856	15,744	−1.7	7.1	15,966	16,496	15,224	600	360	520	3.6	2.1	3.3
Fort Lee borough.........	18,926	18,521	17,033	2.2	8.7	18,391	18,027	16,319	535	494	714	2.8	2.7	4.2
Garfield city	15,665	16,063	14,140	−2.5	13.6	14,666	15,091	13,351	999	972	789	6.4	6.1	5.6
Hackensack city	24,027	24,011	21,880	0.1	9.7	22,828	22,788	20,765	1,199	1,223	1,115	5.0	5.1	5.1
Hoboken city	27,838	26,880	20,089	3.6	33.8	27,113	26,349	19,062	725	531	1,027	2.6	2.0	5.1
Jersey City city	111,108	114,190	114,211	−2.7	(Z)	104,529	107,845	103,861	6,579	6,345	10,350	5.9	5.6	9.1
Kearny town	18,514	19,315	18,875	−4.1	2.3	17,548	18,557	17,900	966	758	975	5.2	3.9	5.2
Linden city	20,624	20,483	19,358	0.7	5.8	19,542	19,651	18,210	1,082	832	1,148	5.2	4.1	5.9
Long Branch city	15,648	15,766	14,751	−0.7	6.9	14,830	14,945	13,723	818	821	1,028	5.2	5.2	7.0
Millville city...........	14,303	13,189	13,026	8.4	1.3	13,202	12,342	12,175	1,101	847	851	7.7	6.4	6.5
Newark city............	104,266	101,808	120,461	2.4	−15.5	95,581	93,676	107,537	8,685	8,132	12,924	8.3	8.0	10.7
New Brunswick city	26,563	23,600	21,829	12.6	8.1	25,407	22,338	20,091	1,156	1,262	1,738	4.4	5.3	8.0
Paramus borough	12,824	12,557	12,854	2.1	−2.3	12,394	12,322	12,439	430	235	415	3.4	1.9	3.2
Passaic city	28,204	28,925	28,848	−2.5	0.3	26,300	26,981	26,003	1,904	1,944	2,845	6.8	6.7	9.9
Paterson city...........	58,944	60,096	68,244	−1.9	−11.9	53,860	55,082	61,455	5,084	5,014	6,789	8.6	8.3	9.9
Perth Amboy city	21,848	21,425	21,342	2.0	0.4	19,983	19,805	19,246	1,865	1,620	2,096	8.5	7.6	9.8
Plainfield city...........	25,329	25,332	26,212	(Z)	−3.4	23,653	23,943	24,196	1,676	1,389	2,016	6.6	5.5	7.7
Rahway city	14,157	13,834	14,198	2.3	−2.6	13,448	13,202	13,524	709	632	674	5.0	4.6	4.7
Sayreville borough.......	22,678	21,789	19,531	4.1	11.6	21,798	21,109	18,827	880	680	704	3.9	3.1	3.6
Trenton city............	38,470	37,293	40,788	3.2	−8.6	34,908	34,623	36,921	3,562	2,670	3,867	9.3	7.2	9.5
Union City city..........	27,816	29,113	30,094	−4.5	−3.3	25,891	27,008	27,357	1,925	2,105	2,737	6.9	7.2	9.1
Vineland city...........	29,359	27,088	26,743	8.4	1.3	27,645	25,691	24,779	1,714	1,397	1,964	5.8	5.2	7.3
Westfield town..........	15,546	15,509	16,025	0.2	−3.2	15,152	15,264	15,601	394	245	424	2.5	1.6	2.6
West New York town	19,995	20,407	20,053	−2.0	1.8	18,814	19,217	18,619	1,181	1,190	1,434	5.9	5.8	7.2
NEW MEXICO...........	935,888	852,293	711,891	9.8	19.7	886,724	810,024	663,698	49,164	42,269	48,193	5.3	5.0	6.8
Alamogordo city..........	15,595	13,711	11,419	13.7	20.1	14,820	13,095	10,713	775	616	706	5.0	4.5	6.2
Albuquerque city.........	259,371	239,107	207,273	8.5	15.4	247,691	229,646	196,013	11,680	9,461	11,260	4.5	4.0	5.4
Carlsbad city............	12,155	11,369	10,799	6.9	5.3	11,551	10,708	9,964	604	661	835	5.0	5.8	7.7
Clovis city..............	15,796	14,009	13,705	12.8	2.2	15,099	13,357	12,847	697	652	858	4.4	4.7	6.3
Farmington city	21,363	18,597	17,072	14.9	8.9	20,450	17,784	16,141	913	813	931	4.3	4.4	5.5
Hobbs city	12,886	11,288	12,304	14.2	−8.3	12,282	10,600	11,673	604	688	631	4.7	6.1	5.1
Las Cruces city..........	40,386	35,749	30,385	13.0	17.7	38,595	33,733	28,061	1,791	2,016	2,324	4.4	5.6	7.6
Rio Rancho city..........	32,165	27,153	16,405	18.5	65.5	30,939	26,292	15,691	1,226	861	714	3.8	3.2	4.4
Roswell city	18,722	18,639	19,496	0.4	−4.4	17,855	17,521	18,329	867	1,118	1,167	4.6	6.0	6.0
Santa Fe city	39,475	34,975	32,216	12.9	8.6	38,043	33,811	31,232	1,432	1,164	984	3.6	3.3	3.1

See footnotes at end of table.

County and City Data Book: 2007

U.S. Census Bureau

Table C-3. Cities — **Civilian Labor Force**—Con.

[Includes states and 1,265 incorporated places of 25,000 or more population as of April 1, 2000, in all states except Hawaii, which has no incorporated places recognized by the U.S. Census Bureau. Two census designated places (CDPs) are also included (Honolulu CDP in Hawaii and Arlington CDP in Virginia). For more information on these areas, see Appendix C, Geographic Information]

City	Total			Percent change		Employed			Unemployed			Unemployment rate[3]		
	2005[1]	2000[1]	1990[2]	2000–2005	1990–2000	2005[1]	2000[1]	1990[2]	2005[1]	2000[1]	1990[2]	2005[1]	2000[1]	1990[2]
NEW YORK.	9,415,861	9,166,972	8,808,856	2.7	4.1	8,943,913	8,751,441	8,339,800	471,948	415,531	469,056	5.0	4.5	5.3
Albany city	47,692	46,319	53,186	3.0	-12.9	45,530	44,589	50,996	2,162	1,730	2,190	4.5	3.7	4.1
Auburn city	13,367	13,050	14,027	2.4	-7.0	12,684	12,504	12,965	683	546	1,062	5.1	4.2	7.6
Binghamton city	20,896	21,534	24,890	-3.0	-13.5	19,745	20,718	23,379	1,151	816	1,511	5.5	3.8	6.1
Buffalo city	124,741	124,751	147,077	(Z)	-15.2	116,523	118,442	134,289	8,218	6,309	12,788	6.6	5.1	8.7
Elmira city	11,938	12,714	13,802	-6.1	-7.9	11,204	12,059	12,797	734	655	1,005	6.1	5.2	7.3
Freeport village	22,717	22,231	22,950	2.2	-3.1	21,587	21,332	21,971	1,130	899	979	5.0	4.0	4.3
Glen Cove city	13,392	13,019	(NA)	2.9	(NA)	12,799	12,567	(NA)	593	452	(NA)	4.4	3.5	(NA)
Hempstead village	25,900	25,140	27,770	3.0	-9.5	24,307	24,001	26,082	1,593	1,139	1,688	6.2	4.5	6.1
Ithaca city	15,183	14,229	13,964	6.7	1.9	14,694	13,683	13,379	489	546	585	3.2	3.8	4.2
Jamestown city	14,751	15,214	16,219	-3.0	-6.2	13,973	14,594	15,195	778	620	1,024	5.3	4.1	6.3
Lindenhurst village	15,185	14,436	14,794	5.2	-2.4	14,447	13,955	14,075	738	481	719	4.9	3.3	4.9
Long Beach city	19,748	19,290	18,222	2.4	5.9	18,949	18,658	17,321	799	632	901	4.0	3.3	4.9
Middletown city	12,163	11,588	(NA)	5.0	(NA)	11,594	11,161	(NA)	569	427	(NA)	4.7	3.7	(NA)
Mount Vernon city	34,438	33,529	35,053	2.7	-4.3	32,604	32,156	33,146	1,834	1,373	1,907	5.3	4.1	5.4
Newburgh city	11,757	11,363	12,064	3.5	-5.8	11,066	10,861	10,973	691	502	1,091	5.9	4.4	9.0
New Rochelle city	37,709	36,442	37,146	3.5	-1.9	35,954	35,042	35,751	1,755	1,400	1,395	4.7	3.8	3.8
New York city	3,733,908	3,665,918	3,335,982	1.9	9.9	3,518,610	3,453,608	3,104,502	215,298	212,310	231,480	5.8	5.8	6.9
Niagara Falls city	24,433	24,470	28,002	-0.2	-12.6	22,734	23,098	25,530	1,699	1,372	2,472	7.0	5.6	8.8
North Tonawanda city	17,863	17,936	18,605	-0.4	-3.6	16,972	17,217	17,757	891	719	848	5.0	4.0	4.6
Port Chester village	14,826	14,416	(NA)	2.8	(NA)	14,187	13,963	(NA)	639	453	(NA)	4.3	3.1	(NA)
Poughkeepsie city	13,803	13,389	14,325	3.1	-6.5	13,154	12,848	13,627	649	541	698	4.7	4.0	4.9
Rochester city	96,446	99,362	111,369	-2.9	-10.8	90,549	94,874	104,732	5,897	4,488	6,637	6.1	4.5	6.0
Rome city	15,126	15,086	17,167	0.3	-12.1	14,345	14,480	16,379	781	606	788	5.2	4.0	4.6
Saratoga Springs city	15,742	14,652	12,614	7.4	16.2	15,214	14,161	12,081	528	491	533	3.4	3.4	4.2
Schenectady city	29,875	29,195	32,282	2.3	-9.6	28,350	28,052	30,500	1,525	1,143	1,782	5.1	3.9	5.5
Spring Valley village	12,366	12,060	(NA)	2.5	(NA)	11,807	11,613	(NA)	559	447	(NA)	4.5	3.7	(NA)
Syracuse city	64,785	65,000	76,769	-0.3	-15.3	61,087	62,235	72,126	3,698	2,771	4,643	5.7	4.3	6.0
Troy city	23,931	23,728	26,596	0.9	-10.8	22,703	22,708	25,062	1,228	1,020	1,534	5.1	4.3	5.8
Utica city	26,258	26,239	30,361	0.1	-13.6	24,847	25,134	28,467	1,411	1,105	1,894	5.4	4.2	6.2
Valley Stream village	19,154	18,832	17,697	1.7	6.4	18,329	18,206	16,962	825	626	735	4.3	3.3	4.2
Watertown city	11,376	11,048	13,028	3.0	-15.2	10,777	10,483	11,854	599	565	1,174	5.3	5.1	9.0
White Plains city	30,698	28,369	28,119	8.2	0.9	29,603	27,485	27,091	1,095	884	1,028	3.6	3.1	3.7
Yonkers city	93,994	91,131	95,784	3.1	-4.9	89,143	87,381	91,242	4,851	3,750	4,542	5.2	4.1	4.7
NORTH CAROLINA	4,332,710	4,123,812	3,497,568	5.1	17.9	4,105,734	3,969,235	3,352,165	226,976	154,577	145,403	5.2	3.7	4.2
Asheville city	36,712	34,904	30,861	5.2	13.1	35,205	33,486	29,612	1,507	1,418	1,249	4.1	4.1	4.0
Burlington city	22,654	23,374	22,199	-3.1	5.3	21,313	22,403	21,240	1,341	971	959	5.9	4.2	4.3
Cary town	56,635	55,574	28,124	1.9	97.6	54,691	54,461	27,612	1,944	1,113	512	3.4	2.0	1.8
Chapel Hill town	26,071	23,083	20,482	12.9	12.7	25,280	22,508	19,893	791	575	589	3.0	2.5	2.9
Charlotte city	329,085	306,662	231,672	7.3	32.4	313,295	296,715	224,758	15,790	9,947	6,914	4.8	3.2	3.0
Concord city	31,387	30,363	14,856	3.4	104.4	30,051	29,308	14,249	1,336	1,055	607	4.3	3.5	4.1
Durham city	108,550	101,013	75,910	7.5	33.1	104,020	97,795	73,558	4,530	3,218	2,352	4.2	3.2	3.1
Fayetteville city	54,968	50,188	32,567	9.5	54.1	52,010	47,699	30,946	2,958	2,489	1,621	5.4	5.0	5.0
Gastonia city	33,073	33,287	28,343	-0.6	17.4	31,028	31,180	27,055	2,045	2,107	1,288	6.2	6.3	4.5
Goldsboro city	13,907	13,955	14,410	-0.3	-3.2	13,040	13,074	13,541	867	881	869	6.2	6.3	6.0
Greensboro city	126,545	122,012	107,446	3.7	13.6	120,055	117,764	103,359	6,490	4,248	4,087	5.1	3.5	3.8
Greenville city	36,952	32,060	24,445	15.3	31.2	35,217	30,575	23,220	1,735	1,485	1,225	4.7	4.6	5.0
Hickory city	19,855	20,319	16,927	-2.3	20.0	18,819	19,645	15,925	1,036	674	1,002	5.2	3.3	5.9
High Point city	48,859	45,983	38,209	6.3	20.3	46,270	44,012	36,511	2,589	1,971	1,698	5.3	4.3	4.4
Huntersville town	19,176	14,408	(NA)	33.1	(NA)	18,580	14,154	(NA)	596	254	(NA)	3.1	1.8	(NA)
Jacksonville city	19,447	16,920	11,480	14.9	47.4	18,257	15,990	10,931	1,190	930	549	6.1	5.5	4.8
Kannapolis city	19,344	19,058	15,253	1.5	24.9	18,338	18,226	14,339	1,006	832	914	5.2	4.4	6.0
Monroe city	14,007	13,618	(NA)	2.9	(NA)	13,314	12,945	(NA)	693	673	(NA)	4.9	4.9	(NA)
Raleigh city	187,050	162,207	125,933	15.3	28.8	179,904	157,665	122,130	7,146	4,542	3,803	3.8	2.8	3.0
Rocky Mount city	25,231	25,928	25,128	-2.7	3.2	23,504	24,165	23,788	1,727	1,763	1,340	6.8	6.8	5.3
Salisbury city	11,435	11,502	11,103	-0.6	3.6	10,700	10,716	10,579	735	786	524	6.4	6.8	4.7
Wilmington city	50,670	39,593	28,580	28.0	38.5	48,835	37,601	26,987	1,835	1,992	1,593	3.6	5.0	5.6
Wilson city	22,429	21,525	18,846	4.2	14.2	20,777	20,080	16,942	1,652	1,445	1,904	7.4	6.7	10.1
Winston-Salem city	96,195	92,860	75,764	3.6	22.6	91,440	89,312	71,769	4,755	3,548	3,995	4.9	3.8	5.3
NORTH DAKOTA	358,960	345,881	318,795	3.8	8.5	346,698	335,780	305,935	12,262	10,101	12,860	3.4	2.9	4.0
Bismarck city	34,907	32,667	27,599	6.9	18.4	33,856	31,927	26,589	1,051	740	1,010	3.0	2.3	3.7
Fargo city	59,760	56,607	44,185	5.6	28.1	58,158	55,361	42,787	1,602	1,246	1,398	2.7	2.2	3.2
Grand Forks city	30,798	28,619	26,387	7.6	8.5	29,887	27,864	25,269	911	755	1,118	3.0	2.6	4.2
Minot city	19,076	18,766	17,417	1.7	7.7	18,323	18,168	16,687	753	598	730	3.9	3.2	4.2

See footnotes at end of table.

Table C-3. Cities — **Civilian Labor Force**—Con.

[Includes states and 1,265 incorporated places of 25,000 or more population as of April 1, 2000, in all states except Hawaii, which has no incorporated places recognized by the U.S. Census Bureau. Two census designated places (CDPs) are also included (Honolulu CDP in Hawaii and Arlington CDP in Virginia). For more information on these areas, see Appendix C, Geographic Information]

City	Total			Percent change		Employed			Unemployed			Unemployment rate[3]		
	2005[1]	2000[1]	1990[2]	2000–2005	1990–2000	2005[1]	2000[1]	1990[2]	2005[1]	2000[1]	1990[2]	2005[1]	2000[1]	1990[2]
OHIO	5,900,354	5,807,036	5,389,113	1.6	7.8	5,550,477	5,573,154	5,079,472	349,877	233,882	309,641	5.9	4.0	5.7
Akron city	107,195	107,208	104,576	(Z)	2.5	100,172	100,749	97,182	7,023	6,459	7,394	6.6	6.0	7.1
Barberton city	13,565	13,565	12,221	–	11.0	12,637	12,804	11,390	928	761	831	6.8	5.6	6.8
Beavercreek city	20,493	20,896	18,002	–1.9	16.1	19,576	20,344	17,473	917	552	529	4.5	2.6	2.9
Bowling Green city	16,089	15,001	15,517	7.3	–3.3	15,376	14,444	14,456	713	557	1,061	4.4	3.7	6.8
Brunswick city	19,710	19,093	15,687	3.2	21.7	18,752	18,514	14,819	958	579	868	4.9	3.0	5.5
Canton city	36,389	37,508	37,448	–3.0	0.2	33,580	34,906	33,772	2,809	2,602	3,676	7.7	6.9	9.8
Cincinnati city	157,193	160,454	174,038	–2.0	–7.8	147,116	151,830	164,168	10,077	8,624	9,870	6.4	5.4	5.7
Cleveland city	191,940	203,665	207,219	–5.8	–1.7	176,789	188,569	185,081	15,151	15,096	22,138	7.9	7.4	10.7
Cleveland Heights city	27,735	28,790	28,800	–3.7	(Z)	26,466	28,075	27,771	1,269	715	1,029	4.6	2.5	3.6
Columbus city	408,548	399,532	350,276	2.3	14.1	386,660	385,108	336,824	21,888	14,424	13,452	5.4	3.6	3.8
Cuyahoga Falls city	28,425	26,907	26,231	5.6	2.6	26,948	26,163	25,305	1,477	744	926	5.2	2.8	3.5
Dayton city	71,169	73,263	79,557	–2.9	–7.9	65,727	68,209	72,648	5,442	5,054	6,909	7.6	6.9	8.7
Delaware city	15,895	13,559	(NA)	17.2	(NA)	15,166	13,048	(NA)	729	511	(NA)	4.6	3.8	(NA)
Dublin city	18,067	16,949	(NA)	6.6	(NA)	17,411	16,626	(NA)	656	323	(NA)	3.6	1.9	(NA)
East Cleveland city	9,959	11,042	14,468	–9.8	–23.7	9,133	9,870	12,682	826	1,172	1,786	8.3	10.6	12.3
Elyria city	29,371	30,184	29,252	–2.7	3.2	27,664	28,675	26,730	1,707	1,509	2,522	5.8	5.0	8.6
Euclid city	26,000	27,294	27,319	–4.7	–0.1	24,383	26,372	26,117	1,617	922	1,202	6.2	3.4	4.4
Fairborn city	16,478	16,823	15,246	–2.1	10.3	15,460	16,088	14,309	1,018	735	937	6.2	4.4	6.1
Fairfield city	25,057	24,591	23,409	1.9	5.0	23,856	23,881	22,487	1,201	710	922	4.8	2.9	3.9
Findlay city	22,138	21,426	19,281	3.3	11.1	21,082	20,697	18,297	1,056	729	984	4.8	3.4	5.1
Gahanna city	18,395	18,529	15,044	–0.7	23.2	17,583	18,122	14,679	812	407	365	4.4	2.2	2.4
Garfield Heights city	15,007	15,709	15,366	–4.5	2.2	14,034	15,159	14,690	973	550	676	6.5	3.5	4.4
Grove City city	16,710	15,044	(NA)	11.1	(NA)	15,922	14,645	(NA)	788	399	(NA)	4.7	2.7	(NA)
Hamilton city	29,771	29,602	28,248	0.6	4.8	27,977	28,046	25,844	1,794	1,556	2,404	6.0	5.3	8.5
Huber Heights city	19,889	20,468	20,846	–2.8	–1.8	18,750	19,713	20,024	1,139	755	822	5.7	3.7	3.9
Kent city	16,719	14,128	15,254	18.3	–7.4	15,939	13,517	14,341	780	611	913	4.7	4.3	6.0
Kettering city	29,632	31,128	32,805	–4.8	–5.1	28,022	30,400	31,974	1,610	728	831	5.4	2.3	2.5
Lakewood city	32,809	34,494	33,402	–4.9	3.3	31,172	33,629	32,192	1,637	865	1,210	5.0	2.5	3.6
Lancaster city	18,286	18,079	17,077	1.1	5.9	17,131	17,332	15,935	1,155	747	1,142	6.3	4.1	6.7
Lima city	17,558	17,662	19,649	–0.6	–10.1	16,311	16,413	17,308	1,247	1,249	2,341	7.1	7.1	11.9
Lorain city	31,475	32,829	31,942	–4.1	2.8	29,298	30,823	28,262	2,177	2,006	3,680	6.9	6.1	11.5
Mansfield city	23,157	22,927	23,309	1.0	–1.6	21,595	21,394	20,967	1,562	1,533	2,342	6.7	6.7	10.0
Maple Heights city	12,872	13,469	13,576	–4.4	–0.8	12,049	12,990	13,045	823	479	531	6.4	3.6	3.9
Marion city	17,407	16,557	16,017	5.1	3.4	16,324	15,678	14,395	1,083	879	1,622	6.2	5.3	10.1
Massillon city	15,750	15,725	14,192	0.2	10.8	14,731	15,065	13,084	1,019	660	1,108	6.5	4.2	7.8
Medina city	14,123	13,565	(NA)	4.1	(NA)	13,490	13,175	(NA)	633	390	(NA)	4.5	2.9	(NA)
Mentor city	29,968	29,580	26,336	1.3	12.3	28,617	28,786	25,114	1,351	794	1,222	4.5	2.7	4.6
Middletown city	26,152	26,027	22,217	0.5	17.1	24,547	24,617	20,353	1,605	1,410	1,864	6.1	5.4	8.4
Newark city	23,373	23,808	21,430	–1.8	11.1	21,932	22,615	19,892	1,441	1,193	1,538	6.2	5.0	7.2
North Olmsted city	18,683	19,385	18,455	–3.6	5.0	17,784	18,978	17,975	899	407	480	4.8	2.1	2.6
North Royalton city	17,397	16,969	12,844	2.5	32.1	16,605	16,597	12,481	792	372	363	4.6	2.2	2.8
Parma city	43,325	44,967	44,168	–3.7	1.8	40,875	43,773	42,988	2,450	1,194	1,180	5.7	2.7	2.7
Reynoldsburg city	18,680	18,581	15,593	0.5	19.2	17,724	18,047	15,275	956	534	318	5.1	2.9	2.0
Sandusky city	14,598	14,814	15,681	–1.5	–5.5	13,546	13,853	14,279	1,052	961	1,402	7.2	6.5	8.9
Shaker Heights city	15,166	16,021	16,533	–5.3	–3.1	14,456	15,635	16,050	710	386	483	4.7	2.4	2.9
Springfield city	29,055	30,226	31,788	–3.9	–4.9	27,004	28,324	29,411	2,051	1,902	2,377	7.1	6.3	7.5
Stow city	19,586	17,775	15,338	10.2	15.9	18,695	17,343	14,964	891	432	374	4.5	2.4	2.4
Strongsville city	24,977	25,123	19,623	–0.6	28.0	24,065	24,637	19,101	912	486	522	3.7	1.9	2.7
Toledo city	146,455	151,434	159,502	–3.3	–5.1	135,478	143,133	144,531	10,977	8,301	14,971	7.5	5.5	9.4
Trotwood city	12,070	12,600	(NA)	–4.2	(NA)	11,108	11,963	(NA)	962	637	(NA)	8.0	5.1	(NA)
Upper Arlington city	16,584	17,608	17,821	–5.8	–1.2	15,890	17,404	17,608	694	204	213	4.2	1.2	1.2
Warren city	19,786	20,197	22,478	–2.0	–10.1	18,318	18,686	19,899	1,468	1,511	2,579	7.4	7.5	11.5
Westerville city	19,439	19,343	16,649	0.5	16.2	18,596	18,999	16,375	843	344	274	4.3	1.8	1.6
Westlake city	16,715	16,912	14,180	–1.2	19.3	15,976	16,597	13,862	739	315	318	4.4	1.9	2.2
Youngstown city	30,249	31,905	35,421	–5.2	–9.9	27,620	29,086	30,996	2,629	2,819	4,425	8.7	8.8	12.5
Zanesville city	10,717	11,879	11,866	–9.8	0.1	9,811	11,046	10,231	906	833	1,635	8.5	7.0	13.8
OKLAHOMA	1,741,753	1,661,045	1,520,852	4.9	9.2	1,665,260	1,609,522	1,434,566	76,493	51,523	86,286	4.4	3.1	5.7
Bartlesville city	17,816	15,953	16,417	11.7	–2.8	17,037	15,409	15,894	779	544	523	4.4	3.4	3.2
Broken Arrow city	42,460	41,633	31,501	2.0	32.2	41,270	40,834	30,600	1,190	799	901	2.8	1.9	2.9
Edmond city	37,970	36,543	28,969	3.9	26.1	37,043	35,983	28,050	927	560	919	2.4	1.5	3.2
Enid city	23,063	22,387	21,199	3.0	5.6	22,178	21,708	20,145	885	679	1,054	3.8	3.0	5.0
Lawton city	35,542	33,097	32,974	7.4	0.4	33,737	31,777	30,661	1,805	1,320	2,313	5.1	4.0	7.0
Midwest City city	27,134	25,890	25,912	4.8	–0.1	25,859	25,119	24,428	1,275	771	1,484	4.7	3.0	5.7
Moore city	23,565	21,801	22,045	8.1	–1.1	22,729	21,308	21,250	836	493	795	3.5	2.3	3.6
Muskogee city	16,354	15,828	16,478	3.3	–3.9	15,305	15,146	15,546	1,049	682	932	6.4	4.3	5.7
Norman city	56,293	51,960	44,285	8.3	17.3	53,958	50,585	42,175	2,335	1,375	2,110	4.1	2.6	4.8
Oklahoma City city	266,655	252,693	231,879	5.5	9.0	254,040	245,068	218,275	12,615	7,625	13,604	4.7	3.0	5.9
Ponca City city	11,541	11,882	13,088	–2.9	–9.2	10,846	11,331	12,426	695	551	662	6.0	4.6	5.1
Shawnee city	13,381	12,819	11,454	4.4	11.9	12,590	12,341	10,691	791	478	763	5.9	3.7	6.7
Stillwater city	20,680	21,031	19,038	–1.7	10.5	19,910	20,513	18,017	770	518	1,021	3.7	2.5	5.4
Tulsa city	209,053	205,394	198,147	1.8	3.7	199,474	198,922	188,974	9,579	6,472	9,173	4.6	3.2	4.6

See footnotes at end of table.

Table C-3. Cities — **Civilian Labor Force**—Con.

[Includes states and 1,265 incorporated places of 25,000 or more population as of April 1, 2000, in all states except Hawaii, which has no incorporated places recognized by the U.S. Census Bureau. Two census designated places (CDPs) are also included (Honolulu CDP in Hawaii and Arlington CDP in Virginia). For more information on these areas, see Appendix C, Geographic Information]

City	Total 2005[1]	Total 2000[1]	Total 1990[2]	Percent change 2000–2005	Percent change 1990–2000	Employed 2005[1]	Employed 2000[1]	Employed 1990[2]	Unemployed 2005[1]	Unemployed 2000[1]	Unemployed 1990[2]	Unemployment rate[3] 2005[1]	Unemployment rate[3] 2000[1]	Unemployment rate[3] 1990[2]
OREGON	1,860,104	1,810,150	1,506,240	2.8	20.2	1,745,811	1,716,954	1,424,864	114,293	93,196	81,376	6.1	5.1	5.4
Albany city	22,578	21,784	15,073	3.6	44.5	21,019	20,338	14,086	1,559	1,446	987	6.9	6.6	6.5
Beaverton city	46,525	45,300	34,329	2.7	32.0	44,169	43,572	33,289	2,356	1,728	1,040	5.1	3.8	3.0
Bend city	36,484	28,855	(NA)	26.4	(NA)	34,666	27,619	(NA)	1,818	1,236	(NA)	5.0	4.3	(NA)
Corvallis city	26,376	25,150	22,573	4.9	11.4	25,140	24,115	21,404	1,236	1,035	1,169	4.7	4.1	5.2
Eugene city	77,530	74,739	62,036	3.7	20.5	73,288	70,977	58,636	4,242	3,762	3,400	5.5	5.0	5.5
Grants Pass city	12,217	9,734	(NA)	25.5	(NA)	11,421	9,112	(NA)	796	622	(NA)	6.5	6.4	(NA)
Gresham city	49,172	49,459	38,033	-0.6	30.0	46,167	46,999	36,609	3,005	2,460	1,424	6.1	5.0	3.7
Hillsboro city	44,283	40,603	21,216	9.1	91.4	42,105	38,837	20,521	2,178	1,766	695	4.9	4.3	3.3
Keizer city	18,301	17,671	(NA)	3.6	(NA)	17,212	16,734	(NA)	1,089	937	(NA)	6.0	5.3	(NA)
Lake Oswego city	19,536	19,971	18,401	-2.2	8.5	18,699	19,442	17,960	837	529	441	4.3	2.6	2.4
McMinnville city	13,215	12,798	(NA)	3.3	(NA)	12,406	12,066	(NA)	809	732	(NA)	6.1	5.7	(NA)
Medford city	34,993	32,009	24,385	9.3	31.3	32,964	30,237	22,876	2,029	1,772	1,509	5.8	5.5	6.2
Oregon City city.	15,622	14,291	(NA)	9.3	(NA)	14,703	13,589	(NA)	919	702	(NA)	5.9	4.9	(NA)
Portland city	294,267	305,797	242,062	-3.8	26.3	276,076	291,197	229,264	18,191	14,600	12,798	6.2	4.8	5.3
Salem city	72,207	68,905	54,292	4.8	26.9	67,596	64,843	51,331	4,611	4,062	2,961	6.4	5.9	5.5
Springfield city.	28,517	28,037	23,349	1.7	20.1	26,532	25,972	21,759	1,985	2,065	1,590	7.0	7.4	6.8
Tigard city	25,870	24,293	18,161	6.5	33.8	24,666	23,343	17,579	1,204	950	582	4.7	3.9	3.2
PENNSYLVANIA.	6,292,282	6,085,833	5,826,666	3.4	4.4	5,979,895	5,830,902	5,510,009	312,387	254,931	316,657	5.0	4.2	5.4
Allentown city	51,278	50,056	53,499	2.4	-6.4	47,898	47,839	50,147	3,380	2,217	3,352	6.6	4.4	6.3
Altoona city.	23,436	23,024	23,390	1.8	-1.6	22,200	21,819	21,571	1,236	1,205	1,819	5.3	5.2	7.8
Bethel Park borough	17,385	17,409	17,605	-0.1	-1.1	16,666	16,809	17,086	719	600	519	4.1	3.4	2.9
Bethlehem city	35,318	34,179	34,314	3.3	-0.4	33,309	32,774	32,351	2,009	1,405	1,963	5.7	4.1	5.7
Chester city	14,834	14,469	17,016	2.5	-15.0	13,661	13,616	15,863	1,173	853	1,153	7.9	5.9	6.8
Easton city	12,764	12,575	12,435	1.5	1.1	12,051	12,026	11,727	713	549	708	5.6	4.4	5.7
Erie city	49,080	48,771	50,836	0.6	-4.1	46,133	46,309	47,249	2,947	2,462	3,587	6.0	5.0	7.1
Harrisburg city.	22,731	22,698	25,095	0.1	-9.6	21,353	21,614	23,650	1,378	1,084	1,445	6.1	4.8	5.8
Lancaster city	27,353	26,326	27,335	3.9	-3.7	25,754	25,394	25,415	1,599	932	1,920	5.8	3.5	7.0
Municipality of Monroeville borough	15,168	15,265	15,778	-0.6	-3.3	14,531	14,698	15,219	637	567	559	4.2	3.7	3.5
New Castle city	10,647	10,978	10,797	-3.0	1.7	9,831	10,244	10,065	816	734	732	7.7	6.7	6.8
Norristown borough	16,061	15,951	16,453	0.7	-3.1	15,131	15,301	15,555	930	650	898	5.8	4.1	5.5
Philadelphia city	626,523	635,138	699,889	-1.4	-9.3	583,709	599,606	655,742	42,814	35,532	44,147	6.8	5.6	6.3
Pittsburgh city	154,578	156,091	164,971	-1.0	-5.4	146,359	149,059	156,977	8,219	7,032	7,994	5.3	4.5	4.8
Plum borough	14,521	14,246	14,334	1.9	-0.6	13,842	13,745	13,797	679	501	537	4.7	3.5	3.7
Reading city	33,620	34,090	37,329	-1.4	-8.7	31,035	32,237	34,524	2,585	1,853	2,805	7.7	5.4	7.5
Scranton city.	35,629	35,295	37,410	0.9	-5.7	33,591	33,650	34,655	2,038	1,645	2,755	5.7	4.7	7.4
State College borough	18,263	17,424	16,075	4.8	8.4	17,689	16,816	15,796	574	608	279	3.1	3.5	1.7
Wilkes-Barre city	19,389	19,359	22,155	0.2	-12.6	18,180	18,282	20,473	1,209	1,077	1,682	6.2	5.6	7.6
Williamsport city	14,362	14,287	14,395	0.5	-0.8	13,443	13,520	13,206	919	767	1,189	6.4	5.4	8.3
York city.	19,102	19,142	20,258	-0.2	-5.5	17,745	18,225	19,101	1,357	917	1,157	7.1	4.8	5.7
RHODE ISLAND.	569,451	543,404	525,851	4.8	3.3	540,709	520,758	493,674	28,742	22,646	32,177	5.0	4.2	6.1
Cranston city.	42,308	40,271	39,175	5.1	2.8	40,148	38,589	36,848	2,160	1,682	2,327	5.1	4.2	5.9
East Providence city.	26,094	25,215	27,032	3.5	-6.7	24,690	24,007	25,388	1,404	1,208	1,644	5.4	4.8	6.1
Newport city	13,585	13,679	14,024	-0.7	-2.5	12,919	13,123	13,254	666	556	770	4.9	4.1	5.5
Pawtucket city.	37,552	36,172	39,518	3.8	-8.5	35,300	34,451	36,662	2,252	1,721	2,856	6.0	4.8	7.2
Providence city	79,616	76,194	74,786	4.5	1.9	74,583	72,220	69,656	5,033	3,974	5,130	6.3	5.2	6.9
Warwick city	49,315	47,574	46,740	3.7	1.8	47,044	45,762	44,178	2,271	1,812	2,562	4.6	3.8	5.5
Woonsocket city	22,035	20,988	21,951	5.0	-4.4	20,794	20,050	20,028	1,241	938	1,923	5.6	4.5	8.8
SOUTH CAROLINA	2,080,517	1,972,850	1,722,150	5.5	14.6	1,938,740	1,902,029	1,638,580	141,777	70,821	83,570	6.8	3.6	4.9
Aiken city.	12,802	11,812	(NA)	8.4	(NA)	12,056	11,382	(NA)	746	430	(NA)	5.8	3.6	(NA)
Anderson city	10,975	10,692	12,467	2.6	-14.2	9,700	10,174	11,491	1,275	518	976	11.6	4.8	7.8
Charleston city	53,436	48,380	39,147	10.5	23.6	50,417	46,794	37,967	3,019	1,586	1,180	5.6	3.3	3.0
Columbia city	52,857	49,463	43,844	6.9	12.8	48,817	47,431	41,635	4,040	2,032	2,209	7.6	4.1	5.0
Florence city	14,582	14,287	13,956	2.1	2.4	13,405	13,782	13,201	1,177	505	755	8.1	3.5	5.4
Goose Creek city	13,045	11,942	7,969	9.2	49.9	12,461	11,628	7,784	584	314	185	4.5	2.6	2.3
Greenville city	29,969	29,213	30,599	2.6	-4.5	27,849	28,246	29,162	2,120	967	1,437	7.1	3.3	4.7
Hilton Head Island town	19,772	16,043	(NA)	23.2	(NA)	19,365	15,817	(NA)	407	226	(NA)	2.1	1.4	(NA)
Mount Pleasant town	28,664	26,336	17,194	8.8	53.2	28,003	25,989	17,001	661	347	193	2.3	1.3	1.1
North Charleston city	38,420	34,248	27,406	12.2	25.0	35,140	32,527	26,324	3,280	1,721	1,082	8.5	5.0	3.9
Rock Hill city.	28,198	25,505	21,625	10.6	17.9	25,997	24,535	20,549	2,201	970	1,076	7.8	3.8	5.0
Spartanburg city	17,920	17,422	20,644	2.9	-15.6	15,946	16,527	19,381	1,974	895	1,263	11.0	5.1	6.1
Summerville town	16,189	14,046	(NA)	15.3	(NA)	15,508	13,709	(NA)	681	337	(NA)	4.2	2.4	(NA)
Sumter city.	16,159	15,328	13,582	5.4	12.9	14,673	14,657	12,800	1,486	671	782	9.2	4.4	5.8
SOUTH DAKOTA	432,032	408,685	350,642	5.7	16.6	415,344	397,678	337,503	16,688	11,007	13,139	3.9	2.7	3.7
Rapid City city.	34,828	32,363	27,401	7.6	18.1	33,506	31,530	26,532	1,322	833	869	3.8	2.6	3.2
Sioux Falls city	80,245	74,664	59,046	7.5	26.5	77,354	72,982	57,390	2,891	1,682	1,656	3.6	2.3	2.8

See footnotes at end of table.

Table C-3. Cities — **Civilian Labor Force**—Con.

[Includes states and 1,265 incorporated places of 25,000 or more population as of April 1, 2000, in all states except Hawaii, which has no incorporated places recognized by the U.S. Census Bureau. Two census designated places (CDPs) are also included (Honolulu CDP in Hawaii and Arlington CDP in Virginia). For more information on these areas, see Appendix C, Geographic Information]

City	Total			Percent change		Employed			Unemployed			Unemployment rate[3]		
	2005[1]	2000[1]	1990[2]	2000–2005	1990–2000	2005[1]	2000[1]	1990[2]	2005[1]	2000[1]	1990[2]	2005[1]	2000[1]	1990[2]
TENNESSEE	2,909,562	2,871,539	2,401,093	1.3	19.6	2,747,618	2,756,498	2,269,015	161,944	115,041	132,078	5.6	4.0	5.5
Bartlett city	23,213	22,585	14,529	2.8	55.4	22,151	22,271	14,307	1,062	314	222	4.6	1.4	1.5
Brentwood city	15,279	12,032	(NA)	27.0	(NA)	14,772	11,845	(NA)	507	187	(NA)	3.3	1.6	(NA)
Bristol city	11,952	11,826	(NA)	1.1	(NA)	11,287	11,431	(NA)	665	395	(NA)	5.6	3.3	(NA)
Chattanooga city	74,039	76,799	71,874	–3.6	6.9	69,892	73,353	68,257	4,147	3,446	3,617	5.6	4.5	5.0
Clarksville city	47,836	44,357	28,879	7.8	53.6	45,203	42,423	26,982	2,633	1,934	1,897	5.5	4.4	6.6
Cleveland city	19,034	18,337	15,341	3.8	19.5	17,449	17,748	14,444	1,585	589	897	8.3	3.2	5.8
Collierville town	18,658	16,816	(NA)	11.0	(NA)	17,845	16,534	(NA)	813	282	(NA)	4.4	1.7	(NA)
Columbia city	15,743	17,184	14,766	–8.4	16.4	14,516	16,381	13,712	1,227	803	1,054	7.8	4.7	7.1
Cookeville city	14,627	12,010	11,321	21.8	6.1	13,667	11,414	10,459	960	596	862	6.6	5.0	7.6
Franklin city	26,816	24,134	11,277	11.1	114.0	25,746	23,396	10,904	1,070	738	373	4.0	3.1	3.3
Germantown city	19,527	20,029	17,030	–2.5	17.6	18,736	19,805	16,787	791	224	243	4.1	1.1	1.4
Hendersonville city	24,301	23,219	18,338	4.7	26.6	23,286	22,462	17,612	1,015	757	726	4.2	3.3	4.0
Jackson city	29,150	28,862	23,601	1.0	22.3	27,165	27,515	22,128	1,985	1,347	1,473	6.8	4.7	6.2
Johnson City city	30,060	27,945	24,045	7.6	16.2	28,556	26,824	22,866	1,504	1,121	1,179	5.0	4.0	4.9
Kingsport city	18,909	19,227	15,721	–1.7	22.3	17,272	18,290	15,021	1,637	937	700	8.7	4.9	4.5
Knoxville city	92,047	86,210	81,063	6.8	6.3	86,266	82,588	76,596	5,781	3,622	4,467	6.3	4.2	5.5
Memphis city	306,481	306,546	284,880	(Z)	7.6	284,613	291,406	268,868	21,868	15,140	16,012	7.1	4.9	5.6
Morristown city	12,332	12,130	(NA)	1.7	(NA)	11,250	11,545	(NA)	1,082	585	(NA)	8.8	4.8	(NA)
Murfreesboro city[3]	44,733	38,321	24,929	16.7	53.7	42,596	36,842	23,516	2,137	1,479	1,413	4.8	3.9	5.7
Nashville-Davidson (balance)[3]	306,463	311,521	275,724	–1.6	13.0	292,348	301,507	265,366	14,115	10,014	10,358	4.6	3.2	3.8
Oak Ridge city	13,204	13,139	13,369	0.5	–1.7	12,576	12,556	12,842	628	583	527	4.8	4.4	3.9
Smyrna town	17,949	14,924	(NA)	20.3	(NA)	17,193	14,578	(NA)	756	346	(NA)	4.2	2.3	(NA)
TEXAS	11,225,882	10,347,847	8,593,724	8.5	20.4	10,629,606	9,896,002	8,041,859	596,276	451,845	551,865	5.3	4.4	6.4
Abilene city	56,972	52,854	49,305	7.8	7.2	54,474	50,615	46,019	2,498	2,239	3,286	4.4	4.2	6.7
Allen city	36,651	25,427	11,063	44.1	129.8	35,277	24,782	10,668	1,374	645	395	3.7	2.5	3.6
Amarillo city	98,293	91,033	81,293	8.0	12.0	94,463	87,280	77,127	3,830	3,753	4,166	3.9	4.1	5.1
Arlington city	204,893	193,871	161,173	5.7	20.3	194,758	187,363	153,660	10,135	6,508	7,513	4.9	3.4	4.7
Austin city	404,479	400,299	270,480	1.0	48.0	386,776	387,285	256,013	17,703	13,014	14,467	4.4	3.3	5.3
Baytown city	31,828	30,983	30,916	2.7	0.2	29,345	29,345	29,086	2,483	1,638	1,830	7.8	5.3	5.9
Beaumont city	53,849	53,758	55,278	0.2	–2.7	49,924	50,282	51,426	3,925	3,476	3,852	7.3	6.5	7.0
Bedford city	31,265	30,896	28,670	1.2	7.8	29,854	30,332	27,731	1,411	564	939	4.5	1.8	3.3
Big Spring city	9,167	9,378	10,110	–2.2	–7.2	8,609	8,848	9,555	558	530	555	6.1	5.7	5.5
Brownsville city	59,454	51,871	39,274	14.6	32.1	55,043	47,729	33,447	4,411	4,142	5,827	7.4	8.0	14.8
Bryan city	36,679	34,250	29,164	7.1	17.4	35,170	32,874	27,561	1,509	1,376	1,603	4.1	4.0	5.5
Carrollton city	70,211	68,348	53,246	2.7	28.4	67,028	66,750	51,402	3,183	1,598	1,844	4.5	2.3	3.5
Cedar Hill city	22,468	18,654	11,247	20.4	65.9	21,325	18,171	10,902	1,143	483	345	5.1	2.6	3.1
Cedar Park city	25,482	15,351	(X)	66.0	(X)	24,793	15,059	(X)	689	292	(X)	2.7	1.9	(X)
Cleburne city	13,632	12,975	10,379	5.1	25.0	12,988	12,369	9,593	644	606	786	4.7	4.7	7.6
College Station city	39,963	33,541	24,500	19.1	36.9	38,482	32,224	23,106	1,481	1,317	1,394	3.7	3.9	5.7
Conroe city	21,586	18,956	14,157	13.9	33.9	20,721	17,894	13,408	865	1,062	749	4.0	5.6	5.3
Coppell city	21,519	20,591	10,622	4.5	93.9	20,617	20,314	10,418	902	277	204	4.2	1.3	1.9
Copperas Cove city	13,327	12,475	8,967	6.8	39.1	12,630	11,700	8,140	697	775	827	5.2	6.2	9.2
Corpus Christi city	142,699	132,371	121,978	7.8	8.5	135,177	125,608	113,687	7,522	6,763	8,291	5.3	5.1	6.8
Dallas city	600,742	619,535	574,614	–3.0	7.8	565,656	590,115	538,104	35,086	29,420	36,510	5.8	4.7	6.4
Deer Park city	16,017	15,795	15,136	1.4	4.4	15,159	15,294	14,538	858	501	598	5.4	3.2	4.0
Del Rio city	15,807	13,587	12,568	16.3	8.1	14,806	12,738	10,837	1,001	849	1,731	6.3	6.2	13.8
Denton city	55,334	46,761	38,388	18.3	21.8	53,350	44,931	36,082	1,984	1,830	2,306	3.6	3.9	6.0
DeSoto city	24,082	21,871	18,595	10.1	17.6	22,726	21,187	17,947	1,356	684	648	5.6	3.1	3.5
Duncanville city	18,972	19,868	20,810	–4.5	–4.5	17,837	19,410	20,002	1,135	458	808	6.0	2.3	3.9
Edinburg city	25,892	20,065	14,091	29.0	42.4	24,688	18,625	11,221	1,204	1,440	2,870	4.7	7.2	20.4
El Paso city	251,665	236,187	232,534	6.6	1.6	234,959	220,696	206,102	16,706	15,491	26,432	6.6	6.6	11.4
Euless city	31,390	29,080	25,253	7.9	15.2	29,976	28,412	24,282	1,414	668	971	4.5	2.3	3.8
Farmers Branch city	14,839	15,791	14,642	–6.0	7.8	14,103	15,403	13,971	736	388	671	5.0	2.5	4.6
Flower Mound town	34,333	29,662	9,133	15.7	224.8	33,041	28,995	8,813	1,292	667	320	3.8	2.2	3.5
Fort Worth city	293,907	268,012	233,730	9.7	14.7	278,363	255,395	217,338	15,544	12,617	16,392	5.3	4.7	7.0
Friendswood city	17,701	15,715	13,285	12.6	18.3	16,942	15,270	12,829	759	445	456	4.3	2.8	3.4
Frisco city	35,390	20,403	3,586	73.5	469.0	34,173	19,930	3,422	1,217	473	164	3.4	2.3	4.6
Galveston city	27,171	27,345	30,057	–0.6	–9.0	25,491	25,558	27,284	1,680	1,787	2,773	6.2	6.5	9.2
Garland city	114,546	118,422	107,916	–3.3	9.7	108,164	114,562	103,434	6,382	3,860	4,482	5.6	3.3	4.2
Georgetown city	17,761	13,782	7,514	28.9	83.4	17,044	13,423	7,118	717	359	396	4.0	2.6	5.3
Grand Prairie city	72,176	68,691	56,302	5.1	22.0	68,355	65,903	53,413	3,821	2,788	2,889	5.3	4.1	5.1
Grapevine city	28,492	25,951	18,060	9.8	43.7	27,349	25,430	17,541	1,143	521	519	4.0	2.0	2.9
Haltom City city	21,639	21,723	17,960	–0.4	21.0	20,532	20,829	17,026	1,107	894	934	5.1	4.1	5.2
Harlingen city	24,513	22,570	21,196	8.6	6.5	22,952	21,362	19,215	1,561	1,208	1,981	6.4	5.4	9.3
Houston city	992,287	963,777	891,617	3.0	8.1	933,057	914,737	836,745	59,230	49,040	54,872	6.0	5.1	6.2
Huntsville city	14,509	13,772	10,654	5.4	29.3	13,775	13,028	10,072	734	744	582	5.1	5.4	5.5
Hurst city	21,221	20,867	20,253	1.7	3.0	20,233	20,207	19,226	988	660	1,027	4.7	3.2	5.1
Irving city	112,884	116,013	100,655	–2.7	15.3	107,232	112,386	96,183	5,652	3,627	4,472	5.0	3.1	4.4

See footnotes at end of table.

Table C-3. Cities — **Civilian Labor Force**—Con.

[Includes states and 1,265 incorporated places of 25,000 or more population as of April 1, 2000, in all states except Hawaii, which has no incorporated places recognized by the U.S. Census Bureau. Two census designated places (CDPs) are also included (Honolulu CDP in Hawaii and Arlington CDP in Virginia). For more information on these areas, see Appendix C, Geographic Information]

City	Total 2005[1]	Total 2000[1]	Total 1990[2]	Percent change 2000–2005	Percent change 1990–2000	Employed 2005[1]	Employed 2000[1]	Employed 1990[2]	Unemployed 2005[1]	Unemployed 2000[1]	Unemployed 1990[2]	Unemployment rate[3] 2005[1]	Unemployment rate[3] 2000[1]	Unemployment rate[3] 1990[2]
TEXAS—Con.														
Keller city	18,841	15,107	(NA)	24.7	(NA)	18,182	14,855	(NA)	659	252	(NA)	3.5	1.7	(NA)
Killeen city	40,515	34,209	23,070	18.4	48.3	38,307	32,167	20,404	2,208	2,042	2,666	5.4	6.0	11.6
Kingsville city	13,303	11,203	10,694	18.7	4.8	12,644	10,573	9,910	659	630	784	5.0	5.6	7.3
Lake Jackson city	13,880	13,603	12,802	2.0	6.3	13,154	13,084	12,417	726	519	385	5.2	3.8	3.0
Lancaster city	15,088	13,605	12,319	10.9	10.4	14,075	12,828	11,754	1,013	777	565	6.7	5.7	4.6
La Porte city	18,330	17,412	15,108	5.3	15.3	17,301	16,821	14,520	1,029	591	588	5.6	3.4	3.9
Laredo city	81,344	66,198	51,690	22.9	28.1	76,796	62,291	45,547	4,548	3,907	6,143	5.6	5.9	11.9
League City city	32,650	25,805	17,530	26.5	47.2	31,336	25,000	16,971	1,314	805	559	4.0	3.1	3.2
Lewisville city	55,268	51,359	30,043	7.6	71.0	53,083	49,842	28,924	2,185	1,517	1,119	4.0	3.0	3.7
Longview city	39,427	35,636	36,060	10.6	−1.2	37,451	33,512	33,032	1,976	2,124	3,028	5.0	6.0	8.4
Lubbock city	115,486	105,670	95,739	9.3	10.4	110,975	101,764	90,739	4,511	3,906	5,000	3.9	3.7	5.2
Lufkin city	16,187	15,535	14,073	4.2	10.4	15,251	14,654	13,196	936	881	877	5.8	5.7	6.2
McAllen city	56,575	46,228	39,841	22.4	16.0	53,612	43,189	33,172	2,963	3,039	6,669	5.2	6.6	16.7
McKinney city	45,373	29,747	11,022	52.5	169.9	43,799	28,769	10,281	1,574	978	741	3.5	3.3	6.7
Mansfield city	19,378	15,986	8,391	21.2	90.5	18,550	15,481	7,984	828	505	407	4.3	3.2	4.9
Mesquite city	71,764	71,440	59,643	0.5	19.8	67,887	69,506	57,246	3,877	1,934	2,397	5.4	2.7	4.0
Midland city	54,953	47,834	45,834	14.9	4.4	52,889	45,858	43,374	2,064	1,976	2,460	3.8	4.1	5.4
Mission city	23,310	17,198	11,547	35.5	48.9	21,992	15,805	9,291	1,318	1,393	2,256	5.7	8.1	19.5
Missouri City city	37,463	29,829	21,536	25.6	38.5	35,704	28,838	21,019	1,759	991	517	4.7	3.3	2.4
Nacogdoches city	16,021	14,509	14,813	10.4	−2.1	15,254	13,783	13,649	767	726	1,164	4.8	5.0	7.9
New Braunfels city	23,241	18,752	13,003	23.9	44.2	22,371	18,151	12,311	870	601	692	3.7	3.2	5.3
North Richland Hills city	35,222	33,291	27,923	5.8	19.2	33,647	32,284	26,785	1,575	1,007	1,138	4.5	3.0	4.1
Odessa city	47,078	42,450	42,811	10.9	−0.8	44,885	40,275	40,413	2,193	2,175	2,398	4.7	5.1	5.6
Paris city	11,770	11,560	10,836	1.8	6.7	10,968	10,956	9,986	802	604	850	6.8	5.2	7.8
Pasadena city	66,953	65,821	61,136	1.7	7.7	62,803	62,552	57,744	4,150	3,269	3,392	6.2	5.0	5.5
Pearland city	29,600	21,553	11,049	37.3	95.1	28,385	20,785	10,733	1,215	768	316	4.1	3.6	2.9
Pharr city	21,825	16,785	13,449	30.0	24.8	20,560	15,432	9,892	1,265	1,353	3,557	5.8	8.1	26.4
Plano city	141,657	134,689	78,793	5.2	70.9	135,298	130,843	76,175	6,359	3,846	2,618	4.5	2.9	3.3
Port Arthur city	22,886	23,455	24,582	−2.4	−4.6	20,602	20,923	21,767	2,284	2,532	2,815	10.0	10.8	11.5
Richardson city	56,858	54,822	45,008	3.7	21.8	54,270	53,492	43,441	2,588	1,330	1,567	4.6	2.4	3.5
Round Rock city	46,177	36,342	17,813	27.1	104.0	44,495	35,084	17,097	1,682	1,258	716	3.6	3.5	4.0
Rowlett city	28,931	25,429	13,733	13.8	85.2	27,597	24,861	13,363	1,334	568	370	4.6	2.2	2.7
San Angelo city	43,998	42,512	39,292	3.5	8.2	42,043	40,825	36,766	1,955	1,687	2,526	4.4	4.0	6.4
San Antonio city	594,644	543,008	443,584	9.5	22.4	565,826	519,568	408,040	28,818	23,440	35,544	4.8	4.3	8.0
San Juan city	11,445	9,285	4,648	23.3	99.8	10,599	8,557	3,661	846	728	987	7.4	7.8	21.2
San Marcos city	25,308	19,905	14,521	27.1	37.1	24,460	18,809	13,421	848	1,096	1,100	3.4	5.5	7.6
Sherman city	17,359	17,056	15,690	1.8	8.7	16,411	16,282	14,704	948	774	986	5.5	4.5	6.3
Socorro city	10,276	10,031	9,667	2.4	3.8	9,452	9,043	7,870	824	988	1,797	8.0	9.8	18.6
Sugar Land city	39,489	34,036	13,698	16.0	148.5	37,872	33,102	13,297	1,617	934	401	4.1	2.7	2.9
Temple city	28,821	26,462	22,094	8.9	19.8	27,488	25,645	20,895	1,333	817	1,199	4.6	3.1	5.4
Texarkana city	16,324	15,445	14,112	5.7	9.4	15,407	14,419	12,981	917	1,026	1,131	5.6	6.6	8.0
Texas City city	20,382	19,524	20,258	4.4	−3.6	18,946	18,358	18,566	1,436	1,166	1,692	7.0	6.0	8.4
The Colony city	20,852	16,174	12,881	28.9	25.6	20,019	15,739	12,309	833	435	572	4.0	2.7	4.4
Tyler city	46,782	41,312	37,916	13.2	9.0	44,534	39,558	35,085	2,248	1,754	2,831	4.8	4.2	7.5
Victoria city	32,042	31,066	26,912	3.1	15.4	30,571	29,860	25,600	1,471	1,206	1,312	4.6	3.9	4.9
Waco city	54,906	50,592	47,462	8.5	6.6	51,922	47,700	43,211	2,984	2,892	4,251	5.4	5.7	9.0
Weslaco city	12,552	10,357	9,924	21.2	4.4	11,622	9,217	7,212	930	1,140	2,712	7.4	11.0	27.3
Wichita Falls city	48,059	46,035	44,000	4.4	4.6	45,659	43,767	40,947	2,400	2,268	3,053	5.0	4.9	6.9
UTAH	1,268,075	1,136,036	820,436	11.6	38.5	1,214,150	1,097,915	784,050	53,925	38,121	36,386	4.3	3.4	4.4
Bountiful city	23,346	20,954	18,041	11.4	16.1	22,554	20,414	17,461	792	540	580	3.4	2.6	3.2
Clearfield city	12,755	11,391	(NA)	12.0	(NA)	12,069	10,924	(NA)	686	467	(NA)	5.4	4.1	(NA)
Draper city	12,241	11,640	(NA)	5.2	(NA)	12,052	11,511	(NA)	189	129	(NA)	1.5	1.1	(NA)
Layton city	34,033	30,457	20,267	11.7	50.3	32,484	29,402	19,408	1,549	1,055	859	4.6	3.5	4.2
Logan city	28,098	23,691	16,649	18.6	42.3	26,925	22,900	15,826	1,173	791	823	4.2	3.3	4.9
Midvale city	16,658	15,702	(NA)	6.1	(NA)	15,892	15,179	(NA)	766	523	(NA)	4.6	3.3	(NA)
Murray city	20,553	19,372	16,981	6.1	14.1	19,599	18,720	16,536	954	652	445	4.6	3.4	2.6
Ogden city	40,892	37,719	30,914	8.4	22.0	38,119	35,494	28,641	2,773	2,225	2,273	6.8	5.9	7.4
Orem city	47,083	41,958	28,891	12.2	45.2	45,064	40,619	27,819	2,019	1,339	1,072	4.3	3.2	3.7
Provo city	62,329	55,526	42,334	12.3	31.2	59,582	53,704	40,214	2,747	1,822	2,120	4.4	3.3	5.0
Riverton city	12,872	12,209	(NA)	5.4	(NA)	12,561	11,997	(NA)	311	212	(NA)	2.4	1.7	(NA)
Roy city	18,714	17,331	(NA)	8.0	(NA)	17,975	16,738	(NA)	739	593	(NA)	3.9	3.4	(NA)
St. George city	31,483	22,105	12,041	42.4	83.6	30,354	21,315	11,521	1,129	790	520	3.6	3.6	4.3
Salt Lake City city	105,604	99,389	84,732	6.3	17.3	100,188	95,691	80,926	5,416	3,698	3,806	5.1	3.7	4.5
Sandy city	50,956	48,267	35,891	5.6	34.5	49,480	47,259	34,866	1,476	1,008	1,025	2.9	2.1	2.9
South Jordan city	15,617	14,798	(NA)	5.5	(NA)	15,184	14,502	(NA)	433	296	(NA)	2.8	2.0	(NA)
Taylorsville city	35,363	33,352	(X)	6.0	(NA)	33,809	32,291	(X)	1,554	1,061	(X)	4.4	3.2	(X)
West Jordan city	39,558	37,329	20,244	6.0	84.4	37,893	36,192	19,648	1,665	1,137	596	4.2	3.0	2.9
West Valley City city	60,910	57,213	44,794	6.5	27.7	57,370	54,795	42,521	3,540	2,418	2,273	5.8	4.2	5.1

See footnotes at end of table.

Table C-3. Cities — **Civilian Labor Force**—Con.

[Includes states and 1,265 incorporated places of 25,000 or more population as of April 1, 2000, in all states except Hawaii, which has no incorporated places recognized by the U.S. Census Bureau. Two census designated places (CDPs) are also included (Honolulu CDP in Hawaii and Arlington CDP in Virginia). For more information on these areas, see Appendix C, Geographic Information]

City	Total			Percent change		Employed			Unemployed			Unemployment rate[3]		
	2005[1]	2000[1]	1990[2]	2000–2005	1990–2000	2005[1]	2000[1]	1990[2]	2005[1]	2000[1]	1990[2]	2005[1]	2000[1]	1990[2]
VERMONT	355,897	335,798	309,280	6.0	8.6	343,520	326,742	294,074	12,377	9,056	15,206	3.5	2.7	4.9
Burlington city	23,032	23,046	22,603	−0.1	2.0	22,317	22,483	21,571	715	563	1,032	3.1	2.4	4.6
VIRGINIA	3,933,949	3,584,037	3,220,117	9.8	11.3	3,797,730	3,502,524	3,076,925	136,219	81,513	143,192	3.5	2.3	4.4
Alexandria city.	83,183	80,458	73,167	3.4	10.0	80,875	79,036	71,129	2,308	1,422	2,038	2.8	1.8	2.8
Arlington CDP.	(NA)	(NA)	(NA)	(NA)	(NA)	(NA)	(NA)	(NA)	(NA)	(NA)	(NA)	(NA)	(NA)	(NA)
Blacksburg town	18,091	16,325	15,541	10.8	5.0	17,611	15,773	14,130	480	552	1,411	2.7	3.4	9.1
Charlottesville city	19,058	19,260	20,473	−1.0	−5.9	18,176	18,694	19,952	882	566	521	4.6	2.9	2.5
Chesapeake city	110,809	97,374	79,366	13.8	22.7	106,921	95,161	75,975	3,888	2,213	3,391	3.5	2.3	4.3
Danville city	21,021	21,255	25,890	−1.1	−17.9	18,913	20,329	23,470	2,108	926	2,420	10.0	4.4	9.3
Hampton city.	68,042	63,944	64,296	6.4	−0.5	64,815	62,225	60,883	3,227	1,719	3,413	4.7	2.7	5.3
Harrisonburg city	21,477	19,539	15,916	9.9	22.8	20,745	19,095	14,934	732	444	982	3.4	2.3	6.2
Leesburg town	20,684	16,588	(NA)	24.7	(NA)	20,276	16,338	(NA)	408	250	(NA)	2.0	1.5	(NA)
Lynchburg city.	31,164	30,601	31,854	1.8	−3.9	29,792	29,861	30,017	1,372	740	1,837	4.4	2.4	5.8
Manassas city.	21,272	19,160	16,355	11.0	17.2	20,669	18,840	15,960	603	320	395	2.8	1.7	2.4
Newport News city	88,653	82,380	80,238	7.6	2.7	84,533	80,245	76,085	4,120	2,135	4,153	4.6	2.6	5.2
Norfolk city.	100,614	92,428	97,518	8.9	−5.2	95,175	89,413	92,910	5,439	3,015	4,608	5.4	3.3	4.7
Petersburg city	14,430	13,832	18,057	4.3	−23.4	13,380	13,362	16,761	1,050	470	1,296	7.3	3.4	7.2
Portsmouth city	45,108	42,693	46,666	5.7	−8.5	42,589	41,247	43,582	2,519	1,446	3,084	5.6	3.4	6.6
Richmond city	97,645	94,849	103,182	2.9	−8.1	92,450	92,351	97,342	5,195	2,498	5,840	5.3	2.6	5.7
Roanoke city.	45,926	46,423	48,469	−1.1	−4.2	44,008	45,290	46,220	1,918	1,133	2,249	4.2	2.4	4.6
Suffolk city	36,985	29,149	24,934	26.9	16.9	35,633	28,421	23,372	1,352	728	1,562	3.7	2.5	6.3
Virginia Beach city	224,128	204,662	190,096	9.5	7.7	216,447	200,133	182,630	7,681	4,529	7,466	3.4	2.2	3.9
WASHINGTON.	3,292,195	3,050,021	2,537,038	7.9	20.2	3,109,921	2,898,677	2,406,444	182,274	151,344	130,594	5.5	5.0	5.1
Auburn city.	23,065	20,936	17,859	10.2	17.2	21,855	19,787	17,029	1,210	1,149	830	5.2	5.5	4.6
Bellevue city.	65,022	61,166	52,185	6.3	17.2	62,407	58,837	50,693	2,615	2,329	1,492	4.0	3.8	2.9
Bellingham city	43,348	36,405	29,188	19.1	24.7	41,521	34,241	27,729	1,827	2,164	1,459	4.2	5.9	5.0
Bothell city	17,780	17,432	(NA)	2.0	(NA)	16,967	16,764	(NA)	813	668	(NA)	4.6	3.8	(NA)
Bremerton city.	15,990	14,917	14,225	7.2	4.9	14,888	13,713	13,331	1,102	1,204	894	6.9	8.1	6.3
Burien city	16,589	16,899	(X)	−1.8	(NA)	15,688	16,283	(X)	901	616	(X)	5.4	3.6	(X)
Des Moines city.	15,002	15,320	(NA)	−2.1	(NA)	14,168	14,468	(NA)	834	852	(NA)	5.6	5.6	(NA)
Edmonds city	21,513	21,149	17,764	1.7	19.1	20,497	20,435	17,135	1,016	714	629	4.7	3.4	3.5
Everett city	47,948	46,149	35,824	3.9	28.8	45,207	42,997	33,363	2,741	3,152	2,461	5.7	6.8	6.9
Federal Way city	44,343	45,457	(X)	−2.5	(NA)	41,999	43,251	(X)	2,344	2,206	(X)	5.3	4.9	(X)
Kennewick city	33,910	29,744	22,919	14.0	29.8	32,122	28,145	21,330	1,788	1,599	1,589	5.3	5.4	6.9
Kent city.	44,066	43,560	23,112	1.2	88.5	42,162	41,272	22,169	1,904	2,288	943	4.3	5.3	4.1
Kirkland city	29,514	28,732	25,320	2.7	13.5	28,279	27,911	24,496	1,235	821	824	4.2	2.9	3.3
Lacey city.	16,729	15,113	(NA)	10.7	(NA)	15,873	14,350	(NA)	856	763	(NA)	5.1	5.0	(NA)
Lakewood city	25,811	25,569	(X)	0.9	(NA)	24,153	23,844	(X)	1,658	1,725	(X)	6.4	6.7	(X)
Longview city	15,977	15,841	14,916	0.9	6.2	14,926	14,811	13,877	1,051	1,030	1,039	6.6	6.5	7.0
Lynnwood city	18,127	18,232	16,513	−0.6	10.4	17,123	17,399	15,702	1,004	833	811	5.5	4.6	4.9
Marysville city	14,449	12,578	(NA)	14.9	(NA)	13,685	12,053	(NA)	764	525	(NA)	5.3	4.2	(NA)
Mount Vernon city	14,647	13,241	(NA)	10.6	(NA)	13,859	12,370	(NA)	788	871	(NA)	5.4	6.6	(NA)
Olympia city	25,448	23,201	17,888	9.7	29.7	24,253	22,413	17,049	1,195	788	839	4.7	3.4	4.7
Pasco city	19,545	14,375	(NA)	36.0	(NA)	18,222	13,191	(NA)	1,323	1,184	(NA)	6.8	8.2	(NA)
Puyallup city	18,927	17,215	11,919	9.9	44.4	17,959	16,442	11,436	968	773	483	5.1	4.5	4.1
Redmond city	28,748	27,584	22,037	4.2	25.2	27,603	26,773	21,443	1,145	811	594	4.0	2.9	2.7
Renton city.	32,281	29,461	24,563	9.6	19.9	30,732	28,199	23,499	1,549	1,262	1,064	4.8	4.3	4.3
Richland city.	24,228	20,742	18,536	16.8	11.9	23,325	20,030	17,609	903	712	927	3.7	3.4	5.0
Sammamish city	18,584	18,222	(X)	2.0	(NA)	17,849	17,883	(X)	735	339	(X)	4.0	1.9	(X)
SeaTac city.	13,568	13,864	(X)	−2.1	(NA)	12,772	13,033	(X)	796	831	(X)	5.9	6.0	(X)
Seattle city	348,371	336,924	302,795	3.4	11.3	332,234	322,292	288,789	16,137	14,632	14,006	4.6	4.3	4.6
Shoreline city	28,104	28,640	(X)	−1.9	(NA)	26,745	27,419	(X)	1,359	1,221	(X)	4.8	4.3	(X)
Spokane city.	102,950	99,348	83,687	3.6	18.7	96,997	93,242	78,516	5,953	6,106	5,171	5.8	6.1	6.2
Spokane Valley city	44,320	(X)	(X)	(NA)	(NA)	42,606	(X)	(X)	1,714	(X)	(X)	3.9	(X)	(X)
Tacoma city	98,739	94,064	83,247	5.0	13.0	92,520	88,753	78,809	6,219	5,311	4,438	6.3	5.6	5.3
University Place city	16,996	16,274	(X)	4.4	(NA)	16,184	15,696	(X)	812	578	(X)	4.8	3.6	(X)
Vancouver city.	78,652	74,553	23,657	5.5	215.1	74,642	70,702	22,239	4,010	3,851	1,418	5.1	5.2	6.0
Walla Walla city.	14,008	13,585	12,077	3.1	12.5	13,207	12,566	11,065	801	1,019	1,012	5.7	7.5	8.4
Wenatchee city	16,183	14,823	(NA)	9.2	(NA)	15,240	13,772	(NA)	943	1,051	(NA)	5.8	7.1	(NA)
Yakima city.	39,711	34,988	29,542	13.5	18.4	37,054	31,985	26,349	2,657	3,003	3,193	6.7	8.6	10.8
WEST VIRGINIA	800,383	808,861	756,306	−1.0	6.9	760,640	764,649	691,184	39,743	44,212	65,122	5.0	5.5	8.6
Charleston city	25,098	26,418	26,851	−5.0	−1.6	24,004	25,241	25,055	1,094	1,177	1,796	4.4	4.5	6.7
Huntington city	22,986	22,944	22,951	0.2	(Z)	21,650	21,515	21,052	1,336	1,429	1,899	5.8	6.2	8.3
Morgantown city	13,715	12,747	11,880	7.6	7.3	13,117	11,994	11,023	598	753	857	4.4	5.9	7.2
Parkersburg city	14,878	15,157	15,561	−1.8	−2.6	13,927	14,333	14,205	951	824	1,356	6.4	5.4	8.7
Wheeling city	13,616	14,332	16,232	−5.0	−11.7	12,841	13,573	15,384	775	759	848	5.7	5.3	5.2

See footnotes at end of table.

Table C-3. Cities — **Civilian Labor Force**—Con.

[Includes states and 1,265 incorporated places of 25,000 or more population as of April 1, 2000, in all states except Hawaii, which has no incorporated places recognized by the U.S. Census Bureau. Two census designated places (CDPs) are also included (Honolulu CDP in Hawaii and Arlington CDP in Virginia). For more information on these areas, see Appendix C, Geographic Information]

City	Total			Percent change		Employed			Unemployed			Unemployment rate[3]		
	2005[1]	2000[1]	1990[2]	2000–2005	1990–2000	2005[1]	2000[1]	1990[2]	2005[1]	2000[1]	1990[2]	2005[1]	2000[1]	1990[2]
WISCONSIN	3,041,470	2,996,091	2,598,898	1.5	15.3	2,897,483	2,894,884	2,486,129	143,987	101,207	112,769	4.7	3.4	4.3
Appleton city	39,770	40,463	40,057	−1.7	1.0	37,488	39,151	38,605	2,282	1,312	1,452	5.7	3.2	3.6
Beloit city	17,307	17,509	17,007	−1.2	3.0	15,930	16,486	16,105	1,377	1,023	902	8.0	5.8	5.3
Brookfield city	20,016	20,297	18,663	−1.4	8.8	19,334	19,790	18,141	682	507	522	3.4	2.5	2.8
Eau Claire city	36,884	36,204	29,633	1.9	22.2	35,246	34,960	27,954	1,638	1,244	1,679	4.4	3.4	5.7
Fond du Lac city	23,514	23,437	19,859	0.3	18.0	22,253	22,627	18,548	1,261	810	1,311	5.4	3.5	6.6
Franklin city	17,921	17,169	(NA)	4.4	(NA)	17,244	16,692	(NA)	677	477	(NA)	3.8	2.8	(NA)
Green Bay city	58,123	58,432	52,368	−0.5	11.6	54,165	56,129	49,501	3,958	2,303	2,867	6.8	3.9	5.5
Greenfield city	20,045	20,572	18,781	−2.6	9.5	19,181	20,031	18,243	864	541	538	4.3	2.6	2.9
Janesville city	33,867	33,532	28,330	1.0	18.4	31,669	32,069	26,623	2,198	1,463	1,707	6.5	4.4	6.0
Kenosha city	48,354	48,004	41,199	0.7	16.5	45,245	45,766	37,726	3,109	2,238	3,473	6.4	4.7	8.4
La Crosse city	28,442	29,047	26,794	−2.1	8.4	27,093	27,959	25,554	1,349	1,088	1,240	4.7	3.7	4.6
Madison city	141,363	132,635	113,858	6.6	16.5	137,029	129,406	111,515	4,334	3,229	2,343	3.1	2.4	2.1
Manitowoc city	18,154	18,484	15,895	−1.8	16.3	17,113	17,804	15,082	1,041	680	813	5.7	3.7	5.1
Menomonee Falls village	18,638	18,699	15,334	−0.3	21.9	17,937	18,261	15,177	701	438	157	3.8	2.3	1.0
Milwaukee city	268,598	283,514	296,053	−5.3	−4.2	249,095	268,433	279,586	19,503	15,081	16,467	7.3	5.3	5.6
New Berlin city	22,052	22,705	20,312	−2.9	11.8	21,230	22,138	19,702	822	567	610	3.7	2.5	3.0
Oak Creek city	19,221	17,900	(NA)	7.4	(NA)	18,447	17,393	(NA)	774	507	(NA)	4.0	2.8	(NA)
Oshkosh city	35,784	35,312	32,725	1.3	7.9	34,018	34,215	31,300	1,766	1,097	1,425	4.9	3.1	4.4
Racine city	38,924	40,139	37,089	−3.0	8.2	35,251	37,827	34,437	3,673	2,312	2,652	9.4	5.8	7.2
Sheboygan city	27,208	28,139	26,221	−3.3	7.3	25,828	27,340	24,972	1,380	799	1,249	5.1	2.8	4.8
Superior city	14,087	14,519	12,587	−3.0	15.3	13,363	13,920	11,912	724	599	675	5.1	4.1	5.4
Waukesha city	38,864	39,149	33,643	−0.7	16.4	37,000	37,805	32,242	1,864	1,344	1,401	4.8	3.4	4.2
Wausau city	19,889	20,317	18,807	−2.1	8.0	18,820	19,495	18,037	1,069	822	770	5.4	4.0	4.1
Wauwatosa city	24,516	26,473	25,670	−7.4	3.1	23,591	25,753	25,100	925	720	570	3.8	2.7	2.2
West Allis city	32,396	34,474	34,291	−6.0	0.5	30,772	33,366	33,018	1,624	1,108	1,273	5.0	3.2	3.7
West Bend city	16,249	16,206	12,993	0.3	24.7	15,272	15,582	12,449	977	624	544	6.0	3.9	4.2
WYOMING	284,538	266,882	236,043	6.6	13.1	274,362	256,685	223,531	10,176	10,197	12,512	3.6	3.8	5.3
Casper city	30,103	27,377	24,255	10.0	12.9	29,128	26,359	22,889	975	1,018	1,366	3.2	3.7	5.6
Cheyenne city	28,319	26,802	25,772	5.7	4.0	27,083	25,737	24,507	1,236	1,065	1,265	4.4	4.0	4.9
Laramie city	16,874	15,446	14,367	9.2	7.5	16,389	14,936	13,630	485	510	737	2.9	3.3	5.1

– Represents zero.   NA Not available.   X Not applicable.   Z Less than .05 percent.

[1]Reflects revised population controls and model reestimation through 2005 for states and revised inputs, reestimation, and new statewide controls through 2005 for cities.
[2]Reflects new modeling approach and reestimation as of March 2005 for states. Reflects 2000 census-based geography and new model-based controls at the state level for cities.
[3]Civilian unemployed as a percent of total civilian labor force.
[4]Data are for Milford (consolidated) city, CT; data for Milford city (balance) not available.
[5]Data are for Athens-Clarke County (consolidated) city, GA; data for Athens-Clark County (balance) not available.
[6]Data are for Augusta-Richmond County (consolidated) city, GA; data for Augusta-Richmond County (balance) not available.
[7]Data are for Columbus (consolidated) city, GA; data for Columbus city not available.
[8]Data are for Honolulu County/city, HI; data for Honolulu CDP not available.
[9]Data are for Indianapolis (incorporated) city, IN; data for Indianapolis city (balance) not available.
[10]Data are for Louisville-Jefferson County (consolidated) city, KY; data for Louisville/Jefferson County (balance) not available.
[11]Data are for West Springfield town, MA; data for West Springfield city not available.
[12]Data are for Butte-Silver Bow (consolidated) city, MT; data for Butte-Silver Bow (balance) not available.
[13]Data are for Nashville-Davidson (consolidated) city, TN; data for Nashville-Davidson (balance) not available.

Survey, Census, or Data Collection Method: Based on the Current Population Survey (CPS), the Current Employment Statistics (CES) survey, and the unemployment insurance (UI) system; for information, see Appendix B, Limitations of the Data and Methodology, and also <http://www.bls.gov/lau/laumthd.htm>.

Source: U.S. Bureau of Labor Statistics, Local Area Unemployment Statistics Program, accessed September 19, 2006 (related Internet site <http://www.bls.gov/lau/>).

Table C-4. Cities — **Manufacturing and Wholesale Trade**

[Includes states and 1,265 incorporated places of 25,000 or more population as of April 1, 2000, in all states except Hawaii, which has no incorporated places recognized by the U.S. Census Bureau. Two census designated places (CDPs) are also included (Honolulu CDP in Hawaii and Arlington CDP in Virginia). For more information on these areas, see Appendix C, Geographic Information]

City	Manufacturing (NAICS 31–33), 2002[1] Establishments[2] Total	Percent with 20 or more employees	All employees Number[3]	Annual payroll (mil. dol.)	Production workers Number[3]	Wages (mil. dol.)	Value added by manufacture (mil. dol.)	Value of shipments (mil. dol.)	Wholesale trade (NAICS 42), 2002[4] Establishments	Sales (mil. dol.) Total	Merchant wholesalers	Paid employees[5]	Annual payroll (mil. dol.)	Operating expenses (mil. dol.)
ALABAMA	5,119	35.4	284,127	9,744.3	220,348	6,650.5	28,641.7	66,686.2	5,747	43,641.4	30,247.9	74,915	2,662.0	4,813.3
Auburn city	40	32.5	[6]1,750	(D)	(D)	(D)	(D)	(D)	23	60.0	(D)	177	6.2	9.9
Bessemer city	45	37.8	1,617	58.0	1,271	39.8	189.7	355.2	76	1,017.7	976.2	1,454	56.0	93.5
Birmingham city	334	38.6	17,671	678.9	12,339	426.3	1,560.9	3,245.6	644	9,705.5	5,102.9	12,468	500.7	884.2
Decatur city	102	41.2	[7]7,500	(D)	(D)	(D)	(D)	(D)	99	607.4	567.0	1,196	44.1	82.5
Dothan city	92	31.5	6,094	200.0	4,609	132.4	544.1	1,091.6	178	(D)	(D)	[6]1,750	(D)	(D)
Florence city	72	34.7	3,076	90.7	2,427	64.2	226.4	525.7	65	(D)	(D)	[8]750	(D)	(D)
Gadsden city	60	40.0	3,820	144.7	3,232	117.0	297.9	654.1	51	158.8	(D)	569	16.9	27.0
Homewood city	35	31.4	1,870	68.0	948	27.1	194.0	571.8	118	534.5	(D)	1,375	54.3	88.2
Hoover city	(NA)	(NA)	(NA)	(NA)	(NA)	(NA)	(NA)	(NA)	138	1,472.3	500.8	1,688	79.9	142.3
Huntsville city	220	41.8	19,179	814.3	12,830	483.6	2,226.4	5,659.9	329	2,235.3	(D)	3,524	148.6	257.1
Madison city	29	41.4	[6]1,750	(D)	(D)	(D)	(D)	(D)	52	363.1	(D)	646	25.9	47.2
Mobile city	166	28.3	8,390	326.9	6,247	228.8	1,169.1	1,915.2	430	2,483.6	2,055.0	5,451	203.9	370.1
Montgomery city	188	41.0	9,514	299.6	7,239	189.6	1,199.5	2,341.1	335	3,279.0	(D)	5,235	188.5	324.6
Phenix City city	23	21.7	1,084	35.8	877	25.8	106.9	182.8	17	174.2	(D)	435	14.7	23.6
Prattville city	17	35.3	1,750	(D)	(D)	(D)	(D)	(D)	23	49.3	(D)	113	2.8	4.9
Prichard city	21	33.3	525	16.6	348	9.3	44.7	104.7	14	65.4	65.4	389	13.5	17.6
Tuscaloosa city	79	36.7	5,274	182.8	4,230	132.6	501.7	1,270.9	90	367.2	(D)	1,028	35.1	60.8
Vestavia Hills city	(NA)	(NA)	(NA)	(NA)	(NA)	(NA)	(NA)	(NA)	44	1,445.4	385.4	638	34.2	75.5
ALASKA	514	19.8	10,933	362.2	9,036	256.6	1,283.6	3,832.0	740	3,616.7	33.7	7,425	313.8	564.8
Anchorage municipality	203	14.8	2,279	82.9	1,679	51.7	209.4	394.7	404	2,629.6	(D)	5,188	222.6	392.5
Fairbanks city	(NA)	(NA)	(NA)	(NA)	(NA)	(NA)	(NA)	(NA)	56	231.6	(D)	596	23.9	46.1
Juneau city and borough	(NA)	(NA)	(NA)	(NA)	(NA)	(NA)	(NA)	(NA)	32	(D)	(D)	[9]175	(D)	(D)
ARIZONA	4,935	26.1	168,155	7,080.6	104,924	3,221.2	25,977.0	41,910.7	6,651	60,977.0	37,936.9	88,568	3,697.8	6,670.0
Apache Junction city	(NA)	(NA)	(NA)	(NA)	(NA)	(NA)	(NA)	(NA)	10	(D)	(D)	[10]60	(D)	(D)
Avondale city	(NA)	(NA)	(NA)	(NA)	(NA)	(NA)	(NA)	(NA)	13	(D)	(D)	[9]175	(D)	(D)
Bullhead City city	(NA)	(NA)	(NA)	(NA)	(NA)	(NA)	(NA)	(NA)	15	(D)	(D)	[10]60	(D)	(D)
Casa Grande city	28	28.6	965	34.6	690	21.6	323.5	434.4	22	76.5	(D)	153	5.3	9.7
Chandler city	164	32.3	11,070	573.5	6,321	258.9	8,362.9	9,320.3	222	3,132.0	1,769.3	4,648	256.7	409.1
Flagstaff city	68	19.1	3,074	139.9	1,800	63.5	486.4	555.7	80	600.8	(D)	955	33.4	67.1
Gilbert town	92	26.1	2,248	91.5	1,277	37.0	156.4	288.6	109	356.6	317.3	698	27.3	57.5
Glendale city	164	25.0	7,277	299.4	3,854	110.4	738.7	1,205.7	142	893.9	(D)	1,532	50.2	95.2
Lake Havasu City city	93	11.8	[6]1,750	(D)	(D)	(D)	(D)	(D)	63	73.3	67.8	280	7.9	13.8
Mesa city	250	22.8	9,955	508.1	5,958	237.2	718.5	2,001.6	345	1,209.0	989.0	2,774	110.4	227.6
Oro Valley town	8	50.0	[6]1,750	(D)	(D)	(D)	(D)	(D)	19	53.8	(D)	133	2.9	4.3
Peoria city	58	22.4	1,154	34.1	839	19.8	84.0	159.3	57	78.7	41.1	239	6.2	9.6
Phoenix city	1,637	30.7	55,675	2,186.7	35,831	1,014.7	6,007.5	10,736.9	2,332	29,631.0	16,261.7	39,681	1,731.8	3,069.5
Prescott city	63	27.0	1,757	45.1	1,279	29.1	121.4	188.9	63	174.0	(D)	468	15.7	27.0
Scottsdale city	262	18.3	4,079	156.8	2,740	83.0	347.2	639.2	642	4,865.9	1,684.4	5,127	279.0	583.2
Sierra Vista city	(NA)	(NA)	(NA)	(NA)	(NA)	(NA)	(NA)	(NA)	16	26.3	26.3	134	3.6	7.8
Surprise city	(NA)	(NA)	(NA)	(NA)	(NA)	(NA)	(NA)	(NA)	12	(D)	(D)	[10]60	(D)	(D)
Tempe city	454	32.2	17,568	775.7	11,014	373.5	1,921.7	3,657.8	641	9,496.5	8,467.6	11,216	529.8	927.6
Tucson city	484	21.5	11,469	404.0	6,858	187.0	1,234.0	2,096.4	529	1,875.9	1,480.2	5,466	189.3	332.0
Yuma city	46	19.6	1,436	42.6	1,246	33.9	134.9	382.3	65	739.0	680.4	2,938	47.9	95.4
ARKANSAS	3,185	34.3	210,394	6,309.3	169,867	4,532.7	21,965.4	46,721.4	3,498	34,470.8	17,398.5	42,875	1,438.0	2,645.9
Conway city	58	36.2	6,451	185.3	5,138	127.2	729.1	1,290.8	51	163.2	(D)	485	13.1	22.7
Fayetteville city	65	38.5	6,299	196.5	4,888	134.1	640.2	1,136.9	80	5,488.1	(D)	1,363	63.4	121.4
Fort Smith city	176	41.5	18,527	548.2	15,594	418.1	1,889.7	4,248.8	197	(D)	(D)	[6]1,750	(D)	(D)
Hot Springs city	50	18.0	1,646	49.7	1,017	31.2	109.9	248.9	61	332.6	(D)	422	12.0	22.2
Jacksonville city	31	41.9	1,419	48.2	982	27.7	139.3	280.3	17	42.4	42.4	123	4.3	7.9
Jonesboro city	107	40.2	6,556	195.9	5,088	130.8	606.3	1,317.8	109	(D)	275.9	[6]1,750	(D)	(D)
Little Rock city	205	32.7	10,061	352.7	7,409	224.9	920.4	3,012.2	512	4,136.8	3,110.8	9,623	378.0	648.7
North Little Rock city	73	39.7	2,981	104.0	2,143	58.2	354.8	656.2	212	4,568.4	(D)	3,246	112.0	255.7
Pine Bluff city	62	46.8	7,500	(D)	(D)	(D)	(D)	(D)	58	173.9	(D)	489	14.5	24.8
Rogers city	56	44.6	5,452	175.9	4,564	133.3	772.4	1,165.0	58	1,149.4	(D)	768	44.7	71.9
Springdale city	106	30.2	8,699	224.4	7,348	162.8	944.7	1,711.3	157	1,296.7	1,142.5	2,119	74.0	144.7
Texarkana city	19	31.6	[11]3,750	(D)	(D)	(D)	(D)	(D)	45	(D)	(D)	[8]750	(D)	(D)
West Memphis city	38	39.5	[6]1,750	(D)	(D)	(D)	(D)	(D)	33	729.8	(D)	497	15.9	32.2
CALIFORNIA	48,478	28.5	1,616,504	66,468.6	1,029,398	31,371.8	197,574.5	378,661.4	58,770	655,954.7	410,148.5	811,344	39,060.9	77,079.8
Alameda city	59	22.0	944	42.7	466	17.1	108.4	165.0	62	1,182.4	(D)	1,020	84.2	249.6
Alhambra city	106	21.7	2,582	79.7	2,047	48.7	136.8	286.3	299	512.6	504.4	1,375	40.9	82.4
Aliso Viejo city	32	40.6	842	37.5	462	13.1	92.3	149.5	85	669.4	589.7	1,093	68.2	120.1
Anaheim city	871	33.4	33,036	1,196.5	22,791	650.3	2,913.5	5,182.0	909	8,072.4	4,401.5	13,332	540.8	1,043.9
Antioch city	(NA)	(NA)	(NA)	(NA)	(NA)	(NA)	(NA)	(NA)	27	(D)	(D)	[8]750	(D)	(D)
Apple Valley town	(NA)	(NA)	(NA)	(NA)	(NA)	(NA)	(NA)	(NA)	14	(D)	(D)	[10]60	(D)	(D)
Arcadia city	72	23.6	1,203	40.3	829	20.8	122.3	185.6	285	545.5	489.2	1,222	43.0	85.1
Atascadero city	(NA)	(NA)	(NA)	(NA)	(NA)	(NA)	(NA)	(NA)	23	(D)	(D)	[9]175	(D)	(D)
Azusa city	121	35.5	5,326	228.3	3,230	87.0	532.2	1,015.6	70	196.2	(D)	757	24.4	45.2
Bakersfield city	152	21.1	3,084	90.9	2,179	54.5	691.4	1,590.7	309	3,826.8	2,990.7	4,094	179.6	353.4

See footnotes at end of table.

Table C-4. Cities — **Manufacturing and Wholesale Trade**—Con.

[Includes states and 1,265 incorporated places of 25,000 or more population as of April 1, 2000, in all states except Hawaii, which has no incorporated places recognized by the U.S. Census Bureau. Two census designated places (CDPs) are also included (Honolulu CDP in Hawaii and Arlington CDP in Virginia). For more information on these areas, see Appendix C, Geographic Information]

City	Manufacturing (NAICS 31–33), 2002[1]								Wholesale trade (NAICS 42), 2002[4]					
	Establishments[2]		All employees		Production workers		Value added by manufacture (mil. dol.)	Value of shipments (mil. dol.)	Estab-lishments	Sales (mil. dol.)		Paid employees[5]	Annual payroll (mil. dol.)	Operating expenses (mil. dol.)
	Total	Percent with 20 or more employees	Number[3]	Annual payroll (mil. dol.)	Number[3]	Wages (mil. dol.)				Total	Merchant wholesalers			
CALIFORNIA—Con.														
Baldwin Park city	138	17.4	2,171	70.4	1,572	41.5	164.3	272.9	155	881.7	881.7	1,461	53.2	105.2
Bell city	29	41.4	906	32.8	654	18.3	92.3	206.8	54	313.6	(D)	752	19.8	41.4
Bellflower city	(NA)	(NA)	(NA)	(NA)	(NA)	(NA)	(NA)	(NA)	36	(D)	(D)	[9]175	(D)	(D)
Bell Gardens city	66	30.3	1,256	41.8	957	26.7	102.2	204.1	35	(D)	(D)	[12]375	(D)	(D)
Belmont city	(NA)	(NA)	(NA)	(NA)	(NA)	(NA)	(NA)	(NA)	35	187.0	(D)	546	42.5	62.6
Benicia city	86	30.2	2,123	86.3	1,396	39.3	666.4	2,092.4	86	626.0	538.3	2,575	98.8	157.3
Berkeley city	160	22.5	4,248	198.8	2,719	114.3	708.6	886.9	136	560.7	499.9	1,579	67.5	132.4
Beverly Hills city	(NA)	(NA)	(NA)	(NA)	(NA)	(NA)	(NA)	(NA)	186	663.9	585.1	945	48.4	104.0
Brea city	187	32.1	7,327	259.3	5,139	148.6	770.3	1,284.4	272	3,866.3	2,875.5	4,389	217.0	725.1
Buena Park city	127	38.6	8,024	260.6	5,373	148.1	678.5	1,442.6	178	1,487.8	1,232.3	2,935	111.4	275.3
Burbank city	263	28.9	6,441	246.9	4,469	136.0	552.4	863.2	237	1,440.9	(D)	2,903	129.9	225.0
Burlingame city	74	31.1	1,949	81.8	1,214	41.9	194.0	339.2	185	2,595.3	2,004.9	1,512	82.6	155.5
Calexico city	(NA)	(NA)	(NA)	(NA)	(NA)	(NA)	(NA)	(NA)	78	407.8	(D)	372	11.5	25.3
Camarillo city	166	39.2	6,933	281.6	4,763	147.7	930.1	1,450.3	132	(D)	(D)	[11]3,750	(D)	(D)
Campbell city	131	22.1	3,065	126.2	1,925	60.0	260.4	405.8	106	622.5	583.9	1,409	94.5	148.2
Carlsbad city	188	40.4	11,405	561.8	4,856	168.4	1,697.3	2,709.8	282	1,699.8	1,520.5	3,822	185.8	338.5
Carson city	305	39.7	14,775	567.1	10,373	327.5	2,766.3	6,594.2	356	5,338.1	(D)	7,446	332.4	654.8
Cathedral City city	(NA)	(NA)	(NA)	(NA)	(NA)	(NA)	(NA)	(NA)	31	(D)	(D)	[12]375	(D)	(D)
Ceres city	32	31.3	1,466	35.9	1,264	22.7	116.2	278.4	18	108.5	(D)	212	7.4	12.6
Cerritos city	103	44.7	4,403	155.6	3,080	86.7	365.7	721.5	288	3,015.4	2,485.6	3,282	147.4	324.7
Chico city	91	30.8	1,994	61.9	1,346	33.3	241.5	385.4	92	347.5	301.6	941	32.4	59.4
Chino city	257	40.5	9,682	313.5	7,336	195.7	798.4	1,629.4	287	1,490.2	1,386.0	3,346	124.6	241.4
Chino Hills city	(NA)	(NA)	(NA)	(NA)	(NA)	(NA)	(NA)	(NA)	62	(D)	(D)	[9]175	(D)	(D)
Chula Vista city	162	25.9	5,602	251.3	3,381	123.5	790.7	1,288.6	301	820.1	751.2	1,833	61.5	124.4
Citrus Heights city	(NA)	(NA)	(NA)	(NA)	(NA)	(NA)	(NA)	(NA)	32	(D)	(D)	[9]175	(D)	(D)
Claremont city	29	41.4	748	23.6	553	14.4	56.8	102.3	29	(D)	(D)	[9]175	(D)	(D)
Clovis city	55	23.6	2,539	83.3	1,706	39.9	248.3	444.8	47	51.3	40.0	186	5.5	9.5
Colton city	64	37.5	2,296	73.7	1,871	48.7	232.7	469.7	50	284.4	(D)	664	20.2	35.2
Compton city	174	46.6	7,514	250.9	5,648	142.9	771.2	1,707.5	127	(D)	(D)	[11]3,750	(D)	(D)
Concord city	136	23.5	3,872	180.6	2,200	74.0	427.0	755.6	182	1,049.2	668.3	2,001	118.1	217.2
Corona city	379	40.6	14,178	505.4	10,744	313.7	1,410.8	2,697.7	293	4,377.5	(D)	5,364	184.0	393.6
Costa Mesa city	300	30.0	7,806	286.7	5,113	126.8	713.6	1,277.2	356	7,689.6	5,458.4	7,056	419.1	797.3
Covina city	123	22.0	2,785	99.0	1,993	55.3	196.1	369.4	85	223.3	176.8	635	19.8	40.0
Culver City city	80	23.8	1,847	71.3	1,308	37.9	173.6	262.7	161	1,195.1	961.9	2,483	133.2	278.5
Cupertino city	44	29.5	1,556	89.7	623	24.2	243.3	408.0	80	(D)	(D)	[11]3,750	(D)	(D)
Cypress city	50	36.0	2,046	73.9	1,114	26.5	251.4	428.7	110	6,001.9	5,284.0	3,505	211.7	981.8
Daly City city	(NA)	(NA)	(NA)	(NA)	(NA)	(NA)	(NA)	(NA)	31	68.5	68.5	288	7.9	11.8
Dana Point city	(NA)	(NA)	(NA)	(NA)	(NA)	(NA)	(NA)	(NA)	61	307.2	(D)	193	8.4	14.3
Danville town	(NA)	(NA)	(NA)	(NA)	(NA)	(NA)	(NA)	(NA)	74	304.2	(D)	286	15.0	23.6
Davis city	(NA)	(NA)	(NA)	(NA)	(NA)	(NA)	(NA)	(NA)	22	(D)	(D)	[9]175	(D)	(D)
Delano city	(NA)	(NA)	(NA)	(NA)	(NA)	(NA)	(NA)	(NA)	17	157.2	(D)	128	5.3	9.6
Diamond Bar city	29	24.1	1,379	47.1	988	24.2	60.2	194.9	179	2,830.3	(D)	1,341	54.2	78.7
Downey city	106	28.3	2,946	98.1	2,171	68.7	409.5	883.7	107	727.9	(D)	1,529	58.2	101.8
Dublin city	35	28.6	1,523	72.1	784	30.4	197.3	310.6	72	730.3	(D)	1,182	94.0	119.9
East Palo Alto city	(NA)	(NA)	(NA)	(NA)	(NA)	(NA)	(NA)	(NA)	5	(D)	(D)	[10]60	(D)	(D)
El Cajon city	192	29.2	6,363	223.4	4,684	137.0	534.1	819.6	134	618.2	(D)	1,264	43.6	76.5
El Centro city	21	28.6	[8]750	(D)	(D)	(D)	(D)	(D)	49	190.8	159.6	394	13.8	26.5
Elk Grove city	37	35.1	1,140	41.9	970	27.8	89.8	176.2	38	252.8	(D)	249	13.0	23.6
El Monte city	223	24.7	6,539	208.8	4,875	126.1	426.0	746.8	309	787.0	(D)	2,038	61.7	115.0
Encinitas city	(NA)	(NA)	(NA)	(NA)	(NA)	(NA)	(NA)	(NA)	103	299.0	186.8	602	24.3	50.2
Escondido city	216	19.9	3,963	131.9	2,943	80.7	334.5	581.7	171	528.5	480.7	1,320	52.8	101.4
Eureka city	35	17.1	627	16.6	509	12.2	38.0	84.4	53	166.8	(D)	588	18.6	33.4
Fairfield city	51	39.2	2,784	124.5	1,889	75.6	539.6	1,038.4	81	1,347.5	(D)	1,887	75.4	118.1
Folsom city	(NA)	(NA)	(NA)	(NA)	(NA)	(NA)	(NA)	(NA)	38	741.7	(D)	1,062	68.8	126.9
Fontana city	107	51.4	5,335	191.8	4,032	119.0	601.5	1,446.2	100	3,209.7	(D)	3,002	97.9	205.7
Foster City city	17	17.6	[6]1,750	(D)	(D)	(D)	(D)	(D)	62	2,665.9	(D)	2,816	301.7	458.3
Fountain Valley city	103	25.2	3,003	122.4	2,387	93.4	1,095.6	1,943.5	162	(D)	(D)	[6]1,750	(D)	(D)
Fremont city	407	44.7	28,230	1,629.6	15,785	737.0	4,502.6	10,784.0	618	10,697.3	8,909.5	12,173	729.9	1,222.3
Fresno city	401	31.2	14,190	458.0	9,884	262.6	1,349.5	3,208.7	616	4,350.1	3,659.1	8,751	308.7	578.3
Fullerton city	247	38.9	8,758	294.4	6,720	191.5	1,087.3	1,949.2	263	2,896.8	1,827.2	4,432	223.6	562.4
Gardena city	316	27.2	7,934	255.2	5,901	158.4	589.4	1,081.1	224	984.7	866.6	2,065	77.5	153.3
Garden Grove city	306	25.2	8,486	287.5	5,980	153.6	713.3	1,262.4	252	1,301.4	1,163.7	2,973	113.2	239.6
Gilroy city	76	27.6	2,005	76.7	1,566	52.7	236.5	471.1	59	(D)	(D)	[8]750	(D)	(D)
Glendale city	274	22.6	4,795	172.9	3,540	109.8	391.8	628.4	256	852.8	714.2	2,102	82.8	150.3
Glendora city	42	28.6	1,285	40.1	898	27.4	167.4	264.6	54	(D)	(D)	[12]375	(D)	(D)
Goleta city	136	33.1	6,784	385.2	2,801	112.2	947.6	1,328.5	57	588.9	(D)	1,330	89.4	162.9
Hanford city	29	27.6	1,190	41.8	1,002	31.2	134.3	272.1	21	(D)	(D)	[9]175	(D)	(D)
Hawthorne city	99	34.3	3,454	143.2	2,444	85.2	333.5	607.1	62	302.1	(D)	1,008	32.3	66.4
Hayward city	387	34.4	13,476	546.4	8,539	256.4	1,262.7	2,728.5	566	5,944.3	3,781.8	9,455	422.0	756.9
Hemet city	29	37.9	1,128	33.8	938	23.4	66.0	132.9	18	(D)	(D)	[9]175	(D)	(D)

See footnotes at end of table.

Table C-4. Cities — **Manufacturing and Wholesale Trade**—Con.

[Includes states and 1,265 incorporated places of 25,000 or more population as of April 1, 2000, in all states except Hawaii, which has no incorporated places recognized by the U.S. Census Bureau. Two census designated places (CDPs) are also included (Honolulu CDP in Hawaii and Arlington CDP in Virginia). For more information on these areas, see Appendix C, Geographic Information]

| City | Manufacturing (NAICS 31–33), 2002[1] | | | | | | | | Wholesale trade (NAICS 42), 2002[4] | | | | | |
| | Establishments[2] | | All employees | | Production workers | | Value added by manufacture (mil. dol.) | Value of shipments (mil. dol.) | Establishments | Sales (mil. dol.) | | Paid employees[5] | Annual payroll (mil. dol.) | Operating expenses (mil. dol.) |
	Total	Percent with 20 or more employees	Number[3]	Annual payroll (mil. dol.)	Number[3]	Wages (mil. dol.)				Total	Merchant wholesalers			
CALIFORNIA—Con.														
Hesperia city	76	21.1	1,154	33.4	987	24.1	70.4	127.3	40	110.1	110.1	252	7.7	12.7
Highland city	(NA)	(NA)	(NA)	(NA)	(NA)	(NA)	(NA)	(NA)	13	(D)	(D)	[9]175	(D)	(D)
Hollister city	47	36.2	1,540	52.2	1,133	33.5	132.7	299.5	29	(D)	(D)	[12]375	(D)	(D)
Huntington Beach city	418	23.2	17,662	974.3	6,823	236.4	2,739.5	4,549.1	474	3,957.3	2,713.7	4,857	209.9	396.3
Huntington Park city	135	40.0	4,115	109.4	3,434	75.1	280.0	520.9	68	407.2	(D)	1,198	41.4	80.5
Imperial Beach city	(NA)	(NA)	(NA)	(NA)	(NA)	(NA)	(NA)	(NA)	11	27.7	27.7	82	2.2	4.4
Indio city	(NA)	(NA)	(NA)	(NA)	(NA)	(NA)	(NA)	(NA)	31	183.1	(D)	555	17.5	33.3
Inglewood city	88	28.4	2,802	105.9	2,025	48.6	242.2	409.8	103	377.4	325.9	1,644	54.7	84.2
Irvine city	454	50.9	33,821	1,522.3	19,502	611.4	4,498.2	9,475.3	911	39,615.2	28,748.7	22,398	1,390.5	3,434.8
Laguna Hills city	84	11.9	828	27.0	669	18.7	54.5	87.7	120	498.5	354.0	798	41.8	72.0
Laguna Niguel city	(NA)	(NA)	(NA)	(NA)	(NA)	(NA)	(NA)	(NA)	114	287.0	150.5	385	16.3	34.4
La Habra city	70	22.9	1,003	37.0	613	18.1	109.0	164.3	61	(D)	(D)	[12]375	(D)	(D)
Lake Elsinore city	59	23.7	932	26.0	755	16.4	67.4	109.0	27	(D)	(D)	[9]175	(D)	(D)
Lake Forest city	115	43.5	4,455	189.7	2,741	80.3	543.0	971.9	232	1,999.9	1,490.5	3,417	203.5	389.5
Lakewood city	(NA)	(NA)	(NA)	(NA)	(NA)	(NA)	(NA)	(NA)	34	(D)	(D)	[9]175	(D)	(D)
La Mesa city	(NA)	(NA)	(NA)	(NA)	(NA)	(NA)	(NA)	(NA)	45	128.5	(D)	286	11.7	14.8
La Mirada city	82	58.5	4,013	160.4	2,898	101.7	486.6	1,009.2	133	2,239.1	(D)	3,355	164.6	386.9
Lancaster city	57	19.3	1,974	56.6	1,359	27.8	113.9	228.0	80	304.7	298.3	1,081	29.1	54.4
La Puente city	(NA)	(NA)	(NA)	(NA)	(NA)	(NA)	(NA)	(NA)	21	(D)	(D)	[12]375	(D)	(D)
La Verne city	52	32.7	1,358	49.9	1,077	34.0	121.8	204.5	68	322.5	237.6	632	25.9	51.2
Lawndale city	(NA)	(NA)	(NA)	(NA)	(NA)	(NA)	(NA)	(NA)	26	70.9	70.9	187	7.2	15.8
Livermore city	144	36.8	4,604	199.2	2,765	91.1	446.9	860.1	192	2,357.7	1,726.1	3,744	190.0	348.7
Lodi city	96	33.3	3,213	109.9	2,579	78.4	271.6	671.2	53	448.9	(D)	560	29.4	45.1
Lompoc city	(NA)	(NA)	(NA)	(NA)	(NA)	(NA)	(NA)	(NA)	10	(D)	(D)	[10]60	(D)	(D)
Long Beach city	318	26.7	19,889	1,159.3	10,209	542.8	2,689.8	5,117.9	413	6,470.7	5,281.2	5,761	290.0	849.5
Los Altos city	(NA)	(NA)	(NA)	(NA)	(NA)	(NA)	(NA)	(NA)	45	319.8	(D)	233	13.8	23.3
Los Angeles city	7,185	22.3	162,210	5,478.4	113,916	2,837.3	14,750.8	28,490.8	9,138	49,019.1	39,291.7	92,274	3,762.7	7,680.0
Los Banos city	(NA)	(NA)	(NA)	(NA)	(NA)	(NA)	(NA)	(NA)	13	(D)	(D)	[10]60	(D)	(D)
Los Gatos town	41	19.5	547	28.1	263	9.2	55.7	105.9	55	(D)	(D)	[8]750	(D)	(D)
Lynwood city	70	34.3	2,024	60.8	1,646	39.8	149.3	263.2	38	(D)	(D)	[8]750	(D)	(D)
Madera city	34	55.9	[6]1,750	(D)	(D)	(D)	(D)	(D)	31	127.0	(D)	400	9.5	18.2
Manhattan Beach city	(NA)	(NA)	(NA)	(NA)	(NA)	(NA)	(NA)	(NA)	47	820.0	(D)	570	44.9	118.7
Manteca city	36	30.6	991	30.9	484	18.3	70.9	134.0	35	(D)	(D)	[9]175	(D)	(D)
Martinez city	23	13.0	[8]750	(D)	(D)	(D)	(D)	(D)	43	494.8	(D)	281	13.7	28.7
Maywood city	33	30.3	604	15.9	522	12.2	44.5	79.0	21	94.7	94.7	254	6.9	13.4
Menlo Park city	51	43.1	3,425	183.1	1,666	70.5	753.9	1,195.7	54	654.1	388.8	1,863	136.6	200.0
Merced city	37	43.2	2,046	72.7	1,665	54.1	299.3	563.5	30	(D)	(D)	[8]750	(D)	(D)
Milpitas city	211	48.8	20,002	1,142.0	7,575	273.3	2,707.9	5,046.2	181	3,609.9	2,281.2	6,266	466.4	733.5
Mission Viejo city	(NA)	(NA)	(NA)	(NA)	(NA)	(NA)	(NA)	(NA)	171	6,441.8	(D)	1,078	55.1	87.8
Modesto city	129	25.6	7,241	348.5	5,017	157.1	1,305.0	2,703.2	153	1,035.7	(D)	1,744	59.4	111.0
Monrovia city	132	33.3	3,692	149.9	2,208	62.7	329.6	545.2	101	216.6	183.4	788	29.3	47.9
Montclair city	70	25.7	1,271	32.6	979	18.7	68.6	126.9	63	175.7	(D)	558	18.0	36.1
Montebello city	97	47.4	5,431	167.1	3,646	95.0	563.4	956.8	132	1,629.1	(D)	2,373	101.9	203.2
Monterey city	55	23.6	959	32.3	594	15.3	69.8	119.0	55	1,031.2	(D)	361	21.2	36.9
Monterey Park city	58	34.5	1,388	47.5	1,041	29.1	108.0	155.6	242	454.6	(D)	1,186	33.6	68.9
Moorpark city	61	29.5	3,673	129.8	2,081	57.6	300.9	547.0	61	(D)	(D)	[6]1,750	(D)	(D)
Moreno Valley city	24	25.0	1,047	37.4	808	21.7	66.9	175.3	29	(D)	(D)	[10]60	(D)	(D)
Morgan Hill city	86	33.7	3,673	179.1	1,927	77.7	253.5	477.3	73	969.7	902.0	2,610	130.0	226.7
Mountain View city	176	25.6	8,003	461.3	3,866	159.3	1,194.2	2,172.5	160	2,283.8	1,025.5	4,085	294.5	441.1
Murrieta city	49	28.6	1,238	41.1	880	24.0	94.2	189.9	47	(D)	(D)	[12]375	(D)	(D)
Napa city	109	14.7	2,917	124.7	1,690	49.3	381.1	546.9	89	506.2	(D)	635	34.9	75.2
National City city	93	23.7	1,954	69.2	1,560	46.3	143.6	249.8	119	728.1	(D)	1,414	50.6	96.4
Newark city	94	41.5	10,480	659.6	2,030	103.0	3,804.9	7,332.1	80	729.3	(D)	1,360	57.6	142.6
Newport Beach city	99	13.1	2,803	112.2	1,988	69.4	255.7	359.1	250	1,835.3	886.6	2,193	123.5	203.2
Norwalk city	73	27.4	1,409	38.8	1,037	23.9	99.3	206.5	94	518.6	(D)	817	29.1	57.8
Novato city	78	15.4	1,229	52.2	668	17.6	144.7	201.9	113	543.8	(D)	951	43.7	79.8
Oakland city	513	23.8	11,065	419.6	7,231	225.4	1,057.3	1,881.5	479	3,565.6	2,512.9	7,460	342.8	592.9
Oakley city	(NA)	(NA)	(NA)	(NA)	(NA)	(NA)	(NA)	(NA)	11	(D)	(D)	[10]60	(D)	(D)
Oceanside city	170	27.1	3,743	115.7	2,859	69.1	286.1	502.0	132	876.9	(D)	1,484	39.9	60.2
Ontario city	474	39.9	16,868	554.9	13,039	351.5	2,021.1	3,661.8	500	9,096.1	7,371.2	11,195	405.1	985.5
Orange city	317	24.9	7,134	248.9	5,077	140.9	562.1	1,071.1	410	4,209.8	2,744.7	6,360	266.4	447.0
Oxnard city	207	33.8	7,914	333.0	5,950	180.4	1,228.4	1,878.2	183	1,542.1	1,465.3	3,794	165.4	349.8
Pacifica city	(NA)	(NA)	(NA)	(NA)	(NA)	(NA)	(NA)	(NA)	18	(D)	(D)	[10]60	(D)	(D)
Palmdale city	40	17.5	4,838	310.7	2,041	106.2	556.1	815.6	37	(D)	(D)	[12]375	(D)	(D)
Palm Desert city	63	17.5	714	21.8	526	12.2	47.1	78.0	91	(D)	(D)	[12]375	(D)	(D)
Palm Springs city	47	19.1	1,142	42.5	809	22.6	89.1	123.9	61	(D)	(D)	[12]375	(D)	(D)
Palo Alto city	98	31.6	8,659	553.9	4,607	285.8	1,296.8	2,463.2	88	841.1	741.7	1,124	74.7	130.5
Paradise town	(NA)	(NA)	(NA)	(NA)	(NA)	(NA)	(NA)	(NA)	6	2.3	2.3	18	0.3	1.0
Paramount city	247	27.1	5,372	199.8	3,909	118.6	492.1	1,529.4	230	991.3	905.4	2,275	86.0	149.3
Pasadena city	121	22.3	1,750	72.9	1,072	33.3	184.1	292.6	182	3,786.4	2,064.7	2,340	130.0	282.1

See footnotes at end of table.

Table C-4. Cities — **Manufacturing and Wholesale Trade**—Con.

[Includes states and 1,265 incorporated places of 25,000 or more population as of April 1, 2000, in all states except Hawaii, which has no incorporated places recognized by the U.S. Census Bureau. Two census designated places (CDPs) are also included (Honolulu CDP in Hawaii and Arlington CDP in Virginia). For more information on these areas, see Appendix C, Geographic Information]

City	Manufacturing (NAICS 31–33), 2002[1]								Wholesale trade (NAICS 42), 2002[4]					
	Establishments[2]		All employees		Production workers		Value added by manu-facture (mil. dol.)	Value of ship-ments (mil. dol.)	Estab-lishments	Sales (mil. dol.)		Paid employ-ees[5]	Annual payroll (mil. dol.)	Operating expenses (mil. dol.)
	Total	Percent with 20 or more employ-ees	Number[3]	Annual payroll (mil. dol.)	Number[3]	Wages (mil. dol.)				Total	Merchant whole-salers			
CALIFORNIA—Con.														
Perris city	37	37.8	2,911	74.9	2,367	49.7	294.8	483.7	11	(D)	(D)	[10]60	(D)	(D)
Petaluma city	136	35.3	5,461	269.0	3,157	108.9	1,179.5	2,088.1	102	797.4	(D)	1,759	84.2	146.3
Pico Rivera city	79	43.0	2,580	84.5	1,811	46.9	201.4	544.9	102	761.5	(D)	1,680	61.5	113.6
Pittsburg city	45	31.1	2,274	112.7	1,677	78.1	426.9	1,122.6	40	206.1	173.8	593	26.5	44.2
Placentia city	131	29.8	3,242	112.1	2,384	68.6	274.9	501.4	132	624.8	531.6	1,276	53.4	97.7
Pleasant Hill city	27	14.8	1,222	43.1	826	31.6	126.3	323.8	41	179.9	79.8	319	15.0	24.7
Pleasanton city	83	22.9	1,772	76.1	1,024	30.4	211.0	350.9	210	9,044.7	2,747.6	5,195	361.8	517.7
Pomona city	259	33.2	9,224	310.1	6,551	187.2	750.8	1,531.7	268	1,403.2	1,183.6	2,964	106.2	218.9
Porterville city	32	18.8	962	24.8	801	18.8	56.3	146.3	20	54.2	(D)	116	2.9	5.3
Poway city	97	40.2	4,278	146.8	2,567	71.2	402.6	724.0	114	890.5	(D)	2,152	106.4	191.3
Rancho Cordova city	(X)	(NA)	(X)	(X)	(X)	(X)	(X)	(X)	(X)	(X)	(X)	(X)	(X)	(X)
Rancho Cucamonga city	253	34.0	8,346	312.2	6,092	190.6	1,125.1	2,210.1	247	2,510.3	(D)	4,014	155.4	300.7
Rancho Palos Verdes city	(NA)	(NA)	(NA)	(NA)	(NA)	(NA)	(NA)	(NA)	54	100.0	(D)	131	5.6	9.7
Rancho Santa Margarita city	46	39.1	1,665	81.7	892	34.2	215.5	371.6	78	344.2	228.1	677	32.7	72.5
Redding city	100	18.0	1,253	40.6	859	23.0	114.8	202.7	143	432.8	(D)	1,408	47.6	83.6
Redlands city	56	23.2	1,141	34.4	898	24.1	89.7	156.2	55	148.8	104.1	612	19.8	33.5
Redondo Beach city	41	12.2	[7]7,500	(D)	(D)	(D)	(D)	(D)	77	314.9	(D)	611	42.8	63.4
Redwood City city	94	24.5	2,917	142.3	1,375	46.4	352.7	522.5	79	829.1	(D)	1,161	79.9	135.9
Rialto city	78	38.5	3,240	111.6	2,398	73.5	311.1	616.6	47	(D)	(D)	[8]750	(D)	(D)
Richmond city	124	31.5	4,854	241.3	3,224	146.3	1,298.8	3,609.7	105	3,733.7	529.5	1,982	90.0	152.0
Riverside city	315	25.4	9,824	367.2	6,969	216.9	888.7	1,806.3	311	3,147.8	(D)	4,572	160.2	298.7
Rocklin city	26	19.2	556	20.0	447	13.7	46.8	97.6	65	581.8	(D)	856	40.8	66.1
Rohnert Park city	41	26.8	956	39.6	561	16.6	84.6	155.4	42	(D)	(D)	[12]375	(D)	(D)
Rosemead city	71	14.1	939	23.2	773	15.7	66.1	105.4	81	940.1	(D)	696	14.8	30.5
Roseville city	64	23.4	1,601	76.5	1,096	47.8	137.7	254.9	104	994.4	(D)	1,393	78.5	116.5
Sacramento city	426	28.6	13,489	511.0	9,021	288.7	1,835.7	3,249.2	548	6,123.4	3,679.9	9,890	396.4	694.9
Salinas city	108	22.2	3,575	112.1	2,677	69.4	531.1	953.8	207	3,814.6	3,085.2	5,403	211.0	363.0
San Bernardino city	152	34.2	3,735	119.8	2,814	76.0	335.9	711.8	175	(D)	(D)	[11]3,750	(D)	(D)
San Bruno city	(NA)	(NA)	(NA)	(NA)	(NA)	(NA)	(NA)	(NA)	32	169.4	(D)	245	17.2	28.5
San Buenaventura (Ventura) city	186	21.5	3,117	111.7	2,190	61.5	290.2	452.7	205	(D)	(D)	[6]1,750	(D)	(D)
San Carlos city	139	24.5	3,041	128.6	2,101	73.1	358.9	600.8	108	595.6	341.8	1,119	62.5	96.0
San Clemente city	87	20.7	2,682	136.2	1,467	55.5	302.5	444.2	162	714.0	(D)	1,324	55.4	103.7
San Diego city	1,363	28.0	56,758	2,578.0	30,698	1,027.1	7,704.6	15,026.6	2,097	21,359.6	16,553.2	34,707	2,345.3	4,108.6
San Dimas city	89	27.0	2,311	78.9	1,761	46.6	540.5	741.1	99	720.2	346.5	923	38.7	92.3
San Francisco city	932	20.5	15,566	488.7	10,512	265.5	1,818.1	3,589.1	1,469	8,896.6	6,341.5	14,996	770.3	1,366.5
San Gabriel city	61	13.1	566	14.8	443	9.9	39.5	63.8	145	183.2	(D)	602	17.7	32.5
San Jose city	1,086	31.4	61,187	3,473.3	25,680	926.2	10,934.9	19,663.9	1,296	24,982.5	16,155.0	27,145	1,798.7	2,931.4
San Juan Capistrano city	37	24.3	980	44.8	527	16.2	108.5	182.3	79	(D)	(D)	[12]375	(D)	(D)
San Leandro city	240	33.8	7,829	297.3	5,611	180.0	848.5	1,866.2	310	2,144.4	1,480.4	5,458	224.9	400.5
San Luis Obispo city	86	23.3	1,658	66.9	997	29.6	144.9	274.5	73	223.2	(D)	719	25.6	49.3
San Marcos city	226	28.8	5,975	217.3	4,014	110.3	554.4	911.3	158	789.2	726.5	1,881	69.8	131.4
San Mateo city	(NA)	(NA)	(NA)	(NA)	(NA)	(NA)	(NA)	(NA)	96	616.7	(D)	1,122	74.2	122.2
San Pablo city	(NA)	(NA)	(NA)	(NA)	(NA)	(NA)	(NA)	(NA)	11	(D)	(D)	[10]60	(D)	(D)
San Rafael city	110	13.6	1,148	44.0	753	26.5	98.6	154.9	189	1,369.8	507.5	1,722	82.4	152.1
San Ramon city	36	19.4	615	31.4	362	13.0	68.5	105.2	144	8,235.6	4,607.7	2,846	179.7	279.4
Santa Ana city	919	30.3	27,657	969.9	20,310	549.3	2,266.6	4,163.3	603	3,615.8	2,724.2	8,050	367.7	674.5
Santa Barbara city	142	16.9	1,523	57.0	1,052	34.4	121.4	200.7	144	582.9	(D)	1,460	66.0	133.8
Santa Clara city	601	30.3	28,753	1,618.5	13,638	527.2	3,946.1	6,182.4	515	9,905.4	6,037.4	15,166	1,395.7	2,532.2
Santa Clarita city	240	34.6	9,470	375.5	6,439	196.9	899.6	1,519.7	198	4,182.7	(D)	2,923	125.4	273.6
Santa Cruz city	112	20.5	1,833	79.7	1,076	32.9	192.3	318.6	75	456.0	(D)	1,300	82.9	126.6
Santa Maria city	80	27.5	2,762	86.5	1,928	46.5	305.4	512.9	124	673.0	369.7	1,527	54.8	101.5
Santa Monica city	111	18.0	2,617	115.5	1,582	46.6	251.7	398.2	195	4,810.5	4,244.7	2,657	185.8	426.4
Santa Paula city	25	20.0	513	15.9	418	10.3	62.2	137.6	18	(D)	(D)	[8]750	(D)	(D)
Santa Rosa city	201	21.9	10,653	534.5	5,824	259.6	1,038.6	1,635.3	165	991.4	826.2	1,898	82.8	145.5
Santee city	131	18.3	1,877	67.6	1,307	41.7	163.3	276.7	59	179.1	143.9	531	19.9	35.5
Saratoga city	(NA)	(NA)	(NA)	(NA)	(NA)	(NA)	(NA)	(NA)	36	(D)	(D)	[9]175	(D)	(D)
Seaside city	(NA)	(NA)	(NA)	(NA)	(NA)	(NA)	(NA)	(NA)	16	13.9	13.9	81	1.8	3.2
Simi Valley city	151	29.8	4,285	168.3	2,804	80.8	555.4	897.3	166	(D)	(D)	[11]3,750	(D)	(D)
South Gate city	168	35.7	7,291	237.2	5,831	162.4	656.2	1,401.0	77	1,784.2	(D)	1,079	41.5	74.3
South San Francisco city	152	40.8	11,001	615.6	4,402	157.9	3,015.2	3,616.0	425	5,872.6	5,007.1	6,708	368.2	766.8
Stanton city	68	16.2	929	31.6	748	21.2	63.4	100.6	48	(D)	(D)	[12]375	(D)	(D)
Stockton city	210	34.8	7,640	269.6	5,868	179.1	895.0	1,645.6	258	2,771.6	2,192.7	4,738	175.6	347.6
Suisun City city	(NA)	(NA)	(NA)	(NA)	(NA)	(NA)	(NA)	(NA)	5	(D)	(D)	[10]60	(D)	(D)
Sunnyvale city	321	44.2	31,425	2,198.6	10,230	451.8	4,519.9	7,947.7	286	6,756.8	5,008.3	10,248	822.9	1,216.4
Temecula city	148	24.3	6,784	260.5	4,134	135.5	1,512.7	2,083.7	145	1,296.0	1,195.7	1,994	80.8	166.0
Temple City city	(NA)	(NA)	(NA)	(NA)	(NA)	(NA)	(NA)	(NA)	84	(D)	(D)	[12]375	(D)	(D)
Thousand Oaks city	170	24.1	4,227	174.0	2,680	78.1	873.3	1,157.8	216	(D)	(D)	[11]3,750	(D)	(D)
Torrance city	323	38.1	16,691	730.2	11,117	423.9	2,550.7	5,073.7	621	32,841.6	(D)	9,192	498.7	2,831.5
Tracy city	58	44.8	2,910	109.8	2,324	76.4	316.3	670.7	54	1,714.8	(D)	918	30.5	52.5
Tulare city	33	36.4	1,944	75.6	1,363	47.1	294.0	1,459.0	42	190.3	151.4	491	17.8	27.9

See footnotes at end of table.

Table C-4. Cities — **Manufacturing and Wholesale Trade**—Con.

[Includes states and 1,265 incorporated places of 25,000 or more population as of April 1, 2000, in all states except Hawaii, which has no incorporated places recognized by the U.S. Census Bureau. Two census designated places (CDPs) are also included (Honolulu CDP in Hawaii and Arlington CDP in Virginia). For more information on these areas, see Appendix C, Geographic Information]

| City | Manufacturing (NAICS 31–33), 2002[1] | | | | | | | | Wholesale trade (NAICS 42), 2002[4] | | | | | |
	Establishments[2] Total	Establishments Percent with 20 or more employees	All employees Number[3]	All employees Annual payroll (mil. dol.)	Production workers Number[3]	Production workers Wages (mil. dol.)	Value added by manufacture (mil. dol.)	Value of shipments (mil. dol.)	Establishments	Sales Total (mil. dol.)	Sales Merchant wholesalers (mil. dol.)	Paid employees[5]	Annual payroll (mil. dol.)	Operating expenses (mil. dol.)
CALIFORNIA—Con.														
Turlock city	72	36.1	3,922	114.6	3,197	80.2	416.6	1,007.6	54	185.2	(D)	490	15.6	26.4
Tustin city	135	25.9	5,467	257.1	2,622	77.4	528.1	1,189.2	235	1,520.9	1,108.2	2,467	134.0	238.1
Twentynine Palms city	(NA)	(NA)	(NA)	(NA)	(NA)	(NA)	(NA)	(NA)	3	(D)	(D)	[13]310	(D)	(D)
Union City city	83	43.4	3,928	163.5	2,766	87.1	529.0	940.1	158	3,276.4	2,993.1	3,831	192.8	366.1
Upland city	105	18.1	1,371	45.6	1,048	28.6	229.1	337.2	90	286.7	(D)	516	18.8	30.9
Vacaville city	61	27.9	2,932	136.0	2,249	88.6	293.3	589.9	27	(D)	(D)	[9]175	(D)	(D)
Vallejo city	46	26.1	817	29.2	537	16.7	100.7	222.8	35	315.2	(D)	539	21.2	38.3
Victorville city	31	32.3	1,002	36.5	797	26.6	195.3	322.1	38	146.1	117.2	453	21.4	34.0
Visalia city	87	32.2	3,320	105.8	2,519	68.0	357.8	683.9	158	1,312.1	1,148.7	1,531	54.4	99.7
Vista city	190	43.7	9,543	313.7	6,456	151.4	978.2	1,698.4	167	914.9	(D)	2,534	92.2	187.3
Walnut city	38	21.1	552	21.4	401	13.7	44.1	68.8	300	648.9	581.6	1,090	33.1	67.5
Walnut Creek city	38	21.1	1,112	58.1	455	17.8	253.6	367.0	122	1,762.2	491.4	1,389	67.0	123.1
Watsonville city	83	31.3	2,801	87.1	2,191	56.3	242.5	385.8	70	1,031.8	(D)	1,471	63.2	125.4
West Covina city	(NA)	(NA)	(NA)	(NA)	(NA)	(NA)	(NA)	(NA)	70	112.2	78.7	198	6.1	12.6
West Hollywood city	(NA)	(NA)	(NA)	(NA)	(NA)	(NA)	(NA)	(NA)	126	502.6	(D)	1,044	46.7	81.6
Westminster city	106	7.5	1,149	26.3	914	17.7	53.6	100.1	98	234.1	(D)	658	17.9	43.3
West Sacramento city	65	24.6	2,483	93.7	1,460	46.6	292.9	558.1	156	5,533.6	(D)	4,535	178.3	329.8
Whittier city	80	25.0	1,646	55.9	1,285	35.5	137.7	241.2	84	(D)	190.6	[8]750	(D)	(D)
Woodland city	65	41.5	2,357	88.2	1,776	55.4	226.4	534.7	79	(D)	(D)	[6]1,750	(D)	(D)
Yorba Linda city	68	25.0	2,081	100.6	1,051	34.0	246.3	411.1	162	2,055.1	(D)	3,983	69.5	142.1
Yuba City city	40	25.0	[6]1,750	(D)	(D)	(D)	(D)	(D)	39	182.7	(D)	544	21.7	37.6
Yucaipa city	(NA)	(NA)	(NA)	(NA)	(NA)	(NA)	(NA)	(NA)	20	(D)	(D)	[10]60	(D)	(D)
COLORADO	5,349	22.3	148,824	6,323.8	94,984	3,249.6	17,798.1	34,661.1	7,339	92,092.2	41,974.3	101,108	4,789.4	8,421.3
Arvada city	113	18.6	[6]1,750	(D)	(D)	(D)	(D)	(D)	126	566.1	(D)	1,063	45.8	75.4
Aurora city	152	23.0	3,715	132.6	2,603	75.9	331.9	655.1	300	5,808.0	3,390.5	6,182	259.0	428.6
Boulder city	251	24.7	7,942	397.2	3,831	133.1	1,055.2	1,618.3	228	958.4	693.5	2,015	108.2	174.0
Broomfield city	77	32.5	5,682	281.4	2,700	84.2	1,079.9	1,722.4	76	(D)	(D)	[8]750	(D)	(D)
Centennial city	70	20.0	1,215	54.8	674	22.6	114.9	219.2	262	12,396.8	(D)	3,420	170.6	343.3
Colorado Springs city	399	24.6	15,695	695.8	9,244	333.6	2,039.8	2,762.4	416	(D)	(D)	[7]7,500	(D)	(D)
Denver city	895	28.8	22,116	767.1	15,091	436.3	2,304.6	4,179.1	1,598	20,041.5	11,119.2	27,570	1,310.9	2,282.2
Englewood city	187	25.7	4,733	186.7	2,811	83.4	475.6	818.3	183	4,082.2	(D)	2,348	108.1	182.5
Fort Collins city	110	20.0	4,965	236.1	2,608	101.3	811.9	1,614.3	126	(D)	(D)	[11]3,750	(D)	(D)
Grand Junction city	102	24.5	2,438	80.6	1,666	44.6	191.6	339.5	157	571.5	(D)	1,550	53.5	86.4
Greeley city	69	20.3	3,821	112.9	3,356	87.7	248.5	1,674.2	83	402.4	292.0	1,127	38.2	64.4
Lakewood city	122	15.6	1,919	97.6	1,370	36.8	278.7	447.7	207	1,297.1	631.7	1,262	66.1	110.3
Littleton city	56	16.1	[7]7,500	(D)	(D)	(D)	(D)	(D)	115	(D)	384.2	[6]1,750	(D)	(D)
Longmont city	131	26.7	3,619	132.5	2,564	77.1	325.9	561.5	84	2,353.3	(D)	1,903	89.8	148.6
Loveland city	82	29.3	4,723	229.0	2,280	89.8	554.3	809.7	63	(D)	(D)	[8]750	(D)	(D)
Northglenn city	39	25.6	706	26.3	504	16.3	62.0	145.9	31	(D)	(D)	[9]175	(D)	(D)
Pueblo city	72	29.2	2,107	90.5	1,505	58.6	261.7	581.5	70	(D)	161.6	[8]750	(D)	(D)
Thornton city	(NA)	(NA)	(NA)	(NA)	(NA)	(NA)	(NA)	(NA)	37	202.7	(D)	414	17.3	29.3
Westminster city	57	26.3	2,277	105.3	1,239	50.9	79.7	532.0	86	1,894.0	(D)	1,872	121.0	168.5
Wheat Ridge city	51	17.6	1,241	52.7	928	35.4	190.7	291.1	65	(D)	(D)	[8]750	(D)	(D)
CONNECTICUT	5,384	31.3	214,910	9,878.0	125,928	4,529.6	27,673.5	45,053.3	4,785	86,932.0	61,726.6	79,072	4,329.0	8,204.2
Bridgeport city	220	28.2	5,991	233.1	4,149	130.9	516.9	856.1	108	542.0	(D)	1,358	61.8	114.5
Bristol city	165	33.9	3,711	159.4	2,647	99.1	323.0	526.7	47	271.7	265.3	711	33.1	58.4
Danbury city	108	45.4	6,553	305.8	3,576	127.3	854.1	1,467.1	103	1,447.6	405.2	1,638	87.4	159.9
Hartford city	94	31.9	1,646	52.9	1,080	28.4	122.6	228.3	182	1,616.8	1,132.6	3,365	170.0	292.7
Meriden city	84	33.3	4,087	172.9	2,257	66.1	325.7	628.4	56	202.7	169.7	556	26.7	45.9
Middletown city	67	34.3	4,670	265.8	2,866	147.7	563.3	1,209.0	47	244.1	205.2	806	30.2	53.2
Milford city (balance)	198	22.2	5,190	269.4	3,360	131.7	699.7	1,193.8	128	758.7	634.4	1,661	74.7	152.6
Naugatuck borough	57	42.1	2,183	84.9	1,548	51.7	283.1	445.4	18	160.1	160.1	281	11.9	24.8
New Britain city	123	33.3	3,603	137.1	2,603	84.4	295.3	576.5	48	267.3	188.8	665	32.3	52.3
New Haven city	94	34.0	3,253	126.6	2,303	76.5	302.8	527.0	107	841.0	487.3	1,416	64.3	112.7
New London city	(NA)	(NA)	(NA)	(NA)	(NA)	(NA)	(NA)	(NA)	22	(D)	(D)	[9]175	(D)	(D)
Norwalk city	147	26.5	6,897	334.3	3,438	114.2	755.6	1,321.5	178	4,112.2	2,719.8	3,053	197.2	556.7
Norwich city	32	28.1	1,019	39.0	628	16.5	130.9	216.2	28	263.6	263.6	598	26.0	45.7
Shelton city	80	47.5	3,884	162.3	2,363	79.9	424.4	690.5	69	623.8	482.7	1,740	82.1	149.7
Stamford city	155	23.2	7,284	322.9	3,181	111.4	2,046.7	2,780.1	295	23,806.4	21,285.7	7,407	702.8	1,297.3
Torrington city	68	39.7	2,623	88.8	1,964	55.3	196.0	332.2	48	(D)	(D)	[12]375	(D)	(D)
Waterbury city	201	30.3	4,808	194.1	3,590	127.7	406.4	773.2	111	(D)	(D)	[6]1,750	(D)	(D)
West Haven city	64	32.8	5,653	209.5	1,394	43.9	982.3	1,417.8	55	531.0	(D)	997	52.5	91.6
DELAWARE	705	32.8	37,287	1,564.8	26,216	937.7	5,063.9	16,417.9	997	17,292.8	4,172.0	21,162	1,286.6	2,375.6
Dover city	26	34.6	2,630	108.7	1,832	73.1	984.5	1,370.3	36	89.3	89.3	242	10.2	18.6
Newark city	53	54.7	6,227	326.4	4,172	194.4	1,144.7	3,398.4	46	517.2	(D)	529	28.6	53.2
Wilmington city	96	22.9	2,186	102.5	1,237	46.3	218.9	473.8	152	12,541.5	(D)	12,120	896.6	1,611.0

See footnotes at end of table.

County and City Data Book: 2007

U.S. Census Bureau

Table C-4. Cities — **Manufacturing and Wholesale Trade**—Con.

[Includes states and 1,265 incorporated places of 25,000 or more population as of April 1, 2000, in all states except Hawaii, which has no incorporated places recognized by the U.S. Census Bureau. Two census designated places (CDPs) are also included (Honolulu CDP in Hawaii and Arlington CDP in Virginia). For more information on these areas, see Appendix C, Geographic Information]

City	Manufacturing (NAICS 31–33), 2002[1]								Wholesale trade (NAICS 42), 2002[4]					
	Establishments[2]		All employees		Production workers		Value added by manufacture (mil. dol.)	Value of shipments (mil. dol.)	Estab-lishments	Sales (mil. dol.)		Paid employees[5]	Annual payroll (mil. dol.)	Operating expenses (mil. dol.)
	Total	Percent with 20 or more employees	Number[3]	Annual payroll (mil. dol.)	Number[3]	Wages (mil. dol.)				Total	Merchant wholesalers			
DISTRICT OF COLUMBIA . . .	146	15.1	2,021	76.1	1,133	39.5	163.1	246.2	381	2,971.5	1,739.2	5,779	278.2	467.2
Washington city	146	15.1	2,021	76.1	1,133	39.5	163.1	246.2	381	2,971.5	1,739.2	5,779	278.2	467.2
FLORIDA	15,202	21.0	377,137	14,082.4	245,216	6,956.2	41,912.6	78,474.8	31,332	219,490.9	153,243.7	299,340	11,884.8	22,866.4
Altamonte Springs city	(NA)	(NA)	(NA)	(NA)	(NA)	(NA)	(NA)	(NA)	129	961.0	461.6	1,132	47.8	95.5
Apopka city	34	32.4	1,334	36.2	824	18.3	140.4	196.9	69	200.7	(D)	548	21.7	43.7
Aventura city	(NA)	(NA)	(NA)	(NA)	(NA)	(NA)	(NA)	(NA)	101	261.5	(D)	324	12.5	29.2
Boca Raton city	162	17.3	3,563	121.4	2,102	59.5	363.0	601.1	517	5,961.2	5,690.1	6,532	379.1	891.2
Bonita Springs city	(NA)	(NA)	(NA)	(NA)	(NA)	(NA)	(NA)	(NA)	43	203.5	(D)	273	11.1	17.7
Boynton Beach city	73	16.4	708	23.4	444	11.9	46.7	84.4	121	660.4	371.0	812	39.3	79.0
Bradenton city	(NA)	(NA)	(NA)	(NA)	(NA)	(NA)	(NA)	(NA)	45	126.2	(D)	344	10.6	17.2
Cape Coral city	92	12.0	749	22.9	532	13.2	43.7	76.3	110	144.3	114.4	445	14.0	24.7
Clearwater city	136	17.6	2,101	70.5	1,187	32.3	185.0	352.4	226	1,386.1	(D)	2,464	94.1	167.2
Coconut Creek city	(NA)	(NA)	(NA)	(NA)	(NA)	(NA)	(NA)	(NA)	67	(D)	(D)	[12]375	(D)	(D)
Cooper City city	(NA)	(NA)	(NA)	(NA)	(NA)	(NA)	(NA)	(NA)	62	183.7	113.3	268	11.4	21.5
Coral Gables city	43	9.3	506	21.2	299	8.2	50.3	75.3	201	2,481.1	1,859.7	1,731	117.0	233.7
Coral Springs city	74	17.6	1,036	36.1	762	21.4	88.9	150.4	297	1,238.2	1,062.3	2,066	74.9	159.3
Dania Beach city	54	9.3	588	22.8	357	9.9	72.9	104.5	153	775.7	(D)	1,371	58.8	112.2
Davie town	98	15.3	1,927	74.1	1,140	32.5	345.7	426.7	287	1,902.8	(D)	1,763	63.1	124.6
Daytona Beach city	58	13.8	1,104	38.1	701	14.3	97.7	193.3	106	808.0	284.5	1,291	42.5	72.0
Deerfield Beach city	108	24.1	2,475	87.4	1,724	46.5	184.5	361.5	262	8,224.7	7,728.8	3,969	191.5	631.4
Delray Beach city	76	14.5	707	26.3	508	16.3	60.8	114.4	141	501.7	312.4	741	28.8	56.9
Deltona city	(NA)	(NA)	(NA)	(NA)	(NA)	(NA)	(NA)	(NA)	10	(D)	(D)	[10]60	(D)	(D)
Dunedin city	(NA)	(NA)	(NA)	(NA)	(NA)	(NA)	(NA)	(NA)	39	(D)	(D)	[9]175	(D)	(D)
Fort Lauderdale city	336	19.0	5,984	236.4	3,628	105.8	537.5	1,033.2	750	6,371.8	3,230.0	7,284	333.8	665.7
Fort Myers city	85	18.8	1,602	52.1	1,203	35.0	156.0	257.1	151	623.7	(D)	1,903	71.0	123.6
Fort Pierce city	29	13.8	556	17.2	362	10.5	52.0	93.9	44	228.4	(D)	534	12.4	20.4
Gainesville city	83	21.7	1,587	59.4	1,081	34.9	210.1	439.3	147	758.1	(D)	1,394	43.4	86.9
Greenacres city	(NA)	(NA)	(NA)	(NA)	(NA)	(NA)	(NA)	(NA)	19	21.4	(D)	73	2.7	4.2
Hallandale Beach city	49	16.3	548	16.5	425	10.5	37.8	65.7	98	206.5	(D)	447	15.5	28.1
Hialeah city	551	17.6	8,667	234.6	6,728	145.4	552.4	1,013.4	559	1,208.7	1,144.0	3,429	99.2	178.3
Hollywood city	144	16.7	2,337	85.9	1,699	49.5	187.4	332.0	395	2,371.5	1,417.2	2,815	118.2	249.8
Homestead city	(NA)	(NA)	(NA)	(NA)	(NA)	(NA)	(NA)	(NA)	36	168.4	146.3	495	12.4	23.4
Jacksonville city	664	32.2	26,932	1,070.6	18,317	577.5	3,918.5	6,831.6	1,264	18,542.7	12,800.8	20,609	870.4	1,544.6
Jupiter town	49	12.2	908	39.2	532	19.1	88.1	153.6	104	235.0	188.6	531	23.0	41.0
Key West city	(NA)	(NA)	(NA)	(NA)	(NA)	(NA)	(NA)	(NA)	25	(D)	(D)	[9]175	(D)	(D)
Kissimmee city	(NA)	(NA)	(NA)	(NA)	(NA)	(NA)	(NA)	(NA)	53	(D)	(D)	[12]375	(D)	(D)
Lakeland city	81	33.3	3,292	105.6	2,349	63.8	383.5	712.7	165	3,060.1	2,820.9	2,206	88.8	157.2
Lake Worth city	54	13.0	519	14.9	397	9.4	37.8	68.9	59	202.3	191.8	549	19.8	35.5
Largo city	96	24.0	3,571	144.2	1,710	50.4	337.2	513.7	86	209.3	110.5	534	16.3	26.7
Lauderdale Lakes city	(NA)	(NA)	(NA)	(NA)	(NA)	(NA)	(NA)	(NA)	24	(D)	(D)	[9]175	(D)	(D)
Lauderhill city	(NA)	(NA)	(NA)	(NA)	(NA)	(NA)	(NA)	(NA)	44	37.5	(D)	122	3.2	8.0
Margate city	(NA)	(NA)	(NA)	(NA)	(NA)	(NA)	(NA)	(NA)	80	138.7	121.3	310	11.1	20.1
Melbourne city	85	27.1	5,412	242.8	2,593	65.9	966.2	1,463.9	130	448.1	308.7	1,106	38.6	61.7
Miami city	473	12.7	6,366	188.3	4,846	116.1	523.6	1,078.4	1,786	6,817.3	6,088.2	11,476	478.3	936.0
Miami Beach city	(NA)	(NA)	(NA)	(NA)	(NA)	(NA)	(NA)	(NA)	154	336.7	185.1	379	25.0	56.2
Miami Gardens city	(X)	(NA)	(X)	(X)	(X)	(X)	(X)	(X)	(X)	(X)	(X)	(X)	(X)	(X)
Miramar city	38	26.3	2,283	55.6	795	18.6	178.1	351.5	131	1,821.6	1,572.6	2,041	87.6	187.4
North Lauderdale city	(NA)	(NA)	(NA)	(NA)	(NA)	(NA)	(NA)	(NA)	14	(D)	(D)	[10]60	(D)	(D)
North Miami city	44	11.4	593	14.8	413	9.9	30.9	49.5	100	787.6	774.6	2,631	71.3	131.7
North Miami Beach city	(NA)	(NA)	(NA)	(NA)	(NA)	(NA)	(NA)	(NA)	90	310.8	310.8	488	17.8	34.5
Oakland Park city	151	11.9	1,830	52.4	1,280	27.0	173.4	309.5	184	795.5	460.1	1,913	138.0	230.9
Ocala city	134	31.3	6,953	212.4	5,330	136.7	573.1	1,057.8	177	868.0	606.9	1,832	61.7	122.3
Orlando city	277	24.9	12,904	640.6	6,366	204.9	2,167.9	3,074.6	644	6,975.8	(D)	9,554	390.2	712.0
Ormond Beach city	54	22.2	1,375	47.6	956	25.2	103.8	169.5	61	192.9	136.1	479	16.7	31.6
Oviedo city	(NA)	(NA)	(NA)	(NA)	(NA)	(NA)	(NA)	(NA)	42	146.9	(D)	173	6.0	10.7
Palm Bay city	56	26.8	7,538	442.5	2,084	98.4	1,163.4	1,695.4	44	101.9	88.7	256	10.9	19.2
Palm Beach Gardens city	(NA)	(NA)	(NA)	(NA)	(NA)	(NA)	(NA)	(NA)	64	186.5	65.6	685	35.4	75.4
Palm Coast city	27	33.3	[6]1,750	(D)	(D)	(D)	(D)	(D)	18	(D)	(D)	[10]60	(D)	(D)
Panama City city	53	18.9	2,071	89.9	1,589	61.9	276.5	557.3	78	237.5	157.7	643	20.3	38.5
Pembroke Pines city	59	10.2	514	17.5	300	9.3	47.6	138.8	186	257.5	206.1	397	15.9	29.9
Pensacola city	65	10.8	892	35.7	631	23.5	121.4	223.6	113	566.0	(D)	1,482	44.7	85.2
Pinellas Park city	254	33.5	10,900	382.2	6,798	171.2	1,003.7	1,674.5	197	916.1	(D)	2,155	81.3	144.1
Plantation city	46	13.0	[6]1,750	(D)	(D)	(D)	(D)	(D)	195	362.7	258.2	715	29.8	49.3
Plant City city	59	49.2	[11]3,750	(D)	(D)	(D)	(D)	(D)	91	867.3	(D)	4,257	89.1	140.2
Pompano Beach city	298	28.2	6,412	224.5	4,488	121.3	596.9	1,048.1	535	3,482.8	3,031.1	7,191	274.7	536.3
Port Orange city	(NA)	(NA)	(NA)	(NA)	(NA)	(NA)	(NA)	(NA)	43	238.2	(D)	336	17.1	23.5
Port St. Lucie city	40	10.0	540	23.0	414	15.5	152.2	246.3	76	112.0	90.8	241	8.0	16.0
Riviera Beach city	75	32.0	1,748	60.8	1,211	35.0	158.0	284.7	102	1,517.4	(D)	2,144	86.5	156.1

See footnotes at end of table.

Table C-4. Cities — **Manufacturing and Wholesale Trade**—Con.

[Includes states and 1,265 incorporated places of 25,000 or more population as of April 1, 2000, in all states except Hawaii, which has no incorporated places recognized by the U.S. Census Bureau. Two census designated places (CDPs) are also included (Honolulu CDP in Hawaii and Arlington CDP in Virginia). For more information on these areas, see Appendix C, Geographic Information]

City	Manufacturing (NAICS 31–33), 2002[1]								Wholesale trade (NAICS 42), 2002[4]					
	Establishments[2]		All employees		Production workers					Sales (mil. dol.)				
	Total	Percent with 20 or more employees	Number[3]	Annual payroll (mil. dol.)	Number[3]	Wages (mil. dol.)	Value added by manufacture (mil. dol.)	Value of shipments (mil. dol.)	Establishments	Total	Merchant wholesalers	Paid employees[5]	Annual payroll (mil. dol.)	Operating expenses (mil. dol.)
FLORIDA—Con.														
St. Petersburg city	176	23.3	7,989	384.2	3,881	124.4	971.8	2,014.3	247	1,092.3	780.9	3,120	138.9	209.1
Sanford city	62	32.3	1,901	57.8	1,436	35.5	205.4	359.3	86	678.8	304.4	1,529	50.4	91.9
Sarasota city	92	14.1	1,267	40.7	939	25.2	108.3	197.9	119	417.1	338.6	693	26.8	53.8
Sunrise city	77	13.0	1,186	38.1	608	18.6	79.5	116.9	289	1,670.6	956.1	2,889	156.9	366.3
Tallahassee city	85	18.8	1,706	63.9	1,004	28.1	141.3	351.3	202	741.2	647.5	2,235	96.2	144.1
Tamarac city	(NA)	(NA)	(NA)	(NA)	(NA)	(NA)	(NA)	(NA)	78	289.2	(D)	609	27.7	43.2
Tampa city	395	24.3	9,760	338.6	6,535	188.0	1,074.7	2,336.9	780	9,746.0	4,024.5	10,263	437.0	786.4
Titusville city	(NA)	(NA)	(NA)	(NA)	(NA)	(NA)	(NA)	(NA)	34	78.8	(D)	270	7.6	15.4
Wellington village	(NA)	(NA)	(NA)	(NA)	(NA)	(NA)	(NA)	(NA)	80	107.5	89.5	233	8.9	17.9
Weston city	(NA)	(NA)	(NA)	(NA)	(NA)	(NA)	(NA)	(NA)	187	2,296.2	2,193.0	1,629	79.1	174.9
West Palm Beach city	142	19.0	1,898	61.2	1,281	34.1	127.3	214.7	189	1,268.8	780.8	1,917	79.5	151.4
Winter Haven city	28	28.6	679	27.7	465	15.9	41.3	210.6	58	238.2	177.2	420	13.6	30.3
Winter Park city	(NA)	(NA)	(NA)	(NA)	(NA)	(NA)	(NA)	(NA)	81	341.0	(D)	703	27.4	45.4
Winter Springs city	(NA)	(NA)	(NA)	(NA)	(NA)	(NA)	(NA)	(NA)	38	36.7	(D)	137	3.8	6.3
GEORGIA	8,805	34.4	452,625	15,709.6	345,762	10,249.7	59,651.3	126,156.6	13,794	201,091.0	90,917.7	201,018	9,177.3	17,428.7
Albany city	67	35.8	7,060	318.4	5,611	235.9	2,528.0	4,220.5	159	847.6	(D)	1,985	69.5	117.2
Alpharetta city	50	26.0	1,404	65.1	833	29.7	150.8	266.7	222	18,262.0	8,168.1	6,831	506.5	876.0
Athens-Clarke County (balance)	98	33.7	6,966	226.0	5,591	157.8	604.0	1,242.9	113	1,311.0	(D)	2,095	76.7	143.0
Atlanta city	411	32.6	15,002	546.7	10,263	322.3	3,487.8	5,158.9	1,060	16,440.3	6,490.9	13,851	625.7	1,194.3
Augusta-Richmond County (balance)	144	40.3	10,672	455.2	7,109	299.6	2,107.0	4,319.5	236	(D)	(D)	[6]1,750	(D)	(D)
Columbus city	141	42.6	11,116	370.9	8,703	259.7	1,213.1	2,420.7	224	1,059.3	(D)	2,508	85.7	193.5
Dalton city	203	45.8	17,718	521.8	15,135	400.2	2,138.7	5,552.7	168	2,372.5	522.3	1,938	82.8	166.8
East Point city	27	33.3	824	31.9	608	17.9	129.4	258.9	28	(D)	(D)	[8]750	(D)	(D)
Gainesville city	93	39.8	[7]7,500	(D)	(D)	(D)	(D)	(D)	102	1,182.2	945.3	1,485	50.3	93.2
Hinesville city	(NA)	(NA)	(NA)	(NA)	(NA)	(NA)	(NA)	(NA)	3	(D)	(D)	[10]60	(D)	(D)
LaGrange city	49	49.0	[11]3,461	120.3	2,518	72.6	326.1	732.6	34	175.0	(D)	407	13.5	23.7
Macon city	104	21.2	[11]3,750	(D)	(D)	(D)	(D)	(D)	174	862.4	725.0	2,320	80.2	154.9
Marietta city	144	32.6	4,945	203.4	3,353	108.4	569.6	1,029.7	362	3,406.9	1,946.1	4,620	231.2	402.4
Peachtree City city	45	60.0	4,074	169.4	2,400	73.3	445.5	1,268.3	95	348.7	(D)	782	33.4	65.3
Rome city	82	35.4	4,825	142.4	3,932	100.5	378.9	939.3	63	201.5	(D)	667	22.5	37.1
Roswell city	59	15.3	809	37.6	482	16.3	106.9	178.1	292	4,375.3	1,190.0	2,929	185.9	313.4
Savannah city	122	27.9	8,679	443.3	6,081	267.0	1,461.1	3,948.3	195	1,425.2	1,209.8	2,086	83.4	159.2
Smyrna city	51	29.4	1,305	61.8	878	35.8	187.7	329.2	117	1,839.6	909.1	9,384	582.6	685.0
Valdosta city	73	41.1	3,784	109.1	2,862	73.2	422.3	1,206.4	99	409.7	(D)	786	26.2	52.9
Warner Robins city	(NA)	(NA)	(NA)	(NA)	(NA)	(NA)	(NA)	(NA)	19	87.6	(D)	169	8.1	11.4
HAWAII	929	16.9	13,200	421.3	8,865	254.7	1,217.7	3,460.2	1,876	9,986.4	6,664.5	19,412	683.4	1,305.5
Honolulu CDP	459	16.8	6,503	190.6	4,494	114.0	462.6	885.6	1,053	6,502.1	3,943.9	11,679	427.7	792.8
IDAHO	1,814	22.9	61,538	2,192.6	47,107	1,437.2	7,440.1	15,174.2	1,989	11,458.0	7,641.0	22,947	768.8	1,429.3
Boise City city	213	18.3	15,640	693.2	10,782	408.8	3,113.7	4,333.0	381	4,159.1	1,969.2	5,511	260.9	480.4
Caldwell city	54	27.8	1,484	39.5	1,147	24.3	100.5	263.7	33	103.0	(D)	384	9.8	12.3
Coeur d'Alene city	60	15.0	958	33.0	751	24.9	75.6	149.9	52	297.7	(D)	578	20.5	34.7
Idaho Falls city	80	21.3	1,422	37.7	1,176	27.5	193.8	340.3	109	923.9	885.9	1,626	50.0	92.8
Lewiston city	40	20.0	[11]3,750	(D)	(D)	(D)	(D)	(D)	51	(D)	(D)	[12]375	(D)	(D)
Meridian city	51	45.1	1,809	56.1	1,351	30.0	128.7	358.5	74	590.8	(D)	1,252	45.3	89.1
Nampa city	83	38.6	5,291	185.0	3,894	114.0	391.8	1,321.5	85	558.4	(D)	1,136	35.2	62.9
Pocatello city	52	21.2	2,087	100.2	1,438	52.5	365.3	555.3	72	264.3	(D)	739	20.6	34.9
Twin Falls city	58	24.1	1,801	53.1	1,425	37.2	164.2	469.4	99	261.8	236.1	924	25.6	45.7
ILLINOIS	16,860	35.1	741,908	29,841.7	511,269	17,002.5	91,825.1	188,365.2	20,520	317,467.1	173,279.6	331,527	15,493.1	29,783.5
Addison village	363	31.4	8,130	305.0	5,948	180.2	641.5	1,121.6	231	1,666.8	1,289.0	3,593	169.8	277.9
Alton city	23	39.1	675	24.1	511	16.8	48.6	150.0	28	75.2	(D)	230	8.2	14.1
Arlington Heights village	111	24.3	2,875	135.8	1,610	57.2	578.9	1,655.8	287	5,200.9	1,639.5	4,480	235.6	425.0
Aurora city	171	42.1	9,484	413.8	5,919	200.6	1,474.6	3,173.0	169	9,068.4	(D)	2,246	118.5	248.0
Bartlett village	25	20.0	968	40.2	679	20.2	98.6	186.2	42	(D)	25.7	[9]175	(D)	(D)
Belleville city	59	28.8	2,383	73.6	1,640	45.0	179.0	347.8	37	166.7	(D)	349	12.9	26.8
Berwyn city	(NA)	(NA)	(NA)	(NA)	(NA)	(NA)	(NA)	(NA)	19	130.6	(D)	145	4.4	7.7
Bloomington city	59	35.6	[6]1,750	(D)	(D)	(D)	(D)	(D)	100	2,040.6	(D)	1,158	61.6	102.5
Bolingbrook village	35	45.7	5,857	319.0	1,972	67.0	534.7	1,227.8	81	2,795.1	(D)	3,540	154.8	294.5
Buffalo Grove village	62	51.6	4,044	167.0	2,804	92.1	612.6	1,040.2	171	2,915.4	1,973.5	2,195	127.3	252.8
Burbank city	(NA)	(NA)	(NA)	(NA)	(NA)	(NA)	(NA)	(NA)	9	8.9	8.9	33	1.0	1.7
Calumet City city	(NA)	(NA)	(NA)	(NA)	(NA)	(NA)	(NA)	(NA)	16	28.5	(D)	82	3.5	4.3
Carbondale city	(NA)	(NA)	(NA)	(NA)	(NA)	(NA)	(NA)	(NA)	15	(D)	(D)	[9]175	(D)	(D)
Carol Stream village	103	49.5	5,589	241.3	3,793	136.0	534.6	1,070.4	133	8,206.2	7,594.1	4,107	171.6	324.7
Carpentersville village	28	32.1	1,780	72.9	1,186	29.6	183.6	265.3	12	19.8	19.8	68	2.5	5.2

See footnotes at end of table.

Table C-4. Cities — **Manufacturing and Wholesale Trade**—Con.

[Includes states and 1,265 incorporated places of 25,000 or more population as of April 1, 2000, in all states except Hawaii, which has no incorporated places recognized by the U.S. Census Bureau. Two census designated places (CDPs) are also included (Honolulu CDP in Hawaii and Arlington CDP in Virginia). For more information on these areas, see Appendix C, Geographic Information]

| City | Manufacturing (NAICS 31–33), 2002[1] | | | | | | | | Wholesale trade (NAICS 42), 2002[4] | | | | |
| | Establishments[2] | | All employees | | Production workers | | | | | Sales (mil. dol.) | | | | |
	Total	Percent with 20 or more employ-ees	Number[3]	Annual payroll (mil. dol.)	Number[3]	Wages (mil. dol.)	Value added by manu-facture (mil. dol.)	Value of ship-ments (mil. dol.)	Estab-lishments	Total	Merchant whole-salers	Paid employ-ees[5]	Annual payroll (mil. dol.)	Operating expenses (mil. dol.)
ILLINOIS—Con.														
Champaign city	57	36.8	2,776	85.6	1,975	56.9	380.7	783.9	75	598.7	(D)	1,837	98.3	186.8
Chicago city	2,617	34.1	97,603	3,502.0	70,123	2,112.0	10,734.2	21,722.1	3,019	29,984.0	(D)	48,062	2,038.6	3,917.0
Chicago Heights city	68	52.9	3,268	123.2	2,162	75.3	428.6	917.6	48	288.3	(D)	623	26.3	47.5
Cicero town	114	46.5	4,435	167.9	3,191	99.8	540.7	947.0	47	430.8	(D)	623	27.3	53.9
Crystal Lake city	90	40.0	3,549	128.9	2,656	83.7	328.9	509.6	101	606.3	(D)	901	38.2	68.6
Danville city	55	41.8	3,632	143.4	2,728	94.8	362.9	1,052.1	46	1,369.3	(D)	1,635	60.7	125.1
Decatur city	97	35.1	7,949	378.4	5,575	248.8	1,627.8	4,325.6	98	(D)	(D)	[6]1,750	(D)	(D)
DeKalb city	47	40.4	2,205	75.2	1,712	49.4	219.1	418.8	23	(D)	(D)	[9]175	(D)	(D)
Des Plaines city	145	46.9	10,199	406.7	6,983	213.8	1,026.4	1,695.2	190	3,309.8	1,688.1	3,949	213.6	380.6
Dolton village	22	36.4	784	27.5	610	20.9	85.0	152.2	14	(D)	(D)	[9]175	(D)	(D)
Downers Grove village	88	35.2	4,454	208.8	2,769	102.6	546.9	824.8	166	10,200.1	(D)	3,534	232.2	314.1
East St. Louis city	(NA)	(NA)	(NA)	(NA)	(NA)	(NA)	(NA)	(NA)	29	322.2	(D)	294	8.9	17.2
Elgin city	194	46.4	9,406	389.1	6,683	236.4	962.1	1,833.0	177	2,791.2	2,063.3	3,278	178.0	342.9
Elk Grove Village village	502	45.8	20,364	806.1	14,567	484.2	1,914.5	3,545.3	579	5,752.8	3,632.3	8,776	433.7	933.2
Elmhurst city	91	38.5	2,290	94.2	1,493	45.3	229.2	403.3	179	1,806.7	(D)	3,417	213.1	366.1
Elmwood Park village	(NA)	(NA)	(NA)	(NA)	(NA)	(NA)	(NA)	(NA)	17	23.0	(D)	68	2.1	3.6
Evanston city	65	24.6	1,939	90.3	1,000	35.6	145.5	280.5	76	321.2	255.7	606	26.4	39.6
Freeport city	44	38.6	3,176	137.9	2,010	67.6	344.7	606.1	29	68.9	(D)	191	6.1	10.5
Galesburg city	39	46.2	[11]3,750	(D)	(D)	(D)	(D)	(D)	33	96.7	(D)	312	9.8	17.9
Glendale Heights village	50	64.0	2,695	104.4	1,836	56.2	253.3	469.0	83	1,635.2	1,425.0	1,978	104.8	184.3
Glen Ellyn village	(NA)	(NA)	(NA)	(NA)	(NA)	(NA)	(NA)	(NA)	66	418.3	(D)	452	23.1	38.4
Glenview village	58	22.4	842	31.8	630	20.7	82.2	129.2	136	1,114.3	513.6	1,802	102.4	195.1
Granite City city	32	53.1	5,400	248.2	4,438	193.6	880.4	1,857.8	37	500.8	(D)	628	21.1	43.7
Gurnee village	68	38.2	2,063	85.3	1,322	45.1	295.5	466.4	82	663.9	469.6	1,283	55.2	111.2
Hanover Park village	16	43.8	533	26.3	349	13.9	77.4	165.4	39	(D)	(D)	[6]1,750	(D)	(D)
Harvey city	32	46.9	1,664	60.0	1,170	39.0	192.7	488.1	31	105.6	(D)	352	14.6	21.8
Highland Park city	39	15.4	854	30.4	545	16.5	117.5	188.6	97	689.9	542.7	318	18.9	42.2
Hoffman Estates village	26	26.9	1,085	70.6	492	26.9	196.7	344.7	99	5,585.6	(D)	1,197	86.1	142.7
Joliet city	86	36.0	4,575	194.0	3,213	122.7	513.9	1,101.8	91	802.4	(D)	1,059	43.0	75.9
Kankakee city	30	53.3	1,952	86.6	1,320	54.8	407.7	843.1	31	142.7	(D)	376	14.8	28.1
Lansing village	35	17.1	1,900	55.3	1,327	25.4	115.3	251.4	34	148.7	121.7	384	20.2	31.6
Lombard village	88	27.3	1,441	52.8	1,023	30.6	104.3	189.2	178	4,934.6	2,668.5	2,513	118.0	224.3
Maywood village	29	31.0	593	22.7	430	13.0	44.7	83.8	11	15.8	15.8	74	2.8	4.0
Moline city	49	34.7	1,935	80.4	1,297	43.7	258.7	467.5	67	2,088.3	(D)	885	50.8	91.0
Mount Prospect village	41	43.9	1,995	98.4	773	28.1	251.7	437.2	128	2,667.6	1,412.6	2,859	159.4	241.0
Mundelein village	76	42.1	2,809	109.4	1,996	60.6	283.6	506.8	86	(D)	(D)	[6]1,750	(D)	(D)
Naperville city	99	26.3	2,513	102.8	1,815	62.4	285.2	490.9	289	15,271.9	1,999.7	2,599	126.0	381.8
Niles village	101	49.5	4,821	183.3	3,399	6.9	562.6	1,103.9	91	646.9	541.0	1,828	79.4	153.4
Normal town	26	26.9	[11]3,750	(D)	(D)	(D)	(D)	(D)	34	(D)	(D)	[12]375	(D)	(D)
Northbrook village	117	30.8	3,470	145.7	2,187	71.1	418.1	690.9	308	5,038.9	1,630.5	3,682	240.3	468.5
North Chicago city	21	38.1	790	30.7	503	15.2	114.6	218.0	15	176.9	176.9	411	19.5	42.1
Oak Forest city	(NA)	(NA)	(NA)	(NA)	(NA)	(NA)	(NA)	(NA)	24	119.0	(D)	200	6.7	15.6
Oak Lawn village	30	20.0	505	19.4	342	12.2	44.3	83.2	35	52.5	(D)	168	5.0	9.4
Oak Park village	(NA)	(NA)	(NA)	(NA)	(NA)	(NA)	(NA)	(NA)	36	170.3	(D)	181	8.3	18.5
Orland Park village	53	20.8	2,384	127.1	1,228	45.3	394.9	552.4	75	171.3	(D)	521	21.7	34.8
Palatine village	68	20.6	2,173	88.1	1,253	35.4	244.4	500.5	137	742.8	(D)	613	31.6	59.2
Park Ridge city	(NA)	(NA)	(NA)	(NA)	(NA)	(NA)	(NA)	(NA)	89	505.2	(D)	421	20.7	38.8
Pekin city	31	38.7	1,193	45.9	845	27.6	263.6	609.8	26	(D)	(D)	[12]375	(D)	(D)
Peoria city	108	43.5	4,763	179.8	3,006	96.4	519.5	1,284.5	204	1,766.5	1,139.5	2,937	118.4	229.7
Quincy city	54	37.0	[11]3,750	(D)	(D)	(D)	(D)	(D)	73	765.2	762.5	1,247	39.0	76.8
Rockford city	421	35.2	21,733	940.1	14,123	528.2	2,955.3	4,773.3	267	1,479.3	918.3	3,453	125.2	221.0
Rock Island city	47	40.4	1,563	43.4	1,230	30.0	114.0	223.2	76	454.7	421.8	962	43.8	78.9
Round Lake Beach village	(NA)	(NA)	(NA)	(NA)	(NA)	(NA)	(NA)	(NA)	4	3.0	(D)	10	0.4	0.6
St. Charles city	126	50.8	6,869	265.8	4,685	145.7	897.6	1,540.3	114	944.4	(D)	1,199	51.5	101.2
Schaumburg village	173	28.9	6,249	251.5	4,204	143.7	1,195.7	1,907.0	372	9,148.6	4,866.7	6,514	431.5	837.0
Skokie village	194	27.8	8,205	284.6	5,787	161.5	644.8	1,190.0	179	4,971.1	4,311.2	2,591	138.5	211.7
Springfield city	78	34.6	2,590	96.2	1,667	51.0	201.3	400.5	142	2,046.8	1,975.3	2,439	106.3	183.7
Streamwood village	36	22.2	1,085	41.5	801	25.4	86.3	175.4	26	107.0	57.1	222	8.7	15.6
Tinley Park village	47	36.2	1,404	52.2	969	31.4	148.8	238.3	59	346.6	201.2	586	24.1	43.2
Urbana city	26	38.5	1,550	47.8	963	24.5	368.5	620.3	29	(D)	(D)	[8]750	(D)	(D)
Waukegan city	86	36.0	4,780	206.0	2,879	89.9	505.7	886.6	92	1,586.8	1,113.3	3,370	142.0	340.7
Wheaton city	36	16.7	1,492	57.5	1,132	37.5	164.3	207.1	92	(D)	(D)	[12]375	(D)	(D)
Wheeling village	182	42.9	8,367	342.3	5,645	188.8	1,035.3	1,992.7	166	1,092.0	(D)	2,464	120.2	214.7
Wilmette village	(NA)	(NA)	(NA)	(NA)	(NA)	(NA)	(NA)	(NA)	48	132.9	(D)	155	6.2	10.5
Woodridge village	30	36.7	1,268	40.5	849	21.3	84.4	194.5	52	1,594.3	(D)	1,932	93.9	195.9

See footnotes at end of table.

Table C-4. Cities — **Manufacturing and Wholesale Trade**—Con.

[Includes states and 1,265 incorporated places of 25,000 or more population as of April 1, 2000, in all states except Hawaii, which has no incorporated places recognized by the U.S. Census Bureau. Two census designated places (CDPs) are also included (Honolulu CDP in Hawaii and Arlington CDP in Virginia). For more information on these areas, see Appendix C, Geographic Information]

| City | Manufacturing (NAICS 31–33), 2002[1] | | | | | | | | Wholesale trade (NAICS 42), 2002[4] | | | | | |
| | Establishments[2] | | All employees | | Production workers | | Value added by manufacture (mil. dol.) | Value of shipments (mil. dol.) | Estab-lishments | Sales (mil. dol.) | | Paid employees[5] | Annual payroll (mil. dol.) | Operating expenses (mil. dol.) |
	Total	Percent with 20 or more employees	Number[3]	Annual payroll (mil. dol.)	Number[3]	Wages (mil. dol.)				Total	Merchant wholesalers			
INDIANA	9,223	39.8	565,559	22,852.7	426,331	15,437.9	78,023.8	160,924.2	8,213	79,806.0	54,802.7	109,600	4,202.1	7,825.6
Anderson city	60	33.3	5,428	272.8	3,922	185.2	582.4	931.7	46	207.0	(D)	700	21.8	39.8
Bloomington city	66	19.7	[11]3,750	(D)	(D)	(D)	(D)	(D)	51	(D)	[8]750	(D)	(D)	(D)
Carmel city	56	23.2	974	37.8	685	21.3	44.7	339.9	159	1,268.9	410.9	1,410	103.9	167.8
Columbus city	98	52.0	10,038	355.3	7,084	227.0	1,254.0	2,890.7	66	389.8	364.0	664	28.0	49.1
East Chicago city	48	56.3	9,324	517.9	6,759	360.4	1,095.4	3,155.5	44	768.9	301.1	775	31.2	75.1
Elkhart city	338	50.3	16,724	558.1	13,071	376.3	1,234.7	2,762.9	156	1,393.8	1,038.3	2,293	83.6	157.8
Evansville city	206	37.9	13,158	524.4	9,657	347.5	1,782.4	3,242.7	254	(D)		[11]3,750	(D)	(D)
Fishers town	23	43.5	733	28.7	450	12.7	68.7	135.0	111	730.6	518.2	1,426	59.5	105.3
Fort Wayne city	377	40.8	17,068	717.2	12,442	472.1	2,074.0	3,665.3	485	3,562.3	2,532.6	8,381	291.1	528.0
Gary city	45	35.6	7,844	405.9	6,277	324.6	1,415.8	2,920.0	58	678.2	(D)	1,096	43.7	82.1
Goshen city	104	55.8	7,763	265.4	6,318	188.4	673.6	1,429.5	31	142.9	125.5	437	14.9	22.9
Greenwood city	47	14.9	833	32.2	567	17.4	89.6	292.7	54	922.9	(D)	696	34.0	54.1
Hammond city	77	41.6	3,879	182.6	2,763	120.7	897.9	1,976.4	82	769.4	(D)	1,302	52.2	93.1
Hobart city	(NA)	(NA)	(NA)	(NA)	(NA)	(NA)	(NA)	(NA)	25	142.6	(D)	247	7.7	17.0
Indianapolis city (balance)	986	36.4	54,226	2,658.5	37,082	1,639.2	12,506.7	20,038.9	1,687	20,707.6	(D)	28,862	1,259.5	2,301.1
Jeffersonville city	74	48.6	4,175	138.3	3,125	92.4	324.8	706.1	39	351.8	(D)	792	24.3	45.6
Kokomo city	65	41.5	15,716	990.0	11,485	700.7	4,054.9	6,927.7	67	(D)	(D)	[8]750	(D)	(D)
Lafayette city	80	48.8	9,944	404.5	7,227	257.5	1,138.3	2,662.7	81	255.0	200.3	1,313	38.1	56.6
Lawrence city	29	27.6	520	17.9	377	10.7	36.0	56.4	48	(D)	(D)	[8]750	(D)	(D)
Marion city	47	48.9	6,105	295.6	5,118	237.8	587.5	1,320.2	25	88.9	(D)	259	8.7	13.5
Merrillville town	37	35.1	851	26.7	642	17.4	59.7	134.3	48	212.5	174.1	380	16.0	27.2
Michigan City city	72	51.4	4,038	156.5	2,858	89.3	476.9	889.7	48	332.4	(D)	630	24.3	47.7
Mishawaka city	110	34.5	5,245	160.8	3,501	104.1	713.2	1,410.9	84	1,327.6	(D)	1,037	36.8	73.0
Muncie city	103	43.7	6,236	284.9	4,462	174.8	653.9	1,317.3	65	420.3	(D)	881	30.0	64.6
New Albany city	91	52.7	[7]7,500	(D)	(D)	(D)	(D)	(D)	63	(D)	893.4	[8]750	(D)	(D)
Noblesville city	42	35.7	1,645	62.0	1,193	36.1	246.3	343.8	93	287.5	(D)	644	26.5	49.8
Portage city	22	50.0	2,241	117.0	1,594	82.9	276.2	1,056.7	28	455.6	(D)	776	31.1	68.9
Richmond city	89	60.7	6,970	256.1	5,544	182.5	893.0	1,629.8	54	445.7	306.1	805	23.1	38.4
South Bend city	196	41.8	7,623	329.5	4,996	173.9	823.4	1,615.6	207	1,874.0	1,507.9	3,833	142.1	257.3
Terre Haute city	88	39.8	6,095	230.6	4,525	153.0	1,251.1	2,026.2	90	280.9	247.6	1,117	32.4	56.3
Valparaiso city	56	25.0	2,158	97.3	1,556	60.8	287.9	630.9	49	258.9	133.6	358	18.0	31.3
West Lafayette city	(NA)	(NA)	(NA)	(NA)	(NA)	(NA)	(NA)	(NA)	10	23.3	(D)	106	3.0	4.0
IOWA	3,804	35.2	222,968	8,125.9	163,122	5,108.3	31,394.3	65,042.0	4,926	33,546.9	26,197.9	62,023	2,145.5	3,941.1
Ames city	41	41.5	2,389	103.9	1,420	47.1	452.9	770.7	45	187.0	160.0	487	17.3	33.3
Ankeny city	22	36.4	1,834	100.7	1,206	57.5	475.7	854.7	50	863.7	830.5	1,129	40.6	74.7
Bettendorf city	35	42.9	1,002	35.0	733	21.8	81.4	130.4	63	439.6	248.8	550	21.5	36.8
Burlington city	35	42.9	2,999	104.0	2,231	73.0	310.5	735.6	30	160.8	(D)	236	7.4	13.9
Cedar Falls city	43	37.2	[6]1,750	(D)	(D)	(D)	(D)	(D)	36	307.4	214.6	610	23.1	38.1
Cedar Rapids city	141	48.2	15,778	798.7	6,851	294.1	2,041.3	4,352.3	276	1,996.8	1,663.4	4,451	190.4	294.5
Clinton city	27	44.4	[11]3,750	114.7	2,281	83.1	1,129.8	2,118.8	27	60.9	(D)	213	5.7	10.6
Council Bluffs city	46	41.3	[11]3,750	(D)	(D)	(D)	(D)	(D)	68	652.7	(D)	1,456	43.7	87.8
Davenport city	114	39.5	7,619	302.1	5,005	177.0	1,398.5	2,497.3	223	1,358.6	1,081.4	2,980	107.0	223.8
Des Moines city	212	30.2	7,350	258.0	4,976	144.0	912.8	2,081.5	375	3,092.2	2,079.6	6,838	262.9	440.0
Dubuque city	91	42.9	4,932	170.0	3,318	104.2	398.4	866.1	94	506.4	396.6	1,295	41.6	73.2
Fort Dodge city	35	28.6	1,039	39.3	800	28.9	311.7	570.0	47	(D)	(D)	[8]750	(D)	(D)
Iowa City city	44	29.5	3,190	115.8	2,203	81.4	2,714.0	3,967.4	33	159.2	118.4	422	12.1	19.7
Marion city	41	22.0	[8]750	(D)	(D)	(D)	(D)	(D)	28	152.4	(D)	264	9.0	21.2
Marshalltown city	40	35.0	[7]7,500	(D)	(D)	(D)	(D)	(D)	30	(D)	(D)	[12]375	(D)	(D)
Mason City city	36	55.6	3,212	102.3	2,435	70.2	343.9	764.7	64	369.5	(D)	723	21.5	40.3
Sioux City city	94	46.8	5,584	168.5	4,113	105.5	560.5	1,827.7	161	917.3	901.0	2,190	75.9	139.7
Urbandale city	29	34.5	1,203	45.4	593	20.1	239.4	455.5	118	1,535.5	(D)	2,227	121.5	178.6
Waterloo city	91	46.2	8,635	376.8	6,305	239.5	1,720.8	3,324.3	84	351.3	(D)	1,492	44.4	74.8
West Des Moines city	38	28.9	1,495	51.4	989	29.1	102.2	212.1	78	1,286.1	(D)	874	48.4	94.2
KANSAS	3,218	33.0	177,825	6,877.3	126,919	4,160.5	21,347.3	50,897.8	4,705	44,117.1	27,259.2	57,926	2,177.1	4,236.8
Dodge City city	22	45.5	[11]3,750	(D)	(D)	(D)	(D)	(D)	39	(D)	(D)	[12]375	(D)	(D)
Emporia city	31	38.7	[11]3,750	(D)	(D)	(D)	(D)	(D)	31	103.1	(D)	378	12.8	19.1
Garden City city	(NA)	(NA)	(NA)	(NA)	(NA)	(NA)	(NA)	(NA)	23	119.7	(D)	192	6.6	10.1
Hutchinson city	47	40.4	1,662	57.2	1,159	32.9	144.8	269.8	60	663.0	(D)	909	28.9	55.0
Kansas City city	233	46.4	[14]17,500	(D)	(D)	(D)	(D)	(D)	258	4,045.9	(D)	6,130	237.3	480.4
Lawrence city	65	33.8	3,187	114.1	2,329	72.5	482.8	804.7	70	302.8	297.7	630	18.4	41.7
Leavenworth city	(NA)	(NA)	(NA)	(NA)	(NA)	(NA)	(NA)	(NA)	12	(D)	(D)	[10]60	(D)	(D)
Leawood city	(NA)	(NA)	(NA)	(NA)	(NA)	(NA)	(NA)	(NA)	74	1,199.7	(D)	494	22.4	42.9
Lenexa city	138	46.4	7,647	286.7	4,621	145.9	672.4	1,463.3	384	3,312.1	1,764.3	6,233	267.8	471.7
Manhattan city	26	34.6	648	18.4	549	1.4	51.4	81.9	35	106.7	(D)	461	12.7	20.9
Olathe city	119	27.7	4,391	191.2	2,695	86.4	494.4	1,104.8	214	2,194.7	1,199.0	3,732	159.4	295.5
Overland Park city	89	19.1	1,207	44.7	808	23.2	94.8	161.1	463	10,969.9	5,213.4	4,507	250.8	463.6
Salina city	67	28.4	3,911	123.0	3,205	85.4	192.4	757.1	76	378.1	(D)	922	30.2	53.6
Shawnee city	47	27.7	1,586	76.3	777	27.1	384.3	536.7	74	669.2	(D)	988	40.2	76.4
Topeka city	99	32.3	6,170	242.8	4,919	185.5	926.6	1,491.2	141	798.4	722.5	1,825	69.7	159.6
Wichita city	487	34.1	34,999	1,475.8	22,122	742.0	4,105.3	8,749.6	648	8,631.3	4,317.1	10,270	412.4	835.6

See footnotes at end of table.

Table C-4. Cities — **Manufacturing and Wholesale Trade**—Con.

[Includes states and 1,265 incorporated places of 25,000 or more population as of April 1, 2000, in all states except Hawaii, which has no incorporated places recognized by the U.S. Census Bureau. Two census designated places (CDPs) are also included (Honolulu CDP in Hawaii and Arlington CDP in Virginia). For more information on these areas, see Appendix C, Geographic Information]

| City | Manufacturing (NAICS 31–33), 2002[1] | | | | | | | | Wholesale trade (NAICS 42), 2002[4] | | | | | |
| | Establishments[2] | | All employees | | Production workers | | Value added by manu-facture (mil. dol.) | Value of ship-ments (mil. dol.) | Estab-lishments | Sales (mil. dol.) | | Paid employ-ees[5] | Annual payroll (mil. dol.) | Operating expenses (mil. dol.) |
	Total	Percent with 20 or more employ-ees	Number[3]	Annual payroll (mil. dol.)	Number[3]	Wages (mil. dol.)				Total	Merchant whole-salers			
KENTUCKY	4,283	39.0	263,202	10,077.0	201,586	6,853.8	34,075.4	88,513.5	4,630	51,838.7	35,903.7	69,192	2,536.6	5,003.2
Bowling Green city	90	51.1	8,189	307.4	6,274	205.1	1,728.7	3,247.3	121	1,797.6	(D)	1,703	59.7	109.3
Covington city	46	32.6	1,255	41.3	1,019	27.8	98.6	243.0	28	521.3	(D)	1,092	40.6	103.3
Frankfort city	15	33.3	629	22.9	440	13.5	145.8	223.8	18	(D)	(D)	[9]175	(D)	(D)
Henderson city	68	45.6	5,511	195.2	4,630	144.7	552.4	1,481.1	37	(D)	(D)	[12]375	(D)	(D)
Hopkinsville city	49	55.1	5,051	165.0	3,980	115.8	398.7	1,038.9	55	(D)	(D)	[8]750	(D)	(D)
Jeffersontown city	105	44.8	4,581	148.5	3,111	80.8	420.0	738.2	202	1,384.2	877.1	3,045	123.0	229.7
Lexington-Fayette	265	34.7	14,025	652.9	7,651	245.0	2,964.9	4,927.7	449	4,011.1	2,556.6	5,667	222.4	403.4
Louisville/Jefferson County (balance)	(X)	(NA)	(X)	(X)	(X)	(X)	(X)	(X)	(X)	(X)	(X)	(X)	(X)	(X)
Owensboro city	78	48.7	4,626	151.1	3,516	101.1	643.6	1,633.8	92	336.1	(D)	1,095	31.8	57.6
Paducah city	34	41.2	[8]750	(D)	(D)	(D)	(D)	(D)	96	2,165.6	(D)	1,872	60.9	123.6
Richmond city	30	50.0	[6]1,750	(D)	(D)	(D)	(D)	(D)	25	(D)	(D)	[9]175	(D)	(D)
LOUISIANA	3,524	30.9	150,401	6,427.4	109,216	4,178.7	28,404.9	89,540.8	5,904	47,192.2	36,525.1	73,548	2,676.9	4,951.0
Alexandria city	35	37.1	1,557	51.9	1,195	34.3	155.3	287.6	78	516.6	278.1	970	31.2	62.6
Baton Rouge city	218	22.0	4,008	143.5	2,689	88.6	420.0	1,168.8	445	2,793.0	1,784.3	6,062	241.4	408.5
Bossier City city	61	32.8	1,640	49.4	1,149	29.2	112.3	224.6	75	436.8	(D)	969	35.2	60.8
Houma city	44	31.8	1,533	54.4	1,310	43.3	132.4	203.6	92	258.2	(D)	792	28.1	49.1
Kenner city	65	12.3	1,174	38.9	896	26.1	76.2	128.7	173	608.6	357.1	1,722	59.8	101.0
Lafayette city	130	23.8	3,899	123.0	2,615	69.6	358.1	741.5	273	1,531.9	1,290.5	4,498	159.4	264.0
Lake Charles city	52	26.9	[11]3,750	(D)	(D)	(D)	(D)	(D)	95	450.6	399.9	1,338	40.4	77.8
Monroe city	53	34.0	2,329	73.1	1,662	43.8	183.7	393.7	110	985.1	906.8	1,381	47.3	93.8
New Iberia city	38	15.8	660	23.4	545	17.0	58.6	141.9	57	(D)	121.6	[8]750	(D)	(D)
New Orleans city	225	27.1	8,584	346.3	5,157	161.8	1,221.9	2,226.2	448	2,792.1	2,280.4	5,693	222.5	429.3
Shreveport city	170	29.4	8,961	389.7	6,930	301.3	1,754.6	4,547.1	348	1,487.1	1,061.8	4,150	138.9	259.8
Slidell city	(NA)	(NA)	(NA)	(NA)	(NA)	(NA)	(NA)	(NA)	52	(D)	(D)	[12]375	(D)	(D)
MAINE	1,880	24.9	67,738	2,627.8	49,524	1,720.9	7,122.3	13,851.9	1,669	10,371.1	8,732.4	19,434	715.0	1,324.1
Bangor city	57	22.8	1,376	53.0	1,043	39.0	92.4	226.4	80	581.7	(D)	1,550	47.3	98.7
Lewiston city	75	34.7	1,993	65.1	1,475	40.3	159.7	254.2	61	(D)	(D)	[8]750	(D)	(D)
Portland city	110	25.5	3,622	123.5	2,658	75.7	444.4	789.0	225	1,434.0	1,132.1	3,215	126.0	218.8
MARYLAND	3,999	29.4	151,294	6,475.2	95,224	3,229.0	19,265.9	36,363.3	6,104	60,679.6	35,945.8	93,474	4,443.8	7,629.7
Annapolis city	(NA)	(NA)	(NA)	(NA)	(NA)	(NA)	(NA)	(NA)	94	465.5	325.1	669	26.1	45.1
Baltimore city	591	35.9	21,042	859.7	14,900	528.0	2,807.4	6,239.4	655	6,047.6	3,855.2	10,817	462.6	847.0
Bowie city	(NA)	(NA)	(NA)	(NA)	(NA)	(NA)	(NA)	(NA)	20	(D)	(D)	[9]175	(D)	(D)
Frederick city	58	34.5	2,396	94.2	1,612	55.4	919.9	1,157.0	86	434.9	(D)	1,153	46.5	75.4
Gaithersburg city	45	37.8	1,901	107.4	798	28.8	388.6	522.6	86	472.2	(D)	1,063	53.4	96.8
Hagerstown city	61	31.1	[11]3,750	(D)	(D)	(D)	(D)	(D)	63	197.7	(D)	607	20.7	35.5
Rockville city	72	18.1	1,418	58.2	969	32.9	121.5	167.5	108	1,021.9	580.4	1,820	116.2	230.8
MASSACHUSETTS	8,859	32.9	349,184	15,573.7	210,629	7,029.9	44,508.8	77,996.6	9,333	127,129.8	73,990.3	154,939	8,536.7	15,425.2
Agawam city	60	35.0	2,030	76.8	1,448	45.7	224.0	408.3	53	406.8	(D)	747	31.3	61.3
Attleboro city	127	37.8	6,633	265.4	4,024	96.9	757.2	1,365.9	40	129.3	(D)	377	16.0	29.4
Barnstable Town city	47	19.1	938	43.0	442	13.4	147.4	222.1	54	162.9	(D)	461	18.6	30.6
Beverly city	65	32.3	3,767	231.1	1,602	73.7	367.9	647.5	55	272.6	(D)	528	32.8	53.4
Boston city	396	31.1	15,955	716.6	9,299	325.4	2,165.9	3,538.9	686	11,392.7	5,508.0	13,719	798.4	1,517.0
Brockton city	113	32.7	2,912	102.2	2,131	62.9	218.8	433.5	87	668.7	446.4	1,232	50.7	87.3
Cambridge city	100	36.0	5,241	263.8	2,761	93.2	870.5	1,234.2	105	1,119.3	(D)	2,007	129.4	201.9
Chelsea city	51	35.3	1,743	64.2	1,225	36.5	181.5	345.8	102	(D)	(D)	[6]1,750	(D)	(D)
Chicopee city	103	37.9	5,321	217.6	3,544	115.8	716.8	1,216.4	38	612.3	(D)	594	34.3	63.0
Everett city	67	25.4	1,543	63.9	1,019	36.2	120.5	222.6	69	1,444.3	(D)	1,740	66.5	159.1
Fall River city	195	37.9	11,707	370.9	9,004	229.7	937.8	1,706.4	84	359.0	(D)	1,346	43.0	74.5
Fitchburg city	83	32.5	2,215	100.1	1,442	53.9	254.2	447.7	33	110.3	(D)	361	14.9	30.0
Franklin city	64	57.8	5,355	263.7	3,055	113.0	1,255.0	2,821.8	51	1,060.6	(D)	901	41.1	116.8
Gloucester city	51	35.3	2,990	152.7	1,674	66.0	436.2	735.8	57	255.9	(D)	360	15.8	32.5
Haverhill city	109	32.1	2,675	102.6	1,782	54.6	214.9	387.9	59	281.9	(D)	820	32.9	53.6
Holyoke city	81	50.6	2,897	111.7	1,978	62.3	278.8	631.1	40	233.1	173.6	745	26.9	46.9
Lawrence city	115	37.4	5,259	202.6	3,621	115.4	458.6	820.1	68	436.0	(D)	1,268	54.3	91.3
Leominster city	118	40.7	4,620	178.3	3,409	104.8	463.2	957.1	44	200.3	(D)	633	23.7	40.2
Lowell city	100	44.0	5,101	225.6	2,833	88.9	511.9	926.1	86	895.6	600.8	1,583	85.6	130.1
Lynn city	63	36.5	6,472	400.6	3,534	192.8	1,519.3	3,211.1	57	357.8	(D)	639	33.5	68.4
Malden city	55	34.5	1,493	61.8	967	34.2	143.4	258.3	44	571.5	(D)	754	35.8	58.5
Marlborough city	88	39.8	5,376	334.9	2,085	80.5	756.1	1,369.3	99	3,646.9	(D)	3,561	234.4	392.1
Medford city	46	17.4	682	24.6	465	12.7	45.6	80.4	63	471.6	(D)	1,083	48.2	91.9
Melrose city	(NA)	(NA)	(NA)	(NA)	(NA)	(NA)	(NA)	(NA)	14	(D)	(D)	[10]60	(D)	(D)
Methuen city	42	35.7	2,093	88.5	1,337	43.4	308.6	513.1	33	822.0	(D)	500	20.0	40.5
New Bedford city	154	37.0	7,386	237.2	5,469	148.0	543.6	1,203.5	125	809.4	696.6	1,999	72.0	136.7
Newton city	70	20.0	1,823	88.4	985	35.8	133.3	377.4	157	1,437.4	500.9	1,676	108.6	167.6
Northampton city	46	43.5	1,466	61.2	953	29.7	168.2	359.7	24	77.2	77.2	317	9.0	16.1
Peabody city	92	32.6	3,589	179.5	1,877	68.3	372.2	708.2	93	3,940.9	(D)	2,286	127.1	263.2
Pittsfield city	61	39.3	2,757	116.0	1,437	44.0	240.1	368.6	52	147.4	(D)	608	17.7	38.1

See footnotes at end of table.

Table C-4. Cities — **Manufacturing and Wholesale Trade**—Con.

[Includes states and 1,265 incorporated places of 25,000 or more population as of April 1, 2000, in all states except Hawaii, which has no incorporated places recognized by the U.S. Census Bureau. Two census designated places (CDPs) are also included (Honolulu CDP in Hawaii and Arlington CDP in Virginia). For more information on these areas, see Appendix C, Geographic Information]

City	Manufacturing (NAICS 31–33), 2002[1]								Wholesale trade (NAICS 42), 2002[4]					
	Establishments[2]		All employees		Production workers		Value added by manufacture (mil. dol.)	Value of shipments (mil. dol.)	Estab-lishments	Sales (mil. dol.)		Paid employ-ees[5]	Annual payroll (mil. dol.)	Operating expenses (mil. dol.)
	Total	Percent with 20 or more employ-ees	Number[3]	Annual payroll (mil. dol.)	Number[3]	Wages (mil. dol.)				Total	Merchant whole-salers			
MASSACHUSETTS—Con.														
Quincy city	67	13.4	727	27.1	535	17.0	98.7	223.1	77	590.8	455.6	736	30.9	53.1
Revere city	(NA)	(NA)	(NA)	(NA)	(NA)	(NA)	(NA)	(NA)	26	(D)	(D)	[9]175	30.9	(D)
Salem city	61	24.6	1,302	50.1	898	28.2	92.5	166.9	53	117.8	(D)	392	14.6	23.5
Somerville city	75	18.7	2,109	87.3	1,326	37.1	174.5	297.5	50	236.4	236.4	561	27.2	45.7
Springfield city	158	33.5	5,929	241.8	4,291	148.2	548.6	1,064.6	138	1,821.5	(D)	2,188	86.3	152.6
Taunton city	75	42.7	4,219	181.9	2,120	60.2	326.1	920.1	59	1,079.7	856.3	1,594	75.9	153.1
Waltham city	141	27.0	5,447	251.3	2,817	102.9	421.2	801.8	141	4,183.1	2,250.6	5,092	409.4	619.9
Watertown city	57	38.6	2,494	107.4	1,511	43.9	388.1	521.5	38	250.9	(D)	526	28.9	47.7
Westfield city	95	37.9	3,358	131.6	2,402	80.6	270.4	514.0	44	1,046.4	969.8	841	32.5	68.9
West Springfield city	77	26.0	2,028	73.0	1,297	40.1	199.3	470.5	83	351.5	318.9	1,135	51.9	96.1
Woburn city	155	36.8	5,356	245.1	3,315	104.9	751.6	1,115.5	272	2,436.8	1,759.5	4,670	222.4	393.1
Worcester city	239	35.1	9,977	442.7	6,343	216.3	948.3	1,616.6	232	1,777.0	1,106.9	3,315	135.0	235.5
MICHIGAN	15,193	33.9	736,259	33,171.2	549,621	22,572.0	97,575.4	221,433.3	12,876	165,958.9	85,024.0	177,963	8,306.5	16,826.2
Allen Park city	18	11.1	[8]750	(D)	(D)	(D)	(D)	(D)	30	(D)	(D)	[12]375	(D)	(D)
Ann Arbor city	75	21.3	2,440	98.8	1,493	48.8	227.2	415.8	113	596.5	419.0	1,048	59.9	102.6
Battle Creek city	80	47.5	7,850	350.2	5,967	240.3	1,529.9	2,793.3	54	519.9	507.0	641	24.2	41.0
Bay City city	57	42.1	3,211	177.4	2,533	134.9	292.7	685.3	54	182.6	140.3	769	24.2	46.5
Burton city	(NA)	(NA)	(NA)	(NA)	(NA)	(NA)	(NA)	(NA)	35	157.5	(D)	391	15.1	27.5
Dearborn city	104	35.6	13,848	664.0	11,775	529.3	1,218.2	4,886.4	142	1,109.4	(D)	2,038	105.2	182.4
Dearborn Heights city	(NA)	(NA)	(NA)	(NA)	(NA)	(NA)	(NA)	(NA)	31	(D)	(D)	[12]375	(D)	(D)
Detroit city	647	28.9	38,019	2,054.0	30,079	1,565.0	8,696.3	22,796.8	611	8,315.9	4,307.3	10,153	439.9	836.0
East Lansing city	(NA)	(NA)	(NA)	(NA)	(NA)	(NA)	(NA)	(NA)	10	(D)	(D)	[10]60	(D)	(D)
Eastpointe city	(NA)	(NA)	(NA)	(NA)	(NA)	(NA)	(NA)	(NA)	26	84.3	84.3	188	5.1	10.8
Farmington Hills city	123	33.3	3,551	156.6	2,118	71.5	346.6	596.6	350	5,130.0	2,308.3	6,172	313.4	540.5
Flint city	88	34.1	[14]17,500	(D)	(D)	(D)	(D)	(D)	109	698.2	414.3	1,875	67.5	112.1
Garden City city	(NA)	(NA)	(NA)	(NA)	(NA)	(NA)	(NA)	(NA)	16	18.6	18.6	90	2.3	4.2
Grand Rapids city	382	41.6	28,760	1,280.8	17,172	617.2	2,710.6	4,960.3	373	4,895.3	4,197.1	8,336	355.1	639.1
Holland city	111	53.2	13,310	472.5	9,297	291.1	1,983.6	3,596.6	50	488.1	(D)	798	37.1	52.0
Inkster city	(NA)	(NA)	(NA)	(NA)	(NA)	(NA)	(NA)	(NA)	10	21.2	21.2	89	3.6	6.8
Jackson city	118	26.3	2,944	114.6	2,148	71.5	363.5	673.9	74	370.2	(D)	1,050	36.1	74.7
Kalamazoo city	134	32.8	5,679	224.6	3,787	117.4	744.0	1,357.1	126	604.8	468.9	1,836	63.5	119.4
Kentwood city	123	55.3	10,110	393.9	7,362	228.0	1,011.1	1,871.5	151	2,075.9	(D)	3,062	126.9	237.7
Lansing city	111	40.5	[14]17,500	(D)	(D)	(D)	(D)	(D)	169	1,742.6	(D)	2,977	114.5	194.3
Lincoln Park city	(NA)	(NA)	(NA)	(NA)	(NA)	(NA)	(NA)	(NA)	9	(D)	(D)	[10]60	(D)	(D)
Livonia city	296	31.4	13,295	692.2	9,936	490.7	1,618.0	3,529.7	367	10,625.6	5,646.4	6,093	311.3	548.5
Madison Heights city	183	40.4	5,360	221.9	3,698	130.3	479.2	888.3	149	1,620.7	793.7	2,460	129.8	236.2
Midland city	42	31.0	[7]7,500	(D)	(D)	(D)	(D)	(D)	51	(D)	(D)	[8]750	(D)	(D)
Mount Pleasant city	23	21.7	805	23.0	648	17.8	51.0	168.1	35	145.3	97.2	431	12.5	29.6
Muskegon city	110	44.5	5,374	216.0	3,977	146.0	598.4	1,136.5	47	241.6	(D)	671	25.6	48.0
Novi city	90	34.4	3,151	129.5	2,040	67.5	301.3	547.1	176	3,999.4	1,955.6	2,995	165.7	314.5
Oak Park city	65	32.3	1,315	53.6	778	31.1	117.3	182.7	83	458.0	367.0	969	44.9	82.6
Pontiac city	63	30.2	[7]7,500	(D)	(D)	(D)	(D)	(D)	66	586.2	306.2	1,782	100.0	167.8
Portage city	78	39.7	4,805	211.7	2,950	102.7	2,955.3	3,392.4	71	867.3	(D)	1,836	122.2	200.0
Port Huron city	67	56.7	4,833	201.1	3,550	124.9	555.3	1,287.2	22	182.2	(D)	182	11.0	21.0
Rochester Hills city	126	45.2	8,883	330.9	6,995	207.8	631.5	1,202.5	124	980.5	(D)	1,234	71.5	121.0
Roseville city	168	30.4	5,120	220.2	3,952	153.3	384.3	615.5	60	(D)	(D)	[8]750	(D)	(D)
Royal Oak city	85	20.0	1,979	82.4	1,410	50.5	219.1	459.2	93	581.9	337.6	789	38.9	65.7
Saginaw city	69	46.4	7,331	400.5	5,887	329.3	1,414.8	2,551.2	53	266.8	(D)	765	28.8	50.7
St. Clair Shores city	52	17.3	2,599	87.0	2,023	55.0	283.2	483.3	72	404.4	(D)	340	15.9	28.9
Southfield city	103	24.3	3,717	190.8	2,132	81.2	395.6	878.3	313	10,822.0	3,136.7	4,381	298.4	512.9
Southgate city	(NA)	(NA)	(NA)	(NA)	(NA)	(NA)	(NA)	(NA)	19	84.7	(D)	188	6.0	12.8
Sterling Heights city	297	34.0	20,847	1,198.5	17,049	948.5	2,760.1	8,048.9	165	1,601.1	(D)	3,643	185.4	291.2
Taylor city	104	33.7	3,018	115.8	2,246	73.1	333.1	756.0	115	906.0	(D)	1,570	73.3	123.1
Troy city	320	37.5	9,211	374.5	6,367	218.4	840.4	1,620.3	466	13,634.4	3,051.2	7,457	423.8	746.0
Warren city	454	31.9	20,144	1,055.7	15,722	801.8	2,439.5	8,480.3	245	1,763.3	1,623.9	4,068	185.9	332.7
Westland city	82	26.8	1,768	74.8	1,355	50.1	159.3	342.4	62	224.1	196.0	577	23.9	43.4
Wyandotte city	43	20.9	1,567	87.7	712	31.4	176.4	443.9	26	33.2	33.2	130	4.5	6.9
Wyoming city	186	44.1	10,097	472.6	7,896	342.7	1,218.7	2,211.6	195	4,013.4	3,522.7	6,893	317.0	620.5
MINNESOTA	8,139	32.4	351,884	14,077.3	233,396	7,598.6	39,610.4	80,623.9	8,884	108,388.8	68,832.7	126,735	6,318.2	11,364.2
Andover city	(NA)	(NA)	(NA)	(NA)	(NA)	(NA)	(NA)	(NA)	22	(D)	(D)	[10]60	(D)	(D)
Apple Valley city	17	29.4	[8]750	(D)	(D)	(D)	(D)	(D)	52	114.8	(D)	129	5.1	10.7
Blaine city	149	26.2	2,992	125.8	1,947	72.0	317.3	529.8	70	490.3	328.5	1,033	49.8	99.0
Bloomington city	156	32.1	7,666	398.2	4,139	138.0	491.3	948.2	363	7,524.4	3,377.2	7,013	400.2	628.0
Brooklyn Center city	44	38.6	1,840	74.3	1,258	41.7	120.8	241.5	46	337.7	248.7	405	16.4	26.2
Brooklyn Park city	121	40.5	5,838	259.8	3,488	125.7	649.1	1,298.9	125	1,026.3	725.9	1,865	84.2	149.3
Burnsville city	117	33.3	3,736	142.3	2,124	57.1	424.3	743.2	198	1,660.3	(D)	2,257	101.7	178.8
Coon Rapids city	60	40.0	3,203	151.7	1,982	73.6	428.8	654.5	44	308.5	179.3	662	28.9	45.3
Cottage Grove city	13	30.8	1,418	71.1	919	40.0	323.0	463.9	14	(D)	(D)	[10]60	(D)	(D)
Duluth city	91	30.8	2,738	112.0	1,822	64.6	279.2	623.2	118	714.7	55.8	1,333	48.3	89.7

See footnotes at end of table.

Table C-4. Cities — **Manufacturing and Wholesale Trade**—Con.

[Includes states and 1,265 incorporated places of 25,000 or more population as of April 1, 2000, in all states except Hawaii, which has no incorporated places recognized by the U.S. Census Bureau. Two census designated places (CDPs) are also included (Honolulu CDP in Hawaii and Arlington CDP in Virginia). For more information on these areas, see Appendix C, Geographic Information]

| City | Manufacturing (NAICS 31–33), 2002[1] | | | | | | | | Wholesale trade (NAICS 42), 2002[4] | | | | | |
| | Establishments[2] | | All employees | | Production workers | | Value added by manufacture (mil. dol.) | Value of shipments (mil. dol.) | Estab-lishments | Sales (mil. dol.) | | Paid employees[5] | Annual payroll (mil. dol.) | Operating expenses (mil. dol.) |
	Total	Percent with 20 or more employees	Number[3]	Annual payroll (mil. dol.)	Number[3]	Wages (mil. dol.)				Total	Merchant wholesalers			
MINNESOTA—Con.														
Eagan city	108	36.1	3,647	143.5	2,521	80.4	403.9	825.6	194	3,775.1	2,978.7	4,524	238.8	402.6
Eden Prairie city	133	45.1	10,242	503.7	5,000	189.3	1,089.1	2,027.1	283	6,488.8	3,012.6	4,387	265.8	508.0
Edina city	80	20.0	2,703	101.1	1,878	56.3	417.9	589.5	255	6,466.7	(D)	2,226	125.6	230.1
Fridley city	127	45.7	7,913	375.7	3,932	138.5	941.3	1,794.4	103	5,067.8	(D)	3,801	501.4	994.1
Inver Grove Heights city	28	39.3	[6]1,750	(D)	(D)	(D)	(D)	(D)	29	67.6	(D)	220	7.1	13.4
Lakeville city	72	33.3	3,113	115.8	2,407	79.1	325.6	557.9	67	457.8	276.1	748	30.2	54.0
Mankato city	53	52.8	2,761	101.0	1,945	60.3	542.8	1,672.3	66	720.9	(D)	1,061	36.9	61.4
Maple Grove city	113	31.0	6,228	305.3	3,385	126.8	588.2	988.0	124	1,858.7	(D)	1,723	69.6	122.8
Maplewood city	30	26.7	573	22.5	379	14.2	51.9	114.9	42	199.9	(D)	296	12.4	24.7
Minneapolis city	581	34.3	19,629	799.8	13,260	453.3	1,772.7	3,336.9	710	9,110.7	4,742.1	12,857	664.1	1,162.7
Minnetonka city	109	34.9	6,561	301.7	3,261	96.6	849.8	1,343.8	258	8,033.6	(D)	3,969	233.8	395.1
Moorhead city	23	26.1	[8]750	(D)	(D)	(D)	(D)	(D)	25	(D)	(D)	[9]175	(D)	(D)
Oakdale city	33	39.4	820	36.3	444	16.8	100.0	237.6	46	830.6	(D)	879	66.7	117.3
Plymouth city	193	50.3	12,249	575.3	6,774	249.6	1,360.9	2,669.7	317	5,329.7	3,092.8	5,833	311.8	542.8
Richfield city	(NA)	(NA)	(NA)	(NA)	(NA)	(NA)	(NA)	(NA)	28	137.7	122.6	356	21.4	31.3
Rochester city	70	48.6	11,227	573.2	4,038	127.2	1,282.1	3,359.2	87	606.1	(D)	941	37.7	63.9
Roseville city	70	38.6	3,065	116.0	1,641	53.1	216.6	413.0	142	1,150.9	607.5	1,877	78.6	127.2
St. Cloud city	79	45.6	7,851	267.2	5,774	176.7	696.9	1,344.1	95	865.1	836.7	2,940	116.2	152.0
St. Louis Park city	88	37.5	3,396	149.6	2,257	78.6	474.9	797.8	190	1,670.2	829.0	1,991	105.7	174.5
St. Paul city	310	34.2	13,588	597.1	9,081	387.9	1,701.3	4,144.8	396	3,831.4	2,596.9	6,203	289.0	506.5
Shoreview city	32	31.3	1,582	68.8	624	21.9	263.2	328.9	47	949.8	(D)	1,260	95.4	158.2
Winona city	75	41.3	3,587	119.8	2,502	68.1	333.1	653.6	45	125.4	(D)	369	11.5	20.4
Woodbury city	28	25.0	1,061	47.2	671	23.4	108.7	283.0	45	155.4	(D)	179	7.5	14.2
MISSISSIPPI	2,796	37.6	182,822	5,476.9	146,003	3,765.6	16,126.6	38,276.1	2,948	19,215.8	14,913.6	35,316	1,170.1	2,218.4
Biloxi city	39	25.6	[8]750	(D)	(D)	(D)	(D)	(D)	52	149.9	(D)	551	13.9	24.3
Clinton city	19	26.3	1,667	58.6	1,408	44.1	54.3	313.1	24	38.0	(D)	[8]80	2.6	4.7
Columbus city	51	43.1	4,964	168.6	3,514	103.8	364.1	920.1	62	(D)	(D)	[8]750	(D)	(D)
Greenville city	39	41.0	2,166	76.6	1,663	50.8	298.5	571.3	52	281.1	(D)	711	17.1	37.6
Gulfport city	66	24.2	1,377	46.2	955	29.6	111.5	202.5	113	417.6	385.1	1,140	37.8	72.1
Hattiesburg city	64	39.1	3,837	112.2	2,870	69.1	436.5	757.2	88	1,033.1	(D)	1,438	40.3	71.0
Jackson city	145	33.1	6,001	198.1	4,603	124.7	503.3	1,050.7	336	2,620.0	1,793.8	5,801	263.5	472.6
Meridian city	54	31.5	2,493	69.4	1,512	44.0	128.0	313.8	74	801.8	(D)	1,692	51.3	94.6
Pascagoula city	31	25.8	[14]17,500	(D)	(D)	(D)	(D)	(D)	37	73.4	(D)	281	8.2	13.9
Southaven city	(NA)	(NA)	(NA)	(NA)	(NA)	(NA)	(NA)	(NA)	33	1,059.1	(D)	1,116	26.6	66.9
Tupelo city	98	41.8	7,139	239.5	5,876	185.8	661.4	1,310.1	145	885.2	567.2	1,667	51.1	92.8
Vicksburg city	35	51.4	[6]1,750	(D)	(D)	(D)	(D)	(D)	38	(D)	(D)	[12]375	(D)	(D)
MISSOURI	7,210	30.4	319,974	12,463.4	239,444	8,095.0	41,528.2	92,909.2	8,491	95,603.6	58,929.7	127,340	4,610.4	8,461.6
Ballwin city	(NA)	(NA)	(NA)	(NA)	(NA)	(NA)	(NA)	(NA)	43	102.5	(D)	133	4.6	9.4
Blue Springs city	38	18.4	826	31.7	558	16.8	33.0	125.8	52	247.0	(D)	324	12.5	27.2
Cape Girardeau city	54	37.0	3,431	122.6	2,808	92.7	1,186.9	1,779.9	99	994.7	973.2	1,412	43.1	80.8
Chesterfield city	38	34.2	1,633	57.1	1,048	29.5	126.2	239.8	187	1,503.1	631.1	1,935	102.9	197.8
Columbia city	63	30.2	3,816	135.3	3,078	95.5	651.0	1,256.1	113	776.6	757.7	2,242	65.9	129.4
Florissant city	(NA)	(NA)	(NA)	(NA)	(NA)	(NA)	(NA)	(NA)	32	25.0	11.9	[10]68	2.2	4.7
Gladstone city	(NA)	(NA)	(NA)	(NA)	(NA)	(NA)	(NA)	(NA)	23	(D)	(D)	[10]60	(D)	(D)
Hazelwood city	33	42.4	6,527	386.1	4,843	275.3	1,314.2	5,104.4	52	2,661.1	(D)	1,538	82.7	152.5
Independence city	110	28.2	3,416	129.9	2,663	91.0	484.0	709.8	99	527.3	(D)	853	28.2	49.7
Jefferson City city	46	37.0	3,206	123.2	2,569	87.1	791.5	1,205.8	62	299.3	(D)	968	31.6	52.4
Joplin city	101	29.7	5,808	190.3	4,616	132.5	603.2	1,244.1	112	(D)	(D)	[6]1,750	(D)	(D)
Kansas City city	498	33.1	21,567	901.2	12,917	424.0	5,083.7	7,276.3	770	21,730.0	9,855.3	30,245	778.5	1,526.8
Kirkwood city	41	29.3	1,232	45.4	868	26.7	102.7	163.8	84	313.1	(D)	511	25.0	41.2
Lee's Summit city	72	34.7	2,726	104.6	1,887	61.5	313.6	534.0	130	1,208.9	(D)	1,860	71.9	118.3
Liberty city	29	34.5	[6]1,750	(D)	(D)	(D)	(D)	(D)	35	(D)	(D)	[12]375	(D)	(D)
Maryland Heights city	118	43.2	4,687	185.6	2,929	95.0	846.3	1,416.8	250	4,821.6	(D)	6,288	287.8	499.5
O'Fallon city	55	50.9	6,346	233.5	4,981	164.1	591.7	1,148.0	73	3,244.3	(D)	782	34.1	85.3
Raytown city	35	20.0	564	20.0	376	10.4	36.8	57.9	51	247.3	(D)	498	22.4	38.8
St. Charles city	75	32.0	[6]1,750	(D)	(D)	(D)	(D)	(D)	88	391.3	281.2	868	36.4	58.7
St. Joseph city	83	53.0	[7]7,500	(D)	(D)	(D)	(D)	(D)	124	1,596.4	1,503.6	1,586	58.6	117.2
St. Louis city	685	38.1	25,531	1,051.9	17,377	593.0	4,870.3	8,399.0	787	10,618.9	8,374.6	14,390	593.0	1,035.4
St. Peters city	49	28.6	1,593	63.9	1,112	38.8	316.5	474.8	66	315.6	237.7	790	28.2	51.7
Springfield city	287	31.0	13,097	444.9	9,066	262.2	1,478.8	3,221.1	433	5,114.0	4,257.6	7,641	250.8	497.1
University City city	(NA)	(NA)	(NA)	(NA)	(NA)	(NA)	(NA)	(NA)	23	119.1	(D)	253	10.3	18.3
Wildwood city	(NA)	(NA)	(NA)	(NA)	(NA)	(NA)	(NA)	(NA)	53	51.8	21.5	117	4.8	8.4
MONTANA	1,234	15.9	18,582	638.8	13,747	421.1	1,674.0	4,987.6	1,485	7,223.4	5,765.5	13,728	430.4	822.5
Billings city	129	14.0	2,254	87.3	1,422	49.7	312.8	1,470.1	291	1,979.1	1,671.7	3,765	132.1	263.3
Bozeman city	73	27.4	997	31.9	680	18.6	79.5	169.3	67	280.7	242.3	842	28.1	56.9
Butte-Silver Bow (balance)	(NA)	(NA)	(NA)	(NA)	(NA)	(NA)	(NA)	(NA)	47	136.3	(D)	429	10.9	18.2
Great Falls city	54	22.2	712	25.0	529	17.0	75.1	245.7	98	874.5	788.8	875	27.6	50.3
Helena city	(NA)	(NA)	(NA)	(NA)	(NA)	(NA)	(NA)	(NA)	42	171.7	(D)	509	27.4	46.6
Missoula city	74	18.9	835	24.6	610	14.6	59.1	132.0	149	546.5	499.7	1,582	48.8	86.9

See footnotes at end of table.

County and City Data Book: 2007

783

U.S. Census Bureau

Table C-4. Cities — **Manufacturing and Wholesale Trade**—Con.

[Includes states and 1,265 incorporated places of 25,000 or more population as of April 1, 2000, in all states except Hawaii, which has no incorporated places recognized by the U.S. Census Bureau. Two census designated places (CDPs) are also included (Honolulu CDP in Hawaii and Arlington CDP in Virginia). For more information on these areas, see Appendix C, Geographic Information]

City	Manufacturing (NAICS 31–33), 2002[1]								Wholesale trade (NAICS 42), 2002[4]					
	Establishments[2]		All employees		Production workers					Sales (mil. dol.)				
	Total	Percent with 20 or more employees	Number[3]	Annual payroll (mil. dol.)	Number[3]	Wages (mil. dol.)	Value added by manufacture (mil. dol.)	Value of shipments (mil. dol.)	Establishments	Total	Merchant wholesalers	Paid employees[5]	Annual payroll (mil. dol.)	Operating expenses (mil. dol.)
NEBRASKA	1,976	30.0	103,029	3,386.5	79,488	2,293.6	11,469.0	30,611.0	2,907	26,155.8	17,979.6	36,805	1,309.9	2,395.9
Bellevue city.	16	37.5	[6]1,750	(D)	(D)	(D)	(D)	(D)	14	16.8	(D)	41	0.9	1.5
Fremont city.	38	42.1	1,318	36.7	915	22.2	100.5	265.3	26	333.5	(D)	350	12.6	19.3
Grand Island city.	67	34.3	[7]7,500	(D)	(D)	(D)	(D)	(D)	81	578.4	494.3	965	36.6	78.2
Kearney city.	(NA)	(NA)	(NA)	(NA)	(NA)	(NA)	(NA)	(NA)	38	364.6	250.5	599	18.3	34.9
Lincoln city.	239	32.2	13,735	495.6	9,745	304.7	1,909.3	3,622.7	264	2,058.9	1,737.1	3,926	140.7	245.3
Omaha city	458	32.1	21,187	740.9	15,773	492.7	2,798.8	6,571.7	838	10,732.3	5,194.8	12,768	558.1	978.6
NEVADA.	1,764	25.3	42,503	1,642.8	28,392	869.2	4,654.7	8,466.2	2,612	16,513.8	11,913.3	31,769	1,278.7	2,240.2
Carson City	163	25.8	3,654	136.8	2,426	72.6	360.7	560.7	110	203.3	180.6	622	22.8	44.0
Henderson city	80	31.3	2,556	92.6	1,767	59.9	545.1	809.3	147	303.8	(D)	728	27.9	49.0
Las Vegas city	225	13.8	3,316	120.6	2,352	75.5	275.6	542.6	449	1,709.5	1,297.6	3,739	146.3	256.8
North Las Vegas city	98	44.9	3,597	124.3	2,668	85.1	445.2	760.8	157	1,540.4	(D)	3,498	144.9	257.9
Reno city.	221	31.2	8,252	371.7	4,746	140.8	834.6	1,773.3	316	2,926.4	(D)	5,150	204.0	372.2
Sparks city	186	26.3	4,229	154.3	2,998	86.8	519.7	958.6	273	2,598.7	2,102.2	4,953	197.6	373.2
NEW HAMPSHIRE.	2,213	32.2	83,545	3,421.1	53,985	1,693.4	8,527.9	15,235.1	2,004	13,741.9	9,968.9	23,539	1,138.7	2,069.6
Concord city.	56	41.1	2,284	88.0	1,519	48.2	198.5	394.5	63	462.9	(D)	1,085	40.6	75.9
Dover city	50	34.0	2,648	114.8	1,462	48.8	212.7	408.7	45	185.5	(D)	305	12.5	23.4
Manchester city.	156	35.3	7,117	274.6	4,737	139.3	672.7	1,267.0	226	2,109.0	1,516.3	3,469	159.0	293.9
Nashua city.	142	36.6	9,905	569.7	3,991	134.3	1,118.0	1,949.6	160	1,425.2	895.5	2,345	129.8	227.4
Rochester city.	38	34.2	1,266	41.1	901	20.9	117.8	219.0	14	131.2	131.2	339	21.3	36.4
NEW JERSEY	10,656	31.1	369,811	15,877.2	236,375	8,057.3	51,602.3	96,599.8	16,803	256,925.5	166,131.6	273,837	14,428.8	29,741.2
Atlantic City city	(NA)	(NA)	(NA)	(NA)	(NA)	(NA)	(NA)	(NA)	15	(D)	(D)	[9]175	(D)	(D)
Bayonne city	50	24.0	3,089	80.5	1,709	42.6	196.3	489.9	56	1,062.3	(D)	1,648	75.7	173.2
Bergenfield borough	(NA)	(NA)	(NA)	(NA)	(NA)	(NA)	(NA)	(NA)	36	(D)	(D)	[9]175	(D)	(D)
Camden city.	81	24.7	2,464	129.4	1,243	45.9	414.2	665.0	86	566.4	(D)	1,160	45.1	85.4
Clifton city	179	43.6	6,340	276.8	4,140	133.6	726.0	1,255.2	203	1,555.6	1,169.0	3,350	158.5	271.2
East Orange city	(NA)	(NA)	(NA)	(NA)	(NA)	(NA)	(NA)	(NA)	17	(D)	(D)	[9]175	(D)	(D)
Elizabeth city	100	34.0	4,587	137.7	3,298	82.2	598.5	986.8	146	(D)	(D)	[11]3,750	(D)	(D)
Englewood city	77	39.0	1,751	72.3	1,127	36.9	172.7	380.5	154	1,221.1	(D)	1,787	103.2	207.2
Fair Lawn borough	46	41.3	2,785	110.7	1,949	65.4	553.6	793.0	79	983.9	863.2	806	38.1	110.7
Fort Lee borough	(NA)	(NA)	(NA)	(NA)	(NA)	(NA)	(NA)	(NA)	212	3,979.0	(D)	1,248	83.1	341.4
Garfield city	77	16.9	1,106	33.2	879	21.2	80.0	152.1	58	(D)	(D)	[8]750	(D)	(D)
Hackensack city	121	19.0	2,181	84.1	1,442	41.3	193.9	424.3	257	3,514.3	1,654.8	3,049	138.4	259.0
Hoboken city	38	36.8	952	31.6	705	19.3	62.4	134.4	52	366.0	(D)	306	13.9	27.5
Jersey City city	139	31.7	3,648	144.6	2,627	89.4	613.6	1,175.0	254	2,606.3	2,482.9	4,574	177.6	340.7
Kearny town.	66	30.3	1,741	59.4	1,238	33.8	228.9	389.9	80	547.7	(D)	1,341	62.4	103.9
Linden city	152	31.6	6,983	325.0	5,208	225.2	1,366.7	5,761.2	124	3,686.3	(D)	2,515	105.6	174.8
Long Branch city	(NA)	(NA)	(NA)	(NA)	(NA)	(NA)	(NA)	(NA)	36	113.2	89.4	271	9.8	14.3
Millville city.	49	44.9	3,581	134.0	2,903	101.2	362.7	675.7	25	218.7	(D)	478	17.6	31.0
Newark city	391	32.7	11,796	447.6	8,375	256.7	1,561.9	2,953.1	402	2,859.6	1,785.4	5,235	240.8	490.8
New Brunswick city	70	28.6	2,239	96.0	1,502	53.5	204.2	436.9	71	629.5	(D)	962	40.2	73.0
Paramus borough	30	30.0	820	29.8	453	10.9	79.2	149.6	147	2,226.3	1,555.0	2,642	188.5	337.6
Passaic city	140	27.9	3,460	92.9	2,636	54.0	235.1	416.8	90	313.8	(D)	806	28.1	51.9
Paterson city	326	28.8	7,100	272.4	5,031	149.1	658.3	1,321.4	200	676.0	(D)	1,922	69.3	121.3
Perth Amboy city	48	35.4	2,017	81.4	1,366	49.4	230.8	661.0	62	410.0	(D)	768	35.6	61.1
Plainfield city	32	34.4	936	29.2	610	16.7	69.3	117.4	23	(D)	(D)	[9]175	(D)	(D)
Rahway city	48	33.3	[11]3,750	(D)	(D)	(D)	(D)	(D)	56	694.6	(D)	859	45.0	98.3
Sayreville borough.	32	28.1	1,451	67.0	1,080	42.0	271.2	432.7	51	217.2	(D)	571	25.6	50.6
Trenton city	75	30.7	2,009	83.2	1,328	45.3	224.2	374.4	75	556.3	406.9	1,542	58.4	106.6
Union City city	102	12.7	1,110	33.9	885	22.2	63.5	142.1	135	1,126.3	(D)	2,544	113.9	212.3
Vineland city.	109	45.0	5,221	174.0	3,976	115.4	732.5	1,183.1	91	589.9	(D)	1,088	42.2	64.5
Westfield town	(NA)	(NA)	(NA)	(NA)	(NA)	(NA)	(NA)	(NA)	28	58.9	37.4	101	5.9	8.9
West New York town	106	9.4	829	19.0	678	13.3	43.9	82.0	64	176.8	(D)	473	19.4	34.8
NEW MEXICO.	1,587	17.8	33,085	1,241.4	23,800	757.1	5,990.6	10,168.1	2,046	8,993.7	6,735.5	19,865	708.1	1,321.2
Alamogordo city	(NA)	(NA)	(NA)	(NA)	(NA)	(NA)	(NA)	(NA)	15	24.7	(D)	90	2.0	3.9
Albuquerque city	562	21.4	14,710	559.5	10,525	344.8	1,507.2	2,818.4	866	4,844.1	3,882.5	10,454	391.3	722.9
Carlsbad city	18	16.7	[8]750	(D)	(D)	(D)	(D)	(D)	24	34.7	34.7	137	4.3	6.1
Clovis city	(NA)	(NA)	(NA)	(NA)	(NA)	(NA)	(NA)	(NA)	42	(D)	(D)	[12]375	(D)	(D)
Farmington city	50	14.0	[8]750	(D)	(D)	(D)	(D)	(D)	119	411.2	320.5	1,025	39.9	64.8
Hobbs city	(NA)	(NA)	(NA)	(NA)	(NA)	(NA)	(NA)	(NA)	75	265.8	242.3	491	14.8	29.4
Las Cruces city	68	22.1	1,290	29.8	1,052	20.0	145.6	337.9	86	203.2	(D)	755	19.5	35.0
Rio Rancho city	34	38.2	[11]3,750	(D)	(D)	(D)	(D)	(D)	24	44.9	(D)	145	6.7	12.9
Roswell city	40	22.5	1,108	42.1	722	20.3	77.5	241.9	49	156.4	136.6	394	9.9	19.9
Santa Fe city	138	8.0	1,028	29.7	722	16.4	56.9	102.2	134	424.0	313.3	1,033	36.3	75.1

See footnotes at end of table.

Table C-4. Cities — **Manufacturing and Wholesale Trade**—Con.

[Includes states and 1,265 incorporated places of 25,000 or more population as of April 1, 2000, in all states except Hawaii, which has no incorporated places recognized by the U.S. Census Bureau. Two census designated places (CDPs) are also included (Honolulu CDP in Hawaii and Arlington CDP in Virginia). For more information on these areas, see Appendix C, Geographic Information]

| City | Manufacturing (NAICS 31–33), 2002[1] | | | | | | | | Wholesale trade (NAICS 42), 2002[4] | | | | | |
| | Establishments[2] | | All employees | | Production workers | | Value added by manu- facture (mil. dol.) | Value of ship- ments (mil. dol.) | Estab- lishments | Sales (mil. dol.) | | Paid employ- ees[5] | Annual payroll (mil. dol.) | Operating expenses (mil. dol.) |
	Total	Percent with 20 or more employ- ees	Number[3]	Annual payroll (mil. dol.)	Number[3]	Wages (mil. dol.)				Total	Merchant whole- salers			
NEW YORK	21,066	25.8	641,434	25,373.8	428,589	13,556.0	83,874.6	147,317.5	35,845	343,663.0	223,576.1	413,226	19,771.9	41,083.4
Albany city	79	34.2	2,310	83.4	1,641	50.9	303.1	560.3	156	1,538.3	695.9	2,415	127.1	213.7
Auburn city	59	39.0	2,599	101.5	1,845	63.6	215.6	575.8	31	84.9	62.6	250	9.9	16.6
Binghamton city	77	42.9	3,886	137.3	2,409	69.9	440.3	831.2	68	282.6	214.8	805	25.5	49.5
Buffalo city	405	37.0	17,158	712.6	12,152	462.4	2,439.9	4,375.0	377	3,757.6	2,081.8	6,138	251.5	449.8
Elmira city	27	44.4	1,828	66.6	1,151	35.6	163.6	274.4	40	117.1	(D)	445	14.8	22.1
Freeport village.	112	28.6	3,484	108.9	2,455	59.2	208.7	395.3	106	401.1	273.8	888	32.7	60.6
Glen Cove city	38	18.4	[6]1,750	(D)	(D)	(D)	(D)	(D)	57	244.5	147.5	446	20.0	32.5
Hempstead village.	(NA)	(NA)	(NA)	(NA)	(NA)	(NA)	(NA)	(NA)	42	181.7	(D)	374	16.8	27.5
Ithaca city	32	25.0	1,101	39.5	796	23.1	178.5	322.6	22	41.5	(D)	129	4.1	8.7
Jamestown city	71	35.2	2,523	87.6	1,909	61.2	170.3	300.8	45	102.8	78.9	363	9.9	19.8
Lindenhurst village.	65	10.8	621	21.5	434	11.9	42.8	71.7	42	184.1	184.1	370	15.4	26.9
Long Beach city	(NA)	(NA)	(NA)	(NA)	(NA)	(NA)	(NA)	(NA)	26	34.2	(D)	52	2.3	4.1
Middletown city	42	31.0	1,284	46.1	928	28.5	109.9	216.9	29	(D)	(D)	[8]750	(D)	(D)
Mount Vernon city	126	34.1	3,859	146.4	2,522	73.5	352.1	680.7	108	(D)	(D)	[6]1,750	(D)	(D)
Newburgh city.	41	31.7	784	21.4	573	11.4	57.6	101.0	68	1,326.6	(D)	1,419	55.2	109.4
New Rochelle city	65	23.1	1,251	43.4	921	25.6	112.4	189.2	122	909.0	876.3	1,262	74.0	151.8
New York city	8,228	20.1	143,211	4,639.4	101,371	2,577.4	13,358.2	25,043.2	17,870	173,539.7	118,232.0	186,600	9,737.8	21,325.6
Niagara Falls city	57	36.8	2,457	124.0	1,590	79.4	376.2	667.8	40	201.8	(D)	480	14.8	33.8
North Tonawanda city.	57	36.8	1,688	63.6	1,213	40.0	154.4	291.9	44	(D)	(D)	[8]750	(D)	(D)
Port Chester village	33	33.3	899	30.1	727	20.5	76.3	125.1	62	320.7	(D)	761	38.5	66.5
Poughkeepsie city	45	40.0	[7]7,500	(D)	(D)	(D)	(D)	(D)	34	146.9	146.9	472	22.4	41.8
Rochester city.	479	31.1	36,282	1,869.9	21,076	884.1	6,562.0	10,889.7	368	4,884.3	1,443.4	6,853	300.6	904.7
Rome city	47	29.8	2,035	75.5	1,458	46.5	194.6	467.7	21	19.1	(D)	134	2.6	3.7
Saratoga Springs city	26	42.3	1,708	64.0	1,379	48.6	241.0	439.9	38	160.5	86.2	229	9.2	15.5
Schenectady city	56	26.8	[11]3,750	(D)	(D)	(D)	(D)	(D)	52	162.4	(D)	593	17.6	30.1
Spring Valley village.	(NA)	(NA)	(NA)	(NA)	(NA)	(NA)	(NA)	(NA)	42	(D)	(D)	[8]750	(D)	(D)
Syracuse city	161	32.3	6,659	265.0	4,231	134.1	806.0	1,469.9	244	1,561.9	1,017.1	3,737	145.7	246.9
Troy city	36	36.1	819	27.0	521	14.5	58.7	127.6	45	326.7	(D)	556	17.5	31.3
Utica city	95	32.6	4,106	134.8	2,880	73.9	388.3	734.3	76	489.9	(D)	1,377	48.6	83.8
Valley Stream village	(NA)	(NA)	(NA)	(NA)	(NA)	(NA)	(NA)	(NA)	99	483.7	370.2	761	37.7	68.3
Watertown city	31	25.8	1,061	42.5	605	20.2	94.5	193.5	40	(D)	(D)	[12]375	(D)	(D)
White Plains city	(NA)	(NA)	(NA)	(NA)	(NA)	(NA)	(NA)	(NA)	159	3,208.2	2,199.7	2,973	201.0	467.4
Yonkers city	125	23.2	3,536	140.0	2,623	82.1	442.1	1,187.8	201	894.9	(D)	1,896	89.4	166.7
NORTH CAROLINA	10,762	36.9	623,333	20,647.6	472,229	13,046.9	87,355.2	156,821.9	11,913	104,331.2	56,350.4	162,230	7,246.0	13,064.9
Asheville city	129	31.8	4,947	172.5	3,507	100.0	531.5	947.8	174	1,197.7	(D)	1,801	64.7	121.1
Burlington city.	99	54.5	7,533	212.5	5,848	135.1	504.8	1,233.3	69	(D)	(D)	[8]750	(D)	(D)
Cary town	82	20.7	2,626	96.3	1,760	48.5	315.4	491.7	160	3,402.4	1,051.6	2,341	152.3	309.3
Chapel Hill town	(NA)	(NA)	(NA)	(NA)	(NA)	(NA)	(NA)	(NA)	33	(D)	(D)	[9]175	(D)	(D)
Charlotte city	756	32.3	31,432	1,194.1	19,813	635.1	3,432.5	6,847.6	2,067	24,165.6	10,043.1	34,805	1,642.3	2,851.9
Concord city	80	31.3	[7]7,500	(D)	(D)	(D)	(D)	(D)	91	478.8	(D)	1,112	46.4	75.1
Durham city	143	27.3	[7]7,500	(D)	(D)	(D)	(D)	(D)	180	(D)	(D)	[6]1,750	(D)	(D)
Fayetteville city	62	33.9	7,296	282.0	5,394	184.5	724.6	1,565.2	128	(D)	383.3	[6]1,750	(D)	(D)
Gastonia city	168	32.7	8,762	267.4	6,752	192.0	903.3	1,712.2	107	577.6	287.1	763	27.5	56.4
Goldsboro city	55	38.2	3,263	105.9	2,462	71.4	229.2	485.6	84	828.9	(D)	1,926	65.5	109.1
Greensboro city	364	40.7	20,348	817.8	14,431	491.9	3,154.5	5,663.4	751	8,234.6	4,179.8	13,648	631.5	1,167.4
Greenville city.	44	31.8	3,005	146.0	1,769	61.1	284.8	484.2	85	259.4	239.5	872	29.0	48.7
Hickory city	232	41.4	13,163	373.5	10,710	255.7	887.8	1,826.0	169	3,266.3	2,083.1	3,786	151.6	358.4
High Point city	282	51.4	15,483	486.5	11,716	307.4	1,079.3	2,613.1	376	2,940.6	(D)	3,247	144.6	349.8
Huntersville town.	25	20.0	609	26.0	356	10.9	95.1	141.9	46	(D)	(D)	[6]1,750	(D)	(D)
Jacksonville city	(NA)	(NA)	(NA)	(NA)	(NA)	(NA)	(NA)	(NA)	24	(D)	(D)	[10]60	(D)	(D)
Kannapolis city	21	14.3	[11]3,750	(D)	(D)	(D)	(D)	(D)	24	(D)	(D)	[9]175	(D)	(D)
Monroe city	84	48.8	7,728	258.5	6,104	174.7	636.1	1,561.4	79	672.4	291.1	1,309	50.1	97.7
Raleigh city	321	22.4	7,437	296.5	4,841	153.7	1,473.2	2,624.0	717	5,406.0	3,016.3	11,802	521.4	829.2
Rocky Mount city.	57	45.6	6,246	216.1	4,561	149.4	1,164.1	1,726.7	92	(D)	(D)	[6]1,750	(D)	(D)
Salisbury city	65	53.8	3,063	102.6	2,315	66.5	209.5	557.1	60	540.9	170.6	868	30.0	52.6
Wilmington city	133	17.3	5,078	257.9	3,526	170.5	759.0	1,250.5	198	786.5	454.4	1,599	55.6	96.9
Wilson city	66	50.0	7,936	295.4	6,103	197.2	4,599.8	5,618.5	86	836.2	(D)	1,371	51.0	99.8
Winston-Salem city	233	38.2	[14]17,500	(D)	(D)	(D)	(D)	(D)	303	3,712.1	2,979.5	4,837	182.8	378.0
NORTH DAKOTA	724	26.8	23,370	757.0	17,017	473.5	2,679.6	6,856.7	1,485	8,806.3	7,455.0	15,958	523.2	953.1
Bismarck city	59	15.3	[6]1,750	(D)	(D)	(D)	(D)	(D)	132	618.5	526.2	1,557	54.6	94.0
Fargo city	132	38.6	5,722	174.6	4,052	98.2	469.8	1,093.8	267	2,333.3	1,905.9	4,400	171.1	290.0
Grand Forks city	47	27.7	1,590	40.4	1,332	29.4	147.6	223.3	77	(D)	364.7	[6]1,750	(D)	(D)
Minot city	(NA)	(NA)	(NA)	(NA)	(NA)	(NA)	(NA)	(NA)	64	(D)	(D)	[8]750	(D)	(D)

See footnotes at end of table.

Table C-4. Cities — **Manufacturing and Wholesale Trade**—Con.

[Includes states and 1,265 incorporated places of 25,000 or more population as of April 1, 2000, in all states except Hawaii, which has no incorporated places recognized by the U.S. Census Bureau. Two census designated places (CDPs) are also included (Honolulu CDP in Hawaii and Arlington CDP in Virginia). For more information on these areas, see Appendix C, Geographic Information]

| City | Manufacturing (NAICS 31–33), 2002[1] | | | | | | | | Wholesale trade (NAICS 42), 2002[4] | | | | |
| | Establishments[2] | | All employees | | Production workers | | | | | Sales (mil. dol.) | | | | |
	Total	Percent with 20 or more employ- ees	Number[3]	Annual payroll (mil. dol.)	Number[3]	Wages (mil. dol.)	Value added by manu- facture (mil. dol.)	Value of ship- ments (mil. dol.)	Estab- lishments	Total	Merchant whole- salers	Paid employ- ees[5]	Annual payroll (mil. dol.)	Operating expenses (mil. dol.)
OHIO	17,494	35.8	868,732	35,301.1	639,821	23,198.1	113,243.4	243,903.9	16,000	166,446.5	90,017.4	234,663	9,635.4	17,416.1
Akron city	352	29.5	11,103	459.6	6,685	231.3	1,329.8	2,304.2	297	2,167.5	1,314.1	4,069	160.0	282.9
Barberton city	74	33.8	3,550	122.2	2,654	74.8	236.5	510.0	33	177.7	(D)	328	13.8	23.5
Beavercreek city	23	26.1	731	21.0	473	12.6	42.5	89.5	35	80.9	(D)	241	13.8	22.7
Bowling Green city	48	50.0	3,055	110.2	2,195	68.8	308.0	584.2	25	47.2	47.2	256	7.2	11.7
Brunswick city	36	52.8	798	32.0	562	20.3	72.8	136.1	57	224.5	198.5	565	23.0	37.0
Canton city	168	32.7	13,210	558.1	10,489	415.4	1,482.5	2,783.3	135	1,216.7	(D)	2,007	66.9	135.0
Cincinnati city	523	33.7	20,014	796.5	13,784	465.2	2,061.6	4,109.4	583	9,356.5	4,767.2	12,355	593.0	967.8
Cleveland city	1,104	30.2	29,898	1,191.3	20,174	661.0	2,950.1	5,582.9	786	5,640.7	3,920.7	12,884	547.2	1,041.8
Cleveland Heights city . . .	(NA)	(NA)	(NA)	(NA)	(NA)	(NA)	(NA)	(NA)	17	36.9	(D)	35	1.5	2.7
Columbus city	675	35.9	32,468	1,295.1	21,041	742.2	5,606.8	10,865.9	1,071	15,680.0	10,123.4	22,921	1,095.5	2,080.9
Cuyahoga Falls city	77	39.0	2,917	101.5	2,440	76.9	386.6	630.1	62	171.0	(D)	565	21.9	33.2
Dayton city	344	36.6	15,000	578.9	11,284	399.3	1,901.7	3,195.5	254	5,453.5	1,245.4	5,159	224.9	511.8
Delaware city	37	48.6	2,461	109.2	1,283	41.0	227.5	655.0	27	53.3	(D)	189	6.6	11.3
Dublin city	29	41.4	1,970	88.6	1,050	32.3	170.2	234.8	107	1,398.2	366.2	2,592	157.3	249.6
East Cleveland city	10	30.0	618	24.2	484	18.7	114.0	128.5	8	16.8	(D)	68	2.0	4.9
Elyria city	126	38.9	8,277	308.0	6,159	193.3	965.3	1,753.4	66	383.3	(D)	646	24.7	56.5
Euclid city	94	40.4	5,215	257.5	3,047	122.3	819.7	1,213.6	60	277.0	(D)	739	31.4	56.9
Fairborn city	10	50.0	[8]750	(D)	(D)	(D)	(D)	(D)	10	(D)	(D)	[9]175	(D)	(D)
Fairfield city	84	39.3	2,780	101.8	2,076	65.2	305.1	546.9	103	1,571.4	1,352.4	1,590	67.1	115.8
Findlay city	60	48.3	6,862	262.2	4,697	153.3	613.8	1,367.7	52	354.7	334.6	640	24.0	50.9
Gahanna city	27	29.6	729	26.7	450	13.7	83.1	153.8	49	411.8	277.4	645	23.4	46.6
Garfield Heights city	43	44.2	1,560	56.8	1,186	36.2	133.0	233.2	46	208.0	(D)	598	22.9	37.6
Grove City city	32	43.8	1,483	65.5	1,129	44.1	169.2	305.9	40	2,508.4	(D)	1,626	44.4	88.6
Hamilton city	84	34.5	[6]1,750	119.9	2,155	72.3	399.6	749.8	45	335.3	(D)	805	32.6	64.3
Huber Heights city	35	42.9	(D)	(D)	(D)	(D)	(D)	(D)	23	172.5	(D)	469	19.2	29.2
Kent city	67	37.3	1,936	63.4	1,477	41.6	101.7	290.2	19	(D)	(D)	[9]175	(D)	(D)
Kettering city	49	28.6	[11]3,750	(D)	(D)	(D)	(D)	(D)	47	204.1	122.4	351	15.6	26.2
Lakewood city	33	24.2	749	34.8	482	18.1	64.4	104.2	52	304.1	(D)	639	24.5	59.5
Lancaster city	59	35.6	3,680	125.4	2,895	86.7	293.7	549.2	41	(D)	(D)	[12]375	(D)	(D)
Lima city	40	32.5	[7]7,500	(D)	(D)	(D)	(D)	(D)	65	(D)	(D)	[8]750	(D)	(D)
Lorain city	53	34.0	5,977	318.9	4,787	270.8	1,162.5	3,707.0	49	207.3	(D)	802	23.7	40.4
Mansfield city	117	47.0	6,940	259.6	5,347	183.7	733.7	1,483.1	91	537.5	427.2	1,308	47.1	81.1
Maple Heights city	(NA)	(NA)	(NA)	(NA)	(NA)	(NA)	(NA)	(NA)	29	196.8	111.4	565	20.8	32.5
Marion city	44	45.5	2,483	81.7	1,879	54.3	365.9	1,073.1	23	138.4	130.2	299	10.7	30.1
Massillon city	70	50.0	4,829	164.8	3,581	109.4	698.1	1,438.0	30	183.8	(D)	533	18.9	31.2
Medina city	78	42.3	3,681	143.2	2,805	95.6	287.9	818.8	54	293.7	232.7	698	25.4	42.2
Mentor city	246	32.1	7,969	308.1	5,327	160.2	784.0	1,415.9	114	393.4	(D)	1,378	56.5	93.9
Middletown city	69	43.5	6,314	331.2	5,049	254.8	487.2	2,278.7	49	1,587.4	(D)	1,506	79.9	140.8
Newark city	47	25.5	2,070	60.0	1,721	42.2	286.7	508.3	32	114.8	(D)	327	13.0	23.1
North Olmsted city	(NA)	(NA)	(NA)	(NA)	(NA)	(NA)	(NA)	(NA)	43	121.9	75.0	156	6.8	10.7
North Royalton city	83	18.1	1,032	35.6	791	22.9	63.5	114.0	72	182.1	154.2	479	18.2	32.2
Parma city	50	24.0	4,107	262.2	3,555	226.8	477.9	868.6	77	393.1	212.8	858	39.7	67.3
Reynoldsburg city	(NA)	(NA)	(NA)	(NA)	(NA)	(NA)	(NA)	(NA)	21	88.3	(D)	88	3.8	5.7
Sandusky city	57	47.4	2,580	111.3	1,670	59.7	233.4	470.8	33	77.8	(D)	269	9.4	14.7
Shaker Heights city	(NA)	(NA)	(NA)	(NA)	(NA)	(NA)	(NA)	(NA)	23	45.0	8.9	54	2.3	4.0
Springfield city	100	43.0	4,019	144.3	2,959	90.4	446.2	771.0	54	1,112.4	(D)	1,175	41.1	67.3
Stow city	52	32.7	1,777	76.1	1,204	43.1	135.2	230.7	49	255.3	244.5	630	29.6	55.0
Strongsville city	89	36.0	3,190	137.3	1,983	69.3	271.1	610.7	85	704.1	564.9	1,837	88.5	126.8
Toledo city	421	33.3	22,933	1,255.6	19,129	1,027.5	2,613.6	9,038.9	407	4,154.2	3,408.8	5,915	227.5	408.1
Trotwood city	(NA)	(NA)	(NA)	(NA)	(NA)	(NA)	(NA)	(NA)	9	13.3	13.3	80	2.3	3.6
Upper Arlington city	(NA)	(NA)	(NA)	(NA)	(NA)	(NA)	(NA)	(NA)	41	105.0	25.7	118	6.1	10.2
Warren city	65	43.1	10,892	519.2	7,873	333.2	937.4	2,650.9	54	786.4	(D)	563	17.1	33.3
Westerville city	42	28.6	1,341	52.5	960	31.7	136.2	236.4	76	1,316.0	931.8	707	32.6	50.3
Westlake city	61	31.1	1,871	64.5	1,332	41.0	200.4	380.0	152	1,460.3	721.7	2,676	117.3	218.1
Youngstown city	128	25.8	3,061	113.5	2,293	75.0	285.2	643.4	131	860.3	(D)	2,244	73.6	120.5
Zanesville city	46	28.3	[6]1,750	(D)	(D)	(D)	(D)	(D)	34	410.6	360.5	802	26.5	52.8
OKLAHOMA	4,027	26.7	149,983	5,355.9	109,230	3,438.2	17,005.4	39,924.1	4,770	30,799.8	23,008.7	54,701	1,886.8	3,383.8
Bartlesville city	30	10.0	1,030	40.2	579	11.5	28.1	117.1	26	(D)	(D)	[10]60	(D)	(D)
Broken Arrow city	132	29.5	4,360	165.3	2,757	82.8	433.5	735.2	131	390.0	334.5	1,057	39.8	70.0
Edmond city	(NA)	(NA)	(NA)	(NA)	(NA)	(NA)	(NA)	(NA)	112	176.2	(D)	467	14.7	28.2
Enid city	50	26.0	951	27.2	709	18.0	76.3	201.6	75	421.3	(D)	725	21.5	39.8
Lawton city	45	22.2	[11]3,750	(D)	(D)	(D)	(D)	(D)	58	149.5	(D)	486	11.8	23.1
Midwest City city	20	15.0	651	23.4	362	11.2	49.5	95.4	24	(D)	(D)	[9]175	(D)	(D)
Moore city	(NA)	(NA)	(NA)	(NA)	(NA)	(NA)	(NA)	(NA)	38	123.7	(D)	486	13.0	23.6
Muskogee city	54	44.4	4,167	161.8	3,419	123.0	554.6	1,038.1	63	290.7	(D)	1,029	27.3	50.3
Norman city	81	21.0	2,665	101.7	1,600	54.5	386.5	727.0	87	400.1	327.9	972	36.4	66.1
Oklahoma City city	715	28.0	29,851	1,176.1	20,797	752.6	4,549.4	10,065.2	1,227	11,936.6	8,737.6	18,454	653.1	1,189.7
Ponca City city	41	31.7	[6]1,750	(D)	(D)	(D)	(D)	(D)	27	90.2	(D)	243	7.6	13.4
Shawnee city	42	35.7	3,030	105.5	2,306	70.2	245.9	528.8	24	69.3	69.3	218	5.4	9.3
Stillwater city	30	30.0	2,039	65.6	1,533	49.5	258.5	933.4	33	189.3	189.3	633	16.6	20.8
Tulsa city	818	30.1	26,495	963.0	16,653	528.3	2,343.2	5,208.2	1,079	8,783.4	6,179.8	14,641	615.4	1,056.9

See footnotes at end of table.

County and City Data Book: 2007

U.S. Census Bureau

Table C-4. Cities — **Manufacturing and Wholesale Trade**—Con.

[Includes states and 1,265 incorporated places of 25,000 or more population as of April 1, 2000, in all states except Hawaii, which has no incorporated places recognized by the U.S. Census Bureau. Two census designated places (CDPs) are also included (Honolulu CDP in Hawaii and Arlington CDP in Virginia). For more information on these areas, see Appendix C, Geographic Information]

City	Manufacturing (NAICS 31–33), 2002[1]								Wholesale trade (NAICS 42), 2002[4]					
	Establishments[2]		All employees		Production workers		Value added by manu-facture (mil. dol.)	Value of ship-ments (mil. dol.)	Estab-lishments	Sales (mil. dol.)		Paid employ-ees[5]	Annual payroll (mil. dol.)	Operating expenses (mil. dol.)
	Total	Percent with 20 or more employees	Number[3]	Annual payroll (mil. dol.)	Number[3]	Wages (mil. dol.)				Total	Merchant whole-salers			
OREGON	5,597	27.1	184,151	7,173.2	130,491	4,275.6	26,440.7	45,864.6	5,770	56,856.0	40,105.6	74,594	3,078.8	5,822.7
Albany city	65	29.2	2,216	77.0	1,771	56.8	157.9	338.9	55	(D)	(D)	[8]750	(D)	(D)
Beaverton city	110	33.6	7,817	412.0	3,702	132.7	1,144.4	1,751.1	282	5,936.0	2,870.4	5,619	283.1	548.0
Bend city	136	24.3	3,420	110.6	2,626	69.1	265.2	490.8	127	554.9	505.5	938	39.1	73.6
Corvallis city	53	17.0	5,001	294.9	2,191	175.9	177.6	339.7	28	32.3	(D)	216	6.1	10.2
Eugene city	313	25.9	8,633	314.9	5,779	164.9	1,246.6	1,990.2	322	1,434.0	1,166.4	3,195	125.0	224.4
Grants Pass city	71	23.9	1,872	54.4	1,518	38.9	128.3	267.3	33	(D)	(D)	[12]375	(D)	(D)
Gresham city	75	36.0	4,822	255.4	3,470	180.7	837.3	1,077.7	73	500.7	467.4	1,101	40.1	70.7
Hillsboro city	163	31.3	6,776	296.1	3,938	122.8	779.4	1,389.5	142	1,396.8	666.7	2,941	189.6	358.3
Keizer city	(NA)	(NA)	(NA)	(NA)	(NA)	(NA)	(NA)	(NA)	16	41.1	41.1	66	2.0	3.4
Lake Oswego city	46	28.3	1,132	55.8	669	19.9	121.7	207.6	150	1,203.4	(D)	1,436	97.1	164.9
McMinnville city	61	27.9	1,595	56.6	1,115	35.1	150.6	383.6	29	133.8	99.1	256	9.5	16.6
Medford city	73	20.5	1,476	50.6	1,174	38.0	131.5	269.2	135	582.1	566.2	1,363	45.5	87.2
Oregon City city	43	20.9	891	37.1	627	22.5	65.8	176.5	27	83.7	83.7	287	11.2	15.5
Portland city	1,099	25.5	30,642	1,111.9	21,760	698.4	3,109.0	6,469.2	1,543	24,168.3	18,704.6	23,700	994.0	1,819.2
Salem city	198	31.8	6,362	216.7	4,804	129.5	593.7	1,156.0	182	948.4	786.9	1,735	63.2	135.5
Springfield city	87	29.9	2,619	111.5	1,977	77.1	417.3	845.5	56	436.1	(D)	952	38.7	65.1
Tigard city	107	28.0	2,699	121.1	1,746	61.6	319.0	539.1	235	2,915.4	1,762.2	2,771	133.7	248.2
PENNSYLVANIA	16,665	34.0	715,453	27,520.0	507,352	16,357.5	92,319.2	181,462.4	15,991	183,741.9	92,034.9	233,934	10,092.1	18,023.6
Allentown city	205	22.4	5,748	272.5	3,526	130.7	350.5	669.1	179	1,956.2	(D)	3,241	155.9	281.7
Altoona city	60	30.0	1,410	40.5	1,127	27.7	149.7	283.5	62	434.1	(D)	966	29.3	54.9
Bethel Park borough	(NA)	(NA)	(NA)	(NA)	(NA)	(NA)	(NA)	(NA)	43	137.1	92.4	289	12.5	21.2
Bethlehem city	76	46.1	5,047	219.3	3,141	109.5	659.7	968.4	72	245.9	154.4	740	29.8	46.8
Chester city	27	48.1	1,705	96.4	1,309	71.5	448.6	880.1	25	79.3	79.3	204	7.8	12.7
Easton city	30	33.3	1,307	52.8	1,022	37.3	110.0	177.8	37	245.2	141.0	743	28.6	54.8
Erie city	193	39.4	7,362	276.1	5,100	167.6	720.8	1,371.0	127	508.0	(D)	1,731	58.8	107.4
Harrisburg city	41	31.7	1,350	47.1	905	27.2	141.5	315.4	74	1,181.2	1,109.3	2,780	99.2	187.2
Lancaster city	99	37.4	7,325	268.5	5,762	188.4	826.2	1,597.4	79	373.0	352.2	956	34.5	62.4
Municipality of Monroeville borough	24	29.2	727	27.0	446	11.7	48.6	75.6	59	761.1	(D)	656	30.9	49.4
New Castle city	78	28.2	1,635	62.0	1,256	41.2	186.0	373.4	48	112.3	(D)	443	12.7	21.1
Norristown borough	38	34.2	[8]750	(D)	(D)	(D)	(D)	(D)	55	(D)	(D)	[8]750	(D)	(D)
Philadelphia city	1,142	28.6	42,922	1,619.4	29,430	904.1	4,738.5	11,639.9	1,296	12,643.5	8,746.4	21,381	969.1	1,791.9
Pittsburgh city	418	28.0	13,416	541.0	8,518	304.7	2,220.9	3,455.3	526	8,341.9	3,896.9	9,825	441.6	747.5
Plum borough	30	26.7	695	23.6	471	11.8	50.7	92.2	46	249.7	91.8	526	24.1	40.4
Reading city	128	43.8	9,852	430.2	7,057	255.6	1,263.7	2,455.7	88	591.4	(D)	1,531	67.7	118.8
Scranton city	112	40.2	3,714	115.0	2,738	73.0	366.9	676.8	106	626.3	564.6	1,869	63.9	123.8
State College borough	(NA)	(NA)	(NA)	(NA)	(NA)	(NA)	(NA)	(NA)	14	12.4	12.4	37	1.5	2.4
Wilkes-Barre city	45	33.3	1,686	59.9	1,278	40.5	132.5	284.2	63	499.1	(D)	1,021	36.3	65.3
Williamsport city	65	46.2	5,499	191.0	4,249	123.7	545.5	1,244.7	46	243.7	(D)	1,506	37.6	64.8
York city	116	38.8	5,648	235.8	3,544	118.0	724.8	1,232.0	93	926.5	(D)	1,121	43.3	88.8
RHODE ISLAND	2,131	27.5	62,285	2,294.6	42,829	1,231.7	6,148.6	10,818.1	1,479	8,566.4	5,827.0	17,688	699.5	1,335.8
Cranston city	210	27.6	6,173	232.2	3,755	100.7	720.4	1,229.4	154	790.3	771.4	2,016	77.7	149.8
East Providence city	124	35.5	3,504	129.7	2,272	64.0	293.3	517.5	115	1,316.6	605.1	1,724	78.2	141.0
Newport city	(NA)	(NA)	(NA)	(NA)	(NA)	(NA)	(NA)	(NA)	31	75.0	(D)	112	4.9	10.2
Pawtucket city	170	36.5	7,894	265.7	5,834	160.4	437.6	1,078.7	78	274.1	264.1	844	30.0	54.2
Providence city	397	20.2	7,015	220.8	4,936	126.3	485.5	818.0	246	1,261.8	774.9	3,547	138.3	242.3
Warwick city	196	30.1	5,281	198.3	3,289	95.5	940.8	1,332.1	180	741.0	(D)	1,489	64.5	113.3
Woonsocket city	80	30.0	2,479	78.1	1,817	44.7	150.4	292.3	44	171.2	144.3	633	26.5	44.3
SOUTH CAROLINA	4,457	37.2	289,933	10,602.6	220,127	6,867.3	38,611.3	81,132.8	4,917	32,989.0	24,543.0	60,376	2,402.8	4,346.9
Aiken city	28	35.7	[6]1,750	(D)	(D)	(D)	(D)	(D)	31	(D)	(D)	[9]175	(D)	(D)
Anderson city	59	39.0	5,838	192.5	4,943	149.6	497.9	1,260.3	57	257.0	163.2	782	22.9	42.1
Charleston city	69	18.8	1,441	50.9	1,017	32.4	164.0	324.9	107	538.7	(D)	1,252	38.8	76.4
Columbia city	102	27.5	5,471	216.9	3,804	134.1	695.2	1,858.1	216	1,395.0	(D)	2,720	121.1	214.5
Florence city	33	48.5	[11]3,750	(D)	(D)	(D)	(D)	(D)	59	285.7	(D)	602	23.0	39.6
Goose Creek city	12	50.0	1,513	82.1	826	35.0	228.3	393.6	11	(D)	(D)	[12]375	(D)	(D)
Greenville city	115	40.9	5,321	175.9	4,030	103.8	402.5	863.1	228	4,243.8	2,945.5	5,744	407.6	673.0
Hilton Head Island town	(NA)	(NA)	(NA)	(NA)	(NA)	(NA)	(NA)	(NA)	68	86.3	64.1	181	7.9	15.8
Mount Pleasant town	(NA)	(NA)	(NA)	(NA)	(NA)	(NA)	(NA)	(NA)	73	170.7	(D)	409	17.3	27.0
North Charleston city	121	36.4	7,735	308.3	5,220	179.3	1,293.4	2,662.0	216	1,618.9	1,050.1	3,114	121.5	224.9
Rock Hill city	59	44.1	2,419	102.2	1,474	48.2	262.9	650.6	70	286.4	156.1	676	29.1	59.9
Spartanburg city	52	30.8	3,010	119.5	2,281	80.7	359.8	812.8	93	1,004.4	898.6	1,258	42.0	80.3
Summerville town	35	28.6	1,204	39.9	926	24.2	78.2	175.7	34	200.1	(D)	404	11.8	22.8
Sumter city	38	44.7	5,401	169.7	4,598	126.4	578.3	989.1	41	115.7	(D)	344	10.6	19.0
SOUTH DAKOTA	926	31.3	37,019	1,096.8	28,584	744.0	5,176.6	10,710.2	1,329	7,845.1	5,580.7	14,973	445.4	811.3
Rapid City city	99	26.3	2,626	72.5	2,116	49.4	201.9	571.9	139	774.4	(D)	1,810	61.9	97.1
Sioux Falls city	135	38.5	9,602	296.9	7,515	207.7	844.6	1,989.5	316	2,175.4	1,672.9	5,362	173.8	290.8

See footnotes at end of table.

Table C-4. Cities — **Manufacturing and Wholesale Trade**—Con.

[Includes states and 1,265 incorporated places of 25,000 or more population as of April 1, 2000, in all states except Hawaii, which has no incorporated places recognized by the U.S. Census Bureau. Two census designated places (CDPs) are also included (Honolulu CDP in Hawaii and Arlington CDP in Virginia). For more information on these areas, see Appendix C, Geographic Information]

City	Manufacturing (NAICS 31–33), 2002[1] Establishments[2] Total	Establishments Percent with 20 or more employees	All employees Number[3]	All employees Annual payroll (mil. dol.)	Production workers Number[3]	Production workers Wages (mil. dol.)	Value added by manufacture (mil. dol.)	Value of shipments (mil. dol.)	Wholesale trade (NAICS 42), 2002[4] Establishments	Sales (mil. dol.) Total	Sales Merchant wholesalers	Paid employees[5]	Annual payroll (mil. dol.)	Operating expenses (mil. dol.)
TENNESSEE	6,948	36.7	411,495	14,824.8	310,738	9,612.3	49,811.0	109,293.5	7,566	97,792.0	59,068.8	121,961	4,895.2	9,349.2
Bartlett city	34	38.2	1,014	39.2	605	19.1	111.6	186.6	71	(D)	(D)	[6]1,750	(D)	(D)
Brentwood city	(NA)	(NA)	(NA)	(NA)	(NA)	(NA)	(NA)	(NA)	122	1,711.6	497.3	2,007	102.1	191.6
Bristol city	49	38.8	1,982	68.4	1,525	41.9	1,227.4	1,891.1	55	(D)	(D)	[6]1,750	(D)	(D)
Chattanooga city	385	39.0	20,669	802.2	14,722	469.9	2,376.5	4,330.3	509	2,714.0	1,747.7	6,652	248.0	438.9
Clarksville city	61	31.1	4,395	149.0	3,444	105.5	713.9	1,217.5	70	337.8	286.9	741	23.6	47.3
Cleveland city	86	43.0	9,232	325.0	7,532	229.8	1,446.9	2,587.5	54	(D)	(D)	[6]1,750	(D)	(D)
Collierville town	33	48.5	2,748	86.5	2,321	66.2	503.2	1,027.7	57	501.0	(D)	977	35.2	59.7
Columbia city	40	30.0	[8]750	(D)	(D)	(D)	(D)	(D)	43	151.7	118.4	392	12.8	20.8
Cookeville city	88	35.2	5,587	154.0	4,424	104.8	582.9	961.4	63	240.3	164.2	789	21.3	45.7
Franklin city	74	25.7	2,423	86.1	1,735	53.1	217.6	432.3	91	1,381.8	434.0	929	60.7	116.8
Germantown city	(NA)	(NA)	(NA)	(NA)	(NA)	(NA)	(NA)	(NA)	71	(D)	(D)	[9]175	(D)	(D)
Hendersonville city	56	12.5	[8]750	(D)	(D)	(D)	(D)	(D)	65	231.9	162.1	465	18.7	30.7
Jackson city	110	50.0	11,113	437.4	8,610	287.3	1,926.2	3,812.8	139	704.1	571.3	1,873	66.4	120.8
Johnson City city	99	47.5	7,458	213.5	5,735	134.5	540.1	1,285.0	106	1,992.6	(D)	1,528	49.1	96.3
Kingsport city	57	33.3	10,629	598.8	6,206	282.2	675.5	2,441.8	88	526.4	475.1	1,330	57.8	106.9
Knoxville city	286	34.3	[7]7,500	(D)	(D)	(D)	(D)	(D)	590	9,070.9	5,724.0	9,049	374.8	656.0
Memphis city	635	34.6	26,586	1,065.7	17,370	567.3	4,154.8	9,585.1	1,372	26,874.1	11,238.8	27,477	1,235.8	2,529.3
Morristown city	88	65.9	13,562	414.4	10,770	288.5	1,258.6	2,388.9	50	(D)	(D)	[8]750	(D)	(D)
Murfreesboro city	85	41.2	4,325	166.2	3,273	110.0	533.0	1,374.1	104	469.4	393.4	1,051	39.3	69.8
Nashville-Davidson (balance)	643	35.1	27,355	1,041.9	19,981	671.4	3,533.0	6,709.3	1,190	19,028.8	10,773.7	21,850	952.7	1,659.8
Oak Ridge city	57	36.8	6,748	370.7	1,992	86.8	853.8	983.3	28	72.5	72.5	196	8.4	13.4
Smyrna town	26	30.8	9,257	455.3	7,080	325.6	235.6	5,280.6	29	431.4	(D)	715	24.3	39.5
TEXAS	21,450	29.5	855,658	34,105.2	588,198	19,226.1	124,462.6	310,816.0	31,832	397,405.1	248,772.7	439,755	18,808.6	34,807.1
Abilene city	103	21.4	[11]3,750	(D)	(D)	(D)	(D)	(D)	183	775.5	714.1	2,225	73.7	145.8
Allen city	21	61.9	1,573	82.9	698	23.1	171.1	341.5	32	(D)	(D)	[9]175	(D)	(D)
Amarillo city	168	20.2	[7]7,500	(D)	(D)	(D)	(D)	(D)	275	1,563.9	1,219.3	3,125	111.8	198.0
Arlington city	274	36.9	13,335	633.0	10,072	448.0	5,244.0	10,592.3	470	6,716.4	5,886.0	6,477	256.7	484.3
Austin city	558	28.7	35,244	1,772.4	20,053	839.7	10,799.7	21,783.5	1,022	(D)	(D)	[14]17,500	(D)	(D)
Baytown city	43	48.8	[11]3,750	(D)	(D)	(D)	(D)	(D)	37	112.5	112.5	370	13.5	25.8
Beaumont city	128	33.6	5,762	310.2	4,029	206.5	1,826.0	8,139.0	233	1,634.8	1,044.9	3,321	123.8	230.9
Bedford city	(NA)	(NA)	(NA)	(NA)	(NA)	(NA)	(NA)	(NA)	57	510.5	162.8	283	20.2	38.1
Big Spring city	23	21.7	[8]750	(D)	(D)	(D)	(D)	(D)	17	(D)	(D)	[9]175	(D)	(D)
Brownsville city	121	25.6	5,351	131.9	4,125	96.1	401.1	760.1	197	578.1	(D)	1,512	35.1	71.8
Bryan city	73	35.6	4,125	112.2	3,321	72.9	279.4	549.8	83	394.7	(D)	1,126	34.7	59.0
Carrollton city	207	40.6	13,897	568.6	9,248	284.2	1,494.6	3,450.7	443	12,003.3	6,177.0	9,661	423.8	783.2
Cedar Hill city	26	42.3	1,279	34.6	1,087	25.4	86.6	146.5	21	58.5	(D)	172	7.2	12.6
Cedar Park city	21	28.6	574	19.1	435	10.5	38.8	71.9	21	(D)	(D)	[10]60	(D)	(D)
Cleburne city	36	22.2	1,345	46.4	1,028	34.3	143.4	313.5	34	141.4	(D)	405	10.2	19.6
College Station city	22	27.3	[8]750	(D)	(D)	(D)	(D)	(D)	20	(D)	(D)	[9]175	(D)	(D)
Conroe city	96	33.3	3,104	121.5	2,159	72.8	438.0	858.8	108	1,227.8	738.4	1,453	56.8	105.1
Coppell city	23	52.2	1,040	37.6	628	17.9	92.9	234.6	60	1,095.3	577.3	1,860	103.6	178.9
Copperas Cove city	(NA)	(NA)	(NA)	(NA)	(NA)	(NA)	(NA)	(NA)	1	(D)	(D)	[13]10	(D)	(D)
Corpus Christi city	197	22.8	6,128	274.4	4,191	161.8	1,142.2	7,286.1	422	1,701.1	1,300.7	4,374	158.5	313.5
Dallas city	1,470	32.1	66,929	2,978.2	38,729	1,237.0	8,971.2	16,476.7	2,957	27,729.5	15,978.6	43,440	1,890.8	3,329.0
Deer Park city	29	48.3	4,485	313.6	2,718	182.7	2,186.0	8,075.9	38	229.5	(D)	600	31.2	48.5
Del Rio city	(NA)	(NA)	(NA)	(NA)	(NA)	(NA)	(NA)	(NA)	31	(D)	(D)	[8]750	(D)	(D)
Denton city	78	33.3	4,250	181.8	3,242	123.4	595.5	1,714.1	95	1,491.4	(D)	1,424	44.5	91.8
DeSoto city	36	33.3	1,459	53.7	1,115	34.8	212.2	357.7	41	158.2	(D)	318	13.5	25.5
Duncanville city	38	21.1	1,547	53.6	1,221	36.1	54.4	130.3	46	97.6	(D)	192	6.4	14.1
Edinburg city	38	26.3	1,007	31.8	552	15.3	83.3	171.2	53	289.4	(D)	1,134	23.5	42.2
El Paso city	579	29.9	24,977	679.3	19,458	443.3	2,897.9	7,659.2	961	4,462.8	3,303.6	8,164	257.5	549.7
Euless city	39	33.3	847	31.7	550	16.4	62.7	103.1	58	332.1	176.6	552	26.6	44.7
Farmers Branch city	125	39.2	6,218	244.9	3,986	118.1	517.3	1,108.4	307	5,751.7	3,170.2	9,491	447.8	771.6
Flower Mound town	26	15.4	748	17.6	613	9.7	28.5	56.7	42	170.1	(D)	223	13.3	18.4
Fort Worth city	785	35.7	48,241	2,434.3	27,448	1,060.0	7,306.0	15,606.7	810	14,042.0	(D)	19,943	1,041.7	2,141.5
Friendswood city	(NA)	(NA)	(NA)	(NA)	(NA)	(NA)	(NA)	(NA)	27	(D)	(D)	[9]175	(D)	(D)
Frisco city	(NA)	(NA)	(NA)	(NA)	(NA)	(NA)	(NA)	(NA)	61	1,012.8	(D)	628	36.4	57.3
Galveston city	35	22.9	701	28.7	532	18.7	56.8	111.8	44	(D)	(D)	[12]375	(D)	(D)
Garland city	337	30.6	14,685	529.3	11,092	324.2	1,895.9	4,000.7	244	2,564.9	1,758.9	4,718	177.4	309.6
Georgetown city	33	27.3	810	30.2	552	15.9	63.1	116.7	34	103.5	103.5	259	10.3	16.3
Grand Prairie city	211	41.7	13,323	620.6	9,243	374.1	1,377.2	2,559.5	328	6,115.5	4,652.6	7,146	293.6	529.5
Grapevine city	38	23.7	1,524	51.9	1,108	26.7	205.7	355.9	89	2,736.1	2,549.0	1,681	74.2	136.3
Haltom City city	121	25.6	2,852	92.3	2,194	57.5	180.1	371.0	111	361.7	341.3	959	36.2	68.4
Harlingen city	60	25.0	2,339	60.9	1,909	44.5	233.1	589.3	87	302.9	281.7	906	23.2	42.0
Houston city	2,674	31.8	88,262	3,430.4	59,917	1,091.9	9,941.6	23,213.0	5,198	122,727.2	100,219.0	77,171	3,676.5	6,673.9
Huntsville city	(NA)	(NA)	(NA)	(NA)	(NA)	(NA)	(NA)	(NA)	31	(D)	(D)	[12]375	(D)	(D)
Hurst city	38	18.4	578	14.6	464	10.1	40.2	95.6	52	197.1	105.2	395	20.0	33.7
Irving city	223	28.7	10,559	450.5	5,793	179.0	1,279.3	2,542.3	476	30,112.5	7,657.9	15,080	783.3	1,615.2

See footnotes at end of table.

Table C-4. Cities — **Manufacturing and Wholesale Trade**—Con.

[Includes states and 1,265 incorporated places of 25,000 or more population as of April 1, 2000, in all states except Hawaii, which has no incorporated places recognized by the U.S. Census Bureau. Two census designated places (CDPs) are also included (Honolulu CDP in Hawaii and Arlington CDP in Virginia). For more information on these areas, see Appendix C, Geographic Information]

City	Manufacturing (NAICS 31–33), 2002[1] Establishments[2] Total	Establishments[2] Percent with 20 or more employees	All employees Number[3]	All employees Annual payroll (mil. dol.)	Production workers Number[3]	Production workers Wages (mil. dol.)	Value added by manufacture (mil. dol.)	Value of shipments (mil. dol.)	Wholesale trade (NAICS 42), 2002[4] Establishments	Sales (mil. dol.) Total	Sales (mil. dol.) Merchant wholesalers	Paid employees[5]	Annual payroll (mil. dol.)	Operating expenses (mil. dol.)
TEXAS—Con.														
Keller city	15	26.7	[8]750	(D)	(D)	(D)	(D)	(D)	20	56.4	(D)	58	2.4	3.7
Killeen city	(NA)	(NA)	(NA)	(NA)	(NA)	(NA)	(NA)	(NA)	17	47.1	(D)	150	3.7	8.4
Kingsville city	(NA)	(NA)	(NA)	(NA)	(NA)	(NA)	(NA)	(NA)	7	(D)	(D)	[10]60	(D)	(D)
Lake Jackson city	(NA)	(NA)	(NA)	(NA)	(NA)	(NA)	(NA)	(NA)	12	17.0	(D)	58	2.3	3.4
Lancaster city	37	32.4	1,454	44.1	1,181	30.5	150.5	246.7	17	(D)	(D)	[9]175	(D)	(D)
La Porte city	31	29.0	1,030	53.4	652	31.9	194.6	539.0	37	165.1	(D)	366	17.3	30.6
Laredo city	94	13.8	[6]1,750	(D)	(D)	(D)	(D)	(D)	382	(D)	(D)	[11]3,750	(D)	(D)
League City city	(NA)	(NA)	(NA)	(NA)	(NA)	(NA)	(NA)	(NA)	42	112.5	(D)	349	14.6	21.1
Lewisville city	95	28.4	2,585	74.7	2,019	49.7	198.8	375.6	126	2,169.4	988.7	2,920	129.2	204.9
Longview city	133	35.3	[7]7,500	(D)	(D)	(D)	(D)	(D)	201	675.0	537.5	2,119	69.5	123.6
Lubbock city	226	25.2	5,246	161.3	3,760	98.8	489.5	1,006.4	415	3,333.0	2,696.5	5,381	181.2	359.1
Lufkin city	52	38.5	[7]7,500	(D)	(D)	(D)	(D)	(D)	59	(D)	(D)	[8]750	(D)	(D)
McAllen city	100	28.0	3,085	87.2	2,043	44.3	425.4	901.0	274	1,652.6	1,156.3	3,269	98.4	180.8
McKinney city	57	40.4	5,839	282.3	2,849	98.4	521.0	1,114.4	77	588.0	503.2	757	32.4	66.1
Mansfield city	73	50.7	2,795	93.4	2,111	56.7	213.6	485.5	61	268.0	199.2	674	24.6	44.1
Mesquite city	78	30.8	3,116	114.7	1,914	54.6	321.8	757.7	89	1,696.8	(D)	2,277	123.6	204.8
Midland city	79	13.9	735	26.8	544	17.7	59.7	97.8	171	709.4	387.5	1,248	49.4	90.8
Mission city	(NA)	(NA)	(NA)	(NA)	(NA)	(NA)	(NA)	(NA)	45	169.6	(D)	419	12.0	24.6
Missouri City city	(NA)	(NA)	(NA)	(NA)	(NA)	(NA)	(NA)	(NA)	49	59.8	49.1	204	6.4	10.7
Nacogdoches city	46	32.6	4,463	108.7	3,643	80.8	443.7	1,084.9	41	(D)	(D)	[12]375	(D)	(D)
New Braunfels city	54	35.2	2,456	71.4	1,639	38.8	228.4	412.6	59	305.1	268.1	440	15.6	32.1
North Richland Hills city	27	22.2	1,465	48.2	1,151	34.0	136.7	254.7	50	198.0	(D)	269	11.7	22.0
Odessa city	134	14.2	2,070	72.9	1,419	42.0	176.6	335.2	219	608.2	515.0	2,043	74.2	124.9
Paris city	40	42.5	4,162	152.6	3,294	112.7	1,551.3	2,187.7	53	118.1	(D)	392	12.0	21.1
Pasadena city	125	37.6	5,969	303.5	4,355	202.2	1,424.5	4,397.9	122	556.4	352.9	1,577	70.5	115.2
Pearland city	63	33.3	1,612	60.6	1,138	35.7	186.5	291.5	49	145.3	(D)	503	17.6	31.6
Pharr city	(NA)	(NA)	(NA)	(NA)	(NA)	(NA)	(NA)	(NA)	76	323.6	276.6	839	25.7	46.8
Plano city	162	27.2	8,596	307.8	3,101	116.4	1,089.3	1,782.7	507	(D)	2,297.8	[7]7,500	(D)	(D)
Port Arthur city	33	45.5	2,436	127.3	1,994	100.1	1,638.6	8,089.5	33	444.3	(D)	730	28.9	54.5
Richardson city	154	29.2	5,252	253.8	2,701	82.5	494.7	1,460.7	393	9,930.5	5,008.8	12,186	837.1	1,698.3
Round Rock city	70	31.4	[11]3,750	(D)	(D)	(D)	(D)	(D)	83	(D)	425.9	[11]3,750	(D)	(D)
Rowlett city	39	15.4	664	19.4	487	12.7	37.6	67.5	44	74.1	(D)	232	8.3	15.0
San Angelo city	86	27.9	3,642	127.8	2,806	81.6	477.9	851.9	109	329.1	208.6	963	29.2	49.6
San Antonio city	903	27.6	33,501	1,056.8	23,394	582.1	2,925.7	6,056.2	1,519	15,310.9	(D)	23,035	923.6	1,679.9
San Juan city	(NA)	(NA)	(NA)	(NA)	(NA)	(NA)	(NA)	(NA)	10	(D)	(D)	[10]60	(D)	(D)
San Marcos city	43	34.9	1,342	48.0	881	24.8	168.9	302.4	21	(D)	(D)	[9]175	(D)	(D)
Sherman city	64	34.4	5,086	230.0	3,512	128.7	1,077.9	1,886.9	57	261.4	(D)	647	20.5	37.6
Socorro city	(NA)	(NA)	(NA)	(NA)	(NA)	(NA)	(NA)	(NA)	12	8.9	8.9	30	0.6	1.2
Sugar Land city	51	37.3	2,837	116.6	1,796	66.0	340.5	879.5	136	5,284.9	(D)	1,620	74.7	132.5
Temple city	64	43.8	6,077	196.7	4,934	146.8	796.7	1,368.7	75	1,650.1	1,415.9	2,286	100.8	138.8
Texarkana city	42	31.0	[6]1,750	(D)	(D)	(D)	(D)	(D)	91	1,068.9	1,009.8	1,328	43.0	75.7
Texas City city	29	41.4	3,783	278.8	2,442	136.4	957.2	5,345.5	38	162.2	(D)	262	10.4	19.5
The Colony city	(NA)	(NA)	(NA)	(NA)	(NA)	(NA)	(NA)	(NA)	13	(D)	(D)	[9]175	(D)	(D)
Tyler city	106	35.8	7,244	272.0	5,351	176.0	868.7	2,213.1	188	896.0	440.6	1,890	73.1	122.9
Victoria city	58	17.2	[6]1,750	(D)	(D)	(D)	(D)	(D)	100	447.3	(D)	1,268	46.0	84.8
Waco city	147	50.3	11,111	369.7	8,432	250.6	2,419.0	3,825.1	171	3,417.9	(D)	2,625	78.9	166.6
Weslaco city	20	30.0	794	19.1	627	12.5	67.0	143.6	30	182.8	(D)	403	12.9	25.4
Wichita Falls city	106	28.3	4,755	170.8	3,610	111.3	528.6	935.4	147	451.7	376.3	1,339	48.2	90.8
UTAH	3,061	26.7	109,944	4,001.3	73,961	2,156.7	12,158.9	25,104.0	3,369	22,905.1	14,936.3	44,061	1,700.5	3,116.8
Bountiful city	(NA)	(NA)	(NA)	(NA)	(NA)	(NA)	(NA)	(NA)	51	(D)	(D)	[9]175	(D)	(D)
Clearfield city	44	54.5	5,262	157.4	4,332	119.7	522.4	901.4	23	299.2	(D)	490	18.2	39.0
Draper city	46	32.6	2,144	96.2	1,295	40.4	287.8	400.4	62	368.4	206.1	965	25.1	42.4
Layton city	38	13.2	556	20.0	441	14.8	87.1	167.5	46	138.8	80.9	415	15.2	27.8
Logan city	90	32.2	6,192	191.2	3,973	105.2	328.5	1,510.7	62	130.1	(D)	476	12.2	21.0
Midvale city	42	16.7	793	27.7	500	12.8	77.1	113.9	88	391.7	349.3	670	26.9	45.8
Murray city	136	20.6	2,148	66.7	1,529	37.6	143.1	239.7	136	682.4	316.7	2,109	72.5	119.3
Ogden city	144	33.3	9,010	323.4	6,418	197.1	1,205.5	2,462.0	132	914.7	(D)	1,404	45.6	81.0
Orem city	113	17.7	2,059	67.5	1,408	36.5	158.5	288.4	125	311.5	286.0	1,030	40.1	77.0
Provo city	82	20.7	1,735	69.6	911	24.4	152.3	262.2	76	679.2	655.1	1,897	81.1	169.1
Riverton city	(NA)	(NA)	(NA)	(NA)	(NA)	(NA)	(NA)	(NA)	20	27.0	(D)	94	4.7	10.0
Roy city	(NA)	(NA)	(NA)	(NA)	(NA)	(NA)	(NA)	(NA)	12	(D)	(D)	[8]750	(D)	(D)
St. George city	75	25.3	1,312	38.8	1,039	27.0	89.7	168.7	81	182.2	(D)	617	17.9	29.6
Salt Lake City city	508	35.6	24,484	966.4	15,100	445.9	2,618.4	5,298.7	676	7,639.1	4,878.8	12,251	515.6	934.9
Sandy city	95	12.6	2,416	95.9	1,518	45.8	299.5	446.9	156	263.2	181.3	653	31.4	49.2
South Jordan city	15	26.7	1,315	55.2	695	15.7	123.3	165.8	26	242.0	(D)	775	29.1	75.5
Taylorsville city	(NA)	(NA)	(NA)	(NA)	(NA)	(NA)	(NA)	(NA)	30	40.0	(D)	155	2.7	4.8
West Jordan city	99	38.4	3,239	110.7	2,546	76.4	332.8	611.7	61	759.9	625.8	1,409	56.4	99.9
West Valley City city	170	34.1	6,220	253.5	3,458	113.0	654.8	1,147.5	177	1,941.8	(D)	3,853	171.9	301.3

See footnotes at end of table.

Table C-4. Cities — **Manufacturing and Wholesale Trade**—Con.

[Includes states and 1,265 incorporated places of 25,000 or more population as of April 1, 2000, in all states except Hawaii, which has no incorporated places recognized by the U.S. Census Bureau. Two census designated places (CDPs) are also included (Honolulu CDP in Hawaii and Arlington CDP in Virginia). For more information on these areas, see Appendix C, Geographic Information]

| City | Manufacturing (NAICS 31–33), 2002[1] | | | | | | | | Wholesale trade (NAICS 42), 2002[4] | | | | | |
| | Establishments[2] | | All employees | | Production workers | | Value added by manufacture (mil. dol.) | Value of shipments (mil. dol.) | Estab-lishments | Sales (mil. dol.) | | Paid employees[5] | Annual payroll (mil. dol.) | Operating expenses (mil. dol.) |
	Total	Percent with 20 or more employees	Number[3]	Annual payroll (mil. dol.)	Number[3]	Wages (mil. dol.)				Total	Merchant wholesalers			
VERMONT	1,176	27.1	43,827	1,757.6	28,429	937.7	5,163.9	9,660.5	869	5,094.4	4,283.3	10,792	418.0	777.6
Burlington city	44	22.7	3,700	176.9	2,262	73.7	418.4	636.2	57	374.4	(D)	462	18.2	33.2
VIRGINIA	5,909	32.2	311,787	11,633.0	229,590	7,294.0	48,261.8	83,952.5	7,712	69,267.8	44,421.1	105,641	4,503.1	7,729.4
Alexandria city	98	19.4	1,504	56.5	1,036	32.6	161.8	272.2	130	902.1	(D)	2,523	109.6	175.4
Arlington CDP[15]	54	14.8	585	16.5	398	10.2	35.9	63.3	97	487.8	308.4	1,232	65.9	107.6
Blacksburg town	28	28.6	1,447	53.2	1,141	36.4	187.4	282.2	18	100.3	100.3	274	11.0	26.8
Charlottesville city	68	22.1	3,630	189.8	1,501	47.6	377.6	640.4	75	232.8	226.0	813	27.7	50.2
Chesapeake city	145	35.2	4,651	185.5	3,213	112.3	460.4	1,139.8	280	2,145.3	1,182.9	4,434	149.4	279.8
Danville city	46	41.3	9,024	299.6	7,459	215.9	640.1	1,389.8	70	203.5	(D)	696	22.0	40.8
Hampton city	85	30.6	4,133	137.1	3,193	84.2	581.7	1,350.1	77	342.1	305.7	914	37.4	67.3
Harrisonburg city	59	33.9	4,774	141.7	3,977	105.8	406.9	769.0	75	(D)	(D)	[6]1,750	(D)	(D)
Leesburg town	16	25.0	511	19.9	315	9.7	34.3	66.2	24	(D)	24.4	[9]175	(D)	(D)
Lynchburg city	118	40.7	9,567	423.2	6,333	227.2	1,186.2	1,758.1	94	585.1	295.9	1,145	42.8	73.9
Manassas city	43	32.6	2,790	162.2	1,243	66.4	558.7	699.0	54	382.0	368.6	799	35.5	64.6
Newport News city	121	34.7	22,213	989.0	14,270	563.3	2,730.8	3,827.7	127	621.3	(D)	1,954	65.7	127.2
Norfolk city	194	36.1	9,752	418.4	7,738	320.8	1,564.2	4,294.1	325	2,862.2	2,148.5	5,687	225.9	375.7
Petersburg city	41	48.8	2,416	106.7	1,755	60.8	328.1	660.1	33	314.1	(D)	759	24.5	43.4
Portsmouth city	66	25.8	1,864	71.9	1,374	48.7	263.3	435.7	65	143.9	(D)	655	23.7	38.1
Richmond city	297	32.7	15,417	749.0	9,995	410.8	11,347.8	13,923.8	441	7,174.0	4,486.8	6,391	260.8	470.9
Roanoke city	126	35.7	4,579	160.3	3,341	98.0	556.9	1,027.0	235	999.8	681.0	2,705	97.6	164.0
Suffolk city	55	38.2	2,229	89.9	1,586	56.1	573.2	1,155.8	58	737.4	578.7	1,317	53.3	88.3
Virginia Beach city	225	17.8	5,067	152.8	3,748	90.7	605.1	1,171.4	444	2,251.1	1,774.1	4,578	174.2	288.7
WASHINGTON	7,535	26.2	265,010	11,163.9	167,547	6,038.2	35,398.6	79,313.9	9,670	84,634.5	52,804.7	121,132	5,157.0	9,398.3
Auburn city	157	26.1	9,997	398.6	6,675	327.7	785.3	1,280.5	175	3,579.0	(D)	3,494	138.3	249.0
Bellevue city	124	21.0	2,071	81.3	1,182	37.3	206.8	566.0	494	10,217.9	2,931.7	6,520	355.9	572.8
Bellingham city	145	29.0	[11]3,750	(D)	(D)	(D)	(D)	(D)	152	509.9	462.7	1,684	64.8	117.0
Bothell city	41	43.9	3,284	194.9	1,117	38.9	477.3	980.3	77	1,737.5	753.9	1,888	129.2	200.2
Bremerton city	(NA)	(NA)	(NA)	(NA)	(NA)	(NA)	(NA)	(NA)	34	124.5	(D)	441	15.2	31.0
Burien city	(NA)	(NA)	(NA)	(NA)	(NA)	(NA)	(NA)	(NA)	39	349.6	39.3	346	13.2	23.6
Des Moines city	(NA)	(NA)	(NA)	(NA)	(NA)	(NA)	(NA)	(NA)	16	75.3	25.3	80	4.2	8.1
Edmonds city	(NA)	(NA)	(NA)	(NA)	(NA)	(NA)	(NA)	(NA)	70	221.2	(D)	310	12.5	23.9
Everett city	138	39.1	33,294	1,770.4	14,395	896.0	7,020.2	15,816.0	141	574.2	460.2	1,479	53.3	101.0
Federal Way city	(NA)	(NA)	(NA)	(NA)	(NA)	(NA)	(NA)	(NA)	79	1,190.5	786.8	584	32.9	85.3
Kennewick city	40	17.5	523	18.3	353	9.5	84.6	146.8	58	246.2	(D)	537	18.2	35.9
Kent city	285	42.5	15,402	894.5	9,174	306.9	1,333.6	2,990.3	452	8,079.5	1,678.3	11,004	473.1	897.0
Kirkland city	70	25.7	[6]1,750	(D)	(D)	(D)	(D)	(D)	175	1,885.5	676.2	2,172	138.0	215.7
Lacey city	(NA)	(NA)	(NA)	(NA)	(NA)	(NA)	(NA)	(NA)	33	60.2	53.8	200	6.5	10.8
Lakewood city	43	18.6	841	26.8	653	19.6	31.5	82.8	70	297.7	(D)	857	29.4	45.0
Longview city	45	40.0	3,467	174.1	2,654	125.4	313.5	1,101.8	44	182.1	(D)	382	13.0	21.8
Lynnwood city	52	25.0	904	33.7	583	17.9	77.3	143.6	73	315.0	(D)	839	37.2	58.3
Marysville city	70	21.4	1,384	55.0	982	34.9	113.3	244.0	36	126.1	(D)	470	14.5	29.8
Mount Vernon city	28	14.3	614	16.2	478	12.5	48.9	100.7	34	(D)	(D)	[12]375	(D)	(D)
Olympia city	41	26.8	[6]1,750	(D)	(D)	(D)	(D)	(D)	55	178.4	(D)	617	25.2	34.1
Pasco city	(NA)	(NA)	(NA)	(NA)	(NA)	(NA)	(NA)	(NA)	76	278.2	(D)	832	28.1	50.0
Puyallup city	42	28.6	727	24.9	538	14.6	66.1	121.4	48	160.9	147.9	276	10.0	19.2
Redmond city	177	35.6	8,394	416.0	4,812	184.7	1,190.2	2,264.6	267	5,091.3	3,656.0	4,719	267.1	608.4
Renton city	64	35.9	[14]17,500	(D)	(D)	(D)	(D)	(D)	120	2,848.3	1,099.5	3,752	157.1	288.1
Richland city	33	12.1	1,450	75.5	956	34.0	145.8	322.8	17	(D)	(D)	[9]175	(D)	(D)
Sammamish city	(NA)	(NA)	(NA)	(NA)	(NA)	(NA)	(NA)	(NA)	52	101.9	43.8	123	5.7	9.8
SeaTac city	(NA)	(NA)	(NA)	(NA)	(NA)	(NA)	(NA)	(NA)	26	63.7	(D)	149	5.4	12.3
Seattle city	1,031	26.1	27,699	1,014.7	18,754	584.4	2,696.0	4,717.1	1,587	14,851.4	9,365.3	21,740	1,038.9	1,899.2
Shoreline city	(NA)	(NA)	(NA)	(NA)	(NA)	(NA)	(NA)	(NA)	40	92.8	74.4	236	6.2	11.0
Spokane city	280	23.6	6,112	212.9	3,866	113.6	621.4	1,094.9	430	3,993.1	2,928.7	6,328	217.1	420.5
Spokane Valley city	(X)	(NA)	(X)	(X)	(X)	(X)	(X)	(X)	(X)	(X)	(X)	(X)	(X)	(X)
Tacoma city	254	39.8	9,286	354.7	6,928	224.0	920.6	2,195.9	272	2,243.4	1,492.0	4,279	160.9	299.9
University Place city	(NA)	(NA)	(NA)	(NA)	(NA)	(NA)	(NA)	(NA)	24	81.5	(D)	164	6.8	13.0
Vancouver city	191	30.9	7,841	315.7	5,504	189.4	900.6	1,878.5	204	1,820.8	594.2	1,843	94.1	170.8
Walla Walla city	65	9.2	[8]750	(D)	(D)	(D)	(D)	(D)	40	(D)	(D)	[12]375	(D)	(D)
Wenatchee city	(NA)	(NA)	(NA)	(NA)	(NA)	(NA)	(NA)	(NA)	73	385.1	319.8	860	28.1	47.4
Yakima city	110	28.2	3,728	132.8	2,862	85.5	253.0	636.4	138	1,407.5	1,054.3	3,072	88.4	167.2
WEST VIRGINIA	1,480	33.0	67,319	2,587.0	50,443	1,695.8	7,983.8	18,911.3	1,699	10,924.3	8,124.1	20,176	669.7	1,186.3
Charleston city	51	27.5	1,056	34.1	703	19.1	74.9	152.2	145	1,820.8	(D)	2,655	105.5	168.8
Huntington city	71	39.4	3,924	152.6	2,657	90.6	374.7	821.0	117	488.2	(D)	1,480	53.0	96.7
Morgantown city	20	40.0	[6]1,750	(D)	(D)	(D)	(D)	(D)	32	(D)	(D)	[12]375	(D)	(D)
Parkersburg city	34	32.4	1,002	34.3	755	21.6	83.4	158.0	66	(D)	(D)	[8]750	(D)	(D)
Wheeling city	46	26.1	806	25.9	625	16.1	116.5	151.5	69	(D)	(D)	[6]1,750	(D)	(D)

See footnotes at end of table.

Table C-4. Cities — **Manufacturing and Wholesale Trade**—Con.

[Includes states and 1,265 incorporated places of 25,000 or more population as of April 1, 2000, in all states except Hawaii, which has no incorporated places recognized by the U.S. Census Bureau. Two census designated places (CDPs) are also included (Honolulu CDP in Hawaii and Arlington CDP in Virginia). For more information on these areas, see Appendix C, Geographic Information]

| City | Manufacturing (NAICS 31–33), 2002[1] | | | | | | | | Wholesale trade (NAICS 42), 2002[4] | | | | | |
| | Establishments[2] | | All employees | | Production workers | | Value added by manufacture (mil. dol.) | Value of shipments (mil. dol.) | Establishments | Sales (mil. dol.) | | Paid employees[5] | Annual payroll (mil. dol.) | Operating expenses (mil. dol.) |
	Total	Percent with 20 or more employees	Number[3]	Annual payroll (mil. dol.)	Number[3]	Wages (mil. dol.)				Total	Merchant wholesalers			
WISCONSIN	9,915	37.5	503,588	19,334.4	365,113	12,054.1	61,501.5	124,664.0	7,557	68,510.7	46,479.2	112,763	4,495.0	8,006.2
Appleton city	110	43.6	7,532	330.0	5,046	199.7	881.0	2,039.9	101	(D)	395.7	[6]1,750	(D)	(D)
Beloit city	56	42.9	3,214	123.4	2,261	76.1	710.5	1,049.3	23	242.7	(D)	232	9.7	25.4
Brookfield city	74	31.1	2,468	104.8	1,614	56.8	200.7	415.1	178	1,420.8	582.5	2,520	113.0	181.0
Eau Claire city	93	40.9	4,657	159.8	3,495	110.9	576.2	959.0	92	894.1	(D)	1,780	63.7	145.2
Fond du Lac city	81	42.0	5,539	240.4	3,764	131.6	662.0	1,408.3	58	506.1	(D)	907	35.0	65.0
Franklin city	53	52.8	2,705	115.9	1,733	53.4	287.2	562.9	36	171.9	108.5	316	14.6	28.7
Green Bay city	157	40.8	12,187	511.8	9,714	375.4	2,776.4	4,882.8	163	2,760.2	(D)	3,053	128.8	209.8
Greenfield city	(NA)	(NA)	(NA)	(NA)	(NA)	(NA)	(NA)	(NA)	25	(D)	(D)	[9]175	(D)	(D)
Janesville city	103	34.0	10,092	556.6	8,060	429.4	4,853.6	10,258.6	75	1,359.8	1,334.7	1,941	81.4	148.6
Kenosha city	126	34.1	5,234	256.7	4,051	191.3	621.1	1,507.6	61	597.3	(D)	726	33.8	85.3
La Crosse city	103	33.0	6,013	223.3	3,839	112.4	443.3	1,168.5	91	5,551.6	(D)	2,814	105.9	180.7
Madison city	224	30.8	10,650	447.3	6,811	232.4	1,670.6	2,903.9	317	1,994.2	1,665.4	5,017	214.3	352.6
Manitowoc city	88	54.5	7,975	289.8	6,035	188.6	868.2	1,575.8	29	177.0	(D)	401	16.3	33.0
Menomonee Falls village	207	43.5	8,727	361.8	5,873	200.2	817.3	1,555.8	138	1,022.1	536.6	1,861	80.6	141.7
Milwaukee city	744	37.9	34,957	1,380.0	22,513	729.2	3,581.9	7,427.8	661	9,277.3	(D)	13,869	616.7	1,061.1
New Berlin city	142	44.4	6,158	250.6	4,054	130.1	608.6	1,210.1	167	1,431.3	1,192.8	2,911	132.1	220.1
Oak Creek city	64	56.3	6,669	325.5	4,100	164.7	1,872.4	2,907.3	34	882.0	882.0	1,335	60.1	114.6
Oshkosh city	117	51.3	8,176	332.3	5,799	201.9	648.3	2,127.6	63	(D)	471.6	[6]1,750	(D)	(D)
Racine city	182	35.2	6,771	296.9	4,461	164.6	936.3	1,531.6	83	841.1	(D)	1,164	58.6	115.6
Sheboygan city	92	56.5	9,150	357.3	6,602	210.3	967.0	1,882.1	53	281.9	(D)	827	24.5	42.5
Superior city	46	30.4	1,005	35.6	648	22.0	108.7	466.9	45	(D)	(D)	[6]1,750	(D)	(D)
Waukesha city	170	40.0	8,954	420.1	5,805	245.6	1,080.5	2,264.1	174	1,352.5	1,099.4	2,147	94.5	165.9
Wausau city	75	45.3	7,065	233.3	5,521	163.3	625.3	1,310.2	64	362.4	(D)	1,114	40.0	67.8
Wauwatosa city	54	29.6	5,013	247.7	3,752	161.9	267.9	936.4	114	1,734.4	(D)	2,127	88.3	167.8
West Allis city	114	28.9	3,981	158.4	2,742	93.1	376.1	570.3	121	832.0	548.6	1,801	80.4	134.9
West Bend city	67	29.9	3,503	121.1	2,542	72.0	256.4	492.1	37	140.1	(D)	397	12.2	22.4
WYOMING	560	18.2	9,608	364.6	7,273	253.2	1,430.0	4,061.5	789	3,331.0	2,542.3	6,256	227.5	396.5
Casper city	46	21.7	536	16.0	436	11.0	52.0	80.9	102	712.1	(D)	790	29.3	54.8
Cheyenne city	38	44.7	1,473	58.4	1,041	34.3	176.1	796.0	72	515.6	(D)	637	22.0	38.8
Laramie city	(NA)	(NA)	(NA)	(NA)	(NA)	(NA)	(NA)	(NA)	19	(D)	(D)	[9]175	(D)	(D)

D Data withheld to avoid disclosure.   NA Not available.   X Not applicable.

[1]Includes data for industry groups and industries with 100 employees or more for states and 500 employees or more for cities.
[2]Includes establishments with payroll at any time during the year.
[3]Number of employees figures represent average number of production workers for pay period that includes the 12th of March, May, August, and November plus other employees for payroll period that includes the 12th of March.
[4]Includes only establishments of firms with payroll.
[5]For pay period including March 12.
[6]1,000 to 2,499 employees. Figure in table represents midpoint of range.
[7]5,000 to 9,999 employees. Figure in table represents midpoint of range.
[8]500 to 999 employees. Figure in table represents midpoint of range.
[9]100 to 249 employees. Figure in table represents midpoint of range.
[10]20 to 99 employees. Figure in table represents midpoint of range.
[11]2,500 to 4,999 employees. Figure in table represents midpoint of range.
[12]250 to 499 employees. Figure in table represents midpoint of range.
[13]0 to 19 employees. Figure in table represents midpoint of range.
[14]10,000 to 24,999 employees. Figure in table represents midpoint of range.
[15]Data are for Arlington County, VA; data for Arlington CDP not available.

Survey, Census, or Data Collection Method: Based on the 2002 Economic Census; for more information, see Appendix B, Limitations of the Data and Methodology, and also <http://www.census.gov/econ/census02/>.

Sources: Manufacturing—U.S. Census Bureau, 2002 Economic Census, *Manufacturing, Geographic Area Series*, accessed October 2006 (related Internet site <http://www.census.gov/econ/census02/>).   Wholesale trade—U.S. Census Bureau, 2002 Economic Census, *Wholesale Trade, Geographic Area Series*, accessed November 2006 (related Internet site <http://www.census.gov/econ/census02/>).

Table C-5. Cities — **Retail Trade and Accommodation and Food Services**

[Includes states and 1,265 incorporated places of 25,000 or more population as of April 1, 2000, in all states except Hawaii, which has no incorporated places recognized by the U.S. Census Bureau. Two census designated places (CDPs) are also included (Honolulu CDP in Hawaii and Arlington CDP in Virginia). For more information on these areas, see Appendix C, Geographic Information]

City	Retail trade (NAICS 44–45), 2002[1]								Accommodation and food services (NAICS 72), 2002[1]				
	Sales					Annual payroll			Sales				
			Per capita[2]		Percent from general merchandise stores								
	Establishments	Total ($1,000)	Amount (dol.)	Percent of national average		Paid employees[3]	Total ($1,000)	Per paid employee (dol.)	Establishments	Total ($1,000)	Percent from food services	Paid employees[3]	Annual payroll ($1,000)
ALABAMA	19,608	43,784,342	9,773	94.8	17.6	222,416	4,094,026	18,407	7,075	4,692,297	85.1	128,327	1,321,326
Auburn city	187	534,307	11,744	113.9	(NA)	3,198	49,352	15,432	130	93,787	81.9	3,188	25,596
Bessemer city	208	588,627	20,082	194.8	(NA)	2,772	58,056	20,944	57	41,938	85.9	1,141	12,227
Birmingham city	1,102	3,536,101	14,895	144.5	5.7	14,518	325,322	22,408	557	443,862	80.6	10,809	131,127
Decatur city	380	956,846	17,720	171.8	20.7	5,127	88,755	17,311	127	89,673	85.3	2,516	25,956
Dothan city	535	1,412,340	23,824	231.0	21.5	6,740	129,310	19,185	179	130,627	(NA)	3,541	35,599
Florence city	308	785,972	21,914	212.5	27.3	4,282	72,723	16,983	104	72,796	95.4	2,316	20,898
Gadsden city	266	571,940	15,056	146.0	22.4	2,908	49,000	16,850	97	67,284	94.4	2,182	20,261
Homewood city	214	682,598	27,647	268.1	33.7	3,528	67,286	19,072	91	100,174	76.1	2,305	27,075
Hoover city	266	1,551,133	24,106	233.8	18.5	6,349	142,935	22,513	136	108,065	85.6	2,954	32,283
Huntsville city	918	2,688,867	16,622	161.2	19.5	13,235	270,118	20,409	406	337,804	83.1	8,859	98,424
Madison city	108	316,593	9,694	94.0	(NA)	1,746	31,786	18,205	69	55,934	(NA)	1,591	16,519
Mobile city	1,040	2,876,090	14,749	143.0	17.9	14,759	276,317	18,722	453	341,495	85.3	9,604	98,843
Montgomery city	981	2,515,081	12,510	121.3	16.5	13,315	249,333	18,726	398	315,444	(NA)	8,362	89,068
Phenix City city	112	185,248	6,480	62.8	(NA)	1,220	19,107	15,661	57	32,998	(NA)	927	8,203
Prattville city	153	492,311	18,062	175.2	(NA)	2,236	43,779	19,579	62	52,870	(NA)	1,432	15,818
Prichard city	67	79,799	2,845	27.6	(NA)	515	11,311	21,963	16	5,775	(NA)	149	1,619
Tuscaloosa city	515	1,416,505	18,094	175.5	19.7	7,431	136,053	18,309	255	194,947	80.2	5,661	51,611
Vestavia Hills city	119	357,474	11,510	111.6	(NA)	1,582	34,248	21,649	50	54,671	67.8	1,554	18,025
ALASKA	2,661	7,437,071	11,608	112.6	25.2	32,984	798,468	24,208	1,849	1,393,225	65.7	23,663	412,784
Anchorage municipality	927	3,781,569	14,128	137.0	28.0	15,412	394,190	25,577	666	745,408	73.4	13,291	234,010
Fairbanks city	224	823,594	26,884	260.7	(NA)	3,412	87,372	25,607	133	101,021	74.6	2,096	28,417
Juneau city and borough	166	375,342	12,197	118.3	33.3	1,823	43,379	23,795	96	61,246	61.6	1,226	19,079
ARIZONA	17,238	56,457,863	10,382	100.7	(NA)	268,584	6,067,994	22,593	9,944	8,612,730	69.2	206,402	2,464,970
Apache Junction city	79	257,920	7,706	74.7	(NA)	1,704	32,986	19,358	55	24,858	(NA)	778	6,826
Avondale city	60	458,281	9,428	91.4	(NA)	1,770	41,552	23,476	27	20,168	83.7	529	5,861
Bullhead City city	117	384,376	10,842	105.1	(NA)	2,041	41,356	20,263	74	34,644	70.6	892	9,266
Casa Grande city	160	416,943	14,612	141.7	(NA)	2,342	44,799	19,129	64	51,274	(NA)	1,327	12,939
Chandler city	501	1,712,106	8,477	82.2	18.2	9,575	202,521	21,151	312	269,567	89.3	6,681	79,361
Flagstaff city	367	914,744	16,649	161.5	(NA)	5,206	103,965	19,970	256	207,662	63.0	5,108	54,606
Gilbert town	207	720,238	5,337	51.8	37.1	3,550	75,848	21,366	131	68,512	(NA)	1,945	18,723
Glendale city	639	2,435,887	10,601	102.8	19.4	11,447	267,799	23,395	331	235,104	97.7	6,439	65,932
Lake Havasu City city	232	642,440	13,771	133.6	14.7	2,976	63,862	21,459	118	74,503	77.4	2,010	19,896
Mesa city	1,361	4,917,279	11,576	112.3	19.6	24,698	546,029	22,108	656	509,169	88.1	14,209	144,323
Oro Valley town	41	201,004	5,607	54.4	(NA)	1,058	22,719	21,474	24	42,541	(NA)	906	14,111
Peoria city	235	1,465,633	11,890	115.3	8.8	5,312	140,096	26,373	121	109,886	87.6	3,262	30,868
Phoenix city	3,946	13,623,483	9,960	96.6	15.3	62,763	1,485,162	23,663	2,386	2,371,268	71.3	52,769	678,383
Prescott city	259	655,649	17,998	174.5	22.3	3,503	74,591	21,293	169	91,260	76.7	2,780	26,166
Scottsdale city	1,279	5,145,204	23,896	231.7	11.5	20,414	564,513	27,653	641	900,258	59.5	19,134	271,430
Sierra Vista city	145	518,495	13,326	129.2	25.3	2,678	56,090	20,945	85	55,002	78.5	1,656	14,744
Surprise city	106	409,029	9,145	88.7	(NA)	2,502	52,249	20,883	54	41,037	88.7	1,061	11,148
Tempe city	754	4,047,639	25,460	246.9	8.7	13,798	356,744	25,855	513	422,756	81.3	10,826	119,060
Tucson city	2,008	6,591,356	13,152	127.5	16.5	32,514	722,787	22,230	1,162	874,815	80.8	23,995	255,035
Yuma city	329	1,086,165	13,569	131.6	27.1	5,260	103,466	19,670	201	146,206	74.2	3,965	38,780
ARKANSAS	12,141	25,611,630	9,463	91.8	20.5	134,197	2,347,757	17,495	4,659	2,766,905	82.1	77,835	751,908
Conway city	266	685,590	14,786	143.4	(NA)	3,770	63,405	16,818	104	69,451	89.5	2,310	18,827
Fayetteville city	412	1,302,695	21,573	209.2	(NA)	6,977	121,431	17,404	239	169,605	81.3	4,569	44,813
Fort Smith city	538	1,411,467	17,337	168.1	27.3	7,058	130,021	18,422	215	155,777	88.3	4,445	43,702
Hot Springs city	389	926,830	25,454	246.9	22.7	4,730	88,401	18,689	176	134,879	70.1	3,740	43,590
Jacksonville city	97	341,758	11,290	109.6	(NA)	1,644	31,317	20,283	48	26,483	86.0	804	7,183
Jonesboro city	394	990,086	17,475	169.5	22.0	5,343	93,794	17,555	131	102,461	92.6	2,989	29,274
Little Rock city	1,020	2,992,029	16,320	158.3	15.8	13,860	273,113	19,705	460	400,524	77.1	10,375	117,902
North Little Rock city	418	1,239,288	20,738	201.1	(NA)	6,594	125,343	19,009	183	157,501	82.7	4,226	44,766
Pine Bluff city	299	677,407	12,538	121.6	(NA)	3,823	66,171	17,309	117	66,823	(NA)	1,878	17,319
Rogers city	229	631,502	15,010	145.6	23.2	3,310	60,042	18,140	77	60,935	90.0	1,610	15,378
Springdale city	249	733,540	14,267	138.4	(NA)	3,413	68,366	20,031	113	80,972	(NA)	2,347	22,691
Texarkana city	131	296,630	10,429	101.1	(NA)	1,626	27,193	16,724	67	91,655	(NA)	1,334	15,203
West Memphis city	143	479,872	17,179	166.6	(NA)	1,945	34,407	17,690	65	45,357	75.3	1,166	13,014
CALIFORNIA	108,941	359,120,365	10,264	99.5	13.0	1,525,113	37,282,032	24,445	66,568	55,559,669	74.4	1,145,536	15,830,563
Alameda city	176	482,438	6,653	64.5	(NA)	2,066	52,796	25,555	148	80,477	88.4	1,790	21,716
Alhambra city	249	1,275,176	14,598	141.6	(NA)	3,767	104,977	27,868	179	108,794	98.2	2,605	32,192
Aliso Viejo city	76	539,082	13,217	128.2	(NA)	1,551	38,643	24,915	51	40,739	(NA)	916	12,878
Anaheim city	855	3,008,129	9,084	88.1	6.4	12,326	324,778	26,349	603	916,207	44.9	17,099	251,765
Antioch city	223	691,533	6,951	67.4	27.6	3,118	71,479	22,925	126	74,462	98.9	1,693	20,959
Apple Valley town	74	245,310	4,242	41.1	(NA)	1,198	25,782	21,521	45	31,883	(NA)	813	8,652
Arcadia city	269	622,902	11,417	110.7	18.2	3,985	80,158	20,115	153	108,391	83.7	2,316	29,645
Atascadero city	120	310,188	11,569	112.2	(NA)	1,502	33,610	22,377	48	23,957	91.2	592	6,480
Azusa city	87	337,056	7,325	71.0	(NA)	1,125	29,228	25,980	67	40,198	95.1	914	11,133
Bakersfield city	981	3,586,569	13,771	133.6	19.5	15,836	344,737	21,769	514	381,952	87.3	9,355	108,190

See footnotes at end of table.

[Includes states and 1,265 incorporated places of 25,000 or more population as of April 1, 2000, in all states except Hawaii, which has no incorporated places recognized by the U.S. Census Bureau. Two census designated places (CDPs) are also included (Honolulu CDP in Hawaii and Arlington CDP in Virginia). For more information on these areas, see Appendix C, Geographic Information]

| City | Retail trade (NAICS 44–45), 2002[1] | | | | | | | | Accommodation and food services (NAICS 72), 2002[1] | | | | |
| | | Sales | | | | Annual payroll | | | | Sales | | | |
	Establishments	Total ($1,000)	Per capita[2] Amount (dol.)	Per capita[2] Percent of national average	Percent from general merchandise stores	Paid employees[3]	Total ($1,000)	Per paid employee (dol.)	Establishments	Total ($1,000)	Percent from food services	Paid employees[3]	Annual payroll ($1,000)
CALIFORNIA—Con.													
Baldwin Park city	127	349,424	4,519	43.8	(NA)	1,824	37,944	20,803	70	45,812	85.1	856	10,715
Bell city	69	187,574	5,047	48.9	(NA)	623	21,338	34,250	48	31,020	94.8	609	7,403
Bellflower city	173	459,377	6,199	60.1	6.3	1,841	47,122	25,596	91	46,408	91.3	1,056	12,147
Bell Gardens city	71	96,505	2,147	20.8	2.8	572	10,823	18,921	43	17,914	88.0	385	4,709
Belmont city	60	296,230	11,974	116.1	(NA)	1,135	41,210	36,308	56	33,449	70.2	669	8,297
Benicia city	70	197,696	7,310	70.9	(NA)	893	28,852	32,309	62	26,901	(NA)	811	7,442
Berkeley city	541	1,156,218	11,208	108.7	0.1	6,877	160,918	23,399	388	249,468	82.5	5,055	72,976
Beverly Hills city	424	1,747,234	50,283	487.6	(NA)	5,554	206,555	37,190	198	423,519	(NA)	7,136	137,148
Brea city	277	919,216	24,962	242.1	24.3	4,999	100,900	20,184	130	143,455	90.7	3,374	39,760
Buena Park city	218	1,382,878	17,531	170.0	8.7	3,383	103,122	30,482	132	98,659	84.9	2,191	27,460
Burbank city	419	1,462,877	14,276	138.5	13.1	7,128	162,921	22,856	249	271,712	84.0	5,377	74,357
Burlingame city	196	668,579	24,098	233.7	(NA)	2,672	77,888	29,150	120	168,673	75.9	2,875	55,421
Calexico city	181	414,464	13,489	130.8	(NA)	2,255	37,035	16,424	50	32,697	96.4	698	8,561
Camarillo city	285	1,103,634	18,625	180.6	5.0	4,817	110,693	22,980	123	89,087	84.7	2,033	24,192
Campbell city	188	654,514	17,560	170.3	(NA)	3,118	76,332	24,481	127	95,060	(NA)	1,956	27,908
Carlsbad city	411	2,019,554	23,418	227.1	13.4	7,720	214,928	27,840	189	293,107	(NA)	5,765	88,350
Carson city	216	1,505,764	16,375	158.8	9.9	4,636	146,231	31,542	116	86,531	80.3	1,755	20,446
Cathedral City city	164	820,851	17,677	171.4	(NA)	2,689	77,866	28,957	79	50,838	88.8	1,221	13,833
Ceres city	74	324,753	8,873	86.0	31.4	1,494	32,912	22,029	48	32,513	(NA)	878	8,387
Cerritos city	257	2,397,507	45,772	443.9	12.3	7,130	193,434	27,130	116	83,237	(NA)	2,045	24,868
Chico city	429	1,383,062	20,313	197.0	(NA)	7,398	146,899	19,857	223	157,884	89.5	4,586	43,154
Chino city	198	784,757	10,839	105.1	(NA)	3,161	78,541	24,847	108	81,496	97.2	2,065	23,580
Chino Hills city	89	373,845	5,177	50.2	(NA)	1,644	38,841	23,626	73	38,962	100.0	1,116	11,262
Chula Vista city	532	1,783,315	9,255	89.8	33.5	8,360	183,412	21,939	296	214,822	89.1	5,074	58,576
Citrus Heights city	319	934,879	10,605	102.8	25.4	5,228	106,443	20,360	141	98,615	99.1	2,449	29,048
Claremont city	88	445,970	12,854	124.7	(NA)	1,004	32,692	32,562	72	58,515	94.2	1,370	15,541
Clovis city	270	1,098,122	14,758	143.1	29.3	4,773	105,934	22,194	135	82,245	(NA)	2,258	22,745
Colton city	105	606,246	12,184	118.2	(NA)	2,052	56,200	27,388	80	42,646	93.7	1,079	11,686
Compton city	153	201,004	2,110	20.5	2.3	873	18,570	21,271	60	39,836	58.7	911	12,802
Concord city	445	2,208,279	17,718	171.8	17.5	8,062	231,394	28,702	234	178,739	87.4	3,628	48,536
Corona city	315	1,661,278	11,802	114.5	21.6	5,680	154,095	27,129	179	138,202	92.8	3,081	35,856
Costa Mesa city	735	2,899,454	26,261	254.7	10.5	13,291	327,525	24,643	362	374,373	74.6	7,355	112,235
Covina city	176	482,335	10,104	98.0	(NA)	2,316	49,905	21,548	102	63,367	(NA)	1,445	18,188
Culver City city	332	1,824,859	46,110	447.2	21.7	5,963	175,736	29,471	163	129,404	77.2	2,478	37,668
Cupertino city	199	1,218,870	23,627	229.1	12.4	4,027	90,384	22,444	114	99,726	87.1	2,116	32,853
Cypress city	101	245,333	5,209	50.5	(NA)	1,224	26,329	21,511	93	67,357	71.8	1,497	18,051
Daly City city	207	768,296	7,564	73.4	(NA)	3,639	78,101	21,462	120	96,056	(NA)	1,977	27,258
Dana Point city	105	202,247	5,666	54.9	(NA)	1,009	22,914	22,710	103	244,507	33.0	3,975	78,371
Danville town	140	313,711	7,401	71.8	(NA)	1,508	36,493	24,200	85	52,401	(NA)	1,105	13,992
Davis city	141	425,096	6,842	66.4	(NA)	2,022	45,478	22,492	124	84,875	90.8	2,354	22,957
Delano city	91	218,015	5,227	50.7	(NA)	1,010	21,880	21,663	48	21,118	87.4	465	4,792
Diamond Bar city	110	259,178	4,493	43.6	(NA)	1,108	27,420	24,747	99	59,937	88.2	1,268	15,595
Downey city	302	1,173,379	10,753	104.3	(NA)	5,073	121,440	23,938	180	129,483	93.0	2,898	35,608
Dublin city	171	1,075,989	31,351	304.0	(NA)	3,471	96,419	27,778	88	91,900	88.5	1,892	27,609
East Palo Alto city	25	164,748	5,221	50.6	(NA)	626	18,654	29,799	9	19,778	100.0	324	4,769
El Cajon city	462	1,643,904	17,320	168.0	11.5	6,589	152,769	23,185	209	134,976	91.7	3,074	37,160
El Centro city	151	589,474	15,605	151.3	(NA)	2,618	58,941	22,514	79	56,939	82.4	1,310	15,671
Elk Grove city	201	1,098,447	12,484	121.1	(NA)	4,632	113,978	24,607	116	92,268	100.0	2,626	27,321
El Monte city	277	1,789,611	15,037	145.8	5.9	3,762	121,183	32,212	136	57,176	97.2	1,201	13,967
Encinitas city	276	973,601	16,395	159.0	(NA)	4,156	100,487	24,179	167	125,682	94.2	2,787	36,731
Escondido city	586	2,261,183	16,732	162.3	9.8	9,858	247,582	25,115	231	147,024	93.1	3,693	40,303
Eureka city	269	704,106	27,183	263.6	22.0	3,227	68,109	21,106	131	78,007	72.6	2,151	22,200
Fairfield city	340	1,243,366	12,258	118.9	24.6	5,777	131,255	22,720	177	130,111	85.7	2,949	35,317
Folsom city	207	1,364,104	22,430	217.5	7.9	4,300	120,194	27,952	137	100,746	(NA)	2,540	30,982
Fontana city	228	999,245	6,964	67.5	14.0	3,565	89,828	25,197	135	88,051	96.2	1,997	22,828
Foster City city	33	249,159	8,552	82.9	(NA)	721	20,769	28,806	50	55,825	(NA)	1,020	19,164
Fountain Valley city	226	948,353	17,100	165.8	(NA)	3,490	84,209	24,129	122	91,161	(NA)	2,044	25,200
Fremont city	446	2,797,428	13,613	132.0	(NA)	7,313	238,507	32,614	295	212,454	84.6	4,547	61,743
Fresno city	1,511	4,743,378	10,683	103.6	15.6	21,474	484,469	22,561	820	544,790	89.7	14,052	149,546
Fullerton city	372	1,420,275	11,042	107.1	22.1	5,725	136,008	23,757	244	173,303	86.8	4,020	50,378
Gardena city	186	620,853	10,439	101.2	(NA)	2,699	76,453	28,326	194	104,907	94.7	2,278	30,006
Garden Grove city	401	1,307,234	7,845	76.1	18.7	4,949	120,399	24,328	291	211,687	71.1	4,350	60,006
Gilroy city	274	813,656	18,940	183.7	(NA)	3,269	79,299	24,258	98	77,325	80.8	1,540	19,979
Glendale city	732	2,625,246	13,204	128.1	7.6	10,440	266,587	25,535	317	231,443	87.4	5,028	64,386
Glendora city	136	584,361	11,629	112.8	(NA)	2,217	53,387	24,081	85	48,383	(NA)	1,166	13,202
Goleta city	131	574,864	19,291	187.1	(NA)	2,139	55,332	25,868	71	56,929	79.9	1,327	15,805
Hanford city	173	492,513	11,135	108.0	(NA)	2,406	53,434	22,209	88	48,979	95.2	1,244	12,947
Hawthorne city	171	753,540	8,812	85.5	(NA)	2,845	68,631	24,123	95	60,850	92.9	1,247	14,660
Hayward city	422	1,751,998	12,374	120.0	14.9	6,963	181,047	26,001	250	132,729	88.5	2,789	34,415
Hemet city	226	822,808	13,029	126.4	(NA)	3,824	88,815	23,226	116	71,450	88.8	1,666	18,186

See footnotes at end of table.

Table C-5. Cities — **Retail Trade and Accommodation and Food Services**—Con.

[Includes states and 1,265 incorporated places of 25,000 or more population as of April 1, 2000, in all states except Hawaii, which has no incorporated places recognized by the U.S. Census Bureau. Two census designated places (CDPs) are also included (Honolulu CDP in Hawaii and Arlington CDP in Virginia). For more information on these areas, see Appendix C, Geographic Information]

City	Retail trade (NAICS 44–45), 2002[1]								Accommodation and food services (NAICS 72), 2002[1]				
	Sales					Annual payroll			Sales				
	Estab-lishments	Total ($1,000)	Per capita[2] Amount (dol.)	Per capita Percent of national average	Percent from general mer-chandise stores	Paid employees[3]	Total ($1,000)	Per paid employee (dol.)	Estab-lishments	Total ($1,000)	Percent from food services	Paid employees[3]	Annual payroll ($1,000)
CALIFORNIA—Con.													
Hesperia city	154	260,914	3,892	37.7	(NA)	1,432	30,597	21,367	72	43,263	95.3	1,082	11,746
Highland city	54	117,597	2,502	24.3	(NA)	646	12,455	19,280	35	15,423	(NA)	395	4,082
Hollister city	115	371,054	10,230	99.2	1,595	40,064	25,118	54	33,258	98.9	811	8,910
Huntington Beach city	548	1,945,786	10,078	97.7	7.4	8,196	205,495	25,073	359	272,862	88.7	6,036	76,823
Huntington Park city	187	420,725	6,725	65.2	1.8	1,953	45,520	23,308	85	58,717	100.0	1,065	13,843
Imperial Beach city	37	42,300	1,564	15.2	(NA)	261	4,157	15,927	34	17,331	85.6	508	4,996
Indio city	144	572,502	10,596	102.8	7.2	2,273	59,794	26,306	78	51,475	83.3	1,104	13,039
Inglewood city	242	636,530	5,562	53.9	27.0	2,627	58,720	22,352	129	78,803	80.7	1,746	20,281
Irvine city	519	2,960,830	18,246	176.9	10.8	9,376	287,868	30,703	396	494,336	75.0	9,666	140,273
Laguna Hills city	235	597,117	18,526	179.7	24.8	3,461	69,375	20,045	87	79,979	92.9	1,918	24,341
Laguna Niguel city	154	901,040	14,120	136.9	(NA)	2,632	81,340	30,904	87	57,680	(NA)	1,365	15,549
La Habra city	177	698,407	11,697	113.4	(NA)	2,693	78,178	29,030	112	74,866	(NA)	1,816	20,410
Lake Elsinore city	119	421,582	13,234	128.3	(NA)	1,697	35,851	21,126	58	46,778	90.8	1,019	11,250
Lake Forest city	234	714,896	9,322	90.4	(NA)	3,078	74,680	24,263	145	105,111	93.1	2,426	30,060
Lakewood city	235	980,801	12,184	118.2	20.5	4,933	100,219	20,316	135	115,850	97.6	2,748	32,279
La Mesa city	273	1,138,377	20,847	202.2	20.7	4,484	108,266	24,145	154	122,904	93.8	2,970	36,114
La Mirada city	83	294,034	6,101	59.2	(NA)	1,299	33,055	25,446	74	61,231	82.6	1,500	17,105
Lancaster city	319	1,228,486	9,923	96.2	22.3	4,809	120,756	25,110	162	121,748	84.7	2,912	30,614
La Puente city	109	263,656	6,318	61.3	3.6	1,188	28,442	23,941	66	26,666	97.3	619	6,839
La Verne city	82	224,691	6,913	67.0	(NA)	1,384	26,709	19,298	67	42,094	(NA)	948	11,204
Lawndale city	93	195,574	6,077	58.9	(NA)	887	19,876	22,408	40	22,463	(NA)	477	6,729
Livermore city	194	932,972	12,254	118.8	25.8	3,769	96,401	25,577	133	103,665	83.7	2,018	28,357
Lodi city	228	724,740	11,973	116.1	(NA)	3,236	73,496	22,712	137	74,535	95.4	1,686	18,818
Lompoc city	126	295,400	7,187	69.7	(NA)	1,519	31,347	20,637	77	49,126	69.0	1,149	12,904
Long Beach city	1,018	2,599,922	5,525	53.6	10.5	12,373	272,778	22,046	731	646,802	73.4	14,000	188,020
Los Altos city	121	203,672	7,508	72.8	(NA)	1,122	27,443	24,459	59	49,572	(NA)	1,007	16,321
Los Angeles city	11,208	30,196,646	7,976	77.4	9.2	131,916	3,173,429	24,056	6,771	5,592,058	81.3	111,071	1,643,262
Los Banos city	76	209,047	7,082	68.7	(NA)	1,022	21,327	20,868	43	21,578	91.1	581	6,207
Los Gatos town	194	641,809	22,816	221.3	(NA)	2,347	68,305	29,103	111	85,590	92.0	1,807	29,146
Lynwood city	98	192,246	2,707	26.3	2.0	969	17,778	18,347	62	37,313	97.4	677	8,290
Madera city	156	374,069	8,135	78.9	(NA)	2,022	40,107	19,835	65	30,958	96.2	843	8,177
Manhattan Beach city	173	594,453	16,848	163.4	(NA)	2,901	65,749	22,664	138	143,766	80.7	3,269	43,578
Manteca city	148	580,779	10,240	99.3	(NA)	2,271	56,014	24,665	93	54,826	93.0	1,408	14,555
Martinez city	58	223,712	6,117	59.3	(NA)	901	27,833	30,891	76	38,740	88.8	856	9,700
Maywood city	51	79,168	2,766	26.8	(NA)	525	10,054	19,150	32	14,932	(NA)	328	3,814
Menlo Park city	143	504,421	16,722	162.2	(NA)	1,987	62,841	31,626	110	84,334	82.6	1,647	29,344
Merced city	244	935,888	13,704	132.9	26.3	3,987	90,681	22,744	123	72,382	90.9	1,863	18,882
Milpitas city	310	777,192	12,260	118.9	12.6	4,778	96,025	20,097	232	231,759	76.3	4,036	66,726
Mission Viejo city	318	1,241,532	12,990	126.0	8.9	5,787	132,864	22,959	148	103,567	(NA)	2,354	30,557
Modesto city	732	2,483,944	12,241	118.7	22.0	11,864	256,074	21,584	383	307,448	89.2	7,922	84,772
Monrovia city	130	708,052	18,770	182.0	(NA)	2,376	64,462	27,130	93	76,078	82.5	1,709	23,595
Montclair city	238	900,103	26,221	254.3	27.4	4,509	102,414	22,713	73	64,575	99.2	1,654	19,328
Montebello city	219	759,281	12,002	116.4	32.2	3,586	76,297	21,276	122	69,110	95.6	1,682	18,685
Monterey city	254	427,420	14,281	138.5	(NA)	2,497	53,017	21,232	225	310,599	45.8	5,346	86,309
Monterey Park city	200	391,124	6,367	61.7	(NA)	1,796	40,174	22,369	146	82,212	93.3	1,867	23,757
Moorpark city	30	80,367	2,331	22.6	(NA)	327	8,915	27,263	34	(D)	(NA)	[4]750	(D)
Moreno Valley city	273	883,999	5,870	56.9	26.2	4,507	98,583	21,873	133	95,061	94.3	2,348	25,301
Morgan Hill city	91	352,383	10,668	103.5	(NA)	1,520	37,873	24,916	83	46,200	76.5	989	13,024
Mountain View city	251	989,828	14,213	137.8	29.0	4,063	99,211	24,418	246	163,052	82.8	2,916	46,357
Murrieta city	111	530,660	8,760	84.9	22.7	2,235	51,165	22,893	67	45,175	(NA)	1,204	12,122
Napa city	335	906,626	12,101	117.4	(NA)	4,300	98,975	23,017	185	146,147	71.8	3,032	43,270
National City city	338	1,308,965	22,072	221.8	6.5	4,928	134,153	27,223	159	105,168	89.2	2,336	27,615
Newark city	203	815,146	18,945	183.7	21.8	4,026	83,106	20,642	128	98,032	75.6	2,017	20,919
Newport Beach city	462	1,791,845	22,621	219.4	(NA)	5,968	184,313	30,884	300	417,205	68.0	7,811	126,541
Norwalk city	156	781,568	7,357	71.3	(NA)	2,874	75,991	26,441	132	75,500	86.2	1,696	19,354
Novato city	191	866,452	18,021	174.8	26.8	2,843	82,913	29,164	121	83,514	85.6	1,772	23,071
Oakland city	1,086	2,518,731	6,276	60.9	3.6	11,255	290,757	25,834	750	535,149	76.5	10,335	161,311
Oakley city	37	101,690	3,901	37.8	(NA)	428	11,685	27,301	24	(D)	(NA)	[5]375	(D)
Oceanside city	375	1,166,531	7,075	68.6	11.3	5,732	125,879	21,961	248	169,514	91.5	3,929	45,782
Ontario city	488	2,422,288	14,707	142.6	6.9	8,803	220,660	25,066	263	320,207	70.6	6,415	86,592
Orange city	566	1,820,968	13,809	133.9	8.7	7,426	185,930	25,038	352	292,327	86.0	6,423	85,934
Oxnard city	443	1,830,608	10,313	100.0	20.2	6,830	168,028	24,601	220	172,831	79.8	3,754	46,521
Pacifica city	70	134,643	3,578	34.7	(NA)	614	13,353	21,748	60	31,307	81.3	686	9,681
Palmdale city	247	947,547	7,648	74.2	20.4	4,457	94,119	21,117	135	105,213	87.7	2,566	29,055
Palm Desert city	400	1,030,662	23,169	224.7	28.2	5,018	113,005	22,520	169	285,256	(NA)	5,611	86,610
Palm Springs city	213	486,157	10,913	105.8	(NA)	2,268	52,771	23,268	241	272,028	51.6	5,657	78,084
Palo Alto city	310	1,400,433	24,425	236.9	(NA)	5,393	160,783	29,813	251	257,241	86.6	5,198	85,964
Paradise town	88	150,754	5,661	54.9	(NA)	823	16,677	20,264	48	18,358	91.0	537	5,499
Paramount city	118	335,764	5,960	57.8	(NA)	1,574	34,846	22,139	66	32,758	100.0	661	8,301
Pasadena city	615	2,198,589	15,765	152.9	9.3	9,520	224,576	23,590	390	455,974	73.2	9,139	131,825

See footnotes at end of table.

County and City Data Book: 2007

U.S. Census Bureau

[Includes states and 1,265 incorporated places of 25,000 or more population as of April 1, 2000, in all states except Hawaii, which has no incorporated places recognized by the U.S. Census Bureau. Two census designated places (CDPs) are also included (Honolulu CDP in Hawaii and Arlington CDP in Virginia). For more information on these areas, see Appendix C, Geographic Information]

City	Retail trade (NAICS 44–45), 2002[1] Estab-lishments	Sales Total ($1,000)	Per capita[2] Amount (dol.)	Per capita[2] Percent of national average	Percent from general mer-chandise stores	Annual payroll Paid employees[3]	Annual payroll Total ($1,000)	Per paid employee (dol.)	Accommodation and food services (NAICS 72), 2002[1] Estab-lishments	Sales Total ($1,000)	Percent from food services	Paid employees[3]	Annual payroll ($1,000)
CALIFORNIA—Con.													
Perris city	70	541,636	14,032	136.1	(NA)	2,157	58,464	27,104	50	27,770	(NA)	645	6,370
Petaluma city	245	780,510	14,170	137.4	(NA)	3,183	84,361	26,504	146	82,347	89.5	1,872	23,637
Pico Rivera city	102	263,171	4,084	39.6	23.5	1,300	35,344	27,188	91	48,153	94.4	1,144	13,393
Pittsburg city	120	587,019	9,755	94.6	(NA)	2,539	70,329	27,699	65	45,500	95.1	972	13,528
Placentia city	103	306,243	6,423	62.3	(NA)	1,223	36,853	30,133	84	51,365	(NA)	1,050	12,858
Pleasant Hill city	145	576,788	17,284	167.6	(NA)	2,498	58,765	23,525	79	71,888	(NA)	1,429	19,593
Pleasanton city	336	1,265,983	19,253	186.7	18.7	6,156	153,185	24,884	199	165,624	79.5	3,286	46,623
Pomona city	271	924,239	6,110	59.3	6.0	3,832	89,660	23,398	167	111,253	86.9	3,280	30,721
Porterville city	156	434,676	10,510	101.9	24.4	2,201	46,482	21,119	66	39,312	87.3	1,031	10,055
Poway city	136	760,892	15,591	151.2	(NA)	2,656	71,831	27,045	98	52,460	(NA)	1,439	16,927
Rancho Cordova city	(X)	(X)	(NA)	(NA)	(NA)	(X)	(X)	(NA)	(X)	(X)	(NA)	(X)	(X)
Rancho Cucamonga city	280	1,033,252	7,200	69.8	25.8	4,937	103,186	20,901	191	147,318	(NA)	3,811	41,895
Rancho Palos Verdes city	46	75,471	1,807	17.5	(NA)	418	9,725	23,266	36	(D)	(NA)	[5]375	(D)
Rancho Santa Margarita city	77	369,395	7,607	73.8	(NA)	1,407	41,120	29,225	64	51,321	(NA)	1,212	13,960
Redding city	484	1,651,811	19,255	186.7	21.4	7,025	166,330	23,677	238	174,339	78.9	4,108	47,478
Redlands city	218	1,168,501	17,538	170.1	13.4	3,966	99,836	25,173	123	71,845	95.3	1,914	20,647
Redondo Beach city	287	637,462	9,744	94.5	10.7	3,751	79,524	21,201	177	161,530	80.1	3,339	47,426
Redwood City city	244	1,301,027	17,523	169.9	14.3	4,787	155,791	32,545	187	130,775	78.5	2,369	34,754
Rialto city	114	378,675	3,930	38.1	(NA)	2,035	44,000	21,622	67	45,688	(NA)	1,065	12,002
Richmond city	238	858,764	8,411	81.6	28.8	3,343	86,548	25,889	111	59,032	89.8	1,130	13,724
Riverside city	789	3,450,302	12,605	122.2	12.8	12,790	323,351	25,282	429	303,952	87.7	7,191	84,519
Rocklin city	104	298,881	6,890	66.8	(NA)	1,279	32,560	25,457	58	29,528	(NA)	747	9,383
Rohnert Park city	116	533,436	12,964	125.7	25.1	2,391	54,017	22,592	76	73,526	76.4	1,618	21,125
Rosemead city	147	230,887	4,232	41.0	(NA)	1,169	22,328	19,100	109	60,074	81.8	1,392	17,305
Roseville city	412	2,932,064	31,956	309.9	16.9	9,135	254,648	27,876	226	223,350	82.6	4,982	62,047
Sacramento city	1,269	3,864,211	8,910	86.4	11.2	18,467	431,136	23,346	869	718,759	73.6	15,118	201,647
Salinas city	470	1,767,414	12,000	116.4	19.7	7,474	184,483	24,683	235	161,692	90.2	3,627	43,325
San Bernardino city	589	2,483,461	12,923	125.3	18.7	8,996	226,468	25,174	316	258,114	90.7	6,249	72,877
San Bruno city	63	163,980	4,170	40.4	(NA)	790	21,056	26,653	43	26,546	66.3	491	6,598
San Buenaventura (Ventura) city	504	1,678,951	16,268	157.8	12.8	7,189	180,234	25,071	268	197,309	83.7	4,840	59,036
San Carlos city	140	433,952	16,031	155.5	(NA)	1,841	55,129	29,945	80	38,296	79.3	780	11,674
San Clemente city	178	368,102	6,593	63.9	(NA)	2,054	48,961	23,837	129	70,063	87.1	1,398	17,242
San Diego city	4,238	13,953,238	11,136	108.0	12.3	62,552	1,490,534	23,829	2,923	3,508,436	60.3	65,314	970,947
San Dimas city	96	223,283	6,253	60.6	(NA)	1,086	23,890	21,998	64	52,494	84.0	1,150	14,076
San Francisco city	3,654	8,883,316	11,658	113.1	7.4	42,032	1,077,957	25,646	3,311	3,546,865	58.8	58,294	1,087,997
San Gabriel city	184	352,320	8,671	84.1	(NA)	1,580	31,526	19,953	157	59,220	99.0	1,373	16,170
San Jose city	2,204	9,091,996	10,146	98.4	12.9	37,837	1,319,449	34,872	1,528	1,167,123	81.5	22,929	332,947
San Juan Capistrano city	132	618,727	17,954	174.1	(NA)	1,884	57,223	30,373	61	48,650	93.3	1,145	14,368
San Leandro city	313	1,803,315	22,537	218.6	22.3	5,916	155,932	26,358	167	95,398	94.6	2,404	25,955
San Luis Obispo city	355	998,648	22,685	220.0	7.1	5,229	107,432	20,545	196	173,065	58.4	4,022	48,724
San Marcos city	217	725,240	11,769	114.1	(NA)	2,622	77,939	29,725	109	77,657	97.5	1,858	22,054
San Mateo city	373	1,291,388	14,085	136.6	13.5	6,806	159,542	23,441	247	244,482	(NA)	4,177	73,197
San Pablo city	91	226,402	7,350	71.3	3.4	1,064	22,744	21,376	50	22,542	(NA)	513	5,572
San Rafael city	362	1,382,569	24,584	238.4	(NA)	5,895	155,625	26,399	201	119,767	82.2	2,446	34,684
San Ramon city	123	441,978	9,448	91.6	(NA)	2,123	52,621	24,786	114	124,628	(NA)	2,449	34,596
Santa Ana city	892	2,972,446	8,707	84.4	7.9	13,307	334,017	25,101	522	363,556	84.8	7,443	99,208
Santa Barbara city	630	1,590,072	17,912	173.7	5.7	7,921	187,508	23,672	396	372,953	68.7	7,665	106,218
Santa Clara city	378	1,653,400	16,316	158.2	11.2	5,732	184,617	32,208	344	370,062	62.2	6,216	105,517
Santa Clarita city	460	2,078,512	13,085	126.9	14.2	8,034	190,977	23,771	245	184,071	(NA)	4,294	55,118
Santa Cruz city	263	693,311	12,548	121.7	(NA)	3,608	77,736	21,545	220	168,117	83.0	4,036	49,401
Santa Maria city	347	1,239,596	15,617	151.5	24.5	5,386	124,185	23,057	165	116,278	82.8	2,888	34,719
Santa Monica city	735	3,081,902	35,614	345.4	2.7	9,335	250,657	26,851	390	591,059	65.3	10,061	172,362
Santa Paula city	66	138,786	4,836	46.9	(NA)	655	12,966	19,795	42	17,879	95.9	451	4,880
Santa Rosa city	744	2,654,904	17,374	168.5	18.7	12,021	305,954	25,452	363	237,069	86.0	5,314	67,405
Santee city	133	496,501	9,406	91.2	37.8	2,186	54,292	24,836	78	43,220	(NA)	1,060	11,652
Saratoga city	50	94,964	3,237	31.4	(NA)	463	11,272	24,346	46	34,901	(NA)	699	9,733
Seaside city	93	565,311	16,634	161.3	(NA)	1,542	47,297	30,673	56	40,145	52.1	786	10,151
Simi Valley city	311	1,181,889	10,174	98.7	21.7	5,054	120,130	23,769	172	133,809	90.7	3,137	39,607
South Gate city	171	591,835	6,010	58.3	(NA)	2,188	53,370	24,392	103	60,955	88.6	1,166	14,292
South San Francisco city	193	681,652	11,409	110.6	(NA)	2,675	72,673	27,167	164	152,217	68.6	2,490	42,116
Stanton city	101	341,484	9,046	87.7	(NA)	1,324	31,330	23,663	76	36,956	91.0	790	9,256
Stockton city	751	2,522,032	9,608	93.2	(NA)	11,165	245,702	22,006	431	284,361	86.9	6,804	75,251
Suisun City city	39	78,667	2,927	28.4	(NA)	395	9,335	23,633	28	(D)	(NA)	[5]375	(D)
Sunnyvale city	316	1,395,768	10,828	105.0	15.6	5,389	150,369	27,903	324	249,481	70.1	4,602	72,474
Temecula city	362	1,599,974	21,691	210.4	22.0	5,872	147,529	25,124	188	183,946	85.1	4,286	52,894
Temple City city	95	128,470	3,632	35.2	(NA)	778	14,450	18,573	47	(D)	(NA)	[4]750	(D)
Thousand Oaks city	527	2,471,333	20,220	196.1	8.8	9,202	237,738	25,835	253	225,945	88.8	5,086	66,707
Torrance city	772	3,977,253	28,283	274.3	14.6	13,719	332,176	24,213	408	377,312	85.0	7,609	106,439
Tracy city	219	825,490	12,170	118.0	(NA)	3,292	80,228	24,371	111	71,501	93.2	1,613	18,338
Tulare city	150	439,407	9,590	93.0	19.6	2,114	45,750	21,641	77	41,007	85.6	1,025	10,069

See footnotes at end of table.

[Includes states and 1,265 incorporated places of 25,000 or more population as of April 1, 2000, in all states except Hawaii, which has no incorporated places recognized by the U.S. Census Bureau. Two census designated places (CDPs) are also included (Honolulu CDP in Hawaii and Arlington CDP in Virginia). For more information on these areas, see Appendix C, Geographic Information]

City	Retail trade (NAICS 44–45), 2002[1]								Accommodation and food services (NAICS 72), 2002[1]				
		Sales					Annual payroll			Sales			
			Per capita[2]		Percent from general mer-chandise stores						Percent from food services		
	Estab-lishments	Total ($1,000)	Amount (dol.)	Percent of national average		Paid employees[3]	Total ($1,000)	Per paid employee (dol.)	Estab-lishments	Total ($1,000)		Paid employees[3]	Annual payroll ($1,000)
CALIFORNIA—Con.													
Turlock city	215	642,300	10,425	101.1	(NA)	3,016	64,091	21,250	115	72,320	95.6	2,080	19,229
Tustin city	258	1,498,837	21,891	212.3	11.6	4,511	124,683	27,640	164	122,082	95.7	2,783	36,029
Twentynine Palms city	33	45,154	1,535	14.9	(NA)	263	5,349	20,338	36	22,110	85.2	609	6,586
Union City city	96	571,561	8,236	79.9	(NA)	2,357	56,822	24,108	96	70,833	(NA)	1,583	18,935
Upland city	232	648,720	9,139	88.6	15.0	3,143	74,739	23,780	99	63,964	(NA)	1,573	19,199
Vacaville city	311	1,031,516	11,065	107.3	(NA)	4,751	103,833	21,855	144	108,261	88.7	2,478	29,648
Vallejo city	264	1,353,032	11,342	110.0	(NA)	4,861	120,854	24,862	179	99,904	89.9	2,331	26,095
Victorville city	304	1,355,160	19,088	185.1	23.5	5,792	128,242	22,141	154	123,606	89.9	3,024	34,005
Visalia city	390	1,325,227	13,655	132.4	25.5	5,821	122,395	21,026	177	116,848	93.3	3,038	32,319
Vista city	247	889,907	9,783	94.9	30.4	3,757	89,950	23,942	147	78,071	99.1	1,774	20,248
Walnut city	86	144,802	4,721	45.8	(NA)	1,025	14,985	14,620	43	11,894	100.0	291	2,768
Walnut Creek city	342	1,565,342	23,984	232.6	9.2	7,267	199,243	27,418	187	184,278	88.0	3,487	54,865
Watsonville city	168	686,994	14,788	143.4	9.0	2,389	53,973	22,592	90	49,966	91.1	1,146	13,205
West Covina city	301	1,393,421	13,010	126.2	15.2	5,978	133,472	22,327	140	114,939	93.6	2,504	29,555
West Hollywood city	335	899,589	24,630	238.9	(NA)	3,536	106,262	30,051	193	286,231	71.7	5,299	86,415
Westminster city	434	1,400,814	15,750	152.7	18.3	6,229	141,392	22,699	220	91,132	92.7	2,188	24,867
West Sacramento city	104	298,170	8,234	79.9	(NA)	1,195	29,991	25,097	66	32,503	(NA)	822	8,856
Whittier city	268	739,283	8,694	84.3	8.2	3,446	82,982	24,081	157	107,715	92.4	2,737	31,142
Woodland city	164	508,046	9,979	96.8	21.0	2,402	51,409	21,403	94	46,112	87.2	1,069	11,900
Yorba Linda city	112	489,133	8,031	77.9	(NA)	1,833	44,974	24,536	67	65,188	(NA)	1,732	19,785
Yuba City city	229	770,487	14,583	141.4	(NA)	3,718	75,313	20,256	96	66,561	(NA)	1,802	17,980
Yucaipa city	72	150,435	3,452	33.5	(NA)	868	17,688	20,378	45	21,610	98.4	536	5,812
COLORADO	18,851	52,226,983	11,610	112.6	14.9	247,264	5,595,862	22,631	10,799	8,808,846	70.2	206,597	2,617,701
Arvada city	281	860,005	8,417	81.6	26.9	4,136	95,769	23,155	160	108,170	(NA)	3,200	31,551
Aurora city	812	3,017,798	10,632	103.1	19.8	13,741	308,318	22,438	449	347,784	83.9	7,767	97,235
Boulder city	617	1,570,817	16,750	162.4	4.5	8,004	190,295	23,775	360	302,153	79.0	7,825	92,682
Broomfield city	206	636,212	15,753	152.8	12.7	3,432	81,111	23,634	95	93,885	75.6	2,061	31,901
Centennial city	294	1,383,018	13,957	135.4	6.2	4,519	110,973	24,557	123	97,740	77.0	2,206	28,216
Colorado Springs city	1,624	5,377,409	14,521	140.8	(NA)	25,289	562,019	22,224	891	833,852	67.3	19,416	244,664
Denver city	2,313	6,405,054	11,486	111.4	9.5	28,934	738,762	25,533	1,641	1,669,129	73.8	34,619	492,023
Englewood city	235	1,116,946	34,074	330.4	(NA)	2,823	84,471	29,922	108	65,692	88.6	1,485	18,984
Fort Collins city	595	1,853,633	14,880	144.3	18.6	9,402	198,104	21,070	348	260,536	88.7	7,288	76,694
Grand Junction city	479	1,440,204	32,482	315.0	(NA)	6,562	146,481	22,323	183	144,360	75.6	3,727	42,712
Greeley city	293	1,055,829	12,782	124.0	18.1	4,604	100,065	21,734	170	103,366	95.0	3,141	29,293
Lakewood city	645	2,122,820	14,781	143.3	9.4	8,281	214,883	25,949	313	254,651	84.9	6,451	76,820
Littleton city	436	1,972,579	49,092	476.1	(NA)	8,049	190,817	23,707	183	(D)	(NA)	[6]3,750	(D)
Longmont city	287	829,409	10,569	102.5	8.7	4,290	91,682	21,371	164	109,130	87.3	2,781	30,987
Loveland city	277	810,291	14,564	141.2	(NA)	3,648	77,904	21,355	127	85,688	95.6	2,297	23,969
Northglenn city	99	438,633	12,993	126.0	(NA)	1,958	46,788	23,896	48	(D)	(NA)	[7]1,750	(D)
Pueblo city	447	1,143,267	11,024	106.9	(NA)	5,883	120,375	20,461	279	154,436	85.9	4,804	43,535
Thornton city	154	812,428	8,625	83.6	32.9	3,622	98,015	27,061	105	83,344	89.7	2,076	23,161
Westminster city	337	984,240	9,479	91.9	19.4	5,518	102,245	18,529	195	189,395	79.5	4,483	54,773
Wheat Ridge city	180	676,717	21,030	203.9	(NA)	2,509	67,861	27,047	93	56,729	86.8	1,391	16,791
CONNECTICUT	13,861	41,952,682	12,131	117.6	10.0	191,807	4,531,064	23,623	7,047	6,681,803	58.4	118,337	1,967,217
Bridgeport city	311	750,616	5,377	52.1	(NA)	3,536	92,731	26,225	185	(D)	(NA)	[7]1,750	(D)
Bristol city	185	666,629	10,993	106.6	(NA)	3,121	61,744	19,783	95	42,543	(NA)	960	12,438
Danbury city	491	1,981,521	25,819	250.4	11.2	8,934	219,373	24,555	193	155,688	79.5	3,142	45,650
Hartford city	367	862,576	6,933	67.2	0.2	3,293	88,641	26,918	310	208,569	79.1	4,777	66,082
Meriden city	276	675,899	11,530	111.8	19.7	4,254	79,066	18,586	109	56,027	74.5	1,070	15,085
Middletown city	149	301,509	8,204	79.6	(NA)	1,982	49,231	24,839	97	48,337	96.9	1,088	15,090
Milford city (balance)	319	1,200,474	23,256	225.5	16.1	5,651	123,722	21,894	150	97,883	84.6	2,143	28,319
Naugatuck borough	84	247,409	7,887	76.5	(NA)	1,254	25,016	19,949	45	13,809	(NA)	339	3,749
New Britain city	156	484,718	6,772	65.7	(NA)	2,214	53,285	24,067	74	38,352	(NA)	934	10,331
New Haven city	370	551,774	4,442	43.1	7.5	3,219	71,959	22,354	282	175,164	81.4	3,584	50,178
New London city	122	483,753	18,403	178.5	(NA)	1,628	51,695	31,754	83	58,227	(NA)	1,332	17,575
Norwalk city	404	2,694,568	32,117	311.5	7.1	7,455	269,868	36,200	201	134,643	87.4	2,147	34,692
Norwich city	171	482,650	13,405	130.0	11.8	2,484	53,561	21,562	75	56,632	(NA)	1,302	17,692
Shelton city	107	511,376	13,175	127.8	(NA)	1,756	50,268	28,626	84	69,243	54.3	1,167	18,552
Stamford city	503	1,429,392	11,952	115.9	7.8	6,477	169,608	26,186	298	263,597	68.0	4,148	82,497
Torrington city	179	530,146	14,877	144.3	16.3	2,486	53,793	21,638	75	40,344	90.7	943	11,647
Waterbury city	461	1,208,169	11,222	108.8	20.2	6,070	123,943	20,419	206	113,403	91.5	2,588	33,613
West Haven city	127	335,034	6,352	61.6	1.2	1,619	42,696	26,372	104	54,326	93.9	1,188	15,270
DELAWARE	3,727	10,912,971	13,544	131.3	14.0	51,889	1,094,288	21,089	1,576	1,231,595	83.7	26,972	355,458
Dover city	284	827,070	25,342	245.8	33.5	4,813	87,027	18,082	121	105,077	75.6	2,616	29,090
Newark city	178	900,477	30,005	291.0	(NA)	3,361	82,779	24,629	115	128,260	96.9	2,803	32,308
Wilmington city	358	1,091,341	15,013	145.6	(NA)	4,518	108,585	24,034	185	162,059	67.3	3,409	52,944

See footnotes at end of table.

Table C-5. Cities — **Retail Trade and Accommodation and Food Services**—Con.

[Includes states and 1,265 incorporated places of 25,000 or more population as of April 1, 2000, in all states except Hawaii, which has no incorporated places recognized by the U.S. Census Bureau. Two census designated places (CDPs) are also included (Honolulu CDP in Hawaii and Arlington CDP in Virginia). For more information on these areas, see Appendix C, Geographic Information]

City	Retail trade (NAICS 44–45), 2002[1]								Accommodation and food services (NAICS 72), 2002[1]				
	Sales					Annual payroll			Sales				
			Per capita[2]		Percent from general mer-chandise stores			Per paid employee (dol.)			Percent from food services		Annual payroll ($1,000)
	Estab-lishments	Total ($1,000)	Amount (dol.)	Percent of national average		Paid employees[3]	Total ($1,000)		Estab-lishments	Total ($1,000)		Paid employees[3]	
DISTRICT OF COLUMBIA . . .	1,877	3,061,401	5,422	52.6	(NA)	18,513	383,878	20,736	1,799	2,943,078	55.1	43,300	873,095
Washington city.	1,877	3,061,401	5,422	52.6	(NA)	18,513	383,878	20,736	1,799	2,943,078	55.1	43,300	873,095
FLORIDA	69,543	191,805,685	11,501	111.5	13.9	902,760	18,371,874	20,351	30,215	29,366,940	65.7	621,207	7,940,944
Altamonte Springs city	340	1,103,307	26,921	261.1	25.0	6,001	117,418	19,566	137	145,485	83.5	3,401	41,963
Apopka city	109	309,883	10,223	99.1	(NA)	1,885	34,203	18,145	44	29,278	(NA)	657	7,368
Aventura city.	193	513,907	19,472	188.8	25.8	3,017	59,573	19,746	67	156,172	(NA)	2,683	48,368
Boca Raton city.	660	1,577,911	18,325	177.7	12.9	9,388	215,271	22,930	291	434,911	52.0	7,728	136,875
Bonita Springs city.	160	436,814	12,479	121.0	(NA)	2,162	44,574	20,617	89	82,710	59.1	1,828	25,645
Boynton Beach city	348	1,043,801	16,435	159.4	32.9	6,256	110,918	17,730	140	108,962	98.4	2,635	31,728
Bradenton city.	253	734,855	14,328	139.0	28.4	3,604	70,671	19,609	105	62,976	89.3	1,767	17,016
Cape Coral city	338	771,176	6,876	66.7	19.9	4,220	79,786	18,907	133	78,340	96.7	2,044	20,062
Clearwater city	703	2,505,488	23,044	223.5	14.7	10,049	221,941	22,086	345	309,629	(NA)	6,784	86,311
Coconut Creek city.	78	721,367	15,146	146.9	(NA)	1,802	64,732	35,922	31	10,415	(NA)	232	2,933
Cooper City city.	85	193,126	6,630	64.3	(NA)	1,257	20,151	16,031	38	22,622	100.0	715	5,984
Coral Gables city.	287	1,018,113	23,603	228.9	(NA)	2,945	101,428	34,441	172	200,400	63.4	4,046	64,365
Coral Springs city	498	1,417,591	11,322	109.8	27.2	8,264	146,998	17,788	222	145,799	92.0	3,571	37,600
Dania Beach city	199	397,852	14,202	137.7	(NA)	2,023	45,007	22,248	75	84,006	(NA)	1,511	26,143
Davie town	355	1,195,502	15,040	145.9	(NA)	4,955	108,595	21,916	166	114,831	95.4	2,563	28,383
Daytona Beach city	484	1,443,006	22,497	218.2	17.9	6,862	132,087	19,249	296	280,849	59.6	6,438	67,595
Deerfield Beach city	285	791,236	10,503	101.9	(NA)	4,053	78,276	19,313	160	147,996	77.0	2,798	38,403
Delray Beach city.	389	3,357,734	54,072	524.4	4.4	5,128	135,030	26,332	176	155,118	75.4	3,153	42,683
Deltona city	82	162,193	2,199	21.3	0.9	1,129	16,997	15,055	34	15,047	100.0	467	3,820
Dunedin city	121	162,361	4,415	42.8	0.9	1,047	17,429	16,647	81	38,169	(NA)	876	9,863
Fort Lauderdale city	1,241	3,216,734	20,385	197.7	5.7	12,703	312,830	24,626	650	759,654	59.6	14,418	205,161
Fort Myers city	562	1,885,256	35,281	342.2	9.8	7,277	183,758	25,252	218	150,916	88.0	3,567	39,859
Fort Pierce city	220	433,868	11,393	110.5	(NA)	2,178	42,123	19,340	100	58,054	86.2	1,555	16,422
Gainesville city	560	1,468,125	13,425	130.2	18.7	8,270	151,205	18,284	295	196,999	80.4	5,500	50,653
Greenacres city	77	424,653	13,980	135.6	(NA)	1,762	33,818	19,193	47	34,986	(NA)	691	7,974
Hallandale Beach city	127	307,614	8,732	84.7	(NA)	1,752	31,628	18,053	59	57,398	70.7	1,634	18,222
Hialeah city.	985	1,511,591	6,691	64.9	10.2	9,343	164,113	17,565	299	169,063	94.4	3,753	42,213
Hollywood city.	567	1,400,131	9,815	95.2	8.3	6,424	143,311	22,309	323	274,269	(NA)	5,746	82,922
Homestead city	132	350,048	10,508	101.9	0.6	1,558	30,754	19,739	57	37,578	82.2	959	9,615
Jacksonville city.	2,886	9,674,514	12,759	123.7	14.0	43,745	947,404	21,657	1,332	1,049,074	81.4	25,682	288,111
Jupiter town	250	541,263	12,486	121.1	(NA)	2,888	59,956	20,760	122	88,864	(NA)	2,148	24,561
Key West city	373	499,964	19,845	192.5	(NA)	3,327	61,957	18,622	262	344,425	46.7	5,117	87,836
Kissimmee city	321	575,257	11,123	107.9	20.4	3,394	65,783	19,382	177	182,979	69.0	3,891	48,322
Lakeland city	536	1,624,361	18,568	180.1	17.6	7,768	158,179	20,363	223	181,296	87.2	4,706	51,991
Lake Worth city	154	278,436	7,757	75.2	(NA)	1,382	29,870	21,614	69	28,959	85.1	604	8,507
Largo city.	324	1,148,892	15,578	151.1	9.0	4,387	94,828	21,616	135	83,024	93.4	2,066	21,733
Lauderdale Lakes city.	77	153,073	4,851	47.0	2.8	667	14,794	22,180	35	23,908	100.0	522	6,386
Lauderhill city	193	330,574	5,634	54.6	(NA)	1,860	34,992	18,813	57	33,038	100.0	760	8,141
Margate city	199	921,207	16,867	163.6	0.6	2,611	58,842	22,536	99	(D)	(NA)	[7]1,750	(D)
Melbourne city.	459	1,471,602	19,839	192.4	16.3	6,642	138,814	20,899	167	127,862	91.4	3,422	37,974
Miami city.	2,659	4,957,125	13,330	129.3	5.3	21,693	439,694	20,269	984	1,021,600	66.5	20,217	291,093
Miami Beach city	483	644,810	7,243	70.2	3.1	4,056	74,541	18,378	454	860,192	44.8	14,159	253,719
Miami Gardens city	(X)	(X)	(NA)	(NA)	(NA)	(X)	(X)	(NA)	(X)	(X)	(NA)	(X)	(X)
Miramar city	144	465,813	5,176	50.2	(NA)	2,292	45,969	20,056	64	27,509	(NA)	799	6,547
North Lauderdale city	52	151,047	3,832	37.2	(NA)	933	16,395	17,572	25	11,709	100.0	323	3,011
North Miami city	204	385,858	6,493	63.0	2.1	2,004	41,609	20,763	86	57,757	95.5	1,502	14,854
North Miami Beach city.	263	692,885	17,135	166.2	35.2	2,973	64,122	21,568	96	83,837	(NA)	1,874	21,848
Oakland Park city	256	604,076	19,266	186.8	(NA)	2,601	61,899	23,798	120	79,190	90.5	1,941	21,426
Ocala city.	540	1,836,770	39,263	380.8	(NA)	8,602	185,060	21,514	205	164,692	93.8	4,268	44,500
Orlando city	1,495	4,140,280	21,007	203.7	8.4	18,641	406,861	21,826	686	971,665	58.5	16,583	257,368
Ormond Beach city	189	407,296	10,954	106.2	(NA)	2,523	46,742	18,526	113	90,608	85.8	2,123	23,352
Oviedo city	125	207,049	7,509	72.8	31.1	1,620	23,490	14,500	39	21,002	(NA)	767	5,653
Palm Bay city	176	526,372	6,341	61.5	5.1	2,531	44,616	17,628	86	47,269	93.1	1,384	12,765
Palm Beach Gardens city	295	911,831	23,268	225.7	26.4	5,432	106,422	19,592	91	110,837	78.0	2,411	30,297
Palm Coast city	93	230,582	6,025	58.4	(NA)	1,306	25,953	19,872	48	42,176	55.1	1,155	13,710
Panama City city	355	1,058,879	28,711	278.4	19.3	4,793	101,393	21,154	153	111,321	75.4	2,826	29,742
Pembroke Pines city.	525	2,077,699	14,207	137.8	18.3	9,958	192,674	19,349	247	204,009	93.3	5,043	56,174
Pensacola city.	415	1,026,368	18,362	178.1	31.8	5,487	101,114	18,428	151	124,082	96.4	3,070	35,295
Pinellas Park city	256	1,500,620	32,221	312.5	(NA)	5,059	131,763	26,045	100	82,942	95.4	1,503	20,288
Plantation city	376	1,211,452	14,339	139.1	17.4	6,296	120,057	19,069	154	132,953	80.2	3,188	36,699
Plant City city	135	543,643	17,637	171.0	(NA)	2,185	47,760	21,858	62	39,974	92.6	1,222	10,584
Pompano Beach city	629	2,364,891	23,301	226.0	11.1	8,118	221,417	27,075	231	148,386	81.7	3,055	37,168
Port Orange city	136	397,759	8,062	78.2	(NA)	2,369	40,224	16,979	68	(D)	(NA)	[7]1,750	(D)
Port St. Lucie city	198	712,055	7,227	70.1	(NA)	3,973	95,881	24,133	107	81,009	69.3	2,313	21,079
Riviera Beach city	113	276,192	9,090	88.2	(NA)	1,039	23,830	22,936	35	40,864	(NA)	756	10,512

See footnotes at end of table.

Table C-5. Cities — **Retail Trade and Accommodation and Food Services**—Con.

[Includes states and 1,265 incorporated places of 25,000 or more population as of April 1, 2000, in all states except Hawaii, which has no incorporated places recognized by the U.S. Census Bureau. Two census designated places (CDPs) are also included (Honolulu CDP in Hawaii and Arlington CDP in Virginia). For more information on these areas, see Appendix C, Geographic Information]

City	Retail trade (NAICS 44–45), 2002[1]								Accommodation and food services (NAICS 72), 2002[1]				
	Estab-lishments	Sales				Paid employees[3]	Annual payroll		Estab-lishments	Sales		Paid employees[3]	Annual payroll ($1,000)
		Total ($1,000)	Per capita[2]		Percent from general merchandise stores		Total ($1,000)	Per paid employee (dol.)		Total ($1,000)	Percent from food services		
			Amount (dol.)	Percent of national average									
FLORIDA—Con.													
St. Petersburg city	915	2,877,143	11,563	112.1	10.4	13,163	282,822	21,486	414	300,862	77.2	7,022	86,494
Sanford city	301	824,401	18,903	183.3	24.3	4,202	83,626	19,901	83	63,122	91.0	1,708	18,589
Sarasota city	503	951,459	17,827	172.9	6.7	4,798	102,369	21,336	233	215,807	(NA)	4,514	62,701
Sunrise city	451	1,541,471	17,478	169.5	18.5	7,344	147,816	20,127	179	147,202	(NA)	3,430	39,977
Tallahassee city	853	2,050,057	13,462	130.6	(NA)	13,409	219,925	16,401	468	370,102	79.7	9,918	97,390
Tamarac city	165	384,179	6,705	65.0	2.5	2,889	65,959	22,831	77	39,998	82.1	909	9,990
Tampa city	1,809	5,141,045	16,320	158.3	9.8	25,074	531,839	21,211	862	1,002,636	68.6	21,263	277,244
Titusville city	154	483,885	11,779	114.2	27.7	2,785	47,136	16,925	73	60,126	93.8	1,829	17,094
Wellington village	167	287,251	6,520	63.2	25.0	2,292	35,984	15,700	60	35,623	100.0	963	9,793
Weston city	138	781,679	12,674	122.9	(NA)	2,062	50,069	24,282	73	61,289	65.0	1,296	19,527
West Palm Beach city	575	2,616,715	30,317	294.0	6.4	9,098	237,914	26,150	304	265,853	82.7	5,549	76,296
Winter Haven city	177	427,105	15,774	153.0	15.4	2,234	44,220	19,794	86	54,866	89.5	1,440	13,649
Winter Park city	221	559,538	19,906	193.0	(NA)	2,752	58,801	21,367	104	109,495	94.4	2,564	31,661
Winter Springs city	40	55,459	1,767	17.1	(NA)	296	5,655	19,105	12	4,087	100.0	192	1,228
GEORGIA	34,050	90,098,578	10,499	101.8	15.1	447,618	8,850,581	19,773	15,463	12,740,423	78.6	293,064	3,515,727
Albany city	491	1,153,334	15,125	146.7	(NA)	6,628	112,316	16,946	195	116,394	(NA)	3,372	31,685
Alpharetta city	343	1,471,117	36,784	356.7	17.8	7,939	152,035	19,150	224	220,177	82.2	4,622	66,745
Athens-Clarke County (balance)	546	1,461,556	14,478	140.4	(NA)	8,446	158,044	18,712	286	217,937	89.0	6,062	58,283
Atlanta city	2,113	4,732,270	10,670	103.5	8.7	27,397	572,320	20,890	1,427	2,119,909	64.8	37,167	598,192
Augusta-Richmond County (balance)	852	2,195,325	11,356	110.1	(NA)	11,815	215,605	18,248	389	(D)	(NA)	[8]7,500	(D)
Columbus city	794	2,329,515	12,569	121.9	15.8	11,366	216,275	19,028	354	319,761	(NA)	7,375	84,678
Dalton city	313	744,672	24,930	241.8	(NA)	4,002	75,937	18,975	132	98,766	(NA)	2,327	28,113
East Point city	61	86,154	2,138	20.7	8.8	540	9,680	17,926	47	67,479	(NA)	1,214	18,951
Gainesville city	295	772,808	27,253	264.3	(NA)	3,806	86,526	22,734	133	104,879	91.0	2,379	28,467
Hinesville city	123	259,171	8,537	82.8	(NA)	1,489	24,474	16,437	56	30,007	86.9	936	7,940
LaGrange city	198	522,567	19,521	189.3	14.4	2,595	48,985	18,877	71	44,936	90.0	1,285	11,714
Macon city	683	1,758,293	18,349	177.9	(NA)	10,186	184,051	18,069	247	181,011	89.2	4,604	48,584
Marietta city	447	1,916,052	31,089	301.5	11.1	6,745	180,098	26,701	238	185,376	71.9	3,797	47,725
Peachtree City city	102	246,902	7,642	74.1	(NA)	1,539	29,589	19,226	67	54,369	(NA)	1,461	17,198
Rome city	320	851,944	23,830	231.1	(NA)	4,012	74,404	18,545	155	112,455	94.3	2,794	28,773
Roswell city	356	1,447,021	17,434	169.1	10.3	5,255	142,519	27,121	190	146,251	91.9	3,547	45,403
Savannah city	860	1,975,688	15,069	146.1	10.5	10,872	211,230	19,429	451	433,907	66.9	10,353	113,378
Smyrna city	204	735,819	15,962	154.8	5.4	3,308	68,365	20,667	131	112,719	91.3	2,529	33,861
Valdosta city	413	930,730	20,872	202.4	(NA)	5,146	94,070	18,280	147	142,992	86.1	3,878	35,028
Warner Robins city	280	848,177	16,159	156.7	(NA)	4,374	81,530	18,640	129	99,750	88.3	2,736	26,641
HAWAII	4,924	13,008,182	10,538	102.2	19.7	63,794	1,333,182	20,898	3,138	5,551,380	42.0	85,641	1,604,706
Honolulu CDP	2,088	5,375,770	14,359	139.3	17.8	25,050	534,189	21,325	1,446	2,385,495	(NA)	37,237	679,399
IDAHO	5,874	13,540,952	10,075	97.7	17.1	69,641	1,372,177	19,704	3,088	1,653,671	72.0	45,435	450,236
Boise City city	969	2,917,363	15,141	146.8	19.9	15,246	312,829	20,519	572	406,385	79.6	10,883	112,629
Caldwell city	119	370,138	12,398	120.2	(NA)	1,703	36,963	21,705	60	25,488	(NA)	860	7,029
Coeur d'Alene city	295	728,522	19,936	193.3	(NA)	3,718	74,869	20,137	168	132,738	63.8	3,085	35,529
Idaho Falls city	364	964,872	18,837	182.7	17.7	4,870	93,061	19,109	177	100,683	(NA)	2,858	26,743
Lewiston city	213	526,110	17,226	167.1	(NA)	2,658	55,897	21,030	96	52,653	80.7	1,566	15,290
Meridian city	121	470,802	11,770	114.1	(NA)	2,250	51,664	22,962	67	46,556	(NA)	1,348	12,558
Nampa city	256	746,090	12,244	118.7	(NA)	3,421	72,444	21,176	115	64,421	94.0	2,022	17,717
Pocatello city	244	525,734	10,090	97.8	(NA)	2,550	52,999	20,784	122	70,905	80.6	2,206	19,293
Twin Falls city	338	801,615	22,469	217.9	(NA)	4,106	87,999	21,432	134	78,652	(NA)	2,187	22,073
ILLINOIS	43,022	131,469,518	10,445	101.3	14.0	601,465	12,514,264	20,806	24,245	19,072,168	75.4	420,801	5,227,014
Addison village	119	1,091,688	30,016	291.1	(NA)	2,751	104,238	37,891	66	52,457	89.5	1,099	14,856
Alton city	185	515,752	17,118	166.0	18.3	2,632	50,967	19,364	92	50,349	93.8	1,422	14,157
Arlington Heights village	288	1,331,671	17,448	169.2	4.5	4,318	91,779	21,255	168	142,027	87.7	3,046	43,395
Aurora city	446	1,266,722	8,083	78.4	19.6	7,345	134,852	18,360	209	157,299	95.0	4,009	46,935
Bartlett village	46	138,773	3,733	36.2	(NA)	575	11,821	20,558	41	21,432	(NA)	462	5,771
Belleville city	218	520,427	12,425	120.5	(NA)	2,863	58,067	20,282	128	58,895	(NA)	1,839	15,728
Berwyn city	129	276,887	5,202	50.4	1.3	1,376	30,157	21,916	100	63,734	(NA)	1,251	16,054
Bloomington city	353	1,066,365	15,804	153.3	13.1	5,389	104,325	19,359	188	156,515	78.2	5,499	47,786
Bolingbrook village	102	480,457	7,889	76.5	38.6	2,426	45,683	18,831	81	71,214	89.1	1,718	20,724
Buffalo Grove village	105	464,712	10,689	103.7	(NA)	1,420	36,538	25,731	75	46,398	(NA)	1,187	12,525
Burbank city	106	265,410	9,526	92.4	8.7	1,315	22,100	16,806	70	35,622	95.6	787	9,091
Calumet City city	197	614,751	15,917	154.4	31.1	3,985	72,973	18,312	96	56,303	100.0	1,436	15,238
Carbondale city	173	494,156	20,042	194.4	(NA)	3,123	50,200	16,074	94	59,571	90.1	1,976	16,100
Carol Stream village	75	247,279	6,142	59.6	(NA)	1,038	20,695	19,937	49	27,851	(NA)	679	6,977
Carpentersville village	34	69,206	2,022	19.6	(NA)	328	6,724	20,500	24	11,182	100.0	335	3,076

See footnotes at end of table.

Table C-5. Cities — **Retail Trade and Accommodation and Food Services**—Con.

[Includes states and 1,265 incorporated places of 25,000 or more population as of April 1, 2000, in all states except Hawaii, which has no incorporated places recognized by the U.S. Census Bureau. Two census designated places (CDPs) are also included (Honolulu CDP in Hawaii and Arlington CDP in Virginia). For more information on these areas, see Appendix C, Geographic Information]

City	Retail trade (NAICS 44–45), 2002[1]								Accommodation and food services (NAICS 72), 2002[1]				
		Sales					Annual payroll			Sales			
			Per capita[2]		Percent from general mer-chandise stores						Percent from food services		
	Estab-lishments	Total ($1,000)	Amount (dol.)	Percent of national average		Paid employees[3]	Total ($1,000)	Per paid employee (dol.)	Estab-lishments	Total ($1,000)		Paid employees[3]	Annual payroll ($1,000)
ILLINOIS—Con.													
Champaign city	376	1,026,224	14,485	140.5	24.4	6,100	106,886	17,522	223	163,185	85.6	5,077	45,069
Chicago city	7,573	17,303,363	5,993	58.1	8.4	83,748	1,802,434	21,522	5,159	5,527,041	68.5	96,874	1,536,112
Chicago Heights city	81	159,527	4,936	47.9	(NA)	867	17,327	19,985	46	26,505	100.0	815	7,238
Cicero town	130	394,587	4,689	45.5	34.7	1,782	32,740	18,373	74	33,576	88.1	785	8,917
Crystal Lake city	221	982,918	24,706	239.6	22.5	4,172	86,464	20,725	92	79,569	95.1	2,034	23,948
Danville city	182	455,553	13,619	132.1	30.5	2,626	47,838	18,217	98	56,272	(NA)	1,821	17,716
Decatur city	334	931,808	11,649	113.0	18.3	4,642	100,349	21,618	176	110,956	(NA)	3,284	32,402
DeKalb city	131	439,044	10,796	104.7	(NA)	2,613	42,847	16,398	78	51,443	84.8	1,656	13,169
Des Plaines city	193	814,706	14,405	139.7	(NA)	2,553	63,594	24,910	144	102,619	78.6	2,544	27,759
Dolton village	46	118,538	4,693	45.5	(NA)	678	12,868	18,979	29	13,625	(NA)	362	3,308
Downers Grove village	225	1,683,305	34,119	330.9	(NA)	4,615	131,189	28,427	116	140,247	79.9	3,325	40,182
East St. Louis city	60	65,854	2,122	20.6	(NA)	509	8,669	17,031	30	(D)	(NA)	[7]1,750	(D)
Elgin city	225	900,661	9,312	90.3	(NA)	3,378	86,051	25,474	139	93,284	87.8	2,260	25,543
Elk Grove Village village	114	507,872	14,597	141.6	(NA)	2,090	55,922	26,757	88	61,681	79.5	1,336	16,351
Elmhurst city	167	847,112	19,599	190.1	(NA)	2,457	68,626	27,931	106	75,564	77.6	1,561	20,804
Elmwood Park village	47	85,550	3,414	33.1	(NA)	469	8,175	17,431	33	23,252	100.0	477	6,978
Evanston city	247	899,128	12,274	119.0	(NA)	4,264	98,689	23,145	184	145,418	88.4	2,977	40,328
Freeport city	131	311,043	11,974	116.1	(NA)	1,670	32,101	19,222	69	25,342	(NA)	820	6,597
Galesburg city	185	469,766	14,182	137.5	(NA)	2,891	48,258	16,692	102	48,960	84.6	1,541	14,276
Glendale Heights village	49	308,656	9,392	91.1	(NA)	1,014	27,346	26,968	48	32,199	(NA)	681	8,368
Glen Ellyn village	113	300,584	11,049	107.2	(NA)	1,543	34,334	22,251	64	38,899	(NA)	977	9,782
Glenview village	178	1,030,707	22,923	222.3	(NA)	3,116	113,361	36,380	109	92,538	78.3	1,813	27,056
Granite City city	89	298,729	9,473	91.9	19.6	1,397	29,618	21,201	57	32,817	96.7	978	8,987
Gurnee village	246	1,011,056	33,385	323.8	22.4	5,045	92,978	18,430	108	117,989	86.5	2,519	32,781
Hanover Park village	67	146,125	3,861	37.4	(NA)	833	17,891	21,478	38	19,636	100.0	408	4,744
Harvey city	69	135,147	4,570	44.3	1.8	495	8,740	17,657	39	17,366	81.0	510	4,220
Highland Park city	214	851,363	27,632	268.0	(NA)	3,156	89,028	28,209	69	46,161	(NA)	991	15,187
Hoffman Estates village	120	769,957	15,308	148.5	(NA)	1,729	44,572	25,779	93	95,725	83.8	2,014	27,580
Joliet city	377	1,520,813	12,760	123.7	17.8	6,931	147,348	21,259	206	675,089	(NA)	7,267	129,268
Kankakee city	103	182,361	6,709	65.1	3.8	1,101	21,642	19,657	58	21,744	98.1	627	5,940
Lansing village	149	558,603	19,967	193.6	(NA)	2,888	53,313	18,460	67	54,516	84.2	1,287	14,459
Lombard village	251	867,521	20,035	194.3	15.3	4,434	91,942	20,736	116	121,960	79.5	2,445	33,954
Maywood village	43	97,256	3,651	35.4	(NA)	308	7,299	23,698	25	(D)	(NA)	[4]750	(D)
Moline city	306	832,275	19,208	186.3	25.6	4,928	91,880	18,644	145	96,810	83.2	2,868	26,782
Mount Prospect village	191	905,230	16,258	157.7	12.2	3,394	77,019	22,693	104	(D)	(NA)	[7]1,750	(D)
Mundelein village	106	235,709	7,359	71.4	(NA)	1,377	28,285	20,541	62	34,481	(NA)	827	9,947
Naperville city	413	2,054,269	15,106	146.5	9.1	8,282	204,990	24,751	248	229,852	85.9	5,823	70,289
Niles village	278	1,299,183	43,511	422.0	25.2	5,651	114,748	20,306	101	79,959	(NA)	1,763	21,642
Normal town	136	497,799	10,393	100.8	(NA)	2,554	45,261	17,722	89	71,862	84.0	2,266	20,579
Northbrook village	223	720,056	21,353	207.1	(NA)	3,550	82,671	23,288	85	78,781	75.6	1,425	21,872
North Chicago city	29	31,237	854	8.3	(NA)	186	3,081	16,565	44	25,513	88.0	466	6,244
Oak Forest city	59	234,569	8,327	80.8	(NA)	765	19,276	25,197	30	23,280	95.6	683	6,651
Oak Lawn village	210	965,191	17,568	170.4	(NA)	3,312	84,851	25,619	91	74,987	81.0	[1]1,929	21,555
Oak Park village	181	228,918	4,434	43.0	(NA)	1,398	26,577	19,011	86	(D)	(NA)	[7]1,750	(D)
Orland Park village	342	1,483,965	27,970	271.2	18.8	7,617	141,633	18,594	135	126,817	(NA)	3,349	35,191
Palatine village	184	609,728	9,150	88.7	(NA)	2,375	54,750	23,053	117	76,128	90.4	1,893	20,847
Park Ridge city	101	341,703	9,091	88.2	(NA)	1,181	26,974	22,840	60	34,105	(NA)	755	9,705
Pekin city	144	451,124	13,476	130.7	16.5	2,178	44,436	20,402	80	40,755	93.0	1,380	11,940
Peoria city	570	1,654,038	14,673	142.3	20.9	8,893	169,703	19,083	323	217,402	(NA)	6,431	63,246
Quincy city	298	819,307	20,270	196.6	(NA)	4,310	79,760	18,506	119	68,106	86.0	2,120	19,385
Rockford city	593	2,041,196	13,495	130.9	20.0	10,661	207,768	19,489	322	244,921	86.4	6,505	67,163
Rock Island city	110	171,755	4,377	42.4	(NA)	1,128	20,532	18,202	78	35,185	(NA)	1,106	10,268
Round Lake Beach village	52	233,350	8,334	80.8	(NA)	1,174	22,915	19,519	31	20,931	100.0	563	5,685
St. Charles city	212	754,692	24,628	238.8	23.2	3,452	73,542	21,304	123	147,558	77.2	2,872	38,304
Schaumburg village	474	2,768,449	37,164	360.4	14.7	12,122	262,938	21,691	240	372,355	64.1	6,719	106,962
Skokie village	357	1,004,539	15,798	153.2	15.1	5,892	118,788	20,161	142	144,108	74.9	2,519	39,378
Springfield city	591	1,909,343	16,919	164.1	21.1	9,650	180,013	18,654	370	279,267	74.9	6,987	79,371
Streamwood village	68	182,747	4,884	47.4	(NA)	929	15,731	16,933	45	29,527	100.0	718	7,142
Tinley Park village	132	783,591	14,927	144.8	(NA)	2,695	62,416	23,160	86	82,234	86.2	2,135	23,032
Urbana city	98	340,455	8,970	87.0	(NA)	1,624	33,540	20,653	92	66,203	67.3	1,902	19,755
Waukegan city	230	611,308	6,705	65.0	9.6	3,027	62,858	20,766	123	87,203	79.7	1,673	19,986
Wheaton city	191	519,253	9,414	91.3	13.0	2,799	49,792	17,789	91	79,661	94.2	1,900	24,089
Wheeling village	114	371,181	10,053	97.5	(NA)	1,922	41,212	21,442	52	57,919	(NA)	1,187	15,173
Wilmette village	133	271,262	9,889	95.9	(NA)	1,462	36,735	25,127	39	31,117	100.0	679	11,673
Woodridge village	65	242,477	7,213	70.0	(NA)	1,152	19,180	16,649	26	23,722	100.0	637	7,580

See footnotes at end of table.

Table C-5. Cities — Retail Trade and Accommodation and Food Services—Con.

[Includes states and 1,265 incorporated places of 25,000 or more population as of April 1, 2000, in all states except Hawaii, which has no incorporated places recognized by the U.S. Census Bureau. Two census designated places (CDPs) are also included (Honolulu CDP in Hawaii and Arlington CDP in Virginia). For more information on these areas, see Appendix C, Geographic Information]

City	Retail trade (NAICS 44–45), 2002[1]								Accommodation and food services (NAICS 72), 2002[1]				
		Sales			Percent from general mer-chandise stores	Annual payroll				Sales			
			Per capita[2]										
	Estab-lishments	Total ($1,000)	Amount (dol.)	Percent of national average		Paid employees[3]	Total ($1,000)	Per paid employee (dol.)	Estab-lishments	Total ($1,000)	Percent from food services	Paid employees[3]	Annual payroll ($1,000)
INDIANA	24,322	67,261,298	10,928	106.0	17.4	343,551	6,403,730	18,640	11,788	9,409,270	70.8	231,071	2,547,617
Anderson city	297	938,508	15,957	154.8	19.8	4,592	84,197	18,336	152	110,882	94.0	3,252	32,221
Bloomington city	383	1,062,278	15,163	147.1	19.4	5,912	100,721	17,037	267	202,461	82.1	6,093	56,740
Carmel city	175	580,618	10,717	103.9	(NA)	2,823	57,561	20,390	104	88,554	79.4	2,250	26,589
Columbus city	221	594,959	15,297	148.4	21.4	3,364	60,064	17,855	100	80,198	84.4	2,244	23,160
East Chicago city	55	88,538	2,788	27.0	(NA)	522	9,817	18,807	54	(D)	(NA)	[6]3,750	(D)
Elkhart city	286	728,532	14,015	135.9	8.0	3,821	74,342	19,456	180	110,213	86.0	3,262	32,089
Evansville city	770	2,380,413	19,990	193.9	(NA)	12,852	238,127	18,528	350	380,130	61.4	9,396	108,359
Fishers town	120	444,048	9,602	93.1	(NA)	2,303	46,304	20,106	88	71,443	85.3	1,732	20,511
Fort Wayne city	1,065	3,200,327	14,258	138.3	21.6	17,386	331,864	19,088	521	380,289	89.2	11,446	119,933
Gary city	215	459,760	4,567	44.3	2.9	2,433	40,102	16,483	96	161,528	(NA)	2,038	34,813
Goshen city	164	615,579	20,658	200.3	(NA)	3,075	60,618	19,713	70	53,397	87.9	1,519	14,662
Greenwood city	289	1,025,876	26,283	254.9	(NA)	6,071	104,326	17,184	122	102,692	(NA)	2,844	30,183
Hammond city	262	714,572	8,790	85.2	12.5	3,225	62,093	19,254	161	(D)	(NA)	[7]1,750	(D)
Hobart city	162	636,147	24,070	233.4	(NA)	3,398	61,348	18,054	56	(D)	(NA)	[7]1,750	(D)
Indianapolis city (balance)	3,071	11,297,126	14,432	140.0	14.1	53,931	1,133,426	21,016	1,776	1,743,771	76.2	41,183	511,383
Jeffersonville city	113	385,544	13,644	132.3	(NA)	1,716	35,468	20,669	71	51,225	(NA)	1,369	15,253
Kokomo city	344	992,706	21,447	208.0	27.8	5,240	92,071	17,571	155	(D)	(NA)	[6]3,750	(D)
Lafayette city	423	1,433,657	23,815	231.0	24.9	7,885	142,705	18,098	185	148,363	90.4	4,368	46,319
Lawrence city	114	255,928	6,365	61.7	(NA)	1,685	32,047	19,019	64	34,234	(NA)	873	10,268
Marion city	212	564,245	17,904	173.6	19.1	2,844	49,543	17,420	104	68,359	(NA)	2,113	19,466
Merrillville town	294	1,135,133	36,825	357.1	26.2	5,975	109,459	18,319	139	(D)	(NA)	[6]3,750	(D)
Michigan City city	250	618,447	19,016	184.4	23.7	3,458	59,329	17,157	90	277,665	(NA)	3,181	47,912
Mishawaka city	391	1,904,908	39,623	384.3	24.5	8,333	149,249	17,911	172	140,774	89.8	3,876	42,459
Muncie city	390	951,971	13,992	135.7	(NA)	5,582	93,034	16,667	178	126,260	91.1	3,918	35,782
New Albany city	169	443,375	11,836	114.8	20.9	2,673	48,939	18,309	73	46,825	(NA)	1,317	13,430
Noblesville city	129	532,792	16,299	158.1	22.0	2,124	45,559	21,450	62	38,488	(NA)	1,150	11,422
Portage city	89	276,090	8,011	77.7	(NA)	1,438	26,317	18,301	60	40,104	88.8	1,165	9,756
Richmond city	226	672,494	17,467	169.4	(NA)	3,537	68,027	19,233	101	73,379	89.1	2,202	21,291
South Bend city	375	927,717	8,694	84.3	(NA)	5,531	103,817	18,770	244	158,308	86.8	4,064	44,942
Terre Haute city	383	1,805,421	30,863	299.3	4.6	6,674	138,057	20,686	219	151,305	(NA)	4,491	42,796
Valparaiso city	202	669,267	23,606	228.9	25.9	3,248	67,085	20,654	96	65,572	93.5	2,179	19,161
West Lafayette city	78	193,572	6,755	65.5	(NA)	1,399	21,806	15,587	93	66,301	76.1	1,832	18,800
IOWA	13,859	31,195,012	10,631	103.1	15.8	176,251	3,175,923	18,019	6,586	3,698,955	70.4	104,638	1,017,109
Ames city	221	672,733	13,067	126.7	(NA)	3,804	64,803	17,035	171	98,762	78.3	3,350	29,634
Ankeny city	94	483,780	16,173	156.8	25.1	2,105	45,122	21,436	70	51,376	85.4	1,423	13,985
Bettendorf city	111	244,727	7,771	75.4	(NA)	1,438	27,527	19,143	66	220,725	15.3	3,433	56,215
Burlington city	126	220,792	8,469	82.1	14.2	1,584	27,191	17,166	79	43,559	84.6	1,381	12,111
Cedar Falls city	161	481,821	13,359	129.6	(NA)	2,646	50,011	18,901	88	57,422	(NA)	2,001	17,162
Cedar Rapids city	570	2,010,908	16,385	158.9	6.0	10,710	211,017	19,703	330	232,873	83.0	6,866	68,516
Clinton city	151	357,403	13,002	126.1	(NA)	1,984	36,030	18,160	82	34,019	80.5	1,201	9,941
Council Bluffs city	261	923,236	15,742	152.7	13.0	4,540	85,165	18,759	137	362,587	20.5	5,577	79,240
Davenport city	545	1,696,768	17,365	168.4	(NA)	8,987	174,712	19,441	239	249,082	63.0	5,713	70,325
Des Moines city	777	2,029,780	10,251	99.4	13.3	12,159	236,389	19,441	476	313,078	79.1	8,129	93,875
Dubuque city	364	896,831	15,715	152.4	2.1	5,158	89,729	17,396	181	100,498	81.5	3,330	29,459
Fort Dodge city	179	436,813	16,765	162.6	30.2	2,569	45,247	17,613	70	42,092	88.2	1,210	12,541
Iowa City city	276	723,258	11,529	111.8	8.9	4,549	82,934	18,231	164	90,624	(NA)	3,407	26,275
Marion city	113	223,516	8,100	78.6	(NA)	1,295	26,740	20,649	33	17,059	(NA)	594	5,548
Marshalltown city	145	325,488	12,577	122.0	(NA)	2,082	35,386	16,996	77	34,088	(NA)	1,015	9,715
Mason City city	200	574,308	20,227	196.2	(NA)	3,259	59,794	18,347	89	46,921	82.8	1,474	13,179
Sioux City city	436	1,100,199	13,067	126.7	(NA)	6,829	117,722	17,239	204	136,968	90.5	4,026	36,479
Urbandale city	140	725,737	23,336	226.3	11.6	3,079	76,203	24,749	66	49,999	71.8	1,254	14,333
Waterloo city	337	960,382	14,339	139.1	24.9	5,850	103,185	17,638	168	92,610	90.2	3,033	27,946
West Des Moines city	231	673,597	13,410	130.1	12.5	4,661	79,168	16,985	126	112,096	72.7	2,835	36,187
KANSAS	11,890	26,505,396	9,772	94.8	17.9	144,874	2,687,657	18,552	5,584	3,196,947	82.6	92,125	910,771
Dodge City city	154	346,779	13,771	133.5	(NA)	1,725	32,808	19,019	75	33,995	82.2	981	9,270
Emporia city	141	316,663	11,892	115.3	(NA)	1,952	33,583	17,204	89	43,633	83.9	1,634	11,727
Garden City city	159	388,570	14,144	137.2	(NA)	2,268	42,020	18,527	59	42,562	71.1	1,176	11,701
Hutchinson city	249	562,619	13,628	132.2	19.7	3,177	57,275	18,028	108	63,771	87.4	1,906	18,357
Kansas City city	358	810,462	5,539	53.7	9.3	3,795	97,237	25,622	198	105,630	(NA)	2,607	29,389
Lawrence city	378	826,968	10,208	99.0	(NA)	5,687	92,121	16,199	235	149,129	83.4	5,206	43,437
Leavenworth city	121	304,699	8,540	82.8	(NA)	1,569	28,130	17,929	49	23,547	94.1	651	6,503
Leawood city	98	265,922	9,425	91.4	(NA)	2,252	33,695	14,962	37	(D)	(NA)	[7]1,750	(D)
Lenexa city	200	793,453	19,264	186.8	17.5	3,288	79,164	24,077	95	72,560	80.6	1,981	22,161
Manhattan city	270	643,158	13,825	134.1	(NA)	3,965	61,846	15,598	145	86,976	77.5	2,897	23,863
Olathe city	371	1,607,085	15,864	153.9	12.7	6,523	142,582	21,858	162	140,628	91.1	3,760	40,820
Overland Park city	750	2,654,325	16,748	162.4	20.7	14,808	308,125	20,808	390	407,398	75.5	9,353	120,010
Salina city	282	758,938	16,490	159.9	(NA)	4,018	71,820	17,875	129	80,972	79.9	2,485	23,647
Shawnee city	167	600,765	11,418	110.7	26.1	3,296	65,957	20,011	84	62,169	(NA)	1,599	17,608
Topeka city	680	1,845,717	15,104	146.5	(NA)	10,132	185,081	18,267	329	(D)	(NA)	[8]7,500	(D)
Wichita city	1,561	4,350,025	12,283	119.1	20.5	22,508	448,881	19,943	865	599,838	84.3	16,308	171,538

See footnotes at end of table.

Table C-5. Cities — **Retail Trade and Accommodation and Food Services**—Con.

[Includes states and 1,265 incorporated places of 25,000 or more population as of April 1, 2000, in all states except Hawaii, which has no incorporated places recognized by the U.S. Census Bureau. Two census designated places (CDPs) are also included (Honolulu CDP in Hawaii and Arlington CDP in Virginia). For more information on these areas, see Appendix C, Geographic Information]

City	Retail trade (NAICS 44–45), 2002[1]								Accommodation and food services (NAICS 72), 2002[1]				
		Sales				Paid employees[3]	Annual payroll			Sales		Paid employees[3]	Annual payroll ($1,000)
			Per capita[2]		Percent from general merchandise stores						Percent from food services		
	Establishments	Total ($1,000)	Amount (dol.)	Percent of national average			Total ($1,000)	Per paid employee (dol.)	Establishments	Total ($1,000)			
KENTUCKY	16,847	40,062,561	9,799	95.0	19.0	214,192	3,827,629	17,870	6,660	4,908,331	84.1	136,442	1,397,143
Bowling Green city	474	1,153,912	23,069	223.7	18.6	6,796	114,315	16,821	179	156,198	84.0	5,312	45,109
Covington city	146	303,471	7,023	68.1	7.5	1,840	36,506	19,840	123	104,500	67.4	2,352	28,320
Frankfort city	138	338,792	12,280	119.1	32.0	1,920	33,625	17,513	86	56,318	(NA)	1,534	16,672
Henderson city	181	480,412	17,503	169.7	(NA)	2,388	45,278	18,961	71	41,380	(NA)	1,404	11,916
Hopkinsville city	192	452,043	15,351	148.9	(NA)	2,436	44,621	18,317	71	46,901	90.8	1,526	13,931
Jeffersontown city	124	549,592	20,876	202.5	(NA)	2,261	53,465	23,647	72	85,328	64.1	2,162	26,297
Lexington-Fayette	1,155	3,912,042	14,895	144.4	19.3	20,462	405,262	19,806	641	599,766	78.9	15,341	175,032
Louisville/Jefferson County (balance)	(X)	(X)	(NA)	(NA)	(NA)	(X)	(X)	(NA)	(X)	(X)	(NA)	(X)	(X)
Owensboro city	362	869,702	15,968	154.9	22.6	4,815	85,869	17,834	127	107,075	82.8	2,983	31,103
Paducah city	356	1,061,079	41,223	399.8	(NA)	5,239	95,603	18,248	144	126,524	81.0	3,560	35,111
Richmond city	185	485,205	17,102	165.9	22.7	2,638	45,423	17,219	85	61,612	88.0	1,855	17,264
LOUISIANA	17,613	41,885,192	9,360	90.8	18.7	228,290	4,069,984	17,828	7,535	7,411,702	62.6	170,158	2,034,265
Alexandria city	379	1,070,936	23,408	227.0	23.0	5,226	97,870	18,728	133	94,942	84.1	2,723	25,312
Baton Rouge city	1,194	3,095,008	13,816	134.0	11.0	16,461	318,056	19,322	548	435,329	85.6	12,024	125,183
Bossier City city	315	1,014,985	17,819	172.8	19.7	4,547	87,792	19,308	155	676,741	(NA)	8,437	164,448
Houma city	234	379,994	11,809	114.5	14.7	2,647	42,524	16,065	84	43,559	92.9	1,241	9,698
Kenner city	370	1,306,617	18,573	180.1	21.0	6,848	122,322	17,862	183	171,640	75.6	4,125	48,310
Lafayette city	781	2,216,845	19,800	192.0	22.6	12,106	229,757	18,979	351	350,844	90.3	9,175	103,723
Lake Charles city	486	1,035,502	14,628	141.9	14.1	6,130	102,302	16,689	183	267,826	(NA)	5,855	68,469
Monroe city	420	1,207,367	23,139	224.4	22.5	6,060	115,954	19,134	149	115,794	86.7	3,008	30,269
New Iberia city	218	553,258	17,055	165.4	(NA)	2,810	53,723	19,119	78	43,335	89.5	1,373	11,155
New Orleans city	1,722	3,158,341	6,686	64.8	(NA)	19,628	354,291	18,050	1,228	1,944,816	48.9	37,141	538,932
Shreveport city	879	2,429,542	12,234	118.6	(NA)	11,500	234,784	20,416	364	625,092	38.5	11,882	154,470
Slidell city	275	811,467	30,680	297.5	(NA)	4,436	74,486	16,791	145	100,109	91.5	2,778	27,963
MAINE	7,050	16,053,515	12,378	120.0	12.2	80,251	1,568,308	19,543	3,726	2,045,841	66.3	44,966	606,880
Bangor city	331	1,259,347	39,789	385.9	18.6	5,818	113,427	19,496	132	113,928	81.0	3,011	8,540
Lewiston city	181	643,768	18,025	174.8	6.4	2,529	46,670	18,454	73	41,443	86.6	1,145	12,283
Portland city	433	1,072,234	16,742	162.4	(NA)	5,132	113,227	22,063	291	191,559	75.0	4,481	62,070
MARYLAND	19,394	60,039,971	11,032	107.0	12.9	285,561	6,208,963	21,743	9,406	7,832,268	79.6	176,495	2,173,737
Annapolis city	320	801,876	22,145	214.8	(NA)	3,276	81,659	24,926	151	183,563	79.0	4,105	57,804
Baltimore city	1,999	3,273,095	5,141	49.9	(NA)	17,814	372,568	20,914	1,341	1,064,895	67.8	19,254	280,586
Bowie city	123	599,059	11,342	110.0	38.7	3,551	59,247	16,685	65	65,634	(NA)	1,909	19,626
Frederick city	353	1,057,156	18,857	182.9	12.4	5,356	115,500	21,565	170	126,733	93.2	3,386	37,305
Gaithersburg city	358	1,816,601	32,482	315.0	23.3	7,619	181,785	23,859	179	184,920	72.4	3,746	50,026
Hagerstown city	243	885,425	23,945	232.2	(NA)	4,361	82,173	18,843	125	85,106	88.1	2,299	25,950
Rockville city	327	1,109,145	21,206	205.7	(NA)	4,196	111,422	26,554	203	160,655	71.1	2,817	42,023
MASSACHUSETTS	25,761	73,903,837	11,527	111.8	9.7	359,149	7,874,188	21,925	15,175	11,789,582	79.0	241,451	3,466,882
Agawam city	83	207,049	7,289	70.7	(NA)	973	21,254	21,844	55	22,283	98.4	791	7,019
Attleboro city	169	762,988	17,686	171.5	21.6	3,434	70,054	20,400	76	61,694	(NA)	1,645	19,478
Barnstable Town city	444	1,294,750	26,646	258.4	(NA)	5,640	136,052	24,123	188	173,889	69.7	2,988	53,207
Beverly city	150	450,585	11,186	108.5	(NA)	2,351	52,594	22,371	97	49,897	44.8	1,095	15,176
Boston city	2,228	5,424,321	9,268	89.9	4.9	28,183	620,654	22,022	1,942	2,581,415	67.4	43,097	750,772
Brockton city	329	1,313,341	13,787	133.7	7.7	6,246	136,007	21,775	155	114,297	86.2	2,922	37,517
Cambridge city	498	1,202,824	11,790	114.3	(NA)	7,206	153,970	21,367	398	485,242	62.3	8,408	145,333
Chelsea city	89	222,296	6,452	62.6	(NA)	1,111	28,206	25,388	61	29,217	(NA)	551	7,996
Chicopee city	151	488,289	8,908	86.4	164.9	2,124	46,003	21,659	120	53,563	90.7	1,490	15,966
Everett city	120	389,121	10,342	100.3	(NA)	1,950	42,474	21,782	72	28,603	(NA)	576	7,646
Fall River city	330	754,439	8,134	78.9	8.9	3,436	76,740	22,334	173	(D)	(NA)	[7]1,750	(D)
Fitchburg city	148	415,735	10,464	101.5	16.2	1,934	38,122	19,711	97	55,615	78.2	1,372	15,163
Franklin city	112	364,570	12,192	118.2	(NA)	1,725	35,542	20,604	58	46,939	89.8	1,151	14,381
Gloucester city	131	254,448	8,278	80.3	(NA)	1,341	26,010	19,396	107	57,369	86.3	1,032	16,592
Haverhill city	145	510,350	8,527	82.7	2.5	2,268	55,374	24,415	124	77,966	(NA)	1,735	22,476
Holyoke city	285	720,495	18,020	174.8	23.9	4,953	79,961	16,144	89	(D)	(NA)	[7]1,750	(D)
Lawrence city	171	392,109	5,429	52.6	1.2	1,561	41,909	26,848	82	33,983	(NA)	677	9,782
Leominster city	223	639,033	15,262	148.0	(NA)	3,724	65,099	17,481	89	64,522	95.5	1,581	18,290
Lowell city	241	517,804	4,957	48.1	3.1	2,560	52,292	20,427	169	(D)	(NA)	[7]1,750	(D)
Lynn city	197	537,913	5,991	58.1	9.9	2,522	56,039	22,220	141	51,679	95.5	1,229	14,560
Malden city	143	425,695	7,614	73.8	(NA)	1,703	34,296	20,139	98	44,780	92.7	1,012	12,808
Marlborough city	214	585,158	15,420	149.5	(NA)	3,304	63,135	19,109	116	105,918	65.3	2,145	31,373
Medford city	173	593,754	10,837	105.1	15.5	2,774	58,081	20,938	73	53,774	(NA)	990	13,826
Melrose city	59	128,388	4,782	46.4	(NA)	741	16,502	22,270	32	15,175	100.0	304	4,057
Methuen city	103	371,798	8,329	80.8	8.5	2,070	37,347	18,042	73	55,697	(NA)	1,392	16,063
New Bedford city	318	574,094	6,098	59.1	2.5	3,030	63,566	20,979	207	(D)	(NA)	[7]1,750	(D)
Newton city	382	1,150,231	13,782	133.7	(NA)	6,323	154,886	24,496	181	189,418	78.6	3,556	59,478
Northampton city	197	437,796	15,111	146.5	(NA)	2,231	47,912	21,476	99	70,578	82.2	1,727	23,915
Peabody city	296	1,133,850	22,836	221.5	17.4	6,075	127,712	21,023	136	118,741	84.2	2,395	32,664
Pittsfield city	218	615,855	13,707	132.9	(NA)	3,079	68,093	22,115	119	69,015	80.3	1,813	20,843

See footnotes at end of table.

[Includes states and 1,265 incorporated places of 25,000 or more population as of April 1, 2000, in all states except Hawaii, which has no incorporated places recognized by the U.S. Census Bureau. Two census designated places (CDPs) are also included (Honolulu CDP in Hawaii and Arlington CDP in Virginia). For more information on these areas, see Appendix C, Geographic Information]

City	Retail trade (NAICS 44–45), 2002[1]								Accommodation and food services (NAICS 72), 2002[1]				
		Sales					Annual payroll			Sales			
			Per capita[2]		Percent from general mer- chandise stores			Per paid employee (dol.)			Percent from food services		Annual payroll ($1,000)
	Estab- lishments	Total ($1,000)	Amount (dol.)	Percent of national average		Paid employees[3]	Total ($1,000)		Estab- lishments	Total ($1,000)		Paid employees[3]	
MASSACHUSETTS—Con.													
Quincy city	260	976,447	10,980	106.5	(NA)	4,658	99,647	21,393	203	161,241	(NA)	3,268	46,402
Revere city	130	299,685	6,346	61.5	(NA)	1,888	34,891	18,480	86	64,237	(NA)	1,180	17,892
Salem city	175	430,315	10,189	98.8	(NA)	2,458	50,561	20,570	121	70,658	88.1	1,552	21,901
Somerville city	176	603,989	7,866	76.3	6.1	2,847	62,172	21,838	155	88,283	(NA)	1,759	25,910
Springfield city	535	1,343,032	8,836	85.7	9.8	7,141	144,067	20,175	284	183,275	82.3	4,802	57,350
Taunton city	256	1,103,482	19,478	188.9	8.3	4,483	85,223	19,010	109	64,500	(NA)	1,550	20,053
Waltham city	219	615,986	10,472	101.6	(NA)	3,055	74,626	24,427	209	181,106	69.9	3,150	53,219
Watertown city	180	668,968	20,453	198.4	(NA)	2,671	83,137	31,126	80	48,923	(NA)	953	14,520
Westfield city	151	532,785	13,214	128.2	26.2	2,793	51,027	18,270	65	32,856	98.1	1,018	9,545
West Springfield city	197	968,259	34,570	335.3	(NA)	3,307	91,663	27,718	111	83,419	81.3	2,045	22,981
Woburn city	191	732,086	19,367	187.8	(NA)	3,285	80,094	24,382	99	100,190	71.7	1,773	27,220
Worcester city	628	1,783,320	10,186	98.8	6.7	8,728	192,343	22,037	394	253,452	90.3	6,221	76,927
MICHIGAN	38,876	109,350,139	10,892	105.6	(NA)	520,958	10,413,480	19,989	19,084	12,248,269	84.3	329,499	3,488,978
Allen Park city	100	113,339	3,900	37.8	(NA)	665	12,303	18,501	66	36,608	82.7	937	9,469
Ann Arbor city	556	1,495,055	13,114	127.2	(NA)	9,151	175,466	19,175	321	300,452	77.7	7,716	91,011
Battle Creek city	272	738,191	13,805	133.9	30.2	4,437	72,998	16,452	146	99,596	93.2	2,972	28,726
Bay City city	203	355,157	9,867	95.7	(NA)	1,791	33,127	18,496	118	49,508	94.8	1,651	14,417
Burton city	196	453,945	15,002	145.5	17.7	2,736	52,741	19,277	66	40,614	96.7	1,066	11,206
Dearborn city	561	1,853,542	19,005	184.3	12.2	8,278	179,717	21,710	284	259,139	65.6	6,023	76,512
Dearborn Heights city	179	383,112	6,619	64.2	(NA)	2,062	39,336	19,077	107	66,927	(NA)	1,869	17,489
Detroit city	2,179	3,268,378	3,543	34.4	2.5	14,760	291,065	19,720	1,037	663,708	83.8	15,918	180,980
East Lansing city	90	300,626	6,462	62.7	(NA)	1,904	27,876	14,641	108	67,349	80.1	2,065	17,967
Eastpointe city	144	382,779	11,325	109.8	2.2	1,702	39,135	22,994	54	26,049	(NA)	813	7,960
Farmington Hills city	284	1,239,439	15,220	147.6	10.7	4,785	136,894	28,609	185	134,904	88.2	3,409	39,872
Flint city	502	972,891	7,985	77.4	22.1	5,560	99,013	17,808	214	108,969	96.2	3,013	27,338
Garden City city	117	415,331	13,941	135.2	(NA)	1,282	35,694	27,842	50	26,368	100.0	633	6,324
Grand Rapids city	638	1,947,343	9,908	96.1	(NA)	9,738	189,891	19,500	373	284,099	82.6	7,460	84,432
Holland city	185	492,833	14,199	137.7	24.8	2,796	51,476	18,411	76	57,391	91.7	1,678	17,626
Inkster city	65	63,187	2,119	20.6	(NA)	387	5,705	14,742	23	8,484	(NA)	360	3,311
Jackson city	206	516,670	14,484	140.5	(NA)	2,802	53,779	19,193	111	62,011	(NA)	1,754	16,503
Kalamazoo city	299	622,816	8,247	80.0	3.8	3,295	67,096	20,363	200	147,352	79.1	4,589	45,693
Kentwood city	299	1,023,057	22,187	215.2	25.7	5,826	110,480	18,963	108	101,717	72.4	2,603	28,314
Lansing city	512	1,688,748	14,279	138.5	17.9	8,196	167,934	20,490	263	193,991	87.0	5,438	57,675
Lincoln Park city	147	325,077	8,221	79.7	28.7	2,123	35,924	16,921	83	41,709	(NA)	1,198	10,449
Livonia city	566	2,014,903	20,136	195.3	24.7	9,373	191,229	20,402	260	247,374	82.7	5,941	69,299
Madison Heights city	184	684,733	22,334	216.6	(NA)	2,950	66,145	22,422	93	77,115	86.1	1,981	20,554
Midland city	256	705,984	16,821	163.1	(NA)	3,858	66,442	17,222	95	89,521	(NA)	2,430	26,386
Mount Pleasant city	139	404,305	15,770	152.9	(NA)	2,360	37,768	16,003	79	70,294	(NA)	2,190	20,721
Muskegon city	177	517,765	13,064	126.7	34.4	2,863	53,295	18,615	86	53,553	(NA)	1,778	16,182
Novi city	338	1,265,004	25,886	251.0	18.7	6,672	129,541	19,416	134	148,591	80.4	3,466	44,975
Oak Park city	147	245,532	7,677	74.5	10.6	1,316	31,568	23,988	38	21,398	(NA)	523	5,921
Pontiac city	202	449,858	6,664	64.6	3.8	2,267	46,769	20,630	128	94,481	(NA)	2,000	24,012
Portage city	324	1,064,271	23,680	229.7	37.3	6,604	105,522	15,978	104	84,997	(NA)	2,826	25,923
Port Huron city	154	277,026	8,691	84.3	3.6	1,524	32,656	21,428	69	42,708	80.6	1,158	11,772
Rochester Hills city	257	1,114,633	16,220	157.3	7.2	4,240	110,859	26,146	96	72,636	(NA)	1,934	21,245
Roseville city	287	1,209,151	25,071	243.1	38.3	5,557	107,481	19,342	112	94,362	90.9	2,868	27,333
Royal Oak city	253	661,260	11,170	108.3	(NA)	3,229	66,127	20,479	142	128,436	97.7	3,043	37,758
Saginaw city	195	295,537	4,910	47.6	(NA)	1,640	30,315	18,485	107	53,622	94.8	1,348	13,070
St. Clair Shores city	229	613,814	9,802	95.1	(NA)	3,010	65,071	21,618	124	(D)	(NA)	[7]1,750	(D)
Southfield city	510	2,413,836	31,029	300.9	6.4	7,449	184,651	24,789	248	214,707	68.8	4,569	59,575
Southgate city	156	898,905	29,754	288.6	27.9	3,179	67,999	21,390	80	75,754	95.0	2,172	22,058
Sterling Heights city	510	2,025,198	16,141	156.5	20.9	8,766	174,511	19,908	219	171,131	91.0	4,726	51,541
Taylor city	354	1,219,332	18,541	179.8	29.0	6,277	117,279	18,684	149	91,230	93.4	2,839	26,442
Troy city	596	3,110,710	38,407	372.5	14.7	13,040	298,819	22,916	253	268,701	80.7	5,837	77,711
Warren city	539	1,768,902	12,897	125.1	8.0	8,441	191,412	22,463	291	207,164	88.0	5,009	53,908
Westland city	347	1,218,875	14,112	136.9	24.0	6,313	109,520	17,348	145	(D)	(NA)	[6]3,750	(D)
Wyandotte city	101	123,044	4,435	43.0	(NA)	619	12,857	20,771	59	24,522	100.0	739	6,591
Wyoming city	283	1,141,000	16,291	158.0	14.3	5,772	123,188	21,342	131	86,902	90.8	2,258	22,986
MINNESOTA	21,129	60,015,531	11,947	115.9	14.3	306,571	6,040,265	19,703	10,232	7,959,590	72.6	203,062	2,362,446
Andover city	51	82,366	2,878	27.9	(NA)	386	7,475	19,365	9	8,407	100.0	216	2,546
Apple Valley city	128	790,642	16,321	158.3	(NA)	3,500	74,914	21,404	52	55,450	(NA)	1,351	14,551
Blaine city	249	699,742	14,401	139.7	12.1	4,199	76,640	18,252	71	67,793	(NA)	1,952	19,238
Bloomington city	585	2,705,068	32,334	313.6	9.1	12,965	317,392	24,481	233	389,329	(NA)	7,718	108,619
Brooklyn Center city	110	679,410	23,791	230.7	15.5	2,924	64,346	22,006	48	53,799	74.0	1,357	17,836
Brooklyn Park city	154	822,127	12,121	117.5	17.7	3,299	80,861	24,511	66	68,919	69.3	1,940	21,126
Burnsville city	372	1,528,162	25,487	247.2	14.0	7,380	158,824	21,521	106	121,330	85.5	2,969	35,949
Coon Rapids city	182	1,065,454	17,072	165.6	(NA)	4,820	102,890	21,346	93	90,568	90.2	2,511	25,999
Cottage Grove city	47	225,219	7,248	70.3	(NA)	1,041	20,351	19,549	22	13,255	(NA)	420	3,743
Duluth city	466	1,067,932	12,359	119.9	16.7	6,701	112,048	16,721	238	192,120	70.2	5,483	55,146

See footnotes at end of table.

[Includes states and 1,265 incorporated places of 25,000 or more population as of April 1, 2000, in all states except Hawaii, which has no incorporated places recognized by the U.S. Census Bureau. Two census designated places (CDPs) are also included (Honolulu CDP in Hawaii and Arlington CDP in Virginia). For more information on these areas, see Appendix C, Geographic Information]

City	Retail trade (NAICS 44–45), 2002[1]							Accommodation and food services (NAICS 72), 2002[1]				
	Estab-lishments	Sales			Paid employees[3]	Annual payroll		Estab-lishments	Sales		Paid employees[3]	Annual payroll ($1,000)
		Total ($1,000)	Per capita[2]			Total ($1,000)	Per paid employee (dol.)		Total ($1,000)	Percent from food services		
			Amount (dol.)	Percent of national average	Percent from general mer-chandise stores								

City	Estab.	Total	Amount	% nat'l	% gen mer	Paid emp	Total payroll	Per emp	Estab.	Total	% food	Paid emp	Annual payroll
MINNESOTA—Con.													
Eagan city	166	748,960	11,696	113.4	(NA)	3,593	70,275	19,559	129	133,120	80.6	3,262	37,909
Eden Prairie city	213	1,723,788	30,165	292.5	8.6	5,680	152,576	26,862	106	120,299	85.0	2,440	33,249
Edina city	334	1,076,875	22,953	222.6	(NA)	6,983	122,026	17,475	104	119,343	(NA)	2,822	37,170
Fridley city	100	601,065	21,962	213.0	(NA)	2,651	59,095	22,292	46	34,817	(NA)	1,065	10,094
Inver Grove Heights city	57	517,169	16,842	163.3	(NA)	1,511	36,995	24,484	35	26,871	87.6	692	7,899
Lakeville city	86	363,534	7,839	76.0	(NA)	1,160	33,876	29,203	42	42,931	90.4	1,246	14,342
Mankato city	283	906,901	27,304	264.8	(NA)	5,093	88,969	17,469	124	109,747	(NA)	3,555	30,446
Maple Grove city	145	588,913	10,422	101.1	(NA)	3,416	57,765	16,910	76	96,363	91.6	2,402	27,694
Maplewood city	249	1,058,482	29,563	286.7	11.5	5,490	107,557	19,591	86	82,187	94.5	2,227	25,066
Minneapolis city	1,276	2,806,708	7,446	72.2	11.3	17,648	355,623	20,151	949	962,837	77.9	21,401	301,878
Minnetonka city	338	1,925,604	37,962	368.2	(NA)	8,900	185,856	20,883	120	127,954	81.8	2,734	38,223
Moorhead city	132	356,258	10,950	106.2	(NA)	1,973	36,020	18,256	63	36,162	(NA)	1,289	10,837
Oakdale city	77	274,890	9,972	96.7	(NA)	1,138	27,086	23,801	29	32,265	(NA)	574	7,788
Plymouth city	182	948,330	14,138	137.1	(NA)	3,892	101,469	26,071	96	104,332	79.0	2,668	30,089
Richfield city	134	387,754	11,297	109.6	(NA)	2,490	42,356	17,010	57	59,116	88.2	1,307	16,808
Rochester city	482	1,822,418	20,148	195.4	29.6	9,665	186,656	19,313	235	240,820	(NA)	6,085	70,425
Roseville city	319	1,372,194	41,142	399.0	15.6	7,435	132,008	17,755	95	128,692	92.2	3,281	39,011
St. Cloud city	393	1,340,969	21,939	212.8	24.2	7,121	131,013	18,398	139	138,469	82.3	4,228	39,986
St. Louis Park city	211	848,609	19,338	187.5	(NA)	3,730	94,725	25,395	79	84,893	(NA)	2,030	26,783
St. Paul city	837	1,985,691	7,001	67.9	(NA)	12,388	246,024	19,860	584	439,668	89.1	11,109	125,211
Shoreview city	47	202,114	7,551	73.2	(NA)	1,274	19,559	15,352	28	20,366	(NA)	491	5,833
Winona city	147	347,382	13,027	126.3	(NA)	2,094	36,131	17,255	81	45,937	(NA)	1,502	13,368
Woodbury city	194	734,385	14,926	144.8	(NA)	3,944	67,088	17,010	63	65,053	91.5	1,792	20,034
MISSISSIPPI	12,561	25,017,531	8,728	84.6	20.7	135,838	2,375,319	17,486	4,329	5,486,105	40.0	109,405	1,473,389
Biloxi city	251	430,124	8,676	84.1	(NA)	3,204	51,162	15,968	167	1,071,898	8.5	14,302	298,825
Clinton city	77	94,564	3,669	35.6	4.4	664	9,173	13,815	43	31,392	(NA)	946	1,915
Columbus city	274	582,113	23,029	223.3	21.9	3,080	55,332	17,965	87	55,017	(NA)	1,860	13,856
Greenville city	234	416,182	10,362	100.5	(NA)	2,326	43,828	18,843	79	79,766	52.8	1,871	19,003
Gulfport city	414	1,123,487	15,567	151.0	19.0	5,299	100,256	18,920	179	312,132	(NA)	5,972	85,021
Hattiesburg city	427	888,035	19,504	189.2	16.5	4,944	89,577	18,118	148	109,690	87.2	3,702	30,808
Jackson city	874	2,804,963	15,579	151.0	14.4	13,129	275,265	20,966	367	318,174	79.1	8,476	91,388
Meridian city	378	880,846	22,417	217.4	(NA)	4,892	89,414	18,278	128	98,512	84.8	2,741	27,419
Pascagoula city	145	413,657	15,990	155.1	(NA)	2,147	38,721	18,035	55	28,257	96.6	858	8,056
Southaven city	129	480,702	14,527	140.9	(NA)	2,251	43,759	19,440	64	54,768	90.3	1,530	15,198
Tupelo city	400	1,028,908	29,488	286.0	27.0	5,471	98,555	18,014	137	93,475	85.6	3,099	27,938
Vicksburg city	244	440,166	16,980	164.7	25.7	2,605	45,827	17,592	88	260,511	(NA)	3,885	54,805
MISSOURI	23,837	61,861,163	10,889	105.6	16.7	311,593	6,072,036	19,487	11,280	8,607,025	73.5	215,792	2,432,448
Ballwin city	115	515,087	16,539	160.4	(NA)	1,937	41,915	21,639	42	27,910	100.0	1,038	8,903
Blue Springs city	158	598,940	11,887	115.3	(NA)	2,480	60,528	24,406	86	56,889	89.4	1,793	16,323
Cape Girardeau city	324	821,082	23,068	223.7	(NA)	4,393	80,746	18,381	107	89,186	85.7	2,806	27,347
Chesterfield city	276	609,330	12,958	125.7	21.6	4,381	76,097	17,370	129	126,752	82.5	3,114	39,844
Columbia city	502	1,521,679	17,490	169.6	22.6	8,114	153,807	18,956	288	220,170	81.7	6,375	61,161
Florissant city	185	723,772	13,608	132.0	10.1	3,634	77,265	21,262	103	77,708	(NA)	2,434	24,570
Gladstone city	98	333,639	12,459	120.8	(NA)	1,413	32,811	23,221	41	30,142	100.0	821	9,885
Hazelwood city	76	468,997	18,091	175.4	(NA)	1,381	46,418	33,612	54	30,585	84.3	879	9,101
Independence city	475	1,707,915	15,161	147.0	24.3	8,809	171,700	19,491	209	166,682	95.1	4,906	51,374
Jefferson City city	298	1,211,551	30,718	297.9	(NA)	7,171	126,341	17,618	139	102,603	(NA)	2,804	29,171
Joplin city	411	1,108,502	23,997	232.7	28.5	5,694	99,877	17,541	174	126,693	83.2	3,958	36,033
Kansas City city	1,657	5,715,628	12,884	125.0	14.0	25,833	574,239	22,229	1,042	1,268,536	55.4	24,772	341,488
Kirkwood city	144	612,752	22,426	217.5	(NA)	2,736	62,717	22,923	48	38,571	(NA)	1,032	12,579
Lee's Summit city	248	914,129	12,237	118.7	15.7	4,083	83,437	20,435	118	90,910	90.5	2,810	27,097
Liberty city	94	332,193	12,073	117.1	(NA)	1,746	34,721	19,886	50	33,248	85.7	1,013	10,216
Maryland Heights city	120	962,844	35,508	344.4	(NA)	2,422	69,858	28,843	86	350,464	18.1	4,800	81,239
O'Fallon city	147	562,970	9,417	91.3	22.4	2,798	56,374	20,148	91	63,763	100.0	2,157	19,614
Raytown city	110	377,282	12,610	122.3	(NA)	1,611	38,324	23,789	41	28,639	100.0	970	7,226
St. Charles city	299	920,734	15,107	146.5	(NA)	4,653	91,554	19,676	162	129,066	92.5	3,736	37,715
St. Joseph city	379	951,224	13,001	126.1	26.8	5,222	97,538	18,678	175	106,383	87.4	3,260	31,090
St. Louis city	1,234	2,821,962	8,092	78.5	(NA)	14,524	329,669	22,698	967	1,033,254	72.6	22,718	305,804
St. Peters city	304	1,308,673	24,385	236.5	14.3	6,159	124,732	20,252	130	95,640	91.7	2,718	28,046
Springfield city	1,069	3,325,640	21,993	213.3	21.4	17,253	321,691	18,646	571	427,936	83.1	12,042	124,656
University City city	91	138,374	3,644	35.3	6.7	980	17,709	18,070	67	38,275	(NA)	1,240	12,533
Wildwood city	27	8,885	263	2.5	(NA)	101	1,626	16,099	21	7,377	(NA)	235	2,109
MONTANA	5,145	10,122,625	11,119	107.8	16.2	52,891	988,009	18,680	3,260	1,537,986	71.9	40,918	408,977
Billings city	624	1,714,236	18,226	176.8	24.8	8,527	173,040	20,293	323	252,144	79.2	6,930	69,490
Bozeman city	313	679,846	23,035	223.4	(NA)	3,841	73,822	19,219	159	92,926	76.0	2,731	26,716
Butte-Silver Bow (balance)	193	432,660	13,211	128.1	(NA)	2,152	39,273	18,250	120	58,863	74.0	1,598	16,321
Great Falls city	387	979,912	17,420	168.9	22.6	5,360	101,867	19,005	210	115,363	80.9	3,561	35,045
Helena city	238	496,570	18,845	182.8	28.7	2,977	56,231	18,888	136	73,050	76.1	2,247	20,988
Missoula city	458	1,237,661	20,831	202.0	(NA)	6,412	121,844	19,002	267	180,431	78.8	4,588	47,640

See footnotes at end of table.

Table C-5. Cities — **Retail Trade and Accommodation and Food Services**—Con.

[Includes states and 1,265 incorporated places of 25,000 or more population as of April 1, 2000, in all states except Hawaii, which has no incorporated places recognized by the U.S. Census Bureau. Two census designated places (CDPs) are also included (Honolulu CDP in Hawaii and Arlington CDP in Virginia). For more information on these areas, see Appendix C, Geographic Information]

City	Retail trade (NAICS 44–45), 2002[1]								Accommodation and food services (NAICS 72), 2002[1]				
		Sales					Annual payroll			Sales			
			Per capita[2]		Percent from general merchandise stores			Per paid employee (dol.)			Percent from food services		Annual payroll ($1,000)
	Establishments	Total ($1,000)	Amount (dol.)	Percent of national average		Paid employees[3]	Total ($1,000)		Establishments	Total ($1,000)		Paid employees[3]	
NEBRASKA	8,157	20,249,200	11,727	113.7	14.0	105,634	1,932,506	18,294	3,992	2,088,710	84.8	62,662	590,533
Bellevue city	118	496,831	10,797	104.7	32.3	2,439	46,687	19,142	77	51,937	91.3	1,423	15,361
Fremont city	141	524,228	20,832	202.0	(NA)	2,361	48,991	20,750	65	36,811	(NA)	1,321	10,397
Grand Island city	296	808,404	18,660	181.0	(NA)	4,193	75,473	18,000	139	77,874	(NA)	2,311	22,477
Kearney city	202	519,811	18,620	180.6	28.3	3,147	54,874	17,437	103	76,085	77.0	2,484	22,703
Lincoln city	990	2,798,920	12,066	117.0	(NA)	16,595	291,695	17,577	524	371,354	(NA)	11,031	103,497
Omaha city	1,785	5,977,329	14,971	145.2	(NA)	32,163	647,849	20,143	1,016	761,216	84.7	20,781	223,814
NEVADA	7,214	26,999,899	12,455	120.8	14.2	112,339	2,646,023	23,554	4,252	19,537,592	16.2	269,098	6,016,270
Carson City	273	861,198	15,788	153.1	(NA)	3,387	89,440	26,407	124	110,119	61.4	2,328	29,979
Henderson city	493	2,750,600	13,413	130.1	17.7	10,494	259,547	24,733	286	660,929	(NA)	9,987	181,244
Las Vegas city	1,563	6,458,407	12,739	123.5	14.4	27,809	671,301	24,140	962	2,416,602	31.5	39,122	779,221
North Las Vegas city	174	514,752	3,802	36.9	(NA)	2,925	58,595	20,032	94	458,361	17.2	5,318	126,817
Reno city	956	3,816,673	20,059	194.5	18.6	15,010	358,004	23,851	580	1,614,303	19.4	28,429	536,029
Sparks city	269	722,462	9,830	95.3	10.5	4,003	88,224	22,039	136	259,892	24.3	4,888	77,775
NEW HAMPSHIRE	6,702	20,830,057	16,342	158.5	13.9	93,804	2,037,551	21,721	3,160	2,082,145	75.3	47,831	632,846
Concord city	324	1,276,470	30,743	298.1	18.5	5,896	117,253	19,887	122	104,194	88.3	2,341	32,362
Dover city	126	345,565	12,404	120.3	2.7	1,828	39,877	21,815	59	47,695	(NA)	1,204	13,473
Manchester city	509	1,738,832	16,055	155.7	(NA)	7,866	167,599	21,307	257	205,813	87.3	4,864	63,447
Nashua city	501	2,335,877	26,644	258.4	15.4	10,058	222,508	22,122	192	173,483	79.4	3,765	56,835
Rochester city	135	503,094	17,195	166.8	(NA)	2,185	48,417	22,159	58	34,123	94.5	934	9,891
NEW JERSEY	34,741	102,153,833	11,911	115.5	10.2	434,574	9,856,227	22,680	17,537	15,715,595	58.7	268,992	4,335,892
Atlantic City city	246	310,130	7,711	74.8	(NA)	1,636	33,900	20,721	193	4,480,402	(NA)	48,136	1,295,782
Bayonne city	230	273,227	4,450	43.2	1.7	1,681	30,720	18,275	110	45,203	(NA)	939	10,476
Bergenfield borough	95	238,307	9,101	88.3	(NA)	913	22,930	25,115	45	15,041	(NA)	330	3,875
Camden city	169	177,577	2,229	21.6	3.7	914	19,487	21,321	88	30,124	100.0	590	7,108
Clifton city	310	941,333	11,818	114.6	15.0	4,129	99,844	24,181	142	(D)	(NA)	[7]1,750	(D)
East Orange city	136	185,042	2,661	25.8	3.7	916	19,505	21,294	51	26,629	(NA)	723	7,227
Elizabeth city	526	1,051,001	8,539	82.8	2.2	5,611	101,231	18,042	238	124,095	61.9	2,312	34,221
Englewood city	179	712,102	27,230	264.1	(NA)	1,563	54,537	34,893	57	34,830	(NA)	634	9,637
Fair Lawn borough	111	335,341	10,616	103.0	(NA)	1,174	33,568	28,593	67	33,039	(NA)	708	9,103
Fort Lee borough	144	545,827	14,776	143.3	(NA)	1,209	33,626	27,813	97	60,076	66.7	999	15,595
Garfield city	70	265,635	8,920	86.5	(NA)	1,018	31,297	30,744	43	18,641	100.0	387	4,890
Hackensack city	431	984,268	22,609	219.3	32.4	4,464	97,221	21,779	113	98,091	(NA)	2,109	29,408
Hoboken city	155	213,375	5,409	52.5	(NA)	1,041	21,960	21,095	154	74,511	99.4	1,390	19,281
Jersey City city	799	1,724,019	7,199	69.8	14.6	7,863	158,335	20,137	379	195,468	78.9	3,261	49,179
Kearny town	120	303,364	7,549	73.2	(NA)	1,478	29,418	19,904	61	20,664	(NA)	433	5,761
Linden city	188	598,890	15,014	145.6	28.8	2,734	60,573	22,155	85	37,032	83.8	724	9,114
Long Branch city	86	188,781	6,007	58.3	0.6	1,091	25,212	23,109	81	32,338	(NA)	689	8,890
Millville city	95	326,781	12,105	117.4	(NA)	1,414	29,377	20,776	43	17,111	(NA)	362	3,966
Newark city	908	1,053,762	3,812	37.0	3.5	5,501	111,091	20,195	488	384,616	74.1	6,530	107,387
New Brunswick city	129	149,659	3,070	29.8	(NA)	898	15,505	17,266	131	91,265	(NA)	1,884	27,334
Paramus borough	644	3,043,805	116,065	1,125.6	16.5	13,965	308,647	22,101	107	121,444	90.3	2,429	33,195
Passaic city	229	332,159	4,848	47.0	11.8	1,870	39,341	21,038	78	(D)	(NA)	[5]375	(D)
Paterson city	427	497,426	3,297	32.0	3.7	2,624	59,851	22,809	170	61,008	(NA)	1,120	14,281
Perth Amboy city	148	319,397	6,683	64.8	(NA)	1,310	26,677	20,364	80	32,416	98.0	649	7,907
Plainfield city	119	170,076	3,532	34.3	(NA)	866	18,009	20,796	47	24,570	(NA)	561	6,319
Rahway city	97	223,496	8,327	80.8	(NA)	818	19,913	24,344	62	32,086	95.9	781	8,697
Sayreville borough	116	187,234	4,514	43.8	(NA)	917	18,674	20,364	70	30,412	90.3	710	8,247
Trenton city	211	315,499	3,702	35.9	(NA)	1,765	37,100	21,020	167	62,362	(NA)	1,239	16,578
Union City city	295	336,818	5,050	49.0	(NA)	1,669	30,647	18,362	134	44,341	(NA)	1,011	11,324
Vineland city	286	895,806	15,882	154.0	(NA)	4,192	90,740	21,646	103	63,147	86.4	1,603	16,632
Westfield town	144	227,161	7,582	73.5	(NA)	1,498	26,619	17,770	57	26,661	100.0	526	7,471
West New York town	247	221,210	4,734	45.9	2.0	1,157	22,192	19,181	60	20,695	100.0	394	4,296
NEW MEXICO	7,227	18,328,637	9,879	95.8	18.3	89,413	1,766,744	19,759	3,756	2,771,474	71.8	69,986	779,512
Alamogordo city	134	344,206	9,798	95.0	(NA)	2,241	32,787	14,631	67	34,517	(NA)	1,144	9,741
Albuquerque city	1,972	6,955,281	14,990	145.4	(NA)	29,599	645,264	21,800	1,096	987,792	79.2	24,289	281,620
Carlsbad city	130	195,230	7,714	74.8	2.4	1,189	21,755	18,297	59	33,981	65.9	1,104	8,738
Clovis city	178	393,743	12,171	118.0	29.4	2,223	40,775	18,342	72	44,221	84.4	1,334	13,440
Farmington city	335	976,065	24,142	234.1	26.8	4,688	93,989	20,049	123	111,468	82.5	2,981	28,612
Hobbs city	145	399,278	13,962	135.4	(NA)	2,083	37,797	18,145	70	36,754	(NA)	1,082	9,453
Las Cruces city	393	1,056,033	14,073	136.5	(NA)	5,232	96,395	18,424	195	125,764	85.4	3,783	34,507
Rio Rancho city	78	438,773	7,824	75.9	(NA)	1,617	40,237	24,884	58	51,483	87.7	1,320	14,425
Roswell city	226	464,872	10,427	101.1	(NA)	2,288	44,305	19,364	86	55,682	78.4	1,689	15,836
Santa Fe city	802	1,594,493	24,032	233.1	(NA)	8,086	180,286	22,296	314	349,013	58.7	7,202	106,080

See footnotes at end of table.

[Includes states and 1,265 incorporated places of 25,000 or more population as of April 1, 2000, in all states except Hawaii, which has no incorporated places recognized by the U.S. Census Bureau. Two census designated places (CDPs) are also included (Honolulu CDP in Hawaii and Arlington CDP in Virginia). For more information on these areas, see Appendix C, Geographic Information]

City	Retail trade (NAICS 44–45), 2002[1]								Accommodation and food services (NAICS 72), 2002[1]				
		Sales					Annual payroll			Sales			
			Per capita[2]		Percent from general merchandise stores						Percent from food services		Annual payroll ($1,000)
	Establishments	Total ($1,000)	Amount (dol.)	Percent of national average		Paid employees[3]	Total ($1,000)	Per paid employee (dol.)	Establishments	Total ($1,000)		Paid employees[3]	
NEW YORK.	76,425	178,067,530	9,291	90.1	11.1	837,806	18,152,597	21,667	39,428	27,835,952	75.5	527,649	7,972,279
Albany city	555	1,676,262	17,864	173.2	16.9	9,340	165,687	17,740	396	238,740	85.4	5,430	67,708
Auburn city	167	414,725	14,663	142.2	(NA)	2,275	41,424	18,208	98	41,835	86.2	1,158	10,911
Binghamton city	193	458,554	9,808	95.1	11.8	2,744	46,791	17,052	168	103,424	88.4	3,236	28,912
Buffalo city	920	1,495,330	5,203	50.5	10.1	10,672	165,659	15,523	636	370,456	85.2	10,130	106,481
Elmira city	111	271,454	8,891	86.2	2.2	1,443	26,403	18,297	75	29,853	(NA)	1,068	8,926
Freeport village	183	545,525	12,456	120.8	(NA)	2,034	52,062	25,596	70	26,603	87.7	522	8,620
Glen Cove city	117	311,550	11,628	112.8	(NA)	1,289	29,447	22,845	64	45,866	88.9	801	13,921
Hempstead village	191	819,498	15,390	149.3	(NA)	2,281	64,924	28,463	71	38,373	(NA)	740	10,489
Ithaca city	196	424,213	14,196	137.7	8.0	2,718	47,568	17,501	206	100,142	81.8	2,523	29,696
Jamestown city	127	336,668	10,766	104.4	(NA)	1,623	31,157	19,197	83	31,226	(NA)	907	8,024
Lindenhurst village	107	205,310	7,346	71.2	(NA)	970	23,982	24,724	61	32,026	(NA)	743	8,342
Long Beach city	91	128,873	3,625	35.2	(NA)	650	14,771	22,725	68	23,280	100.0	502	6,625
Middletown city	202	653,159	25,387	246.2	4.9	2,697	61,049	22,636	78	55,567	(NA)	1,314	15,676
Mount Vernon city	249	350,206	5,102	49.5	1.5	1,726	46,957	27,206	70	22,740	100.0	425	6,060
Newburgh city	138	308,778	10,845	105.2	35.4	1,764	32,491	18,419	88	42,031	99.0	957	11,251
New Rochelle city	278	855,315	11,806	114.5	(NA)	2,835	78,911	27,835	144	105,580	(NA)	1,736	28,687
New York city	30,252	55,518,491	6,848	66.4	7.8	254,183	6,050,555	23,804	15,065	14,280,485	69.3	213,985	4,127,451
Niagara Falls city	184	436,806	8,028	77.9	(NA)	2,564	41,766	16,289	180	99,037	62.1	2,631	26,724
North Tonawanda city	85	118,350	3,632	35.2	5.7	796	12,848	16,141	52	13,227	100.0	582	3,830
Port Chester village	144	400,161	14,320	138.9	12.8	1,660	39,049	23,523	91	47,926	100.0	969	12,610
Poughkeepsie city	185	405,702	13,401	130.0	(NA)	2,442	48,744	19,961	105	47,094	(NA)	1,113	14,069
Rochester city	800	1,309,682	6,056	58.7	15.7	8,594	155,792	18,128	525	283,303	81.6	6,831	81,403
Rome city	161	396,761	11,490	111.4	26.3	2,069	36,905	17,837	74	28,191	(NA)	866	8,079
Saratoga Springs city	186	536,428	19,859	192.6	(NA)	2,624	47,701	18,179	131	99,052	61.6	1,924	28,359
Schenectady city	209	381,214	6,215	60.3	(NA)	2,264	44,141	19,497	155	61,063	86.8	1,527	16,885
Spring Valley village	92	319,814	12,484	121.1	(NA)	900	28,364	31,516	24	9,747	(NA)	213	2,608
Syracuse city	650	1,543,252	10,677	103.5	10.1	8,735	161,812	18,525	415	205,675	85.9	5,880	63,938
Troy city	160	338,127	6,987	67.8	2.6	2,064	38,332	18,572	113	47,947	(NA)	1,381	14,247
Utica city	181	463,898	7,759	75.2	21.2	2,632	57,364	21,795	143	84,609	(NA)	2,156	24,004
Valley Stream village	293	849,921	23,471	227.6	25.4	4,086	84,808	20,756	93	(D)	(NA)	[7]1,750	(D)
Watertown city	262	532,371	19,885	192.8	(NA)	3,272	54,275	16,588	105	62,543	88.7	1,698	17,759
White Plains city	493	1,482,172	26,760	259.5	17.9	6,758	165,112	24,432	168	139,451	73.8	2,117	35,145
Yonkers city	616	2,109,727	10,690	103.7	16.5	8,495	196,425	23,122	271	125,888	93.7	2,791	32,811
NORTH CAROLINA	35,851	88,821,486	10,685	103.6	13.8	435,421	8,453,694	19,415	15,747	11,237,386	78.9	281,788	3,184,887
Asheville city	800	2,069,684	29,279	283.9	18.4	10,546	206,117	19,545	395	391,428	61.5	8,757	115,028
Burlington city	378	1,118,714	24,009	232.8	(NA)	5,437	104,663	19,250	160	124,479	91.7	3,268	32,607
Cary town	468	2,132,327	21,342	207.0	15.7	8,370	170,621	20,385	270	230,667	79.4	5,434	65,887
Chapel Hill town	225	569,656	11,666	113.1	(NA)	3,102	66,608	21,473	182	130,755	70.8	3,345	40,615
Charlotte city	2,298	7,943,719	13,674	132.6	9.7	35,555	792,197	22,281	1,469	1,269,823	78.7	28,934	391,780
Concord city	431	1,320,135	22,578	219.0	14.3	6,531	121,957	18,674	133	134,958	95.7	3,353	39,787
Durham city	856	2,294,799	11,729	113.7	(NA)	13,477	243,993	18,104	484	434,445	74.9	9,906	127,182
Fayetteville city	740	2,350,733	17,842	173.0	(NA)	11,270	227,375	20,175	361	268,498	87.1	7,515	72,424
Gastonia city	415	1,110,179	16,372	158.8	(NA)	6,293	111,694	17,749	157	119,244	93.1	3,163	32,505
Goldsboro city	351	795,775	20,495	198.8	28.0	4,453	74,802	16,798	137	90,025	(NA)	2,799	24,296
Greensboro city	1,198	3,860,010	16,962	164.5	14.7	18,295	394,923	21,586	654	596,949	76.9	14,589	174,129
Greenville city	427	1,181,746	18,002	174.6	14.5	5,752	110,538	19,217	205	167,364	90.5	5,295	47,082
Hickory city	497	1,623,223	41,107	398.7	18.1	7,661	149,254	19,482	229	178,043	90.1	5,072	53,565
High Point city	462	1,314,719	14,503	140.6	10.3	6,011	134,418	22,362	220	144,338	90.8	3,606	39,672
Huntersville town	108	395,637	12,947	125.6	(NA)	1,707	34,627	20,285	63	60,402	85.1	1,403	16,406
Jacksonville city	318	1,053,560	15,813	153.3	21.1	4,698	85,282	18,153	153	128,782	87.0	3,949	32,802
Kannapolis city	192	366,377	9,642	93.5	19.2	2,119	40,696	19,205	56	31,323	(NA)	801	8,851
Monroe city	214	774,798	27,390	265.6	21.8	3,270	65,151	19,924	94	60,884	90.2	1,575	16,149
Raleigh city	1,595	5,250,968	16,985	164.7	11.3	23,574	524,328	22,242	752	638,364	81.7	14,972	185,339
Rocky Mount city	378	874,566	15,625	151.5	18.6	4,639	83,369	17,971	137	98,186	90.4	3,016	27,779
Salisbury city	219	640,973	23,048	223.5	14.4	3,210	61,528	19,168	102	73,663	(NA)	2,051	21,452
Wilmington city	791	2,512,214	27,723	268.9	16.1	11,186	221,499	19,801	349	251,246	85.9	7,206	74,723
Wilson city	304	677,447	14,766	143.2	(NA)	3,425	64,467	18,822	113	84,294	87.3	2,436	23,128
Winston-Salem city	1,027	3,258,599	17,253	167.3	17.0	15,517	316,740	20,412	463	389,048	85.5	10,220	115,879
NORTH DAKOTA	3,433	7,723,945	12,191	118.2	14.6	41,342	729,605	17,648	1,765	854,656	69.9	26,166	244,609
Bismarck city	339	968,000	17,230	167.1	21.1	5,363	97,942	18,263	140	119,636	(NA)	3,730	37,100
Fargo city	493	1,823,127	19,971	193.7	(NA)	9,555	185,075	19,369	241	203,113	74.5	6,356	61,374
Grand Forks city	302	1,041,489	21,450	208.0	(NA)	5,426	97,362	17,944	156	97,690	80.8	3,411	29,172
Minot city	248	747,459	21,094	204.6	(NA)	4,213	73,447	17,433	113	67,041	80.3	2,217	19,670

See footnotes at end of table.

[Includes states and 1,265 incorporated places of 25,000 or more population as of April 1, 2000, in all states except Hawaii, which has no incorporated places recognized by the U.S. Census Bureau. Two census designated places (CDPs) are also included (Honolulu CDP in Hawaii and Arlington CDP in Virginia). For more information on these areas, see Appendix C, Geographic Information]

City		Retail trade (NAICS 44–45), 2002[1]							Accommodation and food services (NAICS 72), 2002[1]				
			Sales					Annual payroll			Sales			
				Per capita[2]		Percent from general merchandise stores			Per paid			Percent from food services		Annual
	Estab-lishments	Total ($1,000)	Amount (dol.)	Percent of national average		Paid employees[3]	Total ($1,000)	employee (dol.)	Estab-lishments	Total ($1,000)		Paid employees[3]	payroll ($1,000)
OHIO	42,280	119,778,409	10,503	101.9	15.0	611,814	11,545,773	18,871	22,663	14,875,890	87.0	418,855	4,259,470
Akron city	820	1,697,740	7,932	76.9	12.6	11,130	197,132	17,712	445	237,773	91.9	6,942	71,639
Barberton city	86	146,320	5,299	51.4	12.1	936	17,023	18,187	50	19,884	(NA)	687	5,626
Beavercreek city	203	764,510	19,806	192.1	24.8	4,019	67,476	16,789	60	61,561	(NA)	1,879	18,171
Bowling Green city	120	371,598	12,595	122.1	28.6	2,035	34,568	16,987	91	52,080	88.1	1,943	15,456
Brunswick city	97	409,560	11,877	115.2	(NA)	1,381	33,088	23,959	48	25,850	(NA)	1,008	6,836
Canton city	303	652,132	8,114	78.7	10.6	3,872	75,930	19,610	171	83,135	99.5	2,608	23,440
Cincinnati city	1,236	3,409,442	10,581	102.6	7.9	15,866	358,474	22,594	797	589,093	82.6	14,903	168,664
Cleveland city	1,451	2,307,009	4,930	47.8	2.8	12,875	242,579	18,841	1,032	732,951	78.7	15,875	194,641
Cleveland Heights city . . .	131	393,818	7,944	77.0	(NA)	2,058	40,302	19,583	79	48,106	(NA)	1,276	13,868
Columbus city	2,641	9,213,094	12,744	123.6	17.9	47,943	937,551	19,556	1,616	1,532,056	80.5	37,523	450,157
Cuyahoga Falls city	196	787,487	15,665	151.9	(NA)	3,595	72,938	20,289	110	94,057	(NA)	2,590	28,904
Dayton city	473	996,427	6,124	59.4	10.9	5,732	112,717	19,665	318	203,571	87.0	5,031	54,204
Delaware city	102	320,009	11,482	111.3	(NA)	1,667	31,173	18,700	76	39,722	93.5	1,187	11,930
Dublin city	143	988,739	30,134	292.2	10.1	3,138	78,781	25,105	105	113,763	70.3	2,589	33,864
East Cleveland city	62	57,808	2,177	21.1	13.2	461	6,390	13,861	29	13,715	(NA)	343	3,383
Elyria city	259	814,077	14,541	141.0	28.6	4,789	82,886	17,308	138	80,402	90.8	2,410	22,878
Euclid city	118	298,990	5,800	56.3	21.4	1,946	33,698	17,317	71	26,971	(NA)	680	6,469
Fairborn city	84	329,847	10,336	100.2	(NA)	1,535	29,941	19,506	78	57,614	73.6	1,621	16,523
Fairfield city	172	827,731	19,494	189.1	(NA)	3,242	83,789	25,845	94	70,611	91.9	2,022	20,667
Findlay city	245	729,455	18,364	178.1	30.0	3,993	69,776	17,475	125	89,036	85.2	2,711	26,074
Gahanna city	85	319,461	9,584	92.9	(NA)	1,300	31,339	24,107	79	61,357	88.4	1,563	15,869
Garfield Heights city	68	174,795	5,809	56.3	13.6	1,004	16,055	15,991	53	27,409	(NA)	813	8,225
Grove City city	81	409,607	14,087	136.6	4.9	1,691	35,813	21,179	86	64,264	86.1	1,827	19,224
Hamilton city	203	581,551	9,564	92.8	27.1	3,565	59,711	16,749	120	70,826	(NA)	2,168	20,222
Huber Heights city	110	296,995	7,792	75.6	40.4	1,725	31,044	17,997	59	47,206	91.8	1,490	13,642
Kent city	79	332,612	11,852	114.9	3.8	1,112	28,195	25,355	76	34,916	94.2	1,165	10,165
Kettering city	186	857,876	15,097	146.4	(NA)	4,093	78,740	19,238	100	75,514	(NA)	2,233	22,024
Lakewood city	133	266,495	4,829	46.8	(NA)	1,511	29,022	19,207	104	48,239	96.8	1,230	12,038
Lancaster city	258	498,333	13,948	135.3	17.9	3,085	53,096	17,211	105	80,604	92.7	2,484	24,376
Lima city	152	331,924	8,124	78.8	(NA)	1,777	38,266	21,534	80	42,609	96.0	1,175	13,349
Lorain city	146	243,930	3,589	34.8	25.6	1,453	26,521	18,253	101	42,941	(NA)	1,330	11,708
Mansfield city	239	631,050	12,331	119.6	2.8	2,942	61,183	20,796	137	76,570	92.5	2,203	22,098
Maple Heights city	111	227,702	8,893	86.2	4.5	1,639	28,167	17,185	41	17,852	100.0	418	4,419
Marion city	107	250,972	6,746	65.4	(NA)	975	22,264	22,835	61	31,987	(NA)	931	8,890
Massillon city	131	412,989	13,038	126.4	(NA)	2,148	40,191	18,711	83	38,712	95.7	1,141	9,956
Medina city	117	299,169	11,421	110.8	(NA)	1,870	30,225	16,163	53	35,995	(NA)	1,180	10,726
Mentor city	366	1,466,132	28,895	280.2	17.3	7,295	139,332	19,100	150	126,835	88.4	3,666	38,238
Middletown city	193	548,077	10,541	102.2	28.6	2,971	54,556	18,363	105	80,197	91.8	2,398	24,636
Newark city	176	354,819	7,666	74.3	19.3	1,809	32,754	18,106	94	65,856	81.1	2,046	19,222
North Olmsted city	277	905,145	26,904	260.9	18.8	5,047	87,364	17,310	113	92,147	88.4	2,551	26,176
North Royalton city	74	117,595	4,039	39.2	(NA)	770	12,601	16,365	40	19,415	100.0	660	5,838
Parma city	342	837,275	9,938	96.4	14.7	5,360	87,488	16,322	175	(D)	(NA)	[6]3,750	(D)
Reynoldsburg city	106	240,345	7,387	71.6	39.7	1,459	24,707	16,934	68	33,836	(NA)	884	9,902
Sandusky city	131	242,135	8,872	86.0	5.1	1,277	25,848	20,241	93	46,830	(NA)	1,136	15,490
Shaker Heights city	80	342,786	11,934	115.7	(NA)	937	17,694	18,884	34	23,570	100.0	665	7,240
Springfield city	266	878,361	13,481	130.7	17.1	4,507	79,610	17,664	169	110,970	90.2	3,554	32,751
Stow city	107	450,472	13,339	129.4	25.9	2,590	42,020	16,224	57	37,394	100.0	1,194	10,658
Strongsville city	231	648,516	14,606	141.7	(NA)	4,421	69,391	15,696	103	72,369	87.6	2,325	20,258
Toledo city	1,164	2,709,938	8,744	84.8	17.5	16,992	306,161	18,092	671	461,192	91.4	13,149	132,998
Trotwood city	119	357,888	13,187	127.9	26.9	2,269	38,890	17,140	28	23,925	100.0	852	6,747
Upper Arlington city	100	151,429	4,617	44.8	(NA)	1,246	20,011	16,060	54	40,104	(NA)	1,069	11,842
Warren city	178	414,294	8,769	85.0	4.4	1,975	39,934	20,220	100	37,965	96.1	1,219	10,136
Westerville city	134	284,932	8,078	78.3	9.7	1,530	28,327	18,514	63	43,460	91.6	1,301	13,040
Westlake city	151	388,895	12,224	118.6	(NA)	2,174	41,408	19,047	82	96,826	83.9	2,469	28,425
Youngstown city	263	353,982	4,461	43.3	2.4	2,413	41,599	17,240	132	57,573	(NA)	1,679	14,935
Zanesville city	241	610,137	24,068	233.4	(NA)	3,282	54,853	16,713	102	70,219	92.7	2,149	20,530
OKLAHOMA	13,922	32,112,960	9,209	89.3	19.5	167,949	2,997,665	17,849	6,506	3,901,754	86.7	111,156	1,113,389
Bartlesville city	186	475,225	13,672	132.6	(NA)	2,590	45,590	17,602	95	49,380	(NA)	1,601	15,538
Broken Arrow city	236	905,164	10,815	104.9	16.6	3,700	77,498	20,945	107	71,341	93.2	2,052	21,080
Edmond city	267	676,926	9,603	93.1	22.7	4,104	69,336	16,895	155	109,459	94.1	3,215	34,303
Enid city	258	549,195	11,804	114.5	(NA)	3,209	55,128	17,179	107	58,643	89.8	1,957	16,370
Lawton city	368	856,931	9,558	92.7	(NA)	4,696	81,735	17,405	166	106,058	(NA)	3,276	27,385
Midwest City city	194	930,725	17,186	166.7	(NA)	4,001	80,074	20,013	110	66,060	(NA)	1,979	18,180
Moore city	107	248,716	5,710	55.4	(NA)	1,510	25,863	17,128	61	41,420	92.5	1,176	11,430
Muskogee city	243	557,323	14,135	137.1	(NA)	3,000	53,857	17,952	107	58,968	(NA)	1,822	16,119
Norman city	416	1,326,871	13,430	130.2	20.0	6,601	120,984	18,328	235	188,552	88.1	5,737	56,222
Oklahoma City city	2,217	6,250,285	12,057	116.9	17.8	31,571	634,091	20,085	1,123	913,309	81.9	23,949	263,481
Ponca City city	173	345,709	13,430	130.2	(NA)	2,020	34,001	16,834	57	35,950	88.3	1,058	9,531
Shawnee city	194	434,251	14,738	142.9	22.4	2,487	41,604	16,729	97	68,631	90.8	2,006	18,877
Stillwater city	203	478,957	11,949	115.9	(NA)	2,830	43,358	15,321	117	81,118	(NA)	2,574	21,867
Tulsa city	1,878	5,598,096	14,322	138.9	16.8	28,677	555,570	19,373	1,041	790,610	83.2	19,938	232,308

See footnotes at end of table.

Table C-5. Cities — **Retail Trade and Accommodation and Food Services**—Con.

[Includes states and 1,265 incorporated places of 25,000 or more population as of April 1, 2000, in all states except Hawaii, which has no incorporated places recognized by the U.S. Census Bureau. Two census designated places (CDPs) are also included (Honolulu CDP in Hawaii and Arlington CDP in Virginia). For more information on these areas, see Appendix C, Geographic Information]

City	Retail trade (NAICS 44–45), 2002[1] Estab-lishments	Sales Total ($1,000)	Per capita[2] Amount (dol.)	Per capita[2] Percent of national average	Percent from general mer-chandise stores	Paid employees[3]	Annual payroll Total ($1,000)	Annual payroll Per paid employee (dol.)	Accommodation and food services (NAICS 72), 2002[1] Estab-lishments	Sales Total ($1,000)	Sales Percent from food services	Paid employees[3]	Annual payroll ($1,000)
OREGON	14,277	37,896,022	10,759	104.3	18.5	183,706	3,983,810	21,686	8,816	5,527,223	75.2	130,010	1,589,959
Albany city	204	490,030	11,595	112.4	24.2	2,747	53,057	19,315	102	57,100	87.9	1,642	16,156
Beaverton city	383	1,671,858	20,840	202.1	10.0	6,503	171,275	26,338	226	182,088	87.4	4,619	56,512
Bend city	498	1,380,382	24,166	234.4	21.5	5,802	132,364	22,814	217	130,699	76.8	3,453	37,264
Corvallis city	224	488,596	9,715	94.2	(NA)	3,035	55,011	18,126	159	90,585	86.4	2,544	25,790
Eugene city	778	2,239,391	15,908	154.3	21.4	11,379	246,569	21,669	441	265,762	85.8	6,868	76,494
Grants Pass city	225	607,723	22,708	220.2	(NA)	2,932	64,417	21,970	130	69,193	80.2	1,602	18,139
Gresham city	249	837,833	8,904	86.4	5.5	3,653	77,982	21,347	201	135,124	95.3	3,471	40,672
Hillsboro city	238	1,050,549	13,885	134.7	8.2	4,138	107,221	25,911	174	124,869	85.1	2,899	38,101
Keizer city	63	101,618	3,030	29.4	(NA)	582	11,760	20,206	46	25,602	(NA)	679	7,384
Lake Oswego city	142	239,712	6,677	64.7	(NA)	1,610	30,051	18,665	86	66,003	86.0	1,573	19,616
McMinnville city	132	341,828	12,219	118.5	(NA)	1,573	32,832	20,872	68	34,702	88.7	951	10,308
Medford city	473	1,462,101	21,855	211.9	23.2	6,678	145,759	21,827	234	165,102	81.5	3,852	45,911
Oregon City city	103	282,585	9,991	96.9	(NA)	1,697	36,213	21,339	58	31,771	(NA)	796	8,598
Portland city	2,500	6,859,207	12,758	123.7	16.6	33,565	792,887	23,622	1,812	1,358,105	77.8	29,701	403,158
Salem city	659	2,017,417	14,140	137.1	22.2	9,542	208,149	21,814	366	232,605	91.0	6,241	67,953
Springfield city	231	554,831	10,230	99.2	28.1	3,216	63,181	19,646	143	103,054	82.6	2,368	28,555
Tigard city	313	1,498,597	33,176	321.7	31.9	6,881	162,326	23,590	151	93,162	94.2	2,306	28,280
PENNSYLVANIA	48,041	130,713,197	10,606	102.9	12.9	661,993	12,669,071	19,138	24,778	15,305,402	79.8	382,019	4,262,263
Allentown city	395	1,162,254	10,963	106.3	9.3	5,794	120,191	20,744	214	124,761	94.5	3,320	35,544
Altoona city	279	882,471	18,213	176.6	33.5	4,692	78,749	16,784	138	81,935	91.0	2,430	22,613
Bethel Park borough	151	478,427	14,498	140.6	21.1	2,974	49,483	16,639	75	57,043	(NA)	1,737	17,630
Bethlehem city	226	441,326	6,130	59.4	3.0	2,666	48,155	18,063	176	101,064	79.3	2,448	26,997
Chester city	59	100,525	2,700	26.2	3.1	416	10,885	26,166	52	16,261	(NA)	309	2,952
Easton city	129	247,929	9,457	91.7	(NA)	1,343	29,215	21,754	86	29,755	89.6	827	8,866
Erie city	487	935,038	8,994	87.2	17.8	6,181	101,861	16,480	243	108,360	95.0	3,593	31,441
Harrisburg city	250	613,160	12,674	122.9	7.7	3,465	60,672	17,510	172	96,523	(NA)	1,866	26,276
Lancaster city	354	805,078	14,458	140.2	(NA)	5,375	96,164	17,891	133	(D)	(NA)	7 1,750	(D)
Municipality of Monroeville borough	310	1,458,611	50,611	490.8	18.7	6,414	128,885	20,094	108	121,844	78.9	3,239	34,933
New Castle city	103	199,038	7,759	75.2	(NA)	771	15,611	20,248	72	22,431	(NA)	662	5,455
Norristown borough	86	173,391	5,577	54.1	(NA)	736	18,855	25,618	53	19,976	(NA)	353	4,077
Philadelphia city	4,522	9,093,922	6,117	59.3	9.1	50,082	965,119	19,271	3,037	2,135,977	73.6	39,973	570,928
Pittsburgh city	1,415	3,561,046	10,872	105.4	13.7	19,576	371,049	18,954	1,054	915,606	73.4	19,722	251,510
Plum borough	52	115,249	4,287	41.6	(NA)	696	12,723	18,280	31	16,419	(NA)	548	4,976
Reading city	320	810,650	10,054	97.5	7.6	3,790	76,773	20,257	154	69,421	92.7	1,559	18,977
Scranton city	408	885,446	11,882	115.2	16.6	5,660	95,399	16,855	204	100,460	85.0	3,252	26,046
State College borough	175	290,204	7,369	71.5	(NA)	2,679	35,740	13,341	136	96,175	74.0	3,141	27,859
Wilkes-Barre city	267	898,656	21,348	207.0	12.2	4,821	77,982	16,175	123	68,271	80.2	1,863	18,678
Williamsport city	144	283,633	9,406	91.2	(NA)	1,922	34,395	17,895	79	32,935	74.6	948	9,284
York city	183	352,751	8,644	83.8	13.0	2,193	40,240	18,349	103	(D)	(NA)	7 1,750	(D)
RHODE ISLAND	4,134	10,342,351	9,679	93.9	9.4	50,665	1,045,721	20,640	2,701	1,731,799	83.1	38,573	502,394
Cranston city	320	947,095	11,692	113.4	7.2	4,839	94,310	19,490	175	96,795	98.4	2,340	28,140
East Providence city	158	454,535	9,177	89.0	2.0	1,925	44,042	22,879	100	56,663	(NA)	1,533	16,459
Newport city	240	305,356	11,628	112.8	(NA)	1,645	33,405	20,307	162	182,215	52.9	3,039	55,716
Pawtucket city	208	441,659	5,979	58.0	2.8	2,431	50,987	20,974	128	54,922	(NA)	1,205	13,514
Providence city	702	1,138,978	6,473	62.8	5.8	6,921	136,485	19,720	490	382,237	80.7	8,075	114,731
Warwick city	471	1,971,529	22,719	220.3	(NA)	9,166	192,053	20,953	252	230,853	76.5	5,334	67,465
Woonsocket city	149	411,603	9,399	91.2	(NA)	2,338	38,035	16,268	83	46,358	(NA)	1,286	12,701
SOUTH CAROLINA	18,416	40,629,089	9,903	96.0	15.4	212,926	3,915,453	18,389	8,135	6,104,316	74.3	152,822	1,728,556
Aiken city	196	351,810	13,619	132.1	12.3	2,129	32,846	15,428	89	58,484	81.7	1,699	15,331
Anderson city	304	604,803	23,441	227.3	12.6	3,760	59,693	15,876	128	81,401	91.9	2,335	23,475
Charleston city	743	1,817,314	18,113	175.7	11.4	9,685	193,844	20,015	400	496,973	(NA)	10,818	138,591
Columbia city	764	2,301,964	19,718	191.2	19.8	12,234	233,475	19,084	398	342,315	82.6	10,050	101,519
Florence city	367	906,790	29,708	288.1	(NA)	4,929	85,347	17,315	121	88,253	92.9	2,560	25,350
Goose Creek city	66	204,155	6,657	64.6	(NA)	1,174	20,003	17,038	43	31,841	(NA)	939	8,310
Greenville city	690	1,833,918	32,586	316.0	11.8	9,852	198,029	20,100	293	252,092	73.8	6,610	77,692
Hilton Head Island town	350	639,361	18,519	179.6	(NA)	3,427	76,147	22,220	202	352,937	(NA)	5,097	100,347
Mount Pleasant town	303	626,800	11,733	113.8	(NA)	3,619	65,410	18,074	150	137,153	79.9	3,516	40,407
North Charleston city	510	1,567,703	19,313	187.3	20.1	7,730	159,604	20,647	223	204,946	70.8	4,698	52,511
Rock Hill city	309	811,332	14,774	143.3	17.5	4,029	75,597	18,763	148	111,512	87.5	3,277	33,874
Spartanburg city	344	891,820	22,684	220.0	14.9	4,906	89,759	18,296	175	122,201	97.1	3,467	36,833
Summerville town	151	409,491	13,555	131.5	15.2	1,997	36,742	18,399	96	62,845	84.6	1,978	17,812
Sumter city	330	614,867	15,318	148.6	17.9	3,706	58,639	15,823	106	66,398	92.4	2,071	18,392
SOUTH DAKOTA	4,249	9,601,175	12,627	122.5	13.2	49,152	903,550	18,383	2,203	1,226,459	64.4	32,226	326,341
Rapid City city	491	1,462,691	24,230	235.0	20.0	6,874	136,822	19,904	227	182,335	68.7	4,576	51,054
Sioux Falls city	722	2,372,408	18,133	175.8	18.4	12,572	239,416	19,044	370	331,068	81.8	8,447	96,490

See footnotes at end of table.

Table C-5. Cities — **Retail Trade and Accommodation and Food Services**—Con.

[Includes states and 1,265 incorporated places of 25,000 or more population as of April 1, 2000, in all states except Hawaii, which has no incorporated places recognized by the U.S. Census Bureau. Two census designated places (CDPs) are also included (Honolulu CDP in Hawaii and Arlington CDP in Virginia). For more information on these areas, see Appendix C, Geographic Information]

City	Retail trade (NAICS 44–45), 2002[1]								Accommodation and food services (NAICS 72), 2002[1]				
		Sales				Annual payroll				Sales			
			Per capita[2]		Percent from general mer-chandise stores						Percent from food services		
	Estab-lishments	Total ($1,000)	Amount (dol.)	Percent of national average		Paid employees[3]	Total ($1,000)	Per paid employee (dol.)	Estab-lishments	Total ($1,000)		Paid employees[3]	Annual payroll ($1,000)
TENNESSEE	24,029	60,136,403	10,386	100.7	17.0	304,652	5,881,592	19,306	10,070	8,024,900	77.9	202,641	2,277,488
Bartlett city	147	624,283	14,933	144.8	(NA)	2,884	55,962	19,404	72	54,914	(NA)	1,404	13,770
Brentwood city	140	580,125	20,973	203.4	(NA)	2,133	54,166	25,394	68	81,081	78.9	2,097	23,280
Bristol city	159	474,497	18,857	182.9	10.2	1,917	44,077	22,993	71	43,786	92.2	1,210	11,643
Chattanooga city	1,109	3,343,297	21,443	207.9	(NA)	16,036	329,407	20,542	534	441,315	80.8	11,575	126,821
Clarksville city	463	1,298,226	12,387	120.1	26.8	7,046	127,576	18,106	223	156,837	88.7	5,087	44,059
Cleveland city	268	622,251	16,610	161.1	24.2	3,278	62,069	18,935	113	87,532	88.4	2,531	24,034
Collierville town	116	546,551	16,006	155.2	(NA)	2,336	54,105	23,161	60	39,349	(NA)	1,306	11,490
Columbia city	238	568,095	17,153	166.3	21.5	2,890	53,192	18,406	90	62,580	(NA)	1,885	17,806
Cookeville city	300	693,719	25,819	250.4	(NA)	3,722	67,394	18,107	111	88,197	(NA)	2,465	24,953
Franklin city	384	1,433,987	29,713	288.2	16.8	6,787	143,822	21,191	153	133,546	83.8	3,212	42,194
Germantown city	173	317,761	8,470	82.1	(NA)	2,266	35,421	15,632	60	54,975	84.7	1,357	16,323
Hendersonville city	148	351,003	8,292	80.4	(NA)	1,738	35,808	20,603	69	43,036	76.9	1,006	12,157
Jackson city	490	1,289,712	21,203	205.6	22.3	6,857	122,553	17,873	175	150,967	(NA)	4,539	43,526
Johnson City city	415	1,326,268	23,238	225.4	(NA)	6,292	122,733	19,506	174	148,171	(NA)	4,582	43,357
Kingsport city	365	1,028,377	23,143	224.4	29.4	5,290	99,558	18,820	169	131,819	83.8	3,750	37,569
Knoxville city	1,361	4,392,149	24,832	240.8	14.5	22,584	455,991	20,191	602	583,370	86.7	15,167	172,926
Memphis city	2,557	7,485,959	11,055	107.2	11.2	36,581	747,596	20,437	1,247	1,163,699	76.5	28,403	345,463
Morristown city	262	790,562	30,700	297.7	(NA)	3,496	81,048	23,183	96	65,148	(NA)	2,001	19,939
Murfreesboro city	440	1,422,425	18,785	182.2	19.9	7,098	138,452	19,506	195	170,265	88.7	4,680	46,565
Nashville-Davidson (balance)	2,656	8,087,333	14,860	144.1	12.1	41,173	879,506	21,362	1,356	1,648,656	60.7	32,017	453,478
Oak Ridge city	156	462,120	16,997	164.8	25.2	2,364	43,583	18,436	70	55,893	85.1	1,522	15,673
Smyrna town	79	266,674	9,018	87.5	(NA)	1,351	23,032	17,048	53	41,501	92.3	883	11,034
TEXAS	75,703	228,694,755	10,528	102.1	15.6	1,026,326	21,104,589	20,563	36,591	29,914,774	81.6	715,844	8,432,938
Abilene city	523	1,445,100	12,620	122.4	22.8	7,022	136,373	19,421	239	173,899	(NA)	5,145	46,273
Allen city	183	416,212	7,248	70.3	11.1	2,506	44,678	17,828	72	54,238	(NA)	1,548	16,804
Amarillo city	852	2,636,353	14,951	145.0	18.6	11,614	237,144	20,419	423	317,319	85.4	8,177	82,576
Arlington city	1,098	4,061,127	11,604	112.5	12.7	18,439	396,736	21,516	585	570,543	83.8	13,634	166,908
Austin city	2,742	9,784,154	14,583	141.4	11.4	43,586	994,948	22,827	1,696	1,784,072	77.3	39,595	531,759
Baytown city	266	902,704	13,434	130.3	22.7	4,364	80,253	18,390	135	91,703	93.0	2,435	25,251
Beaumont city	642	1,806,134	16,047	155.6	18.5	9,041	174,952	19,351	260	222,477	87.8	5,918	64,244
Bedford city	128	538,816	11,143	108.1	(NA)	2,137	43,445	20,330	83	72,319	85.6	1,946	24,271
Big Spring city	127	266,715	10,769	104.4	(NA)	1,508	26,890	17,832	59	24,980	93.2	802	7,366
Brownsville city	525	1,416,563	9,284	90.0	23.7	7,703	127,075	16,497	250	138,784	88.6	3,867	35,961
Bryan city	285	748,201	11,454	111.1	(NA)	3,202	68,398	21,361	118	65,202	(NA)	1,998	17,914
Carrollton city	350	1,244,625	10,843	105.2	8.7	5,119	130,854	25,562	186	125,397	95.0	2,916	34,618
Cedar Hill city	83	258,367	6,954	67.4	23.4	1,351	26,521	19,631	37	(D)	(NA)	[4]750	(D)
Cedar Park city	105	298,864	7,895	76.6	(NA)	1,625	31,284	19,252	41	32,203	94.7	698	8,614
Cleburne city	183	507,317	18,422	178.7	(NA)	2,231	47,166	21,141	62	36,316	93.5	985	9,678
College Station city	272	753,400	10,755	104.3	27.0	4,704	75,720	16,097	185	183,592	81.0	5,140	45,770
Conroe city	374	1,489,714	36,832	357.2	14.9	5,458	130,119	23,840	111	102,238	94.0	2,457	27,236
Coppell city	60	209,974	5,331	51.7	(NA)	933	24,275	26,018	61	42,874	(NA)	912	11,026
Copperas Cove city	70	198,677	6,707	65.0	(NA)	1,051	17,756	16,894	43	28,794	92.8	869	7,420
Corpus Christi city	1,096	3,131,952	11,275	109.3	17.6	15,190	291,386	19,183	649	464,137	84.1	12,713	122,231
Dallas city	4,146	13,141,441	10,914	105.8	11.5	58,504	1,369,124	23,402	2,440	2,784,368	74.2	54,991	815,814
Deer Park city	64	108,760	3,771	36.6	(NA)	594	11,061	18,621	38	23,897	(NA)	614	6,327
Del Rio city	182	393,591	11,385	110.4	22.8	1,993	36,471	18,300	86	(D)	(NA)	[7]1,750	(D)
Denton city	371	1,176,026	12,758	123.7	22.6	5,806	117,191	20,184	175	134,102	90.5	3,667	37,965
DeSoto city	97	288,126	7,335	71.1	(NA)	1,316	26,588	20,204	55	45,927	89.3	1,133	12,930
Duncanville city	121	398,522	11,069	107.4	15.7	1,730	41,631	24,064	54	46,042	(NA)	1,087	12,910
Edinburg city	144	461,099	8,773	85.1	(NA)	2,297	41,566	18,096	79	50,861	88.8	1,387	12,447
El Paso city	1,947	5,545,225	9,653	93.6	25.7	28,110	505,720	17,991	1,009	724,335	86.8	19,624	195,600
Euless city	92	231,989	4,803	46.6	1.9	1,042	23,601	22,650	53	32,810	90.3	796	9,184
Farmers Branch city	182	621,546	22,772	220.8	(NA)	3,065	74,766	24,393	91	81,349	(NA)	1,477	24,944
Flower Mound town	105	284,535	4,854	47.1	(NA)	1,528	24,445	15,998	59	(D)	(NA)	[7]1,750	(D)
Fort Worth city	1,872	5,803,033	10,190	98.8	15.2	26,644	595,365	22,345	991	855,081	83.6	21,013	249,651
Friendswood city	104	225,928	7,193	69.8	(NA)	1,211	22,486	18,568	52	38,577	100.0	1,017	10,138
Frisco city	254	967,719	20,200	195.9	15.8	4,744	101,530	21,402	75	(D)	(NA)	[7]1,750	(D)
Galveston city	246	525,697	9,242	89.6	(NA)	3,038	52,263	17,203	185	184,068	60.6	4,307	54,328
Garland city	554	1,823,402	8,350	81.0	19.1	7,908	186,533	23,588	257	185,546	95.9	4,228	51,285
Georgetown city	129	635,934	19,122	185.4	(NA)	1,763	50,199	28,474	58	37,105	90.3	1,008	11,743
Grand Prairie city	302	1,194,404	8,873	86.0	17.6	4,671	118,552	25,380	166	123,052	92.1	2,911	36,127
Grapevine city	270	1,266,028	27,629	267.9	(NA)	4,286	100,267	23,394	112	281,738	76.6	5,553	84,635
Haltom City city	153	336,940	8,479	82.2	6.7	1,715	39,313	22,923	57	26,775	96.0	741	7,817
Harlingen city	305	792,210	13,359	129.6	19.1	4,142	74,979	18,102	140	103,499	90.3	2,716	28,876
Houston city	7,674	25,813,909	12,889	125.0	11.7	110,706	2,471,944	22,329	4,012	4,155,251	77.0	86,745	1,147,348
Huntsville city	123	298,542	8,557	83.0	(NA)	1,273	26,756	21,018	77	50,266	92.6	1,748	12,324
Hurst city	293	849,863	23,136	224.4	26.6	5,110	99,869	19,544	77	56,554	94.8	1,404	15,489
Irving city	698	3,185,664	16,316	158.2	11.9	13,919	313,500	22,523	462	651,722	(NA)	12,224	194,629

See footnotes at end of table.

[Includes states and 1,265 incorporated places of 25,000 or more population as of April 1, 2000, in all states except Hawaii, which has no incorporated places recognized by the U.S. Census Bureau. Two census designated places (CDPs) are also included (Honolulu CDP in Hawaii and Arlington CDP in Virginia). For more information on these areas, see Appendix C, Geographic Information]

City	Retail trade (NAICS 44–45), 2002[1]								Accommodation and food services (NAICS 72), 2002[1]				
		Sales			Percent from general mer-chandise stores		Annual payroll			Sales			Annual payroll ($1,000)
			Per capita[2]										
	Estab-lishments	Total ($1,000)	Amount (dol.)	Percent of national average		Paid employees[3]	Total ($1,000)	Per paid employee (dol.)	Estab-lishments	Total ($1,000)	Percent from food services	Paid employees[3]	
TEXAS—Con.													
Keller city	77	219,693	6,681	64.8	(NA)	1,132	20,962	18,518	36	17,578	100.0	477	4,962
Killeen city	347	1,129,993	12,240	118.7	19.5	5,216	98,873	18,956	183	129,073	89.8	3,585	35,067
Kingsville city	96	294,024	11,687	113.3	(NA)	1,330	26,372	19,829	62	28,746	(NA)	793	7,584
Lake Jackson city	79	317,509	11,821	114.6	(NA)	1,486	27,306	18,376	33	23,723	(NA)	711	6,618
Lancaster city	63	209,057	7,766	75.3	(NA)	1,144	22,769	19,903	29	10,573	81.6	245	2,860
La Porte city	65	186,765	5,634	54.6	(NA)	690	14,708	21,316	37	24,165	89.6	557	5,451
Laredo city	708	2,008,623	10,516	102.0	(NA)	10,260	183,108	17,847	282	236,884	(NA)	5,578	59,031
League City city	131	428,829	8,361	81.1	(NA)	1,781	38,078	21,380	56	52,304	(NA)	1,283	15,102
Lewisville city	420	1,870,722	22,302	216.3	19.4	7,851	177,220	22,573	176	171,282	90.7	4,576	55,437
Longview city	562	1,431,740	19,303	187.2	23.3	7,241	137,323	18,965	193	139,950	90.0	4,041	40,686
Lubbock city	961	3,056,553	15,011	145.6	17.1	14,626	295,164	20,181	480	399,776	84.1	11,343	108,574
Lufkin city	281	708,338	21,512	208.6	21.5	3,786	69,423	18,337	106	74,029	(NA)	2,094	20,952
McAllen city	727	2,374,947	20,902	202.7	26.3	11,536	225,805	19,574	261	262,908	85.5	6,884	70,064
McKinney city	192	982,359	13,412	130.1	10.1	3,435	85,915	25,012	97	89,396	95.9	2,514	27,472
Mansfield city	76	257,172	8,147	79.0	(NA)	1,464	26,469	18,080	41	26,027	(NA)	715	7,428
Mesquite city	443	1,602,500	12,496	121.2	20.6	8,040	156,303	19,441	187	191,053	92.3	4,677	56,751
Midland city	479	1,219,093	12,709	123.3	(NA)	6,056	116,288	19,202	228	164,121	88.3	4,440	48,399
Mission city	159	483,388	9,410	91.3	(NA)	2,107	38,767	18,399	85	41,645	84.0	977	10,073
Missouri City city	103	322,896	5,472	53.1	32.3	1,805	32,353	17,924	51	(D)	(NA)	[4]750	(D)
Nacogdoches city	228	531,414	17,694	171.6	(NA)	2,601	50,155	19,283	75	54,494	88.1	1,785	15,025
New Braunfels city	245	822,138	19,995	193.9	(NA)	3,432	76,747	22,362	124	92,770	79.0	2,451	27,613
North Richland Hills city	215	1,313,409	22,197	215.3	(NA)	4,942	115,406	23,352	103	86,391	94.7	2,336	26,623
Odessa city	426	1,168,464	12,802	124.1	(NA)	5,606	121,446	21,664	193	137,098	88.8	3,581	39,082
Paris city	215	491,304	18,773	182.1	(NA)	2,455	46,520	18,949	75	48,165	86.6	1,355	14,314
Pasadena city	414	1,261,028	8,752	84.9	25.6	6,442	127,952	19,862	189	126,081	95.2	3,466	35,422
Pearland city	117	454,761	10,419	101.0	26.1	1,992	45,083	22,632	66	36,312	(NA)	1,002	10,338
Pharr city	164	362,724	7,070	68.6	(NA)	1,750	30,208	17,262	63	52,913	73.7	1,060	10,075
Plano city	1,023	4,828,308	20,210	196.0	17.8	18,361	453,888	24,720	495	460,847	87.4	10,499	135,330
Port Arthur city	224	636,917	11,229	108.9	24.8	3,462	60,886	17,587	67	48,538	(NA)	1,238	12,711
Richardson city	400	1,562,543	15,794	153.2	4.4	5,317	146,486	27,550	242	165,948	86.6	3,666	49,852
Round Rock city	196	6,477,701	87,410	847.7	3.4	4,501	111,295	24,727	157	160,726	82.9	3,531	43,694
Rowlett city	70	218,947	4,401	42.7	(NA)	1,082	21,927	20,265	44	23,045	(NA)	591	6,298
San Angelo city	429	1,082,969	12,324	119.5	(NA)	5,475	106,094	19,378	184	120,389	(NA)	3,637	34,365
San Antonio city	3,825	13,828,317	11,598	112.5	15.8	62,196	1,329,522	21,376	2,388	2,537,449	72.5	55,663	712,080
San Juan city	55	74,063	2,634	25.5	3.4	427	5,875	13,759	20	7,214	(NA)	188	1,701
San Marcos city	278	805,559	18,999	184.2	(NA)	3,713	71,505	19,258	144	103,462	(NA)	3,034	30,896
Sherman city	222	816,934	22,891	222.0	(NA)	3,698	76,246	20,618	86	68,874	90.0	1,627	19,527
Socorro city	40	46,930	1,661	16.1	(NA)	304	4,351	14,313	12	5,194	100.0	155	1,168
Sugar Land city	352	1,076,937	15,745	152.7	(NA)	5,249	100,077	19,066	139	117,495	92.9	2,770	32,382
Temple city	277	940,075	17,242	167.2	22.8	4,201	86,449	20,578	120	83,837	83.4	2,146	23,735
Texarkana city	309	894,026	25,573	248.0	23.4	4,168	83,159	19,952	91	74,253	(NA)	2,096	21,177
Texas City city	168	503,784	11,790	114.3	27.5	2,387	44,434	18,615	64	46,286	89.3	1,312	12,464
The Colony city	59	199,410	6,191	60.0	(NA)	971	19,370	19,949	35	23,834	100.0	615	7,389
Tyler city	625	1,925,515	22,169	215.0	(NA)	8,609	186,942	21,715	227	190,395	91.1	5,264	55,513
Victoria city	345	942,915	15,404	149.4	(NA)	4,623	90,284	19,529	133	87,247	(NA)	2,561	24,946
Waco city	544	1,571,587	13,549	131.4	(NA)	8,012	150,837	18,826	276	234,570	86.4	6,106	62,854
Weslaco city	139	508,820	17,193	166.7	16.5	2,204	43,947	19,940	72	52,504	81.3	1,451	12,739
Wichita Falls city	487	1,298,584	12,760	123.7	25.5	6,935	128,448	18,522	220	169,079	(NA)	4,627	51,343
UTAH	8,135	23,675,432	10,132	98.3	16.2	121,745	2,331,772	19,153	4,106	2,984,632	72.6	80,759	846,626
Bountiful city	145	547,743	13,286	128.8	10.9	2,454	49,524	20,181	59	30,412	(NA)	977	9,491
Clearfield city	47	77,417	2,940	28.5	(NA)	549	7,385	13,452	29	13,529	(NA)	504	3,868
Draper city	104	442,855	15,143	146.9	(NA)	2,230	58,659	26,304	45	(D)	(NA)	[4]750	(D)
Layton city	244	887,015	14,790	143.4	26.7	4,443	80,238	18,059	104	86,580	91.3	2,337	22,919
Logan city	229	468,214	10,474	101.6	(NA)	3,315	51,399	15,505	93	59,971	(NA)	1,954	15,712
Midvale city	142	425,473	15,615	151.4	33.9	2,245	43,107	19,201	80	64,801	86.5	1,756	17,029
Murray city	323	1,371,419	30,264	293.5	11.3	5,408	126,700	23,428	98	76,011	93.1	2,312	22,097
Ogden city	336	767,723	9,779	94.8	(NA)	3,985	80,609	20,228	172	99,229	84.4	3,068	28,707
Orem city	410	1,225,543	14,193	137.6	24.2	7,211	127,288	17,652	121	94,864	87.7	2,663	23,681
Provo city	313	854,521	7,746	75.1	17.4	5,273	89,697	17,011	167	138,030	65.2	4,174	42,734
Riverton city	28	70,623	2,496	24.2	(NA)	411	7,197	17,511	23	11,763	100.0	329	3,060
Roy city	58	148,180	4,255	41.3	(NA)	914	15,761	17,244	45	20,388	(NA)	574	5,111
St. George city	345	869,996	16,080	155.9	(NA)	4,544	89,223	19,635	136	108,962	64.0	2,846	29,935
Salt Lake City city	1,025	3,096,678	17,040	165.2	9.7	15,170	293,812	19,368	672	739,365	60.7	16,213	209,632
Sandy city	352	1,623,841	18,115	175.7	17.5	6,473	132,449	20,462	142	130,576	87.0	3,623	37,514
South Jordan city	44	112,541	3,504	34.0	71.5	564	10,834	19,209	17	10,029	(NA)	288	2,785
Taylorsville city	125	371,173	6,330	61.4	23.3	2,041	37,287	18,269	79	59,616	(NA)	1,480	16,594
West Jordan city	166	643,245	7,743	75.1	40.4	3,812	70,560	18,510	80	(D)	(NA)	[7]1,750	(D)
West Valley City city	278	1,131,403	10,253	99.4	12.3	5,154	110,200	21,381	134	97,526	89.6	2,643	26,256

See footnotes at end of table.

[Includes states and 1,265 incorporated places of 25,000 or more population as of April 1, 2000, in all states except Hawaii, which has no incorporated places recognized by the U.S. Census Bureau. Two census designated places (CDPs) are also included (Honolulu CDP in Hawaii and Arlington CDP in Virginia). For more information on these areas, see Appendix C, Geographic Information]

City	Retail trade (NAICS 44–45), 2002[1]								Accommodation and food services (NAICS 72), 2002[1]				
			Sales				Annual payroll			Sales			
			Per capita[2]		Percent from general merchandise stores						Percent from food services		Annual payroll ($1,000)
	Estab-lishments	Total ($1,000)	Amount (dol.)	Percent of national average		Paid employees[3]	Total ($1,000)	Per paid employee (dol.)	Estab-lishments	Total ($1,000)		Paid employees[3]	
VERMONT	3,946	7,623,872	12,371	120.0	7.0	40,105	820,807	20,466	1,950	1,154,048	54.5	29,849	357,265
Burlington city	241	471,189	11,967	116.1	4.9	3,198	61,602	19,263	143	107,031	73.8	2,572	34,017
VIRGINIA	28,914	80,509,062	11,050	107.2	15.6	401,921	8,078,467	20,100	13,305	10,929,429	73.4	256,341	3,094,285
Alexandria city	551	2,053,604	15,269	148.1	0.3	8,578	216,123	25,195	342	395,295	75.6	6,873	114,045
Arlington CDP[9]	647	2,107,505	10,791	104.7	14.3	9,911	231,545	23,362	494	740,062	49.9	11,388	202,687
Blacksburg town	121	193,907	4,929	47.8	(NA)	1,365	19,754	14,472	84	50,992	80.6	1,866	15,142
Charlottesville city	382	901,079	21,997	213.3	3.8	4,884	102,365	20,959	203	153,514	(NA)	3,581	44,076
Chesapeake city	792	2,587,372	12,598	122.2	22.5	12,987	239,258	18,423	322	245,015	85.2	7,199	65,141
Danville city	332	672,723	14,223	137.9	11.1	3,764	64,861	17,232	123	88,898	(NA)	2,586	25,274
Hampton city	480	1,500,977	10,366	100.5	14.2	7,930	139,712	17,618	231	168,280	77.6	4,884	47,276
Harrisonburg city	350	891,822	21,764	211.1	(NA)	4,536	91,052	20,073	150	108,438	(NA)	3,103	30,654
Leesburg town	253	756,533	24,018	232.9	9.0	3,450	73,946	21,434	70	67,537	88.7	1,519	20,696
Lynchburg city	433	1,420,834	21,892	212.3	(NA)	7,579	136,976	18,073	174	130,883	87.1	4,298	38,834
Manassas city	183	712,711	19,464	188.8	(NA)	2,146	64,069	29,855	94	55,896	94.4	1,197	15,262
Newport News city	674	2,078,241	11,569	112.2	21.6	10,366	204,825	19,759	306	214,404	80.0	5,782	59,022
Norfolk city	971	2,231,322	9,365	90.8	15.9	12,948	249,564	19,274	530	424,514	77.0	11,266	114,752
Petersburg city	155	346,861	10,470	101.5	(NA)	1,720	37,007	21,516	61	31,056	77.1	817	8,145
Portsmouth city	291	522,938	5,264	51.1	2.8	3,163	60,893	19,252	157	82,556	76.5	2,456	24,202
Richmond city	1,160	2,526,091	12,863	124.7	14.1	14,039	264,316	18,827	601	430,190	77.8	11,053	126,208
Roanoke city	577	1,712,312	18,384	178.3	14.8	9,013	176,648	19,599	287	214,221	76.5	5,545	63,099
Suffolk city	198	576,240	8,256	80.1	(NA)	3,101	57,127	18,422	71	43,668	84.8	1,342	11,660
Virginia Beach city	1,626	4,168,686	9,679	93.9	17.1	22,883	462,637	20,217	959	875,114	62.5	18,308	206,999
WASHINGTON	22,564	65,262,333	10,758	104.3	15.9	296,507	6,860,587	23,138	13,699	8,642,681	79.5	199,652	2,571,978
Auburn city	317	1,252,712	28,228	273.7	(NA)	5,102	126,712	24,836	122	66,705	91.2	1,767	19,468
Bellevue city	733	2,898,128	25,148	243.9	7.1	11,959	316,178	26,438	313	314,385	67.1	5,947	95,267
Bellingham city	510	1,333,857	18,916	183.4	(NA)	7,001	147,026	21,001	290	167,290	87.7	4,408	50,124
Bothell city	121	764,451	25,055	243.0	(NA)	3,262	66,520	20,392	100	59,226	77.5	1,412	17,926
Bremerton city	165	558,919	13,993	135.7	2.3	2,093	57,663	27,550	111	51,153	85.5	1,377	14,495
Burien city	125	467,744	14,927	144.8	(NA)	1,700	44,780	26,341	79	42,122	100.0	1,008	13,044
Des Moines city	44	102,439	3,510	34.0	(NA)	541	11,705	21,636	42	27,292	95.1	652	8,147
Edmonds city	135	388,125	9,769	94.7	(NA)	1,602	44,660	27,878	91	54,142	96.0	1,452	16,728
Everett city	453	1,544,749	15,918	154.4	21.9	6,566	169,372	25,795	277	179,187	94.0	4,163	50,323
Federal Way city	265	999,014	11,908	115.5	28.8	4,717	99,764	21,150	194	120,925	91.5	3,019	38,699
Kennewick city	357	1,093,818	18,704	181.4	35.1	5,323	106,830	20,070	160	110,518	86.8	2,860	32,907
Kent city	345	1,041,355	12,777	123.9	11.9	5,098	121,981	23,927	213	120,443	85.3	2,909	34,258
Kirkland city	243	1,064,605	23,450	227.4	(NA)	4,018	107,135	26,664	168	143,180	86.1	2,922	44,516
Lacey city	120	452,132	14,035	136.1	35.0	2,220	50,003	22,524	82	52,232	92.1	1,371	14,989
Lakewood city	264	467,373	7,973	77.3	10.4	2,642	57,048	21,593	155	84,646	96.1	2,087	23,389
Longview city	195	575,116	16,189	157.0	20.8	2,774	64,588	23,283	108	56,742	96.5	1,569	16,208
Lynnwood city	403	1,576,939	46,745	453.3	20.7	7,307	172,654	23,629	163	124,565	81.6	2,857	34,800
Marysville city	134	413,382	14,817	143.7	34.4	2,212	46,417	20,984	77	39,089	(NA)	1,078	11,513
Mount Vernon city	156	426,481	15,714	152.4	(NA)	2,112	48,792	23,102	80	43,660	89.7	1,150	13,086
Olympia city	370	1,141,382	26,258	254.6	(NA)	4,887	117,338	24,010	175	124,418	87.2	3,396	38,407
Pasco city	151	564,823	15,426	149.6	(NA)	1,990	53,968	27,120	73	35,395	68.8	880	9,956
Puyallup city	263	1,218,128	34,415	333.8	19.0	4,836	121,202	25,062	118	86,232	94.3	2,186	25,868
Redmond city	255	673,872	14,665	142.2	(NA)	3,442	92,396	26,844	196	160,857	77.2	3,532	51,683
Renton city	211	1,518,772	28,603	277.4	8.7	4,948	144,589	29,222	158	101,479	83.4	2,235	31,239
Richland city	144	360,657	8,682	84.2	(NA)	1,866	38,196	20,469	86	61,395	77.5	1,458	18,255
Sammamish city	31	58,477	1,734	16.8	(NA)	335	6,170	18,418	27	17,806	100.0	514	6,032
SeaTac city	43	94,557	3,765	36.5	(NA)	352	7,919	22,497	61	160,066	31.1	2,748	45,315
Seattle city	2,707	9,029,268	15,833	153.5	9.7	33,779	834,531	24,706	2,232	1,906,344	71.3	36,885	582,376
Shoreline city	134	424,645	8,080	78.4	(NA)	2,094	51,547	24,617	83	51,277	97.1	1,052	13,912
Spokane city	986	2,732,927	13,979	135.6	13.4	14,613	323,779	22,157	565	387,354	79.5	10,009	120,841
Spokane Valley city	(X)	(X)	(NA)	(NA)	(NA)	(X)	(X)	(NA)	(X)	(X)	(NA)	(X)	(X)
Tacoma city	776	2,520,815	12,753	123.7	20.0	11,539	280,056	24,270	446	304,598	88.9	7,488	90,538
University Place city	59	124,491	4,078	39.5	(NA)	795	15,824	19,904	30	14,946	100.0	524	4,949
Vancouver city	473	1,809,783	12,102	117.4	18.4	8,149	184,922	22,693	325	225,035	85.8	5,582	69,830
Walla Walla city	182	376,811	12,324	119.5	(NA)	2,087	41,660	19,962	101	53,068	(NA)	1,493	15,847
Wenatchee city	188	477,924	16,847	163.4	17.1	2,367	52,576	22,212	98	59,935	72.2	1,438	18,219
Yakima city	397	1,060,014	13,238	128.4	19.4	5,199	112,798	21,696	205	121,434	81.8	2,894	33,419
WEST VIRGINIA	7,454	16,747,900	9,281	90.0	18.9	89,340	1,489,064	16,667	3,310	1,974,851	77.4	51,985	555,598
Charleston city	389	872,855	16,826	163.2	14.1	5,622	90,876	16,164	208	180,917	74.7	4,020	48,883
Huntington city	238	483,394	9,615	93.2	7.2	2,810	54,719	19,473	182	112,343	90.5	2,996	29,615
Morgantown city	251	610,994	22,273	216.0	20.2	3,507	55,161	15,729	154	85,696	88.3	2,681	24,107
Parkersburg city	256	620,159	19,020	184.5	12.0	3,229	58,195	18,023	136	76,132	91.2	2,141	21,067
Wheeling city	188	370,120	12,128	117.6	(NA)	2,036	37,714	18,524	104	57,239	(NA)	1,671	16,306

See footnotes at end of table.

County and City Data Book: 2007

U.S. Census Bureau

Table C-5. Cities — **Retail Trade and Accommodation and Food Services**—Con.

[Includes states and 1,265 incorporated places of 25,000 or more population as of April 1, 2000, in all states except Hawaii, which has no incorporated places recognized by the U.S. Census Bureau. Two census designated places (CDPs) are also included (Honolulu CDP in Hawaii and Arlington CDP in Virginia). For more information on these areas, see Appendix C, Geographic Information]

City	Retail trade (NAICS 44–45), 2002[1]								Accommodation and food services (NAICS 72), 2002[1]				
		Sales				Paid employees[3]	Annual payroll			Sales		Paid employees[3]	Annual payroll ($1,000)
	Estab-lishments	Total ($1,000)	Per capita[2]		Percent from general mer-chandise stores		Total ($1,000)	Per paid employee (dol.)	Estab-lishments	Total ($1,000)	Percent from food services		
			Amount (dol.)	Percent of national average									
WISCONSIN	21,360	59,978,700	11,027	106.9	14.7	311,730	6,013,140	19,290	13,268	6,885,765	80.1	200,748	1,954,391
Appleton city	306	852,995	12,075	117.1	20.4	4,832	95,384	19,740	174	109,151	(NA)	3,282	31,343
Beloit city	116	388,654	10,902	105.7	(NA)	1,894	35,763	18,882	95	49,508	94.0	1,350	11,657
Brookfield city	308	1,076,790	27,316	264.9	13.1	6,399	117,568	18,373	99	106,188	74.4	2,362	30,224
Eau Claire city	366	1,136,891	18,191	176.4	(NA)	6,948	115,715	16,654	197	129,710	83.2	4,575	39,024
Fond du Lac city	241	733,618	17,340	168.2	(NA)	4,269	72,944	17,087	124	74,389	88.1	2,513	22,580
Franklin city	60	376,953	12,029	116.7	(NA)	1,671	33,702	20,169	44	23,293	(NA)	690	6,401
Green Bay city	503	1,539,964	15,108	146.5	(NA)	8,568	176,172	20,562	283	147,399	93.7	4,383	42,422
Greenfield city	175	909,708	25,538	247.7	(NA)	3,932	86,536	22,008	68	67,961	(NA)	1,974	19,883
Janesville city	300	1,037,404	17,054	165.4	20.8	5,236	98,676	18,846	162	106,804	89.1	3,141	31,009
Kenosha city	337	975,724	10,533	102.1	(NA)	4,846	91,315	18,843	208	100,772	95.2	3,271	30,544
La Crosse city	298	847,012	16,532	160.3	(NA)	5,192	91,130	17,552	208	116,176	84.1	4,320	34,149
Madison city	1,069	3,475,535	16,136	156.5	17.7	19,562	361,105	18,460	644	505,175	81.7	14,132	149,936
Manitowoc city	167	441,302	12,907	125.2	21.0	2,636	45,015	17,077	98	48,127	82.6	1,583	13,706
Menomonee Falls village	138	708,401	21,310	206.7	(NA)	2,886	66,150	22,921	62	32,033	98.3	1,021	10,295
Milwaukee city	1,513	3,594,429	6,094	59.1	11.4	19,506	390,498	20,019	1,066	781,697	(NA)	19,233	220,658
New Berlin city	97	348,837	9,046	87.7	(NA)	1,712	35,017	20,454	59	33,527	(NA)	959	8,895
Oak Creek city	63	406,324	13,374	129.7	(NA)	1,805	41,564	23,027	51	33,181	80.6	861	8,569
Oshkosh city	290	888,138	13,925	135.0	(NA)	4,725	83,720	17,719	180	99,294	85.4	3,049	29,395
Racine city	356	691,462	8,563	83.0	23.0	4,808	76,208	15,850	150	96,403	(NA)	2,878	28,441
Sheboygan city	210	638,563	12,819	124.3	20.9	3,605	66,125	18,343	133	56,451	90.3	1,837	15,567
Superior city	131	412,643	15,190	147.3	16.5	2,019	39,854	19,739	115	48,551	83.6	1,687	13,560
Waukesha city	230	1,173,495	17,717	171.8	13.8	4,766	105,388	22,112	123	91,518	77.6	2,604	27,071
Wausau city	229	952,621	25,140	243.8	11.7	5,754	102,816	17,869	127	61,468	89.1	2,103	18,856
Wauwatosa city	289	878,993	18,930	183.6	(NA)	5,575	96,438	17,298	105	97,006	89.0	2,558	27,288
West Allis city	285	1,089,939	18,055	175.1	15.0	4,900	108,621	22,168	175	(D)	(NA)	[7]1,750	(D)
West Bend city	151	580,741	20,162	195.5	(NA)	3,164	50,926	16,095	60	33,952	92.0	1,242	9,876
WYOMING	2,861	5,783,756	11,590	112.4	15.3	28,796	554,008	19,239	1,742	984,684	58.2	24,160	270,423
Casper city	309	777,383	15,475	150.1	(NA)	3,935	80,001	20,331	139	81,479	79.4	2,451	23,530
Cheyenne city	300	992,268	18,390	178.3	(NA)	4,562	97,168	21,299	153	127,387	78.7	3,316	37,153
Laramie city	156	349,992	13,103	127.1	(NA)	1,695	29,185	17,218	85	55,041	81.8	1,363	12,205

D Data withheld to avoid disclosure.   NA Not available.   X Not applicable.

[1]Includes only establishments of firms with payroll.
[2]Based on resident population estimated as of July 1, 2002.
[3]For pay period including March 12.
[4]500 to 999 employees. Figure in table represents midpoint of range.
[5]250 to 499 employees. Figure in table represents midpoint of range.
[6]2,500 to 4,999 employees. Figure in table represents midpoint of range.
[7]1,000 to 2,499 employees. Figure in table represents midpoint of range.
[8]5,000 to 9,999 employees. Figure in table represents midpoint of range.
[9]Data are for Arlington County, VA; data for Arlington CDP not available.

Survey, Census, or Data Collection Method: Based on the 2002 Economic Census; for information, see Appendix B, Limitations of the Data and Methodology, and also <http://www.census.gov/econ/census02/>.

Sources: Retail trade—U.S. Census Bureau, 2002 Economic Census, *Retail Trade, Geographic Area Series*, accessed December 2006 (related Internet site <http://www.census.gov/econ/census02/>).   Accommodation and food services—U.S. Census Bureau, 2002 Economic Census, *Accommodation and Food Services, Geographic Area Series*, accessed December 2006 (related Internet site <http://www.census.gov/econ/census02/>).

Table C-6. Cities — **Government and Climate**

[Includes states and 1,265 incorporated places of 25,000 or more population as of April 1, 2000, in all states except Hawaii, which has no incorporated places recognized by the U.S. Census Bureau. Two census designated places (CDPs) are also included (Honolulu CDP in Hawaii and Arlington CDP in Virginia). For more information on these areas, see Appendix C, Geographic Information]

City	City government employment, March 2002 — Total employment	Total payroll ($1,000)	General revenue ($1,000) — Total	General revenue ($1,000) — Taxes	General expenditure Total[1] ($1,000)	Police protection	Sewerage and solid waste management	Highways	Avg daily temp January	Avg daily temp July	Min/max temp January[3]	Min/max temp July[4]	Annual precipitation (inches)	Heating degree days[5]	Cooling degree days[6]
ALABAMA	(X)	(X)	(X)	(X)	(X)	(NA)	(NA)	(NA)	(X)	(X)	(X)	(X)	(X)	(X)	(X)
Auburn city	625	1,016,235	44,673	31,214	39,555	11.3	17.2	12.3	44.7	79.9	34.2	89.7	52.63	2,507	1,932
Bessemer city	(NA)	(NA)	37,205	25,359	37,472	19.7	6.8	4.5	42.9	81.0	30.8	93.6	59.38	2,766	1,943
Birmingham city	(NA)	(NA)	383,847	260,687	466,050	15.3	8.7	2.7	42.6	80.2	32.3	90.6	53.99	2,823	1,881
Decatur city	1,979	5,324,625	185,387	26,884	183,406	4.6	9.4	4.0	38.9	79.2	29.1	90.3	55.31	3,469	1,609
Dothan city	1,068	2,916,856	56,087	39,646	85,571	12.1	18.6	7.0	47.7	81.3	36.2	93.3	56.61	2,058	2,264
Florence city	(NA)	(NA)	(NA)	(NA)	(NA)	(NA)	(NA)	(NA)	39.9	80.2	30.7	90.6	55.80	3,236	1,789
Gadsden city	(NA)	(NA)	51,660	34,805	47,914	17.9	11.9	7.1	40.3	79.8	29.9	90.5	56.10	3,220	1,716
Homewood city	388	1,160,715	36,038	31,456	34,218	19.5	10.0	2.0	42.6	80.2	32.3	90.6	53.99	2,823	1,881
Hoover city	645	2,339,420	71,958	60,160	69,478	17.9	8.8	6.7	42.9	81.0	30.8	93.6	59.38	2,766	1,943
Huntsville city	2,724	8,241,935	220,478	128,087	206,611	13.2	13.0	3.8	39.8	79.5	30.7	89.4	57.51	3,262	1,671
Madison city	(NA)	(NA)	22,367	15,286	23,745	15.1	6.3	28.6	46.6	81.8	35.5	92.7	54.77	2,194	2,252
Mobile city	3,078	7,825,595	274,830	170,421	273,860	13.7	13.7	9.1	50.1	81.5	39.5	91.2	66.29	1,681	2,539
Montgomery city	2,982	7,589,798	154,971	113,777	154,664	18.5	9.5	11.8	46.6	81.8	35.5	92.7	54.77	2,194	2,252
Phenix City city	339	843,739	(NA)	(NA)	(NA)	(NA)	(NA)	(NA)	46.8	82.0	36.6	91.7	48.57	2,154	2,296
Prattville city	(NA)	(NA)	(NA)	(NA)	(NA)	(NA)	(NA)	(NA)	46.6	81.8	35.5	92.7	54.77	2,194	2,252
Prichard city	(NA)	(NA)	(NA)	(NA)	(NA)	(NA)	(NA)	(NA)	50.1	81.5	39.5	91.2	66.29	1,681	2,539
Tuscaloosa city	1,088	2,779,267	85,201	48,297	77,544	18.2	16.3	–	42.9	80.4	32.5	90.8	54.99	2,787	1,893
Vestavia Hills city	(NA)	(NA)	(NA)	(NA)	(NA)	(NA)	(NA)	(NA)	42.6	80.2	32.3	90.6	53.99	2,823	1,881
ALASKA	(X)	(X)	(X)	(X)	(X)	(NA)	(NA)	(NA)	(X)	(X)	(X)	(X)	(X)	(X)	(X)
Anchorage municipality . .	10,423	37,133,902	858,527	321,827	1,042,376	13.2	2.7	18.7	15.8	58.4	9.3	65.3	16.08	10,470	3
Fairbanks city	189	905,250	21,949	11,824	33,217	37.1	–	11.9	-9.7	62.4	-19.0	73.0	10.34	13,980	74
Juneau city and borough	2,244	6,827,974	166,494	64,134	151,829	5.2	3.1	5.6	25.7	56.8	20.7	64.3	58.33	8,574	–
ARIZONA	(X)	(X)	(X)	(X)	(X)	(NA)	(NA)	(NA)	(X)	(X)	(X)	(X)	(X)	(X)	(X)
Apache Junction city	250	792,762	23,056	9,877	26,101	18.0	–	22.9	52.7	89.5	40.0	104.3	12.29	1,542	3,443
Avondale city	(NA)	(NA)	43,455	24,140	31,165	14.9	17.2	13.4	54.7	93.5	41.3	107.6	9.03	1,173	4,166
Bullhead City city	350	1,010,364	36,779	9,025	33,138	27.1	13.1	7.7	54.4	95.6	43.3	111.7	5.84	1,164	4,508
Casa Grande city	336	1,003,682	33,705	15,200	31,779	22.7	14.9	12.3	52.4	90.4	37.3	105.1	9.22	1,572	3,554
Chandler city	1,753	6,111,772	237,380	88,882	222,391	18.3	21.6	12.6	54.3	91.3	41.5	105.7	9.23	1,271	3,798
Flagstaff city	832	2,565,207	92,540	32,998	89,576	10.9	14.7	17.3	29.7	66.1	16.5	82.2	22.91	6,999	126
Gilbert town	741	2,659,295	130,595	70,469	120,841	12.8	18.2	10.6	54.3	91.3	41.5	105.7	9.23	1,271	3,798
Glendale city	1,903	7,137,734	222,143	86,874	236,655	14.9	15.6	10.7	52.5	90.6	39.2	104.2	7.78	1,535	3,488
Lake Havasu City city . . .	577	1,622,119	49,779	24,371	46,355	15.0	20.8	10.5	53.9	95.2	42.9	107.5	6.25	1,230	4,523
Mesa city	3,961	16,587,564	385,546	121,355	480,439	25.6	18.1	11.1	54.3	91.3	41.5	105.7	9.23	1,271	3,798
Oro Valley town	274	897,076	26,237	9,309	25,912	28.9	0.2	19.4	50.6	86.3	34.6	100.7	12.40	1,831	2,810
Peoria city	1,069	3,691,294	139,647	54,767	135,927	11.3	12.0	9.4	54.7	93.5	41.3	107.6	9.03	1,173	4,166
Phoenix city	13,787	58,014,509	2,125,101	750,582	1,981,816	15.2	15.2	4.4	54.2	92.8	43.4	104.2	8.29	1,125	4,189
Prescott city	564	1,521,026	65,469	26,300	56,292	10.5	20.5	31.0	37.1	73.4	23.3	88.3	19.19	4,849	742
Scottsdale city	2,204	8,116,090	354,649	189,317	320,344	15.4	10.5	6.1	54.2	92.8	43.4	104.2	8.29	1,125	4,189
Sierra Vista city	450	1,209,042	31,843	10,406	38,394	13.6	20.0	17.0	47.7	79.1	33.7	92.6	14.02	2,369	1,739
Surprise city	(NA)	(NA)	72,846	34,049	89,583	7.8	6.2	7.8	54.7	93.5	41.3	107.6	9.03	1,173	4,166
Tempe city	2,300	8,010,449	241,164	119,988	223,429	20.8	6.9	7.4	54.1	89.9	40.1	103.6	9.39	1,390	3,655
Tucson city	6,666	21,556,356	598,036	244,614	543,243	18.6	4.8	9.2	54.0	88.5	41.9	100.5	12.00	1,333	3,501
Yuma city	988	2,644,132	76,927	36,270	77,585	18.0	15.0	18.5	58.1	94.1	46.2	107.3	3.01	782	4,540
ARKANSAS	(X)	(X)	(X)	(X)	(X)	(NA)	(NA)	(NA)	(X)	(X)	(X)	(X)	(X)	(X)	(X)
Conway city	394	1,037,102	45,160	15,336	38,568	15.3	22.1	6.8	38.3	82.1	28.1	92.4	48.67	3,320	1,961
Fayetteville city	624	1,753,010	72,545	34,420	60,653	11.9	22.5	10.8	34.3	78.9	24.2	89.1	46.02	4,166	1,439
Fort Smith city	846	2,418,066	99,763	43,808	86,913	13.1	26.7	19.6	38.0	82.2	27.8	92.9	43.87	3,437	1,929
Hot Springs city	501	1,330,450	56,832	24,996	52,213	15.4	20.5	8.9	40.2	82.2	29.6	94.3	57.69	3,133	1,993
Jacksonville city	930	2,239,596	114,858	10,910	93,634	4.0	4.9	2.5	38.2	79.9	27.4	91.1	50.56	3,470	1,699
Jonesboro city	589	1,486,048	64,161	15,119	57,560	8.8	12.5	16.4	35.6	81.6	25.8	92.3	46.18	3,737	1,858
Little Rock city	2,790	7,667,405	239,646	71,911	240,515	17.0	13.4	8.2	40.1	82.4	30.8	92.8	50.93	3,084	2,086
North Little Rock city . . .	941	2,695,027	64,185	22,094	71,311	21.4	21.4	4.3	40.1	82.4	30.8	92.8	50.93	3,084	2,086
Pine Bluff city	423	1,037,056	42,241	14,723	42,148	23.2	21.5	8.5	40.8	82.4	31.5	92.4	52.48	2,935	2,099
Rogers city	364	924,366	36,363	14,143	29,091	18.9	15.2	8.9	32.9	77.5	22.0	88.8	46.92	4,483	1,269
Springdale city	488	1,244,709	38,604	14,578	39,189	16.7	22.2	6.9	34.3	78.9	24.2	89.1	46.02	4,166	1,439
Texarkana city	203	643,779	25,815	9,215	25,056	22.4	14.2	21.1	44.3	82.7	35.6	92.7	47.38	2,421	2,280
West Memphis city	400	957,670	23,943	9,653	22,239	22.1	14.8	9.8	37.5	81.5	28.5	90.9	52.80	3,417	1,903
CALIFORNIA	(X)	(X)	(X)	(X)	(X)	(NA)	(NA)	(NA)	(X)	(X)	(X)	(X)	(X)	(X)	(X)
Alameda city	980	3,825,407	99,057	49,822	113,108	17.3	6.2	7.3	50.9	64.9	44.7	72.7	22.94	2,400	377
Alhambra city	542	2,140,567	78,869	33,474	75,659	18.8	9.3	17.7	56.3	75.6	42.6	89.0	18.56	1,295	1,575
Aliso Viejo city	(NA)	(NA)	(X)	(X)	(X)	(NA)	(NA)	(NA)	56.7	72.4	47.2	82.3	14.03	1,465	1,183
Anaheim city	3,373	13,580,119	436,956	181,353	430,080	16.4	8.8	7.9	56.9	73.2	45.2	84.0	11.23	1,286	1,294
Antioch city	401	1,658,540	60,509	27,069	54,027	29.4	4.6	17.7	45.7	74.4	37.8	90.7	13.33	2,714	1,179
Apple Valley town	86	252,005	26,664	9,750	27,053	18.5	23.3	32.3	45.5	80.0	31.4	99.1	6.20	2,929	1,735
Arcadia city	378	1,722,450	45,635	27,438	42,675	33.6	1.4	12.3	56.3	75.6	42.6	89.0	18.56	1,295	1,575
Atascadero city	149	498,364	18,997	9,714	14,946	25.5	9.9	15.6	47.3	71.6	33.1	91.3	14.71	2,932	785
Azusa city	404	1,509,561	48,369	22,907	40,878	25.0	7.0	8.4	54.6	73.8	41.5	88.7	16.96	1,727	1,191
Bakersfield city	1,294	5,798,120	201,506	84,011	172,860	22.9	22.6	9.1	47.8	83.1	39.3	96.9	6.49	2,120	2,286

See footnotes at end of table.

Table C-6. Cities — **Government and Climate**—Con.

[Includes states and 1,265 incorporated places of 25,000 or more population as of April 1, 2000, in all states except Hawaii, which has no incorporated places recognized by the U.S. Census Bureau. Two census designated places (CDPs) are also included (Honolulu CDP in Hawaii and Arlington CDP in Virginia). For more information on these areas, see Appendix C, Geographic Information]

City	City government employment, March 2002		City government finances, 2001–2002						Climate, 1971–2000[2]						
			General revenue ($1,000)		General expenditure				Average daily temperature (degrees Fahrenheit)		Min. and max. temperatures (degrees Fahrenheit)				
						By selected function, percent of total									
	Total employment	Total payroll ($1,000)	Total	Taxes	Total[1] ($1,000)	Police protection	Sewerage and solid waste management	Highways	January	July	January[3]	July[4]	Annual precipitation (inches)	Heating degree days[5]	Cooling degree days[6]
CALIFORNIA—Con.															
Baldwin Park city	(NA)	(NA)	30,891	12,688	28,671	33.6	0.6	15.8	56.3	75.6	42.6	89.0	18.56	1,295	1,575
Bell city	167	508,423	24,533	10,294	22,698	27.2	6.7	9.7	58.8	76.6	47.9	88.9	14.44	949	1,837
Bellflower city	201	465,283	26,423	15,380	26,247	30.0	–	5.0	57.0	73.8	46.0	82.9	12.94	1,211	1,186
Bell Gardens city	183	798,715	25,122	14,026	27,653	29.6	1.5	18.1	58.8	76.6	47.9	88.9	14.44	949	1,837
Belmont city	143	687,338	29,265	19,265	28,903	23.4	17.2	7.7	48.1	69.7	36.4	88.2	28.71	2,769	569
Benicia city	305	1,025,555	33,237	20,268	28,898	17.0	15.5	9.2	46.3	71.2	38.8	87.4	19.58	2,757	786
Berkeley city	1,755	7,672,679	231,536	93,501	231,268	14.5	14.5	5.3	50.0	62.8	43.6	70.4	25.40	2,857	142
Beverly Hills city	1,022	4,392,183	142,200	86,798	145,446	19.7	8.2	10.4	57.9	69.5	49.4	76.9	18.68	1,379	893
Brea city	529	2,032,506	71,780	45,566	56,647	25.2	3.8	8.6	56.9	73.2	45.2	84.0	11.23	1,286	1,294
Buena Park city	429	1,662,804	62,099	35,993	50,954	28.4	4.6	13.6	57.0	73.8	46.0	82.9	12.94	1,211	1,186
Burbank city	1,482	7,187,000	177,484	88,679	167,184	17.3	16.4	12.0	54.8	75.5	42.0	88.9	17.49	1,575	1,455
Burlingame city	(NA)	(NA)	43,314	26,294	54,170	12.7	9.1	31.4	50.0	62.7	42.9	70.5	23.35	2,720	184
Calexico city	232	698,757	29,600	10,859	24,916	16.4	17.7	12.6	55.8	91.4	41.3	107.0	2.96	1,080	3,952
Camarillo city	150	707,176	53,728	23,586	34,447	17.9	24.4	31.5	55.7	66.0	45.3	74.0	13.61	1,961	389
Campbell city	428	1,169,206	39,359	22,729	52,943	17.4	0.5	15.0	48.7	70.3	38.8	85.4	22.64	2,641	613
Carlsbad city	960	3,435,007	140,968	68,342	94,452	16.4	4.5	16.3	54.7	67.6	45.4	72.1	11.13	2,009	505
Carson city	770	1,904,495	97,461	56,759	90,010	15.9	–	30.8	56.3	69.4	46.2	77.6	14.79	1,526	742
Cathedral City city	230	1,013,562	42,045	30,519	40,658	16.7	–	7.5	57.3	92.1	44.2	108.2	5.23	951	4,224
Ceres city	160	745,540	20,603	10,905	22,547	29.3	12.0	11.8	47.2	77.7	40.1	93.6	13.12	2,358	1,570
Cerritos city	634	1,667,276	96,910	52,614	142,312	6.0	3.0	10.0	57.0	73.8	46.0	82.9	12.94	1,211	1,186
Chico city	(NA)	(NA)	64,007	38,304	51,177	21.1	5.3	9.6	44.5	76.9	35.2	93.0	26.23	2,945	1,334
Chino city	426	1,605,693	71,790	26,698	69,589	23.8	20.0	22.5	54.6	73.8	41.5	88.7	16.96	1,727	1,191
Chino Hills city	164	538,591	57,115	17,033	49,709	7.8	11.3	52.6	56.9	73.2	45.2	84.0	11.23	1,286	1,294
Chula Vista city	1,727	4,680,006	230,496	91,237	202,057	19.4	9.4	16.2	57.3	70.1	46.1	76.1	9.95	1,321	862
Citrus Heights city	52	225,810	46,138	21,324	38,456	32.6	0.5	25.2	46.9	77.7	39.2	94.8	24.61	2,532	1,528
Claremont city	247	823,477	27,437	12,845	26,798	23.7	19.6	13.4	54.6	73.8	41.5	88.7	16.96	1,727	1,191
Clovis city	484	1,840,340	75,384	25,199	69,110	19.4	19.8	19.2	46.0	81.4	38.4	96.6	11.23	2,447	1,963
Colton city	(NA)	(NA)	42,272	17,348	40,970	19.8	10.0	4.0	54.4	79.6	41.8	96.0	16.43	1,599	1,937
Compton city	507	2,068,829	98,020	48,226	90,571	14.7	8.5	13.0	57.0	73.8	46.0	82.9	12.94	1,211	1,186
Concord city	720	3,034,677	104,654	61,556	109,765	24.5	10.5	17.5	46.3	71.2	38.8	87.4	19.58	2,757	786
Corona city	960	3,904,647	158,341	68,818	149,088	16.0	17.3	6.8	54.7	75.9	41.5	92.0	12.00	1,599	1,534
Costa Mesa city	752	4,163,015	80,928	54,386	83,785	36.9	1.0	11.1	55.9	67.3	48.2	71.4	11.65	1,719	543
Covina city	285	937,114	39,224	23,905	43,497	20.2	6.7	6.1	54.6	73.8	41.5	88.7	16.96	1,727	1,191
Culver City city	(NA)	(NA)	118,125	64,801	101,594	20.2	10.4	5.4	56.7	70.8	46.1	80.0	13.32	1,344	959
Cupertino city	211	877,825	47,341	25,181	36,418	16.6	4.7	23.0	48.7	70.3	38.8	85.4	22.64	2,641	613
Cypress city	274	935,373	35,883	23,561	26,356	36.4	0.8	17.6	57.0	73.8	46.0	82.9	12.94	1,211	1,186
Daly City city	745	2,867,198	86,094	32,473	84,476	19.0	18.0	16.4	50.6	57.3	44.6	61.1	19.77	3,665	17
Dana Point city	(NA)	(NA)	24,815	16,883	17,234	31.3	–	27.1	55.4	68.7	43.9	77.3	13.56	1,756	666
Danville town	127	402,988	28,990	13,413	24,198	19.6	–	19.6	47.5	72.4	39.3	85.2	23.96	3,267	983
Davis city	556	1,902,457	80,673	39,017	66,539	13.0	16.4	10.4	45.2	74.3	37.1	92.7	19.05	2,853	1,127
Delano city	296	843,981	26,930	6,879	20,902	19.3	35.2	4.9	46.6	81.1	36.5	99.0	7.34	2,434	1,990
Diamond Bar city	(NA)	(NA)	17,654	9,051	17,442	24.7	1.0	36.7	54.6	73.8	41.5	88.7	16.96	1,727	1,191
Downey city	654	2,499,026	71,458	35,873	63,894	30.0	1.2	18.9	57.0	73.8	46.0	82.9	12.94	1,211	1,186
Dublin city	134	383,938	61,637	46,570	42,289	18.2	2.4	18.8	47.2	72.0	37.4	89.1	14.82	2,755	858
East Palo Alto city	83	362,958	20,923	8,565	17,834	32.1	8.2	7.7	49.0	68.0	40.4	78.8	15.71	2,584	452
El Cajon city	605	2,548,033	73,152	38,234	73,233	27.7	15.8	13.0	54.9	74.7	41.6	87.0	11.96	1,560	1,371
El Centro city	931	2,826,413	89,589	14,498	99,663	5.6	6.0	6.7	55.8	91.4	41.3	107.0	2.96	1,080	3,852
Elk Grove city	(NA)	(NA)	41,708	26,985	25,775	43.9	–	20.3	46.3	75.4	38.8	92.4	17.93	2,666	1,248
El Monte city	564	1,900,524	62,647	40,486	68,878	31.4	–	11.6	56.3	75.6	42.6	89.0	18.56	1,295	1,575
Encinitas city	219	976,185	54,192	28,890	54,509	14.0	5.7	25.5	55.5	75.1	42.5	88.6	15.10	1,464	1,436
Escondido city	(NA)	(NA)	133,792	54,027	118,199	21.5	26.2	11.7	55.5	75.1	42.5	88.6	15.10	1,464	1,436
Eureka city	(NA)	(NA)	30,798	16,022	32,136	18.6	15.4	10.6	47.9	58.1	40.8	63.3	38.10	4,430	7
Fairfield city	702	2,961,897	129,812	69,437	95,234	17.1	0.2	23.8	46.1	72.6	37.5	88.8	23.46	2,649	975
Folsom city	598	2,358,478	96,329	53,596	77,454	14.0	11.7	7.9	46.9	77.7	39.2	94.8	24.61	2,532	1,528
Fontana city	500	2,084,560	156,008	81,692	127,604	15.4	14.3	10.9	56.6	78.3	45.3	95.0	14.77	1,364	1,901
Foster City city	262	1,487,860	49,559	32,789	41,211	16.0	7.5	3.6	48.4	68.0	39.1	80.8	20.16	2,764	422
Fountain Valley city	285	912,684	50,661	29,666	46,508	21.6	5.9	24.9	58.0	72.9	46.6	87.7	13.84	1,153	1,299
Fremont city	1,270	6,347,507	173,024	111,254	186,550	23.3	0.8	12.5	49.8	68.0	42.0	78.3	14.85	2,367	530
Fresno city	3,629	14,654,561	399,504	143,789	433,060	21.4	19.6	9.9	46.0	81.4	38.4	96.6	11.23	2,447	1,963
Fullerton city	(NA)	(NA)	102,127	56,110	90,927	29.3	8.8	13.6	56.9	73.2	45.2	84.0	11.23	1,286	1,294
Gardena city	447	1,578,806	107,741	51,098	96,163	29.7	–	2.4	56.3	69.4	46.2	77.6	14.79	1,526	742
Garden Grove city	(NA)	(NA)	47,589	28,748	30,441	39.0	2.7	32.4	58.0	72.9	46.6	87.7	13.84	1,153	1,299
Gilroy city	336	1,530,855	46,007	22,579	39,337	34.0	12.1	16.0	49.7	72.0	39.4	88.3	20.60	2,278	913
Glendale city	(NA)	(NA)	233,036	91,136	151,128	22.3	10.4	10.0	54.8	75.5	42.0	88.9	17.49	1,575	1,455
Glendora city	306	1,154,995	30,387	15,476	26,219	29.0	11.9	20.3	54.6	73.8	41.5	88.7	16.96	1,727	1,191
Goleta city	(NA)	(NA)	(X)	(X)	(X)	(NA)	(NA)	(NA)	53.1	67.0	40.8	76.7	16.93	2,121	482
Hanford city	255	817,498	30,249	11,446	32,439	13.9	22.2	14.3	44.7	79.6	35.7	95.9	8.58	2,749	1,724
Hawthorne city	468	1,932,294	100,206	29,525	103,019	27.3	10.4	6.5	57.1	69.3	48.6	75.3	13.15	1,274	679
Hayward city	942	5,022,476	140,706	70,872	114,456	29.1	9.4	15.5	49.7	64.6	41.7	75.2	26.30	2,810	261
Hemet city	(NA)	(NA)	42,191	21,665	48,127	23.7	15.5	13.6	52.4	79.9	38.4	97.8	12.55	1,914	1,903

See footnotes at end of table.

Table C-6. Cities — **Government and Climate**—Con.

[Includes states and 1,265 incorporated places of 25,000 or more population as of April 1, 2000, in all states except Hawaii, which has no incorporated places recognized by the U.S. Census Bureau. Two census designated places (CDPs) are also included (Honolulu CDP in Hawaii and Arlington CDP in Virginia). For more information on these areas, see Appendix C, Geographic Information]

City	City government employment, March 2002		City government finances, 2001–2002						Climate, 1971–2000[2]						
			General revenue ($1,000)		General expenditure				Average daily temperature (degrees Fahrenheit)		Min. and max. temperatures (degrees Fahrenheit)				
						By selected function, percent of total									
	Total employ-ment	Total payroll ($1,000)	Total	Taxes	Total[1] ($1,000)	Police pro-tection	Sewer-age and solid waste manage-ment	High-ways	January	July	January[3]	July[4]	Annual precip-itation (inches)	Heat-ing degree days[5]	Cooling degree days[6]
CALIFORNIA—Con.															
Hesperia city	(NA)	(NA)	27,153	17,395	24,156	24.5	–	19.8	45.5	80.0	31.4	99.1	6.20	2,929	1,735
Highland city	36	135,650	22,515	8,575	15,974	23.9	–	29.2	54.4	79.6	41.8	96.0	16.43	1,599	1,937
Hollister city	194	924,544	31,533	14,644	28,147	13.8	14.0	24.8	49.5	66.6	37.8	80.9	13.61	2,724	405
Huntington Beach city	1,581	6,316,966	179,575	93,280	205,268	21.6	5.5	16.9	55.9	67.3	48.2	71.4	11.65	1,719	543
Huntington Park city	232	956,410	40,981	18,922	39,766	29.0	2.5	6.1	58.3	74.2	48.5	83.8	15.14	928	1,506
Imperial Beach city	128	258,614	17,407	5,123	17,455	20.9	27.2	21.5	57.3	70.1	46.1	76.1	9.95	1,321	862
Indio city	(NA)		60,229	21,236	36,476	20.9	–	10.2	56.8	92.8	42.0	107.1	3.15	903	4,388
Inglewood city	916	3,911,514	128,585	49,084	123,265	26.1	8.8	6.5	57.1	69.3	48.6	75.3	13.15	1,274	679
Irvine city	1,060	4,102,847	142,302	81,655	203,360	17.9	–	17.0	54.5	72.1	41.4	83.8	13.87	1,794	1,102
Laguna Hills city	(NA)	(NA)	18,357	12,599	29,855	14.3	–	5.2	56.7	72.4	47.2	82.3	14.03	1,465	1,183
Laguna Niguel city	85	273,287	31,161	19,594	25,903	21.4	–	15.6	55.4	68.7	43.9	77.3	13.56	1,756	666
La Habra city	456	1,428,451	48,453	22,542	44,184	26.6	6.4	16.8	56.9	73.2	45.2	84.0	11.23	1,286	1,294
Lake Elsinore city	64	259,653	28,569	18,408	34,072	11.8	–	19.5	52.2	79.6	38.3	98.1	12.09	1,924	1,874
Lake Forest city	(NA)		34,286	21,852	25,059	27.0	–	37.4	56.7	72.4	47.2	82.3	14.03	1,465	1,183
Lakewood city	352	990,795	43,181	23,396	38,051	16.2	10.0	15.5	57.0	73.8	46.0	82.9	12.94	1,211	1,186
La Mesa city	312	1,249,985	39,684	21,188	38,687	22.2	18.5	17.7	57.1	73.0	45.7	83.6	13.75	1,313	1,261
La Mirada city	213	554,210	37,673	23,055	38,245	16.4	–	14.3	58.8	76.6	47.9	88.9	14.44	949	1,837
Lancaster city	386	941,734	98,307	58,232	99,528	13.1	–	23.6	43.9	80.8	31.0	95.5	7.40	3,241	1,733
La Puente city	61	316,721	11,144	5,280	8,617	44.6	–	15.6	58.8	76.6	47.9	88.9	14.44	949	1,837
La Verne city	(NA)	2,484,544	28,736	15,585	25,641	26.6	1.9	12.1	54.6	73.8	41.5	88.7	16.96	1,727	1,191
Lawndale city	87	316,721	15,154	6,761	14,919	24.7	0.1	9.0	57.1	69.3	48.6	75.3	13.15	1,274	679
Livermore city	542	2,484,544	123,956	37,940	125,054	16.0	10.5	13.4	47.2	72.0	37.4	89.1	14.82	2,755	858
Lodi city	(NA)	(NA)	63,457	28,737	36,183	24.1	13.4	12.7	46.1	73.8	37.5	91.1	18.22	2,710	1,057
Lompoc city	443	1,537,195	30,794	12,121	29,592	19.3	37.8	14.5	53.7	64.5	41.4	75.4	15.85	2,250	322
Long Beach city	6,458	28,839,300	882,844	232,929	936,210	15.9	7.9	9.6	57.0	73.8	46.0	82.9	12.94	1,211	1,186
Los Altos city	(NA)	(NA)	24,582	13,077	22,504	21.2	16.6	10.7	49.0	68.0	40.4	78.8	15.71	2,584	452
Los Angeles city	51,150	259,236,534	6,018,713	2,420,517	6,503,119	17.3	8.8	8.6	58.3	74.2	48.5	83.8	15.14	928	1,506
Los Banos city	167	408,798	17,903	7,179	21,590	18.4	17.4	15.6	45.9	78.1	36.8	94.6	9.95	2,570	1,547
Los Gatos town	205	1,088,504	29,115	19,629	30,730	31.3	2.1	25.6	48.7	70.3	38.8	85.4	22.64	2,641	613
Lynwood city	272	741,040	35,865	15,078	39,441	15.8	8.2	16.0	58.3	74.2	48.5	83.8	15.14	928	1,506
Madera city	279	674,468	34,031	14,145	36,850	19.5	19.0	15.1	45.7	79.6	37.2	96.5	11.94	2,670	1,706
Manhattan Beach city	355	1,370,361	45,920	24,802	38,205	33.0	10.7	13.7	57.1	69.3	48.6	75.3	13.15	1,274	679
Manteca city	309	1,266,579	58,436	22,561	46,352	15.6	32.0	18.2	46.0	77.3	38.1	93.8	13.84	2,563	1,456
Martinez city	(NA)	(NA)	26,659	10,829	19,282	37.4	–	26.2	46.3	71.2	38.8	87.4	19.58	2,757	786
Maywood city	(NA)	(NA)	9,867	4,787	7,769	52.8	–	10.9	58.3	74.2	48.5	83.8	15.14	928	1,506
Menlo Park city	370	1,303,452	47,027	29,952	59,297	14.5	2.4	10.0	49.0	68.0	40.4	78.8	15.71	2,584	452
Merced city	439	1,718,875	52,870	21,020	54,461	20.8	25.1	8.7	46.3	78.6	37.5	96.5	12.50	2,602	1,578
Milpitas city	613	3,238,481	107,642	67,419	123,574	12.7	10.8	12.1	50.5	70.9	41.7	84.3	15.08	2,171	811
Mission Viejo city	195	629,265	60,688	40,032	68,044	11.7	–	25.9	56.7	72.4	47.2	82.3	14.03	1,465	1,183
Modesto city	1,387	5,782,169	177,683	93,720	151,140	25.6	14.8	16.3	47.2	77.7	40.1	93.6	13.12	2,358	1,570
Monrovia city	325	1,360,521	36,401	21,694	30,880	30.3	3.5	10.5	56.1	75.3	44.3	89.4	21.09	1,398	1,558
Montclair city	(NA)		32,457	20,565	29,904	26.7	11.6	10.1	54.6	73.8	41.5	88.7	16.96	1,727	1,191
Montebello city	620	2,437,676	64,901	35,008	58,086	22.5	4.1	2.5	58.8	76.6	47.9	88.9	14.44	949	1,837
Monterey city	(NA)	(NA)	70,103	35,021	61,618	13.6	2.0	8.5	51.6	60.2	43.4	68.1	20.35	3,092	74
Monterey Park city	478	1,601,848	46,952	25,102	45,826	23.7	9.4	10.8	56.3	75.6	42.6	89.0	18.56	1,295	1,575
Moorpark city	72	244,490	24,509	12,429	15,408	18.9	1.1	22.5	54.7	68.3	41.2	80.7	18.41	1,911	602
Moreno Valley city	429	1,261,073	78,628	45,519	75,694	26.2	–	16.9	56.2	77.4	42.0	93.5	10.67	1,674	1,697
Morgan Hill city	(NA)	(NA)	49,770	30,991	47,908	12.3	10.5	10.7	43.5	70.7	37.5	78.2	23.73	4,566	747
Mountain View city	794	4,121,151	139,691	74,501	109,434	14.9	16.8	10.8	49.0	68.0	40.4	78.8	15.71	2,584	452
Murrieta city	152	788,711	68,786	26,813	53,010	27.0	–	26.0	52.2	79.6	38.3	98.1	12.09	1,924	1,874
Napa city	491	2,355,934	63,037	34,291	58,163	23.2	5.6	26.5	47.9	68.6	39.2	82.6	26.46	2,689	529
National City city	429	1,445,404	58,116	27,587	57,809	23.8	12.7	7.0	57.3	70.1	46.1	76.1	9.95	1,321	862
Newark city	(NA)	(NA)	40,510	26,265	37,663	25.8	0.5	12.3	49.8	68.0	42.0	78.3	14.85	2,367	530
Newport Beach city	1,191	3,508,359	131,217	69,815	135,401	17.1	5.4	12.0	55.9	67.3	48.2	71.4	11.65	1,719	543
Norwalk city	409	1,209,694	60,127	29,438	62,048	16.3	–	23.5	57.0	73.8	46.0	82.9	12.94	1,211	1,186
Novato city	338	1,237,810	38,124	19,004	36,894	23.8	–	19.6	48.8	67.7	41.3	80.9	34.29	2,621	451
Oakland city	5,270	33,119,913	920,296	370,456	1,115,357	10.9	1.3	5.9	50.9	64.9	44.7	72.7	22.94	2,400	377
Oakley city	21	69,424	15,540	5,581	7,499	38.0	–	20.5	45.7	74.4	37.8	90.7	13.33	2,714	1,179
Oceanside city	1,076	3,992,863	182,040	50,807	172,335	17.1	19.6	7.1	54.7	67.6	45.4	72.1	11.13	2,009	505
Ontario city	(NA)	(NA)	202,462	104,175	175,302	24.1	13.5	8.7	54.6	73.8	41.5	88.7	16.96	1,727	1,191
Orange city	815	4,132,493	103,618	62,407	99,763	25.0	7.8	12.2	58.0	72.9	46.6	82.7	13.84	1,153	1,299
Oxnard city	(NA)	(NA)	174,755	75,578	172,377	19.9	25.6	9.8	55.6	65.9	45.5	72.7	15.62	1,936	403
Pacifica city	(NA)	(NA)	33,094	11,008	38,593	15.6	14.6	14.8	49.4	62.8	42.9	71.1	20.11	2,862	142
Palmdale city	(NA)	(NA)	79,672	47,468	86,074	14.8	(Z)	9.6	46.6	81.7	34.3	97.5	7.36	2,704	1,998
Palm Desert city	(NA)	(NA)	115,270	76,988	107,697	8.9	–	16.9	56.8	92.8	42.0	107.1	3.15	903	4,388
Palm Springs city	533	2,430,688	110,749	47,273	102,215	15.3	6.2	4.0	57.3	92.1	44.2	108.2	5.23	951	4,224
Palo Alto city	1,313	6,864,390	201,991	52,099	166,188	11.4	29.3	13.9	49.0	68.0	40.4	78.8	15.71	2,584	452
Paradise town	(NA)	(NA)	10,516	5,275	10,304	32.4	2.7	13.9	45.7	77.8	37.7	91.7	56.20	3,145	1,464
Paramount city	(NA)	(NA)	35,369	19,516	33,446	23.4	–	23.0	57.0	73.8	46.0	82.9	12.94	1,211	1,186
Pasadena city	1,881	9,332,736	293,318	121,993	200,422	19.7	4.7	6.2	56.1	75.3	44.3	89.4	21.09	1,398	1,558

See footnotes at end of table.

County and City Data Book: 2007

U.S. Census Bureau

Table C-6. Cities — **Government and Climate**—Con.

[Includes states and 1,265 incorporated places of 25,000 or more population as of April 1, 2000, in all states except Hawaii, which has no incorporated places recognized by the U.S. Census Bureau. Two census designated places (CDPs) are also included (Honolulu CDP in Hawaii and Arlington CDP in Virginia). For more information on these areas, see Appendix C, Geographic Information]

City	City government employment, March 2002		City government finances, 2001–2002							Climate, 1971–2000[2]						
			General revenue ($1,000)		General expenditure					Average daily temperature (degrees Fahrenheit)		Min. and max. temperatures (degrees Fahrenheit)				
						By selected function, percent of total									
	Total employ-ment	Total payroll ($1,000)	Total	Taxes	Total[1] ($1,000)	Police pro-tection	Sewer-age and solid waste manage-ment	High-ways	January	July	January[3]	July[4]	Annual precip-itation (inches)	Heat-ing degree days[5]	Cooling degree days[6]
CALIFORNIA—Con.															
Perris city	54	171,121	24,929	14,182	20,358	27.7	7.3	16.8	51.2	78.3	36.1	97.8	11.40	2,123	1,710
Petaluma city	(NA)	(NA)	64,926	32,269	63,690	16.5	20.6	15.4	48.4	67.3	38.9	82.7	25.85	2,741	385
Pico Rivera city	491	1,002,072	36,983	16,534	37,797	15.9	–	10.8	58.3	74.2	48.5	83.8	15.14	928	1,506
Pittsburg city	354	1,361,497	71,965	38,169	56,460	23.7	1.1	21.8	45.7	74.4	37.8	90.7	13.33	2,714	1,179
Placentia city	246	801,799	32,450	17,998	36,484	25.9	5.1	20.3	58.0	72.9	46.6	82.7	13.84	1,153	1,299
Pleasant Hill city	(NA)	(NA)	25,376	15,799	24,300	27.1	0.3	27.2	46.3	71.2	38.8	87.4	19.58	2,757	786
Pleasanton city	723	3,347,720	121,940	57,333	111,409	13.7	9.8	11.7	47.2	72.0	37.4	89.1	14.82	2,755	858
Pomona city	835	3,432,461	112,237	67,989	113,682	25.3	6.0	16.3	54.6	73.8	41.5	88.7	16.96	1,727	1,191
Porterville city	(NA)	(NA)	29,475	12,169	33,975	13.9	20.4	24.7	48.7	82.8	39.4	98.1	11.49	2,053	2,246
Poway city	282	1,087,853	84,407	41,731	89,221	12.2	9.2	4.0	55.3	70.9	43.5	80.8	11.97	1,808	979
Rancho Cordova city	(X)	(X)	(X)	(X)	(X)	(NA)	(NA)	(NA)	48.2	77.4	41.3	93.8	19.87	2,226	1,597
Rancho Cucamonga city	575	1,540,927	151,333	88,890	104,269	11.9	0.4	17.9	56.6	78.3	45.3	95.0	14.77	1,364	1,901
Rancho Palos Verdes city	61	224,936	21,905	14,606	22,857	12.1	1.0	34.3	56.3	69.4	46.2	77.6	14.79	1,526	742
Rancho Santa Margarita city	9	29,567	18,318	9,782	9,744	14.2	–	44.3	56.7	72.4	47.2	82.3	14.03	1,465	1,183
Redding city	908	3,637,837	116,817	37,890	115,512	14.3	24.6	4.4	45.5	81.3	35.5	98.5	33.52	2,961	1,741
Redlands city	589	2,109,876	70,958	36,107	67,807	21.5	23.8	16.2	52.9	78.0	40.4	94.4	13.62	1,904	1,714
Redondo Beach city	704	2,719,782	79,497	39,808	78,068	21.6	1.3	9.5	57.1	69.3	48.6	75.3	13.15	1,274	679
Redwood City city	775	3,664,181	102,781	58,594	107,020	18.6	8.1	30.3	48.4	68.0	39.1	80.8	20.16	2,764	422
Rialto city	406	1,558,903	62,077	26,199	52,298	28.7	10.8	12.5	54.4	79.6	41.8	96.0	16.43	1,599	1,937
Richmond city	(NA)	(NA)	143,649	77,145	130,066	24.5	7.4	4.9	50.0	62.7	42.9	70.5	23.35	2,720	184
Riverside city	2,250	9,741,403	267,491	100,688	232,499	25.5	8.9	14.6	55.3	78.7	42.7	94.1	10.22	1,475	1,863
Rocklin city	365	1,058,982	41,988	25,093	34,358	15.4	–	9.8	46.9	77.7	39.2	94.8	24.61	2,532	1,528
Rohnert Park city	257	1,089,636	49,680	18,927	57,366	13.3	32.2	4.8	48.7	67.6	39.5	82.2	31.01	2,694	526
Rosemead city	125	216,557	25,772	11,757	30,329	22.1	–	8.7	56.3	75.6	42.6	89.0	18.56	1,295	1,575
Roseville city	(NA)	(NA)	217,996	87,900	221,186	6.4	30.4	23.0	46.9	77.7	39.2	94.8	24.61	2,532	1,528
Sacramento city	4,951	18,564,515	784,978	260,918	666,900	15.8	8.2	8.3	46.3	75.4	38.8	92.4	17.93	2,666	1,248
Salinas city	844	3,475,918	96,063	51,829	87,861	27.2	5.8	13.5	51.2	63.2	41.3	71.3	12.91	2,770	210
San Bernardino city	(NA)	(NA)	196,870	89,647	165,923	25.9	19.6	3.5	54.4	79.6	41.8	96.0	16.43	1,599	1,937
San Bruno city	(NA)	(NA)	38,834	16,208	48,069	17.7	19.1	8.3	49.4	62.8	42.9	71.1	20.11	2,862	142
San Buenaventura (Ventura) city	824	3,346,938	107,873	50,578	95,987	22.5	10.5	18.6	55.6	65.9	45.5	72.7	15.62	1,936	403
San Carlos city	(NA)	(NA)	35,187	19,803	35,955	14.9	8.6	12.5	48.4	68.0	39.1	80.8	20.16	2,764	422
San Clemente city	250	849,757	72,170	40,179	54,561	13.2	7.7	33.8	55.4	68.7	43.9	77.3	13.56	1,756	666
San Diego city	12,190	51,978,374	1,903,319	744,714	1,774,240	14.9	20.6	3.2	57.8	70.9	49.7	75.8	10.77	1,063	866
San Dimas city	98	296,839	23,659	13,229	20,500	19.8	0.1	26.1	54.6	73.8	41.5	88.7	16.96	1,727	1,191
San Francisco city	28,935	165,626,872	4,843,513	1,698,789	4,793,132	7.8	2.5	3.5	52.3	61.3	46.4	68.2	22.28	2,597	163
San Gabriel city	(NA)	(NA)	18,899	11,719	17,721	35.6	(Z)	10.5	56.3	75.6	42.6	89.0	18.56	1,295	1,575
San Jose city	8,175	42,150,868	1,463,484	666,814	1,519,318	12.3	13.8	6.9	50.5	70.9	41.7	84.3	15.08	2,171	811
San Juan Capistrano city	(NA)	(NA)	30,287	19,365	26,478	16.6	7.8	15.9	55.4	68.7	43.9	77.3	13.56	1,756	666
San Leandro city	488	2,050,808	93,737	58,669	94,389	20.8	8.7	8.3	50.0	62.8	43.6	70.4	25.40	2,857	142
San Luis Obispo city	594	2,196,695	59,936	26,826	56,077	15.1	11.0	16.5	53.3	66.5	41.9	80.3	24.36	2,138	476
San Marcos city	268	1,020,863	94,795	47,558	81,839	10.5	–	15.4	56.4	71.6	45.1	82.2	13.69	1,514	1,047
San Mateo city	(NA)	(NA)	109,968	64,435	136,020	15.1	10.8	9.6	48.4	68.0	39.1	80.8	20.16	2,764	422
San Pablo city	(NA)	(NA)	23,766	15,254	21,128	33.6	–	12.2	48.8	67.7	41.3	80.9	34.29	2,621	451
San Rafael city	495	2,276,158	61,047	36,018	68,737	20.4	–	11.9	48.8	67.7	41.3	80.9	34.29	2,621	451
San Ramon city	150	494,858	49,686	28,358	49,782	12.9	0.4	29.4	47.2	72.0	37.4	89.1	14.82	2,755	858
Santa Ana city	2,357	10,801,600	276,195	137,204	283,200	26.9	3.9	11.6	58.0	72.9	46.6	87.7	13.84	1,153	1,299
Santa Barbara city	1,589	5,597,935	163,664	66,328	138,648	16.5	5.9	10.8	53.1	67.0	40.8	76.7	16.93	2,121	482
Santa Clara city	1,309	5,864,177	272,989	103,614	193,437	14.6	12.5	8.6	50.5	70.9	41.7	84.3	15.08	2,171	811
Santa Clarita city	538	1,530,939	107,890	61,539	81,976	13.7	4.4	28.6	50.3	74.1	36.1	94.2	13.96	2,502	1,139
Santa Cruz city	1,163	4,049,595	107,099	41,473	98,358	15.2	27.7	8.6	50.6	63.7	40.2	74.8	30.67	2,836	162
Santa Maria city	517	1,817,550	80,259	32,535	58,502	20.8	23.3	20.2	51.6	63.5	39.3	73.5	14.01	2,783	121
Santa Monica city	2,039	9,638,137	303,239	165,220	231,251	22.8	8.0	5.8	57.0	65.5	50.2	68.8	13.27	1,810	429
Santa Paula city	171	585,498	15,971	5,635	13,369	27.5	14.5	10.7	54.7	68.3	41.2	80.7	18.41	1,911	602
Santa Rosa city	1,481	6,616,220	196,302	69,672	241,239	14.0	42.8	7.8	48.7	67.6	39.5	82.2	31.01	2,694	526
Santee city	158	703,534	30,563	16,845	29,651	26.7	0.7	10.6	57.1	73.0	45.7	83.6	13.75	1,313	1,261
Saratoga city	81	321,345	17,074	8,358	22,782	14.5	–	14.4	50.5	70.9	41.7	84.3	15.08	2,171	811
Seaside city	192	668,351	22,331	16,026	18,967	32.2	–	5.8	51.6	60.2	43.4	68.1	20.35	3,092	74
Simi Valley city	645	2,677,970	91,485	43,498	83,895	22.0	13.4	15.7	53.7	76.0	39.5	95.0	17.79	1,822	1,485
South Gate city	(NA)	(NA)	44,937	21,049	79,785	19.7	4.3	7.1	58.3	74.2	48.5	83.8	15.14	928	1,506
South San Francisco city	709	2,774,760	97,271	49,968	79,597	15.4	10.0	25.0	49.4	62.8	42.9	71.1	20.11	2,862	142
Stanton city	31	92,300	18,919	10,612	16,381	30.2	1.3	22.9	58.0	72.9	46.6	87.7	13.84	1,153	1,299
Stockton city	2,372	8,642,852	253,319	101,810	239,390	25.7	12.7	10.9	46.0	77.3	38.1	93.8	13.84	2,563	1,456
Suisun City city	119	374,750	21,204	12,845	25,644	13.7	0.9	12.7	46.1	72.6	37.5	88.8	23.46	2,649	975
Sunnyvale city	1,032	6,073,756	196,459	75,074	181,059	14.2	32.2	8.0	50.5	70.9	41.7	84.3	15.08	2,171	811
Temecula city	192	670,619	67,951	47,453	64,621	13.3	–	7.8	51.2	78.3	36.1	97.8	11.40	2,123	1,710
Temple City city	76	171,359	12,335	5,577	9,318	30.5	0.2	14.2	56.3	75.6	42.6	89.0	18.56	1,295	1,575
Thousand Oaks city	642	2,316,589	128,958	68,337	127,605	11.9	16.8	20.1	53.7	76.0	39.5	95.0	17.79	1,822	1,485
Torrance city	(NA)	(NA)	195,158	109,945	160,780	26.1	5.0	13.4	56.3	69.4	46.2	77.6	14.79	1,526	742
Tracy city	(NA)	(NA)	121,259	27,392	87,293	9.3	16.8	20.5	47.1	76.4	38.5	92.5	12.51	2,421	1,470
Tulare city	(NA)	(NA)	37,623	15,663	39,258	15.5	26.0	9.5	45.8	79.3	37.4	93.8	11.03	2,588	1,685

See footnotes at end of table.

Table C-6. Cities — **Government and Climate**—Con.

[Includes states and 1,265 incorporated places of 25,000 or more population as of April 1, 2000, in all states except Hawaii, which has no incorporated places recognized by the U.S. Census Bureau. Two census designated places (CDPs) are also included (Honolulu CDP in Hawaii and Arlington CDP in Virginia). For more information on these areas, see Appendix C, Geographic Information]

City	City government employment, March 2002		City government finances, 2001–2002						Climate, 1971–2000[2]						
	Total employment	Total payroll ($1,000)	General revenue ($1,000)		General expenditure				Average daily temperature (degrees Fahrenheit)		Min. and max. temperatures (degrees Fahrenheit)		Annual precipitation (inches)	Heating degree days[5]	Cooling degree days[6]
			Total	Taxes	Total[1] ($1,000)	Police protection	Sewerage and solid waste management	Highways	January	July	January[3]	July[4]			
CALIFORNIA—Con.															
Turlock city	418	1,206,686	49,502	19,783	38,310	24.3	13.1	17.9	46.4	77.6	39.0	93.3	12.43	2,519	1,506
Tustin city	308	1,354,597	47,009	29,155	50,625	28.4	–	23.6	54.5	72.1	41.4	83.8	13.87	1,794	1,102
Twentynine Palms city	(NA)	(NA)	(NA)	(NA)	(NA)	(NA)	(NA)	(NA)	50.0	88.4	36.1	105.8	4.57	1,910	3,064
Union City city	449	1,720,966	51,064	34,252	56,326	24.7	–	8.8	49.8	68.0	42.0	78.3	14.85	2,367	530
Upland city	(NA)	(NA)	56,120	21,664	47,417	19.5	23.9	13.3	54.6	73.8	41.5	88.7	16.96	1,727	1,191
Vacaville city	846	3,200,926	120,758	53,767	134,955	12.7	29.8	8.2	47.2	77.3	38.8	95.8	24.55	2,410	1,498
Vallejo city	(NA)	(NA)	229,427	53,973	191,649	15.3	6.9	7.4	46.3	71.2	38.8	87.4	19.58	2,757	786
Victorville city	424	1,279,837	69,054	35,426	52,771	19.4	21.1	9.4	45.5	80.0	31.4	99.1	6.20	2,929	1,735
Visalia city	(NA)	(NA)	96,924	33,501	80,817	17.6	27.7	11.8	45.8	79.3	37.4	93.8	11.03	2,588	1,685
Vista city	408	1,372,673	71,919	33,088	70,854	15.8	17.3	10.6	56.4	71.6	45.1	82.2	13.69	1,514	1,047
Walnut city	60	206,488	31,905	21,273	31,279	9.2	–	13.4	54.6	73.8	41.5	88.7	16.96	1,727	1,191
Walnut Creek city	525	2,094,195	58,979	34,269	65,738	19.8	–	13.8	47.5	72.4	39.3	85.2	23.96	3,267	983
Watsonville city	404	1,680,583	48,755	22,330	49,042	16.8	17.0	13.7	49.7	62.4	38.7	72.0	23.25	3,080	123
West Covina city	606	2,264,468	73,376	42,111	61,489	33.1	–	8.3	56.3	75.6	42.6	89.0	18.56	1,295	1,575
West Hollywood city	(NA)	(NA)	55,855	28,169	53,468	21.9	2.8	11.8	58.3	74.2	48.5	83.8	15.14	928	1,506
Westminster city	361	1,801,957	58,556	37,296	49,120	39.9	–	51.5	58.0	72.9	46.6	82.7	13.84	1,153	1,299
West Sacramento city	465	1,443,620	58,287	31,843	95,115	10.6	8.1	6.8	46.3	75.4	38.8	92.4	17.93	2,666	1,248
Whittier city	732	1,752,339	60,640	26,737	57,514	36.4	14.0	10.6	56.3	75.6	42.6	89.0	18.56	1,295	1,575
Woodland city	(NA)	(NA)	45,839	23,393	54,295	19.3	5.8	23.9	45.7	76.4	37.6	94.0	20.78	2,683	1,417
Yorba Linda city	(NA)	(NA)	69,850	34,213	63,135	10.4	5.5	31.5	56.9	73.2	45.2	84.0	11.23	1,286	1,294
Yuba City city	267	998,584	39,596	17,235	33,235	18.6	17.9	16.4	46.3	78.9	37.8	96.3	22.07	2,488	1,687
Yucaipa city	64	134,132	21,903	9,342	14,655	23.8	–	23.1	52.9	78.0	40.4	94.4	13.62	1,904	1,714
COLORADO	(X)	(X)	(X)	(X)	(X)	(NA)	(NA)	(NA)	(X)	(X)	(X)	(X)	(X)	(X)	(X)
Arvada city	846	3,408,118	102,003	42,107	85,679	18.4	10.0	24.2	31.2	71.5	15.6	88.3	18.17	5,988	496
Aurora city	2,517	10,166,161	306,243	191,701	287,193	21.1	8.4	16.2	29.2	73.4	15.2	88.0	15.81	6,128	696
Boulder city	(NA)	(NA)	182,259	119,654	179,720	9.2	3.4	14.2	32.5	71.6	19.2	87.2	19.93	5,687	552
Broomfield city	717	2,389,346	95,581	81,050	60,878	27.3	11.7	7.3	32.5	71.6	19.2	87.2	19.93	5,687	552
Centennial city	11	13,108	(X)	(X)	(X)	(NA)	(NA)	(NA)	28.0	66.7	17.1	79.6	21.62	7,337	231
Colorado Springs city	7,634	27,728,449	673,107	166,768	721,444	9.0	8.0	11.9	28.1	69.6	14.5	84.4	17.40	6,480	404
Denver city	13,400	54,179,694	1,912,278	732,592	1,899,756	7.9	2.5	4.3	31.2	71.5	15.6	88.3	18.17	5,988	496
Englewood city	576	2,297,989	55,012	31,435	51,595	14.0	16.4	10.7	28.2	70.2	12.7	85.8	17.06	6,773	435
Fort Collins city	(NA)	(NA)	198,603	91,782	180,310	11.3	6.2	12.4	28.2	71.5	14.5	86.2	13.98	6,256	524
Grand Junction city	(NA)	(NA)	64,557	36,023	73,554	16.6	16.9	26.8	27.4	77.5	16.8	91.9	9.06	5,489	1,098
Greeley city	938	2,680,221	70,670	41,557	76,953	17.3	4.4	11.3	27.8	74.0	15.6	88.7	14.22	5,980	759
Lakewood city	1,265	3,897,024	107,682	61,645	112,101	22.9	2.2	11.8	28.2	70.2	12.7	85.8	17.06	6,773	435
Littleton city	438	1,873,700	56,887	30,758	51,950	15.5	11.8	20.0	28.2	70.2	12.7	85.8	17.06	6,773	435
Longmont city	1,015	3,570,012	103,152	53,384	131,108	9.9	16.4	12.5	27.1	72.2	12.0	88.9	14.15	6,415	587
Loveland city	854	2,595,208	78,392	32,393	70,645	13.8	12.9	7.9	28.2	71.5	14.5	86.2	13.98	6,256	524
Northglenn city	(NA)	(NA)	38,796	21,131	19,498	29.7	13.3	9.9	30.0	72.0	16.2	87.9	13.25	6,074	590
Pueblo city	(NA)	(NA)	89,589	52,958	74,032	19.1	5.1	11.8	30.8	77.0	14.7	93.8	12.60	5,346	997
Thornton city	(NA)	(NA)	95,472	65,347	84,385	8.2	9.3	17.6	30.0	72.0	16.2	87.9	13.25	6,074	590
Westminster city	1,097	3,786,925	158,412	70,080	263,808	34.3	1.4	2.9	29.2	73.4	15.2	88.0	15.81	6,128	696
Wheat Ridge city	(NA)	(NA)	22,742	14,482	26,379	23.2	–	20.1	31.2	71.5	15.6	88.3	18.17	5,988	496
CONNECTICUT	(X)	(X)	(X)	(X)	(X)	(NA)	(NA)	(NA)	(X)	(X)	(X)	(X)	(X)	(X)	(X)
Bridgeport city	5,448	18,961,118	499,396	178,542	504,759	7.1	4.9	1.5	29.9	74.0	22.9	81.9	44.15	5,466	789
Bristol city	2,018	7,321,982	147,086	74,569	149,329	7.4	9.1	5.5	23.4	70.5	12.6	83.3	51.03	6,825	395
Danbury city	2,088	7,049,174	177,979	112,932	165,412	7.9	2.5	3.3	26.5	72.5	17.6	83.9	51.77	6,159	597
Hartford city	(NA)	(NA)	339,806	175,313	301,949	12.3	8.2	5.9	25.9	73.6	16.3	83.8	44.29	6,121	654
Meriden city	(NA)	(NA)	163,950	79,417	159,389	5.8	3.3	1.7	28.3	73.4	20.3	84.2	52.35	5,791	669
Middletown city	(NA)	(NA)	120,781	67,250	121,681	11.5	3.6	2.6	29.9	74.0	22.9	81.9	44.15	5,466	789
Milford city (balance)	(NA)	(NA)	138,251	105,043	130,756	5.9	6.4	1.7	29.9	74.0	22.9	81.9	44.15	5,466	789
Naugatuck borough	1,174	4,044,653	76,610	38,079	76,619	4.9	1.3	1.7	29.9	74.0	22.9	81.9	44.15	5,466	789
New Britain city	2,444	8,955,759	233,855	79,124	200,556	5.9	7.8	2.2	28.3	73.4	20.3	84.2	52.35	5,791	669
New Haven city	(NA)	(NA)	606,927	140,813	713,761	4.3	2.1	2.5	25.9	72.5	16.9	82.8	52.73	6,271	558
New London city	1,045	3,406,785	91,610	30,492	87,335	9.8	6.9	1.4	28.9	71.8	20.0	80.7	48.72	5,799	511
Norwalk city	2,562	10,294,815	240,215	175,029	237,492	6.3	0.1	8.2	27.8	73.4	18.8	84.2	48.38	5,854	652
Norwich city	1,179	3,817,818	104,932	43,948	99,342	8.7	6.5	1.0	27.6	73.2	17.3	83.8	52.73	5,916	627
Shelton city	(NA)	(NA)	89,377	66,090	87,556	4.8	4.2	2.6	29.9	74.0	22.9	81.9	44.15	5,466	789
Stamford city	3,784	18,021,421	381,383	272,702	366,447	11.7	6.5	2.7	28.7	73.5	19.2	85.4	52.79	5,582	692
Torrington city	(NA)	(NA)	(NA)	(NA)	(NA)	(NA)	(NA)	(NA)	23.6	69.5	13.9	80.7	54.59	6,839	323
Waterbury city	(NA)	(NA)	370,576	154,753	310,892	8.2	6.0	1.8	25.9	72.5	16.9	82.8	52.73	6,271	558
West Haven city	(NA)	(NA)	128,833	64,751	124,976	10.3	6.0	2.8	25.9	72.5	16.9	82.8	52.73	6,271	558
DELAWARE	(X)	(X)	(X)	(X)	(X)	(NA)	(NA)	(NA)	(X)	(X)	(X)	(X)	(X)	(X)	(X)
Dover city	368	1,182,649	22,423	9,293	24,551	38.1	25.4	7.9	35.3	77.8	26.9	87.4	46.28	4,212	1,262
Newark city	287	839,846	16,720	5,658	21,659	24.5	25.4	9.5	32.5	76.4	23.5	87.6	45.35	4,746	1,047
Wilmington city	(NA)	(NA)	135,840	81,729	146,318	24.2	11.4	14.2	31.5	76.6	23.7	86.0	42.81	4,888	1,125

See footnotes at end of table.

Table C-6. Cities — **Government and Climate**—Con.

[Includes states and 1,265 incorporated places of 25,000 or more population as of April 1, 2000, in all states except Hawaii, which has no incorporated places recognized by the U.S. Census Bureau. Two census designated places (CDPs) are also included (Honolulu CDP in Hawaii and Arlington CDP in Virginia). For more information on these areas, see Appendix C, Geographic Information]

City	City government employment, March 2002		City government finances, 2001–2002						Climate, 1971–2000[2]						
			General revenue ($1,000)		General expenditure				Average daily temperature (degrees Fahrenheit)		Min. and max. temperatures (degrees Fahrenheit)				
						By selected function, percent of total									
	Total employment	Total payroll ($1,000)	Total	Taxes	Total[1] ($1,000)	Police protection	Sewerage and solid waste management	Highways	January	July	January[3]	July[4]	Annual precipitation (inches)	Heating degree days[5]	Cooling degree days[6]
DISTRICT OF COLUMBIA . . .	(X)	(X)	(X)	(X)	(X)	(NA)	(NA)	(NA)	34.9	79.2	27.3	88.3	39.35	4,055	1,531
Washington city.	36,476	145,396,728	6,237,775	3,227,909	6,378,532	6.0	4.0	1.1	34.9	79.2	27.3	88.3	39.35	4,055	1,531
FLORIDA	(X)	(X)	(X)	(X)	(X)	(NA)	(NA)	(NA)	(X)	(X)	(X)	(X)	(X)	(X)	(X)
Altamonte Springs city	452	1,347,784	46,277	20,559	38,890	20.1	16.4	7.5	58.7	81.5	47.0	91.9	51.31	799	3,017
Apopka city	346	1,205,161	28,259	10,028	25,163	19.8	21.3	8.1	58.7	81.5	47.0	91.9	51.31	799	3,017
Aventura city.	(NA)	(NA)	(NA)	(NA)	(NA)	(NA)	(NA)	(NA)	67.9	82.7	62.6	87.0	46.60	141	4,090
Boca Raton city	1,494	4,955,387	144,930	68,607	118,961	17.6	9.9	5.7	67.2	83.3	57.8	91.8	57.27	219	4,241
Bonita Springs city	25	54,699	(NA)	(NA)	(NA)	(NA)	(NA)	(NA)	64.3	82.0	53.4	91.2	51.90	316	3,646
Boynton Beach city	887	2,991,500	72,409	34,413	63,872	19.2	25.5	1.6	66.2	82.5	57.3	90.1	61.39	246	3,999
Bradenton city.	571	1,477,732	40,487	20,666	36,337	21.0	31.5	5.5	61.6	81.9	50.9	91.3	54.12	538	3,327
Cape Coral city	1,386	3,437,834	132,451	41,026	80,290	18.1	6.3	8.4	62.7	81.3	50.3	91.3	50.07	427	3,287
Clearwater city	1,822	5,931,503	162,311	64,693	181,739	16.5	20.3	2.9	61.3	82.5	52.4	89.7	44.77	591	3,482
Coconut Creek city.	313	1,003,687	30,770	17,151	27,722	29.3	11.4	15.2	67.2	83.3	57.8	91.8	57.27	219	4,241
Cooper City city.	318	744,158	20,080	10,983	22,983	26.4	9.3	6.6	67.5	82.6	59.2	89.8	64.19	167	4,120
Coral Gables city.	881	3,820,469	90,229	54,526	96,308	26.4	14.8	5.0	67.9	82.7	62.6	87.0	46.60	141	4,090
Coral Springs city	974	3,172,329	84,420	47,336	81,425	29.2	3.9	5.5	67.2	83.3	57.8	91.8	57.27	219	4,241
Dania Beach city	(NA)	(NA)	(NA)	(NA)	(NA)	(NA)	(NA)	(NA)	67.5	82.6	59.2	89.8	64.19	167	4,120
Davie town	601	2,524,372	57,005	36,931	59,271	34.1	–	5.7	66.2	82.5	57.3	90.1	61.39	246	3,999
Daytona Beach city	(NA)	(NA)	75,285	32,016	78,332	26.2	22.3	9.5	57.1	81.2	44.5	91.2	57.03	954	2,819
Deerfield Beach city.	618	2,071,394	60,627	26,236	62,169	15.4	23.6	2.8	67.2	83.3	57.8	91.8	57.27	219	4,241
Delray Beach city.	759	2,884,168	77,376	40,059	86,812	22.1	3.0	7.9	66.2	82.5	57.3	90.1	61.39	246	3,999
Deltona city	185	454,686	25,763	11,529	23,079	17.9	16.2	10.2	57.1	81.2	44.5	91.2	57.03	954	2,819
Dunedin city	404	1,140,804	29,066	11,078	26,666	11.1	31.5	2.3	60.9	82.5	50.2	91.3	52.42	623	3,414
Fort Lauderdale city	(NA)	(NA)	237,643	120,530	231,291	28.6	8.8	3.6	67.5	82.6	59.2	89.8	64.19	167	4,120
Fort Myers city	(NA)	(NA)	90,870	30,177	94,313	15.3	19.8	9.4	64.9	83.0	54.5	91.7	54.19	302	3,957
Fort Pierce city	(NA)	(NA)	(NA)	(NA)	(NA)	(NA)	(NA)	(NA)	62.6	81.7	50.7	91.5	53.50	477	3,430
Gainesville city	2,120	6,207,881	109,470	27,890	112,474	19.6	22.7	8.0	54.4	81.1	41.8	92.4	49.56	1,249	2,608
Greenacres city	198	551,131	13,441	8,869	12,262	38.8	5.4	9.0	66.2	82.5	57.3	90.1	61.39	246	3,999
Hallandale Beach city	(NA)	(NA)	(NA)	(NA)	(NA)	(NA)	(NA)	(NA)	68.1	83.7	59.6	90.9	58.53	149	4,361
Hialeah city.	1,658	5,225,130	177,718	88,997	180,928	16.9	20.3	10.1	67.9	82.7	62.6	87.0	46.60	141	4,090
Hollywood city	1,672	7,022,795	160,655	65,422	162,869	30.7	21.5	6.4	67.5	82.6	59.2	89.8	64.19	167	4,120
Homestead city	(NA)	(NA)	(NA)	(NA)	(NA)	(NA)	(NA)	(NA)	67.0	81.8	56.2	90.6	55.55	238	3,923
Jacksonville city.	10,559	37,092,409	1,252,333	589,834	1,478,622	10.1	22.4	3.3	54.5	82.5	42.6	92.7	51.88	1,222	2,810
Jupiter town	360	1,266,007	34,553	17,516	26,297	34.4	7.6	1.9	66.2	82.5	57.3	90.1	61.39	246	3,999
Key West city	454	1,575,745	64,601	13,361	55,905	10.9	29.1	3.8	70.3	84.5	65.2	89.4	38.94	62	4,830
Kissimmee city	(NA)	(NA)	56,073	13,511	45,273	24.5	4.9	12.8	59.7	81.8	47.7	91.6	48.01	694	3,111
Lakeland city	2,278	6,958,729	123,311	28,591	103,816	20.2	14.2	11.7	62.5	84.0	51.1	94.6	49.13	487	3,886
Lake Worth city	576	1,932,804	45,565	13,625	42,692	20.4	22.6	6.9	65.1	81.1	52.5	91.3	58.44	273	3,438
Largo city	(NA)	(NA)	68,177	26,990	70,810	14.7	34.2	2.1	61.3	82.5	52.4	89.7	44.77	591	3,482
Lauderdale Lakes city	176	566,305	20,064	8,692	21,098	24.2	2.3	4.1	67.2	83.3	57.8	91.8	57.27	219	4,241
Lauderhill city	441	1,518,940	26,632	12,469	29,327	28.5	13.4	3.5	67.5	82.6	59.2	89.8	64.19	167	4,120
Margate city	(NA)	(NA)	37,886	22,029	34,910	37.2	2.2	10.7	67.2	83.3	57.8	91.8	57.27	219	4,241
Melbourne city.	910	2,810,074	78,816	28,182	75,468	20.6	22.6	6.7	60.9	81.2	50.0	90.5	48.29	595	3,186
Miami city.	(NA)	(NA)	462,047	231,565	442,108	22.6	7.6	2.2	68.1	83.7	59.6	90.9	58.53	149	4,361
Miami Beach city	1,793	8,162,312	278,098	129,304	253,885	20.0	14.4	2.0	68.1	83.7	59.6	90.9	58.53	149	4,361
Miami Gardens city	(X)	(X)	(X)	(X)	(X)	(NA)	(NA)	(NA)	68.1	83.7	59.6	90.9	58.53	149	4,361
Miramar city	770	2,552,617	65,087	36,853	70,313	19.0	14.8	3.6	68.1	83.7	59.6	90.9	58.53	149	4,361
North Lauderdale city	179	451,558	20,119	9,469	19,966	31.0	5.6	4.3	67.5	82.6	59.2	89.8	64.19	167	4,120
North Miami city	631	2,102,903	44,504	16,442	44,437	23.5	23.6	7.8	68.1	83.7	59.6	90.9	58.53	149	4,361
North Miami Beach city.	(NA)	(NA)	45,214	16,845	44,030	25.0	26.1	5.8	68.1	83.7	59.6	90.9	58.53	149	4,361
Oakland Park city	333	1,194,605	(NA)	(NA)	(NA)	(NA)	(NA)	(NA)	67.5	82.6	59.2	89.8	64.19	167	4,120
Ocala city.	(NA)	(NA)	69,137	24,564	72,266	19.2	32.7	10.0	58.1	81.7	45.7	92.2	49.68	902	2,971
Orlando city	(NA)	(NA)	405,395	142,383	403,996	17.1	20.1	11.6	60.9	82.4	49.9	92.2	48.35	580	3,428
Ormond Beach city	(NA)	(NA)	(NA)	(NA)	(NA)	(NA)	(NA)	(NA)	60.9	82.4	49.9	92.2	48.35	580	3,428
Oviedo city.	261	852,070	20,538	10,299	26,279	58.7	1.5	5.1	58.7	81.5	47.0	91.9	51.31	799	3,017
Palm Bay city	772	2,090,509	49,041	28,386	49,421	22.3	12.5	21.9	60.9	81.2	50.0	90.5	48.29	595	3,186
Palm Beach Gardens city	434	1,347,317	(NA)	(NA)	(NA)	(NA)	(NA)	(NA)	66.2	82.5	57.3	90.1	61.39	246	3,999
Palm Coast city.	98	245,422	16,796	7,581	12,228	6.0	–	11.5	57.4	82.8	46.4	92.0	49.79	909	3,193
Panama City city	530	1,256,990	34,956	19,395	34,081	19.2	9.6	17.3	50.3	80.0	38.7	89.0	64.76	1,810	2,174
Pembroke Pines city.	1,159	4,266,306	116,221	45,353	120,727	17.5	7.8	4.1	67.5	82.6	59.2	89.8	64.19	167	4,120
Pensacola city	1,079	2,869,015	82,951	34,380	93,321	17.6	5.8	6.5	52.0	82.6	42.7	90.7	64.28	1,498	2,650
Pinellas Park city	583	1,847,740	54,612	23,647	42,527	18.8	21.4	14.6	61.7	83.4	54.0	90.2	49.58	548	3,718
Plantation city	894	2,798,042	64,757	36,430	64,932	35.2	6.3	8.9	67.5	82.6	59.2	89.8	64.19	167	4,120
Plant City city	385	1,088,785	34,436	14,298	29,181	18.0	30.8	6.4	61.1	81.5	49.8	90.8	51.17	625	3,261
Pompano Beach city	729	2,748,922	99,987	54,526	86,685	26.5	18.8	4.8	67.2	83.3	57.8	91.8	57.27	219	4,241
Port Orange city	(NA)	(NA)	42,080	16,435	35,494	17.1	21.3	6.8	57.1	81.2	44.5	91.2	57.03	954	2,819
Port St. Lucie city	799	2,199,153	61,917	20,681	66,180	15.4	28.1	15.4	64.5	81.8	54.7	89.5	59.53	315	3,600
Riviera Beach city	434	1,360,035	37,626	22,427	37,660	26.0	8.4	8.0	66.2	82.5	57.3	90.1	61.39	246	3,999

See footnotes at end of table.

Table C-6. Cities — **Government and Climate**—Con.

[Includes states and 1,265 incorporated places of 25,000 or more population as of April 1, 2000, in all states except Hawaii, which has no incorporated places recognized by the U.S. Census Bureau. Two census designated places (CDPs) are also included (Honolulu CDP in Hawaii and Arlington CDP in Virginia). For more information on these areas, see Appendix C, Geographic Information]

City	City government employment, March 2002 — Total employment	Total payroll ($1,000)	General revenue ($1,000) Total	Taxes	General expenditure Total[1] ($1,000)	Police protection	Sewerage and solid waste management	Highways	Avg daily temp January	July	Min/max temp January[3]	July[4]	Annual precipitation (inches)	Heating degree days[5]	Cooling degree days[6]
FLORIDA—Con.															
St. Petersburg city	3,700	10,681,714	339,500	112,122	338,673	16.8	28.6	2.6	61.7	83.4	54.0	90.2	49.58	548	3,718
Sanford city	458	1,313,090	(NA)	(NA)	(NA)	(NA)	(NA)	(NA)	58.7	81.5	47.0	91.9	51.31	799	3,017
Sarasota city	1,014	3,127,461	89,946	42,166	69,023	27.1	24.5	5.0	61.7	83.4	54.0	90.2	49.58	548	3,718
Sunrise city	1,010	9,479,414	109,727	29,022	115,932	13.7	24.5	3.8	67.5	82.6	59.2	89.8	64.19	167	4,120
Tallahassee city	3,312	9,952,245	210,029	58,773	225,388	15.1	23.0	13.4	51.8	82.4	39.7	92.0	63.21	1,604	2,551
Tamarac city	371	1,286,827	44,859	18,072	27,776	27.0	16.3	8.8	67.2	83.3	57.8	91.8	57.27	219	4,241
Tampa city	4,408	15,771,447	507,155	198,641	531,918	19.1	23.5	7.2	61.3	82.5	52.4	89.7	44.77	591	3,482
Titusville city	512	1,363,151	31,878	15,418	31,620	23.8	12.6	3.4	59.9	82.4	49.5	91.4	52.79	677	3,300
Wellington village	(NA)	(NA)	37,392	13,852	27,587	11.7	11.8	6.9	66.2	82.5	57.3	90.1	61.39	246	3,999
Weston city	3	20,313	29,648	14,605	29,977	12.4	11.9	11.7	67.5	82.6	59.2	89.8	64.19	167	4,120
West Palm Beach city	(NA)	(NA)	158,560	68,562	133,191	26.6	5.1	8.8	66.2	82.5	57.3	90.1	61.39	246	3,999
Winter Haven city	547	1,395,716	33,223	14,880	35,956	22.5	43.0	4.9	62.3	82.3	51.0	92.5	50.22	538	3,551
Winter Park city	(NA)	(NA)	(NA)	(NA)	(NA)	(NA)	(NA)	(NA)	60.9	82.4	49.9	92.2	48.35	580	3,428
Winter Springs city	274	764,612	18,330	8,755	15,765	23.1	8.3	15.9	60.9	82.4	49.9	92.2	48.35	580	3,428
GEORGIA	(X)	(X)	(X)	(X)	(X)	(NA)	(NA)	(NA)	(X)	(X)	(X)	(X)	(X)	(X)	(X)
Albany city	1,350	3,188,497	97,867	23,471	92,736	13.0	18.1	7.0	47.5	81.4	35.1	92.5	53.40	2,106	2,264
Alpharetta city	321	772,330	42,849	28,337	50,292	11.6	6.6	14.4	39.5	77.2	29.1	87.5	51.82	3,490	1,327
Athens-Clarke County (balance)	1,614	4,167,491	139,112	46,463	137,097	11.9	12.0	8.5	42.2	79.8	32.9	90.2	47.83	2,861	1,785
Atlanta city	(NA)	(NA)	1,245,450	266,138	1,088,922	12.2	23.3	5.0	41.7	79.5	31.3	90.6	49.10	3,004	1,679
Augusta-Richmond County (balance)	(NA)	(NA)	234,452	70,875	212,572	13.7	13.5	7.5	44.8	80.8	33.1	92.0	44.58	2,525	1,986
Columbus city	3,372	7,908,399	(X)	(X)	(X)	(NA)	(NA)	(NA)	46.8	82.0	36.6	91.7	48.57	2,154	2,296
Dalton city	617	1,546,819	67,159	11,448	80,487	6.4	41.9	11.2	39.4	78.0	28.8	89.8	53.64	3,534	1,393
East Point city	599	1,838,895	32,757	9,969	45,178	19.4	14.8	4.8	42.7	80.0	33.5	89.4	50.20	2,827	1,810
Gainesville city	630	1,667,895	49,232	13,070	58,551	10.5	52.1	4.2	36.0	72.9	24.7	84.0	58.19	4,421	752
Hinesville city	156	450,855	16,102	6,894	15,777	25.1	30.0	12.6	51.6	82.6	40.7	93.3	48.32	1,551	2,539
LaGrange city	390	932,719	29,330	3,779	32,486	17.3	31.3	6.8	42.2	78.7	31.3	89.3	53.38	3,078	1,551
Macon city	1,503	3,576,278	87,054	34,350	88,792	17.0	5.4	3.4	45.5	81.1	34.5	91.8	45.00	2,364	2,115
Marietta city	762	2,607,863	66,120	24,353	85,241	13.6	11.8	6.8	39.4	77.9	28.5	89.3	54.43	3,505	1,403
Peachtree City city	254	752,622	18,283	9,531	19,545	23.1	–	20.6	42.6	79.4	31.8	90.5	50.10	2,958	1,679
Rome city	652	1,735,815	49,659	14,778	47,140	12.0	21.7	5.6	39.4	77.5	29.1	87.7	56.16	3,510	1,360
Roswell city	858	1,940,844	61,745	28,144	66,215	15.6	11.1	15.6	39.5	77.2	29.1	87.5	51.82	3,490	1,327
Savannah city	2,250	6,199,709	198,539	67,247	196,832	14.3	33.0	4.6	49.2	82.1	38.0	92.3	49.58	1,799	2,454
Smyrna city	417	1,104,121	32,849	19,913	35,695	18.9	20.8	9.5	42.7	80.0	33.5	89.4	50.20	2,827	1,810
Valdosta city	597	1,429,994	46,978	13,951	44,433	17.8	21.0	11.4	50.0	80.9	38.0	92.0	53.06	1,782	2,319
Warner Robins city	600	1,223,223	34,757	15,969	33,317	20.5	23.2	9.0	45.5	81.1	34.5	91.8	45.00	2,364	2,115
HAWAII	(X)	(X)	(X)	(X)	(X)	(NA)	(NA)	(NA)	(X)	(X)	(X)	(X)	(X)	(X)	(X)
Honolulu CDP	9,966	32,019,948	1,000,159	534,404	1,181,399	14.2	21.6	9.3	73.0	80.8	65.7	87.8	18.29	–	4,561
IDAHO	(X)	(X)	(X)	(X)	(X)	(NA)	(NA)	(NA)	(X)	(X)	(X)	(X)	(X)	(X)	(X)
Boise City city	1,568	5,014,828	174,897	74,682	191,045	12.6	24.0	1.0	30.2	74.7	23.6	89.2	12.19	5,727	807
Caldwell city	229	475,673	21,978	7,378	23,913	27.7	28.0	9.7	29.3	68.8	19.6	85.7	10.90	6,749	410
Coeur d'Alene city	359	919,007	27,263	11,220	27,805	18.9	18.2	15.0	28.4	68.7	22.1	82.6	26.07	6,540	426
Idaho Falls city	676	1,991,820	53,768	17,087	52,149	14.8	23.4	7.1	19.3	68.4	11.1	85.9	11.02	7,917	322
Lewiston city	(NA)	(NA)	(NA)	(NA)	(NA)	(NA)	(NA)	(NA)	33.7	73.5	28.0	87.6	12.74	5,220	792
Meridian city	183	567,093	17,675	6,923	15,816	26.0	30.5	0.7	29.4	71.8	22.1	89.2	9.94	5,752	579
Nampa city	526	1,351,264	55,762	23,886	47,162	15.8	21.2	9.9	28.9	73.3	20.8	90.5	11.37	5,873	692
Pocatello city	603	1,768,732	43,444	17,378	41,566	16.6	26.1	8.5	24.4	69.2	16.3	87.5	12.58	7,109	387
Twin Falls city	(NA)	(NA)	(NA)	(NA)	(NA)	(NA)	(NA)	(NA)	28.2	72.2	19.7	87.9	9.42	6,300	587
ILLINOIS	(X)	(X)	(X)	(X)	(X)	(NA)	(NA)	(NA)	(X)	(X)	(X)	(X)	(X)	(X)	(X)
Addison village	(NA)	(NA)	31,841	9,901	34,007	24.1	12.4	17.0	22.0	73.3	14.3	83.5	36.27	6,498	830
Alton city	(NA)	(NA)	33,264	7,306	36,376	32.2	11.3	6.8	27.7	78.4	19.4	88.1	38.54	5,149	1,354
Arlington Heights village	711	2,917,103	75,424	40,301	68,331	19.8	2.8	13.8	22.0	73.3	14.3	83.5	36.27	6,498	830
Aurora city	(NA)	(NA)	157,834	73,931	158,699	23.5	5.1	10.9	20.0	72.4	10.5	84.2	38.39	6,859	661
Bartlett village	(NA)	(NA)	21,581	8,851	28,089	21.5	8.1	15.6	19.3	72.6	10.9	83.0	37.22	6,975	679
Belleville city	362	1,079,977	35,823	12,998	35,871	15.8	11.0	14.8	30.9	78.1	22.1	89.6	39.37	4,612	1,339
Berwyn city	531	1,524,352	48,567	25,515	81,149	14.5	4.8	46.8	25.8	75.5	17.3	86.2	40.96	5,555	1,027
Bloomington city	627	2,007,670	73,206	31,826	72,316	15.7	9.3	15.1	22.4	75.2	13.7	85.6	37.45	6,190	998
Bolingbrook village	434	1,444,324	56,728	23,446	85,970	12.4	12.9	14.2	23.1	74.8	14.2	86.8	37.94	6,053	942
Buffalo Grove village	296	1,215,292	38,691	16,737	38,134	22.5	10.1	7.9	18.4	72.1	9.6	82.3	36.56	7,149	624
Burbank city	(NA)	(NA)	17,981	10,265	20,820	22.6	–	8.3	23.5	75.5	16.2	84.7	38.35	6,083	1,001
Calumet City city	(NA)	(NA)	32,477	18,171	37,618	20.2	4.8	15.6	22.0	74.2	14.8	83.7	38.65	6,355	866
Carbondale city	(NA)	(NA)	(NA)	(NA)	(NA)	(NA)	(NA)	(NA)	30.1	76.9	20.8	87.8	45.85	4,930	1,179
Carol Stream village	251	811,253	22,146	6,124	18,821	42.1	8.6	24.9	23.1	74.8	14.2	86.8	37.94	6,053	942
Carpentersville village	(NA)	(NA)	19,662	8,855	23,180	26.5	27.6	6.1	19.3	72.6	10.9	83.0	37.22	6,975	679

See footnotes at end of table.

Table C-6. Cities — **Government and Climate**—Con.

[Includes states and 1,265 incorporated places of 25,000 or more population as of April 1, 2000, in all states except Hawaii, which has no incorporated places recognized by the U.S. Census Bureau. Two census designated places (CDPs) are also included (Honolulu CDP in Hawaii and Arlington CDP in Virginia). For more information on these areas, see Appendix C, Geographic Information]

City	City government employment, March 2002 Total employment	Total payroll ($1,000)	General revenue ($1,000) Total	Taxes	General expenditure Total[1] ($1,000)	By selected function, percent of total Police protection	Sewerage and solid waste management	Highways	Average daily temperature (degrees Fahrenheit) January	July	Min. and max. temperatures (degrees Fahrenheit) January[3]	July[4]	Annual precipitation (inches)	Heating degree days[5]	Cooling degree days[6]
ILLINOIS—Con.															
Champaign city	(NA)	(NA)	63,674	28,445	62,894	15.6	3.9	9.5	33.7	79.0	25.0	89.5	47.93	4,183	1,501
Chicago city	41,432	180,210,052	4,886,942	2,042,303	5,529,215	20.0	8.1	14.7	25.3	75.4	18.3	84.4	38.01	5,787	994
Chicago Heights city	(NA)	(NA)	29,781	15,769	32,605	21.8	9.3	13.7	22.0	74.2	14.8	83.7	38.65	6,355	866
Cicero town	(NA)	(NA)	74,115	41,878	75,900	17.0	4.5	9.2	22.0	73.3	14.3	83.5	36.27	6,498	830
Crystal Lake city	322	1,085,210	32,503	9,517	24,801	23.2	6.8	17.4	28.6	76.3	19.0	87.2	46.96	5,168	1,112
Danville city	(NA)	(NA)	29,444	9,126	28,353	24.6	8.3	10.8	25.8	75.3	17.3	86.2	40.96	5,555	1,027
Decatur city	592	2,239,626	78,028	20,631	58,360	22.6	3.5	15.6	25.8	76.2	17.1	87.8	39.74	5,458	1,142
DeKalb city	291	1,103,214	27,842	12,801	25,537	22.5	4.4	22.3	18.5	73.1	10.3	83.6	37.38	6,979	736
Des Plaines city	585	1,871,636	58,856	32,042	60,310	19.9	8.6	7.4	22.0	73.3	14.3	83.5	36.27	6,498	830
Dolton village	191	487,688	16,978	7,349	19,385	21.4	4.6	15.7	22.0	74.2	14.8	83.7	38.65	6,355	866
Downers Grove village	506	1,962,228	41,937	13,808	45,222	22.5	1.5	20.8	23.1	74.8	14.2	86.8	37.94	6,053	942
East St. Louis city	(NA)	(NA)	39,918	11,520	32,128	20.5	1.9	10.9	29.1	78.6	20.0	88.7	40.33	4,826	1,378
Elgin city	(NA)	(NA)	112,400	33,650	112,985	18.0	4.5	8.7	19.3	72.6	10.9	83.0	37.22	6,975	679
Elk Grove Village village	375	1,639,395	44,898	21,400	36,207	25.8	4.7	21.4	22.0	73.3	14.3	83.5	36.27	6,498	830
Elmhurst city	462	1,693,720	50,111	19,115	54,732	17.5	8.1	20.0	23.1	74.8	14.2	86.8	37.94	6,053	942
Elmwood Park village	219	632,957	19,611	11,882	15,013	21.2	8.0	3.0	22.0	73.3	14.3	83.5	36.27	6,498	830
Evanston city	1,025	3,789,053	125,346	55,226	155,004	10.1	30.6	7.8	22.0	72.9	13.7	83.2	36.80	6,630	702
Freeport city	198	667,188	19,788	5,196	21,461	17.2	17.6	11.1	17.2	71.9	9.0	82.0	34.79	7,317	611
Galesburg city	516	983,504	26,533	9,563	25,667	18.0	4.6	13.3	21.3	74.9	13.5	84.5	37.22	6,347	941
Glendale Heights village	275	864,128	27,694	9,617	25,155	22.8	11.7	26.1	22.0	73.3	14.3	83.5	36.27	6,498	830
Glen Ellyn village	251	718,810	32,284	9,310	26,201	16.3	16.1	16.2	21.7	74.4	12.2	85.7	38.58	6,359	888
Glenview village	484	1,785,568	50,023	19,476	76,094	10.5	2.0	8.3	22.0	73.3	14.3	83.5	36.27	6,498	830
Granite City city	243	886,330	(NA)	(NA)	(NA)	(NA)	(NA)	(NA)	27.7	78.4	19.4	88.1	38.54	5,149	1,354
Gurnee village	224	1,024,524	28,648	7,844	23,005	29.6	4.8	12.6	19.9	72.2	12.1	82.2	35.50	6,955	634
Hanover Park village	(NA)	(NA)	24,806	11,209	24,756	25.2	4.9	17.8	18.4	72.1	9.6	82.3	36.56	7,149	624
Harvey city	(NA)	(NA)	22,230	13,605	19,393	23.4	9.6	13.9	22.0	74.2	14.8	83.7	38.65	6,355	866
Highland Park city	(NA)	(NA)	43,754	22,914	36,049	18.7	1.2	14.5	22.0	72.9	13.7	83.2	36.80	6,630	702
Hoffman Estates village	429	1,813,497	67,866	37,880	57,215	17.9	2.8	7.4	18.4	72.1	9.6	82.3	36.56	7,149	624
Joliet city	(NA)	(NA)	137,370	40,127	147,561	17.1	8.2	24.5	21.7	73.7	13.5	84.6	36.96	6,464	809
Kankakee city	332	1,002,130	33,658	10,065	35,193	16.3	21.4	17.0	21.7	74.4	12.2	85.7	38.58	6,359	888
Lansing village	(NA)	(NA)	27,938	13,342	23,178	30.1	7.0	5.0	21.7	74.4	12.2	85.7	38.58	6,359	888
Lombard village	366	1,406,501	41,531	13,881	39,240	16.5	9.1	27.3	23.1	74.8	14.2	86.8	37.94	6,053	942
Maywood village	(NA)	(NA)	27,385	17,758	34,793	17.1	2.9	7.0	22.0	73.3	14.3	83.5	36.27	6,498	830
Moline city	465	1,723,093	(NA)	(NA)	(NA)	(NA)	(NA)	(NA)	21.8	76.4	13.3	85.1	35.10	6,179	1,100
Mount Prospect village	(NA)	(NA)	44,544	22,893	47,266	20.3	9.3	19.9	22.0	73.3	14.3	83.5	36.27	6,498	830
Mundelein village	199	823,694	23,294	10,723	21,579	25.2	10.6	17.8	18.4	72.1	9.6	82.3	36.56	7,149	624
Naperville city	1,285	5,137,333	130,409	54,934	138,208	18.3	7.9	26.9	23.1	74.8	14.2	86.8	37.94	6,053	942
Niles village	469	1,298,732	37,964	18,288	42,577	18.0	4.9	10.3	22.0	73.3	14.3	83.5	36.27	6,498	830
Normal town	461	1,213,425	35,917	14,980	34,882	17.8	5.3	12.9	25.8	76.2	17.1	87.8	39.74	5,458	1,142
Northbrook village	417	1,398,240	36,117	16,249	41,498	19.7	2.0	26.5	22.0	72.9	13.7	83.2	36.80	6,630	702
North Chicago city	(NA)	(NA)	17,296	6,622	18,911	28.2	7.6	8.9	20.3	71.5	12.0	81.7	34.09	7,031	613
Oak Forest city	230	562,659	14,532	6,569	17,520	24.7	4.5	24.6	22.0	74.2	14.8	83.7	38.65	6,355	866
Oak Lawn village	463	1,897,498	43,364	14,433	42,433	21.9	8.2	10.6	23.5	75.5	16.2	84.7	38.35	6,083	1,001
Oak Park village	558	2,222,238	65,623	34,121	65,620	18.9	4.0	9.3	22.0	73.3	14.3	83.5	36.27	6,498	830
Orland Park village	712	1,703,918	45,176	11,498	53,172	22.6	9.5	5.7	23.5	75.5	16.2	84.7	38.35	6,083	1,001
Palatine village	399	1,826,689	50,909	22,906	58,535	19.1	9.6	11.0	18.4	72.1	9.6	82.3	36.56	7,149	624
Park Ridge city	355	1,314,452	30,810	20,106	36,901	18.1	10.5	15.4	22.0	73.3	14.3	83.5	36.27	6,498	830
Pekin city	(NA)	(NA)	29,647	7,387	34,957	16.0	12.4	11.2	24.4	75.8	15.7	87.4	35.71	5,695	1,088
Peoria city	1,030	3,982,936	121,910	47,003	120,560	15.1	1.5	12.3	22.5	75.1	14.3	85.7	36.03	6,097	998
Quincy city	482	1,325,188	34,311	9,833	32,092	18.5	11.7	14.5	24.9	76.8	16.0	88.0	35.63	5,707	1,117
Rockford city	1,284	5,068,174	130,115	48,790	139,310	22.4	5.7	16.4	19.0	72.9	10.8	83.1	36.63	6,933	768
Rock Island city	529	1,564,357	45,424	12,077	42,506	19.1	11.8	8.7	21.8	76.4	13.3	85.1	35.10	6,179	1,100
Round Lake Beach village	110	335,033	11,691	4,035	7,796	44.4	–	23.8	19.9	72.2	12.1	82.2	35.50	6,955	634
St. Charles city	343	1,367,697	41,441	13,558	54,373	12.9	4.3	26.7	19.3	72.6	10.9	83.0	37.22	6,975	679
Schaumburg village	(NA)	(NA)	86,720	29,293	87,684	26.7	7.0	9.7	18.4	72.1	9.6	82.3	36.56	7,149	624
Skokie village	657	2,523,358	61,344	34,997	51,292	20.3	6.3	8.4	22.0	73.3	14.3	83.5	36.27	6,498	830
Springfield city	(NA)	(NA)	116,364	37,250	155,300	15.8	4.0	15.0	25.1	76.3	17.1	86.5	35.56	5,596	1,165
Streamwood village	218	1,014,082	20,641	10,429	20,821	28.6	–	23.3	19.3	72.6	10.9	83.0	37.22	6,975	679
Tinley Park village	344	967,097	34,402	11,866	23,256	38.1	3.5	16.5	21.8	76.4	13.3	85.1	35.10	6,179	1,100
Urbana city	356	988,951	31,981	12,525	29,554	15.7	2.7	28.9	20.7	73.2	12.4	83.7	34.47	6,606	774
Waukegan city	668	2,541,689	61,598	23,135	58,772	31.8	6.8	10.3	20.3	71.5	12.0	81.7	34.09	7,031	613
Wheaton city	(NA)	(NA)	36,090	14,796	35,509	26.0	4.4	18.5	23.1	74.8	14.2	86.8	37.94	6,053	942
Wheeling village	(NA)	(NA)	29,840	12,197	32,299	25.8	5.6	22.2	18.4	72.1	9.6	82.3	36.56	7,149	624
Wilmette village	220	1,038,062	24,471	13,044	29,760	19.8	10.7	32.5	22.0	73.3	14.3	83.5	36.27	6,498	830
Woodridge village	210	749,954	19,949	8,464	18,298	34.1	2.0	12.0	23.1	74.8	14.2	86.8	37.94	6,053	942

See footnotes at end of table.

Table C-6. Cities — **Government and Climate**—Con.

[Includes states and 1,265 incorporated places of 25,000 or more population as of April 1, 2000, in all states except Hawaii, which has no incorporated places recognized by the U.S. Census Bureau. Two census designated places (CDPs) are also included (Honolulu CDP in Hawaii and Arlington CDP in Virginia). For more information on these areas, see Appendix C, Geographic Information]

City	City government employment, March 2002		City government finances, 2001–2002						Climate, 1971–2000[2]						
			General revenue ($1,000)		General expenditure				Average daily temperature (degrees Fahrenheit)		Min. and max. temperatures (degrees Fahrenheit)				
						By selected function, percent of total									
	Total employment	Total payroll ($1,000)	Total	Taxes	Total[1] ($1,000)	Police protection	Sewerage and solid waste management	Highways	January	July	January[3]	July[4]	Annual precipitation (inches)	Heating degree days[5]	Cooling degree days[6]
INDIANA	(X)	(X)	(X)	(X)	(X)	(NA)	(NA)	(NA)	(X)	(X)	(X)	(X)	(X)	(X)	(X)
Anderson city	977	2,894,384	62,167	29,826	59,986	15.6	19.8	6.6	25.7	74.0	18.4	83.8	39.82	5,807	872
Bloomington city	722	1,973,040	125,922	24,363	135,806	5.9	61.4	6.0	27.9	75.4	19.3	86.0	44.91	5,348	1,017
Carmel city	(NA)	(NA)	49,444	24,359	64,033	10.8	18.2	3.9	25.3	74.2	17.0	84.5	42.85	5,901	873
Columbus city	523	1,350,342	36,969	11,467	38,046	12.4	12.9	6.4	27.9	75.9	19.1	86.4	41.94	5,367	1,059
East Chicago city	933	2,483,338	92,838	41,353	77,642	16.0	25.1	4.1	23.7	74.0	15.3	84.8	38.13	6,055	887
Elkhart city	671	2,116,258	66,272	25,329	67,430	15.0	18.2	5.6	22.8	72.1	14.3	83.3	38.56	6,487	663
Evansville city	1,425	4,084,497	136,823	61,083	150,492	15.8	13.2	3.7	33.2	79.6	24.8	90.5	45.76	4,140	1,616
Fishers town	(NA)	(NA)	26,312	14,606	29,074	16.0	22.0	8.2	25.3	74.2	17.0	84.5	42.85	5,901	873
Fort Wayne city	1,979	6,517,364	144,701	75,910	171,614	18.9	14.1	9.7	23.6	73.4	16.1	84.3	36.55	6,205	830
Gary city	1,827	4,528,028	163,585	65,929	177,292	11.5	14.1	5.6	22.2	73.5	13.9	83.9	38.02	6,497	776
Goshen city	(NA)	(NA)	23,888	7,780	25,889	12.8	18.4	4.7	24.3	73.7	17.0	84.5	36.59	6,075	826
Greenwood city	345	822,810	46,102	8,037	42,545	10.3	4.1	4.9	25.7	74.7	18.0	84.0	40.24	5,783	942
Hammond city	(NA)	(NA)	141,879	29,927	146,241	10.6	8.6	4.1	22.2	73.5	13.9	83.9	38.02	6,497	776
Hobart city	325	743,338	26,031	10,409	30,398	11.1	12.7	5.6	22.2	73.5	13.9	83.9	38.02	6,497	776
Indianapolis city (balance)	(NA)	(NA)	1,643,416	628,805	1,825,830	7.9	9.6	5.3	26.5	75.4	18.5	85.6	40.95	5,521	1,042
Jeffersonville city	231	671,152	(NA)	(NA)	(NA)	(NA)	(NA)	(NA)	31.3	75.8	21.4	88.5	45.47	4,829	1,079
Kokomo city	563	1,735,919	(NA)	(NA)	(NA)	(NA)	(NA)	(NA)	22.8	73.0	15.0	84.1	41.54	6,368	771
Lafayette city	724	2,174,442	74,866	27,324	60,701	13.2	38.9	8.3	23.0	73.5	14.3	84.5	36.90	6,206	842
Lawrence city	192	642,032	20,255	8,890	21,273	20.6	12.9	21.1	25.7	74.7	18.0	84.0	40.24	5,783	942
Marion city	293	687,108	22,545	12,099	23,165	19.2	13.3	9.8	24.2	73.8	16.3	84.5	39.01	6,143	819
Merrillville town	153	426,042	12,478	7,202	17,516	20.7	–	12.2	21.1	72.7	12.1	83.6	40.04	6,642	734
Michigan City city	487	1,531,921	(NA)	(NA)	(NA)	(NA)	(NA)	(NA)	23.4	73.0	15.7	83.1	39.70	6,294	812
Mishawaka city	602	1,764,582	41,750	22,755	43,558	12.6	9.7	9.6	24.3	73.7	17.0	84.5	36.59	6,075	826
Muncie city	670	1,542,432	55,222	30,038	54,336	22.3	26.9	6.9	24.4	72.5	15.9	83.9	41.23	6,215	717
New Albany city	309	877,754	(NA)	(NA)	(NA)	(NA)	(NA)	(NA)	31.3	75.8	21.4	88.5	45.47	4,829	1,079
Noblesville city	(NA)	(NA)	31,762	19,047	36,974	11.2	15.8	9.9	25.3	74.2	17.0	84.5	42.85	5,901	873
Portage city	253	643,254	23,324	10,384	27,369	13.5	17.1	15.0	22.9	73.0	15.5	83.1	40.06	6,270	745
Richmond city	625	1,859,586	(NA)	(NA)	(NA)	(NA)	(NA)	(NA)	25.7	73.1	17.2	84.6	39.55	5,942	769
South Bend city	1,600	100	176,456	62,888	192,496	11.3	21.0	3.9	23.4	73.0	15.7	83.1	39.70	6,294	812
Terre Haute city	685	1,527,406	47,353	25,797	47,148	12.5	14.9	7.4	26.5	76.2	17.7	87.3	42.47	5,433	1,107
Valparaiso city	(NA)	(NA)	24,126	10,036	21,406	12.7	28.7	7.7	22.9	73.0	15.5	83.1	40.06	6,270	745
West Lafayette city	200	596,658	35,054	10,545	32,352	11.5	33.5	6.5	25.2	75.5	17.2	86.3	36.32	5,732	1,024
IOWA	(X)	(X)	(X)	(X)	(X)	(NA)	(NA)	(NA)	(X)	(X)	(X)	(X)	(X)	(X)	(X)
Ames city	807	1,942,492	146,674	17,613	139,513	3.6	4.8	13.5	18.5	73.8	9.6	84.3	34.07	6,791	830
Ankeny city	264	528,526	22,996	12,716	21,363	14.8	6.5	12.8	18.2	74.8	8.7	85.8	33.38	6,961	881
Bettendorf city	340	891,144	34,182	21,189	38,456	12.4	7.9	24.2	21.1	76.2	13.2	85.4	34.11	6,246	1,072
Burlington city	289	783,796	26,094	12,308	29,661	12.4	17.9	25.2	22.8	76.3	15.1	85.4	37.94	5,948	1,095
Cedar Falls city	502	1,405,014	44,143	17,230	39,405	8.0	13.3	29.0	16.1	73.6	6.3	85.0	33.15	7,348	758
Cedar Rapids city	1,467	4,880,435	181,733	65,414	195,494	10.1	20.2	16.6	19.9	74.8	11.5	85.3	36.62	6,488	910
Clinton city	277	692,510	(NA)	(NA)	(NA)	(NA)	(NA)	(NA)	20.4	74.7	12.5	85.0	35.68	6,416	915
Council Bluffs city	533	1,798,529	69,133	39,170	79,319	12.4	24.5	19.8	21.1	76.2	10.4	87.7	33.25	6,323	1,057
Davenport city	935	3,084,468	117,003	53,219	120,335	6.1	11.5	21.7	21.1	76.2	13.2	85.4	34.11	6,246	1,072
Des Moines city	2,330	8,371,160	288,090	101,878	345,444	10.1	13.2	6.5	20.4	76.1	11.7	86.0	34.72	6,436	1,052
Dubuque city	718	1,993,135	73,663	26,433	80,328	11.4	8.9	16.1	17.8	75.1	8.7	85.4	33.96	6,891	908
Fort Dodge city	235	635,174	25,232	11,303	25,932	10.3	14.4	14.7	15.4	73.1	5.8	84.3	34.39	7,513	746
Iowa City city	(NA)	(NA)	78,764	24,616	92,239	7.7	24.5	15.1	21.7	76.9	13.4	87.5	37.27	6,052	1,134
Marion city	(NA)	(NA)	19,613	10,597	17,693	17.6	17.7	21.7	16.8	73.9	7.1	84.4	36.40	7,191	787
Marshalltown city	258	710,728	21,336	10,777	21,029	18.9	15.8	17.9	16.8	73.9	7.1	84.4	36.40	7,191	787
Mason City city	(NA)	(NA)	27,668	13,646	24,167	16.4	13.8	16.1	13.9	72.4	5.1	83.3	34.48	7,765	655
Sioux City city	984	2,908,858	112,354	47,504	112,815	12.0	10.0	11.2	18.6	74.6	8.5	86.2	25.99	6,900	914
Urbandale city	235	573,425	19,912	14,154	18,972	18.1	7.0	15.9	20.4	76.1	11.7	86.0	34.72	6,436	1,052
Waterloo city	698	2,019,855	83,338	39,117	73,388	9.5	18.6	15.2	16.1	73.6	6.3	85.0	33.15	7,348	758
West Des Moines city	494	1,297,775	(NA)	(NA)	(NA)	(NA)	(NA)	(NA)	20.4	76.1	11.7	86.0	34.72	6,436	1,052
KANSAS	(X)	(X)	(X)	(X)	(X)	(NA)	(NA)	(NA)	(X)	(X)	(X)	(X)	(X)	(X)	(X)
Dodge City city	261	575,989	24,369	10,064	25,299	10.5	10.2	4.7	30.1	79.8	18.7	92.8	22.35	5,037	1,481
Emporia city	288	814,470	19,677	7,648	27,407	13.0	31.1	9.0	27.5	78.7	17.3	89.7	35.11	5,187	1,339
Garden City city	297	777,107	22,910	9,543	22,387	16.1	13.7	9.9	28.6	77.8	14.7	92.1	18.77	5,423	1,191
Hutchinson city	402	1,274,400	35,843	15,776	28,766	14.1	20.5	7.5	28.5	79.9	17.0	92.7	30.32	5,146	1,454
Kansas City city	2,756	10,589,627	283,113	117,632	288,195	12.4	5.2	7.2	29.1	79.0	19.9	89.4	40.17	4,847	1,406
Lawrence city	(NA)	(NA)	157,440	29,952	153,717	6.2	8.1	3.7	29.9	80.2	20.5	90.6	39.78	4,685	1,582
Leavenworth city	361	971,014	28,919	14,124	26,498	16.8	11.1	8.2	26.6	79.1	16.4	89.8	40.94	5,331	1,356
Leawood city	255	906,953	34,361	19,005	26,715	20.5	–	25.9	29.1	79.0	19.9	89.4	40.17	4,847	1,406
Lenexa city	418	1,568,665	54,618	33,170	61,482	14.1	–	33.4	29.1	79.0	19.9	89.4	40.17	4,847	1,406
Manhattan city	(NA)	(NA)	25,925	14,664	30,662	22.1	10.3	5.4	27.8	79.9	16.1	92.5	34.80	5,120	1,465
Olathe city	(NA)	(NA)	91,111	35,521	85,804	16.1	13.1	3.1	29.1	79.0	19.9	89.4	40.17	4,847	1,406
Overland Park city	815	3,067,781	103,706	70,466	108,405	19.7	–	11.0	29.1	79.0	19.9	89.4	40.17	4,847	1,406
Salina city	581	1,518,510	50,780	19,958	46,670	11.0	13.8	8.8	29.0	81.3	18.8	93.3	32.19	4,952	1,600
Shawnee city	268	1,138,346	47,914	20,570	60,111	13.1	–	36.5	29.1	79.0	19.9	89.4	40.17	4,847	1,406
Topeka city	(NA)	(NA)	133,948	69,828	121,783	16.6	11.8	8.1	27.2	78.4	17.2	89.1	35.64	5,225	1,357
Wichita city	3,515	10,166,987	350,724	112,172	365,658	12.9	9.3	25.3	30.2	81.0	20.3	92.9	30.38	4,765	1,658

See footnotes at end of table.

Table C-6. Cities — **Government and Climate**—Con.

[Includes states and 1,265 incorporated places of 25,000 or more population as of April 1, 2000, in all states except Hawaii, which has no incorporated places recognized by the U.S. Census Bureau. Two census designated places (CDPs) are also included (Honolulu CDP in Hawaii and Arlington CDP in Virginia). For more information on these areas, see Appendix C, Geographic Information]

City	City government employment, March 2002		City government finances, 2001–2002						Climate, 1971–2000[2]						
			General revenue ($1,000)		General expenditure				Average daily temperature (degrees Fahrenheit)		Min. and max. temperatures (degrees Fahrenheit)				
						By selected function, percent of total									
	Total employment	Total payroll ($1,000)	Total	Taxes	Total[1] ($1,000)	Police protection	Sewerage and solid waste management	Highways	January	July	January[3]	July[4]	Annual precipitation (inches)	Heating degree days[5]	Cooling degree days[6]
KENTUCKY	(X)	(X)	(X)	(X)	(X)	(NA)	(NA)	(NA)	(X)	(X)	(X)	(X)	(X)	(X)	(X)
Bowling Green city	658	1,726,091	57,299	30,677	51,683	10.9	7.9	9.8	34.2	78.5	25.4	89.2	51.63	4,243	1,413
Covington city	(NA)	(NA)	57,657	30,329	56,438	19.1	3.6	12.8	32.0	76.1	24.1	85.9	45.91	4,713	1,154
Frankfort city	(NA)	(NA)	40,271	21,149	42,426	8.4	12.4	3.2	30.3	75.2	20.8	86.9	43.56	5,129	994
Henderson city	485	1,271,703	27,736	8,797	26,633	14.1	28.3	3.9	32.6	77.6	23.6	88.4	44.77	4,374	1,344
Hopkinsville city	(NA)	(NA)	31,615	13,892	28,050	11.9	15.7	6.3	33.2	78.2	24.4	88.5	50.92	4,298	1,433
Jeffersontown city	113	411,264	25,091	12,448	20,744	18.4	9.9	6.7	33.0	78.4	24.9	87.0	44.54	4,352	1,443
Lexington-Fayette	4,128	11,187,113	324,724	197,059	352,891	12.0	18.5	7.0	31.6	75.9	22.5	86.3	46.39	4,769	1,094
Louisville/Jefferson County (balance)	(X)	(X)	(X)	(X)	(X)	(NA)	(NA)	(NA)	33.0	78.4	24.9	87.0	44.54	4,352	1,443
Owensboro city	741	2,183,416	62,056	22,881	66,523	11.4	9.4	4.3	33.5	79.2	24.4	90.7	46.53	4,159	1,565
Paducah city	572	1,540,213	46,145	22,168	45,094	12.0	13.9	10.3	35.2	79.9	27.2	90.8	46.04	3,893	1,635
Richmond city	(NA)	(NA)	25,228	13,081	26,010	8.8	8.7	2.4	34.7	75.8	25.6	87.0	47.33	4,231	1,150
LOUISIANA	(X)	(X)	(X)	(X)	(X)	(NA)	(NA)	(NA)	(X)	(X)	(X)	(X)	(X)	(X)	(X)
Alexandria city	903	2,204,511	54,421	28,383	56,057	17.9	22.5	5.8	48.1	83.3	38.0	92.8	61.44	1,908	2,602
Baton Rouge city	7,215	17,776,617	644,596	335,063	587,865	8.9	12.6	8.1	50.1	81.7	40.2	90.7	63.08	1,689	2,628
Bossier City city	(NA)	(NA)	77,058	49,095	67,248	14.2	12.3	11.6	48.3	81.0	37.4	91.0	61.06	1,981	2,220
Houma city	(NA)	(NA)	(NA)	(NA)	(NA)	(NA)	(NA)	(NA)	53.1	82.5	43.4	90.7	63.67	1,346	2,804
Kenner city	756	1,846,629	67,691	18,734	73,983	23.1	11.5	18.9	52.6	82.7	43.4	91.1	64.16	1,417	2,773
Lafayette city	2,580	5,994,222	197,021	98,329	219,187	12.0	7.9	12.9	51.3	82.2	41.6	91.2	60.54	1,531	2,671
Lake Charles city	879	2,032,679	79,149	51,933	66,011	13.4	12.6	16.2	50.9	82.6	41.2	91.0	57.19	1,546	2,705
Monroe city	1,197	2,448,026	102,637	57,253	112,372	8.6	19.9	14.1	44.6	83.0	33.5	94.1	58.04	2,399	2,311
New Iberia city	309	597,911	22,384	15,441	22,337	18.4	27.8	8.9	51.3	82.3	41.4	91.1	60.89	1,544	2,680
New Orleans city	9,855	24,907,120	946,695	403,252	852,828	12.3	13.6	5.7	52.7	82.2	43.3	90.9	65.15	1,416	2,686
Shreveport city	2,868	7,132,528	272,950	153,001	260,806	13.0	12.5	5.3	46.4	83.4	36.5	93.3	51.30	2,251	2,405
Slidell city	355	858,226	32,381	23,252	34,740	17.7	15.3	15.8	50.7	82.1	40.2	91.1	62.66	1,652	2,548
MAINE	(X)	(X)	(X)	(X)	(X)	(NA)	(NA)	(NA)	(X)	(X)	(X)	(X)	(X)	(X)	(X)
Bangor city	1,467	3,402,587	96,498	41,910	120,975	4.3	5.6	–	18.0	69.2	8.3	79.6	39.57	7,676	313
Lewiston city	1,258	3,399,194	81,895	42,789	82,514	5.1	6.2	7.0	20.5	71.4	11.5	81.5	45.79	7,107	465
Portland city	3,095	8,602,777	217,184	109,196	242,938	2.1	7.2	3.7	21.7	68.7	12.5	78.8	45.83	7,318	347
MARYLAND	(X)	(X)	(X)	(X)	(X)	(NA)	(NA)	(NA)	(X)	(X)	(X)	(X)	(X)	(X)	(X)
Annapolis city	552	1,936,740	46,244	21,512	46,994	23.3	12.1	15.4	32.8	77.5	23.8	87.7	44.78	4,695	1,162
Baltimore city	29,418	101,478,910	2,418,603	806,201	2,159,832	11.8	5.5	5.4	36.8	81.7	29.4	90.6	43.59	4,720	1,147
Bowie city	281	759,146	23,170	10,764	21,348	3.3	30.5	13.1	31.8	75.2	21.2	87.1	44.66	4,970	917
Frederick city	615	1,880,124	54,157	23,572	62,447	20.0	9.0	19.6	33.3	77.9	25.1	88.9	40.64	4,430	1,272
Gaithersburg city	386	993,331	33,219	14,387	33,686	10.5	5.0	5.8	31.8	75.3	23.8	85.4	43.08	4,990	983
Hagerstown city	(NA)	(NA)	42,358	13,999	34,346	26.5	19.0	6.4	29.3	75.2	20.8	86.1	39.45	5,249	902
Rockville city	(NA)	(NA)	58,442	23,781	57,319	7.6	12.1	12.5	31.8	75.3	23.8	85.4	43.08	4,990	983
MASSACHUSETTS	(X)	(X)	(X)	(X)	(X)	(NA)	(NA)	(NA)	(X)	(X)	(X)	(X)	(X)	(X)	(X)
Agawam city	(NA)	(NA)	64,058	34,288	69,377	4.7	4.4	5.3	25.7	73.7	17.2	84.9	46.16	6,104	759
Attleboro city	(NA)	(NA)	95,075	40,080	87,732	5.4	5.4	2.5	27.4	72.2	17.8	83.0	48.34	6,012	558
Barnstable Town city	(NA)	(NA)	119,150	76,825	113,451	7.4	3.3	3.4	29.2	70.5	21.2	77.8	43.03	6,026	413
Beverly city	(NA)	(NA)	93,062	56,621	101,991	5.0	9.7	4.1	28.8	72.6	20.4	82.1	45.51	5,704	582
Boston city	22,630	89,188,595	2,574,620	1,049,473	2,470,901	10.4	6.3	2.1	29.3	73.9	22.1	82.2	42.53	5,630	777
Brockton city	3,512	11,219,747	288,051	84,952	288,214	4.8	4.6	2.6	27.9	72.1	17.8	83.2	48.25	6,008	529
Cambridge city	3,399	10,572,908	728,343	207,804	748,417	3.7	2.8	0.7	29.3	73.9	22.1	82.2	42.53	5,630	777
Chelsea city	(NA)	(NA)	112,495	25,818	113,075	6.4	2.0	1.8	29.3	73.9	22.1	82.2	42.53	5,630	777
Chicopee city	(NA)	(NA)	128,535	49,350	123,618	5.7	5.8	3.8	21.5	68.9	10.4	81.7	48.07	7,312	287
Everett city	1,248	4,338,128	92,565	50,486	118,840	5.4	3.1	2.9	29.3	73.9	22.1	82.2	42.53	5,630	777
Fall River city	3,451	8,577,916	218,994	45,597	253,567	6.5	3.1	5.0	28.5	74.2	20.0	83.1	50.77	5,734	740
Fitchburg city	1,288	4,118,528	104,883	29,562	111,762	5.4	5.9	2.7	24.2	71.9	15.2	81.0	49.13	6,576	548
Franklin city	(NA)	(NA)	75,495	40,150	93,592	3.8	5.5	3.3	25.4	72.3	13.3	84.3	48.75	6,302	534
Gloucester city	(NA)	(NA)	74,854	44,813	73,056	6.6	7.3	1.7	28.8	72.6	20.4	82.1	45.51	5,704	582
Haverhill city	2,052	7,352,164	179,631	58,622	181,871	4.4	4.2	2.1	25.3	72.2	15.6	83.5	46.88	6,435	550
Holyoke city	2,459	7,705,626	152,578	38,133	150,459	6.2	3.8	2.8	21.5	68.9	10.4	81.7	48.07	7,312	287
Lawrence city	(NA)	(NA)	227,406	33,600	235,258	4.5	1.8	1.4	24.5	71.9	14.5	82.9	44.09	6,539	510
Leominster city	1,270	4,472,654	89,139	36,748	85,618	6.0	8.1	5.2	24.2	71.9	15.2	81.0	49.13	6,576	548
Lowell city	4,360	15,906,089	299,973	71,484	289,878	6.8	5.1	2.3	23.6	72.4	14.1	84.5	43.14	6,575	532
Lynn city	3,094	10,468,976	260,159	72,640	257,508	6.0	4.2	2.9	29.3	73.9	22.1	82.2	42.53	5,630	777
Malden city	(NA)	(NA)	128,699	48,564	136,779	5.0	2.3	2.0	29.3	73.9	22.1	82.2	42.53	5,630	777
Marlborough city	(NA)	(NA)	89,972	61,704	86,183	6.5	10.7	6.1	25.9	73.4	16.2	84.0	45.87	6,060	651
Medford city	1,318	4,873,653	124,105	65,296	163,446	5.6	3.8	2.0	29.3	73.9	22.1	82.2	42.53	5,630	777
Melrose city	(NA)	(NA)	58,819	34,110	71,803	5.3	2.2	2.4	29.3	73.9	22.1	82.2	42.53	5,630	777
Methuen city	1,339	4,815,698	98,381	46,988	101,028	5.9	2.6	4.5	24.5	71.8	14.5	82.9	44.09	6,539	510
New Bedford city	(NA)	(NA)	266,889	67,296	302,266	6.4	6.6	2.1	28.5	74.2	20.0	83.1	50.77	5,734	740
Newton city	(NA)	(NA)	243,020	177,317	257,024	5.2	3.6	3.6	25.9	73.4	16.2	84.0	45.87	6,060	651
Northampton city	(NA)	(NA)	68,755	30,686	62,868	5.9	6.9	3.9	22.3	71.2	11.2	83.2	45.57	6,856	452
Peabody city	1,693	5,446,372	116,856	59,457	125,828	4.9	2.8	3.0	28.8	72.6	20.4	82.1	45.51	5,704	582
Pittsfield city	1,724	5,961,931	125,508	49,383	130,843	3.8	5.1	2.0	19.9	67.6	11.2	77.5	48.71	7,689	222

See footnotes at end of table.

Table C-6. Cities — **Government and Climate**—Con.

[Includes states and 1,265 incorporated places of 25,000 or more population as of April 1, 2000, in all states except Hawaii, which has no incorporated places recognized by the U.S. Census Bureau. Two census designated places (CDPs) are also included (Honolulu CDP in Hawaii and Arlington CDP in Virginia). For more information on these areas, see Appendix C, Geographic Information]

City	City government employment, March 2002 — Total employment	City government employment, March 2002 — Total payroll ($1,000)	General revenue ($1,000) — Total	General revenue ($1,000) — Taxes	General expenditure — Total¹ ($1,000)	General expenditure — Police protection	General expenditure — Sewerage and solid waste management	General expenditure — Highways	Average daily temperature — January	Average daily temperature — July	Min. and max. temperatures — January³	Min. and max. temperatures — July⁴	Annual precipitation (inches)	Heating degree days⁵	Cooling degree days⁶
MASSACHUSETTS—Con.															
Quincy city	2,372	8,625,277	213,546	124,052	226,110	9.0	3.8	2.6	26.0	71.6	18.1	81.2	51.19	6,371	558
Revere city	(NA)	(NA)	96,094	45,479	103,489	6.0	2.1	4.3	29.3	73.9	22.1	82.2	42.53	5,630	777
Salem city	1,589	4,998,827	106,724	53,101	107,987	6.5	3.9	2.1	28.8	72.6	20.4	82.1	45.51	5,704	582
Somerville city	2,249	7,818,988	163,687	70,933	189,336	7.3	2.5	3.0	29.3	73.9	22.1	82.2	42.53	5,630	777
Springfield city	7,464	22,891,031	541,779	118,004	603,723	6.6	3.9	1.0	25.7	73.7	17.2	84.9	46.16	6,104	759
Taunton city	(NA)	5,738,146	119,011	47,440	126,560	7.2	3.4	3.4	27.4	72.2	17.8	83.0	48.34	6,012	558
Waltham city	1,817	5,812,146	158,687	106,605	141,804	9.6	10.5	4.3	25.4	71.5	15.7	82.7	46.95	6,370	485
Watertown city	(NA)	(NA)	78,515	50,681	87,140	6.9	4.3	2.6	29.3	73.9	22.1	82.2	42.53	5,630	777
Westfield city	1,564	5,358,961	98,633	41,389	99,610	4.9	4.1	5.4	21.5	68.9	10.4	81.7	48.07	7,312	287
West Springfield city	(NA)	(NA)	(NA)	(NA)	(NA)	(NA)	(NA)	(NA)	25.7	73.7	17.2	84.9	46.16	6,104	759
Woburn city	(NA)	(NA)	96,596	60,412	100,077	6.8	2.9	5.4	25.5	71.5	15.7	82.5	48.31	6,401	472
Worcester city	5,785	23,471,608	494,142	158,403	536,146	5.9	3.6	2.3	23.6	70.1	15.8	79.3	49.05	6,831	371
MICHIGAN	(X)	(X)	(X)	(X)	(X)	(NA)	(NA)	(NA)	(X)	(X)	(X)	(X)	(X)	(X)	(X)
Allen Park city	(NA)	(NA)	28,866	15,237	30,324	16.2	17.0	16.4	24.5	73.5	17.8	83.4	32.89	6,422	736
Ann Arbor city	(NA)	(NA)	137,966	60,658	146,632	14.1	13.9	6.0	23.4	72.6	16.6	83.0	35.35	6,503	691
Battle Creek city	731	2,492,031	77,124	25,849	78,456	16.0	20.2	8.5	23.1	71.0	15.3	82.5	35.15	6,742	559
Bay City city	462	1,634,635	54,708	12,278	50,309	13.4	18.8	16.0	21.0	71.5	13.8	81.5	31.25	7,106	545
Burton city	(NA)	(NA)	18,691	5,096	19,818	21.4	33.2	13.3	21.3	70.6	13.3	82.0	31.61	7,005	555
Dearborn city	(NA)	(NA)	136,874	67,563	152,740	14.9	14.3	13.2	24.7	73.7	16.1	85.7	33.58	6,224	788
Dearborn Heights city	(NA)	(NA)	50,304	23,112	64,791	15.3	25.0	5.8	24.7	73.7	16.1	85.7	33.58	6,224	788
Detroit city	42,873	143,882,576	3,876,160	911,526	4,435,986	7.7	11.6	3.5	24.7	73.7	16.1	85.7	33.58	6,224	788
East Lansing city	555	1,705,186	44,470	14,395	57,545	14.2	22.3	8.8	21.6	70.3	13.9	82.1	31.53	7,098	558
Eastpointe city	318	854,791	27,921	11,843	25,840	23.7	11.7	9.8	25.3	73.6	18.8	83.3	33.97	6,160	757
Farmington Hills city	677	1,913,434	76,123	37,658	86,963	18.3	14.8	13.0	24.7	73.7	16.1	85.7	33.58	6,224	788
Flint city	4,110	12,432,818	–	–	–				21.3	70.6	13.3	82.0	31.61	7,005	555
Garden City city	(NA)	(NA)	29,302	9,844	30,279	15.1	11.4	18.9	24.7	73.7	16.1	85.7	33.58	6,224	788
Grand Rapids city	2,361	8,228,929	235,883	82,730	306,442	20.1	10.5	7.5	22.4	71.4	15.6	82.3	37.13	6,896	613
Holland city	565	1,661,995	41,201	15,637	40,445	17.2	18.3	16.5	24.4	71.4	17.6	82.5	36.25	6,589	611
Inkster city	271	764,718	20,059	8,065	21,057	32.7	1.1	19.7	24.5	73.5	17.8	83.4	32.89	6,422	736
Jackson city	436	1,346,182	39,640	14,077	46,445	16.5	13.2	11.2	22.2	71.3	14.7	82.7	30.67	6,873	570
Kalamazoo city	1,018	3,196,760	116,094	31,654	109,065	24.6	20.8	8.6	24.3	73.2	17.0	84.2	37.41	6,235	773
Kentwood city	270	890,836	30,930	14,597	29,352	24.1	7.3	19.4	22.4	71.4	15.6	82.3	37.13	6,896	613
Lansing city	(NA)	(NA)	222,201	68,507	210,622	8.4	16.1	5.3	21.6	70.3	13.9	82.1	31.53	7,098	558
Lincoln Park city	282	907,353	37,867	17,798	33,565	22.9	17.0	15.4	24.5	73.5	17.8	83.4	32.89	6,422	736
Livonia city	1,044	3,288,185	106,454	43,446	114,729	20.1	20.5	11.9	24.7	73.7	16.1	85.7	33.58	6,224	788
Madison Heights city	283	964,376	35,292	17,749	35,746	20.6	16.1	13.1	24.7	73.7	16.1	85.7	33.58	6,224	788
Midland city	477	1,447,294	62,863	29,691	43,004	9.3	12.8	13.7	22.9	72.7	16.2	83.8	30.69	6,645	679
Mount Pleasant city	205	531,344	18,181	4,872	24,084	13.4	29.0	12.1	20.7	70.6	13.5	82.2	31.57	7,329	492
Muskegon city	349	1,111,161	43,039	15,479	44,016	16.3	10.9	21.3	23.5	69.9	17.1	80.0	32.88	6,943	487
Novi city	419	1,203,843	52,233	25,990	49,428	17.2	1.1	30.2	22.1	71.0	14.3	81.7	29.28	6,989	550
Oak Park city	275	872,141	24,618	13,725	28,603	25.3	14.5	14.1	24.7	73.7	16.1	85.7	33.58	6,224	788
Pontiac city	1,014	3,286,816	149,513	48,697	115,398	16.2	11.5	6.5	22.9	71.9	15.9	82.3	30.03	6,680	626
Portage city	302	984,706	36,247	19,014	41,846	18.9	10.1	22.9	24.3	73.2	17.0	84.2	37.41	6,235	773
Port Huron city	471	1,391,681	49,849	20,820	45,620	15.1	24.4	11.7	22.8	72.2	15.1	81.9	31.39	6,845	626
Rochester Hills city	321	1,006,764	50,913	23,422	53,371	10.9	13.3	23.6	22.0	70.6	13.7	82.7	35.74	7,046	523
Roseville city	(NA)	(NA)	45,328	19,006	42,874	21.3	10.7	10.5	25.3	73.6	18.8	83.3	33.97	6,160	757
Royal Oak city	538	1,805,999	63,272	26,915	70,869	13.9	22.9	4.7	24.7	73.7	16.1	85.7	33.58	6,224	788
Saginaw city	623	2,224,944	72,024	21,967	72,263	18.6	16.0	10.0	21.4	71.2	14.9	81.9	31.61	7,099	548
St. Clair Shores city	421	1,425,288	55,444	24,700	52,762	17.8	18.9	14.6	25.3	73.6	18.8	83.3	33.97	6,160	757
Southfield city	1,027	3,528,389	98,465	55,360	115,999	15.3	2.6	13.6	24.7	73.7	16.1	85.7	33.58	6,224	788
Southgate city	281	801,647	27,392	12,852	27,662	16.9	14.4	9.5	24.5	73.5	17.8	83.4	32.89	6,422	736
Sterling Heights city	(NA)	(NA)	98,053	46,691	94,148	22.3	14.5	14.7	24.4	71.9	18.0	81.8	32.24	6,620	597
Taylor city	(NA)	(NA)	103,613	41,252	117,059	8.9	4.4	36.1	24.5	73.5	17.8	83.4	32.89	6,422	736
Troy city	693	2,338,824	91,542	49,242	127,241	16.2	8.1	26.8	22.9	71.9	15.9	82.3	30.03	6,680	626
Warren city	(NA)	(NA)	129,919	66,702	135,316	23.4	13.7	8.4	24.7	73.7	16.1	85.7	33.58	6,224	788
Westland city	(NA)	(NA)	72,474	22,565	73,978	18.3	17.2	13.0	24.6	73.9	17.6	84.7	32.80	6,167	828
Wyandotte city	(NA)	(NA)	(NA)	(NA)	(NA)	(NA)	(NA)	(NA)	24.5	73.5	17.8	83.4	32.89	6,422	736
Wyoming city	612	1,849,358	62,786	22,195	62,176	20.7	12.2	16.4	22.4	71.4	15.6	82.3	37.13	6,896	613
MINNESOTA	(X)	(X)	(X)	(X)	(X)	(NA)	(NA)	(NA)	(X)	(X)	(X)	(X)	(X)	(X)	(X)
Andover city	61	239,625	18,765	6,348	16,517	6.7	7.2	20.3	10.9	70.4	1.8	80.5	31.36	8,367	500
Apple Valley city	260	831,719	33,495	15,230	33,681	16.3	10.5	16.3	9.2	69.4	-1.1	80.5	29.19	8,805	416
Blaine city	170	701,783	48,265	12,483	46,217	10.1	13.9	2.7	10.9	70.4	1.8	80.5	31.36	8,367	500
Bloomington city	642	2,527,152	116,653	53,623	102,387	13.1	8.9	11.7	13.1	73.2	4.3	83.3	29.41	7,876	699
Brooklyn Center city	(NA)	(NA)	35,343	13,516	33,404	13.9	12.1	15.1	13.0	71.4	2.8	82.8	30.50	7,983	587
Brooklyn Park city	(NA)	(NA)	62,704	29,196	57,914	16.2	8.0	8.2	13.0	71.4	2.8	82.8	30.50	7,983	587
Burnsville city	335	1,295,164	70,124	24,926	66,022	11.6	8.2	18.8	13.8	74.0	3.4	85.8	30.44	7,549	803
Coon Rapids city	(NA)	(NA)	62,256	16,537	46,796	10.5	8.1	17.3	13.0	71.4	2.8	82.8	30.50	7,983	587
Cottage Grove city	202	490,982	24,134	7,815	21,412	16.2	6.5	32.7	12.0	72.1	2.5	82.6	29.95	8,032	617
Duluth city	1,287	4,726,530	175,385	35,770	142,877	10.4	11.9	10.5	8.4	65.5	-1.2	76.3	31.00	9,724	189

See footnotes at end of table.

County and City Data Book: 2007

U.S. Census Bureau

Table C-6. Cities — **Government and Climate**—Con.

[Includes states and 1,265 incorporated places of 25,000 or more population as of April 1, 2000, in all states except Hawaii, which has no incorporated places recognized by the U.S. Census Bureau. Two census designated places (CDPs) are also included (Honolulu CDP in Hawaii and Arlington CDP in Virginia). For more information on these areas, see Appendix C, Geographic Information]

City	City government employment, March 2002		City government finances, 2001–2002							Climate, 1971–2000[2]						
			General revenue ($1,000)		General expenditure					Average daily temperature (degrees Fahrenheit)		Min. and max. temperatures (degrees Fahrenheit)				
						By selected function, percent of total										
	Total employ-ment	Total payroll ($1,000)	Total	Taxes	Total[1] ($1,000)	Police pro-tection	Sewer-age and solid waste manage-ment	High-ways	January	July	January[3]	July[4]	Annual precip-itation (inches)	Heat-ing degree days[5]	Cooling degree days[6]
MINNESOTA—Con.															
Eagan city	(NA)	(NA)	55,884	19,935	54,100	13.7	15.0	3.9	13.1	73.2	4.3	83.3	29.41	7,876	699
Eden Prairie city	402	1,250,105	57,347	25,099	35,443	16.3	14.7	16.5	10.2	71.4	-0.3	82.2	28.82	8,429	567
Edina city	363	1,132,278	55,145	26,650	50,978	8.0	8.7	7.2	13.8	74.0	3.4	85.8	30.44	7,549	803
Fridley city	258	755,812	21,158	8,327	20,198	18.7	15.5	19.7	10.9	70.4	1.8	80.5	31.36	8,367	500
Inver Grove Heights city	271	583,499	26,753	10,125	22,204	14.4	7.0	23.9	10.1	71.0	–	81.3	34.60	8,345	533
Lakeville city	(NA)	(NA)	30,639	11,570	38,537	14.4	14.8	23.6	13.1	72.2	3.8	83.6	31.43	7,773	658
Mankato city	322	924,095	48,320	13,559	51,009	10.5	10.8	26.3	12.5	72.1	2.4	83.4	33.42	8,029	650
Maple Grove city	(NA)	(NA)	79,912	22,592	67,059	6.8	9.6	44.6	13.0	71.4	2.8	82.8	30.50	7,983	587
Maplewood city	(NA)	(NA)	31,109	10,065	36,762	11.7	9.9	15.2	14.5	73.0	6.2	83.2	32.59	7,606	715
Minneapolis city	6,451	24,405,013	750,084	272,790	630,559	14.6	12.8	9.4	13.1	73.2	4.3	83.3	29.41	7,876	699
Minnetonka city	331	1,148,604	35,856	17,245	31,418	18.9	18.4	10.2	13.1	73.2	4.3	83.3	29.41	7,876	699
Moorhead city	375	1,137,764	36,852	4,668	59,539	9.6	9.2	19.8	3.8	69.8	-7.1	81.5	21.56	9,628	478
Oakdale city	99	392,052	22,933	8,686	20,847	14.4	10.7	27.8	14.5	73.0	6.2	83.2	32.59	7,606	715
Plymouth city	376	1,187,052	50,847	17,014	44,297	13.8	12.8	21.3	13.0	71.4	2.8	82.8	30.50	7,983	587
Richfield city	(NA)	(NA)	46,171	13,312	47,177	12.1	5.0	39.1	13.1	73.2	4.3	83.3	29.41	7,876	699
Rochester city	1,074	3,656,648	149,080	37,265	152,327	7.3	7.6	9.9	9.8	70.0	–	80.9	29.10	8,703	474
Roseville city	(NA)	(NA)	39,665	17,666	33,226	12.7	12.5	17.0	14.5	73.0	6.2	83.2	32.59	7,606	715
St. Cloud city	568	1,736,721	92,243	22,271	90,068	10.4	13.8	17.6	8.8	69.8	-1.2	81.7	27.13	8,815	443
St. Louis Park city	(NA)	(NA)	65,166	17,570	62,531	8.4	9.5	9.2	13.0	71.4	2.8	82.8	30.50	7,983	587
St. Paul city	3,396	13,428,259	510,524	127,605	461,460	13.0	5.6	8.5	14.5	73.0	6.2	83.2	32.59	7,606	715
Shoreview city	(NA)	(NA)	18,319	6,962	16,021	7.4	16.7	15.6	14.5	73.0	6.2	83.2	32.59	7,606	715
Winona city	261	700,218	27,648	7,609	22,266	14.7	6.3	11.1	17.6	75.8	9.2	85.3	34.20	6,839	990
Woodbury city	(NA)	(NA)	51,324	15,188	64,622	7.1	6.0	32.7	11.5	72.1	1.9	81.9	29.92	8,104	621
MISSISSIPPI	(X)	(X)	(X)	(X)	(X)	(NA)	(NA)	(NA)	(X)	(X)	(X)	(X)	(X)	(X)	(X)
Biloxi city	640	1,697,336	73,520	18,975	78,316	15.9	12.5	29.8	50.7	81.7	43.5	88.5	64.84	1,645	2,517
Clinton city	(NA)	(NA)	(NA)	(NA)	(NA)	(NA)	(NA)	(NA)	45.0	81.4	35.0	91.4	55.95	2,401	2,264
Columbus city	(NA)	(NA)	25,032	5,337	22,426	20.2	12.9	11.3	42.9	81.5	32.2	92.3	55.91	2,740	2,073
Greenville city	(NA)	(NA)	30,905	10,572	31,139	26.4	11.9	13.2	42.3	82.6	33.0	92.6	54.20	2,715	2,216
Gulfport city	2,807	7,994,679	263,459	24,072	266,142	6.2	4.0	2.4	51.6	82.6	42.6	91.3	65.20	1,514	2,679
Hattiesburg city	739	1,457,137	45,475	16,846	40,972	17.5	11.1	13.4	47.9	81.7	36.0	92.1	62.47	2,024	2,327
Jackson city	(NA)	(NA)	179,326	64,812	168,279	17.2	15.7	10.4	45.0	81.4	35.0	91.4	55.95	2,401	2,264
Meridian city	533	1,099,595	33,507	12,140	30,472	17.5	13.9	20.3	46.1	81.7	34.7	92.9	58.65	2,352	2,173
Pascagoula city	344	801,085	21,897	6,496	24,287	17.5	22.0	10.4	49.4	80.6	39.1	89.7	67.01	1,870	2,286
Southaven city	(NA)	(NA)	(NA)	(NA)	(NA)	(NA)	(NA)	(NA)	37.9	80.4	27.8	90.3	55.06	3,442	1,749
Tupelo city	(NA)	(NA)	44,612	7,363	45,088	17.5	9.9	10.7	40.4	80.4	30.5	91.4	55.86	3,086	1,884
Vicksburg city	681	1,312,506	34,416	8,767	34,038	23.7	9.0	8.3	47.2	81.7	35.5	92.3	57.99	2,089	2,269
MISSOURI	(X)	(X)	(X)	(X)	(X)	(NA)	(NA)	(NA)	(X)	(X)	(X)	(X)	(X)	(X)	(X)
Ballwin city	248	541,112	(NA)	(NA)	(NA)	(NA)	(NA)	(NA)	27.5	78.1	17.3	89.2	38.00	5,199	1,293
Blue Springs city	(NA)	(NA)	31,366	13,189	32,811	23.2	21.1	13.4	24.6	76.6	14.9	87.2	41.18	5,623	1,137
Cape Girardeau city	(NA)	(NA)	39,014	24,837	32,122	15.0	19.2	21.2	32.4	79.5	24.0	90.1	46.54	4,344	1,515
Chesterfield city	193	710,579	31,410	12,640	39,959	15.7	4.2	26.6	27.5	78.1	17.3	89.2	38.00	5,199	1,293
Columbia city	1,356	3,719,910	93,367	42,325	102,277	12.4	24.8	11.0	27.8	77.4	18.2	88.6	40.28	5,177	1,246
Florissant city	(NA)	(NA)	22,859	3,306	23,348	30.1	–	15.6	29.6	80.2	21.2	89.8	38.75	4,758	1,561
Gladstone city	(NA)	(NA)	(NA)	(NA)	(NA)	(NA)	(NA)	(NA)	29.3	81.3	20.7	90.5	35.51	4,734	1,676
Hazelwood city	(NA)	(NA)	20,067	8,703	22,427	23.9	1.0	7.4	29.6	80.2	21.2	89.8	38.75	4,758	1,561
Independence city	(NA)	(NA)	99,640	47,814	120,300	16.2	12.2	9.3	26.6	77.1	17.1	87.5	43.14	5,373	1,176
Jefferson City city	485	1,192,157	34,996	22,060	36,682	16.4	19.1	5.6	28.2	77.9	17.7	89.4	39.59	5,158	1,261
Joplin city	(NA)	(NA)	36,688	22,364	40,556	16.7	10.8	27.5	33.1	79.9	23.7	90.4	46.07	4,253	1,555
Kansas City city	(NA)	(NA)	787,175	466,847	710,202	16.0	6.9	11.4	29.3	81.3	20.7	90.5	35.51	4,734	1,676
Kirkwood city	316	1,054,845	(NA)	(NA)	(NA)	(NA)	(NA)	(NA)	29.6	80.2	21.2	89.8	38.75	4,758	1,561
Lee's Summit city	609	1,952,355	88,329	49,848	82,318	13.9	10.9	20.9	24.6	76.6	14.9	87.2	41.18	5,623	1,137
Liberty city	249	682,666	21,562	11,733	28,115	12.2	21.5	14.4	26.6	77.1	17.1	87.5	43.14	5,373	1,176
Maryland Heights city	249	785,385	37,379	5,505	26,414	24.9	0.4	40.9	29.5	80.7	21.2	90.5	38.84	4,650	1,633
O'Fallon city	(NA)	(NA)	42,550	23,744	50,917	10.9	7.1	10.3	28.3	79.0	19.0	90.2	38.28	5,020	1,399
Raytown city	(NA)	(NA)	(NA)	(NA)	(NA)	(NA)	(NA)	(NA)	24.6	76.6	14.9	87.2	41.18	5,623	1,137
St. Charles city	(NA)	(NA)	84,381	50,691	93,483	18.5	7.0	17.9	27.5	80.7	17.3	89.2	38.00	5,199	1,293
St. Joseph city	665	1,892,337	71,209	34,306	68,722	11.1	10.6	18.8	26.4	78.7	15.9	89.9	35.24	5,345	1,339
St. Louis city	7,425	27,204,390	833,719	427,738	912,131	15.1	2.0	1.9	29.5	80.7	21.2	90.5	38.84	4,650	1,633
St. Peters city	540	1,577,447	48,179	26,248	57,929	13.9	16.3	21.2	28.3	79.0	19.0	90.2	38.28	5,020	1,399
Springfield city	2,918	10,474,899	183,661	85,715	240,616	14.3	13.0	6.3	31.7	78.5	21.8	89.9	44.97	4,602	1,366
University City city	(NA)	(NA)	28,398	11,232	25,771	30.7	9.8	10.6	29.5	80.7	21.2	90.5	38.84	4,650	1,633
Wildwood city	(NA)	(NA)	7,797	1,955	6,702	25.8	–	46.7	27.5	78.1	17.3	89.2	38.00	5,199	1,293
MONTANA	(X)	(X)	(X)	(X)	(X)	(NA)	(NA)	(NA)	(X)	(X)	(X)	(X)	(X)	(X)	(X)
Billings city	865	2,671,514	76,093	18,975	78,221	24.8	15.8	7.3	24.0	72.0	15.1	85.8	14.77	7,006	583
Bozeman city	303	838,841	28,164	8,023	26,662	13.5	19.1	4.8	22.6	65.3	12.0	81.8	16.45	7,984	216
Butte-Silver Bow (balance)	(NA)	(NA)	41,700	16,065	36,033	15.3	9.0	8.6	17.6	62.7	5.4	79.8	12.78	9,399	127
Great Falls city	563	1,308,902	41,493	13,087	42,958	14.8	16.3	20.2	21.7	66.2	11.3	82.0	14.89	7,828	288
Helena city	279	831,756	33,206	6,351	29,585	16.0	24.2	11.2	20.2	67.8	9.9	83.4	11.32	7,975	277
Missoula city	(NA)	(NA)	34,789	15,123	41,735	17.6	10.7	5.0	23.5	66.9	16.2	83.6	13.82	7,622	256

See footnotes at end of table.

Table C-6. Cities — **Government and Climate**—Con.

[Includes states and 1,265 incorporated places of 25,000 or more population as of April 1, 2000, in all states except Hawaii, which has no incorporated places recognized by the U.S. Census Bureau. Two census designated places (CDPs) are also included (Honolulu CDP in Hawaii and Arlington CDP in Virginia). For more information on these areas, see Appendix C, Geographic Information]

City	City government employment, March 2002		City government finances, 2001–2002						Climate, 1971–2000[2]						
			General revenue ($1,000)		General expenditure				Average daily temperature (degrees Fahrenheit)		Min. and max. temperatures (degrees Fahrenheit)				
						By selected function, percent of total									
	Total employ-ment	Total payroll ($1,000)	Total	Taxes	Total[1] ($1,000)	Police pro-tection	Sewer-age and solid waste manage-ment	High-ways	January	July	January[3]	July[4]	Annual precip-itation (inches)	Heat-ing degree days[5]	Cooling degree days[6]
NEBRASKA	(X)	(X)	(X)	(X)	(X)	(NA)	(NA)	(NA)	(X)	(X)	(X)	(X)	(X)	(X)	(X)
Bellevue city	247	690,334	39,943	18,052	37,453	12.7	8.8	25.8	21.7	76.7	11.6	87.4	30.22	6,311	1,095
Fremont city	297	881,070	28,766	15,438	22,951	10.7	32.9	15.8	21.1	76.2	10.4	87.7	29.80	6,444	1,004
Grand Island city	(NA)	(NA)	43,322	18,499	42,875	14.0	12.1	22.6	22.4	75.8	12.2	87.1	25.89	6,385	1,027
Kearney city	248	656,528	25,568	6,916	17,658	22.1	18.7	10.6	22.4	74.7	11.0	85.7	25.20	6,652	852
Lincoln city	2,854	10,159,356	203,404	90,127	192,752	11.8	5.6	20.8	22.4	77.8	11.5	89.6	28.37	6,242	1,154
Omaha city	3,187	11,095,072	389,724	234,317	460,896	15.3	11.2	11.1	21.7	76.7	11.6	87.4	30.22	6,311	1,095
NEVADA	(X)	(X)	(X)	(X)	(X)	(NA)	(NA)	(NA)	(X)	(X)	(X)	(X)	(X)	(X)	(X)
Carson City	(NA)	(NA)	159,979	26,029	143,809	7.4	2.8	6.6	33.7	70.0	21.7	89.2	10.36	5,661	419
Henderson city	2,321	7,667,823	230,798	71,134	247,324	14.7	5.3	3.9	47.0	91.2	36.8	104.1	4.49	2,239	3,214
Las Vegas city	2,719	12,872,693	573,574	168,400	556,002	15.9	5.8	11.1	47.0	91.2	36.8	104.1	4.49	2,239	3,214
North Las Vegas city	1,407	6,021,280	160,465	47,910	164,530	17.8	5.4	7.5	47.0	91.2	36.8	104.1	4.49	2,239	3,214
Reno city	1,734	7,063,853	247,446	83,018	274,681	18.3	6.9	40.2	33.6	71.3	21.8	91.2	7.48	5,600	493
Sparks city	749	2,582,147	77,610	29,206	88,360	15.1	11.9	11.6	33.6	71.3	21.8	91.2	7.48	5,600	493
NEW HAMPSHIRE	(X)	(X)	(X)	(X)	(X)	(NA)	(NA)	(NA)	(X)	(X)	(X)	(X)	(X)	(X)	(X)
Concord city	(NA)	(NA)	46,144	27,440	44,913	12.6	12.1	10.0	20.1	70.0	9.7	82.9	37.60	7,478	442
Dover city	1,169	2,817,928	72,391	36,180	72,576	6.3	5.1	2.5	23.3	70.7	13.1	83.2	42.80	6,748	427
Manchester city	3,467	10,816,040	283,411	83,583	314,739	5.7	2.6	5.4	18.8	68.4	5.2	82.1	39.82	7,742	263
Nashua city	2,929	8,742,113	236,826	121,571	242,653	5.4	5.2	2.6	22.8	70.8	12.1	82.5	45.43	6,834	445
Rochester city	1,008	2,349,686	68,757	34,902	66,714	5.6	6.0	2.6	23.3	70.7	13.1	83.2	42.80	6,748	427
NEW JERSEY	(X)	(X)	(X)	(X)	(X)	(NA)	(NA)	(NA)	(X)	(X)	(X)	(X)	(X)	(X)	(X)
Atlantic City city	1,799	7,339,771	158,385	105,889	164,757	24.2	1.7	2.7	35.2	77.2	29.0	80.6	38.37	4,480	951
Bayonne city	2,534	9,055,493	192,343	102,343	184,903	9.5	5.4	0.7	31.3	77.2	24.4	85.2	46.25	4,843	1,220
Bergenfield borough	233	853,755	(NA)	(NA)	(NA)	(NA)	(NA)	(NA)	28.6	75.0	19.5	85.5	51.50	5,522	824
Camden city	(NA)	(NA)	(NA)	(NA)	(NA)	(NA)	(NA)	(NA)	32.3	76.3	23.2	87.8	48.25	4,801	1,054
Clifton city	754	2,664,538	(NA)	(NA)	(NA)	(NA)	(NA)	(NA)	28.6	75.0	19.5	85.5	51.50	5,522	824
East Orange city	(NA)	(NA)	283,986	68,976	278,933	7.3	4.2	0.6	31.3	77.2	24.4	85.2	46.25	4,843	1,220
Elizabeth city	1,601	6,457,736	162,231	69,285	139,231	23.3	13.2	3.7	29.6	74.5	19.8	85.7	50.94	5,450	787
Englewood city	833	2,770,123	(NA)	(NA)	(NA)	(NA)	(NA)	(NA)	29.6	75.3	22.7	82.5	46.33	5,367	882
Fair Lawn borough	334	1,154,628	(NA)	(NA)	(NA)	(NA)	(NA)	(NA)	28.6	75.0	19.5	85.5	51.50	5,522	824
Fort Lee borough	353	1,622,495	(NA)	(NA)	(NA)	(NA)	(NA)	(NA)	29.6	75.3	22.7	82.5	46.33	5,367	882
Garfield city	(NA)	(NA)	66,739	26,009	61,514	9.7	6.6	3.2	28.6	75.0	19.5	85.5	51.50	5,522	824
Hackensack city	474	2,182,860	54,362	41,336	58,001	18.9	11.8	12.3	28.6	75.0	19.5	85.5	51.50	5,522	824
Hoboken city	(NA)	(NA)	78,704	20,751	73,119	17.6	5.8	1.1	29.6	75.3	22.7	82.5	46.33	5,367	882
Jersey City city	3,658	14,966,667	442,683	120,840	396,502	21.3	14.9	1.8	29.6	75.3	22.7	82.5	46.33	5,367	882
Kearny town	397	1,906,743	67,222	30,186	49,724	25.2	13.7	6.9	31.3	77.2	24.4	85.2	46.25	4,843	1,220
Linden city	(NA)	(NA)	(NA)	(NA)	(NA)	(NA)	(NA)	(NA)	28.5	74.0	18.2	85.8	51.61	5,595	757
Long Branch city	456	1,470,318	49,693	21,075	42,870	16.3	11.8	8.8	31.7	74.1	22.8	82.6	48.63	5,168	750
Millville city	299	987,890	24,047	8,440	22,234	21.9	22.0	3.5	32.7	76.3	24.1	85.9	43.20	4,835	1,009
Newark city	(NA)	(NA)	678,095	163,752	636,597	17.8	9.1	0.1	31.3	77.2	24.4	85.2	46.25	4,843	1,220
New Brunswick city	6,253	13,516,530	190,300	45,026	196,927	6.2	3.0	5.1	29.7	74.8	21.1	85.4	48.78	5,346	816
Paramus borough	(NA)	(NA)	(NA)	(NA)	(NA)	(NA)	(NA)	(NA)	28.6	75.0	19.5	85.5	51.50	5,522	824
Passaic city	(NA)	(NA)	79,553	37,481	76,986	18.6	10.9	2.8	28.6	75.0	19.5	85.5	51.50	5,522	824
Paterson city	2,096	7,084,983	174,915	72,656	185,269	19.0	15.2	4.2	28.6	75.0	19.5	85.5	51.50	5,522	824
Perth Amboy city	549	2,188,421	61,357	20,869	57,313	19.2	10.7	10.1	29.7	74.8	21.1	85.4	48.78	5,346	816
Plainfield city	(NA)	(NA)	(NA)	(NA)	(NA)	(NA)	(NA)	(NA)	30.0	74.9	21.5	86.6	49.63	5,266	854
Rahway city	(NA)	(NA)	34,628	19,303	39,872	20.1	7.5	6.0	29.6	74.5	19.8	85.7	50.94	5,450	787
Sayreville borough	302	1,280,907	39,975	16,366	34,384	23.9	13.9	8.0	29.7	74.8	21.1	85.4	48.78	5,346	816
Trenton city	(NA)	(NA)	390,832	51,806	410,068	7.2	4.7	0.8	30.4	75.2	21.3	86.9	48.83	5,262	903
Union City city	(NA)	(NA)	203,055	37,385	203,803	7.2	2.8	0.5	29.6	75.3	22.7	82.5	46.33	5,367	882
Vineland city	814	2,691,570	52,472	18,313	50,812	17.8	14.0	6.1	26.7	70.4	16.8	81.7	53.28	6,281	438
Westfield town	(NA)	(NA)	(NA)	(NA)	(NA)	(NA)	(NA)	(NA)	30.0	74.9	21.5	86.6	49.63	5,266	854
West New York town	(NA)	(NA)	120,548	33,144	127,770	7.8	4.3	3.2	29.6	75.3	22.7	82.5	46.33	5,367	882
NEW MEXICO	(X)	(X)	(X)	(X)	(X)	(NA)	(NA)	(NA)	(X)	(X)	(X)	(X)	(X)	(X)	(X)
Alamogordo city	372	800,924	27,835	10,841	25,237	20.7	10.9	10.4	42.2	79.7	28.9	93.0	13.20	31	1,715
Albuquerque city	673	20,058,494	705,802	228,698	628,129	15.8	10.5	8.8	35.7	78.5	23.8	92.3	9.47	4,281	1,290
Carlsbad city	346	1,040,052	25,986	9,027	23,542	20.2	19.0	17.0	42.7	81.7	27.5	95.8	14.15	2,823	2,029
Clovis city	364	839,121	26,405	9,928	26,093	18.7	15.5	8.6	37.9	77.5	25.0	91.0	18.50	3,955	1,305
Farmington city	790	2,236,308	114,086	20,034	113,525	6.2	5.5	9.3	29.8	74.9	17.9	90.7	8.39	5,508	805
Hobbs city	(NA)	(NA)	33,892	12,129	36,383	19.8	12.1	6.9	42.9	80.1	29.1	93.5	18.15	2,849	1,842
Las Cruces city	(NA)	(NA)	95,036	52,871	83,375	17.0	14.8	14.8	39.0	78.7	21.1	94.9	11.44	3,818	1,364
Rio Rancho city	(NA)	(NA)	46,201	17,643	36,461	34.1	18.7	12.9	33.8	73.9	19.7	90.0	9.28	4,981	773
Roswell city	(NA)	(NA)	(NA)	(NA)	(NA)	(NA)	(NA)	(NA)	40.0	80.8	24.4	94.8	13.34	3,332	1,814
Santa Fe city	1,331	3,385,598	131,236	50,137	119,651	12.8	13.1	12.1	29.3	69.8	15.5	85.6	14.22	6,073	414

See footnotes at end of table.

Table C-6. Cities — **Government and Climate**—Con.

[Includes states and 1,265 incorporated places of 25,000 or more population as of April 1, 2000, in all states except Hawaii, which has no incorporated places recognized by the U.S. Census Bureau. Two census designated places (CDPs) are also included (Honolulu CDP in Hawaii and Arlington CDP in Virginia). For more information on these areas, see Appendix C, Geographic Information]

City	City government employment, March 2002		City government finances, 2001–2002						Climate, 1971–2000[2]						
			General revenue ($1,000)		General expenditure				Average daily temperature (degrees Fahrenheit)		Min. and max. temperatures (degrees Fahrenheit)				
						By selected function, percent of total									
	Total employment	Total payroll ($1,000)	Total	Taxes	Total[1] ($1,000)	Police protection	Sewerage and solid waste management	Highways	January	July	January[3]	July[4]	Annual precipitation (inches)	Heating degree days[5]	Cooling degree days[6]
NEW YORK	(X)	(X)	(X)	(X)	(X)	(NA)	(NA)	(NA)	(X)	(X)	(X)	(X)	(X)	(X)	(X)
Albany city	1,593	5,228,640	131,779	41,842	141,892	22.8	7.7	9.8	22.2	71.1	13.3	82.2	38.60	6,860	544
Auburn city	(NA)	(NA)	34,258	8,961	35,039	13.3	16.4	10.5	23.7	71.2	16.0	81.5	36.98	6,694	528
Binghamton city	656	2,076,788	55,228	18,805	65,358	13.1	19.0	5.4	21.7	68.7	15.0	78.1	38.65	7,237	396
Buffalo city	12,783	47,316,342	1,007,586	145,851	1,031,838	6.6	4.6	4.7	24.5	70.8	17.8	79.6	40.54	6,692	548
Elmira city	364	1,153,743	26,814	8,249	32,009	17.3	4.2	14.2	23.9	70.3	15.0	82.3	34.95	6,806	446
Freeport village	493	2,008,428	38,896	23,524	45,938	24.0	8.2	11.3	30.7	73.8	24.2	81.0	42.97	5,504	779
Glen Cove city	309	910,747	34,990	17,064	39,480	19.2	11.6	5.9	31.9	74.2	25.4	82.8	46.36	5,231	839
Hempstead village	512	2,145,185	50,547	29,912	55,466	26.3	4.0	8.4	31.9	74.2	25.4	82.8	46.36	5,231	839
Ithaca city	522	1,564,932	36,218	17,437	41,751	14.7	13.3	15.8	22.6	68.7	13.9	80.1	36.71	7,182	312
Jamestown city	(NA)	(NA)	51,955	10,648	57,827	8.3	8.1	4.1	22.3	69.2	14.1	80.1	45.68	7,048	389
Lindenhurst village	141	242,499	8,820	4,310	8,961	–	8.1	30.8	30.7	73.8	24.2	81.0	42.97	5,504	779
Long Beach city	595	1,977,217	53,164	26,312	51,737	22.1	14.4	11.5	31.8	74.8	24.7	82.9	42.46	4,947	949
Middletown city	(NA)	(NA)	24,205	9,793	26,291	20.2	15.8	6.4	26.5	73.0	17.5	84.0	44.00	5,820	674
Mount Vernon city	864	2,989,056	75,102	45,657	71,814	19.2	6.2	2.5	29.7	74.2	20.1	86.0	46.46	5,400	770
Newburgh city	(NA)	(NA)	33,596	11,318	33,630	23.9	12.3	5.4	26.6	74.3	17.1	84.9	45.79	5,813	790
New Rochelle city	655	2,790,560	98,044	58,447	96,266	21.6	4.9	5.1	29.7	74.2	20.1	86.0	46.46	5,400	770
New York city	455,485	201,910,751	52,718,016	22,235,234	54,501,683	6.9	4.5	2.2	32.1	76.5	26.2	84.2	49.69	4,754	1,151
Niagara Falls city	861	2,937,019	90,632	34,291	83,086	15.0	14.5	9.1	24.2	71.4	16.8	81.8	33.93	6,752	508
North Tonawanda city	354	1,214,683	29,622	12,621	30,599	14.4	17.4	13.2	24.2	71.4	16.8	81.8	33.93	6,752	508
Port Chester village	219	824,642	27,766	12,639	32,976	16.6	5.8	25.1	28.4	73.8	21.0	82.5	50.45	5,660	716
Poughkeepsie city	(NA)	953,204	41,602	13,336	45,175	19.7	10.7	9.5	24.5	71.9	14.7	83.6	44.12	6,438	550
Rochester city	12,233	41,801,707	860,615	180,949	882,134	6.5	2.2	2.0	23.9	70.7	16.6	81.4	33.98	6,728	576
Rome city	(NA)	(NA)	39,204	20,621	39,807	13.5	8.2	10.1	20.8	70.2	11.9	81.3	46.27	7,146	416
Saratoga Springs city	(NA)	(NA)	30,125	11,109	28,956	16.4	8.9	13.0	20.9	71.2	11.6	83.0	43.31	6,904	477
Schenectady city	746	2,713,209	61,211	21,209	71,283	17.7	15.4	8.3	22.2	71.1	13.3	82.2	38.60	6,860	544
Spring Valley village	162	714,777	22,584	12,553	24,963	24.4	0.3	5.2	27.3	73.1	18.2	83.8	51.01	5,809	642
Syracuse city	(NA)	(NA)	450,519	26,536	515,520	6.3	1.7	4.4	22.7	70.9	14.0	81.7	40.05	6,803	551
Troy city	694	2,051,150	52,941	16,691	51,186	18.5	8.3	9.1	22.2	71.1	13.3	82.2	38.60	6,860	544
Utica city	821	2,494,080	65,533	27,684	69,730	15.3	3.2	13.3	22.2	70.5	12.6	83.2	41.90	6,855	441
Valley Stream village	431	876,386	23,220	17,983	23,189	0.9	17.8	18.1	22.2	70.5	12.6	83.2	41.90	6,855	441
Watertown city	376	1,140,215	29,213	8,800	33,289	14.7	10.1	10.4	18.6	70.2	9.1	79.4	42.57	7,517	421
White Plains city	(NA)	(NA)	112,282	70,476	110,196	19.4	6.4	7.6	29.7	74.2	20.1	86.0	46.46	5,400	770
Yonkers city	(NA)	(NA)	674,109	247,437	690,183	9.0	2.9	0.9	29.7	74.2	20.1	86.0	46.46	5,400	770
NORTH CAROLINA	(X)	(X)	(X)	(X)	(X)	(NA)	(NA)	(NA)	(X)	(X)	(X)	(X)	(X)	(X)	(X)
Asheville city	(NA)	(NA)	84,250	34,161	84,522	15.2	22.7	9.9	36.4	73.9	26.6	84.3	37.32	4,237	877
Burlington city	734	1,719,245	42,213	15,432	45,504	23.2	24.0	7.2	38.7	79.3	27.6	90.6	45.08	3,588	1,489
Cary town	1,149	3,107,163	116,709	49,904	105,158	9.1	15.9	18.6	39.5	78.7	30.1	87.9	46.49	3,431	1,456
Chapel Hill town	743	1,651,125	55,599	23,243	41,993	21.0	7.8	7.0	38.5	79.4	27.8	88.6	48.04	3,650	1,491
Charlotte city	5,695	20,498,717	957,849	312,819	746,580	19.0	10.3	12.9	41.7	80.3	32.1	90.1	43.51	3,162	1,681
Concord city	862	2,339,248	68,487	26,865	65,560	13.3	22.2	4.4	39.4	79.2	27.9	90.3	47.30	3,463	1,540
Durham city	2,130	6,659,864	207,156	89,076	184,439	18.7	22.1	7.7	39.7	78.8	29.6	89.1	43.05	3,465	1,521
Fayetteville city	1,826	5,085,137	117,307	37,019	110,134	21.8	20.2	10.6	41.7	80.4	31.1	90.4	46.78	3,097	1,721
Gastonia city	1,087	3,152,566	68,145	20,893	71,878	16.9	21.5	5.7	42.0	79.9	31.7	89.9	49.19	3,009	1,701
Goldsboro city	495	1,119,776	45,667	9,759	43,692	13.3	14.2	6.7	43.4	81.2	33.0	91.4	49.84	2,771	1,922
Greensboro city	(NA)	(NA)	269,589	110,268	265,046	18.9	17.1	7.8	39.7	78.6	29.0	88.9	42.89	3,443	1,438
Greenville city	1,235	3,587,820	76,269	20,811	85,045	13.6	16.8	9.7	42.0	78.8	31.9	88.4	49.30	3,113	1,516
Hickory city	697	1,792,889	54,670	24,185	55,782	12.1	19.4	8.2	39.0	77.7	29.2	87.8	48.98	3,608	1,333
High Point city	(NA)	(NA)	110,607	44,286	98,818	14.5	13.2	8.4	39.7	78.2	29.6	89.0	46.19	3,399	1,424
Huntersville town	(NA)	(NA)	(NA)	(NA)	(NA)	(NA)	(NA)	(NA)	39.4	79.2	27.9	90.3	47.30	3,463	1,540
Jacksonville city	448	1,055,341	34,956	11,613	35,295	20.8	25.9	5.6	44.7	80.2	33.9	89.5	54.07	2,656	1,832
Kannapolis city	244	640,050	25,595	11,179	24,528	20.3	21.2	10.8	39.4	79.2	27.9	90.3	47.30	3,463	1,540
Monroe city	504	1,260,952	35,362	10,864	30,011	17.9	19.3	5.4	41.5	79.0	31.0	89.7	48.73	3,125	1,538
Raleigh city	3,519	9,554,157	282,945	122,311	303,071	16.5	15.1	13.9	39.1	79.4	28.1	89.9	45.70	3,514	1,550
Rocky Mount city	802	2,396,100	87,839	15,004	81,080	10.7	16.9	5.7	41.1	79.2	30.8	89.7	46.51	3,215	1,518
Salisbury city	457	1,267,471	35,933	11,682	30,053	18.7	22.0	9.5	40.2	78.7	29.5	89.5	42.86	3,356	1,466
Wilmington city	1,122	3,178,631	105,344	45,586	85,339	18.7	19.8	6.2	44.8	80.1	33.3	90.0	58.44	2,606	1,791
Wilson city	767	1,997,737	49,058	13,879	44,529	17.0	25.2	6.1	40.4	79.2	29.5	90.2	47.18	3,328	1,575
Winston-Salem city	2,310	6,825,571	210,921	75,551	226,389	16.8	19.1	9.0	39.7	78.2	29.6	89.0	46.19	3,399	1,424
NORTH DAKOTA	(X)	(X)	(X)	(X)	(X)	(NA)	(NA)	(NA)	(X)	(X)	(X)	(X)	(X)	(X)	(X)
Bismarck city	644	1,533,226	67,555	21,861	54,383	12.7	10.2	25.1	10.2	70.4	-0.6	84.5	16.84	8,802	471
Fargo city	732	2,441,954	102,001	31,323	118,775	6.6	7.1	4.6	6.8	70.6	-2.3	82.2	21.19	9,092	533
Grand Forks city	519	1,654,781	88,374	23,178	107,239	5.7	18.3	3.8	5.3	69.4	-4.3	81.9	19.60	9,489	420
Minot city	377	852,194	30,381	16,620	33,092	12.5	9.0	8.2	7.5	68.4	-1.8	80.4	18.65	9,479	422

See footnotes at end of table.

Table C-6. Cities — **Government and Climate**—Con.

[Includes states and 1,265 incorporated places of 25,000 or more population as of April 1, 2000, in all states except Hawaii, which has no incorporated places recognized by the U.S. Census Bureau. Two census designated places (CDPs) are also included (Honolulu CDP in Hawaii and Arlington CDP in Virginia). For more information on these areas, see Appendix C, Geographic Information]

City	City government employment, March 2002 Total employment	Total payroll ($1,000)	General revenue ($1,000) Total	Taxes	General expenditure Total[1] ($1,000)	Police protection	Sewerage and solid waste management	Highways	Avg daily temp January	July	Min/max January[3]	July[4]	Annual precipitation (inches)	Heating degree days[5]	Cooling degree days[6]
OHIO	(X)	(X)	(X)	(X)	(X)	(NA)	(NA)	(NA)	(X)	(X)	(X)	(X)	(X)	(X)	(X)
Akron city	2,768	9,477,533	322,893	163,990	336,032	13.9	11.0	12.5	27.2	74.1	20.1	83.9	36.07	5,752	856
Barberton city	(NA)	(NA)	28,392	11,564	29,820	15.7	13.6	10.6	29.1	73.6	20.3	85.0	39.16	5,348	813
Beavercreek city	140	507,051	16,525	7,897	19,249	29.6	–	24.7	27.6	73.1	19.5	83.5	40.06	5,531	768
Bowling Green city	(NA)	(NA)	33,482	15,984	31,432	24.0	16.7	9.2	23.1	72.9	15.2	84.2	33.18	6,492	690
Brunswick city	262	601,193	19,138	10,181	20,613	15.3	8.4	11.8	25.7	71.9	18.8	81.4	38.71	6,121	702
Canton city	1,213	3,671,503	91,403	45,171	86,028	18.7	11.7	6.9	25.2	71.8	17.4	82.3	38.47	6,154	678
Cincinnati city	(NA)	(NA)	792,848	351,732	706,410	13.4	17.3	3.6	30.6	76.8	22.7	86.8	39.57	4,841	1,210
Cleveland city	9,551	32,786,030	954,428	424,781	912,369	19.0	5.4	5.1	25.7	71.9	18.8	81.4	38.71	6,121	702
Cleveland Heights city	649	1,995,967	54,277	33,032	50,987	15.5	9.0	11.4	25.7	71.9	18.8	81.4	38.71	6,121	702
Columbus city	9,053	34,571,485	1,063,945	516,003	1,081,254	18.8	16.8	8.7	28.3	74.7	20.2	85.6	40.03	5,349	935
Cuyahoga Falls city	(NA)	(NA)	54,725	26,159	53,839	14.4	11.1	16.5	29.1	73.6	20.3	85.0	39.16	5,348	813
Dayton city	3,057	10,579,085	307,235	128,712	312,945	16.5	9.5	11.0	26.3	74.3	19.0	84.2	39.58	5,690	935
Delaware city	272	895,271	26,018	11,778	21,363	15.5	16.9	10.4	25.1	73.0	16.6	84.6	37.58	6,178	739
Dublin city	567	1,572,498	72,304	55,518	76,152	8.8	5.3	24.4	28.3	74.7	20.2	85.6	40.03	5,349	935
East Cleveland city	(NA)	(NA)	(NA)	(NA)	(NA)	(NA)	(NA)	(NA)	25.7	71.9	18.8	81.4	38.71	6,121	702
Elyria city	698	2,212,450	48,121	25,113	63,108	17.2	25.0	6.7	27.1	73.8	19.3	85.0	38.02	5,731	818
Euclid city	689	1,993,828	52,963	27,069	56,047	18.3	20.5	5.9	23.0	68.8	14.3	80.0	47.33	6,956	372
Fairborn city	268	977,844	25,941	9,032	24,275	20.2	18.2	6.4	27.9	77.0	20.6	87.2	39.41	5,343	1,214
Fairfield city	360	1,132,805	42,790	23,400	48,758	13.2	16.9	22.5	28.7	76.6	19.9	88.1	43.36	5,261	1,135
Findlay city	413	1,232,638	39,987	17,939	46,616	12.6	37.7	7.8	24.5	73.6	17.4	83.5	36.91	6,194	809
Gahanna city	212	568,866	29,894	14,515	22,370	21.5	8.6	19.6	28.3	75.1	20.3	85.3	38.52	5,492	951
Garfield Heights city	297	812,197	25,957	16,707	25,644	21.3	8.6	6.8	25.7	71.9	18.8	81.4	38.71	6,121	702
Grove City city	144	485,554	26,032	16,873	27,038	21.9	4.6	13.8	28.3	74.7	20.2	85.6	40.03	5,349	935
Hamilton city	743	2,999,553	69,912	25,499	86,077	14.6	14.6	6.1	28.7	76.6	19.9	88.1	43.36	5,261	1,135
Huber Heights city	191	720,145	25,108	14,606	26,822	22.2	10.5	13.5	27.9	77.0	20.6	87.2	39.41	5,343	1,214
Kent city	(NA)	(NA)	24,381	12,161	25,327	19.2	17.0	5.5	27.2	74.1	20.1	83.9	36.07	5,752	856
Kettering city	(NA)	(NA)	54,418	31,999	52,264	17.3	–	25.3	27.9	77.0	20.6	87.2	39.41	5,343	1,214
Lakewood city	681	2,418,632	54,863	30,682	51,825	12.5	15.5	4.9	25.7	71.9	18.8	81.4	38.71	6,121	702
Lancaster city	457	1,442,747	35,714	13,828	38,598	15.6	23.6	10.8	26.5	73.1	17.8	84.4	36.55	5,887	764
Lima city	446	1,456,855	39,824	15,973	43,703	19.2	21.4	8.1	25.5	73.6	18.1	84.0	37.20	5,932	835
Lorain city	(NA)	(NA)	53,038	22,602	59,011	14.4	23.9	5.6	27.1	73.8	19.3	85.0	38.02	5,731	818
Mansfield city	677	1,972,629	49,344	25,842	51,609	18.5	11.5	20.2	24.3	71.0	16.2	81.8	43.24	6,364	653
Maple Heights city	339	1,037,692	21,957	12,636	24,298	23.3	8.0	6.9	25.7	71.9	18.8	81.4	38.71	6,121	702
Marion city	356	1,161,202	28,425	13,643	34,555	15.6	23.7	8.4	24.5	72.7	16.0	83.7	38.35	6,300	703
Massillon city	(NA)	(NA)	30,964	14,215	23,695	15.6	18.4	8.5	25.2	71.8	17.4	82.3	38.47	6,154	678
Medina city	(NA)	(NA)	19,044	10,457	24,356	15.8	9.3	2.7	23.7	71.3	16.2	82.0	38.34	6,525	558
Mentor city	509	1,736,713	51,072	33,413	57,384	15.3	1.1	27.6	23.0	68.8	14.3	80.0	47.33	6,956	372
Middletown city	(NA)	(NA)	56,523	23,455	75,286	12.8	13.0	11.7	27.5	74.2	18.3	86.3	39.54	5,609	879
Newark city	(NA)	(NA)	34,010	16,095	37,438	17.9	12.0	13.3	25.8	72.7	17.3	83.8	41.62	6,084	687
North Olmsted city	(NA)	(NA)	39,057	21,760	46,072	13.2	17.6	13.0	25.7	71.9	18.8	81.4	38.71	6,121	702
North Royalton city	(NA)	(NA)	21,539	12,407	19,163	25.4	22.4	9.1	25.7	71.9	18.8	81.4	38.71	6,121	702
Parma city	(NA)	(NA)	60,444	34,001	59,217	19.0	1.7	9.0	25.7	71.9	18.8	81.4	38.71	6,121	702
Reynoldsburg city	161	541,580	20,497	10,889	24,249	23.9	17.0	3.6	28.3	75.1	20.3	85.3	38.52	5,492	951
Sandusky city	341	1,111,879	27,879	14,151	27,116	17.1	22.2	5.8	25.6	73.8	18.9	81.8	34.46	6,065	785
Shaker Heights city	566	1,825,007	45,171	28,900	43,704	19.7	8.4	7.2	25.7	71.9	18.8	81.4	38.71	6,121	702
Springfield city	708	2,361,586	61,865	31,446	52,572	22.8	11.5	8.6	26.1	73.5	18.2	83.8	37.70	5,921	796
Stow city	254	927,122	26,604	17,634	26,313	12.5	–	25.1	27.2	74.1	20.1	83.9	36.07	5,752	856
Strongsville city	472	1,173,789	46,407	28,117	46,889	18.5	13.4	15.1	25.7	71.9	18.8	81.4	38.71	6,121	702
Toledo city	2,999	11,720,938	347,090	180,418	342,713	20.9	16.6	8.0	27.5	77.6	21.7	87.1	33.52	5,464	1,257
Trotwood city	230	574,481	14,154	7,611	15,193	33.5	12.9	11.1	27.9	77.0	20.6	87.2	39.41	5,343	1,214
Upper Arlington city	325	1,159,926	37,713	26,081	31,332	16.0	8.0	7.3	28.3	75.1	20.3	85.3	38.52	5,492	951
Warren city	459	1,693,023	58,489	18,453	47,669	12.5	16.1	9.2	24.0	70.2	15.3	82.4	37.80	6,678	458
Westerville city	(NA)	(NA)	47,946	25,747	56,768	11.6	11.4	10.9	27.7	74.4	19.7	85.4	39.35	5,434	924
Westlake city	405	983,253	49,384	28,792	47,221	14.0	11.3	5.4	27.1	73.8	19.3	85.0	38.02	5,731	818
Youngstown city	(NA)	(NA)	89,636	35,557	78,989	21.6	18.5	9.8	24.9	69.9	17.4	81.0	38.02	6,451	552
Zanesville city	(NA)	(NA)	26,706	13,517	24,579	33.4	21.8	4.1	24.3	68.4	16.3	78.7	36.91	6,639	373
OKLAHOMA	(X)	(X)	(X)	(X)	(X)	(NA)	(NA)	(NA)	(X)	(X)	(X)	(X)	(X)	(X)	(X)
Bartlesville city	364	994,926	31,094	17,310	30,566	13.5	22.6	10.7	35.4	82.2	23.7	94.5	38.99	3,743	1,894
Broken Arrow city	(NA)	(NA)	53,018	32,501	48,349	19.9	8.5	16.8	34.8	81.3	23.5	92.9	40.46	3,917	1,746
Edmond city	596	1,871,899	55,914	31,575	59,462	19.2	10.6	11.6	36.7	82.0	26.2	93.1	35.85	3,663	1,907
Enid city	(NA)	(NA)	39,033	21,835	26,719	17.6	8.6	18.6	33.1	82.6	21.9	94.4	34.25	4,269	1,852
Lawton city	859	2,304,270	61,577	29,193	46,375	22.4	11.9	6.5	38.2	84.2	26.4	95.7	31.64	3,326	2,199
Midwest City city	511	1,589,023	42,446	20,643	40,959	20.2	10.4	6.4	36.7	82.0	26.2	93.1	35.85	3,663	1,907
Moore city	238	793,790	27,263	14,393	26,618	17.2	6.7	8.8	36.7	82.0	26.2	93.1	35.85	3,663	1,907
Muskogee city	(NA)	(NA)	(NA)	(NA)	(NA)	(NA)	(NA)	(NA)	36.1	82.1	25.2	93.1	43.77	3,667	1,858
Norman city	2,642	7,190,973	226,057	45,335	233,248	6.1	6.3	6.4	35.8	82.1	23.2	93.9	41.65	3,713	1,906
Oklahoma City city	5,002	18,668,804	710,972	350,178	750,567	14.6	14.6	11.5	36.7	82.0	26.2	93.1	35.85	3,663	1,907
Ponca City city	432	1,096,243	20,323	7,924	23,934	14.6	16.6	7.9	33.8	82.9	23.8	94.1	36.41	4,053	1,964
Shawnee city	(NA)	(NA)	(NA)	(NA)	(NA)	(NA)	(NA)	(NA)	37.3	83.0	25.5	94.5	40.87	3,460	2,024
Stillwater city	1,188	3,161,755	34,617	19,562	36,480	17.8	29.2	4.4	34.5	82.3	21.9	93.6	36.71	3,899	1,881
Tulsa city	4,555	14,867,594	615,463	250,217	590,102	15.3	18.6	3.5	37.4	81.9	27.1	92.2	45.10	3,413	1,905

See footnotes at end of table.

Table C-6. Cities — **Government and Climate**—Con.

[Includes states and 1,265 incorporated places of 25,000 or more population as of April 1, 2000, in all states except Hawaii, which has no incorporated places recognized by the U.S. Census Bureau. Two census designated places (CDPs) are also included (Honolulu CDP in Hawaii and Arlington CDP in Virginia). For more information on these areas, see Appendix C, Geographic Information]

City	City government employment, March 2002		City government finances, 2001–2002							Climate, 1971–2000[2]						
			General revenue ($1,000)		General expenditure					Average daily temperature (degrees Fahrenheit)		Min. and max. temperatures (degrees Fahrenheit)				
							By selected function, percent of total									
	Total employ-ment	Total payroll ($1,000)	Total	Taxes	Total[1] ($1,000)	Police pro-tection	Sewer-age and solid waste manage-ment	High-ways	January	July	January[3]	July[4]	Annual precip-itation (inches)	Heat-ing degree days[5]	Cooling degree days[6]
OREGON	(X)	(X)	(X)	(X)	(X)	(NA)	(NA)	(NA)	(X)	(X)	(X)	(X)	(X)	(X)	(X)
Albany city	383	1,252,980	39,541	22,135	45,126	13.4	16.6	11.9	40.3	66.5	33.6	81.2	43.66	4,715	247
Beaverton city	480	1,817,033	50,353	22,972	46,699	22.1	15.9	10.3	40.0	66.8	33.8	79.2	39.95	4,723	287
Bend city	367	1,193,810	46,916	27,637	52,482	22.8	15.3	27.1	31.2	63.5	22.6	80.7	11.73	7,042	147
Corvallis city	570	1,712,806	54,591	21,800	80,321	10.0	8.5	5.7	38.1	63.8	31.6	77.4	67.76	5,501	139
Eugene city	(NA)	(NA)	190,840	81,888	205,368	13.3	11.3	4.6	39.8	66.2	33.0	81.5	50.90	4,786	242
Grants Pass city	(NA)	(NA)	(NA)	(NA)	(NA)	(NA)	(NA)	(NA)	39.3	69.2	31.1	88.8	31.02	4,735	418
Gresham city	558	2,457,678	75,387	37,870	78,899	23.6	15.1	8.6	40.0	68.3	33.5	81.5	45.70	4,491	450
Hillsboro city	652	2,353,984	71,255	40,334	63,790	21.1	21.8	12.4	40.5	67.6	35.1	80.4	38.19	4,532	323
Keizer city	(NA)	(NA)	(NA)	(NA)	(NA)	(NA)	(NA)	(NA)	40.3	66.8	33.5	81.5	40.00	4,784	257
Lake Oswego city	352	1,291,516	43,543	26,775	41,183	11.6	12.7	1.3	41.8	69.3	35.7	82.6	46.05	4,132	475
McMinnville city	291	917,314	31,409	12,589	24,866	15.8	11.7	5.7	39.6	66.6	33.0	81.9	41.66	4,815	288
Medford city	524	1,936,662	51,949	33,935	49,746	23.8	14.8	18.0	39.1	72.7	30.9	90.2	18.37	4,539	711
Oregon City city	295	1,171,516	29,675	12,861	26,374	13.5	18.3	11.2	41.8	69.3	35.7	82.6	46.05	4,132	475
Portland city	6,377	25,536,172	723,890	322,921	875,595	14.4	20.7	12.5	41.8	69.3	35.7	82.6	46.05	4,132	475
Salem city	1,384	5,325,857	138,926	65,115	152,493	14.4	27.3	10.3	40.3	66.8	33.5	81.5	40.00	4,784	257
Springfield city	(NA)	(NA)	58,787	15,989	51,035	17.5	28.5	9.6	39.8	66.2	33.0	81.5	50.90	4,786	242
Tigard city	268	1,005,042	25,270	15,826	23,122	27.4	6.1	10.8	40.0	66.8	33.8	79.2	39.95	4,723	287
PENNSYLVANIA	(X)	(X)	(X)	(X)	(X)	(NA)	(NA)	(NA)	(X)	(X)	(X)	(X)	(X)	(X)	(X)
Allentown city	1,003	3,305,199	82,885	38,241	82,652	21.0	19.2	6.1	27.1	73.3	19.1	83.9	45.17	5,830	787
Altoona city	305	892,723	(NA)	(NA)	(NA)	(NA)	(NA)	(NA)	26.5	71.1	18.2	81.9	42.69	6,055	546
Bethel Park borough	158	419,997	16,628	9,248	19,665	17.9	18.9	15.6	28.6	73.1	19.8	84.5	37.78	5,727	709
Bethlehem city	778	2,184,224	58,196	23,686	64,390	11.8	11.9	16.5	27.1	73.3	19.1	83.9	45.17	5,830	787
Chester city	369	1,130,832	23,495	16,585	27,462	35.8	7.1	9.4	33.7	78.7	27.9	87.5	40.66	4,469	1,333
Easton city	278	846,633	22,094	7,152	31,754	13.3	18.3	3.3	27.1	73.3	19.1	83.9	45.17	5,830	787
Erie city	903	2,861,869	82,228	31,240	69,945	18.4	20.2	8.8	26.9	72.1	20.3	80.4	42.77	6,243	620
Harrisburg city	763	2,762,507	77,322	19,652	85,952	15.7	16.7	8.5	30.3	75.9	23.1	85.7	41.45	5,201	955
Lancaster city	(NA)	(NA)	43,010	18,476	41,058	21.9	14.8	5.4	29.1	74.4	20.7	84.7	43.47	5,448	809
Municipality of Monroeville borough	147	647,431	26,758	17,967	28,270	23.2	15.6	16.3	28.6	73.1	19.8	84.5	37.78	5,727	709
New Castle city	162	441,690	(NA)	(NA)	(NA)	(NA)	(NA)	(NA)	25.9	71.6	16.4	84.5	38.43	6,224	587
Norristown borough	183	669,438	16,959	12,143	19,190	26.0	2.9	10.9	30.2	75.1	20.4	86.6	43.87	5,174	884
Philadelphia city	31,215	121,352,569	4,756,529	2,042,695	4,826,525	10.3	5.6	2.0	32.3	77.6	25.5	85.5	42.05	4,759	1,235
Pittsburgh city	4,294	15,696,717	508,149	275,898	480,474	14.8	4.2	7.1	27.5	72.6	19.9	82.7	37.85	5,829	726
Plum borough	(NA)	(NA)	7,652	5,199	9,183	25.5	9.5	40.8	28.6	73.1	19.8	84.5	37.78	5,727	709
Reading city	827	2,394,994	64,956	24,066	78,932	20.7	14.5	5.9	27.1	73.6	19.1	83.8	45.28	5,876	723
Scranton city	(NA)	(NA)	66,211	36,299	85,824	13.8	2.2	14.1	26.3	72.1	18.5	82.6	37.56	6,234	611
State College borough	267	762,593	19,441	6,304	32,303	13.8	18.4	1.9	25.4	71.2	18.3	80.7	39.76	6,345	538
Wilkes-Barre city	308	1,059,274	(NA)	(NA)	(NA)	(NA)	(NA)	(NA)	21.5	67.7	13.2	77.4	47.89	7,466	234
Williamsport city	211	676,427	18,893	8,154	17,605	24.8	0.1	8.8	25.5	72.4	17.9	83.2	41.59	6,063	709
York city	423	1,407,000	(NA)	(NA)	(NA)	(NA)	(NA)	(NA)	30.0	74.6	20.9	86.5	43.00	5,233	862
RHODE ISLAND	(X)	(X)	(X)	(X)	(X)	(NA)	(NA)	(NA)	(X)	(X)	(X)	(X)	(X)	(X)	(X)
Cranston city	(NA)	(NA)	177,500	110,254	180,860	10.4	9.1	2.5	28.7	73.3	20.3	82.6	46.45	5,754	714
East Providence city	(NA)	(NA)	105,490	59,836	110,486	7.5	5.8	5.1	28.7	73.3	20.3	82.6	46.45	5,754	714
Newport city	964	3,205,885	85,181	50,867	91,022	8.6	6.0	2.3	30.5	71.0	22.6	77.6	46.00	5,624	475
Pawtucket city	2,606	10,098,058	152,218	66,054	146,222	8.9	2.5	1.7	28.7	73.3	20.3	82.6	46.45	5,754	714
Providence city	(NA)	(NA)	530,722	220,453	492,289	7.4	1.7	0.8	28.7	73.3	20.3	82.6	46.45	5,754	714
Warwick city	2,928	10,170,503	228,422	152,849	235,442	6.7	2.6	2.5	28.7	73.3	20.3	82.6	46.45	5,754	714
Woonsocket city	(NA)	(NA)	(NA)	(NA)	(NA)	(NA)	(NA)	(NA)	25.4	72.3	13.3	84.3	48.75	6,302	534
SOUTH CAROLINA	(X)	(X)	(X)	(X)	(X)	(NA)	(NA)	(NA)	(X)	(X)	(X)	(X)	(X)	(X)	(X)
Aiken city	369	875,696	25,710	12,766	31,013	13.3	20.3	4.8	45.6	81.7	33.4	93.7	52.43	2,413	2,081
Anderson city	382	852,433	27,369	13,911	25,352	22.4	20.5	5.4	41.7	79.7	31.3	90.5	46.67	3,087	1,700
Charleston city	2,002	5,357,802	152,505	71,691	101,100	23.5	18.3	2.6	49.8	82.8	42.4	88.5	46.39	1,755	2,473
Columbia city	(NA)	(NA)	148,493	55,764	132,716	19.1	18.6	2.7	47.3	83.6	36.5	95.2	47.14	2,044	2,475
Florence city	444	988,315	26,102	9,536	33,008	16.6	33.2	5.7	45.0	81.2	35.2	90.7	44.76	2,523	2,029
Goose Creek city	148	367,292	9,146	4,271	8,387	33.8	9.2	5.7	47.9	81.7	36.9	90.9	51.53	2,005	2,306
Greenville city	1,033	3,101,103	90,242	53,667	88,365	14.5	6.6	9.2	40.8	78.8	31.4	88.8	50.24	3,272	1,526
Hilton Head Island town	239	916,466	27,231	19,709	31,146	6.8	–	–	47.9	80.5	37.3	88.2	52.52	2,128	2,012
Mount Pleasant town	509	1,229,536	41,160	20,900	38,097	17.8	22.8	6.2	47.1	81.1	37.5	88.5	49.38	2,260	2,124
North Charleston city	888	2,083,482	59,011	33,988	61,372	25.6	7.1	8.2	47.9	81.7	36.9	90.9	51.53	2,005	2,306
Rock Hill city	659	1,531,973	33,638	19,318	34,912	20.4	11.0	3.5	42.2	80.1	32.5	90.1	48.32	2,934	1,721
Spartanburg city	654	1,759,746	33,941	19,565	29,579	28.1	13.1	6.7	42.1	79.3	30.1	91.1	49.95	3,080	1,591
Summerville town	267	699,973	17,928	8,997	14,738	19.7	22.3	9.4	49.1	81.8	38.0	91.8	48.24	1,907	2,251
Sumter city	510	1,068,994	25,069	10,855	19,328	33.9	16.9	4.6	44.9	80.7	33.6	91.8	48.65	2,577	1,913
SOUTH DAKOTA	(X)	(X)	(X)	(X)	(X)	(NA)	(NA)	(NA)	(X)	(X)	(X)	(X)	(X)	(X)	(X)
Rapid City city	(NA)	(NA)	69,891	39,816	66,983	11.6	7.1	19.6	22.3	70.2	10.3	82.7	18.45	7,623	480
Sioux Falls city	1,101	3,528,153	135,661	93,898	116,194	13.8	10.5	20.4	14.0	73.0	2.9	85.6	24.69	7,812	747

See footnotes at end of table.

Table C-6. Cities — **Government and Climate**—Con.

[Includes states and 1,265 incorporated places of 25,000 or more population as of April 1, 2000, in all states except Hawaii, which has no incorporated places recognized by the U.S. Census Bureau. Two census designated places (CDPs) are also included (Honolulu CDP in Hawaii and Arlington CDP in Virginia). For more information on these areas, see Appendix C, Geographic Information]

City	City government employment, March 2002		City government finances, 2001–2002						Climate, 1971–2000[2]						
			General revenue ($1,000)		General expenditure				Average daily temperature (degrees Fahrenheit)		Min. and max. temperatures (degrees Fahrenheit)				
						By selected function, percent of total									
	Total employ-ment	Total payroll ($1,000)	Total	Taxes	Total[1] ($1,000)	Police pro-tection	Sewer-age and solid waste manage-ment	High-ways	January	July	January[3]	July[4]	Annual precip-itation (inches)	Heat-ing degree days[5]	Cooling degree days[6]
TENNESSEE	(X)	(X)	(X)	(X)	(X)	(NA)	(NA)	(NA)	(X)	(X)	(X)	(X)	(X)	(X)	(X)
Bartlett city	(NA)	(NA)	33,791	11,907	31,283	25.6	12.1	15.9	37.3	79.6	27.3	89.9	55.09	3,665	1,635
Brentwood city	(NA)	(NA)	(NA)	(NA)	(NA)	(NA)	(NA)	(NA)	36.8	79.1	27.9	88.7	48.11	3,677	1,652
Bristol city	(NA)	(NA)	(NA)	(NA)	(NA)	(NA)	(NA)	(NA)	34.2	74.2	24.3	84.8	41.33	4,445	956
Chattanooga city	3,264	10,374,844	291,311	113,293	256,469	13.9	12.6	7.2	39.4	79.6	29.9	89.8	54.52	3,427	1,608
Clarksville city	1,105	2,867,220	66,268	24,809	75,990	17.3	9.2	11.3	35.2	79.0	25.0	90.4	51.78	4,058	1,512
Cleveland city	(NA)	(NA)	63,494	13,228	56,831	10.0	10.8	4.9	38.0	77.5	27.7	88.5	55.42	3,782	1,333
Collierville town	423	1,221,361	33,625	15,413	33,166	18.2	14.6	9.5	37.9	81.1	28.2	91.1	53.63	3,491	1,838
Columbia city	486	1,375,948	28,668	6,330	31,252	16.3	34.6	7.4	35.6	77.2	25.0	88.5	56.13	4,183	1,267
Cookeville city	(NA)	(NA)	(NA)	(NA)	(NA)	(NA)	(NA)	(NA)	35.5	76.5	25.3	87.7	57.82	4,229	1,190
Franklin city	483	1,376,476	(NA)	(NA)	(NA)	(NA)	(NA)	(NA)	35.1	77.4	25.2	88.9	54.33	4,199	1,294
Germantown city	(NA)	(NA)	38,582	15,779	39,059	17.1	12.3	5.0	37.9	81.1	28.2	91.1	53.63	3,491	1,838
Hendersonville city	247	697,375	21,061	6,816	22,539	20.6	11.9	25.2	36.8	79.1	27.9	88.7	48.11	3,677	1,652
Jackson city	993	2,857,297	83,113	25,600	72,053	14.0	27.1	10.9	37.1	79.6	28.2	89.4	54.86	3,649	1,648
Johnson City city	1,998	5,246,075	124,823	33,443	115,404	8.8	13.1	6.3	34.2	74.2	24.3	84.8	41.33	4,445	956
Kingsport city	(NA)	(NA)	113,135	38,401	104,171	6.7	12.4	3.6	35.6	76.2	26.2	86.9	44.44	4,178	1,139
Knoxville city	2,939	8,715,038	256,726	123,510	226,504	16.6	12.2	2.9	38.5	78.7	30.3	88.2	48.22	3,531	1,527
Memphis city	26,717	86,792,941	1,601,763	364,395	1,520,287	10.2	4.7	1.6	39.9	82.5	31.3	92.1	54.65	3,041	2,187
Morristown city	(NA)	(NA)	(NA)	(NA)	(NA)	(NA)	(NA)	(NA)	35.5	76.6	26.3	86.7	45.99	4,214	1,191
Murfreesboro city	1,966	4,587,896	99,888	28,010	129,382	7.2	16.8	2.7	35.4	78.1	25.3	89.1	54.98	4,107	1,388
Nashville-Davidson (balance)	20,607	66,769,403	1,711,385	682,890	1,641,965	7.1	5.7	1.9	36.8	79.1	27.9	88.7	48.11	3,677	1,652
Oak Ridge city	(NA)	(NA)	71,825	17,195	70,033	6.2	11.8	3.3	36.6	77.3	27.2	88.1	55.05	3,993	1,301
Smyrna town	(NA)	(NA)	(NA)	(NA)	(NA)	(NA)	(NA)	(NA)	36.8	79.1	27.9	88.7	48.11	3,677	1,652
TEXAS	(X)	(X)	(X)	(X)	(X)	(NA)	(NA)	(NA)	(X)	(X)	(X)	(X)	(X)	(X)	(X)
Abilene city	(NA)	(NA)	84,076	51,679	85,345	16.2	14.7	11.2	43.5	83.5	31.8	94.8	23.78	2,659	2,386
Allen city	468	1,456,478	54,545	33,282	59,710	13.5	7.7	5.6	41.8	82.4	31.1	92.7	41.01	2,843	2,060
Amarillo city	1,939	5,117,286	187,157	77,788	156,896	12.7	13.5	9.1	35.8	78.2	22.6	91.0	19.71	4,318	1,344
Arlington city	(NA)	(NA)	290,984	159,899	276,448	19.2	13.4	12.7	44.1	85.0	34.0	95.4	34.73	2,370	2,568
Austin city	11,646	40,352,129	970,782	406,973	1,028,153	12.0	14.6	2.3	50.2	84.2	40.0	95.0	33.65	1,648	2,974
Baytown city	(NA)	(NA)	63,813	40,176	60,880	31.6	16.1	10.6	51.6	83.6	41.9	91.6	53.75	1,471	2,841
Beaumont city	1,460	4,316,552	104,396	64,104	110,342	19.2	9.2	14.2	51.1	83.1	41.1	92.7	57.38	1,548	2,734
Bedford city	(NA)	(NA)	29,811	21,597	27,465	26.1	9.2	7.7	44.1	85.0	34.0	95.4	34.73	2,370	2,568
Big Spring city	284	686,699	56,686	8,377	57,253	5.1	5.9	2.7	42.7	82.7	29.6	94.3	20.12	2,724	2,243
Brownsville city	1,298	3,541,249	103,527	44,483	110,720	17.3	10.7	7.0	59.6	83.9	50.5	92.4	27.55	644	3,874
Bryan city	884	2,872,772	63,534	26,509	68,246	13.7	19.2	15.1	50.2	84.6	39.8	95.6	39.67	1,616	2,938
Carrollton city	(NA)	(NA)	105,808	70,242	99,873	14.9	6.3	8.8	44.1	85.0	34.0	95.4	34.73	2,370	2,568
Cedar Hill city	240	733,040	24,681	14,839	23,438	20.2	12.7	11.2	43.7	84.3	33.2	94.9	34.54	2,437	2,508
Cedar Park city	(NA)	(NA)	(NA)	(NA)	(NA)	(NA)	(NA)	(NA)	47.2	83.8	35.1	95.7	36.42	1,998	2,584
Cleburne city	296	843,064	26,398	12,451	23,650	14.8	28.4	7.9	45.9	84.5	34.0	97.0	36.25	2,158	2,604
College Station city	832	2,424,468	55,173	27,735	71,474	10.0	19.7	13.5	50.2	84.6	39.8	95.6	39.67	1,616	2,938
Conroe city	450	1,318,208	38,435	29,106	39,502	17.3	8.2	5.7	50.3	83.7	40.0	94.3	49.32	1,647	2,793
Coppell city	347	1,192,372	44,240	31,378	45,414	11.3	3.0	19.9	44.1	85.0	34.0	95.4	34.73	2,370	2,568
Copperas Cove city	218	562,791	14,466	6,637	14,621	27.4	19.1	7.8	46.0	83.5	34.0	95.3	32.88	2,190	2,477
Corpus Christi city	(NA)	(NA)	237,040	111,075	223,553	18.1	19.2	8.0	56.1	83.8	46.2	93.2	32.26	950	3,497
Dallas city	15,451	59,452,335	1,744,086	798,362	2,013,212	11.6	9.6	5.3	45.9	86.5	36.4	96.1	37.05	2,219	2,878
Deer Park city	354	709,914	22,562	16,150	19,574	19.6	27.3	3.5	54.3	84.5	45.2	93.6	53.96	1,174	3,179
Del Rio city	366	815,723	25,353	8,969	24,398	16.6	24.4	6.7	51.3	85.3	39.7	96.2	18.80	1,417	3,226
Denton city	1,120	4,341,615	90,086	40,030	103,419	11.4	25.1	4.0	42.7	83.6	32.0	94.1	37.79	2,650	2,269
DeSoto city	312	1,057,293	34,675	20,859	38,964	14.8	9.8	24.0	46.0	84.6	35.0	96.0	38.81	2,130	2,608
Duncanville city	288	933,575	29,459	18,261	29,302	19.4	22.4	10.3	45.9	86.5	36.4	96.1	37.05	2,219	2,878
Edinburg city	(NA)	(NA)	36,090	18,822	37,341	14.4	19.1	7.1	58.7	85.1	48.2	95.5	22.61	719	3,898
El Paso city	5,545	15,185,442	444,055	208,348	438,238	18.8	11.1	4.1	45.1	83.3	32.9	94.5	9.43	2,543	2,254
Euless city	423	1,413,732	39,683	20,108	56,828	25.0	8.2	9.1	44.1	85.0	34.0	95.4	34.73	2,370	2,568
Farmers Branch city	544	1,869,664	54,337	38,359	48,619	17.2	13.5	10.8	45.9	86.5	36.4	96.1	37.05	2,219	2,878
Flower Mound town	417	1,313,912	27,176	20,125	33,318	13.3	13.2	5.2	44.1	85.0	34.0	95.4	34.73	2,370	2,568
Fort Worth city	6,164	21,379,975	624,201	346,941	566,215	21.4	14.9	11.9	43.3	84.5	31.4	96.6	34.01	2,509	2,466
Friendswood city	203	488,819	18,410	12,486	14,976	26.1	16.9	5.7	54.3	84.5	45.2	93.6	53.96	1,174	3,179
Frisco city	299	1,064,311	(NA)	(NA)	(NA)	(NA)	(NA)	(NA)	41.8	82.4	31.1	92.7	41.01	2,843	2,060
Galveston city	851	2,430,787	88,008	35,117	68,887	17.5	9.9	6.8	55.8	84.3	49.7	88.7	43.84	1,008	3,268
Garland city	2,033	7,521,747	166,728	78,539	194,263	15.0	11.0	13.0	45.9	86.5	36.4	96.1	37.05	2,219	2,878
Georgetown city	(NA)	(NA)	22,975	10,786	38,328	10.3	11.3	3.8	47.2	83.8	35.1	95.7	36.42	1,998	2,584
Grand Prairie city	1,231	4,179,816	136,485	76,523	134,338	16.6	15.1	8.0	44.1	85.0	34.0	95.4	34.73	2,370	2,568
Grapevine city	(NA)	(NA)	(NA)	(NA)	(NA)	(NA)	(NA)	(NA)	42.4	84.0	30.8	95.5	34.66	2,649	2,340
Haltom City city	323	827,827	22,676	16,030	23,423	23.9	17.3	14.6	43.0	84.1	31.4	95.7	34.12	2,608	2,358
Harlingen city	772	1,828,213	61,730	27,556	67,074	12.3	20.0	5.6	58.6	84.4	48.4	94.5	28.13	737	3,736
Houston city	(NA)	(NA)	2,290,340	1,212,296	2,600,871	16.9	13.8	7.3	54.3	84.5	45.2	93.6	53.96	1,174	3,179
Huntsville city	261	759,515	23,050	9,792	35,514	9.1	33.2	25.9	48.5	83.2	39.0	93.8	48.51	1,835	2,600
Hurst city	392	1,337,310	39,271	28,368	33,693	26.4	12.8	10.6	44.1	85.0	34.0	95.4	34.73	2,370	2,568
Irving city	(NA)	(NA)	206,102	142,147	212,473	16.2	12.9	13.6	45.9	86.5	36.4	96.1	37.05	2,219	2,878

See footnotes at end of table.

Table C-6. Cities — **Government and Climate**—Con.

[Includes states and 1,265 incorporated places of 25,000 or more population as of April 1, 2000, in all states except Hawaii, which has no incorporated places recognized by the U.S. Census Bureau. Two census designated places (CDPs) are also included (Honolulu CDP in Hawaii and Arlington CDP in Virginia). For more information on these areas, see Appendix C, Geographic Information]

City	City government employment, March 2002		City government finances, 2001–2002						Climate, 1971–2000[2]						
			General revenue ($1,000)		General expenditure				Average daily temperature (degrees Fahrenheit)		Min. and max. temperatures (degrees Fahrenheit)				
						By selected function, percent of total									
	Total employ-ment	Total payroll ($1,000)	Total	Taxes	Total[1] ($1,000)	Police pro-tection	Sewer-age and solid waste manage-ment	High-ways	January	July	January[3]	July[4]	Annual precip-itation (inches)	Heat-ing degree days[5]	Cooling degree days[6]
TEXAS—Con.															
Keller city	233	785,627	(NA)	(NA)	(NA)	(NA)	(NA)	(NA)	43.0	84.1	31.4	95.7	34.12	2,608	2,358
Killeen city	(NA)	(NA)	55,689	31,228	52,058	21.6	19.1	6.9	46.0	83.5	34.0	95.3	32.88	2,190	2,477
Kingsville city	263	609,093	14,594	8,196	13,714	30.1	18.8	13.4	55.9	84.3	43.4	95.5	29.03	1,001	3,404
Lake Jackson city	261	626,573	21,414	13,193	19,326	17.3	17.0	12.2	54.0	83.7	45.4	90.2	50.66	1,234	3,003
Lancaster city	(NA)	(NA)	26,178	14,903	29,812	9.5	17.4	3.4	44.4	84.0	33.3	95.7	38.69	2,380	2,452
La Porte city	396	1,199,121	33,997	16,362	28,890	22.2	14.4	8.6	51.6	83.6	41.9	91.6	53.75	1,471	2,841
Laredo city	(NA)	(NA)	188,485	65,090	182,194	16.4	9.9	20.0	55.6	88.5	43.7	101.6	21.53	931	4,213
League City city	357	1,033,132	38,149	23,510	31,287	19.6	12.7	10.3	52.7	82.7	43.1	91.2	51.73	1,365	2,815
Lewisville city	723	2,243,474	76,682	43,271	48,981	22.7	5.4	8.4	42.7	83.6	32.0	94.1	37.79	2,650	2,269
Longview city	844	2,091,011	72,006	42,705	74,479	16.6	22.3	8.8	45.4	83.4	33.7	94.5	49.06	2,319	2,355
Lubbock city	1,991	6,174,184	164,091	78,019	171,899	17.5	17.4	8.2	38.1	79.8	24.4	91.9	18.69	3,508	1,769
Lufkin city	479	1,408,187	35,075	18,201	36,976	17.1	16.8	19.4	48.6	82.6	37.9	93.5	46.62	1,900	2,480
McAllen city	1,406	3,320,783	144,719	63,866	121,758	21.6	12.0	8.1	58.7	85.1	48.2	95.5	21.69	719	3,898
McKinney city	489	1,841,886	61,828	38,646	58,718	12.8	10.7	14.8	41.8	82.4	31.1	92.7	41.01	2,843	2,060
Mansfield city	(NA)	(NA)	34,711	21,932	31,352	11.3	9.1	18.1	43.7	84.3	33.2	94.9	34.54	2,437	2,508
Mesquite city	1,030	3,967,353	94,988	59,828	98,687	21.6	9.3	11.3	45.9	86.5	36.4	96.1	37.05	2,219	2,878
Midland city	(NA)	(NA)	83,600	44,819	96,047	15.0	11.4	5.6	44.5	81.8	29.5	95.6	14.84	2,479	2,241
Mission city	(NA)	(NA)	26,780	14,186	28,498	20.9	17.6	16.5	58.8	86.3	47.5	97.7	22.13	740	4,128
Missouri City city	252	879,150	27,022	21,084	28,812	18.5	2.5	20.7	51.8	84.1	41.6	93.7	49.34	1,475	2,950
Nacogdoches city	321	852,244	24,517	12,259	24,171	13.1	21.2	4.1	46.5	83.9	36.4	93.5	48.36	2,150	2,555
New Braunfels city	508	1,329,157	(NA)	(NA)	(NA)	(NA)	(NA)	(NA)	48.6	82.7	35.5	94.7	35.74	1,840	2,545
North Richland Hills city	(NA)	(NA)	59,564	36,141	55,805	21.0	11.8	12.1	44.1	85.0	34.0	95.4	34.73	2,370	2,568
Odessa city	831	2,239,740	61,715	28,268	64,122	21.4	12.8	7.1	43.2	81.7	29.6	94.3	14.80	2,716	2,139
Paris city	(NA)	(NA)	26,761	13,789	28,860	18.2	13.2	17.9	40.6	83.1	29.9	94.3	47.82	2,972	2,197
Pasadena city	1,002	3,416,086	101,793	68,023	91,494	31.0	19.0	7.4	54.3	84.5	45.2	93.6	53.96	1,174	3,179
Pearland city	313	875,815	31,771	22,452	29,542	18.3	15.1	6.4	54.3	84.5	45.2	93.6	53.96	1,174	3,179
Pharr city	375	877,331	(NA)	(NA)	(NA)	(NA)	(NA)	(NA)	60.1	85.9	50.3	96.1	22.96	624	4,181
Plano city	2,349	8,317,767	244,980	155,367	241,975	14.5	17.1	2.0	44.1	85.0	34.0	95.4	34.73	2,370	2,568
Port Arthur city	653	1,989,721	48,179	15,557	51,719	18.9	13.5	11.0	52.2	82.7	42.9	91.6	59.89	1,447	2,823
Richardson city	(NA)	(NA)	119,198	63,612	164,691	10.8	10.3	13.7	45.9	86.5	36.4	96.1	37.05	2,219	2,878
Round Rock city	563	1,881,326	75,547	52,448	81,886	12.2	7.0	36.9	47.2	83.8	35.1	95.7	36.42	1,998	2,584
Rowlett city	316	1,070,921	(NA)	(NA)	(NA)	(NA)	(NA)	(NA)	42.1	82.8	30.8	94.2	40.06	2,710	2,212
San Angelo city	941	2,149,182	64,679	38,925	56,644	21.2	12.8	(NA)	44.9	82.4	31.8	94.4	20.91	2,396	2,383
San Antonio city	17,797	53,864,556	1,079,231	444,765	1,121,493	16.5	12.8	8.3	50.3	84.3	38.6	94.6	32.92	1,573	3,038
San Juan city	154	284,121	7,883	3,747	9,874	16.4	46.8	–	60.1	85.9	50.3	96.1	22.96	624	4,181
San Marcos city	487	1,532,368	37,195	20,974	38,854	17.4	14.0	15.9	49.9	84.4	38.6	95.1	37.19	1,629	2,913
Sherman city	431	1,296,200	31,343	18,383	35,065	13.2	22.9	10.5	41.5	82.8	32.2	92.7	42.04	2,850	2,137
Socorro city	68	123,897	3,486	1,977	2,731	28.5	–	–	44.9	83.6	29.2	98.7	9.71	2,557	2,372
Sugar Land city	445	1,545,709	64,464	46,024	47,123	17.3	12.7	8.1	51.8	84.1	41.6	93.7	49.34	1,475	2,950
Temple city	632	1,653,665	52,870	29,910	55,521	13.7	14.5	4.9	46.1	83.7	34.9	95.0	35.81	2,191	2,551
Texarkana city	577	1,480,549	34,512	19,024	30,943	18.3	19.7	8.8	41.6	82.6	30.7	93.1	51.24	2,893	2,138
Texas City city	484	1,420,946	(NA)	(NA)	(NA)	(NA)	(NA)	(NA)	55.8	84.3	49.7	88.7	43.84	1,008	3,268
The Colony city	282	752,340	17,254	11,831	15,453	20.5	12.6	6.4	42.7	83.6	32.0	94.1	37.79	2,650	2,269
Tyler city	762	2,178,219	72,610	33,608	65,826	21.3	18.0	5.1	47.5	83.4	33.7	93.4	45.27	1,958	2,521
Victoria city	594	1,661,521	57,429	34,547	54,364	15.7	21.6	13.2	53.2	84.2	43.6	93.4	40.10	1,248	3,203
Waco city	1,406	4,349,264	125,754	61,958	117,168	17.6	19.5	5.8	46.1	85.4	35.1	96.7	33.34	2,164	2,840
Weslaco city	310	676,382	23,519	13,732	22,163	17.2	16.2	7.4	58.6	84.5	47.7	95.4	25.37	755	3,791
Wichita Falls city	(NA)	(NA)	85,022	47,931	81,993	17.2	17.0	7.3	40.5	84.8	28.9	97.2	28.83	3,024	2,396
UTAH	(X)	(X)	(X)	(X)	(X)	(NA)	(NA)	(NA)	(X)	(X)	(X)	(X)	(X)	(X)	(X)
Bountiful city	(NA)	(NA)	24,309	10,399	33,112	12.8	48.5	10.2	29.1	75.8	21.6	88.4	22.40	5,937	861
Clearfield city	219	393,225	16,392	8,902	14,613	18.1	17.9	5.8	27.6	74.2	18.6	89.9	20.75	6,142	746
Draper city	108	277,432	19,951	10,890	16,247	20.5	7.7	16.0	31.6	78.0	22.0	95.3	15.76	5,251	1,172
Layton city	385	926,650	30,943	17,782	30,216	19.9	21.0	16.6	27.6	74.2	18.6	89.9	20.75	6,142	746
Logan city	531	1,339,530	38,024	11,823	36,072	15.3	20.6	10.4	21.8	71.6	12.7	88.3	17.86	7,174	522
Midvale city	177	553,759	15,397	9,647	16,023	25.4	6.3	16.6	30.4	78.5	22.1	90.9	26.19	5,441	1,197
Murray city	531	1,580,885	(NA)	(NA)	(NA)	(NA)	(NA)	(NA)	29.2	77.0	21.3	90.6	16.50	5,631	1,066
Ogden city	814	2,349,984	66,202	34,234	69,502	16.4	17.4	8.2	28.1	76.6	20.1	90.0	23.67	5,868	980
Orem city	653	1,585,815	53,805	28,484	62,652	13.6	15.3	13.5	28.6	76.5	20.3	92.3	12.84	5,564	1,016
Provo city	808	2,424,962	74,258	34,437	72,961	16.4	10.3	10.3	30.9	76.9	22.5	93.4	20.13	5,264	1,028
Riverton city	77	153,859	11,307	5,409	11,926	9.4	7.6	16.6	31.6	78.0	22.0	95.3	15.76	5,251	1,172
Roy city	229	460,704	15,100	8,222	14,351	20.3	19.8	13.0	27.6	74.2	18.6	89.9	20.75	6,142	746
St. George city	(NA)	(NA)	52,439	23,134	41,689	14.7	21.9	16.5	41.8	86.3	28.9	102.8	8.77	3,103	2,471
Salt Lake City city	3,516	11,055,310	348,564	147,718	389,666	11.2	8.2	6.7	32.0	78.1	25.4	90.9	17.75	5,095	1,190
Sandy city	(NA)	(NA)	49,255	29,790	54,145	18.3	6.1	17.4	30.4	78.5	22.1	90.9	26.19	5,441	1,197
South Jordan city	187	520,268	19,281	9,564	24,351	9.7	8.9	41.6	31.6	78.0	22.0	95.3	15.76	5,251	1,172
Taylorsville city	30	82,739	17,759	11,707	17,108	18.2	2.3	20.1	29.2	77.0	21.3	90.6	16.50	5,631	1,066
West Jordan city	424	1,176,629	36,406	20,628	54,984	11.0	20.1	22.4	30.4	78.5	22.1	90.9	26.19	5,441	1,197
West Valley City city	741	2,218,410	83,078	37,280	112,764	13.8	2.4	7.4	29.2	77.0	21.3	90.6	16.50	5,631	1,066

See footnotes at end of table.

Table C-6. Cities — **Government and Climate**—Con.

[Includes states and 1,265 incorporated places of 25,000 or more population as of April 1, 2000, in all states except Hawaii, which has no incorporated places recognized by the U.S. Census Bureau. Two census designated places (CDPs) are also included (Honolulu CDP in Hawaii and Arlington CDP in Virginia). For more information on these areas, see Appendix C, Geographic Information]

City	City government employment, March 2002: Total employment	Total payroll ($1,000)	City government finances, 2001–2002 / General revenue ($1,000): Total	Taxes	General expenditure: Total[1] ($1,000)	Police protection	Sewerage and solid waste management	Highways	Climate, 1971–2000[2] / Average daily temperature (°F): January	July	Min. and max. temperatures (°F): January[3]	July[4]	Annual precipitation (inches)	Heating degree days[5]	Cooling degree days[6]
VERMONT	(X)	(X)	(X)	(X)	(X)	(NA)	(NA)	(NA)	(X)	(X)	(X)	(X)	(X)	(X)	(X)
Burlington city	(NA)	(NA)	60,112	21,079	63,883	11.6	8.0	6.1	18.0	70.6	9.3	81.4	36.05	7,665	489
VIRGINIA	(X)	(X)	(X)	(X)	(X)	(NA)	(NA)	(NA)	(X)	(X)	(X)	(X)	(X)	(X)	(X)
Alexandria city	4,787	17,981,409	479,470	293,326	468,357	7.4	4.5	4.1	34.9	79.2	27.3	88.3	39.35	4,055	1,531
Arlington CDP	(NA)	(NA)	(NA)	(NA)	(NA)	(NA)	(NA)	(NA)	34.9	79.2	27.3	88.3	39.35	4,055	1,531
Blacksburg town	523	842,090	21,752	8,436	20,105	20.5	17.3	9.1	30.9	71.1	20.6	82.5	42.63	5,559	533
Charlottesville city	2,181	4,595,813	135,006	59,225	137,709	7.3	4.4	2.7	35.5	76.9	26.2	88.0	48.87	4,103	1,212
Chesapeake city	8,985	24,606,358	595,686	264,098	596,178	6.6	4.1	6.3	40.1	79.1	32.3	86.8	45.74	3,368	1,612
Danville city	2,936	6,530,888	141,957	40,020	147,591	5.7	6.2	5.0	36.6	78.8	25.8	90.0	44.98	3,970	1,418
Hampton city	8,302	17,180,917	374,223	158,411	427,023	5.6	2.6	0.5	39.4	78.5	32.0	85.2	47.90	3,535	1,432
Harrisonburg city	1,302	3,164,731	87,956	40,412	91,930	5.3	7.7	6.4	30.5	73.5	20.4	85.3	36.12	5,333	758
Leesburg town	(NA)	(NA)	32,266	15,784	25,631	16.2	19.1	10.5	31.5	75.2	20.8	87.1	43.21	5,031	911
Lynchburg city	3,208	7,331,804	202,450	80,699	198,092	5.6	4.7	6.8	34.5	75.1	24.5	86.4	43.31	4,354	1,075
Manassas city	1,470	4,655,233	115,452	57,107	109,715	8.2	8.0	7.4	31.7	75.7	21.9	87.4	41.80	4,925	1,075
Newport News city	9,480	23,538,810	604,137	216,931	585,729	5.6	3.2	3.5	41.2	80.3	33.8	87.9	43.53	3,179	1,682
Norfolk city	13,561	33,796,732	886,700	288,216	899,006	5.1	3.5	4.0	40.1	79.1	32.3	86.8	45.74	3,368	1,612
Petersburg city	1,932	4,282,617	(NA)	(NA)	(NA)	(NA)	(NA)	(NA)	39.7	79.6	29.2	91.0	45.26	3,334	1,619
Portsmouth city	(NA)	(NA)	316,883	94,060	317,578	5.9	5.5	1.5	40.1	79.1	32.3	86.8	45.74	3,368	1,612
Richmond city	(NA)	(NA)	886,104	332,288	864,760	6.8	7.7	3.1	36.4	77.9	27.6	87.5	43.91	3,919	1,435
Roanoke city	4,973	12,918,103	337,657	130,974	328,837	4.6	4.3	3.6	35.8	76.2	26.6	87.5	42.49	4,284	1,134
Suffolk city	3,104	7,282,259	181,403	77,140	185,796	4.8	5.7	2.4	39.6	78.5	30.3	88.1	48.71	3,467	1,427
Virginia Beach city	(NA)	(NA)	1,342,140	582,688	1,272,770	4.8	4.0	1.8	40.7	78.8	32.2	86.9	44.50	3,336	1,482
WASHINGTON	(X)	(X)	(X)	(X)	(X)	(NA)	(NA)	(NA)	(X)	(X)	(X)	(X)	(X)	(X)	(X)
Auburn city	472	2,116,580	87,263	36,966	69,260	13.0	23.6	25.7	40.8	66.4	34.6	77.4	39.59	4,624	219
Bellevue city	(NA)	(NA)	194,089	121,514	177,223	10.6	13.2	18.3	41.5	65.5	36.0	74.5	38.25	4,615	192
Bellingham city	983	3,321,864	87,667	45,910	73,607	13.4	9.6	9.5	40.5	63.3	34.8	72.5	34.84	4,980	68
Bothell city	270	1,225,138	39,320	23,518	32,042	24.9	11.7	13.2	40.8	65.2	35.2	75.0	35.96	4,756	174
Bremerton city	398	1,587,052	45,483	18,832	49,628	13.3	20.5	14.9	40.1	64.6	34.7	75.2	53.96	4,994	158
Burien city	63	200,028	15,718	10,063	14,499	34.3	2.4	21.0	40.9	65.3	35.9	75.3	37.07	4,797	173
Des Moines city	(NA)	(NA)	20,693	9,466	18,018	28.0	3.2	21.0	40.9	65.3	35.9	75.3	37.07	4,797	173
Edmonds city	(NA)	(NA)	35,991	18,899	33,403	17.5	4.3	6.1	40.8	65.2	35.2	75.0	35.96	4,756	174
Everett city	1,105	5,516,326	151,010	82,948	155,478	12.8	9.3	15.4	39.7	63.6	33.6	73.0	37.54	5,199	121
Federal Way city	352	1,354,894	49,736	31,117	36,011	28.8	0.9	29.0	41.0	65.6	35.1	76.1	38.95	4,650	167
Kennewick city	409	1,503,274	46,968	26,958	42,942	14.7	8.5	18.2	34.2	75.2	28.0	89.3	8.01	4,731	909
Kent city	996	4,028,734	125,762	58,311	132,508	11.1	18.0	16.2	40.8	66.4	34.6	77.4	39.59	4,624	219
Kirkland city	(NA)	(NA)	66,470	34,024	69,774	10.7	19.3	12.9	40.8	65.2	35.2	75.0	35.96	4,756	174
Lacey city	268	886,554	34,115	16,508	31,023	15.4	19.1	23.3	38.1	62.8	31.8	76.1	50.79	5,531	97
Lakewood city	96	227,176	31,697	18,277	42,168	29.2	—	21.7	41.0	65.6	35.1	76.1	38.95	4,650	167
Longview city	(NA)	(NA)	37,907	18,448	36,611	16.6	24.3	9.8	39.9	64.5	33.8	76.5	48.02	4,900	148
Lynnwood city	444	1,663,967	51,491	25,264	42,707	16.2	6.0	20.9	40.8	65.2	35.2	75.0	35.96	4,756	174
Marysville city	240	886,843	27,221	12,489	29,883	11.1	19.2	10.9	39.7	63.6	33.6	73.0	37.54	5,199	121
Mount Vernon city	279	826,320	41,709	13,127	40,879	9.7	24.8	35.7	39.9	62.3	34.1	73.0	32.70	5,197	47
Olympia city	640	2,633,834	75,144	33,080	64,736	11.3	24.3	15.0	38.1	62.8	31.8	76.1	50.79	5,531	97
Pasco city	185	622,842	30,527	15,146	25,298	17.5	21.3	4.3	34.2	75.2	28.0	89.3	8.01	4,731	909
Puyallup city	379	1,443,748	44,740	27,660	42,352	14.7	11.8	11.8	39.9	64.9	32.9	77.8	40.51	4,991	153
Redmond city	642	2,710,856	86,926	49,582	68,436	9.3	15.7	25.5	25.1	55.0	20.0	65.0	82.86	9,630	12
Renton city	754	2,990,476	91,766	51,961	88,744	11.4	18.9	15.6	40.9	65.3	35.9	75.3	37.07	4,797	173
Richland city	503	2,242,099	52,108	24,705	46,285	10.2	11.4	10.6	33.0	73.2	26.0	87.9	7.55	5,133	739
Sammamish city	54	227,502	28,749	20,080	29,940	10.5	2.4	47.7	40.8	65.2	35.2	75.0	35.96	4,756	174
SeaTac city	167	729,570	37,645	27,386	42,352	13.0	—	25.8	40.9	65.3	35.9	75.3	37.07	4,797	173
Seattle city	12,466	53,245,901	1,297,473	688,510	1,299,838	12.1	19.9	8.0	41.5	65.5	36.0	74.5	38.25	4,615	192
Shoreline city	(NA)	(NA)	31,864	21,230	25,430	24.8	1.7	11.3	40.8	65.2	35.2	75.0	35.96	4,756	174
Spokane city	2,434	8,788,215	238,784	94,651	214,262	14.7	25.9	8.0	27.3	68.6	21.7	82.5	16.67	6,820	394
Spokane Valley city	(X)	(X)	(X)	(X)	(X)	(NA)	(NA)	(NA)	27.3	68.6	21.7	82.5	16.67	6,820	394
Tacoma city	3,554	17,443,347	293,305	124,356	255,254	13.7	26.0	10.3	41.0	65.6	35.1	76.1	38.95	4,650	167
University Place city	98	246,364	17,245	8,686	13,968	23.4	(Z)	48.7	41.0	65.6	35.1	76.1	38.95	4,650	167
Vancouver city	1,294	4,865,225	140,371	64,130	148,485	11.3	13.2	15.0	39.0	65.4	32.4	77.3	41.92	4,990	197
Walla Walla city	(NA)	(NA)	31,723	9,907	30,360	11.6	15.5	13.1	34.7	75.3	28.8	89.9	20.88	4,882	957
Wenatchee city	(NA)	(NA)	24,709	13,083	22,111	15.4	12.1	21.2	29.2	74.4	23.2	87.8	9.12	5,533	832
Yakima city	654	2,606,947	68,477	35,234	59,010	18.1	15.3	9.0	29.1	69.1	20.5	87.2	8.26	6,104	431
WEST VIRGINIA	(X)	(X)	(X)	(X)	(X)	(NA)	(NA)	(NA)	(X)	(X)	(X)	(X)	(X)	(X)	(X)
Charleston city	811	2,094,564	90,122	43,082	83,609	16.9	14.4	6.0	33.4	73.9	24.2	84.9	44.05	4,644	978
Huntington city	(NA)	(NA)	48,409	20,198	47,578	17.7	16.0	3.6	32.1	76.3	23.5	87.1	41.74	4,737	1,128
Morgantown city	(NA)	(NA)	26,886	11,139	26,895	14.0	9.8	8.6	30.8	73.5	22.3	83.4	43.30	5,174	815
Parkersburg city	(NA)	(NA)	—	—	—				30.7	75.4	22.3	85.8	40.69	5,091	1,038
Wheeling city	1,014	1,737,843	27,251	13,910	28,787	16.2	17.3	11.5	29.6	74.8	21.4	85.2	40.34	5,313	926

See footnotes at end of table.

Table C-6. Cities — **Government and Climate**—Con.

[Includes states and 1,265 incorporated places of 25,000 or more population as of April 1, 2000, in all states except Hawaii, which has no incorporated places recognized by the U.S. Census Bureau. Two census designated places (CDPs) are also included (Honolulu CDP in Hawaii and Arlington CDP in Virginia). For more information on these areas, see Appendix C, Geographic Information]

City	City government employment, March 2002		City government finances, 2001–2002							Climate, 1971–2000[2]						
			General revenue ($1,000)		General expenditure					Average daily temperature (degrees Fahrenheit)		Min. and max. temperatures (degrees Fahrenheit)				
						By selected function, percent of total										
	Total employ-ment	Total payroll ($1,000)	Total	Taxes	Total[1] ($1,000)	Police pro-tection	Sewer-age and solid waste manage-ment	High-ways	January	July	January[3]	July[4]	Annual precip-itation (inches)	Heat-ing degree days[5]	Cooling degree days[6]
WISCONSIN	(X)	(X)	(X)	(X)	(X)	(NA)	(NA)	(NA)	(X)	(X)	(X)	(X)	(X)	(X)	(X)
Appleton city.	(NA)	(NA)	84,424	29,015	84,112	15.0	15.4	20.5	16.0	71.6	7.8	81.4	30.16	7,721	572
Beloit city	(NA)	(NA)	53,157	9,712	53,371	16.5	18.1	10.2	19.1	72.4	11.6	82.5	35.25	6,969	664
Brookfield city	450	1,412,463	48,303	26,358	48,803	13.6	24.9	19.9	20.0	74.3	11.5	85.1	32.09	6,886	791
Eau Claire city.	(NA)	(NA)	65,422	22,228	65,564	15.6	7.9	25.3	11.9	71.4	2.5	82.6	32.12	8,196	554
Fond du Lac city	408	1,385,968	45,738	16,232	48,755	19.6	13.7	19.3	16.6	71.8	9.1	81.1	30.15	7,534	586
Franklin city	(NA)	(NA)	28,660	17,065	40,686	29.9	10.5	13.3	20.7	72.0	13.4	81.1	34.81	7,087	616
Green Bay city	1,189	3,737,245	220,391	36,670	225,983	9.2	8.3	9.2	15.6	69.9	7.1	81.2	29.19	7,963	463
Greenfield city	290	963,986	29,761	16,192	27,053	25.9	10.3	22.0	19.9	73.8	12.7	81.9	33.86	6,847	764
Janesville city	524	1,848,717	55,498	20,636	64,240	15.0	20.8	15.5	17.7	72.1	8.6	83.8	32.78	7,238	629
Kenosha city.	925	3,207,916	97,743	39,479	92,980	18.4	13.0	11.1	20.8	71.3	13.2	78.7	34.74	6,999	549
La Crosse city.	902	2,147,789	71,393	23,869	86,693	13.4	9.2	15.6	15.9	74.0	6.3	85.2	32.36	7,340	775
Madison city.	(NA)	(NA)	308,700	121,646	270,544	16.0	15.2	9.7	17.3	71.6	9.3	82.1	32.95	7,493	582
Manitowoc city.	518	1,548,101	41,547	10,149	52,678	10.2	18.9	20.1	18.7	69.9	10.8	79.6	30.49	7,563	425
Menomonee Falls village.	348	956,996	44,210	19,959	49,083	16.7	20.4	18.2	16.5	69.3	8.1	80.2	33.45	7,832	407
Milwaukee city.	(NA)	(NA)	883,790	207,775	862,207	23.0	12.2	12.1	20.0	74.3	11.5	85.1	32.09	6,886	791
New Berlin city	425	945,444	38,707	18,707	36,723	22.5	25.0	16.2	19.9	73.8	12.7	81.9	33.86	6,847	764
Oak Creek city	357	1,004,247	29,501	16,366	33,059	20.1	11.6	29.9	20.7	72.0	13.4	81.1	34.81	7,087	616
Oshkosh city.	(NA)	(NA)	65,706	21,587	67,609	13.8	14.2	19.2	16.1	72.0	7.8	81.8	31.57	7,639	591
Racine city	(NA)	(NA)	114,870	35,037	110,040	22.2	12.4	16.0	20.7	71.3	13.3	78.6	35.35	7,032	567
Sheboygan city	630	1,937,892	56,705	19,853	57,143	15.8	15.3	19.3	20.9	71.4	13.2	81.4	31.90	7,056	559
Superior city	324	947,128	40,550	10,863	36,415	15.3	13.3	15.4	12.1	66.6	3.4	76.2	30.78	9,006	241
Waukesha city.	682	2,383,551	63,076	32,025	71,487	16.5	21.2	10.9	19.5	73.8	11.4	84.2	34.64	6,893	784
Wausau city.	368	1,220,459	45,637	17,118	44,756	12.8	10.9	22.5	13.0	70.1	3.6	80.8	33.36	8,237	464
Wauwatosa city.	508	1,776,559	53,779	27,455	57,168	20.0	14.3	20.8	20.0	74.3	11.5	85.1	32.09	6,886	791
West Allis city	704	2,482,415	70,528	28,567	65,760	23.1	13.0	15.0	19.9	73.8	12.7	81.9	33.86	6,847	764
West Bend city	367	977,852	29,680	14,221	35,497	16.0	13.3	22.0	18.4	70.6	10.7	81.3	32.85	7,371	502
WYOMING	(X)	(X)	(X)	(X)	(X)	(NA)	(NA)	(NA)	(X)	(X)	(X)	(X)	(X)	(X)	(X)
Casper city.	635	1,612,725	58,928	5,180	70,051	13.6	15.1	17.3	22.3	70.0	12.2	86.8	13.03	7,571	428
Cheyenne city.	756	1,618,455	62,374	7,334	58,813	12.2	12.3	28.2	25.9	67.7	14.8	81.9	15.45	7,388	273
Laramie city	315	820,817	26,426	2,166	25,952	18.0	19.2	9.0	20.3	62.9	7.8	79.4	11.19	9,233	75

– Represents zero.   NA Not available.   X Not applicable.   Z Less than .05 percent.

[1]Includes amounts not shown separately.
[2]These data are the 30-year average values computed from the data recorded during the period 1971–2000.
[3]Average daily minimum.
[4]Average daily maximum.
[5]One heating degree day is accumulated for each whole degree that the mean daily temperature (max + min/2) is below 65 degrees Fahrenheit.
[6]One cooling degree day is accumulated for each whole degree that the mean daily temperature (max + min/2) is above 65 degrees Fahrenheit.

Survey, Census, or Data Collection Method: Employment, payroll, and finances—Based on the Census of Governments; for information, see Appendix B, Limitations of the Data and Methodology, and also <http://www.census.gov/govs/www/cog2002.html>.   Climate—Based on data from NOAA weather stations; for information, see Appendix B, Limitations of the Data and Methodology, and also <http://www.ncdc.noaa.gov/oa/climate/normals/usnormalsprods.html#CLIM81>.

Sources: Employment and payroll—U.S. Census Bureau, 2002 Census of Governments, *Volume 3, Number 1, Employment of Major Local Governments*, released May 2004 (related Internet site <http://www.census.gov/govs/www/cog2002.html>).   Finances—U.S. Census Bureau, 2002 Census of Governments, *Volume 4, Number 4, Government Finances*, released April 2005 (related Internet site <http://www.census.gov/govs/www/cog2002.html>).   Climate—U.S. National Oceanic and Atmospheric Administration (NOAA), National Climatic Data Center (NCDC), *Climatography of the United States*, Number 81 (related Internet site <http://cdo.ncdc.noaa.gov/cgi-bin/climatenormals/climatenormals.pl>).

Places

Table D

You may visit us on the Web at
http://www.census.gov/compendia/ccdb

Places

Table D

Table D-1. Places — **Population by Age and Sex**

[Includes states and 242 incorporated places of 100,000 or more population as of April 1, 2000. Two census designated places (CDPs) are also included (Honolulu CDP in Hawaii and Arlington CDP in Virginia). For more information on these areas, see Appendix C, Geographic Information. Seven states (Delaware, Maine, Montana, North Dakota, Vermont, West Virginia, and Wyoming) do not have any incorporated places of 100,000 or more population]

FIPS state and place code[1]	Place	Total population, 2005	Population by age, 2005 Under 5 years	5 to 17 years	18 to 24 years	25 to 34 years	35 to 44 years	45 to 54 years	55 to 64 years	65 to 74 years	75 to 84 years	85 years and over	Males per 100 females, 2005
01 00000	ALABAMA	4,442,558	292,375	793,333	412,216	583,691	640,554	652,826	494,879	325,232	189,350	58,102	93.2
01 07000	Birmingham city	222,154	17,422	40,177	24,135	32,211	31,199	30,486	20,641	13,279	9,359	3,245	89.5
01 37000	Huntsville city	158,618	9,315	26,042	16,552	20,624	24,303	21,018	17,448	14,704	7,156	1,456	95.8
01 50000	Mobile city	193,332	14,480	36,211	19,217	27,335	25,284	23,847	20,801	12,913	10,434	2,810	85.5
01 51000	Montgomery city.	193,042	15,201	36,871	18,928	24,682	27,176	28,518	19,362	12,202	7,471	2,631	87.1
02 00000	ALASKA	641,724	49,204	138,294	66,617	76,278	98,090	106,556	64,529	26,402	12,051	3,703	103.1
02 03000	Anchorage municipality	266,281	21,228	55,955	27,544	33,111	42,004	43,080	26,457	10,524	4,644	1,734	100.0
04 00000	ARIZONA	5,829,839	459,772	1,114,116	552,596	834,828	806,615	747,917	578,598	407,224	261,324	66,849	99.2
04 12000	Chandler city.	225,725	17,711	47,870	18,807	38,403	42,873	30,436	16,368	7,891	4,248	1,118	102.4
04 27400	Gilbert town.	178,539	20,382	43,699	10,786	28,053	33,079	21,909	12,145	5,081	3,157	248	100.9
04 27820	Glendale city	229,913	22,463	46,947	23,368	34,361	33,884	27,866	25,343	9,101	5,097	1,483	100.5
04 46000	Mesa city	442,445	37,267	82,665	44,764	63,547	61,601	51,092	38,299	35,271	22,346	5,593	102.9
04 54050	Peoria city.	141,941	10,235	33,616	10,431	16,456	22,804	19,738	12,584	7,967	6,128	1,982	93.0
04 55000	Phoenix city	1,377,980	121,471	275,000	143,159	239,444	201,219	182,780	111,231	59,230	35,235	9,211	101.8
04 65000	Scottsdale city	215,933	15,216	30,175	13,174	28,386	32,305	33,915	27,805	18,896	11,613	4,448	102.6
04 73000	Tempe city	166,171	8,496	28,125	33,390	29,419	24,220	19,315	12,081	5,641	4,100	1,384	104.7
04 77000	Tucson city	507,362	42,651	86,576	64,080	81,313	69,077	59,335	42,587	31,266	23,109	7,368	95.9
05 00000	ARKANSAS	2,701,431	186,365	485,969	251,855	352,575	382,465	378,702	299,859	206,824	122,066	34,751	94.8
05 41000	Little Rock city	176,924	13,639	28,947	15,851	26,845	26,307	26,434	17,618	11,249	7,008	3,026	92.5
06 00000	CALIFORNIA	35,278,768	2,679,311	6,975,831	3,324,585	5,010,503	5,384,615	4,871,349	3,331,470	1,941,943	1,338,685	420,476	98.4
06 02000	Anaheim city	329,483	32,016	69,071	38,699	47,942	51,000	40,047	24,383	13,987	9,727	2,611	99.5
06 03526	Bakersfield city	286,316	27,736	64,385	28,319	44,764	39,111	34,536	21,613	12,098	10,077	3,677	95.4
06 06000	Berkeley city	90,432	4,064	7,974	15,501	14,254	13,668	12,824	11,562	5,376	3,885	1,324	98.1
06 08954	Burbank city	100,053	6,953	16,891	7,044	14,997	18,116	13,509	10,620	6,453	4,204	1,266	94.6
06 13392	Chula Vista city	212,954	18,278	47,553	16,522	32,017	35,560	26,117	15,730	10,321	9,119	1,737	97.0
06 16000	Concord city	116,782	8,160	18,884	10,170	17,305	19,490	18,968	11,266	7,338	4,253	948	93.8
06 16350	Corona city	162,410	11,429	36,624	16,334	29,114	28,192	22,408	9,217	5,237	2,530	1,325	99.6
06 16532	Costa Mesa city	105,333	8,118	15,831	12,234	20,650	17,885	12,160	9,293	5,122	3,411	629	98.5
06 17918	Daly City city	93,513	6,018	15,573	8,575	13,406	14,115	13,732	10,606	5,230	5,116	1,142	102.5
06 19766	Downey city	111,391	8,607	25,755	10,635	17,816	16,837	10,915	9,689	5,226	4,903	1,008	108.2
06 22230	El Monte city	108,913	8,372	24,110	9,226	20,267	18,210	12,692	7,357	4,336	3,053	1,290	116.9
06 22804	Escondido city	133,017	11,009	27,841	13,142	17,898	21,315	19,723	9,236	6,298	4,693	1,862	100.3
06 24680	Fontana city	158,235	13,917	42,358	18,822	26,847	22,838	20,448	8,292	2,977	1,323	413	106.2
06 26000	Fremont city	210,387	18,875	38,243	13,857	33,887	35,802	31,291	22,278	9,650	5,440	1,064	98.8
06 27000	Fresno city	477,251	44,238	113,181	52,945	75,637	63,240	54,778	36,079	18,166	14,924	4,063	98.6
06 28000	Fullerton city	142,064	8,215	27,899	15,267	19,806	22,620	19,568	15,241	7,279	4,912	1,257	98.1
06 29000	Garden Grove city	192,345	17,064	40,353	18,157	27,185	30,017	28,298	14,766	9,754	5,330	1,421	109.1
06 30000	Glendale city	194,620	9,699	32,954	15,915	24,235	37,245	29,245	20,341	14,313	7,804	2,869	102.0
06 33000	Hayward city	135,474	12,252	23,966	15,260	19,758	21,887	18,841	11,648	6,266	4,404	1,192	106.3
06 36000	Huntington Beach city	189,451	12,447	29,903	13,983	27,989	31,482	29,425	22,751	12,156	7,531	1,784	98.0
06 36546	Inglewood city	120,204	11,569	26,988	12,393	14,914	17,951	14,581	10,885	6,845	2,809	1,269	88.7
06 36770	Irvine city	172,182	11,438	25,759	19,345	26,089	28,942	27,498	19,374	7,339	5,053	1,345	102.2
06 40130	Lancaster city	135,225	11,451	35,387	13,680	17,153	17,427	17,003	12,662	5,326	3,525	1,611	92.2
06 43000	Long Beach city	463,956	34,805	89,644	50,060	66,977	80,135	58,819	40,279	24,260	14,183	4,794	97.3
06 44000	Los Angeles city	3,731,437	287,230	712,862	378,361	594,344	596,361	482,100	334,192	179,082	129,504	37,401	100.0
06 48354	Modesto city	202,971	16,543	42,162	23,285	26,021	30,077	24,922	19,925	9,689	7,281	3,066	91.4
06 49270	Moreno Valley city	162,987	13,817	42,007	16,701	26,079	22,113	21,433	8,767	6,920	4,043	1,107	102.8
06 52526	Norwalk city	103,844	7,670	23,976	10,716	14,806	17,081	14,064	7,644	3,978	3,488	421	98.9
06 53000	Oakland city	373,910	27,039	64,865	31,065	62,548	58,431	50,655	37,946	21,632	14,545	5,184	90.5
06 53322	Oceanside city	162,259	11,731	30,537	17,291	22,691	21,822	22,344	12,513	10,142	10,281	2,907	97.2
06 53896	Ontario city	156,679	11,112	38,140	18,786	24,249	25,424	17,599	9,612	6,205	4,916	636	103.9
06 53980	Orange city	137,994	10,635	25,887	12,532	22,747	21,695	17,846	12,531	7,301	4,801	2,019	94.6
06 54652	Oxnard city	178,871	15,766	44,609	22,227	25,232	26,240	18,595	12,662	6,566	5,634	1,340	104.9
06 55156	Palmdale city	145,800	15,177	37,719	14,912	18,656	19,519	20,982	9,950	4,686	3,689	510	97.9
06 56000	Pasadena city	129,400	8,759	18,690	9,455	23,207	20,870	19,235	12,545	8,458	5,917	2,264	90.8
06 58072	Pomona city	161,257	15,670	37,266	17,142	26,905	23,749	17,332	9,718	8,079	4,238	1,158	102.5
06 59451	Rancho Cucamonga city	144,958	9,914	28,652	13,604	21,561	24,581	21,705	14,618	5,415	4,073	835	89.4
06 62000	Riverside city	294,059	24,116	57,793	39,841	53,498	40,341	32,855	21,472	12,311	8,877	2,955	102.4
06 64000	Sacramento city	445,287	32,112	85,835	44,164	75,497	62,346	58,488	38,783	23,341	19,070	5,651	93.0
06 64224	Salinas city	156,950	15,993	36,857	17,946	27,697	19,207	18,443	9,829	5,504	4,413	1,061	98.8

See footnotes at end of table.

County and City Data Book: 2007

U.S. Census Bureau

Table D-1. Places — **Population by Age and Sex**—Con.

[Includes states and 242 incorporated places of 100,000 or more population as of April 1, 2000. Two census designated places (CDPs) are also included (Honolulu CDP in Hawaii and Arlington CDP in Virginia). For more information on these areas, see Appendix C, Geographic Information. Seven states (Delaware, Maine, Montana, North Dakota, Vermont, West Virginia, and Wyoming) do not have any incorporated places of 100,000 or more population]

FIPS state and place code[1]	Place	Total population, 2005	Population by age, 2005 Under 5 years	5 to 17 years	18 to 24 years	25 to 34 years	35 to 44 years	45 to 54 years	55 to 64 years	65 to 74 years	75 to 84 years	85 years and over	Males per 100 females, 2005
	CALIFORNIA—Con.												
06 65000	San Bernardino city	204,552	19,266	52,015	21,502	33,647	30,056	21,134	12,918	7,256	4,157	2,601	92.5
06 65042	San Buenaventura (Ventura) city	100,154	5,917	18,774	6,934	10,627	16,774	16,501	11,335	7,019	5,069	1,204	90.4
06 66000	San Diego city	1,208,331	93,399	208,163	126,668	211,166	183,516	158,608	103,133	62,781	47,144	13,753	100.1
06 67000	San Francisco city	719,077	39,718	68,952	48,639	133,331	140,775	105,896	76,590	50,928	38,735	15,513	101.9
06 68000	San Jose city	887,330	73,444	166,091	76,007	133,144	155,311	122,112	82,785	45,370	23,408	9,658	104.0
06 69000	Santa Ana city	302,302	31,572	74,616	33,359	49,187	44,954	32,269	17,619	10,370	6,657	1,699	102.5
06 69084	Santa Clara city	102,204	10,840	12,912	9,071	19,284	16,453	13,576	9,192	4,909	4,327	1,640	115.8
06 69088	Santa Clarita city	167,047	13,165	37,637	12,535	19,662	29,848	25,934	14,628	7,446	4,352	1,840	104.0
06 70098	Santa Rosa city	146,500	9,999	24,878	13,546	19,191	22,172	21,319	16,120	7,859	8,127	3,289	95.4
06 72016	Simi Valley city	116,722	10,427	23,707	7,979	14,637	19,517	19,003	12,144	6,059	2,747	502	98.9
06 75000	Stockton city	278,515	22,828	60,967	31,270	42,805	35,724	35,695	22,463	14,163	8,762	3,838	96.1
06 77000	Sunnyvale city	132,725	10,634	19,331	8,185	24,272	23,707	19,711	11,407	9,264	4,822	1,392	98.9
06 78582	Thousand Oaks city	127,895	7,258	24,221	12,406	13,846	18,385	22,461	14,495	8,552	4,398	1,873	98.8
06 80000	Torrance city	138,618	7,901	22,815	9,617	16,524	21,854	25,604	13,362	10,851	8,462	1,628	99.0
06 81666	Vallejo city	115,657	8,609	22,079	9,636	15,092	15,499	19,468	11,882	7,549	3,867	1,976	93.7
06 84200	West Covina city	116,371	9,084	28,616	11,132	19,077	14,400	14,935	9,033	5,483	3,778	833	81.0
08 00000	COLORADO.	4,562,244	338,585	837,578	421,308	707,190	701,751	671,217	441,718	244,896	152,095	45,906	100.2
08 03455	Arvada city	104,766	6,096	22,156	8,092	9,177	17,520	16,333	13,362	6,963	4,177	890	92.2
08 04000	Aurora city	291,317	25,274	56,080	28,750	49,670	44,887	37,918	25,107	13,253	8,532	1,846	96.6
08 12815	Centennial city.	103,482	5,427	23,573	8,303	10,104	15,770	18,810	12,739	5,639	2,699	418	93.9
08 16000	Colorado Springs city	376,985	27,564	69,922	36,777	60,253	57,947	53,178	35,632	19,926	11,823	3,963	96.5
08 20000	Denver city	545,198	51,160	84,045	43,742	102,202	87,998	69,598	47,841	28,264	23,129	7,219	102.7
08 27425	Fort Collins city	122,297	7,558	18,509	23,749	23,926	15,794	14,493	8,815	3,730	4,070	1,653	104.5
08 43000	Lakewood city	142,434	9,060	24,204	13,629	19,147	22,926	21,845	13,218	10,962	5,404	2,039	90.9
08 62000	Pueblo city	101,302	7,448	17,551	11,797	13,752	12,220	13,263	9,694	7,029	6,692	1,856	95.5
08 83835	Westminster city.	99,305	5,959	19,113	11,213	16,903	15,396	14,612	9,094	4,605	2,233	177	108.6
09 00000	CONNECTICUT	3,394,751	210,976	619,914	263,296	390,122	545,007	539,938	382,919	211,281	172,258	59,040	94.1
09 08000	Bridgeport city	132,011	9,634	26,375	12,457	18,788	18,034	18,375	13,607	7,848	4,429	2,464	88.0
09 37000	Hartford city	111,103	9,459	23,737	10,725	18,754	14,870	12,256	9,691	6,470	3,183	1,958	81.8
09 52000	New Haven city	108,412	7,228	18,873	12,515	23,328	16,469	11,120	8,283	6,038	3,355	1,203	87.1
09 73000	Stamford city	118,568	6,846	19,472	8,275	17,220	19,457	20,059	13,087	5,848	6,669	1,635	96.6
09 80000	Waterbury city	104,539	8,299	22,842	10,316	14,148	15,946	13,705	8,554	4,527	4,194	2,008	87.2
10 00000	DELAWARE.	818,587	55,398	140,065	72,045	107,543	126,178	120,477	90,090	58,556	38,626	9,609	94.1
11 00000	DISTRICT OF COLUMBIA . .	515,118	37,723	73,816	31,647	105,606	78,541	69,704	55,587	31,909	23,420	7,165	89.0
11 50000	Washington city	515,118	37,723	73,816	31,647	105,606	78,541	69,704	55,587	31,909	23,420	7,165	89.0
12 00000	FLORIDA.	17,382,511	1,112,350	2,934,500	1,484,879	2,084,375	2,497,219	2,440,996	1,946,979	1,489,260	1,071,963	319,990	95.0
12 10275	Cape Coral city	134,388	10,447	22,931	8,661	19,709	19,696	17,423	14,801	10,393	8,117	2,210	95.1
12 12875	Clearwater city.	108,382	5,517	17,672	8,103	12,555	14,974	16,906	13,372	9,402	6,350	3,531	97.7
12 14400	Coral Springs city	127,654	8,494	28,210	11,449	13,378	23,073	21,602	13,680	4,933	2,182	653	92.2
12 24000	Fort Lauderdale city	141,307	9,777	19,411	10,553	16,428	22,676	24,470	16,018	11,637	7,483	2,854	100.4
12 25175	Gainesville city.	100,879	5,723	12,387	26,902	18,453	9,832	9,757	7,521	5,823	3,738	743	84.0
12 30000	Hialeah city	213,791	12,696	33,314	20,067	22,709	36,635	27,858	23,734	20,765	12,319	3,694	91.5
12 32000	Hollywood city	138,412	7,966	20,886	12,135	20,759	21,568	17,098	15,815	12,090	7,215	2,880	94.4
12 35000	Jacksonville city	768,537	62,072	149,423	67,543	103,230	118,620	112,057	79,254	45,021	24,694	6,623	93.7
12 45000	Miami city	361,701	25,107	57,883	28,972	50,616	46,282	46,537	42,023	34,698	21,785	7,798	91.6
12 45060	Miami Gardens city	91,694	6,841	16,503	10,780	9,287	12,467	13,723	11,018	5,893	3,998	1,184	86.9
12 53000	Orlando city.	221,299	20,124	39,506	18,263	40,846	37,957	26,657	16,800	11,836	6,597	2,713	88.1
12 55775	Pembroke Pines city	159,422	9,086	32,281	10,430	19,625	27,440	22,914	15,052	8,644	10,705	3,245	90.9
12 58050	Pompano Beach city	94,892	3,703	12,098	8,006	10,050	12,703	16,447	12,996	8,710	6,650	3,529	97.1
12 63000	St. Petersburg city	232,960	14,449	33,486	19,285	26,880	36,720	38,052	27,490	18,336	13,791	4,471	92.8
12 70600	Tallahassee city	141,148	8,249	18,554	33,398	23,015	16,333	16,270	12,943	7,464	3,966	956	94.7
12 71000	Tampa city	312,855	22,474	57,725	26,317	43,376	51,926	43,383	32,556	18,700	12,061	4,337	96.2
13 00000	GEORGIA	8,821,142	695,355	1,657,320	836,298	1,323,582	1,420,736	1,223,341	853,007	483,552	255,190	72,761	96.1
13 03440	Athens-Clarke County (balance)	94,125	6,312	11,548	24,963	17,295	11,358	8,485	5,876	4,402	2,656	1,230	97.4
13 04000	Atlanta city	394,929	28,260	62,121	37,921	71,939	65,450	52,194	40,378	20,101	12,279	4,286	91.6
13 04204	Augusta-Richmond County (balance)	181,019	16,001	35,672	16,966	25,474	24,808	24,640	17,529	11,223	6,706	2,000	85.4
13 19000	Columbus city	175,930	14,941	35,376	16,498	23,281	24,487	24,733	16,601	10,826	6,876	2,311	86.9
13 69000	Savannah city	117,478	9,216	21,981	13,948	17,544	13,677	13,749	11,488	7,081	6,912	1,882	90.1

See footnotes at end of table.

Table D-1. Places — **Population by Age and Sex**—Con.

[Includes states and 242 incorporated places of 100,000 or more population as of April 1, 2000. Two census designated places (CDPs) are also included (Honolulu CDP in Hawaii and Arlington CDP in Virginia). For more information on these areas, see Appendix C, Geographic Information. Seven states (Delaware, Maine, Montana, North Dakota, Vermont, West Virginia, and Wyoming) do not have any incorporated places of 100,000 or more population]

| FIPS state and place code[1] | Place | Total population, 2005 | Population by age, 2005 | | | | | | | | | | Males per 100 females, 2005 |
			Under 5 years	5 to 17 years	18 to 24 years	25 to 34 years	35 to 44 years	45 to 54 years	55 to 64 years	65 to 74 years	75 to 84 years	85 years and over	
15 00000	HAWAII	1,238,158	89,827	208,744	110,670	152,593	175,729	185,760	145,940	77,293	69,792	21,810	97.6
15 17000	Honolulu CDP	362,252	22,325	44,335	31,459	45,233	51,280	55,438	48,169	25,901	27,950	10,162	89.6
16 00000	IDAHO	1,395,634	105,906	267,030	145,667	186,132	191,169	200,638	142,372	86,294	53,579	16,847	99.2
16 08830	Boise City city	191,667	12,713	31,587	20,792	30,182	26,842	30,903	18,973	10,366	6,453	2,856	101.3
17 00000	ILLINOIS	12,440,351	899,205	2,332,381	1,128,884	1,745,317	1,861,315	1,792,638	1,244,458	749,624	521,242	165,287	95.9
17 03012	Aurora city	170,490	18,529	32,938	18,477	32,654	29,410	18,295	10,666	5,965	2,734	822	110.4
17 14000	Chicago city	2,701,926	215,448	494,181	264,527	463,236	401,679	343,098	243,672	143,922	97,850	34,313	92.7
17 38570	Joliet city	128,090	10,842	25,435	14,816	23,668	18,082	15,072	9,287	5,669	3,982	1,237	97.5
17 51622	Naperville city	147,779	9,305	35,334	11,194	15,436	27,995	24,811	14,656	5,473	2,998	577	95.9
17 59000	Peoria city	102,136	8,950	18,012	10,801	14,015	12,707	13,573	10,061	7,060	5,605	1,352	91.8
17 65000	Rockford city	139,173	11,791	24,938	12,775	21,588	18,410	18,391	12,282	8,202	8,275	2,521	91.7
17 72000	Springfield city	110,262	7,396	18,158	9,746	17,042	14,624	16,218	12,768	7,443	5,225	1,642	90.3
18 00000	INDIANA	6,093,372	430,123	1,162,893	543,633	814,863	887,673	895,075	631,941	381,799	267,534	77,838	96.5
18 22000	Evansville city	110,708	8,438	18,655	10,482	15,988	15,005	15,103	10,854	7,326	6,484	2,373	93.8
18 25000	Fort Wayne city	219,346	18,920	43,532	20,846	31,738	31,698	28,173	20,070	11,815	9,659	2,895	94.9
18 27000	Gary city	97,057	9,690	21,069	8,034	11,552	12,073	13,518	9,305	6,406	4,475	935	85.8
18 36003	Indianapolis city (balance)	765,310	65,812	144,782	60,409	114,532	119,898	110,253	68,910	42,498	29,516	8,700	94.7
18 71000	South Bend city	97,070	7,197	18,696	11,498	11,579	13,336	13,709	8,094	4,751	6,927	1,283	89.3
19 00000	IOWA	2,862,541	183,179	484,747	267,597	364,979	405,503	440,966	313,403	199,974	152,521	49,672	97.0
19 12000	Cedar Rapids city	119,670	8,722	20,292	10,481	18,729	17,554	17,507	11,719	7,169	6,157	1,340	93.8
19 21000	Des Moines city	196,917	15,927	33,036	16,064	32,640	31,929	27,014	20,271	9,933	7,360	2,743	93.5
20 00000	KANSAS	2,662,616	187,640	483,807	265,344	353,041	376,866	397,830	267,960	167,681	123,473	38,974	97.7
20 36000	Kansas City city	142,341	12,080	28,162	12,549	22,047	20,162	19,445	13,141	7,263	5,691	1,801	96.6
20 53775	Overland Park city	161,901	10,478	30,739	12,763	18,985	28,998	23,535	16,576	10,562	6,958	2,307	96.1
20 71000	Topeka city	117,326	9,647	18,540	10,525	18,582	14,778	16,352	11,763	8,998	5,968	2,173	92.2
20 79000	Wichita city	354,582	29,202	65,272	34,458	52,426	50,327	49,647	32,701	21,314	14,902	4,333	98.8
21 00000	KENTUCKY	4,058,633	271,153	704,958	366,717	545,673	606,671	614,249	453,327	282,308	166,374	47,203	95.8
21 46027	Lexington-Fayette	255,389	19,102	37,837	30,355	39,873	39,986	36,671	25,033	14,686	8,934	2,912	96.0
21 48006	Louisville/Jefferson County (balance)	547,839	39,789	96,058	47,271	69,880	84,856	84,510	59,319	35,767	23,177	7,212	94.9
22 00000	LOUISIANA	4,389,747	318,771	821,857	457,260	574,579	625,693	636,398	456,306	277,936	175,541	45,406	93.2
22 05000	Baton Rouge city	205,442	13,613	36,597	29,518	31,791	21,082	27,791	19,714	12,927	9,353	3,056	90.0
22 40735	Lafayette city	108,175	7,469	18,670	14,429	16,673	12,603	16,248	10,174	6,597	4,339	973	92.0
22 55000	New Orleans city	437,186	34,100	79,880	45,554	58,034	60,640	64,362	46,017	24,660	19,448	4,491	87.4
22 70000	Shreveport city	192,531	15,613	35,870	21,479	26,137	24,780	26,546	17,418	11,807	9,880	3,001	87.4
23 00000	MAINE	1,283,673	67,169	209,050	107,918	141,901	197,425	218,377	160,518	94,313	67,001	20,001	95.3
24 00000	MARYLAND	5,461,318	381,773	1,015,890	480,039	681,885	866,277	833,523	592,481	322,095	221,379	65,976	92.9
24 04000	Baltimore city	608,481	47,091	112,531	58,191	79,932	84,994	89,755	62,693	35,869	28,035	9,390	85.6
25 00000	MASSACHUSETTS	6,182,860	395,070	1,055,601	488,929	844,216	999,788	936,057	666,411	383,730	309,402	103,656	94.1
25 07000	Boston city	520,702	36,035	72,657	60,321	109,780	82,507	61,998	44,033	27,852	18,227	7,292	93.9
25 11000	Cambridge city	81,260	4,152	7,159	7,621	24,988	11,311	8,866	8,107	4,280	3,802	974	95.2
25 37000	Lowell city	96,876	6,230	20,115	6,718	15,934	16,102	12,267	9,327	5,113	3,659	1,411	99.7
25 67000	Springfield city	146,948	9,626	30,501	13,603	23,276	20,196	19,947	12,835	7,978	6,490	2,496	94.0
25 82000	Worcester city	154,398	9,728	25,161	15,039	27,501	20,553	22,032	13,940	8,106	9,005	3,333	91.2
26 00000	MICHIGAN	9,865,583	651,435	1,861,228	898,593	1,248,788	1,469,463	1,494,280	1,047,294	602,291	456,088	136,123	95.7
26 03000	Ann Arbor city	98,743	4,848	12,204	20,434	19,942	13,750	11,343	8,191	4,409	2,371	1,251	98.6
26 22000	Detroit city	836,056	62,231	197,218	79,144	110,579	115,762	110,497	76,191	42,048	32,050	10,336	85.5
26 29000	Flint city	111,948	9,459	24,264	10,707	17,396	14,597	14,786	9,574	5,820	4,402	943	89.4
26 34000	Grand Rapids city	193,568	17,111	36,951	21,724	35,287	25,267	23,376	14,293	8,391	8,141	3,027	96.6
26 46000	Lansing city	119,675	10,480	20,687	15,466	19,259	16,346	16,034	10,304	5,467	4,224	1,408	88.9
26 49000	Livonia city	103,497	4,761	20,254	7,252	8,647	19,874	16,936	11,164	6,966	6,000	1,643	99.8
26 76460	Sterling Heights city	123,368	6,733	20,285	10,956	17,715	18,067	19,269	16,109	6,999	5,642	1,593	100.4
26 84000	Warren city	134,901	9,896	21,378	10,923	20,843	22,266	17,790	11,759	10,721	7,492	1,833	101.4

See footnotes at end of table.

Table D-1. Places — **Population by Age and Sex**—Con.

[Includes states and 242 incorporated places of 100,000 or more population as of April 1, 2000. Two census designated places (CDPs) are also included (Honolulu CDP in Hawaii and Arlington CDP in Virginia). For more information on these areas, see Appendix C, Geographic Information. Seven states (Delaware, Maine, Montana, North Dakota, Vermont, West Virginia, and Wyoming) do not have any incorporated places of 100,000 or more population]

FIPS state and place code[1]	Place	Total population, 2005	Population by age, 2005										Males per 100 females, 2005
			Under 5 years	5 to 17 years	18 to 24 years	25 to 34 years	35 to 44 years	45 to 54 years	55 to 64 years	65 to 74 years	75 to 84 years	85 years and over	
27 00000	MINNESOTA	4,989,848	337,203	889,516	470,955	671,139	774,468	764,182	505,067	297,095	209,131	71,092	98.6
27 43000	Minneapolis city	350,260	27,659	49,261	43,888	74,208	54,312	45,425	28,831	13,010	9,906	3,760	102.1
27 58000	St. Paul city	261,559	22,204	50,071	26,387	39,676	42,042	37,823	21,668	10,078	8,056	3,554	98.7
28 00000	MISSISSIPPI	2,824,156	210,297	533,649	283,126	364,476	405,068	398,835	291,243	195,095	110,042	32,325	92.6
28 36000	Jackson city	163,928	13,741	33,312	17,747	23,706	22,461	22,009	14,595	8,947	5,714	1,696	82.9
29 00000	MISSOURI	5,631,910	378,746	992,398	531,162	734,198	821,179	840,796	612,293	389,406	252,805	78,927	95.2
29 35000	Independence city	111,842	7,763	17,453	9,205	15,212	15,156	17,092	13,329	8,038	6,379	2,215	105.8
29 38000	Kansas City city	440,885	32,120	76,377	43,273	68,060	67,071	61,877	45,569	24,852	17,290	4,396	93.0
29 65000	St. Louis city	333,730	26,160	59,771	30,721	48,137	50,829	48,707	30,237	18,758	15,661	4,749	88.1
29 70000	Springfield city	139,600	8,956	18,233	19,661	21,274	17,902	18,958	14,269	8,524	8,461	3,362	97.0
30 00000	MONTANA	910,651	53,899	149,831	87,375	108,797	124,325	152,894	112,466	66,666	41,360	13,038	98.7
31 00000	NEBRASKA	1,706,976	122,660	306,272	168,208	226,902	236,603	254,461	173,953	109,830	82,241	25,846	98.0
31 28000	Lincoln city	226,062	16,457	34,915	28,847	38,893	30,069	32,019	21,250	11,442	8,691	3,479	96.8
31 37000	Omaha city	373,215	27,502	66,261	39,284	56,428	52,361	52,828	36,922	20,935	15,416	5,278	95.5
32 00000	NEVADA	2,381,281	172,890	445,915	207,553	358,358	362,961	317,139	248,789	159,852	85,558	22,266	102.3
32 31900	Henderson city	223,776	12,603	40,274	20,346	28,949	34,692	33,603	27,747	16,832	7,336	1,394	96.4
32 40000	Las Vegas city	538,653	42,540	102,730	42,085	84,418	85,401	64,654	54,676	36,901	19,704	5,544	100.4
32 51800	North Las Vegas city	165,061	16,399	37,305	16,238	28,246	26,220	17,872	13,244	6,304	2,683	550	108.5
32 60600	Reno city	204,478	15,131	32,217	25,948	31,894	28,745	27,373	20,540	12,523	7,692	2,415	100.8
33 00000	NEW HAMPSHIRE	1,272,486	73,491	229,409	101,892	145,178	210,875	214,829	145,491	80,526	55,187	15,608	97.6
33 45140	Manchester city	109,308	6,580	18,053	11,147	12,685	19,012	18,495	10,314	6,601	4,752	1,669	99.3
34 00000	NEW JERSEY	8,521,427	581,114	1,573,569	699,985	1,030,630	1,373,899	1,285,643	908,577	529,647	411,262	127,101	94.4
34 21000	Elizabeth city	121,137	11,137	23,636	12,995	17,360	17,167	15,368	12,488	6,591	3,123	1,272	86.3
34 36000	Jersey City city	246,335	19,690	44,522	22,878	40,577	41,656	31,140	22,241	13,110	9,032	1,489	98.3
34 51000	Newark city	254,217	24,511	52,683	28,566	37,752	34,529	33,872	20,680	12,776	6,735	2,113	86.5
34 57000	Paterson city	148,353	16,149	30,218	18,888	20,183	19,005	19,936	12,410	5,975	3,916	1,673	89.3
35 00000	NEW MEXICO	1,887,200	131,551	354,810	191,901	232,783	260,587	277,828	210,055	129,604	75,175	22,906	95.4
35 02000	Albuquerque city	488,133	35,037	81,825	52,693	66,925	71,011	71,746	50,757	31,070	20,455	6,614	95.0
36 00000	NEW YORK	18,655,275	1,247,283	3,272,488	1,589,003	2,514,165	2,900,055	2,746,582	2,014,826	1,198,589	879,965	292,319	93.1
36 11000	Buffalo city	256,492	16,265	51,176	28,439	35,572	34,447	37,302	22,204	14,285	13,054	3,748	87.9
36 51000	New York city	7,956,113	589,427	1,335,083	676,440	1,264,189	1,272,179	1,081,910	793,628	479,888	341,659	121,710	90.4
36 63000	Rochester city	189,312	14,054	37,187	20,861	32,857	27,472	26,480	15,572	7,346	5,245	2,238	91.0
36 73000	Syracuse city	132,495	10,231	23,723	17,707	21,601	15,435	16,251	12,113	7,185	5,983	2,266	92.3
36 84000	Yonkers city	193,327	13,428	34,185	16,819	25,400	28,707	25,466	20,733	14,122	10,949	3,518	88.8
37 00000	NORTH CAROLINA	8,411,041	600,652	1,531,365	710,135	1,201,102	1,300,892	1,190,719	890,301	550,826	341,104	93,945	95.7
37 12000	Charlotte city	601,598	50,463	111,103	52,748	100,025	102,673	83,532	55,077	25,782	15,708	4,487	98.0
37 19000	Durham city	191,731	17,319	31,069	18,233	38,477	32,140	23,446	14,915	8,476	5,621	2,035	94.2
37 22920	Fayetteville city	128,777	11,744	23,142	13,356	16,513	18,745	17,225	12,758	9,693	4,302	1,299	89.2
37 28000	Greensboro city	208,552	15,248	34,125	20,903	31,741	32,912	27,379	20,108	14,714	8,680	2,742	86.5
37 55000	Raleigh city	315,249	23,817	45,683	38,054	63,656	50,986	41,668	27,348	11,577	8,867	3,593	100.9
37 75000	Winston-Salem city	183,467	16,446	31,717	15,386	29,774	24,604	24,913	16,878	10,877	9,958	2,914	88.9
38 00000	NORTH DAKOTA	609,645	36,585	98,678	60,367	80,338	83,413	97,914	65,695	41,552	32,966	12,137	99.2
39 00000	OHIO	11,155,606	735,204	2,018,404	996,737	1,419,236	1,636,263	1,707,801	1,210,977	726,116	542,362	162,506	94.6
39 01000	Akron city	200,181	13,894	35,986	20,726	30,436	28,297	26,764	19,843	11,636	9,913	2,686	91.6
39 15000	Cincinnati city	287,540	22,870	49,700	32,921	44,945	37,189	41,437	26,003	14,453	14,164	3,858	87.7
39 16000	Cleveland city	414,534	31,522	83,843	38,926	50,558	63,804	62,057	37,678	23,286	16,830	6,030	87.9
39 18000	Columbus city	693,983	60,740	111,606	77,828	131,641	106,624	88,634	56,727	31,627	21,435	7,121	97.6
39 21000	Dayton city	132,679	9,827	23,388	13,720	18,591	18,277	19,341	14,089	7,196	5,545	2,705	93.1
39 77000	Toledo city	285,937	21,308	52,931	28,401	43,134	38,344	40,552	26,836	16,198	13,754	4,479	94.4

See footnotes at end of table.

[Includes states and 242 incorporated places of 100,000 or more population as of April 1, 2000. Two census designated places (CDPs) are also included (Honolulu CDP in Hawaii and Arlington CDP in Virginia). For more information on these areas, see Appendix C, Geographic Information. Seven states (Delaware, Maine, Montana, North Dakota, Vermont, West Virginia, and Wyoming) do not have any incorporated places of 100,000 or more population]

FIPS state and place code[1]	Place	Total population, 2005	Population by age, 2005										Males per 100 females, 2005
			Under 5 years	5 to 17 years	18 to 24 years	25 to 34 years	35 to 44 years	45 to 54 years	55 to 64 years	65 to 74 years	75 to 84 years	85 years and over	
40 00000	OKLAHOMA	3,433,496	245,018	603,395	340,328	458,896	473,450	499,011	371,635	252,052	149,559	40,152	95.9
40 55000	Oklahoma City city	515,751	40,925	87,301	50,773	79,138	72,973	76,693	52,531	30,476	19,770	5,171	96.1
40 75000	Tulsa city	370,447	28,148	62,796	36,758	55,555	45,845	55,499	39,232	24,511	18,122	3,981	95.3
41 00000	OREGON	3,560,109	226,064	620,397	328,830	495,835	505,058	539,799	396,718	227,961	158,586	60,861	97.8
41 23850	Eugene city	142,716	7,797	21,135	22,699	22,782	19,542	18,750	13,311	6,589	6,693	3,418	93.3
41 59000	Portland city	513,627	33,946	78,784	39,646	90,023	84,148	80,007	53,541	25,784	19,276	8,472	97.1
41 64900	Salem city	142,006	10,702	27,440	13,264	22,656	21,464	17,664	13,335	7,479	5,786	2,216	97.3
42 00000	PENNSYLVANIA	11,979,147	725,577	2,074,197	998,916	1,427,399	1,758,806	1,873,753	1,366,033	828,900	718,791	206,775	93.9
42 02000	Allentown city	105,231	8,215	18,439	9,737	17,674	13,149	12,661	9,517	7,504	5,462	2,873	93.1
42 24000	Erie city	91,423	5,870	18,026	9,894	11,945	11,936	12,455	9,265	4,264	5,722	2,046	91.4
42 60000	Philadelphia city	1,406,415	109,107	261,278	130,743	194,635	200,704	192,782	138,834	83,546	70,817	23,969	86.3
42 61000	Pittsburgh city	284,366	15,708	39,470	35,646	38,744	38,131	44,732	30,512	19,021	17,259	5,143	90.3
44 00000	RHODE ISLAND	1,032,662	64,050	180,281	82,905	136,881	160,021	156,874	111,689	62,459	60,290	17,212	93.1
44 59000	Providence city	160,264	13,662	30,137	18,870	29,307	22,710	17,755	12,069	5,793	7,680	2,281	96.4
45 00000	SOUTH CAROLINA	4,113,961	278,461	743,743	368,452	546,463	606,285	597,108	467,861	291,202	170,279	44,107	93.4
45 16000	Columbia city	88,450	5,630	12,083	11,023	16,327	12,766	10,396	9,358	4,891	4,675	1,301	92.3
46 00000	SOUTH DAKOTA	746,033	53,813	132,432	74,055	93,517	101,753	112,570	76,803	50,779	37,343	12,968	97.8
46 59020	Sioux Falls city	132,358	10,825	20,769	14,560	21,491	19,234	18,588	12,178	7,417	5,692	1,604	96.9
47 00000	TENNESSEE	5,810,590	388,136	994,670	520,118	800,348	881,740	865,581	651,344	409,999	233,902	64,752	95.5
47 14000	Chattanooga city	139,158	9,213	22,589	13,654	18,582	18,145	19,402	17,217	11,174	6,288	2,894	85.5
47 15160	Clarksville city	107,130	10,235	21,992	11,917	19,586	15,716	12,954	7,498	3,462	3,163	607	95.7
47 40000	Knoxville city	168,744	9,239	25,165	24,645	26,225	24,853	22,928	15,336	9,704	8,051	2,598	92.4
47 48000	Memphis city	642,251	53,244	122,434	69,343	96,385	90,453	88,231	59,864	33,640	22,932	5,725	89.7
47 52006	Nashville-Davidson (balance) . .	522,662	41,793	82,743	42,276	85,549	85,867	76,127	52,967	30,362	17,629	7,349	94.4
48 00000	TEXAS	22,270,165	1,866,420	4,433,871	2,198,019	3,260,940	3,297,281	3,031,750	2,034,035	1,217,539	727,411	202,899	97.6
48 01000	Abilene city	105,165	9,421	20,063	12,922	14,178	13,761	13,222	9,017	6,903	4,391	1,287	91.1
48 03000	Amarillo city	176,999	16,133	34,507	17,597	23,117	25,685	25,066	15,149	10,432	7,331	1,982	92.9
48 04000	Arlington city	348,965	32,938	69,185	37,194	55,816	60,181	44,164	28,041	12,678	6,897	1,871	98.1
48 05000	Austin city	678,457	56,130	107,371	84,823	137,523	107,029	90,980	49,487	25,807	14,600	4,707	105.2
48 07000	Beaumont city	107,876	8,491	21,951	11,494	14,635	13,792	13,902	10,009	6,944	5,286	1,372	88.9
48 10768	Brownsville city	171,528	21,368	44,359	19,111	22,650	22,647	15,791	12,583	7,396	4,127	1,496	91.2
48 13024	Carrollton city	122,699	8,605	23,068	11,734	17,164	22,360	19,890	12,658	4,635	2,162	423	103.0
48 17000	Corpus Christi city	280,002	22,736	56,619	30,036	35,503	38,788	39,733	27,363	15,517	11,088	2,619	94.5
48 19000	Dallas city	1,144,946	112,412	194,700	112,029	218,445	172,199	142,271	93,443	56,759	32,161	10,527	103.7
48 24000	El Paso city	583,419	55,972	125,116	63,223	75,497	74,854	76,806	48,607	34,014	23,197	6,133	89.7
48 27000	Fort Worth city	604,538	57,881	117,105	63,701	106,820	84,261	75,287	48,209	27,935	18,179	5,160	100.0
48 29000	Garland city	235,750	18,511	51,152	22,245	36,497	35,994	31,907	20,890	10,987	6,570	997	107.4
48 30464	Grand Prairie city	148,677	14,128	37,015	11,249	23,155	23,776	19,941	11,843	4,532	2,351	687	96.8
48 35000	Houston city	1,941,430	173,274	361,846	198,533	323,010	288,509	260,019	174,020	91,350	56,713	14,156	100.9
48 37000	Irving city	212,262	15,914	40,333	24,684	44,085	34,281	25,679	15,701	6,647	3,453	1,485	100.6
48 41464	Laredo city	207,787	27,758	50,069	22,233	29,135	27,812	20,106	15,069	8,603	5,762	1,240	92.2
48 45000	Lubbock city	199,789	16,645	35,032	31,317	32,268	23,064	23,783	16,568	10,887	8,809	1,416	92.7
48 45384	McAllen city	116,376	12,926	23,575	14,279	19,277	16,045	12,179	6,666	5,634	4,234	1,561	94.6
48 47892	Mesquite city	126,895	11,246	28,570	9,108	15,593	25,968	16,474	10,370	6,029	2,601	936	91.6
48 56000	Pasadena city	150,180	12,728	34,767	14,265	25,675	22,250	17,952	11,511	6,544	3,514	974	101.5
48 58016	Plano city	251,648	17,225	49,957	20,804	35,493	45,257	41,623	24,953	10,601	4,105	1,630	97.7
48 65000	San Antonio city	1,202,223	101,219	240,482	126,736	180,981	176,533	152,692	105,468	63,192	42,928	11,992	95.5
48 76000	Waco city	107,146	9,380	18,873	18,022	14,798	13,326	11,708	8,376	5,092	5,486	2,085	87.9
48 79000	Wichita Falls city	88,861	7,347	16,611	7,619	13,372	11,240	11,872	9,094	6,566	4,066	1,065	96.5
49 00000	UTAH	2,427,350	236,042	502,895	300,588	419,910	298,465	279,130	184,772	113,316	69,518	22,714	100.3
49 62470	Provo city	101,164	10,535	10,979	32,412	24,513	6,291	5,564	5,448	2,342	2,187	893	82.0
49 67000	Salt Lake City city	182,670	16,278	24,583	23,494	41,400	23,557	18,880	15,458	9,237	7,090	2,693	103.2
49 83470	West Valley City city	119,795	13,996	26,803	12,870	21,488	17,561	11,709	8,907	4,234	1,677	550	100.7

See footnotes at end of table.

[Includes states and 242 incorporated places of 100,000 or more population as of April 1, 2000. Two census designated places (CDPs) are also included (Honolulu CDP in Hawaii and Arlington CDP in Virginia). For more information on these areas, see Appendix C, Geographic Information. Seven states (Delaware, Maine, Montana, North Dakota, Vermont, West Virginia, and Wyoming) do not have any incorporated places of 100,000 or more population]

FIPS state and place code[1]	Place	Total popula- tion, 2005	Population by age, 2005										Males per 100 females, 2005
			Under 5 years	5 to 17 years	18 to 24 years	25 to 34 years	35 to 44 years	45 to 54 years	55 to 64 years	65 to 74 years	75 to 84 years	85 years and over	
50 00000	VERMONT.	602,290	32,245	100,324	50,475	69,724	92,152	103,732	76,823	40,641	28,629	7,545	96.6
51 00000	VIRGINIA.	7,332,608	506,004	1,306,584	653,755	961,827	1,151,879	1,115,434	814,077	456,875	284,529	81,644	95.1
51 01000	Alexandria city	133,479	12,164	14,191	6,381	29,819	24,816	18,400	14,335	7,117	5,038	1,218	88.3
51 03000	Arlington CDP	191,852	13,440	21,544	12,133	40,470	37,624	28,138	19,843	9,740	6,106	2,814	98.3
51 16000	Chesapeake city	214,835	14,605	43,658	21,612	24,890	35,565	34,014	21,246	11,071	6,133	2,041	92.8
51 35000	Hampton city	133,584	9,495	25,172	13,288	16,723	19,673	19,941	14,036	8,518	5,112	1,626	90.7
51 56000	Newport News city	176,591	16,059	35,003	16,285	24,929	27,397	23,689	15,801	9,421	6,690	1,317	92.5
51 57000	Norfolk city	206,172	19,795	39,435	20,642	32,082	27,397	27,378	16,986	10,726	9,514	2,217	93.6
51 64000	Portsmouth city	95,183	7,967	18,123	8,231	11,743	13,168	13,662	9,614	6,179	4,718	1,778	87.6
51 67000	Richmond city	180,757	15,465	28,413	17,210	26,765	25,350	24,683	17,432	11,449	10,332	3,658	84.7
51 82000	Virginia Beach city	430,856	32,225	84,745	38,681	60,749	72,829	62,004	39,655	23,108	13,795	3,065	96.7
53 00000	WASHINGTON	6,146,338	395,158	1,082,349	594,212	839,812	946,032	941,950	663,051	361,100	245,118	77,556	98.7
53 05210	Bellevue city	114,748	6,888	17,312	8,655	17,294	18,978	19,499	13,387	6,995	4,600	1,140	103.1
53 63000	Seattle city	536,946	31,852	56,253	50,110	108,525	95,502	75,485	60,703	25,309	22,297	10,910	101.2
53 67000	Spokane city	192,777	11,141	33,170	22,772	28,371	25,224	27,914	18,608	11,932	10,036	3,609	96.4
53 70000	Tacoma city	191,934	13,474	35,980	19,770	30,207	31,720	24,577	15,915	9,301	8,253	2,737	92.3
53 74060	Vancouver city	155,488	10,656	26,876	15,372	25,789	23,165	21,288	16,201	7,929	6,211	2,001	100.3
54 00000	WEST VIRGINIA.	1,771,750	98,936	281,555	152,025	216,671	248,115	283,711	224,352	142,577	93,849	29,959	95.6
55 00000	WISCONSIN	5,375,751	339,983	950,745	505,966	678,571	814,495	840,696	570,831	344,995	251,225	78,244	97.5
55 31000	Green Bay city	94,242	5,575	15,877	9,387	13,226	14,152	15,674	9,316	5,047	4,302	1,686	94.6
55 48000	Madison city	203,704	11,745	26,913	34,466	38,826	29,126	27,463	17,254	9,433	6,349	2,129	95.4
55 53000	Milwaukee city	556,948	48,153	114,003	60,199	82,060	81,053	72,754	46,666	25,234	20,548	6,278	92.8
56 00000	WYOMING.	495,226	31,029	81,848	50,054	61,118	66,131	85,821	60,004	32,193	20,851	6,177	99.7

[1]Federal Information Processing Standards (FIPS) codes for states and places defined as of January 2000.

Survey, Census, or Data Collection Method: Based on the American Community Survey; for information, see Appendix B, Limitations of the Data and Methodology, and also <http://www.census.gov/acs/www/AdvMeth/index.htm>.

Source: U.S. Census Bureau, American Community Survey, "DP-1. General Demographic Characteristics: 2005," using American FactFinder, accessed August 29, 2006 (related Internet site <http://factfinder.census.gov>).

Table D-2. Places — **Population by Race and Hispanic Origin**

[Includes states and 242 incorporated places of 100,000 or more population as of April 1, 2000. Two census designated places (CDPs) are also included (Honolulu CDP in Hawaii and Arlington CDP in Virginia). For more information on these areas, see Appendix C, Geographic Information. Seven states (Delaware, Maine, Montana, North Dakota, Vermont, West Virginia, and Wyoming) do not have any incorporated places of 100,000 or more population]

Place	Number, 2005 — Race[1]						Number, 2005 — Hispanic status[2]		Percent, 2005 — Race[1]						Percent, 2005 — Hispanic status[2]	
	White alone	Black or African American alone	American Indian and Alaska Native alone	Asian alone	Native Hawaiian and Other Pacific Islander alone	Two or more races	Hispanic or Latino origin	Non-Hispanic White alone	White alone	Black or African American alone	American Indian and Alaska Native alone	Asian alone	Native Hawaiian and Other Pacific Islander alone	Two or more races	Hispanic or Latino origin	Non-Hispanic White alone
ALABAMA	3,153,627	1,144,330	23,283	38,444	938	47,293	99,040	3,093,833	71.0	25.8	0.5	0.9	(Z)	1.1	2.2	69.6
Birmingham city	48,852	167,975	114	2,630	–	1,296	6,408	44,002	22.0	75.6	0.1	1.2	–	0.6	2.9	19.8
Huntsville city	101,915	46,581	2,251	4,285	217	1,618	3,479	100,569	64.3	29.4	1.4	2.7	0.1	1.0	2.2	63.4
Mobile city	95,172	90,230	422	3,953	–	1,841	2,946	93,988	49.2	46.7	0.2	2.0	–	1.0	1.5	48.6
Montgomery city	85,229	102,292	316	2,589	–	1,966	2,862	83,269	44.2	53.0	0.2	1.3	–	1.0	1.5	43.1
ALASKA	443,874	22,103	91,013	28,838	3,282	44,426	30,843	428,220	69.2	3.4	14.2	4.5	0.5	6.9	4.8	66.7
Anchorage municipality	185,780	16,547	15,903	18,514	2,297	21,863	18,584	177,540	69.8	6.2	6.0	7.0	0.9	8.2	7.0	66.7
ARIZONA	4,440,804	180,769	275,321	129,197	7,229	138,275	1,668,524	3,507,357	76.2	3.1	4.7	2.2	0.1	2.4	28.6	60.2
Chandler city	171,596	10,991	2,695	15,653	672	7,002	41,314	150,405	76.0	4.9	1.2	6.9	0.3	3.1	18.3	66.6
Gilbert town	151,198	5,873	765	8,574	182	4,025	21,722	138,986	84.7	3.3	0.4	4.8	0.1	2.3	12.2	77.8
Glendale city	175,472	10,378	3,365	4,817	1,178	7,025	69,972	134,741	76.3	4.5	1.5	2.1	0.5	3.1	30.4	58.6
Mesa city	361,116	10,830	9,817	8,845	371	10,216	106,325	301,953	81.6	2.4	2.2	2.0	0.1	2.3	24.0	68.2
Peoria city	118,889	6,486	521	5,600	50	2,394	26,410	100,956	83.8	4.6	0.4	3.9	(Z)	1.7	18.6	71.1
Phoenix city	1,015,038	69,687	29,049	27,724	872	28,882	575,436	665,429	73.7	5.1	2.1	2.0	0.1	2.1	41.8	48.3
Scottsdale city	197,519	3,397	1,481	6,176	–	3,943	17,079	185,066	91.5	1.6	0.7	2.9	–	1.8	7.9	85.7
Tempe city	138,057	4,910	3,837	7,595	–	3,082	36,500	111,319	83.1	3.0	2.3	4.6	–	1.9	22.0	67.0
Tucson city	331,181	19,129	14,848	12,782	759	15,516	206,958	249,370	65.3	3.8	2.9	2.5	0.1	3.1	40.8	49.2
ARKANSAS	2,135,069	414,260	18,481	25,249	4,105	38,848	126,932	2,080,710	79.0	15.3	0.7	0.9	0.2	1.4	4.7	77.0
Little Rock city	92,043	77,171	558	2,220	–	2,758	4,341	89,331	52.0	43.6	0.3	1.3	–	1.6	2.5	50.5
CALIFORNIA	21,491,336	2,163,530	253,774	4,365,548	124,511	1,095,996	12,523,379	15,274,256	60.9	6.1	0.7	12.4	0.4	3.1	35.5	43.3
Anaheim city	199,851	8,542	1,787	41,438	829	6,053	175,418	99,024	60.7	2.6	0.5	12.6	0.3	1.8	53.2	30.1
Bakersfield city	168,271	23,958	3,137	13,132	543	10,115	117,235	125,299	58.8	8.4	1.1	4.6	0.2	3.5	40.9	43.8
Berkeley city	57,873	10,874	122	12,641	51	3,910	8,466	55,148	64.0	12.0	0.1	14.0	0.1	4.3	9.4	61.0
Burbank city	71,161	2,553	566	9,003	113	3,693	23,779	62,125	71.1	2.6	0.6	9.0	0.1	3.7	23.8	62.1
Chula Vista city	124,095	7,396	1,113	29,289	814	8,078	118,805	53,139	58.3	3.5	0.5	13.8	0.4	3.8	55.8	25.0
Concord city	74,604	3,061	171	13,984	950	6,046	30,772	64,358	63.9	2.6	0.1	12.0	0.8	5.2	26.3	55.1
Corona city	116,817	7,596	551	17,163	112	3,058	73,942	61,908	71.9	4.7	0.3	10.6	0.1	1.9	45.5	38.1
Costa Mesa city	71,256	1,316	926	6,451	151	1,900	38,313	56,923	67.6	1.2	0.9	6.1	0.1	1.8	36.4	54.0
Daly City city	23,751	2,875	66	52,883	365	1,893	21,631	14,223	25.4	3.1	0.1	56.6	0.4	2.0	23.1	15.2
Downey city	70,906	2,778	140	9,791	751	2,918	(B)	(B)	63.7	2.5	0.1	8.8	0.7	2.6	(NA)	(NA)
El Monte city	50,344	1,422	781	29,433	–	1,742	(B)	(B)	46.2	1.3	0.7	27.0	–	1.6	(NA)	(NA)
Escondido city	90,904	2,468	1,659	7,424	50	2,592	59,234	60,970	68.3	1.9	1.2	5.6	(Z)	1.9	44.5	45.8
Fontana city	103,581	18,662	880	9,075	452	3,990	101,379	27,256	65.5	11.8	0.6	5.7	0.3	2.5	64.1	17.2
Fremont city	71,227	4,416	925	104,800	1,607	5,296	29,222	64,410	33.9	2.1	0.4	49.8	0.8	2.5	13.9	30.6
Fresno city	255,981	39,396	4,858	58,771	961	11,836	209,487	161,474	53.6	8.3	1.0	12.3	0.2	2.5	43.9	33.8
Fullerton city	70,074	3,582	191	32,030	405	3,984	45,651	58,249	49.3	2.5	0.1	22.5	0.3	2.8	32.1	41.0
Garden Grove city	64,400	4,923	1,361	64,910	1,539	2,802	77,247	43,224	33.5	2.6	0.7	33.7	0.8	1.5	40.2	22.5
Glendale city	136,773	3,633	1,087	28,894	183	2,755	36,158	122,528	70.3	1.9	0.6	14.8	0.1	1.4	18.6	63.0
Hayward city	50,863	23,045	1,166	29,461	2,074	5,620	48,843	28,806	37.5	17.0	0.9	21.7	1.5	4.1	36.1	21.3
Huntington Beach city	142,770	1,268	1,111	20,604	1,318	8,230	31,821	128,235	75.4	0.7	0.6	10.9	0.7	4.3	16.8	67.7
Inglewood city	27,156	47,184	–	322	668	1,521	68,482	3,667	22.6	39.3	–	0.3	0.6	1.3	57.0	3.1
Irvine city	97,112	1,422	420	63,111	271	4,614	14,757	89,443	56.4	0.8	0.2	36.7	0.2	2.7	8.6	51.9
Lancaster city	75,258	27,298	1,106	4,330	834	7,968	43,223	55,305	55.7	20.2	0.8	3.2	0.6	5.9	32.0	40.9
Long Beach city	202,592	60,695	2,206	65,816	2,378	17,703	184,326	141,630	42.7	13.1	0.5	14.2	0.5	3.8	39.7	30.5
Los Angeles city	1,831,467	368,711	15,082	415,652	9,732	87,925	1,824,373	1,063,362	49.1	9.9	0.4	11.1	0.3	2.4	48.9	28.5
Modesto city	148,690	10,141	2,293	14,618	740	5,746	60,083	111,633	73.3	5.0	1.1	7.2	0.4	2.8	29.6	55.0
Moreno Valley city	65,250	28,564	1,346	9,528	203	5,298	79,244	42,653	40.0	17.5	0.8	5.8	0.1	3.3	48.6	26.2
Norwalk city	43,268	5,675	222	15,790	115	4,356	65,577	15,087	41.7	5.5	0.2	15.2	0.1	4.2	63.1	14.5
Oakland city	121,075	115,952	2,072	61,358	3,426	17,784	93,582	88,319	32.4	31.0	0.6	16.4	0.9	4.8	25.0	23.6
Oceanside city	97,018	6,437	767	10,831	2,392	8,518	52,301	85,354	59.8	4.0	0.5	6.7	1.5	5.2	32.2	52.6
Ontario city	90,834	8,222	1,879	5,147	298	4,594	107,180	33,851	58.0	5.2	1.2	3.3	0.2	2.9	68.4	21.6
Orange city	91,486	955	938	12,768	152	3,001	51,130	70,530	66.3	0.7	0.7	9.3	0.1	2.2	37.1	51.1
Oxnard city	108,451	10,646	1,453	12,260	673	4,673	130,034	27,951	60.6	6.0	0.8	6.9	0.4	2.6	72.7	15.6
Palmdale city	92,008	17,827	793	5,175	134	3,586	81,557	39,298	63.1	12.2	0.5	3.5	0.1	2.5	55.9	27.0
Pasadena city	72,385	16,885	463	17,423	–	4,176	40,303	52,986	55.9	13.0	0.4	13.5	–	3.2	31.1	40.9
Pomona city	82,468	11,538	624	16,517	57	5,163	114,004	16,660	51.1	7.2	0.4	10.2	(Z)	3.2	70.7	10.3
Rancho Cucamonga city	101,196	8,043	431	12,114	221	6,471	47,040	72,739	69.8	5.5	0.3	8.4	0.2	4.5	32.5	50.2
Riverside city	160,725	21,346	2,981	16,853	2,614	13,011	131,849	112,209	54.7	7.3	1.0	5.7	0.9	4.4	44.8	38.2
Sacramento city	203,456	72,501	5,739	81,944	3,867	18,707	111,559	160,599	45.7	16.3	1.3	18.4	0.9	4.2	25.1	36.1
Salinas city	88,283	2,090	411	13,133	458	2,768	109,671	29,424	56.2	1.3	0.3	8.4	0.3	1.8	69.9	18.7

See footnotes at end of table.

[Includes states and 242 incorporated places of 100,000 or more population as of April 1, 2000. Two census designated places (CDPs) are also included (Honolulu CDP in Hawaii and Arlington CDP in Virginia). For more information on these areas, see Appendix C, Geographic Information. Seven states (Delaware, Maine, Montana, North Dakota, Vermont, West Virginia, and Wyoming) do not have any incorporated places of 100,000 or more population]

Place	Number, 2005								Percent, 2005							
	Race[1]						Hispanic status[2]		Race[1]						Hispanic status[2]	
	White alone	Black or African American alone	American Indian and Alaska Native alone	Asian alone	Native Hawaiian and Other Pacific Islander alone	Two or more races	Hispanic or Latino origin	Non-Hispanic White alone	White alone	Black or African American alone	American Indian and Alaska Native alone	Asian alone	Native Hawaiian and Other Pacific Islander alone	Two or more races	Hispanic or Latino origin	Non-Hispanic White alone
CALIFORNIA—Con.																
San Bernardino city	122,104	39,923	1,897	7,746	599	3,007	115,070	41,862	59.7	19.5	0.9	3.8	0.3	1.5	56.3	20.5
San Buenaventura (Ventura) city	74,575	1,261	1,599	4,389	139	4,842	30,729	61,512	74.5	1.3	1.6	4.4	0.1	4.8	30.7	61.4
San Diego city	763,661	81,630	6,046	190,893	6,281	42,557	312,767	585,671	63.2	6.8	0.5	15.8	0.5	3.5	25.9	48.5
San Francisco city	382,220	46,779	2,098	238,133	2,726	19,563	98,891	315,394	53.2	6.5	0.3	33.1	0.4	2.7	13.8	43.9
San Jose city	447,079	29,295	3,530	271,900	3,099	24,920	279,420	281,822	50.4	3.3	0.4	30.6	0.3	2.8	31.5	31.8
Santa Ana city	155,335	2,905	945	25,370	546	4,584	238,773	31,426	51.4	1.0	0.3	8.4	0.2	1.5	79.0	10.4
Santa Clara city	44,254	1,786	65	40,408	494	2,567	20,960	36,564	43.3	1.7	0.1	39.5	0.5	2.5	20.5	35.8
Santa Clarita city	115,505	4,140	868	11,197	–	6,115	44,646	103,504	69.1	2.5	0.5	6.7	–	3.7	26.7	62.0
Santa Rosa city	110,302	3,532	1,358	7,536	807	4,981	35,132	94,697	75.3	2.4	0.9	5.1	0.6	3.4	24.0	64.6
Simi Valley city	91,190	1,202	665	10,294	–	2,718	20,072	83,235	78.1	1.0	0.6	8.8	–	2.3	17.2	71.3
Stockton city	148,535	31,744	1,471	63,633	817	11,552	102,441	73,788	53.3	11.4	0.5	22.8	0.3	4.1	36.8	26.5
Sunnyvale city	57,803	4,093	259	50,479	1,053	4,231	22,041	51,272	43.6	3.1	0.2	38.0	0.8	3.2	16.6	38.6
Thousand Oaks city	101,881	2,203	144	10,606	1,524	3,216	17,898	93,806	79.7	1.7	0.1	8.3	1.2	2.5	14.0	73.3
Torrance city	76,805	1,763	971	45,566	253	4,745	18,962	68,473	55.4	1.3	0.7	32.9	0.2	3.4	13.7	49.4
Vallejo city	37,607	30,954	1,119	26,057	2,164	3,810	22,451	29,917	32.5	26.8	1.0	22.5	1.9	3.3	19.4	25.9
West Covina city	49,476	8,136	256	24,236	–	5,080	63,004	18,880	42.5	7.0	0.2	20.8	–	4.4	54.1	16.2
COLORADO	3,809,054	165,729	40,063	117,506	4,476	119,017	891,614	3,281,823	83.5	3.6	0.9	2.6	0.1	2.6	19.5	71.9
Arvada city	94,123	1,025	608	1,726	–	3,841	15,044	84,022	89.8	1.0	0.6	1.6	–	3.7	14.4	80.2
Aurora city	202,340	44,235	3,162	12,459	252	8,398	79,494	147,371	69.5	15.2	1.1	4.3	0.1	2.9	27.3	50.6
Centennial city	91,788	2,268	852	4,705	372	1,654	7,153	87,209	88.7	2.2	0.8	4.5	0.4	1.6	6.9	84.3
Colorado Springs city	302,784	23,831	3,322	9,856	935	14,065	51,755	277,943	80.3	6.3	0.9	2.6	0.2	3.7	13.7	73.7
Denver city	392,164	54,693	6,627	15,905	108	14,237	191,510	271,645	71.9	10.0	1.2	2.9	(Z)	2.6	35.1	49.8
Fort Collins city	110,626	1,314	855	3,193	201	3,073	13,792	100,960	90.5	1.1	0.7	2.6	0.2	2.5	11.3	82.6
Lakewood city	116,165	1,640	894	6,293	65	3,572	30,117	101,868	81.6	1.2	0.6	4.4	(Z)	2.5	21.1	71.5
Pueblo city	78,922	1,894	1,245	651	202	4,350	47,506	48,494	77.9	1.9	1.2	0.6	0.2	4.3	46.9	47.9
Westminster city	86,170	1,625	731	4,823	–	1,622	14,254	77,207	86.8	1.6	0.7	4.9	–	1.6	14.4	77.7
CONNECTICUT	2,756,081	309,769	8,324	108,644	1,480	56,822	371,425	2,555,434	81.2	9.1	0.2	3.2	(Z)	1.7	10.9	75.3
Bridgeport city	58,780	47,041	288	2,717	–	2,672	42,730	35,411	44.5	35.6	0.2	2.1	–	2.0	32.4	26.8
Hartford city	30,511	44,403	1,410	2,512	–	2,971	47,310	16,005	27.5	40.0	1.3	2.3	–	2.7	42.6	14.4
New Haven city	44,498	39,673	596	5,863	–	2,766	26,140	34,896	41.0	36.6	0.5	5.4	–	2.6	24.1	32.2
Stamford city	84,493	14,896	–	7,364	–	1,702	24,447	70,556	71.3	12.6	–	6.2	–	1.4	20.6	59.5
Waterbury city	75,509	14,655	287	2,708	–	7,441	28,721	54,014	72.2	14.0	0.3	2.6	–	7.1	27.5	51.7
DELAWARE	602,213	163,052	2,056	22,376	70	12,071	50,218	570,027	73.6	19.9	0.3	2.7	(Z)	1.5	6.1	69.6
DISTRICT OF COLUMBIA	166,813	292,445	1,386	15,566	242	7,773	45,901	152,879	32.4	56.8	0.3	3.0	(Z)	1.5	8.9	29.7
Washington city	166,813	292,445	1,386	15,566	242	7,773	45,901	152,879	32.4	56.8	0.3	3.0	(Z)	1.5	8.9	29.7
FLORIDA	13,341,532	2,613,628	59,092	371,385	7,523	277,978	3,414,414	10,774,504	76.8	15.0	0.3	2.1	(Z)	1.6	19.6	62.0
Cape Coral city	122,003	2,038	574	3,464	–	1,402	22,557	104,388	90.8	1.5	0.4	2.6	–	1.0	16.8	77.7
Clearwater city	90,852	10,954	276	621	–	3,031	13,784	80,062	83.8	10.1	0.3	0.6	–	2.8	12.7	73.9
Coral Springs city	101,208	12,740	407	6,117	–	3,447	24,881	81,645	79.3	10.0	0.3	4.8	–	2.7	19.5	64.0
Fort Lauderdale city	91,463	42,764	–	3,207	96	1,610	13,459	80,618	64.7	30.3	–	2.3	0.1	1.1	9.5	57.1
Gainesville city	63,931	25,707	225	6,468	–	2,697	7,006	60,194	63.4	25.5	0.2	6.4	–	2.7	6.9	59.7
Hialeah city	195,932	6,160	246	1,340	–	2,066	(B)	(B)	91.6	2.9	0.1	0.6	–	1.0	(NA)	(NA)
Hollywood city	108,270	19,382	191	2,379	288	3,348	39,450	75,765	78.2	14.0	0.1	1.7	0.2	2.4	28.5	54.7
Jacksonville city	471,521	235,582	2,486	28,485	264	11,846	41,556	450,527	61.4	30.7	0.3	3.7	(Z)	1.5	5.4	58.6
Miami city	247,882	79,173	750	2,371	113	8,569	243,874	39,819	68.5	21.9	0.2	0.7	(Z)	2.4	67.4	11.0
Miami Gardens city	11,910	73,913	206	562	226	1,128	(B)	(B)	13.0	80.6	0.2	0.6	0.2	1.2	(NA)	(NA)
Orlando city	118,002	75,436	1,294	5,691	–	4,685	43,978	92,326	53.3	34.1	0.6	2.6	–	2.1	19.9	41.7
Pembroke Pines city	111,720	27,103	73	8,508	–	3,916	57,696	64,606	70.1	17.0	(Z)	5.3	–	2.5	36.2	40.5
Pompano Beach city	63,292	25,950	612	872	–	1,920	11,616	54,325	66.7	27.3	0.6	0.9	–	2.0	12.2	57.2
St. Petersburg city	160,202	59,352	541	7,058	–	4,098	9,943	152,178	68.8	25.5	0.2	3.0	–	1.8	4.3	65.3
Tallahassee city	87,343	46,310	550	4,048	72	1,599	6,116	83,934	61.9	32.8	0.4	2.9	0.1	1.1	4.3	59.5
Tampa city	196,058	89,562	2,224	7,789	1,013	4,800	66,675	144,932	62.7	28.6	0.7	2.5	0.3	1.5	21.3	46.3
GEORGIA	5,516,920	2,571,396	20,223	240,832	4,401	120,531	625,028	5,264,447	62.5	29.2	0.2	2.7	(Z)	1.4	7.1	59.7
Athens-Clarke County (balance)	60,531	25,449	192	3,313	37	1,381	8,402	55,138	64.3	27.0	0.2	3.5	(Z)	1.5	8.9	58.6
Atlanta city	143,112	231,609	502	7,980	83	4,173	18,516	133,508	36.2	58.6	0.1	2.0	(Z)	1.1	4.7	33.8
Augusta-Richmond County (balance)	76,302	96,145	706	2,729	280	3,049	4,591	74,722	42.2	53.1	0.4	1.5	0.2	1.7	2.5	41.3
Columbus city	82,678	80,252	514	3,453	384	4,671	6,989	80,569	47.0	45.6	0.3	2.0	0.2	2.7	4.0	45.8
Savannah city	41,913	70,628	406	1,749	–	2,117	3,590	39,893	35.7	60.1	0.3	1.5	–	1.8	3.1	34.0

See footnotes at end of table.

[Includes states and 242 incorporated places of 100,000 or more population as of April 1, 2000. Two census designated places (CDPs) are also included (Honolulu CDP in Hawaii and Arlington CDP in Virginia). For more information on these areas, see Appendix C, Geographic Information. Seven states (Delaware, Maine, Montana, North Dakota, Vermont, West Virginia, and Wyoming) do not have any incorporated places of 100,000 or more population]

Place	Number, 2005								Percent, 2005							
	Race[1]						Hispanic status[2]		Race[1]						Hispanic status[2]	
	White alone	Black or African American alone	American Indian and Alaska Native alone	Asian alone	Native Hawaiian and Other Pacific Islander alone	Two or more races	Hispanic or Latino origin	Non-Hispanic White alone	White alone	Black or African American alone	American Indian and Alaska Native alone	Asian alone	Native Hawaiian and Other Pacific Islander alone	Two or more races	Hispanic or Latino origin	Non-Hispanic White alone
HAWAII.	308,912	24,239	3,216	520,564	105,042	260,541	98,699	284,455	24.9	2.0	0.3	42.0	8.5	21.0	8.0	23.0
Honolulu CDP.	66,702	6,787	456	212,346	22,804	50,245	13,268	63,537	18.4	1.9	0.1	58.6	6.3	13.9	3.7	17.5
IDAHO	1,281,279	5,931	15,817	15,117	1,054	27,329	126,785	1,212,911	91.8	0.4	1.1	1.1	0.1	2.0	9.1	86.9
Boise City city.	177,851	1,995	1,050	3,801	43	4,826	11,295	169,823	92.8	1.0	0.5	2.0	(Z)	2.5	5.9	88.6
ILLINOIS.	8,986,032	1,803,613	23,175	507,687	3,992	187,242	1,804,619	8,165,057	72.2	14.5	0.2	4.1	(Z)	1.5	14.5	65.6
Aurora city	122,200	17,465	–	10,945	–	2,959	67,715	73,472	71.7	10.2	–	6.4	–	1.7	39.7	43.1
Chicago city	1,042,025	943,752	4,583	128,650	1,940	43,777	778,234	819,215	38.6	34.9	0.2	4.8	0.1	1.6	28.8	30.3
Joliet city	84,457	18,069	644	2,176	39	1,566	30,105	75,803	65.9	14.1	0.5	1.7	(Z)	1.2	23.5	59.2
Naperville city	121,181	3,747	106	18,688	–	2,189	6,246	117,333	82.0	2.5	0.1	12.6	–	1.5	4.2	79.4
Peoria city	66,466	29,270	59	3,842	46	1,174	2,160	65,581	65.1	28.7	0.1	3.8	(Z)	1.1	2.1	64.2
Rockford city.	93,959	26,740	679	2,470	50	2,476	21,068	86,492	67.5	19.2	0.5	1.8	(Z)	1.8	15.1	62.1
Springfield city.	88,300	16,894	34	1,613	–	2,891	1,303	87,778	80.1	15.3	(Z)	1.5	–	2.6	1.2	79.6
INDIANA.	5,247,604	522,377	15,161	72,494	1,610	89,179	277,558	5,131,723	86.1	8.6	0.2	1.2	(Z)	1.5	4.6	84.2
Evansville city	93,260	12,197	245	1,287	–	2,323	1,665	92,797	84.2	11.0	0.2	1.2	–	2.1	1.5	83.8
Fort Wayne city	161,971	35,858	404	4,798	481	7,145	16,438	157,672	73.8	16.3	0.2	2.2	0.2	3.3	7.5	71.9
Gary city	9,864	80,205	–	142	–	3,201	(B)	(B)	10.2	82.6	–	0.1	–	3.3	(NA)	(NA)
Indianapolis city (balance).	507,520	195,044	2,514	12,557	279	18,178	47,764	491,044	66.3	25.5	0.3	1.6	(Z)	2.4	6.2	64.2
South Bend city.	61,762	22,974	1,117	843	–	2,661	10,617	58,391	63.6	23.7	1.2	0.9	–	2.7	10.9	60.2
IOWA	2,675,878	62,827	6,511	41,510	520	31,380	106,052	2,619,948	93.5	2.2	0.2	1.5	(Z)	1.1	3.7	91.5
Cedar Rapids city	108,961	5,917	–	2,068	–	1,812	2,694	107,042	91.1	4.9	–	1.7	–	1.5	2.3	89.4
Des Moines city.	160,212	16,709	564	9,071	44	2,616	18,952	149,786	81.4	8.5	0.3	4.6	(Z)	1.3	9.6	76.1
KANSAS.	2,269,482	147,455	23,647	53,129	1,169	58,934	224,152	2,172,803	85.2	5.5	0.9	2.0	(Z)	2.2	8.4	81.6
Kansas City city.	79,060	44,620	1,064	2,446	–	1,890	32,328	63,650	55.5	31.3	0.7	1.7	–	1.3	22.7	44.7
Overland Park city	139,556	5,347	155	11,080	95	3,450	8,116	134,969	86.2	3.3	0.1	6.8	0.1	2.1	5.0	83.4
Topeka city	89,722	12,953	2,022	1,569	185	3,611	11,653	85,761	76.5	11.0	1.7	1.3	0.2	3.1	9.9	73.1
Wichita city.	261,634	39,470	5,314	15,673	52	10,230	42,928	245,527	73.8	11.1	1.5	4.4	(Z)	2.9	12.1	69.2
KENTUCKY.	3,646,690	292,012	8,343	35,561	3,184	44,148	69,702	3,608,732	89.9	7.2	0.2	0.9	0.1	1.1	1.7	88.9
Lexington-Fayette	205,623	33,879	501	7,392	249	3,858	12,254	197,618	80.5	13.3	0.2	2.9	0.1	1.5	4.8	77.4
Louisville/Jefferson County (balance).	400,504	120,011	1,214	8,499	471	9,289	14,706	393,522	73.1	21.9	0.2	1.6	0.1	1.7	2.7	71.8
LOUISIANA	2,795,263	1,425,685	24,921	58,392	347	48,061	123,066	2,716,471	63.7	32.5	0.6	1.3	(Z)	1.1	2.8	61.9
Baton Rouge city	84,625	110,849	239	5,364	–	2,992	3,354	82,864	41.2	54.0	0.1	2.6	–	1.5	1.6	40.3
Lafayette city	70,800	33,126	243	2,273	–	627	2,734	69,536	65.4	30.6	0.2	2.1	–	0.6	2.5	64.3
New Orleans city	122,622	295,259	1,022	10,655	–	4,237	13,679	114,312	28.0	67.5	0.2	2.4	–	1.0	3.1	26.1
Shreveport city	83,139	104,553	359	2,262	–	1,483	3,624	80,253	43.2	54.3	0.2	1.2	–	0.8	1.9	41.7
MAINE	1,239,525	8,788	7,060	10,907	14	12,607	12,059	1,231,743	96.6	0.7	0.5	0.8	(Z)	1.0	0.9	96.0
MARYLAND.	3,356,489	1,564,914	16,711	258,529	2,554	93,212	316,257	3,228,401	61.5	28.7	0.3	4.7	(Z)	1.7	5.8	59.1
Baltimore city	183,974	396,495	2,507	9,816	136	5,837	13,887	180,834	30.2	65.2	0.4	1.6	(Z)	1.0	2.3	29.7
MASSACHUSETTS.	5,156,426	363,095	13,708	292,537	626	86,904	490,839	4,929,550	83.4	5.9	0.2	4.7	(Z)	1.4	7.0	79.7
Boston city	287,992	128,036	2,048	45,410	–	10,308	76,494	253,237	55.3	24.6	0.4	8.7	–	2.0	14.7	48.6
Cambridge city	56,201	9,184	83	10,989	54	2,153	5,998	53,443	69.2	11.3	0.1	13.5	0.1	2.6	7.4	65.8
Lowell city	63,691	4,405	47	20,604	–	682	15,452	55,814	65.7	4.5	(Z)	21.3	–	0.7	16.0	57.6
Springfield city.	70,402	33,582	338	3,101	59	4,030	52,571	56,673	47.9	22.9	0.2	2.1	(Z)	2.7	35.8	38.6
Worcester city	118,987	16,382	792	8,480	51	2,343	25,946	101,624	77.1	10.6	0.5	5.5	(Z)	1.5	16.8	65.8
MICHIGAN	7,890,608	1,379,010	57,840	227,585	3,546	155,324	371,627	7,699,573	80.0	14.0	0.6	2.3	(Z)	1.6	3.8	78.0
Ann Arbor city	73,568	6,907	48	14,699	34	1,901	3,283	71,521	74.5	7.0	(Z)	14.9	(Z)	1.9	3.3	72.4
Detroit city	92,796	686,241	3,223	9,577	271	12,736	46,993	77,163	11.1	82.1	0.4	1.1	(Z)	1.5	5.6	9.2
Flint city	43,942	62,433	193	208	–	3,571	2,571	43,183	39.3	55.8	0.2	0.2	–	3.2	2.3	38.6
Grand Rapids city	130,745	40,743	1,105	2,997	–	5,564	32,368	113,791	67.5	21.0	0.6	1.5	–	2.9	16.7	58.8
Lansing city	80,686	28,016	520	4,164	85	2,707	12,175	73,005	67.4	23.4	0.4	3.5	0.1	2.3	10.2	61.0
Livonia city	95,941	1,738	212	3,103	–	1,691	3,223	93,679	92.7	1.7	0.2	3.0	–	1.6	3.1	90.5
Sterling Heights city	108,815	4,349	648	7,198	–	1,802	2,414	107,220	88.2	3.5	0.5	5.8	–	1.5	2.0	86.9
Warren city.	114,066	9,800	305	6,907	–	3,722	1,422	112,869	84.6	7.3	0.2	5.1	–	2.8	1.1	83.7

See footnotes at end of table.

Table D-2. Places — **Population by Race and Hispanic Origin**—Con.

[Includes states and 242 incorporated places of 100,000 or more population as of April 1, 2000. Two census designated places (CDPs) are also included (Honolulu CDP in Hawaii and Arlington CDP in Virginia). For more information on these areas, see Appendix C, Geographic Information. Seven states (Delaware, Maine, Montana, North Dakota, Vermont, West Virginia, and Wyoming) do not have any incorporated places of 100,000 or more population]

| | Number, 2005 | | | | | | | | Percent, 2005 | | | | | | | |
| | Race[1] | | | | | | Hispanic status[2] | | Race[1] | | | | | | Hispanic status[2] | |
Place	White alone	Black or African American alone	American Indian and Alaska Native alone	Asian alone	Native Hawaiian and Other Pacific Islander alone	Two or more races	Hispanic or Latino origin	Non-Hispanic White alone	White alone	Black or African American alone	American Indian and Alaska Native alone	Asian alone	Native Hawaiian and Other Pacific Islander alone	Two or more races	Hispanic or Latino origin	Non-Hispanic White alone
MINNESOTA	4,390,040	205,160	53,573	177,645	2,460	73,458	181,959	4,301,409	88.0	4.1	1.1	3.6	(Z)	1.5	3.6	86.2
Minneapolis city.	228,305	58,260	4,510	20,306	196	10,561	37,017	216,975	65.2	16.6	1.3	5.8	0.1	3.0	10.6	61.9
St. Paul city	172,922	35,836	1,897	35,324	87	6,428	22,402	161,329	66.1	13.7	0.7	13.5	(Z)	2.5	8.6	61.7
MISSISSIPPI	1,716,444	1,030,075	12,280	21,523	588	24,567	43,275	1,695,319	60.8	36.5	0.4	0.8	(Z)	0.9	1.5	60.0
Jackson city	34,003	126,908	220	428	149	1,040	(B)	(B)	20.7	77.4	0.1	0.3	0.1	0.6	(NA)	(NA)
MISSOURI	4,760,327	627,978	23,091	78,554	3,100	83,019	148,994	4,675,423	84.5	11.2	0.4	1.4	0.1	1.5	2.6	83.0
Independence city	99,498	4,218	129	689	54	3,159	7,856	96,455	89.0	3.8	0.1	0.6	(Z)	2.8	7.0	86.2
Kansas City city.	271,210	132,187	1,988	10,878	1,054	10,181	35,995	249,123	61.5	30.0	0.5	2.5	0.2	2.3	8.2	56.5
St. Louis city.	147,955	168,909	1,603	7,199	–	4,661	8,268	143,590	44.3	50.6	0.5	2.2	–	1.4	2.5	43.0
Springfield city.	129,115	4,151	755	2,108	107	2,771	3,174	126,792	92.5	3.0	0.5	1.5	0.1	2.0	2.3	90.8
MONTANA	824,721	4,135	55,079	5,508	648	15,801	20,232	812,226	90.6	0.5	6.0	0.6	0.1	1.7	2.2	89.2
NEBRASKA.	1,529,471	68,389	13,250	24,820	557	25,620	122,518	1,457,549	89.6	4.0	0.8	1.5	(Z)	1.5	7.2	85.4
Lincoln city	202,867	7,184	1,668	7,572	–	3,144	9,672	197,287	89.7	3.2	0.7	3.3	–	1.4	4.3	87.3
Omaha city.	288,708	50,452	1,944	6,971	125	7,663	39,674	267,685	77.4	13.5	0.5	1.9	(Z)	2.1	10.6	71.7
NEVADA	1,811,535	170,854	28,163	138,054	11,490	74,460	563,999	1,423,101	76.1	7.2	1.2	5.8	0.5	3.1	23.7	59.8
Henderson city	181,638	11,017	1,850	9,476	2,560	7,193	26,071	168,066	81.2	4.9	0.8	4.2	1.1	3.2	11.7	75.1
Las Vegas city	400,007	60,602	3,845	25,779	2,206	16,298	153,813	281,679	74.3	11.3	0.7	4.8	0.4	3.0	28.6	52.3
North Las Vegas city	110,391	26,766	1,738	8,471	1,061	5,501	65,218	58,755	66.9	16.2	1.1	5.1	0.6	3.3	39.5	35.6
Reno city	155,991	6,025	2,997	12,067	1,783	4,919	45,665	133,009	76.3	2.9	1.5	5.9	0.9	2.4	22.3	65.0
NEW HAMPSHIRE	1,214,616	10,456	4,499	22,850	326	12,468	27,933	1,195,415	95.5	0.8	0.4	1.8	(Z)	1.0	2.2	93.9
Manchester city.	99,760	3,667	271	2,695	–	714	6,679	95,438	91.3	3.4	0.2	2.5	–	0.7	6.1	87.3
NEW JERSEY	5,954,926	1,130,967	20,745	620,588	3,626	125,300	1,307,412	5,371,394	69.9	13.3	0.2	7.3	(Z)	1.5	15.3	63.0
Elizabeth city	58,593	26,462	2,037	3,204	–	868	64,665	25,801	48.4	21.8	1.7	2.6	–	0.7	53.4	21.3
Jersey City city	86,556	67,721	725	44,601	51	5,605	73,265	54,900	35.1	27.5	0.3	18.1	(Z)	2.3	29.7	22.3
Newark city.	55,620	133,867	1,016	3,228	197	2,633	83,567	31,731	21.9	52.7	0.4	1.3	0.1	1.0	32.9	12.5
Paterson city.	44,344	44,428	450	3,199	–	2,134	83,315	18,293	29.9	29.9	0.3	2.2	–	1.4	56.2	12.3
NEW MEXICO	1,311,829	35,604	181,064	22,454	1,711	60,334	822,224	807,552	69.5	1.9	9.6	1.2	0.1	3.2	43.6	42.8
Albuquerque city	352,257	15,368	21,327	10,976	873	16,728	213,289	221,185	72.2	3.1	4.4	2.2	0.2	3.4	43.7	45.3
NEW YORK.	12,508,643	2,858,062	67,460	1,246,567	6,123	283,858	3,028,658	11,315,746	67.1	15.3	0.4	6.7	(Z)	1.5	16.2	60.7
Buffalo city	128,912	105,285	1,008	6,820	–	3,801	19,425	122,466	50.3	41.0	0.4	2.7	–	1.5	7.6	47.7
New York city	3,499,212	2,011,962	33,088	922,978	3,105	130,502	2,221,906	2,746,422	44.0	25.3	0.4	11.6	(Z)	1.6	27.9	34.5
Rochester city	86,392	80,548	418	6,467	–	5,157	25,982	74,153	45.6	42.5	0.2	3.4	–	2.7	13.7	39.2
Syracuse city	80,718	37,768	1,687	5,777	–	4,247	8,225	75,825	60.9	28.5	1.3	4.4	–	3.2	6.2	57.2
Yonkers city	110,407	37,311	1,212	12,086	–	1,792	57,027	85,673	57.1	19.3	0.6	6.3	–	0.9	29.5	44.3
NORTH CAROLINA	6,005,471	1,765,698	106,931	146,795	3,344	125,633	533,087	5,753,812	71.4	21.0	1.3	1.7	(Z)	1.5	6.3	68.4
Charlotte city.	342,761	206,259	2,452	23,560	64	10,285	58,466	302,789	57.0	34.3	0.4	3.9	(Z)	1.7	9.7	50.3
Durham city	82,489	77,775	454	8,402	161	3,111	25,336	77,160	43.0	40.6	0.2	4.4	0.1	1.6	13.2	40.2
Fayetteville city	62,190	52,099	1,077	2,587	216	7,086	6,882	60,187	48.3	40.5	0.8	2.0	0.2	5.5	5.3	46.7
Greensboro city.	107,701	80,937	867	8,754	77	3,772	11,832	102,397	51.6	38.8	0.4	4.2	(Z)	1.8	5.7	49.1
Raleigh city.	195,579	85,116	598	11,954	117	5,338	30,600	182,754	62.0	27.0	0.2	3.8	(Z)	1.7	9.7	58.0
Winston-Salem city	102,573	64,948	868	3,315	–	1,366	26,265	88,194	55.9	35.4	0.5	1.8	–	0.7	14.3	48.1
NORTH DAKOTA	557,952	4,981	29,985	5,459	486	7,277	8,553	554,110	91.5	0.8	4.9	0.9	0.1	1.2	1.4	90.9
OHIO	9,408,020	1,283,908	22,682	162,117	2,652	166,510	253,889	9,284,543	84.3	11.5	0.2	1.5	(Z)	1.5	2.3	83.2
Akron city.	131,244	60,590	369	3,497	61	2,973	3,485	128,976	65.6	30.3	0.2	1.7	(Z)	1.5	1.7	64.4
Cincinnati city	140,285	132,152	188	6,874	–	5,641	3,855	138,486	48.8	46.0	0.1	2.4	–	2.0	1.3	48.2
Cleveland city	160,254	222,837	2,312	6,289	188	6,028	32,085	147,359	38.7	53.8	0.6	1.5	(Z)	1.5	7.7	35.5
Columbus city	454,368	181,977	1,674	27,125	75	18,103	24,607	442,958	65.5	26.2	0.2	3.9	(Z)	2.6	3.5	63.8
Dayton city	68,151	60,290	151	1,827	–	1,281	1,693	67,581	51.4	45.4	0.1	1.4	–	1.0	1.3	50.9
Toledo city	189,641	72,657	546	4,150	–	8,154	18,404	183,746	66.3	25.4	0.2	1.5	–	2.9	6.4	64.3

See footnotes at end of table.

[Includes states and 242 incorporated places of 100,000 or more population as of April 1, 2000. Two census designated places (CDPs) are also included (Honolulu CDP in Hawaii and Arlington CDP in Virginia). For more information on these areas, see Appendix C, Geographic Information. Seven states (Delaware, Maine, Montana, North Dakota, Vermont, West Virginia, and Wyoming) do not have any incorporated places of 100,000 or more population]

| Place | Number, 2005 | | | | | | | | Percent, 2005 | | | | | | | |
| | Race[1] | | | | | | Hispanic status[2] | | Race[1] | | | | | | Hispanic status[2] | |
	White alone	Black or African American alone	American Indian and Alaska Native alone	Asian alone	Native Hawaiian and Other Pacific Islander alone	Two or more races	Hispanic or Latino origin	Non-Hispanic White alone	White alone	Black or African American alone	American Indian and Alaska Native alone	Asian alone	Native Hawaiian and Other Pacific Islander alone	Two or more races	Hispanic or Latino origin	Non-Hispanic White alone
OKLAHOMA	2,589,660	243,094	253,783	54,270	3,598	195,422	227,767	2,491,692	75.4	7.1	7.4	1.6	0.1	5.7	6.6	72.6
Oklahoma City city	345,217	75,983	16,489	22,122	1,108	29,123	66,393	314,322	66.9	14.7	3.2	4.3	0.2	5.6	12.9	60.9
Tulsa city	250,527	57,113	14,956	7,274	687	23,311	38,149	232,041	67.6	15.4	4.0	2.0	0.2	6.3	10.3	62.6
OREGON	3,089,729	58,309	47,805	125,049	6,579	107,365	353,433	2,897,961	86.8	1.6	1.3	3.5	0.2	3.0	9.9	81.4
Eugene city	122,042	1,376	1,345	8,472	178	3,858	9,025	118,777	85.5	1.0	0.9	5.9	0.1	2.7	6.3	83.2
Portland city	408,462	32,009	4,342	36,536	1,890	20,582	43,324	382,033	79.5	6.2	0.8	7.1	0.4	4.0	8.4	74.4
Salem city	113,956	1,397	2,310	4,892	–	3,757	30,734	100,158	80.2	1.0	1.6	3.4	–	2.6	21.6	70.5
PENNSYLVANIA	10,132,144	1,208,536	15,307	266,473	1,812	129,197	484,679	9,908,913	84.6	10.1	0.1	2.2	(Z)	1.1	4.0	82.7
Allentown city	72,903	8,850	156	1,738	–	2,168	35,690	58,569	69.3	8.4	0.1	1.7	–	2.1	33.9	55.7
Erie city	71,764	13,837	115	833	242	2,157	5,312	69,230	78.5	15.1	0.1	0.9	0.3	2.4	5.8	75.7
Philadelphia city	592,159	628,312	3,079	72,898	442	20,971	146,856	545,169	42.1	44.7	0.2	5.2	(Z)	1.5	10.4	38.8
Pittsburgh city	183,078	81,915	938	10,727	–	4,994	5,018	180,725	64.4	28.8	0.3	3.8	–	1.8	1.8	63.6
RHODE ISLAND	856,314	51,843	5,389	26,803	792	19,836	112,722	817,252	82.9	5.0	0.5	2.6	0.1	1.9	10.9	79.1
Providence city	79,427	21,956	1,143	10,824	462	3,666	60,008	64,223	49.6	13.7	0.7	6.8	0.3	2.3	37.4	40.1
SOUTH CAROLINA	2,774,429	1,174,488	13,859	44,560	1,485	45,026	135,041	2,704,013	67.4	28.5	0.3	1.1	(Z)	1.1	3.3	65.7
Columbia city	45,147	38,102	120	2,507	–	2,013	1,616	44,468	51.0	43.1	0.1	2.8	–	2.3	1.8	50.3
SOUTH DAKOTA	656,165	6,166	62,916	4,756	174	11,409	14,140	649,303	88.0	0.8	8.4	0.6	(Z)	1.5	1.9	87.0
Sioux Falls city	119,997	3,450	3,044	2,054	–	1,532	5,136	117,705	90.7	2.6	2.3	1.6	–	1.2	3.9	88.9
TENNESSEE	4,625,715	954,287	15,770	73,824	1,200	67,295	172,704	4,534,901	79.6	16.4	0.3	1.3	(Z)	1.2	3.0	78.0
Chattanooga city	81,136	53,785	165	2,110	–	1,284	2,223	79,485	58.3	38.7	0.1	1.5	–	0.9	1.6	57.1
Clarksville city	71,795	26,093	502	2,559	747	2,395	7,365	69,150	67.0	24.4	0.5	2.4	0.7	2.2	6.9	64.5
Knoxville city	136,561	24,994	411	2,629	53	3,569	2,123	135,144	80.9	14.8	0.2	1.6	(Z)	2.1	1.3	80.1
Memphis city	200,735	404,970	1,228	11,235	–	7,658	26,563	192,413	31.3	63.1	0.2	1.7	–	1.2	4.1	30.0
Nashville-Davidson (balance) . . .	336,731	149,273	1,664	16,943	–	4,858	37,463	314,518	64.4	28.6	0.3	3.2	–	0.9	7.2	60.2
TEXAS	16,021,256	2,442,350	113,898	726,027	12,725	373,440	7,903,079	10,898,613	71.9	11.0	0.5	3.3	0.1	1.7	35.5	48.9
Abilene city	79,843	7,588	755	2,091	–	3,558	23,342	70,542	75.9	7.2	0.7	2.0	–	3.4	22.2	67.1
Amarillo city	138,661	10,580	1,193	2,850	272	3,793	46,588	114,650	78.3	6.0	0.7	1.6	0.2	2.1	26.3	64.8
Arlington city	210,048	59,012	1,345	18,771	784	11,203	82,991	174,668	60.2	16.9	0.4	5.4	0.2	3.2	23.8	50.1
Austin city	469,562	60,683	3,241	35,449	505	11,745	223,361	347,013	69.2	8.9	0.5	5.2	0.1	1.7	32.9	51.1
Beaumont city	41,300	54,013	244	3,988	–	988	12,088	36,288	38.3	50.1	0.2	3.7	–	0.9	11.2	33.6
Brownsville city	138,690	374	754	450	–	1,530	(B)	(B)	80.9	0.2	0.4	0.3	–	0.9	(NA)	(NA)
Carrollton city	82,900	5,887	1,206	18,926	173	1,954	36,809	58,318	67.6	4.8	1.0	15.4	0.1	1.6	30.0	47.5
Corpus Christi city	217,798	11,730	1,444	4,618	–	5,516	161,224	100,105	77.8	4.2	0.5	1.6	–	2.0	57.6	35.8
Dallas city	651,215	271,501	5,305	31,544	355	13,212	482,024	346,876	56.9	23.7	0.5	2.8	(Z)	1.2	42.1	30.3
El Paso city	456,333	16,426	3,132	6,833	260	13,920	465,287	90,656	78.2	2.8	0.5	1.2	(Z)	2.4	79.8	15.5
Fort Worth city	367,444	111,081	5,352	25,337	538	10,579	192,819	266,591	60.8	18.4	0.9	4.2	0.1	1.7	31.9	44.1
Garland city	130,715	40,992	1,471	20,295	239	2,475	82,924	89,269	55.4	17.4	0.6	8.6	0.1	1.0	35.2	37.9
Grand Prairie city	86,340	24,619	2,954	6,735	–	5,844	60,521	52,486	58.1	16.6	2.0	4.5	–	3.9	40.7	35.3
Houston city	1,100,450	455,764	5,913	112,473	1,977	21,608	820,510	539,092	56.7	23.5	0.3	5.8	0.1	1.1	42.3	27.8
Irving city	142,641	25,937	857	21,592	–	5,435	84,638	76,822	67.2	12.2	0.4	10.2	–	2.6	39.9	36.2
Laredo city	179,887	1,012	599	779	–	1,578	197,198	8,890	86.6	0.5	0.3	0.4	–	0.8	94.9	4.3
Lubbock city	155,764	16,960	941	3,678	–	3,291	61,599	116,198	78.0	8.5	0.5	1.8	–	1.6	30.8	58.2
McAllen city	84,169	1,414	796	2,617	–	826	96,852	14,408	72.3	1.2	0.7	2.2	–	0.7	83.2	12.4
Mesquite city	98,406	16,166	629	3,050	–	2,158	30,392	75,034	77.5	12.7	0.5	2.4	–	1.7	24.0	59.1
Pasadena city	109,800	2,935	3,303	5,008	–	2,327	88,469	51,642	73.1	2.0	2.2	3.3	–	1.5	58.9	34.4
Plano city	189,054	12,939	1,259	40,511	–	2,160	29,727	164,296	75.1	5.1	0.5	16.1	–	0.9	11.8	65.3
San Antonio city	768,878	73,540	8,100	21,934	1,184	38,876	735,458	356,420	64.0	6.1	0.7	1.8	0.1	3.2	61.2	29.6
Waco city	74,466	22,436	774	1,439	–	1,566	32,299	49,509	69.5	20.9	0.7	1.3	–	1.5	30.1	46.2
Wichita Falls city	67,464	10,191	498	2,060	47	2,716	13,225	60,852	75.9	11.5	0.6	2.3	0.1	3.1	14.9	68.5
UTAH	2,178,777	18,325	29,875	46,962	14,993	36,328	264,084	2,028,330	89.8	0.8	1.2	1.9	0.6	1.5	10.9	83.6
Provo city	87,597	466	268	2,218	1,314	2,272	12,915	81,982	86.6	0.5	0.3	2.2	1.3	2.2	12.8	81.0
Salt Lake City city	142,877	5,413	2,636	7,235	1,388	2,876	41,745	122,621	78.2	3.0	1.4	4.0	0.8	1.6	22.9	67.1
West Valley City city	85,186	841	973	7,966	3,958	2,496	29,918	74,798	71.1	0.7	0.8	6.6	3.3	2.1	25.0	62.4

See footnotes at end of table.

Table D-2. Places — **Population by Race and Hispanic Origin**—Con.

[Includes states and 242 incorporated places of 100,000 or more population as of April 1, 2000. Two census designated places (CDPs) are also included (Honolulu CDP in Hawaii and Arlington CDP in Virginia). For more information on these areas, see Appendix C, Geographic Information. Seven states (Delaware, Maine, Montana, North Dakota, Vermont, West Virginia, and Wyoming) do not have any incorporated places of 100,000 or more population]

Place	Number, 2005								Percent, 2005							
	Race[1]						Hispanic status[2]		Race[1]						Hispanic status[2]	
	White alone	Black or African American alone	American Indian and Alaska Native alone	Asian alone	Native Hawaiian and Other Pacific Islander alone	Two or more races	Hispanic or Latino origin	Non-Hispanic White alone	White alone	Black or African American alone	American Indian and Alaska Native alone	Asian alone	Native Hawaiian and Other Pacific Islander alone	Two or more races	Hispanic or Latino origin	Non-Hispanic White alone
VERMONT	581,874	2,932	1,168	6,659	65	8,632	5,214	578,212	96.6	0.5	0.2	1.1	(Z)	1.4	0.9	96.0
VIRGINIA	5,259,281	1,397,192	24,261	342,239	4,192	134,315	438,789	5,011,025	71.7	19.1	0.3	4.7	0.1	1.8	6.0	68.3
Alexandria city.	91,052	26,784	374	7,584	–	3,833	18,457	77,301	68.2	20.1	0.3	5.7	–	2.9	13.8	57.9
Arlington CDP	141,864	15,165	378	17,002	–	4,790	31,251	124,055	73.9	7.9	0.2	8.9	–	2.5	16.3	64.7
Chesapeake city	140,461	63,041	1,043	4,413	78	3,891	5,592	137,332	65.4	29.3	0.5	2.1	(Z)	1.8	2.6	63.9
Hampton city.	62,463	63,135	137	3,070	–	3,311	4,502	60,531	46.8	47.3	0.1	2.3	–	2.5	3.4	45.3
Newport News city	90,229	72,849	876	5,017	–	4,783	8,257	85,712	51.1	41.3	0.5	2.8	–	2.7	4.7	48.5
Norfolk city	96,938	92,354	772	5,762	183	6,631	7,692	94,160	47.0	44.8	0.4	2.8	0.1	3.2	3.7	45.7
Portsmouth city	42,246	49,424	744	960	64	1,208	1,766	41,439	44.4	51.9	0.8	1.0	0.1	1.3	1.9	43.5
Richmond city	72,733	99,826	423	2,340	–	4,405	6,796	67,611	40.2	55.2	0.2	1.3	–	2.4	3.8	37.4
Virginia Beach city	302,603	81,841	1,236	22,760	807	15,499	20,803	290,863	70.2	19.0	0.3	5.3	0.2	3.6	4.8	67.5
WASHINGTON.	4,988,017	202,286	88,363	405,030	28,400	204,412	541,722	4,723,932	81.2	3.3	1.4	6.6	0.5	3.3	8.8	76.9
Bellevue city	78,080	3,110	225	28,849	1,324	1,678	6,425	73,074	68.0	2.7	0.2	25.1	1.2	1.5	5.6	63.7
Seattle city	369,689	43,914	6,336	77,363	1,666	21,038	33,707	356,791	68.9	8.2	1.2	14.4	0.3	3.9	6.3	66.4
Spokane city	171,312	3,861	2,899	4,815	367	8,411	6,732	167,269	88.9	2.0	1.5	2.5	0.2	4.4	3.5	86.8
Tacoma city	125,620	22,920	2,498	19,936	2,904	10,038	16,238	121,046	65.4	11.9	1.3	10.4	1.5	5.2	8.5	63.1
Vancouver city	128,837	3,108	2,953	7,258	1,433	7,251	12,957	122,880	82.9	2.0	1.9	4.7	0.9	4.7	8.3	79.0
WEST VIRGINIA	1,682,489	54,270	2,269	7,967	1,121	20,353	10,139	1,676,602	95.0	3.1	0.1	0.4	0.1	1.1	0.6	94.6
WISCONSIN	4,734,357	307,950	45,516	107,517	845	62,410	242,287	4,622,432	88.1	5.7	0.8	2.0	(Z)	1.2	4.5	86.0
Green Bay city	76,902	1,937	2,255	4,577	36	2,210	8,572	74,778	81.6	2.1	2.4	4.9	(Z)	2.3	9.1	79.3
Madison city	167,304	13,096	652	12,708	–	5,058	11,997	161,631	82.1	6.4	0.3	6.2	–	2.5	5.9	79.3
Milwaukee city.	248,855	223,775	4,150	19,854	235	11,565	80,945	219,891	44.7	40.2	0.7	3.6	(Z)	2.1	14.5	39.5
WYOMING	457,681	3,317	9,437	3,148	23	9,548	33,437	439,924	92.4	0.7	1.9	0.6	(Z)	1.9	6.8	88.8

– Represents zero.   B Base figure too small to meet statistical standards.   NA Not available.   Z Less than .05 percent.

[1]Data for some other race not shown.
[2]Data for other Hispanic status categories not shown.

Survey, Census, or Data Collection Method: Based on the American Community Survey; for information, see Appendix B, Limitations of the Data and Methodology, and Internet site <http://www.census.gov/acs/www/AdvMeth/index.htm>.

Source: U.S. Census Bureau, American Community Survey, "DP-1. General Demographic Characteristics: 2005," using American FactFinder, accessed August 29, 2006 (related Internet site <http://factfinder.census.gov>).

Table D-3. Places — **Households**

[Includes states and 242 incorporated places of 100,000 or more population as of April 1, 2000. Two census designated places (CDPs) are also included (Honolulu CDP in Hawaii and Arlington CDP in Virginia). For more information on these areas, see Appendix C, Geographic Information. Seven states (Delaware, Maine, Montana, North Dakota, Vermont, West Virginia, and Wyoming) do not have any incorporated places of 100,000 or more population]

Place	Total households, 2005	Family households — Total[1] Number	Total[1] Percent with own children under 18 years	Married-couple families Number	Married-couple families Percent with own children under 18 years	Female householder, no husband present Number	Female householder, no husband present Percent with own children under 18 years	Nonfamily households Householder living alone Total	Householder living alone Number	Householder living alone Percent 65 years and over	Percent of households with one or more persons Under 18 years	Percent of households with one or more persons 65 years and over	Persons per household, 2005
ALABAMA	1,788,692	1,223,725	44.4	891,157	40.0	261,542	58.8	564,967	495,728	35.3	34.7	23.7	2.48
Birmingham city	93,205	55,859	46.8	26,572	36.0	24,330	58.9	37,346	31,919	25.5	33.9	21.6	2.38
Huntsville city	70,273	41,881	41.4	28,973	32.9	10,980	65.5	28,392	23,289	29.7	27.6	24.1	2.26
Mobile city	78,769	48,761	47.8	28,413	39.2	17,805	63.9	30,008	26,287	33.4	33.4	25.1	2.45
Montgomery city	80,947	52,344	47.2	32,632	41.3	16,631	62.0	28,603	25,433	28.3	35.9	21.9	2.38
ALASKA	233,252	157,187	53.3	116,353	49.3	27,661	65.0	76,065	57,412	17.6	40.0	13.4	2.75
Anchorage municipality	102,277	67,825	52.9	49,577	48.7	12,979	64.9	34,452	25,243	16.7	39.3	12.4	2.60
ARIZONA	2,204,013	1,459,460	47.3	1,078,453	42.9	270,774	61.3	744,553	581,058	31.5	34.9	23.8	2.65
Chandler city	81,634	56,217	56.7	43,664	55.7	9,482	65.4	25,417	17,745	16.6	42.5	12.0	2.77
Gilbert town	54,836	45,256	61.3	37,396	58.5	5,459	73.0	9,580	7,100	22.0	54.3	11.2	3.26
Glendale city	79,828	55,020	52.2	39,663	48.7	10,374	62.5	24,808	18,407	23.1	41.4	14.8	2.88
Mesa city	165,589	110,179	47.3	79,825	42.9	19,229	62.0	55,330	44,498	37.0	35.0	26.0	2.67
Peoria city	47,840	36,837	49.1	29,026	46.0	5,504	64.4	11,003	8,969	46.0	41.7	23.4	2.97
Phoenix city	503,753	314,004	53.7	210,958	50.5	71,415	61.6	189,749	143,573	20.9	37.1	15.4	2.74
Scottsdale city	95,150	54,506	40.8	45,493	38.1	6,451	55.8	40,644	31,345	26.8	24.6	25.6	2.27
Tempe city	66,893	33,272	46.9	22,686	41.2	7,333	61.4	33,621	21,748	13.0	26.9	12.2	2.48
Tucson city	208,342	121,080	49.6	75,845	42.7	33,956	63.3	87,262	69,429	27.5	32.1	21.8	2.44
ARKANSAS	1,087,542	742,444	44.8	555,545	39.7	140,582	61.9	345,098	295,785	35.7	34.1	24.5	2.48
Little Rock city	79,042	44,922	48.7	27,482	42.9	13,435	58.0	34,120	29,291	23.1	30.2	20.5	2.24
CALIFORNIA	12,097,894	8,281,119	50.8	6,011,121	49.4	1,556,125	57.3	3,816,775	2,959,314	32.1	38.7	22.2	2.92
Anaheim city	95,617	71,610	57.6	49,489	58.2	15,040	60.4	24,007	17,578	39.0	48.4	21.1	3.45
Bakersfield city	94,171	65,925	58.2	47,271	54.7	13,841	68.7	28,246	23,100	34.1	45.6	20.8	3.04
Berkeley city	44,260	18,744	34.6	13,485	32.8	3,157	49.9	25,516	17,115	21.8	16.3	18.6	2.04
Burbank city	39,388	23,380	47.3	16,461	51.4	4,491	36.8	16,008	13,176	25.2	31.8	22.1	2.54
Chula Vista city	71,438	53,686	53.4	38,698	55.2	9,947	46.3	17,752	14,840	41.2	46.2	23.4	2.98
Concord city	42,828	28,688	43.6	21,558	44.7	4,776	43.5	14,140	10,491	29.8	31.9	22.0	2.73
Corona city	47,220	38,255	62.3	29,719	64.6	5,304	53.9	8,965	6,343	32.8	52.5	15.6	3.44
Costa Mesa city	39,619	23,492	44.5	15,936	42.7	3,975	49.7	16,127	11,208	19.0	30.1	16.4	2.66
Daly City city	30,911	23,004	48.4	16,558	46.6	3,874	54.4	7,907	6,236	37.5	39.2	27.7	3.03
Downey city	34,853	25,723	53.2	18,753	52.5	4,848	58.7	9,130	7,581	28.8	43.6	21.4	3.20
El Monte city	28,912	23,501	58.3	15,582	60.2	5,155	63.9	5,411	3,728	57.4	54.0	23.8	3.77
Escondido city	43,599	32,702	52.4	24,237	50.6	5,062	59.9	10,897	8,364	46.2	43.4	21.5	3.05
Fontana city	38,838	33,937	64.9	25,106	67.4	6,362	56.5	4,901	3,710	15.6	63.2	9.2	4.07
Fremont city	68,287	52,942	54.5	44,672	55.7	5,122	50.4	15,345	11,494	26.1	45.6	17.5	3.08
Fresno city	154,147	107,226	59.5	68,296	56.0	29,086	68.5	46,921	37,540	31.1	46.1	18.4	3.10
Fullerton city	48,710	33,380	48.5	26,269	46.4	4,865	64.8	15,330	11,851	24.5	36.6	19.2	2.92
Garden Grove city	54,338	43,180	52.9	31,084	54.9	6,932	56.7	11,158	8,610	37.6	46.0	20.9	3.54
Glendale city	70,773	48,444	45.3	35,400	47.2	7,543	49.1	22,329	16,727	39.7	32.7	26.5	2.75
Hayward city	44,255	31,832	48.0	20,255	50.2	7,946	50.6	12,423	8,905	29.8	39.5	19.8	3.06
Huntington Beach city	71,653	47,213	40.4	37,480	39.1	6,644	51.6	24,440	17,810	30.1	29.9	21.2	2.64
Inglewood city	39,125	26,505	56.6	14,944	58.8	8,606	57.9	12,620	10,979	32.4	44.2	21.9	3.07
Irvine city	66,509	41,714	48.0	33,245	48.7	5,041	52.6	24,795	18,659	14.5	32.0	14.2	2.59
Lancaster city	42,245	30,618	55.4	17,210	50.1	11,802	63.9	11,627	9,408	33.6	45.0	17.6	3.20
Long Beach city	163,481	98,272	51.2	63,796	48.8	26,039	58.6	65,209	49,358	22.5	34.8	19.0	2.84
Los Angeles city	1,284,124	784,065	51.5	502,758	51.0	191,232	56.5	500,059	391,780	25.6	35.5	20.0	2.91
Modesto city	68,167	47,702	51.2	33,551	46.0	10,652	66.0	20,465	15,942	35.6	41.9	21.6	2.98
Moreno Valley city	44,380	37,924	59.4	27,111	57.7	7,222	66.9	6,456	4,764	31.6	58.4	17.0	3.67
Norwalk city	27,275	22,986	48.4	16,543	52.5	4,668	39.3	4,289	3,228	29.8	49.4	19.8	3.81
Oakland city	146,282	83,178	47.0	49,793	46.1	24,921	52.0	63,104	48,662	26.3	32.0	21.7	2.56
Oceanside city	58,608	40,344	47.8	30,405	46.9	5,394	53.3	18,264	13,891	47.2	36.9	28.8	2.77
Ontario city	44,754	34,502	60.8	23,821	59.3	7,504	62.9	10,252	6,862	25.2	52.1	18.6	3.50
Orange city	44,779	32,635	47.1	23,499	50.7	6,639	30.9	12,144	9,560	27.2	36.9	21.3	3.08
Oxnard city	45,554	35,827	57.9	25,245	61.4	7,265	59.6	9,727	7,038	40.2	52.7	22.4	3.93
Palmdale city	38,520	30,840	61.4	20,456	56.1	7,381	70.7	7,680	5,777	26.8	56.1	17.0	3.79
Pasadena city	52,610	29,706	43.3	21,356	41.8	5,591	54.2	22,904	18,295	29.5	25.9	22.8	2.46
Pomona city	42,015	32,848	57.1	22,172	62.5	7,423	49.1	9,167	7,195	26.6	52.9	21.8	3.84
Rancho Cucamonga city	49,246	37,038	52.8	27,617	52.3	6,874	68.2	12,208	9,520	28.1	43.0	16.5	2.94
Riverside city	93,405	66,317	54.5	46,305	56.4	13,849	50.8	27,088	19,777	31.0	44.5	18.5	3.15
Sacramento city	168,782	102,167	49.7	62,317	45.0	30,022	59.2	66,615	47,692	29.2	33.8	21.5	2.64
Salinas city	42,134	32,289	61.0	21,908	57.5	8,282	68.5	9,845	7,780	37.7	52.2	18.5	3.73

See footnotes at end of table.

Table D-3. Places — **Households**—Con.

[Includes states and 242 incorporated places of 100,000 or more population as of April 1, 2000. Two census designated places (CDPs) are also included (Honolulu CDP in Hawaii and Arlington CDP in Virginia). For more information on these areas, see Appendix C, Geographic Information. Seven states (Delaware, Maine, Montana, North Dakota, Vermont, West Virginia, and Wyoming) do not have any incorporated places of 100,000 or more population]

Place	Total households, 2005	Households by type, 2005									Percent of households with one or more persons		Persons per house-hold, 2005
		Family households						Nonfamily households					
		Total[1]		Married-couple families		Female householder, no husband present			Householder living alone				
		Number	Percent with own children under 18 years	Number	Percent with own children under 18 years	Number	Percent with own children under 18 years	Total	Number	Percent 65 years and over	Under 18 years	65 years and over	
CALIFORNIA—Con.													
San Bernardino city	63,366	45,400	64.8	26,638	59.8	13,014	75.5	17,966	12,699	31.7	51.0	16.6	3.23
San Buenaventura (Ventura) city.	39,303	24,372	48.1	18,242	44.6	3,492	55.0	14,931	12,084	31.7	32.2	24.5	2.55
San Diego city.	466,579	276,868	48.4	202,923	46.0	52,389	60.3	189,711	135,296	25.6	31.8	19.9	2.59
San Francisco city	322,399	141,327	36.4	102,203	36.9	25,819	37.2	181,072	135,391	26.3	17.7	24.2	2.23
San Jose city	288,339	209,138	53.2	157,914	54.5	34,655	52.4	79,201	61,280	27.7	42.4	19.6	3.08
Santa Ana city	68,790	56,786	61.3	38,907	66.5	11,896	52.6	12,004	8,516	39.0	58.5	20.6	4.39
Santa Clara city.	39,246	24,784	50.0	19,341	50.0	3,881	58.4	14,462	11,236	24.8	32.3	19.6	2.60
Santa Clarita city	53,182	41,136	56.0	32,826	54.1	5,130	59.5	12,046	9,494	28.3	46.8	17.4	3.14
Santa Rosa city.	59,485	35,264	50.9	25,999	46.1	6,404	66.8	24,221	19,184	37.6	32.4	23.9	2.46
Simi Valley city	37,566	29,539	53.2	24,086	51.0	4,058	68.9	8,027	6,605	32.0	43.4	18.1	3.11
Stockton city.	91,327	62,740	56.9	39,565	54.8	16,031	64.9	28,587	22,596	32.3	44.8	21.3	3.05
Sunnyvale city.	52,135	33,164	47.4	26,011	46.7	4,575	52.4	18,971	15,621	26.1	31.4	21.2	2.55
Thousand Oaks city	43,893	30,450	45.3	25,872	45.8	3,140	41.4	13,443	10,249	36.5	33.0	23.8	2.91
Torrance city.	53,921	33,930	47.8	25,913	47.5	5,571	56.2	19,991	15,987	31.8	32.3	27.1	2.57
Vallejo city	40,196	28,502	48.1	19,696	43.1	5,989	63.8	11,694	9,768	35.8	38.5	23.2	2.88
West Covina city	32,999	27,627	56.3	17,979	51.7	7,315	67.0	5,372	4,413	52.7	52.9	21.9	3.53
COLORADO	1,819,037	1,164,221	49.3	907,833	45.5	176,411	66.6	654,816	513,441	25.0	33.9	17.6	2.51
Arvada city.	40,708	28,350	45.5	22,580	41.6	4,190	59.8	12,358	10,516	36.3	33.9	21.4	2.57
Aurora city	111,072	70,685	57.1	49,255	52.4	15,469	71.5	40,387	34,541	23.3	39.2	15.9	2.62
Centennial city	38,078	28,125	48.6	23,088	45.0	3,104	67.1	9,953	7,977	23.5	37.9	15.8	2.72
Colorado Springs city	155,980	95,388	50.9	70,381	44.8	19,378	69.8	60,592	48,004	21.3	33.2	16.8	2.42
Denver city.	241,579	119,873	44.1	83,018	39.2	23,953	61.4	121,706	98,035	22.9	24.7	18.8	2.26
Fort Collins city	52,144	26,821	49.4	20,496	42.7	4,972	79.2	25,323	15,427	19.7	26.2	12.9	2.35
Lakewood city.	62,882	37,532	47.5	24,876	39.0	8,057	65.9	25,350	19,874	23.S	30.2	20.4	2.27
Pueblo city	41,978	26,747	48.0	17,476	38.6	7,533	68.4	15,231	12,733	37.3	33.6	25.6	2.41
Westminster city	38,185	25,289	48.8	20,228	45.9	3,248	70.5	12,896	9,785	22.9	34.7	13.9	2.60
CONNECTICUT	1,323,838	893,288	46.7	675,144	43.7	161,749	59.9	430,550	359,338	37.8	33.9	24.7	2.56
Bridgeport city.	49,095	31,741	47.6	15,339	37.3	13,899	63.0	17,354	15,394	28.8	35.6	22.8	2.69
Hartford city.	43,752	27,091	52.6	9,127	39.3	15,414	64.3	16,661	13,812	36.8	40.1	23.3	2.54
New Haven city.	46,611	23,874	47.4	13,667	41.8	8,119	60.4	22,737	18,052	27.4	29.6	18.8	2.33
Stamford city.	47,412	29,761	47.2	22,505	47.7	4,808	49.1	17,651	15,077	32.7	31.4	23.1	2.50
Waterbury city	40,470	24,263	50.3	15,164	43.1	7,643	70.3	16,207	13,834	34.3	34.4	20.7	2.58
DELAWARE.	317,640	216,182	46.4	159,638	41.1	42,532	65.5	101,458	81,364	35.3	34.9	24.2	2.58
DISTRICT OF COLUMBIA . . .	248,213	108,483	43.3	54,212	34.9	44,193	53.3	139,730	117,044	21.8	22.5	21.0	2.08
Washington city.	248,213	108,483	43.3	54,212	34.9	44,193	53.3	139,730	117,044	21.8	22.5	21.0	2.08
FLORIDA	7,048,800	4,594,803	41.8	3,379,273	37.0	892,578	58.0	2,453,997	1,962,678	37.8	30.6	29.2	2.47
Cape Coral city	54,239	39,935	43.8	30,865	34.2	6,434	70.7	14,304	10,607	39.8	35.1	26.4	2.48
Clearwater city	49,507	26,580	38.5	19,554	30.9	5,470	63.5	22,927	17,722	35.3	22.4	29.5	2.19
Coral Springs city	43,265	34,734	53.3	24,796	49.8	7,142	62.1	8,531	6,949	22.4	44.5	13.8	2.95
Fort Lauderdale city	64,681	30,251	37.6	19,329	34.6	8,523	45.1	34,430	28,461	29.0	22.0	25.9	2.18
Gainesville city	49,301	19,252	43.4	11,425	35.0	7,116	58.6	30,049	18,813	20.3	19.5	16.7	2.05
Hialeah city.	71,504	56,982	42.9	41,025	41.7	12,134	53.0	14,522	12,517	51.5	39.1	36.6	2.99
Hollywood city.	59,170	34,905	43.7	24,286	38.5	7,242	65.0	24,265	18,946	30.0	28.8	27.0	2.34
Jacksonville city.	313,695	199,913	48.4	136,568	44.2	50,842	59.1	113,782	92,685	26.3	34.7	19.2	2.45
Miami city.	144,706	84,750	38.5	45,901	31.4	27,513	52.4	59,956	50,439	37.1	26.5	33.4	2.50
Miami Gardens city	31,076	22,983	34.1	10,512	27.8	8,442	40.5	8,093	7,506	42.9	34.0	27.2	2.95
Orlando city	94,182	51,155	54.0	30,502	48.0	16,757	67.0	43,027	33,058	23.9	33.0	18.4	2.35
Pembroke Pines city.	58,956	41,238	51.8	31,471	50.7	7,914	60.8	17,718	14,770	52.9	38.0	28.1	2.70
Pompano Beach city	43,641	22,784	28.9	16,122	23.6	4,682	47.1	20,857	16,799	38.1	17.7	32.1	2.17
St. Petersburg city	108,808	58,924	39.5	39,161	32.9	15,114	51.8	49,884	40,727	31.5	24.7	26.8	2.14
Tallahassee city.	68,804	33,362	43.4	20,390	36.2	9,487	57.9	35,442	25,132	13.2	23.7	14.4	2.05
Tampa city	135,433	75,645	47.8	46,616	41.6	21,474	64.2	59,788	46,951	26.2	30.2	21.0	2.31
GEORGIA.	3,320,278	2,285,356	49.9	1,643,907	46.5	484,845	61.7	1,034,922	847,535	26.9	38.1	18.3	2.66
Athens-Clarke County (balance).	41,409	18,451	49.4	11,669	37.7	5,445	76.5	22,958	13,737	16.0	25.0	14.3	2.27
Atlanta city	174,130	79,649	45.9	37,886	32.8	33,914	63.6	94,481	77,754	18.7	25.1	16.8	2.27
Augusta-Richmond County (balance).	73,739	48,938	49.0	29,561	42.2	15,802	58.5	24,801	21,350	29.1	38.2	22.2	2.45
Columbus city	70,926	47,567	50.8	28,530	40.3	15,266	66.0	23,359	19,932	33.3	37.8	21.3	2.48
Savannah city.	49,672	29,264	43.4	15,499	34.1	9,974	55.1	20,408	16,143	37.9	29.9	26.0	2.37

See footnotes at end of table.

[Includes states and 242 incorporated places of 100,000 or more population as of April 1, 2000. Two census designated places (CDPs) are also included (Honolulu CDP in Hawaii and Arlington CDP in Virginia). For more information on these areas, see Appendix C, Geographic Information. Seven states (Delaware, Maine, Montana, North Dakota, Vermont, West Virginia, and Wyoming) do not have any incorporated places of 100,000 or more population]

Place	Total households, 2005	Family households Total[1] Number	Percent with own children under 18 years	Married-couple families Number	Percent with own children under 18 years	Female householder, no husband present Number	Percent with own children under 18 years	Nonfamily households Total	Householder living alone Number	Percent 65 years and over	Percent of households with one or more persons Under 18 years	65 years and over	Persons per household, 2005
HAWAII................	430,007	305,789	41.3	229,666	40.9	53,847	45.1	124,218	96,141	32.3	35.3	28.7	2.88
Honolulu CDP...........	146,070	90,942	35.6	65,759	36.0	17,539	36.8	55,128	44,778	33.7	26.8	32.5	2.48
IDAHO................	532,135	372,230	49.5	299,467	45.8	51,593	65.3	159,905	126,582	33.5	37.3	21.4	2.62
Boise City city...........	82,587	50,203	47.1	39,861	44.1	7,327	57.4	32,384	25,389	24.1	31.1	17.9	2.32
ILLINOIS.............	4,691,020	3,126,131	48.3	2,330,118	46.0	593,101	58.1	1,564,889	1,311,567	34.1	35.3	22.8	2.65
Aurora city...........	54,416	40,143	60.6	30,018	62.0	6,647	66.2	14,273	10,973	17.8	48.2	13.0	3.13
Chicago city..........	1,020,605	595,691	47.2	342,941	45.5	195,494	54.1	424,914	349,452	25.7	33.0	21.3	2.65
Joliet city...........	41,764	30,139	54.8	22,635	55.4	5,858	57.2	11,625	9,588	38.0	45.4	19.3	3.07
Naperville city.........	48,655	37,143	59.3	33,569	59.8	3,021	51.6	11,512	8,672	21.7	45.9	12.2	3.04
Peoria city...........	45,053	24,275	44.7	17,136	39.7	5,466	58.5	20,778	17,730	30.2	27.5	23.5	2.27
Rockford city..........	57,071	33,593	48.5	22,454	40.8	8,991	68.1	23,478	20,526	36.9	31.2	24.4	2.44
Springfield city........	49,056	27,572	49.0	18,277	41.2	6,338	66.0	21,484	18,290	34.4	29.1	21.9	2.25
INDIANA.............	2,443,010	1,639,949	46.6	1,261,777	41.9	277,764	63.9	803,061	661,312	35.2	34.4	22.4	2.49
Evansville city........	49,215	29,567	45.8	19,992	37.0	7,516	65.8	19,648	16,878	34.6	31.1	24.5	2.25
Fort Wayne city........	91,447	55,750	51.8	39,805	44.1	12,150	76.1	35,697	27,820	29.6	34.6	20.7	2.40
Gary city............	36,702	22,329	41.6	9,773	19.4	10,685	61.3	14,373	11,245	36.2	35.6	24.5	2.64
Indianapolis city (balance).....	326,261	193,805	48.1	128,933	42.3	50,932	61.7	132,456	108,486	26.8	32.1	19.7	2.35
South Bend city.........	41,409	22,336	50.2	13,912	43.1	6,821	65.5	19,073	15,965	35.2	30.9	24.0	2.34
IOWA................	1,200,833	790,132	45.5	638,800	40.7	113,301	66.6	410,701	336,379	37.5	31.9	24.1	2.38
Cedar Rapids city........	51,850	31,053	48.3	23,239	36.4	6,213	82.2	20,797	15,890	28.5	32.6	20.0	2.31
Des Moines city.........	84,463	50,404	50.4	36,999	46.0	9,639	62.5	34,059	28,399	30.1	33.9	19.4	2.33
KANSAS.............	1,071,938	715,841	47.6	564,704	42.8	110,493	67.5	356,097	298,710	34.0	34.4	22.3	2.48
Kansas City city........	53,597	35,239	49.7	22,659	40.3	9,435	71.6	18,358	16,143	35.9	38.7	20.7	2.66
Overland Park city.......	64,666	40,927	52.9	34,354	50.9	3,968	59.5	23,739	19,442	25.7	34.9	20.5	2.50
Topeka city...........	53,763	31,692	44.0	21,881	35.9	7,492	62.9	22,071	19,264	31.8	29.6	24.7	2.18
Wichita city...........	144,378	89,961	52.7	65,028	46.1	18,157	71.9	54,417	47,584	29.7	35.3	21.0	2.46
KENTUCKY............	1,653,898	1,119,243	45.2	851,851	41.0	202,278	61.6	534,655	460,146	33.9	34.0	22.2	2.45
Lexington-Fayette	114,548	65,647	44.8	49,068	42.5	12,630	57.3	48,901	38,209	22.6	28.9	17.9	2.23
Louisville/Jefferson County (balance)...........	232,883	140,556	46.4	95,434	40.1	36,039	62.3	92,327	78,707	30.5	31.0	21.3	2.35
LOUISIANA............	1,676,599	1,137,005	47.0	768,751	42.2	292,877	59.4	539,594	459,578	33.6	36.6	22.4	2.62
Baton Rouge city........	87,465	50,713	43.4	28,426	34.5	17,460	55.6	36,752	29,217	30.7	29.8	21.9	2.35
Lafayette city..........	45,632	27,779	53.5	18,168	51.3	7,600	57.8	17,853	13,808	21.4	34.3	18.3	2.37
New Orleans city.........	163,334	90,461	45.2	48,301	38.4	36,686	55.9	72,873	61,356	27.1	29.4	20.9	2.68
Shreveport city	77,474	47,367	48.4	25,695	42.5	18,025	56.7	30,107	26,443	34.6	34.7	24.2	2.49
MAINE...............	542,158	355,469	42.4	278,075	36.0	51,806	66.6	186,689	147,288	38.4	30.1	24.7	2.37
MARYLAND............	2,085,647	1,397,971	47.7	1,021,849	45.0	286,217	57.7	687,676	563,801	30.4	35.6	21.6	2.62
Baltimore city	242,978	126,274	43.5	58,187	33.0	55,033	56.0	116,704	99,543	28.2	29.0	22.8	2.50
MASSACHUSETTS........	2,448,032	1,569,672	47.8	1,166,209	45.4	301,432	58.3	878,360	700,377	36.0	33.1	24.2	2.53
Boston city...........	233,028	112,656	46.9	63,557	39.9	39,677	62.8	120,372	87,490	24.7	25.0	18.8	2.23
Cambridge city.........	40,898	16,660	44.8	12,479	43.4	3,095	49.0	24,238	17,902	23.2	19.1	18.7	1.99
Lowell city...........	37,317	23,488	52.3	15,095	44.3	6,353	71.5	13,829	11,034	32.5	37.4	21.2	2.60
Springfield city.........	57,548	34,404	51.3	17,136	40.3	14,381	68.3	23,144	18,633	32.5	34.5	22.6	2.55
Worcester city..........	63,509	35,862	51.1	23,863	42.4	8,664	70.2	27,647	23,221	35.5	31.4	24.0	2.43
MICHIGAN	3,887,994	2,594,228	46.8	1,946,772	42.9	478,630	60.8	1,293,766	1,082,604	33.6	34.0	22.6	2.54
Ann Arbor city.........	44,651	20,250	44.2	15,562	43.2	3,255	52.0	24,401	16,838	16.1	21.8	13.1	2.21
Detroit city...........	311,234	189,728	53.9	74,042	49.0	95,012	59.7	121,506	107,806	28.0	39.0	21.8	2.69
Flint city............	45,054	26,102	51.5	12,161	37.1	10,957	69.0	18,952	16,808	25.2	34.2	18.3	2.48
Grand Rapids city	75,239	43,316	50.9	27,467	44.6	11,697	62.4	31,923	23,212	31.9	33.3	20.1	2.57
Lansing city	49,552	28,429	49.7	18,106	41.4	8,380	64.5	21,123	16,730	29.2	31.0	18.0	2.42
Livonia city	37,560	27,233	45.7	23,618	46.8	2,825	38.2	10,327	9,559	45.0	34.8	26.8	2.76
Sterling Heights city	48,528	32,581	43.7	26,308	41.0	4,859	55.4	15,947	13,628	36.5	31.8	22.6	2.54
Warren city...........	55,326	35,064	44.9	25,725	42.5	6,937	51.3	20,262	17,818	32.3	30.7	26.8	2.44

See footnotes at end of table.

Table D-3. Places — **Households**—Con.

[Includes states and 242 incorporated places of 100,000 or more population as of April 1, 2000. Two census designated places (CDPs) are also included (Honolulu CDP in Hawaii and Arlington CDP in Virginia). For more information on these areas, see Appendix C, Geographic Information. Seven states (Delaware, Maine, Montana, North Dakota, Vermont, West Virginia, and Wyoming) do not have any incorporated places of 100,000 or more population]

		Households by type, 2005											
		Family households						Nonfamily households			Percent of households with one or more persons		
Place	Total households, 2005	Total[1]		Married-couple families		Female householder, no husband present		Total	Householder living alone				Persons per household, 2005
		Number	Percent with own children under 18 years	Number	Percent with own children under 18 years	Number	Percent with own children under 18 years	Total	Number	Percent 65 years and over	Under 18 years	65 years and over	
MINNESOTA	2,020,144	1,329,046	48.4	1,064,228	44.5	183,668	66.7	691,098	555,129	32.2	33.7	20.8	2.47
Minneapolis city	156,970	72,828	48.7	47,442	43.6	17,503	65.0	84,142	63,656	17.0	24.9	13.4	2.23
St. Paul city	107,979	59,504	54.4	39,123	51.6	14,520	64.2	48,475	39,371	20.2	31.7	15.9	2.42
MISSISSIPPI	1,084,034	759,999	46.6	503,632	40.7	204,464	60.1	324,035	281,390	35.9	38.0	23.5	2.61
Jackson city	64,404	40,273	50.9	18,810	42.3	17,481	62.2	24,131	21,282	27.2	38.9	20.0	2.55
MISSOURI	2,285,280	1,520,559	46.0	1,150,439	41.4	274,332	61.8	764,721	634,528	34.1	33.8	23.1	2.46
Independence city	48,796	30,124	42.9	22,078	36.6	5,923	67.5	18,672	15,194	31.5	28.5	24.5	2.29
Kansas City city	187,448	106,267	48.4	70,136	43.4	29,242	57.3	81,181	65,958	22.9	31.5	18.9	2.35
St. Louis city	141,408	69,387	47.0	32,920	36.4	29,434	56.2	72,021	62,472	25.1	26.9	21.5	2.36
Springfield city	67,180	34,936	43.6	24,928	35.8	7,570	69.3	32,244	26,236	36.1	24.8	23.9	2.08
MONTANA	368,268	236,793	43.1	191,961	37.8	31,657	69.4	131,475	105,086	33.4	29.9	23.2	2.47
NEBRASKA	695,592	455,129	48.6	364,290	44.7	66,431	68.3	240,463	201,811	34.9	33.7	22.8	2.45
Lincoln city	97,128	58,465	48.0	46,897	44.6	8,039	69.2	38,663	31,559	26.2	31.3	17.9	2.33
Omaha city	156,292	88,681	51.1	59,251	45.2	22,129	70.3	67,611	56,919	26.9	31.0	20.3	2.39
NEVADA	906,719	589,291	47.1	430,798	42.9	107,178	62.7	317,428	247,009	29.5	34.5	21.5	2.63
Henderson city	86,924	59,476	40.3	45,334	36.8	9,770	53.1	27,448	20,494	28.1	30.0	21.6	2.57
Las Vegas city	204,688	132,735	47.7	91,637	42.5	29,196	62.6	71,953	56,733	30.4	35.2	22.3	2.63
North Las Vegas city	52,061	37,228	58.4	26,681	57.0	6,983	62.6	14,833	11,393	22.6	47.8	13.8	3.17
Reno city	88,118	47,074	48.8	32,298	43.2	10,120	68.3	41,044	32,416	27.9	29.2	19.4	2.32
NEW HAMPSHIRE	497,054	337,615	48.1	269,992	44.5	47,665	63.9	159,439	123,350	35.1	34.8	22.3	2.56
Manchester city	44,354	25,858	48.1	17,457	41.9	5,985	59.0	18,496	14,154	33.7	30.4	23.0	2.46
NEW JERSEY	3,141,956	2,172,279	48.2	1,628,661	47.2	395,401	54.0	969,677	815,879	38.0	36.3	25.1	2.71
Elizabeth city	40,690	28,900	49.0	15,531	48.8	9,188	58.1	11,790	10,612	39.1	41.5	21.5	2.98
Jersey City city	89,572	54,043	51.8	30,417	47.0	18,161	60.4	35,529	28,668	31.2	35.0	23.8	2.75
Newark city	91,927	56,539	54.4	22,456	51.0	26,226	58.8	35,388	30,615	26.2	40.8	19.6	2.77
Paterson city	45,183	33,554	48.6	14,420	49.3	14,793	54.5	11,629	10,251	41.7	44.8	21.7	3.28
NEW MEXICO	727,820	482,759	46.6	348,421	40.7	97,594	63.2	245,061	200,359	32.3	34.8	23.0	2.59
Albuquerque city	208,824	123,804	46.2	87,652	40.3	26,280	64.0	85,020	68,425	27.1	30.4	21.1	2.34
NEW YORK	7,114,431	4,615,803	47.0	3,194,969	44.7	1,066,027	55.5	2,498,628	2,074,637	35.4	33.8	24.9	2.62
Buffalo city	117,124	61,442	54.4	27,613	43.7	27,371	67.3	55,682	45,925	26.2	31.5	21.2	2.19
New York city	3,026,196	1,839,961	47.1	1,075,083	45.8	586,969	52.9	1,186,235	1,001,949	31.2	32.7	23.8	2.63
Rochester city	83,010	43,114	58.4	19,501	44.0	19,724	73.7	39,896	33,326	18.9	34.0	15.2	2.28
Syracuse city	57,835	29,139	52.0	13,429	35.0	13,157	69.5	28,696	21,499	33.1	29.2	20.9	2.29
Yonkers city	72,374	45,380	49.3	29,954	48.3	12,193	56.9	26,994	22,871	43.9	34.2	29.9	2.67
NORTH CAROLINA	3,409,840	2,290,199	46.7	1,680,709	42.1	454,256	63.0	1,119,641	931,418	30.8	34.9	21.6	2.47
Charlotte city	249,403	152,408	50.6	104,530	45.6	36,097	66.2	96,995	79,207	17.6	34.1	14.1	2.41
Durham city	82,567	46,834	49.8	31,301	46.6	11,686	63.8	35,733	29,023	22.2	30.8	15.7	2.32
Fayetteville city	57,143	35,009	43.3	21,773	37.3	10,753	56.5	22,134	18,213	28.1	32.4	22.5	2.25
Greensboro city	93,221	51,511	51.8	34,649	46.2	12,837	63.9	41,710	35,595	26.0	30.6	21.4	2.24
Raleigh city	138,981	75,204	51.3	52,506	46.2	16,337	69.2	63,777	50,251	14.0	30.0	12.7	2.27
Winston-Salem city	79,691	48,780	46.5	31,261	38.3	13,436	64.1	30,911	26,462	29.4	32.1	22.8	2.30
NORTH DAKOTA	270,437	165,806	45.1	137,932	41.8	19,329	65.8	104,631	87,340	33.0	29.3	23.7	2.25
OHIO	4,507,821	2,986,906	46.3	2,228,322	41.6	572,085	62.1	1,520,915	1,275,257	35.3	33.6	23.5	2.47
Akron city	85,558	49,191	47.8	28,523	42.3	16,087	58.3	36,367	28,672	29.4	30.5	21.9	2.34
Cincinnati city	136,949	68,360	50.1	36,153	37.8	25,987	70.1	68,589	59,265	29.1	28.5	19.8	2.10
Cleveland city	177,817	97,659	53.4	45,136	42.6	44,197	65.4	80,158	68,722	27.3	33.7	21.4	2.33
Columbus city	301,325	170,944	50.4	108,790	44.8	46,951	64.0	130,381	101,563	18.7	31.8	15.3	2.30
Dayton city	59,914	31,131	48.4	16,450	36.1	11,783	63.3	28,783	23,526	28.1	29.0	20.6	2.21
Toledo city	120,970	69,197	46.8	43,239	36.9	19,841	65.9	51,773	43,270	30.9	30.0	21.3	2.36

See footnotes at end of table.

Table D-3. Places — **Households**—Con.

[Includes states and 242 incorporated places of 100,000 or more population as of April 1, 2000. Two census designated places (CDPs) are also included (Honolulu CDP in Hawaii and Arlington CDP in Virginia). For more information on these areas, see Appendix C, Geographic Information. Seven states (Delaware, Maine, Montana, North Dakota, Vermont, West Virginia, and Wyoming) do not have any incorporated places of 100,000 or more population]

Place	Total households, 2005	Family households — Total[1] Number	Percent with own children under 18 years	Married-couple families Number	Percent with own children under 18 years	Female householder, no husband present Number	Percent with own children under 18 years	Nonfamily households Total	Householder living alone Number	Percent 65 years and over	Percent of households with one or more persons Under 18 years	65 years and over	Persons per household, 2005
OKLAHOMA	1,380,595	934,124	45.9	704,462	41.1	168,063	64.5	446,471	380,494	35.6	34.8	23.3	2.49
Oklahoma City city	216,838	133,489	48.3	91,988	42.8	30,487	65.3	83,349	70,136	28.3	33.4	19.4	2.38
Tulsa city	160,322	95,796	47.1	62,960	39.4	24,321	67.5	64,526	56,227	28.7	31.2	21.2	2.31
OREGON	1,425,340	908,835	45.9	703,761	41.2	143,531	65.4	516,505	398,789	32.1	31.9	22.4	2.50
Eugene city	63,312	31,731	47.2	22,641	41.1	6,924	68.6	31,581	21,623	30.7	25.0	19.4	2.25
Portland city	228,167	118,471	45.9	87,181	41.9	23,149	58.3	109,696	83,253	22.7	26.2	18.2	2.25
Salem city	55,425	35,009	51.2	24,710	43.4	6,980	74.8	20,416	14,841	33.9	37.5	20.1	2.56
PENNSYLVANIA	4,860,140	3,199,598	44.0	2,419,269	40.5	572,492	57.7	1,660,542	1,400,460	39.4	31.7	26.7	2.46
Allentown city	42,918	25,351	46.8	15,644	41.4	6,891	55.0	17,567	13,865	39.8	34.2	29.1	2.45
Erie city	38,872	21,506	49.0	13,053	39.6	7,340	63.7	17,366	14,146	35.4	30.4	24.3	2.35
Philadelphia city	565,433	321,706	46.3	156,130	39.6	127,888	56.6	243,727	207,903	32.2	31.8	25.2	2.49
Pittsburgh city	136,309	68,844	41.1	42,359	33.9	20,869	59.5	67,465	55,836	30.2	22.8	23.6	2.09
RHODE ISLAND	406,089	259,048	45.9	190,076	42.0	50,935	62.1	147,041	118,456	36.5	31.4	24.7	2.54
Providence city	59,880	35,299	57.4	18,622	54.0	11,810	69.4	24,581	18,755	30.3	35.8	19.3	2.68
SOUTH CAROLINA	1,635,907	1,103,327	44.5	787,694	39.9	248,194	57.3	532,580	445,088	32.6	34.0	22.7	2.51
Columbia city	42,967	21,402	42.2	14,600	35.2	5,610	62.2	21,565	17,765	25.5	23.5	20.5	2.06
SOUTH DAKOTA	310,331	203,891	47.1	161,051	42.1	29,942	68.1	106,440	88,957	36.1	33.1	23.5	2.40
Sioux Falls city	57,108	36,277	53.0	26,598	46.4	7,226	68.0	20,831	17,266	31.0	36.0	18.1	2.32
TENNESSEE	2,366,130	1,604,310	45.3	1,178,184	40.9	319,699	60.7	761,820	644,844	31.8	34.4	22.3	2.46
Chattanooga city	62,655	33,124	41.2	21,233	35.9	10,343	55.0	29,531	25,454	26.1	25.8	24.5	2.22
Clarksville city	40,703	29,468	62.7	22,134	61.5	6,090	64.3	11,235	8,791	25.4	47.4	13.7	2.63
Knoxville city	80,153	41,553	47.5	25,820	39.1	12,506	66.9	38,600	31,164	26.4	27.1	20.4	2.11
Memphis city	261,983	155,875	48.1	75,883	39.2	64,033	59.9	106,108	90,153	22.2	33.7	18.3	2.45
Nashville-Davidson (balance)	233,588	135,214	47.2	83,379	38.2	39,402	68.6	98,374	82,312	23.2	30.5	18.6	2.24
TEXAS	7,978,095	5,597,885	51.0	4,122,975	48.3	1,086,660	62.2	2,380,210	1,973,120	28.2	40.1	19.5	2.79
Abilene city	42,827	28,742	50.0	20,124	45.6	6,902	60.5	14,085	11,554	29.5	36.4	22.6	2.46
Amarillo city	69,103	46,396	51.2	32,616	45.8	10,330	73.4	22,707	19,406	31.7	37.6	20.9	2.56
Arlington city	126,239	85,646	55.8	63,604	52.9	15,873	70.5	40,593	32,922	18.0	41.2	12.3	2.76
Austin city	289,688	149,801	51.1	104,711	47.9	32,827	62.0	139,887	106,195	12.6	29.7	11.7	2.34
Beaumont city	43,256	26,740	44.9	15,979	35.2	8,915	63.1	16,516	13,749	36.9	34.0	25.1	2.49
Brownsville city	47,048	39,322	61.6	25,957	60.2	10,298	68.6	7,726	6,834	18.5	59.2	21.5	3.65
Carrollton city	41,587	30,700	53.2	23,650	51.3	4,291	64.9	10,887	8,295	12.3	43.0	12.2	2.95
Corpus Christi city	103,159	70,302	49.2	46,390	46.2	16,948	62.3	32,857	26,402	27.3	39.5	20.6	2.71
Dallas city	443,764	256,398	50.5	160,685	49.2	69,371	58.9	187,366	153,802	19.4	33.3	16.7	2.58
El Paso city	193,137	146,050	53.2	93,533	49.8	41,448	61.3	47,087	40,978	35.1	45.8	23.8	3.02
Fort Worth city	218,999	148,910	51.4	100,430	48.4	35,462	61.6	70,089	58,813	24.3	39.4	17.2	2.76
Garland city	78,998	58,818	53.4	41,244	50.2	12,456	64.0	20,180	17,229	27.5	44.3	18.2	2.98
Grand Prairie city	47,620	37,102	59.1	27,797	56.9	6,763	71.9	10,518	9,392	13.3	49.3	11.2	3.12
Houston city	733,101	458,219	52.3	303,513	50.4	114,318	58.8	274,882	234,493	20.8	37.0	16.9	2.65
Irving city	76,773	49,483	52.0	35,821	51.1	9,683	57.7	27,290	22,762	11.0	37.6	11.3	2.76
Laredo city	56,247	46,474	60.1	31,058	61.1	12,599	56.7	9,773	8,540	27.0	58.7	20.1	3.69
Lubbock city	81,291	51,180	47.8	35,738	42.3	11,560	62.4	30,111	23,636	25.8	34.8	19.1	2.46
McAllen city	38,830	30,380	60.7	23,745	60.8	5,106	62.7	8,450	7,648	29.1	51.8	20.8	3.00
Mesquite city	44,192	32,670	55.1	22,876	53.7	7,214	63.3	11,522	9,980	24.4	46.8	16.4	2.87
Pasadena city	48,230	35,402	58.7	25,356	59.4	6,491	67.0	12,828	10,228	35.2	47.7	17.6	3.11
Plano city	90,813	64,912	53.1	53,873	50.6	7,872	65.7	25,901	21,972	16.3	41.0	11.9	2.77
San Antonio city	426,227	285,281	51.2	192,709	48.7	69,795	58.2	140,946	114,573	27.5	39.0	19.9	2.82
Waco city	41,354	22,886	50.4	14,753	46.0	6,752	60.8	18,468	13,983	27.7	31.5	21.7	2.59
Wichita Falls city	37,735	23,777	50.7	17,512	47.4	4,870	66.3	13,958	11,575	31.4	36.3	23.3	2.35
UTAH	791,929	593,103	53.8	487,182	52.7	73,382	60.0	198,826	155,914	29.2	43.6	17.8	3.07
Provo city	31,795	20,185	52.0	17,058	54.9	1,933	41.1	11,610	4,994	23.6	34.7	11.5	3.18
Salt Lake City city	75,028	40,038	49.7	28,031	47.8	6,914	55.5	34,990	27,491	24.3	28.9	18.7	2.43
West Valley City city	35,843	28,031	60.0	19,599	55.9	5,336	65.5	7,812	6,096	16.9	52.1	13.0	3.34

See footnotes at end of table.

Table D-3. Places — **Households**—Con.

[Includes states and 242 incorporated places of 100,000 or more population as of April 1, 2000. Two census designated places (CDPs) are also included (Honolulu CDP in Hawaii and Arlington CDP in Virginia). For more information on these areas, see Appendix C, Geographic Information. Seven states (Delaware, Maine, Montana, North Dakota, Vermont, West Virginia, and Wyoming) do not have any incorporated places of 100,000 or more population]

Place	Total households, 2005	Households by type, 2005										Persons per household, 2005
		Family households						Nonfamily households			Percent of households with one or more persons	
		Total¹		Married-couple families		Female householder, no husband present			Householder living alone			
		Number	Percent with own children under 18 years	Number	Percent with own children under 18 years	Number	Percent with own children under 18 years	Total	Number	Percent 65 years and over	Under 18 years	65 years and over	
VERMONT	248,825	156,832	44.8	120,684	38.8	24,632	63.9	91,993	69,050	32.5	30.2	22.6	2.42
VIRGINIA	2,889,688	1,938,966	46.0	1,478,636	43.0	342,995	59.1	950,722	775,237	30.8	34.0	21.3	2.54
Alexandria city	64,054	28,405	35.9	21,445	37.1	3,552	43.9	35,649	28,985	14.1	18.7	15.2	2.08
Arlington CDP	84,133	37,578	40.6	29,886	39.1	4,963	54.6	46,555	35,581	17.7	19.7	16.7	2.28
Chesapeake city	77,821	57,526	51.3	43,552	49.0	10,545	61.5	20,295	17,410	30.8	42.1	18.3	2.76
Hampton city	55,244	34,993	45.9	23,857	39.0	9,011	66.3	20,251	15,662	32.6	32.8	20.9	2.42
Newport News city	73,237	50,174	48.1	35,002	41.5	11,721	64.4	23,063	20,314	30.0	37.1	19.1	2.41
Norfolk city	86,306	50,005	48.8	29,128	40.4	16,864	66.5	36,301	27,780	24.2	32.3	20.1	2.39
Portsmouth city	37,532	23,122	40.6	14,569	32.8	6,997	51.6	14,410	13,355	33.1	30.7	25.6	2.54
Richmond city	82,199	39,205	42.6	21,364	35.6	14,981	55.7	42,994	34,987	31.2	24.2	24.7	2.20
Virginia Beach city	161,353	112,963	50.6	85,345	46.7	22,148	65.8	48,390	37,613	26.8	39.4	17.5	2.67
WASHINGTON	2,450,474	1,574,432	47.7	1,219,685	42.8	250,466	67.3	876,042	677,662	28.5	33.2	20.3	2.51
Bellevue city	48,998	31,482	48.3	26,774	47.9	3,307	60.1	17,516	14,810	23.8	31.6	19.0	2.34
Seattle city	261,433	112,940	43.2	85,797	39.9	17,769	59.4	148,493	113,545	21.6	20.3	17.8	2.05
Spokane city	85,594	47,705	48.3	35,165	42.4	9,231	62.8	37,889	30,409	32.8	29.5	23.2	2.25
Tacoma city	78,806	45,784	54.8	29,566	47.7	13,747	69.1	33,022	26,379	28.5	34.4	20.2	2.44
Vancouver city	63,693	37,726	52.8	25,428	44.7	9,822	73.2	25,967	21,688	28.5	34.2	18.6	2.44
WEST VIRGINIA	740,702	500,147	39.9	388,743	36.4	81,076	52.6	240,555	205,016	41.7	29.8	27.1	2.39
WISCONSIN	2,219,571	1,440,637	46.3	1,127,844	41.6	218,859	66.1	778,934	634,934	34.0	32.2	22.4	2.42
Green Bay city	41,823	25,057	52.7	17,209	45.7	4,923	74.4	16,766	14,122	26.4	32.9	19.5	2.25
Madison city	93,124	44,847	47.4	33,375	43.8	8,088	58.4	48,277	33,698	17.8	24.5	14.3	2.19
Milwaukee city	228,861	128,097	54.2	63,833	44.3	51,748	68.2	100,764	83,639	24.2	34.4	18.0	2.43
WYOMING	204,935	133,902	42.9	109,498	38.1	15,368	67.9	71,033	56,842	31.6	30.5	20.6	2.42

¹Includes male householder, no wife present, not shown separately.

Survey, Census, or Data Collection Method: Based on the American Community Survey; for information, see Appendix B, Limitations of the Data and Methodology, and Internet site <http://www.census.gov/acs/www/AdvMeth/index.htm>.

Source: U.S. Census Bureau, American Community Survey, "DP-1. General Demographic Characteristics: 2005," using American FactFinder, accessed August 29, 2006 (related Internet site <http://factfinder.census.gov>).

Table D-4. Places — **Education**

[Includes states and 242 incorporated places of 100,000 or more population as of April 1, 2000. Two census designated places (CDPs) are also included (Honolulu CDP in Hawaii and Arlington CDP in Virginia). For more information on these areas, see Appendix C, Geographic Information. Seven states (Delaware, Maine, Montana, North Dakota, Vermont, West Virginia, and Wyoming) do not have any incorporated places of 100,000 or more population]

| Place | School enrollment, 2005[1] | | | | Educational attainment, 2005 | | | | | | |
| | Total | Prekinder-garten through grade 8[2] | Grades 9 through 12 | College or graduate school | Population 25 years and over | Percent of persons 25 years and over by highest level completed | | | | | |
						Not a high school graduate	High school graduate	Some college, but no degree	Associate's degree	Bachelor's degree	Graduate or professional degree
ALABAMA	1,107,450	616,334	242,869	248,247	2,944,634	19.7	32.0	20.2	6.7	13.5	7.9
Birmingham city	59,497	32,139	12,614	14,744	140,420	19.4	32.6	21.7	6.0	12.7	7.6
Huntsville city	41,058	19,267	8,113	13,678	106,709	11.4	19.6	20.0	6.5	27.4	15.0
Mobile city	52,720	28,909	10,709	13,102	123,424	15.1	29.1	23.3	6.3	15.9	10.3
Montgomery city	53,048	29,056	12,308	11,684	122,042	16.9	25.8	19.7	5.6	17.9	14.1
ALASKA	186,843	104,568	45,633	36,642	387,609	9.0	28.9	27.2	7.7	17.2	10.1
Anchorage municipality	77,212	42,289	18,297	16,626	161,554	8.3	23.8	28.0	7.6	19.7	12.6
ARIZONA	1,554,918	848,476	339,084	367,358	3,703,355	16.2	25.6	24.6	8.1	16.2	9.3
Chandler city	67,342	35,978	15,883	15,481	141,337	11.0	17.5	26.7	9.5	23.1	12.2
Gilbert town	61,748	36,460	12,362	12,926	103,672	4.7	17.1	29.0	9.8	26.2	13.3
Glendale city	68,595	35,500	15,483	17,612	137,135	16.7	26.3	26.8	9.9	13.8	6.5
Mesa city	115,766	63,101	24,308	28,357	277,749	15.3	26.0	26.5	8.6	16.1	7.6
Peoria city	44,260	26,674	9,801	7,785	87,659	11.4	28.1	28.3	7.3	15.9	9.0
Phoenix city	365,515	210,584	77,852	77,079	838,350	21.4	25.6	22.2	7.6	15.3	7.9
Scottsdale city	46,160	25,593	7,840	12,727	157,368	4.3	17.0	22.4	8.0	29.3	19.1
Tempe city	58,381	22,191	8,155	28,035	96,160	9.8	20.9	21.9	9.0	23.5	14.9
Tucson city	141,954	69,745	25,879	46,330	314,055	17.1	25.0	23.3	8.2	15.8	10.6
ARKANSAS	673,553	373,673	155,963	143,917	1,777,242	19.0	35.6	21.1	5.5	12.6	6.3
Little Rock city	46,218	24,296	8,843	13,079	118,487	8.9	23.6	23.6	5.6	22.8	15.5
CALIFORNIA	10,281,601	5,387,887	2,295,771	2,597,943	22,299,041	19.9	21.8	21.0	7.7	18.9	10.6
Anaheim city	100,526	51,023	25,888	23,615	189,697	29.4	23.1	20.0	6.0	15.1	6.3
Bakersfield city	88,217	47,891	22,281	18,045	165,876	23.0	26.6	21.0	8.0	13.7	7.6
Berkeley city	30,495	6,955	3,196	20,344	62,893	8.0	7.8	12.9	3.8	32.1	35.5
Burbank city	26,606	13,624	5,665	7,317	69,165	15.2	19.3	19.9	10.2	26.5	8.8
Chula Vista city	66,229	35,429	16,598	14,202	130,601	21.5	23.1	22.3	8.3	17.0	7.8
Concord city	31,079	16,376	6,275	8,428	79,568	13.2	25.8	23.1	8.7	19.6	9.5
Corona city	51,630	26,122	12,814	12,694	98,023	21.7	20.9	25.0	8.7	17.3	6.4
Costa Mesa city	28,566	13,575	4,556	10,435	69,150	18.1	19.6	21.2	9.0	21.3	10.9
Daly City city	24,597	10,384	6,169	8,044	63,347	17.8	18.6	20.3	7.8	29.7	5.9
Downey city	38,825	21,771	7,150	9,904	66,394	21.5	31.4	21.5	5.9	15.2	4.5
El Monte city	31,626	18,786	7,107	5,733	67,205	37.7	29.6	17.2	5.3	7.9	2.3
Escondido city	38,746	20,929	9,176	8,641	81,025	24.9	24.4	25.7	5.1	14.5	5.4
Fontana city	56,311	32,025	13,682	10,604	83,138	31.2	25.1	24.0	7.5	9.0	3.3
Fremont city	57,383	31,279	11,213	14,891	139,412	9.7	20.1	15.4	5.8	26.7	22.3
Fresno city	156,618	84,487	38,767	33,364	266,887	29.0	21.9	22.0	8.0	13.2	5.9
Fullerton city	43,943	21,849	8,413	13,681	90,683	14.4	16.7	22.6	7.8	26.6	12.0
Garden Grove city	59,933	31,994	11,333	16,606	116,771	30.3	25.4	18.1	6.9	13.6	5.7
Glendale city	53,757	23,927	12,347	17,483	136,052	19.0	23.2	14.4	10.1	21.4	11.9
Hayward city	38,986	18,665	8,476	11,845	83,996	19.3	31.1	21.1	6.6	16.2	5.7
Huntington Beach city	48,797	23,457	10,887	14,453	133,118	7.2	17.0	27.6	8.1	26.4	13.7
Inglewood city	35,079	20,493	8,810	5,776	69,254	33.4	20.5	25.5	5.3	10.8	4.4
Irvine city	53,450	21,615	7,615	24,220	115,640	3.8	9.9	16.7	6.9	35.8	26.9
Lancaster city	46,229	27,160	10,511	8,558	74,707	18.9	29.4	28.4	9.4	10.3	3.7
Long Beach city	139,085	72,437	26,560	40,088	289,447	24.1	21.7	20.5	7.6	17.6	8.5
Los Angeles city	1,078,165	567,920	237,977	272,268	2,352,984	28.0	20.6	17.0	5.7	19.0	9.7
Modesto city	61,779	30,937	15,110	15,732	120,981	19.4	29.7	25.7	7.7	10.8	6.6
Moreno Valley city	56,165	32,194	13,521	10,450	90,462	30.1	23.7	23.3	9.0	8.9	5.0
Norwalk city	33,934	17,905	8,033	7,996	61,482	30.5	25.6	19.4	9.6	11.8	3.0
Oakland city	98,168	52,048	18,060	28,060	250,941	21.2	20.2	18.1	6.7	20.2	13.6
Oceanside city	44,373	21,710	11,966	10,697	102,700	14.2	24.8	25.7	7.6	19.8	8.0
Ontario city	49,863	27,248	13,045	9,570	88,641	34.2	29.0	21.0	6.1	6.6	3.0
Orange city	39,608	20,632	8,071	10,905	88,940	20.2	21.1	21.8	7.9	19.1	10.0
Oxnard city	59,151	34,546	13,196	11,409	96,269	38.1	20.5	19.8	7.1	10.8	3.7
Palmdale city	45,537	25,944	12,165	7,428	77,992	28.9	30.1	21.8	6.6	8.1	4.6
Pasadena city	34,488	15,841	6,622	12,025	92,496	12.9	16.3	14.6	6.5	26.9	22.8
Pomona city	51,161	29,359	12,214	9,588	91,179	38.7	25.2	16.1	5.8	10.6	3.5
Rancho Cucamonga city	44,910	23,467	8,415	13,028	92,788	10.5	24.0	28.2	11.1	17.3	8.9
Riverside city	93,766	47,532	16,596	29,638	172,309	23.3	24.1	23.5	7.6	13.4	8.0
Sacramento city	131,129	64,548	28,190	38,391	283,176	20.2	19.3	24.4	8.0	18.7	9.4
Salinas city	47,824	28,346	11,016	8,462	86,154	43.1	22.7	15.9	6.4	9.1	2.7

See footnotes at end of table.

Table D-4. Places — **Education**—Con.

[Includes states and 242 incorporated places of 100,000 or more population as of April 1, 2000. Two census designated places (CDPs) are also included (Honolulu CDP in Hawaii and Arlington CDP in Virginia). For more information on these areas, see Appendix C, Geographic Information. Seven states (Delaware, Maine, Montana, North Dakota, Vermont, West Virginia, and Wyoming) do not have any incorporated places of 100,000 or more population]

Place	School enrollment, 2005[1]				Educational attainment, 2005						
						Percent of persons 25 years and over by highest level completed					
	Total	Prekinder-garten through grade 8[2]	Grades 9 through 12	College or graduate school	Population 25 years and over	Not a high school graduate	High school graduate	Some college, but no degree	Associate's degree	Bachelor's degree	Graduate or professional degree
CALIFORNIA—Con.											
San Bernardino city	73,541	43,646	16,338	13,557	111,769	34.7	26.7	19.0	7.4	8.3	4.0
San Buenaventura (Ventura) city	27,714	14,428	5,276	8,010	68,529	10.8	20.1	27.1	12.1	18.2	11.7
San Diego city	355,948	166,302	67,801	121,845	780,101	13.3	17.2	20.9	8.3	24.3	16.1
San Francisco city	149,399	56,104	24,570	68,725	561,768	15.5	14.3	14.9	5.2	31.2	18.9
San Jose city	258,542	137,520	48,633	72,389	571,788	18.5	18.7	18.1	8.6	23.2	12.9
Santa Ana city	98,956	59,306	21,263	18,387	162,755	49.9	21.2	14.1	4.5	6.0	4.2
Santa Clara city	24,281	10,045	3,732	10,504	69,381	10.4	18.0	19.9	7.7	25.7	18.3
Santa Clarita city	53,061	27,476	14,185	11,400	103,710	15.1	23.6	21.5	8.4	22.3	9.0
Santa Rosa city	37,750	19,433	8,316	10,001	98,077	14.9	19.7	28.0	8.2	18.1	11.1
Simi Valley city	36,425	18,602	9,362	8,461	74,609	9.6	22.1	29.0	8.9	20.5	9.9
Stockton city	84,903	44,201	20,496	20,206	163,450	28.0	22.2	23.0	9.8	12.6	4.5
Sunnyvale city	30,196	15,197	5,953	9,046	94,575	9.8	15.3	14.8	5.7	30.2	24.3
Thousand Oaks city	36,069	19,168	8,310	8,591	84,010	6.5	15.8	20.5	8.6	28.9	19.6
Torrance city	37,714	17,483	7,335	12,896	98,285	7.7	17.4	23.1	8.6	28.2	14.9
Vallejo city	33,324	16,901	7,084	9,339	75,333	15.5	25.3	29.4	10.4	15.6	3.7
West Covina city	42,500	21,120	9,508	11,872	67,539	20.7	24.8	23.9	7.5	17.6	5.4
COLORADO	1,203,115	643,400	259,795	299,920	2,964,773	11.3	23.8	21.6	7.8	23.1	12.3
Arvada city	29,769	16,407	7,219	6,143	68,422	7.9	26.1	24.8	8.7	21.9	10.5
Aurora city	74,436	39,948	17,694	16,794	181,213	16.9	27.9	22.3	8.7	17.0	7.1
Centennial city	29,344	17,304	8,049	3,991	66,179	4.2	16.1	21.0	6.4	33.9	18.3
Colorado Springs city	102,922	52,644	22,652	27,626	242,722	8.0	22.7	24.4	9.9	21.6	13.4
Denver city	125,769	69,147	24,070	32,552	366,251	18.5	20.2	17.4	5.0	23.6	15.4
Fort Collins city	42,858	13,576	5,333	23,949	72,481	4.9	15.2	20.4	8.0	32.0	19.5
Lakewood city	35,589	17,842	8,406	9,341	95,541	10.1	26.6	23.3	6.6	21.5	11.9
Pueblo city	25,997	13,406	5,343	7,248	64,506	16.4	29.5	25.2	10.7	12.5	5.8
Westminster city	28,847	15,667	5,112	8,068	63,020	8.8	22.4	26.6	8.7	24.9	8.5
CONNECTICUT	888,842	479,749	209,209	199,884	2,300,565	12.1	29.4	16.5	7.1	20.0	15.0
Bridgeport city	36,921	20,878	9,080	6,963	83,545	28.1	38.1	16.1	5.4	8.3	4.1
Hartford city	34,326	20,706	8,155	5,465	67,182	36.3	32.0	13.2	3.7	9.5	5.4
New Haven city	32,340	15,462	5,784	11,094	69,796	19.7	26.4	14.6	3.5	17.4	18.5
Stamford city	29,519	14,841	6,730	7,948	83,975	10.2	25.4	13.0	5.5	28.3	17.5
Waterbury city	30,714	18,374	7,770	4,570	63,082	17.6	42.9	17.1	7.5	8.5	6.3
DELAWARE	199,582	110,540	42,822	46,220	551,079	14.4	33.0	18.1	6.9	16.4	11.1
DISTRICT OF COLUMBIA	120,339	61,015	23,099	36,225	371,932	16.4	21.0	14.0	3.3	20.0	25.2
Washington city	120,339	61,015	23,099	36,225	371,932	16.4	21.0	14.0	3.3	20.0	25.2
FLORIDA	4,228,051	2,283,485	945,391	999,175	11,850,782	15.4	30.5	20.5	8.4	16.3	8.8
Cape Coral city	29,787	18,193	7,588	4,006	92,349	13.6	32.4	25.7	7.9	14.0	6.4
Clearwater city	23,801	14,113	5,121	4,567	77,090	14.0	28.1	22.5	7.6	19.4	8.3
Coral Springs city	38,844	20,497	9,998	8,349	79,501	8.3	22.9	18.5	11.1	29.0	10.2
Fort Lauderdale city	29,907	15,902	6,243	7,762	101,566	14.1	29.6	19.9	6.9	18.0	11.5
Gainesville city	45,186	10,493	3,275	31,418	55,867	9.2	20.8	15.1	11.8	20.8	22.3
Hialeah city	52,280	23,409	13,583	15,288	147,714	39.8	28.8	12.5	6.9	8.7	3.3
Hollywood city	29,148	15,963	5,841	7,344	97,425	14.5	31.6	18.9	8.7	17.7	8.6
Jacksonville city	206,818	120,245	43,675	42,898	489,499	11.8	33.1	22.2	8.8	16.6	7.5
Miami city	85,555	46,514	17,821	21,220	249,739	36.8	25.7	10.8	6.5	12.6	7.7
Miami Gardens city	26,477	12,674	6,527	7,276	57,570	19.7	41.0	17.3	11.6	7.8	2.6
Orlando city	58,109	34,137	11,594	12,378	143,406	16.2	26.3	19.9	11.5	18.7	7.4
Pembroke Pines city	51,326	25,767	11,124	14,435	107,625	8.5	28.0	22.3	8.9	21.4	10.9
Pompano Beach city	17,622	9,746	4,603	3,273	71,085	19.8	32.2	18.8	6.3	16.1	6.8
St. Petersburg city	53,394	26,424	11,886	15,084	165,740	15.7	27.7	21.3	9.2	17.6	8.5
Tallahassee city	58,561	16,219	5,764	36,578	80,947	6.7	16.1	17.4	9.8	28.6	21.4
Tampa city	80,344	48,213	15,898	16,233	206,339	18.2	29.1	15.8	7.4	18.7	10.8
GEORGIA	2,371,083	1,322,010	518,231	530,842	5,632,169	17.2	29.6	19.6	6.3	17.6	9.5
Athens-Clarke County (balance)	37,240	9,141	3,445	24,654	51,302	14.1	22.7	14.6	5.5	22.8	20.3
Atlanta city	98,885	53,825	18,970	26,090	266,627	17.1	21.8	14.8	3.9	25.3	17.1
Augusta-Richmond County (balance)	50,846	28,039	10,517	12,290	112,380	17.5	32.6	23.8	7.6	11.4	7.2
Columbus city	51,504	27,753	10,700	13,051	109,115	15.9	28.7	22.4	7.4	15.7	9.9
Savannah city	36,188	15,943	7,609	12,636	72,333	18.2	30.2	22.4	7.0	14.6	7.7

See footnotes at end of table.

[Includes states and 242 incorporated places of 100,000 or more population as of April 1, 2000. Two census designated places (CDPs) are also included (Honolulu CDP in Hawaii and Arlington CDP in Virginia). For more information on these areas, see Appendix C, Geographic Information. Seven states (Delaware, Maine, Montana, North Dakota, Vermont, West Virginia, and Wyoming) do not have any incorporated places of 100,000 or more population]

Place	School enrollment, 2005[1]				Educational attainment, 2005						
						Percent of persons 25 years and over by highest level completed					
	Total	Prekinder-garten through grade 8[2]	Grades 9 through 12	College or graduate school	Population 25 years and over	Not a high school graduate	High school graduate	Some college, but no degree	Associate's degree	Bachelor's degree	Graduate or professional degree
HAWAII.	312,471	162,821	69,394	80,256	828,917	11.9	30.5	20.3	9.3	18.8	9.1
Honolulu CDP	82,450	35,565	16,583	30,302	264,133	12.9	25.3	18.6	8.5	22.4	12.4
IDAHO	366,744	196,455	85,737	84,552	877,031	13.3	29.6	25.8	7.9	15.9	7.4
Boise City city	47,470	23,947	9,443	14,080	126,575	7.6	24.2	27.8	6.7	22.5	11.2
ILLINOIS.	3,411,463	1,839,890	729,143	842,430	8,079,881	14.3	28.3	20.9	7.4	18.3	10.9
Aurora city	49,153	28,662	9,432	11,059	100,546	22.4	23.2	16.9	7.0	19.9	10.6
Chicago city	749,942	403,034	150,754	196,143	1,727,770	22.4	23.9	17.9	5.8	17.8	12.1
Joliet city	36,706	20,211	8,141	8,354	76,997	17.0	32.3	22.1	7.9	13.3	7.5
Naperville city	48,642	27,978	10,855	9,809	91,946	2.6	11.7	14.1	5.7	41.6	24.3
Peoria city	29,852	15,444	5,182	9,226	64,373	10.3	25.3	21.0	7.1	23.5	12.9
Rockford city.	33,794	21,072	6,623	6,099	89,669	19.0	35.1	19.9	6.4	13.2	6.4
Springfield city.	28,504	15,098	5,773	7,633	74,962	8.2	30.0	23.1	7.9	18.9	11.9
INDIANA.	1,589,614	901,877	342,323	345,414	3,956,723	14.7	37.1	20.0	7.0	13.5	7.7
Evansville city	24,738	14,210	5,674	4,854	73,133	17.7	35.9	22.5	8.2	9.6	6.1
Fort Wayne city	60,336	34,183	12,148	14,005	136,048	13.4	31.1	23.5	10.5	14.8	6.7
Gary city	27,971	17,302	6,000	4,669	58,264	19.6	34.8	26.0	8.1	7.2	4.4
Indianapolis city (balance)	199,077	116,942	41,184	40,951	494,307	16.4	29.6	20.9	6.6	17.4	9.1
South Bend city	28,629	14,458	5,684	8,487	59,679	19.0	31.8	21.6	5.9	12.1	9.6
IOWA	704,615	368,377	168,530	167,708	1,927,018	10.4	35.9	20.6	9.2	16.5	7.3
Cedar Rapids city	32,750	17,451	6,570	8,729	80,175	8.3	33.6	23.0	9.2	18.6	7.3
Des Moines city.	47,879	26,175	9,959	11,745	131,890	13.4	34.6	20.6	7.0	16.7	7.7
KANSAS	713,998	375,991	155,956	182,051	1,725,825	11.3	30.2	23.2	7.2	18.6	9.6
Kansas City city.	38,215	23,373	8,452	6,390	89,550	23.1	38.5	19.0	6.3	8.9	4.2
Overland Park city	46,703	24,563	10,325	11,815	107,921	3.2	14.9	20.6	5.8	36.5	19.0
Topeka city	27,746	15,741	4,670	7,335	78,614	12.9	34.7	22.1	4.4	17.1	8.8
Wichita city	97,477	51,158	19,804	26,515	225,650	13.9	29.7	23.3	6.6	18.0	8.6
KENTUCKY	989,574	543,822	219,347	226,405	2,715,805	21.0	34.7	18.6	6.4	11.5	7.8
Lexington-Fayette	67,465	30,712	10,896	25,857	168,095	12.9	21.1	18.7	7.6	22.4	17.1
Louisville/Jefferson County (balance).	142,861	76,850	31,111	34,900	364,721	16.4	31.2	22.4	6.5	13.7	9.9
LOUISIANA	1,180,592	655,140	259,588	265,864	2,791,859	19.5	35.0	20.3	4.6	13.4	7.1
Baton Rouge city	63,198	31,889	10,297	21,012	125,714	17.8	24.0	22.2	3.3	19.7	12.9
Lafayette city	31,935	14,904	5,717	11,314	67,607	11.5	27.5	21.6	4.6	24.0	10.8
New Orleans city	120,830	63,273	25,542	32,015	277,652	17.7	26.9	20.9	3.1	18.1	13.3
Shreveport city	52,956	29,573	9,858	13,525	119,569	16.1	32.1	22.3	3.8	18.1	7.5
MAINE	296,233	151,761	73,480	70,992	899,536	11.0	36.2	18.1	9.1	17.0	8.6
MARYLAND.	1,483,858	774,453	331,551	377,854	3,583,616	13.0	26.7	19.6	6.3	19.3	15.2
Baltimore city	164,168	89,083	34,364	40,721	390,668	24.5	30.1	17.7	4.3	12.4	11.0
MASSACHUSETTS.	1,575,699	825,708	351,849	398,142	4,243,260	12.0	27.4	16.0	7.7	21.1	15.7
Boston city	141,396	57,079	27,036	57,281	351,689	16.0	24.3	13.5	5.3	22.7	18.1
Cambridge city	21,951	4,811	3,207	13,933	62,328	5.6	12.0	9.4	3.3	25.9	43.8
Lowell city	27,381	15,856	5,805	5,720	63,813	23.6	33.4	17.7	6.3	10.5	8.5
Springfield city.	40,763	22,649	9,460	8,654	93,218	28.1	31.2	15.2	6.0	11.7	7.8
Worcester city	39,460	19,999	7,560	11,901	104,470	15.9	34.1	15.0	6.5	19.1	9.5
MICHIGAN	2,712,184	1,421,378	614,895	675,911	6,454,327	13.0	31.4	23.0	8.0	15.1	9.5
Ann Arbor city	41,480	9,696	4,314	27,470	61,257	3.2	5.5	11.0	5.1	30.9	44.4
Detroit city	268,311	145,521	68,432	54,358	497,463	23.9	34.3	23.4	6.3	7.4	4.7
Flint city	32,818	17,638	7,834	7,346	67,518	23.7	36.6	22.1	6.4	7.1	4.3
Grand Rapids city	56,428	28,893	11,911	15,624	117,782	18.6	26.3	21.5	7.4	16.6	9.5
Lansing city	36,009	17,825	5,744	12,440	73,042	12.7	29.2	26.1	10.0	14.7	7.3
Livonia city	27,750	14,899	6,552	6,299	71,230	9.7	27.0	20.9	8.5	21.3	12.7
Sterling Heights city	31,702	14,935	7,742	9,025	85,394	14.9	26.9	23.5	9.7	16.5	8.4
Warren city	32,398	17,317	6,297	8,784	92,704	18.5	35.0	22.5	6.3	12.1	5.5

See footnotes at end of table.

Table D-4. Places — **Education**—Con.

[Includes states and 242 incorporated places of 100,000 or more population as of April 1, 2000. Two census designated places (CDPs) are also included (Honolulu CDP in Hawaii and Arlington CDP in Virginia). For more information on these areas, see Appendix C, Geographic Information. Seven states (Delaware, Maine, Montana, North Dakota, Vermont, West Virginia, and Wyoming) do not have any incorporated places of 100,000 or more population]

Place	School enrollment, 2005[1]				Population 25 years and over	Educational attainment, 2005					
						Percent of persons 25 years and over by highest level completed					
	Total	Prekindergarten through grade 8[2]	Grades 9 through 12	College or graduate school		Not a high school graduate	High school graduate	Some college, but no degree	Associate's degree	Bachelor's degree	Graduate or professional degree
MINNESOTA	1,289,951	679,291	303,401	307,259	3,292,174	9.1	28.1	22.6	9.5	21.0	9.7
Minneapolis city.	94,783	40,580	17,365	36,838	229,452	13.4	19.1	18.4	5.9	28.0	15.2
St. Paul city	79,410	40,610	16,258	22,542	162,897	12.7	23.6	20.7	6.6	21.7	14.8
MISSISSIPPI	751,432	429,218	167,628	154,586	1,797,084	21.5	32.0	19.9	7.8	12.2	6.5
Jackson city	50,555	28,891	9,690	11,974	99,128	18.9	24.4	23.7	7.1	16.0	9.9
MISSOURI	1,396,175	762,219	316,106	317,850	3,729,604	15.0	33.5	21.6	6.0	15.4	8.6
Independence city	23,481	13,289	5,593	4,599	77,421	15.4	36.7	23.1	6.2	14.0	4.6
Kansas City city.	109,104	58,355	23,279	27,470	289,115	14.3	28.5	22.3	5.2	18.8	10.9
St. Louis city.	86,417	47,256	18,350	20,811	217,078	22.3	26.9	20.8	5.6	14.7	9.7
Springfield city.	33,992	13,681	6,029	14,282	92,750	14.2	31.8	26.2	5.6	14.4	7.9
MONTANA	209,317	108,883	51,249	49,185	619,546	9.3	31.9	25.0	7.3	18.4	8.0
NEBRASKA.	445,741	234,613	100,542	110,586	1,109,836	10.5	30.6	22.7	8.8	18.8	8.5
Lincoln city	63,878	27,448	10,546	25,884	145,843	7.1	23.6	24.6	9.9	23.2	11.8
Omaha city.	100,555	51,975	20,597	27,983	240,168	12.5	26.1	22.2	7.2	22.0	9.9
NEVADA.	584,893	332,208	128,608	124,077	1,554,923	17.2	30.8	24.4	7.0	14.0	6.6
Henderson city	56,455	31,138	12,665	12,652	150,553	9.4	28.8	27.2	7.1	18.5	9.0
Las Vegas city	127,602	75,548	27,905	24,149	351,298	19.6	30.0	24.3	6.5	13.1	6.5
North Las Vegas city	45,935	29,554	8,319	8,062	95,119	25.0	29.1	23.9	8.1	10.7	3.3
Reno city	53,037	24,169	11,127	17,741	131,182	15.8	28.1	22.3	5.9	18.4	9.5
NEW HAMPSHIRE	318,118	172,830	75,801	69,487	867,694	10.1	30.6	18.4	9.0	20.1	11.7
Manchester city.	24,863	12,498	5,864	6,501	73,528	15.7	32.0	18.3	7.8	16.5	9.8
NEW JERSEY	2,275,052	1,255,535	509,316	510,201	5,666,759	13.7	29.5	16.4	6.2	21.7	12.5
Elizabeth city	32,361	20,233	6,745	5,383	73,369	31.5	30.5	17.4	4.3	13.0	3.3
Jersey City city	66,703	34,381	17,001	15,321	159,245	19.6	27.6	16.4	4.1	23.4	8.9
Newark city.	76,137	44,236	17,266	14,635	148,457	35.3	35.4	12.1	4.7	8.7	3.9
Paterson city.	43,154	21,655	12,603	8,896	83,098	38.6	36.5	11.3	4.2	7.6	1.9
NEW MEXICO	521,618	266,898	118,521	136,199	1,208,938	18.0	28.6	21.4	6.9	14.2	10.9
Albuquerque city	133,117	61,609	25,898	45,610	318,578	13.3	25.2	21.8	7.4	17.5	14.7
NEW YORK.	4,835,203	2,529,835	1,110,415	1,194,953	12,546,501	15.7	29.2	15.6	8.2	17.9	13.4
Buffalo city	75,533	38,859	16,101	20,573	160,612	20.1	32.2	21.0	7.8	10.2	8.7
New York city	2,051,409	1,054,409	460,599	536,401	5,355,163	21.0	26.8	13.7	6.3	19.1	13.1
Rochester city	56,837	30,487	11,548	14,802	117,210	22.9	28.8	16.0	9.8	13.6	8.9
Syracuse city	41,884	19,279	8,068	14,537	80,834	19.5	30.1	15.7	10.0	13.4	11.4
Yonkers city	51,607	27,699	11,980	11,928	128,895	19.9	30.7	15.8	7.0	16.3	10.3
NORTH CAROLINA	2,183,555	1,201,255	473,264	509,036	5,568,889	17.7	29.4	19.6	8.2	17.1	8.0
Charlotte city.	164,211	91,539	33,093	39,579	387,284	11.8	21.9	19.3	8.2	27.4	11.4
Durham city	55,539	26,721	9,217	19,601	125,110	15.4	17.6	16.6	5.9	24.4	20.2
Fayetteville city	34,200	19,448	6,270	8,482	80,535	15.4	27.5	25.7	7.3	15.2	8.9
Greensboro city.	57,092	28,640	10,252	18,200	138,276	16.0	21.9	19.9	5.6	25.5	11.0
Raleigh city.	82,681	37,295	13,353	32,033	207,695	9.3	18.1	16.5	6.0	33.3	16.7
Winston-Salem city	43,822	24,808	9,486	9,528	119,918	17.0	27.4	18.6	6.7	19.1	11.1
NORTH DAKOTA	146,083	73,251	32,969	39,863	414,015	11.8	28.9	22.6	11.2	18.7	6.7
OHIO	2,843,379	1,535,667	646,732	660,980	7,405,261	13.7	36.7	19.4	7.0	14.8	8.5
Akron city.	56,469	29,528	11,121	15,820	129,575	15.4	34.8	22.1	6.0	14.4	7.3
Cincinnati city.	75,163	40,257	13,662	21,244	182,049	19.4	30.0	16.6	6.1	16.3	11.5
Cleveland city	112,136	65,656	26,394	20,086	260,243	25.8	37.9	18.7	5.1	7.9	4.7
Columbus city	184,566	86,522	33,469	64,575	443,809	13.6	28.3	20.7	6.1	20.9	10.6
Dayton city	36,107	19,113	6,781	10,213	85,744	24.5	31.7	22.1	7.3	9.3	5.0
Toledo city	78,683	39,047	16,893	22,743	183,297	18.3	35.5	21.6	7.3	11.5	5.8

See footnotes at end of table.

[Includes states and 242 incorporated places of 100,000 or more population as of April 1, 2000. Two census designated places (CDPs) are also included (Honolulu CDP in Hawaii and Arlington CDP in Virginia). For more information on these areas, see Appendix C, Geographic Information. Seven states (Delaware, Maine, Montana, North Dakota, Vermont, West Virginia, and Wyoming) do not have any incorporated places of 100,000 or more population]

Place	School enrollment, 2005[1]				Population 25 years and over	Educational attainment, 2005 — Percent of persons 25 years and over by highest level completed					
	Total	Prekindergarten through grade 8[2]	Grades 9 through 12	College or graduate school		Not a high school graduate	High school graduate	Some college, but no degree	Associate's degree	Bachelor's degree	Graduate or professional degree
OKLAHOMA	870,176	469,135	189,284	211,757	2,244,755	15.7	32.1	22.9	6.9	15.2	7.2
Oklahoma City city	128,509	67,368	27,536	33,605	336,752	16.5	24.8	26.1	6.3	17.5	8.7
Tulsa city	92,858	49,744	18,516	24,598	242,745	13.9	24.6	22.1	8.7	21.3	9.4
OREGON	877,043	457,847	199,964	219,232	2,384,818	12.5	26.3	26.1	7.3	17.8	10.0
Eugene city	44,196	16,349	6,808	21,039	91,085	6.2	17.7	28.7	6.8	22.8	17.7
Portland city	122,358	59,579	24,561	38,218	361,251	11.2	20.9	23.6	5.5	24.6	14.2
Salem city	36,643	20,639	7,663	8,341	90,600	16.6	24.9	24.5	7.9	16.4	9.7
PENNSYLVANIA	2,922,181	1,559,752	679,232	683,197	8,180,457	13.3	38.6	15.3	7.0	15.9	9.8
Allentown city	23,367	13,595	5,806	3,966	68,840	21.3	39.4	16.7	6.2	10.6	5.8
Erie city	26,250	12,701	6,085	7,464	57,633	12.9	44.1	17.8	5.3	12.9	7.0
Philadelphia city	391,114	198,144	85,451	107,519	905,287	21.5	36.2	15.6	5.0	12.2	9.4
Pittsburgh city	76,541	30,078	13,043	33,420	193,542	13.0	30.3	16.5	7.9	17.1	15.1
RHODE ISLAND	263,678	135,170	58,527	69,981	705,426	16.5	29.2	16.9	8.2	17.9	11.5
Providence city	47,865	24,067	8,975	14,823	97,595	27.6	25.7	13.3	4.9	17.0	11.5
SOUTH CAROLINA	1,025,953	580,115	233,207	212,631	2,723,305	18.3	31.5	19.1	8.2	15.0	7.9
Columbia city	22,546	8,916	4,786	8,844	59,714	13.9	20.2	17.8	5.8	25.4	16.9
SOUTH DAKOTA	184,793	102,377	41,466	40,950	485,733	11.4	32.7	21.7	9.6	17.6	7.0
Sioux Falls city	31,925	17,004	6,120	8,801	86,204	9.5	28.8	21.9	9.8	21.0	9.1
TENNESSEE	1,355,738	755,333	310,605	289,800	3,907,666	18.8	34.5	19.3	5.6	14.1	7.6
Chattanooga city	29,194	16,116	6,968	6,110	93,702	16.8	32.8	21.2	4.6	15.5	9.1
Clarksville city	31,753	17,919	5,373	8,461	62,986	9.4	30.6	30.1	6.6	17.4	5.8
Knoxville city	44,854	19,807	6,925	18,122	109,695	17.6	31.0	17.9	5.6	17.2	10.7
Memphis city	173,420	97,712	36,189	39,519	397,230	18.0	31.9	21.9	6.0	14.1	8.0
Nashville-Davidson (balance)	121,685	64,323	25,540	31,822	355,850	15.4	27.1	19.8	5.9	19.8	11.9
TEXAS	6,241,175	3,510,061	1,375,458	1,355,656	13,771,855	21.2	26.2	21.3	6.1	17.0	8.2
Abilene city	29,828	15,147	6,839	7,842	62,759	16.4	28.7	26.3	4.4	16.1	8.0
Amarillo city	48,450	26,997	10,409	11,044	108,762	18.8	26.0	27.0	6.6	14.8	6.8
Arlington city	101,267	52,108	22,323	26,836	209,648	14.3	23.8	25.7	9.1	18.9	8.1
Austin city	182,821	84,092	30,752	67,977	430,133	14.6	16.7	19.1	5.6	28.5	15.6
Beaumont city	30,643	16,183	7,474	6,986	65,940	18.6	33.1	18.3	5.3	15.3	9.4
Brownsville city	62,506	36,922	14,767	10,817	86,690	40.0	23.1	16.2	6.3	10.4	4.0
Carrollton city	32,007	17,247	8,075	6,685	79,292	15.6	19.1	26.5	7.1	23.4	8.2
Corpus Christi city	83,623	45,981	17,572	20,070	170,611	20.4	27.8	23.4	7.0	13.8	7.6
Dallas city	267,734	160,651	56,198	50,885	725,805	28.9	21.6	17.1	4.0	18.4	10.0
El Paso city	195,043	104,219	41,091	49,733	339,108	29.9	23.8	20.4	6.7	12.8	6.3
Fort Worth city	159,155	93,367	32,728	33,060	365,851	22.6	26.2	20.6	5.4	17.1	8.1
Garland city	66,305	40,084	15,738	10,483	143,842	24.2	25.3	22.6	7.4	15.3	5.2
Grand Prairie city	47,206	29,871	10,229	7,106	86,285	20.0	25.1	23.7	9.0	16.1	6.2
Houston city	519,711	294,436	115,501	109,774	1,207,777	27.8	23.1	17.2	4.2	17.3	10.5
Irving city	61,821	31,417	11,719	18,685	131,331	24.7	21.7	20.1	5.6	18.6	9.3
Laredo city	71,533	44,826	14,581	12,126	107,727	41.3	22.5	12.4	5.5	13.1	5.3
Lubbock city	65,836	29,710	9,511	26,615	116,795	18.5	26.0	22.3	5.5	17.4	10.2
McAllen city	33,810	18,812	7,024	7,974	65,596	26.7	23.5	20.7	5.0	15.3	8.7
Mesquite city	34,743	19,114	10,353	5,276	77,971	21.5	31.6	19.8	8.3	12.2	6.6
Pasadena city	44,347	27,516	10,811	6,020	88,420	30.8	31.4	18.5	4.7	10.8	3.8
Plano city	70,732	37,716	15,705	17,311	163,662	7.5	11.7	20.2	8.4	33.1	19.0
San Antonio city	357,268	192,799	74,617	89,852	733,786	21.2	25.9	22.7	6.8	14.6	8.8
Waco city	35,580	14,473	5,899	15,208	60,871	28.5	22.3	18.8	6.4	15.2	8.8
Wichita Falls city	22,388	13,388	4,536	4,464	57,284	17.3	30.2	23.3	7.2	15.6	6.3
UTAH	751,354	391,688	154,614	205,052	1,387,825	9.9	26.1	26.9	9.3	19.2	8.7
Provo city	45,179	9,231	4,053	31,895	47,238	6.2	14.7	28.8	10.0	26.6	13.8
Salt Lake City city	47,785	20,275	6,648	20,862	118,315	13.1	20.1	23.1	8.0	22.1	13.6
West Valley City city	35,755	21,758	7,584	6,413	66,126	18.9	36.7	24.9	9.4	7.8	2.4

See footnotes at end of table.

Table D-4. Places — **Education**—Con.

[Includes states and 242 incorporated places of 100,000 or more population as of April 1, 2000. Two census designated places (CDPs) are also included (Honolulu CDP in Hawaii and Arlington CDP in Virginia). For more information on these areas, see Appendix C, Geographic Information. Seven states (Delaware, Maine, Montana, North Dakota, Vermont, West Virginia, and Wyoming) do not have any incorporated places of 100,000 or more population]

Place	School enrollment, 2005[1]				Educational attainment, 2005						
						Percent of persons 25 years and over by highest level completed					
	Total	Prekinder-garten through grade 8[2]	Grades 9 through 12	College or graduate school	Population 25 years and over	Not a high school graduate	High school graduate	Some college, but no degree	Associate's degree	Bachelor's degree	Graduate or professional degree
VERMONT	144,829	73,316	35,174	36,339	419,246	10.5	32.0	16.6	8.4	20.2	12.3
VIRGINIA	1,897,723	1,015,420	417,176	465,127	4,866,265	14.6	26.7	19.0	6.5	19.8	13.4
Alexandria city.	24,933	12,328	2,889	9,716	100,743	8.9	14.4	12.9	4.9	30.6	28.2
Arlington CDP.	41,313	19,446	6,530	15,337	144,735	9.4	11.3	9.8	3.1	30.4	35.9
Chesapeake city	61,818	32,729	13,994	15,095	134,960	12.3	26.5	25.5	8.1	17.0	10.7
Hampton city.	35,759	18,487	8,215	9,057	85,629	13.9	26.6	27.2	7.8	15.8	8.6
Newport News city	49,828	28,065	10,363	11,400	109,244	12.5	31.4	28.1	7.0	12.9	8.1
Norfolk city	55,943	31,787	10,323	13,833	126,300	17.3	27.5	24.6	6.4	15.6	8.5
Portsmouth city	24,798	14,237	5,820	4,741	60,862	18.9	29.9	25.1	8.6	12.3	5.3
Richmond city	46,435	24,821	8,555	13,059	119,669	19.9	26.1	17.5	3.5	19.6	13.4
Virginia Beach city	126,095	65,444	28,162	32,489	275,205	7.5	26.0	26.4	9.3	20.5	10.4
WASHINGTON.	1,543,422	806,898	358,464	378,060	4,074,619	11.2	25.1	24.4	9.2	19.6	10.5
Bellevue city	26,472	12,972	5,744	7,756	81,893	5.1	11.1	17.6	7.2	36.6	22.5
Seattle city	117,482	47,837	18,499	51,146	398,731	8.1	14.4	18.4	6.4	32.2	20.5
Spokane city	52,251	23,821	12,103	16,327	125,694	10.3	25.6	28.1	10.9	15.4	9.7
Tacoma city	50,563	29,111	9,970	11,482	122,710	14.3	28.5	24.5	8.9	16.2	7.6
Vancouver city.	35,315	20,297	7,077	7,941	102,584	9.8	26.3	30.0	9.8	16.2	8.0
WEST VIRGINIA	389,179	209,301	87,895	91,983	1,239,234	18.8	41.9	16.9	5.4	10.2	6.8
WISCONSIN	1,381,255	714,109	324,859	342,287	3,579,057	11.2	34.5	20.6	8.8	16.8	8.1
Green Bay city	22,037	11,438	5,413	5,186	63,403	16.3	34.3	19.4	7.9	16.6	5.7
Madison city	66,466	21,872	8,725	35,869	130,580	7.8	17.3	18.2	7.0	28.7	21.0
Milwaukee city.	172,103	92,650	36,873	42,580	334,593	19.5	31.6	22.2	6.3	13.5	6.9
WYOMING	117,997	60,918	28,754	28,325	332,295	8.7	33.7	26.5	8.0	15.5	7.7

[1]For persons 3 years and over.
[2]Includes nursery school, preschool, kindergarten, and grades 1 through 8.

Survey, Census, or Data Collection Method: Based on the American Community Survey; for information, see Appendix B, Limitations of the Data and Methodology, and Internet site <http://www.census.gov/acs/www/AdvMeth/index.htm>.

Source: U.S. Census Bureau, American Community Survey, "DP-2. Selected Social Characteristics in the United States: 2005," using American FactFinder, accessed August 29, 2006 (related Internet site <http://factfinder.census.gov>).

Table D-5. Places — Income and Poverty

[Includes states and 242 incorporated places of 100,000 or more population as of April 1, 2000. Two census designated places (CDPs) are also included (Honolulu CDP in Hawaii and Arlington CDP in Virginia). For more information on these areas, see Appendix C, Geographic Information. Seven states (Delaware, Maine, Montana, North Dakota, Vermont, West Virginia, and Wyoming) do not have any incorporated places of 100,000 or more population]

Place	Median household income, 2005 (dollars)	Median family income, 2005 (dollars)	Per capita income, 2005 (dollars)	Number below poverty in past 12 months, 2005 — Families	Individuals Total	Individuals Under 18 years	Individuals 65 years and over	Percent below poverty in past 12 months, 2005 — Families	Individuals Total	Individuals Under 18 years	Individuals 65 years and over
ALABAMA	36,879	46,086	21,168	167,857	754,258	266,510	75,489	13.7	17.0	24.8	13.2
Birmingham city	27,020	32,162	16,129	14,858	64,135	28,225	5,012	26.6	28.9	49.5	19.4
Huntsville city	44,000	62,179	30,424	4,119	20,665	6,630	1,701	9.8	13.1	19.5	7.3
Mobile city	31,107	37,803	20,532	10,003	46,279	19,910	3,895	20.5	24.0	39.5	14.9
Montgomery city	40,582	47,994	25,122	8,397	32,766	12,556	2,429	16.0	17.0	24.2	10.9
ALASKA	56,234	67,084	26,310	12,968	71,266	26,623	2,955	8.3	11.2	14.5	7.0
Anchorage municipality	61,217	72,931	29,581	4,541	25,040	9,479	703	6.7	9.5	12.5	4.2
ARIZONA	44,282	51,458	23,365	158,604	824,008	314,658	60,518	10.9	14.2	20.3	8.2
Chandler city	62,010	69,406	30,120	3,242	16,853	6,094	777	5.8	7.5	9.4	5.9
Gilbert town	76,171	80,999	28,759	1,411	7,231	3,008	323	3.1	4.1	4.8	3.8
Glendale city	46,713	58,058	20,699	6,783	35,139	15,233	1,758	12.3	15.4	22.4	11.2
Mesa city	44,861	53,730	22,325	9,767	52,067	21,364	4,231	8.9	11.9	18.3	6.7
Peoria city	60,417	67,034	25,658	(NA)	7,625	3,009	952	(NA)	5.4	7.0	5.9
Phoenix city	42,353	47,559	22,471	42,456	225,117	93,893	9,416	13.5	16.4	24.0	9.1
Scottsdale city	60,057	80,218	41,737	(NA)	15,294	4,529	1,419	(NA)	7.1	10.0	4.1
Tempe city	45,644	60,800	24,857	2,387	21,973	4,083	286	7.2	13.5	12.1	2.6
Tucson city	34,241	41,529	18,813	19,754	101,034	35,336	5,004	16.3	20.0	27.9	8.1
ARKANSAS	34,999	43,134	19,325	99,721	461,842	164,510	48,558	13.4	17.2	24.9	13.4
Little Rock city	39,882	55,000	27,122	5,172	26,373	8,669	1,805	11.5	15.0	20.8	8.5
CALIFORNIA	53,629	61,476	26,800	850,405	4,673,274	1,766,647	300,228	10.3	13.3	18.6	8.1
Anaheim city	52,158	56,478	20,794	6,862	38,309	15,949	2,045	9.6	11.7	16.2	7.8
Bakersfield city	45,174	51,601	20,937	9,599	51,617	23,449	2,072	14.6	18.1	26.0	8.0
Berkeley city	48,123	74,852	36,954	(NA)	18,439	1,189	825	(NA)	20.5	10.4	7.8
Burbank city	51,516	70,324	30,654	(NA)	10,096	2,337	467	(NA)	10.1	9.9	3.9
Chula Vista city	55,610	60,032	24,742	4,189	19,155	7,367	2,728	7.8	9.1	11.4	12.9
Concord city	60,458	65,861	27,830	(NA)	10,898	3,328	619	(NA)	9.4	12.6	4.9
Corona city	68,049	71,850	25,499	2,422	11,697	4,449	665	6.3	7.2	9.4	7.3
Costa Mesa city	53,361	54,053	26,762	(NA)	12,531	3,813	469	(NA)	11.9	16.1	5.1
Daly City city	59,199	64,421	22,946	(NA)	6,280	1,990	470	(NA)	6.7	9.3	4.1
Downey city	42,191	51,312	20,898	(NA)	11,393	3,110	1,121	(NA)	10.3	9.1	10.1
El Monte city	36,630	37,882	13,382	4,835	25,527	9,939	1,225	20.6	23.7	31.6	14.1
Escondido city	51,857	56,490	21,851	2,249	12,550	4,485	728	6.9	9.5	11.7	5.7
Fontana city	58,481	61,229	17,627	3,675	22,846	11,497	209	10.8	14.5	20.7	4.4
Fremont city	81,582	94,067	33,706	2,492	13,873	4,568	942	4.7	6.6	8.1	5.8
Fresno city	37,800	42,793	17,586	21,604	115,278	53,801	4,100	20.1	24.3	34.8	11.0
Fullerton city	58,228	68,305	28,111	1,720	11,036	3,384	599	5.2	7.8	9.5	4.5
Garden Grove city	52,229	53,478	18,506	4,988	25,093	10,155	1,141	11.6	13.1	17.8	6.9
Glendale city	49,750	61,315	27,536	3,551	15,842	4,465	1,483	7.3	8.2	10.6	5.9
Hayward city	55,649	66,986	22,168	2,688	16,858	5,731	306	8.4	12.5	15.9	2.6
Huntington Beach city	72,141	85,984	37,125	1,666	11,870	4,264	579	3.5	6.3	10.1	2.7
Inglewood city	34,962	37,509	15,814	4,686	21,589	9,512	760	17.7	18.1	25.1	7.0
Irvine city	82,827	104,707	42,211	2,215	18,139	2,741	1,124	5.3	10.5	7.4	8.2
Lancaster city	44,277	49,108	18,522	4,644	27,132	14,116	297	15.2	20.1	30.2	2.8
Long Beach city	43,746	46,477	23,266	16,125	88,868	33,795	4,050	16.4	19.2	27.6	9.4
Los Angeles city	42,667	47,434	24,587	131,329	747,613	287,699	42,659	16.7	20.1	29.2	12.3
Modesto city	45,769	53,967	21,669	5,106	26,994	10,610	2,255	10.7	13.4	18.6	11.3
Moreno Valley city	56,111	56,190	19,207	4,047	21,287	9,202	2,360	10.7	13.2	17.2	19.6
Norwalk city	51,137	51,780	16,617	2,038	10,429	4,047	777	8.9	10.1	13.0	9.9
Oakland city	44,124	47,283	25,739	14,053	68,148	22,944	6,505	16.9	18.3	25.3	15.7
Oceanside city	55,382	66,929	24,765	(NA)	10,199	2,069	2,186	(NA)	6.3	5.0	9.4
Ontario city	46,344	49,979	17,285	4,867	23,330	9,502	2,405	14.1	14.9	19.5	20.5
Orange city	69,695	74,475	29,365	2,057	10,803	3,217	1,370	6.3	7.8	8.9	9.7
Oxnard city	48,952	50,922	17,099	4,429	29,492	16,058	724	12.4	16.5	26.7	5.3
Palmdale city	46,536	52,320	16,049	4,831	25,264	12,685	672	15.7	17.7	25.4	7.6
Pasadena city	51,233	62,627	36,983	3,062	18,177	5,186	2,244	10.3	14.1	19.2	13.5
Pomona city	41,805	43,328	15,767	3,739	21,525	10,677	538	11.4	13.4	20.2	4.0
Rancho Cucamonga city	71,967	83,958	29,749	(NA)	9,657	2,710	792	(NA)	6.7	7.1	7.7
Riverside city	50,416	57,913	20,924	6,964	41,164	13,412	2,359	10.5	14.1	16.7	9.8
Sacramento city	44,867	50,653	22,841	15,056	85,181	33,944	3,374	14.7	19.2	29.1	7.0
Salinas city	50,165	51,048	16,512	5,553	31,238	13,083	848	17.2	20.1	25.6	7.7

See footnotes at end of table.

Table D-5. Places — **Income and Poverty**—Con.

[Includes states and 242 incorporated places of 100,000 or more population as of April 1, 2000. Two census designated places (CDPs) are also included (Honolulu CDP in Hawaii and Arlington CDP in Virginia). For more information on these areas, see Appendix C, Geographic Information. Seven states (Delaware, Maine, Montana, North Dakota, Vermont, West Virginia, and Wyoming) do not have any incorporated places of 100,000 or more population]

| Place | Median household income, 2005 (dollars) | Median family income, 2005 (dollars) | Per capita income, 2005 (dollars) | Number below poverty in past 12 months, 2005 | | | | Percent below poverty in past 12 months, 2005 | | | |
| | | | | | Individuals | | | | Individuals | | |
				Families	Total	Under 18 years	65 years and over	Families	Total	Under 18 years	65 years and over
CALIFORNIA—Con.											
San Bernardino city	33,915	34,925	14,296	10,814	57,254	27,087	2,151	23.8	28.1	38.3	15.3
San Buenaventura (Ventura) city.	57,574	72,468	30,505	(NA)	10,876	4,240	775	(NA)	10.9	17.2	5.8
San Diego city.	55,637	67,925	29,497	26,935	161,978	58,847	9,412	9.7	13.5	19.8	7.6
San Francisco city	57,496	73,180	39,554	12,626	87,823	14,435	12,608	8.9	12.2	13.4	12.0
San Jose city	70,921	79,413	30,769	15,760	88,182	30,895	6,558	7.5	10.0	13.1	8.4
Santa Ana city	47,438	46,154	14,110	8,969	51,134	22,717	3,133	15.8	17.3	22.7	16.7
Santa Clara city.	71,284	81,861	33,509	(NA)	9,520	2,401	616	(NA)	9.3	10.1	5.7
Santa Clarita city.	74,759	82,628	29,600	2,325	10,682	3,548	707	5.7	6.4	7.0	5.2
Santa Rosa city	51,454	61,134	27,914	3,076	15,987	5,436	1,089	8.7	10.9	15.6	5.6
Simi Valley city	78,692	87,813	31,179	(NA)	4,707	1,119	362	(NA)	4.0	3.3	3.9
Stockton city.	41,118	47,101	18,976	10,093	55,740	23,322	2,656	16.1	20.1	28.1	9.9
Sunnyvale city.	74,449	84,376	38,547	(NA)	10,441	2,940	785	(NA)	7.9	9.9	5.1
Thousand Oaks city	90,503	104,885	43,047	(NA)	10,591	2,606	1,149	(NA)	8.3	8.4	7.8
Torrance city.	66,999	82,048	35,293	(NA)	8,924	2,396	485	(NA)	6.5	7.9	2.3
Vallejo city	54,706	65,362	23,315	(NA)	13,920	5,611	1,609	(NA)	12.1	18.4	12.0
West Covina city	52,603	54,169	19,636	(NA)	16,169	9,426	575	(NA)	14.0	25.6	5.7
COLORADO	50,652	62,470	27,081	96,785	504,106	165,586	38,082	8.3	11.1	14.2	8.6
Arvada city.	61,353	71,614	28,017	(NA)	5,933	2,068	667	(NA)	5.7	7.3	5.5
Aurora city	48,309	56,029	23,060	7,588	38,228	15,304	1,936	10.7	13.1	18.9	8.2
Centennial city	75,313	87,924	36,046	1,019	5,011	2,037	117	3.6	4.9	7.1	1.3
Colorado Springs city	47,854	59,886	26,001	9,297	43,780	15,263	2,587	9.7	11.7	16.0	7.2
Denver city.	42,370	52,139	27,715	14,367	83,044	29,585	7,271	12.0	15.3	22.1	12.4
Fort Collins city	44,261	66,515	25,408	(NA)	21,705	4,301	839	(NA)	17.8	16.6	8.9
Lakewood city.	50,234	60,822	27,890	2,872	14,826	4,845	1,190	7.7	10.4	14.6	6.5
Pueblo city	31,261	37,949	17,723	5,864	23,566	8,749	1,909	21.9	23.3	35.5	12.3
Westminster city	60,265	69,864	28,265	(NA)	5,789	1,299	551	(NA)	5.8	5.3	7.9
CONNECTICUT	60,941	75,541	33,949	55,456	281,408	94,909	33,414	6.2	8.3	11.6	7.5
Bridgeport city.	36,976	44,809	19,333	5,111	23,549	9,652	2,798	16.1	17.9	27.3	19.0
Hartford city.	26,032	28,984	15,947	8,464	35,186	13,670	3,841	31.2	32.0	42.5	33.1
New Haven city	30,603	35,511	20,178	5,730	29,151	9,938	2,265	24.0	27.2	39.8	21.4
Stamford city.	66,638	81,759	44,040	(NA)	10,316	3,172	1,711	(NA)	8.7	12.1	12.1
Waterbury city.	36,120	42,823	18,317	(NA)	18,701	8,107	808	(NA)	18.0	26.8	7.5
DELAWARE.	52,499	63,863	27,650	16,516	84,811	27,780	7,706	7.6	10.4	14.5	7.2
DISTRICT OF COLUMBIA . . .	47,221	51,411	37,569	18,159	97,617	35,310	10,881	16.7	19.0	32.2	17.4
Washington city.	47,221	51,411	37,569	18,159	97,617	35,310	10,881	16.7	19.0	32.2	17.4
FLORIDA	42,433	50,465	24,611	445,037	2,214,381	713,162	289,613	9.7	12.8	17.9	10.1
Cape Coral city . . . . —	46,933	51,017	24,861	(NA)	11,314	3,738	1,216	(NA)	8.5	11.4	5.9
Clearwater city	40,250	50,056	25,052	2,531	11,902	3,910	1,409	9.5	11.0	16.9	7.3
Coral Springs city	63,197	70,723	29,242	1,963	8,157	3,216	598	5.7	6.4	8.9	7.7
Fort Lauderdale city	44,169	50,640	34,443	3,160	23,406	8,246	2,615	10.4	16.6	28.7	11.9
Gainesville city	26,954	41,210	19,535	4,013	32,322	7,311	564	20.8	32.1	40.9	5.5
Hialeah city.	30,271	33,903	13,115	10,590	45,170	11,615	9,893	18.6	21.2	25.9	26.9
Hollywood city.	41,602	47,189	25,630	3,221	17,130	4,488	2,151	9.2	12.4	15.7	9.7
Jacksonville city.	44,173	52,138	23,076	19,179	93,377	32,416	8,092	9.6	12.2	15.7	10.6
Miami city.	25,211	28,784	17,531	20,881	101,883	32,250	21,978	24.6	28.3	39.8	34.2
Miami Gardens city	32,893	38,700	14,730	3,187	15,586	5,416	2,231	13.9	17.0	23.4	20.1
Orlando city.	36,699	40,143	23,157	6,986	33,368	13,166	2,585	13.7	15.1	22.3	12.2
Pembroke Pines city.	55,847	69,267	28,197	3,012	13,923	4,905	2,493	7.3	8.7	11.9	11.0
Pompano Beach city	40,390	46,669	25,784	2,760	13,706	3,686	2,666	12.1	14.4	23.3	14.1
St. Petersburg city	37,947	50,108	26,446	6,726	33,456	9,095	4,555	11.4	14.4	19.2	12.4
Tallahassee city.	35,765	51,688	23,898	3,664	31,372	5,418	1,111	11.0	22.3	20.4	9.0
Tampa city	38,568	47,329	26,265	10,763	57,252	20,828	6,949	14.2	18.3	26.1	19.8
GEORGIA.	45,604	53,744	23,982	264,016	1,266,205	469,302	100,795	11.6	14.4	20.2	12.4
Athens-Clarke County (balance).	29,820	45,746	19,304	3,245	27,913	5,299	892	17.6	29.8	30.6	10.8
Atlanta city	39,752	42,010	33,590	20,349	105,928	44,075	8,018	25.5	26.9	49.1	21.9
Augusta-Richmond County (balance).	37,231	42,761	19,479	9,602	41,196	19,402	3,392	19.6	22.9	38.2	17.0
Columbus city	34,040	41,861	19,821	9,361	34,505	14,973	1,837	19.7	19.6	29.8	9.2
Savannah city	30,887	39,411	17,193	4,284	26,742	9,256	2,424	14.6	22.8	30.1	15.3

See footnotes at end of table.

Table D-5. Places — **Income and Poverty**—Con.

[Includes states and 242 incorporated places of 100,000 or more population as of April 1, 2000. Two census designated places (CDPs) are also included (Honolulu CDP in Hawaii and Arlington CDP in Virginia). For more information on these areas, see Appendix C, Geographic Information. Seven states (Delaware, Maine, Montana, North Dakota, Vermont, West Virginia, and Wyoming) do not have any incorporated places of 100,000 or more population]

Place	Median household income, 2005 (dollars)	Median family income, 2005 (dollars)	Per capita income, 2005 (dollars)	Number below poverty in past 12 months, 2005				Percent below poverty in past 12 months, 2005			
				Families	Individuals			Families	Individuals		
					Total	Under 18 years	65 years and over		Total	Under 18 years	65 years and over
HAWAII...............	58,112	66,472	25,326	23,445	121,418	37,396	15,069	7.7	9.8	12.7	8.9
Honolulu CDP...........	50,793	64,892	27,661	8,583	43,468	9,128	7,911	9.4	12.0	13.9	12.4
IDAHO	41,443	48,775	20,350	38,217	192,390	64,926	13,334	10.3	13.9	17.7	8.5
Boise City city...........	46,342	59,693	24,657	3,816	22,446	6,558	1,130	7.6	11.8	15.4	5.7
ILLINOIS...............	50,260	61,174	26,307	286,603	1,483,873	524,729	128,047	9.2	12.0	16.4	8.9
Aurora city............	55,950	58,218	23,454	4,572	23,195	9,529	1,563	11.4	13.6	18.7	16.4
Chicago city...........	41,015	46,888	23,449	107,418	573,486	215,541	50,194	18.0	21.3	30.8	18.2
Joliet city............	56,175	64,263	23,347	3,060	12,865	5,006	949	10.2	10.1	14.1	8.7
Naperville city.........	93,338	106,464	39,725	(NA)	3,650	545	820	(NA)	2.5	1.2	9.1
Peoria city............	40,276	58,267	25,791	3,145	16,070	7,241	794	13.0	15.8	27.3	5.7
Rockford city..........	35,356	43,185	20,112	5,179	25,409	11,233	1,729	15.4	18.3	31.0	9.1
Springfield city.........	43,054	57,376	27,052	2,904	14,726	5,872	1,173	10.5	13.4	23.3	8.2
INDIANA...............	43,993	54,077	22,519	148,206	740,371	260,496	58,011	9.0	12.2	16.7	8.0
Evansville city.........	34,362	44,034	19,247	3,428	17,118	5,658	1,304	11.6	15.6	21.7	8.1
Fort Wayne city........	38,063	48,462	19,565	7,651	33,868	13,866	1,862	13.7	15.5	22.7	7.6
Gary city.............	25,496	35,125	13,797	5,585	32,945	16,405	1,604	25.0	34.2	54.5	13.6
Indianapolis city (balance).....	41,578	50,584	22,566	22,343	114,963	45,653	5,803	11.5	15.1	22.3	7.2
South Bend city........	31,867	41,101	18,381	3,853	21,931	7,987	1,102	17.3	22.8	32.2	8.5
IOWA................	43,609	54,971	23,340	59,201	310,230	92,227	31,670	7.5	10.9	14.0	7.9
Cedar Rapids city	47,357	57,225	25,029	3,933	17,736	6,783	886	12.7	14.9	24.2	6.0
Des Moines city........	42,690	56,042	23,262	3,192	19,426	6,550	977	6.3	9.9	13.5	4.9
KANSAS..............	42,920	53,998	23,337	60,394	309,561	99,784	24,771	8.4	11.7	15.1	7.5
Kansas City city........	33,157	39,695	16,977	6,217	29,038	13,248	1,407	17.6	20.5	33.6	9.5
Overland Park city	64,804	84,273	35,211	(NA)	6,914	1,809	868	(NA)	4.3	4.5	4.4
Topeka city...........	35,726	48,641	21,992	3,791	17,102	6,606	578	12.0	14.6	23.8	3.4
Wichita city...........	40,115	48,696	22,379	10,968	52,433	17,002	3,517	12.2	14.8	18.2	8.7
KENTUCKY.............	37,369	46,214	20,551	149,521	680,151	215,901	65,822	13.4	16.8	22.5	13.3
Lexington-Fayette	42,442	60,067	26,343	6,450	37,821	9,706	2,565	9.8	14.9	17.5	9.7
Louisville/Jefferson County (balance)...............	38,664	50,098	22,611	17,255	83,386	29,520	6,894	12.3	15.3	22.1	10.4
LOUISIANA.............	36,729	45,730	20,332	183,193	864,277	319,095	73,822	16.1	19.8	28.4	14.8
Baton Rouge city........	31,049	40,516	20,528	12,075	60,605	23,294	3,375	23.8	29.6	47.1	13.3
Lafayette city	39,158	53,109	23,587	3,809	18,438	4,646	1,285	13.7	17.1	18.1	10.8
New Orleans city........	30,711	39,428	21,998	19,748	106,666	43,056	7,999	21.8	24.5	38.1	16.5
Shreveport city.........	32,027	40,346	20,148	8,728	48,485	19,572	3,716	18.4	25.3	38.5	15.1
MAINE	42,801	52,338	23,606	32,066	160,627	46,872	19,302	9.0	12.6	17.5	10.6
MARYLAND.............	61,592	74,879	31,109	83,703	448,038	148,210	46,839	6.0	8.2	10.8	7.7
Baltimore city	32,456	41,542	20,749	23,836	136,256	51,569	13,506	18.9	22.6	33.3	18.4
MASSACHUSETTS........	57,184	71,655	31,007	118,636	637,043	194,294	76,587	7.6	10.3	13.6	9.6
Boston city............	42,562	49,320	30,167	20,086	116,110	35,403	11,897	17.8	22.3	32.8	22.3
Cambridge city.........	59,746	79,201	41,519	1,330	12,665	1,792	1,035	8.0	15.6	15.8	11.4
Lowell city	41,272	46,856	20,419	4,246	19,844	8,715	1,654	18.1	20.7	34.4	16.2
Springfield city.........	29,922	34,985	17,023	9,619	43,215	18,118	3,442	28.0	29.6	46.0	20.3
Worcester city.........	37,797	53,221	22,244	4,371	28,854	9,279	3,239	12.2	18.7	26.8	15.8
MICHIGAN.............	46,039	57,277	24,379	257,314	1,299,688	459,304	99,446	9.9	13.2	18.5	8.3
Ann Arbor city.........	45,798	76,543	30,894	(NA)	22,004	2,081	617	(NA)	22.3	12.2	7.7
Detroit city............	28,069	33,640	15,042	51,145	261,497	114,945	17,341	27.0	31.4	44.9	20.5
Flint city.............	25,972	33,151	15,931	7,200	36,023	14,764	1,814	27.6	32.5	45.3	16.2
Grand Rapids city	38,229	45,897	18,608	6,557	40,082	15,716	1,492	15.1	20.8	29.7	7.6
Lansing city...........	34,367	45,224	17,888	5,138	29,132	11,557	860	18.1	24.4	37.2	7.7
Livonia city............	66,512	77,557	29,389	(NA)	2,576	684	550	(NA)	2.5	2.7	3.8
Sterling Heights city	60,010	70,080	27,098	(NA)	10,095	2,813	1,052	(NA)	8.2	10.5	7.4
Warren city............	44,855	54,761	22,716	3,368	15,696	5,374	2,117	9.6	11.7	17.4	10.6

See footnotes at end of table.

Table D-5. Places — **Income and Poverty**—Con.

[Includes states and 242 incorporated places of 100,000 or more population as of April 1, 2000. Two census designated places (CDPs) are also included (Honolulu CDP in Hawaii and Arlington CDP in Virginia). For more information on these areas, see Appendix C, Geographic Information. Seven states (Delaware, Maine, Montana, North Dakota, Vermont, West Virginia, and Wyoming) do not have any incorporated places of 100,000 or more population]

Place	Median household income, 2005 (dollars)	Median family income, 2005 (dollars)	Per capita income, 2005 (dollars)	Number below poverty in past 12 months, 2005 Families	Individuals Total	Individuals Under 18 years	Individuals 65 years and over	Percent below poverty in past 12 months, 2005 Families	Individuals Total	Individuals Under 18 years	Individuals 65 years and over
MINNESOTA	52,024	63,998	27,248	81,468	456,642	139,801	47,995	6.1	9.2	11.6	8.3
Minneapolis city.	41,829	57,316	26,886	10,643	72,681	23,959	2,967	14.6	20.8	31.7	11.1
St. Paul city	44,103	55,606	23,541	8,467	48,468	18,465	2,495	14.2	18.6	25.8	11.5
MISSISSIPPI.	32,938	40,917	17,971	127,358	600,288	226,148	53,508	16.8	21.3	30.9	15.9
Jackson city	31,177	38,203	19,596	7,832	42,496	16,960	2,576	19.4	26.0	36.4	15.7
MISSOURI	41,974	51,477	23,026	151,576	748,023	256,046	65,991	10.0	13.3	19.0	9.2
Independence city	41,398	47,976	20,949	2,504	11,936	4,302	598	8.3	10.7	17.2	3.6
Kansas City city.	41,069	50,540	24,567	13,758	72,226	27,482	4,382	12.9	16.5	25.8	9.4
St. Louis city.	30,874	36,282	19,153	15,199	84,435	31,837	6,850	21.9	25.4	37.7	17.5
Springfield city.	29,433	41,028	19,699	4,744	25,048	6,614	1,580	13.6	18.0	25.1	7.8
MONTANA	39,301	47,959	21,765	24,840	130,441	40,385	11,071	10.5	14.4	20.1	9.1
NEBRASKA.	43,849	55,073	22,884	37,281	186,178	62,915	19,575	8.2	10.9	14.8	9.0
Lincoln city	45,790	59,855	23,803	4,833	27,513	8,592	1,687	8.3	12.2	17.0	7.1
Omaha city.	40,484	51,637	23,500	11,588	57,020	21,530	3,573	13.1	15.3	23.3	8.6
NEVADA.	49,169	57,079	25,077	52,195	262,092	89,648	23,114	8.9	11.1	14.9	8.6
Henderson city	61,483	72,417	32,335	2,102	14,548	4,278	1,169	3.5	6.5	8.3	4.6
Las Vegas city	47,863	57,471	24,887	12,810	62,678	22,334	8,055	9.7	11.7	15.8	13.0
North Las Vegas city	53,183	54,060	19,198	4,048	20,207	9,162	1,039	10.9	12.4	17.7	10.9
Reno city	42,214	53,390	24,801	5,283	28,047	9,547	1,213	11.2	13.8	20.5	5.4
NEW HAMPSHIRE	56,768	67,354	28,201	17,776	95,090	28,044	11,291	5.3	7.5	9.4	7.5
Manchester city.	50,404	60,602	25,491	2,445	14,032	5,363	1,241	9.5	12.9	22.4	9.5
NEW JERSEY	61,672	75,311	31,471	147,341	738,969	251,999	91,088	6.8	8.7	11.8	8.5
Elizabeth city	40,413	42,377	18,136	4,638	23,728	11,613	1,779	16.0	19.7	34.1	16.2
Jersey City city	40,310	42,267	21,803	9,392	45,129	16,619	4,903	17.4	18.4	26.1	20.7
Newark city.	30,665	34,816	15,346	12,967	62,866	24,044	6,869	22.9	24.8	31.5	31.8
Paterson city.	34,987	37,691	14,341	8,141	35,532	14,559	3,735	24.3	24.1	32.0	32.3
NEW MEXICO	37,492	44,097	20,798	69,023	347,759	124,303	29,879	14.3	18.5	26.0	13.1
Albuquerque city	41,820	54,570	24,576	12,198	66,345	22,516	3,892	9.9	13.7	19.8	6.7
NEW YORK.	49,480	59,686	28,158	513,009	2,565,836	865,102	302,122	11.1	13.8	19.4	12.7
Buffalo city	27,311	33,027	17,348	14,479	68,607	24,943	3,760	23.6	26.9	37.5	12.1
New York city	43,434	49,374	27,233	307,345	1,512,112	526,083	191,653	16.7	19.1	27.7	20.3
Rochester city.	26,650	28,387	16,007	11,884	56,460	21,079	2,809	27.6	30.0	41.8	18.9
Syracuse city	25,935	31,749	16,626	7,651	41,137	14,820	2,250	26.3	31.3	45.0	14.6
Yonkers city	49,304	61,626	25,826	6,260	30,014	8,803	5,761	13.8	15.6	18.9	20.2
NORTH CAROLINA	40,729	49,339	22,519	268,889	1,262,770	448,699	115,331	11.7	15.1	21.3	11.7
Charlotte city.	47,131	56,960	28,875	15,575	78,124	30,198	4,291	10.2	13.0	18.8	9.3
Durham city	42,321	52,081	24,627	5,206	28,278	10,374	2,084	11.1	14.8	21.7	12.9
Fayetteville city	40,778	48,270	22,789	5,005	23,577	9,803	1,262	14.3	18.7	30.5	8.3
Greensboro city.	36,733	50,009	24,540	7,454	36,038	12,010	1,621	14.5	17.3	24.4	6.2
Raleigh city.	48,131	65,033	29,464	7,209	48,612	14,547	1,769	9.6	15.5	21.2	7.4
Winston-Salem city	38,197	46,936	23,125	7,044	35,208	15,496	1,449	14.4	19.2	32.3	6.1
NORTH DAKOTA	41,030	53,103	23,129	12,368	68,199	17,896	10,652	7.5	11.2	13.5	12.3
OHIO	43,493	54,086	23,322	296,649	1,450,650	505,642	119,765	9.9	13.0	18.6	8.4
Akron city.	32,937	38,362	19,497	8,302	40,183	13,501	2,627	16.9	20.1	27.1	10.8
Cincinnati city	29,554	38,763	20,593	13,456	71,767	25,585	6,164	19.7	25.0	35.4	19.0
Cleveland city	24,105	28,990	14,825	27,977	133,886	54,040	9,324	28.6	32.4	47.6	20.2
Columbus city	40,405	47,229	22,134	24,089	128,163	46,273	7,950	14.1	18.5	27.2	13.2
Dayton city	25,928	33,630	16,191	7,856	38,307	14,200	2,329	25.2	28.9	43.2	15.1
Toledo city	33,044	42,179	17,953	12,738	66,606	25,441	3,946	18.4	23.4	34.7	11.5

See footnotes at end of table.

[Includes states and 242 incorporated places of 100,000 or more population as of April 1, 2000. Two census designated places (CDPs) are also included (Honolulu CDP in Hawaii and Arlington CDP in Virginia). For more information on these areas, see Appendix C, Geographic Information. Seven states (Delaware, Maine, Montana, North Dakota, Vermont, West Virginia, and Wyoming) do not have any incorporated places of 100,000 or more population]

Place	Median household income, 2005 (dollars)	Median family income, 2005 (dollars)	Per capita income, 2005 (dollars)	Number below poverty in past 12 months, 2005				Percent below poverty in past 12 months, 2005			
				Families	Individuals			Families	Individuals		
					Total	Under 18 years	65 years and over		Total	Under 18 years	65 years and over
OKLAHOMA	37,063	45,990	20,709	122,312	564,544	192,417	49,436	13.1	16.5	23.0	11.2
Oklahoma City city	37,375	49,769	22,190	19,943	95,947	35,622	5,714	14.9	18.7	28.2	10.3
Tulsa city	35,966	43,802	23,762	14,492	65,140	26,217	4,136	15.1	17.6	29.2	8.9
OREGON	42,944	52,698	23,785	91,400	498,854	152,142	34,244	10.1	14.1	18.4	7.7
Eugene city	33,070	49,212	21,685	3,870	27,415	3,958	830	12.2	19.3	13.9	5.0
Portland city	42,287	55,321	26,677	14,020	90,689	28,471	5,185	11.8	17.8	26.0	9.7
Salem city	39,259	47,380	21,671	3,820	23,556	8,343	1,333	10.9	16.8	22.9	8.6
PENNSYLVANIA	44,537	55,904	24,591	273,725	1,420,396	460,616	156,796	8.6	11.9	16.7	8.9
Allentown city	33,658	37,787	18,139	5,232	24,047	10,497	1,961	20.6	23.0	40.7	12.4
Erie city	31,376	41,177	16,421	3,109	18,390	5,704	1,604	14.5	20.2	24.1	13.3
Philadelphia city	32,573	40,534	19,140	64,162	343,547	129,639	31,514	19.9	24.5	35.4	17.7
Pittsburgh city	30,278	41,633	22,018	11,799	65,726	17,081	6,219	17.1	23.2	31.4	15.0
RHODE ISLAND	51,458	64,657	27,217	24,624	126,150	46,894	11,221	9.5	12.3	19.5	8.0
Providence city	34,202	41,404	20,333	10,339	47,080	18,861	2,634	29.3	29.4	43.4	16.7
SOUTH CAROLINA	39,316	48,100	21,535	138,152	638,643	229,001	58,607	12.5	15.6	22.7	11.6
Columbia city	34,196	47,811	26,416	2,546	17,230	4,529	1,751	11.9	19.5	25.6	16.1
SOUTH DAKOTA	40,310	50,461	21,938	19,721	101,286	33,245	11,338	9.7	13.6	18.2	11.2
Sioux Falls city	44,341	57,196	25,345	3,383	16,288	5,590	1,161	9.3	12.3	17.9	7.9
TENNESSEE	38,874	47,950	22,090	200,166	899,717	290,932	93,064	12.5	15.5	21.4	13.1
Chattanooga city	32,174	47,611	21,893	4,794	26,866	10,636	2,097	14.5	19.3	33.5	10.3
Clarksville city	44,384	50,228	19,622	2,297	11,519	4,194	937	7.8	10.8	13.2	13.0
Knoxville city	30,473	43,485	20,249	7,061	41,980	10,591	3,498	17.0	25.0	31.7	17.2
Memphis city	33,244	40,111	20,279	32,860	150,704	59,328	10,295	21.1	23.6	34.8	16.5
Nashville-Davidson (balance)	40,214	49,748	25,005	15,891	75,968	28,888	5,596	11.8	14.6	23.5	10.1
TEXAS	42,139	49,769	22,216	795,699	3,905,148	1,548,069	273,070	14.2	17.6	24.9	12.7
Abilene city	35,246	42,441	18,544	4,382	21,205	8,195	1,233	15.2	20.2	28.0	9.8
Amarillo city	34,996	42,883	21,487	5,652	26,728	10,635	1,345	12.2	15.2	21.3	6.8
Arlington city	48,992	56,186	22,693	9,028	46,180	17,742	1,341	10.5	13.3	17.5	6.3
Austin city	43,731	60,592	27,760	20,689	122,141	41,091	3,858	13.8	18.1	25.7	8.6
Beaumont city	32,183	43,014	18,663	5,305	24,298	11,113	1,672	19.8	22.6	37.0	12.3
Brownsville city	24,207	24,587	10,669	15,518	72,981	35,722	4,998	39.5	42.6	54.6	38.4
Carrollton city	60,482	65,876	27,117	1,752	7,049	1,956	776	5.7	5.8	6.2	10.7
Corpus Christi city	39,698	44,773	20,039	10,198	51,866	21,189	4,129	14.5	18.6	27.0	14.1
Dallas city	36,403	38,717	24,477	48,157	251,987	102,974	13,208	18.8	22.1	34.1	13.3
El Paso city	32,205	35,562	15,248	34,695	158,216	68,541	11,953	23.8	27.2	38.1	18.9
Fort Worth city	40,663	47,064	21,249	23,414	112,971	46,918	6,934	15.7	18.8	27.2	13.5
Garland city	45,924	51,443	19,327	6,397	35,863	14,212	2,349	10.9	15.3	20.6	12.7
Grand Prairie city	48,865	50,268	19,823	4,019	19,337	9,797	418	10.8	13.1	19.5	5.5
Houston city	36,894	40,172	22,534	91,562	443,757	185,625	23,448	20.0	22.9	35.0	14.5
Irving city	46,543	50,430	23,517	5,352	27,779	10,672	308	10.8	13.1	19.3	2.7
Laredo city	32,019	32,577	12,269	13,577	63,812	30,636	4,271	29.2	30.8	39.6	27.4
Lubbock city	33,853	46,142	19,253	6,719	39,459	12,003	1,198	13.1	19.8	23.6	5.7
McAllen city	35,004	36,183	16,136	7,520	31,386	12,326	3,388	24.8	27.0	34.0	29.6
Mesquite city	47,466	56,375	20,391	2,536	12,572	4,308	805	7.8	9.9	10.9	8.4
Pasadena city	37,642	41,023	16,899	5,875	28,373	12,133	857	16.6	18.9	25.7	7.8
Plano city	71,560	89,972	37,950	3,148	15,733	5,521	896	4.8	6.3	8.3	5.5
San Antonio city	40,186	47,150	20,407	44,091	224,014	90,147	19,996	15.5	18.7	26.7	16.9
Waco city	27,955	40,354	17,344	3,874	27,922	8,430	1,332	16.9	26.3	30.8	10.5
Wichita Falls city	37,255	42,784	20,942	2,527	12,588	4,575	1,275	10.6	14.3	19.6	10.9
UTAH	47,934	54,595	20,814	47,313	246,047	79,854	13,281	8.0	10.2	10.9	6.5
Provo city	31,603	34,085	15,072	(NA)	28,596	3,898	256	(NA)	28.3	18.2	4.7
Salt Lake City city	37,287	44,678	23,286	5,031	30,809	9,300	2,005	12.6	16.9	22.9	10.5
West Valley City city	43,981	44,525	16,249	3,354	16,229	7,506	260	12.0	13.6	18.7	4.0

See footnotes at end of table.

Table D-5. Places — **Income and Poverty**—Con.

[Includes states and 242 incorporated places of 100,000 or more population as of April 1, 2000. Two census designated places (CDPs) are also included (Honolulu CDP in Hawaii and Arlington CDP in Virginia). For more information on these areas, see Appendix C, Geographic Information. Seven states (Delaware, Maine, Montana, North Dakota, Vermont, West Virginia, and Wyoming) do not have any incorporated places of 100,000 or more population]

| Place | Median household income, 2005 (dollars) | Median family income, 2005 (dollars) | Per capita income, 2005 (dollars) | Number below poverty in past 12 months, 2005 | | | | Percent below poverty in past 12 months, 2005 | | | |
| | | | | Families | Individuals | | | Families | Individuals | | |
					Total	Under 18 years	65 years and over		Total	Under 18 years	65 years and over
VERMONT	45,686	57,170	25,469	12,090	68,793	20,194	7,317	7.7	11.5	15.4	9.5
VIRGINIA	54,240	65,174	29,148	142,638	728,947	238,312	79,691	7.4	10.0	13.3	9.7
Alexandria city	66,116	83,934	47,614	(NA)	7,800	899	1,974	(NA)	5.9	3.4	14.8
Arlington CDP	80,433	106,218	49,025	(NA)	15,536	3,448	2,310	(NA)	8.1	9.9	12.4
Chesapeake city	60,817	68,778	26,116	2,309	11,966	4,250	1,087	4.0	5.6	7.4	5.6
Hampton city	45,105	55,635	22,238	3,957	17,603	7,977	1,765	11.3	13.3	23.5	11.6
Newport News city	46,641	54,135	21,212	5,412	24,177	11,138	1,367	10.8	13.8	22.4	7.8
Norfolk city	36,920	42,194	20,903	7,145	36,399	16,406	2,734	14.3	17.7	28.2	12.2
Portsmouth city	40,172	49,624	21,289	2,877	15,896	7,746	1,547	12.4	16.8	30.4	12.2
Richmond city	34,396	45,255	26,284	5,306	33,478	11,693	3,173	13.5	18.5	26.8	12.5
Virginia Beach city	58,545	66,102	28,064	7,125	31,631	13,393	2,682	6.3	7.4	11.7	6.7
WASHINGTON	49,262	60,077	26,662	132,984	729,470	219,214	56,237	8.4	11.9	15.1	8.2
Bellevue city	69,880	85,732	40,843	1,860	9,647	2,067	1,008	5.9	8.4	8.6	7.9
Seattle city	49,297	69,795	36,392	7,468	66,068	10,582	8,115	6.6	12.3	12.2	13.9
Spokane city	34,752	48,064	20,914	5,409	33,235	8,977	2,603	11.3	17.3	20.8	10.2
Tacoma city	40,290	48,183	22,854	6,245	32,340	9,507	3,422	13.6	16.9	19.7	16.9
Vancouver city	40,743	47,277	23,084	5,651	26,275	10,024	2,029	15.0	16.9	27.0	12.6
WEST VIRGINIA	33,452	42,821	19,214	69,897	317,240	95,381	30,572	14.0	18.0	25.6	11.5
WISCONSIN	47,105	58,647	24,761	100,381	545,650	176,832	49,166	7.0	10.2	13.9	7.3
Green Bay city	40,477	49,546	22,843	2,631	13,689	4,706	589	10.5	14.6	22.2	5.3
Madison city	45,928	64,264	27,475	3,690	35,918	6,956	746	8.2	17.7	18.3	4.2
Milwaukee city	32,666	35,675	17,696	27,268	137,760	60,582	6,108	21.3	24.9	38.1	11.7
WYOMING	46,202	55,343	23,936	8,465	46,809	12,311	4,959	6.3	9.5	11.1	8.4

NA Not available.

Survey, Census, or Data Collection Method: Based on the American Community Survey; for information, see Appendix B, Limitations of the Data and Methodology, and also <http://www.census.gov/acs/www/AdvMeth/index.htm>.

Source: U.S. Census Bureau, American Community Survey, "DP-3. Selected Economic Characteristics: 2005," using American FactFinder, accessed August 29, 2006, and "B17001. Poverty Status in the Past 12 Months by Sex by Age," "B17010. Poverty Status of Families by Family Type by Presence and Age of Related Children Under 18 Years," "B19013. Median Household Income (in 2005 Inflation-Adjusted Dollars)," and "B19113. Median Family Income (in 2005 Inflation-Adjusted Dollars)," using American FactFinder, accessed November 29, 2006 (related Internet site <http://factfinder.census.gov>).

Table D-6. Places — Owner- and Renter-Occupied Housing Units and Vehicles Available

[Includes states and 242 incorporated places of 100,000 or more population as of April 1, 2000. Two census designated places (CDPs) are also included (Honolulu CDP in Hawaii and Arlington CDP in Virginia). For more information on these areas, see Appendix C, Geographic Information. Seven states (Delaware, Maine, Montana, North Dakota, Vermont, West Virginia, and Wyoming) do not have any incorporated places of 100,000 or more population]

Place	Owner-occupied housing units, 2005						Renter-occupied housing units, 2005						Percent of occupied housing units by vehicles available, 2005			
	Total units	Median value (dollars)	Value, percent—				Total units	Median gross monthly rent (dollars)	Gross monthly rent, percent[1]—				None	1	2	3 or more
			Less than $100,000	$100,000–$199,999	$200,000–$299,999	$300,000 and over			Less then $300	$300–$499	$500–$749	$750 or more				
ALABAMA	1,261,475	97,500	51.4	32.5	8.9	7.2	527,217	535	13.3	30.1	36.3	20.3	6.8	31.7	38.1	23.4
Birmingham city	47,459	75,800	68.7	24.0	4.1	3.2	45,746	587	8.3	25.9	36.1	29.7	14.0	41.7	30.1	14.2
Huntsville city	41,742	128,700	38.9	35.0	13.8	12.3	28,531	555	4.8	37.5	41.9	15.8	5.8	36.5	38.4	19.2
Mobile city	45,061	97,000	51.9	34.1	7.0	6.9	33,708	557	11.8	22.8	48.3	17.1	8.8	40.7	35.6	14.8
Montgomery city	49,998	100,700	49.7	35.0	7.3	7.9	30,949	590	9.9	22.4	37.8	29.9	10.3	37.9	35.9	15.9
ALASKA	147,019	197,100	16.0	35.1	29.7	19.2	86,233	832	3.3	7.1	28.9	60.6	9.6	32.8	38.8	18.8
Anchorage municipality	62,703	230,600	9.2	28.0	37.3	25.5	39,574	871	1.5	3.8	29.9	64.9	6.8	33.1	43.4	16.7
ARIZONA	1,502,457	185,400	19.4	35.0	20.1	25.4	701,556	717	4.1	12.8	38.5	44.6	6.5	37.6	38.8	17.1
Chandler city	57,625	241,300	4.3	28.4	31.5	35.8	24,009	908	2.1	3.0	24.6	70.2	2.7	32.1	48.0	17.2
Gilbert town	45,022	322,200	(NA)	(NA)	(NA)	(NA)	(B)	1,057	(NA)	(NA)	(NA)	(NA)	(NA)	(NA)	(NA)	(NA)
Glendale city	51,223	196,200	10.8	40.3	26.5	22.5	28,605	699	3.1	9.6	48.4	38.9	7.1	35.4	39.1	18.5
Mesa city	110,364	174,300	20.4	39.2	22.9	17.5	55,145	750	1.7	6.2	42.1	50.0	7.4	43.1	34.4	15.2
Peoria city	37,503	217,900	9.2	34.7	24.4	31.7	(B)	1,090	(NA)	(NA)	(NA)	(NA)	5.1	28.5	45.9	20.5
Phoenix city	298,839	184,300	12.3	42.8	19.2	25.6	204,914	708	3.5	10.0	43.9	42.5	8.3	39.6	37.1	15.0
Scottsdale city	68,775	422,000	2.5	16.9	15.4	65.3	26,375	926	2.1	2.2	21.1	74.5	3.5	41.2	41.7	13.6
Tempe city	32,160	199,300	10.4	39.9	26.8	22.9	34,733	739	1.0	5.7	45.6	47.7	7.5	42.8	32.7	17.0
Tucson city	112,815	144,400	26.1	49.8	16.7	7.4	95,527	605	4.7	20.9	46.1	28.2	11.0	43.6	31.8	13.6
ARKANSAS	736,825	87,400	58.1	29.5	7.2	5.2	350,717	549	11.7	29.0	41.2	18.1	6.6	33.4	40.3	19.7
Little Rock city	47,206	119,900	42.4	35.8	10.3	11.4	31,836	662	6.1	12.3	50.3	31.3	10.1	41.7	36.2	12.0
CALIFORNIA	7,070,138	477,700	6.0	6.6	10.4	77.0	5,027,756	973	3.7	5.6	17.6	73.1	7.6	31.6	38.0	22.7
Anaheim city	48,088	553,400	7.4	1.9	2.6	88.2	47,529	1,092	1.9	3.1	4.5	90.4	6.4	29.8	39.2	24.5
Bakersfield city	59,366	263,000	7.5	19.6	32.6	40.3	34,805	732	3.4	9.5	40.5	46.6	6.2	33.9	38.2	21.7
Berkeley city	19,185	700,300	(NA)	(NA)	(NA)	(NA)	25,075	1,010	2.9	3.3	16.5	77.3	16.0	44.7	29.1	10.2
Burbank city	17,850	590,900	(NA)	(NA)	(NA)	(NA)	21,538	981	2.5	1.6	13.8	82.0	4.1	40.8	40.0	15.1
Chula Vista city	42,006	565,100	7.4	1.9	4.1	86.6	29,432	1,013	2.2	4.3	14.9	78.6	5.5	30.1	40.2	24.2
Concord city	26,388	534,100	(NA)	(NA)	(NA)	(NA)	16,440	1,019	4.1	3.3	9.8	82.9	5.9	32.0	40.4	21.7
Corona city	33,932	491,900	(NA)	(NA)	(NA)	(NA)	13,288	1,065	9.1	2.6	7.7	80.7	5.1	20.6	42.1	32.2
Costa Mesa city	13,921	644,900	(NA)	(NA)	(NA)	(NA)	(B)	1,286	(NA)	(NA)	(NA)	(NA)	7.8	38.2	36.9	17.1
Daly City city	16,896	610,600	(NA)	(NA)	(NA)	(NA)	(B)	1,228	(NA)	(NA)	(NA)	(NA)	9.7	35.0	32.5	22.9
Downey city	18,076	512,900	(NA)	(NA)	(NA)	(NA)	(B)	949	(NA)	(NA)	(NA)	(NA)	4.5	33.3	40.7	21.6
El Monte city	10,693	361,400	(NA)	(NA)	(NA)	(NA)	18,219	905	1.2	6.2	19.2	73.4	8.9	31.7	31.4	28.1
Escondido city	27,124	450,600	7.9	4.5	10.7	77.0	16,475	999	3.5	1.6	11.8	83.2	6.9	31.4	37.3	24.4
Fontana city	28,351	369,000	(NA)	(NA)	(NA)	(NA)	(B)	917	(NA)	(NA)	(NA)	(NA)	3.0	21.4	35.9	39.8
Fremont city	45,809	635,300	4.5	1.2	2.8	91.4	(B)	1,275	(NA)	(NA)	(NA)	(NA)	3.4	24.7	45.1	26.9
Fresno city	77,393	242,500	9.6	23.7	32.2	34.5	76,754	728	4.2	12.3	38.1	45.3	11.4	37.3	36.8	14.6
Fullerton city	27,809	593,100	(NA)	(NA)	(NA)	(NA)	20,901	1,110	1.5	2.9	7.7	88.0	4.0	31.1	41.2	23.7
Garden Grove city	32,684	486,300	8.4	4.9	5.4	81.3	(B)	1,142	(NA)	(NA)	(NA)	(NA)	5.5	22.6	39.3	32.6
Glendale city	27,337	598,900	(NA)	(NA)	(NA)	(NA)	43,436	1,022	3.3	2.0	10.7	84.0	14.1	32.0	37.4	16.5
Hayward city	25,676	531,300	6.3	4.1	2.9	86.6	18,579	1,095	3.2	2.9	9.7	84.1	4.7	27.0	41.6	26.6
Huntington Beach city	44,005	711,000	4.6	2.0	3.2	90.2	(B)	1,362	(NA)	(NA)	(NA)	(NA)	2.8	27.2	46.7	23.3
Inglewood city	13,863	392,900	(NA)	(NA)	(NA)	(NA)	25,262	843	2.7	4.0	26.2	67.2	10.1	46.1	26.4	17.4
Irvine city	37,965	683,400	3.3	1.6	2.8	92.3	(B)	1,528	(NA)	(NA)	(NA)	(NA)	3.5	31.9	45.9	18.7
Lancaster city	24,872	273,100	16.8	11.2	29.5	42.4	17,373	869	2.5	6.5	21.4	69.6	6.2	38.3	36.0	19.5
Long Beach city	66,272	494,200	4.5	2.7	6.2	86.7	97,209	855	4.1	4.8	24.0	67.0	12.0	40.6	32.9	14.5
Los Angeles city	512,799	513,800	2.3	4.0	7.9	85.9	771,325	883	3.7	6.8	23.9	65.6	13.3	38.0	33.3	15.4
Modesto city	41,113	336,900	6.2	9.8	21.6	62.3	27,054	882	4.7	4.6	26.3	64.4	8.0	31.7	38.6	21.6
Moreno Valley city	32,966	341,400	(NA)	(NA)	(NA)	(NA)	(B)	1,060	(NA)	(NA)	(NA)	(NA)	4.9	22.0	41.0	32.1
Norwalk city	18,838	409,000	(NA)	(NA)	(NA)	(NA)	(B)	1,030	(NA)	(NA)	(NA)	(NA)	5.9	19.0	38.5	36.6
Oakland city	67,543	487,300	2.5	3.3	7.1	87.1	78,739	889	7.4	7.5	17.9	67.2	16.3	41.3	29.6	12.8
Oceanside city	38,091	500,500	5.6	3.0	6.0	85.4	(R)	1,091	(NA)	(NA)	(NA)	(NA)	6.4	31.7	40.0	21.9
Ontario city	26,193	347,500	7.2	4.1	22.4	66.3	18,561	961	1.1	3.7	20.2	75.1	5.0	27.7	37.1	30.2
Orange city	28,564	616,900	(NA)	(NA)	(NA)	(NA)	(B)	1,190	(NA)	(NA)	(NA)	(NA)	3.3	27.3	41.6	27.7
Oxnard city	27,396	529,900	8.9	3.7	5.4	82.0	18,158	1,073	2.9	5.2	9.0	82.9	5.1	27.5	38.6	28.8
Palmdale city	27,301	303,800	6.7	10.1	32.0	51.2	11,219	940	5.7	5.5	13.7	75.2	4.3	30.2	35.5	30.0
Pasadena city	24,716	609,200	(NA)	(NA)	(NA)	(NA)	27,894	954	8.6	2.4	14.4	74.5	7.6	42.4	35.1	14.9
Pomona city	26,204	365,400	(NA)	(NA)	(NA)	(NA)	15,811	907	0.8	4.2	20.3	74.8	5.5	30.4	36.3	27.8
Rancho Cucamonga city	32,937	458,700	(NA)	(NA)	(NA)	(NA)	(B)	1,204	(NA)	(NA)	(NA)	(NA)	4.9	23.8	40.0	31.3
Riverside city	52,434	369,900	5.9	6.3	13.1	74.7	40,971	902	2.0	4.1	19.1	74.7	6.0	32.3	36.3	25.4
Sacramento city	89,196	341,400	6.7	9.7	21.4	62.3	79,586	852	5.2	5.9	22.0	66.9	10.5	38.7	35.5	15.4
Salinas city	20,935	560,600	(NA)	(NA)	(NA)	(NA)	21,199	912	8.4	4.0	17.2	70.4	10.7	25.6	37.8	26.0

See footnotes at end of table.

Table D-6. Places — Owner- and Renter-Occupied Housing Units and Vehicles Available—Con.

[Includes states and 242 incorporated places of 100,000 or more population as of April 1, 2000. Two census designated places (CDPs) are also included (Honolulu CDP in Hawaii and Arlington CDP in Virginia). For more information on these areas, see Appendix C, Geographic Information. Seven states (Delaware, Maine, Montana, North Dakota, Vermont, West Virginia, and Wyoming) do not have any incorporated places of 100,000 or more population]

Place	Owner-occupied housing units, 2005						Renter-occupied housing units, 2005						Percent of occupied housing units by vehicles available, 2005			
			Value, percent—					Median gross monthly rent (dol-lars)	Gross monthly rent, percent[1]—							
	Total units	Median value (dollars)	Less than $100,000	$100,000–$199,999	$200,000–$299,999	$300,000 and over	Total units		Less then $300	$300–$499	$500–$749	$750 or more	None	1	2	3 or more
CALIFORNIA—Con.																
San Bernardino city	33,896	243,400	11.0	23.4	34.6	31.1	29,470	769	8.5	6.5	32.2	52.8	10.5	35.7	38.2	15.7
San Buenaventura (Ventura) city	23,820	586,300	(NA)	(NA)	(NA)	(NA)	(B)	1,094	(NA)	(NA)	(NA)	(NA)	5.6	34.4	39.9	20.1
San Diego city	239,409	566,700	3.3	2.0	5.5	89.2	227,170	1,104	2.3	3.1	11.5	83.2	6.6	35.4	39.8	18.2
San Francisco city	122,603	726,700	3.6	0.8	1.8	93.8	199,796	1,118	7.6	6.8	12.7	72.9	31.3	40.3	21.8	6.7
San Jose city	175,828	625,400	6.9	1.7	2.7	88.6	112,511	1,153	2.6	3.4	7.6	86.5	5.1	28.0	40.7	26.1
Santa Ana city	35,938	478,600	6.8	5.0	9.8	78.4	32,852	1,059	2.4	2.2	12.0	83.3	9.4	27.0	36.1	27.5
Santa Clara city	19,913	627,100	(NA)	(NA)	(NA)	(NA)	(B)	1,152	(NA)	(NA)	(NA)	(NA)	5.6	39.4	36.5	18.4
Santa Clarita city	39,373	489,200	(NA)	(NA)	(NA)	(NA)	13,809	1,316	2.1	1.5	6.9	89.5	3.9	22.3	45.5	28.2
Santa Rosa city	33,232	561,200	6.1	2.9	3.7	87.3	26,253	1,025	3.0	1.8	8.4	86.8	8.0	36.4	36.4	19.1
Simi Valley city	29,503	587,600	(NA)	(NA)	(NA)	(NA)	(B)	1,289	(NA)	(NA)	(NA)	(NA)	3.0	20.8	43.4	32.8
Stockton city	49,745	341,800	3.7	11.9	21.2	63.2	41,582	812	6.1	6.3	28.6	59.0	11.6	31.5	36.5	20.4
Sunnyvale city	25,604	677,600	8.2	6.7	1.1	84.0	(B)	1,224	(NA)	(NA)	(NA)	(NA)	3.8	39.7	41.3	15.2
Thousand Oaks city	32,601	703,500	(NA)	(NA)	(NA)	(NA)	(B)	1,446	(NA)	(NA)	(NA)	(NA)	2.3	21.4	45.7	30.6
Torrance city	29,403	632,000	(NA)	(NA)	(NA)	(NA)	24,518	1,183	1.5	1.0	7.6	89.9	3.4	37.0	39.2	20.4
Vallejo city	27,606	436,200	(NA)	(NA)	(NA)	(NA)	(B)	1,065	(NA)	(NA)	(NA)	(NA)	8.6	28.1	37.5	25.7
West Covina city	20,062	458,900	(NA)	(NA)	(NA)	(NA)	(B)	1,171	(NA)	(NA)	(NA)	(NA)	5.1	29.8	35.3	29.7
COLORADO	1,233,695	223,300	9.9	30.9	30.1	29.2	585,342	757	5.2	11.4	32.6	50.8	5.5	31.4	40.5	22.6
Arvada city	31,707	239,300	(NA)	(NA)	(NA)	(NA)	9,001	860	7.6	9.1	22.4	60.8	4.7	27.1	42.9	25.3
Aurora city	72,929	194,600	6.4	47.9	37.1	8.6	38,143	744	2.8	8.1	40.2	49.0	6.5	36.0	38.5	19.0
Centennial city	31,372	280,200	(NA)	(NA)	(NA)	(NA)	(B)	1,030	(NA)	(NA)	(NA)	(NA)	2.0	24.0	48.0	26.0
Colorado Springs city	95,735	190,300	7.7	47.9	26.2	18.2	60,245	716	3.5	14.6	36.9	44.9	6.0	35.1	41.2	17.7
Denver city	132,045	231,900	4.9	31.3	32.0	31.8	109,534	704	8.4	13.2	35.5	42.9	12.4	43.0	32.8	11.7
Fort Collins city	29,090	229,700	(NA)	(NA)	(NA)	(NA)	23,054	784	4.0	9.7	32.1	54.2	5.1	33.5	39.4	22.0
Lakewood city	39,068	237,100	(NA)	(NA)	(NA)	(NA)	23,814	781	1.2	4.7	38.4	55.7	6.5	37.6	39.4	16.5
Pueblo city	26,525	108,800	41.5	49.8	6.5	2.2	15,453	526	15.8	29.9	29.2	25.1	9.0	37.1	33.8	20.1
Westminster city	26,542	223,900	(NA)	(NA)	(NA)	(NA)	11,643	877	2.9	3.2	25.5	68.4	3.9	31.3	38.1	26.7
CONNECTICUT	919,943	271,500	4.2	25.1	26.0	44.8	403,895	839	9.1	7.9	22.1	60.8	8.3	31.1	39.7	20.9
Bridgeport city	23,976	218,800	11.7	29.5	40.3	18.5	25,119	869	14.0	3.2	17.5	65.3	18.2	43.2	27.3	11.3
Hartford city	11,518	173,200	(NA)	(NA)	(NA)	(NA)	32,234	664	15.5	13.4	34.0	37.1	31.7	42.5	18.0	7.8
New Haven city	13,360	188,200	13.7	41.0	25.6	19.7	33,251	814	11.4	8.0	21.7	59.0	27.6	39.8	26.9	5.7
Stamford city	27,343	567,500	(NA)	(NA)	(NA)	(NA)	20,069	1,300	5.6	11.4	7.9	75.0	10.3	37.3	34.4	18.1
Waterbury city	20,303	143,600	16.6	66.4	12.5	4.6	20,167	731	11.5	10.4	30.7	47.3	17.3	39.6	31.2	11.9
DELAWARE	229,860	203,800	16.7	32.1	24.5	26.7	87,780	793	6.7	8.2	28.3	56.7	6.6	33.9	40.5	19.0
DISTRICT OF COLUMBIA	105,518	384,400	2.8	15.5	17.5	64.2	142,695	832	9.4	8.0	24.3	58.3	37.2	42.9	15.6	4.2
Washington city	105,518	384,400	2.8	15.5	17.5	64.2	142,695	832	9.4	8.0	24.3	58.3	37.2	42.9	15.6	4.2
FLORIDA	4,903,949	189,500	21.1	32.0	19.6	27.4	2,144,851	809	4.5	8.4	28.4	58.7	6.6	40.0	39.2	14.3
Cape Coral city	39,854	250,800	3.7	25.7	31.4	39.2	(B)	921	(NA)	(NA)	(NA)	(NA)	3.1	35.3	45.1	16.4
Clearwater city	30,945	166,700	16.2	43.3	14.7	25.7	18,562	790	3.6	10.8	30.8	54.8	9.2	45.7	35.6	9.5
Coral Springs city	29,356	390,800	(NA)	(NA)	(NA)	(NA)	(B)	1,088	(NA)	(NA)	(NA)	(NA)	3.9	26.1	51.0	19.0
Fort Lauderdale city	37,504	344,800	6.2	17.9	17.0	58.9	27,177	815	5.7	3.9	31.5	58.9	11.0	50.8	29.5	8.6
Gainesville city	18,967	133,100	28.0	54.9	10.5	6.7	30,334	679	4.1	15.9	41.3	38.7	7.4	47.0	33.9	11.7
Hialeah city	38,145	202,300	7.2	42.0	30.6	20.2	33,359	776	9.0	7.2	27.1	56.8	10.3	37.9	36.1	15.7
Hollywood city	37,656	239,900	13.0	23.6	26.3	37.1	21,514	874	2.4	4.3	28.9	64.4	8.0	42.8	37.6	11.5
Jacksonville city	201,486	144,600	28.5	44.2	15.3	12.0	112,209	739	6.6	9.1	36.1	48.3	7.5	38.2	39.1	15.2
Miami city	51,489	248,500	13.2	23.3	22.7	40.8	93,217	686	9.9	11.4	36.5	42.3	20.6	49.2	23.3	7.0
Miami Gardens city	22,107	166,300	(NA)	(NA)	(NA)	(NA)	(B)	793	(NA)	(NA)	(NA)	(NA)	12.6	37.3	29.7	20.4
Orlando city	37,368	194,300	15.1	36.2	21.5	27.2	56,814	808	4.8	5.7	24.9	64.6	10.0	47.2	34.5	8.3
Pembroke Pines city	45,966	279,800	9.5	20.8	24.3	45.3	(B)	1,233	(NA)	(NA)	(NA)	(NA)	3.9	38.5	41.4	16.2
Pompano Beach city	28,443	214,500	12.6	32.7	22.8	31.9	15,198	878	1.1	2.6	25.4	70.8	7.5	48.8	33.3	10.5
St. Petersburg city	68,836	166,500	20.3	42.4	18.7	18.6	39,972	714	3.2	12.3	40.5	44.0	13.0	42.4	34.9	9.8
Tallahassee city	33,072	161,300	22.7	44.4	18.6	14.3	35,732	719	2.8	12.5	40.5	44.2	6.6	42.1	37.0	14.3
Tampa city	75,492	168,300	21.0	37.2	15.7	26.1	59,941	720	7.5	8.1	38.3	46.1	10.8	42.8	36.8	9.6
GEORGIA	2,218,217	147,500	28.8	40.8	15.3	15.1	1,102,061	709	7.2	14.8	33.8	44.2	6.9	31.9	39.3	21.9
Athens-Clarke County (balance)	16,459	146,800	21.9	53.3	13.3	11.5	24,950	658	4.0	18.1	42.3	35.6	9.0	36.6	36.4	18.0
Atlanta city	80,605	218,500	13.3	32.7	16.6	37.4	93,525	770	11.7	8.8	26.6	52.9	18.6	45.6	26.5	9.3
Augusta-Richmond County (balance)	42,138	92,200	56.7	33.1	5.9	4.2	31,601	621	7.9	21.3	42.7	28.1	10.2	37.4	33.6	18.7
Columbus city	38,723	113,000	43.8	37.5	10.3	8.3	32,203	594	12.2	19.3	42.2	26.3	11.0	36.7	34.9	17.4
Savannah city	24,838	108,100	45.6	38.6	7.9	7.9	24,834	717	8.2	9.9	36.2	45.7	13.8	40.6	32.8	12.8

See footnotes at end of table.

Table D-6. Places — Owner- and Renter-Occupied Housing Units and Vehicles Available—Con.

[Includes states and 242 incorporated places of 100,000 or more population as of April 1, 2000. Two census designated places (CDPs) are also included (Honolulu CDP in Hawaii and Arlington CDP in Virginia). For more information on these areas, see Appendix C, Geographic Information. Seven states (Delaware, Maine, Montana, North Dakota, Vermont, West Virginia, and Wyoming) do not have any incorporated places of 100,000 or more population]

| Place | Owner-occupied housing units, 2005 | | Value, percent— | | | | Renter-occupied housing units, 2005 | | Gross monthly rent, percent[1]— | | | | Percent of occupied housing units by vehicles available, 2005 | | | |
	Total units	Median value (dollars)	Less than $100,000	$100,000– $199,999	$200,000– $299,999	$300,000 and over	Total units	Median gross monthly rent (dollars)	Less then $300	$300– $499	$500– $749	$750 or more	None	1	2	3 or more
HAWAII	256,578	453,600	2.7	9.2	14.1	73.9	173,429	995	4.2	7.7	14.5	73.7	8.7	34.4	35.9	21.0
Honolulu CDP	72,842	481,000	2.7	8.3	14.5	74.4	73,228	920	5.0	8.6	15.9	70.6	16.3	44.3	26.8	12.6
IDAHO	379,948	134,900	29.9	44.8	13.7	11.6	152,187	594	10.0	23.1	40.7	26.2	4.4	26.3	41.0	28.3
Boise City city	51,816	153,700	14.8	53.3	18.9	12.9	30,771	647	3.5	17.7	46.5	32.3	6.3	33.3	41.0	19.4
ILLINOIS	3,277,573	183,900	23.2	31.3	20.1	25.4	1,413,447	734	7.7	13.1	31.4	47.8	10.2	34.4	37.9	17.5
Aurora city	39,099	186,900	5.2	52.7	24.3	17.8	15,317	944	4.6	5.4	13.5	76.5	5.3	31.6	44.5	18.6
Chicago city	494,985	245,000	8.3	27.2	25.5	38.9	525,620	783	7.3	8.4	29.8	54.5	25.6	43.7	23.4	7.3
Joliet city	30,987	173,400	11.2	51.5	31.7	5.5	10,777	699	8.9	14.1	42.9	34.2	5.1	31.4	41.3	22.2
Naperville city	40,210	382,500	(NA)	(NA)	(NA)	(NA)	(B)	1,009	(NA)	(NA)	(NA)	(NA)	1.4	23.8	54.7	20.1
Peoria city	28,604	105,000	47.1	39.0	7.7	6.2	16,449	604	13.2	14.8	48.1	23.9	13.5	40.3	34.1	12.1
Rockford city	35,470	93,600	57.7	36.7	3.9	1.8	21,601	572	12.9	19.8	37.1	30.2	13.0	41.5	33.9	11.6
Springfield city	31,759	102,200	48.7	37.2	7.1	6.9	17,297	526	10.8	32.7	37.6	18.9	10.0	43.0	34.9	12.1
INDIANA	1,759,089	114,400	41.3	42.7	9.8	6.2	683,921	615	8.1	21.2	42.7	27.9	6.3	31.3	40.3	22.1
Evansville city	29,520	87,000	64.7	28.4	4.2	2.6	19,695	541	10.0	30.3	43.1	16.5	9.5	40.8	37.1	12.5
Fort Wayne city	58,227	87,700	63.1	31.3	4.5	1.1	33,220	568	8.1	30.3	41.0	20.7	7.4	38.2	39.1	15.4
Gary city	19,179	63,000	85.1	14.1	0.5	0.3	17,523	589	15.3	19.1	40.5	25.1	17.7	43.8	27.6	10.9
Indianapolis city (balance)	201,072	117,900	37.6	47.9	8.4	6.0	125,189	643	5.2	16.5	45.4	32.9	9.3	37.2	38.1	15.4
South Bend city	25,249	82,200	68.1	27.8	2.9	1.1	16,160	663	10.0	15.0	37.3	37.7	12.2	43.9	32.2	11.7
IOWA	877,796	106,600	46.1	39.0	9.3	5.5	323,037	559	10.5	27.2	41.3	21.0	5.3	29.4	40.2	25.1
Cedar Rapids city	35,644	116,400	31.3	53.9	11.6	3.3	16,206	610	13.3	20.8	37.0	28.9	8.7	34.3	38.7	18.4
Des Moines city	56,991	106,300	45.2	44.6	5.6	4.6	27,472	618	9.4	16.5	47.8	26.3	7.7	33.5	38.9	19.9
KANSAS	744,580	107,800	46.7	36.1	10.6	6.6	327,358	588	8.5	25.3	38.7	27.4	4.8	30.4	39.5	25.2
Kansas City city	35,270	84,600	64.7	30.4	3.1	1.8	18,327	645	14.7	13.6	33.4	38.3	9.6	37.7	32.5	20.2
Overland Park city	43,461	207,800	3.6	43.0	32.6	20.8	21,205	798	1.3	0.7	37.1	60.9	2.7	33.1	47.7	16.4
Topeka city	33,048	82,600	64.5	30.7	2.6	2.2	20,715	570	6.6	32.5	32.6	28.3	8.7	39.5	36.2	15.6
Wichita city	87,519	99,000	50.8	37.9	7.9	3.3	56,859	581	5.5	27.6	43.0	24.0	7.6	35.6	39.1	17.7
KENTUCKY	1,167,973	103,900	48.0	36.3	9.2	6.4	485,925	527	14.1	30.6	37.9	17.4	7.4	32.6	39.1	20.9
Lexington-Fayette	68,782	142,900	21.0	49.6	16.3	13.1	45,766	585	5.8	26.0	37.2	30.9	7.8	37.4	40.6	14.2
Louisville/Jefferson County (balance)	151,016	125,000	32.1	46.8	11.1	9.9	81,867	582	10.4	22.7	42.9	23.9	10.2	38.2	36.1	15.5
LOUISIANA	1,136,873	101,700	49.2	35.7	8.8	6.3	539,726	569	12.1	24.8	40.9	22.2	9.9	36.4	37.7	15.9
Baton Rouge city	46,171	114,300	42.7	39.8	10.7	6.8	41,294	626	5.7	20.3	46.6	27.4	9.8	45.2	33.1	12.0
Lafayette city	26,326	128,200	35.8	46.5	11.1	6.7	19,306	596	7.8	20.5	49.8	21.9	8.4	36.1	42.8	12.6
New Orleans city	81,670	133,700	32.7	37.2	13.3	16.8	81,664	590	14.4	19.2	39.9	26.5	26.0	42.7	25.0	6.3
Shreveport city	47,942	93,600	53.6	36.2	4.9	5.3	29,532	552	10.5	27.1	44.3	18.2	12.7	39.4	35.1	12.8
MAINE	389,203	155,300	28.8	36.2	18.9	16.1	152,955	623	13.4	19.7	35.4	31.6	5.9	32.5	41.1	20.5
MARYLAND	1,438,614	280,200	10.4	21.5	21.5	46.7	647,033	891	6.2	6.9	20.6	66.3	9.4	32.1	37.2	21.4
Baltimore city	123,532	103,400	48.6	28.3	11.0	12.1	119,446	667	13.4	12.3	36.3	37.9	31.0	42.5	20.8	5.8
MASSACHUSETTS	1,567,885	361,500	2.6	12.2	20.1	65.1	880,147	902	10.9	9.2	16.7	63.2	11.5	35.6	37.3	15.5
Boston city	83,686	420,400	(NA)	(NA)	(NA)	(NA)	149,342	1,075	13.1	9.3	10.8	66.8	35.9	42.9	16.9	4.3
Cambridge city	15,529	527,200	(NA)	(NA)	(NA)	(NA)	25,369	1,265	8.6	3.8	6.5	81.1	31.1	49.1	16.2	3.6
Lowell city	16,975	272,100	(NA)	(NA)	(NA)	(NA)	21,342	850	17.4	4.9	15.8	61.9	15.0	40.4	32.2	12.4
Springfield city	27,684	140,700	(NA)	(NA)	(NA)	(NA)	29,864	603	20.6	19.0	31.1	29.3	24.1	41.6	25.6	8.7
Worcester city	30,049	262,100	(NA)	(NA)	(NA)	(NA)	33,460	780	14.1	9.8	22.7	53.4	17.9	42.4	28.3	11.3
MICHIGAN	2,903,328	149,300	26.7	43.2	16.8	13.4	984,666	655	8.1	17.7	38.7	35.5	6.5	32.9	40.5	20.1
Ann Arbor city	21,098	238,100	5.7	26.1	33.6	34.5	23,553	891	2.2	4.8	24.7	68.3	11.8	42.1	36.3	9.8
Detroit city	169,755	88,300	63.3	31.4	3.6	1.7	141,479	675	7.8	18.0	33.1	41.1	20.4	45.3	25.3	9.0
Flint city	24,184	64,600	86.4	11.4	1.5	0.7	20,870	585	11.6	23.3	44.2	20.9	16.2	41.8	31.8	10.2
Grand Rapids city	46,303	121,100	30.4	60.7	6.1	2.8	28,936	639	8.1	15.8	44.1	31.9	12.0	35.1	38.9	14.1
Lansing city	30,486	104,600	45.7	51.6	2.1	0.6	19,066	602	9.0	27.6	31.0	32.3	11.9	39.0	34.1	15.0
Livonia city	33,589	206,700	5.2	41.4	39.1	14.3	(B)	748	(NA)	(NA)	(NA)	(NA)	4.5	25.5	44.3	25.7
Sterling Heights city	37,255	192,900	6.9	49.7	33.9	9.5	11,273	716	5.3	3.7	50.3	40.7	5.4	33.3	41.6	19.7
Warren city	43,900	147,900	19.8	70.7	9.1	0.3	11,426	683	6.1	5.7	50.1	38.1	6.2	34.7	42.3	16.9

See footnotes at end of table.

[Includes states and 242 incorporated places of 100,000 or more population as of April 1, 2000. Two census designated places (CDPs) are also included (Honolulu CDP in Hawaii and Arlington CDP in Virginia). For more information on these areas, see Appendix C, Geographic Information. Seven states (Delaware, Maine, Montana, North Dakota, Vermont, West Virginia, and Wyoming) do not have any incorporated places of 100,000 or more population]

Place	Owner-occupied housing units, 2005						Renter-occupied housing units, 2005						Percent of occupied housing units by vehicles available, 2005			
			Value, percent—					Median gross monthly rent (dol-lars)	Gross monthly rent, percent[1]—							
	Total units	Median value (dollars)	Less than $100,000	$100,000–$199,999	$200,000–$299,999	$300,000 and over	Total units		Less then $300	$300–$499	$500–$749	$750 or more	None	1	2	3 or more
MINNESOTA	1,530,659	198,800	16.1	34.4	26.9	22.6	489,485	692	10.2	13.4	35.5	40.8	6.3	30.0	41.2	22.5
Minneapolis city.	83,603	226,900	3.6	34.0	35.7	26.7	73,367	705	12.6	8.6	36.7	42.1	15.6	44.1	29.4	10.9
St. Paul city	63,609	200,100	5.0	45.0	29.4	20.7	44,370	732	8.2	7.6	37.5	46.7	13.3	40.0	34.1	12.5
MISSISSIPPI	757,446	82,700	61.2	28.1	6.3	4.3	326,588	538	15.1	28.4	35.8	20.7	7.4	33.4	37.8	21.4
Jackson city	36,477	79,900	66.0	24.5	5.3	4.2	27,927	649	10.6	18.3	41.7	29.3	9.6	40.0	33.0	17.4
MISSOURI	1,614,217	123,100	38.3	40.2	12.6	8.9	671,063	593	9.8	24.3	39.0	26.9	6.8	33.0	39.3	20.9
Independence city	34,276	100,300	49.7	42.1	6.5	1.7	14,520	651	7.1	14.6	45.2	33.1	6.0	34.4	42.4	17.3
Kansas City city.	111,574	124,900	35.8	46.0	11.7	6.5	75,874	664	6.1	15.2	43.1	35.6	10.6	39.8	35.3	14.3
St. Louis city	69,688	103,300	48.2	36.3	9.3	6.2	71,720	567	11.6	23.7	40.9	23.8	21.3	48.4	23.4	6.9
Springfield city.	35,384	91,500	57.8	32.6	5.9	3.7	31,796	549	6.2	34.4	34.9	24.5	9.2	44.6	33.7	12.5
MONTANA	254,458	131,600	35.1	37.9	13.3	13.7	113,810	552	12.2	28.5	37.6	21.7	4.6	28.0	38.6	28.8
NEBRASKA.	474,682	113,200	42.0	41.8	10.7	5.5	220,910	569	10.0	27.2	37.4	25.4	5.1	30.2	39.8	24.8
Lincoln city	58,334	131,700	23.0	58.9	11.9	6.1	38,794	612	5.2	29.3	33.9	31.6	6.0	34.8	38.8	20.4
Omaha city	90,058	124,400	32.1	51.5	10.8	5.6	66,234	623	7.0	21.0	39.7	32.2	8.9	39.9	36.6	14.7
NEVADA.	550,125	283,400	9.5	19.7	24.4	46.4	356,594	861	2.6	7.1	24.0	66.2	7.1	36.4	38.5	17.9
Henderson city	59,256	350,700	3.1	11.4	21.7	63.8	(B)	983	(NA)	(NA)	(NA)	(NA)	3.7	32.5	44.9	18.8
Las Vegas city	120,635	285,200	3.8	20.8	28.8	46.5	84,053	894	2.7	7.6	21.6	68.2	8.4	39.4	38.8	13.5
North Las Vegas city	34,667	263,700	4.2	20.7	39.3	35.8	17,394	888	5.1	6.1	26.3	62.5	10.4	30.0	38.7	20.9
Reno city	40,467	319,400	8.9	14.8	22.0	54.2	47,651	786	4.0	9.8	29.8	56.4	10.3	41.2	34.5	14.0
NEW HAMPSHIRE	362,854	240,100	10.3	24.7	30.1	34.9	134,200	854	7.8	6.9	21.9	63.4	4.6	28.6	42.8	24.0
Manchester city	23,187	227,600	(NA)	(NA)	(NA)	(NA)	21,167	887	6.8	4.5	16.8	71.8	7.7	36.1	38.2	18.1
NEW JERSEY	2,114,072	333,900	5.7	17.0	20.3	57.0	1,027,884	935	6.6	5.1	16.2	72.0	11.6	33.5	37.7	17.3
Elizabeth city	14,546	353,800	(NA)	(NA)	(NA)	(NA)	26,144	871	6.6	8.1	16.5	68.9	31.5	41.6	19.3	7.6
Jersey City city	27,100	299,500	3.3	15.8	31.1	49.8	62,472	861	7.2	10.7	19.9	62.1	37.6	44.3	13.8	4.3
Newark city	21,295	242,600	6.5	29.7	28.6	35.3	70,632	769	15.8	8.6	23.6	51.9	40.5	35.9	18.5	5.1
Paterson city	14,923	307,700	(NA)	(NA)	(NA)	(NA)	30,260	877	8.4	7.6	16.6	67.4	27.2	39.3	23.9	9.7
NEW MEXICO	504,354	125,500	37.7	37.8	12.6	11.8	223,466	587	9.6	26.3	35.9	28.1	5.8	34.2	38.0	22.0
Albuquerque city	130,571	149,900	16.3	58.1	16.1	9.5	78,253	620	4.0	22.1	43.5	30.4	6.8	38.8	37.4	17.0
NEW YORK.	3,936,378	258,900	22.8	19.8	10.7	46.6	3,178,053	841	8.2	10.4	22.9	58.5	28.5	32.3	27.4	11.8
Buffalo city	48,965	60,800	81.5	14.9	1.6	2.0	68,159	586	11.5	22.3	46.0	20.3	31.6	42.1	20.9	5.4
New York city	1,002,272	449,000	5.8	7.8	10.4	76.0	2,023,924	909	8.8	8.1	17.7	65.4	55.1	31.4	10.5	2.9
Rochester city	33,722	62,800	84.4	11.5	2.9	1.2	49,288	656	7.4	19.0	39.7	33.9	23.4	44.7	24.5	7.4
Syracuse city	23,699	75,200	76.5	20.4	2.6	0.2	34,136	588	12.4	20.9	42.6	24.1	24.5	44.5	24.3	6.7
Yonkers city	32,926	391,300	8.5	16.2	11.3	64.1	39,448	939	6.3	6.9	15.9	70.9	26.6	39.3	25.2	8.8
NORTH CAROLINA	2,325,140	127,600	35.6	40.5	12.5	11.4	1,084,700	635	7.7	19.4	41.6	31.3	6.4	32.0	39.0	22.5
Charlotte city	150,185	159,900	15.6	48.7	15.0	20.7	99,218	732	3.6	9.3	40.2	46.9	7.5	40.2	38.2	14.1
Durham city	42,294	157,100	14.3	55.0	19.3	11.4	40,273	724	6.1	8.9	41.5	43.6	8.2	41.6	36.2	13.9
Fayetteville city	28,768	93,000	59.7	28.9	5.4	6.0	28,375	691	4.9	14.2	47.2	33.8	10.9	37.1	37.7	14.3
Greensboro city	49,128	134,900	29.2	45.7	12.8	12.3	44,093	665	3.7	14.2	50.6	31.5	8.6	44.5	33.1	13.8
Raleigh city	74,723	177,200	11.7	46.9	22.3	19.0	64,258	749	3.3	5.2	41.7	49.9	6.7	39.3	39.2	14.8
Winston-Salem city	45,037	125,200	32.2	49.8	7.9	10.2	34,654	619	10.2	20.0	39.1	30.7	8.0	40.2	36.4	15.4
NORTH DAKOTA	182,490	88,600	58.0	33.2	5.9	2.9	87,947	479	15.3	39.8	31.1	13.8	5.0	29.3	38.3	27.5
OHIO	3,152,610	129,600	32.7	46.3	13.1	7.9	1,355,211	613	8.9	20.7	41.1	29.2	7.7	32.4	39.2	20.7
Akron city.	51,874	95,100	53.7	38.1	5.4	2.8	33,684	631	10.0	21.3	34.4	34.4	12.0	40.8	33.9	13.3
Cincinnati city	57,851	121,000	37.0	41.9	9.6	11.4	79,098	524	12.7	31.7	34.7	20.8	22.4	41.6	25.0	11.0
Cleveland city	82,751	86,900	67.1	29.8	2.0	1.0	95,066	582	15.2	18.4	41.0	25.4	24.3	43.1	23.9	8.6
Columbus city	160,324	132,100	30.6	53.8	12.0	3.6	141,001	673	5.4	13.1	44.4	37.0	8.2	41.1	38.6	12.2
Dayton city	31,687	77,200	76.4	21.3	1.2	1.0	28,227	574	18.8	22.3	36.0	22.9	20.3	37.8	29.8	12.0
Toledo city	72,570	94,800	54.9	41.6	2.9	0.7	48,400	571	9.9	27.8	38.6	23.8	12.4	41.8	33.2	12.6

See footnotes at end of table.

Table D-6. Places — **Owner- and Renter-Occupied Housing Units and Vehicles Available**—Con.

[Includes states and 242 incorporated places of 100,000 or more population as of April 1, 2000. Two census designated places (CDPs) are also included (Honolulu CDP in Hawaii and Arlington CDP in Virginia). For more information on these areas, see Appendix C, Geographic Information. Seven states (Delaware, Maine, Montana, North Dakota, Vermont, West Virginia, and Wyoming) do not have any incorporated places of 100,000 or more population]

Place	Owner-occupied housing units, 2005		Value, percent—				Renter-occupied housing units, 2005		Gross monthly rent, percent[1]—				Percent of occupied housing units by vehicles available, 2005			
	Total units	Median value (dollars)	Less than $100,000	$100,000–$199,999	$200,000–$299,999	$300,000 and over	Total units	Median gross monthly rent (dollars)	Less then $300	$300–$499	$500–$749	$750 or more	None	1	2	3 or more
OKLAHOMA	937,051	89,100	57.5	31.8	6.6	4.1	443,544	547	9.0	30.7	39.1	21.3	5.6	33.9	39.4	21.1
Oklahoma City city	130,468	103,800	47.7	40.2	7.6	4.6	86,370	570	4.2	30.8	38.5	26.6	7.1	38.3	37.3	17.4
Tulsa city	89,551	106,600	46.5	35.9	9.6	8.1	70,771	592	8.1	22.1	42.4	27.4	8.1	41.9	37.6	12.3
OREGON	909,113	201,200	12.9	36.7	24.7	25.7	516,227	689	5.2	13.8	40.3	40.7	7.2	31.7	39.3	21.7
Eugene city	32,676	187,000	10.5	45.1	23.1	21.3	30,636	708	4.3	16.6	34.4	44.7	10.2	41.0	36.3	12.6
Portland city	129,055	225,900	3.9	35.3	30.6	30.2	99,112	696	6.2	8.7	43.6	41.5	14.6	37.7	34.1	13.7
Salem city	32,013	156,600	12.1	63.3	17.5	7.1	23,412	617	4.8	19.0	49.5	26.7	6.7	38.6	39.9	14.7
PENNSYLVANIA	3,474,048	131,900	36.3	35.7	14.0	14.1	1,386,092	647	9.1	19.7	35.2	36.0	11.4	33.9	37.0	17.8
Allentown city	21,778	111,500	42.8	44.3	7.7	5.3	21,140	684	11.8	9.0	42.1	37.1	19.9	40.4	29.7	10.0
Erie city	21,937	73,400	80.3	18.0	0.6	1.0	16,935	496	14.6	36.1	37.0	12.3	16.0	45.3	31.5	7.3
Philadelphia city	320,641	100,200	49.9	30.7	10.2	9.2	244,792	725	7.7	10.4	35.8	46.1	34.8	42.6	17.8	4.8
Pittsburgh city	72,803	74,000	72.0	16.6	5.7	5.7	63,506	648	11.2	16.6	38.2	34.0	24.7	43.5	25.0	6.7
RHODE ISLAND	254,639	281,300	2.6	17.3	35.6	44.5	151,450	775	13.1	9.0	24.5	53.4	8.1	35.3	38.8	17.8
Providence city	23,578	245,100	2.8	28.6	40.5	28.1	36,302	817	13.9	9.6	19.8	56.7	17.6	45.0	27.3	10.1
SOUTH CAROLINA	1,146,620	113,100	44.0	34.9	10.6	10.5	489,287	611	8.7	22.3	39.8	29.2	7.6	33.0	38.7	20.7
Columbia city	20,906	139,600	30.9	40.2	12.0	16.9	22,061	621	11.0	16.3	46.2	26.5	18.4	34.8	36.5	10.2
SOUTH DAKOTA	214,246	101,700	49.1	36.4	8.3	6.2	96,085	500	18.8	31.3	34.8	15.1	5.0	27.7	39.0	28.3
Sioux Falls city	35,942	130,600	26.6	55.7	11.2	6.5	21,166	620	7.0	20.3	50.4	22.3	5.6	33.7	42.8	17.9
TENNESSEE	1,638,837	114,000	42.7	38.3	10.4	8.6	727,293	583	10.7	23.6	41.2	24.5	6.4	32.5	38.6	22.6
Chattanooga city	35,171	109,400	44.6	39.5	9.4	6.6	27,484	564	15.3	22.7	36.2	25.8	13.6	43.6	28.8	14.0
Clarksville city	25,667	101,100	49.1	43.1	4.9	2.8	15,036	616	4.6	17.4	55.2	22.9	4.0	33.1	40.7	22.2
Knoxville city	41,314	100,400	49.7	40.1	5.1	5.1	38,839	538	14.1	26.1	40.7	19.1	11.9	41.1	33.0	14.0
Memphis city	142,030	86,200	61.0	26.9	6.2	5.9	119,953	683	5.1	13.1	43.4	38.4	12.9	44.5	30.9	11.7
Nashville-Davidson (balance)	132,396	141,800	23.8	49.7	14.5	12.1	101,192	666	8.8	10.6	47.4	33.2	7.6	43.0	34.7	14.7
TEXAS	5,162,604	106,000	47.0	35.9	9.4	7.7	2,815,491	671	5.9	15.3	40.8	38.0	6.3	35.3	40.8	17.6
Abilene city	24,617	71,500	72.0	21.8	3.6	2.6	18,210	622	3.6	24.0	44.1	28.3	4.5	40.7	38.3	16.5
Amarillo city	45,335	91,600	56.8	35.2	5.9	2.1	23,768	578	5.3	28.0	50.2	16.4	5.1	39.8	39.4	15.6
Arlington city	72,967	121,700	29.4	58.0	8.7	3.8	53,272	718	0.8	9.8	44.7	44.7	3.8	35.0	45.3	15.9
Austin city	139,317	170,900	13.4	47.3	21.6	17.7	150,371	740	2.3	6.9	42.5	48.3	7.9	43.6	36.3	12.1
Beaumont city	23,816	83,300	61.7	30.7	4.2	3.4	19,440	594	13.4	25.1	34.7	26.7	13.8	42.4	29.4	14.4
Brownsville city	29,460	65,000	80.5	15.3	2.8	1.4	17,588	505	24.7	24.4	35.1	15.8	14.0	40.3	33.8	11.9
Carrollton city	26,171	156,900	(NA)	(NA)	(NA)	(NA)	15,416	899	–	0.7	27.0	72.2	2.8	26.0	50.8	20.4
Corpus Christi city	62,338	86,400	61.2	28.4	5.0	5.4	40,821	668	7.8	10.7	41.5	40.0	5.9	40.1	36.6	17.4
Dallas city	203,755	120,900	40.8	29.6	12.9	16.7	240,009	685	5.3	11.2	43.2	40.3	10.1	47.1	32.7	10.2
El Paso city	121,533	81,800	68.7	24.8	3.8	2.7	71,604	514	14.9	32.3	36.2	16.6	11.4	33.8	36.0	18.8
Fort Worth city	127,912	100,000	50.0	37.6	7.0	5.4	91,087	678	4.2	10.8	48.3	36.7	7.3	36.7	40.2	15.8
Garland city	51,131	117,000	31.0	60.9	6.2	1.9	27,867	781	1.4	4.5	36.7	57.3	5.5	33.2	40.8	20.4
Grand Prairie city	32,435	114,800	37.7	57.5	3.7	1.1	15,185	797	5.5	4.9	33.0	56.5	4.4	32.5	44.4	18.7
Houston city	350,459	112,800	42.4	35.8	10.2	11.6	382,642	682	2.9	11.7	47.4	38.1	10.2	43.6	34.7	11.5
Irving city	30,668	128,500	28.5	50.4	11.6	9.5	46,105	764	0.6	5.2	41.5	52.7	4.5	42.7	36.6	16.2
Laredo city	33,832	89,800	59.3	33.5	4.5	2.7	22,415	578	5.5	24.9	44.8	24.8	10.6	36.1	38.6	14.7
Lubbock city	43,796	90,600	59.2	31.4	5.7	3.7	37,495	649	2.4	19.4	40.8	37.4	4.1	39.8	42.7	13.5
McAllen city	22,487	90,200	60.4	30.8	5.6	3.2	16,343	613	8.4	18.1	48.8	24.8	5.6	39.7	39.1	15.6
Mesquite city	31,041	111,200	(NA)	(NA)	(NA)	(NA)	13,151	777	0.8	3.3	41.2	54.6	4.1	33.9	44.7	17.3
Pasadena city	27,143	98,100	52.1	39.8	7.1	0.9	21,087	622	3.0	16.7	54.7	25.6	6.1	39.8	36.1	17.9
Plano city	58,960	196,200	5.6	46.3	27.2	20.9	31,853	857	1.3	0.9	27.7	70.0	3.2	31.0	48.1	17.7
San Antonio city	258,507	89,800	59.1	31.3	5.9	3.7	167,720	649	7.8	15.3	42.2	34.7	8.6	37.2	38.9	15.4
Waco city	19,907	76,000	66.9	21.3	5.6	6.2	21,447	576	7.7	28.6	33.7	30.0	11.8	41.2	32.9	14.1
Wichita Falls city	22,924	78,000	67.7	26.5	1.9	3.8	14,811	622	13.9	12.7	45.2	28.3	7.2	38.2	40.8	13.8
UTAH	558,769	167,200	12.2	53.8	18.8	15.3	233,160	665	4.6	15.4	43.8	36.2	4.3	26.1	41.8	27.8
Provo city	13,634	171,000	(NA)	(NA)	(NA)	(NA)	18,161	630	5.9	14.7	43.2	36.1	3.7	30.0	39.7	26.7
Salt Lake City city	38,947	180,500	7.8	52.7	19.4	20.1	36,081	619	6.3	19.5	48.7	25.5	10.9	38.9	34.7	15.5
West Valley City city	23,997	141,900	10.6	80.5	7.5	1.5	11,846	691	3.5	7.4	55.9	33.2	5.5	30.4	33.2	30.9

See footnotes at end of table.

Table D-6. Places — **Owner- and Renter-Occupied Housing Units and Vehicles Available**—Con.

[Includes states and 242 incorporated places of 100,000 or more population as of April 1, 2000. Two census designated places (CDPs) are also included (Honolulu CDP in Hawaii and Arlington CDP in Virginia). For more information on these areas, see Appendix C, Geographic Information. Seven states (Delaware, Maine, Montana, North Dakota, Vermont, West Virginia, and Wyoming) do not have any incorporated places of 100,000 or more population]

Place	Owner-occupied housing units, 2005						Renter-occupied housing units, 2005						Percent of occupied housing units by vehicles available, 2005			
			Value, percent—						Gross monthly rent, percent[1]—							
	Total units	Median value (dollars)	Less than $100,000	$100,000– $199,999	$200,000– $299,999	$300,000 and over	Total units	Median gross monthly rent (dollars)	Less then $300	$300– $499	$500– $749	$750 or more	None	1	2	3 or more
VERMONT	176,860	173,400	19.4	40.0	21.4	19.2	71,965	683	10.7	12.0	38.7	38.6	6.8	31.9	42.0	19.3
VIRGINIA	2,012,391	212,300	19.6	27.8	16.3	36.3	877,297	812	6.8	11.8	25.3	56.2	6.4	29.9	38.3	25.5
Alexandria city.	27,807	490,700	(NA)	(NA)	(NA)	(NA)	36,247	1,111	6.4	0.8	4.0	88.7	12.3	49.3	30.9	7.5
Arlington CDP.	41,476	581,900	(NA)	(NA)	(NA)	(NA)	42,657	1,261	2.2	0.8	2.7	94.3	10.7	46.7	32.3	10.3
Chesapeake city	56,894	218,400	11.4	32.6	28.6	27.4	20,927	786	3.8	5.0	37.4	53.7	4.1	27.3	39.9	28.7
Hampton city.	33,768	139,300	28.2	47.5	17.5	6.8	21,476	757	6.0	14.6	27.8	51.6	6.0	33.1	38.3	22.6
Newport News city	39,552	152,000	24.4	48.8	19.9	7.0	33,685	793	7.0	7.8	26.9	58.3	10.0	32.7	38.5	18.8
Norfolk city	39,718	152,200	21.3	46.7	14.4	17.6	46,588	697	9.5	7.2	43.0	40.2	11.4	41.9	32.8	13.9
Portsmouth city	24,033	128,600	28.6	54.9	11.8	4.6	13,499	732	11.1	3.0	38.3	47.6	9.7	39.7	34.2	16.4
Richmond city	37,294	149,400	32.6	30.4	17.6	19.5	44,905	697	10.6	9.7	37.7	42.0	19.0	42.6	27.8	10.6
Virginia Beach city	107,472	231,400	5.6	32.9	28.6	33.0	53,881	972	1.8	2.2	11.9	84.2	3.4	30.3	42.1	24.2
WASHINGTON.	1,584,549	227,700	11.5	29.8	25.0	33.7	865,925	741	5.7	11.6	34.1	48.7	6.8	30.4	38.0	24.8
Bellevue city	29,553	434,100	3.5	7.6	11.3	77.7	19,445	910	2.8	2.0	13.0	82.3	5.7	38.0	41.5	14.9
Seattle city	130,552	384,900	1.7	7.4	20.5	70.4	130,881	804	6.9	7.2	28.2	57.7	16.8	40.8	30.6	11.7
Spokane city	47,459	127,500	29.1	53.6	7.9	9.3	38,135	580	6.4	30.7	37.6	25.3	10.0	36.7	36.1	17.2
Tacoma city	41,222	190,000	4.6	51.2	26.6	17.6	37,584	720	7.0	10.4	37.4	45.2	9.8	39.7	30.8	19.6
Vancouver city.	34,484	194,200	5.7	47.6	28.6	18.2	29,209	752	4.5	5.7	39.2	50.6	9.0	38.8	37.3	14.8
WEST VIRGINIA	558,289	84,400	60.8	28.2	6.4	4.6	182,413	483	17.2	36.2	32.9	13.6	8.5	33.7	39.2	18.6
WISCONSIN	1,556,441	152,600	23.1	46.4	18.4	12.1	663,130	643	7.6	17.9	41.8	32.7	6.7	31.3	41.1	20.9
Green Bay city	23,204	127,700	(NA)	(NA)	(NA)	(NA)	18,619	558	8.2	31.7	40.9	19.2	9.6	36.1	39.3	15.1
Madison city	45,020	200,000	4.0	46.0	32.8	17.2	48,104	751	4.3	7.1	38.4	50.2	11.3	39.6	38.2	10.9
Milwaukee city.	113,122	119,000	37.9	51.8	7.3	3.0	115,739	657	7.1	14.4	44.1	34.4	17.7	45.2	28.3	8.9
WYOMING	146,504	135,000	32.1	43.8	12.3	11.9	58,431	537	10.2	30.1	39.1	20.6	4.1	26.4	37.9	31.5

- Represents zero.   B Number of sample cases is too small to meet statistical standards.   NA Not available.

[1]For units with cash rent.

Survey, Census, or Data Collection Method: Based on the American Community Survey; for information, see Appendix B, Limitations of the Data and Methodology, and also <http://www.census.gov/acs/www/AdvMeth/index.htm>.

Source: U.S. Census Bureau, American Community Survey, "DP-4. Selected Housing Characteristics in the United States: 2005," using American FactFinder, accessed October 3, 2006 (related Internet site <http://factfinder.census.gov>).

Source Notes and Explanations

Appendix A

You may visit us on the Web at
http://www.census.gov/compendia/ccdb

Appendix A.
Source Notes and Explanations

This appendix presents general notes on population, economic, and government censuses followed by source notes and explanation of the data items presented in table sets A/B, C, and D of this publication. Tables A/B, state/county contain identical data items, but Tables C and D vary in both geographic and data coverage.

Each table set begins with information on the number of data items and tables, as well as specific geographic coverage. For each table, the table number and title are given followed by a brief listing of the data items on that table, the source citation for these items, and related definitions and other explanatory text on the source.

GENERAL NOTES

Population

Decennial censuses. The population statistics for 2000 and earlier are based on results from the censuses of population and housing, conducted by the U.S. Census Bureau as of April 1 in each of those years. As provided by article 1, section 2, of the U.S. Constitution, adopted in 1787, a census has been taken every 10 years commencing with 1790. The original purposes of the census were to apportion the seats in the U.S. House of Representatives based on the population of each state and to derive an equitable tax on each state for the payment of the Revolutionary War debt. Through the years, the nation's needs and interests have become more complex, and the content of the decennial census has changed accordingly. Presently, census data not only are used to apportion seats in the House and to aid legislators in the realignment of legislative district boundaries, but are also used in the distribution of billions of federal dollars each year and are vital to state and local governments and to private firms for such functions as market analysis, site selection, and environmental impact studies.

The decennial census uses both short- and long-form questionnaires to gather information. The short form asks a limited number of basic questions. These questions are asked of all people and housing units and are often referred to as 100-percent questions because they are asked of the entire population. The population items include sex, age, race, Hispanic or Latino, household relationship, and group quarters. Housing items include occupancy status, vacancy status, and tenure (owner occupied or renter occupied). The long form asks more detailed

information on a sample basis and includes the 100-percent questions, as well as questions on education, employment, income, ancestry, homeowner costs, units in a structure, number of rooms, plumbing facilities, etc. For a more detailed discussion of the information available from the 2000 census, see "Introduction to Census 2000 Data Products" available at <http://www.census.gov/mso /www/prodprof/census2000.pdf>.

Persons enumerated in the census were counted as inhabitants of their usual place of residence, which generally means the place where a person lives and sleeps most of the time. This place is not necessarily the same as the legal residence, voting residence, or domicile. In the vast majority of cases, however, the use of these different bases of classification would produce substantially the same statistics, although appreciable differences may exist for a few areas.

The implementation of this usual-residence practice has resulted in the establishment of residence rules for certain categories of persons whose usual place of residence is not immediately apparent (e.g., college students were counted at their college residence). As in the above example, persons were not always counted as residents of the place where they happened to be staying on census day. However, persons without a usual place of residence were counted where they were enumerated.

For information on procedures and concepts used for the 2000 Census of Population and Housing, as well as a facsimile of the questionnaires, and descriptions of the data products resulting from the census, see U.S. Census Bureau, *2000 Census of Population and Housing: Summary File 1, Technical Documentation*, Series SF1/01(RV), released June 2001 and available on the Census Bureau's Web site at <http://www.census.gov/prod/cen2000 /doc/sf1.pdf> and 2000 Census of Population and Housing, Profiles of General Demographic Characteristics, Technical Documentation, released May 2001 and available at <http://www.census.gov/prod/cen2000/doc/ProfilesTD.pdf>.

Population estimates. The Census Bureau annually produces estimates of total resident population for each state and county. County population estimates are produced with a component of population change method, while the state population estimates are solely the sum of the county populations.

The Census Bureau develops county population estimates with a demographic procedure called an administrative records component of population change method. A major assumption underlying this approach is that the components of population change are closely approximated by administrative data in a demographic change model. In order to apply the model, Census Bureau demographers estimate each component of population change separately. For the population residing in households, the components of population change are births, deaths, and net migration, including net international migration. For the nonhousehold population, change is represented by the net change in the population living in group quarters facilities.

Each component in this model is represented with data that are symptomatic of some aspect of population change. For example, birth certificates are symptomatic of additions to the population resulting from births, so the Census Bureau uses these data to estimate the birth component for a county. Some other components are derived from death certificates, Internal Revenue Service (IRS) data, Medicare enrollment records, Armed Forces data, group quarters population data, and data from the American Community Survey (ACS).

In cases where the Census Bureau does not have data for all counties for the current estimate year, components of population change are estimated based on one or more simplifying assumptions. When initial population estimates are prepared, the same variant of the component model with these simplifying assumptions is used. In the creation of current vintage population estimates, the initial population estimates from the previous vintage are replaced with revised population estimates calculated with the actual data for all components of population change. Calculations of revised population estimates also incorporate updates to components of change from previous years.

The estimates of the county populations are produced by starting with the base populations from either Census 2000 or the revised population estimate for the most recent year and then adding or subtracting the demographic components of population change calculated for the time period. Basically, the Census Bureau adds the estimated number of births and subtracts the estimated number of deaths for the time period. The Census Bureau then accounts for net migration, which is calculated using several components including net internal migration, net foreign-born international migration, net movement to or from Puerto Rico, net Armed Forces movement to or from overseas, the change in group quarters population, and native emigration from the United States.

The Census Bureau produces separate population estimates for the populations under age 65 and aged 65 and older, mainly because different data are used to measure the internal migration of these two populations. For the population under age 65, data from individual IRS tax returns are used to calculate measures of migration.

Medicare enrollment is used to calculate measures of migration for the population aged 65 and older because this population is not always well-represented on tax returns.

The first step in estimating the population under age 65 is to establish the base populations under age 65. The total base population for the estimate of the population under age 65 is either the April 1, 2000, population estimates base or the revised county population estimate for the prior estimate year. For official population estimates, the April 1, 2000, population estimates base is not adjusted for census undercount. In general, the April 1, 2000, population estimates base uses Census 2000 data as its base but includes certain modifications (geographic updates, Count Question Resolution [CQR] changes to the Census Bureau's program TIGER® database). The group quarters population component is primarily a combination of military personnel living in barracks, college students living in dormitories, and persons residing in institutions. The Census Bureau subtracts the base group quarters population under age 65 from the base total population under age 65 to calculate the base household population under age 65.

The components of population change are calculated using resident births, resident deaths to the population under age 65, net internal migration for the population under age 65, and net international migration for the population under age 65. Resident births are recorded by residence of mother, regardless of where the birth occurred; hence, a county need not have a hospital in order to have resident births. Resident deaths to the population under age 65 use death data tabulated by the most recent residence of the decedent, not by the place where the death occurred. Net internal migration for population under age 65 is estimated using household migration derived from federal income tax returns and the change in the group quarters population.

Net international migration for the population under age 65 is estimated from several sources, including the net foreign-born international migration, net movement to or from Puerto Rico, net Armed Forces movement to or from overseas, and native emigration. National-level data on the net foreign-born international migration of the population under 65 for the current estimate period are distributed to counties based on the county distribution of the noncitizen foreign-born population who entered the United States during the 5 years prior to April 1, 2000, from Census 2000. National-level data on the total net movement of the population under age 65 to or from Puerto Rico for the current estimate period are distributed to counties based on the county distribution of the Puerto Rican population who entered the United States during the 5 years prior to April 1, 2000. The national-level total Armed Forces station strength data are distributed to states using Armed

Forces data originally supplied by each branch of the service, and these state-level data are distributed to counties using the military employment data from Census 2000. National-level data on the total number of emigrants from the United States under age 65 for the current estimate period are distributed to counties based on the county distribution of the native-born population from Census 2000.

The first step in estimating the population aged 65 and older is to establish the base populations. The total base population for the estimate of the population aged 65 and older is either the Census 2000 base (for July 1 population estimate in the decennial year) or the revised county population estimate for the prior estimate year. The base group quarters population aged 65 and older is primarily a combination of persons aged 65 and older residing in nursing homes and other facilities and persons residing in institutions. This population is subtracted from the total base population to calculate the base household population aged 65 and older.

The components of population change for the population 65 and older are resident deaths to the population aged 65 and older, net internal migration for the population aged 65 and older, and net international migration for the population aged 65 and over. Resident deaths to the population aged 65 and older use death data tabulated by the most recent residence of the decedent, not by the place where the death occurred. Net internal migration for the population aged 65 and older includes household migration derived from Medicare enrollment records and the change in the group quarters population. The process used to derive the net international migration for the population aged 65 and older is similar to that used for the population under age 65.

A detailed explanation of how population estimates are produced can be found at <http://www.census.gov /popest/topics/methodology/2006_st_co_meth.html>.

American Community Survey

The American Community Survey (ACS) is a nationwide survey designed to provide communities a fresh look at how they are changing. It is intended to eliminate the need for the long form in the 2010 census. The ACS collects information from U.S. households similar to what was collected on the Census 2000 long form, such as income, commute time to work, home value, veteran status, and other important data. As with the official U.S. census, information about individuals will remain confidential.

The ACS collects and produces population and housing information every year instead of every 10 years. About three million households are surveyed each year. Collecting data every year will reduce the cost of the official decennial census and will provide more up-to-date information throughout the decade about trends in the U.S. population at the local community level.

The ACS will provide estimates of demographic, housing, social, and economic characteristics every year for all states, as well as for all cities, counties, metropolitan areas, and population groups of 65,000 people or more.

For smaller areas, it will take 3 to 5 years to accumulate a sufficient sample to produce data for areas as small as census tracts. For example, areas of 20,000 to 65,000 can use data averaged over 3 years. For rural areas and city neighborhoods or population groups of less than 20,000 people, it will take 5 years to accumulate a sample that is similar to that of the decennial census. These averages can be updated every year.

Economic Census

The economic census is the major source of facts about the structure and functioning of the nation's economy. It provides essential information for government, business, industry, and the general public. It furnishes an important part of the framework for such composite measures as gross domestic product estimates, input/output measures, production and price indexes, and other statistical series that measure short-term changes in economic conditions. Title 13 of the United States Code (Sections 131, 191, and 224) directs the Census Bureau to take the economic census every 5 years, covering years ending in 2 and 7. The economic censuses form an integrated program at 5-year intervals since 1967 and before that for 1963, 1958, and 1954. Prior to that time, the individual censuses were taken separately at varying intervals. Prior to 1997, the Census Bureau took the census of agriculture, but beginning in 1997, that census has been done under the direction of the U.S. Department of Agriculture. Beginning with the 1997 Economic Census, the census presents data based on the North American Industry Classification System (NAICS). Previous census data were presented based on the Standard Industrial Classification (SIC) system developed some 60 years ago. Due to this change, comparability between census years and data found in previous books will be limited. This new system of industrial classification was developed by experts on classification in government and private industry under the guidance of the Office of Information and Regulatory Affairs, Office of Management and Budget (OMB).

There are 20 NAICS sectors, which are subdivided into 100 subsectors (three-digit codes), 317 industry groups (four-digit codes), and, as implemented in the United States, 1,904 industries (five- and six-digit codes). While many of the individual NAICS industries correspond directly to industries as defined under the SIC system, most of the higher-level groupings do not.

The economic censuses are collected on an establishment basis. A company operating at more than one location is required to file a separate report for each store, factory, shop, or other location. Each establishment is assigned a separate industry classification based on its primary activity and not that of its parent company. Establishments responding to the establishment survey are classified into industries on the basis of their principal product or activity (determined by annual sales volume) in accordance with the North American Industry Classification System—United States, 2002 manual available from the National Technical Information Service.

More detailed information about the scope, coverage, classification system, data items, and publications for each of the economic censuses and related surveys is published in the *Guide to the Economic Censuses and Related Statistics*. More information on the methodology, procedures, and history of the censuses is available in the "Guide to the 2002 Economic Census" found on the Census Bureau's Web site at <http://www.census.gov/econ/census02/guide/index.html>.

Data from the 2002 Economic Census were released through the Census Bureau's American FactFinder service, on CD-ROM, and in Adobe Acrobat PDF reports available on the Census Bureau's Web site. For more information on these various media of release, see <http://www.census.gov/econ/census02/>.

Census of Governments

The census of governments provides the only source of periodic, comprehensive, and uniform information that identifies and describes all units of state and local government.

The Census Bureau conducts a census of governments at 5-year intervals as required by law under Title 13, United States Code, Section 161. The 2002 Census of Governments, similar to those taken since 1957, covers three major subject fields: government organization, public employment, and government finances. Organization data include location, type, and characteristics of local governments. Finances and employment data include revenue, expenditure, debt, assets, employee counts, payroll, and benefits.

The census covers all local governments in the United States. Local governments as defined by the Census Bureau include three general-purpose governments (county, municipal, and township) and two limited-purpose governments (school district and special district). For information on the history, methodology, and concepts for the census of governments, see the "Government Finance and Employment Classification Manual" found at <http://www.census.gov/govs/www/class.html>.

TABLE A/B—STATES/COUNTIES

Table A presents 15 tables with 188 items of data for each state, the United States as a whole, and the District of Columbia. On the first page of the table, the stub presents

Federal Information Processing Standard (FIPS) state codes for the 50 states and the District of Columbia. For a discussion of the codes, see Appendix C, Geographic Information.

Table B presents the same 15 tables with the same items of data as in table A for each state and for each of the 3,141 counties and county equivalents (boroughs, independent cities, parishes, etc.).

Counties and county equivalents are presented in alphabetical order within states, which are also presented in alphabetical order. Independent cities, which are found in Maryland, Missouri, Nevada, and Virginia, are placed at the end of the county listing for those states.

FIPS codes for states and counties, with applicable metropolitan area codes, are shown in tables A-1 and B-1, respectively. These codes are given to facilitate cross-reference with other publications and to provide information for access to data available in electronic format. For more information regarding these code numbers, see Appendix C, Geographic Information.

Table A/B-1. Area and Population

Area, 2000: Total and Rank. Population: 2006, 2005, 2000, and 1990; Rank: 2006, 2000, and 1990; Persons per square mile of land area: 2006, 2000, and 1990.

Sources: **Area**—U.S. Census Bureau, 2000 Summary File 1 (SF1), GCT-PH1 Population, Housing Units, Area, and Density: 2000 (related Internet site <http://www.census.gov/Press-Release/www/2001/sumfile1.html>). **Population, 2006, 2005, and 2000**—U.S. Census Bureau, Population Estimates, Annual County Population Estimates and Components of Change: April 1, 2000 to July 1, 2006 (related Internet site <http://www.census.gov/popest/counties/files/CO-EST2006-alldata.txt>). **Population, 1990**—U.S. Census Bureau archive 1990 to 1999, "County Population Estimates for July 1, 1999 and Population Change for April 1, 1990 to July 1, 1999" (related Internet site <http://www.census.gov/popest/archives/1990s/CO-99-02.html>).

Area measurement data provide the size, in square units, of geographic entities for which the Census Bureau tabulates and disseminates data. Area is calculated from the specific boundary recorded for each entity (in this case, states and counties) in the Census Bureau's geographic database.

Area measurements may disagree with the information displayed on Census Bureau maps and in the TIGER® database because, for area measurement purposes, features identified as intermittent water and glaciers are reported as land area. TIGER® is an acronym for the new digital (computer-readable) geographic database that automates the mapping and related geographic activities required to support the Census Bureau's census and survey programs; TIGER® stands for Topologically Integrated Geographic Encoding and Referencing system.

The accuracy of any area measurement data is limited by the accuracy inherent in (1) the location and shape of the various boundary information in the database, (2) the location and shapes of the shorelines of water bodies in that database, and (3) rounding affecting the last digit in all operations that compute and/or sum the area measurements. Identification of land and inland, coastal, and territorial is for statistical purposes and does not necessarily reflect legal definitions thereof.

Population estimate is the estimated population from the calculated number of people living in an area as of July 1. The estimated population is calculated from a component of change model that incorporates information on natural change (births, deaths) and net migration (net internal migration, net international migration) that has occurred in an area since a Census 2000 reference date.

The Census Bureau develops county population estimates with a demographic procedure called an "administrative records component of population change" method. A major assumption underlying this approach is that the components of population change are closely approximated by administrative data in a demographic change model. In order to apply the model, Census Bureau demographers estimate each component of population change separately.

In cases where we do not have data for all counties for the current estimate year, we estimate the components of population change based on one or more simplifying assumptions. When we prepare our initial population estimates, we use the same variant of the component model with these simplifying assumptions. In the creation of current vintage population estimates, we replace the initial population estimates from the previous vintage with revised population estimates calculated with the actual data for all components of population change. Calculations of revised population estimates also incorporate updates to components of change from previous years.

The 2000 and 1990 decennial population counts are from the short-form questionnaires that were asked of all people and housing units and are often referred to as 100-percent questions because they are asked of the entire population.

Persons enumerated in the census were counted as inhabitants of their usual place of residence, which generally means the place where a person lives and sleeps most of the time. This place is not necessarily the same as the legal residence, voting residence, or domicile. In the vast majority of cases, however, the use of these different bases of classification would produce substantially the same statistics, although appreciable differences may exist for a few areas.

Rank numbers are assigned on the basis of population size, with each county area placed in descending order, largest to smallest. Where ties occur—two or more areas with identical populations—the same rank is assigned to each of the tied county areas. In such cases, the following rank number(s) is omitted so that the lowest rank is usually equal to the number of county areas ranked.

Persons per square mile of land area, also known as population density, is the average number of inhabitants per square mile of land area. These figures are derived by dividing the total number of residents by the number of square miles of land area in the specified geographic area. To determine population per square kilometer, multiply the population per square mile of land area by .3861. The figures for persons per square mile for 2006 and 2000 were calculated on the basis of land area data from the 2000 census. The figures for persons per square mile for 1990 were calculated on the basis of land area data from the 1990 census.

Table A/B-2. Components of Population Change

Components of population change, April 1, 2000, to July 1, 2006: Number—Total population change, Natural increase (Total, Births, and Deaths), Net international migration; Percent change. Population change, April 1, 1990, to April 1, 2000: Number and Percent change.

Sources: **Components of population change**—U.S. Census Bureau, Components of Population Change, "Population Estimates, Cumulative Estimates of the Components of Population Change for Counties: April 1, 2000 to July 1, 2006" (related Internet site <http://www.census.gov /popest/counties/files/CO-EST2006-alldata.txt>). **Population change**—Census 2000, Demographic Profiles 1; 1990 census, 100 percent data, STF1 (related Internet site <http://www.census.gov/main/www/cen2000.html>).

For information on **components of population change**, see the General Notes.

Natural increase refers to the excess of births over deaths.

Net international migration. International migration, in its simplest form, is defined as any movement across U.S. (50 states and District of Columbia) borders. The Census Bureau makes estimates of net international migration for the nation, states, and counties. We estimate net international migration as (1) net migration of the foreign born, (2) net movement from Puerto Rico, (3) net movement of the U.S. Armed Forces, and (4) emigration of the native born. The largest component, net migration of the foreign born, includes lawful permanent residents (immigrants), temporary migrants (such as students), humanitarian migrants (such as refugees), and people illegally present in the United States. Currently, we do not estimate these components individually.

Percent population change refers to the difference between the population of an area at the beginning and end of a time period, expressed as a percentage of the beginning population.

Table A/B-3. Population by Age, Race, Hispanic Origin, and Sex

Population characteristics, 2005: Age (percent)— Under 5 years, 5 to 14 years, 15 to 24 years, 25 to 34 years, 35 to 44 years, 45 to 54 years, 55 to 64 years, 65 to 74 years, and 75 years and over; One race (percent)—White alone, Black or African American alone, Asian alone, American Indian and Alaska Native alone, Native Hawaiian and Other Pacific Islander alone; Percent Hispanic or Latino origin; Males per 100 females.

Source: **Population characteristics**—U.S. Census Bureau, "County Population Estimates by Age, Sex, Race, and Hispanic Origin: April 1, 2000 to July 1, 2005," released August 4, 2006 (related Internet site <http://www.census.gov/popest/datasets.html>).

The **age** classification is based on the age of the person in complete years as of July 1, 2005.

The **race** classifications used by the Census Bureau adhere to the December 15, 2000 (revised from October 30, 1997) *Federal Register Notice* entitled "Revisions to the Standards for the Classification of Federal Data on Race and Ethnicity" and issued by OMB (available online at <http://www.whitehouse.gov/omb/inforeg/re _guidance2000update.pdf>). These standards govern the categories used to collect and present federal data on race and ethnicity. OMB required federal agencies to use a minimum of five race categories: White, Black or African American, American Indian and Alaska Native, Asian, and Native Hawaiian and Other Pacific Islander. For respondents unable to identify with any of these five race categories, OMB approved a sixth category—Some Other Race.

The Census 2000 question on race included three areas where respondents could write in a more specific race group. The response categories and write-in answers can be combined to create the five minimum OMB race categories plus Some Other Race. People who responded to the question on race by indicating only one race are referred to as the race-alone population, or the group that reported only one race category.

The concept of race, as used by the Census Bureau, reflects self-identification by people according to the race or races with which they most closely identify. These categories are sociopolitical constructs and should not be interpreted as being scientific or anthropological in nature. Furthermore, the race categories include both racial and national-origin groups. Caution must be used when interpreting changes in the racial composition of the U.S. population over time.

White. A person having origins in any of the original peoples of Europe, the Middle East, or North Africa. It includes people who indicate their race as White or report entries such as Irish, German, Italian, Lebanese, Near Easterner, Arab, or Polish.

Black or African American. A person having origins in any of the Black racial groups of Africa. It includes people who indicate their race as Black, African American, or Negro or who provide written entries such as African American, Afro American, Kenyan, Nigerian, or Haitian.

American Indian and Alaska Native. A person having origins in any of the original peoples of North and South America (including Central America) and who maintain tribal affiliation or community attachment. It includes people who classify themselves as described below.

American Indian includes people who indicate their race as American Indian, entered the name of an Indian tribe, or report such entries as Canadian Indian, French-American Indian, or Spanish-American Indian.

Alaska Native includes written responses of Eskimos, Aleuts, and Alaska Indians as well as entries such as Arctic Slope, Inupiat, Yupik, Alutiiq, Egegik, and Pribilovian. The Alaska tribes are the Alaskan Athabascan, Tlingit, and Haida.

Asian. A person having origins in any of the original peoples of the Far East, Southeast Asia, or the Indian subcontinent including, for example, Cambodia, China, India, Japan, Korea, Malaysia, Pakistan, the Philippine Islands, Thailand, and Vietnam. It includes Asian Indian, Chinese, Filipino, Korean, Japanese, Vietnamese, and Other Asian.

Native Hawaiian and Other Pacific Islander. A person having origins in any of the original peoples of Hawaii, Guam, Samoa, or other Pacific Islands. It includes people who indicate their race as Native Hawaiian, Guamanian or Chamorro, Samoan, and Other Pacific Islander.

Hispanic or Latino origin. People who identify with the terms Hispanic or Latino are those who classify themselves in one of the specific Hispanic or Latino categories listed on the questionnaire—Mexican, Puerto Rican, or Cuban—as well as those who indicate that they are other Spanish, Hispanic, or Latino. Origin can be viewed as the heritage, nationality group, lineage, or country of birth of the person or the person's parents or ancestors before their arrival in the United States. People who identify their origin as Spanish, Hispanic, or Latino may be any race.

The federal government considers race and Hispanic origin to be two separate and distinct concepts. For Census 2000, the questions on race and Hispanic origin were asked of every individual living in the United States. The question on Hispanic origin asked respondents if they were Spanish, Hispanic, or Latino. The question on race asked respondents to report the race or races they considered themselves to be. Both questions are based on self-identification. The question on Hispanic origin for Census 2000 was similar to the 1990 census question, except for its placement on the questionnaire. For Census 2000, the question on Hispanic origin was asked directly before the question on race.

Table A/B-4. Population Characteristics

Households, 2000: Total and With individuals under 18 years (percent of total). Educational attainment, 2000: Total persons, High school graduate or higher (percent), and Bachelor's degree or higher (percent). Foreign-born population, 2000 (percent). Persons 5 years and over: Speaking a language other than English at home, 2000 (percent) and Residing in same house in 1995 and 2000 (percent). Workers who drove alone to work, 2000 (percent). Households with income of $75,000 or more in 1999 (percent). Persons in poverty (percent): 2004 and 2000.

Sources: **Households**—U.S. Census Bureau, 2000 Census of Population and Housing, "Census 2000 Profiles of General Demographic Characteristics," data files, (DP1) accessed June 14, 2002 (related Internet site <http://www.census.gov/Press-Release/www/2002/demoprofiles.html>). **Educational attainment, foreign-born population, language, residence, commuting, and income**—U.S. Census Bureau, "Census 2000 Profiles of General Demographic Characteristics," data files, (DP2) accessed June 14, 2002 (related Internet site <http://www.census.gov/Press-Release/www/2002/demoprofiles.html>). **Poverty**—U.S. Census Bureau, Small Area Income and Poverty Estimates, accessed December 4, 2006 (related Internet site <http://www.census.gov/hhes/www/saipe/index.html>).

A **household** includes all of the people who occupy a housing unit. People not living in households are classified as living in group quarters.

Data on **educational attainment** in 2000 were derived from answers to the questionnaire, which was asked of a sample of persons. Data are tabulated as attainment for persons 25 years old and over. Persons are classified according to the highest level of school completed or the highest degree received. Respondents were asked to report the level of the previous grade attended or the highest degree received for the persons currently enrolled in school. The question included response categories that allowed persons to report completing the twelfth grade without receiving a high school diploma and that instructed respondents to report as "high school graduate(s)" persons who received either a high school diploma or the equivalent; for example, passed the Test of General Educational Development (GED) and did not attend college. The category "High school graduate or higher" covers persons whose highest degree was a high school

diploma or its equivalent; persons who attended college or professional school; and persons who received a college, university, or professional degree. Persons who reported completing the twelfth grade but not receiving a diploma are not included.

Foreign-born population. The Census Bureau separates the U.S. resident population into two groups based on whether or not a person was a U.S. citizen at the time of birth. Anyone born in the United States or U.S. island area (such as Puerto Rico) or born abroad to a U.S. citizen parent is a U.S. citizen at the time of birth and, consequently, included in the native population. The term "foreign-born population" refers to anyone who is not a U.S. citizen at birth. This includes naturalized U.S. citizens, legal permanent resident aliens (immigrants), temporary migrants (such as students), humanitarian migrants (such as refugees), and people illegally present in the United States.

For the 2000 census, persons were asked to report whether they sometimes or always **spoke a language other than English** at home. People who knew languages other than English but did not use them at home, who only used them elsewhere, or whose usage was limited to a few expressions or slang were excluded. Most people who reported speaking a language other than English at home also speak English. Tabulations of language spoken at home include only the responses of persons 5 years old and over. The percentage shown is obtained by dividing the number of persons speaking a language other than English at home by the total number of persons 5 years and over.

Persons **living in the same house in 1995 and 2000** are those who responded "Yes, this house" to the 2000 census question, "Did this person live in this house or apartment five years ago (on April 1, 1995)?" The category includes not only persons who did not move during the 5 years, but also those who had moved but by census day had returned to their 1995 residence. Census questions also asked for the state (or foreign country), U.S. county, city or town, and ZIP code of residence on April 1, 1995, for those people who reported that on that date they lived in a different house than their current residence. Residence 5 years earlier is used in conjunction with location of current residence to determine the extent of residential mobility of the population. Data were tabulated for persons 5 years old and over, and the percentage shown is derived by dividing the number of persons living in the same house by the total number of persons 5 years old and over.

Data on **driving alone to work** in 2000 are derived from questions asked to workers 16 years and over who were employed and at work during the reference week. Respondents who answered "Car, truck, or van" to the 2000 census question, "How did this person usually get to work last week?" were also asked, "How many people, including this person, usually rode in the car, truck, or van last week?" Data from respondents who answered "Drove alone" to this latter question are included in the tabulation.

Household income and poverty. Data for 2000 household income and persons below poverty level are based on the Small Area Income and Poverty Estimates (SAIPE) program. This program was started by the Census Bureau with support from other federal agencies in order to provide more current estimates of selected income and poverty statistics than the most recent decennial census. Estimates are created for states, counties, and school districts (not shown in this publication). These updated estimates of income and poverty statistics are used for the administration of federal programs and the allocation of federal funds to local jurisdictions.

The estimates are not direct counts from enumerations or administrative records, nor direct estimates from sample surveys. Data from these sources are not adequate to provide intercensal estimates for all counties. Instead, a model is employed that utilizes the relation between income or poverty and tax and program data for the states and a subset of counties using estimates of income or poverty from the Current Population Survey (CPS). The models involved use selected variables based on survey and administrative sources including income and poverty estimates derived from the March CPS; direct estimates of income and poverty from the 1990 decennial census data; data summarized from federal individual income tax returns; number of food stamp recipients; information from the Bureau of Economic Analysis (BEA), in the form of personal income estimates; supplemental security income recipients; and demographic intercensal estimates of the population of states and counties by age and group quarters status.

Household income is total money income received in a calendar year by all household members 15 years and over. Total money income is the sum of amounts reported separately for income from wages or salaries; nonfarm self-employment; farm self-employment; social security; public assistance; and all other regularly received income such as veterans' payments, pensions, unemployment compensation, and alimony. Receipts not counted as income include various "lump-sum" payments such as capital gains or inheritances. The total represents the amount of income received before deductions for personal income taxes, social security, bond purchases, union dues, Medicare deductions, etc. Household income differs from family income by including income received by all household members, not just those related to the householder, and by persons living alone or in other nonfamily households. Income is derived on a sample basis.

Poverty is defined in relation to family income. Families and unrelated individuals are classified as above or below the poverty level by comparing their total income to an income cutoff or "poverty threshold." The income cutoffs vary by family size, number of children, and age of the family householder or unrelated individual. Poverty status is determined for all families (and, by implication, all family members). Poverty status is also determined for persons not in families, except for inmates of institutions, members of the Armed Forces living in barracks, college students living in dormitories, and unrelated individuals under 15 years. Poverty status is derived on a sample basis.

Table A/B-5. Births, Deaths, and Infant Deaths

Births: Number—2004 and 2000 and Rate per 1,000 population—2004 and 2000. Deaths: Number—2004 and 2000 and Rate per 1,000 population—2004 and 2000. Infant deaths: Number—2004, 2000, and 1990 and Rate per 1,000 live births—2004, 2000, and 1990.

Source: **Births, deaths, and infant deaths**—U.S. National Center for Health Statistics, Division of Vital Statistics, accessed January 25, 2007 (related Internet site <http://www.cdc.gov>), and unpublished data.

Through the National Vital Statistics System, the National Center for Health Statistics (NCHS) collects and publishes data on **births** and **deaths** in the United States. The Division of Vital Statistics obtains information on births and deaths from the registration offices of all states, New York City, and the District of Columbia. In most areas, practically all births and deaths are registered. The most recent test of the completeness of birth registration, conducted on a sample of births from 1964 to 1968, showed that 99.3 percent of all births in the United States during that period were registered. No comparable information is available for deaths, but it is generally believed that death registration in the United States is at least as complete as birth registration.

Births and deaths statistics are limited to events occurring during the year. The data are by place of residence and exclude events occurring to nonresidents of the United States. Births or deaths that occur outside the United States are excluded. **Birth** and **death rates** represent the number of births and deaths per 1,000 resident population. **Infant death rates** represent the number of deaths of infants under 1 year of age per 1,000 live births. They exclude fetal deaths.

Table A/B-6. Physicians, Community Hospitals, Medicare, Social Security, and Supplemental Security Income

Physicians, 2004: Number and Rate per 100,000 persons. Community hospitals, 2004: Number and Beds—Number and Rate per 100,000 persons. Medicare program enrollment, 2005: Total, Percent change, 2000–2005, and Rate per 100,000 persons.

Social Security program beneficiaries, December 2005: Number, Rate per 100,000 persons, Percent change, 2000–2005, and Retired workers, number. Supplemental Security Income program recipients, 2005: Number and Rate per 100,000 persons.

Sources: **Physicians**—American Medical Association, Chicago, IL, *Physician Characteristics and Distribution in the U.S.*, annual (copyright), accessed May 17, 2006. **Community hospitals**—Health Forum LLC, an American Hospital Association (AHA) Company, Chicago, IL, *Hospital Statistics*, and unpublished data (copyright), e-mail accessed May 4, 2006 (related Internet site <http://www.healthforum.com>). **Medicare program enrollment**—Centers for Medicare and Medicaid Services, CMS Statistics, Medicare Enrollment, accessed February 8, 2006 (related Internet site <http://www.cms.hhs.gov/>). **Social Security program**—U.S. Social Security Administration, Office of Research, Evaluation, and Statistics, OASDI Beneficiaries by State and County, accessed October 24, 2006 (related Internet site <http://www.ssa.gov/policy/docs/statcomps/oasdi_sc/2005/>). **Supplementary Security Income program**—U.S. Social Security Administration, Office of Research, Evaluation, and Statistics, *SSI Recipients by State and County, 2005*, accessed July 24, 2006 (related Internet site <http://www.ssa.gov/policy/docs/statcomps/ssi_sc/2005/>).

The number of **physicians** covers active, nonfederal physicians, as of December 31 of the year shown. The figures are based on information contained in the American Medical Association (AMA) Physician Masterfile. The file has been maintained by the AMA since 1906 and includes information on every physician in the country and on those graduates of American medical schools who are temporarily practicing overseas. The file also includes members and nonmembers of the AMA and graduates of foreign medical schools who are in the United States and meet U.S. education standards for primary recognition as physicians. Thus, all physicians comprising the total manpower pool are included on the file. However, this publication excludes data for all federal physicians and nonfederal physicians who are temporarily in foreign locations.

Masterfile data are obtained from both AMA surveys and inputs from physicians, other organizations, and institutions. Primary sources are as follows: medical schools, hospitals, medical societies, national boards, state licensing agencies, the Educational Commission for Foreign Medical Graduates, the Surgeon General of the U.S. Government, the American Board of Medical Specialties, and physicians.

The physician rate per 100,000 persons is based on the resident population estimated as of July 1, 2004.

Community hospitals are defined as nonfederal, short-term (average length of stay less than 30 days), general, or other special hospitals whose facilities and services are available to the public; psychiatric and tuberculosis hospitals and hospital units of institutions are excluded. Data for beds are based on the average number of beds in the facilities over the reporting period. The rate is per 100,000 resident population estimated as of July 1, 2004.

Medicare enrollment. When first implemented in 1966, Medicare covered only most persons aged 65 and over. By the end of 1966, 3.7 million persons had received at least some health care services covered by Medicare. In 1973, other groups became eligible for Medicare benefits: persons who are entitled to social security or Railroad Retirement disability benefits for at least 24 months; persons with end stage renal disease (ESRD) requiring continuing dialysis or kidney transplant; and certain otherwise noncovered aged persons who elect to buy into Medicare. Medicare consists of two primary parts: Hospital Insurance (HI), also known as Part A, and Supplementary Medical Insurance (SMI), also known as Part B. Health care services covered under Medicare's Hospital Insurance include inpatient hospital care, skilled nursing facility care, home health agency care, and hospice care. SMI coverage is optional and required payment of a monthly premium. SMI helps pay for physician, outpatient hospital, home health, and other services for the aged and disabled who have voluntarily enrolled.

Social security. The Old-Age, Survivors, and Disability Insurance Program (OASDI) provides monthly benefits for retired and disabled insured workers and their dependents and to survivors of insured workers. To be eligible for benefits, a worker must have had a specified period of employment in which OASDI taxes were paid. A worker becomes eligible for full retirement benefits at age 65, although reduced benefits may be obtained up to 3 years earlier; the worker's spouse is under the same limitations. Survivor benefits are payable to dependents of deceased insured workers. Disability benefits are payable to an insured worker under age 65 with a prolonged disability and to that person's dependents on the same basis as dependents of a retired worker. Also, disability benefits are payable at age 50 to the disabled widow or widower of a deceased worker who was fully insured at the time of death. A lump-sum benefit is generally payable on the death of an insured worker to a spouse or minor children.

The data were derived from the Master Beneficiary Record (MBR), the principal administrative file of social security beneficiaries. Data for total recipients and retired workers include persons with special age-72 benefits. Special age-72 benefit represents the monthly benefit payable to men who attained age 72 before 1972 and for women who attained age 72 before 1970 and who do not have sufficient quarters to qualify for a retired-worker benefit under either the fully or the transitionally insured status provision.

The **Supplemental Security Income** (SSI) program provides cash payments in accordance with nationwide eligibility requirements to persons who are aged, blind, or disabled with limited income and resources. Under the SSI program, each person living in his or her own household is provided a cash payment from the federal government that is sufficient, when added to the person's countable income (the total gross money income of an individual less certain exclusions), to bring the total monthly income up to a specified level (the federal benefit rate). If the individual or couple is living in another household, the guaranteed level is reduced by one-third.

An aged person is defined as an individual who is 65 years or over. A blind person is anyone with vision of 20/200 or less with the use of correcting lens in the better eye or with tunnel vision of 20 degrees or less. The disabled classification refers to any person unable to engage in any substantial gainful activity by reason of any medically determinable physical or mental impairment expected to result in death or that has lasted or can be expected to last for a continuous period of at least 12 months. For a child under 18 years, eligibility is based on disability or severity comparable with that of an adult, since the criterion of "substantial gainful activity" is inapplicable for children.

Table A/B-7. Housing Units and Building Permits

Housing units: 2005, 2000, and 1990; Net change, 2000–2005—Number and Percent; Units per square mile of land area—2005 and 1990. Housing 2000, percent: Owner-occupied housing units and Units in multiunit structures. New private housing units authorized by building permits: Cumulative, 2000–2005 period, 2005, and 2004.

Sources: **Housing units, 2005 and 2000**—U.S. Census Bureau, "Annual Estimates of Housing Units for Counties: April 1, 2000 to July 1, 2005," accessed November 14, 2005 (related Internet site <http://www.census.gov /popest/housing/HU-EST2005-4.html>). **Housing units, 1990**—U.S. Census Bureau, 1990 Census of Population and Housing, Summary Tape File (STF) 1C on CD-ROM (archive). **Housing 2000**—U.S. Census Bureau, 2000 Census of Population and Housing, Census 2000 Profiles of General Demographic Characteristics data files, accessed July 19, 2005 (related Internet site <http://censtats.census .gov/pub/Profiles.shtml>). **Building permits**—U.S. Census Bureau, "New Residential Construction—Building Permits," May 24, 2006, e-mail from Manufacturing, Mining, and Construction Statistics Branch, subject: Annual Place Level Data 2000–2005 (related Internet site <http://www.census.gov/const/www/permitsindex .html>).

A **housing unit** is a house, apartment, mobile home or trailer, group of rooms, or single room occupied or, if

vacant, intended for occupancy as separate living quarters. Separate living quarters are those in which the occupants do not live and eat with any other persons in the structure and which have direct access from the outside of the building through a common hall. A housing unit is classified as occupied if it is the usual place of residence of the person or group of people living in it at the time of census enumeration or if the occupants are only temporarily absent; that is, away on vacation or business. All occupied housing units are classified as either owner occupied or renter occupied. A housing unit is **owner occupied** if the owner or co-owner lives in the unit even if it is mortgaged or not fully paid for. All occupied housing units, which are not owner occupied, whether they are rented for cash rent or occupied without payment of cash rent, are classified as renter occupied. **Multiunit structures** are structures containing two or more housing units.

Units per square mile of land area is the average number of housing units per square mile of land area. These figures are derived by dividing the total number of housing units by the number of square miles of land area in the specified geographic area. To determine housing units per square kilometer, multiply the units per square mile of land area by .3861. The figures for units per square mile of land area for 2005 were calculated on the basis of land area data from the 2000 census. The figures for units per square mile of land area for 1990 were calculated on the basis of land area data from the 1990 census.

Building permits data are based on reports submitted by local building permit officials in response to a Census Bureau mail survey. They are obtained using Form C-404, "Report of New Privately Owned Residential Building or Zoning Permits Issued." Data are collected from individual permit offices, most of which are municipalities; the remainder are counties, townships, or New England and Middle Atlantic-type towns. Currently, there are 19,000 permit-issuing places. When a report is not received, missing data are either (1) obtained from the Survey of Use of Permits, which is used to collect information on housing starts, or (2) imputed.

The data relate to new private housing units intended for occupancy on a housekeeping basis. They exclude mobile homes (trailers), hotels, motels, and group residential structures, such as nursing homes and college dormitories. They also exclude conversions of and alterations to existing buildings. A housing unit consists of a room or group of rooms intended for occupancy as separate living quarters by a family, by a group of unrelated persons living together, or by a person living alone.

Table A/B-8. Crime—Number of Offenses

Violent crimes: 2004—Total, Murder and non-negligent manslaughter, Forcible rape, Robbery, and

Aggravated assault; 2000. Property crimes: 2004—Total, Burglary, Larceny-theft, and Motor vehicle theft; 2000.

Source: **Crime**—U.S. Department of Justice, Federal Bureau of Investigation, Uniform Crime Reporting Program, unpublished data, annual (related Internet site <http://www.fbi.gov/>).

Data presented on **crime** are through the voluntary contribution of crime statistics by law enforcement agencies across the United States. The Uniform Crime Reporting (UCR) Program provides periodic assessments of crime in the nation as measured by offenses coming to the attention of the law enforcement community. The Committee of Uniform Crime Records of the International Association of Chiefs of Police initiated this voluntary national data-collection effort in 1930. UCR program contributors compile and submit their crime data in one of two means: either directly to the Federal Bureau of Investigation (FBI) or through the state UCR programs.

Users of these data are cautioned about comparing data between areas based on these respective Crime Index figures. Assessing criminality and law enforcement's responses from area to area should encompass many elements (i.e., population density and urbanization, population composition, stability of population, modes of transportation, commuting patterns and highway systems, economic conditions, cultural conditions, family conditions, climate, effective strength and emphasis of law enforcement agencies, attitudes of citizenry toward crime, and crime reporting practices). These elements may have a significant impact on crime reporting. Also, not all law enforcement agencies provide data for all 12 months of the year, and some agencies fail to report at all. Data are as reported to the FBI.

Seven offenses, because of their seriousness, frequency of occurrence, and likelihood of being reported to police, were initially selected to serve as an index for evaluating fluctuations in the volume of crime. These crimes, known as the Crime Index offenses, were murder and non-negligent manslaughter, forcible rape, robbery, aggravated assault, burglary, larceny-theft, and motor vehicle theft. By congressional mandate, arson was added as the eighth index offense in 1979. Only the Modified Index includes arson. In 2004, the FBI discontinued the use of the Crime Index in the UCR Program and decided to publish a violent crime total and a property crime total until a more viable index is developed.

Violent crimes include four crime categories: (1) Murder and nonnegligent manslaughter, as defined in the UCR program, is the willful (nonnegligent) killing of one human being by another. This offense excludes deaths caused by negligence, suicide, or accident; justifiable homicides; and attempts to murder or assaults to murder. (2) Forcible rape is the carnal knowledge of a female forcibly and against

her will. Assaults or attempts to commit rape by force or threat of force are also included; however, statutory rape (without force) and other sex offenses are excluded. (3) Robbery is the taking or attempting to take anything of value from the car, custody, or control of a person or persons by force or threat of force or violence and/or by putting the victim in fear. (4) Aggravated assault is an unlawful attack by one person upon another for the purpose of inflicting severe or aggravated bodily injury. This type of assault is usually accompanied by the use of a weapon or by means likely to produce death or great bodily harm. Attempts are included since an injury does not necessarily have to result when a gun, knife, or other weapon is used, which could and probably would result in a serious personal injury if the crime were successfully completed.

In general, **property crimes** include four crime categories: (1) Burglary is the unlawful entry of a structure to commit a felony or theft. (2) Larceny-theft is the unlawful taking, carrying, leading, or riding away of a property from the possession or constructive possession of another. It includes crimes such as shoplifting, pocket picking, purse snatching, thefts from motor vehicles, thefts of motor vehicle parts and accessories, and bicycle thefts, in which no use of force, violence, or fraud occurs. This crime category does not include embezzlement, "con" games, forgery, worthless checks, and motor vehicle theft. (3) Motor vehicle theft is the theft or attempted theft of a motor vehicle. This definition excludes the taking of a motor vehicle for temporary use by those persons having lawful access. (4) Arson is any willful or malicious burning or attempt to burn, with or without intent to defraud, a dwelling house, public building, motor vehicle or aircraft, personal property of another, etc. Only fires determined through investigation to have been willfully or maliciously set are classified as arson. Fires of suspicious or unknown origins are excluded. In this publication, arson is not included in property crime figures.

Table A/B-9. Personal Income and Earnings by Industries

Personal income: Total, by place of residence—2005, 2004, and 2000; Percent change: 2004–2005 and 2000–2005; Per capita—2005 and 2000; Earnings, by place of work, 2005—Total and Percent by selected major industries (Construction, Retail trade, Professional and technical services, Health care and social assistance, and Government).

Source: **Personal income and earnings**—U.S. Bureau of Economic Analysis, Regional Economic Information System (REIS), downloaded estimates and software, accessed June 5, 2007 (related Internet site <http://www.bea.gov/regional/docs/reis2005dvd.cfm>).

The **personal income** of an area is defined as the income received by, or on behalf of, all the residents of that area. It consists of the income received by persons from all sources, that is, from participation in production, from both government and business transfer payments, and from government interest. Personal income is the sum of wage and salary disbursements, other labor income, proprietors' income, rental income of persons, personal dividend income, personal interest income, and transfer payments, less personal contributions for social insurance.

Personal income differs by definition from money income, which is prepared by the Census Bureau, in that money income is measured before deduction of personal contributions for social insurance and does not include imputed income, lump-sum payments, and income received by quasi-individuals. Money income does include income from private pensions and annuities and from interpersonal transfer, such as child support; therefore it is not comparable to personal income. Total personal income is adjusted to place of residence.

About 90 percent of the state and county estimates of personal income are based on census data and on administrative-records data that are collected by other federal agencies. The data from censuses are mainly collected from the recipient of the income. The most important source of census data for state and county estimates is the census of population and housing that is conducted by the Census Bureau. The data from administrative records may originate either from the recipients of the income or from the source of the income. These data are a by-product of the administration of various federal and state government programs. The most important sources of these data are as follows: the state unemployment insurance programs of the Employment and Training Administration, U.S. Department of Labor; the social insurance programs of the Social Security Administration (SSA) and the Health Care Financing Administration, U.S. Department of Health and Human Services; the federal income tax program of the IRS, U.S. Department of the Treasury; the veterans' benefit programs of the U.S. Department of Veterans Affairs; and the military payroll systems of the U.S. Department of Defense (DoD). The remaining 10 percent of the estimates are based on data from other sources. For example, the estimates of the components of farm proprietors' income, a component of personal income, are partly based on the state estimates of farm income and the county estimates of cash receipts, crop production, and livestock inventory that are prepared by the U.S. Department of Agriculture, which uses sample surveys, along with census data and administrative-records data, to derive its estimates.

Total **earnings** cover wage and salary disbursements, other labor income, and proprietors' income. Wage and salary disbursements are defined as monetary remuneration of employees, including corporate officers; commissions, tips, and bonuses; and pay-in-kind that represents income to the recipient. They are measured before such deductions as social security contributions and union

dues. All disbursements in the current period are covered. "Pay-in-kind" represents allowances for food, clothing, and lodging paid in kind to employees, which represent income to them, valued at the cost to the employer. Other labor income consists of employer contributions to privately administered pension and welfare funds and a few small items such as directors' fees, compensation of prison inmates, and miscellaneous judicial fees. Proprietors' income is the monetary income and income in-kind of proprietorships and partnerships, including the independent professions, and of tax-exempt cooperatives.

Table A/B-10. Labor Force and Private Business Establishments and Employment

Civilian labor force: Total—2006, 2000 and Net change, 2000–2006; Number of unemployed—2006 and 2000; Unemployment rate—2006 and 2000. Private nonfarm businesses: Establishments—2004 and Net change, 2000–2004; Employment—2004 and Net change, 2000–2004; Annual payroll per employee, 2004—Amount and Percent of U.S. average.

Sources: **Civilian labor force**—U.S. Bureau of Labor Statistics, *Local Area Unemployment Statistics, Annual Averages*, accessed April 17, 2007 (related Internet site <http://www.bls.gov/lau>). **Private nonfarm businesses**—U.S. Census Bureau, *County Business Patterns*, accessed July 12, 2006 (related Internet site <http://www.census.gov/epcd/cbp/view/cbpview.html>).

Civilian labor force data are the product of a federal-state cooperative program in which state employment security agencies prepare labor force and unemployment estimates under concepts, definitions, and technical procedures established by the Bureau of Labor Statistics (BLS). These data for substate areas are produced by BLS primarily for use in allocating funds under various federal legislative programs. Users of these data are cautioned that, because of the small size of many of the areas, as well as limitations of the data inputs, the estimates are subject to considerable, but nonquantifiable, error. An explanation of the technical procedures used to develop monthly and annual local area labor force estimates appears monthly in the explanatory note for state and area unemployment data in the BLS periodical, *Employment and Earnings*. Additional information may also be found at the BLS Web site at <http://www.bls.gov/opub/hom>.

The civilian labor force comprises all civilians 16 years and over classified as employed or unemployed. Employed persons are all civilians who, during the survey week, did any work at all as paid employees in their own business, profession, or on their own farm or who worked 15 hours or more as unpaid workers in an enterprise operated by a member of the family. It also includes all those who were not working but who had jobs or businesses from which they were temporarily absent because of illness, bad weather, vacation, labor-management disputes, job training, or personal reasons, whether they were paid for the time off or were seeking other jobs. Each employed person is counted only once. Those who held more than one job are counted in the job at which they worked the greatest number of hours during the survey week, the calendar week including the 12th of the month.

Unemployed persons are all civilians 16 years and over who had no employment during the survey week and were available for work, except for temporary illness, and had made specific efforts to find employment some time during the prior 4 weeks. Persons who were laid off or were waiting to report to a new job within 30 days did not need to be looking for work to be classified as unemployed. The unemployment rate for all civilian workers represents the number of unemployed as a percent of the civilian labor force.

Private business establishments and employment. County Business Patterns (CBP) is an annual series that provides subnational economic data by industry. The series is useful for studying the economic activity of small areas; analyzing economic changes over time; and as a benchmark for statistical series, surveys, and databases between economic censuses. CBP covers most of the country's economic activity. The series excludes data on self-employed individuals, employees of private households, railroad employees, agricultural production employees, and most government employees. Data for 1997 and earlier years are based on the SIC system.

CBP data are extracted from the Business Register, the Census Bureau's file of all known single and multiestablishment companies. The Annual Company Organization Survey and quinquennial economic censuses provide individual establishment data for multilocation firms. Data for single-location firms are obtained from various program censuses, the Annual Survey of Manufactures, and Current Business Surveys, as well as from administrative records of the IRS, SSA, and BLS.

This series has been published annually since 1964 and at irregular intervals dating back to 1946. The comparability of data over time may be affected by definitional changes in establishments, activity status, and industrial classifications.

An **establishment** is a single physical location at which business is conducted or services or industrial operations are performed. It is not necessarily identical with a company or enterprise, which may consist of one or more establishments. When two or more activities are carried on at a single location under a single ownership, all activities generally are grouped together as a single establishment. The entire establishment is classified on the basis of its major activity and all data are included in that classification.

Establishment counts represent the number of locations with paid employees any time during the year. This series excludes governmental establishments except for wholesale liquor establishments (NAICS 4248), retail liquor stores (NAICS 44531), federally chartered savings institutions (NAICS 522120), federally chartered credit unions (NAICS 522130), and hospitals (NAICS 622).

Total **payroll** includes all forms of compensation, such as salaries, wages, reported tips, commissions, bonuses, vacation allowances, sick-leave pay, employee contributions to qualified pension plans, and the value of taxable fringe benefits. For corporations, it includes amounts paid to officers and executives; for unincorporated businesses, it does not include profit or other compensation of proprietors or partners. Payroll is reported before deductions for social security, income tax, insurance, union dues, etc. First-quarter payroll consists of payroll during the January-to-March quarter.

Table A/B-11. Banking, Retail Trade, and Accommodation and Food Services

Banking, 2005: Offices—Number and Rate per 10,000 people; Total deposits. Retail trade, 2002: Establishments; Sales—Total, Per capita, and General merchandise stores, percent of total. Accommodation and food services, 2002: Establishments; Sales—Total, Per capita, Percent change, 1997–2002, and Food services, percent of total.

Sources: **Banking**—U.S. Federal Deposit Insurance Corporation (FDIC) and Office of Thrift Supervision (OTS), 2005 Bank and Thrift Branch Office Data Book: Summary of Deposits, accessed August 9, 2006 (related Internet site <http://www2.fdic.gov/sod/index.asp>). **Retail trade**—U.S. Census Bureau, 2002 Economic Census, *Retail Trade, Geographic Area Series*, accessed June 21, 2005 (related Internet site <http://www.census.gov/econ /census02/>). **Accommodation and food services**—U.S. Census Bureau, 1997 and 2002 Economic Censuses, *Accommodation and Food Services, Geographic Area Series*, accessed June 21, 2005 (related Internet site <http://www.census.gov/econ/census02/>).

Banking. The FDIC and OTS collect deposit data on each office of every FDIC-insured bank and savings institution as of June 30 of each year in the Summary of Deposits (SOD) survey. The FDIC surveys all FDIC-insured commercial banks, savings banks, and U.S. branches of foreign banks, and the OTS surveys all savings associations. Data presented here exclude U.S. branch offices of foreign banks. For all counties, individual banking offices—not the combined totals of the bank—are the source of the data.

Insured savings institutions include all FDIC-insured (OTS-Regulated and FDIC-Regulated) financial institutions that operate under federal or state banking charters.

The number of **banking offices** in any given area includes every location at which deposit business is transacted. Banking office is defined to include all offices and facilities that actually hold deposits, but to exclude loan production offices, computer centers, and other nondeposit installations, such as automated teller machines (ATMs). The term "offices" includes both main offices and branches. An institution with four branches operates a total of five offices.

Retail trade data presented are based on NAICS for 2002 and are not entirely comparable with previous data for earlier economic censuses (see "General Note for Economic Censuses"). The data cover only establishments with payroll. The Retail Trade sector (NAICS codes 44–45) comprises establishments engaged in retailing merchandise, generally without transformation, and rendering services incidental to the sale of merchandise. The retailing process is the final step in the distribution of merchandise; retailers are, therefore, organized to sell merchandise in small quantities to the general public. This sector comprises two main types of retailers: store (operate fixed point-of-sale locations, located and designed to attract a high volume of walk-in customers) and nonstore retailers (establishments of this subsector reach customers and market merchandise with methods, such as the broadcasting of "infomercials," the broadcasting and publishing of direct-response advertising, the publishing of paper and electronic catalogs, door-to-door solicitation, in-home demonstration, selling from portable stalls [street vendors, except food], and distribution through vending machines). For more detailed information on subsectors of the retail trade industry, see the list of codes with definitions at Internet site <http://www.census.gov/epcd /www/naics.html>.

An **establishment** is a single physical location at which business is conducted or where services or industrial operations are performed. It is not necessarily identical with the company or enterprise, which may consist of one or more establishments. The count of establishments represents the number in business at any time during the year.

Sales for the Retail Trade sector includes merchandise sold for cash or credit at retail and wholesale by establishments primarily engaged in retail trade; amounts received from customers for layaway purchases; receipts from rental of vehicles, equipment, instruments, tools, etc.; receipts for delivery, installation, maintenance, repair, alteration, storage, and other services; the total value of service contracts; gasoline, liquor, tobacco, and other excise taxes that are paid by the manufacturer or wholesaler and passed on to the retailer; and shipping and handling receipts. Sales are net after deductions for refunds and allowances for merchandise returned by customers. Trade-in allowances are not deducted from sales. Sales do not include carrying or other credit charges; sales and

other taxes (including Hawaii's General Excise Tax) collected from customers and forwarded to taxing authorities; gross sales and receipts of departments or concessions operated by other companies; and commissions or receipts from the sale of government lottery tickets. Sales do not include retail sales made by manufacturers, wholesalers, service establishments, or other businesses whose primary activity is other than retail trade. They do include receipts other than from the sale of merchandise at retail, e.g., service receipts, sales to industrial users, and sales to other retailers, by establishments primarily engaged in retail trade. Sales figures represent the sales of all establishments in business at any time during the year.

Accommodation and food services data presented are based on NAICS for 2002. The data cover only establishments with payroll. The Accommodation and Food Services sector (NAICS code 72) comprises establishments providing customers with lodging and/or prepared meals, snacks, and beverages for immediate consumption. This sector is comprised of hotels and other lodging places that were formerly classified in the SIC system in Division I, Services, and eating and drinking places and mobile food services that were classified in SIC Division G, Retail Trade. This new sector includes both accommodation and food services establishments because the two activities are often combined at the same establishment. Excluded from this sector are civic and social organizations, amusement and recreation parks, theaters, and other recreation or entertainment facilities providing food and beverage services.

For the definition of establishments, see "Retail trade" above.

Sales for the Accommodation and Food Services sector includes sales from customers for services rendered, from the use of facilities, and from merchandise sold. If tax-exempt, includes dues and assessments from members and affiliates. Sales do not include carrying or other credit charges; sales and other taxes (including Hawaii's General Excise Tax) collected from customers and forwarded to taxing authorities; gross sales and receipts of departments or concessions operated by other companies; and commissions or receipts from the sale of government lottery tickets.

Sales in the food services sector cover the industries in the Food Services and Drinking Places subsector that prepare meals, snacks, and beverages to customer order for immediate on-premises and off-premises consumption. There is a wide range of establishments in these industries. Some provide food and drink only; while others provide various combinations of seating space, waiter/ waitress services, and incidental amenities, such as limited entertainment. The industries in the subsector are grouped based on the type and level of services provided.

The industry groups are full-service restaurants; limited-service eating places; special food services, such as food service contractors, caterers, and mobile food services, and drinking places.

Table A/B-12. Government Expenditure, Earnings, and Employment

Federal government expenditure: 2004—Total, Percent change, 2000–2004, Per capita, and Direct payments to individuals, percent of total; 2000. Federal, state, and local governments: Earnings—2005 (Total, Percent of total, and Percent change, 2000–2005) and 2000; Employment—2005 (Total, Percent of total, and Percent change, 2000–2005) and 2000.

Sources: **Federal government expenditure**—U.S. Census Bureau, *Consolidated Federal Funds Report*, accessed February 28, 2006 (related Internet site <http://www.census.gov/govs/www/cffr.html>). **Government earnings and employment**—U.S. Bureau of Economic Analysis, Regional Economic Information System (REIS), downloaded estimates and software, accessed June 5, 2007 (related Internet site <http://www.bea.gov/regional/docs/reis2005dvd.cfm>).

Data on **federal expenditure** and obligations were obtained from a report prepared in accordance with the Consolidated Federal Funds Report (CFFR) Act of 1982 (P.L. 97-326) (1983–1985), amended Act of 1986 (P.L. 99-547) (1986–1994), which specified that the following reporting systems and agencies be used as data sources: Federal Assistance Award Data System (FAADS), Federal Procurement Data Center (FPDC), Office of Personnel Management (OPM), DoD, U.S. Postal Service (USPS), IRS, U.S. Coast Guard (USCG), Public Health Service (PHS), National Oceanic and Atmospheric Administration (NOAA), and Federal Bureau of Investigation (FBI). In addition, several other agencies were requested to provide data, usually for selected programs. For more information on the methodology and sources of data utilized, see the introduction and Appendix D of the *Consolidated Federal Funds Report for Fiscal Year 1999* found on the Census Bureau's Web site at <http://www.census.gov/prod/2000pubs/cffr-99.pdf>.

The CFFR covers federal government expenditure or obligation for direct payments for individuals, procurement, grants, salaries and wages, direct loans, and guaranteed loans and insurance. The dollar amounts reported under these categories can represent actual expenditures or obligations. The grants and procurement data represent obligated funds, while salaries, wages, and direct payments represent actual expenditures. Data on loan and insurance programs generally represent the contingent liability of the federal government.

Most data covering **direct payments for individuals** were taken from information reported to the FAADS. The two object areas of direct payments for individuals are (1) direct payments for retirement and disability benefits and (2) all other direct payments for individuals.

Government earnings consist of the wages and salaries of civilian employees of the federal government, cash wages (including allowances) of full-time military personnel and of the members of the Military Reserves including the National Guard and pay-in-kind provided to enlisted personnel, and wages and salaries of state and local government employment. Wages and salaries paid to employees of the USPS are included in federal civilian earnings. Employer contributions to government employee retirement plans and employer contributions for government social insurance, which are part of supplements to wages and salaries, are also included in government earnings.

Government employment estimates are a companion series to the personal income estimates from BEA (see text, Table A/B-9. Personal Income and Earnings by Industries). The estimates are constructed primarily from the BLS ES-202 program and the Unemployment Compensation for Federal Employees program. The employment estimates are the average of 12 monthly observations of a number of full-time and part-time employees. BEA adjusts data from these programs based on information from other sources, such as the DoD, U.S. Department of Education, and Census Bureau. Government includes the executive, legislative, judicial, administrative, and regulatory activities of federal, state, and local governments.

Table A/B-13. Local Government Finances and Elections

Local government employment, March 2002: Total employment and Total payroll. Local government finances, 2002: General revenue—Total, Per capita, and Taxes (Total and Property, percent of total); Total debt outstanding—Amount and Per capita. Elections, 2004: Votes cast for President—Total, Percent change, 2000–2004, Republican candidate, percent of total, and Democratic candidate, percent of total.

Sources: **Local government employment and finances**—U.S. Census Bureau, 2000 Census of Governments, Compendium of Government Employment, accessed November 20, 2006; Finances, accessed August 6, 2006 (related Internet site <http://www.census.gov/govs/www/cog2002.html>). **Elections, 2004**—CQ Press, 2005, *America Votes 2003–2004*, Washington, DC (copyrighted and printed with permission of CQ Press) (related Internet site <http://www.cqpress.com>).

A census of governments is taken at 5-year intervals as required by law under Title 13, United States Code, Section 161. This 2002 census, similar to those taken since 1957, covers three major subject fields—government organization, public employment, and government finances. The concept of local governments as defined by the Census Bureau covers three general purpose governments (county, municipal, and township) and two special purpose (school district and special district) governments. For information on the history, methodology, and concepts for the census of governments, see the *Government Finance and Employment Classification Manual* found at <http://www.census.gov/govs/www/class.html>.

Local government employment refers to all persons gainfully employed by and performing services for a county, municipal, township, special district, school district, or public school system government. Employees include all persons paid for personal services performed, including persons paid from federally funded programs, paid elected officials, persons in paid-leave status, and persons paid on a per-meeting, annual, semiannual, or quarterly basis.

Payroll amounts represent gross payrolls for the 1-month period of March (31 days). The gross payroll includes all salaries, wages, fees, commissions, bonuses, or awards paid to employees during the pay period that included the date of March 12. Payroll amounts reported for a period other than 1 month were converted to represent an amount for the month of March. All payroll figures are in current whole dollars and have not been adjusted for inflation. Conversion of a reported payroll to a payroll amount that would have been paid during a 31-day month is accomplished by multiplying the reported payroll by an appropriate factor. For example, a two-week payroll is multiplied by 2.214, a 1-week payroll is multiplied by 4.429, and a twice-a-month payroll is multiplied by 2.

General revenue covers all government revenue except liquor stores' revenue, insurance trust revenue, and utility revenue. **Taxes** are compulsory contributions exacted by a government for public purposes except employee and employee assessments for retirement and social insurance purposes, which are classified as insurance trust revenue. All tax revenue is classified as general revenue and comprises amounts received (including interest and penalties but excluding protested amounts and refunds) from all taxes imposed by a government. Local government tax revenue excludes any amounts from shares of state imposed and collected taxes, which are classified as Intergovernmental Revenue. **Property taxes** are taxes conditioned on ownership of property and measured by its value. This category includes general property taxes related to property as a whole, real and personal, tangible or intangible, whether taxed at a single rate or at classified rates, and taxes on selected types of property, such as motor vehicles, or on certain or all intangibles.

Total debt outstanding refers to the par value of long-term obligations remaining unpaid at the close of the fiscal year, including obligations past due but not yet presented for payment.

Elections data for 2004 are comprised of total **votes cast for President**, which include votes cast for Republican and Democratic candidates, as well as candidates representing minor political parties.

Table A/B-14. Farm Earnings, Agriculture, and Water Use

Farm earnings, 2005: Total and Percent of total. Agriculture 2002: Farms—Number, and Percent (Less than 50 acres and 500 acres or more); Land in farms—Total acres and Average size of farm; Value of farm products sold—Total, Average per farm, and Percent from (Crops and Livestock and poultry). Water use, 2000: Total; Ground water, percent of total; By selected major use (Irrigation and Public supply).

Sources: **Farm earnings**—U.S. Bureau of Economic Analysis, Regional Economic Information System (REIS), downloaded estimates and software, accessed June 5, 2007 (related Internet site <http://www.bea.gov/regional /docs/reis2005dvd.cfm>). **Agriculture**—U.S. Department of Agriculture, National Agricultural Statistics Service, *2002 Census of Agriculture, Volume 1, Geographic Area Series*, accessed April 9, 2007 (related Internet site <http://www.agcensus.usda.gov/>). **Water use,**—U.S. Geological Survey (USGS), *Water Use in the United States*, individual state/county and United States by state, accessed May 19, 2006 (related Internet site <http://water.usgs.gov /watuse>).

Farm earnings include the income of farm workers (wages and salaries and other labor income) and farm proprietors. The estimation of farm proprietors' income starts with the computation of the realized net income of all farms, which is derived as farm gross receipts less production expenses. This measure is then modified to reflect current production through a change-in-inventory adjustment and to exclude the income of corporate farms and salaries paid to corporate officers. Farm proprietors' income includes only the income of sole proprietorships and partnerships. Therefore, an adjustment is made to exclude the net farm income of corporate farms, including the salaries of officers of corporate farms.

Agriculture. The current definition of a **farm**, in use since 1974, covers any place from which $1,000 or more of agricultural products were produced and sold, or normally would have been sold, during the census year. Farms were classified into selected size groups according to the total land area in the farm. The land area of a farm is an operating unit concept and includes land owned and operated as well as land rented from others. Land rented to or assigned to a tenant was considered the tenant's farm and not that of the owner. The acreage designated as **land in farms** consists primarily of agricultural land used for crops, pasture, or grazing. It also includes woodland

and wasteland not actually under cultivation or used for pasture or grazing, provided it was part of the farm operator's total operation. Land in farms is an operating-unit concept and includes land owned and operated, as well as land rented from others. Land used rent free was to be reported as land rented from others. Land rented or assigned to a tenant was considered the tenant's farm and not that of the owner. All land in Indian reservations used for growing crops or grazing livestock was to be included as land in farms. With few exceptions, the land in each farm was tabulated as being in the operator's principal county. The principal county was defined as the one where agricultural products of the greatest value were raised or produced. It was usually the county containing all or the largest proportion of the land in the farm. For a limited number of Midwestern and Western states, this procedure resulted in the allocation of more land in farms to a county than the total land area of the county.

Value of farm products sold represents the gross market value before taxes and production expenses of all agricultural products sold or removed from the place in 2002 regardless of who received the payment. It includes sales by the operator as well as the value of any shares received by partners, landlords, contractors, or others associated with the operation. In addition, it includes receipts from placing commodities in the Commodity Credit Corporation (CCC) loan program. It does not include payments received for participation in federal farm programs, nor does it include income from farm-related sources, such as custom work and other agricultural services, or income from nonfarm sources. Data may include sales from crops produced in earlier years and exclude some crops produced in a given year but held in storage. The value of agricultural products sold was requested of all operators. If the operator failed to report this information, estimates were made based on the amount of crops harvested, livestock or poultry inventory, or number sold. Extensive estimation was required for operators growing crops or livestock under contract.

Water use. The USGS National Water-Use Information Program is responsible for compiling and disseminating the nation's water-use data. The USGS works in cooperation with local, state, and federal environmental agencies to collect water-use information at a site-specific level, such as the amount of water used to produce power at a fossil-fuel power-generation plant in Georgia. USGS also compiles the data from hundreds of thousands of these sites to produce water-use information aggregated up to the county, state, and national levels. Every 5 years, data at the state and hydrologic region level are compiled into a national water-use data system. The data were most recently published in USGS Circular 1268, *Estimated Use of Water in the United States in 2000*. For more information

on methodology and procedures, see the *National Handbook of Recommended Methods for Water Data Acquisition* found on the USGS Web site at <http://pubs.usgs.gov /chapter11>.

Water use, in the broadest sense, pertains to the interaction of human activity with and their influence on the hydrologic cycle, and includes elements such as self-supplied withdrawal, public supply delivery, consumptive use, wastewater release, reclaimed wastewater, return flow, and instream use. In a restrictive sense, water use refers to water that is actually used for a specific purpose, such as for domestic use, irrigation, or industrial processing. The quantity of water used for a specific category is determined by combining self-supplied withdrawals and public water-supply deliveries. **Withdrawals** include water removed from the ground or diverted from a surface-water source for use. **Ground water withdrawals** cover generally all subsurface water as distinct from surface water; specifically, that part of the subsurface water in the saturated zone (a zone in which all voids are filled with water) where the water is under pressure greater than atmospheric.

Data are presented for irrigation and public supply water withdrawals. Other water use categories available from USGS include domestic, commercial, livestock, industrial mining, thermoelectric power, hydroelectric power, and wastewater treatment. **Irrigation** covers the artificial application of water on lands to assist in the growing of crops and pastures or to maintain vegetative growth in recreational lands such as parks and golf courses. **Public supply** use covers water withdrawn by public and private water suppliers and delivered to users. Public suppliers provide water for a variety of uses, such as domestic, commercial, thermoelectric power, industrial, and public water use.

Table A/B-15. Manufacturing

Manufacturing: Establishments, 2002—Total and Percent change, 1997–2002; Employment, 2005—Total, Percent of all employees, and Percent change, 2001–2005; Earnings, 2005—Total and Percent of all earnings; Value added by manufactures, 2002—Total and Percent change, 1997–2002; Capital expenditures, 2002—Total and Percent change, 1997–2002.

Sources: **Establishments**—U.S. Census Bureau, 2002 Economic Census (related Internet site <http://www.census .gov/econ/census02/>). **Employment and earnings**—U.S. Bureau of Economic Analysis, Regional Economic Information System (REIS), downloaded estimates and software, accessed June 5, 2007 (related Internet site <http://www.bea.gov/regional/docs /reis2005dvd.cfm>). **Value added and capital expenditures**—U.S. Census Bureau, 2002 Economic Census, *Manufacturing, Geographic Area Series*, accessed December 2005 (related Internet site <http://www.census .gov/econ/census02/>).

Manufacturing establishments, value added, and capital expenditures data presented are based on NAICS. The Manufacturing sector (NAICS codes 31–33) comprises establishments engaged in the mechanical, physical, or chemical transformation of materials, substances, or components into new products. The assembling of component parts of manufactured products is considered manufacturing, except in cases where the activity is appropriately classified in the Construction sector. Establishments in the Manufacturing sector are often described as plants, factories, or mills and characteristically use power-driven machines and materials-handling equipment. However, establishments that transform materials or substances into new products by hand or in the worker's home and those engaged in selling to the general public products made on the same premises from which they are sold, such as bakeries, candy stores, and custom tailors, may also be included in this sector. Manufacturing establishments may process materials or may contract with other establishments to process their materials for them. Both types of establishments are included in manufacturing.

An **establishment** is a single physical location at which business is conducted or where services or industrial operations are performed. It is not necessarily identical with the company or enterprise, which may consist of one or more establishments. The count of establishments represents the number in business at any time during the year.

The **manufacturing employment** number is the average number of production workers plus the number of other employees in mid-March. Included are all persons on paid sick leave, paid holidays, and paid vacations during the pay period. Officers of corporations are included as employees; proprietors and partners of unincorporated firms are excluded.

Manufacturing earnings cover earnings by employees in the manufacturing industry, which covers establishments primarily engaged in the mechanical or chemical transformation of substances or materials into new products. The assembly of component parts of products also is considered to be manufacturing if the resulting product is neither a structure nor other fixed improvement. These activities are usually carried on in plants, factories, or mills that characteristically use power-driven machines and materials-handling equipment.

TABLE C—CITIES

Table C comprises six individual tables with 82 items of data. These tables present data for states and 1,265 incorporated places of 25,000 or more population as of April 1, 2000. Hawaii has no incorporated places recognized by the Census Bureau. Two census designated places (CDPs) are also included (Honolulu CDP in Hawaii and Arlington CDP in Virginia). The stub for Table C-1 presents the FIPS two-digit state codes and five-digit place codes. For a discussion of the codes, see Appendix C, Geographic Information.

Table C-1. Area and Population

Land area, 2000: Total and Rank. Population: 2005—Number and Per square mile; 2000 and 1990; Rank—2005, 2000, and 1990; Percent change—2000–2005 and 1990–2000.

Sources: **Land area**—U.S. Census Bureau, 2000 Census of Population and Housing, Summary Population and Housing Characteristics, Series PHC-1, using American FactFinder, accessed August 21, 2006 (related Internet site <http://factfinder.census.gov>). **Population, 2005 and 2000**—U.S. Census Bureau, "Subcounty Population Estimates, April 1, 2000 to July 1, 2005 (SUB-EST2005)," released June 21, 2006 (related Internet site <http://www.census.gov/popest/cities/>). **Population, 1990**—U.S. Census Bureau, "Population Estimates for States, Counties, Places and Minor Civil Divisions: Annual Time Series, April 1, 1990 Census to July 1, 2000 Estimate (SU-2000-10)," released November 1, 2005 (related Internet site <http://www.census.gov/popest/eval-estimates /subcounty/subcounty-2000c4.html>).

The Census Bureau provides **land area** data for the decennial censuses. Area was calculated from the specific set of boundaries recorded for the entity (in this case, cities) in the Census Bureau's geographic database. For more information, see Table A/B-1.

The Census Bureau develops subcounty **population** estimates using the "Distributive Housing Method," which uses housing unit estimates to distribute the county population to subcounty areas within the county. Housing unit estimates use building permits, mobile home shipments, and estimates of housing unit loss to update housing unit change since the last census. Census counts of housing units are geographically updated each year to reflect legal changes reported in the Boundary and Annexation Survey (BAS), census corrections, and other administrative revisions.

Population data from 1990 to 2000 reflect governmental unit boundaries legally effective as of January 1, 2000, including any post-1990 corrections and other changes due to annexations, new incorporations, or mergers.

Table C-2. Crime

Number: Violent—2005 (Total, Murder and non-negligent manslaughter, Forcible rape, Robbery, and Aggravated assault) and 2000; Property—2005 (Total, Burglary, Larceny-theft, Motor vehicle theft) and 2000. Rate per 100,000 population: Violent—2005 and 2000; Property—2005 and 2000.

Source: **Crime**—U.S. Department of Justice, Federal Bureau of Investigation, *Crime in the United States*, annual, accessed September 18, 2006 (related Internet site <http://www.fbi.gov/ucr/ucr.htm>).

For information on **crime**, see Table A/B-8.

Rates are based on resident population enumerated as of April 1 for decennial census years and estimated as of July 1 for other years. Population figures used for these rates are from the FBI.

Table C-3. Civilian Labor Force

Total: 2005, 2000, and 1990; Percent change—2000–2005 and 1990–2000. Employed: 2005, 2000, and 1990. Unemployed: 2005, 2000, and 1990. Unemployment rate: 2005, 2000, and 1990.

Source: **Civilian labor force**—U.S. Bureau of Labor Statistics, Local Area Unemployment Statistics Program, accessed September 19, 2006 (related Internet site <http://www.bls.gov/lau/>).

For information on **civilian labor force** data, see Table A/B-10.

Table C-4. Manufacturing and Wholesale Trade

Manufacturing, 2002: Establishments—Total and Percent with 20 or more employees; All employees—Number and Annual payroll; Production workers—Number and Wages; Value added by manufacture and Value of shipments. Wholesale trade, 2002: Establishments; Sales—Total and Merchant wholesalers; Paid employees, Annual payroll, and Operating expenses.

Sources: **Manufacturing**—U.S. Census Bureau, 2002 Economic Census, *Manufacturing, Geographic Area Series*, accessed October 2006 (related Internet site <http://www.census.gov/econ/census02/>). **Wholesale trade**—U.S. Census Bureau, 2002 Economic Census, *Wholesale Trade, Geographic Area Series*, accessed November 2006 (related Internet site <http://www.census.gov/econ/census02/>).

Manufacturing

An **establishment** is a single physical location at which business is conducted. It is not necessarily identical with a company or enterprise, which may consist of one establishment or more. The count of establishments represents those in business at any time during the year.

The **all employees** number is the average number of production workers plus the number of other employees in mid-March. Included are all persons on paid sick leave, paid holidays, and paid vacation; not included are proprietors and partners of unincorporated businesses. For some cities, the source provides only range values to avoid disclosure for individual companies. In these cases,

the figure we provide in the table is the midpoint of this range value and is footnoted with the range value. For more detailed information on employment-size ranges, see the online report at <http://www.census.gov/econ/census02>.

The number of **production workers** is the average for the payroll periods including the 12th of March, May, August, and November. Production workers include workers (up through the line-supervisor level) engaged in fabricating, processing, assembling, inspecting, receiving, storing, handling, packing, warehousing, shipping (but not delivering), maintenance, repair, janitorial and guard services, product development, auxiliary production for plants own use (e.g., power plant), record keeping, and other services closely associated with these production operations at the establishment covered by the report. Employees above the working-supervisor level are excluded from this item.

Value added by manufacture is a measure of manufacturing activity derived by subtracting the cost of materials, supplies, containers, fuel, purchased electricity, and contract work from the value of shipments (products manufactured plus receipts for services rendered). The result of this calculation is adjusted by the addition of value added by merchandising operations (i.e., the difference between the sales value and the cost of merchandise sold without further manufacture, processing, or assembly) plus the net change in finished goods and work-in-process between the beginning- and end-of-year inventories. Value added avoids the duplication in the figure for value of shipments that results from the use of products of some establishments as materials by others. Value added is considered to be the best value measure available for comparing the relative economic importance of manufacturing among industries and geographic areas.

Value of shipments includes the received or receivable net selling values, "Free on Board" (FOB) plant (exclusive of freight and taxes), of all products shipped, both primary and secondary, as well as all miscellaneous receipts, such as receipts for contract work performed for others, installation and repair, sales of scrap, and sales of products bought and sold without further processing. Included are all items made by or for the establishments from material owned by it, whether sold, transferred to other plants of the same company, or shipped on consignment. The net selling value of products made in one plant on a contract basis from materials owned by another is reported by the plant providing the materials. In the case of multiunit companies, the manufacturer is requested to report the value of products transferred to other establishments of the same company at full economic or commercial value, including not only the direct cost of production, but also a reasonable proportion of "all other costs" (including company overhead) and profit.

Wholesale Trade

Paid employees consist of full-time and part-time employees, including salaried officers and executives of corporations, who were on the payroll during the pay period including March 12. Included are employees on paid sick leave, paid holidays, and paid vacations. Not included are proprietors and partners of unincorporated businesses, employees of departments or concessions operated by other companies at the establishment, full- and part-time leased employees whose payroll was filed under an employee leasing companys Employer Identification Number (EIN), and temporary staffing obtained from a staffing service. For some cities, the source provides only range values to avoid disclosure for individual companies. In these cases, the figure we provide in the table is the midpoint of this range value and is footnoted with the range value. For more detailed information on employment-size ranges, see the online report at <http://www.census.gov /econ/census02>.

Wholesale trade sales include merchandise sold for cash or credit by establishments primarily engaged in wholesale trade; receipts from rental of vehicles, equipment, instruments, tools, etc.; receipts for delivery, installation, maintenance, repair, alteration, storage, and other services; gasoline, liquor, tobacco, and other excise taxes that are paid by the manufacturer and passed on to the wholesaler; and shipping and handling receipts. Sales are net after deductions for refunds and allowances for merchandise returned by customers. Trade-in allowances are not deducted from sales. Sales do not include carrying or other credit charges; sales and other taxes (including Hawaii's General Excise Tax) collected from customers and forwarded to taxing authorities; and nonoperating income from such sources as investments, rental or sales of real estate, and interest. Sales do not include wholesale sales made by manufacturers, retailers, service establishments, or other businesses whose primary activity is other than wholesale trade. They do include receipts other than from the sale of merchandise at wholesale (service receipts, retail sales, etc.) by establishments primarily engaged in wholesale trade.

Annual payroll includes all forms of compensation, such as salaries, wages, commissions, dismissal pay, bonuses, vacation allowances, sick-leave pay, and employee contributions to qualified pension plans, paid during the year to all employees and reported on IRS Form 941 as taxable Medicare wages and tips (even if not subject to income or FICA tax). Includes tips and gratuities received by employees from patrons and reported to employers. Excludes payrolls of departments or concessions operated by other companies at the establishment. For corporations, payroll includes amounts paid to officers and executives; for unincorporated businesses, it does not include profit or other compensation of proprietors or partners. Payroll is reported before deductions for social security, income tax, Insurance, union dues, etc.

Operating expenses include payroll, employee benefits, interest and rent expenses, payroll taxes, cost of supplies used for operation, depreciation expenses, fundraising expenses, contracted or purchased services, and other expenses charged to operations during 2002. Expenses exclude cost of goods sold, income taxes, and interest for wholesale establishments; outlays for the purchase of real estate; construction and all other capital improvements; funds invested; assessments or dues paid to the parent or other chapters of the same organization; and, for fundraising organizations, funds transferred to charities and other organizations.

Table C-5. Retail Trade and Accommodation and Food Services

Retail trade, 2002: Establishments; Sales—Total, Per capita (Amount and Percent of national average), and Percent from general merchandise stores; Paid employees; Annual payroll—Total and Per paid employee. Accommodation and food services, 2002: Establishments; Sales—Total and Percent from food services; Paid employees and Annual payroll.

Sources: **Retail trade**—U.S. Census Bureau, 2002 Economic Census, *Retail Trade, Geographic Area Series*, accessed December 2006 (related Internet site <http://www.census.gov/econ/census02/>). **Accommodation and food services**—U.S. Census Bureau, 2002 Economic Census, *Accommodation and Food Services, Geographic Area Series*, accessed December 2006 (related Internet site <http://www.census.gov/econ/census02/>).

For information on **retail trade** and **accommodation and food services**, see Table A/B-11. For definitions of **paid employees and annual payroll**, see the notes for Table C-4.

Table C-6. Government and Climate

City government employment, March 2002: Total employment and Payroll. City government finances, 2001–2002: General revenue—Total and Taxes; General expenditure—Total and By selected function, percent of total (Police protection, Sewerage and solid waste management, and Highways). Climate, 1971–2000: Average daily temperature—January and July; Min. and max. temperatures—January and July; Annual precipitation, Heating degree days, and Cooling degree days.

Sources: **Employment and payroll**—U.S. Census Bureau, 2002 Census of Governments, *Volume 3, Number 1, Employment of Major Local Governments*, released May 2004 (related Internet site <http://www.census.gov /govs/www/cog2002.html>). **Finances**—U.S. Census Bureau, 2002 Census of Governments, *Volume 4, Number 4, Government Finances*, released April 2005 (related Internet site <http://www.census.gov/govs/www

/cog2002.html>). **Climate**—U.S. National Oceanic and Atmospheric Administration (NOAA), National Climatic Data Center (NCDC), *Climatography of the United States*, Number 81 (related Internet site <http://cdo.ncdc.noaa .gov/cgi-bin/climatenormals/climatenormals.pl>).

City Government

For information on **employment, payroll, and general revenue**, see Table A/B-13.

General expenditure covers all government expenditures other than the specifically enumerated kinds of expenditures classified as liquor stores expenditures, utility expenditures, and insurance trust expenditures. **Police protection** expenditures are for preservation of law and order and traffic safety and include police patrols and communications, crime prevention activities, detention and custody of persons awaiting trial, traffic safety, and vehicular inspection. **Sewerage and solid waste management** expenditures are for provision of sanitary and storm sewers and sewage disposal facilities and services, and payments to other governments for such purposes. **Highway** expenditures are for construction, maintenance, and operation of highways, streets, and related structures, including toll highways, bridges, tunnels, ferries, street lighting, and snow and ice removal.

Climate

All climate data presented are average values for the 30-year period, 1971–2000. The average value of a meteorological element over 30 years is defined as a climatological normal. The normal climate helps in describing the climate and is used as a base to which current conditions can be compared. Every 10 years, the NCDC computes new 30-year climate normals for selected temperature and precipitation elements for a large number of U.S. climate and weather stations. Climate normals are a useful way to describe the average weather of a location. Over the decades the term "normal," to the layperson, has come to be most closely associated with the mean or average. In this context, a "climatic normal" is simply the arithmetic average of the values over a 30-year period (generally, three consecutive decades). A person unfamiliar with climate and climate normals may perceive the normal to be the climate that one should "expect" to happen. It is important to note that the normal may, or may not, be what one would expect to happen. This is especially true with precipitation in dry climates, such as the desert southwestern region of the United States, and with temperatures at continental locations that frequently experience large swings from cold air masses to warm air masses.

The **average daily temperatures**, or mean temperatures, for January and July were determined by adding the average daily maximum temperatures and average daily minimum temperatures and dividing by 2. Temperature limits represent average daily minimum for January and average daily maximum for July.

Annual precipitation values are the average annual water equivalent of all precipitation for the 30-year period. Precipitation totals include rain and the liquid equivalent of frozen and freezing precipitation such as snow, sleet, freezing rain, and hail.

Heating and cooling degree-days are used as relative measures of the energy required for heating and cooling buildings. One **heating-degree day** is accumulated for each whole degree that the mean daily temperature is below 65 F (i.e., a mean daily temperature of 62 F will produce three heating-degree days). **Cooling-degree day** are accumulated in similar fashion for deviations of the mean daily temperature above 65 F.

TABLE D—PLACES

Table D comprises six individual tables with 79 items of data. These tables present data for states and 242 incorporated places of 100,000 or more population as of April 1, 2000. Hawaii has no incorporated places recognized by the Census Bureau. Two CDPs are also included (Honolulu CDP in Hawaii and Arlington CDP in Virginia). For a discussion of the codes, see Appendix C, Geographic Information.

Table D-1. Population by Age and Sex

Total population, 2005. Population by age, 2005: Under 5 years, 5 to 17 years, 18 to 24 years, 25 to 34 years, 35 to 44 years, 45 to 54 years, 55 to 64 years, 65 to 74 years, 75 to 84 years, 85 years and over. Males per 100 females, 2005.

Source: **Population by age and sex**—U.S. Census Bureau, American Community Survey, "DP-1. General Demographic Characteristics: 2005," using American FactFinder, accessed August 29, 2006 (related Internet site <http://factfinder.census.gov>).

Data for the ACS are collected from a sample of housing units and used to produce estimates of the actual figures that would have been obtained by interviewing the entire population using the same methodology. The estimate base from the Population Estimate Program (PEP) is the population count or estimate used as the starting point in the estimates process. It can be the last census count or the estimate for a previous date. Also referred to as the "base population," ACS and PEP data would not be expected to be the same because they are based on different methodologies.

The **age** classification is based on the age of the person in complete years at the time of the interview. Both age and date of birth were used in combination to calculate the most accurate age at the time of the interview.

Table D-2. Population by Race and Hispanic Origin

Number, 2005: Race—White alone, Black or African American alone, American Indian and Alaska Native alone, Asian alone, Native Hawaiian and Other Pacific Islander alone, and Two or more races; Hispanic status—Hispanic or Latino origin and Non-Hispanic White alone. Percent, 2005: Race—White alone, Black or African American alone, American Indian and Alaska Native alone, Asian alone, Native Hawaiian and Other Pacific Islander alone, Two or more races; Hispanic status—Hispanic or Latino origin and Non-Hispanic White alone.

Source: **Population by race and Hispanic origin**—U.S. Census Bureau, American Community Survey, "DP-1. General Demographic Characteristics: 2005," using American FactFinder, accessed August 29, 2006 (related Internet site <http://factfinder.census.gov>).

Refer to the notes for D-1 for information regarding the differences between ACS data and PEP data.

The concept of race, as used by the Census Bureau, reflects self-identification by people according to the race or races with which they most closely identify. These categories are sociopolitical constructs and should not be interpreted as being scientific or anthropological in nature. Furthermore, the race categories include both racial and national-origin groups. For more information, see Table A/B-3.

Table D-3. Households

Total households, 2005. Households by type, 2005: Family households—Total (Number and Percent with own children under 18 years), Married-couple families (Number and Percent with own children under 18 years), and Female householder, no husband present (Number and Percent with own children under 18 years); Nonfamily households—Total and Householder living alone (Number and Percent 65 years and over); Percent of households with one or more persons—Under 18 years and 65 years and over. Persons per household, 2005.

Source: **Households**—U.S. Census Bureau, American Community Survey, "DP-1. General Demographic Characteristics: 2005," using American FactFinder, accessed August 29, 2006 (related Internet site <http://factfinder .census.gov>).

Household. A household includes all of the people who occupy a housing unit. A housing unit may be a house, an apartment, a mobile home or trailer, a group of rooms, or a single room that is occupied as separate living quarters. Separate living quarters are those in which the occupants live separately from any other individuals in the building and that have direct access from outside the building or through a common hall. People not living in households

are classified as living in group quarters. **Persons per household** (or average household size) is a measure obtained by dividing the number of people in households by the total number of households (or householders).

Family household (family). A family includes a householder and one or more people living in the same household who are related to the householder by birth, marriage, or adoption. All people in a household who are related to the householder are regarded as members of his or her family. A family household may contain people not related to the householder, but those people are not included as part of the householder's family in census tabulations. Thus, the number of family households is equal to the number of families, but family households may include more members than do families. A household can contain only one family for purposes of census tabulations. Not all households contain families, since a household may comprise a group of unrelated people or one person living alone. **Married-couple family** is a family in which the householder and his or her spouse are enumerated as members of the same household. **Female householder, no husband present** includes a family with a female who maintains a household with no husband of the householder present. **Nonfamily household** is a household in which the householder lives alone or with nonrelatives only.

Own child category is a never-married child under 18 years old who is a son or daughter of the householder by birth, marriage (a stepchild), or adoption.

Table D-4. Education

School enrollment, 2005: Total, Prekindergarten through grade 8, Grades 9 through 12, and College or graduate school. Educational attainment, 2005: Population 25 years and over and Percent of persons 25 years and over, by highest level completed—Not a high school graduate, High school graduate, Some college, but no degree, Associate's degree, Bachelor's degree, and Graduate or professional degree.

Source: **Education**—U.S. Census Bureau, American Community Survey, "DP-2. Selected Social Characteristics in the United States: 2005," using American FactFinder, accessed August 29, 2006 (related Internet site <http://factfinder .census.gov>).

School enrollment. People were classified as enrolled in school if they were attending a "regular" public or private school or college at any time during the 3 months prior to the time of interview. The question included instructions to "include only nursery or preschool, kindergarten, elementary school, and schooling which leads to a high school diploma, or a college degree" as regular school or college. Respondents who did not answer the enrollment question were assigned the enrollment status and type of school of a person with the same age, sex, and race/Hispanic or Latino origin whose residence was in the same or nearby area. A regular school advances a person toward an elementary school certificate, a high school diploma, or a college, university, or professional school (such as law or medicine) degree. Tutoring or correspondence schools are included if credit can be obtained in a "regular school." People enrolled in "vocational, technical, or business school" were not reported as enrolled in regular school.

Data on **educational attainment** are derived from questions asked of all respondents to the ACS , and data presented here are tabulated for people 25 years old and over. Respondents are classified according to the highest degree or the highest level of school completed. Persons currently enrolled in school are asked to report the level of the previous grade attended or the highest degree received. **High school graduate** refers to respondents who received a high school diploma or the equivalent, such as passing the GED, and did not attend college. **Some college, but no degree** refers to respondents who have attended college for some amount of time but have no degree. The category **associate's degree** includes people whose highest degree is an associate's degree, which generally requires 2 years of college-level work and is either in an occupational program that prepares them for a specific occupation, or an academic program primarily in the arts and sciences. The course work may or may not be transferable to a **bachelor's degree**.

Table D-5. Income and Poverty

Median household income, 2005, Median family income, 2005, and Per capita income, 2005. Number below poverty in past 12 months, 2005: Families; Individuals—Total, Under 18 years, and 65 years and over. Percent below poverty in past 12 months, 2005: Families; Individuals—Total, Under 18 years, and 65 years and over.

Source: **Income and poverty**—U.S. Census Bureau, American Community Survey, "DP-3. Selected Economic Characteristics: 2005," using American FactFinder, accessed August 29, 2006, and "B17001. Poverty Status in the Past 12 Months by Sex by Age," "B17010. Poverty Status of Families by Family Type by Presence and Age of Related Children Under 18 Years," "B19013. Median Household Income (in 2005 Inflation-Adjusted Dollars)," and "B19113. Median Family Income (in 2005 Inflation-Adjusted Dollars)," using American FactFinder, accessed November 29, 2006 (related Internet site <http://factfinder.census.gov>).

Income of households includes the income of the householder and all other individuals 15 years old and over in the household, whether they are related to the householder or not. Because many households consist of only one person, average household income is usually less than average family income. Although the household income statistics cover the past 12 months, the characteristics of individuals and the composition of households refer to the time of enumeration. Thus, the income of the household does not include amounts received by individuals who were members of the household during all or part of the past 12 months if these individuals no longer resided in the household at the time of enumeration. Similarly, income amounts reported by individuals who did not reside in the household during the past 12 months but who were members of the household at the time of enumeration are included. However, the composition of most households was the same during the past 12 months as at the time of enumeration. Median income divides the income distribution into two equal parts: one-half of the cases falling below the median income and one-half above the median. The **median household income** is based on the distribution of the total number of households including those with no income.

In compiling statistics on family income, the incomes of all members 15 years old and over related to the householder are summed and treated as a single amount. Although the family income statistics cover the past 12 months, the characteristics of individuals and the composition of families refer to the time of enumeration. Thus, the income of the family does not include amounts received by individuals who were members of the family during all or part of the past 12 months if these individuals no longer resided with the family at the time of enumeration. Similarly, income amounts reported by individuals who did not reside with the family during the past 12 months but who were members of the family at the time of enumeration are included. However, the composition of most families was the same during the past 12 months as at the time of enumeration. Median income divides the income distribution into two equal parts: one-half of the cases falling below the median income and one-half above the median. The **median family income** is based on the distribution of the total number of families including those with no income.

Per capita income is the mean income computed for every man, woman, and child in a particular group. It is derived by dividing the aggregate income of the group by the total population of the group.

Poverty status is determined using thresholds arranged in a two-dimensional matrix. The matrix consists of family size cross-classified by presence and number of family members under age 18 years old. Unrelated individuals and two-person families are further differentiated by age of reference person. To determine a person's poverty status, one compares the person's total family income in the last 12 months with the poverty threshold appropriate for that person's family size and composition. If the total income of that person's family is less than the threshold appropriate for that family, then the person is considered poor or "below the poverty level," together with every member of his or her family. If a person is not living with anyone related by birth, marriage, or adoption, then the person's own income is compared with his or her poverty threshold. The total number of people below the poverty level was the sum of people in families and the number of unrelated individuals with incomes in the last 12 months below the poverty level.

Table D-6. Owner- and Renter-Occupied Housing Units and Vehicles Available

Owner-occupied housing units, 2005: Total units and Median value; Value, percent—Less than $100,000, $100,000–$199,999, $200,000–$299,999, and $300,000 and over. Renter-occupied housing units, 2005: Total units and Median gross monthly rent; Gross monthly rent, percent—Less than $300, $300–$499, $500–$749, and $750 or more. Percent of occupied housing units by vehicles available, 2005: None, 1, 2, and 3 or more.

Source: **Housing units and vehicles**—U.S. Census Bureau, American Community Survey, "DP-4. Selected Housing Characteristics in the United States: 2005," using American FactFinder, accessed October 3, 2006 (related Internet site <http://factfinder.census.gov>).

A housing unit is **owner occupied** if the owner or co-owner lives in the unit even if it is mortgaged or not fully paid for. The unit is "Owned by you or someone in this household with a mortgage or loan" if it is being purchased with a mortgage or some other debt arrangement, such as a deed of trust, trust deed, contract to purchase, land contract, or purchase agreement. The unit also is considered owned with a mortgage if it is built on leased land and there is a mortgage on the unit. Mobile homes occupied by owners with installment loan balances also are included in this category. A housing unit is "Owned by you or someone in this household free and clear (without a mortgage)" if there is no mortgage or other similar debt on the house, apartment, or mobile home including units built on leased land if the unit is owned outright without a mortgage.

All occupied housing units that are not owner occupied, whether they are rented for cash rent or occupied without payment of cash rent, are classified as **renter occupied.**

Data on **vehicles available** show the number of passenger cars, vans, and pickup or panel trucks of 1-ton capacity or less kept at home and available for the use of household members. Vehicles rented or leased for 1 month or more, company vehicles, and police and government vehicles are included if kept at home and used for non-business purposes. Dismantled or immobile vehicles are excluded. Vehicles kept at home but used only for business purposes also are excluded.

Limitations of the Data and Methodology

Appendix B

Page

You may visit us on the Web at
http://www.census.gov/compendia/ccdb

Limitations of the Data
and Methodology

Appendix B

Appendix B.
Limitations of the Data and Methodology

Introduction

The data presented in this *County and City Data Book* came from many sources. The sources include not only the U.S. Census Bureau, but also other organizations that collect and issue statistics. Consequently, the data vary considerably as to reference periods, definitions of terms, and, for ongoing series, the number and frequency of time periods for which data are available.

The statistics presented were obtained and tabulated by various means. Some statistics are based on complete enumerations or censuses while others are based on samples.

Each set of data relates to a group of individuals or units of interest referred to as the *target universe* or *target population*, or simply as the *universe* or *population*. Prior to data collection the target universe should be clearly defined. For example, if data are to be collected for the universe of households in the United States, it is necessary to define a "household." The target universe may not be completely tractable. Cost and other considerations may restrict data collection to a survey universe based on some available list, which may be inaccurate or out of date. This list is called a *survey frame* or *sampling frame*.

The data in many tables are based on data obtained for all population units, a census, or on data obtained for only a portion, or sample, of the population units. When the data presented are based on a sample, the sample is usually a scientifically selected probability sample. This is a sample selected from a list or sampling frame in such a way that every possible sample has a known chance of selection and usually each unit selected can be assigned a number, greater than 0 and less than or equal to 1, representing its likelihood or probability of selection.

For large-scale sample surveys, the probability sample of units is often selected as a multistage sample. The first stage of a multistage sample is the selection of a probability sample of large groups of population members, referred to as primary sampling units (PSUs). For example, in a national multistage household sample, PSUs are often counties or groups of counties. The second stage of a multistage sample is the selection, within each PSU selected at the first stage, of smaller groups of population units, referred to as secondary sampling units. In subsequent stages of selection, smaller and smaller nested groups are chosen until the ultimate sample of population units is obtained. To qualify a multistage sample as a probability sample, all stages of sampling must be carried out using probability sampling methods.

Prior to selection at each stage of a multistage (or a single-stage) sample, a list of the sampling units or sampling frame for that stage must be obtained. For example, for the first stage of selection of a national household sample, a list of the counties and county groups that form the PSUs must be obtained. For the final stage of selection, lists of households, and sometimes persons within the households, have to be compiled in the field. For surveys of economic entities and for the economic censuses, the Census Bureau generally uses a frame constructed from the Census Bureau's Business Register. The Business Register contains all establishments with payroll in the United States, including small single-establishment firms as well as large multiestablishment firms.

Wherever the quantities in a table refer to an entire universe, but are constructed from data collected in a sample survey, the table quantities are referred to as *sample estimates*. In constructing a sample estimate, an attempt is made to come as close as is feasible to the corresponding universe quantity that would be obtained from a complete census of the universe. Estimates based on a sample will, however, generally differ from the hypothetical census figures. Two classifications of errors are associated with estimates based on sample surveys: (1) *sampling error*—the error arising from the use of a sample, rather than a census, to estimate population quantities and (2) *nonsampling error*—those errors arising from nonsampling sources. As discussed below, the magnitude of the sampling error for an estimate can usually be estimated from the sample data. However, the magnitude of the nonsampling error for an estimate can rarely be estimated. Consequently, actual error in an estimate exceeds the error that can be estimated.

The particular sample used in a survey is only one of a large number of possible samples of the same size, which could have been selected using the same sampling procedure. Estimates derived from the different samples would, in general, differ from each other. The *standard error* (SE) is a measure of the variation among the estimates derived from all possible samples. The SE is the most commonly used measure of the sampling error of an estimate. Valid estimates of the SEs of survey estimates can usually be calculated from the data collected in a probability sample.

For convenience, the SE is sometimes expressed as a percent of the estimate and is called the relative standard error or *coefficient of variation* (CV). For example, an estimate of 200 units with an estimated SE of 10 units has an estimated CV of 5 percent.

A sample estimate and an estimate of its SE or CV can be used to construct interval estimates that have a prescribed confidence that the interval includes the average of the estimates derived from all possible samples with a known probability. To illustrate, if all possible samples were selected under essentially the same general conditions, and using the same sample design, and if an estimate and its estimated standard error were calculated from each sample, then: 1) approximately 68 percent of the intervals from one SE below the estimate to one SE above the estimate would include the average estimate derived from all possible samples; 2) approximately 90 percent of the intervals from 1.6 SEs below the estimate to 1.6 SEs above the estimate would include the average estimate derived from all possible samples; and 3) approximately 95 percent of the intervals from two SEs below the estimate to two SEs above the estimate would include the average estimate derived from all possible samples.

Thus, for a particular sample, one can say with the appropriate level of confidence (e.g., 90 percent or 95 percent) that the average of all possible samples is included in the constructed interval. Example of a confidence interval: An estimate is 200 units with a SE of 10 units. An approximate 90 percent confidence interval (plus or minus 1.6 standard errors) is from 184 to 216.

All surveys and censuses are subject to nonsampling errors. Nonsampling errors are of two kinds: *random* and *nonrandom*. Random nonsampling errors arise because of the varying interpretation of questions (by respondents or interviewers) and varying actions of coders, keyers, and other processors. Some randomness is also introduced when respondents must estimate. Nonrandom nonsampling errors result from total nonresponse (no usable data obtained for a sampled unit), partial or item nonresponse (only a portion of a response may be usable), inability or unwillingness on the part of respondents to provide correct information, difficulty interpreting questions, mistakes in recording or keying data, errors of collection or processing, and coverage problems (overcoverage and undercoverage of the target universe). Random nonresponse errors usually, but not always, result in an understatement of sampling errors and, thus, an overstatement of the precision of survey estimates. Estimating the magnitude of nonsampling errors would require special experiments or access to independent data and, consequently, the magnitudes are seldom available.

Nearly all types of nonsampling errors that affect surveys also occur in complete censuses. Since surveys can be conducted on a smaller scale than censuses, nonsampling

errors can presumably be controlled more tightly. Relatively more funds and effort can perhaps be expended toward eliciting responses, detecting and correcting response error, and reducing processing errors. As a result, survey results can sometimes be more accurate than census results.

To compensate for suspected nonrandom errors, adjustments of the sample estimates are often made. For example, adjustments are frequently made for nonresponse, both total and partial. Adjustments made for either type of nonresponse are often referred to as *imputations*. Imputation for total nonresponse is usually made by substituting for the questionnaire responses of the nonrespondents the "average" questionnaire responses of the respondents. These imputations usually are made separately within various groups of sample members, formed by attempting to place respondents and nonrespondents together that have "similar" design or ancillary characteristics. Imputation for item nonresponse is usually made by substituting for a missing item the response to that item of a respondent having characteristics that are "similar" to those of the nonrespondent.

For an estimate calculated from a sample survey, the *total error* in the estimate is composed of the sampling error, which can usually be estimated from the sample, and the nonsampling error, which usually cannot be estimated from the sample. The total error present in a population quantity obtained from a complete census is composed of only nonsampling errors. Ideally, estimates of the total error associated with data given in these tables should be given. However, due to the unavailability of estimates of nonsampling errors, only estimates of the levels of sampling errors, in terms of estimated SEs or CVs, are available. To obtain estimates of the estimated SEs from the sample of interest, obtain a copy of the referenced report, which appears at the end of each table.

Source of Additional Material: The Federal Committee on Statistical Methodology (FCSM) is an interagency committee dedicated to improving the quality of federal statistics <http://fcsm.ssd.census.gov>.

Principal Databases: Beginning below are brief descriptions of some of the sample surveys, censuses, and administrative collections that provide a substantial portion of the data contained in this publication.

U.S. DEPARTMENT OF AGRICULTURE

National Agricultural Statistics Service (NASS)

Census of Agriculture

Universe, Frequency, and Types of Data: Complete count of U.S. farms and ranches conducted once every 5 years with data at the national, state, and county level. Data published on farm numbers and related items/ characteristics.

Type of Data Collection Operation: Complete census for number of farms; land in farms; agriculture products sold; total cropland; irrigated land; farm operator characteristics; livestock and poultry inventory and sales; and selected crops harvested. Market value of land and buildings, total farm production expenses, machinery and equipment, fertilizer and chemicals, and farm labor are estimated from a sample of farms.

Data Collection and Imputation Procedures: Data collection takes place by mailing questionnaires to all farmers and ranchers. Nonrespondents are contacted by telephone and correspondence follow-ups. Imputations were made for all nonresponse items/characteristics. Coverage adjustments were made to account for missed farms and ranches.

Estimates of Sampling Error: Variability in the estimates is due to the sample selection and estimation for items collected by sample and census nonresponse and coverage estimation procedures. The CVs for national and state estimates are generally very small. The response rate is approximately 81 percent.

Other (nonsampling) Errors: Nonsampling errors are due to incompleteness of the census mailing list, duplications on the list, respondent reporting errors, errors in editing reported data, and in imputation for missing data. Evaluation studies are conducted to measure certain nonsampling errors such as list coverage and classification error. Results from the evaluation program for the 2002 census indicate the net undercoverage amounted to about 18 percent of the nation's total farms.

Sources of Additional Material: U.S. Department of Agriculture, National Agricultural Statistics Service, *2002 Census of Agriculture*, Volume 1, *Subject Series C* Part 1, *Agriculture Atlas of the U.S.*; Part 2, *Coverage Evaluation*; Part 3, *Rankings of States and Counties*. See also the *2002 Census of Agriculture*, Volume 1, Chapter 1, U.S. National Level Data, Appendix C, Statistical Methodology at <http://www.nass.usda.gov/census/census02/volume1/us/us2appxc.pdf>.

U.S. BUREAU OF LABOR STATISTICS (BLS)

Current Employment Statistics (CES) Program

Universe, Frequency, and Types of Data: Monthly survey drawn from a sampling frame of over 8 million unemployment insurance tax accounts in order to obtain data by industry on employment, hours, and earnings.

Type of Data Collection Operation: In 2006, the CES sample included about 160,000 businesses and government agencies, which represent approximately 400,000 individual work sites.

Data Collection and Imputation Procedures: Each month, the state agencies cooperating with BLS, as well as BLS Data Collection Centers, collect data through various automated collection modes and mail. BLS-Washington staff prepares national estimates of employment, hours, and earnings, while states use the data to develop state and area estimates.

Estimates of Sampling Errors: The relative SE for total nonfarm employment is 0.2 percent.

Other (nonsampling) Errors: Estimates of employment adjusted annually to reflect complete universe. The average adjustment is 0.2 percent over the last decade, with an absolute range from less than 0.05 percent to 0.5 percent.

Sources of Additional Material: U.S. Bureau of Labor Statistics, *Employment and Earnings*, monthly, Explanatory Notes and Estimates of Errors, Tables 2-A through 2-F. See also the *BLS Handbook of Methods*, Chapter 1, Labor Force Data Derived from the Current Population Survey, and Chapter 2, Employment, Hours, and Earnings from the Establishment Survey. The BLS Handbook may be found at <http://www.bls.gov/opub/hom>.

U.S. DEPARTMENT OF COMMERCE

U.S. Bureau of Economic Analysis (BEA)

Regional Economic Information System (REIS)

Universe, Frequency, and Types of Data: REIS contains estimates of personal income and its components and employment for local areas such as states, counties, metropolitan areas, and micropolitan areas.

Type of Data Collection Operation: The estimates of personal income are primarily based on administrative records data, census data, and survey data.

Data Collection and Imputation Procedures: The data are collected from administrative records, which may come from the recipients of the income or from the sources of the income. These data are a by-product of the administration of various federal and state government programs. The most important sources of these data are the state unemployment insurance programs of BLS, the social insurance programs of the Centers for Medicare and Medicaid Services, federal income tax program of the Internal Revenue Service (IRS), veterans' benefit programs of the U.S. Department of Veterans Affairs, and military payroll systems of the U.S. Department of Defense.

The data from censuses are mainly collected from the recipients of income. The most important sources for these data are the Census of Agriculture at USDA and the Census of Population and Housing conducted by the Census Bureau. Other sources may include estimates of farm proprietors' income by USDA, wages and salaries from County Business Patterns from the Census Bureau, and the Quarterly Census of Employment and Wages by the U.S. Department of Labor.

Estimates of Sampling Error: Not applicable, except component variables may be subject to error.

Other (nonsampling) Errors: Nonsampling errors in the administrative datasets may affect personal income estimates.

Sources of Additional Material: U.S. Bureau of Economic Analysis, *Local Area Personal Income and Employment Methodology, 2005.* See also <http://www.bea.gov/regional/docs/lapi2005>. Methodological information on other BEA datasets, such as state personal income and gross state product, may be found at <http://www.bea.gov/bea/regional/articles.cfm?section=methods>.

U.S. CENSUS BUREAU

American Community Survey (ACS)

Universe, Frequency, and Types of Data: Nationwide survey to obtain data about demographic, social, economic, and housing characteristics of people, households, and housing units. Covers household population and excludes the population living in institutions, college dormitories, and other group quarters.

Type of Data Collection Operation: Two-stage stratified annual sample of approximately 838,000 housing units. The ACS samples housing units from the Master Address File (MAF). The first stage of sampling involves dividing the United States into primary sampling units PSUs, most of which comprise a metropolitan area, a large county, or a group of smaller counties. Every PSU falls within the boundary of a state. The PSUs are then grouped into strata on the basis of independent information, that is, information obtained from the decennial census or other sources. The strata are constructed so that they are as homogeneous as possible with respect to social and economic characteristics that are considered important by ACS data users. A pair of PSUs were selected from each stratum. The probability of selection for each PSU in the stratum is proportional to its estimated 1996 population. In the second stage of sampling, a sample of housing units within the sample PSUs is drawn. Ultimate sampling units (USUs) are housing units. The USUs sampled in the second stage consist of housing units that are systematically drawn from sorted lists of addresses of housing units from the MAF.

Data Collection and Imputation Procedures: The ACS is conducted every month on independent samples. Each housing unit in the independent monthly sample is mailed a prenotice letter announcing the selection of the address to participate, a survey questionnaire package, and a reminder postcard. These sample units receive a second (replacement) questionnaire package if the initial questionnaire is not returned by a scheduled date. In the mailout/mailback sites, sample units for which a questionnaire is not returned in the mail and for which a telephone

number is available are defined as the telephone nonresponse follow-up universe. Interviewers attempt to contact and interview these mail nonresponse cases. Sample units from all sites that are still unresponsive 2 months after the mailing of the survey questionnaires and directly after the completion of the telephone follow-up operation are subsampled at a rate of 1 in 3. The selected nonresponse units are assigned to field representatives, who visit the units, verify their existence or declare them nonexistent, determine their occupancy status, and conduct interviews. After data collection is completed, any remaining incomplete or inconsistent information was imputed during the final automated edit of the collected data.

Estimates of Sampling Error: The data in the ACS products are estimates of the actual figures that would have been obtained by interviewing the entire population using the same methodology. The estimates from the chosen sample also differ from other samples of housing units and persons within those housing units.

Other (nonsampling) Errors: In addition to sampling error, data users should realize that other types of errors may be introduced during any of the various complex operations used to collect and process survey data. An important goal of the ACS is to minimize the amount of nonsampling error introduced through nonresponse for sample housing units. One way of this is by following up on mail nonrespondents.

Sources of Additional Material: U.S. Census Bureau, American Community Survey Web site available at <http://www.census.gov/acs/www/index.html> and the American Community Survey, Accuracy of the Data documents available at <http://www.census.gov/acs/www/UseData/Accuracy/Accuracy1.htm>.

2002 Census of Governments

Universe, Frequency, and Types of Data: The universe of local governments enumerated for the 2002 Census of Governments includes county, municipal, town, township, and special-purpose local governments. The census of governments is taken every 5 years. The 2002 Census of Governments, similar to those taken since 1957, covers three major subject fields: government organizations, public employment, and government finances.

Type of Data Collection Operation: The census of governments includes more than 87,000 local government units and in 2002 covered 3,034 county governments, 19,429 municipal governments, 16,504 town or township governments, 35,052 special district governments, and 13,506 school district governments. The universe list used as the mail and control file for all phases of the census of governments is updated periodically to add newly established units that meet Census Bureau criteria for independent governments and to delete dissolved or inactive units.

Data Collection and Imputation Procedures: There are three phases of state and local government data collection. Phase 1 is precensus research to classify and identify all 87,525 local governments. It includes extensive legal research into government structure by state, as well as a mailout/mailback survey, and produces and updated list of all local governments and selected data. Phase 2 covers all of the state and local governments and expands the census year annual finance survey from about 14,000 to 87,575 state and local governments. It uses in-house data compilations of source documents for many of the state and largest local governments, consolidated data submissions (usually electronic files) for about 55,000 local governments, Internet data collection capabilities, and a mailout/mailback survey of the remaining governments. Phase 3 covers all of the federal civilian, state, and local governments and expands the census-year annual employment survey from about 10,000 to all 87,575 local governments. It relies on consolidated submissions from more than 30 state respondents and an Internet data collection capability, with the remainder obtained through a mailout/mailback survey.

For counties, municipalities, and townships that failed to respond, missing data were imputed by using the most recently reported prior census or annual survey data. These data were adjusted by median growth rates calculated from similar types of governments, i.e., in the same state, same type, and about the same size. The appropriate growth rate was applied to the nonreporting government's year data to get a current year imputed value. For general purpose governments that failed to report in the prior census or subsequent annual surveys, a responding county, municipality, or township from the same group as the nonrespondent was randomly selected and per capita values for the respondent were multiplied by the population of the nonrespondent to get imputed values for the nonrespondent. For special districts, because of an initial lower response to the mail canvass than for general purpose governments, the special district government portion of the 2002 Census of Governments employed secondary sources and follow-ups more extensively. These efforts included using 2001 fiscal year data if they were available; summary financial data obtained during the organization phase of the 2002 Census of Governments, the American Hospital Association, Mergent Municipal and Government Manual, Bond Buyer's database, and various state agencies and departments.

Estimates of Sampling Error: Since the census of governments is based on a survey whose coverage extends to all governments in the universe, there is no sampling error to be accounted for.

Other (nonsampling) Errors: Only 10.7 percent of counties, and 18.5 percent of the municipalities and townships, and 35.3 percent of the special districts were total nonrespondents to the census. Other nonsampling errors

include response errors and processing errors, many of which are corrected through computer and analyst checks.

Sources of Additional Material: U.S. Census Bureau, 2002 Census of Governments, various reports and Web site at <http://www.census.gov/govs/www/cog2002.html> and the "Federal, State, and Local Governments, Government Finance and Employment Classification Manual" found at <http://ftp2.census.gov/govs/class/classfull.pdf>.

2002 Economic Census

Universe, Frequency, and Types of Data: Conducted every 5 years to obtain data on number of establishments, number of employees, total payroll size, total sales/receipts/revenues, and other industry-specific statistics. In 2002, the universe was all employer and nonemployer establishments primarily engaged in wholesale, retail, utilities, finance and insurance, real estate, transportation and warehousing, information, education, health care, and other service industries.

Type of Data Collection Operation: All large employer firms were surveyed (i.e., all employer firms above payroll size cutoffs established to separate large from small employers) plus a 5 percent to 25 percent sample of the small employer firms. Firms with no employees were not required to file a census return.

Data Collection and Imputation Procedures: Mail questionnaires were used with both mail and telephone follow-ups for nonrespondents. Data for nonrespondents and for small employer firms not mailed a questionnaire were obtained from administrative records of other federal agencies or imputed. Nonemployer data were obtained exclusively from IRS 2002 income tax returns.

Estimates of Sampling Error: Not applicable for basic data such as sales, revenue, receipts, and payroll.

Other (nonsampling) Errors: Establishment response rates by North American Industry Classification System (NAICS) sector in 2002 ranged from 80 percent to 89 percent. Item response rates generally ranged from 50 percent to 90 percent with lower rates for the more detailed questions. Nonsampling errors may occur during the collection, reporting, and keying of data, and due to industry misclassification.

Sources of Additional Material: U.S. Census Bureau, 2002 Economic Census, Geographic Area Series Reports (by NAICS sector), Appendix C and <http://www.census.gov/econ/census02/guide/index.html>.

Census of Population

Universe, Frequency, and Types of Data: Complete count of U.S. population conducted every 10 years since 1790. Data obtained on number and characteristics of people in the United States.

Type of Data Collection Operation: In 1980, 1990, and 2000, complete census for some items—age, date of birth, sex, race, and relationship to householder. In 1980, approximately 19 percent of the housing units were included in the sample; in 1990 and 2000, approximately 17 percent were included.

Data Collection and Imputation Procedures: In 1980, 1990, and 2000, mail questionnaires were used extensively with personal interviews in the remainder. Extensive telephone and personal follow-up for nonrespondents was done in the censuses. Imputations were made for missing characteristics.

Estimates of Sampling Error: Sampling errors for data are estimated for all items collected by sample and vary by characteristic and geographic area. The CVs for national and state estimates are generally very small.

Other (nonsampling) Errors: Since 1950, evaluation programs have been conducted to provide information on the magnitude of some sources of nonsampling errors such as response bias and undercoverage in each census. Results from the evaluation program for the 1990 census indicated that the estimated net undercoverage amounted to about 1.5 percent of the total resident population. For Census 2000, the evaluation program indicated a net over-count of 0.5 percent of the resident population.

Sources of Additional Material: U.S. Census Bureau, *1990 Census of Population and Housing, Content Reinterview Survey: Accuracy of Data for Selected Population and Housing Characteristics as Measured by Reinterview*, CPH-E-1; *1990 Census of Population and Housing, Effectiveness of Quality Assurance*, CPH-E-2; Programs to Improve Coverage in the 1990 Census, CPH-E-3. For Census 2000, see <http://www.census.gov/pred/www>.

County Business Patterns

Universe, Frequency, and Types of Data: County Business Patterns is an annual tabulation of basic data items extracted from the Business Register, a file of all known single- and multilocation companies maintained and updated by the Census Bureau. Data include number of establishments, number of employees, first quarter and annual payrolls, and number of establishments by employment size class. Data are excluded for self-employed persons, domestic service workers, railroad employees, agricultural production workers, and most government employees.

Type of Data Collection Operation: The annual Company Organization Survey provides individual establishment data for multilocation companies. Data for single establishment companies are obtained from various Census Bureau programs, such as the Annual Survey of Manufactures and Current Business Surveys, as well as from administrative records of the IRS and the Social Security Administration.

Estimates of Sampling Error: Not applicable.

Other (nonsampling) Error: The data are subject to nonsampling errors, such as industry classification errors, as well as errors of response, keying, and nonreporting.

Sources of Additional Materials: U.S. Census Bureau, *General Explanation of County Business Patterns*. See also "Frequently Asked County Business Patterns (CBP) Questions" at <http://www.census.gov/epcd/cbp/view/cbpfaq.html>.

Monthly Survey of Construction

Universe, Frequency, and Types of Data: Survey conducted monthly of newly constructed housing units (excluding mobile homes). Data are collected on the start, completion, and sale of housing. (Annual figures are aggregates of monthly estimates.)

Type of Data Collection Operation: For permit-issuing places, probability sample of 850 housing units obtained from 19,000 permit-issuing places. For nonpermit places, multistage probability sample of new housing units selected in 169 PSUs. In those areas, all roads are canvassed in selected enumeration districts.

Data Collection and Imputation Procedures: Data are obtained by telephone inquiry and field visit.

Estimates of Sampling Error: Estimated CV of 3 percent to 4 percent for estimates of national totals but may be higher for estimated totals of more detailed characteristics, such as housing units in multiunit structures.

Other (nonsampling) Errors: Response rate is over 90 percent for most items. Nonsampling errors are attributed to definitional problems, differences in interpretation of questions, incorrect reporting, inability to obtain information about all cases in the sample, and processing errors.

Sources of Additional Material: U.S. Census Bureau, "New Residential Construction" at <http://www.census.gov/const/www/newresconstindex.html>.

Population Estimates

Universe, Frequency, and Types of Data: The Census Bureau annually produces estimates of total resident population for each state and county. County population estimates are produced with a component of population change method, while the state population estimates are solely the sum of the county populations.

Type of Data Collection Operation: The Census Bureau develops county population estimates with a demographic procedure called an "administrative records component of population change" method. A major assumption underlying this approach is that the components of population change are closely approximated by administrative data in a demographic change model. In order to apply the model, Census Bureau demographers estimate each component of population change separately. For the population residing in households, the components of population change are births, deaths, and net migration, including net international migration. For the nonhousehold population, change is represented by the net change in the population living in group quarters facilities.

Estimates of Sampling Error: Not applicable.

Other (nonsampling) Errors: Not available.

Sources of Additional Material: U.S. Census Bureau, "State and County Total Resident Population Estimates Method: July 1, 2006," at <http://www.census.gov/popest /topics/methodology/2006_st_co_meth.html>.

For methodological information on other population estimates datasets, such as housing unit estimates and state population estimates by age, sex, race, and Hispanic origin, see <http://www.census.gov/popest/topics /methodology>.

U.S. FEDERAL BUREAU OF INVESTIGATION (FBI)

Uniform Crime Reporting (UCR) Program

Universe, Frequency, and Types of Data: Monthly reports on the number of criminal offenses that become known to law enforcement agencies. Data are collected on crimes cleared by arrest; by age, sex, and race of arrestees and for victims and offenders for homicides; on fatal and nonfatal assaults against law enforcement officers; and on hate crimes reported.

Type of Data Collection Operation: Crime statistics are based on reports of crime data submitted either directly to the FBI by contributing law enforcement agencies or through cooperating state UCR programs.

Data Collection and Imputation Procedures: States with UCR programs collect data directly from individual law enforcement agencies and forward reports, prepared in accordance with UCR standards, to the FBI. Accuracy and consistency edits are performed by the FBI.

Estimates of Sampling Error: Not applicable.

Other (nonsampling) Errors: Coverage of 94 percent of the population (95 percent in metropolitan statistical areas [MSAs], 84 percent in cities outside of metropolitan areas, and 89 percent in nonmetropolitan counties) by UCR program through a varying number of agencies reporting.

Sources of Additional Material: U.S. Federal Bureau of Investigation, *Crime in the United States*, annual. For most recent report, see Web site at <http://www.fbi.gov/ucr /ucr.htm#cius>.

For additional information, see Appendix I "Methodology" at <http://www.fbi.gov/ucr/cius_03/pdf/03sec7.pdf>.

U.S. INTERNAL REVENUE SERVICE (IRS)

Individual Income Tax Returns

Universe, Frequency, and Types of Data: Annual study of unaudited individual income tax returns, forms 1040, 1040A, and 1040EZ, filed by U.S. citizens and residents. Data provided on various financial characteristics by size of adjusted gross income, marital status, and by taxable and nontaxable returns. Data by state, based on 100 percent file, also include returns from 1040NR, filed by nonresident aliens, plus certain self-employment tax returns.

Type of Data Collection Operation: Annual 2002 stratified probability sample of approximately 176,000 returns broken into sample strata based on the larger of total income or total loss amounts as well as the size of business plus farm receipts. Sampling rates for sample strata varied from 0.05 percent to 100 percent.

Data Collection and Imputation Procedures: Computer selection of sample of tax return records. Data adjusted during editing for incorrect, missing, or inconsistent entries to ensure consistency with other entries on return.

Estimates of Sampling Error: Estimated CVs for tax year 2002—adjusted gross income less deficit 0.12 percent; salaries and wages 0.21 percent; and tax exempt interest received 1.78 percent. (State data not subject to sampling error.)

Other (nonsampling) Errors: Processing errors and errors arising from the use of tolerance checks for the data.

Sources of Additional Material: U.S. Internal Revenue Service, *Statistics of Income, Individual Income Tax Returns*, annual. For recent report, see Web site at <http://www.irs.gov/taxstats/index.html>. For information about methodology and sample, see "Description of the Sample" at <http://www.irs.gov/pub/irs-soi /02insec2.pdf>.

NATIONAL CENTER FOR HEALTH STATISTICS (NCHS)

National Vital Statistics System

Universe, Frequency, and Types of Data: Annual data on births and deaths in the United States.

Type of Data Collection Operation: Mortality data based on complete file of death records, except 1972, based on 50 percent sample. Natality statistics 1951–1971, based on 50 percent sample of birth certificates, except a 20 percent to 50 percent sample in 1967, received by NCHS. Beginning 1972, data from some states received through Vital Statistics Cooperative Program

(VSCP) and complete file used; data from other states based on 50 percent sample. Beginning 1986, all reporting areas participated in the VSCP.

Data Collection and Imputation Procedures: Reports based on records from registration offices of all states, District of Columbia, New York City, Puerto Rico, Virgin Islands, Guam, American Samoa, and Northern Mariana Islands.

Estimates of Sampling Error: For recent years, there is no sampling for these files; the files are based on 100 percent of events registered.

Other (nonsampling) Errors: Data on births and deaths believed to be at least 99 percent complete.

Sources of Additional Material: U.S. National Center for Health Statistics, *Vital Statistics of the United States*, Vol. I and Vol. II, annual; and *National Vital Statistics Reports*. See NCHS Web site at <http://www.cdc.gov/nchs/nvss.htm>.

For more information about the National Vital Statistics System, see <http://www.cdc.gov/nchs/data/misc/usvss.pdf>.

Geographic Information

Appendix C

Page

You may visit us on the Web at
http://www.census.gov/compendia/ccdb

Appendix C

Appendix C.
Geographic Information

Table A—States

States are the primary governmental divisions of the United States. The District of Columbia is treated as a statistical equivalent of a state for census purposes. A map showing the United States with census regions and divisions and their constituent states appears on the inside front cover.

Each state and the District of Columbia is assigned a two-digit Federal Information Processing Standards (FIPS) code. The FIPS state code is a sequential numbering, with some gaps, of the alphabetical arrangement of the states and the District of Columbia: Alabama (01) to Wyoming (56). These codes are presented in the first column of table A-1.

FIPS codes are issued by the National Institute of Standards and Technology for a variety of geographical entities, including states, counties, metropolitan areas, and places. The objective of the FIPS codes is to improve the transferability of the data resources within the federal government and to avoid unnecessary duplication and incompatibilities in the collection, processing, and dissemination of data. FIPS code documentation is available from the National Technical Information Service, Springfield, VA, 22161 (703-487-4650). State FIPS codes can be viewed at Internet site <http://www.itl.nist.gov/fipspubs/fip5-2.htm>.

Table B—Counties

The primary political divisions of most states are termed "counties." In Louisiana, these divisions are known as "parishes." In Alaska, which has no counties, the county equivalents are the organized "boroughs" and the "census areas" that are delineated for statistical purposes by the State of Alaska and the U.S. Census Bureau. In four states (Maryland, Missouri, Nevada, and Virginia), there are one or more cities that are independent of any county organization and, thus, constitute primary divisions of their states. These cities are known as "independent cities" and are treated as equivalent to counties for statistical purposes. The District of Columbia has no primary divisions, and the entire area is considered equivalent to a county for statistical purposes. Maps for each state showing counties and equivalent areas can be found in Appendix D.

Each county and statistically equivalent entity is assigned a three-digit FIPS code that is unique within a state. These codes are assigned in alphabetical order of county or county equivalents except for the independent cities, which are assigned codes higher than and following the listing of counties. The combination of a FIPS two-digit state code followed by a FIPS three-digit county code provides a unique geographic identifier for each county and equivalent area. These codes are presented in the third column of table C-2 at the end of this appendix. County codes can be viewed at Internet site <http://www.itl.nist.gov/fipspubs/fip6-4.htm>.

Metropolitan areas. The first column of table C-2 presents the five-digit core based statistical area (CBSA) code for the metropolitan area (MA) in which the county is located. The codes represent metropolitan areas defined by the Office of Management and Budget as of December 5, 2005. An MA containing a single core with a population of 2.5 million or more may be subdivided into smaller groupings of counties referred to as metropolitan divisions (MDs). The second column of table C-2 presents the five-digit MD.

A complete listing of these MAs with their component counties and 2006 population can be found at the end of this appendix in table C-2. For a discussion of metropolitan area concepts, see Internet site <http://www.census.gov/population/www/estimates/metroarea.html>. Other data for these areas are not presented in this volume but are published in another *Statistical Abstract* supplement, the *State and Metropolitan Area Data Book*. For a complete description, see the inside back cover.

County and county equivalent changes. Counties and equivalent areas shown in tables B-1 through B-15 of this publication total 3,141 as of November 15, 2001, when Bloomfield County was created from parts of Adams, Boulder, Jefferson, and Weld Counties. The boundaries of Broomfield County reflect the boundaries of Broomfield city legally in effect on that date. Between January 1, 1992, when the number of counties was previously defined, and November 15, 2001, there have been a number of changes to counties and equivalent areas. These changes are summarized below.

In Alaska: Effective September 22, 1992, the Yakutat Borough was established; this new borough was created from part of the Skagway-Yakutat-Angoon Census Area (CA) with the remaining area being renamed the Skagway-Hoonah-Angoon CA. Effective January 1, 1994, Juneau Borough gained territory from Skagway-Hoonah-Angoon CA.

In Maryland: Effective July 1, 1997, Montgomery County expanded to include all of the former Prince George's County part of Takoma Park city and Prince George's County decreased as a result of the county boundary shift excluding Takoma Park city.

In Montana: Effective November 7, 1997, Gallatin County was expanded by addition of territory from the former county equivalent of Yellowstone National Park. Park County was also expanded by addition of territory from the former county equivalent of Yellowstone National Park. This change eliminates Yellowstone National Park as a county equivalent.

In Virginia: Effective July 1, 1993, the independent city of Bedford gained area annexed from Bedford County; the independent city of Galax gained area annexed from Carroll County; and the independent city of Fairfax gained area annexed from Fairfax County. Effective July 1, 1994, the independent city of Waynesboro gained area annexed from Augusta County. Effective June 30, 1995, the independent city of South Boston no longer exists; it became a dependent town within Halifax County. Effective December 31, 1995, the independent city of Franklin gained area annexed from Southampton County. Effective July 1, 2001, the independent city of Clifton Forge no longer exists; it became a dependent town within Alleghany County.

Table C—Cities

As used in this publication, the term "city" refers to incorporated places with a 2000 population of 25,000 or more and the Honolulu and Arlington census designated places (CDPs) of Hawaii and Virginia, respectively. Incorporated places presented in this table are those reported to the Census Bureau as legally in existence on January 1, 2005, under the laws of their respective states, as cities, boroughs, municipalities, towns, and villages, with the following exceptions: the boroughs in Alaska and New York and the towns in the New England states, New York, and Wisconsin. The boroughs in Alaska are county equivalents and are shown in table B. The boroughs in New York and the towns in the states noted above are treated as minor civil divisions (MCDs) for decennial purposes. For those cities that legally came into existence after January 1, 2000, the estimated 2000 population for that area was used to determine inclusion in table C. Incorporated places can cross both county and MCD boundaries.

In table C, the two-digit FIPS state codes and five-digit FIPS place codes are presented in the first column of table C-1. Each place is assigned a five-digit FIPS place code that is unique within the state based on alphabetical order within the state. Together with the two-digit FIPS state code, this code provides a unique identifier for each place in the country. To view place codes see, Internet site <http://geonames.usgs.gov/domestic/download_data.htm>.

Also in table C, the name of the county or county equivalent in which the city is located is shown in the column following the area name in table C-1. If a city crosses county boundaries, all counties in which the city is located are listed alphabetically.

Consolidated cities. As of 2005, the Census Bureau recognized seven entities that had consolidated their city governmental function with a county or MCD but continue to contain governmentally active incorporated places within and as part of those consolidated cities. These areas with their components and 2005 population are listed below in table C-1. In table C, the data for cities shown in tables C-1 through C-6 of this publication cover only the portion of the consolidated city not in any other place, e.g., "Milford city (balance)."

Table C-1. Consolidated Cities and Components

Area name	2005 population
Milford city, CT	54,802
(coextensive with Milford town)	
Milford city (balance)	53,045
Woodmont borough	1,757
Athens-Clarke County, GA	104,439
(coextensive with Clarke County)	
Athens-Clarke County (balance)	103,238
Bogart town (part)	142
Winterville city	1,059
Augusta-Richmond County, GA	195,769
(coextensive with Richmond County)	
Augusta-Richmond County (balance)	190,782
Blythe city	777
Hephzibah city	4,210
Indianapolis, IN	793,968
(not coextensive with Marion County due to exclusion of following four places:	
Beech Grove city 14,069	
Lawrence city 40,959	
Southport city 1,729	
Speedway town 12,408)	
Clermont town	1,461
Crows Nest town	101
Cumberland town	2,726
Homecroft town	733
Indianapolis city (balance)	784,118
Meridian Hills town	1,695
North Crows Nest town	42
Rocky Ripple town	697
Spring Hill town	96
Warren Park town	1,620
Williams Creek town	408
Wynnedale town	271
Louisville/Jefferson County, KY	699,827
(coextensive with Jefferson County)	
Anchorage city	2,529
Audubon Park city	1,535
Bancroft city	542
Barbourmeade city	1,272
Beechwood Village city	1,170
Bellemeade city	873
Bellewood city	303
Blue Ridge Manor city	627
Briarwood city	554
Broeck Pointe city	297
Brownsboro Farm city	678
Brownsboro Village city	316
Cambridge city	192

Table C-1. **Consolidated Cities and Components**—Con.

Area name	2005 population
Louisville/Jefferson County, KY—Con.	
Coldstream city	966
Creekside city	353
Crossgate city	252
Douglass Hills city	5,597
Druid Hills city	317
Fincastle city	833
Forest Hills city	507
Glenview city	636
Glenview Hills city	341
Glenview Manor city	194
Goose Creek city	273
Graymoor-Devondale city	2,937
Green Spring city	773
Hickory Hill city	145
Hills and Dales city	158
Hollow Creek city	821
Hollyvilla city	494
Houston Acres city	491
Hurstbourne city	3,939
Hurstbourne Acres city	1,505
Indian Hills city	2,977
Jeffersontown city	26,100
Kingsley city	424
Langdon Place city	980
Lincolnshire city	154
Louisville/Jefferson County (balance)	556,429
Lyndon city	10,248
Lynnview city	960
Manor Creek city	223
Maryhill Estates city	176
Meadowbrook Farm city	147
Meadow Vale city	770
Meadowview Estates city	421
Middletown city	6,072
Minor Lane Heights city	1,526
Mockingbird Valley city	199
Moorland city	463
Murray Hill city	618
Norbourne Estates city	457
Northfield city	984
Norwood city	397
Old Brownsboro Place city	389
Parkway Village city	706
Plantation city	903
Poplar Hills city	402
Prospect city	4,774
Richlawn city	452
Riverwood city	477
Rolling Fields city	653
Rolling Hills city	907
St. Matthews city	17,309
St. Regis Park city	1,526
Seneca Gardens city	695
Shively city	15,212
South Park View city	201
Spring Mill city	384
Spring Valley city	677
Strathmoor Manor city	330
Strathmoor Village city	619
Sycamore city	159
Ten Broeck city	143
Thornhill city	176
Watterson Park city	1,046
Wellington city	556
West Buechel city	1,323

Table C-1. **Consolidated Cities and Components**—Con.

Area name	2005 population
Westwood city	614
Wildwood city	248
Windy Hills city	2,504
Woodland Hills city	661
Woodlawn Park city	1,034
Worthington Hills city	1,602
Butte-Silver Bow, MT	32,982
(coextensive with Silver Bow County)	
Butte-Silver Bow (balance)	32,282
Walkerville town	700
Nashville-Davidson, TN	575,261
(coextensive with Davidson County)	
Belle Meade city	3,100
Berry Hill city	684
Forest Hills city	5,168
Goodlettsville city	10,007
Lakewood city	2,388
Nashville-Davidson (balance)	549,110
Oak Hill city	4,747
Ridgetop city	57

Table D—Places

The term "place," for the purposes of this publication, refers to incorporated places with a 2000 population of 100,000 or more and the Honolulu and Arlington CDPs of Hawaii and Virginia, respectively. Seven states (Delaware, Maine, Montana, North Dakota, Vermont, West Virginia, and Wyoming) do not have any incorporated places of 100,000 or more population. Incorporated places presented in this table are those reported to the Census Bureau as legally in existence on January 1, 2005, under the laws of their respective states, as cities, boroughs, municipalities, towns, and villages, with the following exceptions: the boroughs in Alaska and New York and the towns in the New England states, New York, and Wisconsin. The boroughs in Alaska are county equivalents and are shown in table B. The boroughs in New York and the towns in the states noted above are treated as MCDs for decennial purposes. For those places that legally came into existence after January 1, 2005, the estimated 2000 population for that area was used to determine inclusion in table D. Incorporated places can cross both county and MCD boundaries.

Consolidated cities. As of 2005, the Census Bureau recognized five entities with a population of 100,000 or more that had consolidated their city governmental function with a county or MCD but continue to contain governmentally active incorporated places within and as part of those consolidated cities. These areas with their components and 2005 population are listed above in table C-1. In table D, the data for places shown in tables D-1 through D-6 of this publication cover only the portion of the consolidated city not in any other place, e.g., "Indianapolis city (balance)."

In table D, the two-digit FIPS state codes and five-digit FIPS place codes are presented in the first column of table D-1. Each place is assigned a five-digit FIPS place code that is unique within the state based on alphabetical order within the state. Together with the two-digit FIPS state code, this code provides a unique identifier for each place in the country. To view place codes, see Internet site <http://geonames.usgs.gov/domestic/download_data.htm>.

Table C-2. **Metropolitan Areas and Component Counties**

[Metropolitan areas (MAs) defined as of December 18, 2006. CBSA = Core based statistical area; FIPS = Federal Information Processing Standards]

CBSA	Metro-politan divi-sion	State and county FIPS	Metropolitan statistical area / *Metropolitan division* / Component county	2006 population
10180			**Abilene, TX**	**158,063**
		48059	Callahan County, TX	13,491
		48253	Jones County, TX	19,645
		48441	Taylor County, TX	124,927
10420			**Akron, OH**	**700,943**
		39133	Portage County, OH	155,012
		39153	Summit County, OH	545,931
10500			**Albany, GA**	**163,961**
		13007	Baker County, GA	4,098
		13095	Dougherty County, GA	94,773
		13177	Lee County, GA	32,495
		13273	Terrell County, GA	10,657
		13321	Worth County, GA	21,938
10580			**Albany-Schenectady-Troy, NY**	**850,957**
		36001	Albany County, NY	297,556
		36083	Rensselaer County, NY	155,292
		36091	Saratoga County, NY	215,473
		36093	Schenectady County, NY	150,440
		36095	Schoharie County, NY	32,196
10740			**Albuquerque, NM**	**816,811**
		35001	Bernalillo County, NM	615,099
		35043	Sandoval County, NM	113,772
		35057	Torrance County, NM	17,551
		35061	Valencia County, NM	70,389
10780			**Alexandria, LA**	**150,080**
		22043	Grant Parish, LA	19,879
		22079	Rapides Parish, LA	130,201
10900			**Allentown-Bethlehem-Easton, PA-NJ**	**800,336**
		34041	Warren County, NJ	110,919
		42025	Carbon County, PA	62,567
		42077	Lehigh County, PA	335,544
		42095	Northampton County, PA	291,306
11020			**Altoona, PA**	**126,494**
		42013	Blair County, PA	126,494
11100			**Amarillo, TX**	**241,515**
		48011	Armstrong County, TX	2,120
		48065	Carson County, TX	6,595
		48375	Potter County, TX	121,328
		48381	Randall County, TX	111,472
11180			**Ames, IA**	**80,145**
		19169	Story County, IA	80,145
11260			**Anchorage, AK**	**359,180**
		02020	Anchorage Municipality, AK	278,700
		02170	Matanuska-Susitna Borough, AK	80,480
11300			**Anderson, IN**	**130,575**
		18095	Madison County, IN	130,575
11340			**Anderson, SC**	**177,963**
		45007	Anderson County, SC	177,963
11460			**Ann Arbor, MI**	**344,047**
		26161	Washtenaw County, MI	344,047
11500			**Anniston-Oxford, AL**	**112,903**
		01015	Calhoun County, AL	112,903
11540			**Appleton, WI**	**217,313**
		55015	Calumet County, WI	44,579
		55087	Outagamie County, WI	172,734
11700			**Asheville, NC**	**398,009**
		37021	Buncombe County, NC	222,174
		37087	Haywood County, NC	56,447
		37089	Henderson County, NC	99,033
		37115	Madison County, NC	20,355
12020			**Athens-Clarke County, GA**	**185,479**
		13059	Clarke County, GA	112,787
		13195	Madison County, GA	27,837
		13219	Oconee County, GA	30,858
		13221	Oglethorpe County, GA	13,997
12060			**Atlanta-Sandy Springs-Marietta, GA**	**5,138,223**
		13013	Barrow County, GA	63,702
		13015	Bartow County, GA	91,266
		13035	Butts County, GA	23,561
		13045	Carroll County, GA	107,325
		13057	Cherokee County, GA	195,327
		13063	Clayton County, GA	271,240
		13067	Cobb County, GA	679,325
		13077	Coweta County, GA	115,291
		13085	Dawson County, GA	20,643
		13089	DeKalb County, GA	723,602
		13097	Douglas County, GA	119,557
		13113	Fayette County, GA	106,671
		13117	Forsyth County, GA	150,968
		13121	Fulton County, GA	960,009
		13135	Gwinnett County, GA	757,104
12060			**Atlanta-Sandy Springs-Marietta, GA—Con.**	
		13143	Haralson County, GA	28,616
		13149	Heard County, GA	11,472
		13151	Henry County, GA	178,033
		13159	Jasper County, GA	13,624
		13171	Lamar County, GA	16,679
		13199	Meriwether County, GA	22,881
		13217	Newton County, GA	91,451
		13223	Paulding County, GA	121,530
		13227	Pickens County, GA	29,640
		13231	Pike County, GA	16,801
		13247	Rockdale County, GA	80,332
		13255	Spalding County, GA	62,185
		13297	Walton County, GA	79,388
12100			**Atlantic City, NJ**	**271,620**
		34001	Atlantic County, NJ	271,620
12220			**Auburn-Opelika, AL**	**125,781**
		01081	Lee County, AL	125,781
12260			**Augusta-Richmond County, GA-SC**	**523,249**
		13033	Burke County, GA	22,986
		13073	Columbia County, GA	106,887
		13189	McDuffie County, GA	21,917
		13245	Richmond County, GA	194,398
		45003	Aiken County, SC	151,800
		45037	Edgefield County, SC	25,261
12420			**Austin-Round Rock, TX**	**1,513,565**
		48021	Bastrop County, TX	71,684
		48055	Caldwell County, TX	36,720
		48209	Hays County, TX	130,325
		48453	Travis County, TX	921,006
		48491	Williamson County, TX	353,830
12540			**Bakersfield, CA**	**780,117**
		06029	Kern County, CA	780,117
12580			**Baltimore-Towson, MD**	**2,658,405**
		24003	Anne Arundel County, MD	509,300
		24005	Baltimore County, MD	787,384
		24013	Carroll County, MD	170,260
		24025	Harford County, MD	241,402
		24027	Howard County, MD	272,452
		24035	Queen Anne's County, MD	46,241
		24510	Baltimore city, MD	631,366
12620			**Bangor, ME**	**147,180**
		23019	Penobscot County, ME	147,180
12700			**Barnstable Town, MA**	**224,816**
		25001	Barnstable County, MA	224,816
12940			**Baton Rouge, LA**	**766,514**
		22005	Ascension Parish, LA	97,335
		22033	East Baton Rouge Parish, LA	429,073
		22037	East Feliciana Parish, LA	20,922
		22047	Iberville Parish, LA	32,974
		22063	Livingston Parish, LA	114,805
		22077	Pointe Coupee Parish, LA	22,648
		22091	St. Helena Parish, LA	10,759
		22121	West Baton Rouge Parish, LA	22,463
		22125	West Feliciana Parish, LA	15,535
12980			**Battle Creek, MI**	**137,991**
		26025	Calhoun County, MI	137,991
13020			**Bay City, MI**	**108,390**
		26017	Bay County, MI	108,390
13140			**Beaumont-Port Arthur, TX**	**379,640**
		48199	Hardin County, TX	51,483
		48245	Jefferson County, TX	243,914
		48361	Orange County, TX	84,243
13380			**Bellingham, WA**	**185,953**
		53073	Whatcom County, WA	185,953
13460			**Bend, OR**	**149,140**
		41017	Deschutes County, OR	149,140
13740			**Billings, MT**	**148,116**
		30009	Carbon County, MT	9,903
		30111	Yellowstone County, MT	138,213
13780			**Binghamton, NY**	**247,554**
		36007	Broome County, NY	196,269
		36107	Tioga County, NY	51,285
13820			**Birmingham-Hoover, AL**	**1,100,019**
		01007	Bibb County, AL	21,482
		01009	Blount County, AL	56,436
		01021	Chilton County, AL	41,953
		01073	Jefferson County, AL	656,700
		01115	St. Clair County, AL	75,232
		01117	Shelby County, AL	178,182
		01127	Walker County, AL	70,034

Table C-2. **Metropolitan Areas and Component Counties**—Con.

[Metropolitan areas (MAs) defined as of December 18, 2006. CBSA = Core based statistical area; FIPS = Federal Information Processing Standards]

Geographic codes			Metropolitan statistical area *Metropolitan division* Component county	2006 population	Geographic codes			Metropolitan statistical area *Metropolitan division* Component county	2006 population
CBSA	Metropolitan division	State and county FIPS			CBSA	Metropolitan division	State and county FIPS		
13900			**Bismarck, ND.**	**101,138**	16700			**Charleston-North Charleston, SC**	**603,178**
		38015	Burleigh County, ND	75,384			45015	Berkeley County, SC	152,282
		38059	Morton County, ND	25,754			45019	Charleston County, SC	331,917
13980			**Blacksburg-Christiansburg-Radford, VA** . .	**151,524**			45035	Dorchester County, SC	118,979
		51071	Giles County, VA	17,403	16740			**Charlotte-Gastonia-Concord, NC-SC**	**1,583,016**
		51121	Montgomery County, VA	84,541			37007	Anson County, NC	25,472
		51155	Pulaski County, VA	35,055			37025	Cabarrus County, NC	156,395
		51750	Radford city, VA	14,525			37071	Gaston County, NC	199,397
14020			**Bloomington, IN.**	**178,714**			37119	Mecklenburg County, NC	827,445
		18055	Greene County, IN	33,360			37179	Union County, NC	175,272
		18105	Monroe County, IN	122,613			45091	York County, SC	199,035
		18119	Owen County, IN.	22,741	16820			**Charlottesville, VA**	**190,278**
14060			**Bloomington-Normal, IL**	**161,202**			51003	Albemarle, County, VA	92,035
		17113	McLean County, IL	161,202			51065	Fluvanna County, VA	25,058
14260			**Boise City-Nampa, ID**	**567,640**			51079	Greene County, VA	17,709
		16001	Ada County, ID.	359,035			51125	Nelson County, VA	15,161
		16015	Boise County, ID.	7,641			51540	Charlottesville city, VA	40,315
		16027	Canyon County, ID	173,302	16860			**Chattanooga, TN-GA.**	**496,704**
		16045	Gem County, ID	16,558			13047	Catoosa County, GA	62,016
		16073	Owyhee County, ID	11,104			13083	Dade County, GA	16,233
14460			**Boston-Cambridge-Quincy, MA-NH**	**4,455,217**			13295	Walker County, GA	64,606
	14484		*Boston-Quincy, MA.*	*1,835,986*			47065	Hamilton County, TN	312,905
		25021	Norfolk County, MA	654,753			47115	Marion County, TN	27,942
		25023	Plymouth County, MA	493,623			47153	Sequatchie County, TN	13,002
		25025	Suffolk County, MA	687,610	16940			**Cheyenne, WY**	**85,384**
	15764		*Cambridge-Newton-Framingham, MA. . . .*	*1,467,016*			56021	Laramie County, WY	85,384
		25017	Middlesex County, MA	1,467,016	16980			**Chicago-Naperville-Joliet, IL-IN-WI**	**9,505,748**
	37764		*Peabody, MA.*	*735,958*		16974		*Chicago-Naperville-Joliet, IL.*	*7,929,775*
		25009	Essex County, MA	735,958			17031	Cook County, IL.	5,288,655
	40484		*Rockingham County-* *Strafford County, NH*	*416,257*			17037	DeKalb County, IL.	100,139
		33015	Rockingham County, NH	296,267			17043	DuPage County, IL.	932,670
		33017	Strafford County, NH	119,990			17063	Grundy County, IL.	45,828
14500			**Boulder, CO.**	**282,304**			17089	Kane County, IL.	493,735
		08013	Boulder County, CO	282,304			17093	Kendall County, IL.	88,158
14540			**Bowling Green, KY**	**113,320**			17111	McHenry County, IL.	312,373
		21061	Edmonson County, KY	12,054			17197	Will County, IL.	668,217
		21227	Warren County, KY	101,266		23844		*Gary, IN*	*700,896*
14740			**Bremerton-Silverdale, WA**	**240,604**			18073	Jasper County, IN	32,296
		53035	Kitsap County, WA	240,604			18089	Lake County, IN	494,202
14860			**Bridgeport-Stamford-Norwalk, CT**	**900,440**			18111	Newton County, IN	14,293
		09001	Fairfield County, CT.	900,440			18127	Porter County, IN	160,105
15180			**Brownsville-Harlingen, TX.**	**387,717**		29404		*Lake County-Kenosha County, IL-WI . . . .*	*875,077*
		48061	Cameron County, TX.	387,717			17097	Lake County, IL	713,076
15260			**Brunswick, GA.**	**100,613**			55059	Kenosha County, WI	162,001
		13025	Brantley County, GA	15,735	17020			**Chico, CA**	**215,881**
		13127	Glynn County, GA	73,630			06007	Butte County, CA	215,881
		13191	McIntosh County, GA.	11,248	17140			**Cincinnati-Middletown, OH-KY-IN**	**2,104,218**
15380			**Buffalo-Niagara Falls, NY**	**1,137,520**			18029	Dearborn County, IN	49,663
		36029	Erie County, NY	921,390			18047	Franklin County, IN	23,373
		36063	Niagara County, NY.	216,130			18115	Ohio County, IN	5,826
15500			**Burlington, NC.**	**142,661**			21015	Boone County, KY	110,080
		37001	Alamance County, NC	142,661			21023	Bracken County, KY	8,655
15540			**Burlington-South Burlington, VT**	**206,007**			21037	Campbell County, KY.	86,866
		50007	Chittenden County, VT.	150,069			21077	Gallatin County, KY	8,153
		50011	Franklin County, VT.	48,187			21081	Grant County, KY	24,769
		50013	Grand Isle County, VT	7,751			21117	Kenton County, KY	154,911
15940			**Canton-Massillon, OH.**	**409,764**			21191	Pendleton County, KY	15,334
		39019	Carroll County, OH	29,189			39015	Brown County, OH	44,423
		39151	Stark County, OH	380,575			39017	Butler County, OH	354,992
15980			**Cape Coral-Fort Myers, FL**	**571,344**			39025	Clermont County, OH	192,706
		12071	Lee County, FL.	571,344			39061	Hamilton County, OH	822,596
16180			**Carson City, NV**	**55,289**			39165	Warren County, OH	201,871
		32510	Carson City, NV	55,289	17300			**Clarksville, TN-KY**	**240,500**
16220			**Casper, WY**	**70,401**			21047	Christian County, KY	66,989
		56025	Natrona County, WY	70,401			21221	Trigg County, KY.	13,399
16300			**Cedar Rapids, IA**	**249,320**			47125	Montgomery County, TN	147,114
		19011	Benton County, IA	26,962			47161	Stewart County, TN	12,998
		19105	Jones County, IA.	20,505	17420			**Cleveland, TN**	**109,477**
		19113	Linn County, IA.	201,853			47011	Bradley County, TN	93,538
16580			**Champaign-Urbana, IL**	**216,581**			47139	Polk County, TN	15,939
		17019	Champaign County, IL	185,682	17460			**Cleveland-Elyria-Mentor, OH**	**2,114,155**
		17053	Ford County, IL.	14,211			39035	Cuyahoga County, OH	1,314,241
		17147	Piatt County, IL.	16,688			39055	Geauga County, OH	95,676
16620			**Charleston, WV**	**305,526**			39085	Lake County, OH	232,892
		54005	Boone County, WV	25,512			39093	Lorain County, OH.	301,993
		54015	Clay County, WV.	10,256			39103	Medina County, OH.	169,353
		54039	Kanawha County, WV	192,419	17660			**Coeur d'Alene, ID.**	**131,507**
		54043	Lincoln County, WV	22,357			16055	Kootenai County, ID.	131,507
		54079	Putnam County, WV	54,982	17780			**College Station-Bryan, TX.**	**192,152**
							48041	Brazos County, TX	159,006
							48051	Burleson County, TX	16,932
							48395	Robertson County, TX	16,214
					17820			**Colorado Springs, CO.**	**599,127**
							08041	El Paso County, CO	576,884
							08119	Teller County, CO	22,243
					17860			**Columbia, MO**	**155,997**
							29019	Boone County, MO	146,048
							29089	Howard County, MO	9,949

U.S. Census Bureau

Table C-2. **Metropolitan Areas and Component Counties**—Con.

[Metropolitan areas (MAs) defined as of December 18, 2006. CBSA = Core based statistical area; FIPS = Federal Information Processing Standards]

CBSA	Metropolitan division	State and county FIPS	Metropolitan statistical area / *Metropolitan division* / Component county	2006 population
17900			**Columbia, SC**	**703,771**
		45017	Calhoun County, SC	15,026
		45039	Fairfield County, SC	23,810
		45055	Kershaw County, SC	57,490
		45063	Lexington County, SC	240,160
		45079	Richland County, SC	348,226
		45081	Saluda County, SC	19,059
17980			**Columbus, GA-AL**	**288,847**
		01113	Russell County, AL	50,085
		13053	Chattahoochee County, GA	14,041
		13145	Harris County, GA	28,785
		13197	Marion County, GA	7,276
		13215	Muscogee County, GA	188,660
18020			**Columbus, IN**	**74,444**
		18005	Bartholomew County, IN	74,444
18140			**Columbus, OH**	**1,725,570**
		39041	Delaware County, OH	156,697
		39045	Fairfield County, OH	140,591
		39049	Franklin County, OH	1,095,662
		39089	Licking County, OH	156,287
		39097	Madison County, OH	41,496
		39117	Morrow County, OH	34,529
		39129	Pickaway County, OH	53,606
		39159	Union County, OH	46,702
18580			**Corpus Christi, TX**	**415,810**
		48007	Aransas County, TX	24,831
		48355	Nueces County, TX	321,457
		48409	San Patricio County, TX	69,522
18700			**Corvallis, OR**	**79,061**
		41003	Benton County, OR	79,061
19060			**Cumberland, MD-WV**	**99,759**
		24001	Allegany County, MD	72,831
		54057	Mineral County, WV	26,928
19100			**Dallas-Fort Worth-Arlington, TX**	**6,003,967**
	19124		*Dallas-Plano-Irving, TX*	*4,019,499*
		48085	Collin County, TX	698,851
		48113	Dallas County, TX	2,345,815
		48119	Delta County, TX	5,561
		48121	Denton County, TX	584,238
		48139	Ellis County, TX	139,300
		48231	Hunt County, TX	83,338
		48257	Kaufman County, TX	93,241
		48397	Rockwall County, TX	69,155
	23104		*Fort Worth-Arlington, TX*	*1,984,468*
		48251	Johnson County, TX	149,016
		48367	Parker County, TX	106,266
		48439	Tarrant County, TX	1,671,295
		48497	Wise County, TX	57,891
19140			**Dalton, GA**	**134,397**
		13213	Murray County, GA	41,398
		13313	Whitfield County, GA	92,999
19180			**Danville, IL**	**81,941**
		17183	Vermilion County, IL	81,941
19260			**Danville, VA**	**107,087**
		51143	Pittsylvania County, VA	61,501
		51590	Danville city, VA	45,586
19340			**Davenport-Moline-Rock Island, IA-IL**	**377,291**
		17073	Henry County, IL	50,339
		17131	Mercer County, IL	16,786
		17161	Rock Island County, IL	147,545
		19163	Scott County, IA	162,621
19380			**Dayton, OH**	**838,940**
		39057	Greene County, OH	152,298
		39109	Miami County, OH	101,914
		39113	Montgomery County, OH	542,237
		39135	Preble County, OH	42,491
19460			**Decatur, AL**	**149,549**
		01079	Lawrence County, AL	34,312
		01103	Morgan County, AL	115,237
19500			**Decatur, IL**	**109,309**
		17115	Macon County, IL	109,309
19660			**Deltona-Daytona Beach-Ormond Beach, FL**	**496,575**
		12127	Volusia County, FL	496,575
19740			**Denver-Aurora, CO**	**2,408,750**
		08001	Adams County, CO	414,338
		08005	Arapahoe County, CO	537,197
		08014	Broomfield County, CO	45,116
		08019	Clear Creek County, CO	9,130
		08031	Denver County, CO	566,974
		08035	Douglas County, CO	263,621
19740			**Denver-Aurora, CO—Con.**	
		08039	Elbert County, CO	23,181
		08047	Gilpin County, CO	5,042
		08059	Jefferson County, CO	526,994
		08093	Park County, CO	17,157
19780			**Des Moines-West Des Moines, IA**	**534,230**
		19049	Dallas County, IA	54,525
		19077	Guthrie County, IA	11,344
		19121	Madison County, IA	15,547
		19153	Polk County, IA	408,888
		19181	Warren County, IA	43,926
19820			**Detroit-Warren-Livonia, MI**	**4,468,966**
	19804		*Detroit-Livonia-Dearborn, MI*	*1,971,853*
		26163	Wayne County, MI	1,971,853
	47644		*Warren-Troy-Farmington Hills, MI*	*2,497,113*
		26087	Lapeer County, MI	93,761
		26093	Livingston County, MI	184,511
		26099	Macomb County, MI	832,861
		26125	Oakland County, MI	1,214,255
		26147	St. Clair County, MI	171,725
20020			**Dothan, AL**	**138,234**
		01061	Geneva County, AL	25,868
		01067	Henry County, AL	16,706
		01069	Houston County, AL	95,660
20100			**Dover, DE**	**147,601**
		10001	Kent County, DE	147,601
20220			**Dubuque, IA**	**92,384**
		19061	Dubuque County, IA	92,384
20260			**Duluth, MN-WI**	**274,244**
		27017	Carlton County, MN	34,116
		27137	St. Louis County, MN	196,067
		55031	Douglas County, WI	44,061
20500			**Durham, NC**	**464,389**
		37037	Chatham County, NC	60,052
		37063	Durham County, NC	246,896
		37135	Orange County, NC	120,100
		37145	Person County, NC	37,341
20740			**Eau Claire, WI**	**155,041**
		55017	Chippewa County, WI	60,300
		55035	Eau Claire County, WI	94,741
20940			**El Centro, CA**	**160,301**
		06025	Imperial County, CA	160,301
21060			**Elizabethtown, KY**	**110,878**
		21093	Hardin County, KY	97,087
		21123	Larue County, KY	13,791
21140			**Elkhart-Goshen, IN**	**198,105**
		18039	Elkhart County, IN	198,105
21300			**Elmira, NY**	**88,641**
		36015	Chemung County, NY	88,641
21340			**El Paso, TX**	**736,310**
		48141	El Paso County, TX	736,310
21500			**Erie, PA**	**279,811**
		42049	Erie County, PA	279,811
21660			**Eugene-Springfield, OR**	**337,870**
		41039	Lane County, OR	337,870
21780			**Evansville, IN-KY**	**350,356**
		18051	Gibson County, IN	33,396
		18129	Posey County, IN	26,765
		18163	Vanderburgh County, IN	173,356
		18173	Warrick County, IN	57,090
		21101	Henderson County, KY	45,666
		21233	Webster County, KY	14,083
21820			**Fairbanks, AK**	**86,754**
		02090	Fairbanks North Star Borough, AK	86,754
22020			**Fargo, ND-MN**	**187,001**
		27027	Clay County, MN	54,476
		38017	Cass County, ND	132,525
22140			**Farmington, NM**	**126,473**
		35045	San Juan County, NM	126,473
22180			**Fayetteville, NC**	**341,363**
		37051	Cumberland County, NC	299,060
		37093	Hoke County, NC	42,303
22220			**Fayetteville-Springdale-Rogers, AR-MO**	**420,876**
		05007	Benton County, AR	196,045
		05087	Madison County, AR	15,361
		05143	Washington County, AR	186,521
		29119	McDonald County, MO	22,949

Table C-2. **Metropolitan Areas and Component Counties**—Con.

[Metropolitan areas (MAs) defined as of December 18, 2006. CBSA = Core based statistical area; FIPS = Federal Information Processing Standards]

CBSA	Metropolitan division	State and county FIPS	Metropolitan statistical area / *Metropolitan division* / Component county	2006 population
22380		04005	**Flagstaff, AZ**	**124,953**
			Coconino County, AZ	124,953
22420		26049	**Flint, MI**	**441,966**
			Genesee County, MI	441,966
22500			**Florence, SC**	**198,848**
		45031	Darlington County, SC	67,551
		45041	Florence County, SC	131,297
22520			**Florence-Muscle Shoals, AL**	**142,657**
		01033	Colbert County, AL	54,766
		01077	Lauderdale County, AL	87,891
22540		55039	**Fond du Lac, WI**	**99,243**
			Fond du Lac County, WI	99,243
22660		08069	**Fort Collins-Loveland, CO**	**276,253**
			Larimer County, CO	276,253
22900			**Fort Smith, AR-OK**	**288,818**
		05033	Crawford County, AR	58,785
		05047	Franklin County, AR	18,276
		05131	Sebastian County, AR	120,322
		40079	Le Flore County, OK	50,079
		40135	Sequoyah County, OK	41,356
23020			**Fort Walton Beach-Crestview-Destin, FL**	**180,291**
		12091	Okaloosa County, FL	180,291
23060			**Fort Wayne, IN**	**408,071**
		18003	Allen County, IN	347,316
		18179	Wells County, IN	28,199
		18183	Whitley County, IN	32,556
23420		06019	**Fresno, CA**	**891,756**
			Fresno County, CA	891,756
23460		01055	**Gadsden, AL**	**103,362**
			Etowah County, AL	103,362
23540			**Gainesville, FL**	**243,985**
		12001	Alachua County, FL	227,120
		12041	Gilchrist County, FL	16,865
23580		13139	**Gainesville, GA**	**173,256**
			Hall County, GA	173,256
24020			**Glens Falls, NY**	**129,455**
		36113	Warren County, NY	66,087
		36115	Washington County, NY	63,368
24140		37191	**Goldsboro, NC**	**113,847**
			Wayne County, NC	113,847
24220			**Grand Forks, ND-MN**	**96,523**
		27119	Polk County, MN	31,088
		38035	Grand Forks County, ND	65,435
24300		08077	**Grand Junction, CO**	**134,189**
			Mesa County, CO	134,189
24340			**Grand Rapids-Wyoming, MI**	**774,084**
		26015	Barry County, MI	59,899
		26067	Ionia County, MI	64,821
		26081	Kent County, MI	599,524
		26123	Newaygo County, MI	49,840
24500		30013	**Great Falls, MT**	**79,385**
			Cascade County, MT	79,385
24540		08123	**Greeley, CO**	**236,857**
			Weld County, CO	236,857
24580			**Green Bay, WI**	**299,003**
		55009	Brown County, WI	240,213
		55061	Kewaunee County, WI	20,832
		55083	Oconto County, WI	37,958
24660			**Greensboro-High Point, NC**	**685,378**
		37081	Guilford County, NC	451,905
		37151	Randolph County, NC	140,410
		37157	Rockingham County, NC	93,063
24780			**Greenville, NC**	**165,776**
		37079	Greene County, NC	20,157
		37147	Pitt County, NC	145,619
24860			**Greenville-Mauldin-Easley, SC**	**601,986**
		45045	Greenville County, SC	417,166
		45059	Laurens County, SC	70,374
		45077	Pickens County, SC	114,446
25060			**Gulfport-Biloxi, MS**	**227,904**
		28045	Hancock County, MS	40,421
		28047	Harrison County, MS	171,875
		28131	Stone County, MS	15,608
25180			**Hagerstown-Martinsburg, MD-WV**	**257,619**
		24043	Washington County, MD	143,748
		54003	Berkeley County, WV	97,534
		54065	Morgan County, WV	16,337
25260		06031	**Hanford-Corcoran, CA**	**146,153**
			Kings County, CA	146,153
25420			**Harrisburg-Carlisle, PA**	**525,380**
		42041	Cumberland County, PA	226,117
		42043	Dauphin County, PA	254,176
		42099	Perry County, PA	45,087
25500			**Harrisonburg, VA**	**113,449**
		51165	Rockingham County, VA	72,564
		51660	Harrisonburg city, VA	40,885
25540			**Hartford-West Hartford-East Hartford, CT**	**1,188,841**
		09003	Hartford County, CT	876,927
		09007	Middlesex County, CT	163,774
		09013	Tolland County, CT	148,140
25620			**Hattiesburg, MS**	**134,744**
		28035	Forrest County, MS	76,372
		28073	Lamar County, MS	46,240
		28111	Perry County, MS	12,132
25860			**Hickory-Lenoir-Morganton, NC**	**359,856**
		37003	Alexander County, NC	36,177
		37023	Burke County, NC	90,054
		37027	Caldwell County, NC	79,841
		37035	Catawba County, NC	153,784
25980			**Hinesville-Fort Stewart, GA**	**74,023**
		13179	Liberty County, GA	62,571
		13183	Long County, GA	11,452
26100		26139	**Holland-Grand Haven, MI**	**257,671**
			Ottawa County, MI	257,671
26180		15003	**Honolulu, HI**	**909,863**
			Honolulu County, HI	909,863
26300		05051	**Hot Springs, AR**	**95,164**
			Garland County, AR	95,164
26380			**Houma-Bayou Cane-Thibodaux, LA**	**202,902**
		22057	Lafourche Parish, LA	93,554
		22109	Terrebonne Parish, LA	109,348
26420			**Houston-Sugar Land-Baytown, TX**	**5,539,949**
		48015	Austin County, TX	26,407
		48039	Brazoria County, TX	287,898
		48071	Chambers County, TX	28,779
		48157	Fort Bend County, TX	493,187
		48167	Galveston County, TX	283,551
		48201	Harris County, TX	3,886,207
		48291	Liberty County, TX	75,685
		48339	Montgomery County, TX	398,290
		48407	San Jacinto County, TX	24,760
		48473	Waller County, TX	35,185
26580			**Huntington-Ashland, WV-KY-OH**	**285,475**
		21019	Boyd County, KY	49,371
		21089	Greenup County, KY	37,374
		39087	Lawrence County, OH	63,179
		54011	Cabell County, WV	93,904
		54099	Wayne County, WV	41,647
26620			**Huntsville, AL**	**376,753**
		01083	Limestone County, AL	72,446
		01089	Madison County, AL	304,307
26820			**Idaho Falls, ID**	**116,980**
		16019	Bonneville County, ID	94,630
		16051	Jefferson County, ID	22,350
26900			**Indianapolis-Carmel, IN**	**1,666,032**
		18011	Boone County, IN	53,526
		18013	Brown County, IN	15,071
		18057	Hamilton County, IN	250,979
		18059	Hancock County, IN	65,050
		18063	Hendricks County, IN	131,204
		18081	Johnson County, IN	133,316
		18097	Marion County, IN	865,504
		18109	Morgan County, IN	70,290
		18133	Putnam County, IN	36,978
		18145	Shelby County, IN	44,114
26980			**Iowa City, IA**	**139,567**
		19103	Johnson County, IA	118,038
		19183	Washington County, IA	21,529
27060		36109	**Ithaca, NY**	**100,407**
			Tompkins County, NY	100,407
27100		26075	**Jackson, MI**	**163,851**
			Jackson County, MI	163,851

Table C-2. **Metropolitan Areas and Component Counties**—Con.

[Metropolitan areas (MAs) defined as of December 18, 2006. CBSA = Core based statistical area; FIPS = Federal Information Processing Standards]

CBSA	Metropolitan division	State and county FIPS	Metropolitan statistical area / *Metropolitan division* / Component county	2006 population
27140			**Jackson, MS**	**529,456**
		28029	Copiah County, MS	29,223
		28049	Hinds County, MS	249,012
		28089	Madison County, MS	87,419
		28121	Rankin County, MS	135,830
		28127	Simpson County, MS	27,972
27180			**Jackson, TN**	**111,937**
		47023	Chester County, TN	16,043
		47113	Madison County, TN	95,894
27260			**Jacksonville, FL**	**1,277,997**
		12003	Baker County, FL	25,203
		12019	Clay County, FL	178,899
		12031	Duval County, FL	837,964
		12089	Nassau County, FL	66,707
		12109	St. Johns County, FL	169,224
27340			**Jacksonville, NC**	**150,673**
		37133	Onslow County, NC	150,673
27500			**Janesville, WI**	**159,153**
		55105	Rock County, WI	159,153
27620			**Jefferson City, MO**	**144,958**
		29027	Callaway County, MO	43,072
		29051	Cole County, MO	73,296
		29135	Moniteau County, MO	15,092
		29151	Osage County, MO	13,498
27740			**Johnson City, TN**	**191,136**
		47019	Carter County, TN	59,157
		47171	Unicoi County, TN	17,663
		47179	Washington County, TN	114,316
27780			**Johnstown, PA**	**146,967**
		42021	Cambria County, PA	146,967
27860			**Jonesboro, AR**	**113,330**
		05031	Craighead County, AR	88,244
		05111	Poinsett County, AR	25,086
27900			**Joplin, MO**	**168,552**
		29097	Jasper County, MO	112,505
		29145	Newton County, MO	56,047
28020			**Kalamazoo-Portage, MI**	**319,738**
		26077	Kalamazoo County, MI	240,720
		26159	Van Buren County, MI	79,018
28100			**Kankakee-Bradley, IL**	**109,090**
		17091	Kankakee County, IL	109,090
28140			**Kansas City, MO-KS**	**1,967,405**
		20059	Franklin County, KS	26,513
		20091	Johnson County, KS	516,731
		20103	Leavenworth County, KS	73,628
		20107	Linn County, KS	9,962
		20121	Miami County, KS	30,900
		20209	Wyandotte County, KS	155,509
		29013	Bates County, MO	17,116
		29025	Caldwell County, MO	9,313
		29037	Cass County, MO	95,781
		29047	Clay County, MO	206,957
		29049	Clinton County, MO	20,671
		29095	Jackson County, MO	664,078
		29107	Lafayette County, MO	33,186
		29165	Platte County, MO	83,061
		29177	Ray County, MO	23,999
28420			**Kennewick-Richland-Pasco, WA**	**226,033**
		53005	Benton County, WA	159,463
		53021	Franklin County, WA	66,570
28660			**Killeen-Temple-Fort Hood, TX**	**351,322**
		48027	Bell County, TX	257,897
		48099	Coryell County, TX	72,667
		48281	Lampasas County, TX	20,758
28700			**Kingsport-Bristol-Bristol, TN-VA**	**302,451**
		47073	Hawkins County, TN	56,850
		47163	Sullivan County, TN	153,239
		51169	Scott County, VA	22,882
		51191	Washington County, VA	51,984
		51520	Bristol city, VA	17,496
28740			**Kingston, NY**	**182,742**
		36111	Ulster County, NY	182,742
28940			**Knoxville, TN**	**667,384**
		47001	Anderson County, TN	73,579
		47009	Blount County, TN	118,186
		47093	Knox County, TN	411,967
		47105	Loudon County, TN	44,566
		47173	Union County, TN	19,086
29020			**Kokomo, IN**	**100,877**
		18067	Howard County, IN	84,500
		18159	Tipton County, IN	16,377
29100			**La Crosse, WI-MN**	**129,236**
		27055	Houston County, MN	19,832
		55063	La Crosse County, WI	109,404
29140			**Lafayette, IN**	**185,745**
		18007	Benton County, IN	9,050
		18015	Carroll County, IN	20,526
		18157	Tippecanoe County, IN	156,169
29180			**Lafayette, LA**	**254,432**
		22055	Lafayette Parish, LA	203,091
		22099	St. Martin Parish, LA	51,341
29340			**Lake Charles, LA**	**192,316**
		22019	Calcasieu Parish, LA	184,524
		22023	Cameron Parish, LA	7,792
29420			**Lake Havasu City-Kingman, AZ**	**193,035**
		04015	Mohave County, AZ	193,035
29460			**Lakeland, FL**	**561,606**
		12105	Polk County, FL	561,606
29540			**Lancaster, PA**	**494,486**
		42071	Lancaster County, PA	494,486
29620			**Lansing-East Lansing, MI**	**454,044**
		26037	Clinton County, MI	69,909
		26045	Eaton County, MI	107,237
		26065	Ingham County, MI	276,898
29700			**Laredo, TX**	**231,470**
		48479	Webb County, TX	231,470
29740			**Las Cruces, NM**	**193,888**
		35013	Dona Ana County, NM	193,888
29820			**Las Vegas-Paradise, NV**	**1,777,539**
		32003	Clark County, NV	1,777,539
29940			**Lawrence, KS**	**112,123**
		20045	Douglas County, KS	112,123
30020			**Lawton, OK**	**109,181**
		40031	Comanche County, OK	109,181
30140			**Lebanon, PA**	**126,883**
		42075	Lebanon County, PA	126,883
30300			**Lewiston, ID-WA**	**59,571**
		16069	Nez Perce County, ID	38,324
		53003	Asotin County, WA	21,247
30340			**Lewiston-Auburn, ME**	**107,552**
		23001	Androscoggin County, ME	107,552
30460			**Lexington-Fayette, KY**	**436,684**
		21017	Bourbon County, KY	19,839
		21049	Clark County, KY	35,275
		21067	Fayette County, KY	270,789
		21113	Jessamine County, KY	44,790
		21209	Scott County, KY	41,605
		21239	Woodford County, KY	24,386
30620			**Lima, OH**	**105,788**
		39003	Allen County, OH	105,788
30700			**Lincoln, NE**	**283,970**
		31109	Lancaster County, NE	267,135
		31159	Seward County, NE	16,835
30780			**Little Rock-North Little Rock-Conway, AR**	**652,834**
		05045	Faulkner County, AR	100,685
		05053	Grant County, AR	17,493
		05085	Lonoke County, AR	62,902
		05105	Perry County, AR	10,411
		05119	Pulaski County, AR	367,319
		05125	Saline County, AR	94,024
30860			**Logan, UT-ID**	**111,156**
		16041	Franklin County, ID	12,494
		49005	Cache County, UT	98,662
30980			**Longview, TX**	**203,367**
		48183	Gregg County, TX	117,090
		48401	Rusk County, TX	48,354
		48459	Upshur County, TX	37,923
31020			**Longview, WA**	**99,905**
		53015	Cowlitz County, WA	99,905
31100			**Los Angeles-Long Beach-Santa Ana, CA**	**12,950,129**
	31084		*Los Angeles-Long Beach-Glendale, CA*	*9,948,081*
		06037	Los Angeles County, CA	9,948,081
	42044		*Santa Ana-Anaheim-Irvine, CA*	*3,002,048*
		06059	Orange County, CA	3,002,048

Table C-2. **Metropolitan Areas and Component Counties**—Con.

[Metropolitan areas (MAs) defined as of December 18, 2006. CBSA = Core based statistical area; FIPS = Federal Information Processing Standards]

Geographic codes			Metropolitan statistical area / *Metropolitan division* / Component county	2006 population	Geographic codes			Metropolitan statistical area / *Metropolitan division* / Component county	2006 population
CBSA	Metro-politan divi-sion	State and county FIPS			CBSA	Metro-politan divi-sion	State and county FIPS		
31140			**Louisville-Jefferson County, KY-IN**	**1,222,216**	33460			**Minneapolis-St. Paul-Bloomington, MN-WI**—Con.	
		18019	Clark County, IN	103,569			27171	Wright County, MN	114,787
		18043	Floyd County, IN	72,570			55093	Pierce County, WI	39,373
		18061	Harrison County, IN	36,992			55109	St. Croix County, WI	80,015
		18175	Washington County, IN. .	28,062	33540			**Missoula, MT**	**101,417**
		21029	Bullitt County, KY	72,851			30063	Missoula County, MT	101,417
		21103	Henry County, KY	16,025	33660			**Mobile, AL**	**404,157**
		21111	Jefferson County, KY	701,500			01097	Mobile County, AL.	404,157
		21163	Meade County, KY	27,994	33700			**Modesto, CA**	**512,138**
		21179	Nelson County, KY	42,102			06099	Stanislaus County, CA	512,138
		21185	Oldham County, KY	55,285	33740			**Monroe, LA**	**172,223**
		21211	Shelby County, KY	39,717			22073	Ouachita Parish, LA	149,259
		21215	Spencer County, KY	16,475			22111	Union Parish, LA.	22,964
		21223	Trimble County, KY	9,074	33780			**Monroe, MI**	**155,035**
31180			**Lubbock, TX**	**261,411**			26115	Monroe County, MI	155,035
		48107	Crosby County, TX	6,549	33860			**Montgomery, AL**.	**361,748**
		48303	Lubbock County, TX	254,862			01001	Autauga County, AL	49,730
31340			**Lynchburg, VA**.	**239,510**			01051	Elmore County, AL	75,688
		51009	Amherst County, VA	32,239			01085	Lowndes County, AL	12,759
		51011	Appomattox County, VA	14,128			01101	Montgomery County, AL	223,571
		51019	Bedford County, VA	66,507	34060			**Morgantown, WV**	**115,136**
		51031	Campbell County, VA	52,667			54061	Monongalia County, WV	84,752
		51515	Bedford city, VA	6,249			54077	Preston County, WV	30,384
		51680	Lynchburg city, VA	67,720	34100			**Morristown, TN**	**132,851**
31420			**Macon, GA**	**229,326**			47057	Grainger County, TN	22,453
		13021	Bibb County, GA	154,903			47063	Hamblen County, TN	61,026
		13079	Crawford County, GA. . . .	12,823			47089	Jefferson County, TN	49,372
		13169	Jones County, GA	26,973	34580			**Mount Vernon-Anacortes, WA**	**115,700**
		13207	Monroe County, GA	24,443			53057	Skagit County, WA	115,700
		13289	Twiggs County, GA	10,184	34620			**Muncie, IN**.	**114,879**
31460			**Madera, CA**	**146,345**			18035	Delaware County, IN	114,879
		06039	Madera County, CA.	146,345	34740			**Muskegon-Norton Shores, MI**	**175,231**
31540			**Madison, WI**.	**543,022**			26121	Muskegon County, MI	175,231
		55021	Columbia County, WI	55,440	34820			**Myrtle Beach-Conway-North Myrtle Beach, SC**.	**238,493**
		55025	Dane County, WI	463,826			45051	Horry County, SC	238,493
		55049	Iowa County, WI	23,756	34900			**Napa, CA**.	**133,522**
31700			**Manchester-Nashua, NH**	**402,789**			06055	Napa County, CA	133,522
		33011	Hillsborough County, NH	402,789	34940			**Naples-Marco Island, FL**	**314,649**
31900			**Mansfield, OH**	**127,010**			12021	Collier County, FL.	314,649
		39139	Richland County, OH.	127,010	34980			**Nashville-Davidson—Murfreesboro—Franklin, TN**.	**1,455,097**
32580			**McAllen-Edinburg-Mission, TX.**	**700,634**			47015	Cannon County, TN	13,448
		48215	Hidalgo County, TX	700,634			47021	Cheatham County, TN	39,018
32780			**Medford, OR**	**197,071**			47037	Davidson County, TN	578,698
		41029	Jackson County, OR	197,071			47043	Dickson County, TN	46,583
32820			**Memphis, TN-MS-AR.**	**1,274,704**			47081	Hickman County, TN	23,812
		05035	Crittenden County, AR	52,083			47111	Macon County, TN	21,726
		28033	DeSoto County, MS	144,706			47147	Robertson County, TN	62,187
		28093	Marshall County, MS	35,853			47149	Rutherford County, TN	228,829
		28137	Tate County, MS	26,723			47159	Smith County, TN	18,753
		28143	Tunica County, MS	10,419			47165	Sumner County, TN	149,416
		47047	Fayette County, TN	36,102			47169	Trousdale County, TN.	7,811
		47157	Shelby County, TN	911,438			47187	Williamson County, TN.	160,781
		47167	Tipton County, TN	57,380			47189	Wilson County, TN	104,035
32900			**Merced, CA**	**245,658**	35300			**New Haven-Milford, CT**.	**845,244**
		06047	Merced County, CA.	245,658			09009	New Haven County, CT	845,244
33100			**Miami-Fort Lauderdale-Pompano Beach, FL**.	**5,463,857**	35380			**New Orleans-Metairie-Kenner, LA.**	**1,024,678**
	22744		*Fort Lauderdale-Pompano Beach-Deerfield Beach, FL*	*1,787,636*			22051	Jefferson Parish, LA	431,361
		12011	Broward County, FL. . . .	1,787,636			22071	Orleans Parish, LA	223,388
	33124		*Miami-Miami Beach-Kendall, FL*	*2,402,208*			22075	Plaquemines Parish, LA	22,512
		12086	Miami-Dade County, FL. .	2,402,208			22087	St. Bernard Parish, LA	15,514
	48424		*West Palm Beach-Boca Raton-Boynton Beach, FL*	*1,274,013*			22089	St. Charles Parish, LA	52,761
		12099	Palm Beach County, FL. .	1,274,013			22095	St. John the Baptist Parish, LA	48,537
33140			**Michigan City-LaPorte, IN**	**110,479**			22103	St. Tammany Parish, LA	230,605
		18091	LaPorte County, IN	110,479	35620			**New York-Northern New Jersey-Long Island, NY-NJ-PA**	**18,818,536**
33260			**Midland, TX**	**124,380**		20764		*Edison, NJ*	*2,308,777*
		48329	Midland County, TX	124,380			34023	Middlesex County, NJ	786,971
33340			**Milwaukee-Waukesha-West Allis, WI.**	**1,509,981**			34025	Monmouth County, NJ	635,285
		55079	Milwaukee County, WI	915,097			34029	Ocean County, NJ.	562,335
		55089	Ozaukee County, WI	86,321			34035	Somerset County, NJ	324,186
		55131	Washington County, WI	127,578		35004		*Nassau-Suffolk, NY.*	*2,795,377*
		55133	Waukesha County, WI	380,985			36059	Nassau County, NY	1,325,662
33460			**Minneapolis-St. Paul-Bloomington, MN-WI.**	**3,175,041**			36103	Suffolk County, NY	1,469,715
		27003	Anoka County, MN	327,005		35084		*Newark-Union, NJ-PA*	*2,152,757*
		27019	Carver County, MN	87,545			34013	Essex County, NJ	786,147
		27025	Chisago County, MN	50,344			34019	Hunterdon County, NJ	130,783
		27037	Dakota County, MN	388,001			34027	Morris County, NJ	493,160
		27053	Hennepin County, MN	1,122,093			34037	Sussex County, NJ	153,384
		27059	Isanti County, MN	38,576			34039	Union County, NJ	531,088
		27123	Ramsey County, MN	493,215			42103	Pike County, PA	58,195
		27139	Scott County, MN	124,092					
		27141	Sherburne County, MN. . . .	84,995					
		27163	Washington County, MN. . . .	225,000					

Table C-2. **Metropolitan Areas and Component Counties**—Con.

[Metropolitan areas (MAs) defined as of December 18, 2006. CBSA = Core based statistical area; FIPS = Federal Information Processing Standards]

CBSA	Metropolitan division	State and county FIPS	Metropolitan statistical area / Metropolitan division / Component county	2006 population	CBSA	Metropolitan division	State and county FIPS	Metropolitan statistical area / Metropolitan division / Component county	2006 population
35620			New York-Northern New Jersey-Long Island, NY-NJ-PA—Con.		37900			Peoria, IL.	370,194
	35644		New York-White Plains-Wayne, NY-NJ	11,561,625			17123	Marshall County, IL	13,003
		34003	Bergen County, NJ	904,037			17143	Peoria County, IL	182,495
		34017	Hudson County, NJ	601,146			17175	Stark County, IL	6,233
		34031	Passaic County, NJ	497,093			17179	Tazewell County, IL	130,559
		36005	Bronx County, NY	1,361,473			17203	Woodford County, IL	37,904
		36047	Kings County, NY	2,508,820	37980			Philadelphia-Camden-Wilmington, PA-NJ-DE-MD.	5,826,742
		36061	New York County, NY	1,611,581		15804		Camden, NJ	1,249,659
		36079	Putnam County, NY	100,603			34005	Burlington County, NJ	450,627
		36081	Queens County, NY	2,255,175			34007	Camden County, NJ	517,001
		36085	Richmond County, NY	477,377			34015	Gloucester County, NJ	282,031
		36087	Rockland County, NY	294,965		37964		Philadelphia, PA	3,885,395
		36119	Westchester County, NY	949,355			42017	Bucks County, PA	623,205
35660			Niles-Benton Harbor, MI	161,705			42029	Chester County, PA	482,112
		26021	Berrien County, MI	161,705			42045	Delaware County, PA	555,996
35980			Norwich-New London, CT	263,293			42091	Montgomery County, PA	775,688
		09011	New London County, CT	263,293			42101	Philadelphia County, PA	1,448,394
36100			Ocala, FL	316,183		48864		Wilmington, DE-MD-NJ	691,688
		12083	Marion County, FL	316,183			10003	New Castle County, DE	525,587
36140			Ocean City, NJ	97,724			24015	Cecil County, MD	99,506
		34009	Cape May County, NJ	97,724			34033	Salem County, NJ	66,595
36220			Odessa, TX	127,462	38060			Phoenix-Mesa-Scottsdale, AZ	4,039,182
		48135	Ector County, TX	127,462			04013	Maricopa County, AZ	3,768,123
36260			Ogden-Clearfield, UT	497,640			04021	Pinal County, AZ	271,059
		49011	Davis County, UT	276,259	38220			Pine Bluff, AR	103,638
		49029	Morgan County, UT	8,134			05025	Cleveland County, AR	8,858
		49057	Weber County, UT	213,247			05069	Jefferson County, AR	80,655
36420			Oklahoma City, OK	1,172,339			05079	Lincoln County, AR	14,125
		40017	Canadian County, OK	101,335	38300			Pittsburgh, PA	2,370,776
		40027	Cleveland County, OK	228,594			42003	Allegheny County, PA	1,223,411
		40051	Grady County, OK	50,490			42005	Armstrong County, PA	70,096
		40081	Lincoln County, OK	32,645			42007	Beaver County, PA	175,736
		40083	Logan County, OK	36,971			42019	Butler County, PA	182,901
		40087	McClain County, OK	31,038			42051	Fayette County, PA	145,760
		40109	Oklahoma County, OK	691,266			42125	Washington County, PA	206,432
36500			Olympia, WA	234,670			42129	Westmoreland County, PA	366,440
		53067	Thurston County, WA	234,670	38340			Pittsfield, MA	131,117
36540			Omaha-Council Bluffs, NE-IA	822,549			25003	Berkshire County, MA	131,117
		19085	Harrison County, IA	15,745	38540			Pocatello, ID	86,357
		19129	Mills County, IA	15,595			16005	Bannock County, ID	78,443
		19155	Pottawattamie County, IA	90,218			16077	Power County, ID	7,914
		31025	Cass County, NE	25,963	38860			Portland-South Portland-Biddeford, ME	513,667
		31055	Douglas County, NE	492,003			23005	Cumberland County, ME	274,598
		31153	Sarpy County, NE	142,637			23023	Sagadahoc County, ME	36,837
		31155	Saunders County, NE	20,344			23031	York County, ME	202,232
		31177	Washington County, NE	20,044	38900			Portland-Vancouver-Beaverton, OR-WA	2,137,565
36740			Orlando-Kissimmee, FL	1,984,855			41005	Clackamas County, OR	374,230
		12069	Lake County, FL	290,435			41009	Columbia County, OR	49,163
		12095	Orange County, FL	1,043,500			41051	Multnomah County, OR	681,454
		12097	Osceola County, FL	244,045			41067	Washington County, OR	514,269
		12117	Seminole County, FL	406,875			41071	Yamhill County, OR	94,678
36780			Oshkosh-Neenah, WI	160,593			53011	Clark County, WA	412,938
		55139	Winnebago County, WI	160,593			53059	Skamania County, WA	10,833
36980			Owensboro, KY	112,093	38940			Port St. Lucie, FL	392,117
		21059	Daviess County, KY	93,613			12085	Martin County, FL	139,393
		21091	Hancock County, KY	8,636			12111	St. Lucie County, FL	252,724
		21149	McLean County, KY	9,844	39100			Poughkeepsie-Newburgh-Middletown, NY	671,538
37100			Oxnard-Thousand Oaks-Ventura, CA	799,720			36027	Dutchess County, NY	295,146
		06111	Ventura County, CA	799,720			36071	Orange County, NY	376,392
37340			Palm Bay-Melbourne-Titusville, FL	534,359	39140			Prescott, AZ	208,014
		12009	Brevard County, FL	534,359			04025	Yavapai County, AZ	208,014
37380			Palm Coast, FL	83,084	39300			Providence-New Bedford-Fall River, RI-MA	1,612,989
		12035	Flagler County, FL	83,084			25005	Bristol County, MA	545,379
37460			Panama City-Lynn Haven, FL	163,505			44001	Bristol County, RI	52,256
		12005	Bay County, FL	163,505			44003	Kent County, RI	170,053
37620			Parkersburg-Marietta-Vienna, WV-OH	161,724			44005	Newport County, RI	82,144
		39167	Washington County, OH	61,867			44007	Providence County, RI	635,596
		54073	Pleasants County, WV	7,280			44009	Washington County, RI	127,561
		54105	Wirt County, WV	5,980	39340			Provo-Orem, UT	474,180
		54107	Wood County, WV	86,597			49023	Juab County, UT	9,420
37700			Pascagoula, MS	152,405			49049	Utah County, UT	464,760
		28039	George County, MS	21,828	39380			Pueblo, CO	152,912
		28059	Jackson County, MS	130,577			08101	Pueblo County, CO	152,912
37860			Pensacola-Ferry Pass-Brent, FL	439,987	39460			Punta Gorda, FL	154,438
		12033	Escambia County, FL	295,426			12015	Charlotte County, FL	154,438
		12113	Santa Rosa County, FL	144,561	39540			Racine, WI	196,096
							55101	Racine County, WI	196,096
					39580			Raleigh-Cary, NC	994,551
							37069	Franklin County, NC	55,886
							37101	Johnston County, NC	152,143
							37183	Wake County, NC	786,522

County and City Data Book: 2007

C–11

U.S. Census Bureau

Table C-2. **Metropolitan Areas and Component Counties**—Con.

[Metropolitan areas (MAs) defined as of December 18, 2006. CBSA = Core based statistical area; FIPS = Federal Information Processing Standards]

Geographic codes			Metropolitan statistical area / *Metropolitan division* / Component county	2006 population	Geographic codes			Metropolitan statistical area / *Metropolitan division* / Component county	2006 population
CBSA	Metro-politan divi-sion	State and county FIPS			CBSA	Metro-politan divi-sion	State and county FIPS		
39660			**Rapid City, SD**	**118,763**	41180			St. Louis, MO-IL[1]—Con.	
		46093	Meade County, SD	24,425			17163	St. Clair County, IL	260,919
		46103	Pennington County, SD	94,338			29071	Franklin County, MO	100,067
39740			**Reading, PA**	**401,149**			29099	Jefferson County, MO	216,469
		42011	Berks County, PA	401,149			29113	Lincoln County, MO	50,123
39820			**Redding, CA**	**179,951**			29183	St. Charles County, MO	338,719
		06089	Shasta County, CA	179,951			29189	St. Louis County, MO.	1,000,510
39900			**Reno-Sparks, NV**	**400,560**			29219	Warren County, MO.	29,685
		32029	Storey County, NV.	4,132			29221	Washington County, MO	24,182
		32031	Washoe County, NV	396,428			29510	St. Louis city, MO	347,181
40060			**Richmond, VA**	**1,194,008**	41420			**Salem, OR**.	**384,600**
		51007	Amelia County, VA	12,502			41047	Marion County, OR	311,304
		51033	Caroline County, VA	26,731			41053	Polk County, OR	73,296
		51036	Charles City County, VA	7,221	41500			**Salinas, CA**	**410,206**
		51041	Chesterfield County, VA	296,718			06053	Monterey County, CA.	410,206
		51049	Cumberland County, VA	9,465	41540			**Salisbury, MD**	**117,761**
		51053	Dinwiddie County, VA.	25,695			24039	Somerset County, MD	25,774
		51075	Goochland County, VA	20,085			24045	Wicomico County, MD	91,987
		51085	Hanover County, VA	98,983	41620			**Salt Lake City, UT**.	**1,067,722**
		51087	Henrico County, VA	284,399			49035	Salt Lake County, UT.	978,701
		51097	King and Queen County, VA	6,903			49043	Summit County, UT	35,469
		51101	King William County, VA	15,381			49045	Tooele County, UT.	53,552
		51109	Louisa County, VA	31,226	41660			**San Angelo, TX**	**105,752**
		51127	New Kent County, VA	16,852			48235	Irion County, TX	1,814
		51145	Powhatan County, VA	27,649			48451	Tom Green County, TX	103,938
		51149	Prince George County, VA	36,184	41700			**San Antonio, TX**.	**1,942,217**
		51183	Sussex County, VA	12,249			48013	Atascosa County, TX	43,876
		51570	Colonial Heights city, VA.	17,676			48019	Bandera County, TX	20,203
		51670	Hopewell city, VA	22,731			48029	Bexar County, TX	1,555,592
		51730	Petersburg city, VA	32,445			48091	Comal County, TX.	101,181
		51760	Richmond city, VA	192,913			48187	Guadalupe County, TX.	108,410
40140			**Riverside-San Bernardino-Ontario, CA** . . .	**4,026,135**			48259	Kendall County, TX	30,213
		06065	Riverside County, CA.	2,026,803			48325	Medina County, TX	43,913
		06071	San Bernardino County, CA	1,999,332			48493	Wilson County, TX.	38,829
40220			**Roanoke, VA**	**295,050**	41740			**San Diego-Carlsbad-San Marcos, CA**	**2,941,454**
		51023	Botetourt County, VA	32,228			06073	San Diego County, CA.	2,941,454
		51045	Craig County, VA	5,179	41780			**Sandusky, OH**	**78,116**
		51067	Franklin County, VA	50,784			39043	Erie County, OH	78,116
		51161	Roanoke County, VA	90,482	41860			**San Francisco-Oakland-Fremont, CA**	**4,180,027**
		51770	Roanoke city, VA	91,552		36084		*Oakland-Fremont-Hayward, CA*.	*2,481,745*
		51775	Salem city, VA	24,825			06001	Alameda County, CA	1,457,426
40340			**Rochester, MN**.	**179,573**			06013	Contra Costa County, CA	1,024,319
		27039	Dodge County, MN	19,770		41884		*San Francisco-San Mateo-*	
		27109	Olmsted County, MN	137,521				*Redwood City, CA*.	*1,698,282*
		27157	Wabasha County, MN	22,282			06041	Marin County, CA	248,742
40380			**Rochester, NY**	**1,035,435**			06075	San Francisco County, CA	744,041
		36051	Livingston County, NY	64,173			06081	San Mateo County, CA.	705,499
		36055	Monroe County, NY	730,807	41940			**San Jose-Sunnyvale-Santa Clara, CA**	**1,787,123**
		36069	Ontario County, NY	104,353			06069	San Benito County, CA	55,842
		36073	Orleans County, NY	43,213			06085	Santa Clara County, CA	1,731,281
		36117	Wayne County, NY	92,889	42020			**San Luis Obispo-Paso Robles, CA**	**257,005**
40420			**Rockford, IL**.	**348,252**			06079	San Luis Obispo County, CA.	257,005
		17007	Boone County, IL	52,617	42060			**Santa Barbara-Santa Maria-**	
		17201	Winnebago County, IL	295,635				**Goleta, CA**.	**400,335**
40580			**Rocky Mount, NC**	**146,276**			06083	Santa Barbara County, CA	400,335
		37065	Edgecombe County, NC	53,964	42100			**Santa Cruz-Watsonville, CA**	**249,705**
		37127	Nash County, NC	92,312			06087	Santa Cruz County, CA	249,705
40660			**Rome, GA**	**95,322**	42140			**Santa Fe, NM**	**142,407**
		13115	Floyd County, GA	95,322			35049	Santa Fe County, NM	142,407
40900			**Sacramento—Arden-**		42220			**Santa Rosa-Petaluma, CA**	**466,891**
			Arcade—Roseville, CA	**2,067,117**			06097	Sonoma County, CA	466,891
		06017	El Dorado County, CA	178,066	42260			**Sarasota-Bradenton-Venice, FL**	**682,833**
		06061	Placer County, CA.	326,242			12081	Manatee County, FL	313,298
		06067	Sacramento County, CA	1,374,724			12115	Sarasota County, FL	369,535
		06113	Yolo County, CA	188,085	42340			**Savannah, GA**	**320,013**
40980			**Saginaw-Saginaw Township North, MI** . . .	**206,300**			13029	Bryan County, GA.	29,648
		26145	Saginaw County, MI.	206,300			13051	Chatham County, GA	241,411
41060			**St. Cloud, MN**	**182,784**			13103	Effingham County, GA	48,954
		27009	Benton County, MN	38,688	42540			**Scranton—Wilkes-Barre, PA**	**550,841**
		27145	Stearns County, MN	144,096			42069	Lackawanna County, PA	209,728
41100			**St. George, UT**	**126,312**			42079	Luzerne County, PA	313,020
		49053	Washington County, UT	126,312			42131	Wyoming County, PA.	28,093
41140			**St. Joseph, MO-KS**	**122,306**	42660			**Seattle-Tacoma-Bellevue, WA**	**3,263,497**
		20043	Doniphan County, KS.	7,865		42644		*Seattle-Bellevue-Everett, WA*	*2,496,619*
		29003	Andrew County, MO	17,177			53033	King County, WA.	1,826,732
		29021	Buchanan County, MO	84,955			53061	Snohomish County, WA	669,887
		29063	DeKalb County, MO	12,309		45104		*Tacoma, WA*	*766,878*
41180			**St. Louis, MO-IL[1]**	**2,796,368**			53053	Pierce County, WA	766,878
		17005	Bond County, IL	18,055	42680			**Sebastian-Vero Beach, FL**	**130,100**
		17013	Calhoun County, IL	5,177			12061	Indian River County, FL	130,100
		17027	Clinton County, IL	36,633					
		17083	Jersey County, IL	22,628					
		17117	Macoupin County, IL	48,841					
		17119	Madison County, IL	265,303					
		17133	Monroe County, IL.	31,876					

Table C-2. **Metropolitan Areas and Component Counties**—Con.

[Metropolitan areas (MAs) defined as of December 18, 2006. CBSA = Core based statistical area; FIPS = Federal Information Processing Standards]

CBSA	Geographic codes — Metropolitan division	State and county FIPS	Metropolitan statistical area / *Metropolitan division* / Component county	2006 population
43100			**Sheboygan, WI.**	**114,756**
		55117	Sheboygan County, WI.	114,756
43300			**Sherman-Denison, TX.**	**118,478**
		48181	Grayson County, TX	118,478
43340			**Shreveport-Bossier City, LA**	**386,778**
		22015	Bossier Parish, LA.	107,270
		22017	Caddo Parish, LA	253,118
		22031	De Soto Parish, LA	26,390
43580			**Sioux City, IA-NE-SD**	**143,474**
		19193	Woodbury County, IA.	102,972
		31043	Dakota County, NE	20,587
		31051	Dixon County, NE	6,170
		46127	Union County, SD	13,745
43620			**Sioux Falls, SD**	**212,911**
		46083	Lincoln County, SD	35,239
		46087	McCook County, SD	5,851
		46099	Minnehaha County, SD	163,281
		46125	Turner County, SD	8,540
43780			**South Bend-Mishawaka, IN-MI.**	**318,007**
		18141	St. Joseph County, IN	266,678
		26027	Cass County, MI	51,329
43900			**Spartanburg, SC**	**271,087**
		45083	Spartanburg County, SC.	271,087
44060			**Spokane, WA.**	**446,706**
		53063	Spokane County, WA.	446,706
44100			**Springfield, IL**	**206,112**
		17129	Menard County, IL.	12,588
		17167	Sangamon County, IL	193,524
44140			**Springfield, MA**	**686,174**
		25011	Franklin County, MA	72,183
		25013	Hampden County, MA	460,520
		25015	Hampshire County, MA	153,471
44180			**Springfield, MO**	**407,092**
		29043	Christian County, MO.	70,514
		29059	Dallas County, MO	16,696
		29077	Greene County, MO	254,779
		29167	Polk County, MO.	29,596
		29225	Webster County, MO	35,507
44220			**Springfield, OH**	**141,872**
		39023	Clark County, OH	141,872
44300			**State College, PA.**	**140,953**
		42027	Centre County, PA.	140,953
44700			**Stockton, CA.**	**673,170**
		06077	San Joaquin County, CA	673,170
44940			**Sumter, SC**	**104,430**
		45085	Sumter County, SC	104,430
45060			**Syracuse, NY.**	**650,051**
		36053	Madison County, NY	70,197
		36067	Onondaga County, NY	456,777
		36075	Oswego County, NY	123,077
45220			**Tallahassee, FL**	**336,502**
		12039	Gadsden County, FL	46,658
		12065	Jefferson County, FL	14,677
		12073	Leon County, FL.	245,625
		12129	Wakulla County, FL	29,542
45300			**Tampa-St. Petersburg-Clearwater, FL**	**2,697,731**
		12053	Hernando County, FL.	165,409
		12057	Hillsborough County, FL.	1,157,738
		12101	Pasco County, FL	450,171
		12103	Pinellas County, FL	924,413
45460			**Terre Haute, IN.**	**168,217**
		18021	Clay County, IN	27,021
		18153	Sullivan County, IN	21,542
		18165	Vermillion County, IN	16,645
		18167	Vigo County, IN	103,009
45500			**Texarkana, TX-Texarkana, AR**	**134,510**
		05091	Miller County, AR	43,055
		48037	Bowie County, TX	91,455
45780			**Toledo, OH**	**653,695**
		39051	Fulton County, OH.	42,900
		39095	Lucas County, OH.	445,281
		39123	Ottawa County, OH	41,331
		39173	Wood County, OH	124,183
45820			**Topeka, KS**	**228,894**
		20085	Jackson County, KS	13,500
		20087	Jefferson County, KS.	18,848
		20139	Osage County, KS.	16,958
		20177	Shawnee County, KS	172,693
		20197	Wabaunsee County, KS	6,895
45940			**Trenton-Ewing, NJ**	**367,605**
		34021	Mercer County, NJ	367,605
46060			**Tucson, AZ**	**946,362**
		04019	Pima County, AZ.	946,362
46140			**Tulsa, OK**	**897,752**
		40037	Creek County, OK.	69,146
		40111	Okmulgee County, OK	39,670
		40113	Osage County, OK	45,549
		40117	Pawnee County, OK	16,844
		40131	Rogers County, OK	82,435
		40143	Tulsa County, OK.	577,795
		40145	Wagoner County, OK.	66,313
46220			**Tuscaloosa, AL**	**198,769**
		01063	Greene County, AL	9,374
		01065	Hale County, AL	18,236
		01125	Tuscaloosa County, AL.	171,159
46340			**Tyler, TX.**	**194,635**
		48423	Smith County, TX.	194,635
46540			**Utica-Rome, NY.**	**297,286**
		36043	Herkimer County, NY.	63,332
		36065	Oneida County, NY.	233,954
46660			**Valdosta, GA**	**126,305**
		13027	Brooks County, GA.	16,464
		13101	Echols County, GA	4,274
		13173	Lanier County, GA.	7,723
		13185	Lowndes County, GA.	97,844
46700			**Vallejo-Fairfield, CA**	**411,680**
		06095	Solano County, CA	411,680
47020			**Victoria, TX.**	**114,088**
		48057	Calhoun County, TX	20,705
		48175	Goliad County, TX.	7,192
		48469	Victoria County, TX.	86,191
47220			**Vineland-Millville-Bridgeton, NJ.**	**154,823**
		34011	Cumberland County, NJ	154,823
47260			**Virginia Beach-Norfolk-Newport News, VA-NC.**	**1,649,457**
		37053	Currituck County, NC.	23,770
		51073	Gloucester County, VA.	38,293
		51093	Isle of Wight County, VA	34,723
		51095	James City County, VA.	59,741
		51115	Mathews County, VA.	9,184
		51181	Surry County, VA	7,119
		51199	York County, VA	61,879
		51550	Chesapeake city, VA	220,560
		51650	Hampton city, VA.	145,017
		51700	Newport News city, VA.	178,281
		51710	Norfolk city, VA.	229,112
		51735	Poquoson city, VA.	11,918
		51740	Portsmouth city, VA.	101,367
		51800	Suffolk city, VA.	81,071
		51810	Virginia Beach city, VA.	435,619
		51830	Williamsburg city, VA.	11,793
47300			**Visalia-Porterville, CA.**	**419,909**
		06107	Tulare County, CA.	419,909
47380			**Waco, TX.**	**226,189**
		48309	McLennan County, TX.	226,189
47580			**Warner Robins, GA**	**127,530**
		13153	Houston County, GA.	127,530
47900			**Washington-Arlington-Alexandria, DC-VA-MD-WV.**	**5,290,400**
	13644		*Bethesda-Gaithersburg-Frederick, MD*	*1,155,069*
		24021	Frederick County, MD	222,938
		24031	Montgomery County, MD	932,131
	47894		*Washington-Arlington-Alexandria, DC-VA-MD-WV.*	*4,135,331*
		11001	District of Columbia, DC.	581,530
		24009	Calvert County, MD.	88,804
		24017	Charles County, MD.	140,416
		24033	Prince George's County, MD.	841,315
		51013	Arlington County, VA.	199,776
		51043	Clarke County, VA.	14,565
		51059	Fairfax County, VA	1,010,443
		51061	Fauquier County, VA.	66,170
		51107	Loudoun County, VA.	268,817
		51153	Prince William County, VA.	357,503
		51177	Spotsylvania County, VA.	119,529
		51179	Stafford County, VA.	120,170
		51187	Warren County, VA.	36,102
		51510	Alexandria city, VA.	136,974
		51600	Fairfax city, VA.	22,422
		51610	Falls Church city, VA.	10,799
		51630	Fredericksburg city, VA.	21,273
		51683	Manassas city, VA.	36,638
		51685	Manassas Park city, VA.	11,642
		54037	Jefferson County, WV	50,443

Table C-2. **Metropolitan Areas and Component Counties**—Con.

[Metropolitan areas (MAs) defined as of December 18, 2006. CBSA = Core based statistical area; FIPS = Federal Information Processing Standards]

Geographic codes			Metropolitan statistical area *Metropolitan division* Component county	2006 population	Geographic codes			Metropolitan statistical area *Metropolitan division* Component county	2006 population
CBSA	Metro-politan divi-sion	State and county FIPS			CBSA	Metro-politan divi-sion	State and county FIPS		
47940			**Waterloo-Cedar Falls, IA**	**162,263**	49020			**Winchester, VA-WV**	**118,932**
		19013	Black Hawk County, IA.	126,106			51069	Frederick County, VA	71,187
		19017	Bremer County, IA.	23,837			51840	Winchester city, VA	25,265
		19075	Grundy County, IA.	12,320			54027	Hampshire County, WV	22,480
48140			**Wausau, WI**	**130,223**	49180			**Winston-Salem, NC**	**456,614**
		55073	Marathon County, WI.	130,223			37059	Davie County, NC	40,035
48260			**Weirton-Steubenville, WV-OH**	**125,168**			37067	Forsyth County, NC	332,355
		39081	Jefferson County, OH.	70,125			37169	Stokes County, NC	46,168
		54009	Brooke County, WV.	24,132			37197	Yadkin County, NC	38,056
		54029	Hancock County, WV.	30,911	49340			**Worcester, MA**	**784,992**
48300			**Wenatchee, WA**	**106,806**			25027	Worcester County, MA	784,992
		53007	Chelan County, WA.	71,034	49420			**Yakima, WA**	**233,105**
		53017	Douglas County, WA	35,772			53077	Yakima County, WA.	233,105
48540			**Wheeling, WV-OH**	**147,329**	49620			**York-Hanover, PA**	**416,322**
		39013	Belmont County, OH	68,771			42133	York County, PA	416,322
		54051	Marshall County, WV	33,896	49660			**Youngstown-Warren-Boardman, OH-PA** . .	**586,939**
		54069	Ohio County, WV	44,662			39099	Mahoning County, OH	251,026
48620			**Wichita, KS**	**592,126**			39155	Trumbull County, OH	217,362
		20015	Butler County, KS	63,147			42085	Mercer County, PA	118,551
		20079	Harvey County, KS	33,643	49700			**Yuba City, CA**	**161,806**
		20173	Sedgwick County, KS.	470,895			06101	Sutter County, CA.	91,410
		20191	Sumner County, KS.	24,441			06115	Yuba County, CA	70,396
48660			**Wichita Falls, TX**	**145,528**	49740			**Yuma, AZ**	**187,555**
		48009	Archer County, TX.	9,266			04027	Yuma County, AZ	187,555
		48077	Clay County, TX	11,104					
		48485	Wichita County, TX	125,158					
48700			**Williamsport, PA**	**117,668**					
		42081	Lycoming County, PA.	117,668					
48900			**Wilmington, NC**	**326,166**					
		37019	Brunswick County, NC	94,945					
		37129	New Hanover County, NC.	182,591					
		37141	Pender County, NC	48,630					

[1]The portion of Sullivan city in Crawford County, MO, is legally part of the St. Louis, MO–IL MSA. That portion is not included in these figures for the St. Louis MSA.

County Maps by State

Appendix D

Page

You may visit us on the Web at
http://www.census.gov/compendia/ccdb

County Maps by State

Appendix D

ALABAMA - Core Based Statistical Areas, Counties, and Selected Places

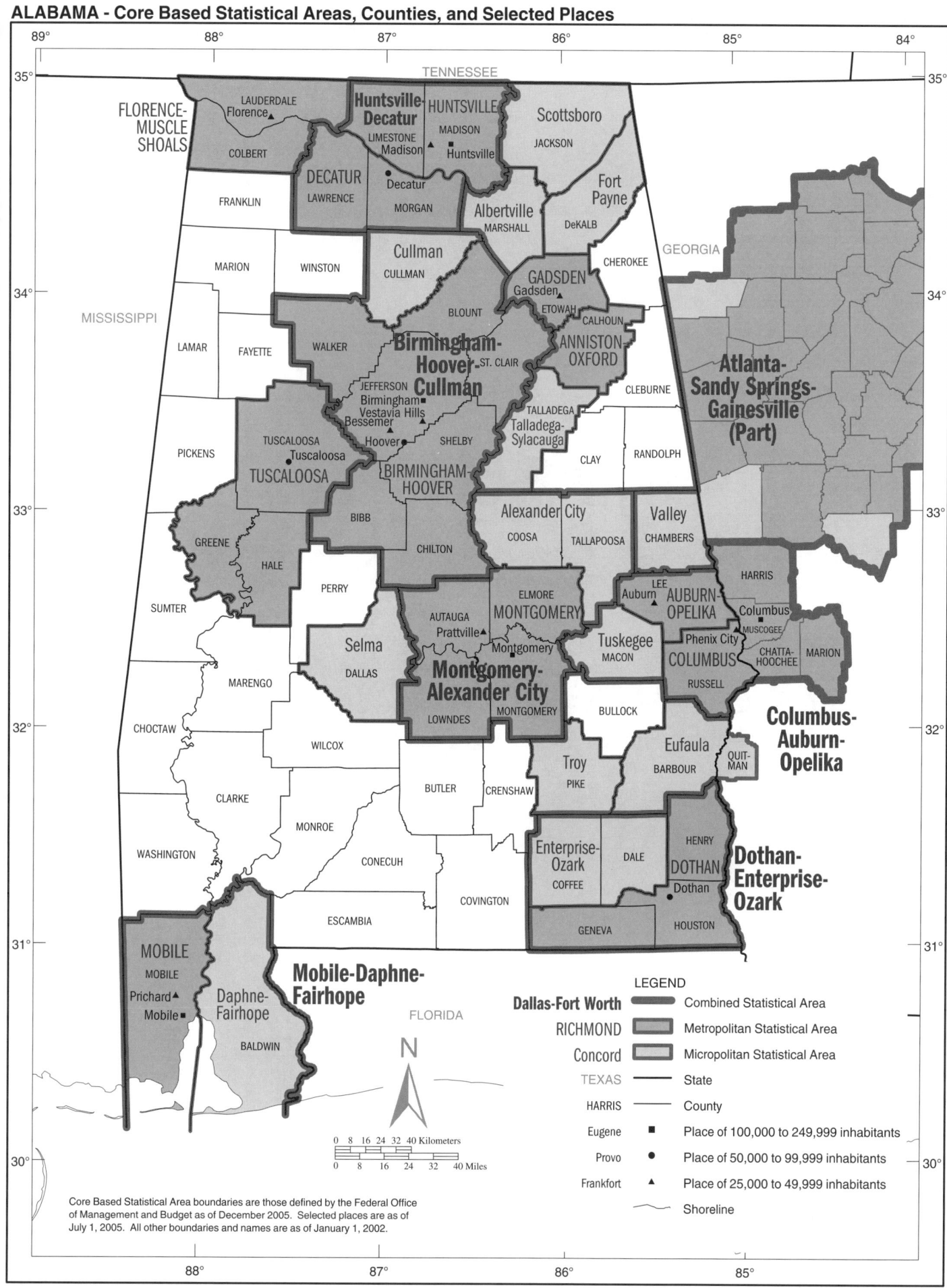

LEGEND

Dallas-Fort Worth	Combined Statistical Area
RICHMOND	Metropolitan Statistical Area
Concord	Micropolitan Statistical Area
TEXAS	State
HARRIS	County
Eugene ■	Place of 100,000 to 249,999 inhabitants
Provo ●	Place of 50,000 to 99,999 inhabitants
Frankfort ▲	Place of 25,000 to 49,999 inhabitants
	Shoreline

Core Based Statistical Area boundaries are those defined by the Federal Office of Management and Budget as of December 2005. Selected places are as of July 1, 2005. All other boundaries and names are as of January 1, 2002.

0 8 16 24 32 40 Kilometers

0 8 16 24 32 40 Miles

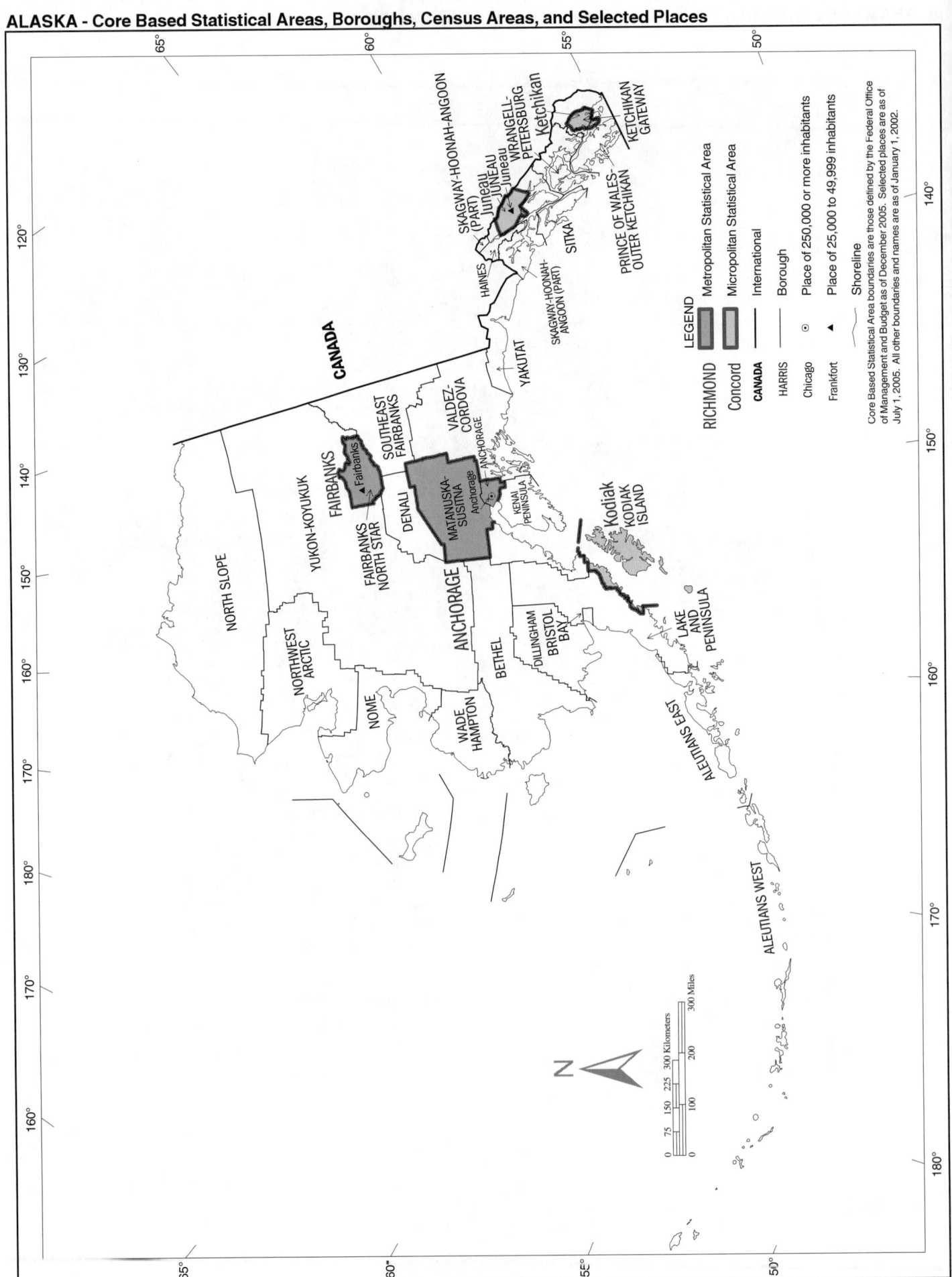

LEGEND

	Metropolitan Statistical Area
RICHMOND	
	Micropolitan Statistical Area
Concord	
CANADA	International
HARRIS	Borough
Chicago ⊙	Place of 250,000 or more inhabitants
Frankfort ◄	Place of 25,000 to 49,999 inhabitants
	Shoreline

Core Based Statistical Area boundaries are those defined by the Federal Office of Management and Budget as of December 2005. Selected places are as of July 1, 2005. All other boundaries and names are as of January 1, 2002.

CANADA

SKAGWAY-HOONAH-ANGOON

Ketchikan

KETCHIKAN GATEWAY

WRANGELL-PETERSBURG

Juneau

Juneau

SKAGWAY-HOONAH-ANGOON (PART)

HAINES

SITKA

PRINCE OF WALES-OUTER KETCHIKAN

SKAGWAY-HOONAH-ANGOON (PART)

YAKUTAT

SOUTHEAST FAIRBANKS

VALDEZ-CORDOVA

FAIRBANKS

Fairbanks

ANCHORAGE

DENALI

FAIRBANKS NORTH STAR

MATANUSKA-SUSITNA

Anchorage

KENAI PENINSULA

YUKON-KOYUKUK

NORTH SLOPE

NORTHWEST ARCTIC

NOME

WADE HAMPTON

BETHEL

DILLINGHAM

BRISTOL BAY

Kodiak

KODIAK ISLAND

LAKE AND PENINSULA

ANCHORAGE

ALEUTIANS EAST

ALEUTIANS WEST

N

| 0 | 75 | 150 | 225 | 300 Kilometers |
| 0 | | 100 | 200 | 300 Miles |

ARIZONA - Core Based Statistical Areas, Counties, and Selected Places

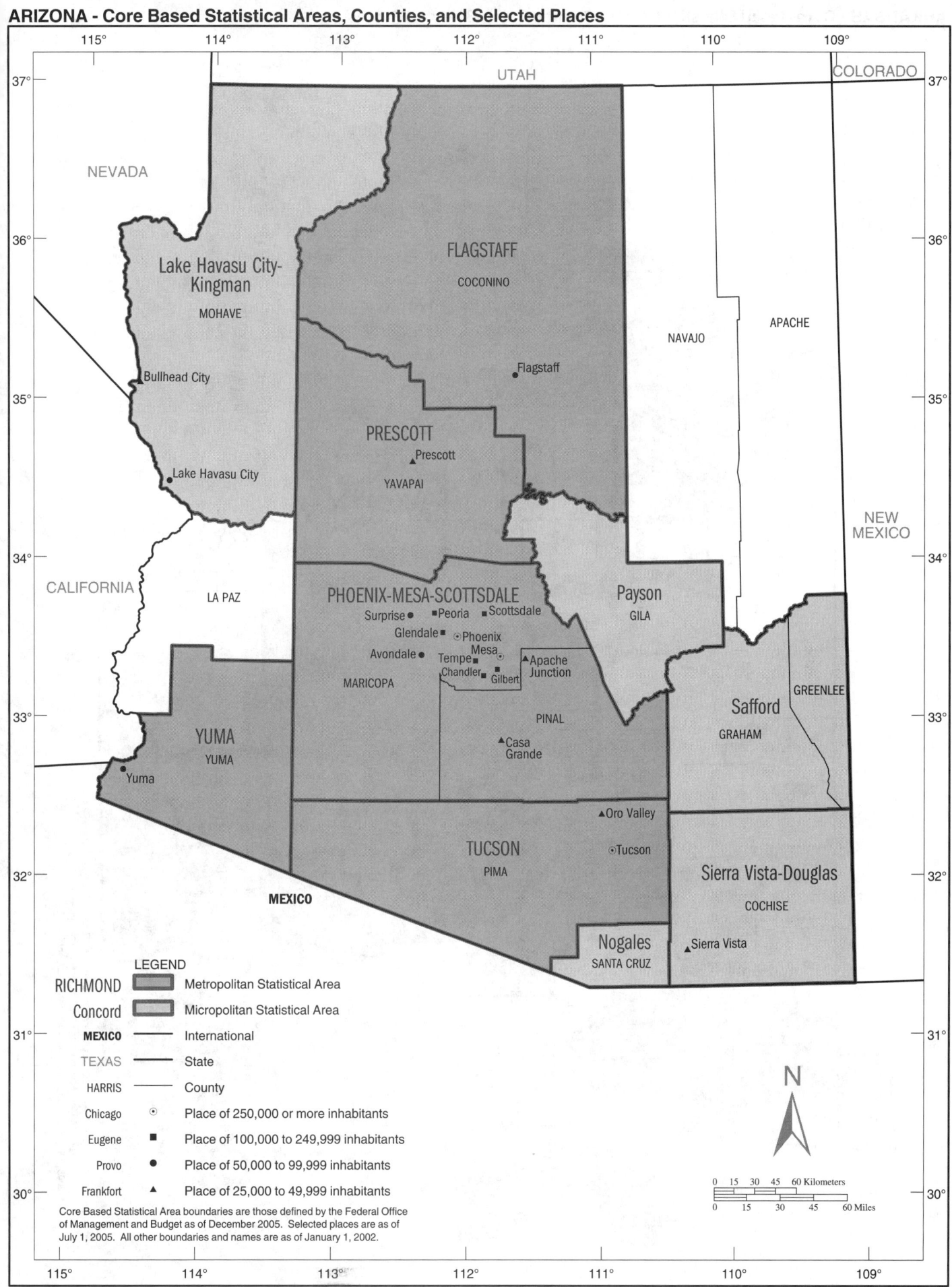

UTAH

COLORADO

NEVADA

Lake Havasu City-Kingman

MOHAVE

Bullhead City ▲

FLAGSTAFF

COCONINO

NAVAJO

APACHE

Lake Havasu City

Flagstaff ●

PRESCOTT

Prescott ▲

YAVAPAI

NEW MEXICO

CALIFORNIA

LA PAZ

PHOENIX-MESA-SCOTTSDALE

Surprise ● ■ Peoria ■ Scottsdale

Glendale ■ ⊙ Phoenix

Avondale ● Mesa ⊙

Tempe ■

Chandler ■ ■ Gilbert

▲ Apache Junction

Payson

GILA

MARICOPA

Safford

GREENLEE

GRAHAM

YUMA

YUMA

PINAL

Yuma ●

▲ Casa Grande

▲ Oro Valley

MEXICO

TUCSON

PIMA

⊙ Tucson

Sierra Vista-Douglas

COCHISE

Nogales

SANTA CRUZ

● Sierra Vista

LEGEND

RICHMOND		Metropolitan Statistical Area
Concord		Micropolitan Statistical Area
MEXICO	—	International
TEXAS	—	State
HARRIS	—	County
Chicago	⊙	Place of 250,000 or more inhabitants
Eugene	■	Place of 100,000 to 249,999 inhabitants
Provo	●	Place of 50,000 to 99,999 inhabitants
Frankfort	▲	Place of 25,000 to 49,999 inhabitants

N

0 15 30 45 60 Kilometers

0 15 30 45 60 Miles

Core Based Statistical Area boundaries are those defined by the Federal Office of Management and Budget as of December 2005. Selected places are as of July 1, 2005. All other boundaries and names are as of January 1, 2002.

U.S. DEPARTMENT OF COMMERCE Economics and Statistics Administration U.S. Census Bureau

County and City Data Book: 2007

U.S. Census Bureau

ARKANSAS - Core Based Statistical Areas, Counties, and Selected Places

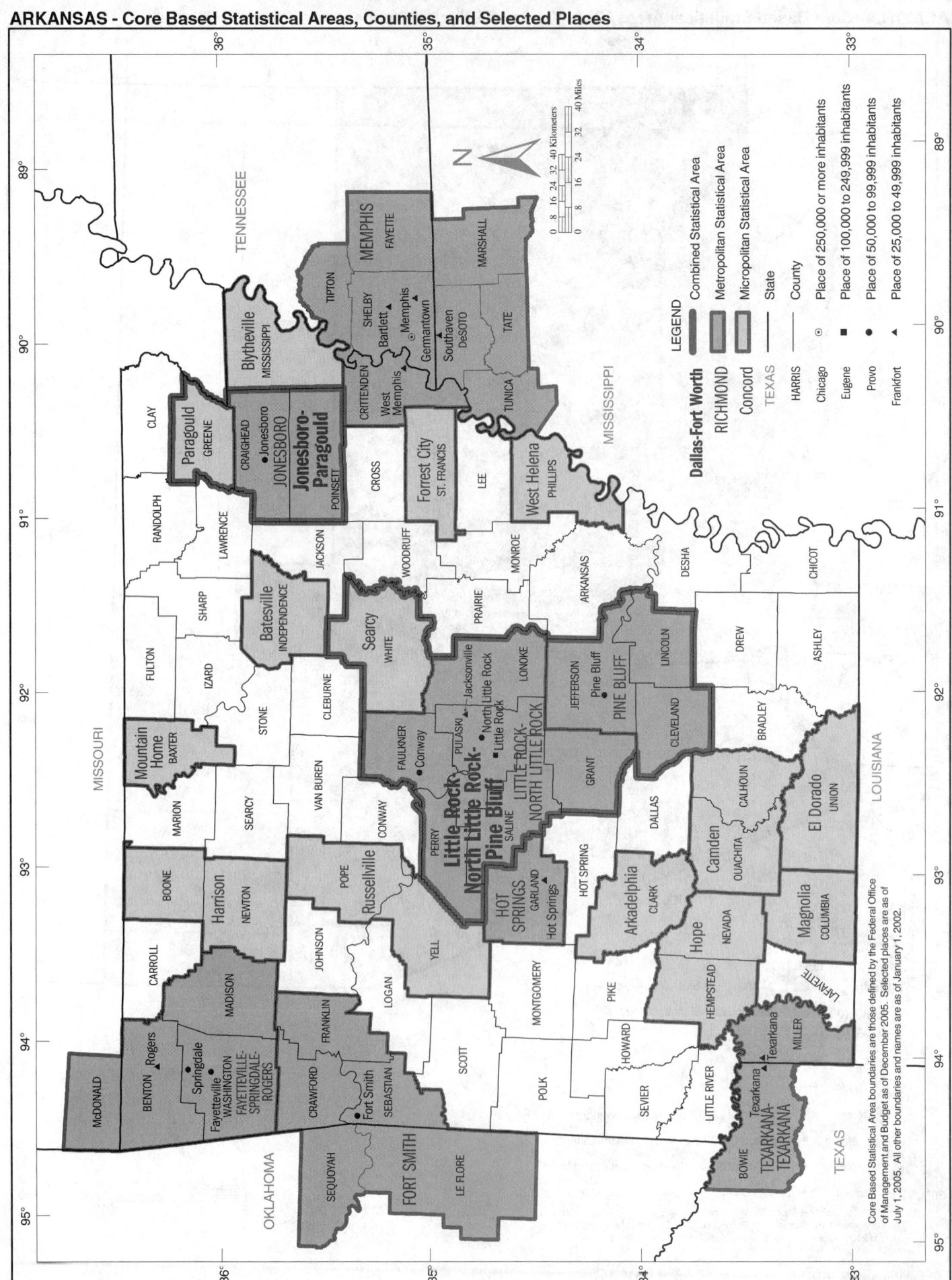

CALIFORNIA - Core Based Statistical Areas, Counties, and Selected Places

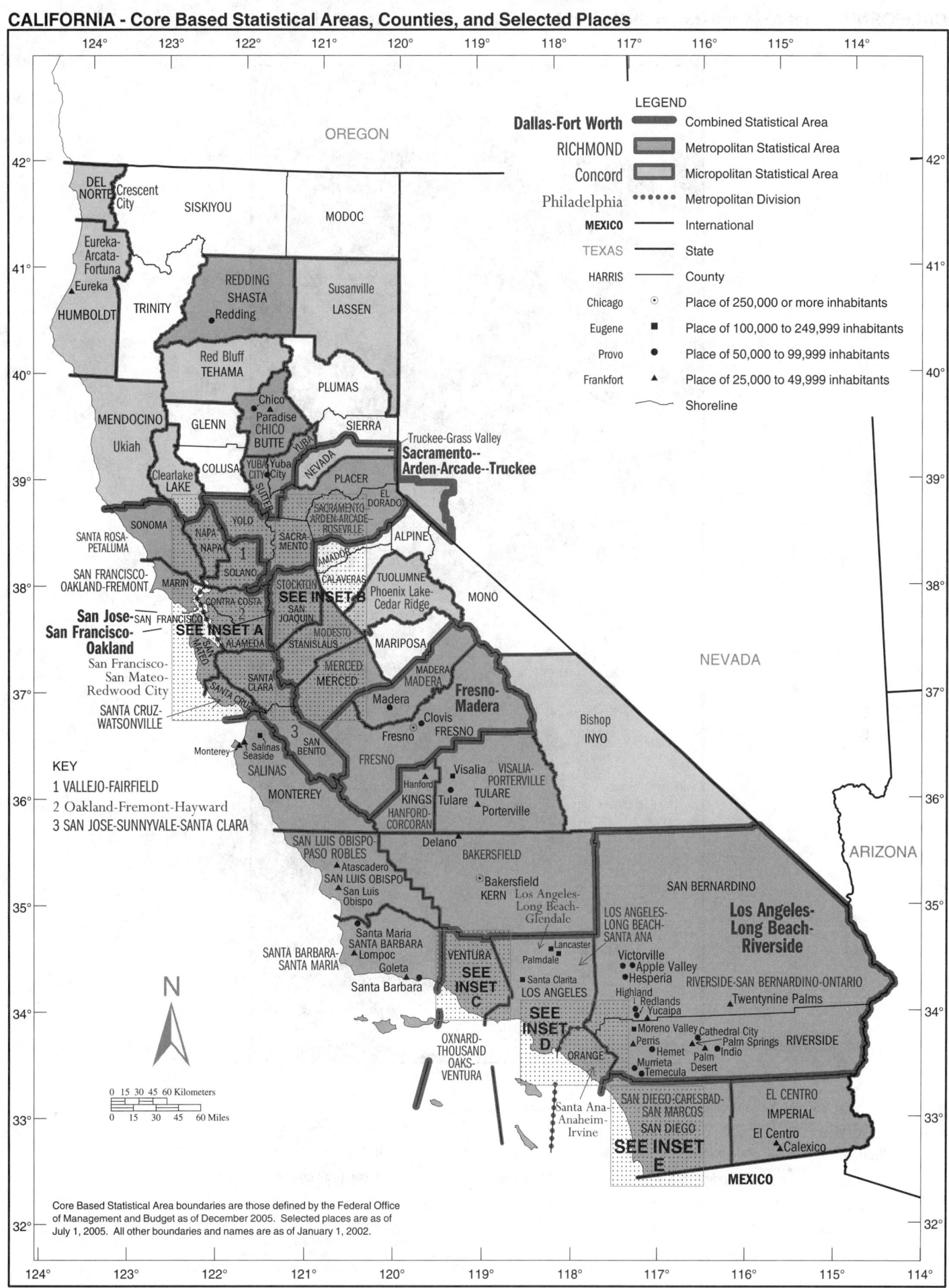

LEGEND

Dallas-Fort Worth ▬▬▬ Combined Statistical Area
RICHMOND ▬▬ Metropolitan Statistical Area
Concord ▭ Micropolitan Statistical Area
Philadelphia •••••• Metropolitan Division
MEXICO ▬▬ International
TEXAS ▬ State
HARRIS ▬ County
Chicago ⊙ Place of 250,000 or more inhabitants
Eugene ■ Place of 100,000 to 249,999 inhabitants
Provo ● Place of 50,000 to 99,999 inhabitants
Frankfort ▲ Place of 25,000 to 49,999 inhabitants
〰 Shoreline

KEY
1 VALLEJO-FAIRFIELD
2 Oakland-Fremont-Hayward
3 SAN JOSE-SUNNYVALE-SANTA CLARA

N

0 15 30 45 60 Kilometers
0 15 30 45 60 Miles

Core Based Statistical Area boundaries are those defined by the Federal Office of Management and Budget as of December 2005. Selected places are as of July 1, 2005. All other boundaries and names are as of January 1, 2002.

Map

122°30′ 122°00′

YUBA CITY
(PART)

Clearlake
(Part)

LAKE
(PART)

Sacramento--
Arden-Arcade--
Truckee
(Part)

SUTTER
(PART)

YOLO
(PART)

SACRAMENTO--
ARDEN-ARCADE--
ROSEVILLE
(PART)

• Woodland

NAPA

NAPA

38°30′

Davis •   West
Sacramento

38°30′

Santa Rosa

SONOMA
(PART)

▲ Rohnert Park

Vacaville •

SANTA
ROSA-
PETALUMA
(PART)

• Napa

Fairfield
• • Suisun City

VALLEJO-
FAIRFIELD

Petaluma •

SOLANO

Novato •

• Vallejo

SACRAMENTO
(PART)

MARIN
(PART)

• Benicia

38°00′

San Rafael •

Pittsburg •

▲ Martinez

38°00′

• San Pablo
Richmond ■

Concord ▲
Pleasant Hill ▲

Antioch

• Oakley

CONTRA COSTA

Walnut Creek ▲

Oakland-
Fremont-
Hayward

■ Berkeley

• Danville

SAN JOAQUIN
(PART)

SAN FRANCISCO
(PART)

San
Francisco ⊙

Oakland ⊙
• Alameda

• San Ramon

Daly •
City

▲ Dublin

• Livermore

South
San
Francisco

San •
Leandro

San Bruno ▲

Burlingame

• Pleasanton

Pacifica ▲

• Hayward

STOCKTON
(PART)

• Union City

ALAMEDA

San •
Mateo

Foster
City ▲

Newark ▲
Fremont •

SAN
MATEO

San ▲
Carlos

Redwood ▲
City

Menlo Park •
East Palo Alto

San Francisco-
San Mateo-
Redwood City
(Part)

37°30′

Palo
Alto •

• Milpitas

37°30′

Mountain View •
Sunnyvale •

SAN
FRANCISCO-
OAKLAND-
FREMONT
(PART)

Los ▲
Altos

• Santa Clara

Cupertino •

⊙ San Jose

SAN JOSE-
SUNNYVALE-
SANTA CLARA
(PART)

Saratoga •

▲ Campbell

Los Gatos ▲

SANTA
CLARA
(PART)

• Morgan Hill

San Jose-
San Francisco-
Oakland
(Part)

SANTA CRUZ

SANTA CRUZ-
WATSONVILLE

• Gilroy

37°00′

• Santa Cruz

37°00′

Watsonville •

SALINAS
(PART)

SAN BENITO
(PART)

MONTEREY (PART)

122°30′ 122°00′ 121°30′

N

0 5 10 15 20 Kilometers

0 5 10 15 20 Miles

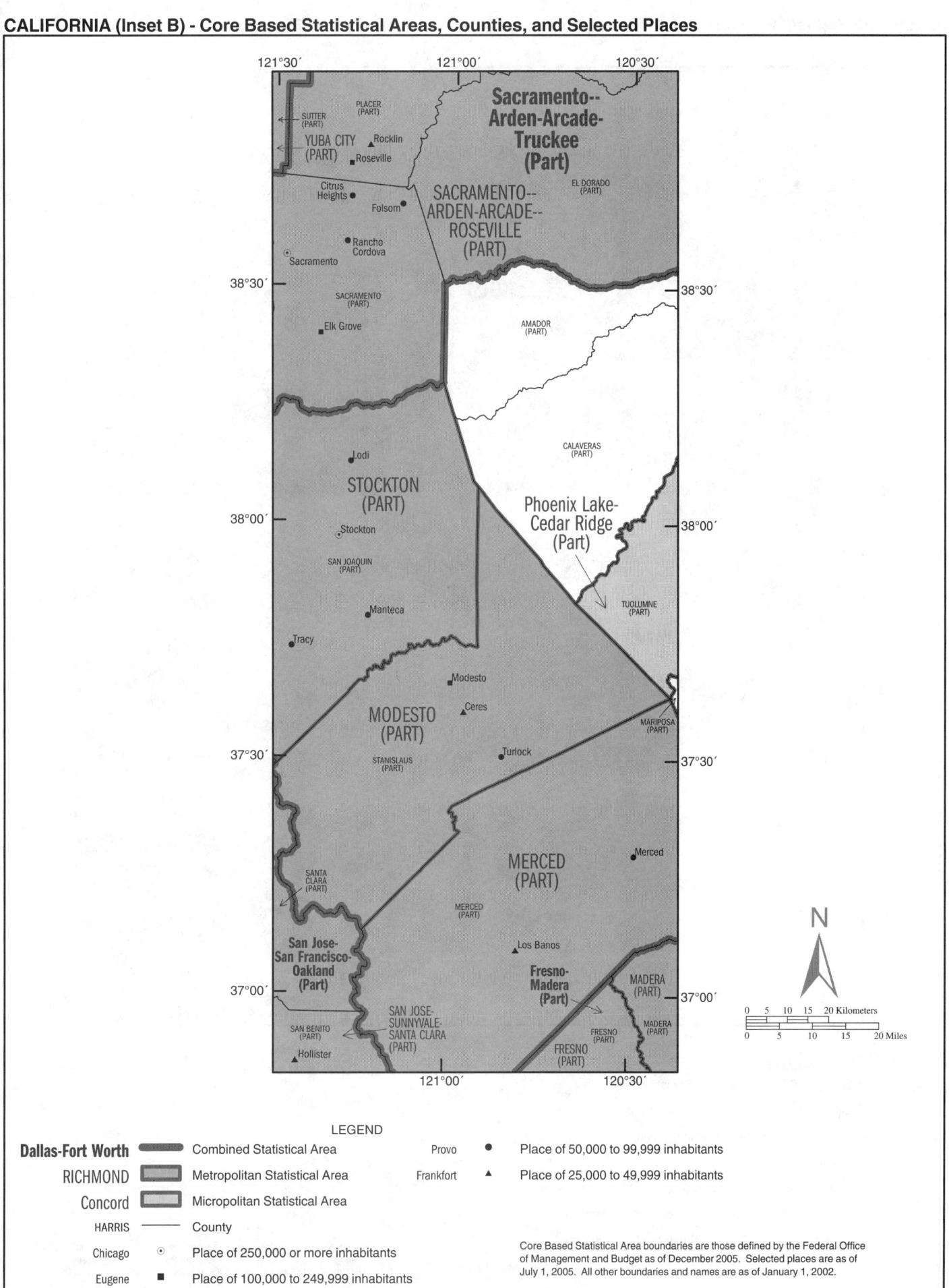

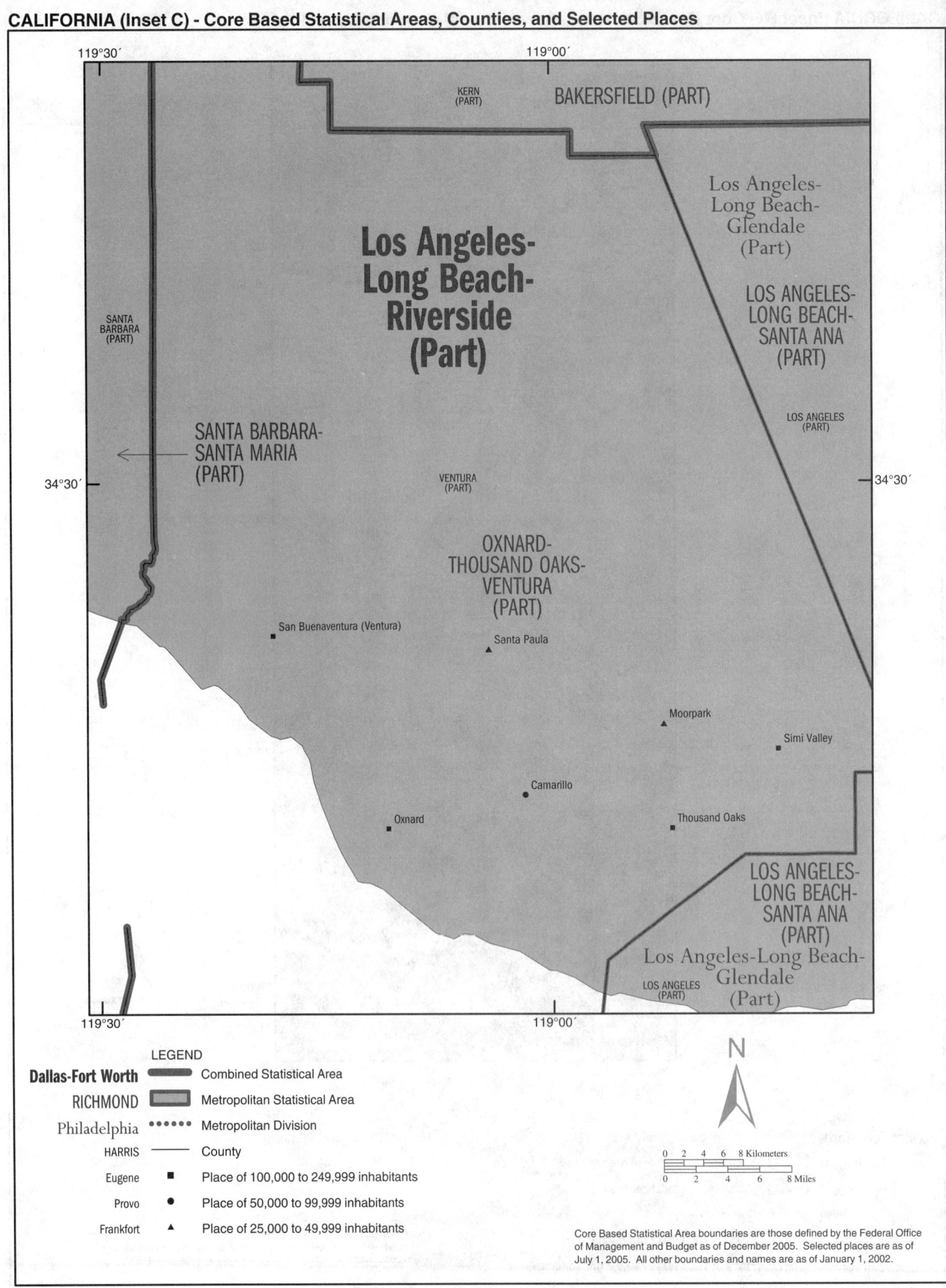

119°30′   119°00′

KERN
(PART)

BAKERSFIELD (PART)

Los Angeles-
Long Beach-
Glendale
(Part)

LOS ANGELES-
LONG BEACH-
SANTA ANA
(PART)

Los Angeles-
Long Beach-
Riverside
(Part)

SANTA
BARBARA
(PART)

LOS ANGELES
(PART)

SANTA BARBARA-
SANTA MARIA
(PART)

34°30′

VENTURA
(PART)

OXNARD-
THOUSAND OAKS-
VENTURA
(PART)

34°30′

■ San Buenaventura (Ventura)

▲ Santa Paula

▲ Moorpark

■ Simi Valley

● Camarillo

■ Thousand Oaks

■ Oxnard

LOS ANGELES-
LONG BEACH-
SANTA ANA
(PART)

Los Angeles-Long Beach-
Glendale
(Part)

LOS ANGELES
(PART)

119°30′   119°00′

LEGEND

Dallas-Fort Worth	Combined Statistical Area
RICHMOND	Metropolitan Statistical Area
Philadelphia	•••••• Metropolitan Division
HARRIS	—— County
Eugene	■ Place of 100,000 to 249,999 inhabitants
Provo	● Place of 50,000 to 99,999 inhabitants
Frankfort	▲ Place of 25,000 to 49,999 inhabitants

N

0 2 4 6 8 Kilometers

0 2 4 6 8 Miles

Core Based Statistical Area boundaries are those defined by the Federal Office
of Management and Budget as of December 2005. Selected places are as of
July 1, 2005. All other boundaries and names are as of January 1, 2002.

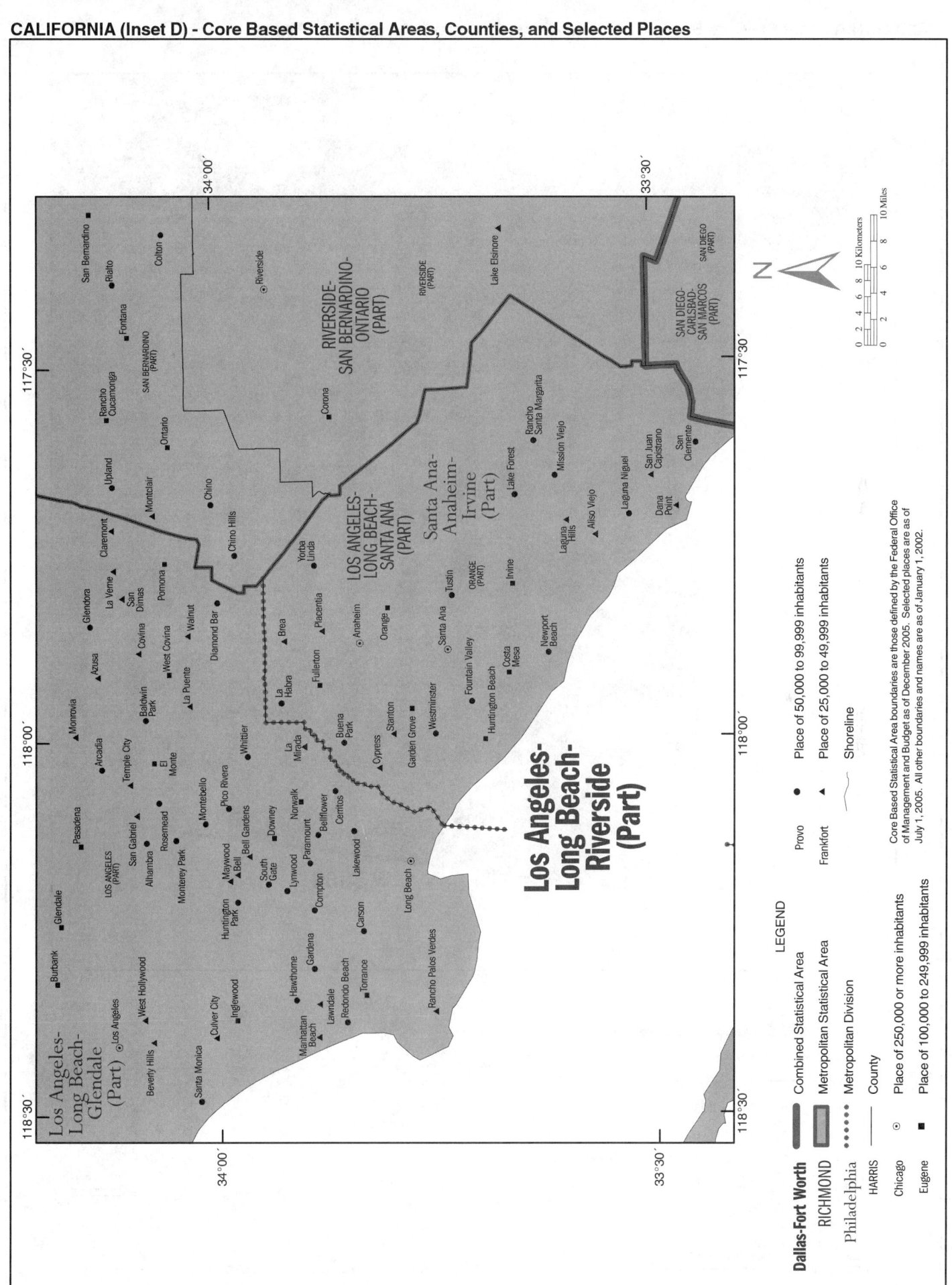

LEGEND

Dallas-Fort Worth	Combined Statistical Area
RICHMOND	Metropolitan Statistical Area
Philadelphia	Metropolitan Division
HARRIS	County
Chicago ⊙	Place of 250,000 or more inhabitants
Eugene ■	Place of 100,000 to 249,999 inhabitants

Provo ●	Place of 50,000 to 99,999 inhabitants
Frankfort ▲	Place of 25,000 to 49,999 inhabitants
	Shoreline

Core Based Statistical Area boundaries are those defined by the Federal Office of Management and Budget as of December 2005. Selected places are as of July 1, 2005. All other boundaries and names are as of January 1, 2002.

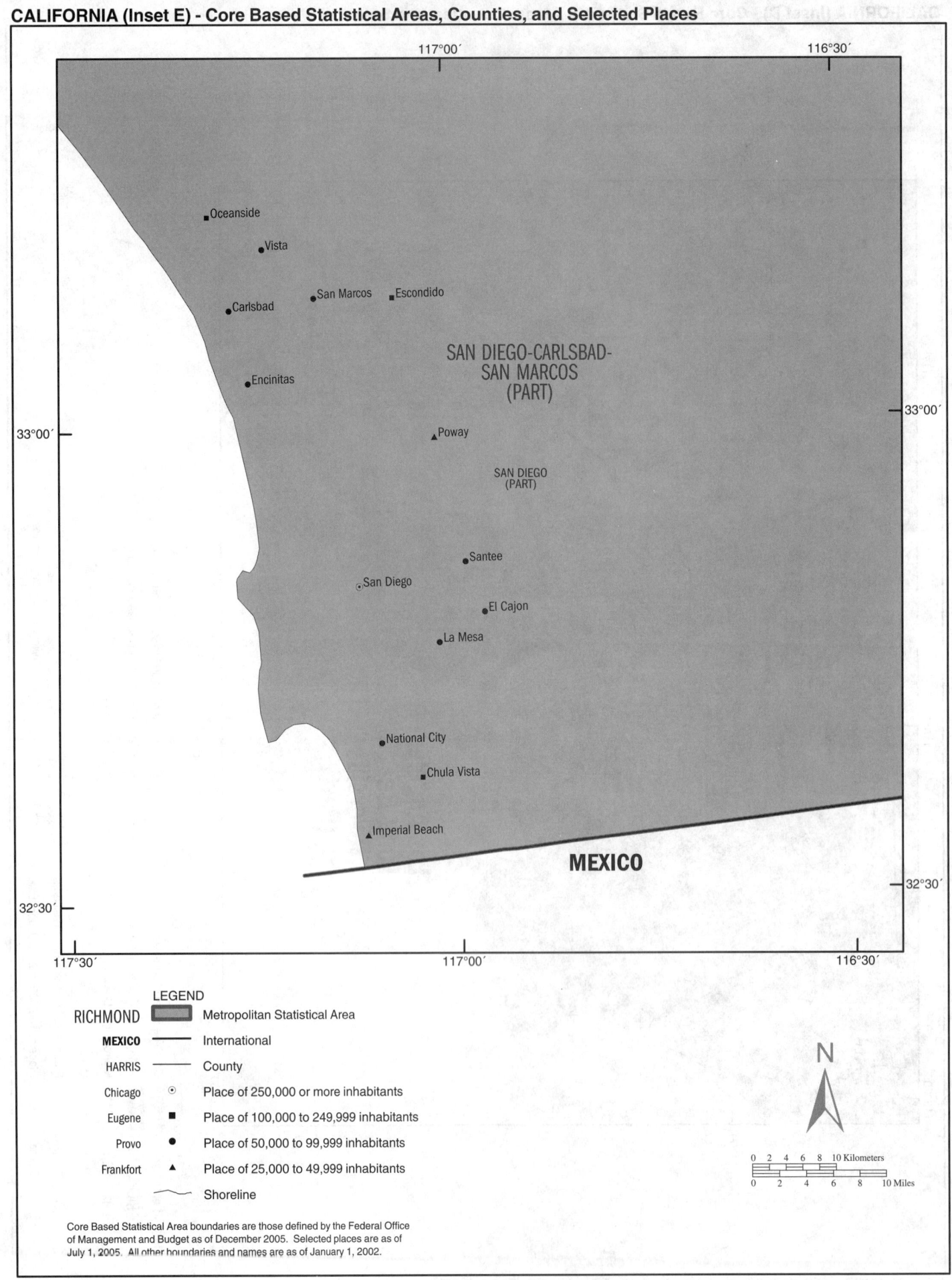

117°00´

116°30´

33°00´

33°00´

Oceanside

Vista

Carlsbad

San Marcos

Escondido

SAN DIEGO-CARLSBAD-
SAN MARCOS
(PART)

Encinitas

Poway

SAN DIEGO
(PART)

Santee

San Diego

El Cajon

La Mesa

National City

Chula Vista

Imperial Beach

MEXICO

32°30´

32°30´

33°00´

117°30´

117°00´

116°30´

LEGEND

RICHMOND ▨ Metropolitan Statistical Area

MEXICO —— International

HARRIS —— County

Chicago ⊙ Place of 250,000 or more inhabitants

Eugene ▪ Place of 100,000 to 249,999 inhabitants

Provo ● Place of 50,000 to 99,999 inhabitants

Frankfort ▲ Place of 25,000 to 49,999 inhabitants

〜 Shoreline

N

0 2 4 6 8 10 Kilometers
0 2 4 6 8 10 Miles

Core Based Statistical Area boundaries are those defined by the Federal Office
of Management and Budget as of December 2005. Selected places are as of
July 1, 2005. All other boundaries and names are as of January 1, 2002.

COLORADO - Core Based Statistical Areas, Counties, and Selected Places

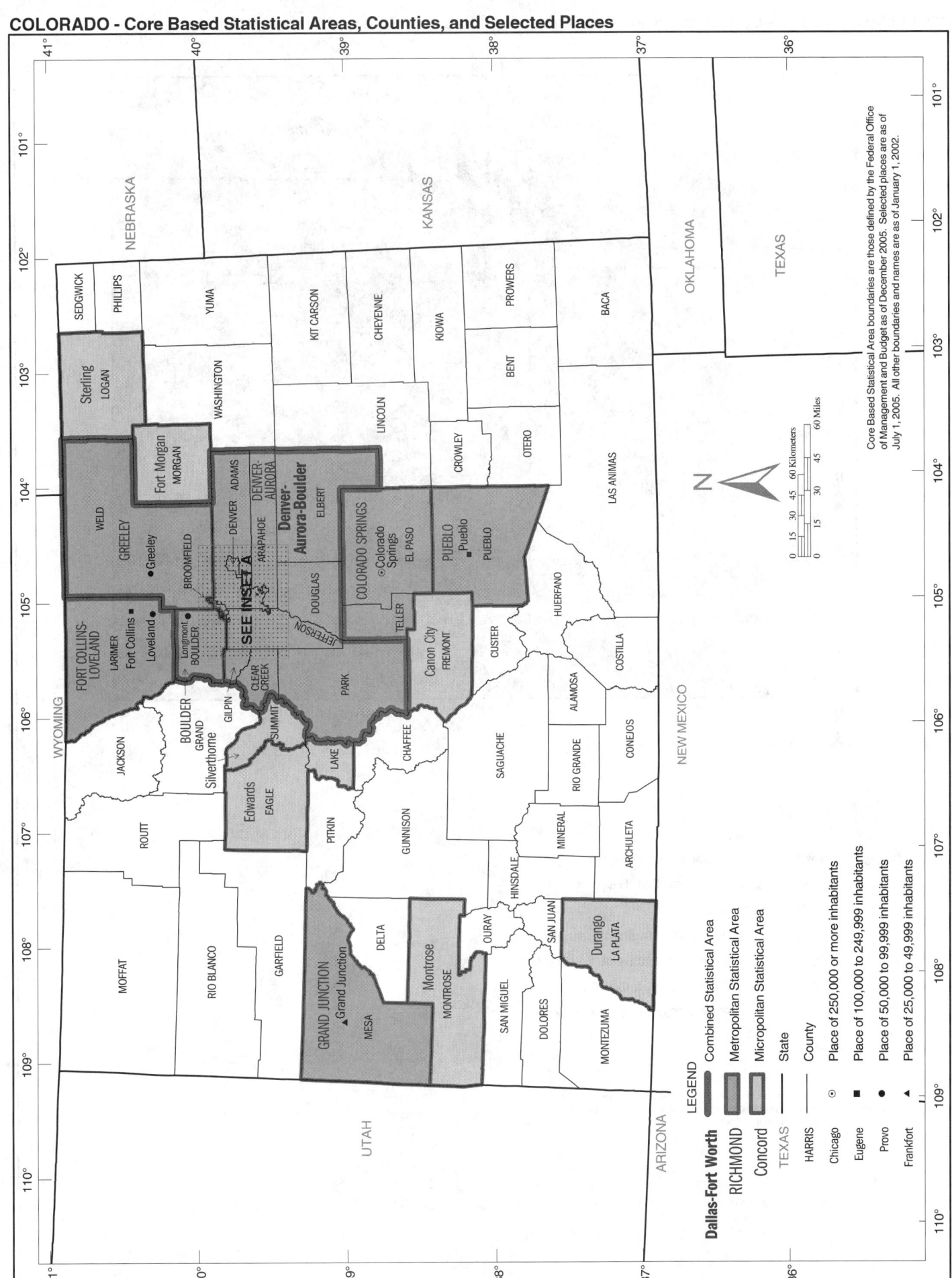

Core Based Statistical Area boundaries are those defined by the Federal Office of Management and Budget as of December 2005. Selected places are as of July 1, 2005. All other boundaries and names are as of January 1, 2002.

LEGEND

Dallas-Fort Worth — Combined Statistical Area

RICHMOND — Metropolitan Statistical Area

Concord — Micropolitan Statistical Area

TEXAS — State

HARRIS — County

Chicago ⊙ — Place of 250,000 or more inhabitants

Eugene ■ — Place of 100,000 to 249,999 inhabitants

Provo ● — Place of 50,000 to 99,999 inhabitants

Frankfort ▲ — Place of 25,000 to 49,999 inhabitants

U.S. DEPARTMENT OF COMMERCE Economics and Statistics Administration U.S. Census Bureau

County and City Data Book: 2007

COLORADO (Inset A) - Core Based Statistical Areas, Counties, and Selected Places

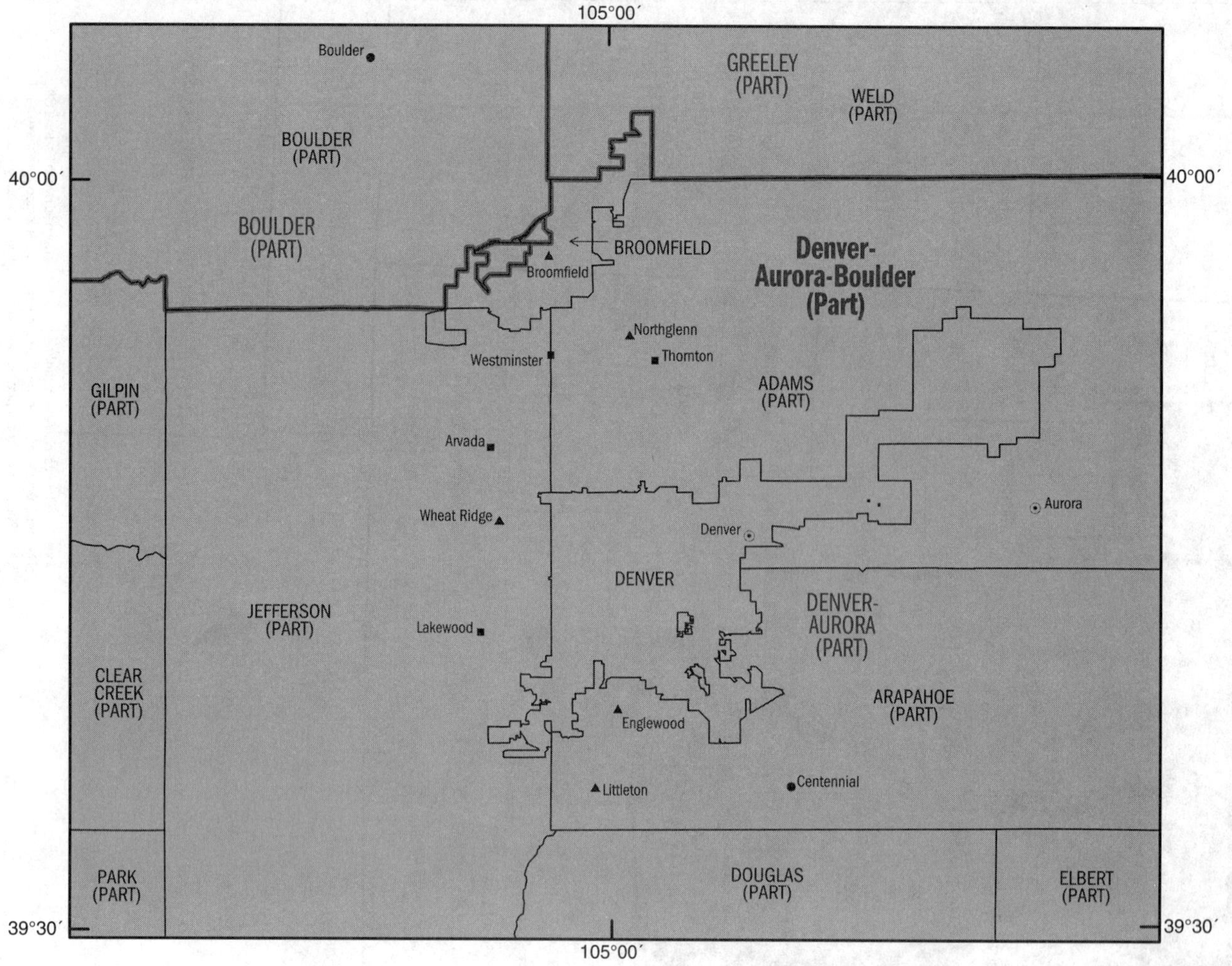

105°00´

Boulder •

GREELEY
(PART)

WELD
(PART)

BOULDER
(PART)

40°00´

40°00´

BOULDER
(PART)

Denver-
Aurora-Boulder
(Part)

▲ BROOMFIELD

Broomfield

BROOMFIELD

▲ Northglenn

Westminster ■

■ Thornton

ADAMS
(PART)

GILPIN
(PART)

Arvada ■

Aurora ⊙

Wheat Ridge ▲

Denver ⊙

JEFFERSON
(PART)

DENVER

DENVER-
AURORA
(PART)

CLEAR
CREEK
(PART)

Lakewood ■

Englewood ▲

ARAPAHOE
(PART)

▲ Littleton

● Centennial

PARK
(PART)

DOUGLAS
(PART)

ELBERT
(PART)

39°30´

39°30´

105°00´

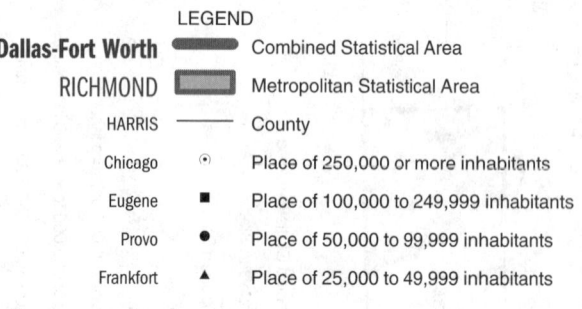

LEGEND

Dallas-Fort Worth ▬▬▬ Combined Statistical Area

RICHMOND ▬▬▬ Metropolitan Statistical Area

HARRIS ——— County

Chicago ⊙ Place of 250,000 or more inhabitants

Eugene ■ Place of 100,000 to 249,999 inhabitants

Provo ● Place of 50,000 to 99,999 inhabitants

Frankfort ▲ Place of 25,000 to 49,999 inhabitants

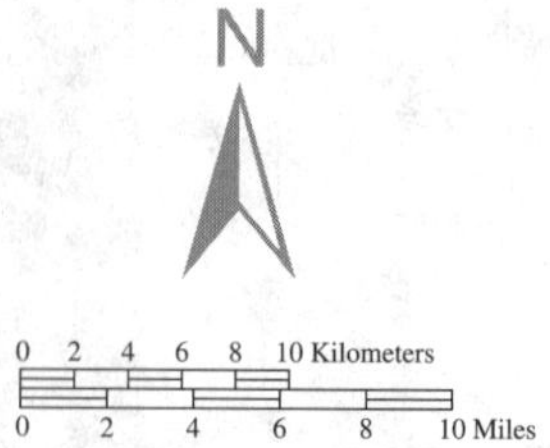

N

0 2 4 6 8 10 Kilometers

0 2 4 6 8 10 Miles

Core Based Statistical Area boundaries are those defined by the Federal Office
of Management and Budget as of December 2005. Selected places are as of
July 1, 2005. All other boundaries and names are as of January 1, 2002.

CONNECTICUT - Core Based Statistical Areas, Counties, and Selected Places

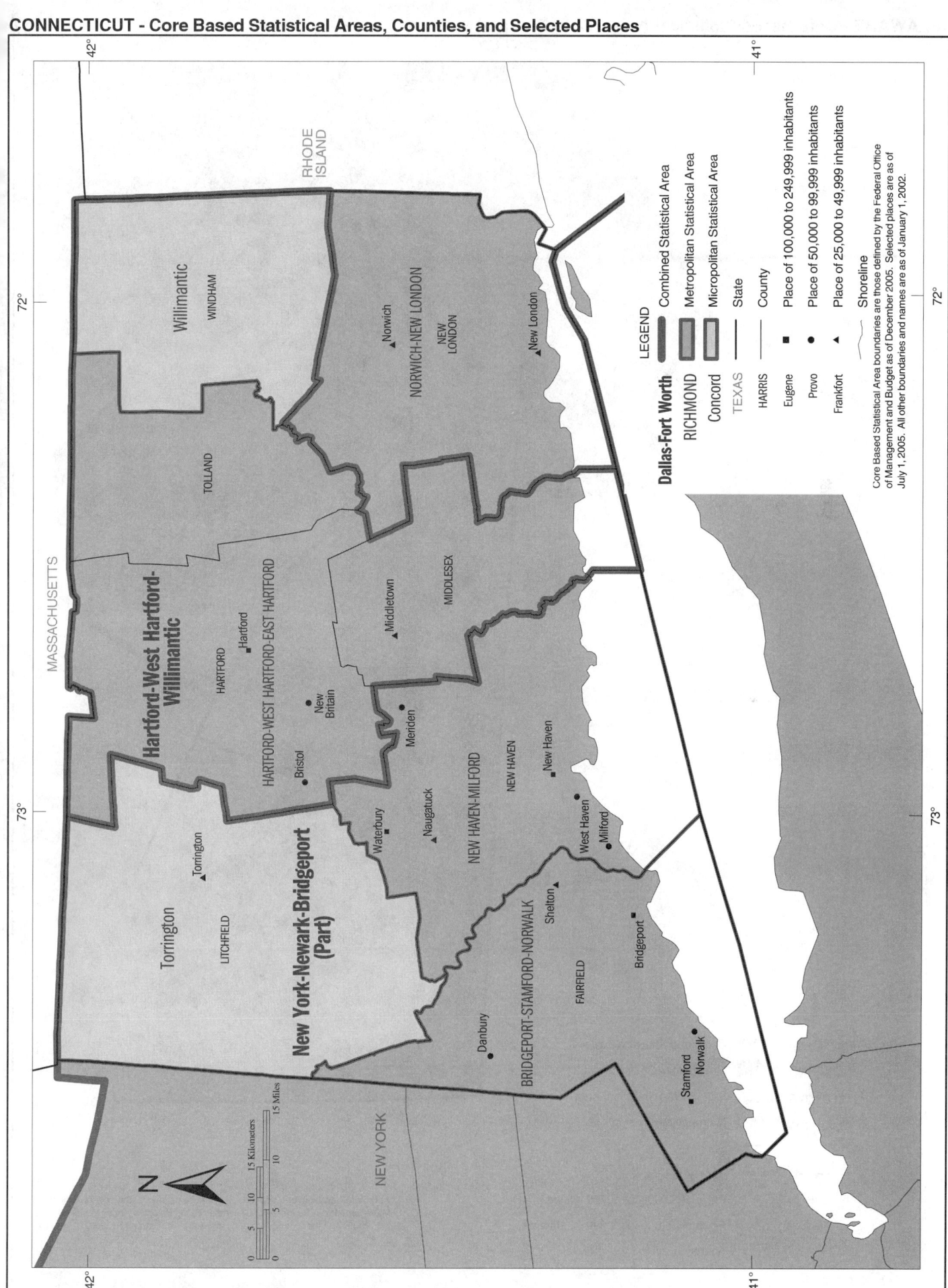

LEGEND

Dallas-Fort Worth   Combined Statistical Area

RICHMOND   Metropolitan Statistical Area

Concord   Micropolitan Statistical Area

TEXAS   State

HARRIS   County

Eugene ■   Place of 100,000 to 249,999 inhabitants

Provo ●   Place of 50,000 to 99,999 inhabitants

Frankfort ◄   Place of 25,000 to 49,999 inhabitants

Shoreline

Core Based Statistical Area boundaries are those defined by the Federal Office of Management and Budget as of December 2005. Selected places are as of July 1, 2005. All other boundaries and names are as of January 1, 2002.

PENNSYLVANIA

76°

75°

40°

40°

Wilmington

Wilmington ●

Philadelphia-Camden-Vineland (Part)

▲ Newark

CECIL

NEW CASTLE

PHILADELPHIA-
CAMDEN-
WILMINGTON
(PART)

SALEM

NEW JERSEY

MARYLAND

DOVER

Dover ▲

KENT

N

39°

39°

0 5 10 15 Kilometers

0 5 10 15 Miles

Seaford

SUSSEX

LEGEND

Dallas-Fort Worth	Combined Statistical Area
RICHMOND	Metropolitan Statistical Area
Concord	Micropolitan Statistical Area
Philadelphia	•••••• Metropolitan Division
TEXAS	—— State
HARRIS	—— County
Provo ●	Place of 50,000 to 99,999 inhabitants
Frankfort ▲	Place of 25,000 to 49,999 inhabitants
	Shoreline

Core Based Statistical Area boundaries are those defined by the Federal Office
of Management and Budget as of December 2005. Selected places are as of
July 1, 2005. All other boundaries and names are as of January 1, 2002.

76°

75°

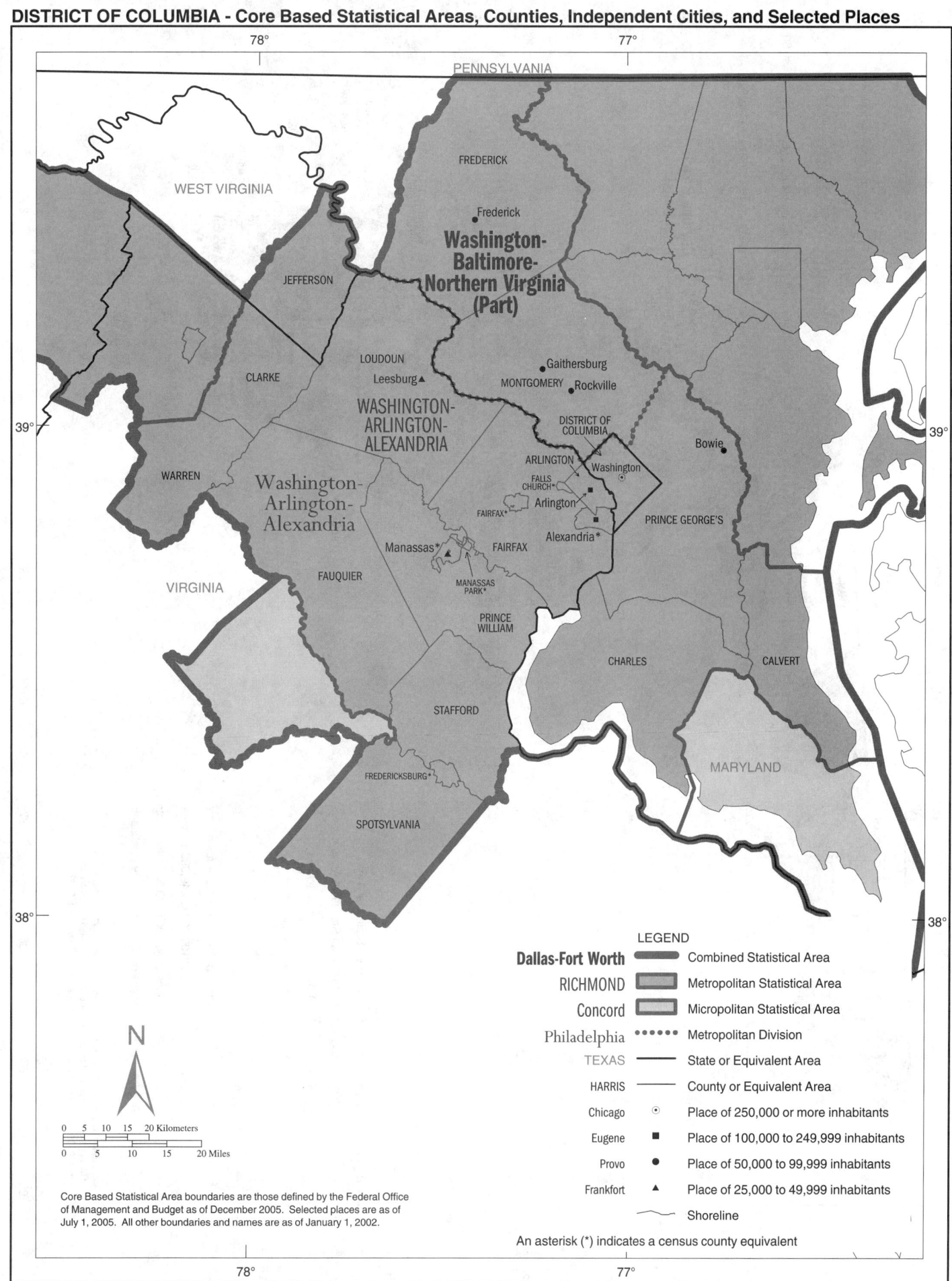

LEGEND

Dallas-Fort Worth	Combined Statistical Area
RICHMOND	Metropolitan Statistical Area
Concord	Micropolitan Statistical Area
Philadelphia	•••••• Metropolitan Division
TEXAS	State or Equivalent Area
HARRIS	County or Equivalent Area
Chicago ⊙	Place of 250,000 or more inhabitants
Eugene ■	Place of 100,000 to 249,999 inhabitants
Provo ●	Place of 50,000 to 99,999 inhabitants
Frankfort ▲	Place of 25,000 to 49,999 inhabitants
	Shoreline

An asterisk (*) indicates a census county equivalent

Core Based Statistical Area boundaries are those defined by the Federal Office of Management and Budget as of December 2005. Selected places are as of July 1, 2005. All other boundaries and names are as of January 1, 2002.

0 5 10 15 20 Kilometers
0 5 10 15 20 Miles

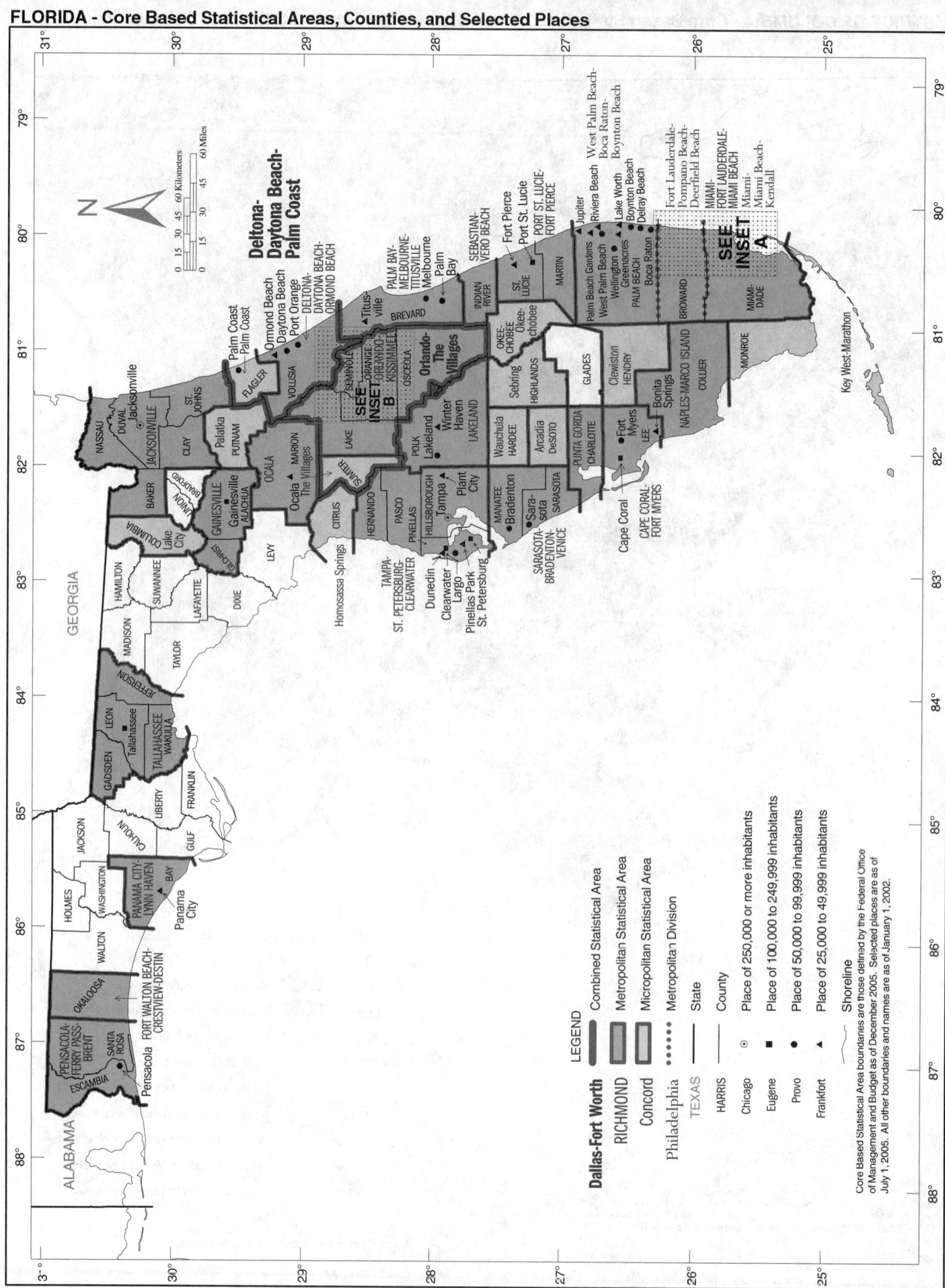

Deltona-
Daytona Beach-
Palm Coast

LEGEND

Dallas-Fort Worth   Combined Statistical Area

RICHMOND   Metropolitan Statistical Area

Concord   Micropolitan Statistical Area

Philadelphia   Metropolitan Division

TEXAS   State

HARRIS   County

Chicago   Place of 250,000 or more inhabitants

Eugene   Place of 100,000 to 249,999 inhabitants

Provo   Place of 50,000 to 99,999 inhabitants

Frankfort   Place of 25,000 to 49,999 inhabitants

   Shoreline

Core Based Statistical Area boundaries are those defined by the Federal Office
of Management and Budget as of December 2005. Selected places are as of
July 1, 2005. All other boundaries and names are as of January 1, 2002.

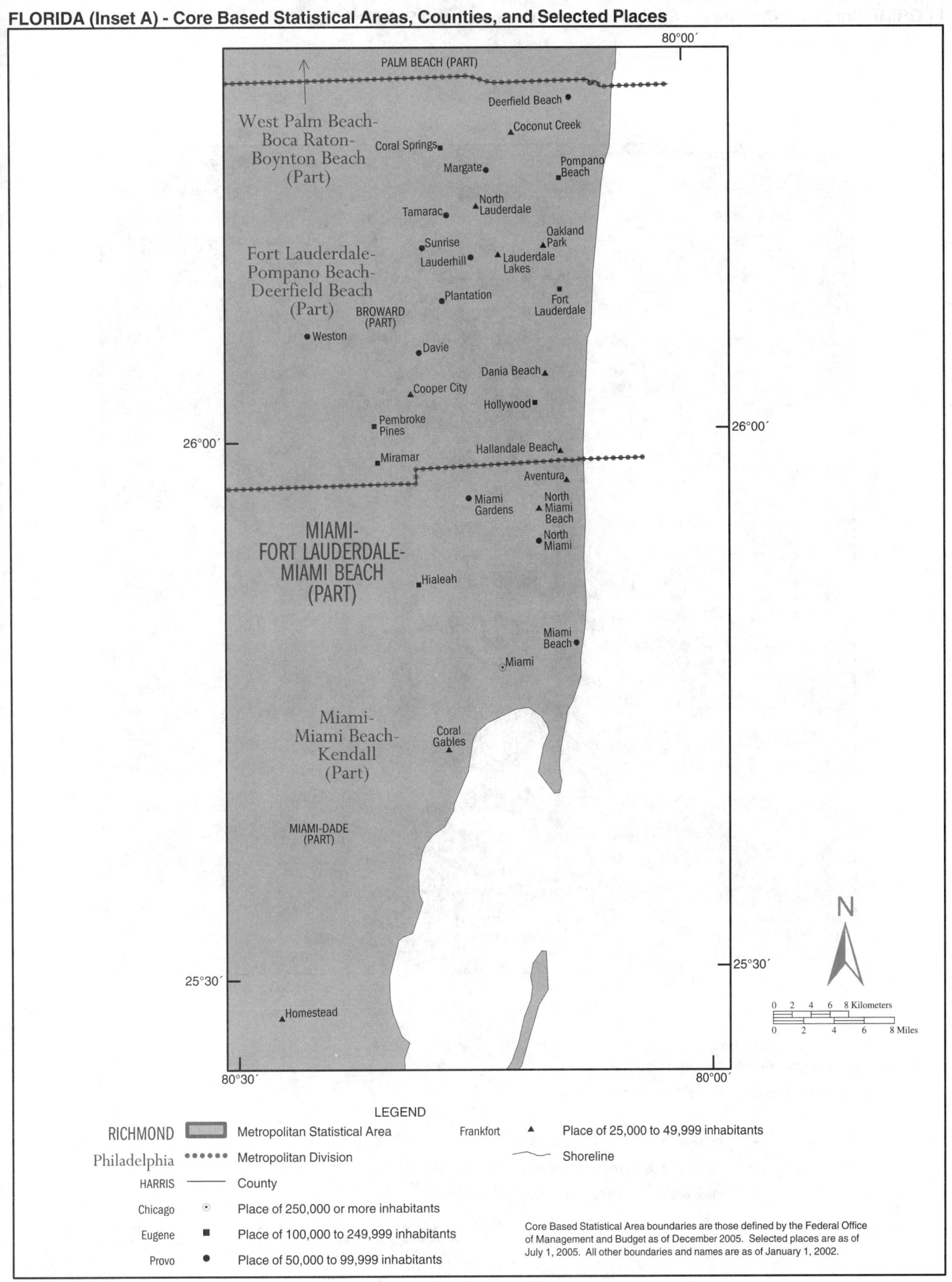

80°00′

PALM BEACH (PART)

West Palm Beach-
Boca Raton-
Boynton Beach
(Part)

Deerfield Beach

Coconut Creek

Coral Springs

Margate

Pompano
Beach

North
Lauderdale

Tamarac

Oakland
Park

Fort Lauderdale-
Pompano Beach-
Deerfield Beach
(Part)

Sunrise
Lauderhill

Lauderdale
Lakes

Plantation

Fort
Lauderdale

BROWARD
(PART)

Weston

Davie

Dania Beach

Cooper City

Hollywood

Pembroke
Pines

26°00′

Miramar

Hallandale Beach

Aventura

MIAMI-
FORT LAUDERDALE-
MIAMI BEACH
(PART)

Miami
Gardens

North
Miami
Beach

North
Miami

Hialeah

Miami
Beach

Miami

Miami-
Miami Beach-
Kendall
(Part)

Coral
Gables

MIAMI-DADE
(PART)

26°00′

25°30′

Homestead

N

0 2 4 6 8 Kilometers

0 2 4 6 8 Miles

80°30′   80°00′

25°30′

U.S. DEPARTMENT OF COMMERCE Economics and Statistics Administration U.S. Census Bureau

81°30′   81°00′

OCALA (PART)
MARION (PART)

LAKE
(PART)

• Deltona

VOLUSIA
(PART)

**Deltona-
Daytona Beach-
Palm Coast
(Part)**

DELTONA-
DAYTONA BEACH-
ORMOND BEACH
(PART)

▲ Sanford

PALM BAY-
MELBOURNE-
TITUSVILLE
(PART)

SEMINOLE

▲ Winter Springs

BREVARD
(PART)

▲Apopka

▲ Altamonte
Springs

▲ Oviedo

Winter Park▲

**Orlando-
The Villages
(Part)**

ORANGE
(PART)

■ Orlando

28°30′

28°30′

ORLANDO-
KISSIMMEE
(PART)

LAKELAND
(PART)

• Kissimmee

OSCEOLA
(PART)

POLK (PART)

81°30′   81°00′

N

LEGEND

Dallas-Fort Worth   Combined Statistical Area

RICHMOND   Metropolitan Statistical Area

HARRIS   County

Eugene   ■   Place of 100,000 to 249,999 inhabitants

Provo   ●   Place of 50,000 to 99,999 inhabitants

Frankfort   ▲   Place of 25,000 to 49,999 inhabitants

   Shoreline

0   2   4   6   8 Kilometers

0   2   4   6   8 Miles

Core Based Statistical Area boundaries are those defined by the Federal Office
of Management and Budget as of December 2005. Selected places are as of
July 1, 2005. All other boundaries and names are as of January 1, 2002.

GEORGIA - Core Based Statistical Areas, Counties, and Selected Places

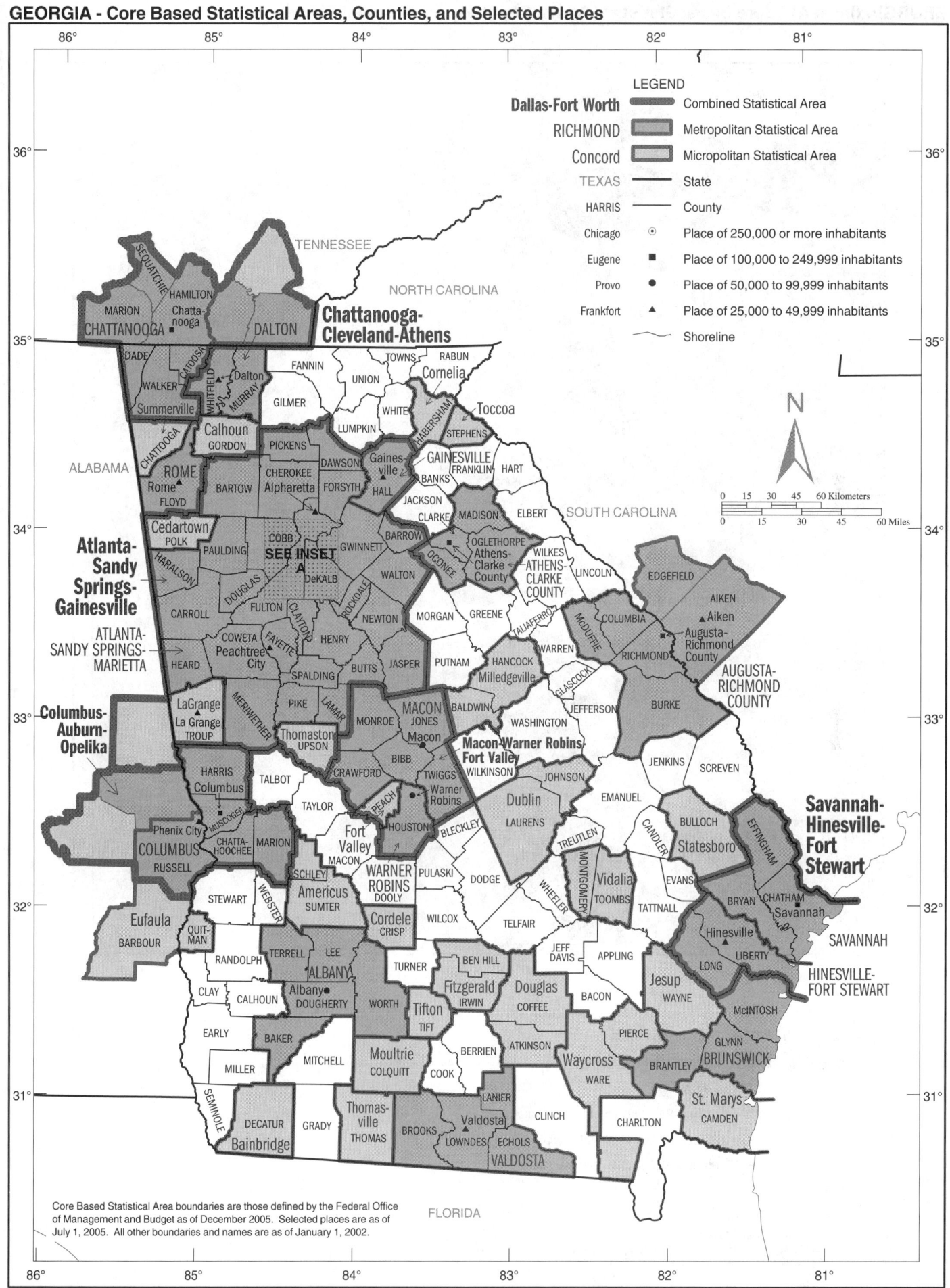

LEGEND

Dallas-Fort Worth — Combined Statistical Area

RICHMOND — Metropolitan Statistical Area

Concord — Micropolitan Statistical Area

TEXAS — State

HARRIS — County

Chicago ⊙ Place of 250,000 or more inhabitants

Eugene ■ Place of 100,000 to 249,999 inhabitants

Provo ● Place of 50,000 to 99,999 inhabitants

Frankfort ▲ Place of 25,000 to 49,999 inhabitants

— Shoreline

Core Based Statistical Area boundaries are those defined by the Federal Office of Management and Budget as of December 2005. Selected places are as of July 1, 2005. All other boundaries and names are as of January 1, 2002.

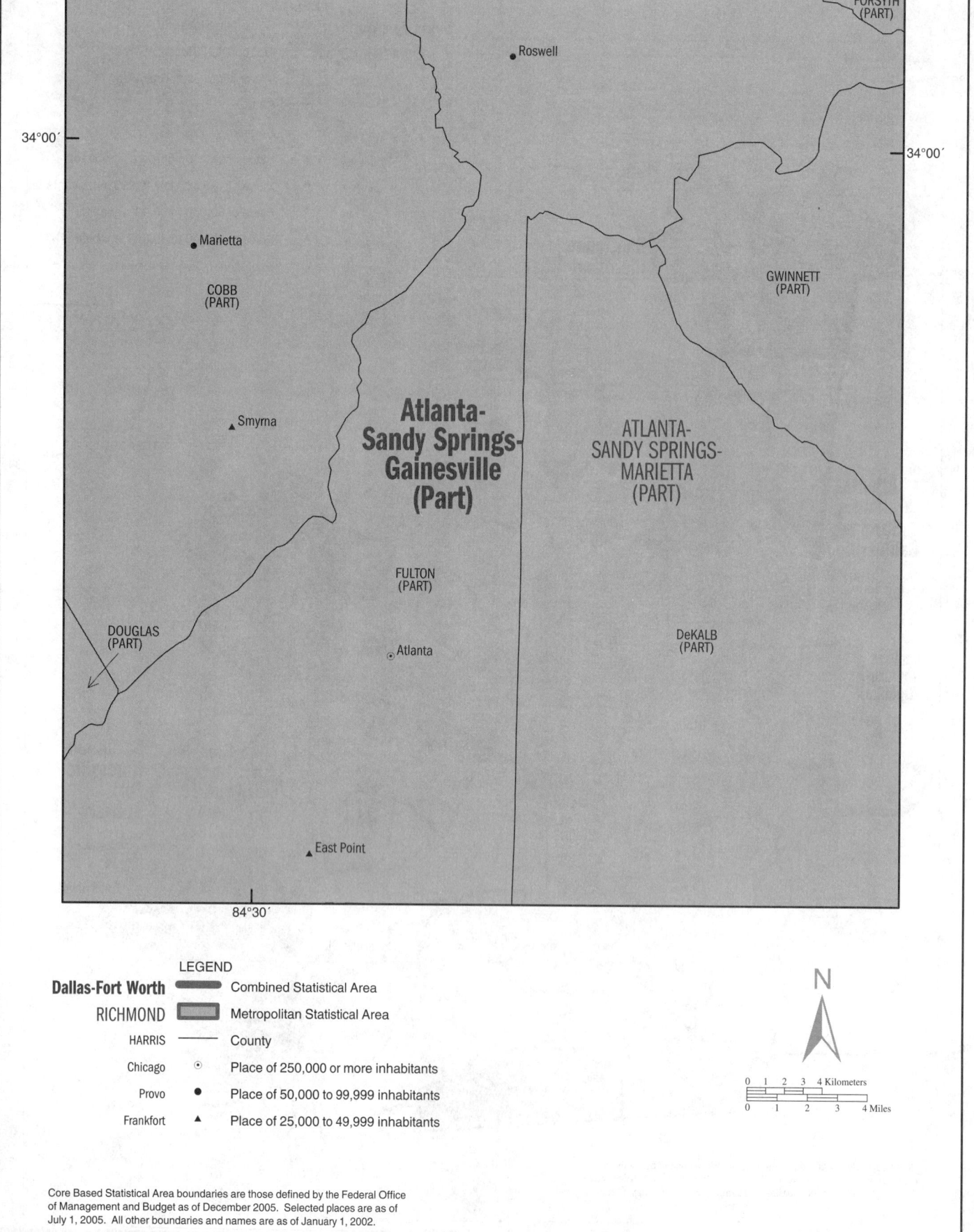

FORSYTH (PART)

84°30´

• Roswell

34°00´

34°00´

• Marietta

COBB (PART)

GWINNETT (PART)

▲ Smyrna

Atlanta-Sandy Springs-Gainesville (Part)

ATLANTA-SANDY SPRINGS-MARIETTA (PART)

FULTON (PART)

DOUGLAS (PART)

⊙ Atlanta

DeKALB (PART)

▲ East Point

84°30´

LEGEND

Dallas-Fort Worth ▬▬▬ Combined Statistical Area

RICHMOND ▭ Metropolitan Statistical Area

HARRIS ── County

Chicago ⊙ Place of 250,000 or more inhabitants

Provo ● Place of 50,000 to 99,999 inhabitants

Frankfort ▲ Place of 25,000 to 49,999 inhabitants

N

0 1 2 3 4 Kilometers
0 1 2 3 4 Miles

Core Based Statistical Area boundaries are those defined by the Federal Office of Management and Budget as of December 2005. Selected places are as of July 1, 2005. All other boundaries and names are as of January 1, 2002.

U.S. DEPARTMENT OF COMMERCE Economics and Statistics Administration U.S. Census Bureau

HAWAII - Core Based Statistical Areas, Counties, and Selected Places

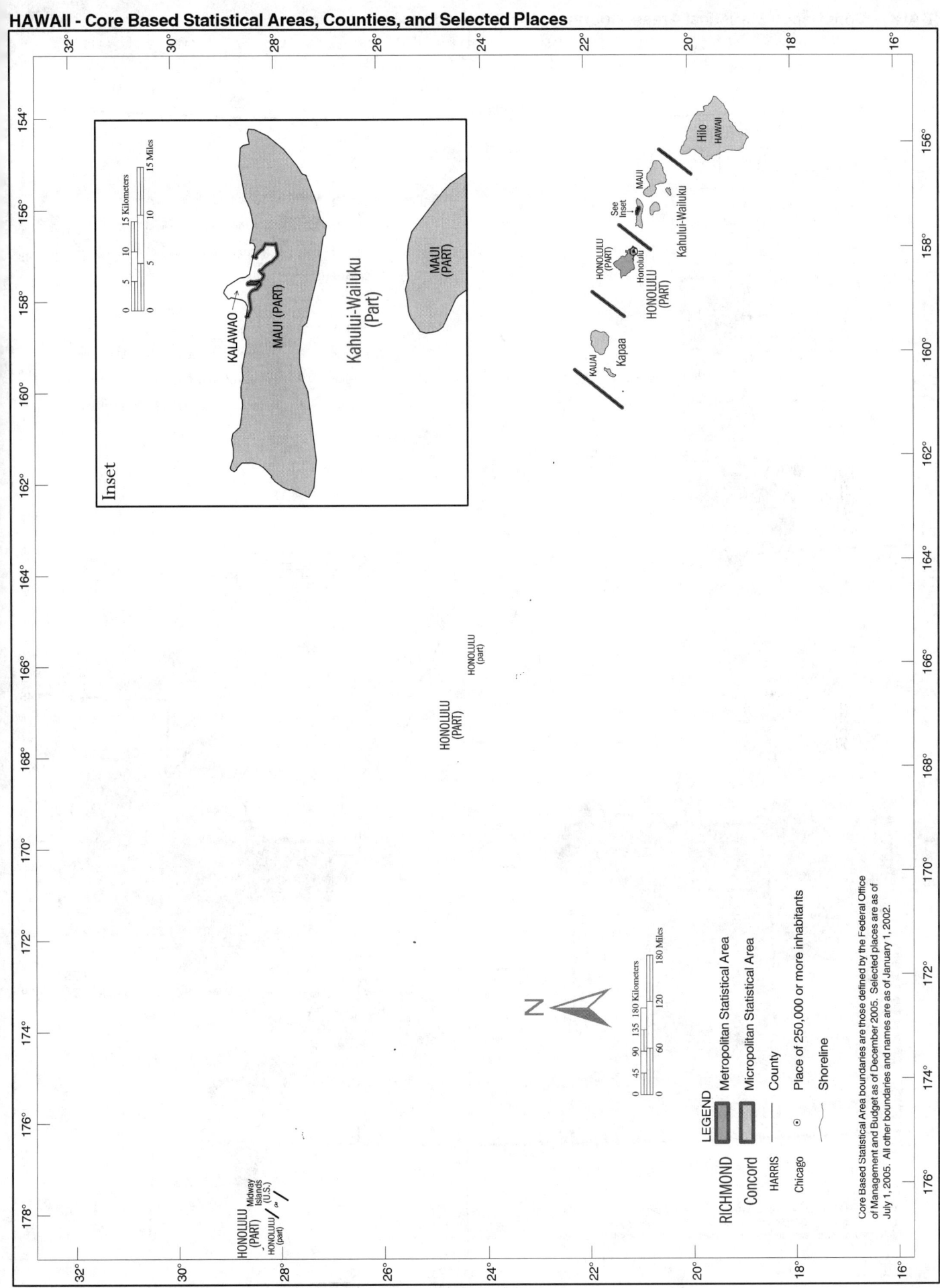

Inset

KALAWAO

MAUI (PART)

Kahului-Wailuku (Part)

MAUI (PART)

15 Kilometers   15 Miles
10
5
0   5   10   15
0

HONOLULU (PART)

HONOLULU (part)

KAUAI
Kapaa

HONOLULU (PART)
Honolulu

HONOLULU (PART)

See Inset

MAUI
Kahului-Wailuku

Hilo
HAWAII

HONOLULU (PART)   Midway Islands (U.S.)
HONOLULU (part)

N

180 Kilometers   180 Miles
0   45   90   135   120
0   60

LEGEND

RICHMOND   Metropolitan Statistical Area

Concord   Micropolitan Statistical Area

HARRIS   County

Chicago ⊙   Place of 250,000 or more inhabitants

Shoreline

Core Based Statistical Area boundaries are those defined by the Federal Office of Management and Budget as of December 2005. Selected places are as of July 1, 2005. All other boundaries and names are as of January 1, 2002.

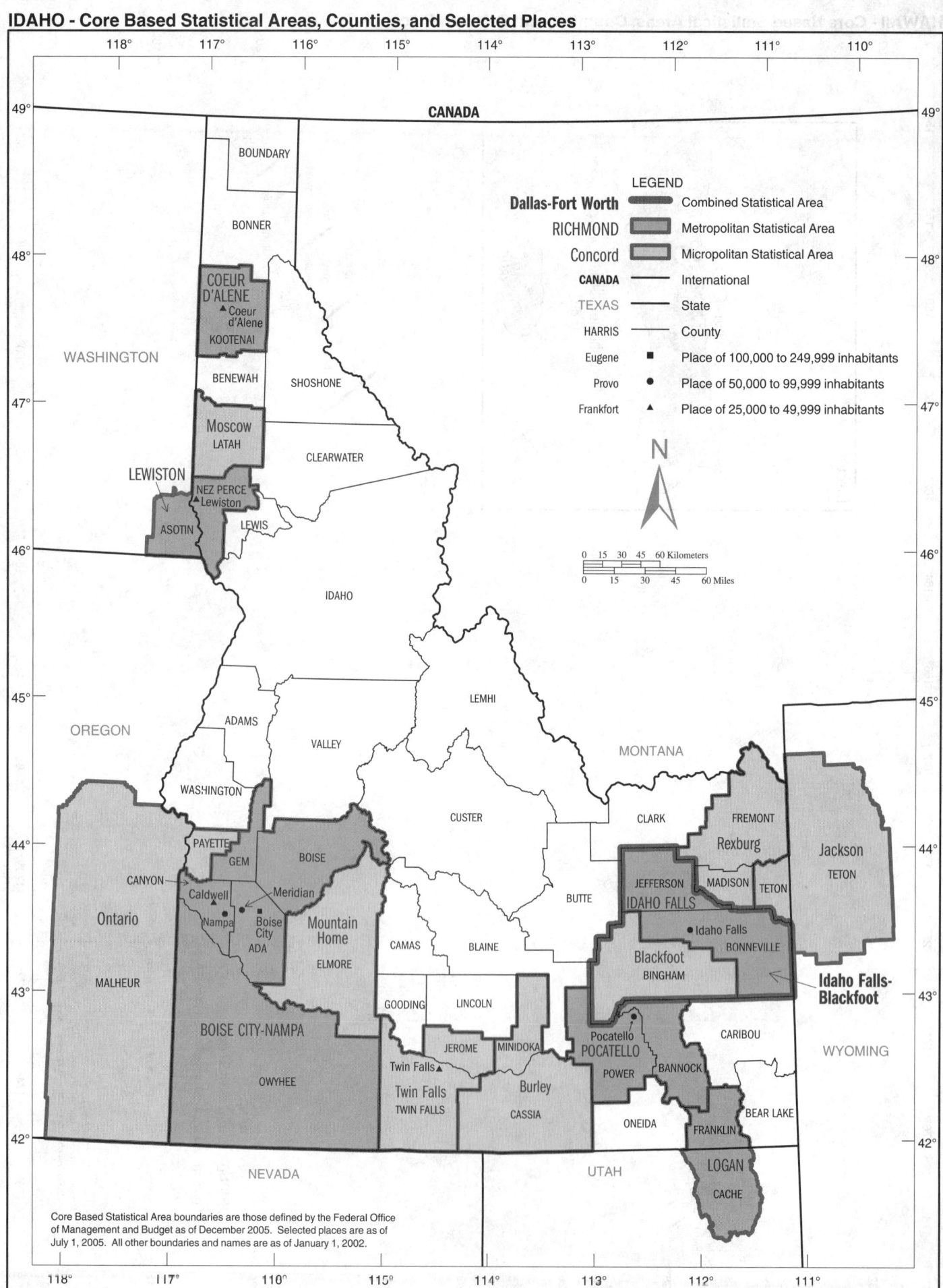

ILLINOIS - Core Based Statistical Areas, Counties, Independent City, and Selected Places

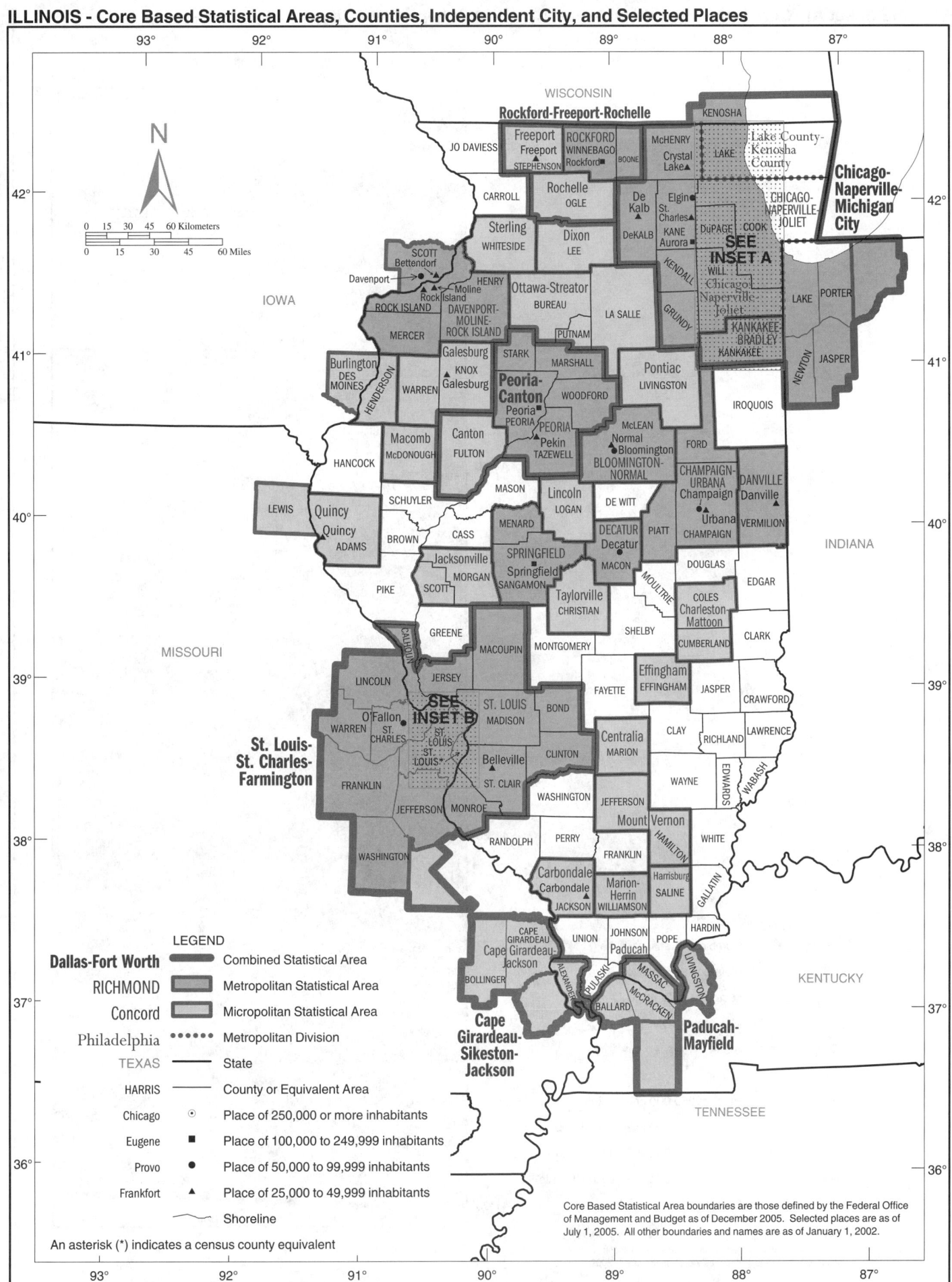

LEGEND

Dallas-Fort Worth   Combined Statistical Area

RICHMOND   Metropolitan Statistical Area

Concord   Micropolitan Statistical Area

Philadelphia   ••••• Metropolitan Division

TEXAS   —— State

HARRIS   —— County or Equivalent Area

Chicago   ⊙ Place of 250,000 or more inhabitants

Eugene   ■ Place of 100,000 to 249,999 inhabitants

Provo   ● Place of 50,000 to 99,999 inhabitants

Frankfort   ▲ Place of 25,000 to 49,999 inhabitants

—— Shoreline

An asterisk (*) indicates a census county equivalent

Core Based Statistical Area boundaries are those defined by the Federal Office of Management and Budget as of December 2005. Selected places are as of July 1, 2005. All other boundaries and names are as of January 1, 2002.

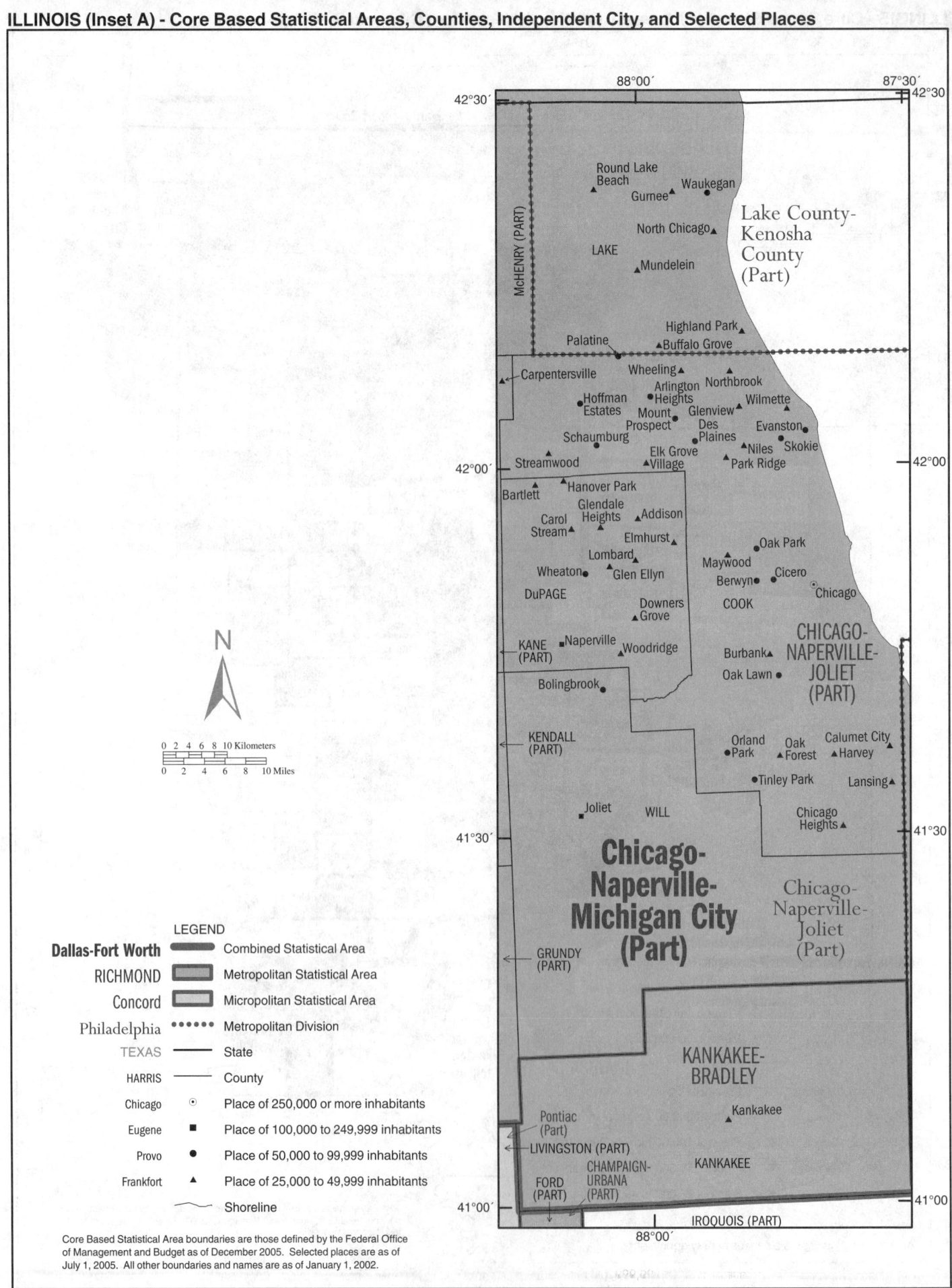

LEGEND

Dallas-Fort Worth ▬▬▬ Combined Statistical Area

RICHMOND ▭ Metropolitan Statistical Area

Concord ▭ Micropolitan Statistical Area

Philadelphia •••••• Metropolitan Division

TEXAS ▬▬▬ State

HARRIS ▬▬▬ County

Chicago ⊙ Place of 250,000 or more inhabitants

Eugene ■ Place of 100,000 to 249,999 inhabitants

Provo ● Place of 50,000 to 99,999 inhabitants

Frankfort ▲ Place of 25,000 to 49,999 inhabitants

∼∼∼ Shoreline

Core Based Statistical Area boundaries are those defined by the Federal Office
of Management and Budget as of December 2005. Selected places are as of
July 1, 2005. All other boundaries and names are as of January 1, 2002.

ILLINOIS (Inset B) - Core Based Statistical Areas, Counties, Independent City, and Selected Places

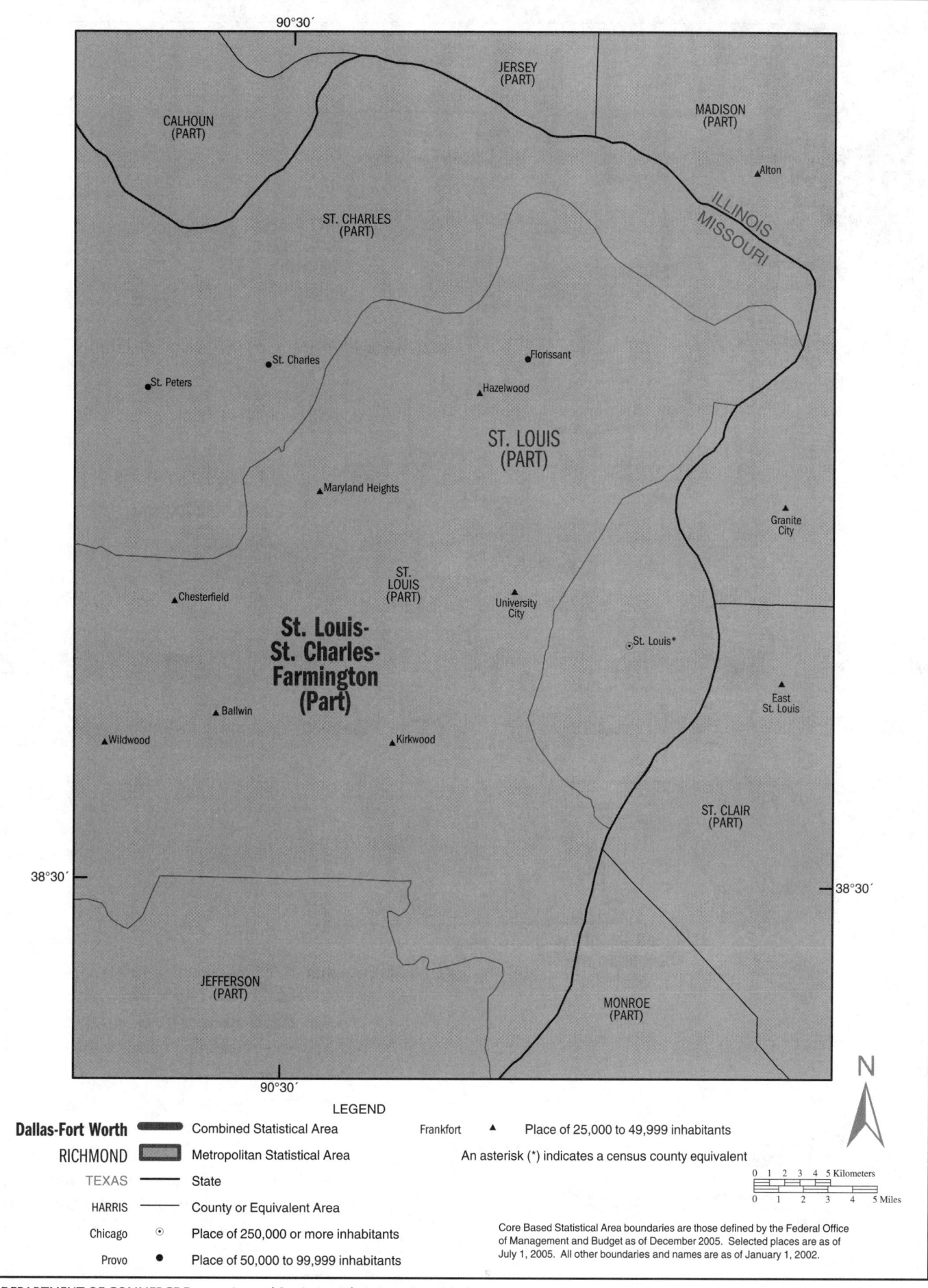

90°30′

JERSEY
(PART)

CALHOUN
(PART)

MADISON
(PART)

▲Alton

ST. CHARLES
(PART)

ILLINOIS
MISSOURI

●Florissant

●St. Charles

▲Hazelwood

●St. Peters

ST. LOUIS
(PART)

▲Maryland Heights

Granite
City ▲

ST.
LOUIS
(PART)

▲Chesterfield

University
City ▲

⊙St. Louis*

St. Louis-
St. Charles-
Farmington
(Part)

▲Ballwin

East
St. Louis ▲

▲Wildwood

▲Kirkwood

ST. CLAIR
(PART)

38°30′

38°30′

JEFFERSON
(PART)

MONROE
(PART)

N

LEGEND

Dallas-Fort Worth ▬▬▬ Combined Statistical Area

Frankfort ▲ Place of 25,000 to 49,999 inhabitants

RICHMOND ▭ Metropolitan Statistical Area

An asterisk (*) indicates a census county equivalent

TEXAS ─── State

HARRIS ─── County or Equivalent Area

0 1 2 3 4 5 Kilometers

Chicago ⊙ Place of 250,000 or more inhabitants

0 1 2 3 4 5 Miles

Provo ● Place of 50,000 to 99,999 inhabitants

Core Based Statistical Area boundaries are those defined by the Federal Office
of Management and Budget as of December 2005. Selected places are as of
July 1, 2005. All other boundaries and names are as of January 1, 2002.

INDIANA - Core Based Statistical Areas, Counties, and Selected Places

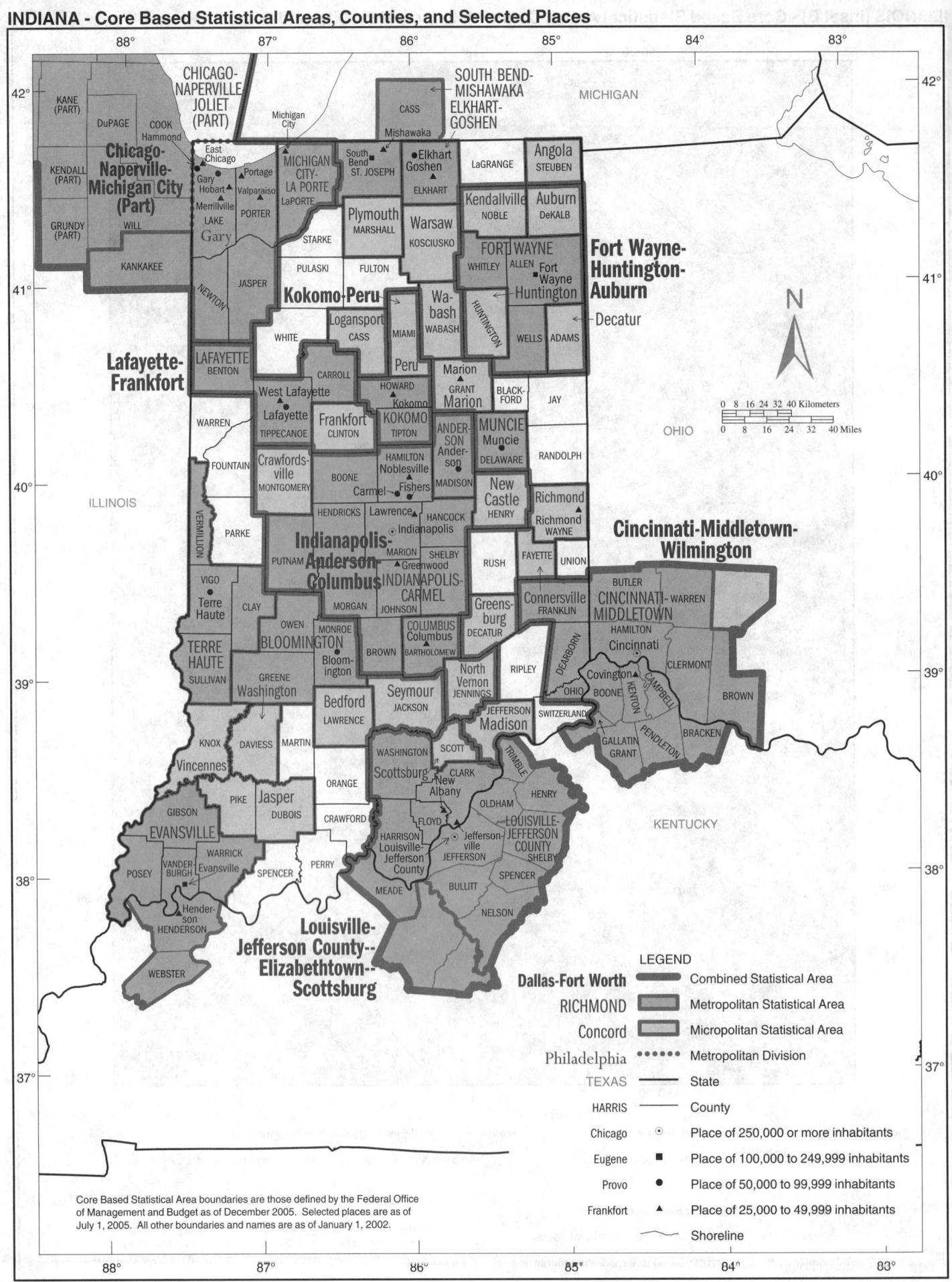

LEGEND

Dallas-Fort Worth	Combined Statistical Area
RICHMOND	Metropolitan Statistical Area
Concord	Micropolitan Statistical Area
Philadelphia	Metropolitan Division
TEXAS	State
HARRIS	County
Chicago ⊙	Place of 250,000 or more inhabitants
Eugene ■	Place of 100,000 to 249,999 inhabitants
Provo ●	Place of 50,000 to 99,999 inhabitants
Frankfort ▲	Place of 25,000 to 49,999 inhabitants
	Shoreline

Core Based Statistical Area boundaries are those defined by the Federal Office of Management and Budget as of December 2005. Selected places are as of July 1, 2005. All other boundaries and names are as of January 1, 2002.

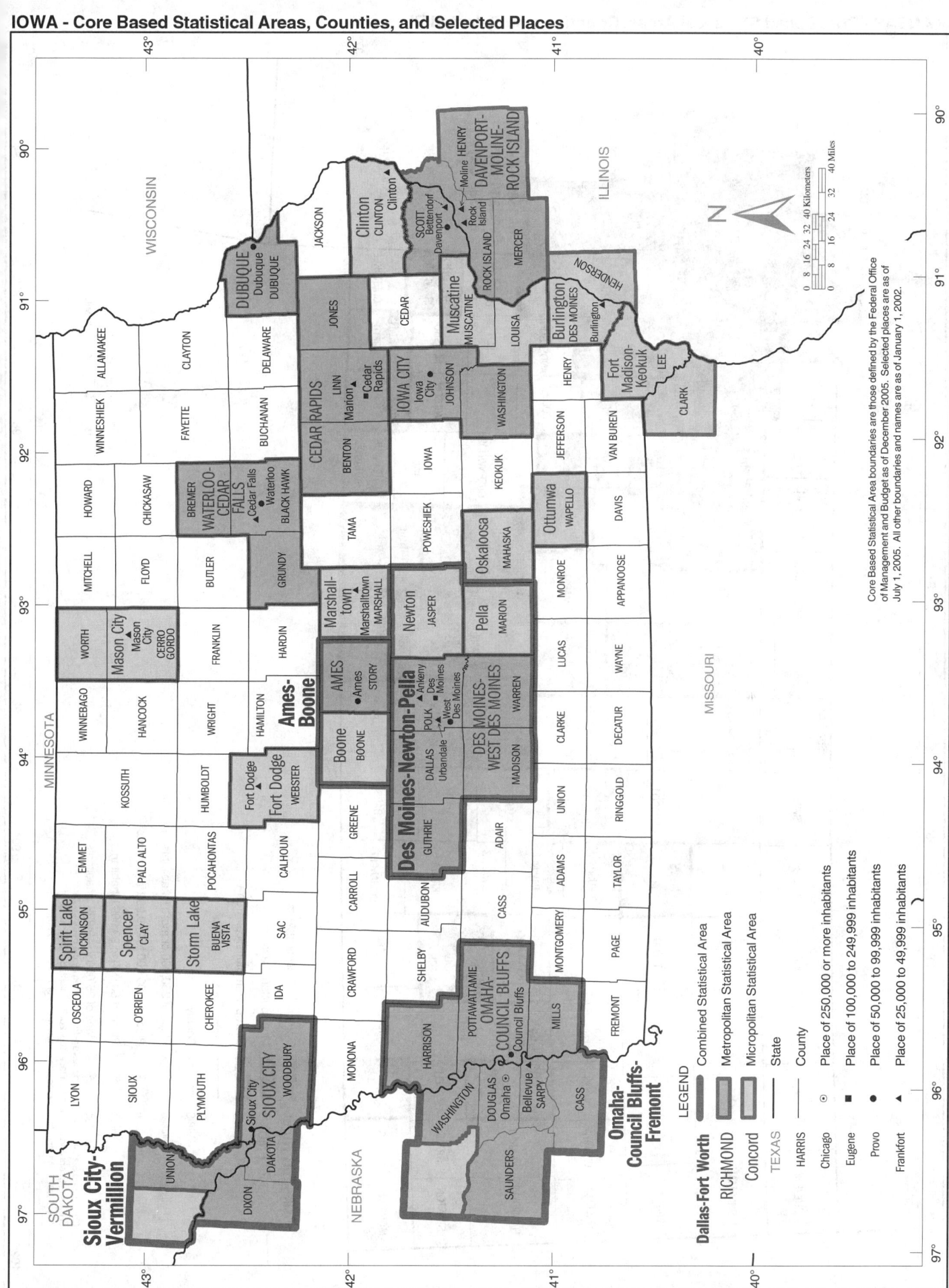

LEGEND

Dallas-Fort Worth	Combined Statistical Area
RICHMOND	Metropolitan Statistical Area
Concord	Micropolitan Statistical Area
	State
	County
⊙	Place of 250,000 or more inhabitants
■	Place of 100,000 to 249,999 inhabitants
●	Place of 50,000 to 99,999 inhabitants
▲	Place of 25,000 to 49,999 inhabitants

TEXAS
HARRIS
Chicago
Eugene
Provo
Frankfort

Core Based Statistical Area boundaries are those defined by the Federal Office of Management and Budget as of December 2005. Selected places are as of July 1, 2005. All other boundaries and names are as of January 1, 2002.

KANSAS - Core Based Statistical Areas, Counties, and Selected Places

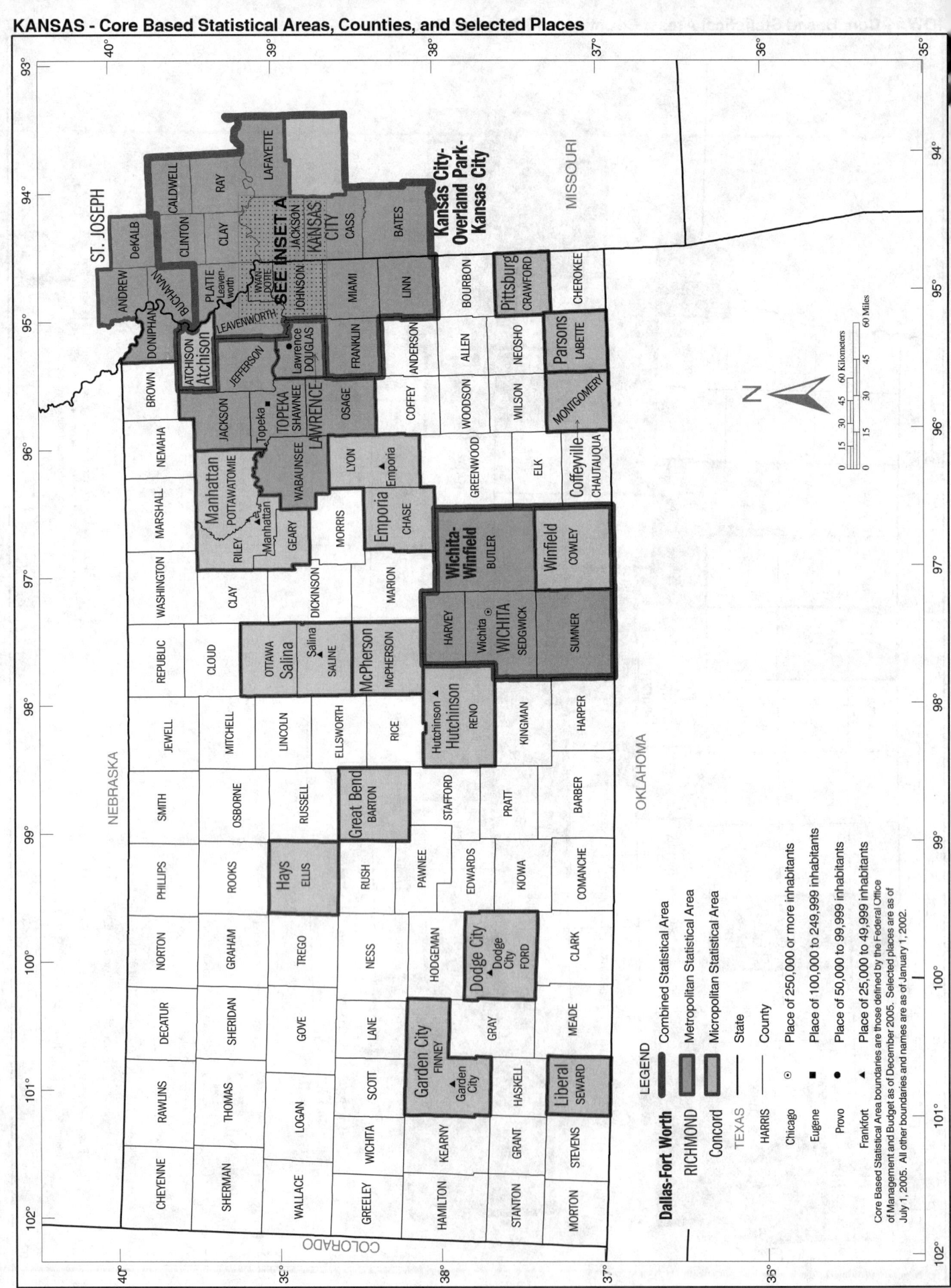

LEGEND

Dallas-Fort Worth Combined Statistical Area

RICHMOND Metropolitan Statistical Area

Concord Micropolitan Statistical Area

State

County

⊙ Chicago Place of 250,000 or more inhabitants

■ Eugene Place of 100,000 to 249,999 inhabitants

● Provo Place of 50,000 to 99,999 inhabitants

▲ Frankfort Place of 25,000 to 49,999 inhabitants

Core Based Statistical Area boundaries are those defined by the Federal Office of Management and Budget as of December 2005. Selected places are as of July 1, 2005. All other boundaries and names are as of January 1, 2002.

Kansas City-Overland Park-Kansas City

RAY
(PART)

LAFAYETTE
(PART)

39°00´

Blue Springs

Independence

JACKSON

Lee's Summit

CASS
(PART)

CLAY
(PART)

Raytown

Gladstone

Kansas City

94°30´

KANSAS CITY
(PART)

MISSOURI
KANSAS

Overland Park
Leawood

PLATTE
(PART)

Kansas City

Kansas City-
Overland Park-
Kansas City
(Part)

WYANDOTTE

Shawnee

Lenexa

JOHNSON

LEAVENWORTH
(PART)

Olathe

MIAMI (PART)

DOUGLAS
(PART)

LAWRENCE
(PART)

FRANKLIN (PART)

95°00´

39°00´

LEGEND

Dallas-Fort Worth	Combined Statistical Area
RICHMOND	Metropolitan Statistical Area
Concord	Micropolitan Statistical Area
TEXAS	State
HARRIS	County
Chicago ⊙	Place of 250,000 or more inhabitants

Eugene ■	Place of 100,000 to 249,999 inhabitants
Provo ●	Place of 50,000 to 99,999 inhabitants
Frankfort ▲	Place of 25,000 to 49,999 inhabitants

Core Based Statistical Area boundaries are those defined by the Federal Office of Management and Budget as of December 2005. Selected places are as of July 1, 2005. All other boundaries and names are as of January 1, 2002.

N

0 2 4 6 Kilometers
0 2 4 6 Miles

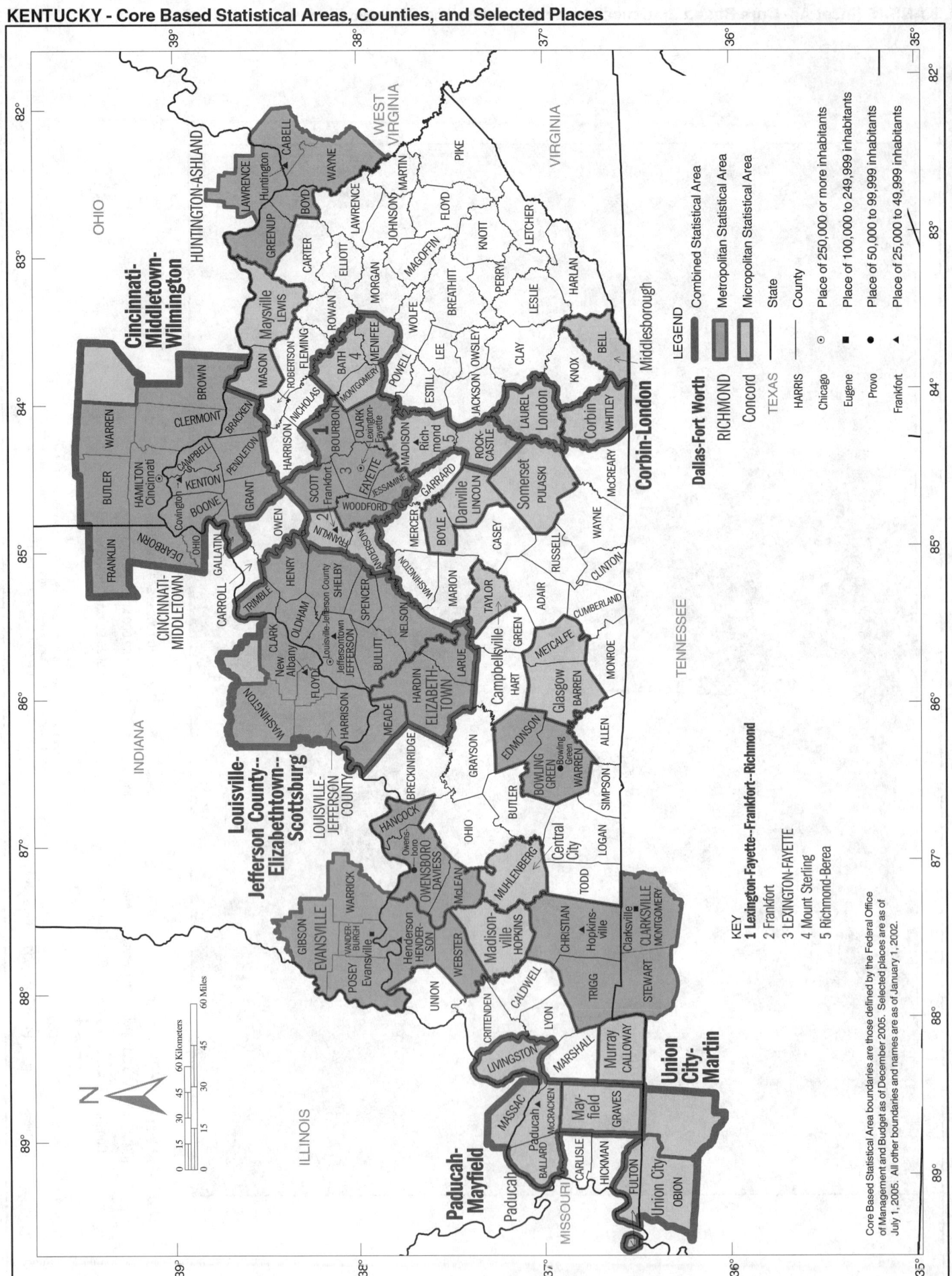

LEGEND

Combined Statistical Area
Metropolitan Statistical Area
Micropolitan Statistical Area
State
County

Place of 250,000 or more inhabitants
Place of 100,000 to 249,999 inhabitants
Place of 50,000 to 99,999 inhabitants
Place of 25,000 to 49,999 inhabitants

TEXAS — State
HARRIS — County
Chicago — Place of 250,000 or more inhabitants
Eugene — Place of 100,000 to 249,999 inhabitants
Provo — Place of 50,000 to 99,999 inhabitants
Frankfort — Place of 25,000 to 49,999 inhabitants

KEY
1 Lexington-Fayette--Frankfort--Richmond
2 Frankfort
3 LEXINGTON-FAYETTE
4 Mount Sterling
5 Richmond-Berea

Core Based Statistical Area boundaries are those defined by the Federal Office of Management and Budget as of December 2005. Selected places are as of July 1, 2005. All other boundaries and names are as of January 1, 2002.

LOUISIANA - Core Based Statistical Areas, Parishes, and Selected Places

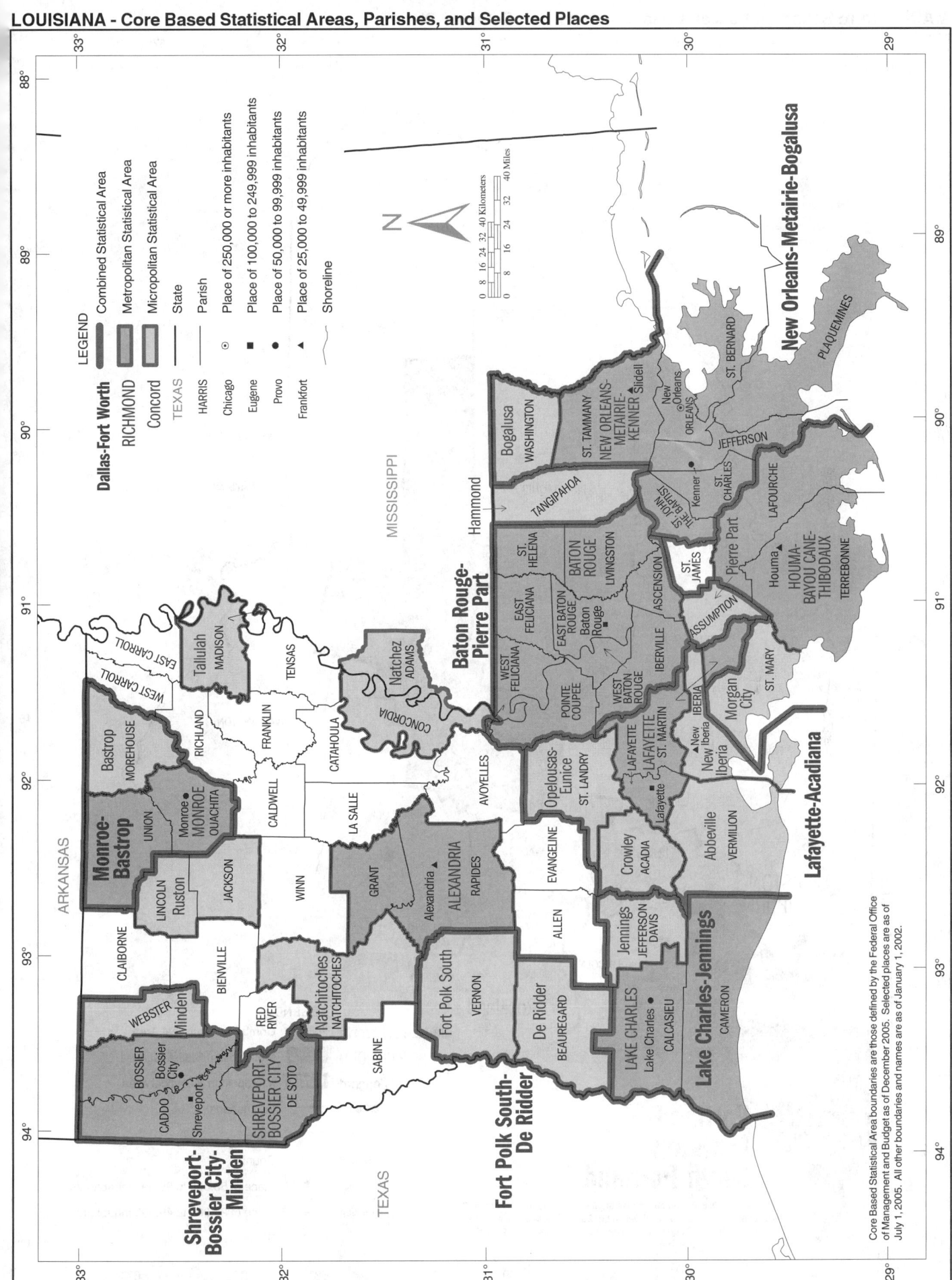

Core Based Statistical Area boundaries are those defined by the Federal Office of Management and Budget as of December 2005. Selected places are as of July 1, 2005. All other boundaries and names are as of January 1, 2002.

U.S. DEPARTMENT OF COMMERCE Economics and Statistics Administration U.S. Census Bureau

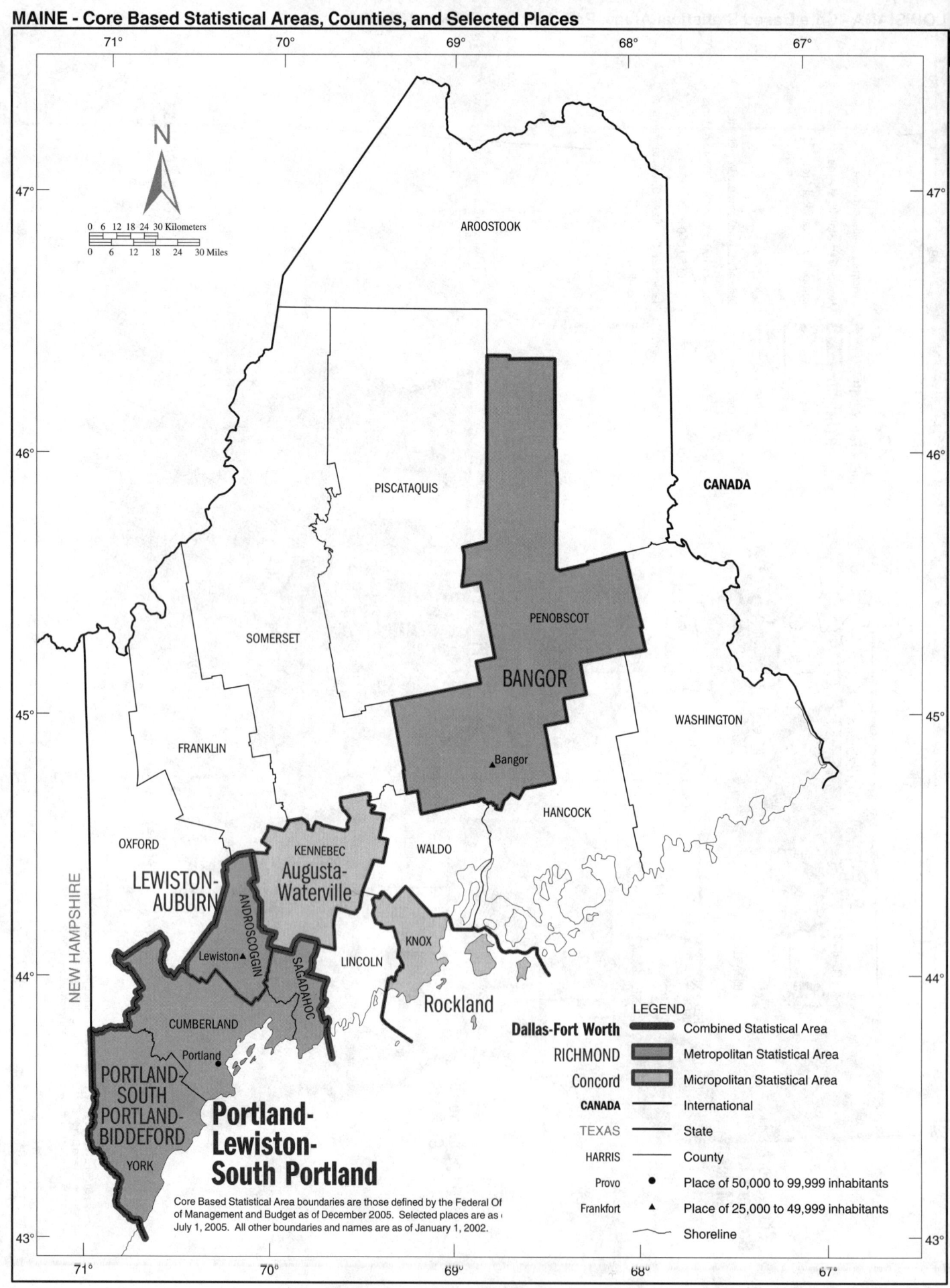

LEGEND

Dallas-Fort Worth — Combined Statistical Area

RICHMOND — Metropolitan Statistical Area

Concord — Micropolitan Statistical Area

CANADA — International

TEXAS — State

HARRIS — County

Provo ● Place of 50,000 to 99,999 inhabitants

Frankfort ▲ Place of 25,000 to 49,999 inhabitants

⌇ Shoreline

Core Based Statistical Area boundaries are those defined by the Federal Of
of Management and Budget as of December 2005. Selected places are as
July 1, 2005. All other boundaries and names are as of January 1, 2002.

U.S. DEPARTMENT OF COMMERCE Economics and Statistics Administration U.S. Census Bureau

MARYLAND - Core Based Statistical Areas, District of Columbia, Counties, Independent Cities, and Selected Places

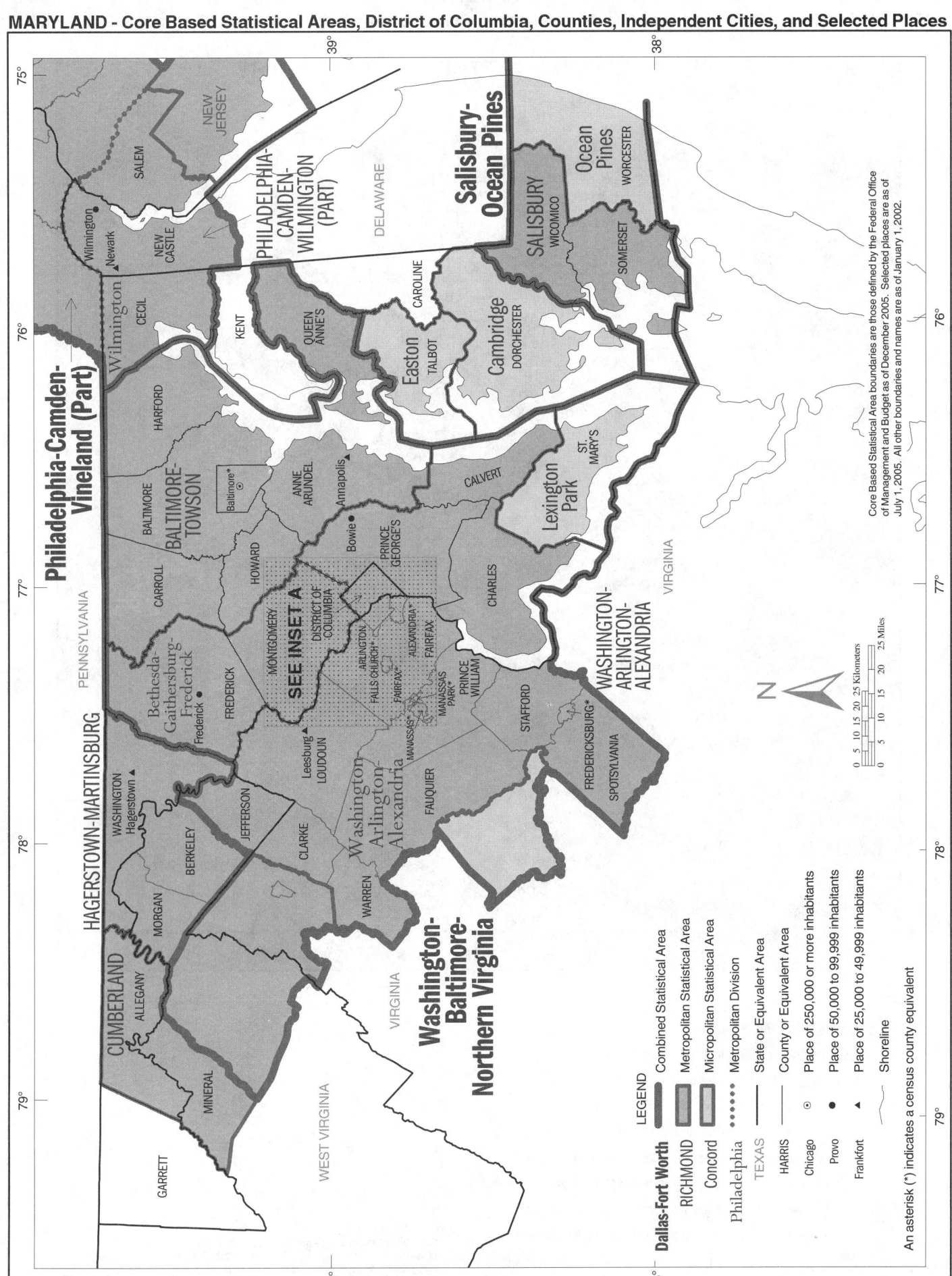

Core Based Statistical Area boundaries are those defined by the Federal Office of Management and Budget as of December 2005. Selected places are as of July 1, 2005. All other boundaries and names are as of January 1, 2002.

LEGEND

Dallas-Fort Worth Combined Statistical Area
RICHMOND Metropolitan Statistical Area
Concord Micropolitan Statistical Area
Philadelphia Metropolitan Division
TEXAS State or Equivalent Area
HARRIS County or Equivalent Area
⊙ Chicago Place of 250,000 or more inhabitants
● Provo Place of 50,000 to 99,999 inhabitants
◄ Frankfort Place of 25,000 to 49,999 inhabitants
Shoreline

An asterisk (*) indicates a census county equivalent

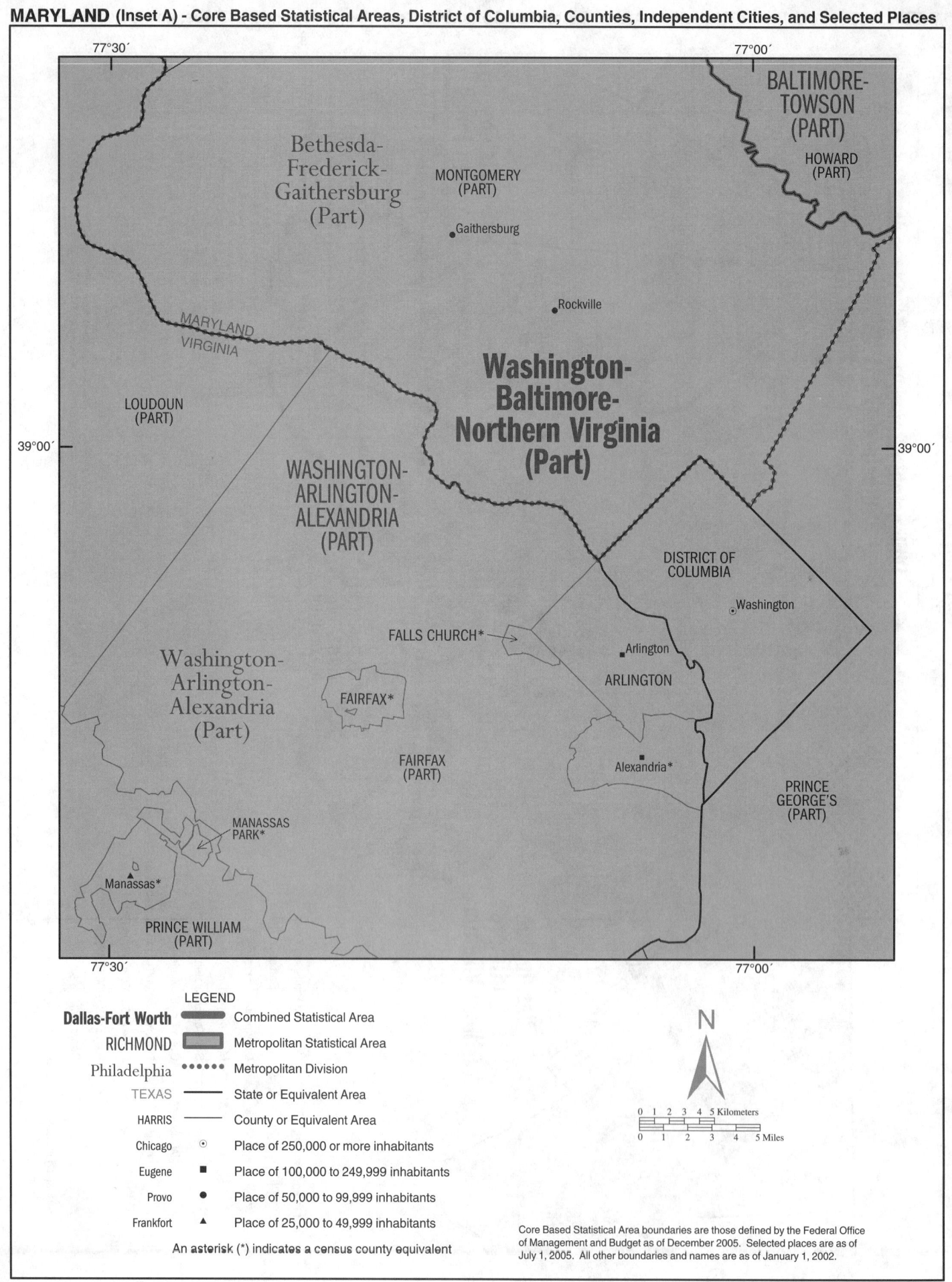

77°30′

77°00′

BALTIMORE-
TOWSON
(PART)

HOWARD
(PART)

Bethesda-
Frederick-
Gaithersburg
(Part)

MONTGOMERY
(PART)

●Gaithersburg

●Rockville

MARYLAND
VIRGINIA

LOUDOUN
(PART)

**Washington-
Baltimore-
Northern Virginia
(Part)**

39°00′

39°00′

WASHINGTON-
ARLINGTON-
ALEXANDRIA
(PART)

DISTRICT OF
COLUMBIA

⊙Washington

Washington-
Arlington-
Alexandria
(Part)

FALLS CHURCH*

■Arlington

ARLINGTON

FAIRFAX*

FAIRFAX
(PART)

■Alexandria*

PRINCE
GEORGE'S
(PART)

MANASSAS
PARK*

▲Manassas*

PRINCE WILLIAM
(PART)

77°30′

77°00′

LEGEND

Dallas-Fort Worth	▬▬▬	Combined Statistical Area
RICHMOND	▭	Metropolitan Statistical Area
Philadelphia	••••••	Metropolitan Division
TEXAS	▬	State or Equivalent Area
HARRIS	▬	County or Equivalent Area
Chicago	⊙	Place of 250,000 or more inhabitants
Eugene	■	Place of 100,000 to 249,999 inhabitants
Provo	●	Place of 50,000 to 99,999 inhabitants
Frankfort	▲	Place of 25,000 to 49,999 inhabitants

An asterisk (*) indicates a census county equivalent

N

0 1 2 3 4 5 Kilometers
0 1 2 3 4 5 Miles

Core Based Statistical Area boundaries are those defined by the Federal Office
of Management and Budget as of December 2005. Selected places are as of
July 1, 2005. All other boundaries and names are as of January 1, 2002.

MASSACHUSETTS - Core Based Statistical Areas, Counties, and Selected Places

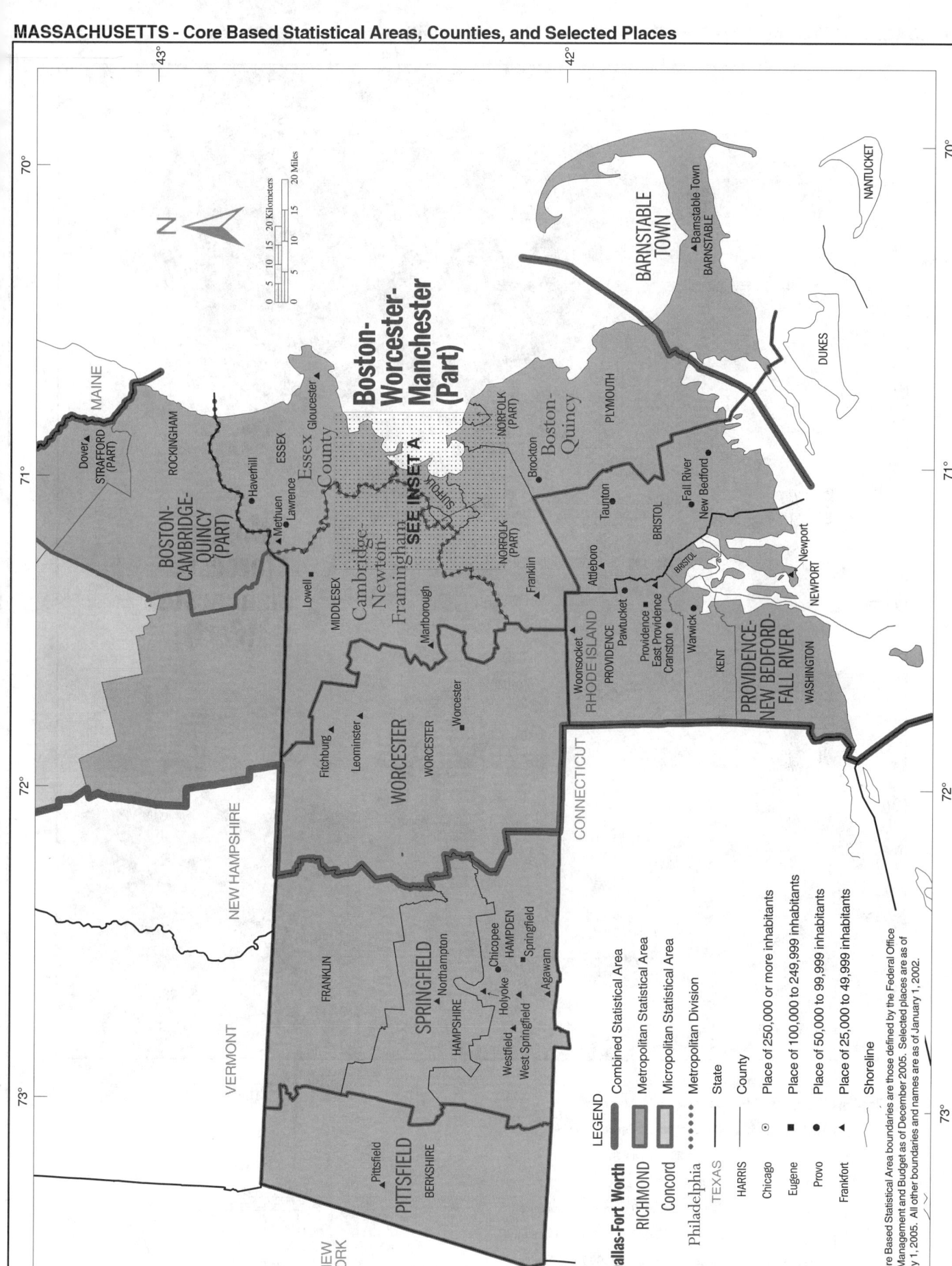

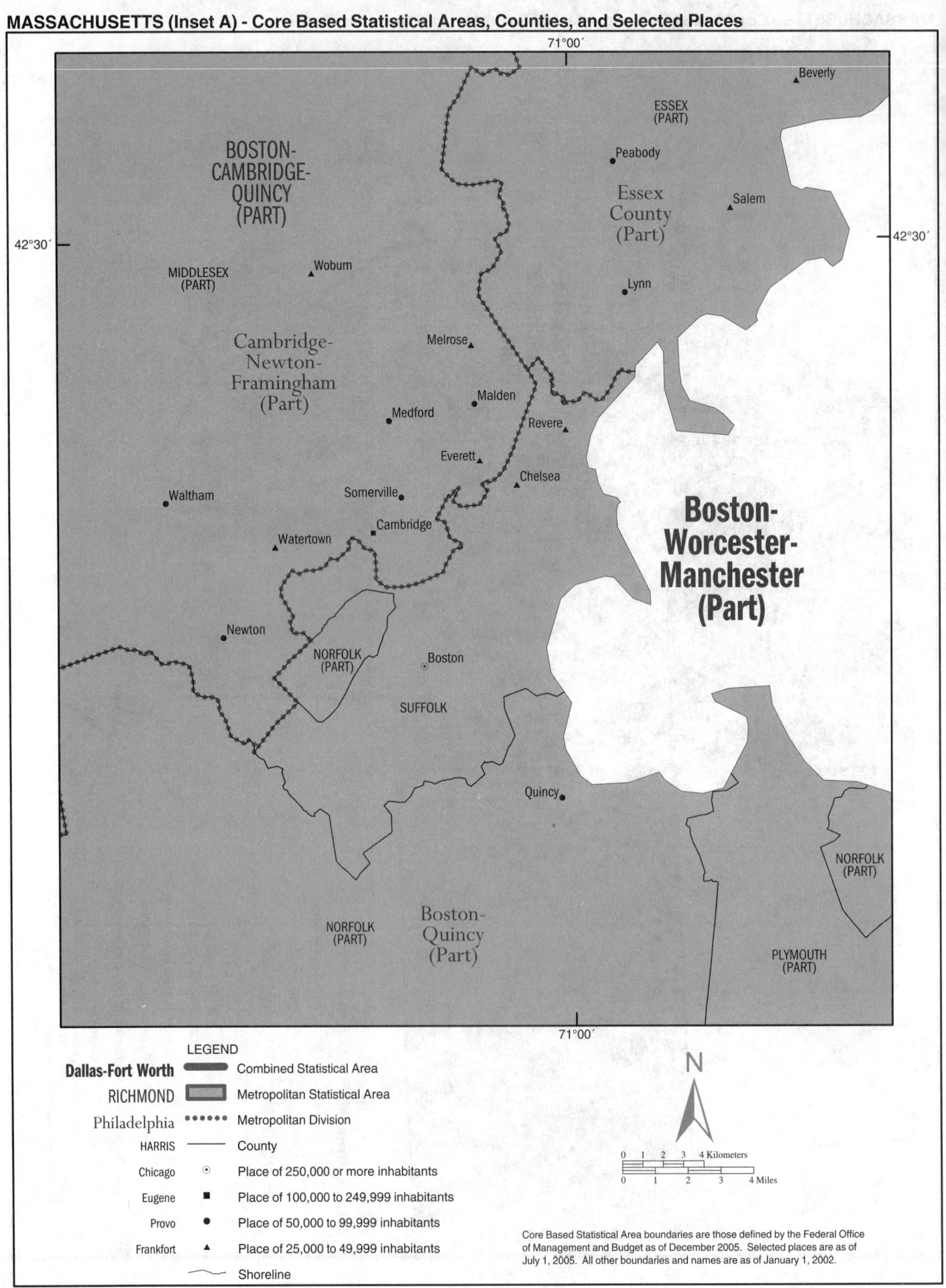

71°00´

BOSTON-
CAMBRIDGE-
QUINCY
(PART)

ESSEX
(PART)

• Beverly

• Peabody

Essex
County
(Part)

▲ Salem

42°30´

MIDDLESEX
(PART)

▲ Woburn

• Lynn

42°30´

Cambridge-
Newton-
Framingham
(Part)

Melrose ▲

• Malden

• Medford

Revere ▲

Everett ▲

Waltham •

Somerville •

Chelsea ▲

Boston-
Worcester-
Manchester
(Part)

Watertown ▲

■ Cambridge

Newton •

NORFOLK
(PART)

⊙ Boston

SUFFOLK

Quincy •

NORFOLK
(PART)

NORFOLK
(PART)

Boston-
Quincy
(Part)

PLYMOUTH
(PART)

71°00´

LEGEND

Dallas-Fort Worth ▬▬▬ Combined Statistical Area

RICHMOND ▭ Metropolitan Statistical Area

Philadelphia ●●●●●● Metropolitan Division

HARRIS ── County

Chicago ⊙ Place of 250,000 or more inhabitants

Eugene ■ Place of 100,000 to 249,999 inhabitants

Provo ● Place of 50,000 to 99,999 inhabitants

Frankfort ▲ Place of 25,000 to 49,999 inhabitants

── Shoreline

N

0 1 2 3 4 Kilometers

0 1 2 3 4 Miles

Core Based Statistical Area boundaries are those defined by the Federal Office
of Management and Budget as of December 2005. Selected places are as of
July 1, 2005. All other boundaries and names are as of January 1, 2002.

U.S. DEPARTMENT OF COMMERCE Economics and Statistics Administration U.S. Census Bureau

MICHIGAN - Core Based Statistical Areas, Counties, and Selected Places

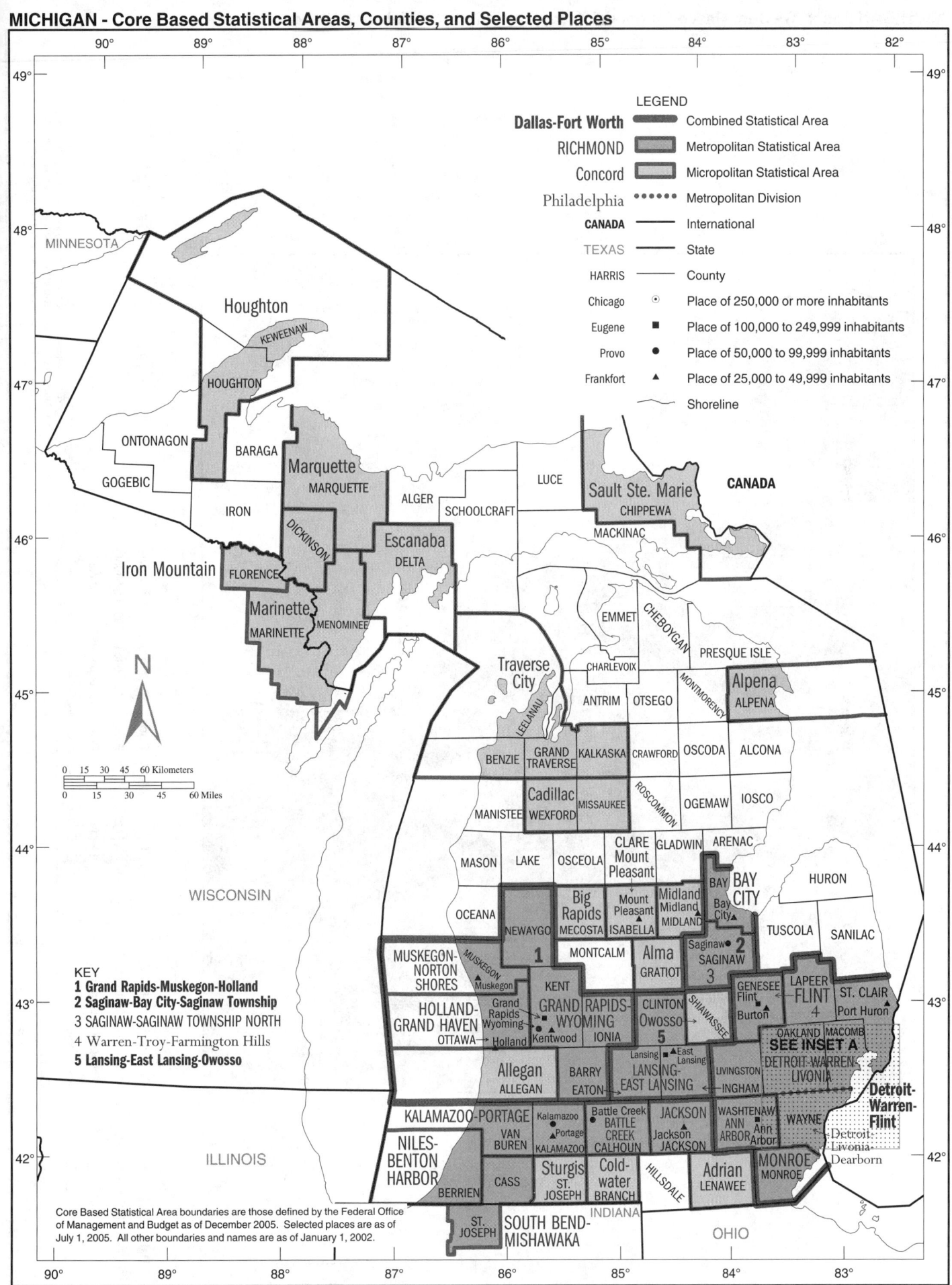

LEGEND

Dallas-Fort Worth	Combined Statistical Area
RICHMOND	Metropolitan Statistical Area
Concord	Micropolitan Statistical Area
Philadelphia	Metropolitan Division
CANADA	International
TEXAS	State
HARRIS	County
Chicago ⊙	Place of 250,000 or more inhabitants
Eugene ■	Place of 100,000 to 249,999 inhabitants
Provo ●	Place of 50,000 to 99,999 inhabitants
Frankfort ▲	Place of 25,000 to 49,999 inhabitants
	Shoreline

KEY
1 **Grand Rapids-Muskegon-Holland**
2 **Saginaw-Bay City-Saginaw Township**
3 SAGINAW-SAGINAW TOWNSHIP NORTH
4 Warren-Troy-Farmington Hills
5 **Lansing-East Lansing-Owosso**

Core Based Statistical Area boundaries are those defined by the Federal Office of Management and Budget as of December 2005. Selected places are as of July 1, 2005. All other boundaries and names are as of January 1, 2002.

N

10 Miles
10 Kilometers
0 2 4 6 8
0 2 4 6 8

Core Based Statistical Area boundaries are those defined by the Federal Office of Management and Budget as of December 2005. Selected places are as of July 1, 2005. All other boundaries and names are as of January 1, 2002.

82°30´

42°30´

ST. CLAIR (PART)

82°30´

MACOMB (PART)

Sterling Heights

Roseville
St. Clair Shores
Eastpointe

CANADA

Warren-Troy-Farmington Hills (Part)

Rochester Hills

Troy

Madison Heights

Warren

Detroit

83°00´

83°00´

Pontiac

Detroit-Warren-Flint (Part)

Royal Oak
Southfield
Oak Park

Dearborn Heights
Dearborn

Lincoln Park

Allen Park
Wyandotte
Southgate

OAKLAND (PART)

Farmington Hills

Livonia

Garden City
Inkster

Taylor

Westland

WAYNE (PART)

Detroit-Livonia-Dearborn (Part)

MONROE (PART)

Novi

MONROE (PART)

DETROIT-WARREN-LIVONIA (PART)

LIVINGSTON (PART)

GENESEE (PART)

FLINT (PART)

ANN ARBOR (PART)

WASHTENAW (PART)

83°30´

83°30´

42°30´

LEGEND

Dallas-Fort Worth — Combined Statistical Area
RICHMOND — Metropolitan Statistical Area
Philadelphia ••••• Metropolitan Division
CANADA —— International
HARRIS —— County
Chicago ⊙ Place of 250,000 or more inhabitants

Eugene ■ Place of 100,000 to 249,999 inhabitants
Provo ● Place of 50,000 to 99,999 inhabitants
Frankfort ▲ Place of 25,000 to 49,999 inhabitants
Shoreline

MINNESOTA - Core Based Statistical Areas, Counties, and Selected Places

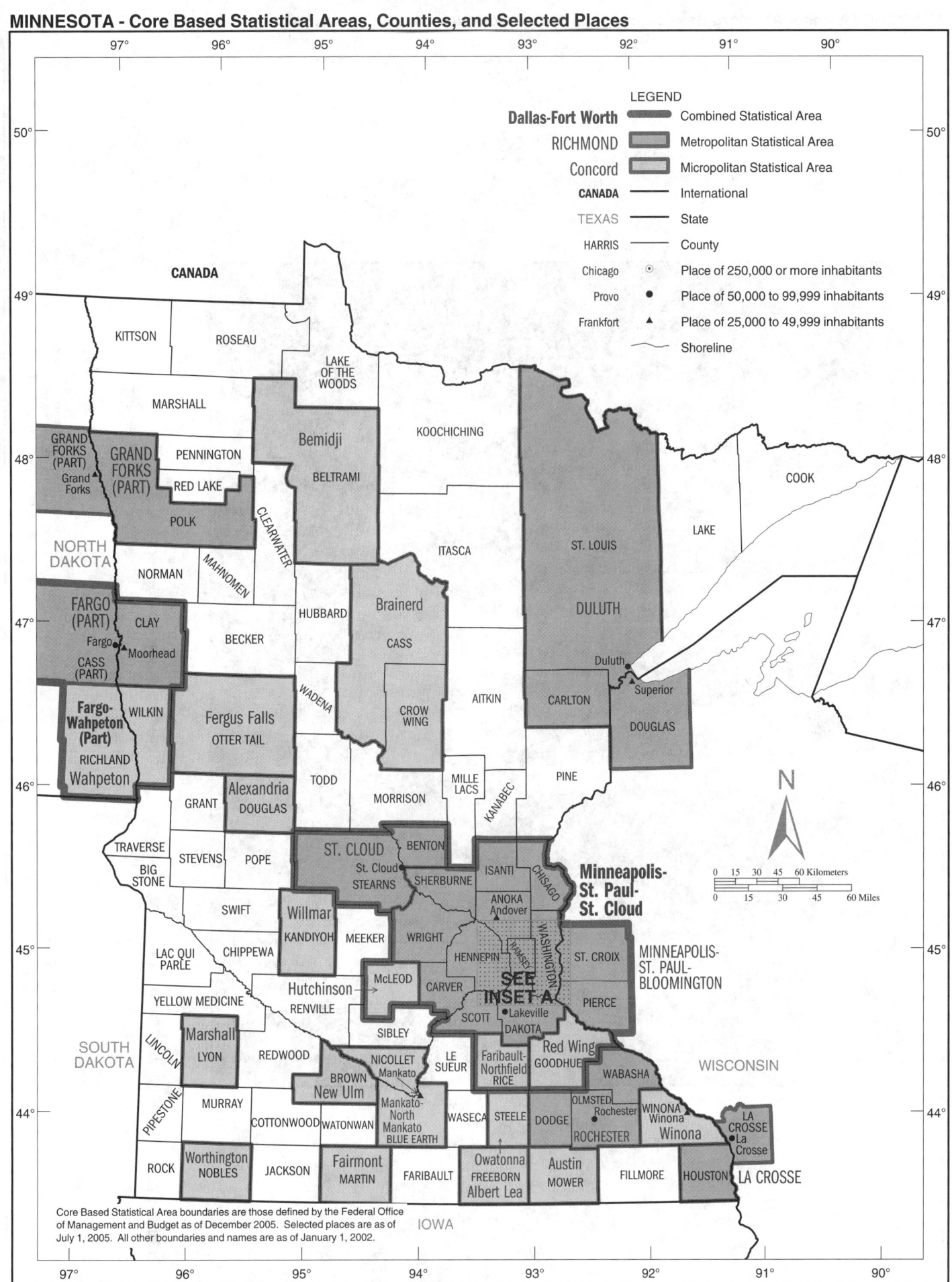

LEGEND

Dallas-Fort Worth	Combined Statistical Area
RICHMOND	Metropolitan Statistical Area
Concord	Micropolitan Statistical Area
CANADA	International
TEXAS	State
HARRIS	County
Chicago ⊙	Place of 250,000 or more inhabitants
Provo ●	Place of 50,000 to 99,999 inhabitants
Frankfort ▲	Place of 25,000 to 49,999 inhabitants
	Shoreline

CANADA

NORTH DAKOTA

SOUTH DAKOTA

WISCONSIN

IOWA

KITTSON, ROSEAU, LAKE OF THE WOODS, MARSHALL, PENNINGTON, RED LAKE, POLK, BEMIDJI, BELTRAMI, KOOCHICHING, GRAND FORKS (PART), Grand Forks, NORMAN, MAHNOMEN, CLEARWATER, HUBBARD, BECKER, COOK, LAKE, ST. LOUIS, DULUTH, FARGO (PART), Fargo, CLAY, Moorhead, CASS (PART), WILKIN, Fergus Falls, OTTER TAIL, WADENA, Brainerd, CASS, AITKIN, Duluth, Superior, CARLTON, DOUGLAS, Fargo-Wahpeton (Part), RICHLAND, Wahpeton, GRANT, Alexandria, DOUGLAS, TODD, MORRISON, CROW WING, MILLE LACS, PINE, TRAVERSE, STEVENS, POPE, BIG STONE, ST. CLOUD, BENTON, St. Cloud, STEARNS, SHERBURNE, KANABEC, CHISAGO, SWIFT, Willmar, KANDIYOHI, MEEKER, WRIGHT, ISANTI, ANOKA, Andover, Minneapolis-St. Paul-St. Cloud, LAC QUI PARLE, CHIPPEWA, Hutchinson, McLEOD, CARVER, HENNEPIN, RAMSEY, WASHINGTON, ST. CROIX, SEE INSET A, MINNEAPOLIS-ST. PAUL-BLOOMINGTON, YELLOW MEDICINE, RENVILLE, SIBLEY, SCOTT, Lakeville, DAKOTA, PIERCE, LINCOLN, Marshall, LYON, REDWOOD, NICOLLET, LE SUEUR, Faribault-Northfield, RICE, Red Wing, GOODHUE, WABASHA, WISCONSIN, PIPESTONE, MURRAY, BROWN, New Ulm, Mankato, Mankato-North Mankato, BLUE EARTH, WASECA, STEELE, DODGE, OLMSTED, Rochester, ROCHESTER, WINONA, Winona, LA CROSSE, ROCK, Worthington, NOBLES, JACKSON, COTTONWOOD, WATONWAN, Fairmont, MARTIN, FARIBAULT, Owatonna, FREEBORN, Albert Lea, Austin, MOWER, FILLMORE, HOUSTON, La Crosse

N

| 0 | 15 | 30 | 45 | 60 Kilometers |
| 0 | 15 | 30 | 45 | 60 Miles |

Core Based Statistical Area boundaries are those defined by the Federal Office of Management and Budget as of December 2005. Selected places are as of July 1, 2005. All other boundaries and names are as of January 1, 2002.

Core Based Statistical Area boundaries are those defined by the Federal Office of Management and Budget as of December 2005. Selected places are as of July 1, 2005. All other boundaries and names are as of January 1, 2002.

LEGEND

Dallas-Fort Worth	Combined Statistical Area
RICHMOND	Metropolitan Statistical Area
TEXAS	State
HARRIS	County
Chicago ⊙	Place of 250,000 or more inhabitants
Provo ●	Place of 50,000 to 99,999 inhabitants
Frankfort ▲	Place of 25,000 to 49,999 inhabitants

MISSISSIPPI - Core Based Statistical Areas, Counties, and Selected Places

LEGEND

Dallas-Fort Worth — Combined Statistical Area
RICHMOND — Metropolitan Statistical Area
Concord — Micropolitan Statistical Area
TEXAS — State
HARRIS — County
Chicago ⊙ Place of 250,000 or more inhabitants
Eugene ■ Place of 100,000 to 249,999 inhabitants
Provo ● Place of 50,000 to 99,999 inhabitants
Frankfort ▲ Place of 25,000 to 49,999 inhabitants
— Shoreline

N

0 8 16 24 32 40 Kilometers
0 8 16 24 32 40 Miles

TENNESSEE
ARKANSAS
LOUISIANA
ALABAMA
TISHOMINGO

TIPTON (PART)
CRITTENDEN
SHELBY
MEMPHIS (PART)
West Memphis
Bartlett
Memphis
Germantown
FAYETTE

Southaven
DeSOTO
BENTON
Corinth
ALCORN
MARSHALL
TIPPAH
PRENTISS

Clarksdale
TUNICA
TATE
PANOLA
Oxford
LAFAYETTE
UNION
Tupelo
Tupelo
LEE
ITAWAMBA
PONTOTOC

COAHOMA
QUITMAN
YALOBUSHA
CALHOUN
CHICKASAW
MONROE

Cleveland
BOLIVAR
TALLAHATCHIE
Grenada
GRENADA
WEBSTER
CLAY
West Point
Starkville
OKTIBBEHA
Columbus
LOWNDES

SUNFLOWER
Indian-ola
Greenwood
LEFLORE
CARROLL
MONTGOMERY
CHOCTAW

Greenville
WASHINGTON
Columbus-West Point

Greenville
HUMPHREYS
HOLMES
ATTALA
WINSTON
NOXUBEE

ISSAQUENA
SHARKEY
Yazoo City
YAZOO
LEAKE
NESHOBA
KEMPER

MADISON
JACKSON
Meridian
Meridian
LAUDERDALE

WARREN
Vicks-burg
HINDS
Clinton
Jackson
RANKIN
SCOTT
NEWTON

Vicksburg
Jackson-Yazoo City
SMITH
JASPER
CLARKE

CLAIBORNE
COPIAH
SIMPSON

JEFFERSON
Laurel
LAWRENCE
COVINGTON
JONES
WAYNE

Natchez
CONCORDIA
ADAMS
FRANKLIN
Brook-haven
LINCOLN
JEFFERSON DAVIS

McComb
AMITE
PIKE
MARION
LAMAR
FORREST
PERRY
GREENE
WALTHALL

WILKINSON
Hattiesburg
HATTIESBURG

Picayune
PEARL RIVER
STONE
GEORGE
GULFPORT-BILOXI
PASCAGOULA
HARRISON
JACKSON
Gulfport
Biloxi
Pascagoula
HANCOCK

Gulfport-Biloxi-Pascagoula

Core Based Statistical Area boundaries are those defined by the Federal Office of Management and Budget as of December 2005. Selected places are as of July 1, 2005. All other boundaries and names are as of January 1, 2002.

MISSOURI - Core Based Statistical Areas, Counties, Independent City, and Selected Places

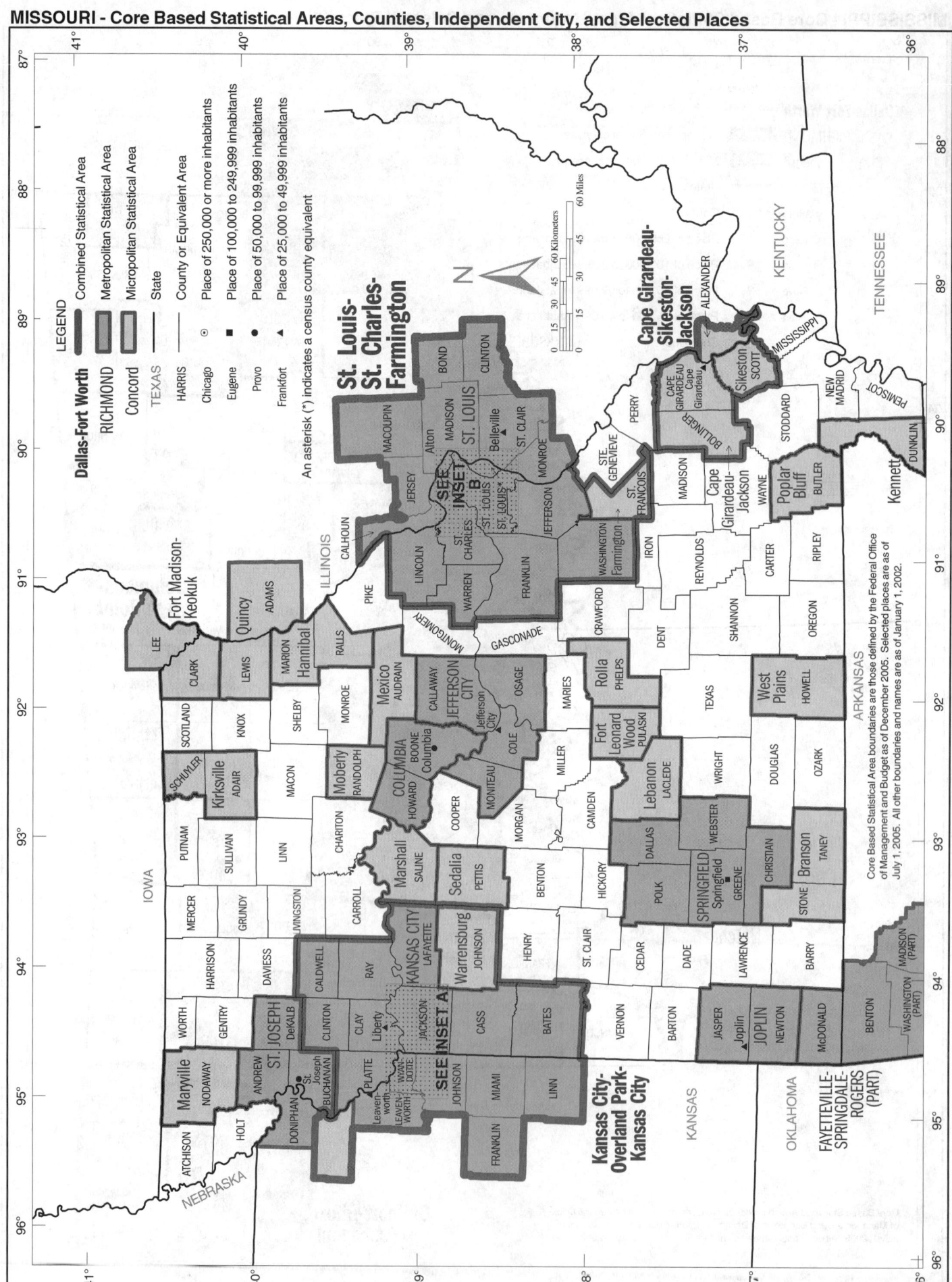

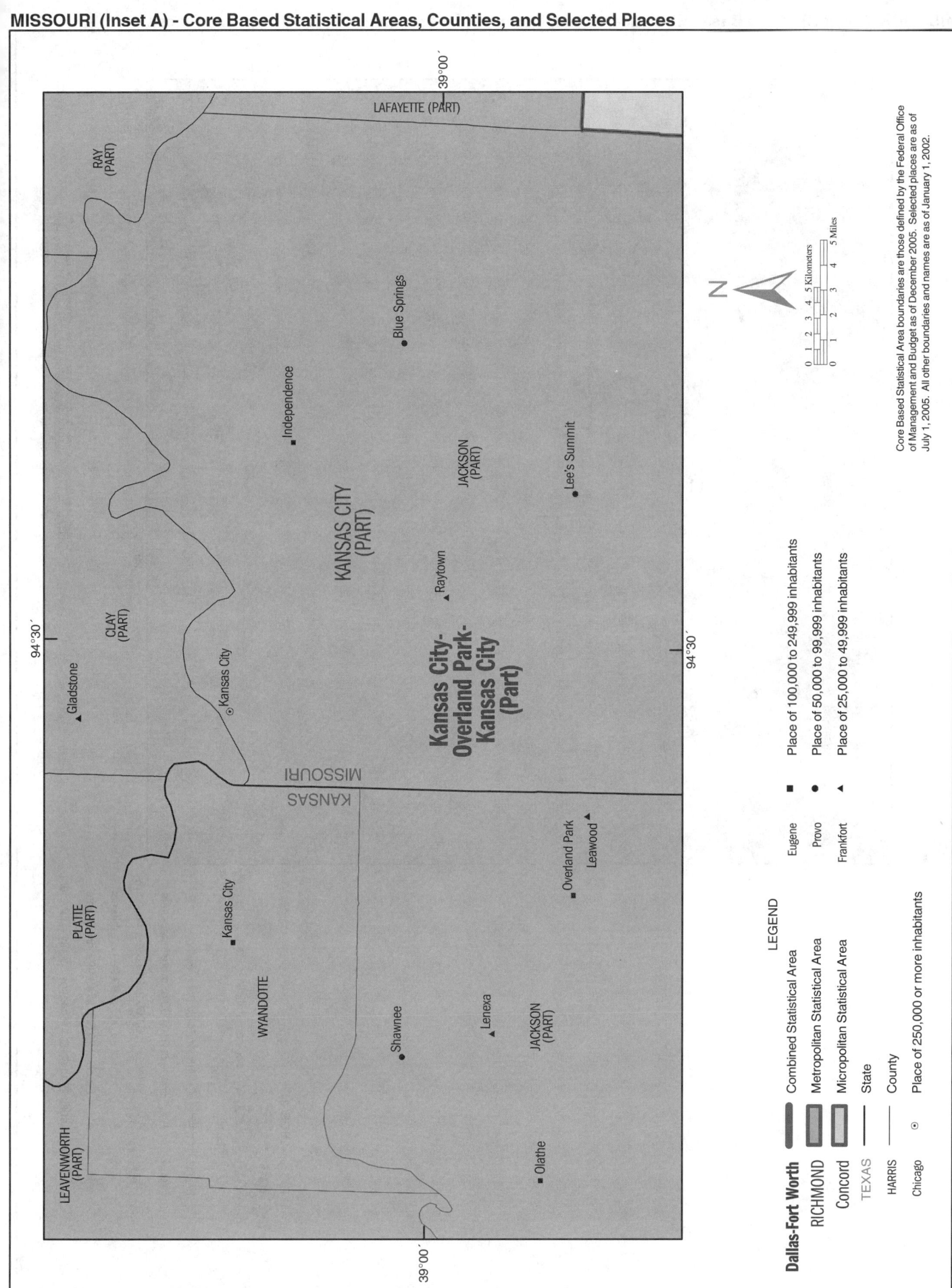

LAFAYETTE (PART)

RAY (PART)

Blue Springs

Independence

KANSAS CITY (PART)

JACKSON (PART)

Lee's Summit

CLAY (PART)

Raytown

Gladstone

Kansas City

Kansas City-Overland Park-Kansas City (Part)

MISSOURI
KANSAS

Overland Park
Leawood

PLATTE (PART)

Kansas City

WYANDOTTE

Lenexa

JACKSON (PART)

Shawnee

LEAVENWORTH (PART)

Olathe

94°30´

94°30´

39°00´

39°00´

N

0 1 2 3 4 5 Kilometers
0 1 2 3 4 5 Miles

Core Based Statistical Area boundaries are those defined by the Federal Office of Management and Budget as of December 2005. Selected places are as of July 1, 2005. All other boundaries and names are as of January 1, 2002.

LEGEND

Dallas-Fort Worth	Combined Statistical Area
RICHMOND	Metropolitan Statistical Area
Concord	Micropolitan Statistical Area
——	State
HARRIS	County
⊙ Chicago	Place of 250,000 or more inhabitants
■ Eugene	Place of 100,000 to 249,999 inhabitants
● Provo	Place of 50,000 to 99,999 inhabitants
▲ Frankfort	Place of 25,000 to 49,999 inhabitants

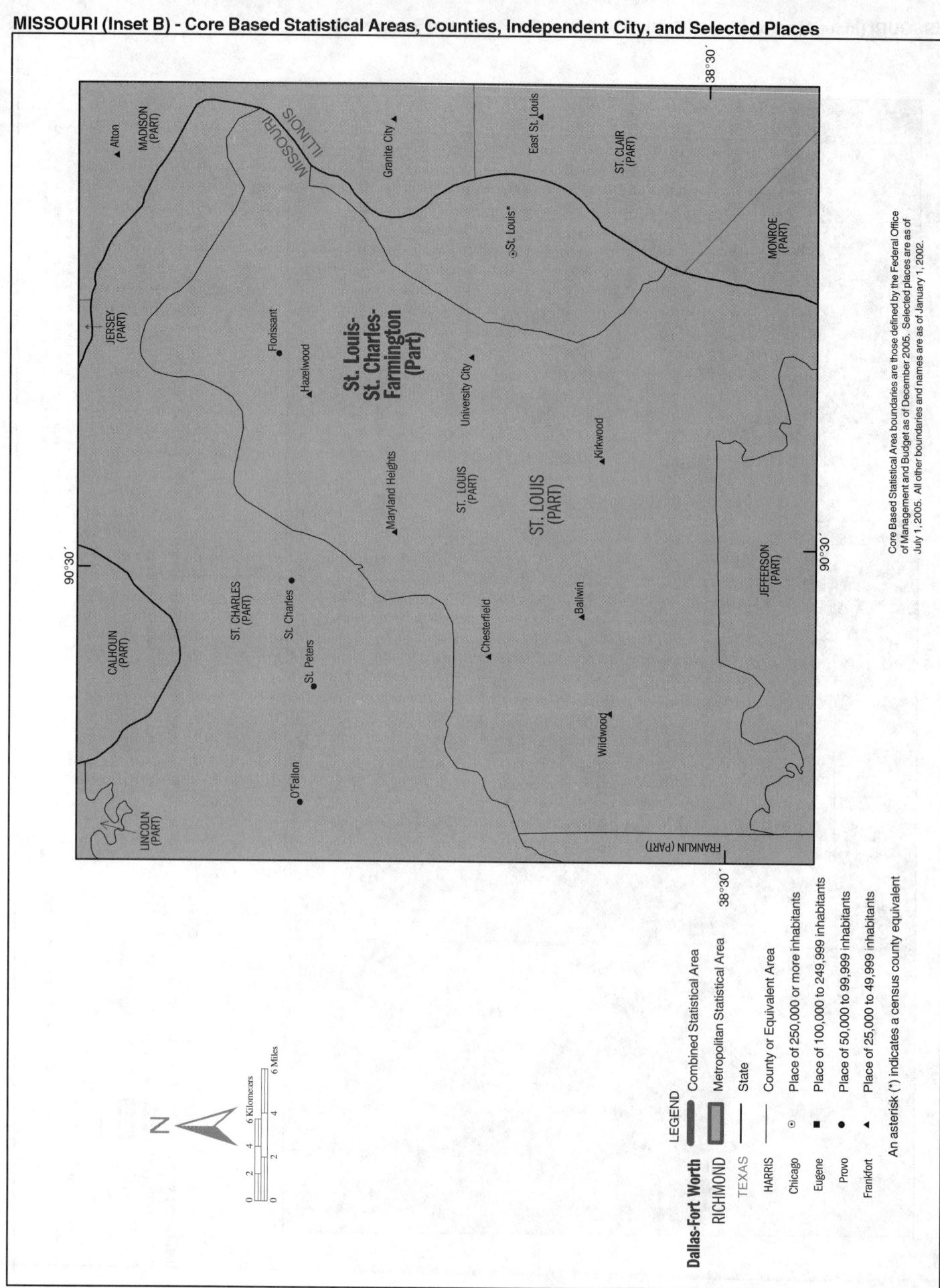

Core Based Statistical Area boundaries are those defined by the Federal Office of Management and Budget as of December 2005. Selected places are as of July 1, 2005. All other boundaries and names are as of January 1, 2002.

LEGEND

Dallas-Fort Worth	Combined Statistical Area
RICHMOND	Metropolitan Statistical Area
	State
TEXAS	
HARRIS	County or Equivalent Area
⊙ Chicago	Place of 250,000 or more inhabitants
■ Eugene	Place of 100,000 to 249,999 inhabitants
● Provo	Place of 50,000 to 99,999 inhabitants
▲ Frankfort	Place of 25,000 to 49,999 inhabitants

An asterisk (*) indicates a census county equivalent

MONTANA - Core Based Statistical Areas, Counties, and Selected Places

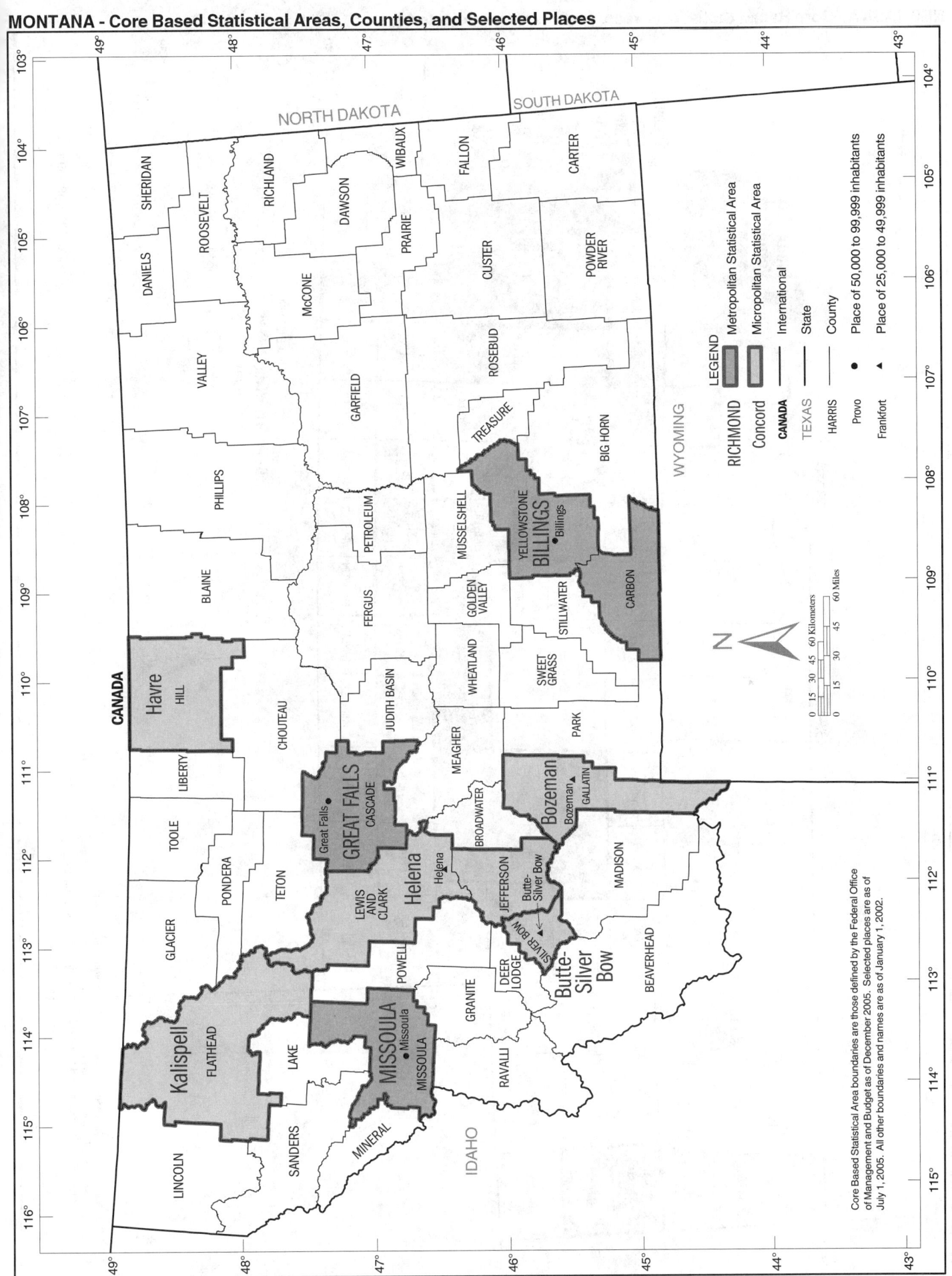

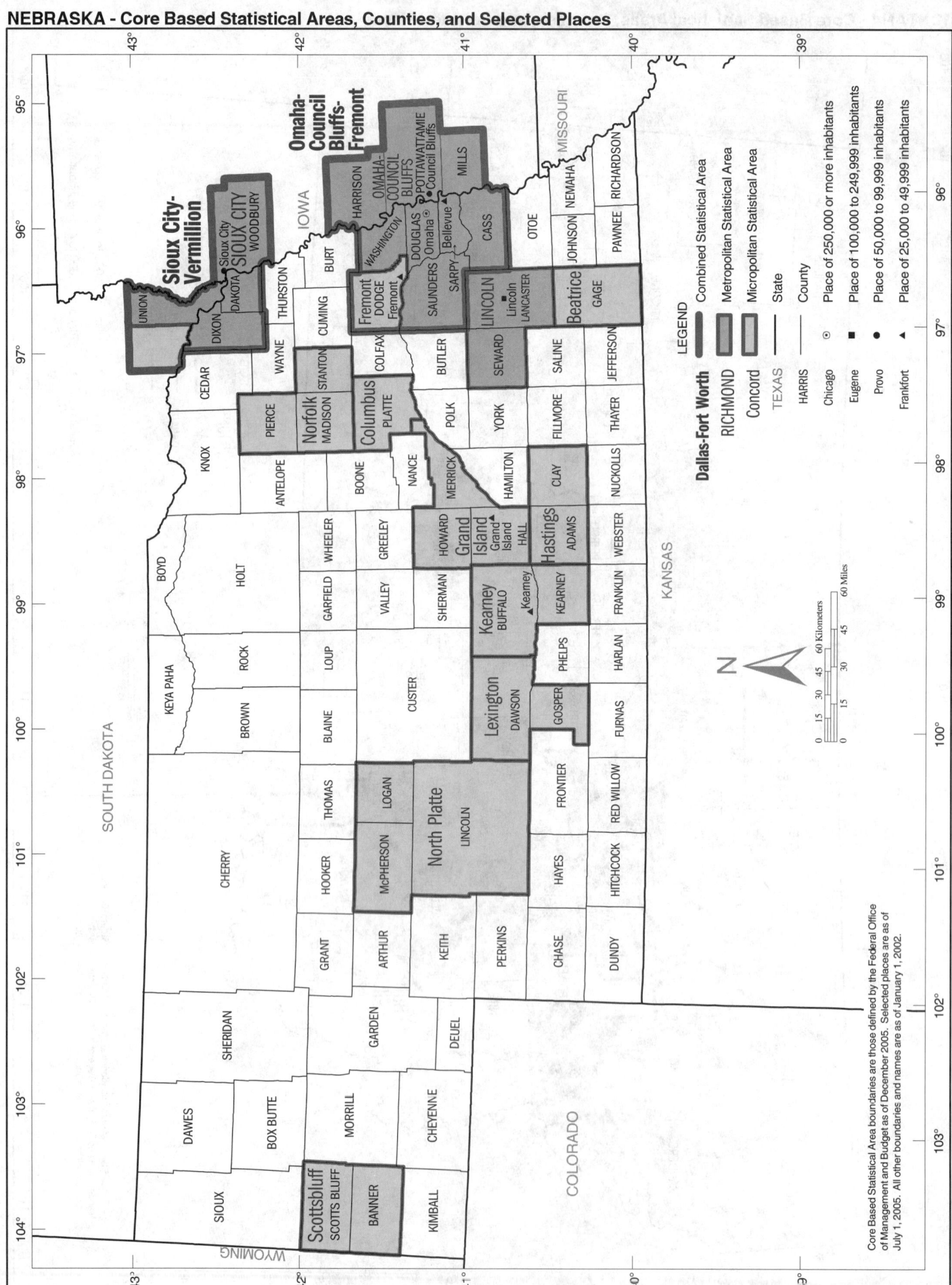

NEVADA - Core Based Statistical Areas, Counties, Independent City, and Selected Places

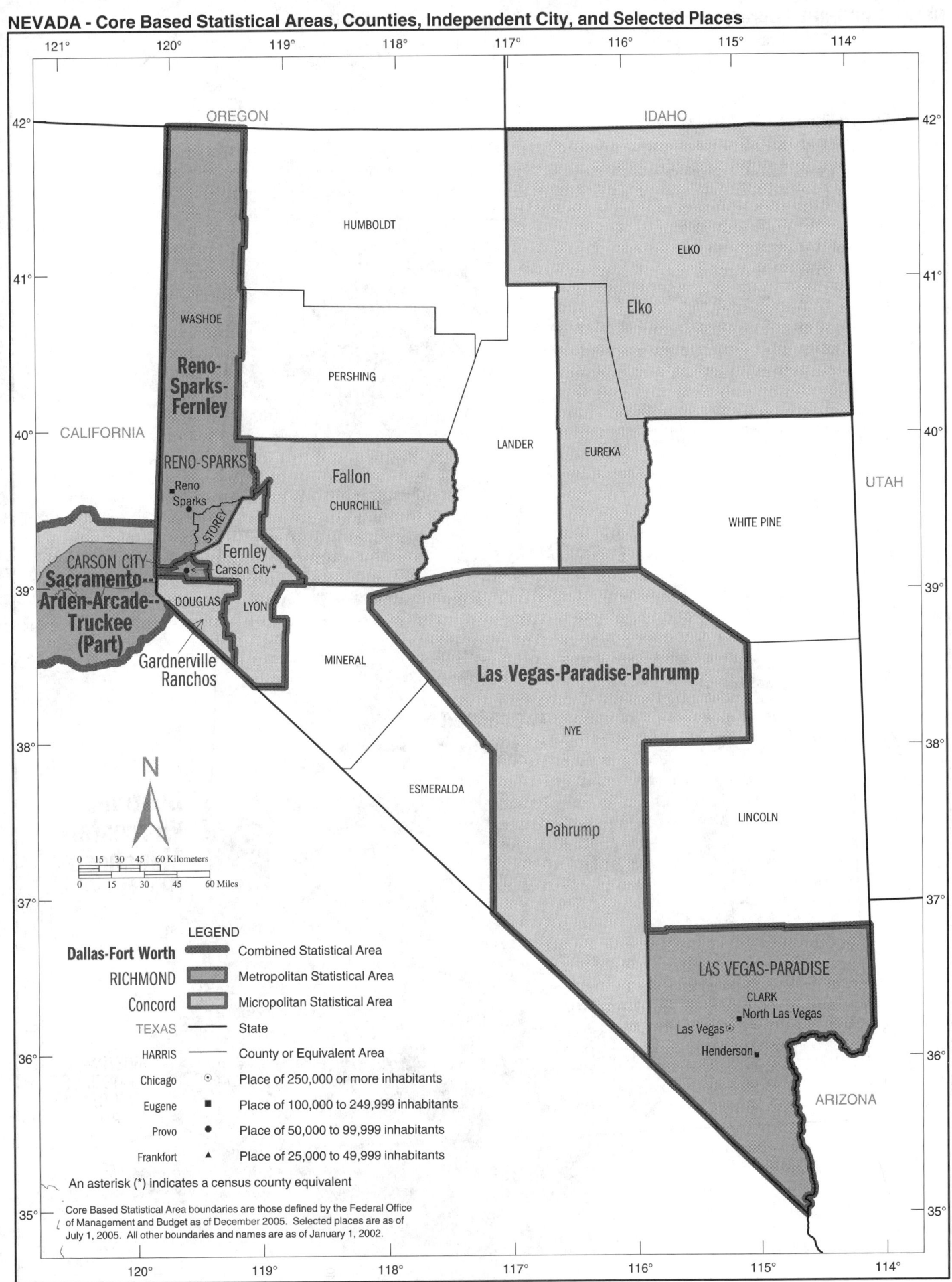

LEGEND

Dallas-Fort Worth	Combined Statistical Area
RICHMOND	Metropolitan Statistical Area
Concord	Micropolitan Statistical Area
TEXAS	State
HARRIS	County or Equivalent Area
Chicago ⊙	Place of 250,000 or more inhabitants
Eugene ■	Place of 100,000 to 249,999 inhabitants
Provo ●	Place of 50,000 to 99,999 inhabitants
Frankfort ▲	Place of 25,000 to 49,999 inhabitants

An asterisk (*) indicates a census county equivalent

Core Based Statistical Area boundaries are those defined by the Federal Office
of Management and Budget as of December 2005. Selected places are as of
July 1, 2005. All other boundaries and names are as of January 1, 2002.

73°   72°   71°

45°   45°

LEGEND

Dallas-Fort Worth ▭ Combined Statistical Area

RICHMOND ▭ Metropolitan Statistical Area

Concord ▭ Micropolitan Statistical Area

Philadelphia ···· Metropolitan Division

CANADA —— International

TEXAS —— State

HARRIS —— County

Eugene ■ Place of 100,000 to 249,999 inhabitants

Provo ● Place of 50,000 to 99,999 inhabitants

Frankfort ▲ Place of 25,000 to 49,999 inhabitants

〜 Shoreline

Core Based Statistical Area boundaries are those defined by the Federal Office of Management and Budget as of December 2005. Selected places are as of July 1, 2005. All other boundaries and names are as of January 1, 2002.

N

0 5 10 15 20 Kilometers
0 5 10 15 20 Miles

CANADA

Berlin

ESSEX

COOS

VERMONT

MAINE

44°   44°

ORANGE

Lebanon

GRAFTON

CARROLL

Claremont-Lebanon

WINDSOR

Laconia

BELKNAP

Boston-Worcester-Manchester (Part)

Claremont

SULLIVAN

Concord

MERRIMACK

Rochester▲

STRAFFORD

● Concord

Dover▲

43°   Rockingham County Strafford County   43°

Keene

CHESHIRE

Manchester ■

MANCHESTER-NASHUA

HILLSBOROUGH

ROCKINGHAM

BOSTON-CAMBRIDGE-QUINCY (PART)

● Nashua

● Haverhill

▲Methuen

●Lawrence

Lowell ■

ESSEX (PART)

Gloucester ▲

MASSACHUSETTS

MIDDLESEX (PART)

Beverly

Peabody ▲

Woburn▲

Salem ▲

Melrose▲

● Lynn

Malden▲

73°   72°   71°

NEW YORK-
Newark-
Bridgeport
(Part)

New York-
White Plains-
Wayne

PUTNAM

ROCKLAND

WESTCHESTER   CONNECTICUT

▲Spring
Valley

White
Plains

Port Chester

Yonkers New
Rochelle

BERGEN

Mount
Vernon
BRONX

Glen
Cove

NASSAU

SUFFOLK
(PART)

Hempstead

▲Lindenhurst

QUEENS

Valley Stream Freeport
▲   ▲

ESSEX

SEE
INSET
A

HUDSON

NEW YORK

UNION

New York

RICHMOND

KINGS

Long
Beach

PIKE

NEW YORK

Newark-
Union

SUSSEX

PASSAIC

MORRIS

WARREN

CARBON

ALLENTOWN-
BETHLEHEM-
EASTON

PENNSYLVANIA

NORTHAMPTON

LEHIGH

HUNTERDON

SOMERSET

MIDDLESEX

Perth
Amboy ▲

New
Brunswick ●

Sayreville ▲

NEW YORK-
NORTHERN NEW JERSEY-
LONG ISLAND
(PART)

PHILADELPHIA-
CAMDEN-
WILMINGTON
(PART)

BUCKS

TRENTON-
EWING

MERCER

Trenton ●

Long Branch ▲

MONMOUTH

Elizabeth

Edison

OCEAN

CHESTER
(PART)

Norristown ▲

MONTGOMERY

Philadelphia

Philadelphia-
Camden-
Vineland
(Part)

DELAWARE

PHILADELPHIA

Camden ●

Camden

CAMDEN

BURLINGTON

Chester ●

Wilmington ●

▲Newark

CECIL
(PART)

NEW CASTLE

Wilmington
(Part)

SALEM

GLOUCESTER

ATLANTIC
CITY

MARYLAND

DELAWARE

VINELAND-
MILLVILLE-
BRIDGETON

Vineland ●

▲Millville

ATLANTIC

Atlantic City ▲

OCEAN
CITY

CUMBERLAND

CAPE
MAY

N

| 0 | 5 | 10 | 15 | 20 | 25 Kilometers |

| 0 | 5 | 10 | 15 | 20 | 25 Miles |

LEGEND

Dallas-Fort Worth	▬▬▬	Combined Statistical Area
RICHMOND		Metropolitan Statistical Area
Philadelphia	••••••	Metropolitan Division
TEXAS	▬▬▬	State
HARRIS	▬▬▬	County
Chicago	⊙	Place of 250,000 or more inhabitants
Eugene	■	Place of 100,000 to 249,999 inhabitants
Provo	●	Place of 50,000 to 99,999 inhabitants
Frankfort	▲	Place of 25,000 to 49,999 inhabitants
		Shoreline

Core Based Statistical Area boundaries are those defined by the Federal Office
of Management and Budget as of December 2005. Selected places are as of
July 1, 2005. All other boundaries and names are as of January 1, 2002.

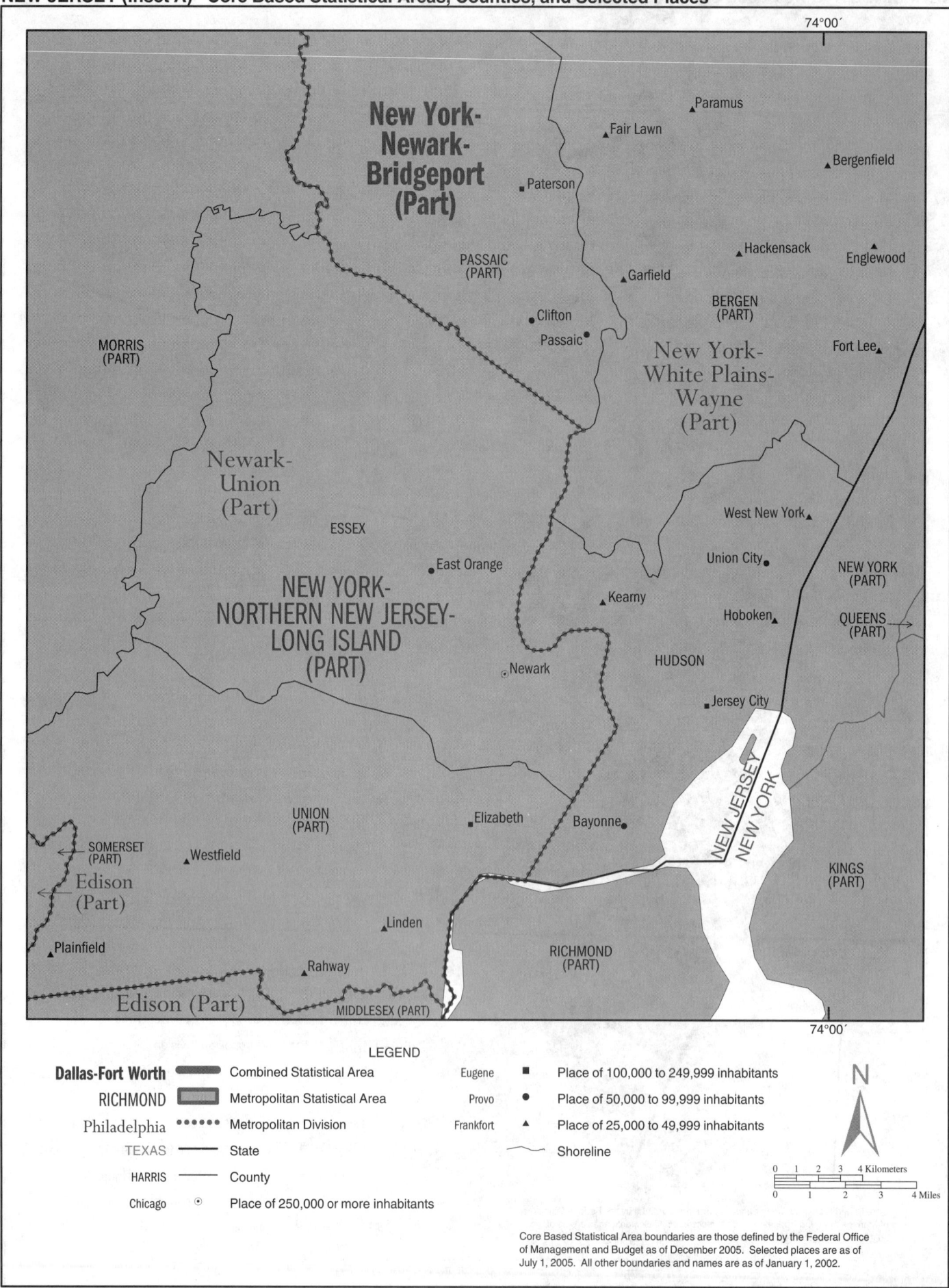

74°00′

**New York-
Newark-
Bridgeport
(Part)**

▲ Paramus

▲ Fair Lawn

▲ Bergenfield

PASSAIC
(PART)

■ Paterson

▲ Hackensack

Englewood ▲

● Garfield

BERGEN
(PART)

MORRIS
(PART)

● Clifton

Passaic ●

**New York-
White Plains-
Wayne
(Part)**

Fort Lee ▲

*Newark-
Union
(Part)*

ESSEX

West New York ▲

● East Orange

Union City ●

NEW YORK
(PART)

**NEW YORK-
NORTHERN NEW JERSEY-
LONG ISLAND
(PART)**

▲ Kearny

Hoboken ▲

QUEENS
(PART) →

HUDSON

◉ Newark

■ Jersey City

UNION
(PART)

● Bayonne

NEW JERSEY
NEW YORK

KINGS
(PART)

SOMERSET
(PART)

▲ Westfield

● Elizabeth

*Edison
(Part)* ←

▲ Linden

RICHMOND
(PART)

▲ Plainfield

▲ Rahway

Edison (Part)

MIDDLESEX (PART)

74°00′

LEGEND

Dallas-Fort Worth	▬▬ Combined Statistical Area	Eugene	■	Place of 100,000 to 249,999 inhabitants
RICHMOND	▬ Metropolitan Statistical Area	Provo	●	Place of 50,000 to 99,999 inhabitants
Philadelphia	•••• Metropolitan Division	Frankfort	▲	Place of 25,000 to 49,999 inhabitants
TEXAS	▬ State		〜	Shoreline
HARRIS	▬ County			
Chicago	◉ Place of 250,000 or more inhabitants			

N

0 1 2 3 4 Kilometers
0 1 2 3 4 Miles

Core Based Statistical Area boundaries are those defined by the Federal Office
of Management and Budget as of December 2005. Selected places are as of
July 1, 2005. All other boundaries and names are as of January 1, 2002.

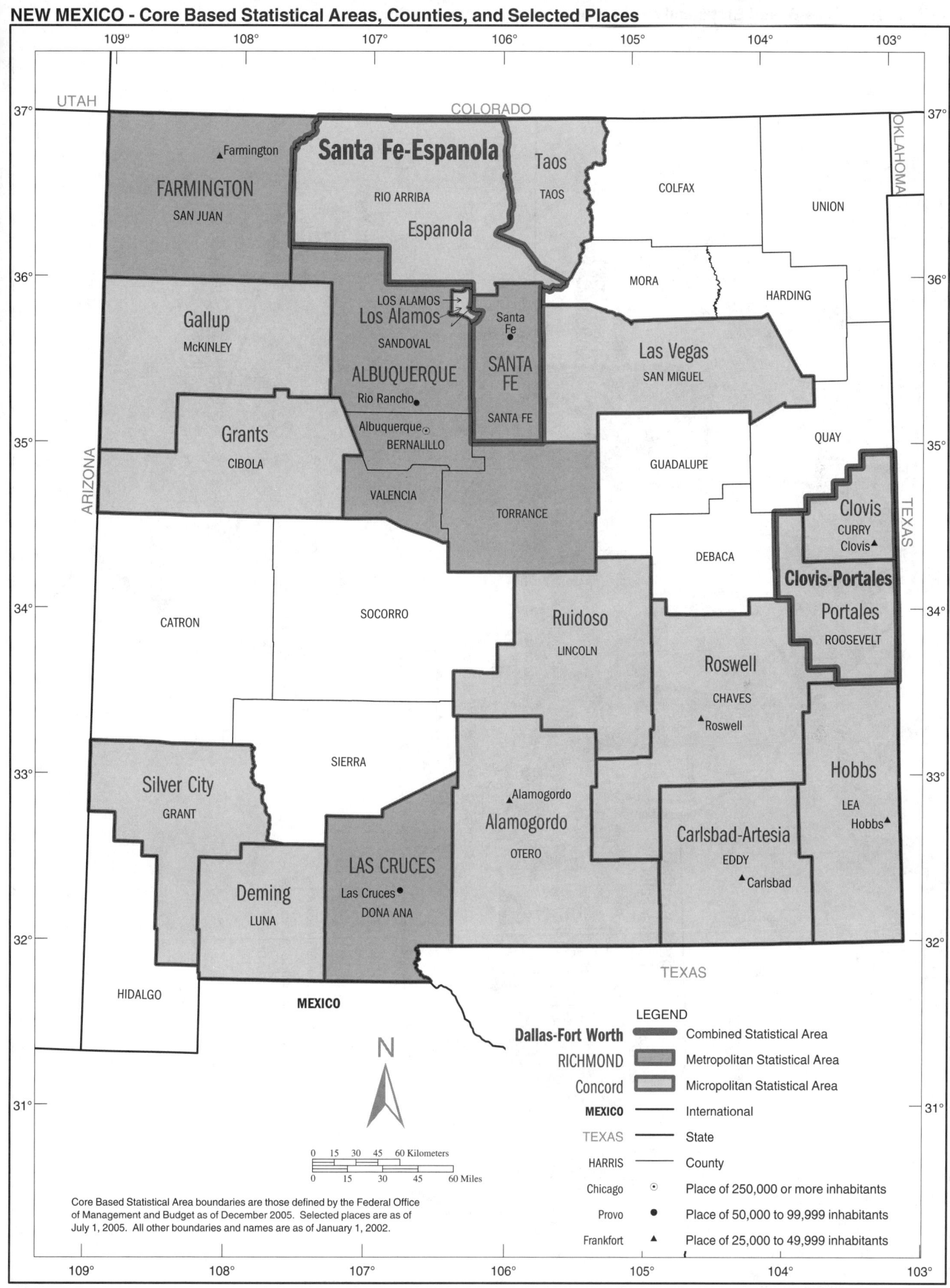

NEW MEXICO - Core Based Statistical Areas, Counties, and Selected Places

UTAH
COLORADO

Farmington
Santa Fe-Espanola
Taos

FARMINGTON
RIO ARRIBA
TAOS

SAN JUAN
Espanola

COLFAX
UNION

Gallup
McKINLEY

LOS ALAMOS
Los Alamos
Santa Fe

MORA
HARDING

SANDOVAL

ALBUQUERQUE
SANTA FE

Rio Rancho
Las Vegas
SAN MIGUEL

ARIZONA

Grants
Albuquerque
BERNALILLO

CIBOLA

SANTA FE

QUAY

VALENCIA
TORRANCE
GUADALUPE

CATRON
SOCORRO

Ruidoso
LINCOLN

DEBACA

Clovis
CURRY
Clovis

Clovis-Portales
Portales
ROOSEVELT

Roswell
CHAVES
Roswell

SIERRA

Silver City
GRANT

Alamogordo
Alamogordo
OTERO

Hobbs
LEA
Hobbs

Carlsbad-Artesia
EDDY
Carlsbad

Deming
LUNA

LAS CRUCES
Las Cruces
DONA ANA

HIDALGO

MEXICO

TEXAS

TEXAS

N

0   15   30   45   60 Kilometers
0   15   30   45   60 Miles

LEGEND

Dallas-Fort Worth — Combined Statistical Area
RICHMOND — Metropolitan Statistical Area
Concord — Micropolitan Statistical Area
MEXICO — International
TEXAS — State
HARRIS — County
Chicago ⊙ Place of 250,000 or more inhabitants
Provo ● Place of 50,000 to 99,999 inhabitants
Frankfort ▲ Place of 25,000 to 49,999 inhabitants

Core Based Statistical Area boundaries are those defined by the Federal Office
of Management and Budget as of December 2005. Selected places are as of
July 1, 2005. All other boundaries and names are as of January 1, 2002.

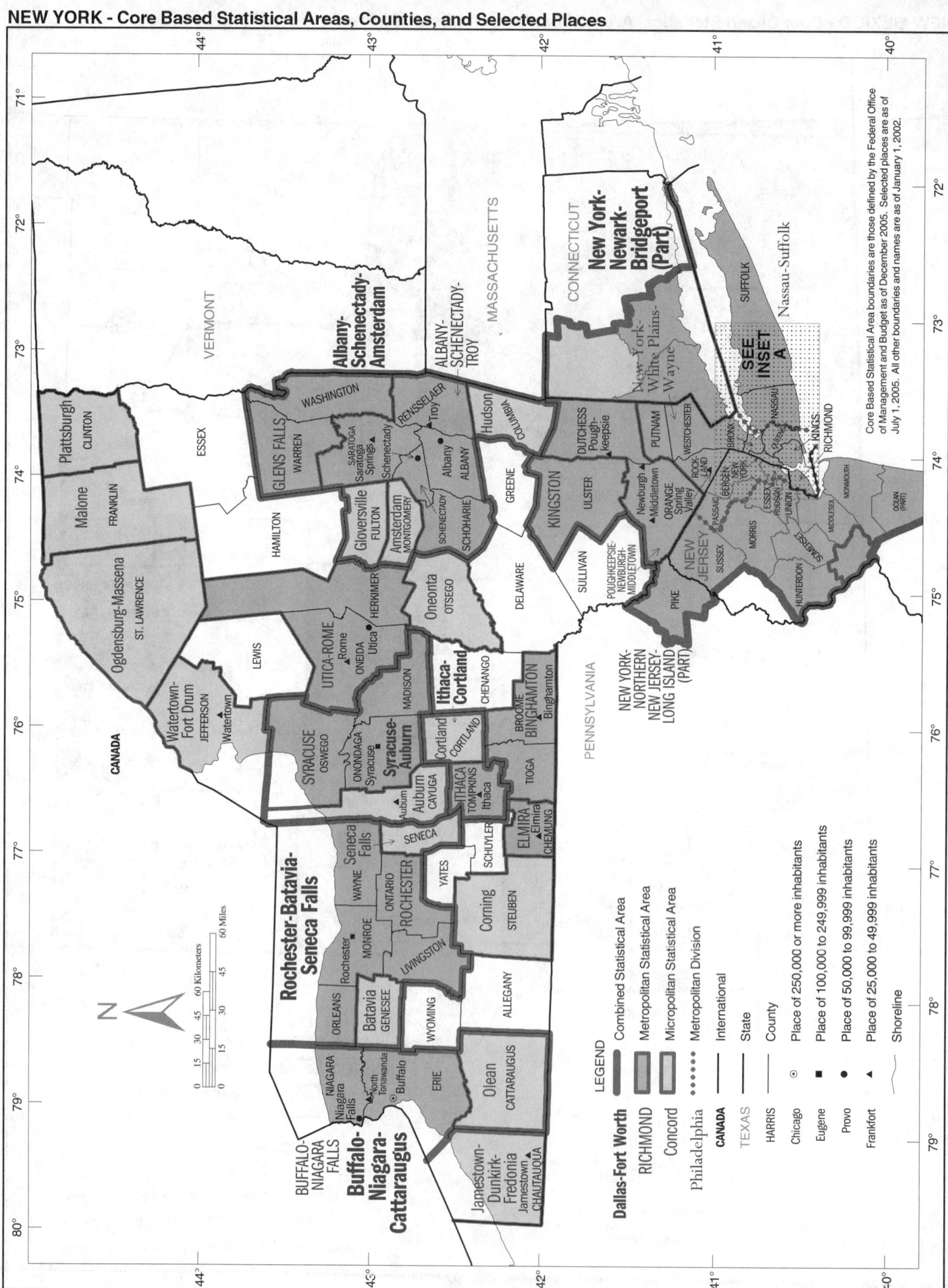

Core Based Statistical Area boundaries are those defined by the Federal Office of Management and Budget as of December 2005. Selected places are as of July 1, 2005. All other boundaries and names are as of January 1, 2002.

LEGEND

Dallas-Fort Worth	Combined Statistical Area
RICHMOND	Metropolitan Statistical Area
Concord	Micropolitan Statistical Area
Philadelphia	Metropolitan Division
CANADA	International
TEXAS	State
HARRIS	County
Chicago ⊙	Place of 250,000 or more inhabitants
Eugene ■	Place of 100,000 to 249,999 inhabitants
Provo ●	Place of 50,000 to 99,999 inhabitants
Frankfort ▲	Place of 25,000 to 49,999 inhabitants
	Shoreline

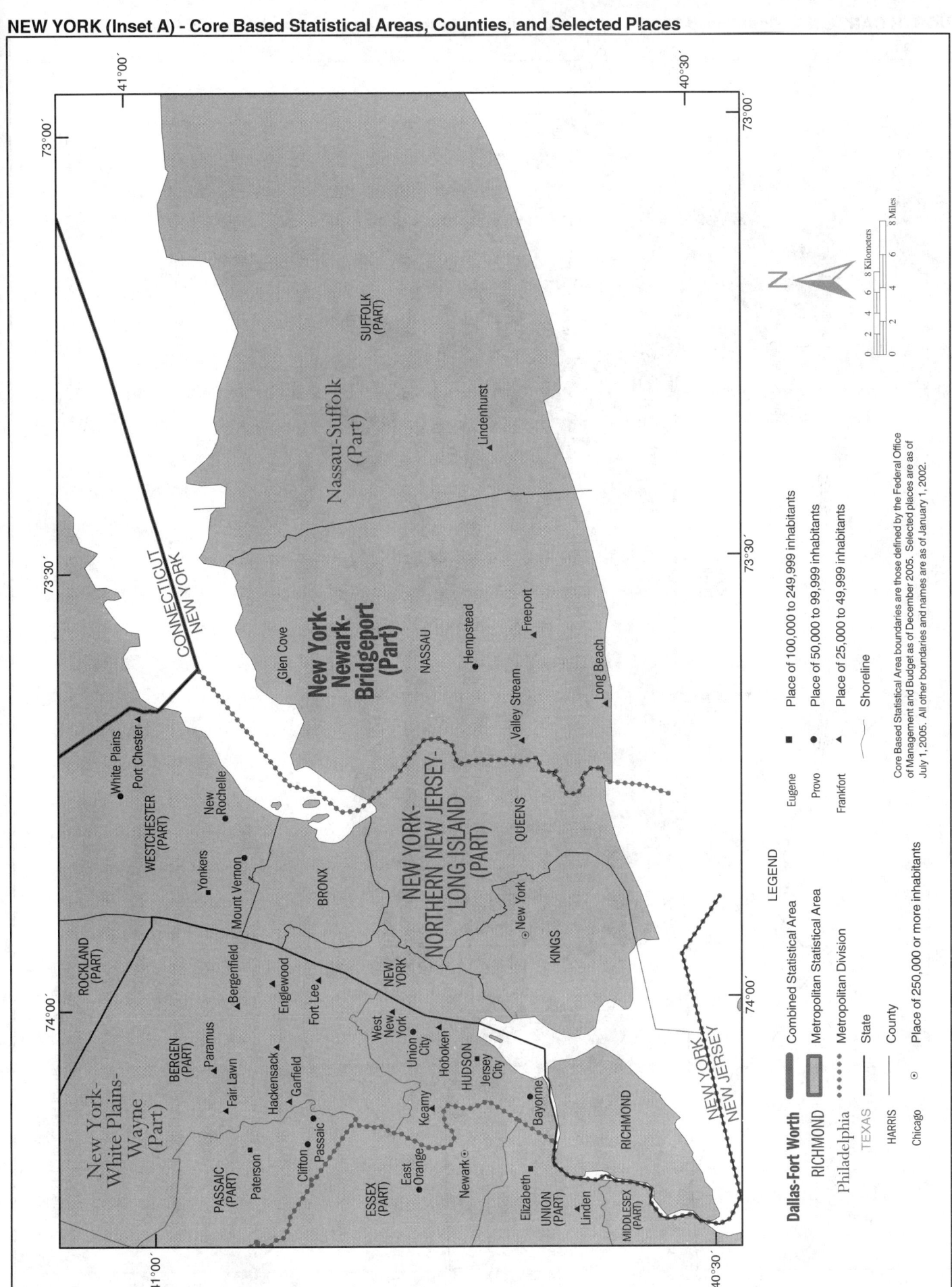

LEGEND

Dallas-Fort Worth	Combined Statistical Area	
RICHMOND	Metropolitan Statistical Area	
Philadelphia	Metropolitan Division	
TEXAS	State	
HARRIS	County	
Chicago ⊙	Place of 250,000 or more inhabitants	

Eugene ■	Place of 100,000 to 249,999 inhabitants
Provo ●	Place of 50,000 to 99,999 inhabitants
Frankfort ▲	Place of 25,000 to 49,999 inhabitants
	Shoreline

Core Based Statistical Area boundaries are those defined by the Federal Office of Management and Budget as of December 2005. Selected places are as of July 1, 2005. All other boundaries and names are as of January 1, 2002.

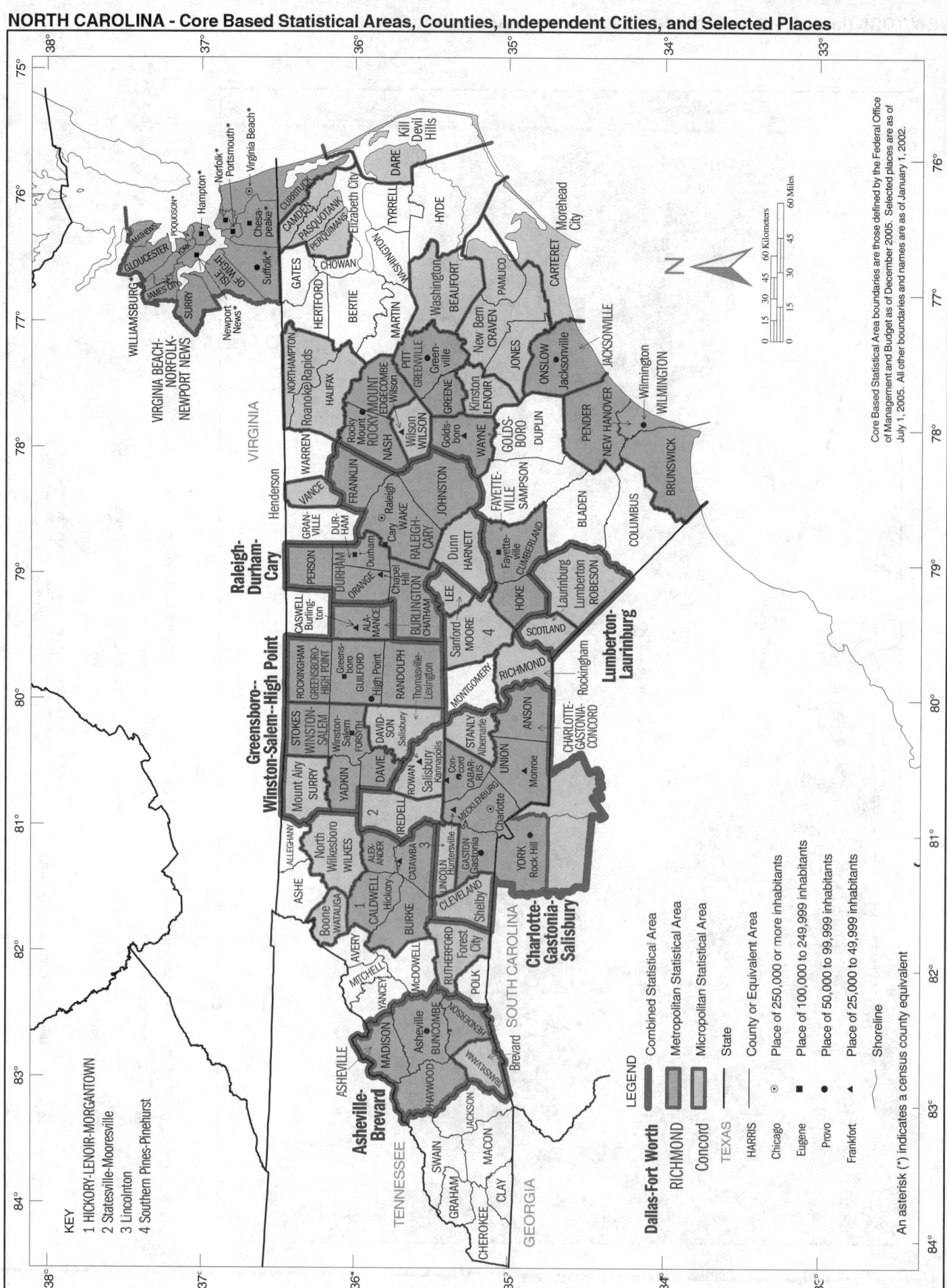

LEGEND

Combined Statistical Area
Metropolitan Statistical Area
Micropolitan Statistical Area
State
County or Equivalent Area

⊙ Place of 250,000 or more inhabitants
■ Place of 100,000 to 249,999 inhabitants
● Place of 50,000 to 99,999 inhabitants
▲ Place of 25,000 to 49,999 inhabitants
Shoreline

An asterisk (*) indicates a census county equivalent

Dallas-Fort Worth
RICHMOND
Concord
TEXAS
HARRIS
Chicago
Eugene
Provo
Frankfort

KEY
1 HICKORY-LENOIR-MORGANTOWN
2 Statesville-Mooresville
3 Lincolnton
4 Southern Pines-Pinehurst

Core Based Statistical Area boundaries are those defined by the Federal Office of Management and Budget as of December 2005. Selected places are as of July 1, 2005. All other boundaries and names are as of January 1, 2002.

0 15 30 45 60 Kilometers
0 15 30 45 60 Miles

NORTH DAKOTA - Core Based Statistical Areas, Counties, and Selected Places

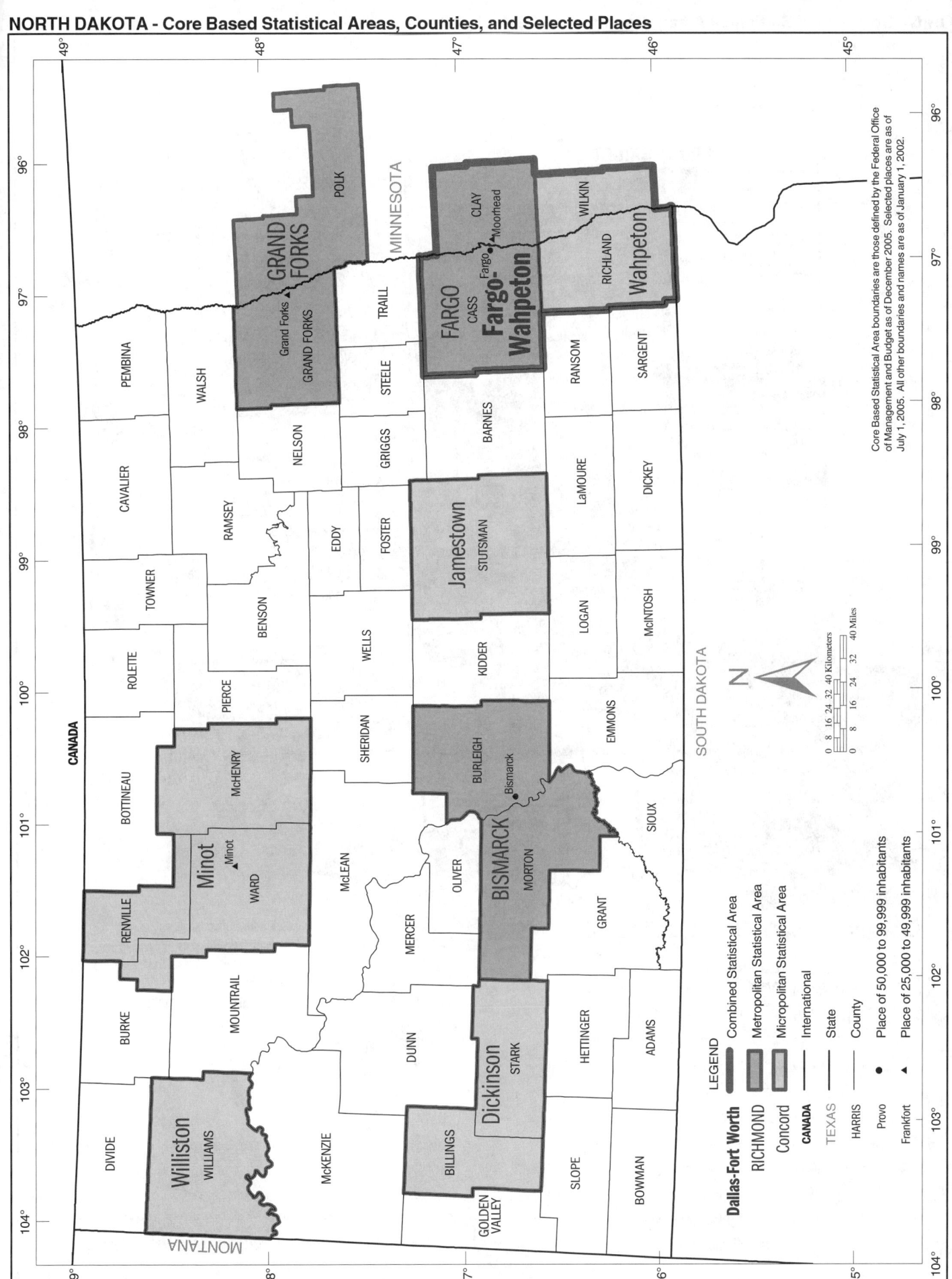

Core Based Statistical Area boundaries are those defined by the Federal Office of Management and Budget as of December 2005. Selected places are as of July 1, 2005. All other boundaries and names are as of January 1, 2002.

LEGEND

Dallas-Fort Worth	Combined Statistical Area
RICHMOND	Metropolitan Statistical Area
Concord	Micropolitan Statistical Area
CANADA	International
TEXAS	State
HARRIS	County
● Provo	Place of 50,000 to 99,999 inhabitants
▲ Frankfort	Place of 25,000 to 49,999 inhabitants

U.S. DEPARTMENT OF COMMERCE Economics and Statistics Administration U.S. Census Bureau

OHIO - Core Based Statistical Areas, Counties, and Selected Places

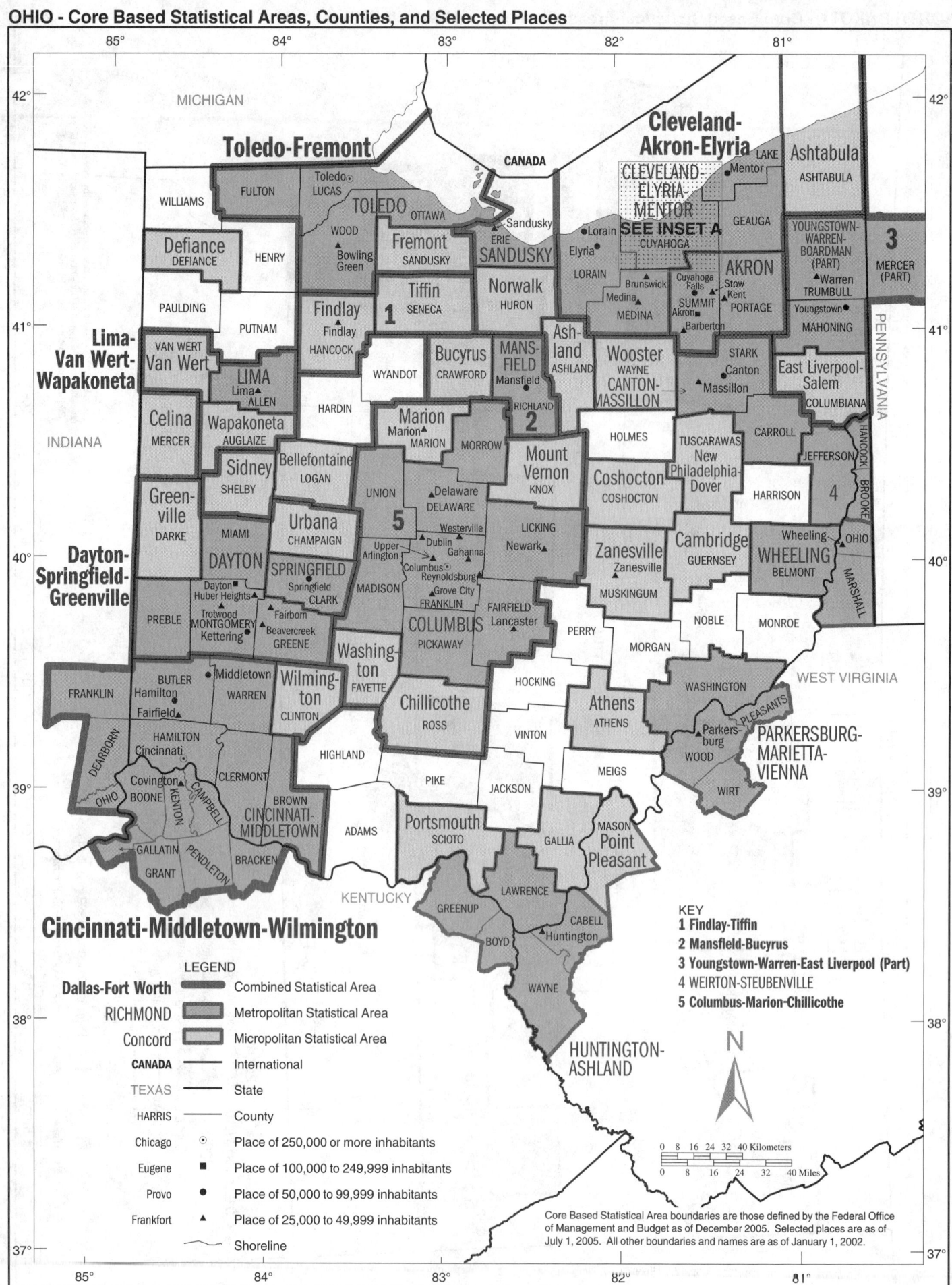

Toledo-Fremont

Cleveland-Akron-Elyria

Ashtabula

Lima-Van Wert-Wapakoneta

INDIANA

Dayton-Springfield-Greenville

Cincinnati-Middletown-Wilmington

KENTUCKY

WEST VIRGINIA

PARKERSBURG-MARIETTA-VIENNA

HUNTINGTON-ASHLAND

PENNSYLVANIA

KEY
1 Findlay-Tiffin
2 Mansfield-Bucyrus
3 Youngstown-Warren-East Liverpool (Part)
4 WEIRTON-STEUBENVILLE
5 Columbus-Marion-Chillicothe

LEGEND

Dallas-Fort Worth   Combined Statistical Area

RICHMOND   Metropolitan Statistical Area

Concord   Micropolitan Statistical Area

CANADA   International

TEXAS   State

HARRIS   County

Chicago ⊙ Place of 250,000 or more inhabitants

Eugene ■ Place of 100,000 to 249,999 inhabitants

Provo ● Place of 50,000 to 99,999 inhabitants

Frankfort ▲ Place of 25,000 to 49,999 inhabitants

Shoreline

N

0 8 16 24 32 40 Kilometers
0 8 16 24 32 40 Miles

Core Based Statistical Area boundaries are those defined by the Federal Office of Management and Budget as of December 2005. Selected places are as of July 1, 2005. All other boundaries and names are as of January 1, 2002.

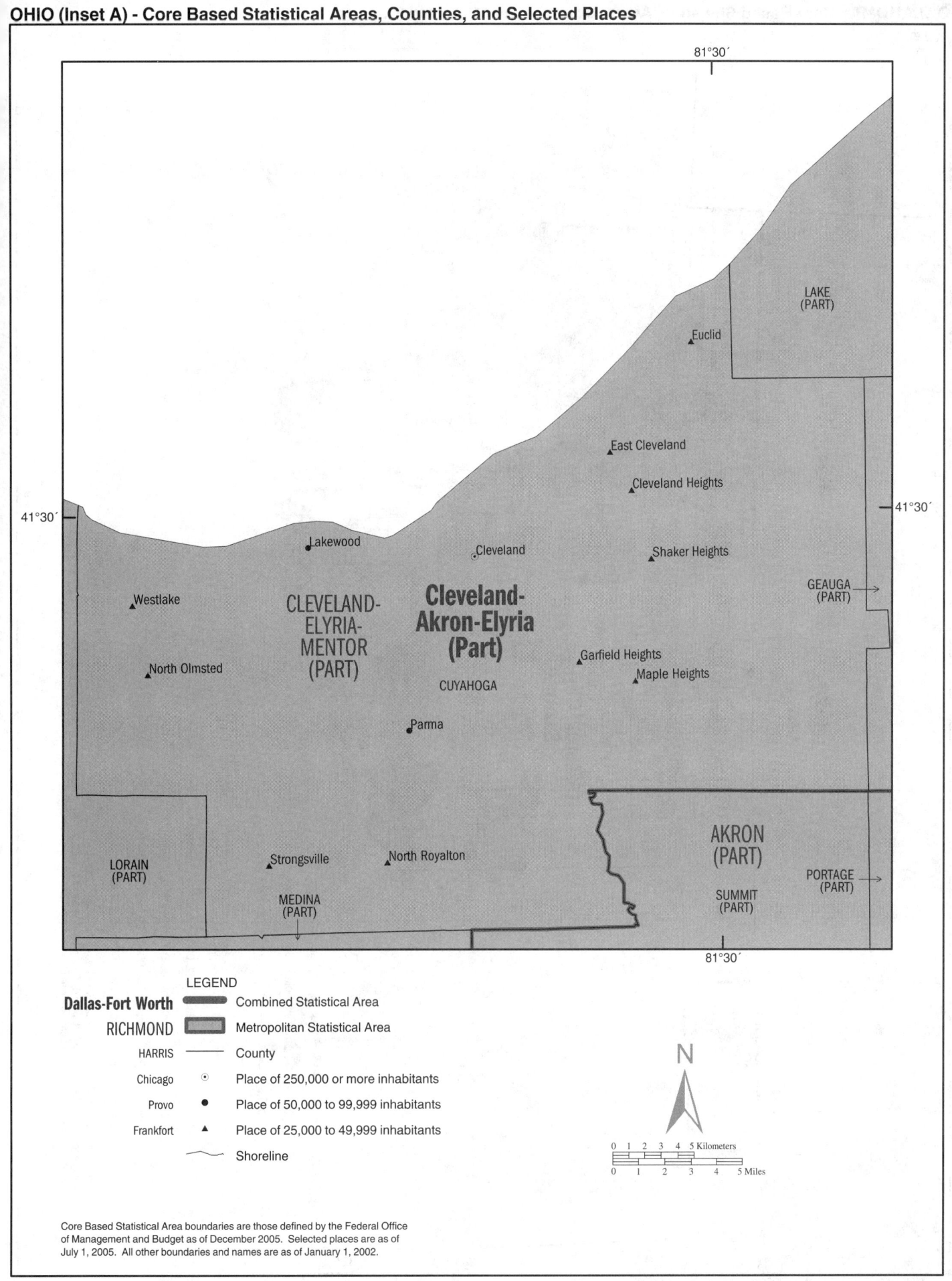

81°30′

LAKE
(PART)

▲Euclid

▲East Cleveland

▲Cleveland Heights

41°30′   41°30′

▲Lakewood   ⊙Cleveland   ▲Shaker Heights

GEAUGA →
(PART)

Westlake
▲   CLEVELAND-   Cleveland-
                     ELYRIA-   Akron-Elyria
                     MENTOR   (Part)
                     (PART)

North Olmsted   ▲Garfield Heights
▲   ▲Maple Heights
                                              CUYAHOGA

●Parma

AKRON
(PART)

LORAIN   Strongsville   North Royalton   PORTAGE →
(PART)   ▲   ▲   (PART)

              MEDINA   SUMMIT
              (PART)   (PART)

81°30′

LEGEND

Dallas-Fort Worth ▬▬▬ Combined Statistical Area

RICHMOND ▭ Metropolitan Statistical Area

HARRIS ─── County

Chicago ⊙ Place of 250,000 or more inhabitants

Provo ● Place of 50,000 to 99,999 inhabitants

Frankfort ▲ Place of 25,000 to 49,999 inhabitants

〜 Shoreline

N

0 1 2 3 4 5 Kilometers

0 1 2 3 4 5 Miles

Core Based Statistical Area boundaries are those defined by the Federal Office
of Management and Budget as of December 2005. Selected places are as of
July 1, 2005. All other boundaries and names are as of January 1, 2002.

OKLAHOMA - Core Based Statistical Areas, Counties, and Selected Places

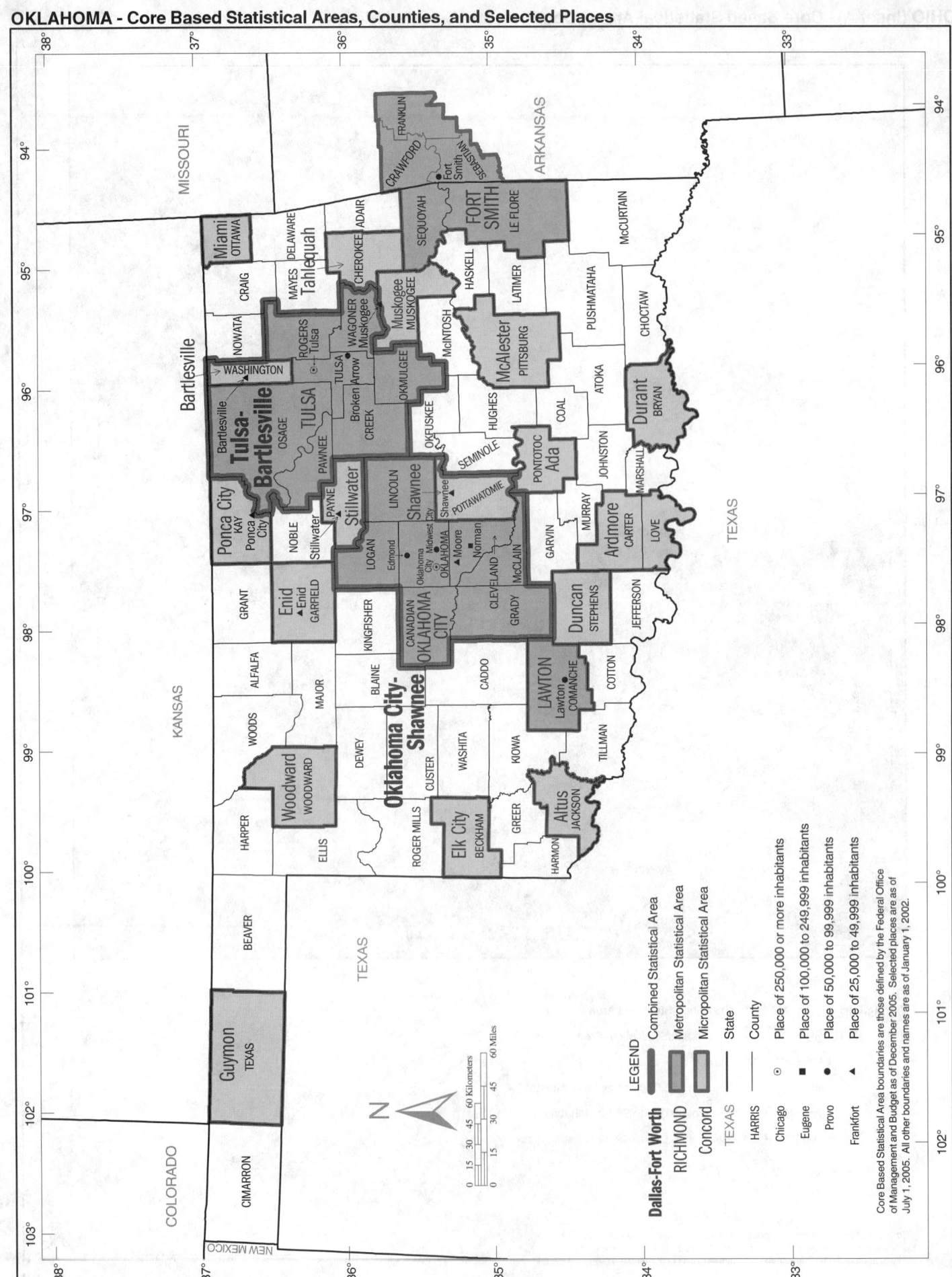

U.S. DEPARTMENT OF COMMERCE Economics and Statistics Administration U.S. Census Bureau

OREGON - Core Based Statistical Areas, Counties, and Selected Places

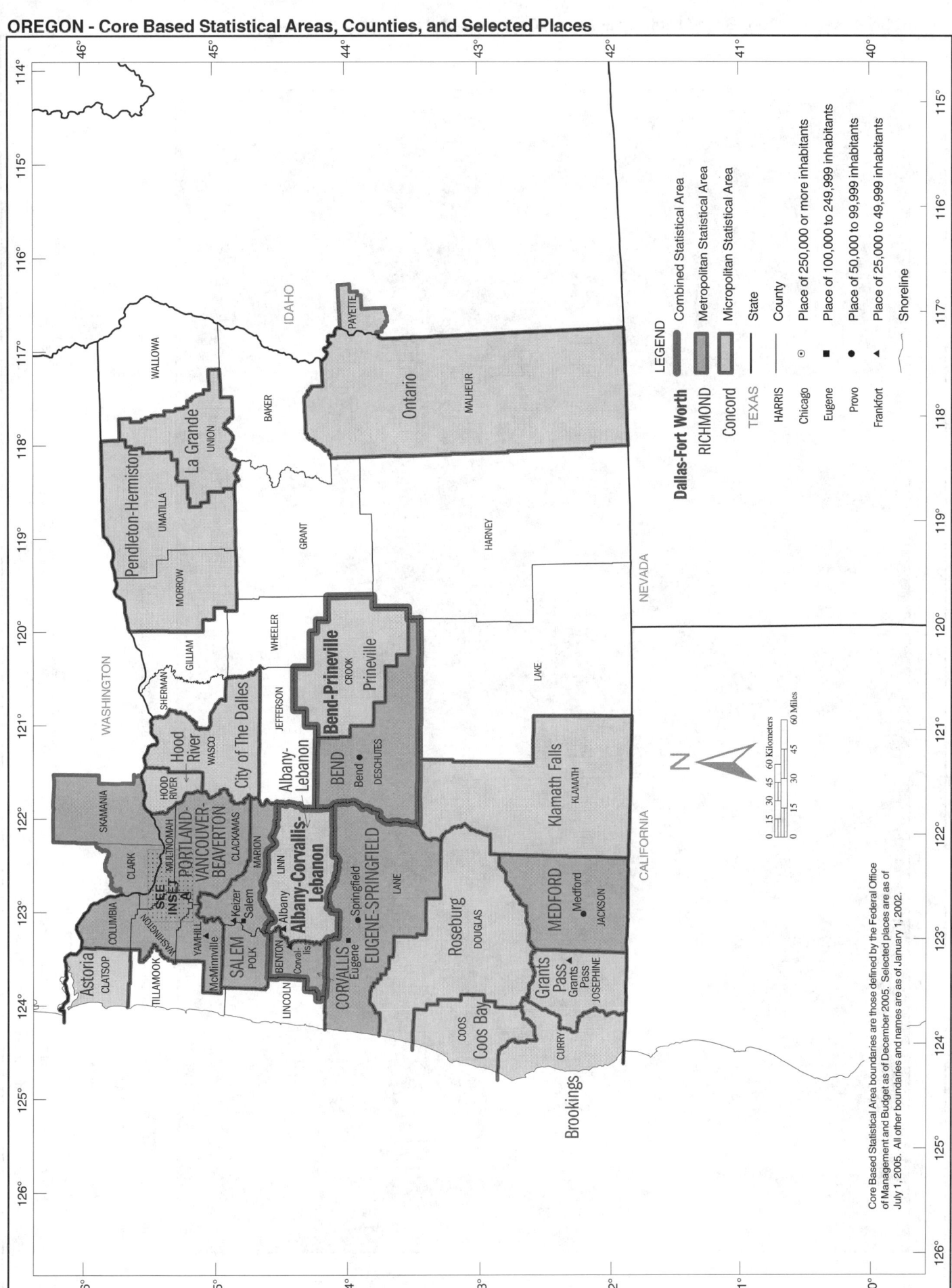

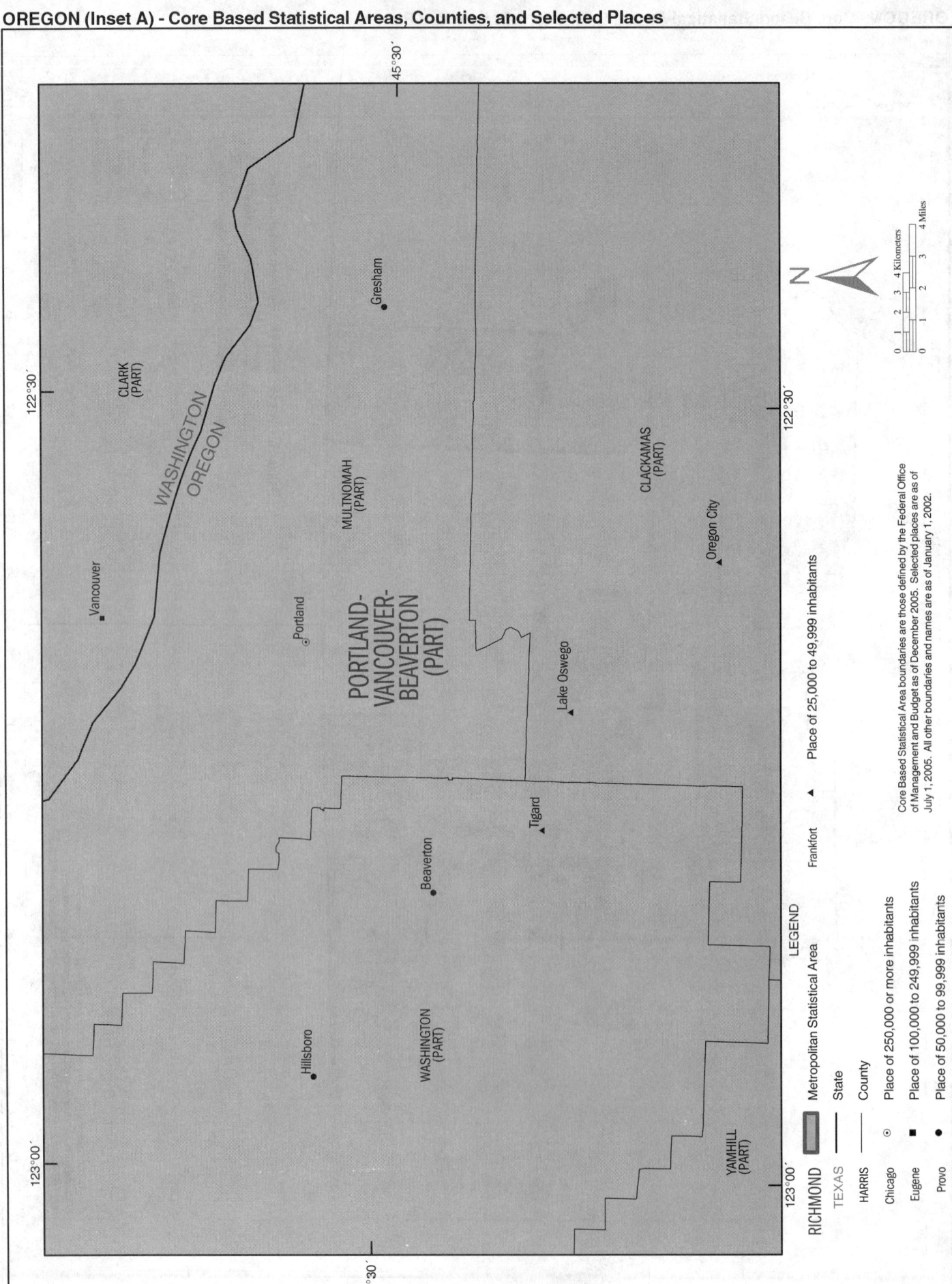

LEGEND

RICHMOND	Metropolitan Statistical Area
TEXAS	State
HARRIS	County
Chicago ⊙	Place of 250,000 or more inhabitants
Eugene ■	Place of 100,000 to 249,999 inhabitants
Provo ●	Place of 50,000 to 99,999 inhabitants
Frankfort ▲	Place of 25,000 to 49,999 inhabitants

Core Based Statistical Area boundaries are those defined by the Federal Office of Management and Budget as of December 2005. Selected places are as of July 1, 2005. All other boundaries and names are as of January 1, 2002.

CLARK (PART)

WASHINGTON
OREGON

Vancouver

Gresham

MULTNOMAH (PART)

Portland

PORTLAND-
VANCOUVER-
BEAVERTON
(PART)

CLACKAMAS (PART)

Oregon City

Lake Oswego

Tigard

Beaverton

Hillsboro

WASHINGTON (PART)

YAMHILL (PART)

N

PENNSYLVANIA - Core Based Statistical Areas, Counties, and Selected Places

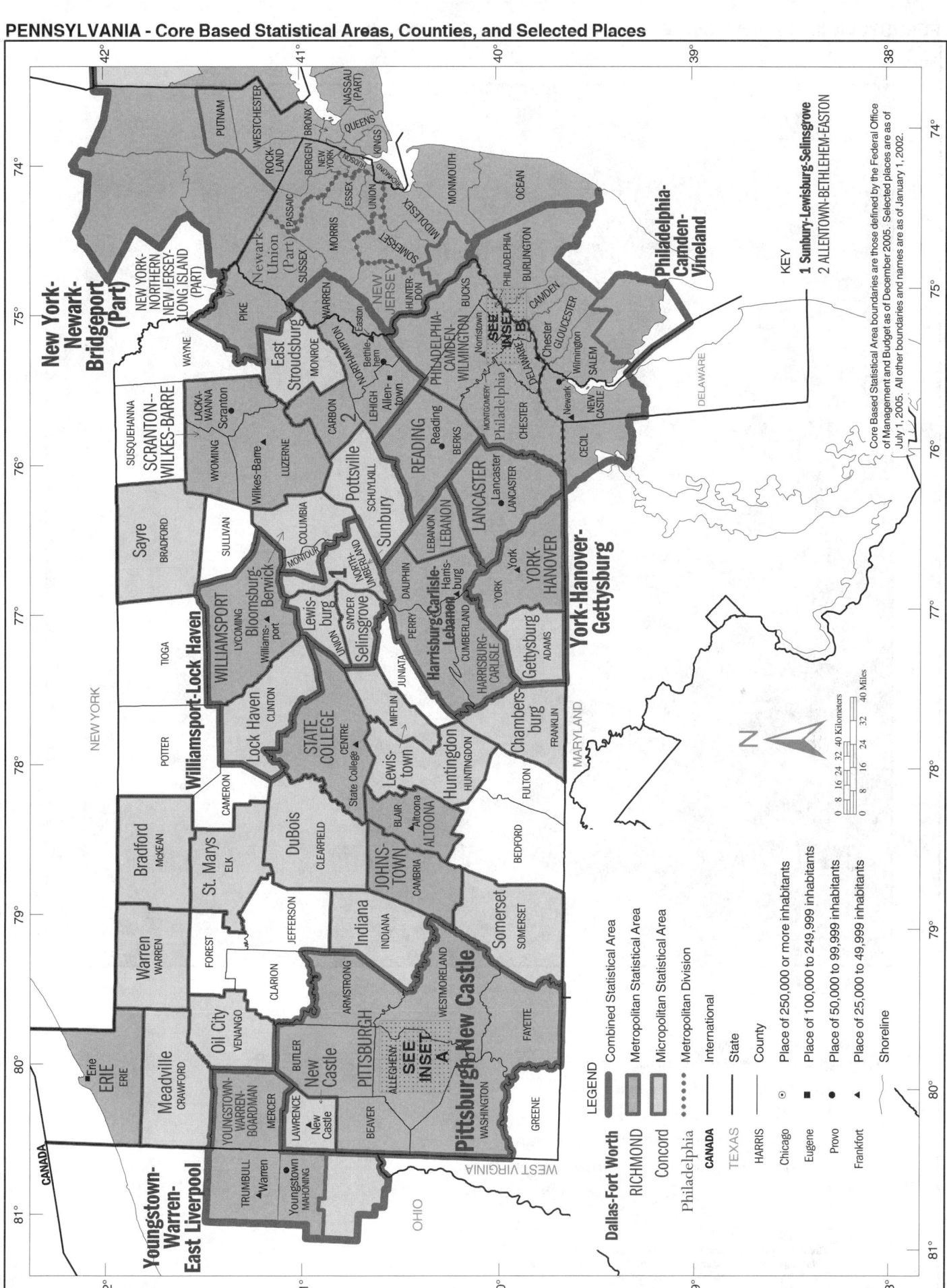

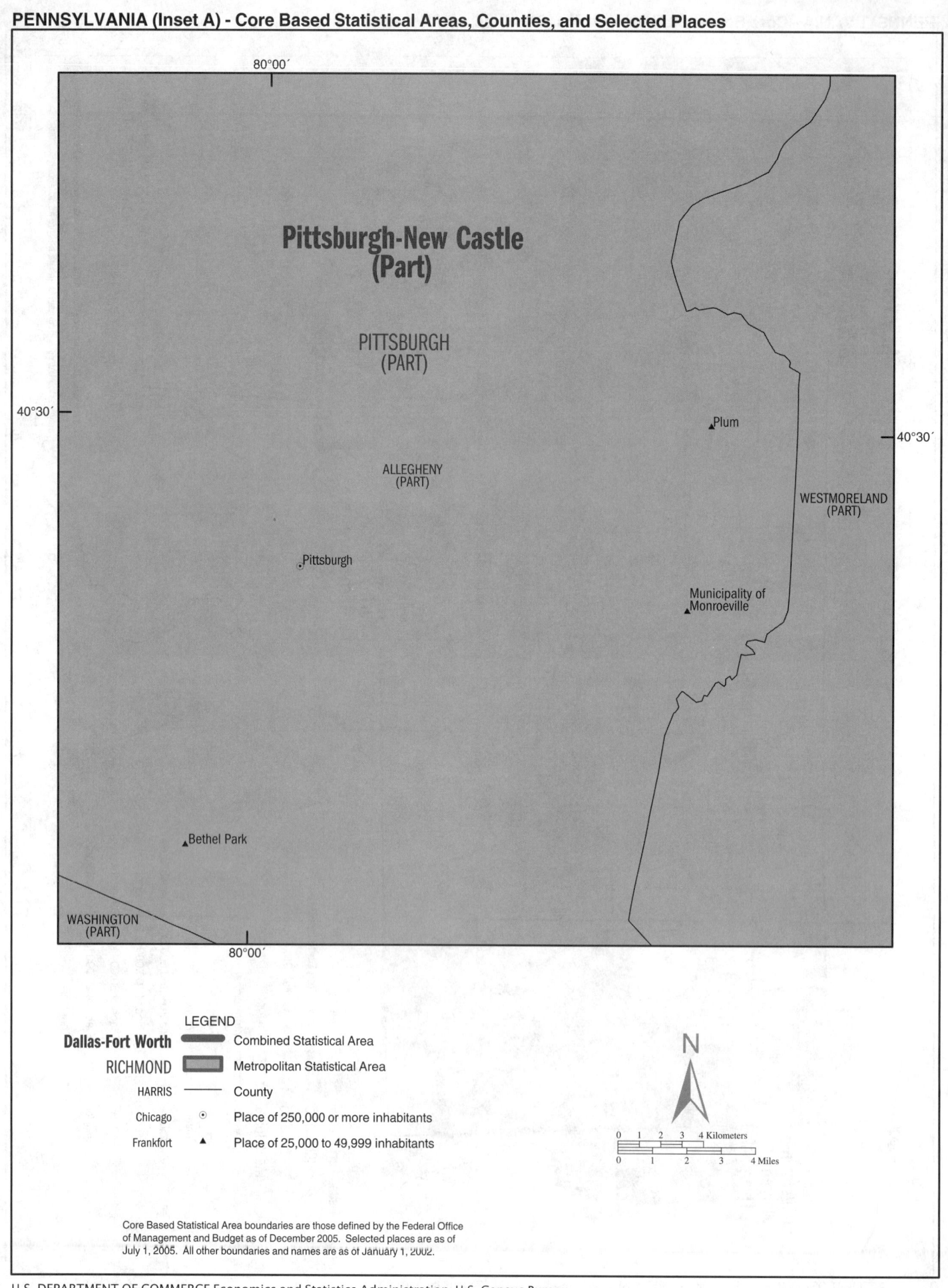

80°00′

**Pittsburgh-New Castle
(Part)**

PITTSBURGH
(PART)

40°30′

Plum

40°30′

ALLEGHENY
(PART)

WESTMORELAND
(PART)

Pittsburgh

Municipality of
Monroeville

Bethel Park

WASHINGTON
(PART)

80°00′

LEGEND

Dallas-Fort Worth ▬▬▬ Combined Statistical Area

RICHMOND ▭ Metropolitan Statistical Area

HARRIS ── County

Chicago ⊙ Place of 250,000 or more inhabitants

Frankfort ▲ Place of 25,000 to 49,999 inhabitants

N

0 1 2 3 4 Kilometers

0 1 2 3 4 Miles

Core Based Statistical Area boundaries are those defined by the Federal Office
of Management and Budget as of December 2005. Selected places are as of
July 1, 2005. All other boundaries and names are as of January 1, 2002.

BUCKS
(PART)

40°00´

75°00´

BURLINGTON
(PART)

PHILADELPHIA-
CAMDEN-
WILMINGTON
(PART)

75°00´

CAMDEN
(PART)

PENNSYLVANIA
NEW JERSEY

·Camden

⊙Philadelphia

**Philadelphia-
Camden-
Vineland (Part)**

PHILADELPHIA
(PART)

Philadelphia
(Part)

MONTGOMERY
(PART)

DELAWARE
(PART)

CHESTER
(PART)

40°00´

N

3 Kilometers
3 Miles

Core Based Statistical Area boundaries are those defined by the Federal Office of Management and Budget as of December 2005. Selected places are as of July 1, 2005. All other boundaries and names are as of January 1, 2002.

LEGEND

Dallas-Fort Worth — Combined Statistical Area

RICHMOND — Metropolitan Statistical Area

Philadelphia ••••• Metropolitan Division

TEXAS — State

HARRIS — County

Chicago ⊙ Place of 250,000 or more inhabitants

Provo • Place of 50,000 to 99,999 inhabitants

U.S. DEPARTMENT OF COMMERCE Economics and Statistics Administration U.S. Census Bureau

71°

42°   42°

MASSACHUSETTS

▲ Woonsocket

▲ Attleboro

● Taunton

PROVIDENCE

Pawtucket ●

Boston-Worcester-Manchester (Part)

PROVIDENCE-NEW BEDFORD-FALL RIVER

■ Providence

East Providence ▲

BRISTOL

● Cranston

BRISTOL

● Fall River

Warwick ●

CONNECTICUT

New Bedford ●

KENT

WASHINGTON

Newport
▲

NEWPORT

N

| 0 | 2 | 4 | 6 | 8 | 10 Kilometers |
| 0 | 2 | 4 | 6 | 8 | 10 Miles |

LEGEND

Dallas-Fort Worth ▬▬▬ Combined Statistical Area

RICHMOND ▬▬▬ Metropolitan Statistical Area

TEXAS ———— State

HARRIS ———— County

Eugene ■ Place of 100,000 to 249,999 inhabitants

Provo ● Place of 50,000 to 99,999 inhabitants

Frankfort ▲ Place of 25,000 to 49,999 inhabitants

〜〜〜 Shoreline

Core Based Statistical Area boundaries are those defined by the Federal Office of Management and Budget as of December 2005. Selected places are as of July 1, 2005. All other boundaries and names are as of January 1, 2002.

41°   41°

71°

NORTH CAROLINA

N

40 Miles

40 Kilometers
0 8 16 24 32 40
0 8 16 24 32

Charlotte-Gastonia-Salisbury (Part)

CHARLOTTE-GASTONIA-CONCORD

Bennettsville

MYRTLE BEACH-CONWAY-NORTH MYRTLE BEACH

Myrtle Beach-Conway-Georgetown

LEGEND

	Combined Statistical Area
	Metropolitan Statistical Area
	Micropolitan Statistical Area
	State
	County
⊙	Place of 250,000 or more inhabitants
■	Place of 100,000 to 249,999 inhabitants
●	Place of 50,000 to 99,999 inhabitants
▲	Place of 25,000 to 49,999 inhabitants
	Shoreline

Dallas-Fort Worth
RICHMOND
Concord

TEXAS
HARRIS

Chicago
Eugene
Provo
Frankfort

HORRY

DILLON
Dillon

MARION

MARLBORO

GEORGETOWN
Georgetown

CHESTERFIELD

DARLINGTON

Florence
FLORENCE

WILLIAMSBURG

Mount Pleasant
Charleston

CHARLESTON-NORTH CHARLESTON

BERKELEY
Goose Creek

LEE

Sumter
SUMTER

CLARENDON

Summer-ville
North Charleston

DORCHESTER

Kannapolis
Concord
CABARRUS

UNION
Monroe

ANSON

MECKLENBURG
Charlotte

LANCASTER
Lancaster

KERSHAW

RICHLAND
Columbia
COLUMBIA

CALHOUN

ORANGEBURG
Orangeburg

Walterboro

COLLETON

Hilton Head Island-Beaufort

BEAUFORT

Hilton Head Island

Gastonia
GASTON

YORK
Rock Hill

CHESTER
Chester

FAIRFIELD

LEXINGTON

Columbia-Newberry

NEWBERRY
Newberry

BAMBERG

JASPER

CHEROKEE
Gaffney

UNION
Union

SPARTANBURG
Spartanburg
SPARTAN-BURG

LAURENS

GREEN-VILLE

Green-wood
GREENWOOD

SALUDA

AIKEN
Aiken

Augusta-Richmond County

EDGEFIELD

BARNWELL

ALLENDALE

HAMPTON

GEORGIA

Greenville-Spartanburg-Anderson

GREENVILLE
Green-ville

PICKENS

ANDERSON
Anderson

ABBEVILLE

McCORMICK

COLUMBIA

McDUFFIE

RICHMOND

BURKE

AUGUSTA-RICHMOND COUNTY

OCONEE
Seneca

Core Based Statistical Area boundaries are those defined by the Federal Office of Management and Budget as of December 2005. Selected places are as of July 1, 2005. All other boundaries and names are as of January 1, 2002.

SOUTH DAKOTA - Core Based Statistical Areas, Counties, and Selected Places

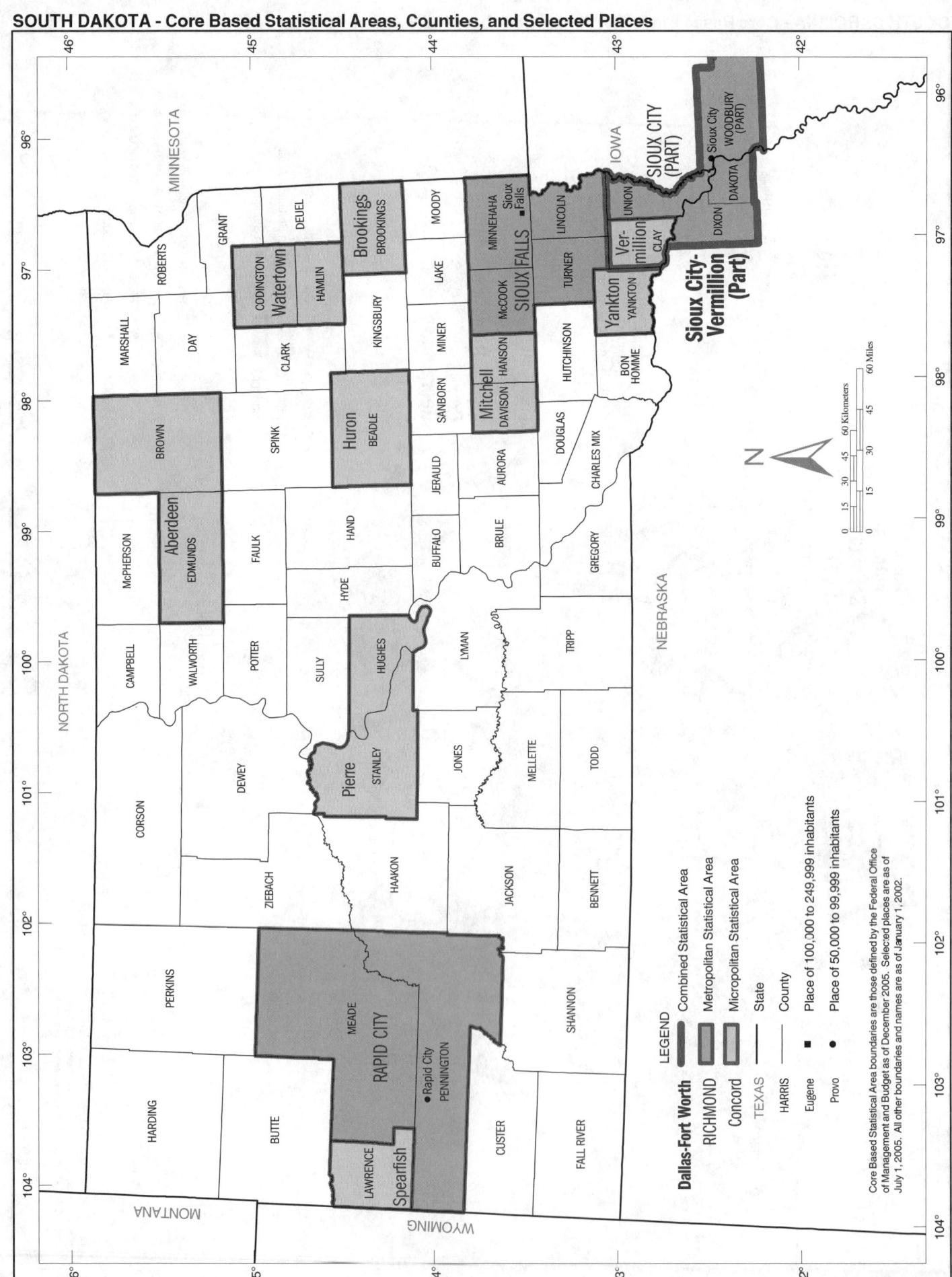

TENNESSEE - Core Based Statistical Areas, Counties, Independent City, and Selected Places

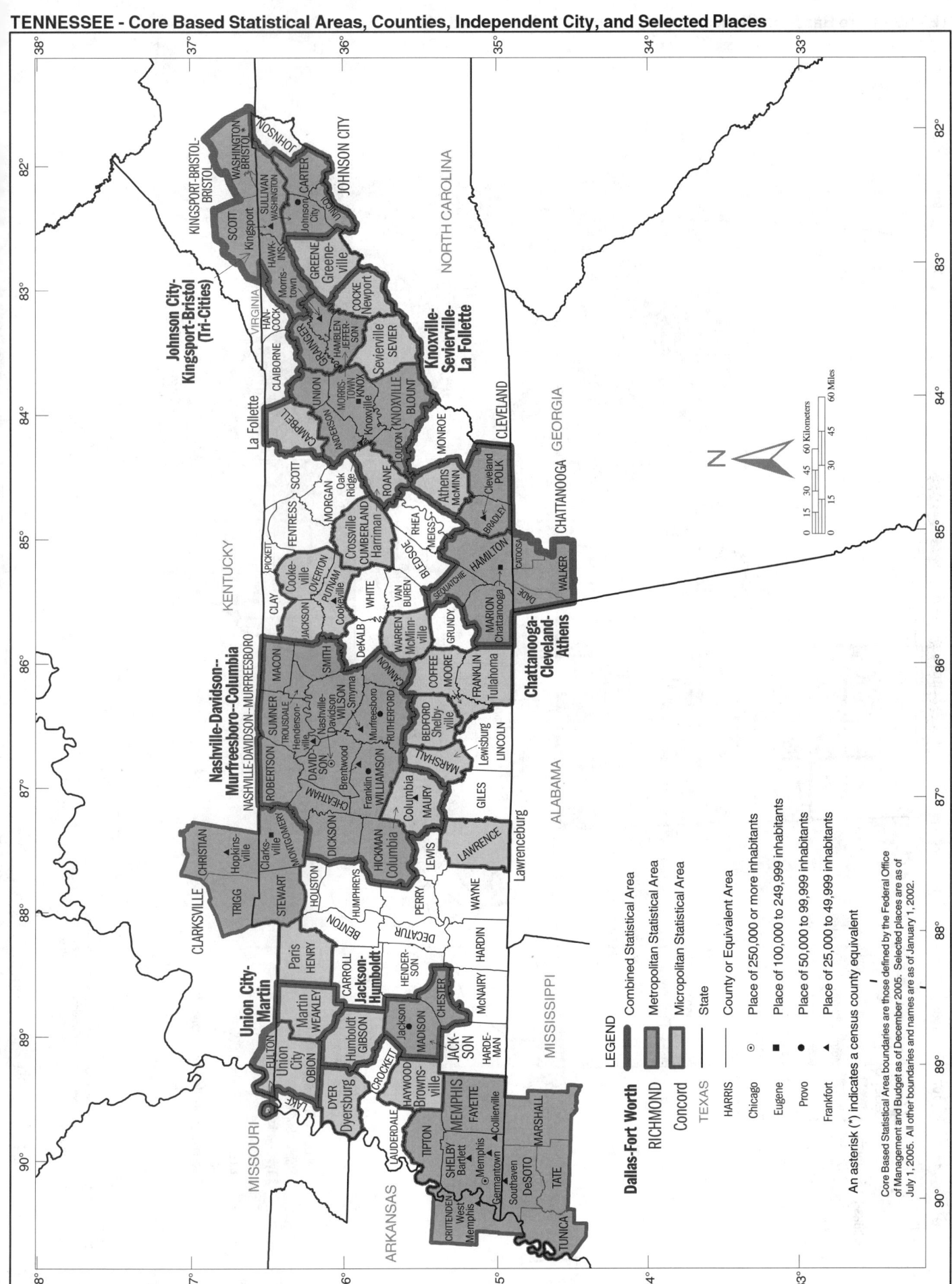

LEGEND

Dallas-Fort Worth Combined Statistical Area

RICHMOND Metropolitan Statistical Area

Concord Micropolitan Statistical Area

— State

— County or Equivalent Area

HARRIS

Chicago ⊙ Place of 250,000 or more inhabitants

Eugene ■ Place of 100,000 to 249,999 inhabitants

Provo ● Place of 50,000 to 99,999 inhabitants

Frankfort ◀ Place of 25,000 to 49,999 inhabitants

An asterisk (*) indicates a census county equivalent

Core Based Statistical Area boundaries are those defined by the Federal Office of Management and Budget as of December 2005. Selected places are as of July 1, 2005. All other boundaries and names are as of January 1, 2002.

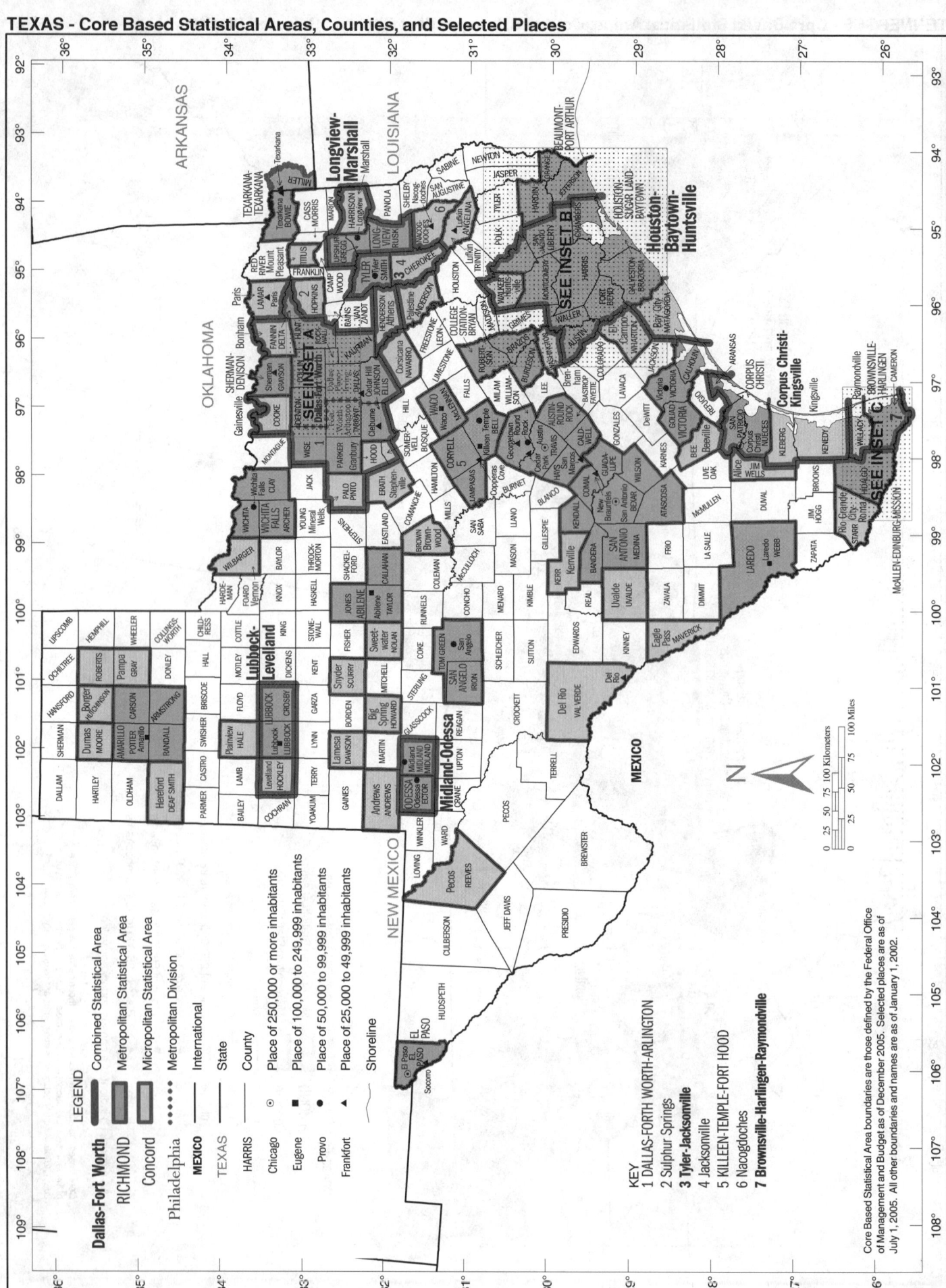

LEGEND

Dallas-Forth Worth — Combined Statistical Area
RICHMOND — Metropolitan Statistical Area
Concord — Micropolitan Statistical Area
Philadelphia •••••• — Metropolitan Division
— International
MEXICO — State
HARRIS — County
Chicago ⊙ — Place of 250,000 or more inhabitants
Eugene ■ — Place of 100,000 to 249,999 inhabitants
Provo ● — Place of 50,000 to 99,999 inhabitants
Frankfort ▲ — Place of 25,000 to 49,999 inhabitants
— Shoreline

KEY
1 DALLAS-FORTH WORTH-ARLINGTON
2 Sulphur Springs
3 Tyler-Jacksonville
4 Jacksonville
5 KILLEEN-TEMPLE-FORT HOOD
6 Nacogdoches
7 Brownsville-Harlingen-Raymondville

Core Based Statistical Area boundaries are those defined by the Federal Office of Management and Budget as of December 2005. Selected places are as of July 1, 2005. All other boundaries and names are as of January 1, 2002.

33°00´

96°00´

DELTA (PART)

HOPKINS (PART)

Sulphur Springs (Part)

RAINS (PART)

VAN ZANDT (PART)

FANNIN (PART)

Bonham (Part)

HUNT

96°00´

SHERMAN-DENISON (PART)

DALLAS-FORT WORTH-ARLINGTON (PART)

96°30´

Garland

Dallas

ROCKWALL

KAUFMAN (PART)

GRAYSON (PART)

McKinney

COLLIN

Allen

Plano

Richardson

Rowlett

Mesquite

Frisco

Gainesville (Part)

97°00´

The Colony

Lewisville

Carrollton

Coppell

Farmers Branch

DALLAS (PART)

Irving

Dallas-Plano-Irving (Part)

Lancaster

Duncanville

DeSoto

Grand Prairie

Denton

Flower Mound

DENTON

Dallas-Fort Worth (Part)

Keller

Grapevine

North Richland Hills

Hurst

Euless

Bedford

Haltom City

Arlington

Mansfield

Fort Worth

TARRANT (PART)

COOKE (PART)

MONTAGUE (PART)

97°30´

WISE (PART)

Fort Worth-Arlington (Part)

33°00´

96°30´

97°00´

97°30´

LEGEND

Place of 100,000 to 249,999 inhabitants		
Place of 50,000 to 99,999 inhabitants		
Place of 25,000 to 49,999 inhabitants		

Eugene

Provo

Frankfort

Core Based Statistical Area boundaries are those defined by the Federal Office of Management and Budget as of December 2005. Selected places are as of July 1, 2005. All other boundaries and names are as of January 1, 2002.

Dallas-Fort Worth   Combined Statistical Area

RICHMOND   Metropolitan Statistical Area

Concord   Micropolitan Statistical Area

Philadelphia   Metropolitan Division

HARRIS   County

Chicago   Place of 250,000 or more inhabitants

Core Based Statistical Area boundaries are those defined by the Federal Office of Management and Budget as of December 2005. Selected places are as of July 1, 2005. All other boundaries and names are as of January 1, 2002.

LOUISIANA
TEXAS

NEWTON (PART)
JASPER (PART)
ORANGE
BEAUMONT-PORT ARTHUR
JEFFERSON
Port Arthur
Beaumont
HARDIN
TYLER (PART)
CHAMBERS
LIBERTY
POLK (PART)
SAN JACINTO
Baytown
HOUSTON-SUGAR LAND-BAYTOWN
Pasadena
La Porte
Deer Park
League City
Texas City
Galveston
HARRIS
Houston
TRINITY (PART)
Conroe
MONTGOMERY
Houston-Baytown-Huntsville (Part)
Pearland
Friendswood
BRAZORIA
Lake Jackson
Huntsville (Part)
Huntsville
WALKER (PART)
HOUSTON (PART)
Sugar Land
Missouri City
FORT BEND
MADISON (PART)
GRIMES
WALLER
Bay City (Part)
MATAGORDA (PART)
COLLEGE STATION-BRYAN (PART)
LEON (PART)
AUSTIN
El Campo
WHARTON
Bryan
College Station
BRAZOS
ROBERTSON (PART)
BURLESON (PART)
Brenham (Part)
WASHINGTON (PART)
COLORADO (PART)
JACKSON (PART)
FAYETTE (PART)
LAVACA (PART)

LEGEND

Dallas-Fort Worth	Combined Statistical Area
RICHMOND	Metropolitan Statistical Area
Concord	Micropolitan Statistical Area
HARRIS	County
Chicago ⊙	Place of 250,000 or more inhabitants
Eugene ■	Place of 100,000 to 249,999 inhabitants
Provo ●	Place of 50,000 to 99,999 inhabitants
Frankfort ▲	Place of 25,000 to 49,999 inhabitants
	Shoreline

26°30' 26°00'

Kingsville (Part)

Brownsville-
Harlingen-
Raymondville

CAMERON

BROWNSVILLE-
HARLINGEN

Brownsville

97°30'

WILLACY
(PART)

Raymondville

WILLACY

Harlingen

MEXICO

98°00'

Weslaco

Corpus Christi-
Kingsville
(Part)

HIDALGO
(PART)

San Juan

Edinburg

McALLEN-EDINBURG-MISSION
(PART)

McAllen

Pharr

Mission

98°30'

Rio Grande
City-
Roma
(Part)

STARR
(PART)

26°30' 26°00'

N

15 Kilometers 15 Miles
10
5
0   0

Core Based Statistical Area boundaries are those defined by the Federal Office
of Management and Budget as of December 2005. Selected places are as of
July 1, 2005. All other boundaries and names are as of January 1, 2002.

LEGEND

Dallas-Fort Worth   Combined Statistical Area

RICHMOND   Metropolitan Statistical Area

Concord   Micropolitan Statistical Area

MEXICO   International

HARRIS   County

Eugene   ■   Place of 100,000 to 249,999 inhabitants

Provo   ●   Place of 50,000 to 99,999 inhabitants

Frankfort   ▲   Place of 25,000 to 49,999 inhabitants

Shoreline

UTAH - Core Based Statistical Areas, Counties, and Selected Places

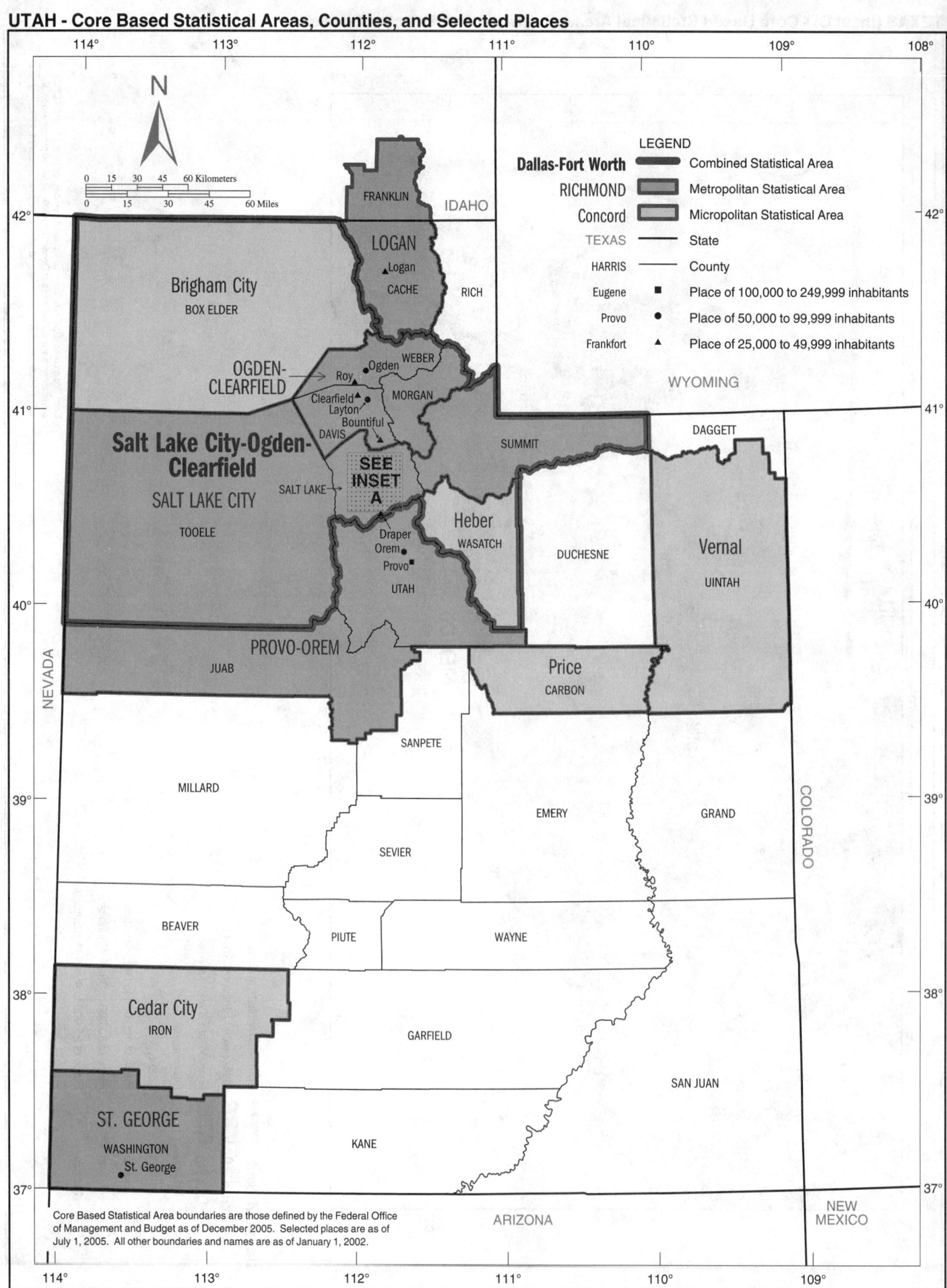

LEGEND

Dallas-Fort Worth — Combined Statistical Area
RICHMOND — Metropolitan Statistical Area
Concord — Micropolitan Statistical Area
TEXAS — State
HARRIS — County
Eugene ■ Place of 100,000 to 249,999 inhabitants
Provo ● Place of 50,000 to 99,999 inhabitants
Frankfort ▲ Place of 25,000 to 49,999 inhabitants

Core Based Statistical Area boundaries are those defined by the Federal Office of Management and Budget as of December 2005. Selected places are as of July 1, 2005. All other boundaries and names are as of January 1, 2002.

U.S. DEPARTMENT OF COMMERCE Economics and Statistics Administration U.S. Census Bureau

County and City Data Book: 2007

U.S. Census Bureau

112°00´

.Salt Lake City

Salt Lake City-
Ogden-Clearfield
(Part)

.West Valley City

SALT LAKE CITY
(PART)

● Taylorsville   ▲Murray

SALT LAKE
(PART)

▲Midvale

.West Jordan

.Sandy

▲South Jordan

.Riverton

UTAH
(PART)   PROVO-OREM
(PART)

112°00´

LEGEND

Dallas-Fort Worth   Combined Statistical Area

RICHMOND   Metropolitan Statistical Area

HARRIS   County

Eugene   ■   Place of 100,000 to 249,999 inhabitants

Provo   ●   Place of 50,000 to 99,999 inhabitants

Frankfort   ▲   Place of 25,000 to 49,999 inhabitants

N

0 1 2 3 Kilometers
0 1 2 3 Miles

Core Based Statistical Area boundaries are those defined by the Federal Office
of Management and Budget as of December 2005. Selected places are as of
July 1, 2005. All other boundaries and names are as of January 1, 2002.

73°
72°
71°

45°
45°

CANADA

GRAND
ISLE

**BURLINGTON-
SOUTH
BURLINGTON**

ORLEANS

Berlin

FRANKLIN

ESSEX

COOS

LAMOILLE

▲Burlington

CALEDONIA

CHITTENDEN

MAINE

Barre

WASHINGTON

Lebanon

44°
44°

ADDISON

ORANGE

GRAFTON

**Claremont-
Lebanon**

Rutland

N

0 5 10 15 20 Kilometers
0 5   10   15   20 Miles

RUTLAND

WINDSOR

NEW YORK

Claremont

SULLIVAN

Bennington

LEGEND

Dallas-Fort Worth ▬▬▬ Combined Statistical Area

BENNINGTON

RICHMOND � Metropolitan Statistical Area

Concord ▭ Micropolitan Statistical Area

NEW HAMPSHIRE

CANADA ——— International

WINDHAM

43°
43°

TEXAS ——— State

HARRIS ——— County

Frankfort ▲ Place of 25,000 to 49,999 inhabitants

Core Based Statistical Area boundaries are those defined by the Federal Office
of Management and Budget as of December 2005. Selected places are as of
July 1, 2005. All other boundaries and names are as of January 1, 2002.

MASSACHUSETTS

73°
72°
71°

U.S. DEPARTMENT OF COMMERCE Economics and Statistics Administration U.S. Census Bureau

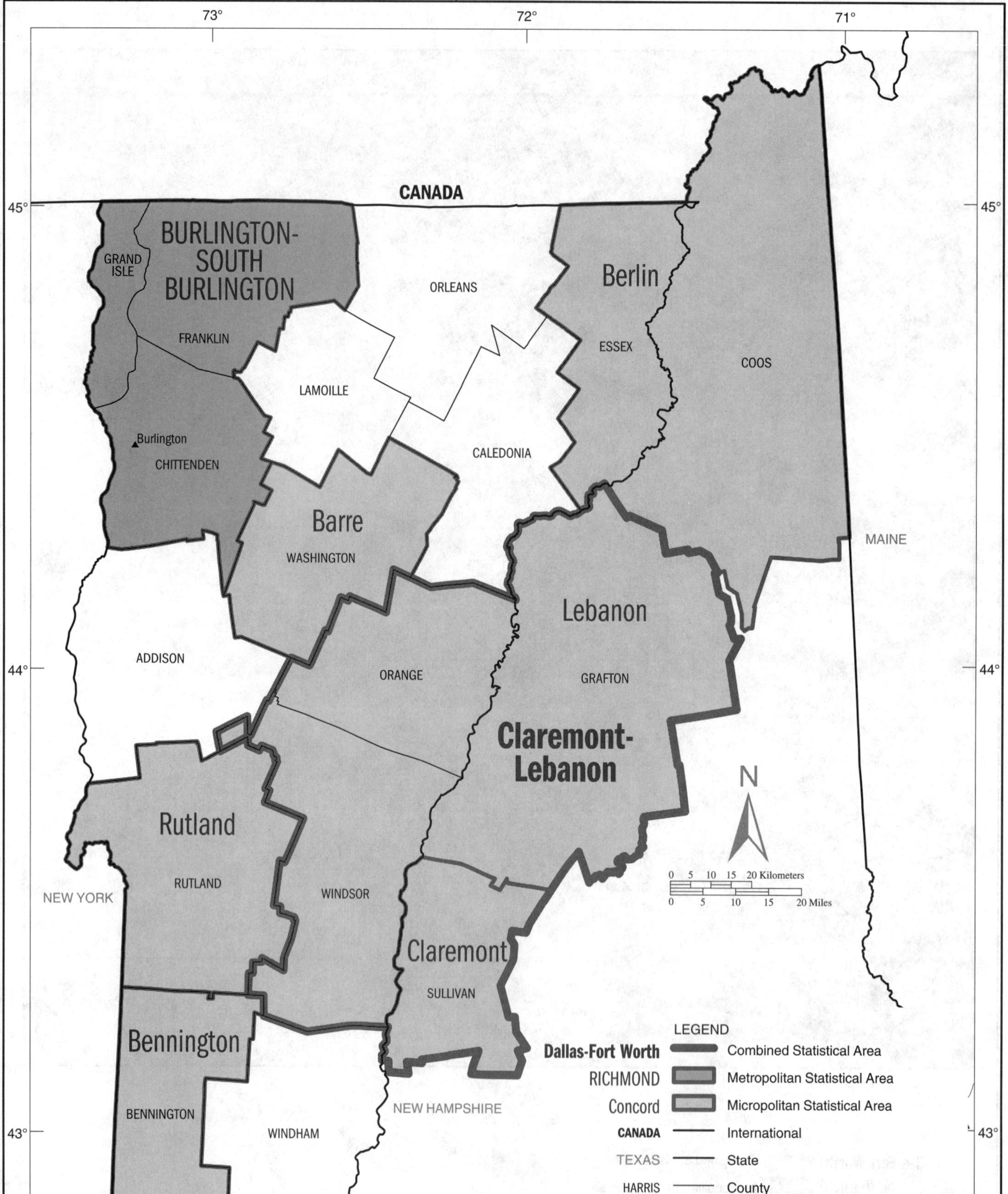

VIRGINIA - Core Based Statistical Areas, District of Columbia, Counties, Independent Cities, and Selected Places

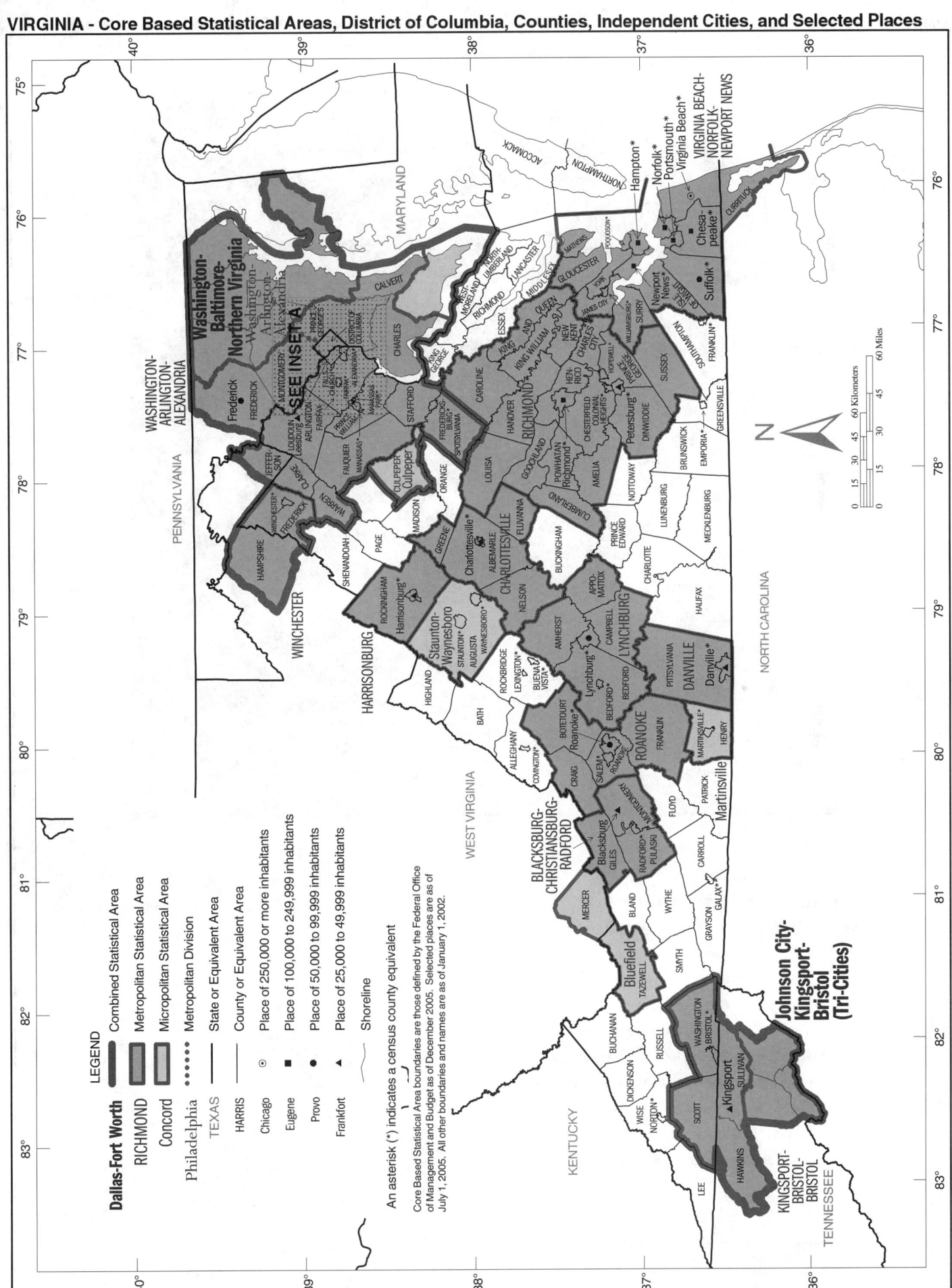

LEGEND

Dallas-Fort Worth Combined Statistical Area
RICHMOND Metropolitan Statistical Area
Concord Micropolitan Statistical Area
Philadelphia Metropolitan Division
TEXAS State or Equivalent Area
HARRIS County or Equivalent Area
Chicago ⊙ Place of 250,000 or more inhabitants
Eugene ■ Place of 100,000 to 249,999 inhabitants
Provo ● Place of 50,000 to 99,999 inhabitants
Frankfort ◄ Place of 25,000 to 49,999 inhabitants
••••• Shoreline

An asterisk (*) indicates a census county equivalent

Core Based Statistical Area boundaries are those defined by the Federal Office of Management and Budget as of December 2005. Selected places are as of July 1, 2005. All other boundaries and names are as of January 1, 2002.

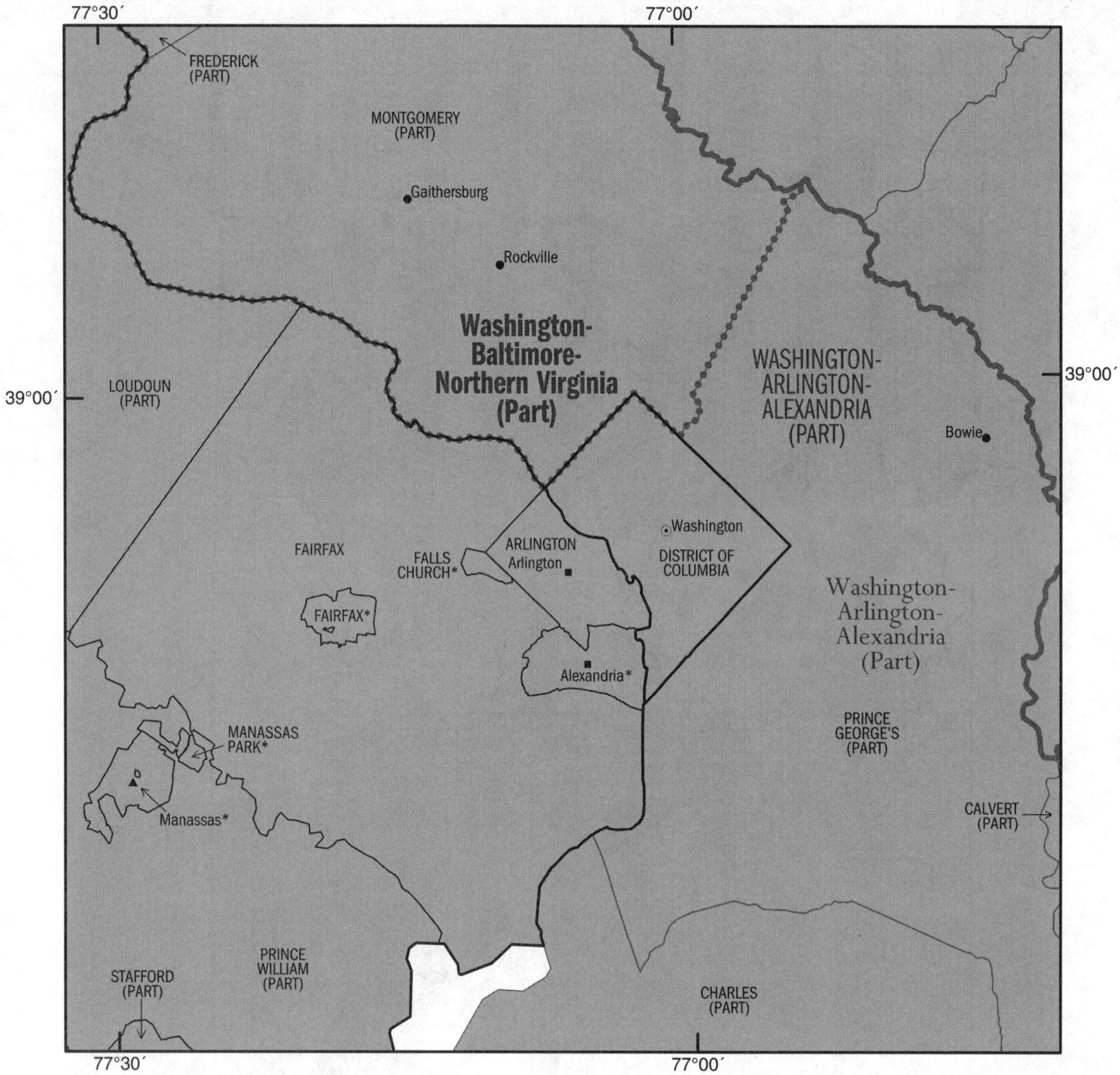

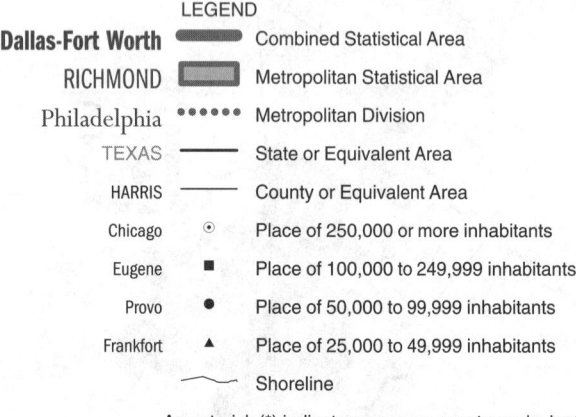

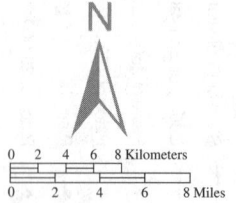

FREDERICK
(PART)

MONTGOMERY
(PART)

Gaithersburg

Rockville

**Washington-
Baltimore-
Northern Virginia
(Part)**

WASHINGTON-
ARLINGTON-
ALEXANDRIA
(PART)

39°00′

LOUDOUN
(PART)

39°00′

Bowie

FAIRFAX

FALLS
CHURCH*

ARLINGTON
Arlington

Washington

DISTRICT OF
COLUMBIA

Washington-
Arlington-
Alexandria
(Part)

FAIRFAX*

Alexandria*

PRINCE
GEORGE'S
(PART)

MANASSAS
PARK*

CALVERT
(PART)

Manassas*

STAFFORD
(PART)

PRINCE
WILLIAM
(PART)

CHARLES
(PART)

77°30′

77°00′

77°30′

77°00′

LEGEND

Dallas-Fort Worth	Combined Statistical Area
RICHMOND	Metropolitan Statistical Area
Philadelphia	Metropolitan Division
TEXAS	State or Equivalent Area
HARRIS	County or Equivalent Area
Chicago ⊙	Place of 250,000 or more inhabitants
Eugene ■	Place of 100,000 to 249,999 inhabitants
Provo ●	Place of 50,000 to 99,999 inhabitants
Frankfort ▲	Place of 25,000 to 49,999 inhabitants
	Shoreline

An asterisk (*) indicates a census county equivalent

N

0 2 4 6 8 Kilometers

0 2 4 6 8 Miles

Core Based Statistical Area boundaries are those defined by the Federal Office
of Management and Budget as of December 2005. Selected places are as of
July 1, 2005. All other boundaries and names are as of January 1, 2002.

WASHINGTON - Core Based Statistical Areas, Counties, and Selected Places

LEGEND

- Combined Statistical Area — Dallas-Fort Worth
- Metropolitan Statistical Area — RICHMOND
- Micropolitan Statistical Area — Concord
- Metropolitan Division — Philadelphia
- International — CANADA
- State — TEXAS
- County — HARRIS
- ⊙ Place of 250,000 or more inhabitants — Chicago
- ■ Place of 100,000 to 249,999 inhabitants — Eugene
- ● Place of 50,000 to 99,999 inhabitants — Provo
- ▲ Place of 25,000 to 49,999 inhabitants — Frankfort
- Shoreline

Core Based Statistical Area boundaries are those defined by the Federal Office of Management and Budget as of December 2005. Selected places are as of July 1, 2005. All other boundaries and names are as of January 1, 2002.

U.S. DEPARTMENT OF COMMERCE Economics and Statistics Administration U.S. Census Bureau

County and City Data Book: 2007

U.S. Census Bureau

D–77

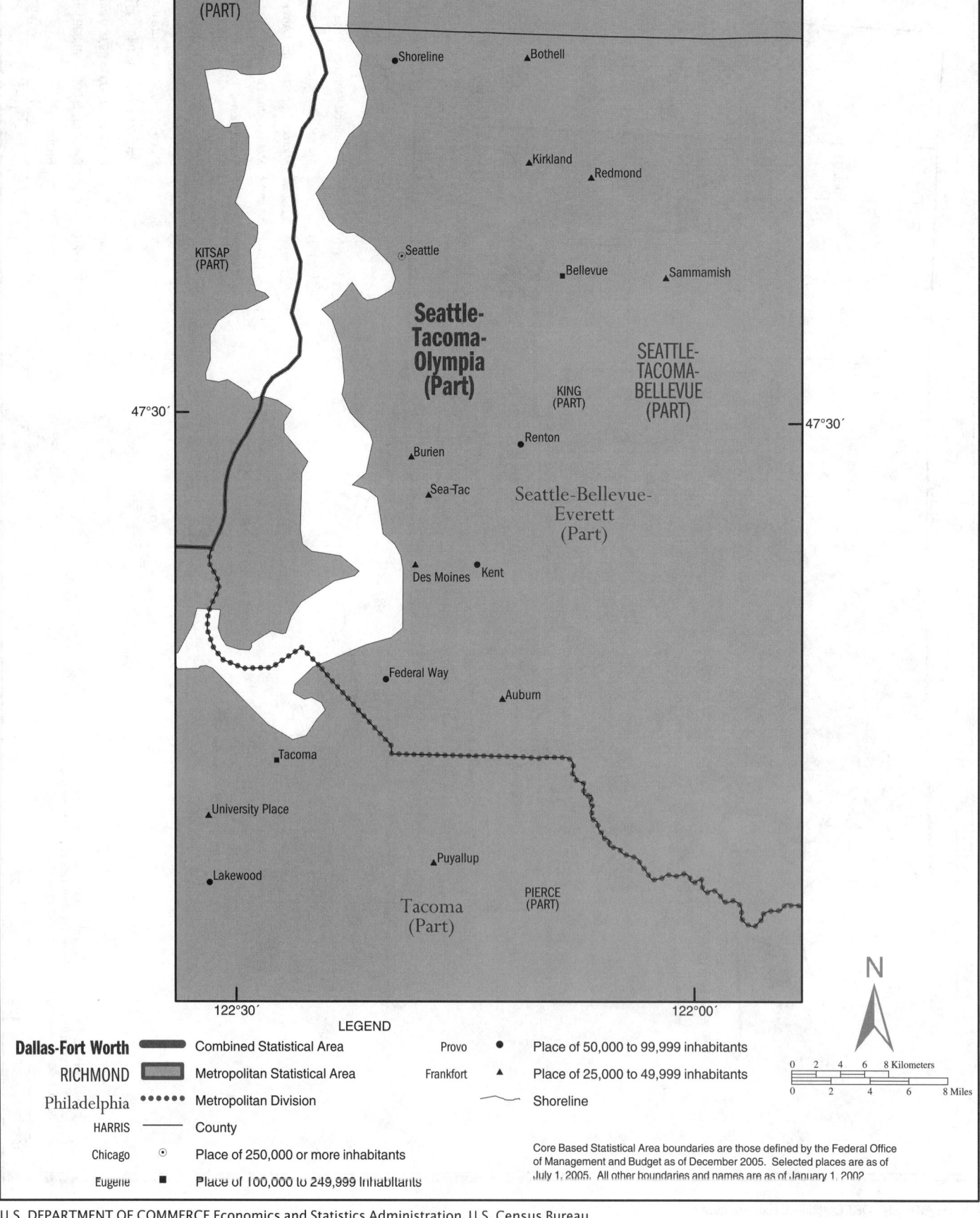

LEGEND

Dallas-Fort Worth	Combined Statistical Area	Provo ●	Place of 50,000 to 99,999 inhabitants	
RICHMOND	Metropolitan Statistical Area	Frankfort ▲	Place of 25,000 to 49,999 inhabitants	
Philadelphia	Metropolitan Division		Shoreline	
HARRIS	County			
Chicago ⊙	Place of 250,000 or more inhabitants			
Eugene ■	Place of 100,000 to 249,999 inhabitants			

Core Based Statistical Area boundaries are those defined by the Federal Office of Management and Budget as of December 2005. Selected places are as of July 1, 2005. All other boundaries and names are as of January 1, 2002.

0 2 4 6 8 Kilometers
0 2 4 6 8 Miles

WEST VIRGINIA - Core Based Statistical Areas, District of Columbia, Counties, Independent Cities, and Selected Places

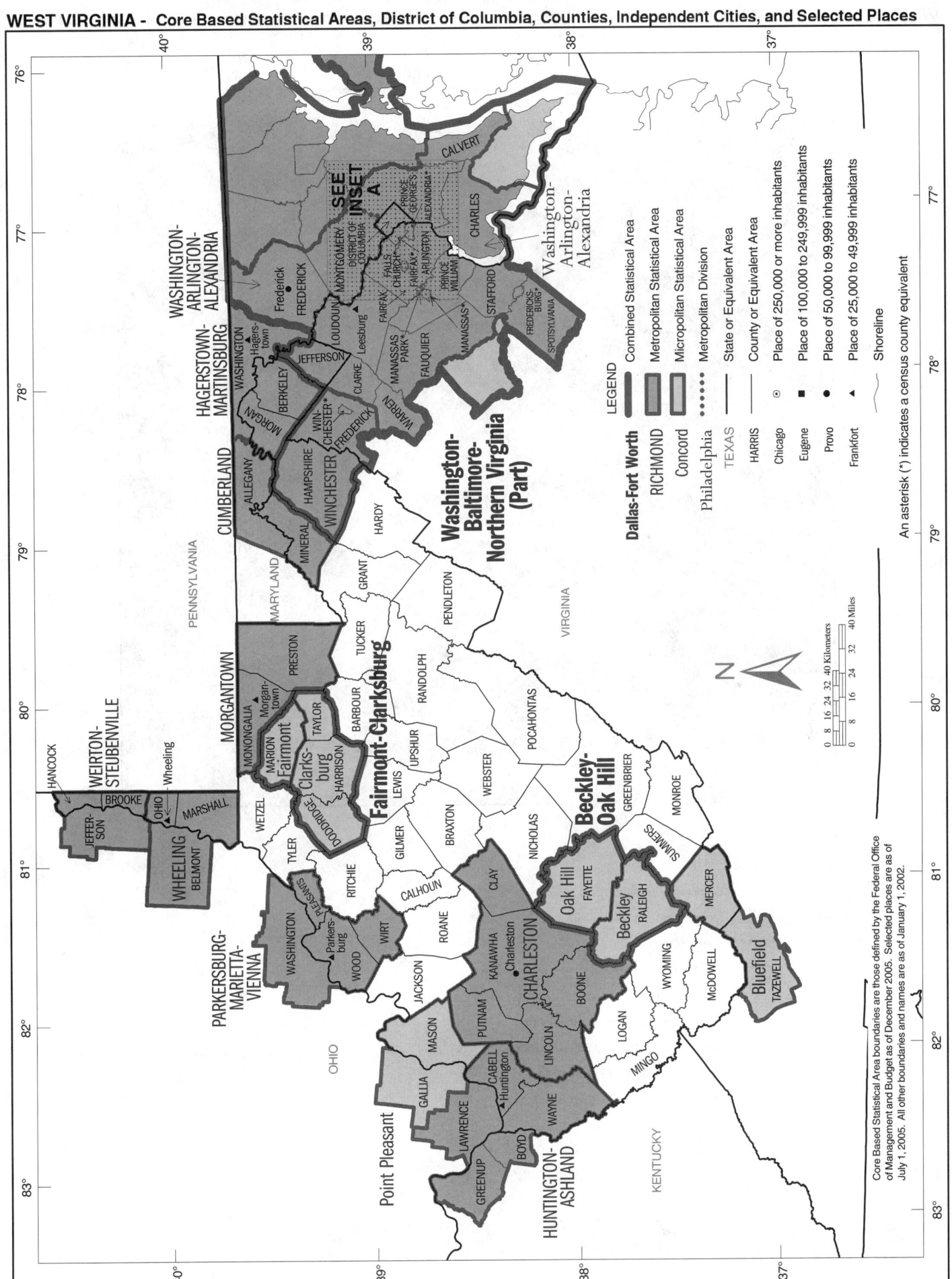

LEGEND

Combined Statistical Area	
Metropolitan Statistical Area	
Micropolitan Statistical Area	
Metropolitan Division	
State or Equivalent Area	
County or Equivalent Area	

Dallas-Fort Worth
RICHMOND
Concord
Philadelphia

TEXAS
HARRIS
Chicago
Eugene
Provo
Frankfort

Place of 250,000 or more inhabitants
Place of 100,000 to 249,999 inhabitants
Place of 50,000 to 99,999 inhabitants
Place of 25,000 to 49,999 inhabitants
Shoreline

An asterisk (*) indicates a census county equivalent

Core Based Statistical Area boundaries are those defined by the Federal Office of Management and Budget as of December 2005. Selected places are as of July 1, 2005. All other boundaries and names are as of January 1, 2002.

0 8 16 24 32 40 Kilometers
0 8 16 24 32 40 Miles

N

Washington-Baltimore-Northern Virginia (Part)

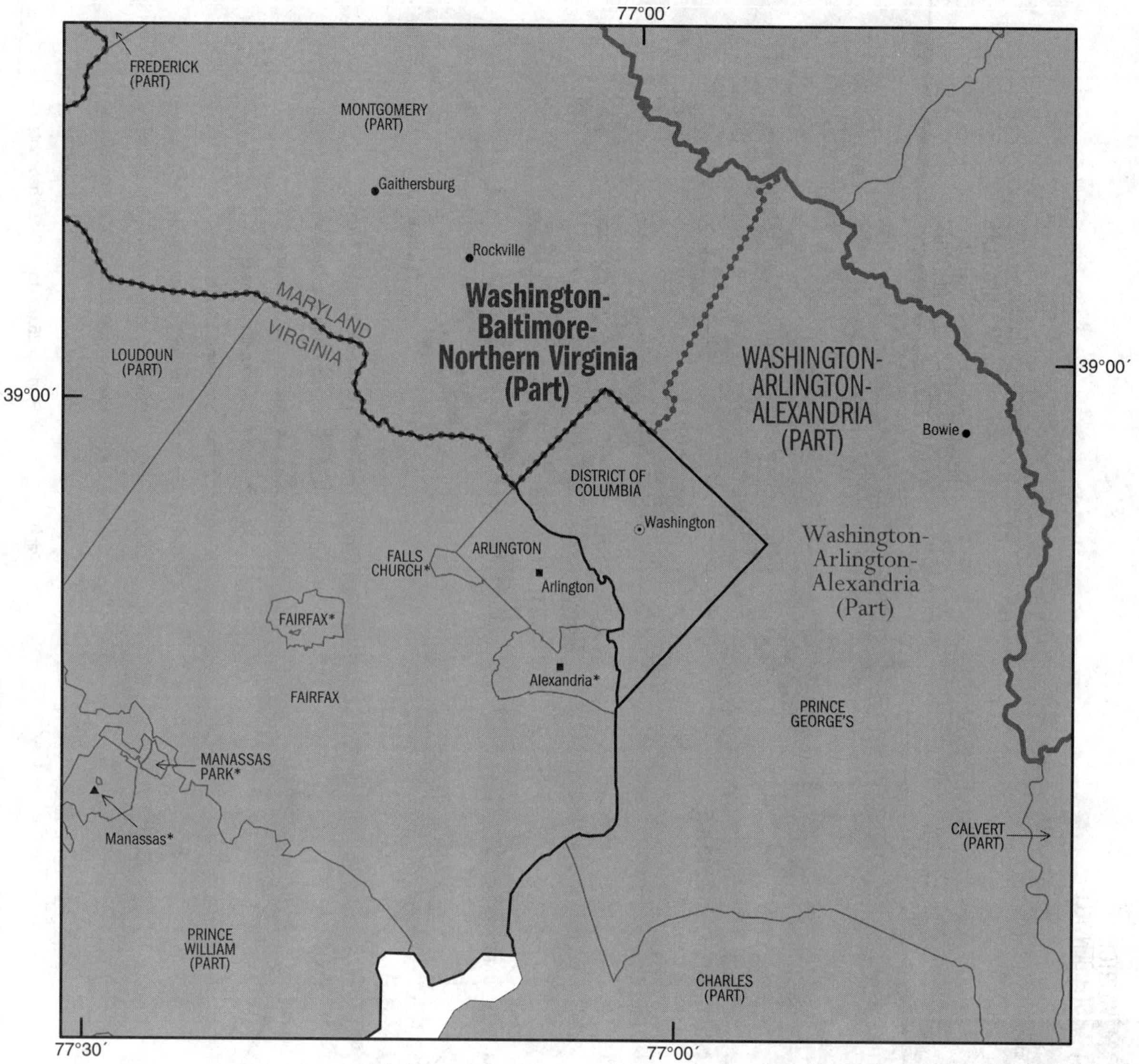

77°00′

FREDERICK
(PART)

MONTGOMERY
(PART)

●Gaithersburg

●Rockville

MARYLAND

VIRGINIA

**Washington-
Baltimore-
Northern Virginia
(Part)**

WASHINGTON-
ARLINGTON-
ALEXANDRIA
(PART)

LOUDOUN
(PART)

39°00′

Bowie ●

39°00′

DISTRICT OF
COLUMBIA

⊙Washington

FALLS
CHURCH*

ARLINGTON

■
Arlington

Washington-
Arlington-
Alexandria
(Part)

FAIRFAX*

FAIRFAX

Alexandria*
■

PRINCE
GEORGE'S

MANASSAS
PARK*

▲
Manassas*

CALVERT
(PART)

PRINCE
WILLIAM
(PART)

CHARLES
(PART)

77°30′

77°00′

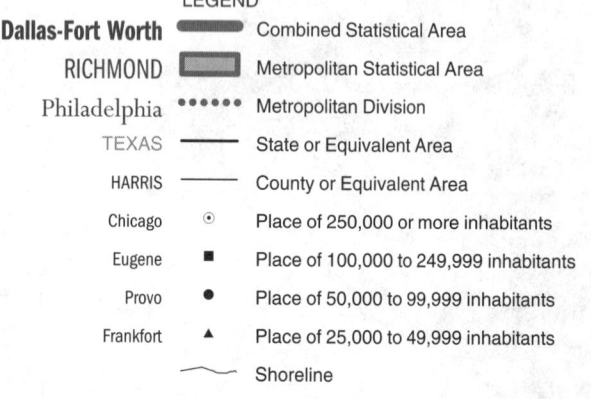

LEGEND

Dallas-Fort Worth	Combined Statistical Area
RICHMOND	Metropolitan Statistical Area
Philadelphia	Metropolitan Division
TEXAS	State or Equivalent Area
HARRIS	County or Equivalent Area
Chicago ⊙	Place of 250,000 or more inhabitants
Eugene ■	Place of 100,000 to 249,999 inhabitants
Provo ●	Place of 50,000 to 99,999 inhabitants
Frankfort ▲	Place of 25,000 to 49,999 inhabitants
	Shoreline

An asterisk (*) indicates a census county equivalent

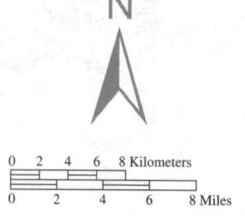

N

0 2 4 6 8 Kilometers

0 2 4 6 8 Miles

Core Based Statistical Area boundaries are those defined by the Federal Office
of Management and Budget as of December 2005. Selected places are as of
July 1, 2005. All other boundaries and names are as of January 1, 2002.

WISCONSIN - Core Based Statistical Areas, Counties, and Selected Places

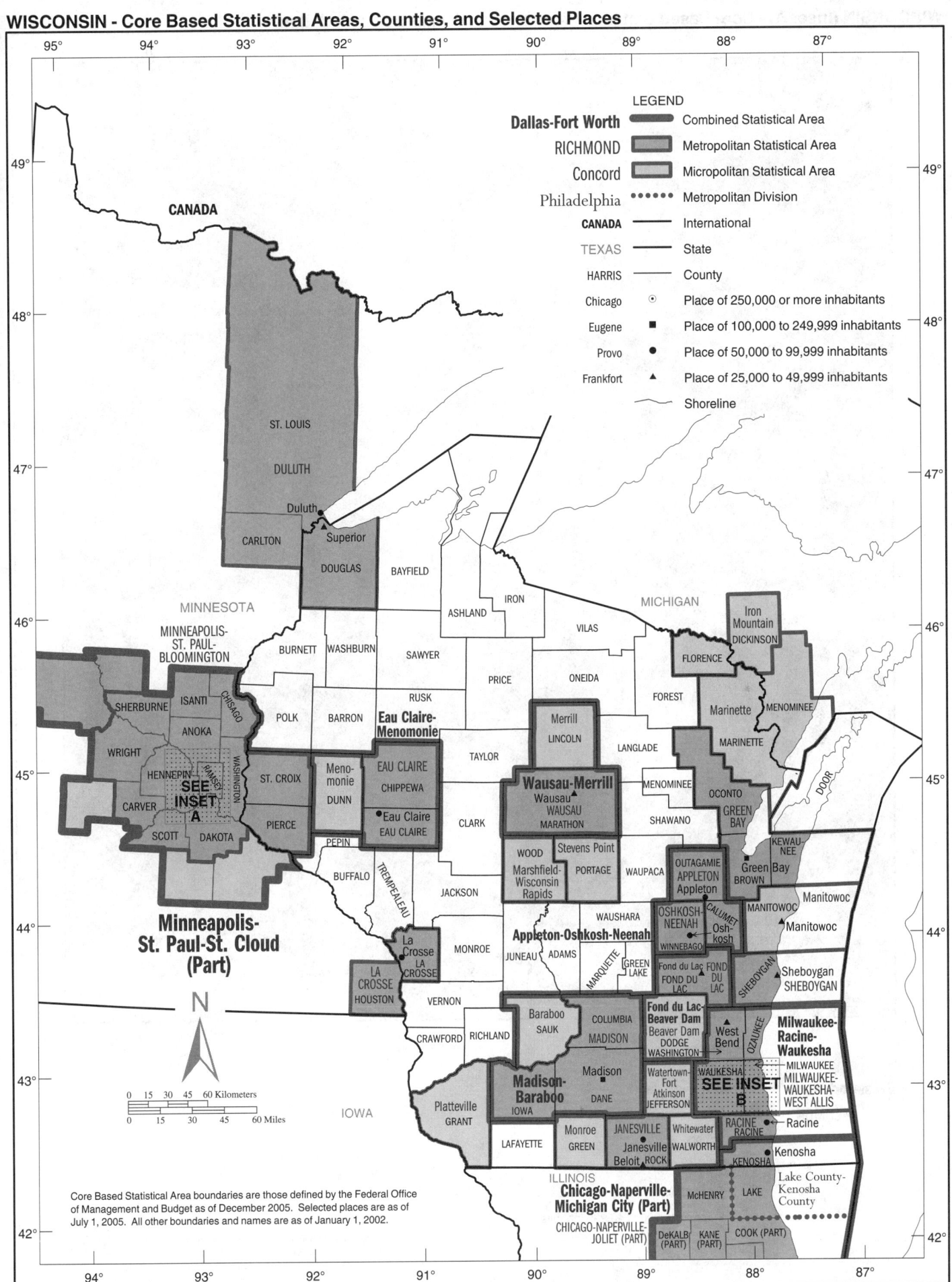

LEGEND

Dallas-Fort Worth — Combined Statistical Area
RICHMOND — Metropolitan Statistical Area
Concord — Micropolitan Statistical Area
Philadelphia ••••• Metropolitan Division
CANADA — International
TEXAS — State
HARRIS — County
Chicago ⊙ Place of 250,000 or more inhabitants
Eugene ■ Place of 100,000 to 249,999 inhabitants
Provo ● Place of 50,000 to 99,999 inhabitants
Frankfort ▲ Place of 25,000 to 49,999 inhabitants
— Shoreline

Core Based Statistical Area boundaries are those defined by the Federal Office of Management and Budget as of December 2005. Selected places are as of July 1, 2005. All other boundaries and names are as of January 1, 2002.

93°30′   93°00′

Coon Rapids

Blaine

ANOKA
(PART)

Maple Grove   Brooklyn Park

**Minneapolis-
St. Paul-
St. Cloud
(Part)**

Fridley   Shoreview

Brooklyn Center

WASHINGTON
(PART)

Plymouth   RAMSEY

45°00′   MINNEAPOLIS-
ST. PAUL-
BLOOMINGTON
(PART)   Roseville   Maplewood   45°00′

HENNEPIN
(PART)   Oakdale

Minneapolis

St. Louis Park   St. Paul

Minnetonka

Edina   Woodbury

Richfield

Eden Prairie   Inver
Grove
Heights

Bloomington   Eagan   Cottage Grove

DAKOTA
(PART)

SCOTT
(PART)   Burnsville

Apple Valley

93°30′   93°00′

N

0 1 2 3 4 5 Kilometers
0 1 2 3 4 5 Miles

Core Based Statistical Area boundaries are those defined by the Federal Office
of Management and Budget as of December 2005. Selected places are as of
July 1, 2005. All other boundaries and names are as of January 1, 2002.

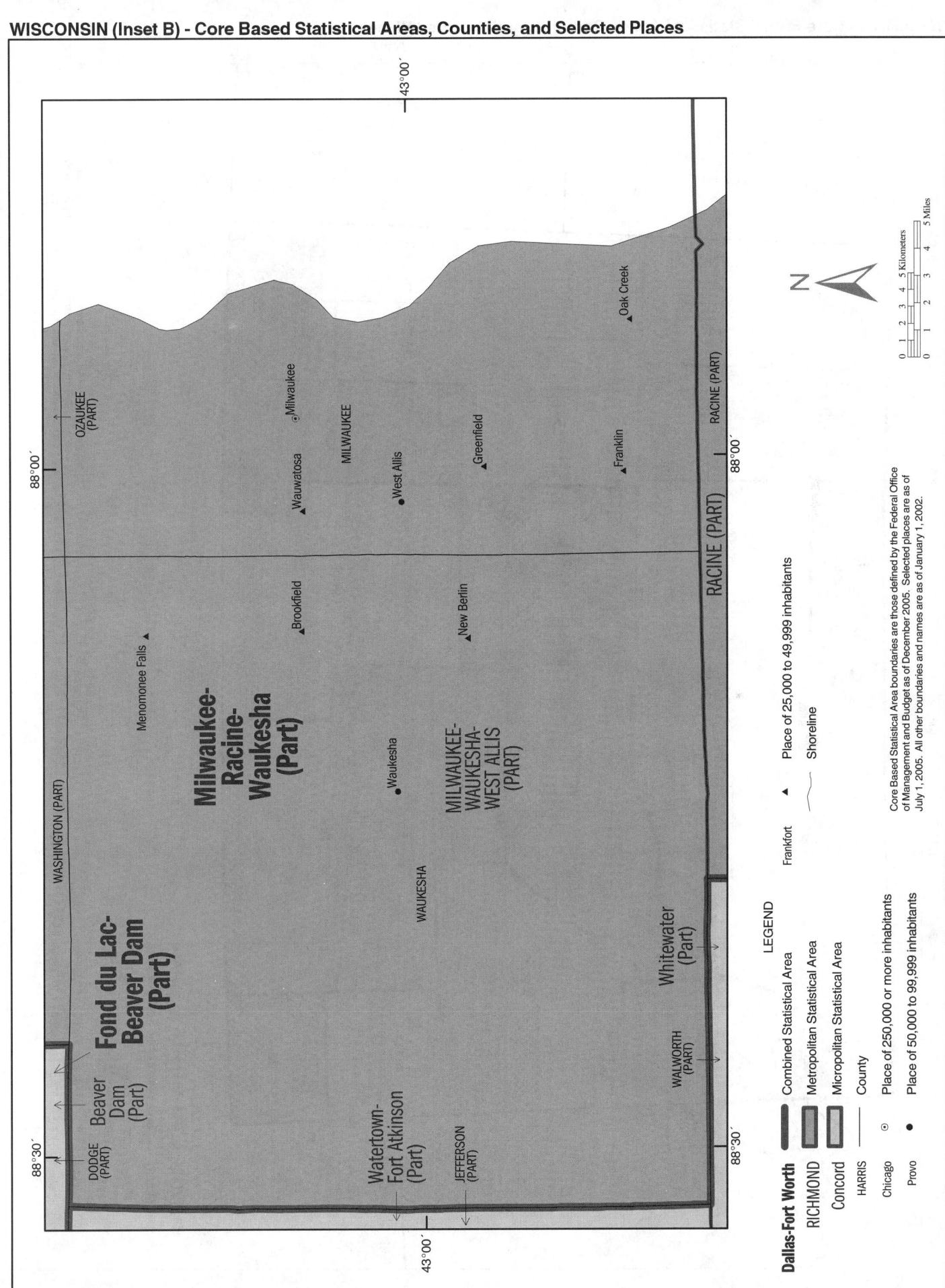

LEGEND

Dallas-Fort Worth	Combined Statistical Area
RICHMOND	Metropolitan Statistical Area
Concord	Micropolitan Statistical Area
HARRIS	County
⊙ Chicago	Place of 250,000 or more inhabitants
● Provo	Place of 50,000 to 99,999 inhabitants
▲ Frankfort	Place of 25,000 to 49,999 inhabitants
Shoreline	

Core Based Statistical Area boundaries are those defined by the Federal Office of Management and Budget as of December 2005. Selected places are as of July 1, 2005. All other boundaries and names are as of January 1, 2002.

Fond du Lac-Beaver Dam (Part)

Beaver Dam (Part)

DODGE (PART)

WASHINGTON (PART)

OZAUKEE (PART)

Milwaukee-Racine-Waukesha (Part)

Menomonee Falls ▲

Brookfield ▲

▲ Wauwatosa

⊙ Milwaukee

MILWAUKEE

● West Allis

Waukesha ●

WAUKESHA

MILWAUKEE-WAUKESHA-WEST ALLIS (PART)

New Berlin ▲

Greenfield ▲

Franklin ▲

▲ Oak Creek

RACINE (PART)

RACINE (PART)

Watertown-Fort Atkinson (Part)

JEFFERSON (PART)

WALWORTH (PART)

Whitewater (Part)

88°30´

88°00´

43°00´

N

0 1 2 3 4 5 Kilometers
0 1 2 3 4 5 Miles

WYOMING - Core Based Statistical Areas, Counties, and Selected Places

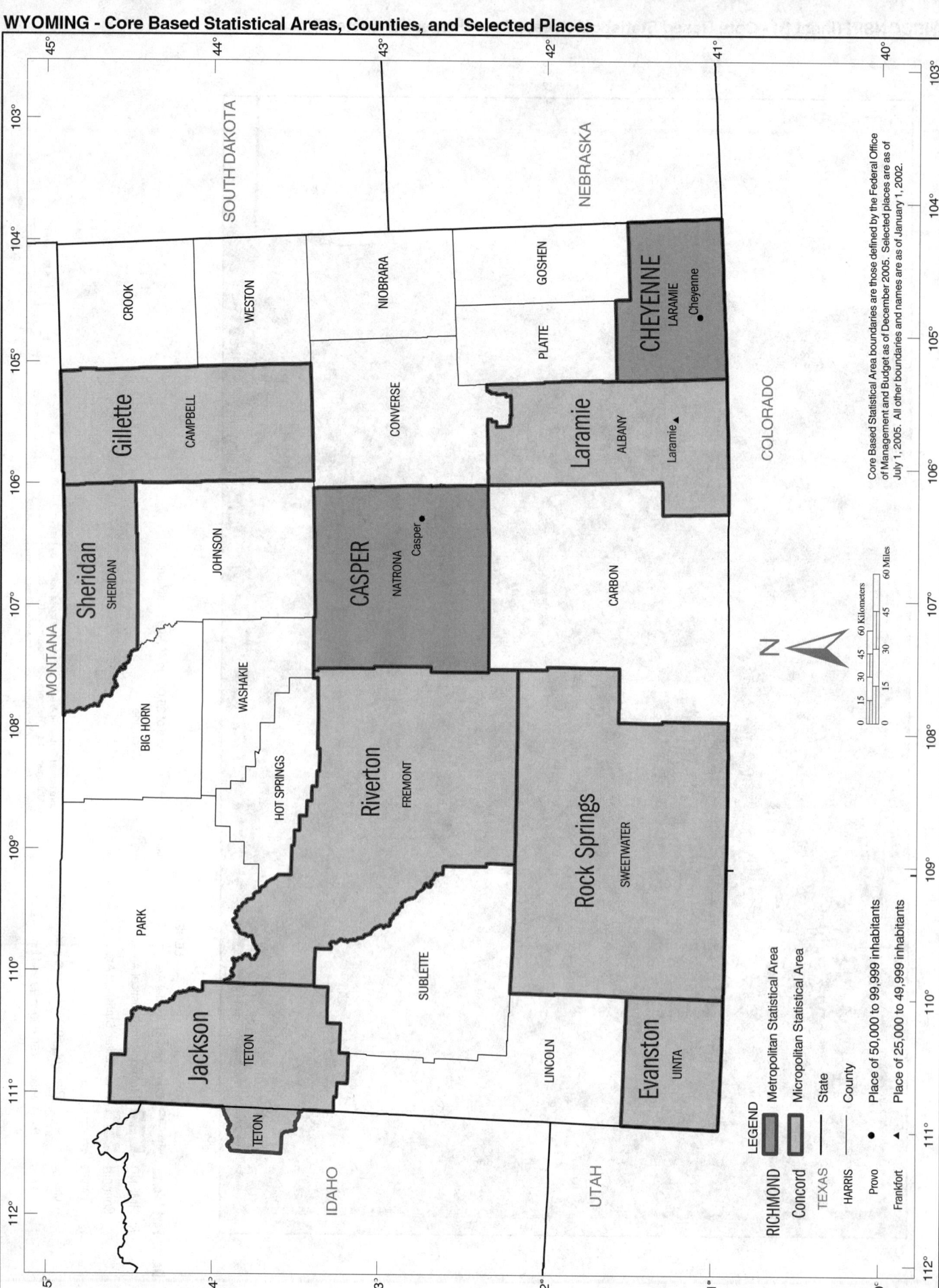

Core Based Statistical Area boundaries are those defined by the Federal Office of Management and Budget as of December 2005. Selected places are as of July 1, 2005. All other boundaries and names are as of January 1, 2002.

LEGEND

RICHMOND	Metropolitan Statistical Area
Concord	Micropolitan Statistical Area
TEXAS	State
HARRIS	County
• Provo	Place of 50,000 to 99,999 inhabitants
▲ Frankfort	Place of 25,000 to 49,999 inhabitants

Subject Guide

Appendix E

Subjects covered in this publication are shown down the left side of this guide in alphabetical order. Types of geographic areas are shown across the top. Page and table references are given where applicable. For information on subjects, see Appendix A. For definitions of geographic areas, see Appendix C.

You may visit us on the Web at
http://www.census.gov/compendia/ccdb

Appendix E.
Subject Guide

Item	Table A. States		Table B. Counties		Table C. Cities		Table D. Places	
	Page	Table	Page	Table	Page	Table	Page	Table
A								
Accommodation and food services:								
Annual payroll					792–811	C-5		
Employees, paid					792–811	C-5		
Establishments.	13	A-11	480–525	B-11	792–811	C-5		
Sales, total	13	A-11	480–525	B-11	792–811	C-5		
Food services.	13	A-11	480–525	B-11	792–811	C-5		
Acreage, farm.	16	A-14	618–663	B-14				
African-American population	5	A-3	112–157	B-3			840–845	D-2
Age of population	5	A-3	112–157	B-3			834–839	D-1
Aggravated assault	10	A-8	342–387	B-8	732–751	C-2		
Agriculture:								
Acreage.	16	A-14	618–663	B-14				
Earnings	16	A-14	618–663	B-14				
Farms.	16	A-14	618–663	B-14				
Land in farms	16	A-14	618–663	B-14				
Value of farm products sold.	16	A-14	618–663	B-14				
American Indian and Alaska Native population . . .	5	A-3	112–157	B-3			840–845	D-2
Annual payroll:								
Accommodation and food services					792–811	C-5		
Manufacturing.					772–791	C-4		
Private nonfarm business	12	A-10	434–479	B-10				
Retail trade					792–811	C-5		
Wholesale trade.					772–791	C-4		
Area, land	3	A-1	20–65	B-1	712–731	C-1		
Asian population	5	A-3	112–157	B-3			840–845	D-2
B								
Banking:								
Deposits	13	A-11	480–525	B-11				
Offices	13	A-11	480–525	B-11				
Births:								
Rates.	7	A-5	204–249	B-5				
Total	4, 7	A-2, 5	66–111, 204–249	B-2, 5				
Black or African-American population	5	A-3	112–157	B-3			840–845	D-2
Building permits	9	A-7	296–341	B-7				
Burglary.	10	A-8	342–387	B-8	732–751	C-2		
C								
City government:								
Employment					812–831	C-6		
Finances:								
General expenditure					812–831	C-6		
General revenue, total					812–831	C-6		
Taxes					812–831	C-6		
Payroll					812–831	C-6		
Civilian labor force.	12	A-10	434–479	B-10	752–771	C-3		
Climate:								
Annual precipitation.					812–831	C-6		
Average daily temperature.					812–831	C-6		
Cooling degree days.					812–831	C-6		
Heating degree days.					812–831	C-6		
Community hospitals.	8	A-6	250–295	B-6				
Commuting alone to work	6	A-4	158–203	B-4				
Construction, earnings	11	A-9	388–433	B-9				

Item	Table A. States		Table B. Counties		Table C. Cities		Table D. Places	
	Page	Table	Page	Table	Page	Table	Page	Table
L—Con.								
Livestock...............................	16	A-14	618–663	B-14				
Local government:								
Employment............................	15	A-13	572–617	B-13				
Finances:								
Debt................................	15	A-13	572–617	B-13				
General revenue......................	15	A-13	572–617	B-13				
Taxes..............................	15	A-13	572–617	B-13				
Payroll................................	15	A-13	572–617	B-13				
M								
Males per 100 females...................	5	A-3	112–157	B-3			834–839	D-1
Manufacturing:								
Capital expenditure......................	17	A-15	664–709	B-15				
Earnings..............................	17	A-15	664–709	B-15				
Employment...........................	17	A-15	664–709	B-15	772–791	C-4		
Establishments.........................	17	A-15	664–709	B-15	772–791	C-4		
Production workers.....................					772–791	C-4		
Value added...........................	17	A-15	664–709	B-15	772–791	C-4		
Value of shipments....................					772–791	C-4		
Wages...............................					772–791	C-4		
Married-couple households...............							846–851	D-3
Medicare program enrollment.............	8	A-6	250–295	B-6				
Merchant wholesalers, sales.............					772–791	C-4		
Murder.................................	10	A-8	342–387	B-8	732–751	C-2		
N								
Native Hawaiian and Other Pacific Islander								
population............................	5	A-3	112–157	B-3			840–845	D-2
New private housing units.................	9	A-7	296–341	B-7				
Nonfamily households....................							846–851	D-3
O								
Owner-occupied housing.................							864–869	D-6
P								
Payroll:								
Accommodation and food services...........					792–811	C-5		
Government:								
City.................................					812–831	C-6		
Local.................................	15	A-13	572–617	B-13				
Manufacturing..........................					772–791	C-4		
Private nonfarm businesses.................	12	A-10	434–479	B-10				
Retail trade............................					792–811	C-5		
Wholesale trade.........................					772–791	C-4		
Personal income:								
Earnings:								
Construction..........................	11	A-9	388–433	B-9				
Government..........................	11, 14	A-9, 12	388–433, 526–571	B-9, 12				
Health care and social assistance..........	11	A-9	388–433	B-9				
Manufacturing.........................	17	A-15	664–709	B-15				
Professional and technical services.........	11	A-9	388–433	B-9				
Retail trade..........................	11	A-9	388–433	B-9				
Per capita..............................	11	A-9	388–433	B-9			858–863	D-5
Total..................................	11	A-9	388–433	B-9				
Physicians..............................	8	A-6	250–295	B-6				
Population:								
Age groups............................	5	A-3	112–157	B-3			834–839	D-1
Change...............................	4	A-2	66–111	B-2	712–731	C-1		
Density................................	3	A-1	20–65	B-1	712–731	C-1		
Foreign born...........................	6	A-4	158–203	B-4				
Hispanic or Latino population.............	5	A-3	112–157	B-3			840–845	D-2
Households............................	6	A-4	158–203	B-4			846–851	D-3
Males per 100 females....................	5	A-3	112–157	B-3			834–839	D-1
Race..................................	5	A-3	112–157	B-3			840–845	D-2

Item	Table A. States		Table B. Counties		Table C. Cities		Table D. Places	
	Page	Table	Page	Table	Page	Table	Page	Table
W—Con.								
Water use:								
Ground water	16	A-14	618–663	B-14				
Irrigation	16	A-14	618–663	B-14				
Public supply	16	A-14	618–663	B-14				
Withdrawals	16	A-14	618–663	B-14				
White population	5	A-3	112–157	B-3			840–845	D-2
Wholesale trade:								
Annual payroll					772–791	C-4		
Employees, paid					772–791	C-4		
Establishments					772–791	C-4		
Operating expenses					772–791	C-4		
Sales, total					772–791	C-4		
Merchant wholesalers					772–791	C-4		

County and City Data Book: 2007

U.S. Census Bureau